DUE

PATTERSON'S

ELEMENTARY EDUCATION

1990 Edition

VOLUME II

DISCARD

Edited by **Douglas Moody**

edi

EDUCATIONAL DIRECTORIES INC.

Educational Directories Inc.
P.O. Box 199
Mount Prospect, IL 60056-0199
(708) 459-0605

First edition published 1989. Second edition 1990

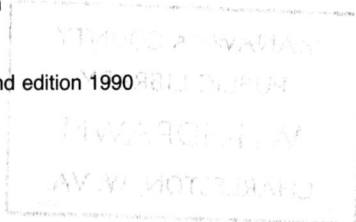

ISBN 0-910536-47-3
ISSN 1044-1417

Printed in the United States of America

CONTENTS

HOW TO USE THIS DIRECTORY

Patterson's ELEMENTARY EDUCATION (published annually since 1989) is the first, single volume, comprehensive, national directory to elementary education and the third in a series of school directories published by Educational Directories Inc. Patterson's AMERICAN EDUCATION (published annually since 1904) is THE standard directory to secondary education; and Patterson's SCHOOLS CLASSIFIED (published annually since 1951) is the most comprehensive directory to post secondary education available. The three volumes combined fulfill the need for a single, systemized, comprehensive directory to our nation's schools from first grade through post graduate collegiate studies.

Patterson's ELEMENTARY EDUCATION contains 13,642 public school districts, 59,984 public elementary schools and 10,562 private and church affiliated elementary schools in an easy to use and consistent format. It is an invaluable resource to anyone involved in education or education research. Public libraries, school registrars, principals, guidance counselors, director of admissions, schools of education, financial aid offices, the military, governmental agencies and business people find it a welcome replacement to the multitude of other directories required for national coverage of our nation's school systems (with their variation in size, content, format and publishing dates).

One of the primary objectives of this directory is to make available the latest, most comprehensive information about elementary education in an easily accessible format. Its general organization is geographical. Entries are arranged alphabetically, by state, then by community (post office) and then by school type. Each state begins with a listing of the officials in its Department of Education followed by the head of the State Board of Education. If a state has intermediate superintendents (a level of superintendent between the state superintendent of schools and the superintendents who actually operate the schools) they appear in a table preceding the community listings. Community listings follow and include the county name, community population, district name, total district student enrollment, the superintendent's name and address and a listing of the community schools, their principals and their addresses. A district may be responsible for schools in more than one community. To achieve consistency, the district office is listed in the community in which it is located. A cross reference is provided to and from the schools of the district located in other communities. A short line may appear at the end of the listing of public elementary schools. This line separates the public schools from the private and church affiliated elementary schools located in the community. Please refer to page vi Guide to Editorial Style for an example of how these elements work together to provide an easy to use format.

Public School Types (Names)

All currently open graded public elementary schools have been included in this book except kindergarten only and special needs schools.

To avoid repetition, the name of the school is omitted when its name is the same as the community name.

The grade spans of many schools are in a state of flux. The greatest changes taking place between intermediate, middle, and junior high schools. Editors have for the most part resisted the temptation to "rename" a school where their published name does not reflect the grades currently being taught. Where the school system provided a modifier (primary, elementary, intermediate, etc.) in the school name editors felt obligated to use the provided modifier. Where no modifier is supplied or where the modifier is clearly non-descriptive of the grades taught or is inconsistent with other school names in the same district editors have changed or added a modifier for purposes of clarity.

For the most part, as used in this book:

* *Primary Schools* teach any combination of grades one through four.

* *Elementary Schools* teach grades one through five, six, seven, eight or nine.

* *Middle Schools* teach any combination of grades four through eight.

* *Schools* teach grades one through twelve.

This volume does not include secondary schools (see Patterson's AMERICAN EDUCATION):

* *Junior High Schools* teach any combination of

grades not including one or twelve but including eight and nine.

* *Mid High Schools* teach nine but not eight or twelve.

* *Junior-Senior High Schools* teach any combination of grades not including one but including eight, nine and twelve.

* *High Schools* teach grades nine through twelve.

* *Senior High Schools* teach twelve but not nine.

Private and Church Affiliated Schools

Private and church affiliated schools with less than 100 students and special needs schools have not been included in this book.

Private and church affiliated school names have received minimum modification.

Addresses

Since the majority of our users view the directory as a source of mailing addresses rather than visiting addresses, it is editorial practice to list the official United States Postal Service mailing address whenever possible. When a school district chooses to route all of the mail for its schools through a central post office box, we follow its practice and provide the district address for each of its schools.

ABBREVIATIONS

AU	Administrative Unit
CCSD	Community Consolidated School District
CESD	Consolidated Elementary School District
CISD	City Independent School District
CSD	City School District
CUSD	Community Unit School District
ECCSD	Elementary Community Consolidated School District
EHSD	Elementary-High School District
ES	Elementary School
ESD	Elementary School District
EVD	Exempted Village District
HSD	High School District
IS	Intermediate School
ISD	Independent School District
JESD	Joint Elementary School District
JHS	Junior High School
JSD	Joint School District
JSHS	Junior-Senior High School
JUESD	Joint Unified Elementary School District
JUHSD	Joint Unified High School District
JUn. ESD	Joint Union Elementary School District
JUSD	Joint Unified School District
JUn. HSD	Joint Union High School District
JVSD	Joint Vocational School District
MS	Middle School
PS	Primary School
RHSD	Rural High School District
RISD	Rural Independent School District
RSD	Reorganized School District
S	School
SAD	School Administrative District
SD	School District
SHS	Senior High School
SSD	Separate School District
UESD	Unified Elementary School District
UHSD	Unified High School District
Un. ESD	Union Elementary School District
USD	Unified School District
UFD	Union Free District
Un. HSD	Union High School District
Un. SD	Union School District

ENROLLMENT/POPULATION CODES

Code	From-To	Code	From-To
1	0-100	7	10,001-25,000
2	101-500	8	25,001-100,000
3	501-1,000	9	100,001-250,000
4	1,001-2,500	10	250,001-500,000
5	2,501-5,000	11	500,001-1,000,000
6	5,001-10,000	12	Over 1,000,000

Dallas, Polk Co., Pop. Code 6
Dallas SD 2
Sch. Sys. Enr. Code 4
Supt. – Gary Burton, 111 SW ASH ST 97338
LaCreole JHS, 701 SE LACREOLE DRIVE 97338
  John LaFountaine, prin.
Bridgeport ES, 17475 BRIDGEPORT ROAD 97338

- **State shown at the top of each page; applicable to all addresses below.**

- **City, county, city population**
  City – Elmira
  County – Lane
  City population – 4*
  Refer to page v for population code table.

Dayton, Yamhill Co., Pop. Code 4
Dayton SD 8
Sch. Sys. Enr. Code 3
Supt. – Steve Johnson, 526 FERRY ST 97114
ES, 526 FERRY ST 97114 – Robert Dittmer, prin.

- **School district name**
  Enterprise SD 21
  (see table for abbreviations)
- **Total school district enrollment**
  Sch. Sys. Enr. Code – 3*
  (Estimated total school enrollment for entire school district)

  Refer to page v for enrollment code table

ES 97722 – A. Rushton, prin.

Dillard, Douglas Co., Pop. Code 3
Winston-Dillard SD 116
Sch. Sys. Enr. Code 4
Supt. – Raymond Hajduk, P O BOX 288 97432
ES, P O BOX 288 97432 – Kathleen Mathson, prin.
Lookingglass ES, P O BOX 288 97432
  Gary Frazier, prin.
McGovern ES, P O BOX 288 97432
  Richard Fulwyler, prin.
Tennile ES, P O BOX 288 97432
  Chalmers Blatch, prin.
Other Schools – See Winston

Drain, Douglas Co., Pop. Code 4
North Douglas SD 22
Sch. Sys. Enr. Code 3
Supt. – Charles Jackson, P O BOX 428 97435
North Douglas ES, P O BOX 338 97435
  Dorothy Keechi, prin.

- **Name and address of superintendent**
  Superintendent – Kent Hunsaker
  Street Address – 4640 Barger Drive
  City – Eugene *(shown at the beginning of entry)*
  State – Oregon *(shown at the top of page)*
  Zip Code – 97402
  If school district office is not located in this city, a cross reference will show office location: example –
  Supt. – See Monks Corner

ES 97115 – Larry Derry, prin.

Eagle Creek, Clackamas Co.
Estacada SD 108
Supt. – See Estacada
ES, 30391 SW HIGHWAY 211 97022
  Eugene Harper, prin.

Eagle Point, Jackson Co., Pop. Code 5
Eagle Point SD 9
Sch. Sys. Enr. Code 5
Supt. – Stephen Miller, P O BOX 548 97524
JHS, P O BOX 218 97524 – Jan Donnelly, prin.
Hale ES, P O BOX 197 97524
  Sam Chimento, prin.
Little Butte IS, P O BOX 549 97524
  Eleanor Mitchell, prin.
Other Schools – See Shady Cove, Trail, White City

Eastside, Coos Co., Pop. Code 4

Eddyville, Lincoln Co., Pop. Code 4
Lincoln County SD
Supt. – See Newport
ES 97343 – (—), prin.

Elgin, Union Co., Pop. Code 4
Elgin SD 23
Sch. Sys. Enr. Code 3
Supt. – Ralph Reed, P O BOX 68 97827
Mayfield ES, P O BOX 638 97827
  Joy Delgado, prin.

Elkton, Douglas Co., Pop. Code 2
Elkton SD 34
Sch. Sys. Enr. Code 2
Supt. – Bill Karwacki, P O BOX 390 97436
ES, P O BOX 440 97436 – Bill Karwacki, prin.

Elmira, Lane Co., Pop. Code 2
Fern Ridge SD 28J
Sch. Sys. Enr. Code 4
Supt. – Les Wolfe
  88834 TERRITORIAL ROAD 97437
Fern Ridge MS
  88834 TERRITORIAL ROAD 97437
  Donna Hein, prin.
ES, 88960 TERRITORIAL ROAD 97437
  Bonnie Swan, prin.
Other Schools – See Eugene, Noti, Veneta

Enterprise, Wallowa Co., Pop. Code 4
Enterprise SD 21
Sch. Sys. Enr. Code 3
Supt. – Larry Christman, P O BOX 520 97828
ES, P O BOX 520 97828 – Robert Eddy, prin.

Troy SD 54
Sch. Sys. Enr. Code 1
Supt. – (—), HCR 62 BOX 76 97828
Troy ES, HCR 62 BOX 76 97828
  Theodore Zeller, prin.

- **Community schools, their principals and their addresses.**
  (School name is omitted when its name is the same as the city name)

Three Lynx ES, 55550 E HIGHWAY 224 97623
  Dianne Cole, prin.
Other Schools – See Eagle Creek

Eugene, Lane Co., Pop. Code 9
Bethel SD 52
Sch. Sys. Enr. Code 5
Supt. – Kent Hunsaker
  4640 BARGER DRIVE 97402
Cascade MS, 1525 ECHO HOLLOW ROAD 97402
  Max Garrett, prin.
Shasta MS, 4656 BARGER DRIVE 97402
  Randy Harvey, prin.
Clear Lake ES, 4646 BARGER DRIVE 97402
  Mary Louise Noble, prin.
Danebo ES, 1265 CANDELIGHT DRIVE 97402
  Pamela Ellis, prin.
Fairfield ES, 3455 ROYAL AVE 97402
  Jim Winger, prin.
Irving ES, 3200 HYACINTH ST 97404
  Fred Merten, prin.
Malabon ES, 1380 TANEY ST 97402
  Lee Holden, prin.

- **Private and church affiliated elementary schools appear below a short line in the cities where they are located.**

Other Schools – See Lorane

Eugene SD 4J
Sch. Sys. Enr. Code 7
Supt. – Margaret Nichols
  200 N MONROE ST 97402
Butte MS, 500 E 43RD AVE 97405
  Cecil Kribs, prin.
Jefferson MS, 1650 W 22ND AVE 97405
  Jeannine Bertrand, prin.
Kelly MS, 850 HOWARD AVE 97404
  Ted Calhoun, prin.
Kennedy MS, 2200 BAILEY HILL ROAD 97405
  Dick Hicks, prin.
Madison MS, 875 WILKES DRIVE 97404
  L. George, prin.
Monroe MS, 2800 BAILEY LANE 97401
  James Slemp, prin.
Roosevelt MS, 680 E 24TH AVE 97405
  Jerry Henderson, prin.
Young MS, 2555 GILHAM ROAD 97401
  Evelyn Matthews, prin.
Adams ES, 950 W 22ND AVE 97405

Edison ES, 1328 E 22ND AVE 97403
  Karrin Emmert, prin.
Gilham ES, 3147 GILHAM ROAD 97401
  Tom Hochstatter, prin.
Harris ES, 1150 E 29TH AVE 97403
  Cliff Lind, prin.
Howard ES, 700 HOWARD AVE 97404
  Nancy Hunsdon, prin.
McCornack ES, 1968 BRITTANY ST 97405
  Margaret Johnson, prin.
Meadowlark ES, 1500 QUEENS WAY 97401
  Ernest Carbajal, prin.
Parker ES, 3875 KINCAID ST 97405
  Earl Harris, prin.
Patterson ES, 1510 W 15TH AVE 97402
  Virgil Erickson, prin.
River Road ES, 120 HILLIARD LANE 97404
  Roger Diddock, prin.
Santa Clara ES, 2685 RIER ROAD 97404
  Virginia Schwartzrock, prin.
Spring Creek ES, 560 IRVINGTON DRIVE 97404
  Harry Jahnke, prin.
Twin Oaks ES, 85916 BAILEY HILL ROAD 97405
  Paul Murphy, prin.
Washington ES, 3515 HARLOW ROAD 97401
  Dennis Arendt, prin.
Westmoreland ES, 1717 CITY VIEW ST 97402
  Gerald Keener, prin.
Whiteaker ES, 21 N GRAND ST 97402
  Paul Randall, prin.
Willagillespie ES
  1125 WILLAGILLESPIE ROAD 97401
  Amanda Seabloom, prin.
Willakenzie ES, 3057 WILLAKENZIE ROAD 97401
  Gordon Quigley, prin.
Willard ES, 2855 LINCOLN ST 97405
  Arline DeFrank, prin.

Fern Ridge SD 28J
Supt. – See Elmira
Central ES, 87230 CENTRAL ROAD 97402
  Steve Tritten, prin.

Springfield SD 19
Supt. – See Springfield
Goshen ES, 34020 B ST 97405
  Dallas Lommen, prin.

Eugene Montessori School
  2255 OAKMONT WAY 97401
Eugene Waldorf ES
  3411-A WILLAMETTE ST 97405
O'Hara Catholic ES, 715 W 18TH AVE 97402
Pioneer Montessori Children School
  1475 FERRY ST 97401
St. Paul Catholic School, 1201 SATRE ST 97401
Williamette Christian School
  P O BOX 10399 97440

Fairview, Multnomah Co., Pop. Code 4
Reynolds SD 7
Supt. – See Troutdale
ES, SECOND & MAIN STS 97024
  David Reynolds, prin.

Falls City, Polk Co., Pop. Code 3
Falls City SD 57
Sch. Sys. Enr. Code 2
Supt. – E. Jambura, 81 E NORTH MAIN ST 97344
ES, 177 PROSPECT AVE 97344
  Patricia Sowby, prin.

Fields, Harney Co.
Fields Trout Creek SD 33
Sch. Sys. Enr. Code 1
Supt. – Dee Fowler 97710
ES 97710 – (—), prin.

Finn Rock, Lane Co., Pop. Code 1
McKenzie SD 68
Sch. Sys. Enr. Code 2
Supt. – Edward Curtis
  51187 BLUE RIVER DRIVE 97488
McKenzie River ES
  51187 BLUE RIVER DRIVE 97488
  Anne Raftree, prin.

Florence, Lane Co., Pop. Code 5
Siuslaw SD 97J
Sch. Sys. Enr. Code 4
Supt. – Glenn Butler
  RURAL ROUTE 02 BOX 4 97439
Siuslaw MS 97439 – J. Browne, prin.
Rhododendron ES 97439 – Duane Wright, prin.
Siuslaw ES 97439 – Emmett Devereux, prin.

Forest Grove, Washington Co., Pop. Code 7
Washington County SD 15
Sch. Sys. Enr. Code 5
Supt. – Gary Lucas, 1343 PACIFIC AVE 97116
Armstrong MS, 1777 MOUNT VIEW LANE 97116
  Georgia Deetz, prin.
McCall MS, 1341 PACIFIC AVE 97116
  Daniel Rodriguez, prin.
Central ES, 1728 MAIN ST 97116

ELEMENTARY SCHOOLS

ALABAMA

STATE DEPARTMENT OF EDUCATION
483 State Office Building
501 Dexter Avenue, Montgomery 36130
(205) 261-5156

State Superintendent of Education	Dr. Wayne Teague
Deputy State Superintendent of Education	Dr. William Mellown, Jr.
Assistant State Superintendent for Professional Services	Dr. C. C. Baker
Assistant State Superintendent for Instructional Services	Martha Barton
Assistant State Superintendent for Admin. & Financial Services	William Rutherford
Assistant State Superintendent for General Administrative Services	J. Maurice Persall

STATE BOARD OF EDUCATION
Governor Guy Hunt, *President*   Montgomery 36104

DEPARTMENT OF POSTSECONDARY EDUCATION
Fred Gainous, *Chancellor*   4505 Executive Park, Montgomery 36116

PUBLIC, PRIVATE, AND PAROCHIAL ELEMENTARY SCHOOLS

Abbeville, Henry Co., Pop. Code 5
Henry County SD
Sch. Sys. Enr. Code 4
Supt. – William Covington, P O BOX 635 36310
IS, P O BOX 547 36310 – George Keith, prin.
PS, 100 ELM ST 36310 – Ted Seay, prin.
Other Schools – See Headland

Adamsville, Jefferson Co., Pop. Code 4
Jefferson County SD
Supt. – See Birmingham
ES, P O BOX K 35005 – Danny Salmon, prin.

Addison, Winston Co., Pop. Code 3
Winston County SD
Supt. – See Double Springs
S, P O BOX 241 35540 – Olen Bolzle, prin.

Akron, Hale Co., Pop. Code 3
Hale County SD
Supt. – See Greensboro
Akron West ES, P O BOX 48 35441
Fredricka Waiters, prin.

Alabaster, Shelby Co., Pop. Code 5
Shelby County SD
Supt. – See Columbiana
Thompson MS, P O BOX 584 35007
Randal McDonald, prin.
Thompson ES, P O BOX 989 35007
Leslie Harrison, prin.

Alberta, Wilcox Co., Pop. Code 4
Wilcox County SD
Supt. – See Camden
ES, P O BOX 145 36720 – William Smith, prin.

Albertville, Marshall Co., Pop. Code 6
Albertville CSD
Sch. Sys. Enr. Code 5
Supt. – James Pratt, P O BOX 1487 35950
Alabama Avenue MS
600 E ALABAMA AVE 35950 – Cecil Wright, prin.
Big Spring Lake ES, RURAL ROUTE 07 35950
Kathryn Reed, prin.
Evans MS, 900 W MCKINNEY ST 35950
John Slivka, prin.
McCord Avenue MS, E MCCORD AVE 35950
Bob Rice, prin.
West End ES, 1100 HORTON RD 35950
Nona Proctor, prin.

Marshall County SD
Supt. – See Guntersville
Asbury ES, HCR 35950 – A. Bonds, prin.

Alexander City, Tallapoosa Co., Pop. Code 7
Alexander City CSD
Sch. Sys. Enr. Code 5
Supt. – Paul Fanning, P O BOX 1205 35010
JHS, P O BOX 817 35010 – Jere Lawrence, prin.
Laurel ES, LAUREL ST 35010
Randal Willis, prin.
Pearson ES, SCOTT ROAD 35010
Richard Wagoner, prin.
Radney MS, 1109 ALLISON DR 35010
Barbara Young, prin.

Tallapoosa County SD
Supt. – See Dadeville

Hackneyville S
RURAL ROUTE 03 BOX 329 35010
Henry Hunter, prin.
New Site S, RURAL ROUTE 04 35010
Terry Speake, prin.

Alexandria, Calhoun Co.
Calhoun County SD
Supt. – See Anniston
S, P O BOX 180 36250 – Grover Whaley, prin.
ES, P O BOX 121 36250 – Gary Holaway, prin.

Aliceville, Pickens Co., Pop. Code 5
Pickens County SD
Supt. – See Carrollton
MS, P O BOX G 35442 – Carl Brooks, prin.
ES, P O BOX 430 35442 – William Rice, prin.

Alpine, Talladega Co.
Talladega County SD
Supt. – See Talladega
Winterboro S, RURAL ROUTE 01 35014
Wallis Schuessler, prin.

Altoona, Etowah Co., Pop. Code 3
Etowah County SD
Supt. – See Gadsden
West End ES, RURAL ROUTE 01 BOX 211B 35952
Glen Miller, prin.

Andalusia, Covington Co., Pop. Code 7
Andalusia CSD
Sch. Sys. Enr. Code 4
Supt. – Timothy Alford, 122 6TH AVE 36420
MS, 1201 8TH AVE 36420 – Kim Dyess, prin.
Church Street ES, 420 CHURCH ST 36420
Sonny Steele, prin.
Three Notch ES, 505 E THREE NOTCH ST 36420
Patricia Wenum, prin.

Covington County SD
Sch. Sys. Enr. Code 5
Supt. – James King, P O BOX 460 36420
Pleasant Home S
RURAL ROUTE 07 BOX 10 36420
James Garner, prin.
Straughn S, RURAL ROUTE 06 36420
James Odom, prin.
Other Schools – See Lockhart, Opp, Red Level

Anderson, Lauderdale Co., Pop. Code 2
Lauderdale County SD
Supt. – See Florence
ES, P O BOX 97 35610 – Ronald Killen, prin.

Anniston, Calhoun Co., Pop. Code 8
Anniston CSD
Sch. Sys. Enr. Code 5
Supt. – Hughey Wright, P O BOX 1500 36202
MS, 4800 MCCLELLAN BLVD 36206
Jacky Sparks, prin.
Constantine ES, 1200 JOHNSON AVE 36201
June Allred, prin.
Cooper MS, 2025 COOPER AVE 36201
Mattie Miller, prin.
Golden Springs ES, 100 FEARY DR 36201
Teresa Nichols, prin.
Johnston ES, 710 LEIGHTON AVE 36201
Richard Hooks, prin.
Norwood ES, 420 W 29TH ST 36201
Joe Steele, prin.

Randolph Park ES, 2200 W 17TH ST 36201
Cornell Howard, prin.
Tenth Street ES, 1525 E 10TH ST 36201
Jan Hurd, prin.

Calhoun County SD
Sch. Sys. Enr. Code 7
Supt. – Jim Winn, P O BOX 2084 36202
White Plains S
RURAL ROUTE 06 BOX 343 36201
Benny Character, prin.
Coldwater ES, RURAL ROUTE 10 BOX 694 36201
Ralph Turley, prin.
Saks ES, 31 WATSON ST 36206
Huey Brown, prin.
Saks MS, 32 WATSON ST 36206
W. Connell, prin.
Wellborn ES, RURAL ROUTE 03 BOX 15 36201
Therman Smith, prin.
Other Schools – See Alexandria, Bynum, De
Armanville, Jacksonville, Ohatchee, Weaver

Oxford CSD
Supt. – See Oxford
Hanna PS, 715 PARK AVE 36201
William Hutchings, prin.

Donoho School, 2501 HENRY ROAD 36201
Sacred Heart ES, 1821 MCCALL DR 36201

Arab, Marshall Co., Pop. Code 5
Arab CSD
Sch. Sys. Enr. Code 5
Supt. – T. Larry Davis, P O BOX O 35016
JHS, 125 OLD CULLMAN ROAD 35016
Coy Mills, prin.
MS, 899 8TH AVE NE 35016
Lurlene Barron, prin.
PS, NORTHGATE DR 35016
Robert Pritchett, prin.

Marshall County SD
Supt. – See Guntersville
Grassy ES, RURAL ROUTE 01 35016
Jackie Thrower, prin.

Ardmore, Limestone Co., Pop. Code 4
Limestone County SD
Supt. – See Athens
S, 4TH ST 35739 – Ronnie Holt, prin.

Ariton, Dale Co., Pop. Code 3
Dale County SD
Supt. – See Ozark
S, P O BOX 248 36311 – Ronnie Jackson, prin.

Arley, Winston Co., Pop. Code 2
Winston County SD
Supt. – See Double Springs
Meek S, P O BOX 168 35541
Danny Springer, prin.

Arlington, Wilcox Co.

Ephiphany Lutheran School, P O BOX 309 36722

Ashford, Houston Co., Pop. Code 4
Houston County SD
Supt. – See Dothan
ES, P O BOX 469 36312 – William Godwin, prin.

Ashland, Clay Co., Pop. Code 4
Clay County SD
Sch. Sys. Enr. Code 5
Supt. – James Fulbright, P O BOX 278 36251
ES, P O BOX 516 36251 – M. Thompson,Jr., prin.
Other Schools – See Cragford, Lineville, Millerville

Ashville, St. Clair Co., Pop. Code 3
St. Clair County SD
Sch. Sys. Enr. Code 6
Supt. – Charles Ray,Jr., P O BOX 248 35953
ES, P O BOX 250 35953 – Jimmy Ray Nixon, prin.
Yancy MS, P O BOX 340 35953
  M. Gladden, prin.
Other Schools – See Leeds, Odenville, Ragland,
  Springville, Steele

Athens, Limestone Co., Pop. Code 7
Athens CSD
Sch. Sys. Enr. Code 2
Supt. – R. Weizenecker
  313 E WASHINGTON ST 35611
MS, 601 S CLINTON ST 35611
  Cecil Armstrong, prin.
ES, 515 N MADISON ST 35611
  Daniel Brett, prin.
Cowart ES, 1701 W HOBBS ST 35611
  Gerald Perry, prin.
Newman ES, E SOUTH ST 35611
  Nancy Cutts, prin.

Limestone County SD
Sch. Sys. Enr. Code 6
Supt. – Ernest Adams
  300 N JEFFERSON ST 35611
Clements S, RURAL ROUTE 05 BOX 344 35611
  Robert Tinnon, prin.
East Limestone S, RURAL ROUTE 03 35611
  Glenn Johnson, prin.
Johnson ES, RURAL ROUTE 01 BOX 204 35611
  Richard Phillips, prin.
Owens ES, RURAL ROUTE 08 35611
  Donald Osborne, prin.
Piney Chapel ES
  RURAL ROUTE 09 BOX 342 35611
  Harold Nash, prin.
Reid ES, RURAL ROUTE 02 BOX 535 35611
  Henry White, prin.
Other Schools – See Ardmore, Elkmont, Lester, Tanner

Atmore, Escambia Co., Pop. Code 6
Escambia County SD
Supt. – See Brewton
Escambia County MS, P O BOX 1236 36504
  Herbert Payne, prin.
Moore ES, 501 BECK ST 36502
  Glenn Taylor, prin.
Patterson ES, 1102 W CRAIG ST 36502
  Louis Bell, prin.

Attalla, Etowah Co., Pop. Code 6
Attalla CSD
Sch. Sys. Enr. Code 4
Supt. – Billy J. Rains, 101 CASE AVE SE 35954
Etowah MS, 429 4TH ST SW 35954
  Mike Brown, prin.
Curtiston ES, CULLMAN AVE 35954
  Fred Rogers, prin.
Stowers Hill MS, 404 9TH AVE SW 35954
  Robert Turk, prin.

Etowah County SD
Supt. – See Gadsden
Duck Springs ES
  RURAL ROUTE 03 BOX 63 35954
  Barry Bottoms, prin.
Ivalee ES, RURAL ROUTE 02 BOX 54A 35954
  Kirby Hubbard, prin.

Auburn, Lee Co., Pop. Code 7
Auburn CSD
Sch. Sys. Enr. Code 5
Supt. – Ed Richardson, P O BOX 2208 36831
JHS, 332 E SAMFORD AVE 36830
  Clima White, prin.
Dean Road ES, 335 DEAN ROAD 36830
  June Spooner, prin.
Drake MS, 655 SPENCER AVE 36830
  Robert Miller, prin.
Woods ES, 715 SANDERS ST 36830
  Michael Melvin, prin.
Wrights Mill Road ES
  807 WRIGHTS MILL RD 36830 – Emily Lacy, prin.

Autaugaville, Autauga Co., Pop. Code 3
Autauga County SD
Supt. – See Prattville
ES, P O BOX 69 36003 – Charles Cooper,Sr., prin.

Baileyton, Cullman Co., Pop. Code 2
Cullman County SD
Supt. – See Cullman
ES, P O BOX C 35019 – James Meherg, prin.

Baker Hill, Barbour Co., Pop. Code 4
Barbour County SD
Supt. – See Clayton
ES, P O BOX 26 36004 – Lester Price, prin.

Banks, Pike Co., Pop. Code 2
Pike County SD
Supt. – See Troy
ES, RURAL ROUTE 02 BOX 3 36005
  Mark Bazzell, prin.

Bay Minette, Baldwin Co., Pop. Code 6
Baldwin County SD
Sch. Sys. Enr. Code 7
Supt. – J. Larry Newton
  175 COURTHOUSE SQ 36507
MS, 1000 TRACK ST 36507 – Owen Liles, prin.
ES, 800 BLACKBURN AVE 36507
  Beverly Hultz, prin.
Cross Roads ES, RURAL ROUTE 01 36507
  Robert Hazelwood, prin.
Pine Grove ES, RURAL ROUTE 02 BOX 204 36507
  Beatrice Sheldon, prin.
White House Fork ES, RURAL ROUTE 01 36507
  Joseph Hendrickson, prin.
Other Schools – See Bon Secour, Daphne, Elberta,
  Fairhope, Foley, Gulf Shores, Loxley, Perdido,
  Robertsdale, Silverhill, Spanish Fort, Stapleton,
  Summerdale

Bayou La Batre, Mobile Co., Pop. Code 5
Mobile County SD
Supt. – See Mobile
Alba ES, P O BOX 367 36509
  Carolyn Taylor, prin.

St. Margaret School, 26 S WINTZELL 36509

Bear Creek, Marion Co., Pop. Code 2
Marion County SD
Supt. – See Hamilton
Phillips ES, P O BOX 68 35543 – Billy Dixon, prin.

Beatrice, Monroe Co., Pop. Code 2
Monroe County SD
Supt. – See Monroeville
ES, P O BOX 68 36425 – Leon Stallworth, prin.

Berry, Fayette Co., Pop. Code 3
Fayette County SD
Supt. – See Fayette
ES, P O BOX 162 35546 – Maurice Manning, prin.

Bessemer, Jefferson Co., Pop. Code 8
Bessemer CSD
Sch. Sys. Enr. Code 6
Supt. – Larry Wilson, 412 17TH ST N 35020
Davis MS, 1224 CLAREDON AVE 35020
  Tolton Rosser, prin.
Abrams ES, 1200 23RD ST N 35020
  Hazel Smith, prin.
Greenwood ES, 5012 ROSELYN RD 35023
  John Bush, prin.
Hard ES, 2801 ARLINGTON AVE 35020
  Grover Dunn, prin.
Jonesboro PS, 125 OWEN AVE 35020
  Judith Butzman, prin.
Westhills PS, 710 GLENN RD 35023
  Carolyn Tingle, prin.

Jefferson County SD
Supt. – See Birmingham
Oak Grove S, RURAL ROUTE 05 BOX 307 35023
  Richard Humber, prin.
Alliance ES, 1175 ALLIANCE RD 35023
  Charles Turner,Jr., prin.
Concord ES, 6015 WARRIOR RIVER RD 35023
  Jasper Faulkner, prin.
Greenwood ES, 1219 SCHOOL RD SE 35023
  Terry Sanders, prin.
Lipscomb ES, 605 10TH ST N 35020
  James Andrews, prin.
McNeil ES, 1923 13TH ST N 35020
  Hugh Colston, prin.

St. Aloysius ES, 1701 6TH AVE N 35020
St. Francis of Assisi School
  2410 7TH AVE N 35020

Billingsley, Autauga Co., Pop. Code 2
Autauga County SD
Supt. – See Prattville
S, RURAL ROUTE 01 36006 – Collier Hunt, prin.

Birmingham, Jefferson Co., Pop. Code 10
Birmingham CSD
Sch. Sys. Enr. Code 8
Supt. – Cleveland Hammonds
  P O BOX 10007 35202
Alabama Fine Arts JHS, 820 18TH ST N 35203
  James Nelson, prin.
Arrington MS, 2101 JEFFERSON AVE SW 35211
  Mallory Coats, prin.
Brown MS, 4811 COURT S #J 35208
  Gary Leeman, prin.
Glenn MS, 901 16TH ST W 35208
  Julian Todd, prin.
Huffman Magnet MS
  517 HUFFMAN ROAD 35215
  Albert Morton, prin.
Kennedy MS, 125 63RD ST N 35212
  Thomas Nilsen, prin.
Kirby MS, 1328 28TH ST N 35234
  Robert Hill, prin.
Payne MS, 1500 DANIEL PAYNE DRIVE 35214
  Sylvia Pierce, prin.
Phileo MS, P O BOX 10007 35202 – (—), prin.
Putman Magnet MS
  1757 MONTCLAIR ROAD 35210
  David Newell, prin.
Smith MS, 1124 FIVE MILE ROAD 35215
  Michael Curry, prin.
South East Lake MS, 720 86TH ST S 35206
  Nancy Howard, prin.
Arthur ES, 625 14TH AVE NW 35215
  Kenneth Clemmons, prin.

Avondale ES, 4000 8TH CT S 35222
  Barbara Jones, prin.
Barrett ES, 7601 DIVISION AVE 35206
  Jerry White, prin.
Calloway ES, 3417 34TH TER N 35207
  Margaret Starks, prin.
Center Street ES, 1832 CENTER WAY S 35205
  China Sykes, prin.
Central Park ES, 4915 AVENUE Q 35208
  Kathryn Donovan, prin.
Christian Alternative ES
  725 MOUNTAIN DR 35206
  Linda Houghton, prin.
Comer ES, 1220 50TH ST S 35222
  William Shepherd, prin.
Council ES, 1400 AVE M ENSLEY 35218
  Charles Warren, prin.
Curry ES, 7900 8TH AVE N 35206
  Joy Stewart, prin.
Davis ES, 417 29TH ST S 35233
  Sylvester Hollis, prin.
Dupuy ES, 4500 14TH AVE N 35212
  Rosa Hanks, prin.
Eagan ES, 1716 31ST AVE N 35207
  Aquilla Washington, prin.
Elyton ES, 6 TUSCALOOSA AVE SW 35211
  Addie Pugh, prin.
Epic ES, 1000 10TH AVE 35228
  Louise Caskey, prin.
Fairview ES, 2623 29TH ST N 35234
  Don Orton, prin.
Finley Avenue ES, 135 FINLEY AVE W 35204
  Gwendolyn Goodwyn, prin.
Gate City ES
  6910 GEORGIA ROAD GATE CITY 35212
  William Clemons, prin.
Gibson ES, 956 50TH ST N 35212
  Ted Fuller, prin.
Going Magnet ES
  1015 N MARTINWOOD DR 35235
  Betty Dooley, prin.
Graymont ES, 300 8TH AVE W 35204
  Jesse Watts,Jr., prin.
Green Acres ES, 945 PINEVIEW RD 35228
  Katherine Brown, prin.
Hemphill ES, 1240 COTTON AVE SW 35211
  Willie Wilder, prin.
Hill ES, 507 3RD ST N 35204
  Carolyn Purofoy, prin.
Hudson ES, 3300 HUNTSVILLE RD 35207
  Errol Pharris, prin.
Inglenook ES, 4120 INGLENOOK ST 35217
  Craig Smiley, prin.
Iris ES, 1115 11TH ST S 35205
  James Moreno, prin.
Jackson ES, 1401 16TH WAY SW 35211
  Willie Maye, prin.
Jones Valley ES, 2921 DOWELL AVE SW 35211
  Ronald Bell, prin.
Kingston ES, 801 46TH ST N 35212
  Allen Lewis, prin.
Lee ES, 630 18TH ST SW 35211
  Robert Atkins, prin.
Lewis ES, 2015 26TH AVE N 35234
  Gladys McGee, prin.
Lincoln ES, 901 9TH AVE N 35204
  Barbara McDonald, prin.
McArthur ES, 2418 17TH AVE N 35234
  Cora Huggins, prin.
McCaw ES, 1020 AVE M ENSLEY 35214
  Anita Skipwith, prin.
McElwain Magnet ES
  4447 MONTEVALLO RD S 35213
  Buford Carter III, prin.
Moore ES, 1401 AVE G ENSLEY 35218
  Pinnie Yarbrough, prin.
North Birmingham ES, 2620 35TH AVE N 35207
  Albert McDanal,Jr., prin.
North Roebuck ES, 300 RED LANE RD 35215
  Romona Shannon, prin.
Norwood ES, 3136 NORWOOD BLVD 35234
  Columbus Hasberry, prin.
Oliver ES, 6871 6TH CT S 35212
  Alfred Bell, prin.
Patterson ES, 210 64TH ST S 35212
  Mims McCarroll, prin.
Powderly ES
  DAWSON 7TH 20TH AVE ST SW 35211
  Michael Wesley, prin.
Powell ES, 2331 6TH AVE N 35203
  Eva Jones, prin.
Pratt ES, 306 AVENUE U 35214
  Raymond Horn, prin.
Price ES, 532 28TH ST SW 35211
  Billy Flynn, prin.
Princeton Alternative ES, 1425 2ND AVE W 35208
  Mary Hardy, prin.
Riggins ES, 3177 44TH CT N 35207
  Alvin Washington, prin.
Riley ES, 3420 HICKORY AVE SW 35221
  George Lewis, prin.
Robinson ES, 8400 1ST AVE S 35206
  K. Tortorice, prin.
Scott ES, 572 CHERRY AVE 35214
  Doremus Wallace, prin.
Shields ES, 3969 14TH AVE N 35234
  James Pharris, prin.
Spaulding ES, 1720 12TH ST SW 35211
  Carolyn Francisco, prin.
Tuggle ES, 412 12TH CT N 35204
  Theodore Hawkins, prin.
Tuxedo ES, 2009 AVENUE Q 35218
  Eddie Dansby, prin.

Washington ES, 115 4TH AVE S   35205
   Freddie Shepherd, prin.
Wenonah ES, 3008 WILSON RD SW   35221
   Herman Williams, prin.
Whatley ES, 549 43RD ST N   35222
   Norman Bester, prin.
Wilkerson ES, 116 11TH CT N   35204
   Clifton Howard, prin.
Wilson ES, 1030 4TH TER W   35204
   Leslie Springer, prin.
Wright Magnet ES, 1212 CHEYENNE BLVD   35215
   James Moran, prin.
Other Schools – See Ensley, Wylam

Hoover CSD
Sch. Sys. Enr. Code 3
Supt. – C. Mitchell
   1855 DATA DRIVE #205   35244
Simmons JHS
   1575 PATTONS CHAPEL ROAD   35226
   Barb McDonald, prin.
Bluff Park ES, 569 PARK AVE   35226
   Pat Decker, prin.
Green Valley ES
   3200 OLD COLUMBIANA ROAD   35226
   Patricia Lovelady, prin.
Gwin ES, 1580 PATTONS CHAPEL ROAD   35226
   Linda Griggs, prin.
Rocky Ridge ES, 2876 OLD ROCKY RIDGE   35243
   Anne Jordan, prin.
Shades Mountain ES
   2250 SUMPTER STREET   35226
   Brenda Carraway, prin.

Jefferson County SD
Sch. Sys. Enr. Code 8
Supt. – William Burkett
   A-400 COURTHOUSE   35263
Minor ES, 3015 MULGA LOOP RD   35224
   Tom Denton,Jr., prin.
Cahaba Heights ES, 4401 DOLLY RIDGE RD   35243
   G. Richard Lazenby, prin.
Center Point ES, 2209 CENTER POINT RD   35215
   Harold Reese, prin.
Chalkville ES
   940 CHALKVILLE SCHOOL RD   35215
   Jerry Mitchell, prin.
Crumly Chapel ES, 2201 PERSHING RD   35214
   Ellen Harris, prin.
Erwin ES, 528 23RD AVE NW   35215
   John Edwards, prin.
Grantswood Community ES
   RURAL ROUTE 04 BOX 858   35210
   Ilene Egerman, prin.
Hillview ES, 1520 CHERRY AVE   35214
   Ann Jones, prin.
Phileo ES, 6001 CRESTWOOD BLVD   35212
   (—), prin.
Rocky Ridge ES
   2876 OLD ROCKY RIDGE RD   35243
   Anne Jordan, prin.
Other Schools – See Adamsville, Bessemer, Brighton,
   Clay, Dolomite, Dora, Fultondale, Gardendale,
   Graysville, Hueytown, Irondale, Leeds, Mc Calla,
   Morris, Mount Olive, Pinson, Pleasant Grove,
   Quinton, Trussville, Warrior

Mountain Brook CSD
Supt. – See Mountain Brook
Cherokee Bend ES, 4400 FAIR OAKS DR   35213
   Janice Wolfe, prin.
Crestline ES, 3785 JACKSON BLVD   35213
   Joyce McCollum, prin.

Shelby County SD
Supt. – See Columbiana
Riverchase MS, 853 WILLOW OAK DRIVE   35244
   Charlotte Lusco, prin.
Inverness ES, 5251 VALLEY DALE ROAD   35243
   Elizabeth Smith, prin.

Vestavia Hills CSD
Supt. – See Vestavia Hills
Vestavia Hills Central MS
   1289 MONTGOMERY HWY   35216
   James Jeffers, prin.
Vestavia Hills PS East, 2109 PARKVIEW PL   35216
   James Williams, prin.
Vestavia Hills PS West
   1965 MERRYVALE RD   35216
   Ozilene Cartee, prin.

Advent Episcopal Day School
   2019 6TH AVE N   35203
All Saints Episcopal School
   110 W HAWTHORNE RD   35209
Briarwood Christian School
   3005 HIGHWAY 280 S   35243
Highland Day School, 4801 OLD LEEDS RD   35213
Holy Family ES, 1916 19TH ST   35218
Our Lady of Fatima School, 630 1ST ST S   35205
Our Lady of Sorrows School
   1720 OXMOOR RD   35209
Our Lady of the Valley School
   5510 DOUBLE OAK LN   35242
Pilgrim Lutheran School, 447 FIRST ST N   35204
St. Barnabas School, 7901 FIRST AVE N   35206
St. Francis Xavier School
   2 XAVIER CIRCLE   35213
St. Joseph Parochial School, 1105 30TH ST   35218
St. Paul Inter. Parochial School
   2121 FOURTH AVE N   35203
St. Rose of Lima ES, 1401 22ND ST S   35205

Blountsville, Blount Co., Pop. Code 4
Blount County SD
Supt. – See Oneonta
Moore S, RURAL ROUTE 3 BOX 190   35031
   Robert Harris, prin.
ES, P O BOX 160   35031 – Frank Carr, prin.

Boaz, Marshall Co., Pop. Code 6
Etowah County SD
Supt. – See Gadsden
Carlisle ES, RURAL ROUTE 03 BOX 310   35957
   Amelia Cartrett, prin.
Whitesboro ES, RURAL ROUTE 01   35957
   Doris Leftwich, prin.

Marshall County SD
Supt. – See Guntersville
ES, 502 SPARKS AVE   35957
   William Aaron, prin.
Corley MS, P O BOX 526   35957
   Mike Matthews, prin.

Boligee, Greene Co., Pop. Code 2
Greene County SD
Supt. – See Eutaw
Paramount S, P O BOX 188   35443
   Cleophus Gaines, prin.

Bon Secour, Baldwin Co.
Baldwin County SD
Supt. – See Bay Minette
Swift Consolidated ES, P O BOX 7   36511
   Connie West, prin.

Boykin, Wilcox Co.
Wilcox County SD
Supt. – See Camden
ES   36723 – Ollie Mingo, prin.

Brantley, Crenshaw Co., Pop. Code 4
Crenshaw County SD
Supt. – See Luverne
S, P O BOX 86   36009 – James Head, prin.

Bremen, Cullman Co., Pop. Code 6
Cullman County SD
Supt. – See Cullman
Cold Springs S, P O BOX 130   35033
   Larry Carroll, prin.

Brent, Bibb Co., Pop. Code 5
Bibb County SD
Supt. – See Centreville
MS, 118 4TH ST   35034 – Bobby McAfee, prin.

Brewton, Escambia Co., Pop. Code 6
Brewton CSD
Sch. Sys. Enr. Code 4
Supt. – Dale T. Garner, P O BOX 59   36427
MS, 301 LILES BLVD   36426
   Vernon Baggett, prin.
ES, 901 BELLEVIEW   36426 – Jerry Murphree, prin.

Escambia County SD
Sch. Sys. Enr. Code 6
Supt. – M. Brantley, P O BOX 307   36427
McCall ES, RURAL ROUTE 02   36426
   Danny Norwood, prin.
Neal ES, P O BOX 2250   36427
   Murray Stinson, prin.
North Brewton ES, RURAL ROUTE 05   36426
   Leon Hartley, prin.
Other Schools – See Atmore, East Brewton, Flomaton,
   Huxford

Bridgeport, Jackson Co., Pop. Code 5
Jackson County SD
Supt. – See Scottsboro
MS   35740 – Elizabeth Mountain, prin.
PS, 704R JACOBS AVE   35740 – James Bain, prin.

Brighton, Jefferson Co., Pop. Code 4
Jefferson County SD
Supt. – See Birmingham
ES, 3300 BROWNS CIR   35020 – Leroy Goree, prin.

Brilliant, Marion Co., Pop. Code 3
Marion County SD
Supt. – See Hamilton
ES, RURAL ROUTE 01 BOX 10-ABC   35548
   David Sexton, prin.

Brookwood, Tuscaloosa Co., Pop. Code 2
Tuscaloosa County SD
Supt. – See Tuscaloosa
ES, RURAL ROUTE 01 BOX 3500   35444
   Lee Boozer, prin.

Brundidge, Pike Co., Pop. Code 5
Pike County SD
Supt. – See Troy
Pike County ES   36010 – Eddie Capleton, prin.

Bryant, Jackson Co.
Jackson County SD
Supt. – See Scottsboro
ES   35958 – Dana Moore, prin.

Buhl, Tuscaloosa Co.
Tuscaloosa County SD
Supt. – See Tuscaloosa
ES, P O BOX 97   35446 – Robin Runcie, prin.

Butler, Choctaw Co., Pop. Code 4
Choctaw County SD
Sch. Sys. Enr. Code 5
Supt. – Toreatha Johnson
   914 RIDERWOOD DRIVE   36904

ES, 211 PUSHMATAHA   36904
   Miriam Heaton, prin.
East Choctaw ES, RURAL ROUTE   36904
   David Johnson, prin.
Other Schools – See Gilbertown, Lisman, Silas

Bynum, Calhoun Co.
Calhoun County SD
Supt. – See Anniston
ES, P O BOX 338   36253 – Georgia Emerson, prin.

Calera, Shelby Co., Pop. Code 4
Shelby County SD
Supt. – See Columbiana
ES, P O BOX AA   35040 – Philip Haynie, prin.

Camden, Wilcox Co., Pop. Code 4
Wilcox County SD
Sch. Sys. Enr. Code 4
Supt. – Odell Tumblin, P O BOX 160   36726
Camden Academy MS   36726
   Palmer Williams, prin.
Hobbs ES   36726 – Ora Gulley Colston, prin.
Other Schools – See Alberta, Boykin, Coy, Millers
   Ferry, Pine Apple, Pine Hill

Camp Hill, Tallapoosa Co., Pop. Code 4
Tallapoosa County SD
Supt. – See Dadeville
Bell S, P O BOX 457   36850 – Frank Holley, prin.

Carbon Hill, Walker Co., Pop. Code 4
Carbon Hill CSD
Sch. Sys. Enr. Code 4
Supt. – Don Stovall, P O BOX 370   35549
JHS, P O BOX 609   35549 – David Beason, prin.
ES, P O BOX 609   35549 – David Beason, prin.

Carrollton, Pickens Co., Pop. Code 3
Pickens County SD
Sch. Sys. Enr. Code 5
Supt. – Ralph Smith, P O BOX 32   35447
S, P O BOX 320   35447 – Edwina Burks, prin.
Other Schools – See Aliceville, Gordo, Reform

Castleberry, Conecuh Co., Pop. Code 3
Conecuh County SD
Supt. – See Evergreen
Conecuh County S, RURAL ROUTE 2   36432
   Louise Bradley, prin.

Cedar Bluff, Cherokee Co., Pop. Code 3
Cherokee County SD
Supt. – See Centre
S, P O BOX 8   35959 – Jimmy Glenn Dean, prin.

Centre, Cherokee Co., Pop. Code 4
Cherokee County SD
Sch. Sys. Enr. Code 5
Supt. – H. E. Arnold,Jr., 130 E MAIN ST   35960
MS, 350 E MAIN ST   35960 – Ed Miller, prin.
ES, 725 E MAIN ST   35960 – Billy Tillery, prin.
Other Schools – See Cedar Bluff, Gaylesville,
   Leesburg, Spring Garden

Centreville, Bibb Co., Pop. Code 4
Bibb County SD
Sch. Sys. Enr. Code 5
Supt. – Joe Elliot,Jr.
   103 SW DAVIDSON DRIVE   35042
ES, 661 MONTGOMERY RD   35042
   Rebecca Pratt, prin.
Other Schools – See Brent, Randolph, West Blocton,
   Woodstock

Chatom, Washington Co., Pop. Code 4
Washington County SD
Sch. Sys. Enr. Code 5
Supt. – Vivian Dearmon, P O BOX L   36518
MS, P O BOX B   36518 – George Holcomb, prin.
ES, P O BOX J   36518 – Lilybel Bounds, prin.
Other Schools – See Fruitdale, Leroy, Mc Intosh,
   Millry, Wagarville

Chelsea, Shelby Co., Pop. Code 2
Shelby County SD
Supt. – See Columbiana
S, P O BOX 39   35043 – Glen Frederick, prin.

Cherokee, Colbert Co., Pop. Code 4
Colbert County SD
Supt. – See Tuscumbia
MS, P O BOX H   35616 – Polie Reynolds, prin.
ES, RURAL ROUTE 01 BOX 2   35616
   James Mills, prin.
Littleville ES, RURAL ROUTE 03   35616
   Norman Hubbard, prin.

Chickasaw, Mobile Co., Pop. Code 6
Mobile County SD
Supt. – See Mobile
Clark MS, 12 12TH AVE   36611 – Alfred July, prin.
ES, 201 N CRAFT HWY   36611
   Lexie Barnett, prin.
Hamilton ES, 80 GRANT ST   36611
   Sandra Byrd, prin.

St. Thomas Catholic School
   255 N CRAFT HWY   36611

Childersburg, Talladega Co., Pop. Code 5
Talladega County SD
Supt. – See Talladega
Childersburg MS, 800 4TH ST SE   35044
   John Ragland, prin.
ES, 50 PINECREST RD   35044 – Vickie Oliver, prin.
Watwood ES, P O BOX 406   35044
   Peggy Hayes, prin.

Citronelle, Mobile Co., Pop. Code 4
Mobile County SD
Supt. – See Mobile
MS, P O BOX 97   36522 – William Clark, prin.
Lott ES, RURAL ROUTE 01 BOX 331   36522
   Geraldine Powley, prin.

Clanton, Chilton Co., Pop. Code 6
Chilton County SD
Sch. Sys. Enr. Code 5
Supt. – Joseph Daniel, 1705 LAY DAM RD   35045
Adair MS, 102 1ST ST S   35045
   James Popwell, prin.
ES, 1000 CLOVERLEAF DR   35045
   Robert Carden, prin.
Other Schools – See Jemison, Maplesville, Thorsby,
   Verbena

Clay, Jefferson Co., Pop. Code 6
Jefferson County SD
Supt. – See Birmingham
ES, P O BOX 100   35048 – Roy Hornsby, prin.

Clayton, Barbour Co., Pop. Code 4
Barbour County SD
Sch. Sys. Enr. Code 4
Supt. – Bob Baker, P O BOX 186   36016
ES, P O BOX 407   36016 – Yamandu Acosta, prin.
Other Schools – See Baker Hill, Clio, Eufaula,
   Louisville

Cleveland, Blount Co., Pop. Code 2
Blount County SD
Supt. – See Oneonta
S, P O BOX 127   35049 – Bobby Ellis, prin.

Clio, Barbour Co., Pop. Code 4
Barbour County SD
Supt. – See Clayton
ES, P O BOX 158   36017 – Horace Teal, prin.

Coffee Springs, Geneva Co., Pop. Code 2
Geneva County SD
Supt. – See Geneva
S, P O BOX 68   36318 – John Williams, prin.

Coffeeville, Clarke Co., Pop. Code 2
Clarke County SD
Supt. – See Grove Hill
ES, P O BOX 38   36524 – Patricia Pugh, prin.

Coker, Tuscaloosa Co., Pop. Code 6
Tuscaloosa County SD
Supt. – See Tuscaloosa
Westwood ES, RURAL ROUTE 02 BOX 307   35452
   Patricia Davis, prin.

Collinsville, De Kalb Co., Pop. Code 4
Dekalb County SD
Supt. – See Fort Payne
S, P O BOX 269   35961 – Samuel Clanton, prin.

Columbia, Houston Co., Pop. Code 3
Houston County SD
Supt. – See Dothan
Houston County S, 202 W CHURCH ST   36319
   Douglas Dease, prin.

Columbiana, Shelby Co., Pop. Code 4
Shelby County SD
Sch. Sys. Enr. Code 7
Supt. – Ellie Glasscox, 410 E COLLEGE ST   35051
MS, P O BOX 306   35051 – Q. L. Bentley, prin.
Hill ES, 201 WASHINGTON ST   35051
   Ann Head, prin.
Other Schools – See Alabaster, Birmingham, Calera,
   Chelsea, Helena, Montevallo, Pelham, Shelby,
   Vincent, Wilsonville

Cordova, Walker Co., Pop. Code 5
Walker County SD
Supt. – See Jasper
Bankhead MS, 500 SCHOOL ROAD   35550
   Steve Adkins, prin.
ES, 99 NORTH ST   35550 – Johnny Barnett, prin.

Cottondale, Tuscaloosa Co.
Tuscaloosa County SD
Supt. – See Tuscaloosa
ES, RURAL ROUTE 04 BOX 215   35453
   William Niles, prin.

Cottonwood, Houston Co., Pop. Code 4
Houston County SD
Supt. – See Dothan
S, RURAL ROUTE 01 BOX 700   36320
   John Tew, prin.

Courtland, Lawrence Co., Pop. Code 3
Lawrence County SD
Supt. – See Moulton
Hubbard ES, P O BOX E   35618
   Patrick Graham, prin.

Coy, Wilcox Co.
Wilcox County SD
Supt. – See Camden
Tates Chapel ES   36435 – James Gildersleeve, prin.

Cragford, Clay Co.
Clay County SD
Supt. – See Ashland
Mellow Valley S, RURAL ROUTE 01   36255
   James McCullers, prin.

Crane Hill, Cullman Co., Pop. Code 4
Cullman County SD
Supt. – See Cullman

Dowling ES, RURAL ROUTE 01   35053
   Larry Rutledge, prin.

Cropwell, St. Clair Co.
Pell City CSD
Supt. – See Pell City
Coosa Valley ES
   RURAL ROUTE 01 BOX 110   35054
   Thelma Jones, prin.

Crossville, De Kalb Co., Pop. Code 4
Dekalb County SD
Supt. – See Fort Payne
S, P O BOX 38   35962 – Joseph Owens, prin.

Cuba, Sumter Co., Pop. Code 2
Sumter County SD
Supt. – See Livingston
Kinterbish ES, RURAL ROUTE 01 BOX 102   36907
   Robert Smith, prin.

Cullman, Cullman Co., Pop. Code 7
Cullman CSD
Sch. Sys. Enr. Code 4
Supt. – Edwin Allen, P O BOX 887   35056
MS, 800 2ND AVE NE   35055 – Don Dossey, prin.
East ES, 608 4TH AVE SE   35055
   Joe Maddox, prin.
West ES, 303 ROSEMONT AVE SW   35055
   Terry Smith, prin.

Cullman County SD
Sch. Sys. Enr. Code 6
Supt. – Jim Boyd, P O BOX 518   35056
Fairview S, RURAL ROUTE 07 BOX 1905   35055
   Keith Pattillo, prin.
Good Hope S, RURAL ROUTE 06 BOX 33   35055
   Billy Joe Pugh, prin.
West Point S, RURAL ROUTE 05 BOX 500   35055
   Jan Farley, prin.
Jones Chapel ES
   RURAL ROUTE 10 BOX 2265   35055
   Edward Cornelius, prin.
Welti ES, RURAL ROUTE 03 BOX 845   35055
   Harold Ballew, prin.
Other Schools – See Baileyton, Bremen, Crane Hill,
   Garden City, Hanceville, Holly Pond, Joppa, Logan,
   Vinemont

Sacred Heart School Cullman
   112 2ND AVE SE   35055
St. Paul's Lutheran School
   510 3RD AVE SE   35055

Dadeville, Tallapoosa Co., Pop. Code 5
Tallapoosa County SD
Sch. Sys. Enr. Code 5
Supt. – Jimmy Sanford, COURTHOUSE   36853
ES   36853 – Donald Black, prin.
Other Schools – See Alexander City, Camp Hill,
   Notasulga

Daleville, Dale Co., Pop. Code 6
Daleville CSD
Sch. Sys. Enr. Code 4
Supt. – J. F. Moore III
   323 N DALEVILLE AVE   36322
ES, 323 N DALEVILLE AVE   36322
   William Burns, prin.
Windham ES, 200 HERITAGE DR   36322
   William Burns, prin.

Danville, Morgan Co., Pop. Code 5
Lawrence County SD
Supt. – See Moulton
Speake S, RURAL ROUTE 02 BOX 174   35619
   Vernon Hurn, prin.

Morgan County SD
Supt. – See Decatur
S, RURAL ROUTE 02   35619
   Mitchell Owens, prin.
Neel ES, RURAL ROUTE 03   35619
   Kenneth Thompson, prin.

Daphne, Baldwin Co., Pop. Code 5
Baldwin County SD
Supt. – See Bay Minette
ES, P O BOX 220   36526 – William Yokel, prin.

Bayside Academy, P O BOX 130   36526
Christ the King School, P O BOX 1890   36526

Dauphin Island, Mobile Co.
Mobile County SD
Supt. – See Mobile
ES, GENEREAL DELIVERY   36528
   Nancy Burnett, prin.

De Armanville, Calhoun Co.
Calhoun County SD
Supt. – See Anniston
ES, P O BOX 237   36257 – Frank Douthit, prin.

Deatsville, Elmore Co., Pop. Code 5
Elmore County SD
Supt. – See Wetumpka
Holtville S, RURAL ROUTE 02   36022
   William Earnest, prin.

Decatur, Morgan Co., Pop. Code 8
Decatur CSD
Sch. Sys. Enr. Code 6
Supt. – Dr. Byron Nelson, 302 4TH AVE NE   35601
Brookhaven MS, 1302 5TH AVE SW   35601
   James Webster, prin.
Oak Park MS, 1100 16TH AVE SE   35601
   Lawrence Walters, prin.

Austinville ES, 2320 CLARA AVE SW   35601
   David Livingston, prin.
Bibb ES, 211 GORDON DR SE   35601
   Ann Harris, prin.
Carver Developmental ES
   809 CHURCH ST NE   35601
   Thomas Maynor, prin.
Eastwood ES, 1802 26TH AVE SE   35601
   Jane Knight, prin.
Harris ES, 1922 MCAULIFFE DR SW   35603
   Alan Jeffreys, prin.
Jackson ES, 1950 PARK ST SE   35601
   Jill Eaton, prin.
Nungester ES, 726 TAMMY ST SW   35603
   M. Foster, prin.
Sheffield ES, 801 WILSON ST NW   35601
   Lorenzo Jackson, prin.
Somerville Road ES
   910 SOMERVILLE RD SE   35601
   Barbara Sittason, prin.
West Decatur ES, 708 MEMORIAL DR SW   35601
   Ronnie Beans, prin.
Westlawn ES, 417 MONROE DR NW   35601
   Anita Buckley, prin.
Woodmeade ES, 1500 19TH AVE SW   35601
   James West, prin.

Morgan County SD
Sch. Sys. Enr. Code 4
Supt. – Charles Thompson
   1325 POINT MALLARD PARKWAY   35601
Flint ES, RURAL ROUTE 06 BOX 209   35603
   Roland Oden, prin.
Priceville ES, RURAL ROUTE 04 BOX 90   35603
   Howard Morris, prin.
Other Schools – See Danville, Eva, Falkville,
   Hartselle, Joppa, Laceys Spring, Somerville, Trinity

St. Ann ES, 240 JOHNSTON ST SE   35601

Demopolis, Marengo Co., Pop. Code 6
Demopolis CSD
Sch. Sys. Enr. Code 4
Supt. – W. Wesley Hill, P O BOX 700   36732
Jones MS, 715 E JACKSON ST   36732
   Joseph McDaniel, prin.
Westside ES, 1724 MAUVILLA DR   36732
   James Henderson, prin.

Marengo County SD
Supt. – See Linden
Essex S, RURAL ROUTE 01 BOX 433   36732
   Flora Kennard, prin.

Dixon's Mills, Marengo Co.
Marengo County SD
Supt. – See Linden
Marengo S, RURAL ROUTE 01 BOX 154   36736
   Dock Harper, Jr., prin.

Dolomite, Jefferson Co.
Jefferson County SD
Supt. – See Birmingham
Woodward MS, 1101 ALEXANDER ST   35061
   James Hankins, prin.

Dora, Walker Co., Pop. Code 4
Jefferson County SD
Supt. – See Birmingham
Bagley ES, 8581 TATE MILL RD   35062
   Jerry Vines, prin.

Walker County SD
Supt. – See Jasper
Boyd ES, P O BOX A   35062 – James Gann, prin.

Dothan, Houston Co., Pop. Code 8
Dothan CSD
Sch. Sys. Enr. Code 6
Supt. – Gene Watson, 500 DUSY ST   36301
Beverlye MS, 427 S BEVERLY ROAD   36301
   James Daniels, prin.
Carver MS, 801 E NORTH ST   36303
   James Kelley, prin.
Girard MS, 600 GIRARD AVE   36303
   J. Roland, prin.
Honeysuckle MS
   1407 HONEYSUCKLE ROAD   36301
   Sam Nichols, prin.
Cloverdale ES, ROLLINS AVE   36301
   Betty Armstrong, prin.
Girard Avenue ES, 522 GIRARD AVE   36303
   Ila Flowers, prin.
Grandview ES, 800 6TH AVE   36301
   Theodore Whiting, prin.
Heard ES, 201 DANIEL CIR   36301
   Jacqueline Bridges, prin.
Highland MS, 900 W POWELL ST   36303
   Crawford Drake, prin.
Montana Street MS, 1001 MONTANA ST   36303
   Michael Patton, prin.
Selma Street ES, 1301 W SELMA ST   36301
   Roger Smith, prin.
Southside MS, 813 S ST ANDREWS ST   36301
   William Van Tassel, prin.
Stringer Street MS, 1020 STRINGER ST   36303
   Jerry Faine, prin.
Wilson Street MS, 201 WILSON ST   36303
   Ray Hargrove, prin.

Houston County SD
Sch. Sys. Enr. Code 6
Supt. – Julian Layton, P O BOX 1688   36302
Rehobeth S, P O BOX 105   36302
   Donald Holman, prin.

Other Schools – See Ashford, Columbia, Cottonwood,
Newton, Pansey, Webb

Double Springs, Winston Co., Pop. Code 3
Winston County SD
Sch. Sys. Enr. Code 5
Supt. – William Reeves, P O BOX 9 35553
ES, P O BOX 305 35553 – Jackie Herron, prin.
Other Schools – See Addison, Arley, Lynn

Douglas, Marshall Co., Pop. Code 2
Marshall County SD
Supt. – See Guntersville
ES, P O BOX 300 35964 – Robert Sloman, prin.

Dozier, Crenshaw Co., Pop. Code 2
Crenshaw County SD
Supt. – See Luverne
S, P O BOX 8 36028 – Howard Davis, prin.

Duncanville, Tuscaloosa Co.
Tuscaloosa County SD
Supt. – See Tuscaloosa
Maxwell ES, RURAL ROUTE 01 BOX 231 35456
Carolyn Price, prin.

Dutton, Jackson Co., Pop. Code 2
Jackson County SD
Supt. – See Scottsboro
ES, RURAL ROUTE 01 BOX 38 35744
Bruce Pickett, prin.

East Brewton, Escambia Co., Pop. Code 4
Escambia County SD
Supt. – See Brewton
Neal MS, P O BOX 193 36427 – John Baxter, prin.

East Tallassee, Elmore Co.
Tallassee CSD
Supt. – See Tallassee
ES, CENTRAL BLVD 36023 – James Jones, prin.

Eclectic, Elmore Co., Pop. Code 4
Elmore County SD
Supt. – See Wetumpka
Elmore County ES, P O BOX 690 36024
Tony McGhee, prin.

Eight Mile, Mobile Co.
Mobile County SD
Supt. – See Mobile
ES, 5110 ST STEPHENS RD 36613
Richard Zitnik, prin.
Indian Springs ES, P O BOX C 36613
Isum Richardson, prin.

Elba, Coffee Co., Pop. Code 5
Coffee County SD
Sch. Sys. Enr. Code 4
Supt. – Clayton Bryant, P O BOX D 36323
Other Schools – See Jack, Kinston, New Brockton

Elba CSD
Sch. Sys. Enr. Code 4
Supt. – Lamar Foley, P O BOX F 36323
ES, 716 TROY HWY 36323 – Sara Sharpless, prin.
MS, 720 N DIXON ST 36323 – Dale Crowe, prin.

Elberta, Baldwin Co., Pop. Code 2
Baldwin County SD
Supt. – See Bay Minette
ES, 324 E CHREAGO ST 36530 – John Cobb, prin.

St. Benedict School, P O BOX A 36530

Eldridge, Walker Co., Pop. Code 2
Walker County SD
Supt. – See Jasper
ES, P O BOX 68 35554 – Mamie Noles, prin.

Elkmont, Limestone Co., Pop. Code 2
Limestone County SD
Supt. – See Athens
Limestone County S, P O BOX 150 35620
F. Dawson, prin.

Empire, Walker Co.
Walker County SD
Supt. – See Jasper
ES, RURAL ROUTE 02 BOX 32A 35063
James Morgan, prin.

Ensley, Jefferson Co.
Birmingham CSD
Supt. – See Birmingham
Bush Magnet MS, 1112 25TH ST N 35218
Deborah Horn, prin.
Baker ES, 3013 AVENUE F 35218
Ronnie McFarling, prin.
Minor ES, 2425 AVE S ENSLEY 35218
Linda Whatley, prin.

Enterprise, Coffee Co., Pop. Code 7
Enterprise CSD
Sch. Sys. Enr. Code 6
Supt. – Thad Morgan, 502 E WATTS ST 36330
College Street ES, W COLLEGE ST 36330
Charles Henderson, prin.
Coppinville MS, 413 N OUIDA ST 36330
Z. Fleming,Jr., prin.
Harrand Creek ES, MORGAN LN 36330
Colleen Gordan, prin.
Hillcrest ES, E WATTS AVE 36330
Hugh Williams, prin.
Holly Hill ES, HOLLY HILL ROAD 36330
Ron Blair, prin.
Pinedale ES, 207 DOTHAN HWY 36330
Sam Thompson,Jr., prin.

Rucker Boulevard ES, P O BOX 1274 36331
Milton Trawick, prin.

Eufaula, Barbour Co., Pop. Code 6
Barbour County SD
Supt. – See Clayton
Comer ES, RURAL ROUTE 03 36027
McDonald Comer, prin.

Eufaula CSD
Sch. Sys. Enr. Code 5
Supt. – Dr. Daniel Parker
420 SANFORD AVE 36027
Moorer MS, 101 SAINT FRANCIS ROAD 36027
Wayne Fiquett, prin.
Bluff City ES, STATE DOCKS ROAD 36027
John Hart, prin.
Sanford Avenue ES, 420 SANFORD AVE 36027
Frances Davis, prin.
Western Heights ES
520 PUMP STATION RD 36027
Vic Adkison, prin.

Eutaw, Greene Co., Pop. Code 5
Greene County SD
Sch. Sys. Enr. Code 4
Supt. – Charles Miles, P O BOX 569 35462
Carver ES, P O BOX 659 35462
Robert Young, prin.
Eatman ES, RURAL ROUTE 03 BOX 16 35462
Harvey Johnson,Jr., prin.
Other Schools – See Boligee, Forkland

Eva, Morgan Co., Pop. Code 2
Morgan County SD
Supt. – See Decatur
ES, P O BOX 8 35621 – Jasper Jones, prin.

Evergreen, Conecuh Co., Pop. Code 5
Conecuh County SD
Sch. Sys. Enr. Code 5
Supt. – William Coker, P O BOX 548 36401
Marshall MS, 504 REYNOLDS AVE 36401
Jim Burden, prin.
Evergreen City ES, 101 PERRYMAN ST 36401
Gene McDonald, prin.
Lyeffion ES, RURAL ROUTE 01 36401
Wilson Morgan, prin.
Southside MS, 220 S SHIPP ST 36401
Alex Johnson, prin.
Other Schools – See Castleberry, Repton

Excel, Monroe Co., Pop. Code 2
Monroe County SD
Supt. – See Monroeville
S, P O BOX 429 36439 – John Ross, prin.

Fairfield, Jefferson Co., Pop. Code 7
Fairfield CSD
Sch. Sys. Enr. Code 4
Supt. – Don Byrd, P O BOX 110 35064
Forest Hills MS, 700 GRASELI ROAD 35064
Harold Boykin, prin.
Donald ES, 715 VALLEY RD 35064
Howard Segars, prin.
Glen Oaks ES, 1301 HIGHLAND DR 35064
Yvette McPherson, prin.
Robinson ES, 301 61ST ST 35064
Arthur Jones, prin.

St. Mary's ES
6124 MYRON MASSEY BLVD 35064

Fairhope, Baldwin Co., Pop. Code 6
Baldwin County SD
Supt. – See Bay Minette
MS, RURAL ROUTE 01 BOX 371 36532
Lyle Underwood, prin.
ES, 2 N BISHOP ROAD 36532
Martha Bigby, prin.

Falkville, Morgan Co., Pop. Code 3
Morgan County SD
Supt. – See Decatur
S, P O BOX 388 35622 – Don Murphy, prin.

Fayette, Fayette Co., Pop. Code 5
Fayette County SD
Sch. Sys. Enr. Code 5
Supt. – Terry Dillard, P O BOX 599 35555
Hubbertville S, RURAL ROUTE 03 35555
Caldwell Hollingsworth, prin.
ES, 509 2ND ST NE 35555
Lohrone Cannon, prin.
Other Schools – See Berry

Five Points, Chambers Co., Pop. Code 2
Chambers County SD
Supt. – See Lafayette
ES, P O BOX 68 36855 – Raynard Grady, prin.

Flat Rock, Jackson Co.
Jackson County SD
Supt. – See Scottsboro
ES 35966 – Charles Starkey, prin.

Flomaton, Escambia Co., Pop. Code 4
Escambia County SD
Supt. – See Brewton
ES, RURAL ROUTE 02 BOX 80P 36441
David Curran, prin.

Florala, Covington Co., Pop. Code 5
Florala CSD
Sch. Sys. Enr. Code 2
Supt. – Erskine Ziglar, P O BOX 386 36442
Florala City ES, P O BOX 386 36442
Erskine Ziglar, prin.

Florence, Lauderdale Co., Pop. Code 8
Florence CSD
Sch. Sys. Enr. Code 6
Supt. – Thomas Taylor
541 RIVERVIEW DRIVE 35630
Brandon ES, 1701 COLE ST 35630
Dempsey Rutherford, prin.
Forest Hills ES, 101 STOVALL DR 35633
Floyd Parker, prin.
Harlan ES, 2233 MCBURNEY DR 35630
Fred Hendon, prin.
Hibbett ES, 1601 APPLEBY BLVD 35630
Roy Duncan, prin.
Powell ES, 1640 TUNE AVE 35630
Howard Robinson, prin.
Weeden ES, 500 BALDWIN ST 35630
Gloria Staggs, prin.

Lauderdale County SD
Sch. Sys. Enr. Code 6
Supt. – O. Linville, P O BOX 278 35631
Central S, RURAL ROUTE 04 BOX 126 35633
George Miller, prin.
Rogers S, RURAL ROUTE 01 BOX 300 35630
William Valentine, prin.
Wilson S, RURAL ROUTE 05 BOX 109 35630
Ralph Thompson, prin.
Cloverdale ES, RURAL ROUTE 12 BOX 63 35633
Roy Abston,Jr., prin.
Kilby Laboratory ES
UNIV OF NORTH ALABAMA 35630
Earl Gardner, prin.
Underwood ES
RURAL ROUTE 15 BOX 305 35633
Brenda Pool, prin.
Other Schools – See Anderson, Killen, Lexington,
Rogersville, Waterloo

St. Joseph School, 115 PLUM ST 35630

Foley, Baldwin Co., Pop. Code 5
Baldwin County SD
Supt. – See Bay Minette
MS, 2001 S CEDAR ST 36535
Tommie Conaway, prin.
ES, 200 N CEDAR ST 36535 – Brenda Pierce, prin.

Forkland, Greene Co., Pop. Code 2
Greene County SD
Supt. – See Eutaw
Birdine ES, RURAL ROUTE 01 BOX 327 36740
Abraham Kennard, prin.

Fort Deposit, Lowndes Co., Pop. Code 4
Lowndes County SD
Supt. – See Hayneville
Lowndes County MS, P O BOX P 36032
Willie Hill, prin.
ES, P O BOX 189 36032 – Dale Braxton, prin.

Fort Payne, De Kalb Co., Pop. Code 6
Dekalb County SD
Sch. Sys. Enr. Code 6
Supt. – Franklin Kellett, P O BOX 777 35967
Adamsburg ES
RURAL ROUTE 08 BOX 166 35967
Jim Cordell, prin.
Ruhuma ES, P O BOX 367M 35967
Larry McCallie, prin.
Other Schools – See Collinsville, Crossville, Fyffe,
Geraldine, Groveoak, Henagar, Ider, Mentone,
Rainsville, Sylvania, Valley Head

Ft. Payne CSD
Sch. Sys. Enr. Code 4
Supt. – John Holtzclaw, P O BOX 61 35967
MS, 4910 MARTIN AVE NE 35967
Quentin Benn, prin.
Forest Avenue ES, 101 FOREST AVE N 35967
John Culver, prin.
Williams Avenue MS
1700 WILLIAMS AVE NE 35967
Ronald Bell, prin.

Fosters, Tuscaloosa Co.
Tuscaloosa County SD
Supt. – See Tuscaloosa
Myrtlewood ES, P O BOX 130 35463
James Cain,Jr., prin.

Frisco City, Monroe Co., Pop. Code 4
Monroe County SD
Supt. – See Monroeville
ES, P O BOX 160 36445 – William Royster, prin.

Fruitdale, Washington Co., Pop. Code 2
Washington County SD
Supt. – See Chatom
S, P O BOX 381 36539 – Otis James, prin.

Fruithurst, Cleburne Co., Pop. Code 2
Cleburne County SD
Supt. – See Heflin
ES, P O BOX 128 36262 – Danny Mobley, prin.

Fulton, Clarke Co., Pop. Code 3
Clarke County SD
Supt. – See Grove Hill
ES, P O BOX 25 36446 – Tony Counselman, prin.

Fultondale, Jefferson Co., Pop. Code 6
Jefferson County SD
Supt. – See Birmingham
ES, 1500 WALKERS CHAPEL RD 35068
Lee Morton, prin.

Fyffe, De Kalb Co., Pop. Code 2
Dekalb County SD
Supt. – See Fort Payne
S, P O BOX 7   35971 – Nelson Ellis, prin.

Gadsden, Etowah Co., Pop. Code 8
Etowah County SD
Sch. Sys. Enr. Code 6
Supt. – Ralph Cain, 800 FORREST AVE   35901
Gaston S, RURAL ROUTE 06   35901
   Dennis Simmons, prin.
Hokes Bluff MS
   RURAL ROUTE 11 BOX 162   35903
   H. Reeves, prin.
Rainbow MS, RURAL ROUTE 13 BOX 18-A   35901
   Harriet McMeckin, prin.
Hokes Bluff ES, RURAL ROUTE 11   35903
   Francis Walton, prin.
Jones ES, RURAL ROUTE 13 BOX 18   35901
   Ralph Muskett, prin.
Lookout Mountain ES, RURAL ROUTE 08   35901
   Harold Gautney, prin.
Southside ES, RURAL ROUTE 01 BOX 721   35901
   Anita Hill, prin.
Other Schools – See Altoona, Attalla, Boaz, Glencoe

Gadsden CSD
Sch. Sys. Enr. Code 6
Supt. – Fred Taylor, P O BOX 184   35999
Cory MS, 715 RALEY ST   35903
   June Longshore, prin.
Disque MS, 612 TRACY ST   35901
   Elaine Campbell, prin.
Forrest MS, 2000 KYLE AVE   35904
   Wendell Traylor, prin.
Adams ES, 919 RALEY ST   35903
   Elaine Williams, prin.
Brown ES, 1231 ALCOTT RD   35901
   Sarah Pettus, prin.
Donehoo ES, 1109 E BROAD ST   35903
   Roszell Gadson, prin.
Floyd ES, 601 BLACK CREEK RD   35904
   Stanley Parrish, prin.
Mitchell ES, 1501 NOCCALULA RD   35901
   Barbara Overholtzer, prin.
Smith ES, 2000 S 11TH ST   35901
   Anthony Knowles, prin.
Striplin ES, 600 CLEVELAND AVE   35901
   James Bridges, prin.
Thompson ES, 236 GOLDENROD AVE   35901
   Elaine Mayes, prin.
Walnut Park ES, 3200 WALNUT ST   35904
   Eulene Sheffield, prin.

St. James Catholic School
   700 ALBERT RAINS BLVD   35901

Garden City, Cullman Co., Pop. Code 3
Cullman County SD
Supt. – See Cullman
ES, P O BOX 185   35070 – Rollan Edwards, prin.

Gardendale, Jefferson Co., Pop. Code 6
Jefferson County SD
Supt. – See Birmingham
Bragg JHS, 840 ASH AVE   35071
   Robert Chapman, prin.
ES, 860 BAUERS LN   35071 – George Park,Jr., prin.
Rogers ES, P O BOX 70   35071
   Clayton Reid,Jr., prin.

Gaylesville, Cherokee Co., Pop. Code 2
Cherokee County SD
Supt. – See Centre
S, P O BOX 8   35973 – Bill Wilson, prin.

Geneva, Geneva Co., Pop. Code 5
Geneva CSD
Sch. Sys. Enr. Code 4
Supt. – Wynnton Melton
   505 N CHEROKEE ST   36340
Mulkey ES, W MAPLE AVE   36340
   Dewey Spears, prin.

Geneva County SD
Sch. Sys. Enr. Code 5
Supt. – James Reeder, P O BOX 250   36340
Other Schools – See Coffee Springs, Hartford,
   Samson, Slocomb

Georgiana, Butler Co., Pop. Code 4
Butler County SD
Supt. – See Greenville
Austin ES, P O BOX 519   36033
   John Peagler, prin.

Geraldine, De Kalb Co., Pop. Code 3
Dekalb County SD
Supt. – See Fort Payne
S, P O BOX 145   35974 – B. Morris, prin.

Gilbertown, Choctaw Co., Pop. Code 2
Choctaw County SD
Supt. – See Butler
ES, P O BOX C   36908 – John White, prin.

Glencoe, Etowah Co., Pop. Code 5
Etowah County SD
Supt. – See Gadsden
MS, 1000 LONESOME BEND ROAD   35905
   Scarlett Farley, prin.
ES, 207 N COLLEGE ST   35905
   Martha Tumlin, prin.

Goodsprings, Walker Co., Pop. Code 3
Walker County SD
Supt. – See Jasper

Martin S, P O BOX 157   35560 – Ted Craven, prin.

Goodwater, Coosa Co., Pop. Code 4
Coosa County SD
Supt. – See Rockford
ES   35072 – Robert Armour, prin.

Gordo, Pickens Co., Pop. Code 4
Pickens County SD
Supt. – See Carrollton
SE, P O BOX J   35466 – Barry Smitherman, prin.

Goshen, Pike Co., Pop. Code 2
Pike County SD
Supt. – See Troy
ES, RURAL ROUTE 01 BOX 284   36035
   Elaine Carmichael, prin.

Grand Bay, Mobile Co., Pop. Code 3
Mobile County SD
Supt. – See Mobile
Castlen ES, P O BOX 276   36541
   O. Annette Rehm, prin.

Grant, Marshall Co., Pop. Code 2
Marshall County SD
Supt. – See Guntersville
Smith ES, RURAL ROUTE 03   35747
   Thomas Little, prin.

Graysville, Jefferson Co., Pop. Code 5
Jefferson County SD
Supt. – See Birmingham
Brookville ES, RURAL ROUTE 01 BOX 599   35073
   Zsolt Batizy, prin.

Greensboro, Hale Co., Pop. Code 5
Hale County SD
Sch. Sys. Enr. Code 5
Supt. – Dan Butler, P O BOX 360   36744
Greensboro East S, P O BOX 460   36744
   Clinton Brasfield, prin.
Greensboro West S, P O BOX 490   36744
   Victor Scott, prin.
Other Schools – See Akron, Moundville, Newbern

Greenville, Butler Co., Pop. Code 6
Butler County SD
Sch. Sys. Enr. Code 5
Supt. – Jimmie Lawrence
   101 BUTLER CIRCLE   36037
JHS, 300 OVERLOOK ROAD   36037
   Gerald Benson, prin.
Baptist Hill PS, SIMPSON ST   36037
   Estelle Womack, prin.
MS, BUTLER CIR   36037 – Allin Whittle, prin.
Parmer ES, BUTLER CIR   36037
   Mary Funderburk, prin.
Other Schools – See Georgiana, Mc Kenzie

Grove Hill, Clarke Co., Pop. Code 4
Clarke County SD
Sch. Sys. Enr. Code 5
Supt. – Melvin Joiner, P O BOX 936   36451
Wilson Hall MS, P O BOX 458   36451
   Constance Bowen, prin.
ES   36451 – Terry Foster, prin.
Other Schools – See Coffeeville, Fulton, Jackson

Groveoak, De Kalb Co.
Dekalb County SD
Supt. – See Fort Payne
ES   35975 – R. Simpson, prin.

Guin, Marion Co., Pop. Code 4
Marion County SD
Supt. – See Hamilton
ES, P O BOX 10   35563 – Jimmy Atkinson, prin.

Gulf Shores, Baldwin Co., Pop. Code 4
Baldwin County SD
Supt. – See Bay Minette
ES, P O BOX 1339   36542 – Robert Zeanah, prin.

Guntersville, Marshall Co., Pop. Code 6
Guntersville CSD
Sch. Sys. Enr. Code 4
Supt. – Harold Patterson, P O BOX 129   35976
Carlisle Park MS, 801 SUNSET DRIVE   35976
   Bobby Erwin, prin.
Cherokee MS, 3300 HIGHWAY 79   35976
   Sue Morgan, prin.
ES, 1800 LUSK ST   35976 – Margaret Daniel, prin.

Marshall County SD
Sch. Sys. Enr. Code 6
Supt. – Charles Edmonds
   RURAL ROUTE 02 BOX 403-B   35976
Claysville ES, HCR 62 BOX 14   35976
   Andrew Lee, prin.
Other Schools – See Albertville, Arab, Boaz, Douglas,
   Grant, Union Grove

Gurley, Madison Co., Pop. Code 3
Madison County SD
Supt. – See Huntsville
Madison County S, P O BOX 158   35748
   Betty Burch, prin.

Hackleburg, Marion Co., Pop. Code 3
Marion County SD
Supt. – See Hamilton
ES, P O BOX 340   35564 – Charles Estes, prin.

Haleyville, Winston Co., Pop. Code 5
Haleyville CSD
Sch. Sys. Enr. Code 4
Supt. – Dr. Boyce Albright, 1800 20TH ST   35565

14th Avenue ES, 14TH AVE   35565
   Howard Lyons, prin.
21st Street MS, 21ST ST   35565
   Howard Lyons, prin.

Hamilton, Marion Co., Pop. Code 5
Marion County SD
Sch. Sys. Enr. Code 5
Supt. – Roberta Goggans, P O BOX 67   35570
MS, P O BOX 156   35570 – Virginia Stovall, prin.
ES, P O BOX 10   35570 – William Clark, prin.
Other Schools – See Bear Creek, Brilliant, Guin,
   Hackleburg

Hanceville, Cullman Co.
Cullman County SD
Supt. – See Cullman
S, 801 COMMERCE ST   35077 – Bill Lay, prin.

Hartford, Geneva Co., Pop. Code 5
Geneva County SD
Supt. – See Geneva
Geneva County S, 310 LILY ST   36344
   Mike Whitaker, prin.

Hartselle, Morgan Co., Pop. Code 6
Hartselle CSD
Sch. Sys. Enr. Code 5
Supt. – Lee Hartsell, P O BOX 97   35640
JHS, 101 PETAIN ST SW   35640
   Frank Parker, prin.
Burleson ES, 305 E COLLEGE ST   35640
   E. Stewart Bennett, prin.
Crestline ES, 208 CRESTLINE ST SW   35640
   Loy Greenhill,Jr., prin.

Morgan County SD
Supt. – See Decatur
Sparkman ES, RURAL ROUTE 03 BOX 281   35640
   Ferrell Clemons, prin.

Harvest, Madison Co.
Madison County SD
Supt. – See Huntsville
ES, P O BOX 57   35749 – Nancy Hughes, prin.

Hayden, Blount Co., Pop. Code 2
Blount County SD
Supt. – See Oneonta
ES, 160 BRACKEN LN   35079
   W. Dale Thomas, prin.

Hayneville, Lowndes Co., Pop. Code 2
Lowndes County SD
Sch. Sys. Enr. Code 5
Supt. – Eli Seaborn, P O BOX 755   36040
MS, P O BOX 307   36040 – Theresa Douglas, prin.
Central ES, RURAL ROUTE 02 BOX 49A   36040
   Percy Miller, prin.
Russell ES, RURAL ROUTE 02 BOX 103   36040
   Larue Pringle, prin.
White Hall ES, RURAL ROUTE 01 BOX 193   36040
   Ed King, prin.
Other Schools – See Fort Deposit

Hazel Green, Madison Co., Pop. Code 5
Madison County SD
Supt. – See Huntsville
S, P O BOX 108   35750 – E. Deason, prin.

Headland, Henry Co., Pop. Code 5
Henry County SD
Supt. – See Abbeville
MS, P O BOX 324   36345 – George Davis, prin.
ES, 305 MITCHELL ST   36345
   Sherrill Singleton, prin.

Heflin, Cleburne Co., Pop. Code 5
Cleburne County SD
Sch. Sys. Enr. Code 4
Supt. – Scott Dennis
   RURAL ROUTE 04 BOX 24   36264
Cleburne County ES
   RURAL ROUTE 04 BOX 24   36264
   Robert Chambless, prin.
Pleasant Grove ES
   RURAL ROUTE 03 BOX 374   36264
   Don Chandler, prin.
Other Schools – See Fruithurst, Ranburne

Helena, Shelby Co., Pop. Code 4
Shelby County SD
Supt. – See Columbiana
ES, P O BOX 271   35080 – Billy Bramblett, prin.

Henagar, De Kalb Co., Pop. Code 4
Dekalb County SD
Supt. – See Fort Payne
ES, P O BOX 98   35978 – Buman Hulsey, prin.

Higdon, Jackson Co., Pop. Code 2
Jackson County SD
Supt. – See Scottsboro
North Sand Mountain S, P O BOX 128   35979
   Jim Kirby, prin.

Highland Home, Crenshaw Co.
Crenshaw County SD
Supt. – See Luverne
S, HIGHWAY 331   36041 – C. Richardson, prin.

Hillsboro, Lawrence Co., Pop. Code 2
Lawrence County SD
Supt. – See Moulton
Tennessee Valley ES, P O BOX 97   35643
   Jewell Satchel, prin.

Holly Pond, Cullman Co., Pop. Code 2
Cullman County SD
Supt. – See Cullman
S, P O BOX 70 35083 – David Rogers, prin.

Hollywood, Jackson Co., Pop. Code 2
Jackson County SD
Supt. – See Scottsboro
ES 35752 – Bruce Money, prin.

Holt, Tuscaloosa Co., Pop. Code 5
Tuscaloosa County SD
Supt. – See Tuscaloosa
ES, 1001 CRESCENT RIDGE RD NE 35404
Barbara Spencer, prin.

Holy Trinty, Russell Co.

St. Joseph ES, C/O POST OFFICE 36859

Homewood, Jefferson Co., Pop. Code 8
Homewood CSD
Sch. Sys. Enr. Code 5
Supt. – Robert Bumpus, P O BOX 6066 35259
MS, 1108 FRISCO ST 35209
Donald Cornutt, prin.
Edgewood ES, 901 COLLEGE AVE 35209
Martha Robbins, prin.
Kent ES, 213 HALL AVE 35209
Donald Burgess, prin.
Shades Cahaba ES
3001 MONTGOMERY HWY 35209
Michael Miller, prin.

Hope Hull, Montgomery Co., Pop. Code 6
Montgomery County SD
Supt. – See Montgomery
Pintlala ES, RURAL ROUTE 01 36043
Robert Belser, prin.

Hueytown, Jefferson Co., Pop. Code 6
Jefferson County SD
Supt. – See Birmingham
ES, 112 FOREST RD 35023 – Stephen Bailey, prin.
North Highland ES, 2021 29TH AVE N 35023
Sybil Reese, prin.
Zinnerman ES, 126 JOHNSON DR 35023
Ray Bellew, prin.

Huntsville, Madison Co., Pop. Code 9
Huntsville CSD
Sch. Sys. Enr. Code 7
Supt. – Mary Caylor, P O BOX 1256 35807
Chapman MS, 2006 REUBEN DRIVE NE 35811
John Calvarese, prin.
Davis Hills MS
3221 MASTIN LAKE ROAD NW 35810
Charles Ford, prin.
MS, 817 ADAMS ST SE 35801
Louise Amos, prin.
Mountain Gap MS
821 MOUNTAIN GAP ROAD SE 35803
Robert Ballinger, prin.
Stone MS, 2620 CLINTON AVE W 35805
Alta Morrison, prin.
Westlawn MS, 4217 9TH AVE SW 35805
Earline Pinckley, prin.
White MS, 4800 SPARKMAN DRIVE NW 35810
Jack Anthony, prin.
Whitesburg MS, 107 SANDERS ROAD SW 35802
James Puckett, prin.
Academy for Academics\Arts ES
2800 POPLAR ST NW 35805
Dorothy Davis, prin.
Academy for Science\Foreign Language ES
3221 MASTIN LAKE RD NW 35810
Ollye Doyle, prin.
Blossomwood ES
1321 WOODMONT AVE SE 35801
Nancy Rooks, prin.
Chaffee ES, 7900 WHITTIER RD SW 35802
Jo Ann Burchfield, prin.
Chapman ES, 2006 REUBEN DR NE 35811
Ina Hucks, prin.
Colonial Hills ES, 3112 MERIDIAN ST N 35811
Jane Kelly, prin.
East Clinton ES
605 CLINTON AVEAKE ROAD 35801
Larry Tessman, prin.
Farley ES, 12820 S MEMORIAL PKY 35803
Rosalie Horton, prin.
Highlands ES, 2500 BARNEY TER NW 35810
Norma Harris, prin.
Jones Valley ES, 4908 GARTH RD SE 35802
Marilyn Dawson, prin.
Lakewood ES, 3501 KENWOOD DR NW 35810
Norton Webb, prin.
Lincoln ES, 1110 MERIDIAN ST N 35801
Joe McFerrin, prin.
McDonnell ES, 4010 BINDERTON PL SW 35805
Julia Wickwire, prin.
Monte Sano ES
1107 MONTE SANO BLVD SE 35801
Juanita Hillis, prin.
Montview ES, 2600 GARVIN RD NW 35810
Evelyn Pratt, prin.
Morris ES, 4801 BOB WALLACE AVE SW 35805
Nellie Berry, prin.
Mountain Gap ES
821 MOUNTAIN GAP RD SE 35803
Jo Ann Sturdivant, prin.
Ridgecrest ES, 3505 CERRO VISTA DR SW 35805
Mildred Haga, prin.
Rolling Hills ES, 2109 HILLTOP TERR 35810
Teri Stokes, prin.

Terry Heights ES, 2820 BARBARA DR NW 35816
Ann Moore, prin.
University Place ES
4503 UNIVERSITY AVE NW 35805
Norman Sharp, prin.
Weatherly Heights ES
1307 CANNSTATT DR SE 35803
Clarence Herring, prin.
West Huntsville ES, 3001 9TH AVE SW 35805
Earnest Horton, prin.
West Mastin Lake ES
5308 MASTIN LAKE RD NW 35810
Helen Jamar, prin.
Whitesburg ES, 6810 WHITESBURG DR S 35802
Ellen Brusick, prin.

Madison County SD
Sch. Sys. Enr. Code 7
Supt. – Richard Chapman, P O BOX 226 35804
Central ES, 990 RYLAND PIKE NE 35811
Larry Sharp, prin.
Monrovia ES, 1030 JEFF RD NW 35806
Carl Barnes, prin.
Riverton ES, 2615 WINCHESTER RD NE 35811
Lloyd Humphrey, prin.
Other Schools – See Gurley, Harvest, Hazel Green,
Madison, Meridianville, New Hope, New Market,
Owens Cross Roads, Toney

Oakwood Academy 35802
Randolph School, 1005 DRAKE AVE SE 35802
Westminster Christian Academy
1400 EVANGEL DR NW 35816
Grace Lutheran School
3321 S MEMORIAL PKY 35801
Holy Family School
2300 BEASLEY AVE NW 35816
Holy Spirit Catholic School
619 AIRPORT RD SW 35802

Hurtsboro, Russell Co., Pop. Code 3
Russell County SD
Supt. – See Phenix City
Russell ES, P O BOX 257 36860
Larry Screws, prin.

Huxford, Escambia Co.
Escambia County SD
Supt. – See Brewton
ES, P O BOX 549 36543 – Milner Donald, prin.

Ider, De Kalb Co., Pop. Code 3
Dekalb County SD
Supt. – See Fort Payne
S 35981 – Wayne Hardman, prin.

Irondale, Jefferson Co., Pop. Code 6
Jefferson County SD
Supt. – See Birmingham
ES, 301 18TH ST S 35210 – Dennis Duncan, prin.

Irvington, Mobile Co.
Mobile County SD
Supt. – See Mobile
Dixon ES, IRVINGTON-BLB HWY 36544
Martha Peek, prin.

Jack, Coffee Co.
Coffee County SD
Supt. – See Elba
Zion Chapel S, RURAL ROUTE 01 36346
Nelson Whitehurst, prin.

Jackson, Clarke Co., Pop. Code 6
Clarke County SD
Supt. – See Grove Hill
MS, P O BOX 397 36545 – Ronald Powe, prin.
Gillmore ES, P O BOX 867 36545
Wanda Roberts, prin.

Jacksonville, Calhoun Co., Pop. Code 6
Calhoun County SD
Supt. – See Anniston
Pleasant Valley S
RURAL ROUTE 02 BOX 498 36265
Wayne Wigley, prin.

Jacksonville CSD
Sch. Sys. Enr. Code 4
Supt. – Anita Hardin
520 PELHAM ROAD N 36265
Stone ES, 115 COLLEGE ST 36265
Mark Washington, prin.

Jasper, Walker Co., Pop. Code 7
Jasper CSD
Sch. Sys. Enr. Code 5
Supt. – Bobby Neighbors, P O BOX 500 35502
Maddox MS, 1602 2ND AVE 35501
Wayne Henslee, prin.
Memorial Park ES, 800 10TH AVE W 35501
Howard Norris, prin.
Simmons ES, 1001 19TH ST E 35501
Brack Orear,Jr., prin.
West Jasper ES, 1500 19TH ST W 35501
Patricia Robertson, prin.

Walker County SD
Sch. Sys. Enr. Code 6
Supt. – John Brown, P O BOX 311 35502
Curry MS, RURAL ROUTE 13 BOX 66 35501
George Miller, prin.
Curry ES, RURAL ROUTE 13 BOX 66 35501
Jimmy Stephenson, prin.
Farmstead ES, RURAL ROUTE 11 BOX 2 35501
Percy Goode, prin.

Valley ES, RURAL ROUTE 12 BOX 81B 35501
Gwin Wells, prin.
Other Schools – See Cordova, Dora, Eldridge, Empire,
Goodsprings, Nauvoo, Oakman, Parrish, Sipsey,
Sumiton, Townley

Jemison, Chilton Co., Pop. Code 4
Chilton County SD
Supt. – See Clanton
ES, P O BOX 162 35085 – Gene Cost, prin.

Joppa, Morgan Co.
Cullman County SD
Supt. – See Cullman
ES, P O BOX 8 35087 – Bobby Moody, prin.

Morgan County SD
Supt. – See Decatur
Ryan ES, RURAL ROUTE 01 35087
Ted Mauldin, prin.

Kellyton, Coosa Co.
Coosa County SD
Supt. – See Rockford
ES 35089 – James McClellan, prin.

Killen, Lauderdale Co., Pop. Code 3
Lauderdale County SD
Supt. – See Florence
Brooks ES, P O BOX 8 35645
John Winchester, prin.

Kinston, Coffee Co., Pop. Code 3
Coffee County SD
Supt. – See Elba
S, P O BOX 158 36453 – Ruffin Cain, prin.

Laceys Spring, Morgan Co., Pop. Code 2
Morgan County SD
Supt. – See Decatur
ES, P O BOX 10 35754 – David McAnally, prin.

Lafayette, Chambers Co., Pop. Code 5
Chambers County SD
Sch. Sys. Enr. Code 6
Supt. – Jerry Milner, P O BOX 408D 36862
Chambers County S
RURAL ROUTE 01 BOX 146 36862
Dwight Sanderson, prin.
Lafayette Eastside ES, 300 AVENUE A SE 36862
Beatrice Walton, prin.
Lafayette Southside MS, 621 1ST ST SE 36862
Mack Smith, prin.
Other Schools – See Five Points, Lanett, Valley

Lanett, Chambers Co., Pop. Code 6
Chambers County SD
Supt. – See Lafayette
Huguley ES, RURAL ROUTE 03 BOX 926 36863
Douglas Hubbard,Jr., prin.

Lanett CSD
Sch. Sys. Enr. Code 4
Supt. – Daniel Washburn, P O BOX 329 36863
JHS, P O BOX 349 36863 – Rose Williams, prin.
Lanett Central ES, P O BOX 448 36863
Athan Eiland, prin.
Lanett MS South, P O BOX 427 36863
H. Malcom Gilchrist,Jr., prin.

Springwood School, CHERRY DR 36863

Leeds, Jefferson Co., Pop. Code 6
Jefferson County SD
Supt. – See Birmingham
JHS, RURAL ROUTE 04 BOX 557 35094
James Roberson, prin.
ES, 201 ASHVILLE RD SE 35094
Jean Clark, prin.

St. Clair County SD
Supt. – See Ashville
Moody ES, RURAL ROUTE 03 BOX 811 35094
James Lawley, prin.

Leesburg, Cherokee Co., Pop. Code 1
Cherokee County SD
Supt. – See Centre
Sand Rock S, RURAL ROUTE 01 35983
L. Pearson, prin.

Leighton, Colbert Co., Pop. Code 4
Colbert County SD
Supt. – See Tuscumbia
MS, P O BOX 309 35646 – Walter Davis, prin.
Hatton ES, RURAL ROUTE 01 35646
Hagan Cooper, prin.
ES, P O BOX 399 35646 – Joe Sandlin, prin.

Leroy, Washington Co.
Washington County SD
Supt. – See Chatom
S, P O BOX 40 36548 – Cleophus Stephens, prin.

Lester, Limestone Co., Pop. Code 1
Limestone County SD
Supt. – See Athens
West Limestone S
RURAL ROUTE 01 BOX 99 35647
Aubry Privett, prin.

Lexington, Lauderdale Co., Pop. Code 2
Lauderdale County SD
Supt. – See Florence
S, P O BOX 70 35648 – Patrick Brown, prin.

Lincoln, Talladega Co., Pop. Code 4
Talladega County SD
Supt. – See Talladega

S, P O BOX 197   35096 – Jimmy Nash, prin.
Drew MS, RURAL ROUTE 01 BOX 177D   35096
    James Coleman, prin.

Linden, Marengo Co., Pop. Code 5
    Linden CSD
    Sch. Sys. Enr. Code 3
    Supt. – Paul Whitcomb, P O BOX C   36748
    Austin JHS, P O BOX 577   36748
      Walter Davis, prin.
    ES, P O BOX 557   36748 – Larry Huckabee, prin.

    Marengo County SD
    Sch. Sys. Enr. Code 4
    Supt. – Marcus Walters, P O BOX 398   36748
    Other Schools – See Demopolis, Dixon's Mills, Sweet
      Water, Thomaston

Lineville, Clay Co., Pop. Code 4
    Clay County SD
    Supt. – See Ashland
    Barfield ES, RURAL ROUTE 02   36266
      Horace Mattox, prin.
    ES, P O BOX 207   36266 – Jo Ann Blair, prin.

Lisman, Chotaw Co., Pop. Code 2
    Choctaw County SD
    Supt. – See Butler
    ES, P O BOX 127   36912 – Lee Edwards,Jr., prin.

Livingston, Sumter Co., Pop. Code 4
    Sumter County SD
    Sch. Sys. Enr. Code 5
    Supt. – David Jones, P O BOX 10   35470
    ES, P O BOX 370   35470 – Eddie Dawson, prin.
    Other Schools – See Cuba, Panola, York

Loachapoka, Lee Co., Pop. Code 2
    Lee County SD
    Supt. – See Opelika
    S, P O BOX 187   36865 – George Ervin, prin.

Lockhart, Covington Co., Pop. Code 3
    Covington County SD
    Supt. – See Andalusia
    Harlan ES, P O BOX 267   36455
      Terry Holley, prin.

Locust Fork, Blount Co., Pop. Code 2
    Blount County SD
    Supt. – See Oneonta
    S, P O BOX 46   35097 – Gene Vinson, prin.

Logan, Cullman Co.
    Cullman County SD
    Supt. – See Cullman
    ES, P O BOX 120   35098 – Billy Pugh, prin.

Louisville, Barbour Co., Pop. Code 3
    Barbour County SD
    Supt. – See Clayton
    ES   36048 – William Dean, prin.

Lower Peach Tree, Monroe Co.
    Monroe County SD
    Supt. – See Monroeville
    Monroe S, RURAL FREE DELIVERY   36751
      H. Williams, prin.

Loxley, Baldwin Co., Pop. Code 3
    Baldwin County SD
    Supt. – See Bay Minette
    MS, P O BOX 38   36551 – Dudley Howell, prin.
    ES, P O BOX 8   36551 – Mickael Wade, prin.

Luverne, Crenshaw Co., Pop. Code 4
    Crenshaw County SD
    Sch. Sys. Enr. Code 5
    Supt. – Samuel Carr, P O BOX 167   36049
    S, P O BOX 272   36049 – Elton Mitchell, prin.
    Other Schools – See Brantley, Dozier, Highland Home

Lynn, Winston Co., Pop. Code 2
    Winston County SD
    Supt. – See Double Springs
    S, P O BOX 128   35575 – Danny Hogan, prin.

Mc Calla, Jefferson Co., Pop. Code 3
    Jefferson County SD
    Supt. – See Birmingham
    McAdory S, RURAL ROUTE 01   35111
      Nell Salamone, prin.

Mc Intosh, Washington Co., Pop. Code 2
    Washington County SD
    Supt. – See Chatom
    Boykin ES, P O BOX 357   36553 – Vera Dean, prin.
    Reeds Chapel ES, P O BOX 209   36553
      Gallasneed Weaver, prin.

Mc Kenzie, Butler Co., Pop. Code 2
    Butler County SD
    Supt. – See Greenville
    S, P O BOX 158   36456 – Dwight Vickery, prin.

Madison, Madison Co., Pop. Code 5
    Madison County SD
    Supt. – See Huntsville
    MS, 17 COLLEGE ST   35758 – Henry Bradley, prin.
    West Madison ES
      4976 WALL TRIANA HWY   35758
      Dee Fowler, prin.

Maplesville, Chilton Co., Pop. Code 3
    Chilton County SD
    Supt. – See Clanton
    Isabelle S, RURAL ROUTE 02   BOX 239   36750
      Martha Mims, prin.
    S, P O BOX 146   36750 – George Walker,Jr., prin.

Marbury, Autauga Co., Pop. Code 5
    Autauga County SD
    Supt. – See Prattville
    S, P O BOX A   36051 – Kerwin Carson, prin.

Marion, Perry Co., Pop. Code 5
    Perry County SD
    Sch. Sys. Enr. Code 4
    Supt. – Willie Carr, GREENSBORO ST   36756
    West Side MS, P O BOX 1020   36756
      Albert Nelson, prin.
    ES, P O BOX 960   36756 – Jerildine Melton, prin.
    Other Schools – See Selma, Uniontown

Marion Junction, Dallas Co.
    Dallas County SD
    Supt. – See Selma
    Harrell ES, RURAL ROUTE 01 BOX 102   36759
      Henry Ketton, prin.

Mentone, De Kalb Co., Pop. Code 2
    Dekalb County SD
    Supt. – See Fort Payne
    Moon Lake ES, P O BOX 444   35984
      Charles Bell, prin.

Meridianville, Madison Co.
    Madison County SD
    Supt. – See Huntsville
    Moores Mill ES, 8861 MOORES MILL RD   35759
      Lynn Fanning, prin.

Midfield, Jefferson Co., Pop. Code 6
    Midfield CSD
    Sch. Sys. Enr. Code 2
    Supt. – Andy Rowell, P O BOX 7889   35228
    Rutledge MS, 1221 8TH ST   35228
      Herbert Alexander, prin.
    ES, 416 PARKWOOD ST   35228
      Joel Roberts, prin.

Midland City, Dale Co., Pop. Code 4
    Dale County SD
    Supt. – See Ozark
    ES, P O BOX A   36350 – Bobby Moon, prin.

Midway, Bullock Co., Pop. Code 3
    Bullock County SD
    Supt. – See Union Springs
    Merritt ES, P O BOX 10   36053
      Ruby Swanson, prin.

Millbrook, Elmore Co., Pop. Code 4
    Elmore County SD
    Supt. – See Wetumpka
    MS, P O BOX 487   36054 – Theodore Jackson, prin.
    Robinson Springs ES
      RURAL ROUTE 02 BOX 616   36054
      Carol McGalliard, prin.

Millers Ferry, Wilcox Co.
    Wilcox County SD
    Supt. – See Camden
    Wilcox Co. Training ES   36760
      Mildred Sanders, prin.

Millerville, Clay Co.
    Clay County SD
    Supt. – See Ashland
    ES, P O BOX 17   36267 – Bobby Joe Vinson, prin.

Millport, Lamar Co., Pop. Code 4
    Lamar County SD
    Supt. – See Vernon
    South Lamar S, P O BOX 127   35576
      Doug Cash, prin.

Millry, Washington Co., Pop. Code 3
    Washington County SD
    Supt. – See Chatom
    S, P O BOX 65   36558 – W. A. Taylor,Jr., prin.

Mobile, Mobile Co., Pop. Code 9
    Mobile County SD
    Sch. Sys. Enr. Code 8
    Supt. – Billy Salter, P O BOX 1327   36633
    Azalea MS
      3800 PLEASANT VALLEY ROAD   36609
      Thomas Greene, prin.
    Chastang MS, 2800 BERKELY AVE   36617
      James Buskey, prin.
    Dunbar MS, 500 SAINT ANTHONY ST   36603
      Freddie Sigler, prin.
    Eanes MS, 1901 HURTEL ST   36605
      Charles Potts, prin.
    Hillsdale MS, 6301 BILOXI AVE   36608
      Jackie Birindelli, prin.
    Phillips MS, 3255 OLD SHELL ROAD   36607
      John Sklopan, prin.
    Pillans MS, 2051 MILITARY ROAD   36605
      Annette Sanders, prin.
    Scarborough MS, 1800 PHILLIPS LANE   36618
      Vance Allen, prin.
    Washington MS, 1961 ANDREWS ST   36617
      Eddie Butler, prin.
    Austin ES, 150 PROVIDENT LN   36608
      Glenys Mason, prin.
    Baker ES, RURAL ROUTE 05 BOX 87   36695
      Sarah Morrow, prin.
    Brazier ES, 2161 BUTLER ST   36617
      Ralph Wilson, prin.
    Council ES, 751 WILKINSON ST   36603
      Gloria York, prin.
    Crichton ES, 2825 SPRINGHILL AVE   36607
      Carrie Lee, prin.
    Dickson ES, 4645 BIT & SPUR RD   36608
      Betty Lee, prin.

Dodge ES, 2615 LONGLEAF DR   36693
    John Myrick, prin.
Fonde ES, 3956 COTTAGE HILL RD   36609
    James Hamner,Jr., prin.
Fonvielee ES, 461 DONALD ST   36617
    Jo Ann Harris, prin.
Forest Hill ES, 4501 MOFFAT RD   36618
    Grace Daniels, prin.
Griggs ES, THREE NOTCH ROAD   36619
    Lois Stevenson, prin.
Hall ES, 1108 ANTWERP ST   36605
    Marilyn Howell, prin.
Hollingers Island ES
    RURAL ROUTE 01 BOX 151A   36605
    Mona Girby, prin.
Holloway ES, 625 STANTON RD   36617
    Gertrude Baker, prin.
Leinkauf ES, 1451 CHURCH ST   36604
    Terry Knight, prin.
Maryvale ES, 1901 N MARYVALE ST   36605
    Joyce Hunter, prin.
Meadowlake ES
    8115 3 NOTCH KRONER ROAD   36609
    Claretha Finley, prin.
Mertz ES, 950 MCRAE AVE   36606
    Fred Fendley, prin.
Morningside ES, 2700 S GREENBRIER DR   36605
    Thomas Stokes, prin.
Old Shell Road ES, 1706 OLD SHELL RD   36604
    Bobby Smith, prin.
Orchard ES, RURAL ROUTE 08 BOX 241   36618
    Charles Downey, prin.
Shephard ES, 1176 AZALEA RD   36693
    Lionel Alexander, prin.
South Brookley ES, 1600 BOYKIN BLVD   36605
    Tina Nelson, prin.
Thomas ES, 743 ALVAREZ AVE   36612
    Claire Quinlivan, prin.
Westlawn ES, 3071 RALSTON RD   36606
    Susan McRae, prin.
ES, 265 N WASSON AVE   36612
    Pauline Essary, prin.
Will ES, 5750 SUMMIT AVE   36608
    Tommy Knight, prin.
Williams ES, 2173 DAUPHIN ISLAND PKY   36605
    Louise Trimble, prin.
Woodcock ES, 261 RICKARBY ST   36606
    Sallie Knight, prin.
Other Schools – See Bayou La Batre, Chickasaw,
    Citronelle, Dauphin Island, Eight Mile, Grand Bay,
    Irvington, Mount Vernon, Prichard, Saint Elmo,
    Saraland, Satsuma, Semmes, Theodore, Wilmer

Julius T. Wright School, 65 N MOBILE ST   36609
St. Paul's Episcopal School
    161 DOGWOOD LANE   36608
UMS Preparatory School, 65 N MOBILE ST   36607
Corpus Christi School, 6300 MCKENNA DR   36608
Holy Family School, 1400 JOYCE RD   36618
Little Flower ES, 2103 GOVERNMENT ST   36606
Most Pure Heart of Mary School
    310 SENGSTAK ST   36603
Our Lady of Lourdes School
    1624 BOYKIN BLVD   36605
St. Dominics ES, 4160 BURMA RD   36693
St. Ignatius ES, 3650 SPRING HILL AVE   36608
St. Lukes Episcopal School
    980 AZALEA RD   36693
St. Mary ES, 107 N LAFAYETTE ST   36604
St. Monica ES, 1950 ST MONICA DR   36605
St. Pius X School, 217 S SAGE AVE   36606
St. Vincent De Paul School
    450 LARKSPUR DR   36619

Monroeville, Monroe Co., Pop. Code 5
    Monroe County SD
    Sch. Sys. Enr. Code 6
    Supt. – B. Grissette, P O BOX 159   36461
    JHS, 315 YORK ST   36460 – Terry Wilkerson, prin.
    ES, 420 S MOUNT PLEASANT AVE   36460
      Clayton Hale, prin.
    MS, 518 PICKENS ST   36460
      Darenell Payne, prin.
    Other Schools – See Beatrice, Excel, Frisco City,
    Lower Peach Tree, Uriah

Montevallo, Shelby Co., Pop. Code 5
    Shelby County SD
    Supt. – See Columbiana
    MS, 195 SANFORD ST   35115
      Johnny McClain, prin.
    ES, 279 JETER CIR   35115 – James Jones, prin.

Montgomery, Montgomery Co., Pop. Code 9
    Montgomery County SD
    Sch. Sys. Enr. Code 8
    Supt. – Thomas Bobo, P O BOX 1991   36197
    Bear ES, 2525 CHURCHHILL DR   36111
      Pamela Morgan, prin.
    Bellingrath ES, 3488 S COURT ST   36105
      Willie Thomas, prin.
    Brewbaker IS, 4455 BREWBAKER DR   36116
      Walter Bibbins, prin.
    Brewbaker PS, 4455 BREWBAKER DR   36116
      Robert Harry, prin.
    Carver ES, 2001 W FAIRVIEW AVE   36108
      Cindy McKenzie, prin.
    Catoma ES
      1780 MITHCELL YOUNG ROAD   36108
      Emily Segers, prin.
    Chisholm ES, 307 E VANDIVER BLVD   36110
      Frank Goolsby, prin.
    Crump ES, 3510 WOODLEY RD   36116
      Marvorene Tucker, prin.

Dalraida ES, 440 DALRAIDA RD   36109
  Anne Jones, prin.
Dannelly ES, 3425 CARTER HILL RD   36111
  Joesph Armistead, prin.
Davis ES, 3605 CLEVELAND AVE   36105
  Maggie Stringer, prin.
Davis Learning ES, 309 N CALIFORNIA ST   36107
  June Ferguson, prin.
Dozier ES, 200 EASTERN BY-PASS   36109
  Beatrice Sexton, prin.
Fews ES, 321 EARLY ST   36104
  Essie Braggs, prin.
Flowers ES, 3510 HARRISON RD   36109
  Sandra Pugh, prin.
Floyd ES, 630 AUGUSTA AVE   36111
  Arthur McKnatt, prin.
Forest Avenue ES, 1700 W FIFTH ST   36106
  Margaret Compton, prin.
Harrison ES, 164 S BLVD E   36105
  Bennie Smith, prin.
Hayneville Road ES
  3315 HAYNEVILLE RD   36108
  Vernon Baker, prin.
Head ES, 3950 ATLANTA HWY   36109
  Bertha Tiller, prin.
Highland Avenue ES
  2024 HIGHLAND AVE   36107
  Carolyn Jackson, prin.
Highland Gardens ES, 2801 WILLENA AVE   36107
  Sammie Kennedy, prin.
Johnson ES, 4550 NARROW LANE RD   36116
  Brenda Jordan, prin.
Lawrence ES, 2124 BEACH ST   36104
  Ronald Stewart, prin.
Loveless ES, 921 W JEFF DAVIS AVE   36108
  Paul Werking, prin.
MacMillan ES, 25 COVINGTON ST   36104
  Mary Zeigler, prin.
Morningview ES, 2849 PELZER AVE   36109
  Eloise Moseley, prin.
Paterson ES, 1015 E JEFFERSON ST   36104
  Phyllis Thompson, prin.
Peterson ES, 201 PENDAR ST   36104
  Jean Berry, prin.
Southlawn ES, 5225 PATRICIA LN   36108
  James Nuckles, prin.
Vaughn Road ES, 4407 VAUGHN RD   36106
  Don Oswald, prin.
Wares Ferry Road ES
  6425 WARES FERRY RD   36117 – Kay Fuller, prin.
Other Schools – See Hope Hull, Ramer

The Montgomery Academy
  3240 VAUGHN ROAD   36194
Our Lady Queen of Mercy School
  4421 NARROW LANE RD   36116
Resurrection Catholic School
  2815 FORBES RD   36199
St. Bede School, 3850 ATLANTA HWY   36109
St. John the Baptist School
  533 S UNION ST   36104
St. Jude Elementary School
  2048 W FAIRVIEW AVE   36196
Trinity Lutheran Church School
  1104 ROSA PARKS DR   36108

Morris, Jefferson Co., Pop. Code 3
Jefferson County SD
Supt. – See Birmingham
Bryan ES, 600 KIMBERLY CUT OFF RD   35116
  James Hart,Jr., prin.

Moulton, Lawrence Co., Pop. Code 4
Lawrence County SD
Sch. Sys. Enr. Code 6
Supt. – Dewayne Key, 602 MARKET ST S   35650
ES, 515 MAIN ST S   35650 – Cindy Collins, prin.
MS, 601 MAIN ST S   35650 – Charles Garner, prin.
Other Schools – See Courtland, Danville, Hillsboro,
  Mount Hope, Town Creek, Trinity

Moundville, Hale Co., Pop. Code 3
Hale County SD
Supt. – See Greensboro
ES, RURAL ROUTE 01 BOX 589   35474
  Joseph Stegall,Jr., prin.

Mountain Brook, Jefferson Co., Pop. Code 7
Mountain Brook CSD
Sch. Sys. Enr. Code 5
Supt. – Dr. Darrell McClain, P O BOX 9036   35213
Brookwood Forest ES
  3701 S BROOKWOOD RD   35223
  Marie Taylor, prin.
ES, 3020 CAMBRIDGE RD   35223
  Kathleen Shivers, prin.
Other Schools – See Birmingham

Mount Hope, Lawrence Co., Pop. Code 4
Lawrence County SD
Supt. – See Moulton
S, RURAL ROUTE 01 BOX 23-B   35651
  Dennis Gilbreath, prin.

Mount Olive, Jefferson Co.
Jefferson County SD
Supt. – See Birmingham
ES, 1301 BROOKSIDE RD   35117
  Terry Garrett, prin.

Mount Vernon, Mobile Co., Pop. Code 4
Mobile County SD
Supt. – See Mobile
Belsaw-Mt. Vernon ES, P O BOX 150   36560
  Ina Tillman, prin.

Calcedeaver ES, RURAL ROUTE 01   36560
  Thomas Stokes, prin.
Munford, Talladega Co., Pop. Code 3
Talladega County SD
Supt. – See Talladega
Hill ES, P O BOX 218   36268
  Alice Huddleston, prin.

Muscle Shoals, Colbert Co., Pop. Code 6
Muscle Shoals CSD
Sch. Sys. Enr. Code 4
Supt. – Martha Livingston, P O BOX 2730   35662
Avalon MS, 1400 E AVALON AVE   35661
  Maudine Smith, prin.
Highland Park ES, 710 ELMHURST ST   35661
  Jimmy Howard, prin.
Webster ES, 200 WEBSTER ST   35561
  Sam Brewer, prin.

Nauvoo, Walker Co., Pop. Code 2
Walker County SD
Supt. – See Jasper
Lupton ES, RURAL ROUTE 01 BOX 220   35578
  Glenn Braden, prin.

Newbern, Hale Co., Pop. Code 2
Hale County SD
Supt. – See Greensboro
Sunshine S, RURAL ROUTE 01 BOX 312   36765
  Jenkins Bryant, prin.

New Brockton, Coffee Co., Pop. Code 4
Coffee County SD
Supt. – See Elba
ES, P O BOX 190   36351 – Charles Cole, prin.

New Hope, Madison Co., Pop. Code 4
Madison County SD
Supt. – See Huntsville
S, 5300 MAIN DRIVE   35760
  Dennis Stephens, prin.

New Market, Madison Co., Pop. Code 3
Madison County SD
Supt. – See Huntsville
ES, P O BOX 94   35761 – Sandra Rhodes, prin.
Walnut Grove ES, 1961 JOE QUICK RD   35761
  David King, prin.

Newton, Houston Co., Pop. Code 4
Dale County SD
Supt. – See Ozark
ES, 401 COLLEGE ST   36352 – Evelyn Collier, prin.

Houston County SD
Supt. – See Dothan
Wicksburg S, RURAL ROUTE 01   36352
  James Johnson, prin.

Northport, Tuscaloosa Co., Pop. Code 6
Tuscaloosa County SD
Supt. – See Tuscaloosa
Crestmont ES, 2400 34TH AVE   35476
  Samuel Key, prin.
Flatwoods ES, 3800 66TH AVE   35476
  Charlene True, prin.
Huntington Place ES
  RURAL ROUTE 08 BOX 105A   35476
  David Gray, prin.
Matthews ES, 1225 RICE MINE RD   35476
  John Davis, prin.
Regional Education Center
  1324 RICE MINE RD   35476
  Michael Middleton, prin.
Vestavia ES   35476 – Roger Ballard, prin.
Walker ES, RURAL LROUTE 05 BOX 66   35476
  Gary Mims, prin.

Notasulga, Macon Co., Pop. Code 3
Macon County SD
Supt. – See Tuskegee
S, P O BOX 8   36866 – Robert Anderson, prin.

Tallapoosa County SD
Supt. – See Dadeville
Reeltown S, RURAL ROUTE 01   36866
  Michael Walton, prin.

Oakman, Walker Co., Pop. Code 3
Walker County SD
Supt. – See Jasper
ES, P O BOX 287   35579 – Ray Tidwell, prin.

Odenville, St. Clair Co., Pop. Code 3
St. Clair County SD
Supt. – See Ashville
St. Clair Co. S, BURGESS DRIVE   35120
  Edward Moseley, prin.

Ohatchee, Calhoun Co., Pop. Code 2
Calhoun County SD
Supt. – See Anniston
S, RURAL ROUTE 01 BOX 18   36271
  Jerry Ellard, prin.

Oneonta, Blount Co., Pop. Code 5
Blount County SD
Sch. Sys. Enr. Code 6
Supt. – J. M. Hazelrig, P O BOX 578   35121
Appalachian S
  RURAL ROUTE 04 BOX 227-A   35121
  James Carr, prin.
Other Schools – See Blountsville, Cleveland, Hayden,
  Locust Fork, Remlap

Oneonta CSD
Sch. Sys. Enr. Code 4
Supt. – Bill Burdette
  RURAL ROUTE 01 BOX 14   35121
Oneonta City S, RURAL ROUTE 01 BOX 14   35121
  Bill Burdette, prin.

Opelika, Lee Co., Pop. Code 7
Lee County SD
Sch. Sys. Enr. Code 6
Supt. – Tennis Britton,Jr., P O BOX 120   36803
Beauregard S, RURAL ROUTE 05 BOX 157   36801
  Richard Brown, prin.
Sanford MS, RURAL ROUTE 02 BOX 283   36801
  James Sasser, prin.
Other Schools – See Loachapoka, Salem, Smiths,
  Valley

Opelika CSD
Sch. Sys. Enr. Code 5
Supt. – J. Phillip Raley, P O BOX 2469   36803
Opelika JHS, 1206 DENSON DRIVE   36801
  W. Parker, prin.
Brown IS, GLENN ST   36802
  Larry Strickland, prin.
Carver PS, 307 CARVER AVE   36801
  James Blair, prin.
Jeter PS, 214 JETER AVE   36801
  William James, prin.
Martin MS, N 5TH ST   36802
  Barbara Walters, prin.
Morris Avenue IS, MORRIS AVE   36802
  Ray Winegar, prin.
Pepperell IS, 2111 PEPPERELL PKY   36801
  Cheryl Deaton, prin.

Russell County SD
Supt. – See Phenix City
Dixie ES, RURAL ROUTE 01 BOX 291   36801
  Jerel Gunter, prin.

Opp, Covington Co., Pop. Code 6
Covington County SD
Supt. – See Andalusia
Fleeta ES, RURAL ROUTE 03   36467
  John Thomasson, prin.

Opp CSD
Sch. Sys. Enr. Code 4
Supt. – Allen Miller, P O BOX 428   36467
MS, 303 E STEWART AVE   36467
  Kenneth Short, prin.
South Highlands ES, 503 BROWN ST   36467
  John Dee, prin.

Orrville, Dallas Co., Pop. Code 2
Dallas County SD
Supt. – See Selma
Five Points ES, RURAL ROUTE 02 BOX 139   36767
  George Poole, prin.
Salem ES, RURAL ROUTE 02 BOX 333   36767
  Melvin Miller, prin.

Owens Cross Roads, Madison Co., Pop. Code 3
Madison County SD
Supt. – See Huntsville
ES, P O BOX 187   35763 – William Patrick,Jr., prin.

Oxford, Calhoun Co., Pop. Code 5
Oxford CSD
Sch. Sys. Enr. Code 4
Supt. – Bill B. Cassidy, 310 E 2ND ST   36203
ES, 1401 CAFFEY DR   36203
  Debbie Nothdurft, prin.
Other Schools – See Anniston

Ozark, Dale Co., Pop. Code 7
Dale County SD
Sch. Sys. Enr. Code 5
Supt. – L. Dansby, P O BOX 978   36361
Other Schools – See Ariton, Midland City, Newton,
  Pinckard, Skipperville

Ozark CSD
Sch. Sys. Enr. Code 5
Supt. – Dr. Ron Moseley, P O BOX 788   36361
East Gate MS, RURAL ROUTE 04   36360
  Sonny Raley, prin.
Smith MS, 159 ENTERPRISE ROAD   36360
  James Jarmon,Jr., prin.
Lisenby ES, FAUST AVE   36360
  Robert Steed, prin.
Mixon ES, HOLIDAY LN   36360
  Charles Burg, prin.

Panola, Tuscaloosa Co.
Sumter County SD
Supt. – See Livingston
North Sumter ES, P O BOX 98   35477
  Darrow Jones,Jr., prin.

Pansey, Houston Co.
Houston County SD
Supt. – See Dothan
Harmon ES, RURAL ROUTE 01   36370
  Reuben Thomas, prin.

Parrish, Walker Co., Pop. Code 4
Walker County SD
Supt. – See Jasper
ES, P O BOX 109   35580 – Jerome Smith, prin.

Pelham, Shelby Co., Pop. Code 3
Shelby County SD
Supt. – See Columbiana
Valley ES, RURAL ROUTE 02 BOX 310   35124
  Norma Rogers, prin.

Pell City, St. Clair Co., Pop. Code 6
Pell City CSD
Sch. Sys. Enr. Code 5
Supt. – Hoyt Washington, 25 12TH ST S 35125
Eden S, 412 WOLF CREEK ROAD N 35125
    Barbara Vaughn, prin.
Duran JHS, 309 12TH ST S 35125
    Robert Hand, prin.
Kennedy MS, 813 16TH ST S 35125
    Troy Taylor, prin.
Roberts ES, 810 MARTIN ST N 35125
    Andrew Wright, prin.
Other Schools – See Cropwell

Perdido, Baldwin Co.
Baldwin County SD
Supt. – See Bay Minette
ES, P O BOX 28 36562 – Ellison McDuffie, prin.

Phenix City, Russell Co., Pop. Code 8
Phenix City CSD
Sch. Sys. Enr. Code 5
Supt. – Clifford S. Smith, P O BOX 460 36868
Allen ES, 1502 11TH AVE 36867
    Brenda Alexander, prin.
Central ES, 1700 17TH AVE 36867
    Ronald Plauche, prin.
Meadowlane ES, 709 MEADOWLANE DR 36867
    George Alexander, prin.
Phenix City Annex Building MS
    1501 17TH AVE 36867 – Marvin Pierce, prin.
MS, 1500 14TH ST 36867 – Howard Walker, prin.
Ridgecrest ES, 1806 8TH PL S 36867
    Janett Peoples, prin.
Sherwood ES, 906 IDLE HOUR DR 36867
    Pansy Slocumb, prin.
Westview ES, 1012 23RD AVE 36867
    Hattie Nathan, prin.

Russell County SD
Sch. Sys. Enr. Code 5
Supt. – William Siniard, P O BOX 908 36868
Ladonia ES, RURAL ROUTE 04 BOX 682 36867
    Aubrey Holliman, prin.
Other Schools – See Hurtsboro, Opelika, Pittsview,
    Seale

Mother Mary Mission School
    318 SEALE RD 36867
St. Patrick's ES, 3910 LAKEWOOD DR 36867

Phil Campbell, Franklin Co., Pop. Code 4
Franklin County SD
Supt. – See Russellville
S, P O BOX G 35581 – Mike Graham, prin.
East Franklin ES, RURAL ROUTE 01 35581
    William Smith, prin.

Piedmont, Clahoun Co., Pop. Code 6
Piedmont CSD
Sch. Sys. Enr. Code 4
Supt. – Hazel Kisor, P O BOX 232 36272
Willard MS, P O BOX 226 36272
    Betty Lou Lusk, prin.
Southside ES, P O BOX 359 36272
    Sherman Meers, prin.

Pinckard, Dale Co., Pop. Code 3
Dale County SD
Supt. – See Ozark
South Dale JHS, P O BOX D 36371
    Robert Woodham, prin.

Pine Apple, Wilcox Co., Pop. Code 2
Wilcox County SD
Supt. – See Camden
Moore Academy ES, P O BOX 38 36768
    Claude Ezell, prin.

Pine Hill, Wilcox Co., Pop. Code 3
Wilcox County SD
Supt. – See Camden
MS 36769 – Joe Kirkland, prin.
ES 36769 – Booker Booker, prin.

Pinson, Jefferson Co., Pop. Code 4
Jefferson County SD
Supt. – See Birmingham
Rudd JHS, 370 HIGHWAY 75 N 35126
    Ken Moses, prin.
Johnson ES, 8300 KERMIT JOHNSON RD 35126
    Jack Phillips, prin.
ES, 4200 SCHOOL DR 35126
    Norma Bumpus, prin.

Pisgah, Jackson Co., Pop. Code 3
Jackson County SD
Supt. – See Scottsboro
S 35765 – Sam Kenimer, prin.
Rosalie ES, RURAL ROUTE 01 35765
    Rayford Green, prin.

Pittsview, Russell Co.
Russell County SD
Supt. – See Phenix City
ES, P O BOX 157 36871 – Herman Stephens, prin.

Plantersville, Dallas Co., Pop. Code 3
Dallas County SD
Supt. – See Selma
Terry ES, RURAL ROUTE 02 BOX 1 36758
    Charles Levins, prin.

Pleasant Grove, Jefferson Co., Pop. Code 6
Jefferson County SD
Supt. – See Birmingham
ES, 601 PARK RD 35127 – Ben Burger, prin.

Prattville, Autauga Co., Pop. Code 7
Autauga County SD
Sch. Sys. Enr. Code 6
Supt. – David Weedon, P O BOX 130 36067
JHS, P O BOX D 36067 – John Schremser, prin.
ES, 134 PATRICK ST 36067
    Edwina Johnes, prin.
IS, 1020 HONEYSUCKLE DR 36067
    Malcolm Cain, prin.
PS, 216 WETUMPKA ST 36067
    Geilda Clark, prin.
Other Schools – See Autaugaville, Billingsley,
    Marbury

Prichard, Mobile Co., Pop. Code 8
Mobile County SD
Supt. – See Mobile
Mobile County Training MS
    P O BOX 10097 36610 – Charles Sellers, prin.
MS, 528 SIPSEY ST 36610 – Booker Davis, prin.
Glendale ES, 22 FLOCK AVE 36610
    Dorothy Scruggs, prin.
Palmer ES, 628 S CRAFT HWY 36610
    Palmer Richardson, prin.
Robbins ES, 2416 W MAIN ST 36610
    Annie Crandle, prin.
Whitley ES, 799 EDWARDS ST 36610
    Betty Salfford, prin.

St. James Major ES, 927 W PRICHARD AVE 36610

Princeton, Jackson Co., Pop. Code 4
Jackson County SD
Supt. – See Scottsboro
Paint Rock Valley S 35766
    Grant Barham,Jr., prin.

Quinton, Jefferson Co.
Jefferson County SD
Supt. – See Birmingham
West Jefferson S
    RURAL ROUTE 02 BOX 1560 35130
    Ronald Cooper, prin.

Ragland, St. Clair Co., Pop. Code 4
St. Clair County SD
Supt. – See Ashville
S, P O BOX 8 35131 – Joan Ford, prin.

Rainsville, De Kalb Co., Pop. Code 4
Dekalb County SD
Supt. – See Fort Payne
Plainview S, P O BOX 469 35986 – Bob Gray, prin.

Ramer, Montgomery Co., Pop. Code 2
Montgomery County SD
Supt. – See Montgomery
Dunbar ES 36069 – Neill Cowles,Jr., prin.

Ranburne, Cleburne Co., Pop. Code 2
Cleburne County SD
Supt. – See Heflin
ES, RURAL ROUTE 01 BOX 2 36273
    Charles Hendrix, prin.

Randolph, Bibb Co.
Bibb County SD
Supt. – See Centreville
ES 36792 – David Conway, prin.

Red Bay, Franklin Co., Pop. Code 4
Franklin County SD
Supt. – See Russellville
S, P O BOX H 35582 – Bobby Forsythe, prin.

Red Level, Covington Co., Pop. Code 3
Covington County SD
Supt. – See Andalusia
S, P O BOX D 36474 – Johnny Taylor, prin.

Reform, Pickens Co., Pop. Code 4
Pickens County SD
Supt. – See Carrollton
ES, RURAL ROUTE 01 BOX 212 35481
    Hal Luse, prin.

Remlap, Blount Co.
Blount County SD
Supt. – See Oneonta
Southeastern ES
    RURAL ROUTE 02 BOX 888 35133
    Robert Nichols, prin.

Repton, Conecuh Co., Pop. Code 2
Conecuh County SD
Supt. – See Evergreen
S, HIGHWAY 84 36475 – David Johnson, prin.

Roanoke, Randolph Co., Pop. Code 6
Roanoke CSD
Sch. Sys. Enr. Code 4
Supt. – Thomas E. Turner, P O BOX 312 36274
Handley MS, W POINT ST 36274
    Joe Ammons, prin.
Knight Enlow ES, P O BOX 685 36274
    Thomas Cato, prin.

Robertsdale, Baldwin Co., Pop. Code 4
Baldwin County SD
Supt. – See Bay Minette
Elsanor ES, RURAL ROUTE 01 36567
    Joseph Erlandson, prin.
ES, P O BOX 529 36567 – Ronald Green, prin.
Rosinton ES, RURAL ROUTE 01 36567
    Joseph Erlandson, prin.

St. Patrick's Catholic School, P O BOX 609 36567

Rockford, Coosa Co., Pop. Code 3
Coosa County SD
Sch. Sys. Enr. Code 4
Supt. – Larry Hardman, P O BOX 37 35136
ES 35136 – David Touart, prin.
Other Schools – See Goodwater, Kellyton, Sylacauga,
    Weogufka

Rock Mills, Chambers Co.
Randolph County SD
Supt. – See Wedowee
ES 36274 – Frederick Walker, prin.

Rogersville, Lauderdale Co., Pop. Code 3
Lauderdale County SD
Supt. – See Florence
Lauderdale County S, P O BOX 220 35652
    J. Johnson, prin.

Russellville, Franklin Co., Pop. Code 6
Franklin County SD
Sch. Sys. Enr. Code 5
Supt. – Hoyt Dillard, P O BOX 610 35653
Belgreen S, RURAL ROUTE 06 35653
    Eddie Britton, prin.
Tharptown ES, RURAL ROUTE 01 35653
    Gary Smith, prin.
Other Schools – See Phil Campbell, Red Bay, Vina

Russellville CSD
Sch. Sys. Enr. Code 4
Supt. – R. Courington, P O BOX 880 35653
MS, P O BOX 1213 35653 – Jerry Baker, prin.
College Avenue MS, 313 COLLEGE AVE 35653
    Joe Pride, prin.
West ES, P O BOX 458 35653 – Rocky Stone, prin.

Saint Elmo, Mobile Co.
Mobile County SD
Supt. – See Mobile
ES, P O BOX 158 36568 – Marie King, prin.

Salem, Lee Co.
Lee County SD
Supt. – See Opelika
Wacoochee JHS, P O BOX 100 36874
    Robert Ellis, prin.

Samson, Geneva Co., Pop. Code 4
Geneva County SD
Supt. – See Geneva
S, 209 N BROAD ST 36477 – D. Wells, prin.

Saraland, Mobile Co., Pop. Code 6
Mobile County SD
Supt. – See Mobile
Adams MS, 401 BALDWIN ROAD 36571
    Frank Coleman, prin.
ES, 229 MCKEOUGH AVE 36571
    James Kimbrell, prin.

Sardis, Dallas Co., Pop. Code 3
Dallas County SD
Supt. – See Selma
Shiloh ES, RURAL ROUTE 01 BOX 424 36775
    Jesse Todd,Jr., prin.

Satsuma, Mobile Co., Pop. Code 4
Mobile County SD
Supt. – See Mobile
Lee ES, P O BOX 519 36572 – Gail Vinocur, prin.

Scottsboro, Jackson Co., Pop. Code 6
Jackson County SD
Sch. Sys. Enr. Code 6
Supt. – W. Townson
    COURTHOUSE SUITE 20 35768
Skyline S, RURAL ROUTE 01 35768
    Wade Gentle, prin.
Other Schools – See Bridgeport, Bryant, Dutton, Flat
    Rock, Higdon, Hollywood, Pisgah, Princeton,
    Section, Stevenson, Woodville

Scottsboro CSD
Sch. Sys. Enr. Code 5
Supt. – J. Balentine, 906 S SCOTT ST 35768
JHS, 1601 JEFFERSON DRIVE 35768
    Roy Durham, prin.
Brownwood ES, 305 BINGHAM ST 35768
    Nesbitt Sanford, prin.
Caldwell ES, 833 S MARKET ST 35768
    Edith Hambrick, prin.
Nelson ES, 202 IDA MOODY DR 35768
    Jerry Chrisman, prin.
Page MS, 305 S SCOTT ST 35768
    Ella Lamberth, prin.

Seale, Russell Co.
Russell County SD
Supt. – See Phenix City
Mt. Olive ES, RURAL ROUTE 01 BOX 149 36875
    Alphonso Johnson, prin.
Oliver ES, RURAL ROUTE 01 BOX 1 36875
    Cherry Page, prin.

Section, Jackson Co., Pop. Code 3
Jackson County SD
Supt. – See Scottsboro
S 35771 – B. Laney, prin.
Macedonia ES 35771 – James Jones, prin.

Selma, Dallas Co., Pop. Code 8
Dallas County SD
Sch. Sys. Enr. Code 6
Supt. – Marvin Warren,Jr., P O BOX 1056 36702
Brantley ES, RURAL ROUTE 03 BOX 362 36701
    Willie Thomas, prin.

Southside ES
   3104 OLD MONTGOMERY RD   36701
   Carolyn Trolinger, prin.
Tipton ES, 2500 TIPTON ST E   36701
   Finis Sanders, prin.
Valley Grande ES
   RURAL ROUTE 04 BOX 59   36701
   Kathalene Singley, prin.
Other Schools – See Marion Junction, Orrville,
   Plantersville, Sardis

Perry County SD
Supt. – See Marion
East Perry ES, RURAL ROUTE 06 BOX 252   36701
   Joe Ivey, prin.

Selma CSD
Sch. Sys. Enr. Code 6
Supt. – Norward Roussell, P O BOX F   36702
East Side JHS, 400 WASHINGTON ST   36701
   F. Reese, prin.
Westside MS, 1701 SUMMERFIELD ROAD   36701
   James Carter, prin.
Byrd ES, 625 LAPSLEY ST   36701
   Allen Hobbs, prin.
Cedar Park ES, 1101 WOODROW AVE   36701
   Carolina Maenza, prin.
Clark ES, 405 LAWRENCE ST   36701
   Aubrey Larkin, prin.
East End ES, 501 PLANT ST   36701
   Benjamin Givan, prin.
Edgewood ES, 709 HIGHLAND AVE   36701
   Don Raybon, prin.
Knox ES, 1002 MABRY ST   36701
   Rebecca Bunch, prin.
Meadowview ES, 1816 ORRVILLE ROAD   36701
   Raymond Howard, prin.
Payne ES, 1529 FRANKLIN ST   36701
   Benice Miller, prin.

Semmes, Mobile Co., Pop. Code 3
Mobile County SD
Supt. – See Mobile
MS, WOLF ROAD   36575 – William Foster, prin.
ES, WOLF ROAD   36575 – Louise Smith, prin.

Sheffield, Colbert Co., Pop. Code 7
Sheffield CSD
Sch. Sys. Enr. Code 4
Supt. – Roger Tomberlin, P O BOX 460   35660
Willson MS, 2200 E 31ST ST   35660
   Carl Owens, prin.
Blake ES, 12TH AVE   35660 – Eddie Myrick, prin.
Brewster ES, 200 CHICKAMAUGA ST   35660
   Jesse Joiner, prin.
Southeast ES, 701 E 17TH ST   35660
   Glenn Rikard, prin.
Threadgill ES, 900 ANNAPOLIS AVE   35660
   Joe McCullough, prin.

Shelby, Shelby Co.
Shelby County SD
Supt. – See Columbiana
ES, P O BOX 238   35143 – Samuel Arledge, prin.

Shorter, Macon Co., Pop. Code 2
Macon County SD
Supt. – See Tuskegee
Wolfe-Shorter S, RURAL ROUTE 01   36075
   Ollie Beasley, prin.

Silas, Choctaw Co., Pop. Code 2
Choctaw County SD
Supt. – See Butler
Shady Grove ES, P O BOX 212   36919
   Johnny Dixon,Jr., prin.
ES   36919 – B. Smith,Jr., prin.

Silverhill, Baldwin Co., Pop. Code 3
Baldwin County SD
Supt. – See Bay Minette
ES, P O BOX 248   36576 – James Comer, prin.

Sipsey, Walker Co., Pop. Code 3
Walker County SD
Supt. – See Jasper
ES, PARK ST   35584 – Maury Fowler, prin.

Skipperville, Dale Co.
Dale County SD
Supt. – See Ozark
Long S, RURAL ROUTE 01 BOX 1   36374
   Charles Kelly, prin.

Slocomb, Geneva Co., Pop. Code 4
Geneva County SD
Supt. – See Geneva
S   36375 – Jerry Glover, prin.

Smiths, Lee Co., Pop. Code 3
Lee County SD
Supt. – See Opelika
Smiths Station PS, P O BOX 339   36877
   David Henry, prin.

Somerville, Morgan Co., Pop. Code 2
Morgan County SD
Supt. – See Decatur
Cotaco ES, RURAL ROUTE 03 BOX 340   35670
   William Ellinger, prin.
Union Hill ES, RURAL ROUTE 02   35670
   John Tomlinson, prin.

Spanish Fort, Baldwin Co.
Baldwin County SD
Supt. – See Bay Minette
ES, P O BOX 77   36527 – Agnes Smith, prin.

Spring Garden, Cherokee Co.
Cherokee County SD
Supt. – See Centre
S, P O BOX 31   36275 – Ecil Chandler, prin.

Springville, St. Clair Co., Pop. Code 4
St. Clair County SD
Supt. – See Ashville
S, P O BOX 207   35146 – Ernest Bagley, prin.

Stapleton, Baldwin Co.
Baldwin County SD
Supt. – See Bay Minette
ES, P O BOX 155   36578 – Steve Thomas, prin.

Steele, St. Clair Co., Pop. Code 3
St. Clair County SD
Supt. – See Ashville
ES, P O BOX 367   35987
   Fredrick Honeycutt, prin.

Stevenson, Jackson Co., Pop. Code 4
Jackson County SD
Supt. – See Scottsboro
MS   35772 – Angela Guess, prin.
PS   35772 – Steve Durham, prin.

Sulligent, Lamar Co., Pop. Code 4
Lamar County SD
Supt. – See Vernon
S, P O BOX 367   35586 – C. Elliott, prin.

Sumiton, Walker Co., Pop. Code 4
Walker County SD
Supt. – See Jasper
ES, RURAL ROUTE 01 BOX 478   35148
   Benny Rowe, prin.

Summerdale, Baldwin Co., Pop. Code 3
Baldwin County SD
Supt. – See Bay Minette
ES, 405 JACKSON ROAD   36580
   Connie West, prin.

Sweet Water, Marengo Co., Pop. Code 2
Marengo County SD
Supt. – See Linden
S, P O BOX 127   36782 – Sidney Atkins, prin.

Sycamore, Talladega Co.
Talladega County SD
Supt. – See Talladega
ES, P O BOX 128   35149 – Donald Fields, prin.

Sylacauga, Talladega Co., Pop. Code 7
Coosa County SD
Supt. – See Rockford
Stewartville ES
   RURAL ROUTE 02 BOX 148K   35150
   Thomas Ham, prin.

Sylacauga CSD
Sch. Sys. Enr. Code 4
Supt. – Dr. Joseph B. Morton, P O BOX 1127   35150
East Highland MS, P O BOX 450   35150
   Jesse L. Cleveland, prin.
Indian Valley ES, P O BOX 6   35150
   Clara Montgomery, prin.
Mountainview ES, P O BOX G   35150
   James Embry, prin.
Pinecrest ES, RURAL ROUTE 07 BOX 460   35150
   Dan Deese, prin.

Talladega County SD
Supt. – See Talladega
Comer S, SEMINOLE AVE & 8TH ST   35150
   Dwight Rayfield, prin.
Fayetteville S, RURAL ROUTE 05 BOX 241   35150
   Daniel Payant, prin.

Sylvania, De Kalb Co., Pop. Code 2
Dekalb County SD
Supt. – See Fort Payne
S, P O BOX 20   35988 – Weldon Parrish, prin.

Talladega, Talladega Co., Pop. Code 7
Talladega CSD
Sch. Sys. Enr. Code 5
Supt. – Billy Mills, P O BOX 946   35160
Ellis JHS, 414 ELM ST   35160 – M. Floyd,Jr., prin.
Dixon MS, 414 ELM ST   35160
   Dolia Patterson, prin.
Graham ES, 403 CEDAR ST   35160
   Richard Nelson, prin.
Henderson ES, 400 SPRING ST N   35160
   Joyce Hutchinson, prin.
Houston ES, RURAL ROUTE 03 BOX 8   35160
   Joan Landham, prin.
Salter ES, BRECON ACCESS ROAD   35160
   Sebron Harmon, prin.
Young ES, E DAMON   35160
   Carolyn Roberts, prin.

Talladega County SD
Sch. Sys. Enr. Code 6
Supt. – L. Grissett, P O BOX 887   35160
Talladega County Training S
   RURAL ROUTE 08 BOX 212   35160
   John Stamps, prin.
Idalia ES, RURAL ROUTE 06 BOX 172   35160
   Cora Williamson, prin.
Jonesview ES, RURAL ROUTE 05   35160
   Doris Stamps, prin.
Other Schools – See Alpine, Childersburg, Lincoln,
   Munford, Sycamore, Sylacauga

Tallassee, Elmore Co., Pop. Code 5
Tallassee CSD
Sch. Sys. Enr. Code 4
Supt. – James Street, P O BOX 488   36078
Southside MS, P O BOX 608   36078
   Russell H. Stokes, prin.
ES, 502 BARNETT BLVD   36078
   Robert Meadows, prin.
Other Schools – See East Tallassee

Tanner, Limestone Co.
Limestone County SD
Supt. – See Athens
S, RURAL ROUTE 07   35671 – John Black, prin.
Mooresville Belle Mina ES
   RURAL ROUTE 01   35671 – Harvey Craig, prin.

Tarrant City, Jefferson Co., Pop. Code 6
Tarrant CSD
Sch. Sys. Enr. Code 4
Supt. – Wayne Reynolds
   1318 ALABAMA ST   35217
MS, 1425 E LAKE BLVD   35217
   James Graham, prin.
ES, 1269 PORTLAND ST   35217
   Marcell Burchfield, prin.

Theodore, Mobile Co., Pop. Code 3
Mobile County SD
Supt. – See Mobile
MS, 5760 THEODORE-DAWES ROAD   36582
   Tom Legros, prin.
Burroughs ES, 345 BURROUGHS LN   36582
   William Lawrence, prin.
Davis ES, 6900 NAN GRAY DAVIS RD   36582
   Eveleen Lathan, prin.

Thomaston, Marengo Co., Pop. Code 3
Marengo County SD
Supt. – See Linden
Johnson S, P O BOX 67   36783
   Rayvell Smith, prin.

Thomasville, Clarke Co., Pop. Code 5
Thomasville CSD
Sch. Sys. Enr. Code 4
Supt. – David Hulsey, 3001 GATES DRIVE   36784
ES, 527 W FRONT ST N   36784
   Howard Jackson, prin.
MS, 3001 GATES DRIVE   36784
   Carvel Rowell, prin.

Thorsby, Chilton Co., Pop. Code 3
Chilton County SD
Supt. – See Clanton
S, P O BOX 386   35171 – Peggy Murrah, prin.

Toney, Madison Co.
Madison County SD
Supt. – See Huntsville
Madison Cross Road ES
   11548 PULASKI PIKE   35773 – Ken Hogan, prin.

Town Creek, Lawrence Co., Pop. Code 4
Lawrence County SD
Supt. – See Moulton
Hatton ES, RURAL ROUTE 01 BOX 455   35672
   Thomas Smith, prin.
Hazlewood ES, P O BOX K   35672
   Claud Russell, prin.

Townley, Walker Co., Pop. Code 5
Walker County SD
Supt. – See Jasper
ES, P O BOX B   35587 – Gary Aultman, prin.

Trinity, Morgan Co., Pop. Code 3
Lawrence County SD
Supt. – See Moulton
East Lawrence ES
   RURAL ROUTE 01 BOX 900   35673
   Larry Hancock, prin.

Morgan County SD
Supt. – See Decatur
West Morgan S
   RURAL ROUTE 02 BOX 218   35673
   Tommy Tomlinson, prin.

Troy, Pike Co., Pop. Code 7
Pike County SD
Sch. Sys. Enr. Code 5
Supt. – John Key, 109 E CHURCH ST   36081
Shellhorn ES, RURAL ROUTE 07 BOX 81   36081
   Elizabeth Grubbs, prin.
Spring Hill ES, RURAL ROUTE 02 BOX 159   36081
   Kelley Wilson, prin.
Other Schools – See Banks, Brundidge, Goshen

Troy CSD
Sch. Sys. Enr. Code 4
Supt. – John Vaughan, P O BOX 529   36081
Henderson JHS, P O BOX 925   36081
   Willie Thomas, prin.
College View MS, 300 PELL AVE   36081
   Toni Stetson, prin.
Henderson ES, P O BOX 926   36081
   Geoffrey Spann, prin.
Oakland Heights ES, P O BOX 945   36081
   Henry Jones, prin.

Trussville, Jefferson Co., Pop. Code 5
Jefferson County SD
Supt. – See Birmingham
Hewitt MS, 301 PARKWAY DR   35173
   Connie Williams, prin.
Hewitt ES, 425 CHEROKEE DR   35173
   Gloria Solomon, prin.

Tuscaloosa, Tuscaloosa Co., Pop. Code 8
Tuscaloosa CSD
Sch. Sys. Enr. Code 7
Supt. – Dr. Thomas Ingram, 1100 21ST ST E 35405
Eastwood MS, 2301 14TH ST E 35404
  Dennis Bryant, prin.
Alberta ES, 2700 UNIVERSITY BLVD E 35404
  Marcia Burke, prin.
Arcadia ES, 3740 14TH ST E 35404
  Betty Pilegge, prin.
Central ES, 3015 15TH ST 35401
  Phyllis Rodgers, prin.
King ES, 2430 MARTIN L KING JR BLVD 35401
  Louise Crawford, prin.
Northington ES, 1300 21ST ST E 35405
  Tulane Duke, prin.
Oakdale ES, 5001 25TH ST 35401
  Jo Ann Bassett, prin.
Skyland ES, 408 SKYLAND BLVD 35405
  Johnnie Payne, prin.
Stafford ES, 1614 15TH ST 35401
  Dorothy Johnson, prin.
Stillman Heights ES, 3834 21ST ST 35401
  Daphine Ferguson, prin.
MS, 1210 21ST AVE 35401 – Joan Dowdle, prin.
University Place ES, 221 18TH ST 35401
  Jeanette Harpole, prin.
Verner ES, 1701 N RIDGE ROAD 35406
  Johnnie Hitson, prin.
Westlawn MS
  2800 MARTIN L KING JR BLVD 35401
  Elizabeth Cheshire, prin.
Woodland Forrest ES
  6001 HARGROVE RD E 35405 – Shelly Jones,
  prin.

Tuscaloosa County SD
Sch. Sys. Enr. Code 7
Supt. – Neil Hyche, P O BOX 2568 35403
Englewood ES, RURAL ROUTE 06 BOX 200 35405
  Tommy Wood, prin.
Other Schools – See Brookwood, Buhl, Coker,
  Cottondale, Duncanville, Fosters, Holt, Northport,
  Vance

Tuscaloosa Academy, 420 26TH ST N 35406
Holy Spirit Regional Catholic School
  711 37TH ST E 35405

Tuscumbia, Colbert Co., Pop. Code 6
Colbert County SD
Sch. Sys. Enr. Code 5
Supt. – Roger L'don Moore, P O BOX 270 35674
Colbert Heights ES, 210 SUNSET DR 35674
  Howard Wright, prin.
New Bethel ES, RURAL ROUTE 02 35674
  James Hovater, prin.
Other Schools – See Cherokee, Leighton

Tuscumbia CSD
Sch. Sys. Enr. Code 4
Supt. – Dr. Robert Clemmons, P O BOX 149 35674
Northside MS, 600 N HIGH ST 35674
  Johnnie Smith, prin.
Southside ES, 1408 JOE WHEELER HWY 35674
  Clarence Blankenship, prin.
Thompson MS, FRANKFORD ROAD 35674
  James Wilson, prin.

Tuskegee, Macon Co., Pop. Code 7
Macon County SD
Sch. Sys. Enr. Code 5
Supt. – Raymond Handy, P O BOX 90 36083
Chisholm ES, RURAL ROUTE 01 BOX 135 36083
  Joseph Asberry, prin.
ES, 321 S MAIN ST 36083
  Walter Bowers,Jr., prin.
Washington ES, P O BOX 708 36083
  Robert Ivey,Jr., prin.
Other Schools – See Notasulga, Shorter, Tuskegee
  Institute, Union Springs

Tuskegee Institute, Macon Co.
Macon County SD
Supt. – See Tuskegee
Adams ES, P O BOX RR 36088
  Lifus Johnson, prin.

St. Joseph School, 2009 MONTGOMERY RD 36088

Union Grove, Marshall Co., Pop. Code 2
Marshall County SD
Supt. – See Guntersville
ES, P O BOX 7 35175 – Thomas Pluckett, **prin.**

Union Springs, Bullock Co., Pop. Code 5
Bullock County SD
Sch. Sys. Enr. Code 5
Supt. – Feagin Johnson, P O BOX 231 36089
South Highlands MS, P O BOX 111 36089
  Julius Thomas, prin.
ES, 211 W CONECUH AVE 36089
  Hoover Burney, prin.
Other Schools – See Midway

Macon County SD
Supt. – See Tuskegee
South Macon S
  RURAL ROUTE 02 BOX 224 36089
  Theodore Samuel, prin.

Uniontown, Perry Co., Pop. Code 4
Perry County SD
Supt. – See Marion
ES, P O BOX 570 36786 – Herbert McFadden, prin.
MS, P O BOX 539 36786 – Edwin Dial,Jr., prin.

Uriah, Monroe Co., Pop. Code 2
Monroe County SD
Supt. – See Monroeville
Blacksher S, P O BOX 68 36480
  Bennie Rhodes, prin.

Valley, Chambers Co.
Chambers County SD
Supt. – See Lafayette
JHS, P O BOX 327 36854 – Larry Newton, prin.
Fairfax ES, 502 BLVD CIR 36854
  Carey Philpott, prin.
Lanier ES, 6001 20TH AVE 36854
  Danny Berry, prin.
Riverview ES, P O BOX 300 36872
  Thomas Moore, prin.
Shawmut ES, 3301 23RD DR 36854
  Samuel Bradford, prin.

Lee County SD
Supt. – See Opelika
Beulah S, RURAL ROUTE 02 BOX 150 36854
  Jerry Southwell, prin.

Valley Head, De Kalb Co., Pop. Code 2
Dekalb County SD
Supt. – See Fort Payne
S, P O BOX 145 35989 – Elaine Keith, prin.

Vance, Tuscaloosa Co., Pop. Code 2
Tuscaloosa County SD
Supt. – See Tuscaloosa
ES, P O BOX 208 35490 – William Noe, prin.

Verbena, Chilton Co., Pop. Code 2
Chilton County SD
Supt. – See Clanton
S, P O BOX 128 36091 – Donald Hand, prin.

Vernon, Lamar Co., Pop. Code 4
Lamar County SD
Sch. Sys. Enr. Code 5
Supt. – Laverne Steedley, P O BOX 469 35592
S, P O BOX 369 35592 – John Boman, prin.
Other Schools – See Millport, Sulligent

Vestavia Hills, Jefferson Co., Pop. Code 6
Vestavia Hills CSD
Sch. Sys. Enr. Code 5
Supt. – J. Carlton Smith
  1204 MONTGOMERY HIGHWAY 35216
Pizitz MS, 2020 PIZITZ DRIVE 35216
  Bill Anderson, prin.
Other Schools – See Birmingham

Vina, Franklin Co., Pop. Code 2
Franklin County SD
Supt. – See Russellville
S, P O BOX 36 35593 – Wayne Bolton, prin.

Vincent, Shelby Co., Pop. Code 4
Shelby County SD
Supt. – See Columbiana
MS, P O BOX B 35178 – Betty Edwards, prin.
ES, RURAL ROUTE 01 35178 – Calvin Smith, prin.

Vinemont, Cullman Co., Pop. Code 2
Cullman County SD
Supt. – See Cullman
S, P O BOX 189 35179 – Huelee Adams, prin.

Wadley, Randolph Co., Pop. Code 3
Randolph County SD
Supt. – See Wedowee
S, P O BOX 49 36276 – Paul Hodge, prin.

Wagarville, Washington Co., Pop. Code 5
Washington County SD
Supt. – See Chatom
ES, RURAL ROUTE 01 BOX 321 36585
  John Wood, prin.

Warrior, Jefferson Co., Pop. Code 5
Jefferson County SD
Supt. – See Birmingham
Corner S, 10005 CORNER SCHOOL ROAD 35180
  Charles Burkett, prin.
S, 300 MONTGOMERY ST 35180
  John Strickland, prin.

Waterloo, Lauderdale Co., Pop. Code 2
Lauderdale County SD
Supt. – See Florence
S, P O BOX 68 35677 – Thomas Glasgow, prin.

Weaver, Calhoun Co., Pop. Code 4
Calhoun County SD
Supt. – See Anniston
ES, 700 SCHOOL DR 36277 – Ralph Taylor, prin.

Webb, Houston Co., Pop. Code 2
Houston County SD
Supt. – See Dothan
ES, P O BOX 100 36376 – James Bond, prin.

Wedowee, Randolph Co., Pop. Code 3
Randolph County SD
Sch. Sys. Enr. Code 4
Supt. – James Holmes, P O BOX 288 36278
Randolph County S, P O BOX 696 36278
  Hulond Humphries, prin.
MS, RURAL ROUTE 01 BOX 670 36278
  Wyoleen Sikes, prin.
Other Schools – See Rock Mills, Wadley, Woodland

Weogufka, Coosa Co.
Coosa County SD
Supt. – See Rockford
ES 35183 – Roy Green, prin.

West Blocton, Bibb Co., Pop. Code 4
Bibb County SD
Supt. – See Centreville
ES, P O BOX 248 35184 – Sarah Lunsford, prin.

Wetumpka, Elmore Co., Pop. Code 5
Elmore County SD
Sch. Sys. Enr. Code 6
Supt. – Fordyce Tatum, P O BOX 617 36092
JHS, 300 W OSCEOLA ST 36092
  Fred Dickerson, prin.
ES, 510 MICANOPY ST 36092
  Robert Murchinson, prin.
Other Schools – See Deatsville, Eclectic, Millbrook

Wilmer, Mobile Co., Pop. Code 3
Mobile County SD
Supt. – See Mobile
Williams ES, RURAL ROUTE 01 BOX 78 36587
  Dian Beitel, prin.
ES, WILMER AVE 36587 – Elinor Crowe, prin.

Wilsonville, Shelby Co., Pop. Code 3
Shelby County SD
Supt. – See Columbiana
ES, P O BOX 216 35186 – Rosemary Liveoak, prin.

Winfield, Marion Co., Pop. Code 5
Winfield CSD
Sch. Sys. Enr. Code 4
Supt. – Dale Brasher, P O BOX 70 35594
ES, P O BOX 70 35594 – Terrell Kirkpatrick, prin.

Woodland, Randolph Co., Pop. Code 2
Randolph County SD
Supt. – See Wedowee
S, P O BOX 157 36280 – James McCord, prin.

Woodstock, Bibb Co.
Bibb County SD
Supt. – See Centreville
New Woodstock ES 35188 – Lee Major, prin.

Woodville, Jackson Co., Pop. Code 2
Jackson County SD
Supt. – See Scottsboro
S, RURAL ROUTE 02 35776 – Tony Baker, prin.

Wylam, Jefferson Co.
Birmingham CSD
Supt. – See Birmingham
ES, 701-41ST ST 35224 – Claud Vaughn, prin.

York, Sumter Co., Pop. Code 5
Sumter County SD
Supt. – See Livingston
York West End ES, P O BOX 127 36925
  Larry Yates, prin.

ALASKA

PUBLIC, PRIVATE, AND PAROCHIAL ELEMENTARY SCHOOLS

Akhiok, Kodiak Co., Pop. Code 2
Kodiak Island Borough SD
Supt. – See Kodiak
S, AKHIOK RURAL STA 99615
  Steven Rounsaville, prin.

Akiachak, Central Co., Pop. Code 2
Yupiit SD
Sch. Sys. Enr. Code 2
Supt. – Bradley Raphel, P O BOX 100 99551
ES, P O BOX 100 99551 – Clayton Carnes, prin.
Other Schools – See Akiak, Tuluksak

Akiak, Central Co., Pop. Code 2
Yupiit SD
Supt. – See Akiachak
ES, P O BOX 52227 99552 – (—), prin.

Akutan, Southcentral Co., Pop. Code 2
Aleutian Region SD
Supt. – See Anchorage
S, GENERAL DELIVERY 99553
  Richard Little, prin.

Alakanuk, Northwestern Co., Pop. Code 3
Lower Yukon SD
Supt. – See Mountain Village
S, LOWER YUKON RIVER 99554
  Mike Hull, prin.

Aleknagik, Central Co., Pop. Code 2
Southwest Region SD
Supt. – See Dillingham
Aleknagik North Shore S 99555
  Mariam Chapman, prin.
Aleknagik South Shore ES 99555 – (—), prin.

Allakaket, Central Co., Pop. Code 2
Yukon-Koyukuk SD
Supt. – See Nenana
S, GENERAL DELIVERY 99720
  Wayne Young, prin.

Ambler, Northwestern Co., Pop. Code 2
Northwest Arctic SD
Supt. – See Kotzebue
S 99786 – Marlies Kruse, prin.

Anaktuvuk Pass, Northwestern Co., Pop. Code 2
North Slope Borough SD
Supt. – See Barrow
Nunamuit S, GENERAL DELIVERY 99721
  Lehaman Burrow, prin.

Anchorage, Southcentral Co., Pop. Code 9
Aleutian Region SD
Sch. Sys. Enr. Code 1
Supt. – Robert Mutch
  4000 OLD SEWARD HWY #301 99503
Other Schools – See Akutan, Atka, Cold Bay, False
  Pass, Nikolski

Anchorage SD
Sch. Sys. Enr. Code 8
Supt. – William Coats, P O BOX 196614 99519
Central ABC JHS, 1405 E ST 99501
  Beverly Bailey, prin.
Clark JHS, 150 S BRAGAW ST 99508
  Kathleen Carmody, prin.
Hanshew JHS, 10121 LAKE OTIS PKWY 99507
  Lance Campbell, prin.
Mears JHS, 2700 W 100TH AVE 99515
  Marilyn Cunningham, prin.
Romig JHS, 2500 MINNESOTA DR 99503
  Marilyn Conaway, prin.
Wendler JHS, 2905 LAKE OTIS PKWY 99508
  Lance Bowie, prin.
Abbott Loop ES
  8427 LAKE OTIS PARKWAY 99507
  Lloyd Arterburn, prin.
Airport Heights ES, 1510 ALDER DRIVE 99508
  Eugene Burke, prin.
Baxter ES, 2991 BAXTER ROAD 99504
  Carol Hussey, prin.
Bayshore ES, 11500 BAYSHORE DRIVE 99515
  Gilbert Cragen, prin.
Bear Valley ES
  15001 MOUNTAIN AIR DRIVE 99516
  Darleen Starry, prin.
Campbell ES, 7206 ROVENNA 99518
  Charles Booth, prin.
Chester Valley ES, 1750 PATTERSON ST 99504
  Mary Flynn, prin.
Chinook ES, 3101 W 88TH AVE 99502
  Nancy Farmer, prin.
Chugach Optional ES, 1205 E ST 99501
  Sandra Guerrieri, prin.
College Gate ES, 3101 SUNFLOWER ST 99508
  Robyn Rehmann, prin.
Creekside Park ES, 7500 E 6TH AVE 99504
  Earl Williams, prin.
Denali Fundamental ES, 148 E 9TH AVE 99501
  Larry Newland, prin.
Fairview ES, 1327 NELCHINA ST 99501
  David Combs, prin.
Government Hill ES, 525 E BLUFF DRIVE 99501
  Sonya Lamarr, prin.
Huffman ES, 12000 LORRAINE ST 99516
  Marilyn Barnett, prin.
Inlet View ES, 1219 N ST 99501
  George Rakos, prin.
Klatt ES, 11900 JUNIPER ST 99515
  John Kito, prin.
Lake Otis ES, 3331 LAKE OTIS PARKWAY 99508
  James Cox, prin.
Mountain View ES, 4005 MEHPHEE 99508
  Linda Black, prin.
Muldoon ES, 515 CHERRY ST 99504
  Toni McDermott, prin.
North Star ES, 605 W FIREWEED LANE 99503
  Shannon Jones, prin.

Northern Lights ABC ES
  1705 W 32ND AVE 99517 – Elizabeth Barner,
  prin.
Northwood ES, 4807 NORTHWOOD DRIVE 99517
  Susan Usher, prin.
Nunaka Valley ES, 1905 TWINING DR 99504
  Leeann Crumbley, prin.
Ocean View ES
  11911 JOHN ROAD #3117-A 99515
  Robert Rood, prin.
O'Malley ES, 11100 ROCK RIDGE DR 99516
  John Murphy, prin.
Ptarmigan ES, 888 EDWARD ST 99504
  Mary Boxx, prin.
Rabbit Creek ES, 13650 LAKE OTIS PKWY 99516
  Gary Cannon, prin.
Rogers Park ES
  1400 E NORTHERN LIGHTS BLVD 99508
  LeRoy Jeffery, prin.
Russian Jack ES, 4420 E 20TH AVE 99508
  Donna Johnson, prin.
Sand Lake ES, 7500 JEWEL LAKE ROAD 99502
  M. Denice Clyne, prin.
Scenic Park ES, 3933 PATTERSON ST 99504
  Orriene Denslow, prin.
Spring Hill ES
  9911 LAKE OTIS PARKWAY 99507
  Jay Meineman, prin.
Sustina ES, 7500 TYONE CT 99504
  Barbara Weil, prin.
Taku ES, 701 E 72ND AVE 99518
  John Donohue, prin.
Tudor ES, 1666 CACHE DRIVE 99507
  James Kurka, prin.
Turnagain ES
  3500 W NORTHERN LIGHTS BLVD 99517
  James Graham, prin.
Williwaw ES, 550 S BRAGAW ST 99508
  Carolyn Lyons, prin.
Willow Crest ES, 1004 W TUDOR ROAD 99503
  William Breeden, prin.
Wonder Park ES, 5100 E 4TH AVE 99508
  Marsha Buck, prin.
Wood ES, 7001 CRANBERRY ST 99502
  Colleen Stevens, prin.
Other Schools – See Chugiak, Eagle River, Elmendorf
  A F B, Fort Richardson, Girdwood

Lake & Peninsula SD
Supt. – See King Salmon
Ivanof Bay S 99502 – Myrna Sovde, prin.

Abbott Loop Christian School
  2626 ABBOTT ROAD 99507
Anchorage Christian School
  6401 E NORTHERN LIGHTS BLVD 99504
Harvester Christian Academy
  9101 BRAYTON DR 99507
Muldoon Christian School
  7041 DE BARR ROAD 99504

Anchorage Lutheran School Assoc.
  8100 ARTIC BLVD 99502
St. Elizabeth Ann Seton School
  2901 HUFFMAN RD 99516

Anchor Point, Southcentral Co., Pop. Code 2
Kenai Peninsula Borough SD
Supt. – See Soldotna
Nikolaevsk S, P O BOX S129 NIKOLAEVSK 99556
  Kenneth Moore, prin.
Chapman ES, P O BOX 156 99556
  Serve Wilson, prin.

Anderson, Central Co., Pop. Code 3
Railbelt SD
Supt. – See Healy
S, P O BOX 3120 99760 – Robert Murray, prin.

Angoon, Southeastern Co., Pop. Code 2
Chatham SD
Sch. Sys. Enr. Code 2
Supt. – Darrell Moore, P O BOX 109 99820
S, P O BOX 209 99820 – Ronald Gleason, prin.
Other Schools – See Elfin Cove, Gustavus, Haines,
  Hobart Bay, Juneau, Tenakee Springs

Aniak, Central Co., Pop. Code 2
Kuspuk SD
Sch. Sys. Enr. Code 2
Supt. – Bob McHenry, P O BOX 108 99557
Nicoll ES, P O BOX 29 99557
  Lamont Albertson, prin.
Other Schools – See Chuathbaluk, Crooked Creek,
  Lower Kalskag, Red Devil, Sleetmute, Stony River,
  Upper Kalskag

Anvik, Central Co., Pop. Code 2
Iditarod Area SD
Supt. – See McGrath
Blackwell S 99558 – Steve Pine, prin.

Arctic Village, Central Co., Pop. Code 1
Yukon Flats SD
Supt. – See Fort Yukon
S 99722 – Dan Kitchin, prin.

Atka, Southcentral Co.
Aleutian Region SD
Supt. – See Anchorage
S, ATKA RURAL BRANCH 99502
  Peggy Baker, prin.

Atmautluak, Bethel Co., Pop. Code 2
Lower Kuskokwim SD
Supt. – See Bethel
Alexie Memorial S, GENERAL DELIVERY 99559
  Stephen O'Brien, prin.

Atqasuk, Northwestern Co.
North Slope Borough SD
Supt. – See Barrow
Meade River S, GENERAL DELIVERY 99791
  Linda Shepard, prin.

Barrow, Northwestern Co., Pop. Code 4
North Slope Borough SD
Sch. Sys. Enr. Code 4
Supt. – Shirley Holloway, P O BOX 169 99723
Ipalook ES, P O BOX 450 99723 – (—), prin.
Other Schools – See Anaktuvuk Pass, Atqasuk,
  Kaktovik, Nuiqsut, Point Hope, Point Lay,
  Wainwright

Beaver, Central Co.
Yukon Flats SD
Supt. – See Fort Yukon
S 99724 – Margaret Fisher, prin.

Bethel, Central Co., Pop. Code 5
Lower Kuskokwim SD
Sch. Sys. Enr. Code 5
Supt. – Sue Hare, P O BOX 305 99559
Bethel-Kilbuck ES, P O BOX 305 99559
  Elinor Hernandez, prin.
Bethel-Mikelnguut Eitnauvit ES
  P O BOX 350 99559 – Michael Murray, prin.
Other Schools – See Atmautluak, Chefornak, Eek,
  Goodnews Bay, Kasigluk, Kipnuk, Kongiganak,
  Kwethluk, Kwigillingok, Mekoryuk, Napakiak,
  Napaskiak, Newtok, Nightmute, Nunapitchuk,
  Oscarville, Platinum, Quinhagak, Toksook Bay,
  Tuntutuliak, Tununak

Bettles Field, Central Co.
Yukon-Koyukuk SD
Supt. – See Nenana
Bettles S, GENERAL DELIVERY 99726
  George Nicholson, prin.

Brevig Mission, Northwestern Co., Pop. Code 2
Bering Strait SD
Supt. – See Unalakleet
S 99785 – Douglas New, prin.

Buckland, Northwestern Co., Pop. Code 2
Northwest Arctic SD
Supt. – See Kotzebue
ES 99727 – William Grubbs, prin.

Cantwell, Central Co., Pop. Code 1
Railbelt SD
Supt. – See Healy
S, P O BOX 29 99729 – Patricia McRae, prin.

Central, Central Co.
Yukon Flats SD
Supt. – See Fort Yukon
S 99730 – Earla Hutchinson, prin.

Chalkyitsik, Ft. Yukon Co., Pop. Code 2
Yukon Flats SD
Supt. – See Fort Yukon
S 99788 – William Fischer, prin.

Chefornak, Central Co., Pop. Code 2
Lower Kuskokwim SD
Supt. – See Bethel
Chaptnquak S, GENERAL DELIVERY 99561
  Glen Rutherford, prin.

Chenega Bay, Southcentral Co.
Chugach SD
Supt. – See Whittier
S 99562 – Kim Berg, prin.

Chevak, Northwestern Co., Pop. Code 2
Kashunamiut SD
Sch. Sys. Enr. Code 2
Supt. – Alex Tatum, 985 KSD WAY 99563
S, 985 KSD WAY 99563 – James Reynolds, prin.

Chignik, Southcentral Co.
Lake & Peninsula SD
Supt. – See King Salmon
Chignik Bay S 99564 – Robert Whicker, prin.

Chignik Lagoon, Southcentral Co.
Lake & Peninsula SD
Supt. – See King Salmon
S 99565 – Lloyd Chery, prin.

Chignik Lake, Chignik Co., Pop. Code 2
Lake & Peninsula SD
Supt. – See King Salmon
S 99564 – Sara Hornberger, prin.

Chiniak, Kodiak Island Co.
Kodiak Island Borough SD
Supt. – See Kodiak
ES, P O BOX 5529 99615 – Elaine Griffin, prin.

Chistochina, Southcentral Co.
Copper River SD
Supt. – See Glennallen
S, MILE 32 1/2 TOK HWY 99586
  Doyle Traw, prin.

Chuathbaluk, Aniak Co., Pop. Code 1
Kuspuk SD
Supt. – See Aniak
S 99557 – Deborah Grigg, prin.

Chugiak, Anchorage Co.
Anchorage SD
Supt. – See Anchorage
ES, MILE 20 OLD GLENN HWY BX 30 99567
  Floyd Sucher, prin.

Circle, Central Co., Pop. Code 1
Yukon Flats SD
Supt. – See Fort Yukon
S 99733 – Michael Doppler, prin.

Clarks Point, Central Co., Pop. Code 1
Southwest Region SD
Supt. – See Dillingham
S 99569 – Robert Sackrison, prin.

Clear, Yukon-Koyukuk Co.
Railbelt SD
Supt. – See Healy
Browns ES, P O BOX 78829 99704
  Eleanor McKee, prin.

Cold Bay, Southcentral Co., Pop. Code 2
Aleutian Region SD
Supt. – See Anchorage
S, GENERAL DELIVERY 99571
  Theresa Mercer, prin.
Nelson Lagoon S 99571 – Thomas Grimes, prin.

Cooper Landing, Kenai Peninsula Co.
Kenai Peninsula Borough SD
Supt. – See Soldotna
ES, P O BOX 515 99572 – Jean Romig, prin.

Copper Center, Southcentral Co., Pop. Code 2
Copper River SD
Supt. – See Glennallen
ES, P O BOX D 99573 – Rita Dishman, prin.
Kenny Lake ES, P O BOX 274 99573
  (—), prin.

          ——————

Sapa Christian School, P O BOX 289 99573

Cordova, Southcentral Co., Pop. Code 4
Chugach SD
Supt. – See Whittier
Icy Bay S, P O BOX 488 99574
  Charles Rains, prin.

Cordova CSD
Sch. Sys. Enr. Code 2
Supt. – William Fairall, P O BOX 140 99574
Mount Eccles ES, P O BOX 140 99574
  James Bruseth, prin.

Craig, Southeastern Co., Pop. Code 2
Craig CSD
Sch. Sys. Enr. Code 2
Supt. – William Milhorn, P O BOX 71 99921
ES, P O BOX 800 99921 – (—), prin.

Crooked Creek, Central Co., Pop. Code 1
Kuspuk SD
Supt. – See Aniak
John S 99575 – Gary Kleven, prin.

Deering, Northwestern Co., Pop. Code 2
Northwest Arctic SD
Supt. – See Kotzebue
S 99736 – Thomas Matheson, prin.

Delta Junction, Central Co., Pop. Code 3
Delta-Greely SD
Sch. Sys. Enr. Code 3
Supt. – Larry Huxel, P O BOX 527 99737
ES, POUCH 1 99737 – Ronald Beck, prin.
Ft. Greely ES 99737 – Bill Barron, prin.

Dillingham, Central Co., Pop. Code 4
Dillingham CSD
Sch. Sys. Enr. Code 2
Supt. – Henry Kilmer, P O BOX 202 99576
ES, P O BOX 3202 99576 – Thomas Troxell, prin.

Southwest Region SD
Sch. Sys. Enr. Code 2
Supt. – John Anttonen, P O BOX 196 99576
Other Schools – See Aleknagik, Clarks Point, Ekwok,
  Koliganek, Levelock, Manokotak, New Stuyahok,
  Togiak, Twin Hills

Diomede, Northwestern Co., Pop. Code 2
Bering Strait SD
Supt. – See Unalakleet
S 99762 – Franklin Adreon, prin.

Dot Lake, Delta Junction Co., Pop. Code 1
Alaska Gateway SD
Supt. – See Tok
S 99737 – Timothy MacDonald, prin.

Eagle, Central Co., Pop. Code 2
Alaska Gateway SD
Supt. – See Tok
Eagle Community S 99738 – Terry McMullin, prin.

Eagle River, Southcentral Co.
Anchorage SD
Supt. – See Anchorage
Gruening JHS, P O BOX 770200 99577
  Debbie Stafford, prin.
Birchwood ABC ES
  BIRCHWOOD LOOP RD BOX 400 99577
  Frank Randazzo, prin.
ES, OLD EAGLE RIVER RD BOX 300 99577
  William Lester, prin.
Fire Lake ES, P O BOX 772569 99577
  James Starry, prin.
Homestead ES, P O BOX 500 99577
  Sharon Meacham, prin.
Ravenwood ES, P O BOX 773049 99577
  Jeffery Argil, prin.

Edna Bay, Southeastern Co.
Southeast Island SD
Supt. – See Ketchikan
S 99950 – Gordon Vernon, prin.

Eek, Central Co., Pop. Code 2
Lower Kuskokwim SD
Supt. – See Bethel
S, GENERAL DELIVERY 99578 – (—), prin.

Egegik, Central Co.
Lake & Peninsula SD
Supt. – See King Salmon
S 99579 – Lance Blackwood, prin.

Eielson A F B, Fairbanks North Co.
Fairbanks-North Star Borough SD
Supt. – See Fairbanks
Anderson ES, BLDG 5227 KODIAK ST 99702
  Joseph Caciari, prin.
Pennell ES, BLDG 5226 COMAN DRIVE 99702
  Carole Hemphill, prin.
Taylor MS, 5270 ARCTIC AVE 99702
  Frederica Buffmire, prin.

Ekwok, Central Co., Pop. Code 1
Southwest Region SD
Supt. – See Dillingham
Nelson ES 99580 – Todd Overby, prin.

Elmendorf A F B, Anchorage Co.
Anchorage SD
Supt. – See Anchorage
Aurora ES, BLDG 21-295 ELDER ST 99506
  Terry Stimson, prin.
Mount Spurr ES, 7-500 I ST 99506
  Michele Stickney, prin.
Orion ES, 21595 LEMON AVE 99506
  Carol Comeau, prin.

Elfin Cove, Skagway-yakutata Co.
Chatham SD
Supt. – See Angoon
S 99825 – Rod Pruitt, prin.

Elim, Northwestern Co., Pop. Code 2
Bering Strait SD
Supt. – See Unalakleet
Aniguin S 99739 – Tom Genne, prin.

Emmonak, Northwestern Co., Pop. Code 3
Lower Yukon SD
Supt. – See Mountain Village
S 99581 – Shirley Peverall, prin.

F P O Seattle
Adak Region SD
Sch. Sys. Enr. Code 3
Supt. – LeRoy Key, ADAK ISLAND 98791
Stevens ES
  ADAK NAS BOX 40 INTRA-AK 98791
  Kenneth Tahfs, prin.

Fairbanks, Central Co., Pop. Code 7
Fairbanks-North Star Borough SD
Sch. Sys. Enr. Code 7
Supt. – Richard Cross, P O BOX 1250 99707
North Pole MS, P O BOX 1250 99707
  Lee Solis, prin.
Ryan MS, P O BOX 1250 99707
  Yvonne Ryans, prin.
Tanana JHS, P O BOX 1250 99707
  Mark Bergemann, prin.
Badger Road ES, P O BOX 1250 99707
  John Haverlik, prin.
Barnette ES, 1000 BARNETTE ST 99701
  Sandra Gamble, prin.
Brown ES 99701 – John Pile, prin.
Chena ES, P O BOX 1250 99707
  Darlene Haymon, prin.
Denali ES, 1042 LATHROP ST 99701
  (—), prin.
Hunter ES, 1630 GILLIAM WAY 99701
  Roger Griffin, prin.
Joy ES, P O BOX 1250 99707
  Robert Curran, prin.
Nordale ES, P O BOX 1250 99707 – (—), prin.
North Pole ES, P O BOX 1250 99707
  (—), prin.
Pearl Creek ES, P O BOX 1250 99707
  Elizabeth Farni, prin.
Rosamond Weller ES, P O BOX 1250 99707
  Mark Shellinger, prin.
Salcha ES, P O BOX 1250 99707
  Russell Griffin, prin.
Two Rivers ES, P O BOX 12501 99707
  Randall Swenson, prin.
University Park ES, P O BOX 1250 99707
  William Rogers, prin.
Woodriver ES, P O BOX 1250 99707
  Ruth Hurlburt, prin.
Other Schools – See Eielson A F B, Fort Wainwright

Yukon Flats SD
Supt. – See Fort Yukon
Northern Lights S, P O BOX 10410 99710
  Priscilla Delgado, prin.

Immaculate Conception School
  715 MONROE ST 99701

False Pass, Southcentral Co., Pop. Code 1
Aleutian Region SD
Supt. – See Anchorage
S, GENERAL DELIVERY 99583
  Joe Newman, prin.

Fort Richardson, Anchorage Co.
Anchorage SD
Supt. – See Anchorage
Kennedy ES, 540 DYEA AVE 99505
  David Cusato, prin.
Ursa Major ES, 454 DYEA AVE 99505
  Anna Seabrook, prin.
Ursa Minor ES, 6TH AVE & HOONAH 99505
  Joseph Ivey, prin.

Fortuna Ledge, Wade Hampton Co.
Lower Yukon SD
Supt. – See Mountain Village
Marshall S, FORTUNA LEDGE P O 99585
  Courtland Ofelt, prin.

Fort Wainwright, Fairbanks North Co.
Fairbanks-North Star Borough SD
Supt. – See Fairbanks
Aurora ES, BLDG 4165 NEELY ST 99703
  Stanley Lujan, prin.
MS, BLDG 4166 NEELY ST 99703
  Patricia Benally, prin.

Fort Yukon, Yukon-Koyukuk Co.
Yukon Flats SD
Sch. Sys. Enr. Code 2
Supt. – Robert McConnell, P O BOX 359 99740
Birch Creek S, BIRCH CREEK VILLAGE 99740
  Thomas Sorenson, prin.
S 99740 – Peter Van Borkulo, prin.
Other Schools – See Arctic Village, Beaver, Central,
  Chalkyitsik, Circle, Fairbanks, Rampart, Stevens
  Village, Venetie

Gakona, Valdez-Cordova Co.
Copper River SD
Supt. – See Glennallen
ES, P O BOX 228 99586 – Robert Carnahan, prin.
Slana ES, SLANA VIA 99586 – Linda Bates, prin.

Galena, Central Co., Pop. Code 3
Galena CSD
Sch. Sys. Enr. Code 2
Supt. – Harry Purdy, P O BOX 299 99741
ES, P O BOX 299 99741 – (—), prin.

Gambell, Northwestern Co., Pop. Code 2
Bering Strait SD
Supt. – See Unalakleet
S 99742 – Nancy Thomas, prin.

Girdwood, Anchorage Co.
Anchorage SD
Supt. – See Anchorage
ES, P O BOX 189 99587 – Bruce Lamm, prin.

Glennallen, Southcentral Co., Pop. Code 2
Copper River SD
Sch. Sys. Enr. Code 3
Supt. – Leland Dishman, P O BOX 103 99588
ES, P O BOX 66 99588 – (—), prin.

Sparks ES, P O BOX 108 99588
  Laura Mann, prin.
Other Schools – See Chistochina, Copper Center,
  Gakona, Paxson

Golovin, Nome Co., Pop. Code 1
Bering Strait SD
Supt. – See Unalakleet
Olson S 99762 – Richard Dine, prin.

Goodnews Bay, Central Co., Pop. Code 2
Lower Kuskokwim SD
Supt. – See Bethel
Rocky Mountain S, GENERAL DELIVERY 99589
  Sharon Weatherford, prin.

Grayling, Central Co., Pop. Code 2
Iditarod Area SD
Supt. – See McGrath
David-Lewis Memorial S
  GENERAL DELIVERY 99590
  Phyllis Kardos, prin.

Gustavus, Southeastern Co.
Chatham SD
Supt. – See Angoon
S, P O BOX 17 99826 – Dennis Coffield, prin.

Haines, Southeastern Co., Pop. Code 4
Chatham SD
Supt. – See Angoon
Klukwan ES, P O BOX 1409 99827
  Robert Nelson, prin.

Haines Borough SD
Sch. Sys. Enr. Code 2
Supt. – Nancy Billingsley, P O BOX 636 99827
JHS, P O BOX 636 99827 – (—), prin.
ES, P O BOX 1289 99827 – Alan Heinrich, prin.
Mosquito Lake ES, P O BOX 2189 99827
  Ronald Weishahn, prin.

Covenant Life School, P O BOX 598 99827

Healy, Central Co., Pop. Code 1
Railbelt SD
Sch. Sys. Enr. Code 2
Supt. – James Paul, P O BOX 280 99743
Tri-Valley S, P O BOX 400 99743
  Scott Iverson, prin.
Other Schools – See Anderson, Cantwell, Clear

Hobart Bay, Southeastern Co.
Chatham SD
Supt. – See Angoon
S 99805 – (—), prin.

Holy Cross, Central Co., Pop. Code 2
Iditarod Area SD
Supt. – See McGrath
S, P O BOX 99 99602 – Allen Reinhart, prin.

Homer, Southcentral Co., Pop. Code 4
Kenai Peninsula Borough SD
Supt. – See Soldotna
English Bay S 99603 – Sharon Radtke, prin.
JHS, 320 PIONEER 99603 – (—), prin.
Banks ES, 1340 EAST ROAD 99603
  Lewis McLin, prin.
IS, 450 STERLING HIGHWAY 99603
  Roderick Ladd, prin.
McNeil Canyon ES
  FRITZ CREEK VLY RD #15015 99603
  Diane Borgman, prin.
Razdolna ES
  FRITZ CREEK VLY RD #15015 99603
  Robert Bell, prin.

Hoonah, Southeastern Co., Pop. Code 3
Hoonah CSD
Sch. Sys. Enr. Code 2
Supt. – Dr. Thomas Brown, P O BOX 157 99829
ES, P O BOX 157 99829 – (—), prin.

Hooper Bay, Northwestern Co., Pop. Code 3
Lower Yukon SD
Supt. – See Mountain Village
S 99604 – David Harrison, prin.

Hope, Southcentral Co.
Kenai Peninsula Borough SD
Supt. – See Soldotna
S, P O BOX 47 99605 – Louis Kustin, prin.

Hughes, Yukon-Koyukuk Co., Pop. Code 1
Yukon-Koyukuk SD
Supt. – See Nenana
ES, GENERAL DELIVERY 99745
  Howard Cloud, prin.

Huslia, Central Co., Pop. Code 2
Yukon-Koyukuk SD
Supt. – See Nenana
S 99746 – Teresa Rovig, prin.

Hydaburg, Southeastern Co.
Hydaburg CSD
Sch. Sys. Enr. Code 2
Supt. – Nancy Schave, P O BOX 109 99922
ES, P O BOX 109 99922 – (—), prin.

Iliamna, Central Co., Pop. Code 1
Lake & Peninsula SD
Supt. – See King Salmon
Newhalen S 99606 – Walter Scott, prin.

Juneau, Southeastern Co., Pop. Code 8
Chatham SD
Supt. – See Angoon

Cube Cove S, 8995 YANDUKIN DR 99801
  Michael Schroeder, prin.
Eight Fathom Bight S, 8995 YANDUKIN DR 99801
  Maryanne Dickey, prin.
Freshwater Bay S, P O BOX 34738 99803
  Brenda Patterson, prin.

Juneau Borough SD
Sch. Sys. Enr. Code 5
Supt. – Bruce Johnson
  10014 CRAZY HORSE DRIVE 99801
Drake MS, 10014 CRAZY HORSE DRIVE 99801
  Susan Derse, prin.
Dryden MS, 10014 CRAZY HORSE DRIVE 99801
  Lynn Divelbess, prin.
Auke Bay ES, 10014 CRAZY HORSE DRIVE 99801
  Judy Franklet, prin.
Gastineau ES, 10014 CRAZY HORSE DRIVE 99801
  Christine Crooks, prin.
Glacier Valley ES
  10014 CRAZY HORSE DRIVE 99801
  Kathleen Wayne, prin.
Harborview ES
  10014 CRAZY HORSE DRIVE 99801
  Susan Horton, prin.
Mendenhall River Community ES
  10014 CRAZY HORSE DRIVE 99801
  Jacqueline Sparks, prin.

Southeast Island SD
Supt. – See Ketchikan
Gildersleeve S, P O BOX 33626 99803
  Dave Gordon, prin.

Life Covenant Fellowship School
  P O BOX 2013 99803

Kake, Southeastern Co., Pop. Code 3
Kake CSD
Sch. Sys. Enr. Code 2
Supt. – George White, P O BOX 450 99830
JHS, P O BOX 450 99830 – (—), prin.
ES, P O BOX 450 99830 – Leo Kondro, prin.

Kaktovik, Central Co., Pop. Code 2
North Slope Borough SD
Supt. – See Barrow
Kaveolook S, P O BOX 10 99747
  Maurice Pearson, prin.

Kaltag, Central Co., Pop. Code 2
Yukon-Koyukuk SD
Supt. – See Nenana
S 99748 – Kevin LeFevour, prin.

Karluk, Southcentral Co.
Kodiak Island Borough SD
Supt. – See Kodiak
S 99608 – Gerald Sheehan, prin.

Kasigluk, Central Co.
Lower Kuskokwim SD
Supt. – See Bethel
Akula-Elitnaurvit S, GENERAL DELIVERY 99609
  William Ferguson, prin.

Kasilof, Kenai Peninsula Co.
Kenai Peninsula Borough SD
Supt. – See Soldotna
Tustumena ES, P O BOX 177 99610
  Al Besch, prin.

Kenai, Southcentral Co., Pop. Code 5
Kenai Peninsula Borough SD
Supt. – See Soldotna
JHS, 201 N TINKER LANE 99611
  Richard Hultberg, prin.
Mount View MS, 315 SWIRES ROAD 99611
  Richard Boudreau, prin.
Sears ES, 549 N FOREST DRIVE 99611
  Jacqueline Imle, prin.

Ketchikan, Southeastern Co., Pop. Code 6
Ketchikan Gateway Borough SD
Sch. Sys. Enr. Code 4
Supt. – Edward McNulty, P O BOX Z 99901
Schoenbar JHS, 217 SCHOENBAR ROAD 99901
  Richard Clement, prin.
Houghtaling ES, 2940 BRANOF AVE 99901
  Robert Vincent, prin.
Point Higgins ES 99901 – Dan Michalsen, prin.
Valley Park ES, 410 SCHOENBAR RD 99901
  Karen Pennington, prin.
White Cliff ES, 1900 1ST AVE 99901
  Ronald Hamberger, prin.

Southeast Island SD
Sch. Sys. Enr. Code 2
Supt. – Robert Weinstein, P O BOX 8340 99901
Fire Cove S, P O BOX B 99901
  Donald Robbins, prin.
Green S, P O BOX LI 99901 – Phyllis Ulrich, prin.
Hill S, P O BOX N 99901 – Jody Luger, prin.
S, GENERAL DELIVERY 99901
  Judith Jones, prin.
Kasaan S 99924 – Barry Stewart, prin.
LaBouchere Bay S, P O BOX E 99901
  Rosemary Waide, prin.
Polk Inlet ES, P O BOX K 99901
  Amelia Dilworth, prin.
Smith Cove S, P O BOX 6220 99901
  Paul Hepler, prin.
Valentine S, P O BOX L 99901
  Michael Williams, prin.
Whale Pass S, P O BOX A 99950
  Patricia McDonald, prin.

Nichen Cove ES, POUCH C 99950
Amelia Dilworth, prin.
Other Schools – See Edna Bay, Juneau, Meyers
Chuck, Point Baker, Port Alexander, Sitka, Thorne
Bay

Ketchikan Christian Academy
P O BOX 7400 99901
Holy Name School, 433 JACKSON ST 99901

Kiana, Northwestern Co., Pop. Code 2
Northwest Arctic SD
Supt. – See Kotzebue
ES 99749 – Gerald Clancy, prin.

King Cove, Southcentral Co., Pop. Code 2
King Cove CSD
Sch. Sys. Enr. Code 1
Supt. – Benjamin Kirker, P O BOX 6 99612
King Cove City S, P O BOX 6 99612
Kenneth Satre, prin.

King Salmon, Central Co.
Lake & Peninsula SD
Sch. Sys. Enr. Code 2
Supt. – Frank Hill, P O BOX 498 99613
Igiugig S 99613 – Mike Roberts, prin.
Other Schools – See Anchorage, Chignik, Chignik
Lagoon, Chignik Lake, Egegik, Iliamna, Kokhanok,
Nondalton, Pedro Bay, Perryville, Pilot Point, Port
Alsworth, Port Heiden

Kipnuk, Central Co., Pop. Code 2
Lower Kuskokwim SD
Supt. – See Bethel
S, GENERAL DELIVERY 99614
John Kaufman, prin.

Kivalina, Northwestern Co., Pop. Code 2
Northwest Arctic SD
Supt. – See Kotzebue
McQueen ES 99750 – Thomas Hanifan, prin.

Klawock, Southeastern Co., Pop. Code 2
Klawock CSD
Sch. Sys. Enr. Code 2
Supt. – Morris Ververs, P O BOX 9 99925
ES, P O BOX 9 99925 – (—), prin.

Kobuk, Kobuk Co., Pop. Code 1
Northwest Arctic SD
Supt. – See Kotzebue
ES 99751 – Jackie Bowling, prin.

Kodiak, Southcentral Co., Pop. Code 5
Kodiak Island Borough SD
Sch. Sys. Enr. Code 4
Supt. – David Witteveen, P O BOX 886 99615
JHS, P O BOX 886 99615 – Betty Walters, prin.
East ES, 722 MILL BAY ROAD 99615
Gale Holfert, prin.
Main ES, 722 MILL BAY ROAD 99615
Thomas Wischer, prin.
Peterson ES, 722 MILL BAY ROAD 99615
Marcia Oswalt, prin.
Other Schools – See Akhiok, Chiniak, Karluk, Larsen
Bay, Old Harbor, Ouzinkie, Port Lions

Kokhanok, Iliamna Co.
Lake & Peninsula SD
Supt. – See King Salmon
S 99606 – Daniel Hill, prin.

Koliganek, Dillingham Co., Pop. Code 2
Southwest Region SD
Supt. – See Dillingham
ES 99576 – Pamela Winkelman, prin.

Kongiganak, Bethel Co., Pop. Code 2
Lower Kuskokwim SD
Supt. – See Bethel
S, GENERAL DELIVERY 99559
Pat Kennedy, prin.

Kotlik, Northwestern Co., Pop. Code 2
Lower Yukon SD
Supt. – See Mountain Village
S 99620 – Gerald Gates, prin.

Kotzebue, Northwestern Co., Pop. Code 4
Northwest Arctic SD
Sch. Sys. Enr. Code 4
Supt. – Gerald Covey, P O BOX 51 99752
JHS 99752 – (—), prin.
ES 99752 – Larry Villars, prin.
Other Schools – See Ambler, Buckland, Deering,
Kiana, Kivalina, Kobuk, Noatak, Noorvik, Selawik,
Shungnak

Koyuk, Northwestern Co., Pop. Code 2
Bering Strait SD
Supt. – See Unalakleet
Koyuk-Malemute S 99753
Donald Gillespie, prin.

Koyukuk, Central Co., Pop. Code 1
Yukon-Koyukuk SD
Supt. – See Nenana
S 99754 – Timothy Cline, prin.

Kwethluk, Central Co., Pop. Code 2
Lower Kuskokwim SD
Supt. – See Bethel
S, GENERAL DELIVERY 99621
Robert Medinger, prin.

Kwigillingok, Central Co., Pop. Code 2
Lower Kuskokwim SD
Supt. – See Bethel

S, GENERAL DELIVERY 99622
Mike Smith, prin.

Larsen Bay, Southcentral Co., Pop. Code 2
Kodiak Island Borough SD
Supt. – See Kodiak
S 99624 – Roberta Ward, prin.

Levelock, Central Co., Pop. Code 1
Southwest Region SD
Supt. – See Dillingham
S 99625 – Joe Schreiber, prin.

Lime Village, Central Co.
Iditarod Area SD
Supt. – See McGrath
ES, GENERAL DELIVERY 99627
Shirley Moses, prin.

Lower Kalskag, Bethel Co., Pop. Code 2
Kuspuk SD
Supt. – See Aniak
ES 99626 – Wayne Ayers, prin.

Manley Hot Springs, Yukon-Koyukuk Co.
Yukon-Koyukuk SD
Supt. – See Nenana
ES 99756 – Damaris Mortvedt, prin.

Manokotak, Central Co., Pop. Code 2
Southwest Region SD
Supt. – See Dillingham
S 99628 – James Moras, prin.

McGrath, Central Co., Pop. Code 2
Iditarod Area SD
Sch. Sys. Enr. Code 2
Supt. – Sarah Hanuske-Hamilton
P O BOX 105 99627
S, P O BOX 105 99627 – Robert Maguire, prin.
Telida ES 99627 – Katherine Holbrook, prin.
Other Schools – See Anvik, Grayling, Holy Cross,
Lime Village, Nikolai, Shageluk

Mekoryuk, Central Co., Pop. Code 2
Lower Kuskokwim SD
Supt. – See Bethel
Nunivaarmiut S, GENERAL DELIVERY 99630
Les Daenzer, prin.

Metlakatla, Southeastern Co., Pop. Code 4
Annette Island SD
Sch. Sys. Enr. Code 2
Supt. – Walter Bromenschenkel, P O BOX 7 99926
ES, P O BOX 7 99926 – Dona Ruth Ross, prin.

Meyers Chuck, Ketchikan Co.
Southeast Island SD
Supt. – See Ketchikan
S 99903 – Marie Wierema, prin.

Minto, Central Co., Pop. Code 2
Yukon-Koyukuk SD
Supt. – See Nenana
S 99578 – John Stone, prin.

Moose Pass, Kenai Peninsula Co.
Kenai Peninsula Borough SD
Supt. – See Soldotna
ES, P O BOX 46 99631 – (—), prin.

Mountain Village, Northwestern Co., Pop. Code 3
Lower Yukon SD
Sch. Sys. Enr. Code 4
Supt. – Jim Riedlinger, P O BOX 200 99632
S, P O BOX 201 99632 – David Rhodes, prin.
Other Schools – See Alakanuk, Emmonak, Fortuna
Ledge, Hooper Bay, Kotlik, Pilot Station, Pitkas
Point, Russian Mission, Scammon Bay, Sheldon
Point

Naknek, Central Co., Pop. Code 2
Bristol Bay Borough SD
Sch. Sys. Enr. Code 2
Supt. – Richard Leath, P O BOX 169 99633
ES, P O BOX 169 99633 – Robert Swanson, prin.
South Naknek ES, P O BOX 169 99633
James Hopkins, prin.

Napakiak, Central Co., Pop. Code 2
Lower Kuskokwim SD
Supt. – See Bethel
S, GENERAL DELIVERY 99634 – Gene Hulse, prin.

Napaskiak, Bethel Co., Pop. Code 2
Lower Kuskokwim SD
Supt. – See Bethel
Williams Memorial S, GENERAL DELIVERY 99559
Alfred Knutsen, prin.

Nenana, Central Co., Pop. Code 2
Nenana CSD
Sch. Sys. Enr. Code 2
Supt. – Steven Yates, P O BOX 10 99760
Nenana Highway Attendance Area
P O BOX 309 99760 – (—), prin.
S, P O BOX 10 99760 – (—), prin.

Yukon-Koyukuk SD
Sch. Sys. Enr. Code 2
Supt. – Fred Lau, P O BOX 309 99760
Northwind S, P O BOX 309 99760 – (—), prin.
Other Schools – See Allakaket, Bettles Field, Hughes,
Huslia, Kaltag, Koyukuk, Manley Hot Springs,
Minto, Nulato, Ruby

New Stuyahok, Central Co., Pop. Code 2
Southwest Region SD
Supt. – See Dillingham
S 99636 – Nels Nichols, prin.

Newtok, Tununak Co., Pop. Code 2
Lower Kuskokwim SD
Supt. – See Bethel
Ayaprun S, GENERAL DELIVERY 99559
Barbara Jones, prin.

Nightmute, Tununak Co., Pop. Code 2
Lower Kuskokwim SD
Supt. – See Bethel
S, GENERAL DELIVERY 99690
James Hyska, prin.

Nikiski, Kenai Peninsula Co.
Kenai Peninsula Borough SD
Supt. – See Soldotna
ES, P O BOX 8229 99635 – Jack Albaugh, prin.
North Star ES, P O BOX 8629 99635
Janice Hall, prin.

Nikolai, Yukon-Koyukuk Co.
Iditarod Area SD
Supt. – See McGrath
Top of the Kuskokwim ES
GENERAL DELIVERY 99601 – Dennis Bonie, prin.

Nikolski, Southcentral Co.
Aleutian Region SD
Supt. – See Anchorage
S, GENERAL DELIVERY 99638
Ronald Edwards, prin.

Ninilchik, Southcentral Co., Pop. Code 2
Kenai Peninsula Borough SD
Supt. – See Soldotna
S, P O BOX 145 99639 – Kenneth Satre, prin.

Noatak, Northwestern Co., Pop. Code 2
Northwest Arctic SD
Supt. – See Kotzebue
ES 99761 – Peter Flisock, prin.

Nome, Northwestern Co., Pop. Code 4
Nome CSD
Sch. Sys. Enr. Code 3
Supt. – Robert Shigley, P O BOX 131 99762
ES, P O BOX 131 99762 – David Newton, prin.

Nondalton, Central Co., Pop. Code 2
Lake & Peninsula SD
Supt. – See King Salmon
S 99640 – David Smith, prin.

Noorvik, Northwestern Co., Pop. Code 2
Northwest Arctic SD
Supt. – See Kotzebue
ES 99763 – (—), prin.

Northway, Central Co., Pop. Code 1
Alaska Gateway SD
Supt. – See Tok
S, P O BOX B 99764 – Willaim Bryson, prin.

Nuiqsut, Barrow Co.
North Slope Borough SD
Supt. – See Barrow
S, GENERAL DELIVERY 99723
Robert Miller, prin.

Nulato, Central Co., Pop. Code 2
Yukon-Koyukuk SD
Supt. – See Nenana
Demoski S, P O BOX 65029 99765
Glenn Olson, prin.

Nunapitchuk, Central Co.
Lower Kuskokwim SD
Supt. – See Bethel
Tobeluk Memorial S, GENERAL DELIVERY 99641
Jacqueline Slaughter, prin.

Old Harbor, Southcentral Co., Pop. Code 2
Kodiak Island Borough SD
Supt. – See Kodiak
S, P O BOX 49 99643 – Charles Coons, prin.

Oscarville, Central Co.
Lower Kuskokwim SD
Supt. – See Bethel
S, GENERAL DELIVERY 99559
Francis Neal, prin.

Ouzinkie, Southcentral Co., Pop. Code 2
Kodiak Island Borough SD
Supt. – See Kodiak
S, P O BOX 93 99644 – Patricia Gibbs, prin.

Palmer, Southcentral Co., Pop. Code 4
Matanuska-Susitna Borough SD
Sch. Sys. Enr. Code 6
Supt. – Bruce DeMond, P O BOX AB 99645
Glacier View S, P O BOX 8454 99645
Dewey Taylor, prin.
JHS, P O BOX AB 99645 – (—), prin.
Big Lake ES, P O BOX 1688 99645
Jim Bitney, prin.
Butte ES, P O BOX 1688 99645
David Spear, prin.
Cottonwood Creek ES, P O BOX 1688 99645
Chester Anderson, prin.
Finger Lake ES, P O BOX 1688 99645
Martin Laster, prin.
Iditarod ES, P O BOX 1688 99645
Donald Chicarell, prin.
Pioneer Peak ES, P O BOX 1688 99645
John Norman, prin.
Point MacKenzie ES, P O BOX 1688 99645
James Bitney, prin.
Sherrod MS, P O BOX AB 99645
Stephen Glauner, prin.

Snowshoe ES, P O BOX 1688 99645
  Robert Seims, prin.
Sutton ES, P O BOX 1688 99645
  Linda Connelly, prin.
Swanson ES, P O BOX 1688 99645
  Rose Anderson, prin.
Talkeetna ES, P O BOX 1688 99645
  Erin Aulman, prin.
Tanaina ES, P O BOX 1688 99645
  Lawrence Healy, prin.
Trappers Creek ES, P O BOX 1688 99645
  Karen Faerber, prin.
Willow ES, P O BOX 1688 99645
  William Lorentzen, prin.
Other Schools – See Skwentna, Wasilla

Paxson, Delta Junction Co.
Copper River SD
Supt. – See Glennallen
S 99737 – Dale Judge, prin.

Pedro Bay, Dillingham Co.
Lake & Peninsula SD
Supt. – See King Salmon
S 99647 – Barbara Jacko, prin.

Pelican, Southeastern Co., Pop. Code 2
Pelican CSD
Sch. Sys. Enr. Code 1
Supt. – Kenneth Siderius, P O BOX 603 99832
S, P O BOX 603 99832 – (—), prin.

Perryville, Southcentral Co., Pop. Code 1
Lake & Peninsula SD
Supt. – See King Salmon
S 99648 – Kenneth Eggleston, prin.

Petersburg, Southeastern Co., Pop. Code 5
Petersburg CSD
Sch. Sys. Enr. Code 3
Supt. – William Creger, P O BOX 289 99833
MS, P O BOX 289 99833 – (—), prin.
ES, P O BOX 289 99833 – Melissa Carraway, prin.

Pilot Point, Dillingham Co.
Lake & Peninsula SD
Supt. – See King Salmon
S 99649 – Michelle Gasper, prin.

Pilot Station, Northwestern Co., Pop. Code 2
Lower Yukon SD
Supt. – See Mountain Village
S 99650 – Patricia Brady, prin.

Pitkas Point, St. Marys Co.
Lower Yukon SD
Supt. – See Mountain Village
S 99658 – Kirk Pearson, prin.

Platinum, Central Co., Pop. Code 1
Lower Kuskokwim SD
Supt. – See Bethel
Arvuq S, GENERAL DELIVERY 99651
  Dennis Ronsse, prin.

Point Baker, Prince of Wales-Outer Ketchikan Co.
Southeast Island SD
Supt. – See Ketchikan
Port Protection S, GENERAL DELIVERY 99927
  Tracy Jones, prin.

Point Hope, Northwestern Co., Pop. Code 2
North Slope Borough SD
Supt. – See Barrow
Tikigaq S, P O BOX 125 99766
  Nathaniel Good, prin.

Point Lay, Barrow Co.
North Slope Borough SD
Supt. – See Barrow
Cully S, GENERAL DELIVERY 99790
  Andrew Fields, prin.

Port Alexander, Sitka Co., Pop. Code 1
Southeast Island SD
Supt. – See Ketchikan
S 99836 – Peter Kimzey, prin.

Port Alsworth, Dillingham Co.
Lake & Peninsula SD
Supt. – See King Salmon
S 99653 – (—), prin.

Port Graham, Homer Co., Pop. Code 2
Kenai Peninsula Borough SD
Supt. – See Soldotna
S 99603 – DeEtta Scarborough, prin.

Port Heiden, King Salmon Co., Pop. Code 1
Lake & Peninsula SD
Supt. – See King Salmon
S 99549 – John Sandidge, prin.

Port Lions, Southcentral Co., Pop. Code 2
Kodiak Island Borough SD
Supt. – See Kodiak
S, P O BOX 248 99550 – William Biehl, prin.

Quinhagak, Central Co., Pop. Code 2
Lower Kuskokwim SD
Supt. – See Bethel
S 99655 – Kenneth Groves, prin.

Rampart, Fairbanks Co., Pop. Code 1
Yukon Flats SD
Supt. – See Fort Yukon
S, 199 RAMPART AVE 99701 – Irene Bowie, prin.

Red Devil, Central Co., Pop. Code 1
Kuspuk SD
Supt. – See Aniak
Willis S 99656 – Deanna Cole, prin.

Ruby, Central Co., Pop. Code 2
Yukon-Koyukuk SD
Supt. – See Nenana
Kangas S, P O BOX 18 99768
  Richard Strick, prin.

Russian Mission, Central Co., Pop. Code 2
Lower Yukon SD
Supt. – See Mountain Village
S, GENERAL DELIVERY 99657
  Dr. Virginia Kendall, prin.

Saint George Island, Aleutian Islands Co.
Pribilof Islands SD
Supt. – See Saint Paul Island
ES 99833 – Robert Winston, prin.

Saint Mary's, Northwestern Co., Pop. Code 2
St. Mary's SD
Sch. Sys. Enr. Code 2
Supt. – James Zuelow, P O BOX 171 99658
Elicarvicuar ES, P O BOX 171 99658
  (—), prin.

Saint Michael, Northwestern Co., Pop. Code 2
Bering Strait SD
Supt. – See Unalakleet
Andrews S 99659 – Bruce Currie, prin.

Saint Paul Island, Southcentral Co., Pop. Code 2
Pribilof Islands SD
Sch. Sys. Enr. Code 2
Supt. – Denver Bowen 99660
S 99660 – G. Daryl Brown, prin.
Other Schools – See Saint George Island

Sand Point, Aleutian Islands Co., Pop. Code 3
Sand Point CSD
Sch. Sys. Enr. Code 2
Supt. – John Davis, P O BOX 158 99661
ES, P O BOX 269 99661 – Charles Beckley, prin.

Savoonga, Northwestern Co., Pop. Code 2
Bering Strait SD
Supt. – See Unalakleet
Kingeekuk Memorial S 99769 – Steven Jones, prin.

Scammon Bay, Northwestern Co., Pop. Code 2
Lower Yukon SD
Supt. – See Mountain Village
S 99662 – Roger Bak, prin.

Selawik, Northwestern Co., Pop. Code 2
Northwest Arctic SD
Supt. – See Kotzebue
ES 99770 – Alex Hazelton, prin.

Seldovia, Southcentral Co.
Kenai Peninsula Borough SD
Supt. – See Soldotna
English S, P O BOX 171 99663
  Paul Sorenson, prin.

Seward, Southcentral Co., Pop. Code 4
Kenai Peninsula Borough SD
Supt. – See Soldotna
ES, P O BOX 247 99664 – Roger Sampson, prin.

Shageluk, Central Co., Pop. Code 2
Iditarod Area SD
Supt. – See McGrath
Innoko River S, GENERAL DELIVERY 99665
  Howard Diamond, prin.

Shaktoolik, Northwestern Co., Pop. Code 2
Bering Strait SD
Supt. – See Unalakleet
S 99771 – Gerald Girv, prin.

Sheldon Point, Emmonak Co., Pop. Code 2
Lower Yukon SD
Supt. – See Mountain Village
S 99666 – Charles Wihger, prin.

Shishmaref, Northwestern Co., Pop. Code 2
Bering Strait SD
Supt. – See Unalakleet
S 99772 – James Wack, prin.

Shungnak, Northwestern Co., Pop. Code 2
Northwest Arctic SD
Supt. – See Kotzebue
S 99773 – Donald Haile, prin.

Sitka, Southeastern Co., Pop. Code 6
Sitka Borough SD
Sch. Sys. Enr. Code 4
Supt. – Arthur Woodhouse, P O BOX 179 99835
Blatchley JHS, P O BOX 179 99835
  Walter Clark, prin.
Baranof ES, 305 BARANOF ST 99835
  Cliff Schadler, prin.
Etolin Street MS, 601 ETOLIN ST 99835
  Terry Coon, prin.
Lincoln Street ES, 601 ETOLIN ST 99835
  (—), prin.
Mount Edgecumbe ES, 450 KRUZOF AVE 99835
  (—), prin.
Verstovia MS, P O BOX 179 99835 – (—), prin.

Southeast Island SD
Supt. – See Ketchikan
Rowan Bay S 99835 – James Guenther, prin.

Skagway, Southeastern Co., Pop. Code 3
Skagway CSD
Sch. Sys. Enr. Code 2
Supt. – Gordon Tope, P O BOX 497 99840
S, P O BOX 497 99840 – (—), prin.

Skwentna, Southcentral Co.
Matanuska-Susitna Borough SD
Supt. – See Palmer
S 99667 – Greg Miller, prin.

Sleetmute, Central Co., Pop. Code 2
Kuspuk SD
Supt. – See Aniak
S 99668 – Bambi Phipps, prin.

Soldotna, Southcentral Co., Pop. Code 4
Kenai Peninsula Borough SD
Sch. Sys. Enr. Code 6
Supt. – Fred Pomeroy, 144 N BINKLEY ST 99669
JHS, 426 W REDOUBT AVE 99669
  Daryl Kellum, prin.
Kalifornsky Beach ES, 1049 POPPY LN 99669
  Gary Jackson, prin.
Redoubt ES, 426 W REDOUBT AVE 99669
  Larry Nauta, prin.
ES, 162 PARK AVE 99669 – David Dickerson, prin.
Other Schools – See Anchor Point, Cooper Landing,
  Homer, Hope, Kasilof, Kenai, Moose Pass, Nikiski,
  Ninilchik, Port Graham, Seldovia, Seward, Sterling,
  Tyonek

Cook Inlet Academy, P O BOX 50 99669
Kalifonsky Christian School, P O BOX 857 99669

Stebbins, Northwestern Co., Pop. Code 2
Bering Strait SD
Supt. – See Unalakleet
Tukurngnailguq S 99671 – Ron Magee, prin.

Sterling, Southcentral Co.
Kenai Peninsula Borough SD
Supt. – See Soldotna
ES, HCR 02 BOX 215 99672 – Victor Varick, prin.

Resurrection Christian Academy
  P O BOX 384 99672

Stevens Village, Central Co.
Yukon Flats SD
Supt. – See Fort Yukon
S 99774 – Jon Laughlin, prin.

Stony River, Aniak Co., Pop. Code 1
Kuspuk SD
Supt. – See Aniak
Michael S 99673 – (—), prin.

Tanacross, Southeast Fairbanks Co.
Alaska Gateway SD
Supt. – See Tok
Tanacross ES, GENERAL DELIVERY 99776
  Russ Johnston, prin.

Tanana, Central Co., Pop. Code 2
Tanana CSD
Sch. Sys. Enr. Code 1
Supt. – Vincent Barry, P O BOX 89 99777
Tanana City S, P O BOX 89 99777 – (—), prin.

Tatitlek, Cordova Co.
Chugach SD
Supt. – See Whittier
Tatitlek Community S, P O BOX 167 99677
  Joe McGowan, prin.

Teller, Northwestern Co., Pop. Code 2
Bering Strait SD
Supt. – See Unalakleet
Isabell S 99778 – Laurence Dunn, prin.

Tenakee Springs, Southeastern Co., Pop. Code 2
Chatham SD
Supt. – See Angoon
S, P O BOX 62 99841 – Katy White, prin.

Tetlin, Southeast Fairbanks Co.
Alaska Gateway SD
Supt. – See Tok
Mentaska Lake S 99780 – John Rusyniak, prin.
S, GENERAL DELIVERY 99779
  Thomas Nash, prin.

Thorne Bay, Ketchikan Co.
Southeast Island SD
Supt. – See Ketchikan
S, P O BOX 05 99950 – Michael Walker, prin.

Togiak, Central Co., Pop. Code 2
Southwest Region SD
Supt. – See Dillingham
S 99678 – Dorian Ross, prin.

Tok, Central Co., Pop. Code 2
Alaska Gateway SD
Sch. Sys. Enr. Code 2
Supt. – Spike Jorgensen, P O BOX 226 99780
S, P O BOX 249 99780 – Doug Hosken, prin.
Other Schools – See Dot Lake, Eagle, Northway,
  Tanacross, Tetlin

Toksook Bay, Tununak Co., Pop. Code 2
Lower Kuskokwim SD
Supt. – See Bethel
Nelson Island S, GENERAL DELIVERY 99637
  Joseph O'Neill, prin.

Tuluksak, Bethel Co., Pop. Code 2
Yupiit SD
Supt. – See Akiachak
ES, GENERAL DELIVERY   99679 – (—), prin.

Tuntutuliak, Bethel Co.
Lower Kuskokwim SD
Supt. – See Bethel
Angapak Memorial S, GENERAL DELIVERY   99680
Frank Barnett, prin.

Tununak, Central Co., Pop. Code 2
Lower Kuskokwim SD
Supt. – See Bethel
Albert Memorial S, GENERAL DELIVERY   99681
Ian Parks, prin.

Twin Hills, Dillingham Co.
Southwest Region SD
Supt. – See Dillingham
ES   99576 – Mary Alexie, prin.

Tyonek, Southcentral Co., Pop. Code 2
Kenai Peninsula Borough SD
Supt. – See Soldotna
Bartlett S   99682 – Thomas Maughn, prin.

Unalakleet, Northwestern Co., Pop. Code 3
Bering Strait SD
Sch. Sys. Enr. Code 4
Supt. – Ed Gonion, P O BOX 225   99684
S   99684 – Timothy Doran, prin.
Other Schools – See Brevig Mission, Diomede, Elim,
Gambell, Golovin, Koyuk, Saint Michael, Savoonga,
Shaktoolik, Shishmaref, Stebbins, Teller, Wales,
White Mountain

Unalaska, Southcentral Co., Pop. Code 4
Unalaska CSD
Sch. Sys. Enr. Code 2
Supt. – John Novak, P O BOX 260   99685
ES, P O BOX 260   99685 – (—), prin.

Upper Kalskag, Bethel Co., Pop. Code 2
Kuspuk SD
Supt. – See Aniak
Gregory ES   99607 – Ralph Steeves, prin.

Valdez, Southcentral Co., Pop. Code 4
Valdez CSD
Sch. Sys. Enr. Code 3
Supt. – Harry Rogers, P O BOX 398   99686
Gilson JHS, P O BOX 398   99686 – (—), prin.
Hutchens ES, P O BOX 398   99686
James Barra, prin.

Venetie, Central Co., Pop. Code 2
Yukon Flats SD
Supt. – See Fort Yukon
S   99781 – Terry Myrick, prin.

Wainwright, Northwestern Co., Pop. Code 2
North Slope Borough SD
Supt. – See Barrow
Alak S, P O BOX 10   99782 – Don Emberlin, prin.

Wales, Northwestern Co., Pop. Code 2
Bering Strait SD
Supt. – See Unalakleet
Wales-Kingikme S   99783 – Thomas Briscoe, prin.

asilla, Southcentral Co., Pop. Code 4
Matanuska-Susitna Borough SD
Supt. – See Palmer
JHS, P O BOX 871686   99687 – Stephen Chin, prin.

White Mountain, Northwestern Co., Pop. Code 2
Bering Strait SD
Supt. – See Unalakleet
S   99784 – George Ihly, prin.

Whittier, Anchorage Co., Pop. Code 2
Chugach SD
Sch. Sys. Enr. Code 1
Supt. – Robert Brown, P O BOX 638   99693
Whittier Community S, P O BOX 638   99693
Patrick Ireland, prin.
Other Schools – See Chenega Bay, Cordova, Tatitlek

Wrangell, Southeastern Co., Pop. Code 4
Wrangell CSD
Sch. Sys. Enr. Code 3
Supt. – Mary Francis, P O BOX 651   99929
ES, P O BOX 736   99929 – David Dirksen, prin.

Yakutat, Southeastern Co., Pop. Code 2
Yakutat CSD
Sch. Sys. Enr. Code 2
Supt. – Leland Clune, P O BOX 427   99689
ES, P O BOX 427   99689 – Jerry Schoenberger, prin.

W

ARIZONA

STATE DEPARTMENT OF EDUCATION
1535 W. Jefferson St., Phoenix 85007
(602) 542-5198

Superintendent of Public Instruction	C. Diane Bishop
Deputy Superintendent	Ray Borane
Deputy Superintendent, Vocational Education	Barbara Border
Associate Superintendent, Educational Services	Paul Koehler
Associate Superintendent, General Operations	Thomas Neel

STATE BOARD OF EDUCATION
Karin Kirksey Zander, *President*   1535 W. Jefferson St. #418, Phoenix   85007

ARIZONA BOARD OF REGENTS
Herman Chanen, *President*   3030 N. Central #1400, Phoenix   85012

COUNTY SUPERINTENDENTS OF SCHOOLS

Apache County, David Silva, Supt.
P O BOX 548, Saint Johns   85936
Cochise County, Tom Campbell, Supt.
P O BOX 208, Bisbee   85603
Coconino County, Mary Nackard, Supt.
COURTHOUSE, Flagstaff   86001
Gila County, Armida Bittner, Supt.
1400 ASH ST, Globe   85501
Graham County, Clay Larson, Supt.
800 MAIN STREET, Safford   85546

Greenlee County, Thomas Wright, Supt.
P O BOX 1595, Clifton   85533
Lapaz County, Bruce Kulp, Supt.
P O BOX 1147, Parker   85344
Maricopa County, Sandra Dowling, Supt.
111 S 3RD AVE # 401, Phoenix   85003
Mohave County, Betty Bell, Supt.
515 W BEALE ST, Kingman   86401
Navajo County, B. Bennett, Supt.
P O BOX 668, Holbrook   86025

Pima County, Anita Lohr, Supt.
131 W CONGRESS ST, Tucson   85701
Pinal County, Sherry Ferguson, Supt.
P O BOX 769, Florence   85232
Santa Cruz County, Gonazlo Galindo, Supt.
P O BOX 1150, Nogales   85628
Yavapai County, Paul Street, Supt.
255 E GURLEY, Prescott   86301
Yuma County, Raymond Drysdale, Supt.
210 S 1ST AVE, Yuma   85364

PUBLIC, PRIVATE, AND PAROCHIAL ELEMENTARY SCHOOLS

Aguila, Maricopa Co.
Aguila ESD 63
Sch. Sys. Enr. Code 1
Supt. – (—), P O BOX 218   85320
ES, P O BOX 218   85320 – Jamie Vest, prin.

Ajo, Pima Co., Pop. Code 6
Ajo USD 15
Sch. Sys. Enr. Code 3
Supt. – James Powell, P O BOX 68   85321
JHS, P O BOX 68   85321 – Gail McClelland, prin.
ES, P O BOX 68   85321 – Cindy Orr, prin.

Alpine, Apache Co.
Alpine ESD 7
Sch. Sys. Enr. Code 1
Supt. – (—), P O BOX 170   85920
ES, P O BOX 170   85920 – John Ligon, prin.

Amado, Santa Cruz Co.
Continental ESD 39
Sch. Sys. Enr. Code 2
Supt. – Jerry McEuen
TUSCON NOGALES HCR BOX 469C   85640
Continental ES, HCR BOX 469C   85645
(—), prin.

Apache Junction, Pinal Co., Pop. Code 6
Apache Junction USD 43
Sch. Sys. Enr. Code 5
Supt. – Wm. F. Wright, P O BOX 879   85220
JHS, P O BOX 879   85220 – Gary Nine, prin.
Four Peaks ES, P O BOX 879   85217
Gary Loutzenheiser, prin.
Gold Canyon ES, P O BOX 879   85217
Vincent Frillici, prin.
Superstition Mountain ES, P O BOX 879   85217
Frank Reed, prin.

Mesa USD 4
Supt. – See Mesa
Sousa ES, 616 NORTH MOUNTAIN RD   85220
Robert Stiffler, prin.

Arlington, Maricopa Co.
Arlington ESD 47
Sch. Sys. Enr. Code 2
Supt. – Ben Travis, HCR BOX 125   85322
ES, HCR 03 BOX 125   85322 – (—), prin.
Other Schools – See Buckeye

Ash Fork, Yavapai Co., Pop. Code 4
Ash Fork USD 31
Sch. Sys. Enr. Code 2
Supt. – Dennis DeGutes, P O BOX 247   86320
ES, P O BOX 247   86320 – Dennis Degutes, prin.

Avondale, Maricopa Co., Pop. Code 6
Avondale ESD 44
Sch. Sys. Enr. Code 5
Supt. – Dr. Douglas DelBarto
235 W WESTERN AVE   85323
JHS, CENTRAL AVE & LA PASADA   85323
Dr. Terry Rowles, prin.
PS, 237 W WESTERN AVE   85323
George Tewksbury, prin.
Coor MS, 220 W LA CANADA BLVD   85323
Dick Koontz, prin.
Other Schools – See Goodyear

Bagdad, Yavapai Co., Pop. Code 4
Bagdad USD 20
Sch. Sys. Enr. Code 3
Supt. – Sylvester Krell, P O BOX 427   86321
Lincoln ES, P O BOX 427   86321
Julie Hibbard, prin.

Hillside ESD 35
Sch. Sys. Enr. Code 1
Supt. – (—)
BAGDAD ROUTE HILLSIDE STA   86321
Hillside ES, BAGDAD ROUTE   86321
Janet Jones, prin.

Bapchule, Pinal Co.

Casa Blanca Day School, P O BOX 1112   85221

Benson, Cochise Co., Pop. Code 5
Benson ESD 9
Sch. Sys. Enr. Code 3
Supt. – Larry Stout, P O BOX 2030   85602
MS, P O BOX 2030   85602 – Roland Dendy, prin.
PS, P O BOX 2030   85602
Richard Valentine, prin.

Full Gospel Assembly School
P O BOX 2137   85602

Bisbee, Cochise Co., Pop. Code 6
Bisbee USD 2
Sch. Sys. Enr. Code 2
Supt. – Dr. Ed Czuppa, P O BOX G   85603
Lowell MS, P O BOX G   85603 – Carl Sjogren, prin.
Greenway ES, P O BOX G   85603
Kent Kelling, prin.

Black Canyon City, Yavapai Co., Pop. Code 3
Canon ESD 50
Sch. Sys. Enr. Code 2
Supt. – Gary Rathgeber, P O BOX 89   85324
Canon JHS, P O BOX 89   85324
Gary Rathgeber, prin.
Canon ES, P O BOX 89   85324
Gary Rathgeber, prin.

Blue, Greenlee Co.
Blue ESD 22
Sch. Sys. Enr. Code 1
Supt. – (—)   85922
ES   85922 – Sally Hulsey, prin.

Bouse, La Paz Co.
Bouse ESD 26
Sch. Sys. Enr. Code 1
Supt. – (—), P O BOX S   85325
ES, P O BOX S   85325 – Alan Crossland, prin.

Bowie, Cochise Co., Pop. Code 4
Bowie USD 14
Sch. Sys. Enr. Code 2
Supt. – Bruce Brown, P O BOX 157   85605
ES, P O BOX 157   85605 – (—), prin.

Buckeye, Maricopa Co., Pop. Code 5
Arlington ESD 47
Supt. – See Arlington
Harquahala Valley ES, HCR 02 BOX 364   85326
Charlls Wentz, prin.

Buckeye ESD 33
Sch. Sys. Enr. Code 4
Supt. – Thomas Godfrey, 210 S 6TH ST   85326
ES, 210 S 6TH ST   85326 – James Stephens, prin.

Liberty ESD 25
Sch. Sys. Enr. Code 3
Supt. – Gary Spiker
RURAL ROUTE 03 BOX 145   85326
Liberty ES, RURAL ROUTE 03 BOX 145   85326
Peter Turner, prin.

Bullhead City, Mohave Co.
Bullhead City ESD 15
Sch. Sys. Enr. Code 3
Supt. – Douglas Lutz, 1004 HANCOCK RD   86442
JHS, 1004 HANCOCK ROAD   86442
Ray Stevens, prin.
IS, 1004 E HACOCK ROAD   86442
Glen Scholl, prin.
Bullhead PS, 1004 HANCOCK ROAD   86442
Mary Ellen Adams, prin.

Camp Verde, Yavapai Co., Pop. Code 3
Camp Verde USD 28
Sch. Sys. Enr. Code 4
Supt. – Phillip England, P O BOX 728   86322
ES, P O BOX 728   86322 – Frank Tompkins, prin.

SDA Church School, P O BOX 2119   86322

Casa Grande, Pinal Co., Pop. Code 7
Casa Grande ESD 4
Sch. Sys. Enr. Code 5
Supt. – Dr. W. Dean Skaggs
1460 N PINAL AVE   85222
Casa Grande JHS
300 W MACMURRAY BLVD   85222
Jody Summerford, prin.
Cholla ES, 1180 E KORTSEN ROAD   85222
Jack Bliss, prin.
Cottonwood ES, 1667 N KADOTA AVE   85222
Linda Irvin, prin.
Evergreen ES, 1000 N AMARILLO   85222
Jon Sheldahl, prin.
Ironwood ES, 1500 N COLORADO   85222
Donald Dermody, prin.
Ocotillo ES, 501 N FLORENCE ST   85222
Marcus Cox, prin.
Palo Verde ES, 1000 E DOAN ST   85222
David Hernandez, prin.
Saguaro ES, 1501 N CENTER AVE   85222
Claire Davis, prin.

O'Brien ESD 90
Sch. Sys. Enr. Code 1
Supt. – Sherry Ferguson
RURAL ROUTE BOX 3125   85222
O'Brien ES, RURAL ROUTE BOX 3125   85222
Brenda Glatt, prin.

St. Anthony School, 501 E SECOND ST   85222

Cashion, Maricopa Co., Pop. Code 5
Littleton ESD 65
Sch. Sys. Enr. Code 4
Supt. – Quentin Aycock, P O BOX 280   85329
Underdown JHS, P O BOX 280   85329
Fred Fox, prin.
Littleton ES, P O BOX 280   85329
Harold Yost, prin.

Cave Creek, Maricopa Co., Pop. Code 4
Cave Creek USD 93
Sch. Sys. Enr. Code 4
Supt. – David Alexander, P O BOX 426   85331
Cactus Shadows MS, P O BOX 426   85331
William Wicevich, prin.
Black Mountain MS, P O BOX 426   85331
Lewis Smith, prin.
PS, P O BOX 426   85331 – Nancy Clarke, prin.

Chambers, Apache Co.

Wide Ruins Boarding School   86502

Chandler, Maricopa Co., Pop. Code 8
Chandler USD 80
Sch. Sys. Enr. Code 6
Supt. – Dr. James T. Perry
1525 W FRYE RD   85224
Andersen ES, 1351 N DOBSON ROAD   85224
Ronald Black, prin.
Erie ES, 1150 W ERIE ST   85224
Maria Worth, prin.
Frye ES, 801 E FRYE ROAD   85225
Raymond Polvani, prin.
Galveston ES, 661 E GALVESTON ST   85225
James Estes, prin.
Goodman ES, 2600 W KNOX RD   85224
Ronald Brown, prin.
Hartford ES, 700 N HARTFORD ST   85224
Pat Cuendet, prin.
Humphrey ES, 125 S 132ND ST   85225
Joanne Hock, prin.
Knox ES, 700 W ORCHID LN   85224
Mary Lou Carpenter, prin.
San Marcos ES, 451 W FRYE ROAD   85224
Dale Hancock, prin.
Shumway ES, 1325 N SHUMWAY AVE   85225
Joe Pena, prin.
Weinberg ES, 21221 S VALVISTA ROAD   85224
Janet Langer, prin.

Kyrene ESD 28
Supt. – See Tempe
Kyrene Del Cielo ES
1350 N LAKESHORE DR   85226 – Beth Hill, prin.
Kyrene Del Sureno ES
3375 W GALVESTON   85226 – Janis Richau, prin.

Mesa USD 4
Supt. – See Mesa
Frost ES, 1560 W SUMMIT PL   85224
Martin Calvert, prin.
Jordan ES, 3320 N CARRIAGE LN   85224
Jane Ann Hughes, prin.
Pomeroy ES, 1507 W SHAWNEE DR   85224
Louise McCance, prin.
Sirrine ES, 591 W MESQUITE ST   85224
Dr. Phelps Wilkins, prin.

Chandler Christian School
310 N HARTFORD ST   85224
Del Ray Christian Academy
830 W RAY ROAD   85224
Saint Marys Basha
200 W GALVESTON ST   85224

Chinle, Apache Co., Pop. Code 7
Chinle USD 24
Sch. Sys. Enr. Code 5
Supt. – Darryl Doss, P O BOX 587   86503
JHS, P O BOX 587   86503 – Patrick Macy, prin.
MS, P O BOX 587   86503 – Eddie Scott, prin.
PS, P O BOX 587   86503 – Mary Ann Hunter, prin.

Many Farms ES, P O BOX 587   86503
Joan Gilmore, prin.
Tsaile ES, P O BOX 587   86503 – Troy Stark, prin.

Cottonwood Day School, CHINLE AGENCY   86503
Low Mountain Boarding School   86503

Chino Valley, Yavapai Co., Pop. Code 5
Chino Valley USD 51
Sch. Sys. Enr. Code 3
Supt. – Ronald Minnich, P O BOX 225   86323
Del Rio ES, P O BOX 225   86323
Nancy Helm, prin.

Cibecue, Navajo Co.

Cibecue Day School   85911

Clarkdale, Yavapai Co., Pop. Code 4
Clarkdale-Jerome ESD 3
Sch. Sys. Enr. Code 2
Supt. – Dr. John Tavasci, P O BOX 248   86324
Clarkdale-Jerome ES, P O BOX 248   86324
(—), prin.

Clifton, Greenlee Co., Pop. Code 5
Clifton USD 3
Sch. Sys. Enr. Code 3
Supt. – Luis Montoya, P O BOX 1567   85533
Laugharn ES, P O BOX 1567   85533
Steve Hudgens, prin.

Eagle ESD 45
Sch. Sys. Enr. Code 1
Supt. – (—), P O BOX 1595   85533
Eagle ES, P O BOX 631   85533 – Reed Adler, prin.

Cochise, Cochise Co.
Cochise ESD 26
Sch. Sys. Enr. Code 1
Supt. – (—), P O BOX 1088   85606
ES, P O BOX 1088   85606 – Betty Pinnell, prin.

Colorado City, Mohave Co., Pop. Code 2
Colorado City USD 14
Sch. Sys. Enr. Code 3
Supt. – Alvin Barlow, P O BOX 268   86021
ES, P O BOX 268   86021 – Warren Johnson, prin.

Concho, Apache Co.
Concho ESD 6
Sch. Sys. Enr. Code 2
Supt. – Pam Bennett, P O BOX 198   85924
ES, P O BOX 198   85924 – (—), prin.

Coolidge, Pinal Co., Pop. Code 6
Coolidge USD 21
Sch. Sys. Enr. Code 5
Supt. – Dr. Robert Arends
520 W LINDBERGH   85228
Coolidge Central MS, P O BOX 1499   85228
Sam Heeringa, prin.
North ES, P O BOX 1499   85228
Sam Heeringa, prin.
West ES, P O BOX 1499   85228
Judith Bobbitt, prin.

Cornville, Yavapai Co.
Cottonwood-Oak Creek ESD 6
Supt. – See Cottonwood
Oak Creek ES, P O BOX 204   86325
David Osborn, prin.

Cottonwood, Yavapai Co., Pop. Code 5
Cottonwood-Oak Creek ESD 6
Sch. Sys. Enr. Code 5
Supt. – Linda Lawrence, P O BOX 57   86326
JHS, P O BOX 57   86326 – Sarah Hartley, prin.
Bright ES, P O BOX 57   86326
Jeanne Wright, prin.
ES, P O BOX 57   86326 – Baltazar Lozano, prin.
Other Schools – See Cornville, West Sedona

Montezuma Schs., P O BOX 428   86326

Crown King, Yavapai Co.
Crown King ESD 41
Sch. Sys. Enr. Code 1
Supt. – (—), P O BOX 172   86343
ES, P O BOX 172   86343 – Patricia Cruz, prin.

Dateland, Maricopa Co.
Hyder ESD 16
Sch. Sys. Enr. Code 2
Supt. – Jack Aldridge, P O BOX 1   85333
ES, P O BOX 1   85333 – (—), prin.

Sentinel ESD 71
Sch. Sys. Enr. Code 1
Supt. – (—), HCR BOX 57   85333
Sentinel ES, HCR BOX 57   85333
Gail Ridgely, prin.

Dennehotso, Apache Co.

Dennehotso Boarding School, P O BOX LL   86535

Dewey, Yavapai Co.
Humboldt USD 22
Sch. Sys. Enr. Code 4
Supt. – Laurence Dodd, P O BOX A   86327
Bradshaw Mountain JHS, P O BOX A   86327
Craig Angalich, prin.
Humboldt ES, P O BOX A   86327
Roger Williams, prin.
Lake Valley ES, P O BOX A   86327
Christopher Reynolds, prin.

Dolan Springs, Mohave Co.
Chloride ESD 11
Sch. Sys. Enr. Code 2
Supt. – (—), P O BOX 248 86441
Mt. Tipton ES, P O BOX 248 86441
Betty Bell, prin.

Douglas, Cochise Co., Pop. Code 7
Apache ESD 42
Sch. Sys. Enr. Code 1
Supt. – (—), P O BOX 1118 85608
Apache ES, P O BOX 1118 85608
Rose Levno, prin.

Douglas USD 27
Sch. Sys. Enr. Code 5
Supt. – Armando DeLucas, P O BOX 1237 85608
JHS, 842 12TH ST 85607 – Ray Crespin, prin.
Huber JHS, 15TH ST & WASHINGTON 85607
Mike Foster, prin.
A Avenue ES, 15TH ST & A AVE 85607
Guadalupe Mejia, prin.
Carlson ES, 1132 12TH ST 85607
John Clark, prin.
Clawson ES, 7TH & BONITA AVE 85607
Gloria Keith, prin.
Fifteenth Street ES, 15TH ST & D AVE 85607
Guadalupe Mejia, prin.
Marley ES, 7TH & D AVE 85607
Camille La Forge, prin.
Stevenson ES, 2200 11TH ST 85607
Jay St. John, prin.
Other Schools – See Pirtleville

Lorreto Catholic School, 1200 14TH ST 85607

Duncan, Greenlee Co., Pop. Code 3
Duncan USD 2
Sch. Sys. Enr. Code 3
Supt. – Erwin Crotts, P O BOX Q 85534
ES, P O BOX Q 85534 – Curtis Brown, prin.

Ehrenberg, La Paz Co.
Quartzside ESD 4
Sch. Sys. Enr. Code 2
Supt. – James Lamb, P O BOX 130 85334
ES, P O BOX 130 85334 – (—), prin.

Elfrida, Cochise Co., Pop. Code 4
Elfrida ESD 12
Sch. Sys. Enr. Code 2
Supt. – (—), P O BOX 328 85610
ES, P O BOX 328 85610 – Betty Nitka, prin.

Elgin, Santa Cruz Co.
Sonoita ESD 25
Sch. Sys. Enr. Code 1
Supt. – Barry Levitt, P O BOX 36 85611
ES, P O BOX 36 85611 – Barry Levitt, prin.

Eloy, Pinal Co., Pop. Code 6
Eloy ESD 11
Sch. Sys. Enr. Code 4
Supt. – Lawrence Dunton, P O BOX 728 85231
JHS, PHOENIX & SANTA CRUZ STS 85231
James Russum, prin.
Curiel ES, 11TH ST & CURIEL 85231
Dorothy Erdman, prin.
IS, 1005 N SANTA CRUZ AVE 85231
Gene Stouffer, prin.

Toltec ESD 22
Sch. Sys. Enr. Code 2
Supt. – Rex Deputy
RURAL ROUTE 01 BOX 390 85231
Toltec ES, RURAL ROUTE 01 BOX 390 85231
(—), prin.

Flagstaff, Coconino Co., Pop. Code 8
Flagstaff USD 1
Sch. Sys. Enr. Code 7
Supt. – Bill Williams, 701 N KENDRICK ST 86001
Christensen ES, 4000 N CUMMINGS DR 86001
Pat Horn, prin.
Cromer ES, KOCH FIELD ROAD 86004
Larry Peterson, prin.
Killip ES, 2300 E 6TH ST 86001
Kathleen Karol, prin.
Kinsey ES, 607 E KINSEY ST 86001
Carl Coffelt, prin.
Knoles ES, 4005 E BUTLER 86001
David McKay, prin.
Marshall ES, 850 N BONITO ST 86001
R. Mares, prin.
Sechrist ES, 2230 N FT VALLEY ROAD 86001
Robert Boothe, prin.
South Beaver ES, 506 N BEAVER ST 86001
Paul Hubbard, prin.
Thomas ES, 3300 LOCKETT ROAD 86004
Hazel Robinson, prin.
Weitzel ES, 3401 N 4TH ST 86004
Mike Flick, prin.
Other Schools – See Sedona, Winslow

Montessori Discovery School
2212 E CEDAR AVE 86004
Mountain Elementary School
510 N LEROUX ST 86001
Saint Marys School
320 N HUMPHREYS ST 86001

Florence, Pinal Co., Pop. Code 5
Florence USD 1
Sch. Sys. Enr. Code 4
Supt. – Paul Hanley, P O BOX 829 85232
MS, P O BOX 829 85232
Clarence L. Martin, prin.

ES, P O BOX 829 85232 – Shirley Stouffer, prin.

Fort Defiance, Apache Co., Pop. Code 7
Window Rock USD 8
Sch. Sys. Enr. Code 5
Supt. – Guy Archambeau, P O BOX 559 86504
Tso Ho Tso MS, P O BOX 559 86504
D'Wayne Farr, prin.
ES, P O BOX 559 86504 – Marie Arviso, prin.
Window Rock ES, P O BOX 559 86504
Marion Maxwell, prin.

Fort Huachuca, Cochise Co., Pop. Code 6
Ft. Huachuca Accommodation SD 00
Sch. Sys. Enr. Code 4
Supt. – Dr. Paul Bohardt, P O BOX Q 85613
Smith MS, P O BOX Q 85613
Ben Rutherford, prin.
Myer MS, P O BOX Q 85613
Ronald Swackhamer, prin.
Johnston ES, P O BOX Q 85613
Gary Slocum, prin.

Fort Thomas, Graham Co., Pop. Code 2
Ft. Thomas USD 7
Sch. Sys. Enr. Code 2
Supt. – Jerry Hancock, P O BOX 28 85536
ES, P O BOX 28 85536 – Billie Kay Hinton, prin.

Fountain Hills, Maricopa Co.
Fountain Hills USD 98
Sch. Sys. Enr. Code 3
Supt. – Dr. Lenora Jarrett, P O BOX 18049 85268
Four Peaks MS, P O BOX 18049 85268
Joanne Meehan, prin.
McDowell Mountain ES, P O BOX 18049 85268
David Finley, prin.

Horse Mesa Accommodation Dist 509
Supt. – See Williams AFB
Ft. McDowell Accommodation PS
P O BOX 17779 85268 – Diane Ludeman, prin.

Fredonia, Coconino Co., Pop. Code 4
Fredonia-Moccasin USD 6
Sch. Sys. Enr. Code 3
Supt. – Charles Eberhard, P O BOX 247 86022
Fredonia-Moccasin ES, P O BOX 247 86022
Vaughn Williams, prin.
Moccasin PS 86022 – Vaughn Williams, prin.

Gadsden, Yuma Co.
Gadsden ESD 32
Sch. Sys. Enr. Code 4
Supt. – James Wombacher, P O BOX 128 85336
MS, P O BOX 128 85336 – Charles Juenger, prin.
Rio Colorado ES, P O BOX 128 85336
Alicia Valdez, prin.

Ganado, Apache Co., Pop. Code 3
Ganado USD 20
Sch. Sys. Enr. Code 5
Supt. – Albert Yazzie 86505
MS 86505 – Phillip Bluehouse, prin.
PS 86505 – Sigmund Boloz, prin.
IS 86505 – William Soder, prin.

Kinilichee Boarding School 86505
Nazlini Boarding School 86505

Gila Bend, Maricopa Co., Pop. Code 4
Gila Bend USD 24
Sch. Sys. Enr. Code 3
Supt. – Dr. Buel Bowlan, P O BOX V 85337
ES, P O BOX V 85337 – Susan Steinour, prin.

Paloma ESD 94
Sch. Sys. Enr. Code 2
Supt. – Ronald Fletcher, HCR BOX 172 85337
Paloma ES, HCR BOX 172 85337 – (—), prin.

Gilbert, Maricopa Co., Pop. Code 6
Gilbert USD 41
Sch. Sys. Enr. Code 6
Supt. – Dr. Walter Delecki, P O BOX 1 85234
JHS, 1016 N BURK ST 85234
Charles Santa Cruz, prin.
Mesquite JHS, 130 W MESQUITE ST 85234
Jill Wagner, prin.
Burk ES, 1000 E MESQUITE 85234
Nancy Cooledge, prin.
ES, 175 W ELLIOT RD 85234 – John Quinby, prin.
Greenfield ES, 10629 S GREENFIELD ROAD 85234
Robert Rimer, prin.
Houston ES, 1000 E MESQUITE 85234
Sherryl Heard, prin.
Islands ES, 245 S MCQUEEN 85234
Dr. Susan Harrison, prin.
Neely ES, 321 W JUNIPER AVE 85234
Barbara Osland, prin.
Patterson ES, 1211 W GUADALUPE RD 85234
Dr. Steven Nance, prin.
Pioneer ES, 7815 S GREENFIELD ROAD 85234
William Salisbury, prin.

Glendale, Maricopa Co., Pop. Code 8
Alhambra ESD 68
Supt. – See Phoenix
Barcelona ES, 4432 W MARYLAND AVE 85301
Donna Dobbin, prin.

Deer Valley USD 97
Supt. – See Phoenix
Desert Sky JHS, 5130 W GROVERS 85308
Janet Altersitz, prin.
Bellair ES, 4701 W GROVERS AVE 85308
Diane Hamilton, prin.

Greenbrier ES, 6150 W GREENBRIER DR 85308
Kit Wood, prin.
Mirage ES, 3910 W GROVERS AVE 85308
Larry Bauer, prin.
Mountain Shadows ES, 19602 N 45TH AVE 85308
Nick Portonova, prin.
Park Meadows ES, 20012 N 35TH AVE 85308
Kent Davis, prin.

Glendale ESD 40
Sch. Sys. Enr. Code 6
Supt. – Dr. Ron Crates
5734 W GLENDALE AVE 85301
Challenger MS, 6905 W MARYLAND AVE 85303
Tom Heck, prin.
Glendale Landmark MS
5730 W MYRTLE AVE 85301 – Judy Smith, prin.
Bicentennial ES-South, 5260 N 72ND AVE 85303
Robert Dooley, prin.
Bicentennial MS-North
7237 W MISSOURI AVE 85303
Robert Dooley, prin.
Burton ES, 4801 W MARYLAND AVE 85301
Merrill Harlan, prin.
Glendale American ES, 8530 N 55TH AVE 85302
Dick Thomas, prin.
Horizon ES, 8520 N 47TH AVE 85302
Al Sulka, prin.
Imes ES, 6625 N 56TH AVE 85301
Roger Jackson, prin.
Mensendick/Jack ES-South
6600 W MISSOURI AVE 85301
Thomas Freehill, prin.
Mensendick/Jack MS-North
5535 N 67TH AVE 85301 – Tom Freehill, prin.
Sine ES, 4932 W MYRTLE AVE 85301
Colleen Longstrom, prin.
Smith ES, 6534 N 63RD AVE 85301
Joe Casillas, prin.

Peoria USD 11
Supt. – See Peoria
Copperwood ES, 11232 N 65TH AVE 85304
Robert Holzmiller, prin.
Desert Palms ES, 11441 N 55TH AVE 85304
Denton Santarelli, prin.
Desert Valley ES, 12901 N 63RD AVE 85306
Janel Becker, prin.
Foothills ES, 15808 N 63RD AVE 85306
Laura White, prin.
Heritage ES, 5312 W MOUNTAIN VIEW RD 85302
Dr. Vincent Howard, prin.
Kachina ES, 5304 W CROCUS DR 85306
Karen Kundin, prin.
Pioneer ES, 6315 W PORT AU PRINCE LN 85306
Steve Highlen, prin.
Sahuaro Ranch ES, 10401 N 63RD AVE 85302
Al Sinclair, prin.

Washington ESD 6
Supt. – See Phoenix
Arroyo ES, 4535 W CHOLLA ST 85304
Steve Salomone, prin.
Sunburst ES, 14218 N 47TH AVE 85306
Connie Gibbons, prin.
Sunset ES
4626 W MOUNTAIN VIEW ROAD 85302
Terry Clark, prin.
Sweetwater ES
4602 W SWEETWATER AVE 85304
Betty Hart, prin.

New World Educational Ctr.
511 W MARYLAND AVE 85301
Northwest Christian Academy
14240 N 43RD AVE 85306
Grace Lutheran School, 7161 N 56TH AVE 85301
Our Lady Of Perpetual Help School
7521 N 57TH AVE 85301
Saint Louis The King School
4331 W MARYLAND AVE 85301
West Side Private School
7614 N 43RD AVE 85301

Globe, Gila Co., Pop. Code 6
Globe USD 1
Sch. Sys. Enr. Code 5
Supt. – Orval Nutting, 501 ASH ST 85501
MS, 501 ASH ST 85501 – Michael Minton, prin.
Copper Rim ES, 501 ASH ST 85501
Forrest McKelvy, prin.
East Globe MS, 501 ASH ST 85501
Carol Warren, prin.

Holy Angels School, 1300 E CEDAR ST 85501
Holy Angels School, 1300 E CEDAR ST 85501

Goodyear, Maricopa Co.
Avondale ESD 44
Supt. – See Avondale
Pioneer ES, 540 E LA PASADA BLVD 85338
Larry Evearitt, prin.

Grand Canyon, Coconino Co., Pop. Code 4
Grand Canyon USD 4
Sch. Sys. Enr. Code 2
Supt. – John L. Vest, P O BOX 519 86023
ES, P O BOX 519 86023 – John Vest, prin.

Guadalupe, Maricopa Co., Pop. Code 5
Tempe ESD 3
Supt. – See Tempe
Frank ES, 8409 S 56TH ST 85284
Mary Lou Torres, prin.

Hackberry, Mohave Co.
Hackberry ESD 3
Sch. Sys. Enr. Code 1
Supt. – (—), P O BOX 22 86411
ES, P O BOX 22 86411 – Maria O'Dell, prin.

Heber, Navajo Co.
Heber-Overgaard USD 6
Sch. Sys. Enr. Code 2
Supt. – Larry Brewer, P O BOX 547 85928
Capps ES, P O BOX 847 85928
Franklin Greer, prin.

Hereford, Cochise Co.
Palominas ESD 49
Sch. Sys. Enr. Code 3
Supt. – Gene Brust, P O BOX 38 85615
Palominas ES, P O BOX 38 85615
Shirley Loiselle, prin.

Higley, Maricopa Co.
Higley ESD 60
Sch. Sys. Enr. Code 2
Supt. – Larry Likes, P O BOX 59 85236
ES, P O BOX 59 85236 – (—), prin.

Holbrook, Navajo Co., Pop. Code 6
Holbrook USD 3
Sch. Sys. Enr. Code 4
Supt. – Frank Turley, P O BOX 640 86025
JHS, P O BOX 640 86025 – Van Palmer, prin.
Hulet ES, P O BOX 640 86025 – Jim Cassidy, prin.
Park ES, P O BOX 640 86025 – Midge Cole, prin.

Holbrook SDA Indian School, P O BOX 880 86025
New Covenant Christian School
307 N 1ST AVE 86025

Hotevilla, Navajo Co.

Hotevilla-Becavi Community School
P O BOX 48 86030

Houck, Apache Co.

Pine Springs Boarding School, P O BOX 198 86506

Huachuca City, Cochise Co., Pop. Code 4
Tombstone USD 1
Supt. – See Tombstone
ES, P O BOX 4468 85616 – David Hrach, prin.

Joseph City, Navajo Co., Pop. Code 2
Joseph City USD 2
Sch. Sys. Enr. Code 2
Supt. – Dr. David McLaren, P O BOX 8 86032
ES, P O BOX 8 86032 – Duane Jones, prin.

Kaibito, Coconino Co.

Kaibito Boarding School 86053

Kayenta, Navajo Co., Pop. Code 3
Kayenta USD 27
Sch. Sys. Enr. Code 4
Supt. – Dr. Joseph Martin, P O BOX 337 86033
MS, P O BOX 337 86033 – Carolyn Stewart, prin.
IS, P O BOX 337 86033 – Eugene Charley, prin.
PS, P O BOX 337 86033 – Richard Russell, prin.

Chilchinbato Day School, P O BOX 547 86033
Kayenta Boarding School, P O BOX 188 86033

Keams Canyon, Navajo Co.
Cedar USD 25
Sch. Sys. Enr. Code 3
Supt. – Loren Joseph, P O BOX 367 86034
Jeddito ES, P O BOX 367 86034
Adelbert Goldtooth, prin.

Keams Canyon Boarding School
P O BOX 397 86034

Kearny, Pinal Co., Pop. Code 5
Ray USD 3
Sch. Sys. Enr. Code 4
Supt. – R. W. Chastain, P O BOX 427 85237
Ray MS, P O BOX 427 85237 – Fred Howe, prin.
Ray PS, P O BOX 427 85237
M. Wayne Cude, prin.

Kingman, Mohave Co., Pop. Code 6
Kingman ESD 4
Sch. Sys. Enr. Code 5
Supt. – Patrick Carlin
3033 MCDONALD AVE 86401
JHS, 1969 DETROIT AVE 86401
Lester Byram, prin.
Hualapai ES, 350 EASTERN ST 86401
Betty Rowe, prin.
La Senita ES, 3175 GORDON DR 86401
Patcy Byfield, prin.
Manzanita ES, 2901 DETROIT AVE 86401
Homer Johnston, prin.
Palo Christi ES, 500 MAPLE ST 86401
Frances Blalock, prin.

Manzanita Christian School, 2040 GOLDEN 86401

Kirkland, Yavapai Co.
Kirkland ESD 23
Sch. Sys. Enr. Code 1
Supt. – (—), P O BOX 50 86332
ES, P O BOX 50 86332 – Allison Smith, prin.

Kykotsmovi Village, Coconino Co.

Hopi Day School, P O BOX 42 86039

Hopi Mission School, P O BOX 39 86039
Navajo Bible Academy, P O BOX 41 86039
Rocky Ridge Boarding School, P O BOX 299 86039

Lake Havasu City, Mohave Co., Pop. Code 7
Lake Havasu USD 1
Sch. Sys. Enr. Code 5
Supt. – Ray Lange, 750 HAVASUPAI BLVD 86403
JHS, 98 SWANSON AVE 86403
Melvin Scarbrough, prin.
Havasupai ES, 880 CASHMERE DR 86403
Lana Banker, prin.
Nautilus ES, 1425 PATRICIAN DR 86403
James Conley, prin.
Oro Grande ES, 1250 PAWNEE DR 86403
Jack Crews, prin.
Smoketree ES, 2395 N SMOKETREE AVE 86403
Burton Binenfeld, prin.
Starline ES, 215 STARLINE DR 86403
Ronald Liesen, prin.

Lakeside, Navajo Co., Pop. Code 3
Blue Ridge USD 32
Sch. Sys. Enr. Code 4
Supt. – Gordon Meredith, P O BOX 885 85929
Blue Ridge JHS, P O BOX 885 85929
Ted Dost, prin.
Blue Ridge ES, P O BOX 885 85929
Paul Pullin, prin.
Blue Ridge MS, P O BOX 885 85929
Diana Butler, prin.

Laveen, Maricopa Co.
Laveen ESD 59
Sch. Sys. Enr. Code 4
Supt. – Fred Miller, P O BOX 29 85339
ES, P O BOX 29 85339 – Gene Giesaking, prin.
Other Schools – See Phoenix

Saint Johns Indian ES
RURAL ROUTE 01 BOX 752 85339

Litchfield Park, Maricopa Co.
Litchfield ESD 79
Sch. Sys. Enr. Code 4
Supt. – Bill Matthews
553 E PLAZA CIRCLE #A 85340
Libby ES, 553 E PLAZA CIR # A 85340
Gary Ewert, prin.
ES, 553 E PLAZA CIR # A 85340
Steven Terry, prin.

Littlefield, Mohave Co.
Littlefield ESD 9
Sch. Sys. Enr. Code 1
Supt. – (—) 86432
ES 86432 – Jack Sullivan, prin.

Lukachukai, Apache Co.

Lukachukai Boarding School 86507

Marana, Pima Co., Pop. Code 4
Marana USD 6
Sch. Sys. Enr. Code 6
Supt. – Dr. Scott Foster
11279 W GRIER ROAD 85238
JHS, 11279 W GRIER ROAD 85238
Bruce G. Dewey, prin.
Estes ES, 11279 W GRIER ROAD 85653
Julia Thayer, prin.
Ironwood ES, 3300 W FREER DR 85741
Jane Ballesteros, prin.
Roadrunner ES
16651 W CALLE CARMELA 85653
Michael Dayton, prin.
Other Schools – See Tucson

Maricopa, Pinal Co., Pop. Code 5
Maricopa USD 20
Sch. Sys. Enr. Code 3
Supt. – Gail Pew, P O BOX 310 85239
ES, P O BOX 310 85239 – Diana Likes, prin.

Mobile ESD 86
Sch. Sys. Enr. Code 1
Supt. – (—), P O BOX 209 85239
Mobile ES, P O BOX 209 85239
Jerry Begalman, prin.

Mayer, Yavapai Co., Pop. Code 3
Mayer USD 43
Sch. Sys. Enr. Code 2
Supt. – James Rhoades, P O BOX 189 86333
ES, P O BOX 189 86333 – Terry Head, prin.

Mc Nary, Apache Co.
Mc Nary ESD 23
Sch. Sys. Enr. Code 1
Supt. – (—), P O BOX 598 85930
ES, P O BOX 598 85930 – Joel Tudor, prin.

Mc Neal, Cochise Co.
Double Adobe ESD 45
Sch. Sys. Enr. Code 1
Supt. – (—)
RURAL ROUTE 01 BOX 72 85617
Double Adobe ES
RURAL ROUTE 01 BOX 72 85617
Pamela Sanders, prin.

Mc Neal ESD 55
Sch. Sys. Enr. Code 1
Supt. – (—)
ES, P O BOX 397 85617
Carole Breckenridge, prin.

Mesa, Maricopa Co., Pop. Code 9
Mesa USD 4
Sch. Sys. Enr. Code 8
Supt. – Dr. James Zaharis
549 N STAPLEY DRIVE 85203
Rhodes JHS, 1860 S LONGMORE ST 85202
Linda Rottman, prin.
Adams ES, 738 S LONGMORE ST 85202
Dorothy Levy, prin.
Alma ES, 1313 W MEDINA AVE 85202
David Mullins, prin.
Crismon ES, 825 W MEDINA AVE 85202
Beverly Cooper, prin.
Edison ES, 545 N HOME 85203
Joann Pearman, prin.
Eisenhower ES, 858 N MESA DR 85201
Richard Finlinson, prin.
Emerson ES, 940 W UNIVERSITY DR 85201
Trudy Kinkade, prin.
Field ES, 2325 E ADOBE ROAD 85203
Dr. Donald Blair, prin.
Franklin ES, 236 S SIRRINE ST 85202
Marc Mason, prin.
Hale ES, 1425 N 23RD ST 85203
Julia Kelly, prin.
Hawthorne ES, 630 N HUNT DRIVE 85203
Gerald Kempf, prin.
Highland ES, 3042 E ADOBE ROAD 85203
Lloyd Gregory, prin.
Holmes ES, 948 S HORNE ST 85204
Harold Fuller, prin.
Irving ES, 3220 E PUEBLO AVE 85204
Betty Bendure, prin.
Ishikawa ES, 2635 N 32ND ST 85203
Pauline Shelby, prin.
Jefferson ES, 120 S JEFFERSON ST 85208
Rhonda Moffit, prin.
Johnson ES, 3807 E PUEBLO AVE 85206
Dan Young, prin.
Keller ES, 1445 E HILTON AVE 85204
Frank Wilson, prin.
Lehi ES, 2555 N STAPLEY DR 85203
Ronald Skon, prin.
Lincoln ES, 930 S SIRRINE ST 85202
Charlotte Culley, prin.
Lindbergh ES, 930 S LAZONA DR 85204
Don Streets, prin.
Longfellow ES, 345 S HALL ST 85204
Donald Erickson, prin.
Lowell ES, 920 E BROADWAY RD 85204
Ron Schreer, prin.
MacArthur ES, 1435 E MCLELLAN ROAD 85203
Judy Niederkruger, prin.
Madison ES, 849 S SUNNYVALE 85206
Henry Hasebe, prin.
Mendoza ES, 5831 E MCLELLAN 85205
Bob Meko, prin.
O'Connor ES, 4840 E ADOBE RD 85205
Susan Hubbard, prin.
Redbird ES, 1020 S EXTENSION ROAD 85202
Mark Bankhead, prin.
Robson ES, 2122 E PUEBLO AVE 85204
Dr. Jerry Edwards, prin.
Roosevelt ES, 828 S VALENCIA ST 85202
Hector Benitez, prin.
Salk ES, 7029 E BROWN ROAD 85207
Carol Taylor, prin.
Stevenson ES, 638 S 96TH ST 85208
Reid Wilcox, prin.
Taft ES, 9800 E QUARTERLINE ROAD 85207
Robert Stiffler, prin.
Washington ES, 2260 W ISABELLA AVE 85202
Sharon Hamilton, prin.
Webster ES, 202 N SYCAMORE ST 85201
Robert Fleischmann, prin.
Whitman ES, 1829 N GRAND ST 85201
Blair Ressler, prin.
Whittier ES, 733 N LONGMORE ST 85201
Ken Piotro, prin.
Other Schools – See Apache Junction, Chandler

East Mesa Christian Academy
752 S ELLSWORTH ROAD 85208
Casa De Montessori School
745 S EXTENSION RD 85202
Central Christian School, 933 N LINDSAY 85203
Christ The King School, 1545 E DANA AVE 85204
Good Shepherd Academy, 950 W 8TH AVE 85202
John Hancock Academy Inc.
1456 E BROADWAY RD 85204
Montessori Tempe School
410 S EL DORADO ROAD 85202
Queen Of Peace School
109 N MACDONALD ST 85201
Redeemer Christian School
719 N STAPLEY DRIVE 85203
Trinity Christian School
2402 N USERY PASS ROAD 85207
Trivium Christian School, 1556 N MESA DRIVE 85201

Miami, Gila Co., Pop. Code 5
Miami USD 40
Sch. Sys. Enr. Code 4
Supt. – Lawrence Lemons, P O BOX H 85539
Kornegay JHS, P O BOX H 85539
Jane Emde, prin.
Bullion Plaza MS, P O BOX H 85539
Gillen Emde, prin.
Central Heights PS, P O BOX H 85539
James Sterr, prin.
Inspiration Addition PS, P O BOX H 85539
Gillen Emde, prin.
Las Lomas PS, P O BOX H 85539
James Sterr, prin.

Mohave Valley, Mohave Co.
Mohave Valley ESD 16
Sch. Sys. Enr. Code 5
Supt. – Emmett Brown, P O BOX 5070 86440
JHS, P O BOX 5070 86440 – Craig Vallon, prin.
Fort Mojave ES, P O BOX 5070 86440
  Lee Robinson, prin.
ES, P O BOX 5070 86440 – Emmett Brown, prin.

Christian Academy, P O BOX 6076 86440

Morenci, Greenlee Co., Pop. Code 3
Morenci USD 18
Sch. Sys. Enr. Code 4
Supt. – Tony Boling, P O BOX 1060 85540
Fairbanks ES, P O BOX 1060 85540
  Robert Epperson, prin.

Morristown, Yavapai Co.
Morristown ESD 75
Sch. Sys. Enr. Code 1
Supt. – (—), P O BOX 98 85342
ES, P O BOX 98 85342 – Lucille Thompson, prin.

Naco, Cochise Co.
Naco ESD 23
Sch. Sys. Enr. Code 2
Supt. – Kenneth McElyea, P O BOX 397 85620
ES, P O BOX 397 85620 – (—), prin.

Nogales, Santa Cruz Co., Pop. Code 7
Nogales USD 1
Sch. Sys. Enr. Code 6
Supt. – James Clark, 222 PLUM ST 85621
Carpenter MS, 704 KINO BLVD 85621
  Jerry Barnett, prin.
Pierson MS, ARROYO BLVD 85621
  Ramon Paz, prin.
Challenger ES, 2685 CALLE MAYER 85621
  Tom Ralls, prin.
Lincoln ES, PERKINS ST 85621
  Rina Gotsis, prin.
Mitchell ES, MARTINEZ ST 85621
  Elinora Baffert, prin.
Welty ES, CALLE CANADA 85621
  Annette Barber, prin.

Santa Cruz ESD 28
Sch. Sys. Enr. Code 2
Supt. – Lel Newlon, P O BOX 105 85628
Santa Cruz ES, PATAGONIA HCR bOX 105 85621
  (—), prin.

Nogales SDA School
  4514 E FRONTAGE ROAD 85621
Sacred Heart School, 333 ARROYO BLVD 85621

Oracle, Pinal Co., Pop. Code 4
Oracle ESD 2
Sch. Sys. Enr. Code 3
Supt. – Jack Harmon, P O BOX 588 85623
Mountain Vista MS, P O BOX 588 85623
  Kathleen Parkhurst, prin.
Oracle Ridge PS, P O BOX 588 85623
  Loretta Wood, prin.

Page, Coconino Co., Pop. Code 5
Page USD 8
Sch. Sys. Enr. Code 5
Supt. – Patrick Schrader, P O BOX 1927 86040
MS, P O BOX 1927 86040 – Marvin Lamer, prin.
Desert Veiw ES, P O BOX 1927 86040
  Jack Wade, prin.
Lake View ES, P O BOX 1927 86040
  Gerald Stone, prin.

Palo Verde, Maricopa Co.
Palo Verde ESD 49
Sch. Sys. Enr. Code 2
Supt. – Larry Baker, P O BOX 108 85343
ES, P O BOX 108 85343 – (—), prin.

Paradise Valley, Maricopa Co., Pop. Code 7

Camelback Desert School
  6050 N INVERGORDON ROAD 85253

Parker, LaPaz Co., Pop. Code 5
Parker USD 27
Sch. Sys. Enr. Code 4
Supt. – H. F. Dick, P O BOX 1089 85344
Wallace MS, P O BOX 1089 85344
  Robert Sells, prin.
Blake ES, P O BOX 1089 85344
  Rudy Gonzales, prin.
Lepera ES, RURAL ROUTE 01 BOX 169 85344
  James Lotts, prin.

Parks, Coconino Co.
Maine Cons. ESD 10
Sch. Sys. Enr. Code 1
Supt. – Lyman Jackson, P O BOX 7 86018
Maine Cons. ES, P O BOX 7 86018 – (—), prin.

Patagonia, Santa Cruz Co., Pop. Code 3
Patagonia ESD 6
Sch. Sys. Enr. Code 2
Supt. – (—), P O BOX 295 85624
ES, P O BOX 295 85624 – Jac Heiss, prin.

Payson, Gila Co., Pop. Code 6
Payson USD 10
Sch. Sys. Enr. Code 5
Supt. – Laverne Baker, P O BOX 919 85547
JHS, P O BOX 919 85547 – Bill Lawson, prin.
ES, P O BOX 919 85547 – Johnny Ketchem, prin.

Randall ES, P O BOX 919 85547
  Johnny Ketchem, prin.

Peach Springs, Coconino Co.
Peach Springs ESD 8
Sch. Sys. Enr. Code 2
Supt. – Michael Reed, P O BOX 138 86434
ES, P O BOX 138 86434 – (—), prin.

Valentine ESD 22
Sch. Sys. Enr. Code 1
Supt. – (—), HCR BOX 50 86434
Valentine ES, HCR BOX 50 86435
  Ronnie McPherson, prin.

Pearce, Cochise Co.
Ash Creek ESD 53
Sch. Sys. Enr. Code 1
Supt. – (—), HCR BOX 260 85625
Ash Creek ES, HCR BOX 260 85625
  (—), prin.

Pearce ESD 22
Sch. Sys. Enr. Code 2
Supt. – Ronald Smith, P O BOX 127 85625
ES, P O BOX 127 85625 – (—), prin.

Peoria, Maricopa Co., Pop. Code 7
Dysart USD 89
Sch. Sys. Enr. Code 5
Supt. – Dr. William L. Jones
  RURAL ROUTE 01 BOX 703 85345
JHS, RURAL ROUTE 01 BOX 703 85345
  Saundra Harmon, prin.
El Mirage ES, RURAL ROUTE 01 BOX 703 85345
  Vic Mondino, prin.
Luke ES, RURAL ROUTE 01 BOX 703 85345
  Marsha Baney, prin.
Surprise ES, RURAL ROUTE 01 BOX 703 85345
  Fernando De La Ossa, prin.

Peoria USD 11
Sch. Sys. Enr. Code 7
Supt. – Dr. Raymond S. Kellis, P O BOX 39 85345
Alta Loma ES, 9750 N 87TH AVE 85345
  Terri Mainwaring, prin.
Cotton Boll ES, 8540 W BUTLER 85345
  Robert Heinle, prin.
Murphy ES, 7231 W NORTH LN 85345
  Robert Johnson, prin.
Oakwood ES, 12900 N 71ST AVE 85345
  Russell Snider, prin.
Oasis ES, 7841 W SWEETWATER 85345
  Charlene Joehnk, prin.
ES, 11501 N 79TH DR 85345 – Jane Coady, prin.
Sundance ES, 7051 W CHOLLA ST 85345
  Steve Gillett, prin.
Sun Valley ES, 8361 N 95TH AVE 85345
  Sally Jamsa, prin.
Other Schools – See Glendale

Southwest Indian School
  14202 N 73RD AVE 85345

Phoenix, Maricopa Co., Pop. Code 11
Alhambra ESD 68
Sch. Sys. Enr. Code 6
Supt. – Carol Grosse
  3001 W HAZELWOOD ST 85017
Alhambra Traditional ES
  3736 W OSBORN ROAD 85031 – Jess Bass, prin.
Andalucia ES, 4702 W CAMPBELL AVE 85031
  Jacqueline Doerr, prin.
Catalina ES, 3845 W MARYLAND AVE 85019
  Shirley Howell, prin.
Cordova ES, 3455 W MONTEBELLO AVE 85017
  Dr. Robert Troidl, prin.
Granada ES, 3106 W CAMPBELL AVE 85017
  Frank Terbush, prin.
Sevilla ES, 3801 W MISSOURI AVE 85019
  Larry Wingate, prin.
Simpson MS, 2301 W MISSOURI AVE 85015
  Frank Tunnell, prin.
Westwood PS, 2225 W PIERSON ST 85015
  Martha Braly, prin.
Other Schools – See Glendale

Balsz ESD 31
Sch. Sys. Enr. Code 4
Supt. – Raymond Miller
  4309 E BELLEVIEW ST 85008
Balsz ES, 4309 E BELLEVIEW ST 85008
  Pat Murphy, prin.
Crockett ES, 501 N 36TH ST 85008
  Raul Disarufino, prin.
Griffith ES, 4505 E PALM LN 85008
  Sandra Cox, prin.
Orangedale ES, 5048 E OAK ST 85008
  Ben McGrady, prin.

Cartwright ESD 83
Sch. Sys. Enr. Code 7
Supt. – Dr. William R. Dabb
  3401 N 67TH AVE 85033
Borman JHS, 3637 N 55TH AVE 85031
  Jack Kensler, prin.
Desert Sands JHS, 6308 W CAMPBELL AVE 85033
  Jeffery Graham, prin.
Estrella JHS, 3733 N 75TH AVE 85033
  John Woollums, prin.
Barry ES, 2533 N 60TH AVE 85035
  Fred Thompson, prin.
Cartwright ES, 5833 W THOMAS ROAD 85031
  Rubi Magdalena, prin.
Downs ES, 3611 N 47TH AVE 85031
  George Hoefflin, prin.

Harris ES, 2252 N 55TH AVE 85035
  John Ryan, prin.
Heatherbrae ES
  7070 W HEATHERBRAE DR 85033
  Lynn Butler, prin.
Holiday Park ES, 4417 N 66TH AVE 85033
  James Futch, prin.
Long ES, 4407 N 55TH AVE 85031
  Emil Goimarac, prin.
Palm Lane ES, 2043 N 64TH DR 85035
  Jerrold Rankin, prin.
Peralta ES, 7125 W ENCANTO BLVD 85035
  William Titus, prin.
Spitalny ES, 3201 N 46TH DR 85031
  Sue Enright, prin.
Starlight Park ES, 7960 W OSBORN ROAD 85033
  Edward Kunkel, prin.
Sunset, 6602 W OSBORN ROAD 85033
  (—), prin.
Tomahawk ES, 7820 W TURNEY 85033
  William Sullivan, prin.

Creighton ESD 14
Sch. Sys. Enr. Code 5
Supt. – Donald Covey, 2702 E FLOWER ST 85016
Creighton MS, 2802 E MCDOWELL 85008
  Michael Helminski, prin.
Kennedy ES, 2702 E OSBORN ROAD 85016
  Earl Mendenhall, prin.
Loma Linda ES, 2002 E CLARENDON AVE 85016
  Bruce Johnson, prin.
Machan ES, 2140 E VIRGINIA AVE 85006
  Dr. Lynn Davey, prin.
Monte Vista ES, 3501 E OSBORN ROAD 85018
  Kathryn Frankel, prin.
Papago ES, 2013 N 36TH ST 85008
  Jim Heard, prin.
Squaw Peak ES, 4601 N 34TH ST 85018
  Timothy Moe, prin.

Deer Valley USD 97
Sch. Sys. Enr. Code 5
Supt. – Dr. Edgar Sims, 20402 N 15TH AVE 85027
Deer Valley JHS, 21100 N 27TH AVE 85027
  Jean Gallaugher, prin.
Constitution ES, 18440 N 15TH AVE 85023
  Murray White, prin.
Desert Winds ES, 19825 N 15TH AVE 85027
  Freddy Craig, prin.
New River ES, 2720 NEW RIVER STAGE 85029
  Pat Crisp, prin.
Sunrise ES, 17624 N 31ST AVE 85023
  Kenneth Neumann, prin.
Village Meadows ES
  2020 W MORNINGSIDE DR 85023
  Clifford Henkel, prin.
Other Schools – See Glendale

Fowler ESD 45
Sch. Sys. Enr. Code 4
Supt. – Jack Null, 6707 W VAN BUREN ST 85043
Fowler MS, 6707 W VAN BUREN ST 85043
  Kathleen Kaderlick, prin.
Sunridge PS, 6244 W ROOSEVELT ST 85043
  Linda South, prin.

Isaac ESD 5
Sch. Sys. Enr. Code 6
Supt. – Dr. Carol Wilson, 1701 N 35TH AVE 85009
Isaac JHS, 3402 W MCDOWELL ROAD 85009
  Mary Radcliffe, prin.
Butler ES, 3843 W ROOSEVELT ST 85009
  Dolores Herrera, prin.
Coe ES, 3801 W ROANOKE AVE 85009
  Gerald Behrle, prin.
Mitchell ES, 1700 N 41ST AVE 85009
  Albert Bowler, prin.
Sutton ES, 1001 N 31ST AVE 85009
  Lee Privee, prin.
Zito ES, 4525 W ENCANTO BLVD 85035
  Mary Rosales, prin.

Kyrene ESD 28
Supt. – See Tempe
Kyrene De Las Lomas ES
  11820 S WARNER ELLIOTT LOOP 85044
  Dixie Shirley, prin.

Laveen ESD 59
Supt. – See Laveen
Cash ES, 3851 W ROESER ROAD 85041
  Steve Chambers, prin.

Madison ESD 38
Sch. Sys. Enr. Code 5
Supt. – Dr. William Schaefer
  5601 N 16TH ST 85016
Madison I MS, 5525 N 16TH ST 85016
  Robert Chartier, prin.
Madison Meadows MS
  225 W OCOTILLO ROAD 85013
  Dr. Peter Spang, prin.
Madison Heights ES, 7150 N 22ND ST 85020
  Claudette Gronski, prin.
Madison Park II ES
  1431 E CAMPBELL AVE 85014
  Scott Meyers, prin.
Madison Rose Lane ES, 6124 N 12TH ST 85014
  Margaret Kesler, prin.
Madison Simis ES, 7302 N 10TH ST 85020
  Joanne Johnson, prin.

Murphy ESD 21
Sch. Sys. Enr. Code 5
Supt. – Robert Donofrio
  2625 W BUCKEYE ROAD 85009

Garcia ES, 1441 S 27TH AVE 85009
  Barbara Ortega, prin.
Hamilton ES, 2020 W DURANGO ST 85009
  Paul Mohr, prin.
Kuban ES, 3201 W SHERMAN ST 85009
  John Bartell, prin.
Sullivan ES, 2 N 31ST AVE 85009
  Deborah Hull, prin.

Osborn ESD 8
Sch. Sys. Enr. Code 5
Supt. – Wilma Basnett
  1220 W OSBORN ROAD 85013
Clarendon MS, 1225 W CLARENDON AVE 85013
  Del Merrill, prin.
Grandview MS, 11TH AVE 85013
  Vanice French, prin.
Longview MS
  1209 E INDIAN SCHOOL ROAD 85014
  Karen Lindberg, prin.
Encanto ES, 1226 W OSBORN ROAD 85013
  Anna Maie Murphy, prin.
Longview PS
  1209 E INDIAN SCHOOL ROAD 85014
  Wendy Ong, prin.
Solano ES, 1500 W MISSOURI AVE 85015
  Brad Swanson, prin.

Paradise Valley USD 69
Sch. Sys. Enr. Code 8
Supt. – Majorie Kaplan
  3012 E GREENWAY ROAD 85032
Greenway MS, 3003 E GREENWAY ROAD 85032
  Donald Skawski, prin.
Shea MS, 10849 N 27TH ST 85028
  Carl Shutts, prin.
Aire Libre ES, 16428 N 21ST ST 85022
  David Zuckerman, prin.
Arrowhead ES, 3820 E NISBET RD 85032
  David Bane, prin.
Campo Bello ES
  2650 E CONTENTION MINE ROAD 85032
  Lee Daly, prin.
Desert Cove ES, 11020 N 28TH ST 85028
  Robert McClarin, prin.
Eagle Ridge ES, 19801 N 13TH ST 85024
  G. Thomas Krebs, prin.
Echo Mountain ES, 1811 E MICHIGAN AVE 85022
  Judith DeWalt, prin.
Foothills ES, 17835 N 44TH ST 85032
  Joseph Bunting, prin.
Gold Dust MS, 3602 E CHOLLA ST 85028
  Brian Gilchrist, prin.
Indian Bend ES
  3633 E THUNDERBIRD ROAD 85032
  Richard Buscher, prin.
Larkspur ES, 2450 E LARKSPUR DR 85032
  Thomas Edwards, prin.
Liberty ES, 5020 E ACOMA DR 85254
  Margo Seck, prin.
Mercury Mine ES, 9640 N 28TH ST 85028
  Jack Bierman, prin.
Palomino ES, 15833 N 29TH ST 85032
  Richard Ebert, prin.
Quail Run ES, 3303 E UTOPIA 85032
  Lloyd Aycock, prin.
Village Vista ES, 4215 E ANDORA DR 85032
  Steven Walters, prin.
Other Schools – See Scottsdale

Pendergast ESD 92
Supt. – See Tolleson
Desert Horizon ES, 8525 W OSBORN RD 85037
  Harold Waltman, prin.
Villa De Paz ES, 4940 N 103RD AVE 85039
  Gary Rooker, prin.
Westwind ES, 9040 W CAMPBELL AVE 85037
  Elaine Whissen, prin.

Phoenix ESD 1
Sch. Sys. Enr. Code 6
Supt. – Gerald Cuendet, 125 E LINCOLN ST 85004
Capitol ES, 333 N 17TH AVE 85007
  Patricia Williams, prin.
Dunbar ES, 701 S 9TH AVE 85007
  Phillip Kinsey, prin.
Edison ES, 1742 E MCKINLEY ST 85006
  Louis Salcido, prin.
Emerson ES, 915 E PALM LN 85006
  Linda Floyd, prin.
Garfield ES, 811 N 13TH ST 85006
  Camerino Lopez, prin.
Heard ES, 2301 W THOMAS ROAD 85015
  Tom Luster, prin.
Herrera ES, 1450 S 11TH ST 85034
  Dr. Ruth Ann Marston, prin.
Kenilworth ES, 1210 N 5TH AVE 85003
  Joe Tameron, prin.
Lowell ES, 1120 S 1ST AVE 85003
  Debra Gomez, prin.
McLeod Bethune ES, 1510 S 15TH AVE 85007
  Shirley Johnson, prin.
Ott ES, 1801 S 12TH ST 85034
  Richard Valdez, prin.
Shaw ES, 20 N 14TH ST 85034
  Thomas Dean, prin.
Whittier ES, 2000 N 16TH ST 85006
  Estelle Greenberg, prin.

Riverside ESD 2
Sch. Sys. Enr. Code 2
Supt. – (—), 1414 S 51ST AVE 85043
Riverside, 1414 S 51ST AVE 85043
  (—), prin.

Roosevelt ESD 66
Sch. Sys. Enr. Code 7
Supt. – Dr. Alejandro Perez, 6000 S 7TH ST 85040
Greenfield MS, 7009 S 10TH ST 85040
  Louis Williams, prin.
Julian MS, 2149 E CARVER DR 85040
  Raymond Jackson, prin.
Barr ES, 2041 E VINEYARD ROAD 85040
  Dewey Jefferies,Jr., prin.
Bush ES, 602 E SIESTA WAY 85040
  Eddie Lewis, prin.
Conchos ES, 1718 W VINEYARD RD 85041
  Saul Solis, prin.
Davis ES, 6209 S 15TH AVE 85041
  Anthony Morell, prin.
Jorgensen ES, 1701 W ROESER ROAD 85041
  Michael Martinez, prin.
Kennedy ES, 6825 S 10TH ST 85040
  Daniel Bonow, prin.
King ES, 4615 S 22ND ST 85040
  Wellington Swindall, prin.
Lassen ES, 909 W VINEYARD RD 85041
  Barbara Johnson, prin.
Linda ES, 4610 S 12TH ST 85040
  Louis Grijalva, prin.
Palmdale ES, 3146 E WIER AVE 85040
  Laverne White, prin.
Rio Vista ES, 4001 S 3RD ST 85040
  Frank Solano, prin.
Sierra Vista ES, 6401 S 16TH ST 85040
  Jose Leyba, prin.
Southwest ES, 1111 W DOBBINS 85041
  Tak Nakamura, prin.
Sunland ES, 5401 S 7TH AVE 85041
  Murle Williams, prin.
Valley View ES, 8220 S 7TH AVE 85041
  Ralph Ludders, prin.

Scottsdale USD 48
Sch. Sys. Enr. Code 7
Supt. – Dr. Duane Sheldon, P O BOX 15428 85060
Ingleside MS, 5402 E OSBORN ROAD 85018
  John Weimer, prin.
Hopi ES, 5110 E LAFAYETTE BLVD 85018
  John Butts, prin.
Tavan ES, 4610 E OSBORN ROAD 85018
  Bruce Burns, prin.
Other Schools – See Scottsdale

Tempe ESD 3
Supt. – See Tempe
Nevitt ES, 4525 E SAINT ANNE AVE 85040
  Edna Maciekowich, prin.

Washington ESD 6
Sch. Sys. Enr. Code 7
Supt. – Dr. Gerald Olson, 8610 N 19TH AVE 85021
Cholla MS, 3120 W CHOLLA ST 85029
  Gary Batsell, prin.
Desert Foothills MS, 3333 W BANFF LANE 85023
  Kenneth Wamsley, prin.
Mountain Sky MS, 16225 N 7TH AVE 85023
  Dr. Ace Faust, prin.
Palo Verde JHS, 7502 N 39TH AVE 85051
  Dr. Judy Kennedy, prin.
Royal Palm JHS, 8520 N 19TH AVE 85021
  Mary Beyda, prin.
Acacia ES, 3021 W EVANS DR 85023
  Richard Boyer, prin.
Alta Vista ES, 8710 N 31ST AVE 85051
  Ken Anger, prin.
Cactus Wren ES, 9650 N 39TH AVE 85051
  Dr. Sally Solberg, prin.
Chaparral ES, 3808 W JOAN D'ARC AVE 85029
  Terry Hammon, prin.
Desert View ES, 8621 N 3RD ST 85020
  John Carroll, prin.
Ironwood ES, 14850 N 39TH AVE 85023
  Leonard Sweeney, prin.
Jacobs ES, 14402 N 23RD AVE 85023
  Marilyn Holroyd, prin.
Lakeview ES, 3040 W YUCCA ST 85029
  Dr. Gloria Grossman, prin.
Lookout Mountain ES
  15 W GREENWAY ROAD 85023
  Betty Kent, prin.
Manzanita ES, 8430 N 39TH AVE 85051
  Charles Debenon, prin.
Maryland ES, 6503 N 21ST AVE 85015
  Patricia Andazola, prin.
Miller ES, 2021 W ALICE AVE 85021
  Sonia Karp, prin.
Moon Mountain ES, 13425 N 19TH AVE 85029
  Paul Gissel, prin.
Mountain View ES
  1502 W MOUNTAIN VIEW ROAD 85021
  Dr. Joel Davidson, prin.
Ocotillo ES, 3225 W OCOTILLO ROAD 85017
  Yvonne Carter, prin.
Orangewood ES, 7337 N 19TH AVE 85021
  Dr. Peggy George, prin.
Roadrunner ES, 7702 N 39TH AVE 85051
  William Hanlon, prin.
Sahuaro ES, 12835 N 33RD AVE 85029
  Ralph Friedly, prin.
Senita ES, 10444 N 39TH AVE 85051
  Marilyn Czerny, prin.
Shaw Butte ES, 12202 N 21ST AVE 85029
  Muriel Lundy, prin.
Sunnyslope ES, 240 E VOGEL AVE 85020
  Pam Clark, prin.
Tumbleweed ES, 4001 W LAUREL LN 85029
  James Carlson, prin.
Washington ES, 8033 N 27TH AVE 85051
  Lyn Bailey, prin.

Other Schools – See Glendale

Wilson ESD 7
Sch. Sys. Enr. Code 3
Supt. – Raymond Argel
  3025 E FILLMORE ST 85008
Wilson MS, 2929 E FILLMORE ST 85008
  Thomas Butler, prin.
Wilson PS, 415 N 30TH ST 85008
  Manuel Madrid, prin.

Christian Challenge Academy
  2030 N 36TH ST 85008
Landmark Christian Academy
  7040 S 40TH ST 85040
Phoenix Country Day School
  P O BOX 15087 85060
Scottsdale Christian Academy
  9827 N 32ND ST 85028
Western Christian School
  4030 N 67TH AVE 85033
All Saints Episcopal Day School
  6300 N CENTRAL AVE 85012
Calvary Academy, 1625 W DOBBINS ROAD 85041
Christ Lutheran School
  3901 E INDIAN SCHOOL ROAD 85018
Covenant Christian School
  1117 E DEVONSHIRE AVE 85014
Grace Christian School
  2940 W BETHANY HOME ROAD 85017
Greenway Christian Academy
  3033 W CARIBBEAN LANE 85023
Light & Life Christian School
  4002 N 18TH AVE 85015
Martin Luther School
  1830 W GLENROSA AVE 85015
Most Holy Trinity School
  535 E ALICE AVE 85020
New Horizons Private School
  3018 N 7TH AVE 85013
Phoenix Christian Grade School
  2425 N 26TH ST 85008
SS. Simon & Jude ES, 6351 N 27TH AVE 85017
Saint Agnes School, 2311 E PALM LANE 85006
Saint Catherines School
  6413 S CENTRAL AVE 85040
Saint Francis Xavier School
  4715 N CENTRAL AVE 85012
Saint Gregory School, 3437 N 18TH AVE 85015
Saint Jeromes School, 10815 N 35TH AVE 85029
Saint Marys ES, 231 N 3RD ST 85004
Saint Matthew School
  2038 W VAN BUREN ST 85009
Saint Theresa School
  5001 E THOMAS ROAD 85018
Saint Vincent De Paul School
  3130 N 51ST AVE 85031
St. Thomas the Apostle School
  4510 N 24TH ST 85016
Valley Cathedral Christian School
  6225 N CENTRAL AVE 85012
Valley Christian School
  1055 E HEARN ROAD 85022
Valley Jewish Day School
  P O BOX C4200 STE 363 85261

Picacho, Pinal Co.
Picacho ESD 33
Sch. Sys. Enr. Code 2
Supt. – Robert Noe, P O BOX 8 85241
ES, P O BOX 8 85241 – (—), prin.

Pima, Graham Co., Pop. Code 4
Pima USD 6
Sch. Sys. Enr. Code 3
Supt. – Stan Smith, P O BOX 429 85543
ES 85543 – Steven John, prin.

Pine, Gila Co.
Pine ESD 12
Sch. Sys. Enr. Code 2
Supt. – Sue Myers, P O BOX 328 85544
ES, P O BOX 1150 85544 – (—), prin.

Pinon, Navajo Co.
Pinon USD 4
Sch. Sys. Enr. Code 3
Supt. – Marilyn Galt, P O BOX 839 86510
ES, P O BOX 839 86510
  Adelbert Goldtooth, prin.

Pirtleville, Cochise Co.
Douglas USD 27
Supt. – See Douglas
Faras ES 85607 – Gloria Keith, prin.

Polacca, Navajo Co.

Polacca Day School 86042

Pomerene, Cochise Co.
Pomerene ESD 64
Sch. Sys. Enr. Code 1
Supt. – (—), P O BOX 7 85627
ES, P O BOX 7 85627 – Stephen Webb, prin.

Prescott, Yavapai Co., Pop. Code 7
Prescott USD 1
Sch. Sys. Enr. Code 6
Supt. – Dr. James Howard
  146 S GRANITE ST 86303
Granite Mountain JHS
  1800 WILLIAMSON VALLEY ROAD 86301
  Don Aycock, prin.
JHS, 300 S GRANITE ST 86301 – Jay Collier, prin.

Dexter ES, 551 1ST ST 86301
  William Munson, prin.
Hicks ES, 1845 CAMPBELL AVE 86301
  Kelton Aker, prin.
Judd ES, 1749 WILLIAMSON VALLEY RD 86301
  Mary Anne Kapp, prin.
Lincoln ES, 201 PARK AVE 86303
  Floyd James, prin.
Miller Valley ES
  900 IRON SPRINGS ROAD 86301
  Robert Williams, prin.
Washington ES, 300 E GURLEY ST 86301
  Kent Evans, prin.

Christian Academy, P O BOX 226 86302
Sacred Heart Grade School
  131 N SUMMIT ST 86303

Queen Creek, Maricopa Co., Pop. Code 1
J. O. Combs ESD 44
Sch. Sys. Enr. Code 2
Supt. – Thomas Robinette
  RURAL ROUTE 02 BOX 33 85242
Combs ES, RURAL ROUTE 02 BOX 33 85242
  (—), prin.

Queen Creek USD 95
Sch. Sys. Enr. Code 3
Supt. – Ralph Pomeroy
  RURAL ROUTE 01 BOX 24 85242
JHS, RURAL ROUTE 01 BOX 24 85242
  Carolyn Tanner, prin.
ES, RURAL ROUTE 01 BOX 24 85242
  Katherine Cue, prin.

Red Rock, Pinal Co.
Red Rock ESD 5
Sch. Sys. Enr. Code 1
Supt. – (—), P O BOX 56 85245
ES, P O BOX 56 85245 – Frank Klell, prin.

Red Valley, Apache Co.

Red Rock Day School, P O BOX 10 86544

Rimrock, Yavapai Co.
Beaver Creek ESD 26
Sch. Sys. Enr. Code 2
Supt. – (—), P O BOX 8 86335
Beaver Creek ES, P O BOX 8 86335
  Judy McBride, prin.

Riviera, Mohave Co., Pop. Code 4

Riviera Christian School
  805 MARINA BLVD 86442

Roll, Maricopa Co.
Mohawk Valley ESD 17
Sch. Sys. Enr. Code 2
Supt. – Andrew Dail, P O BOX 67 85347
Mohawk Valley ES, P O BOX 67 85347
  (—), prin.

Sacaton, Pinal Co., Pop. Code 3
Sacaton ESD 18
Sch. Sys. Enr. Code 3
Supt. – Jacob Garcia, P O BOX 98 85247
MS, P O BOX 98 85247 – Mary Jo Walter, prin.
ES, P O BOX 98 85247 – Marilyn Atcitty, prin.

Safford, Graham Co., Pop. Code 6
Safford USD 1
Sch. Sys. Enr. Code 5
Supt. – John Sinclair, P O BOX 960 85548
JHS, P O BOX 960 85548 – John Vail, prin.
Nelson MS, 612 W 11TH ST 85546
  Mark Tregaskes, prin.
Stinson PS, 612 W 11TH ST 85546
  Ann Markle, prin.

Sahuarita, Pima Co.
Sahuarita USD 30
Sch. Sys. Enr. Code 4
Supt. – Stephen Lebrecht, P O BOX 26 85629
JHS, P O BOX 26 85629 – Charles Oldham, prin.
ES, P O BOX 26 85629 – Nancy Harrington, prin.
Sopori ES, P O BOX 26 85629
  Frank Hansen, prin.

Saint David, Cochise Co.
St. David USD 21
Sch. Sys. Enr. Code 2
Supt. – Dr. Ronald Nelson, P O BOX 70 85630
ES, P O BOX 70 85630 – Jim Crawford, prin.

Saint Johns, Apache Co., Pop. Code 5
St. Johns USD 1
Sch. Sys. Enr. Code 4
Supt. – Lee Cook, P O BOX 3030 85936
JHS, P O BOX 3060 85936 – Ken Crosby, prin.
Coronado PS, P O BOX 609 85936
  Mervin Jarvis, prin.

Saint Michaels, Apache Co.

St.Michaels Indian HS, P O BOX M 86511
Hunters Point Boarding School, P O BOX N 86511
St. Michael ES, P O BOX M 86511

Salome, LaPaz Co., Pop. Code 2
Salome Consolidated ESD 30
Sch. Sys. Enr. Code 2
Supt. – (—), P O BOX 358 85348
Salome Consolidated ES, P O BOX 358 85348
  Charles Antoni, prin.

San Carlos, Gila Co.
San Carlos USD 20
Sch. Sys. Enr. Code 3
Supt. – Thomas Morgan, P O BOX 207 85550
Rice ES, P O BOX 207 85550 – John Bush, prin.

Saint Charles School, P O BOX 338 85550

Sanders, Apache Co., Pop. Code 2
Sanders USD 18
Sch. Sys. Enr. Code 3
Supt. – Peter Belletto, P O BOX 250 86512
JHS, P O BOX 68 86512 – L. Ridley, prin.
ES, P O BOX 68 86512 – Irene Guilbert, prin.

San Manuel, Pinal Co., Pop. Code 7
Mammoth/San Manuel USD 8
Sch. Sys. Enr. Code 4
Supt. – Carl Nuhn, P O BOX 406 85631
Gardner MS, P O BOX 406 85631
  Don McClure, prin.
Avenue B MS, P O BOX 406 85631
  J. Simminger, prin.
First Avenue ES, P O BOX 406 85631
  Jane Taylor, prin.
Mammoth ES, P O BOX 406 85631
  Hank Payton, prin.

San Simon, Cochise Co., Pop. Code 2
San Simon USD 18
Sch. Sys. Enr. Code 2
Supt. – Billy McDowell, P O BOX 38 85632
ES, P O BOX 38 85632 – (—), prin.

Sasabe, Pima Co.
San Fernando ESD 35
Sch. Sys. Enr. Code 1
Supt. – (—), P O BOX 306 85633
San Fernando ES, P O BOX 306 85633
  Nancy Turner, prin.

Scottsdale, Maricopa Co., Pop. Code 8
Paradise Valley USD 69
Supt. – See Phoenix
Desert Shadows MS
  5858 E SWEETWATER AVE 85254
  William Cooper, prin.
Sunrise MS, 4960 E ACOMA DR 85254
  Thomas Cultice, prin.
Desert Shadows ES
  5902 E SWEETWATER AVE 85254
  Barbara Hollenbeck, prin.
Desert Springs MS, 6010 EAST ACOMA DR 85254
  Donald Hiemstra, prin.
North Ranch ES, 16406 N 61ST PLACE 85254
  James DeWalt, prin.
Sandpiper ES, 6724 E HEARN ROAD 85254
  Tacy Ashby, prin.

Scottsdale USD 48
Supt. – See Phoenix
Cocopah MS, 6615 E CHOLLA ST 85254
  Leslie Hurst, prin.
Mohave MS, 5520 N 86TH ST 85253
  Leonard Barcelona, prin.
Supai MS, 6720 E CONTINENTAL DR 85257
  Corwin Ellsworth, prin.
Anasazi ES, 11130 E CHOLLA ST 85259
  Ken Moore, prin.
Cherokee ES, 8801 N 56TH ST 85253
  Dorothy Totten, prin.
Cochise ES, 9405 N 84TH ST 85258
  Barry Weiler, prin.
Hohokam ES, 8451 E OAK ST 85257
  Lois Barnes, prin.
Kiva ES, 6911 E MCDONALD DR 85253
  Jackie Taylor, prin.
Laguna ES, 10475 E LAKEVIEW 85258
  Corrine Hochgraef, prin.
Navajo ES, 4525 N GRANITE REEF ROAD 85251
  Gloria Hallowell, prin.
Pima ES, 8330 E OSBORN ROAD 85251
  Richard Orson, prin.
Pueblo ES, 6320 N 82ND ST 85253
  Robert Colby, prin.
Sequoya ES, 11808 N 64TH ST 85254
  Bobbie Sferra, prin.
Tonalea ES, 6801 E OAK ST 85257
  Dr. Keith Powell, prin.
Yavapai ES, 701 N MILLER ROAD 85257
  Vicki Durbin, prin.

Judson School, P O BOX 1569 85252
Our Lady Of Perpetual Help School
  3801 N MILLER ROAD 85251
Saint Daniel The Prophet School
  1030 N HAYDEN ROAD 85257

Second Mesa, Navajo Co.

Second Mesa Day School, P O BOX 728 86043

Sedona, Coconino Co., Pop. Code 4
Flagstaff USD 1
Supt. – See Flagstaff
ES, P O BOX 0 86336 – Wanda James, prin.

Seligman, Yavapai Co., Pop. Code 3
Seligman USD 40
Sch. Sys. Enr. Code 2
Supt. – James McLaney, P O BOX 278 86337
ES, P O BOX 278 86337 – James McLaney, prin.

Sells, Pima Co., Pop. Code 3
Indian Oasis-Baboquivari USD 40
Sch. Sys. Enr. Code 4
Supt. – Michael Ryan, P O BOX 248 85634
Baboquivari JHS, P O BOX 248 85634
  Sharon Walker, prin.
Sells Primary School, P O BOX 248 85634
  Ann Francisco, prin.
Topawa MS, P O BOX 248 85634
  Marie Dorn, prin.

San Simon School, HCR 01 BOX 92 85634
Santa Rosa Boarding School 85634

Shonto, Coconino Co.

Shonto Boarding School 86054

Show Low, Navajo Co., Pop. Code 5
Show Low USD 10
Sch. Sys. Enr. Code 4
Supt. – Norlis McKay
  500 W OLD LINDEN RD 85901
MS, 500 W OLD LINDEN ROAD 85901
  Norman Ehmke,Jr., prin.
Clay Springs ES
  500 W OLD LINDEN ROAD 85901
  Lavell Owens, prin.
Linden ES, 500 W OLD LINDEN ROAD 85901
  Lavell Owens, prin.
Pinedale ES, 500 W OLD LINDEN ROAD 85901
  Norlis McKay, prin.
ES, 500 W OLD LINDEN ROAD 85901
  Norlis McKay, prin.

Sierra Vista, Cochise Co., Pop. Code 8
Sierra Vista USD 68
Sch. Sys. Enr. Code 6
Supt. – Jon Lokensgard, 4001 E FRY BLVD 85635
MS, 4001 E FRY BLVD 85635
  Donald Rothery, prin.
Bella Vista ES, 4001 E FRY BLVD 85635
  Cathy Hernandez, prin.
Carmichael ES, 4001 E FRY BLVD 85635
  Elaine Newton, prin.
Huachuca Mountain ES, 3555 FRY BLVD 85635
  David Chaffin, prin.
Pueblo Del Sol ES, 4001 E FRY BLVD 85635
  Patricia Nygaard-Ross, prin.
Town & Country ES, 4001 E FRY BLVD 85635
  Robert Sadorf, prin.
Village Meadows ES, 4001 E FRY BLVD 85635
  John Wilson, prin.

Shiloh Christian School
  200 N NORTH AVE 85635

Skull Valley, Yavapai Co.
Skull Valley ESD 15
Sch. Sys. Enr. Code 1
Supt. – (—), P O BOX 127 86338
ES, P O BOX 127 86338 – Dick Bowerman, prin.

Snowflake, Navajo Co., Pop. Code 5
Snowflake USD 5
Sch. Sys. Enr. Code 5
Supt. – Monty Harris, P O BOX 1100 85937
JHS, P O BOX 1100 85937 – Gary McEwen, prin.
Capps ES, P O BOX 1100 85937
  Franklin Greer, prin.
Highland PS, P O BOX 1100 85937
  J. Raymond McGrath, prin.
IS, P O BOX 1100 85937 – Terry Austin, prin.
Taylor ES, P O BOX 1100 85937
  Dennis Evans, prin.

Solomon, Graham Co.
Solomonville ESD 5
Sch. Sys. Enr. Code 2
Supt. – Sharon Friauf, P O BOX 167 85551
ES, P O BOX 167 85551 – (—), prin.

Somerton, Yuma Co., Pop. Code 6
Somerton ESD 11
Sch. Sys. Enr. Code 4
Supt. – Louise Kleinstiver, P O BOX E 85350
Carlisle JHS, P O BOX E 85350 – Francis Irr, prin.
Desert Sonora IS, P O BOX E 85350
  Patsy Howerton, prin.
Orange Grove ES, P O BOX E 85350
  Celine Fernandez, prin.
PS, P O BOX E 85350 – Ron Corona, prin.

Springerville, Apache Co., Pop. Code 4
Round Valley USD 10
Sch. Sys. Enr. Code 4
Supt. – Dr. Robert McKenzie, P O BOX 610 85938
Round Valley MS, P O BOX 610 85938
  Clyde Hamblin, prin.
Round Valley PS, P O BOX 610 85938
  Phyllis Colter, prin.

Stanfield, Pinal Co.
Stanfield ESD 24
Sch. Sys. Enr. Code 2
Supt. – Charles Brown, P O BOX 578 85272
ES, P O BOX 578 85272 – (—), prin.

Sun Valley, Navajo Co.

Twin Wells Indian School
  1H40 & SUN VALLEY EXIT 86029

Supai, Coconino Co.

Havasupai School, P O BOX 40 86435

Superior, Pinal Co., Pop. Code 5
Superior USD 15
Sch. Sys. Enr. Code 5
Supt. – Russell Hoffman, 199 N LOBB AVE 85273
Roosevelt MS, 199 N LOBB AVE 85273
Barney McIlvoy, prin.
Kennedy ES, 1500 SUNSET DR 85273
Barney McIlvoy, prin.

Teec Nos Pos, Apache Co., Pop. Code 2
Red Mesa USD 27
Sch. Sys. Enr. Code 3
Supt. – Dr. Jim Franklin, HCR 01 BOX 41 86514
Red Mesa ES, HCR 01 BOX 40 86514
Charles Bent, prin.
Round Rock ES, HCR 01 BOX 40 86514
Robert Roessel, prin.

Immanuel Mission School, P O BOX C 86514
Teec Nos Pos Boarding School 86514

Tempe, Maricopa Co., Pop. Code 9
Kyrene ESD 28
Sch. Sys. Enr. Code 6
Supt. – Dr. William Poston,Jr.
8700 S KYRENE ROAD 85284
Kyrene JHS, 1050 E CARVER ROAD 85284
Patricia Weegar, prin.
Kyrene Del Pueblo JHS, 8700 S KYRENE RD 85284
Robert Brown, prin.
Kyrene De La Mariposa ES
50 E KNOX ROAD 85284 – Wanda Land, prin.
Kyrene de los Lagos ES
17001 S 34TH WAY 85044 – Sheila Spinn, prin.
Kyrene De Los Ninos ES, 1330 E DAVA DR 85283
Carol Parish, prin.
Kyrene Del Norte ES
1331 E REDFIELD ROAD 85283
Gary Murphy, prin.
Waggoner ES, 1050 E CARVER ROAD 85284
Julie Weimer, prin.
Kyrene De La Paloma ES
8700 S KYRENE RD 85284 – Patrick O'Brien, prin.
Other Schools – See Chandler, Phoenix

Tempe ESD 3
Sch. Sys. Enr. Code 7
Supt. – Augustin Orci, P O BOX 27708 85282
Getz S, 625 W CORNELL DR 85283
Connie Thomas, prin.
Connolly IS, 2002 E CONCORDA DRIVE 85282
John Reinhold, prin.
Fees IS, 1600 E WATSON DR 85283
Dr. Dale Despain, prin.
Gilliland IS, 1025 S BECK AVE 85281
Paul Chavarria, prin.
McKemy IS, 2250 S COLLEGE AVE 85281
Joseph Spracale, prin.
Aguilar ES, 5800 S FOREST AVE 85283
Loretta Pacheco, prin.
Arredondo ES, 1330 E CARSON DR 85282
Calli Merrick, prin.
Broadmor ES, 311 E AEPLI DR 85282
Eddie Casillas, prin.
Bustoz ES, 2020 E CARSON DR 85282
Paula Visser, prin.
Carminati ES, 4001 S MCALLISTER AVE 85282
Dr. Mary Ann Lawson, prin.
Curry ES, 1974 E MEADOW DR 85282
Louise Conti, prin.
Evans ES, 4525 S COLLEGE AVE 85282
Al Jauregui, prin.
Fuller ES, 1975 E CORNELL DR 85283
Dr. John Laidlaw, prin.
Holdeman ES, 1326 W 18TH ST 85281
Dr. Michael Fidler, prin.
Hudson ES, 1325 E MALIBU DR 85282
Robert Harrison, prin.
Laird ES, 1500 N SCOVEL ST 85281
Dr. Duane Whitfield, prin.
Meyer ES, 2615 S DORSEY LN 85282
Orpha Brown, prin.
Rover ES, 1300 E WATSON DR 85283
Sharon Bryant, prin.
Scales ES, 1115 W 5TH ST 85281
Leonard Gallardo, prin.
Thew ES, 2130 E HOWE ST 85281
Nina Burkhardt, prin.
Wood ES, 727 W CORNELL DR 85283
Michael Walsh, prin.
Other Schools – See Guadalupe, Phoenix

Tri-City Christian Academy
2150 E SOUTHERN AVE 85282
Gethsemane Christian School
1035 E GUADELUPE ROAD 85283
Grace Community Christian School
3201 S TERRACE ROAD 85282
Our Lady Of Mount Carmel School
2115 S RURAL ROAD 85282
Seventh Day Adventist School
630 W 17TH PLACE 85281

Thatcher, Graham Co., Pop. Code 5
Thatcher USD 4
Sch. Sys. Enr. Code 4
Supt. – Max Peck, P O BOX 610 85552
Daley PS, P O BOX 610 85552
Glenn Woods, prin.
MS, P O BOX 610 85552 – Glenn Woods, prin.

New Life Christian School
8TH & 1ST AVES 85552

Tolleson, Maricopa Co., Pop. Code 5
Pendergast ESD 92
Sch. Sys. Enr. Code 5
Supt. – Richard Terbush, 3802 S 91ST AVE 85353
Pendergast ES, 3802 S 91ST AVE 85353
Bernny Valdez, prin.
Other Schools – See Phoenix

Tolleson ESD 17
Sch. Sys. Enr. Code 3
Supt. – Dr. Christa Metzger, P O BOX 278 85353
MS, 9407 W GARFIELD ST 85353
Manny Silva, prin.
Unit 1 ES, 9255 W MONROE ST #1 85353
Mary Stewart, prin.

Union ESD 62
Sch. Sys. Enr. Code 1
Supt. – (—), 3834 S 91ST AVE 85353
Union ES, 3834 S 91ST AVE 85353
Ronald Anglemyer, prin.

Tombstone, Cochise Co., Pop. Code 4
Tombstone USD 1
Sch. Sys. Enr. Code 4
Supt. – D. B. Forrest, P O BOX 1000 85638
Meyer ES, P O BOX 1000 85638
Conney Mcquerry, prin.
Other Schools – See Huachuca City

Tonalea, Coconino Co.

Red Lake School, P O BOX 62 86044

Tonopah, Maricopa Co.
Ruth Fisher ESD 90
Sch. Sys. Enr. Code 2
Supt. – (—), HCR 02 BOX 583 85354
Fisher ES, HCR 02 BOX 583 85354
G. Sanders, prin.

Tonto Basin, Gila Co.
Tonto Basin SD 33
Sch. Sys. Enr. Code 1
Supt. – (—), P O BOX 337 85553
ES, P O BOX 337 85553 – (—), prin.

Tortilla Flat, Pinal Co.
Horse Mesa Accommodation Dist 509
Supt. – See Williams AFB
Horse Mesa Accommodation ES, P O BOX 2 85290
Diane Ludeman, prin.

Tubac, Santa Cruz Co.
Santa Cruz Valley USD 35
Supt. – See Tumacacori
Tubac ES No 2, P O BOX 1925 85646
Elaine Lewis, prin.

Tuba City, Coconino Co., Pop. Code 7
Tuba City USD 15
Sch. Sys. Enr. Code 5
Supt. – Alice Weekley, P O BOX 67 86045
JHS, P O BOX 67 86045 – Hector Tahu, prin.
Cameron PS, P O BOX 67 86045
Patrick Konopasek, prin.
Eagles Nest MS, P O BOX 67 86045
Oscar Tso, prin.
Gap/Bodeway PS, P O BOX 67 86045
Ray Vernon, prin.
PS, P O BOX 67 86045 – Ray Vernon, prin.

Tucson, Pima Co., Pop. Code 10
Altar Valley ESD 51
Sch. Sys. Enr. Code 2
Supt. – Jerry Bergmans
SELLS HCR BOX 870 85735
Altar Valley ES
SELLS STAR ROUTE BOX 870 85735
(—), prin.

Amphitheater USD 10
Sch. Sys. Enr. Code 7
Supt. – Rick Wilson
701 W WETMORE ROAD 85705
Amphitheater JHS, 315 E PRINCE ROAD 85705
Robert Smith, prin.
Cross JHS, 1000 W CHAPALA DRIVE 85704
Don Bridges, prin.
Copper Creek ES
11620 N COPPER SPRING TR 85704
Robert Lenihan, prin.
Coronado ES, 3401 E WILDS ROAD 85737
Dr. Edwin MacBeth, prin.
Donaldson ES, 2040 W OMAR DR 85704
James Paterson, prin.
Harelson ES, 826 W CHAPALA DR 85704
Cathy Esposito, prin.
Holaway ES, 3500 N CHERRY AVE 85719
Dr. William Cihon, prin.
Keeling ES, 435 E GLENN ST 85705
Gerry Hernbrode, prin.
Mesa Verde ES, 1661 W SAGE ST 85704
John Ritchie, prin.
Nash ES, 515 W KELSO ST 85705
Katherine Fischer, prin.
Prince ES, 125 E PRINCE ROAD 85705
Timothy Doyle, prin.
Rio Vista ES, 1351 E LIMBERLOST 85919
James Fogltance, prin.
Walker ES
1750 N ROLLER COASTER ROAD 85704
Paul Ritz, prin.

Catalina Foothills USD 16
Sch. Sys. Enr. Code 4
Supt. – Robert Hetzel, 2101 E RIVER ROAD 85718

Orange Grove JHS
1911 E ORANGE GROVE ROAD 85718
Mary Scheetz, prin.
Canyon View ES
5725 N SABINO CANYON ROAD 85715
Chris Ahearn, prin.
Manzanita ES, 3000 E MANZANITA AVE 85718
Elizabeth Goettl, prin.
Sunrise Drive ES, 5301 E SUNRISE DR 85718
Gary Londer, prin.

Flowing Wells USD 8
Sch. Sys. Enr. Code 6
Supt. – Dr. Robert Hendricks
1556 W PRINCE ROAD 85705
Flowing Wells JHS
4545 N LA CHOLLA BLVD 85705
Robert Hamil, prin.
Davis ES, 4250 N ROMERO ROAD 85705
Shirley Fisher, prin.
Douglas ES
3302 N FLOWING WELLS ROAD 85705
Eric Abrams, prin.
Laguna ES, 5001 N SHANNON ROAD 85705
Tom Kappler, prin.
Richardson ES
6901 N CAMINO DE LA TIERRA 85704
Renate Krompasky, prin.

Marana USD 6
Supt. – See Marana
Tortolita MS, 4101 W HARDY ROAD 85741
David Santa Maria, prin.
Butterfield ES
3400 W MASSINGALE ROAD 85741
Lee Lance, prin.
Degrazia ES, 5051 W OVERTON RD 85741
Joel Perry, prin.
Desert Winds ES, 12675 W RUDASILL RD 85743
Richard Lesko, prin.
Thornydale ES, 7751 N OLD FATHER RD 85741
Donald Pierson, prin.

Sunnyside USD 12
Sch. Sys. Enr. Code 7
Supt. – Fred T. Bull, 2238 E GINTER ROAD 85706
Apollo MS, 265 W NEBRASKA ST 85706
Judson Jones, prin.
Chaparrel MS, 3700 E ALVORD ROAD 85706
Norma Garcia, prin.
Sierra MS, 5801 S DEL MORAL BLVD 85706
Susan Masek, prin.
Craycroft ES, 5455 E VALENCIA RD 85706
Dr. Mary Bergman, prin.
Drexel ES, 801 E DREXEL ROAD 85706
Dan Goitia, prin.
Elvira ES, 150 W ELVIRA ROAD 85706
Mary Jane Santos, prin.
Esperanza ES, 2353 E BANTAM RD 85706
Bob Lomas, prin.
Gallego ES, 5102 S CHERRY AVE 85706
Mary Musgrave, prin.
Liberty ES, 5101 S LIBERTY AVE 85706
Olivia Schaad, prin.
Los Amigos ES, 2200 E DREXEL RD 85706
Robert Lowe, prin.
Los Ninos ES, 5445 S ALVERNON WAY 85706
John Flores, prin.
Los Ranchitos ES, 2054 E GINTER ROAD 85706
Kathleen Baker, prin.
Mission Manor ES
6115 S SANTA CLARA AVE 85706
Madelon Alpert, prin.
Santa Clara ES
6910 S SANTA CLARA AVE 85706
Marty Cortez, prin.

Tanque Verde USD 13
Sch. Sys. Enr. Code 4
Supt. – Lewis Sorensen
4201 N MELPOMENE WAY 85749
Agua Caliente ES
11420 E LIMBERLOST DR 85749
Marion Wilson, prin.
Tanque Verde ES
11420 E LIMBERLOST DR 85749
Arnold Bianco, prin.

Tucson USD 1
Sch. Sys. Enr. Code 8
Supt. – Paul Houston, P O BOX 40400 85711
Basic Curriculum MS, 5350 E 16TH ST 85711
James Moffett, prin.
Carson MS, 7777 E STELLA ROAD 85730
Carol Smith, prin.
Doolen MS
2400 N COUNTRY CLUB ROAD 85716
Bob Davis, prin.
Fickett MS, 7240 E CALLE ARTURO 85710
John Michel, prin.
Gridley MS, 350 S HARRISON ROAD 85748
Betsy Hansen, prin.
Hohokam MS, 7400 S SETTLER 85746
Judith Hokett, prin.
Magee MS, 8300 E SPEEDWAY BLVD 85710
Mary Carr, prin.
Mansfield MS, 1300 E 6TH ST 85719
Arnie Adler, prin.
Maxwell MS, 2802 W ANKLAM ROAD 85745
Daniel Lupo, prin.
Naylor MS, 1701 S COLUMBUS BLVD 85711
Mike Schwanenberger, prin.
Pistor JHS, 2840 W CANADA ST 85746
E. Virginia Romero, prin.

Safford Magnet MS, 300 S 5TH AVE 85701
  Pi Irwin, prin.
Secrist MS, 3400 S HOUGHTON ROAD 85730
  Dorthi Woodward, prin.
Townsend MS, 2120 N BEVERLY AVE 85712
  Roy Baker, prin.
Utterback MS, 3233 S PINAL VISTA 85713
  Ross Sheard, prin.
Vail MS, 5350 E 16TH ST 85711
  Janet Kaufman, prin.
Wakefield MS, 101 W 44TH ST 85713
  Al Rivera, prin.
Blenman ES
  1695 N COUNTRY CLUB ROAD 85716
  Mary Lou Harvey, prin.
Bloom ES, 8310 E PIMA ST 85715
  Linda Arrington, prin.
Bonillas Basic Curriculum ES
  4711 E 16TH ST 85711 – Jo Carpenter, prin.
Booth ES, 7255 E KENYON DR 85710
  John Michel, prin.
Borman ES, 6630 E LIGHTNING DR 85708
  Michael Casey, prin.
Borton ES, 700 E 22ND ST 85713
  Mary Belle McCorkle, prin.
Brichta ES, 2110 W BRICHTA DR 85745
  Denise Hines, prin.
Carrillo IS, 440 S MAIN AVE 85701
  Henry Vega, prin.
Cavett ES, 2120 E NACO VISTA 85713
  Betty Brown, prin.
Collier ES, 3900 N BEAR CANYON ROAD 85749
  Pamela Roberts, prin.
Corbett ES, 5949 E 29TH ST 85711
  Harriet Johnson, prin.
Cragin ES, 2945 N TUCSON BLVD 85716
  Howard Kennedy, prin.
Davidson ES, 3915 E FT LOWELL ROAD 85712
  Vicki Balentine, prin.
Davis Bilingual ES, 500 W ST MARYS RD 85705
  Conrado Gomez, prin.
Dietz ES, 7575 E PALMA ST 85710
  Betty Hauser, prin.
Drachman PS, 549 S CONVENT AVE 85701
  Rosanna Gallagher, prin.
Duffy ES, 5145 E 5TH ST 85711
  Adalena Comeaux, prin.
Dunham ES, 9850 E 29TH ST 85748
  Ed McEuen, prin.
Erickson ES, 6750 E STELLA ROAD 85730
  Elizabeth Warfield, prin.
Ford ES, 8001 E STELLA ROAD 85730
  Bert Ronsick, prin.
Fruchthendler ES, 7470 E CLOUD ROAD 85715
  Frank Valenzuela, prin.
Fort Lowell ES, 5151 E PIMA ST 85712
  Robert Hooper, prin.
Gale ES, 666 S GOLLOB ROAD 85710
  Diane Carrillo, prin.
Grijalva ES, 1795 W DREXEL 85746
  Diane Quevedo, prin.
Henry ES, 650 N IGO WAY 85710
  Ned Levine, prin.
Holladay IS, 1110 E 33RD ST 85713
  Nora Grigg, prin.
Hollinger ES, 150 W AJO WAY 85713
  Miguel Ortega, prin.
Howell ES, 401 N IRVING AVE 85711
  Armando Alday, prin.
Hudlow ES, 502 N CARIBE AVE 85710
  Jessie Zander, prin.
Hughes ES, 700 N WILSON AVE 85719
  Chuck Tyree, prin.
Jefferson Park ES, 1701 E SENECA ST 85719
  Arthur DeFilippo, prin.
Keen ES, 3538 E ELLINGTON PL 85713
  Eloise Carrillo, prin.
Kellond ES, 6606 E LEHIGH DR 85710
  John Garbini, prin.
Lawrence ES, 6855 S MARK ROAD 85746
  Ruth Gedeon, prin.
Lineweaver ES, 461 S BRYANT AVE 85711
  Kathy Hayes, prin.
Lynn ES, 1573 W AJO WAY 85713 – E. West, prin.
Lyons ES, 7555 E DOGWOOD ST 85730
  Ed Crawford, prin.
Maldonado ES, 3535 W MESSALA WAY 85746
  Rose Garcia, prin.
Manzo ES, 1301 W ONTARIO ST 85745
  Andy Diaz, prin.
Marshall ES, 9066 E 29TH ST 85710
  Ernie Galaz, prin.
Menlo Park ES, 1100 W FRESNO ST 85745
  Richard Martinez, prin.
Miles Exploratory ES, 1400 E BROADWAY 85719
  Robert Garitano, prin.
Miller ES, 6951 S CAMINO DE LA TIERRA 85746
  Caroline Tompkins, prin.
Mission View ES, 2600 S 8TH AVE 85713
  Yolanda Saldate, prin.
Myers ES, 5000 E ANDREW ST 85711
  Sara Conrad, prin.
Ochoa ES, 101 W 25TH ST 85713
  Hector Placencia, prin.
Pueblo Gardens ES, 2210 E 33RD ST 85713
  Eloise Carrillo, prin.
Reynolds ES, 7450 E STELLA ROAD 85730
  Margaret Romero, prin.
Richey ES, 2209 N 15TH AVE 85705
  Betty Garcia, prin.
Roberts ES, 4355 E CALLE AURORA 85711
  Leonard Basurto, prin.
Robison ES, 2745 E 18TH ST 85716
  Esperanza Bejerano, prin.

Rogers ES, 6000 E 15TH ST 85711
  Jean Larson, prin.
Rose ES, 710 W MICHIGAN DR 85714
  Avelina Trujillo, prin.
Roskruge ES, 501 E 6TH ST 85705
  Jesus De La Garza, prin.
Safford ES, 300 S 5TH AVE 85701 – Pi Irwin, prin.
Schumaker ES, 501 N MAGUIRE AVE 85710
  Joyce Jennings, prin.
Sewell ES, 425 N SAHUARA AVE 85711
  Arthur Solomon, prin.
Smith ES, 5741 E IRONWOOD ST 85708
  John Joe, prin.
Steele ES, 700 S SARNOFF DR 85710
  Harold Pierce, prin.
Tolson ES, 1000 S GREASEWOOD ROAD 85745
  Adriana Herman, prin.
Tully ES, 1701 W EL RIO DR 85745
  Dr. Ann Shaeffer, prin.
Van Buskirk ES, 725 E FAIR ST 85714
  Duane Courson, prin.
Van Horne ES, 7550 E PIMA ST 85715
  William Gordon, prin.
Vesey ES, 5005 S BUTTS ROAD 85746
  David Geesey, prin.
Warren ES, 3505 W MILTON ROAD 85746
  Ron DeWitt, prin.
Wheeler ES, 1818 S AVENIDA DEL SOL 85710
  Beverly Beadle, prin.
White ES, 2315 W CANADA ST 85746
  Abe Aragon, prin.
Whitmore ES, 5330 E GLENN ST 85712
  Dr. Richard Sherfey, prin.
Wright ES, 4311 E LINDEN ST 85712
  Martha Preston, prin.
Wrightstown ES
  8950 E WRIGHTSTOWN ROAD 85715
  Richard Daglio, prin.

Zimmerman SD
Sch. Sys. Enr. Code 1
Supt. – Anita Lohr, 130 W CONGRESS ST 85701
Zimmerman ES, 130 W CONGRESS ST 85701
  Mary Wendel, prin.

Amphitheater Christian School
  226 W PRINCE ROAD 85705
Golf Links Christian Academy
  6902 E GOLF LINKS ROAD 85730
Kino Learning Center
  6625 NORTH FIRST AVENUE 85718
Tuller School, 5877 E 14TH ST 85711
Broadway Christian School
  6700 E BROADWAY 85710
Casas Adobes Baptist School
  2131 W INA ROAD 85741
Faith Lutheran Parish School
  3925 E 5TH ST 85711
First Southern Christian School
  445 E SPEEDWAY BLVD 85705
Fountain Of Life Lutheran School
  710 S KOLB ROAD 85710
Garden Of Tucson Inc. School
  5260 N ROYAL PALM DRIVE 85705
Good Christian School, 6188 E PIMA ST 85712
Ironwood Hills School
  2745 W IRONWOOD HILLS DR 85745
Our Mother Of Sorrows School
  1800 S KOLB ROAD 85710
SS. Peter & Paul School
  1436 N CAMBELL AVE 85719
Saint Ambrose School
  300 S TUCSON BLVD 85716
Saint Cyrils School, 4725 E PIMA ST 85712
Saint John The Evangelist School
  600 W AJO WAY 85713
Saint Josephs School
  215 S CRAYCROFT ROAD 85711
San Zavier Indian Mission School
  RURAL ROUTE 11 BOX 644 85746
Santa Cruz School, 29 W 22ND ST 85713
Tucson Country Day School
  3231 N CRAYCROFT 85712
Tucson SDA Jr. Academy
  3225 N MARTIN AVE 85719
Tuscon Hebrew Academy, 5550 E 5TH ST 85711

Tumacacori, Santa Cruz Co.
Santa Cruz Valley USD 35
Sch. Sys. Enr. Code 3
Supt. – William Horie, P O BOX 187 85640
Calabasas MS No. 1, P O BOX 187 85640
  Charles Bier, prin.
Mountain View MS #3, P O BOX 187 85640
  Guy Bake, prin.
Other Schools – See Tubac

Vail, Pima Co.
Vail ESD 20
Sch. Sys. Enr. Code 3
Supt. – Calvin Baker, P O BOX D8 85641
Vail ES, P O BOX D8 85641
  Jack St. Amand, prin.

Vernon, Apache Co.
Vernon ESD 9
Sch. Sys. Enr. Code 1
Supt. – (—), P O BOX 6 85940
ES, P O BOX 6 85940 – Ronald Schlaback, prin.

Wellton, Yuma Co., Pop. Code 3
Wellton ESD 24
Sch. Sys. Enr. Code 2
Supt. – Dr. R. Mutterer, P O BOX 517 85356
ES, P O BOX 517 85356 – Eric Kleinstiver, prin.

Wenden, La Paz Co.
Wenden ESD 19
Sch. Sys. Enr. Code 2
Supt. – (—) P O BOX 8 85357
ES, P O BOX 8 85357 – Herbert Tillapaugh, prin.

West Sedona, Yavapai Co.
Cottonwood-Oak Creek ESD 6
Supt. – See Cottonwood
ES, P O BOX 3429 86340 – Daniel Stephens, prin.

Whiteriver, Navajo Co., Pop. Code 3
Whiteriver USD 20
Sch. Sys. Enr. Code 4
Supt. – Joseph Landavazo, P O BOX 190 85941
MS, P O BOX 190 85941 – Gene R. Nelson, prin.
Seven Mile ES, P O BOX 190 85941
  John Brach, prin.
ES, P O BOX 190 85941 – Myrna Hillyard, prin.

Wickenburg, Maricopa Co., Pop. Code 5
Wickenburg USD 9
Sch. Sys. Enr. Code 4
Supt. – H. Suverkrup, P O BOX 1418 85358
Vulture Peak MS, P O BOX 1418 85358
  Dennis Pittman, prin.
MacLennan ES, P O BOX 1418 85358
  Nancy Brooks, prin.

Wikieup, Mohave Co.
Owens Whitney ESD 6
Sch. Sys. Enr. Code 1
Supt. – (—) 85360
Owens Whitney ES 85360 – Susan Burdsal, prin.

Willcox, Cochise Co., Pop. Code 5
Bonita ESD 16
Sch. Sys. Enr. Code 1
Supt. – (—), SUNSET ROUTE BOX 1 85643
Bonita ES, SUNSET ROUTE BOX 1 85643
  Dr. Mary Lou Gammon, prin.

Willcox USD 13
Sch. Sys. Enr. Code 4
Supt. – Dr. J. H. Eikenberry
  480 N BISBEE AVE 85643
MS, 360 N BISBEE AVE 85643
  Richard Williams, prin.
ES, 501 W DELOS ST 85643 – Ellen Duhon, prin.

Williams, Coconino Co., Pop. Code 4
Williams USD 2
Sch. Sys. Enr. Code 3
Supt. – Roger Short, 515 S 9TH ST 86046
ES, 601 N 7TH ST 86046 – Dennis Finch, prin.

Williams AFB, Maricopa Co.
Horse Mesa Accommodation Dist 509
Sch. Sys. Enr. Code 2
Supt. – Hank Diulus, 11 COOLIDGE ST 85225
Other Schools – See Fountain Hills, Tortilla Flat

Winkelman, Gila Co., Pop. Code 4
Hayden/Winkelman USD 41
Sch. Sys. Enr. Code 3
Supt. – Lalo Serrano, P O BOX 409 85292
Hambly JHS, P O BOX 409 85292
  Charles Odom, prin.
IS, P O BOX 409 85292 – Jack Rostal, prin.
PS, P O BOX 409 85292 – Jack Rostal, prin.

Winslow, Navajo Co., Pop. Code 6
Chevelon Butte ESD 5
Sch. Sys. Enr. Code 1
Supt. – (—), P O BOX 1090 86047
Chevelon Butte ES, P O BOX 1090 86047
  (—), prin.

Flagstaff USD 1
Supt. – See Flagstaff
Leupp ES, HCR 86047 – Michael Mares, prin.

Winslow USD 1
Sch. Sys. Enr. Code 5
Supt. – W. E. Peters, P O BOX 580 86047
JHS, P O BOX 580 86047 – Allen Cardon, prin.
Brennan ES, P O BOX 580 86047
  Gary Calhoun, prin.
Jefferson ES, P O BOX 580 86047
  Ted Wilcox, prin.
Washington ES, P O BOX 580 86047
  Bob Mansell, prin.

Leupp Boarding School, HCR 61 86047

Wittmann, Maricopa Co.
Nadaburg ESD 81
Sch. Sys. Enr. Code 3
Supt. – Steven Yokobosky, P O BOX 100 85361
Nadaburg ES, P O BOX 100 85361 – (—), prin.

Yarnell, Yavapai Co.
Yarnell ESD 52
Sch. Sys. Enr. Code 3
Supt. – (—), P O BOX 488 85362
ES, P O BOX 575 85362 – Sam Weinschenk, prin.

Young, Gila Co.
Young ESD 5
Sch. Sys. Enr. Code 1
Supt. – Valerie Sullivan, P O BOX 123 85554
ES, P O BOX 390 85554 – Valerie Sullivan, prin.

Yucca, Mohave Co.
Yucca ESD 13
Sch. Sys. Enr. Code 1
Supt. – (—), P O BOX 128 86438
ES, P O BOX 128 86438 – (—), prin.

Yuma, Yuma Co., Pop. Code 8
 Crane ESD 13
  Sch. Sys. Enr. Code 5
  Supt. – Gary Knox, 4250 W 16TH ST 85364
 Crane JHS, 4480 W 32ND ST 85364
  Phil Blais, prin.
 Pueblo ES, 2903 W 20TH ST 85364
  Judith Bishop, prin.
 Rancho Viejo IS, 930 S AVENUE C 85364
  Cindy Didway, prin.
 Rancho Viejo PS, 930 AVENUE C 85364
  Dan Branine, prin.
 Reagan Fundamental ES, 3200 W 16TH ST 85364
  Scott Jackson, prin.
 Suverkrup ES, 1590 AVE C 85364
  Kathy Fleenor, prin.

 Yuma ESD 1
  Sch. Sys. Enr. Code 6
  Supt. – Dr. Thomas McCraley
   450 W 6TH ST 85364

 Fourth Avenue JHS, 450 S 4TH AVE 85364
  William Roberts, prin.
 Gila Vista JHS, 2245 S ARIZONA AVE 85364
  Ed Robinson, prin.
 Woodard JHS, 2250 S 8TH AVE 85364
  Wes Vandenburg, prin.
 Byrne ES, 16TH ST & 9TH AVE 85364
  Audine Powell, prin.
 Carver ES, 1300 W 5TH ST 85364
  Alfred Guerrero, prin.
 Ham ES, 22ND ST & KENNEDY LN 85364
  Jane Dunham, prin.
 Johnson ES, 12TH ST & A AVE 85364
  Robert Garcia, prin.
 McGraw ES, ARIZONA AVE & 24TH ST 85364
  Wayne Amon, prin.
 Palmcroft ES, 8TH AVE & PALMCROFT DR 85364
  Jon Daugherty, prin.
 Pecan Grove ES, 21ST AVE & 7TH ST 85364
  Ken Waters, prin.

 Post IS, 400 W 5TH ST 85364
  Jerry Cauthen, prin.
 Price ES, YUMA PROVING GROUNDS 85365
  Eula Baumgarner, prin.
 Rolle ES, E 28TH ST & ENGLER AVE 85364
  Hal Siel, prin.
 Roosevelt PS, 550 W 5TH ST 85364
  Tom Wells, prin.

 Immaculate Conception School
  501 S AVENUE B 85364
 Saint Francis Of Assisi School
  700 W 18TH ST 85364
 Seventh Day Adventist School
  17TH ST & SIXTH AVE 85364
 Yuma Lutheran School
  2555 S ENGLER AVE 85365

ARKANSAS

STATE DEPARTMENT OF EDUCATION
State Education Building
4 State Capitol Mall, Little Rock 72201
(501) 682-4204

Director of Education	Ruth Steele
Deputy Director of Education	Herbert Cleek
Associate Director Federal Programs	Clearence Lovell
Associate Director Administrative Services	Robert Shaver
Associate Director Instructional Services	Emma Bass
Associate Director Planning & Development	Sterling Ingram
Associate Director Personnel	Fred Dawson
Associate Director Special Education	Diane Sydoriak

STATE BOARD OF EDUCATION
Jeff Starling, *Chairperson*   P.O. Box 8509, Pine Bluff   71611

ARKANSAS DEPARTMENT OF HIGHER EDUCATION
Paul Marion, *Director*   1220 W. 3rd St., Little Rock   72201

PUBLIC, PRIVATE, AND PAROCHIAL ELEMENTARY SCHOOLS

Alma, Crawford Co., Pop. Code 5
 Alma SD
  Sch. Sys. Enr. Code 4
  Supt. – Charles Dyer, P O BOX 1018 72921
 MS, P O BOX 455 72921 – Ronnie Newton, prin.
 IS, P O BOX 417 72921 – John Ewing, prin.
 PS, P O BOX 2267 72921 – Marsha Wooly, prin.

Alpena, Boone Co., Pop. Code 2
 Alpena SD
  Sch. Sys. Enr. Code 2
  Supt. – Norman Marvell, P O BOX 270 72611
 ES, P O BOX 270 72611 – Mike Forney, prin.

Altheimer, Jefferson Co., Pop. Code 4
 Altheimer-Sherrill SD
  Sch. Sys. Enr. Code 3
  Supt. – Randy Crowder, P O BOX N 72004
 Martin ES, P O BOX M 72004 – Thomas Holt, prin.

Altus, Franklin Co., Pop. Code 2
 Altus-Denning SD
  Sch. Sys. Enr. Code 2
  Supt. – Virgil Coy Hammons 72821
  Altus-Denning ES 72821 – Shirley Little, prin.

Amity, Clark Co., Pop. Code 3
 Amity SD
  Sch. Sys. Enr. Code 2
  Supt. – Vaughn Wright, P O BOX 67 71921
 ES 71921 – Jackie Robertson, prin.

Arkadelphia, Clark Co., Pop. Code 7
 Arkadelphia SD
  Sch. Sys. Enr. Code 4
  Supt. – James Ford, 235 N 11TH ST 71923
 Central PS, 233 N 11TH ST 71923
  Patti Jarvis, prin.

 Peake MS, 1609 PINE ST 71923
  Carroll Forte, prin.
 Perritt PS, 1900 WALNUT ST 71923
  Wanda O'Quinn, prin.

Arkansas City, Desha Co., Pop. Code 3
 Arkansas City SD
  Sch. Sys. Enr. Code 2
  Supt. – Gene Gregory, P O BOX 217 71630
 ES, P O BOX 217 71630 – Alvis Hooks, prin.

Armorel, Mississippi Co., Pop. Code 2
 Armorel SD
  Sch. Sys. Enr. Code 2
  Supt. – James Thomas, P O BOX 7 72310
 ES, P O BOX 7 72310 – Donald McGohan, prin.

Ashdown, Little River Co., Pop. Code 5
 Ashdown SD
  Sch. Sys. Enr. Code 4
  Supt. – William Stringer, 511 N 2ND ST 71822
 Burke Street ES, 140 BURKE ST 71822
  Patsy Matthews, prin.
 Franks IS, HIGHWEAY 32 WEST 71822
  L. F. Henderson, prin.

Atkins, Pope Co., Pop. Code 5
 Atkins SD
  Sch. Sys. Enr. Code 4
  Supt. – Bobby Broach, P O BOX 156 72823
 ES, P O BOX 156 72823 – Louise Thompson, prin.

Augusta, Woodruff Co., Pop. Code 5
 Augusta SD
  Sch. Sys. Enr. Code 3
  Supt. – Hershel Hooks, 222 LOCUST ST 72006
 ES, 905 N 4TH ST 72006 – Bobby Brown, prin.

Bald Knob, White Co., Pop. Code 5
 Bald Knob SD
  Sch. Sys. Enr. Code 4
  Supt. – James Staggs
   RURAL ROUTE 03 BOX 33 72010
 Lubker ES, RURAL ROUTE 03 BOX 33 72010
  Jack Parks, prin.

Batesville, Independence Co., Pop. Code 6
 Batesville SD
  Sch. Sys. Enr. Code 4
  Supt. – W. Coop, 330 E COLLEGE AVE 72501
 IS, 955 WATER 72501 – Betty Harrison, prin.
 Central ES, SEVENTH & OAK STS 72501
  Joyce Richey, prin.
 Desha ES, P O BOX 188 72503
  Charles O'Brien, prin.
 East ES, 19TH & LYON STS 72501
  Gerald Harris, prin.
 West ES, HILL & PINE STS 72501
  Ovie Lawrence, prin.

 Southside SD
  Sch. Sys. Enr. Code 3
  Supt. – Bobby Smith, P O BOX 162 72501
 Southside ES, RURAL ROUTE 05 BOX 162 72501
  Tim Sisk, prin.

Bauxite, Saline Co., Pop. Code 2
 Bauxite SD
  Sch. Sys. Enr. Code 3
  Supt. – J. Ford, P O BOX 345 72011
 Pine Haven ES, P O BOX 136 72011
  William Browning, prin.

Bay, Craighead Co., Pop. Code 4
 Bay-Brown SD
  Sch. Sys. Enr. Code 3
  Supt. – Forrest Jackson, P O BOX 39 72411

ES, P O BOX 39 72411 – Janis Roberts, prin.

Bearden, Ouachita Co., Pop. Code 4
Bearden SD
Sch. Sys. Enr. Code 3
Supt. – Don Cain, P O BOX 195 71720
ES, P O BOX 195 71720 – George Goree, prin.
Other Schools – See Thornton

Beebe, White Co., Pop. Code 5
Beebe SD
Sch. Sys. Enr. Code 4
Supt. – Floyd Lee Marshall
1201 W CENTER ST 72012
ES, 1201 W CENTER ST 72012 – Bill Hefner, prin.

Bee Branch, Van Buren Co., Pop. Code 1
South Side SD
Sch. Sys. Enr. Code 2
Supt. – Dick Lefler, RURAL ROUTE 01 72013
Southside ES, RURAL ROUTE 01 72013
Doylene Bintliff, prin.

Belleville, Yell Co., Pop. Code 3
Western Yell County SD
Supt. – See Havana
Western Yell County ES, P O BOX 307 72824
Mary Alean Newton, prin.

Benton, Saline Co., Pop. Code 7
Benton SD
Sch. Sys. Enr. Code 5
Supt. – Frank Chenault, P O BOX 939 72015
MS, RIVER ST 72015 – Carl Merrick, prin.
Caldwell ES, 1800 W SEVIER ST 72015
Carolyn Arick, prin.
Grant ES, 1800 W SEVIER ST 72015
Dorothy Richards, prin.
Perrin ES, 1201 SMITHERS DR 72015
Mary Lou McKinley, prin.
Ringgold ES, 536 RIVER ST 72015
Mary Slatton, prin.

Harmony Grove SD
Sch. Sys. Enr. Code 3
Supt. – Hollis Simpson
RURAL ROUTE 06 BOX 673 72015
Westbrook ES
614 N HWY 229 HASKELL ST 72015
Jerry Franks, prin.

Bentonville, Benton Co., Pop. Code 6
Bentonville SD
Sch. Sys. Enr. Code 5
Supt. – Carl Barger, 400 NW 2ND ST 72712
Baker ES, 301 NW 3RD ST 72712
James Beckloff, prin.
Jefferson ES, 810 BELLA VISTA ROAD 72712
Mike Mumma, prin.
Old High MS, 405 NW 2ND ST 72712
Dennis Snider, prin.

Bergman, Boone Co., Pop. Code 2
Bergman SD
Sch. Sys. Enr. Code 3
Supt. – Verlin Breedlove
GENERAL DELIVERY 72615
ES, GENERAL DELIVERY 72615
Larry Hunter, prin.

Berryville, Carroll Co., Pop. Code 5
Berryville SD
Sch. Sys. Enr. Code 4
Supt. – Richard Paul, P O BOX 408 72616
ES, P O BOX 408 72616 – Gene Ary, prin.

Bigelow, Perry Co., Pop. Code 2
East End SD
Sch. Sys. Enr. Code 2
Supt. – John Jordan, P O BOX B 72016
Watson ES, P O BOX B 72016
Connie Davison, prin.

Big Flat, Baxter Co., Pop. Code 2
Tri-County Consolidated SD
Sch. Sys. Enr. Code 1
Supt. – Hugh Pace, P O BOX 1 72617
Other Schools – See Fifty-Six

Biggers, Randolph Co., Pop. Code 2
Biggers-Reyno SD
Sch. Sys. Enr. Code 2
Supt. – Herschel Smith, P O BOX 82 72413
Biggers-Reyno ES, P O BOX 82 72413
Sam Becerra, prin.

Bismarck, Hot Spring Co., Pop. Code 4
Bismark SD
Sch. Sys. Enr. Code 3
Supt. – James Guffey, P O BOX 311 71929
ES, RURAL ROUTE 01 BOX 208 71929
Scott Henderson, prin.

Black Rock, Lawrence Co., Pop. Code 3
Black Rock SD
Sch. Sys. Enr. Code 2
Supt. – B. Maxwell, P O BOX 240 72415
ES, P O BOX 240 72415 – Edie Allen, prin.

Blevins, Hempstead Co., Pop. Code 2
Blevins SD
Sch. Sys. Enr. Code 2
Supt. – Randy Hughes, P O BOX 98 71825
ES, P O BOX 98 71825 – Larry Elrod, prin.

Blytheville, Mississippi Co., Pop. Code 7
Blytheville SD
Sch. Sys. Enr. Code 5
Supt. – Frank Ladd, 200 SOUTH LAKE ST 72315

Central IS, MOULTRIE & DIVISION 72315
Oscar Ford Jr., prin.
Fairview IS, 415 TENNESSEE ST 72315
Terry Gabrielson, prin.
Franklin PS, 1007 S FRANKLIN ST 72315
Mildred Long, prin.
Robinson PS, 1700 W MCHANEY DR 72315
Gene Henton, prin.
Other Schools – See Burdette

Booneville, Logan Co., Pop. Code 5
Booneville SD
Sch. Sys. Enr. Code 4
Supt. – Cyrus Underwood
690 N KENNEDY ST 72927
Hederick ES, 401 W 4TH ST 72927
Vernon Crawley, prin.

Bradford, White Co., Pop. Code 3
Bradford SD
Sch. Sys. Enr. Code 3
Supt. – Arthur Dunn, P O BOX B 72020
ES, P O BOX B 72020 – Rudolph Amann, prin.

Bradley, Lafayette Co., Pop. Code 3
Bradley SD
Sch. Sys. Enr. Code 3
Supt. – Travis Gore, P O BOX 308 71826
ES, P O BOX 308 71826 – John Black, prin.

Branch, Franklin Co., Pop. Code 2
County Line SD
Sch. Sys. Enr. Code 3
Supt. – Bryan Spillers, P O BOX 158 72928
County Line ES, P O BOX 158 72928
Kay Johnson, prin.

Briggsville, Yell Co., Pop. Code 2
Fourche Valley SD
Sch. Sys. Enr. Code 1
Supt. – Vernon Morrison
RURAL ROUTE 01 72853
Fourche Valley ES, P O BOX 60 72853
(—), prin.

Brinkley, Monroe Co., Pop. Code 5
Brinkley SD
Sch. Sys. Enr. Code 4
Supt. – Dewey Snowden, 800 S MAIN ST 72021
Partee ES, CARTER & LYNN ST 72021
Roenna Devore, prin.

Brookland, Craighead Co., Pop. Code 3
Brookland SD
Sch. Sys. Enr. Code 3
Supt. – Leon Christenberry, P O BOX 35 72417
ES, P O BOX 35 72417 – Geraline South, prin.

Bryant, Saline Co., Pop. Code 5
Bryant SD
Sch. Sys. Enr. Code 5
Supt. – Edward Love, 200 NW 4TH ST 72022
ES, 200 NW FOURTH ST 72022
William Spencer, prin.
Davis ES, 200 NW 4TH ST 72022
Diana Julian, prin.
Salem ES, 200 NW FOURTH ST 72022
Ricki Bailey, prin.

Burdette, Mississippi Co., Pop. Code 2
Blytheville SD
Supt. – See Blytheville
ES 72321 – John Davis, prin.

Cabot, Lonoke Co., Pop. Code 5
Cabot SD 4
Sch. Sys. Enr. Code 5
Supt. – Donald Turney, 504 E LOCUST ST 72023
JHS, 504 E LOCUST ST 72023
Brooks Nash, prin.
Eastside ES, 17 BELLAMY ST 72023
David Babb, prin.
Northside ES, 814 W LOCUST ST 72023
Mary Johnson, prin.
Southside ES, HIGHWAY 89 SOUTH 72023
Jim Lewis, prin.
Westside ES, 1701 S SECOND ST 72023
Randy Dorrough, prin.
Other Schools – See Ward

Caldwell, St. Francis Co., Pop. Code 2
Forrest City SD
Supt. – See Forrest City
ES, P O BOX 178 72322 – Rita Ferguson, prin.

Cale, Nevada Co., Pop. Code 2
Nevada SD 1
Sch. Sys. Enr. Code 3
Supt. – Barney Kyzar, P O BOX 101 71828
Other Schools – See Rosston

Calico Rock, Izard Co., Pop. Code 4
Calico Rock SD
Sch. Sys. Enr. Code 2
Supt. – F. Lee Mears, P O BOX 226 72519
ES, P O BOX 226 72519 – Patsy Henderson, prin.

Camden, Ouachita Co., Pop. Code 7
Camden SD
Sch. Sys. Enr. Code 4
Supt. – Jerry Daniel, P O BOX 578 71701
MS, 255 POPE AVE 71701 – Frank Adcock, prin.
Ivory PS, 575 JEFFERSON DR NW 71701
Mary Gibbs, prin.
Whiteside MS, 1201 MAUL ROAD 71701
Charles Marino, prin.

Fairview SD
Sch. Sys. Enr. Code 4
Supt. – George Branch
2708 MOUNT HOLLY ROAD 71701
Fairview MS, 2708 MOUNT HOLLY ROAD 71701
Bertha Kennedy, prin.
Fairview ES, 2708 MOUNT HOLLY ROAD 71701
Billy Green, prin.

Harmony Grove SD
Sch. Sys. Enr. Code 3
Supt. – Carlos Price
RURAL ROUTE 03 BOX 644 71701
Harmony Grove ES
RURAL ROUTE 03 BOX 644 71701
Terry Teutsch, prin.

Caraway, Craighead Co., Pop. Code 4
Riverside SD
Supt. – See Lake City
Riverside East ES, P O BOX 699 72419
Gerald Jennings, prin.

Carlisle, Lonoke Co., Pop. Code 5
Carlisle SD
Sch. Sys. Enr. Code 3
Supt. – Leon Miles, P O BOX O 72024
ES, P O BOX O 72024 – David Faucett, prin.

Carthage, Dallas Co., Pop. Code 3
Carthage SD
Sch. Sys. Enr. Code 2
Supt. – James Cash, P O BOX 16 71725
ES, P O BOX 16 71725 – Ethel Halton, prin.

Casa, Perry Co., Pop. Code 2
Perry-Casa SD
Sch. Sys. Enr. Code 2
Supt. – Joe Zarlingo, P O BOX B 72025
Perry-Casa ES, P O BOX B 72025
Nelson Adams, prin.

Cave City, Sharp Co., Pop. Code 4
Cave City SD
Sch. Sys. Enr. Code 3
Supt. – Billy Boyle, P O BOX 125 72521
ES, P O BOX 125 72521 – Larry Brown, prin.

Cedarville, Crawford Co., Pop. Code 4
Cedarville SD
Sch. Sys. Enr. Code 3
Supt. – Melvin Landers, P O BOX 97 72932
ES, P O BOX 97 72932 – John Borntrager, prin.

Center Ridge, Conway Co., Pop. Code 2
Nemo Vista SD
Sch. Sys. Enr. Code 2
Supt. – Thomas Flowers
RURAL ROUTE 01 BOX 8 72027
Nemo Vista ES, RURAL ROUTE 01 BOX 8 72027
Norma Hazel, prin.

Charleston, Franklin Co., Pop. Code 4
Charleston SD
Sch. Sys. Enr. Code 3
Supt. – Charles Harris, P O BOX 188 72933
ES, HIGHWAY 22 WEST 72933
Carl Underwood, prin.

Charlotte, Independence Co.
Cord-Charlotte SD
Sch. Sys. Enr. Code 2
Supt. – Jerrell Lillard, P O BOX 7 72522
Cord-Charlotte ES, P O BOX 7 72522
Ron Brooks, prin.

Cherry Valley, Cross Co., Pop. Code 3
Cross County SD
Sch. Sys. Enr. Code 3
Supt. – Harold Algee, P O BOX 158 72324
ES 72324 – James Martin, prin.
Other Schools – See Hickory Ridge, Vanndale

Clarendon, Monroe Co., Pop. Code 4
Clarendon SD
Sch. Sys. Enr. Code 3
Supt. – Lee Vent, P O BOX 248 72029
ES, P O BOX 248 72029 – Ervin Kulbeth, prin.

Clarksville, Johnson Co., Pop. Code 6
Clarksville SD
Sch. Sys. Enr. Code 4
Supt. – Dean Pitts, 1701 CLARK ROAD 72830
ES, 1903 CLARK ROAD 72830
Mike McNabb, prin.

Clinton, Van Buren Co., Pop. Code 4
Alread SD
Sch. Sys. Enr. Code 1
Supt. – James McGaha, RURAL ROUTE 03 72031
Alread ES, RURAL ROUTE 03 72031
Sue Simpson, prin.

Clinton SD
Sch. Sys. Enr. Code 3
Supt. – Homer Burnley
RURAL ROUTE 02 BOX 98 72031
MS, RURAL ROUTE 02 BOX 103-2 72031
Polly Johnson, prin.
Cowsert ES, RURAL ROUTE 02 BOX 103-1 72031
Jimmy Smith, prin.

Coal Hill, Johnson Co., Pop. Code 3
Westside SD
Sch. Sys. Enr. Code 3
Supt. – Jerry Smith, P O BOX 189 72832
Westside ES, P O BOX 127 72832
David Sosebee, prin.

College Station, Pulaski Co.
Pulaski Co Special SD
Supt. – See Little Rock
ES, P O BOX 428 72053 – Robert Evans, prin.

Concord, Cleburne Co., Pop. Code 2
Concord SD
Sch. Sys. Enr. Code 3
Supt. – Jerry Beggs, P O BOX 10 72523
ES, P O BOX 10 72523 – Howard Allen, prin.

Conway, Faulkner Co., Pop. Code 7
Conway SD
Sch. Sys. Enr. Code 5
Supt. – James Clark, PRINCE ST W 72032
Burns ES, 1201 DONAGHEY AVE 72032
 Robert Anthony, prin.
Cone ES, SOUTH BOULEVARD 72032
 Anne Irby, prin.
MS, 1001-23 DAVIS ST 72032
 Steve Fulmer, prin.
Mattison ES, HIGHWAY 286 EAST 72032
 Cecil Boothe, prin.
Moore ES, COUNTRY CLUB ROAD 72032
 Mary Wells, prin.
Smith ES, HARKRIDER ST 72032
 Tom Ratliff, prin.
Vann ES, HUBBARD ST AT SALEM ROAD 72032
 Janie Naylor, prin.

St. Joseph ES, 375 HARKRIDER ST 72032

Corning, Clay Co., Pop. Code 5
Corning SD
Sch. Sys. Enr. Code 4
Supt. – Jim Kimbrell, P O BOX 479 72422
Central MS, FOURTH ST 72422
 Jackie Crawford, prin.
Park ES, HARB ST 72422 – Terry Rapert, prin.

Cotter, Baxter Co., Pop. Code 3
Cotter SD
Sch. Sys. Enr. Code 3
Supt. – Jimmy Sutterfield, P O BOX 70 72626
Gist ES, P O BOX 70 72626
 Eric Richardson, prin.

Cotton Plant, Woodruff Co., Pop. Code 4
Cotton Plant SD
Sch. Sys. Enr. Code 2
Supt. – J. Babbs, P O BOX 40 72036
ES, RUTH ST 72036 – James Marsh, prin.

Cove, Polk Co., Pop. Code 2
Van Cove SD
Sch. Sys. Enr. Code 2
Supt. – Jerry Shinn, P O BOX 69 71937
Other Schools – See Vandervoort

Crawfordsville, Crittenden Co., Pop. Code 3
Crawfordsville SD
Sch. Sys. Enr. Code 3
Supt. – Don Bailey, P O BOX 47 72327
ES, P O BOX 47 72327 – Carlton Young, prin.

Crossett, Ashley Co., Pop. Code 6
Crossett SD
Sch. Sys. Enr. Code 5
Supt. – John Fincher, 301 W 9TH AVE 71635
Anderson ES, CAMP ROAD 71635
 Mary Bell, prin.
Daniel MS, 203 W 6TH ST 71635
 David Barnes, prin.
Hastings ES, 305 OAK ST 71635
 Janice Warren, prin.
North Crossett ES, BINNS LOOP 71635
 J. McCormick, prin.
Price ES, 1300 S MISSISSIPPI ST 71635
 Jim Knighton, prin.

Cushman, Independence Co., Pop. Code 3
Cushman SD
Sch. Sys. Enr. Code 2
Supt. – Gary Anderson, P O BOX 128 72526
Cushman ES, P O BOX 128 72526
 Oma Jean Brown, prin.

Danville, Yell Co., Pop. Code 4
Danville SD
Sch. Sys. Enr. Code 2
Supt. – David Craig, P O BOX 548 72833
Tucker ES, P O BOX 939 72833
 Melba Boyd, prin.

Dardanelle, Yell Co., Pop. Code 5
Dardanelle SD
Sch. Sys. Enr. Code 4
Supt. – B. Chandler, P O BOX Q 72834
MS, RURAL ROUTE 02 BOX 2 72834
 Diane Thomas, prin.
IS, 900 N 4TH 72834 – Roger Massey, prin.
PS, 900 N 5TH ST 72834 – Roger Massey, prin.

Decatur, Benton Co., Pop. Code 4
Decatur SD
Sch. Sys. Enr. Code 2
Supt. – Ray Watson, P O BOX 97 72722
ES, P O BOX 97 72722 – Linda Rogers, prin.

Deer, Newton Co., Pop. Code 1
Deer SD
Sch. Sys. Enr. Code 2
Supt. – J. McConnaughhay, P O BOX 56 72628
ES, P O BOX 56 72628 – Junior Edgmon, prin.

Delaplaine, Greene Co., Pop. Code 2
Delaplaine SD
Sch. Sys. Enr. Code 2
Supt. – Wm. Wilkinson, P O BOX 68 72425
ES, P O BOX 68 72425 – Phyllis Wilkinson, prin.

Delight, Pike Co., Pop. Code 2
Delight SD
Sch. Sys. Enr. Code 2
Supt. – Curtis Turner, P O BOX 8 71940
ES, P O BOX 8 71940 – Wallace Tarpley, prin.

Dell, Mississippi Co., Pop. Code 2
Gosnell SD
Supt. – See Gosnell
ES, P O BOX 236 72426 – Sandra Hughey, prin.

De Queen, Sevier Co., Pop. Code 5
De Queen SD
Sch. Sys. Enr. Code 4
Supt. – Billy Bob Blackwood
 812 W STILWELL AVE 71832
ES, ROUTE 04 71832 – Janice Duggan, prin.

Dermott, Chicot Co., Pop. Code 5
Dermott SD
Sch. Sys. Enr. Code 4
Supt. – Jimmy Jones, HIGHWAY 35 E 71638
ES, P O BOX 368 71638 – Bennie Adams, prin.
Dermott Upper MS, P O BOX 368 71638
 Archie Nimmer, prin.

Des Arc, Prairie Co., Pop. Code 4
Des Arc SD
Sch. Sys. Enr. Code 2
Supt. – Jim Galloway
 RURAL ROUTE 02 BOX A 72040
ES, RURAL ROUTE 02 BOX S 72040
 Mike Mertens, prin.

De Valls Bluff, Prairie Co., Pop. Code 3
De Valls Bluff SD
Sch. Sys. Enr. Code 2
Supt. – L. Gershner, P O BOX 298 72041
ES, P O BOX 298 72041 – Frank Allen, prin.

De Witt, Arkansas Co., Pop. Code 5
De Witt SD
Sch. Sys. Enr. Code 4
Supt. – Tom Cox, P O BOX 471 72042
MS, 301 N JACKSON ST 72042
 James Emerson, prin.
Southside ES, 601 S UNION ST 72042
 Robert Franks, prin.
Westside MS, 422 W 1ST ST 72042
 Marlyn Smith, prin.

Dierks, Howard Co., Pop. Code 4
Dierks SD
Sch. Sys. Enr. Code 3
Supt. – Wayne Freppon, P O BOX 124 71833
ES, P O BOX 70 71833 – Jo Ann Walters, prin.

Doddridge, Miller Co., Pop. Code 2
Bright Star SD
Sch. Sys. Enr. Code 2
Supt. – Leo Garrison
 RURAL ROUTE 01 BOX 222 71834
Bright Star ES, RURAL ROUTE 01 BOX 222 71834
 Elizabeth Stewart, prin.

Donaldson, Hot Spring Co., Pop. Code 2
Ouachita SD
Sch. Sys. Enr. Code 2
Supt. – James Sutherland
 RURAL ROUTE 01 BOX 12 71941
Ouachita ES, RURAL ROUTE 01 BOX 12 71941
 Betty Tidwell, prin.

Dover, Pope Co., Pop. Code 3
Dover SD
Sch. Sys. Enr. Code 3
Supt. – Danny Taylor, P O BOX 325 72837
ES, P O BOX 331 72837 – Earl Humphreys, prin.

Dumas, Desha Co., Pop. Code 6
Dumas SD
Sch. Sys. Enr. Code 4
Supt. – Don McHan, 701 MEADOW DR 71639
Central ES, 101 COURT ST 71639
 Mildred Sizemore, prin.
Reed MS, 710 S CHERRY ST 71639
 Gerald Shepherd, prin.

Dyess, Mississippi Co., Pop. Code 2
South Mississippi County SD
Supt. – See Wilson
ES 72330 – Albert Williams, prin.

Earle, Crittenden Co., Pop. Code 5
Earle SD
Sch. Sys. Enr. Code 4
Supt. – Bobby Clark, P O BOX 637 72331
MS, P O BOX 637 72331 – Levi Davis, prin.
ES, P O BOX 637 72331 – Johnny Neeley, prin.

Edmondson, Crittenden Co., Pop. Code 2
West Memphis SD
Supt. – See West Memphis
Wedlock ES, P O BOX 445 72332
 Vernard Davis, prin.

Elaine, Phillips Co., Pop. Code 3
Elaine SD
Sch. Sys. Enr. Code 3
Supt. – Kenneth Parker, P O BOX 179 72333
Wood ES, P O BOX 479 72333
 Izora Hilliard, prin.

El Dorado, Union Co., Pop. Code 8
El Dorado SD
Sch. Sys. Enr. Code 6
Supt. – Bob Watson, 700 COLUMBIA AVE 71730
Brown ES, DIXIE DR 71730 – F. Coy Henley, prin.
Goodwin ES, 201 E 5TH ST 71730
 Geneva Moss, prin.
Murmil Heights ES
 RIPLEY & CHEROKEE STS 71730
 Dorothy Shirey, prin.
Northwest ES, 1600 N COLLEGE AVE 71730
 Eugene Johnson,Jr., prin.
Southside ES, S JACKSON ST 71730
 Glynn Calahan, prin.
Watson MS, 1400 E CENTER ST 71730
 Dennis Tucker, prin.
West Woods ES, N BRADFORD ST 71730
 Jene Dumas, prin.
Yocum ES, S COLLEGE ST 71730
 June Smith, prin.

Parkers Chapel SD
Sch. Sys. Enr. Code 2
Supt. – John Gross
 401 PARKERS CHAPEL ROAD 71730
Parkers Chapel ES
 401 PARKERS CHAPEL ROAD 71730
 Jeanne Ford, prin.

Union SD
Sch. Sys. Enr. Code 2
Supt. – James Jones
 RURAL ROUTE 03 BOX 121 71730
Union ES, RURAL ROUTE 03 BOX 121 71730
 Marcelle Gulledge, prin.

Holy Redeemer Catholic ES
 1103 W CEDAR ST 71730

Elkins, Washington Co., Pop. Code 3
Elkins SD
Sch. Sys. Enr. Code 3
Supt. – Donald Lee, P O BOX 322 72727
ES, P O BOX 322 72727 – Edgar Warren,Jr., prin.

Emerson, Columbia Co., Pop. Code 2
Emerson SD
Sch. Sys. Enr. Code 2
Supt. – Arthur Pharr, P O BOX 128 71740
ES, P O BOX 129 71740 – Bobbie Stevens, prin.

Emmet, Neveda Co., Pop. Code 2
Emmet SD
Sch. Sys. Enr. Code 2
Supt. – Gene Ross, P O BOX 334 71835
ES, P O BOX 334 71835 – Merle Sanford, prin.

England, Lonoke Co., Pop. Code 5
England SD
Sch. Sys. Enr. Code 4
Supt. – Carroll King, P O BOX 10 72046
ES, P O BOX 10 72046 – Mary Wyatt, prin.

Enola, Faulkner Co., Pop. Code 2
Enola SD
Sch. Sys. Enr. Code 2
Supt. – Jim Chism, P O BOX 99 72047
ES, P O BOX 99 72047 – Ed Bradshaw, prin.

Eudora, Chicot Co., Pop. Code 5
Eudora SD
Sch. Sys. Enr. Code 3
Supt. – Frank Grimes, 111 N ARCHER ST 71640
Johns ES, 111 N ARCHER ST 71640
 Johnette Walker, prin.

Eureka Springs, Carroll Co., Pop. Code 4
Eureka Springs SD
Sch. Sys. Enr. Code 3
Supt. – Billy Don Meggenberg
 44 KINGS HIGHWAY 72632
ES 72632 – Gerald Plank, prin.

Evening Shade, Sharp Co., Pop. Code 2
Evening Shade SD
Sch. Sys. Enr. Code 2
Supt. – John Walker, P O BOX 68 72532
ES, P O BOX 68 72532 – Lorraine Belote, prin.

Everton, Marion Co., Pop. Code 2
Marion County SD
Sch. Sys. Enr. Code 2
Supt. – Tom Stokes, P O BOX 45 72633
Bruno-Pyatt ES, RURAL ROUTE 01 BOX 45 72633
 Jerry Bridges, prin.

Farmington, Washington Co., Pop. Code 4
Farmington SD
Sch. Sys. Enr. Code 3
Supt. – Randall Lynch, P O BOX 120 72730
Ledbetter ES, P O BOX 120 72730
 Joseph Kisner, prin.

Fayetteville, Washington Co., Pop. Code 8
Fayetteville SD
Sch. Sys. Enr. Code 6
Supt. – Winston Simpson, P O BOX 849 72702
Asbell ES, 1500 N SANS AVE 72701
 James Paul, prin.
Bates ES, 601 S BUCHANAN AVE 72701
 Art Hanna, prin.
Butterfield Trail ES
 3050 OLD MISSOURI ROAD 72701
 Bert Stark, prin.
Happy Hollow ES, ROUTE 10 RAY ST 72701
 Gerald Harriman, prin.
Jefferson ES, 612 S COLLEGE AVE 72701
 John Colbert, prin.

Leverett ES, 1124 W CLEVELAND ST 72701
  Sandra Wiebe, prin.
Root ES, 1529 MISSION BLVD 72701
  Oma Blackwell, prin.
Washington ES, 425 N HIGHLAND AVE 72701
  Kathleen Meistrell, prin.

St. Joseph ES, 313 E LAFAYETTE ST 72701

Fifty-Six, Stone Co., Pop. Code 2
Tri-County Consolidated SD
Supt. – See Big Flat
Tri-County ES, P O BOX 1 72560
  John Jarboe, prin.

Flippin, Marion Co., Pop. Code 4
Flippin SD
Sch. Sys. Enr. Code 3
Supt. – George Lewis, P O BOX 256 72634
ES, P O BOX 239 72634 – Curtis Bryant, prin.

Floral, Independence Co.
Midland SD
Supt. – See Pleasant Plains
Midland ES, P O BOX 119 72534
  Glynn Sharp, prin.

Fordyce, Dallas Co., Pop. Code 6
Fordyce SD
Sch. Sys. Enr. Code 4
Supt. – Jerry Bush, 1800 W COLLEGE ST 71742
MS, W COLLEGE ST 71742 – Leon Hays, prin.
Patterson ES, W COLLEGE ST 71742
  Richard Nickels, prin.
Wallace MS, EDEN ST 71742 – Vada Adams, prin.

Foreman, Little River Co., Pop. Code 4
Foreman SD
Sch. Sys. Enr. Code 3
Supt. – Stewart Scoggins, P O BOX 280 71836
ES, P O BOX 280 71836 – Elaine Cowling, prin.

Forrest City, St. Francis Co., Pop. Code 7
Forrest City SD
Sch. Sys. Enr. Code 6
Supt. – James Laws, 334 GRAHAM ST 72335
MS, 1133 N DIVISION ST 72335
  Clarence Chambers, prin.
Evans ES, RURAL ROUTE 02 BOX 46 72335
  Issac Wilburn, prin.
Forrest City PS Central, 845 N ROSSER ST 72335
  Virginia Gattinger, prin.
Lincoln Fifth MS, 149 N WATER ST 72335
  Bettye Jones, prin.
Lincoln Sixth MS, 149 N WATER ST 72335
  Mary Ann Parker, prin.
Stewart ES, 625 IRVING ST 72335
  Tempie Moorehead, prin.
Other Schools – See Caldwell, Madison

Fort Smith, Sebastian Co., Pop. Code 8
Ft. Smith SD
Sch. Sys. Enr. Code 7
Supt. – Benny Gooden, P O BOX 1384 72902
Ballman ES, 2601 S Q ST 72901
  Margherita Morgan, prin.
Barling ES, 1400 S D ST 72923
  Rex Cochran, prin.
Beard ES, 1600 CAVANAUGH ROAD 72903
  David Rathbun, prin.
Belle Point ES, 1501 DODSON AVE 72901
  Joann Molett, prin.
Bonneville ES, 2500 S WALDRON ROAD 72903
  Van Howell, prin.
Carnall ES, 2524 S TULSA ST 72901
  Brenda Sellers, prin.
Cavanaugh ES, 1025 SCHOOL ST 72903
  David Rathbun, prin.
Cook ES, 3517 BROOKEN HILL ROAD 72903
  Billy Spicer, prin.
Euper Lane ES, 6601 EUPER LANE 72903
  Darline McNeil, prin.
Fairview ES, 2400 S DALLAS ST 72901
  Ralph Williams, prin.
Howard ES, 1301 N 8TH ST 72901
  Yvonne Keaton, prin.
Morrison ES, 3515 NEWLON ROAD 72904
  Donald Weaver, prin.
Orr ES, 3609 S PHOENIX ST 72903
  Marvin Aaron, prin.
Parker ES, 811 N T ST 72904
  Berthena Nunn, prin.
Pike ES, 4111 PARK AVE 72903
  Barbara Kell, prin.
Spradling ES, 4949 SPRADLING AVE 72904
  Gay Presley, prin.
Sunnymede ES, 4201 N O ST 72904
  Jane Wiswall, prin.
Sutton ES, 5001 KELLEY HWY 72904
  Linda Riley, prin.
Tilles ES, 815 N 16TH ST 72901 – Eddy Hill, prin.
Trusty ES, 3300 HARRIS AVE 72904
  Lynn Ellison, prin.
Woods ES, 3201 S MASSARD ROAD 72903
  William Freeman, prin.

Ft. Smith Christian School
  4201 WINDSOR DRIVE 72914
Christ the King ES
  1920 S GREENWOOD AVE 72901
First Lutheran School
  2407 S MASSARD ROAD 72903
Immaculate Conception ES
  SOUTH 14TH & B STS 72901
Metro Christian ES, P O BOX 4127 72914
St. Boniface ES, 201 N 19TH ST 72901

St. Scholastica Montessori ES
  P O BOX 3489 72913

Fouke, Miller Co., Pop. Code 3
Fouke SD
Sch. Sys. Enr. Code 3
Supt. – Lynn Nix, P O BOX 20 71837
ES, P O BOX 20 71837 – J. Belin, prin.

Fountain Hill, Ashley Co., Pop. Code 2
Fountain Hill SD
Sch. Sys. Enr. Code 2
Supt. – Joseph Lindsey, P O BOX 147 71642
ES, P O BOX 147 71642 – Marilyn Carpenter, prin.

Garfield, Benton Co., Pop. Code 2
Rogers SD
Supt. – See Rogers
ES 72732 – Jennie Brooks, prin.

Garland City, Miller Co., Pop. Code 3
Garland SD
Sch. Sys. Enr. Code 2
Supt. – Kenneth Allbritton, P O BOX 220 71839
ES, P O BOX 220 71839 – Martha Baker, prin.

Gentry, Benton Co., Pop. Code 4
Gentry SD
Sch. Sys. Enr. Code 3
Supt. – Buddy Auman, P O BOX 159 72734
MS, P O BOX 159 72734 – Nick Tschepikow, prin.
ES, P O BOX 159 72734 – Patsy Hastings, prin.

Gillett, Arkansas Co., Pop. Code 3
Gillett SD
Sch. Sys. Enr. Code 2
Supt. – Tom Wilson, P O BOX 98 72055
ES, P O BOX 98 72055 – Vicki Reed, prin.

Glenwood, Pike Co., Pop. Code 4
Glenwood SD
Sch. Sys. Enr. Code 2
Supt. – Bill Livingston, P O BOX 27 71943
ES, P O BOX 27 71943 – Gail Parker, prin.

Gosnell, Mississippi Co., Pop. Code 5
Gosnell SD
Sch. Sys. Enr. Code 4
Supt. – Lynn Cox, 600 HIGHWAY 181 72315
ES, 600 HIGHWAY 181 72315
  Sandra Hughey, prin.
Other Schools – See Dell

Gould, Lincoln Co., Pop. Code 4
Gould SD
Sch. Sys. Enr. Code 2
Supt. – Melvin Brown, P O BOX S 71643
ES, P O BOX S 71643 – Betty Brewer, prin.

Grady, Lincoln Co., Pop. Code 2
Grady SD
Sch. Sys. Enr. Code 2
Supt. – Abel White, P O BOX 238 71644
ES, P O BOX 238 71644 – Vaughn McGaha, prin.

Grapevine, Grant Co.
Sheridan SD
Supt. – See Sheridan
ES 72057 – Bobby Daniel, prin.

Gravette, Benton Co., Pop. Code 4
Gravette SD
Sch. Sys. Enr. Code 3
Supt. – Paul Human, P O BOX J 72736
MS, P O BOX 480 72736 – Doug Albertson, prin.
Duffy ES, P O BOX 480 72736
  Bob Williamson, prin.

Greenbrier, Faulkner Co., Pop. Code 4
Greenbrier SD
Sch. Sys. Enr. Code 4
Supt. – Dean Mallett, P O BOX 68 72058
MS, P O BOX 68 72058 – Hoyt Rowden, prin.
ES, P O BOX 68 72058 – Rick Whitley, prin.

Green Forest, Carroll Co., Pop. Code 4
Green Forest SD
Sch. Sys. Enr. Code 3
Supt. – James Johnston, P O BOX AO 72638
ES, P O BOX AO 72638 – Lyle Sparkman, prin.

Greenland, Washington Co., Pop. Code 3
Greenland SD
Sch. Sys. Enr. Code 3
Supt. – Wesley Cannon, P O BOX 57 72737
ES, P O BOX 57 72737 – Joette Folsom, prin.

Greenway, Clay Co., Pop. Code 2
Clay County Central SD
Supt. – See Rector
Clay County North MS, P O BOX 367 72430
  Kelly Scobey, prin.

Greenwood, Sebastian Co., Pop. Code 5
Greenwood SD
Sch. Sys. Enr. Code 4
Supt. – Bob Evans, P O BOX 460 72936
Wells MS, 700 RAYMOND WELLS DR 72936
  Larry Bridges, prin.
ES, P O BOX 640 72936 – Robert Turner, prin.

Greers Ferry, Cleburne Co., Pop. Code 3
West Side Greers Ferry SD
Sch. Sys. Enr. Code 2
Supt. – Gay Horton
  RURAL ROUTE 03 BOX 10 72067
West Side ES, RURAL ROUTE 03 72067
  Boyce Watkins, prin.

Griffithville, White Co., Pop. Code 2
Griffithville SD
Sch. Sys. Enr. Code 2
Supt. – Leon McClure, P O BOX 45 72060
ES, P O BOX 45 72060 – William Leach, prin.

Grubbs, Jackson Co., Pop. Code 3
Grubbs SD
Sch. Sys. Enr. Code 3
Supt. – William Lackey, P O BOX 78 72431
ES, P O BOX 78 72431 – Randy Ham, prin.

Gurdon, Clark Co., Pop. Code 5
Gurdon SD
Sch. Sys. Enr. Code 3
Supt. – Bob Thompson, 314 SCHOOL ST 71743
MS, 504 S FIFTH ST 71743
  Gaines Thompson, prin.
PS, TENTH AND PINE ST 71743
  Jo Anne Shaver, prin.

Guy, Faulkner Co., Pop. Code 2
Guy-Perkins SD
Sch. Sys. Enr. Code 2
Supt. – Mark Willborg, P O BOX 96 72061
Guy-Perkins ES, P O BOX 96 72061
  Refus Caldwell, prin.

Hackett, Sebastian Co., Pop. Code 3
Hackett SD
Sch. Sys. Enr. Code 3
Supt. – Donal Webb, P O BOX 188 72937
ES, P O BOX 188 72937 – Tom Carson, prin.

Hamburg, Ashley Co., Pop. Code 5
Hamburg SD
Sch. Sys. Enr. Code 4
Supt. – Charles Allen, 503 E LINCOLN AVE 71646
Hamburg Lower ES, EAST BAKER ST 71646
  John Dillard, prin.
Hamburg Upper MS, BARTLETT ST 71646
  Jerry Janes, prin.
Other Schools – See Portland, Wilmot

Hampton, Calhoun Co., Pop. Code 4
Hampton SD
Sch. Sys. Enr. Code 3
Supt. – Darrell Donaldson, P O BOX 628 71744
ES, P O BOX 628 71744 – Don McKinnie, prin.

Hardy, Sharp Co., Pop. Code 3
Highland SD
Sch. Sys. Enr. Code 4
Supt. – Jack Kimbrell, P O BOX 419 72542
Cherokee ES, P O BOX 419 72542
  Clayta Ballard, prin.
Highland MS, P O BOX 419 72542
  Danny Lusk, prin.

Harrisburg, Poinsett Co., Pop. Code 4
Harrisburg SD
Sch. Sys. Enr. Code 4
Supt. – Rick Saunders, P O BOX 47 72432
MS, P O BOX 47 72432 – Ronald Bishop, prin.
ES, P O BOX 47 72432 – Mary Brooks, prin.

Harrison, Boone Co., Pop. Code 6
Harrison SD
Sch. Sys. Enr. Code 5
Supt. – Charles Adair
  400 S SYCAMORE ST 72601
Central MS, 110 S CHERRY 72601
  Mary Purseley, prin.
Eagle Heights ES, 500 N CHESTNUT ST 72601
  Mary Wilson, prin.
Forest Heights ES, 1124 S TAMARIND ST 72601
  Rex DePriest, prin.
Skyline Heights ES, 1120 W HOLT AVE 72601
  Faye Tilley, prin.
Woodland Heights ES, 520 E WOMACK ST 72601
  Viki White, prin.

Hartford, Sebastian Co., Pop. Code 3
Hartford SD
Sch. Sys. Enr. Code 2
Supt. – Robert Lafevers, P O BOX 128 72938
ES, P O BOX 489 72938 – Bertha Bills, prin.

Hatfield, Polk Co., Pop. Code 2
Hatfield SD
Sch. Sys. Enr. Code 2
Supt. – Thomas McCormick, P O BOX 130 71945
ES, P O BOX 130 71945 – Sharon Rowland, prin.

Hattieville, Conway Co., Pop. Code 2
Wonderview SD
Sch. Sys. Enr. Code 2
Supt. – Ron Wilson
  RURAL ROUTE 01 BOX 219 72063
Wonderview ES
  RURAL ROUTE 01 BOX 219 72063
  Dean Roach, prin.

Havana, Yell Co., Pop. Code 2
Western Yell County SD
Sch. Sys. Enr. Code 2
Supt. – Robert Smalley, P O BOX 214 72842
Other Schools – See Belleville

Hazen, Prairie Co., Pop. Code 4
Hazen SD
Sch. Sys. Enr. Code 3
Supt. – Forrest Kyle, P O BOX 358 72064
ES, P O BOX 358 72064 – Larry Anthony, prin.

Heber Springs, Cleburne Co., Pop. Code 5
Heber Springs SD
Sch. Sys. Enr. Code 4
Supt. – Richard Reavis, 800 W MOORE ST 72543

MS, 800 W MOORE ST 72543
   Stanley Wildman, prin.
ES, 800 W MOORE ST 72543 – John Mueller, prin.

Hector, Pope Co., Pop. Code 2
Hector SD
Sch. Sys. Enr. Code 3
Supt. – Tommy Tyler
   RURAL ROUTE 01 BOX 24 72843
ES, RURAL ROUTE 01 BOX 24 72843
   Roy Pearson, prin.

Helena, Phillips Co., Pop. Code 6
Helena SD
Sch. Sys. Enr. Code 5
Supt. – Tom Cheney, P O BOX 369 72342
Helena Crossing ES
   RURAL ROUTE 01 BOX 368 72342
   Betty Medford, prin.
Jefferson ES, COLUMBIA ST 72342
   Patricia Dean, prin.
Wahl MS, HICKORY HILL DR 72342
   Roy Bridges, prin.
Other Schools – See West Helena

Lakeview SD
Sch. Sys. Enr. Code 2
Supt. – Leon Phillips, RURAL ROUTE 01 72342
Lakeview ES, RURAL ROUTE 01 72342
   Barbara Davis, prin.

Hermitage, Bradley Co., Pop. Code 2
Hermitage SD
Sch. Sys. Enr. Code 3
Supt. – Carroll Morgan, P O BOX 38 71647
ES, P O BOX 38 71647 – Richard Rankin, prin.

Hickory Ridge, Cross Co., Pop. Code 2
Cross County SD
Supt. – See Cherry Valley
ES 72347 – Peggy Burnett, prin.

Holly Grove, Monroe Co., Pop. Code 3
Holly Grove SD
Sch. Sys. Enr. Code 2
Supt. – Wm. Dowell, P O BOX G 72069
ES, P O BOX AA 72069 – Pamela Scales, prin.

Hope, Hempstead Co., Pop. Code 7
Hope SD
Sch. Sys. Enr. Code 5
Supt. – Dale Franks, 117 E 2ND ST 71801
Yerger MS, 500 E NINTH STREET 71801
   Jack Brown, prin.
Brown ES, 500 SOUTH SPRUCE ST 71801
   Wendel McCorkle, prin.
Garland ES, WEST SIXTH ST 71801
   Steve Bradshaw, prin.
Henry ES, SOUTH MAIN ST 71801
   Billie Whitmarsh, prin.

Spring Hill SD
Sch. Sys. Enr. Code 2
Supt. – Robert Morgan
   RURAL ROUTE 01 BOX 834 71801
Spring Hill ES
   RURAL ROUTE 01 BOX 834 71801
   James Martin, prin.

Horatio, Sevier Co., Pop. Code 3
Horatio SD
Sch. Sys. Enr. Code 2
Supt. – Pat Adcock, P O BOX 435 71842
ES, P O BOX 435 71842 – Tricia Hays, prin.

Hot Springs, Garland Co., Pop. Code 8
Cutter-Morning Star SD
Sch. Sys. Enr. Code 3
Supt. – Alton Gaston
   RURAL ROUTE 02 BOX 315 71901
Cutter-Morning Star ES, 2901 SPRING ST 71901
   Don Roberts, prin.

Fountain Lake SD
Sch. Sys. Enr. Code 3
Supt. – Irvin Bass
   RURAL ROUTE 07 BOX 220 71901
Fountain Lake ES
   RURAL ROUTE 07 BOX 220 71901
   Charles Clark, prin.

Hot Springs SD
Sch. Sys. Enr. Code 5
Supt. – Maurice Dunn, 140 E BORDER ST 71901
Gardner ES, 525 GARDNER LANE 71913
   J. Burroughs, prin.
Greenwood MS, 1625 GREENWOOD ST 71913
   J Burroughs, prin.
MS, OAK & ORANGE STS 71901
   Charles Butler, prin.
Jones MS, HOBSON AVE 71913
   Gary Burroughs, prin.
Langston ES, 120 CHESTNUT ST 71901
   Alyce Robinson, prin.
Oaklawn ES, 301 OAKLAWN BLVD 71913
   George Robinson, prin.
Park ES, 220 GLEN ST 71901
   Mozella Rosbourough, prin.

Lakeside SD
Sch. Sys. Enr. Code 4
Supt. – Steve Floyd
   4429 MALVERN ROAD 71901
Lakeside IS, 4421 MALVERN RD 71901
   LaDell Doss, prin.
Lakeside PS, 4419 MALVERN ROAD 71901
   Jim Bledsoe, prin.

St. Johns ES, 583 W GRAND AVE 71901
St. Michael's ES, 1125 MALVERN AVE 71901

Hoxie, Lawrence Co., Pop. Code 5
Hoxie SD
Sch. Sys. Enr. Code 3
Supt. – David Cook, P O BOX 40 72433
ES, P O BOX 40 72433 – Jane Barnhill, prin.

Hughes, St. Francis Co., Pop. Code 4
Hughes SD
Sch. Sys. Enr. Code 4
Supt. – Nelson Wall, P O BOX 9 72348
ES, P O BOX 9 72348 – Michael Haynie, prin.

Humnoke, Lonoke Co., Pop. Code 2
Humnoke SD
Sch. Sys. Enr. Code 2
Supt. – Paula Henderson, P O BOX 47 72072
ES, P O BOX 47 72072 – Paula Henderson, prin.

Humphrey, Jefferson Co., Pop. Code 3
Humphrey SD
Sch. Sys. Enr. Code 2
Supt. – Robert Davis, P O BOX 190 72073
ES, P O BOX 190 72073 – Monica Bausom, prin.

Huntsville, Madison Co., Pop. Code 4
Huntsville SD
Sch. Sys. Enr. Code 4
Supt. – Chester Woodruff, P O BOX F 72740
MS, P O BOX G 72740 – David Fox, prin.
Watson ES, P O BOX H 72740
   Dana Samples, prin.

Huttig, Union Co., Pop. Code 3
Huttig SD
Sch. Sys. Enr. Code 2
Supt. – Bob Mathis, P O BOX 407 71747
ES, HIGHWAY 129 BOX 407 71747
   Frankie Futch, prin.

Imboden, Lawrence Co., Pop. Code 3
Sloan-Hendrix SD
Sch. Sys. Enr. Code 3
Supt. – L. Davis, P O BOX 188 72434
Sloan-Hendrix ES, P O BOX 188 72434
   Ann Burrow, prin.

Jacksonville, Pulaski Co., Pop. Code 8
Pulaski Co Special SD
Supt. – See Little Rock
Adkins ES, 500 CLOVERDALE ROAD 72076
   Melvin Goodrum, prin.
Arnold Drive ES, 798 ARNOLD DRIVE 72076
   Toney Abbott, prin.
Bayou Meto ES
   RURAL ROUTE 02 BOX 200 72076
   George Petry, prin.
DuPree ES, GREGORY ST 72076 – Jo Husson, prin.
ES, 108 S OAK ST 72076 – Doug Ask, prin.
Pinewood ES, 1919 NORTHEASTERN AVE 72076
   Diane Vogler, prin.
Taylor ES, RURAL ROUTE 01 BOX 43-A 72076
   Truett McCurry, prin.
Tolleson ES, 601 HARRIS ROAD 72076
   Wanda Williams, prin.

Jasper, Newton Co., Pop. Code 3
Jasper SD
Sch. Sys. Enr. Code 2
Supt. – Lindsey Parks, P O BOX 446 72641
ES, P O BOX 446 72641 – William Clayborn, prin.

Jessieville, Garland Co., Pop. Code 5
Jessieville SD
Sch. Sys. Enr. Code 3
Supt. – Gene Glazener, P O BOX 4 71949
ES, P O BOX 4 71949 – George Foshee, prin.

Joiner, Mississippi Co., Pop. Code 3
South Mississippi County SD
Supt. – See Wilson
Shawnee ES, RURAL ROUTE 01 BOX 177 72350
   Albert Williams, prin.

Jonesboro, Craighead Co., Pop. Code 8
Jonesboro SD
Sch. Sys. Enr. Code 5
Supt. – Bill Beasley
   1300 E MATTHEWS AVE 72401
East ES, 1218 COBB ST 72401
   Wilbur Green, prin.
Hillcrest ES, HILLCREST DRIVE 72401
   Leon Lee, prin.
North ES, 613 N FISHER 72401
   Jackie McBride, prin.
South ES, 1001 ROSEMOND ST 72401
   Rose Marie Barrett, prin.
West ES, 1110 W WASHINGTON AVE 72401
   Reams Walls, prin.

Nettleton SD
Sch. Sys. Enr. Code 4
Supt. – Danny Slay, 4201 RACE ST 72401
Nettleton MS, 3801 VERA ST 72401
   Clarence Higgins, Jr., prin.
Nettleton ES, 4207 RACE ST 72401
   Al Fisher, prin.
University Heights ES
   RURAL ROUTE 10 BOX 23 72401
   Kay Darby, prin.

Valley View SD
Sch. Sys. Enr. Code 3
Supt. – Radius Baker, RURAL ROUTE 06 72401

Valley View ES
   RURAL ROUTE 09 BOX 208 72401
   Jimmy Wilson, prin.

Westside SD
Sch. Sys. Enr. Code 4
Supt. – Grover Cooper
   RURAL ROUTE 04 BOX 104 72401
Westside ES, RURAL ROUTE 04 BOX 105 72401
   Alice Baugh, prin.
Westside MS, RURAL ROUTE 04 BOX 105 72401
   Joe Morrow, prin.

Blessed Sacrament ES, 720 S CHURCH ST 72401

Judsonia, White Co., Pop. Code 4
Central SD
Sch. Sys. Enr. Code 2
Supt. – Stanley Gibson
   RURAL ROUTE 01 BOX 382 72081
Central ES, RURAL ROUTE 01 BOX 383 72081
   Curtis Anderson, prin.

Judsonia SD
Sch. Sys. Enr. Code 3
Supt. – Eddie Wood
   RURAL ROUTE 02 BOX 206 72081
ES, RURAL ROUTE 02 BOX 206 72081
   Michael Lincoln, prin.

Junction City, Union Co., Pop. Code 3
Junction City SD
Sch. Sys. Enr. Code 3
Supt. – Paul Muse, P O BOX H 71749
ES, P O BOX H 71749 – Wayne Barrett, prin.

Keiser, Mississippi Co., Pop. Code 3
South Mississippi County SD
Supt. – See Wilson
ES 72351 – Ronald Martin, prin.

Kensett, White Co., Pop. Code 4
Kensett SD
Sch. Sys. Enr. Code 2
Supt. – Tony Wood, P O BOX 419 72082
ES, P O BOX 419 72082 – Pat Bashaw, prin.

Kingsland, Cleveland Co., Pop. Code 2
Kingsland SD
Sch. Sys. Enr. Code 2
Supt. – Gene Franklin, P O BOX 126 71652
ES, P O BOX 126 71652 – Frankie Hall, prin.

Kingston, Madison Co., Pop. Code 2
Kingston SD
Sch. Sys. Enr. Code 2
Supt. – S. Steele, P O BOX 149 72742
ES, P O BOX 149 72742 – Johnny Hunter, prin.

Kirby, Pike Co., Pop. Code 2
Kirby SD
Sch. Sys. Enr. Code 2
Supt. – Donnie Davis, P O BOX 8 71950
ES, P O BOX 9 71950 – Joyce Smith, prin.

Lake City, Craighead Co., Pop. Code 4
Riverside SD
Sch. Sys. Enr. Code 2
Supt. – Charles Owens, P O BOX 178 72437
Riverside West ES, P O BOX 178 72437
   Gerald Jennings, prin.
Other Schools – See Caraway

Lake Village, Chicot Co., Pop. Code 5
Lakeside SD
Sch. Sys. Enr. Code 4
Supt. – Dale Diemer
   600 S LAKESHORE DRIVE 71653
Central MS, 600 S LAKESHORE DRIVE 71653
   Edward Briggs, prin.
Central ES, 600 S LAKESHORE DR 71653
   Jeanette Buckner, prin.

St. Mary School, 204 LAKE SHORE DR 71653

Lamar, Johnson Co., Pop. Code 3
Lamar SD
Sch. Sys. Enr. Code 4
Supt. – W. Langrell, P O BOX 208 72846
ES, P O BOX 208 72846 – Larry Bacchus, prin.

Lavaca, Sebastian Co., Pop. Code 4
Lavaca SD
Sch. Sys. Enr. Code 3
Supt. – Carl Steward, P O BOX 8 72941
ES, P O BOX 8 72941 – Warren Shade, prin.

Leachville, Mississippi Co., Pop. Code 4
Buffalo Island Central SD
Supt. – See Monette
Buffalo Island Central East ES, P O BOX 110 72438
   Joe Jones, prin.

Lead Hill, Boone Co., Pop. Code 2
Lead Hill SD
Sch. Sys. Enr. Code 2
Supt. – William Ernst, P O BOX A 72644
ES, P O BOX A 72644 – Mary Hopkin, prin.

Lepanto, Poinsett Co., Pop. Code 4
East Poinsett County SD
Sch. Sys. Enr. Code 3
Supt. – William Craig, P O BOX 4760 72354
East Poinsett County ES, P O BOX 4760 72354
   Joyce Lamb, prin.
Other Schools – See Tyronza

Leslie, Searcy Co., Pop. Code 3
Leslie SD
Sch. Sys. Enr. Code 2
Supt. – Ed Bradberry, P O BOX 160   72645
ES   72645 – David Campbell, prin.

Lewisville, Lafayette Co., Pop. Code 4
Lewisville SD
Sch. Sys. Enr. Code 3
Supt. – Larry Hudson, P O BOX 400   71845
ES, P O BOX 550   71845 – Loretta Corbin, prin.

Lexa, Phillips Co., Pop. Code 2
Barton-Lexa SD
Sch. Sys. Enr. Code 3
Supt. – Roy Kirkland
   RURAL ROUTE 02 BOX 200   72355
Barton ES, RURAL ROUTE 02 BOX 200   72355
   Clifton Harrington, prin.

Lincoln, Washington Co., Pop. Code 4
Lincoln SD
Sch. Sys. Enr. Code 4
Supt. – Loyd Jones, P O BOX 479   72744
MS, P O BOX 479   72744 – James Gregory, prin.
ES, P O BOX 479   72744 – W. Vafakos, prin.

Little Rock, Pulaski Co., Pop. Code 9
Little Rock SD
Sch. Sys. Enr. Code 7
Supt. – George Cannon
   810 W MARKHAM ST   72201
Badgett ES, 6900 PECAN LANE   72206
   Mary Golston, prin.
Bale ES, 6501 W 32ND ST   72204
   Levanna Wilson, prin.
Baseline ES, 3623 BASELINE ROAD   72209
   Robert Brown, prin.
Booker Magnet ES, 2016 BARBER ST   72206
   William Finn, prin.
Brady ES, 7915 W MARKHAM ST   72205
   Karen Buchanan, prin.
Carver ES, 800 APPERSON ST   72202
   Bob Goodwin, prin.
Cloverdale ES, 6500 HINKSON ROAD   72209
   Jacqualine Dedman, prin.
Dodd ES, 6423 STAGECOACH ROAD   72204
   Mary Cheatham, prin.
Fair Park ES, 616 N HARRISON ST   72205
   Catherine Gill, prin.
Forest Park ES, 1600 N TYLER ST   72207
   Virginia Ashley, prin.
Franklin ES, 1701 S HARRISON ST   72204
   Connie Aston, prin.
Fulbright ES, 300 PLEASANT VALLEY DR   72212
   Mac Huffman, prin.
Garland ES, 3615 W 25TH ST   72204
   Cheryl Simmons, prin.
Geyer Springs ES, 5240 MABELVALE PIKE   72209
   Eleanor Cox, prin.
Gibbs ES, 1115 W 16TH ST   72202
   Donna Davis, prin.
Ish ES, 3001 S PULASKI ST   72206
   Lonnie Dean, prin.
Jefferson ES, 2600 N MCKINLEY ST   72207
   Margaret Gremillion, prin.
McDermott ES, 1200 RESERVOIR ROAD   72207
   Michael Oliver, prin.
Meadowcliff ES, 25 SHERATON DR   72209
   Jerry Worm, prin.
Mitchell ES, 2410 S BATTERY ST   72206
   Donita Hudspeth, prin.
Otter Creek ES
   16000 OTTER CREEK PARKWAY   72209
   Pat Price, prin.
Pulaski Heights ES, 319 N PINE ST   72205
   Eddie McCoy, prin.
Rightsell ES, 911 W 19TH ST   72206
   Kay Loss, prin.
Rockefeller ES, 700 E 17TH STREET   72206
   Anne Mangan, prin.
Romine ES, 3400 ROMINE ROAD   72204
   Lionel Ward, prin.
Stephens ES, 3700 W 18TH ST   72204
   Stan Strauss, prin.
Terry ES, 10800 MARA LYNN ROAD   72211
   Nancy Volsen, prin.
Wakefield ES, 75 WESTMINSTER DR   72209
   Lloyd Black, prin.
Washington IS, 1800 E 6TH ST   72202
   Lonnie Dean, prin.
Watson ES, 7000 VALLEY DR   72209
   Diana Glaze, prin.
Western Hills ES
   4901 WESTERN HILLS AVE   72204
   Margie Puckett, prin.
Williams Magnet ES, 7301 EVERGREEN DR   72207
   Ed Jackson, prin.
Wilson ES, 4015 STANNUS ST   72204
   Reine Price, prin.
Woodruff ES, 3010 W 7TH ST   72205
   Pat Higginbotham, prin.
Other Schools – See Mabelvale

Pulaski Co Special SD
Sch. Sys. Enr. Code 8
Supt. – Bob Lester, P O BOX 6409   72216
Baker ES, 14001 W 12TH ST   72211
   Ila Newberry, prin.
Bates ES, 7000 MURRAY   72209
   Cherrie Johnson, prin.
Fuller ES, 1702 DIXON ROAD   72206
   Cynthia Ballard, prin.
Landmark ES, 19824 ARCH ST PIKE   72206
   Bonni Shearer, prin.

Lawson ES, 19901 LAWSON ROAD   72210
   Peggy Bates, prin.
Robinson ES
   RURAL ROUTE 05 BOX 493A   72212
   Virginia Kindervater, prin.
Other Schools – See College Station, Jacksonville,
   Maumelle, North Little Rock, Scott

Sheridan SD
Supt. – See Sheridan
East End ES, RURAL ROUTE 04 BOX 1111   72206
   Bruce Schrader, prin.

Cathedral ES, 3110 W 17TH STREET   72206
Christ Lutheran ES, 315 S HUGHES ST   72205
Christ the King School
   4000 N RODNEY PARHAM RD   72212
Educare ES, 7501 ASHER AVE   72204
Good Counsel ES, 1204 S JACKSON ST   72204
Holy Souls ES, N TYLER & H ST   72205
Mitchell Child Center ES, 6601 W 12TH ST   72204
Pulaski Academy, 12701 HINSON ROAD   72212
St. Edward's ES, E 9TH & FERRY STS   72202
St. Theresa ES, 6311 BASELINE ROAD   72209

Lockesburg, Sevier Co., Pop. Code 3
Lockesburg SD
Sch. Sys. Enr. Code 2
Supt. – Victor Rettmann, P O BOX 88   71846
ES, P O BOX 89   71846 – Velma Owens, prin.

London, Pope Co., Pop. Code 3
Russellville SD
Supt. – See Russellville
ES, RURAL ROUTE 01   72847
   Frankie Casey, prin.

Lonoke, Lonoke Co., Pop. Code 5
Lonoke SD
Sch. Sys. Enr. Code 4
Supt. – Charles Knox, 501 W ACADEMY ST   72086
MS, 501 W ACADEMY ST   72086
   Steven Lilly, prin.
PS, 800 LINCOLN ST   72086 – Ross Moore, prin.

Lowell, Benton Co., Pop. Code 4
Rogers SD
Supt. – See Rogers
ES, 202 MCCLURE ST   72745
   Jayne Granger, prin.

Luxora, Mississippi Co., Pop. Code 4
South Mississippi County SD
Supt. – See Wilson
ES, P O BOX 130   72358 – Joann Baker, prin.

Lynn, Lawrence Co., Pop. Code 2
Lynn SD
Sch. Sys. Enr. Code 2
Supt. – Larry Glenn, P O BOX 338   72440
ES, P O BOX 338   72440 – Willie Jones, prin.

Mabelvale, Pulaski Co., Pop. Code 2
Little Rock SD
Supt. – See Little Rock
Chicot ES, P O BOX 405   72103 – Otis Preslar, prin.
ES, P O BOX 207   72103 – Dorothy Faulkner, prin.

Mc Crory, Woodruff Co., Pop. Code 4
McCrory SD
Sch. Sys. Enr. Code 3
Supt. – Charles Vondran, 517 N SEAMAN   72101
ES, 605 E THIRD ST   72101 – Billy Duncan, prin.

Mc Gehee, Desha Co., Pop. Code 6
McGehee SD
Sch. Sys. Enr. Code 4
Supt. – Jerome Wesson, 104 S 5TH ST   71654
MS, P O BOX 767   71654 – Virginia Williams, prin.
PS, P O BOX 767   71654 – Donna Somervell, prin.

Mc Neil, Columbia Co., Pop. Code 3
McNeil SD
Sch. Sys. Enr. Code 2
Supt. – Glen Nichols, P O BOX 167   71752
ES, P O BOX 167   71752 – James Berry, prin.

Mc Rae, White Co., Pop. Code 3
McRae SD
Sch. Sys. Enr. Code 2
Supt. – Calvin Estes, P O BOX C   72102
ES, P O BOX C   72102 – Robin Hopper, prin.

Madison, St. Francis Co., Pop. Code 4
Forrest City SD
Supt. – See Forrest City
Forrest Hills ES, 2505 SYCAMORE DR   72335
   Martha Pigue, prin.
Madison-Butler ES, GENERAL DELIVERY   72359
   Vhaness Chambers, prin.

Magazine, Logan Co., Pop. Code 3
Magazine SD
Sch. Sys. Enr. Code 2
Supt. – Henry Jenkins, P O BOX 128   72943
ES   72943 – Joan Jones, prin.

Magnolia, Columbia Co., Pop. Code 7
Magnolia SD
Sch. Sys. Enr. Code 5
Supt. – Ed McKinney, P O BOX 649   71753
Central MS, 456 E NORTH ST   71753
   Joe Thomason, prin.
East West ES, 1310 HOLLENSWORTH ST   71753
   Roger Loper, prin.

Walker SD
Sch. Sys. Enr. Code 2
Supt. – W. Moss,Jr., P O BOX 1149   71753

Walker ES, P O BOX 1149   71753
   Kiril Jones, prin.

Malvern, Hot Spring Co., Pop. Code 7
Glen Rose SD
Sch. Sys. Enr. Code 3
Supt. – Don Ray Henson, P O BOX 300   72104
Glen Rose ES, RURAL ROUTE 03 BOX 300   72104
   Don Henson, prin.

Magnet Cove SD
Sch. Sys. Enr. Code 5
Supt. – Glen Coston
   HARVER HILLS BOX 1   72104
Magnet Cove ES
   RURAL ROUTE 07 BOX 400   72104
   Kenneth Hammons, prin.

Malvern SD
Sch. Sys. Enr. Code 5
Supt. – William Hunt, 1517 S MAIN ST   72104
Fields ES, 955 DIVISION ST   72104
   Randall Muse, prin.
Pratt ES, 339 DONNELL ST   72104
   Pat Sexton, prin.
Smith ES, 1735 E SULLENBERGER AVE   72104
   C. C. Hunt, prin.
Wilson MS, 404 N BANKS ST   72104
   Louanne Rowe, prin.

Mammoth Spring, Fulton Co., Pop. Code 4
Mammoth Spring SD
Sch. Sys. Enr. Code 3
Supt. – Arliss Powell, P O BOX 370   72554
ES, P O BOX 370   72554 – Ruth Shaw, prin.

Manila, Mississippi Co., Pop. Code 5
Manila SD
Sch. Sys. Enr. Code 3
Supt. – William Clark,Jr., OLYMPIA ST   72442
ES, P O BOX 670   72442 – Herbert Adkins, prin.
Other Schools – See West Ridge

Mansfield, Sebastian Co., Pop. Code 3
Mansfield SD
Sch. Sys. Enr. Code 3
Supt. – Larry Austin, P O BOX 307   72944
ES, P O BOX 417   72944 – D. Wallace, prin.

Marianna, Lee Co., Pop. Code 6
Lee County 1
Sch. Sys. Enr. Code 5
Supt. – Charles Moore, P O BOX 309   72360
Strong MS, 214 S ALABAMA ST   72360
   James McCoy, prin.
Nunnally ES, 188 W CHESTNUT ST   72360
   Ora Barnes, prin.
Strong MS, 214 S ALABAMA ST   72360
   Alma Clemmer, prin.
Whitten ES, 175 WALNUT ST   72360
   Ora Stevens, prin.
Other Schools – See Moro

Lee Academy
   RURAL ROUTE 02 BOX 2101   72360

Marion, Crittenden Co., Pop. Code 2
Marion SD
Sch. Sys. Enr. Code 4
Supt. – James Carter, 76 ELM ST   72364
MS, 65 W MILITARY ROAD   72364
   John Heath, prin.
MS, 117 MILITARY ROAD   72364
   Jane McGinnis, prin.
Phelix ES, HIGHWAY 77 NORTH   72364
   Beth Poe, prin.

Marked Tree, Poinsett Co., Pop. Code 5
Marked Tree SD
Sch. Sys. Enr. Code 3
Supt. – Charles Sims
   406 SAINT FRANCIS ST   72365
Normandy ES, 703 NORMANDY ST   72365
   Paulete Smith, prin.

Marmaduke, Greene Co., Pop. Code 4
Marmaduke SD
Sch. Sys. Enr. Code 3
Supt. – Jerry McIntosh, 1010 GREYHOUND   72443
Lafe MS, 1010 GREYHOUND   72443
   Jim Lentz, prin.
ES, 1010 GREYHOUND   72443 – Jim Lentz, prin.

Marshall, Searcy Co., Pop. Code 4
Marshall SD
Sch. Sys. Enr. Code 3
Supt. – Reck Wallis, P O BOX 310   72650
ES, P O BOX 310   72650 – Franklin Lewis, prin.

Marvell, Phillips Co., Pop. Code 4
Marvell SD
Sch. Sys. Enr. Code 4
Supt. – Wayne Corkran, P O BOX 126   72366
MS, P O BOX 126   72366 – Ruth Denson, prin.
ES, P O BOX 126   72366 – Susan Clark, prin.

Marvell Academy ES, P O BOX 277   72366

Maumelle, Pulaski Co.
Pulaski Co Special SD
Supt. – See Little Rock
Pine Forest ES, 400 PINE FOREST DR   72118
   Mary Cole, prin.

Mayflower, Faulkner Co., Pop. Code 4
Mayflower SD
Sch. Sys. Enr. Code 3
Supt. – Thurman Ford, P O BOX 127   72106

ES, P O BOX 127 72106 – Wesley Whitley, prin.

Maynard, Randolph Co., Pop. Code 2
Maynard SD
Sch. Sys. Enr. Code 3
Supt. – Harmon Seawel, P O BOX 98 72444
ES, P O BOX 499 72444 – Wayne Gould, prin.

Melbourne, Izard Co., Pop. Code 4
Melbourne SD
Sch. Sys. Enr. Code 2
Supt. – John Sawyer, P O BOX 125 72556
ES, P O BOX 125 72556 – Ferris Crawford, prin.

Mena, Polk Co., Pop. Code 6
Acorn SD
Sch. Sys. Enr. Code 2
Supt. – John Thompson
   RURAL ROUTE 03 BOX 450 71953
Acorn ES, RURAL ROUTE 03 BOX 450 71953
   Doris Lott, prin.

Mena SD
Sch. Sys. Enr. Code 4
Supt. – Lonnie Barron, 304 MENA ST 71953
MS, 304 MENA ST 71953 – Al Gathright, prin.
Durham ES, 106 N REINE ST 71953
   Larry Atchley, prin.
Harshman MS, 720 HORNBECK AVE 71953
   Judith Roberson, prin.

Menifee, Conway Co., Pop. Code 2
South Conway County SD
Supt. – See Morrilton
East Side MS 72107 – Sherrye Shipp, prin.

Mineral Springs, Howard Co., Pop. Code 3
Mineral Springs SD
Sch. Sys. Enr. Code 3
Supt. – Donald Rowlett, P O BOX 188 71851
ES, P O BOX 188 71851 – Jeanie Gorham, prin.

Monette, Craighead Co., Pop. Code 4
Buffalo Island Central SD
Sch. Sys. Enr. Code 3
Supt. – Roland Wells, P O BOX N 72447
Buffalo Island Central West ES, P O BOX N 72447
   Darrell Collier, prin.
Other Schools – See Leachville

Monticello, Drew Co., Pop. Code 6
Drew Central SD
Sch. Sys. Enr. Code 3
Supt. – Norman Hill, P O BOX 10 71655
Drew Central ES
   RURAL ROUTE 04 BOX 10 71655
   Mike Johnston, prin.

Monticello SD
Sch. Sys. Enr. Code 4
Supt. – J. Jordan, P O BOX 517 71655
City Park ES, P O BOX 517 71655
   Peggy Doss, prin.
IS, P O BOX 517 71655 – Sue Hickman, prin.
Whaley ES, 621 N MAIN ST 71655
   Tommy Matthews, prin.

Montrose, Ashley Co., Pop. Code 3

Montrose Academy, P O BOX 368 71658

Moro, Lee Co., Pop. Code 2
Lee County SD 1
Supt. – See Marianna
ES 72368 – Wayne Thompson, prin.

Morrilton, Conway Co., Pop. Code 6
South Conway County SD
Sch. Sys. Enr. Code 5
Supt. – Ray Fullerton
   CHURCH & FLETCHER STS 72110
Northside ES, 1203 N SAINT JOSEPH ST 72110
   H. Turner, prin.
Reynolds ES, 410 BRIDGE ST 72110
   David Garrett, prin.
Other Schools – See Menifee

Sacred Heart Schools
   500 E BROADWAY ST 72110
Sacred Heart ES, 106 N SAINT JOSEPH ST 72110

Mountainburg, Crawford Co., Pop. Code 3
Mountainburg SD
Sch. Sys. Enr. Code 3
Supt. – Kenneth Redding, P O BOX 15 72946
ES, P O BOX 15 72946 – David Crotts, prin.

Mountain Home, Baxter Co., Pop. Code 6
Mountain Home SD
Sch. Sys. Enr. Code 5
Supt. – Roy Ragsdale, 1230 MAPLE ST 72653
Berry IS, 1001 S MAIN ST 72653
   John Prysock, prin.
Herron PS, 610 N COLLEGE ST 72653
   Cecil Tilley, prin.
Pinkston MS, 1301 S COLLEGE ST 72653
   Mike Breton, prin.
Wilks ES, 618 N COLLEGE ST 72653
   James Simmons, prin.

Mountain Pine, Garland Co., Pop. Code 4
Mountain Pine SD
Sch. Sys. Enr. Code 3
Supt. – Roy Karr, P O BOX 1 71956
ES, P O BOX 1 71956 – Darwin Foshee, prin.

Mountain View, Stone Co., Pop. Code 4
Mountain View SD
Sch. Sys. Enr. Code 4
Supt. – Darrell Shelton
   RURAL ROUTE 71 BOX 159 72560
ES, ROUTE 71 BOX 154 72560
   Joe Stewart, prin.

Mount Holly, Union Co., Pop. Code 2
Mount Holly SD
Sch. Sys. Enr. Code 2
Supt. – Curtis Pharr, P O BOX 68 71758
ES, P O BOX 68 71758 – Teresa Lindsey, prin.

Mount Ida, Montgomery Co., Pop. Code 4
Mount Ida SD
Sch. Sys. Enr. Code 3
Supt. – Bobby Barrett, P O BOX 345 71957
Craven ES, P O BOX 345 71957 – Jerry Beggs, prin.

Mount Judea, Newton Co.
Mount Judea SD
Supt. – Ford Ewing, P O BOX 40 72655
ES, P O BOX 40 72655 – Jether Raney, prin.

Mount Pleasant, Izard Co., Pop. Code 2
Mount Pleasant SD
Sch. Sys. Enr. Code 2
Supt. – Howard Lamb, P O BOX 144 72561
ES, P O BOX 144 72561 – Alvin Wiles, prin.

Mount Vernon, Faulkner Co., Pop. Code 2
Mount Vernon SD
Sch. Sys. Enr. Code 2
Supt. – Carroll Denton, P O BOX 118 72111
ES, P O BOX 118 72111
   Charles Van Winkle, prin.

Mulberry, Crawford Co., Pop. Code 4
Mulberry SD
Sch. Sys. Enr. Code 2
Supt. – Charles Waldrip, P O BOX D 72947
Marvin ES, P O BOX D 72947
   Roger Benham, prin.

Murfreesboro, Pike Co., Pop. Code 4
Murfreesboro SD
Sch. Sys. Enr. Code 3
Supt. – Jim Dalton, P O BOX 339 71958
ES, P O BOX 339 71950 – Gary Turner, prin.

Nashville, Howard Co., Pop. Code 5
Nashville SD
Sch. Sys. Enr. Code 4
Supt. – Danny Howard
   1301 MOUNT PLEASANT DRIVE 71852
MS, 415 W 4TH ST 71852 – Arthur Tucker, prin.
Nashville PS, 1201 N 8TH ST 71852
   Paul Tollett, prin.

Newark, Independence Co., Pop. Code 4
Newark SD
Sch. Sys. Enr. Code 3
Supt. – Bob DePoyster, P O BOX 280 72562
ES, P O BOX 336 72562 – Mike Flynn, prin.

Newport, Jackson Co., Pop. Code 6
Newport SD
Sch. Sys. Enr. Code 4
Supt. – Steve Castleberry, REMMEL PARK 72112
JHS, REMMEL PARK 72112 – Rick Rana, prin.
Castleberry ES, 400 N PECAN ST 72112
   D. Everett Patton, prin.
Gibbs Albright MS, REASEL PARK 72112
   Deedy Simmons, prin.

Norfork, Baxter Co., Pop. Code 2
Norfork SD
Sch. Sys. Enr. Code 2
Supt. – Lyndle McCurley
   HCR 62 BOX 13-B 72658
ES, RURAL ROUTE 01 P O BOX A 72658
   Don Weaver, prin.

Norman, Montgomery Co., Pop. Code 3
Caddo Hills SD
Sch. Sys. Enr. Code 3
Supt. – John Bass, P O BOX 249 71960
Caddo Hills ES
   RURAL ROUTE 01 BOX 249 71960
   Burl Roark, prin.

Norphlet, Union Co., Pop. Code 3
Norphlet SD
Sch. Sys. Enr. Code 3
Supt. – Winfred May, P O BOX E 71759
ES, P O BOX E 71759 – Auby McEachern, prin.

North Little Rock, Pulaski Co., Pop. Code 8
North Little Rock SD
Sch. Sys. Enr. Code 6
Supt. – Joe Austin, P O BOX 687 72115
Amboy ES, 2400 W 58TH ST 72118
   Jane Ford, prin.
Argenta ES, 1301 MAIN ST 72114
   Pat Coomes, prin.
Belwood ES, 3902 VIRGINIA DR 72118
   Susie Jackson, prin.
Boone Park ES, 1400 CRUTCHER ST 72114
   Pat Siegel, prin.
Central MS, 23RD & POPLAR STS 72114
   Kathy Morledge, prin.
Crestwood ES, 1901 CRESTWOOD ROAD 72116
   Linda Wilson, prin.
Glenview ES, EAST 19 & EDMOND ROAD 72117
   Harold Allen, prin.

Indian Hills ES, 6800 INDIAN HILLS DR 72116
   Alice Stovall, prin.
Lakewood ES, 4400 FAIRWAY AVE 72116
   Portia Power, prin.
Lynch Drive ES, 5800 ALPHA ST 72117
   Diane Crites, prin.
Meadow Park ES
   2300 EUREKA GARDENS ROAD 72117
   James Zeigler, prin.
North Heights ES, 4901 ALLEN ST 72118
   Judy Binz, prin.
Park Hill ES
   3801 JOHN F KENNEDY BLVD 72116
   Betty Murray, prin.
Pike View ES, 441 MCCAIN BLVD 72116
   Deborah Austin, prin.
Pine ES, 1900 N PINE ST 72114
   Fran Jackson, prin.
Redwood ES, FOURTH & REDWOOD 72114
   Dorisene Hill, prin.
Rose City ES, EARL & SCHOOL STS 72117
   Kathryn Harvey, prin.
Seventh Street ES, 7TH & BEECH STS 72114
   Marsha Paul, prin.

Pulaski Co Special SD
Supt. – See Little Rock
Cato Road ES, 2901 CATO ROAD 72116
   Doug Newkirk, prin.
Harris ES, 4400 JACKSONVILLE HIGHWAY 72217
   Raymond Green, prin.
Oak Grove ES, RURAL ROUTE 05 BOX 158 72118
   Ronnie Duke, prin.
Oakbrooke ES, 2200 THORNHILL DR 72116
   Karl Brown, prin.
Sherwood ES, 307 VERONA AVE 72116
   Larry Fuller, prin.
Sylvan Hills ES, 402 FOREST RIDGE ROAD 72116
   Doug Hoffmann, prin.

Central Arkansas Christian ES
   117 W MARYLAND AVE 72116
Immaculate Conception ES
   7000 JOHN F KENNEDY BLVD 72116
St. Mary's ES, 1518 PARKER ST 72114
St. Patrick's ES, 1900 ORANGE ST 72114

Oark, Johnson Co.
Oark SD 7
Sch. Sys. Enr. Code 2
Supt. – Bill Gilmore, GENERAL DELIVERY 72852
ES, GENERAL DELIVERY 72852
   Jan Bridges, prin.

Oden, Montgomery Co., Pop. Code 2
Oden SD
Sch. Sys. Enr. Code 2
Supt. – Claude Berry, P O BOX 150 71961
Maddox ES, P O BOX 150 71961
   Don Hamilton, prin.

Oil Trough, Independence Co., Pop. Code 2
Oil Trough SD
Sch. Sys. Enr. Code 2
Supt. – Thomas Smith, P O BOX 177 72564
ES, P O BOX 177 72564 – Barbara Reynolds, prin.

Ola, Yell Co., Pop. Code 4
Ola SD
Sch. Sys. Enr. Code 3
Supt. – Phillip Young, P O BOX 736 72853
ES, P O BOX 736 72853 – Rick Kinzey, prin.

Omaha, Boone Co., Pop. Code 2
Omaha SD
Sch. Sys. Enr. Code 2
Supt. – David Land, P O BOX 249 72662
ES, P O BOX 249 72662 – John Barron, prin.

Osceola, Mississippi Co., Pop. Code 6
Osceola SD
Sch. Sys. Enr. Code 4
Supt. – Carol Smith, P O BOX 628 72370
East ES, P O BOX 628 72370
   Don McGohan, prin.
North ES, P O BOX 628 72370
   Madeline Givens, prin.
MS, P O BOX 628 72370
   Milton Washington, prin.
West ES, P O BOX 628 72370
   Nelda Adams, prin.

Ozark, Franklin Co., Pop. Code 5
Ozark SD
Sch. Sys. Enr. Code 4
Supt. – Scott Stone, 1200 W SCHOOL ST 72949
MS, 1601 WALDEN DR 72949 – Mike Boyd, prin.
Ozark Upper ES, 1601 WALDEN DR 72949
   Mike Boyd, prin.

Pleasant View SD
Sch. Sys. Enr. Code 2
Supt. – Gary Moon, RURAL ROUTE 02 72949
Pleasant View ES, RURAL ROUTE 02 72949
   Larry McCain, prin.

Palestine, St. Francis Co., Pop. Code 3
Palestine/Wheatley SD
Sch. Sys. Enr. Code 3
Supt. – Fred Johnson, P O BOX 8 72372
ES, 103 W WOOD 72372 – Linda Hamilton, prin.
Other Schools – See Wheatley

Pangburn, White Co., Pop. Code 3
Pangburn SD
Sch. Sys. Enr. Code 3
Supt. – Jerome Browning, P O BOX 68 72121

ES, P O BOX 68 72121 – James Williams, prin.

Paragould, Greene Co., Pop. Code 7
Green County Tech. SD
Sch. Sys. Enr. Code 4
Supt. – Gerald Dickinson
   4633 W KINGSHIGHWAY 72450
Green County Technical JHS
   4635 W KINGSHIGHWAY 72450
   Chester Key, prin.
East ES, RURAL ROUTE 05 72450
   Lee Ross, prin.
South ES, RURAL ROUTE 01 72450
   Joe Ed Smith, prin.
West ES, 4637 W KINGSHIGHWAY 72450
   Jimmy Ballard, prin.

Northeast Arkansas SD
Sch. Sys. Enr. Code 4
Supt. – Edward Teeter, P O BOX 37 72450
Baldwin ES, P O BOX 37 72450
   Christy Blackshear, prin.
Elmwood ES, P O BOX 37 72450
   Jesse Howard, prin.
Oak Grove ES, RURAL ROUTE 02 BOX 159 72450
   Leon Lowe, prin.
Oakwood ES, P O BOX 37 72450
   Jesse Howard, prin.
Wilson ES, SOUTH 10TH ST 72450
   U. Austin Hagan, prin.

Stanford SD
Sch. Sys. Enr. Code 2
Supt. – Harold Baker
   ROURAL ROUTE 07 BOX 240 72450
Stanford ES, RURAL ROUTE 07 BOX 240 72450
   Marvin Clark, prin.

Crowley's Ridge Academy
   626 ACADEMY DRIVE 72450

Paris, Logan Co., Pop. Code 5
Paris SD
Sch. Sys. Enr. Code 4
Supt. – William Chambers, 602 N 100TH ST 72855
MS, 2000 WOOD ST 72855 – Larry Cozens, prin.
ES, ELEMENTARY AVE 72855
   Maxwell Crowe, prin.

St. Joseph ES, 25 S SPRUCE ST 72855

Parkdale, Ashley Co., Pop. Code 2
Parkdale SD
Sch. Sys. Enr. Code 2
Supt. – Edward Akin, P O BOX 97 71661
ES, P O BOX 97 71661 – Dewayne Haynes, prin.

Parkin, Cross Co., Pop. Code 4
Parkin SD
Sch. Sys. Enr. Code 3
Supt. – Joseph Whitby, P O BOX 7 72373
ES, P O BOX 37 72373 – Jeannett Bennett, prin.

Paron, Saline Co., Pop. Code 1
Paron SD
Sch. Sys. Enr. Code 2
Supt. – John Smith, GENERAL DELIVERY 72122
ES, GENERAL DELIVERY 72122
   Karen Metcalf, prin.

Pearcy, Garland Co.
Lake Hamilton SD
Sch. Sys. Enr. Code 3
Supt. – Ken Turner
   RURAL ROUTE 01 BOX 106 71964
Lake Hamilton IS, 107 N WOLFE DR 71964
   Jim Ashcraft, prin.
Lake Hamilton PS, 106 S WOLFE DR 71964
   John Smalling, prin.

Pea Ridge, Benton Co., Pop. Code 4
Pea Ridge SD
Sch. Sys. Enr. Code 3
Supt. – Marvin Higginbottom, P O BOX 6 72751
ES, P O BOX 6 72751 – Ozy Murphey, prin.

Perryville, Perry Co., Pop. Code 4
Perryville SD
Sch. Sys. Enr. Code 3
Supt. – Bobby Joe Hibbard, P O BOX 129 72126
ES, P O BOX 129 72126 – Homer Chitwood, prin.

Piggott, Clay Co., Pop. Code 5
Piggott SD
Sch. Sys. Enr. Code 4
Supt. – Don Montgomery, P O BOX 387 72454
MS, P O BOX 387 72454 – Lendell Vennada, prin.
ES, P O BOX 387 72454 – Betty Sue Payne, prin.

Pine Bluff, Jefferson Co., Pop. Code 8
Dollarway SD
Sch. Sys. Enr. Code 4
Supt. – Terry Smith
   4900 DOLLARWAY ROAD 71602
Matthews ES, 4900 DOLLARWAY ROAD 71602
   Celestine Cross, prin.
Pinecrest ES, 5601 CALHOUN ST 71602
   Ron Smead, prin.
Townsend Park MS, 2601 FLUKER ST 71601
   James Raby, prin.

Pine Bluff SD
Sch. Sys. Enr. Code 6
Supt. – Willis Alderson, P O BOX 7678 71611
Pine Bluff JHS Eighth, 4101 S OLIVE ST 71603
   Otis Brown, prin.
Belair MS, 1303 COMMERCE ROAD 71601
   Mark Willett, prin.

Broadmoor ES, 1800 E 11TH AVE 71601
   Earl Chanay, prin.
Carver ES, 300 N LINDEN ST 71601
   Gwendolyn Dancy, prin.
First Ward ES, 1300 E FIFTH AVE 71601
   Charles Sowell, prin.
Forrest Park ES, 1903 W 34TH AVE 71603
   Karlynn Roberts, prin.
Greenville ES, 2501 W 10TH AVE 71603
   Joe Hall, prin.
Indiana Street ES, 1519 S INDIANA ST 71601
   Clara Stover, prin.
Lakeside ES, 609 W 15TH AVE 71601
   Marlene Ferguson, prin.
Meyer ES, 2319 S LINDEN ST 71603
   Bobbie Hodge, prin.
Oak Park MS, 30TH & ORANGE STS 71603
   Duane Edwards, prin.
Southeast MS
   RURAL ROUTE 03 BOX 2001 71601
   Jerry Hilton, prin.
Southwood ES, 4200 S FIR ST 71603
   Charles Cone, prin.
Taylor MS, 1415 W 13TH AVE 71603
   Joe Simpson, prin.
Thirty-Fourth Avenue MS
   34TH & MISSOURI ST 71601
   Bettye Wright, prin.

Watson Chapel SD
Sch. Sys. Enr. Code 5
Supt. – Charles Knight
   RURAL ROUTE 07 BOX 500 71603
Coleman MS, 4600 W 13TH AVE 71603
   Steve Smith, prin.
Edgewood ES, 31ST & ORLANDO STS 71603
   Charles Bell, prin.
Owen ES, RURAL ROUTE 07 BOX 451 71603
   Johnny Reid, prin.

White Hall SD
Sch. Sys. Enr. Code 5
Supt. – Michael Crowley
   RURAL ROUTE 04 BOX 889 71602
Other Schools – See Redfield, White Hall

Jefferson Preparatory ES
   2206 RIDGEWAY ROAD 71603
St. Peters School, 1515 STATE ST 71601
Trinity Episcopal Day ES
   708 W 2ND AVE #8069 71601

Plainview, Yell Co., Pop. Code 3
Plainview-Rover SD
Sch. Sys. Enr. Code 2
Supt. – Richard Holbert, P O BOX 157 72857
Plainview-Rover ES, P O BOX 157 72857
   John James, prin.

Pleasant Plains, Independence Co., Pop. Code 2
Midland SD
Sch. Sys. Enr. Code 2
Supt. – Richard Blevins, P O BOX 258 72568
Other Schools – See Floral

Pocahontas, Randolph Co., Pop. Code 6
Pocahontas SD
Sch. Sys. Enr. Code 4
Supt. – Marcus Van Camp
   2300 N PARK ST 72455
MS, 2301 N PARK ST 72455 – Bryon Busby, prin.
Spikes ES, 1713 HIGHLAND BLVD 72455
   Marvin Riddle, prin.

St. Paul ES, 311 CEDAR ST 72455

Portland, Ashley Co., Pop. Code 3
Hamburg SD
Supt. – See Hamburg
ES, P O BOX 8 71663 – Novilla Frazer, prin.

Pottsville, Pope Co., Pop. Code 3
Pottsville SD
Sch. Sys. Enr. Code 3
Supt. – Dain Duvall, P O BOX 70 72858
ES, P O BOX 70 72858 – Howard Caudle, prin.

Poughkeepsie, Sharp Co., Pop. Code 1
Poughkeepsie SD
Sch. Sys. Enr. Code 2
Supt. – Susan Metcalf
   GENERAL DELIVERY 72569
ES, GENERAL DELIVERY 72569
   Lee Roy Baird, prin.

Poyen, Grant Co., Pop. Code 2
Poyen SD
Sch. Sys. Enr. Code 2
Supt. – Jerry Newton, P O BOX 209 72128
ES, P O BOX 209 72128 – Bobby Daniel,Jr., prin.

Prairie Grove, Washington Co., Pop. Code 4
Prairie Grove SD
Sch. Sys. Enr. Code 4
Supt. – Ben Winborn, P O BOX 247 72753
ES, P O BOX 247 72753 – J. Lyman, prin.

Prattsville, Grant Co., Pop. Code 2
Prattsville SD
Sch. Sys. Enr. Code 2
Supt. – Cecil Holt, P O BOX 48 72129
ES, P O BOX 48 72129 – Jay Ramick, prin.

Prescott, Nevada Co., Pop. Code 5
Prescott SD
Sch. Sys. Enr. Code 4
Supt. – Don Johnston, 762 MARTIN ST 71857

MS, 1030 E 5TH ST 71858
   Donald Mitchell, prin.
ES, 335 SCHOOL T 71857 – Howard Austin, prin.

Quitman, Cleburne Co., Pop. Code 3
Quitman SD
Sch. Sys. Enr. Code 3
Supt. – Hubert Long, Jr., P O BOX 178 72131
ES, P O BOX 178 72131 – James Fielder, prin.

Ravenden Springs, Randolph Co., Pop. Code 2
Randolph County SD
Sch. Sys. Enr. Code 2
Supt. – Clifford Adams, RURAL ROUTE 01 72460
Oak Ridge Central ES, RURAL ROUTE 01 72460
   Scott James, prin.

Rector, Clay Co., Pop. Code 4
Clay County Central SD
Sch. Sys. Enr. Code 3
Supt. – Bob Guess, P O BOX 367 72461
Clay County South ES, P O BOX 367 72461
   Kelly Scobey, prin.
Other Schools – See Greenway

Redfield, Jefferson Co., Pop. Code 3
White Hall SD
Supt. – See Pine Bluff
Hardin ES, P O BOX 159 72132 – Dan Mincy, prin.

Rison, Cleveland Co., Pop. Code 4
Rison SD
Sch. Sys. Enr. Code 3
Supt. – Grady Cathey, P O BOX 307 71665
ES, P O BOX 307 71665 – Annette Rawls, prin.

Woodlawn SD
Sch. Sys. Enr. Code 2
Supt. – Max Watts
   RURAL ROUTE 02 BOX 56-A 71665
Woodlawn ES
   RURAL ROUTE 02 BOX 56-A 71665
   Joy Boydston, prin.

Rogers, Benton Co., Pop. Code 7
Rogers SD
Sch. Sys. Enr. Code 6
Supt. – Frank Tillery, 220 S 5TH ST 72756
Eastside ES, 505 E NEW HOPE ROAD 72756
   Mitzi Bardrick, prin.
Grace Hill ES, 901 N DIXIELAND ROAD 72756
   Jane Scott, prin.
Grimes ES, 1801 S 13TH 72756
   Judith Carmical, prin.
Northside ES, 807 N 6TH ST 72756
   Ruby Clark, prin.
Westside ES, 2200 W OAK ST 72756
   Delores Bartizal, prin.
Other Schools – See Garfield, Lowell

St. Vincent De Paul School
   1305 W CYPRESS 72756

Rohwer, Desha Co., Pop. Code 1
Delta Special SD
Sch. Sys. Enr. Code 2
Supt. – Robert Gunn, P O BOX 41 71654
Delta ES, P O BOX 41 71666
   Renee Treadwell, prin.

Rose Bud, White Co., Pop. Code 2
Rose Bud SD
Sch. Sys. Enr. Code 2
Supt. – Rodger Harlan, P O BOX 9 72137
ES, P O BOX 9 72137 – Doug Langston, prin.

Rosston, Nevada Co., Pop. Code 2
Nevada SD 1
Supt. – See Cale
Nevada ES, P O BOX 50 71858
   Natalie Sherwood, prin.

Russellville, Pope Co., Pop. Code 7
Russellville SD
Sch. Sys. Enr. Code 5
Supt. – Gene Lavender, P O BOX 928 72801
Center Valley ES
   RURAL ROUTE 07 BOX 227 72801
   Thomas Doan, prin.
Crawford ES, N PARKER ROAD 72801
   Georganne Peel, prin.
Dwight ES, W SECOND & MUSKOGEE ST 72801
   Sue Frueauff, prin.
Oakland Heights ES, 15TH & S DETROIT 72801
   Howard Ritchie, prin.
MS, 1100 S ARKANSAS AVE 72801
   John Thaxton, prin.
Sequoyah ES, WEST 12 ST 72801
   Richard Payne, prin.
Other Schools – See London

St. John's School, 1914 W MAIN ST 72801

Saint Joe, Searcy Co., Pop. Code 3
St. Joe SD
Sch. Sys. Enr. Code 2
Supt. – Chuck Archer, P O BOX 69 72675
ES, P O BOX 69 72675 – John Szitar, prin.

Saint Paul, Madison Co., Pop. Code 2
St. Paul SD
Sch. Sys. Enr. Code 2
Supt. – Bill Schafer, P O BOX 125 72760
ES, P O BOX 125 72760 – Dora Rogers, prin.

Salem, Fulton Co., Pop. Code 4
Salem SD
Sch. Sys. Enr. Code 3
Supt. – Don Baker, P O BOX 517 72576
ES, P O BOX 455 72576 – Beverly Shell, prin.

Saratoga, Hempstead Co., Pop. Code 2
Saratoga SD
Sch. Sys. Enr. Code 2
Supt. – Michael Deal, P O BOX 90 71859
ES, P O BOX 90 71859 – Angela Piggee, prin.

Scotland, Van Buren Co., Pop. Code 2
Scotland SD
Sch. Sys. Enr. Code 2
Supt. – Larry Gibby, P O BOX 204 72141
ES, P O BOX 204 72141 – Jesse Huffman, prin.

Scott, Pulaski Co.
Pulaski Co Special SD
Supt. – See Little Rock
ES, RURAL ROUTE 01 BOX 300 72142
  Carl Hill, prin.

Scranton, Logan Co., Pop. Code 2
Scranton SD
Sch. Sys. Enr. Code 2
Supt. – Bill Horne, P O BOX 86 72863
ES, P O BOX 86 72863 – Leona Cleveland, prin.

Searcy, White Co., Pop. Code 7
Searcy SD
Sch. Sys. Enr. Code 5
Supt. – Al Hunter, 801 N ELM ST 72143
Deener ES, 133 CLOVERDALE BLVD 72143
  Morse Mallett, prin.
McRae ES, 801 E MOORE AVE 72143
  Mickey Pounders, prin.
Southwest MS, 1103 W WOODRUFF AVE 72143
  Danny Barnett, prin.
Other Schools – See West Point

Harding Academy, P O BOX 775 72143

Sheridan, Grant Co., Pop. Code 5
Sheridan SD
Sch. Sys. Enr. Code 5
Supt. – David Robinson, 400 N ROCK ST 72150
ES, 510 W CHURCH ST 72150 – Angela Belt, prin.
Other Schools – See Grapevine, Little Rock

Sherwood, Pulaski Co., Pop. Code 7

Victory Baptist ES, 515 SHERWOOD AVE 72116

Shirley, Van Buren Co., Pop. Code 2
Shirley SD
Sch. Sys. Enr. Code 3
Supt. – Charles Bane, P O BOX 66 72153
ES, P O BOX 40 72153 – Mark Gammill, prin.

Siloam Springs, Benton Co., Pop. Code 6
Siloam Springs SD
Sch. Sys. Enr. Code 4
Supt. – Burton Elliott, P O BOX 798 72761
Maple MS, 825 S MAPLE ST 72761
  Sara Ford, prin.
Northside ES, 501 W ELGIN ST 72761
  Anne Ruble, prin.
Southside ES, 850 S WRIGHT ST 72761
  J. Long, prin.

Smackover, Union Co., Pop. Code 4
Smackover SD
Sch. Sys. Enr. Code 3
Supt. – Bob Hood
  RURAL ROUTE 1 BOX 123-B 71762
ES, 303 W 7TH ST 71762 – Lewis Gardner, prin.

Sparkman, Dallas Co., Pop. Code 3
Sparkman SD
Sch. Sys. Enr. Code 2
Supt. – Jerry Moore, P O BOX 37 71763
ES, P O BOX 37 71763 – William Bennett, prin.

Springdale, Washington Co., Pop. Code 7
Springdale SD
Sch. Sys. Enr. Code 6
Supt. – Jim Rollins, P O BOX 8 72765
Elmdale ES, 420 N WEST END ST 72764
  Donald Johnson, prin.
Jones ES, 900 S POWELL ST 72764
  Don Bishop, prin.
Lee ES, 400 QUANDT ST 72764 – Peggy Hill, prin.
Parsons Hills ES, 2200 CARDINAL DR 72764
  Mary Littrell, prin.
Smith ES, 40TH & FALCON 72764
  Linda Childers, prin.
Tyson ES, 2400 ROBINSON LANE 72764
  Lola Malone, prin.
Walker ES, 1701 S 40TH 72764
  Joan Fratzke, prin.
Westwood ES, 1800 MCRAY ST 72764
  Jerry Rogers, prin.

Ozark Christian Academy
  1506 W ROBINSON AVE 72764

Stamps, Lafayette Co., Pop. Code 5
Stamps SD
Sch. Sys. Enr. Code 3
Supt. – Cecil Daves, P O BOX 309 71860
ES, P O BOX 309 71860 – William Hanson, prin.

Star City, Lincoln Co., Pop. Code 4
Star City SD
Sch. Sys. Enr. Code 4
Supt. – Dalda Womack, P O BOX 39 71667

MS, P O BOX 39 71667 – Charlie Baggett, prin.
ES, P O BOX 39 71667 – Patricia Harper, prin.

Stephens, Ouachita Co., Pop. Code 4
Stephens SD
Sch. Sys. Enr. Code 3
Supt. – Leo Johnson, P O BOX 427 71764
ES, P O BOX 426 71764 – John McWilliams, prin.

Strawberry, Lawrence Co., Pop. Code 2
Strawberry SD
Sch. Sys. Enr. Code 2
Supt. – Dean Fugett, P O BOX 49 72469
ES, P O BOX 49 72469 – Charles Fraser, prin.

Strong, Union Co., Pop. Code 3
Strong SD
Sch. Sys. Enr. Code 3
Supt. – Travis Wedgeworth, P O BOX 8 71765
ES, P O BOX 736 71765 – Gerrald Koonce, prin.

Stuttgart, Arkansas Co., Pop. Code 7
Stuttgart SD
Sch. Sys. Enr. Code 5
Supt. – Joe Williams, P O BOX 928 72160
Clary ES, P O BOX 928 72160
  Sharon Konecny, prin.
Ginserich ES, P O BOX 928 72160
  Melvin Bryant, prin.
Shannon ES, P O BOX 928 72160
  Gay Fisher, prin.
Stuttgart-Meekins MS, P O BOX 928 72160
  David Wood, prin.

Holy Rosary School, 1814 S CROCKETT 72160
St. John's Lutheran ES
  2019 S BUERKLE ST 72160

Sulphur Rock, Independence Co., Pop. Code 2
Sulphur Rock SD
Sch. Sys. Enr. Code 2
Supt. – Robert Calvery, P O BOX 98 72579
ES, P O BOX 98 72579 – Jack Sanders, prin.

Swifton, Jackson Co., Pop. Code 3
Swifton SD
Sch. Sys. Enr. Code 2
Supt. – Glenn Fugatt, P O BOX 188 72471
ES, P O BOX 188 72471 – John Fuller, prin.

Taylor, Columbia Co., Pop. Code 3
Taylor SD
Sch. Sys. Enr. Code 2
Supt. – Ben Smith
  RURAL ROUTE 02 BOX 1 71861
ES, RURAL ROUTE 02 BOX 1 71861
  Robert Hardy, prin.

Texarkana, Miller Co., Pop. Code 7
Genoa Central SD
Sch. Sys. Enr. Code 3
Supt. – Gary Cobb
  RURAL ROUTE 07 BOX 518 75502
Genoa Central ES
  RURAL ROUTE 07 BOX 518 75502
  Frank McFerrin, prin.

Texarkana SD
Sch. Sys. Enr. Code 6
Supt. – Ross Beck, 1500 JEFFERSON AVE 75502
College Hill ES, ARTESIAN ROSE 75502
  Mary Russell, prin.
Fairview ES, 801 E SIXTEENTH ST 75502
  Vera Humphrey, prin.
Kilpatrick ES, 1002 E 35TH ST 75502
  Janie Pumphrey, prin.
Trice ES, 4505 PINSON DR 75502
  Wilbur Howard, prin.
Union ES, 1701 LINE FERRY ROAD 75502
  Daniel Hammock, prin.
Washington IS, 1900 MARIETTA ST 75502
  Lewis Thompson, prin.

Thornton, Calhoun Co., Pop. Code 3
Bearden SD
Supt. – See Bearden
ES, P O BOX 37 71766 – James O'Dell, prin.

Tillar, Desha Co., Pop. Code 2
Desha-Drew SD
Sch. Sys. Enr. Code 2
Supt. – Opal Crow, P O BOX 8 71670
Prewitt ES, P O BOX 8 71670 – Curtis Harris, prin.

Timbo, Stone Co., Pop. Code 2
Stone County SD
Sch. Sys. Enr. Code 2
Supt. – Ronnie Lee, P O BOX 40 72680
ES, HIGHWAY 263 72680
  Elaine Branscum, prin.

Trumann, Poinsett Co., Pop. Code 6
Trumann SD
Sch. Sys. Enr. Code 4
Supt. – Jim Cole, 221 PINE ST 72472
Cedar Park ES, 221 PINE ST 72472
  Ed Richardson, prin.
Central ES/Harrisburg, 221 PINE ST 72472
  Rebecca Russell, prin.

Tuckerman, Jackson Co., Pop. Code 4
Tuckerman SD
Sch. Sys. Enr. Code 3
Supt. – Gene Fletcher, P O BOX 10 72473
ES, P O BOX 10 72473 – Don Douglas, prin.

Turrell, Crittenden Co., Pop. Code 4
Turrell SD
Sch. Sys. Enr. Code 3
Supt. – M. McFatridge, P O BOX 369 72384
ES, P O BOX 369 72384 – Gladiola Hughey, prin.

Tyronza, Poinsett Co., Pop. Code 3
East Poinsett County SD
Supt. – See Lepanto
East Poinsett County ES
  RURAL ROUTE 02 BOX 184 72386
  Luther Robinson, prin.

Umpire, Howard Co., Pop. Code 2
Umpire SD
Sch. Sys. Enr. Code 2
Supt. – Charles McConnell 71971
ES 71971 – Jeanette McConnell, prin.

Valley Springs, Boone Co., Pop. Code 2
Valley Springs SD
Sch. Sys. Enr. Code 3
Supt. – Roy Norvell, P O BOX 86 72682
ES, P O BOX 86 72682 – Joe Hefley, prin.

Van Buren, Crawford Co., Pop. Code 7
Van Buren SD
Sch. Sys. Enr. Code 5
Supt. – Billy Mitchell
  2001 POINTER TRAIL 72956
City Heights ES, 301 MOUNT VISTA ST 72956
  James Starbird, prin.
Izard ES, 24TH & BALDWIN STS 72956
  Phillip Hays, prin.
King ES, 400 N 19TH ST 72956
  Linda Rorie, prin.
Parkview ES, 617 PARKVIEW 72956
  Alvy Hays, prin.
Tate ES, RURAL ROUTE 03 BOX 186A 72956
  Jerry Faught, prin.
MS, 913 N 24TH ST 72956
  Edmond Brewer, prin.

Vandervoort, Polk Co., Pop. Code 1
Van Cove SD
Supt. – See Cove
Van Cove ES, P O BOX 878 71972
  Leon Goss, prin.

Vanndale, Cross Co.
Cross County SD
Supt. – See Cherry Valley
ES 72387 – James Martin, prin.

Vilonia, Faulkner Co., Pop. Code 6
Vilonia SD
Sch. Sys. Enr. Code 4
Supt. – Frank Mitchell, P O BOX 160 72173
ES 72173 – Barbara Fuller, prin.

Viola, Fulton Co., Pop. Code 2
Viola SD
Sch. Sys. Enr. Code 3
Supt. – Marvin Newton 72583
ES 72583 – Jerry Taylor, prin.

Violet Hill, Izard Co., Pop. Code 2
Izard County Consolidated Schools
Sch. Sys. Enr. Code 2
Supt. – Otey Greene, P O BOX 588 72584
Izard County Consolidated ES, P O BOX 8 72584
  Richard Billingsley, prin.

Wabbaseka, Jefferson Co., Pop. Code 2
Wabbeseka-Tucker SD
Sch. Sys. Enr. Code 2
Supt. – Caleb Brunson, P O BOX 210 72175
ES, P O BOX 210 72175 – Sam Nelson, prin.

Waldo, Columbia Co., Pop. Code 4
Waldo SD
Sch. Sys. Enr. Code 3
Supt. – Manuel Whitley, 498 LOCUST ST 71770
ES, 500 LOCUST ST 71770 – Laura Wilson, prin.

Waldron, Scott Co., Pop. Code 5
Waldron SD
Sch. Sys. Enr. Code 4
Supt. – James Regnier, P O BOX 1397 72958
MS, RURAL ROUTE 01 BOX 100-A 72958
  Larry Pugh, prin.
ES, P O BOX 476 72958
  Wallace Aspinwall, prin.

Walnut Ridge, Lawrence Co., Pop. Code 5
Walnut Ridge SD
Sch. Sys. Enr. Code 5
Supt. – Glen Murphy, STATE & FREE STS 72476
MS, SE 6TH ST 72476 – Aaron Hosman, prin.
ES, 510 E FREE ST 72476 – Jean Edmondson, prin.

Ward, Lonoke Co., Pop. Code 3
Cabot SD 4
Supt. – See Cabot
ES, P O BOX 336 72176 – Mary Ramey, prin.

Warren, Bradley Co., Pop. Code 6
Warren SD
Sch. Sys. Enr. Code 4
Supt. – Frank Anthony, 803 N WALNUT ST 71671
Eastside ES, N BRADLEY ROAD 71671
  Billy Watson, prin.
Westside MS, 208 N BRASS ST 71671
  Edward Parham, prin.

Washington, Hempstead Co., Pop. Code 2
Washington SD
Sch. Sys. Enr. Code 2
Supt. – Mildred Smith, P O BOX 128 71862

Lincoln ES, P O BOX 129   71862
   Thurston Hulsey, prin.

Weiner, Poinsett Co., Pop. Code 3
   Weiner SD
   Sch. Sys. Enr. Code 2
   Supt. – Charlotte Wright, P O BOX 408   72479
   ES, P O BOX 408   72479 – Tom Knight, prin.

Western Grove, Newton Co., Pop. Code 2
   Western Grove SD
   Sch. Sys. Enr. Code 2
   Supt. – Carl Jones, P O BOX 50   72685
   ES, P O BOX 50   72685 – Joe Adams, prin.

West Fork, Washington Co., Pop. Code 4
   West Fork SD
   Sch. Sys. Enr. Code 3
   Supt. – John Self, P O BOX 319   72774
   MS, P O BOX 319   72774 – D. Mullins, prin.
   ES, P O BOX 319   72774 – Roy Keyes,Jr., prin.

West Helena, Phillips Co., Pop. Code 7
   Helena SD
   Supt. – See Helena
   Miller JHS, HIGHWAY 49   72390
    Bob Farrah, prin.
   Beech Crest ES, 2 RICHMOND HILL ST   72390
    Charles Hopson, prin.
   West Side ES, 339 S ASHLEY   72390
    Ernest Simes, prin.
   Woodruff MS, CLEBURNE AVE   72390
    Kenneth Murphree, prin.

Desoto ES, N FOURTH ST   72390

West Memphis, Crittenden Co., Pop. Code 8
   West Memphis SD
   Sch. Sys. Enr. Code 6
   Supt. – Bill Kissinger, 301 S AVALON ST   72301
   Bragg ES, 309 W BARTON AVE   72301
    Lynne Barber, prin.
   Faulk ES, 908 VANDERBILT AVE   72301
    Gary Adams, prin.
   Jackson ES, 2395 S L HENRY ST   72301
    Joyce Williams, prin.
   Maddux ES, 2100 E BARTON AVE   72301
    Jim Naylor, prin.
   Richland ES, 1011 W BARTON AVE   72301
    Gerald Park, prin.
   Weaver ES, 1280 E BARTON AVE   72301
    Sarah Kirkley, prin.

Wonder ES, 901 S SEVENTEENTH ST   72301
   Ora Breckinridge, prin.
   Other Schools – See Edmondson

St. Michael's ES, 405 N MISSOURI ST   72301

West Point, White Co., Pop. Code 2
   Searcy SD
   Supt. – See Searcy
   ES   72178 – Carol Sicks, prin.

West Ridge, Mississippi Co.
   Manila SD
   Supt. – See Manila
   ES, HIGHWAY 140 #5   72391
    Norma Anderson, prin.

Wheatley, St. Francis Co., Pop. Code 3
   Palestine/Wheatley SD
   Supt. – See Palestine
   ES, P O BOX 255   72392
    Kathleen Hamilton, prin.

White Hall, Jefferson Co., Pop. Code 4
   White Hall SD
   Supt. – See Pine Bluff
   Gandy ES, 7400 CLAUD ROAD   71602
    Delbert Bond, prin.
   Moody ES, MOODY SCHOOL DR   71602
    Dorothy Welch, prin.
   Taylor ES, 1001 WEST ST   71602
    George Connell, prin.

Wickes, Polk Co., Pop. Code 2
   Wickes SD
   Sch. Sys. Enr. Code 2
   Supt. – Mickey Lewis, P O BOX C   71973
   ES, P O BOX C   71973 – Pat Stewart, prin.

Wilburn, Cleburne Co., Pop. Code 2
   Wilburn SD
   Sch. Sys. Enr. Code 2
   Supt. – Bill Hunt, P O BOX 1000   72179
   ES, P O BOX 1000   72179 – Gale Koening, prin.

Williford, Sharp Co., Pop. Code 2
   Williford SD
   Sch. Sys. Enr. Code 2
   Supt. – J. Evans, P O BOX 137   72482
   ES, P O BOX 137   72482 – Linda Bassham, prin.

Wilmar, Drew Co., Pop. Code 3
   Wilmar SD
   Sch. Sys. Enr. Code 2
   Supt. – Lamar Jones, P O BOX 88   71675
   ES, P O BOX 88   71675 – Thomas Reaves, prin.

Wilmot, Ashley Co., Pop. Code 4
   Hamburg SD
   Supt. – See Hamburg
   ES, P O BOX 127   71676 – Ernest Smith, prin.

Wilson, Mississippi Co., Pop. Code 4
   South Mississippi County SD
   Sch. Sys. Enr. Code 4
   Supt. – Harvey Barton, P O BOX 159   72395
   ES, 1 LEE STREET   72395 – Ron Martin, prin.
   Other Schools – See Dyess, Joiner, Keiser, Luxora

Winslow, Washington Co., Pop. Code 2
   Winslow SD
   Sch. Sys. Enr. Code 2
   Supt. – Mary Sallee, P O BOX 140   72959
   ES, P O BOX 140   72959 – Barbara Kutko, prin.

Winthrop, Little River Co., Pop. Code 2
   Winthrop SD
   Sch. Sys. Enr. Code 2
   Supt. – James Reed, P O BOX 8   71866
   ES, P O BOX 8   71866 – Frank Cockrell, prin.

Witts Springs, Searcy Co., Pop. Code 1
   Witts Springs SD
   Sch. Sys. Enr. Code 2
   Supt. – Edgar Loftin, GENERAL DELIVERY   72686
   ES   72686 – Bennie Docekal, prin.

Wynne, Cross Co., Pop. Code 6
   Wynne SD
   Sch. Sys. Enr. Code 3
   Supt. – Leon Wigginton, P O BOX 69   72396
   JHS, P O BOX 69   72396 – Charles Cobb, prin.
   IS, P O BOX 69   72396 – James Pitchford, prin.
   PS, P O BOX 69   72396 – Odell McCallum, prin.

Yellville, Marion Co., Pop. Code 4
   Yellville-Summit SD
   Sch. Sys. Enr. Code 3
   Supt. – Jerry Cunningham
    RURAL ROUTE 01   72687
   Yellville-Summit ES, RURAL ROUTE 01   72687
    John Dwyer, prin.

CALIFORNIA

STATE DEPARTMENT OF EDUCATION
721 Capitol Mall, Sacramento 95814
(916) 445-4688

Superintendent of Public Instruction	Bill Honig
Executive Deputy Superintendent	William Dawson
Chief Management Services	Robert LaLiberte
General Counsel Legal & Audits	Joseph Symkowick
Deputy Superintendent Curriculum & Instructional Leadership	James Smith
Deputy Superintendent Field Services	Robert Agee
Deputy Superintendent Governmental Policy	Joe Holsinger
Deputy Superintendent Specialized Programs	Shirley Thornton
Deputy Superintendent Program Assistance & Compliance	David Gordon

STATE BOARD OF EDUCATION
Francis Laufenberg, *President*   2625 Hillcrest Ave., Orange   92667

CALIFORNIA POSTSECONDARY EDUCATION COMMISSION
Ken O'Brien, *Executive Director*   1020 12th St., Sacramento   95814

COUNTY SUPERINTENDENTS OF SCHOOLS

Alameda County, William Berck, Supt.
   224 W WINTON AVE, Hayward   94544
Alpine County, James Parsons, Supt.
   RURAL ROUTE 01   BOX 42 B, Markleeville   96120
Amador County, Clifford Tyler, Supt.
   217 REX AVE, Jackson   95642
Butte County, Eugene Even, Supt.
   1859 BIRD ST, Oroville   95965

Calaveras County, Marjorie Geiszler, Supt.
   P O BOX 760, Altaville   95221
Colusa County, JoAn Salzen, Supt.
   146 7TH ST, Colusa   95932
Contra Costa County, Ronald Stewart, Supt.
   77 SANTA BARBARA ROAD, Pleasant Hill   94523
Del Norte County, Robert Appel, Supt.
   301 W WASHINGTON BLVD, Crescent City   95531

El Dorado County, Ken Lowry, Supt.
   6767 GREEN VALLEY ROAD, Placerville   95667
Fresno County, John Taylor, Supt.
   2314 MARIPOSA ST, Fresno   93721
Glenn County, Lloyd Hubbard, Supt.
   525 W SYCAMORE ST, Willows   95988
Humboldt County, Louis Bucher, Supt.
   901 MYRTLE AVE, Eureka   95501

Imperial County, Herbert Farrar, Supt.
　1398 SPERBER ROAD, El Centro   92243
Inyo County, Ken Baker, Supt.
　135 S JACKSON ST, Independence   93526
Kern County, Kelly Blanton, Supt.
　5801 SUNDALE AVE, Bakersfield   93309
Kings County, Gene Billingsley, Supt.
　1144 W LACEY BLVD, Hanford   93230
Lake County, Judith Luchsinger, Supt.
　1152 S MAIN ST, Lakeport   95453
Lassen County, William Gillaspie, Supt.
　472-013 JOHNSTONVILLE ROAD, Susanville   96130
Los Angeles County, Stuart Gothold, Supt.
　9300 IMPERIAL HIGHWAY, Downey   90242
Madera County, Sally Frazier, Supt.
　28123 AVE 14, Madera   93638
Marin County, Byron Mauzy, Supt.
　P O BOX 4925, San Rafael   94913
Mariposa County, George J. Barendse, Supt.
　P O BOX 8, Mariposa   95338
Mendicino County, James Spence, Supt.
　2240 EASTSIDE ROAD, Ukiah   95482
Merced County, William Stockard, Supt.
　632 W 13TH ST, Merced   95340
Modoc County, Lewis Foster, Supt.
　139 HENDERSON ST, Alturas   96101
Mono County, Edward Inwood, Supt.
　P O BOX 477, Bridgeport   93517
Monterey County, Troy Bramlett, Supt.
　P O BOX 80851, Salinas   93912
Napa County, Edgar Henderson, Supt.
　4032 MAHER ST, Napa   94558

Nevada County, Jerome Hund, Supt.
　11745 MALTMAN DRIVE, Grass Valley   95945
Orange County, Robert Peterson, Supt.
　P O BOX 9050, Costa Mesa   92628
Placer County, John Reinking, Supt.
　360 NEVADA ST, Auburn   95603
Plumas County, Floyd Warren, Supt.
　P O BOX 10330, Quincy   95971
Riverside County, Dale Holmes, Supt.
　P O BOX 868, Riverside   92502
Sacramento County, Nick Floratos, Supt.
　9738 LINCOLN VILLAGE DRIVE, Sacramento   95827
San Benito County, James Lowry, Supt.
　460 5TH ST, Hollister   95023
San Bernardino County, Charles Terrell, Supt.
　201 NORTH E ST, San Bernardino   92410
San Diego County, Thomas Boysen, Supt.
　6401 LINDA VISTA ROAD, San Diego   92111
San Francisco County, Ramon Cortines, Supt.
　135 VAN NESS AVE, San Francisco   94102
San Joaquin County, Gaylord Nelson, Supt.
　P O BOX 213030, Stockton   95213
San Luis Obispo County, Salvatore Canale, Supt.
　P O BOX 8105, San Luis Obispo   93403
San Mateo County, William Jennings, Supt.
　333 MAIN ST, Redwood City   94063
Santa Barbara County, William Cirone, Supt.
　P O BOX 6307, Santa Barbara   93160
Santa Clara County, Thomas Goodman, Supt.
　100 SKYPORT DRIVE, San Jose   95110
Santa Cruz County, Frank Cooper, Supt.
　809 BAY AVE, Capitola   95010

Shasta County, Majorie Gates, Supt.
　1644 MAGNOLIA AVE, Redding   96001
Sierra County, Michael Moore, Supt.
　P O BOX 959, Loyalton   96118
Siskiyou County, Frank Tallerico, Supt.
　609 S GOLD ST, Yreka   96097
Solano County, Wendall Kuykendall, Supt.
　655 WASHINGTON ST, Fairfield   94533
Sonoma County, Marv Adams, Supt.
　410 FISCAL DRIVE, Santa Rosa   95401
Stanislaus County, John Allard, Supt.
　801 CO CENTER III COURT, Modesto   95355
Sutter County, William Robinson, Supt.
　463 2ND ST, Yuba City   95991
Tehama County, Louis Bosetti, Supt.
　P O BOX 810, Red Bluff   96080
Trinity County, Donald Stewart, Supt.
　P O BOX AH, Weaverville   96093
Tulare County, Dean Hall, Supt.
　202 COUNTY CIVIC CENTER, Visalia   93291
Tuolumne County, Orville Millhollin, Supt.
　175 FAIRVIEW LANE, Sonora   95370
Ventura County, James Cowan, Supt.
　535 E MAIN ST, Ventura   93001
Yolo County, John Graf, Supt.
　175 WALNUT ST, Woodland   95695
Yuba County, Victor Pulsifer, Supt.
　938 14TH ST, Marysville   95901

PUBLIC, PRIVATE, AND PAROCHIAL ELEMENTARY SCHOOLS

Acampo, San Joaquin Co.
Lodi USD
Supt. – See Lodi
Houston ES, 4600 E ACAMPO ROAD   95220
　Carolyn Wilson, prin.

Oak View Un. ESD
Sch. Sys. Enr. Code 2
Supt. – William Chiechi
　7474 E COLLIER ROAD   95220
Oak View ES, 7474 E COLLIER ROAD   95220
　William Chiechi, prin.

Mokelumne River ES, 18950 N HWY 99   95220

Acton, Los Angeles Co., Pop. Code 3
Soledad-Agua Dulce Un. ESD
Sch. Sys. Enr. Code 4
Supt. – Tom Brown, P O BOX 68   93510
High Desert MS
　3710 ANTELOPE WOODS RD   93510
　Elizabeth Gowling, prin.
ES, 32248 N CROWN VALLEY ROAD   93510
　Margaret Odell, prin.
Other Schools – See Agua Dulce

Adelanto, San Bernardino Co., Pop. Code 4
Adelanto ESD
Sch. Sys. Enr. Code 4
Supt. – David Kincaid, P O BOX 70   92301
ES, 17931 JONATHAN ST   92301
　Derral Lee, prin.
Westside Park ES, 18270 CADABA   92301
　James Naranjo, prin.
Other Schools – See George A F B

Adin, Modoc Co.
Big Valley JUSD
Supt. – See Bieber
Big Valley PS, P O BOX 186   96006
　Boyce McClain, prin.

Agoura Hills, Los Angeles Co., Pop. Code 2
Las Virgenes USD
Supt. – See Westlake
Lindero Canyon MS
　5844 LARBOARD LANE   91301
　E. Joseph Nardo, prin.
Sumac ES, 6050 CALMFIELD AVE   91301
　Patricia Vincent, prin.
Willow ES, 5920 RUSTLING OAKS DRIVE   91301
　Renee Lamkay, prin.
Yerba Buena ES, 5844 LARBOARD LANE   91301
　Dorothy Penney, prin.

Oak Park USD
Sch. Sys. Enr. Code 4
Supt. – Marilyn Corey, 5801 CONIFER ST   91301
Medea Creek MS, 899 KANAN ROAD   91301
　Larry Misel, prin.
Brookside ES, 165 SATINWOOD AVE   91301
　Jeff Hamlin, prin.
Oak Hills ES, 1010 KANAN RD   91301
　Mary George, prin.

Agua Dulce, Los Angeles Co.
Soledad-Agua Dulce Un. ESD
Supt. – See Acton
ES, 11311 W FRASCATI ST   91350
　Carol Urban, prin.

Ahwahnee, Madera Co.
Wasuma Un. ESD
Sch. Sys. Enr. Code 2
Supt. – Leonard Brown, P O BOX 98   93601
Wasuma ES, P O BOX 98   93601
　Leonard Brown, prin.

Alameda, Alameda Co., Pop. Code 8
Alameda City USD
Sch. Sys. Enr. Code 6
Supt. – John Searles, 2200 CENTRAL AVE   94501
Chipman MS, 401 PACIFIC AVE   94501
　Jeffrey Daley, prin.
Lincoln MS, 1250 FERNSIDE BLVD   94501
　Nicholas O'Donnell, prin.
Wood MS, 420 GRAND ST   94501
　Robert Reeves, prin.
Earhart ES, 400 PACKET LANDING ROAD   94501
　Marlene Grcevich, prin.
Edison ES, 2700 BUENA VISTA AVE   94501
　Rosemary Holmes, prin.
Haight ES, 2025 SANTA CLARA AVE   94501
　David Dierking, prin.
Longfellow ES, 500 PACIFIC AVE   94501
　Patricia Klaus, prin.
Lum ES, 1801 SANDCREEK WAY   94501
　James Lynch, prin.
Miller ES, 250 SINGLETON AVE   94501
　William Horlbeck, prin.
Otis ES, 3010 FILLMORE ST   94501
　Barbara Manning, prin.
Washington ES, 825 TAYLOR AVE   94501
　Carole Robie, prin.
Woodstock ES, 1900 3RD ST   94501
　Raymond Sheriff, prin.

Carden Redwood ES
　1433 SAN ANTONIO AVE   94501
Peter Pan Academy, 3171 MECARTNEY RD   94501
St. Barnabas ES, 1400 6TH ST   94501
St. Joseph ES, 1910 SAN ANTONIO AVE   94501
St. Philip Neri ES, 1335 HIGH ST   94501

Alamo, Contra Costa Co.
San Ramon Valley USD
Supt. – See Danville
Stone Valley MS, 3001 MIRANDA AVE   94507
　Ronald Loos, prin.
ES, 100 WILSON ROAD   94507 – (—), prin.
Rancho Romero ES, 180 HEMME AVE   94507
　Bonnie Solberg, prin.

Albany, Alameda Co., Pop. Code 7
Albany City USD
Sch. Sys. Enr. Code 4
Supt. – J. Dale Hudson, 904 TALBOT AVE   94706
MS, 1000 JACKSON ST   94706
　Teresa Corpuz, prin.
Cornell ES, 920 CORNELL AVE   94706
　Craig Boyan, prin.
Marin ES, 1001 SANTA FE AVE   94706
　Gary Amado, prin.
Vista ES, 720 JACKSON ST   94706
　Helen Laird, prin.

Alderpoint, Humboldt Co.
Southern Humbolt JUSD
Supt. – See Garberville
Jewett ES   95411 – Don Swanson, prin.

Alhambra, Los Angeles Co., Pop. Code 8
Alhambra City SD
Sch. Sys. Enr. Code 7
Supt. – B. H. Peppin, P O BOX 110   91802
Baldwin ES, 900 S ALMANSOR ST   91801
　Charles Hanawalt, prin.
Emery Park ES
　2821 W COMMONWEALTH AVE   91803
　Barbra Randolph, prin.
Fremont ES, 2001 ELM ST   91803
　Susan Tenorio, prin.
Garfield ES, 110 W MCLEAN ST   91801
　Garnet Stewart, prin.
Granada ES, 100 S GRANADA AVE   91801
　Lavonne Wood, prin.

Marguerita ES
　1603E S MARGUERITA AVE   91803
　Gary Fox, prin.
Northrup ES, 409 S ATLANTIC BLVD   91801
　Marsha Gilbert, prin.
Park ES, 301 N MARENGO AVE   91801
　Cristina Witham, prin.
Ramona ES, 509 W NORWOOD PLACE   91803
　Amy Shields, prin.
Other Schools – See Monterey Park

All Souls ES, 29 S ELECTRIC AVE   91801
Emmaus Lutheran ES
　840 S ALMANSOR ST   91801
St. Therese ES, 515 N VEGA ST   91801
St. Thomas More Catholic ES
　2510 S FREMONT AVE   91803

Alpaugh, Tulare Co., Pop. Code 3
Alpaugh USD
Sch. Sys. Enr. Code 1
Supt. – Walter Terrio, P O BOX 7   93201
ES, P O BOX 7   93201 – Walter Terrio, prin.

Alpine, San Diego Co., Pop. Code 6
Alpine Un. SD
Sch. Sys. Enr. Code 4
Supt. – John Ancell
　1323 ADMINISTRATION WAY   92001
McQueen MS
　8770 HARBISON CANYON ROAD   92201
　Richard Miller, prin.
ES, 1850 ALPINE BLVD   92001
　Sharon Justeson, prin.
Shadow Hills MS
　8818 HARBISON CANYON ROAD   92001
　Jonathan Knight, prin.

Alta, Placer Co.
Alta-Dutch Flat Un. ESD
Sch. Sys. Enr. Code 2
Supt. – Lorna Winter, P O BOX 958   95701
Alta-Dutch Flat ES, BONNIE NOOK ROAD   95701
　Lorna Winter, prin.

Altadena, Los Angeles Co., Pop. Code 8
Pasadena USD
Supt. – See Pasadena
Eliot MS, 2184 LAKE AVE   91001
　Delano Yarbrough, prin.
ES, 743 E CALAVERAS ST   91001 – J. Ridout, prin.
Burbank ES, 2046 ALLEN AVE   91001
　Linda Talbert, prin.
Edison ES, 3126 GLENROSE AVE   91001
　Larry Raymond, prin.
Franklin ES, 527 VENTURA ST   91001
　Virgie Edwards, prin.
Jackson ES, 593 W WOODBURY ROAD   91001
　Antoinette Dunbar, prin.
Loma Alta ES, 3544 CANON BLVD   91001
　Carmen Rosser, prin.
Noyes ES, 1919 PINECREST DRIVE   91001
　Elyse Sullivan, prin.

Sahag-Mesrob Armenian Christian School
　2501 MAIDEN LN   91001
St. Elizabeth ES, 1840 LAKE AVE   91001
St. Mark's ES, 1014 E ALTADENA DR   91001

Alta Loma, San Bernardino Co., Pop. Code 5
Alta Loma ESD
Sch. Sys. Enr. Code 6
Supt. – J. McMurtry, P O BOX 370   91701
JHS, 9000 LEMON AVE   91701 – James Dyer, prin.
ES, 7085 AMETHYST ST   91701
　Arcila Aleman, prin.
Carnelian ES, 7105 CARNELIAN ST   91701
　Mary Burke, prin.
Deer Canyon ES, 10225 HAMILTON ST   91701
　Gary Hall, prin.

Hermosa ES, 10133 WILSON AVE 91701
  Blanche Steinaker, prin.
Jasper ES, 6881 S GILBERT ST 91701
  Michael Doyle, prin.
Stork ES, 5646 JASPER ST 91701
  Peter Watson, prin.
Victoria Groves ES, 10950 EMERSON 91701
  Joseph Laponis, prin.

Altaville, Calaveras Co.
Mark Twain Un. ESD
  Sch. Sys. Enr. Code 2
  Supt. – Keith Bell, P O BOX 1239 95221
  Twain ES, P O BOX 1239 95221 – Keith Bell, prin.

Alturas, Modoc Co., Pop. Code 5
Modoc JUSD
  Sch. Sys. Enr. Code 4
  Supt. – Frank Burk, 906 W 4TH ST 96101
  Modoc JHS, 906 W 4TH ST 96101
    Patricia Neal, prin.
  ES, 809 W 8TH ST 96101 – Kenneth Bushey, prin.
  Other Schools – See Canby, Likely

Alviso, Santa Clara Co.
Santa Clara USD
  Supt. – See Santa Clara
  Mayne ES, P O BOX 187 95002
    Ruth Costanzo, prin.

Amboy, San Bernardino Co.
Needles USD
  Supt. – See Needles
  ES, P O BOX 66 92304 – David Renquest, prin.

Anaheim, Orange Co., Pop. Code 9
Anaheim ESD
  Sch. Sys. Enr. Code 7
  Supt. – Meliton Lopez, 890 S OLIVE ST 92805
  Barton ES, 1926 W CLEARBROOK LANE 92804
    Ervin Hass, prin.
  Edison ES, 1526 E ROMNEYA DRIVE 92805
    Consuelo Raley, prin.
  Franklin ES, 521 W WATER ST 92805
    Carolyn Johnson, prin.
  Gauer ES, 810 N GILBERT ST 92801
    Jack Dales, prin.
  Guinn ES, 1051 S SUNKIST ST 92806
    Myron Okimoto, prin.
  Henry ES, 1123 W ROMNEYA DRIVE 92801
    Maureen Kaneko, prin.
  Jefferson ES, 504 E SOUTH ST 92805
    Loretta Barthrop, prin.
  Juarez ES, 841 S SUNKIST ST 92806
    Evelyn Weisman, prin.
  Key ES, 2000 W BALL ROAD 92804
    Stella Marquez, prin.
  Lincoln ES, 1413 E BROADWAY 92805
    Ruth Sorensen, prin.
  Loara ES, 1601 W BROADWAY 92802
    Patrick Hart, prin.
  Madison ES, 1510 S NUTWOOD ST 92804
    Lynn Crutchley, prin.
  Mann ES, 920 N JANSS ST 92805
    Robert Gasio, prin.
  Marshall ES, 2066 W FALMOUTH AVE 92801
    Greta Nagel, prin.
  Palm Lane ES, 1646 W PALM LANE 92802
    Joyce Holmes, prin.
  Price ES, 1516 W NORTH ST 92801
    Randall Wiethorn, prin.
  Revere ES, 131 W MIDWAY DRIVE 92805
    Phillip Perez, prin.
  Roosevelt ES, 1600 E VERMONT AVE 92805
    Dana McClanahan, prin.
  Ross ES, 535 S WALNUT ST 92802
    Sandra Englander, prin.
  Stoddard ES, 1841 S NINTH ST 92802
    Roberta Thompson, prin.
  Sunkist ES, 500 N SUNKIST ST 92806
    Dorothy Ver Wys, prin.

Anaheim Un. HSD
  Sch. Sys. Enr. Code 7
  Supt. – Cynthia Grennan, P O BOX 3520 92803
  Ball JHS, 1500 W BALL ROAD 92802
    Miles Brakke, prin.
  Brookhurst JHS, 601 N BROOKHURST ST 92801
    Ken McGee, prin.
  Dale JHS, 900 S DALE AVE 92804
    Bennett Looney, prin.
  Orangeview JHS, 3715 W ORANGE AVE 92804
    Thomas Kenaley, prin.
  South JHS, 2320 E SOUTH ST 92806
    Kenneth Moulton, prin.
  Sycamore JHS, 1801 E SYCAMORE ST 92805
    LaFrance Terrell, prin.
  Other Schools – See Cypress, La Palma

Centralia ESD
  Supt. – See Buena Park
  Danbrook ES, 320 S DANBROOK DRIVE 92804
    Leroy Green, prin.

Magnolia ESD
  Sch. Sys. Enr. Code 5
  Supt. – Arch Haskins
    2705 W ORANGE AVE 92804
  Baden-Powell ES
    2911 W STONYBROOK DRIVE 92804
    L. Smith, prin.
  Disney ES, 2323 W ORANGE AVE 92804
    Susan Harris, prin.
  Marshall ES, 2627 W CRESCENT AVE 92801
    June Tait, prin.

Maxwell ES, 2613 W ORANGE AVE 92804
  Richard Turrentine, prin.
Salk ES, 1411 S GILBERT ST 92804
  Daniel Copple, prin.
Schweitzer ES, 229 S DALE AVE 92804
  John Allison, prin.
Walter ES, 10802 RUSTIC LANE 92804
  Steve Dunn, prin.
Other Schools – See Stanton

Orange USD
  Supt. – See Orange
  El Rancho MS, 181 S DEL GIORGIO ROAD 92808
    Ralph Jameson, prin.
  Anaheim Hills ES, 6450 E SERRANO AVE 92807
    Sharon Adele, prin.
  Crescent IS, 5001 GERDA DR 92807
    William Colley, prin.
  Crescent PS, 5125 E GERDA DRIVE 92807
    Anne Schrader, prin.
  Imperial ES, 400 S IMPERIAL HIGHWAY 92807
    Marilyn Buchtel, prin.
  Nohl Canyon ES
    4100 NOHL RANCH ROAD 92807
    Gordon Schott, prin.
  Riverdale ES, 4540 E RIVERDALE AVE 92807
    Jim Luft, prin.

Placentia USD
  Supt. – See Placentia
  Glenview ES, 1775 N GLENVIEW AVE 92807
    Judith Glick, prin.
  Rio Vista ES, 310 N RIO VISTA ST 92806
    John McClanahan, prin.
  Woodsboro ES, 7575 E WOODSBORO AVE 92807
    Bonnie Drolet, prin.

Savanna ESD
  Sch. Sys. Enr. Code 4
  Supt. – Thomas Halvorsen
    1330 S KNOTT AVE 92804
  Cerritos ES, 3731 W CERRITOS AVE 92804
    Marilyn Warner, prin.
  Hansen ES, 1300 S KNOTT AVE 92804
    Victoria Hernandez, prin.
  Reid ES, 720 S WESTERN AVE 92804
    Donald Hill, prin.
  Other Schools – See Buena Park

St. Catherines Military School
  P O BOX 3070 92803
Anaheim Discovery Christian School
  720 S MAGNOLIA AVE 92804
Fairmont Private ES, 1557 W MABLE ST 92802
Hepatha Lutheran ES
  5800 E SANTA ANA CANYON RD 92807
Heritage ES, 227 N MAGNOLIA AVE 92801
Prince of Peace Lutheran ES
  1421 W BALL RD 92802
Southern California Christian ES
  1026 S EAST ST 92805
St. Anthony Claret ES
  1450 E LA PALMA AVE 92805
St. Boniface ES, 500 W CHARTRES ST 92805
St. Justin Martyr ES, 2030 W BALL RD 92804
Trinity Lutheran Christian ES
  4101 E NOHL RANCH RD 92807
Zion Lutheran ES, 1244 E CYPRESS ST 92805

Anderson, Shasta Co., Pop. Code 6
Cascade Un. ESD
  Sch. Sys. Enr. Code 4
  Supt. – Joseph Cresto,Jr., 1645 MILL ST 96007
  MS, 1646 FERRY ST 96007 – Fred Ides, prin.
  Anderson Heights ES, 1530 SPRUCE ST 96007
    Richard Schafer, prin.
  Meadow Lane ES
    2770 BALLS FERRY ROAD 96007
    Tom Worthen, prin.
  Verde Vale ES, 1661 JACQUELINE ST 96007
    James Carroll, prin.

Happy Valley Un. ESD
  Sch. Sys. Enr. Code 3
  Supt. – David Taylor, 17480 PALM AVE 96007
  Happy Valley MS, 17480 PALM AVE 96007
    Robert Ferrera, prin.
  Happy Valley PS
    16300 CLOVERDALE ROAD 96007
    Jim Amour, prin.

Pacheco Un. ESD
  Supt. – See Redding
  Prairie ES, RURAL ROUTE 01 BOX 3012 96007
    Spencer Smith, prin.

Sacred Heart ES, P O BOX 547 96007

Angwin, Napa Co., Pop. Code 6
Howell Mountain ESD
  Sch. Sys. Enr. Code 2
  Supt. – Lenore Mercer
    525 WHITE COTTAGE ROAD N 94508
  Howell Mountain ES
    525 WHITE COTTAGE ROAD N 94508
    Lenore Mercer, prin.

Pacific Union College ES, 135 NEILSEN CT 94508

Annapolis, Sonoma Co.
Horicon ESD
  Sch. Sys. Enr. Code 2
  Supt. – Clarence DePew
    35555 ANNAPOLIS ROAD 95412
  Horicon ES, ANNAPOLIS ROAD 95412
    Clarence DePew, prin.

Antioch, Contra Costa Co., Pop. Code 8
Antioch USD
  Sch. Sys. Enr. Code 7
  Supt. – Alan Newell, 510 G ST 94509
  Belshaw ES, 2801 ROOSEVELT LANE 94509
    Larry Mori, prin.
  Bidwell ES, 800 GARY AVE 94509
    Luann Duggan, prin.
  Fremont ES, 1413 F ST 94509
    Joseph Wallace, prin.
  Kimball ES, 1310 AUGUST WAY 94509
    Karlis Veidins, prin.
  Marsh ES, 2304 H ST 94509 – William Reed, prin.
  Mission ES, 1711 MISSION DRIVE 94509
    Ralph Richardson, prin.
  Sutter ES, 3410 LONGVIEW ROAD 94509
    Carol Burcio, prin.
  Turner ES, 4207 DELTA FAIR BLVD 94509
    Jeannie Rhodes, prin.

Holy Rosary ES, 25 E 15TH ST 94509

Anza, Riverside Co.
Hemet USD
  Supt. – See Hemet
  Hamilton ES, P O BOX 97 92306
    Carlyle Cripe, prin.

Apple Valley, San Bernardino Co., Pop. Code 6
Apple Valley USD
  Sch. Sys. Enr. Code 6
  Supt. – June Schmieder
    22974 BEAR VALLEY ROAD 92308
  JHS, 12555 NAVAJO ROAD 92308
    Robert Turner, prin.
  Desert Knolls ES, 18213 SYMERON DRIVE 92307
    (—), prin.
  Mariana ES, 10601 MANHASSET ROAD 92308
    Rick Wolf, prin.
  Mojave Mesa ES, Q5552 WICHITA ROAD 92308
    Doug Jenison, prin.
  Rancho Verde ES, 14334 PIONEER ROAD 92307
    Edward Barrington, prin.
  Sandia ES, 21331 SANDIA RD 91701
    William Quimby, prin.
  Yucca Loma ES
    21351 YUCCA LOMA ROAD 92307
    Mary Jenkins, prin.

Apple Valley Christian School
  22434 NISQUALLY ROAD 92308
Our Lady of the Desert ES
  18350 HIGHWAY 18 92307

Aptos, Santa Cruz Co., Pop. Code 6
Pajaro Valley USD
  Supt. – See Watsonville
  JHS, 1001 HUNTINGTON DR 95003
    Paul Owen, prin.
  Mar Vista ES, 6860 SOQUEL DR 95003
    Cathy Stefanki, prin.
  Rio Del Mar ES, 819 DINEHURST 95001
    Carlene Gundersgaard, prin.
  Valencia ES, 250 APTOS SCHOOL ROAD 95003
    Yida Nogueda, prin.

Mid County Christian ES
  2701 CABRILLO COLLEGE DR 95003
Santa Cruz Montessori School
  6230 SOQUEL DR 95003

Arbuckle, Colusa Co., Pop. Code 4
Pierce JUSD
  Sch. Sys. Enr. Code 3
  Supt. – Dean Crechriou
    RURAL ROUTE 01 BOX 20 95912
  Johnson JHS, RURAL ROUTE 01 BOX 22 95912
    Keith Williams, prin.
  ES, P O BOX 100 95912 – Thomas Hamilton, prin.
  Other Schools – See Grimes

Arcadia, Los Angeles Co., Pop. Code 8
Arcadia USD
  Sch. Sys. Enr. Code 6
  Supt. – Stephen Goldstone
    234 CAMPUS DRIVE 91006
  Camino Grove ES, P O BOX 2 91006
    William Robertson, prin.
  Highland Oaks ES, 10 VIRGINIA DRIVE 91006
    Paul Kearns, prin.
  Holly Avenue ES, 360 W DUARTE ROAD 91006
    Aideen Honzay, prin.
  Longley Way ES, 2601 LONGLEY WAY 91006
    John Hart, prin.
  Reid ES, 1000 HUGO REID DRIVE 91006
    Tim Brown, prin.
  Stocker ES, 422 W LEMON AVE 91006
    Mary Sund, prin.

El Monte ESD
  Supt. – See El Monte
  Rio Hondo ES, 11425 WILDFLOWER ROAD 91006
    Armene Chavdarian, prin.

Rio Hondo Preparatory School
  P O BOX 118 91006
Annunciation ES, 1307 E LONGDEN AVE 91006
Anoakia ES, 758 ANOAKIA LN 91006
Arcadia Christian ES
  1900 S SANTA ANITA AVE 91006
Barnhart ES, 226 W COLORADO BLVD 91006
Holy Angels ES, 360 CAMPUS DR 91006

Arcata, Humboldt Co., Pop. Code 7
Arcata ESD
Sch. Sys. Enr. Code 3
Supt. – Lawrence McCarty, 1897 S ST 95521
Sunny Brae MS, 1430 BUTTERMILK LANE 95521
  David Hochman, prin.
Bloomfield ES, 1897 S ST 95521
  Diana Hendry, prin.
Sunset ES, 2400 BALDWIN ST 95521
  Lynda Kime, prin.

Fieldbrook ESD
Sch. Sys. Enr. Code 2
Supt. – William Werner
  4070 FIELDBROOK ROAD 95521
Fieldbrook ES, 4070 FIELDBROOK RD 95521
  William Werner, prin.

Pacific Un. ESD
Sch. Sys. Enr. Code 3
Supt. – Sarie Toste, 3001 JANES ROAD 95521
Pacific ES, 3001 JANES ROAD 95521
  Sarie Toste, prin.

Christian School of Arcata, 1700 UNION ST 95521

Armona, Kings Co., Pop. Code 4
Armona Un. ESD
Sch. Sys. Enr. Code 3
Supt. – Joe Looney, P O BOX 368 93202
Parkview MS, 11075 C ST 93202
  Phil Holloway, prin.
ES, 14045 PIMO ST 93202
  Gerry Collinwood, prin.

Armona Union Academy, P O BOX 397 93202

Arnold, Calaveras Co.
Vallecito Un. ESD
Supt. – See Murphys
Fischer ES, P O BOX 807 95247
  Walter O'Neill, prin.

Aromas, Monterey Co.
Pajaro Valley USD
Supt. – See Watsonville
ES, P O BOX 216 95004 – Rowland Baker, prin.

Arroyo Grande, San Luis Obispo Co., Pop. Code 7
Lucia Mar USD
Sch. Sys. Enr. Code 6
Supt. – Joseph Boeckx, 602 ORCHARD AVE 93420
Paulding IS, 600 CROWN HILL ST 93420
  James Miller, prin.
Branch ES, 970 SCHOOL ROAD 93420
  Martha Silva, prin.
Harloe ES, 901 FIAR OAKS AVE 93420
  David Wilson, prin.
North Oceano ES, 2101 THE PIKE 93420
  Sandra Lebens, prin.
Ocean View ES, 1208 LINDA DRIVE 93420
  Raenna Thomasson, prin.
Other Schools – See Grover City, Nipomo, Oceano,
  Pismo Beach

Coastal Christian Academy, 227 BRIDGE ST 93420
St. Patrick's Parochial ES
  900 W BRANCH ST 93420
Valley View Advent Academy
  230 VERNON ST 93420

Artesia, Los Angeles Co., Pop. Code 7
ABC USD
Supt. – See Cerritos
Ross JHS, 17707 ELAINE AVE 90701
  Joe Baird, prin.
Burbank ES, 17711 ROSETON AVE 90701
  Donald Bolton, prin.
Elliott ES, 18415 CORTNER AVE 90701
  Ginny Trapani, prin.
Kennedy ES, 17500 BELSHIRE AVE 90701
  Judi McEvers, prin.
Niemes ES, 16715 JERSEY AVE 90701
  Karin Newlin, prin.

Our Lady of Fatima ES
  18626 CLARKDALE AVE 90701

Arvin, Kern Co., Pop. Code 6
Arvin Un. ESD
Sch. Sys. Enr. Code 4
Supt. – John Davis
  737 BEAR MOUNTAIN BLVD 93203
Haven Drive JHS
  737 BEAR MOUNTAIN BLVD 93203
  Kenneth Randolph, prin.
Haven Drive IS
  737 BEAR MOUNTAIN BLVD 93203
  Clifford Turk, prin.
Sierra Vista ES
  737 BEAR MOUNTAIN BLVD 93203
  Donald Olague, prin.

Di Giorgio ESD
Sch. Sys. Enr. Code 2
Supt. – Carl Delfino
  RURAL ROUTE 01 BOX 34 93203
Di Giorgio ES, RURAL ROUTE 01 BOX 34 93203
  Carl Delfino, prin.

Atascadero, San Luis Obispo Co., Pop. Code 7
Atascadero USD
Sch. Sys. Enr. Code 5
Supt. – Anthony Avina, 6800 LEWIS AVE 93422
JHS, 6501 LEWIS AVE 93422
  Dianne Brokaw, prin.

Lewis Avenue ES, 6495 LEWIS AVE 93422
  Mike Clark, prin.
Monterey Road ES
  3355 MONTEREY ROAD 93422
  Fred McGaughey, prin.
San Gabriel ES, 8500 SAN GABRIEL RD 93422
  Charles Wilbur, prin.
Santa Rosa Road ES
  8655 SANTA ROSA ROAD 93422
  Greg Howe, prin.
Other Schools – See Creston, Santa Margarita

North County Christian School
  P O BOX 6017 93423

Atherton, San Mateo Co., Pop. Code 6
Las Lomitas ESD
Supt. – See Menlo Park
Los Lomitas ES
  299 ALAMEDA DE LAS PULGAS 94025
  Marsha Gilpatrick, prin.

Menlo Park City ESD
Supt. – See Menlo Park
Encinal MS, 195 ENCINAL AVE 94025
  Leon Johnson, prin.
Laurel ES, 95 EDGE ROAD 94025
  Jhea McCloskey, prin.

Redwood City ESD
Supt. – See Redwood City
Selby Lane ES, 170 SELBY LANE 94025
  Judith Daher, prin.

Atwater, Merced Co., Pop. Code 7
Atwater ESD
Sch. Sys. Enr. Code 5
Supt. – Dr. Donald DeLong, P O BOX 775 95301
Mitchell IS, 1753 5TH ST 95301
  Sandra Lenker, prin.
Bellevue ES, P O BOX 775 95301
  Mona Adkins, prin.
Colburn ES, P O BOX 775 95301 – Earl Gotts, prin.
Mitchell ES, 1761 GROVE AVE 95301
  Randy Cross, prin.
Olaeta ES, P O BOX 775 95301
  Andrew Tolsma, prin.
Shaffer ES, P O BOX 775 95301
  Blandford Jones, prin.
Wood ES, P O BOX 775 95301
  Michael Kelly, prin.

St. Anthony ES, 1801 WINTON WAY 95301

Auberry, Fresno Co.
Auberry Un. ESD
Sch. Sys. Enr. Code 2
Supt. – Ward Stewart
  33367 AUBERRY ROAD 93602
ES, 33367 AUBERRY ROAD # 539 93602
  Ward Stewart, prin.

Chawanakee JESD
Supt. – See North Fork
Chawanakee ES
  46964 LOWER REDINGER RD 93602
  June Richie, prin.

Pine Ridge ESD
Sch. Sys. Enr. Code 2
Supt. – Beverly Hauss
  45828 AUBERRY ROAD 93602
Pine Ridge ES, 45828 AUBERRY ROAD 93602
  Beverly Hauss, prin.

Auburn, Placer Co., Pop. Code 6
Ackerman ESD
Sch. Sys. Enr. Code 2
Supt. – David Westsmith
  13777 BOWMAN ROAD 95603
Bowman ES, 13777 BOWMAN ROAD 95603
  David Westsmith, prin.

Auburn Un. ESD
Sch. Sys. Enr. Code 4
Supt. – Del Alberti
  1225 LINCOLN WAY #3 95603
Cain MS, 150 PALM AVE 95603
  Catherine Barbo, prin.
Alta Vista ES, 173 OAK ST 95603
  Audrey Mueller, prin.
Lincoln Way ES, 1215 LINCOLN WAY 95603
  Walter Adamson, prin.
Rock Creek ES, 3050 BELL ROAD 95603
  Bill Van Nort, prin.

Forest Lake Christian School
  12515 COMBIE ROAD 95603
St. Joseph's Parish ES, 11610 ATWOOD RD 95603

Avalon, Los Angeles Co., Pop. Code 4
Long Beach USD
Supt. – See Long Beach
ES, P O BOX 557 90704 – Clifford Meyer, Jr., prin.

Avenal, Kings Co., Pop. Code 5
Reef-Sunset USD
Sch. Sys. Enr. Code 4
Supt. – Tony Thornburg, 205 N PARK ST 93204
ES, 500 S 1ST AVE 93204 – Alan Dyar, prin.
Other Schools – See Kettleman City

Azusa, Los Angeles Co., Pop. Code 8
Azusa USD
Sch. Sys. Enr. Code 6
Supt. – Duane Stiff, P O BOX 500 91702

Center IS, 5500 S CERRITOS AVE 91702
  Jon Blickenstaff, prin.
Foothill IS, 151 N FENIMORE AVE 91702
  Peter Baum, prin.
Slauson IS, 340 W 5TH ST 91702 – Art Hiett, prin.
Dalton ES, 500 E 10TH ST 91702
  Carolyn Wertz, prin.
Gladstone Street ES
  1040 E GLADSTONE ST 91702
  George Siordia, prin.
Hodge ES, 700 W 11TH ST 91702
  Arturo Delgado, prin.
Lee ES, 550 N CERRITOS AVE 91702
  Bettina Hunt, prin.
Magnolia ES, 945 E NEARFIELD ST 91702
  Lee Baker, prin.
Mountain View ES, 201 N VERNON AVE 91702
  Sandra Miller, prin.
Murray ES, 505 E RENWICK ROAD 91702
  Kenneth Colbert, prin.
Paramount ES, 409 W PARAMOUNT ST 91702
  Adele McCready, prin.
Powell ES, 1035 E MAUNA LOA AVE 91702
  Susan Mummert, prin.
Valleydale ES, 701 S LARK ELLEN AVE 91702
  Mariann Zamary, prin.
Other Schools – See Covina

Alpha Christian ES, P O BOX 1238 91702
Light & Life Christian ES
  777 E ALOSTA AVEVE 91702
St. Frances of Rome ES
  734 N PASADENA AVE 91702

Badger, Fresno Co.
Cutler-Orosi USD
Supt. – See Orosi
Sierra ES, P O BOX 170 93603
  Ramon Oyervidez, prin.

Baker, San Bernardino Co., Pop. Code 2
Baker Valley USD
Sch. Sys. Enr. Code 2
Supt. – Chuck Gehrke, P O BOX 460 92309
ES, P O BOX 460 92309 – Chuck Gehrke, prin.
Other Schools – See Mountain Pass

Bakersfield, Kern Co., Pop. Code 9
Bakersfield City ESD
Sch. Sys. Enr. Code 7
Supt. – Herbert Cole, 1300 BAKER ST 93305
Chipman JHS, 2905 EISSLER ST 93306
  Jerry Tate, prin.
Compton JHS, 3200 PICO AVE 93306
  Linda Mapes, prin.
Curran JHS, 1116 LYMRIC WAY 93309
  Leroy Kroeker, prin.
Emerson JHS, 801 4TH ST 93304
  Donald Londquist, prin.
Sierra JHS, 3017 CENTER ST 93306
  Hugh McGowan, prin.
Washington JHS, 1101 NOBLE AVE 93305
  Barb Sutliff, prin.
Casa Loma ES, 525 E CASA LOMA DRIVE 93307
  Marguerite Lewis, prin.
College Heights ES, 2551 SUNNY LANE 93305
  Palmira McBride, prin.
Eissler ES, 2901 EISSLER ST 93306
  Clarence Medders, prin.
Franklin ES, 2400 TRUXTUN AVE 93301
  Donna McKay, prin.
Fremont ES, 607 TEXAS ST 93307
  Shirley Walston, prin.
Harding ES, 3201 PICO AVE 93306
  Matthew Michael, prin.
Harris ES, 4110 GARNSEY LAND 93309
  Martin DeLeon, prin.
Hort ES, 2301 PARK DRIVE 93306
  Dennis Patrick, prin.
Jefferson ES, 816 LINCOLN ST 93305
  Manuel Ruiz, prin.
Longfellow ES, 12 LINCOLN ST 93305
  Darrow Baker, prin.
Mann ES, 2710 NILES ST 93306
  Genevieve Fabrizius, prin.
McKinley ES, 601 4TH ST 93304
  Vashti Sherrill, prin.
Mt. Vernon ES, 2162 POTOMAC AVE 93307
  Lillian Tafoya, prin.
Munsey ES, 3801 BRAVE AVE 93309
  Ruth McBride, prin.
Nichols ES, 3401 RENEGADE AVE 93306
  Dena Brown, prin.
Noble ES, 1015 NOBLE AVE 93305
  Rodney Edgmon, prin.
Owens ES, 815 POTOMAC AVE 93307
  Fred Haynes, prin.
Pauly ES, 313 PLANZ ROAD 93304
  Helen Poloynis, prin.
Penn ES, 2201 SAN EMIDIO ST 93304
  William McCullough, prin.
Pioneer Drive ES, 4404 PIONEER DRIVE 93306
  Leroy Wallace, prin.
Roosevelt ES, 2324 VERDE ST 93304
  Kathryn Ramey, prin.
Voorhies ES, 6001 PIONEER DRIVE 93306
  Lorenza Hughes, prin.
Wayside ES, 1000 MING AVE 93307
  Shirley Durrett, prin.
West ES, 2400 BENTON ST 93304
  Herbert Nealy, prin.
Williams ES, 1201 WILLIAMS ST 93305
  Al Capilla, prin.

Beardsley ESD
Sch. Sys. Enr. Code 4
Supt. – Bill Luehe, 1001 ROBERTS LN 93308
Beardsley JHS, 1001 ROBERTS LN 93308
  Ronald Seckler, prin.
Beardsley IS, 1005 ROBERTS LANE 93308
  Patricia Alexander, prin.
North Beardsley ES, 900 SANDORD DR 93308
  Randall Jolin, prin.

Edison ESD
Sch. Sys. Enr. Code 3
Supt. – Gary Bray, 9600 EUCALPTUS ST 93306
Edison MS, RURAL ROUTE 05 BOX 532X 93307
  Gary Carlson, prin.
Orangewood ES
  VINELAND AND EUCALYPTUS STS 93307
  Louis Fisher, prin.

Fairfax ESD
Sch. Sys. Enr. Code 4
Supt. – Bill Gibson
  1501 S FAIRFAX ROAD 93307
Fairfax ES, 1501 S FAIRFAX ROAD 93307
  Dale Countryman, prin.
Virginia Avenue ES, 3301 VIRGINIA AVE 93307
  Frank Heath, prin.

Fruitvale ESD
Sch. Sys. Enr. Code 3
Supt. – Carl Olsen
  2114 CALLOWAY DRIVE 93312
Fruitvale JHS, 2114 CALLOWAY DRIVE 93312
  John Hefner, prin.
Greenacres ES, 2114 CALLOWAY DRIVE 93312
  John Hefner, prin.
Quailwood ES, 7310 REMINGTON AVE 93309
  Kay Antongiovanni, prin.

General Shafter ESD
Sch. Sys. Enr. Code 1
Supt. – Jeff Rice, 1316 SHAFTER RD 93313
General Shafter ES
  RURAL ROUTE 07 BOX 713 93313
  (—), prin.

Greenfield Un. ESD
Sch. Sys. Enr. Code 5
Supt. – Don Williams
  16245 FAIRVIEW ROAD 93307
Greenfield JHS, 1109 PACHECO ROAD 93307
  Dwight Walsh, prin.
Fairview ES, 425 E FAIRVIEW ROAD 93307
  Bertha Boullion, prin.
McKee IS, 205 MCKEE ROAD 93307
  David Gehrke, prin.
Plantation ES, 901 PLANTATION AVE 93304
  Dick Smith, prin.
Planz ES, 2400 PLANZ ROAD 93304
  Jim Maberry, prin.

Lakeside Un. ESD
Sch. Sys. Enr. Code 2
Supt. – Raberta Rous
  RURAL ROUTE 03 BOX 1053 93311
Lakeside ES, RURAL ROUTE 03 BOX 1053 93311
  Raberta Rous, prin.

Lerdo ESD
Sch. Sys. Enr. Code 2
Supt. – George Bury
  RURAL ROUTE 11 BOX 650 93312
Lerdo ES, RURAL ROUTE 11 BOX 650 93312
  William Cummings, prin.

Norris SD
Sch. Sys. Enr. Code 4
Supt. – Alvin Sandrini
  RURAL ROUTE 11 BOX 258 93312
Norris JHS, RURAL ROUTE 11 BOX 258 93312
  Steven Shelton, prin.
Norris ES, RURAL ROUTE 11 BOX 258 93312
  Sharron Wennihan, prin.

Panama-Buena Vista Un. SD
Sch. Sys. Enr. Code 6
Supt. – Bill Williams, 4200 ASHE ROAD 93313
Actis JHS, 2400 WESTHOLME BLVD 93309
  Jerry Owen, prin.
Tevis JHS, 3901 PIN OAK PARK BLVD 93311
  Frances Seaman, prin.
Thompson JHS, 4200 PLANZ ROAD 93309
  Paul White, prin.
Buena Vista ES, 6547 BUENA VISTA RD 93311
  Doris DuQuette, prin.
Castle ES, 6001 EDGEMONT DRIVE 93309
  Chris Beck, prin.
Hart ES, 9501 RIDGE ROAD DR 93311
  Larry Stephens, prin.
Laurelglen ES, 2601 EL PORTAL DIRVE 93309
  Jerald Kirkland, prin.
Panama ES, RURAL ROUTE 07 BOX 300 93313
  Kenneth Niblett, prin.
Sandrini ES, 4100 ALUM AVE 93313
  Brian Mark, prin.
Seibert ES, 2800 AGATE ST 93304
  John Birkhauser, prin.
Sing Lum ES, 4600 CHANEY LANE 93311
  John Flippen, prin.
Stine ES, 4300 WILSON ROAD 93309
  Gene Durrett, prin.
Stockdale ES, 7801 KROLL WAY 93309
  Ron Madding, prin.
Van Horn ES, 5501 KEINPELL AVE 93309
  Dolores Whitley, prin.

Rio Bravo-Greeley ESD
Sch. Sys. Enr. Code 2
Supt. – Gerald Higbee
  RURAL ROUTE 04 BOX 500 93312
Rio Bravo-Greeley ES
  ENOS LANE AND KRATZMEYER RD 93308
  David Reese, prin.

Rosedale Un. ESD
Sch. Sys. Enr. Code 4
Supt. – Gary Mullhofer
  RURAL ROUTE 08 BOX 188 93312
Rosedale MS, 33567 ROSEDALE HIGHWAY 93309
  James Henderson, prin.
Rosedale-North ES, 11500 MEACHAM AVE 93308
  Max Souder, prin.

Standard ESD
Supt. – See Oildale
Highland ES, 2900 BARNETT ST 93308
  Tom Lewis, prin.
Wingland ES, 2000 DIANE DRIVE 93308
  Erich Kwek, prin.

Vineland ESD
Sch. Sys. Enr. Code 3
Supt. – Glen Worrell
  RURAL ROUTE 06 BOX 317 93307
Sunset MS, RURAL ROUTE 06 BOX 317 93307
  Stephen Greenfield, prin.
Vineland ES
  VINELAND ROAD AND SUNSET BL 93307
  Phyllis Beene, prin.

—————

Bakersfield SDA Academy
  3333 BERNARD ST 93306
Carden School,Inc., 7900 NILES ST 93306
Friends-Othr ES, 7300 MING AVE 93309
Heritage Academy, 2401 BERNARD ST 93306
Our Lady of Guadalupe ES
  609 E CALIFORNIA AVE 93307
Our Lady of Perpetual Help ES
  2750 LOMA LINDA DR 93305
St. Francis ES, 2516 PALM ST 93304
St. John's Lutheran ES, 912 NEW STINE RD 93309
Stockdale Christian ES
  4901 CALIFORNIA AVE 93309
Sunrise Christian ES
  2600 ROSE MARIE DR 93304

Baldwin Park, Los Angeles Co., Pop. Code 8
Baldwin Park USD
Sch. Sys. Enr. Code 7
Supt. – Jerry Holland, 3699 HOLLY AVE 91706
Holland JHS, 4733 LANDIS AVE 91706
  James Kidwell, prin.
Jones JHS, 14250 MERCED AVE 91706
  Marcus Beasley, prin.
Olive JHS, 13701 OLIVE ST 91706
  Elmer Erdmann, prin.
Sierra Vista JHS, 3600 FRAZIER ST 91706
  Morris Sawyer, prin.
Bursch ES, 4245 MERCED AVE 91706
  R. Hepner, prin.
Central ES, 14741 CENTRAL AVE 91706
  Diana Dobrenen, prin.
Deanza ES, 12820 BESS AVE 91706
  Cyril Koch, prin.
Elwin ES, 13010 WACO ST 91706
  Kathleen Braithwaite, prin.
Foster ES, 13900 FOSTER AVE 91706
  Irene Lewis, prin.
Geddes ES, 14600 CAVETTE PLACE 91706
  Jean Nelson, prin.
Heath ES, 14321 SCHOOL ST 91706
  Gayle Hughes, prin.
Kenmore ES, 3823 KENMORE AVE 91706
  Gloria Orozco, prin.
Pleasant View ES, 14900 NUBIA ST 91706
  Juan Diaz, prin.
Tracy ES, 13350 TRACY ST 91706
  Gerald Robison, prin.
Vineland ES, 3609 VINELAND AVE 91706
  Carolyn Biggle, prin.
Walnut ES, 4701 WALNUT ST 91706
  Marilyn Pina, prin.

Baldwin Park Christian Baptist School
  13940 MERCED AVE 91706
St. John the Baptist ES
  3870 STEWART AVE 91706

Ballico, Merced Co.
Ballico-Cressey ESD
Sch. Sys. Enr. Code 2
Supt. – John Simkins, P O BOX 49 95303
MS, P O BOX 49 95303 – John Simkins, prin.
Cressey ES, P O BOX 49 95303
  John Simkins, prin.

Bangor, Butte Co.
Bangor Un. ESD
Sch. Sys. Enr. Code 1
Supt. – Larry McWilliams, P O BOX 340 95914
ES, ORO-BANGOR HIGHWAY 95914
  Larry McWilliams, prin.

Banning, Riverside Co., Pop. Code 7
Banning USD
Sch. Sys. Enr. Code 5
Supt. – Steve Wilson, 161 W WILLIAMS ST 92220
Coombs IS, 1151 W WILSON ST 92220
  Olivia Hershey, prin.
Cabazon ES, 161 WILLIAMS ST 92220
  (—), prin.

Central ES, 295 N SAN GORGONIO AVE 92220
  Larry Phelps, prin.
Hemmerling ES, 1928 W NICOLET ST 92220
  Laurence Silverman, prin.
Hoffer ES, 1115 E HOFFER ST 92220
  Jessie Wall, prin.

—————

Precious Blood ES, 117 W NICOLET ST 92220

Barstow, San Bernardino Co., Pop. Code 7
Barstow USD
Sch. Sys. Enr. Code 6
Supt. – Eugene Feerick, 551 AVENUE H 92311
JHS, 1000 ARMORY ROAD 92311
  Willard Roberson, prin.
Cameron ES, 801 S MURIEL DRIVE 92311
  James Treese, prin.
Crestline ES, MONTEREY AND RIMROCK 92311
  Ruth Dawson, prin.
Henderson ES, 400 AVENUE E 92311
  Thomas Galvin, prin.
Lenwood ES, 34374 ASH ROAD 92311
  Donald Langille, prin.
Montara ES, 700 MONTARA ROAD 92311
  Phillip Chavez, prin.
Skyline North ES
  36968 CAMARILLIO AVE 92311
  Julia Layden, prin.
Thomson ES, 310 W MOUNTAIN VIEW ST 92311
  Shirley Kelso, prin.
Other Schools – See Hinkley

—————

Barstow Christian ES, 800 YUCCA AVE 92311
St. Joseph's ES
  555 E MOUNTAIN VIEW AVE 92311

Bass Lake, Madera Co.
Bass Lake SD
Supt. – See Oakhurst
ES, P O BOX 157 93604 – Glen Rose, prin.

Bayside, Humboldt Co.
Jacoby Creek ESD
Sch. Sys. Enr. Code 2
Supt. – Ron Bank
  1617 OLD ARCATA ROAD 95524
Jacoby Creek ES, 1617 OLD ARCATA RD 95524
  Ron Bank, prin.

Bear Valley, Calaveras Co.
Alpine County USD
Supt. – See Markleeville
ES, P O BOX 5095 95223 – James Parsons, prin.

Beaumont, Riverside Co., Pop. Code 6
Beaumont USD
Sch. Sys. Enr. Code 5
Supt. – John Wood, P O BOX 187 92223
Mountain View JHS, 1575 CHERRY AVE 92223
  Victor Kezer, prin.
Palm ES, 701 PALM AVE 92223
  Joyce Gonzales, prin.
Summit MS, 650 MAGNOLIA AVE 92223
  Earl Weideman, prin.
Wellwood ES, 715 WELLWOOD AVE 92223
  (—), prin.

—————

Cherry Valley Brethren ES, P O BOX 3153 92223

Bell, Los Angeles Co., Pop. Code 8
Los Angeles USD
Supt. – See Los Angeles
Corona Avenue ES, 3825 BELL AVE 90201
  Edward Losch, prin.
Woodlawn Avenue ES
  6314 WOODLAWN AVE 90201
  Geraldine Herrera, prin.

Bella Vista, Shasta Co.
Bella Vista ESD
Sch. Sys. Enr. Code 2
Supt. – Marvin Steinberg, P O BOX 70 96008
ES, P O BOX 1070 96008 – Marvin Steinberg, prin.

Bellflower, Los Angeles Co., Pop. Code 8
Bellflower USD
Sch. Sys. Enr. Code 6
Supt. – Kenneth Davis, 16703 CLARK AVE 90706
Jefferson ES, 10027 ROSE ST 90706
  Ed Krucli, prin.
Pyle ES, 14500 WOODRUFF AVE 90706
  Warren Binzley, prin.
Ramona ES, 9351 LAUREL ST 90706
  Judy Rafferty, prin.
Washington ES, 9725 JEFFERSON ST 90706
  Michael Medlen, prin.
Woodruff ES, 15332 EUCALYPTUS AVE 90706
  Jeanie Cash, prin.
Other Schools – See Lakewood

—————

Advent Union-Bellflower ES
  15548 SANTA ANA AVE 90706
Bellflower Christian ES
  17408 GRAND AVE 90706
St. Bernard ES, 9647 BEACH ST 90706
St. Dominic Savio ES, 9750 FOSTER RD 90706
Wonderland PS, 10440 ARTESIA BLVD 90706
Woodruff Christian ES
  16400 WOODRUFF AVE 90706

Bell Gardens, Los Angeles Co., Pop. Code 8
Montebello USD
Supt. – See Montebello
IS, 5841 LIVE OAK ST 90201
  Bruce Matsui, prin.
Suva IS, 6660 SUVA ST 90201 – Lary Weiss, prin.

ES, 5620 QUINN ST 90201 – Tom Valdiviez, prin.
Colmar ES, 6139 LOVELAND ST 90201
  Jerome Horkin, prin.
Garfield ES, 7425 GARFIELD AVE 90201
  Janet Torncello, prin.
Suva ES, 6740 SUVA ST 90201
  Margaret Hangartner, prin.

Bell Gardens Christian ES, 6262 GAGE AVE 90201
St. Gertrude ES, 6824 TOLER AVE 90201

Belmont, San Mateo Co., Pop. Code 7
  Belmont ESD
  Sch. Sys. Enr. Code 4
  Supt. – Forrest Shigley
    2960 HALLMARK DRIVE 94002
  Ralston IS, 2675 RALSTON AVE 94002
    Joseph Fruhwirth, prin.
  Central ES, 525 MIDDLE ROAD 94002
    Gretchen Ross, prin.
  Fox ES, 3100 SAINT JAMES ROAD 94002
    Trudy Schoneman, prin.
  Nesbit ES, 500 BIDDULPH WAY 94002
    Forrest Shigley, prin.

Belmont Oaks Academy Kindergarten
  2200 CARLMONT DR 94002
Immaculate Heart of Mary ES
  1000 ALAMEDA DE LAS PULGAS 94002
Notre Dame ES, 1500 RALSTON AVE 94002

Belvedere-Tiburon, Marin Co., Pop. Code 4

St. Hilarys ES, 765 HILARY DR 94920

Benicia, Solano Co., Pop. Code 7
  Benicia USD
  Sch. Sys. Enr. Code 5
  Supt. – John Slezak, 350 E K ST 94510
  MS, 1100 SOUTHAMPTON ROAD 94510
    Carole Hiltman, prin.
  Farmar ES, 901 MILITARY WEST 94510
    Terry Jensen, prin.
  Henderson ES, 650 HASTINGS DR 94510
    Marian Susnjar, prin.
  Mills ES, 401 EAST K ST 94510 – Jane West, prin.
  Semple ES, 2015 E THIRD ST 94510
    Dan Dempsey, prin.

St. Dominic's ES, 935 E 5TH ST 94510

Benton, Inyo Co.
  Eastern Sierra USD
  Supt. – See Bridgeport
  Beaman ES 93512 – Dora Hruda, prin.

Berkeley, Alameda Co., Pop. Code 9
  Berkeley USD
  Sch. Sys. Enr. Code 6
  Supt. – Andrew Viscovich, 2134 GROVE ST 94704
  King JHS, 1781 ROSE ST 94703
    Kathleen Denst, prin.
  Willard JHS, 2425 STUART ST 94705
    Christine Lim, prin.
  Columbus IS, 2211 7TH ST 94710
    Lorna Neill, prin.
  Cragmont PS, 830 REGAL ROAD 94708
    Beverly Miller, prin.
  Emerson PS, 2800 FOREST AVE 94705
    Carolyn Gaertner, prin.
  Jefferson PS, 1400 ADA ST 94702
    Marian Altman, prin.
  LeConte PS, 2241 RUSSELL ST 94705
    Barbara James, prin.
  Longfellow IS, 1500 DERBY ST 94703
    Connie Whitehurst, prin.
  Malcolm X IS, 1731 PRINCE ST 94703
    Ronald Williams, prin.
  Model ES, 2955 CLAREMONT AVE 94705
    (—), prin.
  Oxford PS, 1130 OXFORD ST 94707
    Kathleen Lewis, prin.
  Thousand Oaks PS, 840 COLUSA AVE 94707
    Keith Nomura, prin.
  Washington PS, 2300 GROVE ST 94704
    Frank Fisher, prin.

Richmond USD
  Supt. – See Richmond
  Kensington ES, 90 HIGHLAND BLVD 94708
    Barbara Herold, prin.

Berkeley Christian ES, 1 WINDSOR AVE 94708
Berkeley Montessori School
  2030 FRANCISCO ST 94709
Berkwood ES, 1809 BANCROFT WAY 94703
Black Pine Circle ES, 2027 7TH ST 94710
Ecole Bilingue ES, 1009 HEINZ AVE 94710
School of the Madeleine ES
  1225 MILVIA ST 94709
Sheltons PS, 3339 M L KING JR WAY 94703
St. Joseph ES, 2125 JEFFERSON AVE 94703

Berry Creek, Butte Co.
  Pioneer Un. ESD
  Sch. Sys. Enr. Code 2
  Supt. – Paul McKillop, P O BOX 37 95916
  ES, P O BOX 37 95916 – Paul McKillop, prin.

Beverly Hills, Los Angeles Co., Pop. Code 8
  Beverly Hills USD
  Sch. Sys. Enr. Code 5
  Supt. – Robert French, 255 S LASKY DRIVE 90212
  Beverly Vista ES, 200 S ELM DRIVE 90212
    Nadine Bendit, prin.

El Rodeo ES, 605 N WHITTIER DRIVE 90210
  Dolores Fitchman, prin.
Hawthorne ES, 624 N REXFORD DRIVE 90210
  Ann Picker, prin.
Mann ES, 8701 CHARLEVILLE BLVD 90211
  Arthur Fields, prin.

Good Shepherd ES, 148 S LINDEN DR 90212
Hillel Hebrew Academy
  9120 W OLYMPIC BLVD 90212
Temple Emmanuel Community Day ES
  8844 BURTON WAY 90211

Bieber, Lassen Co., Pop. Code 2
  Big Valley JUSD
  Sch. Sys. Enr. Code 2
  Supt. – Dennis O'Brien, P O BOX 157 96009
  Big Valley IS, P O BOX 157 96009
    Boyce McClain, prin.
  Other Schools – See Adin

Big Bar, Trinity Co.
  Cox Bar ESD
  Sch. Sys. Enr. Code 1
  Supt. – (—), P O BOX 529 96010
  Cox Bar ES, P O BOX 529 96010
    H. Biggers,Jr., prin.

Big Bear Lake, San Bernardino Co., Pop. Code 5
  Bear Valley USD
  Sch. Sys. Enr. Code 4
  Supt. – Rudy Macioge, P O BOX 1529 92315
  MS, 40940 PENNYSLVANIA AVE 92315
    John Niederkorn, prin.
  Big Bear MS, P O BOX 1627 92315
    Tony Kerst, prin.
  Martin ES, P O BOX 1887 92315
    Tony Kerst, prin.
  North Shore ES, P O BOX 1887 92315
    Joelle DeLandtsheer, prin.

Big Bend, Shasta Co.
  Indian Springs ESD
  Sch. Sys. Enr. Code 1
  Supt. – Bill Cullingford, P O BOX P 96011
  Indian Springs ES, P O BOX P 96011
    Bill Cullingford, prin.

Big Creek, Fresno Co.
  Big Creek ESD
  Sch. Sys. Enr. Code 1
  Supt. – Edwin Swanson, P O BOX 98 93605
  ES, P O BOX 98 93605 – Edwin Swanson, prin.

Biggs, Butte Co., Pop. Code 4
  Biggs USD
  Sch. Sys. Enr. Code 3
  Supt. – Wayne Boulding, P O BOX 397 95917
  ES, P O BOX 397 95917 – Lavonne Brown, prin.
  Other Schools – See Richvale

Big Pine, Inyo Co., Pop. Code 3
  Big Pine USD
  Sch. Sys. Enr. Code 2
  Supt. – Layton Dixon, 500 S MAIN ST 93513
  ES, P O BOX 347 93513 – Bonnie Parks, prin.

Big Sur, Monterey Co., Pop. Code 2
  Carmel USD
  Supt. – See Carmel
  Cooper ES, P O BOX 250 93920
    Robert Douglas, prin.

Pacific ESD
  Sch. Sys. Enr. Code 1
  Supt. – William Raebee, P O BOX 1 93920
  Pacific Valley S, P O BOX 1 93920
    William Raebee, prin.

Bishop, Inyo Co., Pop. Code 5
  Bishop JSD
  Sch. Sys. Enr. Code 4
  Supt. – Jeffrey Blackwell, 800 W PINE ST 93514
  Home Street MS, 201 HOME ST 93514
    George Lozito, prin.
  Elm Street ES, 800 W ELM ST 93514
    Gail Koske, prin.
  Pine Street MS, 800 W PINE ST 93514
    George Lozito, prin.

Round Valley JESD
  Sch. Sys. Enr. Code 2
  Supt. – Mary Kilpatrick, RURAL ROUTE 02 93514
  Round Valley ES, RURAL ROUTE 02 93514
    (—), prin.

Blocksburg, Humboldt Co.
  Southern Humboldt USD
  Supt. – See Garberville
  Casterlin MS, HCR ROUTE 95414
    Don Swanson, prin.

Bloomington, San Bernardino Co., Pop. Code 7
  Colton JUSD
  Supt. – See Colton
  JHS, 18829 ORANGE ST 92316
    Patricia Gupperton, prin.
  Crestmore ES, 18870 JURUPA AVE 92316
    Doris Groves, prin.
  Grimes ES, 10009 SPRUCE AVE 92316
    Hal Ensey, prin.
  Lewis ES, 18040 SAN BERNARDINO AVE 92316
    Marilynn Jordan, prin.
  Smith ES, 9551 LINDEN AVE 92316
    Dotti Garcia, prin.
  Zimmerman ES, 11050 LINDEN AVE 92316
    Charlotte Naugle, prin.

Bloomington Christian School
  P O BOX 355 92316

Blue Lake, Humboldt Co., Pop. Code 4
  Blue Lake Un. ESD
  Sch. Sys. Enr. Code 2
  Supt. – Joseph Brewer, P O BOX 268 95525
  ES, P O BOX 268 95525 – Joseph Brewer, prin.

Green Point ESD
  Sch. Sys. Enr. Code 1
  Supt. – (—), 180 VALKENSAR LANE 95525
  Green Point ES, 180 VALKENSAR LANE 95525
    Marie Twibell, prin.

Blythe, Riverside Co., Pop. Code 6
  Palo Verde USD
  Sch. Sys. Enr. Code 5
  Supt. – Leamon Hanson, 187 N 7TH ST 92225
  JHS, 825 N LOVEKIN BLVD 92225
    Thomas Truax, prin.
  Appleby ES, 401 S 3RD ST 92225
    Robert Palmer, prin.
  Brown ES, 241 N 7TH ST 92225
    Norman Baker, prin.
  White ES, 201 N 1ST ST 92225
    Marilee Moore, prin.

Zion Lutheran ES, 721 E CHANSLOR WAY 92225

Bolinas, Marin Co.
  Bolinas-Stinson Un. ESD
  Sch. Sys. Enr. Code 2
  Supt. – Sarah Pusey, HCR 94924
  Bolinas-Stinson ES, HCR 94924
    Sarah Pusey, prin.

Bonita, San Diego Co., Pop. Code 4
  Chula Vista City SD
  Supt. – See Chula Vista
  Allen ES, 4300 ALLEN SCHOOL ROAD 92002
    Jack Geving, prin.
  Sunnyside ES, 5430 SAN MIGUEL ROAD 92002
    Jerry January, prin.
  Valley Vista ES, 3724 VALLEY VISTA WAY 92002
    Barb Boucher, prin.

Bonsall, San Diego Co., Pop. Code 3
  Bonsall Un. ESD
  Sch. Sys. Enr. Code 3
  Supt. – Terry Ryan, P O BOX 3 92003
  ES, OLD RIVER ROAD 92003
    James Hutcherson, prin.

Boonville, Mendocino Co., Pop. Code 3
  Anderson Valley USD
  Sch. Sys. Enr. Code 3
  Supt. – James Johnson, P O BOX 457 95415
  Anderson Valley ES, P O BOX 457 95415
    Damon Dickinson, prin.

Boron, Kern Co., Pop. Code 4
  Muroc JUSD
  Supt. – See North Edwards
  West Boron ES, 12300 DEL ORO ST 93516
    (—), prin.

Borrego Springs, San Diego Co., Pop. Code 3
  Borrego Springs USD
  Sch. Sys. Enr. Code 2
  Supt. – David West, P O BOX 235 92004
  ES, P O BOX 235 92004 – Shanda Smith, prin.

Boulevard, San Diego Co.
  Mountain Empire USD
  Supt. – See Pine Valley
  Clover Flats ES, P O BOX 1088 92005
    Anna Sullivan, prin.

Boyes Hot Springs, Sonoma Co., Pop. Code 5
  Sonoma Valley USD
  Supt. – See Sonoma
  Flowery ES, P O BOX 367 95416
    Greg Aldridge, prin.

Bradley, Monterey Co.
  Bradley Un. ESD
  Sch. Sys. Enr. Code 1
  Supt. – (—), P O BOX 60 93426
  ES, P O BOX 60 93426 – (—), prin.

Brawley, Imperial Co., Pop. Code 7
  Brawley ESD
  Sch. Sys. Enr. Code 5
  Supt. – John Anderson, 261 D ST 92227
  Worth JHS, IMPERIAL AVE & D ST 92227
    Barbara Layaye, prin.
  Hildalgo/Witter ES, TENTH AND K STS 92227
    Beatrice Arce, prin.
  Oakley/Swing ES
    B ST AND EASTERN AVE 92227
    Raymond Spencer, prin.

Magnolia Un. ESD
  Sch. Sys. Enr. Code 1
  Supt. – (—), 4502 CASEY ROAD 92227
  Magnolia ES, 4502 CASEY ROAD 92227
    Blaine Smith, prin.

Mulberry ESD
  Sch. Sys. Enr. Code 1
  Supt. – (—), 1391 RUTHERFORD ROAD 92227
  Mulberry ES, 1391 RUTHERFORD ROAD 92227
    Patrick Casey, prin.

Sacred Heart ES, 428 S IMPERIAL AVE 92227

Brea, Orange Co., Pop. Code 8
Brea-Olinda USD
Sch. Sys. Enr. Code 5
Supt. – Edgar Seal
    1 CIVIC CENTER CIRCLE 92621
JHS, 400 N BREA BLVD 92621
    Mike Condiff, prin.
Arovista ES, 900 EADINGTON DRIVE 92621
    Mark Goldband, prin.
Brea County Hills ES
    150 N ASSOCIATED ROAD 92621
    Eileen Moore, prin.
Fanning ES, 650 APRICOT AVE 92621
    Timothy Harvey, prin.
Laurel ES, 200 FLOWER AVE 92621
    Patricia Ahern, prin.
Mariposa ES, 1111 MARIPOSA DRIVE 92621
    Howard Bryden, prin.
Olinda ES, 109 LILAC LANE 92621
    Joan Lewis, prin.

Brea-Olinda Friends Christian School
    200 ASSOCIATED ROAD 92621
Christ Lutheran ES, 820 W IMPERIAL HWY 92621
St. Angela Merici ES, 575 WALNUT AVE 92621

Brentwood, Contra Costa Co., Pop. Code 5
Brentwood Un. SD
Sch. Sys. Enr. Code 4
Supt. – William Bristow, 250 1ST ST 94513
Hill MS, 140 BIRCH ST 94513
    Jack England, prin.
ES, 929 2ND ST 94513 – Carol Dessaussois, prin.
Garin ES, 250 1ST ST 94513
    Shirley Winthrop, prin.

Bridgeport, Mono Co., Pop. Code 2
Eastern Sierra USD
Sch. Sys. Enr. Code 3
Supt. – Mark Evans, P O BOX 575 93517
ES, P O BOX 577 93517 – Donna Smyth, prin.
Other Schools – See Benton, Coleville, Lee Vining

Bridgeville, Humboldt Co.
Bridgeville ESD
Sch. Sys. Enr. Code 2
Supt. – Lola Cathey, P O BOX 98 95526
ES, P O BOX 98 95526 – (—), prin.

Southern Trinity JUSD
Sch. Sys. Enr. Code 2
Supt. – Richard Plater
    RURAL ROUTE BOX 156 95526
Van Duzen ES, HCR BOX 156 95526
    Richard Plater, prin.
Other Schools – See Zenia

Brisbane, San Mateo Co., Pop. Code 5
Brisbane ESD
Sch. Sys. Enr. Code 2
Supt. – Anne Ladd, 1 SOLANO ST 94005
Lipman IS, 1 SOLANO ST 94005
    Marilyn Marino, prin.
ES, 550 SAN BRUNO AVE 94005
    Marilyn Marino, prin.
Other Schools – See Daly City

Broderick, Yolo Co., Pop. Code 6
Washington USD
Supt. – See West Sacramento
Golden State MS, 1100 CARRIE ST 95605
    A. Woolnough, prin.
Elkhorn Village ES, 750 CUMMINS WAY 95605
    Mary Brewer, prin.
Norman ES, 1200 ANNA ST 95605
    Jeannie Pierson, prin.

Holy Cross ES, 800 TODHUNTER AVE 95605

Browns Valley, Yuba Co.
Marysville JUSD
Supt. – See Marysville
ES 95918 – Dennis McGuire, prin.

Buellton, Santa Barbara Co., Pop. Code 4
Buellton Un. ESD
Sch. Sys. Enr. Code 2
Supt. – Richard O'Mara, P O BOX S 93427
Jonata ES, P O BOX S 93427
    Barbara Hallum, prin.

Buena Park, Orange Co., Pop. Code 8
Buena Park ESD
Sch. Sys. Enr. Code 5
Supt. – Richard Cochran
    6885 ORANGETHORPE AVE 90620
JHS, 6931 ORANGETHORPE AVE 90620
    Ronald Barry, prin.
Beatty ES, 8201 COUNTRY CLUB DRIVE 90621
    Jerry Horton, prin.
Corey ES, 7351 HOLDER ST 90620
    Richard Martin, prin.
Emery ES, 8600 SOMERSET ST 90621
    Carol Jeanson, prin.
Gilbert ES, 7255 8TH ST 90621
    George Cottrell, prin.
Pendleton ES, 7101 STANTON AVE 90621
    Margaret Berry, prin.
Whitaker ES, 8401 MONTANA AVE 90621
    Gloria Gregorek, prin.

Centralia ESD
Sch. Sys. Enr. Code 5
Supt. – Patricia White
    6625 LA PALMA AVE 90620
Buena Terra ES, 8299 HOLDER ST 90620
    Diana Frost, prin.

Dysinger ES, 7770 CAMELLIA DRIVE 90620
    Lidna Rader, prin.
Knott ES, 7300 LA PALMA AVE 90620
    Jefrey Schleiger, prin.
San Marino ES, 6215 SAN ROLANDO WAY 90620
    Richard Hoss, prin.
Temple ES, 7800 HOLDER ST 90620
    Jackie Parkhill, prin.
Other Schools – See Anaheim, La Palma

Cypress ESD
Supt. – See Cypress
Dickerson ES, 10051 BERNADETTE AVE 90620
    Lawrence Spaulding, prin.

Savanna ESD
Supt. – See Anaheim
Holder ES, 9550 HOLDER ST 90620
    Mark Dolter, prin.

Crescent Avenue Christian ES
    5600 CRESCENT AVE 90620
St. Pius V ES, 7681 ORANGETHORPE AVE 90621

Burbank, Los Angeles Co., Pop. Code 8
Burbank USD
Sch. Sys. Enr. Code 7
Supt. – Arthur Pierce
    330 N BUENA VISTA ST 91505
Disney ES, 1220 W ORANGE GROVE AVE 91506
    Linda Reksten, prin.
Edison ES, 2110 W CHESTNUT ST 91506
    Caroline Kirven, prin.
Emerson ES, 720 E CYPRESS AVE 91501
    Marilyn Ramsey, prin.
Harte ES, 3200 W JEFFRIES AVE 91505
    Barbara Oslund, prin.
Jefferson ES, 1900 N 6TH ST 91504
    Leslie Frank, prin.
McKinley ES, 349 W VALENCIA AVE 91506
    Susan Andrews, prin.
Miller ES, 720 E PROVIDENCIA AVE 91501
    Gail Copeland, prin.
Providencia ES, 1919 N ONTARIO ST 91505
    Harold Vences, prin.
Roosevelt ES, 850 N CORDOIVA ST 91505
    Yvonne Powers, prin.
Stevenson ES, 3333 W OAK ST 91505
    Joan Maxwell, prin.
Washington ES, 2322 N LINCOLN ST 91504
    Joan Baca, prin.

American Lutheran ES
    755 N WHITNALL HWY 91505
First Lutheran ES
    1001 S GLENOAKS BLVD 91502
St. Finbar ES, 2120 W OLIVE AVE 91506
St. Francis Xavier ES, 3601 SCOTT RD 91504
St. Robert Bellarmine ES, 154 N 5TH ST 91501

Burlingame, San Mateo Co., Pop. Code 8
Burlingame ESD
Sch. Sys. Enr. Code 4
Supt. – James Black
    2303 TROUSDALE DRIVE 94010
Burlingame IS, 1715 QUESADA WAY 94010
    Robert Welch, prin.
Franklin ES, 2385 TROUSDALE DRIVE 94010
    Martin Harrington, prin.
Lincoln ES, 1801 DEVEREUX DRIVE 94010
    Ellen Haas, prin.
McKinley ES, 701 PALOMA AVE 94010
    Frederick Heron, prin.
Washington ES, 801 HOWARD AVE 94010
    Catherine Jamentz, prin.

Carden ES, P O BOX 1667 94011
Nueva Learning School
    6565 SKYLINE BLVD 94010
Our Lady of Angels ES
    1328 CABRILLO AVE 94010
St. Catherine of Siena ES
    1300 BAYSWATER AVE 94010

Burney, Shasta Co., Pop. Code 4
Fall River JUSD
Supt. – See Cassel
East Burney ES, TORONTO ST 96013
    Charles Condry,Jr., prin.
Mt. Burney MS, TAMARACK AVE 96013
    Charles Condry,Jr., prin.

Burnt Ranch, Trinity Co.
Burnt Ranch ESD
Sch. Sys. Enr. Code 2
Supt. – (—), P O BOX 39 95527
ES, P O BOX 176 95527 – Phyllis Stockel, prin.

Burrel, Fresno Co.
Burrel Un. ESD
Sch. Sys. Enr. Code 2
Supt. – Mildred Wylie
    16704 JAMESON AVE 93656
ES, 16704 JAMESON AVE 93656
    Mildred Wylie, prin.

Buttonwillow, Kern Co., Pop. Code 4
Buttonwillow Un. ESD
Sch. Sys. Enr. Code 2
Supt. – Lamont Skiby
    400 MCKITTRICK HIGHWAY 93206
ES, 400 MCKITTRICK HIGHWAY 93206
    Laura Hubbard, prin.

Byron, Contra Costa Co.
Byron Un. ESD
Sch. Sys. Enr. Code 3
Supt. – Katherine Himelhoch
    RURAL ROUTE 01 BOX 48 94514
MS, RURAL ROUTE 01 BOX 48 94514
    Margaret Rodgers, prin.
Discovery Bay ES
    1700 WILLOW LAKE ROAD 94514
    Katherine Himelhoch, prin.

Mountain House ESD
Sch. Sys. Enr. Code 1
Supt. – (—)
    RURAL ROUTE 01 BOX 32F 94514
Mountain House ES
    3950 MOUNTAIN HOUSE ROAD 94514
    (—), prin.

Calabasas, Los Angeles Co., Pop. Code 8
Las Virgenes USD
Supt. – See Westlake
Wright MS, 4029 LAS VIRGENES ROAD 91302
    Rob Fraisse, prin.
Lupin Hill ES, 26210 ADAMOR ROAD 91302
    Richard Malfatti, prin.
Round Meadow ES
    5151 ROUND MEADOW ROAD 91302
    Lisa Dritz, prin.

Viewpoint School
    23620 MULHOLLAND HIGHWAY 91302
Meadow Oaks ES
    23456 MULHOLLAND HWY 91302

Calexico, Imperial Co., Pop. Code 7
Calexico USD
Sch. Sys. Enr. Code 6
Supt. – Gerald Dadey, P O BOX 792 92231
De Anza JHS, 824 BLAIR AVE 92231
    Mickey Western, prin.
Charles ES, 1201 KOKE ROAD 92231
    Belia Cruz, prin.
Dool ES, 800 ENCINAS AVE 92231
    William Cudog, prin.
Jefferson ES, 1120 E 7TH ST 92231
    Luis Pacheco, prin.
Kennedy Garden ES
    2300 ROCKWOOD AVE 92231
    Cecelia Castaneda, prin.
Mains ES, 655 SHERIDAN ST 92231
    Emily Palacio, prin.
Rockwood ES, 1000 ROCKWOOD AVE 92231
    Simon Lopez, prin.

Calexico Mission School, P O BOX 1067 92231
Our Lady of Guadalupe Academy
    536 ROCKWOOD AVE 92231

Caliente, Kern Co.
Caliente Un. ESD
Sch. Sys. Enr. Code 1
Supt. – C. McElroy, P O BOX 128 93518
ES, P O BOX 128 93518 – C. McElroy, prin.
Piute Mountain ES, HCR ROUTE BOX 64-B 93518
    C. McElroy, prin.

California City, Kern Co., Pop. Code 5
Mojave USD
Supt. – See Mojave
Ulrich ES, 9124 CATALPA AVE 93505
    Larry Adams, prin.

California Hot Springs, Tulare Co.
Hot Springs ESD
Sch. Sys. Enr. Code 1
Supt. – (—), P O BOX 38 93207
Hot Springs ES, P O BOX 38 93207
    (—), prin.

Calimesa, Riverside Co., Pop. Code 4

Mesa Grande Junior Academy
    975 FREMONT ST #A 92320

Calipatria, Imperial Co., Pop. Code 5
Calipatria USD
Sch. Sys. Enr. Code 4
Supt. – Jim Hanks, 601 W MAIN ST 92233
Fremont MS, 601 W MAIN ST 92233
    Harman Bonniksen, prin.
Fremont PS, 601 W MAIN ST 92233
    Robin Lilywhite, prin.
Other Schools – See Niland

Calistoga, Napa Co., Pop. Code 5
Calistoga JUSD
Sch. Sys. Enr. Code 3
Supt. – John Burke, P O BOX 498 94515
ES, P O BOX 498 94515 – Elizabeth Alt, prin.

Calpella, Mendocino Co., Pop. Code 3
Ukiah USD
Supt. – See Ukiah
ES, 151 MOORE ST 95418 – Barbara Hopper, prin.

Mt. Meadow Waldorf ES, P O BOX 313 95418

Camarillo, Ventura Co., Pop. Code 8
Pleasant Valley ESD
Sch. Sys. Enr. Code 6
Supt. – Shirley Carpenter
    600 TEMPLE AVE 93010
Los Altos IS, 700 TEMPLE AVE 93010
    Jim Williams, prin.
Monte Vista IS, 888 LANTANA ST 93010
    Milo Spracklen, prin.

Bedford Open ES, 1099 BEDFORD DR 93010
　Julie Cavaliere, prin.
Camarillo Heights ES
　35 CATALINA DRIVE 93010 – Fred Phipps, prin.
Dos Caminos ES, 3635 APPIAN WAY 93010
　Al Lane, prin.
El Descanso ES, 1099 BEDFORD DRIVE 93010
　Richard Mahlke, prin.
El Rancho ES, 550 TEMPLE AVE 93010
　Carol Vines, prin.
Las Colinas ES, 5750 FIELDCREST DR 93010
　William Lamp, prin.
Las Posas ES, 75 E CALLE LA GUERRA 93010
　Ralph Alamillo, prin.
Los Nogales ES, 1555 KENDALL AVE 93010
　Charles Warda, prin.
Los Primeros ES, 2222 VENTURA BLVD 93010
　Ruben Jimenez, prin.
Santa Rosa ES, 13282 SANTA ROSA ROAD 93010
　Dianne Anders, prin.
Valle Lindo ES, 777 AILEEN ST 93010
　Paige Fisher, prin.

Christian Church School
　1777 ARNEILL ROAD 93010
Camarillo Christian ES, P O BOX 130 93011
Carden School of Camarillo
　1915 LAS POSAS RD 93010
St. Mary Magdalen ES
　2534 VENTURA BLVD 93010

Cambria, San Luis Obispo Co., Pop. Code 4
Cambria Un. ESD
　Sch. Sys. Enr. Code 3
　Supt. – Thomas Garnella, 1350 MAIN ST 93428
Santa Lucia MS
　2850 SCHOOLHOUSE LANE 93428
　Denis deClercq, prin.
ES, 1350 MAIN ST 93428 – Carol Stoner, prin.

Camino, El Dorado Co., Pop. Code 3
Camino Un. ESD
　Sch. Sys. Enr. Code 3
　Supt. – John Nordquist, P O BOX 505 95709
ES, P O BOX 505 95709 – John Nordquist, prin.

Campbell, Santa Clara Co., Pop. Code 8
Campbell Un. ESD
　Sch. Sys. Enr. Code 6
　Supt. – Marcia Plumleigh, 155 N 3RD ST 95008
MS, 295 CHERRY LANE 95008
　Edward McCauley, prin.
Capri ES, 850 CHAPMAN DR 95008
　Stan Johnson, prin.
Castlemont ES, 3040 PAYNE AVE 95008
　Marilyn Lane, prin.
Hazelwood ES, 775 WALDO ROAD 95008
　Myra Castner, prin.
Rosemary ES, 401 W HAMILTON AVE 95008
　Don Bergstrom, prin.
Other Schools – See Los Gatos, San Jose, Saratoga

Campbell Christian ES
　1125 W CAMPBELL AVE 95008
Old Orchard ES, 400 W CAMPBELL AVE 95008
San Jose Christian ES
　1300 SHEFFIELD AVE #8 95008
St. Lucy's ES, 76 KENNEDY AVE 95008
West Valley SDA ES, 95 DOT AVE 95008

Campo, Calaveras Co.
Mountain Empire USD
　Supt. – See Pine Valley
ES, 31360 HIGHWAY 94 92006
　Anna Sullivan, prin.

Camp Pendleton, San Diego Co.
Fallbrook Un. ESD
　Supt. – See Fallbrook
Pendleton ES, 110 MARINE DRIVE 92055
　Talmage Cowan, prin.

Camptonville, Yuba Co.
Camptonville ESD
　Sch. Sys. Enr. Code 2
　Supt. – Peter Clark, P O BOX 278 95922
ES, P O BOX 278 95922 – Peter Clark, prin.

Canby, Modoc Co.
Modoc JUSD
　Supt. – See Alturas
Arlington ES, P O BOX 7 96015
　Kenneth Bushey, prin.

I'Sot School, P O BOX 125 96015

Canoga Park, Los Angeles Co.
Los Angeles USD
　Supt. – See Los Angeles
Columbus JHS, 22250 ELKWOOD ST 91304
　Jay Peterman, prin.
Sutter JHS, 7330 WINNETKA AVE 91306
　Edward Moreno, prin.
ES, 7438 TOPANGA CANYON BLVD 91303
　Charles Molina, prin.
Capistrano Avenue ES
　8118 CAPISTRANO AVE 91304
　Petronella Montante, prin.
Fullbright Avenue ES
　6940 FULLBRIGHT AVE 91306
　Gayle Biava, prin.
Hamlin Street ES, 22627 HAMLIN ST 91307
　James Grover, prin.
Hart Street ES, 21040 HART ST 91303
　Diana Villafana, prin.

Justice Street ES, 23350 JUSTICE ST 91304
　James Grover, prin.
Limerick Avenue ES, 8530 LIMERICK AVE 91306
　Juana Smerigan, prin.
Pomelo Drive ES, 7633 MARCH AVE 91304
　Barbara Baugh, prin.
Sunny Brae Avenue ES
　20620 ARMINTA ST 91306 – Robert Dixon, prin.
Welby Way ES, 23456 WELBY WAY 91307
　Kenneth Fields, prin.
Winnetka Avenue ES
　8240 WINNETKA AVE 91306 – Jean Lau, prin.

Coutin School, 7119 OWENSMOUTH AVE 91303
Faith Baptist School
　7644 FARRALONE AVE 91304
St. Peter Agbu American Day School
　6844 OAKDALE AVE 91306
West Valley Christian School
　6624 LOCKHURST DRIVE 91307
Canoga Park Lutheran ES
　7357 JORDAN AVE 91303
Our Lady of Valley ES, 22041 GAULT ST 91303
Shepherd/Valley Lutheran ES
　23838 KITTRIDGE ST 91307
St. Joseph the Worker ES
　19812 CANTLAY ST 91306
St. Martin of Fields Parish Day School
　7136 WINNETKA AVE 91306
West Valley Christian Academy
　7911 WINNETKA AVE 91306

Cantil, Kern Co.
Mojave USD
　Supt. – See Mojave
Red Rock ES, P O BOX 45 93519
　Larry Adams, prin.

Cantua Creek, Fresno Co.
Cantua ESD
　Sch. Sys. Enr. Code 2
　Supt. – Stewart Fisher, P O BOX 618 93608
Cantua ES, P O BOX 618 93608 – (—), prin.

Canyon, Contra Costa Co.
Canyon ESD
　Sch. Sys. Enr. Code 1
　Supt. – (—), P O BOX 141 94516
ES, P O BOX 141 94516 – (—), prin.

Canyon Country, Los Angeles Co.
Saugus Un. ESD
　Supt. – See Saugus
Cedarcreek ES
　27792 CAMP PLENTY ROAD 91351
　Candace Clark, prin.
Honby ES, 19059 VICCI ST 91351
　Russell Cochran, prin.
Rio Vista ES, 20417 CEDARCREEK ST 91351
　Nadine Elswick, prin.
Skyblue Mesa ES, 28040 HARDESTY AVE 91351
　Kathleen Wolfson, prin.

Sulphur Springs Un. ESD
　Sch. Sys. Enr. Code 5
　Supt. – Robert Nolet
　18830 SOLEDAD CANYON ROAD 91351
Cox ES, 18643 OAKMOOR ST 91351
　Frank Ford, prin.
Mint Canyon Community ES
　16400 SIERRA HIGHWAY 91351 – (—), prin.
Mitchell Community ES
　16821 GOODVALE ROAD 91351
　Bernard Camenson, prin.
Pinetree Community ES
　29156 LOTUSGARDEN DR 91351
　Nick Teeter, prin.
Soledad Canyon Community ES
　18801 MANDAN ST 91351 – Judy Heyn, prin.
Sulphur Springs Community ES
　16628 LOST CANYON ROAD 91351
　Rochelle Glassberg, prin.
Other Schools – See Newhall

William S. Hart Un. HSD
　Supt. – See Newhall
Sierra Vista JHS, 19425 STILLMORE ST 91351
　Michael Allmandinger, prin.

Santa Clarita Christian ES
　27249 LUTHER DR 91351

Capistrano Beach, Orange Co., Pop. Code 5
Capistrano USD
　Supt. – See San Juan Capistrano
Palisades ES, 26462 VIA SACRAMENTO 92624
　Joel Drew, prin.

Capitola, Santa Cruz Co., Pop. Code 6
Soquel Un. ESD
　Sch. Sys. Enr. Code 4
　Supt. – Richard Patterson
　620 MONTEREY AVE 95010
New Brighton MS, 250 WASHBURN AVE 95010
　Dave Schumaker, prin.
ES, 504 MONTEREY AVE 95010
　Barry Vitcov, prin.
Other Schools – See Santa Cruz, Soquel

Cardiff By Sea, San Diego Co., Pop. Code 6
Cardiff ESD
　Sch. Sys. Enr. Code 3
　Supt. – Joseph Fazio
　1888 MONTGOMERY AVE 92007
Cardiff ES, 18888 MONTGOMERY AVE 92007
　Sandra Freeman, prin.

Harris MS, 1508 WINDSOR ROAD 92007
　Sandra Freeman, prin.

Carlotta, Humboldt Co.
Cuddeback Un. ESD
　Sch. Sys. Enr. Code 2
　Supt. – Ron Ferrando, P O BOX 7 95528
Cuddeback ES, P O BOX 7 95528
　Ron Ferrando, prin.

Carlsbad, San Diego Co., Pop. Code 8
Carlsbad USD
　Sch. Sys. Enr. Code 6
　Supt. – Thomas Brierley, 801 PINE AVE 92008
Valley JHS, 1645 MAGNOLIA AVE 92008
　Don Le May, prin.
Buena Vista ES, 1330 BUENA VISTA WAY 92008
　Marielena Erickson, prin.
Hope ES, 3010 TAMARACK AVE 92008
　Betty Lahr, prin.
Jefferson ES, 3743 JEFFERSON ST 92008
　Sally Mattes, prin.
Kelly ES, 4885 KELLY DR 92008
　Carol Herrera, prin.
Magnolia ES, 1905 MAGNOLIA AVE 92008
　James Boone, prin.
Pine ES, 3333 HARDING ST 92008
　Stephen Ahle, prin.

Encinitas Un. ESD
　Supt. – See Encinitas
La Costa Height ES, 3035 LEVANTE AVE 92008
　Jennifer Jeffries, prin.

San Marcos USD
　Supt. – See San Marcos
La Costa Meadows ES, 6889 EL PUERTE 92009
　Fred Wise, prin.

St. Patrick's ES, P O BOX 249 92008

Carmel, Monterey Co., Pop. Code 5
Carmel USD
　Sch. Sys. Enr. Code 4
　Supt. – Robert Infelise, P O BOX 22270 93922
MS, P O BOX 222740 93922
　Karl Pallastrini, prin.
Carmel River ES, P O BOX 222700 93922
　Sharron Douglas, prin.
Other Schools – See Big Sur, Carmel Valley

All Saints Episcopal Day ES
　RURAL ROUTE 02 BOX 763 93923
Briarcliff ES, P O BOX AP 93921
Junipero Serra ES, 2992 LASUEN DR 93923

Carmel Valley, Monterey Co., Pop. Code 5
Carmel USD
　Supt. – See Carmel
Tularcitos ES, 35 FORD ROAD 93924
　James Kohnke, prin.

Carmichael, Sacramento Co., Pop. Code 8
San Juan USD
　Sch. Sys. Enr. Code 8
　Supt. – George Jeffers, P O BOX 4001 95609
Barrett IS, 4243 BARRETT ROAD 95608
　Linda Ferrick, prin.
Churchill IS, 4900 WHITNEY AVE 95608
　Dee Ward, prin.
ES, 6141 SUTTER AVE 95608
　Gary Blaisdell, prin.
Coyle Avenue ES, 6330 COYLE AVE 95608
　John Rabe, prin.
Del Dayo ES, 1301 MCLLAREN DRIVE 95608
　Jan Dahl, prin.
Deterding ES, 6000 STANLEY AVE 95608
　Penny Scribner, prin.
Garfield ES, 3700 GARFIELD AVE 95608
　Trudy Erickson, prin.
Kelly ES, 6301 MORAGA DRIVE 95608
　James Ontjes, prin.
Mission Avenue ES, 2925 MISSION AVE 95608
　Karen Nemetz, prin.
Peck ES, 6230 RUTLAND DRIVE 95608
　Steve Brush, prin.
Schweitzer ES, 4350 GLENRIDGE DRIVE 95608
　Lois Wilson, prin.
Star King Exceptional ES
　4848 COTTAGE WAY 95608 – Wilma Bower, prin.
Starr King Regular ES
　4848 COTTAGE WAY 95608 – Dave Cowles, prin.
Other Schools – See Citrus Heights, Fair Oaks,
　Orangevale, Sacramento

Sacramento Union Academy
　5601 WINDING WAY 95608
Our Lady of Assumption ES
　5055 COTTAGE WAY 95608
St. John Evangelist ES, 5701 LOCUST AVE 95608
St. Michael's Episcopal Day ES
　2140 MISSION AVE 95608
Victory Christian ES, 3045 GARFIELD AVE 95608

Carpinteria, Santa Barbara Co., Pop. Code 7
Carpinteria USD
　Sch. Sys. Enr. Code 4
　Supt. – Robert Barbot, 1400 LINDEN AVE 93013
JHS, 5351 CARPINTERIA AVE 93013
　Tyson Willson, prin.
Aliso MS, 4545 CARPINTERIA AVE 93013
　Josephine Costantini, prin.
Canalina ES, 1480 LINDEN AVE 93013
　Mary Lamp, prin.
Main MS, 5241 8TH ST 93013
　Barbara Fileto, prin.

Other Schools – See Summerland

Carson, Los Angeles Co., Pop. Code 8
Compton USD
Supt. – See Compton
Bunche ES, 16223 HASKIN LANE 90746
  Bettye Walker, prin.

Los Angeles USD
Supt. – See Los Angeles
232nd Place ES, 23240 ARCHIBALD AVE 90745
  Marshall Sisca, prin.
Ambler Avenue ES
  319 E SHERMAN DRIVE 90746
  Daniel Lawson, prin.
Annalee Avenue ES, 19410 ANNALEE AVE 90746
  Edison Griffin, prin.
Bonita Street ES, 21929 BONITA ST 90745
  Josephine Brown, prin.
Broadacres Avenue ES
  19424 BROADACRES AVE 90746
  Teri Abbott, prin.
Caroldale Avenue ES
  22424 CAROLDALE AVE 90745
  Joseph Scollo, prin.
Carson Street ES, 161 E CARSON ST 90745
  Richard Taylor, prin.
Catskill Avenue ES, 23536 CATSKILL AVE 90745
  Don Scott, prin.
Del Amo ES, 21228 WATER ST 90745
  Phyllis Hughes, prin.
Dolores Street ES, 22526 DOLORES ST 90745
  Patrice Velasquez, prin.
Leapwood Avenue ES
  19302 LEAPWOOD AVE 90746
  David Nelson,Jr., prin.
Towne Avenue ES, 18924 TOWNE AVE 90746
  Dorothy Akashi, prin.

Paris Christian Education Academy
  17625 CENTRAL AVE #F 90746
Peninsula Christian ES
  22507 FIGUEROA ST 90745
St. Philomena ES, 21832 MAIN ST 90745

Caruthers, Fresno Co., Pop. Code 3
Alvina ESD
Sch. Sys. Enr. Code 2
Supt. – Guy Wilson, 295 W SAGINAW AVE 93609
Alvina ES, 295 W SAGINAW AVE 93609
  Guy Wilson, prin.

Caruthers Un. ESD
Sch. Sys. Enr. Code 3
Supt. – Judy Statler, P O BOX 7 93609
ES, P O BOX 7 93609 – Mary Bailey, prin.

Casmalia, Santa Barbara Co.
Casmalia ESD
Sch. Sys. Enr. Code 1
Supt. – (—), P O BOX K 93429
ES, 3491 POINT SAL ROAD 93429
  Kenneth McCalip, prin.

Cassel, Shasta Co.
Fall River JUSD
Sch. Sys. Enr. Code 4
Supt. – Ivan Keys, P O BOX 89 96016
Other Schools – See Burney, Fall River Mills

Castaic, Los Angeles Co.
Castaic Un. SD
Sch. Sys. Enr. Code 3
Supt. – Scott Brown
  31616 N RIDGE ROUTE RD 91310
MS, 31634 N RIDGE ROUTE RD 91310
  Beverly Silsbee, prin.
ES, 31700 RIDGE ROUTE 91350
  Beverly Knutson, prin.
Live Oak ES, 27715 SADDLERIDGE RD 91384
  Sharon Millen, prin.

Castella, Shasta Co.
Castle Rock Un. ESD
Sch. Sys. Enr. Code 1
Supt. – Raymond Kermode, P O BOX 146 96017
Castle Rock ES, P O BOX 146 96017
  Raymond Kermode, prin.

Castro Valley, Alameda Co., Pop. Code 8
Castro Valley USD
Sch. Sys. Enr. Code 6
Supt. – Robert Hagler, P O BOX 2146 94546
Canyon MS, 19600 CULL CANYON ROAD 94552
  Donald Gelles, prin.
ES, 20185 SAN MIGUEL AVE 94546
  Nancy Crans, prin.
Chabot ES, 19014 LAKE CHABOT ROAD 94546
  Darlene Santos, prin.
Independent ES
  4070 E CASTRO VALLEY BLVD 94546
  Jack McKay, prin.
Marshall ES, 20111 MARSHALL ST 94546
  Virginia Hubbard, prin.
Palomares ES, 6395 PALO VERDE ROAD 94552
  Robin Olivier, prin.
Proctor ES, 17520 REDWOOD ROAD 94546
  Allen Honda, prin.
Vannoy ES, 5100 VANNOY AVE 94546
  Taylor Lyen, prin.

Hayward USD
Supt. – See Hayward
Strobridge ES, 21400 BEDFORD DR 94546
  Dick Panzica, prin.

Our Lady of Grace ES, 19920 ANITA AVE 94546

Redwood Christian ES
  19300 REDWOOD RD 94546
Redwood Christian ES, 20600 JOHN DR 94546

Castroville, Monterey Co., Pop. Code 5
North Monterey County USD
Supt. – See Moss Landing
Gambetta MS, 10301 SEYMOUR ST 95012
  Claudette Beaty, prin.
ES, 11161 MERRITT ST 95012
  Keith Parkhurst, prin.
Elkhorn ES, 2235 ELKHORN ROAD 95012
  John Simpson, prin.

Cathedral City, Riverside Co., Pop. Code 5
Palm Springs USD
Supt. – See Palm Springs
ES, SECOND & VAN FLEET STS 92234
  Molly Schecter, prin.
Landau ES, 30-310 LANDAU BLVD 92234
  Joan Cole, prin.

Cathey's Valley, Mariposa Co.
Mariposa County USD
Supt. – See Mariposa
ES 95306 – Bill McKay, prin.

Cayucos, San Luis Obispo Co., Pop. Code 4
Cayucos ESD
Sch. Sys. Enr. Code 2
Supt. – Vera Wallen, 301 CAYUCOS DRIVE 93430
ES, 301 CAYUCOS DRIVE 93430
  Vera Wallen, prin.

Cazadero, Sonoma Co.
Ft. Ross ESD
Sch. Sys. Enr. Code 1
Supt. – Marjorie Johnson
  30600 SEA VIEW ROAD 95421
Ft. Ross ES, 30600 SEA VIEW ROAD 95421
  Marjorie Johnson, prin.

Montgomery ESD
Sch. Sys. Enr. Code 2
Supt. – Irwin Karp, P O BOX 286 95421
Montgomery ES, P O BOX 286 95421
  Irwin Karp, prin.

Cedarville, Modoc Co., Pop. Code 3
Surprise Valley JUSD
Sch. Sys. Enr. Code 2
Supt. – Richard Cunnison, P O BOX 28F 96104
Surprise Valley ES, WALLACE & HIGH STS 96104
  Richard Cunnison, prin.

Central Valley, Shasta Co., Pop. Code 4
Shasta Lake Un. ESD
Sch. Sys. Enr. Code 4
Supt. – Kenneth Matias, P O BOX 757 96019
Central Valley IS, HARDENBROOK & MAIN 96019
  Robert Stathem, prin.
Deer Creek MS
  VALLECITO & DEER CREEK 96019
  Richard Ferguson, prin.
Project City ES, P O BOX 757 96019
  Donna Myers, prin.
Other Schools – See Summit City

Ceres, Stanislaus Co., Pop. Code 7
Ceres USD
Sch. Sys. Enr. Code 6
Supt. – M. Robert Adkison, P O BOX 307 95307
Hensley JHS, 1806 MOFFETT ROAD 95307
  Sharon Brenneise, prin.
Caswell ES, 1800 CENTRAL AVE 95307
  Jan Beekman, prin.
Don Pedro ES, 2300 DON PEDRO AVE 95307
  Jerry Panella, prin.
Fowler ES, 2611 GARRISON ST 95307
  Patricia De Bora, prin.
White ES, 2904 6TH ST 95307 – Diane Scott, prin.
Other Schools – See Modesto

Cerritos, Los Angeles Co., Pop. Code 8
ABC USD
Sch. Sys. Enr. Code 7
Supt. – Larry Lucas
  16700 NORWALK BLVD 90701
Carmenita JHS, 13435 166TH ST 90701
  Linda Caillet, prin.
Haskell JHS, 11525 DEL AMO BLVD 90701
  Ronald Murphy, prin.
Tetzlaff JHS, 12351 DEL AMO BLVD 90701
  Jerry Perez, prin.
Bragg ES, 11501 BOS ST 90701
  Janet Morey, prin.
Carver ES, 19200 ELY AVE 90701
  Suzanne Soo Hoo, prin.
ES, 13600 183RD ST 90701 – Paulette Fuller, prin.
Gonsalves ES, 13650 PARK ST 90701
  Andrew Washington, prin.
Juarez ES, 11939 ACLARE ST 90701
  Craig Peck, prin.
Leal ES, 12920 DROXFORD ST 90701
  (—), prin.
Nixon ES, 19600 JACOB AVE 90701
  Kristen Powell, prin.
Stowers ES, 13350 BEACH ST 90701
  Decla Johnson, prin.
Wittmann ES, 16801 YVETTE AVE 90701
  Jesus Lopez, prin.
Other Schools – See Artesia, Hawaiian Gardens,
Lakewood

Valley Christian JHS, 18100 DUMONT AVE 90701
Concordia Lutheran ES, 13633 183RD ST 90701

Challenge, Yuba Co.
Marysville JUSD
Supt. – See Marysville
Yuba Feather ES, P O BOX 1458 95925
  Kay Heath, prin.

Chatsworth, Los Angeles Co.
Los Angeles USD
Supt. – See Los Angeles
Chatsworth Park ES
  22005 DEVONSHIRE ST 91311
  Dora Golden, prin.
Germain Street ES, 20730 GERMAIN ST 91311
  Patricia Dunbar, prin.
Superior Street ES, 9756 OSO AVE 91311
  Jean Hilliard, prin.

Chatsworth Hill Academy, P O BOX 4135 91313
Egremont ES, 19850 DEVONSHIRE ST 91311
Pinecrest ES, 19750 MAYALL ST 91311
Sierra Canyon ES
  11052 INDEPENDENCE AVE 91311
St. John Eudes ES, 9925 MASON AVE 91311

Chester, Plumas Co., Pop. Code 4
Plumas USD
Supt. – See Quincy
ES, P O BOX 826 96020 – Rita Wolenik, prin.

Chicago Park, Nevada Co.
Chicago Park ESD
Sch. Sys. Enr. Code 2
Supt. – Robert Walter
  MOUNT OLIVE ROAD 95717
ES, P O BOX 20 95712 – Robert Walter, prin.

Chico, Butte Co., Pop. Code 8
Chico USD
Sch. Sys. Enr. Code 7
Supt. – Robert Purvis, 1163 E 7TH ST 95928
Chapman ES, 1071 E 16TH ST 95928
  Jim Sands, prin.
Citrus Ave. ES, 1350 CITRUS AVE 95926
  Robert Gamette, prin.
Cohasset ES, COHASSET STAGE 95926
  Arthur Neumann, prin.
Dow ES, 1420 NEAL DOW AVE 95926
  W. Stephenson, prin.
Hooker Oak ES, 1238 ARBUTUS AVE 95926
  David Reise, prin.
Marigold ES, 2446 MARIGOLD AVE 95926
  Patricia Spear, prin.
McMannus ES, 988 EAST AVE 95926
  Jerry McGuire, prin.
Nord ES, RURAL ROUTE 01 BOX 660 95926
  Arthur Neumann, prin.
Parkview ES, 1770 E 8TH ST 95928
  William Lathrop, prin.
Partridge ES, 290 EAST AVE 95926
  Richard Aguilera, prin.
Rosedale ES, 100 OAK ST 95928
  Paul Oxley, prin.
Shasta ES, 169 LEORA COURT 95926
  Beulah Robinson, prin.
Sierra View ES, 1598 HOOKER OAK AVE 95926
  Charles Fullmer, prin.
Other Schools – See Forest Ranch

Chico Christian ES
  2801 NOTRE DAME BLVD 95928
Notre Dame ES, 435 HAZEL ST 95928

Chinese Camp, Tuolumne Co.
Chinese Camp ESD
Sch. Sys. Enr. Code 1
Supt. – (—), P O BOX 100 95309
ES, P O BOX 100 95309 – Betty Buchler, prin.

Chino, San Bernardino Co., Pop. Code 8
Chino USD
Sch. Sys. Enr. Code 7
Supt. – Mike Dirksen
  5130 RIVERSIDE DRIVE 91710
Magnolia JHS, 13150 MOUNTAIN AVE 91710
  Leonard McGinnis, prin.
Ramona JHS, 4575 WALNUT AVE 91710
  Glenna Ramsey, prin.
Townsend JHS, 15359 ILEX DRIVE 91709
  Phil Hiatt, prin.
Borba Fundamental ES, 12970 THIRD ST 91710
  Sue Roche, prin.
Briggs Fundamental ES
  11800 ROSWELL AVE 91710 – Richard Bray, prin.
Cattle ES, 13590 CYPRESS 91710
  Bill Westbrook, prin.
Cortez ES, 12750 CARRISSA AVE 91710
  Lucian Carpenter, prin.
Dickson ES, 3930 PAMELA DRIVE 91710
  Dick Barboza, prin.
Eagle Canyon ES
  13435 EAGLE CANYON DR 91709
  Doreen Daley, prin.
El Rancho ES, 5862 C ST 91710
  Richard Cira, prin.
Gird ES, 4980 RIVERSIDE DRIVE 91710
  Nancy McDonald, prin.
Glenmeade ES, 15000 WHIRLAWAY LANE 91709
  Patricia Miller, prin.
Litel ES, 3425 EUCALYPTUS AVE 91709
  Jerry Hartman, prin.
Los Serranos ES, 15650 PIPE LINE AVE 91709
  Lynette Forte, prin.
Marshall ES, 12045 TELEPHONE AVE 91710
  Mike Finkbiner, prin.

Newman ES, 4150 WALNUT AVE 91710
  Richard Pattison, prin.
Oakridge ES, 15452 VALLE VISTA DR 91710
  Don Berg, prin.
Walnut Avenue ES, 5550 WALNUT AVE 91710
  Sue Stoeber, prin.
Other Schools – See Ontario

Communty Free Methodist ES
  13333 RAMONA AVE 91710
St. Margaret's ES, 12664 CENTRAL AVE 91710

Chowchilla, Madera Co., Pop. Code 6
Alview-Dairyland Un. ESD
Sch. Sys. Enr. Code 2
Supt. – Lee Roy Tatom
  12861 AVENUE 18 1/2 93610
Dairyland MS, 12861 AVENUE 18 1/2 93610
  Lee Roy Tatom, prin.
Alview ES, 20513 ROAD 4 93610
  Lee Roy Tatom, prin.

Chowchilla ESD
Sch. Sys. Enr. Code 4
Supt. – Charles Jacobs, P O BOX 907 93610
Wilson MS, P O BOX 907 93610
  Henry Burton, prin.
Fairmead MS, P O BOX 907 93610
  Jean Upton, prin.
Fuller ES, P O BOX 907 93610 – Kay Donner, prin.

Chualar, Monterey Co.
Chualar Un. ESD
Sch. Sys. Enr. Code 2
Supt. – Richard Jukes, P O BOX 188 93925
ES, P O BOX 188 93925 – Tomas Guajardo, prin.

Chula Vista, San Diego Co., Pop. Code 8
Chula Vista City SD
Sch. Sys. Enr. Code 7
Supt. – Robert McCarthy, 84 EAST J ST 92010
Castle Park ES, 25 EMERSON ST 92011
  Shirley Helleis, prin.
Cook ES, 875 CUYAMACA AVE 92011
  Patricia Roth, prin.
Feaster ES, 670 FLOWER ST 92010
  Edward Aceves, prin.
Halecrest ES, 475 E J ST 92010
  Robert Montgomery, prin.
Harborside ES, 681 NAPLES ST 92011
  William Hall, prin.
Hilltop Drive ES, 30 MURRAY ST 92010
  Michael Humphrey, prin.
Kellogg ES, 229 E NAPLES ST 92011
  Robert French, prin.
Lauderbach ES, 390 PALOMAR ST 92011
  George Bjornstad, prin.
Loma Verde ES, 1450 LOMA LANE 92011
  Betty Walsh, prin.
Montgomery MS, 1601 HERMOSA AVE 92011
  Ruben Castaneda, prin.
Mueller ES, 715 I ST 92010 – Don Jeffries, prin.
Otay ES, 1651 ALBANY AVE 92011
  John Harder, prin.
Palomar ES, 300 E PALOMAR ST 92011
  Ginger Hovenic, prin.
Parkview ES, 575 JUNIPER ST 92011
  Sandra Edwin, prin.
Rice ES, 915 4TH AVE 92011
  Kathleen Stevens, prin.
Rogers ES, 510 E NAPLES ST 92011
  Dorothy Stimson, prin.
Rohr ES, 1540 MALTA AVE 92011
  Larry Blocker, prin.
Rosebank ES, 80 FLOWER ST 92010
  Sam Snyder, Jr., prin.
South Western Satellite ES, 1468 E H ST 92010
  Dick Slaker, prin.
Tiffany ES, 1691 ELMHURST ST 92013
  Alfred Madison, prin.
Valle Lindo ES, 1515 OLEANDER AVE 92011
  Harry Roux, prin.
Vista Square ES, 540 G ST 92010
  Elivinia Degarmo, prin.
Other Schools – See Bonita, San Diego

Sweetwater Un. HSD
Sch. Sys. Enr. Code 8
Supt. – Anthony Trujillo, 1130 5TH AVE 92011
Castle Park MS, 160 QUINTARD ST 92011
  Elizabeth Lebron, prin.
Other Schools – See San Diego

Chula Vista Christian ES, 960 5TH AVE 92011
Covenant Christian ES, 505 E NAPLES ST 92011
Pilgrim Lutheran ES, 497 E ST 92010
Southwestern Christian ES, 482 L ST 92011
St. John's Episcopal ES, 760 1ST AVE 92010
St. Pius X ES, 37 E EMERSON ST 92011
St. Rose of Lima ES, 473 3RD AVE 92010

Citrus Heights, Sacramento Co., Pop. Code 7
San Juan USD
Supt. – See Carmichael
Sylvan IS, 7137 AUBURN BLVD 95610
  Joe Dion, prin.
Arlington Heights ES
  6401 TRENTON WAY 95621
  Joann Hammer, prin.
Cambridge Heights ES
  5555 FLEETWOOD DRIVE 95621
  Dale Pingree, prin.
Carriage Drive ES, 7519 CARRIAGE DR 95621
  Richard Battistessa, prin.

ES, 7085 AUBURN BLVD 95621
  Ernestine Smith, prin.
Grand Oaks ES, 7901 ROSSWOOD DRIVE 95621
  Jack Woo, prin.
Kingswood ES, 5700 PRIMROSE DRIVE 95610
  Don Caldiera, prin.
Lichen ES, 8319 LICHEN DRIVE 95621
  Ray Gonzales, prin.
Mariposa Avenue ES
  7940 MARIPOSA AVE 95610
  Timothy McCarty, prin.
Skycrest ES, 5641 MARIPOSA AVE 95610
  Clifton Oakes, prin.
Sunrise ES, 7400 SUNRISE BLVD 95610
  Rubye Martin, prin.
Woodside ES, 8248 VILLA OAK DRIVE 95610
  Joseph Hayes, prin.

Carden Sunrise ES, P O BOX 2270 95611
Holy Family ES, 7817 OLD AUBURN RD 95610

City of Commerce, Los Angeles Co.
Montebello USD
Supt. – See Montebello
Bandini ES, 2318 COUTS AVE 90040
  Raymond Rivera, prin.
Rosewood Park ES, 2353 COMMERCE WAY 90040
  Robert Capps, prin.

City of Industry, Los Angeles Co., Pop. Code 3
Basset USD
Supt. – See La Puente
Torch MS, 751 VINELAND AVE 91746
  Carmella Franco, prin.

Claremont, Los Angeles Co., Pop. Code 8
Claremont USD
Sch. Sys. Enr. Code 6
Supt. – Thomas Peeler
  2080 N MOUNTAIN AVE 91711
El Roble IS, 665 N MOUNTAIN AVE 91711
  Ralph Patterson, prin.
Chaparral ES, 451 CHAPARRAL DRIVE 91711
  Dave Paul, prin.
Condit ES, 1750 N MOUNTAIN AVE 91711
  Charles Freitas, prin.
Mountain View ES
  851 SANTA CLARA AVE 91711
  Jocelyn Lyon, prin.
Oakmont ES, 120 W GREEN ST 91711
  Eric Andrew, prin.
Sumner ES, 1770 SUMNER AVE 91711
  Gyle Tague, prin.
Sycamore ES, 225 W EIGHTH ST 91711
  Clare Eckhardt, prin.
Vista Del Valle ES, 550 VISTA DR 91711
  Duane Jackman, prin.

Foothill Country Day ES
  1035 HARRISON AVE 91711
Our Lady of Assumption ES
  611 W BONITA AVE 91711

Clarksburg, Yolo Co., Pop. Code 2
River Delta USD
Supt. – See Rio Vista
ES, P O BOX 99 95612 – Julia Rinne, prin.

Clayton, Contra Costa Co., Pop. Code 5
Mt. Diablo USD
Supt. – See Concord
Mount Diablo ES
  5880 MOUNT ZION DRIVE 94517
  Ted Beard, prin.

Clearlake, Lake Co., Pop. Code 5
Konocti USD
Sch. Sys. Enr. Code 5
Supt. – William Cornelison, P O BOX 6630 95422
Burns Valley ES, P O BOX 6420 95422
  Christine Thomas, prin.
Other Schools – See Clearlake Oaks, Lower Lake

Clearlake Oaks, Lake Co., Pop. Code 3
Konocti USD
Supt. – See Clearlake
East Lake ES, P O BOX 577 95423
  Howard Smith, prin.

Clements, San Joaquin Co.
Lodi USD
Supt. – See Lodi
ES, P O BOX 106 95227 – Tad Ishihara, prin.

Cloverdale, Sonoma Co., Pop. Code 5
Cloverdale USD
Sch. Sys. Enr. Code 4
Supt. – Scott Brown, 97 SCHOOL ST 95425
Washington Street MS
  129 S WASHINGTON ST 95425
  Tim Justus, prin.
Jefferson ES, 315 NORTH ST 95425
  Claud Williams, prin.

Clovis, Fresno Co., Pop. Code 8
Clovis USD
Sch. Sys. Enr. Code 7
Supt. – Floyd Buchanan
  5545 W HERNDON AVE 93612
Clark IS, 902 5TH ST 93612 – Hank Brown, prin.
Cole ES, 615 W STUART AVE 93612
  Terry Allen, prin.
Cox ES, 2191 SIERRA AVE 93612
  Lloyd Harline, prin.
Dry Creek ES, 8098 N ARMSTRONG AVE 93612
  Ann Lindsey, prin.

Jefferson ES, 1880 FOWLER AVE 93612
  Gary Giannoni, prin.
Miramonte ES, 1590 BELLAIRE AVE 93612
  Virginia Thomas, prin.
Sierra Vista ES, 510 BARSTOW AVE 93612
  Richard Smith, prin.
Tarpey ES, MINNEWAWA AVE 93612
  Norman McTeer, prin.
Weldon ES, 150 DEWITT AVE 93612
  Susan Vandoren, prin.
Other Schools – See Fresno, Friant, Palmdale, Pinedale

Our Lady of Perpetual Help ES
  859 HARVARD AVE 93612

Coachella, Riverside Co., Pop. Code 6
Coachella Valley USD
Supt. – See Thermal
Duke JHS, 85-358 BAGDAD AVE 92236
  Amparo Barrera, prin.
Palm View ES, 1390 SEVENTH ST 92236
  John Molina, prin.
Pendleton ES, 84-750 CALLE ROJO 92236
  Tully Valmassoi, prin.
Valley View ES, 85-270 VALLEY ROAD 92236
  Joe Ceja, prin.

Coalinga, Fresno Co., Pop. Code 6
Coalinga/Huron JUSD
Sch. Sys. Enr. Code 5
Supt. – Harold Moore, 657 SUNSET ST 93210
JHS, 516 BAKER ST 93210 – Vern Apple, prin.
ES, 657 SUNSET ST 93210 – Patricia Lewis, prin.
Other Schools – See Huron

Coarsegold, Madera Co.
Coarsegold Un. ESD
Sch. Sys. Enr. Code 3
Supt. – Michael Wagenleitner, P O BOX 338 93614
Coarsegold Union ES, P O BOX 338 93614
  Susan Macy, prin.

Coleville, Mono Co., Pop. Code 1
Eastern Sierra USD
Supt. – See Bridgeport
Antelope ES, P O BOX 200 96107
  Kathryn Winebarger, prin.

Colfax, Placer Co., Pop. Code 3
Colfax ESD
Sch. Sys. Enr. Code 2
Supt. – Alan Shuttleworth, P O BOX 699 95713
ES, SCHOOL AND PLEASANT ST 95713
  Alan Shuttleworth, prin.
Iowa Hill ES, P O BOX 699 95713
  Alan Shuttleworth, prin.

Colma, San Mateo Co., Pop. Code 2
Jefferson ESD
Supt. – See Daly City
Franklin IS, 700 STEWART AVE 94015
  Thomas Zach, prin.
Columbus ES, 700 STEWART AVE 94015
  Glenn Forcum, prin.
Garden Village ES, 208 GARDEN LANE 94015
  Bobby Allen, prin.

Colton, San Bernardino Co., Pop. Code 8
Colton JUSD
Sch. Sys. Enr. Code 7
Supt. – Russell Dickinson
  1212 VALENCIA DRIVE 92324
JHS, 670 W LAUREL ST 92324
  Pete Carrasco, prin.
Terrace Hills JHS, 22579 DE BERRY ST 92324
  Pat Ensey, prin.
Birney ES, 1050 E OLIVE PL 92324
  James Jackson, prin.
Grant ES, 550 W OLIVE ST 92324
  Opal Thompson, prin.
Lincoln ES, 444 E OLIVE ST 92324
  Therese Martinez, prin.
McKinley ES, 600 JOHNSTON ST 92324
  Jolyne Patten, prin.
Reche Canyon ES, 3101 CANYON VISTA 92324
  Gary Roberts, prin.
Rogers ES, 955 W LAUREL ST 92324
  Mike Brown, prin.
Wilson ES, 750 S 8TH ST 92324
  Dale Chilson, prin.
Other Schools – See Bloomington, Grand Terrace

Colton Christian School, P O BOX 865 92324

Columbia, Stanislaus Co., Pop. Code 3
Columbia Un. SD
Sch. Sys. Enr. Code 3
Supt. – Ray Enos
  22540 PARROTS FERRY ROAD 95310
ES, 22540 PARROTTS FERRY ROAD 95310
  Mike Raleigh, prin.
Other Schools – See Pinecrest

Colusa, Colusa Co., Pop. Code 5
Colusa USD
Sch. Sys. Enr. Code 4
Supt. – Jim Mark, 745 10TH ST 95932
Egling MS, 813 WEBSTER ST 95932
  Ed Conrado, prin.
Burchfield PS, 400 FREMONT ST 95932
  Susan St. John, prin.

Our Lady of Lourdes School
  745 WARE AVE 95932

Comptche, Mendocino Co.
Mendocino USD
Supt. – See Mendocino
ES, P O BOX 144 95427 – Susan Franklin, prin.

Compton, Los Angeles Co., Pop. Code 8
Compton USD
Sch. Sys. Enr. Code 8
Supt. – Ted Kimbrough
604 S TAMARIND ST 90220
Bunche MS, 12338 S MONA BLVD 90222
Betty Smith, prin.
Davis MS, 621 W POPLAR ST 90220
Delores Holmes, prin.
Enterprise MS, 2800 W COMPTON BLVD 90220
Richard Banton, prin.
Roosevelt MS, 1200 E ALONDRA BLVD 90221
Mary Randle, prin.
Walton MS, 900 W GREENLEAF BLVD 90220
Prentiss Ellis, prin.
Whaley MS, 14401 S GIBSON AVE 90221
Estelle Schultz, prin.
Willowbrook MS
2601 N WILMINGTON AVE 90222
Henry Jennings, prin.
Anderson ES, 2210 E 130TH ST 90222
Doris Lee, prin.
Bursch ES, 2505 W 156TH ST 90220
Carmen Stewart, prin.
Caldwell Street ES, 2300 W CALDWELL ST 90220
Leslie Wilcox, prin.
Dickison ES, 905 N ARANBE AVE 90220
Calvyn Brown, prin.
Emerson ES, 1011 E CALDWELL ST 90221
William English, prin.
Foster ES, 1620 N PANNES AVE 90221
Eva Spight, prin.
Jefferson ES, 2508 E 133RD ST 90222
Alfredia Nabors, prin.
Kelly ES, 2320 E ALONDRA BLVD 90221
Althea Jenkins, prin.
Kennedy ES, 1305 S OLEANDER AVE 90220
Helen Drye, prin.
King ES, 2270 E 122ND ST 90222
Lavonne Johnson, prin.
Laurel Street ES, 1321 W LAUREL ST 90220
Naomi Ferns, prin.
Longfellow ES, 1101 S DWIGHT AVE 90220
Thelma Williams, prin.
Mayo ES, 915 N MAYO AVE 90221
Edna Allen, prin.
McKinley ES, 14431 S STANFORD AVE 90220
Joyce Bagsby, prin.
McNair ES, 1450 W EL SEGUNDO BLVD 90222
Charles Barnett, prin.
Riles ES, 12501 N WILMINGTON AVE 90222
Ernest Cash, prin.
Roosevelt ES, 700 N BRADFIELD AVE 90221
Lowell Winston, prin.
Rosecrans ES, 1301 N ACACIA AVE 90222
Versie Burns, prin.
Tibby ES, 1400 W POPLAR ST 90220
Mattye Goins, prin.
Washington ES
1421 N WILMINGTON AVE 90222
Peter Danna, prin.
Other Schools – See Carson, Los Angeles

Christian Foundation ES
440 S SANTA FE AVE 90221
First Christian Day ES of Compton
225 S SANTA FE AVE 90221
Optimal Christian Academy
1300 E PALMER ST 90221
Our Lady of Victory ES, 601 E PALMER ST 90221
St. Albert the Great ES
804 E COMPTON BLVD 90220

Concord, Contra Costa Co., Pop. Code 9
Mt. Diablo USD
Sch. Sys. Enr. Code 8
Supt. – Frank Abbott
1936 CARLOTTA DRIVE 94519
El Dorado IS, 1750 WEST ST 94521
Ken Duckert, prin.
Glenbrook MS, 2351 OLIVERA ROAD 94520
Dan Corsetti, prin.
Oak Grove MS, 2050 MINERT ROAD 94518
Audrey Wayman, prin.
Pine Hollow IS
5522 PINE HOLLOW ROAD 94521
Marcie Brown, prin.
Ayers ES, 5120 MYRTLE DRIVE 94521
Scott Grange, prin.
El Monte ES, 1400 DINA DRIVE 94518
Christine Peterson, prin.
Highlands ES
1326 PENNSYLVANIA BLVD 94521
Robert Boone, prin.
Holbrook ES, 3333 RONALD WAY 94519
Marlene Sipes, prin.
Meadow Homes ES, 1371 DETROIT AVE 94520
Leonard Boone, prin.
Monte Gardens ES, 3841 LARKSPUR DR 94519
Barbara Blankenship, prin.
Mountain View ES
1705 THORNEWOOD DRIVE 94521
Sharon Russon, prin.
Silverwood ES, 1649 CLAYCOARD AVE 94521
James Kaar, prin.
Sun Terrace ES, 2448 FLOYD LAND 94520
Janet Gatti, prin.
Westwood ES, 1748 WEST ST 94521
Michael Martinez, prin.

Woodside ES, 761 SAN SIMEON DRIVE 94518
Linda Henderson, prin.
Wren Avenue ES, 3339 WREN AVE 94519
Joan Evans, prin.
Ygnacio Valley ES
2217 CHALOMAR ROAD 94518
Don Williams, prin.
Other Schools – See Clayton, Martinez, Pittsburg,
Pleasant Hill, Walnut Creek

Concord Christian School
2120 OLIVERA COURT 94520
Discovery Christian Schs.
5547 ALABAMA DR 94521
Bianchi ES, 4347 COWELL RD 94518
Kings Valley Christian ES
4255 CLAYTON RD 94521
Queen of Sts. ES, 2391 GRANT ST 94520
St. Agnes ES, 3886 CHESTNUT AVE 94519
St. Francis of Assisi ES
866 OAK GROVE RD 94518
Tabernacle Baptist ES
4380 CONCORD BLVD 94521
Ygnacio Valley Christian ES
4977 CONCORD BLVD 94521

Cool, El Dorado Co.
Black Oak Mine USD
Supt. – See Georgetown
Northside ES, PO BOX 217 95614
Bruce Leiper, prin.

Copperopolis, Calaveras Co.
Calaveras USD
Supt. – See San Andreas
ES, P O BOX 145 95228 – Timothy Hicks, prin.

Corcoran, Kings Co., Pop. Code 6
Corcoran JUSD
Sch. Sys. Enr. Code 4
Supt. – Allan Asplund
1520 PATTERSON AVE 93212
Muir JHS, LETTS AND BELL AVES 93212
Steven Brown, prin.
Fremont ES, BELL AND JOSEPHINE AVES 93212
Gloria Graville, prin.
Harte ES, WHITLEY & JEPSON AVES 93212
Roy Randles, prin.
Mark Twain MS
OREGON AND LETTS AVES 93212
Manuel Porras, prin.

Corning, Tehama Co., Pop. Code 5
Corning Un. ESD
Sch. Sys. Enr. Code 4
Supt. – Lloyd Ludu, 900 WEST ST 96021
Maywood IS, 1666 MARGUEITE 96021
Ronald Mongini, prin.
Olive View MS, 1402 FIG ST 96021
Thomas Armosino, prin.
West Street ES, 900 WEST ST 96021
John LaLaguna, prin.

Kirkwood ESD
Sch. Sys. Enr. Code 1
Supt. – (—)
RURAL ROUTE 01 BOX 250A 96021
Kirkwood ES
RURAL ROUTE 01 BOX 250A 96021
Cynthia McConnell, prin.

Richfield ESD
Sch. Sys. Enr. Code 2
Supt. – (—)
RURAL ROUTE 01 BOX 429 96021
Richfield ES, RURAL ROUTE 01 BOX 429 96021
Richard McBrayer, prin.

Corona, Riverside Co., Pop. Code 8
Alvord USD
Supt. – See Riverside
Promenade ES, 550 HAMILTON AVE 91719
Kristin Lasher, prin.

Corona-Norco USD
Sch. Sys. Enr. Code 7
Supt. – Donald Helms
300 S BUENA VISTA AVE 91720
Adams ES, 2350 BORDER AVE 91720
Cyndy Schurr, prin.
Coronita ES, 1757 VIA DEL RIO 91719
Paul Loesch, prin.
El Cerrito ES, 7581 RUDELL ROAD 91719
Keith Bauer, prin.
Foothill ES, 2601 BUENA VISTA AVE 91720
Patricia Scott, prin.
Garretson ES, 1650 GARRETSON AVE 91719
Frank Ware, prin.
Home Gardens ES, 13550 TOLTON AVE 91719
George Wilcox, prin.
Jefferson ES, 1040 S VICENTIA AVE 91720
Warren Juola, prin.
Lincoln Alter ES, 1041 FULLERTON ST 91720
Robert McCall, prin.
Parkridge ES, 750 CORONA AVE 91720
Dennis Crane, prin.
Prado View ES, 2800 RIDGELINE DR 91710
Linda Joyce, prin.
Stallings ES, 1980 FULLERTON AVE 91719
Lydia Wells, prin.
Vicentia ES, 2005 S VICENTIA AVE 91720
Robert Stephenson, prin.
Other Schools – See Norco

Corona Christian School
1901 W ONTARIO AVE 91720

Corona Heights Christian Baptist School
930 E ONTARIO AVE 91719
Crossroads Christian ES, P O BOX 1296 91718
Grace Luthern Church Christian Day Schoo
1811 S LINCOLN AVE 91720
St. Edward ES, 500 S MERRILL ST 91720

Corona Del Mar, Orange Co.
Newport-Mesa USD
Supt. – See Newport Beach
Harbor View ES, 900 GOLDENROD AVE 92625
Larry Alford, prin.

Harbor Day ES, 3443 PACIFIC VIEW DR 92625

Coronado, San Diego Co., Pop. Code 7
Coronado USD
Sch. Sys. Enr. Code 4
Supt. – David Blumenthal, 706 6TH ST 92118
MS, 911 7TH ST 92118 – Gary Davidson, prin.
Central ES, 803 7TH ST 92118
Maureen McGrath, prin.
Crown ES, 201 6TH ST 92118
Maureen McGrath, prin.
Silver Strand ES, 1350 LEYTE ROAD 92118
Hugh Watson, Jr., prin.

Sacred Heart ES, 706 C AVE 92118

Corralitos, Santa Cruz Co.

Salesian Sisters ES, 605 ENOS LN 95076

Corte Madera, Marin Co., Pop. Code 6
Larkspur ESD
Supt. – See Larkspur
Cummins ES, 58 MOHAWK AVE 94925
Michael Fanning, prin.

Marin Country Day ES, 5221 PARADISE DR 94925
Marin Horizon ES
330 GOLDEN HIND PASSAGE 94925

Costa Mesa, Orange Co., Pop. Code 8
Newport-Mesa USD
Supt. – See Newport Beach
TeWinkle IS, 3224 CALIFORNIA ST 92626
Scott Paulsen, prin.
California ES, 3232 CALIFORNIA ST 92626
Scott Paulsen, prin.
College Park ES, 2380 NOTRE DAME ROAD 92626
Dick Clarke, prin.
Kaiser ES, 2130 SANTA ANA AVE 92627
William Knight, prin.
Killybrooke ES, 3155 KILLYBROOKE LANE 92626
Frank Feller, prin.
Paularino ES, 1060 PAULARINO AVE 92626
Ken Killian, prin.
Pomona ES, 2051 POMONA AVE 92627
Sandy Bundy, prin.
Sonora ES, 966 SONORA ROAD 92626
Ned Hall, prin.
Whittier ES, 1800 WHITTIER AVE 92627
Tom Carr, prin.
Wilson ES, 801 W WILSON ST 92627
Charles Godshall, prin.

Christ Lutheran ES, 760 VICTORIA ST 92627
Page ES of Costa Mesa, 657 VICTORIA ST 92627
Page School of Beverly Hills
657 VICTORIA ST 92627
Page School of Hancock Park
657 VICTORIA ST 92627
Park Private Day ES
261 MONTE VISTA AVE 92627
Prince of Peace Lutheran ES
2987 MESA VERDE DR E 92626
St. Joachim ES, 1964 ORANGE AVE 92627
St. John The Baptist ES, 1021 BAKER ST 92626

Cotati, Sonoma Co., Pop. Code 5
Cotati-Rohnert Park USD
Supt. – See Rohnert Park
MS, 216 E SCHOOL ST 94928 – Rick Brewer, prin.
Page ES, 1075 MADRONE AVE 94928
Bob Earnest, prin.

Cottonwood, Shasta Co., Pop. Code 4
Cottonwood Un. ESD
Sch. Sys. Enr. Code 3
Supt. – Kenneth Osborn, 20512 W 1ST ST 96022
West Cottonwood JHS, P O BOX 500 96022
Dale Hansen, prin.
East Cottonwood ES, 3425 BRUSH ST 96022
Andrew Hinds, prin.

Evergreen Un. ESD
Sch. Sys. Enr. Code 3
Supt. – Harley North
19415 HOOKER CREEK ROAD 96022
Evergreen ES, 19415 HOOKER CREEK RD 96022
Mike Leonard, prin.

Coulterville, Mariposa Co.
Mariposa County USD
Supt. – See Mariposa
Coulterville-Greeley ES
10326 FISKE ROAD 95311
Eldon Henderson, prin.

Courtland, Sacramento Co.
River Delta USD
Supt. – See Rio Vista
Bates ES, P O BOX 308 95615
Donald Fenocchio, prin.

Covelo, Mendocino Co., Pop. Code 3
Round Valley USD
Sch. Sys. Enr. Code 3
Supt. – Donald Cook, P O BOX 276 95428
Round Valley ES, P O BOX 276 95428
  James Hatfield, prin.

Covina, Los Angeles Co., Pop. Code 8
Azusa USD
Supt. – See Azusa
Ellington ES, 5034 N CLYDEBANK AVE 91722
  Sharron Lindsay, prin.

Charter Oak USD
Sch. Sys. Enr. Code 6
Supt. – Michael Caston, P O BOX 9 91723
Royal Oak IS, 303 GLENDORA AVE 91723
  Richard Evers, prin.
Badillo ES, 1771 E OLD BADILLO ST 91724
  Donna Patrick, prin.
Cedargrove ES, 1209 N GLENDORA AVE 91724
  Roger Klinkhart, prin.
Glen Oak ES, 1000 N SUNFLOWER AVE 91723
  Ronald Bunte, prin.
Washington ES, P O BOX 9 91723
  Paul Morrow, prin.
Other Schools – See Glendora

Covina-Valley USD
Sch. Sys. Enr. Code 7
Supt. – Jack Rankin, P O BOX 269 91723
Las Palmas IS, 641 N LARK ELLEN AVE 91722
  Peter Maldonado, prin.
Sierra Vista IS, 777 E PUENTE AVE 91723
  Robert Shivers, prin.
Traweek JHS, P O BOX 269 91723
  John Schlenz, prin.
Barranca ES, 727 S BARRANCA AVE 91723
  Georgia Florentine, prin.
Ben Lomond ES, 621 E COVINA BLVD 91722
  Ronald Cytryn, prin.
ES, 160 N BARRANCA AVE 91723
  Ronald Iannone, prin.
Cypress ES, 351 W CYPRESS AVE 91723
  C. Wilson, prin.
Lark Ellen ES, 4555 N LARK ELLEN AVE 91722
  Russell Manzone, prin.
Manzanita ES, 4131 N NORA AVE 91722
  Jeneane Shield, prin.
Rowland Avenue ES, P O BOX 269 91723
  Richard Mooneyham, prin.
Valencia ES, 758 W GRONDAHL ST 91722
  William Brown, prin.
Other Schools – See Irwindale, West Covina

Baldwin Park Sonrse Christian ES
  1220 E RUDDOCK ST 91724
Sacred Heart ES, 360 W WORKMAN AVE 91723
St. John Lutheran ES, 304 E COVINA BLVD 91722
St. Louise De Marillac ES
  1728 E COVINA BLVD 91724

Crescent City, Del Norte Co., Pop. Code 5
Del Norte County USD
Sch. Sys. Enr. Code 5
Supt. – Gene Edinger
  301 W WASHINGTON BLVD 95531
Crescent Elk MS, 994 G STREET 95531
  Sherry Smith, prin.
Hamilton ES, 1050 E ST 95531
  Patrick Finley, prin.
Maxwell ES, 1124 EL DORADO ST 95531
  Barbara Clausen, prin.
Pine Grove ES, 900 NORTHCREST DR 95531
  Rick Smith, prin.
Other Schools – See Fort Dick, Gasquet, Klamath, Smith River

St. Joseph School, 440 THIRD ST 95501

Creston, San Luis Obispo Co.
Atascadero USD
Supt. – See Atascadero
ES 93432 – Joan Sando, prin.

Crockett, Contra Costa Co., Pop. Code 5
John Swett USD
Sch. Sys. Enr. Code 4
Supt. – Harold Zuckerman, P O BOX 847 94525
Carquinez MS, 1099 POMONA ST 94525
  Phyllis Hunt, prin.
Other Schools – See Rodeo

Crows Landing, Stanislaus Co.
Newman-Crows Landing USD
Supt. – See Newman
Bonita ES, 425 FINK ROAD 95313
  Jack Mayer, prin.

Cucamonga, San Bernardino Co., Pop. Code 6
Cucamonga ESD
Sch. Sys. Enr. Code 4
Supt. – John Costello
  8776 ARCHIBALD AVE 91730
Rancho Cucamonga MS, 10022 FERON ST 91730
  Geraldine Gordon, prin.
ES, 8677 ARCHIBALD AVE 91730
  Joyce Wolfe, prin.
Los Amigos ES, 8646 BAKER AVE 91730
  Donald Nicholson, prin.

Cudahy, Los Angeles Co., Pop. Code 7
Los Angeles USD
Supt. – See Los Angeles
Clara Streer PS, 4740 CLARA ST 90201
  John Kershaw, prin.

Elizabeth Street ES, 4811 ELIZABETH ST 90201
  John Kershaw, prin.
Park Avenue ES, 8020 PARK AVE 90201
  Lloyd Johnson, prin.

Blair ES, 4433 SANTA ANA ST 90201
Community Christian ES, 4235 CLARA ST 90201

Culver City, Los Angeles Co., Pop. Code 8
Culver City USD
Sch. Sys. Enr. Code 5
Supt. – C. Rethmeyer, 4034 IRVING PLACE 90232
MS, 4601 ELENDA ST 90230 – Bruce Farr, prin.
El Rincon ES, 11177 OVERLAND AVE 90230
  Dennis Fox, prin.
Farragut ES, 10820 FARRAGUT DRIVE 90230
  Marilyn Miller, prin.
Howe ES, 4100 IRVING PLACE 90232
  Jeffrey Russell, prin.
La Ballona ES, 10915 WASHINGTON BLVD 90232
  Diane Wallace, prin.

Los Angeles USD
Supt. – See Los Angeles
Braddock Drive ES
  4711 INGLEWOOD BLVD 90230
  John Manken, prin.
Playa Del Rey ES, 12221 JUNIETTE ST 90230
  Betsy Warren, prin.
Stoner Avenue ES
  11735 BRADDOCK DRIVE 90230
  Jerrolyn Hogue, prin.

Horizon ES, 3430 MCMANUS AVE 90232
St. Augustine Catholic ES
  3819 CLARINGTON AVE 90232

Cupertino, Santa Clara Co., Pop. Code 8
Cupertino Un. ESD
Sch. Sys. Enr. Code 7
Supt. – Yvette del Prado
  10301 VISTA DRIVE 95014
Hyde JHS, 19325 BOLLINGER ROAD 95014
  Marilyn Miller, prin.
Kennedy JHS, 821 BUBB ROAD 95014
  Larry Curb, prin.
Collins ES, 10401 VISTA DRIVE 95014
  Sharon Skold, prin.
Faria ES, 10155 BARBARA LANE 95014
  K. Fisk, prin.
Garden Gate ES, 10500 ANN ARBOR AVE 95014
  Joy Weiss, prin.
Lincoln ES, 21710 MCCLELLAN ROAD 95014
  James Harriman, prin.
Older ES, 19500 CALLE DE BARCELONA 95014
  Ruth Spadafore, prin.
Regnart ES, 1170 YORKSHIRE DRIVE 95014
  (—), prin.
Stevens Creek ES
  10300 AINSWORTH DRIVE 95014
  Sheila Tiedt, prin.
Other Schools – See Los Altos, San Jose, Santa Clara, Saratoga, Sunnyvale

Montebello ESD
Sch. Sys. Enr. Code 1
Supt. – Janet Schwind
  15101 MONTEBELLO ROAD 95014
Montebello ES
  15101 MONTEBELLO ROAD 95014
  Janet Schwind, prin.

Our Savior Lutheran School
  5825 BOLLINGER ROAD 95014
St. Joseph of Cupertino ES
  10120 N DE ANZA BLVD 95014

Cutten, Humboldt Co.
Cutten ESD
Sch. Sys. Enr. Code 3
Supt. – Arnie Ziegler, P O BOX 188 95534
MS, 4182 WALNUT DRIVE 95501
  Arnie Ziegler, prin.
Ridgewood ES, RIDGEWOOD DRIVE 95534
  Ron Pontoni, prin.

Cypress, Orange Co., Pop. Code 8
Anaheim Un. HSD
Supt. – See Anaheim
Lexington JHS, 4351 ORANGE AVE 90630
  Patricia Savage, prin.

Cypress ESD
Sch. Sys. Enr. Code 5
Supt. – William Calton, 9470 MOODY ST 90630
Arnold ES, 9281 DENNI ST 90630
  Betty Harlan, prin.
Cawthon ES, 4545 MYRA AVE 90630
  Shelby Williamson, prin.
Damron ES, 5400 MYRA AVE 90630
  James Owen, prin.
King ES, 8710 MOODY ST 90630
  John Lawson, prin.
Morris ES, 9952 GRAHAM ST 90630
  J. Collings, prin.
Swain ES, 5851 NEWMAN ST 90630
  J. Collings, prin.
Vessels ES, 5900 CATHY AVE 90630
  M. Beatty, prin.
Other Schools – See Buena Park, La Palma

Harvest Christian Academy, P O BOX 869 90630
Calvary Chapels ES, 5202 LINCOLN AVE 90630
Orange County Christian ES, P O BOX 2426 90630

St. Irenaeus Catholic ES
  9201 GRINDLAY ST 90630

Daly City, San Mateo Co., Pop. Code 8
Bayshore ESD
Sch. Sys. Enr. Code 2
Supt. – Winifred Kum, 1 MARTIN ST 94014
Robertson IS, 1 MARTIN ST 94014
  Kate Scholz, prin.
Bayshore ES, 155 ORIENTE ST 94014
  Kate Scholz, prin.

Brisbane ESD
Supt. – See Brisbane
Panorama ES, 25 BELLEVUE AVE 94014
  Frank Piro, prin.

Jefferson ESD
Sch. Sys. Enr. Code 6
Supt. – Joseph DiGeronimo
  101 LINCOLN AVE 94015
Pollicita MS, 550 E MARKET ST 94014
  Bobby Allen, prin.
Rivera IS, 1255 SOUTHGATE AVE 94015
  George Grant, prin.
Brown ES, 305 EASTMOOR AVE 94015
  Ann Hale, prin.
Colma ES, 444 E MARKET ST 94014
  Harriet Jones, prin.
Edison ES, 1267 SOUTHGATE AVE 94015
  Jose Nieto, prin.
Kennedy ES, 785 PRICE ST 94014
  June Moorehead, prin.
Roosevelt ES, 1200 SKYLINE DRIVE 94015
  Gladys Regan, prin.
Tobias ES, 725 SOUTHGATE AVE 94015
  Burt Norall, prin.
Washington ES, 251 WHITTIER ST 94014
  Carl Pileri, prin.
Webster ES, 425 EL DORADO DRIVE 94015
  Winifred Noble, prin.
Westlake ES, 80 FIELDCREST DRIVE 94015
  Donald Robertson, prin.
Wilson ES, 43 MIRIAM ST 94014
  Dan Cafferata, prin.
Other Schools – See Colma

South San Francisco USD
Supt. – See South San Francisco
Junipero Serra ES, 151 VICTORIA DR 94015
  Ed Pitcock, prin.
Skyline ES, 55 CHRISTEN AVE 94015
  Elisa Noonan, prin.

Bayshore Christian Academy
  310 OTTILIA ST 94014
Hilldale ES, 79 FLORENCE ST 94014
Holy Angels ES, 20 REINER ST 94014
Our Lady of Mercy ES, 7 ELMWOOD DR 94015
Our Lady of Perpertual Help ES
  80 WELLINGTON AVE 94014

Dana Point, Orange Co., Pop. Code 5
Capistrano USD
Supt. – See San Juan Capistrano
Dana ES, 24242 LA CRESTA DRIVE 92629
  Douglas Kramer, prin.

Dana Point Christian ES, 33732 BIG SUR 92629
St. Edward ES
  33866 CALLE LA PRIMAVERA 92629

Danville, Contra Costa Co., Pop. Code 6
San Ramon Valley USD
Sch. Sys. Enr. Code 7
Supt. – William Streshly
  699 OLD ORCHARD ROAD 94526
Los Cerros MS, 968 BLEMER ROAD 94526
  Duff Danilovich, prin.
Wood IS, 566 S HARTZ AVE 94526
  Richard Boschetti, prin.
Baldwin ES, 741 BROOKSIDE DRIVE 94526
  Tom Lotz, prin.
Green Valley ES, 1001 DIABLO ROAD 94526
  Bernard De Costa, prin.
Greenbrook ES, 1475 HARLAN DRIVE 94526
  Marie Schmidt, prin.
Montair ES, 300 QUINTERRA LANE 94526
  Robert Scott, prin.
Vista Grande ES, 667 DIABLO ROAD 94526
  Don Irvine, prin.
Other Schools – See Alamo, San Ramon

San Ramon Valley Christian Academy
  222 W EL PINTADO 94526
St. Isidore ES, 435 LA GONDA WAY 94526

Davenport, Santa Cruz Co.
Pacific ESD
Sch. Sys. Enr. Code 1
Supt. – (—), OCEAN ST 95017
Pacific ES, P O BOX H 95017 – Joy Monahan, prin.

Davis, Yolo Co., Pop. Code 8
Davis JUSD
Sch. Sys. Enr. Code 6
Supt. – Darrel Taylor, 526 B ST 95616
Birch Lane ES, 1600 BIRCH LANE 95616
  Velma Lagerstrom, prin.
North Davis ES, 555 E 14TH ST 95616
  Mary Dolcini, prin.
Pioneer ES, 5215 HAMEL ST 95616
  Barbara Wells, prin.
Valley Oak ES, 1400 E 8TH ST 95616
  Fred Diel, prin.

West Davis ES, 1221 ANDERSON ROAD   95616
 Norman Enfield, prin.
West Davis IS, 1207 SYCAMORE LANE   95616
 Diane Zimmerman, prin.

St. James ES, 1215 B ST   95616

Delano, Kern Co., Pop. Code 7
Columbine ESD
 Sch. Sys. Enr. Code 2
 Supt. – (—)
  RURAL ROUTE 01 BOX 735   93215
 Columbine ES
  RURAL ROUTE 01 BOX 735   93215
  Gary Giraudi, prin.

Delano Un. ESD
 Sch. Sys. Enr. Code 5
 Supt. – David Yetter, 1405 12TH AVE   93215
 Cecil Avenue JHS
  CECIL AVE & NORWALK   93215 – Al Watts, prin.
 Albany Park ES, 20TH AND CLARK   93215
  Michael Radsick, prin.
 Del Vista ES
  QUINCY ST AND SEVENTH PLACE   93215
  Sue Rozum, prin.
 Fremont ES, 12TH AND CLINTON STS   93215
  Rosemarie Bans, prin.
 Terrace ES, 20TH AND NORWALK   93215
  Judy Tucker, prin.
 Valle Vista ES
  GRACES HWY & CLINTON ST   93215
  Marcos Ramirez, prin.

St. Mary ES, P O BOX 819   93216

Delhi, Merced Co., Pop. Code 4
Delhi ESD
 Sch. Sys. Enr. Code 3
 Supt. – Kirk McCandless, P O BOX 338   95315
 El Capitan MS, P O BOX 338   95315
  Sandra Nerlin, prin.
 Schendel ES, P O BOX 338   95315
  Elmano Costa, prin.

Del Mar, San Diego Co., Pop. Code 6
Del Mar Un. ESD
 Sch. Sys. Enr. Code 3
 Supt. – Robert Harriman, 225 NINTH ST   92014
 Del Mar Heights ES
  13555 BOQUITA DRIVE   92014
  Stewart Seaward, prin.
 Del Mar Hills ES, 14085 MANGO DRIVE   92014
  Jeffrey Swenerton, prin.

Del Rey, Fresno Co.
Sanger USD
 Supt. – See Sanger
 ES, P O BOX 68   93616 – Robert Ward, prin.

Denair, Stanislaus Co., Pop. Code 4
Denair USD
 Sch. Sys. Enr. Code 4
 Supt. – Wayne Kidwell, P O BOX 368   95316
 MS, 3773 MADERA AVE   95316 – Larry Hoyt, prin.
 ES, 3773 MADERA AVE   95316 – Bill Gandy, prin.

Gratton ESD
 Sch. Sys. Enr. Code 1
 Supt. – Richard Cox
  4500 N GRATTON ROAD   95316
 Gratton ES, 4500 N GRATTON ROAD   95316
  Richard Cox, prin.

Descanso, San Diego Co.
Mountain Empire USD
 Supt. – See Pine Valley
 ES, 24842 VIEJAS BLVD   92016 – Roy Radke, prin.

Desert Center, Riverside Co.
Desert Center USD
 Sch. Sys. Enr. Code 1
 Supt. – Roy Savage, P O BOX 106   92239
 Eagle Mountain ES, P O BOX 106   92239
  Roy Savage, prin.

Desert Hot Springs, Riverside Co., Pop. Code 6
Palm Springs USD
 Supt. – See Palm Springs
 Corsini ES, 68750 HACIENDA DRIVE   92240
  Diane Franco, prin.
 ES, 11-625 WEST DRIVE   92240
  Edward Wenzlaff, prin.

Diamond Bar, Los Angeles Co., Pop. Code 7
Pomona USD
 Supt. – See Pomona
 Lorbeer JHS, 501 DIAMOND BAR BLVD   91765
  Jack Housen, prin.
 Armstrong ES, 22750 BEAVERHEAD DRIVE   91765
  Eugene Domeno, prin.
 Diamond Point ES
  24150 SUNSET CROSSING ROAD   91765
  Richard Rodriguez, prin.
 Golden Springs ES, 245 BALLENA DRIVE   91765
  Tom Mangham, prin.

Walnut Valley USD
 Supt. – See Walnut
 Chaparral MS, 1405 SPRUCE TREE DRIVE   91765
  Roger Skinner, prin.
 Castle Rock ES, 2975 CASTLE ROCK ROAD   91765
  Marshall Manthorne, prin.
 Evergreen ES
  2450 EVERGREEN SPRINGS DR   91765
  Albert Stone, prin.

Maple Hill ES, 1350 MAPLE HILL ROAD   91765
 Sandra Skinner, prin.
Quail Summit ES
 23330 E QUAIL SUMMIT DR   91765
 Carolyn Haugen, prin.

Mt. Calvary Lutheran ES
 23300 GOLDEN SPRINGS DR   91765

Diamond Springs, El Dorado Co., Pop. Code 3
Mother Lode Un. ESD
 Supt. – See Placerville
 Brown ES, 6520 OAK DELL ROAD   95619
  Stan Shiba, prin.

Dinuba, Tulare Co., Pop. Code 6
Dinuba SD
 Sch. Sys. Enr. Code 5
 Supt. – Mark Fabrizio, P O BOX 125   93618
 Washington IS, 1250 N HAYES AVE   93618
  Thomas Ayers, prin.
 Grand View ES, 39746 ROAD 64   93618
  Jodie Rhea, prin.
 Jefferson ES
  BRAWFORD AND SIERRA WAY   93618
  Ronald Jefferson, prin.
 Lincoln ES, EATON & SAGINAW AVES   93618
  Phillip Stovall, prin.
 Wilson ES, GREEN & KAMM AVES   93618
  Anne Raymond, prin.

Dixon, Solano Co., Pop. Code 6
Dixon USD
 Sch. Sys. Enr. Code 5
 Supt. – J. Gerry Laird, 305 N ALMOND ST   95620
 Jacobs IS, 200 N LINCOLN ST   95620
  Gabriel Alvarado, prin.
 Anderson MS, 415 EAST C ST   95620
  Dorcas Alarcon, prin.
 Silveyville PS, 355 N ALMOND ST   95620
  George Tognetti, prin.

Dobbins, Yuba Co.
Marysville JUSD
 Supt. – See Marysville
 ES, P O BOX 127   95935 – Amy Stewart, prin.

Dorris, Siskiyou Co., Pop. Code 3
Butte Valley USD
 Sch. Sys. Enr. Code 2
 Supt. – Max Harrell, P O BOX 709   96023
 ES, P O BOX 748   96023 – Larry Butler, prin.
 Other Schools – See Macdoel

Dos Palos, Merced Co., Pop. Code 5
Dos Palos J Un. ESD
 Sch. Sys. Enr. Code 4
 Supt. – Van Sweet, 2041 ALMOND ST   93620
 Bryant MS, BRYANT ROAD   93620
  Charles Ratliff, prin.
 ES, 2041 ALMOND ST   93620 – Gayle Bonds, prin.

Douglas City, Trinity Co.
Douglas City ESD
 Sch. Sys. Enr. Code 2
 Supt. – (—), P O BOX 280   96024
 ES, P O BOX 280   96024 – Robert Gravette, prin.

Downey, Los Angeles Co., Pop. Code 8
Downey USD
 Sch. Sys. Enr. Code 7
 Supt. – Ed Sussman, P O BOX 75   90241
 East MS, 10301 WOODRUFF AVE   90241
  Teresa Shuck, prin.
 Griffiths MS, 9633 TWEEDY LANE   90240
  Wendy Lopour, prin.
 South MS, 12500 BIRCHDALE AVE   90242
  Dale Lostetter, prin.
 West MS
  11985 OLD RIVER SCHOOL ROAD   90242
  Earl Haugen, prin.
 Alameda ES, 8613 E ALAMEDA ST   90242
  Karen Nadell, prin.
 Carpenter ES, 9439 FOSTER ROAD   90242
  Denise Takano, prin.
 Gallatin ES, 9513 BROOKSHIRE AVE   90240
  Gloria Widmann, prin.
 Gauldin ES, 9724 SPRY ST   90242
  Georgia Ananias, prin.
 Imperial ES, 8133 IMPERIAL HIGHWAY   90242
  Richard Edwards, prin.
 Price ES, 9525 TWEEDY LANE   90240
  Pamela Box, prin.
 Rio Hondo ES, 7731 MULLER ST   90241
  Wendy McKinsey, prin.
 Rio San Gabriel ES, 9338 GOTHAM ST   90241
  Judith Fisher, prin.
 Ward ES, 8851 E ADOREE AVE   90242
  Linda Kennedy, prin.
 Williams ES, 7530 ARNETT ST   90241
  Paula Barnes, prin.

Calvary Chapel Christian ES
 12808 WOODRUFF AVE   90242
Good Shepherd Lutheran ES
 13200 CLARK AVE   90242
Our Lady of Perpetual Help ES
 10441 DOWNEY AVE   90241
St. Mark's ES, 10354 DOWNEY AVE   90241
St. Raymond ES
 12320 PARAMOUNT BLVD   90242

Downieville, Sierra Co., Pop. Code 2
Sierra-Plumas JUSD
 Sch. Sys. Enr. Code 3
 Supt. – Beverly Back, P O BOX E   95936

ES, P O BOX B   95936 – Lou Phillippi, prin.
Other Schools – See Loyalton, North San Juan,
 Sierraville

Doyle, Lassen Co.
Fort Sage USD
 Supt. – See Herlong
 Long Valley ES, P O BOX 7   96109
  Griff Nelson, prin.

Duarte, Los Angeles Co., Pop. Code 7
Duarte USD
 Sch. Sys. Enr. Code 5
 Supt. – Robert Packer
  1427 BUENA VISTA AVE   91010
 Northview MS, 1137 CENTRAL AVE   91010
  Robert Ortega, prin.
 Andres Duarte ES
  1433 CRESTFIELD DRIVE   91010
  Dennis Trzeciak, prin.
 Beardslee ES, 1212 KELLWILL WAY   91010
  Ross Haws, prin.
 Maxwell ES, 733 EUCLID AVE   91010
  Sylvia Whitlock, prin.
 Royal Oaks ES, 2499 ROYAL OAKS DRIVE   91010
  Diane Gerson, prin.
 Valley View ES, 237 MEL CANYON ROAD   91010
  Janet Trostle, prin.

Dublin, Alameda Co., Pop. Code 7
Dublin JUSD
 Sch. Sys. Enr. Code 5
 Supt. – Heinz Gewing
  7471 LARKDALE AVE   94568
 Wells IS, 6800 PENN DRIVE   94568
  Linda Pearson, prin.
 Fredericksen ES, 7243 TAMARACK DR   94568
  Brian McBride, prin.
 Murray ES, 8435 DAVONA DRIVE   94568
  Mark Stott, prin.
 Nielsen ES, 7500 AMARILLO DRIVE   94568
  Diane Griffiths, prin.

Christian Center ES, 7997 VOMAC RD   94568
St. Raymond ES, 11555 SHANNON AVE   94568

Ducor, Tulare Co.
Ducor Un. ESD
 Sch. Sys. Enr. Code 2
 Supt. – Warren Rankins, P O BOX 87   93218
 Ducor Union ES   93218 – Warren Rankins, prin.

Dunlap, Fresno Co.
Kings Canyon JUSD
 Supt. – See Reedley
 ES, P O BOX 100   93621 – Dan Kenney, prin.

Dunsmuir, Siskiyou Co., Pop. Code 4
Dunsmuir ESD
 Sch. Sys. Enr. Code 2
 Supt. – Robert Wilson
  4760 SISKIYOU AVE   96025
 ES, 4760 SISKIYOU AVE   96025 – (—), prin.

Durham, Butte Co., Pop. Code 3
Durham USD
 Sch. Sys. Enr. Code 3
 Supt. – Donald McNelis, P O BOX 300   95938
 IS, 9420 PUTNEY DRIVE   95938
  Linda Brown, prin.
 ES, P O BOX 700   95938 – Noel Buehler, prin.

Earlimart, Tulare Co., Pop. Code 5
Allensworth ESD
 Sch. Sys. Enr. Code 1
 Supt. – (—), HCR 01 BOX 136   93219
 Allensworth ES, YOUNG ROAD   93219
  Julia Lupo, prin.

Earlimart ESD
 Sch. Sys. Enr. Code 4
 Supt. – Sandra Torchia, P O BOX 27   93219
 Earlimart IS, SUTTER AVE   93219
  Michael Sawyer, prin.
 ES, 192 S CHURCH ROAD   93219 – (—), prin.

East Highlands, San Bernardino Co.
Redlands USD
 Supt. – See Redlands
 Cram ES, 29111 BASELINE ST   92346
  Emil Aznar, prin.

East Nicolaus, Sutter Co.
Marcum-Illinois Un. ESD
 Sch. Sys. Enr. Code 2
 Supt. – Gavin Huffmater, P O BOX 116   95622
 Marcum-Illinois Union ES, P O BOX 116   95622
  Gavin Huffmater, prin.

East Palo Alto, Santa Clara Co.
Ravenswood City ESD
 Supt. – See Palo Alto
 McNair IS, 2033 PULGAS AVE   94303
  Ida Carveth, prin.

Edwards, Kern Co., Pop. Code 7
Muroc JUSD
 Supt. – See North Edwards
 Bailey ES   93523 – Diane Walters, prin.
 Branch ES   93523 – Mollie Graham, prin.
 Forbes Avenue MS   93523 – Tony Monetti, prin.

El Cajon, San Diego Co., Pop. Code 8
Cajon Valley Un. ESD
 Sch. Sys. Enr. Code 7
 Supt. – Ron Hockwalt, P O BOX 1007   92022
 Cajon Valley IS, 395 BALLANTYNE ST   92020
  James Raymond, prin.

Emerald IS, 1221 EMERALD AVE 92020
 Patricia Parlin, prin.
Greenfield IS, 1495 GREENFIELD DRIVE 92021
 Nancy Girvin, prin.
Montgomery MS, 570 MELODY LANE 92021
 Stephanie Troncone, prin.
Anza ES, 1005 S ANZA ST 92020
 Alfred Dominico, prin.
Ballantyne ES, 165 ROANOKE ROAD 92020
 Candace Marr, prin.
Bostonia ES, 1390 BROADWAY 92021
 Sylvia Casas, prin.
Chase ES, 195 E CHASE AVE 92020
 Marilyn Skordas, prin.
Crest ES, 2000 SUNCREST BLVD 92021
 Paul Preddy, prin.
Cuyamaca ES, 851 S JOHNSON AVE 92020
 Jeanne Koelln, prin.
Flying Hills ES, 1251 FINCH ST 92020
 Lupe Buell, prin.
Fuerte ES, 11625 FUERTE DRIVE 92020
 Alison Cummings, prin.
Hall ES, 1376 PEPPER DRIVE 92021
 Margo Taylor, prin.
Johnson Avenue ES, 575 N JOHNSON AVE 92020
 Lynn Spiller, prin.
Lexington ES, 533 S 1ST ST 92019
 Alice Rodriguez, prin.
Madison Avenue ES
 1615 E MADISON AVE 92019
 Estelle Womack, prin.
Magnolia ES, 650 GREENFIELD DRIVE 92021
 Stephen Boyle, prin.
Meridian ES, 651 S 3RD ST 92019
 Cindi Britton, prin.
Naranca ES, 1030 NARANCA AVE 92021
 J. Pangborn, prin.
Rancho San Diego ES
 12151 CALLE ALBARA 92020 – Paul Nelson,
 prin.
Rios ES, 14314 RIOS CANYON ROAD 92021
 Andrea Elliott, prin.
Vista Grade ES, 1908 VISTA GRANDE RD 92020
 Lisbeth Johnson, prin.
Other Schools – See La Mesa

Dehesa ESD
Sch. Sys. Enr. Code 2
Supt. – Anne Johnson
 4612 DEHESA ROAD 92021
Dehesa ES, 4612 DEHESA ROAD 92019
 Anne Johnson, prin.

La Mesa-Spring Valley ESD
Supt. – See La Mesa
Fletcher Hills ES, 2330 CENTER PLACE 92020
 John Bley, prin.

Christian JHS, 211 S 3RD ST 92019
Bostonia Christian ES, 1025 N 2ND ST 92021
El Cajon Valley Christian ES
 728 PEPPER DR 92021
Holy Trinity ES, 509 BALLARD ST 92019
Lad and Lassie Childrens Learning School
 1052 E MADISON AVE 92019
Meridian Christian ES, 660 S 3RD ST 92019
Our Lady of Grace Catholic ES
 2760 NAVAJO RD 92020
St. Kierans ES, 1465 CAMILLO CT 92021

El Centro, Imperial Co., Pop. Code 7
El Centro ESD
Sch. Sys. Enr. Code 6
Supt. – Bill Criman, 1256 BROADWAY ST 92243
Kennedy JHS, 900 N 6TH ST 92243
 Michael Welish, prin.
Wilson ES, 666 S WILSON ST 92243
 David Watson, prin.
De Anza ES, 1530 S WATERMAN AVE 92243
 Alicia Armenta, prin.
Desert Garden MS, 1900 S 6TH ST 92243
 Sharon Anderholt, prin.
Harding ES, 950 S 7TH ST 92243
 Fred Rooney, prin.
Hedrick ES, 550 S WATERMAN AVE 92243
 Pat Rudolph, prin.
Lincoln ES, 200 N 12TH ST 92243
 Neil Bock, prin.
McKinley ES, 1177 N 8TH ST 92243
 Pat Lara, prin.
Washington ES, 223 S 1ST ST 92243
 Rosalynne Young, prin.

Imperial USD
Supt. – See Imperial
Westside ES, 2294 W VAUGHN ROAD 92243
 (—), prin.

McCabe Un. ESD
Sch. Sys. Enr. Code 2
Supt. – George Blek, 701 W MCCABE ROAD 92243
McCabe ES, 701 W MCCABE ROAD 92243
 George Blek, prin.

Meadows Un. ESD
Sch. Sys. Enr. Code 2
Supt. – Larry Kelly, 2059 BOWKER ROAD 92243
Meadows ES, 2059 BOWKER ROAD 92243
 Larry Kelly, prin.

St. Mary's Catholic ES
 700 S WATERMAN AVE 92243

El Cerrito, Contra Costa Co., Pop. Code 7
Richmond USD
Supt. – See Richmond

Portola JHS, 1021 NAVELLIER ST 94530
 Bill Parnell, prin.
Castro ES, 7125 DONAL AVE 94530
 (—), prin.
Fairmont ES, 724 KEARNEY ST 94530
 Chris Bennett, prin.
Harding ES, 7230 FAIRMONT AVE 94530
 Barbara Whitaker, prin.
Madera ES, 8500 MADERA DRIVE 94530
 Judith Boehm, prin.

Prospect ES, 2060 TAPSCOFT AVE 94530
St. Jerome ES, 320 SAN CARLOS AVE 94530
St. John the Baptist ES
 11156 SAN PABLO AVE 94530
Tehiyah Day ES, 2603 TASSAJARA AVE 94530
East Bay Sierra ES, 960 AVIS DR 94530

El Dorado Hills, El Dorado Co.
Buckeye Un. ESD
Supt. – See Shingle Springs
Brooks ES, 3610 PARK DRIVE 95630
 Margaret Stripe, prin.

Rescue Un. ESD
Supt. – See Rescue
Jackson ES, 1490 FRANCISCO DRIVE 95630
 Bill Prange, prin.

El Granada, San Mateo Co., Pop. Code 4
Cabrillo USD
Supt. – See Half Moon Bay
ES, SANTIAGO ST 94018 – Jan Parrillo, prin.

Elk, Mendocino Co.
Mendocino USD
Supt. – See Mendocino
Greenwood ES, P O BOX 39 95432
 Susan Franklin, prin.

Elk Creek, Glenn Co.
Stoney Creek JUSD
Sch. Sys. Enr. Code 2
Supt. – Earnie Graham, P O BOX 68 95939
ES, SANHEDRIN ROAD 95939
 Thomas Rutherglen, prin.
Other Schools – See Stonyford

Elk Grove, Sacramento Co., Pop. Code 5
Elk Grove USD
Sch. Sys. Enr. Code 7
Supt. – Robert Trigg
 8820 ELK GROVE BLVD 95624
Kerr JHS, 8865 ELK GROVE BLVD 95624
 Arnold Adreani, prin.
ES, 8828 ELK GROVE BLVD 95624
 Joan Deboy, prin.
Feickert ES, 9351 FEICKERT DRIVE 95624
 Eunice Del Buono, prin.
Foulks Ranch ES, 6211 LAGUNA PARK DR 95624
 John Mattingly, prin.
Franklin ES
 4011 HOOD-FRANKLIN ROAD 95624
 Irene West, prin.
Markofer ES, 9759 TRALEE WAY 95624
 Pacita Dean, prin.
McKee ES, 8701 HALVERSON DRIVE 95624
 Carole Sacre, prin.
Pleasant Grove ES
 10760 PLEASANT GROVE SCH RD 95624
 Kimi Kaneko, prin.
Other Schools – See Sacramento, Sloughhouse, Wilton

El Monte, Los Angeles Co., Pop. Code 8
El Monte ESD
Sch. Sys. Enr. Code 7
Supt. – Jeffrey Seymour
 3540 LEXINGTON AVE 91731
Cherrylee ES, 5025 BUFFINGTON ROAD 91732
 Michael Raymond, prin.
Columbia ES, 3400 CALIFORNIA AVE 91731
 (—), prin.
Cortada ES, 3111 POTRERO AVE 91733
 Martha Surbida, prin.
Durfee ES, 12233 STAR ST 91732
 Harold Roy, prin.
Gidley ES, 10226 LOWER AZUSA ROAD 91731
 Stuart Dunn, prin.
Le Gore ES, 11121 BRYANT ROAD 91731
 Suzanne Seymour, prin.
Mulhall ES, 10900 MULHALL ST 91731
 Lillian Prince, prin.
New Lexington ES, 10410 BODGER ST 91733
 Sally Yarbray, prin.
Norwood ES, 4520 WHISTLER AVE 91732
 Donna Robinson, prin.
Potrero ES, 2611 POTRERO AVE 91733
 Suzette Johnston, prin.
Rio Vista ES, 4300 ESTO AVE 91731
 Anna Phipps, prin.
Shirpser ES, 4020 GIBSON ROAD 91731
 Lawrence Herrera, prin.
Wilkerson ES, 2700 DOREEN AVE 91733
 Virginia Nicholl, prin.
Wright ES, 11317 MCGIRK AVE 91732
 John Ross, prin.
Other Schools – See Arcadia, South El Monte, Temple City

Mountain View ESD
Sch. Sys. Enr. Code 6
Supt. – Julian Lopez
 2850 MOUNTAIN VIEW ROAD 91732
Baker MS, 12043 EXLINE ST 91732
 Wally Cook, prin.

Kranz IS, 12460 FINEVIEW ST 91732
 Sharon Baker, prin.
Cogswell IS, 11050 FINEVIEW ST 91733
 Al Gasparian, prin.
La Primaria ES, 4220 GILMAN ROAD 91732
 Patricia Jorgensen, prin.
Maxson ES, 12380 FELIPE ST 91732
 Gloria Diaz, prin.
Miramonte ES, 10620 SCHMIDT ROAD 91733
 Ed Marquez, prin.
Monte Vista ES, 11111 THIENES AVE 91733
 Andy Salcido, prin.
Parkview ES, 12044 ELLIOTT AVE 91732
 Annzella Curry, prin.
Payne ES, 2850 MOUNTAIN VIEW ROAD 91732
 Robert Caraveo, prin.
Twin Lakes ES, 3900 GILMAN ROAD 91732
 Rosa Alvidrez, prin.
Voorhis ES, 3501 DURFEE AVE 91732
 Roberta Vincent, prin.

El Monte Christian ES
 2400 SANTA ANITA AVE 91733
First Lutheran ES
 3351 SANTA ANITA AVE 91731
Nativity ES, 10907 SAINT LOUIS DR 91731

El Nido, Merced Co.
El Nido ESD
Sch. Sys. Enr. Code 2
Supt. – (—), P O BOX 141 95317
ES, 161 E EL NIDO ROAD 95317 – C. Davis, prin.

El Portal, Mariposa Co.
Mariposa County USD
Supt. – See Mariposa
ES, P O BOX 190 95318 – George Heiss, prin.

El Segundo, Los Angeles Co., Pop. Code 7
El Segundo USD
Sch. Sys. Enr. Code 4
Supt. – Richard Bertain, 641 SHELDON ST 90245
MS, 615 RICHMOND ST 90245
 Ronald Braunstein, prin.
Center Street ES, 700 CENTER ST 90245
 Virginia Gembica, prin.

St. Anthony ES, 233 LOMITA ST 90245

El Sobrante, Contra Costa Co.
Richmond USD
Supt. – See Richmond
Crespi JHS, 1121 ALLVIEW AVE 94803
 George Crews, prin.
ES, 1060 MANOR ROAD 94803
 Pearl Lewis, prin.
Murphy ES, 4350 VALLEY VIEW ROAD 94803
 Henry Hopkins, prin.
Olinda ES, 5855 OLINDA ROAD 94803
 Dean Karahalios, prin.
Sheldon ES, 2601 MAY ROAD 94803
 Robert Cone, prin.

Apostolic Christian Pentacostal Academy
 P O BOX 699 94803
Bethel Christian Academy, 431 RINCON RD 94803
El Sobrante Christian ES, 5100 ARGYLE RD 94803

El Toro, Orange Co., Pop. Code 6
Saddleback Valley USD
Supt. – See Mission Viejo
Serrano IS, 24642 JERONIMO ROAD 92630
 Barbara Smith, prin.
Aliso ES, 22882 LOUMONT DRIVE 92630
 Phil Riley, prin.
Gates ES, 23882 LANDISVIEW AVE 92630
 Cal Burt, prin.
La Madera ES, 25350 SERRANO ROAD 92630
 Viva McBride, prin.
Olivewood ES, 23391 DUNE MEAR ROAD 92630
 Dave Whitcher, prin.
Rancho Canada ES, 21801 WINDING WAY 92630
 Evelyn Menzel, prin.
Santiago ES, 24982 RIVENDELL DRIVE 92630
 Don Snyder, prin.

Abiding Savior Lutheran ES
 23262 EL TORO RD 92630

El Verano, Sonoma Co.
Sonoma Valley USD
Supt. – See Sonoma
ES, P O BOX 430 95433 – Larry Westlake, prin.

Elverta, Sacramento Co.
Elverta JESD
Sch. Sys. Enr. Code 2
Supt. – Fred Warchol, P O BOX 222 95626
Alpha IS, 8920 ELWYN AVE 95626
 (—), prin.
ES, 7900 ELOISE AVE 95626 – (—), prin.

Emeryville, Alameda Co., Pop. Code 5
Emery USD
Sch. Sys. Enr. Code 3
Supt. – Peter Corona
 4727 SAN PABLO AVE 94608
Yates ES, 1070 41ST ST 94608 – Aron Cargo, prin.

East Bay Waldorf ES, 1275 61ST ST 94608

Emigrant Gap, Placer Co.
Emigrant Gap ESD
Sch. Sys. Enr. Code 1
Supt. – (—)
 1067 EMIGRANT GAP ROAD 95715

ES, P O BOX 87   95715 – Margaret Goodell, prin.

Empire, Stanislaus Co., Pop. Code 4
Empire Un. ESD
Sch. Sys. Enr. Code 5
Supt. – Donald Brownell, P O BOX U   95319
Teel MS, P O BOX U   95319 – John Casey, prin.
ES, 5210 FIRST ST   95319 – Cindy Murray, prin.
Other Schools – See Modesto

Encinitas, San Diego Co., Pop. Code 6
Encinitas Un. ESD
Sch. Sys. Enr. Code 5
Supt. – Donald Lindstrom, 189 UNION ST   92024
Capri ES, 941 CAPRI ROAD   92024
   Nancy Austin, prin.
Ecke Central ES, 185 UNION ST   92024
   Lorraine Boyle, prin.
Flora Vista ES, 1690 WANDERING ROAD   92024
   Raymond O'Toole, prin.
Ocean Knoll ES, 910 MELBA ROAD   92024
   Bruce DeMitchell, prin.
Pacific View ES, 608 3RD ST   92024
   Katherine North, prin.
Park Dale Lane ES, 2050 PARK DALE LANE   92024
   Gregory Ryan, prin.
Other Schools – See Carlsbad

San Dieguito Un. HSD
Sch. Sys. Enr. Code 6
Supt. – William Berrier
   625 N VULCAN AVE   92024
Other Schools – See Solana Beach

Rhoades ES, 2210 ENCINITAS BLVD   92024
St. John's ES, P O BOX 457   92024

Encino, Los Angeles Co.
Los Angeles USD
Supt. – See Los Angeles
Emelita Street ES, 17931 HATTERAS ST   91316
   Naomi Michaels, prin.
ES, 16941 ADDISON ST   91316
   Orlando Miller, prin.
Lanai Road ES, 4241 LANAI ROAD   91436
   Ronald Ferrier, prin.

Holy Martyrs School
   5300 WHITE OAK AVE   91316
Bethel Lutheran ES
   17500 BURBANK BLVD   91316
Egremont ES, 5461 LOUISE AVE   91316
Our Lady of Grace ES
   17720 VENTURA BLVD   91316
St. Cyril of Jerusalem ES
   4548 HASKELL AVE   91436
Valley Beth Shalom Day ES
   15739 VENTURA BLVD   91436

Escalon, San Joaquin Co., Pop. Code 5
Escalon USD
Sch. Sys. Enr. Code 4
Supt. – Bob Wallace, 1520 YOSEMITE AVE   95320
El Portal MS, 805 1ST ST   95320
   Pete Keeslar, prin.
Dent ES, 1998 YOSEMITE AVE   95320
   Judy Wentworth, prin.
Van Allen ES, 21051 E HIGHWAY 120   95320
   Donna Hollander, prin.
Other Schools – See Farmington, Stockton

Escondido, San Diego Co., Pop. Code 8
Escondido Un. ESD
Sch. Sys. Enr. Code 7
Supt. – Robert Fisher, 980 N ASH ST   92027
Del Dios MS, 1400 W 9TH AVE   92025
   Virginia Krauszer, prin.
Grant MS, 939 E MISSION AVE   92025
   Mary Jo Bechtold, prin.
Hidden Valley MS, 2700 REED ROAD   92027
   Royce Moore, prin.
Central ES, 122 W 4TH AVE   92025
   Ronald Smith, prin.
Conway ES, 1325 CONWAY DRIVE   92027
   Peggy Wozniak, prin.
Felicita ES, 737 W 13TH AVE   92025
   Stan Reid, prin.
Glen View ES, 2201 E MISSION AVE   92027
   Hank Nadeau, prin.
Juniper ES, 1809 S JUNIPER ST   92025
   John Stubbs, prin.
Lincoln ES, 1029 N BROADWAY   92026
   Martha Edwards, prin.
Miller ES, 1975 MILLER AVE   92025
   Judith Adams, prin.
North Broadway ES, 2301 N BROADWAY   92026
   David Tew, prin.
Oak Hill ES, 1820 OAK HILL DRIVE   92027
   Thomas French, prin.
Orange Glen ES
   2861 E VALLEY PARKWAY   92027
   Wilfrid Bailie, prin.
Rincon ES, 2301 N BROADWAY   92026
   Ronald Guiles, prin.
Rose ES, 906 N ROSE ST   92027
   Marlin Brossart, prin.

San Pasqual Un. SD
Sch. Sys. Enr. Code 2
Supt. – J. Christensen
   16666 SAN PASQUAL VALLEY RD   92027
San Pasqual Union ES
   16666 SAN PASQUAL VALLEY RD   92027
   J. Christensen, prin.

Calvin Christian School
   1868 N BROADWAY   92026
Escondido Adventist Academy
   1233 W 9TH AVE   92025
Orange Glen Christian School
   2081 BEAR VALLEY PKWY   92027
Childrens Montessori School
   2950 BEAR VALLEY PKY S   92025
Escondido Christian ES, P O BOX 27157   92027
Grace Lutheran ES, 643 W 13TH AVE   92025
Light & Life Christian ES, 120 N ASH ST   92027
St. Mary's ES, 130 E 13TH AVE   92025

Esparto, Yolo Co., Pop. Code 4
Esparto USD
Sch. Sys. Enr. Code 3
Supt. – Jerry Elmore, P O BOX 69   95627
ES, P O BOX 69   95627 – Brenda Taylor, prin.

Essex, San Bernardino Co.
Needles USD
Supt. – See Needles
ES, NATIONAL TRAILS HWY   92332
   David Renquest, prin.

Etiwanda, San Bernardino Co.
Etiwanda ESD
Sch. Sys. Enr. Code 3
Supt. – Carleton Lightfoot, P O BOX 248   91739
IS, P O BOX 248   91739 – Heidi Soehnel, prin.
Caryn ES, 6290 SIERRA CREST LOOP   91739
   John Golden, prin.
Summit ES, 13394 SUMMIT AVE   91739
   Neil Westlotorn, prin.
Windrows ES
   6855 VICTORIA PARK LANE   91739
   John Golden, prin.

Slomsek ES, 12704 FOOTHILL BLVD   91739

Etna, Siskiyou Co., Pop. Code 3
Etna Un. ESD
Sch. Sys. Enr. Code 2
Supt. – Ray Cameron, P O BOX 490   96027
ES, P O BOX 490   96027 – Ray Cameron, prin.

Eureka, Humboldt Co., Pop. Code 7
Eureka City SD
Sch. Sys. Enr. Code 6
Supt. – Jack Cottongim
   3200 WALFORD AVE   95501
Winship JHS, 2500 CYPRESS ST   95501
   Larry Olson, prin.
Zane JHS, 2155 S STREET   95501 – Jim Scott, prin.
Birney ES
   SOUTH AVE AND PROSPECT ST   95501
   Roger Lorenzetti, prin.
Grant ES, OAK AND H STS   95501
   Russell Bradford, prin.
Jefferson ES, GRANT AND B STS   95501
   Joann Davenport, prin.
LaFayette ES, 3100 PARK ST   95501
   Philip Kirby, prin.
Lincoln ES, HARRIS & PINE STS   95501
   Marty Walker, prin.
Marshall ES, HUMBOLDT AND J STS   95501
   (—), prin.
Washington ES, 3322 DOLBEER ST   95501
   Brian Sanders, prin.

Freshwater ESD
Sch. Sys. Enr. Code 2
Supt. – Jack Persson
   75 GREENWOOD HEIGHTS DRIVE   95501
Freshwater ES, 75 GREENWOOD HTS DR   95501
   Jack Persson, prin.

Garfield ESD
Sch. Sys. Enr. Code 1
Supt. – (—)
   2200 FRESHWATER ROAD   95501
Garfield ES, RURAL ROUTE 01 BOX 60YA   95501
   Christine Gordon, prin.

South Bay Un. ESD
Sch. Sys. Enr. Code 3
Supt. – Sarah Turner
   6077 N HIGHWAY 101   95501
Pine Hill ES, 5230 VANCE ST   95501
   Sarah Turner, prin.
South Bay ES, 6077 N HIGHWAY 101   95501
   Cynthia Van Vleck, prin.

St. Bernards ES, 115 HENDERSON ST   95501

Exeter, Tulare Co., Pop. Code 6
Exeter Un. SD
Sch. Sys. Enr. Code 4
Supt. – Donald Gercich, 233 E MAPLE ST   93221
Wilson MS, 265 ALBERT AVE   93221
   Gary Cascarano, prin.
Lincoln ES, 333 D ST   93221
   Renee Whitson, prin.

Sierra View Junior Academy
   19933 AVENUE 256   93221

Fairfax, Marin Co., Pop. Code 6
Ross Valley SD
Supt. – See San Anselmo
White Hill IS, 101 GLEN DRIVE   94930
   Joseph Turnage, prin.
Manor ES, 150 OAK MANOR DRIVE   94930
   Gail Loucks, prin.

St. Rita ES, 102 MARINDA DR   94930

Fairfield, Solano Co., Pop. Code 8
Fairfield-Suisun USD
Sch. Sys. Enr. Code 7
Supt. – Ernest Moretti
   1025 DELAWARE ST   94533
Grange MS, 1975 BLOSSOM AVE   94533
   Richard Watson, prin.
Sullivan MS, 2195 UNION AVE   94533
   Ernest McClelland, prin.
Blanc ES, 230 ATLANTIC AVE   94533
   Sam Tracas, prin.
Bransford ES, 900 TRAVIS BLVD   94533
   Eugene Ellis, prin.
Dover ES, 301 E ALASKA AVE   94533
   Margaret Renn, prin.
Fairview ES, 830 1ST ST   94533
   Kathi Megyeri, prin.
Gordon ES, 1950 DOVER AVE   94533
   Robert Perkins, prin.
Jones ES, 2001 WINSTON DRIVE   94533
   Herschel Bolton, prin.
Kyle ES, 1600 KIDDER AVE   94533
   John Mealley, prin.
Richardson ES
   1069 MEADOWLARK DRIVE   94533
   Gwen Lawton, prin.
Sheldon ES, 1901 WOOLNER AVE   94533
   Preston Garmire, prin.
Tolenas ES, RURAL ROUTE 01 BOX 161A   94533
   Gene Thomas, prin.
Weir ES, 1975 PENNSYLVANIA AVE   94533
   James Blackwell, prin.
Other Schools – See Suisun City

Holy Spirit ES, 1050 N TEXAS ST   94533
Solano Christian Academy, P O BOX 2409   94533

Fair Oaks, Sacramento Co., Pop. Code 7
San Juan USD
Supt. – See Carmichael
Rogers IS, 4924 DEWEY DRIVE   95628
   Don Tipton, prin.
Dewey Fundamental ES
   7025 FALCON ROAD   95628
   Beverley Hendrickson, prin.
ES, 10700 FAIR OAKS BLVD   95628
   Robert Pritchard, prin.
Holst ES, 4501 BANNISTER ROAD   95628
   Jack Schott, prin.
LeGette ES, 4623 KENNETH AVE   95628
   Lynn Montgomery, prin.
Littlejohn ES, 6838 KERMIT LANE   95628
   Pamela Costa, prin.
Northridge ES, 5150 COCOA PALM WAY   95628
   George Zarzana, prin.
Roberts ES, 5630 ILLINOIS AVE   95628
   Carl Ahlberg, prin.

Sacramento Waldorf School
   3750 VANNISTER ROAD   95628
Faith Lutheran ES, 9133 FAIR OAKS BLVD   95628
St. Mel's Parochial ES
   4745 PENNSYLVANIA AVE   95628

Fallbrook, San Diego Co., Pop. Code 6
Fallbrook Un. ESD
Sch. Sys. Enr. Code 6
Supt. – William Diedrich, P O BOX 698   92028
Potter IS, 1743 RECHE ROAD   92028
   Robert Bauersfeld, prin.
Fallbrook Street ES, P O BOX 698   92028
   Faus Smyth, prin.
La Paloma MS, P O BOX 698   92028
   James Choate, prin.
Male Ellis ES, P O BOX 698   92028
   Roberta DeLuca, prin.
San Onofre ES, P O BOX 698   92028
   Lawrence Lawson, prin.
Other Schools – See Camp Pendleton

Vallecitos SD
Sch. Sys. Enr. Code 2
Supt. – Marie Corr, 5211 FIFTH ST   92028
Vallecitos ES, 5211 FIFTH ST   92028
   Marie Corr, prin.

St. Peters School, 450 S STAGE COACH LN   92028
Zion Lutheran ES, 1405 E FALLBROOK ST   92028

Fall River Mills, Shasta Co.
Fall River JUSD
Supt. – See Cassel
ES, P O BOX 310   96028 – Pegian Cecil, prin.

Farmersville, Tulare Co., Pop. Code 6
Farmersville ESD
Sch. Sys. Enr. Code 4
Supt. – Don Sato
   281 S FARMERSVILLE BLVD   93223
JHS, 650 VIRGINIA AVE   93223 – Janet Jones, prin.
Hester ES, 477 ASH   93223 – Ronald Garcia, prin.
Snowden MS, 301 S FARMERSVILLE BLVD   93223
   James Carter, prin.

Farmington, Stanislaus Co.
Escalon USD
Supt. – See Escalon
ES, P O BOX 68   95230 – Jeanette Meduena, prin.

Feather Falls, Butte Co.
Feather Falls Un. ESD
Sch. Sys. Enr. Code 1
Supt. – Tim Shannon, P O BOX A   95940

ES, P O BOX A 95940 – Tim Shannon, prin.

Fellows, Kern Co.
Midway ESD
Sch. Sys. Enr. Code 2
Supt. – Robert Mickelson, P O BOX 39 93224
Midway ES, P O BOX 39 93224
Grant Peterson, prin.

Felton, Santa Cruz Co., Pop. Code 4
San Lorenzo Valley USD
Sch. Sys. Enr. Code 5
Supt. – John Prieskorn, 6134 HIGHWAY 9 95018
San Lorenzo Valley JHS, 6134 HIGHWAY 9 95018
Dave Weiss, prin.
Boulder Creek ES, 6134 HIGHWAY 9 95018
Craig Barker, prin.
Quail Hollow ES, 6134 HWY 9 95018
Paula Simmons, prin.
San Lorenzo Valley ES, 6134 HIGHWAY 9 95018
Karren Inman, prin.

Ferndale, Humboldt Co., Pop. Code 4
Ferndale ESD
Sch. Sys. Enr. Code 2
Supt. – Alan Jorgensen, P O BOX 667 95536
ES, P O BOX 667 95536 – Alan Jorgensen, prin.

Fillmore, Ventura Co., Pop. Code 6
Fillmore USD
Sch. Sys. Enr. Code 5
Supt. – Marlene Davis, P O BOX 697 93015
JHS, 2ND & PALM STS 93015
Mario Contini, prin.
San Cayetano ES, P O BOX 697 93015
Karen Cooksey, prin.
Sespe MS, P O BOX 697 93015
Walter Weiss III, prin.
Other Schools – See Piru

Firebaugh, Fresno Co., Pop. Code 5
Firebaugh-Las Deltas USD
Sch. Sys. Enr. Code 4
Supt. – Violet Chuck
1976 MORRIS KYLE DRIVE 93622
JHS, 1976 MORRIS KYLE DRIVE 93622
Allan Gordon, prin.
Bailey PS, 1691 Q ST 93622 – Agnes Clark, prin.
Mills IS, 1191 P ST 93622 – Agnes Clark, prin.

Oro Loma ESD
Sch. Sys. Enr. Code 2
Supt. – Patricia Dennis
5609 N RUSSELL AVE 93622
Oro Loma ES, 5609 N RUSSELL AVE 93622
(—), prin.

St. Joseph's ES, 1900 SAIPAN AVE 93622

Five Points, Fresno Co.
Westside ESD
Sch. Sys. Enr. Code 2
Supt. – Charles McManaman
19191 EXCELSIOR AVE 93624
Westside ES, 19191 EXCELSIOR AVE 93624
Charles McManaman, prin.

Flournoy, Tehama Co.
Flournoy Un. ESD
Sch. Sys. Enr. Code 1
Supt. – (—)
OSBORNE AND PASKENTA ROADS 96029
ES, OSBORNE & PASKENTA ROADS 96029
(—), prin.

Folsom, Sacramento Co., Pop. Code 7
Folsom-Cordova USD
Sch. Sys. Enr. Code 7
Supt. – David Benson, 1091 COLOMA ST 95630
JHS, 500 BLUE RAVINE ROAD 95630
Robert Mange, prin.
Judah ES, 101 DEAN WAY 95630
Bill Hooker, prin.
Sprentz ES, 249 FLOWER DRIVE 95630
Cliff Highley, prin.
Sundahl ES, 9932 INWOOD ROAD 95630
Sandra Gallardo, prin.
Other Schools – See Mather A F B, Rancho Cordova

Rescue Un. ESD
Supt. – See Rescue
Marina Village MS
1901 FRANCISCO DRIVE 95630
Anthony DeVille, prin.

St. John Notre Dame ES
309 MONTROSE DR 95630

Fontana, San Bernardino Co., Pop. Code 8
Fontana USD
Sch. Sys. Enr. Code 7
Supt. – Anthony Lardieri
9680 CITRUS AVE 92335
Southridge MS, 14500 LIVE OAK 92335
Gary Soto, prin.
Chaparral ES, 1400 SHADOW DR 92335
Patricia Browning, prin.
Cypress ES, 9751 CYPRESS AVE 92335
Richard Bentley, prin.
Juniper ES, 7655 JUNIPER AVE 92336
Harriet Beck, prin.
Jurupa Hills ES, 10755 OLEANDER AVE 92335
Tom Hogan, prin.
Live Oak ES, 9522 LIVE OAK AVE 92335
Bill Olinger, prin.
Locust ES, 7420 LOCUST AVE 92336
Esmael Velasquez, prin.

Maple ES, 751 S MAPLE AVE 92335
William Hartman, prin.
North Tamarind ES, 7961 TAMARIND AVE 92336
Christopher Vanzee, prin.
Oleander ES, 8650 OLEANDER AVE 92335
Michael Martin, prin.
Palmetto ES, 9325 PALMETTO AVE 92335
Patricia Peoples, prin.
Pepper ES, 16613 RANDALL AVE 92335
Patsy Etheredge, prin.
Poplar ES, 9937 POPLAR AVE 92335
Ray Banks, prin.
Redwood ES, 8570 REDWOOD AVE 92335
Jean Carns, prin.
South Tamarind ES, 8561 TAMARIND AVE 92335
Frederick Ortman, prin.
Tokay ES, 7846 TOKAY AVE 92336
Lawrence Boldt, prin.
West Randall ES, 15620 RANDALL AVE 92335
Carolyn Kezsely, prin.

Ambassador Baptist Schs., P O BOX 338 92334
First Lutheran Christian Day ES
9315 CITRUS AVE 92335
Fontana Christian ES, 17777 MERRILL AVE 92335
Resurrestion Academy, P O BOX 816 92334
St. Joseph Academy, 8460 MANGO AVE 92335

Forest Falls, San Bernardino Co.
Redlands USD
Supt. – See Redlands
Fallsvale ES
40600 VALLEY OF FALLS DRIVE 92339
(—), prin.

Foresthill, Placer Co., Pop. Code 3
Foresthill ESD
Sch. Sys. Enr. Code 3
Supt. – Dan Elliott, P O BOX 609 95631
Foresthill Divide MS
22888 FORESTHILL RD 95631 – (—), prin.
ES, P O BOX 609 95631 – David Vegas, prin.

Forest Ranch, Butte Co.
Chico USD
Supt. – See Chico
Forest ES 95942 – Roger Steel, prin.

Forestville, Sonoma Co., Pop. Code 3
Forestville Un. ESD
Sch. Sys. Enr. Code 3
Supt. – Milton Bonzeli
6321 HIGHWAY 116 95436
ES, 6321 HIGHWAY 116 95436
Scott Humble, prin.

Forks of Salmon, Siskiyou Co.
Forks of Salmon ESD
Sch. Sys. Enr. Code 1
Supt. – (—), SALMON RIVER ROAD 96031
Forks ES 96031 – Suzanne Jennings, prin.

Fort Bragg, Mendocino Co., Pop. Code 6
Fort Bragg USD
Sch. Sys. Enr. Code 5
Supt. – Robert Maddux, 312 S LINCOLN ST 95437
MS, 500 N HAROLD ST 95437
Mark Bibbens, prin.
Gray Dana MS, 1197 CHESTNUT ST 95437
Robert Dawes, prin.
Redwood ES, 324 S LINCOLN ST 95437
Olive McArdle, prin.
Other Schools – See Leggett

Fort Dick, Del Norte Co.
Del Norte County USD
Supt. – See Crescent City
Redwood ES, P O BOX 155 95538
Al Peyton, prin.

Fort Irwin, San Barnardino Co.
Silver Valley USD
Supt. – See Yermo
MS, NATIONAL TRAINING CENTER 92310
(—), prin.
ES, NATIONAL TRAINING CENTER 92310
Thomas Reynolds, prin.

Fort Jones, Siskiyou Co., Pop. Code 3
Ft. Jones Un. ESD
Sch. Sys. Enr. Code 2
Supt. – Jeffrey Hamilton
11501 MATHEWS ST 96032
ES, P O BOX 249 96032 – Jeffrey Hamilton, prin.

Quartz Valley ESD
Sch. Sys. Enr. Code 1
Supt. – (—)
11033 QUARTZ VALLEY ROAD 96032
Quartz Valley ES
11033 QUARTZ VALLEY RD 96032
Marilyn Seward, prin.

Fort Ord, Monterey Co.
Monterey Peninsula USD
Supt. – See Monterey
Fitch MS
NORTH-SOUTH ROAD AT ANZA 93941
Stanley Cook, prin.
Hayes ES, COE & NAPIER 93941
Ray Stevenson, prin.
Marshall ES
NORMANDY & CARENTAN ROADS 93941
Iva McDuffy, prin.
Patton ES, 350 RENDOVA ROAD 93941
Anne Bagby, prin.

Stilwell ES
NORMANDY & NORTH-SOUTH ROAD 93941
Bob Biddy, prin.

Fortuna, Humboldt Co., Pop. Code 6
Fortuna Un. ESD
Sch. Sys. Enr. Code 3
Supt. – Albert Keller, Jr., 843 L ST 95540
MS, 843 L ST 95540 – Jane DeHaan, prin.
South Fortuna ES
NEWBURG AND FORTUNA BLVD 95540
Dale Stockly, prin.

Rohnerville ESD
Sch. Sys. Enr. Code 2
Supt. – Kenneth Lytle, 2800 THOMAS ST 95540
Thomas MS, 2800 THOMAS ST 95540
Anne Nicksic, prin.
Ambrosini ES, 3850 ROHNERVILLE ROAD 95540
Kenneth Lytle, prin.

Foster City, San Mateo Co., Pop. Code 7
San Mateo City SD
Supt. – See San Mateo
Bowditch MS, 1450 TARPON ST 94404
John Belforte, prin.
Audubon ES, 841 GULF AVE 94404
Warren Kofler, prin.
ES, 461 BEACH PARK BLVD 94404
Charles Moorer, prin.

Fountain Valley, Orange Co., Pop. Code 8
Fountain Valley ESD
Sch. Sys. Enr. Code 6
Supt. – Ruben Ingram, 17210 OAK ST 92708
Fulton MS, 8778 EL LAGO CIRCLE 92708
Peter Murphy, prin.
Masuda MS, 17415 LOS JARDINES W 92708
Marc Ecker, prin.
Courreges ES, 18313 SANTA CARLOTTA 92708
Ed Lavelle, prin.
Cox ES, 17615 LOS JARDINES EAST 92708
Carole Anderson, prin.
ES, 17911 BUSHARD ST 92708
Steve Enoch, prin.
Gisler ES, 18720 LAS FLORES ST 92708
Nancy Young, prin.
Moiola ES, 9790 FINCH AVE 92708
Carl Dane, prin.
Plavan ES, 9675 WARNER AVE 92708
Catherine Follett, prin.
Tamura ES, 17340 SANTA SUZANNE ST 92708
Ned Powell, prin.
Other Schools – See Huntington Beach

Garden Grove USD
Supt. – See Garden Grove
Allen ES, 16200 BUSHARD ST 92708
James Smith, prin.
Northcutt ES, 11303 SANDSTONE AVE 92708
Dwain Leach, prin.

Ocean View ESD
Supt. – See Huntington Beach
Vista View ES, 16250 HICKORY ST 92708
Patrick Monahan, prin.

First Southern Baptist Christian School
10350 ELLIS AVE 92708
Hawthorne Christian ES
16835 BROOKHURST ST 92708

Fowler, Fresno Co., Pop. Code 4
Fowler USD
Sch. Sys. Enr. Code 4
Supt. – Thomas Crow, 658 E ADAMS AVE 93625
Fremont ES, 306 E TUOLUMNE ST 93625
Eric Cederquist, prin.
Marshall ES, 142 N ARMSTRONG AVE 93625
Mary Vaughan, prin.
Other Schools – See Fresno

Freedom, Santa Cruz Co.
Pajaro Valley USD
Supt. – See Watsonville
ES, 25 HOLLY DRIVE 95019 – (—), prin.

Fremont, Alameda Co., Pop. Code 9
Fremont USD
Sch. Sys. Enr. Code 8
Supt. – Raphael Bellumini, P O BOX 5008 94537
Centerville JHS, 37720 FREMONT BLVD 94536
Garo Mirigian, prin.
Hopkins JHS, 600 DRISCOLL ROAD 94539
Tim Reichert, prin.
Horner JHS, 41365 CHAPEL WAY 94538
E. McCoy, prin.
Thornton JHS, 4357 THORNTON AVE 94536
Jim Butler, prin.
Walters JHS, 39600 LOGAN DRIVE 94538
Suzon Kornblum, prin.
Ardenwood ES, 33955 AMELIA LANE 94536
Ed Childress, prin.
Azevada ES, 39450 ROYAL PALM DRIVE 94538
Charles Adcock, prin.
Blacow ES, 40404 SUNDALE DRIVE 94538
John Melendez, prin.
Brier ES, 39201 SUNDALE DRIVE 94538
Vickey Rinehart, prin.
Brookvale ES, 3400 NICOLET AVE 94536
Norma Speer, prin.
Cabrillo ES, 36700 SAN PEDRO DRIVE 94536
Allan Petersdorf, prin.
Chadbourne ES, 801 PLYMOUTH AVE 94539
Marie Martin, prin.

Durham ES, 40292 LESLIE ST 94538
  William Bryant, prin.
Glenmoor ES, 4620 MATTOS DRIVE 94536
  Mary Stone, prin.
Gomes ES, 555 LEMOS LANE 94539
  Bill Senning, prin.
Green ES, 42875 GATEWOOD ST 94538
  Paul Messner, prin.
Grimmer ES, 43030 NEWPORT DRIVE 94538
  Paul Wagner, prin.
Hirsch ES, 41399 CHAPEL WAY 94538
  Susan de Girolamo, prin.
Leitch ES, 41700 FERNALD COURT 94539
  Clinton Ingram, prin.
Maloney ES, 38700 LOGAN DRIVE 94536
  Halleine Morrison, prin.
Mattos ES, 37944 FARWELL DRIVE 94536
  Nancy Curteman, prin.
Millard ES, 5200 VALPEY PARK AVE 94538
  Nancy Harrington, prin.
Mission San Jose ES, 43545 BRYANT ST 94539
  Ann Lord, prin.
Mission Valley ES, 41700 DENISE ST 94539
  Gail Pagan, prin.
Niles ES, 37141 2ND ST 94536
  Angela Upchurch, prin.
Oliveira ES, 4180 ALDER AVE 94536
  Tom Lord, prin.
Parkmont ES, 2601 PARKSIDE DRIVE 94536
  Lorene Hirsch, prin.
Patterson ES, 35521 CABRILLO DRIVE 94536
  William Wright, prin.
Vallejo Mill ES
  38569 CANYON HEIGHTS DRIVE 94536
  Wayne Haro, prin.
Vista Alternative ES
  4455 SENECA PARK AVE 94538
  Wayne Crow, prin.
Warm Springs MS
  47370 WARM SPRINGS BLVD 94539
  Jerry Hennings, prin.
Warwick ES, 3375 WARWICK ROAD 94555
  Marie Troiano, prin.
Weibel ES, 45135 S GRIMMER BLVD 94539
  George Pfaffenberger, prin.

Fremont Christian JHS
  4760 THORNTON AVE 94536
Christian Community ES
  39700 MISSION BLVD 94539
Free to be Private ES
  35985 MISSION BLVD 94536
Fremont Christian IS, 4360 HANSEN AVE 94536
Fremont Christian PS
  4760 THORNTON AVE 94536
Holy Spirit ES, 3930 PARISH AVE 94536
Prince of Peace Lutheran ES
  38451 FREMONT BLVD 94536
St. Joseph ES, P O BOX 3246 94539
St. Leonard ES
  3635 SAINT LEONARDS WAY 94538

French Camp, San Joaquin Co.
Manteca USD
Supt. – See Manteca
ES, P O BOX 285 95231 – Gary Dei Rossi, prin.

French Gulch, Shasta Co.
French Gulch-Whiskeytown Un. ESD
Sch. Sys. Enr. Code 1
Supt. – Ardeth Zoll, P O BOX 368 96033
French Gulch Whiskeytown ES
  P O BOX 5B 96033 – Ardeth Zoll, prin.

Fresno, Fresno Co., Pop. Code 9
American Un. ESD
Sch. Sys. Enr. Code 2
Supt. – Richard Rhodes
  2801 W ADAMS AVE 93706
American ES, 2801 W ADAMS AVE 93706
  Richard Rhodes, prin.

Central USD
Sch. Sys. Enr. Code 5
Supt. – George Keledjian
  4605 N POLK AVE 93711
El Capitan MS, 4443 W WELDON AVE 93722
  Douglas Perry, prin.
Biola-Pershing ES, 4885 N BIOLA AVE 93722
  Luis Pannarale, prin.
Herndon-Barstow ES
  6265 N GRANTLAND AVE 93722
  Rayna Perry, prin.
Houghton-Kearney ES
  8905 W KEARNEY BLVD 93706
  Douglas Atwood, prin.
Madison ES, 330 S BRAWLEY AVE 93706
  Cathleen Self, prin.
Roosevelt ES, 2600 N GARFIELD AVE 93722
  Michael MacChesney, prin.
Teague ES, 4725 N POLK AVE 93722
  Dennis Wegley, prin.

Clovis USD
Supt. – See Clovis
Kastner IS, 7676 N 1ST ST 93710
  Virginia Boris, prin.
Fort Washington ES, 960 E TEAGUE AVE 93710
  Richard Sparks, prin.
Lincoln ES, 774 E ALLUVIAL AVE 93710
  Tom Lutton, prin.
Temperance-Kutner ES
  1448 N ARMSTRONG AVE 93727
  Pete Reyes, prin.

Fowler USD
Supt. – See Fowler
Malaga ES, 3910 S WARD AVE 93725
  Leslie Emerzian, prin.

Fresno USD
Sch. Sys. Enr. Code 8
Supt. – Glen Rathwick, TULARE & M STS 93722
Ahwahnee MS, 1127 E ESCALON AVE 93710
  Meher Chekerdemian, prin.
Cooper MS, 2277 W BELLAIRE WAY 93705
  Dolphus Trotter, prin.
Ft. Miller MS, 1302 E DAKOTA AVE 93704
  Julie Adams, prin.
Irwin Computech MS
  555 E BELGRAVIA AVE 93706
  Vurdell Newsome, prin.
Kings Canyon MS, 5117 E TULARE AVE 93727
  Don Beauregard, prin.
Scandinavian MS
  3232 N SIERRA VISTA AVE 93726
  Jenna Reynolds, prin.
Tehipite MS, 630 N AUGUSTA ST 93701
  Richard Shore, prin.
Tenaya MS, 1239 W MESA AVE 93711
  Jeannette Phillips, prin.
Tioga MS, 3232 E FAIRMONT AVE 93726
  Diane Gilbert, prin.
Wawona MS, 4524 N THORNE AVE 93704
  Paul Creel, prin.
Yosemite MS, 1292 N 9TH ST 93703
  Jon Adams, prin.
Addams ES, 2117 W MCKINLEY 93728
  Elizabeth Johnston, prin.
Ayer ES, 5272 E LOWE AVE 93727
  Leo Franz, prin.
Aynesworth ES, 4765 E BURNS AVE 93725
  J. Powers, prin.
Baird ES, 5500 N MAROA AVE 93704
  Wayne Snell, prin.
Bethune ES, 1616 S FRUIT AVE 93706
  Erlinda Griffin, prin.
Birney ES, 3034 E CORNELL AVE 93703
  Bob Edmond, prin.
Bullard Project Talent ES
  4750 N HARRISON AVE 93704
  Jean Bastien, prin.
Burroughs ES, 166 N SIERRA VISTA AVE 93702
  Jim Newton, prin.
Calwa ES, 4303 E JENSEN AVE 93725
  Larry Garcia, prin.
Carver ES, 2463 S FIG AVE 93706
  Bobby Lee, prin.
Centennial ES, 3830 E SAGINAW WAY 93726
  Sandra Carsten, prin.
Columbia ES, 1025 S TRINITY ST 93706
  Mary Montgomery, prin.
Dailey ES, 3135 N HARRISON ST 93705
  Harold Massey, prin.
Del Mar ES, 4122 N DEL MAR AVE 93704
  Richard Alexander, prin.
Easterby ES, 5211 E TULARE AVE 93727
  Richard Andrade, prin.
Eaton ES, 1451 E SIERRA AVE 93710
  Lynn Freeman, prin.
Ericson ES, 4774 E YALE AVE 93703
  Al Hooper, prin.
Ewing ES, 4873 E OLIVE AVE 93727
  Don Irvin, prin.
Forkner ES, 7120 N VALENTINE AVE 93711
  Randy Hein, prin.
Fremont ES, 1005 W WELDON AVE 93705
  David Sinner, prin.
Gibson ES, 1266 W BARSTOW AVE 93711
  Celeste Cusumano, prin.
Heaton ES, 1533 N SAN PABLO AVE 93728
  Theodore Tukloff, prin.
Hidalgo ES, 900 N 1ST ST 93721
  Al Psenner, prin.
Holland ES, 4676 N FRESNO ST 93726
  Sandra Lacroix, prin.
Homan ES, 1602 W HARVARD AVE 93705
  Seth Atamian, prin.
Jackson ES, 3733 E KERCKHOFF AVE 93702
  James Harris, prin.
Jefferson ES, 202 N MARIPOSA ST 93701
  Ruben Barrios, prin.
King ES, 1001 E FLORENCE AVE 93706
  Rae Aldredge, prin.
Kirk ES, 2000 E BELGRAVIA AVE 93706
  Jean Williams, prin.
Kratt ES, 650 W SIERRA AVE 93704
  Glenn Stafford, prin.
Lane ES, 4730 E LOWE AVE 93702
  George Marsh, prin.
Lawless ES, 5255 N REESE AVE 93722
  Ginny Dow, prin.
Lincoln ES, 651 B ST 93706
  Moses Dominguez, prin.
Lowell ES, 171 N POPLAR AVE 93701
  Larry Luna, prin.
Malloch ES, 2251 W MORRIS AVE 93711
  John Edmondson, prin.
Manchester Gate MS, 2307 E DAKOTA AVE 93726
  Gary Christensen, prin.
Mayfair ES, 3305 E HOME AVE 93703
  Al Sanchez, prin.
McCardle ES, 577 E SIERRA AVE 93710
  Diane Buckalew, prin.
Muir ES, 410 E DENNETT AVE 93728
  Carlos Encinas, prin.
Norseman ES, 4636 E WELDON AVE 93703
  Glenna Encinas, prin.

Powers ES, 110 E SWIFT AVE 93704
  Alan Harrison, prin.
Pyle ES, 4140 N AUGUSTA ST 93726
  Larry Calvert, prin.
Robinson ES, 555 E BROWNING AVE 93710
  John Maurer, prin.
Roeding ES, 1225 W DAKOTA AVE 93705
  Vera Pettus, prin.
Rowell ES, 3460 E MCKENZIE AVE 93702
  Arthur Carlson, prin.
Slater ES, 4472 N EMERSON AVE 93705
  George Marsh, prin.
Starr ES, 1780 W SIERRA AVE 93711
  Richard Emerson, prin.
Sunset ES, 1755 S CRYSTAL AVE 93706
  Karen Matthews, prin.
Thomas ES, 4444 N MILLBROOK AVE 93726
  Pumphrey McBride, prin.
Turner ES, 5218 E CLAY AVE 93727
  Mary Marcelletti, prin.
Viking ES, 4251 N WINERY AVE 93726
  Neil Unruh, prin.
Vinland ES, 4666 N MAPLE AVE 93726
  Richard Corsaro, prin.
Webster ES, 930 N AUGUSTA ST 93701
  Adina Janzen, prin.
Wilson ES, 2131 W ASHLAN AVE 93705
  Diane Tukloff, prin.
Winchell ES, 3722 E LOWE AVE 93702
  Bob Quintana, prin.
Wishon ES, 3857 E HARVARD AVE 93703
  Doug Jackson, prin.
Wolters ES, 5174 N 1ST ST 93710
  Olivia Palacio, prin.

Monroe ESD
Sch. Sys. Enr. Code 2
Supt. – Robert Condoian
  11842 S CHESTNUT AVE 93725
Monroe ES, 11842 S CHESTNUT AVE 93725
  Robert Condoian, prin.

Orange Center ESD
Sch. Sys. Enr. Code 2
Supt. – Russell Yorke, 3530 S CHERRY AVE 93706
Orange Center ES, 3530 S CHERRY AVE 93706
  Russell Yorke, prin.

Pacific Un. ESD
Sch. Sys. Enr. Code 2
Supt. – Warren Jennings
  2065 E BOWLES AVE 93725
Pacific Union ES, 2065 E BOWLES AVE 93725
  Warren Jennings, prin.

Sanger USD
Supt. – See Sanger
Lone Star ES, 2617 S FOWLER AVE 93725
  James Trapp, prin.
Wash ES, 6350 E LANE AVE 93727
  Wilma Ewert, prin.

Washington Colony ESD
Sch. Sys. Enr. Code 2
Supt. – Olin Mosher, 130 E LINCOLN AVE 93706
Washington Colony ES
  130 E LINCOLN AVE 93706
  Olin Mosher, Jr., prin.

West Fresno ESD
Sch. Sys. Enr. Code 3
Supt. – Norman Douglas, 2888 S IVY AVE 93706
West Fresno MS, 2888 S IVY AVE 93706
  Gerald Pierce, prin.
West Fresno ES, 2910 S IVY ST 93706
  James Rhodes, prin.

West Park ESD
Sch. Sys. Enr. Code 2
Supt. – Bernie Hanlon
  2695 S VALENTINE AVE 93706
West Park ES, 2695 S VALENTINE AVE 93706
  Bernie Hanlon, prin.

Chestnut Avenue Baptist Academy
  1461 N CHESTNUT AVE 93703
Fresno Adventist Academy
  5397 E OLIVE AVE 93727
Fresno Christian School
  7280 N CEDAR AVE 93710
Truth Taberncle Christian Academy
  P O BOX 5393 93755
Carden School of Fresno Inc.
  5550 N FRESNO ST 93710
Northwest School System
  5415 N WEST AVE 93711
Our Lady of Victory ES
  1626 W PRINCETON AVE 93705
Sacred Heart ES, 4460 E YALE AVE 93703
St. Anthony ES, 5680 N MAROA AVE 93704
St. Helen ES, 4870 E BELMONT AVE 93727

Friant, Fresno Co.
Clovis USD
Supt. – See Clovis
ES, P O BOX 223 93626 – Marshall Doris, prin.

Fullerton, Orange Co., Pop. Code 9
Fullerton ESD
Sch. Sys. Enr. Code 7
Supt. – Duncan Johnson
  1401 W VALENCIA DRIVE 92633
Ladera Vista JHS, 1700 E WILSHIRE AVE 92631
  Richard Blough, prin.
Nicholas JHS, 1100 W OLIVE AVE 92633
  Mary Dalessi, prin.

Parks JHS, 1710 W ROSECRANS AVE 92633
 LeNelle Cittadin, prin.
Acacia ES, 1200 N ACACIA AVE 92631
 Georgia Menges, prin.
Commonwealth ES
 2200 E COMMONWEALTH AVE 92631
 Barbara Moore, prin.
Fern Drive ES, 1400 W FERN DRIVE 92633
 Kenneth MacKay, prin.
Golden Hill ES, 732 BARRIS DRIVE 92632
 Patricia Puleo, prin.
Hermosa Drive ES, 400 E HERMOSA DRIVE 92635
 Marilyn Korostoff, prin.
Laguna Road ES, 300 W LAGUNA ROAD 92635
 Harold Sullivan, prin.
Orangethorpe ES
 1400 S BROOKHURST ROAD 92633
 Patrick Backus, prin.
Pacific Drive ES, 1501 W VALENCIA DRIVE 92633
 Garrett Rutherford, prin.
Raymond ES, 517 N RAYMOND AVE 92631
 Carolee Michael, prin.
Richman ES, 700 S RICHMAN AVE 92632
 Minard Duncan, prin.
Rolling Hills ES
 1460 E ROLLING HILLS DRIVE 92635
 Mary Turner, prin.
Sunset Lane ES, S030 SUNSET LANE 92633
 Sue Faassen, prin.
Valencia Park ES
 3441 W VALENCIA DRIVE 92633
 Larry Beaver, prin.
Woodcrest ES, 455 W BAKER AVE 92632
 Judith Gibbs, prin.

Placentia USD
 Supt. – See Placentia
Topaz ES, 3232 E TOPAZ LANE 92631
 Kjell Taylor, prin.

Carden Country Day ES
 1620 N PLACENTIA AVE 92631
Eastside Christian ES, P O BOX 4178 92634
St. Juliana Falconieri ES
 1320 N ACACIA AVE 92631
St. Mary's Catholic ES
 400 W COMMONWEALTH AVE 92632
St. Philip Benizi ES, 215 S PINE DR 92633

Galt, Sacramento Co., Pop. Code 6
 Galt J Un. ESD
 Sch. Sys. Enr. Code 4
 Supt. – R. L. McCaffrey, 21 C ST 95632
 Galt MS, 1011 C ST 95632 – June Gillis, prin.
 Fairsite ES, 902 CAROLINE ST 95632
 Gerald Keen, prin.
 Valley Oaks ES, 21 C ST 95632
 Jeffery Jennings, prin.

Garberville, Humboldt Co., Pop. Code 3
 Southern Humbolt JUSD
 Sch. Sys. Enr. Code 4
 Supt. – Roger C. Adams, P O BOX 129 95440
 Other Schools – See Alderpoint, Blocksburg, Miranda,
 Redway, Weott, Whitethorn

Gardena, Los Angeles Co., Pop. Code 8
 Los Angeles USD
 Supt. – See Los Angeles
 135th Street ES, 801 W 135TH ST 90247
 Joseph Jewell, prin.
 153rd Street ES, 1605 W 153RD ST 90247
 Patricia McKenna, prin.
 156th Street ES, 2100 W 156TH ST 90249
 Marjorie Van Swearingen, prin.
 186th Street ES, 1581 W 186TH ST 90248
 Marilyn Steuben, prin.
 Amestoy ES, 1048 W 149TH ST 90247
 Dorothy Gaither, prin.
 Chapman ES, 1947 W COMPTON BLVD 90249
 James Clark, prin.
 Denker Avenue ES, 1620 W 162ND ST 90247
 Narvia Shannon, prin.
 ES, 647 W GARDENA BLVD 90247
 Mercedes Le Brun, prin.
 Purche Avenue ES, 13210 PURCHE AVE 90249
 Jessie Kendrick, prin.

Calvary Baptist ES
 2818 MANHATTAN BEACH BLVD 90249
Gardena Valley Christian ES
 1473 W 182ND ST 90248
Regina ES, 13510 VAN NESS AVE 90249
St. Anthony of Padua ES, 1003 W 163RD ST 90247

Garden Grove, Orange Co., Pop. Code 9
 Garden Grove USD
 Sch. Sys. Enr. Code 8
 Supt. – Ed Dundon
 10331 STANFORD AVE 92640
 Alamitos IS, 12381 DALE ST 92641
 Lou Drexel, prin.
 Bell IS, 12345 SPRINGDALE ST 92645
 Gerald Stanley, prin.
 Doig IS, 12752 TRASK AVE 92643
 John Barriga, prin.
 Irvine IS, 10552 HAZARD AVE 92643
 Ron Porter, prin.
 Jordan IS, 9821 WOODBURY AVE 92644
 Bill Langan, prin.
 Ralston IS, 10851 LAMPSON AVE 92640
 Denny Pace, prin.
 Barker ES, 12565 SPRINGDALE ST 92645
 Barbara Gibbons, prin.

Bryant ES, 8371 ORANGEWOOD AVE 92641
 Sharon Wiggins, prin.
Clinton ES, 13641 CLINTON ST 92643
 Barbara Batson, prin.
Cook ES, 9802 WOODBURY AVE 92644
 Lee Kolb, prin.
Crosby ES, 12181 WEST ST 92640
 Joan Watral, prin.
Eisenhower ES, 13221 LILLY ST 92643
 Frances Murphy, prin.
Enders ES, 12302 SPRINGDALE ST 92645
 Fred Clair, prin.
Evans ES, 12281 NELSON ST 92640
 Victoria Weber, prin.
Excelsior ES, 10421 WOODBURY ROAD 92643
 Rosemary Davis, prin.
Faylane ES, 11731 MORRIE LANE 92640
 Frank Branda, prin.
Gilbert ES, 9551 ORANGEWOOD AVE 92641
 Ed Raphael, prin.
Hill ES, 9681 11TH ST 92644
 Judith Roseberry, prin.
Lawrence ES, 12521 MONROE ST 92641
 Larry Hartman, prin.
Mitchell ES, 13451 TAFT ST 92643
 DeWayne Terry, prin.
Monroe ES, 10552 HAZARD AVE 92643
 Don Ewoldt, prin.
Morningside ES
 10521 MORNINGSIDE DRIVE 92643
 Linda Futchik, prin.
Murdy ES, 14841 DONEGAL DRIVE 92644
 Jessie Thacker, prin.
Paine ES, 15792 WARD ST 92643
 Tom Williams, prin.
Parkview ES, 12272 WILKEN WAY 92640
 Margaret Ferguson, prin.
Patton ES, 6861 SANTA RITA AVE 92645
 Carol Patterson, prin.
Post ES, 14641 WARD ST 92643
 Janet Kurtz, prin.
Riverdale ES, 13222 LEWIS ST 92643
 Anker Christensen, prin.
Stanford ES, 12721 MAGNOLIA ST 92641
 Jean Clifford, prin.
Stanley ES, 12201 ELMWOOD ST 92640
 Ray Fry, prin.
Sunnyside ES, 9972 RUSSELL AVE 92644
 Phil Reber, prin.
Violette ES, 12091 LAMPSON AVE 92640
 Bruce Hankins, prin.
Wakeham ES, 7772 CHAPMAN AVE 92641
 Vince Spinosa, prin.
Warren ES, 12871 ESTOCK DRIVE 92640
 Judi Smith, prin.
Woodbury ES, 11362 WOODBURY ROAD 92643
 Al Sims, prin.
Zeyen ES, 12081 MAGNOLIA ST 92641
 Don Marshall, prin.
Other Schools – See Fountain Valley, Santa Ana,
 Stanton, Westminster

Orange USD
 Supt. – See Orange
 Lampson ES, 13321 LAMPSON AVE 92640
 Carolyn Reichert, prin.

Westminster ESD
 Supt. – See Westminster
 Anderson ES, 8902 HEWITT PLACE 92644
 John Sessums, prin.
 Meairs ES, 8441 TRASK AVE 92644
 Sally Gilmore, prin.

Orangewood SDA Academy
 13732 CLINTON ST 92643
Garden Grove Christian ES
 13201 CENTURY BLVD 92643
King of Kings Lutheran ES
 13431 NEWHOPE ST 92643
St. Callistus ES, 12901 LEWIS ST 92640
St. Columban ES, 10855 STANFORD AVE 92640
St. Paul's Lutheran ES, 13072 BOWEN ST 92643

Garden Vall, El Dorado Co.
 Black Oak Mine USD
 Supt. – See Georgetown
 Creekside ES, P O BOX 63302 95633
 (–), prin.

Gasquet, Del Norte Co.
 Del Norte County USD
 Supt. – See Crescent City
 Mountain ES 95543 – Dennis Louy, prin.

Gazelle, Siskiyou Co.
 Gazelle Un. ESD
 Sch. Sys. Enr. Code 1
 Supt. – (–), P O BOX 6 96034
 ES, P O BOX 6 96034 – Abner Weed,Jr., prin.

George A F B, San Bernardino Co.
 Adelanto ESD
 Supt. – See Adelanto
 ES, 620 NEVADA AVE 92394
 Victoria Magathan, prin.
 Sheppard ES, 930 MCCOY CIRCLE 92394
 Billy Forde, prin.

Georgetown, El Dorado Co.
 Black Oak Mine USD
 Sch. Sys. Enr. Code 4
 Supt. – Charles Pryor, P O BOX 349001 95634
 ES, P O BOX 349002 95634 – Ralph Friend, prin.
 Other Schools – See Cool, Garden Vall

Gerber, Tehama Co., Pop. Code 3
 Gerber Un. ESD
 Sch. Sys. Enr. Code 2
 Supt. – Joseph Harrop, 23014 CHARD AVE 96035
 ES, 23014 CHARD AVE 96035 – (–), prin.

Geyserville, Sonoma Co., Pop. Code 3
 Geyserville USD
 Sch. Sys. Enr. Code 2
 Supt. – Emanuel Scrafani, P O BOX 108 95441
 MS, 1300 MOODY LANE 95441
 Carolyn Kieser, prin.
 ES, 21699 GEYSERVILLE AVE 95441
 Gail Guidici, prin.

Gilroy, Santa Clara Co., Pop. Code 7
 Gilroy USD
 Sch. Sys. Enr. Code 6
 Supt. – Kenneth Noonan, 7663 CHURCH ST 95020
 South Valley JHS, 385 I O O F AVE 95020
 Roger Cornia, prin.
 Brownell Fundamental ES
 7800 CARMEL ST 95020 – Rich Imler, prin.
 El Roble ES, 930 3RD ST 95020
 Saundra Bruemmer, prin.
 Eliot ES, 470 SEVENTH ST 95020
 Chris Waller, prin.
 Glen View ES, 600 W 8TH ST 95020
 George Heiss, prin.
 Jordan ES, 7743 HANNA ST 95020
 Linda Piceno, prin.
 Kelley ES, 8755 KERN AVE 95020
 Gene Sakahara, prin.
 Las Animas ES, 8450 WREN AVE 95020
 M. Lopez, prin.
 Rucker ES, 325 SANTA CLARA AVE 95020
 Dom Galu, prin.
 San Ysidro ES, 2220 PACHECO PASS HWY 95020
 Esther Carlson, prin.

St. Mary's ES, 7900 CHURCH ST 95020

Glendale, Los Angeles Co., Pop. Code 9
 Glendale USD
 Sch. Sys. Enr. Code 7
 Supt. – Rob Sanchis, 223 N JACKSON ST 91206
 Balboa ES, 1844 BEL AIRE DR 91201
 Diane Hawley, prin.
 Cerritos ES, 120 E CERRITOS AVE 91205
 Jeannie Flint, prin.
 Columbus ES, 425 MILFORD ST 91203
 Terry Dutton, prin.
 Edison ES, 440 W LOMITA AVE 91204
 Mary Arevalo, prin.
 Franklin ES, 1610 LAKE ST 91201 – (–), prin.
 Fremont ES, 3320 LAS PALMAS AVE 91208
 Eleanor Schaubel, prin.
 Glenoaks ES, 2015 E GLENOAKS BLVD 91206
 Richard Martin, prin.
 Jefferson ES, 1540 FIFTH ST 91201
 Paul Estep, prin.
 Keppel ES, 730 GLENWOOD ROAD 91202
 Gordon Morse, prin.
 Mann ES, 501 E ACACIA AVE 91205
 Wayne Sparks, prin.
 Marshall ES, 1201 E BROADWAY ST 91205
 Nancy Jude, prin.
 Muir ES, 912 S CHEVY CHASE DRIVE 91205
 Kenneth Henisey, prin.
 Verdugo Woodlands ES
 1751 N VERDUGO ROAD 91208
 Lemore Lacey, prin.
 White ES, 744 E DORAN ST 91206
 Glenn Franklin, prin.
 Other Schools – See La Crescenta

Glendale Adventist Academy
 700 KIMLIN DRIVE 91206
Calvary Christian ES
 610 N GLENDALE AVE 91206
Chamlian Armenian ES
 4444 LOWELL AVE 91214
Crescenta Valley SDA ES
 6245 HONOLULU AVE 91214
First Lutheran ES, 1300 E COLORADO ST 91205
Holy Family ES, 400 S LOUISE ST 91205
Incarnation ES, 123 W GLENOAKS BLVD 91202
Lutheran School of the Foothills Mt. Oli
 3561 FOOTHILL BLVD 91214
Mekhitarist Armenian ES
 4900 MARYLAND AVE 91214
Salem Lutheran ES, 1211 N BRAND BLVD 91202
St. James the Less ES
 4625 DUNSMORE AVE 91214
Zion Lutheran ES, 301 N ISABEL ST 91206

Glendora, Los Angeles Co., Pop. Code 8
 Charter Oak USD
 Supt. – See Covina
 Willow ES, 1427 WILLOW AVE 91740
 Richard Bishop, prin.

Glendora ESD
 Sch. Sys. Enr. Code 6
 Supt. – Patrick Bushman
 500 N LORAINE AVE 91740
 Goddard MS, 859 E SIERRA MADRE AVE 91740
 Ted McNevin, prin.
 Sandburg MS, 819 W BENNETT AVE 91740
 Bennett Conner, prin.
 Cullen ES, 440 N LIVE OAK AVE 91740
 Shirleen Smith, prin.
 La Fetra ES, 547 W BENNETT AVE 91740
 Beverly Hoy, prin.

Sellers ES, 500 N LORAINE AVE   91740
  Lois Green, prin.
Stanton ES, 725 S VECINO DRIVE   91740
  Paul Miller, prin.
Sutherland ES, 1330 N AMELIA AVE   91740
  Andrew Mulhall, prin.
Williams ES, 301 S LORAINE AVE   91740
  Georgia Maurizio, prin.

Foothill Christian ES, 901 S GRAND AVE   91740
Hope Lutheran ES
  1041 E FOOTHILL BLVD   91740
St. Dorothy's ES, 215 S VALLEY CTR   91740

Glen Ellen, Sonoma Co., Pop. Code 4
Sonoma Valley USD
Supt. – See Sonoma
Dunbar ES, 11700 DUNBAR ROAD   95442
  Ken Limon, prin.

Glennville, Kern Co.
Linns Valley-Poso Flat SD
Sch. Sys. Enr. Code 1
Supt. – (—), P O BOX 547   93226
Linns Valley-Poso Flat Union ES
  P O BOX 547   93226 – John Barnes, prin.

Goleta, Santa Barbara Co., Pop. Code 6
Goleta Un. ESD
Sch. Sys. Enr. Code 5
Supt. – Rich Shelton
  401 N FAIRVIEW AVE   93117
El Rancho ES, 7421 MIRANO DRIVE   93117
  Carol Johansen, prin.
Ellwood ES, 7686 HOLLISTER AVE   93117
  Robert Pearce, prin.
Isla Vista ES, 6875 EL COLEGIO ROAD   93117
  Ed Armstrong, prin.
Kellogg ES, 475 CAMBRIDGE DR   93117
  Ronald Wilmot, prin.
La Patera ES, 555 LA PATERA LANE   93117
  Bryan McCabe, prin.
Other Schools – See Santa Barbara

Santa Barbara SD
Supt. – See Santa Barbara
Goleta Valley JHS
  6100 STOW CANYON ROAD   93117
  Linton Roberts, prin.

Vista Del Mar Un. ESD
Sch. Sys. Enr. Code 1
Supt. – Marianne Caston
  RURAL ROUTE 01   BOX 268   93117
Vista Del Mar ES
  RURAL ROUTE 01   BOX 268   93117
  Marianne Caston, prin.

Gonzales, Monterey Co., Pop. Code 5
Gonzales Un. ESD
Sch. Sys. Enr. Code 4
Supt. – Gordon Piffero, 401 4TH ST   93926
Fairview MS, 401 4TH ST   93926
  Francisco Santana, prin.
La Gloria ES, SECOND AND ELKO   BOX G   93926
  Bill Amen, prin.

Gorman, Los Angeles Co.
Gorman ESD
Sch. Sys. Enr. Code 1
Supt. – Wesley Thomas, HCR 02   BOX 104   93243
Gorman ES, HCR ROUTE 02   BOX 104   93243
  Wesley Thomas, prin.

Goshen, Tulare Co., Pop. Code 4
Visalia USD
Supt. – See Visalia
ES, P O BOX 133   93227 – Frank Netto, prin.

Granada Hills, Los Angeles Co.
Los Angeles USD
Supt. – See Los Angeles
Danube Avenue ES, 11220 DANUBE AVE   91344
  Jacqueline Harris, prin.
El Oro Way ES, 12230 EL ORO WAY   91344
  Linda Pacheco, prin.
Granada ES, 17170 TRIBUNE ST   91344
  Ronald Felt, prin.
Haskell ES, 15850 TULSA ST   91344
  Marilyn Erickson, prin.
Knollwood ES, 11822 GERALD AVE   91344
  Charles Strole,Jr., prin.
Tulsa Street ES
  10900 HAYVENHURST AVE   91344
  Martha Figueroa, prin.
Van Gogh Street ES, 17160 VAN GOGH ST   91344
  Clay Brown, prin.

De La Salle ES, 16535 CHATSWORTH ST   91344
Granada Hills Baptist ES
  10949 ZELZAH AVE   91344
Hillcrest Christian ES, 17351 RINALDI ST   91344
Our Savior First Lutheran School
  16603 SAN FERNANDO MSN   91344
St. Euphrasia ES, 17637 MAYERLING ST   91344

Grand Terrace, San Bernardino Co., Pop. Code 6
Colton JUSD
Supt. – See Colton
ES, 12066 VIVIENDA AVE   92324
  Marcia Johnson, prin.
Terrace View ES
  22731 GRAND TERRACE ROAD   92324
  Maryetta Ferre, prin.

Grass Valley, Nevada Co., Pop. Code 6
Clear Creek ESD
Sch. Sys. Enr. Code 2
Supt. – Ken Gammelgard
  17700 MCCOURTNEY ROAD   95949
Clear Creek ES
  17700 MCCOURTNEY ROAD   95949
  Kenneth Gammelgard, prin.

Grass Valley ESD
Sch. Sys. Enr. Code 4
Supt. – Robert Hufford, 225 S AUBURN ST   95945
Gilmore IS, 10837 STATE HIGHWAY 20   95945
  Linda Breninger, prin.
Bell Hill ES, 324 S SCHOOL ST   95945
  Carol Judd, prin.
Scotten MS
  10821 SQUIRREL CREEK ROAD   95945
  Jon Cohee, prin.
Hennessy ES, 225 S AUBURN ST   95945
  Marilyn Morais, prin.

Pleasant Ridge Un. ESD
Sch. Sys. Enr. Code 4
Supt. – James Meshwert
  22580 KINGSTON LANE   95949
Magnolia IS, 22431 KINGSTON LANE   95949
  David Rosenquist, prin.
Alta Sierra ES, 185 ANNIE DR   95949
  Linda Gallagher, prin.
Cottage Hill ES, 22600 KINGSTON LANE   95949
  Gail Maloney, prin.
Pleasant Ridge Union MS
  16229 DUGGAN ROAD   95949
  Fran Madison, prin.

Union Hill ESD
Sch. Sys. Enr. Code 2
Supt. – Marvin Odom
  11638 COLFAX HIGHWAY   95945
Union Hill ES, 11638 COLFAX HIGHWAY   95945
  Marvin Odom, prin.

Mt. St. Mary's ES
  CHURCH AND CHAPEL STS   95945

Greenfield, Monterey Co., Pop. Code 5
Greenfield Un. ESD
Sch. Sys. Enr. Code 4
Supt. – Dan Owens, P O BOX 97   93927
MS, P O BOX 97   93927 – Paul Griffin, prin.
Oak Avenue ES, P O BOX 97   93927
  Joe Clark, prin.

Greenville, Plumas Co., Pop. Code 4
Plumas USD
Supt. – See Quincy
ES, P O BOX 689   95947 – Kest Porter, prin.

Grenada, Siskiyou Co.
Grenada ESD
Sch. Sys. Enr. Code 2
Supt. – Edward Butler, P O BOX 10   96038
ES, P O BOX 10   96038 – Edward Butler, prin.

Gridley, Butte Co., Pop. Code 5
Gridley Un. ESD
Sch. Sys. Enr. Code 4
Supt. – J. Underhill, 429 MAGNOLIA ST   95948
Sycamore MS, 1125 SYCAMORE ST   95948
  Dennis Wilson, prin.
McKinley ES, 1045 SYCAMORE ST   95948
  Jacob Van Ruiten, prin.
Wilson MS, 409 MAGNOLIA ST   95948
  James King, prin.

Manzanita ESD
Sch. Sys. Enr. Code 2
Supt. – Nancy Barnes
  627 E EVANS REIMER ROAD   95948
Manzanita ES, 627 EVANS-REIMER ROAD   95948
  Nancy Barnes, prin.

Grimes, Colusa Co.
Pierce JUSD
Supt. – See Arbuckle
Grand Island ES, LEVEN ST   95950
  Patricia Hamilton, prin.

Groveland, Mariposa Co.
Big Oak Flat-Groveland UESD
Sch. Sys. Enr. Code 2
Supt. – Duncan Hobbs, P O BOX 377   95321
Tenaya ES, P O BOX 377   95321
  Duncan Hobbs, prin.

Grover City, San Luis Obispo Co., Pop. Code 6
Lucia Mar USD
Supt. – See Arroyo Grande
ES, 365 S 10TH ST   93433 – Harvey White, prin.
Grover Heights ES
  770 N 8TH ST & RITCHIE ROAD   93433
  Richard Simpson, prin.

Guadalupe, Santa Barbara Co., Pop. Code 5
Guadalupe Un. ESD
Sch. Sys. Enr. Code 3
Supt. – Hugo Lara, P O BOX 788   93434
McKenzie JHS, P O BOX 788   93434
  Hugo Lara, prin.
Buren ES, P O BOX 788   93434
  Jose Nichols, prin.

Guerneville, Sonoma Co., Pop. Code 3
Guerneville ESD
Sch. Sys. Enr. Code 3
Supt. – Sam Pullaro
  14630 ARMSTRONG WOODS ROAD   95446

ES, 14630 ARMSTRONG WOODS RD   95446
  David Wax, prin.

Gustine, Merced Co., Pop. Code 5
Gustine USD
Sch. Sys. Enr. Code 4
Supt. – John Simas, 286 5TH ST   95322
ES, 701 WALLIS AVE   95322 – Richard Lentz, prin.

Our Lady of Miracles ES, 370 LINDEN AVE   95322

Hacienda Heights, Los Angeles Co., Pop. Code 8
Hacienda La Puente USD
Supt. – See La Puente
Cedarlane JHS, 16333 CEDARLANE DRIVE   91745
  Ted Hornstra, prin.
Newton IS, 15616 NEWTON ST   91745
  Gabe Parodi, prin.
Orange Grove IS
  14505 ORANGE GROVE AVE   91745
  Robert Dickey, prin.
Bixby ES, 16446 WEDGEWORTH DRIVE   91745
  Joanne Nahmias, prin.
Glenelder ES, 16234 FOLGERT ST   91745
  Gene Eddings, prin.
Grazide ES, 2850 LEOPOLD AVE   91745
  Jack Nahmias, prin.
Kwis ES, 1925 KWIS AVE   91745
  Harold Brunsdon, prin.
Los Altos ES, 15565 LOS ALTOS DRIVE   91745
  Roy Gosen, prin.
Los Molinos ES, 3112 LAS MARIAS DRIVE   91745
  Penny Fraumeni, prin.
Los Robles ES, 1530 RIDLEY AVE   91745
  Alice Hatch, prin.
Mesa Robles ES
  16060 MESA ROBLES DRIVE   91745
  Albert Campbell, prin.
Palm ES, 14740 PALM AVE   91745
  William McKinney, prin.
Shadybend ES, 15430 SHADYBEND DR   91745
  Amy Baumann, prin.
Wedgeworth ES, 16949 WEDGEWORTH DR   91745
  Robert Saxton, prin.

Hacienda Christian ES, 15518 GALE AVE   91745
St. Mark's Lutheran ES
  2323 LAS LOMITAS DR   91745

Half Moon Bay, San Mateo Co., Pop. Code 6
Cabrillo USD
Sch. Sys. Enr. Code 5
Supt. – Richard Tubbs, 498 KELLY AVE   94019
Cunha IS, KELLY & CHURCH STS   94019
  Mary Ellen Powell, prin.
Hatch ES, MIRAMONTES ST   94019
  James Lianides, prin.
Kings Mountain ES, 498 KELLY AVE   94019
  Lorraine Scott, prin.
Other Schools – See El Granada, Montara

Hamilton A F B, Marin Co.
Novato USD
Supt. – See Novato
Hamilton ES, 601 BOILING DRIVE   94934
  Rick Lorraine, prin.

Hamilton City, Glenn Co., Pop. Code 3
Hamilton Un. ESD
Sch. Sys. Enr. Code 2
Supt. – Phyllis Manning, P O BOX 227   95951
Hamilton ES, P O BOX 277   95951
  Phyllis Manning, prin.

Hanford, Kings Co., Pop. Code 7
Delta View JUn. ESD
Sch. Sys. Enr. Code 1
Supt. – (—), 1201 LACEY BLVD   93230
Delta View ES, 1201 LACEY BLVD   93230
  Genavra Williamson, prin.

Hanford ESD
Sch. Sys. Enr. Code 5
Supt. – Joe Simas, P O BOX G-1067   93232
Wilson Elem. S, 11TH AVE & FLORINDA   93230
  Kay VanAndel, prin.
Jefferson MS, 511 W MALONE ST   93230
  Douglas Bartsch, prin.
Lincoln ES, 807 S IRWIN ST   93230
  Mike Mendoza, prin.
Monroe ES, MONROE DRIVE   93230
  Dean Osterling, prin.
Richmond ES
  BEULAH AND CAMERON STS   93230
  Robert Uldall, prin.
Roosevelt ES, DAVIS AND GRANT STS   93230
  Rebecca Presley, prin.

Kings River-Hardwick UESD
Sch. Sys. Enr. Code 2
Supt. – Walt Hanline
  10300 EXCELSIOR AVE   93230
Kings River-Hardwick ES
  10300 EXCELSIOR AVE   93230
  Walt Hanline, prin.

Kit Carson Un. SD
Sch. Sys. Enr. Code 2
Supt. – Joseph Wilimek, 9895 7TH AVE   93230
Kit Carson Union ES, 9895 7TH AVE   93230
  Joseph Wilimek, prin.

Lakeside Un. ESD
Sch. Sys. Enr. Code 2
Supt. – Ron Madruga, 9100 JERSEY AVE   93230
Lakeside MS, 9100 JERSEY AVE   93230
  Dale Drew, prin.

Gardenside ES, 9615 TEMPLE DR   93230
  Dale Drew, prin.

Pioneer Un. ESD
  Sch. Sys. Enr. Code 2
  Supt. – Hugh Lee, 8810 14TH AVE   93230
  Pioneer ES, 8810 14TH AVE   93230
    Hugh Lee, prin.

Central Valley Christian ES
    11948 FLINT AVE   93230
McCarthy Memorial ES, 1000 N HARRIS ST   93230
Western Christian ES
    1594 W GRANGEVILLE BLVD   93230

Happy Camp, Siskiyou Co., Pop. Code 3
  Happy Camp Un. ESD
  Sch. Sys. Enr. Code 2
  Supt. – Gayle Jackson, 64236 SECOND AVE   96039
  ES, P O BOX 467   96039 – (—), prin.

Harbor City, Los Angeles Co.
  Los Angeles USD
  Supt. – See Los Angeles
  ES, 1508 254TH ST   90710 – Charles Norton, prin.
  Normont ES, 1001 253RD ST   90710
    Ralph Martucci, prin.
  President Avenue ES, 1465 243RD ST   90710
    Mary Pasic, prin.

Harbor City Christian School
    840 W 255TH ST   90710
Southland Christian ES
    1050 STONEBRYN DR   90710
Western Avenue Baptist ES
    25226 WESTERN AVE   90710

Hawaiian Gardens, Los Angeles Co., Pop. Code 7
  ABC USD
  Supt. – See Cerritos
  Killingsworth JHS, 21409 ELAINE AVE   90716
    Pat Mascorro, prin.
  Furgeson ES, 22215 ELAINE AVE   90716
    George Dominguez, prin.
  Hawaiian ES, 12350 226TH ST   90716
    Harvey Hoyo, prin.

Hawthorne, Los Angeles Co., Pop. Code 8
  Hawthorne ESD
  Sch. Sys. Enr. Code 6
  Supt. – Roger Bly, 4301 W 129TH ST   90250
  Hawthorne IS, 4366 W 129TH ST   90250
    Cheryl Lampe, prin.
  Yukon IS, 13838 YUKON AVE   90250
    Steven Tabor, prin.
  Eucalyptus ES, 12044 EUCALYPTUS AVE   90250
    Roberta Bowman, prin.
  Jefferson ES, 4091 W 139TH ST   90250
    Royal Lord, Jr., prin.
  Ramona ES, 4617 W 136TH ST   90250
    Kenneth Jacobson, prin.
  Washington ES, 4339 W 129TH ST   90250
    Donald Carrington, prin.
  Williams MS, 13434 YUKON AVE   90250
    Robert Cardwell, prin.
  York ES, 11838 YORK AVE   90250
    Terry Moore, prin.
  Zela Davis ES, 13435 YUKON AVE   90250
    Pamela Fees, prin.

  Wiseburn ESD
  Sch. Sys. Enr. Code 4
  Supt. – Arthur Margolese
    13530 AVIATION BLVD   90250
  Dana MS, 13500 AVIATION BLVD   90250
    Carol Greenhalgh, prin.
  Anza ES, 5234 W 120TH ST   90250
    Kay Plush, prin.
  Cabrillo ES, 5309 W 125TH ST   90250
    Kay Plush, prin.

Acacia Baptist Day ES
    4712 W EL SEGUNDO BLVD   90250
Assembly of God Hawthorne ES
    3841 W 130TH ST   90250
Hawthorne Christian ES
    13600 PRAIRIE AVE   90250
St. Joseph ES, 4311 W 119TH ST   90250
Trinity Lutheran ES, 4783 W 130TH ST   90250

Hayfork, Trinity Co., Pop. Code 3
  Mountain Valley USD
  Sch. Sys. Enr. Code 3
  Supt. – Marvin Stewart, P O BOX 339   96041
  Hayfork ES, P O BOX C   96041
    Kenneth Harbord, prin.
  Other Schools – See Hyampom

Hayward, Alameda Co., Pop. Code 8
  Hayward USD
  Sch. Sys. Enr. Code 7
  Supt. – Joel Thornley, P O BOX 5000   94540
  Harte IS, 1047 E ST   94541 – Fran Krug, prin.
  King IS, 26890 HOLLY HILL AVE   94545
    Sue Parker, prin.
  La Vista IS, 27845 WHITMAN ST   94544
    Nellie Gardere, prin.
  Winton IS, 119 WINTON AVE   94544
    Gillian Cole, prin.
  Bowman ES, 520 JEFFERSON ST   94544
    James Rowley, prin.
  Burbank MS, 353 B ST   94541 – Gloria Tejeda, prin.
  Cherryland ES, 585 WILLOW AVE   94541
    Joanne Robinson, prin.
  East Avenue ES, 2424 EAST AVE   94541
    Flo Lofgren, prin.

Eden ES, 27790 PORTSMOUTH AVE   94545
    Patricia Holder, prin.
Eden Gardens ES, 2184 THAYER AVE   94545
    Kathleen Goldman, prin.
Eldridge ES, 26825 ELDRIDGE AVE   94544
    John Matthews, prin.
Fairview ES, 23515 MAUD ST   94541
    Elizabeth Eades, prin.
Glassbrook ES, 975 SCHAFER ROAD   94544
    Marc Guerrero, prin.
Harder ES, 495 WYETH ROAD   94544
    Linda Fulvio, prin.
Highland ES, 2021 HIGHLAND BLVD   94542
    Cheryl Milner, prin.
Longwood ES, 850 LONGWOOD AVE   94541
    Sharon Ough, prin.
Markham ES, 1570 WARD ST   94541
    Jon Hassell, prin.
Muir ES, 24823 DOTO ROAD   94544
    Jeanne Armas, prin.
Palma Ceia ES, 27679 MELBOURNE AVE   94545
    Carol Pike, prin.
Park ES, 411 LARCHMONT ST   94544
    Lynn Kau, prin.
Ruus ES, 28027 DICKENS AVE   94544
    Robert Costa, prin.
Schafer Park ES, 26268 FLAMINGO AVE   94544
    Gene Dennett, prin.
Shepherd ES, 27211 TYRRELL AVE   94544
    Celestine Villa, prin.
Southgate ES, 26601 CALORAGA AVE   94545
    Nancy Sheridan, prin.
Treeview ES, 30565 TREEVIEW ST   94544
    Meedie Monegan, prin.
Tyrrell MS, 27000 TYRRELL AVE   94544
    Don Dickson, prin.
Other Schools – See Castro Valley

New Haven USD
  Supt. – See Union City
  Hillview Crest ES, 31410 WHEELON AVE   94544
    Julia Strong, prin.

San Lorenzo USD
  Supt. – See San Lorenzo
  Colonial Acres ES, 17115 MEEKLAND AVE   94541
    Ernest Jaramillo, prin.
  Lorenzo Manor ES, 18250 BENGAL AVE   94541
    Victoria Srago, prin.

American Heritage Christian School
    425 GRESEL ST   94544
All Saints ES, 22870 2ND ST   94541
Good Shepherd Lutheran ES
    166 W HARDER RD   94544
Hayward Christian ES, 354 B ST   94541
St. Bedes ES, 26900 PATRICK AVE   94544
St. Clement ES, 790 CALHOUN ST   94544
St. Joachims ES, 21250 HESPERIAN BLVD   94541

Healdsburg, Sonoma Co., Pop. Code 6
  Alexander Valley Un. ESD
  Sch. Sys. Enr. Code 2
  Supt. – Michael McEvoy
    8511 HIGHWAY 128   95448
  Alexander Valley ES, 8511 HIGHWAY 128   95448
    Michael McEvoy, prin.

  Healdsburg SD
  Sch. Sys. Enr. Code 4
  Supt. – Lawrence Machi
    925 UNIVERSITY ST   95448
  JHS, 315 GRANT ST   95448 – Stewart Fox, prin.
  Fitch Mountain ES, 565 SANNS LANE   95448
    Nancy Baker, prin.
  MS, 400 1ST ST   95448 – Stephen Rosenthal, prin.

  West Side Un. ESD
  Sch. Sys. Enr. Code 2
  Supt. – Daniel Levine, 1201 FELTA ROAD   95448
  West Side ES, 1201 FELTA ROAD   95448
    Daniel Levine, prin.

St. John's ES, 212 TUCKER ST   95448

Heber, Imperial Co., Pop. Code 3
  Heber ESD
  Sch. Sys. Enr. Code 2
  Supt. – Jesse Silva, P O BOX B   92249
  JHS, P O BOX B   92249 – Jesse Silva, prin.
  ES, P O BOX B   92249 – Jesse Silva, prin.

Helendale, San Bernardino Co.
  Helendale SD
  Sch. Sys. Enr. Code 2
  Supt. – David LaQuay
    15350 RIVERVIEW ROAD   92342
  Riverview MS, P O BOX 249   92342
    James Brown, prin.
  ES, HCR BOX 83   92342 – James Brown, prin.

Helm, Fresno Co.
  Helm ESD
  Sch. Sys. Enr. Code 1
  Supt. – Gary Groth, P O BOX 38   93627
  ES, LARSEN AVE   93627 – Richard Robinson, prin.

Hemet, Riverside Co., Pop. Code 7
  Hemet USD
  Sch. Sys. Enr. Code 7
  Supt. – Jack McLaughlin
    2350 W LATHAM AVE   92343
  Acacia MS, 1200 E ACACIA AVE   92343
    Karen Doshier, prin.
  Cottonwood ES, 44260 SAGE ROAD   92343
    Alejandro Ochoa, prin.

ES, 633 E KIMBALL AVE   92343
    Kennedy Rocker, prin.
Little Lake ES, 26091 MERIDIAN ST   92344
    Joseph Picchiottino, prin.
Ramona ES, 41051 WHITTIER AVE   92344
    Myrna Rohr, prin.
Valle Vista ES, 26400 DARTMOUTH ST   92344
    Richard Jeffrey, prin.
Whittier ES, 400 W WHITTIER AVE   92343
    Clark Merrill, prin.
Other Schools – See Anza, Idyllwild, Winchester

Baptist Christian School, 26089 GIRARD ST   92344
St. John Lutheran School
    26410 COLUMBIA   92344

Herald, Sacramento Co.
  Arcohe ESD
  Sch. Sys. Enr. Code 2
  Supt. – Donald Morris, P O BOX 93   95638
  Arcohe ES, P O BOX 93   95638
    Conrad Mizuno, prin.

Hercules, Conta Costa Co., Pop. Code 6
  Richmond USD
  Supt. – See Richmond
  ES, 1919 LUPINE ROAD   94547
    Charles Forcier, prin.
  Ohlone ES, 1616 PHEASANT DRIVE   94547
    Larry Collison, prin.

Herlong, Lassen Co., Pop. Code 3
  Fort Sage USD
  Sch. Sys. Enr. Code 3
  Supt. – Leonard Shipley, P O BOX 35   96113
  Fort Sage MS, P O BOX 97   96113
    Griff Nelson, prin.
  Sierra ES, P O BOX 35   96113 – Griff Nelson, prin.
  Other Schools – See Doyle

Hermosa Beach, Los Angeles Co., Pop. Code 7
  Hermosa Beach City ESD
  Sch. Sys. Enr. Code 3
  Supt. – Shalee Cunningham, P O BOX 338   90254
  Hermosa Valley ES, 1800 PROSPECT AVE   90254
    Shalee Cunningham, prin.

International Bilingual School
    425 VALLEY DR   90254
Our Lady of Guadalupe ES
    340 MASSEY ST   90254

Hesperia, San Bernardino Co., Pop. Code 6
  Hesperia USD
  Sch. Sys. Enr. Code 7
  Supt. – David Haney, 9144 3RD ST   92345
  JHS, 10275 CYPRESS AVE   92345
    Brenda McGinnis, prin.
  Cottonwood ES, 8850 COTTONWOOD AVE   92345
    Cherry Dobbs, prin.
  Eucalyptus ES, 9144 3RD AVE   92345
    Scott Meier, prin.
  Josua Circle ES, 10140 8TH AVE   92345
    Keith McCaffrey, prin.
  Juniper ES, 9400 1ST AVE   92345
    Larry Anderson, prin.
  Kingston ES, 7473 KINGSTON AVE   92345
    Ann Bernal, prin.
  Lime Street ES, 16852 LIME ST   92345
    Len Knapp, prin.
  Maple ES, 10616 MAPLE AVE   92345
    Gary Thomas, prin.
  Mesa Grande ES, 9172 3RD AVE   92345
    Robert Fore, prin.

Faith Christian School, P O BOX 1205   92345
Hesperia Christian School, 16775 OLIVE ST   92345
New Life Christian ES, P O BOX 2809   92345

Hickman, Stanislaus Co.
  Hickman ESD
  Sch. Sys. Enr. Code 2
  Supt. – Richard Ferriera, P O BOX 37   95323
  ES, 13306 I ST   95323 – Richard Ferriera, prin.

Highland, San Bernardino Co., Pop. Code 7
  San Bernardino City USD
  Supt. – See San Bernardino
  Belvedere ES, 2501 MARSHALL BLVD   92346
    Mildredan Ward, prin.
  Cole Avenue ES, 1331 COLE AVE   92346
    Ginger Hodge, prin.
  Cypress ES, 26825 CYPRESS ST   92346
    Hannah Ward, prin.
  Highland-Pacific ES, 3340 E PACIFIC AVE   92346
    Bonnie Everett, prin.
  Lankershim ES, 7499 LANKERSHIM AVE   92346
    Arlan Anderson, prin.
  Oehl ES, 2525 PALM AVE   92346
    Harold Volkommer, prin.
  Thompson ES, 7401 CHURCH AVE   92346
    Barb Pregmon, prin.

Fairview Junior Academy, 26200 DATE ST   92346
St. Adelaide ES, 27487 BASELINE ST   92346

Hillsborough, San Mateo Co., Pop. Code 7
  Hillsborough CSD
  Sch. Sys. Enr. Code 4
  Supt. – Quentin Taylor
    300 EL CERRITO AVE   94010
  Crocker MS, 2600 RALSTON AVE   94010
    Marilyn Loushin-Miller, prin.
  South Hillsborough ES
    303 EL CERRITO AVE   94010
    Ruthann Taylor, prin.

West Hillsborough ES, 376 BARBARA WAY   94010
Julie Ryan, prin.

Hilmar, Merced Co., Pop. Code 3
Hilmar USD
Sch. Sys. Enr. Code 4
Supt. – Victor Norton, 7807 LANDER AVE   95324
Eilim ES, 7677 LANDER AVE   95324
David Fliflet, prin.
Other Schools – See Stevinson

Hinkley, San Bernardino Co., Pop. Code 3
Barstow USD
Supt. – See Barstow
ES, 37600 HINKLEY RD   92347
Wayne Costa, prin.

Hollister, San Benito Co., Pop. Code 7
Cienega Un. ESD
Sch. Sys. Enr. Code 1
Supt. – (—), 11936 CIENAGA ROAD   95023
Cienega ES, 11936 CIENEGA ROAD   95023
Claudia Libby, prin.

Hollister ESD
Sch. Sys. Enr. Code 5
Supt. – Donald Slezak, P O BOX 1067   95024
Rancho San Justo MS
1201 RANCHO DRIVE   95023
Nicholas Ferrero, prin.
Calaveras MS, 1151 BUENA VISTA ROAD   95023
Emilio Uccello, prin.
Cerra Vista PS, 2151 CERRA VISTA DR   95023
Susan Winn, prin.
Fremont ES, 335 WEST ST   95023
Chuck Bradley, prin.
Hardin MS, 881 LINE ST   95023
Robert Hammond, prin.
Sunnyslope ES, 1475 MEMORIAL DRIVE   95023
Mary Guerrero, prin.

North County JUn. ESD
Sch. Sys. Enr. Code 2
Supt. – David Evans
500 SPRING GROVE ROAD   95023
Spring Grove ES
500 SPRING GROVE ROAD   95023
Donald Carter, prin.

Southside ESD
Sch. Sys. Enr. Code 1
Supt. – (—), 4991 SOUTHSIDE ROAD   95023
Southside ES, 4991 SOUTHSIDE ROAD   95023
John Pavlovich, prin.

Sacred Heart ES, 670 COLLEGE ST   95023

Hollywood, Los Angeles Co.

Bethany Lutheran School
1518 N ALEXANDRIA AVE   90027

Holtville, Imperial Co., Pop. Code 5
Holtville USD
Sch. Sys. Enr. Code 4
Supt. – Jack Tevault, 621 E 6TH ST   92250
JHS, 800 BEALE AVE   92250
John Kirchenbauer, prin.
Finley ES, 627 E 6TH ST   92250
Patricia Salcedo, prin.
Pine ES, 3295 HOLT ROAD   92250
Jo Thornburg, prin.

Hoopa, Humboldt Co., Pop. Code 3
Klamath-Trinity JUSD
Sch. Sys. Enr. Code 4
Supt. – Ted Toreson, P O BOX 1308   95546
Hoopa Valley ES, P O BOX 1308   95546
Todd Clark, prin.
Norton ES, WEITCHPEC ROUTE   95546
Joyce Rich, prin.
Weitchpec ES, WEITCHPEC ROUTE   95546
Joyce Rich, prin.
Other Schools – See Orleans, Willow Creek

Hopland, Mendocino Co., Pop. Code 3
Ukiah USD
Supt. – See Ukiah
ES, P O BOX 368   95449 – Naomi Engstrom, prin.

Hornbrook, Siskiyou Co.
Hornbrook ESD
Sch. Sys. Enr. Code 1
Supt. – (—), P O BOX 169   96044
ES, P O BOX 169   96044 – Robert Schaller, prin.

Horse Creek, Siskiyou Co.
Klamath River Un. ESD
Sch. Sys. Enr. Code 1
Supt. – (—), P O BOX 190   96045
Klamath River ES   96045 – Curtis Neitsch, prin.

Hughson, Stanislaus Co., Pop. Code 5
Hughson Un. ESD
Sch. Sys. Enr. Code 3
Supt. – Carrolyn Nicholas, P O BOX 189   95326
Ross MS, P O BOX 189   95326
Carrolyn Nicholas, prin.
ES, 7201 E WHITMORE AVE   95326
Gary Lampella, prin.

Huntington Beach, Orange Co., Pop. Code 9
Fountain Valley ESD
Supt. – See Fountain Valley
Talbert MS, 9101 BRABHAM DRIVE   92646
Judy Blankinship, prin.
Newland ES, 8787 DOLPHIN DRIVE   92646
Myron Morper, prin.

Oka ES, 9800 YORKTOWN AVE   92646
Waldo Price, prin.

Huntington Beach City ESD
Sch. Sys. Enr. Code 6
Supt. – Diana Peters, P O BOX 71   92648
Dwyer MS, P O BOX 71   92648
Alan Rasmussen, prin.
Sowers MS, P O BOX 71   92648 – Ian Collins, prin.
Eader ES, 9291 BANNING AVE   92646
Dareen Yonts, prin.
Hawes ES, 9682 YELLOWSTONE DRIVE   92646
Marie Smith, prin.
Kettler ES, 8750 DORSETT DRIVE   92646
Clyde Glasser, prin.
Moffett ES, 8800 BURLCREST DRIVE   92646
Paul Morrow, prin.
Perry ES, 1931 HARDING LANE   92646
John Magnuson, prin.
Smith ES, 770 17TH ST   92648 – Don Pate, prin.

Ocean View ESD
Sch. Sys. Enr. Code 6
Supt. – Dale Coogan, 16940 B ST   92647
Circle View ES, 6261 HOOKER DRIVE   92647
Dan Moss, prin.
College View ES, 6582 LENNOX DRIVE   92647
Michel Hsiang, prin.
Crest View ES, 18052 LISA LANE   92646
James Enderson, prin.
Golden View ES
17251 GOLDEN VIEW LANE   92647
Mike Merz, prin.
Harbour View ES, 4343 PICKWICK CR   92649
Marilyn Koeller, prin.
Haven View ES, 16081 WAIKIKI LANE   92649
Pam Wheless, prin.
Hope View ES, 17622 FLINTSTONE LANE   92647
Gayle Bowles, prin.
Lake View ES, 17451 ZEIDER LANE   92647
Diane Hobbensiefken, prin.
Marine View ES, 5682 TILBURG DRIVE   92649
Robert Vouga, prin.
Mesa View ES, 17601 AVILLA LANE   92647
Janet Reece, prin.
Oak View ES, 17241 OAK LANE   92647
Joan Buffehr, prin.
Spring View ES, 16662 TRUDY LANE   92647
William Lescher, prin.
Sun View ES, 7721 JULIETTE LOW DRIVE   92647
Barbara O'Connor, prin.
Village View ES, 5361 SISSON DRIVE   92649
Don Devor, prin.
Other Schools – See Fountain Valley, Midway City,
Westminster

Westminster ESD
Supt. – See Westminster
Stacy IS, 6311 LARCHWOOD DRIVE   92647
Genia Pickett, prin.
Clegg ES, 6311 LARCHWOOD DRIVE   92647
Clarence Owen, prin.
Franklin ES, 14422 HAMMON LANE   92647
Gary Lewis, prin.
Schroeder ES, 15151 COLUMBIA LANE   92647
Harlan Kelley, prin.

Liberty Christian School
7661 WARNER AVE   92647
Carden School, 721 E UTICA AVE   92648
Huntington Christian ES, 1207 MAIN ST   92648
St. Bonaventure ES, 16377 BRADBURY LN   92647
Sts. Simon and Jude ES
20400 MAGNOLIA ST   92646

Huntington Park, Los Angeles Co., Pop. Code 8
Los Angeles USD
Supt. – See Los Angeles
Gage JHS, 2880 E GAGE AVE   90255
Soledad Garcia, prin.
Nimitz JHS, 6021 CARMELITA AVE   90255
Guadalupe Simpson, prin.
Middleton Street ES, 6537 MALABAR ST   90255
Takako Suzuki, prin.
Miles Avenue ES, 6720 MILES AVE   90255
Emma Rodriguez, prin.

Huntington Park Baptist ES
2662 CLARENDON AVE   90255
St. Matthias ES, 7130 CEDAR ST   90255

Huron, Fresno Co., Pop. Code 5
Coalinga/Huron JUSD
Supt. – See Coalinga
ES, 12TH AND N STS   93234
Robin Hutchison, prin.

Hyampom, Trinity Co.
Mountain Valley USD
Supt. – See Hayfork
ES, P O BOX 146   96046 – (—), prin.

Hydesville, Humboldt Co., Pop. Code 3
Hydesville ESD
Sch. Sys. Enr. Code 2
Supt. – (—), P O BOX 551   95547
ES, P O BOX 551   95547 – James Hendry, prin.

Idyllwild, Riverside Co., Pop. Code 3
Hemet USD
Supt. – See Hemet
ES, P O BOX 97   92349 – (—), prin.

Igo, Shasta Co.
Igo-Ono-Platina Un. ESD
Sch. Enr. Code 2
Supt. – Marvin Peterson, P O BOX A   96047
Igo-Ono ES, P O BOX A   96047
Marvin Peterson, prin.
Other Schools – See Platina

Imperial, Imperial Co., Pop. Code 5
Imperial USD
Sch. Sys. Enr. Code 4
Supt. – Frank Cranley, 10TH & E STS   92251
Wright IS, 515 W 10TH ST   92251
Joseph Kinder, prin.
Hulse ES, 303 S D ST   92251 – Bobby Haney, prin.
Other Schools – See El Centro

Imperial Beach, San Diego Co., Pop. Code 7
South Bay Un. ESD
Sch. Sys. Enr. Code 6
Supt. – Philip Grignon, 601 ELM AVE   92032
Bayside ES, 490 EMORY ST   92032
Ronald Bechtel, prin.
Central ES, 1290 EBONY AVE   92032
John Hollingsworth, prin.
Harbort View ES, 650 CORONADO AVE   92032
Marilyn Wheeler, prin.
ES, 990 CONNECTICUT ST   92032
Stephen Baity, prin.
Oneonta ES, 1311 10TH ST   92032
Robert Eaton, prin.
West View ES, 525 3RD ST   92032
Lowell Billings, prin.
Other Schools – See San Diego

Independence, Inyo Co., Pop. Code 3
Owens Valley USD
Sch. Sys. Enr. Code 2
Supt. – William Nance, P O BOX E   93526
Owens Valley ES, P O BOX E   93526
(—), prin.

Indio, Riverside Co., Pop. Code 7
Desert Sands USD
Sch. Sys. Enr. Code 7
Supt. – Ken Meberg, 82879 HIGHWAY 111   92201
Jefferson MS, 83089 AVENUE 46   92201
Robert Block, prin.
Wilson MS, 83501 DILLON AVE   92201
Anthony Virga, prin.
Eisenhower ES, 83-391 DILLON AVE   92201
Maureen Mendoza, prin.
Hoover MS, 44-300 MONROE ST   92201
Luis Maestre, prin.
Jackson ES, 82-850 KENNER AVE   92201
Diane Kellar, prin.
Kennedy ES, 45-100 CLINTON ST   92201
Jo Davidian, prin.
Roosevelt MS, 83-200 AVENUE 47   92201
(—), prin.
Van Buren ES, 47-733 VAN BUREN ST   92201
Stan Little, prin.
Other Schools – See La Quinta, Palm Desert

Christian School of the Desert
40-700 YUCCA LN   92201
Our Lady of Perpetual Help ES
82-470 BLISS AVE   92201

Inglewood, Los Angeles Co., Pop. Code 8
Inglewood USD
Sch. Sys. Enr. Code 7
Supt. – George McKenna
401 S INGLEWOOD AVE   90301
Crozier JHS, 151 N GREVILLEA AVE   90301
James Crowe, prin.
Monroe JHS, 10711 S 10TH AVE   90303
Gladys Evans, prin.
Bennett Kew ES, 11710 CHERRY AVE   90303
Nancy Ichinaga, prin.
Centinela ES, 1123 MARLBOROUGH AVE   90302
Vivian Shannon, prin.
Freeman ES, 2602 W 79TH ST   90305
Roberta Carroll, prin.
Highland ES, 430 VENICE WAY   90302
Betty Steward, prin.
Hudnall ES, 331 W OLIVE ST   90301
Nancy Young, prin.
Kelso ES, 809 E KELSO ST   90301
Marjorie Thompson, prin.
La Tijera ES, 1415 LA TIJERA BLVD   90302
Vera Stevens, prin.
Lane ES, 9330 S 8TH AVE   90305
Jacqueline Atkins, prin.
Oak Street ES, 633 S OAK ST   90301
Ruby Nelson, prin.
Parent ES, 5354 W 64TH ST   90302
Marie Stricklin, prin.
Payne ES, 215 W 94TH ST   90301
Wendy Peretz, prin.
Woodworth ES, 3200 W 104TH ST   90303
Lacy Alexander, prin.
Worthington ES, 11101 YUKON AVE   90303
Joann Foster, prin.

Los Angeles USD
Supt. – See Los Angeles
Century Park ES, 10935 SPINNING AVE   90303
Helen Ketch, prin.

Anthony's ES, 8420 CRENSHAW BLVD   90305
Calvary Christian ES, 2400 W 85TH ST   90305
Chapel of Peace Lutheran ES
1009 N MARKET ST   90302

Christian Academy
8420 CRENSHAW BLVD 90305
Faith Lutheran ES, 3320 W 85TH ST 90305
Good Shepherd Lutheran ES
901 MAPLE ST 90301
Inglewood Christian ES
215 E HILLCREST BLVD 90301
Scott Christian ES, 930 S OSAGE AVE 90301
St. John Chrysostom ES
530 E FLORENCE AVE 90301

Inyokern, Kern Co., Pop. Code 3
Sierra Sands USD
Supt. – See Ridgecrest
ES 93527 – Kenneth Holan, prin.

Ione, Amador Co., Pop. Code 4
Amador County USD
Supt. – See Jackson
Ione MS 95640 – Grant Sandro, prin.
ES 95640 – James Vardy, prin.

Irvine, Orange Co., Pop. Code 8
Irvine USD
Sch. Sys. Enr. Code 7
Supt. – David Brown, P O BOX 19535 92713
Lakeside MS, 3 LEMONGRASS 92714
Don Erger, prin.
Rancho San Joaquin IS
4861 MICHELSON DRIVE 92715
Judy Cunningham, prin.
Sierra Vista MS, 2 LIBERTY 92720
Dave Holmes, prin.
Venado MS, 4 DEERFIELD AVE 92714
John Tennant, prin.
Alderwood Basics ES, 2 ALDERWOOD 92714
Lynn Bogart, prin.
Bonita Canyon ES, 1 SUNDANCE DRIVE 92715
Dorothea Maas, prin.
Brywood ES, NO 1 WESTWOOD 92720
Stuart Cunningham, prin.
College Park ES, 3700 CHAPARRAL AVE 92714
Beverley Khalil, prin.
Culverdale ES, 2 THIEL AVE 92714
Tom Perrie, prin.
Deerfield ES, 2 DEERFIELD AVE 92714
Susanne Wiegand, prin.
Eastshore ES, 155 EASTSHORE 92714
Sharon Denisi, prin.
El Camino Real ES
4782 KAREN ANN LANE 92714
Eugene Bedley, prin.
Greentree ES, 4200 MANZANITA 92714
Clay White, prin.
Los Naranjos ES, 1 SMOKETREE 92714
(—), prin.
Meadow Park ES, 50 BLUE LAKE SOUTH 92614
Dennis Gibbs, prin.
Northwood ES, 28 CARSON 92720
Joanne Hodder, prin.
Santiago Hills ES, 29 CHRISTAMON WEST 92720
John Inmon, prin.
Springbrook ES, 31-A W YALE LOOP 92714
Patricia Mulhaupt, prin.
Stone Creek ES, TWO STONE CREEK 92714
Marilyn Boyd, prin.
Turtle Rock ES, 5151 AMALFI DRIVE 92715
Ron Moreland, prin.
University Park ES, 4572 SANDBURG WAY 92715
Craig Ritter, prin.
Vista Verde ES, 5144 MICHELSON ROAD 92715
Bruce Terry, prin.
Westwood Basics ES, ONE LIBERTY 92720
Dan Thomas, prin.
Other Schools – See Santa Ana

Liberty Christian Academy
5108 BONITA CANYON DR 92715

Irwindale, Los Angeles Co., Pop. Code 4
Covina-Valley USD
Supt. – See Covina
Merwin ES, 16125 E CYPRESS ST 91722
Sandra Simon, prin.

Isleton, Sacramento Co., Pop. Code 3
River Delta USD
Supt. – See Rio Vista
ES, P O BOX 528 95641 – Brenda Golubski, prin.

Ivanhoe, Tular Co.
Visalia USD
Supt. – See Visalia
ES, 16030 AVE 332 93235 – James Moore, prin.

Jackson, Amador Co., Pop. Code 4
Amador County USD
Sch. Sys. Enr. Code 5
Supt. – Clifford Tyler, 217 REX AVE 95642
Jackson MS 95642 – Rick Carder, prin.
ES, 220 CHURCH ST 95642 – Gerald Herrick, prin.
Pioneer MS, 217 REX AVE 95642
Mark Mathany, prin.
Plymouth ES, 217 REX AVE 95642
Frank Tortorich, prin.
Sutter Creek ES, 217 REX AVE 95642
Bruce Peccianti, prin.
Other Schools – See Ione, Pine Grove

Jacumba, San Diego Co.
Mountain Empire USD
Supt. – See Pine Valley
ES, 44343 OLD HIGHWAY 80 92034
Roy Radke, prin.

Jamestown, Tuolumne Co., Pop. Code 3
Jamestown ESD
Sch. Sys. Enr. Code 2
Supt. – Dan White, P O BOX 657 95327
ES, P O BOX 657 95327 – Randy Panietz, prin.

Jamul, San Diego Co., Pop. Code 3
Jamul-Dulzura Un. USD
Sch. Sys. Enr. Code 3
Supt. – Thomas Bishop
14581 LYONS VALLEY ROAD 92035
Oak Grove MS
14585 LYONS VALLEY ROAD 92035
Larry Gillham, prin.
ES, 14581 LYONS VALLEY ROAD 92035
Diana Damschen, prin.

Janesville, Lassen Co.
Janesville Un. ESD
Sch. Sys. Enr. Code 2
Supt. – Wallace McCormick, P O BOX 280 96114
ES, P O BOX 280 96114
Wallace McCormick, prin.

Johannesburg, Kern Co.
Sierra Sands USD
Supt. – See Ridgecrest
Rand ES, P O BOX 157 93528
Kenneth Holan, prin.

Joshua Tree, San Bernardino Co., Pop. Code 4
Morongo USD
Supt. – See Twentynine Palms
Friendly Hills ES, 7252 SUNNY VISTA 92252
Betty Barnes, prin.
ES, 6051 SUNBURST ST 92252
Daniel Mosunich, prin.

Julian, San Diego Co., Pop. Code 2
Julian Un. ESD
Sch. Sys. Enr. Code 2
Supt. – C. Kevin Ogden, P O BOX 337 92036
Julian JHS, P O BOX 337 92036 – (—), prin.
ES, P O BOX 337 92036 – C. Ogden, prin.

Junction City, Trinity Co.
Junction City ESD
Sch. Sys. Enr. Code 1
Supt. – (—), P O BOX 40 96048
ES, P O BOX 40 96048 – Donna Moore, prin.

Kelseyville, Lake Co., Pop. Code 3
Kelseyville USD
Sch. Sys. Enr. Code 4
Supt. – Robert Gomez, P O BOX 308 95451
Gard Street MS, P O BOX 308 95451
Howard Chase, prin.
ES, 5065 KONOCTI ROAD 95451
Jan Patten, prin.

Kentfield, Marin Co., Pop. Code 5
Kentfield ESD
Sch. Sys. Enr. Code 3
Supt. – Robert B. Caine
699 SIR FRANCIS DRAKE BLVD 94904
Kent MS, 250 STADIUM WAY 94904
Nancy Schlobohm, prin.
Bacich ES, 25 MCALLISTER AVE 94904
Katherine Tusler, prin.

Kenwood, Sonoma Co., Pop. Code 3
Kenwood ESD
Sch. Sys. Enr. Code 2
Supt. – Rob Harper, P O BOX 220 95452
ES, P O BOX 220 95452 – Robert Harper, prin.

Kerman, Fresno Co., Pop. Code 5
Kerman USD
Sch. Sys. Enr. Code 5
Supt. – John B. Burns, 151 S 1ST ST 93630
JHS, 601 S 1ST ST 93630 – Jack Booher, prin.
Kerman-Floyd ES, 14655 W F ST 93630
Nancy Newsome, prin.
Sun Empire ES, 2649 N MODOC AVE 93630
Dale Sutherland, prin.

Kettleman City, Kings Co.
Reef-Sunset USD
Supt. – See Avenal
ES, P O BOX 248 93239 – John Wight, prin.

Keyes, Stanislaus Co., Pop. Code 4
Keyes Un. ESD
Sch. Sys. Enr. Code 2
Supt. – Jack Harlan, P O BOX 549 95328
ES, SEVENTH AND KEYES ROAD 95328
Glenn Reed, prin.

King City, Monterey Co., Pop. Code 6
Bitterwater-Tully Un. ESD
Sch. Sys. Enr. Code 1
Supt. – (—), LONOAK ROUTE 93930
Bitterwater-Tully ES, LONOAK ROUTE 93390
Carol Roeder, prin.

King City Un. ESD
Sch. Sys. Enr. Code 4
Supt. – Stephen Young, 415 PEARL ST 93930
San Lorenzo MS, 415 PEARL ST 93930
Ralph Burgess, prin.
Del Rey MS, 502 KING ST 93930
Carolyn McCombs, prin.
Santa Lucia ES, RUSS & COLLINS STS 93930
L. Brown, prin.

Kingsburg, Fresno Co., Pop. Code 6
Clay JESD
Sch. Sys. Enr. Code 2
Supt. – (—), 12449 S SMITH AVE 93631
Clay ES, 12449 S SMITH AVE 93631
Gary Johnson, prin.

Kings River Un. ESD
Sch. Sys. Enr. Code 3
Supt. – T. Moshier, 3961 AVENUE 400 93631
Kings River ES, 3961 AVE 400 93631
T. Moshier, prin.

Kingsburg J Un. ESD
Sch. Sys. Enr. Code 4
Supt. – Gary J. Andreis, P O BOX 217 93631
Roosevelt MS, 10TH & DRAPER STS 93631
Donald Tow, prin.
Lincoln MS, 19TH AND MARIPOSA STS 93631
Ronald Allvin, prin.
Washington ES, SMITH AND ELLIS STS 93631
Ronald Montoro, prin.

Klamath, Del Norte Co.
Del Norte County USD
Supt. – See Crescent City
Keating ES, P O BOX 65 95548
Dennis Burns, prin.

Kneeland, Humboldt Co.
Kneeland ESD
Sch. Sys. Enr. Code 1
Supt. – (—), 9313 KNEELAND ROAD 95549
ES, 9313 KNEELAND ROAD # 12 95549
Wayne Schmalz, prin.

Knightsen, Conta Costa Co.
Knightsen ESD
Sch. Sys. Enr. Code 2
Supt. – Roland Johnson, P O BOX 265 94548
ES, P O BOX 265 94548 – (—), prin.

Knights Ferry, Stanislaus Co.
Knights Ferry ESD
Sch. Sys. Enr. Code 1
Supt. – (—), P O BOX 840 95361
ES, P O BOX 840 95361 – Yanik Ruley, prin.

Knights Landing, Yolo Co., Pop. Code 3
Woodland JUSD
Supt. – See Woodland
Grafton ES, P O BOX 458 95645
Gayle Ramey, prin.

Korbel, Humboldt Co.
Maple Creek ESD
Sch. Sys. Enr. Code 1
Supt. – Cathleen Carnes
15933 MAPLE CREEK ROUTE 95550
Maple Creek ES, MAPLE CREEK ROUTE 95550
Cathleen Carnes, prin.

Kyburz, El Dorado Co.
Silver Fork ESD
Sch. Sys. Enr. Code 1
Supt. – (—), P O BOX 45 95720
Silver Fork ES, P O BOX 45 95720
Richard Crow, prin.

La Canada-Flintridge, Los Angeles Co., Pop. Code 7
La Canada USD
Sch. Sys. Enr. Code 5
Supt. – Judith Glickman
5039 PALM DRIVE 91011
La Canada ES, 4540 ENCINAS DRIVE 91011
C. Holman, prin.
Palm Crest ES, 5025 PALM DR 91011
Don Hingst, prin.
Paradise Canyon ES, 471 KNIGHT WAY 91011
Gloria McGehee, prin.

Delphi Academy, 4490 CORNISHON AVE 91011
Ribet Academy, 4025 PALM DR 91011
Crestview Preparatory ES
140 FOOTHILL BLVD 91011
St. Bede the Venerable ES
217 FOOTHILL BLVD 91011

La Crescenta, Los Angeles Co., Pop. Code 7
Glendale USD
Supt. – See Glendale
Rosemont JHS, 4725 ROSEMONT AVE 91214
Lois Neil, prin.
Dunsmore ES, 4717 DUNSMORE AVE 91214
David Smith, prin.
ES, 4343 LA CRESCENTA AVE 91214
Cathleen Lawless, prin.
Lincoln ES, 3333 ALTURA AVE 91214
Sally Buckley, prin.
Monte Vista ES, 2620 ORANGE AVE 91214
Linda Milano, prin.
Mountain Avenue ES
2307 MOUNTAIN AVE 91214
Mabel Morse, prin.

Lafayette, Contra Costa Co., Pop. Code 7
Lafayette ESD
Sch. Sys. Enr. Code 5
Supt. – James Martin, P O BOX 1029 94549
Stanley IS, 3455 SCHOOL ST 94549
Camille Moore, prin.
Burton Valley ES
561 MERRIEWOOD DRIVE 94549
Benjamin Shaw, prin.
Happy Valley ES
3855 HAPPY VALLEY ROAD 94549
Carol Blackburn, prin.

ES, 950 MOROGA ROAD   94549
  Paula Dausman, prin.
Springhill ES, 3301 SPRINGHILL ROAD   94549
  Bruce Wodhams, prin.

Basic Education School, 957 DEWING AVE   94549
Temple Isaiah School
  3800 MOUNT DIABLO BLVD   94549
St. Perpetua ES, 3445 HAMLIN RD   94549
White Pony & Meher ES, 999 LELAND DR   94549

La Grange, Tuolumne Co.
La Grange ESD
Sch. Sys. Enr. Code 1
Supt. – (—), P O BOX 66   95329
ES, 30237 FLOTO ST   95329
  David Ginsberg, prin.

Mariposa County USD
Supt. – See Mariposa
Pedro ES, 4311 HILDAGO   95329
  Russell Livingston, prin.

Laguna Beach, Orange Co., Pop. Code 7
Laguna Beach USD
Sch. Sys. Enr. Code 4
Supt. – Dennis Smith, 550 BLUMONT ST   92651
Thurston MS, 2100 PARK AVE   92651
  Cheryl Baughn, prin.
El Morro ES, 8681 COAST HIGHWAY   92651
  Gwen Gross, prin.
Top of the World ES
  21601 TREETOP LANE   92651
  Robert Klempen, prin.

St. Catherine ES, 3090 S COAST HWY   92651

Laguna Hills, Orange Co., Pop. Code 7
Saddleback Valley USD
Supt. – See Mission Viejo
Lomarena ES, 25100 EARHART ROAD   92653
  Chris Appel, prin.
San Joaquin ES, 22182 BARBERA   92653
  Larry Callison, prin.
Valencia ES, 25661 PASEO DE VALENCIA   92653
  Kathy Dick, prin.

Mission Hills Christian School
  25292 MCINTYRE ST   92653

Laguna Niguel, Orange Co., Pop. Code 5
Capistrano USD
Supt. – See San Juan Capistrano
Niguel Hills JHS, 29070 PASEO ESCUELA   92677
  Jean Trygstad, prin.
Bergeson ES, 25302 RANCHO NIGUEL   92677
  Ellen Fine, prin.
Crown Valley ES
  29292 CROWN VALLEY PARKWAY   92677
  Pam Cariker, prin.
Moulton ES, 29851 HIGHLANDS AVE   92677
  Patricia Griggs, prin.

La Habra, Orange Co., Pop. Code 8
La Habra City ESD
Sch. Sys. Enr. Code 5
Supt. – Richard Hermann, P O BOX 307   90633
Imperial MS, P O BOX 307   90633
  Betty Bidwell, prin.
Washington MS, P O BOX 307   90633
  Gary Mantey, prin.
El Cerrito ES, 1051 N HILLSIDE   90631
  Albert Peraza, prin.
Ladera Palma ES, 2151 BROOKDALE AVE   90631
  Judy Wolfe, prin.
Las Lomas ES, 301 LAS LOMAS DRIVE   90631
  Mary Anderson, prin.
Las Positas MS
  1400 SCHOOLWOOD DRIVE   90631
  Tony Gianetto, prin.
Sierra Vista MS, 1800 E WHITTIER BLVD   90631
  Myrna Klose, prin.
Walnut Street MS, 625 N WALNUT ST   90631
  Patricia Miller, prin.

Carden School of La Habra, 200 NADA ST   90631
Our Lady of Guadalupe ES
  920 W LA HABRA BLVD   90631

La Honda, San Mateo Co.
La Honda-Pescadero USD
Supt. – See Pescadero
ES, SEARS RANCH ROAD   94020
  Melba Rhodes, prin.

La Jolla, San Diego Co.
San Diego City USD
Supt. – See San Diego
Bird Rock ES, 5371 LA JOSSA HERMOSA   92037
  Sandra Harding, prin.
ES, 1111 MARINE ST   92037
  Trudy Campbell, prin.
Torrey Pines ES, 8350 CLIFFRIDGE AVE   92037
  Barry Bernstein, prin.

La Jolla Country Day School
  9490 GENESEE AVE   92037
All Hallows Academy, 2390 NAUTILUS ST   92037
Evans ES, 6510 S LA JOLLA SCENIC DR   92037
Stella Maris Academy
  7704 HERSCHEL AVE   92037

Lake Arrowhead, San Bernardino Co., Pop. Code 5
Rim of the World USD
Sch. Sys. Enr. Code 5
Supt. – Reed Montgomery, P O BOX 430   92352

Henck IS, P O BOX 430   92352
  David Cathalinat, prin.
Hoffman ES   92352 – James Sims, prin.
ES   92352 – Kenneth Newton, prin.
Tone MS   92352 – John Fenn, prin.
Valley of Enchantment ES   92352
  Karen Bryan, prin.

Lake Elsinore, Riverside Co., Pop. Code 6
Elsinore Un. HSD
Sch. Sys. Enr. Code 5
Supt. – Larry Maw, 1201 W GRAHAM AVE   92330
Elsinore JHS, 1201 W GRAHAM AVE   92330
  Cheryl Bass, prin.
Terra Cotta JHS, 29251 ROBB RD   92330
  Ron Foland, prin.

Lake Elsinore SD
Sch. Sys. Enr. Code 6
Supt. – Barb Nelson, 545 CHANEY ST   92330
Butterfield ES, 16275 GRAND AVE   92330
  Cheryl Eining, prin.
Elsinore ES, 512 W SUMNER ST   92330
  Chris Petersen, prin.
Hayman ES, 21-440 LEMON ST   92330
  Jerry Winant, prin.
Machado ES, 15-150 JOY AVE   92330
  Jacquie Buchanan, prin.
Railroad Canyon ES, 1300 MILL ST   92330
  Colleen Anderson, prin.
Other Schools – See Wildomar

Bundy Canyon Christian School
  23411 BUNDY CANYON ROAD   92330

Lakehead, Shasta Co.
Canyon Un. ESD
Sch. Sys. Enr. Code 2
Supt. – Bill Hopkins, P O BOX 376   96051
Canyon ES, P O BOX 376   96051
  Bill Hopkins, prin.

Lake Hughes, Los Angeles Co.
Hughes-Elizabeth Lakes Un. ESD
Sch. Sys. Enr. Code 2
Supt. – James Windle
  16633 ELIZABETH LAKE ROAD   93532
Hughes-Lakes ES
  16633 ELIZABETH LAKE ROAD   93532
  Roberta Zapf, prin.

Lake Isabella, Kern Co., Pop. Code 3
Kernville Un. ESD
Sch. Sys. Enr. Code 4
Supt. – Douglas Halloran, HCR 01 BOX 136   93240
Wallace JHS, RURAL ROUTE 02 BOX 1012   93240
  Shirley Russom, prin.
Wallace ES, RURAL ROUTE 02 BOX 1012   93240
  Larry Holochwost, prin.

Lakeport, Lake Co., Pop. Code 5
Lakeport USD
Sch. Sys. Enr. Code 4
Supt. – Dale Jensen, 100 LANGE ST   95453
Terrace MS, 250 LANGE ST   95453
  Timothy Hoff, prin.
ES, 150 LANGE ST   95453 – Donald Mcguire, prin.

Lakeside, San Diego Co., Pop. Code 7
Lakeside Un. ESD
Sch. Sys. Enr. Code 5
Supt. – Jacquelyn Spacek, P O BOX 578   92040
Lakeside MS, P O BOX 578   92040
  Rich Henderson, prin.
Tierra Del Sol MS, P O BOX 578   92040
  Diana Adams, prin.
Eucalyptus Hills ES, P O BOX 578   92040
  K. Ackley, prin.
Lakeside Farms ES, P O BOX 578   92040
  K. Ackley, prin.
Lakeview ES, P O BOX 578   92040
  Constance Fish, prin.
Lindo Park ES, P O BOX 578   92040
  Joyce Byrne, prin.
Riverview ES, P O BOX 578   92040
  Nancy Frick, prin.
Winter Gardens ES, P O BOX 578   92040
  Nancy Frick, prin.

Our Lady of Perpetual Help ES
  9825 PINO DR   92040

Lakeview Terrace, Los Angeles Co.
Los Angeles USD
Supt. – See Los Angeles
Brainard Avenue ES
  11407 BRAINARD AVE   91342
  Cheryl Sparti, prin.
Fenton Avenue ES, 11828 GAIN ST   91342
  Herman Christopher, prin.

Lakewood, Los Angeles Co., Pop. Code 8
ABC USD
Supt. – See Cerritos
Aloha ES, 11737 214TH ST   90715
  Margaret Skilling, prin.
Melbourne ES, 21314 CLARETTA AVE   90715
  Gloria Aguilar, prin.
Palms ES, 12445 207TH ST   90715
  Marjorie Wall, prin.
Willow ES, 11733 205TH ST   90715
  Robert Quezada, prin.

Bellflower USD
Supt. – See Bellflower
Foster ES, 5223 BIGELOW ST   90712
  Jean Keleman, prin.

Lindstrom ES, 5900 CANEHILL AVE   90713
  Rick Kemppainen, prin.
Williams ES, 6144 N CLARK AVE   90712
  Kirk Real, prin.

Long Beach USD
Supt. – See Long Beach
Cleveland ES, 4760 HACKETT AVE   90713
  Lue MaGee, prin.
Gompers ES, 5206 BRIERCREST AVE   90713
  John Folsom, prin.
Holmes ES, 5020 BARLIN AVE   90712
  William Alban, prin.
MacArthur ES, 6011 CENTRALIA ST   90713
  Mary Goshert, prin.
Madison ES, 2801 BOMBERRY ST   90712
  James Churchill, prin.
Monroe ES, 4400 LADOGA AVE   90713
  Kenneth Mendonca, prin.
Riley ES, 3319 SANDWOOD ST   90712
  Steven Fish, prin.

St. Pancratius ES
  3601 SAINT PANCRATIUS PL   90712

La Mesa, San Diego Co., Pop. Code 8
Cajon Valley Un. ESD
Supt. – See El Cajon
Avocado ES
  3845 AVACADO SCHOOL ROAD   92041
  Robyn Perlin, prin.

La Mesa-Spring Valley ESD
Sch. Sys. Enr. Code 7
Supt. – Warren Hogarth, 4750 DATE AVE   92041
MS, 4200 PARKS AVE   92041
  Nevelle Deveraux, prin.
Parkway MS, 9009 PARK PLAZA   92041
  Calvin Strickland, prin.
La Mesa Dale ES, 4370 PARKS AVE   92041
  William Yakubik, prin.
Lemon Avenue ES, 8787 LEMON AVE   92041
  Lois DeKock, prin.
Maryland Avenue ES
  5400 MARYLAND AVE   92042
  Sandra Pineda, prin.
Murdock ES, 4354 CONRAD DRIVE   92041
  Joan Heraty, prin.
Murray Manor ES, 8305 EL PASO ST   92042
  Marilynn Prouty, prin.
Northmont ES, 9405 GREGORY ST   92042
  Jack Reed, prin.
Rolando ES, 6925 TOWER ST   92041
  Shirley Panish, prin.
Other Schools – See El Cajon, Spring Valley

Lemon Grove ESD
Supt. – See Lemon Grove
Vista La Mesa ES, 3900 VIOLET ST   92041
  Daniel Heiserman, prin.

Christ Lutheran ES, 7929 LA MESA BLVD   92041
La Mesa Christian ES, 9407 JERICHO RD   92042
St. Luke's Lutheran Christian Day School
  5150 WILSON ST   92041
St. Martin Academy, 7708 EL CAJON BLVD   92041

La Mirada, Los Angeles Co., Pop. Code 8
Norwalk-La Mirada USD
Supt. – See Norwalk
Dulles ES, 12726 MEADOW GREEN ROAD   90638
  Robert Vieth, prin.
Eastwood ES, 15730 PESCADOS DRIVE   90638
  George Christian, prin.
Escalona ES, 15135 ESCALONA ROAD   90638
  Donald Henry, prin.
Foster Road ES, 13930 FOSTER ROAD   90638
  Patricia Almada, prin.
Gardenhill ES, 14607 GARDENHILL DRIVE   90638
  George Keplinger, prin.
Hutchinson ES, 13900 ESTERO ROAD   90638
  Jeannine Goenne, prin.
La Pluma ES, 14420 LA PLUMA DRIVE   90638
  Christine Reasin, prin.

Beatitudes of Our Lord ES
  13021 SANTA GERTRUDES AVE   90638
Brethren ES, 12200 OXFORD DR   90638
St. Paul of the Cross ES, 14030 FOSTER RD   90638
Whittier Christian School
  15709 OLIVE BRANCH DR   90638

Lamont, Kern Co., Pop. Code 6
Lamont ESD
Sch. Sys. Enr. Code 4
Supt. – Robert Lasley, 8201 PALM AVE   93241
Mountain View MS, 8201 PALM AVE   93241
  James Bates, prin.
Alicante Avenue ES
  ALICANTE AVE AND STOBAUGH   93241
  Robert Hentges, prin.
ES, PALM AVE AND MAIN ST   93241
  Joan Shannon, prin.
Myrtle Avenue MS
  HALF ROAD AND MYRTLE AVE   93241
  Larry Wilkins, prin.

Lancaster, Los Angeles Co., Pop. Code 8
Eastside Un. ESD
Sch. Sys. Enr. Code 4
Supt. – Robert Wakeling
  6742 E AVENUE H   93535
Eastside ES, 6742 E AVENUE H   93535
  Barbara Walkington, prin.
Tierra Bonita ES, 6742 E AVENUE H   93535
  Patricia McMurrin, prin.

Lancaster ESD
Sch. Sys. Enr. Code 6
Supt. – E. Wright, 44711 CEDAR AVE 93534
Park View IS, 44711 CEDAR AVE 93534
 James Schettig, prin.
Piute IS, 44711 CEDAR AVE 93534
 Robert Lloyd, prin.
Desert View ES, 1555 W AVENUE H #10 93534
 E. Premer, prin.
El Dorado ES, 361 E PONDERA ST 93535
 Howard Sundberg, prin.
Joshua ES, 43926 2ND ST E 93535
 Alyce Ellis, prin.
Linda Verde ES, 4424 N FIFTH ST EAST 93535
 Michael Kurth, prin.
Mariposa ES, 737 W AVENUE H #6 93534
 Diane Palmer, prin.
Monte Vista ES, 1235 W KETTERING ST 93534
 William Wilson, prin.
Sierra ES, 747 W AVENUE J #12 93534
 Irvine Wheeler, prin.
Sunnydale ES, 1233 W AVENUE J #8 93534
 Howard Horn, prin.

Westside Un. ESD
Sch. Sys. Enr. Code 5
Supt. – George Reams, 46809 70TH ST W 93536
Del Sur ES, 9023 W AVENUE H 93536
 William Sullivan, prin.
Valley View ES, 3310 W AVENUE L-8 93536
 Regina Rossall, prin.
Other Schools – See Leona Valley, Quartz Hill

Wilsona SD
Sch. Sys. Enr. Code 4
Supt. – Chester Caldeira
 41625 N 170TH ST 93535
Challenger MS, 41625 N 170TH ST 93535
 Greg Gerard, prin.
Wilsona ES, 41625 170TH ST E 93535
 Mary Sumption, prin.
Other Schools – See Palmdale

Bethel Christian Baptist Academy
 3100 W AVE K 93536
Landmark Christian School, 836 E AVE 1 93534
Grace Lutheran ES, 856 W NEWGROVE ST 93534
Lancaster Christian ES, 44339 BEECH AVE 93534
Learning Village/Valley Chrstn MS
 44648 15TH ST W 93534
Sacred Heart ES, 45002 DATE AVE 93534

La Palma, Orange Co., Pop. Code 7
Anaheim Un. HSD
Supt. – See Anaheim
Walker JHS, 6131 WALKER ST 90620
 Elizabeth Jackman, prin.

Centralia ESD
Supt. – See Buena Park
Los Coyotes ES, 8122 MOODY ST 90623
 Gene Starr, prin.
Miller ES, 7751 FURMAN ROAD 90623
 Karen Kawai, prin.

Cypress ESD
Supt. – See Cypress
Luther ES, 4631 LA PALMA AVE 90623
 Jeannette Lohrman, prin.

La Porte, Yuba Co.
Plumas USD
Supt. – See Quincy
ES, SCHOOL ST 95981 – Fran Efird, prin.

La Puente, Los Angeles Co., Pop. Code 8
Basset USD
Sch. Sys. Enr. Code 6
Supt. – Ronald Raya, 904 WILLOW AVE 91746
Edgewood MS, 904 WILLOW AVE 91746
 Susan Naeve, prin.
Don Julian ES, 13855 DON JULIAN ROAD 91746
 Cliff Duck, prin.
Erwin ES, 943 SUNKIST AVE 91746
 Margaret Lutz, prin.
Sunkist ES, 935 MARYLAND AVE 91746
 Robert Watanabe, prin.
Vanwig ES, 1151 VAN WIG AVE 91746
 John Sharp, prin.
Other Schools – See City of Industry

Hacienda La Puente USD
Sch. Sys. Enr. Code 8
Supt. – James Johnson, P O BOX 1217 91749
Sierra Vista IS
 15801 SIERRA VISTA COURT 91744
 Bob Twitchell, prin.
Sparks IS, 15100 GIORDANO ST 91744
 Barbara Nakaoka, prin.
Baldwin ES, 1616 GRIFFITH AVE 91744
 Harry Davis, prin.
California ES, 1111 CALIFORNIA AVE 91744
 Jon Robinson, prin.
Del Valle ES, 801 DEL VALLE AVE 91744
 Howard Heinrichs, prin.
Grandview ES, 795 GRANDVIEW LANE 91744
 Gare Herrington, prin.
LasSalette ES, 14333 LASSALETTE ST 91744
 Dave McDonnell, prin.
Nelson ES, 330 CALIFORNIA AVE 91744
 Mike Gomez, prin.
Sparks ES, 15151 E TEMPLE AVE 91744
 Sandee Roberts, prin.
Sunset ES, 800 TONOPAH AVE 91744
 Frank Keohane, prin.

Temple ES, 635 CALIFORNIA AVE 91744
 Ken Quon, prin.
Valinda ES, 1030 INDIAN SUMMER AVE 91744
 Virginia Bower, prin.
Wing Lane ES, 16605 WING LANE 91744
 Alan Cushnie, prin.
Workman ES, 16000 WORKMAN ST 91744
 Mary Ann Shuler, prin.
Other Schools – See Hacienda Heights

Rowland USD
Supt. – See Rowland Heights
Giano IS, 3223 S GIANO ST 91744
 Bill Weirich, prin.
Hurley ES, 535 LAURA AVE 91744
 Artemisa Garcia, prin.
La Seda ES, 341 LA SEDA ROAD 91744
 Helen Paulette, prin.
Northam ES, 17800 RENAULT ST 91744
 Van Windham, prin.
Rorimer ES, 18750 RORIMER ST 91744
 Victoria Fisher, prin.
Villacorta ES, 17840 VILLA CORTA ST 91744
 Margot Napper, prin.
Yorbita ES, 502 VIDALIA AVE 91744
 Robert Wertz, prin.

Montessori School/Rowland Heights
 18760 COLIMA RD 91748
St. Joseph ES, 15650 TEMPLE AVE 91744
St. Louis of France ES, 13901 TEMPLE AVE 91746
St. Marthas ES, 444 N AZUSA AVE 91744
Sunset Christian ES, 400 N SUNSET AVE 91744

La Quinta, Riverside Co., Pop. Code 3
Desert Sands USD
Supt. – See Indio
MS, 78-900 AVENUE 50 92253
 Milton Jones, prin.
Adams ES, 78-880 AVENIDA 50 92253
 Carole Horlock, prin.
Truman ES, 78-870 AVENIDA 50 92253
 John Sherwood, prin.

Larkspur, Marin Co., Pop. Code 7
Larkspur ESD
Sch. Sys. Enr. Code 3
Supt. – Richard Derby, 18 MAGNOLIA AVE 94939
Hall MS, 200 DOHERTY DRIVE 94939
 Jeffrey Plotnick, prin.
Other Schools – See Corte Madera

St. Patrick's ES, 120 KING ST 94939

Lathrop, San Joaquin Co., Pop. Code 4
Manteca USD
Supt. – See Manteca
ES, P O BOX 168 95330 – Rebecca Rector, prin.

Laton, Fresno Co., Pop. Code 4
Laton JUSD
Sch. Sys. Enr. Code 3
Supt. – David Vaughn, P O BOX 278 93242
Conejo MS, P O BOX 7 93242 – Barry Dew, prin.
ES, P O BOX 7 93242 – Michael Decker, prin.

La Verne, Los Angeles Co., Pop. Code 7
Bonita USD
Supt. – See San Dimas
Ramona IS, 3490 RAMONA AVE 91750
 Jerry Ray, prin.
Laverne Heights ES, 1550 BASELINE RD 91750
 Tom Milligan, prin.
Roynon ES, 2715 E ST 91750 – John Johnson, prin.

Calvary Baptist School, 2990 DAMIEN AVE 91750

Lawndale, Los Angeles Co., Pop. Code 7
Lawndale ESD
Sch. Sys. Enr. Code 5
Supt. – James Waters, 4161 W 147TH ST 90260
Rogers IS, 4161 W 147TH ST 90260
 Martha Shaw, prin.
Addams ES, 4353 W 153RD ST 90260
 Yolanda Mendoza, prin.
Anderson ES, 4110 W 154TH ST 90260
 Frank Noyes, prin.
Green ES, 4520 W 168TH ST 90260
 Dianna Taylor, prin.
Mitchell ES, 14429 CONDON AVE 90260
 Evelyn Chidsey, prin.
Roosevelt ES, 3633 W COMPTON BLVD 90260
 Fred Huntington, prin.
Twain ES, 3728 W 154TH ST 90260
 Cynthia Geraghty, prin.

Laytonville, Medocino Co., Pop. Code 3
Laytonville USD
Sch. Sys. Enr. Code 3
Supt. – Brian Buckley, P O BOX 868 95454
ES, P O BOX 325 95454 – Richard Matlock, prin.
Spy Rock ES, P O BOX 325 95454
 Richard Matlock, prin.

Lebec, Los Angeles Co.
El Tejon Un. ESD
Sch. Sys. Enr. Code 3
Supt. – Laverne Carlson, P O BOX 876 93243
El Tejon MS, 35272 LEBEC ROAD 93243
 Joel Hampton, prin.
Mettler ES, P O BOX 876 93243
 Rommie Lewis, prin.
Frazier Park ES, P O BOX 876 93243
 Barbara Sorenson, prin.

Lee Vining, Mono Co., Pop. Code 2
Eastern Sierra USD
Supt. – See Bridgeport
ES, P O BOX 70 93541 – Nancy Lampson, prin.

Leggett, Mendocino Co., Pop. Code 2
Fort Bragg USD
Supt. – See Fort Bragg
Leggett Valley ES, P O BOX 158 95455
 Denis Bossetti, prin.

Le Grand, Merced Co., Pop. Code 3
Le Grand Un. ESD
Sch. Sys. Enr. Code 2
Supt. – Charles Alsberg, P O BOX 27 95333
ES, 13071 E LE GRAND ROAD 95333
 Charles Alsberg, prin.

Lemoncove, Tulare Co.
Sequoia USD
Sch. Sys. Enr. Code 2
Supt. – Robert Ecker, P O BOX 327 93244
Sequoia ES, 23958 AVENUE 324 93244
 Robert Ecker, prin.

Lemon Grove, San Diego Co., Pop. Code 7
Lemon Grove ESD
Sch. Sys. Enr. Code 5
Supt. – James Justeson, 8025 LINCOLN ST 92045
MS, 7866 LINCOLN ST 92045
 Joseph Farley, prin.
Palm MS, 8425 PALM ST 92045
 Barb Allen, prin.
Golden Avenue ES, 7885 GOLDEN AVE 92045
 William Baucher, prin.
Monterey Heights ES
 7550 CANTON DRIVE 92045
 Gordon Newton, prin.
Mt. Vernon ES, 8350 MOUNT VERNON ST 92045
 Ronald Clayton, prin.
San Altos ES, 1750 MADERA ST 92045
 Donald Griffitts, prin.
San Miguel ES, 7059 SAN MIGUEL AVE 92045
 Frank Patrick, prin.
Other Schools – See La Mesa

St. John of the Cross ES
 8175 LEMON GROVE WAY 92045

Lemoore, Kings Co., Pop. Code 6
Central Un. ESD
Sch. Sys. Enr. Code 4
Supt. – Carl Carlson, 15783 18TH AVE 93245
Central ES, 15783 S 18TH AVE 93245
 Patricia Ehda, prin.
Neutra ES
 HAWKEYE AND ORISKANY AVES 93245
 Robert Marienau, prin.
Other Schools – See Stratford

Island Un. ESD
Sch. Sys. Enr. Code 2
Supt. – Thomas Bates, 7799 21ST AVE 93245
Island ES, 7799 21ST AVE 93245
 Thomas Bates, prin.

Lemoore Un. ESD
Sch. Sys. Enr. Code 4
Supt. – Idanna Aaron, P O BOX 40 93245
Engvall JHS, P O BOX 40 93245 – Tom Lasek, prin.
ES, 573 BUSH ST 93245 – Thomas Hewitt, prin.
Meadow Lane ES
 MEADOW LANE AND QUANDT 93245
 Michael Fetterhoff, prin.

Kings Christian School, 900 E D ST 93245
Mary Immaculate Queen ES
 884 N LEMOORE AVE 93245

Lennox, Los Angeles Co., Pop. Code 7
Lennox ESD
Sch. Sys. Enr. Code 6
Supt. – Kenneth Moffett
 10319 FIRMONA AVE 90304
MS, 11033 S BUFORD AVE 90304
 Larry Kennedy, prin.
Buford ES, 4919 W 109TH ST 90304
 Jessie Sawyer, prin.
Felton ES, 10417 FELTON AVE 90304
 Marlene Wilson, prin.
Jefferson ES, 10322 CONDON AVE 90304
 Joann Isken, prin.
Larch ES, 11200 LARCH AVE 90304
 Brian Johnson, prin.
Whelan ES, 4125 W 105TH ST 90304
 Sandra Calderon, prin.

Leona Valley, Los Angeles Co.
Westside Un. ESD
Supt. – See Lancaster
ES, 9063 W LEODNA AVE 93550
 Julie Matzke, prin.

Lewiston, Trinity Co., Pop. Code 3
Lewiston ESD
Sch. Sys. Enr. Code 2
Supt. – Sharon MacKenzie, P O BOX 182 96052
ES, P O BOX 120 96052 – Sharon MacKenzie, prin.

Likely, Modoc Co.
Modoc JUSD
Supt. – See Alturas
South Fork ES, P O BOX 115 96116
 Kenneth Bushey, prin.

Lincoln, Placer Co., Pop. Code 5
Western Placer USD
Sch. Sys. Enr. Code 5
Supt. – John Bozzo, 1070 6TH ST   95648
Coppin ES, 150 E 12TH ST   95648
Yvonne Nunes, prin.
Edwards ES, 204 L ST   95648
Leonard Valasek, prin.
Other Schools – See Sheridan

Linden, San Joaquin Co., Pop. Code 3
Linden USD
Sch. Sys. Enr. Code 4
Supt. – John Fitzgerald, P O BOX 539   95236
ES, 18100 E FRONT ST   95236
Mark Calonico, prin.
Other Schools – See Stockton

Lindsay, Tulare Co., Pop. Code 6
Lindsay USD
Sch. Sys. Enr. Code 5
Supt. – Robert Mohr, 519 E HONOLULU ST   93247
Garvey JHS, 340 N HARVARD AVE   93247
Wanda Crawford, prin.
Jefferson ES, 333 N WESTWOOD AVE   93247
Michael McQuary, prin.
Lincoln ES, 851 N STANFORD   93247
Thomas Hendricks, prin.
Washington ES, 451 E SAMOA ST   93247
Cheryl Cook, prin.

Litchfield, Lassen Co.
Shaffer Un. SD
Sch. Sys. Enr. Code 2
Supt. – M. Lavell Deese, P O BOX 52   96117
Shaffer ES, P O BOX 52   96117 – M. Deese, prin.

Littlerock, Los Angeles Co., Pop. Code 4
Keppel Un. ESD
Sch. Sys. Enr. Code 4
Supt. – Emerson Hall, 35118 82ND ST E   93543
Almondale MS, 9330 AVE U   93543
Merle Fowler, prin.
Alpine ES
8244 PEARBLOSSOM HIGHWAY   93543
John Adams, prin.
Antelope MS, 37237 100TH ST E   93543
Marcus Pospisil, prin.
Gibson MS, 9655 E AVENUE Q-10   93543
James Lott, prin.
Mountain View MS, 35118 N 82ND ST E   93543
James Lott, prin.
Sunset View ES, 37237 N 100TH ST E   93543
Catherine Sorenson, prin.
Other Schools – See Pearblossom

Live Oak, Sutter Co., Pop. Code 5
Live Oak USD
Sch. Sys. Enr. Code 4
Supt. – Don Witzansky
2341 PENNINGTON ROAD   95953
MS, 2082 PENNINGTON ROAD   95953
Paulla McIntire, prin.
Encinal ES, 6484 LARKIN ROAD   95953
Margo Schullerts, prin.
Luther ES, 10123 CONNECTICUT AVE   95953
Edward Changus, prin.

Nuestro ESD
Sch. Sys. Enr. Code 1
Supt. – James Crowhurst
3934 BROADWAY ROAD   95953
Nuestro ES, 3934 BROADWAY ROAD   95953
James Crowhurst, prin.

Livermore, Alameda Co., Pop. Code 8
Livermore Valley JUSD
Sch. Sys. Enr. Code 7
Supt. – Leo Croce, 685 LAS POSITAS BLVD   94550
East Avenue MS, 3951 EAST AVE   94550
Gerald Stunkel, prin.
Junction Ave. MS, 298 JUNCTION AVE   94550
Leslie Imel, prin.
Mendenhall MS, 1701 EL PADRO DRIVE   94550
Charles DePaoli, prin.
Arroyo Seco ES, 5280 IRENE WAY   94550
(—), prin.
Christenson ES
5757 HAGGIN OAKS DRIVE   94550
Arnold Moore, prin.
Jackson Avenue ES, 554 JACKSON AVE   94550
Michael Hazelhofer, prin.
Marylin Avenue ES, 800 MARYLIN AVE   94550
Carol Howell, prin.
Michell ES, 1001 ELAINE AVE   94550
Elden Williams, prin.
Portola ES, 2451 PORTOLA AVE   94550
Linda Maguire, prin.
Rancho Las Positas ES
401 LAS POSITAS BLVD   94550
David Cooper, prin.
Smith ES, 391 ONTARIO DRIVE·   94550
Diane Everett, prin.
Sunset ES, 1671 FRANKFURT WAY   94550
Patricia Heineman, prin.

Patterson JUSD
Supt. – See Patterson
Harney ES, DEL PUERTO CANYON ROAD   94550
Daniel Barton, prin.

Calvary Christian ES, 2200 ARROYO RD   94550
Our Saviors Lutheran ES, 3820 EAST AVE   94550
St. Micheals ES, 372 MAPLE ST   94550

Livingston, Merced Co., Pop. Code 6
Livingston Un. SD
Sch. Sys. Enr. Code 6
Supt. – Harold Thompson, 922 B ST   95334
IS, 922 B ST   95334 – Henry Escobar, prin.
Campus Park ES, 922 B ST   95334
Kathy Berkeley, prin.
Herndon MS, 922 B ST   95334 – Victor Zuber, prin.

Longview Mennonite ES
12725 W LONGVIEW AVE   95334

Lockeford, San Joaquin Co., Pop. Code 4
Lodi USD
Supt. – See Lodi
ES, P O BOX 106   95237 – Tad Ishihara, prin.

Lockwood, Monterey Co.
San Antonio Un. ESD
Sch. Sys. Enr. Code 2
Supt. – Gary Gerbrandt
HRC LOCKWOOD-SAN LUCAS ROAD   93932
San Antonio ES   93932 – Gary Gerbrandt, prin.

Lodi, San Joaquin Co., Pop. Code 8
Lodi USD
Sch. Sys. Enr. Code 7
Supt. – Neil Schmidt
815 W LOCKEFORD ST   95240
Senior MS, 945 S HAM LANE   95240
Richard Ferrara, prin.
Children's Center ES, 701 CALAVERAS ST   95240
(—), prin.
Garfield ES, 1001 S GARFIELD ST   95240
Beverly Gabrielson, prin.
Henderson MS
13451 N EXTENSION ROAD   95242
Linda Nook, prin.
Heritage ES, 509 EDEN ST   95240
Ken Allen, prin.
Lakewood ES, 1100 N HAM LANE   95242
Frank Garcia, prin.
Lawrence ES, 721 CALAVERAS ST   95240
Beverly Gabrielson, prin.
Live Oak ES, 5099 BEAR CREEK ROAD   95240
James Benevides, prin.
Nichols ES, 1301 S CRESCENT AVE   95240
Joe Lobb, prin.
Reese ES, 1800 W ELM ST   95242
Millard Fore, prin.
Tokay Colony ES
13520 E LIVE OAK ROAD   95240
Christine Muzik, prin.
Turner ES, 18051 N RAY ROAD   95242
James Thomas, prin.
Vinewood ES, 1600 W TOKAY ST   95242
Brenda Kosaka, prin.
Washington ES, 831 W LOCKEFORD ST   95240
James Thomas, prin.
Other Schools – See Acampo, Clements, Lockeford,
Stockton, Victor, Woodbridge

Century Christian ES
550 W CENTURY BLVD   95240
Lodi SDA ES, 1240 S CENTRAL AVE   95240
St. Anne ES, 200 S PLEASANT AVE   95240
St. Peter's Lutheran ES
2400 OXFORD WAY   95242

Loleta, Humboldt Co., Pop. Code 3
Loleta Un. ESD
Sch. Sys. Enr. Code 2
Supt. – Frank Trone, P O BOX 547   95551
ES, LOLETA DRIVE BOX 547   95551
Frank Trone, prin.

Loma Linda, San Bernardino Co., Pop. Code 7

Loma Linda SDA Academy
10656 ANDERSON ST   92354

Lomita, Los Angeles Co., Pop. Code 7
Los Angeles USD
Supt. – See Los Angeles
Eshelman Avenue ES
25902 ESHELMAN AVE   90717
William Bennett, prin.
Lomita Fundamental Magnet ES
2211 247TH ST   90717 – Meno Phillips, prin.

St. Margaret Mary ES
25515 ESHELMAN AVE   90717

Lompoc, Santa Barbara Co., Pop. Code 8
Lompoc USD
Sch. Sys. Enr. Code 6
Supt. – James Brown, P O BOX H   93438
Lompoc MS, P O BOX H   93438
John Lemon, prin.
Fillmore ES, 1211 E PINE AVE   93436
Wyland Fuller, prin.
Hapgood ES, 324 S A ST   93436
Carl Krugmeier, prin.
La Canada ES, 620 W NORTH AVE   93436
Gerald Schockmel, prin.
La Honda ES, 1213 N A ST   93436
Tonya Opfermann, prin.
Los Berros ES, 3745 VIA LATO   93436
James Swartz, prin.
Miguelito ES, 1600 W OLIVE AVE   93436
David Manship, prin.
Ruth ES, 501 NORTH W ST   93436
Dorothy Jackson, prin.
Other Schools – See Vandenburg A F B

La Purisima Concepcion ES
219 W OLIVE AVE   93436

Lone Pine, Inyo Co., Pop. Code 4
Lone Pine USD
Sch. Sys. Enr. Code 2
Supt. – William Schmidt, P O BOX 159   93545
Lo-Inyo ES, P O BOX 159   93545
Nancy Sonke, prin.
Other Schools – See Olancha

Long Beach, Los Angeles Co., Pop. Code 10
Long Beach USD
Sch. Sys. Enr. Code 8
Supt. – E. Giugni, 701 LOCUST AVE   90813
Addams ES, 5320 PINE AVE   90805
Beryl Brooks, prin.
Barton ES, 1100 E DEL AMO BLVD   90807
David Meacham, prin.
Birney ES, 710 W SPRING ST   90806
Duane Maeda, prin.
Bixby ES, 5251 E STEARNS ST   90815
Naomi Blackmore, prin.
Bryant ES, 4101 E FOUNTAIN ST   90804
Martha Estrada, prin.
Burbank ES, 501 JUNIPERO AVE   90814
Jean Evans, prin.
Burcham ES, 5610 E MONIACO ROAD   90808
Marnos Lelesi, prin.
Burnett ES, 565 E HILL ST   90806
Anne Cook, prin.
Burroughs ES, 1260 E 33RD ST   90807
Christine Cook, prin.
Carver ES, 5335 E PAWO ST   90808
James Garren, prin.
College IS, 1890 ORANGE AVE   90806
Barbara Richardson, prin.
Cubberley ES, 3200 MONOGRAM AVE   90808
Jan Leight, prin.
Edison ES, 625 MAINE AVE   90802
David Short, prin.
Emerson ES, 2625 JOSIE AVE   90815
Louella Woo, prin.
Fremont ES, 4000 E 4TH ST   90814
Dolores Reynolds, prin.
Gant ES, 1854 N BRITTON DRIVE   90815
Rowena Anderson, prin.
Garfield ES, 2240 VBALTIC AVE   90810
Ronald Howarth, prin.
Grant ES, 1225 E 64TH ST   90805
Julia Mendell, prin.
Harte ES, 1671 E PHILLIPS ST   90805
A. Skare, prin.
Henry ES, 3720 CANEHILL AVE   90808
Janice McNab, prin.
Hudson ES, 2335 WEBSTER AVE   90810
Drucilla Grenier, prin.
Keller ES, 7020 E BRITTAIN ST   90808
Betty Wilson, prin.
Kettering ES, 550 SILVERA AVE   90803
Patricia Jernigan, prin.
King ES, 145 E ARTESIA ST   90806
Martha Dauway, prin.
LaFayette ES, 2445 CHESTNUT AVE   90806
Casey Shim, prin.
Lee ES, 1620 TEMPLE AVE   90804
Bobby Robertson, prin.
Lincoln ES, 1175 E 11TH ST   90813
Elizabeth Ash, prin.
Longfellow ES, 3800 OLIVE AVE   90807
Jacquelyn Dodge, prin.
Los Cerritos ES
515 W SAN ANTONIO DRIVE   90807
Stephen Smith, prin.
Lowell ES, 5201 E BROADWAY   90803
Shirley Black, prin.
Mann ES, 257 CORONADO AVE   90803
Mary Steinhauer, prin.
McKinley ES, 6822 N PARAMOUNT BLVD   90805
A. Phillips, prin.
Muir ES, 3038 DELTA AVE   90810
Rozanne Churchill, prin.
Naples ES, 5537 #E THE TOLEDO   90803
Cynthia Terry, prin.
Newcomb ES, 3351 VAL VERDE AVE   90808
John Frangesch, prin.
Nightingale ES, 3701 E WILLOW ST   90815
Brian Cowie, prin.
Prisk ES, 2375 FANWOOD AVE   90815
Gwendolyn Matthews, prin.
Roosevelt ES, 1574 LINDEN AVE   90813
Robert Montague, prin.
Signal Hill ES, 2285 WALNUT AVE   90806
Bruce Woods, prin.
Stevenson ES, 515 LIME AVE   90802
Marilyn Montgomery, prin.
Sutter ES, 5075 DAISY AVE   90805
Nancy Henry, prin.
Tincher ES, 1701 PETALUMA AVE   90815
Suzanne Fellenzer, prin.
Tucker ES, 2221 ARGONNE AVE   90815
Mary Steinhauer, prin.
Twain ES, 5021 E CENTRALIA ST   90808
Joan Taylor, prin.
Webster ES, 1755 W 32ND WAY   90810
Benjamin Holzman, prin.
Whittier ES, 1761 WALNUT AVE   90813
Raoul Ramos, prin.
Willard ES, 1055 FREEMAN AVE   90804
Selena Sutherland, prin.
Other Schools – See Avalon, Lakewood, Los Alamitos

Los Angeles USD
Supt. – See Los Angeles
Dominguez ES, 21250 S SANTA FE AVE   90810
  Joyce Zikas, prin.

Paramount USD
Supt. – See Paramount
Collins ES, 6125 COKE AVE   90805
  Arthur La Cues, prin.

Calvary Chapel Paramount School
  132 ARTESIA BLVD   90805
Longview Private School
  4747 DAISY AVE AVE   90805
Bethany Baptist ES, 2244 CLARK AVE   90815
Bethany Lutheran ES, 5100 E ARBOR RD   90808
First Baptist of Lakewood ES
  5336 E ARBOR RD   90808
First Lutheran ES, 946 LINDEN AVE   90813
Holy Innocents ES, 2500 PACIFIC AVE   90806
Huntington ES, 2935 E SPAULDING ST   90804
Light & Life Christian ES
  5951 DOWNEY AVE   90805
Long Beach Advent ES, 4951 OREGON AVE   90805
Long Beach Brethren ES
  3601 LINDEN AVE   90807
Los Altos Brethren ES, 6565 E STEARNS ST   90815
McKinney ES, 2650 PACIFIC AVE   90806
Nazarene Christian School/Long Beach
  5253 E LOS COYOTES DIAGONAL   90815
Our Lady of Refuge ES
  5210 E LOS COYOTES DIAGONAL   90815
Southern Caifornia Military Academy
  2065 CHERRY AVE   90806
St. Anthony ES, 855 E 5TH ST   90802
St. Athanasius ES, 5369 LINDEN AVE   90805
St. Barnabas ES, 3980 MARRON AVE   90807
St. Cornelius ES
  3330 N BELLFLOWER BLVD   90808
St. Cyprian ES, 5133 E ARBOR RD   90808
St. John Lutheran ES, 6650 ORANGE AVE   90805
St. Joseph ES, 6200 E WILLOW ST   90815
St. Lucy ES, 2320 COTA AVE   90810
St. Maria Goretti ES
  3950 PALO VERDE AVE   90808

Loomis, Placer Co., Pop. Code 4
Loomis Un. ESD
Sch. Sys. Enr. Code 4
Supt. – D. Kent Ashworth, P O BOX 104   95650
Franklin ES
  7050 FRANKLIN SCHOOL ROAD   95650
  David Dominguez, prin.
ES, P O BOX 104   95650 – Glenn Lockwood, prin.
Placer ES, 8650 HORSESHOE BAR ROAD   95650
  Joseph Silva, prin.

Los Alamitos, Orange Co., Pop. Code 7
Long Beach USD
Supt. – See Long Beach
Lee-Rossmoor MS, 11481 FOSTER ROAD   90720
  Sue Lagerborg, prin.
Oak Academy, 10821 OAK ST   90720
  Robert Hedges, prin.

Los Alamitos USD
Sch. Sys. Enr. Code 6
Supt. – Michael Miller, 10652 REAGAN ST   90720
McAuliffe MS, 4112 CERRITOS AVE   90720
  Anne Klentz, prin.
Hopkinson ES, 12582 KENSINGTON RAOD   90720
  Patricia Simmons, prin.
ES, 10862 BLOOMFIELD ST   90720
  Karen Lovelace, prin.
Rossmoor ES, 3272 SHAKESPEARE DRIVE   90720
  Pennie Pyscher, prin.
Other Schools – See Seal Beach

Grace Christian ES, 3021 BLUME DR   90720
St. Hedwig ES, 3591 ORANGEWOOD AVE   90720

Los Alamos, Santa Barbara Co.
Los Alamos ESD
Sch. Sys. Enr. Code 2
Supt. – Marilyn Cumiford, P O BOX 318   93440
Reed ES, P O BOX 318   93440
  Marilyn Cumiford, prin.

Los Altos, Santa Clara Co., Pop. Code 8
Cupertino Un. ESD
Supt. – See Cupertino
Montclaire ES, 1160 SAINT JOSEPH AVE   94022
  John Erkman, prin.

Los Altos ESD
Sch. Sys. Enr. Code 5
Supt. – Margaret Gratiot
  201 COVINGTON ROAD   94022
Blach IS, 1120 COVINGTON ROAD   94022
  Patricia Wool, prin.
Egan IS, 100 W PORTOLA AVE   94022
  Michael O'Kane, prin.
Almond ES, 550 ALMOND AVE   94022
  Daniel Haley, prin.
Loyola ES, 770 BERRY AVE   94022
  Diane Finch, prin.
Oak Avenue ES, 1501 OAK AVE   94022
  Martin St. John, prin.
Santa Rita ES, 700 LOS ALTOS AVE   94022
  David McNulty, prin.
Other Schools – See Los Altos Hills, Mountain View

Los Altos Christian ES
  625 MAGDALENA AVE   94022
Miramonte ES, 1175 ALTAMEAD DR   94022

Pinewood School, 327 FREMONT AVE   94022
Pinewood Private School Lower Campus
  477 FREMONT AVE   94022
St. Nicholas ES, 12816 EL MONTE AVE   94022
St. Simon ES, 1840 GRANT RD   94022
St. William ES, 401 ROSITA AVE   94022

Los Altos Hills, Santa Clara Co., Pop. Code 6
Los Altos ESD
Supt. – See Los Altos
Bullis-Purissima ES
  25890 W FREMONT RD   94022
  Charlene Luks, prin.

Los Angeles, Los Angeles Co., Pop. Code 12
Compton USD
Supt. – See Compton
Vanguard MS, 13305 S SAN PEDRO ST   90061
  Flora Young, prin.
Carver ES, 1425 E 120TH ST   90059
  Ann Cooper, prin.
Lincoln ES, 1667 E 118TH ST   90059
  Doris Ayers, prin.
Twain ES, 13024 SALINAS AVE   90059
  Eugene Albright, prin.

Los Angeles USD
Sch. Sys. Enr. Code 8
Supt. – Leonard Britton
  450 N GRAND AVE   90012
Berendo JHS, 1157 S BERENDO ST   90006
  Cecillia Duran, prin.
Gompers IS, 234 E 112TH ST   90061
  John Rupert, prin.
Harte Prep IS, 9301 S HOOVER ST   90044
  Charles Palmer, prin.
Virgil JHS, 152 N VERMONT AVE   90004
  Alan Wexler, prin.
Wright JHS, 6550 W 80TH ST   90045
  Jacqueline Tucker, prin.
102nd Street ES, 1963 E 103RD ST   90002
  Melba Coleman, prin.
107th Street ES, 147 E 107TH ST   90003
  Gwendolyn Wykoff, prin.
109th Street ES, 10915 MCKINLEY AVE   90059
  Matilde MacReady, prin.
112th Street ES, 1265 E 112TH ST   90059
  Robert Woodson, prin.
116th Street ES, 11610 STANFORD AVE   90059
  Lawrence Foley, prin.
118th Street ES, 144 E 118TH ST   90061
  Chere Talbert, prin.
122nd Street ES, 405 E 122ND ST   90061
  LeMuel Mossett,Jr., prin.
24th Street ES, 2055 W 24TH ST   90018
  Margaret Jones, prin.
Albion Street ES, 322 S AVE 18   90031
  Candida Fernandez, prin.
Aldama ES, 632 N AVE 50   90042
  Allyn Shapiro, prin.
Alexandria Avenue ES
  4211 OAKWOOD AVE   90004
  Carol Labrow, prin.
Allesandro ES, 2210 RIVERSIDE DRIVE   90039
  Lynn Andrews, prin.
Alta Loma ES, 1745 VINEYARD AVE   90019
  C. Carlson, prin.
Angeles Mesa ES, 26Y11 W 52ND ST   90043
  Bertha Jackson, prin.
Ann Street ES, 126 BLOOM ST   90012
  Anne Elder, prin.
Annandale ES, 6125 POPPY PEAK DRIVE   90042
  Barbara Gee, prin.
Aragon Avenue ES, 1118 ARAGON AVE   90065
  Sandra Wilkins, prin.
Ascot Avenue ES, 1447 E 45TH ST   90011
  Carol Heard, prin.
Atwater Avenue ES
  3271 SILVER LAKE BLVD   90039
  Annette Seydel, prin.
Avalon Gardens ES
  13940 S SAN PEDRO ST   90061
  Steven Freedman, prin.
Baldwin Hills ES, 5421 RODEO ROAD   90016
  Ruth Oates, prin.
Beethoven Street ES, 3711 BEETHOVEN ST   90066
  Lemuel Chavis, prin.
Bellevue Avenue PS
  610 N MICHELTORENA ST   90026
  Ingrid Isaksen, prin.
Belvedere ES, 3724 E 1ST ST   90063
  Robert Quihuis, prin.
Breed Street ES, 2226 E 3RD ST   90033
  Virginia Dominguez, prin.
Bridge Street ES, 605 N BOYLE AVE   90033
  Sam Ramirez, prin.
Brockton Avenue ES
  1309 ARMACOST AVE   90025
  Elaine Gourley, prin.
Brooklyn Avenue ES
  4620 BROOKLYN AVE   90022
  Mona Riddall, prin.
Bryson Avenue ES, 4470 MISSOURI AVE   90280
  Jorge Garcia, prin.
Buchanan Street ES, 5024 BUCHANAN ST   90042
  Mary Shambra, prin.
Budlong Avenue ES, 5940 BUDLONG AVE   90044
  Steven Bell, prin.
Bushnell Way ES, 5507 BUSHNELL WAY   90042
  Dore Wong, prin.
Cahuenga ES, 220 S HOBART BLVD   90004
  Lloyd Houske, prin.
Canfield Avenue ES, 9233 AIRDROME ST   90035
  Gaile Cazenave, prin.

Carthay Center ES, 6351 W OLYMPIC BLVD   90048
  La Verne Van Zant, prin.
Castelar Street ES, 840 YALE ST   90012
  William Chun Hoon, prin.
Castle Heights Avenue ES
  9755 CATTARAUGUS AVE   90034
  Delores Spiva, prin.
Cheremoya Avenue ES
  6017 FRANKLIN AVE   90028
  Margaret Young, prin.
Cienega ES, 2611 S ORANGE DRIVE   90016
  Kay Jeffries, prin.
Cimarron Avenue ES
  11559 CIMARRON ST   90047
  Helen Clemmons, prin.
City Terrace ES
  4350 CITY TERRACE DRIVE   90063
  Dennis Martinez, prin.
Clifford Street ES, 2150 DUANE ST   90039
  Alma Sanchez, prin.
Clover Avenue ES, 11020 CLOVER AVE   90034
  Eva Holmes, prin.
Coliseum Street ES, 4400 COLISEUM ST   90016
  Sandra Porter, prin.
Commonwealth Avenue ES
  215 S COMMONWEALTH AVE   90004
  Rosalyn Carlton, prin.
Compton Avenue ES, 1515 E 104TH ST   90002
  Victoria Verches, prin.
Cowan Avenue ES, 7615 COWAN AVE   90045
  Richard Schopf, prin.
Crescent Heights Boulevard MS
  1661 S CRESCENT HTS BLVD   90035
  Jeffrey Felz, prin.
Dacatah Street ES, 1314 S DACOTAH ST   90023
  Joan Mezori, prin.
Dahlia Heights ES, 5063 FLORISTAN AVE   90041
  Edward Burton, prin.
Dayton Heights ES
  607 N WESTMORELAND AVE   90004
  Beatrice McClendon, prin.
Delevan Drive ES, 4168 W AVE 42   90065
  Roland Lewis, prin.
Dorris Place ES, 2225 DORRIS PLACE   90031
  Javier Sandoval, prin.
Dublin Avenue Fundamental Center
  3875 DUBLIN AVE   90008
  Genevieve Shepherd, prin.
Eagle Rock ES, 2057 FAIR PARK AVE   90041
  Bernice Hallam, prin.
Eastman Avenue ES
  4112 E OLYMPIC BLVD   90023
  Mirta Feinberg, prin.
El Sereno ES, 3838 ROSEMEAD AVE   90032
  Edward Decarbo, prin.
Elysian Heights ES, 1562 BAXTER ST   90026
  Evelyn Florio, prin.
Euclid Avenue ES, 806 EUCLID AVE   90023
  Frank Serrano, prin.
Evergreen Avenue ES, 2730 GANAHL ST   90033
  Javier Centeno, prin.
Fairburn Avenue ES, 1403 FAIRBURN AVE   90024
  Christine Curtis, prin.
Farmdale ES, 2660 FITHIAN AVE   90032
  Zena Schaffer, prin.
Fifty-Fourth Street ES, 5501 EILEEN AVE   90043
  Joyce Cooper, prin.
Fifty-Ninth Street ES, 5939 2ND AVE   90043
  Lawrence James, prin.
Fifty-Second Street ES, 816 W 51ST ST   90037
  Kattie Gaspard, prin.
Figueroa Street ES, 510 W 111TH ST   90044
  Elzie James Jr., prin.
First Street ES, 2820 E 1ST ST   90033
  Mary Morin, prin.
Fletcher Drive ES, 3350 FLETCHER DRIVE   90065
  Le Roy Christensen, prin.
Florence Avenue ES, 7211 BELL AVE   90001
  Barbara Espinosa, prin.
Flournoy ES, 1630 E 111TH ST   90059
  Albert Davis, prin.
Ford Boulevard ES, 1112 S FORD BLVD   90022
  Irma Kearney, prin.
Forty-Ninth Street ES, 750 E 49TH ST   90011
  Andrea Roberts, prin.
Forty-Second Street ES, 4231 4TH AVE   90008
  Victor Kimbell, prin.
Fourth Street ES, 420 AMALIA AVE   90022
  May Arakaki, prin.
Franklin Avenue ES
  1910 N COMMONWEALTH AVE   90027
  Verna Dauterive, prin.
Gardner Street ES, 7450 HAWTHORN AVE   90046
  Marta Acosta, prin.
Garvanza ES, 317 N AVE 62   90042
  Juliette Thompson, prin.
Gates Street ES, 3333 MANITOU AVE   90031
  Anthony Beltran, prin.
Glassell Park ES, 2211 W AVE 30   90065
  Herbert Leong, prin.
Glen Alta ES, 3410 SIERRA ST   90031
  Phillipa Brown, prin.
Glenfeliz Boulevard ES
  3955 GLENFELIZ BLVD   90039
  Rita Caldera, prin.
Graham ES, 8407 S FIR AVE   90001
  Kenneth Johnson, prin.
Grand View Boulevard ES
  3951 GRAND VIEW BLVD   90066
  Catherine Kennedy, prin.
Grant ES, 1530 N WILTON PLACE   90028
  Beverly Neu, prin.
Grape Street ES, 1940 E 111TH ST   90059
  Ramona Arnold, prin.

Griffin Avenue ES, 2025 GRIFFIN AVE   90031
  Yvonne Davis, prin.
Hammel Street ES, 438 N BRANNICK AVE   90063
  Walton Ragan, prin.
Hancock Park ES, 408 S FAIRFAX AVE   90036
  Brenda Steppes, prin.
Harrison Street ES
  3529 CITY TERRACE DRIVE   90063
  Michael Jeffers, prin.
Hillcrest Drive ES
  4041 HILLSCREST DRIVE   90008
  Carole Gentry, prin.
Hillside ES, 120 E AVE 35   90031
  Robert Tafoya, prin.
Hobart Boulevard ES, 980 S HOBART BLVD   90006
  Jim Messrah, prin.
Holmes Avenue ES, 5108 HOLMES AVE   90058
  Charles Stewart, prin.
Hooper Avenue ES, 1225 E 52ND ST   90011
  Gerald Regnier,Jr., prin.
Hoover Street ES, 2726 FRANCIS AVE   90005
  Gerald Huber, prin.
Humphreys Avenue ES
  500 S HUMPHREYS AVE   90022
  Fanny Johnson, prin.
Huntington Drive ES
  4435 N HUNTINGTON DRIVE   90032
  Edmundo Aguilar, prin.
Hyde Park ES, 3140 HYDE PARK BLVD   90043
  Berniece Earley, prin.
Ivanhoe ES, 2828 HERKIMER ST   90039
  Martha Powell, prin.
Kennedy ES, 4010 RAMBOZ DRIVE   90063
  Dennis Martinez, prin.
Kenter Canyon ES, 645 N KENTER AVE   90049
  Ella Yee Quan, prin.
Kentwood ES, 8401 EMERSON AVE   90045
  Marguerette Smith, prin.
King ES, 3989 S HOBART BLVD   90062
  Judy Burton, prin.
La Salle Avenue ES, 8715 LA SALLE AVE   90047
  Helen McKnight, prin.
Latona Avenue ES, 4312 BERENICE AVE   90031
  Anthony Ugliano, prin.
Laurel ES, 925 N HAYWORTH AVE   90046
  Nancy Dean, prin.
Lillian Street ES, 5909 LILLIAN ST   90001
  Donald Taylor, prin.
Lockwood Avenue ES
  4345 LOCKWOOD AVE   90029
  Dean Shelly, prin.
Logan Street ES, 1711 MONTANA ST   90026
  George Devall,Jr., prin.
Lorena Street ES, 1015 S LORENA ST   90023
  Lucille Derrig, prin.
Loreto Street ES, 3408 ARROYO SECO AVE   90065
  John Shambra, prin.
Los Angeles New ES, 3330 W PICO BLVD   90019
  Joe Miraglia, prin.
Los Feliz ES
  1740 N NEW HAMPSHIRE AVE   90027
  Jack Sarkisian, prin.
Loyola Village ES, 8821 VILLANOVA ST   90045
  Daniel Basalone, prin.
Magnola Avenue ES, 1626 ORCHARD AVE   90006
  Patricia Miller, prin.
Main Street ES, 129 E 53RD ST   90011
  Marvin McMahan, prin.
Malabar Street ES, 3200 MALABAR ST   90063
  Conrad Boubion, prin.
Manchester Avenue ES, 661 W 87TH ST   90044
  Bernie Goldstein, prin.
Manhattan Place ES, 1850 W 96TH ST   90047
  Joenicey Titus, prin.
Mar Vista ES, 3330 GRANVILLE AVE   90066
  Consuelo Garcia, prin.
Marianna Avenue ES, 4215 GLEASON ST   90063
  Robert Venegas, prin.
Marvin ES, 2411 S MARVIN AVE   90016
  Barbara Boudreaux, prin.
Mayberry Street ES, 2414 MAYBERRY ST   90026
  Andrea Allen, prin.
McKinley Avenue ES
  7812 MCKINLEY AVE   90001
  Alvis Andrews, prin.
Melrose Avenue ES, 731 N DETROIT ST   90046
  Helen Lomax, prin.
Menlo Avenue ES, 4156 MENLO AVE   90037
  Donald Marzullo, prin.
Micheltorena Street ES
  1511 MICHELTORENA ST   90026
  Eugene Sabin, prin.
Miller ES, 830 W 77TH ST   90044
  Ray Jones, prin.
Miramonte ES, 1400 E 68YH ST   90001
  Elma LaPointe, prin.
Monte Vista Street ES
  5423 MONTE VISTA ST   90042
  Emil Espinosa,Jr., prin.
Mt. Washington ES
  3981 SAN RAFAEL AVE   90065
  Patrcia Cobb, prin.
Multonomah Street ES
  2101 N INDIANA ST   90032
  Gilbert Gillogly, prin.
Murchison Street ES
  1501 MURCHISON ST   90033
  Jeanne Yamamoto, prin.
Nevada Avenue ES, 1569 E 32ND ST   90011
  David Sanchez, prin.
Nevin Avenue ES, 1569 E 32ND ST   90011
  Louis Owens, prin.
Ninety-Eighth Street ES, 5431 W 98TH ST   90045
  James Campbell, prin.

Ninety-Fifth Street ES, 1109 W 96TH ST   90044
  Orpheus Jones, prin.
Ninety-Ninth Street ES
  9900 WADSWORTH AVE   90002
  Mattye Fegan, prin.
Ninety-Second Street ES, 9211 GRAPE ST   90002
  Michael Martin, prin.
Ninety-Seventh Street ES, 419 W 98TH ST   90003
  Charles Barrett, prin.
Ninety-Sixth Street ES, 1471 E 96TH ST   90002
  Carol Epting, prin.
Ninety-Third Street ES, 330 E 93RD ST   90003
  Arne Rubenstein, prin.
Ninth Street ES, 829 TOWNE AVE   90021
  Betty Peifer, prin.
Normandie Avenue ES
  4505 RAYMOND AVE   90037 – Judith Willis, prin.
Norwood Street ES, 2020 OAK ST   90007
  Angelene Kasza, prin.
Overland Avenue ES, 10650 ASHBY AVE   90064
  Suzanne DiJulio, prin.
Palms ES, 3520 MOTOR AVE   90034
  Joseph Stock, prin.
Parmelee Avenue ES, 1338 E 76TH PLACE   90001
  Dorothy Padilla, prin.
Plasencia ES, 1321 CORTEZ ST   90026
  Lawrence Gonzales, prin.
Queen Anne Place ES
  1212 QUEEN ANNE PLACE   90019
  James Smith, prin.
Ramona ES, 1133 N MARIPOSA AVE   90029
  Susan Arcaris, prin.
Raymond Avenue ES
  7511 RAYMOND AVE   90044
  Eloise Pritchett, prin.
Richland Avenue ES
  11562 RICHLAND AVE   90064
  Melanie Deutsch, prin.
Riggin ES, 4865 E 1ST ST   90022
  Morris Hamasaki, prin.
Ritter ES, 11108 WATTS AVE   90059
  Eloise Blanton, prin.
Rockdale ES, 1321 YOSEMITE DRIVE   90041
  Elizabeth Castaneda, prin.
Roscomare Road ES
  2425 ROSCOMARE ROAD   90077
  Rosemary Lucente, prin.
Rosemont Avenue ES
  421 ROSEMONT AVE   90026
  Elmen Langham, prin.
Rosewood Avenue ES, 503 N CROFT AVE   90048
  Jack Silas, prin.
Rowan ES, 600 S ROWAN AVE   90023
  Harold Bertrand,Jr., prin.
Russell ES, 1263 FIRESTONE BLVD   90001
  Paul Carson, prin.
San Pascual Avenue ES
  815 SAN PASCUAL AVE   90042
  Marjorie Heppner, prin.
San Pedro Street ES
  1635 S SAN PEDRO ST   90015
  Amparo Cazares, prin.
Santa Monica Boulevard ES
  1022 N VAN NESS AVE   90038
  Albert Arnold, prin.
Saturn Street ES, 5360 SATURN ST   90019
  Joan Humphrey, prin.
Second Street ES, 1942 E 2ND ST   90033
  Alma Monroe, prin.
Selma Avenue ES, 6611 SELMA AVE   90028
  Santa Campuzano, prin.
Seventh-Fourth Street ES, 2112 W 74TH ST   90047
  Ann Hayes, prin.
Seventy-Fifth Street ES, 142 W 75TH ST   90003
  Patricia Turner, prin.
Shenandoah Street ES
  2450 S SHENANDOAH ST   90034
  Nathalee Evans, prin.
Sheridan Street ES, 416 CORNWELL ST   90033
  Maria Ott, prin.
Short Avenue ES, 12814 MAXELLA AVE   90066
  Harold Klein, prin.
Sierra Park ES, 3170 BUDAU AVE   90032
  John Schroeder, prin.
Sierra Vista MS, 4342 ALPHA ST   90032
  Seth Sandberg, prin.
Sixth Avenue ES, 3109 6TH AVE   90018
  Willa Davis, prin.
Sixty Eighth Street ES, 612 W 68TH ST   90044
  Louvenia Jenkins, prin.
Sixty-First Street ES, 6020 S FIGUEROA ST   90003
  Dolores Kaneshina, prin.
Sixty-Sixth Street ES
  6600 S SAN PEDRO ST   90003
  Carmen Garner, prin.
Solano Avenue ES, 615 SOLANO AVE   90012
  Judith Lazzarini, prin.
Soto Street ES, 1020 S SOTO ST   90023
  Natalie Gamex, prin.
South Park ES, 8510 TOWNE AVE   90003
  Barbara Langford, prin.
Sterry ES, 1730 CORINTH AVE   90025
  Sumoy Quon, prin.
Sunrise ES, 2821 E 7TH ST   90023
  Esther McShane, prin.
Tenth Street ES, 1000 GRATTAN ST   90015
  Diana Johnston, prin.
Third Street ES, 201 S JUNE ST   90004
  Barbara Lake, prin.
Thirty-Sixth Street ES, 17731 W 36TH ST   90018
  Marvin Silver, prin.
Toland Way ES, 4545 TOLAND WAY   90041
  Chester Ambrose, prin.

Trinity Street ES, 3736 TRINITY ST   90011
  Ruth Drye, prin.
Twentieth Street ES, 1353 E 20TH ST   90011
  Josephine Miles, prin.
Twenty-Eighth Street ES
  2807 STANFORD AVE   90011
  Haruko Morita, prin.
Union Avenue ES
  150 S BURLINGTON AVE   90057
  Richard Torchia, prin.
Utah Street ES, 255 N CLARENCE ST   90033
  Cynthia Carter, prin.
Valley View ES
  6921 WOODROW WILSON DRIVE   90068
  Sandra Coffey, prin.
Van Ness Avenue ES
  501 N VAN NESS AVE   90004 – Alan McCall, prin.
Vermont Avenue ES, 1435W W 27TH ST   90007
  Madelon Yamamoto, prin.
Vernon City ES, 2360 E VERNON AVE   90058
  Esther Macias, prin.
Vine Street ES, 955 VINE ST   90038
  Edwina Fields, prin.
Virginia Road ES, 2925 VIRGINIA ROAD   90016
  Adron Brown, prin.
Wadsworth Avenue ES, 981 E 41ST ST   90011
  Victor Placeres, prin.
Walgrove Avenue ES
  1630 WALGROVE AVE   90066
  Doshia Monroe, prin.
Warner Avenue ES, 615 HOLMBY AVE   90024
  Sheila Newman, prin.
Weemes ES, 1260 W 36TH PLACE   90007
  Mary Latimore, prin.
Weigand Avenue ES, 10401 WEIGAND AVE   90002
  Jose Velazquez, prin.
West Athens ES, 1110 W 119TH ST   90044
  Willie Washington,Jr., prin.
West Vernon Avenue ES
  4312 S GRAND AVE   90037 – Elyse Sullivan, prin.
Western Avenue ES, 1724 W 53RD ST   90062
  Linda Kim, prin.
Westport Heights ES, 6011 W 79TH ST   90045
  James Campbell, prin.
Westwood ES, 2050 SELBY AVE   90025
  Michelle Bennett, prin.
Wilshire Crest ES, 5241 W OLYMPIC BLVD   90036
  Evelyn Osborne, prin.
Wilton Place ES, 745 S WILTON PLACE   90005
  Emmett Dorough, prin.
Windsor Hills ES, 5215 OVERDALE DRIVE   90043
  Genova Moore, prin.
Wonderland Avenue ES
  8510 WONDERLAND AVE   90046
  Julia Tyler, prin.
Woodcrest ES, 1151 W 109TH ST   90044
  Renee Jackson, prin.
Yorkdale ES, 5657 MERIDIAN ST   90042
  Raymond Halverson, prin.
Other Schools – See Bell, Canoga Park, Carson,
  Chatsworth, Cudahy, Culver City, Encino, Gardena,
  Granada Hills, Harbor City, Huntington Park,
  Inglewood, Lakeview Terrace, Lomita, Long Beach,
  Maywood, Mission Hills, Monterey Park, North
  Hollywood, Northridge, Pacific Palisades, Pacoima,
  Panorama City, Reseda, San Fernando, San Pedro,
  Santa Monica, Sepulveda, Sherman Oaks, South
  Gate, Studio City, Sunland, Sun Valley, Sylmar,
  Tarzana, Topanga, Torrance, Tujunga, Van Nuys,
  Venice, West Hollywood, Wilmington, Woodland
  Hills

Montebello USD
Supt. – See Montebello
Eastmont ES, 630 LEONARD AVE   90022
  Joseph Gascon, prin.
Montebello Park ES
  6300 NORTHSIDE DRIVE   90022
  Anita Quintanar, prin.
Winter Gardens ES, 1277 CLELA AVE   90022
  Naomi Katayama, prin.

Alex Pilibos Armenian School
  1615 N ALEXANDRIA AVE   90027
Holy Cross School, 104 W 47TH PL   90037
Hughes Christian Baptist School
  1017 W 60TH PL   90044
Immaculate Heart MS
  5515 FRANKLIN AVE   90028
Le Lycee Francias De Los Angeles
  3261 OVERLAND AVE   90034
Los Feliz Hills School, 4155 RUSSELL AVE   90027
Mace Kingsley Prep Academy
  650 MICHELTORENA ST   90026
Newbridge School
  1619 S ROBERTSON BLVD   90035
Pilgrim School
  540 S COMMONWEALTH AVE   90020
St. Mary Magdalen ES
  1223 S CORNING ST   90035
West Coast Talmudical-Seminary
  7215 WARING AVE   90046
All Saints ES, 3420 PORTOLA AVE   90032
Arshag Dickranian Armenian School
  1200 N CAHUENGA BLVD   90038
Ascension Catholic ES, 500 W 111TH PL   90044
Ascension Lutheran ES, 5820 WEST BLVD   90043
Assumption ES, 3016 WINTER ST   90063
Berkeley Hall ES
  16000 MULHOLLAND DR   90049
Beverly Christian ES, 345 S WOODS AVE   90022
Blessed Sacrament ES
  6641 W SUNSET BLVD   90028
Cathedral Chapel ES, 755 S COCHRAN AVE   90036

Center for Early Education ES
  563 N ALFRED ST 90048
Christ the King ES, 617 N ARDEN BLVD 90004
Covenant Lutheran ES, 310 W 95TH ST 90003
Creative Learning ES
  2320 W MARTIN L KING BLVD 90008
Curtis School Foundation
  15871 MULHOLLAND DR 90049
Divine Savior ES, 624 CYPRESS AVE 90065
Dolores Mission ES, 170 S GLESS ST 90033
East Los Angeles Light & Life Christn ES
  207 S DACOTAH ST 90063
First Church of God Christian ES
  2941 W 70TH ST 90043
First Lutheran ES, 3119 W 6TH ST 90020
First Lutheran ES of Culver City
  3754 DUNN DR 90034
Fryer Yavneh Hebrew Academy
  7353 BEVERLY BLVD 90036
Good Shepherd Lutheran ES
  6338 N FIGUEROA ST 90042
Grace Lutheran ES, 936 W VERNON AVE 90037
Hollywood Little Red School House
  1248 N HIGHLAND AVE 90038
Holy Name of Jesus Catholic ES
  1955 W JEFFERSON BLVD 90018
Holy Spirit ES, 1418 S BURNSIDE AVE 90019
Holy Trinity ES, 3716 BOYCE AVE 90039
Immaculate Conception ES
  830 GREEN AVE 90017
Immaculate Heart of Mary ES
  1055 N ALEXANDRIA AVE 90029
International Childrens ES
  2325 THURMAN AVE 90016
Los Angeles Hankook Academy
  4900 WILSHIRE BLVD 90010
Los Angeles Union SDA ES
  846 E EL SEGUNDO BLVD 90059
Marina Light of Life ES
  12606 CULVER BLVD 90066
Maryknoll ES, 222 S HEWITT ST 90012
Marymount JHS, 12001 W SUNSET BLVD 90049
Miracle Baptist Christian ES
  8300 S CENTRAL AVE 90001
Mirman School for Gifted Children
  16180 MULHOLLAND DR 90049
Mother of Sorrows ES, 100 W 87TH PL 90003
Nativity ES, 943 W 57TH ST 90037
Noahs Ark Christian ES
  221 S JUANITA AVE 90004
Normandie Christian Schoolof Los Angeles
  6306 S NORMANDIE AVE 90044
Notre Dame Academy
  2911 OVERLAND AVE 90064
Our Lady Help of Christian ES
  2024 DARWIN AVE 90031
Our Lady of Guadalupe School Rosehill
  4522 BROWNE AVE 90032
Our Lady of Guadalupe ES
  436 N HAZARD AVE 90063
Our Lady of Loretto ES, 258 N UNION AVE 90026
Our Lady of Lourdes ES
  315 S EASTMAN AVE 90063
Our Lady of Rosary Talpa ES
  411 S EVERGREEN AVE 90033
Our Lady of Soledad ES, 4545 DOZIER AVE 90022
Our Mother of Good Counsel ES
  4622 AMBROSE AVE 90027
Our Saviors Lutheran ES, 4270 W 6TH ST 90020
Precious Blood ES
  307 S OCCIDENTAL BLVD 90057
Redeemer Alternative ES
  900 E ROSECRANS AVE 90059
Redeemer Baptist ES
  10792 NATIONAL BLVD 90064
Resurrection ES, 3360 OPAL ST 90023
Sacred Heart ES, 2109 SICHEL ST 90031
San Antonio Da Padua ES, 1500 BRIDGE ST 90033
San Miguel ES, 2270 E 108TH ST 90059
Santa Isabel ES, 2424 WHITTIER BLVD 90023
Santa Teresita ES, 2646 ZONAL AVE 90033
Sephardic Hebrew Academy
  310 HUNTLEY DR 90048
Sinai Akiba Academy
  10400 WILSHIRE BLVD 90024
St. Agnes ES, 1428 W ADAMS BLVD 90007
St. Aloysius ES, 2037 NADEAU ST 90001
St. Alphonsus ES, 552 AMALIA AVE 90022
St. Ambrose ES, 1265 N FAIRFAX AVE 90046
St. Anastasia ES, 8631 STANMOOR DR 90045
St. Anselm ES, 7019 S VAN NESS AVE 90047
St. Bernadette ES, 4196 MARLTON AVE 90008
St. Bernard ES, 3254 VERDUGO RD 90065
St. Brendan Catholic ES
  238 S MANHATTAN PL 90004
St. Casimir ES, 2714 ST GEORGE ST 90027
St. Cecilia ES, 4224 S NORMANDIE AVE 90037
St. Columbkilles ES, 131 W 64TH ST 90003
St. Dominic ES, 2005 MERTON AVE 90041
St. Eugene ES, 9521 HAAS AVE 90047
St. Frances Cabrini ES
  1428 W IMPERIAL HWY 90047
St. Francis of Assisi ES
  1550 MALTMAN AVE 90026
St. Gerard Majella ES
  4451 INGLEWOOD BLVD 90066
St. Gregory Nazianzen ES
  911 S NORTON AVE 90019
St. Ignatius of Loyola ES
  6025 MONTE VISTA ST 90042
St. James Wilshire ES
  625 S ST ANDREWS PL 90005
St. Jerome ES, 5580 THORNBUM ST 90045
St. Joan of Arc ES, 11561 GATEWAY BLVD 90064

St. John the Evangel ES
  6102 S VICTORIA AVE 90043
St. Lawrence of Brindisi ES
  10044 COMPTON AVE 90002
St. Malachy Catholic ES, 1228 E 81ST ST 90001
St. Martin of Tours ES
  11955 W SUNSET BLVD 90049
St. Mary Catholic ES, 416 S ST LOUIS ST 90033
St. Michael ES, 1027 W 87TH ST 90044
St. Odilia ES, 5300 HOOPER AVE 90011
St. Paul the Apostle ES, 1536 SELBY AVE 90024
St. Paul's ES, 1908 S BRONSON AVE 90018
St. Raphael ES, 924 W 70TH ST 90044
St. Sebastian ES, 1430 FEDERAL AVE 90025
St. Teresa of Avila ES, 2215 FARGO ST 90039
St. Thomas the Apostle ES
  2632 W 15TH ST 90006
St. Timothy ES, 10479 W PICO BLVD 90064
St. Turibius ES, 1524 ESSEX ST 90021
St. Vincent ES, 2333 S FIGUEROA ST 90007
Sycamore Grove ES, 4900 N FIGUEROA ST 90042
Transfiguration ES, 4020 ROXTON AVE 90008
Trinity Lutheran School
  987 S GRAMERCY PL 90019
United World International Learning Scho
  5125 CRENSHAW BLVD 90043
Victory Baptist Day ES, P O BOX 11038 90011
Visitation ES, 8740 EMERSON AVE 90045
West Angeles Christian Academy
  3010 CRENSHAW BLVD 90016
Westchester Lutheran ES
  7831 S SEPULVEDA BLVD 90045
Westchester Neighborhood ES
  5820 W MANCHESTER AVE 90045
Westland ES, 16200 MULHOLLAND DR 90049
Westminster Academy
  1495 COLORADO BLVD 90041
White Memorial Advent ES
  1605 NEW JERSEY ST 90033
Wise Temple Day ES
  15500 STEPHEN S WISE DR 90077
Woodcrest Nazarene Chrstian ES
  10936 S NORMANDIE AVE 90044
Yeshiva Isacsohn/Torath Emeth Academy
  540 N LA BREA AVE 90036

Los Banos, Merced Co., Pop. Code 7
Los Banos USD
  Sch. Sys. Enr. Code 5
  Supt. – Robert Brickman
    901 E PACHECO BLVD 93635
  JHS, 659 K ST 93635 – Michael Villalta, prin.
  Charleston ES, P O BOX 991 93635
    Janine Brauer, prin.
  ES, 1260 7TH ST 93635 – Janis Barr, prin.
  Miano ES, 1129 B ST 93635 – Richard Miller, prin.
  Miller ES, 545 W L ST 93635
    Betty Meacham, prin.
  Volta ES, 24307 INGOMAR GRADE 93635
    Sarah Sturgeon, prin.

Our Lady of Fatima ES, 1625 CENTER AVE 93635

Los Gatos, Santa Clara Co., Pop. Code 8
Campbell Un. ESD
  Supt. – See Campbell
  Rolling Hills MS, 1585 MORE AVE 95030
    Philip Short, prin.
Lakeside JESD
  Sch. Sys. Enr. Code 2
  Supt. – Hal Kelban, 19621 BLACK ROAD 95030
  Lakeside ES, 19621 BLACK ROAD 95030
    Hal Kelban, prin.
Loma Prieta J Un. ESD
  Sch. Sys. Enr. Code 3
  Supt. – Kenneth Simpkins
    23845 SUMMIT ROAD 95030
  English MS, 23800 SUMMIT ROAD 95030
    Ken Simpkins, prin.
  Loma Prieta ES, 23845 SUMMIT ROAD 95030
    Carole Carpenter, prin.
Los Gatos Un. ESD
  Sch. Sys. Enr. Code 4
  Supt. – Stephen Benbow, P O BOX 367 95031
  Fisher JHS, P O BOX 367 95031 – Rob Lowry, prin.
  Blossom Hill ES
    16400 BLOSSOM HILL ROAD 95032
    Sue Russ, prin.
  Daves Avenue ES, 17770 DAVES AVE 95030
    Maury Nelson, prin.
  Lexington ES
    19700 SANTA CRUZ HIGHWAY 95030
    Wendy Feltham, prin.
  Van Meter ES, 16445 LOS GATOS BLVD 95032
    Ron Harder, prin.
Union ESD
  Supt. – See San Jose
  Alta Vista ES, 200 BLOSSOM VALLEY RD 95030
    Lucius Jenkins, prin.

Los Gatos Christian JHS, 16845 HICKS RD 95032
Carden School of Almaden South Valley
  220 BELGATOS RD 95032
Hillbrook ES, 16000 MARCHMONT DR 95032
Los Gatos Christian School/Williams Camp
  16845 HICKS RD 95032
St. Mary's ES, 30 LYNDON AVE 95030
Valley Christian ES
  220 KENSINGTON WAY 95032

Los Molinos, Tehama Co., Pop. Code 3
Lassen View Un. ESD
  Sch. Sys. Enr. Code 2
  Supt. – Raymond Barber
    10818 HIGHWAY 99 E 96055
  Lassen View ES, 10818 HIGHWAY 99 E 96055
    Raymond Barber, prin.

Los Molinos USD
  Sch. Sys. Enr. Code 3
  Supt. – A. R. Tolman, P O BOX 609 96055
  ES, P O BOX 7 96055 – David Pilger, prin.
  Other Schools – See Vina

Los Nietos, Los Angeles Co., Pop. Code 6
Los Nietos ESD
  Supt. – See Whittier
  MS, 11425 RIVERA ROAD 90606
    Charles Menzies, prin.

Los Olivos, Santa Barbara Co., Pop. Code 2
Los Olivos ESD
  Sch. Sys. Enr. Code 2
  Supt. – Gates Foss, P O BOX 208 93441
  ES, P O BOX 208 93441 – Gates Foss, prin.

Los Osos, San Luis Obispo Co., Pop. Code 4
San Luis Coastal USD
  Supt. – See San Luis Obispo
  JHS, 1555 EL MORRO AVE 93402
    Greg Pruitt, prin.
  Sunnyside ES, 880 MANZANITA DRIVE 93402
    F. Lacey, prin.

Lost Hills, Kern Co.
Lost Hills Un. ESD
  Sch. Sys. Enr. Code 2
  Supt. – John Bogie, P O BOX 158 93249
  MS, P O BOX 158 93249 – David Day, prin.
  ES, P O BOX 158 93249 – David Day, prin.

Lower Lake, Lake Co., Pop. Code 3
Konocti USD
  Supt. – See Clearlake
  Oak Hill MS, P O BOX 719 95457
    Susan Daly, prin.
  ES, P O BOX 719 95457 – Scott Mahoney, prin.

Loyalton, Sierra Co., Pop. Code 4
Sierra-Plumas JUSD
  Supt. – See Downieville
  IS, P O BOX 127 96118 – Michael Filippini, prin.
  ES, P O BOX 127 96118 – Joe Nocero, prin.

Lucerne, Lake Co., Pop. Code 4
Lucerne ESD
  Sch. Sys. Enr. Code 2
  Supt. – Ed Costa, P O BOX 1083 95458
  ES, P O BOX 1083 95458 – Ed Costa, prin.

Lucerne Valley, San Bernardino Co.
Lucerne Valley Un. SD
  Sch. Sys. Enr. Code 3
  Supt. – Ron Peavy, HCR BOX 900 92356
  MS, P O BOX 900 92356 – Rob Weaver, prin.
  ES, P O BOX 900 92356 – Howard Collins, prin.

Lynwood, Los Angeles Co., Pop. Code 8
Lynwood USD
  Sch. Sys. Enr. Code 7
  Supt. – LaVoneia Steele, 11331 PLAZA ST 90262
  Hosler JHS, 11300 SPRUCE ST 90262
    Rob Schmidt, prin.
  Abbott ES, 5260 CLARK ST 90262
    Louis Byrd, prin.
  Lincoln ES, 11031 STATE ST 90262
    Joyce Ortiz, prin.
  Lindbergh ES, 3300 CEDAR AVE 90262
    Paul Rourman, prin.
  Lugo ES, 4345 PENDLETON AVE 90262
    Armando Rocchi, prin.
  Rogers ES, 11220 DUNCAN AVE 90262
    Cheryl White, prin.
  Roosevelt ES, 10835 MALLISON AVE 90262
    Bernice Jacobs, prin.
  Twain ES, 12315 THORSON AVE 90262
    Louis Garcia, prin.
  Washington ES, 4225 SANBORN AVE 90262
    Gary Furuno, prin.
  Wilson ES, 11700 SCHOOL ST 90262
    Robert Simpson, prin.

Lynwood Adventist ES
  11011 HARRIS AVE 90262
St. Emydius ES, 10990 CALIFORNIA AVE 90262
St. Paul Lutheran ES, 3801 CORTLAND ST 90262
St. Philip Neri ES, 12522 STONEACRE AVE 90262

Mc Cloud, Siskiyou Co., Pop. Code 4
McCloud Un. ESD
  Sch. Sys. Enr. Code 2
  Supt. – William Mashburn
    332 HAMILTON WAY 96057
  ES, P O BOX 700 96057 – William Mashburn, prin.

Macdoel, Siskiyou Co.
Butte Valley USD
  Supt. – See Dorris
  ES, P O BOX 153 96058 – Larry Butler, prin.

Mc Farland, Kern Co., Pop. Code 6
McFarland USD
  Sch. Sys. Enr. Code 4
  Supt. – Ronald Huebert, 401 5TH ST 93250
  MS, 356 KERN AVE 93250 – Earl Guinn, prin.
  Browning Road ES, 410 E PERKINS AVE 93250
    Roberto Cardenas, prin.

Kern Avenue ES, 356 KERN AVE 93250
Tim Scanlon, prin.

Mc Kinleyville, Humboldt Co., Pop. Code 4
Mc Kinleyville Un.ESD
Sch. Sys. Enr. Code 4
Supt. – Larry Georgianna, P O BOX 2067 95521
JHS, P O BOX 2067 95521
Denis Chamberlain, prin.
Dows Prairie ES 95521 – Roy Fields, prin.
Morris ES 95521 – Bill Guimond, prin.

Mc Kittrick, Kern Co.
Belridge ESD
Sch. Sys. Enr. Code 1
Supt. – Gary Peterson, HRC BOX 900 93251
Belridge ES, HCR ROUTE BOX 900 93251
Gary Peterson, prin.

McKittrick ESD
Sch. Sys. Enr. Code 1
Supt. – Alyce Willis, P O BOX 277 93251
ES, P O BOX 277 93251 – Alyce Willis, prin.

Madera, Madera Co., Pop. Code 7
Madera USD
Sch. Sys. Enr. Code 7
Supt. – Thomas Riley
1902 HOWARD ROAD 93637
Jefferson JHS, 1407 SUNSET AVE 93637
James Morgan, prin.
Adams ES, 1822 NATIONAL AVE 93637
Donald Knox, prin.
Alpha ES, 900 STADIUM ROAD 93637
Jack Netherton, prin.
Berenda ES, 26820 CLUB DR 93638
Alvin Stansell, prin.
Dixieland ES, 18440 ROAD 19 93637
Carles Beckett, prin.
Eastin-Arcola ES, 29551 AVE 8 93637
Angela Hill, prin.
Howard ES, 13878 ROAD 21 1/2 93637
(—), prin.
La Vina ES, 8594 ROAD 23 93637
Betty Scalise, prin.
Millview ES, 1609 CLINTON ST 93638
Jerry English, prin.
Monroe ES, 1819 N LAKE ST 93638
Marisa Moger, prin.
Ripperdan ES, 26133 AVE 7 93637
Jean Belanger, prin.
Sierra Vista ES, 917 E OLIVE AVE 93638
Larry Goossen, prin.
Washington ES, 509 E SOUTH ST 93638
J. Adams, prin.
Webster ES, 36477 RUTH AVE 93638
C. Wachtel, prin.

Spring Valley ESD
Supt. – See O'Neals
Sierra View ES, 16436 PAULA ROAD 93638
William Scheidt, prin.

St. Joachim ES, 400 W 4TH ST 93637

Magalia, Butte Co.
Paradise USD
Supt. – See Paradise
Pines ES, P O BOX 1696 95954
Laura Dearden, prin.

Malibu, Los Angeles Co., Pop. Code 6
Santa Monica-Malibu USD
Supt. – See Santa Monica
Malibu Park ES, 30215 MORNINGVIEW DR 90265
Bill Bonozo, prin.
Webster ES, 3602 WINTER CANYON ROAD 90265
Ron Merriman, prin.

Our Lady of Malibu ES
3625 WINTER CANYON RD 90265

Mammoth Lakes, Mono Co.
Mammoth USD
Sch. Sys. Enr. Code 3
Supt. – Richard McAteer, P O BOX 1320 93546
Mammoth ES, P O BOX 1320 93546
Dianne Daugherty, prin.

Manchester, Mendocino Co.
Manchester Un. ESD
Sch. Sys. Enr. Code 1
Supt. – (—), P O BOX 98 95459
ES, P O BOX 98 95459 – William Borofka, prin.

Manhattan Beach, Los Angeles Co., Pop. Code 8
Manhattan Beach City ESD
Sch. Sys. Enr. Code 4
Supt. – Douglas Keeler, 1501 REDONDO DR 90266
IS, 1431 15TH ST 90266 – Billie Jean Knight, prin.
Grand View ES, 455 25TH ST 90266
Anita Robertson, prin.
Meadows Avenue ES
1200 MEADOWS AVE 90266
Ernest Donlou, prin.
Pacific ES, 110 S ROWELL 90266
Christine Norvell, prin.
Pennekamp ES, 110 S ROWELL 90266
Lois Woodall, prin.

American Martyrs ES, 1701 LAUREL AVE 90266

Manteca, San Joaquin Co., Pop. Code 7
Manteca USD
Sch. Sys. Enr. Code 7
Supt. – Harold Hughes, P O BOX 32 95336

Golden West ES, 1111 N MAIN ST 95336
Joann Flinn, prin.
Hafley ES, 848 NORTHGATE DRIVE 95336
Joseph Wickham, prin.
Lincoln ES, 750 E YOSEMITE AVE 95336
Marion Elliott, prin.
Mcparland ES, 1601 NORTHGATE DR 95336
Delmer Derrick, prin.
New Haven ES, 14600 S AUSTIN ROAD 95336
Norman Hixon, prin.
Nile Garden ES, 5700 NILE ROAD 95336
Joe Cook, prin.
Sequoia ES, 710 MARTHA ST 95336
Donald Vos, prin.
Shasta ES, 7505 E EDISON ST 95336
Richard Mello, prin.
Yosemite ES, 737 W YOSEMITE AVE 95336
Harriet Myrick, prin.
Other Schools – See French Camp, Lathrop

Manteca Christian School
486 BUTTON AVE 95336
St. Anthony's ES, 525 E NORTH ST 95336

Manton, Tehama Co.
Manton JUn. ESD
Sch. Sys. Enr. Code 1
Supt. – (—), P O BOX 2 96059
ES, P O BOX 2 96058 – R. Morrall, prin.

Maricopa, Kern Co., Pop. Code 3
Maricopa USD
Sch. Sys. Enr. Code 2
Supt. – Richard Tucker
RURAL ROUTE 02 BOX 618 93252
ES, HCR ROUTE 02 BOX 618 93252
Pamela Sanders, prin.

Marina, Monterey Co., Pop. Code 7
Monterey Peninsula USD
Supt. – See Monterey
Los Arboles MS, 294 HILLCREST AVE 93933
J. Wiles, prin.
Crumpton ES, 460 CARMEL AVE 93933
Diane Lingle, prin.
Marina Del Mar ES, 3066 LAKE DRIVE 93933
Amy Jones, prin.
Marina Vista MS, 390 CARMEL AVE 93933
Tyrus Laster, prin.
Olson ES, 261 BEACH ROAD 93933
Robert Stadille, prin.

Mariposa, Mariposa Co., Pop. Code 3
Mariposa County USD
Sch. Sys. Enr. Code 4
Supt. – George Barandse, P O BOX 8 95338
JHS, P O BOX 8 95338 – Judy Eppler, prin.
ES, P O BOX 8 95338 – Dale Alger, prin.
Woodland ES, 3394 WOODLAND DRIVE 95338
James Archer, prin.
Other Schools – See Cathey's Valley, Coulterville, El
Portal, La Grange, Yosemite Park

Markleeville, Alpine Co.
Alpine County USD
Sch. Sys. Enr. Code 2
Supt. – James Parsons
RURAL ROUTE 01 BOX 42B 96120
Diamond Valley ES
RURAL ROUTE 01 BOX 42B 96120
Gerald Herrich, prin.
Other Schools – See Bear Valley

Martinez, Contra Costa Co., Pop. Code 7
Martinez USD
Sch. Sys. Enr. Code 5
Supt. – Patricia Crocker, 921 SUSANA ST 94553
JHS, COURT & WARREN STS 94553
J. Adams, prin.
Las Juntas ES, 4105 PACHECO BLVD 94553
Robert Buoncristiani, prin.
ES, 850 JONES ST 94553
Richard McLaughlin, prin.
Swett ES
4955 ALHAMBRA VALLEY ROAD 94553
Charles Fereira, prin.

Mt. Diablo USD
Supt. – See Concord
Hidden Valley ES, 500 GLACIER DRIVE 94553
Bill Redman, prin.

Patchins ES, 1200 PALM AVE 94553
St. Catherine of Siena ES, 604 MELLUS ST 94553

Marysville, Yuba Co., Pop. Code 6
Marysville JUSD
Sch. Sys. Enr. Code 6
Supt. – Paul Britton, 1919 B ST 95901
Alicia IS, 1208 PASADO ROAD 95901
Jack Stokes, prin.
Foothill MS, 5351 FRUITLAND ROAD 95901
Robert Wilkerson, prin.
McKenney IS, 19TH & HUSTON STS 95901
Kitty Tedrick, prin.
Arboga ES, 1686 BROADWAY ST 95901
Lee Limonoff, prin.
Cedar Lane ES, 841 CEDAR LANE 95901
Efton Pritchard, prin.
Cordua ES, 2830 HIGHWAY 20 95901
James Covert, prin.
Covillaud ES, SEVENTH & F STS 95901
James Covert, prin.
Kynoch ES, 19TH & AHERN STS 95901
Nancy Mack, prin.

Loma Rica ES
RURAL ROUTE 03 BOX 1750 95901
Dennis McGuire, prin.
Linda ES, 6180 DUNNING AVE 95901
Russell Killingsworth, prin.
Other Schools – See Browns Valley, Challenge,
Dobbins, Olivehurst, Smartville

Plumas ESD
Sch. Sys. Enr. Code 1
Supt. – Harvey Hurtt
2548 HOFFMAN-PLUMAS ROAD 95901
Plumas ES
2548 HOFFMAN-PLUMAS ROAD 95901
Harvey Hurtt, prin.

Notre Dame ES, 715 C ST 95901

Mather A F B, Sacramento Co.
Folsom-Cordova USD
Supt. – See Folsom
Kitty Hawk ES 95655 – Loretta Ashizawa, prin.
Mather Heights ES 95655
Loretta Ashizawa, prin.

Maxwell, Colusa Co., Pop. Code 3
Maxwell USD
Sch. Sys. Enr. Code 2
Supt. – Patrick Sinclair, P O BOX 788 95955
ES, 146 W NORTH ST 95955
Patrick Sinclair, prin.

Maywood, Los Angeles Co., Pop. Code 7
Los Angeles USD
Supt. – See Los Angeles
Fishburn Avenue ES, 5701 FISHBURN AVE 90270
Donald Fisher, prin.
Heliotrope Avenue ES
5911 WOODLAWN AVE 90270
Kenneth Miller, prin.
Loma Vista Avenue ES, 3629 E 58TH ST 90270
Joseph Bethel, prin.

Maywood Baptist Pilgrim School
3759 E 57TH ST 90270
St. Rose of Lima ES, 4422 E 60TH ST 90270

Meadow Vista, Placer Co.
Placer Hills Un. ESD
Sch. Sys. Enr. Code 4
Supt. – George Dunham, P O BOX 68 95722
Placer Hills ES, P O BOX 68 95722
Gary Cranfill, prin.
Other Schools – See Weimar

Mecca, Riverside Co.
Coachella Valley USD
Supt. – See Thermal
ES, P O BOX 747 92254 – Henry Gunter, prin.

Mendocino, Mendocino Co., Pop. Code 3
Mendocino USD
Sch. Sys. Enr. Code 3
Supt. – D. Kirkpatrick, P O BOX 1154 95460
MS, P O BOX 226 95460 – John Stafford, prin.
ES, P O BOX 226 95460 – Susan Franklin, prin.
Other Schools – See Comptche, Elk

Mendota, Fresno Co., Pop. Code 5
Mendota Un. ESD
Sch. Sys. Enr. Code 4
Supt. – Kulwant Singh Sidhu, 115 MCCABE 93640
McCabe JHS, 115 MCCABE 93640
Gilbert Rossette, prin.
McCabe MS, 115 MCCABE 93640
Joan Dallin, prin.
Washington ES, 1599 5TH ST 93640
Barbara Ward, prin.

Menlo Park, San Mateo Co., Pop. Code 8
Las Lomitas ESD
Sch. Sys. Enr. Code 3
Supt. – Charla Rolland
1011 ALTSCHUL AVE 94025
La Entrada MS, 2200 SHARON ROAD 94025
Duke Williams, prin.
Other Schools – See Atherton

Menlo Park City ESD
Sch. Sys. Enr. Code 4
Supt. – Martha Symonds, 1102 ELDER AVE 94025
Hillview MS, 1100 ELDER AVE 94025
Michael Moore, prin.
Oak Knoll ES, 1895 OAK KNOLL LANE 94025
Marilyn Franklin, prin.
Other Schools – See Atherton

Ravenswood City ESD
Supt. – See Palo Alto
Menlo Oaks MS, 475 POPE ST 94025
Vera Clark, prin.
Belle Haven ES, 415 IVY DRIVE 94025
Othene Thomas, prin.
Flood ES, 320 SHERIDAN DR 94025
Adela Cook, prin.
Willow Oaks ES, 620 WILLOW ROAD 94025
Gwen Gholson, prin.

Bethany Lutheran School
1095 CLOUD AVE 94025
Brooks ES, 2245 AVY AVE 94025
Nativity ES, 1250 LAUREL ST 94025
Peninsula School, Ltd.
920 PENINSULA WAY 94025
St. Joseph's ES, 50 EMILIE AVE 94025
St. Raymond's ES, 1211 ARBOR RD 94025
Woodland ES, 360 LA CUESTA DR 94025

Mentone, San Bernardino Co., Pop. Code 4
Redlands USD
Supt. – See Redlands
ES, 1320 CRAFTON AVE 92359
Carol Sanchez, prin.

Merced, Merced Co., Pop. Code 8
McSwain Un. ESD
Sch. Sys. Enr. Code 3
Supt. – Charles Galatro, 926 SCOTT ROAD 95340
McSwain ES, 926 SCOTT ROAD 95340
(—), prin.

Merced City ESD
Sch. Sys. Enr. Code 7
Supt. – Ronald Dangaran, 444 W 23RD ST 95340
Hoover IS, 800 E 26TH ST 95340
Kathleen Crookham, prin.
Rivera IS, 945 BUENA VISTA DRIVE 95348
Robert Wendel, prin.
Tenaya IS, 760 W 8TH ST 95340
Tom Parker, prin.
Burbank ES, 609 E ALEXANDER AVE 95340
Gil Garcia, prin.
Chenoweth ES, 3200 N PARSONS AVE 95340
Susan Peterson, prin.
Franklin ES, 2736 FRANKLIN ROAD 95348
Don Stowell, prin.
Fremont ES, 1120 W 22ND ST 95340
Audrey Robinson, prin.
Givens ES, 2900 GREEN ST 95340
Rosemary Duran, prin.
Gracey ES, 945 WEST AVE 95340
Judy Doyle, prin.
Muir ES, 300 W 26TH ST 95340 – Lou Exum, prin.
Peterson ES, 848 PIER ROAD 95340
Gloria Thomas, prin.
Sheehy ES, 1240 W 6TH ST 95340
Don Davey, prin.
Wright ES, 900 E 20TH ST 95340
Sylvia Fuller, prin.

Plainsburg ESD
Sch. Sys. Enr. Code 1
Supt. – James Tesone
3708 PLAINSBURG ROAD 95340
Plainsburg ES, 3708 PLAINSBURG ROAD 95340
James Tesone, prin.

Weaver Un. ESD
Sch. Sys. Enr. Code 4
Supt. – Steve Becker, 3076 E CHILDS AVE 95340
Weaver ES, 3076 E CHILDS AVE 95340
Everett Jones, prin.

Merced Christian ES, 3312 G ST 95340
Our Lady of Mercy ES, 1400 E 27TH ST 95340

Meridian, Sutter Co.
Meridian ESD
Sch. Sys. Enr. Code 1
Supt. – Harry Herkert, P O BOX 147 95957
ES, P O BOX 147 95957 – Harry Herkert, prin.

Winship ESD
Sch. Sys. Enr. Code 1
Supt. – John Leal, 4305 S MERIDIAN ROAD 95957
Winship ES, 4305 S MERIDIAN ROAD 95957
John Leal, prin.

Middletown, Lake Co., Pop. Code 3
Middletown USD
Sch. Sys. Enr. Code 4
Supt. – Robert Slaby, P O BOX 338 95461
MS, 15846 WARDLAW ST 95461
Linda Close, prin.
Cannon ES, 15846 WARDLAW ST 95461
Richard Giovannoli, prin.
Cobb Mountain ES, P O BOX 338 95461
Keller McDonald, prin.

Midway City, Orange Co., Pop. Code 4
Ocean View ESD
Supt. – See Huntington Beach
Star View ES, 8411 WORTHY DRIVE 92655
Karan Spane, prin.

Westminster ESD
Supt. – See Westminster
Demille ES, 15400 VAN BUREN ST 92655
Harvey Morris, prin.

Bethany Christian Academy
14782 EDEN ST 92655

Millbrae, San Mateo Co., Pop. Code 7
Millbrae ESD
Sch. Sys. Enr. Code 4
Supt. – Eve Bressler
825 MURCHISON DRIVE 94030
Taylor IS, 850 TAYLOR BLVD 94030
Sharon Fritz, prin.
Green Hills ES, 401 LUDEMAN LANE 94030
R. Edwards, prin.
Lomita Park ES, 200 SANTA HELENA AVE 94030
Marilyn Koczor, prin.
Meadows ES, 1101 HELEN DRIVE 94030
Eugene Van Duyn, prin.
Spring Valley ES, 817 MURCHISON DRIVE 94030
Leonard Sarkon, prin.

St. Dunstan's ES, 1150 MAGNOLIA AVE 94030

Mill Valley, Marin Co., Pop. Code 7
Mill Valley ESD
Sch. Sys. Enr. Code 4
Supt. – James McDonough, P O BOX 1089 94942

MS, P O BOX 1089 94942 – John Moulthrop, prin.
Old Mill ES, 352 THROCKMORTON AVE 94941
Ron Davis, prin.
Park ES, 360 E BLITHEDALE AVE 94941
James Derich, prin.
Strawberry Point ES
117 E STRAWBERRY DRIVE 94941
Judy Cooper, prin.
Tamalpais Valley ES, 350 BELL LANE 94941
Janie Teitelbaum, prin.

Mt. Tamalpais ES, 100 HARVARD AVE 94941

Millville, Shasta Co.
Millville ESD
Sch. Sys. Enr. Code 2
Supt. – Angela Davies
10650 BROOKDALE ROAD 96062
ES, 10650 BROOKDALE ROAD 96062
Angela Davis, prin.

Milpitas, Santa Clara Co., Pop. Code 6
Milpitas USD
Sch. Sys. Enr. Code 6
Supt. – John MacKay
1331 CALAVERAS BLVD 95035
Rancho Milpitas MS
1331 E CALAVERAS BLVD 95035
Patricia Dell, prin.
Russell MS, 1500 ESCUELA PKWY 95035
Charles Perotti, prin.
Burnett ES, 400 FANYON ST 95035
Michael Schadeck, prin.
Curtner ES, 275 REDWOOD AVE 95035
Judy Boyer, prin.
Pomery ES, 1505 ESCUELA PARKWAY 95035
Frank Hinebaugh, prin.
Randall ES, 1300 ESDEL 95035
Lawrence Lovato, prin.
Rose ES, 250 ROSWELL DR 95035
Lynne McCall, prin.
Sinnott ES, 2025 YELLOWSTONE AVE 95035
Martha Olivo, prin.
Spangler ES, 140 ABBOTT AVE 95035
Sandra MacKey, prin.
Weller ES, 345 BOULDER ST 95035
Frank Hill, prin.
Zanker ES, 1585 FALLEN LEAF DR 95035
Charles Starr, prin.

Calvary Assembly of God Foothill School
1115 AYER ST 95035
Rainbow Bridge School
1500 YOSEMITE DR 95035
St. John the Baptist School, 279 S MAIN ST 95035

Mineral, Tehama Co.
Mineral ESD
Sch. Sys. Enr. Code 1
Supt. – (—), P O BOX 130 96063
ES, P O BOX 11 96063 – David Harp, prin.

Mira Loma, Riverside Co.
Jurupa USD
Supt. – See Riverside
Sky Country ES, 5520 LUCRETIA AVE 91752
Laz Barreiro, prin.
Troth Street ES, 5565 TROTH ST 91752
Dick Sevaly, prin.

Miramonte, Fresno Co., Pop. Code 3
Kings Canyon JUSD
Supt. – See Reedley
ES, P O BOX 64 93641 – Walter Todd, prin.

Miranda, Humboldt Co.
Southern Humbolt JUSD
Supt. – See Garberville
JHS 95553 – Harlan Tucker, prin.

Mission Hills, Los Angeles Co., Pop. Code 5
Los Angeles USD
Supt. – See Los Angeles
San Jose Street ES, 14928 CLYMER ST 91345
James Owen, prin.

Mission Viejo, Orange Co., Pop. Code 8
Capistrano USD
Supt. – See San Juan Capistrano
Barcelona Hills ES
23000 VIA SANTA MARIA 92691
Don McNeff, prin.
Castille ES, 24042 VIA LA CORUNA 92691
Merle Smith, prin.
Hankey ES, 27252 NUBLES 92692
Shirley Martin, prin.
Newhart ES, 25001 OSO VIEJO 92692
James Henderson, prin.
Viejo ES, 26782 VIA GRANDE 92691
Richard Campbell, prin.

Saddleback Valley USD
Sch. Sys. Enr. Code 7
Supt. – P. Hartman, 25631 DISENO DRIVE 92691
La Paz IS, 25151 PRADERA DRIVE 92691
Robert McQueen, prin.
Los Alisos IS, 25171 MOOR AVE 92691
Tom Tullar, prin.
Cordillera ES, 25952 CORDILLERA DRIVE 92691
Mardell Skaggs, prin.
De Portola ES, 27031 PRELADOS DRIVE 92691
Chuck Prince, prin.
Del Cerro ES, 24382 REGINA ST 92691
George Schroer, prin.
Del Largo ES, 27181 ENTIDAD 92691
Tony Ignoffo, prin.

La Tierra ES, 24150 LINDLEY ST 92691
Bob Gaebel, prin.
Linda Vista ES, 25222 PERCIA DRIVE 92691
Patricia Insley, prin.
Montevideo ES, 24071 CARRILLO 92691
Jim Hamilton, prin.
O'Neil ES, 24701 SAN DOVAL LANE 92691
Waneta Norton, prin.
Yermo ES, 26400 TRABUCO RD 92691
Mike Delaney, prin.
Other Schools – See El Toro, Laguna Hills, Rancho
Santa Margarita, Trabuco Canyon

Stoneybrook Christian ES
26300 VIA ESCOLAR 92692

Modesto, Stanislaus Co., Pop. Code 9
Ceres USD
Supt. – See Ceres
Westport ES, 5218 S CARPENTER ROAD 95351
Bea Lingenfelter, prin.

Empire Un. ESD
Supt. – See Empire
Capistrano ES, 400 CAPISTRANO DRIVE 95354
Lynn McPeak, prin.
Sipherd ES, 3420 E ORANGEBURG AVE 95355
Gary McDaniel, prin.

Hart-Ransom Un. ESD
Sch. Sys. Enr. Code 2
Supt. – Dennis Boyer
3930 SHOEMAKE AVE 95351
Hart-Ransom ES, 3930 SHOEMAKE AVE 95351
Dennis Boyer, prin.

Modesto CSD
Sch. Sys. Enr. Code 8
Supt. – James Enochs, 426 LOCUST ST 95351
La Loma IS, 1800 ENCINA AVE 95354
Bruce Urban, prin.
Roosevelt IS, 1330 COLLEGE AVE 95350
Cameron McCune, prin.
Twain IS, 707 S EMERALD AVE 95351
Charles Darr, prin.
Beard ES, 915 BOWEN AVE 95350
Ken Arnold, prin.
Bret Harte ES, 909 BRET HARTE PLACE 95351
Ramiro Nava, prin.
Burbank ES, 1135 PARADISE ROAD 95351
Fred Rich, prin.
El Vista ES, 450 EL VISTA AVE 95354
Mark Lewis, prin.
Enslen ES, 515 COLDWELL AVE 95354
Dorothy David, prin.
Everett ES, 1530 MOUNT VERNON DRIVE 95350
Ken Narita, prin.
Fairview ES, 1937 W WHITMORE AVE 95351
Charles Dunning, prin.
Franklin MS, 120 S EMERALD AVE 95351
Lenore Shively, prin.
Franklin PS, 500 LOCUST ST 95351
Brad Vaughan, prin.
Fremont ES, 1220 W ORANGEBURG AVE 95350
Lynn Jamison, prin.
Garrison ES, 1811 TERESA ST 95350
Donella Silveira, prin.
Kirschen ES, 1111 HAMMOND ST 95351
Jerry Cooper, prin.
Lakewood ES, 2920 MIDDLEBORO PLACE 95355
Phil Hennessey, prin.
Marshall MS, 515 SUTTER AVE 95351
Robert Lee, prin.
Muir ES, 1215 LUCERN AVE 95350
James Martinez, prin.
Robertson Road ES
1821 ROBERTSON ROAD 95351
Leslie McPeak, prin.
Rose Avenue ES, 1120 ROSE AVE 95355
Marye Martinez, prin.
Shackelford ES, 100 SCHOOL AVE 95351
Tony Ramos, prin.
Sonoma ES, 1325 SONOMA AVE 95355
Marie Bairey, prin.
Tuolumne ES, 707 HERNDON AVE 95351
Lana Tuemmler, prin.
Wilson ES, 201 WILSON AVE 95354
Jim White, prin.
Wright ES, 1602 MONTEREY AVE 95354
Dan Cruz, prin.

Paradise ESD
Sch. Sys. Enr. Code 2
Supt. – (—), 3361 CALIFORNIA AVE 95351
Paradise ES, 3361 CALIFORNIA AVE 95351
Robert York, prin.

Riverbank ESD
Supt. – See Riverbank
Milnes ES, 6437 MINES ROAD 95355
Guy Miceli, prin.

Salida Un. ESD
Supt. – See Salida
Perkins ES, 3900 BLUE BIRD DRIVE 95356
Wayne Beck, prin.
Sisk ES, 5250 TAMARA LANE 95356
John Campopiano, prin.

Shiloh ESD
Sch. Sys. Enr. Code 2
Supt. – (—), 6633 PARADISE ROAD 95351
Shiloh ES, 6633 PARADISE ROAD 95351
E. Beasley, prin.

Stanislaus Un. ESD
Sch. Sys. Enr. Code 5
Supt. – Andy Schindler
   3601 CARVER ROAD   95356
Prescott Sr. MS, 2243 W RUMBLE ROAD   95350
  James Shively, prin.
Chrysler ES, 2818 CONANT AVE   95350
  Chet Jensen, prin.
Eisenhut ES, 1809 SHELDON DRIVE   95350
  Anthony Damore, prin.
Muncy ES, 2410 JANNA AVE   95350
  Jerald Rhine, prin.
Stanislaus ES, 1931 KIERNAN AVE   95356
  Lamar Dodson, prin.

Sylvan Un. ESD
Sch. Sys. Enr. Code 6
Supt. – Michael Sibitz, 605 SYLVAN AVE   95350
Somerset MS, 1037 FLOYD AVE   95350
  Robert Dunbar, prin.
Brown ES, 2024 VERA CRUZ DRIVE   95355
  William Stires, prin.
Coffee ES, 3900 NORTHVIEW DRIVE   95355
  Martha Gausman, prin.
Sherwood ES, 819 E RUMBLE ROAD   95350
  L. Lovell, prin.
Standiford ES, 605 TOKAY AVE   95350
  Mary Sanders, prin.
Sylvan ES, 2908 COFFEE ROAD   95355
  Pat Dimond, prin.
Woodrow ES, 800 WOODROW AVE   95350
  Randy Klinkenfus, prin.

Brethren Heritage School
  2524 FINNEY ROAD   95351
Modesto Christian School
  3200 TULLY ROAD   95350
Big Valley Christian ES
  605 STANDIFORD AVE   95350
Calvary Temple Christian ES
  P O BOX 6248   95355
Modesto Adventist ES, 2008 E HATCH RD   95351
Our Lady of Fatima ES
  501 W GRANGER AVE   95350
St. Stanislaus ES, 1416 MAZE BLVD   95351

Mojave, Kern Co., Pop. Code 5
Mojave USD
Sch. Sys. Enr. Code 4
Supt. – E. Baldwin, 3500 DOUGLAS AVE   93501
Joshua MS, 3200 PAT ST   93501
  Joe Honeycutt, prin.
ES, 15800 0 ST   93501 – Betty Giblin, prin.
Other Schools – See California City, Cantil

Mokelumne Hill, Calaveras Co.
Calaveras USD
Supt. – See San Andreas
ES, WEST POINT ROAD   95245
  Rob Williams, prin.

Monrovia, Los Angeles Co., Pop. Code 8
Monrovia USD
Sch. Sys. Enr. Code 6
Supt. – Donald Montgomery
  325 E HUNTINGTON DRIVE   91016
Clifton MS, 226 S IVY AVE   91016
  Rhuenette Montle, prin.
Santa Fe MS, 148 W DUARTE ROAD   91016
  Nelius Ronning, prin.
Bradoaks ES, 930 E LEMON AVE   91016
  Richard Brandes, prin.
Mayflower ES, 210 N MAYFLOWER AVE   91016
  Joan Buhler, prin.
Monroe ES, 402 W COLORADO BLVD   91016
  Joanne Spring, prin.
Plymouth ES, 1300 BOLEY ST   91016
  Deborah Collins, prin.
Wild Rose ES, 232 JASMINE AVE   91016
  Bruce Jorgensen, prin.

First Lutheran ES, 1323 S MAGNOLIA AVE   91016
Immaculate Conception ES
  726 S SHAMROCK AVE   91016

Montague, Siskiyou Co., Pop. Code 4
Big Springs Un. ESD
Sch. Sys. Enr. Code 2
Supt. – Joe Funderburg, 7405A-12   96064
Big Springs ES, 7405 A-12   96064
  Joe Funderburg, prin.

Bogus ESD
Sch. Sys. Enr. Code 1
Supt. – (—), HCR BOX 95   96064
Bogus ES, 13735 AGER BESWICK ROAD   96064
  Leigh Andreatta, prin.

Delphic ESD
Sch. Sys. Enr. Code 1
Supt. – (—)
  RURAL ROUTE 01 BOX 465   96064
Delphic ES, RURAL ROUTE 01 BOX 465   96064
  Cliff Lantz, prin.

Little Shasta ESD
Sch. Sys. Enr. Code 1
Supt. – (—)
  8409 LITTLE SHASTA ROAD   96064
Little Shasta ES, 8409 LITTLE SHASTA RD   96064
  Kathleen Koon, prin.

Montague ESD
Sch. Sys. Enr. Code 2
Supt. – Dan Laney, P O BOX 308   96064
ES, 740 PRATHER ST   96064 – Dan Laney, prin.

Willow Creek ESD
Sch. Sys. Enr. Code 1
Supt. – Patty George, 9839 AGER ROAD   96064
Willow Creek ES, 9839 AGER ROAD   96064
  Patty George, prin.

Montara, San Mateo Co., Pop. Code 4
Cabrillo USD
Supt. – See Half Moon Bay
Farallone View ES
  LACONTE AND KANOFF   94037
  Paul Cannon, prin.

Montclair, San Bernardino Co., Pop. Code 7
Ontario-Montclair ESD
Supt. – See Ontario
Serrano JHS, 4725 SAN JOSE ST   91763
  Gary Whitcanack, prin.
Vernon MS, 9775 VERNON AVE   91763
  Betty Normand, prin.
Kingsley ES, 5625 KINGSLEY ST   91763
  Jim Zajicek, prin.
Lehigh ES, 10200 LEHIGH ST   91763
  Albert Mooney, prin.
Margarita ES, 9550 MONTE VISTA AVE   91763
  Sally Martinez, prin.
Monte Vista ES, 4900 ORCHARD ST   91763
  John Duncan, prin.
Moreno ES, 4825 MORENO ST   91763
  Sari Kustner, prin.

Our Lady of Lourdes ES
  5303 ORCHARD ST   91763

Montebello, Los Angeles Co., Pop. Code 8
Montebello USD
Sch. Sys. Enr. Code 8
Supt. – John Cook
  123 S MONTEBELLO BLVD   90640
Eastmont IS, 400 BRADSHAWE ST   90640
  Frederick Johnson, prin.
La Merced IS
  215 E AVENIDA DE LA MERCED   90640
  Stephen Stanton, prin.
IS, 1600 WHITTIER BLVD   90640
  Louis Ayala, prin.
Freemont ES, 200 W MADISON AVE   90640
  Donald McOwen, prin.
Greenwood ES, 900 S GREENWOOD AVE   90640
  Eugene Kerr, prin.
La Merced ES, 724 N POPLAR AVE   90640
  William Erwin, prin.
Washington ES, 1400 W MADISON AVE   90640
  Judi Petersen, prin.
Wilcox ES, 816 DONNA WAY   90640
  Doris Kerkes, prin.
Other Schools – See Bell Gardens, City of Commerce,
  Los Angeles, Monterey Park, Pico Rivera, South San
  Gabriel

Marian ES, 840 N GARFIELD AVE   90640
Montebello Baptist ES, 136 S 7TH ST   90640
St. Benedict ES, 127 N 10TH ST   90640
St. John's Lutheran ES, 417 N 18TH ST   90640

Monterey, Monterey Co., Pop. Code 8
Monterey Peninsula USD
Sch. Sys. Enr. Code 7
Supt. – James Harrison, P O BOX 1031   93942
Colton MS, P O BOX 1031   93942
  Tad Kumagai, prin.
Bay View ES, BELDON & PRESCOTT STS   93940
  Curt Parker, prin.
Foothill ES, VIA CASOLI   93940
  Joe Cardinale, prin.
La Mesa ES, SYLVAN ROAD   93940
  Peter Krasa, prin.
Monte Vista ES, SOLEDAD DRIVE   93940
  Gene Tolhurst, prin.
Other Schools – See Fort Ord, Marina, Seaside

Santa Catalina School
  1500 MARK THOMAS DRIVE   93940
San Carlos ES, 450 CHURCH ST   93940

Monterey Park, Los Angeles Co., Pop. Code 8
Alhambra City SD
Supt. – See Alhambra
Brightwood ES, 1701 W BRIGHTWOOD ST   91754
  Jacinth Cisneros, prin.
Monterey Highlands ES
  400 CADUDA CANYON DRIVE   91754
  William Carroll, prin.
Repetto ES, 650 S GRANDRIDGE AVE   91754
  Mary Hall, prin.
Ynez ES, 120 S YNEZ AVE   91754
  Edward Aguirre, prin.

Garvey ESD
Supt. – See Rosemead
Hillcrest ES, 795 E PEPPER ST   91754
  Harvey Wyma, prin.
Monterey Vista ES, 901 E GRAVES AVE   91754
  Ray Sparks, prin.

Los Angeles USD
Supt. – See Los Angeles
Lane ES, 1500 W BROOKLYN AVE   91754
  Dennis Dulyea, prin.

Montebello USD
Supt. – See Montebello
Macy IS, 2101 S LUPINE AVE   91754
  Nicholas Monsour, prin.
Bella Vista ES, 2410 S FINDLAY AVE   91754
  John Franson, prin.

Childrens Village Day ES
  415 S GARFIELD AVE   91754
New Avenue Educatioanl School
  126 N NEW AVE   91754
St. Stephen Martyr ES
  119 S RAMONA AVE   91754
St. Thomas Aquinas ES
  1501 S ATLANTIC BLVD   91754

Monte Rio, Sonoma Co., Pop. Code 3
Monte Rio Un. ESD
Sch. Sys. Enr. Code 2
Supt. – Jane McDonough, P O BOX 340   95462
ES, P O BOX 340   95462 – Jane McDonough, prin.

Montgomery Creek, Shasta Co.
Mountain Un. ESD
Sch. Sys. Enr. Code 2
Supt. – Stan Caspary, P O BOX 368   96065
MS, P O BOX 368   96065 – Stan Caspary, prin.
Cedar Creek ES, P O BOX 368C   96065
  Stan Caspary, prin.

Montrose, Los Angeles Co.

Holy Redeemer ES, 2361 DEL MAR RD   91020

Moorpark, Ventura Co., Pop. Code 5
Moorpark USD
Sch. Sys. Enr. Code 5
Supt. – Thomas Duffy, 30 FLORY AVE   93021
Chaparral MS, 280 POINDEXTER AVE   93021
  Charles Smith, prin.
Campus Canyon ES, 15300 MONROE AVE   93021
  Frank DePasquale, prin.
Flory MS, 240 FLORY AVE   93021
  Vishna Herrity, prin.
Mountain Meadows ES
  4200 MOUNTAIN MEADOW DR   93021
  Ellen Smith, prin.
Peach Hill ES
  13400 CHRISTIAN BARRETT DR   93021
  Juanita Suarez, prin.

Moraga, Contra Costa Co., Pop. Code 7
Moraga ESD
Sch. Sys. Enr. Code 4
Supt. – John Cooley, P O BOX 158   94556
IS, 1010 CAMINO PABLO   94556
  William Walters, prin.
Camino Pablo ES, 1111 CAMINO PABLO   94556
  Neil Jennings, prin.
Rheem ES, 90 LAIRD DRIVE   94556
  Paul Ricciardi, prin.

Moreno Valley, Riverside Co.
Moreno Valley USD
Sch. Sys. Enr. Code 7
Supt. – Robert Lee, 13911 PERRIS BLVD   92388
Alessandro MS, 23301 DRACEA   92388
  Patrick Kelleher, prin.
Valley View MS, 24551 DRACAEA ST   92388
  Mary Bruce, prin.
Armada ES, 25201 KENNEDY DRIVE   92388
  Irene Shapkaroff, prin.
Badger Springs ES, 24551 DRACAEA ST   92388
  James Dutton, prin.
Butterfield ES, 13400 KITCHING ST   92388
  Rose Roberson, prin.
Cloverdale ES, 12050 KITCHING ST   92388
  Diana Shannon, prin.
Creekside ES, 16563 HEACOCK ST   92388
  Chuck Jones, prin.
Honey Hollow ES, 11765 HONEY HOLLOW   92388
  Robert Romero, prin.
Midland ES, 11440 DAVIS ST   92388
  Claudia Maidenberg, prin.
Moreno ES, 26700 COTTONWOOD AVE   92360
  Steve Comadena, prin.
Ramona ES, 24801 BAY AVE   92388
  Darlene Chodan, prin.
Serrano ES, 24100 DELPHINIUM   92388
  Don Hardy, prin.
Sugar Hill ES
  24455 OLD COUNTRY ROAD   92387
  Louise Bigbie, prin.
Sunnymead ES, 12875 HEACOCK ST   92388
  Terri Atkinson, prin.
Sunnymeadows ES
  23200 EUCALYPTUS AVE   92388
  Charles Kahlert, prin.
Vista Heights ES, 23049 OLD LAKE DR   92387
  Ernie Raugewitz, prin.
Other Schools – See Riverside

Morgan Hill, Santa Clara Co., Pop. Code 7
Morgan Hill USD
Sch. Sys. Enr. Code 6
Supt. – H. Crow, P O BOX 927   95037
Burnett ES, 85 TILTON AVE   95037
  James McDonald, prin.
Encinal MS, MONTEREY HIGHWAY   95037
  James Yinger, prin.
Jackson ES, 2700 FOUNTAIN OAKS DRIVE   95037
  Robert Davis, prin.
Machado ES, 15130 SYCAMORE AVE   95037
  Brendan White, prin.
Nordstrom ES, 1425 E DUNNE AVE   95037
  Doris Cross, prin.
Paradise Valley ES
  1400 LA CROSSE DRIVE   95037
  Brendan White, prin.
Walsh ES, 353 W MAIN AVE   95037
  Barbara Schaller, prin.
Other Schools – See San Jose, San Martin

South Valley Christian ES
145 WRIGHT AVE 95037
St. Catherine ES, 17500 PEAK AVE 95037

Morongo Valley, San Bernardino Co., Pop. Code 4
Morongo USD
Supt. – See Twentynine Palms
ES, 10951 HESS BLVD 92256
Donald Vanmeter, prin.

Morro Bay, San Luis Obispo Co., Pop. Code 6
San Luis Coastal USD
Supt. – See San Luis Obispo
Morro ES, 1130 NAPA AVE 93442
David Moore, prin.

Moss Landing, Monterey Co., Pop. Code 3
North Monterey County USD
Sch. Sys. Enr. Code 5
Supt. – Leo St. John, P O BOX 41A 95039
Other Schools – See Castroville, Salinas, Watsonville

Mountain Pass, San Bernardino Co.
Baker Valley USD
Supt. – See Baker
ES, P O BOX 105 92366 – Chuck Gehrke, prin.

Mountain View, Santa Clara Co., Pop. Code 6
Los Altos ESD
Supt. – See Los Altos
Springer ES, 1120 ROSE AVE 94040
Darla Tupper, prin.

Mountain View ESD
Sch. Sys. Enr. Code 4
Supt. – William Grafft, 220 VIEW ST 94041
Graham MS, 220 VIEW ST 94041
Lonnie Hartman, prin.
Bubb ES, 525 HANS AVE 94040
Gwen Bindon, prin.
Castro ES, 505 ESCUELA AVE 94040
Shirley Hooser, prin.
Landels ES, 115 W DANA ST 94041
Daniel Meyerson, prin.
Slater ES, 325 GLADYS AVE 94043
Maria Loya, prin.

Whisman ESD
Sch. Sys. Enr. Code 4
Supt. – Tim Cuneo
750 SAN PIERRE WAY #A 94043
Crittenden MS, 1701 ROCK ST 94043
Jack Boterenbrood, prin.
Monta Loma ES, 460 THOMPSON AVE 94043
June Banta, prin.
Theurkauf ES, 1625 SAN LUIS AVE 94043
June Banta, prin.
Whisman ES, 310 EASY ST 94043
Ann Muto, prin.

Southbay Christian School
1134 MIRAMONTE AVE 94040
St. Joseph's ES, 1120 MIRAMONTE AVE 94040

Mount Baldy, Los Angeles Co.
Mt. Baldy JESD
Sch. Sys. Enr. Code 1
Supt. – Thelma Edmundson, P O BOX 489 91759
ES, P O BOX 489 91759
Thelma Edmundson, prin.

Mount Hamilton, Santa Clara Co.
Alum Rock Un. ESD
Supt. – See San Jose
ES, P O BOX 37 95140 – (—), prin.

Mount Shasta, Siskiyou Co., Pop. Code 5
Mt. Shasta Un. SD
Sch. Sys. Enr. Code 3
Supt. – Robert Krausse, 501 CEDAR ST 96067
Sisson MS, 601 E ALMA ST 96067
Greg Gunkel, prin.
ES, 501 CEDAR ST 96067 – Robert Krausse, prin.

Murphys, Calaveras Co., Pop. Code 3
Vallecito Un. ESD
Sch. Sys. Enr. Code 4
Supt. – Rex Wetzel, P O BOX 807 95247
Michelson ES, P O BOX 748 95247
Jack Pickens, prin.
Other Schools – See Arnold

Murrieta, Riverside Co.
Murrieta ESD
Sch. Sys. Enr. Code 3
Supt. – Charles Vandewetering
24725 ADAMS AVE 92362
Avaxat ES
24300 RANCHO LAS BRISAS DR 92362
Guy Romero, prin.
ES, 24725 ADAMS ST 92362
Susan Reynolds, prin.

Napa, Napa Co., Pop. Code 8
Napa Valley USD
Sch. Sys. Enr. Code 7
Supt. – John Gyves, 2425 JEFFERSON ST 94558
Redwood MS, 3600 OXFORD ST 94558
Harrall Miller, prin.
Silverado MS, 1133 COOMBSVILLE ROAD 94558
David Wildman, prin.
Alta Heights ES, 15 MONTECITO BLVD 94559
Kathryn Martin, prin.
Bel Aire Park ES
3580 BECKWORTH DRIVE 94558
Evelyn Agnew, prin.

Browns Valley ES, 1001 BUHMAN AVE 94558
John Nelson, prin.
Capell ES, 1191 CAPELL VALLEY ROAD 94558
Richard Dunn, prin.
Carneros ES, 1680 LOS CARNEROS AVE 94559
Bonnie Broxton, prin.
El Centro ES, 1480 EL CENTRO AVE 94558
Willard Curry, prin.
McPherson ES, 2670 YAJOME ST 94558
G. Murray, prin.
Mt. George ES, 1019 2ND AVE 94558
Richard Dunn, prin.
Northwood ES, 2214 BERKS ST 94558
Betty Lambert, prin.
Phillips ES, 1210 SHETLER AVE 94559
Alice Jackson, prin.
Pueblo Vista ES, 1600 BARBARA ROAD 94558
Beverly Efishoff, prin.
Salvador ES, 1850 SALVADOR AVE 94558
Jan Farrington, prin.
Shearer ES, 1590 ELM ST 94559
Louis Martin, prin.
Snow ES, 1130 FOSTER ROAD 94558
John Holder, prin.
Vichy ES, 3261 VICHY AVE 94558
Margaret Wetterlund, prin.
West Park ES, 2700 KILBURN AVE 94558
Carol Vironda, prin.
Westwood ES, 2700 KILBURN AVE 94558
Phillip Moreno, prin.
Wooden Valley ES
1340 WOODEN VALLEY ROAD 94558
Richard Dunn, prin.
Other Schools – See Vallejo, Yountville

St. Helena USD
Supt. – See Saint Helena
Monticello ES, 8333 KNOXVILLE ROAD 94558
Ruth Reynolds, prin.

Napa Advent Junior Academy
2201 PINE ST 94559
Napa Valley Christian ES, P O BOX 4288 94558
St. Apollinaris ES, 3700 LASSEN ST 94558
St. John's ES, 983 NAPA ST 94559
St. John's Lutheran ES
3521 LINDA VISTA AVE 94558

National City, San Diego Co., Pop. Code 8
National ESD
Sch. Sys. Enr. Code 6
Supt. – Gary Smith, P O BOX Y 92050
Central ES, 933 E AVE 92050
Arleen Nelson, prin.
El Toyon ES, 2000 DIVISION ST 92050
Arlen Hurt, prin.
Harbison ES, 3235 E 8TH ST 92050
Carole Sabin, prin.
Kimball ES, 302 W 18TH ST 92050
Suzanne De La Vergne, prin.
Las Palmas ES, 1900 E 18TH ST 92050
Mary Daugherty, prin.
Lincoln Acres ES, 2200 S LANOITAN AVE 92050
Wayne Brandon, prin.
Olivewood ES, 2505 F AVE 92050
Nelo Whidby, prin.
Otis ES, 621 E 18TH ST 92050
Armida Gonzalez, prin.
Palmer Way ES, 2900 PALMER ST 92050
Dale Jones, prin.

San Diego Academy, 2700 E 4TH ST 92050
Southport Christian Academy
142 E 16TH ST 92050

Needles, San Bernardino Co., Pop. Code 5
Needles USD
Sch. Sys. Enr. Code 4
Supt. – K. Getschow, 1900 ERIN DRIVE 92363
Chemehuevi Valley ES, 1900 ERIN DRIVE 92363
Dennis Murray, prin.
D Street ES, 1900 ERIN DRIVE 92363
Dennis Murray, prin.
Vista Colorado ES, 1900 ERIN DRIVE 92363
David Renquest, prin.
Other Schools – See Amboy, Essex, Parker Dam

Nevada City, Nevada Co., Pop. Code 4
Nevada City SD
Sch. Sys. Enr. Code 4
Supt. – Dennis Dobbs
215 WASHINGTON ST 95959
Seven Hills IS, 700 HOOVER LANE 95959
Gary Winning, prin.
Deer Creek ES, 805 LINDLEY AVE 95959
Michael McGarr, prin.
ES, 505 MAIN ST 95959 – George Olive, prin.

Newark, Alameda Co., Pop. Code 8
Newark USD
Sch. Sys. Enr. Code 6
Supt. – Ruben Peterson, P O BOX 385 94560
Bunker ES, 6071 SMITH AVE 94560
Kenneth Stange, prin.
Graham ES, 36270 CHERRY ST 94560
Esther Hoag, prin.
Kennedy ES, 35430 BLACKBURN DRIVE 94560
Marcella Smith, prin.
Lincoln ES, 36111 BETTENCOURT ST 94560
Jan Goodman, prin.
Milani ES, 37490 BIRCH ST 94560
Mary Dunn, prin.
Musick ES, 5736 MUSICK AVE 94560
Cheryl McElhany, prin.

Schilling ES, 36901 SPRUCE ST 94560
Leo Hinkel, prin.
Snow ES, 6580 MIRABEAU DRIVE 94560
Nancy Villarreal, prin.

St. Edwards ES, 5788 THORNTON AVE 94560

Newberry Springs, San Bernardino Co., Pop. Code 3
Silver Valley USD
Supt. – See Yermo
ES, 33713 NEWBERRY ROAD 92365
Patricia Wilson, prin.

Newbury Park, Ventura Co., Pop. Code 6
Conejo Valley USD
Supt. – See Thousand Oaks
Sequoia IS, 2655 BORCHARD ROAD 91320
James Scarpino, prin.
Banyan ES, 1120 KNOLLWOOD DRIVE 91320
Loren Grossi, prin.
Cypress ES, 4200 KIMBER DRIVE 91320
Patricia Grant, prin.
Manzanita ES, 1626 MICHAEL DRIVE 91320
Philip Parish, prin.
Maple ES, 3501 KIMBER DRIVE 91320
Marilyn Bayles, prin.
Walnut ES, 581 DANA DRIVE 91320
Bradley Baker, prin.

Conejo Adventist ES
2645 W HILLCREST DR 91320

Newcastle, Placer Co., Pop. Code 3
Newcastle ESD
Sch. Sys. Enr. Code 2
Supt. – Edward Gilligan, P O BOX 197 95658
ES, P O BOX 197 95658 – Edward Gilligan, prin.

Ophir ESD
Sch. Sys. Enr. Code 2
Supt. – John Bliss, 1373 LOZANOS ROAD 95658
Ophir ES, 1373 LOZANOS ROAD 95658
John Bliss, prin.

New Cuyama, Santa Barbara Co., Pop. Code 4
Cuyama JUn. SD
Sch. Sys. Enr. Code 2
Supt. – Gary Glover, P O BOX 271 93254
Cuyama ES, P O BOX 271 93254 – John Kidd, prin.

Newhall, Los Angeles Co., Pop. Code 6
Newhall ESD
Sch. Sys. Enr. Code 5
Supt. – J. Michael McGrath
25022 HAWKBRYN AVE 91321
ES, 24607 WALNUT ST 91321
Joyce Watterau, prin.
Peachland Avenue ES
24800 PEACHLAND AVE 91321
Barbara O'Rear, prin.
Wiley Canyon ES
24240 W GLORITA CIRCLE 91321
Geraldene Morey, prin.
Other Schools – See Valencia

Sulphur Springs Un. ESD
Supt. – See Canyon Country
Valley View ES
19414 SIERRA ESTATES DRIVE 91321
Linda Short, prin.

William S. Hart Un. HSD
Sch. Sys. Enr. Code 6
Supt. – Hamilton Smyth
24823 WALNUT ST 91321
Placerita JHS, 25015 NEWHALL AVE **91321**
James Tanner, prin.
Other Schools – See Canyon Country, Valencia

Our Lady of Perpetual Help ES
23225 LYONS AVE 91321

Newman, Stanislaus Co., Pop. Code 5
Newman-Crows Landing USD
Sch. Sys. Enr. Code 4
Supt. – Ed Williams, 890 O ST 95360
Yolo MS, 907 R ST 95360 – Rick Hennes, prin.
Von Renner ES, 1388 PATCHETT DRIVE 95360
Alex Marshall, prin.
Other Schools – See Crows Landing

Newport Beach, Orange Co., Pop. Code 8
Newport-Mesa USD
Sch. Sys. Enr. Code 7
Supt. – John Nicoll, P O BOX 1368 92663
Ensign IS, P O BOX 1368 92663
Paul Twedt, prin.
Anderson ES
1900 PORT SEABOURNE PLACE 92660
Bruce Crockard, prin.
Mariners ES, 2100 MARINERS DRIVE 92660
Alvin Zeidman, prin.
Newport ES, 14TH ST AND BALBOA BLVD 92663
Bob Miller, prin.
Newport Heights ES, 300 E 15TH ST 92663
Cheryle Markel, prin.
Other Schools – See Corona Del Mar, Costa Mesa

Carden Hall ES, 1541 MONROVIA AVE 92663
Co Pre'Christian ES, 883 W 15TH ST 92663
Our Lady Queen of Angels ES
750 DOMINGO DR 92660

Nicasio, Marin Co.
Nicasio ESD
Sch. Sys. Enr. Code 1
Supt. – (—)
PETALUMA-NICASIO VALLEY RD 94946
ES, PETALUMA-NICASIO VALLEY RD 94946
Jeffry Pflugrath, prin.

Niland, Imperial Co., Pop. Code 3
Calipatria USD
Supt. – See Calipatria
ES, FOURTH AND ISIS STS 92257
Choh Brister, prin.

Nipomo, San Luis Obispo Co., Pop. Code 5
Lucia Mar USD
Supt. – See Arroyo Grande
Dana MS, 920 W TEFFT RD 93444
Juan Olivarria, prin.
ES, P O BOX 385 93444 – Loleta Hamlett, prin.

Norco, Riverside Co., Pop. Code 7
Corona-Norco USD
Supt. – See Corona
Highland ES, 2301 ALHAMBRA ST 91760
Lorri Young, prin.
ES, 1700 TEMESCAL AVE 91760
Sharon Haddy, prin.
Riverview ES, 4600 PEDLEY AVE 91760
Eddie Soto, prin.
Sierra Vista ES, 3560 CORONA AVE 91760
A. Scanlon, prin.
Washington ES, 1220 PARKRIDGE AVE 91760
James Allen, prin.

St. Mel ES, P O BOX 220 91760

North Edwards, Kern Co.
Muroc JUSD
Sch. Sys. Enr. Code 5
Supt. – Robert Deckard, P O BOX 833 93523
Lynch ES 93523 – Peter Anderson, prin.
Other Schools – See Boron, Edwards

North Fork, Madera Co., Pop. Code 3
Chawanakee JESD
Sch. Sys. Enr. Code 2
Supt. – Grant Sturm, P O BOX 707 93643
ES, P O BOX 707 93643 – Cory Aboudara, prin.
Other Schools – See Auberry

North Highlands, Sacramento Co., Pop. Code 8
Center USD
Sch. Sys. Enr. Code 5
Supt. – Rex Fortune, 8408 WATT AVE 95660
Center JHS, 8725 WATT AVE 95660
Tom Wright, prin.
Center ES, P O BOX 1550 95660
Mary Anderson, prin.
Dudley ES, 8000 AZTEC WAY 95660
Denise Hexom, prin.
Spinelli ES, 3401 SCOTLAND DRIVE 95660
R. Loehr, prin.

Grant JUn. HSD
Supt. – See Sacramento
Julio JHS, 6444 WALERGA ROAD 95660
Sheila Curtis, prin.

Rio Linda Un. ESD
Supt. – See Rio Linda
Aero Haven ES, 5450 GEORGIA DRIVE 95660
Lillie Campbell, prin.
Allison ES, 4315 DON JULIO BLVD 95660
Ralph Scott, prin.
Hillsdale ES, 6469 GUTHRIE ST 95660
Hal Higgins, prin.
Holmes ES, 7201 ARUTAS DRIVE 95660
Leanne Mitchell, prin.
Joyce ES, 6050 WATT AVE 95660
Gordon Fergusson, prin.
Kohler ES, 4004 BRUCE WAY 95660
Roberta Hooker, prin.
Larchmont ES, 6560 MELROSE DRIVE 95660
James Potter, prin.
Madison ES, 5241 HARRISON ST 95660
Sonya Boyle, prin.
Oakdale ES, 3708 MYRTLE AVE 95660
Paul Harrington, prin.
Sierra View ES, 3638 BAINBRIDGE DRIVE 95660
Gary Henderson, prin.
Village ES, 6845 LARCHMONT DRIVE 95660
Judith Flint, prin.

St. Lawrence ES, 4325 DON JULIO BLVD 95660

North Hollywood, Los Angeles Co.
Los Angeles USD
Supt. – See Los Angeles
Arlington Heights ES
11530 STRATHERN ST 91605
Mona Kantor, prin.
Arminta Street ES, 11530 STRATHERN ST 91605
Thomas Stevens, prin.
Burbank Boulevard ES, 12215 ALBERS ST 91607
Rita Frost, prin.
Camellia Avenue ES, 7451 CAMELLIA AVE 91605
Shirley Reed, prin.
Coldwater Canyon ES
6850 COLDWATER CANYON AVE 91605
Jilanne Fager, prin.
Colfax Avenue ES, 11724 ADDISON ST 91607
Elisabeth Norton, prin.
Fair Avenue ES, 6501 FAIR AVE 91606
Mary Bardsley, prin.

Lankershim ES, 5250 BAKMAN AVE 91601
Anna McLinn, prin.
Monlux ES, 6051 BELLAIRE AVE 91606
Gary Parks, prin.
Oxnard Street ES, 10912 OXNARD ST 91606
Dennis Hovey, prin.
Rio Vista ES, 4243 SATSUMA AVE 91602
Beverly Bittle, prin.
Saticoy ES, 7850 ETHEL AVE 91605
Sandra Mcguern, prin.
Strathern Street ES
7939 SAINT CLAIR AVE 91605
Kathryn Henry, prin.
Toluca Lake ES, 4840 CAHUENGA BLVD 91601
John Colton, prin.
Victory Boulevard ES, 6315 RADFORD AVE 91606
Charles Webb, prin.

Campbell Hall School
4533 LAUREL CANYON BLVD 91607
Adat Ari El Day ES
5540 LAUREL CANYON BLVD 91607
Country ES, 5243 LAUREL CANYON BLVD 91607
Emek Hebrew Academy
12732 CHANDLER BLVD 91607
Laurel Hall ES, 11919 OXNARD ST 91606
Oakwood ES, 11230 MOORPARK ST 91602
St. Charles Borromeo ES
10850 MOORPARK ST 91602
St. Jane Frances De Chantal ES
12950 HAMLIN ST 91606
St. Patricks ES, 10626 ERWIN ST 91606
St. Paul First Lutheran ES
11330 MCCORMICK ST 91601

Northridge, Los Angeles Co.
Los Angeles USD
Supt. – See Los Angeles
JHS, 17960 CHASE ST 91325
Doris Williams, prin.
Andasol Avenue ES, 10126 ENCINO AVE 91325
Loretta Norwalt, prin.
Beckford Avenue ES, 19130 TULSA ST 91326
William Snow, prin.
Calahan Street ES, 18722 KNAPP ST 91324
Diane Island, prin.
Castlebay Lane ES
19010 CASTLEBAY LANE 91326
Robert Miller, prin.
Darby Avenue ES, 10818 DARBY AVE 91326
Earl Lewis, prin.
Dearborn Street ES, 9240 WISH AVE 91325
Richard Lioy, prin.
Lorne Street ES, 17440 LORNE ST 91325
Sid Carp, prin.
Napa Street ES, 19010 NAPA ST 91324
John McClure, prin.
Topeka Drive ES, 9815 TOPEKA DRIVE 91324
Frank McKendall, prin.

Highland Hall School, 17100 SUPERIOR ST 91325
San Fernando Valley SDA Academy
17601 LASSEN ST 91325
Countryside Preparatory ES
8756 CANBY AVE 91325
First Lutheran ES, 18355 ROSCOE BLVD 91325
First Presbyterian ES of Granada Hills
10400 ZELZAH AVE 91326
Heschel Day ES, 17701 DEVONSHIRE ST 91325
Our Lady of Lourdes ES
18437 SUPERIOR ST 91325
Pinecrest ES, 17081 DEVONSHIRE ST 91325
St. Nicholas ES, 9501 BALBOA BLVD 91325

North San Juan, Nevada Co.
Sierra-Plumas JUSD
Supt. – See Downieville
Pliocene Ridge ES, ALLEGHANY HCR 95960
Stephen Lebbert, prin.

Twin Ridges ESD
Sch. Sys. Enr. Code 2
Supt. – Paul Alderete, P O BOX 529 95960
Grizzly Hill MS, P O BOX 529 95960
Randy Wise, prin.
Oak Tree ES, P O BOX 529 95960
Paul Alderete, prin.
Other Schools – See Washington

Norwalk, Los Angeles Co., Pop. Code 8
Little Lake City ESD
Supt. – See Santa Fe Springs
Lakeside JHS, 11000 KENNEY ST 90650
Judith Dutcher, prin.
Cresson ES, 11650 CRESSON ST 90650
Thomas Noesen, prin.
Lakeland ES, 11224 BOMBARDIER AVE 90650
Philip Morse, prin.
Orr ES, 12130 JERSEY AVE 90650
Yolanda Venegas, prin.
Paddison ES, 12100 CREWE ST 90650
Edna Morales, prin.
Studebaker ES, 11800 HALCOURT AVE 90650
Sheila Wells, prin.

Norwalk-La Mirada USD
Sch. Sys. Enr. Code 7
Supt. – Bruce Newlin
12820 PIONEER BLVD 90650
Dolland ES, 15021 BLOOMFIELD AVE 90650
Michael Newcomb, prin.
Edmondson ES, 15121 GRAYLAND AVE 90650
Alexis Alessi, prin.
Glazier ES, 10932 EXCELSIOR DRIVE 90650
Mary McCuistion, prin.

Hargitt ES, 12940 FOSTER ROAD 90650
Stephen Gertz, prin.
Johnston ES, 13421 FAIRFORD AVE 90650
Henry Mothner, prin.
Lampton ES, 14716 ELMCROFT AVE 90650
(—), prin.
Moffitt ES, 13323 GOLLER AVE 90650
Phyllis Pringle, prin.
Morrison ES, 13510 MAIDSTONE AVE 90650
Debbie McKenzie, prin.
New River ES, 13432 HALCOURT AVE 90650
John Hively, prin.
Nottingham ES, 11960 162ND ST 90650
Marilyn Smith, prin.
Nuffer ES, 14821 JERSEY AVE 90650
Kathy Stolhand, prin.
Waite ES, 14320 NORWALK BLVD 90650
Angela Henderson, prin.
Walnut ES, 12100 E WALNUT ST 90650
Christopher Forehan, prin.
Other Schools – See La Mirada

Pioneer Baptist School
11717 PIONEER BLVD 90650
Brethren ES, 11005 FOSTER RD 90650
Nazarene Christian ES
15014 STUDEBAKER RD 90650
Norwalk Christian ES
11129 PIONEER BLVD 90650
St. John of God ES, 13817 PIONEER BLVD 90650
St. Linus ES, 13913 SHOEMAKER AVE 90650
Temple Baptist ES, 12722 WOODS AVE 90650
Trinity Lutheran ES
11507 STUDEBAKER RD 90650

Novato, Marin Co., Pop. Code 8
Novato USD
Sch. Sys. Enr. Code 6
Supt. – Dan Thompson, 1015 7TH ST 94947
San Jose MS, 1000 SUNSET PARKWAY 94947
Ken Hansen, prin.
Sinaloa MS, 2045 VINEYARD ROAD 94947
Richard Gerhardt, prin.
Loma Verde ES
399 ALAMEDA DE LA LOMA 94949
Joanne Wheeler, prin.
Lu Sutton ES, 1800 CENTER ROAD 94947
Kathleen Bond, prin.
Lynwood ES, 1320 LYNWOOD DRIVE 94947
Jill Rosenquist, prin.
Olive ES, 629 PLUM ST 94945
Richard Melendy, prin.
Pleasant Valley ES, 755 SUTRO AVE 94947
Harry Moore, prin.
Rancho ES, 1430 JOHNSON ST 94947
Mary Sinkkonen, prin.
San Ramon ES, 45 SAN RAMON WAY 94945
Michael Ingerson, prin.
Other Schools – See Hamilton A F B

Christian Life ES, 1370 S NOVATO BLVD 94947
Our Lady of Loretto ES
1811 VIRGINIA AVE 94945

Nuevo, Riverside Co.
Nuview Un. SD
Sch. Sys. Enr. Code 3
Supt. – David Wiebe
29780 LAKEVIEW AVE 92367
Nuview ES, 29680 LAKEVIEW AVE 92367
Helen Fulton, prin.

Oakdale, Stanislaus Co., Pop. Code 6
Oakdale Un. ESD
Sch. Sys. Enr. Code 4
Supt. – Kenneth Kennedy, P O BOX 199 95361
JHS, 739 MAGNOLIA ST 95361
David Cook, prin.
Cloverland ES, JOHNSON & E STS 95361
Marilyn Lane, prin.
Fair Oaks ES, 151 N LEE AVE 95361
Michael Keefe, prin.
Magnolia ES, 739 MAGNOLIA ST 95361
Pam Antinetti, prin.

Oakhurst, Madera Co.
Bass Lake SD
Sch. Sys. Enr. Code 3
Supt. – Angelo Pizelo, P O BOX 395 93644
Oak Creek IS, P O BOX 395 93644
Clint Bletscher, prin.
ES, P O BOX 395 93644 – Sam Garamendi, prin.
Other Schools – See Bass Lake

Oakland, Alameda Co., Pop. Code 10
Oakland USD
Sch. Sys. Enr. Code 8
Supt. – Joe Coto, 1025 2ND AVE 94606
Arts S, 5263 BROADWAY TERRACE 94618
Albert Andrews, prin.
Carter MS, 4521 WEBSTER ST 94609
George Jasper, prin.
Claremont MS, 5750 COLLEGE AVE 94618
Gail Hojo, prin.
Elmhurst MS, 1800 98TH AVE 94603
Geraldine Goree, prin.
Foster MS, 2850 WEST ST 94608
Mildred Gardner, prin.
Lowell MS, 991 14TH ST 94607
Robert Taylor, prin.
Madison MS, 400 CAPISTRANO DRIVE 94603
Paul Randall, prin.
Allendale ES, 3670 PENNIMAN AVE 94619
Clarence Stevens, prin.

Bella Vista ES, 1025 E 28TH ST 94610
  Vivian Jefferson, prin.
Brookfield Village ES, 401 JONES AVE 94603
  Yolanda Peeks, prin.
Burbank ES, 3550 64TH AVE 94605
  Robert Smith, prin.
Burckhalter ES, 3994 BURCKHALTER AVE 94605
  Phyllis Flory, prin.
Chabot ES, 6686 CHABOT ROAD 94618
  Patricia Christiansen, prin.
Cleveland ES, 745 CLEVELAND AVE 94606
  Helen Fong, prin.
Cole MS, 1011 UNION ST 94607
  Jacqueline Woods, prin.
Cox ES, 9860 SUNNYSIDE ST 94603
  John Cooke, prin.
Crocker Highlands ES
  525 MIDCREST ROAD 94610
  Marilyn Jones, prin.
Emerson ES, 4803 LAWTON AVE 94609
  Lottye Scott, prin.
Franklin Year Round ES
  915 FOOTHILL BLVD 94606 – Jay Cleckner, prin.
Fruitvale ES, 3200 BOSTON AVE 94602
  Carole Scott, prin.
Garfield ES, 1640 22ND ST 94606
  Dale Shaw, prin.
Glenview ES, 4215 LA CRESTA AVE 94602
  Glenna Yee, prin.
Golden Gate ES, 6200 SAN PABLO AVE 94608
  Leon Washington, prin.
Grass Valley ES, 4720 DUNKIRK AVE 94605
  Yetive Bradley, prin.
Hawthorne Year Round ES, 1700 28TH AVE 94601
  Arlene Graham, prin.
Highland ES, 8521 A ST 94621
  William Riley, prin.
Hillcrest ES, 30 MARGUERITE DRIVE 94618
  Gary Yee, prin.
Hoover ES, 890 BROCKHURST ST 94608
  Dolores Ward, prin.
Howard ES, 8755 FONTAINE ST 94605
  Terry Brock, prin.
Jefferson ES, 2035 40TH AVE 94601
  Burton Yin, prin.
Kaiser ES, 25 S HILL COURT 94618
  James DuFloth, prin.
King ES, 960 10TH ST 94607
  Michael Hopkins, prin.
La Escuelita ES, 1100 3RD AVE 94606
  George Lerma, prin.
Lafayette ES, 1700 MARKET ST 94607
  Charles Jones, prin.
Lakeview ES, 746 GRAND AVE 94610
  Anson Scott, prin.
Laurel ES, 3750 BROWN AVE 94619
  Belen Balaba, prin.
LaZear ES, 824 29TH AVE 94601
  Yolanda Ross, prin.
Lincoln ES, 225 11TH ST 94607
  Gilbert Cho, prin.
Lockwood ES, 6701 E 14TH ST 94621
  Alfred Gordon, prin.
Longfellow ES, 3877 LUSK ST 94608
  Don Thomas, prin.
Mann ES, 5222 YGNACIO AVE 94601
  Ilene Linssen, prin.
Manzanita ES, 2409 E 27TH ST 94601
  Tommie Clay, prin.
Markham ES, 7220 KRAUSE AVE 94605
  Laverda Henderson, prin.
Marshall ES, 3400 MALCOLM AVE 94605
  Shirley Kelly, prin.
Maxwell Park ES, 4730 FLEMING AVE 94619
  Wendy Caporicci, prin.
Melrose ES, 1325 53RD AVE 94601
  Delia Ruiz, prin.
Miller ES, 5525 ASCOT DRIVE 94611
  Linda Lu, prin.
Montclair ES, 1757 MOUNTAIN BLVD 94611
  Connie White, prin.
Munck ES, 11900 CAMPUS DRIVE 94619
  Christina Owyang, prin.
Parker ES, 7929 NEY AVE 94605
  Gwen DeBow, prin.
Peralta Year Round ES, 460 63RD ST 94609
  Stanley Kistner, prin.
Piedmont Avenue ES
  4314 PIEDMONT AVE 94611 – Mary Sams, prin.
Prescott ES, 920 CAMPBELL ST 94607
  Isao Nishijima, prin.
Redwood Heights ES, 4401 39TH AVE 94619
  Voncile Wilson, prin.
Santa Fe ES, 915 54TH ST 94608
  Dorothy Norwood, prin.
Sequoia ES, 3730 LINCOLN AVE 94602
  Cheryl Rodby, prin.
Sherman ES, 5328 BRANN ST 94619
  Laverne Moore, prin.
Sobrante Park ES, 470 EL PASEO DRIVE 94603
  William Self, prin.
Stonehurst ES, 10315 E ST 94603
  Martin Worth, prin.
Swett ES, 4551 STEELE ST 94619
  Margaret Hauben, prin.
Thornhill ES, 5880 THORNHILL DRIVE 94611
  James DuFloth, prin.
Toler Heights ES, 9736 LAWLOR ST 94605
  Shirley Kelly, prin.
Washington ES, 581 61ST ST 94609
  Claude Jenkins, prin.
Webster ES, 8000 BIRCH ST 94621
  Willie Hamilton, prin.

Whittier ES, 6328 E 17TH ST 94621
  Jeanette MacDonald, prin.
Whitton ES, 3031 E 18TH ST 94601
  (—), prin.

Golden Gate SDA Academy
  3800 MOUNTAIN BLVD 94619
Head-Royce School, 4315 LINCOLN AVE 94602
Patten Academy of Christian Education
  2433 COOLIDGE AVE 94601
Pentecostal Way Truth Academy
  1575 7TH ST 94607
Shiloh Chrstian Schs., 3295 SCHOOL ST 94602
Bentley ES, 1 HILLER DR 94618
Corpus Christi ES, 1 ESTATES DR 94611
Hope Academy, 8411 MACARTHUR BLVD 94605
Park Day ES, 368 42ND ST 94609
Sacred Heart ES, 675 41ST ST 94609
St. Andrew Mission Baptist ES
  2624 WEST ST 94612
St. Anthony ES, 1500 E 15TH ST 94606
St. Augustine ES, 410 ALCATRAZ AVE 94609
St. Benedict ES, 8030 ATHERTON ST 94605
St. Bernard ES, 1630 62ND AVE 94621
St. Columba ES, 1086 ALCATRAZ AVE 94608
St. Cyril ES, 3200 62ND AVE 94605
St. Elizabeth ES, 1516 33RD AVE 94601
St. Jarlath ES, 2634 PLEASANT ST 94602
St. Lawrence Otoole ES, 3695 HIGH ST 94619
St. Leo ES, 4238 HOWE ST 94611
St. Louis Bertrand ES, 1445 101ST AVE 94603
St. Paschals ES, 3710 DORISA AVE 94605
St. Patricks ES, 1630 10TH ST 94607
St. Pauls Episcopal ES
  116 MONTECITO AVE 94610
St. Theresa ES, 4850 CLAREWOOD DR 94618
Zion Lutheran ES, 5201 PARK BLVD 94611

Oakley, Contra Costa Co.
Oakley Un. ESD
  Sch. Sys. Enr. Code 4
  Supt. – Frank Hengel, P O BOX 7 94561
  MS, P O BOX 7 94561 – Ann Stevenson, prin.
  Gehringer PS, P O BOX 7 94561
    Hilario Puente, prin.

Oak Run, Shasta Co.
Oak Run ESD
  Sch. Sys. Enr. Code 1
  Supt. – (—), P O BOX 48 96069
  ES, P O BOX 48 96069 – Angela Davis, prin.

Oak View, Ventura Co., Pop. Code 5
Ventura USD
  Supt. – See Ventura
  Arnaz ES, 400 SUNSET AVE 93022
    David Gomez, prin.
  ES, 555 MAHONEY AVE 93022
    Jose Montano, prin.

Occidental, Sonoma Co.
Harmony Un. ESD
  Sch. Sys. Enr. Code 3
  Supt. – Rich Fischer, P O BOX 279 95465
  Harmony ES, BOHEMIAN HIGHWAY 95465
    Rod Buchignani, prin.

Oceano, San Luis Obispo Co., Pop. Code 5
Lucia Mar USD
  Supt. – See Arroyo Grande
  ES, P O BOX 308 93445 – Phillip Gallegos, prin.

Oceanside, San Diego Co., Pop. Code 8
Oceanside City USD
  Sch. Sys. Enr. Code 7
  Supt. – Steven Speach, 2111 MISSION AVE 92054
  Jefferson JHS, 823 ACACIA AVE 92054
    Michael Walker, prin.
  Lincoln JHS, 2000 CALIFORNIA ST 92054
    Pat Barnes, prin.
  Burgener ES, 707 CAREY ROAD 92054
    Ronald Briggs, prin.
  Del Rio ES, 5207 E PARKER ST 92056
    Joseph Timilione, prin.
  Ditmar ES, 1125 S DITMAR ST 92054
    Lidna Hess, prin.
  Garrison ES, 333 GARRISON ST 92054
    Timothy Keane, prin.
  Laurel ES, 1410 LAUREL ST 92054
    Bruce Montgomery, prin.
  Libby ES, 423 W REDONDO DRIVE 92056
    James Cosman, prin.
  Mission ES, 2100 MISSION AVE 92054
    Gordon Hoard, prin.
  North Terrace ES, 940 CAPISTRANO DRIVE 92054
    Melody Huelsebusch, prin.
  Pacifica ES, 4991 MACARIO DRIVE 92056
    Hurley Dodd, prin.
  Palmquist ES, 1999 CALIFORNIA ST 92054
    Mary Gleisberg, prin.
  Reynolds ES, 4575 DOUGLAS DR 92056
    Larry Layton, prin.
  San Luis Rey ES, 3535 HACIENDA DRIVE 92054
    Margaret Cowman, prin.
  San Rafael ES, 1616 SAN RAFAEL DRIVE 92054
    Linda Goldstein, prin.
  Santa Margarita ES, 1 OFFICERS ROAD 92054
    Dorothy Faulkner, prin.
  South Oceanside ES, 1806 S HORNE ST 92054
    William Wagner, prin.

Oceanside Christian ES, 1836 DIXIE ST 92054
St. Mary Star of the Sea ES
  515 WISCONSIN AVE 92054

Oildale, Kern Co., Pop. Code 7
Standard ESD
  Sch. Sys. Enr. Code 4
  Supt. – Edward Moon
    1200 N CHESTER AVE 93308
  Standard JHS, 1200 N CHESTER AVE 93308
    Richard Moon, prin.
  Standard ES, 115 E MINNER AVE 93308
    William Goff, prin.
  Other Schools – See Bakersfield

Ojai, Ventura Co., Pop. Code 6
Ojai USD
  Sch. Sys. Enr. Code 5
  Supt. – Andrew Smidt, P O BOX 878 93023
  Matilija JHS, 703 EL PASEO ROAD 93023
    James Berube, prin.
  Meiners Oaks ES, 400 S LOMITA AVE 93023
    Marvin Vanwagner, prin.
  Mira Monte ES, 1216 LOMA DRIVE 93023
    Lawrence Hartmann, prin.
  San Antonio ES, 650 CARTNE ROAD 93023
    Joseph DeVito, prin.
  Summit ES
    12525 OJAI SANTA PAULA ROAD 93023
    David Brown, prin.
  Topa Topa ES, 916 MOUNTAIN VIEW AVE 93023
    Pamela Martens, prin.

Ojai Valley School, 723 EL PASEO ROAD 93023
St. Thomas Aquinas ES, 210 CANADA ST 93023

Olancha, Inyo Co.
Lone Pine USD
  Supt. – See Lone Pine
  ES, P O BOX 157 93549 – Nancy Sonke, prin.

Olivehurst, Yuba Co., Pop. Code 6
Marysville JUSD
  Supt. – See Marysville
  Yuba Gardens IS, 1964 11TH ST 95961
    Dave Favro, prin.
  Ella ES, 4850 OLIVEHURST AVE 95961
    Richard Teagarden, prin.
  Johnson Park ES, 4364 LEVER AVE 95961
    Lee Limonoff, prin.
  ES, 1778 MCGOWAN PKWY 95961
    Herschel Todd, prin.

O'Neals, Madera Co.
Spring Valley ESD
  Sch. Sys. Enr. Code 2
  Supt. – William Scheidt, P O BOX 9 93645
  Spring Valley ES, P O BOX 9 93645
    William Scheidt, prin.
  Other Schools – See Madera

Ontario, San Bernardino Co., Pop. Code 8
Chino USD
  Supt. – See Chino
  Dickey ES, 2840 S PARCO AVE 91761
    Rod Nelson, prin.

Mountain View ESD
  Sch. Sys. Enr. Code 4
  Supt. – Ed Peltz, 2947 S TURNER AVE A 91761
  Yokley JHS, 2947 S TURNER AVE 91761
    Rand Shumway, prin.
  Creek View ES, 3742 LYTLE CREEK LOOP 91761
    Craig Newby, prin.
  Mountain View ES, 2825 E WALNUT ST 91761
    Burt Bradshaw, prin.

Ontario-Montclair ESD
  Sch. Sys. Enr. Code 7
  Supt. – Frank Cosca, P O BOX 313 91762
  De Anza JHS, 1450 S SULTANA AVE 91761
    Sam Brown, prin.
  Imperial JHS, 1460 E G ST 91764
    James Broecker, prin.
  Vina Danks MS, 1020 N VINE AVE 91762
    Kenneth Gabel, prin.
  Arroyo ES, 17700 E SEVENTH ST 91764
    Chuck Morris, prin.
  Berlyn ES, 1320 N BERLYN AVE 91764
    Sharon McGehee, prin.
  Bon View ES, 1515 S BON VIEW AVE 91761
    John Neiuber, prin.
  Central ES, 415 EAST G ST 91764
    Walter Schaefer, prin.
  Corona ES, 1140 N CORONA AVE 91764
    Martin Olsky, prin.
  Cypress ES, 1825 S CYPRESS AVE 91762
    Jeraldine Roth, prin.
  Del Norte ES, 850 N DEL N ST 91764
    Mark Douglas, prin.
  Edison ES, 515 E 6TH ST 91764
    Benjamin Ramirez, prin.
  El Camino ES, 1525 W 5TH ST 91762
    George Willmore, prin.
  Elderberry ES, 950 N ELDERBERRY AVE 91762
    Mary Gonzales, prin.
  Euclid ES, 1120 S EUCLID AVE 91762
    Loel Miller, prin.
  Hawthorne ES, 715 W HAWTHORNE ST 91762
    Karen Reiter, prin.
  Howard MS, 4650 HOWARD ST 91761
    Dennis Williams, prin.
  Mariposa ES, 1605 E D ST 91764 – (—), prin.
  Mission ES, 5555 HOWARD ST 91761
    Norm Steinker, prin.
  Sultana ES, 1845 S SULTANA AVE 91761
    Bette Lovein, prin.
  Vineyard ES, 1500 E 6TH ST 91764
    David Jones, prin.
  Other Schools – See Montclair, Pomona

Calvary Christian ES, 1430 N GROVE AVE 91764
Mountian Avenue Christian ES
    1951 S MOUNTAIN AVE 91762
Ontario Christian ES, 1907 S EUCLID AVE 91762
Redeemer Lutheran ES, 920 W 6TH ST 91762
St. George ES, 322 W D ST 91762

Orange, Orange Co., Pop. Code 8
Orange USD
Sch. Sys. Enr. Code 7
Supt. – John Ikerd, 370 N GLASSELL ST 92666
McPherson MS, 333 S PROSPECT ST 92669
    Mary Ann Owsley, prin.
Portola MS, 270 N PALM DRIVE 92668
    A. Neil Smith, prin.
Santiago MS
    515 N RANCHO SANTIAGO BLVD 92669
    Dennis Miller, prin.
Yorba MS, 935 N CAMBRIDGE ST 92667
    Dave Gunderson, prin.
California ES, 1080 N CALIFORNIA ST 92667
    Ewell Gunter, prin.
Cambridge ES, 425 N CAMBRIDGE ST 92666
    Doyle Schmidt, prin.
Esplanade ES, 381 N ESPLANADE ST 92669
    Louise Saladino, prin.
Fletcher ES, 515 W FLETCHER AVE 92665
    Maralynn Frasure, prin.
Handy ES, 860 N HANDY ST 92667
    Robert Joy, prin.
Jordan ES, 4319 E JORDAN AVE 92669
    Forrest Shattuck, prin.
Laveta ES, 2800 E LA VETA AVE 92669
    Eddie Salgado, prin.
Linda Vista ES, 1200 N CANNON ST 92669
    Thomas Cooper, prin.
Palmyra ES, 1325 E PALMYRA AVE 92666
    Gordon Mitchell, prin.
Prospect ES, 379 N PROSPECT ST 92669
    Carol Stiff, prin.
Sycamore ES, 340 N MAIN ST 92668
    (—), prin.
Taft ES, 1829 N CAMBRIDGE ST 92665
    Ray Brooks, prin.
West Orange ES, 243 S BUSH ST 92668
    James Barton, prin.
Other Schools – See Anaheim, Garden Grove, Santa
    Ana, Silverado, Villa Park

Jubilation Bible School
    8612 S ORANGE OLIVE ROAD 92665
Covenant Christian ES
    1855 N ORANGE OLIVE RD 92665
Crystal Cathedral Academy
    4201 W CHAPMAN AVE 92668
Far Horizons Montessori School
    264 N MAIN ST 92668
Holy Family ES, 530 S GLASSELL ST 92666
Immanuel Lutheran ES, 147 S PINE ST 92666
Independence Christian ES
    1820 E MEATS AVE 92665
La Purisima ES, 18801 E SPRING ST 92669
Oak Ridge Private ES, 1459 N HANDY ST 92667
Orange Christian ES, 2830 N GLASSELL ST 92665
Salem Lutheran ES, 19921 E FRANK AVE 92669
St. John's Lutheran ES
    515 E ALMOND AVE 92666
St. Norbert ES, 300 E TAFT ST 92665
St. Paul's Lutheran ES, 901 N HEIM AVE 92665

Orange Cove, Fresno Co., Pop. Code 5
Kings Canyon JUSD
Supt. – See Reedley
Citrus MS, 222 4TH ST 93646
    Roger Trujillo, prin.
McCord MS, 333 CENTER ST 93646
    Al Uribe, prin.
Sheridan ES, TENTH AND J STS 93646
    Edwina Waide, prin.

Orangevale, Sacramento Co., Pop. Code 7
San Juan USD
Supt. – See Carmichael
Carnegie IS, 5820 ILLINOIS AVE 95662
    Dave Ferencik, prin.
Pasteur IS, 8935 ELM AVE 95662
    Dennis Haggard, prin.
Coleman ES, 6545 BEECH AVE 95662
    Dean Neeley, prin.
Green Oaks Fundamental ES
    7145 FILBERT AVE 95662 – Ella Deleon, prin.
Oakview Community ES, 7229 BEECH AVE 95662
    Christina Zarzana, prin.
ES, 6550 FILBERT AVE 95662
    Georgia Lastar, prin.
Ottomon Way ES, 9460 OTTOMON WAY 95662
    Karen Hunter, prin.
Pallisades ES, 9601 LAKE NATOMA DRIVE 95662
    Janice Moore, prin.
Pershing ES, 9010 PERSHING AVE 95662
    Jean Crim, prin.
Trajan ES, 6601 TRAJAN DRIVE 95662
    Ruth Michon, prin.
Twin Lakes ES, 9380 TWIN LAKES AVE 95662
    Charlene Mathews, prin.

Orcutt, Santa Barbara Co., Pop. Code 6
Orcutt Un. ESD
Sch. Sys. Enr. Code 5
Supt. – Jack Garvin, P O BOX 2310 93455
Lakeview JHS, P O BOX 2310 93455
    Dale Hyatt, prin.
JHS, P O BOX 2310 93455 – Ralph Tilton, prin.

Dunlap ES, 1220 OAK KNOLL ROAD 93455
    Tony Brancato, prin.
Grisham ES, PINAL & NORRIS STS 93455
    Donald Brown, prin.
Nightingale ES, 255 WINTER ROAD 93455
    Pat Eggleton, prin.
Patterson Road ES, 400 PATTERSON ROAD 93455
    Richard Makela, prin.
Pine Grove ES, 1050 E RICE RANCH ROAD 93455
    Jean Dunham, prin.
Shaw ES, 759 DAHLIA PLACE 93455
    Keith Martindale, prin.

Orick, Humboldt Co., Pop. Code 3
Orick ESD
Sch. Sys. Enr. Code 1
Supt. – Beverly Cottingham, P O BOX 128 95555
ES, P O BOX 128 95555
    Beverly Cottingham, prin.

Orinda, Contra Costa Co., Pop. Code 6
Orinda Un. ESD
Sch. Sys. Enr. Code 4
Supt. – Laurie Halsey
    8 ALTARINDA ROAD 94563
Orinda IS, 80 IVY DRIVE 94563
    Jean Hyland, prin.
Del Rey ES, 25 EL CAMINO MORAGA 94563
    Barbara Doyal, prin.
Glorietta ES, 15 MARTHA ROAD 94563
    Janet Horner, prin.
Sleepy Hollow ES
    20 WASHINGTON LANE 94563
    Linda Morehouse, prin.

Orland, Glenn Co., Pop. Code 5
Capay JUn. ESD
Sch. Sys. Enr. Code 2
Supt. – (—)
    RURAL ROUTE 02 BOX 2472 95963
Capay Joint Union ES
    RURAL ROUTE 02 BOX 2472 95963
    Charles Schaffert, prin.

Lake ESD
Sch. Sys. Enr. Code 2
Supt. – (—)
    RURAL ROUTE 04 BOX 4306 95963
Lake ES, RURAL ROUTE 04 BOX 4306 95963
    Leroy Dean, prin.

Orland JSD
Sch. Sys. Enr. Code 4
Supt. – Leeds Lacy,Jr., 1320 6TH ST 95963
Price IS, 1320 6TH ST 95963 – David Fase, prin.
Fairview MS
    COUNTY ROAD L AND SOUTH ST 95963
    Elizabeth Lawrence, prin.
Mill Street ES, 102 MILL ST 95963
    Larry Long, prin.

Plaza ESD
Sch. Sys. Enr. Code 2
Supt. – (—)
    RURAL ROUTE 01 BOX 1529 95963
Plaza ES, RURAL ROUTE 01 BOX 1529 95963
    Michael Kimberley, prin.

Orleans, Humboldt Co.
Klamath-Trinity JUSD
Supt. – See Hoopa
ES, P O BOX 215 95556 – Joyce Rich, prin.

Oro Grande, San Bernardino Co., Pop. Code 3
Oro Grande ESD
Sch. Sys. Enr. Code 2
Supt. – Ken Larson, P O BOX 386 92368
ES, 19175 THIRD ST 92368 – Ken Larson, prin.

Orosi, Tulare Co., Pop. Code 5
Cutler-Orosi USD
Sch. Sys. Enr. Code 5
Supt. – Eddie Ikard, 41855 ROAD 128 93647
Palm MS, 12915 AVE 419 93647
    Bob Cumiford, prin.
Yettem MS, 41855 ROAD 128 93647
    Sue Saunders, prin.
Other Schools – See Badger

Oroville, Butte Co., Pop. Code 6
Golden Feather Un. ESD
Sch. Sys. Enr. Code 2
Supt. – Saddie Nishitani
    11679 NELSON BAR RD 95965
Concow MS, 11679 NELSON BAR ROAD 95965
    Sam Dresser, prin.
Spring Valley ES, 2271 PENTZ ROAD 95965
    Marlene Oberdorf, prin.

Oroville City ESD
Sch. Sys. Enr. Code 5
Supt. – Donald Remley, 2795 YARD ST 95966
Central MS, 2795 YARD ST 95966
    Michael Trenton, prin.
Bird Street ES, 1421 BIRD ST 95965
    Robin Little, prin.
Eastside ES, 2775 YARD ST 95966
    Robin Little, prin.
Oakdale Heights ES
    2255 LAS PLUMAS AVE 95966
    Raymond Sehorn, prin.
Ophir ES, 210 OAKVALE AVE 95966
    Lee Hutchins, prin.
Stanford Avenue ES, 1801 STANFORD AVE 95966
    D. Fuller, prin.

Wyandotte Avenue ES
    2800 WYANDOTTE AVE 95966
    Weldon Papa, prin.

Palermo Un. SD
Supt. – See Palermo
Wilcox ES, 5737 AUTREY LANE 95966
    Jeanne Purcell, prin.

Thermalito Un. ESD
Sch. Sys. Enr. Code 4
Supt. – Gordon Lemky, 1050 SIERRA AVE 95965
Nelson Avenue ES, 1050 SIERRA AVE 95965
    Hedrick Light, prin.
Poplar Avenue ES, 1050 SIERRA AVE 95965
    Bruno Zancanella, prin.
Sierra Avenue ES, 1050 SIERRA AVE 95965
    Bruno Zancanella, prin.

Oroville Christian ES, 3785 OLIVE HWY 95966
St. Thomas Catholic ES, 1380 BIRD ST 95965

Oxnard, Ventura Co., Pop. Code 9
Hueneme ESD
Supt. – See Port Hueneme
Blackstock MS, 701 E ROAD ROAD 93033
    Tom Haas, prin.
Green MS, 3739 S C ST 93033 – Rich Froyen, prin.
Hathaway ES, 405 E DOLLIE ST 93033
    Robin Freeman, prin.
Haycox ES, 5400 PERKINS ROAD 93033
    William Davis, prin.
Hollywood Beach ES, 4000 SUNSET LANE 93035
    Jeffrey Baarstad, prin.
Larsen ES
    E THOMAS AVE MCMILLAN MANOR 93033
    James Pardue, prin.
Sunkist ES, 1400 TEAKWOOD ST 93033
    Don Barnes, prin.
Williams ES, 4300 ANCHORAGE ST 93033
    Deloris Carn, prin.

Ocean View ESD
Sch. Sys. Enr. Code 4
Supt. – Robert Allen, 2382 ETTING ROAD 93033
Ocean View JHS, 4300 OLDS ROAD 93033
    Frank Samuels, prin.
Laguna Vista ES, 5084 ETTING ROAD 93033
    Hugh Pickrel, prin.
Mar Vista ES, 2382 ETTING ROAD 93033
    Nancy Cuellar, prin.
Tierra Vista ES, 2001 SANFORD ST 93033
    Sam Ballinger, prin.

Oxnard ESD
Sch. Sys. Enr. Code 7
Supt. – Norman Brekke, 831 S B ST 93030
Fremont IS, 831 S B ST 93030
    Richard Duarte, prin.
Haydock IS, 831 S B ST 93030
    Ronald D'Incau, prin.
Nueva Vista IS, 831 S B ST 93030
    Ruth Battle, prin.
Curren MS, 1101 N F ST 93030
    Richard Canady, prin.
Driffill ES, 910 SOUTH E ST 93030
    Peter Nichols, prin.
Elm Street MS, 450 E ELM ST 93033
    Loretta Carter, prin.
Harrington ES, 2501 GISLER AVE 93033
    Peter Chapa, prin.
Juanita ES, 224 N JUANITA AVE 93030
    Juanita Valdez, prin.
Kamala ES, 634 W KAMALA ST 93033
    Mexie Duff, prin.
Lemonwood ES, 2200 CARNEGIE CT 93033
    Dennis Williams, prin.
Marina West ES, 2501 CAROB ST 93035
    Frank Rodriguez, prin.
McAuliffe ES, 3300 W VIA MARINA AVE 93030
    Paul Kirk, prin.
McKinna ES, 1611 S J ST 93033
    Constance Hershkowitz, prin.
Ramona ES, 804 COOPER ROAD 93030
    Dennis Johnson, prin.
Rose Avenue MS, 220 S DRISKILL ST 93030
    Ernest Morrison, prin.
Sierra Linda MS, 2201 JASMINE ST 93030
    Edmundo Chavez, prin.

Rio ESD
Sch. Sys. Enr. Code 4
Supt. – John McGarry, 3300 CORTEZ ST 93030
Rio Del Valle MS, 3100 N ROSE AVE 93030
    Gary Martino, prin.
El Rio ES, 2714 E VINEYARD AVE 93030
    Rafael Perez, prin.
Rio Lindo ES, 2131 SNOW AVE 93030
    Carol Taylor, prin.
Rio Plaza ES, 600 SIMON WAY 93030
    Diann Depasquale, prin.
Rio Real ES, 1140 KENNY ST 93030
    David Lopez, prin.

Community Christian ES, 723 S D ST 93030
Law Private ES, 2931 ALBANY DR 93033
Our Lady of Guadalupe ES
    530 N JUANITA AVE 93030
Santa Clara ES, 324 SOUTH E ST 93030
St. Anthony's ES, 2421 S C ST 93033
St. John's Lutheran ES, 1500 N C ST 93030
Vineyard Christian ES
    2700 BUCKAROO WAGON WHEEL 93030

Pacifica, San Mateo Co., Pop. Code 8
Laguna Salada Un. ESD
Sch. Sys. Enr. Code 5
Supt. – Ronald Gilpatrick
  375 REINA DEL MAR   94044
Cabrillo ES, 601 CRESPI DRIVE   94044
  Leslie Linhares, prin.
Fairmont ES, 290 EDGEWOOD DRIVE   94044
  John Perry, prin.
Linda Mar ES, 830 ROSITA ROAD   94044
  Raymond Gomes, prin.
Oddstad ES, 930 ODDSTAD BLVD   94044
  Karen Warner, prin.
Ortega ES, 1283 TERRA NOVA BLVD   94044
  Marilyn Krassner, prin.
Pacific Manor ES, 411 OCEANA BLVD   94044
  Ron Lewis, prin.
Sharp Park ES, 1427 PALMETTO AVE   94044
  Alberta Freitas, prin.
Vallemar ES, 377 REINA DEL MAR AVE   94044
  Brian Connor, prin.
Westview ES, 367 GLENCOURT WAY   94044
  Kitty Mindel, prin.
Other Schools – See San Bruno

Alma Heights Christian Academy
  1295 SEVILLE DR   94044
Good Shepherd ES, 909 OCEANA BLVD   94044

Pacific Grove, Monterey Co., Pop. Code 7
Pacific Grove USD
Sch. Sys. Enr. Code 4
Supt. – Richard Rigg, 555 SINEX AVE   93950
MS, 835 FOREST AVE   93950 – (—), prin.
Down ES, 485 PINE AVE   93950
  Howard Cobb, prin.
Forest Grove ES, 1065 CONGRESS AVE   93950
  Denise Rowe, prin.

Pacific Palisades, Los Angeles Co.
Los Angeles USD
Sch. Sys. Enr. Code
Supt. – See Los Angeles
Marquez Avenue ES
  16821 MARQUEZ AVE   90272
  Jacqueline Ota, prin.
Pacific Palisades ES, 800 VIA DE LA PAZ   90272
  Terri Arnold, prin.

Corpus Christi ES, 890 TOYOPA DR   90272
St. Matthew's Parish ES, P O BOX 37   90272
Village School, Inc.
  780 SWARTHMORE AVE   90272

Pacoima, Los Angeles Co.
Los Angeles USD
Sch. Sys. Enr. Code
Supt. – See Los Angeles
Beachy Avenue ES, 9757 BEACHY AVE   91331
  Lurline Hemphill, prin.
Broadous ES, 12561 FILMORE ST   91331
  Ora Parker, prin.
Canterbury Avenue ES
  13670 MONTAGUE ST   91331
  Karen Robertson, prin.
Haddon Avenue ES, 10115 HADDON AVE   91331
  Albert Roque, prin.
Montague Street ES, 13000 MONTAGUE ST   91331
  Alvin Parde, prin.
Pacoima ES, 11016 NORRIS AVE   91331
  Robert Owens, prin.
Sharp Avenue ES, 13800 PIERCE ST   91331
  Ricardo Sosapavon, prin.
Telfair Avenue ES, 10975 TELFAIR AVE   91331
  Dolores Soll, prin.
Vena Avenue ES, 9377 VENA AVE   91331
  Diane Pritchard, prin.

Calvary Lutheran ES
  8800 WOODMAN AVE   91331
Guardian Angel ES, 10919 NORRIS AVE   91331
Mary Immaculate Catholic ES
  10390 REMICK AVE   91331
Panorama Baptist ES
  8755 WOODMAN AVE   91331

Paicines, San Benito Co.
Jefferson ESD
Sch. Sys. Enr. Code 1
Supt. – (—)
  221 OLD HERNANDEZ ROAD   95043
Jefferson ES, 221 OLD HERNANDEZ ROAD   95043
  Marvin Langsam, prin.

Panoche ESD
Sch. Sys. Enr. Code 1
Supt. – (—), 31441 PANOCHE ROAD   95043
Panoche ES, 31441 PANOCHE ROAD   95043
  John Light, prin.

Willow Grove Un. ESD
Sch. Sys. Enr. Code 1
Supt. – (—), P O BOX 46   95043
Willow Grove ES, P O BOX 46   95043
  Rosemary Grassi, prin.

Pala, San Diego Co.

Mission San Antonio de Pala ES
  P O BOX 80   92059

Palermo, Butte Co., Pop. Code 6
Palermo Un. SD
Sch. Sys. Enr. Code 4
Supt. – Glenn Tabor
  2261 ESPERANZA AVE   95968
MS, 2261 ESPERANZA AVE   95968
  David Kramer, prin.

Honcut PS, 2261 ESPERANZA AVE   95968
  Jeanne Purcell, prin.
Other Schools – See Oroville

Palmdale, Los Angeles Co., Pop. Code 7
Clovis USD
Supt. – See Clovis
Gettysburg ES, 2155 BARSTOW   93612
  Tony Petersen, prin.

Palmdale ESD
Sch. Sys. Enr. Code 6
Supt. – Forrest McElroy, 38260 10TH ST E   93550
Juniper IS, 38260 10TH ST E   93550
  Mary Wright, prin.
Sage IS, 38260 10TH ST E   93550
  David Millen, prin.
Cactus ES, 4037 E AVENUE P-8   93550
  Judy Fish, prin.
Chaparral ES, 37510 50TH ST E   93550
  Greg Cary, prin.
Desert Rose ES, 2801 E AVENUE R-6   93550
  Lonel Herrera, prin.
Joshua Hills ES, 3030 FAIRFIELD   93550
  Robert Berlinger, prin.
Manzanita ES, P O BOX 218   93550
  Joyce Inman, prin.
Ocotillo ES
  1330 W ELIZABETH LAKE ROAD   93551
  Leonard Tahsuda, prin.
Tamarisk ES, P O BOX 218   93550
  Betty Stiers, prin.
Tumbleweed ES, P O BOX 218   93550
  Fredrick Strasburg, prin.
Yucca ES, P O BOX 218   93550
  Darwyne Vickers, prin.

Wilsona SD
Supt. – See Lancaster
Vista San Gabriel ES, 18020 E AVENUE O   93551
  Rex Comer, prin.

Bethel Christian Academy, 2714 E AVE R   93550
St. Mary Catholic ES, P O BOX 1000   93550

Palm Desert, Riverside Co., Pop. Code 7
Desert Sands USD
Supt. – See Indio
MS, 74-200 RUTLEDGE WAY   92260
  Margaret Steen, prin.
Lincoln MS, 74-100 RUTLEDGE WAY   92260
  Larry Taylor, prin.
Washington ES, 45-768 PORTOLA AVE   92260
  Joan Schiffling, prin.

Palm Desert Learning Tree School
  42-675 WASHINGTON ST   92260

Palm Springs, Riverside Co., Pop. Code 8
Palm Springs USD
Sch. Sys. Enr. Code 7
Supt. – Wilber Hawkins
  333 S FARRELL DRIVE   92262
Coffman MS, 34-603 PLUMLEY ROAD   92260
  Terri Simon, prin.
Cree MS, 1011 E VISTA CHINO   92262
  Nancy Gravette, prin.
Agua Caliente ES
  30-800 SAN LUIS REY PLAZA   92262
  James Hurst, prin.
Cahuilla ES, 833 MESQUITE ROAD   92262
  Steve Mahoney, prin.
Cielo Vista ES, 650 S PASEO DOROTEA   92264
  Joanne Burkett, prin.
Finchy ES, 777 E TACHEVAH DRIVE   92262
  William Rogers, prin.
Vista Del Monte ES
  2744 N VIA MIRALESTE   92262
  Andy Bellomo, prin.
Other Schools – See Cathedral City, Desert Hot
  Springs, Rancho Mirage, Thousand Palms

Desert Chapel Christian ES
  630 S SUNRISE WAY   92264
Palm Valley ES, 67675 BOLERO DR   92264
St. Theresa ES, 2850 E RAMON RD   92264

Palo Alto, Santa Clara Co., Pop. Code 8
Palo Alto USD
Sch. Sys. Enr. Code 6
Supt. – Julian Crocker, 25 CHURCHILL AVE   94306
Stanford MS, 480 E MEADOW DRIVE   94306
  James Mathiott, prin.
Addison ES, 650 ADDISON AVE   94301
  Donna Elder, prin.
Briones ES, 4100 ORME AVE   94306
  Gerald Schmidt, prin.
Duveneck ES, 705 ALESTER AVE   94303
  Champlin Heilman, prin.
El Carmelo ES, 3024 BRYANT ST   94306
  Elayne Goodman, prin.
Fairmeadow ES, 500 E MEADOW DRIVE   94306
  William White, prin.
Hays ES, 1525 MIDDLEFIELD ROAD   94301
  Harold Jones, prin.
Hoover ES, 800 BARRON AVE   94306
  Kay Van Der Burg, prin.
Ohlone ES, 950 AMARILLO AVE   94303
  (—), prin.
Palo Verde ES, 3450 LOUIS ROAD   94303
  Thomas Steege, prin.
Other Schools – See Stanford

Ravenswood City ESD
Sch. Sys. Enr. Code 5
Supt. – Charlie Knight, 2160 EUCLID AVE   94303
Ravenswood MS, 2450 RALMAR AVE   94303
  James Logan, prin.
Brentwood Oaks ES, 2086 CLARK AVE   94303
  Brenda Corbin, prin.
Costano ES, 2695 FORDHAM ST   94303
  Joseph Davis, prin.
Other Schools – See East Palo Alto, Menlo Park

Keys ES, 2890 MIDDLEFIELD RD   94306
St. Elizabeth of Seton Catholic ES
  1095 CHANNING AVE   94301

Palo Cedro, Shasta Co.
Junction ESD
Sch. Sys. Enr. Code 2
Supt. – Barry Reed
  3801 DESCHUTES ROAD   96073
Junction IS, 3999 DESCHUTES ROAD   96073
  John Wilson, prin.
Junction ES, 3801 DESCHUTES ROAD   96073
  Berry Reed, prin.

North Cow Creek ESD
Sch. Sys. Enr. Code 2
Supt. – William Quinn
  10619 SWEDE CREEK ROAD   96073
North Cow Creek ES
  10619 SWEDE CREEK ROAD   96073
  William Quinn, prin.

Country Christian ES, 21945 OLD 44 DR   96073

Palomar Mountain, San Diego Co.
Pauma ESD
Supt. – See Pauma Valley
ES   92060 – Michael Stuckhardt, prin.

Palos Verdes Estates, Los Angeles Co., Pop. Code 7
Palos Verdes Peninsula USD
Supt. – See Rolling Hills Estates
Malaga Cove IS, 300 PASEO DEL MAR   90274
  Carl Lane, prin.
Ridgecrest IS, 28915 NORTHBAY RD   90274
  William Erickson, prin.
Lunada Bay ES, 520 PASEO LUNADO   90274
  Norma Poling, prin.
Montemalaga ES, 1121 VIA NOGALES   90274
  Roger Gartland, prin.

Palos Verdes Peninsula, Los Angeles Co., Pop. Code 8
Chadwick School, 26800 ACADEMY DRIVE   90274
Rolling Hills Country Day ES
  26444 CRENSHAW BLVD   90274
St. John Fisher ES, 5446 CREST RD W   90274

Panorama City, Los Angeles Co.
Los Angeles USD
Supt. – See Los Angeles
Charnock Road IS, 14041 CHASE ST   91402
  Evelyn Barker, prin.
Chase Street ES, 14041 CHASE ST   91402
  Roger Buss, prin.
Liggett Street ES, 9373 MOONBEAM AVE   91402
  Ed Krojansky, prin.
Ranchito Avenue ES, 7940 RANCHITO AVE   91402
  Norman Bernstein, prin.

College d'Etudes Francaises, P O BOX 4839   91412
St. Genevieve ES, 14024 COMMUNITY ST   91402

Paradise, Butte Co., Pop. Code 7
Paradise USD
Sch. Sys. Enr. Code 5
Supt. – Richard Landess
  5665 RECREATION DRIVE   95969
IS, 5657 RECREATION DRIVE   95969
  James Kyle, prin.
ES, 588 PEARSON ROAD   95969
  Stephen Jennings, prin.
Ponderosa ES, 6593 PENTZ ROAD   95969
  Abe Memeo, prin.
Other Schools – See Magalia, Stirling City

Paradise Adventist School, P O BOX 2169   95969
St. Thomas More School
  771 ELLIOTT ROAD   95969

Paramount, Los Angeles Co., Pop. Code 8
Paramount USD
Sch. Sys. Enr. Code 7
Supt. – Richard Caldwell
  15110 CALIFORNIA AVE   90723
Alondra IS, 16200 DOWNEY AVE   90723
  John Thomas, prin.
Clearwater IS, 14708 PARAMOUNT BLVD   90723
  Ralph Anaya, prin.
Gaines ES, 7340 JACKSON ST   90723
  Olga Okell, prin.
Keppel ES, 6630 MARK KEPPEL ST   90723
  Howard Bryan, prin.
Lincoln ES, 15324 CALIFORNIA AVE   90723
  Bertha Forsythe, prin.
Los Cerritos ES, 14626 GUNDRY AVE   90723
  Sara Thurber, prin.
Mokler ES, 8571 FLOWER AVE   90723
  Sumie Imada, prin.
Roosevelt ES, 13451 MERKEL AVE   90723
  Gloria Alkire, prin.
Other Schools – See Long Beach, South Gate

Gethsemane Baptist School
   15363 ORANGE AVE   90723
Our Lady of Rosary ES
   14813 PARAMOUNT BLVD   90723

Parker Dam, San Bernardino Co.
Needles USD
   Supt. – See Needles
   ES, CALIFORNIA AND UTAH STS   92667
      Dennis Murray, prin.

Parlier, Fresno Co., Pop. Code 5
Kings Canyon JUSD
   Supt. – See Reedley
   Riverview ES, 8662 S LAC JAC AVE   93648
      John Panzak, prin.

Parlier USD
   Sch. Sys. Enr. Code 4
   Supt. – Fernando Elizondo
      900 S NEWMARK AVE   93648
   Martinez JHS, 900 S NEWMARK AVE   93648
      Jim Daddino, prin.
   Central MS, 601 3RD ST   93648
      Mathew Brletic, prin.
   Tuolumne ES, 500 TUOLUMNE ST   93648
      Chris Wilson, prin.

Pasadena, Los Angeles Co., Pop. Code 9
Pasadena USD
   Sch. Sys. Enr. Code 7
   Supt. – Phillip Jordan, 351 S HUDSON AVE   91101
   Wilson MS, 300 S MADRE AVE   91107
      Joanne Foland, prin.
   Allendale ES, 1135 S EUCLID AVE   91106
      Jean Mills, prin.
   Benito Fundamental ES, 3700 DENAIR ST   91107
      Anna Hession, prin.
   Cleveland ES, 524 PALISADE ST   91103
      Pamela Powell, prin.
   Field ES, 3600 E SIERRA MADRE BLVD   91107
      Timothy Hack, prin.
   Hamilton ES, 2089 ROSE VILLA ST   91107
      Zakkiyah Williams, prin.
   Jefferson ES, 1500 E VILLA ST   91106
      Susan Ballantyne, prin.
   Linda Vista ES, 1259 LINDA VISTA AVE   91103
      Lonnie Urbina, prin.
   Longfellow ES
      1065 E WASHINGTON BLVD   91104
      Isaac Hammond, prin.
   Madison ES, 515 E ASHTABULA ST   91104
      Gloria Delaney, prin.
   San Rafael ES, 1090 NITHSDALE ROAD   91105
      Robert Densford, prin.
   Washington MS, 1520 N RAYMOND AVE   91103
      Willis Charles, prin.
   Webster ES, 2101 E WASHINGTON BLVD   91104
      Geraldyne Filhart, prin.
   Williard ES, 301 MADRE ST   91107
      Regenia Moses, prin.
   Other Schools – See Altadena, Sierra Madre

Polytechnic School
   1030 E CALIFORNIA BLVD   91106
Reynolds Christian Academy
   1612 E ELIZABETH ST   91104
Assumption of the Blessed Virgin Mary ES
   2660 E ORANGE GROVE BLVD   91107
Calvary Christian ES
   1555 E COLORADO BLVD   91106
Chandler ES, 1005 ARMADA DR   91103
High Point Academy
   1720 KINNELOA CANYON RD   91107
Imperial ES, 254 S PASADENA AVE   91129
Mayfield JHS/Holy Child Jesus
   405 S EUCLID AVE   91101
Pasadena Christian ES
   1515 N LOS ROBLES AVE   91104
Pasadena Towne/Country ES
   200 S SIERRA MADRE BLVD   91107
San Marino Montessori School
   444 S SIERRA MADRE BLVD   91107
St. Andrew ES, 42 CHESTNUT ST   91103
St. Philip the Apostle ES, 161 S HILL AVE   91106

Paskenta, Tehama Co.
Elkins ESD
   Sch. Sys. Enr. Code 1
   Supt. – (—), TOOMES CAMP ROAD   96074
   Elkins ES, P O BOX 407   96074
      Marla Martz, prin.

Paso Robles, San Luis Obispo Co., Pop. Code 6
Paso Robles SD
   Sch. Sys. Enr. Code 5
   Supt. – Richard Herzberg, 504 1/2 28TH ST   93446
   Flamson MS, 24TH & SPRING STS   93446
      Noel Lacayo, prin.
   Bauer/Speck ES, 18TH & VINE STS   93446
      Gary Hoskins, prin.
   Brown ES, 36TH & OAK STS   93446
      Bart Ellerbroek, prin.
   Pifer ES, 900 CRESTON ROAD   93446
      Dawn Aiken, prin.

Phillips ESD
   Sch. Sys. Enr. Code 1
   Supt. – (—), 4725 RIVERGROVE DR   93446
   Phillips ES, SHANDO HCR ROUTE   93446
      Grace Wittstrom, prin.

St. Rose ES, 900 TUCKER AVE   93446

Trinity Lutheran School
   940 CRESTON ROAD   93446

Patterson, Stanislaus Co., Pop. Code 5
Patterson JUSD
   Sch. Sys. Enr. Code 4
   Supt. – Keith Daniel, P O BOX 547   95363
   JHS, 201 N 9TH ST   95363 – Ronald Hartman, prin.
   Las Palmas MS, 624 W LAS PALMAS AVE   95363
      Daniel Barton, prin.
   Northmead ES, 625 L ST   95363
      Joanne Stewart, prin.
   Other Schools – See Livermore, Vernails, Westley

Pauma Valley, San Diego Co.
Pauma ESD
   Sch. Sys. Enr. Code 2
   Supt. – Michael Stuckhardt
      33158 COLE GRADE ROAD   92061
   Pauma ES, 33158 COLE GRADE RAOD   92061
      Michael Stuckhardt, prin.
   Other Schools – See Palomar Mountain

Paynes Creek, Tehama Co.
Plum Valley ESD
   Sch. Sys. Enr. Code 1
   Supt. – (—), PLUM CREEK ROAD   96075
   Plum Valley ES   96075 – Evan Gittelsohn, prin.

Pearblossom, Los Angeles Co.
Keppel Un. ESD
   Supt. – See Littlerock
   Lake Los Angeles ES, P O BOX 186   93553
      Catherine Sorenson, prin.

Penngrove, Sonoma Co.
Petaluma SD
   Supt. – See Petaluma
   ES, P O BOX 480   94951 – Charol Weiss, prin.

Penn Valley, Nevada Co.
Pleasant Valley ESD
   Sch. Sys. Enr. Code 3
   Supt. – Wayne Padover
      14685 PLEASANT VALLEY ROAD   95946
   ES, 14685 PLEASANT VALLEY ROAD   95946
      Karen Boettcher, prin.

Ready Springs Un. SD
   Sch. Sys. Enr. Code 2
   Supt. – Larry Babcock
      10862 SPENCEVILLE RD   95946
   Ready Springs ES, 10862 SPENCEVILLE RD   95946
      Larry Babcock, prin.

Penryn, Placer Co.
Penryn ESD
   Sch. Sys. Enr. Code 2
   Supt. – Sarah Peterson, P O BOX 349   95663
   ES, P O BOX 349   95663 – Sarah Peterson, prin.

Perris, Riverside Co., Pop. Code 6
Perris ESD
   Sch. Sys. Enr. Code 4
   Supt. – Elaine Rowen, 143 E FIRST ST   92370
   Good Hope IS, 24-050 THEDA ST   92370
      Charles Martin, prin.
   PS, 500 N A ST   92370 – Richard Shepler, prin.
   Sanders ES, 146 N A ST   92370 – (—), prin.

Perris Un. HSD
   Sch. Sys. Enr. Code 5
   Supt. – J. Hane, 1151 N A ST   92370
   Perris Valley MS, 501 N A ST   92370
      Lou Ann Archbold, prin.
   Pinacate MS, 1990 S A ST   92370
      Walter Otto, prin.

Val Verde ESD
   Sch. Sys. Enr. Code 4
   Supt. – Leona Williams
      20340 INDIAN AVE   92370
   Mead Valley ES, 21-100 OLEANDER AVE   92370
      Andy Fisher, prin.
   Val Verde ES, 2656 INDIAN AVE   92370
      Robert Baker, prin.

Temple Christian Schs.
   745 N PERRIS BLVD   92370
St. James ES, 250 E 3RD ST   92370

Pescadero, San Mateo Co., Pop. Code 2
La Honda-Pescadero USD
   Sch. Sys. Enr. Code 2
   Supt. – Judith Robertson, P O BOX 189   94060
   ES, 620 NORTH ST   94060 – Judi Robertson, prin.
   Other Schools – See La Honda

Petaluma, Sonoma Co., Pop. Code 8
Cinnabar ESD
   Sch. Sys. Enr. Code 2
   Supt. – Gary Vickers-Barr, P O BOX 750399   94975
   Cinnabar ES, 286 SKILLMAN LN   94975
      Gary Barr, prin.

Dunham ESD
   Sch. Sys. Enr. Code 1
   Supt. – Tom Wolf, 4111 ROBLAR ROAD   94952
   Dunham ES, 4111 ROBLAR ROAD   94952
      Tom Wolf, prin.

Laguna JESD
   Sch. Sys. Enr. Code 1
   Supt. – (—)
      3286 CHILENO VALLEY ROAD   94952
   Laguna ES, 3286 CHILENO VALLEY ROAD   94952
      Barbara Armington, prin.

Liberty ESD
   Sch. Sys. Enr. Code 2
   Supt. – Jim Currie, 170 LIBERTY ROAD   94952
   Liberty ES, 170 LIBERTY ROAD   94952
      Jim Currie, prin.

Lincoln ESD
   Sch. Sys. Enr. Code 1
   Supt. – (—)
      1300 HICKS VALLEY ROAD   94952
   Lincoln ES, 1300 HICKS VALLEY ROAD   94952
      Patty Pomi, prin.

Old Adobe Un. ESD
   Sch. Sys. Enr. Code 4
   Supt. – Don Brann, 845 CRINELLA DRIVE   94952
   Eldredge ES, 207 MARIA DRIVE   94952
      Carolyn Coyman, prin.
   La Tecera ES, 1600 ALBIN WAY   94952
      Tom Eggert, prin.
   Miwok Valley ES
      1010 SAINT FRANCIS DRIVE   94952
      Patricia Raney, prin.
   Old Adobe ES, 2856 ADOBE ROAD   94952
      Dan Longaker, prin.

Petaluma SD
   Sch. Sys. Enr. Code 5
   Supt. – Charles Cadman, 11 5TH ST   94952
   Kenilworth JHS, 998 E WASHINGTON ST   94952
      Richard Clecak, prin.
   JHS, 700 BANTAM WAY   94952
      Sharon Carrick, prin.
   Cherry Valley ES, 1001 CHERRY ST   94952
      Carolyn Magliulo, prin.
   Grant ES, 200 GRANT AVE   94952
      Mogens Kristensen, prin.
   McDowell ES, 1425 MCGREGOR DRIVE   94952
      Robert Foster, prin.
   McKinley ES, 110 ELLIS ST   94952
      Robert Alpert, prin.
   McNear ES, 605 SUNNYSLOPE AVE   94952
      William Wurzburg, prin.
   Valley Vista ES, 730 N WEBSTER ST   94952
      Nancy Smith, prin.
   Other Schools – See Penngrove

Two Rock Un. ESD
   Sch. Sys. Enr. Code 2
   Supt. – (—), 5001 SPRINGHILL ROAD   94952
   Two Rock ES, 5001 SPRING HILL ROAD   94952
      Colleen Richardson, prin.

Union JESD
   Sch. Sys. Enr. Code 1
   Supt. – (—), 5225 RED HILL ROAD   94952
   Union ES, 5225 RED HILL ROAD   94952
      Elaine Boling, prin.

Waugh ESD
   Sch. Sys. Enr. Code 1
   Supt. – (—), 1060 CORONA ROAD   94952
   Waugh ES, 1060 CORONA ROAD   94952
      Irwin Karp, prin.

Wilmar Un. ESD
   Sch. Sys. Enr. Code 2
   Supt. – Monica Fagan, 3775 BODEGA AVE   94952
   Wilson ES, 3775 BODEGA AVE   94952
      Monica Fagan, prin.

Reid ES, P O BOX 750549   94975
St. Vincent ES, UNION & HOWARD STS   94952

Petrolia, Humboldt Co.
Mattole Un. ESD
   Sch. Sys. Enr. Code 2
   Supt. – Raymond Azevedo, P O BOX 32   95558
   Honeydew ES, P O BOX 32   95545
      Raymond Azevedo, prin.
   Mattole Union ES, P O BOX 32   95558
      Raymond Azevedo, prin.

Phelan, San Bernardino Co.
Snowline JUSD
   Sch. Sys. Enr. Code 5
   Supt. – Arthur Townley, P O BOX 1188   92371
   Pinon Mesa MS, 9298 SHEEP CREEK ROAD   92371
      Joe Womack, prin.
   Baldy Mesa ES, P O BOX 1188   92371
      Edward Conrad, prin.
   ES, P O BOX 78   92371 – Steve Mereness, prin.
   Other Schools – See Wrightwood

Pico Rivera, Los Angeles Co., Pop. Code 8
El Rancho USD
   Sch. Sys. Enr. Code 7
   Supt. – Thomas Sakalis
      9333 LOCH LOMOND DRIVE   90660
   Burke MS, 8101 ORANGE AVE   90660
      Tom Cunningham, prin.
   North Park MS, 4450 DURFEE AVE   90660
      Ron Colosimo, prin.
   Rivera MS, 7200 CITRONELL AVE   90660
      Manford Mainer, prin.
   Birney ES, 8501 ORANGE AVE   90660
      Steve Kennedy, prin.
   Durfee ES, 4220 DURFEE AVE   90660
      Andrew Sermeno, prin.
   Magee ES, 8200 SERAPIS AVE   90660
      David Verdugo, prin.
   North Ranchito ES, 8837 OLYMPIC BLVD   90660
      Linda Vargas, prin.
   Pio Pico ES, 4211 COLUMBIA AVE   90660
      Alice Baeza, prin.
   Rio Vista ES, 8809 COFFMAN PICO ROAD   90660
      Robert Martinez, prin.

Rivera ES, 7520 CITRONELL AVE 90660
  Fernando Reyes, prin.
South Ranchito ES, 5241 PASSONS BLVD 90660
  Raul Almada, prin.
Valencia ES, 9241 COSGROVE ST 90660
  Carmen Ruiz, prin.

Montebello USD
Supt. – See Montebello
Montebello Gardens ES, 4700 PINE ST 90660
  Delia Montes, prin.

Armenian Mesrobian School
  8420 BEVERLY ROAD 90660
St. Hilary ES, 5401 CITRONELL AVE 90660
St. Marianne De Paredes ES
  7911 BUHMAN AVE 90660

Piedmont, Alameda Co., Pop. Code 7
Piedmont City USD
Sch. Sys. Enr. Code 4
Supt. – Gail Anderson
  780 MAGNOLIA AVE 94611
MS, 740 MAGNOLIA AVE 94611
  John Morrison, prin.
Beach ES, 100 LAKE AVE 94611
  Nancy McHugh, prin.
Havens ES, 1800 OAKLAND AVE 94611
  Ruth Helgeson, prin.
Wildwood ES, 301 WILDWOOD AVE 94611
  Carolyn Raffo, prin.

Pinecrest, Tuolumne Co.
Columbia Un. SD
Supt. – See Columbia
ES, P O BOX 1218 95364 – (—), prin.

Pinedale, Fresno Co., Pop. Code 4
Clovis USD
Supt. – See Clovis
Nelson ES, 1336 W SPRUCE AVE 93650
  Linda Hauser, prin.
ES, 7171 N SUGARPINE AVE 93650
  Janice Davis, prin.

Pine Grove, Amador Co., Pop. Code 3
Amador County USD
Supt. – See Jackson
ES 95665 – Mark Mathany, prin.

Community Christian ES, P O BOX 809 95665

Pine Valley, San Diego Co.
Mountain Empire USD
Sch. Sys. Enr. Code 4
Supt. – Jerome Miller
  RURAL ROUTE BOX 8 92062
Mountain Empire JHS
  3305 BUCKMAN SPRINGS ROAD 92062
  Fred Kamper, prin.
ES, 7454 PINE BLVD 92062 – Roy Radke, prin.
Other Schools – See Boulevard, Campo, Descanso,
  Jacumba, Potrero

Pinole, Contra Costa Co., Pop. Code 7
Richmond USD
Supt. – See Richmond
JHS, 1575 MANN DRIVE 94564 – John Nules, prin.
Collins ES
  PINOLE VALLEY AND TENNENT 94564
  Evelyn Beckford, prin.
Ellerhorst ES, 3501 PINOLE VALLEY ROAD 94564
  Marilyn McCartney, prin.
Shannon ES, 685 MARLESTA ROAD 94564
  Sheila Farley, prin.
Stewart ES, 2040 HOKE DRIVE 94564
  William Wire, prin.

St. Joseph ES, 1961 PLUM ST 94564

Piru, Ventura Co., Pop. Code 3
Fillmore USD
Supt. – See Fillmore
ES, P O BOX 215 93040 – Lynn Edmonds, prin.

Pismo Beach, San Luis Obispo Co., Pop. Code 6
Lucia Mar USD
Supt. – See Arroyo Grande
Judkins IS, 680 WADSWORTH AVE 93449
  John Hobberlin, prin.
Shell Beach ES, SHELL BEACH ROAD 93449
  Nora Anderson, prin.

Pittsburg, Contra Costa Co., Pop. Code 8
Mt. Diablo USD
Supt. – See Concord
Riverview MS, 205 PACIFICA AVE 94565
  Jo Fyfe, prin.
Bel Air ES, 663 CANAL ROAD 94565
  Dolores Totman, prin.
Rio Vista ES, 611 PACIFICA AVE 94565
  Ron Walters, prin.
Shore Acres ES, 351 MARINA ROAD 94565
  Gary Vanerstrom, prin.

Pittsburg USD
Sch. Sys. Enr. Code 6
Supt. – Salvatore Cardinale
  2000 RAILROAD AVE 94565
Central JHS, 1201 STONEMAN AVE 94565
  Christopher Franklin, prin.
Hillview JHS, 333 YOSEMITE DRIVE 94565
  Robert Guthrie, prin.
Foothill ES, 1200 JENSEN DRIVE 94565
  Lee Arevalo, prin.
Heights ES, 163 WEST BLVD 94565
  Steve Gair, prin.

Highlands ES, 4141 HARBOR ST 94565
  Edith Carlston, prin.
Los Medanos ES, 610 CROWLEY AVE 94565
  Peter Cardinale, prin.
Parkside ES, 985 W 17TH ST 94565
  Patricia Lasarte, prin.
Village ES, 350 SCHOOL ST 94565
  Ila Warner, prin.

Christian Center School
  1210 STONEMAN AVE 94565
St. Peter Martyr ES
  FIFTH AND MONTEZUMA 94565

Pixley, Tulare Co., Pop. Code 4
Pixley Un. ESD
Sch. Sys. Enr. Code 3
Supt. – W. Wayne Clark, P O BOX P 93256
ES, P O BOX P 93256 – Wayne Swanson, prin.

Placentia, Orange Co., Pop. Code 8
Placentia USD
Sch. Sys. Enr. Code 7
Supt. – James Fleming
  1301 E ORANGETHORPE AVE 92670
Kraemer JHS
  1301 E ORANGETHORPE AVE 92670
  Adrianne Trontz, prin.
Tuffree JHS, 1301 E ORANGETHORPE AVE 92670
  George Bowman, prin.
Brookhaven ES, 1851 BROOKHAVEN AVE 92670
  Sally Morton, prin.
Golden ES, 740 GOLDEN AVE 92670
  Ann Test, prin.
Morse Avenue ES, 431 MORSE AVE 92670
  Paula Emry, prin.
Ruby Drive ES, 1811 N PLACENTIA AVE 92670
  Barb Vignone, prin.
Sierra Vista ES, 1811 N PLACENTIA AVE 92670
  Sharon Jackson, prin.
Tynes ES, 735 STANFORD DRIVE 92670
  Kathy Linden, prin.
Van Buren ES, 1245 N VAN BUREN ST 92670
  Kenneth Lorge, prin.
Wagner ES, 717 YORBA LINDA BLVD 92670
  Dale Downey, prin.
Other Schools – See Anaheim, Fullerton, Yorba Linda

St. Joseph ES, 801 N BRADFORD AVE 92670

Placerville, El Dorado Co., Pop. Code 6
Gold Oak Un. ESD
Sch. Sys. Enr. Code 3
Supt. – Bruce Hahn
  3171 PLEASANT VALLEY ROAD 95667
Gold Oak ES
  3171 PLEASANT VALLEY ROAD 95667
  Mark Rickabaugh, prin.

Gold Trail Un. SD
Sch. Sys. Enr. Code 3
Supt. – Steven Herrington
  1336 COLD SPRINGS ROAD 95667
Gold Trail ES, 1336 COLD SPRINGS ROAD 95667
  Donald Schaefer, prin.

Mother Lode Un. ESD
Sch. Sys. Enr. Code 4
Supt. – Larry Acheatel, 3783 FORNI ROAD 95667
Green MS, 3781 FORNI ROAD 95667
  David Soper, prin.
Indian Creek MS, 6701 GREEN VALLEY RD 95667
  Daniel McPherson, prin.
Other Schools – See Diamond Springs

Placerville Un. ESD
Sch. Sys. Enr. Code 4
Supt. – Cynthia Simms
  1032 THOMPSON WAY 95667
Markham JHS, 2800 MOULTON DRIVE 95667
  Nute Momberg, prin.
Schnell ES
  2871 SCHNELL SCHOOL ROAD 95667
  Cathryn Morgan, prin.
Sierra MS, 1100 THOMPSON WAY 95667
  David Baker, prin.

El Dorado Junior Academy
  1900 BROADWAY 95667

Planada, Merced Co., Pop. Code 5
Planada ESD
Sch. Sys. Enr. Code 3
Supt. – John Chavez, P O BOX 236 95365
ES, P O BOX 236 95365 – John Chavez, prin.

Platina, Shasta Co.
Igo-Ono-Platina Un. ESD
Supt. – See Igo
ES, P O BOX 6 96076 – Marvin Peterson, prin.

Pleasant Grove, Sutter Co.
Pleasant Grove JUn. ESD
Sch. Sys. Enr. Code 2
Supt. – A. Hyatt, 3075 HOWSLEY ROAD 95668
ES, 3075 HOWSLEY ROAD 95668 – A. Hyatt, prin.

Pleasant Hill, Contra Costa Co., Pop. Code 8
Mt. Diablo USD
Supt. – See Concord
Sequoia MS, 277 BOYD ROAD 94523
  Jim Pflinger, prin.
Valley View MS, 181 VIKING DRIVE 94523
  Jeff McCreary, prin.
Fair Oaks ES, 2400 LISA LANE 94523
  Gary Holt, prin.

ES, 2097 OAK PARK BLVD 94523
  Dick Taylor, prin.
Sequoia ES, 277 BOYD ROAD 94523
  Gail Brekke, prin.
Strandwood ES, 416 GLADYS DRIVE 94523
  Robert Corritone, prin.
Valhalla ES, 530 KIKI DRIVE 94523
  Charles Cline, prin.

Christ the King ES, 195 BRANDON RD 94523
Pleasant Hill Junior Academy
  796 GRAYSON RD 94523

Pleasanton, Alameda Co., Pop. Code 8
Pleasanton USD
Sch. Sys. Enr. Code 6
Supt. – Bill James, 4665 BERNAL AVE 94566
Harvest Park IS, 4900 VALLEY AVE 94566
  Sally Rayhill, prin.
Alisal ES, 1454 SANTA RITA ROAD 94566
  Steven Maher, prin.
Donlon ES, 4150 DORMAN RD 94566
  Ken Whipple, prin.
Fairlands ES, 4151 W LAS POSITAS BLVD 94566
  John Bristow, prin.
Lydiksen ES, 7700 HIGHLAND OAKS RD 94566
  Cheri Joyce, prin.
Valley View ES, 480 ADAMS WAY 94566
  Randy Zern, prin.
Vintage Hills ES, 1125 CONCORD ST 94566
  Cathy Alden, prin.
Walnut Grove ES, 19999 HARVEST ROAD 94566
  Gerald Shelley, prin.

Point Arena, Mendocino Co., Pop. Code 2
Arena Un. ESD
Sch. Sys. Enr. Code 2
Supt. – D. Kim Jamieson, P O BOX 87 95468
Arena ES, P O BOX 45 95468
  Dolores Roberts, prin.

Point Reyes Station, Marin Co.
Shoreline USD
Supt. – See Tomales
Inverness ES, P O BOX 300 94956
  Sandy Neumann, prin.
West Marin ES, P O BOX 300 94956
  Sandy Neumann, prin.

Pollock Pines, El Dorado Co., Pop. Code 3
Pollock Pines ESD
Sch. Sys. Enr. Code 3
Supt. – William Kramer, 6181A PINE ST 95726
Sierra Ridge MS, 2700 AMBER TRAIL 95726
  Ralph Haslam, prin.
Pinewood MS, 6181 PINE ST 95726
  Stanton Miller, prin.
ES, 6290 PONY EXPRESS TRAIL 95726
  Stephen Malkemus, prin.

Pomona, Los Angeles Co., Pop. Code 8
Ontario-Montclair ESD
Supt. – See Ontario
Ramona ES, 4225 E 9TH ST 91766
  Von Richardson, prin.

Pomona USD
Sch. Sys. Enr. Code 7
Supt. – Timothy Graves, P O BOX 2900 91769
Emerson JHS, 635 LINCOLN AVE 91767
  Catherine Chamberlain, prin.
Fremont JHS, 725 W FRANKLIN AVE 91766
  Frank Garcia, prin.
Marshall JHS, 1921 ARROYO AVE 91768
  Warren Veasey, prin.
Palomares JHS
  2211 N ORANGE GROVE AVE 91767
  Erma Walks, prin.
Simons JHS, 900 E FRANKLIN AVE 91766
  Wayne Joseph, prin.
Alcott ES, 1600 S TOWNE AVE 91766
  James Stewart, prin.
Allison ES, 1011 RUSSELL PLACE 91767
  Gary Clark, prin.
Arroyo ES, 1605 ARROYO AVE 91768
  Brenda Erby, prin.
Barfield ES, 2181 N SAN ANTONIO AVE 91767
  Gloria Marquez, prin.
Decker ES, 20 VILLAGE LOOP ROAD 91766
  Virginia Scott, prin.
Harrison ES, 425 E HARRISON AVE 91767
  Louise Ehresman, prin.
Kellogg ES, 610 MEDINA ST 91768
  John Avila, prin.
Kingsley ES, 1170 WASHINGTON ST 91767
  (—), prin.
Lexington ES, 550 W LEXINGTON AVE 91766
  Tina Clausen, prin.
Lincoln ES, 1200 N GORDON ST 91768
  Amauri Rodriguez, prin.
Madison ES, 351 W PHILLIPS BLVD 91766
  Julian Villasenor, prin.
Mendoza ES, 851 S HAMILTON BLVD 91766
  Jo Roberts, prin.
Montvue ES, 1440 SAN BERNARDINO AVE 91767
  Cecelia Hale, prin.
Philadelphia ES, 600 E PHILADELPHIA ST 91766
  Robert Rodman, prin.
Roosevelt ES, 701 N HUNTINGTON BLVD 91768
  Samuel Tharpe, prin.
San Jose ES, 2015 CADILLAC DRIVE 91767
  Rodolpho Flores, prin.
Washington ES, 975 E 9TH ST 91766
  Vera Harrison, prin.

Westmont ES, 1780 W 9TH ST 91766
Fernando Canedo, prin.
Yorba ES, 250 W LA VERNE AVE 91767
Gwendolyn Tucker, prin.
Other Schools – See Diamond Bar

Arrow Highway Christian ES
305 E ARROW HWY 91767
First Baptist ES, 521 N GAREY AVE 91767
Oak Tree Day ES
456 W ORANGE GROVE AVE 91768
Pomona Adventist Jr. Academy
P O BOX 2543 91769
Pomona Valley Christian ES, P O BOX 2331 91769
Sacred Heart ES, 1263 S HAMILTON BLVD 91766
St. Joseph ES, 1200 W HOLT AVE 91768
St. Madeleine ES, 935 E KINGSLEY AVE 91767

Pond, Kern Co.
Pond Un. ESD
Sch. Sys. Enr. Code 2
Supt. – John Leonard, P O BOX 527 93280
ES, POND ROAD AND BENNER AVE 93280
John Leonard, prin.

Pope Valley, Napa Co.
Pope Valley Un. ESD
Sch. Sys. Enr. Code 1
Supt. – Susan Eakle, P O BOX 167 94567
ES, P O BOX 167 94567 – Susan Eakle, prin.

Porterville, Tulare Co., Pop. Code 7
Alta Vista ESD
Sch. Sys. Enr. Code 2
Supt. – Marlowe Hammer
2293 CRABTREE AVE 93257
Alta Vista ES, 2293 CRABTREE AVE 93257
Mary Fratini, prin.

Burton ESD
Sch. Sys. Enr. Code 4
Supt. – William Buckley
264 N WESTWOOD ST 93257
Burton IS, 264 N WESTWOOD ST 93257
Ernest Williams, prin.
Burton ES, 264 N WESTWOOD ST 93257
Jim Segrue, prin.
Oak Grove ES, 264 N WESTWOOD ST 93257
Betty Jones, prin.

Citrus South Tule ESD
Sch. Sys. Enr. Code 1
Supt. – Dave Kimble
31374 SUCCESS VALLEY DRIVE 93257
Citrus South Tule ES
31374 SUCCESS VALLEY DRIVE 93257
Dave Kimble, prin.

Hope ESD
Sch. Sys. Enr. Code 1
Supt. – (—)
816 W TEAPOT DOME AVE 93257
Hope ES, 816 W TEAPOT DOME AVE 93257
Robert Rodgers,Jr., prin.

Pleasant View ESD
Sch. Sys. Enr. Code 2
Supt. – Richard Stewart, 14004 ROAD 184 93257
Pleasant View ES, 14004 ROAD 184 93257
Richard Stewart, prin.

Porterville SD
Sch. Sys. Enr. Code 6
Supt. – Jacob Rankin, 589 W VINE AVE 93257
Bartlett IS, 589 W VINE AVE 93257
Katherine Whitley, prin.
Pioneer IS, 589 W VINE AVE 93257
Don Erwin, prin.
Belleview ES, 197 W BELLEVIEW AVE 93257
Pat Contreras, prin.
Doyle ES, 1045 E ORANGE AVE 93257
John Watkins, prin.
Olive Street ES, 255 W OLIVE AVE 93257
Hector Villicana, prin.
Roche ES, 388 N ROCHE ST 93257
Bill Drumright, prin.
Vandalia ES, 271 E COLLEGE AVE 93257
Lillian Durbin, prin.
West Putnam ES, 1345 W PUTNAM AVE 93257
Evelyn Lane, prin.
Westfield ES, 1151 W PIONEER AVE 93257
David Huchingson, prin.

Rockford ESD
Sch. Sys. Enr. Code 2
Supt. – Tom Michaelson, 14983 ROAD 208 93257
Rockford ES, 14983 ROAD 208 93257
Tom Michaelson, prin.

Woodville ESD
Sch. Sys. Enr. Code 3
Supt. – Maebelle Flannery
16541 ROAD 168 93257
Woodville ES, 16541 ROAD 168 93257
Frank Chavez, prin.

St. Anne ES, 385 N F ST 93257

Port Hueneme, Ventura Co., Pop. Code 7
Hueneme ESD
Sch. Sys. Enr. Code 6
Supt. – Ronald Rescigno, 354 N 3RD ST 93041
Bard ES, 622 E PLEASANT VALLEY RD 93041
Pamela Martens, prin.
Hueneme ES, 344 N THIRD ST 93041
Eldon Mrstik, prin.

Parkview ES, 1416 N SIXTH PLACE 93041
Al Nishino, prin.
Other Schools – See Oxnard

Hueneme Christian ES
312 N VENTURA RD 93041

Portola, Plumas Co., Pop. Code 4
Plumas USD
Supt. – See Quincy
ES, P O BOX 2020 96122 – Robert Balzan, prin.

Portola Valley, San Mateo Co., Pop. Code 5
Portola Valley ESD
Sch. Sys. Enr. Code 3
Supt. – James Shroyer, 4575 ALPINE ROAD 94025
Corte Madera MS, 4575 ALPINE ROAD 94025
Gerald Krumbein, prin.
Ormondale ES, 200 SHAWNEE PASS 94025
Eva Gal, prin.

Potrero, San Diego Co.
Mountain Empire USD
Supt. – See Pine Valley
ES, P O BOX 120 92063 – Anna Sullivan, prin.

Potter Valley, Mendocino Co., Pop. Code 2
Potter Valley Comm. USD
Sch. Sys. Enr. Code 2
Supt. – Michael Warych, P O BOX 219 95469
ES, P O BOX 219 95469 – Kay Schultz, prin.

Poway, San Diego Co., Pop. Code 7
Poway USD
Sch. Sys. Enr. Code 5
Supt. – Robert Reeves
13626 TWIN PEAKS ROAD 92064
Meadowbrook MS
13626 TWIN PEAKS ROAD 92064
Don Hurst, prin.
Twin Peaks MS
13626 TWIN PEAKS ROAD 92064
Carol Everett, prin.
Chaparrel ES, 17250 TANNIN DRIVE 92064
Yvonne Lux, prin.
Garden Road ES, 14614 GARDEN ROAD 92064
Diane Cantelli, prin.
Midland ES, 13910 MIDLAND ROAD 92064
Fred Vanhouten, prin.
Painted Rock ES
16711 MARTINCOIT ROAD 92064
E. Noetzel, prin.
Pomerado ES, 12321 9TH ST 92064
Susan Van Zant, prin.
Tierra Bonita ES
14678 TIERRA BONITA ROAD 92064
Sam Blank, prin.
Valley ES, 13000 BOWRON ROAD 92064
Bill Chiment, prin.
Other Schools – See San Diego

Cornerstne Christian ES, P O BOX 927 92064
St. Michael's ES, 15542 POMERADO RD 92064

Princeton, Glenn Co., Pop. Code 2
Princeton JUSD
Sch. Sys. Enr. Code 2
Supt. – Michael vonKleist, P O BOX 8 95970
ES, P O BOX 8 95970 – Michael vonKleist, prin.

Quartz Hill, Los Angeles Co., Pop. Code 5
Westside Un. ESD
Supt. – See Lancaster
Walker MS, 5632 W AVE L-8 93536
Steve Kalish, prin.
ES, 41820 50TH ST W 93536 – Paul Brunner, prin.

Quincy, Plumas Co., Pop. Code 4
Plumas USD
Sch. Sys. Enr. Code 5
Supt. – Floyd Warren, P O BOX 330 95971
Indian Jim ES, 40246 ALDER 95971
Clyde Bryan, prin.
Pioneer ES, 175 MILL CREEK ROAD 95971
Pete Melhus, prin.
ES, P O BOX 180 95971 – Marilyn Gilbert, prin.
Other Schools – See Chester, Greenville, La Porte,
Portola, Taylorsville

Rail Road Flat, Calaveras Co.
Calaveras USD
Supt. – See San Andreas
ES, P O BOX 217 95248 – Michael Chimente, prin.

Raisin, Fresno Co.
Raisin City ESD
Sch. Sys. Enr. Code 2
Supt. – Earl Gordon, P O BOX 68 93652
Raisin City ES, P O BOX 68 93652
Earl Gordon, prin.

Ramona, San Diego Co., Pop. Code 5
Ramona USD
Sch. Sys. Enr. Code 5
Supt. – Donald Haught, 20 9TH ST 92065
Peirce JHS, 1521 HANSON LANE 92065
Tom Cruz, prin.
Dukes ES, 24908 ABAIR WAY 92065
Dave Wilson, prin.
Hanson Lane ES
HANSON LANE & RAMONA ST 92065
Darrel Cheely, prin.
ES, EIGHTH & D STS 92065 – Doris Engberg, prin.

Ramona Lutheran ES, 520 16TH STREET 92065

Rancho Cordova, Sacramento Co., Pop. Code 8
Folsom-Cordova USD
Supt. – See Folsom
Cordova Gardens ES, 2400 DAWES ST 95670
Dale Ingvardsen, prin.
Cordova Lane ES, 2460 CORDOVA LANE 95670
Liz Bartlett, prin.
Cordova Meadows ES
2550 WHITE ROCK DRIVE 95670
Daryl Hackbarth, prin.
Cordova Villa ES
10359 S WHITE ROCK ROAD 95670
Walter Olsen, prin.
ES, 2562 CHASELIA WAY 95670
Ray Kerekes, prin.
Riverview ES
10700 AMBASSADOR DRIVE 95670
Joe Mathew, prin.
Shields ES, 10434 GEORGETOWN DRIVE 95670
Anne Zeman, prin.
Walnutwood ES, 10850 GADSTEN WAY 95670
Marilyn Sugimoto, prin.
White Rock ES, 10487 WHITE ROCK ROAD 95670
Martin Baumann, prin.
Williamson ES, 2275 BENITA WAY 95670
Barbara Sims, prin.

St. John Vianney ES, 10499 COLOMA RD 95670

Rancho Cucamonga, San Bernadino Co., Pop. Code 8
Central ESD
Sch. Sys. Enr. Code 5
Supt. – (—), 9457 FOOTHILL BLVD 91730
Cucamonga IS, 7611 HELLMAN AVE 91730
Paul Taylor, prin.
Bear Gulch ES, 8355 BEAR GULCH PLACE 91730
Andrew Carlmark, prin.
Central ES, 7955 ARCHIBALD AVE 91730
David Soden, prin.
Coyote Canyon ES
11075 TERRA VISTA PARKWAY 91730
Patt Hatcher, prin.
Dona Merced ES, 10333 PALO ALTO ST 91730
Robert Hatcher, prin.
Valle Vista ES, 7727 VALLE VISTA DIRVE 91730
Randy Keeth, prin.

Rancho Mirage, Riverside Co., Pop. Code 6
Palm Springs USD
Supt. – See Palm Springs
ES, 42-985 INDIAN TRAIL 92270
Martin Russell, prin.

Rancho Palos Verdes, Los Angeles Co., Pop. Code 6
Palos Verdes Peninsula USD
Supt. – See Rolling Hills Estates
Mira Catalina ES, 30511 LUCANIA DRIVE 90274
Michael McIntyre, prin.
Point Vicente ES
30540 RUE DE LA PIERRE 90274
Pamela Lopez, prin.
Silver Spur ES, 5500 IRONWOOD ST 90274
Forest Brown, prin.
Soleado ES, 27800 LONGHILL DR 90274
Patrick Corwin, prin.
Vista Grande ES
7032 PURPLE RIDGE DRIVE 90274
Patricia Wright, prin.

Rancho Santa Fe, San Diego Co., Pop. Code 4
Rancho Sante Fe ESD
Sch. Sys. Enr. Code 2
Supt. – R. Roger Rowe, P O BOX 809 92067
MS, LA GRANADA & AVE DE ACACIAS 92067
R. Roger Rowe, prin.
ES, P O BOX 809 92067 – R. Rowe, prin.

Rancho Santa Margarita, Orange Co.
Saddleback Valley USD
Supt. – See Mission Viejo
Trabuco Mesa ES
21301 AVENIDA DE LAS FLORES 92688
Jeff Herdman, prin.

Ravendale, Lassen Co.
Ravendale ESD
Sch. Sys. Enr. Code 1
Supt. – (—), P O BOX 25 96123
ES, P O BOX 25 96123 – Carl McGrew, prin.

Raymond, Madera Co.
Raymon-Knowles Un. ESD
Sch. Sys. Enr. Code 1
Supt. – (—), P O BOX 47 93653
Raymond-Knowles ES, P O BOX 47 93653
Stella Pizelo, prin.

Red Bluff, Tehama Co., Pop. Code 6
Antelope ESD
Sch. Sys. Enr. Code 2
Supt. – Richard Dedrick
22630 ANTELOPE BLVD 96080
Berrendos MS, 401 CHESTNUT AVE 96080
John Fenton, prin.
Antelope ES, RURAL ROUTE 01 BOX 893 96080
Richard Dedrick, prin.

Bend ESD
Sch. Sys. Enr. Code 1
Supt. – (—)
RURAL ROUTE 03 BOX 3520 96080
Bend ES, 22270 BEND FERRY ROAD 96080
Charles Williams, prin.

Red Bluff Un. ESD
Sch. Sys. Enr. Code 4
Supt. – George Russell
1535 DOUGLASS ST 96080
Vista MS, 1535 DOUGLASS ST 96080
James Smith, prin.
Bidwell MS, 1256 WALNUT ST 96080
Richard White, prin.
Jackson Heights ES, 225 JACKSON ST 96080
Lorna Bonham, prin.
Metteer ES, 695 KIMBALL ROAD 96080
Ray Morris, prin.

Reeds Creek ESD
Sch. Sys. Enr. Code 2
Supt. – (—)
RURAL ROUTE 02 BOX 2238 96080
Reeds Creek ES, 18335 JOHNSON ROAD 96080
Cindy Nellums, prin.

———

Community Christian ES
598 ROUNDUP AVE 96080
Sacred Heart ES, 2225 MONROE ST 96080

Redding, Shasta Co., Pop. Code 8
Bass ESD
Sch. Sys. Enr. Code 2
Supt. – Linda Matias, 7420 BASS DRIVE 96003
Bass ES, 7420 BASS DRIVE 96003
Linda Matias, prin.

Buckeye ESD
Sch. Sys. Enr. Code 3
Supt. – Charles Menoher
3407 HIATT DRIVE 96003
Buckeye JHS, 3407 HIATT DRIVE 96003
Roy Reddin, prin.
Buckeye ES, 3407 HIATT DRIVE 96003
William Tonkin, prin.

Columbia ESD
Sch. Sys. Enr. Code 2
Supt. – Anthony Huff
1700 OLD OREGON TRAIL 96003
Columbia ES, 1700 OLD OREGON TRAIL 96003
Anthony Huff, prin.

Enterprise ESD
Sch. Sys. Enr. Code 4
Supt. – Lee Jenkins
1155 MISTLETOE LANE 96002
Parsons JHS, 750 HARTNELL AVE 96002
Don Bagley, prin.
Alta Mesa ES, 2301 SATURN SKYWAY 96002
Glenn Eaton, prin.
Lassen View ES, LOMA VISTA DRIVE 96002
Bill Rich, prin.
Mistletoe ES, 1225 MISTLETOE LANE 96002
(—), prin.
Rother ES, 795 HARTNELL AVE 96002
Jay Johnson, prin.
Shasta Meadows ES, 2825 YANA AVE 96002
Carol Kelly, prin.

Grant ESD
Sch. Sys. Enr. Code 2
Supt. – Steven Lund, 4419 SWASEY DRIVE 96001
Grant ES, 8835 SWASEY DRIVE 96001
Steven Lund, prin.

Pacheco Un. ESD
Sch. Sys. Enr. Code 3
Supt. – Hugh Beaton
8101 CHURN CREEK ROAD 96002
Pacheco MS, 8101 CHURN CREEK ROAD 96002
Spencer Smith, prin.
Other Schools – See Anderson

Redding ESD
Sch. Sys. Enr. Code 5
Supt. – William Kipp, P O BOX 2418 96099
Sequoia MS, P O BOX 2418 96099
James Weaver, prin.
Bonny View ES, P O BOX 2418 96099
William Parr, prin.
Cedar Meadows ES
5885 E BONNYVIEW ROAD 96001
J. Engelhardt, prin.
Cypress ES, 901 W CYPRESS AVE 96001
Jerry Blancett, prin.
Juniper ES, 3005 ANITA ST 96001
Dennis Brichacek, prin.
Manzanita ES
1301 MANZANITA HILLS ROAD 96001
Molly Ranken, prin.
Sycamore ES, 1926 SYCAMORE DRIVE 96001
Cora McMahan, prin.

———

Grace Baptist School
3782 CHURN CREEK ROAD 96002
North Valley Christian School
2960 HARTNELL AVE 96002
Redding SDA ES, 1356 E CYPRESS AVE 96002
St. Joseph's ES, 2460 GOLD ST 96001
Trinity Lutheran ES, 2440 HILLTOP DR 96002

Redlands, San Bernardino Co., Pop. Code 8
Redlands USD
Sch. Sys. Enr. Code 7
Supt. – Ron Franklin, P O BOX 1008 92373
Crafton ES, 311 N WABASH AVE 92374
Roy Cencirulo, prin.
Franklin ES, 850 E COLTON AVE 92374
Ken Tolar, prin.
Kimberly ES, 301 W SOUTH AVE 92373
Jerry Meeker, prin.

Kingsbury ES, 600 CAJON ST 92373
Marcia Hazlett, prin.
Lugonia ES, 202 W PENNSYLVANIA AVE 92374
David Regalado, prin.
Mariposa ES, 30800 PALO ALTO DRIVE 92373
Ron Warren, prin.
McKinley ES, 645 W OLIVE AVE 92373
Manuel Espinosa, prin.
Mission ES, RURAL ROUTE 01 BOX 102 92373
Jack Robinson, prin.
Smiley ES, 1210 W CYPRESS AVE 92373
James Pearce, prin.
Other Schools – See East Highlands, Forest Falls,
Mentone, San Bernardino

———

Calvary Chapel Christian ES
9700 ALABAMA ST 92374
Redlands Christian ES, 1145 CHURCH ST 92374
Redlands Junior Academy
130 TENNESSEE ST 92373
Sacred Heart ES, 215 S EUREKA ST 92373
Temple Baptist ES, 615 E CYPRESS AVE 92374
Valley Preparatory School, 1605 FORD ST 92373

Redondo Beach, Los Angeles Co., Pop. Code 8
Redondo Beach City ESD
Sch. Sys. Enr. Code 5
Supt. – Nick Parras
1401 INGLEWOOD AVE 90278
Adams MS, 1401 INGLEWOOD AVE 90278
Mary Ann Stott, prin.
Hillcrest MS, 1401 INGLEWOOD AVE 90278
Michael Trownsell, prin.
Alta Vista ES, 815 KNOB HILL AVE 90277
Nancy Spence, prin.
Beryl Heights ES, 920 BERYL ST 90277
Leonard Boedeker, prin.
Birney ES, 1600 GREEN LANE 90278
James McDonald, prin.
Jefferson ES, 600 HARKNESS LANE 90278
Jeff Bordofsky, prin.
Lincoln ES, 2223 PLANT AVE 90278
Leonard Stoll, prin.
Madison ES, 2200 MACKAY LANE 90278
Thomas Dase, prin.
Tulita ES, 1520 PROSPECT AVE 90254
Leonard Boedeker, prin.
Washington ES, 1100 LILIENTHAL LANE 90278
Sandra Hanna, prin.

———

Le Lycee Francais de Los Angeles
220 VIA RIVIERA 90277
Redondo Christian Schs.
P O BOX 7000 268 90277
St. James ES, 122 N PACIFIC COAST HWY 90277
Coast Christian ES, 525 EARLE LN 90278
Riviera Hall ES, 330 PALOS VERDES BLVD 90277
St. Lawrence Martyr ES
1950 S PROSPECT AVE 90277

Redway, Humboldt Co., Pop. Code 3
Southern Humbolt JUSD
Supt. – See Garberville
ES, P O BOX 369 95560 – Susan Jennings, prin.

Redwood City, San Mateo Co., Pop. Code 5
Redwood City ESD
Sch. Sys. Enr. Code 6
Supt. – Kenneth Hill, 815 ALLERTON ST 94063
Kennedy IS, 815 ALLERTON ST 94063
Derald Blackmore, prin.
McKinley IS, 815 ALLERTON ST 94063
Gary Prehn, prin.
Clifford ES, CLIFFORD & SCENIC DRIVE 94062
Dale Dana, prin.
Cloud ES, 3790 RED OAK WAY 94061
Catherine Hauck, prin.
Fair Oaks ES, 2950 FAIR OAKS AVE 94063
Robert Costa, prin.
Ford ES, 2498 MASSACHUSETTS AVE 94061
Edward Glazer, prin.
Garfield ES
MIDDLEFIELD & SEMI-CIRCULAR 94063
Rafael Ramirez, prin.
Gill ES, 555 AVENUE DEL ORA 94062
Linda Denman, prin.
Hawes ES, 909 ROOSEVELT AVE 94061
Nancy Hendry, prin.
Hoover ES, CHARTER & STAMBAUGH STS 94063
Mike Fernandez, prin.
Orion ES, 3150 GRANGER WAY 94061
(—), prin.
Roosevelt ES, VERA AVE AT UPTON ST 94061
Stephen Rowley, prin.
Taft ES, TENTH AVE & BAY ROAD 94063
Mary Lairon, prin.
Other Schools – See Atherton

———

Our Lady of Mt. Carmel ES, 301 GRAND ST 94062
Peninsula Christian ES
1305 MIDDLEFIELD RD 94063
Redeemer Lutheran ES, 468 GRAND ST 94062
St. Pius ES, 1100 WOODSIDE RD 94061
Waldorf School of the Penninsula
2434 MCGARVEY AVE 94061

Redwood Valley, Mendocino Co.
Ukiah USD
Supt. – See Ukiah
MS, 700 SCHOOL WAY 95470
Gary Brawley, prin.

———

Deep Valley Christian ES, 8555 UVA DDR 95470

Reedley, Fresno Co., Pop. Code 7
Kings Canyon JUSD
Sch. Sys. Enr. Code 6
Supt. – John Rogalsky, P O BOX 552 93654
Grant MS, 360 N EAST AVE 93654
Robert Yohn, prin.
Navelencia ES, 22620 WAHTOKE AVE 93654
Carol Lopez-Doerksen, prin.
Alta MS, 21771 E PARLIER AVE 93654
Jean Clemons, prin.
Great Western ES
5051 S FRANKWOOD AVE 93654
Jim Toews, prin.
Jefferson ES, 1037 E DUFF AVE 93654
Marlow Ens, prin.
Lincoln ES, 374 E NORTH AVE 93654
Johnnie Willems, prin.
Washington ES, 12TH AND K STS 93654
Sandra Byrd, prin.
Other Schools – See Dunlap, Miramonte, Orange Cove,
Parlier

———

St. La Salle ES, 404 E MANNING AVE 93654

Rescue, El Dorado Co.
Rescue Un. ESD
Sch. Sys. Enr. Code 4
Supt. – Donna Soldano
2390 BASS LAKE ROAD 95672
Green Valley ES, 2390 BASS LAKE ROAD 95672
Gary Brockett, prin.
MS, 3880 GREEN VALLEY ROAD 95672
William Plumb, prin.
Other Schools – See El Dorado Hills, Folsom

Reseda, Los Angeles Co.
Los Angeles USD
Supt. – See Los Angeles
Bertrand Avenue ES, 7021 BERTRAND AVE 91335
Margaret Davis, prin.
Blythe Street ES, 18730 BLYTHE ST 91335
Marueen Banks, prin.
Cantara Street ES, 17950 CANTARA ST 91335
Sue Beever, prin.
Melvin Avenue ES, 7700 MELVIN AVE 91335
Judy Hergesheimer, prin.
ES, 7265 AMIGO AVE 91335 – Janie Taylor, prin.
Shirley Avenue ES, 19452 HART ST 91335
James Scupine, prin.
Vanalden Avenue ES, 19019 DELANO ST 91335
Floyd Cottam, prin.

———

First Baptist of Reseda ES
18644 SHERMAN WAY 91335
St. Catherine of Siena ES
7311 LINDLEY AVE 91335
Valley Trinity Early Education School
8055 RESEDA BLVD 91335

Rialto, San Bernardino Co., Pop. Code 8
Rialto USD
Sch. Sys. Enr. Code 7
Supt. – David Andrews
182 E WALNUT AVE 92376
Bemis ES, 774 E ETIWANDA AVE 92376
Irene Newton, prin.
Boyd ES, 310 E MERRILL AVE 92376
W. Williams, prin.
Casey ES, 219 N EUCALYPTUS AVE 92376
Mitchell Hovey, prin.
Dollahan ES, 1060 W ETIWANDA AVE 92376
Jay Higgs, prin.
Dunn ES, 830 N LILAC AVE 92376
Zelpha Gentry, prin.
Henry ES, 470 E ETIWANDA AVE 92376
Robbin Hawkins, prin.
Hughbanks ES, 2241 N APPLE AVE 92376
Robert Seikel, prin.
Kelley ES, 380 S MERIDIAN AVE 92376
Michael Brown, prin.
Morgan ES, 1571 N SYCAMORE AVE 92376
Robert Hayden, prin.
Myers ES, 975 N MERIDIAN AVE 92376
Jerry Rucker, prin.
Preston ES, 1750 N WILLOW AVE 92376
Stephen White, prin.
Simpson ES, 1050 S LILAC AVE 92376
Howard Williams, prin.
Trapp ES, 5751 RIVERSIDE AVE 92376
Robin Valles, prin.

———

Community Baptist ES, 275 E GROVE ST 92376
Peppercreek ES, 304 N PEPPER AVE 92376
St. Catherine of Siena ES
335 N SYCAMORE AVE 92376

Richgrove, Tulare Co., Pop. Code 4
Richgrove ESD
Sch. Sys. Enr. Code 2
Supt. – James Logsdon, P O BOX 201 93261
ES, P O BOX 201 93261 – James Logsdon, prin.

Richmond, Contra Costa Co., Pop. Code 8
Richmond USD
Sch. Sys. Enr. Code 7
Supt. – Walter Marks, 1108 BISSELL AVE 94801
Coronado ES, 2001 VIRGINIA AVE 94804
Irene Kirby, prin.
Ford ES, 2711 MARICOPA AVE 94804
Erma Hollinquest, prin.
Grant ES, 2400 DOWNER AVE 94804
Richard Tracy, prin.
King ES, 234 S 39TH ST 94804
Nadine Mathis, prin.

Lincoln ES, 29 6TH ST   94801
  William Henderson, prin.
Mira Vista ES
  HAZEL AVE AND MIRA VISTA DR   94805
  Frank Bianchi, prin.
Nystrom ES, 230 S TENTH ST   94804
  Darlene Jones, prin.
Peres ES, 719 5TH ST   94801
  Lindalee Ausejo, prin.
Riverside ES, 1300 AMADOR ST   94806
  Kenneth Stewart, prin.
Stege ES, 4949 CYPRESS AVE   94804
  Morine Hill, prin.
Valley View ES, 3416 MAYWOOD DRIVE   94803
  Jane Cathcart, prin.
Verde ES, 2000 GIARAMITA ST   94801
  Frank Carson, prin.
Washington ES, 565 WINE ST   94801
  Calvin Auten, prin.
Wilson ES, 629 42ND ST   94805
  Melvin Silverman, prin.
Other Schools – See Berkeley, El Cerrito, El Sobrante,
  Hercules, Pinole, San Pablo

St. Cornelius ES, 201 28TH ST   94804
St. Davids ES, 871 SONOMA ST   94805

Richvale, Butte Co.
Biggs USD
Supt. – See Biggs
ES, P O BOX 8   95974 – Lavonne Brown, prin.

Ridgecrest, Kern Co., Pop. Code 7
Sierra Sands USD
Sch. Sys. Enr. Code 6
Supt. – Anthony Magliari
  113 W FELSPAR AVE   93555
Faller ES, GUAM AND UPJOHN STS   93555
  Dianne Braithwaite, prin.
Groves ES   93555 – John Condos, prin.
Las Flores ES, 720 W LAS FLORES AVE   93555
  Patricia Kleinschmidt, prin.
Pierce ES   93555 – Gary Speegle, prin.
Richmond ES   93555 – Beverly Estis, prin.
Vieweg ES   93555 – Perry Hayes, prin.
Other Schools – See Inyokern, Johannesburg

Immanuel Christian Baptist School
  201 W GRAAF AVE   93555
Ridgecrest Lutheran School
  725 N FAIRVIEW   93555
St. Ann ES, 446 W CHURCH AVE   93555

Rio Dell, Humboldt Co., Pop. Code 5
Rio Dell ESD
Sch. Sys. Enr. Code 2
Supt. – Steven Lowder, 95 CENTER ST   95562
MS, 95 CENTER ST   95562 – Dale McGrew, prin.
PS, 95 CENTER ST   95562 – Steven Lowder, prin.

Rio Linda, Sacramento Co., Pop. Code 6
Grant JUn. HSD
Supt. – See Sacramento
JHS, 1101 G ST   95673 – Luana Duarte, prin.

Rio Linda Un. ESD
Sch. Sys. Enr. Code 6
Supt. – Dale Faust, 627 L ST   95673
Dry Creek ES, 1230 G ST   95673 – Bill Bybee, prin.
Orchard ES, 1040 Q ST   95673 – Mary Lester, prin.
ES, 631 L ST   95673 – Jay Baumgartner, prin.
Other Schools – See North Highlands, Sacramento

Rio Oso, Sutter Co.
Browns ESD
Sch. Sys. Enr. Code 2
Supt. – Debra Pearson, 1248 PACIFIC AVE   95674
Browns ES, 1248 PACIFIC AVE   95674
  Debra Pearson, prin.

Rio Vista, Sacramento Co., Pop. Code 5
River Delta USD
Sch. Sys. Enr. Code 4
Supt. – Robert Tomasini
  445 MONTEZUMA ST   94571
Riverview MS, 525 S 2ND ST   94571
  Jerry Rubier, prin.
White ES, 500 ELM WAY   94571
  John Littleton, prin.
Other Schools – See Clarksburg, Courtland, Isleton,
  Walnut Grove

Ripon, San Joaquin Co., Pop. Code 5
Ripon USD
Sch. Sys. Enr. Code 4
Supt. – Joseph O'Leary
  301 N ACACIA AVE   95366
ES, 509 W MAIN ST   95366 – Willis Burgess, prin.
Ripona ES, 415 OREGON ST   95366
  Robert Prewitt, prin.
Weston ES, 1660 STANLEY DR   95366
  Leo Zuber, prin.

Ripon Christian School, 435 MAPLE AVE   95366

Riverbank, Stanislaus Co., Pop. Code 6
Riverbank ESD
Sch. Sys. Enr. Code 4
Supt. – Paul Hewitt, 3651 SANTA FE ST   95367
Cardoza MS, 3525 SANTA FE ST   95367
  Joseph Galindo, prin.
California Avenue MS
  3800 CALIFORNIA AVE   95367 – Guy Miceli,
  prin.

Rio Altura ES
  STANISLAUS ST & ESTELLE AVE   95367
  Bonnie Santos, prin.
Other Schools – See Modesto

Riverdale, Fresno Co., Pop. Code 4
Riverdale JUn. ESD
Sch. Sys. Enr. Code 3
Supt. – James Brooks, P O BOX 338   93656
MS, 3700 STATHEM ST   93656 – Liz Motta, prin.
PS, FELAND AT KRUGER AVE   93656
  (—), prin.

Riverside, Riverside Co., Pop. Code 9
Alvord USD
Sch. Sys. Enr. Code 7
Supt. – Norman Guith, 10365 KELLER AVE   92505
Arizona IS, 10365 KELLER AVE   92505
  William Crocker, prin.
Loma Vista IS, 10365 KELLER AVE   92505
  Herbert Bice, prin.
Wells IS, 10365 KELLER AVE   92505
  Larry Alexander, prin.
Arlanza ES, 5891 RUTLAND AVE   92503
  Zack Earp, prin.
Collett ES, 10850 COLLETT AVE   92505
  Reynaldo Majia, prin.
Foothill ES, 8230 WELLS AVE   92503
  Eugene Vaughan, prin.
La Granada ES, 10346 KELLER AVE   92505
  Frank Snook, prin.
McAuliffe ES, 4100 GOLDEN AVE   92505
  Gretchen Hanson, prin.
Myra Linn ES, 10435 BRANIGAN WAY   92505
  Larry Holliday, prin.
Orrenmaa ES, 3350 FILLMORE ST   92503
  Lucinda Brouwer, prin.
Terrace ES, 6601 RUTLAND AVE   92503
  Philip Prouix, prin.
Twinhill ES, 11000 CAMPBELL AVE   92505
  Susan Navarro, prin.
Other Schools – See Corona

Jurupa USD
Sch. Sys. Enr. Code 7
Supt. – John Wilson
  3924 RIVERVIEW DRIVE   92509
Jurupa JHS, 8700 GALENA ST   92509
  Linda Lenertz, prin.
Mission JHS, 5961 OSO LANE   92509
  Donald Manzo, prin.
Arbuckle ES, 3600 PACKARD ST   92509
  Michelle Johnson, prin.
Camino Real ES, 4655 CAMINO REAL   92509
  Ellen Raher, prin.
Glen Avon ES, 4352 PYRITE ST   92509
  Anne Swick, prin.
Indian Hills ES, 7750 LINARES AVE   92509
  Laverne Manns, prin.
Mission Bell ES, 4020 CONNING ST   92509
  Donald McCall, prin.
Pacific Avenue ES, 6110 45TH ST   92509
  Donna Henderson, prin.
Pedley ES, 5871 HUDSON ST   92509
  Ellen Kinnear, prin.
Rustic Lane ES, 6420 RUSTIC LANE   92509
  Walter Lancaster, prin.
Sunnyslope ES, 7050 38TH ST   92509
  Gary Hale, prin.
Van Buren ES, 9501 JURUPA ROAD   92509
  Carmen Hernandez, prin.
West Riverside ES
  3972 RIVERVIEW DRIVE   92509
  Erasmo Mendez, prin.
Other Schools – See Mira Loma

Moreno Valley USD
Supt. – See Moreno Valley
Arnold Heights ES, 15801 HARMON ST   92508
  Patrick Heacock, prin.
Edgemont ES, 21790 EUCALYPTUS ST   92508
  Willie Hasson, prin.

Riverside USD
Sch. Sys. Enr. Code 8
Supt. – George Lantz, P O BOX 2800   92516
Riverside Independent Study
  6735 MAGNOLIA   92506 – William Vernon, prin.
Central MS, 4795 MAGNOLIA AVE   92506
  Lewis Vanderzyl, prin.
Chemawa MS, 8830 MAGNOLIA AVE   92503
  Georgia Renne, prin.
Gage MS, 6400 LINCOLN AVE   92506
  Barbara Carpenter, prin.
Sierra MS, 4950 CENTRAL AVE   92504
  Christopher Cordner, prin.
University Heights MS
  1155 MASSACHUSETTS AVE   92507
  Ignacio Alfaro, prin.
Adams ES, 8362 COLORADO AVE   92504
  Jess Cruz, prin.
Alcott ES, 2433 CENTRAL AVE   92506
  Glenn King, prin.
Bryant ES, 4324 3RD ST   92501
  Jackie Williams, prin.
Castle View ES, 6201 SHAKER DRIVE   92506
  Michael Cunningham, prin.
Emerson ES, 4660 OTTAWA AVE   92507
  Neva Ringwald, prin.
Fremont ES, 1925 N ORANGE ST   92501
  Susan Toscano, prin.
Grant ES, 4011 14TH ST   92501
  Robert Murphy, prin.
Harrison ES, 2901 HARRISON ST   92503
  Rheanette Lee, prin.

Hawthorne ES, 9174 INDIANA AVE   92503
  James Hazlett, prin.
Highgrove ES, 690 CENTER ST   92507
  Brenda Clark, prin.
Highland ES, 700 HIGHLANDER DRIVE   92507
  Naomi Lawrence, prin.
Hyatt ES, 4466 MOUNT VERNON AVE   92507
  Elois Brooks, prin.
Jackson ES, 4585 JACKSON ST   92503
  Stuart Bernhard, prin.
Jefferson ES, 4285 JEFFERSON ST   92504
  Lloyd Dowell, prin.
Liberty ES, 9631 HAYES ST   92503
  Raul Hernandez, prin.
Longfellow ES, 3610 EUCALYPTUS AVE   92507
  Alta Balow, prin.
Madison ES, 3635 MADISON ST   92504
  Dolores Luhrs, prin.
Magnolia ES, 3975 MAPLEWOOD PLACE   92506
  Rosemarie Hocker, prin.
Monroe ES, 8535 GARFIELD ST   92504
  Corinne Law, prin.
Mountain View ES, 6180 STREETER AVE   92504
  Christena Peterson, prin.
Pachappa ES, 6200 RIVERSIDE AVE   92506
  Cathy Taylor, prin.
Victoria ES, 2910 ARLINGTON AVE   92506
  Georgia Hill, prin.
Washington ES, 2760 JANE ST   92506
  Leila Bloomberg, prin.
Woodcrest ES, 16940 DRAMERIA   92504
  Christopher McGinn, prin.

Bethel Christian Schs.
  2425 VAN BUREN BLVD   92503
La Sierra Academy, P O BOX 8050   92515
Riverside Christian HS, 3532 MONROE ST   92504
Agape Christian ES, 8775 MAGNOLIA AVE   92503
Grace Baptist ES, 8223 CALIFORNIA AVE   92504
Harvest Christian ES
  6151 ARLINGTON AVE   92504
Hawarden Hills Academy
  6696 VIA VISTA DR   92506
Immanuel Lutheran ES
  5545 ALESSANDRO BLVD   92506
Our Lady of Perpetual Help ES
  6686 STREETER AVE   92504
Queen of Angels ES, 4824 JONES AVE   92505
Riverside Christian Day ES
  3612 ARLINGTON AVE   92506
Riverside Garden ES, 1085 W LINDEN ST   92507
St. Catherine's ES, 3728 ARLINGTON AVE   92506
St. Francis De Sals ES, 4205 MULBERRY ST   92501
St. Thomas of Apostle ES
  9136 MAGNOLIA AVE   92503

Robbins, Sutter Co.
Yuba City USD
Supt. – See Yuba City
ES, P O BOX 238   95676 – Wayne Perkins, prin.

Rocklin, Placer Co., Pop. Code 6
Rocklin ESD
Sch. Sys. Enr. Code 4
Supt. – John Anderson, 5175 MEYERS ST   95677
Spring View MS, 5040 5TH ST   95677
  Les Atchison, prin.
Parker Whitney ES, 5145 TOPAZ AVE   95677
  John Lehmann, prin.
MS, 5025 MEYERS ST   95677 – (—), prin.

Rodeo, Contra Cosa Co.
John Swett USD
Supt. – See Crockett
Garretson MS, 545 GARRETSON AVE   94572
  Roger Martin, prin.
Hillcrest ES
  CALIFORNIA AND MAHONEY   94572
  Daniel Archuleta, prin.

St. Patrick's ES
  SEVENTH ST & VAQUEROS AVE   94572

Rohnert Park, Sonoma Co., Pop. Code 7
Cotati-Rohnert Park USD
Sch. Sys. Enr. Code 6
Supt. – John Haro, 325 E COTATI AVE   94928
JHS, 7165 BURTON AVE   94928
  Ron Kincaid, prin.
Crane ES, 1290 SOUTHWEST BLVD   94928
  Andy Carciere, prin.
Evergreen ES, 1125 EMILY AVE   94928
  Ann Huber, prin.
Gold Ridge ES, 1455 GOLF COURSE DRIVE   94928
  Julan Pekkain, prin.
Hahn ES, 825 HUDIS ST   94928 – Jack Miller, prin.
La Fiesta ES, 8511 LIMAN WAY   94928
  Lou Colby, prin.
Reed ES, 390 ARLEN DRIVE   94928
  Jane Wheeler, prin.
Rohnert ES, 550 BONNIE AVE   94928
  Barbara Vrankovich, prin.
Other Schools – See Cotati

Rolling Hills Estates, Los Angeles Co., Pop. Code 6
Palos Verdes Peninsula USD
Sch. Sys. Enr. Code 6
Supt. – Jack Price, 38 CREST RD W   90274
Rancho Vista ES
  4323 PALOS VERDES DRIVE N   90274
  Jan Knickerbocker, prin.
Other Schools – See Palos Verdes Estates, Rancho
  Palos Verdes

Romoland, Riverside Co.
Romoland ESD
Sch. Sys. Enr. Code 3
Supt. – Roland Skumawitz, P O BOX 1368 92380
ES, P O BOX 1368 92380 – Margaret Reed, prin.

Rosamond, Kern Co., Pop. Code 4
Southern Kern USD
Sch. Sys. Enr. Code 4
Supt. – Robert Scherer, P O BOX CC 93560
Hamilton JHS, P O BOX CC 93560 – (—), prin.
ES, P O BOX CC 93560 – Rod Van Norman, prin.
Tropico MS, P O BOX CC 93560
   Duane Kamstra, prin.

Rosemead, Los Angeles Co., Pop. Code 8
Garvey ESD
Sch. Sys. Enr. Code 6
Supt. – Roger Temple, 2730 DEL MAR AVE 91770
Fern IS, 8470 FERN AVE 91770
   Joe Aguerrebere, prin.
Garvey IS, 2720 JACKSON AVE 91770
   Bob Diaz, prin.
Bitely ES, 7501 E FERN AVE 91770
   Barbara Niewola, prin.
Duff ES, 7830 DOROTHY ST 91770
   Chris Hunt, prin.
Emerson ES, 7544 EMERSON PLACE 91770
   Bruce Davis, prin.
Fern ES, 8470 FERN AVE 91770
   Joyce Metevia, prin.
Rice ES, 2150 ANGELUS AVE 91770
   Amelia Goddard, prin.
Willard ES, 3152 WILLARD AVE 91770
   Bonnie Boman, prin.
Williams ES, 2444 DEL MAR AVE 91770
   Mary Binch, prin.
Other Schools – See Monterey Park, San Gabriel

Rosemead ESD
Sch. Sys. Enr. Code 5
Supt. – Walter Ermerson
   3640 RIO HONDO AVE 91770
Muscatel IS, 4201 IVAR AVE 91770
   (—), prin.
Encinta ES, 4515 ENCINITA AVE 91770
   Maribeth Jacobs, prin.
Janson ES, 8628 MARSHALL ST 91770
   Georgianna Donnelly, prin.
Savannah ES, 3720 RIO HONDO AVE 91770
   Georgianna Donnelly, prin.
Shuey ES, 8472 WELLS ST 91770
   Judith Chapman, prin.

Grace Garden Education ES
   2662 WALNUT GROVE AVE 91770

Roseville, Placer Co., Pop. Code 7
Dry Creek ESD
Sch. Sys. Enr. Code 2
Supt. – Kelvin Lee, 2955 P F EAST ROAD 95678
Dry Creek ES, 2955 P F E ROAD 95678
   Kelvin Lee, prin.

Eureka Un. ESD
Sch. Sys. Enr. Code 4
Supt. – Ken Poulsen, 5477 EUREKA ROAD 95678
Cavitt IS, 7200 FULLER DRIVE 95678
   Janet Schimpf, prin.
Eureka Union MS, 5477 EUREKA ROAD 95661
   Ronald Walker, prin.
Greenhills ES, 8200 GREENHILLS WAY 95678
   David Freeman, prin.

Roseville City ESD
Sch. Sys. Enr. Code 5
Supt. – Suellen Skeen, P O BOX 1059 95661
Eich IS, 1509 SIERRA GARDENS DRIVE 95678
   Richard Pierucci, prin.
Cirby ES, 814 DARLING WAY 95678
   Millard Hamel, prin.
Crestmont ES, 1501 SHERIDAN AVE 95661
   Curtis Casey, prin.
Kaseberg ES, 1040 MAIN ST 95678
   Robert Edwards, prin.
Sargeant ES, 1200 RIDGECREST WAY 95661
   Boyce Baldwin, prin.
Sierra Gardens ES, 711 OAK RIDGE DRIVE 95661
   Carole Kane, prin.
Woodbridge ES, 515 NILES AVE 95678
   Mollie Gelder, prin.

Foothill Christian ES, 200 CIRBY WAY 95678
St. Albans Country Day ES
   2312 VERNON ST 95678
St. Rose ES, 633 VINE AVE 95678

Ross, Marin Co., Pop. Code 5
Ross ESD
Sch. Sys. Enr. Code 2
Supt. – Catherine Townsley, P O BOX 1058 94957
ES, P O BOX 1058 94957
   Catherine Townsley, prin.

Rowland Heights, Los Angeles Co., Pop. Code 7
Rowland USD
Sch. Sys. Enr. Code 7
Supt. – Sharon Robison, 1830 NOGALES ST 91748
Alvarado IS, 1901 DESIRE AVE 91748
   Burl Hunt, prin.
Blandford ES, 2601 BLANDFORD DRIVE 91748
   Sue Brewer, prin.
Farjardo ES, 18550 FARJARDO ST 91748
   Gay Carnello, prin.
Jellick ES, 1400 JELLICK AVE 91748
   Sandra Johnson, prin.

Killian ES, 19100 KILLIAN AVE 91748
   Arlene Simmonds, prin.
Rowland ES, 2036 FULLERTON ROAD 91748
   Catherine Carter, prin.
Shelyn ES, 19500 NACORA ST 91748
   Georgina Califf, prin.
Other Schools – See La Puente, Walnut, West Covina

Sacramento, Sacramento Co., Pop. Code 10
Del Paso Heights ESD
Sch. Sys. Enr. Code 4
Supt. – Carl Mack, Jr., 575 KESNER AVE 95838
Del Paso Heights ES, 590 MOREY AVE 95838
   Otto Isaac, prin.
Fairbanks ES, 227 FAIRBANKS AVE 95838
   Diann Smooth, prin.
Garden Valley ES
   3601 NORTHGATE BLVD 95834
   Lezell Williams, prin.
North Avenue ES, 1281 NORTH AVE 95838
   Doug Moore, prin.

Elk Grove USD
Supt. – See Elk Grove
Las Flores S, 5900 BAMFORD DRIVE 95823
   James Fales, prin.
Rutter JHS, 7350 PALMER HOUSE DRIVE 95828
   Bill Giachino, prin.
Florin ES, 7300 KARA DRIVE 95828
   David Givens, prin.
Jackson ES, 8351 CUTLER WAY 95828
   Joseph Way, prin.
Kennedy ES, 7037 BRIGGS DRIVE 95828
   Sheila Gibson, prin.
Kirchgater ES, 8141 STEVENSON AVE 95828
   Mary Fitch, prin.
Leimbach ES, 8101 GRANDSTAFF DRIVE 95823
   Milly Schrader, prin.
Mack ES, 4701 BROOKFIELD DRIVE 95823
   Ray Viramontes, prin.
Prairie ES, 5251 VALLEY HI DRIVE 95823
   Walker Munson, Jr., prin.
Reese ES, 7600 LINDALE DRIVE 95828
   Gayle Moore, prin.
Sierra-Enterprise ES, 5501 HEDGE AVE 95826
   Dean Springer, prin.

Grant JUn. HSD
Sch. Sys. Enr. Code 7
Supt. – Hazel Mahone, 1333 GRAND AVE 95838
Foothill Farms JHS, 5001 DIABLO DRIVE 95842
   Carl Brown, prin.
King JHS, 3051 FAIRFIELD ST 95815
   Jerry Payne, prin.
Other Schools – See North Highlands, Rio Linda

Natomas Un. ESD
Sch. Sys. Enr. Code 4
Supt. – Raff McDonald
   1515 SPORTS DR #1 95834
Natomas JHS, 3700 DE PASO ROAD 95834
   Jay Barry, prin.
American Lakes ES
   2800 STONECREEK DRIVE 95833
   Charles Kilbourne, prin.
Jefferson ES, 2001 PEBBLEWOOD 95833
   Judy Harder, prin.

North Sacramento ESD
Sch. Sys. Enr. Code 5
Supt. – Deloy Barrus, 670 DIXIEANNE AVE 95815
Babcock ES, 2400 CORMORANT WAY 95815
   Morris Malan, prin.
Castori ES, 1801 SOUTH AVE 95838
   Jeffrey Holland, prin.
Dos Rios ES, 700 DOS RIOS ST 95814
   Lawrence Lester, prin.
Hagginwood ES, 1418 PALO VERDE AVE 95815
   Amy Stewart, prin.
Johnson ES, 2591 EDGEWATER ROAD 95815
   Alice Lonczak, prin.
Northwood ES, 2630 TAFT ST 95815
   Jana Fields, prin.
Rogers ES, 477 LAS PALMAS AVE 95815
   John Brewer, prin.
Smythe ES, 2781 NORTHGATE BLVD 95833
   Kathleen Seabourne, prin.
Strauch ES, 3141 NORTHSTEAD DRIVE 95833
   Christine Rodrigues, prin.
Woodlake ES, 700 SOUTHGATE ROAD 95815
   Margaret Kirchgater, prin.

Rio Linda Un. ESD
Supt. – See Rio Linda
Frontier ES, 6691 SILVERTHORNE CIRCLE 95842
   Bruce Mitchell, prin.
Pioneer ES, 5816 PIONEER WAY 95841
   Frank Porter, prin.
Ridgepoint ES, 4680 MONUMENT DR 95842
   John Long, prin.
Woodridge ES, 5761 BRETT DRIVE 95842
   Barbara Baxter, prin.

Robla ESD
Sch. Sys. Enr. Code 4
Supt. – Paul Rahe, 5248 ROSE ST 95838
Bell Avenue ES, 1900 BELL AVE 95838
   Rita Wirtz, prin.
Main Avenue ES, 1400 MAIN AVE 95838
   Don Fuller, prin.
Robla ES, 5248 ROSE ST 95838
   Ted Hutchison, prin.
Taylor Street ES, 4350 TAYLOR ST 95838
   Dick Tomlinson, prin.

Sacramento City USD
Sch. Sys. Enr. Code 8
Supt. – Keith Larick, P O BOX 2271 95810
Bacon MS, 4140 CUNY AVE 95823
   William Hallett, prin.
Brannan MS, 5301 ELMER WAY 95822
   Barbara Chimento, prin.
California MS, 1600 VALLEJO WAY 95818
   Jay Kenagy, prin.
Carson MS, 5301 N ST 95819 – L. Johnson, prin.
Einstein MS, 9325 MIRANDY DRIVE 95826
   Carolyn Stewart, prin.
Goethe MS, 2250 68TH AVE 95822
   Mario Soberanis, prin.
Still MS, 2250 JOHN STILL DRIVE 95832
   Rachel Wallin, prin.
Sutter MS, 3150 I ST 95816 – Ed Marquez, prin.
Wood MS, 6201 LEMON HILL AVE 95824
   Raymond Valdez, prin.
Anderson ES, 2850 49TH ST 95817
   June Okamoto, prin.
Anthony ES, 7864 DETROIT BLVD 95832
   Shirley Gimmey, prin.
Baker ES, 5717 LAURINE WAY 95824
   James De Leon, prin.
Bancroft ES, 2929 BELMAR ST 95826
   Oscar Satow, prin.
Bear Flag ES, 6620 GLORIA DRIVE 95831
   Denise Verbeck, prin.
Bidwell ES, 1730 65TH AVE 95822
   Francis McNamara, prin.
Birney ES, 6251 13TH ST 95831
   Robert Hernandez, prin.
Bonnheim ES, 7300 MARIN AVE 95820
   David Fiscus, prin.
Bowling Green ES
   4211 TURNBRIDGE DRIVE 95823
   Brenda Drumm, prin.
Bret Harte ES, 2751 9TH AVE 95818
   Lois Ford, prin.
Burnett ES, 6032 36TH AVE 95824
   Ray Patterson, prin.
Cabrillo ES, 1141 SEAMAS AVE 95822
   John DeRuiter, prin.
Camellia Basic ES
   7400 ELDER CREEK ROAD 95824
   Jerry Houseman, prin.
Cohen ES, 9025 SALMON FALLS DRIVE 95826
   Thomas McAllister, prin.
Crocker/Riverside ES
   2970 RIVERSIDE BLVD 95818 – Billie Egolf, prin.
Didion ES, 6490 HARMON DRIVE 95831
   Ernest Shaffer, prin.
Elder Creek ES, 7934 LEMON HILL AVE 95824
   Evan Lum, prin.
Erlewine ES, 2441 STANSBERRY WAY 95826
   Burton Smith, prin.
Freeport ES, 2118 MEADOWVIEW ROAD 95832
   Lorraine Collins, prin.
Fruit Ridge ES, 4625 44TH ST 95820
   Delila Delancey, prin.
Golden Empire ES
   9045 CANABERRA DRIVE 95826
   Harris Perry, prin.
Greenwood ES, 5457 CARLSON DRIVE 95819
   Sandra Green, prin.
Harkness ES, 2147 54TH AVE 95822
   Linda Sain, prin.
Hearst Basic ES, 1410 60TH ST 95819
   Ruth Brown, prin.
Hollywood Park ES, 4915 HARTE WAY 95822
   William Welsh, prin.
Hopkins ES, 2221 MATSON DRIVE 95822
   Elaine Freedman, prin.
Huntington ES, 5921 26TH ST 95822
   Ronald Nishimura, prin.
Jefferson ES, 2635 CHESTNUT HILL DRIVE 95826
   Jean Davis, prin.
Judah ES, 3919 MCKINLEY BLVD 95819
   Clyde Kidd, prin.
Kemble ES, 7495 29TH ST 95822
   Rovida Mott, prin.
King ES, 480 LITTLE RIVER WAY 95831
   Frances Oda, prin.
Lincoln ES, 3324 GLENMOOR DRIVE 95827
   William Waller, prin.
Lisbon ES, 7555 S LAND PARK DR 95831
   Oliver Hughes, prin.
Lubin ES, 3535 M ST 95816 – Michael Hall, prin.
Maple ES, 3301 37TH AVE 95824
   Gene Carey, prin.
Marshall ES, 9525 GOETHE ROAD 95827
   Pam Ingalls, prin.
Morse ES, 1901 60TH AVE 95822
   Francis O'Connor, prin.
Newcomer Center ES
   5201 STRAWBERRY LANE 95820
   Ishmael Rasul, prin.
Nicholas ES, 6601 STEINER DRIVE 95823
   Sue Nelson, prin.
Oak Ridge ES, 4501 SACRAMENTO BLVD 95820
   Lena Del Campo, prin.
Pacific ES, 6201 41ST ST 95824 – Joe Bernal, prin.
Parkway ES, 4720 G PARKWAY 95823
   William Chase, prin.
Phillips ES, 2930 21ST AVE 95820
   Ventura Cardona, prin.
Pony Express ES, 1250 56TH AVE 95831
   Akio Iwanaga, prin.
Sequoia ES, 3333 ROSEMONT DRIVE 95826
   Robert Green, prin.
Sloat ES, 7525 CANDLEWOOD WAY 95822
   Gordon Westover, prin.

Smith ES, 401 MCCLATCHY WAY   95818
    William Ellerbee, prin.
Sutterville ES, 4967 MONTEREY WAY   95822
    Edna Mikell, prin.
Tahoe ES, 3110 60TH ST   95820
    Richard Cisneros, prin.
Twain ES, 4914 58TH ST   95820 – G. Hatley, prin.
Warren ES, 5420 LOWELL ST   95820
    Mark Helsley, prin.
Washington ES, 520 18TH ST   95814
    Guadalupe Lewis, prin.
Wenzel ES, 6870 GREENHAVEN DR   95831
    Shyrlee Freeman, prin.
William Land ES, 2120 12TH ST   95818
    Lucienne Wong, prin.
Winn ES, 3351 EXPLORER DRIVE   95827
    William Geisreiter, prin.
Wire ES, 5100 EL PARAISO AVE   95824
    George Robertson, prin.
Woodbine ES, 2500 52ND AVE   95822
    Olivia Rodriguez, prin.

San Juan USD
Supt. – See Carmichael
Arcade Fundamental MS
    3500 EDISON AVE   95821 – John Gabriel, prin.
Arden IS, 1640 WATT AVE   95864
    Joyce Howard, prin.
Salk Alternative MS, 2950 HURLEY WAY   95864
    Cheryl Magee, prin.
Cottage ES, 2221 MORSE AVE   95825
    Marge Tarbell, prin.
Cowan Fundamental ES
    3350 BECERRA WAY   95821 – Ron Johnson, prin.
Creekside ES, 2641 KENT DRIVE   95821
    Gerald Fassett, prin.
Del Paso Manor ES, 2700 MARYAL DRIVE   95821
    Dennis Pedersen, prin.
Dyer-Kelly ES, 2236 EDISON AVE   95821
    Gary Darrow, prin.
Edison ES, 1500 DOM WAY   95864
    Ernie Tavella, prin.
Greer ES, 2301 HURLEY WAY   95825
    Linda Winthers, prin.
Howe Avenue ES, 2404 HOWE AVE   95825
    Randy Bobby, prin.
Mariemont ES, 1401 CORTA WAY   95864
    Karla Dellner, prin.
Mitchell ES, 4425 LAURELWOOD WAY   95864
    John Sessarego, prin.
Pasadena Avenue ES
    4330 PASADENA AVE   95821 – Kay Valler, prin.
Sierra Oaks ES, 171 MILLS ROAD   95864
    Barbara Kennedy, prin.
Whitney Avenue ES, 4248 WHITNEY AVE   95821
    Jon Sadowski, prin.

American Heritage Christian School
    9027 CALVINE ROAD   95829
Calvary Christian School, 5051 47TH AVE   95824
Calvary School, 2665 DEL PASO BLVD   95815
Capital Christian Education Center
    9470 MICRON AVE   95827
Colonial Christian Academy, 4865 63RD ST   95820
Liberty Towers Christian School
    5132 ELKHORN BLVD   95842
Sacramento Country Day School
    2636 LATHAM DRIVE   95864
Sacramento State Prep School
    3600 FAIR OAKS BLVD   95864
Trinity Christian School
    5225 HILLSDALE BLVD   95842
All Hallows ES, 5700 13TH AVE   95820
Brookfield ES, P O BOX 22220   95822
Courtyard Private ES, 2324 L ST   95816
Florin Christian Academy, P O BOX 28545   95828
Gloria Dei Lutheran ES
    4910 LEMON HILL AVE   95824
Holy Spirit ES, 3920 W LAND PARK DR   95822
Immaculate Conception ES, 2549 32ND ST   95817
Merryhill Country School
    2730 EASTERN AVE   95821
Merryhill Country School-Natomas
    2401 NORTHVIEW DR   95833
Our Lady of Fatima ES
    1718 EL MONTE AVE   95815
Our Savior Lutheran ES, 5461 44TH ST   95820
Presentation ES, 3100 NORRIS AVE   95821
Sacred Heart ES, 3933 I ST   95816
Shalom Day ES, 2351 WYDA WAY   95825
St. Anne's ES, 7720 24TH ST   95832
St. Charles Borromeo ES
    7580 CENTER PKY   95823
St. Francis of Assisi ES, 2500 K ST   95816
St. Ignatius ES, 3249 ARDEN WAY   95825
St. Mary's ES, 5815 N ST   95819
St. Patrick ES, 5945 FRANKLIN BLVD   95824
St. Peter's ES, 6200 MCMAHON ST   95824
St. Philomene ES, 2320 EL CAMINO AVE   95821
St. Robert ES, 2251 IRVIN WAY   95822
Town and Country Lutheran ES
    4049 MARCONI AVE   95821

Saint Helena, Napa Co., Pop. Code 5
St. Helena USD
Sch. Sys. Enr. Code 4
Supt. – Frank Raney, 465 MAIN ST   94574
Stevenson IS, 1316 HILLVIEW PLACE   94574
    Rich Svendsen, prin.
ES, 1325 ADAMS ST   94574 – Ruth Reynolds, prin.
Other Schools – See Napa

Foothills Advent ES, 711 SUNNYSIDE RD   94574

St. Helena Parochial School
    1255 OAK AVE   94574

Salida, Stanislaus Co., Pop. Code 4
Salida Un. ESD
Sch. Sys. Enr. Code 4
Supt. – Robert Meade, P O BOX 1329   95368
ES, COVERT & FINNEY ROADS   95368
    John Campopiano, prin.
Other Schools – See Modesto

Salinas, Monterey Co., Pop. Code 8
Alisal Un. ESD
Sch. Sys. Enr. Code 5
Supt. – Robert Flores, 1205 E MARKET ST   93905
Alisal ES, 1437 DEL MONTE AVE   93905
    Henry Karrer, prin.
Bardin ES, BARDIN AND ALISAL ROADS   93905
    Verdan Glenn, prin.
Fremont ES, 1255 E MARKET ST   93905
    Mary Jane Kamm, prin.
Paul ES, 1300 RIDER AVE   93905
    Anastacio Cabral, prin.
Rocca Barton ES, 680 LAS CASITAS DR   93905
    E. Jordan, prin.
Sanborn ES, 901 N SANBORN ROAD   93905
    David Bazan, prin.

Graves ESD
Sch. Sys. Enr. Code 1
Supt. – Elaine Osborn, P O BOX 885   93902
Graves ES, P O BOX 885   93902
    Elaine Osborn, prin.

Lagunita ESD
Sch. Sys. Enr. Code 1
Supt. – John Lalley
    975 SAN JUAN GRADE ROAD   93907
Lagunita ES, 975 SAN JUAN GRADE ROAD   93907
    John Lalley, prin.

North Monterey County USD
Supt. – See Moss Landing
Echo Valley ES, 147 ECHO VALLEY ROAD   93907
    Benita Low, prin.
Prunedale ES, 17719 PESANTE ROAD   93907
    Karen Baker, prin.

Salinas City ESD
Sch. Sys. Enr. Code 6
Supt. – William Pollard, 431 W ALISAL ST   93901
Boronda ES, 1114 FONTES LANE   93907
    Mary Randall, prin.
El Gabilan ES, 1256 LINWOOD DRIVE   93906
    Steve Bradley, prin.
Kammann ES, 521 ROCHEX AVE   93906
    Mark Schwartz, prin.
Lincoln ES, 705 CALIFORNIA ST   93901
    Manuel Palato, prin.
Loma Vista ES, 757 SAUSAL DRIVE   93906
    Ream Lochry, prin.
Los Padres ES, 1130 JOHN ST   93905
    Frances Berry, prin.
Mission Park ES, 403 W ACACIA ST   93901
    Bernice Winter, prin.
Monterey Park ES, 401 SAN MIGUEL AVE   93901
    Roy Michaels, prin.
Natividad ES, 1465 MODOC AVE   93906
    Michael Trujillo, prin.
Roosevelt ES, 120 CAPITOL ST   93901
    Barbara Henares, prin.
Sherwood ES, 110 S WOOD ST   93905
    Rollie Dick, prin.
University Park ES, 833 W ACACIA ST   93901
    Patricia Willingham, prin.

Salinas Un. HSD
Sch. Sys. Enr. Code 6
Supt. – Lawrence Lekander
    431 W ALISAL ST   93901
El Sausal JHS, 1155 E ALISAL ST   93905
    Roger Anton, prin.
Washington JHS, 560 IVERSON ST   93901
    Y. Suzuki, prin.

Santa Rita Un. ESD
Sch. Sys. Enr. Code 4
Supt. – Harold Blythe
    303 SAN JUAN GRADE ROAD   93906
Gavilan View MS, 55 ROGGE ROAD   93906
    Thomas Dietrich, prin.
La Joya ES, 55 ROGGE ROAD   93906
    Mary Stefan, prin.
Santa Rita ES, 2014 SANTA RITA ST   93906
    James Fontana, prin.

Washington Un. ESD
Sch. Sys. Enr. Code 3
Supt. – Jerry Tollefson
    43 SAN BENANCIO ROAD   93908
San Benancio MS
    43 SAN BENANCIO ROAD   93908 – Rex Tift, prin.
Toro Park ES, 22500 PORTOLA DRIVE   93908
    Bonnie Tinder, prin.
Washington ES
    340 CORRAL DE TIERRA ROAD   93908
    Bonnie Tinder, prin.

Winham Street Christian Academy
    P O BOX 176   93902
Madonna Del Sasso ES
    20 SANTA TERESA WAY   93906
Sacred Heart ES, 123 W MARKET ST   93901
Salinas Christian ES, 345 E ALVIN DR   93906

Salton City, Riverside Co.
Coachella Valley USD
Supt. – See Thermal
Sea View ES, P O BOX 162   92274
    Paula Daniel, prin.

Samoa, Humboldt Co.
Peninsula Un. ESD
Sch. Sys. Enr. Code 1
Supt. – Truman Davidson, P O BOX 175   95564
Peninsula Union ES, P O BOX 175   95564
    Truman Davidson, prin.

San Andreas, Calaveras Co., Pop. Code 4
Calaveras USD
Sch. Sys. Enr. Code 5
Supt. – Herbert Hemington, P O BOX 788   95249
Toyon MS, P O BOX 1510   95249
    Walter Vater, prin.
ES, P O BOX 67   95249 – Barbara McInturf, prin.
Other Schools – See Copperopolis, Mokelumne Hill,
    Rail Road Flat, Valley Springs, West Point

San Anselmo, Marin Co., Pop. Code 7
Ross Valley SD
Sch. Sys. Enr. Code 4
Supt. – Frank Elliott
    46 GREEN VALLEY COURT   94960
Brookside ES, 116 BUTTERFIELD ROAD   94960
    Keith McPherson, prin.
Thomas ES, ROSS AT KENSINGTON RAOD   94960
    Geraldine Anderson, prin.
Other Schools – See Fairfax

San Domenico Lower ES
    150 BUTTERFIELD RD   94960
St. Anselm ES, 40 BELLE AVE   94960

San Ardo, Monterey Co.
San Ardo Un. ESD
Sch. Sys. Enr. Code 2
Supt. – David Austin, P O BOX 170   93450
ES, P O BOX 170   93450 – David Austin, prin.

San Bernardino, San Bernardino Co., Pop. Code 9
Redlands USD
Supt. – See Redlands
Victoria ES, 9963 RICHARDSON ST   92408
    Stanley Snyder, prin.

San Bernardino City USD
Sch. Sys. Enr. Code 8
Supt. – E. Neal Roberts, 777 F ST   92410
Arrowview IS, 2299 G ST   92405
    Jim Alvarado, prin.
Curtis MS, 1472 E 6TH ST   92410
    Susan Romo, prin.
Del Vallejo MS, 1855 E LYNWOOD DR   92404
    Delfina Bryant, prin.
Golden Valley MS
    3800 N WATERMAN AVE   92404
    James Dilday, prin.
Richardson Prep JHS, 455 S K ST   92410
    Kathy Krause, prin.
Serrano MS, 3131 PIEDMONT DRIVE   92346
    Edith Krache, prin.
Shandin Hills MS
    4301 LITTLE MOUNTAIN DRIVE   92407
    Don Simpson, prin.
Arrowhead ES
    3825 N MOUNTAIN VIEW AVE   92405
    Marion Blackwell, prin.
Barton ES, 2214 PUMALO ST   92404
    Olivette Miller, prin.
Bradley ES, 1300 VALENCIA AVE   92404
    Santosh Trikha, prin.
Burbank ES, 198 MILL ST   92408
    Maryhelen Anderson, prin.
California ES, 2699 N CALIFORNIA ST   92405
    Manuel Salinas, prin.
Davidson ES, 2844 DAVIDSON AVE   92405
    Marcia Draper, prin.
Del Rosa ES, 3395 MOUNTAIN AVE   92404
    Joe Liner, prin.
Emmerton ES, 1888 ARDEN AVE   92404
    Wayne Tully, prin.
Gilbert Street ES, 700 E GILBERT ST   92404
    David Brown, prin.
Hillside ES, 4975 N MAYFIELD AVE   92407
    Martha Pinckey, prin.
Hunt ES, 1342 PUMALO ST   92404
    Carol Cowan, prin.
Kendall ES, 4951 N STATE ST   92407
    Patricia Imbriorski, prin.
Kimbark ES, 18021 W KENWOOD AVE   92407
    Zoneth Overbey, prin.
King MS, 1250 N MUSCOTT ST   92411
    Susan Brown, prin.
Lincoln ES, 255 W 13TH ST   92405
    Joyce Payne, prin.
Lytle Creek ES, 275 S K ST   92410
    Sharon Sedrowski, prin.
Marshall ES, 3288 N G ST   92405
    Pauline Farhar, prin.
Monterey ES, 24644 MONTEREY AVE   92410
    Jerry Reece, prin.
Mt. Vernon ES, 1271 W 10TH ST   92411
    Guadalupe Cardoza, prin.
Muscoy ES, 2119 BLAKE ST   92405
    William Shupe, prin.
Newmark ES, 4121 N 3RD AVE   92407
    Wilton Pate, prin.
North Park ES, 5378 N H ST   92407
    James Marinis, prin.

Parkside ES, 3775 N WATERMAN AVE   92404
   Linda Campbell, prin.
Ramona-Alesandro ES, 670 RAMONA AVE   92411
   Tom Crist, prin.
Riley ES, 1266 N G ST   92405
   James Tanner, prin.
Rio Vista ES, 1451 N CALIFORNIA ST   92411
   Mary McCoy, prin.
Roosevelt ES, 1554 GARNER AVE   92411
   Narciso Cardona, prin.
Urbita ES, 771 S J ST   92410 – Janice Downs, prin.
Vermont ES, 3695 VERMONT ST   92405
   David Coleman, prin.
Warm Springs ES, 7497 STERLING AVE   92410
   Gloria Carlson, prin.
Wilson ES, 2894 BELLE ST   92404
   Ellase Stiggers, prin.
Other Schools – See Highland

───────────

Banner ES, 2372 E LYNWOOD DR   92404
Del Rosa Christian ES, 1333 E 39TH ST   92404
Holy Rosary ES
   2620 N ARROWHEAD AVE   92405
Mountain View Christian ES
   2102 E FOOTHILL DR   92404
New Life Christian Academy
   P O BOX 6012   92412
Our Lady of Assumptn ES, 796 W 48TH ST   92407
Our Lady of Guadalupe ES, 1475 W 7TH ST   92411
San Bernardino Christian ES, 2898 N G ST   92405
St. Anne ES, 6886 DEL ROSA AVE   92404
St. Anthony ES, 1510 W 16TH ST   92411
Valley Christian ES, 1671 N SIERRA WAY   92405

San Bruno, San Mateo Co., Pop. Code 8
Laguna Salada Un. ESD
Supt. – See Pacifica
Pacific Heights ES
   3791 PACIFIC HEIGHTS BLVD   94066
   Alberta Freitas, prin.
Portola ES, 300 AMADOR AVE   94066
   Sylvia Gappa, prin.

San Bruno Park ESD
Sch. Sys. Enr. Code 4
Supt. – John Mehl, 500 ACACIA AVE   94066
Parkside IS, 1801 NILES AVE   94066
   Anthony Cidonio, prin.
Allen ES, 875 ANGUS AVE W   94066
   Gary Barsocchini, prin.
Belle Air ES, 450 3RD AVE   94066
   Ernestine Forcum, prin.
Crestmoor ES, 2322 CRESTMOOR DRIVE   94066
   John Savage, prin.
El Crystal ES, 201 BALBOA WAY   94066
   Gus Xerogeanes, prin.
Muir ES, 130 CAMBRIDGE LANE   94066
   Raymond Stagnaro, prin.
Rollingwood ES
   2500 COTTONWOOD DRIVE   94066
   (—), prin.

South San Francisco USD
Supt. – See South San Francisco
Monte Verde ES
   2551 SAINT CLOUD DRIVE   94066
   Shelley Brown, prin.

───────────

Highlands Christian School
   1900 MONTEREY DR   94066
St. Robert's ES, 349 OAK AVE   94066

San Carlos, San Mateo Co., Pop. Code 7
San Carlos ESD
Sch. Sys. Enr. Code 4
Supt. – James Stanfill, 826 CHESTNUT ST   94070
Central MS, 826 CHESTNUT ST   94070
   Beverly Badgley, prin.
Arundel ES, PHELPS & ARUNDEL ROAD   94070
   William Hartley, prin.
Brittan Acres ES, TAMARACK & BELLE   94070
   Richard Smith, prin.
Heather ES, 2757 MELENDY DRIVE   94070
   Richard Irizary, prin.
White Oaks ES
   CEDAR & WHITE OAK WAY   94070
   Charles Calderhead, prin.

───────────

Alpha Beacon Christian School
   750 DARTMOUTH AVE   94070
St. Charles ES, 850 TAMARACK AVE   94070

San Clemente, Orange Co., Pop. Code 8
Capistrano USD
Supt. – See San Juan Capistrano
Shorecliffs JHS, 240 VIA SOCORRO   92672
   Christopher Cairns, prin.
Benedict ES, 1251 SARMENTOSO   92672
   John Hopkins, prin.
Concordia ES
   3120 AVENIDA DEL PRESIDENTE   92672
   Jeffrey Bristow, prin.
Hansen ES, 189 LA CUESTA   92672
   Nancy Smith, prin.
Las Palmas ES, 1101 CALLE PUENTE   92672
   Linda Purrington, prin.

───────────

Our Lady of Fatima ES
   105 N LA ESPERANZA   92672

San Diego, San Diego Co., Pop. Code 11
Chula Vista City SD
Supt. – See Chula Vista
Finney ES, 3950 BYRD ST   92154
   Clifford Johnson, prin.

Juarez-Lincoln ES, 849 TWINING AVE   92154
   William Collins, prin.
Los Altos ES, 1332 KENALAN DRIVE   92154
   Fred Elliott, prin.
Silver Wing ES, 3730 AREY DRIVE   92154
   John Pletcher, prin.

Poway USD
Supt. – See Poway
Black Mountain MS, 9353 OVIEDO ST   92129
   Louise Dunbar, prin.
Canyon View ES, 9225 ADOLPHIA ST   92129
   Jack Troxell, prin.
Los Penasquitos ES, 14125 CUCA ST   92129
   Marjorie Postel, prin.
Rolling Hills ES
   15255 PENASQUITOS DRIVE   92129
   Raymon Wilson, prin.
Sundance ES, 8944 TWIN TRAILS DRIVE   92129
   Earl Scull, prin.
Sunset Hills ES, 9291 OVIEDO ST   92129
   Steve Hodge, prin.
Westwood ES, 17449 MATINAL ROAD   92127
   Charlene Bishop, prin.

San Diego City USD
Sch. Sys. Enr. Code 9
Supt. – Thomas Payzant, 4100 NORMAL ST   92103
Correia JHS, 4302 VALETA ST   92107
   Michael Lorch, prin.
De Portola MS
   11010 CLAIREMONT MESA BLVD   92124
   Russell Vowinkle, prin.
Farb MS, 4880 LA CUENTA DRIVE   92124
   Charles Freebern, prin.
Keiller MS, 7270 LISBON ST   92114
   Jon Curry, prin.
Kroc MS, 5050 CONRAD AVE   92117
   Isabelle Skidmore, prin.
Mann MS, 4345 54TH ST   92115
   Maruta Gardner, prin.
Marston MS, 3799 CLAIREMONT DRIVE   92117
   Robert Quon, prin.
Pacific Beach MS, 4676 INGRAHAM ST   92109
   Mary Worthington, prin.
Wilson MS, 3838 ORANGE AVE   92105
   Kimiko Fukuda, prin.
Adams ES, 4672 35TH ST   92116
   John Jones, prin.
Alcott ES, 4680 HIDALGO AVE   92117
   Virginia Dinsdale, prin.
Angier ES, 8450 HURIBUT ST   92123
   Ted Janette, prin.
Audubon ES, 8111 SAN VICENTE ST   92114
   Harold Black, prin.
Baker ES, 4041 T ST   92113 – Maria Garcia, prin.
Balboa ES, 1844 S 40TH ST   92113
   Margarita Carmona, prin.
Barnard ES, 2930 BARNARD ST   92110
   Jerry Hopper, prin.
Bay Park ES, 2433 DENVER ST   92110
   Barbara Coates, prin.
Bayview Terrace ES, 2445 FOGG ST   92109
   Grace Sherr, prin.
Benchley/Weinberger ES
   6269 TWIN LAKE DRIVE   92119
   Marita Saunders, prin.
Bethune ES, 6835 BENJAMIN HOLT ROAD   92114
   Ann Bolton, prin.
Birney ES, 4345 CAMPUS AVE   92103
   William Conner, prin.
Boone ES, 7330 BROOKHAVEN RD   92114
   Janice Kaneko, prin.
Breen ES, 11131 POLARIS DRIVE   92126
   Bennye Seraile, prin.
Brooklyn ES, 3035 ASH ST   92102
   Jane Senour, prin.
Burbank ES, 2146 JULIAN AVE   92113
   Mary Saylor, prin.
Cabrillo ES, 3120 TALBOT ST   92106
   Robert Jones, prin.
Cadman ES, 4370 KAMLOOP AVE   92117
   Patricia McGann, prin.
Carson ES, 6905 KRAMER ST   92111
   Linda Buffington, prin.
Carver ES, 3251 JUANITA ST   92105
   Harold Russell, prin.
Central ES, 4063 POLK AVE   92105
   Mary Martin, prin.
Chesterton MS, 7335 WHEATLEY ST   92111
   Paul Yap, prin.
Chollas MS, 545 45TH ST   92102
   Richard Camacho, prin.
Clay ES, 6506 SOLITA AVE   92115
   Edward McFadd, prin.
Crown Point ES, 4033 INGRAHAM ST   92109
   Ralph Green, prin.
Cubberley ES, 3201 MARATHON DRIVE   92123
   J. Aftreth, prin.
Curie ES, 4080 GOVERNOR DRIVE   92122
   Ronald Hertzberg, prin.
Dailard ES, 6425 CIBOLA RD   92120
   Daniel Ellis, prin.
Dewey ES, 3251 ROSECRANS PL   92110
   Gloria Coleman, prin.
Doyle ES, 3950 BERINO COURT   92122
   Jerry Jordan, prin.
Edison ES, 4077 35TH ST   92104
   Connie Akashian, prin.
Emerson ES, 3510 NEWTON AVE   92113
   Jerry Hill, prin.
Encanto ES, 822 65TH ST   92114
   Mary McClain, prin.

Ericson ES, 11174 WESTONHILL DRIVE   92126
   Stewart Brown, prin.
Euclid ES, 4166 EUCLID AVE   92105
   Eugene Ernst, prin.
Field ES, 4375 BANNOCK AVE   92117
   Margie Foelber, prin.
Fletcher ES, 7666 BOBOLINK WAY   92123
   Lanell Alston, prin.
Florence ES, 3914 1ST AVE   92103
   Sarah Olinde, prin.
Foster MS, 65550 51ST ST   92120
   Deanna Ibarra, prin.
Franklin ES, 4481 COPELAND AVE   92116
   Joseph Mercurio, prin.
Freese ES, 8140 GREENLAWN DR   92114
   Maggie Gunner, prin.
Fremont ES, 2375 CONGRESS ST   92110
   Tomaline Lenox, prin.
Fulton ES, 7055 SKYLINE DRIVE   92114
   August Castille, prin.
Gage ES, 6811 BISBY LAKE AVE   92119
   Freddie Jackson, prin.
Grant ES, 1425 WASHINGTON PLACE   92103
   Barbara Bethel, prin.
Green ES, 7030 WANDERMERE DR   92119
   Carol Voelker, prin.
Hamilton ES, 2807 FAIRMOUNT AVE   92105
   Carrie Perry, prin.
Hancock ES, 3303 TAUSSIG ST   92124
   Sally Collier, prin.
Hardy ES, 5420 MONTEZUMA ROAD   92115
   Gail Guth, prin.
Hawthorne ES, 4750 LEHRER DRIVE   92117
   Helen Dillon, prin.
Hearst ES, 6230 DEL CERRO BLVD   92120
   Julia Taylor, prin.
Hickman ES, 10850 MONTONGO   92126
   Philip Smith, prin.
Holmes ES, 4902 MOUNT ARARAT DRIVE   92111
   Jeannie Steeg, prin.
Horton ES, 5050 GUYMON ST   92102
   James Hensley, prin.
Jackson ES, 4365 54TH ST   92115
   Roger Cunningham, prin.
Jefferson ES, 3770 UTAH ST   92104
   Diana Shipley, prin.
Jerabeck ES, 10050 AVENIDA MAGNIFICA   92131
   Josephine Wraith, prin.
Johnson ES, 1355 KELTON ROAD   92114
   Carol Pike, prin.
Jones ES, 2751 GREYLING DRIVE   92123
   Clifford Mendoza, prin.
Juarez ES, 2633 MELBOURNE DRIVE   92123
   Kenneth Chappell, prin.
Kennedy ES, 445 S 47TH ST   92113
   Edward Cain, prin.
King ES, 415 31ST ST   92102
   Anita Calhoun, prin.
Knox ES, 1098 S 49TH ST   92113
   Myrtle Faucette, prin.
Lafayette ES, 6125 PRINTWOOD WAY   92117
   Joseph Coit, prin.
Lee ES, 6196 CHILDS AVE   92139
   Robert Holmes, prin.
Linda Vista ES, 2772 ULRIC ST   92111
   Adel Nadeau, prin.
Lindbergh ES
   4133 MOUNT ALBERTINE AVE   92111
   Mervin Nerling, prin.
Logan MS, 2875 OCEAN VIEW BLVD   92113
   Delores Celia, prin.
Loma Portal ES, 3341 BROWNING ST   92106
   Patricia Rath, prin.
Longfellow ES, 5055 UULY ST   92110
   Lydia Ulloa, prin.
Lowell ES, 1110 BEARDSLEY   92113
   Consuelo Gills, prin.
Marshall ES, 3550 ALTADENA AVE   92105
   Barb Wyatt, prin.
Marvin ES, 5720 BRUNSWICK AVE   92120
   Dianette Mitchell, prin.
Mason ES, 10340 SABN RAMON DRIVE   92126
   Thomas Crellin, prin.
McKinley ES, 3045 FELTON ST   92104
   Bridget Ferrentino, prin.
Mead ES, 730 45TH ST   92102
   Marcos Mendoza, prin.
Miller ES, 4343 SHIELDS ST   92124
   Rosary Nepi, prin.
Miramar Ranch ES
   10805 RED CEDAR DRIVE   92131
   Bruce McKay, prin.
Oak Park ES, 2606 54TH ST   92105
   Joshua Tull, prin.
Ocean Beach ES
   4741 SANTA MONICA AVE   92107
   Frank Petersen, prin.
Pacific Beach ES, 1234 TOURMALINE ST   92109
   Judith Ernst, prin.
Paradise Hills ES, 5816 ALLEGHANY ST   92139
   D. Hill, prin.
Penn ES, 2797 UTICA DRIVE   92139
   Vladamier Batza, prin.
Perry ES, 6195 RANGER ROAD   92139
   Roger Challberg, prin.
Rolando Park ES, 6620 MARLOWE DRIVE   92115
   Richard Six, prin.
Ross ES, 7470 BAGDAD ST   92111
   John Weld, prin.
Rowan ES, 1755 ROWAN ST   92105
   Mable Wigfall, prin.
Sandburg ES, 11230 AVENIDA DEL GATO   92126
   Michael Giafaglione, prin.

Sequoia ES, 4690 LIMERICK AVE 92117
  Juel Moore, prin.
Sessions ES, 2150 BERYL ST 92109
  Karen Marshall, prin.
Sherman ES, 450 24TH ST 92102
  Cecilia Estrada, prin.
Silver Gate ES, 1499 VENICE ST 92107
  William Tellous, prin.
Spreckels ES, 6033 STADIUM ST 92122
  David Johnson, prin.
Sunset View ES, 4365 HILL ST 92107
  Judith Uriostegui, prin.
Tierrasanta ES, 5450 LA CUENTA DRIVE 92124
  James Noel,Jr., prin.
Toler ES, 3350 BAKER ST 92117
  Patricia Tisdale, prin.
Valencia Park ES, 5880 SKYLINE DRIVE 92114
  Carolyn Dubuque, prin.
Vista Grande ES, 5606 ANTIGUA BLVD 92124
  Alexander Cremidan, prin.
Walker ES, 9165 HILLERY DRIVE 92126
  Gilbert Gutierrez, prin.
Washington ES, 1734 UNION ST 92101
  Raul Contreras, prin.
Webster ES, 4801 ELM ST 92102
  Dimple Morrison, prin.
Wedgeforth ES, 3443 EDIWHAR AVE 92123
  Lyle Rangel, prin.
Whitman ES, 4050 APPLETON ST 92117
  John Sullivan, prin.
Zamorano ES, 2655 CASEY ST 92139
  Rachel Flanagan, prin.
Other Schools – See La Jolla

Solana Beach ESD
Supt. – See Solana Beach
Solana Highlands ES
  3520 LONG RUN ROAD 92130
  Karen Clark, prin.

South Bay Un. ESD
Supt. – See Imperial Beach
Barry ES, 2001 RIMBEY AVE 92154
  Victor Resendez, prin.
Emory ES, 1915 CORONADO AVE 92154
  R. Walters, prin.
Nestor ES, 1455 HOLLISTER ST 92154
  Valerie Galfat, prin.
Nicoloff ES, 1777 HOWARD AVE 92073
  David Flint, prin.
Pence ES, 877 VIA TONGA COURT 92154
  Celia Ramirez, prin.
Sunnyslope ES, 2500 ELM AVE 92154
  Lynda Schultheis, prin.

Sweetwater Un. HSD
Supt. – See Chula Vista
Mar Vista MS, 1267 17TH ST 92154
  William Hawes, prin.

Clairemont Christian School
  3811 MOUNT ACADIA BLVD 92111
New Life Academy, 4445 LAURAL ST 92105
St. Stephens Christian S
  5825 IMPERIAL AVE 92114
All Saints Episcopal ES, 3674 7TH AVE 92103
Beth Israel Day ES, 2512 3RD AVE 92103
Blessed Sacrament ES, 4551 56TH ST 92115
Carden ES, 12635 EL CAMINO REAL 92130
Childrens Creative/Performing Arts Acad.
  4431 MT HERBERT AVE 92117
Christ Cornerstone Lutheran School
  9028 WESTMORE ROAD 92126
Christian ES, 6747 AMHERST ST 92115
City Tree ES, 320 DATE ST 92101
Coleman Day ES
  6460 BOULDER LAKE AVE 92119
Faith Community ES
  2285 MURRAY RIDGE RD 92123
First Southern Baptist ES
  3219 CLAIREMONT MESA BLVD 92117
Good Shepherd ES, 8180 GOLD COAST DR 92126
Grace Lutheran ES, 3967 PARK BLVD 92103
Holy Family ES, 1945 COOLIDGE ST 92111
Holy Spirit ES, 2755 55TH ST 92105
Horizon Christian ES, P O BOX 17480 92117
Mission Bay Montessori Academy
  2640 SODERBLOM AVE 92122
Montessori School House
  4544 POCAHONTAS AVE 92117
Nazareth ES
  10728 SAN DIEGO MISSN ROAD 92108
Our Lady of Sacred Heart ES
  4106 42ND ST 92105
Our Lady's ES, 650 24TH ST 92102
Parker ES, 4201 RANDOLPH ST 92103
Reformation Lutheran ES
  4670 MT ABERNATHY AVE 92117
Sacred Heart Academy
  4895 SARATOGA AVE 92107
San Diego Hebrew Day ES
  6365 LAKE ATLIN AVE 92119
San Diego Jewish Academy
  6660 COWLES MOUNTAIN BLVD 92119
School of the Madeleine, 1875 ILLION ST 92110
Soledad Christian ES
  4747 SOLEDAD MOUNTAIN RD 92109
St. Charles Borromeo Academy
  2808 CADIZ ST 92110
St. Charles ES, 929 18TH ST 92154
St. Columba ES, 3365 GLENCOLUM DR 92123
St. Didacus Parochial ES, 4630 34TH ST 92116
St. Jude Academy, P O BOX 13601 92113
St. Michael ES, 2637 HOMEDALE ST 92139

St. Patrick's ES, 3014 CAPPS ST 92104
St. Paul Lutheran School
  1376 FELSPAR STREET 92109
St. Rita's ES, 5165 IMPERIAL AVE 92114
St. Therese Academy, 6046 CAMINO RICO 92120
St. Vincent ES, 4077 IBIS ST 92103
Tierrasanta Chrstian ES, 5850 SANTO RD 92124
Trinity Lutheran School, 7210 LISBON 92114
Warren-Walker School, Inc.
  4605 PT LOMA AVE 92107

San Dimas, Los Angeles Co., Pop. Code 7
Bonita USD
Sch. Sys. Enr. Code 6
Supt. – Duane Dishno, 115 W ALLEN AVE 91773
Lone Hill MS, 700 S LONE HILL AVE 91773
  Adolphus Carter, prin.
Allen Avenue ES, 740 E ALLEN AVE 91773
  Lorna Horton, prin.
Ekstrand ES, 400 N WALNUT AVE 91773
  Elvin Bartel, prin.
Gladstone ES, 1314 W GLADSTONE ST 91773
  David Trost, prin.
Miller ES, 115 W ALLEN AVE 91773
  Elaine Harper, prin.
Shull ES, 825 N AMELIA AVE 91773
  Parket Sutton, prin.
Other Schools – See La Verne

Holy Name of Mary ES
  124 S SAN DIMAS CANYON RD 91773

San Fernando, Los Angeles Co., Pop. Code 7
Los Angeles USD
Supt. – See Los Angeles
Gridley Street ES, 1907 8TH ST 91340
  Paul Martinez, prin.
Morningside ES, 576 N MACLAY AVE 91340
  William Schiff, prin.
O'Melveny ES, 728 WOODWORTH ST 91340
  Nancy Orozco, prin.
ES, 1130 MOTT ST 91340 – Sylvia Perea, prin.
Vaughn Street ES, 13330 VAUGHN ST 91340
  Emma Wilson, prin.

First Lutheran School
  777 N MACLAY AVE 91340
First Church of Christ Day ES
  727 KEWEN ST 91340
Santa Rosa De Lima ES, 1309 MOTT ST 91340
St. Ferdinand ES, 1012 CORONEL ST 91340

San Francisco, San Francisco Co., Pop. Code 11
San Francisco USD
Sch. Sys. Enr. Code 8
Supt. – Ramon Cortines
  135 VAN NESS AVE 94102
Court S, 375 WOODSIDE AVE 94127
  Gloria Burchard, prin.
Aptos MS, 105 APTOS AVE 94127
  Mary Beth Barrett, prin.
Burbank MS, 325 LA GRANDE AVE 94112
  Olivia Martinez, prin.
Denman MS, 241 ONEIDA AVE 94112
  Renee French, prin.
Everett MS, 450 CHURCH ST 94114
  Joseph Crivello, prin.
Francisco MS, 2190 POWELL ST 94133
  Benson Wong, prin.
Franklin MS, 1430 SCOTT ST 94115
  Steve Hirabayashi, prin.
Giannini MS, 3151 ORTEGA ST 94122
  Bennett Fonsworth, prin.
Hoover MS, 2290 14TH AVE 94116
  Maureen Petiti, prin.
King Academic MS, 350 GIRARD 94134
  Lynette Porteous, prin.
Lick MS, 1220 NOE ST 94114
  Mary Lou Mason, prin.
Mann MS, 3351 23RD ST 94110
  Carlos Garcia, prin.
Marina MS, 3500 FILLMORE ST 94123
  Lana Toy, prin.
Potrero Hill MS, 655 DE HARO ST 94107
  Sam Rodriguez, prin.
Presidio MS, 450 30TH AVE 94121
  Betty Gandel, prin.
Roosevelt MS, 460 ARGUELLO BLVD 94118
  Susan Wong, prin.
Visitacion Valley MS, 450 RAYMOND AVE 94134
  Fannie Phaegler, prin.
Alamo ES, 250 23RD AVE 94121
  Dorothy Lynch, prin.
Alvarado ES, 625 DOUGLASS ST 94114
  Rose Barragan, prin.
Argonne ES, 675 17TH AVE 94121
  Myrna Tsukamoto, prin.
Bret Harte ES, 1035 GILMAN AVE 94124
  Owen Dallas, prin.
Bryant ES, 1050 YORK ST 94110
  Barbara Karvelis, prin.
Buena Vista Annex ES, 1670 NOE ST 94131
  (—), prin.
Cabrillo ES, 735 24TH AVE 94121
  Vermuta Morris, prin.
Carmichael ES, 55 SHERMAN ST 94103
  Kathleen Loughlin, prin.
Carver ES, 1360 OAKDALE AVE 94124
  Louise Jones, prin.
Chinese Education ES, 657 MERCHANT ST 94111
  Carolyn Hee, prin.
Clarendon/Second Community ES
  500 CLARENDON AVE 94131
  Beverly Jimenez, prin.

Cleveland ES, 455 ATHENS ST 94112
  Gerhard Lowenthal, prin.
Cobb ES, 2725 CALIFORNIA ST 94115
  Marion Maginnis, prin.
Commodore Sloat ES, 50 DARIEN WAY 94127
  Lida Opalenik, prin.
Commodore Stockton ES, 950 CLAY ST 94108
  Lai Ming-Meyer, prin.
Douglas Traditional ES, 4235 19TH ST 94114
  Dolores Nice, prin.
Drake ES, 350 HARBOR ROAD 94124
  John Bernard, prin.
Drew ES, 50 POMONA ST 94124
  Davida Desmond, prin.
Edison ES, 3531 22ND ST 94114
  Graciela Spreitz, prin.
El Dorado ES, 70 DELTA ST 94134
  Mae Threadgill, prin.
Fairmount ES, 65 CHENERY ST 94131
  Judy Coenen, prin.
Filipino Education ES, 824 HARRISON ST 94107
  Ross Quema, prin.
Flynn ES, 3125 ARMY ST 94110
  Helen Chin, prin.
Garfield ES, 420 FILBERT ST 94133
  May Huie, prin.
Glen Park ES, 151 LIPPARD AVE 94131
  Marion Grady, prin.
Golden Gate ES, 1601 TURK ST 94115
  Sam Louie, prin.
Grattan ES, 165 GRATTAN ST 94117
  Robert Smirle, prin.
Guadalupe ES, 859 PRAGUE ST 94112
  Betty Dilg, prin.
Hawthorne ES, 825 SHOTWELL ST 94110
  Judith Kell, prin.
Hillcrest ES, 810 SILVER AVE 94134
  Joseph Miller, prin.
Jefferson ES, 1725 IRVING ST 94122
  Judith Rosen, prin.
Junipero Serra ES
  625 HOLLY PARK CIRCLE 94110
  Warren Cane, prin.
Key ES, 1530 43RD AVE 94122
  Patricia Crocker, prin.
Lafayette ES, 4545 ANZA ST 94121
  Joan Hepperly, prin.
Lakeshore ES, 220 MIDDLEFIELD DRIVE 94132
  Sharon Guillestegui, prin.
Lawton ES, 1570 31ST AVE 94122
  Mike Holway, prin.
Lilienthal ES, 3950 SACRAMENTO ST 94118
  Kathleen King, prin.
Longfellow ES, 755 MORSE ST 94112
  David Plyer, prin.
Marshall ES, 1575 15TH ST 94103
  Rosendo Marin, prin.
McCoppin ES, 651 6TH AVE 94118
  Marge Manko, prin.
McKinley ES, 1025 14TH ST 94114
  Sally Smith, prin.
Miraloma ES, 175 OMAR WAY 94127
  Elaine Fong, prin.
Mission Education ES, 2641 25TH ST 94110
  Avelina Nicholas, prin.
Monroe ES, 260 MADRID ST 94112
  George Ryan, prin.
Moscone ES, 2355 FOLSOM ST 94110
  Nora Haymond, prin.
Muir ES, 380 WEBSTER ST 94117
  Jon Lucero, prin.
New Traditions ES, 1501 OFARRELL ST 94115
  Marilyn Stepney, prin.
Ortega ES, 400 SARGENT ST 94132
  Deborah Sims, prin.
Parker ES, 840 BROADWAY ST 94133
  Claudia Jeung, prin.
Peabody ES, 251 6TH AVE 94118
  Cecil Casey, prin.
Redding ES, 1421 PINE ST 94109
  Darlene Lau, prin.
Revere ES, 555 TOMPKINS AVE 94110
  Louise Look, prin.
Sanchez ES, 325 SANCHEZ ST 94114
  Kathleen Shimuzu, prin.
Sheridan ES, 431 CAPITOL AVE 94112
  Audrey Davis, prin.
Sherman ES, 1651 UNION ST 94123
  Sam Cohen, prin.
Spring Valley ES, 1451 JACKSON ST 94109
  Lonnie Chinn, prin.
Starr King ES, 1215 CAROLINA ST 94107
  Thomas Alexander, prin.
Stevenson ES, 2051 34TH AVE 94116
  Joyce Stewart, prin.
Sunnyside ES, 250 FOERSTER ST 94112
  Margaret Penn, prin.
Sutro ES, 235 12TH AVE 94118
  Jolie Wineroth, prin.
Swett ES, 727 GOLDEN GATE AVE 94102
  Lois Sims, prin.
Taylor ES, 423 BURROWS ST 94134
  Carol Tucker, prin.
Ulloa ES, 2650 42ND AVE 94116
  Richard Smith, prin.
Visitacion Valley ES, 55 SCHWERIN ST 94134
  Carol Belle, prin.
Webster ES, 465 MISSOURI ST 94107
  Wilhelmina Santamaria, prin.
Weill ES, 1501 OFARRELL ST 94115
  Marilyn Stepney, prin.
West Portal ES, 5 LENOX WAY 94127
  Jeanne Villafuerte, prin.

William De Avila ES, 1351 HAIGHT ST 94117
 Duncan Hodel, prin.
Yick Wo ES, 2245 JONES ST 94133
 Shirlene Tong, prin.
Other Schools – See Treasure Island

French American International School
 220 BUCHANAN ST 94102
Lycee Francais De San Fran, 834 28TH AVE 94121
Voice Pentecost Christian School
 1970 OCEAN AVE 94127
All Hollows ES, 1601 LANE ST 94124
Brandeis-Hillel Day ES
 655 BROTHERHOOD WAY 94132
Cathedral School for Boys
 1275 SACRAMENTO ST 94108
Convent of the Sacred Heart ES
 2200 BROADWAY ST 94115
Corpus Christi ES, 75 FRANCIS ST 94112
Discovery School, 65 OCEAN AVE 94112
Ecole Notre Dame des Victoires School
 659 PINE ST 94108
Epiphany ES, 600 ITALY AVE 94112
Fellowship Academy, 501 CAMBRIDGE ST 94134
First Baptist Church ES, 42 WALLER ST 94102
Hamlin ES, 2120 BROADWAY ST 94115
Hebrew Academy of San Francisco
 645 14TH AVE 94118
Holy Name ES, 1560 40TH AVE 94122
Immaculate Conception ES
 1550 TREAT AVE 94110
Katherine Delmar Burke ES
 7070 CALIFORNIA ST 94121
Krouzian-Zekarian of St. Gregory Armen
 825 BROTHERHOOD WAY 94132
Live Oak ES, 117 DIAMOND ST 94114
Mission Dolores ES, 3371 16TH ST 94114
Our Lady of Visitacion ES
 785 SUNNYSIDE AVE 94134
Sacred Heart ES, 735 FELL ST 94117
San Francisco Chinese Parents Comm. Scho
 843 STOCKTON ST 94108
San Francisco Christian ES
 25 WHITTIER ST 94112
San Francisco Day ES
 2266 CALIFORNIA ST 94115
San Francisco Junior Academy
 66 GENEVA AVE 94112
San Francisco Montessori School
 300 GREEN ST 94133
San Francisco Waldorf ES
 2938 WASHINGTON ST 94115
St. Anne ES, 1320 14TH AVE 94122
St. Anthony's ES, 299 PRECITA AVE 94110
St. Brendan ES
 940 LAGUNA HONDA BLVD 94127
St. Brigid ES, 2250 FRANKLIN ST 94109
St. Cecilia ES
 18TH AVENUE AND VICENTE ST 94116
St. Charles ES, 3250 18TH ST 94110
St. Dominic ES, 2445 PINE ST 94115
St. Elizabeth's ES, 450 SOMERSET ST 94134
St. Emydius ES, 301 DE MONTFORT AVE 94112
St. Finn Barr ES, 419 HEARST AVE 94112
St. Gabriel ES, 2550 41ST AVE 94116
St. James ES, 321 FAIR OAKS ST 94110
St. John's Memorial ES, 925 CHENERY ST 94131
St. Joseph ES, 220 10TH ST 94103
St. Mary's Chinese Day ES
 902 STOCKTON ST 94108
St. Michael ES, 55 FARALLONES ST 94112
St. Monica ES, 5920 GEARY BLVD 94121
St. Paul of the Shipwreck ES, 6475 3RD ST 94124
St. Paul's ES, 1660 CHURCH ST 94131
St. Paulus Lutheran ES, 888 TURK ST 94102
St. Peter's Parish ES, 1266 FLORIDA ST 94110
St. Philip ES, 665 ELIZABETH ST 94114
St. Stephen's ES, 401 EUCALYPTUS DR 94132
St. Thomas More ES
 50 THOMAS MORE WAY 94132
St. Thomas the Apostle ES
 3801 BALBOA ST 94121
St. Vincent De Paul ES, 2305 GREEN ST 94123
Star of the Sea ES, 360 9TH AVE 94118
Sts. Peter & Paul ES, 632-666 FILBET ST 94133
Stuart Hall for Boys School
 2252 BROADWAY ST 94115
Town School for Boys, 2750 JACKSON ST 94115
West Portal Lutheran ES, 200 SLOAT BLVD 94132
Zion Lutheran ES, 495 9TH AVE 94118

San Gabriel, Los Angeles Co., Pop. Code 8
Garvey ESD
 Supt. – See Rosemead
Dewey Avenue ES, 525 DEWEY AVE 91776
 Dolores Preciado, prin.
Marshall ES, 1817 JACKSON AVE 91776
 Marilyn Malmquist, prin.

San Gabriel ESD
 Sch. Sys. Enr. Code 5
 Supt. – Gary Goodson, 102 E BROADWAY 91776
Jefferson IS, 1440 LAFAYETTE ST 91776
 Jonathan Greenberg, prin.
Coolidge ES, 421 N MISSION DRIVE 91775
 Harold Frost, prin.
Madison ES, 1340 E LIVE OAK ST 91776
 Roger Stokka, prin.
McKinley ES, 1425 MANLEY DRIVE 91776
 Susan Crum, prin.
Roosevelt ES, 401 S WALNUT GROVE AVE 91776
 Joseph Hovard, prin.
Washington ES, 300 N SAN MARINO AVE 91775
 John Kemp, prin.

Wilson ES, 8317 SHEFFIELD ROAD 91775
 Leon Crabb, prin.

Temple City USD
 Supt. – See Temple City
Emperor ES, 6415 N MUSCATEL AVE 91775
 Tad Root, prin.

San Gabriel SDA Academy
 8827 E BROADWAY 91776
Clairbourn ES, 8400 HUNTINGTON DR 91775
San Gabriel Christian ES, 117 N PINE ST 91775
San Gabriel Mission ES
 547 W MISSION DR 91776
St. Anthony ES
 1905 S SAN GABRIEL BLVD 91776

Sanger, Fresno Co., Pop. Code 7
Sanger USD
 Sch. Sys. Enr. Code 6
 Supt. – Robert Jones, 1905 7TH ST 93657
Washington JHS, 2207 9TH ST 93657
 Henry Vasquez, prin.
Centerville ES, 48 S SMITH AVE 93657
 Richard Larimer, prin.
Fairmont ES, 3095 N GREENWOOD AVE 93657
 Jack Sutherland, prin.
Jackson ES, 1810 3RD ST 93657
 Glenn Corwin, prin.
Jefferson ES, 1110 TUCKER AVE 93657
 Leon Sarkisian, prin.
Lincoln ES, 1700 14TH ST 93657
 Rosemarie Sancho, prin.
Madison ES, 2324 CHERRY AVE 93657
 Sherrey Bishop, prin.
Wilson ES, 610 FALLER AVE 93657
 Jim Simpson, prin.
Other Schools – See Del Rey, Fresno

San Geronimo, Marin Co.
Lagunitas ESD
 Sch. Sys. Enr. Code 2
 Supt. – M. Dale Lambert, P O BOX 208 94963
Lagunitas ES, P O BOX 308 94963
 Larry Enos, prin.
San Geronimo Valley ES, P O BOX 208 94963
 Larry Enos, prin.

San Jacinto, Riverside Co., Pop. Code 6
San Jacinto USD
 Sch. Sys. Enr. Code 5
 Supt. – Sandra Shackelford, 600 E MAIN ST 92383
Monte Vista MS, 181 N RAMONA BLVD 92383
 Frederick Richardson, prin.
De Anza ES, 1189 DE ANZA DR 92383
 Penny Harrison, prin.
Hyatt ES, 400 E SHAVER ST 92383
 Deborah DeForge, prin.
ES, 136 N RAMONA BLVD 92383
 Mike Salinas, prin.

St. Hyacinth Academy
 275 S VICTORIA AVE 92383

San Joaquin, Fresno Co., Pop. Code 4
San Joaquin ESD
 Sch. Sys. Enr. Code 3
 Supt. – Paul Johnson, P O BOX 408 93660
ES, P O BOX 408 93660 – Paul Johnson, prin.

San Jose, Santa Clara Co., Pop. Code 11
Alum Rock Un. ESD
 Sch. Sys. Enr. Code 7
 Supt. – Walter Symons, 2930 GAY AVE 95127
Fischer MS, 1720 HOPKINS DRIVE 95122
 Gregorio Gutierrez, prin.
George MS, 277 MAHONEY DRIVE 95127
 James O'Berg, prin.
Mathson MS, 2050 KAMMERER AVE 95116
 Ricardo Trevino, prin.
Ocala MS, 2800 OCALA AVE 95148
 Donald Ayers, prin.
Pala MS, 149 N WHITE ROAD 95127
 Arthur Harris, prin.
Sheppard MS
 480 ROUGH & READY ROAD 95133
 Gloria Loventhal, prin.
Arbuckle ES, 1970 CINDERELLA LANE 95116
 Louis Henry, prin.
Cassell ES, 1300 TALLAHASSEE DRIVE 95122
 Ronald Fredericks, prin.
Cureton ES, 3720 EAST HILLS DRIVE 95127
 Anita Canul, prin.
Dorsa ES, 1290 BAL HARBOR WAY 95122
 Susan Tacke, prin.
Goss ES, 2475 VAN WINKLE LANE 95116
 Earsie Mike, prin.
Hubbard ES, 1745 JUNE AVE 95122
 (—), prin.
Linda Vista ES, 100 KIRK AVE 95127
 Robert Denike, prin.
Lyndale ES, 13901 NORDYKE DRIVE 95127
 James Collett, prin.
Mayfair ES, 3311 LUCIAN AVE 95116
 Andrew Jimenez, prin.
McCollam ES, 3311 LUCIAN AVE 95127
 Frank Wilkens, prin.
Meyer ES, 1824 DAYTONA DRIVE 95122
 Mario Sanchez, prin.
Miller ES, 1250 S KING ROAD 95122
 Helen Ramirez, prin.
Painter ES
 500 ROUGH AND READY ROAD 95133
 Tom Nichols, prin.

Rogers ES, 2999 RIDGEMONT DRIVE 95127
 (—), prin.
Ryan ES, 1241 MCGINNESS AVE 95127
 Mary Ann Forbes, prin.
San Antonio ES, 1855 E SAN ANTONIO ST 95116
 Elena Portillo, prin.
Shields ES, 2851 GAY AVE 95127
 Elizabeth Schaefer, prin.
Slonaker ES, 1601 CUNNINGHAM AVE 95122
 Robert Bird, prin.
Other Schools – See Mount Hamilton

Berryessa Un. ESD
 Sch. Sys. Enr. Code 6
 Supt. – Thomas Sullivan
 1376 PIEDMONT ROAD 95132
Morrill MS, 1970 MORRILL AVE 95132
 Al Moe, prin.
Piedmont MS, 955 PIEDMONT ROAD 95132
 Patricia Stelwagon, prin.
Sierramont MS, 3155 KIMLEE DRIVE 95132
 (—), prin.
Brooktree ES, 1781 OLIVETREE DRIVE 95131
 Corwin Barfield, prin.
Cherrywood ES, 2550 GREENGATE DRIVE 95132
 Carolyn Keagle, prin.
Laneview ES, 2095 WARMWOOD LANE 95132
 Arthur Villarruz, prin.
Majestic ES, 1855 MAJESTIC WAY 95132
 Estella Quintanilla, prin.
Noble ES, 3466 GROSSMONT DRIVE 95132
 Gloria Lewis, prin.
Northwood ES, 2760 E TRIMBLE ROAD 95132
 Carol Dillard, prin.
Ruskin ES, 1401 TURLOCK LANE 95132
 Joan Fischer, prin.
Summerdale ES
 1100 SUMMERDALE DRIVE 95132
 Katie Kaufman, prin.
Toyon ES, 995 BARD ST 95127
 Michael Pascal, prin.
Vinci Park ES, 1311 VINCI PARK WAY 95131
 Patrick Allen, prin.

Cambrian ESD
 Sch. Sys. Enr. Code 4
 Supt. – P. Barone, 4115 JACKSOL DRIVE 95124
Price MS, 2650 NEW JERSEY AVE 95124
 Catherine Gallegos, prin.
Bagby ES, 1840 HARRIS AVE 95124
 Fran Gelb, prin.
Fammatre ES, 2800 NEW JERSEY AVE 95124
 Robert Custer, prin.
Farnham ES, 15711 WOODARD ROAD 95124
 Michael Demko, prin.
Sartorette ES, 3850 WOODFORD DRIVE 95124
 Richard Wendell, prin.

Campbell Un. ESD
 Supt. – See Campbell
Monroe ES, 1055 S MONROE ST 95128
 Lois Adams, prin.
Blackford ES, 1970 WILLOW ST 95125
 Elizabeth Denny, prin.
Forest Hill ES, 4450 MCCOY AVE 95130
 Eugene Smith, prin.
Lynhaven ES, 881 S CYPRESS AVE 95117
 Jocelyn Zona, prin.

Cupertino Un. ESD
 Supt. – See Cupertino
Miller JHS, 6151 RAINBOW DRIVE 95129
 Andrew Garrido, prin.
De Vargas ES, 5050 MOORPARK AVE 95129
 Suzanne Godshall, prin.
Dilworth ES, 1101 STRAYER DRIVE 95129
 Robert Adams, prin.
Meyerholtz ES, 6990 MELVIN DRIVE 95129
 Bob Downer, prin.
Muir ES, 6560 HANOVER DRIVE 95129
 Patricia Demarlo, prin.

Evergreen ESD
 Sch. Sys. Enr. Code 6
 Supt. – James Smith, 3188 QUIMBY ROAD 95148
Leyva IS, 1865 MONROVIA DRIVE 95122
 Tom Andrade, prin.
Quimby Oak IS, 3190 QUIMBY ROAD 95148
 Bette Samdahl, prin.
Cadwallader ES
 3799 CADWALLADER AVE 95121
 Carole Martin, prin.
Cedar Grove ES, 2702 SUGARPLUM DRIVE 95148
 Lali Morales, prin.
Dove Hill ES, 1460 COLT WAY 95121
 Phyllis Lindstrom, prin.
Evergreen ES, 3010 FOWLER ROAD 95135
 Judith Rule, prin.
Holly Oak ES, 2995 ROSSMORE WAY 95148
 (—), prin.
Laurelwood ES, 4280 PARTRIDGE DRIVE 95121
 Robert Pruitt, prin.
Millbrook ES, 3200 MILLBROOK DRIVE 95148
 Peter Gutierrez, prin.
Montgomery ES
 2010 DANIEL MALONEY DRIVE 95121
 Sue Fettchenhauer, prin.
Norwood Creek ES
 3241 REMINGTON WAY 95148 – E. Milde, prin.
Smith ES, 2025 CLARICE DRIVE 95122
 Will Ector, prin.
Whaley ES, 2655 ALVIN AVE 95121
 Jennie Collett, prin.

Franklin-McKinley ESD
Sch. Sys. Enr. Code 6
Supt. – Dolores Ballesteros
  2072 LUCRETIA AVE 95122
Fair JHS, 1702 MCLAUGHLIN AVE 95122
  Ken Morgan, prin.
Sylvandale JHS, 653 SYLVANDALE AVE 95111
  Nancy McLaurin, prin.
Franklin ES, 420 TULLY ROAD 95111
  Kenneth Rice, prin.
Hellyer ES, 725 HELLYER AVE 95111
  Kenneth Van Otten, prin.
Hillsdale ES, 3100 WATER ST 95111
  John Delgado, prin.
Kennedy ES, 1602 LUCRETIA AVE 95122
  Lynne Hopkins, prin.
Los Arboles ES, 455 LOS ARBOLES ST 95111
  Diane Cooper, prin.
McKinley ES, 651 MACREDES CT 95116
  Rod Cryer, prin.
Santee ES, 1313 AUDUBON DRIVE 95122
  Barbara Anderson, prin.
Seven Trees ES, 3975 MIRA LOMA WAY 95111
  Charlene Berg, prin.
Stonegate ES, 2605 GASSMANN DRIVE 95121
  Virginia Mirrione, prin.
Windmill Springs ES, 2880 AETNA WAY 95121
  James Shock, prin.

Luther Burbank ESD
Sch. Sys. Enr. Code 2
Supt. – Richard Foley, 4 WABASH AVE 95128
Burbank ES, 4 WABASH AVE 95128
  Richard Foley, prin.

Moreland ESD
Sch. Sys. Enr. Code 5
Supt. – Robert Reasoner
  4710 CAMPBELL AVE 95130
Castro MS, 4600 STUDENT LANE 95130
  Laurie LeDuc, prin.
Rogers MS, 4835 DOYLE ROAD 95129
  Angie Fredrick, prin.
Anderson ES, 4000 RHODA DRIVE 95117
  Norman VanWoerkom, prin.
Baker ES, 4845 BUCKNALL ROAD 95130
  Paul Madarang, prin.
Country Lane ES, 5140 COUNTRY LANE 95129
  Dan Kueuzer, prin.
Easterbrook ES, 4660 EASTUS DRIVE 95129
  James Gomes, prin.
Latimer ES, 4250 LATIMER AVE 95130
  Marguerite Weiner, prin.
Payne ES, 3750 GLEASON AVE 95130
  Jerry Thornton, prin.

Morgan Hill USD
Supt. – See Morgan Hill
Los Paseos ES, 121 AVENIDA GRANDE 95139
  Robert Pedretti, prin.

Mt. Pleasant ESD
Sch. Sys. Enr. Code 4
Supt. – Ida Jew, 14265 STORY ROAD 95127
Boeger MS, 1944 FLINT AVE 95148
  James Ross, prin.
Marten ES, 14271 STORY ROAD 95127
  Frank Cream, prin.
Mt. Pleasant ES, 14275 CANDLER AVE 95127
  Roy Shiba, prin.
Sanders Traditional ES
  3411 ROCKY MOUNTAIN DRIVE 95127
  Kathleen Hess, prin.
Valle Vista ES, 2400 FLINT AVE 95148
  Mary Tidwell, prin.

Oak Grove ESD
Sch. Sys. Enr. Code 7
Supt. – Anthony Russo
  6578 SANTA TERESA BLVD 95119
Bernal IS, 6610 SAN IGNACIO AVE 95119
  Tom Burgei, prin.
Davis IS, 5035 EDENVIEW DRIVE 95111
  Emmanuel Barbara, prin.
Herman IS, 5955 BLOSSOM AVE 95123
  Oscar Donahue, prin.
Baldwin ES, 280 MARTINVALE LN 95119
  Margaret Bonanno, prin.
Blossom Valley ES, 420 ALLEGAN CIRCLE 95123
  Ralph Shonack, prin.
Christopher ES, 565 COYOTE ROAD 95111
  Sue Mills, prin.
Del Roble ES
  5345 AVENIDA ALMENDROS 95123
  Richard Belgum, prin.
Edenvale ES, 285 AZUCAR AVE 95111
  Meril Smith, prin.
Frost ES, 530 GETTYSBURG DRIVE 95123
  John Aguilar, prin.
Glider ES, 511 COZY DRIVE 95123
  Anita Karsen, prin.
Hayes ES, 5035 POSTON DRIVE 95136
  Lawrence Dauch, prin.
Miner ES, 5629 LEAN AVE 95123
  Burns Srigley, prin.
Oak Ridge ES, 5920 BUFKIN DRIVE 95123
  Jackie Dobbins, prin.
Parkview ES, 330 BLUEFIELD DRIVE 95136
  Denise Stephens, prin.
Sakamoto ES, 6280 SHADELANDS DRIVE 95123
  Patsy VanEttinger, prin.
San Anselmo ES
  6670 SAN ANSELMO WAY 95119
  Henry Castaniada, prin.

Santa Teresa ES, 6200 ENCINAL DRIVE 95119
  Judith Hetzel, prin.
Stipe ES, 5000 LYNG DRIVE 95111
  Charles Cook, prin.
Taylor ES, 410 SAUTNER DRIVE 95123
  Charles Caldwell, prin.

Orchard SD
Sch. Sys. Enr. Code 2
Supt. – Larry Todd, 711 E GISH ROAD 95112
Orchard ES, 711 E GISH ROAD 95112
  Donna Hajduk, prin.

San Jose USD
Sch. Sys. Enr. Code 8
Supt. – Hilda Beck, 1605 PARK AVE 95126
Burnett MS, 850 N 2ND ST 95112
  Cotine Weltzin, prin.
Castillero MS
  6384 LEYLAND PARK DRIVE 95120
  Doloras Rodriguez, prin.
Harte MS, 7050 BRET HARTE DRIVE 95120
  Harry Davis, prin.
Hoover MS, 1635 PARK AVE 95126
  George Romero, prin.
Markham MS, 2105 COTTLE AVE 95125
  Harold Garrett, prin.
Muir MS, 1260 BRANHAM LANE 95118
  Jesse Rizzo, prin.
Steinbeck MS, 820 STEINBECK DRIVE 95123
  Oreen Gernreich, prin.
Allen ES, 5845 ALLEN AVE 95123
  Linda Gonzalez, prin.
Almaden ES, 1295 DENTWOOD DRIVE 95118
  Rosemary Young, prin.
Bachrodt ES, 102 SONORA AVE 95110
  Tom Nanamura, prin.
Booksin ES, 1590 DRY CREEK ROAD 95125
  Roberta Bondelie, prin.
Carson ES, 4245 MEG DRIVE 95136
  Nancy Locke, prin.
Cory ES, 2280 KENWOOD AVE 95128
  Bonnie Piche, prin.
Darling ES, 333 N 33RD ST 95133
  Jerome Kristal, prin.
Empire Gardens ES, 1060 E EMPIRE ST 95112
  Corky Conway, prin.
Gardner ES, 502 ILLINOIS AVE 95125
  Lydia Dague, prin.
Grant ES, 470 E JACKSON ST 95112
  Patricia Gregory, prin.
Graystone ES, 6982 SHEARWATER DRIVE 95120
  Cecilia Huffman, prin.
Hester ES, 1460 THE ALAMEDA 95126
  Susan Valdez, prin.
Los Alamitos ES, 6164 SILBERMAN DRIVE 95120
  Roger Banta, prin.
Lowell ES, 625 S 7TH ST 95112
  Emerita Camilleri, prin.
Mann ES, 55 N 7TH ST 95112
  Mary Maxwell, prin.
Olinder ES, 890 E WILLIAM ST 95116
  Monica Olds, prin.
Randol ES, 762 SUNSET GLEN DRIVE 95123
  Carol Garcia, prin.
Reed ES, 1524 JACOB AVE 95118
  Gerald Weltzin, prin.
Schallenberger ES, 1280 KOCH LANE 95125
  Cheryl Petermann, prin.
Simonds ES, 6515 GRAPEVINE WAY 95120
  Sverre Knapstad, prin.
Terrell ES, 3925 PEARL AVE 95136
  Jack Fix, prin.
Trace MS, 651 DANA AVE 95126
  Rose Dunnigan, prin.
Washington ES, 100 OAK ST 95110
  Lorie Rizzo, prin.
Willow Glen ES, 1425 LINCOLN AVE 95125
  Nate Wilson, prin.

Union ESD
Sch. Sys. Enr. Code 5
Supt. – Janis Roan, 5175 UNION AVE 95124
Dartmouth MS, 5575 DARTMOUTH DRIVE 95118
  Henry Warkentin, prin.
Union MS
  2130 LOS GATOS-ALMADEN ROAD 95124
  Mary Glaviano, prin.
Athenour ES, 5200 DENT AVE 95118
  Linda Ramsey, prin.
Carlton ES, 2421 CARLTON AVE 95124
  William Stanton, prin.
Guadalupe ES, 6044 VERA CRUZ DRIVE 95120
  Karen Mullaly, prin.
Lietz ES, 5300 CARTER AVE 95118
  Sidney Aronson, prin.
Lone Hill ES, 4949 HARWOOD ROAD 95124
  Camille Karlson, prin.
Noddin ES, 1755 GILDA WAY 95124
  Marvin Kidwiler, prin.
Oster ES, 1855 LENCAR WAY 95124
  Elvin Mardock, prin.
Other Schools – See Los Gatos

Christian Community Academy
  1523 MCLAUGHLIN AVE 95122
Liberty Baptist School, 2790 S KING ROAD 95122
Achiever Christian ES, 800 IRONWOOD DR 95125
Challenger ES, 1325 BOURET DR 95118
Challenger ES, 4455 UNION AVE 95124
Country ES of Almaden
  6835 TRINIDAD DR 95120
Five Wounds ES, 1390 FIVE WOUNDS LN 95116
Harker Academy, 500 SARATOGA AVE 95129

Holy Family Education School
  4848 PEARL AVE 95136
Learning Academy, 5670 CAMDEN AVE 95124
Milpitas Christian ES
  3435 BIRCHWOOD LN 95132
Most Holy Trinity ES
  1940 CUNNINGHAM AVE 95122
Primary Plus School, 3500 AMBER DR 95117
Queen of Apostles ES, 4950 MITTY WAY 95129
Small World ES, 730 CAMINA ESCUELA 95129
St. Christopher ES, 2278 BOOKSIN AVE 95125
St. Frances Cabrini ES
  15325 WOODARD RD 95124
St. John Vianney ES, 4601 HYLAND AVE 95127
St. Leo the Great ES
  1051 W SAN FERNANDO ST 95126
St. Martin of Tours ES, 300 OCONNOR DR 95128
St. Patrick ES, 51 N 9TH ST 95112
St. Stephen's ES, 500 SHAWNEE LN 95123
St. Timothy ES, 5100 CAMDEN AVE 95124
St. Victor ES, 3150 SIERRA RD 95132
Valley Christian ES, 1175 HILLSDALE AVE 95118

San Juan Bautista, San Benito Co., Pop. Code 4
San Juan Un. ESD
Sch. Sys. Enr. Code 3
Supt. – David Evans, P O BOX A 95045
San Juan ES, P O BOX A 95045
  Lewis Becker, prin.

San Juan Capistrano, Orange Co., Pop. Code 7
Capistrano USD
Sch. Sys. Enr. Code 7
Supt. – Jerome Thornsley
  32972 CALLE PERFECTO 92675
Forster JHS, 25601 CAMINO DEL AVION 92675
  Richard Johnson, prin.
Ambuehl ES
  28001 SAN JUAN CREEK ROAD 92675
  David Gerhard, prin.
Del Obispo ES
  25591 CAMINO DEL AVION 92675
  Marcia Jones, prin.
San Juan ES, 31642 EL CAMINO REAL 92675
  Carol Holmes, prin.
Other Schools – See Capistrano Beach, Dana Point,
  Laguna Niguel, Mission Viejo, San Clemente

Capistrano Valley Christian School
  32032 DEL OBISPO ST 92675
St. Margarets School
  31641 LA NOVIA AVE 92675
Mission ES, 31641 EL CAMINO REAL 92675

San Leandro, Alameda Co., Pop. Code 8
San Leandro USD
Sch. Sys. Enr. Code 6
Supt. – Richard Tubbs, 14735 JUNIPER ST 94579
Garfield ES, 13050 AURORA DRIVE 94577
  Garry Loeffler, prin.
Jefferson ES, 14311 LARK ST 94578
  Karen Short, prin.
McKinley ES, 2150 E 14TH ST 94577
  Pamela Goode, prin.
Monroe ES, 3750 MONTEREY BLVD 94578
  Tom Carman, prin.
Roosevelt ES, 951 DOWLING BLVD 94577
  Mary Beth Barloga, prin.
Washington ES, 250 DUTTON AVE 94577
  James Bolar, prin.
Wilson ES, 1300 WILLIAMS ST 94577
  Bob Thomas, prin.

San Lorenzo USD
Supt. – See San Lorenzo
Corvallis ES, 14790 CORVALLIS ST 94579
  Leslie Anderson, prin.
Hillside ES, 15980 MARCELLA ST 94578
  James Wilson, prin.
Washington Manor ES, 1170 FARGO AVE 94579
  Joanne Ellgas, prin.

Chinese Christian Schs., 750 FARGO AVE 94579
Assumption ES, 1851 136TH AVE 94578
Manor Baptist Christian ES
  1845 LEWELLING BLVD 94579
Montessori School of San Leandro
  16292 FOOTHILL BLVD 94578
St. Felicitas ES, 1650 MANOR BLVD 94579
St. Leander ES, 451 DAVIS ST 94577

San Lorenzo, Alameda Co., Pop. Code 7
San Lorenzo USD
Sch. Sys. Enr. Code 6
Supt. – Alden Badal, P O BOX 37 94580
Bay ES, 2001 BROCKMAN ROAD 94580
  Donald Victor, prin.
Del Rey ES, 1510 VIA SONYA 94580
  Caryl Laniewski, prin.
Edendale ES, 16160 ASHLAND AVE 94580
  Gary Baca, prin.
Hesperian ES, 620 DREW ST 94580
  Kathleen Ratto, prin.
Other Schools – See Hayward, San Leandro

Calvary Lutheran ES
  17200 VIA MAGDALENA 94580
St. John ES, 270 E LEWELLING BLVD 94580
Stivers ES, 1000 PASEO GRANDE 94580

San Lucas, Monterey Co.
San Lucas Un. ESD
Sch. Sys. Enr. Code 2
Supt. – Stanley Stark, SAN BENITO ST 93954
ES, SAN BENITO ST 93954 – Stanley Stark, prin.

San Luis Obispo, San Luis Obispo Co., Pop. Code 8
San Luis Coastal USD
Sch. Sys. Enr. Code 6
Supt. – Irvin Nikolai, P O BOX 8124 93403
Laguna JHS
  1050 LOS OSOS VALLEY ROAD 93402
  Richard Andrus, prin.
Baywood ES, P O BOX 8124 93403
  Michael Simkins, prin.
Bellevue-Sante Fe ES
  1401 SAN LUIS BAY DRIVE 93401
  Richard Pierce, prin.
Bishop's Peak ES, P O BOX 8124 93403
  Edward Riley, prin.
Hawthorne ES, P O BOX 8124 93403
  Richard Pierce, prin.
Los Ranchos ES, 5785 LOS RANCHOS RD 93401
  Janet Wentz, prin.
Pacheco ES, 165 GRAND AVE 93401
  Marianne Michels, prin.
Sinsheimer ES, P O BOX 8124 93401
  James Miller, prin.
Smith ES, 1375 BALBOA ST 93401
  Herb Alloway, prin.
Teach MS, P O BOX 8124 93401
  John Pisula, prin.
Other Schools – See Los Osos, Morro Bay

Old Mission ES, 761 BROAD ST 93401

San Luis Rey, San Diego Co.

Old Mission Montessori School
  4070 MISSION AVE 92068

San Marcos, San Diego Co., Pop. Code 7
San Marcos USD
Sch. Sys. Enr. Code 6
Supt. – Mac Bernd
  270 W SAN MARCOS BLVD 92069
JHS, 650 W MISSION ROAD 92069
  Susan Maki, prin.
Dunn ES
  300 S RANCHO SANTA FE ROAD 92069
  Janet Bernard, prin.
Knob Hill ES, 1825 KNOB HILL RD 92069
  Patricia Arendt, prin.
Richland ES, 910 BORDEN ROAD 92069
  Marge Hobbs, prin.
ES, 300 W SAN MARCOS BLVD 92069
  Sara Johnson, prin.
Woodland Park ES
  1220 ROCK SPRINGS ROAD 92069
  Dennis Stokes, prin.
Other Schools – See Carlsbad

San Marino, Los Angeles Co., Pop. Code 7
San Marino USD
Sch. Sys. Enr. Code 5
Supt. – Gary Richards, 1665 WEST DRIVE 91108
Huntington IS, 1700 HUNTINGTON DRIVE 91108
  Charles Johnson, prin.
Carver ES, 1300 S SAN GABRIEL BLVD 91108
  William Langton, prin.
Valentine ES, 1650 HUNTINGTON DRIVE 91108
  Mary Meye, prin.

Southwestern Academy
  2800 MONTEREY ROAD 91108
Sts. Felicitas & Pereptua ES
  2955 HUNTINGTON DR 91108

San Martin, Santa Clara Co., Pop. Code 4
Morgan Hill USD
Supt. – See Morgan Hill
Gwinn MS, 95 NORTH ST 95046
  Arlene Machado, prin.
ES, 100 NORTH ST 95046
  Arlene Machado, prin.

San Mateo, San Mateo Co., Pop. Code 8
San Mateo City SD
Sch. Sys. Enr. Code 6
Supt. – Joyce Mahdesian, P O BOX K 94402
Abbott MS, 600 36TH AVE 94403
  William Kramer, prin.
Bayside MS, 2025 KEHOE AVE 94403
  Murry Schekman, prin.
Borel MS, 425 BARNESON AVE 94402
  Clathel Zach, prin.
Baywood ES
  600 ALAMEDA DE LAS PULGAS 94402
  Basil Willett Jr., prin.
Hall ES, 130 SAN MIGUEL AVE 94403
  Charles Pierce, prin.
Highlands ES, 2320 NEWPORT ST 94402
  Ronald Veronda, prin.
Horrall ES, 949 OCEAN VIEW AVE 94401
  Patricia Cartwright, prin.
Laurel ES, 316 36TH AVE 94403
  Richard Morgan, prin.
Meadow Heights ES, 2619 DOLORES ST 94403
  Shirley Seitz, prin.
North Shoreview ES, 1301 CYPRESS AVE 94401
  Evelyn Hamer, prin.
Park ES, 161 CLARK DRIVE 94402
  Elbert Colum, prin.
Parkside ES, 1685 EISENHOWER ST 94403
  Ellen Hancock, prin.
Sunnybrae ES, 1031 S DELAWARE ST 94402
  Anthony Rose, prin.
Other Schools – See Foster City

Carey ES
  2101 ALAMEDA DE LAS PULGAS 94403

Grace Lutheran ES
  2825 ALAMEDA LAS PULGAS 94403
San Mateo Christian Academy
  525 42ND AVE 94403
St. Gregory ES, 2701 HACIENDA ST 94403
St. Matthew's ES, 900 S EL CAMINO REAL 94402
St. Matthew's Episcopal ES
  900 S EL CAMINO REAL 94402
St. Timothy ES, 1515 DOLAN AVE 94401

San Miguel, San Luis Obispo Co., Pop. Code 3
Pleasant Valley JUn. ESD
Sch. Sys. Enr. Code 1
Supt. – (—), P O BOX 4390 93451
Pleasant Valley ES, P O BOX 4390 93451
  Judy Bidell, prin.

San Miguel JUn. ESD
Sch. Sys. Enr. Code 2
Supt. – Robert McLaughlin, P O BOX 299 93451
Larsen ES, P O BOX 299 93451
  Robert McLaughlin, prin.

Shandon JUSD
Supt. – See Shandon
Parkfield ES
  PARKFIELD HCR RT BOX 3510 93451
  Duane Hamann, prin.

San Pablo, Contra Costa Co., Pop. Code 7
Richmond USD
Supt. – See Richmond
Helms JHS, 2500 ROAD 20 94806
  Jim Reno, prin.
Bayview ES, 3001 16TH ST 94806
  Karen Hancox, prin.
Dover ES, 1871 21ST ST 94806
  Irene Hightower, prin.
Downer ES, 1777 SANFORD AVE 94806
  Clyde Wallace, prin.
El Portal ES, 2600 MORAGA ROAD 94806
  Dyane Marks, prin.
Lake ES, 2700 11TH ST 94806
  Patricia Dennett, prin.
Montalvin Manor ES
  300 CHRISTINE DRIVE 94806
  Byron Lambie, prin.
Seaview ES, 2000 STOUTHWOOD DRIVE 94806
  Marian O'Connell, prin.
Tara Hills ES, 2300 DOLAN WAY 94806
  Masa Gin, prin.

St. Paul ES, 1825 CHURCH LN 94806

San Pedro, Los Angeles Co., Pop. Code 8
Los Angeles USD
Supt. – See Los Angeles
Bandini Street ES, 425 N BANDINI ST 90731
  Steven Smith, prin.
Barton Hill ES, 423 N PACIFIC AVE 90731
  Dale Armstrong, prin.
Cabrillo Avenue ES, 732 S CABRILLO AVE 90731
  Jeanne Holmes, prin.
Crestwood Street ES
  1946 W CRESTWOOD ST 90732
  Thelma Ortega, prin.
Fifteenth Street ES, 1527 S MESA ST 90731
  Stanley Bunyan, prin.
Leland Street ES, 2120 S LELAND ST 90731
  Julia Migliaccio, prin.
Park Western Place ES
  1214 PARK WESTERN PLACE 90732
  Albert Stebinger, prin.
Point Fermin ES, 3333 S KERCKHOFF AVE 90731
  Charles Hall, prin.
Seventh Street ES, 1570 W 7TH ST 90732
  Patricia Kinnan, prin.
Taper Avenue ES, 1824 N TAPER AVE 90731
  Albert Fasani, prin.
White Point ES, 1410 SILVIUS AVE 90731
  Jack Zannella, prin.

Christ Lutheran ES
  28850 S WESTERN AVE 90732
Holy Trinity ES, 1226 W SANTA CRUZ ST 90732
Mary Star of the Sea ES
  717 S CABRILLO AVE 90731
St. Peter's Episcopal Day ES
  1648 W 9TH ST 90732

San Rafael, Marin Co., Pop. Code 8
Dixie ESD
Sch. Sys. Enr. Code 4
Supt. – Larry Lyon
  380 NOVA ALBION WAY 94903
Miller Creek MS
  2255 LAS GALLINAS AVE 94903
  Linda Sheppard, prin.
Dixie ES, 1175 IDYLBERRY ROAD 94903
  Charles Warfield, prin.
Vallecito ES, 50 NOVA ALBION WAY 94903
  Robert Lawrence, prin.

San Rafael CSD
Sch. Sys. Enr. Code 5
Supt. – Nancy Dalton
  225 WOODLAND AVE 94901
Davidson MS, 280 WOODLAND AVE 94901
  Jarold Warren, prin.
Bahia Vista ES, 125 BAHIA WAY 94901
  Shirley Voller, prin.
Coleman ES, 140 RAFAEL DRIVE 94901
  Hoyt Howlett, prin.
Gallinas ES, 177 N SAN PEDRO ROAD 94903
  Harry Holland, prin.

Glenwood ES, 25 CASTLEWOOD DRIVE 94901
  Val Travaglini, prin.
Sun Valley ES, 75 HAPPY LANE 94901
  Jan Derby, prin.

Marin Waldorf ES, 755 IDYLBERRY RD 94903
St. Isabellas Parochial ES, P O BOX 6188 94903
St. Mark's ES, 375 BLACKSTONE DR 94903
St. Raphael's ES, 1100 5TH AVE 94901

San Ramon, Contra Costa Co., Pop. Code 2
San Ramon Valley USD
Supt. – See Danville
Pine Valley IS, 3000 PINE VALLEY ROAD 94583
  Steve Ow, prin.
Armstrong ES, 2849 CALAIS DRIVE 94583
  Lizanne Kendall, prin.
Bolinger Canyon ES
  2300 TALAVERA DRIVE 94583
  Joan Diamond, prin.
Country Club ES, 7534 BLUE FOX WAY 94583
  Carol Rowley, prin.
Disney ES, 3250 PINE VALLEY ROAD 94583
  David Beery, prin.
Montevideo ES
  13000 BROADMOOR DRIVE 94583
  Roger Tovey, prin.
Twin Creeks ES, 2785 MARSH DR 94583
  Susan Burleson, prin.

Santa Ana, Orange Co., Pop. Code 9
Garden Grove USD
Supt. – See Garden Grove
Fitz IS, 4600 W MCFADDEN AVE 92704
  Michael Lombardi, prin.
Hazard ES, 4218 HAZARD AVE 92703
  Gene Takach, prin.
Heritage ES, 426 S ANDRES PLACE 92704
  Robert Gresham, prin.
Newhope ES, 4419 W REGENT DRIVE 92704
  Dick Lane, prin.
Rosita ES, 4726 HAZARD AVE 92703
  James Franklin, prin.
Russell ES, 600 S JACKSON ST 92704
  Dick Mobley, prin.

Irvine USD
Supt. – See Irvine
El Toro Marine ES
  8171 S E TRABUCO ROAD 92709
  Dan Graham, prin.

Orange USD
Supt. – See Orange
Fairhaven ES, 1415 FAIRHAVEN AVE 92701
  Lynn Cook, prin.
Panorama ES
  10512 CRAWFORD CANYON DRIVE 92705
  Maggie VanEck, prin.

Santa Ana USD
Sch. Sys. Enr. Code 8
Supt. – Ed Krass, 1405 FRENCH ST 92701
Carr IS, 2120 W EDINGER AVE 92704
  Vincent Tafolla, prin.
Lathrop IS, 1111 S BROADWAY 92707
  Greg Rankin, prin.
MacArthur IS, 600 W ALTON AVE 92707
  Thomas Reasin, prin.
McFadden IS, 2701 S RAITT ST 92704
  (—), prin.
Sierra IS, 1901 N MCCLAY 92701
  Daniel Salcedo, prin.
Spurgeon IS, 2701 W 5TH ST 92703
  Cathy Makin, prin.
Willard IS, 1342 N ROSS ST 92706
  Howard Haas, prin.
Adams ES, 2130 S RAITT ST 92704
  Martha Baker, prin.
Diamond ES, 2305 W EDINGER AVE 92704
  Mark Davis, prin.
Edison ES, 2063 ORANGE AVE 92707
  Helen Stainer, prin.
Franklin ES, 210 W CUBBON ST 92701
  Lupe O'Leary, prin.
Fremont ES, 1930 W 10TH ST 92703
  Jacquin Terry, prin.
Grant ES, 333 E WALNUT ST 92701
  Reginald Villamil, prin.
Greenville Fundamental ES
  3600 S RAITT ST 92704 – Joyce Horowitz, prin.
Hoover ES, 408 E SANTA CLARA AVE 92706
  Helen Romeo, prin.
Jackson ES, 1143 S NAKOMA DRIVE 92704
  Susan Johns, prin.
Jefferson ES, 15232 W ADAMS ST 92704
  Susan Despenas, prin.
Lincoln ES, 425 S SULLIVAN ST 92704
  Joseph Randazzo, prin.
Lowell ES, 915 RICHLAND AVE 92703
  Ann Reed, prin.
Madison ES, 1124 HOBART ST 92707
  Diana Blazey, prin.
Martin ES, 939 W WILSHIRE AVE 92707
  Helen Matthews, prin.
Monroe ES, 417 E CENTRAL AVE 92707
  Thomas Lagano, prin.
Monte Vista ES
  2116 N MONTE VISTA AVE 92704
  Donald Tibbetts, prin.
Muir Fundamental ES, 1951 MABURY ST 92701
  Betty Wagner, prin.
Remington ES, 1325 E 4TH ST 92701
  Serene Stokes, prin.

Roosevelt ES, 501 HALLADAY ST   92701
  Robert Deberry, prin.
Roosevelt Annex ES, 820 E CAMILE   92701
  Terry Araujo, prin.
Santiago ES, 2212 N BAKER ST   92706
  Joan Stone, prin.
Sepulveda ES, 1818 S BRISTOL ST   92704
  Betty Nickel, prin.
Taft ES, 500 KELLER AVE   92707
  William Hart, prin.
Washington ES, 910 W ANAHURST PLACE   92707
  Nadine Rodriguez, prin.
Wilson ES, 1317 N BAKER ST   92706
  Donald Guenzler, prin.

Tustin USD
Supt. – See Tustin
Hewes MS, 13232 HEWES AVE   92705
  Julie Hume, prin.
Arroyo ES, 1111 CORONEL ROAD   92705
  Gerald Aust, prin.
Loma Vista ES, 13822 PROSPECT AVE   92705
  Pete Schaefer, prin.
Tustin Memorial ES
  12712 BROWNING AVE   92705
  Angelo Dimino, prin.

Bethel Baptist Church School
  901 S EUCLID ST   92704
Calvary Church Christian ES
  1010 N TUSTIN AVE   92705
Edgewood Private ES
  12421 NEWPORT AVE   92705
Grand Avenue Christian ES
  2121 N GRAND AVE   92701
Immaculate Heart of Mary ES
  2204 W MCFADDEN AVE   92704
Maranatha Christian Academy
  3800 S FAIRVIEW ST   92704
Our Lady of Pillar ES
  601 N WESTERN AVE   92703
Peace Lutheran ES
  18542 VANDERLIP AVE   92705
St. Anne ES, P O BOX 2427   92707
St. Barbara ES, 5306 W MCFADDEN AVE   92704
St. Joseph ES, 608 CIVIC CENTER DR E   92701
Trinity Lutheran ES, 906 S BROADWAY   92701

Santa Barbara, Santa Barbara Co., Pop. Code 8
Cold Spring ESD
Sch. Sys. Enr. Code 2
Supt. – Lawrence Fisher
  2243 SYCAMORE CANYON ROAD   93108
Cold Spring ES
  2243 SYCAMORE CANYON ROAD   93108
  Lawrence Fisher, prin.

Goleta Un. ESD
Supt. – See Goleta
Foothill ES, 711 RIBERA DIRVE   93111
  Tully Johnson, prin.
Hollister ES, 4950 ANITA LANE   93111
  Dennis Naiman, prin.
Mountain View ES
  5465 QUEEN ANNE LANE   93111
  Albert Zonana, prin.

Hope ESD
Sch. Sys. Enr. Code 3
Supt. – Bryan Dixon
  3970 LA COLINA ROAD   93110
Monte Vista ES, 730 N HOPE AVE   93110
  Carl Doerfler, prin.
Vieja Valley ES, 434 NOGAL DRIVE   93110
  Richard Blowers, prin.

Montecito Un. ESD
Sch. Sys. Enr. Code 2
Supt. – Bronte Reynolds
  385 SAN YSIDRO ROAD   93108
Montecito ES, 385 SAN YSIDRO ROAD   93108
  Bronte Reynolds, prin.

Santa Barbara SD
Sch. Sys. Enr. Code 7
Supt. – Mike McLaughlin, 723 E COTA ST   93103
La Colina JHS, 4025 FOOTHILL ROAD   93110
  Robert Bowen, prin.
La Cumbre JHS, 2255 MODOC ROAD   93101
  Nancy O'Leary, prin.
JHS, 721 E COTA ST   93103 – Rudy Aguilera, prin.
Adams ES, 2701 LAS POSITAS ROAD   93105
  Jennie Dearmin, prin.
Cleveland ES
  123 ALAMEDA PADRE SERRA   93103
  Nancy Hill, prin.
Franklin ES, 1111 E MASON ST   93103
  Blas Garza Jr., prin.
Harding ES, 1625 ROBBINS ST   93101
  Marten Mailes, prin.
McKinley ES, 350 LOMA ALTA DR   93109
  Juanita Carney, prin.
Monroe ES, 431 FLORA VISTA DRIVE   93109
  Stanley Zaletel, prin.
Peabody ES, 3018 CALLE NOGUERA   93105
  Paul Cordeiro, prin.
Roosevelt ES, 1990 LAGUNA ST   93101
  Julio Corella, prin.
Washington ES, 290 LIGHTHOUSE ROAD   93109
  Clay Dunaway, prin.
Other Schools – See Goleta

Laguna Blanca School
  4125 PALOMA DRIVE   93110
Crane ES, 1795 SAN LEANDRO LN   93108

Marymount ES, 2130 MISSION RIDGE RD   93103
Montessori Center School
  3970 LA COLINA RD   93110
Norte Dame ES, 33 E MICHELTORENA ST   93101
Our Lady of Mt. Carmel ES
  530 HOT SPRINGS RD   93108
San Roque ES, 3214 CALLE CEDRO   93105
Santa Barbara Christian ES
  5020 SAN SIMEON DR   93111
St. Raphael ES, 160 JOSEPH ST   93111

Santa Clara, Santa Clara Co., Pop. Code 8
Cupertino Un. ESD
Supt. – See Cupertino
Eisenhower ES, 277 RODONOVAN DRIVE   95051
  (—), prin.

Santa Clara USD
Sch. Sys. Enr. Code 7
Supt. – R Gatti, P O BOX 397   95052
Buchser MS, 1111 BELLOMY ST   95050
  Donald Flohr, prin.
Bowers ES, 2755 BARKLEY AVE   95051
  Robert Feliciano, prin.
Bracher ES, 2700 CHROMITE DRIVE   95051
  Sherry Garvey, prin.
Briarwood ES, 1930 TOWNSEND AVE   95051
  Norman Landess, prin.
Haman ES, 865 LOS PADRES BLVD   95050
  Luverne Welykholowa, prin.
Hughes ES, 4949 CALLE DE ESCUELA   95054
  Joseph Passarello, prin.
Laurelwood ES, 955 TEAL DRIVE   95051
  Hilliard Polk, prin.
Millikin ES, 2720 SONOMA PLACE   95051
  Dean Latter, prin.
Montague ES, 750 LAURIE AVE   95054
  Willis Laine, prin.
Pomeroy ES, 1250 POMEROY AVE   95051
  Michael Masiello, prin.
Scott Lane ES, 1925 SCOTT BLVD   95050
  Saverio Arella, prin.
Sutter ES, 3200 FORBES AVE   95051
  Jay Wagner, prin.
Westwood ES, 435 SARATOGA AVE   95050
  Earl Davidson, prin.
Other Schools – See Alviso, Sunnyvale

Carden El Encanto Day ES
  615 HOBART TER   95051
Kinderwood Child Development School
  270 WASHINGTON ST   95050
Rainbow Montessori Child Develpmnt. Scho
  3421 MONROE ST   95051
St. Clare ES, P O BOX 178   95052
St. Justin's ES, 2655 HOMESTEAD RD   95051
St. Lawrence ES
  1971 SAINT LAWRENCE DR   95051

Santa Cruz, Santa Cruz Co., Pop. Code 8
Bonny Doon Un. ESD
Sch. Sys. Enr. Code 2
Supt. – Michael DiStefano
  1492 PINE FLAT ROAD   95060
Bonny Doon ES, 1492 PINE FLAT RD   95060
  Michael DiStefano, prin.

Happy Valley ESD
Sch. Sys. Enr. Code 2
Supt. – (—)
  3125 BRANCIFORTE DRIVE   95065
Happy Valley ES
  3125 BRANCIFORTE DRIVE   95065
  (—), prin.

Live Oak ESD
Sch. Sys. Enr. Code 4
Supt. – Rudy Carino, 966 BOSTWICK LANE   95062
Del Mar MS, 1959 MERRILL ST   95062
  S. Nathan Cross, prin.
Green Acres ES, 966 BOSTWICK LANE   95062
  Donn Shallenberger, prin.
Live Oak ES, 1916 CAPITOLA ROAD   95062
  Sesario Escoto, prin.

Santa Cruz CSD
Sch. Sys. Enr. Code 6
Supt. – Dale Kinsley, 133 MISSION ST   95060
Branciforte JHS, 315 POPLAR ST   95062
  Richard Wood, prin.
Mission Hill JHS, 425 KING ST   95060
  Joan Roberts, prin.
Bay View ES, 1231 BAY ST   95060
  Roy Nelson, prin.
Branciforte ES, 840 N BRANCIFORTE AVE   95062
  Jean Willis, prin.
De Lavearga ES, 1145 MORRISSEY BLVD   95065
  Bob Bush, prin.
Gault ES, 1320 SEABRIGHT AVE   95062
  Charlotte Moore, prin.
Natural Bridges ES, 255 SWIFT ST   95060
  Tom Sutkus, prin.
Westlake ES, 1000 HIGH ST   95060
  Don Iglesias, prin.

Scotts Valley Un. ESD
Supt. – See Scotts Valley
Brook Knoll ES, 150 TREETOP DRIVE   95060
  Donna Hellewell, prin.

Soquel Un. ESD
Supt. – See Capitola
Santa Cruz Gardens ES, 8005 WINKLE AVE   95065
  Carl Pearson, prin.

Gateway ES, 1051 CAYUGA ST   95062

Good Shepherd ES, 2727 MATTISON LN   95065
Hauselt Memorial Junior Academy
  427 CAPITOLA ROAD EXT   95062
Holy Cross ES, 150 EMMETT ST   95060
Santa Cruz Waldorf ES
  2190 EMPIRE GRADE   95060

Santa Fe Springs, Los Angeles Co., Pop. Code 7
Little Lake City ESD
Sch. Sys. Enr. Code 5
Supt. – John Pulice, 10515 PIONEER BLVD   90670
Lake Center JHS, 10503 PIONEER BLVD   90670
  E. Madrid, prin.
Jersey Avenue ES, 9400 JERSEY AVE   90670
  Martha Maya, prin.
Lakeview ES, 11500 JOSLIN ST   90670
  Pauline Dolinski, prin.
Other Schools – See Norwalk

Los Nietos ESD
Supt. – See Whittier
Rancho Santa Gertrudes ES
  11233 CHARLESWORTH ROAD   90670
  Raymond Chapman, prin.

Santa Fe Springs Christian ES
  11457 FLORENCE AVE   90670
St. Pius X ES, 10855 PIONEER BLVD   90670

Santa Margarita, San Luis Obispo Co., Pop. Code 3
Atascadero USD
Supt. – See Atascadero
Carrisa Plains ES, HCR ROUTE BOX 88-A   93453
  Joan Sando, prin.
ES, P O BOX X   93453 – Judy Randazzo, prin.

Santa Maria, Santa Barbara Co., Pop. Code 8
Blochman Un. ESD
Sch. Sys. Enr. Code 2
Supt. – Richard Blanchard
  RURAL ROUTE 01 BOX 206   93454
Foxen ES, RURAL ROUTE 01 BOX 206   93454
  Richard Blanchard, prin.

Santa Maria-Bonita Un. ESD
Sch. Sys. Enr. Code 6
Supt. – Leroy Small, P O BOX 460   93456
El Camino MS, 219 W EL CAMINO ST   93454
  Art Delgadillo, prin.
Fesler MS, 1100 E FESLER ST   93454
  Anna Hamner, prin.
Adam ES, 500 WINDSOR ST   93454
  Roland Anderson, prin.
Alvin ES, 301 E ALVIN AVE   93454
  Raymond Torres, prin.
Arellanes ES, 1890 SANDALWOOD DRIVE   93455
  Ann Kemper, prin.
Battles ES, 605 E BATTLES ROAD   93454
  David Hutt, prin.
Bonita ES, 2715 W MAIN ST   93454
  Ann Kemper, prin.
Bruce ES, 601 W ALVIN AVE   93454
  Herbert Talledge, prin.
Fairlawn ES, 120 N MARY DRIVE   93454
  Phillip Alvarado, prin.
Miller ES, 410 E CAMINO COLEGIO   93454
  Steve Fabula, prin.
Oakley ES, 1120 W HARDING AVE   93454
  Henry Grennan, prin.
Rice ES, 700 VICKIE AVE   93454
  Ron Elwell, prin.
Tunnell ES, 1248 E DENA WAY   93454
  Thomas Karling, prin.

Valley Christian Academy
  2970 SANTA MARIA WAY   93455
Christian Life ES, 709 N CURRYER   93454
Pacific Christian ES, 550 E STOWELL RD   93454
St. Louis of Montfort ES, 5095 HARP RD   93455
St. Mary of Assumption ES, P O BOX 1965   93456

Santa Monica, Los Angeles Co., Pop. Code 8
Los Angeles USD
Supt. – See Los Angeles
Canyon ES, 421 N ENTRADA DRIVE   90402
  Walter Young, prin.

Santa Monica-Malibu USD
Sch. Sys. Enr. Code 6
Supt. – Eugene Tucker, 1651 16TH ST   90404
Adams MS, 2425 16TH ST   90405
  Jerry Kantor, prin.
Lincoln MS, 1501 CALIFORNIA AVE   90403
  Ilene Straus, prin.
Alternative ES, 2802 FOURTH ST   90405
  William Shea, prin.
Edison ES, 2425 KANSAS AVE   90404
  Ruth Odell, prin.
Franklin ES, 2400 MONTANA AVE   90403
  Dale Petrulis, prin.
Grant ES, 2368 PEARL ST   90405
  Mary Cheetham, prin.
McKinley ES, 2401 SANTA MONICA BLVD   90404
  Nancy Crawford, prin.
Muir ES, 721 OCEAN PARK BLVD   90405
  Jon Campbell, prin.
Rogers ES, 2401 14TH ST   90405
  Julianne Di Chiro, prin.
Roosevelt ES, 801 MONTANA AVE   90403
  Jerry Harris, prin.
Other Schools – See Malibu

Carlthorp ES, 438 SAN VICENTE BLVD   90402
Crossroads ES, 1229 4TH ST   90401
Pilgrim Lutheran ES, 1730 WILSHIRE BLVD   90403

Santa Monica Montessori School
1619 20TH ST 90404
St. Anne ES, 2015 COLORADO AVE 90404
St. Monica ES, 1039 7TH ST 90403
Wildwood ES, 3111 OLYMPIC BLVD 90404

Santa Paula, Ventura Co., Pop. Code 7
Briggs ESD
Sch. Sys. Enr. Code 2
Supt. – J. Alex Pulido
14438 W TELEGRAPH ROAD 93060
Briggs MS, 14438 W TELEGRAPH ROAD 93060
J. Alex Pulido, prin.
Olivelands ES, 12465 FOOTHILL ROAD 93060
Chrisann Weeks, prin.

Mupu ESD
Sch. Sys. Enr. Code 2
Supt. – (—)
4410 N SANTA PAULA-OJAI RD 93060
Mupu ES, 4410 N SANTA PAULA OJAI RD 93060
Mark Stevens, prin.

Santa Clara ESD
Sch. Sys. Enr. Code 1
Supt. – (—)
20030 W TELEGRAPH ROAD 93060
Santa Clara ES
20030 E TELEGRAPH ROAD 93060
Valerie Sare, prin.

Santa Paula ESD
Sch. Sys. Enr. Code 5
Supt. – James Turner, P O BOX 710 93060
Isbell MS, P O BOX 710 93060 – Jeff Chancer, prin.
Bedell ES, 1305 LAUREL ROAD 93060
Glenn Deines, prin.
Blanchard ES, 115 N PECK ROAD 93060
Wilma Turchik, prin.
Glen City ES, 141 STECKEL DRIVE 93060
Bonnie Switack, prin.
McKevett ES, 955 E PLEASANT ST 93060
David Luna, prin.
Thille ES, 1144 E VENTURA ST 93060
Ricardo Amador, prin.
Webster ES, 1150 SATICOY ST 93060
Sema English, prin.

Santa Rosa, Sonoma Co., Pop. Code 8
Bellevue Un. ESD
Sch. Sys. Enr. Code 4
Supt. – Armando Flores
3223 PRIMROSE AVE 95407
Bellevue ES, 3223 PRIMROSE AVE 95407
Armando Flores, prin.
Kawana ES, 2121 MORAGA DRIVE 95404
Nancy Padden, prin.

Bennett Valley Un. ESD
Sch. Sys. Enr. Code 3
Supt. – Lyle Graf, 2250 MESQUITE DRIVE 95405
Bennett Valley MS
4580 BENNETT VIEW DRIVE 95404
Sanford Brousseau, prin.
Strawberry ES, 2311 HORSESHOE DRIVE 95405
Kitten Keith, prin.
Yulupa ES, 2250 MESQUITE DRIVE 95405
Lyle Graf, prin.

Mark West Un. ESD
Sch. Sys. Enr. Code 3
Supt. – Ida Victorson
5187 OLD REDWOOD HIGHWAY 95401
San Miguel ES, 5350 FAUGHT ROAD 95403
Jeffrey Heller, prin.
West MS, 5187 OLD REDWOOD HIGHWAY 95403
Sharon Boschen, prin.

Oak Grove Un. ESD
Supt. – See Sebastopol
Willowside MS, 5285 HALL ROAD 95401
Terry Kneisler, prin.

Piner-Olivet Un. ESD
Sch. Sys. Enr. Code 4
Supt. – Jack Hansen, 2590 PINER ROAD 95401
Olivet ES, 1825 WILLOWSIDE ROAD 95401
Marion Guillen, prin.
Piner ES, 2590 PINER ROAD 95401
Kris Krause, prin.

Rincon Valley Un. ESD
Sch. Sys. Enr. Code 5
Supt. – Rich Scardamaglia
1000 YULUPA AVE 95405
Binkley MS, 4965 CANYON DRIVE 95405
William Moberly, prin.
Madrone ES, 4550 RINCONADA DRIVE 95405
Delmar Reid, prin.
Mantanzas MS, 1687 YULUPA AVE 95405
James Witchey, prin.
Sequoia ES, 5305 DUPOINT DRIVE 95405
Peggy Christiansen, prin.
Spring Creek ES, 4676 MAYETTE AVE 95405
Anthony Pimentel, prin.
Village ES, 900 YULUPA AVE 95405
Thomas Crawford, prin.
Whited ES, 4995 SONOMA HIGHWAY 95405
Robert Stanley, prin.

Roseland ESD
Sch. Sys. Enr. Code 3
Supt. – Leslie Crawford
950 SEBASTOPOL ROAD 95407
Roseland ES, 950 SEBASTOPOL ROAD 95407
Margaret Sarubbi, prin.

Sheppard ES, 1777 WEST AVE 95407
Liv Fjosne, prin.

Santa Rosa CSD
Sch. Sys. Enr. Code 7
Supt. – J. Landis, P O BOX 940 95402
Brook Hill ES, 1850 VALLEJO ST 95404
Byron Fisher, prin.
Burbank ES, 203 S A ST 95401
Wallace Trujillo, prin.
Doyle Park ES, 1350 SONOMA AVE 95405
Ellie Lowry, prin.
Fremont ES, 756 HUMBOLDT ST 95404
Ray Ferro, prin.
Hidden Valley ES, 3435 BONITA VISTA LN 95404
Robert Burt, prin.
Lehman ES, 1700 JENNINGS AVE 95401
Anna Evers, prin.
Lincoln ES, 850 W 9TH ST 95401
Akiko Yonemoto, prin.
Monroe ES, 2567 MARLOW ROAD 95403
Gerald Hill, prin.
Proctor Terrace ES, 1711 BRYDEN LANE 95404
Vernon Calsy, prin.
Steele Lane ES, 301 STEELE LANE 95403
Vicki Lockner, prin.

Wright ESD
Sch. Sys. Enr. Code 4
Supt. – Patsy Barnes, 4389 PRICE AVE 95407
Wilson ES, 246 BRITTAIN LANE 95401
Phillip Smith, prin.
Wright ES, 4389 PRICE AVE 95407
Donna Penrose, prin.

Covenant Community School
1315 PACIFIC AVE 95404
Redwood Junior Academy
385 MARK WEST SPRINGS ROAD 95404
Rincon Valley Christian School
697 BENICIA DRIVE 95405
Santa Rosa Christian ES, 950 S WRIGHT RD 95407
Sonoma Country Day ES
50 MARK WEST SPRINGS RD 95403
St. Eugenes ES, 300 FARMERS LN 95405
St. Luke Lutheran Day ES.
905 MENDOCINO AVE 95401
St. Rose ES, 4300 OLD REDWOOD HWY 95403
Summerfld Waldorf ES
155 WILLOWSIDE RD 95401

Santa Ynez, Santa Barbara Co., Pop. Code 2
College School
Sch. Sys. Enr. Code 3
Supt. – Dianne Howe, 3325 PINE ST 93460
Santa Ynez MS 93460 – K. McLaughlin, prin.
College ES, 3525 PINE ST 93460
Dianne Howe, prin.

Santa Ysabel, San Diego Co.
Spencer Valley ESD
Sch. Sys. Enr. Code 1
Supt. – (—) P O BOX 208 92070
Spencer Valley ES, P O BOX 159 92070
Jane Wingrove, prin.

Santee, San Diego Co., Pop. Code 7
Santee ESD
Sch. Sys. Enr. Code 6
Supt. – Douglas Giles, P O BOX 220 92071
Cajon Park ES, 10300 N MAGNOLIA AVE 92071
William Warwick, prin.
Carlton Hills ES, 9353 PIKE ROAD 92071
Wilford Hall, prin.
Carlton Oaks ES
9353 WETHERSFIELD ROAD 92071
John Fleming, prin.
Harritt ES, 8120 ARLETTE ST 92071
Cindy Slatinsky, prin.
Hill Creek ES, 9665 JEREMY ST 92071
Thomas White, prin.
Pepper Drive ES, 1935 MARLINDA WAY 92071
Calvin Metz, prin.
Prospect Avenue ES, 9303 PROSPECT AVE 92071
Elizabeth Bodge, prin.
Rio Seco ES, 9545 CUYAMACA ST 92071
Sue Peters, prin.
ES, 10445 MISSION GORGE ROAD 92071
John Tofflemire, prin.
Sycamore Canyon ES
10201 SETTLE ROAD 92071
Richard Hausam, prin.

B.M.F. Christian Day School
8836 PROSPECT AVE 92071
Carlton Hills Christian ES
9735 HALBERNS BLVD 92071

San Ysidro, San Diego Co.
San Ysidro ESD
Sch. Sys. Enr. Code 5
Supt. – Gilberto Anzaldua
4350 OTAY MESA ROAD 92073
MS, 4345 OTAY MESA ROAD 92073
John Gugerty, prin.
Beyer ES, 2312 E BEYER BLVD 92073
Carolina Wittman, prin.
La Mirada ES
222 AVENIDA DE LA MADRID 92073
Jose Valdivia, prin.
Smythe ES, 1880 SMYTHE AVE 92073
Michael Marques, prin.
Sunset ES, 3825 SUNSET LANE 92073
Manuel Paul, prin.

Willow ES, 226 WILLOW ROAD 92073
Georgia Grijalva, prin.

Our Lady of Mt. Carmel ES
109 W SEAWARD AVE 92073

Saratoga, Santa Clara Co., Pop. Code 8
Campbell Un. ESD
Supt. – See Campbell
Marshall Lane ES, 14114 MARILYN LANE 95070
David Gillies, prin.

Cupertino Un. ESD
Supt. – See Cupertino
Blue Hills ES, 12300 DE SANKA AVE 95070
Jerd Ferraiuolo, prin.

Saratoga Un. ESD
Sch. Sys. Enr. Code 4
Supt. – Michael Filice,Jr.
14675 ALOHA AVE 95070
Redwood IS, 13925 FRUITVALE AVE 95070
Gail Wasserman, prin.
Argonaut ES, SHADOW MOUNTAIN ROAD 95070
William Colton, prin.
Foothill ES, 13919 LYNDE AVE 95070
Louise Klayman, prin.
ES, 14592 OAK ST 95070 – Lisa Akers, prin.

Sacred Heart ES, 13718 SARATOGA AVE 95070
St. Andrew's ES, P O BOX 2789 95070

Saticoy, Ventura Co.
Ventura USD
Supt. – See Ventura
ES, 560 JAZMIN ST 93004 – Nancy Bradford, prin.

Saugus, Los Angeles Co., Pop. Code 6
Saugus Un. ESD
Sch. Sys. Enr. Code 5
Supt. – Charles Helmers
26590 BOUQUET CANYON ROAD 91350
Emblem ES, 22635 ESPUELLA DRIVE 91350
Justin Caulfield, prin.
Highlands ES, 27332 CATALA AVE 91350
Albert Nocciolo, prin.
Rosedell ES, 27853 URBANDALE AVE 91350
James Dixon, prin.
Santa Clarita ES
27177 SECO CANYON ROAD 91350
Gerald Hugger, prin.
Other Schools – See Canyon Country, Valencia

Sausalito, Marin Co., Pop. Code 6
Sausalito ESD
Sch. Sys. Enr. Code 2
Supt. – Donald Johnson, 630 NEVEDA ST 94965
Bayside ES, 630 NEVADA ST 94965
Juanita Gaskins, prin.

Sawyers Bar, Siskiyou Co.
Sawyers Bar ESD
Sch. Sys. Enr. Code 1
Supt. – (—), SAWYERS BAR ROAD 96027
ES 96027 – (—), prin.

Scotia, Humboldt Co., Pop. Code 3
Scotia Un. ESD
Sch. Sys. Enr. Code 2
Supt. – Richard Barsanti, P O BOX 217 95565
Murphy ES, P O BOX 217 95565
Richard Barsanti, prin.

Scotts Valley, Santa Cruz Co., Pop. Code 6
Scotts Valley Un. ESD
Sch. Sys. Enr. Code 4
Supt. – Andy La Couture
155 TREETOP DRIVE 95060
MS, 8 BEAN CREEK ROAD 95066
Chris McGriff, prin.
Vine Hill ES, 101 TABOR DRIVE 95066
Stan Evers, prin.
Other Schools – See Santa Cruz

Baymonte Christian ES
5000-B GRANITE CREEK RAOD 95066

Seal Beach, Orange Co., Pop. Code 8
Los Alamitos USD
Supt. – See Los Alamitos
McGaugh ES, 1698 BOLSA AVE 90740
John Blaydes, prin.

Seaside, Monterey Co., Pop. Code 6
Monterey Peninsula USD
Supt. – See Monterey
King MS, 1713 BROADWAY AVE 93955
Ron Breding, prin.
Del Rey Woods ES, 1281 PLUMAS AVE 93955
James Manning, prin.
Highland ES
SONOMA AVE & YOSEMITE ST 93955
Carol Starks, prin.
Manzanita ES, 1720 YOSEMITE ST 93955
John Lamb, prin.
Ord Terrace ES, 1755 LA SALLE AVE 93955
Rodger Smith, prin.

Sebastopol, Sonoma Co., Pop. Code 6
Gravenstein Un. ESD
Sch. Sys. Enr. Code 3
Supt. – Joseph Carnation, 3840 TWIG AVE 95472
Hillcrest MS, 725 BLOOMFIELD ROAD 95472
MaryLou Herrera, prin.

Oak Grove Un. ESD
Sch. Sys. Enr. Code 2
Supt. – Terry Kneisler, 8760 BOWER ST   95472
Oak Grove ES, 8760 BOWER ST   95472
  Jim Waliszewski, prin.
Other Schools – See Santa Rosa

Sebastopol Un. ESD
Sch. Sys. Enr. Code 4
Supt. – Mike Carey, 7905 VALENTINE AVE   95472
Brook Haven MS, 7905 VALENTINE AVE   95472
  James Pascoe, prin.
Park Side ES, 7450 BODEGA AVE   95472
  Thomas Steinhofer, prin.
Pine Crest MS, 7285 HAYDEN AVE   95472
  Frank Putnam, prin.

Twin Hills Un. ESD
Sch. Sys. Enr. Code 3
Supt. – Robert Perkins
  1685 WATERTROUGH ROAD   95472
Twin Hills MS
  700 WATERTROUGH ROAD   95472
  Ronald Larsen, prin.
Apple Blossom ES
  1685 WATER TROUGH RD   95472
  L. Watson, prin.

Seeley, Imperial Co., Pop. Code 3
Seeley Un. ESD
Sch. Sys. Enr. Code 2
Supt. – Jim Hughes, P O BOX 868   92273
ES, P O BOX 868   92273 – Jim Hughes, prin.

Seiad Valley, Siskiyou Co.
Seiad ESD
Sch. Sys. Enr. Code 1
Supt. – (—), P O BOX 647   96086
Seiad ES, P O BOX 647   96086
  Philip Campbell, prin.

Selma, Fresno Co., Pop. Code 7
Selma USD
Sch. Sys. Enr. Code 5
Supt. – Steve Bojorquez
  3036 THOMPSON AVE   93662
Roosevelt JHS, FLORAL & B STS   93662
  Guy Evans, prin.
Garfield ES, 2535 B ST   93662
  Christine Williams, prin.
Indianola ES, 11524 E DINUBA AVE   93662
  Jean Fetterhoff, prin.
Jackson ES, 2220 HUNTSMAN AVE   93662
  William Mannlein, prin.
Terry ES, 12906 S FOWLER AVE   93662
  Donald Turpin, prin.
Washington ES, 1420 2ND ST   93662
  Peggi Adams, prin.
White ES, NEBRASKA AND MITCHELL   93662
  Mark Ford, prin.
Wilson ES, 1325 STILLMAN ST   93662
  (—), prin.

Sepulveda, Los Angeles Co., Pop. Code 8
Los Angeles USD
Supt. – See Los Angeles
Gledhill Street ES, 16030 GLEDHILL ST   91343
  Selma Alpert, prin.
Langdon Avenue ES, 8817 LANGDON AVE   91343
  Gerald Gottlieb, prin.
Lassen ES, 15017 SUPERIOR ST   91343
  Suzanne Hofmann, prin.
Mayall Street ES, 16701 MAYALL ST   91343
  Patricia Abney, prin.
Noble Avenue ES, 8329 NOBLE AVE   91343
  Willard Kearney, prin.
Plummer ES, 9340 NOBLE AVE   91343
  Pamela Worden, prin.

California Christian School, P O BOX 2457   91343
Our Lady of Peace ES
  9028 LANGDON AVE   91343
Valley Park Baptist ES
  16514 NORDHOFF ST   91343
Valley Presbyterian ES
  9240 HASKELL AVE   91343

Shafter, Kern Co., Pop. Code 6
Maple ESD
Sch. Sys. Enr. Code 2
Supt. – Ann Paslay, 29151 FRESNO AVE   93263
Maple ES, 29161 FRESNO AVE   93263
  Ann Paslay, prin.

Richland ESD
Sch. Sys. Enr. Code 4
Supt. – George Bury
  331 N SHAFTER HIGHWAY   93263
Richland JHS, 331 N SHAFTER HIGHWAY   93263
  Ronald Adams, prin.
Richland IS, 331 SHAFTER AVE   93263
  Lyle Mack, prin.
Richland PS, 331 SHAFTER AVE   93263
  Chris Frazier, prin.

Shandon, San Luis Obispo Co., Pop. Code 2
Shandon JUSD
Sch. Sys. Enr. Code 2
Supt. – Richard Summers, P O BOX 79   93461
JHS, P O BOX 79   93461 – Richard Summers, prin.
ES, P O BOX 79   93461 – Linda Matlock, prin.
Other Schools – See San Miguel

Shasta, Shasta Co., Pop. Code 3
Shasta Un. ESD
Sch. Sys. Enr. Code 2
Supt. – Pete Seiler, P O BOX 1125   96087

ES, P O BOX 1125   96087 – Pete Seiler, prin.

Shaver Lake, Fresno Co.
Sierra Un. SD
Supt. – See Tollhouse
Balch Camp ES
  57800 MCKINLEY GROVE ROAD   93664
  C. Sparrow, prin.
Pole Corral ES, 57800 MCKINLEY GROVE   93664
  C. Sparrow, prin.

Sheridan, Placer Co.
Western Placer USD
Supt. – See Lincoln
ES, P O BOX 268   95681 – Harry Leffmann, prin.
Valley View ES, P O BOX 268   95681
  Harry Leffmann, prin.

Sherman Oaks, Los Angeles Co.
Los Angeles USD
Supt. – See Los Angeles
Dixie Canyon Avenue ES
  4220 DIXIE CANYON AVE   91423
  Robert Fishman, prin.
Riverside ES, 13061 RIVERSIDE DRIVE   91423
  Constance Lue, prin.
ES, 14755 GREENLEAF ST   91403
  Sally Shane, prin.

Buckley School, 3900 STANSBURY AVE   91423
C&F Merdinian Armenian Evangelical ES
  13330 RIVERSIDE DR   91423
St. Francis De Sals ES
  13368 VALLEYHEART DR   91423

Shingle Springs, El Dorado Co.
Buckeye Un. ESD
Sch. Sys. Enr. Code 4
Supt. – Joyce Flanigan, P O BOX 547   95682
Camerado Springs JHS
  2480 MERRYCHASE DRIVE   95682
  Gary Pogue, prin.
Blue Oak ES, 2391 MERRYCHASE DR   95682
  Cathy Bean, prin.
Buckeye ES, 4561 BUCKEYE ROAD   95682
  Sharon Kirklin, prin.
Other Schools – See El Dorado Hills

Latrobe ESD
Sch. Sys. Enr. Code 2
Supt. – Bonnie Allen
  7900 S SHINGLE ROAD   95682
Millers Hill MS, 7900 S SHINGLE ROAD   95682
  Bonnie Allen, prin.
Blue Oak ES, 2391 MERRYCHASE DR   95682
  Cathy Bean, prin.
Latrobe ES, 7680 S SHINGLE ROAD   95682
  Bonnie Allen, prin.

Shingletown, Shasta Co.
Black Butte Un. ESD
Sch. Sys. Enr. Code 2
Supt. – John Brickner
  7752 PONDEROSA WAY   96088
Black Butte ES, 7752 PONDEROSA WAY   96088
  William Howell, prin.

Shoshone, Inyo Co., Pop. Code 2
Death Valley USD
Sch. Sys. Enr. Code 1
Supt. – James Copeland, P O BOX 217   92384
Death Valley ES   92384 – James Copeland, prin.
Tecopa-Francis ES   92384 – James Copeland, prin.

Sierra Madre, Los Angeles Co., Pop. Code 7
Pasadena USD
Supt. – See Pasadena
ES, 141 W HIGHLAND AVE   91024
  William Rosecrans, prin.

Bethany Christian ES, 93 N BALDWIN AVE   91024
St. Rita ES, 322 N BALDWIN AVE   91024

Sierraville, Sierra Co.
Sierra-Plumas JUSD
Supt. – See Downieville
ES, P O BOX 147   96126 – Mary Genasci, prin.

Silverado, Orange Co., Pop. Code 3
Orange USD
Supt. – See Orange
ES, 7531 SANTIAGO CANYON ROAD   92676
  Ed Berriman, prin.

Simi Valley, Ventura Co., Pop. Code 8
Simi Valley USD
Sch. Sys. Enr. Code 7
Supt. – J. Duncan, 875 COCHRAN ST   93065
Atherwood ES, 2350 GREENSWARD ST   93065
  Dianne Opp, prin.
Berylwood ES, 2300 HEYWOOD ST   93065
  Charles Bock, prin.
Big Springs ES, 3401 BIG SPRINGS AVE   93063
  Richard Henderson, prin.
Crestview ES, 200 CROSBY AVE   93065
  Sheila Robbins, prin.
Hollow Hills ES, 828 GIBSON AVE   93065
  Susan Parks, prin.
Justin ES, 2245 N JUSTIN AVE   93065
  Ann Ecklund, prin.
Katherine ES, 5455 KATHERINE ST   93063
  Ian McKenzie, prin.
Knolls ES, 6334 KATHERINE ROAD   93063
  Shari Wohlstattar, prin.
Lincoln ES, 1220 4TH ST   93065
  James Lian, prin.

Madera ES, 250 ROYAL AVE   93065
  Michael Traxler, prin.
Mountain View ES, 2925 FLETCHER ST   93065
  Frank Chapman, prin.
Park View ES, 1500 ALEXANDER ST   93065
  Rob Hunter, prin.
Santa Susana ES, 4300 APRICOT ROAD   93063
  Richard Hamilton, prin.
Simi ES, 2956 SCHOOL ST   93065
  Les Adelson, prin.
Sycamore ES, 2100 RAVENNA ST   93065
  Robert Chall, prin.
Township ES, 4101 TOWNSHIP AVE   93063
  William Myers, prin.
Vista ES, 2175 WISTERIA ST   93065
  Laurence Cates, prin.
White Oak ES, 2201 ALSCOT AVE   93063
  Robert Gottschalk, prin.

Good Shepherd Lutheran ES
  2949 ALAMO ST   93063
Grace Brethren ES, 1717 ARCANE AVE   93065
Pinecrest ES, 4974 COCHRAN ST   93065
Simi Valley Christian Day ES
  4200 TOWNSHIP AVE   93063
Simi Valley SDA ES, 1636 SINALOA RD   93065
St. Rose of Lima ES, 1325 ROYAL AVE   93065
West Simi Christian School
  1350 CHERRY AVE   93065

Sloughhouse, Sacramento Co.
Elk Grove USD
Supt. – See Elk Grove
Cosumnes ES, 13580 JACKSON ROAD   95683
  Judy Hunt, prin.

Smartville, Nevada Co.
Marysville JUSD
Supt. – See Marysville
Rose Bar ES   95977 – Dennis McGuire, prin.

Smith River, Del Norte Co.
Del Norte County USD
Supt. – See Crescent City
Smith River ES, P O BOX 194   95567
  Roy Magnuson, prin.

Snelling, Merced Co., Pop. Code 4
Merced River Un. ESD
Sch. Sys. Enr. Code 2
Supt. – L. Glen Fowler
  2241 TURLOCK ROAD   95369
Hopeton ES, 2241 TURLOCK ROAD   95369
  L. Fowler, prin.
Other Schools – See Winton

Snelling-Merced Falls Un. SD
Sch. Sys. Enr. Code 1
Supt. – Bette Woolstenhulme, P O BOX 198   95369
Snelling-Merced Falls ES, P O BOX 198   95369
  Bette Woolstenhulme, prin.

Solana Beach, San Diego Co., Pop. Code 6
San Dieguito Un. HSD
Supt. – See Encinitas
Warren JHS, 155 STEVENS AVE   92075
  Penny Francisco, prin.

Solana Beach ESD
Sch. Sys. Enr. Code 4
Supt. – Raymond Edman, 309 N RIOS AVE   92075
Skyline MS, 606 LOMAS SANTA FE DRIVE   92075
  Berge Minasian, prin.
Solana Vista ES, 780 SANTA VICTORIA   92075
  Berge Minasian, prin.
Other Schools – See San Diego

Santa Fe Christian Schs.
  838 ACADEMY DRIVE   92075
St. James Academy, 623 S NARDO AVE   92075

Soledad, Monterey Co., Pop. Code 6
Mission Un. ESD
Sch. Sys. Enr. Code 1
Supt. – Richard Hackbert
  RURAL ROUTE 01 BOX R   93960
Mission ES, RURAL ROUTE 01 BOX 4   93960
  Richard Hackbert, prin.

Soledad Un. ESD
Sch. Sys. Enr. Code 4
Supt. – John Alioto, 335 MARKET ST   93960
Main Street ES, 441 MAIN ST   93960
  Yolanda LeNoble, prin.
Gabilan ES, 900 WALKER DRIVE   93960
  Rose Ferrero, prin.
San Vincente ES, 1300 METZ ROAD   93960
  Judi Wing, prin.

Solvang, Santa Barbara Co., Pop. Code 4
Ballard ESD
Sch. Sys. Enr. Code 1
Supt. – (—), 2425 SCHOOL ST   93463
Ballard ES, 2425 SCHOOL ST   93463
  Kathleen Sherrill, prin.

Solvang ESD
Sch. Sys. Enr. Code 2
Supt. – Scott Purdy, 565 ATTERDAG ROAD   93463
MS, 565 ATTERDAG ROAD   93463
  Scott Purdy, prin.
ES, 565 ATTERDAG ROAD   93463
  Scott Purdy, prin.

Santa Ynez Valley Chrstian Academy
  1693 LAUREL AVE   93463

Somerset, El Dorado Co.
Indian Diggings ESD
Sch. Sys. Enr. Code 1
Supt. – (—), 6020 OMO RANCH ROAD 95684
Indian Diggings ES, STAR ROUTE 95684
Benjamin Moran, prin.

Pioneer Un. ESD
Sch. Sys. Enr. Code 3
Supt. – Paul Porter, P O BOX 8 95684
Pioneer ES, P O BOX 8 95684
Richard Williams, prin.

Somesbar, Humboldt Co.
Junction ESD
Sch. Sys. Enr. Code 1
Supt. – Christine Margarian, HIGHWAY 96 95568
Junction ES 95568 – Christine Magarian, prin.

Somis, Ventura Co.
Mesa Un. ESD
Sch. Sys. Enr. Code 2
Supt. – Dennis Convery
  3901 MESA SCHOOL ROAD 93066
Mesa ES, 3901 MESA SCHOOL ROAD 93066
  Larry Birdsell, prin.

Somis Un. ESD
Sch. Sys. Enr. Code 2
Supt. – Dale Forgey, P O BOX 900 93066
ES, 5268 NORTH ST 93066 – Dale Forgey, prin.

Sonoma, Sonoma Co., Pop. Code 6
Sonoma Valley USD
Sch. Sys. Enr. Code 5
Supt. – William Levinson, 721 W NAPA ST 95476
Altimira IS, 17805 ARNOLD DRIVE 95476
  Marilyn Kelly, prin.
Prestwood ES, 343 E MACARTHUR ST 95476
  Tom Smeltzer, prin.
Sassarini ES, 652 5TH ST W 95476
  John Woolley, prin.
Other Schools – See Boyes Hot Springs, El Verano,
  Glen Ellen

Sonoma Valley Christian ES, P O BOX 731 95476
St. Francis Solano ES, 342 W NAPA ST 95476

Sonora, Tuolumne Co., Pop. Code 5
Belleview ESD
Sch. Sys. Enr. Code 2
Supt. – Norman Wiley
  22736 KUEIN MILL ROAD 95370
Belleview ES, 22736 KUEIN MILL ROAD 95370
  Norman Wiley, prin.

Curtis Creek ESD
Supt. – See Standard
Sullivan Creek ES, 16331 HIDDEN VALLEY 95370
  David Delgardo, prin.

Sonora ESD
Sch. Sys. Enr. Code 3
Supt. – Ron Meade, 830 GUZZI LANE 95370
ES, 830 GREENLEY ROAD 95370
  Judy Borgquist, prin.

Mother Lode Advent Junior Academy
  80 N FOREST RD 95370

Soquel, Santa Cruz Co., Pop. Code 6
Mountain ESD
Sch. Sys. Enr. Code 2
Supt. – (—)
  3042 OLD SAN JOSE ROAD 95073
Mountain ES, 3042 OLD SAN JOSE ROAD 95073
  (—), prin.

Soquel Un. ESD
Supt. – See Capitola
ES, 2700 PORTER ST 95073 – Thom Dunks, prin.

Soulsbyville, Tuolumne Co.
Soulsbyville ESD
Sch. Sys. Enr. Code 3
Supt. – Lawrence Naegeli, P O BOX 158 95372
ES, P O BOX 158 95372 – Lawrence Naegeli, prin.

South El Monte, Los Angeles Co., Pop. Code 4
El Monte ESD
Supt. – See El Monte
Loma ES, 2131 LOMA AVE 91733
  Regina Luke, prin.

Valle Lindo ESD
Sch. Sys. Enr. Code 4
Supt. – Patrick Sayne, 1431 CENTRAL AVE 91733
Shively MS, 1431 CENTRAL AVE 91733
  Ed Madrid, prin.
New Temple ES, 11033 CENTRAL AVE 91733
  Mary Piaz, prin.

Epiphany ES, 10915 MICHAEL HUNT DR 91733

South Gate, Los Angeles Co., Pop. Code 8
Los Angeles USD
Supt. – See Los Angeles
JHS, 4100 FIRESTONE BLVD 90280
  Peter Ferry, prin.
Liberty Boulevard ES, 2728 LIBERTY BLVD 90280
  James Abbott, prin.
San Gabriel Avenue ES
  8628 SAN GABRIEL AVE 90280
  David Abernethy, prin.
Stanford Avenue ES, 2833 ILLINOIS AVE 90280
  De Whayne Gallups, prin.
State Street ES, 3211 SANTA ANA ST 90280
  Michael Rosales, prin.

Tweedy ES, 5115 SOUTHERN AVE 90280
  Sylvia Ruiz, prin.
Victoria Avenue ES, 3320 MISSOURI AVE 90280
  Duane Barrett, prin.

Paramount USD
Supt. – See Paramount
Hollydale ES, 5511 CENTURY BLVD 90280
  Hortencia Torres, prin.

Redeemer Lutheran ES
  2626 LIBERTY BLVD 90280
St. Helen ES, 9329 MADISON AVE 90280

South Lake Tahoe, El Dorado Co., Pop. Code 7
Lake Tahoe USD
Sch. Sys. Enr. Code 5
Supt. – Bruce Hauger, P O BOX 14426 95702
MS, P O BOX 14426 95702
  George Nettleman, prin.
Al Tahoe ES, P O BOX 14426 95702
  Kenneth Wrye, prin.
Bijou ES, P O BOX 14426 95702
  Virginia Glenn, prin.
Meyers ES, P O BOX 14426 95702
  Karen Tinlin, prin.
Sierra House ES, P O BOX 14426 95702
  Doug Forte, prin.
Tahoe Valley ES, P O BOX 14426 95702
  James Ellis, prin.

South Pasadena, Los Angeles Co., Pop. Code 7
South Pasadena USD
Sch. Sys. Enr. Code 5
Supt. – Louie Joseph, 1020 EL CENTRO ST 91030
JHS, 1600 OAK ST 91030 – Edward Tucker, prin.
Arroyo Vista ES, 335 EL CENTRO ST 91030
  Joe Johnson, prin.
Marengo ES, 1400 MARENGO AVE 91030
  Marsha Aguirre, prin.
Monterey Hills ES, 1624 VIA DEL REY ST 91030
  Vivien Hutton, prin.

Holy Family Catholic ES
  1519 FREMONT AVE 91030
Stancliff ES, 1101 ARROYO VERDE RD 91030

South San Francisco, San Mateo Co., Pop. Code 8
South San Francisco USD
Sch. Sys. Enr. Code 6
Supt. – Thomas Gaffney, 398 B ST 94080
Alta Loma JHS, 398 B ST 94080
  Mark Avelar, prin.
Parkway JHS, 398 B ST 94080
  Angelo Carmassi, prin.
Westborough JHS, 398 B ST 94080
  Marlowe Tyler, prin.
Buri Buri ES, 120 EL CAMPO DRIVE 94080
  Timothy Sullivan, prin.
Foxridge ES, 2525 WEXFORD AVE 94080
  Constance Smith, prin.
Hillside ES, 1400 HILLSIDE BLVD 94080
  Dennis Dawson, prin.
Los Cerritos ES, 210 W ORANGE AVE 94080
  Tracey Walsh, prin.
Martin ES, 35 SCHOOL ST 94080
  Mary Meissner, prin.
Ponderosa ES, 295 PONDEROSA ROAD 94080
  Karen Engel, prin.
Serra Vista ES, 257 LONGFORD DRIVE 94080
  Ivor Satero, prin.
Spruce ES, 501 SPRUCE AVE 94080
  Michael Vince, prin.
Sunshine Gardens ES, 1200 MILLER AVE 94080
  Laurie Sanders, prin.
Other Schools – See Daly City, San Bruno

All Souls Catholic ES, 479 MILLER AVE 94080
Master Dolorosa ES, 1040 MILLER AVE 94080
St. Veronica's ES, 434 ALIDA WAY 94080

South San Gabriel, Los Angeles Co.
Montebello USD
Supt. – See Montebello
Potrero Heights ES, 8026 HILL DRIVE 91770
  (—), prin.

Spreckels, Monterey Co.
Spreckels Un. ESD
Sch. Sys. Enr. Code 2
Supt. – John McFall, P O BOX 7308 93962
ES, P O BOX 7308 93962 – Margaret Lancina, prin.

Spring Valley, San Diego Co., Pop. Code 8
La Mesa-Spring Valley ESD
Supt. – See La Mesa
La Presa MS, 1001 LELAND ST 92077
  Steven Coover, prin.
MS, 3900 CONRAD DRIVE 92077
  Patrick Holland, prin.
Avondale ES, 8401 STANSBURY ST 92077
  Janet McQuaid, prin.
Bancroft ES, 8805 TYLER ST 92077
  Frank Murphy, prin.
Casa De Oro ES
  AGUA DULCE BLVD & RAMONA DR 92077
  Linda Ashley, prin.
Highlands ES, 3131 S BARCELONA ST 92077
  Edward Stokes, prin.
Kempton Street ES, 740 KEMPTON ST 92077
  Ronald Begley, prin.
La Presa ES, 519 LA PRESA AVE 92077
  Janice Cook, prin.
Loma ES, 10355 LOMA LANE 92078
  Duane Keiser, prin.

Rancho ES, 8845 NOELINE AVE 92077
  Alice Tanner, prin.
ES, 3845 SPRING DRIVE 92077
  Norma Reed, prin.

Mt. Helix Country Day ES
  3327 KENORA DR 92077
Santa Sophia Academy
  9810 SAN JUAN ST 92077
Trinity Christian ES, 3902 KENWOOD DR 92077

Springville, Tulare Co., Pop. Code 3
Springville Un. ESD
Sch. Sys. Enr. Code 2
Supt. – Jack Wallen, P O BOX 349 93265
ES, P O BOX 349 93265 – Jack Wallen, prin.

Standard, Tuolumne Co.
Curtis Creek ESD
Sch. Sys. Enr. Code 3
Supt. – Dan Wood, P O BOX 116 95373
Curtis Creek ES, P O BOX 116 95373
  Donna Dodge, prin.
Other Schools – See Sonora

Stanford, Palo Alto Co.
Palo Alto USD
Supt. – See Palo Alto
Escondido ES, 890 ESCONDIDO ROAD 94305
  Robert French, prin.
Nixon ES, 1711 STANFORD AVE 94305
  Ruth Malen, prin.

Stanton, Orange Co., Pop. Code 7
Garden Grove USD
Supt. – See Garden Grove
Carver ES, 11150 SANTA ROSALIA ST 90680
  Karen Jensen, prin.

Magnolia ESD
Supt. – See Anaheim
Pyles ES, 10411 DALE AVE 90680
  Elizabeth Hillon, prin.

St. Polycarp ES, 8182 CHAPMAN AVE 90680

Stevinson, Merced Co.
Hilmar USD
Supt. – See Hilmar
Merquin ES, THIRD AVE 95374
  Melinda Hennes, prin.

Stewarts Point, Sonoma Co.
Reservation ESD
Sch. Sys. Enr. Code 1
Supt. – (—), SKAGGS SPRING ROAD 95480
Reservation ES, P O BOX 2 95480
  Shirley Parrish, prin.

Stirling City, Butte Co.
Paradise USD
Supt. – See Paradise
Brakebill ES, P O BOX 8 95978
  Laura Dearden, prin.

Stockton, San Joaquin Co., Pop. Code 8
Delta Island Un. ESD
Sch. Sys. Enr. Code 2
Supt. – Jim Roberts
  11022 HOWARD ROAD 95206
Delta Island ES, 11022 HOWARD ROAD 95206
  Jim Roberts, prin.

Escalon USD
Supt. – See Escalon
Collegeville ES, 6701 S JACK TONE RD 95205
  Don Adams, prin.

Holt Union ESD
Sch. Sys. Enr. Code 1
Supt. – (—), 1545 S HOLT ROAD 95206
Holt ES, 1545 S HOLT ROAD 95206
  Milton Handley, prin.

Lincoln USD
Sch. Sys. Enr. Code 6
Supt. – Tod Anton, 2010 W SWAIN ROAD 95207
Pacific MS, 6768 ALEXANDRIA PLACE 95207
  Bill McKeever, prin.
Sierra MS, 6776 ALEXANDRIA PLACE 95207
  Bill Toledo, prin.
Barron ES, 6835 CUMBERLAND PLACE 95209
  Kelleen Yocum, prin.
Colonial Heights ES, 8135 BALBOA AVE 95209
  Will Pool, prin.
Knoles ES, 6511 CLARKSBURG PLACE 95207
  Linda Myers, prin.
Landeen ES, 4128 FEATHER RIVER DRIVE 95207
  Jim Ellis, prin.
Lincoln ES, 818 W LINCOLN ROAD 95207
  Bob Riefe, prin.
Village Oaks ES, 1900 W SWAIN ROAD 95207
  A. Bird, prin.
Williams ES, 2450 MEADOW AVE 95207
  William Lina, prin.

Linden USD
Supt. – See Linden
Waterloo MS, 7007 N PEZZI ROAD 95205
  Charles Gritts, prin.
Glenwood ES, 2005 N ALPINE ROAD 95205
  Ron Estes, prin.
Waverly ES, 3507 WILMARTH ROAD 95205
  (—), prin.

Lodi USD
Supt. – See Lodi

Delta Sierra MS, 2255 WAGNER HTS   95209
  (—), prin.
Morada MS, 5001 EASTVIEW DRIVE   95212
  Janet Dillon, prin.
Clairmont ES, 8282 LE MANS AVE   95210
  Jerry Abatangle, prin.
Clairmont Mini ES, 8121 BURGUNDY DR   95210
  Jerry Abatangle, prin.
Creekside ES, 2515 ESTATE DRIVE   95209
  Ed Cattuzzo, prin.
Davis ES, 5224 E MORADA LANE   95212
  Kathleen Scott, prin.
Elkhorn ES, 10505 DAVIS ROAD   95209
  Bill Mackey, prin.
Oakwood ES, 1315 WOODCREEK WAY   95209
  Duane Ostgaard, prin.
Otto Drive ES, 3810 OTTO DRIVE   95209
  Linda Nook, prin.
Parklane ES, 8405 TAM OSHANTER DRIVE   95210
  David Hinchman, prin.

Stockton City USD
Sch. Sys. Enr. Code 8
Supt. – Mary Mend, 701 N MADISON ST   95202
Fremont MS, 2021 E FLORA ST   95205
  Floyd Weaver, prin.
Hamilton MS, 2245 E 11TH ST   95206
  Edna Ramos, prin.
Marshall MS, 1141 LEVER BLVD   95206
  John Casey, prin.
Webster MS, 2725 MICHIGAN AVE   95204
  Vernon Uyeda, prin.
Adams ES, 6402 INGLEWOOD AVE   95207
  Vaness Moll, prin.
August MS, 2101 SUTRO AVE   95205
  Clark Redfield, prin.
Cleveland ES, 20 E FULTON ST   95204
  Patricia Busher, prin.
El Dorado ES, 1540 N LINCOLN ST   95204
  Antonio Morales, prin.
Elmwood ES, 840 S CARDINAL AVE   95205
  Carl Burger, prin.
Fillmore ES, 2644 E POPLAR ST   95205
  Margarito Ortega, prin.
Garfield MS, 1670 E 6TH ST   95206
  Syble Johnson, prin.
Grant ES, 1800 S SUTTER ST   95206
  Al Fields, prin.
Grunsky ES, 1550 SCHOOL ST   95205
  Marshall Dunlap, prin.
Hazelton MS, 535 W JEFFERSON ST   95206
  Petrina Romo, prin.
Hoover ES, 2900 KIRK ST   95204
  Priscilla Lopez, prin.
Kennedy MS, 630 PONCE DE LEON AVE   95210
  Floretta Bush, prin.
King ES, 2640 E LAFAYETTE ST   95205
  Gracie Madrid, prin.
Kohl Open ES, 6234 N ALTURAS AVE   95207
  Bud West, prin.
Madison MS, 2939 MISSION ROAD   95204
  Mae Hill, prin.
McKinley ES, 30 W 9TH ST   95206
  Joaquin Hagedorn, prin.
Monroe ES, 2236 E 11TH ST   95206
  Barbara Chan, prin.
Montezuma ES, 2843 FARMINGTON ROAD   95205
  Janie Reddish, prin.
Nightingale ES, 1721 CARPENTER ROAD   95206
  Barbara Davis, prin.
Pulliam ES, 230 PRESIDIO WAY   95207
  Anna Moreno, prin.
Roosevelt MS, 776 S BROADWAY AVE   95205
  Arturo Vasquez, prin.
Stockton Skills ES, 349 E VINE ST   95202
  Cordie Simpson, prin.
Taylor Skills MS, 1101 LEVER BLVD   95206
  Cecilia Moran, prin.
Tyler Skills ES, 3830 WEBSTER AVE   95204
  Robert Cossey, prin.
Valenzuela Multilingual ES
  419 DOWNING AVE   95206 – Robert Cain, prin.
Van Buren MS, 1628 E 10TH ST   95206
  Robert Eustis, prin.
Victory ES, 1838 W ROSE ST   95203
  Cheri Conaway, prin.

Calvary Baptist School
  703 E SWAIN ROAD   95207
Stockton Christian School
  9025 WEST LANE   95210
Annunciation ES, 1110 N LINCOLN ST   95203
Carden School of Stockton
  1200 W HAMMER LN   95209
Evangelical Methodist Christian ES
  P O BOX 5096   95205
Lincoln Christian Academy
  211 QUAIL LAKES DR   95207
Nazarene Christian ES
  915 ROSEMARIE LN   95207
Northside Christian Academy
  10300 N HWY 99   95212
Presentation ES
  1635 W BENJAMIN HOLT DR   95207
St. George's Primary and Senior ES
  144 W 5TH ST   95206
St. Gertrude ES, 1701 E MAIN ST   95205
St. Luke ES, 4005 N SUTTER ST   95204
Trinity Lutheran ES, 444 N AMERICAN ST   95202

Stonyford, Colusa Co.
Stoney Creek JUSD
Supt. – See Elk Creek
Indian Valley ES   95979 – Nancy Gardner, prin.

Stratford, Kings Co., Pop. Code 3
Central Un. ESD
Supt. – See Lemoore
ES, P O BOX 148   93266 – Deane Villa, prin.

Strathmore, Tulare Co., Pop. Code 4
Strathmore Un. ESD
Sch. Sys. Enr. Code 3
Supt. – Stan Halperin, P O BOX 247   93267
ES, P O BOX 198   93267 – Johnny Jones, prin.

Sunnyside Un. ESD
Sch. Sys. Enr. Code 2
Supt. – Herbert Bonds, 21644 AVENUE 196   93267
Sunnyside ES, 21644 AVE 196   93267
  Herbert Bonds, prin.

Studio City, Los Angeles Co.
Los Angeles USD
Supt. – See Los Angeles
Carpenter Avenue ES
  3909 CARPENTER AVE   91604 – Joan Marks, prin.

St. Michael of Angels Parish Day School
  3646 COLDWATER CANYON AVE   91604

Suisun City, Solano Co., Pop. Code 7
Fairfield-Suisun USD
Supt. – See Fairfield
Green Valley MS
  RURAL ROUTE 01   BOX 277   94585
  Gary Keeter, prin.
Crescent ES, 400 MULBERRY ST   94585
  Karen Dyer, prin.
Crystal MS, 100 CORDELIA ST   94585
  Mayrene Bates, prin.
Falls ES, 1634 ROCKVILLE ROAD   94585
  (—), prin.
Oakbrook ES, 700 OAKBROOK DR   94586
  Larry Carr, prin.
ES, 725 GOLDEN EYE WAY   94585
  Ella Blackmon, prin.
Suisun Valley ES
  RURAL ROUTE 01   BOX 117-A   94585
  Julie Martin, prin.

Sultana, Tulare Co.
Monson-Sultana JUESD
Sch. Sys. Enr. Code 2
Supt. – D. Atkinson, P O BOX 25   93666
Monson-Sultana ES, 10643 AVE 416   93666
  Bill Fulmer, prin.

Summerland, Santa Barbara Co., Pop. Code 3
Carpinteria USD
Supt. – See Carpinteria
MS, 135 VALENCIA   93067 – Barbara Fileto, prin.

Summit City, Shasta Co., Pop. Code 3
Shasta Lake Un. ESD
Supt. – See Central Valley
Toyon ES, SHASTA DAM BLVD   96089
  Donald Goodykoontz, prin.

Sun City, Riverside Co., Pop. Code 6
Menifee Un. ESD
Sch. Sys. Enr. Code 4
Supt. – Glen Newman
  26301 GARBONI ROAD   92380
Menifee ES, 26301 GARBONI ROAD   92380
  Laraine Hair, prin.
Menifee Valley MS, 26255 GARBONI RD   92381
  Gerald Hillman, prin.

Sunland, Los Angeles Co.
Los Angeles USD
Supt. – See Los Angeles
Apperson Street ES
  10233 WOODWARD AVE   91040
  Audrey Flanders, prin.
Sunland ES, 8350 HILLROSE ST   91040
  Robert Romer, prin.

Sunnyvale, Santa Clara Co., Pop. Code 9
Cupertino Un. ESD
Supt. – See Cupertino
Cupertino JHS, 1650 S BERNARDO AVE   94087
  Steve Parker, prin.
Nimitz ES, 545 CHEYENNE DRIVE   94087
  Mary Fisher, prin.
Stockmeir-Ortega MS
  592 DUNHOLME WAY   94087
  Dick Anderson, prin.
Stockmeir-Ortega PS
  572 DUNHOLME WAY   94087
  Dick Anderson, prin.
West Valley ES, 1635 BELLEVILLE WAY   94087
  Andy Mortensen, prin.

Santa Clara USD
Supt. – See Santa Clara
Peterson MS, 1380 ROSALIA AVE   94087
  Louis Pastorini, prin.
Ponderosa ES, 804 PONDEROSA AVE   94086
  Francis Rodeo, prin.

Sunnyvale ESD
Sch. Sys. Enr. Code 6
Supt. – Gary Mills, P O BOX 217   94088
Sunnyvale JHS, 1080 MANGO AVE   94087
  Barry Groves, prin.
Bishop ES, 450 N SUNNVALE AVE   94086
  Boyd Haley, prin.
Cherry Chase ES
  1138 HEATHERSTONE WAY   94087
  Philip Shoff, prin.

Columbia Community ES, 739 MORSE AVE   94086
  Michael Peregrin, prin.
Cumberland ES, 824 CUMBERLAND AVE   94087
  G. Pelkey, prin.
Ellis ES, 550 E OLIVE AVE   94086
  Lawrence Dismuke, prin.
Hollenbeck ES, 1185 HOLLENBECK AVE   94087
  Robert Lammers, prin.
Lakewood ES, 750 LAKECHIME DRIVE   94089
  Donna Myers, prin.

Resurrection ES, 1395 HOLLENBECK AVE   94087
South Penninsula Hebrew Day ES
  1030 ASTORIA DR   94087
St. Cyprian ES, 195 LEOTA AVE   94086
St. Martin's ES, 597 CENTRAL AVE   94086

Sunol, Alameda Co.
Sunol Glen ESD
Sch. Sys. Enr. Code 2
Supt. – Robert Wakeling, P O BOX 569   94586
Sunol Glen ES, P O BOX 569   94586
  Robert Wakeling, prin.

Sun Valley, Los Angeles Co.
Los Angeles USD
Supt. – See Los Angeles
Fernangeles ES, 12001 ART ST   91352
  Dolores Bousequeto, prin.
Glenwood ES, 8001 LEDGE AVE   91352
  Arthur Chandler, prin.
Roscoe ES, 10765 STRATHERN ST   91352
  Sharon Lee, prin.
Stonehurst Avenue ES
  9851 STONEHURST AVE   91352
  Janice Gonzales, prin.
Vinedale ES
  10150 LA TUNA CANYON ROAD   91352
  Norene Charnofsky, prin.

Grace Community Church School
  13248 ROSCOE BLVD   91352
Village Christian School
  8930 VILLAGE AVE   91352
Our Lady of Holy Rosary ES
  7802 VINELAND AVE   91352

Susanville, Lassen Co., Pop. Code 6
Johnstonville ESD
Sch. Sys. Enr. Code 2
Supt. – David Urbanac
  704-795 BANGHAM LANE   96130
Johnstonville ES
  704-795 BANGHAM LANE   96130
  David Urbanac, prin.

Richmond ESD
Sch. Sys. Enr. Code 2
Supt. – Sandra Pearson
  700-585 RICHMOND ROAD E   96130
Richmond ES, 700 RICHMOND ROAD #585   96130
  Sandra Pearson, prin.

Susanville ESD
Sch. Sys. Enr. Code 4
Supt. – Marshall Leve, 1324 CORNELL ST   96130
Diamond View ES, 850 RICHMOND ROAD   96130
  Jud Jensen, prin.
McKinley ES, FOURTH ST   96130
  David Burriel, prin.

Calvary Academy, 995 PAIUTE LN   96130

Sutter, Sutter Co., Pop. Code 4
Brittan ESD
Sch. Sys. Enr. Code 2
Supt. – Sandra Ellinwood, 2340 PEPPER ST   95982
Brittan ES, 2340 PEPPER ST   95982
  Sandra Ellinwood, prin.

Sylmar, Los Angeles Co.
Los Angeles USD
Supt. – See Los Angeles
Dyer Street ES, 14500 DYER ST   91342
  Ferol White, prin.
El Dorado Avenue ES
  12749 EL DORADO AVE   91342
  Elizabeth Sullivan, prin.
Harding Street ES, 13060 HARDING ST   91342
  David Vidaurrazaga, prin.
Herrick Avenue ES, 13350 HERRICK AVE   91342
  Allen Sussman, prin.
Hubbard Street ES, 13325 HUBBARD ST   91342
  Sidney Yukelson, prin.
Osceola Street ES, 14940 OSCEOLA ST   91342
  Loraine Mason, prin.
ES, 13291 PHILLIPPI AVE   91342
  Yvonne Chan, prin.

Foothill Baptist Day ES, 13550 HERRON ST   91342
St. Didacus ES, 14325 ASTORIA ST   91342
Sylmar Light & Life Christian School
  14019 SAYRE ST   91342

Taft, Kern Co., Pop. Code 6
Taft City ESD
Sch. Sys. Enr. Code 4
Supt. – Floyd Davis, 820 6TH ST   93268
Lincoln MS, 820 6TH ST   93268
  Linda LaMarre, prin.
Conley ES, ROSE AVE & SOUTH ST   93268
  Sylvia Hazel, prin.
Jefferson ES, DATE AND TAYLOR STS   93268
  Mike Harris, prin.
Parkview ES, A ST AND SIXTH AVE   93268
  Charlotte Blum, prin.

Roosevelt ES, 811 N 6TH ST 93268
  Lynda Brooks, prin.
ES, 212 LUCARD ST 93268 – James Murphy, prin.

Tahoe City, Placer Co., Pop. Code 4
  Tahoe-Truckee USD
  Supt. – See Truckee
  North Tahoe IS 95730 – Bill Ellisen, prin.

Tarzana, Los Angeles Co.
  Los Angeles USD
  Supt. – See Los Angeles
  Nestle Avenue ES, 5060 NESTLE AVE 91356
    Jacklyn Thompson, prin.
  ES, 5726 TOPEKA DRIVE 91356
    Carol Albright, prin.
  Wilbur Avenue ES, 5213 CREBS AVE 91356
    Frank Specchierla, prin.

  Castlemont ES, 5562 RESEDA BLVD 91356
  Lindley Avenue Baptist ES
    5901 LINDLEY AVE 91356
  Woodcrest Schs., 6043 TAMPA AVE 91356

Taylorsville, Plumas Co.
  Plumas USD
  Supt. – See Quincy
  ES, P O BOX 202 95983 – Marilyn McArthur, prin.

Tehachapi, Kern Co., Pop. Code 5
  Tehachapi USD
  Sch. Sys. Enr. Code 5
  Supt. – George Wolters
    400 S SNYDER AVE 93561
  Jacobsen JHS, 126 S SYNDER AVE 93561
    Richard Dieterle, prin.
  Golden Hills ES
    HCR ROUTE 04 BOX 5042-E 93561
    (—), prin.
  Tompkins ES, 1120 S CURRY ST 93561
    Judy Nobles, prin.
  Wells ES, 300 ROBINSON ST 93561
    Larry Blaylock, prin.

Temecula, Riverside Co., Pop. Code 2
  Temecula Un.ESD
  Sch. Sys. Enr. Code 5
  Supt. – Patricia Novotney
    43172 BUSINESS PARK DR 92390
  Margarita MS, 30600 MARGARITA RD 92390
    Linnea Clark, prin.
  MS, 41951 MORAGA ROAD 92390
    Karen Dubrule, prin.
  Rancho ES, 31530 LA SERENA WAY 92390
    William Robinson, prin.
  Sparkman ES, 43750 MARGARITA RD 92390
    Susan Warwick, prin.
  Vail ES, 29915 MIRA LOMA DRIVE 92390
    Michael Runyen, prin.

  Linfield Christian School
    31950 PAUBA ROAD 92390

Temple City, Los Angeles Co., Pop. Code 8
  El Monte ESD
  Supt. – See El Monte
  Cleminson ES, 5213 DALEVIEW AVE 91780
    Richard Willis, prin.

  Temple City USD
  Sch. Sys. Enr. Code 5
  Supt. – Wesley A. Bosson
    9516 LONGDEN AVE 91780
  Oak Avenue IS, 6623 OAK AVE 91780
    Jerry Childs, prin.
  Cloverly MS, 5476 N CLOVERLY AVE 91780
    Eleanor Vracin, prin.
  La Rosa ES, 9301 LA ROSA DRIVE 91780
    Richard Tauer, prin.
  Longden ES, 9501 WENDON ST 91780
    Karen Kallay, prin.
  Other Schools – See San Gabriel

  First Lutheran ES, 9123 BROADWAY 91780
  St. Luke ES, 5521 CLOVERLY AVE 91780

Templeton, San Luis Obispo Co., Pop. Code 6
  Templeton USD
  Sch. Sys. Enr. Code 3
  Supt. – Richard Scheider
    RURAL ROUTE 02 BOX 1 93465
  MS, RURAL ROUTE 02 BOX 2 93465
    Thomas Novak, prin.
  ES, RURAL ROUTE 02 BOX 12 93465
    Mary Bush, prin.

Terra Bella, Tulare Co., Pop. Code 4
  Saucelito ESD
  Sch. Sys. Enr. Code 1
  Supt. – David De Paoli, 17615 AVENUE 104 93270
  Saucelito ES, 17615 AVE 104 93270
    David De Paoli, prin.

  Terra Bella Un. ESD
  Supt. – See Three Rivers
  ES, 9364 ROAD 238 93270
    Theodore Thomas, prin.

  Zion Lutheran ES, 10368 ROAD 256 93270

Thermal, Riverside Co., Pop. Code 3
  Coachella Valley USD
  Sch. Sys. Enr. Code 6
  Supt. – David Alvarez, P O BOX 847 92274
  Kelley ES, 87-163 CENTER ST 92274
    Foch Pensis, prin.

Oasis ES, 88-775 AVENUE 76 92274
  Maria Ramos, prin.
Westside ES, 82-225 AIRPORT BLVD 92274
  Bob Bailey, prin.
Other Schools – See Coachella, Mecca, Salton City

Thornton, San Joaquin Co., Pop. Code 3
  New Hope ESD
  Sch. Sys. Enr. Code 2
  Supt. – Charles Boice, P O BOX 238 95686
  New Hope ES
    26675 N SACRAMENTO BLVD 95686
    Charles Boice, prin.

Thousand Oaks, Ventura Co., Pop. Code 8
  Conejo Valley USD
  Sch. Sys. Enr. Code 7
  Supt. – William Seaver
    1400 E JANSS ROAD 91362
  Colina IS, 1500 E HILLCREST DRIVE 91362
    Linda Musella, prin.
  Los Cerritos IS
    2100 E AVNDA DEL LAS FLORES 91362
    Bernie Carr, prin.
  Redwood IS
    233 W GAINSBOROUGH ROAD 91360
    Richard Johnson, prin.
  Acacia ES, 55 W NORMAN AVE 91360
    Gail Lowe, prin.
  Aspen ES, 1870 OBERLIN AVE 91360
    Margaret Badoud, prin.
  Conejo ES, 280 N CONEJO SCHOOL ROAD 91362
    Neil Snyder, prin.
  Glenwood ES, 1135 WINDSOR DRIVE 91360
    Frances Smith, prin.
  Ladera ES, 1211 CALLE ALMENDRO 91360
    Donald Holstrom, prin.
  Madrona ES, 612 CAMINO MANZANAS 91360
    Patricia Adams, prin.
  Meadows ES, 2000 LA GRANADA DRIVE 91362
    Timothy Stephens, prin.
  Park Oaks ES, 1335 CALLE BOUGANVILLA 91360
    Rachelle Morga, prin.
  University ES, 2801 ATLAS DRIVE 91360
    Susan Magnone, prin.
  Weathersfield ES
    3151 DARLINGTON DRIVE 91360
    Deanna Roth, prin.
  Wildwood ES, 620 VELARDE DRIVE 91360
    Linda Hensley, prin.
  Other Schools – See Newbury Park, Westlake

  Hillcrest Christian School
    384 ERBES ROAD 91362
  Ascension Lutheran ES
    1600 E HILLCREST DR 91362
  Bethany Christian ES, 200 BETHANY CT 91360
  Carden Conejo ES, 975 EVENSTAR AVE 91361
  First Baptist Academy, 1250 ERBES RD 91362
  Pinecrest ES, 449 E WILBUR RD 91360
  St. Jude the Apostle ES
    32036 LINDERO CANYON RD 91361
  St. Paschal Baylon ES, 154 E JANSS RD 91360
  St. Patrick's Parish Day ES, 1 CHURCH RD 91362

Thousand Palms, Riverside Co.
  Palm Springs USD
  Supt. – See Palm Springs
  Lindley ES, 31495 ROBERT ROAD 92276
    Myron Theilman, prin.

Three Rivers, Madera Co., Pop. Code 3
  Terra Bella Un. ESD
  Sch. Sys. Enr. Code 3
  Supt. – Robert Uphoff, P O BOX 99 93271
  Other Schools – See Terra Bella

  Three Rivers Un. ESD
  Sch. Sys. Enr. Code 2
  Supt. – Larry Horton, P O BOX 99 93271
  ES, P O BOX 99 93271 – Larry Horton, prin.

Tiburon, Marin Co., Pop. Code 6
  Reed Un. ESD
  Sch. Sys. Enr. Code 3
  Supt. – Judith Foster
    277 A KAREN WAY #A 94920
  Del Mar IS, 105 AVENIDA MIRAFLORES 94920
    Rob Kessler, prin.
  Bel Aire MS, 277 KAREN WAY 94920
    Marylee Fisher, prin.
  Reed ES, 1199 TIBURON BLVD 94920
    Sheila Puckett, prin.

Tipton, Tulare Co., Pop. Code 3
  Tipton ESD
  Sch. Sys. Enr. Code 2
  Supt. – Linord Cameron, P O BOX 150 93272
  ES, 370 N EVANS ROAD 93272
    Linord Cameron, prin.

Tollhouse, Fresno Co.
  Sierra Un. SD
  Sch. Sys. Enr. Code 3
  Supt. – C. Sparrow
    27444 TOLLHOUSE ROAD 93667
  Sierra ES, 27444 TOLLHOUSE ROAD 93667
    C. Sparrow, prin.
  Other Schools – See Shaver Lake

Tomales, Marin Co., Pop. Code 2
  Shoreline USD
  Sch. Sys. Enr. Code 3
  Supt. – Patrick Kennedy, P O BOX 198 94971
  Bodega Bay ES, P O BOX 198 94971
    Paul Olson, prin.

ES, P O BOX 198 94971 – James Patterson, prin.
Other Schools – See Point Reyes Station

Topanga, Los Angeles Co., Pop. Code 4
  Los Angeles USD
  Supt. – See Los Angeles
  ES, 141 N TOPANGACYN BLVD 90290
    Paula Benjamin, prin.

Torrance, Los Angeles Co., Pop. Code 9
  Los Angeles USD
  Supt. – See Los Angeles
  Halldale ES, 21514 HALLDALE AVE 90501
    Diane Spitzkeit, prin.
  Meyler Street ES, 1123 W 223RD ST 90502
    Helen Friedman, prin.
  Van Deene Avenue ES, 826 JAVELIN ST 90502
    Roberta Burk, prin.

  Torrance USD
  Sch. Sys. Enr. Code 7
  Supt. – Edward Richardson
    2335 PLAZA DEL AMO 90501
  Calle Mayor MS, 4800 CALLE MAYOR 90505
    William Colby, prin.
  Casimir MS, 17220 CASIMIR AVE 90504
    Richard Leibovitz, prin.
  Hull MS, 2080 W 231ST ST 90501
    Barry Gross, prin.
  Lynn MS, 5038 HALISON ST 90503
    Richard Long, prin.
  Madrona MS, 21364 MADRONA AVE 90503
    Cecil Paschall, prin.
  Magruder MS, 4100 W 185TH ST 90504
    Sidney Morrison, prin.
  Adams ES, 2121 W 238TH ST 90501
    Cyma Early, prin.
  Anza ES, 21400 ELLINWOOD DRIVE 90503
    Warren Carver, prin.
  Arlington ES, 17800 VAN NESS AVE 90504
    Michael Brajevich, prin.
  Arnold ES, 4100 W 227TH ST 90505
    Janice Schultz, prin.
  Carr ES, 3404 W 168TH ST 90504
    Paul Harenski, prin.
  Edison ES, 3800 W 182ND ST 90504
    Craig Kimball, prin.
  Fern ES, 1314 FERN AVE 90503
    Robert Scharf, prin.
  Hickory ES, 2800 W 227TH ST 90505
    Nancy Raiche, prin.
  Lincoln ES, 2418 W 166TH ST 90504
    Daniel Kelly, prin.
  Riviera ES, 365 PASEO DE ARENA 90505
    Michael Bartelt, prin.
  Seaside ES, 4651 SHARYNNE LANE 90505
    Jeanne Gelwicks, prin.
  ES, 2125 LINCOLN AVE 90501 – J. Shearer, prin.
  Towers ES, 5600 TOWERS ST 90503
    Grant Logan, prin.
  Victor ES, 4820 SPENCER ST 90503
    Laurie Love, prin.
  Walteria ES, 24456 MADISON ST 90505
    Lora Hester, prin.
  Wood ES, 2250 W 235TH ST 90501
    Alice Lucas, prin.
  Yukon ES, 17815 YUKON AVE 90504
    Donald Credell, prin.

  Ascension Lutheran ES
    17910 PRAIRIE AVE 90504
  First Lutheran Christian ES
    2900 W CARSON ST 90503
  Nativity ES, 2371 W CARSON ST 90501
  South Bay Junior Academy
    4400 DEL AMO BLVD 90503
  St. Catherine Laboure ES
    3846 REDONDO BEACH BLVD 90504
  St. James ES, 4625 GARNET ST 90503

Trabuco Canyon, Orange Co.
  Saddleback Valley USD
  Supt. – See Mission Viejo
  Trabuco ES, P O BOX 277 92678
    Ray Leverich, prin.

Tracy, San Joaquin Co., Pop. Code 7
  Banta ESD
  Sch. Sys. Enr. Code 2
  Supt. – Janet Watkins
    22345 EL RANCHO ROAD 95376
  Banta ES, 22345 EL RANCHO RD 95376
    Janet Watkins, prin.

  Jefferson ESD
  Sch. Sys. Enr. Code 2
  Supt. – Mary Church, P O BOX 1029 95378
  Jefferson ES, 7500 W LINNE ROAD 95376
    Mary Church, prin.

  Lammersville ESD
  Sch. Sys. Enr. Code 2
  Supt. – Kenneth Olds
    16555 VON SOSTEN ROAD 95376
  Lammersville ES
    16555 VON SOSTEN ROAD 95376
    Kenneth Olds, prin.

  New Jerusalem ESD
  Sch. Sys. Enr. Code 2
  Supt. – Thomas Guthrie
    31400 S KOSTER ROAD 95376
  New Jerusalem ES, 31400 S KOSTER ROAD 95376
    Thomas Guthrie, prin.

Tracy SD
Sch. Sys. Enr. Code 5
Supt. – Robert Baum, 315 E 11TH ST   95376
Clover MS, 315 E 11TH ST   95376
  Melva Rush, prin.
Monte Vista MS, 315 E 11TH ST   95376
  James Franco, prin.
Central ES, 1370 PARKER AVE   95376
  Jon Fine, prin.
McKinley ES, 800 W CARLTON WAY   95376
  Harold Kushins, prin.
North ES, 2820 HOLLY DRIVE   95376
  Warren Twitchell, prin.
South ES, 10460 MOUNT DIABLO ROAD   95376
  John Vaille, prin.
Villalovoz ES, 1550 CYPRESS DR   95376
  Jacquelyn Gobel, prin.
West Park ES, 750 W 10TH ST   95376
  Tony Serna, prin.

St. Bernard's ES, 165 W EATON AVE   95376

Tranquillity, Fresno Co., Pop. Code 3
Tranquillity ESD
Sch. Sys. Enr. Code 2
Supt. – John Crider, P O BOX 337   93668
ES, 6116 S DANIELS   93668 – John Crider, prin.

Traver, Tulare Co.
Traver JESD
Sch. Sys. Enr. Code 2
Supt. – George Nord, P O BOX 69   93673
ES, 36736 CANAL DRIVE   93673
  George Nord, prin.

Travis A F B, Solano Co.
Travis USD
Sch. Sys. Enr. Code 5
Supt. – Robert McLennan
  DE RONDE DRIVE   94535
Golden West IS, DE RONDE DRIVE   94535
  Ulysses Harvey, prin.
Center ES, ARMSTRONG & KELLY STS   94535
  Roger Berg, prin.
Scandia ES, 100 BROADWAY ST   94535
  Jake Catado, prin.
Travis ES, HICKAM AVE   94535
  Mabel Hockett, prin.
Other Schools – See Vacaville

Treasure Island, San Francisco Co.
San Francisco USD
Supt. – See San Francisco
ES, 13TH & E STS US NAVAL STA   94130
  John Whisman, prin.

Tres Pinos, San Benito Co.
Tres Pinos Un. ESD
Sch. Sys. Enr. Code 1
Supt. – (—), 5635 AIRLINE HIGHWAY   95075
ES, 5635 AIRLINE HIGHWAY   95075
  Sharon Johnston, prin.

Trinidad, Humboldt Co., Pop. Code 2
Big Lagoon Un. ESD
Sch. Sys. Enr. Code 1
Supt. – (—)
  269 BIG LAGOON PARK ROAD   95570
Big Lagoon ES
  269 BIG LAGOON PARK ROAD   95570
  William Hawkins, prin.

Trinidad Un. ESD
Sch. Sys. Enr. Code 2
Supt. – Ron Flenner, P O BOX 3030   95570
ES, P O BOX 3030   95570 – Ron Flenner, prin.

Trinity Center, Siskiyou Co.
Coffee Creek ESD
Sch. Sys. Enr. Code 1
Supt. – (—), HCR 02 BOX 4740   96091
Coffee Creek ES, HCR 02 BOX 4740   96091
  Rosalie Collins, prin.

Trinity Center ESD
Sch. Sys. Enr. Code 1
Supt. – (—), P O BOX 127   96091
ES, P O BOX 127   96091 – Terry Karlin, prin.

Trona, San Bernardino Co., Pop. Code 4
Trona JUSD
Sch. Sys. Enr. Code 3
Supt. – James W. Triplett, P O BOX 307   93562
ES, TRONA ROAD   93562 – Alan Tsubota, prin.

Truckee, Nevada Co., Pop. Code 4
Tahoe-Truckee USD
Sch. Sys. Enr. Code 5
Supt. – Francis Mulholland, P O BOX 458   95734
Donner Trail ES, P O BOX 458   95734
  Larry Robins, prin.
Kings Beach ES, P O BOX 458   95734
  Larry Robins, prin.
Sierra Mountain MS, P O BOX 458   95734
  Rodney Hisken, prin.
Tahoe Lake ES, P O BOX 458   95734
  Frank Evans, prin.
ES, P O BOX 458   95734 – Sandra Stewart, prin.
Other Schools – See Tahoe City

Tujunga, Los Angeles Co., Pop. Code 7
Los Angeles USD
Supt. – See Los Angeles
Mountain View ES, 6410 OLCOTT ST   91042
  Myra Morewitz, prin.

Pinewood Avenue ES
  10111 SILVERTON AVE   91042
  Clayton Brown, prin.
Plainview Avenue ES
  10819 PLAINVIEW AVE   91042
  Pedro Ortiz, prin.

Our Lady of Lourdes ES
  7324 APPERSON ST   91042

Tulare, Tulare Co., Pop. Code 7
Buena Vista ESD
Sch. Sys. Enr. Code 2
Supt. – Ronald Levine, 21660 ROAD 60   93274
Buena Vista ES, 21660 ROAD 60   93274
  Ronald Levine, prin.

Oak Valley Un. ESD
Sch. Sys. Enr. Code 2
Supt. – Douglas Henderson
  24500 ROAD 68   93274
Oak Valley ES, 24500 ROAD 68   93274
  Douglas Henderson, prin.

Palo Verde Un. ESD
Sch. Sys. Enr. Code 2
Supt. – Davis Harp, 9637 AVENUE 196   93274
Palo Verde ES, 9637 AVE 196   93274
  Davis Harp, prin.

Sundale Un. ESD
Sch. Sys. Enr. Code 2
Supt. – Nancy Ruel, 13990 AVENUE 240   93274
Sundale ES, 13990 AVE 240   93274
  Nancy Ruel, prin.

Tulare City ESD
Sch. Sys. Enr. Code 6
Supt. – Bill Postlewaite
  600 N CHERRY AVE   93274
Cherry Avenue JHS, 540 N CHERRY AVE   93274
  Gary Smith, prin.
Mulcahy JHS, 1001 W SONORA AVE   93274
  John Caudle, prin.
Cypress ES, 1870 S LASPINA ST   93274
  James Henderson, prin.
Garden ES, 640 E PLEASANT AVE   93274
  Steve Stafford, prin.
Kohn ES, 500 S LASPINA ST   93274
  A. Gordon, prin.
Lincoln ES, 909 E CEDAR AVE   93274
  Pauline Friedman, prin.
Maple ES, 640 W CROSS AVE   93274
  Pam Canby, prin.
Pleasant ES, 1855 W PLEASANT   93274
  Robert James, prin.
Roosevelt ES, 1046 W SONORA AVE   93274
  Cyndi Silva, prin.
Wilson ES, 955 E TULARE AVE   93274
  Mike Wenn, prin.

St. Aloysius ES, 627 N BEATRICE DR   93274

Tulelake, Modoc Co., Pop. Code 3
Tulelake Basin JUSD
Sch. Sys. Enr. Code 3
Supt. – Charles Binderup, P O BOX 547   96134
Newell ES, P O BOX 788   96134
  Bryce Dethlefs, prin.
Tulelake Basin MS, P O BOX 788   96134
  Bryce Dethlefs, prin.

Tuolumne, Tuolumne Co., Pop. Code 4
Summerville ESD
Sch. Sys. Enr. Code 2
Supt. – Ronald Parker, P O BOX 938   95379
Summerville ES, P O BOX 938   95379
  Ronald Parker, prin.

Mother Lode Christian School
  P O BOX 757   95379

Tupman, Kern Co.
Elk Hills ESD
Sch. Sys. Enr. Code 1
Supt. – Belton Banks, P O BOX 128   93276
Elk Hills ES, P O BOX 128   93276
  Belton Banks, prin.

Turlock, Stanislaus Co., Pop. Code 7
Chatom Un. ESD
Sch. Sys. Enr. Code 3
Supt. – Richard Pritchard
  7201 CLAYTON ROAD   95380
Chatom MS, 7201 CLAYTON ROAD   95380
  M. Bayless, prin.
Mountain View ES
  CROWS LANDING AT W MAIN   95380
  Richard Pritchard, prin.

Turlock JSD
Sch. Sys. Enr. Code 6
Supt. – J. Denton Palmer, P O BOX 1105   95381
JHS, 1441 COLORADO AVE   95380
  Thomas Hoy, prin.
Brown ES, 1400 GEORGETOWN AVE   95380
  Wray Hardock III, prin.
Crane PS, 1100 CAHILL AVE   95380
  Patricia McGuire, prin.
Crowell ES, 118 NORTH AFVE   95380
  Annarae Luevano, prin.
Cunningham ES, 324 W LINWOOD AVE   95380
  George King, prin.
Julien ES, 1924 E CANAL DRIVE   95380
  Marvin Dutcher, prin.

Osborn ES, 201 N SODERQUIST ROAD   95380
  William Parks, prin.
Wakefield ES, 400 SOUTH AVE   95380
  Marta Kyte, prin.

Sacred Heart ES, 1225 COOPER AVE   95380
Turlock Christian ES, P O BOX 944   95381

Tustin, Orange Co., Pop. Code 8
Tustin USD
Sch. Sys. Enr. Code 6
Supt. – Maurice Ross, 300 S C ST   92680
Columbus Tustin MS, 17952 BENETA WAY   92680
  Regina Cain, prin.
Currie MS, 300 S C ST   92680
  William Wingo, prin.
Beswick ES, 1362 MITCHELL AVE   92680
  Pete Brower, prin.
Estock ES, 14741 N B ST   92680
  Christine Gregg, prin.
Heideman ES, 15571 WILLIAMS ST   92680
  Pat James, prin.
Nelson ES, 14392 BROWNING AVE   92680
  Dan Brooks, prin.
Thorman ES, 1402 SYCAMORE AVE   92680
  William Wingo, prin.
Veeh ES, 1701 SAN JUAN ST   92680
  Nancy Baker, prin.
Other Schools – See Santa Ana

Colonial Bible Church ES
  13601 BROWNING AVE   92680
Red Hill Lutheran ES
  13200 RED HILL AVE   92680
St. Cecilia ES, 1311 SYCAMORE AVE   92680
St. Jeanne of Lestonnc ES
  16791 E MAIN ST   92680

Twain Harte, Tuolumne Co., Pop. Code 4
Twain Harte-Long Barn UESD
Sch. Sys. Enr. Code 3
Supt. – James Haslip, P O BOX 339   95383
ES, P O BOX 339   95383 – Madeline Sharp, prin.

Twentynine Palms, San Bernardino Co., Pop. Code 6
Morongo USD
Sch. Sys. Enr. Code 6
Supt. – John Dempsey, P O BOX 1209   92277
JHS, 5798 UTAH TRAIL   92277
  Frank Simone, prin.
Oasis ES, 73175 EL PASEO DR   92277
  Pauline Orson, prin.
Palm Vista ES, 74350 BASE LINE AVE   92277
  Jean Johnson, prin.
ES, 5498 UTAH TRAIL   92277
  Douglas Lawson, prin.
Other Schools – See Joshua Tree, Morongo Valley,
  Yucca Valley

Blessed Sacrament School, 6785 SAGE AVE   92277

Twin Peaks, San Bernardino Co.

Calvary Chapel Christian ES, P O BOX 1210   92391

Ukiah, Mendocino Co., Pop. Code 7
Ukiah USD
Sch. Sys. Enr. Code 6
Supt. – Donald De Martini
  925 N STATE ST   95482
Pomolita JHS, 740 N SPRING ST   95482
  Michael Lauletta, prin.
Nokomis ES, 495 WASHINGTON AVE   95482
  Meg Scrofani, prin.
Oak Manor ES, 400 OAK MANOR DRIVE   95482
  Marilyn Boulanger, prin.
Yokayo ES, 790 S DORA ST   95482
  Bruce Devries, prin.
Zeek ES, 500 LOW GAP ROAD   95482
  Carl Morgensen, prin.
Other Schools – See Calpella, Hopland, Redwood
  Valley

St. Mary of Angels ES, 991 S DORA ST   95482
Ukiah Junior Academy, 180 STRIPP LN   95482

Union City, Alameda Co., Pop. Code 8
New Haven USD
Sch. Sys. Enr. Code 7
Supt. – Guy Emanuele
  34200 ALVARADO NILES ROAD   94587
Alvarado MS, 31102 FREDI ST   94587
  Kevin Brodehl, prin.
Barnard-White MS, 725 WHIPPLE ROAD   94587
  Linda MacLaren, prin.
New Haven MS, 2801 HOP RANCH ROAD   94587
  Gladys Gause, prin.
Alvarado ES, 31100 FREDI ST   94587
  Hector Caraballo, prin.
Cabello ES, 4500 CABELLO DRIVE   94587
  Mei Kamenik, prin.
Decoto ES, 600 G ST   94587 – Rod Fivelstad, prin.
Pioneer ES, 32737 BEL AIRE ST   94587
  Carla Elde, prin.
Searles ES, 33629 15TH ST   94587
  Susan Hunt, prin.
Other Schools – See Hayward

Our Lady of Rosary ES, 678 B ST   94587

Upland, San Bernardino Co., Pop. Code 8
Upland USD
Sch. Sys. Enr. Code 6
Supt. – Loren Sanchez, P O BOX 1239   91785

Pioneer JHS, P O BOX 1239 91785
  Roger Schulte, prin.
JHS, P O BOX 1239 91785 – William Smith, prin.
Baldy View ES, 979 W 11TH ST 91786
  Robert Clarke, prin.
Cabrillo ES, 1562 W 11TH ST 91786
  Frank Migaiolo, prin.
Citrus ES, 925 W 7TH ST 91786 – Jan Cowin, prin.
Foothill Knolls ES
  1245 VETERANS COURT 91786
  Marylouise Lau, prin.
Magnolia ES, 465 W 15TH ST 91786
  Molly King, prin.
Sierra Vista ES, 253 E 14TH ST 91786
  Sandra Hughes, prin.
Sycamore ES, 1075 W 13TH ST 91786
  John Temple, prin.
ES, 601 N 5TH AVE 91786 – David Bardin, prin.
Valencia ES, 541 W 22ND ST 91786
  Carolyn Ruis, prin.

Ninth Street Christian ES, 100 W 9TH ST 91786
St. Joseph ES, 905 N CAMPUS AVE 91786

Upper Lake, Lake Co., Pop. Code 3
Upper Lake Un. ESD
Sch. Sys. Enr. Code 3
Supt. – Richard Detton, P O BOX 36 95485
ES, P O BOX 36 95485 – Steve Dunlop, prin.

Vacaville, Solano Co., Pop. Code 8
Travis USD
Supt. – See Travis A F B
Cambridge ES, 100 CAMBRIDGE DRIVE 95688
  Kathleen Scott, prin.

Vacaville USD
Sch. Sys. Enr. Code 7
Supt. – Lyle Welch, 752 SCHOOL ST 95688
Alamo ES, 500 S ORCHARD AVE 95688
  Julia Busher, prin.
Elm ES, 129 ELM ST 95688 – Jerry Clark, prin.
Elmira ES, 751 SCHOOL ST 95688
  Richard Ashley, prin.
Fairmont ES, 1355 MARSHALL ROAD 95688
  Gerviece Brown, prin.
Hemlock ES, 400 HEMLOCK ST 95688
  Leon Spiegel, prin.
Markham ES, 101 MARKHAM AVE 95688
  Raymond Posey, prin.
Orchard ES, 805 N ORCHARD AVE 95688
  Cynthia Walker, prin.
Padan ES, 200 PADAN SCHOOL ROAD 95688
  Patricia Bradanini, prin.
Sierra Vista ES, 301 BEL AIR DRIVE 95688
  Warren Sheldon, prin.
Ulatis ES, 100 MCCLELLAN ST 95688
  Marcia Rooney, prin.
Vaca Pena IS, 200 KEITH WAY 95688
  John Westermann, prin.

Christian Academy, 1117 DAVIS ST 95688
Notre Dame School, 1781 MARSHALL RD 95687

Valencia, Saugus Co., Pop. Code 5
Newhall ESD
Supt. – See Newhall
Meadows ES, 25577 FEDALA ROAD 91355
  Larry Heath, prin.
Old Orchard ES, 25141 AVENIDA RONDEL 91355
  Betty Granger, prin.
Valencia Valley ES, 23601 CARRIZO DR 91355
  Geraldene Morey, prin.

Saugus Un. ESD
Supt. – See Saugus
Seco Canyon ES
  27827 SECO CANYON ROAD 91355
  J. Blankenship, prin.

William S. Hart Un. HSD
Supt. – See Newhall
Arroyo Seco JHS
  27171 VISTA DELGADO DRIVE 91355
  Lew White, prin.

Pinecrest ES
  25443 N ORCHARD VILLGE ROAD 91355

Vallejo, Solano Co., Pop. Code 8
Napa Valley USD
Supt. – See Napa
Donaldson Way ES
  430 DONALDSON WAY 94589
  Ron Goldberg, prin.
Napa Junction ES, 300 NAPA ST 94590
  Marilyn McCurdy, prin.

Vallejo City USD
Sch. Sys. Enr. Code 7
Supt. – M. Dale Welsh
  211 VALLE VISTA AVE 94590
Beverly Hills ES, 1450 CORONEL AVE 94591
  Chris Jordan, prin.
Cave ES, 770 TREGASKIS AVE 94591
  Dayle Kerstad, prin.
Cooper ES, 612 DEL MAR AVE 94589
  Ellen Nims, prin.
Davidson ES, 436 DEL SUR ST 94591
  Sylvia Harris, prin.
Farragut ES, 301 FARRAGUT AVE 94590
  A. Humphreys, prin.
Federal Terrace ES, 415 DANIELS AVE 94590
  Elona Meyer, prin.
Glen Cove ES, 501 GLEN COVE PKWY 94591
  Kathy Howard, prin.

Highland ES, 1309 ENSIGN AVE 94590
  William Tschida, prin.
Lincoln ES, 620 CAROLINA ST 94590
  Jane Stern, prin.
Loma Vista ES, 146 RAINIER ST 94590
  Donna Dailey, prin.
Mare Island ES, NINTH & TISDALE ROAD 94592
  Geneva Watts, prin.
Mini ES, 1530 LORENZO DRIVE 94589
  Susan Straight, prin.
Patterson ES, 1080 PORTER ST 94590
  Linda Beckstrom, prin.
Pennycook ES, 3620 FERNWOOD ST 94591
  Lee Cockrum, prin.
Steffan Manor ES, 815 CEDAR ST 94591
  Carolyn Jackson, prin.
Widenmann ES, 100 WHITNEY AVE 95489
  James Warfield, prin.

Hilltop Christian ES, 210 LOCUST DR 94591
North Hills Christian ES
  200 ADMIRAL CALLAGHAN LANE 94591
Reignierd ES, 380 CONTRA COSTA ST 94590
St. Basil ES, 1230 NEBRASKA ST 94590
St. Catherine of Siena Catholic ES
  3460 TENNESSEE ST 94591
St. Vincent Ferrer ES, 420 FLORIDA ST 94590

Valley Center, San Diego Co.
Valley Center Un. ESD
Sch. Sys. Enr. Code 4
Supt. – Harry Weinberg
  28751 COLE GRADE ROAD 92082
MS, 28751 COLE GRADE ROAD 92082
  Paul White, prin.
ES, 28751 COLE GRADE ROAD 92082
  Gary Wilson, prin.
PS, 14249 FRUITVALE RD 92082
  Paul Lahr, prin.

Valley Home, Stanislaus Co.
Valley Home JESD
Sch. Sys. Enr. Code 2
Supt. – (—), P O BOX 127 95384
ES, 4600 TEXAS AVE 95384 – Harold Pope, prin.

Valley Springs, Calaveras Co., Pop. Code 3
Calaveras USD
Supt. – See San Andreas
ES, P O BOX 187 95252 – John Hofstetter, prin.

Vandenburg A F B, Santa Barbara Co., Pop. Code 7
Lompoc USD
Supt. – See Lompoc
MS, MOUNTAINVIEW BLVD 93437
  Robert Forinash, prin.
Buena Vista ES, 100 ALDEBARAN AVE 93436
  Donald Civerolo, prin.
Crestview ES, 100 UTAH AVE 93437
  Donald Ribble, prin.
Los Padres ES, MOUNTAIN VIEW BLVD 93437
  Norman Ellertson, prin.

Van Nuys, Los Angeles Co., Pop. Code 9
Los Angeles USD
Supt. – See Los Angeles
Mulholland JHS, 17120 VANOWEN ST 91406
  Carolyn Baker, prin.
Anatola Avenue ES, 7364 ANATOLA AVE 91406
  Kiyo Fukumoto, prin.
Bassett Street ES, 15756 BASSETT ST 91406
  Barbara Kamon, prin.
Chandler ES, 14030 WEDDINGTON ST 91401
  Alvaro Cortes, prin.
Cohasset Street ES, 15810 SATICOY ST 91406
  Maria Villasenor, prin.
Erwin Street ES, 13400 ERWIN ST 91401
  Kassaye Makuria, prin.
Gault Street ES, 17000 GAULT ST 91406
  John Kinnon, prin.
Hazeltine Avenue ES
  7150 HAZELTINE AVE 91405
  Nathan Glickman, prin.
Kester Avenue ES, 5353 KESTER AVE 91411
  William Fukuhara, prin.
Kittridge Street ES, 13619 KITTRIDGE ST 91401
  Donald Watson, prin.
LeMay Street ES, 17520 VANOWEN ST 91406
  Gabriel Tumin, prin.
Stagg Street ES, 7839 AMESTOY AVE 91406
  Sallye Gauthier, prin.
Sylvan Park ES, 6238 NOBLE AVE 91411
  Evelyn Bautista, prin.
Valerio Street ES, 15035 VALERIO ST 91405
  Walton Greene, prin.
ES, 6464 SYLMAR AVE 91401
  Dorothy Hawe, prin.

Childrens Community ES
  14702 SYLVAN ST 91411
Fairfield ES, 16945 SHERMAN WAY 91406
First Baptist Van Nuys Day ES
  14800 SHERMAN WAY 91405
First Lutheran ES, 6952 VAN NUYS BLVD 91405
Laurence ES, 6428 WOODMAN AVE 91401
Pinecrest ES, 14111 SHERMAN WAY 91405
St. Bridget of Sweden ES
  7120 WHITAKER AVE 91406
St. Elizabeth ES, 6635 TOBIAS AVE 91405
Valley School, 15700 SHERMAN WAY 91406

Venice, Los Angeles Co.
Los Angeles USD
Supt. – See Los Angeles

Broadway ES, 1015 LINCOLN BLVD 90291
  Magdalena Guajardo, prin.
Coeur D'Alene Avenue ES
  810 COEUR D ALENE AVE 90291
  Beth Ojena, prin.
Westminster Avenue ES
  1010 WASHINGTON BLVD 90291
  Cleo Binghan, prin.

First Lutheran School, 815 VENICE BLVD 90291
St. Mark ES, 912 COEUR D ALENE AVE 90291

Ventura, Ventura Co., Pop. Code 8
Ventura USD
Sch. Sys. Enr. Code 7
Supt. – Cesare Caldarelli,Jr.
  120 E SANTA CLARA ST 93001
Anacapa MS, 100 S MILLS ROAD 93003
  Charlotte McElroy, prin.
Balboa MS, 247 S HILL ROAD 93003
  Edward Valentine, prin.
Cabrillo MS, 1426 E SANTA CLARA ST 93001
  Norman Diebel, prin.
De Anza MS, 2060 CAMERON ST 93001
  Lorraine Becker, prin.
Elmhurst ES, 5080 ELMHURST ST 93003
  Kenneth Coffey, prin.
Foster ES, 20 PLEASANT PLACE 93001
  Gregory Kampf, prin.
Juanamaria ES, 100 CROCKER AVE 93004
  Gerald Dannenberg, prin.
Lincoln ES, 1107 E SANTA CLARA ST 93001
  Jeffrey Nelsen, prin.
Loma Vista ES, 300 LYNN DRIVE 93003
  Fannie Hutchison, prin.
Montalvo ES, 2050 GRAND AVE 93003
  I. Munday, prin.
Pierpont ES
  MARTHA'S VINEYARD COURT 93003
  Diane Peterson, prin.
Poinsettia ES, 350 N VICTORIA AVE 93003
  JoAnn VanderMolen, prin.
Portola ES, 1350 PARTRIDGE DRIVE 93003
  Phyllis Robertson, prin.
Reynolds ES, 450 VALMORE AVE 93003
  Beverly McCaslin, prin.
Rogers ES, 316 HOWARD ST 93003
  Thomas Smith, prin.
Serra ES, 8880 HALIFAX ST 93004
  Tom Carmody, prin.
Sheridan Way ES, 573 SHERIDAN WAY 93001
  Robert Fraser, prin.
Other Schools – See Oak View, Saticoy

Temple Christian Baptist School
  5415 RALSTON ST 93003
College Heights Christian ES
  6360 TELEPHONE RD 93003
Friends ES, 3503 ARUNDELL CIR 93003
Holy Cross ES, 183 E MAIN ST 93001
Our Lady of Assumptn ES
  3169 TELEGRAPH RD 93003
Sacred Heart ES, 10770 HENDERSON RD 93004
St. Paul's Parish Day ES
  3290 LOMA VISTA RD 93003
Ventura Mission Christian Day School
  500 HIGH POINT DR 93003

Vernails, San Joaquin Co.
Patterson JUSD
Supt. – See Patterson
Rising Sun ES, WELTY & SPENCER ROADS 95385
  William Johnson, prin.

Victor, San Joaquin Co.
Lodi USD
Supt. – See Lodi
ES, P O BOX L 95253 – Christine Muzik, prin.

Victorville, San Bernardino Co., Pop. Code 7
Victor ESD
Sch. Sys. Enr. Code 5
Supt. – Ralph Baker, 16821 A ST 92392
Del Rey ES, 15332 DEL REY ST 92392
  Conny Ridgeway, prin.
Irwin ES, 15907 MOJAVE DRIVE 92392
  (—), prin.
Liberty ES, 12900 AMETHYST 92392
  Marie Miller, prin.
Mojave Vista ES, 16100 BURWOOD AVE 92392
  Diane Wilkinson, prin.
Park View ES, 13427 CAHUENGA ST 92392
  Martha McCarthy, prin.
Village ES, 14711 MOJAVE DR 92392
  Karren Fechner, prin.

Victor Valley Un. HSD
Sch. Sys. Enr. Code 5
Supt. – George Davis
  16350 MOJAVE DRIVE 92392
Hook JHS, 15000 HOOK ROAD 92392
  Mark LeBrun, prin.
Victor Valley JHS, 16925 FORREST AVE 92392
  Gabriel Escalera, prin.

Victor Valley Christian School
  16125 LORENE DR 92392

Villa Park, Orange Co., Pop. Code 6
Orange USD
Supt. – See Orange
Cerro Villa MS, 17852 SERRANO AVE 92667
  Don Buck, prin.
Serrano ES, 17741 SERRANO AVE 92667
  Joe Fortier, prin.

ES, 10551 CENTER DRIVE   92667
   A. Roland, prin.

Vina, Tehama Co.
Los Molinos USD
Supt. – See Los Molinos
ES, P O BOX 287   96092 – Carolyn Steffan, prin.

Visalia, Tulare Co., Pop. Code 8
Liberty ESD
Sch. Sys. Enr. Code 2
Supt. – David DeLong, 11535 AVENUE 264   93277
Liberty ES, 11535 AVENUE 264   93277
   David DeLong, prin.

Outside Creek ESD
Sch. Sys. Enr. Code 2
Supt. – (—), 26452 ROAD 164   93277
Outside Creek ES, 26452 ROAD 164   93277
   Kyle Weisenberger, prin.

Stone Corral ESD
Sch. Sys. Enr. Code 2
Supt. – Weldon Brumley
   15590 AVENUE 383   93291
Stone Corral ES, 15590 AVE 383   93291
   Weldon Brumley, prin.

Visalia USD
Sch. Sys. Enr. Code 7
Supt. – Robert Line, 315 E ACEQUIA AVE   93291
Divisadero MS, 1200 S DIVISADERO ST   93277
   Thomas Biscotti, prin.
Green Acres MS, 1147 N MOONEY BLVD   93291
   Geraldine Murphy, prin.
Valley Oak MS, 2000 N LOVERS LANE   93291
   William Adams, prin.
Conyer ES, 814 S SOWELL ST   93277
   Myron Skeklian, prin.
Crestwood ES, 3001 W WHITENDALE AVE   93277
   Noah Williamson, prin.
Crowley ES, 214 E FERGUSON AVE   93291
   Jesus Alaniz, prin.
Elbow Creek ES, 32747 ROAD 138   93291
   John McCarthy, prin.
Elbow ES, 31411 ROAD 160   93291
   John McCarthy, prin.
Fairview ES, 1051 ROBIN DRIVE   93291
   John Crenshaw, prin.
Golden Oak ES, 1700 N LOVERS LANE   93291
   Miguel Granillo, prin.
Highland ES, 701 N STEVENSON   93291
   Martin Ruby, prin.
Houston ES, 1200 N GIDDINGS   93291
   Gary Mekeel, prin.
Linwood ES, 3129 S LINWOOD   93277
   Arthur Simon, prin.
Mineral King ES, 3333 E KAWEAH AVE   93277
   Frances Holdbrooks, prin.
Mountain View ES, 2021 S ENCINA   93277
   Lynne Brumit, prin.
Packwood ES, 67832 AVENUE 280   93277
   Arthur Simon, prin.
Pinkham ES, 2200 E TULARE AVE   93277
   Phillip Nava, prin.
Royal Oaks ES, 1323 CLOVER DR   93277
   Verna Crookshanks, prin.
Union ES, 28050 ROAD 148   93277
   Michael Bishop, prin.
Veva Blunt ES, 1119 S CHINOWTH ROAD   93277
   Clifford Denham, prin.
Washington ES, 500 S GARDEN ST   93277
   Larry Schryer, prin.
Willow Glen ES, 310 N AKERS ST   93291
   Betty Kapheim, prin.
Other Schools – See Goshen, Ivanhoe
_____

Central Valley Christian School
   5600 W TULARE AVE   93277
McCann ES, 200 E RACE ST   93277
Visalia Christian Academy
   3737 W WALNUT AVE   93277

Vista, San Diego Co., Pop. Code 8
Vista USD
Sch. Sys. Enr. Code 7
Supt. – Rene Townsend
   1234 ARCADIA AVE   92084
Lincoln MS, 1234 ARCADIA AVE   92084
   Patricia Campbell, prin.
Washington MS, 1234 ARCADIA AVE   92084
   Stephanie Tarkington, prin.
Alamosa ES, 5130 ALAMOSA PARK DR   92083
   James Charnholm, prin.
Beaumont ES, 550 BEAUMONT DRIVE   92084
   Eric Monce, prin.
Bobier ES, 220 W BOBIER DRIVE   92083
   Jacqueline Bracamonte, prin.
Casita ES, 260 CEDAR RD   92083
   Olympio Matos, prin.
Crestview ES, 510 SUNSET DRIVE   92083
   Julie Larson, prin.
Grapevine ES, 630 GRAPEVINE ROAD   92083
   Raymond Lanoue, prin.
Monte Vista ES
   1720 MONTE VISTA DRIVE   92084
   Ronald Arnold, prin.
Olive ES, 836 OLIVE AVE   92083
   Eileen Howard, prin.
_____

National University School
   2022 UNIVERSITY DR   92083
Tri City Christian Schs.
   302 N EMERALD DR   92083
Faith Lutheran ES, 700 E BOBIER DR   92084

St. Francis of Assisi ES, 525 W VISTA WAY   92083
Vista Christian ES, P O BOX 1869   92083

Walnut, Los Angeles Co., Pop. Code 6
Rowland USD
Supt. – See Rowland Heights
Oswalt ES, 19501 SHADOW OAK DRIVE   91789
   Harold Moe, prin.
Ybarra ES
   1300 S BREA CANYON CUTOFF   91789
   Ralph Pagan, prin.

Walnut Valley USD
Sch. Sys. Enr. Code 7
Supt. – David Brown, P O BOX 469   91789
Suzanne MS, 525 SUZANNE ROAD   91789
   Laurel Kanthak, prin.
Collegewood ES
   20725 COLLEGEWOOD DRIVE   91789
   Jack Lebrun, prin.
Morris ES, 19875 CALLE BAJA   91789
   Clifford Wellington, prin.
Vejar ES, 20222 VEJAR ROAD   91789
   Truman Collins, prin.
ES, 841 GLENWICK AVE   91789
   Sandra Miller, prin.
Other Schools – See Diamond Bar
_____

Christian Chapel ES
   1920 BREA CANYON CUT-OFF RD   91789

Walnut Creek, Contra Costa Co., Pop. Code 8
Mt. Diablo USD
Supt. – See Concord
Foothill MS, 2775 CEDRO LANE   94598
   Walter Quinn, prin.
Bancroft ES, 2200 PARISH DRIVE   94598
   Margaret Allen, prin.
Valle Verde ES
   3275 PEACHWILLOW LAND   94598
   Leslie Anderson, prin.
Walnut Acres ES, 180 CEREZO DRIVE   94598
   Ken Magruda, prin.

Walnut Creek ESD
Sch. Sys. Enr. Code 4
Supt. – Kenneth Meinecke
   960 YGNACIO VALLEY ROAD   94596
IS, 2425 WALNUT BLVD   94596
   Daniel Leary, prin.
Buena Vista ES, 2355 SAN JUAN AVE   94596
   Charles Adams, prin.
Indian Valley ES, 551 MARSHALL DRIVE   94598
   Paul Sheckler, prin.
Murwood ES, 2050 VANDERSLICE AVE   94596
   Allan Bartlett, prin.
Walnut Heights ES, 4064 WALNUT BLVD   94596
   Nancy Rivara, prin.
_____

Dorris-Eaton ES, 1847 NEWELL AVE   94595
Palmer School for Boys & Girls
   2740 JONES RD   94596
Seven Hills ES, P O BOX 3300   94598
St. Mary's ES, 1158 BONT LN   94596
Walnut Creek Christian Academy
   2336 BUENA VISTA AVE   94596
Woodlands Christian ES, 2721 LARKEY LN   94596

Walnut Grove, Sacramento Co., Pop. Code 3
River Delta USD
Supt. – See Rio Vista
ES, P O BOX 145   95690 – Sonya Boyle, prin.

Warner Springs, San Diego Co.
Warner Un. ESD
Sch. Sys. Enr. Code 2
Supt. – (—), P O BOX 8   92086
Warner ES, P O BOX 8   92086
   Robbie Blackwood, prin.

Wasco, Kern Co., Pop. Code 6
Semitropic ESD
Sch. Sys. Enr. Code 2
Supt. – Michael Rucks, HCR BOX 82   93280
Semitropic ES, HCR ROUTE BOX 82   93280
   Michael Rucks, prin.

Wasco Un. ESD
Sch. Sys. Enr. Code 4
Supt. – Allen Walker, 639 BROADWAY ST   93280
Jefferson MS, 305 GRIFFITH AVE   93280
   Refugio Martinez, prin.
Clemens ES, 1101 5TH ST   93280
   Peggy Clemens, prin.
Palm Avenue MS, 1017 PALM AVE   93280
   James Forrest, prin.
_____

St. John ES, 909 BROADWAY ST   93280

Washington, Los Angeles Co.
Twin Ridges ESD
Supt. – See North San Juan
Malakoff ES   95986 – Randy Wise, prin.
ES   95986 – Randy Wise, prin.

Waterford, Stanislaus Co., Pop. Code 5
Roberts Ferry Un. ESD
Sch. Sys. Enr. Code 1
Supt. – William Lebo
   101 ROBERTS FERRY ROAD   95386
Roberts Ferry Union ES
   101 ROBERTS FERRY ROAD   95386
   William Lebo, prin.

Waterford ESD
Sch. Sys. Enr. Code 3
Supt. – Martin Petersen, P O BOX 270   95386

MS, P O BOX 270   95386 – Evan Smith, prin.
Moon ES, P O BOX 270   95386
   Robert Chrisman, prin.

Watsonville, Santa Cruz Co., Pop. Code 7
North Monterey County USD
Supt. – See Moss Landing
Moss Landing MS, 1815 SALINAS ROAD   95076
   Don Pedroni, prin.

Pajaro Valley USD
Sch. Sys. Enr. Code 7
Supt. – James Baker, P O BOX 630   95077
Hall MS, 201 BREWINGTON AVE   95076
   Norbert Kowalkowski, prin.
Rolling Hills MS, 130 HERMAN AVE   95076
   George Clark, prin.
Alianza ES, 440 ARTHUR ROAD   95076
   Patrick Sweeney, prin.
Amesti ES, 25 AMESTI ROAD   95076
   Gil Hayward, prin.
Bradley ES, 321 CORRALITOS ROAD   95076
   Edwin Leach, prin.
Calabasas ES, 202 CALABASAS ROAD   95076
   David Bilardello, prin.
Hall District ES, 300 SILL ROAD   95076
   Dan Cooperman, prin.
Hyde ES, 125 ALTA VISTA ST   95076
   Robert Duran, prin.
MacQuiddy ES, 330 MARTINELLI ST   95076
   Susan Hill, prin.
Pajaro ES, 250 SALINAS ROAD   95076
   Norma Fierro, prin.
Salsipuedes ES, 115 CASSERLY ROAD   95076
   Doug Hoff, prin.
White ES, 515 PALM AVE   95076
   Gary Bloom, prin.
Other Schools – See Aptos, Aromas, Freedom
_____

Monte Vista Christian School
   2 SCHOOL WAY   95076
Green Valley Christian ES
   376 GREEN VALLEY ROAD EXT   95076
Moreland Notre Dame ES
   133 BRENNAN ST   95076

Waukena, Tulare Co.
Waukena JUn. ESD
Sch. Sys. Enr. Code 2
Supt. – Steven Hatakeyama, P O BOX 86   93282
Waukena Joint Union ES, P O BOX 86   93282
   Steven Hatakeyama, prin.

Weaverville, Trinity Co., Pop. Code 4
Weaverville ESD
Sch. Sys. Enr. Code 2
Supt. – Gerald Boosinger, P O BOX 1000   96093
ES, P O BOX 100   96093 – Gerald Boosinger, prin.

Weed, Siskiyou Co., Pop. Code 5
Butteville Un. ESD
Sch. Sys. Enr. Code 1
Supt. – (—), P O BOX 4489   96094
Butteville Union ES, P O BOX 4489   96094
   Eugene Barbier, prin.

Weed Un. ESD
Sch. Sys. Enr. Code 3
Supt. – Aldo Zanotto, 575 WHITE AVE   96094
ES, 575 WHITE AVE   96094 – (—), prin.

Weimar, Placer Co.
Placer Hills Un. ESD
Supt. – See Meadow Vista
Weimar Hills JHS, P O BOX 255   95736
   Michael Bossi, prin.

Weldon, Kern Co.
South Fork Un. ESD
Sch. Sys. Enr. Code 2
Supt. – Gary Bray, P O BOX 1239   93283
South Fork ES   93283 – Charles Smith, prin.

Weott, Humboldt Co.
Southern Humbolt JUSD
Supt. – See Garberville
Johnson ES   95571 – Don Swanson, prin.

West Covina, Los Angeles Co., Pop. Code 8
Covina-Valley USD
Supt. – See Covina
Grovecenter ES, 775 N LARK ELLEN AVE   91791
   Kathryn Contreras, prin.
Mesa ES, 409 S BARRANCA ST   91791
   William Schulte, prin.
Workman Avenue ES
   1941 E WORKMAN AVE   91790
   Constance Brown, prin.

Rowland USD
Supt. – See Rowland Heights
Rincon IS, 2800 E HOLLINGWORTH ST   91792
   Ray Warner, prin.
Hollingworth ES
   3003 E HOLLINGWORTH ST   91792
   Keith McGlothlin, prin.

West Covina USD
Sch. Sys. Enr. Code 6
Supt. – Jane Gawronski
   1717 W MERCED AVE   91790
Hollencrest IS, 2101 E MERCED AVE   91791
   Kenji Kinoshita, prin.
Willowood IS, 2021 W ALWOOD ST   91790
   Douglas Koel, prin.
California ES, 1125 W BAINBRIDGE AVE   91790
   Sibylla Law, prin.

Cameron ES, 1225 E CAMERON AVE 91790
  Mike Popoff, prin.
Cortez ES, 2226 E RIO VERDE DRIVE 91791
  Robert Signer, prin.
Merced ES, 1545 E MERCED AVE 91791
  Maria Caterinicchio, prin.
Merlinda ES, 1120 S VALINDA AVE 91790
  Phyllis McDonald, prin.
Monte Vista ES, 1615 W ELDRED AVE 91790
  Ronald Preston, prin.
Orangewood ES, 1440 S ORANGE AVE 91790
  Barbara Lamoure, prin.
Vine ES, 1901 E VINE AVE 91791
  Gary Lawson, prin.
Wescove ES, 1010 W VINE AVE 91790
  Frances Bennie, prin.

Christ Lutheran ES, 311 S CITRUS AVE 91791
Dove Day ES, 502 S LARK ELLEN AVE 91791
Immanuel First Lutheran ES
  512 S VALINDA AVE 91790
South Hills Academy
  1600 E FRANCISQUITO AVE 91791
St. Christopher ES
  900 W CHRISTOPHER ST 91790
St. Martha Episcopal Day ES
  520 S LARK ELLEN AVE 91791
West Covina Christian ES
  763 N SUNSET AVE 91790
West Covina Hills Adventist ES
  3528 E TEMPLE WAY 91791

West Hollywood, Los Angeles Co., Pop. Code 8
Los Angeles USD
Supt. – See Los Angeles
ES, 970 HAMMOND ST 90069
  Grace Snipper, prin.

Westlake, Los Angeles Co., Pop. Code 5
Conejo Valley USD
Supt. – See Thousand Oaks
ES, 1571 E POTERO ROAD 91361
  Michael Waters, prin.
Westlake Hills ES
  2797 PANAMINT COURT 91362
  Everett Eaton, prin.

Las Virgenes USD
Sch. Sys. Enr. Code 6
Supt. – Albert Marley
  30961 AGOURA ROAD #100 91361
White Oak ES
  31761 VILLAGE SCHOOL ROAD 91361
  Robert DeBoise, prin.
Other Schools – See Agoura Hills, Calabasas,
  Woodland Hills

Westley, Stanislaus Co., Pop. Code 3
Patterson JUSD
Supt. – See Patterson
Grayson ES, P O BOX 7 95387
  William Johnson, prin.

Westminster, Orange Co., Pop. Code 8
Garden Grove USD
Supt. – See Garden Grove
McGarvin IS, 9802 BISHOP PLACE 92683
  Tom Holler, prin.
Anthony ES, 15320 PICKFORD ST 92683
  Bruce Johnson, prin.
Carrillo ES, 15270 BUSHARD ST 92683
  Stephanie Paggi, prin.
Marshall ES, 15791 BUSHARD ST 92683
  Gary Lewis, prin.

Ocean View ESD
Supt. – See Huntington Beach
Westmont ES, 8251 HEIL AVE 92683
  Julie Stein, prin.

Westminster ESD
Sch. Sys. Enr. Code 6
Supt. – Barney Davis
  14121 CEDARWOOD ST 92683
Johnson IS, 13603 EDWARDS ST 92683
  Dale Bischof, prin.
Warner IS, 14171 NEWLAND ST 92683
  Joan Read, prin.
Boos ES, 13890 HAMMON PLACE 92683
  Hodge Hill, prin.
Eastwood ES, 13552 UNIVERSITY ST 92683
  Richard Sturges, prin.
Fruberger ES, 6952 HOOD DRIVE 92683
  Duane Collier, prin.
Midway City ES, 8521 HAZARD AVE 92683
  Richard Richards, prin.
Schmitt ES, 7200 TRASK AVE 92683
  Joe Costa, prin.
Sequoia ES, 5900 IROQUOIS ROAD 92683
  Guy Carrozzo, prin.
Webber ES, 14142 HOOVER ST 92683
  Richard Weaver, prin.
Other Schools – See Garden Grove, Huntington
  Beach, Midway City

Hebrew Academy, 14401 WILLOW LANE 92683
Blessed Sacrament Catholic ES
  14146 OLIVE ST 92683
St. Luke's Christian ES
  13552 GOLDENWEST ST 92683
Westminster Christian ES
  14061 CHESTNUT ST 92683

Westmorland, Imperial Co., Pop. Code 4
Westmorland Un. ESD
Sch. Sys. Enr. Code 2
Supt. – Jimmie Hughes, P O BOX 88 92281
ES, P O BOX 88 92281 – Jimmie Hughes, prin.

West Point, Calaveras Co., Pop. Code 3
Calaveras USD
Supt. – See San Andreas
ES, P O BOX 96 95255 – Bill Hamilton, prin.

West Sacramento, Yolo Co., Pop. Code 7
Washington USD
Sch. Sys. Enr. Code 5
Supt. – K. Kobayashi, 930 W ACRES ROAD 95691
Evergreen ES, 919 W ACRES ROAD 95691
  Ardeen Westvik, prin.
Westfield Village ES, 508 POPLAR AVE 95691
  Nancy Brynelson, prin.
Westmore Oaks ES, 1504 FALLBROOK ST 95691
  Elaine Madsen, prin.
Other Schools – See Broderick

Our Lady of Grace ES
  RURAL ROUTE 01 BOX 370 95691

Westwood, Lassen Co., Pop. Code 4
Westwood USD
Sch. Sys. Enr. Code 2
Supt. – Herold Sinclair, P O BOX H 96137
Walker ES, FIFTH AND DELWOOD 96137
  Terry Ferguson, prin.

Wheatland, Yuba Co., Pop. Code 4
Wheatland USD
Sch. Sys. Enr. Code 4
Supt. – Gerald Arnold, P O BOX 818 95692
Bear River MS, P O BOX 818 95692
  Kenneth Kaiser, prin.
Far West MS, S BEALE RD 95692
  Larry Westcamp, prin.
Lone Tree ES, S BEALE RD 95692
  Anne Osmond, prin.
ES, 200 MAIN ST 95692 – Lee Springer, prin.

Whitethorn, Humboldt Co.
Southern Humbolt JUSD
Supt. – See Garberville
Ettersburg ES, HCR ROUTE ETTERSBURG 95489
  Michael Leonard, prin.
ES 95489 – Michael Leonard, prin.

Whitmore, Shasta Co.
Whitmore Un. ESD
Sch. Sys. Enr. Code 1
Supt. – David Klasson, P O BOX 10 96096
ES, P O BOX 10 96096 – David Klasson, prin.

Whittier, Los Angeles Co., Pop. Code 8
East Whittier City ESD
Sch. Sys. Enr. Code 6
Supt. – Dorothy Fagan
  14535 WHITTIER BLVD 90605
East Whittier MS, 14421 WHITTIER BLVD 90605
  John Stoddard, prin.
Granada MS, 15337 LEMON DRIVE 90604
  Charles Royce, prin.
Hillview MS, 10931 STAMY ROAD 90604
  (—), prin.
Ceres ES, 10601 CERES AVE 90604
  Terre Delgado, prin.
Evergreen ES, 12915 HELMER DRIVE 90602
  Dorka Duron, prin.
La Colima ES, 11225 MILLER ROAD 90604
  Marlene Carabello, prin.
Laurel ES, 13550 LAMBERT ROAD 90605
  Tom Lewis, prin.
Mulberry ES, 14029 ULBERRY DRIVE 90605
  Leon Kampa, prin.
Murphy Ranch ES, 16021 JANINE DRIVE 90603
  Laurie Eastwood, prin.
Ocean View ES, 145359 E SECOND ST 90605
  Larry Bobst, prin.
Orchard Dale ES, 10625 COLE ROAD 90604
  Kathy Grubbs, prin.
Scott Avenue ES, 11701 SCOTT AVE 90604
  Ann Reno, prin.

Los Nietos ESD
Sch. Sys. Enr. Code 4
Supt. – Terry Giboney
  8324 WESTMAN AVE 90606
Aeolian ES, 11600 AEOLIAN ST 90606
  Mercedes Parks, prin.
Nelson ES, 8140 VICKI DRIVE 90606
  Peter Nichols, prin.
Other Schools – See Los Nietos, Santa Fe Springs

Lowell JESD
Sch. Sys. Enr. Code 4
Supt. – Ronald Randolph
  11019 VALLEY HOME AVE 90603
Rancho-Starbuck IS
  16430 WOODBRIER DRIVE 90604
  Fred Wright, prin.
Jordan ES, 11019 VALLEY HOME AVE 90603
  Ernest Thompson, prin.
Macy ES, 11019 VALLEY HOME AVE 90603
  Bob Hardcastle, prin.
Meadow Green ES
  11019 VALLEY HOME AVE 90603
  Wayne Anderson, prin.
Olita ES, 11019 VALLEY HOME AVE 90603
  Cynthia Makowski, prin.

South Whittier ESD
Sch. Sys. Enr. Code 5
Supt. – Richard Graves, P O BOX 3057 90605
South Whittier IS
  13243 LOS NIETOS ROAD 90605
  David Morton, prin.
Lake Marie ES, 10001 CARMENITA ROAD 90605
  Virginia Berg, prin.
Loma Vista ES, 13463 MEYER ROAD 90605
  Mike Madrid, prin.
Los Altos ES, 12001 BONA VISTA LANE 90604
  Cecelia Laidemitt, prin.
McKibben ES, 10550 MILLS AVE 90604
  Dorothy Smith, prin.
Monte Vista MS, 12000 LOMA DR 90604
  Celia Lebel, prin.
Telechron ES, 112200 TELECHRON AVE 90605
  Patricia Mikuta, prin.

Whittier City ESD
Sch. Sys. Enr. Code 6
Supt. – Neal Avery, 7211 WHITTIER AVE 90602
Dexter IS, 11532 FLORAL DRIVE 90601
  Donald Hoagland, prin.
Edwards IS, 6812 NORWALK BLVD 90606
  Paz Enciso, prin.
Andrews Northwest ES
  1010 S CARAWAY DR 90601
  Alex Gasporra, prin.
Hoover ES, 6302 ALTA AVE 90601
  Margaret Leon, prin.
Jackson ES, 8015 PAINTER AVE 90602
  Robert Mazzeo, prin.
Lincoln ES, 12620 BROADWAY 90601
  Paul Moore, prin.
Longfellow ES, 6005 MAGNOLIA AVE 90601
  Nancy Pittman, prin.
Mill ES, 4030 WORKMAN MILL ROAD 90601
  Janet Garcia, prin.
Orange Grove ES
  10626 ORANGE GROVE AVE 90601
  Jeanette Kelly, prin.
Phelan ES, 7150 CULLY AVE 90606
  Kirk Reeve, prin.
Sorensen ES, 11493 ROSEHEDGE DRIVE 90606
  Claude Traylor, prin.
Washington MS, 7804 S THORNLAKE AVE 90606
  William Blake, prin.
West Whittier ES, 6411 NORWALK BLVD 90606
  Dora Buchner, prin.

Painter Avenue Christian School
  13713 PUTNAM ST 90605
Whittier Christian JHS, 14625 KEESE DR 90604
Bethany Baptist ES, 10252 MILLS AVE 90604
Brethren ES, 8101 VICKI DR 90606
Faith Lutheran ES, 9920 MILLS AVE 90604
Primanti Montessori Schs.
  10947 VALLEY HOME AVE 90603
St. Bruno ES, 15700 CITRUSTREE RD 90603
St. Gregory the Great ES
  13925 TELEGRAPH RD 90604
St. Mary of Assumption ES
  7203 NEWLIN AVE 90602
Trinity Lutheran ES, 11716 FLORAL DR 90601
Whittier Christian ES, 6548 NEWLIN AVE 90601

Wildomar, Riverside Co.
Lake Elsinore SD
Supt. – See Lake Elsinore
ES, 21-575 PALOMAR ROAD 92395
  Corene Barr, prin.

Williams, Colusa Co., Pop. Code 4
Williams USD
Sch. Sys. Enr. Code 3
Supt. – Robert Dial, P O BOX 7 95987
MS, P O BOX 7 95987 – Anthony Katsaris, prin.
ES, 1404 E ST 95987 – Anthony Katsaris, prin.

Willits, Mendocino Co., Pop. Code 5
Willits USD
Sch. Sys. Enr. Code 4
Supt. – James Roberts, 249 N MAIN ST 95490
Baechtel Grove MS, 1150 MAGNOLIA AVE 95490
  Shirley Schott, prin.
Brookside ES
  SPRUCE AND LINCOLN WAY 95490
  David Taxis, prin.
Mill Creek ES, 139 N MAIN ST 95490
  Paul Ubelhart, prin.
Sherwood ES, P O BOX 814 95490
  Paul Ubelhart, prin.
Vineyard ES
  16500 HEARST WILLIS ROAD 95490
  Paul Ubelhart, prin.

Willow Creek, Humboldt Co., Pop. Code 3
Klamath-Trinity JUSD
Supt. – See Hoopa
Trinity Valley ES, P O BOX 638 95573
  Darline Giddings, prin.

Willows, Glenn Co., Pop. Code 5
Willows USD
Sch. Sys. Enr. Code 4
Supt. – Gary Kemp, 334 W SYCAMORE ST 95988
IS, 1145 W CEDAR ST 95988
  Wayne Weatherford, prin.
Murdock ES, 655 FRENCH ST 95988
  John Woolley, prin.

Wilmington, Los Angeles Co., Pop. Code 8
Los Angeles USD
Supt. – See Los Angeles

Broad Avenue ES, 24815 BROAD AVE　90744
　Patricia Hardy, prin.
Fries Avenue ES, 1301 N FRIES AVE　90744
　Judith Newman, prin.
Gulf Avenue ES, 828 W L ST　90744
　Delores Buettgenbach, prin.
Hawaiian Avenue ES, 540 HAWAIIAN AVE　90744
　Tommye Keenan, prin.
Wilmington Park ES, 1140 MAHAR AVE　90744
　Claire Sizgorich, prin.

Wilmington Christian School
　931 FRIGATE AVE　90744
Holy Family ES, 1122 E ROBIDOUX ST　90744
Pacific Harbor Christian ES
　1530 N WILMINGTON BLVD　90744
Sts. Peter & Paul ES, 706 BAY VIEW AVE　90744

Wilton, Sacramento Co.
Elk Grove USD
Sch. Sys. Enr. Code 4
Supt. – See Elk Grove
Dillard ES, 9721 DILLARD ROAD　95693
　Karen Hayashi, prin.

Winchester, Riverside Co.
Hemet USD
Supt. – See Hemet
ES, 28751 WINCHESTER ROAD　92396
　Donald Akkerman, prin.

Windsor, Sonoma Co.
Windsor Un. SD
Sch. Sys. Enr. Code 4
Supt. – Norman Ginsburg
　7650 BELL ROAD　95492
MS, 7650 BELL RD　95492 – Virginia Rieffel, prin.
Brooks ES, 7650 BELL RD　95492
　Joe Taylor, prin.
ES, 7650 BELL RD　95492
　Wayne Yamagishi, prin.

Winterhaven, Imperial Co., Pop. Code 3
San Pasqual Valley USD
Sch. Sys. Enr. Code 3
Supt. – Gus Headington
　676 BASE LINE ROAD　92283
San Pasqual Valley ES　92283
　Richard Winch, prin.

Winters, Yolo Co., Pop. Code 5
Winters JUSD
Sch. Sys. Enr. Code 4
Supt. – Michael Roberts, 47 MAIN ST　95694
MS, 425 ANDERSON AVE　95694
　David Inns, prin.
Waggoner ES, 500 EDWARDS ST　95694
　Marjorie Hein, prin.

Winton, Merced Co., Pop. Code 2
Merced River Un. ESD
Supt. – See Snelling
Washington MS, 4402 OAKDALE ROAD　95388
　L. Glen Fowler, prin.

Winton ESD
Sch. Sys. Enr. Code 4
Supt. – Raymond Fitchett, P O BOX 8　95388
Sparkes MS, 7265 ALMOND AVE　95388
　Mark Walker, prin.
Crookham ES, 7160 W WALNUT AVE　95388
　Agnes Sietsema, prin.

Woodbridge, San Joaquin Co., Pop. Code 4
Lodi USD
Supt. – See Lodi
MS, P O BOX P　95258 – Ralph Blumenthal, prin.

Woodlake, Tulare Co., Pop. Code 6
Woodlake Un. SD
Sch. Sys. Enr. Code 4
Supt. – Brian Vaccaro
　400 W WHITNEY AVE　93286
Woodlake IS, 497 N PALM ST　93286
　Evelyn Hodel, prin.
White Learning ES, 700 N CYPRESS ST　93286
　Tom Vanwoerkom, prin.

Woodland, Yolo Co., Pop. Code 8
Woodland JUSD
Sch. Sys. Enr. Code 6
Supt. – Robert Watt, 526 MARSHALL AVE　95695
Beamer ES, 525 BEAMER ST　95695
　Lois Serrano, prin.
Dingle ES, 625 ELM ST　95695 – Ilse Grant, prin.
Freeman ES, 126 N WEST ST　95695
　Edward Markel, prin.
Gibson ES, 312 GIBSON ROAD　95695
　Patricia Reimer, prin.
Laugenour ES, RURAL ROUTE 02 BOX 465　95695
　Don Darby, prin.
Maxwell ES, 50 ASHLEY ST　95695
　Reinaldo Genera, prin.
Plainfield ES, RURAL ROUTE 01 BOX 706　95695
　Craig Beller, prin.

Whitehead ES
　624 W SOUTHWOOD DRIVE　95695
　Peder Matthews, prin.
Willow Spring ES
　RURAL ROUTE 04 BOX 187　95695
　Michael Parker, prin.
Woodland Prairie ES, 1444 STETSON ST　95695
　Judy Rose, prin.
Zamora ES, 1716 COTTONWOOD ST　95695
　Jill Casanega, prin.
Other Schools – See Knights Landing

Holy Rosary ES, 505 CALIFORNIA ST　95695
Woodland Christian ES, 1616 WEST ST　95695

Woodland Hills, Los Angeles Co.
Las Virgenes USD
Supt. – See Westlake
Chaparral ES, 22601 LIBERTY BELL ROAD　91364
　Martha Mutz, prin.

Los Angeles USD
Supt. – See Los Angeles
Hale JHS, 23830 CALIFA ST　91367
　Rich Bell, prin.
Parkman JHS, 20800 BURBANK BLVD　91367
　Andrew Anderson, prin.
Calabash Street ES, 23055 EUGENE ST　91364
　Paula Benjamin, prin.
Calvert Street ES, 19850 DELANO ST　91367
　Gerald Dodge, prin.
Lockhurst Drive ES
　6170 LOCKHURST DRIVE　91367
　Cermella Trbovich, prin.
Serrania Avenue ES, 5014 SERRANIA AVE　91364
　Alphonse Edwards, prin.
Woodlake Avenue ES
　23231 HATTERAS ST　91367
　Donald Foster, prin.
ES, 22201 SAN MIGUEL ST　91364
　Sandra Argast, prin.

Kadima Hebrew Academy, 5724 OSO AVE　91367
Pinecrest-Woodland Hills ES
　5975 SHOUP AVE　91367
St. Bernardne of Siena ES
　6061 VALLEY CIRCLE BLVD　91367
St. Mel ES, 20820 VENTURA BLVD　91364

Woodside, San Mateo Co., Pop. Code 6
Woodside ESD
Sch. Sys. Enr. Code 2
Supt. – Bruce Thompson
　3195 WOODSIDE ROAD　94062
ES, 3195 WOODSIDE ROAD　94062
　Bruce Thompson, prin.

Woody, Kern Co.
Blake ESD
Sch. Sys. Enr. Code 1
Supt. – (—), P O BOX 53　93287
Blake ES, P O BOX 53　93287
　Robin Lindsey, prin.

Wrightwood, San Bernardino Co., Pop. Code 3
Snowline JUSD
Supt. – See Phelan
ES, P O BOX 368　92397 – Janet Vondra, prin.

Yermo, San Bernardino Co., Pop. Code 4
Silver Valley USD
Sch. Sys. Enr. Code 4
Supt. – Joanne Duncan, P O BOX 847　92398
Daggett MS, P O BOX 847　92398
　Everett McCullough, prin.
ES, P O BOX 847　92398 – Frank Baca, prin.
Other Schools – See Fort Irwin, Newberry Springs

Yorba Linda, Orange Co., Pop. Code 8
Placentia USD
Supt. – See Placentia
Yorba JHS, 5350 FAIRMONT BLVD　92686
　Richard Vouga, prin.
Fairmont ES, 5241 FAIRMONT LBVD　92686
　Donna Jones, prin.
Glenknoll Drive ES
　6361 GLENKNOLL DRIVE　92686
　Pauline Schara, prin.
Travis Ranch ES
　5200 VIA DE LA ESCUELA　92686
　Earl Pratt, prin.

Yorba Linda ESD
Sch. Sys. Enr. Code 4
Supt. – Mary Ellen Blanton
　4999 CASA LOMA AVE　92686
MS, 4777 CASA LOMA AVE　92686
　Larry Mauzey, prin.
Linda Vista ES, 5600 OHIO ST　92686
　Ken Darby, prin.
Paine ES, 4444 PLUMOSA DRIVE　92686
　John Best, prin.
Rose Drive ES, 4700 ROSE DRIVE　92686
　Audell Jackson, prin.

Calvary Christian Baptist School
　18821 YORBA LINDA BLVD　92686
Friends Christian ES, 5211 LAKEVIEW AVE　92686

Yosemite Park, Mariposa Co.
Mariposa County USD
Supt. – See Mariposa
Wawona ES, P O BOX 72　95389
　Michelle Horner, prin.
Yosemite ES, P O BOX 485　95389
　Dennis Carlock, prin.

Yountville, Napa Co., Pop. Code 5
Napa Valley USD
Supt. – See Napa
ES, P O BOX 2440　94599 – Jan Farrington, prin.

Yreka, Siskiyou Co., Pop. Code 6
Yreka Un. ESD
Sch. Sys. Enr. Code 4
Supt. – Robert Singleton, 405 JACKSON ST　96097
Jackson Street MS, 405 JACKSON ST　96097
　James Birdsong, prin.
Evergreen ES, 416 EVERGREEN LANE　96097
　(—), prin.
Gold Street ES, 321 N GOLD ST　96097
　Gerald Giardino, prin.

Yuba City, Sutter Co., Pop. Code 7
Franklin ESD
Sch. Sys. Enr. Code 2
Supt. – William Messick
　332 N TOWNSHIP ROAD　95991
Franklin ES, 332 N TOWNSHIP ROAD　95991
　William Messick, prin.

Yuba City USD
Sch. Sys. Enr. Code 6
Supt. – A. Karperos, 750 N PALORA AVE　95991
Gray Avenue JHS, 808 GRAY AVE　95991
　Douglas Usedom, prin.
April Lane ES, 800 APRIL LANE　95991
　Howard Anthony, prin.
Barry ES, 1255 BARRY ROAD　95991
　Bob Chiechi, prin.
Bridge Street ES, 500 BRIDGE ST　95991
　Marlene Barber, prin.
Central-Gaither ES, 8403 BAILEY ROAD　95991
　Richard Garmire, prin.
King Avenue ES, 630 KING AVE　95991
　Robert Kruse, prin.
Lincoln ES, 1582 LINCOLN ROAD　95991
　William Zeller, prin.
Lincrest ES, 1400 PHILLIPS ROAD　95991
　Robert Jacoby, prin.
Park Avenue ES, 100 MORTON ST　95991
　Linda Cohee, prin.
Tierra Buena ES, 1794 VILLA AVE　95991
　Stephanie Cross, prin.
Other Schools – See Robbins

Faith Christian Schs., P O BOX 1690　95992
Grace Christian Academy
　1980 S WALTON AVE　95991
St. Isidores ES, 200 CLARK AVE　95991

Yucaipa, San Bernardino Co., Pop. Code 7
Yucaipa JUSD
Sch. Sys. Enr. Code 6
Supt. – John Wilde, 12797 3RD ST　92399
IS, 12358 6TH ST　92399 – Alfred Rezendes, prin.
Calimesa ES, 13523 2ND ST　92399
　Mollie Vanderzyl, prin.
Dunlap ES, 32870 AVENUE E　92399
　J. McGinn, prin.
Valley ES, 12333 8T ST　92399
　Nancy Greening, prin.
ES, 12375 CALIFORNIA ST　92399
　Ellen Garretson, prin.

Panorama Christian School
　33981 YUCAIPA BLVD　92399
Yucaipa Christian ES
　34784 YUCAIPA BLVD　92399

Yucca Valley, San Bernardino Co., Pop. Code 5
Morongo USD
Supt. – See Twentynine Palms
La Contenta JHS
　7050 LA CONTENTA ROAD　92284
　Kathleen Croy, prin.
Yucca Mesa ES, P O BOX 1779　92286
　Beverly Willard, prin.
ES, 7601 HOPI TRAIL　92284 – Char Allen, prin.

Zenia, Trinity Co.
Southern Trinity JUSD
Supt. – See Bridgeville
Hoaglin-Zenia ES　95495 – Lois Hall, prin.

COLORADO

STATE DEPARTMENT OF EDUCATION
State Office Building
201 E. Colfax Ave., Denver 80203
(303) 866-6806

Commissioner of Education	William Randall
Deputy Commissioner	Ray Kilmer
Asst. Commissioner Federal Relations & Instructional Services	Dr. Arvin Blome
Assistant Commissioner Management Services	Dan Stewart
Assistant Commissioner Accountability & Accreditation Services	Arthur Ellis
Assistant Commissioner Library Services	Nancy Bolt

STATE BOARD OF EDUCATION
Dr. Tom Howerton, *Chairperson*   Colorado Springs

COLORADO COMMISSION ON HIGHER EDUCATION
David Longanecker, *Executive Director*   1300 Broadway, Denver   80203

PUBLIC, PRIVATE, AND PAROCHIAL ELEMENTARY SCHOOLS

Agate, Elbert Co., Pop. Code 2
Agate SD 300
Sch. Sys. Enr. Code 1
Supt. – Larry Ranney 80101
S 80101 – Larry Ranney, prin.

Aguilar, Las Animas Co., Pop. Code 3
Aguilar Reorganized SD 6
Sch. Sys. Enr. Code 2
Supt. – Lillian Stanton, P O BOX 567 81020
ES, P O BOX 567 81020 – Joan Crittenden, prin.

Akron, Washington Co., Pop. Code 4
Akron SD R-1
Sch. Sys. Enr. Code 2
Supt. – Delano Arnold, 600 ELM AVE 80720
ES, 251 E 5TH ST 80720 – Charles Johnson, prin.

Alamosa, Alamosa Co., Pop. Code 6
Alamosa SD Re-11J
Sch. Sys. Enr. Code 4
Supt. – Janet Makris, 209 VICTORIA ST   81101
Ortega MS, 1301 MAIN ST 81101
   Timothy Snyder, prin.
Boyd ES, 11TH & HUNT AVE 81101
   Naomi Salazar, prin.
Evans MS, 108 LA VETA AVE 81101
   Waldo Herrera, prin.
Polston ES, 6935 HIGHWAY 17 81101
   Charlotte Bobicki, prin.

Anton, Washington Co.
Arickaree SD R-2
Sch. Sys. Enr. Code 2
Supt. – Ralph Foster, P O BOX 20 80801
Arickaree ES 80801 – Ralph Foster, prin.

Antonito, Conejos Co., Pop. Code 4
South Conejos SD Re-10
Sch. Sys. Enr. Code 3
Supt. – Polinario Lucero, P O BOX 398 81120
Antonito MS, P O BOX 398 81120
   Herman Gallegos, prin.
Guadalupe ES, P O BOX 398 81120
   Angelo Velasquez, prin.

Arvada, Jefferson Co., Pop. Code 8
Jefferson County SD R-1
Supt. – See Golden
Moore JHS, 8455 W 88TH AVE 80005
   Dr. Ken Nakauchi, prin.
Allendale ES, 5900 OAK ST 80004
   Tim Brethauer, prin.
Campbell ES, 6500 OAK ST 80004
   Tom Trembath, prin.
Fitzmorris ES, 6250 INDEPENDENCE ST 80004
   Dorothy Jochim, prin.
Foster ES, 5300 SAULSBURY CT 80002
   Wayne Scantland, prin.
Fremont ES, 11955 W 64TH AVE 80004
   Tom Thorne, prin.
Hackberry Hill ES, 7300 W 76TH AVE 80003
   Ronald Goostree, prin.
Lawrence ES, 5611 ZEPHYR ST 80002
   Merle Jornod, prin.
Little ES, 8448 OTIS DR 80003
   Kent Schnurbusch, prin.
Parr ES, 5800 W 84TH AVE 80003
   James Hixson, prin.

Peck ES, 6495 CARR ST 80004
   Kathryn Frank, prin.
Russell ES, 5150 ALLISON ST 80002
   Michael Cussen, prin.
Secrest ES, 6875 W 64TH AVE 80003
   Richard Markov, prin.
Sierra ES, 7751 OAK ST 80005
   Jacquelin Medina, prin.
Stott ES, 6600 YANK WAY 80004
   Mary Schaefer, prin.
Swanson ES, 6055 W 68TH AVE 80003
   Louise Colvert, prin.
Thompson ES, 7750 HARLAN ST 80003
   B. J. Meadows, prin.
Vanderhoof ES, 7840 CARR DR 80005
   Anne Barr, prin.
Warder ES, 7840 CARR DR 80005
   James Cramer, prin.
Weber ES, 8725 W 81ST PL 80005
   Jean Scharfenberg, prin.

Westminster SD 50
Supt. – See Westminster
Tennyson Knolls ES, 6330 TENNYSON ST 80003
   Jan Riess, prin.

Arvada Christian School
   11706 W 82ND AVE 80005
Jesus Center School, 6210 WARD ROAD 80004
Maranatha Christian Center, 7180 OAK ST 80004
St. Anne School, 7320 GRANT PL 80002

Aspen, Pitkin Co., Pop. Code 4
Aspen SD 1
Sch. Sys. Enr. Code 3
Supt. – Frank Betts, P O BOX 300 81612
MS, P O BOX 300 81612 – Betsy Hill, prin.
ES, P O BOX 300 81612 – Barbara Tarbet, prin.

Aspen Country Day School, P O BOX 2466 81612

Ault, Weld Co., Pop. Code 3
Ault-Highland SD Re-9
Sch. Sys. Enr. Code 3
Supt. – Kenneth Frisbie, P O BOX 68 80610
Highland JHS, P O BOX 68 80610
   David Faulkner, prin.
Highland MS, P O BOX 68 80610
   Dave Faulkner, prin.
Other Schools – See Pierce

Aurora, Arapahoe Co., Pop. Code 8
Aurora SD 28J
Sch. Sys. Enr. Code 8
Supt. – Dr. Victor Ross, 1085 PEORIA ST 80011
Aurora Hills MS, 1009 S UVALDA ST 80012
   Dr. Cecil Matthews, prin.
Columbia MS, 17600 E COLUMBIA AVE 80013
   Ronald Hultquist, prin.
East MS, 1275 FRASER ST 80011
   Harold Pyper, prin.
Mrachek MS, 1955 S TELLURIDE ST 80013
   Dr. Nancy Pokorny, prin.
North MS, 12095 MONTVIEW BLVD 80010
   Richard Rusak, prin.
South MS, 12310 E PARKVIEW DRIVE 80011
   Dr. Dan Colvin, prin.
West MS, 10100 E 13TH AVE 80010
   John Basham, prin.

Altura ES, 1650 ALTURA BLVD 80011
   Norman Maki, prin.
Arkansas ES, 17301 E ARKANSAS AVE 80017
   Jerry Lemons, prin.
Boston PS, 1365 BOSTON ST 80010
   Rosalee Pleis, prin.
Century ES, 2500 S GRANBY WAY 80014
   Anita Jarks, prin.
Crawford ES, 1600 FLORENCE ST 80010
   Vern Martin, prin.
Dalton ES, 17401 E DARTMOUTH AVE 80013
   Dianne Dugan, prin.
Dartmouth ES, 3050 S LAREDO 80013
   Barbara Larsen, prin.
Elkhart ES, 1020 EAGLE ST 80011
   John Ahlenius, prin.
Fulton ES, 755 FULTON 80010
   Richard Wells, prin.
Iowa ES, 16701 E IOWA AVE 80017
   Ann Willis, prin.
Jamaica PS, 800 JAMAICA ST 80010
   Rosalee Pleis, prin.
Jewell ES, 14601 E JEWELL AVE 80012
   Helen O'Malley, prin.
Kenton ES, 1255 KENTON ST 80010
   Ann Thomas, prin.
Knoll ES, 12455 E 2ND AVE 80011
   Suzanne Johnson, prin.
Lansing ES, 551 LANSING ST 80010
   Barbara Weaver, prin.
Laredo ES, 1350 LAREDO ST 80011
   Sarah Kelzenberg, prin.
Miller ES, 1701 ESPANA 80011
   Jack Nelson, prin.
Montview ES, 2055 MOLINE ST 80010
   Deborah Backus, prin.
Paris ES, 1635 PARIS ST 80010
   Suzanne Johnson, prin.
Park Lane ES, 13001 E 30TH AVE 80011
   Judith Griswold, prin.
Sable ES, 2601 SABLE BLVD 80011
   Lawrence Mudron, prin.
Side Creek ES, 19191 E ILLIF PLACE 80017
   Helen Pryor, prin.
Sixth Avenue ES, 560 VAUGHN ST 80011
   John Dale, prin.
Tollgate ES, 701 S KALISPELL WAY 80017
   Al Curtis, prin.
Vassar ES, 18101 E VASSAR AVE 80013
   Mary Skitt, prin.
Vaughn ES, 1155 VAUGHN AVE 80010
   David Prok, prin.
Virginia Center ES, 395 S TROYN AVE 80012
   Ann Craig, prin.
Wheeling ES, 472 S WHEELING 80012
   Wilbur Smith, prin.
Yale ES, 16001 E YALE AVE 80013
   Barbara Zahn, prin.

Cherry Creek SD 5
Supt. – See Englewood
Horizon MS, 3961 S RESERVOIR ROAD 80013
   Fred Henderson, prin.
Laredo MS, 5000 S LAREDO ST 80015
   Dr. Galen Crowder, prin.
Prairie MS, 12600 E JEWELL AVE 80012
   Catherine Canny, prin.

Arrowhead ES, 19100 E BATES AVE 80013
Susan Henderson, prin.
Cimarron ES, 17373 E LEHIGH PL 80013
Jim McDermott, prin.
Creekside ES, 19993 E LONG AVE 80016
Nancy Flaming, prin.
Eastridge Community ES
11777 E WESLEY AVE 80014
Henry Taylor, prin.
Independence ES, 4700 S MEMPHIS ST 80015
Michael Duff, prin.
Indian Ridge ES, 16501 E PROGRESS DR 80015
Orville Turner, prin.
Meadow Point ES, 17901 E GRAND AVE 80015
Bob Villarreal, prin.
Mission Viejo ES, 3855 S ALICIA PKWY 80013
Thomas Balakas, prin.
Polton Community ES
2985 S OAKLAND ST 80014
David Livingston, prin.
Ponderosa ES, 1885 S LIMA ST 80012
Jean Capillupo, prin.
Sagebrush ES, 14700 E TEMPLE PL 80015
Douglas Gowler, prin.
Summit ES, 18201 E QUINCY AVE 80015
George Mansfield, prin.
Sunrise ES, 4050 S GENOA WAY 80013
Linda Markus, prin.
Timberline ES, 5500 S KILLARNEY ST 80015
Gary Steck, prin.
Trails West ES, 5400 S WACO ST 80015
Jerome Kalamen, prin.
Village East Community ES
1433 S OAKLAND ST 80012 – Al Lemieux, prin.

Christian Way ES
14700 E MISSISSIPPI AVE 80012
Hope Lutheran ES, 1345 MACON ST 80010
St. Pius Tenth ES, 13680 E 14TH PL 80011
St. Therese School, 1200 KENTON ST 80010

Avon, Eagle Co., Pop. Code 3
Eagle County SD Re-50(J)
Supt. – See Eagle
Meadow Mountain PS, P O BOX 5810 81620
Ann Sanders, prin.

Avondale, Pueblo Co., Pop. Code 5
Pueblo County Rural SD 70
Supt. – See Pueblo
ES, 213 HWY 50 E 81022 – Kathy Mauro, prin.

Bailey, Park Co., Pop. Code 2
Platte Canyon SD 1
Sch. Sys. Enr. Code 4
Supt. – Richard Laughlin, P O BOX 295 80421
Fitzsimmons MS, P O BOX 295 80421
Marilyn Morris, prin.
Deer Creek ES, P O BOX 295 80421
Bob Pritchett, prin.

Basalt, Garfield Co., Pop. Code 2
Roaring Fork SD Re-1J
Supt. – See Glenwood Springs
ES, P O BOX Z 81621 – Richard Hayes, prin.

Bayfield, La Plata Co., Pop. Code 2
Bayfield SD 10-Jt-R
Sch. Sys. Enr. Code 3
Supt. – Richard Heger, P O BOX 258 81122
MS, P O BOX 258 81122 – Betty Kutzleb, prin.
ES, P O BOX 258 81122 – Donald Magill, prin.

Bellvue, Larimer Co., Pop. Code 2
Poudre SD R-1
Supt. – See Fort Collins
Poudre Canyon ES
POUDRE CANYON ROUTE 80512
Mary Kay Sommers, prin.
Stove Prairie ES 80512 – Mary Kay Sommers, prin.

Bennett, Adams Co., Pop. Code 3
Bennett SD 29J
Sch. Sys. Enr. Code 3
Supt. – James Lathrop, P O BOX 68 80102
MS, P O BOX 68 80102 – Paul Read, prin.
ES, P O BOX 68 80102 – Mark Collins, prin.

Berthoud, Larimer Co., Pop. Code 4
Thompson SD R-2J
Supt. – See Loveland
Turner MS, 950 MASSACHUSETTS 80513
Dennis Kuehl, prin.
ES, P O BOX 115 80513 – William Rigsby, prin.
Stockwell ES, 5TH ST & INDIANA AVE 80513
Charles Schoonover, prin.

Bethune, Kit Carson Co., Pop. Code 1
Bethune SD R-5
Sch. Sys. Enr. Code 2
Supt. – James M. Poole, P O BOX 43 80805
S, P O BOX 43 80805 – James Poole, prin.

Beulah, Pueblo Co., Pop. Code 2
Pueblo County Rural SD 70
Supt. – See Pueblo
MS, RURAL ROUTE 01 BOX 149A 81023
Mike Gregorich, prin.
ES, RURAL ROUTE 01 BOX 149A 81023
Mike Gregorich, prin.

Black Hawk, Gilpin Co., Pop. Code 2
Gilpin County SD Re-1
Sch. Sys. Enr. Code 2
Supt. – Paul Coleman
10595 HIGHWAY 119 80422

Gilpin County S, 10595 HIGHWAY 119 80422
John Weishaar, prin.

Blanca, Costilla Co., Pop. Code 2
Sierra Grande SD R-30
Sch. Sys. Enr. Code 2
Supt. – John Roybal
RURAL ROUTE 01 BOX 15 81123
Sierra Grande S
RURAL ROUTE 01 BOX 15 81123
Lauren Bussey, prin.

Boulder, Boulder Co., Pop. Code 8
Boulder Valley SD Re-2(J)
Sch. Sys. Enr. Code 7
Supt. – Dr. James Hager, P O BOX 9011 80301
Aurora 7 ES, 3995 AURORA AVE 80303
Eugene Rodriquez, prin.
Bear Creek ES, 2500 TABLE MESA DR 80303
John Ferree, prin.
Columbine ES, 3130 REPPLIER ST 80302
Jack Kaufman, prin.
Crest View ES, 1879 SUMAC AVE 80302
Ed Schriner, prin.
Douglass ES, 840 75TH ST 80303
Marilyn Helpenstell, prin.
Eisenhower ES, 1220 EISENHOWER DR 80303
Pamela Hurt, prin.
Flatirons ES, 1150 7TH ST 80302
Robert Rea, prin.
Foothill ES, 1001 HAWTHORN AVE 80302
Kathy Berman, prin.
Gold Hill ES, GOLD HILL HCR 80302
Betsey Krill, prin.
Heatherwood ES, 7750 CONCORD DR 80301
Craig Christopher, prin.
Majestic Heights ES, 4655 HANOVER AVE 80303
John Konx, prin.
Mapleton ES, 840 MAPLETON AVE 80302
Betsey Krill, prin.
Martin Park ES, 3740 MARTIN DR 80303
Phyillis Perry, prin.
Mesa ES, 1575 LEHIGH ST 80303
Carolyn Topping, prin.
University Hill ES, 956 16TH ST 80302
Naomi Grothjan, prin.
Whittier ES, 2008 PINE ST 80302
Barbara Spriggs, prin.
Other Schools – See Broomfield, Jamestown,
Lafayette, Louisville, Nederland

Jarrow Montessori School
3900 ORANGE COURT 80302
Sacred Heart ES, 1317 MAPLETON AVE 80302

Branson, Las Animas Co., Pop. Code 1
Branson Reorganized SD 82
Sch. Sys. Enr. Code 1
Supt. – James Matthews 81027
ES, P O BOX 128 81027 – James Matthews, prin.

Breckenridge, Summit Co., Pop. Code 3
Summit SD Re-1
Supt. – See Frisco
ES, P O BOX 1213 80424 – Jack Hart, prin.

Briggsdale, Weld Co., Pop. Code 2
Briggsdale SD Re-10J
Sch. Sys. Enr. Code 2
Supt. – Richard Hodgson, P O BOX 125 80611
ES, P O BOX 125 80611 – Richard Hodgson, prin.

Brighton, Adams Co., Pop. Code 6
Brighton SD 27J
Sch. Sys. Enr. Code 5
Supt. – John Meyer, 630 S 8TH AVE 80601
Overland Trail MS, 445 N 19TH AVE 80601
Roger Quist, prin.
Vikan MS, 879 JESSUP ST 80601 – G. Neely, prin.
North ES, 525 E BRIDGE ST 80601
Donna Jones, prin.
Northeast ES, 1605 E LONGS PEAK ST 80601
Neil Fleischauer, prin.
South ES, 305 S 5TH AVE 80601
William Sarchet, prin.
Southeast ES, 1690 SKEEL ST 80601
Carol Sarchet, prin.
Other Schools – See Henderson

Zion Lutheran School, 1400 SKEEL ST 80601

Broomfield, Boulder Co., Pop. Code 6
Boulder Valley SD Re-2(J)
Supt. – See Boulder
Broomfield Heights MS, 1555 DAPHNE ST 80020
Walt Grebing, prin.
Birch ES, 10TH & BIRCH ST 80020
Bill Swartsfager, prin.
Emerald ES, 755 ELMHURST PL 80020
John Ortner, prin.
Kohl ES, 10TH & KOHL ST 80020
Woodrow Spriggs, prin.

Jefferson County SD R-1
Supt. – See Golden
Adams ES, 9955 YARROW ST 80020
Cynthia Stevenson, prin.
Juchem ES, 10951 N HARLAN ST 80020
Heather Clifton, prin.
Lukas ES, 9650 W 97TH AVE 80020
Gretchen Vasquez, prin.
Witt ES, 10255 W 104TH DR 80020
Fred Chaffe, prin.

Northglenn-Thornton SD 12
Supt. – See Northglenn

Centennial ES, 13200 WESTLAKE DR 80020
D. Viers, prin.
Mountain View ES, 12401 PERRY ST 80020
George Moyer, prin.

Beautiful Savior Lutheran School
P O BOX 8 80020
Nativity of Our Lord School
900 W MIDWAY BLVD 80020

Brush, Morgan Co., Pop. Code 5
Brush SD Re-2(J)
Sch. Sys. Enr. Code 4
Supt. – William Weatherill, P O BOX 585 80723
MS, P O BOX 585 80723 – John Gotto, prin.
Central MS, P O BOX 585 80723
Ervin Hammond, prin.
Thomson ES, P O BOX 585 80723
Warren Lashor, prin.

Buena Vista, Chaffee Co., Pop. Code 4
Buena Vista SD R-31
Sch. Sys. Enr. Code 3
Supt. – D. Smith, P O BOX O 81211
McGinnis MS, P O BOX O 81211
Edd Brown, prin.
Avery ES, P O BOX O 81211 – Warren Witler, prin.

Burlington, Kit Carson Co., Pop. Code 5
Burlington SD Re-6J
Sch. Sys. Enr. Code 3
Supt. – Harvey Billington
MS 80807 – Ray Rhoades, prin.
ES 80807 – Eric Talla, prin.

Byers, Arapahoe Co., Pop. Code 2
Byers SD 32J
Sch. Sys. Enr. Code 2
Supt. – George Sauter, P O BOX 420 80103
ES, P O BOX 420 80103
Michael Grandstaff, prin.

Calhan, El Paso Co., Pop. Code 2
Calhan SD R-J1
Sch. Sys. Enr. Code 2
Supt. – Dennis Disario, P O BOX 21 80808
ES, 800 BULLDOG DR 80808
Ricardo Concha, prin.

Ellicott SD 22
Sch. Sys. Enr. Code 3
Supt. – Lionel Robertson
RURAL ROUTE 02 80808
Ellicott ES, RURAL ROUTE 02 80808
Robert Danielson, prin.

Campo, Baca Co., Pop. Code 2
Campo SD Re-6
Sch. Sys. Enr. Code 1
Supt. – Lyle Bliss, P O BOX 70 81029
ES, P O BOX 70 81029 – Lyle Bliss, prin.

Canon City, Fremont Co., Pop. Code 6
Canon City SD Re-1
Sch. Sys. Enr. Code 5
Supt. – Dr. W. David Whitehead
1104 ROYAL GORGE BLVD 81212
MS, 12TH & MAIN ST 81212
Keith Thomas, prin.
Harrison ES, 485 N COTTONWOOD AVE 81212
Tom Hinkle, prin.
Lincoln ES, 420 MYRTLE AVE 81212
Kathryn Kulsick, prin.
McKinley ES, 1240 MCKINLEY ST 81212
Gary Wilson, prin.
Skyline ES, 2855 N 9TH K ST 81212
Conrad Miller, prin.
Washington ES, N 9TH & FLORAL ST 81212
Mike Schwab, prin.

Capulin, Conejos Co.
North Conejos SD Re-1J
Supt. – See La Jara
Centauri JHS, P O BOX 67 81124
La Mont Morgan, prin.

Carbondale, Garfield Co., Pop. Code 3
Roaring Fork SD Re-1J
Supt. – See Glenwood Springs
MS, 455 S 3RD ST 81623 – Tom Brown, prin.
ES, P O BOX 188 81623 – James Phillips, prin.

Castle Rock, Douglas Co., Pop. Code 4
Douglas County SD Re-1(J)
Sch. Sys. Enr. Code 7
Supt. – Dr. Richard O'Connell
131 WILCOX ST 80104
ES, 1103 CANYON DR 80104
Clark Milsom, prin.
Douglas ES 15, 1103 CANON DR 80104
Jo Ann McCall, prin.
South Street ES, 1100 SOUTH ST 80104
Raymond Kinter, prin.
Other Schools – See Franktown, Highlands Ranch,
Larkspur, Littleton, Parker, Sedalia

Cedaredge, Delta Co., Pop. Code 3
Delta County SD 50 (J)
Supt. – See Delta
MS, RURAL ROUTE 02 BOX 1 81413
Richard Hanson, prin.
ES, 230 NW CEDAR AVE 81413
Fred Beard, prin.

Center, Saguache Co., Pop. Code 4
Center SD 26Jt
Sch. Sys. Enr. Code 3
Supt. – Philip Varoz, P O BOX 730 81125

JHS, P O BOX 730 81125 – Richard Varrati, prin.
ES, P O BOX 730 81125 – Fred Cordova, prin.

Cheraw, Otero Co., Pop. Code 2
Cheraw SD 31
Sch. Sys. Enr. Code 2
Supt. – Joe Howard 81030
MS 81030 – Joe Howard, prin.
ES 81030 – Joe Howard, prin.

Cheyenne Wells, Cheyenne Co., Pop. Code 3
Cheyenne County SD RE-5
Sch. Sys. Enr. Code 2
Supt. – Haim Calderon, P O BOX 577 80810
MS, P O BOX 577 80810 – Herman Martin, prin.
Cheyenne Wells PS, P O BOX 577 80810
Herman Martin, prin.

Clifton, Mesa Co., Pop. Code 7
Mesa County Valley SD 51
Supt. – See Grand Junction
Mt. Garfield MS, 3476 HIGHWAY 24 81520
Gerald Reynolds, prin.
ES, 3276 F ROAD 81520 – Wallace Gross, prin.

Collbran, Mesa Co., Pop. Code 2
Plateau Valley SD 50
Sch. Sys. Enr. Code 2
Supt. – Lester Mundy, P O BOX 425 81624
Plateau Valley ES
RURAL ROUTE 01 BOX 26 81624
Lester Mundy, prin.

Colorado City, Pueblo Co., Pop. Code 2
Pueblo County Rural SD 70
Supt. – See Pueblo
Craver MS, P O BOX 267 81019
William Bregar, prin.

Colorado Springs, El Paso Co., Pop. Code 9
Academy SD 20
Sch. Sys. Enr. Code 6
Supt. – Dr. Thomas S. Crawford
7610 N UNION BLVD 80920
Challenger MS, 10215 LEXINGTON DRIVE 80908
Donald Joiner, prin.
Eagleview MS, 1325 VINDICATOR DRIVE 80919
Dominic Mollica, prin.
Timberview MS, 8680 SCARBOROUGH DR 80920
William Shell, prin.
Foothills ES, 825 ALLEGHENY DR 80919
Linda Macey, prin.
Frontier ES, 3755 MEADOW RIDGE DR 80920
Dr. Caroline Jackson, prin.
High Plains ES, 2248 VINTAGE DR 80920
Gail Smartt, prin.
Mountain View ES, 9495 OTERO AVE 80920
Judith Casey, prin.
Pioneer ES, 3663 WOODLAND HILLS DR 80918
Suzanne Loughran, prin.
Rockrimmon ES, 194 MIKADO DR W 80919
Sharon DeWeese, prin.
Wolford ES, 13710 BLACK FOREST ROAD 80908
Kay Frunzi, prin.
Woodmen ES, 1130 W WOODMEN ROAD 80919
Lew Davis, prin.
Other Schools – See USAF Academy

Cheyenne Mountain SD 12
Sch. Sys. Enr. Code 4
Supt. – Dr. Loren Thompson
1118 W CHEYENNE ROAD 80906
Broadmoor ES, MARLAND & POURTALES 80906
Robert Jones, prin.
Canon ES, 1201 W CHEYENNE ROAD 80906
Sylvia Nolte, prin.
Cheyenne Mountain ES
5250 FARTHING DR 80906 – Steven Benson, prin.
Skyway Park ES, 1100 MERCURY DR 80906
David Starritt, prin.

Colorado Springs SD 11
Sch. Sys. Enr. Code 8
Supt. – Kenneth Burnley
1115 N EL PASO ST 80903
Adams ES, 2101 MANITOBA DR 80910
Newgene Ray, prin.
Audubon ES, 2400 E VAN BUREN ST 80909
Douglas Christensen, prin.
Bates ES, 702 CRAGMOR ROAD 80907
John O'Brien, prin.
Bristol ES, 890 N WALNUT ST 80905
Philip Frye, prin.
Buena Vista ES, 1620 W BIJOU ST 80904
Alan Rasmussen, prin.
Carver ES, 4740 ARTISTIC CIR 80917
Rosemary Emerick, prin.
Chipeta ES, 2340 RAMSGATE TERRACE 80919
John Kerr, prin.
Columbia ES, 835 E SAINT VRAIN ST 80903
Nadyne Guzman, prin.
Edison ES, 3125 N HANCOCK AVE 80907
Richard Osika, prin.
Fremont ES, 5110 EL CAMINO DR 80918
Blaine Peterson, prin.
Grant ES, 3215 WESTWOOD BLVD 80918
Gary Beard, prin.
Henry ES, 1310 LEHMBERG BLVD 80915
Dorothy Candea, prin.
Howbert ES, 1023 N 31ST ST 80904
Robert McAllister, prin.
Hunt ES, 917 E MORENO AVE 80903
Richard Gallegos, prin.
Ivywild ES, 1604 S CASCADE AVE 80906
Ida Liebert, prin.

Jackson ES, 4340 EDWINSTOWE AVE 80907
Kay Branine, prin.
Jefferson ES, 1801 HOWARD AVE 80909
Terrance Linnan, prin.
Keller ES, 3730 MONTEBELLO DR W 80918
Tim Callahan, prin.
King ES, 6110 SAPPORO DR 80918
Alfredo Nevarez, prin.
Lincoln ES, 2727 N CASCADE AVE 80907
Joseph Thrutchley, prin.
Longfellow ES, 3302 MAIZELAND ROAD 80909
Diane Walden, prin.
Madison ES, 4120 CONSTITUTION AVE 80909
Sherry Baker, prin.
Martinez ES, 6450 VICKERS DR 80919
Ron Sebben, prin.
Midland ES, 2110 BROADWAY 80904
Elizabeth Johnson, prin.
Monroe ES, 15 S CHELTON RD 80910
Sherry Ramirez, prin.
Palmer ES, 1921 E YAMPA ST 80909
Karen Ballek, prin.
Penrose ES, 4285 NONCHALANT CIR S 80917
John Griego, prin.
Pike ES, 2510 N CHESTNUT ST 80907
Charles Hideman, prin.
Rogers ES, 110 S CIRCLE DR 80910
Tim Conner, prin.
Roosevelt ES, 205 BYRON DR 80910
James Barron, prin.
Rudy ES, 5370 CRACKER BARREL CIR 80917
Thomas Dairy, prin.
Steele ES, 1720 N WEBER ST 80907
Jean Keeley, prin.
Stratton ES, 2460 PASEO ROAD 80907
Kristina Post, prin.
Taylor ES, 900 E BUENA VENTURA ST 80907
Areatha Clair, prin.
Twain ES, 3402 E SAN MIGUEL ST 80909
James Pierson, prin.
Washington ES, 924 W PIKES PEAK AVE 80905
Robbie Hardaway, prin.
Whittier ES, 2904 W KIOWA ST 80904
Kenneth Bailey, prin.
Wilson ES, 1409 DE REAMER CIR 80915
Evelyn Lucero, prin.

Falcon SD 49
Supt. – See Peyton
Evans ES, 1675 WINNEBAGO ROAD 80915
Jon Maroon, prin.
Stetson ES, 4970 JEDEDIAH SMITH RD 80922
Shirley Trees, prin.

Hanover SD 28
Sch. Sys. Enr. Code 1
Supt. – Joe Huber
17050 S PEYTON HIGHWAY 80909
Hanover S, 17050 S PEYTON HIGHWAY 80909
Joe Huber, prin.

Harrison SD 2
Sch. Sys. Enr. Code 6
Supt. – Dr. Harold Terry
1060 HARRISON ROAD 80906
Carmel MS, 1740 PEPPERWOOD DRIVE 80910
Richard Price, prin.
Gorman MS, 2883 S CIRCLE DRIVE 80906
Ken Jackson, prin.
Panorama MS, 2145 S CHELTON ROAD 80916
Criss Tausan, prin.
Bricker ES, 4880 DOVER PLACE 80916
Paul Jackson, prin.
Centennial ES, 1860 S CHELTON RD 80910
Gerry Coufal, prin.
Chamberlin ES, 2400 SLATER AVE 80906
Sal Turner, prin.
Giberson ES, 2880 FERBER DR 80916
James Ensign, prin.
Monterey ES, 2311 MONTEREY ROAD 80910
Anne O'Rourke, prin.
Oak Creek ES, 3333 W OAK CREEK DR 80906
Dieter Rein, prin.
Otero ES, 1650 CHARMWOOD DR 80906
Lee Cope, prin.
Pikes Peak ES, 1520 VERDE DR 80910
Gary Langenhuizen, prin.
Stratmoor Hills ES, 200 LOOMIS AVE 80906
Charles Haitz, prin.
Stratton Meadows ES, 605 WARREN AVE 80906
Sue Harrison, prin.
Turman ES, 3245 SPRINGRITE DR 80916
Mary Ellen Burciago, prin.
Wildflower ES, 1160 KEITH DR 80916
Brooks Nelson, prin.

Widefield SD 3
Sch. Sys. Enr. Code 6
Supt. – Dr. Leonard Bartel, 1820 MAIN ST 80911
French ES, 5225 ALTURAS DR 80911
William Mullane, prin.
King ES, 6910 DEFOE AVE 80911
Charlene Seaney, prin.
North ES, 209 LETA DR 80911
Donald Castle, prin.
Pinello ES, 2515 CODY DR 80911
Elizabeth Salvo, prin.
Sunrise ES, 7070 GRAND VALLEY DR 80911
David Fussell, prin.
Talbott ES, DEAN & FORDHAM STS 80911
James Goodwin, prin.
Venetucci ES, 405 WILLIS DR 80911
Caesar Gutierrez, prin.
Webster ES, 445 JERSEY LN 80911
James Yorke, prin.

Widefield ES, 509 WIDEFIELD DR 80911
Kathlyn Hutchison, prin.

Colorado Springs Christian School
301 AUSTIN BLUFFS PARKWAY 80907
Colorado Springs School
21 BROADMOOR AVE 80906
Hilltop Christian School
6915 PALMER PARK BLVD 80915
Corpus Christie School
2410 N CASCADE AVE 80907
Divine Redeemer ES, 901 N LOGAN AVE 80909
Evangelical Christian Academy
2511 N LOGAN AVE 80907
Holy Trinity School, 3115 LARKSPUR DR 80907
Immanuel Lutheran School
828 E PIKES PEAK AVE 80903
Pauline Memorial ES, 1601 MESA AVE 80906
Redeemer Luther School
2221 N WAHSATCH AVE 80907

Commerce City, Adams Co., Pop. Code 7
Adams County SD 14
Sch. Sys. Enr. Code 6
Supt. – Dr. Richard Weber
4720 E 69TH AVE 80022
Adams City MS, 4451 E 72ND AVE 80022
Karen Lewis, prin.
Kearney MS, 6160 KEARNEY ST 80022
J. Keith Lusk, prin.
Alsup ES, 7101 BIRCH ST 80022
Ernestine Garcia, prin.
Central ES, 6450 HOLLY ST 80022
Michael Cummings, prin.
Dupont ES, 7970 KIMBERLY ST 80022
Thoams Sandhei, prin.
Hanson ES, 7133 E 73RD AVE 80022
Cathleen Braiman, prin.
Kemp ES, 6775 ONEIDA ST 80022
Harvey Hoffman, prin.
Monaco ES, 7631 MONACO ST 80022
Elaine Bramow, prin.
Rose Hill ES, 6900 E 58TH AVE 80022
Daniel Montoya, prin.

Conifer, Jefferson Co., Pop. Code 2
Jefferson County SD R-1
Supt. – See Golden
West Jefferson ES, 26501 BARKLEY ROAD 80433
Cynthia Smrz, prin.

Cortez, Montezuma Co., Pop. Code 6
Montezuma-Cortez SD Re-1
Sch. Sys. Enr. Code 5
Supt. – Roy Johnson, P O BOX R 81321
JHS, P O BOX R 81321 – Roger Braaten, prin.
Battle Rock ES, P O BOX R 81321
Bradley Wayt, prin.
Downey ES, P O BOX R 81321
Martin Hopkins, prin.
Kemper ES, P O BOX R 81321
Eugene Sparks, prin.
Lakeview ES, P O BOX R 81321
Victor Bruce, prin.
Lewis-Arriola ES, P O BOX R 81321
Martin Hopkins, prin.
Manaugh ES, P O BOX R 81321
Victor Bruce, prin.
Mesa ES, P O BOX R 81321 – Bradley Wayt, prin.
Pleasant View ES, P O BOX R 81321
Eugene Sparks, prin.

Cotopaxi, Fremont Co., Pop. Code 2
Cotopaxi SD Re-3
Sch. Sys. Enr. Code 2
Supt. – Larry Coleman, P O BOX 385 81223
ES, P O BOX 385 81223 – Goeffrey Gerk, prin.

Craig, Moffat Co., Pop. Code 5
Moffat County SD Re-1
Sch. Sys. Enr. Code 5
Supt. – Dr. Charles Grove, 775 YAMPA AVE 81625
MS, 915 YAMPA AVE 81625 – F. Little, prin.
East ES, 600 TEXAS AVE 81625
James Covalt, prin.
Powder Wash ES, POWDER WASH CAMP 81625
Oliver Phillips, prin.
Ridgview ES, 655 WESTRIDGE ROAD 81625
Paul Duzenack, prin.
Sunset ES, 800 W 7TH ST 81625
Carl Rohnke, prin.
Other Schools – See Dinosaur, Maybell

Crawford, Delta Co., Pop. Code 2
Delta County SD 50 (J)
Supt. – See Delta
ES, P O BOX 98 81415 – Gerry Neill, prin.

Creede, Mineral Co., Pop. Code 3
Creede Cons. SD 1
Sch. Sys. Enr. Code 2
Supt. – Lonnie Rogers, P O BOX 429 81130
ES, P O BOX 429 81130 – Edward Skroch, prin.

Crested Butte, Gunnison Co., Pop. Code 3
Gunnison Watershed SD Re-1J
Supt. – See Gunnison
ES 81224 – Susan Lebow, prin.

Cripple Creek, Teller Co., Pop. Code 2
Cripple Creek-Victor SD Re-1
Sch. Sys. Enr. Code 2
Supt. – R. Clifford Young, P O BOX 97 80813
Cripple Creek-Victor ES, P O BOX 97 80813
Don McGill, prin.

Crowley, Crowley Co., Pop. Code 2
Crowley County SD Re-1-J
Supt. – See Ordway
Crowley County MS, P O BOX 338 81033
  Gary Frickell, prin.

De Beque, Mesa Co., Pop. Code 2
De Beque SD 49Jt
Sch. Sys. Enr. Code 1
Supt. – Ray Griffith, P O BOX 88 81630
ES, P O BOX 88 81630 – Ray Griffith, prin.

Deer Trail, Arapahoe Co., Pop. Code 2
Deer Trail SD 26J
Sch. Sys. Enr. Code 2
Supt. – Stephen Beaber, P O BOX 129 80105
ES, P O BOX 129 80105 – Stephen Beaber, prin.

Del Norte, Rio Grande Co., Pop. Code 4
Del Norte SD C7
Sch. Sys. Enr. Code 3
Supt. – Marlin Janas, P O BOX 159 81132
MS, P O BOX 159 81132 – Charles Moore, prin.
Mesa ES, P O BOX 159 81132 – (—), prin.
Underwood MS, P O BOX 159 81132
  Larry Slade, prin.

Delta, Delta Co., Pop. Code 5
Delta County SD 50 (J)
Sch. Sys. Enr. Code 5
Supt. – Laddie Livingston, 765 2075 ROAD 81416
MS, 822 GRAND AVE 81416 – Earle Wise, prin.
Garnet Mesa ES, 600 A ST 81416
  Jay Alsdorf, prin.
Lincoln ES, 1050 HASTINGS ST 81416
  Fred Zamarripa, prin.
Other Schools – See Cedaredge, Crawford, Hotchkiss, Paonia

Denver, Denver Co., Pop. Code 11
Cherry Creek SD 5
Supt. – See Englewood
Cunningham ES, 9659 E MISSISSIPPI AVE 80231
  James Brickey, prin.
Holly Hills ES, 6161 E CORNELL AVE 80222
  Don Waldera, prin.

Denver County SD 1
Sch. Sys. Enr. Code 8
Supt. – Richard Koeppe, 900 GRANT ST 80203
Baker MS, 574 W 6TH AVE 80204
  George Diedrich, prin.
Cole MS, 3240 HUMBOLDT ST 80205
  Barbara Batey, prin.
Gove MS, 4050 E 14TH AVE 80220
  Marjorie Noel, prin.
Grant MS, 1751 S WASHINGTON ST 80210
  Patricia De Leon, prin.
Hamilton MS, 8600 E DARTMOUTH AVE 80231
  Glenn Leyden, prin.
Henry MS, 3005 S GOLDEN WAY 80227
  Bill Oller, prin.
Hill MS, 451 CLERMONT ST 80220
  Farrell Howell, prin.
Kepner MS, 911 S HAZEL COURT 80219
  Marjorie Tepper, prin.
King MS, 19535 E 46TH AVE 80249
  Nadine Fuller, prin.
Kunsmiller MS, 2250 S QUITMAN WAY 80219
  Moises Martinez, prin.
Lake MS, 1820 LOWELL BLVD 80204
  Willard Smith, prin.
Mann MS, 4130 NAVAJO ST 80211
  Martha Guevara, prin.
Merrill MS, 1551 S MONROE ST 80210
  John Wilson, prin.
Morey MS, 840 E 14TH AVE 80218
  Rhoda Imhoff, prin.
Place MS
  7125 CHERRY CREEK NORTH DR 80224
  Wanda Taylor, prin.
Rishel MS, 451 S TEJON ST 80223
  Irene Martinez-Jordan, prin.
Skinner MS, 3435 W 40TH AVE 80211
  Mikyo Matsuura, prin.
Smiley MS, 2540 HOLLY ST 80207
  Cheryl Betz, prin.
Amesse ES, 5440 SCRANTON ST 80239
  Alberta Alston, prin.
Asbury ES, 1320 E ASBURY AVE 80210
  Janet Jackson, prin.
Ashley ES, 1914 SYRACUSE ST 80220
  Evelyn Bryant, prin.
Barnum ES, 85 HOOKER ST 80219
  Donald Wilson, prin.
Barrett ES, 2900 RICHARD ALLEN CT 80205
  Julia Hazzard, prin.
Beach Court ES, 4950 BEACH CT 80221
  Phillip Fresquez, prin.
Bradley MS, 3051 S ELM ST 80222
  Patricia Castro, prin.
Bromwell ES, 2500 E 4TH AVE 80206
  Ned Modica, prin.
Brown ES, 2550 LOWELL BLVD 80211
  Alberto Corrales, prin.
Bryant-Webster ES, 3635 QUIVAS ST 80211
  Mary Strandburg, prin.
Carson ES, 5420 E 1ST AVE 80220
  Carleane English, prin.
Centennial ES, 4665 RALEIGH ST 80212
  Gerald Gilmore, prin.
Cheltenham ES, 1580 JULIAN ST 80204
  Patricia Carpio, prin.
Colfax ES, 1526 TENNYSON ST 80204
  Mary Romero, prin.

College View ES, 2680 S DECATUR ST 80219
  Zelma Ray, prin.
Columbian ES, 2925 W 40TH AVE 80211
  Rachel Starks, prin.
Columbine MS, 2540 E 29TH AVE 80205
  Wilma Gillespie, prin.
Cory MS, 1550 S STEELE ST 80210
  Ronald Gist, prin.
Cowell ES, 4540 W 10TH AVE 80204
  Gerald Prud'Homme, prin.
Crofton MS, 2409 ARAPAHOE ST 80205
  William Abbey, prin.
Del Pueblo ES, 750 GALAPAGO ST 80204
  Florence Arellano, prin.
Doull ES, 2520 S UTICA ST 80219
  Betty Freeland, prin.
Eagleton ES, 880 HOOKER ST 80204
  John Merz, prin.
Ebert ES, 410 23RD ST 80205 – Abie Duarte, prin.
Edison ES, 3350 QUITMAN ST 80212
  Joyce Martinez, prin.
Ellis ES, 1651 S DAHLIA ST 80222
  Dean Kornelsen, prin.
Fairmont ES, 520 W 3RD AVE 80223
  Mary Sours, prin.
Fairview ES, 2715 W 11TH AVE 80204
  Carol Genera, prin.
Fallis MS, 6700 E VIRGINIA AVE 80224
  H. Sondra Harris, prin.
Force MS, 1550 S WOLFF ST 80219
  Anthony Makowski, prin.
Ford ES, 14500 MAXWELL PL 80239
  Barbara Dwight, prin.
Garden Place ES, 4425 LINCOLN ST 80216
  Joy Wilson, prin.
Gilpin ES, 2949 CALIFORNIA ST 80205
  Betty Germany, prin.
Godsman ES, 2120 W ARKANSAS AVE 80223
  Ben Nuanes, prin.
Goldrick ES, 1050 S JUNI ST 80223
  Arthur McQueary, prin.
Greenlee Met Lab ES, 1150 LIPAN ST 80204
  Evangeline Sena, prin.
Gust ES, 3440 W YALE AVE 80219
  Ann Misun, prin.
Hallett ES, 2950 JASMINE ST 80207
  Hiram Haynes, prin.
Harrington MS, 3230 E 38TH AVE 80205
  Sally Edwards, prin.
Holm MS, 3185 S WILLOW ST 80231
  Patricia Ford, prin.
Johnson ES, 1850 S IRVING ST 80219
  Phillip Miyazawa, prin.
Kaiser ES, 4500 S QUITMAN ST 80236
  James Vandever, prin.
Knapp ES, 500 S UTICA ST 80219
  Doris Burns, prin.
Knight Fundamental MS
  3245 E EXPOSITION AVE 80209
  Nicanor Garcia, prin.
Lincoln ES, 715 S PEARL ST 80209
  Ann Pena, prin.
Marrama ES, 19100 E 40TH AVE 80239
  Maceo Brodnax, prin.
McGlone MS, 4500 CROWN BLVD 80239
  Max Rodriquez, prin.
McKinley-Thatcher ES, 1230 S GRANT ST 80210
  Beverly Gunst, prin.
McMeen MS, 1000 S HOLLY ST 80222
  (—), prin.
Mitchell ES, 1350 E 33RD AVE 80205
  Martha Urioste, prin.
Montclair ES, 1151 NEWPORT ST 80220
  Barbara Baker, prin.
Moore ES, 846 CORONA ST 80218
  Judy Fontius, prin.
Munroe ES, 3440 W VIRGINIA AVE 80219
  Claudia Martinez, prin.
Newlon ES, 361 VRAIN ST 80219
  Katherine Adolph, prin.
Oakland ES, 4580 DEARBORN ST 80239
  Twila Norman, prin.
Palmer ES, 995 GRAPE ST 80220
  Marilyn Goldstein, prin.
Park Hill ES, 5050 E 19TH AVE 80220
  Carla Santorno, prin.
Philips ES, 6550 E 21ST AVE 80207
  Cora Redden, prin.
Remington ES, 4735 PECOS ST 80211
  Teresa Salazar, prin.
Rosedale MS, 2330 S SHERMAN ST 80210
  Robert McConnell, prin.
Sabin ES, 3050 S VRAIN ST 80236
  Ronald Makowski, prin.
Samuels MS, 3985 S VINCENNES CT 80237
  Richard Dutton, prin.
Schenck ES, 1300 S LOWELL BLVD 80219
  Thomas Mc Callin, prin.
Schmitt ES, 1820 S VALLEJO ST 80223
  Noble Jenkins, prin.
Smedley ES, 4250 SHOSHONE ST 80211
  Veronica Benavidez, prin.
Smith ES, 3590 JASMINE ST 80207
  David Thompson, prin.
Southmoor MS, 3755 S MAGNOLIA WAY 80237
  Ronald Mohr, prin.
Steck ES, 425 ASH ST 80220
  Priscella Gifford, prin.
Stedman ES, 2940 DEXTER ST 80207
  Ron Cabrera, prin.
Steele MS, 320 S MARION PKWY 80209
  E. Kate Deal, prin.
Stevens ES, 1140 COLUMBINE ST 80206
  Thelma Gash, prin.

Swansea ES, 4650 COLUMBINE ST 80216
  Carlos Beer, prin.
Teller MS, 1150 GARFIELD ST 80206
  Joy Wilson, prin.
Traylor MS, 2900 S IVAN WAY 80227
  Leo Goettelman, prin.
University Park ES
  2300 S SAINT PAUL ST 80210
  Karen Harvey, prin.
Valdez ES, 2525 W 29TH AVE 80211
  Joann Estrada-Mast, prin.
Valverde ES, 2030 W ALAMEDA AVE 80223
  Richard Smith, prin.
Westwood ES, 3615 W KENTUCKY AVE 80219
  Patricia Schmidt, prin.
Whiteman MS, 451 NEWPORT ST 80220
  Michael Wilson, prin.
Whittier MS, 2480 DOWNING ST 80205
  Brenda Higdon, prin.
Wyman ES, 1690 WILLIAMS ST 80218
  Mary Taylor, prin.

Mapleton SD 1
Sch. Sys. Enr. Code 5
Supt. – Jack Blendinger, 591 E 80TH AVE 80229
Dewey JHS, 7480 CONIFER ROAD 80221
  Betty Inhelder, prin.
Meadow ES, 9150 MONROE ST 80229
  Sam Molinaro, prin.
Monterey ES, 2200 MCELWAIN BLVD 80229
  Robert Seno, prin.
Valley View ES, 660 W 70TH AVE 80221
  Sharon Wood, prin.
Western Hills ES, 7700 DELTA ST 80221
  Dennis McDaniel, prin.
Other Schools – See Thornton

Northglenn-Thornton SD 12
Supt. – See Northglenn
Coronado Hills ES, 8300 DOWNING DR 80229
  David Gavin, prin.
Federal Heights ES, 2500 W 96TH AVE 80221
  Richard Flint, prin.
McElwain ES, 1020 DAWSON DR 80229
  Dane Hansen, prin.

Westminster SD 50
Supt. – See Westminster
Carpenter MS, 7000 LIPAN ST 80221
  Bruce Spinney, prin.
Clear Lake MS, 1940 ELMWOOD LANE 80221
  Carol Proffitt, prin.
Hodgkins MS, 3475 W 67TH AVE 80221
  Peter Golden, prin.
Baker ES, 3555 W 64TH AVE 80221
  Donald Anderson, prin.
Berkeley Gardens ES, 5301 LOWELL BLVD 80221
  Kathy Madigan, prin.
Day ES, 1740 JORDAN DR 80221
  Ann Heim, prin.
Fairview ES, 7826 FAIRVIEW AVE 80221
  Joseph Laterra, prin.
Metz ES, 2341 SHERRELWOOD DR 80221
  Arden Harms, prin.
Sherrelwood ES, 8095 KALAMATH ST 80221
  Steve Vande Ven, prin.

Beth Eden Baptist School
  2600 WADSWORTH BLVD 80215
Colorado Academy, 3800 S PIERCE ST 80235
Denver Christian School, 2135 S PEARL ST 80210
Mile High Adventist Academy
  711 E YALE AVE 80210
Randell-Moore School of Denver
  2160 S COOK ST 80210
Temple Baptist Academy
  2727 S SHERIDAN BLVD 80227
Annunciation ES, 3536 LAFAYETTE ST 80205
Assumption ES, 2341 E 78TH AVE 80229
Blessed Sacrament School, 1973 ELM ST 80220
Christ the King ES, 860 ELM ST 80220
Faith Lutheran ES, 4780 ELIOT ST 80211
Good Shepherd Catholic School
  940 FILLMORE ST 80206
Grace Lutheran ES, 880 FAIRFAX ST 80220
Graland Country Day School, 30 BIRCH ST 80220
Guardian Angels ES, 1843 W 52ND AVE 80211
Hillel Academy, 450 S HUDSON ST 80222
Holy Family ES, 4380 UTICA ST 80212
Loyola ES, 2350 GAYLORD ST 80205
Montessori School of Denver
  1460 S HOLLY ST 80222
Most Precious Blood School
  3959 E ILIFF AVE 80211
Notre Dame ES, 2165 S ZENOBIA ST 80219
Our Lady of Lourdes School
  2256 S LOGAN ST 80210
Presentation ES, 660 JULIAN ST 80204
Redeemer Lutheran ES
  3400 W NEVADA PL 80219
St. Andrew Lutheran ES
  12150 ANDREWS DR 80239
St. Anne's Episcopal ES, 2701 S YORK ST 80210
St. Catherine's ES, 4200 FEDERAL BLVD 80211
St. Francis ES, 320 S SHERMAN ST 80209
St. James ES, 1250 NEWPORT ST 80220
St. John's Lutheran ES
  750 S FRANKLIN ST 80209
St. Joseph ES, 605 W 6TH AVE 80204
St. Rosa of Lima ES, 1345 W DAKOTA AVE 80223
St. Vincent De Paul ES
  2401 E ARIZONA AVE 80210
Theodore Herzel ES, 2450 S WABASH ST 80231
University Hills ES, 4949 E EASTMAN AVE 80222

Van Dellen Christian School
4200 E WARREN AVE 80222
Waldorf School of Denver
735 E FLORIDA AVE 80210

Dinosaur, Moffat Co., Pop. Code 2
Moffat County SD Re-1
Supt. – See Craig
ES, P O BOX 240 81610 – Oliver Phillips, prin.

Dolores, Montezuma Co., Pop. Code 3
Dolores SD 4A
Sch. Sys. Enr. Code 3
Supt. – Charles Ewan, P O BOX 757 81323
JHS, P O BOX 757 81323 – Bob Gotthelf, prin.
ES, P O BOX 757 81323 – Janie Kratz, prin.

Dove Creek, Dolores Co., Pop. Code 3
Dolores County SD Re NO.2
Sch. Sys. Enr. Code 2
Supt. – Douglas Johnson, P O BOX 457 81324
JHS, P O BOX 457 81324 – Jim Buffington, prin.
Seventh Street ES, P O BOX 457 81324
Max Dicken, prin.
Other Schools – See Egnar, Rico

Durango, La Plata Co., Pop. Code 7
Durango SD 9-R
Sch. Sys. Enr. Code 5
Supt. – Harvie Guest, P O BOX 2467 81302
Florida Mesa ES, P O BOX 2467 81302
John Welcher, prin.
Ft. Lewis Mesa ES, P O BOX 2467 81302
(—), prin.
Needham ES, P O BOX 2467 81302
Reynaldo Santa Cruz, prin.
Park/Mason ES, P O BOX 2467 81302
Nyla Gruver, prin.
Riverview ES, P O BOX 2467 81302
Kathy Deaderick, prin.
Sunnyside ES, P O BOX 2467 81302
John Welcher, prin.

New Life Academy, 860 PLYMOUTH DR 81301
St. Columba School, 1801 E THIRD AVE 81301

Eads, Kiowa Co., Pop. Code 3
Eads SD Re-1
Sch. Sys. Enr. Code 2
Supt. – Max Bridgeman, P O BOX 877 81036
JHS, P O BOX 877 81036 – (—), prin.
ES, P O BOX 877 81036 – B. Wiser, prin.
Other Schools – See Haswell

Eagle, Eagle Co., Pop. Code 3
Eagle County SD Re-50(J)
Sch. Sys. Enr. Code 4
Supt. – Dr. Charles Schwahn, P O BOX 740 81631
Eagle Valley MS, P O BOX 1019 81631
Nicholas Seaver, prin.
Eagle Valley ES, P O BOX 769 81631
John Riemers, prin.
Other Schools – See Avon, Mc Coy, Minturn, Red
Cliff, Vail

Eaton, Weld Co., Pop. Code 4
Eaton SD Re-2
Sch. Sys. Enr. Code 4
Supt. – Bill Powell, P O BOX 127 80615
MS, P O BOX 37 80615 – Jon Campbell, prin.
ES, P O BOX 906 80615 – Oren Nero, prin.
Other Schools – See Galeton

Edgewater, Denver Co., Pop. Code 5
Jefferson County SD R-1
Supt. – See Golden
ES, 2280 DEPEW ST 80214
Pauline Bustamante, prin.
Lumberg ES, 6705 W 22ND AVE 80214
Dan Lewis, prin.

Egnar, San Miguel Co.
Dolores County SD Re NO.2
Supt. – See Dove Creek
ES, P O BOX 37 81325 – Patsy Spier, prin.

Elbert, Elbert Co., Pop. Code 2
Elbert SD 200
Sch. Sys. Enr. Code 2
Supt. – Charles Dvorak, P O BOX 38 80106
ES, P O BOX 38 80106 – Charles Dvorak, prin.

Elizabeth, Elbert Co., Pop. Code 2
Elizabeth SD C-1
Sch. Sys. Enr. Code 4
Supt. – Walter Way, P O BOX 610 80107
ES, P O BOX 550 80107 – Nel Little, prin.

Empire, Clear Creek Co., Pop. Code 2
Clear Creek SD Re-1
Supt. – See Idaho Springs
ES, P O BOX 667 80438 – Donald Weber, prin.

Englewood, Arapahoe Co., Pop. Code 8
Cherry Creek SD 5
Sch. Sys. Enr. Code 8
Supt. – Jim Huge, 4850 S YOSEMITE ST 80111
Campus MS, 4785 S DAYTON ST 80111
(—), prin.
Belleview ES, 4851 S DAYTON ST 80111
Karen Campbell, prin.
Cherry Hills Village ES
2400 E QUINCY AVE 80110 – Jerry Kral, prin.
Cottonwood Creek ES
11200 E ORCHARD AVE 80111
Joanne Ihrig, prin.
Dry Creek ES, 7686 E HINSDALE AVE 80112
Bob Dye, prin.

Greenwood ES, 5550 S HOLLY ST 80111
Carl Guthals, prin.
Heritage ES, 6867 E HERITAGE PL S 80111
Charles Stanely, prin.
High Plains ES, 6100 S FULTON ST 80111
Mike Volkl, prin.
Homestead ES
7451 S HOMESTEAD PKWY 80112
Russ Lofthouse, prin.
Walnut Hills Community ES
8295 E COSTILLA BLVD 80112
Mary Terch, prin.
Willow Creek ES, 7855 S WILLOW WAY 80112
Deena Brooks, prin.
Other Schools – See Aurora, Denver, Littleton

Englewood SD 1
Sch. Sys. Enr. Code 5
Supt. – Dr. Roscoe L. Davidson
4101 S BANNOCK ST 80110
Flood MS, 3695 S LINCOLN ST 80110
Steven Cohen, prin.
Sinclair MS, 300 W CHENANGO AVE 80110
Larry Nisbet, prin.
Bishop ES, 3100 S ELATI ST 80110
James Hess, prin.
Cherrelyn ES, 4500 S LINCOLN ST 80110
Frank Hammond, prin.
Clayton ES, 4600 S FOX ST 80110
Barbara LaFray, prin.
Hay ES, 3195 S LAFAYETTE ST 80110
Charles Grimes, prin.
Maddox ES, 700 W MANSFIELD AVE 80110
Keith Whisenand, prin.

Sheridan SD 2
Sch. Sys. Enr. Code 4
Supt. – Vicky Brooks
4000 S LOWELL BLVD 80110
Sheridan MS, P O BOX 1198 80150
James Taylor, prin.
Ft. Logan ES, 3700 S KNOX COURT 80150
Clark Bond, prin.
Terry ES, 4485 S IRVING ST 80110
John Gordon, prin.

St. Marys Academy
4545 S UNIVERSITY BLVD 80110
All Souls ES, 4951 S PENNSYLVANIA ST 80110
Collegiate School of Denver
3501 S COLORADO BLVD 80110
St. Louis ES, 3301 S SHERMAN ST 80110

Erie, Boulder Co., Pop. Code 4
St. Vrain Valley SD Re-1J
Supt. – See Longmont
ES, 4137 N 127TH 80516
Debby Shaffer-Meyer, prin.

Estes Park, Larimer Co., Pop. Code 4
Park SD R-3(J)
Sch. Sys. Enr. Code 4
Supt. – Bill Fears, P O BOX 1140 80517
MS, P O BOX 1140 80517 – Nola Gill, prin.
ES, P O BOX 1140 80517 – Steve Peterson, prin.

Evans, Weld Co., Pop. Code 6
Greeley SD 6
Supt. – See Greeley
Chappelow MS, 2001 34TH ST 80620
Ken Bennett, prin.
Centennial ES, 1400 37TH ST 80620
Joanne Andrade, prin.
Dos Rios ES, 2201 34TH ST 80620
Helen Rosales, prin.

Evergreen, Jefferson Co., Pop. Code 4
Clear Creek SD Re-1
Supt. – See Idaho Springs
King-Murphy ES, 425 CIRCLE K ROAD 80439
William Madouros, prin.

Jefferson County SD R-1
Supt. – See Golden
Bergen ES, 1892 COLORADO HWY 74 80439
Sondra Jackson, prin.
Marshdale ES
26663 N TURKEY CREEK ROAD 80439
Mike Warner, prin.
Wilmot ES, RURAL ROUTE 04 BOX 723 80439
Larry Fayer, prin.

Fairplay, Park Co., Pop. Code 2
Park County SD Re-2
Sch. Sys. Enr. Code 2
Supt. – William Granlund, P O BOX 188 80440
Teter ES, P O BOX 189 80440 – David Hoss, prin.
Other Schools – See Guffey, Lake George

Flagler, Kit Carson Co., Pop. Code 3
Arriba-Flagler SD C-20
Sch. Sys. Enr. Code 2
Supt. – Mark Ricken, P O BOX L 80815
S, P O BOX L 80815 – Richard Wilkinson, prin.

Fleming, Logan Co., Pop. Code 2
Frenchman SD Re-3
Sch. Sys. Enr. Code 2
Supt. – Richard Shively, P O BOX 468 80728
ES, P O BOX 468 80728 – Richard Hoeppner, prin.

Florence, Fremont Co., Pop. Code 5
Florence SD Re-2J
Sch. Sys. Enr. Code 4
Supt. – Victor Becco, 403 W 5TH ST 81226
MS, 500 W 5TH ST 81226 – Charles Picco, prin.

Fremont ES, 500 W 5TH ST 81226
Karen Kahn, prin.
Other Schools – See Penrose

Fort Carson, El Paso Co., Pop. Code 7
Fountain SD 8
Supt. – See Fountain
Abrams ES, BLDG 600 80913 – Jon Mahoney, prin.
Freedoms Trail ES, BLDG 5510 80913
Michael O'Neil, prin.

Fort Collins, Larimer Co., Pop. Code 8
Poudre SD R-1
Sch. Sys. Enr. Code 7
Supt. – Dr. Lee Hansen
2407 LA PORTE AVE 80521
Barton ES, 703 E PROSPECT RD 80525
David Hodge, prin.
Bauder ES, 2345 W PROSPECT RD 80526
William Bruss, prin.
Beattie ES, 3000 MEADOWLARK AVE 80526
Lois Schmitt, prin.
Bennett ES
1125 BENNETT SCHOOL ROAD 80521
David Benson, prin.
Dunn ES, 501 S WASHINGTON AVE 80521
Les Olson, prin.
Fullana MS, 220 N GRANT AVE 80521
Richard Clark, prin.
Harris ES, 501 E ELIZABETH ST 80524
Sherry Ritch, prin.
Irish ES, 515 IRISH DR 80521 – Paul Ehni, prin.
Johnson ES, 4101 SENECA ST 80526
Paul Ehni, prin.
Laurel MS, 1000 LOCUST ST 80524
Sherry Ritch, prin.
Lopez ES, 637 WABASH ST 80526
Richard Ellerby, prin.
Moore ES, 1905 ORCHARD PL 80521
Russell Fulton, prin.
O'Dea ES, 312 PRINCETON ROAD 80525
Paul Havenar, prin.
Putnam PS, 1400 MAPLE ST 80521
Richard Clark, prin.
Riffenburgh ES, 1320 E STUART ST 80525
Paul Huff, prin.
Shepardson ES, 1501 SPRINGWOOD DR 80525
Bruce Bartlett, prin.
Tavelli ES, 1118 MIRAMONT DR 80524
Bernard Long, prin.
Washington ES, 223 S SHIELDS ST 80521
Les Olson, prin.
Waverly ES
10431 N COUNTY ROAD NO 15 80524
Mary Kay Sommers, prin.
Werner ES, 5400 MAIL CREEK LANE 80525
Bill Chenoweth, prin.
Other Schools – See Bellvue, Laporte, Livermore, Red
Feather Lakes, Timnath, Wellington

Heritage Christian School, 1500 ELLIS ST 80524
St. Joseph's ES, 127 N HOWES ST 80521

Fort Lupton, Weld. Co., Pop. Code 4
Ft. Lupton SD Re-8
Sch. Sys. Enr. Code 4
Supt. – Dr. Harlan Else, 301 REYNOLDS ST 80621
IS, 201 S MCKINLEY AVE 80621
Dan Vallez, prin.
Butler ES, 411 MCKINLEY AVE 80621
Robert Libhart, prin.
Twombly PS, 1600 9TH ST 80621
Rosalie Martinez, prin.

Fort Morgan, Morgan Co., Pop. Code 6
Ft. Morgan SD Re-3
Sch. Sys. Enr. Code 5
Supt. – Jack Geckler, 230 WALNUT ST 80701
MS, 300 DEUEL ST 80701 – Dan Carlson, prin.
Baker ES, 300 LAKE ST 80701
Esther Bocock, prin.
Columbine ES, 815 WEST ST 80701
Clair Leibhart, prin.
Green Acres ES, 930 SHERMAN ST 80701
Betty Nida, prin.
Sherman MS, 300 SHERMAN ST 80701
Randy Zila, prin.

Trinity Lutheran School, 1215 W 7TH AVE 80701

Fountain, El Paso Co., Pop. Code 5
Fountain SD 8
Sch. Sys. Enr. Code 5
Supt. – Michael Martin
400 W ALABAMA AVE 80817
Fountain Mesa ES
400 CAMINO DEL REY ST 80817
William Steer, prin.
Jordahl ES, 800 PROGRESS DR 80817
William Weeks, prin.
Lorraine ES, 301 E IOWA AVE 80817
Joe Carter, prin.
Other Schools – See Fort Carson

Fowler, Otero Co., Pop. Code 4
Fowler SD R4J
Sch. Sys. Enr. Code 2
Supt. – Dr. Larry Vibber, P O BOX 218 81039
JHS, P O BOX 218 81039 – Al Lotrich, prin.
Park ES, P O BOX 218 81039
Suzanne Treece, prin.
West MS, P O BOX 218 81039
Suzanne Treece, prin.

Franktown, Douglas Co.
Douglas County SD Re-1(J)
Supt. – See Castle Rock
Cherry Valley ES
  RURAL ROUTE 01 BOX 510   80116
  Gary Antisdel, prin.
ES, 1384 N COLO HIGHWAY 83   80116
  Gary Antisdel, prin.

Fraser, Grand Co., Pop. Code 2
East Grand SD 2
Supt. – See Granby
Fraser Valley ES, P O BOX 128   80442
  Gary Harris, prin.

Frederick, Boulder Co., Pop. Code 3
St. Vrain Valley SD Re-1J
Supt. – See Longmont
ES, P O BOX 178   80530 – Karen Yacono, prin.

Frisco, Summit Co., Pop. Code 2
Summit SD Re-1
Sch. Sys. Enr. Code 4
Supt. – Dr. Walter Jackson, P O BOX 7   80443
Summit County MS, P O BOX 7   80443
  David Johnson, prin.
Dillon Valley ES, P O BOX 7   80443
  Keith Thompson, prin.
ES, P O BOX 7   80443 – Jane Gibson, prin.
Silverthorne ES, P O BOX 7   80443
  Judy Rodgers, prin.
Other Schools – See Breckenridge

Fruita, Mesa Co., Pop. Code 4
Mesa County Valley SD 51
Supt. – See Grand Junction
MS, 239 N MAPLE ST   81521 – James Bailey, prin.
Shelledy ES, 353 N MESA ST   81521
  Byron Pulliam, prin.

Galeton, Weld Co., Pop. Code 2
Eaton SD Re-2
Supt. – See Eaton
ES, P O BOX 758   80622 – Walter Jeffers, prin.

Gardner, Huerfano Co., Pop. Code 3
Huerfano SD Re-1
Supt. – See Walsenburg
ES, 25421 ST HWY 69   81040
  Julia Marchant, prin.

Gateway, Mesa Co., Pop. Code 2
Mesa County Valley SD 51
Supt. – See Grand Junction
S   81522 – Charles Everett, prin.

Georgetown, Clear Creek Co., Pop. Code 3
Clear Creek SD Re-1
Supt. – See Idaho Springs
ES, P O BOX 457   80444 – Donald Weber, prin.

Gilcrest, Weld Co., Pop. Code 2
Gilcrest SD Re-1
Sch. Sys. Enr. Code 4
Supt. – Dr. Clifford Brookhart, P O BOX 157   80623
ES, P O BOX 158   80623 – Lendon Shotts, prin.
Other Schools – See La Salle, Platteville

Glenwood Springs, Garfield Co., Pop. Code 5
Roaring Fork SD Re-1J
Sch. Sys. Enr. Code 5
Supt. – Dwight Helm, P O BOX 820   81602
JHS, P O BOX 820   81602 – Stan Johnson, prin.
ES, P O BOX 1580   81602 – Bernard Selting, prin.
Other Schools – See Basalt, Carbondale

St. Stephen School
  414 S HYLAND PARK DR   81601

Golden, Jefferson Co., Pop. Code 6
Jefferson County SD R-1
Sch. Sys. Enr. Code 8
Supt. – John Peper
  1829 DENVER WEST DR   80401
Bell JHS, 1001 ULYSSES ST   80401
  John Peery, prin.
Coal Creek ES, 11719 RANCH ELSIE ROAD   80403
  Sharon Hulby, prin.
Fairmount ES, 15975 W 50TH AVE   80403
  Vivian Elliott, prin.
Johnson ES, 701 JOHNSON DR   80401
  Bob Mc Cullough, prin.
Kyffin ES, 205 FLORA WAY   80401
  Marion Summervill, prin.
Maple Grove ES, 3085 ALKIRE ST   80401
  Dennis Nocton, prin.
Mitchell ES, 700 12TH ST   80401
  Vicki Hall, prin.
Pleasant View ES, 15920 W 10TH AVE   80401
  Diana Wolf, prin.
Ralston ES, 25856 COLUMBINE GLEN AVE   80401
  Cheryl White, prin.
Welchester ES, 13000 W 10TH AVE   80401
  Karla Byrd, prin.
Other Schools – See Arvada, Broomfield, Conifer,
  Edgewater, Evergreen, Indian Hills, Lakewood,
  Littleton, Morrison, Westminster, Wheat Ridge

Granada, Prowers Co., Pop. Code 3
Granada SD Re-1
Sch. Sys. Enr. Code 2
Supt. – Ian DeBono, P O BOX 259   81041
ES, P O BOX 259   81041 – Ian DeBono, prin.

Granby, Grand Co., Pop. Code 3
East Grand SD 2
Sch. Sys. Enr. Code 4
Supt. – Gary Sibigtroth, P O BOX 125   80446

East Grand JHS, P O BOX 125   80446
  H. Ashton, prin.
ES, P O BOX 125   80446 – Robb Rankin, prin.
Grand Lake ES, P O BOX 125   80446
  J. Young, prin.
Other Schools – See Fraser

Grand Junction, Mesa Co., Pop. Code 7
Mesa County Valley SD 51
Sch. Sys. Enr. Code 7
Supt. – Louis Grasso,Jr., 2115 GRAND AVE   81501
Bookcliff MS, 2935 ORCHARD AVE   81504
  Eldon Beard, prin.
East MS, 830 GUNNISON AVE   81501
  Sandra McGuire, prin.
Orchard Mesa MS, 2736 C ROAD   81503
  Jolynn Mc Dermott, prin.
West MS, 123 ORCHARD AVE   81501
  Beverly Johnson, prin.
Appleton ES, 2358 H ROAD   81505
  Kathleen Drogos, prin.
Broadway ES, 2248 BROADWAY   81503
  Robin Peckham, prin.
Chatfield ES, 3188 D 1/2 ROAD   81504
  Gary Anderson, prin.
Columbine ES, 624 N 9TH ST   81501
  Pearl Adams, prin.
Columbus ES, 2660 UNAWEEP AVE   81503
  Jeffrey Phillips, prin.
Fruitvale ES, 585 30 ROAD   81504
  Virginia Bergen, prin.
Lincoln Orchard Mesa ES
  2888 B 1/2 ROAD   81503 – William Lewis, prin.
Lincoln Park ES, 600 N 14TH ST   81501
  Corine Hesslink, prin.
Mesa View ES, 2967 B ROAD   81503
  Jerry Jordan, prin.
Nisley ES, 543 28 3/4 ROAD   81501
  Ernest Lax, prin.
Orchard Avenue ES, 1800 ORCHARD AVE   81501
  John Fulham, prin.
Pomona ES, 588 25 1/2 ROAD   81505
  James Maguire, prin.
Scenic ES, 451 W SCENIC DR   81503
  Tom Parrish, prin.
Thunder Mountain ES, 3063 F 1/2 ROAD   81504
  Dennis Svaldi, prin.
Tope ES, 2220 N 7TH ST   81501
  Russell Conner, prin.
Wingate ES, 334 S CAMP ROAD   81503
  Gilbert Roberts, prin.
Other Schools – See Clifton, Fruita, Gateway, Loma,
  Palisade

Holy Family School, 800 BOOKCLIFF AVE   81501

Greeley, Weld Co., Pop. Code 8
Greeley SD 6
Sch. Sys. Enr. Code 7
Supt. – J. Timothy Waters, 811 15TH ST   80631
Brentwood MS, 2600 24TH AVE CT   80631
  Carol Hildebrand, prin.
Franklin MS, 818 35TH AVE   80631
  Ralph Rangel, prin.
Maplewood MS, 1210 21ST AVE   80631
  Donna Newton, prin.
Cameron ES, 1424 13TH AVE   80631
  Ben Rohnke, prin.
East Memorial ES, 614 E 20TH ST   80631
  John Helwick, prin.
Jackson ES, 2002 25TH ST   80631
  Joe Vickarelli, prin.
Jefferson ES, 1315 4TH AVE   80631
  Richard Urban, prin.
McAuliffe ES, 600 51ST AVE   80634
  Jerry Christian, prin.
Madison ES, 24TH AVE & 5TH ST   80631
  Sue Anschutz, prin.
Martinez ES, 341 14TH AVE   80631
  Alice Leal, prin.
Meeker ES, 2221 28TH AVE   80631
  Fred Tjardes, prin.
Monfort ES, 2101 47TH AVE   80634
  Mark Lubbers, prin.
Scott ES, 29TH AVE & 13TH ST   80631
  Bill Gillenwater, prin.
Shawsheen ES, 4020 7TH ST   80634
  Bruce Messinger, prin.
Other Schools – See Evans

Dayspring Christian School
  9TH AVE & 23RD ST   80631
Greeley Catholic School, 915 12TH ST   80631
Trinity Lutheran School, 3000 35TH AVE   80634

Green Mountain Falls, El Paso Co., Pop. Code 3
Manitou Springs SD 14
Supt. – See Manitou Springs
Ute Pass ES, 9230 CHIPITA PARK ROAD   80819
  Rhonda Richer, prin.

Grover, Weld Co., Pop. Code 2
Grover SD Re-12
Sch. Sys. Enr. Code 2
Supt. – Richard Kimmel, P O BOX 38   80729
Pawnee ES, P O BOX 38   80729
  Richard Kimmel, prin.

Guffey, Park Co.
Park County SD Re-2
Supt. – See Fairplay
ES   80820 – William Granlund, prin.

Gunnison, Gunnison Co., Pop. Code 5
Gunnison Watershed SD Re-1J
Sch. Sys. Enr. Code 4
Supt. – Thomas Jacobson
  216 GEORGIA AVE   81230
Ruland JHS, 700 E VIRGINIA AVE   81230
  Greg Kruthaupt, prin.
Blackstock MS, 212 N PINE ST   81230
  Keith Foote, prin.
Lake ES, 800 N BLVD   81230 – Susan LeBow, prin.
O'Leary ES, 225 N PINE ST   81230
  Keith Foote, prin.
Other Schools – See Crested Butte

Haswell, Kiowa Co., Pop. Code 2
Eads SD Re-1
Supt. – See Eads
ES   81045 – B. Wiser, prin.

Haxtun, Phillips Co., Pop. Code 3
Haxtun SD Re-2J
Sch. Sys. Enr. Code 2
Supt. – Michael Blake, P O BOX 548   80731
ES, P O BOX 548   80731 – Paul Olson, prin.

Hayden, Routt Co., Pop. Code 3
Hayden SD Re-1
Sch. Sys. Enr. Code 2
Supt. – Bruce Yoast, P O BOX 70   81639
MS, P O BOX 70   81639 – Donald Santee, prin.
Hayden Valley ES, P O BOX 70   81639
  Donald McClaskey, prin.

Henderson, Adams Co.
Brighton SD 27J
Supt. – See Brighton
ES, 12301 E 124TH AVE   80640 – David Rose, prin.

Highlands Ranch, Douglas Co.
Douglas County SD Re-1(J)
Supt. – See Castle Rock
Douglas ES 17, 8898 MAPLEWOOD DR   80126
  David Bebell, prin.
Northridge ES, 555 S PARK ROAD   80126
  F. Douglas McFarland, prin.
Sand Creek ES, 8898 W MAPLEWOOD DR   80123
  Charles Denis, prin.

Hoehne, Las Animas Co., Pop. Code 3
Hoehne Reorganized SD 3
Sch. Sys. Enr. Code 2
Supt. – Jasper Butero, P O BOX 91   81046
JHS, P O BOX 91   81046 – Jasper Butero,Jr., prin.
ES, P O BOX 91   81046 – Jasper Butero,Jr., prin.

Holly, Prowers Co., Pop. Code 3
Holly SD Re-3
Sch. Sys. Enr. Code 2
Supt. – Larry Eklund, P O BOX 608   81047
Shanner ES, P O BOX 608   81047
  Albert McCorkle, prin.

Holyoke, Phillips Co., Pop. Code 4
Holyoke SD Re-1J
Sch. Sys. Enr. Code 3
Supt. – Dennis Krominga, 435 S MORLAN   80734
ES, 336 E KELLOGG   80734 – Jim Yakel, prin.

Hooper, Alamosa Co.
Sangre De Cristo SD Re-22J
Supt. – See Mosca
Sangre De Cristo ES   81136 – Walter Paulson, prin.

Hotchkiss, Delta Co., Pop. Code 3
Delta County SD 50 (J)
Supt. – See Delta
MS, P O BOX 60   81419 – Jim Kent, prin.
ES, P O BOX 309   81419 – James Carter, prin.

Hudson, Weld Co., Pop. Code 3
Keenesburg SD Re-3J
Supt. – See Keenesburg
ES, P O BOX 278   80642 – Frederick Syman, prin.

Hugo, Lincoln Co., Pop. Code 3
Genoa-Hugo Consolidated SD C113
Sch. Sys. Enr. Code 2
Supt. – Red Mosier, P O BOX 247   80821
ES, P O BOX 247   80821 – Robert Houska, prin.

Hygiene, Boulder Co., Pop. Code 2
St. Vrain Valley SD Re-1J
Supt. – See Longmont
ES   80533 – Tom McIntosh, prin.

Idaho Springs, Clear Creek Co., Pop. Code 4
Clear Creek SD Re-1
Sch. Sys. Enr. Code 4
Supt. – Daniel Johnson, P O BOX 3399   80452
Carlson ES, P O BOX 3399   80452
  Linda Fowler, prin.
Other Schools – See Empire, Evergreen, Georgetown

Idalia, Yuma Co., Pop. Code 1
East Yuma County SD RJ-2
Supt. – See Wray
ES, 26845 CO RD 9.2   80735
  M. Kim Vanderheiden, prin.

Ignacio, La Plata Co., Pop. Code 3
Ignacio SD 11 Jt
Sch. Sys. Enr. Code 3
Supt. – Bryce Fauble, P O BOX 446   81137
JHS, P O BOX 446   81137 – Jake Candelaria, prin.
Ignacio IS, P O BOX 399   81137 – Roy Lyons, prin.
PS, P O BOX 293   81137 – Roy Lyons, prin.

Iliff, Logan Co., Pop. Code 2
Valley SD Re-1
Supt. – See Sterling
Caliche ES, RURAL ROUTE 01 80736
  Fred Rasmussen, prin.

Indian Hills, Jefferson Co., Pop. Code 3
Jefferson County SD R-1
Supt. – See Golden
Parmalee ES, 4470 S PARMALEE GULCH 80454
  Earl Painter, prin.

Jamestown, Boulder Co., Pop. Code 2
Boulder Valley SD Re-2(J)
Supt. – See Boulder
ES 80455 – John Knox, prin.

Joes, Yuma Co., Pop. Code 2
West Yuma County SD R-J-1
Supt. – See Yuma
Liberty ES, P O BOX 112 80822
  Bruce Yearous, prin.

Johnstown, Weld Co., Pop. Code 4
Johnstown-Milliken SD Re-5J
Sch. Sys. Enr. Code 4
Supt. – Fred Palmer, LOCK DRAWER G 80534
Letford MS, W CHARLOTTE ST CIR 80534
  Dudley Sweet, prin.
Other Schools – See Milliken

Julesburg, Sedgwick Co., Pop. Code 4
Julesburg SD Re-1
Sch. Sys. Enr. Code 2
Supt. – James Howitt, P O BOX 359 80737
ES, P O BOX 359 80737 – Giles Lowden, prin.

Karval, Lincoln Co., Pop. Code 1
Karval SD Re-23
Sch. Sys. Enr. Code 1
Supt. – John Pierce, P O BOX 272 80823
ES, P O BOX 272 80823 – John Pierce, prin.

Keenesburg, Weld Co., Pop. Code 2
Keenesburg SD Re-3J
Sch. Sys. Enr. Code 4
Supt. – Bob Gudka, P O BOX 269 80643
ES, P O BOX 269 80643 – Landon Shotts, prin.
Prospect Valley ES, 33318 HIGHWAY 52 80643
  William Knies, prin.
Other Schools – See Hudson

Kersey, Weld Co., Pop. Code 2
Platte Valley SD Re-7
Sch. Sys. Enr. Code 3
Supt. – Glen Hanson, P O BOX 487 80644
Platte Valley ES, P O BOX 487 80644
  Bill Edwards, prin.

Kim, Las Animas Co., Pop. Code 2
Kim Reorganized SD 88
Sch. Sys. Enr. Code 1
Supt. – Milton Roeder, P O BOX 100 81049
ES, P O BOX 100 81049 – Milton Roeder, prin.

Kiowa, Elbert Co., Pop. Code 2
Kiowa SD C-2
Sch. Sys. Enr. Code 2
Supt. – William Kendrick, P O BOX 128 80117
ES, P O BOX 128 80117 – Bill Kendrick, prin.

Kit Carson, Cheyenne Co., Pop. Code 2
Kit Carson SD R-1
Sch. Sys. Enr. Code 2
Supt. – Kenneth O'Mara, P O BOX 185 80825
S, P O BOX 185 80825 – Kenneth O'Mara, prin.

Kremmling, Grand Co., Pop. Code 3
West Grand SD 1 JT
Sch. Sys. Enr. Code 3
Supt. – Eldred Chicoine, P O BOX 515 80459
West Grand MS, P O BOX 515 80459
  Raymond Mann, prin.
West Grand ES, P O BOX 515 80459
  Paul Reese, prin.

Lafayette, Boulder Co., Pop. Code 5
Boulder Valley SD Re-2(J)
Supt. – See Boulder
Angevine MS, 101 BASELINE ROAD 80026
  Lois Hay, prin.
ES, 101 N BERMONT AVE 80026
  Mark Sparn, prin.
Ryan ES, 1405 CENTAUR VLG DR 80026
  Jane Daniels, prin.
Sanchez ES, 655 SIR GALAHAD DR 80026
  Carol Silva, prin.

La Jara, Conejos Co., Pop. Code 3
North Conejos SD Re-1J
Sch. Sys. Enr. Code 4
Supt. – Chris Martinez, P O BOX 72 81140
ES, P O BOX 470 81140 – Marvene Lobato, prin.
Other Schools – See Capulin, Manassa, Romeo

La Junta, Otero Co., Pop. Code 6
East Otero SD R1
Sch. Sys. Enr. Code 4
Supt. – Dr. Donald White, P O BOX 439 81050
JHS, 9TH & SMITHLAND 81050
  Tano Paolucci, prin.
Columbian ES, 800 GRACE AVE 81050
  Ron Nordin, prin.
East ES, EAST SIXTH 81050 – Harold Reese, prin.
West ES, 6TH & TOPEKA 81050
  James Herrell, prin.

Lake City, Hinsdale Co., Pop. Code 2
Hinsdale County SD Re 1
Sch. Sys. Enr. Code 1
Supt. – Noreen Thibault, P O BOX 115 81235
ES, P O BOX 115 81235 – Noreen Thibault, prin.

Lake George, Park Co., Pop. Code 3
Park County SD Re-2
Supt. – See Fairplay
ES 80827 – David Hoss, prin.

Lakewood, Jefferson Co., Pop. Code 9
Jefferson County SD R-1
Supt. – See Golden
Carmody JHS, 2050 S KIPLING ST 80227
  Marcia Goldin, prin.
Creighton JHS, 75 INDEPENDENCE ST 80226
  Gerald Michels, prin.
Dunstan JHS, 1855 S WRIGHT ST 80228
  Richard Ransom, prin.
JHS, 7655 W 10TH AVE 80215 – Dean Huber, prin.
O'Connell JHS, 1275 S TELLER ST 80226
  Dean Larson, prin.
Bear Creek ES, 3125 S KIPLING ST 80227
  Margaret Doll, prin.
Belmar ES, 885 S GARRISON ST 80226
  Darrell Erlewine, prin.
Deane ES, 580 S HARLAN ST 80226
  Dr. Ray Nielson, prin.
DeVinny ES, 1725 S WRIGHT ST 80228
  Walt Skillern, prin.
Eiber ES, 1385 INDEPENDENCE ST 80215
  Robert Wallace, prin.
Foothills ES, 13165 W OHIO AVE 80228
  Gene Swenson, prin.
Glennon Heights ES, 11025 GLENNON DR 80226
  Kenneth Vendena, prin.
Green Gables ES, 8701 W WOODARD DR 80227
  Elizabeth Lindeman, prin.
Green Mountain ES
  12250 W KENTUCKY DR 80228
  Leo Lohman, prin.
Hutchinson ES, 12900 W UTAH AVE 80228
  Curt Rokala, prin.
Irwin ES, 1505 S PIERSON ST 80226
  Linda Glanot, prin.
Kendrick Lakes ES, 1350 S HOYT ST 80226
  Landon Lyons, prin.
Lasley ES, 1401 S KENDALL ST 80226
  Karen Fitzpatrick, prin.
Molholm ES, 6000 W 9TH AVE 80214
  Georgia Peterson, prin.
Patterson ES, 1263 S DUDLEY ST 80226
  Peggy Taylor, prin.
Slater ES, 8605 W 23RD AVE 80215
  Leslie Mason, prin.
South Lakewood ES, 8425 W 1ST AVE 80226
  Muriel Brainard, prin.
Stein ES, 80 S TELLER ST 80226 – Ron Rich, prin.
Stober ES, 2300 URBAN ST 80215
  Jerry Jones, prin.
Vivian ES, 10500 W 25TH AVE 80215
  Christine Best, prin.
Westgate ES, 8550 W VASSAR DR 80227
  Mary Jane Kipp, prin.

Silver State Baptist School
  875 S SHERIDAN BLVD 80226
Bethlehem Lutheran School
  7470 W 22ND AVE 80215
Our Lady of Fatima Catholic School
  10530 W 20TH AVE 80215
St. Bernadette School, 1100 UPHAM ST 80215

Lamar, Prowers Co., Pop. Code 6
Lamar SD Re-2
Sch. Sys. Enr. Code 4
Supt. – Bill Van Buskirk, 210 W PEARL ST 81052
MS, 606 S MAIN ST 81052
  Philip McDowell, prin.
Alta Vista ES, RURAL ROUTE 01 BOX 240 81052
  Dana Eudaley, prin.
Lincoln ES, 200 N 10TH ST 81052
  Dana Eudaley, prin.
Parkview ES, 1105 S 2ND 81052
  Robert Hodge, prin.
Washington ES, 600 W PEARL ST 81052
  Wayne Stokke, prin.

Laporte, Larimer Co., Pop. Code 3
Poudre SD R-1
Supt. – See Fort Collins
Cache-La Poudre ES, P O BOX 488 80535
  Ronald Maulsby, prin.

Larkspur, Douglas Co., Pop. Code 2
Douglas County SD Re-1(J)
Supt. – See Castle Rock
ES, 1103 W PERRY PARK AVE 80118
  Cheryl Dunkle, prin.

La Salle, Weld Co., Pop. Code 4
Gilcrest SD Re-1
Supt. – See Gilcrest
North Valley MS, P O BOX 248 80645
  Robert Stark, prin.
ES, P O BOX 248 80645 – Robert Stark, prin.

Las Animas, Bent Co., Pop. Code 5
Las Animas SD Re-1
Sch. Sys. Enr. Code 3
Supt. – Edward Schelhaas
  1214 THOMPSON BLVD 81054
MS, 1214 7TH ST 81054 – Lenard Smith, prin.
Columbian MS, 1026 6TH ST 81054
  Connie Donovan, prin.

Memorial ES, 136 6TH ST 81054
  Lawrence Sena, prin.

La Veta, Huerfano Co., Pop. Code 3
La Veta SD Re-2
Sch. Sys. Enr. Code 2
Supt. – Roger Brunelli, P O BOX 85 81055
ES, P O BOX 85 81055 – Roger Brunelli, prin.

Leadville, Lake Co., Pop. Code 5
Lake County SD R-1
Sch. Sys. Enr. Code 4
Supt. – James McCabe, P O BOX 977 80461
Lake County IS, P O BOX 977 80461
  Tom Wilson, prin.
Westpark ES, P O BOX 977 80461
  Larry Marriott, prin.

Limon, Lincoln Co., Pop. Code 4
Limon SD Re-4J
Sch. Sys. Enr. Code 2
Supt. – Donald Weber, P O BOX 249 80828
ES, P O BOX 249 80828 – Joan Marley, prin.

Littleton, Arapahoe Co., Pop. Code 8
Cherry Creek SD 5
Supt. – See Englewood
West MS, 5151 S HOLLY ST 80121
  (—), prin.

Douglas County SD Re-1(J)
Supt. – See Castle Rock
Acres Green ES, 13524 ACRES GREEN DR 80124
  Joann Alam, prin.
Plum Creek ES, 8236 W CARDER CT 80125
  John Miller, prin.

Jefferson County SD R-1
Supt. – See Golden
Caryl JHS, 6509 W KEN CARYL AVE 80123
  Barbara Sibold, prin.
Deer Creek JHS
  9201 W COLUMBINE DRIVE 80123
  DeWayne Neel, prin.
Colorow ES, 6317 S ESTES ST 80123
  Jerald Watson, prin.
Columbine Hills ES, 6005 W CANYON AVE 80123
  Judy Eichman, prin.
Dutch Creek ES, 7304 W ROXBURY PL 80123
  James Burke, prin.
Leawood ES, 6155 W LEAWOOD DR 80123
  Cynthia Foster, prin.
Normandy ES, 6750 S KENDALL BLVD 80123
  Cynthia Haws, prin.
Peiffer ES, 4997 S MILLER WAY 80127
  Harry Morgan, prin.
Shaffer ES, 7961 S SANGRE DE CRISTO RD 80127
  Michael De Guire, prin.
Stony Creek ES, 7203 S EVERETT ST 80123
  Mike Connors, prin.
Ute Meadows ES, 11050 W MEADOWS DR 80127
  Roy Burley, prin.
Westridge ES, 10785 W ALAMO PLACE 80127
  Ron Horn, prin.

Littleton SD 6
Sch. Sys. Enr. Code 7
Supt. – Robert Tschirki, 6558 S ACOMA ST 80120
Euclid MS, 777 W EUCLID AVE 80120
  John Schaecher, prin.
Goddard MS, 3800 W BERRY AVE 80123
  Lowell Ensey, prin.
Newton MS, 4001 E ARAPAHOE ROAD 80122
  Flo Bullock, prin.
Powell MS, 8000 S CORONA WAY 80122
  Michael Farrell, prin.
Ames ES, 7300 S CLERMONT DR 80122
  Ken Coddington, prin.
Centennial ES, 3306 W BERRY AVE 80123
  Colin Conway, prin.
East ES, 5933 S FAIRFIELD ST 80120
  Darlene Dougherty, prin.
Field ES, 5402 S SHERMAN WAY 80121
  Henry Wyeno, prin.
Franklin ES, 1603 E EUCLID AVE 80121
  Diane Lewis, prin.
Highland ES, 711 E EUCLID AVE 80121
  Judith Husbands, prin.
Hopkins ES, 7171 S PENNSYLVANIA ST 80122
  Michael Camelio, prin.
Lenski ES, 6350 S FAIRFAX WAY 80121
  Howard Huddleston, prin.
Moody ES, 6390 S WINDEMERE ST 80120
  Steve McGrath, prin.
Peabody ES, 3128 E MAPLEWOOD AVE 80121
  Rose Marie Grove, prin.
Runyon ES, 7455 S ELATI ST 80120
  John Rotter, prin.
Sandburg ES, 6900 S ELIZABETH ST 80122
  Helene Anderson, prin.
Twain ES, 6901 S FRANKLIN ST 80122
  Monte Moses, prin.
Whitman ES, 6557 S ACOMA ST 80120
  Donald Lodice, prin.
Wilder ES, 4300 W 3-PONDS CIR 80120
  Christopher Wilson, prin.

St. Mary MS, 6833 S PRINCE ST 80120
St. Mary's ES, 5592 S NEVADA ST 80120
Shepherd of the Hills School
  7691 S UNIVERSITY BLVD 80122

Livermore, Larimer Co., Pop. Code 4
Poudre SD R-1
Supt. – See Fort Collins
ES 80536 – Mary Kay Sommers, prin.

Loma, Mesa Co.
Mesa County Valley SD 51
Supt. – See Grand Junction
ES, 1360 13 ROAD 81524 – Joann Yount, prin.

Longmont, Boulder Co., Pop. Code 7
St. Vrain Valley SD Re-1J
Sch. Sys. Enr. Code 7
Supt. – Dr. Keith Blue
395 S PRATT PARKWAY 80501
Olde Columbine S, 620 BAKER 80501
Bill Blick, prin.
Burlington ES, 1051 S PRATT PKWY 80501
Will Masters, prin.
Central/Lincoln ES, 425 N BROSS ST 80501
Isabel Romero, prin.
Columbine MS, 620 N ATWOOD ST 80501
Jo Jacobson, prin.
Indian Peaks ES, 1335 S JUDSON ST 80501
Lillian Weyand, prin.
Loma Linda ES, 333 E MT VIEW 80501
Noelle Branch, prin.
Longmont Estates ES
1601 NORTHWESTERN ROAD 80501
Richard Montoya, prin.
Main Street MS, 820 N MAIN ST 80501
Ivan Peterson, prin.
Mountain View ES, 1415 14TH ST 80501
Frank LaMirand, prin.
Niwot ES, 8778 MORTON ROAD 80501
Ivan Adams, prin.
Northridge ES, 1200 W 19TH AVE 80501
Claudine Garby, prin.
Rocky Mountain ES, 800 E 5TH AVE 80501
Carol Cook, prin.
Sanborn ES, 2235 N VIVIAN ST 80501
Charles Anderson, prin.
Spangler ES, 1440 COLLYER ST 80501
Tom Gibbons, prin.
Other Schools – See Erie, Frederick, Hygiene, Lyons, Mead

Faith Baptist School, 833 W 15TH AVE 80501
St. John the Baptist School
350 N EMERY ST 80501

Louisville, Boulder Co., Pop. Code 6
Boulder Valley SD Re-2(J)
Supt. – See Boulder
MS, 1341 MAIN ST 80027 – Mel Beayprez, prin.
Coal Creek ES, 801 W TAMARISK ST 80027
Ellen Goering, prin.
ES, 400 HUTCHINSON ST 80027
Arnold Levihn, prin.

St. Louis ES, 841 GRANT AVE 80027

Loveland, Larimer Co., Pop. Code 7
Thompson SD R-2J
Sch. Sys. Enr. Code 7
Supt. – Jack Hale, 535 N DOUGLAS AVE 80537
Big Thompson ES
7702 W U S HIGHWAY 34 80537
David Leech, prin.
Blair ES, 860 E 29TH ST 80538
Julia Goettsch, prin.
Centennial ES, 1555 W 37TH ST 80538
Samuel Simonetta, prin.
Edmondson ES, 307 W 49TH ST 80538
Barbara Miller, prin.
Garfield ES, 720 N COLORADO AVE 80537
Dale Osborn, prin.
Kitchen ES, 915 DEBORAH DR 80537
Linda Glecker, prin.
Lincoln ES, 33RD & DOUGLAS 80537
James Sendek, prin.
Martin ES, 4129 JONI LN 80537
Richard Christie, prin.
Milner ES, 743 JOCELYN DR 80537
Linda Edwards, prin.
Monroe ES, 1500 N MONROE AVE 80538
Ken Rethmeier, prin.
Namaqua ES, 209 N COUNTY ROAD 19 E 80537
Charles Raisch, prin.
Stansberry ES, 407 E 42ND ST 80538
David Mathias, prin.
Truscott ES, 211 W 6TH ST 80537
Roger Dailey, prin.
Van Buren ES, 1811 W 15TH ST 80538
Gregory Voelz, prin.
Winona ES, 201 BOISE AVE 80537
Merle Roberts, prin.
Other Schools – See Berthoud

Immanuel Lutheran School
1101 HILLTOP DR 80537
St. John the Evangelist School
1730 W 12TH ST 80537

Lyons, Boulder Co., Pop. Code 3
St. Vrain Valley SD Re-1J
Supt. – See Longmont
ES, 338 HIGH ST 80540 – Loretts Hamilton, prin.

Mc Clave, Bent Co., Pop. Code 2
McClave SD Re-2
Sch. Sys. Enr. Code 2
Supt. – Dale Curley, P O BOX 1 81057
ES, P O BOX 1 81057 – Dale Curley, prin.

Mc Coy, Eagle Co.
Eagle County SD Re-50(J)
Supt. – See Eagle
PS, P O BOX 576 80463 – Nancy Alley, prin.

Manassa, Conejos Co., Pop. Code 3
North Conejos SD Re-1J
Supt. – See La Jara
MS, P O BOX 98 81141 – Eva Marie Salas, prin.

Mancos, Montezuma Co., Pop. Code 3
Mancos SD Re-6
Sch. Sys. Enr. Code 2
Supt. – Julio Archuleta, P O BOX 428 81328
JHS, P O BOX 428 81328 – Jack Curran, prin.
ES, P O BOX 420 81328 – Howard Culp, prin.

Manitou Springs, El Paso Co., Pop. Code 5
Manitou Springs SD 14
Sch. Sys. Enr. Code 4
Supt. – Gary Miller, 701 DUCLO AVE 80829
MS, 415 EL MONTE PLACE 80829
Keith Elsberry, prin.
ES, 701 DUCLO AVE 80829 – Anne Standley, prin.
Other Schools – See Green Mountain Falls

Manzanola, Otero Co., Pop. Code 2
Manzanola SD 3j
Sch. Sys. Enr. Code 2
Supt. – Paul Price, P O BOX 148 81058
ES, P O BOX 148 81058 – Natalie Oakes, prin.

Maybell, Moffat Co.
Moffat County SD Re-1
Supt. – See Craig
Browns Park ES, 14305 HWY 318 81640
Oliver Phillips, prin.
ES, P O BOX 38 81640 – Oliver Phillips, prin.

Mead, Boulder Co., Pop. Code 2
St. Vrain Valley SD Re-1J
Supt. – See Longmont
ES, P O BOX 248 80542 – Wayne Stone, prin.

Meeker, Rio Blanco Co., Pop. Code 4
Meeker SD Re-1
Sch. Sys. Enr. Code 3
Supt. – Robert Ash, P O BOX 1089 81641
Barone JHS, P O BOX 690 81641
Richard Flaherty, prin.
ES, P O BOX 988 81641 – Steve Balloga, prin.
Other Schools – See Rifle

Merino, Logan Co., Pop. Code 2
Buffalo SD Re-4(J)
Sch. Sys. Enr. Code 2
Supt. – Charles Hauer, P O BOX 198 80741
ES, P O BOX 198 80741 – Bruce Gentry, prin.

Milliken, Weld Co., Pop. Code 3
Johnstown-Milliken SD Re-5J
Supt. – See Johnstown
MS, 66 IRENE AVE 80543
Vaughn Griswold, prin.
ES, COUNTY ROAD 21 & BROAD ST 80543
Dennis Thompson, prin.

Minturn, Eagle Co., Pop. Code 3
Eagle County SD Re-50(J)
Supt. – See Eagle
MS, P O BOX U 81645 – Glen Gallegos, prin.

Moffat, Saguache Co., Pop. Code 1
Moffat SD 2
Sch. Sys. Enr. Code 2
Supt. – Don Nichols, P O BOX 127 81143
ES, P O BOX 127 81143 – Charles Grant, prin.

Monte Vista, Rio Grande Co., Pop. Code 5
Monte Vista SD C-8
Sch. Sys. Enr. Code 4
Supt. – Dr. Bill Metz, 1444 HUXLEY AVE 81144
JHS, 3720 SHERMAN 81144 – Gil Gonzales, prin.
ES, 1444 HUXLEY AVE 81144 – Gary Kidd, prin.

Sargent SD Re-33J
Sch. Sys. Enr. Code 2
Supt. – Ronald Pincheon
1967 HIGHWAY 374 E 81144
Sargent ES, 1967 HIGHWAY 374 E 81144
D. Anna Mayfield, prin.

Montrose, Montrose Co., Pop. Code 6
Montrose County SD Re-1J
Sch. Sys. Enr. Code 5
Supt. – Robert Cito, P O BOX 219 81402
Johnson ES, P O BOX 219 81402
Robert Balerio, prin.
Morgan ES, P O BOX 219 81402
Richard Brown, prin.
North Side ES, P O BOX 219 81402
Russ Stone, prin.
Oak Grove ES, P O BOX 219 81402
Richard Baker, prin.
Pomona ES, P O BOX 219 81402
Paul Hedges, prin.
Riverside ES, P O BOX 219 81402
Phillip Diller, prin.
Uncompahgre MS, P O BOX 219 81402
Phillip Diller, prin.
Other Schools – See Olathe

Monument, El Paso Co., Pop. Code 2
Lewis-Palmer SD 38
Sch. Sys. Enr. Code 4
Supt. – James Smith, P O BOX B 80132
Lewis-Palmer MS, 66 JEFFERSON ST 80132
Thomas Hayes, prin.
Kilmer ES, 4285 WALKER RD 80132
Dwight Bauman, prin.
Lewis-Palmer ES
1315 LAKE WOODMOOR DR 80132
George Parsons, prin.

Other Schools – See Palmer Lake

Morrison, Jefferson Co., Pop. Code 2
Jefferson County SD R-1
Supt. – See Golden
Kendallvue ES, 1365 W MARLOWE AVE 80465
Steve Cline, prin.
Red Rocks ES, 17199 hWY 74 80465
Jorge-Ayn Riley, prin.

Mosca, Alamosa Co., Pop. Code 2
Sangre De Cristo SD Re-22J
Sch. Sys. Enr. Code 2
Supt. – Walter Paulson, P O BOX 145 81146
Other Schools – See Hooper

Naturita, Montrose Co., Pop. Code 3
West End SD Re-2
Sch. Sys. Enr. Code 2
Supt. – Larry Swain, P O BOX 7 81422
MS, P O BOX 14 81422 – Larry Swain, prin.
Other Schools – See Nucla, Paradox

Nederland, Boulder Co., Pop. Code 2
Boulder Valley SD Re-2(J)
Supt. – See Boulder
ES 80466 – Holly Hultgren, prin.

New Castle, Garfield Co., Pop. Code 3
Garfield SD Re-2
Supt. – See Rifle
Riverside JHS, P O BOX 198 81647
Charles Shupe, prin.
ES, P O BOX 199 81647 – Charles Shupe, prin.

New Raymer, Weld Co., Pop. Code 2
Prairie SD Re-11J
Sch. Sys. Enr. Code 1
Supt. – Larry Rewerts, P O BOX 68 80742
Prairie ES, P O BOX 68 80742
Larry Rewerts, prin.

Northglenn, Adams Co., Pop. Code 8
Northglenn-Thornton SD 12
Sch. Sys. Enr. Code 7
Supt. – Dr. James Mitchell
11285 HIGHLINE DRIVE 80233
Hillcrest ES, 10335 CROKE DR 80221
Ronald Roloff, prin.
Hulstrom ES, 10604 GRANT DR 80233
Laurence Marchant, prin.
Leroy Drive ES, 1451 LEROY DR 80233
Roger Brown, prin.
Malley Drive ES, 1300 MALLEY DR 80233
Suzanne Miller, prin.
North Mor ES, 9580 DAMON DR 80221
James Van Wert, prin.
Stukey ES, 11080 GRANT DR 80233
Laurence Marchant, prin.
Westview ES, 1300 ROSEANNA DR 80234
Richard Eslinger, prin.
Wyco Drive ES, 11551 WYCO DR 80233
David Sautte, prin.
Other Schools – See Broomfield, Denver, Thornton, Westminster

Gethsemane Lutheran ES
10675 WASHINGTON ST 80233

Norwood, San Miguel Co., Pop. Code 2
Norwood SD R-2J
Sch. Sys. Enr. Code 2
Supt. – Bruce Cannell, P O BOX 448 81423
Basin ES, P O BOX 448 81423
Donald Davis, prin.
ES, P O BOX 448 81423 – Donald Davis, prin.

Nucla, Montrose Co., Pop. Code 3
West End SD Re-2
Supt. – See Naturita
ES, P O BOX 489 81424 – Bette Hendrickson, prin.

Oak Creek, Routt Co., Pop. Code 2
South Routt SD Re-3J
Sch. Sys. Enr. Code 2
Supt. – William Meek, P O BOX 158 80467
Sorocco JHS, P O BOX 158 80467
Richard Coleman, prin.
Other Schools – See Yampa

Olathe, Montrose Co., Pop. Code 3
Montrose County SD Re-1J
Supt. – See Montrose
MS, P O BOX 505 81425 – Jerome Suppes, prin.
ES, P O BOX 505 81425 – J. Hartmangruber, prin.

Ordway, Crowley Co., Pop. Code 4
Crowley County SD Re-1-J
Sch. Sys. Enr. Code 3
Supt. – Dick Michael, P O BOX 338 81063
Crowley County ES, P O BOX 338 81063
Gary Frickell, prin.
Other Schools – See Crowley

Otis, Washington Co., Pop. Code 3
Lone Star SD 101
Sch. Sys. Enr. Code 1
Supt. – Don Montgomery
RURAL ROUTE 02 80743
Lone Star ES, RURAL ROUTE 02 80743
Don Montgomery, prin.

Otis SD R-3
Sch. Sys. Enr. Code 2
Supt. – Durell Thompson, P O BOX 105 80743
ES, P O BOX 101 80743 – Durell Thompson, prin.

Ouray, Ouray Co., Pop. Code 3
Ouray SD R-1
Sch. Sys. Enr. Code 2
Supt. – Ron Kelton, P O BOX N 81427
ES, P O BOX N 81427 – Ginny Ficco, prin.

Ovid, Sedgwick Co., Pop. Code 2
Platte Valley SD Re-3
Sch. Sys. Enr. Code 2
Supt. – Keith Sommerfeld, P O BOX 369 80744
Other Schools – See Sedgwick

Pagosa Springs, Archuleta Co., Pop. Code 4
Archuleta County SD 50 Jt
Sch. Sys. Enr. Code 4
Supt. – Terry Alley, P O BOX 1498 81147
JHS, P O BOX 1498 81147 – Larry Lister, prin.
ES, P O BOX 1498 81147 – Henry Smith, prin.

Palisade, Mesa Co., Pop. Code 3
Mesa County Valley SD 51
Supt. – See Grand Junction
Taylor ES, 689 BRENTWOOD DR 81526
Delores Crane, prin.

Palmer Lake, El Paso Co., Pop. Code 4
Lewis-Palmer SD 38
Supt. – See Monument
ES, P O BOX 10 80133 – Genevieve Garcia, prin.

Paonia, Delta Co., Pop. Code 4
Delta County SD 50 (J)
Supt. – See Delta
MS, P O BOX 10 81428 – Floyd Beard, prin.
ES, P O BOX 1179 81428 – Willa Sorenson, prin.

Parachute, Garfield Co., Pop. Code 2
Garfield SD 16
Sch. Sys. Enr. Code 2
Supt. – John Pennington, P O BOX 68 81635
St. John MS, P O BOX 68 81635
John Miller, prin.
Underwood ES, P O BOX 68 81635
Ronald Hinz, prin.

Paradox, Montrose Co.
West End SD Re-2
Supt. – See Naturita
PS 81429 – Larry Swain, prin.

Parker, Douglas Co., Pop. Code 3
Douglas County SD Re-1(J)
Supt. – See Castle Rock
Mountain View PS, 8502 E PINERY PKWY 80134
Jane Ellison, prin.
Northeast IS, 6598 N HWY 83 80134
Mary Schueler, prin.
Pine Lane IS, 6450 E PINE LANE AVE 80134
Michael Dubrovich, prin.
Pine Lane PS, 6475 E PONDEROSA DR 80134
George Jurata, prin.

Peetz, Logan Co., Pop. Code 2
Plateau SD Re-5
Sch. Sys. Enr. Code 2
Supt. – Leonard Wiss, P O BOX B 80747
ES, P O BOX B 80747 – Leonard Wiss, prin.

Penrose, Freemont Co., Pop. Code 4
Florence SD Re-2J
Supt. – See Florence
ES, 100 ILLINOIS 81240 – Tom Gribben, prin.

Peyton, El Paso Co., Pop. Code 2
Falcon SD 49
Sch. Sys. Enr. Code 4
Supt. – Dr. Alan Hafer
10850 E WOODMAN ROAD 80831
Falcon ES, 12050 FALCON HWY 80831
Tom Fitch, prin.
Other Schools – See Colorado Springs

Peyton SD 23 Jt
Sch. Sys. Enr. Code 2
Supt. – Dr. David Trujillo 80831
MS, P O BOX 98 80831 – Katrina Robinson, prin.
ES, P O BOX 98 80831 – Katrina Robinson, prin.

Pierce, Weld Co., Pop. Code 3
Ault-Highland SD Re-9
Supt. – See Ault
Highland ES, P O BOX 39 80650 – Sue Reid, prin.

Platteville, Weld Co., Pop. Code 3
Gilcrest SD Re-1
Supt. – See Gilcrest
South Valley MS, P O BOX 427 80651
Bernie Martinez, prin.
ES, P O BOX 427 80651 – Judith Yamaguchi, prin.

Pritchett, Baca Co., Pop. Code 2
Pritchett SD Re-3
Sch. Sys. Enr. Code 1
Supt. – James Boydstun, P O BOX 7 81064
ES, P O BOX 7 81064 – James Boydstun, prin.

Pueblo, Pueblo Co., Pop. Code 8
Pueblo CSD 60
Sch. Sys. Enr. Code 7
Supt. – Dr. M. Vallejo, P O BOX 575 81002
Corwin MS, 1500 LAKEVIEW AVE 81004
Fred Ingo, prin.
Freed MS, 715 W 20TH ST 81003
Frank DeLeon, prin.
Heaton MS, 6 ADAIR ROAD 81001
Robert Moore, prin.
Pitts MS, 29 LEHIGH AVE 81005
Edmund Romero, prin.

Risley MS, E 7TH & LACROSSE 81001
Lee Roy Martinez, prin.
Roncalli MS, 4202 HIGHWAY 76 81005
Frank Zerfas, prin.
Belmont ES, 31 MCNAUGHTON ROAD 81001
Frank Taulli, prin.
Bessemer ES, 1125 E ROUTT AVE 81004
Rose Marie Prewett, prin.
Beulah Heights ES, 2670 DELPHINIUM ST 81005
Dorothy Bjork, prin.
Bradford ES, E 1ST & LACROSSE 81001
Lucia Martinez, prin.
Carlile ES, 736 W EVANS AVE 81004
Richard Gonzales, prin.
Columbian ES, 1202 BRAGDON AVE 81004
Kenton Burger, prin.
Eastwood ES, E 17TH & NEILSON 81001
Kathy West, prin.
Fountain ES, 916 N FOUNTAIN AVE 81001
Joyce Anderson, prin.
Franklin ES, 1315 HORSESHOE DR 81001
Henry Gonzales, prin.
Goodnight ES, WINDY WAY & SAGE ST 81005
Linda Ballas, prin.
Haaff ES, 15 CHINOOK LN 81001
Stephen Hiza, prin.
Hellbeck ES, 3000 LAKEVIEW AVE 81005
Roy Franklin, prin.
Highland Park ES, 2701 VINEWOOD LN 81005
Norma Vice, prin.
Hyde Park ES, 2500 W 18TH ST 81003
Marcos Berumen, prin.
Irving ES, 1629 W 21ST ST 81003
Robert Cason, prin.
Jefferson ES, NUCKOLLS & PRAIRIE AVES 81005
Dorothy Buksar, prin.
Minnequa ES, 1708 E ORMAN AVE 81004
J. Arthur Sanches, prin.
Morton ES, W 31ST & COLFAX 81003
Donald Nelson, prin.
Park View ES, E 9TH & MONUMENT 81001
Edward Lujan, prin.
Somerlid ES, 705 W 27TH ST 81003
Mary Ann Roldan, prin.
South Park ES, 3100 HOLLYWOOD DR 81005
Mary Lou Cummings, prin.
Spann ES, 2300 E 10TH ST 81001
William Vensor, prin.
Sunset Park ES, 110 UNIVERSITY CIR 81005
Cheryl Bronn, prin.

Pueblo County Rural SD 70
Sch. Sys. Enr. Code 3
Supt. – Michael Johnson
24951 E HIGHWAY 50 81006
Pleasant View MS, 23531 EVERETT ROAD 81006
Rudolph Bonan, prin.
Vineland MS, 1132 36TH LANE 81006
Charles Carmichael, prin.
North Mesa ES, 28881 GALE ROAD 81006
John Musso, prin.
South Mesa ES, 23701 PRESTON ROAD 81006
Richard Vivoda, prin.
Vineland ES, 35777 IRIS ROAD 81006
Ron Petkosek, prin.
Other Schools – See Avondale, Beulah, Colorado City,
Pueblo West, Rye

John Neuman ES, 2415 E ORMAN AVE 81004
Trinity Evangelist Lutheran School
715 W EVANS AVE 81004

Pueblo West, Pueblo Co., Pop. Code 5
Pueblo County Rural SD 70
Supt. – See Pueblo
MS, 484 S MAHER DRIVE 81007
Rick Thielbar, prin.
ES, 386 W HAHNS PEAK AVE 81007
Ione Miller, prin.

Rangely, Rio Blanco Co., Pop. Code 4
Rangely SD Re-4
Sch. Sys. Enr. Code 3
Supt. – James Burks, 402 W MAIN ST 81648
JHS, 550 RIVER ROAD 81648
William McDaniel, prin.
Parkview ES, 609 S STANOLIND AVE 81648
William Palmer, prin.

Red Cliff, Eagle Co., Pop. Code 2
Eagle County SD Re-50(J)
Supt. – See Eagle
ES, P O BOX 154 81649 – Lorraine Lopez, prin.

Red Feather Lakes, Larimer Co., Pop. Code 2
Poudre SD R-1
Supt. – See Fort Collins
ES 80545 – Mary Kay Sommers, prin.

Rico, Dolores Co., Pop. Code 1
Dolores County SD Re NO.2
Supt. – See Dove Creek
ES, P O BOX 38 81332 – Doug Johnson, prin.

Ridgway, Ouray Co., Pop. Code 2
Ridgway SD R-2
Sch. Sys. Enr. Code 2
Supt. – Aaron Weatherby, P O BOX 230 81432
ES, P O BOX 230 81432 – Aaron Weatherby, prin.

Rifle, Garfield Co., Pop. Code 4
Garfield SD Re-2
Sch. Sys. Enr. Code 4
Supt. – Lennard Eckhardt
839 WHITE RIVER 81650

MS, 839 WHITE RIVER 81650
Max Wheeler, prin.
Lewis ES, 839 WHITE RIVER 81650
George Hesse, prin.
Other Schools – See New Castle, Silt

Meeker SD Re-1
Supt. – See Meeker
Rock ES, PICEANCE CREEK ROUTE 81650
Richard Flaherty, prin.

Rocky Ford, Otero Co., Pop. Code 5
Rocky Ford SD R-2
Sch. Sys. Enr. Code 4
Supt. – Dr. Douglas Brown, P O BOX 311 81067
Jefferson MS, P O BOX 311 81067
Melvyn Davy, prin.
Liberty MS, P O BOX 311 81067
James Wilkins, prin.
Washington ES, P O BOX 311 81067
Georgetta Driskell, prin.

Romeo, Conejos Co., Pop. Code 2
North Conejos SD Re-1J
Supt. – See La Jara
ES, P O BOX 158 81148 – Eva Marie Salas, prin.

Rush, El Paso Co.
Miami-Yoder SD 60 JT
Sch. Sys. Enr. Code 2
Supt. – Yvonne Robertson 80833
Miami/Yoder ES 80833 – Jeff Hatter, prin.

Rye, Pueblo Co., Pop. Code 2
Pueblo County Rural SD 70
Supt. – See Pueblo
ES, P O BOX 239 81069 – Elizabeth Trujillo, prin.

Saguache, Saguache Co., Pop. Code 3
Mountain Valley SD Re-1
Sch. Sys. Enr. Code 2
Supt. – James McDermott, P O BOX 127 81149
Mountain Valley S, P O BOX 127 81149
Wesley Brewer, prin.

Salida, Chaffee Co., Pop. Code 5
Salida SD R-32 J
Sch. Sys. Enr. Code 4
Supt. – C. Robertson, P O BOX 70 81201
Kesner JHS, P O BOX 70 81201
Mike Baldino, prin.
Longfellow ES, P O BOX 512 81201
Jerre Doss, prin.

Sanford, Conejos Co., Pop. Code 3
Sanford SD 6 J
Sch. Sys. Enr. Code 2
Supt. – Warren Reed, P O BOX 248 81151
ES, P O BOX 248 81151 – Arnold Mortensen, prin.

San Luis, Costilla Co., Pop. Code 3
Centennial SD R-1
Sch. Sys. Enr. Code 2
Supt. – Robert Rael, P O BOX 347 81152
Centennial JHS, P O BOX 347 81152
Herman Martinez, prin.
Centennial ES, P O BOX 347 81152
Herman Martinez, prin.

Sedalia, Douglas Co., Pop. Code 2
Douglas County SD Re-1(J)
Supt. – See Castle Rock
ES, 5449 N HUXTABLE ST 80135
Karen Kay Close, prin.

Sedgwick, Sedgwick Co., Pop. Code 2
Platte Valley SD Re-3
Supt. – See Ovid
Platte Valley ES, P O BOX 128 80749
James Jeffers, prin.

Sheridan Lake, Kiowa Co., Pop. Code 5
Plainview SD Re-2
Sch. Sys. Enr. Code 1
Supt. – Orrin Oppliger, P O BOX 1268 81071
Plainview S, P O BOX 1268 81071
Orrin Oppliger, prin.

Silt, Garfield Co., Pop. Code 3
Garfield SD Re-2
Supt. – See Rifle
ES, P O BOX 245 81652 – William Vitany, prin.

Silverton, San Juan Co., Pop. Code 3
Silverton SD 1
Sch. Sys. Enr. Code 2
Supt. – Dan Salifsberg, P O BOX 156 81433
ES, P O BOX 128 81433 – Dan Salfisberg, prin.

Simla, Elbert Co., Pop. Code 2
Big Sandy SD 100J
Sch. Sys. Enr. Code 2
Supt. – Richard Ullom, P O BOX 68 80835
JHS, P O BOX 68 80835 – Philip Thomas, prin.
ES, P O BOX 68 80835 – Marcella Ruch, prin.

Springfield, Baca Co., Pop. Code 4
Springfield SD Re-4
Sch. Sys. Enr. Code 2
Supt. – William Zitterkopf, 389 TIPTON ST 81073
JHS, 389 TIPTON ST 81073 – James Walton, prin.
ES, 389 TIPTON ST 81073
William Zitterkopf, prin.

Steamboat Springs, Routt Co., Pop. Code 4
Steamboat Springs SD Re-2
Sch. Sys. Enr. Code 4
Supt. – Dr. J. Alan Aufderheide
51 E MAPLE 80477

JHS, P O BOX 1177   80477 – Alfred Root, prin.
Soda Creek ES, 639 PARK AVE   80477
  Steve Kaufman, prin.
Strawberry Park MS, P O BOX 1177   80477
  John DeVincentis, prin.

Sterling, Logan Co., Pop. Code 7
Valley SD Re-1
Sch. Sys. Enr. Code 5
Supt. – Dr. Roger Blake, P O BOX 910   80751
JHS, 1177 PAWNEE AVE   80751
  Martin Foster, prin.
Campbell ES, CLARK & 9TH AVE   80751
  Robert Jesson, prin.
Franklin ES, 916 S 4TH AVE   80751
  Gloria Corbin, prin.
Hagen ES, VERDE AVE   80751
  Frank Bargell, prin.
Stevens ES, 1215 N 5TH ST   80751
  Keith Gentry, prin.
Other Schools – See Iliff

St. Anthony's ES, 324 S 3RD ST   80751

Strasburg, Adams Co., Pop. Code 3
Strasburg SD 31J
Sch. Sys. Enr. Code 2
Supt. – Delmer Hemphill, P O BOX 207   80136
ES, P O BOX 207   80136 – Pat Banks, prin.

Stratton, Kit Carson Co., Pop. Code 3
Stratton SD R-4
Sch. Sys. Enr. Code 2
Supt. – David Cockerham, P O BOX 266   80836
Stratton Elementary School, P O BOX 266   80836
  Kathleen Pickard, prin.

Swink, Otero Co., Pop. Code 2
Swink SD 33
Sch. Sys. Enr. Code 2
Supt. – Bernie Sachs, P O BOX 487   81077
ES, P O BOX 487   81077 – Pat Lesar, prin.

Telluride, San Miguel Co., Pop. Code 3
Telluride SD R-1
Sch. Sys. Enr. Code 2
Supt. – P. Cleve Penberthy, P O BOX 187   81435
MS, P O BOX 187   81435 – Marc Hankin, prin.
ES, P O BOX 187   81435 – Gordon Gibson, prin.

Thornton, Adams Co., Pop. Code 7
Mapleton SD 1
Supt. – See Denver
Clayton MS, 2410 POZE BLVD   80229
  Elizabeth Bieber, prin.
York JHS, 9200 YORK ST   80229
  Cheryl Tufly, prin.
Heid ES, E 91ST & POZE BLVD   80229
  Mary Truitt, prin.

Northglenn-Thornton SD 12
Supt. – See Northglenn
Cherry Drive ES, 11500 CHERRY DR   80233
  Nancy Jo Johnson, prin.
Hunter's Glen ES, 13222 CORONA ST   80241
  John Virgil, prin.
North Star ES, 8740 N STAR DR   80221
  John Fajardo, prin.
Riverdale ES, 10724 ELM DRIVE   80030
  Robert Huckins, prin.
Skyview ES, 5021 E 123RD AVE   80241
  Michael Lentz, prin.
Tarver ES, 3500 SUMMIT GROVE PKWY   80241
  David Usechek, prin.
ES, 901 EPPINGER BLVD   80229
  J. Sam Thornham, prin.
Woodglen ES, 11717 MADISON ST   80233
  Kathleen Rust, prin.

Timnath, Larimer Co., Pop. Code 2
Poudre SD R-1
Supt. – See Fort Collins
ES, P O BOX 10   80547 – Ruth Herron, prin.

Trinidad, Las Animas Co., Pop. Code 6
Trinidad SD 1
Sch. Sys. Enr. Code 4
Supt. – James Murlless, P O BOX 766   81082
JHS, 614 PARK ST   81082 – Joseph Reorda, prin.
East Street ES, 206 EAST ST   81082
  Patricia Festi, prin.
Eckhart ES, 1021 PIERCE ST   81082
  Charles Simpleman, prin.
Park Street MS, 612 PARK ST   81082
  A. Sanchez, prin.

Holy Trinity ES, 135 CHURCH   81032

USAF Academy, El Paso Co., Pop. Code 6
Academy SD 20
Supt. – See Colorado Springs
Douglass Valley ES   80840 – Wendy Crist, prin.
Pine Valley ES   80840 – Sharon Rice, prin.

Vail, Eagle Co., Pop. Code 2
Eagle County SD Re-50(J)
Supt. – See Eagle

Red Sandstone ES, P O BOX 1428   81658
  Beverly Golden, prin.

Vail Mountain School
  3160 KATSOS RANCH ROAD   81657

Vilas, Baca Co., Pop. Code 1
Vilas SD Re-5
Sch. Sys. Enr. Code 2
Supt. – Melvin Scarrow   81087
ES   81087 – Melvin Scarrow, prin.

Vona, Kit Carson Co., Pop. Code 1
Hi-Plaines SD R-23
Sch. Sys. Enr. Code 2
Supt. – Anthon Leon Sant, P O BOX 8   80861
Hi-Plains ES, P O BOX 8   80861
  Anthon Leon Sant, prin.

Walden, Jackson Co., Pop. Code 3
North Park SD R-1
Sch. Sys. Enr. Code 2
Supt. – Harry Masinton, P O BOX 798   80480
ES, P O BOX 798   80480 – Melanie Wood, prin.

Walsenburg, Huerfano Co., Pop. Code 5
Huerfano SD Re-1
Sch. Sys. Enr. Code 3
Supt. – Gary Upchurch, 611 W 7TH ST   81089
MS, 415 WALSEN AVE   81089
  Joe Donahue, prin.
Washington ES, 611 W 7TH ST   81089
  William Duran, prin.
Other Schools – See Gardner

St. Mary's School, 7TH & RUSSELL   81089

Walsh, Baca Co., Pop. Code 3
Walsh SD Re-1
Sch. Sys. Enr. Code 2
Supt. – Terry Cates, P O BOX 68   81090
ES, P O BOX 68   81090 – Carlyn Yokum, prin.

Weldona, Morgan Co., Pop. Code 2
Weldon Valley SD Re-20 (J)
Sch. Sys. Enr. Code 2
Supt. – Lawrence Stukey, P O BOX 668   80653
Weldon Valley S, P O BOX 668   80653
  Lawrence Stukey, prin.

Wellington, Larimer Co., Pop. Code 3
Poudre SD R-1
Supt. – See Fort Collins
Eyestone ES, 4000 WILSON AVE   80549
  Kim Nohava, prin.

Westcliffe, Custer Co., Pop. Code 2
Custer County Cons. SD C-1
Sch. Sys. Enr. Code 2
Supt. – Richard Wilson, P O BOX 211   81252
Custer County Consolidated S, P O BOX 211   81252
  Richard Graham, prin.

Westminster, Adams Co., Pop. Code 7
Jefferson County SD R-1
Supt. – See Golden
Zerger ES, 9050 FIELD ST   80030
  Irene Griego, prin.

Northglenn-Thornton SD 12
Supt. – See Northglenn
Cotton Creek ES, 11100 VRAIN ST   80030
  Patricia Brown, prin.
Rocky Mountain ES, 3350 W 99TH AVE   80030
  George Moyer, prin.

Westminster SD 50
Sch. Sys. Enr. Code 7
Supt. – Michael Massarotti
  4476 W 68TH AVE   80030
Shaw Heights MS, 8780 CIRCLE DRIVE   80030
  Barbara Arnett, prin.
Flynn ES, 8731 LOWELL BLVD   80030
  Jincy Fletcher, prin.
Harris Park ES, 4300 W 75TH AVE   80030
  Ben Martinez, prin.
Mesa ES, 9100 LOWELL BLVD   80030
  Mark Whitney, prin.
Skyline Vista ES, 7395 ZUNI ST   80030
  John Bellomo, prin.
Sunset Ridge ES, 9451 HOOKER ST   80030
  Cynthia Watson, prin.
Vista Grande ES, 8845 WAGNER DR   80030
  Mary Lou Zarlengo, prin.
ES, 7482 IRVING ST   80030 – Patricia Ireland, prin.
Westminster Hills ES, 4105 W 80TH AVE   80030
  Marlys White, prin.
Other Schools – See Arvada, Denver

Belleview School, 3455 W 83RD AVE   80030
Holy Trinity ES, 7595 FEDERAL BLVD   80030
Shepherd of the Valley School
  8820 FIELD ST   80020

Weston, Las Animas Co., Pop. Code 2
Primero Reorganized SD 2
Sch. Sys. Enr. Code 2
Supt. – Felix Garcia, RURAL ROUTE 01   81091
ES, RURAL ROUTE 01   81091
  Shirley Tomsic, prin.

Wheat Ridge, Jefferson Co., Pop. Code 8
Jefferson County SD R-1
Supt. – See Golden
Everitt JHS, 3900 KIPLING ST   80033
  Russell Ramsey, prin.
JHS, 7101 W 38TH AVE   80033
  P. Carl Schiele, prin.
Kullerstrand ES, 12225 W 38TH AVE   80033
  Ralph Bartlett, prin.
Martensen ES, 6625 W 45TH PL   80033
  Diane Ullman, prin.
Pennington ES, 4645 INDEPENDENCE ST   80033
  Susan Loving, prin.
Prospect Valley ES, 3400 PIERSON ST   80033
  Arleyne Morgan, prin.
Stevens ES, 4001 REED ST   80033
  Norman Oliver, prin.
Wilmore-Davis ES, 7975 W 41ST AVE   80033
  George Lauterbach, prin.

Janus Wilmont School, 32ND & KIPLING   80033
Sts. Peter and Paul School, 3920 PIERCE   80033

Wiggins, Morgan Co., Pop. Code 2
Wiggins SD Re-50 (J)
Sch. Sys. Enr. Code 2
Supt. – Gene Brubacher, P O BOX 128   80654
JHS, P O BOX 128   80654 – Robert Sachs, prin.
ES, P O BOX 128   80654 – Steve Neel, prin.

Wiley, Prowers Co., Pop. Code 2
Wiley SD Re-13 Jt
Sch. Sys. Enr. Code 2
Supt. – Norman Blake, P O BOX 247   81092
ES, P O BOX 247   81092 – William Elam, prin.

Windsor, Weld Co., Pop. Code 4
Windsor SD Re-4
Sch. Sys. Enr. Code 4
Supt. – Dr. James Raine, 301 WALNUT ST   80550
MS, P O BOX 609   80550 – Arlen Koehler, prin.
Mountain View MS, P O BOX 609   80550
  Verdell Lessman, prin.
Skyview ES, P O BOX 609   80550
  Brian Lessman, prin.
Tozer PS, P O BOX 609   80550
  William Miles, prin.

Woodland Park, Teller Co., Pop. Code 4
Woodland Park SD Re-2
Sch. Sys. Enr. Code 4
Supt. – Dr. Steven McKee, P O BOX 99   80866
MS, P O BOX 99   80866 – Charles Lutgen, prin.
Columbine ES, P O BOX 99   80866
  Russell Tomlin, prin.
Gateway ES, P O BOX 99   80866 – Rob Danin, prin.

Woodrow, Washington Co.
Woodlin SD R-104
Sch. Sys. Enr. Code 2
Supt. – Robert Butler, P O BOX 185   80757
Woodlin S, P O BOX 185   80757
  Tom George, prin.

Wray, Yuma Co., Pop. Code 4
East Yuma County SD RJ-2
Sch. Sys. Enr. Code 3
Supt. – Ken Fritz, P O BOX 157   80758
Buchanan MS, 620 W 7TH ST   80758
  Robert Selle, prin.
ES, 30204 CO RD 35   80758
  David Leadabrand, prin.
Other Schools – See Idalia

Yampa, Routt Co., Pop. Code 2
South Routt SD Re-3J
Supt. – See Oak Creek
South Routt ES, P O BOX 97   80483
  William Alley, prin.

Yoder, El Paso Co., Pop. Code 1
Edison SD 54 Jt
Sch. Sys. Enr. Code 1
Supt. – LeRoy Reams
  14550 EDISON ROAD   80864
S, 14550 EDISON RD   80864 – LeRoy Reams, prin.

Yuma, Yuma Co., Pop. Code 4
West Yuma County SD R-J-1
Sch. Sys. Enr. Code 3
Supt. – Wayne Brown, 1101 S ASH ST   80759
Yuma West MS, 500 S ELM ST   80759
  Wayne Laut, prin.
Morris PS, P O BOX 327   80759
  Darlene Korf, prin.
Other Schools – See Joes

CONNECTICUT

STATE DEPARTMENT OF EDUCATION
P.O. Box 2219, Hartford 06145
(203) 566-5061

Commissioner of Education	Gerald Tirozzi
Deputy Commissioner Finance & Operations	Frank Altieri
Deputy Commissioner Program & Support Services	Scott Brohinsky
Director Curriculum Professional Development	Betty Sternberg
Director Education Support Services	Robert Margolin
Director Management & Budget	John Coroso
Director Rehabilitation Services	Marilyn Campbell
Director Research, Evaluation, Assessment	Pascal Forgione
Director Vocational, Technical & Adult Education	Theodore Sergi

STATE BOARD OF EDUCATION
Abraham Glassman, *Chairperson*   44 Berlow Rd., South Windsor   06074

BOARD OF GOVERNORS FOR HIGHER EDUCATION
Dr. Norma Foreman Glasgow, *Commissioner*   61 Woodland St., Hartford   06105

PUBLIC, PRIVATE, AND PAROCHIAL ELEMENTARY SCHOOLS

Andover, Tolland Co., Pop. Code 4
Andover SD
Supt. – See Hebron
ES, SCHOOL ROAD   06232 – Fred Ashton, prin.

Ansonia, New Haven Co., Pop. Code 7
Ansonia SD
Sch. Sys. Enr. Code 4
Supt. – R. E. Zuraw, 42 GROVE   06401
Prendergast MS, 59 FINNEY ST   06401
 Peter Sosnovich, prin.
Willis MS, 85 CLIFTON AVE   06401
 John O'Brien, prin.
Lincoln-Hayes ES, 83 COTTAGE AVE   06401
 Peter Stamos, prin.
Mead ES, FORD ST   06401 – Michael Dalton, prin.
Peck ES, 34 HOLBROOK ST   06401
 John D'Alexander, prin.

Assumption ES, 51 N CLIFF ST   06401
St. Joseph ES, 36 JEWETT ST   06401
SS Peter & Paul School, 60 HOWARD AVE   06401

Ashford, Windham Co., Pop. Code 5
Ashford SD
Sch. Sys. Enr. Code 2
Supt. – Richard Butler, P O BOX 128   06278
ES, P O BOX 128   06278 – Clay Jordan, prin.

Avon, Hartford Co., Pop. Code 7
Avon SD
Sch. Sys. Enr. Code 4
Supt. – Dr. Herbert F. Pandiscio
 34 SIMSBURY ROAD   06001
MS, 375 W AVON ROAD   06001
 Jerome Cramp, prin.
Roaring Brook ES, 30 OLD WHEELER LN   06001
 Anthony Segretario, prin.
Towpath ES, 50 SIMSBURY RD   06001
 John Fleming, prin.

Baltic, New London Co., Pop. Code 4
Sprague SD
Sch. Sys. Enr. Code 2
Supt. – Aram Damarjian, ROUTE 97   06330
Sayles ES, P O BOX 693   06330
 John Bennett, prin.

St. Joseph ES, SCHOOL HILL RD   06330

Beacon Falls, New Haven Co., Pop. Code 5
Regional SD 16
Supt. – See Prospect
Laurel Ledge ES   06403 – Michael Dance, prin.

Berlin, Hartford Co., Pop. Code 7
Berlin SD
Sch. Sys. Enr. Code 4
Supt. – Theodore Rokicki
 240 KENSINGTON ROAD   06037
McGee MS, 899 NORTON ROAD   06037
 Guy Parillo, prin.
Willard ES, 1088 NORTON RD   06037
 Maureen Walsh, prin.
Other Schools – See East Berlin, Kensington

Bethany, New Haven Co., Pop. Code 5
Bethany SD
Sch. Sys. Enr. Code 2
Supt. – Franklin Plummer, 44 PECK ROAD   06525
Other Schools – See New Haven

Bethel, Fairfield Co., Pop. Code 6
Bethel SD
Sch. Sys. Enr. Code 5
Supt. – Robert Gilchrest, P O BOX 253   06801
MS, 1 SCHOOL ST   06801 – Emil Fusek, prin.
Berry ES, 58 WHITTLESEY DR   06801
 Michael Giarratano, prin.
Johnson ES, WHITTLESEY DR   06801
 John Boyle, prin.
Rockwell ES, 59 WHITTLESEY DR   06801
 Herbert Fane, prin.

St. Mary ES, 24 DODGINGTOWN RD   06801

Bethlehem, Litchfield Co., Pop. Code 5
Regional SD 14
Supt. – See Woodbury
ES, 22 EAST ST   06751 – Claire Hines, prin.

Bloomfield, Hartford Co., Pop. Code 7
Bloomfield SD
Sch. Sys. Enr. Code 5
Supt. – L. Copes, 785 PARK AVE   06002
JHS, 330 PARK AVE   06002 – James Cronin, prin.
MS, 390 PARK AVE   06002
 Edward Simmons, prin.
Laurel ES, 1 FILLEY ST   06002 – John Seidell, prin.
Metacomet ES, 185 SCHOOL ST   06002
 Portia Mendez, prin.
Vincent ES, 25 TURKEY HILL RD   06002
 Doreen Doren, prin.

Sigel Hebrew ES, 53 GABB RD   06002

Bolton, Hartford Co., Pop. Code 2
Bolton SD
Sch. Sys. Enr. Code 3
Supt. – Richard Packman
 106 NOTCH ROAD   06040
ES, 104 NOTCH RD   06043 – Anne Rash, prin.

Bozrah, New London Co., Pop. Code 4
Bozrah SD
Sch. Sys. Enr. Code 2
Supt. – David Easterly, P O BOX 52   06334
Fields Memorial ES, P O BOX 52   06334
 David Easterly, prin.

Branford, New Haven Co., Pop. Code 7
Branford SD
Sch. Sys. Enr. Code 5
Supt. – Armand Fusco, 33 LAUREL ST   06405
IS, 185 DAMASCUS ROAD   06405
 Francis Walsh, prin.
Branford Hills ES, 80 BURBAN DR   06405
 Mary O'Brien, prin.
Brushy Plain ES, BRUSHY PLAIN ROAD   06405
 Mary O'Brien, prin.
Indian Neck ES, 12 MELROSE AVE   06405
 Mary O'Brien, prin.

Pine Orchard ES, BIRCH ROAD   06405
 Mary O'Brien, prin.
Sliney ES, EADES ST   06405
 Mark Rabinowitz, prin.
Tisko ES, 118 DAMASCUS RD   06405
 Mary O'Brien, prin.

St. Mary ES, 62 CEDAR ST   06405

Bridgeport, Fairfield Co., Pop. Code 9
Bridgeport SD
Sch. Sys. Enr. Code 7
Supt. – James Connelly
 45 LYON TERR RM 303   06604
Cross MS, 1775 RESERVOIR AVE   06606
 Gladys Hill, prin.
East Side ES, 700 PALISADE AVE   06610
 Ralph Veneruso, prin.
Barnum ES, 529 NOBLE AVE   06608
 Virginia Martinez, prin.
Beardsley ES, 500 HUNTINGTON RD   06610
 Edward Kovac, prin.
Black Rock ES, 545 BREWSTER ST   06605
 Charlene Carter, prin.
Blackham ES, 425 THORME ST   06606
 Joanne D'Onofrio, prin.
Bryant ES, 865 MAPLEWOOD AVE   06605
 Robert Marconi, prin.
Clemente ES, 1055 PEMBROKE ST   06608
 Virginia Lity, prin.
Columbus ES, 275 GEORGE ST   06604
 Milagros Vizcarrondo, prin.
Curiale ES, 300 LAUREL AVE   06605
 Michael Koperwhats, prin.
Dunbar ES, 445 UNION AVE   06607
 James Hodge, prin.
Edison ES, 115 BOSTON TER   06610
 Joan Nobriga, prin.
Garfield ES, 655 STILLMAN ST   06608
 Jose Vizcarrondo, prin.
Hall ES, CLERMONT AVE   06610
 Joseph Rutkosky, prin.
Hallen ES, 68 OMEGA AVE   06606
 Charles O'Hara, prin.
High Horizons ES, 700 PALISADE AVE   06610
 Michael Hanna, prin.
Hooker ES, 159 ROGER WILLIAMS RD   06610
 Anne Walsh, prin.
Howe ES, 287 CLINTON AVE   06605
 Aida Comulada, prin.
Longfellow MS, 139 OCEAN TER   06605
 Bruce Posey, prin.
Madison ES, 376 WAYNE ST   06606
 Steven Balgach, prin.
Maplewood ES, 240 LINWOOD AVE   06604
 William Holsworth, prin.
McKinley ES, 345 LOGAN ST   06607
 Jettie Tisdale, prin.
Multicultural ES, 700 PALISADE AVE   06610
 William Quintana, prin.
Newfield ES, 405 NEWFIELD AVE   06607
 Ruth Gunter, prin.
Park City ES, 1526 CHOPSEY HILL RD   06606
 Ralph Council, prin.

Read ES, 130 EZRA ST 06606
  M. Gloria Maina, prin.
Roosevelt ES, 680 PARK AVE 06604
  William Tinkler, prin.
Waltersville ES, 95 GILMORE ST 06608
  Roberto Rodriguez, prin.
Webster ES, 1375 NORTH AVE 06604
  Katherine Brady, prin.
Winthrop ES, 85 ECKART ST 06606
  Henry Kelly, prin.

Blessed Sacrament of St. Mary Es
  276 UNION AVE 06607
Holy Rosary ES, 391 E WASHINGTON AVE 06608
Sacred Heart of St. Anthony ES
  637 PARK AVE 06604
St. Ambrose ES, 461 MILL HILL AVE 06610
St. Andrew ES, 395 ANTON ST 06606
St. Ann ES, 521 BREWSTER ST 06605
St. Augustine ES, 63 PEQUONNOCK ST 06604
St. Michael ES, 286 PULASKI ST 06608
St. Patrick ES, 322 WELLS ST 06606
St. Raphael ES, 324 FRANK ST 06604
Zion ES, 612 GRAND ST 06604

Bridgewater, Litchfield Co., Pop. Code 4
Regional SD 12
Supt. – See Washington Depot
The Burnham ES, MAIN ST 06752
  Richard Hoffman, prin.

Bristol, Hartford Co., Pop. Code 8
Bristol SD
Sch. Sys. Enr. Code 6
Supt. – Ed Maher, 129 CHURCH ST 06010
Memorial Boulevard MS
  70 MEMORIAL BLVD 06010 – Walter Ives, prin.
Northeast MS, 530 STEVENS ST 06010
  Frederick Mascola, prin.
Bingham ES, 3 NORTH ST 06010
  Carolyn Cistulli, prin.
Edgewood ES, 15 MIX ST 06010
  John Reardon,Jr., prin.
Greene-Hills ES, 718 PINE ST 06010
  Ronald Stockman, prin.
Hubbell ES, 90 W WASHINGTON ST 06010
  Gerard Lefevre, prin.
Ivy Drive ES, 160 IVY DR 06010
  Anthony Acampora, prin.
Jennings ES, 291 BURLINGTON AVE 06010
  Karen Bailey, prin.
Mountain View ES, 71 VERA DR 06010
  Geraldine Pelegano, prin.
O'Connell ES, 120 PARK ST 06010
  Willard Lewis, prin.
South Side ES, TUTTLE ROAD 06010
  Armand Hudon, prin.
Stafford ES, 212 LOUISIANA AVE 06010
  Ketih Simpson, prin.

Immanuel Lutheran ES, 154 MEADOW ST 06010
St. Ann ES, 241 WEST ST 06010
St. Anthony ES, 20 PLEASANT ST 06010
St. Joseph ES, 335 CENTER ST 06010
St. Matthew ES, WELCH DR 06010

Broad Brook, Hartford Co., Pop. Code 4
East Windsor SD
Supt. – See East Windsor
East Windsor MS, 38 MAIN ST 06016
  Judith Fuqua, prin.
ES, 14 RYE ST 06016 – Albert Via, prin.

Brookfield, Fairfield Co., Pop. Code 7
Brookfield SD
Supt. – See Brookfield Center
Huckleberry MS
  100 CANDLEWOOD LAKE RD 06804
  Gary Alger, prin.

Brookfield Center, Fairfield Co., Pop. Code 3
Brookfield SD
Sch. Sys. Enr. Code 4
Supt. – Michael Perrone 06805
Whisconier MS, 17 W WHISCONIER ROAD 06805
  Richard Bellesheim, prin.
Center ES, 8 OBTUSE HL 06805
  Linda Fredrickson, prin.
Other Schools – See Brookfield

St. Joseph ES, ROUTE 133 06805

Brooklyn, Windham Co., Pop. Code 6
Brooklyn SD
Sch. Sys. Enr. Code 3
Supt. – Louise Berry, GORMAN ROAD 06234
ES, GORMAN ROAD 06234
  Stanley Meiela,Jr., prin.

Burlington, Hartford Co., Pop. Code 6
Regional SD 10
Sch. Sys. Enr. Code 4
Supt. – James Schmidt, RURAL ROUTE 01 06013
Har-Bur MS, RURAL ROUTE 01 06013
  Joseph Scheideler, prin.
Lake Garda ES, RURAL ROUTE 03 06013
  Lucy Menta, prin.
Other Schools – See Harwinton

Canaan, Litchfield Co., Pop. Code 4
North Canaan SD
Supt. – See Falls Village
North Canaan ES 06018 – Linda Lackner, prin.

Canterbury, Windham Co., Pop. Code 5
Canterbury SD
Sch. Sys. Enr. Code 3
Supt. – James Gallow
  RURAL ROUTE 14 BOX 28 06331
Baldwin ES, 45 WESTMINSTER RD 06331
  Mary Porter Price, prin.

Canton Center, Hartford Co.
Canton SD
Supt. – See Collinsville
Cherry Brook ES, 4 BARBOURTOWN RD 06020
  Geraldine Smith, prin.

Centerbrook, Middlesex Co.
Essex SD
Supt. – See Deep River
Essex ES, SCHOOL CIR 06409
  Thomas James, prin.

Central Village, Windham Co., Pop. Code 4
Plainfield SD
Sch. Sys. Enr. Code 5
Supt. – Albert DePetrillo, P O BOX 218 06332
Other Schools – See Moosup, Plainfield

Chaplin, Windham Co., Pop. Code 4
Chaplin SD
Sch. Sys. Enr. Code 2
Supt. – A. Wutzl, P O BOX 277 06235
ES, CHAPLIN ST 06235 – Robert Rifenburg, prin.

Hampton SD
Sch. Sys. Enr. Code 2
Supt. – A. Wutzl, P O BOX 277 06235
Other Schools – See Hampton

Scotland SD
Sch. Sys. Enr. Code 2
Supt. – A. Wutzl, P O BOX 277 06235
Other Schools – See Scotland

Cheshire, New Haven Co., Pop. Code 7
Cheshire SD
Sch. Sys. Enr. Code 5
Supt. – John Barnes, 29 MAIN ST 06410
Dodd JHS, 100 PARK PL 06410
  Patricia Bellini, prin.
Chapman ES, 38 COUNTRY CLUB RD 06410
  Gerald Corcoran, prin.
Doolittle ES, 735 CORNWALL AVE 06410
  Mark Nolan, prin.
Highland ES, 490 HIGHLAND AVE 06410
  Charles Hague, prin.
Norton ES, 414 N BROOKSVALE RD 06410
  George Kenyon, prin.

Chester, Middlesex Co., Pop. Code 5
Chester SD
Supt. – See Deep River
ES, RIDGE ROAD 06412 – Claudia Kane, prin.

Clinton, Middlesex Co., Pop. Code 7
Clinton SD
Sch. Sys. Enr. Code 4
Supt. – Joseph Cirasuolo
  112 GLENWOOD ROAD 06413
Eliot MS, 69 FAIRY DELL ROAD 06413
  Geraldine Andrew, prin.
Joel ES, GLENWOOD CIR 06413
  Kopi Saltman, prin.
Pierson MS, 75 E MAIN ST 06413
  James Snow, prin.

Colchester, New London Co., Pop. Code 5
Colchester SD
Sch. Sys. Enr. Code 4
Supt. – Edward Favolise, 5 S MAIN ST 06415
Central MS, 70 NORWICH AVE 06415
  W. H. Harris, prin.
Jackter ES, HALLS HILL ROAD 06415
  Carol Wheeler, prin.

Salem SD
Sch. Sys. Enr. Code 2
Supt. – Jefferson Prestridge
  200 HARTFORD ROAD 06415
Salem ES, 200 HARTFORD RD 06415
  Jefferson Prestridge, prin.

Colebrook, Litchfield Co., Pop. Code 4
Colebrook SD
Supt. – See Winsted
Colebrook Consolodated ES, P O BOX 9 06021
  Evelyn Burnham, prin.

Collinsville, Hartford Co., Pop. Code 5
Canton SD
Sch. Sys. Enr. Code 4
Supt. – David Quattropani, 39 DYER AVE 06022
Canton ES, 40 DYER AVE 06022
  Geraldine Smith, prin.
Canton MS, 39 DYER AVE 06022
  Edward Handi, prin.
Other Schools – See Canton Center

Columbia, Tolland Co., Pop. Code 5
Columbia SD
Sch. Sys. Enr. Code 3
Supt. – John Vitale, P O BOX 166 06237
Porter ES, SCHOOLHOUSE RD 06237
  Robert Choiniere, prin.

Cos Cob, Fairfield Co.
Greenwich SD
Supt. – See Greenwich
ES, BOSTON POST ROAD 06807
  Dominic Butera, prin.

Coventry, Tolland Co., Pop. Code 6
Coventry SD
Sch. Sys. Enr. Code 4
Supt. – Nathan Chesler
  78 RIPLEY HILL ROAD 06238
Hale MS, 1776 MAIN ST 06238
  Edward Mahoney, prin.
ES, 3453 MAIN ST 06238
  Mary Margaret Piazza, prin.
Robertson ES, 227 CROSS ST 06238
  William Carpenter, prin.

Cromwell, Middlesex Co., Pop. Code 7
Cromwell SD
Sch. Sys. Enr. Code 4
Supt. – Dr. K. Alexander Paddyfote
  MANN MEMORIAL DR 06416
MS, MANN MEMORIAL DR 06416
  Harry Dumeer, prin.
Stevens ES, 25 COURT ST 06416
  Richard Frank, prin.

Danbury, Fairfield Co., Pop. Code 8
Danbury SD
Sch. Sys. Enr. Code 6
Supt. – Anthony Singe
  ADM BLDG MILL RIDGE 06810
Great Plain ES, 10 STADLEY ROUGH RD 06811
  Anthony Molinaro, prin.
Hayestown Avenue ES
  HAYESTOWN AVE & TAMARACK RD 06811
  Richard Lucas, prin.
King Street IS, SOUTH KING ST 06811
  John Del Grego, prin.
King Street PS, SOUTH KING ST 06811
  Beverly White, prin.
Mill Ridge IS, MILL RIDGE ROAD 06811
  Pierre Lachance, prin.
Mill Ridge PS, MILL RIDGE ROAD 06811
  Kathleen Dzubak, prin.
Morris Street ES, 28 MORRIS ST 06810
  Norman Kaback, prin.
Park Avenue ES, 82 PARK AVE 06810
  Robert Simonelli, prin.
Pembroke ES, 32 PEMBROKE RD 06811
  Levi Newsome, prin.
Roberts Avenue ES, 2 ROBERTS AVE 06810
  Anthony Kirmil, prin.
Shelter Rock ES, SHELTER ROCK ROAD 06810
  John Eriquez, prin.
South Street ES, 129 SOUTH ST 06810
  Julia Horne, prin.
Stadley Rough ES, 25 KAREN RD 06811
  Nancy Sailer, prin.

Immanuel Lutheran ES, 35 FOSTER ST 06810
Sacred Heart ES, 17 COTTAGE ST 06810
St. Gregory the Great ES
  85 GREAT PLAINES ROAD 06810
St. Joseph ES, 370 MAIN ST 06810
St. Peter ES, 98 MAIN ST 06810

Danielson, Windham Co., Pop. Code 5
Killingly SD
Sch. Sys. Enr. Code 5
Supt. – David Cressy, 190 MAIN ST 06239
Killingly JHS, 52 BROAD ST 06239
  Jerre Filmore, prin.
Killingly Memorial ES
  CORNER MAIN & HUTCHINS ST 06239
  Brenda Keefe, prin.
Other Schools – See Dayville

St. James ES, WATER ST 06239

Darien, Fairfield Co., Pop. Code 7
Darien SD
Sch. Sys. Enr. Code 5
Supt. – James J. Loughran, P O BOX 1167 06820
Middlesex MS
  204 HOLLOW TREE RIDGE ROAD 06820
  Phillip Nelson, prin.
Hindley MS, 10 NEARWATER LN 06820
  Mary Cushman, prin.
Ox Ridge ES, 395 MANSFIELD AVE 06820
  John Rechi, prin.
Royle MS, 133 MANSFIELD AVE 06820
  Robert Valuk, prin.
Tokeneke ES, 7 OLD FARM RD 06820
  Ira Friedland, prin.

Dayville, Windham Co.
Killingly SD
Supt. – See Danielson
Killingly Central ES, P O BOX 365 06241
  Elizabeth Forrest, prin.

Deep River, Middlesex Co., Pop. Code 5
Chester SD
Sch. Sys. Enr. Code 2
Supt. – John Proctor, P O BOX 187 06417
Other Schools – See Chester

Deep River SD
Sch. Sys. Enr. Code 2
Supt. – John Proctor, P O BOX 187 06417
ES, 12 RIVER ST 06417
  Edward Weselcouch, prin.

Essex SD
Sch. Sys. Enr. Code 2
Supt. – John Proctor, WINTHROP ROAD 06417
Other Schools – See Centerbrook

Regional SD 4
Sch. Sys. Enr. Code 3
Supt. – John Proctor, P O BOX 187 06417
Winthrop JHS, WINTHROP ROAD 06417
Timothy Doyle, prin.

Derby, New Haven Co., Pop. Code 7
Derby SD
Sch. Sys. Enr. Code 4
Supt. – Michael Ippolito, P O BOX 373 06418
Bradley ES, 155 DAVID HUMPHREYS RD 06418
William Duggan, prin.
Irving ES, 9 GARDEN PL 06418
Henry Jemioto, prin.
Lincoln MS, 187 MINERVA ST 06418
Howard Manco, prin.

St. Mary ES, 14 SEYMOUR AVE 06418

Durham, Middlesex Co., Pop. Code 6
Regional SD 13
Sch. Sys. Enr. Code 4
Supt. – Howard F. Kelley, MAIDEN LANE 06422
Strong MS, 76 MAIN ST 06422
Earle Bidwell, prin.
Brewster ES, TUTTLE ROAD 06422
Valerie Huydie, prin.
Korn ES, MAIDEN LN 06422 – Daniel Perley, prin.
Other Schools – See Middlefield

East Berlin, Hartford Co.
Berlin SD
Supt. – See Berlin
Hubbard ES, 135 GROVE ST 06023
Robert Chamness, prin.

Eastford, Windham Co., Pop. Code 4
Eastford SD
Sch. Sys. Enr. Code 2
Supt. – Francis Stevens, WESTFORD ROAD 06242
ES, WESTFORD ROAD 06242
Francis Stevens, prin.

East Granby, Hartford Co., Pop. Code 5
East Granby SD
Sch. Sys. Enr. Code 3
Supt. – Dr. A. T. Lederman
33 TURKEY HILLS ROAD 06026
MS, 95 S MAIN ST 06026 – Daniel Michael, prin.
Allgrove ES, 33 TURKEY HILLS RD 06026
James Johnson, prin.
Seymour MS, 185 HARTFORD AVE 06026
James Johnson, prin.

East Hampton, Middlesex Co., Pop. Code 6
East Hampton SD
Sch. Sys. Enr. Code 4
Supt. – Dorothea Isleib, 39 N MAPLE ST 06424
Center ES, 9 SUMMIT ST 06424
Dorothea Isleib, prin.
MS, 39 N MAPLE ST 06424
Richard Huelsmann, prin.
Memorial ES, 20 SMITH ST 06424
Joanne Andershonis, prin.

East Hartford, Hartford Co., Pop. Code 8
East Hartford SD
Sch. Sys. Enr. Code 6
Supt. – Sam Leone, 110 LONG HILL DR 06108
MS, 777 BURNSIDE AVE 06108
James Fallon, prin.
Other Schools – See Hartford

St. Rose ES, 21 CHURCH ST 06108

East Hartland, Hartford Co.
Hartland SD
Sch. Sys. Enr. Code 2
Supt. – Alfred Tracy, SOUTH ROAD 06027
Hartland ES, SOUTH ROAD 06027
Alfred Tracy, prin.

East Haven, New Haven Co., Pop. Code 8
East Haven SD
Sch. Sys. Enr. Code 5
Supt. – Stephen Casner, HUDSON ST 06512
MS, 67 HUDSON ST 06512 – Henry Luzzi, prin.
Deer Run ES, ROUTE 80 06512
Philip Madonna, prin.
Momauguin ES, COSEY BEACH ROAD 06512
Philip Costello, prin.
Moore ES, HOOP POLE LN 06512
John Mezzanotte, prin.
Overbrook ES, 54 GERRISH AVE 06512
John Marcucci, prin.
Tuttle ES, 108 PROSPECT RD 06512
John Villano, prin.
Other Schools – See New Haven

St. Vincent De Paul ES, 35 BISHOP ST 06512

East Lyme, New London Co., Pop. Code 7
East Lyme SD
Sch. Sys. Enr. Code 5
Supt. – Robert Minor, P O BOX 176 06333
Flanders ES, P O BOX 32 06333
Cherry Jones, prin.
Other Schools – See Niantic

Easton, Fairfield Co., Pop. Code 6
Easton SD
Sch. Sys. Enr. Code 3
Supt. – Lawrence R. Miller
215 CENTER ROAD 06612
Keller MS, 360 SPORT HILL ROAD 06612
Lynda Cox, prin.

Staples ES, 215 CENTER RD 06612
Nancy Lischko, prin.

Redding SD
Sch. Sys. Enr. Code 3
Supt. – Lawrence Miller
215 CENTER ROAD 06612
Other Schools – See Redding, West Redding

East Windsor, Hartford Co., Pop. Code 6
East Windsor SD
Sch. Sys. Enr. Code 4
Supt. – Richard Teller, 74 S MAIN ST 06088
Other Schools – See Broad Brook

Ellington, Tolland Co., Pop. Code 6
Ellington SD
Sch. Sys. Enr. Code 4
Supt. – Dr. Joseph Delucia, 47 MAIN 06029
Center ES, MAIN ST 06029 – Ross Zabel, prin.
Crystal Lake ES, SANDY BEACH ROAD 06029
Frank Milbury, prin.
Windermere ES, ABBOTT ROAD 06029
Joseph Florentine, prin.
Other Schools – See Vernon-Rockville

Elmwood, Hartford Co.

St. Brigid ES, 100 MAYFLOWER ST 06110

Enfield, Hartford Co., Pop. Code 8
Enfield SD
Sch. Sys. Enr. Code 6
Supt. – Louis Mager, 27 SHAKER ROAD 06082
Kennedy MS, 155 RAFFLE ROAD 06082
James Mahoney, prin.
Alcorn ES, 1010 ENFIELD ST 06082
Carol Circosta, prin.
Barnard ES, 27 SHAKER RD 06082
George Perry, prin.
Crandall ES, BRAINARD ROAD 06082
John Pedace, prin.
Enfield Street ES, 1318 ENFIELD ST 06082
John Mack, prin.
Hale ES, TAYLOR ROAD 06082
Elaine Parakilas, prin.
Hazardville Memorial ES, 68 N MAPLE ST 06082
Patricia McKiernan, prin.
Parkman ES, 165 WEYMOUTH RD 06082
Ronald Orlandi, prin.
Stowe ES, 117 POST OFFICE RD 06082
Dennis Balsewicz, prin.
Whitney ES, MIDDLE ROAD 06082
William Kennedy, prin.

Enfield Montessori ES, 1370 ENFIELD ST 06082
St. Adalbert ES, 90 ALDEN AVE 06082
St. Bernard ES, 424 HAZARD AVE 06082
St. Joseph ES, 256 PEARL ST 06082
St. Martha ES, 224 BRAINARD RD 06082

Fairfield, Fairfield Co., Pop. Code 8
Fairfield SD
Sch. Sys. Enr. Code 6
Supt. – Larry Dougherty, P O BOX 220 06430
Fairfield Woods MS
1115 FAIRFIELD WOODS ROAD 06430
Brian Fagan, prin.
Tomlinson MS, 240 UNQUOWA ROAD 06430
Raymond Agostino, prin.
Dwight ES, 1600 REDDING RD 06430
Antone Andrade, prin.
Holland Hill ES, 200 MEADOWCROFT RD 06430
Margaret Fitzgerald, prin.
Jennings ES, 31 PALM DR 06430
Jack Shapiro, prin.
McKinley ES, 60 THOMPSON ST 06430
Vincent Antezzo, prin.
North Stratfield ES
190 PUTTING GREEN RD 06432
Anne McGrath, prin.
Riverfield ES, 1525 MILL PLAIN RD 06430
Joseph Ricciotti, prin.
Sherman ES, 250 FERN ST 06430
Joseph Walsh, prin.
Stratfield ES, 1407 MELVILLE AVE 06432
Roger Previs, prin.

Fairfield Country Day ES
2970 BRONSON RD 06430
Holy Family ES, 140 EDISON AVE 06430
Our Lady of Assumption School
605 STRATFIELD RD 06432
St. Pius X ES, 834 BROOKSIDE DR 06430
St. Thomas Aquinas ES, 118 RUANE ST 06430
Tuller ES, 157 TULLER RD 06430
Unquowa ES, 981 STRATFIELD RD 06432

Falls Village, Litchfield Co., Pop. Code 3
Canaan SD
Sch. Sys. Enr. Code 2
Supt. – Val Bernardoni
WARREN TURNPIKE ROAD 06031
Kellogg ES 06031 – Diane Marino, prin.

Cornwall SD
Sch. Sys. Enr. Code 2
Supt. – Val Bernardoni
WARREN TURNPIKE ROAD 06031
Other Schools – See West Cornwall

Kent SD
Sch. Sys. Enr. Code 2
Supt. – Val Bernardoni
WARREN TURNPIKE ROAD 06031
Other Schools – See Kent

North Canaan SD
Sch. Sys. Enr. Code 2
Supt. – Val Bernardoni
WARREN TURNPIKE ROAD 06031
Other Schools – See Canaan

Salisbury SD
Sch. Sys. Enr. Code 2
Supt. – Val Bernardoni
WARREN TURNPIKE ROAD 06031
Other Schools – See Salisbury

Sharon SD
Sch. Sys. Enr. Code 2
Supt. – Val Bernardoni
WARREN TURNPIKE ROAD 06031
Other Schools – See Sharon

Farmington, Hartford Co., Pop. Code 7
Farmington SD
Sch. Sys. Enr. Code 5
Supt. – Dr. Wm. Streich, MONTIETH DR 06032
Robbins MS, WOLF PIT ROAD 06032
Dr. James Aseltine, prin.
East Farms ES, 25 WOLF PIT RD 06032
Michael Galluzzo, prin.
Wallace ES, SCHOOL ST 06032
Helen McMullen, prin.
West District ES, WEST DISTRICT ROAD 06032
Harvey Dutil, prin.
Other Schools – See Unionville

Gales Ferry, New London Co., Pop. Code 3
Ledyard SD
Supt. – See Ledyard
Ledyard JHS, 1860 ROUTE 12 06335
Trent Alexopoulos, prin.
ES, 7 HURLBUTT RD 06335 – Sally Keating, prin.
Gallup Hill ES, 169 GALLUP HILL RD 06339
Stephen Panikoff, prin.
Ledyard Center ES
740 COLONEL LEDYARD HWY 06339
Elizabeth Fenn, prin.
Long ES, 1854 ROUTE 12 06335
Ronald Walling, prin.

Glastonbury, Hartford Co., Pop. Code 7
Glastonbury SD
Sch. Sys. Enr. Code 5
Supt. – R. Tegarden, 232 WILLIAMS ST 06033
Welles MS, 1029 NEIPSIC ROAD 06033
Mark Cohan, prin.
Academy MS, 2141 MAIN ST 06033
Carol Schmidt, prin.
Buttonball Lane ES, 376 BUTTONBALL LN 06033
Patricia DaSilva, prin.
Eastbury ES, 1389 NEIPSIC RD 06033
William McDermott, prin.
Hebron Avenue ES, 1323 HEBRON AVE 06033
Mary Ann Manchester, prin.
Hopewell ES
1050 CHESTNUT HILL ROAD 06033
Peter Maluk, prin.
Naubuc ES, 82 GRISWOLD ST 06033
Patricia Hatch, prin.

Goshen, Litchfield Co., Pop. Code 4
Regional SD 6
Supt. – See Litchfield
Goshen Center ES 06756
Arthur McCormack, prin.

Granby, Hartford Co., Pop. Code 6
Granby SD
Sch. Sys. Enr. Code 4
Supt. – Ralph Wallace
15 N GRANBY ROAD 06035
Memorial MS, 309 SALMON BROOK ST 06035
Stanley Pestka, prin.
Kearns ES, 5 CANTON RD 06035
Marie Edwards, prin.
Kelly Lane ES, 60 KELLY LN 06035
Robert Barba, prin.
Wells Road ES, 134 WELLS RD 06035
Richard LaMitie, prin.

Greens Farms, Fairfield Co.

Greens Farms Academy
35 BEACHSIDE AVE 06436

Greenwich, Fairfield Co., Pop. Code 8
Greenwich SD
Sch. Sys. Enr. Code 6
Supt. – Dr. Ernest Fleishman
P O BOX 1249 06836
Curtiss ES, 180 E ELM ST 06830
Linda Egener Hartzer, prin.
Glenville ES, 33 RIVERSVILLE RD 06831
Thomas Brown, prin.
Hamilton Avenue ES, 184 HAMILTON AVE 06830
Hazel Hobbs, prin.
New Lebanon ES, 25 MEAD AVE 06830
Carol Sarabun, prin.
North Street ES, 381 NORTH ST 06830
Sandra Mond, prin.
Other Schools – See Cos Cob, Old Greenwich,
Riverside

Brunswick School, 100 MAHER AVE 06830
Convent of Sacred Heart School
1177 KING ST 06830
Greenwich Academy, 200 N MAPLE AVE 06830
Greenwich Catholic ES, 257 STANWICH RD 06830
Greenwich Country Day ES
OLD CHURCH RD 06830

Whitby ES, 969 LAKE AVE   06831

Groton, New London Co., Pop. Code 6
Groton SD
Sch. Sys. Enr. Code 6
Supt. – Joan Stipetic, P O BOX K   06340
Barnum ES, BRIAR HILL ROAD   06340
    Carl Missal, prin.
Chester ES, 130 FORT HILL RD   06340
    Harrison Day, prin.
Eastern Point ES
    225 SHENNECOSSETT RD   06340
    Thomas O'Connor, prin.
Groton Heights MS, 244 MONUMENT ST   06340
    Donna Purdy, prin.
Ledyard ES, 120 WEST ST   06340
    Donna Purdy, prin.
Morrison ES, TOLL GATE ROAD   06340
    Russell Leonard, prin.
Noank ES, SMITH LN   06340 – Edward Volle, prin.
Pleasant Valley ES
    380 PLEASANT VALLEY RD S   06340
    Raymond Fanning, prin.
Seely ES, 55 SEELY SCHOOL DR   06340
    Richard Raymond, prin.
Other Schools – See Mystic

Sacred Heart ES, 50 SACRED HEART DR   06340

Guilford, New Haven Co., Pop. Code 7
Guilford SD
Sch. Sys. Enr. Code 5
Supt. – Thomas Giblin
    NEW ENGLAND ROAD   06437
Adams MS, 200 CHURCH ST   06437
    Duncan Craig, prin.
Baldwin MS, 68 BULLARD DRIVE   06437
    Peter Madonia, prin.
Cox ES, 3 MILL RD   06437 – Robert Pleasure, prin.
Guilford Lakes ES, MAUPAS ROAD   06437
    James Rook, prin.
Jones ES, LONG HILL ROAD   06437
    Charlotte Nelson, prin.
Leete ES, SOUTH UNION   06437
    Rosemary Waldron, prin.

Hamden, New Haven Co., Pop. Code 8
Hamden SD
Sch. Sys. Enr. Code 6
Supt. – David Shaw, 60 PUTNAM AVE   06517
MS, 550 NEWHALL ST   06517
    Salvatore Cavallaro, prin.
Bear Path ES, 10 KIRK RD   06514
    Frank Pinto, prin.
Church Street ES, 670 WINTERGREEN AVE   06514
    Cherly Townsend, prin.
Dunbar Hill ES, 315 LANE ST   06514
    JoAnne Young, prin.
Helen Street ES, 285 HELEN ST   06514
    Joyce Kossman, prin.
Shepherd Glen ES, SKIFF ST EXT   06514
    Richard Palleria, prin.
Other Schools – See New Haven

Barry ES, 306 CIRCULAR AVE   06514
Hamden Hall Country Day School
    1108 WHITNEY AVE   06517

Hampton, Windham Co., Pop. Code 4
Hampton SD
Supt. – See Chaplin
Hampton Consolodated ES, ROUTE 97   06247
    Deborah Fritz, prin.

Hartford, Hartford Co., Pop. Code 9
East Hartford SD
Supt. – See East Hartford
Goodwin ES, 1235 FORBES ST   06118
    Donald Cohen, prin.
Hockanum ES, 191 MAIN ST   06118
    Anthony Picano, prin.
Langford ES, 61 ALPS DR   06108
    Anthony Krawczyk, prin.
Mayberry ES, 101 GREAT HILL RD   06108
    Roch Girard, prin.
Norris ES, 40 REMINGTON RD   06108
    Mary Lou Ruggiero, prin.
O'Brien ES, 52 FARM DR   06108
    Stanley Smith, prin.
O'Connell ES, 301 MAY RD   06118
    George Dunn, prin.
Pitkin ES, 330 HILLS ST   06118
    George Drumm, prin.
Silver Lane ES, 15 MERCER AVE   06118
    Paula Erickson, prin.

Hartford SD
Sch. Sys. Enr. Code 7
Supt. – Hernan LaFontaine, 249 HIGH ST   06103
Fox MS, 305 GREENFIELD ST   06112
    Jimmie Hill, prin.
Quirk MS, 85 EDWARDS ST   06120
    David Lawrence, prin.
Barbour ES, 150 TOWER AVE   06120
    Leonard Berliner, prin.
Barnard-Brown ES, 1304 MAIN ST   06103
    Frederick Tracy, prin.
Batchelder ES, 757 NEW BRITAIN AVE   06106
    Richard Spurling, prin.
Betances ES, 42 CHARTER OAK AVE   06106
    Edna Negron, prin.
Burns ES, 195 PUTNAM ST   06106
    Herbert Shedroff, prin.
Burr ES, 400 WETHERSFIELD AVE   06114
    Donald DeFemia, prin.

Clark ES, 75 CLARK ST   06120
    Vernal Davis, prin.
Dwight ES, 585 WETHERSFIELD AVE   06114
    Frederick Maher, prin.
Fisher ES, 280 PLAINFIELD ST   06112
    Lloyd Foster, prin.
Fox ES, 470 MAPLE AVE   06114
    Nelio Nanni, prin.
Hooker ES, 200 SHERBROOKE AVE   06106
    Nancy Maldonado, prin.
Kennelly ES, 180 WHITE ST   06114
    Robert Andrew, prin.
King ES, 25 RIDGEFIELD ST   06112
    Harold Barrow, prin.
Kinsella ES, 65 VAN BLOCK AVE   06106
    Charles Boornazian, prin.
McDonough ES, 100 WILSON ST   06106
    Donald Carso, prin.
Naylor ES, 639 FRANKLIN AVE   06114
    Ernest Cermola, prin.
Parkville Community ES, 1755 PARK ST   06106
    David Mulholland, prin.
Rawson ES, 260 HOLCOMB ST   06112
    Henderson Duval, prin.
Sand Everywhere ES, 1700 MAIN ST   06120
    Baxter Atkinson, prin.
Simpson-Waverly ES, 55 WAVERLY ST   06112
    James Thompson, prin.
Twain ES, 395 LYME ST   06112
    Walter Gordy, prin.
Vine Street ES, 104 VINE ST   06112
    Everette Chandler, prin.
Webster ES, 5 CONE ST   06105
    Susie Hinton, prin.
West ES, 927 ASYLUM AVE   06105
    Roland Harris, prin.
Wish ES, 350 BARBOUR ST   06120
    Freddie Morris, prin.

West Hartford SD
Supt. – See West Hartford
Bugbee ES, 1943 ASYLUM AVE   06117
    June Webber, prin.
Charter Oak ES, 30 PARKER ST   06110
    Gwen Rustin, prin.
Duffy ES, 95 WESTMINSTER ST   06112
    Susan Jojin, prin.
King Philip ES, 100 KING PHILIP DR   06117
    Alan Coriaty, prin.
Morley ES, 77 BRETTON RD   06119
    Pauline Brading, prin.
Nordeldt ES, 35 BARKSDALE RD   06117
    Karen List, prin.
Whiting Lane ES, 47 WHITING LN   06119
    Carol Perotta, prin.
Wolcott ES, 71 WOLCOTT RD   06110
    Plato Karafelis, prin.

St. Christopher ES, 570 BREWER ST   06118
Cathedral Regional ES, 809 ASYLUM AVE   06105
Our Lady of Sorrows ES, 39 GRACE ST   06106
Renbrook ES, 2865 ALBANY AVE   06117
SS. Cyril Methodius ES, 35 GROTON ST   06106
Schechter ES, 160 MOHEGAN DR   06117
St. Augustine ES, 20 CLIFFORD ST   06114
St. Justin ES, 250 BLUE HILLS AVE   06112
St. Thomas the Apostle ES, 25 DOVER RD   06119
St. Timothy ES, 225 KING PHILIP DR   06117

Harwinton, Litchfield Co., Pop. Code 5
Regional SD 10
Supt. – See Burlington
Harwinton Consolodated ES
    EAST LITCHFIELD ROAD   06791
    Bobby Gioscia, prin.

Hebron, Tolland Co., Pop. Code 6
Andover SD
Sch. Sys. Enr. Code 2
Supt. – Pat Hayden, RURAL ROUTE 85   06248
Other Schools – See Andover

Hebron SD
Sch. Sys. Enr. Code 3
Supt. – Patrick Hayden, 21 PENDLETON DR   06248
Gilead Hill ES, 180 GILEAD ST   06248
    Joseph Reardon, prin.
ES, ROUTE 85   06248 – Paul White, prin.

Marlborough SD
Sch. Sys. Enr. Code 3
Supt. – Pat Hayden, RURAL ROUTE 85   06248
Other Schools – See Marlborough

Regional SD 8
Sch. Sys. Enr. Code 4
Supt. – Patrick Hayden, 21 PENDLETON DR   06248
RHAM JHS, RHAM RD   06248
    Henry Grabber, prin.

Higganum, Middlesex Co., Pop. Code 3
Regional SD 17
Sch. Sys. Enr. Code 4
Supt. – Charles Sweetman
    LITTLE CITY ROAD   06441
Haddam-Killingworth MS
    LITTLE CITY ROAD   06441 – Virginia Rebar, prin.
Haddam ES, RURAL ROUTE 9A   06441
    Edward Lewis, prin.
Other Schools – See Killingworth

Jewett City, New London Co., Pop. Code 5
Griswold SD
Sch. Sys. Enr. Code 4
Supt. – H. McLaughlin, 50 SCHOOL ST   06351

Griswold ES, SLATER AVE   06351
    Cheryl Veilleux, prin.

Lisbon SD
Sch. Sys. Enr. Code 3
Supt. – Lawrence Fenn, 15 NEWENT ROAD   06351
Lisbon Central ES, 15 NEWENT RD   06351
    Lawrence Fenn, prin.

St. Mary ES, 54 N MAIN ST   06351

Kensington, Hartford Co.
Berlin SD
Supt. – See Berlin
Griswold ES, 133 HEATHER LN   06037
    Anthony Rigazio-Digilio, prin.

St. Paul ES, 461 ALLING ST   06037

Kent, Litchfield Co., Pop. Code 5
Kent SD
Supt. – See Falls Village
Kent Center ES   06757 – Edward Epstein, prin.

Killingworth, Middlesex Co., Pop. Code 5
Regional SD 17
Supt. – See Higganum
Burr District ES, ROUTE 81   06417
    Robert Smalley, prin.
ES, ROUTE 81   06417
    William Cieslukowski, prin.

Lebanon, New London Co., Pop. Code 5
Lebanon SD
Sch. Sys. Enr. Code 4
Supt. – Corrine Berglund, P O BOX 88   06249
ES, ROUTE 207   06249 – Albert Vertefeuille, prin.

Ledyard, New London Co., Pop. Code 7
Ledyard SD
Sch. Sys. Enr. Code 5
Supt. – Henry Ashmore
    130 GALLUP HILL ROAD   06339
Other Schools – See Gales Ferry

Litchfield, Litchfield Co., Pop. Code 4
Litchfield SD
Sch. Sys. Enr. Code 4
Supt. – Allan Walker, PLUMB HILL   06759
MS, PLUMB HILL   06759 – Michael Malley, prin.
Center ES, WEST ST   06759
    Robert Lindgren, prin.

Regional SD 6
Sch. Sys. Enr. Code 3
Supt. – Vincent Ferrandino   06759
Other Schools – See Goshen, Morris, Warren

Lyme, New London Co., Pop. Code 4
Regional SD 18
Supt. – See Old Lyme
Lyme Consolidated ES, ROUTE 156   06371
    Mary Lou Bargnesi, prin.

Madison, New Haven Co., Pop. Code 7
Madison SD
Sch. Sys. Enr. Code 5
Supt. – Peter Barile, Jr., P O BOX 71   06443
Brown MS, 980 DURHAM ROAD   06443
    James Coyne, prin.
Academy Street MS, 4 SCHOOL ST   06443
    Robert Wolfe, prin.
Island Avenue ES, 20 ISLAND AVE   06443
    Alexis Christina, prin.
Jeffrey MS, 331 COPSE RD   06443
    Jerome Greenberg, prin.
Ryerson ES, 982 DURHAM RD   06443
    Paul Sinicrope, prin.

Our Lady of Mercy ES, 149 NECK RD   06443
The Country School
    341 OPENING HILL RD   06443

Manchester, Hartford Co., Pop. Code 6
Manchester SD
Sch. Sys. Enr. Code 6
Supt. – Dr. James Kennedy
    45 N SCHOOL ST   06040
Bowers ES, 141 PRINCETON ST   06040
    Anthony Spino, prin.
Buckley ES, 250 VERNON ST   06040
    Edward Timbrell, prin.
Hale ES, 160 SPRUCE ST   06040 – Leo Diana, prin.
Keeney ES, 179 KEENEY ST   06040
    Francis Amara, prin.
Martin ES, 140 DARTMOUTH RD   06040
    Raymond Whinnem, prin.
Robertson ES, 65 N SCHOOL ST   06040
    Rochelle Abraitis, prin.
Verplanck ES, 126 OLCOTT ST   06040
    Douglas Townsend, prin.
Waddell ES, 163 BROAD ST   06040
    Gail Rowe, prin.
Washington ES, 94 CEDAR ST   06040
    Ray Gardiner, prin.

Assumption JHS, 27 ADAMS ST S   06040
St. Bridget ES, 74 MAIN ST   06040
St. James ES, 73 PARK ST   06040

Mansfield Center, Windham Co.
Mansfield SD
Supt. – See Storrs/Mansfield
Southeast ES, 134 WARRENVILLE RD   06250
    Harry Mangle, prin.
Vinton ES, 306 STAFFORD RD   06250
    James Palmer, prin.

Marlborough, Middlesex Co.
Marlborough SD
Supt. – See Hebron
ES, SCHOOL DR 06447 – Walter Machowski, prin.

Meriden, New Haven Co., Pop. Code 8
Meriden SD
Sch. Sys. Enr. Code 6
Supt. – John DeGennaro, 142 E MAIN ST 06450
Lincoln MS, 164 CENTENNIAL AVE 06450
  Thomas Cioffi, prin.
Washington MS, 1225 N BROAD ST 06450
  Michael Ferry, prin.
Barry ES, 124 COLUMBIA ST 06450
  Richard Dangelo, prin.
Franklin ES, 426 W MAIN ST 06450
  Maureen Kane, prin.
Hale ES, ATKINS ST EXT 06450
  Nena Nanfeldt, prin.
Hanover ES, 208 MAIN ST 06450
  Leverett Stocking, prin.
Hooker ES, OVERLOOK ROAD 06450
  Thomas Hall, prin.
Pulaski ES, 100 CLEARVIEW AVE 06450
  Joseph Borriello, prin.
Putnam ES, 161 PARKER AVE 06450
  Robert Galbraith, prin.
Sherman ES, 60 N PEARL ST 06450
  Robert Smith, prin.

Our Lady Mt. Carmel ES, 115 LEWIS AVE 06450
St. Joseph ES, 159 W MAIN ST 06450
St. Laurent ES, 125 CAMP ST 06450
St. Mary ES, 97 GROVE ST 06450
St. Rose ES, 35 CENTER ST 06450
St. Stanislaus ES, 81 AKRON ST 06450

Middlebury, New Haven Co., Pop. Code 6
Regional SD 15
Sch. Sys. Enr. Code 5
Supt. – Donald Crowell, P O BOX 665 06762
Memorial MS, 73 KELLY ROAD 06762
  Judith Dooling, prin.
ES, WHITTEMORE ROAD 06762
  Margaret Clark, prin.
Other Schools – See Southbury

Middlefield, Middlesex Co., Pop. Code 5
Regional SD 13
Supt. – See Durham
Lyman ES, WAY ROAD 06455 – Janet Yuse, prin.
Middlefield Memorial MS, HUBBARD ST 06455
  Charles Rogers, prin.

Independent Day ES, LAUREL BROOK RD 06455

Middletown, Middlesex Co., Pop. Code 8
Middletown SD
Sch. Sys. Enr. Code 5
Supt. – Dr. Alfred B. Tychsen
  310 HUNTING HILL AVE 06457
Bielefield ES, 70 MAYNARD ST 06457
  Eugene Nocera, prin.
Farm Hill ES, 390 RIDGE RD 06457
  Richard Thompson, prin.
Keigwin Annex MS, 99 SPRUCE ST 06457
  John Ryan, prin.
Lawrence ES, MILE LN 06457
  Harold Kaplan, prin.
MacDonough ES, 66 SPRING ST 06457
  Pamela Muraca, prin.
Moody ES, 300 COUNTRY CLUB RD 06457
  E. Joensuu, prin.
Snow ES, WADSWORTH ST 06457
  Edward Pehota, prin.
Wesley ES, WESLEYAN HILLS ROAD 06457
  James Downey, prin.

St. John ES, 5 ST JOHNS SQ 06457
St. Mary of Czestochowa ES, 87 S MAIN ST 06457
St. Sebastian ES, 61 DUANT TERRACE 06457

Milford, New Haven Co., Pop. Code 8
Milford SD
Sch. Sys. Enr. Code 6
Supt. – Robert Blake, EELS HILL ROAD 06460
Calf Pen Meadow ES
  395 WELCHES POINT RD 06460
  Patricia Breen, prin.
Central ES, HIGH ST 06460
  Richard Wronski, prin.
Kay Avenue ES, 50 KAY AVE 06460
  Charles Hayden, prin.
Kennedy ES, 398 WEST AVE 06460
  Richard Salerno, prin.
Live Oaks ES, 575 MERWIN AVE 06460
  Raymond Vitali, prin.
Mathewson ES, WEST RIVER ST 06460
  George Lopes, prin.
Meadowside ES, SEEMANS LN 06460
  Paul Overchuk, prin.
Orange Avenue ES, 260 ORANGE AVE 06460
  Frank Santino, prin.
Orchard Hills ES, 181 MARINO DR 06460
  Robert Cummings, prin.
Pumpkin Delight ES, 20 ART ST 06460
  Robert Dambrose, prin.
Seabreeze ES, 240 CHAPEL ST 06460
  Patricia Barrett, prin.
Simon Lake ES, 59 DEVONSHIRE RD 06460
  Mario Gradoia, prin.

St. Ann ES, 64 RIDGE ST 06460
St. Gabriel ES, 1 TUDOR ST 06460
St. Mary ES, 70 GULF ST 06460

Monroe, Fairfield Co., Pop. Code 7
Monroe SD
Sch. Sys. Enr. Code 5
Supt. – Don Maloney
  375 MONROE TRNPK 06468
Chalk Hill MS, 345 FAN HILL ROAD 06468
  Ralph DeGruttola, prin.
Fawn Hollow ES, 345 FAN HILL RD 06468
  John Galla, prin.
ES, 375 MONROE TPKE 06468
  Patrick Walsh, prin.
Stepney ES, 180 OLD NEWTOWN RD 06468
  G. Gustaitis, prin.

St. Jude ES, 707 MONROE TPKE 06468

Montville, New London Co., Pop. Code 7
Montville SD
Supt. – See Oakdale
Palmer Memorial ES, MAPLE AVE 06353
  Rosemarie Payne, prin.

Moodus, Middlesex Co., Pop. Code 4
East Haddam SD
Sch. Sys. Enr. Code 4
Supt. – Samuel Roth, PLAINS ROAD 06469
East Haddam ES, JOE WILLIAMS ROAD 06469
  James Cannata, prin.

Moosup, Windham Co.
Plainfield SD
Supt. – See Central Village
ES, 35 CHURCH ST 06354 – Joseph Pempek, prin.

All Hallows ES, 120 PROSPECT ST 06354

Morris, Litchfield Co., Pop. Code 4
Regional SD 6
Supt. – See Litchfield
ES 06763 – Andrew Mozelak, prin.

Mystic, New London Co., Pop. Code 6
Groton SD
Supt. – See Groton
Butler ES, 155 OCEAN VIEW AVE 06355
  John Wilson, prin.
Hathaway ES, 115 OSLO ST 06355
  James Shaughnessy, prin.
Mystic Academy MS, 24 BANK ST 06355
  James Shaughnessy, prin.

Stonington SD
Supt. – See Old Mystic
MS, MISTUXET AVE 06355
  Donald Ascare, prin.

Naugatuck, New Haven Co., Pop. Code 8
Naugatuck SD
Sch. Sys. Enr. Code 5
Supt. – Raymond E. Dowling
  380 CHURCH ST 06770
City Hill MS, 441 CITY HILL ST 06770
  Joseph Connolly, prin.
Hillside MS, 51 HILLSIDE AVE 06770
  Robert Markovic, prin.
Andrew Avenue ES, 164 ANDREW AVE 06770
  Edward Mariano, prin.
Central Avenue ES, 28 CENTRAL AVE 06770
  Regina Birdsell, prin.
Cross Street ES, CROSS ST 06770
  Raymond Powell, prin.
Hop Brook ES, 75 CROWN ST 06770
  Robert Sullivan, prin.
Prospect Street ES, 100 PROSPECT ST 06770
  Robert Aquavia, prin.
Salem ES, 124 MEADOW ST 06770
  Robert Cronin, prin.
Western ES, PINE ST 06770 – Ralph Wilkins, prin.

St. Francis ES, 294 CHURCH ST 06770
St. Hedwig ES, 32 GOLDEN HILL ST 06770

New Britain, Hartford Co., Pop. Code 8
New Britain SD
Sch. Sys. Enr. Code 6
Supt. – Dr. Marie S. Gustin
  27 HILLSIDE PL 06051
Pulaski MS, 757 FARMINGTON AVE 06053
  Joseph Hogan, prin.
Roosevelt MS, 40 GOODWIN ST 06051
  William Ostapchuk, prin.
Slade MS, 183 STEELE ST 06052
  Armand Regalbuti, prin.
Chamberlain ES, 120 NEWINGTON AVE 06051
  Sharon Cicio, prin.
Diloreto ES, 732 SLATER RD 06053
  Joseph Perrotta, prin.
Gaffney ES, 322 SLATER RD 06053
  John Putinski, prin.
Holmes ES, NYE ROAD 06053
  Jeannette Carpinteri, prin.
Jefferson ES, 140 HORSE PLAIN ROAD 06053
  James Rhinesmith, prin.
Lincoln ES, 145 STEELE ST 06052
  M. Martinez, prin.
Northend ES, 160 BASSETT ST 06051
  Mary Jennings, prin.
Smalley ES, 175 WEST ST 06051
  Vincent Mercadante, prin.
Smith ES, 142 RUTHERFORD ST 06051
  Dominick DiNino, prin.
Vance ES, 183 VANCE ST 06052
  Michael Cicchetti, prin.

St. Ann MS, 114 NORTH ST 06051

St. Franics of Assisi MS
  30 PENDLETON RD 06053
Holy Cross ES, 221 FARMINGTON AVE 06053
Sacred Heart ES, 35 ORANGE ST 06053
St. Joseph ES, 29 EDSON ST 06051
St. Matthew's ES, 87 FRANKLIN SQ 06051

New Canaan, Fairfield Co., Pop. Code 7
New Canaan SD
Sch. Sys. Enr. Code 5
Supt. – John Fitzsimons, 156 SOUTH AVE 06840
Saxe MS, 468 SOUTH AVE 06840
  Arvid Anderson, prin.
East ES, LITTLE BROOK ROAD 06840
  Robert Groeschner, prin.
South ES, GOWER ROAD 06840
  Russell Firlik, prin.
West ES, 769 PONUS RDG 06840
  Leonard Tomasello, prin.

New Canaan Counrty ES
  PONUS RIDGE AND FROGTOWN RD 06840
St. Aloysius ES, 33 SOUTH AVE 06840

New Fairfield, Fairfield Co., Pop. Code 7
New Fairfield SD
Sch. Sys. Enr. Code 4
Supt. – John Gawrys, 24 GILLOTTI ROAD 06812
Consolidated ES, 12 GILLOTTI RD 06812
  Kathleen Kelly, prin.
Meeting House Hill MS, 24 GILLOTTI RD 06812
  David Green, prin.

New Hartford, Litchfield Co., Pop. Code 5
New Hartford SD
Sch. Sys. Enr. Code 3
Supt. – Mario Dei Dolori, P O BOX 315 06057
Antolini MS, ROUTE 202 06057
  Donald Lovley, prin.
Bakerville ES, CEDAR LN 06057
  Louis Casinghino, prin.
ES, WICKETT ST 06057 – Louis Casinghino, prin.

New Haven, New Haven Co., Pop. Code 9
Bethany SD
Supt. – See Bethany
Bethany Community ES, 44 PECK RD 06525
  Marjorie Sherman, prin.

East Haven SD
Supt. – See East Haven
Ferrara ES, 22 MAYNARD RD 06513
  George Dayharsh, prin.

Hamden SD
Supt. – See Hamden
Ridge Hill ES, 120 CAREW RD 06517
  Richard Balisciano, prin.
Spring Glen ES, 1908 WHITNEY AVE 06517
  Beverly Damen, prin.
West Woods ES, 350 W TODD ST 06518
  Gilbert Rebhun, prin.

New Haven SD
Sch. Sys. Enr. Code 7
Supt. – John Dow, 200 ORANGE ST 06510
Clemente ES, 360 COLUMBUS AVE 06519
  Andrew Alberino, prin.
Fair Haven MS, 164 GRAND AVE 06513
  Alexander Esposito, prin.
Robinson MS, 150 FOURNIER ST 06511
  Charles Warner, prin.
Ross Arts Magnet MS, 185 BARNES AVE 06513
  Marion Inman, prin.
Sheridan MS, 191 FOUNTAIN ST 06515
  Louis Puglisi, prin.
Troup MS, 259 EDGEWOOD AVE 06511
  William Beaty, prin.
Barnard ES, 170 DERBY AVE 06511
  Kathleen Parker, prin.
Beecher ES, 100 JEWELL ST 06515
  Ramona Gatison, prin.
Bishop Woods ES, 1481 QUINNIPIAC AVE 06513
  Richard Denardis, prin.
Brennan ES, 200 WILMOT RD 06515
  Dietria Wells, prin.
Clinton Avenue ES, 293 CLINTON AVE 06513
  Patricia Derenzo, prin.
Columbus ES, 255 BLATCHLEY AVE 06513
  Carmen Polanco, prin.
Davis ES, 35 DAVIS ST 06515 – John Leary, prin.
Dwight ES, 130 EDGEWOOD AVE 06511
  Willie Freeman, prin.
East Rock Community ES, 133 NASH ST 06511
  Salvatore Punzo, prin.
Edgewood ES, 737 EDGEWOOD AVE 06515
  Ronald Jakubowski, prin.
Grant ES, 185 GOFFE ST 06511
  Jeffie Frazier, prin.
Hale ES, 480 TOWNSEND AVE 06512
  Peter Villano, prin.
Hill Central ES, 140 DEWITT ST 06519
  Gerald Baldino, prin.
Hooker ES, 180 CANNER ST 06511
  Joseph Angeletti, prin.
King ES, 580 DIXWELL AVE 06511
  Edward Ferrucci, prin.
Lincoln-Bassett ES, 130 BASSETT ST 06511
  Verdell Roberts, prin.
Mauro ES, 130 ORCHARD ST 06519
  Joseph Montagna, prin.
Prince ES, 22 GOLD ST 06519
  David Rubin, prin.
Quinnipiac ES, 460 LEXINGTON AVE 06513
  Harry Hines, prin.

Strong ES, 69 GRAND AVE 06513
  Sylvia Olinsky, prin.
Truman ES, 114 TRUMAN ST 06519
  Cosby Marable, prin.
Welch Annex ES, 49 PRINCE ST 06519
  Paul Piantino, prin.
West Hills ES, 311 VALLEY ST 06515
  Audrey Tiani, prin.
Wexler ES, 209 DIXWELL AVE 06511
  James Courtney, prin.
Woodward ES, 455 FORBES AVE 06512
  Frank Palmieri, prin.

Ezra Academy, 75 RIMMON RD 06525
Sacred Heart ES, 208 COLUMBUS AVE 06519
St. Aedan ES, 351 MCKINLEY AVE 06515
St. Bernadette ES, 20 BURR ST 06512
St. Brendan ES, 342 ELLSWORTH AVE 06511
St. Francis ES, 423 FERRY ST 06513
St. Michael ES, 234 GREENE ST 06511
St. Peter ES, ST PETER AVE 06519
St. Rita ES, 1601 WHITNEY AVE 06517
St. Rose ES, 12 RICHARD ST 06513
St. Stanislaus ES, 15 ELD ST 06511
St. Stephen ES, 418 RIDGE RD 06517
St. Thomas Day ES, 830 WHITNEY AVE 06511

Newington, Hartford Co., Pop. Code 8
  Newington SD
  Sch. Sys. Enr. Code 5
  Supt. – Wm. P. Ward, 131 CEDAR ST 06111
  Kellogg MS, 155 HARDING AVE 06111
    Robert Buganski, prin.
  Wallace MS, 71 HALLERAN ROAD 06111
    David McCain, prin.
  Chaffee ES, 160 SUPERIOR AVE 06111
    David Gowell, prin.
  Green ES, 30 THOMAS ST 06111
    Paul Gionfriddo, prin.
  Paterson ES, 120 CHURCH ST 06111
    Christian Decker, prin.
  Reynolds ES, 85 RESERVOIR RD 06111
    Richard Frank, prin.

  St. Mary ES, 652 WILLARD AVE 06111

New London, New London Co., Pop. Code 8
  New London SD
  Sch. Sys. Enr. Code 5
  Supt. – Dr. Rene Racette, 134 WILLIAMS ST 06320
  JHS, LINCOLN AVE 06320 – John Bassett, prin.
  Edgerton ES, 120 CEDAR GROVE AVE 06320
    Edwin McDonough, prin.
  Hale ES, BEECH DR 06320 – Joel Movitch, prin.
  Harbor ES, 432 MONTAUK AVE 06320
    James DeVine, prin.
  Jennings ES, 50 MERCER ST 06320
    John Sullivan, prin.
  Winthrop ES, 74 GROVE ST 06320
    Bettye Fletcher, prin.

  St. Joseph ES, 25 SQUIRE ST 06320
  St. Mary ES, 28 HUNTINGTON ST 06320

New Milford, Litchfield Co., Pop. Code 7
  New Milford SD
  Sch. Sys. Enr. Code 5
  Supt. – Stephen Tracy, 50 EAST ST 06776
  Schaghticoke MS, 23 HIPP ROAD 06776
    Don Fiftal, prin.
  Hill & Plain ES, 60 OLD TOWN PARK RD 06776
    Thomas Atticks, prin.
  Northville ES, 22 HIPP RD 06776
    Cheryl Dickinson, prin.
  Pettibone MS, 2 PICKETT DISTRICT RD 06776
    William Burley, prin.

Newtown, Fairfield Co., Pop. Code 4
  Newtown SD
  Sch. Sys. Enr. Code 5
  Supt. – John Reed, 11 QUEEN ST 06470
  MS, 11 QUEEN ST 06470 – Louis Villamana, prin.
  Hawley ES, 29 CHURCH HILL RD 06470
    Doris Bushaw, prin.
  Head Omeadow ES, BOOGS HILL ROAD 06470
    Edgar Rodrigues, prin.
  Middle Gate ES, COLD SPRING ROAD 06470
    William Bircher, prin.
  Other Schools – See Sandy Hook

  St. Rose ES, 40 CHURCH HILL RD 06470

Niantic, New London Co.
  East Lyme SD
  Supt. – See East Lyme
  East Lyme JHS, 25 SOCIETY ROAD 06357
    Jerome Belair, prin.
  Haynes ES, 29 SOCIETY RD 06357
    Linda Horowitz, prin.
  ES, 7 W MAIN ST 06357
    Richard Spindler-Virgin, prin.

Norfolk, Litchfield Co., Pop. Code 4
  Norfolk SD
  Supt. – See Winsted
  Botelle ES, GREENWOODS ROAD 06058
    Michael Day, prin.

North Branford, New Haven Co., Pop. Code 7
  North Branford SD
  Supt. – See Northford
  IS, 675 FOXON ROAD 06471
    Nicholas Bauer, prin.
  Harrison ES, 335 FOXON RD 06471
    Richard Belfonti, prin.

Northford, New Haven Co.
  North Branford SD
  Sch. Sys. Enr. Code 4
  Supt. – John Mulrain, P O BOX 129 06472
  IS, MIDDLETOWN AVE 06472
    Frederic Dambrose, prin.
  Williams ES, MIDDLETOWN AVE 06472
    Robin Blaschke, prin.
  Other Schools – See North Branford

North Franklin, New London Co.
  Franklin SD
  Sch. Sys. Enr. Code 2
  Supt. – James McCarthy, ROUTE 207 06254
  Franklin ES, ROUTE 207 06254
    James McCarthy, prin.

North Grosvenordale, Windham Co., Pop. Code 4
  Thompson SD
  Sch. Sys. Enr. Code 4
  Supt. – Donald Hardy, RURAL ROUTE 12 06255
  Thompson MS, RURAL ROUTE 12 06255
    David Johnson, prin.
  Thompson Memorial ES, ROUTE 12 06255
    Mary Fisher, prin.

  St. Joseph ES, MAIN ST 06255

North Haven, New Haven Co., Pop. Code 7
  North Haven SD
  Sch. Sys. Enr. Code 5
  Supt. – Frank Samuelson, Sr.
    5 LINSLEY ST 06473
  Clintonville ES, 456 CLINTONVILLE RD 06473
    Gerald Nolan, prin.
  Green Acres ES, 146 UPPER STATE ST 06473
    Anthony Caprio, prin.
  Montowese ES, 145 FITCH ST 06473
    John Pinto, prin.
  Ridge Road ES, 1341 RIDGE RD 06473
    Jane Moncheski, prin.

North Stonington, New London Co., Pop. Code 5
  North Stonington SD
  Sch. Sys. Enr. Code 3
  Supt. – Kenneth Shaw, P O BOX 313 06359
  ES, P O BOX 6001 06359 – Ronald Rymash, prin.

North Windham, Windham Co.
  Windham SD
  Supt. – See Willimantic
  North Windham MS, 112 JORDAN LANE 06256
    Paul Kaminski, prin.

Norwalk, Fairfield Co., Pop. Code 8
  Norwalk SD
  Sch. Sys. Enr. Code 6
  Supt. – Ralph Sloan, 105 MAIN ST 06851
  Hale MS, STRAWBERRY HILL AVE 06851
    J. White, prin.
  Ponus Ridge MS, 19 HUNTERS LANE 06850
    Leroy Vaughn, prin.
  Roton MS, 201 HIGHLAND AVE 06853
    Fred Foldeak, prin.
  West Rocks MS, 81 ROCKS ROAD 06851
    Thomas Rietano, prin.
  Brookside ES, 382 HIGHLAND AVE 06854
    Jason Edgecomb, prin.
  Columbus ES, 46 CONCORD ST 06854
    Arthur Perschino, prin.
  Cranbury ES, 5 KNOWALOT LN 06851
    Marie Iannazzi, prin.
  Fox Run ES, 228 FILLOW ST 06850
    June Carroll, prin.
  Jefferson ES, 75 VAN BUREAU AVE 06850
    Geno Eriquezzo, prin.
  Kendall ES, 57 FILLOW ST 06850
    Patricia Tingle, prin.
  Marvin ES, CALF PASTURE BEACH ROAD 06855
    Walter Reck, prin.
  Naramake ES, 16 KING ST 06851
    Thomas Grace, prin.
  Rowayton ES, 145 ROWAYTON AVE 06853
    Robert Bottomley, prin.
  Silvermine ES, 194 PERRY AVE 06850
    Fred Urban, prin.
  Tracey ES, 24 CAMP ST 06851
    Joseph Quick, prin.
  Wolfpit ES, 1 STARLIGHT DR 06851
    William Bray, prin.

  Parkway Christian Academy
    260 NEW CANAAN AVE 06850
  St. Joseph ES, 10 CHESTNUT ST 06854
  St. Phillip ES, 25 FRANCE ST 06851
  St. Thomas the Apostle ES, 208 EAST AVE 06855

Norwich, New London Co., Pop. Code 8
  Norwich SD
  Sch. Sys. Enr. Code 5
  Supt. – Walt Juzwic, 23 MAHAN DRIVE 06360
  Kelly JHS, 15 MAHAN DR 06360
    James Horan, prin.
  Teachers Memorial JHS, STARR ST 06360
    William Peckham, prin.
  Bishop ES, 526 MAIN ST 06360
    Marlene Seder, prin.
  Buckingham ES, 182 CEDAR ST 06360
    Gary Gelmini, prin.
  Greeneville ES, 182 GOLDEN ST EXT 06360
    Donald Steinman, prin.
  Huntington ES, 80 W TOWN ST 06360
    John DeStefano, prin.
  Mahan ES, SALEM TPKE 06360
    Alton Button, prin.

Moriarty ES, LAWLER LN 06360
  Nancy Buckley, prin.
Stanton ES, 386 NEW LONDON TPKE 06360
  Robert Henseler, prin.
Uncas ES, 280 ELIZABETH ST EXT 06360
  Wilmer Stevens, prin.
Veterans Memorial ES, CROUCH AVE 06360
  Barbara Bielecki, prin.
Other Schools – See Taftville

  Preston SD
  Sch. Sys. Enr. Code 2
  Supt. – Alvin McNeill
    RURAL ROUTE 01 RT 164 06360
  Preston Plains MS
    RURAL ROUTE 01 RT 164 06360
    A. J. McNeill, prin.
  Poquetanuck ES, RURAL ROUTE 05 06360
    Harold Karsten, prin.
  Preston City MS, RURAL ROUTE 03 06360
    Joseph Grillo, prin.

  St. Joseph ES, 120 CLIFF ST 06360
  St. Patrick Cathedral ES, 213 BROADWAY 06360

Oakdale, New London Co., Pop. Code 2
  Montville SD
  Sch. Sys. Enr. Code 5
  Supt. – Leonard Tyl
    OLD COLCHESTER ROAD 06370
  Murphy MS, CHESTERFIELD ROAD 06370
    Robert Lamperelli, prin.
  Fair Oaks ES, 836 CHESTERFIELD ROAD 06370
    Robert Lee, prin.
  ES, OFF INDIANA CIR 06370
    Emory Merrill, prin.
  Other Schools – See Montville, Uncasville

Oakville, Litchfield Co., Pop. Code 6
  Watertown SD
  Supt. – See Watertown
  Swift JHS, 250 COLONIAL ST 06779
    Joseph Mercier, prin.

  St. Mary Magdalen School
    140 BUCKINGHAM ST 06779

Old Greenwich, Fairfield Co.
  Greenwich SD
  Supt. – See Greenwich
  ES, 285 SOUND BEACH AVE 06870
    Sylvia Morency Wahl, prin.

Old Lyme, New London Co., Pop. Code 6
  Regional SD 18
  Sch. Sys. Enr. Code 4
  Supt. – Julius D'Agostino, LYME STREET 06371
  Lyme-Old Lyme MS, LYME ST 06371
    Richard Finlaw, prin.
  Center ES, LYME ST 06371 – Adam Burrows, prin.
  Mile Creek ES, MILE CREEK ROAD 06371
    Ronald Martino, prin.
  Other Schools – See Lyme

Old Mystic, New London Co.
  Stonington SD
  Sch. Sys. Enr. Code 4
  Supt. – Lyman F. Root, P O BOX 296 06372
  Other Schools – See Mystic, Pawcatuck, Stonington,
    Westerly

Old Saybrook, Middlesex Co., Pop. Code 6
  Old Saybrook SD
  Sch. Sys. Enr. Code 4
  Supt. – John Burgess, 50 SHEFFIELD ST 06475
  Main Street MS, 308 MAIN ST 06475
    James Crowley, prin.
  Goodwin ES, 80 OLD BOSTON POST RD 06475
    John Walsh, prin.

Oneco, Windham Co.
  Sterling SD
  Sch. Sys. Enr. Code 2
  Supt. – John Kivela, P O BOX 159 06373
  Sterling Memorial ES, ROUTE 14-A 06373
    John Kivela, prin.

Orange, New Haven Co., Pop. Code 7
  Orange SD
  Sch. Sys. Enr. Code 4
  Supt. – Dorothy Berger
    605 ORANGE CENTER ROAD 06477
  Peck Place ES, 500 PECK LN 06477
    John Kowal, prin.
  Race Brook ES, 107 GRANNIS RD 06477
    Alphonse Russo, prin.
  Turkey Hill ES, 441 TURKEY HILL RD 06477
    Kenneth Geigle, prin.

  Beth Chana-Hannah Academy
    P O BOX 587 06477

Oxford, New Haven Co., Pop. Code 6
  Oxford SD
  Sch. Sys. Enr. Code 4
  Supt. – Vincent Mustaro, P O BOX 548 06483
  Great Oak MS
    222 GOVERNORS HILL ROAD 06483
    Barb Denver, prin.
  Oxford Center ES, 462 OXFORD RD 06483
    Robert Martino, prin.

Pawcatuck, New London Co., Pop. Code 6
  Stonington SD
  Supt. – See Old Mystic
  West Broad Street ES, 131 W BROAD ST 06379
    Sandra McKenna, prin.

West Vine Street ES, 27 W VINE ST 06379
Joseph Bibbo, prin.

St. Michael ES, 63 LIBERTY ST 06379

Plainfield, Windham Co., Pop. Code 5
Plainfield SD
Supt. – See Central Village
Plainfield Central MS
RURAL ROUTE 02 BOX 308 06374
Robert McHale, prin.
ES, P O BOX 187 06374 – Melanie Robeda, prin.
Plainfield Memorial MS
RURAL ROUTE 02 BOX 308 06374
Mary Ann Dumas, prin.

St. John the Apostle ES, 12 RAILROAD AVE 06374

Plainville, Hartford Co., Pop. Code 7
Plainville SD
Sch. Sys. Enr. Code 4
Supt. – James Ritchie
ROBT HOLCOMB WAY 06062
JHS, 74 EAST ST 06062 – Paul Cavaliere, prin.
Linden Street ES, 69 LINDEN ST 06062
Robert Proulx, prin.
Toffolon ES, 501 NORTHWEST DR 06062
Joseph Maggipinto, prin.
Wheeler ES, CLEVELAND MEMORIAL DR 06062
James Graffam, prin.

Our Lady of Mercy ES, 35 S CANAN ST 06062

Plantsville, Hartford Co., Pop. Code 6
Southington SD
Supt. – See Southington
ES, 70 CHURCH ST 06479 – Robert Wood, prin.
South End ES, MAXWELL-NOBLE DR 06479
John Alusitz, prin.
Strong ES, 820 MARION AVE 06479
Mary Connelly, prin.

Pleasant Valley, Litchfield Co.
Barkhamsted SD
Supt. – See Winsted
Barkhamsted ES, P O BOX 162 06063
Anthony Mirizzi, prin.

Plymouth, Litchfield Co., Pop. Code 7
Plymouth SD
Supt. – See Terryville
Plymouth Center ES, 41 NORTH ST 06782
Lawrence Amara, prin.

Pomfret Center, Windham Co.
Pomfret SD
Sch. Sys. Enr. Code 2
Supt. – Robert Glenn 06259
Pomfret Community ES 06259
Robert Glenn, prin.

Portland, Middlesex Co., Pop. Code 6
Portland SD
Sch. Sys. Enr. Code 4
Supt. – LeRoy Dyer, P O BOX 231 06480
JHS, 314 MAIN ST 06480
Margaret Downey, prin.
Gildersleeve MS, 575 MAIN ST 06480
Donald Rixon, prin.
Valley View ES, 81 HIGH ST 06480
Deborah Barton, prin.

Prospect, New Haven Co., Pop. Code 6
Regional SD 16
Sch. Sys. Enr. Code 4
Supt. – John Buck, 30 COER ROAD 06712
Long River MS 06712 – Michael Abdalla, prin.
Algonquin ES 06712 – John O'Connor, prin.
Community MS 06712 – John O'Connor, prin.
Other Schools – See Beacon Falls

Putnam, Windham Co., Pop. Code 6
Putnam SD
Sch. Sys. Enr. Code 4
Supt. – Donald Nicoletti, 126 CHURCH ST 06260
MS, WICKER ST 06260 – Gerard Cotnoir, prin.
ES, WICKER ST 06260 – Gerard Cotnoir, prin.

St. Mary ES, 15 MARSHALL ST 06260

Quaker Hill, New London Co.
Waterford SD
Supt. – See Waterford
ES, P O BOX 438 06375 – Wilfred Gladue, prin.

Redding, Fairfield Co., Pop. Code 6
Redding SD
Supt. – See Easton
ES, LONETOWN RD 06875
Robert Bernstein, prin.

Ridgefield, Fairfield Co., Pop. Code 7
Ridgefield SD
Sch. Sys. Enr. Code 5
Supt. – Joseph Leheny, 40 FLORIDA RD 06877
East Ridge MS, 10 E RIDGE ROAD 06877
Mary Gorman, prin.
Farmingville ES, 324 FARMINGVILLE RD 06877
Robert McDonald, prin.
Ridgebury ES, 112 BENNETTS FARM RD 06877
William Monti, prin.
Scotland ES, 111 BARLOW MOUNTAIN RD 06877
Barbara Depencier, prin.
Veterans Park ES, 8 GOVERNOR ST 06877
Arnold Finaldi, prin.

Riverside, Fairfield Co.
Greenwich SD
Supt. – See Greenwich
North Mianus ES, 309 PALMER HILL RD 06878
Susanne Holloman, prin.
ES, 90 HENDRIE AVE 06878
Elizabeth Ehik, prin.

Rocky Hill, Hartford Co., Pop. Code 7
Rocky Hill SD
Sch. Sys. Enr. Code 4
Supt. – Paul Calaluce, 33 CHURCH ST 06067
Griswold JHS, 144 BAILEY ROAD 06067
Charles Stewart, prin.
Moser ES, SCHOOL ST 06067
Bente Pedersen, prin.
Stevens ES, 322 ORCHARD ST 06067
Bente Pedersen, prin.
West Hill ES, CRONIN DR 06067
William Evans, prin.

Roxbury, Litchfield Co., Pop. Code 4
Regional SD 12
Supt. – See Washington Depot
Booth Free ES, SOUTH ST 06783
Richard Hoffman, prin.

Salisbury, Litchfield Co., Pop. Code 5
Salisbury SD
Supt. – See Falls Village
Salisbury Central ES 06068
Thomas Bradley, prin.

Sandy Hook, Fairfield Co., Pop. Code 3
Newtown SD
Supt. – See Newtown
ES, 12 DICKENSON DR 06482
Ronald Vitarelli, prin.

Scotland, Windham Co., Pop. Code 4
Scotland SD
Supt. – See Chaplin
ES, BROOK ROAD 06264 – Scott Johnson, prin.

Seymour, New Haven Co., Pop. Code 7
Seymour SD
Sch. Sys. Enr. Code 4
Supt. – Eugene Coppola
98 BANK ST ANNEX BLDG 06483
MS, 25 PINE ST 06483 – Paul Porter, prin.
Bungay ES, 35 BUNGAY RD 06483
Violet Brennan, prin.
Chatfield ES, 51 SKOKORAT ST 06483
Salvatore Giannone, prin.
Lopresti ES, 29 MAPLE ST 06483
Theresa Rasmussen, prin.

Sharon, Litchfield Co., Pop. Code 5
Sharon SD
Supt. – See Falls Village
Sharon Center ES 06069
Patricia Chamberlain, prin.

Shelton, Fairfield Co., Pop. Code 8
Shelton SD
Sch. Sys. Enr. Code 5
Supt. – Anthony Pagliaro
60 PERRY HILL ROAD 06484
IS, 60 PERRY HILL ROAD 06484
Timothy Walsh III, prin.
Booth Hill ES, 544 BOOTH HILL RD 06484
Frank Skoronski, prin.
LaFayette ES, 54 GROVE ST 06484
Louis Dagostine, prin.
Long Hill ES, 565 LONG HILL AVE 06484
Charles Turecek, prin.
Mohegan ES, 29-31 MOHEGAN RD 06484
John Larsen, prin.
ES, 138 WILLOUGHBY RD 06484
Stephen Fusti, prin.

St. Joesph ES, 420 CORAM AVE 06484
St. Lawrence ES, 505 SHELTON AVE 06484

Sherman, Fairfield Co., Pop. Code 4
Sherman SD
Sch. Sys. Enr. Code 2
Supt. – Angelo Dirienco 06784
ES, SHERMAN SCHOOL 06784
Angelo Dirienzo, prin.

Simsbury, Hartford Co., Pop. Code 7
Simsbury SD
Sch. Sys. Enr. Code 5
Supt. – Joseph Townsley
933 HOPMEADOW ST 06070
James Memorial MS, 155 FIRETOWN ROAD 06070
Robert Pelletier, prin.
Central ES, 29 MASSACO ST 06070
William Marshall, prin.
Squadron Line ES, 44 SQUADRON LINE RD 06070
Steven Sedlack, prin.
Other Schools – See Tariffville, Weatogue, West Simsbury

St. Mary ES, 946 HOPMEADOW ST 06070

Somers, Tolland Co., Pop. Code 6
Somers SD
Sch. Sys. Enr. Code 4
Supt. – Paul Gagliarducci
9TH DISTRICT ROAD 06071
Avery ES, 9TH DISTRICT RD 06071
Kenneth Sullivan, prin.
Kibbe-Fuller ES, 619 MAIN ST 06071
Richard Quinn, prin.
Other Schools – See Somersville

Somersville, Tolland Co.
Somers SD
Supt. – See Somers
ES, 43 SCHOOL ST 06072 – Richard Quinn, prin.

Southbury, New Haven Co., Pop. Code 7
Regional SD 15
Supt. – See Middlebury
Rochambeau MS, 100 PETER ROAD 06488
Aldro Jenks, prin.
Gainfield ES, 307 OLD FIELD RD 06488
John Mudry, prin.
Pomperaug ES, 607 MAIN ST 06488
Richard Gusenburg, prin.

Southington, Harfford Co., Pop. Code 8
Southington SD
Sch. Sys. Enr. Code 6
Supt. – Louis Saloom, 49 BEECHER ST 06489
Central ES, 240 MAIN ST 06489
John Fiondella, prin.
Flanders ES, VICTORIA DR 06489
Louis Fabri, prin.
Hatton ES, 70 SPRING LAKE RD 06489
Joann Colvin, prin.
Kelley ES, RIDGEWOOD ROAD 06489
Thomas Gramitt, prin.
North Center ES, 200 N MAIN ST 06489
Nancy Arnold, prin.
Thalberg ES, 145 DUNHAM ROAD 06489
Paul Baillargeon, prin.
Other Schools – See Plantsville

St. Thomas ES, 133 BRISTOL ST 06489
St. Dominic PS, 1050 FLANDER RD 06489

South Windsor, Hartford Co., Pop. Code 7
South Windsor SD
Sch. Sys. Enr. Code 5
Supt. – Joseph Wood, 1737 MAIN ST 06074
Edwards MS, 100 ARNOLD WAY 06074
Laura Boutilier, prin.
Orchard Hill ES, 350 FOSTER ST 06074
Lawrence Mickel, prin.
Pleasant Valley ES, 591 ELLINGTON RD 06074
Orville Rowley, prin.
Smith ES, 949 AVERY ST 06074
Geoffrey McCarthy, prin.
Terry ES, 569 GRIFFIN RD 06074
Marvin Eisenberg, prin.

Stafford Springs, Tolland Co., Pop. Code 5
Stafford SD
Sch. Sys. Enr. Code 4
Supt. – Wayne Senecal, P O BOX 147 06076
Witt MS, P O BOX 106 06076
James Prenetta, prin.
Borough ES, 50 PROSPECT ST 06076
Rose Robichaud, prin.
West Stafford ES, 413 W MAIN ST 06076
Michael Magrone, prin.
Other Schools – See Staffordville

Union SD
Supt. – See Union City
Union ES, 9 KINNEY HOLLOW RD 06076
Jerrold Baggish, prin.

St. Edward ES, 11 CHURCH ST 06076

Staffordville, Tolland Co.
Stafford SD
Supt. – See Stafford Springs
ES, P O BOX 216 06077 – Marcia Veshia, prin.

Stamford, Fairfield Co., Pop. Code 9
Stamford SD
Sch. Sys. Enr. Code 7
Supt. – William Papallo
195 HILLANDALE AVE 06902
Cloonan MS, 11 W NORTH ST 06902
Ed Mathews, prin.
Dolan MS, 51 TOMS ROAD 06906
Lynda Hautala, prin.
Turn-of-River MS, 117 VINE ROAD 06905
Jerry Wanosky, prin.
Davenport Ridge ES, 1300 NEWFIELD AVE 06905
Theodore Boccuzzi, prin.
Hart ES, 61 ADAMS AVE 06902
Marion Inman, prin.
Murphy ES, 19 HORTON ST 06902
Nadine Schultz, prin.
Newfield ES, 349 PEPPER RIDGE RD 06905
Mary Savage, prin.
Northeast ES, 82 SCOFIELDTOWN RD 06903
Pauline Rauh, prin.
Rogers ES, 83 LOCKWOOD AVE 06902
John Gilchrist, prin.
Roxbury ES, 751 WESTHILL RD 06902
Ethan Margolis, prin.
Springdale ES, 1127 HOPE ST 06907
Harvey Okun, prin.
Stark ES, 398 GLENBROOK RD 06906
Walter Goodwin, prin.
Stillmeadow ES, 800 STILLWATER RD 06902
Margaret Schneider, prin.
Westover ES, 412 STILLWATER AVE 06902
Edmund Barbieri, prin.

King School, 1450 NEWFIELD AVE 06905
St. Gabriel MS, 948 NEWFIELD AVE 06905
Bi-Cultural Day ES, 2186 HIGH RIDGE RD 06903
Holy Name of Jesus ES
305 WASHINGTON BLVD 06902
Holy Spirit ES, 403 SCOFIELDTOWN RD 06903
Long Ridge ES, 478 ERSKINE RD 06903

Our Lady Star of Sea ES
   1170 SHIPPAN AVE   06902
Sacred Heart ES, 1 SCHUYLER AVE   06902
St. Cecilia ES, 1186 NEWFIELD AVE   06905

Stonington, New London Co., Pop. Code 4
Stonington SD
Supt. – See Old Mystic
Deans Mill ES, RURAL ROUTE 01 BOX 63   06378
   Conrad Berdeen, prin.

Pine Point ES, P O BOX 392   06378

Storrs/Mansfield, Tolland Co.
Mansfield SD
Sch. Sys. Enr. Code 4
Supt. – Gordon Schimmel
   4 S EAGLEVILLE RD   06268
Mansfield MS, 205 SPRING HILL RD   06268
   Carole Iwanick, prin.
Northwest ES, 321 HUNTING LODGE RD   06268
   Barbara Lasher, prin.
Other Schools – See Mansfield Center

Stratford, Fairfield Co., Pop. Code 8
Stratford SD
Sch. Sys. Enr. Code 6
Supt. – Walter Dunbar, 1000 E BROADWAY   06497
Flood IS, 490 CHAPEL ST   06497
   Carol Rose, prin.
Wooster IS, 150 LINCOLN AVE   06497
   George Hames, prin.
Center ES, 55 SUTTON AVE   06497
   Basil Chaltas, prin.
Chapel ES, 380 CHAPEL ST   06497
   John Knudsen, prin.
Franklin ES, 1895 BARNUM AVE   06497
   Albert Bushinsky, prin.
Honeyspot House ES, 400 HONEYSPOT RD   06497
   Edward Bizub, prin.
Johnson House MS, 719 BIRDSEYE ST   06497
   Richard Hageman, prin.
Lordship ES, 254 CROWN ST   06497
   Elliot David, prin.
Nichols ES, 396 NICHOLS AVE   06497
   John Hartnett, prin.
Second Hill Lane ES, 65 SECOND HILL LN   06497
   Joseph DiMenna, prin.
Whitney ES, 1130 HUNTINGTON RD   06497
   James Cashavelly, prin.
Wilcoxson ES, 600 WILCOXSON AVE   06497
   Sandra Michaelides, prin.

Holy Name of Jesus ES, 3 MARY AVE   06497
St. James ES, 1 MONUMENT PL   06497
St. Mark ES, 500 WIGWAM LN   06497

Suffield, Hartford Co., Pop. Code 6
Suffield SD
Sch. Sys. Enr. Code 4
Supt. – Bernard Ellis
   260 MOUNTAIN ROAD   06078
McAlister MS, 260 MOUNTAIN ROAD   06078
   Anthony Kula, prin.
Bridge Street ES, 90 BRIDGE ST   06078
   Melvin Chafetz, prin.
Spaulding ES, 945 MOUNTAIN ROAD   06078
   Melvin Chafetz, prin.

Taftville, New London Co.
Norwich SD
Supt. – See Norwich
Wequonnoc ES, PROVIDENCE ST   06380
   Albert Wojtcuk, prin.

Sacred Heart ES, 15 HUNTERS AVE   06380

Tariffville, Hartford Co.
Simsbury SD
Supt. – See Simsbury
ES, 42 WINTHROP ST   06081
   Patricia Fienemann, prin.

Terryville, Litchfield Co., Pop. Code 5
Plymouth SD
Sch. Sys. Enr. Code 4
Supt. – Virginia Grzymkowski
   19 E MAIN ST   06786
Fisher MS, 75 N MAIN ST   06786
   Derald DeMerchant, prin.
East Main Street MS, 22 E MAIN ST   06786
   William Wyshner, prin.
Prospect Street ES, 12 PROSPECT ST   06786
   Louis Rascoe, prin.
Other Schools – See Plymouth

Thomaston, Litchfield Co., Pop. Code 6
Thomaston SD
Sch. Sys. Enr. Code 4
Supt. – Eugene Diggs, P O BOX 166   06787
MS, 49 THOMAS AVE   06787
   Nancy Vandeventer, prin.
Black Rock ES, 59 BRANCH RD   06787
   Raymond Giannamore, prin.

Tolland, Tolland Co., Pop. Code 6
Tolland SD
Sch. Sys. Enr. Code 4
Supt. – Joseph Matava
   51 TOLLAND GREEN   06084
MS, OLD POST RD   06084 – Vene Harding, prin.
Parker Memorial ES, OLD POST ROAD   06084
   Stephen Schachner, prin.

Torrington, Litchfield Co., Pop. Code 8
Torrington SD
Sch. Sys. Enr. Code 5
Supt. – Dr. Louis J. Esparo
   355 MIGEON AVE   06790
Vogel MS, 68 CHURCH ST   06790
   Michael Buzzi, prin.
East ES, 215 HOGAN DR   06790
   Robert Doyle, prin.
Forbes ES, 500 MIGEON AVE   06790
   Josephine Radocchio, prin.
Forest Court ES, 57 FOREST CT   06790
   Grace Michnevitz, prin.
Southwest ES, 340 LITCHFIELD ST   06790
   John Pelchat, prin.
ES, 631 TORRINGFORD WEST ST   06790
   John Dunne, prin.
Wetmore MS, 51 CHURCH ST   06790
   Michael Buzzi, prin.

St. Francis of Assisi ES, 360 PROSPECT ST   06790
St. Peter ES, 28 SAINT JOHNS PL   06790

Trumbull, Fairfield Co., Pop. Code 8
Trumbull SD
Sch. Sys. Enr. Code 5
Supt. – Edwin Merritt, 6254 MAIN ST   06611
Hillcrest MS, 530 DANIELS FARM ROAD   06611
   David Erwin, prin.
Madison MS, 4630 MADISON AVE   06611
   Rob Gabriel, prin.
Booth Hill ES, 545 BOOTH HILL RD   06611
   Michael Ward, prin.
Daniels Farm ES, 710 DANIELS FARM RD   06611
   Matthew Hunyadi, prin.
Middlebrook ES
   220 MIDDLEBROOKS AVE   06611
   Richard Witten, prin.
Ryan ES, 210 PARK LN   06611
   Robert DeCerbo, prin.
Tashua ES, 401 STONEHOUSE RD   06611
   Jacqueline Norcel, prin.

Christian Heritage ES
   575 WHITE PLAINS RD   06611
St. Catherine of Siena ES
   190 SHELTON RD   06611
St. Teresa ES, 55 ROSEMOND TER   06611

Uncasville, New London Co., Pop. Code 4
Montville SD
Supt. – See Oakdale
Mohegan ES, 49 GOLDEN RD   06382
   Philip Mountain, prin.

Union City, New Haven Co.
Union SD
Sch. Sys. Enr. Code 1
Supt. – Richard Butler
   9 KINNEY HOLLOW ROAD   06076
Other Schools – See Stafford Springs

Unionville, Hartford Co.
Farmington SD
Supt. – See Farmington
Union ES, SCHOOL STREET   06085
   Roberta Kurlantzick, prin.

Vernon-Rockville, Tolland Co., Pop. Code 8
Ellington SD
Supt. – See Ellington
Longview MS
   46 MIDDLE BUTCHER ROAD   06066
   Anthony Manizza, prin.

Vernon SD
Sch. Sys. Enr. Code 5
Supt. – Albert Kerkin, SCHOOL & PARK ST   06066
Vernon Center MS, 777 HARTFORD TRNPK   06066
   Dennis Beiu, prin.
Center Road ES, 20 CENTER RD   06066
   David Engelson, prin.
Lake Street ES, RFD LAKE ST   06066
   Donald Ellwood, prin.
Maple Street ES, MAPLE AND UNION STS   06066
   Gerald Griffin, prin.
Northeast ES, EAST ST   06066
   Edward Litke, prin.
Skinner Road ES, 90 SKINNER RD   06066
   Blaine Girard, prin.

St. Bernard ES, 20 SCHOOL ST   06066
St. Joseph School, 31 WEST ST   06066

Voluntown, New London Co., Pop. Code 4
Voluntown SD
Sch. Sys. Enr. Code 2
Supt. – Robert Danehy, P O BOX 128   06384
ES, P O BOX 128   06384 – Robert Danehy, prin.

Wallingford, New Haven Co., Pop. Code 8
Wallingford SD
Sch. Sys. Enr. Code 6
Supt. – Robert Nicoletti
   18 KONDRACKI LANE   06492
Hammarskjold MS, 106 POND HILL ROAD   06492
   James Whalen, prin.
Moran MS, 141 HOPE HILL ROAD   06492
   Walter Schipke, prin.
Beach ES, 304 N MAIN ST   06492
   Richard O'Connor, prin.
Cook Hill ES, 50 SCHOOL HOUSE RD   06492
   Patricia Cronin, prin.
Highland ES, 200 HIGHLAND AVE   06492
   Joseph Proto, prin.

Parker Farms ES, PARKER FARMS ROAD   06492
   Walter Serbent, prin.
Pond Hill ES, 301 POND HILL RD   06492
   John Hackett, prin.
Rock Hill ES, 911 DURHAM RD   06492
   Richard Fitzsimmons, prin.
Stevens ES, 18 KONDRACKI LN   06492
   John Sheehy, prin.

Holy Trinity ES, 11 N WHITTLESEY AVE   06492

Warren, Litchfield Co., Pop. Code 4
Regional SD 6
Supt. – See Litchfield
ES   06754 – Frank Colangelo, prin.

Washington, Litchfield Co., Pop. Code 5
Regional SD 12
Supt. – See Washington Depot
Shepaug Valley MS, SOUTH ST   06793
   Eugene Horrigan, prin.

Washington Depot, Litchfield Co., Pop. Code 3
Regional SD 12
Sch. Sys. Enr. Code 3
Supt. – Joseph Bickford, SCHOOL ST   06794
Washington ES, SCHOOL ST   06794
   Anne George, prin.
Other Schools – See Bridgewater, Roxbury,
   Washington

Rumsey Hall ES, 201 ROMFORD RD   06794
Washington Montessori ES   06793

Waterbury, New Haven Co., Pop. Code 9
Waterbury SD
Sch. Sys. Enr. Code 7
Supt. – Guy DiBiasio, 236 GRAND ST   06702
North End MS, 460 BUCKS HILL ROAD   06704
   Joseph Cavanaugh, prin.
Wallace MS, 3465 E MAIN ST   06705
   John Cleary, prin.
West Side MS, 483 CHASE PKWY   06708
   Lucian Mannello, prin.
Barnard ES, 11 DRAHER ST   06702
   John Cicchitto, prin.
Bucks Hill ES, 330 BUCKS HILL RD   06704
   Theresa Guay, prin.
Bunker Hill ES, 170 BUNKER HILL AVE   06708
   Joseph Meaney, prin.
Carrington ES, 26 KENMORE AVE   06708
   Anthony Russo, prin.
Chase ES
   CORNER MERIDEN/WOODTICK RDS   06705
   Edmund Malaspina, prin.
Cross ES, 1255 HAMILTON AVE   06706
   William Moriarty, prin.
Driggs ES, 77 WOODLAWN TER   06710
   Annie Booker, prin.
East Farms ES, 3196 E MAIN ST   06705
   George Roberts, prin.
Gilmartin ES, 107 WYOMING AVE   06706
   Antoinette McKnack, prin.
Hoperville ES
   CORNER PIEDMONT/CYPRESS STS   06706
   John Theriault, prin.
Kingsbury ES, 220 COLUMBIA BLVD   06710
   John Bolan, prin.
Maloney ES, 233 S ELM ST   06706
   Richard Cherubino, prin.
Regan ES, 2780 N MAIN ST   06704
   William Synnott, prin.
Rotella ES, 440 PIERPONT RD   06705
   Phyllis Coviello, prin.
Sprague ES, 1448 THOMASTON AVE   06704
   William Monagan, prin.
Tinker ES, 809 HIGHLAND AVE   06708
   Paul Ciochetti, prin.
Walsh ES, 29 ASHLEY ST   06704
   Robert Hurley, prin.
Washington ES, 658 BALDWIN ST   06706
   Daniel Dalessio, prin.

St. Margaret's-McTavern School
   585 CHASE PKWY   06708
Blessed Sacrament ES
   386 ROBINWOOD RD   06708
Our Lady of Mt. Carmel ES
   645 CONGRESS AVE   06708
SS Peter & Paul ES, 116 BEECHER AVE   06705
Sacred Heart ES, 31 WOLCOTT ST   06702
St. Anne ES, 28 E CLAY ST   06706
St. Francis Xavier ES, 605 BALDWIN ST   06706
St. Joseph ES, 29 JOHN ST   06708
St. Lucy ES, 58 GRIGGS ST   06704
St. Margaret ES, 289 WILLOW ST   06710
St. Mary ES, 65 COLE ST   06706

Waterford, New London Co., Pop. Code 7
Waterford SD
Sch. Sys. Enr. Code 4
Supt. – David Cattanach, P O BOX 284   06385
Clark Lane JHS, 105 CLARK LANE   06385
   D. Harold Goldberg, prin.
Cohanzie ES, 48 DAYTON RD   06385
   J. Miner, prin.
Great Neck ES, 165 GREAT NECK RD   06385
   Constance Giordano, prin.
Oswegatchie ES, 470 BOSTON POST RD   06385
   Vincent Lanzalotta, prin.
Southwest ES, 51 DANIELS AVE   06385
   Victor Ferry, prin.
Other Schools – See Quaker Hill

Watertown, Litchfield Co., Pop. Code 7
Watertown SD
Sch. Sys. Enr. Code 5
Supt. – Blaise Salerno, 10 DEFOREST ST   06795
Baldwin ES, 68 NORTH ST   06795
   Bernard Beauchamp, prin.
Griffin ES, 26 DAVIS ST   06779
   Donald Mitchell, prin.
Heminway Park MS
   37 HEMINWAY PARK RD   06795
   William Norwood, prin.
Judson ES, 124 HAMILTON LN   06795
   J. Henry, prin.
Polk ES, 435 BUCKINGHAM ST   06779
   Raymond Cwick, prin.
Other Schools – See Oakville

St. John the Evangelist ES, 760 MAIN ST   06795

Weatogue, Hartford Co.
Simsbury SD
Supt. – See Simsbury
Latimer Lane ES, 33 MOUNTAIN VIEW DR   06089
   Thomas Jefferson, prin.

Westbrook, Middlesex Co., Pop. Code 6
Westbrook SD
Sch. Sys. Enr. Code 3
Supt. – Dr. Robert Schreck
   ROGER GOODSPEED DR   06498
Ingraham ES, ROGER GOODSPEED DR   06498
   Katharine Bishop, prin.
Mulvey MS, 866 BOSTON POST RD   06498
   Katharine Bishop, prin.

West Cornwall, Litchfield Co.
Cornwall SD
Supt. – See Falls Village
Cornwall Consolidated ES   06796
   William Oros, prin.

Westerly, New London Co.
Stonington SD
Supt. – See Old Mystic
Pawcatuck MS, 100 FIELD ST   06379
   John Walsh, prin.

West Hartford, Hartford Co., Pop. Code 8
West Hartford SD
Sch. Sys. Enr. Code 6
Supt. – Lloyd Calvert, 28 SOUTH MAIN ST   06107
King Philip MS, 100 KING PHILIP DR   06117
   Paul Berkel, prin.
Sedgwick MS, 128 SEDGWICK ROAD   06107
   Robert Donahue, prin.
Braeburn ES, 45 BRAEBURN RD   06107
   Gerald Sandler, prin.
Webster Hill ES, 125 WEBSTER HILL BLVD   06107
   Thomas Karpeichik, prin.
Other Schools – See Hartford

West Haven, New Haven Co., Pop. Code 8
West Haven SD
Sch. Sys. Enr. Code 6
Supt. – John Onofrio, 25 OGDEN ST   06516
Bailey MS, 106 MORGAN LANE   06516
   Ralph Carrano, prin.
Carrigan MS, OGDEN & TETLOW ST   06516
   Frank Raffone, prin.
Forest ES, BURWELL ROAD   06516
   Matthew Brandon, prin.
Haley ES, 148 SOUTH ST   06516
   Robert Rocco, prin.
Mackrille ES
   JONES HILL ROAD AT CHASE LN   06516
   Bonnie Jo Nelson, prin.
Molloy ES, MELOY ROAD   06516
   Wilfred Fournier, prin.
Pagels ES, 26 BENHAM HILL RD   06516
   Laurence Frattini, prin.
Savin Rock Community ES, 50 PARK ST   06516
   Peter Florio, prin.
Stiles ES, 575 MAIN ST   06516 – Billie Ladd, prin.
Thompson ES, 165 RICHARD ST   06516
   Lynne Farrell, prin.
Washington ES, 369 WASHINGTON AVE   06516
   James Acabbo, prin.

Our Lady of Victory ES
   620 JONES HILL RD   06516
St. Lawrence ES, 231 MAIN ST   06516
St. Louis ES, 89 BULL HILL LN   06516

Weston, Fairfield Co., Pop. Code 6
Weston SD
Sch. Sys. Enr. Code 4
Supt. – Otty Norwood, 37 SCHOOL ROAD   06883

MS, 135 SCHOOL ROAD   06883
   Richard Miller, prin.
Hurlbutt ES, 9 SCHOOL RD   06883
   Jean McNeill, prin.

Westport, Fairfield Co., Pop. Code 8
Westport SD
Sch. Sys. Enr. Code 5
Supt. – Judith Shook, 110 MYRTLE AVE   06880
Bedford MS, 170 RIVERSIDE AVE   06880
   Glenn Hightower, prin.
Coleytown MS, 255 NORTH AVE   06880
   Daniel Christianson, prin.
Coleytown ES, 65 EASTON RD   06880
   Daniel Sullivan, prin.
Kings Highway ES, 125 POST RD W   06880
   Angela Wormser-Reid, prin.
Long Lots ES, 13 HYDE LN   06880
   Stuart Sellinger, prin.

Assumption ES, 15 BURR RD   06880

West Redding, Fairfield Co.
Redding SD
Supt. – See Easton
Read MS, ROUTE 53   06896
   Dianne Otteson, prin.

West Simsbury, Hartford Co., Pop. Code 4
Simsbury SD
Supt. – See Simsbury
Tootin Hills ES, 25 NIMROD RD   06092
   Russell Butterworth, prin.

West Willington, Tollard Co., Pop. Code 5
Willington SD
Sch. Sys. Enr. Code 3
Supt. – Michael McKee, ROUTE 32   06279
Hall Memorial MS, ROUTE 32   06279
   Robert McGray, prin.
Center ES, OLD FARMS ROAD   06279
   Rita Mannebach, prin.

Wethersfield, Hartford Co., Pop. Code 8
Wethersfield SD
Sch. Sys. Enr. Code 5
Supt. – Richard Zanini, 51 WILLOW ST   06109
Deane MS, 551 SILAS DEANE HWY   06109
   Kenneth Edwards, prin.
Emerson-Williams ES, 461 WELLS RD   06109
   J. Cushman, prin.
Hanmer ES, 50 FRANCIS ST   06109
   John Ferguson, prin.
Highcrest ES, 95 HIGHCREST RD   06109
   William Murphy, prin.
Wright ES, 186 NOTT ST   06109
   Robert McCarthy, prin.

Corpus Christi ES, 581 SILAS DEANE HWY   06109

Willimantic, Windham Co., Pop. Code 7
Windham SD
Sch. Sys. Enr. Code 5
Supt. – Mary Kramer, 322 PROSPECT ST   06226
Kramer MS, 322 PROSPECT ST   06226
   Ann Richardson, prin.
Natchaug ES, 124 JACKSON ST   06226
   Susan Webb, prin.
Sweeney ES, OAK HILL DR   06226
   Ralph Marshall, prin.
Other Schools – See North Windham, Windham

St. Mary and Jospeh ES, 35 VALLEY ST   06226

Wilton, Fairfield Co., Pop. Code 7
Wilton SD
Sch. Sys. Enr. Code 5
Supt. – David Clune, P O BOX 277   06897
Middlebrook MS, 363 DANBURY ROAD   06897
   Robert Shook, prin.
Cider Mill MS, 365 DANBURY RD   06897
   James Remler, prin.
Driscoll ES, 336 BELDEN HILL RD   06897
   Helen Martin, prin.
Miller ES, 217 WOLFPIT RD   06897
   Alfred Karpinski, prin.

Our Lady of Fatima School
   225 DANBURY RD   06897

Windham, Windham Co., Pop. Code 7
Windham SD
Supt. – See Willimantic
Windham Center ES, P O BOX 138   06280
   William Haddad, prin.

Windsor, Hartford Co., Pop. Code 8
Windsor SD
Sch. Sys. Enr. Code 5
Supt. – James Myers
   150 BLOOMFIELD AVE   06095
Sage Park MS, 25 SAGE PARK ROAD   06095
   William Sanders, prin.
Clover Street ES, 57 CLOVER ST   06095
   Robert Kiely, prin.
Ellsworth ES, 730 KENNEDY RD   06095
   Warren Logee, prin.
Kennedy ES, 530 PARK AVE   06095
   Arthur Beckius, prin.
Poquonock ES, 1760 POQUONOCK AVE   06095
   Grandon Willet, prin.
Wolcott ES, 57 E WOLCOTT AVE   06095
   Maurice Smith, prin.

St. Gabriel ES, 77 BLOOMFIELD AVE   06095

Windsor Locks, Hartford Co., Pop. Code 7
Windsor Locks SD
Sch. Sys. Enr. Code 4
Supt. – Dr. Peter D'Arrigo, 50 CHURCH ST   06096
MS, 7 CENTER ST   06096 – Carol Janssen, prin.
North Street ES, NORTH ST   06096
   John Byron, prin.
South Street ES, SOUTH ST   06096
   Edward Lanati, prin.

Winsted, Litchfield Co., Pop. Code 6
Barkhamsted SD
Sch. Sys. Enr. Code 2
Supt. – Leonard Lanza, CENTRAL AVE   06098
Other Schools – See Pleasant Valley

Colebrook SD
Sch. Sys. Enr. Code 2
Supt. – Leonard Lanza, CENTRAL AVENUE   06098
Other Schools – See Colebrook

Norfolk SD
Sch. Sys. Enr. Code 2
Supt. – Leonard Lanza, CENTRAL AVE   06098
Other Schools – See Norfolk

Winchester SD
Sch. Sys. Enr. Code 4
Supt. – Norman Michaud, 101 N MAIN ST   06098
Pearson MS, 2 WETMORE AVE   06098
   Francis Savage, prin.
Batcheller ES, 201 PRATT ST   06098
   Arthur Dobos, prin.
Hinsdale MS, 15 HINSDALE AVE   06098
   Richard Conrad, prin.

St. Anthony ES, 55 OAK ST   06098

Wolcott, New Haven Co., Pop. Code 7
Wolcott SD
Sch. Sys. Enr. Code 5
Supt. – Thomas Jakubaitis, 154 CENTER ST   06716
Alcott MS, 1490 WOODTICK ROAD   06716
   Robert Gerace, prin.
Frisbie ES, 24 TODD RD   06716
   Michael Palmerie, prin.
Tyrrell ES, 500 TODD RD   06716
   Russell Emons, prin.
Wakelee ES, 12 HEMPLE DR   06716
   Robert Carroll, prin.

Woodbridge, New Haven Co., Pop. Code 6
Woodbridge SD
Sch. Sys. Enr. Code 3
Supt. – Alex Warren, BEECHER ROAD   06525
Beecher ES, 40 BEECHER RD   06525
   Marie Oddi, prin.

Woodbury, Litchfield Co., Pop. Code 6
Regional SD 14
Sch. Sys. Enr. Code 4
Supt. – Vincent Ganci
   MINORTOWN ROAD   06798
MS, SCHOOL ST   06798 – Vincent Iezzi, prin.
Mitchell ES, 14 SCHOOL ST   06798
   Robert Lynam, prin.
Other Schools – See Bethlehem

Woodstock, Windham Co., Pop. Code 6
Woodstock SD
Sch. Sys. Enr. Code 3
Supt. – Anthony Perrelli, P O BOX 237   06281
ES, P O BOX 237   06281 – Victoria Scheufler, prin.

DELAWARE

STATE DEPARTMENT OF PUBLIC INSTRUCTION
Townsend Building
P.O. Box 1402, Dover 19903
(302) 736-4629

Superintendent of Public Instruction	Dr. William Keene
Deputy Superintendent Administration	Dr. John Ryan
Assistant Superintendent Administrative Services	Dr. James Spartz
Deputy Superintendent Instruction	Sidney Collison
Assistant Superintendent Instructionl Services	Primo Toccafondi

STATE BOARD OF EDUCATION
Charles Welch, *President*   P.O. Box 1402, Dover   19903

DELAWARE POSTSECONDARY EDUCATION COMMISSION
Robert McBride, *Chairperson*   820 N. French St., Wilmington   19801

PUBLIC, PRIVATE, AND PAROCHIAL ELEMENTARY SCHOOLS

Arden, New Castle Co., Pop. Code 3

The Arden ES, THE HIGHWAY   19810

Bear, New Castle Co.
Christina SD
Supt. – See Newark
Leasure ES, BEAR CORBITT ROAD   19701
 Donald Schneck, prin.

Caravel Academy, 2801 DEL LAWS ROAD   19701
Fairwinds Baptist Church School
 P O BOX 128   19701

Bridgeville, Sussex Co., Pop. Code 4
Woodbridge SD
Sch. Sys. Enr. Code 4
Supt. – J. Alan Ferner, 120 EDGEWOOD ST   19933
Woodbridge Early Childhood Ctr.
 48 CHURCH ST   19933 – Peggy Horton, prin.
Other Schools – See Greenwood

Camden, Kent Co., Pop. Code 4
Caesar Rodney SD
Sch. Sys. Enr. Code 6
Supt. – F. Postlethwait, P O BOX 188   19934
Other Schools – See Camden-Wyoming, Dover,
 Magnolia

Camden-Wyoming, Kent Co., Pop. Code 4
Caesar Rodney SD
Supt. – See Camden
Rodney JHS
 25 E CAMDEN WYOMING AVE   19934
 Gerald Buckworth, prin.
Frear ES, RURAL ROUTE 02   19934
 Johnny Smith, prin.
Simpson MS, P O BOX 219   19934
 Robert Knarr, prin.
Stokes ES, 11 E CAMDEN WYOMING AVE   19934
 William Gale, prin.

Claymont, New Castle Co., Pop. Code 7
Brandywine SD
Sch. Sys. Enr. Code 7
Supt. – Dr. Frank J. Furgele
 1000 PENNSYLVANIA AVE   19703
Darley Road ES, DARLEY ROAD   19703
 Ben Ellis, prin.
Maple Lane ES, MAPLE LANE   19703
 Dr. John Szczechowski, prin.
Other Schools – See Wilmington

Holy Rosary ES, 3210 PHILADELPHIA PIKE   19703

Clayton, Kent Co., Pop. Code 4
Smyrna SD
Supt. – See Smyrna
ES, MAIN ST   19938 – Harriett Burris, prin.

Delaware City, New Castle Co., Pop. Code 4
Colonial SD
Supt. – See New Castle
Gunning Bedford MS, COX NECK ROAD   19706
 Daniel Poorman, prin.
ES, 5TH AND BAYNARD STS   19706
 Charles Haegele, prin.

Dover, Kent Co., Pop. Code 7
Caesar Rodney SD
Supt. – See Camden
Arnold ES, CENTER ROAD   19901
 Conlyn Hart, prin.
Brown ES, 360 WEBBS LN   19901
 Charles Wilt, prin.
Star Hill MS, RURAL ROUTE 01   19901
 Clarence Dyer, prin.
Welch ES, HAWTHORNE DR   19901
 Frani Melda, prin.

Capital SD
Sch. Sys. Enr. Code 6
Supt. – Dr. Edward Goate, 945 FOREST ST   19901
Central MS, DELAWARE AVE   19901
 John Leone, prin.
East ES, 852 S LITTLE CREEK RD   19901
 Ronald Bogia, prin.
Fairview ES, PEAR ST & WALKER ROAD   19901
 Martin Burns, prin.
Henry MS, CARVER ROAD   19901
 Joseph Feichtl, prin.
South ES, 955 S STATE ST   19901
 Donald Buckland, prin.
Towne Point ES, 629 BUCKSON DR   19901
 William Denbrock, prin.
West ES, 901 FOREST ST   19901
 Dr. Danny Kingery, prin.
Other Schools – See Hartly

Capitol Baptist School
 402 KESSELRING AVE   19901
Central Christian School
 RURAL ROUTE 02 BOX 300   19901
Kent Christian Academy
 1761 N DUPONT HIGHWAY   19901
Victory Chapel Christian School
 RURAL ROUTE 02 BOX 327   19901
Holy Cross ES, 631 S STATE ST   19901

Felton, Kent Co., Pop. Code 2
Lake Forest SD
Supt. – See Harrington
Lake Forest North ES, MAIN ST   19943
 Frank Young, prin.

Frankford, Sussex Co., Pop. Code 3
Indian River SD
Sch. Sys. Enr. Code 6
Supt. – Charles Hudson
 RURAL ROUTE 02 BOX 236   19945
ES   19945 – David Shugard, prin.
Other Schools – See Georgetown, Millsboro, Ocean
 View, Selbyville

Frederica, Kent Co., Pop. Code 3
Lake Forest SD
Supt. – See Harrington
Lake Forest East ES, FRONT ST   19946
 Richard Seyler, prin.

Georgetown, Sussex Co., Pop. Code 4
Indian River SD
Supt. – See Frankford
ES, 301 W MARKET ST   19947
 Theodore Fleetwood, prin.

Greenville, New Castle Co.
Red Clay Cons. SD
Supt. – See Wilmington
DuPont MS, 3130 KENNETT PIKE   19807
 Phillip Reed, prin.

Greenwood, Sussex Co., Pop. Code 3
Woodbridge SD
Supt. – See Bridgeville
Woodbridge ES, GOVERNORS AVE   19950
 David Winski, prin.

Greenwood Mennonite School
 RURAL ROUTE 01 BOX 62-C   19950
Hickory Ridge Christian School
 P O BOX 186   19950
Spirit and Life Christian Academy
 RURAL ROUTE 02 BOX 136A   19950

Harrington, Kent Co., Pop. Code 4
Lake Forest SD
Sch. Sys. Enr. Code 5
Supt. – Dr. James VanSciver, DORMAN ST   19952
Chipman JHS, 101 W CENTER ST   19952
 Marjorie Davis, prin.
-ake Forest South ES, DORMAN ST   19952
 Earl Griffin, prin.
Other Schools – See Felton, Frederica

Hartly, Kent Co., Pop. Code 2
Capital SD
Supt. – See Dover
ES, P O BOX 25   19953 – Betty Penrod, prin.

Hockessin, New Castle Co., Pop. Code 3
Red Clay Cons. SD
Supt. – See Wilmington
DuPont MS
 BENGE & MEETING HOUSE ROADS   19707
 Francis Ryan, prin.

Sanford School   19707
Wilmington Christian School, P O BOX 626   19707

Laurel, Sussex Co., Pop. Code 4
Laurel SD
Sch. Sys. Enr. Code 4
Supt. – Robert Hupp, 815 S CENTRAL AVE   19956
Laurel Central MS, 801 S CENTRAL AVE   19956
 Edward Taylor II, prin.
North Laurel ES, 300 WILSON ST   19956
 Karol Powers, prin.
West Laurel ES, 499 W SIXTH ST   19956
 Karol Powers, prin.

Baptist Christian Academy, P O BOX 326   19956
El Shaddai Academy
 RURAL ROUTE 01 BOX 115   19956
Epworth Christian School
 RURAL ROUTE 01 BOX 65   19956

Lewes, Sussex Co., Pop. Code 5
Cape Henlopen SD
Sch. Sys. Enr. Code 5
Supt. – Dr. James Wilson
 1270 KINGS HWY   19958
Savannah Road MS, 810 SAVANNAH RD   19958
 Nancy Feichtl, prin.

115

Shields ES, SUSSEX DR 19958
Philip Mancini, prin.
Other Schools – See Milton, Rehoboth Beach

Lewes Christian Academy, P O BOX 25 19958

Lincoln, Sussex Co., Pop. Code 2

Christian Tabernacle Academy
P O BOX 148 19960

Magnolia, Kent Co., Pop. Code 2
Caesar Rodney SD
Supt. – See Camden
McIlvaine ES 19962 – Johnny Smith, prin.

Middletown, New Castle Co., Pop. Code 5
Appoquinimink SD
Supt. – See Odessa
Redding MS, 201 NEW ST 19709
Jacqueline Robinson, prin.
Silver Lake ES, 200 E COCHRAN ST 19709
Howard Gaines, prin.

Broadmeadow School, 500 S BROAD ST 19709
Great Commission Academy
225 SUGAR PINE DRIVE 19709

Milford, Kent Co., Pop. Code 6
Milford SD
Sch. Sys. Enr. Code 5
Supt. – Charles Moses
906 LAKEVIEW AVE 19963
Milford-Lakeview MS, 612 LAKEVIEW AVE 19963
Dr. Gary Annett, prin.
Banneker ES, 449 NORTH ST 19963
Dr. Kae Keister, prin.
Ross ES, 310 LOVERS LN 19963
Dr. Joanne New, prin.

Milford First Baptist Christian School
P O BOX 238 19963
The Family Learning Academy
306 S WASHINGTON STREET 19963

Millsboro, Sussex Co., Pop. Code 4
Indian River SD
Supt. – See Frankford
East Millsboro ES, 500 E STATE ST 19966
William Burton, prin.

Milton, Sussex Co., Pop. Code 4
Cape Henlopen SD
Supt. – See Lewes
Brittingham ES, 400 MULBERRY ST 19968
F. Matthes, prin.
Milton Federal Street MS, FEDERAL ST 19968
William Howell, prin.

Newark, New Castle Co., Pop. Code 7
Christina SD
Sch. Sys. Enr. Code 7
Supt. – Dr. Michael Walls, 83 E MAIN ST 19711
Gauger MS, GENDER ROAD 19713
Shirley Saunders, prin.
Kirk MS, 140 BRENNEN DRIVE 19713
Dr. Jane Barfield, prin.
Shue MS, 1500 CAPITOL TRAIL 19711
Dr. D. Hugh Ferguson, prin.
Brookside ES, 65 MARROWS RD 19713
Marlene James, prin.
Cobbs ES, BROADFIELD DR 19713
Thomas Cobley, prin.
Downes ES, 200 CASHO MILL RD 19711
(—), prin.
Gallaher ES, 800 N BROWNLEAF RD 19713
Barbara Holladay, prin.
MacLary ES, 300 SAINT REGIS DR 19711
Dr. Byron Chandler, prin.
McVey ES, 908 JANICE DR 19713
William Murray, prin.
Christiana-Salem ES, HCR 273 19702
Martin Groundland, prin.
Smith ES, 142 BRENNEN DR 19713
James Hill, prin.
West Park Place ES
193 WEST PARK PLACE 19711
Thelma Carr, prin.
Wilson ES, 14 FORGE RD 19711
Dr. Peter Idstein, prin.
Other Schools – See Bear, Wilmington

Red Clay Cons. SD
Supt. – See Wilmington
Forest Oak ES, 55 S MEADOWOOD DR 19711
William Cooke, prin.

Faith City Christian School
179 CHRISTIANA MALL 19702
Great Commission Academy
602 BIRCHWOOD DR 19713
Holy Angels ES, 82 POSSUM PARK RD 19711
The Independence ES
1300 PAPER MILL RD 19711

New Castle, New Castle Co., Pop. Code 5
Colonial SD
Sch. Sys. Enr. Code 6
Supt. – Ray Christian, 20 BLOUNT ROAD 19720
MS, 9TH & DELAWARE STS 19720
Delvin Burns, prin.
Read MS, 400 E BASIN ROAD 19720
George Meney, prin.
Castle Hills ES, MOORES LANE 19720
Donald Lacey, prin.
Colwyck MS, LANDERS LN 19720
John Gray, prin.
Downie ES, FRENCHTOWN ROAD 19720
Dolores Higgins, prin.
Eisenberg MS, LANDERS LN 19720
Keith Dorman, prin.
McCullough MS, CHASE AVE 19720
Dr. Richard Gochnauer, prin.
Pleasantville ES, PLEASANT PL 19720
Raymond Martin, prin.
Wilmington Manor ES
200 E ROOSEVELT AVE 19720
Meridith Roberts, prin.
Other Schools – See Delaware City, Saint Georges,
Wilmington

New Castle Baptist Academy
901 W BASIN ROAD 19720
Holy Spirit ES, CHURCH DR 19720
Our Lady Fatima ES
HARRISON AVE & DUPONT PKWY 19720
St. Peter's ES, 6TH & HARMONY STS 19720

Ocean View, Sussex Co., Pop. Code 2
Indian River SD
Supt. – See Frankford
Lord Baltimore ES 19970 – John Young, prin.

Odessa, New Castle Co., Pop. Code 3
Appoquinimink SD
Sch. Sys. Enr. Code 4
Supt. – Dr. Ronald Mersky, P O BOX 158 19730
Other Schools – See Middletown, Townsend

Rehoboth Beach, Sussex Co., Pop. Code 4
Cape Henlopen SD
Supt. – See Lewes
ES, 500 STOCKLEY ST 19971 – O. Basinski, prin.

Saint Georges, New Castle Co.
Colonial SD
Supt. – See New Castle
MacDonough ES 19733 – Charles Haegele, prin.

Seaford, Sussex Co., Pop. Code 6
Seaford SD
Sch. Sys. Enr. Code 5
Supt. – Dr. Russell Knorr
ADMIN BLDG DELAWARE PLACE 19973
MS, STEIN HIGHWAY 19973 – Earl Cannon, prin.
Douglass IS, SWAIN ROAD 19973
Daniel Jones, prin.
Seaford Central ES, DELAWARE PLACE 19973
George Stone, prin.
West Seaford ES, SUSSEX AVE 19973
Philip Nixon, prin.

Seaford Christian Academy
110 HOLLY STREET 19973

Selbyville, Sussex Co., Pop. Code 4
Indian River SD
Supt. – See Frankford
Showell ES, RURAL ROUTE 02 BOX 5 19975
Sandra Bunting, prin.

Smyrna, Kent Co., Pop. Code 5
Smyrna SD
Sch. Sys. Enr. Code 5
Supt. – Wayne Barton, 22 S MAIN ST 19977
ES, S SAINT AND SCHOOL LN 19977
William Wells, prin.
MS, W FRAZIER ST 19977
Randall Hansen, prin.
Smyrna North ES, MAIN ST EXT 19977
Sally Ann Orr, prin.
Other Schools – See Clayton

Townsend, New Castle Co., Pop. Code 2
Appoquinimink SD
Supt. – See Odessa
ES 19734 – Charles Atkinson, prin.

Wilmington, New Castle Co., Pop. Code 8
Brandywine SD
Supt. – See Claymont
Burnett JHS, 37TH & FRANKLIN PLACE 19802
Wilbert Miller, prin.
Hanby JHS, 2525 BERWYN ROAD 19810
Thomas Adams, prin.
Talley JHS, 1110 CYPRESS ROAD 19810
Robert Cline, prin.
Brandywood ES, 2115 ANSON RD 19810
Diane Young, prin.

Carrcroft ES, 503 CREST RD 19803
David Moore, prin.
Dupont MS, 34TH & VAN BUREN STS 19802
Dr. Ann Houseman, prin.
Forwood ES, 1400 WESTMINSTER DR 19810
James Rauhe, prin.
Harlan MS, 36TH & JEFFERSON STS 19802
Andrew Ricketts, prin.
Lancashire ES, 2000 NAAMANS RD 19810
Patricia McCarthy, prin.
Lombardy ES, 412 FOULK RD 19803
Kathleen Overstreet, prin.
Mt.Pleasant ES, PHILADELPHIA PIKE AND 19809
Nick Cofrancesco, prin.

Christina SD
Supt. – See Newark
Bancroft MS, 8TH AND LOMBARD STS 19801
Maurice Pritchett, prin.
Bayard MS, DUPONT & CHESTNUT STS 19805
Major Hairston,Jr., prin.
Drew MS, 7TH & LOMBARD STS 19801
Milton Markley, prin.
Pulaski MS, CEDAR & BROOM STS 19805
Edward Smith, prin.
Pyle MS, 5TH & LOMBARD STS 19801
Milton Markley, prin.
Stubbs MS, 11TH & PINE STS 19801
Leslie Morrill, prin.

Colonial SD
Supt. – See New Castle
King MS, 3000 N CLAYMONT ST 19802
Paul Biery, prin.

Red Clay Cons. SD
Sch. Sys. Enr. Code 7
Supt. – Dr. Joseph Johnson
1400 N WASHINGTON ST 19801
Conrad MS, WOODCREST 19804 – Louis Ott, prin.
Skyline MS, 2900 SKYLINE DRIVE 19808
John Tentromono, prin.
Stanton MS, 1800 LIMESTONE ROAD 19804
T. Edwin Conard, prin.
Baltz ES, SPRUCE AVE 19805
Edward Hagarty, prin.
Heritage ES, 2815 HIGHLANDS LN 19808
Judith Stranch, prin.
Highlands ES, 2100 GILPIN AVE 19806
Carolyn Williams, prin.
Lewis ES, 10TH & VAN BUREN STS 19805
Samuel Lewis, prin.
Marbrook ES, 2101 CENTERVILLE RD 19808
Dr. Linda Poole, prin.
Mote MS
EDWARD AVE & KIRKWOOD HWY 19808
V. Schurr, prin.
Richardson Park ES, IDELLA AVE 19804
Paul Loper, prin.
Shortlidge ES, 18TH & WEST STS 19802
Paul Julian, prin.
Warner MS, 18TH & VAN BUREN STS 19802
Paul Carlson, prin.
Other Schools – See Greenville, Hockessin, Newark

Concord Christian Academy
2510 MARSH ROAD 19810
St. Edmond's Academy, 2120 VEALE RD 19810
Tatnall School, 1501 BARLEY MILL ROAD 19807
Tower Hill School, 2813 W 17TH ST 19806
Wilmington Friends School
101 SCHOOL ROAD 19803
Christ our King ES
28TH AND MADISON STS 19802
Corpus Christi ES, 907 NEW RD 19805
Immaculate Heart of Mary ES
1000 SHIPLEY RD 19803
St. Ann's ES, 2006 SHALLCROSS AVE 19806
St. Anthony Padua ES, 9TH & SCOTT STS 19805
St. Catherine Siena ES
2501 CENTERVILLE RD 19808
St. Elizabeth's ES, CEDAR & RODNEY STS 19805
St. Hedwig's ES
LINDEN AND HARRISON STS 19805
St. Helena's ES, 210 BELLEFONTE AVE 19809
St. John Beloved ES, 905 MILLTOWN RD 19808
St. Mary Magdalen ES, 9 SHARPLEY RD 19803
St. Matthew's ES, 1 FALLON AVE 19804
St. Paul's ES, 3RD AND VAN BUREN STS 19805
St. Peter's Cathedral ES
6TH AND TATNALL STS 19801
St. Thomas Apostle ES
PYLE & BAYARD AVE 19805
Ursuline Academy JHS
1102 PENNSYLVANIA AVE 19806

DISTRICT OF COLUMBIA

PUBLIC SCHOOLS OF THE DISTRICT OF COLUMBIA
415 12th St., N.W., Washington 20004
(202) 724-4222

Superintendent of Schools	Andrew Jenkins
Deputy Superintendent	William Brown
Associate Superintendent of Instruction	Dr. James Guines
Associate Superintendent Career & Adult Education	Otho Jones
Associate Superintendent Management Services	James Brown
Associate Superintendent Special Services & State Affairs	Wilbur Millard

PUBLIC, PRIVATE, AND PAROCHIAL ELEMENTARY SCHOOLS

Washington, Pop. Code 11
Bunker Hill Administrative Unit
Sch. Sys. Enr. Code 7
Supt. – Barbara Jackson
   14TH ST & MICHIGAN AVE NE 20017
Adams ES, 19TH & CALIFORNIA STS NW 20005
   Alexander Brown, prin.
Bancroft ES, 18TH & NEWTON STRS NW 20010
   Thomas Jones, prin.
Brookland ES
   MICHIGAN AVE & RNDLPH ST NE 20017
   Marguerite Pettigrew, prin.
Bunker Hill ES
   14TH & MICHIGAN AVE NE 20017
   Carolyn Preston, prin.
Burroughs ES, 18TH & MONROE STS NE 20018
   Nae Davis, prin.
Cleveland ES, 8TH AND T STS NW 20045
   Annie Mair, prin.
Cook ES, N CAPITOL & P STS NW 20001
   Thomas Kelly, prin.
Cooke ES, 17TH & EUCLID STS NW 20009
   Josephine Teague, prin.
Emery ES, LINCOLN RD & S ST NE 20002
   Michael Holloman, prin.
Ft. Lincoln ES
   31ST PL & FT LINCOLN DR NE 20018
   Louise Buckner, prin.
Gage Eckington ES, 3RD & ELM STS NW 20001
   Mary Thompson, prin.
Harrison ES, 13TH & V STS NW 20009
   Jerome Shelton, prin.
Langdon ES, 20TH AND EVARTS STS NE 20018
   Ralph Briscoe, prin.
Lewis ES, 300 BRYANT ST NW 20001
   Joyce Thompson, prin.
Meyer ES, 11TH & CLIFTON ST NW 20009
   Barbara Lyles, prin.
Monroe ES, 3012 GEORGIA AVE NW 20001
   J. Barnes, prin.
Noyes ES, 10TH & F STS NE 20002
   Charles Epps, prin.
Park View ES
   WARDER ST & NEWTON PL NW 20010
   Shirley Hayes, prin.
Reed ES, 2200 CHAMPLAIN ST NW 20009
   John Sparrow, prin.
Shaed ES
   LINCOLN RD & DOUGLAS ST NE 20002
   Brenda Richards, prin.
Slater-Langston ES
   P ST N CAPITOL & 1ST STS NW 20001
   Thomas Kelly, prin.
Slowe ES, 14TH AND JACKSON STS NE 20017
   Alvira Travis, prin.
Tubman ES, 13TH & KENYON STS NW 20011
   Peggy Wines, prin.
Webb ES, 1375 MOUNT OLIVET RD NE 20002
   John Anthony, prin.
Wheatley ES
   MONTELLO AVE & NEAL ST NE 20002
   Marjorie Haigler, prin.
Woodridge ES
   CARLTON AND CENTRAL AVES NE 20018
   Leonard Sanders, prin.
Young ES, 26TH ST & BENNING RD NE 20002
   Eurah Collins, prin.

Carver Administrative Unit
Sch. Sys. Enr. Code 8
Supt. – Earnest Devoe, 45TH & LEE STS NE 20019
Kramer JHS, 17TH & Q STS SE 20020
   Zavolia Willis, prin.
Stuart-Hobson MS, 4TH & E STS NE 20002
   Veola Jackson, prin.
Aiton ES, 533 48TH PL NE 20019
   Thomas Brown, prin.
Beers ES, 36TH PL & ALABAMA AVE SE 20020
   Michael Hammond, prin.

Benning ES, 41ST AND E CAPITOL STS NE 20019
   Geneva Williams, prin.
Blow ES, 725 19TH ST NE 20002
   Clyde Gray, prin.
Brent ES, 3RD & D STS SE 20003
   Frances Plummer, prin.
Bryan ES, 13TH ST & INDPDNCE AVE SE 20003
   Gretchen Lofland, prin.
Burrville ES
   DIVISION AVE & HAYES ST NE 20019
   Walter Henry, prin.
Carver ES, 45TH & LEE ST NE 20019
   Ronald Hasty, prin.
Davis ES, 44TH & H ST SE 20019
   Alice Jones, prin.
Drew ES, 56TH & EADS ST NE 20019
   Regina Rutledge, prin.
Fletcher-Johnson ES
   BENNING RD & C ST SE 20019
   George Rutherford, prin.
Gibbs ES, 19TH & E STS NE 20002
   Ray Bledsoe, prin.
Giddings ES, 3RD & G STS SE 20003
   Perry Handy, prin.
Goding ES, 10TH & F ST NE 20002
   Gloria Smith, prin.
Harris ES, 53RD & C ST SE 20019
   Florence Dagner, prin.
Houston ES, 1100 50TH PL NE 20019
   Dene Pendleton, prin.
Kenilworth ES
   44TH ST NASH & ORD STS NE 20019
   Warren Simms, prin.
Ketcham ES, 15TH & U STS SE 20020
   Romaine Thomas, prin.
Kimball ES
   MINNESOTA AVE & ELY PL SE 20019
   Janie Prue, prin.
Kingsman ES, 14TH & R ST SE 20020
   Margaret Saxon, prin.
Ludlow-Taylor ES, 7TH & G STS NE 20002
   Valerie Green, prin.
Maury ES, 13TH ST & CONSTITUTION NE 20002
   LeGrande Baldwin, prin.
Merritt ES, 50TH & HAYES ST NE 20019
   Ronald Hasty, prin.
Miner ES, 601 15TH ST NE 20002
   Bernard Braddock, prin.
Nalle ES, 50TH & BASS PL SE 20019
   Shirley Williams, prin.
Orr ES, MINNESOTA AVE/NAYLOR RD SE 20020
   Lawrence Boone, prin.
Payne ES, 15TH & C STS SE 20003
   Gretchen Lofland, prin.
Peabody ES, 5TH & C STS NE 20003
   Veola Jackson, prin.
Plummer ES, TEXAS AVE & C ST SE 20019
   Henryetta Gray, prin.
Randle Highlands ES, 30TH & R ST SE 20020
   Tony Jones, prin.
Richardson ES, 53RD & BLAINE ST NE 20019
   Marline Guy, prin.
River Terrace ES, 34TH & DIX ST NE 20019
   Constance Clark, prin.
Shadd ES, 5600 E CAPITOL ST NE 20019
   William Birchette, prin.
Smothers ES, 44TH & BROOKS ST NE 20019
   Constance Clark, prin.
Stanton ES
   NAYLOR RD & ALABAMA AVE SE 20020
   Elbie Davis, prin.
Thomas ES, 650 ANACOSTIA AVE NE 20019
   Patricia McCrimmon, prin.
Tyler ES, 10TH & F ST NE 20002
   Joan Kelly, prin.
Watkins ES, 12TH & E STS SE 20003
   Veola Jackson, prin.
Weatherless ES, BURNS & C STS 20019
   Shirley McGaillaria, prin.

Winston ES, 31ST & ERIE STS SE 20020
   Marie Marshall, prin.

Savoy Administrative Unit
Sch. Sys. Enr. Code 7
Supt. – Thomas Harper
   2400 SHANNON PL SE 20020
Amidon ES, 4TH AND EYE STRS SW 20024
   Pauline Hamlette, prin.
Birney ES, KING AVE & SUMNER RD SE 20020
   James Tillery, prin.
Bowen ES, DELAWARE AVE & M ST SW 20024
   Edward Wells, prin.
Draper ES
   WAHLER PL WHLR RD & 9TH SE 20032
   Edward Stewart, prin.
Friendship ES
   S CAPITOL ST & LVGSTN RD SE 20032
   Tyrone Hopkins, prin.
Garfield ES
   ALABAMA AVE & IRVING PL SE 20020
   William Pitts, prin.
Garrison ES, 12TH & S STS NW 20009
   Andrea Irby, prin.
Green ES, 15TH ST & MSISPPI AVE SE 20032
   Vandy Jamison, prin.
Hendley ES, 6TH & CHESAPEAKE STS SE 20032
   Clark Stewart, prin.
King ES, 6TH ST & ALABAMA AVE SE 20032
   William Dalton, prin.
Leckie ES
   KING AVE & CHESAPEAKE ST SW 20032
   Gloria Blaylock, prin.
Malcolm X ES
   ALABAMA AVE & CNGRS ST SE 20032
   Sandra Coates, prin.
McGogney ES, 3400 WHEELER RD SE 20032
   Joyce Jamison, prin.
Montgomery ES
   P ST 5TH ST NEW JERSEY NW 20001
   Harriette Freeman, prin.
Moten MS, MORRIS & ELVANS RDS SE 20020
   Isaac Jackson, prin.
Patterson ES, S CAPITOL & ELMIR ST SW 20032
   Bessie Wells, prin.
Ross ES, 1730 R ST NW 20009
   Erasmo Garza, prin.
Savoy ES, 2400 SHANNON PL SE 20020
   Betty Larkins, prin.
Seaton ES
   10TH ST & RHODE ISLAND NW 20001
   Martha Anderson, prin.
Simon ES, 4TH & MISSISSIPPI AVE SE 20032
   Helen Ferguson, prin.
Stevens ES, 21ST & K STS NW 20036
   Juanita Braddock, prin.
Syphax ES, HALF & N STS SW 20024
   Mary Williams, prin.
Terrell ES
   WHEELER RD & SAVANNAH ST SE 20032
   Dennis Johnson, prin.
Thomson ES, 12TH & L STS NW 20005
   Robert Bracy, prin.
Turner ES
   STANTON RD & ALABAMA AVE SE 20020
   Francis Cook, prin.
Van Ness ES, 5TH & M ST SE 20003
   Cassandra Butler, prin.
Walker Jones ES, 1ST & T ST NE 20002
   William Blylock, prin.
Washington Highland ES
   8TH & YUMA ST SE 20032
   Shirley Mitchell, prin.
Wilkinson ES, POMEROY RD & ERIE ST SE 20020
   Myra Spriggs, prin.
Wilson ES, 6TH & K STS NE 20002
   Erma Fields, prin.

West Administrative Unit
Sch. Sys. Enr. Code 7
Supt. – Shelia Handy
  FARRAGUT BTWN 13TH-14TH NW   20066
Hardy MS
  FOXHALL ROAD & VOLTA PL NW   20007
  Amanda Garnett, prin.
Barnard ES, 5TH & DECATUR STS NW   20011
  Edward Norris, prin.
Brightwood ES
  13TH & NICHOLSON ST NW   20011
  William Moore, prin.
Clark ES, 7TH & WEBSTER STS NW   20011
  Myrtle Lewis, prin.
Eaton ES, 34TH & LOWELL STS NW   20016
  Patricia Greer, prin.
Fillmore Art Center ES, 35TH & R ST NW   20007
  Patricia Mitchell, prin.
Hearst ES, 37TH & TILDEN STS NW   20008
  Patricia Greer, prin.
Hyde ES, 32ND & O STS NW   20007
  Betty Brooks, prin.
Janney ES
  42ND AND ALBEMARLE STS NW   20016
  Emily Crandall, prin.
Keene ES
  ROCK CRK CHURCH & RIGGS NE   20011
  Alexzene Williams, prin.
Key ES, HURST TERRACE & DANA PL NW   20016
  Betty Brooks, prin.
LaFayette ES
  NORTHAMPTON & BRD BRC RD   20015
  Sandra Bond, prin.
LaSalle ES, RIGGS RD & MADISON ST NE   20011
  Earle Bannister, prin.
Mann ES, 44TH & NEWARK STS NW   20015
  Patricia Patton, prin.

Murch ES, 36TH & ELLICOTT STS NW   20008
  Mary Gill, prin.
Oyster ES, 29TH & CALVERT ST NW   20008
  Elena Izquierdo, prin.
Petworth ES, 8TH & SHEPHERD STS NW   20011
  Harriet Weatherspoon, prin.
Powell ES
  UPSHUR ST/13TH/14TH STS NW   20011
  Harriet Weatherspoon, prin.
Raymond ES, 10TH & SPRING RD NW   20010
  Debra Jackson Nesmith, prin.
Rudolph ES, 2ND & T ST NE   20002
  Dolores Talley, prin.
Shepherd ES, 14TH ST & KALMIA RD NW   20012
  Edith Smith, prin.
Stoddert ES, 39TH & CALVERT STS NW   20007
  Patricia Patton, prin.
Takoma ES
  PINEY BRANCH & DAHLIA ST NW   20012
  Elsie Mitchell, prin.
Truesdell ES, 8TH & INGRAHAM ST NW   20011
  Katie Jones, prin.
West ES, FARRAGUT ST/13TH/14/STS NW   20011
  Mildred Musgrove, prin.
Whittier ES, 5TH & SHERIDAN ST NW   20011
  John Simpson, prin.

———————————————

Georgetown Day School
  4530 MACARTHUR BLVD NW   20007
Maret School, 3000 CATHEDRAL AVE NW   20068
Our Lady of Perpetual Help ES
  1604 MORRIS RD SE   20020
Washington Internationl School
  3100 MACOMB ST NW   20008
Annunciation ES, 3825 KLINGLE PL NW   20016
Assumption ES, 220 HIGH VIEW PL SE   20032
Blessed Sacrament ES
  5841 CHEVY CHASE PKY NW   20015

Capital Hill Day School
  210 S CAROLINA AVE SE   20003
Holy Comforter ES
  15TH & E CAPITOL ST SE   20003
Holy Name ES, 1217 W VIRGINIA AVE NE   20002
Holy Redeemer ES
  1135 NEW JERSEY AVE NW   20001
Holy Trinity ES, 1325 36TH ST NW   20007
Immaculate Conception ES, 711 N ST NW   20001
National Presbyterian ES
  4121 NEBRASKA AVE NW   20016
Nativity ES, 6008 GEORGIA AVE NW   20011
Our Lady Queen of Peace ES
  3740 ELY PL SE   20019
Our Lady of Perpetual Help ES
  1409 V ST SE   20020
Our Lady of Victory ES
  4755 WHITEHAVEN PKY NW   20007
Sacred Heart ES, 1625 PARK RD NW   20010
Sheridan ES, 4400 36TH ST NW   20008
St. Ann ES, 4404 WISCONSIN AVE NW   20016
St. Anthony ES, 1222 MONROE ST NE   20017
St. Augustine ES, 1421 V ST NW   20009
St. Benedict of Moor ES, 330 21ST ST NE   20002
St. Francis DeSales ES
  2019 RHODE ISLAND AVE NE   20018
St. Francis Xavier ES, 2700 O ST SE   20020
St. Gabriel ES, 510 WEBSTER ST NW   20011
St. Martin's ES, 62 T ST NE   20002
St. Patrick's Episcopal ES
  4700 WHITEHAVEN PKY NW   20007
St. Peter's Interparochal ES, 422 3RD ST SE   20003
St. Thomas More ES, 4265 4TH ST SE   20032

FLORIDA

STATE DEPARTMENT OF EDUCATION
PL 08, The Capitol, Tallahassee 32301
(904) 487-1785

Commissioner of Education	Betty Castor
Deputy Commissioner of Education	William Golden
Director Division of Administration	Lanny Larson
Director Division of Blind Services	Donald Wedewer
Director Division of Human Resource Development	Ida Baker
Director Division of Public Schools	Donald Van Fleet
Director Division of Vocational/Adult Education	Robert Howell
Director Division of Community Colleges	Clark Maxwell
Director Division of Universities	Charles Reed

STATE BOARD OF EDUCATION
Governor Bob Martinez, *Chairperson*   Tallahassee   32301

FLORIDA BOARD OF REGENTS
Joan Ruffier, *Chairperson*   Orlando

PUBLIC, PRIVATE, AND PAROCHIAL ELEMENTARY SCHOOLS

Alachua, Alachua Co., Pop. Code 5
Alachua SD 1
Supt. – See Gainesville
Mebane MS, RURAL ROUTE 01 BOX 4   32615
  Terry Stechmiller, prin.
ES, P O BOX 69   32615 – Pansy Post, prin.

Alford, Jackson Co., Pop. Code 3
Jackson SD 32
Supt. – See Marianna
ES, P O BOX 188   32420 – Joe Houston, prin.

Altamonte Springs, Seminole Co., Pop. Code 7
Seminole SD 59
Supt. – See Sanford
Teague MS, 1000 SAND LAKE ROAD   32714
  Sidney Boyette, prin.
Altamonte ES, 300 PINEVIEW ST   32701
  Mildred Bell, prin.
Forest City ES, 2245 SAND LAKE RD   32714
  Peter Barnett, prin.

Lake Orienta ES, 612 NEWPORT AVE   32701
  Leroy Johnson, prin.
Spring Lake ES, 695 W ORANGE AVE   32714
  James Neville, prin.

———————————————

Altamonte Christian School
  601 PALM SPRINGS DRIVE   32701
St. Mary Magdalen ES
  851 MAITLAND AVE   32701

Altha, Calhoun Co., Pop. Code 2
Calhoun SD 7
Supt. – See Blountstown
S, P O BOX 67   32421 – Harriett Peacock, prin.

Altoona, Lake Co.
Lake SD 35
Supt. – See Tavares
ES, HWY 19   32702 – Jerry Hatfield, prin.

Alturas, Polk Co.
Polk SD 53
Supt. – See Bartow
ES, P O BOX 97   33820 – Jack Cline, prin.

Alva, Lee Co., Pop. Code 2
Lee SD 36
Supt. – See Fort Myers
MS, P O BOX 128   33920 – Charles Watson, prin.
ES, P O BOX 278   33920 – James Donmoyer, prin.

Anthony, Marion Co.
Marion SD 42
Supt. – See Ocala
ES, P O BOX 69   32617 – Wendy Staley, prin.

Apalachicola, Franklin Co., Pop. Code 5
Franklin SD 19
Sch. Sys. Enr. Code 4
Supt. – Gloria Tucker, 155 AVENUE EAST   32320

Chapman ES, 12TH ST AND AVE E 32320
  Rose McCoy, prin.
Other Schools – See Carrabelle, Eastpoint

Apollo Beach, Hillsborough Co.
Hillsborough SD 29
Supt. – See Tampa
ES, 501 APOLLO BEACH BLVD 33570
  Barbara MacLamma, prin.

Apopka, Orange Co., Pop. Code 6
Orange SD 48
Supt. – See Orlando
MS, 425 S PARK AVE 32703 – Wesley Aman, prin.
ES, 675 W DIXIE HWY 32712
  Patricia Hollingsworth, prin.
Clarcona ES, 3607 DAYMOND RD 32703
  Nicholas Gledich, prin.
Dream Lake ES, 500 N PARK AVE 32712
  Dr. Karen Werrenrath, prin.
Lovell ES, 815 S ROGER WILLIAMS RD 32703
  Don Mapel, prin.
Rock Springs ES, 2400 ROCK SPRINGS RD 32712
  Susan Kiffe, prin.
Wheatley ES, 2 W 18TH ST 32703
  Leonard Ingram, prin.

Seminole SD 59
Supt. – See Sanford
Bear Lake ES, 3399 GLEAVES CT 32703
  Chris Colwell, prin.

Arcadia, De Soto Co., Pop. Code 6
De Soto SD 14
Sch. Sys. Enr. Code 5
Supt. – Lawrence Browning
  530 LASALONA AVE 33821
De Soto MS, 420 W GIBSON ST 33821
  David Dunlap, prin.
Memorial ES, 851 E HICKORY ST 33821
  Don Knoche, prin.
West ES, 304 W IMOGENE ST 33821
  James Abraham, prin.
Other Schools – See Nocatee

Archer, Alachua Co., Pop. Code 4
Alachua SD 1
Supt. – See Gainesville
Archer Community ES
  RURAL ROUTE 01 BOX 115 32618
  Jahala Stirling, prin.

Atlantic Beach, Duval Co., Pop. Code 6
Duval SD 16
Supt. – See Jacksonville
ES, 298 SHERRY DR 32233 – Doris Le Prell, prin.
Finegan ES, 555 WONDERWOOD DR 32233
  John Gornto, prin.
Mayport ES, 2753 SHANGRILA DR 32233
  Elizabeth McNamara, prin.

Auburndale, Polk Co., Pop. Code 6
Polk SD 53
Supt. – See Bartow
Auburndale Central ES, 320 LEMON ST 33823
  Lora Williams, prin.
Boswell ES, 2820 K-VILLE AVE 33823
  Robert Donaway, prin.
Caldwell ES, 141 DAIRY RD 33823
  Dan Pierce, prin.
Lena Vista ES, 208 S BERKLEY RD 33823
  Ferris French, prin.
Stambaugh MS, 226 N BARTOW AVE 33823
  Gerald Winsett, prin.

Avon Park, Highlands Co., Pop. Code 6
Highlands SD 28
Supt. – See Sebring
MS, 312 S LAKE AVE 33825
  James Bradley, prin.
Avon ES, 705 W WINTHROP ST 33825
  Charles Johnson,Jr., prin.

Babson Park, Polk Co., Pop. Code 3
Polk SD 53
Supt. – See Bartow
ES, 815 U S HWY ALT 27 33827 – Dale Fair, prin.

Bagdad, Santa Rosa Co.
Santa Rosa SD 57
Supt. – See Milton
ES, P O BOX 255 32530 – Roderick Gracey, prin.

Baker, Okaloosa Co., Pop. Code 2
Okaloosa SD 46
Supt. – See Crestview
S, RURAL ROUTE 02 BOX 231 32531
  Wayne Ansley, prin.

Baldwin, Duval Co., Pop. Code 4
Duval SD 16
Supt. – See Jacksonville
Jones ES, 700 ORANGE AVE 32234
  James Hurst, prin.

Bartow, Polk Co., Pop. Code 7
Polk SD 53
Sch. Sys. Enr. Code 8
Supt. – Dr. John Stewart, P O BOX 391 33830
ES, 590 S WILSON AVE 33830
  Thomas Meeks, prin.
Floral Avenue ES, 1530 S FLORAL AVE 33830
  Ruth Bodenheimer, prin.
Gause ES, 1395 POLK ST 33830
  Ernest Dodson, prin.
Gibbons Street ES, 1869 GIBBONS ST 33830
  Ora Greene, prin.

Stephens ES, 1350 N MAPLE AVE 33830
  (—), prin.
Union Academy JHS, 1195 E WABASH ST 33830
  Harold Barker, prin.
Other Schools – See Alturas, Auburndale, Babson
  Park, Davenport, Dundee, Eagle Lake, Eaton Park,
  Fort Meade, Frostproof, Haines City, Highland City,
  Lake Alfred, Lakeland, Lake Wales, Mulberry, Polk
  City, Winter Haven

Bay Harbor Islands, Dade Co., Pop. Code 5
Dade SD 13
Supt. – See Miami
Bay Harbor ES, 1165 94TH ST 33154
  Nicholas Rinaldi, prin.

Bell, Gilchrist Co., Pop. Code 2
Gilchrist SD 21
Supt. – See Trenton
S, RURAL ROUTE 01 BOX 35 32619
  Robert Irvin, prin.

Belle Glade, Palm Beach Co., Pop. Code 7
Palm Beach SD 50
Supt. – See West Palm Beach
Lake Shore MS, 1101 SW AVE E 33430
  Barbara Altman, prin.
ES, 7TH AND CANAL STS NW 33430
  Harry Davis, prin.
Glade View ES, 1100 SW AVENUE G 33430
  Gary Hagermann, prin.
Gove ES, 900 SE AVENUE G 33430
  Ruth Irvin, prin.
Lake Shore MS, 1102 W AVENUE A 33430
  Gary Hagermann, prin.

Christian Day School, 17 NW AVENUE B 33430
Glades Day School, 400 NE AVENUE L 33430

Belleview, Marion Co., Pop. Code 4
Marion SD 42
Supt. – See Ocala
ES, 5556 S E AGNEW ROAD 32620
  Jane McClellan, prin.
Belleview-Santos ES, 9600 SE US HWY 441 32620
  John Livingston, prin.

Blountstown, Calhoun Co., Pop. Code 5
Calhoun SD 7
Sch. Sys. Enr. Code 4
Supt. – Howard Johnson
  425 E CENTRAL AVE 32424
MS, 611 MAYHAW DRIVE 32424
  James Dunn, prin.
ES, 300 FULLER WARREN DR 32424
  Jimmy Suggs, prin.
Other Schools – See Altha, Clarksville

Bethel Mennonite Christian School
  356 GASKIN ST 32424

Boca Raton, Palm Beach Co., Pop. Code 8
Palm Beach SD 50
Supt. – See West Palm Beach
MS, 1251 NW 8TH ST 33486
  Dr. Dick Reed, prin.
Loggers Run Community MS
  11584 W PALMETTO PARK ROAD 33428
  Juanita Lampi, prin.
Addison Mizner ES, 199 SW 12TH AVE 33486
  (—), prin.
ES, 103 SW 1ST AVE 33432
  Raymond Garvey, prin.
Calusia Community ES
  2051 CLINT MOORE RD 33496
  Betty Thomas, prin.
Coral Sunset ES, 22400 HAMMOCK ST 33428
  Mary Smith, prin.
Mitchell ES, 2401 NW 3RD AVE 33431
  Joanne Cripps, prin.
Verde ES, 6590 VERDE TRL 33433
  Susan Marshall, prin.
Whispering Pines ES
  9090 SPANICH ISLES BLVD 33496
  (—), prin.

Boca Raton Academy
  2700 SAINT ANDREWS BLVD 33434
St. Joan of Arc ES, 501 SW 3RD AVE 33432
St. Jude Academy School
  21689 TOLEDO RD 33433
St. Paul Lutheran ES
  701 W PALMETTO PARK RD 33486

Bokeelia, Lee Co.
Lee SD 36
Supt. – See Fort Myers
Pine Island MS, 5360 RIDGEWOOD DR 33922
  Dr. James Mosher, prin.
Pine Island ES, 5360 RIDGEWOOD AVE 33922
  Dr. J. Douglas Mosher, prin.

Bonifay, Holmes Co., Pop. Code 5
Holmes SD 30
Sch. Sys. Enr. Code 5
Supt. – Jack Jones, 211 W IONA AVE 32425
Bethlehem S, RURAL ROUTE 03 BOX 118 32425
  W. Odell Paul, prin.
ES, 307 W NORTH AVE 32425
  Kenneth Yates, prin.
Other Schools – See Graceville, Ponce De Leon,
  Westville

Bonita Springs, Lee Co., Pop. Code 4
Lee SD 36
Supt. – See Fort Myers

MS, 10140 W TERRY ST 33923
  Robert Durham, prin.
ES, 10701 DEAN ST 33923 – James Johnson, prin.
Spring Creek ES, 25571 U S HWY 41 S E 33923
  Tommy Halgrim, prin.

Bowling Green, Hardee Co., Pop. Code 4
Hardee SD 25
Supt. – See Wauchula
ES, P O BOX 158 33834 – Jack Liames, prin.

Manatee SD 41
Supt. – See Bradenton
Duette ES, HWY 62 33834 – Ada Bilbrey, prin.

Boynton Beach, Palm Beach Co., Pop. Code 8
Palm Beach SD 50
Supt. – See West Palm Beach
Congress ES, 101 S CONGRESS AVE 33426
  William Pinder, prin.
McAliffe MS, 6500 LE CHALET BLVD 33437
  Jane Vowell, prin.
Forest Park ES, 1201 SW 3RD ST 33435
  Lois Lesslie, prin.
Galaxy ES, 461 W BOYNTON BEACH BLVD 33435
  Michael Borowski, prin.
Hagen Road ES, 10439 HAGEN RANCH RD 33437
  Jack Thompson, prin.
Poinciana ES, 1400 NW 1ST ST 33435
  (—), prin.
Rolling Green ES, 550 MINER RD 33435
  Gay Voss, prin.

St. Joseph's School, P O BOX 550 33425
St. Mark ES, 730 NE 6TH AVE 33435

Bradenton, Manatee Co., Pop. Code 8
Manatee SD 41
Sch. Sys. Enr. Code 7
Supt. – Gene Witt, P O BOX 9069 34206
MS, 202 13TH AVE E 34208
  George Douglas, Jr., prin.
Harllee MS, 6423 9TH ST E 34203 – C. King, prin.
King MS, 600 75TH ST NW 34209
  Nancy Carson, prin.
Sugg MS, 3801 50TH ST W 34205
  Judy Bills, prin.
Ballard ES, 912 18TH ST W 34205
  Dr. Altamese McPherson, prin.
Bashaw ES, 3515 MORGAN JOHNSON RD 34208
  Thomas Walker, prin.
Bayshore ES, 6120 26TH ST W 34207
  Sally Shuford, prin.
Daughtrey ES, 515 63RD AVE E 34203
  Larry Simmons, prin.
Manatee ES, 1609 6TH AVE E 34208
  Ozell Ackerman, prin.
Miller ES, 4201 MANATEE AVE W 34205
  Barbara Harvey, prin.
Moody ES, 5425 38TH AVE W 34209
  Jack Dietrich, prin.
Orange Ridge ES, 400 30TH AVE W 34205
  Philip Joachim, prin.
Palma Sola ES, 6806 5TH AVE NW 34209
  Douglas De Gruchy, prin.
Prine ES, 3801 SOUTHERN PKY W 34205
  Roland Montanus, prin.
Samoset ES, 1720 33RD AVE E 34208
  Hillard Story, prin.
Stewart ES, 7905 15TH AVE NW 34209
  Michael Sicard, prin.
Wakeland ES
  1812 ROBERTO CLEMENTE BLVD 34208
  Roy Larson, prin.
Other Schools – See Bowling Green, Brandonton
  Beach, Myakka City, Oneco, Palmetto, Sarasota

Bradenton Academy, 6210 17TH AVE W 34209
Bradenton Christian School
  3304 43RD ST W 34209
Nicholson School of Bradenton
  3700 32ND ST W 34205
St. Stephen's Episcopal School
  4030 MANATEE AVE W 34205
Trinity Baptist Academy, 5116 26TH ST W 34207
St. Joseph ES, 2990 26TH ST W 34205

Brandonton Beach, Sarasota Co., Pop. Code 4
Manatee SD 41
Supt. – See Bradenton
Anna Maria ES, P O BOX 188 34217
  James Kronus, prin.

Brandon, Hillsborough Co., Pop. Code 7
Hillsborough SD 29
Supt. – See Tampa
Brooker ES, 812 DEWOLF RD 33511
  Milton Lovelace, prin.
Kingswood ES, 3102 S KINGS AVE 33511
  Mary Ann Metrick, prin.
Limona ES, 1115 TELFAIR RD 33511
  J. Robert Harre, prin.
Yates ES, 301 N KINGSWAY RD 33511
  Robert Wheeler, prin.

Immanuel Lutheran ES
  2913 JOHN MOORE RD 33511
Nativity ES, 705 E BRANDON BLVD 33511

Branford, Suwannee Co., Pop. Code 3
Suwannee SD 61
Supt. – See Live Oak
S, P O BOX 387 32008 – Mary Daniels, prin.

Bristol, Liberty Co., Pop. Code 4
Liberty SD 39
Sch. Sys. Enr. Code 4
Supt. – Jerry M. Johnson, P O BOX 429 32321
ES, P O BOX 609 32321 – Gordon Revell, prin.
Other Schools – See Hosford

Bronson, Levy Co., Pop. Code 3
Levy SD 38
Sch. Sys. Enr. Code 5
Supt. – William Irby, P O BOX 128 32621
ES, P O BOX 220 32621 – Cliff Norris, prin.
Other Schools – See Cedar Key, Chiefland, Williston,
  Yankeetown

Brooker, Bradford Co., Pop. Code 2
Bradford SD 4
Supt. – See Starke
ES, P O BOX 7 32622 – William McRae, prin.

Brooksville, Hernando Co., Pop. Code 6
Hernando SD 27
Sch. Sys. Enr. Code 7
Supt. – Dr. James Austin
  919 US ROUTE HWY 41 N 34601
Parrott MS, 19220 YOUTH DR 34601
  Willie Stephens, prin.
Powell MS, 14400 POWELL ROAD 34609
  Clarence Wingrove, prin.
Black MS, 916 VARSITY DR 34601
  Howard Wade, prin.
PS, 602 BELL AVE 34601 – W. C. Hutto, prin.
Eastside ES, 27151 ROPER RD 34602
  Dwain Erickson, prin.
Moton Center ES, 841 SCHOOL ST 34601
  Yvonne Brewer, prin.
Other Schools – See Spring Hill

Pasco SD 51
Supt. – See Land O'Lakes
Shady Hills ES, 1900 SHADY HILLS RD 34610
  Jospeh Souto, prin.

Bryceville, Nassau Co.
Nassau SD 45
Supt. – See Fernandina Beach
ES, P O BOX 3 32009 – June Page, prin.

Bunnell, Flagler Co., Pop. Code 4
Flagler SD 18
Sch. Sys. Enr. Code 5
Supt. – Donn Kaupke, P O BOX 755 32010
Belle Terre MS, P O BOX 815 32010
  Elmer Taylor, prin.
ES, P O BOX 937 32010 – Hanneke Jevons, prin.
Other Schools – See Palm Coast

Bushnell, Sumter Co., Pop. Code 3
Sumter SD 60
Sch. Sys. Enr. Code 5
Supt. – Joe Strickland, 202 N FLORIDA ST 33513
ES, 218 W FLANNERY AVE 33513
  John Dixon, prin.
Other Schools – See Lake Panasoffkee, Webster,
  Wildwood

Callahan, Nassau Co., Pop. Code 3
Nassau SD 45
Supt. – See Fernandina Beach
MS, P O BOX AA 32011 – Ben Rice, prin.
ES, 100 BOOTH ST S 32011 – Carolyn Parks, prin.
IS, P O BOX 1440 32011 – Glenn Long, prin.

Canal Point, Palm Beach Co.
Palm Beach SD 50
Supt. – See West Palm Beach
ES, 300 EVERGLADES ST 33438
  Kathryn Cunningham, prin.

Cantonment, Escambia Co., Pop. Code 5
Escambia SD 17
Supt. – See Pensacola
Ransom MS, 648 MUSCOGEE ROAD 32533
  Richard Harper, prin.
Allen ES, 1051 HWY 95A-N 32533
  Hubert Williford, prin.
Barrineau Park ES, 6055 BARINEAU PARK 32533
  Martin Reeves, prin.
Molino ES, 6450 N HIGHWAY 95-A 32533
  Ruth Gordon, prin.

Cape Canaveral, Brevard Co., Pop. Code 6
Brevard SD 5
Supt. – See Rockledge
Cape View ES, 8440 ROSALIND AVE 32920
  Susie Fleming, prin.

Cape Coral, Lee Co., Pop. Code 8
Lee SD 36
Supt. – See Fort Myers
Caloosa MS, 610 SE DEL PRADO BLVD 33904
  Dr. Alfred Willie, prin.
Gulf MS, 1809 SW 36TH TERRACE 33904
  Dr. Lois Timberlake, prin.
Caloosa ES, 620 S DEL PRADO BLVD 33904
  Dr. Mary Santini, prin.
Cape ES, 4519 VINCENNES BLVD 33904
  Jon Looney, prin.
Gulf ES, 3400 SW 17TH PL 33914
  Dr. Douglas Santini, prin.
Pelican ES, 3525 SW 3RD AVE 33914
  Richard Ivill, prin.
Skyline ES, 620 SW 19TH ST 33911
  Stephen Foust, prin.

Carrabelle, Franklin Co., Pop. Code 4
Franklin SD 19
Supt. – See Apalachicola

S, P O BOX 549 32322 – Clayton Wooten, prin.

Casselberry, Seminole Co., Pop. Code 7
Seminole SD 59
Supt. – See Sanford
S. Seminole MS
  101 S WINTER PARK DRIVE 32707
  Curtis Hughes, prin.
ES, 1075 CRYSTAL BOWL CIR 32707
  Paul Murphy, prin.
Red Bug ES, 4000 RED BUG LAKE RD 32707
  Patricia Milliot, prin.
Sterling Park ES, 501 EAGLE CIR S 32707
  Michael Townsley, prin.

Cedar Key, Levy Co., Pop. Code 3
Levy SD 38
Supt. – See Bronson
S, P O BOX 369 32625 – Mary Wells, prin.

Century, Escambia Co., Pop. Code 2
Escambia SD 17
Supt. – See Pensacola
Carver MS, P O BOX 207 32535
  Robert Smith, Jr., prin.
Bratt ES, RURAL ROUTE 02 BOX 250A 32535
  Wayne Odom, prin.
Byrneville ES, P O BOX 192 32535
  Roy Ikner, prin.
ES, P O BOX 428 32535 – Thomas McGinty, prin.

Charlotte Harbor, Charlotte Co.

Charlotte Christian Academy
  24044 HERITAGE PLACE 33950

Chattahoochee, Gadsden Co., Pop. Code 6
Gadsden SD 20
Supt. – See Quincy
ES, P O BOX 218 32324 – Corbin Scott, prin.

Chiefland, Levy Co., Pop. Code 4
Levy SD 38
Supt. – See Bronson
ES, P O BOX 40 32626 – (—), prin.

Chipley, Washington Co., Pop. Code 5
Washington SD 67
Sch. Sys. Enr. Code 5
Supt. – Kelly Brock, 206 N 3RD ST 32428
Roulhac MS 32428 – Calvin Stevenson, prin.
Smith ES 32428 – Gladys Stephens, prin.
Other Schools – See Vernon

Citra, Marion Co., Pop. Code 2
Marion SD 42
Supt. – See Ocala
North Marion MS
  RURAL ROUTE 01 BOX 1970 32627
  Rudy Bedform, prin.

Clarksville, Calhoun Co.
Calhoun SD 7
Supt. – See Blountstown
Carr ES 32430 – Jimmy Cox, prin.

Clearwater, Pinellas Co., Pop. Code 8
Pinellas SD 52
Sch. Sys. Enr. Code 8
Supt. – Dr. Scott Rose, P O BOX 4688 34618
Clearwater Comprehensive MS
  1220 PALMETTO ST 34615 – Charles Baker, prin.
Kennedy MS, 1660 PALMETTO ST 34615
  Kate Herrington, prin.
Oak Grove MS, 1370 BELCHER ROAD S 34624
  Pegoty Lopez, prin.
Belcher ES, 1839 BELCHER RD S 34624
  Franklin Tennian, prin.
Belleair ES, 1156 LAKEVIEW RD 34616
  Brenda Leasure, prin.
Curtis Fundamental ES, 1210 HOLT ST 34615
  Joan Minnis, prin.
Davis ES, 2630 LANDMARK DR 34621
  John Dileo, prin.
De Leon ES, 1301 PONCE DE LEON BLVD 34616
  Lillie McGarrah, prin.
Eisenhower ES, 2800 DREW ST 34619
  Saro Ficarrotta, prin.
High Point ES, 6033 150TH AVE N 34620
  Charles Eubanks, prin.
Kings Highway ES, 1715 KINGS HWY 34615
  John Day, prin.
North Ward ES-Clearwater
  900 FT HARRISON AVE N 34615
  Marcia Morgan, prin.
Plumb ES, 1920 LAKEVIEW RD 34624
  Mike Skaroulis, prin.
Sandy Lane ES, 1360 SANDY LN 34615
  A. Garcia, prin.
Skycrest ES, 10 CORONA AVE N 34625
  George Tosh, prin.
South Ward ES, 610 FT HARRISON AVE S 34616
  E. Eubanks, prin.
Other Schools – See Dunedin, Gulfport, Largo,
  Madeira Beach, Oldsmar, Palm Harbor, Pinellas
  Park, Safety Harbor, Saint Petersburg, Seminole,
  Tarpon Springs

Clearwater-Largo Christian School
  1739 GREENWOOD AVE S 34616
Lakeside Christian School
  1897 SUNSET POINT ROAD 34625
First Lutheran ES, 1644 NURSERY RD 34616
St. Cecelia IS, 400 HILLCREST AVE S 34616
St. Paul's ES, 1600 ST PAULS DR 34624

Clermont, Lake Co., Pop. Code 6
Lake SD 35
Supt. – See Tavares
JHS, 680 E HIGHLAND AVE 32711
  Bill Cockcroft, prin.
ES, 245 2ND ST 32711 – Sharon Powell, prin.
Minneola ES, 300 PEARL ST E 32711
  John Currie, prin.

Clewiston, Hendry Co., Pop. Code 6
Hendry SD 26
Supt. – See La Belle
MS, RURAL ROUTE 01 BOX 5 33440
  John Sullivan, prin.
IS, 435 E CIRCLE DR 33440
  Richard Shearer, prin.
Clewiston 3rd & 4th Grade Center
  ARROYO AVE 33440 – C. Swaggerty, Jr., prin.
PS, P O BOX 10 33440 – Howard McKire, prin.

Cocoa, Brevard Co., Pop. Code 7
Brevard SD 5
Supt. – See Rockledge
Clearlake MS, 1225 CLEARLAKE ROAD 32922
  Ralph Beckett, Jr., prin.
McNair MS, 501 POINSETT DRIVE 32922
  Rob Manning, prin.
Cambridge ES, 2000 CAMBRIDGE DR 32922
  William Weeks, prin.
Challenger 7 ES, 6135 RENA AVE 32927
  Julia Bumgarner, prin.
Fairglen ES, 201 INDIAN TRL 32927
  James Clark, prin.
Pineda ES, 905 PINEDA ST 32922
  Michael Horne, prin.
Saturn ES, 880 N RANGE RD 32926
  George Pickel, prin.

Bethel Christian Academy, P O BOX 3147 32924
St. Mark's Episcopal Day School
  4 CHURST ST 32922

Cocoa Beach, Brevard Co., Pop. Code 7
Brevard SD 5
Supt. – See Rockledge
Roosevelt ES, 1400 MINUTEMEN CSWY 32931
  Robert Fritz, prin.

Our Saviours ES, 5301 N ATLANTIC AVE 32931

Coconut Creek, Broward Co., Pop. Code 6
Broward County SD 6
Supt. – See Fort Lauderdale
ES, 500 NW 45TH AVE 33066
  Christine Miller, prin.

Coconut Grove, Dade Co.
Dade SD 13
Supt. – See Miami
Carver ES, 238 GRAND AVE 33133
  Rexford Darrow, prin.
ES, 3351 MATILDA ST 33133 – Jose Carbia, prin.

St. Stephen's Episocpal ES
  3439 MAIN HWY 33133

Cooper City, Broward Co., Pop. Code 7
Broward County SD 6
Supt. – See Fort Lauderdale
Pioneer MS, 5350 SW 90TH AVE 33328
  Kenneth Black, prin.
ES, 5080 SW 92ND AVE 33328
  Dr. Samuel Williams, prin.
Griffin ES, 5050 SW 116TH AVE 33330
  Dolores Hardison, prin.

Coral Gables, Dade Co., Pop. Code 8
Dade SD 13
Supt. – See Miami
Carver ES, 4901 LINCOLN DRIVE 33133
  Samuel Gay, prin.
MS, 105 MINORCA AVE 33134
  George Bowker, prin.
West Laboratory ES, 5300 CARILLO ST 33146
  Patricia Frost, prin.

St. Philip's Episcopal ES
  1142 CORAL WAY 33134
St. Theresa Catholic ES
  2701 INDIAN MT TRL 33134

Coral Springs, Broward Co., Pop. Code 8
Broward County SD 6
Supt. – See Fort Lauderdale
MS, 10300 WILES ROAD 33067
  Frances Vandiver, prin.
Forest Glen MS, 6400 WILES RD 33067
  Thomas Geismar, prin.
Ramblewood MS
  8585 W ATLANTIC BLVD 33065
  James Flynn, prin.
Coral Park ES, 7400 PARKSIDE DR 33067
  John Van Boven, prin.
ES, 3601 NW 110TH AVE 33065
  Verda Farrow, prin.
Forest Hills ES, 3100 NW 85TH AVE 33065
  James Thomas, prin.
Hunt ES, 7800 NW 35TH CT 33065
  Dr. Joel Keiter, prin.
Maplewood ES, 9850 RAMBLEWOOD DR 33071
  Nancy Moore, prin.
Ramblewood ES, 8950 W ATLANTIC BLVD 33071
  Patricia Yaffa, prin.
Riverside ES, 101 CORAL RIDGE DR 33071
  George Gott, prin.

Westchester ES
12495 ROYAL PALM BLVD   33065
Janet Bedell, prin.

Coral Springs Christian ES
2251 RIVERSIDE DR   33065
St. Andrew Catholic ES, 9990 NW 29TH ST   33065
University School Nova University ES
3251 NW 101ST AVE   33065

Cottondale, Jackson Co., Pop. Code 4
Jackson SD 32
Supt. – See Marianna
ES, P O BOX 529   32431 – Richard Wheatley, prin.

Crawfordville, Wakulla Co., Pop. Code 3
Wakulla SD 65
Sch. Sys. Enr. Code 5
Supt. – Roger Stokley, P O BOX 100   32327
Wakulla MS, RURAL ROUTE 02 BOX 4800   32327
Robert Myhre, prin.
ES, P O BOX 367   32327 – Randall Anderson, prin.
Shadeville ES
RURAL ROUTE 03 BOX 5401   32327
David Miller, prin.
Other Schools – See Sopchoppy

Crescent City, Putnam Co., Pop. Code 4
Putman SD 54
Supt. – See Palatka
Miller MS, 210 S PROSPECT ST   32012
Robert Pugh, prin.
Crescent City Community ES
950 HUNTINGTON RD   32012 – John Milton, prin.

Crestview, Okaloosa Co., Pop. Code 6
Okaloosa SD 46
Sch. Sys. Enr. Code 7
Supt. – Pledger Sullivan
COUNTY COURTHOUSE   32536
Northwood ES, 501 E 4TH AVE   32536
Emmett Windham, prin.
Sikes ES, 425 ADAMS DR   32536
Rodney Storey, prin.
Southside ES, 650 S PEARL ST   32536
Tommy Grandstaff, prin.
Other Schools – See Baker, Destin, Eglin AFB, Fort
Walton Beach, Laurel Hill, Mary Esther, Niceville,
Shalimar, Valparaiso

Cross City, Dixie Co., Pop. Code 4
Dixie SD 15
Sch. Sys. Enr. Code 4
Supt. – H. Allen Harden, P O BOX G   32628
Anderson ES, P O BOX K   32628
Garry Durham, prin.
Other Schools – See Old Town

Crystal River, Citrus Co., Pop. Code 5
Citrus SD 9
Supt. – See Inverness
MS, 705 NE 3RD AVE   32629 – Martin Lewis, prin.
PS, 947 NE 6TH ST   32629 – Carrick Branch, prin.

Central Catholic School
6751 W GULF TO LAKE HWY   32629

Dade City, Pasco Co., Pop. Code 5
Pasco SD 51
Supt. – See Land O'Lakes
Pasco MS, 505 S 14TH ST   33525
George Avadikian, prin.
Centennial ES, 975 MADILL RD   33525
Sandra Ramos, prin.
Cox ES, 201 W MAIN AVE   33525
Rozalyne Wright, prin.
LaCoochee ES, 805 CUMMER RD   33525
Renee Sedlack, prin.
Pasco ES, 524 W FLORIDA AVE   33525
Barbara Munz, prin.
San Antonio ES, 374 DARBY RD   33525
Katherine Piersall, prin.

Dania, Broward Co., Pop. Code 7
Broward County SD 6
Supt. – See Fort Lauderdale
Olsen MS, 1301 SE 2ND AVE   33004
James Vanover, prin.
Collins ES, 1050 NW 2ND ST   33004
Ora Hollinger, prin.
ES, 300 SE 2ND AVE   33004
William Mauger, prin.

Davenport, Polk Co., Pop. Code 4
Polk SD 53
Supt. – See Bartow
ES, P O BOX 728   33837 – Sharon Knowles, prin.

Davie, Broward Co., Pop. Code 7
Broward County SD 6
Supt. – See Fort Lauderdale
ES, 7025 SW 39TH ST   33314
June Hilton-Hantula, prin.
Eisenhower ES, 6501 SW 39TH ST   33314
Mary Mitchell, prin.

Daytona Beach, Volusia Co., Pop. Code 8
Volusia SD 64
Supt. – See De Land
Bonner ES, 868 CYPRESS ST   32014
Minnie Harris, prin.
Highlands ES, 323 HEINEMAN ST   32014
Edna Fields, prin.
Longstreet ES, 2745 PENINSULA DR S   32018
Earnest Davies,Jr., prin.
Ortona ES, 1265 GRANDVIEW AVE N   32018
William Bottom, prin.

Small ES, 800 SOUTH ST   32014
Lawrence Broxton, prin.
Westside ES, 1210 JIMMY ANN DR   32017
Gwendolyn Carson, prin.

Daytona Beach Baptist School
P O BOX 4670   32021
Wise Private School, 250 POINCIANA AVE   32019
Our Lady of Lourdes ES
1014 HALIFAX AVE N   32018
St. Paul's ES, 314 1ST AVE   32014

Deerfield Beach, Broward Co., Pop. Code 8
Broward County SD 6
Supt. – See Fort Lauderdale
MS, 701 SE 6TH AVE   33441
Rayfield Henderson, prin.
ES, 650 NE 1ST ST   33441 – John Civettini, prin.
Deerfield Park ES, 627 SW 2ND AVE   33441
Willie Latson, prin.

Zion Lutheran Christian School
859 SE 6TH AVE   33441
St. Ambrose ES, P O BOX 999   33441

De Funiak Springs, Walton Co., Pop. Code 6
Walton SD 66
Sch. Sys. Enr. Code 5
Supt. – Teddy R. Deshazo
CO COURTHOUSE   32433
Walton MS, 105 GEORGIA ST   32433
David Drake, prin.
Saunders ES, RURAL ROUTE 08 BOX 595   32433
Roddy Harrison, prin.
West Defuniak ES, 1900 LINCOLN AVE   32433
P. C. Rutherford, prin.
Other Schools – See Freeport, Paxton, Point
Washington

De Land, Volusia Co., Pop. Code 7
Volusia SD 64
Sch. Sys. Enr. Code 8
Supt. – Dr. James Surratt, P O BOX 2118   32721
MS, 1400 S AQUARIUS AVE   32724
Joseph Reed,Jr., prin.
Southwestern MS
605 W NEW HAMPSHIRE AVE   32720
Robert Milby, prin.
Blue Lake ES, 282 N BLUE LAKE AVE   32724
Rowena Reddix, prin.
Marks ES, 1000 N GARFIELD AVE   32724
James Clements,Jr., prin.
Starke ES, 730 S PARSONS AVE   32720
Carolyn Lawrence, prin.
Woodward Avenue ES
1201 S WOODWARD AVE   32720
Earle Hunt,Jr., prin.
Other Schools – See Daytona Beach, De Leon Springs,
Deltona, Edgewater, Enterprise, Holly Hill, Lake
Helen, New Smyrna Beach, Oak Hill, Orange City,
Ormond Beach, Osteen, Pierson, Port Orange,
Seville, South Daytona

Lake Gertie Christian Academy
401 W LAKE GERTIE ROAD   32720
St. Peter's Catholic ES
421 W NEW YORK AVE   32720

De Leon Springs, Volusia Co.
Volusia SD 64
Supt. – See De Land
McInnis ES, HWY 17   32028
Joseph Faircloth, prin.

Delray Beach, Palm Beach Co., Pop. Code 8
Palm Beach SD 50
Supt. – See West Palm Beach
Carver MS, 301 SW 14TH AVE   33444
Kelly Brown, prin.
Banyan Creek ES, 51 N SWINTON AVE   33444
Barbara Brown, prin.
Pine Grove ES, 400 SW 10TH ST   33444
Judith Kurzawski, prin.
Plumosa ES, 1712 NE 2ND AVE   33444
William Stanfield, prin.
Spady ES, 330 NW 8TH AVE   33444
Mavis Allred, prin.

St. Vincent Ferrer ES, 715 NE 8TH AVE   33483
Trinity Lutheran ES, 400 N SWINTON AVE   33444

Deltona, Volusia Co., Pop. Code 5
Volusia SD 64
Supt. – See De Land
MS, 250 ENTERPRISE ROAD   32725
Albert Guenther, prin.
Deltona Lakes ES, 2022 ADELIA BLVD   32725
Ronald McPherson, prin.
Discovery ES, 975 ABIGAIL DR   32725
Roxanne Gill, prin.

Deltona Christian School
1200 PROVIDENCE BLVD   32725

Destin, Okaloosa Co., Pop. Code 5
Okaloosa SD 46
Supt. – See Crestview
ES, 633 KELLY ST   32541 – Eugene Walls, prin.

Doctors Inlet, Clay Co.
Clay SD 10
Supt. – See Green Cove Springs
ES, 2634 STATE ROAD 220   32030
Fred Fedorowich, prin.

Dover, Hillsborough Co.
Hillsborough SD 29
Supt. – See Tampa
ES, 3035 NELSON AVE   33527
Willis Peters, prin.

Dundee, Polk Co., Pop. Code 4
Polk SD 53
Supt. – See Bartow
ES, 215 FREDERICK AVE   33838
Evelyn Powell, prin.

Dunedin, Pinellas Co., Pop. Code 8
Pinellas SD 52
Supt. – See Clearwater
Dunedin Highland MS, 896 UNION ST   34698
Paul Sullivan, prin.
ES, 531 BELTREES ST   34698
Forunato Maglietta, prin.
San Jose ES, 1670 SAN HELEN DR   34698
Anthony Reidy, prin.

Our Lady of Lourdes ES
1701 SAN HELEN DR   34698

Dunnellon, Marion Co., Pop. Code 4
Citrus SD 9
Supt. – See Inverness
Citrus Springs ES, 3570 W CENTURY BLVD   32630
Archie Dabney, prin.

Marion SD 42
Supt. – See Ocala
MS, P O BOX 609   32630 – Walter Miller, prin.
ES, P O BOX 220   32630 – Bruce Foster, prin.

Eagle Lake, Polk Co., Pop. Code 4
Polk SD 53
Supt. – See Bartow
ES, 400 CRYSTAL BEACH RD   33839
Charles Streeter, prin.

East Palatka, Putnam Co.
Putman SD 54
Supt. – See Palatka
Browning-Pearch Community ES
P O BOX 398   32031 – William Ivey, prin.

Eastpoint, Franklin Co.
Franklin SD 19
Supt. – See Apalachicola
Brown ES, P O BOX 608   32328
Janis Gordon, prin.

Eaton Park, Polk Co.
Polk SD 53
Supt. – See Bartow
Pope ES, P O BOX 70   33840 – Jay Erwin, prin.

Eatonville, Orange Co., Pop. Code 4
Orange SD 48
Supt. – See Orlando
Hungerford ES, 230 COLLEGE AVE   32751
Rufus Brooks, prin.

Edgewater, Volusia Co., Pop. Code 6
Volusia SD 64
Supt. – See De Land
ES, 550 S OLD COUNTY RD   32032
John Nadal, prin.

Eglin AFB, Okaloosa Co.
Okaloosa SD 46
Supt. – See Crestview
Cherokee ES, 200 GAFFNEY RD   32542
John Bludworth,Jr., prin.
Oak Hill ES, 101 CHINQUAPIN DR   32542
Robert Snaith, prin.

Elfers, Pasco Co.
Pasco SD 51
Supt. – See Land O'Lakes
Anclote ES, P O BOX 446   34680
Lonne Tatum, prin.
Locke ES, P O BOX 307   34680
Dennis Taylor, prin.

Englewood, Sarasota Co., Pop. Code 6
Sarasota SD 58
Supt. – See Sarasota
ES, 150 N MCCALL RD   34223 – Robert Cox, prin.

A. G. Christian Academy
240 N PINE ROAD   34223
Heritage Christian HS, 75 N PINE ROAD   34223

Enterprise, Volusia Co.
Volusia SD 64
Supt. – See De Land
ES, 211 MAIN ST   32725 – Gynell Bott, prin.

Eustis, Lake Co., Pop. Code 6
Lake SD 35
Supt. – See Tavares
MS, 1801 E BATES AVE   32726
Dr. Thomas Sanders, prin.
ES, 714 E CITRUS AVE   32726
Shirley Whitmore, prin.
Eustis Heights ES, 310 W TAYLOR AVE   32726
Joseph Rivers, prin.

Faith Lutheran ES, P O BOX 1108   32727

Everglades City, Collier Co., Pop. Code 2
Collier SD 11
Supt. – See Naples
Everglades S, SCHOOL DR   33929
T Chambers, prin.

Fellsmere, Indian River Co., Pop. Code 4
Indian River SD 31
Supt. – See Vero Beach
ES, 50 N CYPRESS ST 32948
Patricia Donovan, prin.

Fernandina Beach, Nassau Co., Pop. Code 6
Nassau SD 45
Sch. Sys. Enr. Code 6
Supt. – Craig Marsh, 1201 ATLANTIC AVE 32034
MS, 1205 ATLANTIC AVE 32034
Linda Mooris, prin.
Hardee MS, 300 SUSAN DR 32034
Blanca Lee, prin.
Southside ES, 1112 JASMINE ST 32034
Mildred Campbell, prin.
Other Schools – See Bryceville, Callahan, Hilliard,
Yulee

Fern Park, Seminole Co.
Seminole SD 59
Supt. – See Sanford
English Estates ES, 299 OXFORD RD 32730
Betty Stanley, prin.

Floral City, Citrus Co., Pop. Code 3
Citrus SD 9
Supt. – See Inverness
ES, P O BOX 340 32636 – Linda Kelley, prin.

New Testament Christian HS, P O BOX 490 32636

Florida City, Dade Co., Pop. Code 6
Dade SD 13
Supt. – See Miami
ES, 364 NW 6TH AVE 33034 – E. Chandler, prin.

Fort Lauderdale, Broward Co., Pop. Code 9
Broward County SD 6
Sch. Sys. Enr. Code 9
Supt. – Virgil Morgan, P O BOX 5408 33310
Everglades MS, 2400 NW 26TH ST 33311
Joseph Eddings, prin.
Lauderhill MS, 1901 NW 49TH AVE 33313
Moses Barnes, prin.
New River MS, 3100 RIVERLAND ROAD 33312
James Moller, prin.
Nova MS, 3600 COLLEGE AVE 33314
Suzanne Alvord, prin.
Parkway MS, 3600 NW 5TH COURT 33311
Benjamin Williams, prin.
Rogers MS, 700 SW 26TH ST 33315
Gregory Clark, prin.
Sunrise MS, 1750 NE 14TH ST 33304
Mick Gancitano, prin.
Bayview ES, 1175 MIDDLE RIVER DR 33304
Kathleen Goldstein, prin.
Bennett ES, 1755 NE 14TH ST 33304
Ronald Mayhew, prin.
Broward Estates ES, 441 NW 35TH AVE 33311
Bruce Voelkel, prin.
Country Isles ES
2300 COUNTRY ISLES RD 33326
Thomas Bardash, prin.
Croissant Park ES, 1800 SW 4TH AVE 33315
Harvey Bullock, prin.
Dillard ES, 2365 NW 11TH ST 33311
Jacqueline Box, prin.
Edgewood ES, 1300 SW 32ND CT 33315
Collins Plummer, prin.
Flamingo ES, 1130 SW 133RD AVE 33325
Dr. Gian Berchielli, prin.
Floranada ES, 5251 NE 14TH WAY 33334
Marcia Pann, prin.
Forman ES, 3521 DAVIE RD 33314
Larry Katz, prin.
Foster ES, 3471 SW 22ND ST 33312
Sandra Levenson, prin.
Harbordale ES, 900 SE 15TH ST 33316
Dr. Roy Campbell, prin.
King ES, 591 NW 31ST AVE 33311
Winifred Graham, prin.
Larkdale ES, 3250 NW 12TH PL 33311
Sandra Murray, prin.
Lauderdale Manors ES, 1400 NW 14TH CT 33311
Sandra Kip, prin.
Lauderhill Turner ES, 4747 NW 14TH ST 33313
Michael Cassaw, prin.
Meadowbrook ES, 2300 SW 46TH AVE 33317
Lynn Wills, prin.
North Andrews Gardens ES
345 NE 56TH ST 33334 – James Meyer, prin.
North Fork ES, 101 NW 15TH AVE 33311
John Sands, prin.
North Side ES, 120 NE 11TH ST 33304
Roger Allee, prin.
Oriole ES, 3081 NW 39TH ST 33309
William Nocerini, prin.
Riverland ES, 2600 SW 11TH CT 33312
Jill Wilson, prin.
Rock Island ES, 2301 NW 26TH ST 33311
Janie Stewart, prin.
Sunland Park ES, 919 NW 13TH AVE 33311
Robert Smith, prin.
Walker ES, 1001 NW 4TH ST 33311
Lucy Thomas, prin.
Westwood Heights ES, 2861 SW 9TH ST 33312
Richard Bartfay, prin.
Other Schools – See Coconut Creek, Cooper City,
Coral Springs, Dania, Davie, Deerfield Beach,
Hallandale, Hollywood, Lauderdale Lakes,
Lauderhill, Margate, Miramar, North Lauderdale,
Oakland Park, Pembroke, Pembroke Pines,
Plantation, Pompano Beach, Sunrise, Tamarac,
Wilton Manors

Ft. Lauderdale Christian School
6330 NW 31ST AVE 33309
Ft. Lauderdale Winter School
P O BOX 6145 33310
Pine Crest School, 1501 NE 62ND ST 33334
University School of Nova University
7500 SW 36TH ST 33314
Westminster Academy, 5620 NE 22ND AVE 33308
Faith Lutheran ES, 1161 SW 30TH AVE 33312
Lutheran Central ES, 100 SW 11TH ST 33315
O. L. Queen Martyrs ES, 2785 SW 11TH CT 33312
Peace Lutheran ES
1901 E COMMERCIAL BLVD 33308
St. Ambrose Episcopal ES
2250 SW 31ST AVE 33312
St. Andony ES, 820 NE 3RD ST 33301
St. Clement ES, 301 NW 29TH ST 33311
St. David School, 3900 S UNIVERSITY DR 33328
St. Helen ES
3340 W OAKLAND PARK BLVD 33311
St. Jerome ES, 2601 SW 9TH AVE 33315
St. Mark's Episcopal ES
1750 E OAKLAND PARK BLVD 33334

Fort Mc Coy, Marion Co.
Marion SD 42
Supt. – See Ocala
ES, P O BOX 68 32637 – Linda Tuck, prin.

Fort Meade, Polk Co., Pop. Code 6
Polk SD 53
Supt. – See Bartow
MS, 610 S CHARLESTON AVE 33841
Billy Flanagan, prin.
Lewis ES, 115 S OAK AVE 33841
James Kilbourn, prin.
Riverside MS, 1002 6TH ST NE 33841
Claxton Pittman, prin.

Fort Myers, Lee Co., Pop. Code 8
Lee SD 36
Sch. Sys. Enr. Code 8
Supt. – Karl Engel, 2055 CENTRAL AVE 33901
Cypress Lake MS
1421 CYPRESS LAKE DRIVE SW 33907
Cecil Hatfield, prin.
Dunbar MS, 3800 EDISON AVE 33901
Charles Bell, prin.
MS, 3015 CENTRAL AVE 33901
Judi Hughes, prin.
Lee MS, 4203 BALLARD ROAD SE 33905
Dr. Douglas Whittaker, prin.
Allen Park ES, 3345 CANELO DR 33901
Don Campbell, prin.
Edgewood ES, 3464 EDGEWOOD AVE 33916
James Garrison,Jr., prin.
Edison Park ES, 2401 EUCLID AVE 33901
Linda Caruso, prin.
Franklin Park ES, 2323 FORD ST 33916
Marie Vawter, prin.
Heights ES, 7114 SCHOOL ST 33908
R. Paul Cochrane, prin.
Michigan ES, 4312 MICHIGAN AVE 33905
Robert Grumley, prin.
Orange River ES, 310 UNDERWOOD DR 33905
Richard Herring, prin.
Orangewood ES, 4001 DELEON ST 33901
Patricia Patrizi, prin.
San Carlos Park ES, P O BOX 5000 33912
Elbert Tolbert, prin.
Suncoast ES, 1858 SUNCOAST LN 33917
David Short, prin.
Tanglewood ES, 1620 MANCHESTER BLVD 33919
Elizabeth LaFuze, prin.
Three Oaks ES, 19600 CYPRESS VIEW DR 33912
Constance Jones, prin.
Tice ES, 4524 TICE ST 33905
David Richards, prin.
Villas ES, 8595 BEACON BLVD 33907
Jack Barnett, prin.
Other Schools – See Alva, Bokeelia, Bonita Springs,
Cape Coral, Fort Myers Beach, Lehigh Acres, North
Fort Myers, Sanibel Island

Canterbury School
1400 COLLEGE PARKWAY SW 33907
Evangelical Christian School
2367 BEACON BLVD SE 33907
Ft. Myers Christian School
1550 COLONIAL BLVD SW 33907
Good Shepherd Lutheran ES
4770 ORANGE GROVE BLVD 33903
St. Francis Xavier ES, 2055 HEITMAN ST 33901
St. Michael Lutheran ES, 3595 BROADWAY 33901

Fort Myers Beach, Lee Co.
Lee SD 36
Supt. – See Fort Myers
ES, 2751 OAK ST 33931 – Toni Sindler, prin.

Fort Pierce, St. Lucie Co., Pop. Code 8
St. Lucie SD 56
Sch. Sys. Enr. Code 7
Supt. – George Hill, 2909 DELAWARE AVE 34947
McCarty MS, 1201 MISSISSIPPI AVE 34950
Jerry Barlowe, prin.
Fairlawn ES, 1900 S 33RD ST 34947
Louise Deal, prin.
ES, 1100-1200 DELAWARE AVE 33450
Herbert Dickerson, prin.
Garden City ES, 1801 N 21ST ST 34950
Cleon Middleton, prin.
Lakewood Park ES, 7800 INDRIO RD 34951
Alan Edwards, prin.
Lawnwood ES, 1900 S 23RD ST 34950
Lois Watts, prin.
Moore ES, 827 N 29TH ST 34947
George Rahming, prin.
Port St. Lucie ES, 198 NW MARION AVE 34983
Jane Grinsted, prin.
St. Lucie ES, 1800 S 13TH ST 34950
Norman Behling, prin.
Sweet ES, 1400 AVENUE Q 34950
Wynel Granitz, prin.
White City ES, 905 W 2ND ST 34982
Kenneth Burleson, prin.
Other Schools – See Port Saint Lucie

Palm Vista Christian School, 700 S 33RD ST 34947
St. Anastasia ES, 401 S 33RD ST 34947
St. Andrew's Episcopal ES
210 S INDIAN RIVER DR 34950

Fort Walton Beach, Okaloosa Co., Pop. Code 7
Okaloosa SD 46
Supt. – See Crestview
Edwins ES, 7 WRIGHT PKWY 32548
Allen Dunn, prin.
Elliott Point ES, 301 HUGHES ST NE 32548
Benny Bowen, prin.
Kenwood ES, 634 EAGLE ST NE 32548
Zella Tobin, prin.
New Heights ES, 720 LOVEJOY RD NW 32548
Dr. Bill Thompson, prin.
Ocean City ES, 720 ESSEX RD 32548
Dr. Philip Cummings, prin.
Wright ES, 305 LANG RD 32548
Terry Hecker, prin.

Ft. Walton Christian School
535 CLIFFORD ST 32548
St. Mary ES, 110 ROBINWOOD DR SW 32548

Fort White, Columbia Co., Pop. Code 2
Columbia SD 12
Supt. – See Lake City
ES, P O BOX 129 32038 – Kenneth Herring, prin.

Freeport, Walton Co., Pop. Code 3
Walton SD 66
Supt. – See De Funiak Springs
ES, HWY 331 32439 – Keith Miller,Jr., prin.

Frostproof, Polk Co., Pop. Code 5
Polk SD 53
Supt. – See Bartow
ES, 118 W 3RD ST 33843 – Joy Shepard, prin.

Fruitland Park, Lake Co., Pop. Code 4
Lake SD 35
Supt. – See Tavares
ES, 304 VICTORIA AVE 32731
Shirley Johnston, prin.

Gainesville, Alachua Co., Pop. Code 8
Alachua SD 1
Sch. Sys. Enr. Code 7
Supt. – Dr. Douglas Magann
1817 E UNIVERSITY AVE 32601
Lanier Center S, 312 NW 16TH AVE 32601
Cathy Costello, prin.
Bishop ES, 1901 NE 9TH ST 32609
William Cake, prin.
Ft. Clarke MS, 9301 NW 23RD AVE 32606
William Cliett, Jr., prin.
Lincoln MS, 1001 SE 12TH ST 32601
Virginia Childs, prin.
Westwood MS, 3215 NW 15TH AVE 32605
Michael Joyner, prin.
Duval ES, 2106 NE 8TH AVE 32601
Dewitt Lewis, prin.
Finley ES, 1912 NW 5TH AVE 32603
Christine Hirsch, prin.
Foster ES, 3800 NW 6TH ST 32609
Debra Krank, prin.
Glen Springs ES, 2826 NW 31ST AVE 32605
Patsy Kinney, prin.
Hidden Oak ES, 9205 NW 23RD AVE 32606
Doris Richardson, prin.
Idylwild ES, 4601 SW 20TH TER 32608
Dr. Robert Craig, Jr., prin.
Lake Forest ES, 427 SE 43RD ST 32601
Marvin Nelson, prin.
Littlewood ES, 812 NW 34TH ST 32605
Ann Mullally, prin.
Metcalfe ES, 1905 NE 12TH ST 32609
Dean Niederkohr, prin.
Prairie View ES, 1801 SE 32ND PL 32601
Lougene Hill, prin.
Rawlings ES, 3500 NE 15TH ST 32609
Elizabeth Parker, prin.
Talbot ES, 5701 NW 43RD ST 32606
Barbara Buys, prin.
Terwilliger ES, 301 NW 62ND ST 32607
Richard Westfall, prin.
Wiles ES, 4601 SW 75TH ST 32608
Robert VanWinkle, prin.
Williams ES, 1245 SE 7TH AVE 32601
Shirley McCray, prin.
Other Schools – See Alachua, Archer, Hawthorne,
High Springs, Newberry, Waldo

St. Patricks ES, 550 NE 16TH AVE 32601

Geneva, Seminole Co.
Seminole SD 59
Supt. – See Sanford
ES, P O BOX 328 32732 – Nancy McNamara, prin.

Gibsonton, Hillsborough Co., Pop. Code 4
Hillsborough SD 29
Supt. – See Tampa
Eisenhower JHS
  RURAL ROUTE 01 BOX 527 33534
  John Owens, prin.
ES, 7723 GIBSONTON DR 33534
  Barbara Ammirati, prin.

Glen Saint Mary, Baker Co., Pop. Code 2
Baker SD 2
Supt. – See Macclenny
Westside ES, P O BOX 610 32040
  Rita Rhoden, prin.

Graceville, Jackson Co., Pop. Code 5
Holmes SD 30
Supt. – See Bonifay
Poplar Springs S
  RURAL ROUTE 02 BOX 88 32440
  Myron Hudson, prin.

Jackson SD 32
Supt. – See Marianna
ES, 605 ALABAMA ST 32440
  Patricia Segrest, prin.

Grand Ridge, Jackson Co., Pop. Code 3
Jackson SD 32
Supt. – See Marianna
S, P O BOX 208 32442 – James Dickson, prin.

Greenacres City, Palm Beach Co., Pop. Code 6
Palm Beach SD 50
Supt. – See West Palm Beach
Greenacres ES, 405 JACKSON AVE 33463
  Bettye Bryant, prin.

Green Cove Springs, Clay Co., Pop. Code 5
Clay SD 10
Sch. Sys. Enr. Code 7
Supt. – See Ann Wiggins, P O BOX 488 32043
Bennett ES, 1 OAKRIDGE AVE S 32043
  Ray Jenner, prin.
MS, P O BOX 308 32043
  George Dunnavant, Jr., prin.
Lake Asbury ES, 2901 SANDRIDGE RD 32043
  Anne Poidevant, prin.
Other Schools – See Doctors Inlet, Jacksonville,
  Keystone Heights, Middleburg, Orange Park

Greenville, Madison Co., Pop. Code 5
Madison SD 40
Supt. – See Madison
MS, P O BOX 428 32331 – Colleen Campbell, prin.
PS, P O BOX 398 32331 – George Pridgeon, prin.

Groveland, Lake Co., Pop. Code 4
Lake SD 35
Supt. – See Tavares
MS, 205 E MAGNOLIA ST 32736
  Cecil Gray, prin.
ES, 930 PARKWOOD ST 32736
  Dr. Edward Pauley, prin.

Gulf Breeze, Santa Rosa Co., Pop. Code 6
Santa Rosa SD 57
Supt. – See Milton
MS, 639 GULF BREEZE PARKWAY 32561
  Walter Karr, prin.
ES, 549 GULF BREEZE PKY 32561
  Nancy Welch, prin.
Holley-Navarre ES
  8000 GULF BREEZE PKY 32561
  Sandra Williams, prin.
Oriole Beach ES, 1260 ORIOLE BEACH RD 32561
  George Dahlgren, prin.

Gulfport, Pinellas Co., Pop. Code 7
Pinellas SD 52
Supt. – See Clearwater
Disston Gifted ES, 1001 51ST ST S 33707
  (—), prin.
ES, 2014 52ND ST S 33707
  Richard Snyder, prin.

Gulf Stream, Palm Beach Co., Pop. Code 2

Gulf Stream ES, 3600 GULFSTREAM RD 33483

Haines City, Polk Co., Pop. Code 7
Polk SD 53
Supt. – See Bartow
Boone MS, 225 S 22ND ST 33844
  Joseph Brow, prin.
Jenkins MS, 701 LEDWITH AVE 33844
  Delmus Davis, prin.
Alta Vista ES, 801 SCENIC HWY 33844
  Russell Teisinger, prin.
Bethune MS, 900 AVENUE F 33844
  Josephine Howard, prin.
Eastside ES, 1820 E JOHNSON AVE 33844
  Jimmie Myers, prin.

Landmark Christian School
  2020 E HINSON AVE 33844

Hallandale, Broward Co., Pop. Code 8
Broward County SD 6
Supt. – See Fort Lauderdale
ES, 120 SW 4TH AVE 33009
  Ruthie Coachman, prin.

Hampton, Bradford Co., Pop. Code 2
Bradford SD 4
Supt. – See Starke
ES, P O BOX 200 32044 – Mary Ann Kyle, prin.

Hastings, St. Johns Co., Pop. Code 3
St. John's SD 55
Supt. – See Saint Augustine
ES, P O BOX 336 32045 – Ethel McNeil, prin.

Havana, Gadsden Co., Pop. Code 5
Gadsden SD 20
Supt. – See Quincy
MS, 420 E 6TH AVE 32333 – Ken Maclean, prin.
ES, 705 US 27 S 32333 – Julius Fisher, prin.

Hawthorne, Alachua Co., Pop. Code 4
Alachua SD 1
Supt. – See Gainesville
Shell ES, P O BOX 70 32640
  Gladys Wright, prin.

Hernando, Citrus Co.
Citrus SD 9
Supt. – See Inverness
ES, GENERAL DELIVERY 32642
  Keven Banks, prin.

Hialeah, Dade Co., Pop. Code 9
Dade SD 13
Supt. – See Miami
Bright ES, 2530 W 10TH AVE 33010
  William Rosenberg, prin.
Dupuis ES, 1150 W 59TH PL 33012
  Dr. Edmund Burck, prin.
Earhart ES, 5987 E 7TH AVE 33013
  Patsy Mason, prin.
Flamingo ES, 701 E 33RD ST 33013
  Katherine Astley, prin.
ES, 550 E 8TH ST 33010 – Jessie Stinson, prin.
Meadowlane ES, 4280 W 8TH AVE 33012
  George Kovachy, prin.
Milam ES, 6020 W 16TH AVE 33012
  Diana Urbizu, prin.
North Hialeah ES, 4251 E 5TH AVE 33013
  Allen Starke, prin.
North Twin Lakes ES, 625 W 74TH PL 33014
  Diana Esposito, prin.
Palm Lakes ES, 7450 W 16TH AVE 33014
  Steven Lovelass, prin.
Palm Springs ES, 6304 E 1ST AVE 33013
  Henry Haddon, prin.
Palm Springs North ES
  17615 NW 82ND AVE 33015 – Robert Gray, prin.
Shepard ES, 5700 W 24TH AVE 33016
  Paul Papier, prin.
South Hialeah ES, 265 E 5TH ST 33010
  Helen Stolte, prin.
Twin Lakes ES, 6735 W 5TH PL 33012
  Samella Gaines, prin.
Walters ES, 650 W 33RD ST 33012
  William Kennedy, prin.

Dade Christian School, 6601 NW 167TH ST 33015
Immaculate Conception Catholic ES
  125 W 45TH ST 33012
Our Lady of the Lakes School
  6600 MIAMI LAKEWAY N 33014
St. John Apostle ES, 479 E 4TH ST 33010

Highland City, Polk Co.
Polk SD 53
Supt. – See Bartow
ES, P O BOX 1327 33846
  Katheryn Ricketts, prin.

High Springs, Alachua Co., Pop. Code 4
Alachua SD 1
Supt. – See Gainesville
Spring Hill MS, P O BOX 907 32643
  Thomas Diedeman, prin.
ES, P O BOX 386 32643 – Darla McCrea, prin.

Hilliard, Nassau Co., Pop. Code 4
Nassau SD 45
Supt. – See Fernandina Beach
ES, P O BOX 1109 32046 – Carl Kane, prin.

Hobe Sound, Martin Co., Pop. Code 4
Martin SD 43
Supt. – See Stuart
ES, 11555 SE GOMEZ AVE 33455
  Deana England, prin.

Hobe Sound Bible Academy, P O BOX 1065 33455

Holiday, Pinellas Co.
Pasco SD 51
Supt. – See Land O'Lakes
Gulfside ES, 2329 ANCLOTE BLVD 34691
  Henry Wichmanowski, prin.

Holly Hill, Volusia Co., Pop. Code 6
Volusia SD 64
Supt. – See De Land
ES, 1500 CENTER ST 32017 – Mary Pyles, prin.
Hurst ES, 1340 WRIGHT ST 32017
  Steven Johnston, prin.

Hollywood, Broward Co., Pop. Code 9
Broward County SD 6
Supt. – See Fort Lauderdale
Apollo MS, 6800 ARTHUR ST 33024
  George Schafer, prin.
Attucks MS, 3500 N 22ND AVE 33020
  David Goldstein, prin.
Driftwood MS, 2751 N 70TH TERRACE 33024
  Frank Campana, prin.
McNicol MS, 1411 S 28TH AVE 33020
  Jacob Greene, prin.
Bethune ES, 2400 MEADE ST 33020
  Andrew Luciani, prin.

Boulevard Heights ES, 7201 JOHNSON ST 33024
  Gerald Talton, prin.
Colbert ES, 2701 PLUNKETT ST 33020
  Frank Schachner, prin.
Driftwood ES, 2700 N 69TH AVE 33024
  Edmund Cannon, prin.
Hollywood Central ES, 1700 MONROE ST 33020
  Ben Price, prin.
Hollywood Hills ES, 3501 TAFT ST 33021
  Warren Gassman, prin.
Hollywood Park ES, 901 N 69TH WAY 33024
  Gayle Benz, prin.
Lake Forest ES, 3550 SW 58TH AVE 33023
  Dr. Everett Putney, prin.
Oakridge ES, 1507 N 28TH AVE 33020
  Jane Muehlberg, prin.
Orange Brook ES, 715 S 46TH AVE 33021
  Bob Watts, prin.
Sheridan Hills ES, 5001 THOMAS ST 33021
  Ralph DeFino, prin.
Sheridan Park ES, 2310 N 70TH TER 33024
  Marilyn Foertmeyer, prin.
Stirling ES, 5500 STIRLING RD 33021
  John Drag, prin.
Watkins ES, 3601 SW 56TH WAY 33023
  Robert Sulcer, prin.
West Hollywood ES
  6301 HOLLYWOOD BLVD 33024
  Maureen Bethel, prin.

Faith Tabernacle Christian School
  P O BOX 4874 33083
Hollywood Christian School
  1708 N 60TH AVE 33021
Annunciation ES, 3751 SW 39TH ST 33023
Little Flower ES, 1843 PIERCE ST 33020
Nativity ES, 5200 JOHNSON ST 33021
St. Bernadett ES, 7450 STIRLING RD 33024
St. Mark's Lutheran ES, 502 N 28TH AVE 33020

Homestead, Dade Co., Pop. Code 7
Dade SD 13
Supt. – See Miami
JHS, 650 NW 2ND AVE 33030
  James Chandler, prin.
Air Base ES, 12829 SW 272ND ST 33032
  Eugene Turano, prin.
Avocado ES, 16969 SW 294TH ST 33030
  Rita White, prin.
Campbell Drive ES, 30700 SW 157TH AVE 33033
  Delno Oliver, prin.
Chapman ES, 27190 SW 140TH AVE 33032
  Frazier Cheyney, prin.
Leisure City ES, 14950 SW 288TH ST 33033
  Robert McKay, prin.
Lewis ES, 505 SW 85H ST 33030
  Gwendolyn Hines, prin.
Redland ES, 24701 SW 162ND AVE 33031
  Dr. Bruce Booher, prin.
Redondo ES, 18480 SW 304TH ST 33030
  Estela Santiago, prin.
West Homestead ES, 1550 SW 6TH ST 33030
  Esther Fernandez, prin.

Sacred Heart ES, 300 SE 1ST DR 33030
St. John's Episcopal ES, P O BOX 1030 33090

Homosassa, Citrus Co.
Citrus SD 9
Supt. – See Inverness
ES, P O BOX 498 32646 – Robert Brust, prin.

Hosford, Liberty Co.
Liberty SD 39
Supt. – See Bristol
ES, GENERAL DELIVERY 32334
  Glen Moore, prin.

Hudson, Pasco Co., Pop. Code 4
Pasco SD 51
Supt. – See Land O'Lakes
MS, 14540 COBRA WAY 34669
  Max Ramos, prin.
ES, 313 HUDSON AVE 34667 – Dalne Dola, prin.
Northwest ES, 14302 COBRA WAY 34669
  Betty Crary, prin.

Immokalee, Collier Co., Pop. Code 5
Collier SD 11
Supt. – See Naples
MS, 508 N 9TH ST 33934 – Cecilia Bates, prin.
Highlands ES, 1101 LAKE TRAFFORD RD 33934
  David Vanveld, prin.
Lake Trafford ES
  3500 LAKE TRAFFORD RD 33934
  Jacob Lieb, prin.
Pinecrest ES, 213 S 9TH ST 33934
  Florence Jelks, prin.
Village Oaks ES, 1501 STATE ROAD 29 N 33934
  Norma Merricks, prin.

Indialantic, Brevard Co., Pop. Code 5
Brevard SD 5
Supt. – See Rockledge
ES, 1050 N PALM AVE 32903
  Ned Straehla, prin.

Holy Name Jesus Catholic ES
  3060 HWY AIA 32903

Indian Harbor Beach, Brevard Co., Pop. Code 6
Brevard SD 5
Supt. – See Rockledge
Ocean Breeze ES, 1101 CHEYENNE DR 32937
  Diane Okoniewski, prin.

Especially for Children ES
1230 BANANA RIVER DR 32937

Indiantown, Martin Co., Pop. Code 4
Martin SD 43
Supt. – See Stuart
MS, P O BOX 728 34956 – David George, prin.
Warfield ES, P O BOX 248 34956
John Clyde, prin.

Interlachen, Putnam Co., Pop. Code 3
Putman SD 54
Supt. – See Palatka
Price MS, RURAL ROUTE 01 BOX 15 32048
Howard Alred, prin.
Interlachen Community ES
RURAL ROUTE 01 BOX 5 32048
Floyd West, prin.

Inverness, Citrus Co., Pop. Code 5
Citrus SD 9
Sch. Sys. Enr. Code 7
Supt. – Carl Austin, 1007 W MAIN ST 32650
MS, 1950 US 41 N 32650 – William Eldridge, prin.
PS, 206 S LINE ST 32652 – Bonnie Skrove, prin.
Pleasant Grove ES
631 PLEASANT GROVE RD 32652
Mark Brunner, prin.
Other Schools – See Crystal River, Dunnellon, Floral
City, Hernando, Homosassa, Lecanto

Islamorada, Monroe Co., Pop. Code 4

Island Christian School
83250 OVERSEAS HIGHWAY 33036

Jacksonville, Duval Co., Pop. Code 11
Clay SD 10
Supt. – See Green Cove Springs
Clay Hill ES, RURAL ROUTE 15 BOX 2070 32234
Stephen Lowe, prin.

Duval SD 16
Sch. Sys. Enr. Code 9
Supt. – Herb Sang
1701 PRUDENTIAL DRIVE 32207
Brentwood MS, 3750 SPRINGFIELD BLVD 32206
Hortense Brewington, prin.
Brown MS, 1535 MILNOR AVE 32206
William Permenter, prin.
Butler 7th Grade Center, 900 ACORN ST 32209
Kenneth Manuel, prin.
Carver MS, 2854 45TH ST W 32209
Dorethea Haynes, prin.
Daniels MS, 1951 15TH ST W 32209
Josephine Fiveash, prin.
Gilbert 7th Grade Center
1424 FRANKLIN ST 32206
Curtis Randolph, prin.
Hull MS, 7528 HULL ST 32219
Dr. Jon Thompson, prin.
Jacksonville Beach MS, 315 10TH ST S 32250
Gail Brinson, prin.
Johnson 7th Grade Center, 1840 9TH ST W 32209
Johnnie Williams, prin.
Livingston MS, 1128 BARBER ST 32209
Robert Strauss, prin.
Long Branch MS, 3723 FRANKLIN ST 32206
Selinda Keyes, prin.
McLeod Bethune MS, 4330 PEARCE ST 32209
Dorothy Mitchell, prin.
Moncrief MS, 5443 MONCRIEF RD 32209
Joseph Sanchez, prin.
Oceanway 7th Grade Center
143 OCEANWAY AVE 32218 – Walter Carr, prin.
Paxon MS, 3276 5TH ST W 32205
Ray Mitchell, prin.
Payne MS, 6725 HEMA RD 32209
Jessie Boddie, prin.
Pine Forest MS, 3929 GRANT RD 32207
Gerald Benton, prin.
Sherwood Forest MS
4346 ROANOKE BLVD 32208
Dr. James Hurst, prin.
Tolbert MS, 1925 13TH ST W 32209
Mark Sweeney, prin.
West Jacksonville MS
2115 COMMONWEALTH AVE 32209
Evelyn Anderson, prin.
Woodson MS, 2334 BUTLER AVE 32209
Dr. Robert Thweatt, prin.
Arlington ES, 1201 UNIVERSITY BLVD N 32211
Helen McCall, prin.
Arlington Heights ES, 1520 SPRINKLE DR 32211
Donna Kellam, prin.
Axson ES, 1221 16TH ST E 32206
Edna Bell, prin.
Bayview ES, 3257 LAKE SHORE BLVD 32210
Dr. Alvenia Scriven, prin.
Beal ES, 330 9TH ST W 32206
Dr. Erma Mitchell, prin.
Beauclerc ES, 4555 CRAVEN RD W 32257
Dr. Nancy Snyder, prin.
Biltmore ES, 2101 PALM AVE 32205
Marilyn Daly, prin.
Brookview ES, 10450 THERESA DR 32216
Estelle McKissick, prin.
Cedar Hills ES, 6534 ISH BRANT RD 32210
Kay Knowlton, prin.
Central Riverside ES, 2555 GILMORE ST 32204
(—), prin.
Crown Point ES, 3800 CROWN POINT RD 32257
Mildred Logan, prin.

Crystal Springs ES, 1200 HAMMOND BLVD 32221
Barbara Price, prin.
Culver ES, 580 LAWTON AVE 32208
David Theus, prin.
Dinsmore ES, 7126 CIVIC CLUB DR 32219
Michael Akers, prin.
Englewood ES, 4359 SPRING PARK RD 32207
Susan Heavner, prin.
Fishweir ES, 3977 HERSCHEL ST 32205
Sharon Broderick, prin.
Forest Hills ES, 3501 WINSTON DR 32208
Ken Stewart, prin.
Ft. Caroline ES, 3925 ATHORE DR 32211
Barbara Gross, prin.
Garden City ES, 2814 DUNN AVE 32218
Caroline Rademacher, prin.
Greenfield ES, 6343 KNIGHTS LN N 32216
Jerry Powers, prin.
Gregory Drive ES, 7800 GREGORY DR 32210
Marilyn Morrow, prin.
Hendricks Avenue ES
3400 HENDRICKS AVE 32207
Juanita Wilson, prin.
Highlands ES, 1000 DEPAUL DR 32218
Barbara Langley, prin.
Hogan-Spring Glen ES, 6736 BEACH BLVD 32216
Elizabeth Scudder, prin.
Holiday Hill ES, 6900 ALTAMA RD 32216
Mildred Marshall, prin.
Hyde Grove ES, 2056 LANE AVE S 32210
Lorraine Gallagher, prin.
Hyde Park ES, 5300 PARK ST 32205
Virginia Greene, prin.
Jackson ES, 6127 CEDAR HILLS BLVD 32210
Sandra Pittman, prin.
Jacksonville Heights ES
7750 TEMPEST ST S 32244 – Jane Patterson, prin.
Jefferson ES, 8233 NEVADA ST 32220
Margaret McCaughey, prin.
Justina Road ES, 3101 JUSTINA RD 32211
Lorraine Long, prin.
King ES, 8801 LAKE PLACID DR 32208
Joan Spaulding, prin.
Kings Trail ES, 7401 OLD KINGS RD S 32217
Jim Kitchens, prin.
Kite ES, 9430 LEM TURNER RD 32208
Dr. Carolyn Chambliss, prin.
Lackawanna ES, 3108 LENOX AVE 32205
Kenneth Lewis, prin.
Lake Forest ES, 901 KENNARD ST 32208
Charles Meide, prin.
Lake Lucina ES, 6527 MERRILL RD 32211
Ray Johnson, prin.
Lone Star ES, 10400 LONE STAR RD 32225
Ennis Woodley, prin.
Loretto ES, 3900 LORETTO RD 32223
Josie Doty, prin.
Love ES, 1531 WINTHROP ST 32206
Lily Smith, prin.
Love Grove ES, 2446 UNIVERSITY BLVD S 32216
Lewellyn Sadler, prin.
Merrill Road ES, 8239 MERRILL RD 32211
Voncile Jackson, prin.
Morgan ES, 964 SAINT CLAIR ST 32205
Christine Solomon, prin.
Morse Avenue ES, 6084 MORSE AVE 32244
William Hatcher, prin.
Normandy ES, 6803 ARQUES RD 32205
Joanne Ragans, prin.
Normandy Village ES, 8257 HERLONG RD 32210
Patricia Martin, prin.
North Shore ES, 5701 SILVER PLZ 32208
Cynthia Anderson, prin.
Norwood ES, 6720 NORWOOD AVE 32208
Mary Brown, prin.
Oak Hill ES, 6910 DAUGHTRY BLVD S 32210
Barbara Spurlin, prin.
Oceanway ES, 143 OCEANWAY AVE 32218
Marilyn Myrick, prin.
Ortega ES, 4010 BALTIC ST 32210
Ruth Hoyle, prin.
Parkwood Heights ES
1709 LANSDOWNE DR 32211
Sherron Kenski, prin.
Pickett ES, 6305 OLD KINGS RD 32205
(—), prin.
Pine Estates ES, 10741 PINE ESTATES RD E 32218
Bernard Gannon, prin.
Pinedale ES, 4229 EDISON AVE 32205
Jan Starr, prin.
Ramona ES, 5540 RAMONA BLVD 32205
W. West, prin.
Reynolds Lane ES, 840 REYNOLDS LN 32205
R. Lauzon, prin.
Rutherford ES, 1514 HUBBARD ST 32206
Sara Hollander, prin.
San Jose ES, 5805 OLD ST AUGUSTINE RD 32207
Janis Bourne, prin.
San Mateo ES, 600 BAISDEN RD 32218
Florence Drury, prin.
San Pablo ES, 801 18TH AVE N 32250
Montelle Trammell, prin.
Scott ES, 1951 MARKET ST N 32206
Jeannette Robinson, prin.
Seabreeze ES, 1400 SEABREEZE AVE 32250
Susan Schondelmaier, prin.
Sheffield ES, 13333 LANIER RD 32226
Irving Huffingham, prin.
Southside Estates ES, 9775 IVEY RD 32216
Ronald Van Pelt, prin.
Spring Park ES, 2250 SPRING PARK RD 32207
William Dutter, prin.
Stockton ES, 4827 CARLISLE RD 32210
Dr. Janice Hunter, prin.

Timucuan ES, 5429 110TH ST 32244
Donna Darby, prin.
Upson ES, 1090 DANCY ST 32205
Raymond Williams, prin.
Venetia ES, 4300 TIMUQUANA RD 32210
Sandra Elliott, prin.
Wesconnett ES, 5710 WESCONNETT BLVD 32244
Carole Walker, prin.
West Riverside ES, 2801 HERSCHEL ST 32205
Jill Leinhauser, prin.
Windy Hill ES, 3831 FOREST BLVD 32216
Verna Fields, prin.
Woodland Acres ES, 328 BOWLAN ST N 32211
Bill Reynolds, prin.
Other Schools – See Atlantic Beach, Baldwin,
Neptune Beach, Whitehouse

St. John's SD 55
Supt. – See Saint Augustine
Julington Creek ES, 2316 RACETRACK RD 32259
Glenn Smith, prin.

Bolles School, 7400 SAN JOSE BLVD 32217
Greater Jacksonville Chrisitan School
P O BOX 7129 32238
Harvest Christian Academy
1057 ARLINGTON ROAD N 32211
Temple Christian School
4200 GEORGETOWN DRIVE 32210
Victory Christian Academy
10613 LEM TURNER ROAD 32218
Assumption ES, 2431 ATLANTIC BLVD 32207
Christ the King Catholic ES
6822 LARKIN RD 32211
Holy Cross Lutheran ES
6620 ARLINGTON EXPY 32211
Holy Rosary ES, 4920 BRENTWOOD AVE 32206
Jacksonville Country ES, P O BOX 16309 32245
Resurrection Parish ES, 3406 JUSTINA RD 32211
Riverside Presbyterian ES, 830 OAK ST 32204
Sacred Heart ES, 5752 BLANDING BLVD 32244
San Jose Catholic ES, 3619 TOLEDO RD 32217
San Jose Episcopal Day ES
7423 SAN JOSE BLVD 32217
Solomon Schechter ES, P O BOX 23886 32241
St. Andrew's Episcopal ES
7801 LONE STAR RD 32211
St. Joseph's ES
11600 OLD SAINT AUGUSTINE 32223
St. Mark's Episcopal ES
4114 OXFORD AVE 32210
St. Matthew's Catholic ES
1767 BLANDING BLVD 32210
St. Patrick's ES, 1429 BROWARD RD 32218
St. Paul's School, 2609 PARK ST 32204
St. Pius Catholic ES, 1470 13TH ST W 32209

Jacksonville Beach, Duval Co., Pop. Code 7

St. Paul's by the Sea Episcopal ES
1150 5TH ST N 32250
St. Paul's School, 428 N 2ND AVE 32250

Jasper, Hamilton Co., Pop. Code 4
Hamilton SD 24
Sch. Sys. Enr. Code 4
Supt. – Owen Hinton, Jr., P O BOX 1059 32052
Hamilton MS, RURAL ROUTE 04 BOX 177 32052
Brenda Graham, prin.
Central Hamilton ES, P O BOX 136 32052
Ronald Hobbs, prin.
Other Schools – See Jennings, White Springs

Jay, Santa Rosa Co., Pop. Code 3
Santa Rosa SD 57
Supt. – See Milton
ES, 702 S ALABAMA ST 32565
Elton Nowling, prin.

Jennings, Hamilton Co., Pop. Code 3
Hamilton SD 24
Supt. – See Jasper
North Hamilton ES, P O BOX 6 32053
Harry Pennington, prin.

Jensen Beach, Martin Co.
Martin SD 43
Supt. – See Stuart
ES, 2525 NE SAVANNAH RD 34957
Doris Burke, prin.

Jupiter, Palm Beach Co., Pop. Code 6
Palm Beach SD 50
Supt. – See West Palm Beach
MS, 15245 N MILITARY TRAIL 33458
Samuel Watson, prin.
ES, 200 S LOXAHATCHEE DR 33458
Jack Meeds, prin.
Thomas ES, 800 MAPLEWOOD DR 33458
Doris George, prin.

Jupiter Christian School, P O BOX 968 33468

Key Biscayne, Dade Co.
Dade SD 13
Supt. – See Miami
ES, 150 W MCINTYRE ST 33149
Elisabeth Carroll, prin.

Key Largo, Monroe Co.
Monroe SD 44
Supt. – See Key West
ES, P O BOX 195 33037 – Dale Wolgast, prin.

Keystone Heights, Clay Co., Pop. Code 3
Clay SD 10
Supt. – See Green Cove Springs

ES, 335 PECAN ST   32656 – Hubert White, prin.

Key West, Monroe Co., Pop. Code 7
Monroe SD 44
Sch. Sys. Enr. Code 6
Supt. – Dr. Armando Henriquez
  P O BOX 1430   33041
Obryant MS, 1105 LEON ST   33040
  Robert Walker, prin.
Adams ES, JUNIOR COLLEGE ROAD   33040
  Phyllis Allen, prin.
Archer ES, 1302 WHITE ST   33040
  William Cabanas, prin.
Poinciana ES, 1212 14TH ST   33040
  Gerald Braden, prin.
Sigsbee ES, FELTON ROAD   33040
  Bill Quinn, prin.
Other Schools – See Key Largo, Marathon, Sugar Loaf
  Key, Tavernier

Grace Lutheran ES, 2713 FLAGLER AVE   33040
Mary Immaculate Star of the Sea School
  700 TRUMAN AVE   33040

Kissimmee, Osceola Co., Pop. Code 7
Osceola SD 49
Sch. Sys. Enr. Code 7
Supt. – Max Waters, P O BOX 1948   32742
Beaumont MS, BEAUMONT & AULTMAN   32741
  Mike Smith, prin.
John MS, 2001 DENN JOHN LANE   32743
  Tommy Tate, prin.
Parkway MS, 857 FLORIDA PKY   32743
  Charles Bryan, prin.
Boggy Creek ES, 810 FLORIDA PKY   32743
  Dean Cherry, prin.
Central Avenue ES, 1502 N CENTRAL AVE   32741
  Chris Colombo, prin.
Highlands ES, 800 W DONEGAN AVE   32741
  Roberta Vogel, prin.
Mill Creek ES, 1700 MILL SLOUGH RD   32743
  Jim Scott, prin.
Pleasant Hill ES, 1253 PLEASANT HILL RD   32741
  Shelley Ducharme, prin.
Reedy Creek ES, 2300 BROOK CT   32758
  Kenneth Meyers, prin.
Thacker Avenue ES, 301 N THACKER AVE   32741
  Sylvia Evans, prin.
Other Schools – See Saint Cloud

La Belle, Hendry Co., Pop. Code 4
Hendry SD 26
Sch. Sys. Enr. Code 6
Supt. – William Burke, P O BOX 1980   33935
MS, P O BOX 1920   33935 – William Perry, prin.
ES, P O BOX 1860   33935 – Joann Patterson, prin.
IS, 2052 NW EUCALYPTUS BLVD   33935
  Michael Gasz, prin.
Other Schools – See Clewiston

Lake Alfred, Polk Co., Pop. Code 5
Polk SD 53
Supt. – See Bartow
ES, 550 E CUMMINGS ST   33850
  Eileen Castle, prin.

Lake Butler, Union Co., Pop. Code 4
Union SD 63
Sch. Sys. Enr. Code 4
Supt. – James H. Cason III, 55 SW 6TH ST   32054
MS, 150 SW 6TH ST   32054 – Marsan Boyd, prin.
ES, 800 SW 6TH ST   32054 – Lowell Dukes, prin.

Lake City, Columbia Co., Pop. Code 6
Columbia SD 12
Sch. Sys. Enr. Code 6
Supt. – Dr. Silas Pittman, P O BOX 1148   32056
Eastside ES, 225 DEFENDER AVE   32055
  Norman Steadman, prin.
Five Points ES
  RURAL ROUTE 08 BOX 276   32056
  Grady Markham, prin.
Melrose ES, 1500 E PUTNAM ST   32055
  Roy Dicks, prin.
Niblack MS, 1500 BROADWAY ST   32055
  William Orr, prin.
Summers ES, 2688 MCFARLANE AVE   32055
  Arthur Holiday, prin.
Other Schools – See Fort White

Epiphany Catholic ES
  RURAL ROUTE 10 BOX 161   32055

Lake Helen, Volusia Co., Pop. Code 4
Volusia SD 64
Supt. – See De Land
Long-Lake Helen ES, 307 S LAKEVIEW DR   32744
  Nancy Roberts, prin.

Lakeland, Polk Co., Pop. Code 8
Polk SD 53
Supt. – See Bartow
Carlton Palmore ES
  3725 CLEVELAND HEIGHTS BLVD   33813
  Anice McElroy, prin.
Central Avenue ES, 604 S CENTRAL AVE   33801
  Diane Herring, prin.
Churchwell ES, 8201 PARK BYRD RD   33809
  Delores Brundidge, prin.
Cleveland Court ES, 328 E EDGEWOOD DR   33803
  Joseph Thomas, prin.
Combee ES, 2805 MORGAN COMBEE RD   33801
  Larry Poorbaugh, prin.
Cox ES, 1005 N MASSACHUSETTS AVE   33805
  Latha Speed, prin.

Crystal Lake ES, GALVIN & LANGFORD   33801
  W. Pace, prin.
Dixieland ES, 416 ARIANA ST   33803
  Brenda Satchel, prin.
Griffin ES, 3315 KATHLEEN RD   33809
  Roy Burt,Jr., prin.
Kathleen ES, 3515 SHERETZ RD   33809
  Susan Jones, prin.
Keen ES, 815 PATEAU AVE   33801
  John Luposello, prin.
Lime Street ES, 1225 E LIME ST   33801
  Phillip Obrien, prin.
Lincoln Avenue MS, 1130 N LINCOLN AVE   33805
  Lucille Richardson, prin.
Medulla ES, 850 SCHOOLHOUSE RD   33813
  Nancy Bailey, prin.
North Lakeland ES, 410 ROBSON ROAD   33805
  Debra Painter, prin.
Padgett ES, 110 LEELON RD   33809
  Joseph Gillen, prin.
Rochelle MS, 1501 S DAKOTA AVE   33803
  Jesse Johnson, prin.
Scott Lake ES, 1140 E S R 540A   33813
  Elizabeth Miles, prin.
Sikes ES, 2727 SHEPHERD RD   33811
  Flora Haire, prin.
Southwest ES, 2250 SOUTHWEST AVE   33803
  Diana Myrick, prin.
Winston ES, 3415 SWINDELL RD   33809
  Roy Thompkins, prin.

Evangel Christian School, 1360 E MAIN ST   33801
Lakeland Christian School
  111 FOREST PARK ST   33803
Pathway Christian Academy
  1942 W MEMORIAL BLVD   33801
St. Joseph's ES, 223 S MISSOURI AVE   33801
St. Paul Lutheran ES, 3020 S FLORIDA AVE   33803

Lake Mary, Seminole Co., Pop. Code 5
Seminole SD 59
Supt. – See Sanford
Greenwood Lakes MS
  601 LAKE PARK DRIVE   32746
  Teddy Barker, prin.
ES, 132 S COUNTRY CLUB RD   32746
  Elizabeth Paul, prin.

Lake Panasoffkee, Sumter Co.
Sumter SD 60
Supt. – See Bushnell
ES, P O BOX 329   33538 – Gloria Hodges, prin.

Lake Park, Palm Beach Co., Pop. Code 6
Palm Beach SD 50
Supt. – See West Palm Beach
Eisenhower ES, 2926 LONE PINE RD   33410
  Betty Mason, prin.
Grove Park ES, 8330 N MILITARY TRL   33410
  Tommy Turner, prin.
ES, 410 3RD ST   33403 – John Johnson, prin.

Lake Placid, Highlands Co., Pop. Code 3
Highlands SD 28
Supt. – See Sebring
MS, 328 E INTERLAKE BLVD   33852
  Robert Peavy, prin.
Lake Country ES, 516 COUNTY RD 29   33852
  Majel Bowerman, prin.
ES, 101 LAKE DR W   33852 – Billy Cason, prin.

Lake Wales, Polk Co., Pop. Code 6
Polk SD 53
Supt. – See Bartow
McLaughlin JHS, 800 S 4TH ST   33853
  Jimmy Chambers, prin.
Hillcrest ES, 1051 HESPERIDES RD   33853
  H. Hiers,Jr., prin.
Polk Avenue ES, 110 E POLK AVE   33853
  Max Linton, prin.
Spook Hill ES, 321 E NORTH AVE   33853
  James Beaver, prin.
Wilson ES, 306 FLORIDA AVE   33853
  Jerome Mack, prin.

Lake Wales Lutheran ES, 411 ALVINA AVE   33853

Lake Worth, Palm Beach Co., Pop. Code 8
Palm Beach SD 50
Supt. – See West Palm Beach
JHS, 301 S A ST   33460 – Sharon Walker, prin.
Barton ES, 1700 BARTON RD   33460
  Nora Rosensweig, prin.
Highland ES, 1735 7TH AVE N   33460
  Elizabeth Taylor, prin.
North Grade ES, 824 N K ST   33460
  (—), prin.
Palm Springs ES, 3563 10TH AVE N   33461
  Lenore Dupee, prin.

Troywood Learning Environment School
  1200 N G ST   33460
Lake Worth Christian ES, 1325 N A ST   33460
Sacred Heart ES, 410 N M ST   33460
St. Luke Catholic ES, 2892 CONGRESS AVE   33461

Land O'Lakes, Pasco Co., Pop. Code 3
Pasco SD 51
Sch. Sys. Enr. Code 8
Supt. – Thomas E. Weightman
  7727 US HIGHWAY 41   34639
Pine View MS, 1500 PARKWAY BLVD   34639
  Robert Dorn, prin.
Lake Myrtle ES, 2775 COLLIER PKY   34639
  Monica Joiner, prin.

Sanders Memorial ES, 2170 SCHOOL RD   34639
  Marti Meacher, prin.
Other Schools – See Brooksville, Dade City, Elfers,
  Holiday, Hudson, New Port Richey, Zephyrhills

Lantana, Palm Beach Co., Pop. Code 6
Palm Beach SD 50
Supt. – See West Palm Beach
MS, 1225 W DREW ST   33462
  G. Bruce Mitchell, prin.
ES, 710 W OCEAN AVE   33462
  Ronald Armstrong, prin.

Lake Worth Christian School
  7592 HIGH RIDGE ROAD   33462

Largo, Pinellas Co., Pop. Code 8
Pinellas SD 52
Supt. – See Clearwater
Fitzgerald MS, 6410 118TH AVE   34643
  Linda Tucker, prin.
MS, 155 8TH AVE SW   34641
  Carl Mostellar, prin.
Anona ES, 12010 INDIAN ROCKS RD S   34640
  Stephen Micklo, prin.
Bardmoor ES, 8900 GREENBRIAR RD   34647
  Dr. Jack Taylor, prin.
Bauder ES, 12755 86TH ST   34646
  Anne Stuckey, prin.
Fuguitt ES, 13010 101ST ST   34643
  Charlie Carr, prin.
Helms ES, 561 CLEARWATER LARGO RD S   34640
  Mary Athanson, prin.
Largo Central ES, 250 1ST AVE NE   34640
  Archie Miller,Jr., prin.
Oakhurst ES, 10535 137TH ST   34644
  James Barker, prin.
Ridgecrest ES, 1901 119TH ST   34648
  John Lash, prin.
Starkey ES, 9300 86TH AVE   34647
  Winifred Halstead, prin.
Walsingham ES, 9099 WALSINGHAM RD   34643
  Faye Kerrigan, prin.

Harvest Temple Christian School
  13301 WALSINGHAM ROAD   34644
St. Patrick ES, 1501 TROTTER RD   34640

Lauderdale Lakes, Broward Co., Pop. Code 8
Broward County SD 6
Supt. – See Fort Lauderdale
MS, 3911 NW 30TH AVE   33309
  Dr. Jerutha Ford, prin.

Lauderhill, Broward Co., Pop. Code 8
Broward County SD 6
Supt. – See Fort Lauderdale
Castle Hill ES, 2640 NW 46TH AVE   33313
  Mary Ellen Van Pelt, prin.
Royal Palm ES, 1951 NW 56TH AVE   33313
  Samuel Truitt, prin.

Laurel Hill, Okaloosa Co., Pop. Code 3
Okaloosa SD 46
Supt. – See Crestview
S, P O BOX 188   32567 – Grover Hicks, prin.

Lawtey, Clay Co., Pop. Code 3
Bradford SD 4
Supt. – See Starke
ES, P O BOX D   32058 – Buddy Paterson, prin.

Lecanto, Citrus Co.
Citrus SD 9
Supt. – See Inverness
MS, P O BOX T   32661 – James Halcomb, prin.
ES, 3790 W EDUCATIONAL PATH   32661
  Stephen Guyler, prin.

Lee, Madison Co., Pop. Code 2
Madison SD 40
Supt. – See Madison
ES, P O BOX 188   32059 – Dennis Miller, prin.

Leesburg, Lake Co., Pop. Code 7
Lake SD 35
Supt. – See Tavares
Carver MS, 1200 BEECHER ST   32748
  James Polk, Jr., prin.
Oak Park MS, 2101 W SOUTH ST   32748
  Dorothy Carrier, prin.
Beverly Shores ES, 1108 W GRIFFIN RD   32748
  Kenneth Hollingsworth, prin.
Dabney ES, 910 E DIXIE AVE   32748
  John Johnson, prin.
Rimes ES, P O BOX 307   32749 – Ted Wolf, prin.
Skeen ES, 401 S MOSS ST   32748
  Noel Hansen, prin.
Treadway ES
  10619 TREADWAY SCHOOL RD   32788
  James Gant, prin.

Lehigh Acres, Lee Co., Pop. Code 5
Lee SD 36
Supt. – See Fort Myers
MS, 104 ARTHUR AVE   33936 – Roger Jones, prin.
Lehigh ES, 200 SCHOOLWAY CT   33936
  Allen Humfleet, prin.
Sunshine ES, 601 SARA AVE   33936
  Shirley Watson, prin.

Leisure City, Dade Co., Pop. Code 5
Dade SD 13
Supt. – See Miami
Campbell Drive MS, 31110 SW 157TH AVE   33033
  Onetha Gilliard, prin.

Lithia, Hillsborough Co.
Hillsborough SD 29
Supt. – See Tampa
Pinecrest ES, P O BOX 474   33547
Martha Hood, prin.

Live Oak, Suwannee Co., Pop. Code 6
Suwannee SD 61
Sch. Sys. Enr. Code 5
Supt. – Frank Stankunas
224 PARSHLEY ST SW   32060
Suwannee MS, 617 ONTARIO AVE SW   32060
Wyman Harvard, prin.
Suwannee ES East, 1625 WALKER AVE SW   32060
Charles Blalock, prin.
Suwannee ES West
1419 WALKER AVE SW   32060
Nancy Roberts, prin.
Other Schools – See Branford

Longwood, Seminole Co., Pop. Code 7
Seminole SD 59
Supt. – See Sanford
Milwee MS, 1725 STATE ROAD 427 S   32750
Willie Hold, prin.
Rock Lake MS, 250 SLADE DRIVE   32750
Richard Rost, prin.
ES, 830 ORANGE AVE E   32750
David Scott, prin.
Sabal Point ES, 960 WEKIVA SPRINGS RD   32779
Elizabeth Waterhouse, prin.
Wekiva ES, 1450 E WEKIVA TRL   32779
Rita Ramsey, prin.
Woodlands ES
1429 E E WILLIAMSON ROAD   32750
Jewell Morgan, prin.

Forest Lake Education Ctr. ES
2801 SAND LAKE RD   32779
Sweetwater Episcopal Academy
251 E LAKE BRANTLEY DR   32779

Loxahatchee, Palm Beach Co.
Palm Beach SD 50
Supt. – See West Palm Beach
Loxahatchee Groves ES
16020 OKEECHOBEE BLVD E   33470
Walter Murray, prin.

Lutz, Hillsborough Co., Pop. Code 3
Hillsborough SD 29
Supt. – See Tampa
ES, 202 5TH AVE SE   33549
Eulah McWilliams, prin.

Lynn Haven, Bay Co., Pop. Code 6
Bay SD 3
Supt. – See Panama City
Mowat MS, 1903 HIGHWAY 390   32444
Joel Creel, prin.
ES, 301 W 9TH ST   32444 – Allen Comerford, prin.

Macclenny, Baker Co., Pop. Code 5
Baker SD 2
Sch. Sys. Enr. Code 5
Supt. – Tim Starling, 392 S BOULEVARD E   32063
Baker County MS, 420 S 8TH ST   32063
William Baker, Jr., prin.
ES, 301 S BOULEVARD E   32063
Joann Bath, prin.
Other Schools – See Glen Saint Mary

Mac Dill AFB, Hillsborough Co.
Hillsborough SD 29
Supt. – See Tampa
Tinker ES, 1 KAYVEE LOOP   33621
N. Jean Leone, prin.

Madeira Beach, Pinellas Co., Pop. Code 5
Pinellas SD 52
Supt. – See Clearwater
MS, 591 TOM STUART CAUSEWAY   33708
Ronald Cinnamon, prin.
ES, 749 TOM STUART CSWY   33708
Marcia Gibbs, prin.

Madison, Madison Co., Pop. Code 5
Madison SD 40
Sch. Sys. Enr. Code 5
Supt. – Randall M. Buchanan, P O BOX 449   32340
MS, RURAL ROUTE 01 BOX 225   32340
Larry Alderman, prin.
PS, 500 W HAYNES ST   32340
Frank Galbraith, prin.
Other Schools – See Greenville, Lee, Pinetta

Maitland, Orange Co., Pop. Code 6
Orange SD 48
Supt. – See Orlando
MS, 1901 CHOCTAW TRAIL   32751
Howard Fleming, prin.
Dommerich ES, 1900 CHOCTAW TRL   32751
Richard Weidley, prin.
Lake Sybelia ES, 600 SANDSPUR RD   32751
Donna Smith, prin.

Malone, Jackson Co., Pop. Code 3
Jackson SD 32
Supt. – See Marianna
S, P O BOX 68   32445 – Frank Waller, prin.

Mango, Hillsborough Co.
Hillsborough SD 29
Supt. – See Tampa
ES, P O BOX 8   33550 – Guy Cacciatore, prin.

Marathon, Monroe Co., Pop. Code 5
Monroe SD 44
Supt. – See Key West
Switlik ES, 3400 OVERSEAS HWY   33050
Joe Orr, prin.

Marco, Collier Co.
Collier SD 11
Supt. – See Naples
Barfield ES, RURAL ROUTE 92   33937
Carol Gossard, prin.

Margate, Broward Co., Pop. Code 8
Broward County SD 6
Supt. – See Fort Lauderdale
MS, 500 NW 65TH AVE   33060
Robert Gillette, prin.
Atlantic West ES, 301 NW 69TH TER   33063
Ellen Flynn, prin.
ES, 6300 NW 18TH ST   33063 – Al Capuano, prin.

Faith Christian School
6950 ROYAL PALM BLVD   33063

Marianna, Jackson Co., Pop. Code 6
Jackson SD 32
Sch. Sys. Enr. Code 6
Supt. – Tim Chase, P O BOX 5958   32446
MS, 1600 W SOUTH ST   32446
Lillie Speights, prin.
Golson ES, 800 2ND AVE   32446
Virginia Braxton, prin.
Riverside MS, 604 CHEROKEE ST   32446
Harry Bell,Jr., prin.
Other Schools – See Alford, Cottondale, Graceville, Grand Ridge, Malone, Sneads

Mary Esther, Okaloosa Co., Pop. Code 5
Okaloosa SD 46
Supt. – See Crestview
Florosa ES, P O BOX 2   32569 – James Hill, prin.
ES, HWY 98   32569 – Dr. Jack Garnett, prin.

Mascotte, Lake Co., Pop. Code 4
Lake SD 35
Supt. – See Tavares
ES, P O BOX 429   32753 – Carmen Arnold, prin.

Mayo, Lafayette Co., Pop. Code 3
LaFayette SD 34
Sch. Sys. Enr. Code 4
Supt. – Milton Ceraso, P O BOX 58   32066
LaFayette ES, P O BOX 260   32066
William Hart, prin.

Melbourne, Brevard Co., Pop. Code 8
Brevard SD 5
Supt. – See Rockledge
Stone MS, 1101 E UNIVERSITY BLVD   32901
Donald Albert, prin.
Allen ES, 2601 FOUNTAINHEAD BLVD   32935
Estle White, prin.
Creel ES, 1566 PALMWOOD DR   32935
Kathryn Eward, prin.
Croton ES, 1449 CROTON RD   32935
Ella Greenwade, prin.
Harbor City ES, 1377 SARNO RD   32935
William Murray, prin.
Meadowlane ES, 2255 MINTON RD   32904
Edward Midgett, Jr., prin.
Port Malabar ES, 301 PIONEER AVE NE   32907
Johnny Harper, Jr., prin.
Sabal ES, 1400 N WICKHAM RD   32935
Bill Campbell, prin.
Sherwood ES, 2541 POST RD   32935
John Stinson, prin.
University Park ES
500 W UNIVERSITY BLVD   32901
Clenton Taylor, prin.

Brevard Christian School
1100 DORCHESTER AVE   32904
Ascension Catholic ES, P O BOX 360937   32936
Our Lady of Lourdes ES, 420 E FEE AVE   32901
Wade Christian Academy, P O BOX 1113   32902

Melbourne Beach, Brevard Co., Pop. Code 5
Brevard SD 5
Supt. – See Rockledge
Gemini ES, 2100 OAK ST   32951
Lynne Blackwood, prin.

Melrose, Alachua Co., Pop. Code 3
Putman SD 54
Supt. – See Palatka
Melrose Community ES, P O BOX 186   32666
Donald Williams, prin.

Merritt Island, Brevard Co., Pop. Code 8
Brevard SD 5
Supt. – See Rockledge
Audubon ES, 1201 N BANANA RIVER DR   32952
Edward Powell, prin.
Carroll ES, 1 SKYLINE BLVD   32953
Walter Taylor, prin.
Gardendale ES, 301 GROVE BLVD   32953
Albert Narvaez, Jr., prin.
Mila ES, 288 W MERRITT AVE   32953
Lynda Smith, prin.
Tropical ES, 885 S COURTENAY PKY   32952
Gene Brock, prin.

Divine Mercy Catholic ES
1940 N COURTENAY PKY   32953

Miami, Dade Co., Pop. Code 10
Dade SD 13
Sch. Sys. Enr. Code 8
Supt. – Dr. Joseph Fernandez
1410 NE 2ND AVE   33132
Allapattah JHS, 1331 NW 46TH ST   33142
Maria Jenkins, prin.
Drew JHS, 1801 NW 60TH ST   33142
William Clark, prin.
Lake Stevens JHS, 18484 NW 48TH PLACE   33055
Tom Smith, prin.
Lee JHS, 3100 NW 5TH AVE   33127
William Jones, prin.
Mann JHS, 8950 NW 2ND AVE   33150
Dr. Marshall Stearns, prin.
Mays JHS, 11700 HAINLIN MILL DRIVE   33170
Robert Stinson, prin.
Miami Edison MS, 6101 NW 2ND AVE   33127
Sandra Powell, prin.
Allapattah MS, 4700 NW 12TH AVE   33127
Harold Jones, Sr., prin.
Arcola Lake ES, 1037 NW 81ST ST   33150
Shirlee Shateen, prin.
Auburndale ES, 3255 SW 6TH ST   33135
Olga Miyar, prin.
Banyan ES, 3060 SW 85TH AVE   33155
Gloria Aguila-Fisher, prin.
Bel-Aire ES, 10205 SW 194TH ST   33157
Maurice Sullivan, prin.
Bent Tree ES, 4861 SW 140TH AVE   33175
Donald Lape, prin.
Biscayne Gardens ES, 560 NW 151ST ST   33169
Dr. Lynda Jollivette, prin.
Blanton ES, 10327 NW 11TH AVE   33150
Alice Harrison, prin.
Blue Lakes ES, 9250 SW 52ND TER   33165
Christine Garnett, prin.
Broadmoor ES, 3401 NW 83RD ST   33147
Maxine Sconiers, prin.
Buena Vista ES, 3001 NW 2ND AVE   33127
Sylvia Cordero, prin.
Calusa ES, 9580 W CALUSA CLUB DR   33186
James Gould, Jr., prin.
Caribbean ES, 11990 SW 200TH ST   33177
Carmen Suarez, prin.
Citrus Grove ES, 2121 NW 5TH ST   33125
Minnie Eckles, prin.
Colonial Drive ES, 10755 SW 160TH ST   33157
Bettye Meares, prin.
Comstock ES, 2420 NW 18TH AVE   33142
Merwyn Levin, prin.
Coral Park ES, 1225 SW 97TH AVE   33174
Dr. Louis Manganiello, prin.
Coral Reef ES, 7955 SW 152ND ST   33157
Clarence Maschinot, Jr., prin.
Coral Terrace ES, 6801 SW 24TH ST   33155
Michael Wagner, prin.
Coral Way ES, 1950 SW 13TH AVE   33145
Julia Lopez, prin.
Crowder ES, 757 NW 66TH ST   33150
Otto McQueen, prin.
Cutler Ridge ES, 20210 CORAL SEA RD   33189
Beaulah Richards, prin.
Cypress ES, 5400 SW 112TH CT   33165
Gary Morehouse, prin.
Devon Aire ES, 10501 SW 122ND AVE   33186
Gloria Gray, prin.
Douglas ES, 314 NW 12TH ST   33136
Robert Kalinsky, prin.
Drew ES, 1775 NW 60TH ST   33142
Frederick Morley, prin.
Dunbar ES, 505 NW 20TH ST   33127
Maybelline Truesdell, prin.
Earlington Heights ES, 4750 NW 22ND AVE   33142
Marietta Mischia, prin.
Edison Park ES, 500 NW 67TH ST   33150
Arletha Walton, prin.
Emerson ES, 8001 SW 36TH ST   33155
Livia Alonso, prin.
Evans ES, 1895 NW 75TH ST   33147
Willie Brown, prin.
Everglades ES, 8375 SW 16TH ST   33155
Bobby Friedman, prin.
Fairchild ES, 5757 SW 45TH ST   33155
Ana Driggs, prin.
Fairlawn ES, 444 SW 60TH AVE   33144
Laura Bethel, prin.
Flagami ES, 920 SW 76TH AVE   33144
Stanley Dansky, prin.
Flagler ES, 5252 NW 1ST ST   33126
Leticia Lauredo, prin.
Floral Heights ES, 5120 NW 24TH AVE   33142
Fannie Thurston, prin.
Floyd ES, 12650 SW 109TH AVE   33176
Johanna Teague, prin.
Franklin ES, 13100 NW 12TH AVE   33168
Dr. David Felton, prin.
Gratigny ES, 11905 N MIAMI AVE   33168
Bernard Nissman, prin.
Greenglade ES, 3060 SW 127TH AVE   33175
Jenisu Ainsley, prin.
Gulfstream ES, 20900 SW 97TH AVE   33189
John Gardner, prin.
Hadley ES, 8400 NW 7TH ST   33126
Menia Stone, prin.
Hall ES, 1901 SW 134TH AVE   33175
Barbara Bell, prin.
Hibiscus ES, 18701 NW 1ST AVE   33169
Robert Butts, prin.
Holmes ES, 1175 NW 67TH ST   33150
Jeanette Goa, prin.
Hoover ES, 9050 MANNOCK BLVD   33196
Samuel Jerkins, prin.

Howard Drive ES, 7750 SW 136TH ST   33156
   Anthony Houghton, prin.
Kendale ES, 10693 SW 93RD ST   33176
   Donna Lozar, prin.
Kendale Lakes ES, 8000 SW 142ND AVE   33183
   Leonard Greenbaum, prin.
Kensington Park ES, 711 NW 30TH AVE   33125
   America Bermudez, prin.
Kenwood ES, 9300 SW 79TH AVE   33156
   Harold Schmitt, prin.
King ES, 7124 NW 12TH AVE   33150
   Beverly Nixon, prin.
Kinloch Park ES, 4275 NW 1ST ST   33126
   Charles Collard, prin.
Lakeview ES, 1290 NW 115TH ST   33167
   Henry Crawford,Jr., prin.
Leewood ES, 10343 SW 124TH ST   33176
   Charlene Houghton, prin.
Liberty City ES, 1855 NW 71ST ST   33147
   Ruby Poiter, prin.
Little River ES, 514 NW 77TH ST   33150
   Fredric Zerlin, prin.
Lorah Park ES, 5160 NW 31ST AVE   33142
   Agenoira Paschal, prin.
Martin MS, 14250 BOGGS DR   33176
   Ossie Hollis, prin.
Melrose MS, 3050 NW 35TH ST   33142
   Dorothy Blake, prin.
Miami Heights ES, 17661 SW 117TH AVE   33177
   Rosemary Brady, prin.
Miami Park ES, 2225 NW 103RD ST   33147
   Merry Schrage, prin.
Miramar MS, 109 NE 19TH ST   33132
   Barbara Moss, prin.
Morningside ES, 6620 NE 5TH AVE   33138
   Dr. Paul Madsen, prin.
Moton MS, 18050 HOMESTEAD AVE   33157
   Dr. Rasamma Nyberg, prin.
Norland ES, 19450 NW 8TH CT   33169
   Leo Strousberg, prin.
Norwood ES, 19010 NW 14TH CT   33169
   Benedict Balser, prin.
Ojus ES, 18600 W DIXIE HWY   33180
   Jeanne Friedman, prin.
Olinda ES, 5536 NW 21ST AVE   33142
   Lenora Smith, prin.
Olympia Heights ES, 9797 SW 40TH ST   33156
   Clifford Herrman, prin.
Orchard Villa ES, 5720 NW 13TH AVE   33142
   Henry Mingo, prin.
Palmetto ES, 12401 SW 74TH AVE   33156
   Lawrence Feldman, prin.
Parkway ES, 1320 NW 188TH ST   33169
   Jack Silberman, prin.
Perrine ES, 8851 SW 168TH ST   33157
   Lillie Harris, prin.
Pharr MS, 2000 NW 46TH ST   33142
   June Day, prin.
Pine Lake ES, 16700 SW 109TH AVE   33157
   Clemencia Waddell, prin.
Pine Villa ES, 21799 SW 117TH CT   33170
   Dr. William Wright, prin.
Pinecrest ES, 10250 SW 57TH AVE   33156
   Bonnie Wheatley, prin.
Poinciana Park ES, 6745 NW 23RD AVE   33147
   Lawrence Crawford, prin.
Richmond MS, 16929 SW 104TH AVE   33157
   Clarence Jones,Jr., prin.
Riverside MS, 221 SW 12TH AVE   33130
   Jesselyn Brown, prin.
Rockway ES, 2790 SW 83RD CT   33165
   Tessa Gold, prin.
Royal Green ES, 13047 SW 47TH ST   33175
   Carol Delaurier, prin.
Royal Palm ES, 4200 SW 112TH CT   33165
   Herbert Jacobson, prin.
Santa Clara ES, 1051 NW 29TH TER   33127
   Robert Heath, prin.
Scott Lake ES, 1160 NW 175TH ST   33169
   David Dobbs, prin.
Seminole ES, 121 SW 78TH PL   33144
   George Suarez, prin.
Shadowlawn ES, 149 NW 49TH ST   33127
   Brenda Edwards, prin.
Shenandoah ES, 1023 SW 21ST AVE   33135
   Judith Richardson, prin.
Silver Bluff ES, 2609 SW 25 AVE   33133
   Elba Machin, prin.
Snapper Creek ES, 10151 SW 64TH ST   33173
   Linda Stuart, prin.
South Miami Heights ES
   12231 SW 190TH TER   33177
   Maria Gonzalez, prin.
Southside ES, 45 SW 13TH ST   33130
   James McKenna, prin.
Stirrup ES, 330 NW 97TH AVE   33172
   Jack Gibson, prin.
Sunset ES, 5120 SW 72ND ST   33143
   Roberta Granville, prin.
Sunset Park ES, 10235 SW 84TH ST   33173
   Dr. Elizabeth Faust, prin.
Sweetwater ES, 10655 SW 4TH ST   33174
   Maria Rodriguez, prin.
Sylvania Heights ES, 5901 SW 16TH ST   33155
   Lucy Williams, prin.
Tropical ES, 4545 SW 104TH AVE   33165
   Carolyn Bonner, prin.
Tucker ES, 3500 S DOUGLAS RD   33133
   Von Beebe, prin.
Village Green ES, 12265 SW 34TH ST   33175
   Camille King, prin.
Vineland ES, 8455 SW 119TH ST   33156
   Dr. Betty Nowlin, prin.

West Little River MS, 2450 NW 84TH ST   33147
   Glenda Harris, prin.
Westview ES, 2101 NW 127TH ST   33167
   Richard Artmeier, prin.
Wheatley ES, 1801 NW 1ST PL   33136
   Charlie Williams, prin.
Whispering Pines ES, 18929 SW 89TH RD   33157
   Nereida Santa Cruz, prin.
Winston Park ES, 13200 79TH ST   33183
   Michael Liebman, prin.
Other Schools – See Bay Harbor Islands, Coconut
   Grove, Coral Gables, Florida City, Hialeah,
   Homestead, Key Biscayne, Leisure City, Miami
   Beach, Miami Lakes, Miami Shores, Miami Springs,
   Naranja, North Bay Village, North Miami, North
   Miami Beach, Opa-Locka, South Miami

Miami Shores Prep School
   1850 79TH ST CSWAY   33141
Carrollton School of the Sacred Heart
   3747 MAIN HIGHWAY   33133
Florida Christian School
   4200 SW 89TH AVE   33165
Gables Academy, 7700 MILLER ROAD   33155
Greater Miami Academy
   3100 NW 18TH AVE   33142
Interamerican Military Academy
   3525 NW 7TH ST   33125
Kendall Acres Academy
   7700 MILLER ROAD   33155
La Luz School, 931 SW 1ST ST   33130
LaProgresiva Presbyterian School
   P O BOX 350866   33135
Lear School, 11211 BISCAYNE BLVD   33181
Lincoln-Marti School, 904 SW 23RD AVE   33135
Miami Aerospace Academy
   P O BOX 350490   33135
Miami Christian School
   200 NW 109TH AVE   33172
Miami Country Day School
   601 NE 107TH ST   33161
Northwest Christian Academy
   951 NW 136TH ST   33168
Alexander School,Inc., 6050 SW 57TH AVE   33143
Blessed Trinity ES, 4020 CURTISS PKY   33166
Corpus Christi ES, 795 NW 32ND ST   33127
Emes Academy Miami ES
   7902 CARLYLE AVE   33141
Epiphany School, 5555 S W 84TH ST   33143
Holy Cross Academy, 12425 SW 72 ST   33183
Holy Redeemer ES, 1301 NW 71ST ST   33147
Kendall Christian ES, 8485 SW 112TH ST   33156
Kings Christian ES, 8951 SW 44TH ST   33165
Mt. Olive Lutheran ES
   10875 QUAIL ROOST DR   33157
Our Lady of Divine Providence School
   10205 W FLAGLER ST   33174
St. Agatha ES, 1111 SW 107TH AVE   33174
St. Brendan ES, 8755 SW 32ND ST   33165
St. Francis Xavier ES, 1682 NW 4TH AVE   33136
St. Hugh ES, 3460 ROYAL RD   33133
St. James Catholic ES, 601 NW 131ST ST   33168
St. John Neumann ES
   12125 SW 107TH AVE   33186
St. Kevin Catholic ES, 4001 SW 127TH AVE   33175
St. Mary's Cathedral ES
   7485 NW 2ND AVE   33150
St. Matthew Lutheran School
   621 BEACON BLVD   33135
St. Michael Archangel ES
   300 NW 28TH AVE   33125
St. Thomas Apostle ES, 7303 SW 64TH ST   33143
St. Thomas Episcopal ES
   5690 SW 88TH ST   33156
St. Timothy ES, 5400 SW 102ND AVE   33165
Sts. Peter Paul ES, 1435 SW 12TH AVE   33129
Visitation Catholic ES, 100 NE 191ST ST   33179

Miami Beach, Dade Co., Pop. Code 8
Dade SD 13
Supt. – See Miami
Nautilus JHS, 4301 MICHIGAN AVE   33140
   Martin Zigler, prin.
Biscayne ES, 800 77TH ST   33141
   Harriet Glick, prin.
Fienberg ES, 1420 WASHINGTON AVE   33139
   Marjorie Santayana, prin.
North Beach ES, 4100 PRAIRIE AVE   33140
   Michael Kesselman, prin.

Rabbi Gross Hebrew Academy
   2400 PINE TREE DRIVE   33140
Landow Yeshiva ES, 1140 ALTON RD   33139
Lehrman Day ES Temple Emanu-El
   727 77TH ST   33141
St. Joseph ES, 8625 BYRON AVE   33141
St. Patrick ES, 3700 GARDEN AVE   33140

Miami Lakes, Dade Co.
Dade SD 13
Supt. – See Miami
ES, 14250 NW 67TH AVE   33014
   Margarita Davis, prin.

Miami Shores, Dade Co., Pop. Code 6
Dade SD 13
Supt. – See Miami
ES, 10351 NE 5TH AVE   33138 – Della Zaher, prin.

St. Rose of Lima ES, 10690 NE 5TH AVE   33138

Miami Springs, Dade Co., Pop. Code 7
Dade SD 13
Supt. – See Miami

JHS, 150 S ROYAL POINCIANA BLVD   33166
   Steven Ladd, prin.
ES, 51 PARK ST   33166 – Susan Lehrman, prin.
Springview ES, 1122 BLUEBIRD AVE   33166
   Juan Lengomin, prin.

Middleburg, Clay Co., Pop. Code 3
Clay SD 10
Supt. – See Green Cove Springs
ES, 3958 MAIN ST   32068
   Twila Shrewsbury, prin.

Milton, Santa Rosa Co., Pop. Code 6
Santa Rosa SD 57
Sch. Sys. Enr. Code 7
Supt. – Bennett C. Russell, 603 CANAL ST   32570
Hobbs MS, 309 GLOVER LANE   32570
   Nancy Padgett, prin.
King MS, 2499 STEWART ST NW   32570
   Jack Taylor, prin.
Berryhill ES, P O BOX 628   32572
   Terry Neustaedter, prin.
Chumuckla ES, RURAL ROUTE 02   32571
   Thelma Dukes, prin.
East Milton ES, 26 WARD BASIN RD   32570
   John Rogers, prin.
Jackson ES, 623 SUSAN ST   32570
   Junius Williams III, prin.
Munson ES, RURAL ROUTE 01 BOX 75   32570
   Gene Fleming, prin.
Pea Ridge ES, 250 SCHOOL LN   32571
   Wayland Foster, prin.
Rhodes ES, 800 BYROM ST   32570
   Hilda Worley, prin.
Other Schools – See Bagdad, Gulf Breeze, Jay, Pace

Santa Rosa Christian School, P O BOX 643   32572

Mims, Brevard Co.
Brevard SD 5
Supt. – See Rockledge
ES, 2582 US HIGHWAY 1   32754
   Evelyn Smith, prin.
Pinewood ES, P O BOX 737   32754
   Gerald Beverly II, prin.

Miramar, Broward Co., Pop. Code 8
Broward County SD 6
Supt. – See Fort Lauderdale
Perry MS, 3400 SW 69TH AVE   33023
   Roberta Insel, prin.
Fairway ES, 7850 FAIRWAY BLVD   33023
   Joan Banashak, prin.
ES, 6831 SW 26TH ST   33023
   Joseph Schapiro, prin.
Perry ES, 6850 SW 34TH ST   33023
   Robert Morgan, Jr., prin.
Sunshine ES, 7737 W LASALLE BLVD   33023
   Francis McKeon, prin.

St. Bartholomew ES, 8001 MIRAMAR PKY   33025
St. Stephen Protomartyr ES
   2000 STATE ROAD #7   33023

Monticello, Jefferson Co., Pop. Code 5
Jefferson SD 33
Sch. Sys. Enr. Code 4
Supt. – Stephen Walker
   1490 W WASHINGTON ST   32344
Howard MS, 1145 SECOND ST   32344
   Pink Hightower,Jr., prin.
Jefferson County ES
   960 ROCKY BRANCH RD   32344
   William McRae,Jr., prin.

Aucilla Christian Academy
   RURAL ROUTE 01 BOX 56   32344

Moore Haven, Glades Co., Pop. Code 4
Glades SD 22
Sch. Sys. Enr. Code 3
Supt. – Linda Taylor, P O BOX 459   33471
ES, P O BOX 160   33471 – Gary Clark, prin.

Mount Dora, Lake Co., Pop. Code 6
Lake SD 35
Supt. – See Tavares
MS, 1250 GRAND AVE E   32757
   James Hollins, prin.
Roseborough ES, 751 E 5TH AVE   32757
   Carolyn Samuel, prin.
Triangle ES, 1707 EUDORA RD   32757
   Robert Burnham, prin.

Christian Home & Bible School
   P O BOX 1017   32757

Mulberry, Polk Co., Pop. Code 5
Polk SD 53
Supt. – See Bartow
JHS, 500 SE 9TH AVE   33860 – Frank Satchel, prin.
Kingsford ES, 1400 DEAN ST   33860
   Daniel Mihlfeld, prin.
Purcell MS, 305 NE 1ST AVE   33860
   William Hendrick, prin.

Myakka City, Manatee Co.
Manatee SD 41
Supt. – See Bradenton
ES, P O BOX 38   34251 – Thomas Redmon, prin.

Naples, Collier Co., Pop. Code 7
Collier SD 11
Sch. Sys. Enr. Code 7
Supt. – Dr. Thomas L. Richey
   3710 ESTEY AVE   33942

East Naples MS, 4100 ESTEY AVE   33942
  Mary Brown, prin.
Golden Gate MS, 2701 48TH TERRACE SW   33999
  Birgil Morar, prin.
Gulfview MS, 709 3RD AVE S   33940
  Gene Nara, prin.
Pine Ridge MS, 1515 PINE RIDGE ROAD   33942
  Santo Pino, prin.
Avalon ES, 3300 THOMASSON DR   33962
  Jerry Primus, prin.
Big Cypress ES
  3250 GOLDEN GATE BLVD W   33964
  Jerry Hartwig, prin.
Golden Gate ES, 4911 20TH PL SW   33999
  John Kelly, prin.
Lake Park ES, 1446 12TH ST N   33940
  Gene Olliff, prin.
Naples Park ES, 685 11TH ST N   33940
  Dr. Larry Cunningham, prin.
Poinciana ES, 2825 AIRPORT RD   33942
  Noreen Masterson, prin.
Sea Gate ES, 650 SEAGATE DR   33940
  Dr. Patricia Woodruff, prin.
Shadowlawn ES, 2161 SHADOWLAWN DR   33962
  Dr. Karla Singer, prin.
Other Schools – See Everglades City, Immokalee,
  Marco

Naples Christian Academy
  3050 SANTA BARBARA BLVD   33999
St. Ann ES, 542 8TH AVE S   33999
St. Elizabeth Seton ES, 2760 52ND TER SW   33999

Naranja, Dade Co.
Dade SD 13
Supt. – See Miami
ES, 13990 SW 264TH ST   33032
  Dr. Andrea Rosenblatt, prin.

Neptune Beach, Duval Co., Pop. Code 6
Duval SD 16
Supt. – See Jacksonville
ES, 1515 FLORIDA BLVD   32233
  Marilyn Duncan, prin.

Beaches Chapel Christian School
  610 FLORIDA BLVD   32233

Newberry, Alachua Co., Pop. Code 4
Alachua SD 1
Supt. – See Gainesville
ES, P O BOX 498   32669 – Diana Lagotic, prin.

New Port Richey, Pasco Co., Pop. Code 7
Pasco SD 51
Supt. – See Land O'Lakes
Bayonet Point MS, 990 PLAZA DRIVE   34653
  Tom Rulison, prin.
Gulf MS, 900 E LOUISIANA AVE   34653
  Richard Koop, prin.
Calusa ES, 2301 ORCHID LAKE ROAD   34653
  Richard Tauber, prin.
Cypress ES, 6704 DOGWOOD CT   34654
  Sharyn Disabato, prin.
Moon Lake ES, 12019 TREE BREEZE DR   34654
  Kathleen Lane, prin.
Richey Fundamental ES
  800 N MADISON ST   34652 – Joan Palma, prin.
Schrader ES, 11041 LITTLE RD   34654
  Sherry Heyden, prin.
Seven Springs ES
  8025 MITCHEL RANCH RD   34655
  Richard Wendlek, prin.

New Smyrna Beach, Volusia Co., Pop. Code 7
Volusia SD 64
Supt. – See De Land
New Smyrna Beach MS
  1200 S MYRTLE AVE   32069 – Dolores Sapp, prin.
Chisholm ES, 557 RONNOC LN   32069
  David Fisher, prin.
Coronado Beach ES, 3550 MICHIGAN AVE   32069
  Kathleen Reed, prin.
Read-Pattilo ES, 300 6TH ST   32069
  Paul Finn, prin.
Samsula ES, 248 N SAMSULA DR   32069
  Robert Orebaugh, prin.

Sacred Heart ES, P O BOX 729   32070

Niceville, Okaloosa Co., Pop. Code 6
Okaloosa SD 46
Supt. – See Crestview
Edge ES, 300 HIGHWAY 85 N   32578
  S. Majors, prin.
Plew ES, HWY 20 E   32578
  Donald Dearman, prin.

Rocky Bayou Christian School
  2101 N PARTIN DRIVE   32578

Nocatee, De Soto Co.
De Soto SD 14
Supt. – See Arcadia
ES, P O BOX 188   33864 – Robert Kujawa, prin.

Nokomis, Sarasota Co.
Sarasota SD 58
Supt. – See Sarasota
ES, P O BOX 759   34274 – William Stenger, prin.

North Bay Village, Dade Co., Pop. Code 5
Dade SD 13
Supt. – See Miami
Treasure Island ES, 7540 E TREASURE DR   33141
  Beverly Karrenbauer, prin.

North Fort Myers, Lee Co., Pop. Code 6
Lee SD 36
Supt. – See Fort Myers
Suncoast MS, 1856 SUNCOAST LANE NE   33903
  Richard Burton, prin.
Bayshore ES, RT 41 BOX 601   33903
  Dr. Carrie Robinson, prin.
English ES, 120 PINE ISLAND RD   33903
  Dr. Edward Steinwand, prin.
Tropic Islands ES
  1145 ORANGE GROVE BLVD   33903
  Sharon Benner, prin.

New Testament Baptist School
  736 PINE ISLAND ROAD   33903

North Lauderdale, Broward Co., Pop. Code 7
Broward County SD 6
Supt. – See Fort Lauderdale
Morrow ES, 408 SW 76TH TER   33068
  Robert Collins, prin.
ES, 7500 KIMBERLY BLVD   33068
  Lois Giuffreda, prin.
Pinewood ES, 1600 SW 83RD AVE   33068
  Robert Latcham, prin.

North Miami, Dade Co., Pop. Code 8
Dade SD 13
Supt. – See Miami
Bryan ES, 1200 NE 125TH ST   33161
  Joe Brusco, prin.
Natural Bridge ES, 1650 NE 141ST ST   33181
  Juanita Lane, prin.
ES, 665 NE 145TH ST   33161
  Patricia Parham, prin.

Holy Cross Lutheran ES, 650 NE 135TH ST   33161
Holy Family Catholic ES
  14650 NE 12TH AVE   33161

North Miami Beach, Dade Co., Pop. Code 8
Dade SD 13
Supt. – See Miami
Fulford ES, 16140 NE 18TH AVE   33162
  Alberta Godfrey, prin.
Greynolds Park ES, 1536 NE 179TH ST   33162
  Pearl Hornstein, prin.
Highland Oaks ES, 20500 NE 24TH AVE   33180
  Virginia Boone, prin.
Ives ES, 20770 NE 14TH AVE   33179
  Sally Blonder, prin.
Oak Grove ES, 15640 NE 8TH AVE   33162
  Robert Russell, prin.
Sabal Palm ES, 17101 NE 7TH AVE   33162
  Gertrude Edelman, prin.

St. Lawrence ES, 2200 NE 191ST ST   33180

North Palm Beach, Palm Beach Co., Pop. Code 7
Palm Beach SD 50
Supt. – See West Palm Beach
ES, 401 ANCHORAGE DR   33408
  Victor Schott, prin.

St. Clare's ES
  821 PROSERITY FARMS ROAD   33408

North Port, Sarasota Co., Pop. Code 6
Sarasota SD 58
Supt. – See Sarasota
ES, 1000 GLENALLEN BLVD   34287
  George McGuire, prin.

Oak Hill, Volusia Co., Pop. Code 3
Volusia SD 64
Supt. – See De Land
Burns Oak Hill ES, 104 RIDGE RD   32759
  Carl Persis, prin.

Oakland Park, Broward Co., Pop. Code 7
Broward County SD 6
Supt. – See Fort Lauderdale
Lloyd Estates ES, 750 NW 41ST ST   33309
  Barbara Barrs, prin.
ES, 936 NE 33RD ST   33334
  Richard Wohlfarth, prin.

Ocala, Marion Co., Pop. Code 8
Marion SD 42
Sch. Sys. Enr. Code 8
Supt. – Ralph Archibald, P O BOX 670   32678
Fort King MS, 545 NE 17TH AVE   32670
  Elaine Lane, prin.
Howard MS, 1108 NW 16TH AVE   32675
  Clyde Folsom, prin.
Osceola MS, 526 SE TUSCAVILLA AVE   32671
  Charles Glanzer, prin.
College Park PS, 3155 SW 26TH ST   32674
  Warren Hope, prin.
Eighth Street ES, 513 SE 8TH ST   32671
  Helen Ingrao, prin.
Fessenden ES, 4200 NW 90TH ST   32675
  Bob James, prin.
Jones Upper MS, 1900 SW 5TH ST   32674
  Glynn Murphy, prin.
Madison Street ES, 1239 NW 4TH ST   32675
  Ruth Marcos, prin.
Oakcrest ES, 1112 NE 28TH ST   32670
  Margaret Harper, prin.
Ocala Springs ES
  5757 NE 40TH AVENUE RD   32670
  Paul Conley, prin.
Shady Hill ES, 5959 S MAGNOLIA AVE   32674
  Charles McAuley, prin.
South Ocala ES, 2831 SE LAKE WEIR AVE   32671
  Joel Weldon, prin.

Ward-Highlands ES, 537 SE 36TH AVE   32671
  James Gallimore, prin.
Wyomina Park ES, 511 NE 12TH AVE   32670
  Christopher Mendola, prin.
Other Schools – See Anthony, Belleview, Citra,
  Dunnellon, Fort Mc Coy, Reddick, Silver Springs,
  Sparr, Summerfield, Weirsdale

Ocala Christian Academy
  1714 SE 36TH AVE   32671
St. John Lutheran School
  1915 SE LAKE WEIR AVE   32671
Blessed Trinity ES, 5 SE 17TH ST   32671

Ocoee, Orange Co., Pop. Code 6
Orange SD 48
Supt. – See Orlando
MS, 300 S BLUFORD AVE   32761
  Robert Williams, prin.
ES, 400 S LAKEWOOD AVE   32761
  Jewell Bovis, prin.
Spring Lake ES, 115 SPRING LAKE CIR   32761
  Rudolph James, prin.

Okeechobee, Okeechobee Co., Pop. Code 5
Okeechobee SD 47
Sch. Sys. Enr. Code 6
Supt. – Danny Mullins, 100 SW 5TH AVE   34974
JHS, 800 NW 27TH ST   33472
  Barry Linville, prin.
Central ES, 610 SW 5TH AVE   34974
  Linda King, prin.
Everglades ES, 650 SE 36TH TER   34974
  Milo McCranie, prin.
North ES, 3000 NW 10TH TER   34972
  Roland Clericuzio, prin.
MS, 610 SW 2ND AVE   34974 – Gans Earnest, prin.
Okeechobee South ES, 575 SW 28TH ST   34974
  Sam Smith, prin.

Oldsmar, Pinellas Co., Pop. Code 5
Pinellas SD 52
Supt. – See Clearwater
ES, 300 ST PETERSBURG DR W   34677
  Sadie Brown, prin.

Old Town, Dixie Co.
Dixie SD 15
Supt. – See Cross City
ES, RURAL ROUTE 03 BOX 1   32680
  Lacy Vaughan, prin.

Oneco, Manatee Co., Pop. Code 5
Manatee SD 41
Supt. – See Bradenton
ES, P O BOX 668   34264 – Tim Kolbe, prin.

Community Christian School, P O BOX 968   34264

Opa-Locka, Dade Co., Pop. Code 7
Dade SD 13
Supt. – See Miami
Carol City JHS, 3737 NW 188TH ST   33055
  Robert Smith, prin.
Parkway JHS, 2349 NW 175TH ST   33056
  Fridolin Damianos, prin.
Brentwood ES, 3101 NW 191ST ST   33056
  Rosemarie Jaworski, prin.
Bunche Park ES, 16001 BUNCHE PARK DR   33054
  Ruby Johnson, prin.
Carol City ES, 4375 NW 173RD DR   33055
  Jimmie Brown, prin.
Crestview ES, 2201 NW 187TH ST   33056
  Jill Witlin, prin.
Golden Glades ES, 16520 NW 28TH AVE   33176
  Anna Jackson, prin.
Lake Stevens ES, 5101 NW 183RD ST   33055
  Robert Keiser, prin.
Miami Gardens ES, 4444 NW 195TH ST   33055
  Lew Leon, prin.
Myrtle Grove ES, 3125 NW 176TH ST   33056
  Cecil Daniels, prin.
North Carol City ES, 19010 NW 37TH AVE   33056
  Dorothy Sawyer, prin.
North County ES, 3250 NW 207TH ST   33056
  Gertrude Pope, prin.
North Glade ES, 5000 NW 177TH ST   33055
  Herbert Day, prin.
ES, 600 AHMAD ST   33054 – Ada Barnes, prin.
Parkview ES, 17631 NW 20TH AVE   33056
  Paul Shannon, prin.
Rainbow Park ES, 15355 NW 19TH AVE   33054
  Robert Thomas, prin.
Skyway ES, 4555 NW 206TH TER   33055
  Frederica Wilson, prin.
Young ES, 14120 NW 24TH AVE   33054
  Annie Brown, prin.

Our Lady of Perpetual Help ES
  13400 NW 28TH AVE   33054
St. Monica ES, 3490 NW 191ST ST   33056

Orange City, Voulsia Co., Pop. Code 5
Volusia SD 64
Supt. – See De Land
ES, 555 E UNIVERSITY AVE   32763
  Gerald Gill, prin.

Orange Park, Clay Co., Pop. Code 6
Clay SD 10
Supt. – See Green Cove Springs
Cherry ES, 420 EDSON DR   32073
  Roy Philemon, prin.
Grove Park ES, 1643 MILLER ST   32073
  Dale Eichorn, prin.

Jennings ES, 215 CORONA DR   32073
  William Turner, prin.
Lakeside ES, 2752 MOODY RD   32073
  Mary Bethea, prin.
Montclair ES, 2398 MOODY RD   32073
  Don Thmpson, prin.
ES, 1401 PLAINFIELD AVE   32073
  Donald Sohm, prin.
Ridgeview ES, 421 JEFFERSON AVE   32065
  Lucian Paulk, prin.

St. Johns Country Day School
  3100 DOCTORS LAKE DRIVE   32073

Orlando, Orange Co., Pop. Code 9
Orange SD 48
  Sch. Sys. Enr. Code 8
Supt. – Dr. James Schott, P O BOX 271   32802
Carver ES, 4500 COLUMBIA ST   32811
  Ernest Bradley, prin.
Conway MS, 4600 ANDERSON ROAD   32806
  Beth Provancha, prin.
Howard MS, 800 E ROBINSON ST   32801
  Glennis Terry, prin.
Jackson MS
  1103 STONEWALL JACKSON ST   32807
  Jones Dabbs, prin.
Lee MS, 1201 MAURY ROAD   32804
  Lynn Lyons, prin.
Liberty MS, 3405 S CHICASAW TRAIL   32825
  Rex Hart, prin.
Lockhart MS, 3411 DOCTOR LOVE ROAD   32810
  Otto Dickman, prin.
Meadowbrook MS, 6000 NORTH LANE   32808
  Jack Holton, prin.
Memorial MS, 2220 W MICHIGAN ST   32805
  Mary Bailey, prin.
Robinswood MS, 6305 BALBOA DRIVE   32818
  Myron Singhaus, prin.
Union Park MS, 1844 WESTFALL DRIVE   32817
  Robert Bruce, prin.
Walker MS, 150 AMIDON LANE   32809
  Edward Makovec, prin.
Westridge MS, 3800 W OAK RIDGE ROAD   32809
  Ralph Smith, prin.
Audubon Park ES, 1500 FALCON DR   32803
  Peggy Rivers, prin.
Azalea Park ES, 1 CAROL AVE   32807
  Ralph Hewitt, prin.
Blankner ES, 720 E KALEY AVE   32806
  Cynthia Kiffer, prin.
Bonneville ES, 13020 SUSSEX DR   32826
  Mary Fedler, prin.
Catalina ES, 2510 GULFSTREAM RD   32805
  Anthony Hollimon, prin.
Cheney ES, 2000 N FORSYTH RD   32807
  Bill McDaniels, prin.
Chickasaw ES, 6900 AUTUMNVALE DR   32822
  Lucinda Waldron, prin.
Columbia ES
  16850 COLUMBIA SCHOOL ROAD   32820
  Donald Richardson, prin.
Conway ES, 4100 LAKE MARGARET DR   32812
  Charlotte Barolet, prin.
Cypress Park ES, 9601 11TH AVE   32824
  Leon Henderson,Jr., prin.
Deerwood ES
  1356 S ECONLOCKHATCHEE TRL   32825
  Lois Begley, prin.
Dover Shores ES
  1200 GASTON FOSTER RD   32812
  James Kaiser, prin.
Durrance ES, 7700 BENRUS ST   32827
  William James, prin.
Eccleston ES, 1500 AARON AVE   32811
  John Lang, prin.
Englewood ES, 900 ENGEL DR   32807
  Mildred Dunlap, prin.
Fern Creek ES, 1121 N FERNCREEK AVE   32803
  Edwina Carter, prin.
Grand Avenue ES, 800 GRAND ST   32805
  Gustav Roess, prin.
Hiawassee ES, 6800 HENNEPIN BLVD   32818
  Jeraldine Ware, prin.
Hillcrest ES, 1010 E CONCORD ST   32803
  Preston Kizer, prin.
Ivey Lane ES, 209 SILVERTON ST   32811
  Lorraine Harris, prin.
Kaley ES, 1600 E KALEY AVE   32806
  Amilda Hogue, prin.
Lake Como ES, 901 S BUMBY AVE   32806
  Janice Weems, prin.
Lake Silver ES, 2401 N RIO GRANDE AVE   32804
  Dr. Stephen Leggett, prin.
Lake Weston ES, 5500 MILAN DR   32810
  Zada Hamilton, prin.
Lancaster ES, 6700 SHERYL ANN DR   32809
  Donald Richardson, prin.
Lockhart ES, 7500 EDGEWATER DR   32810
  Joanne Loggins, prin.
McCoy ES, 5225 S SEMORAN BLVD   32822
  Dr. Marie Davis, prin.
Metor West ES, 1801 LAKE VILMA DR   32811
  Vicki Brooks, prin.
Oak Hill ES, 11 S HIAWASSEE RD   32811
  Cleveland Henry, prin.
Orange Center ES, 621 S TEXAS AVE   32805
  Felton Johnson, prin.
Orlo Vista ES, 3 N HASTINGS ST   32811
  Frank Keller, prin.
Palmetto ES, 2015 DUSKIN AVE   32809
  Cora Shellman, prin.
Palm Lake ES, 8000 PINE OAK DR   32819
  Carolyn Cappleman, prin.

Pershing ES, 1800 PERSHING AVE   32806
  Patricia Maher, prin.
Phillips ES, 6909 DR PHILLIPS BLVD   32819
  Dell Shadgett, prin.
Pinar ES, 3701 ANTHONY LN   32822
  Jalna O'Neil, prin.
Pine Castle ES, 905 WALTHAM AVE   32809
  Peter Gabel, prin.
Pine Hills ES, 1006 FERNDELL RD   32808
  Rosa Lee Hutchinson, prin.
Pineloch ES, 3101 WOODS AVE   32805
  Minnie Woodruff, prin.
Princeton ES, 311 W PRINCETON ST   32804
  Andrew Taylor, prin.
Ray ES, 200 BEECHER ST   32808
  Paul Mitchell, prin.
Richmond Heights ES
  2500 S VINELAND RD   32805
  Sylvester Harris,Jr., prin.
Ridgewood Park ES, 3401 PIONEER RD   32808
  Susan Kiffe, prin.
Riverside ES, 3125 PEMBROOK DR   32810
  Marlene Jackson, prin.
Rock Lake ES, 408 N TAMPA AVE   32805
  Shelia Smalley, prin.
Rolling Hills ES, 4903 DONOVAN ST   32808
  Norma Masterson, prin.
Sadler ES, 4000 W OAK RIDGE RD   32809
  Melanie Craig, prin.
Shenandoah ES, 4827 S CONWAY RD   32812
  Sylvia Boyd, prin.
Tangelo Park ES, 5115 ANZIO ST   32819
  Roy Brooks, prin.
Union Park ES, 1600 N DEAN RD   32825
  David Collins, prin.
Washington Shores ES
  944 W LAKE MANN DR   32805
  Katie Vereen, prin.
Winegard ES, 7055 WINEGARD RD   32809
  John Rowland, prin.
Other Schools – See Apopka, Eatonville, Maitland,
  Ocoee, Windermere, Winter Garden, Winter Park,
  Zellwood

Downey Christian School, P O BOX 27040   32867
Eastland Christian School
  6000 E COLONIAL DRIVE   32807
Heritage Prep School
  6000 W COLONIAL DRIVE   32808
Lake Highland Prep School
  901 HIGHLAND AVE   32803
Orlando Christian School
  4161 N POWERS DRIVE   32818
Pine Hills Christian Academy
  5020 DEAUVILLE DRIVE   32808
Good Shepherd ES, 5902 OLEANDER DR   32807
Orlando Jr. Academy, 30 E EVANS ST   32804
St. Andrew ES, 877 N HASTINGS ST   32808
St. Charles ES, 4005 EDGEWATER DR   32804
St. James Cathedral ES
  505 E RIDGEWOOD ST   32803
St. John Vianney ES
  6200 S ORANGE BLOSSOM TRL   32809
Trinity Lutheran ES
  123 E LIVINGSTON ST   32801
West Orlando Chrstian ES
  2332 N HIAWASSEE RD   32818

Ormond Beach, Volusia Co., Pop. Code 7
Volusia SD 64
  Supt. – See De Land
ES, 100 CORBIN AVE   32074
  Margaret Hyman, prin.
Osceola ES, 100 OSCEOLA AVE   32074
  Jimmy Hogan, prin.
Pine Trail ES, 300 AIRPORT RD   32074
  Thomas Vitale, prin.
Tomoka ES, 999 OLD TOMOKA RD   32074
  W. L. Mullens, prin.

St. Brendan ES, 136 BANYAN DR   32074

Osteen, Volusia Co.
Volusia SD 64
  Supt. – See De Land
ES, P O BOX 2022AA   32764
  Marcella Osteen, prin.

Oviedo, Seminole Co.
Seminole SD 59
  Supt. – See Sanford
Jackson Heights MS, 141 ACADEMY AVE   32765
  Bobby Rainey, prin.
Tuskawilla MS, 1801 TUSKAWILLA ROAD   32765
  Gene Brewer, prin.
Lawton ES, 151 GRAHAM AVE   32765
  Michael Mizwicki, prin.
Stenstrom ES
  1800 ALAFAYA WOODS BLVD   32765
  Norman Ragsdale, prin.

St. Luke's Lutheran ES
  2025 W ST ROAD 426   32765

Pace, Milton Co.
Santa Rosa SD 57
  Supt. – See Milton
MS, P O BOX 2000   32570 – Thomas Sims, prin.
Dixon ES, 401 PACE RD   32571
  Larry Blackwell, prin.

Pahokee, Palm Beach Co., Pop. Code 6
Palm Beach SD 50
  Supt. – See West Palm Beach
ES, 560 E MAIN PL   33476 – Barbara Case, prin.

Palatka, Putnam Co., Pop. Code 7
Putman SD 54
  Sch. Sys. Enr. Code 7
Supt. – C. L. Overturf, Jr., 200 S 7TH ST   32077
Beasley MS, 900 S 18TH ST   32077
  William Black, prin.
Jenkins MS, 1100 N 19TH ST   32077
  Robert Holiday, prin.
Long ES, RURAL ROUTE 06 BOX 5600   32077
  Wayne Mangum, prin.
Mellon ES, 301 MELLON RD   32077
  Janice Browning, prin.
Moseley ES, 1100 HUSSON AVE   32077
  Jim Holt, prin.
Smith Community ES
  RURAL ROUTE 04 BOX 460   32077
  Douglas Grant, prin.
Other Schools – See Crescent City, East Palatka,
  Interlachen, Melrose

Palm Bay, Brevard Co., Pop. Code 7
Brevard SD 5
  Supt. – See Rockledge
Columbia ES, 1225 WACO ST SE   32907
  Larry Kuhn, prin.
Lockmar ES, 1789 SW PEPPER   32905
  Donald Grabach, prin.
McAuliffe ES, 155 DEL MUNDO ST NW   32907
  Norma Murphy, prin.
ES, 1200 ALAMANDA RD NE   32905
  Joseph Padula, Jr., prin.
Turner ES, 3175 JUPITER BLVD SE   32909
  Joseph Obrien, prin.

St. Joseph's Catholic ES
  5320 BABCOCK ST NE   32905

Palm Beach, Palm Beach Co., Pop. Code 6
Palm Beach SD 50
  Supt. – See West Palm Beach
ES, COCONUT ROW AND SEAVIEW AVE   33480
  (—), prin.

Palm Beach Day ES, 241 SEAVIEW AVE   33480

Palm Beach Gardens, Palm Beach Co., Pop. Code 7
Palm Beach SD 50
  Supt. – See West Palm Beach
Watkins JHS, 9480 MCARTHUR BLVD   33403
  Donalt Rott, prin.
Allamanda ES, 10300 ALAMANDA DR   33410
  Amelia Murgio, prin.
ES, 10060 RIVERSIDE DR   33410
  Victoria Gibson, prin.

St. Mark's Episcopal ES, 3395 BURNS RD   33410

Palm City, Martin Co.
Martin SD 43
  Supt. – See Stuart
ES, 1951 SW 34TH ST   34990 – Nancy Marin, prin.

Palm Coast, Flagler Co.
Flagler SD 18
  Supt. – See Bunnell
Wadsworth MS, P O BOX 3010   32037
  Nancy Willis, prin.

Palmetto, Manatee Co., Pop. Code 6
Manatee SD 41
  Supt. – See Bradenton
Lincoln MS, 1400 1ST AVE E   34221
  Richard Bills, prin.
Blackburn ES, 3904 17TH ST E   34221
  Cecilia Hysmith, prin.
Palm View ES, 6025 BAYSHORE RD   34221
  Robert Doyle, prin.
ES, 719 9TH AVE W   34221 – Glenna Shields, prin.
Tillman MS, 1415 29TH ST E   34221
  Ted Williams, prin.

Palm Harbor, Pinellas Co., Pop. Code 5
Pinellas SD 52
  Supt. – See Clearwater
MS, 1800 STATE ROAD 584   33563
  (—), prin.
Curlew Creek ES, 3030 CURLEW RD   34684
  David Morrow, prin.
Cypress Woods ES
  4900 CYPRESS WOODS BLVD   34685
  Robert Bouffard, prin.
Ozona ES, 525 PENNSYLVANIA AVE   34683
  Mary Sanchez, prin.
ES, 415 15TH ST   34683 – Ralph Mays, prin.
Sutherland ES, 3150 BELCHER RD   34683
  Dr. Richard Bernard, prin.

Palm Harbor Montessori ES
  2313 NEBRASKA AVE   34683

Palm Springs, Palm Beach Co., Pop. Code 6
Palm Beach SD 50
  Supt. – See West Palm Beach
Kirklane ES, 4200 PURDY LN   33461
  Clifford Taylor, prin.

Panama City, Bay Co., Pop. Code 8
Bay SD 3
  Sch. Sys. Enr. Code 7
Supt. – Leonard Hall, P O BOX 820   32401
Brown MS, S HIGHWAY 231   32404
  Thomas Bowers, prin.
Everitt MS, 608 SCHOOL AVE   32401
  David Creel, prin.
Jinks MS, 600 W 11TH ST   32401
  Shirley Jackson, prin.

Rosenwald MS, 924 BAY AVE 32401
  Eli Campbell, prin.
Callaway ES, 7115 E HIGHWAY 22 32404
  George Cornett, prin.
Cedar Grove ES, 2826 E 15TH ST 32405
  Dr. Sue Cochran, prin.
Harris MS, 819 E 11TH ST 32401
  Mary McLain, prin.
Hiland Park ES, 2507 E BALDWIN RD 32405
  A. Richbourg, prin.
Hutchinson Beach ES, 560 STATE RD 30-C 32407
  Joel Armstrong, prin.
Merriam Cherry Street ES
  1125 CHERRY STREET 32401 – Joe Bullock, prin.
Milville ES, 203 N EAST AVE 32401
  Dr. Stephanie Gall, prin.
Moore ES, 1900 MICHIGAN AVE 32405
  Dewey McQuagge, prin.
Northside ES, 2001 NORTHSIDE DR 32405
  Gerald Taylor, prin.
Oakland Terrace ES, 2010 W 12TH ST 32401
  Curtis Pittman, prin.
Parker ES, 640 S HIGHWAY 22-A 32404
  Herbert McFatter, prin.
Patterson ES, 1025 REDWOOD AVE 32401
  Mary McLain, prin.
Springfield ES, 520 SCHOOL AVE 32401
  Robert Cain, prin.
Other Schools – See Lynn Haven, Southport, Tyndall
  Air Base, West Bay, Youngstown

Good Shepherd Lutheran ES
  P O BOX 10322 32404
St. John Catholic ES, 1005 FORTUNE AVE 32401

Paxton, Walton Co., Pop. Code 3
Walton SD 66
Supt. – See De Funiak Springs
S, P O BOX 1168 32538 – Virginia Pridgen, prin.

Pembroke, Fort Meade Co.
Broward County SD 6
Supt. – See Fort Lauderdale
Pembroke Pines ES, 6700 SW 9TH ST 33032
  Ronald Adderley, prin.

Pembroke Pines, Broward Co., Pop. Code 1
Broward County SD 6
Supt. – See Fort Lauderdale
Pines MS, 200 N DOUGLAS ROAD 33024
  Fran Bolden, prin.
Pasadena Lakes ES
  8801 PASADENA BLVD 33024
  Frances Lewis, prin.
Pembroke Lakes ES, 11251 TAFT ST 33026
  Harold Osborn, prin.
Pines Lake ES, 10300 JOHNSON ST 33026
  Ronald Herbert, prin.

Pensacola, Escambia Co., Pop. Code 8
Escambia SD 17
Sch. Sys. Enr. Code 8
Supt. – Mike Holloway, P O BOX 1470 32597
Bellview MS, 6201 MOBILE HIGHWAY 32506
  Charles Mccurley, prin.
Brentwood MS, 201 HANCOCK LANE 32503
  Dr. C. Payton, prin.
Brown-Barge Magnet MS
  151 E FAIRFIELD DR 32503 – Camille Barr, prin.
Brownsville MS, 1800 N KIRK ST 32505
  Thomas Frazier, prin.
Ferry Pass MS, 8355 YANCEY AVE 32514
  Jerome Watson, prin.
Wedgewood MS
  3420 W PINESTEAD ROAD 32505
  Elvin McCorvey, prin.
Workman MS, 6299 LANIER DRIVE 32504
  Janice Wiliamson, prin.
Bellview ES, 4425 BELLVIEW AVE 32506
  Edgar Massey, prin.
Beulah ES, 6201 HELMS RD 32506
  (—), prin.
Bibbs MS, 2005 N 6TH AVE 32503
  Debbie Rees, prin.
Brentwood ES, 4820 N PALAFOX ST 32505
  Otha Leverette III, prin.
Cook ES, 1100 E CERVANTES ST 32501
  Sharon Pugh, prin.
Cordova Park ES, 2250 SEMUR RD 32503
  Charles Thomas, prin.
Dixon MS, 1201 N H ST 32501
  Suzanne Angstadt, prin.
Edgewater ES, 100 BOEING ST 32507
  Dr. Virginia Abercrombie, prin.
Ensley ES, 501 E JOHNSON AVE 32514
  Robert Cary, prin.
Ferry Pass ES, 8310 N DAVIS HWY 32514
  Gene Dunn, prin.
Goulding ES, 1403 W CROSS ST 32501
  Robert Powell, prin.
Hallmark ES, 115 S E ST 32501
  Marjorie Anderson, prin.
Holm ES, 6101 LANIER DR 32504
  Mary Stanley, prin.
Lincoln Park ES, 7600 KERSHAW DR 32514
  Malachi Williams, prin.
Longleaf ES, RURAL ROUTE 10 BOX 538 32506
  Douglas Garber, prin.
McArthur ES
  RURAL ROUTRE 03 BOX 170 32504
  Martha Lyle, prin.
Montclair ES, 820 MASSACHUSETTS AVE 32505
  Joan Ennis, prin.
Myrtle Grove ES, 6116 LILLIAN HWY 32506
  Jo Alice Tarwater, prin.

Navy Point ES, 1050 GULF BEACH HWY 32507
  Betty Thorson, prin.
Oakcrest ES, 1820 HOLLYWOOD ST 32505
  Carl Ashby, prin.
Pine Meadow ES, 10001 OMAR AVE 32514
  Larry Rich, prin.
Pleasant Grove ES, 3000 OWEN BELL LN 32507
  (—), prin.
Scenic Heights ES
  3801 CHERRY LAUREL DR 32504
  Dr. Clarence Ladner, prin.
Semmes ES, 1250 E TEXAR DR 32503
  Lawrence Scott, prin.
Sherwood ES, P O BOX 3357 32516
  James Pace, prin.
Suter ES, 2900 E STRONG ST 32503
  Dr. Gavin Thorsen, prin.
Weis MS, 2701 N Q ST 32505
  Robert Hatcher, prin.
West Pensacola ES, 801 N 49TH AVE 32506
  Ernest Thorne, prin.
Yniestra ES, 2315 W JACKSON ST 32505
  Gwendol Talbot, prin.
Other Schools – See Cantonment, Century, Warrington

Liberty Christian School, P O BOX 3138 32506
Pensacola Christian School, P O BOX 18000 32523
Little Flower Catholic ES, P O BOX 3008 32516
Sacred Heart ES, 1603 N 12TH AVE 32503
St. John Evangelist ES, 325 S NAVY BLVD 32507
St. Michael ES, 601 N PALAFOX ST 32501
St. Paul ES, 3121 HYDE PARK RD 32503

Perrine, Dade Co.

Our Lady of Holy Rosary ES
  18455 FRANJO RD 33157

Perry, Taylor Co., Pop. Code 6
Taylor SD 62
Sch. Sys. Enr. Code 5
Supt. – Glenda Hamby, P O BOX 509 32347
Taylor County JHS, 318 N CLARK ST 32347
  James Bowden, prin.
Morse ES, 800 W ASH ST 32347
  Tim Tripp, prin.
MS, 508 AQUANALDO AVE 32347
  C. T. Burgess, prin.
PS, 400 N CLARK ST 32347 – Clyde Cruce, prin.
Other Schools – See Steinhatchee

Pierson, Volusia Co., Pop. Code 4
Volusia SD 64
Supt. – See De Land
ES, 1 W 1ST AVE 32080 – Geneva Sylvester, prin.

Pinellas Park, Pinellas Co., Pop. Code 8
Pinellas SD 52
Supt. – See Clearwater
MS, 6940 70TH AVE 34665
  Patricia Goodwin, prin.
Cross Bayou ES, 6886 102ND AVE 34666
  Craig Anderson, prin.
Pinellas Central ES, 10501 58TH ST 34666
  Marie Shipley, prin.
ES, 7575 53RD ST 34665 – Sally Smith, prin.
Skyview ES, 8601 60TH ST 34666
  Ernest Pierce,Jr., prin.

Sacred Heart ES, 7951 46TH WAY 34665

Pinetta, Madison Co.
Madison SD 40
Supt. – See Madison
ES, P O BOX 98 32350 – Donald Winterton, prin.

Plantation, Broward Co., Pop. Code 8
Broward County SD 6
Supt. – See Fort Lauderdale
MS, 6000 W SUNRISE BLVD 33313
  Kenneth Perkins, prin.
Seminole ES, 6200 SW 16TH ST 33317
  Douglas Parrish, prin.
Mirror Lake ES, 1200 NW 72ND AVE 33313
  Ronald Broman, prin.
Peters ES, 851 NW 68TH AVE 33317
  Linda Freebairn, prin.
ES, 301 NW 46TH AVE 33317
  Andrew O'Connell, prin.
Plantation Park ES, 875 SW 54TH AVE 33317
  Fran Welch, prin.
Tropical ES, 1500 SW 66TH AVE 33317
  Melanie Hiatt, prin.

American Heritage School
  12200 W BROWARD BLVD 33325
Broward Christian School
  1490 N FLAMINGO ROAD 33323
St. Gregory ES, 200 N UNIVERSITY DR 33324

Plant City, Hillsborough Co., Pop. Code 7
Hillsborough SD 29
Supt. – See Tampa
Bryan ES-Plant City, 2006 W OAK AVE 33566
  Barbara Franques, prin.
Burney-Simmons ES, 903 S EVERS ST 33566
  Joyce Haines, prin.
Cork ES, 3501 CORK RD 33566
  Constance Gilbert, prin.
Jackson ES, 502 E GILCHRIST ST 33566
  James Rodgers, prin.
Knights ES, 4815 N KEEN RD 33566
  Sadye Martin, prin.
Lincoln MS, 1207 E RENFRO ST 33566
  Robert Hall, prin.

Marshall JHS, 18 S MARYLAND AVE 33566
  George Montzt, prin.
Robinson ES
  4801 S TURKEY CREEK ROAD 33566
  Dennis Higgins, prin.
Springhead ES, 3208 S NESMITH RD 33566
  George Snapp, prin.
Trapnell ES, 1605 W TRAPNELL RD 33566
  Ruth Tyre, prin.
Wilson ES, 1602 N FRANKLIN ST 33566
  R. Joyce Gatlin, prin.

Hope Lutheran School, 2001 PARK ROAD 33566

Point Washington, Walton Co.
Walton SD 66
Supt. – See De Funiak Springs
Bay ES 32454 – Delene Sholes, prin.

Polk City, Polk Co., Pop. Code 3
Polk SD 53
Supt. – See Bartow
ES, 125 S BOUGAINVILLEA AVE 33868
  Darlene Bruner, prin.

Pompano Beach, Broward Co., Pop. Code 8
Broward County SD 6
Supt. – See Fort Lauderdale
Crystal Lake MS, 3551 NE 3RD AVE 33064
  Norbert Williams, prin.
MS, 310 NE 6TH ST 33060 – Dan Okeefe, prin.
Silverlakes MS
  7600 TAM O'SHANTER BLVD 33068
  Paulette McLane, prin.
Broadview ES, 1800 SW 62ND AVE 33068
  Warren Smith, prin.
Cresthaven ES, 801 NE 25TH ST 33064
  Stephen Wolner, prin.
Cypress ES, 851 SW 3RD AVE 33060
  Jacquelyn Vernon, prin.
Drew ES, 2600 NW 9TH CT 33069
  Hubert Lee, prin.
Markham ES, 1501 NW 15TH AVE 33069
  Dorothy Wooten, prin.
McNab ES, 1350 SE 9TH AVE 33060
  Elda Corby, prin.
Norcrest ES, 3951 NE 16TH AVE 33064
  Penny Keiter, prin.
Palmview ES, 2601 NE 1ST AVE 33064
  Pernell Wright, prin.
Park Ridge ES, 5200 NE 9TH AVE 33064
  Nathaniel Hankerson, prin.
ES, 700 NE 13TH AVE 33060 – William Bell, prin.
Sanders Park ES, 800 NW 16TH ST 33060
  Sidney Ditkowski, prin.
Tedder ES, 4157 NE 1ST TER 33064
  William Smith, prin.

Highlands Christian Academy
  501 NE 48TH ST 33064
Hope Lutheran ES, 1840 NE 41ST ST 33064
St. Coleman ES, 2250 SE 12TH ST 33064
St. Elizabeth ES, 901 NE 33RD ST 33064

Ponce De Leon, Holmes Co., Pop. Code 2
Holmes SD 30
Supt. – See Bonifay
ES, RURAL ROUTE 02 BOX 232C 32455
  Gerald Commander, prin.

Ponte Vedra Beach, Saint Johns Co.
St. John's SD 55
Supt. – See Saint Augustine
Ponte Verda-Palm Valley ES, P O BOX 658 32082
  Robert Allten,Jr., prin.

Port Charlotte, Charlotte Co., Pop. Code 7
Charlotte SD 8
Supt. – See Punta Gorda
JHS, 700 MIDWAY BLVD NE 33952
  David Holt, prin.
Armstrong ES, 22100 BREEZESWEPT AVE 33952
  Joan Stancil, prin.
Meadow Park ES, 3131 LAKE VIEW BLVD 33948
  Thomas Herdtner, prin.

St. Charles Borromeo ES
  21505 AUGUSTA AVE 33952

Port Orange, Volusia Co., Pop. Code 7
Volusia SD 64
Supt. – See De Land
ES, 402 DUNLAWTON AVE 32019
  Sharon Porter, prin.
Spruce Creek ES, 642 TAYLOR RD 32019
  Albert Bouie, prin.
Sugar Mill ES, 1101 CHARLES ST 32019
  David Morgan, prin.

Port Saint Joe, Gulf Co., Pop. Code 5
Gulf SD 23
Sch. Sys. Enr. Code 4
Supt. – B. Walter Wilder
  CO COURTHOUSE 32456
Highland View ES, 102 SEVENTH ST 32456
  Sara Joe Wooten, prin.
ES, 2201 LONG AVE 32456 – Gerald Lewter, prin.
Other Schools – See Wewahitchka

Port Saint Lucie, St. Lucie Co., Pop. Code 4
St. Lucie SD 56
Supt. – See Fort Pierce
Northport MS, 250 NW FLORESTA DRIVE 34983
  John Townsend, prin.
Bayshore ES, 1661 SW BAYSHORE DR 34983
  Henry Parish, prin.

Floresta ES, 1501 SE FLORESTA DR 34983
  Gordon Archer, prin.
Morningside ES, 2300 SE GOWIN DR 34952
  David Owens, prin.
Village Green ES, 1700 SE LENNARD RD 34952
  Mary Mosley, prin.
Windmill Point ES, 700 SW DARWIN BLVD 34953
  Charles Hill, prin.

Princeton, Dade Co.

Princeton Christian School, P O BOX 4299 33092

Punta Gorda, Charlotte Co., Pop. Code 6
Charlotte SD 8
Sch. Sys. Enr. Code 7
Supt. – Robert Bedford
  1016 EDUCATION ST 33950
JHS, 825 CARMALITA ST 33950
  Rene DesJardins, prin.
East ES, 27050 FAIRWAY DR 33982
  Jack Stroup, prin.
Jones ES, 1221 COOPER ST 33950
  Gayle Dean, prin.
Liberty ES, 370 ATWATER ST 33954
  Robert Alwood, prin.
Peace River ES, 22400 HANCOCK AVE 33980
  Peggy Jividen, prin.
Other Schools – See Port Charlotte, Rotonda West

Quincy, Gadsden Co., Pop. Code 6
Gadsden SD 20
Sch. Sys. Enr. Code 6
Supt. – Robert Bryant, P O BOX 818 32351
Carter-Paramore MS, 631 S STEWART ST 32351
  Napolia White, prin.
Greensboro ES
  RURAL ROUTE 01 BOX 172 32351
  Lester Black, prin.
Gretna ES, RURAL ROUTE 01 BOX 34 32351
  Rosa Barkely, prin.
Munroe ES, 1850 W KING ST 32351
  Charles Boyd, prin.
St. John's ES, P O BOX 186 32351
  Vivian Kelly, prin.
Stewart Street ES, 831 S STEWART ST 32351
  Douglas Black, prin.
Other Schools – See Chattahoochee, Havana

Munroe Day School
  RURAL ROUTE 05 BOX 35 32351

Reddick, Marion Co., Pop. Code 3
Marion SD 42
Supt. – See Ocala
Reddick-Collier ES, P O BOX 159 32686
  Gary Miller, prin.

Riverview, Hillsborough Co., Pop. Code 4
Hillsborough SD 29
Supt. – See Tampa
ES, 10809 HANNAWAY DR 33569
  Sheila Jarsonbeck, prin.

Providence Christian School
  5416 PROVIDENCE ROAD 33569

Riviera Beach, Palm Beach Co., Pop. Code 8
Palm Beach SD 50
Supt. – See West Palm Beach
Kennedy JHS, 1901 AVENUE S 33404
  Clifford Durden, prin.
Lincoln ES, 1160 W 10TH ST 33404
  Thomas Smith, prin.
ES, 200 W 12TH ST 33404 – Edward Bohne, prin.
Washington ES, 1709 W 30TH ST 33404
  Dr. David Horan, prin.
West Riviera ES, 1057 W 6TH ST 33404
  Michael Murgio, prin.

St. Francis Assisi ES, 100 W 20TH ST 33404

Rockledge, Brevard Co., Pop. Code 7
Brevard SD 5
Sch. Sys. Enr. Code 8
Supt. – Lloyd Soughers
  1260 FLORIDA AVE S 32955
Kennedy MS, 2100 FISKE BLVD S 32955
  James Adams, prin.
Anderson ES, 3011 FISKE BLVD S 32955
  Audrey Sullivan, prin.
Golfview ES, 1530 FISKE BLVD S 32955
  Vicki Osborne, prin.
Other Schools – See Cape Canaveral, Cocoa, Cocoa
  Beach, Indialantic, Indian Harbor Beach,
  Melbourne, Melbourne Beach, Merritt Island,
  Mims, Palm Bay, Satellite Beach, Titusville

St. Mary's Catholic School
  1152 SEMINOLE DR 32955

Rotonda West, Charlotte Co.
Charlotte SD 8
Supt. – See Punta Gorda
Ainger JHS, 245 CONCORD ROAD 33946
  William Strickland, prin.
Vineland ES, 467 BOUNDARY BLVD 33947
  Barbara Hargrove, prin.

Royal Palm Beach, Palm Beach Co., Pop. Code 5
Palm Beach SD 50
Supt. – See West Palm Beach
Crestwood Community MS
  64 SPARROW DRIVE 33411
  William Hagan, prin.

Johnson Community ES, 100 REDWOOD DR 33411
  Elizabeth Killetts, prin.

Ruskin, Hillsborough Co., Pop. Code 4
Hillsborough SD 29
Supt. – See Tampa
ES, 101 COLLEGE AVE E 33570
  Jospeh Green, prin.

Ruskin Christian School
  820 COLLEGE AVE W 33570

Safety Harbor, Pinellas Co., Pop. Code 6
Pinellas SD 52
Supt. – See Clearwater
MS, 125 7TH ST N 34695 – Sally Barker, prin.
ES, 535 5TH AVE N 34695 – Elaine Cutler, prin.

Saint Augustine, St. Johns Co., Pop. Code 7
St. John's SD 55
Sch. Sys. Enr. Code 7
Supt. – Otis Mason, P O BOX 500 32085
Ketterlinus MS, 75 ORANGE ST 32084
  Lionel Key,Jr., prin.
Murray MS, P O BOX 3588 32085
  Harriette Coffee, prin.
Crookshank ES, 250 N WHITNEY ST 32084
  Delores Rowley, prin.
Fullerwood ES, 10 HILDRETH DR 32084
  Gwen Reichert, prin.
Hamblen ES, 16 ISABEL ST 32084
  Frederic Allen, prin.
Hartley ES, 260 RIVERA BLVD 32086
  Patricia Roberson, prin.
Hunt ES, MAGNOLIA DR 32084
  Robert Taylor, prin.
Mill Creek ES, 3720 NINE MILE RD 32092
  Charles Moore, prin.
Webster ES, 146 N ORANGE ST 32084
  James Coffee, prin.
Other Schools – See Hastings, Jacksonville, Ponte
  Vedra Beach

Cathedral Parish ES
  259 SAINT GEORGE ST 32084

Saint Cloud, Osceola Co., Pop. Code 6
Osceola SD 49
Supt. – See Kissimmee
MS, 1975 MICHIGAN AVE 32769
  Gary Morgensen, prin.
Hickory Tree ES, 2801 HICKORY TREE RD 32769
  Virginia Phillips, prin.
Jeffries ES, 1200 VERMONT AVE 32769
  John Beall, prin.
Lakeview ES, 2900 W 5TH ST 32769
  Jim Digiacomo, prin.
Michigan Avenue ES
  2015 MICHIGAN AVE 32769
  Boscom Fawbush, prin.

Saint Petersburg, Pinellas Co., Pop. Code 9
Pinellas SD 52
Supt. – See Clearwater
Azalea MS, 7855 22ND AVE N 33710
  John Leanes, prin.
Bay Point MS, 2151 62ND AVE S 33712
  Ronald Zay, prin.
Lealman Comprehensive MS
  4100 35TH ST N 33714 – Scotty East, prin.
Meadowlawn MS, 5900 16TH ST N 33703
  John Singletary, prin.
Riviera MS, 501 62ND AVE NE 33702
  Lou Graves, prin.
Sixteenth Street MS, 701 16TH ST S 33705
  Victoria Desmond, prin.
Tyrone MS, 6421 22ND AVE N 33710
  Paul Brown, prin.
Azalea ES, 1680 74TH ST N 33710
  Merrill Dietzer, prin.
Bay Point ES, 2051 62ND AVE S 33712
  Robert Welch, prin.
Bay Vista ES, 5900 9TH ST S 33705
  Dr. Robert Lavely, prin.
Bear Creek ES, 350 61ST ST S 33707
  Cyrus Everette, prin.
Blanton ES, 6400 54TH AVE N 33709
  Roberts Evers, prin.
Campbell Park ES, 1101 7TH AVE S 33705
  James Steen, prin.
Childs Park Fundamental ES
  3836 21ST AVE S 33711 – Elizabeth Danner, prin.
Clearview Avenue ES, 3815 43RD ST N 33714
  Frank Martin, prin.
Fairmount Park ES, 575 41ST ST S 33711
  Virginia Ammon, prin.
Gulf Beaches ES, 8600 BOCA CIEGA DR 33706
  Robert Sokolowski, prin.
Lakeview Fundamental ES, 2229 25TH ST S 33712
  John Thompson, prin.
Lakewood ES, 4151 6TH ST S 33705
  Willene Givens, prin.
Lealman Avenue ES, 4001 58TH AVE N 33714
  Clarice Pennington, prin.
Lynch ES, 1901 71ST AVE N 33702
  Arthur Fernandez, prin.
Maximo ES, 4850 31ST ST S 33712
  Paula Lamb, prin.
Melrose ES, 1752 13TH AVE S 33712
  Ronald Hallam, prin.
Mt. Vernon ES, 4629 13TH AVE N 33713
  James Lott, prin.
North Ward ES-St. Petersburg
  11TH AVE & 4TH ST N 33701 – Ann Rainey, prin.

North Shore ES, 3500 OAK ST NE 33704
  Johnny Welch, prin.
Northwest ES, 5601 22ND AVE N 33710
  Lorraine Meister, prin.
Norwood ES, 2154 27TH AVE N 33713
  Ken Obryant, prin.
Pasadena ES, 95 72ND ST N 33710
  Winifred Pfister, prin.
Perkins ES, 2400 QUEENSBORO AVE S 33712
  Larry Kelley, prin.
Rio Vista ES, 8131 MACOMA DR NE 33702
  Marion Plichcinski, prin.
Seventy-Fourth Street ES, 3801 74TH ST N 33709
  Robert Riel, prin.
Shore Acres ES, 1800 62ND AVE NE 33702
  Louis McCoy, prin.
Tyrone ES, 2401 66TH ST N 33710
  Gail Morrison, prin.
Westgate ES, 35609 58TH ST N 33710
  Olney Arnold, prin.
Woodlawn ES, 1600 16TH ST N 33704
  Leonard Kizner, prin.

Bible Speaks Christian School
  P O BOX 12728 33733
Canterbury School of Florida
  901 58TH AVE NE 33703
Keswick Christian School
  10101 54TH AVE N 33708
Northside Christian School
  7777 62ND AVE N 33709
Shorecrest Prep School, 5101 1ST ST NE 33703
Thom Howard Academy, 4500 43RD ST N 33714
Grace Lutheran ES, 4301 16TH ST N 33703
Holy Family ES, 250 78TH AVE NE 33702
Most Holy Name of Jesus School
  5825 17TH AVE S 33706
St. John ES, 500 84TH AVE 33706
St. Jude Cathedral ES, 600 58TH ST N 33710
St. Paul Catholic ES, 1900 12TH ST N 33704
St. Raphael ES, 1376 SNELL ISLE BLVD NE 33704
Transfiguration Parish ES, 4000 43RD ST N 33714

San Antonio, Pasco Co., Pop. Code 3

St. Anthony ES, P O BOX 847 33576

Sanford, Seminole Co., Pop. Code 7
Seminole SD 59
Sch. Sys. Enr. Code 8
Supt. – Robert W. Hughes
  1211 S MELLONVILLE AVE 32771
Lakeview MS, 100 LAKEVIEW AVE 32771
  Richard Mossman, prin.
MS, 1700 S FRENCH AVE 32771
  Dan Pellham, prin.
Goldsboro ES, 1300 W 20TH ST 32771
  Lorraine Offer, prin.
Hamilton ES, 1501 E 8TH ST 32771
  Carem Gager, prin.
Idyllwilde ES, 430 VIHLEN RD 32771
  Carolyn Towles, prin.
Midway ES, 2321 JITWAY AVE 32771
  Leroy Hampton, prin.
Pine Crest ES, 405 W 27TH ST 32773
  Tim Seibert, prin.
Wilson ES, 985 S ORANGE BLVD 32771
  Terry Rabun, prin.
Other Schools – See Altamonte Springs, Apopka,
  Casselberry, Fern Park, Geneva, Lake Mary,
  Longwood, Oviedo, Winter Park, Winter Springs

All Souls ES, 810 S OAK AVE 32771

Sanibel Island, Lee Co., Pop. Code 5
Lee SD 36
Supt. – See Fort Myers
Sanibel ES, 3840 SANIBEL-CAPTIVA RD 33957
  Barbara Ward, prin.

Sarasota, Sarasota Co., Pop. Code 8
Manatee SD 41
Supt. – See Bradenton
Abel ES, 7100 MADONNA PL 34243
  Joyce Hurkman, prin.

Sarasota SD 58
Sch. Sys. Enr. Code 8
Supt. – Dr. Charles W. Fowler
  2418 HATTON ST 34237
Booker MS, 3601 N ORANGE AVE 34234
  Diane Riva, prin.
Brookside MS, 3636 S SHADE AVE 34239
  Dr. Tom Bohlinger, prin.
McIntosh MS, 701 MCINTOSH ROAD 34232
  Allen Wilson, prin.
MS, 1001 S SCHOOL AVE 34237
  Mary Moore, prin.
Alta Vista ES, 2589 ALTA VISTA ST 34237
  Barry Napshin, prin.
Ashton ES, 5110 ASHTON RD 34233
  John Zoretich, prin.
Bay Haven ES, 2901 W TAMIAMI CIR 34234
  Marilyn Highland, prin.
Booker ES, 3400 N ORANGE AVE 34234
  Jerome Dupree, prin.
Brentwood ES, 2500 VINSON AVE 34232
  Sandra Russell, prin.
Fruitville ES, 601 HONORE AVE 34232
  Vincent Laurini, prin.
Gocio ES, 3450 GOCIO RD 34235
  Carlotta Cooley, prin.
Gulf Gate ES
  6500 S LOCKWOOD RIDGE RD 34231
  Barbara Stahlschmidt, prin.

Lakeview ES, 7299 PROCTOR RD 34241
  Jan Coleman, prin.
Philippi Shores ES, 4747 S TAMIAMI TRL 34231
  Lowell Hockett, prin.
Southside ES, 1901 WEBBER ST 34239
  John Spielman III, prin.
Tuttle ES, 925 N BRINK AVE 34237
  Charlotte Hartwell, prin.
Wilkinson ES, 3400 WILKINSON RD 34231
  William Muth, prin.
Other Schools – See Englewood, Nokomis, North Port, Venice

Sarasota Christian School
  5415 BABIA VISTA ST 34232
West Florida Christian School
  4311 WILKINSON ROAD 34233
Incarnation ES, 2911 BEE RIDGE RD 34239
St. Martha ES, 801 N ORANGE AVE 34236

Satellite Beach, Brevard Co., Pop. Code 6
  Brevard SD 5
  Supt. – See Rockledge
  Holland ES, 50 HOLLAND CT 32937
    Constance St. John, prin.
  Sea Park ES, 300 SEA PARK BLVD 32937
    H. Sylvester, prin.
  Surfside ES, 401 CASSIA BLVD 32937
    William Hall, prin.

Sebastian, Indian River Co., Pop. Code 5
  Indian River SD 31
  Supt. – See Vero Beach
  Pelican Island ES, 1355 SCHUMANN DR 32958
    William Kulp, prin.
  ES, COUNTY ROAD 512 32958
    Mark Dugan, prin.

Sebring, Highland Co., Pop. Code 6
  Highlands SD 28
  Sch. Sys. Enr. Code 6
  Supt. – Ruth Handley, 426 SCHOOL ST 33870
  MS, 500 E CENTER AVE 33870
    Wallace Cox, prin.
  Sun N Lake ES, 4515 PONCE DE LEON 33870
    Edward Pipon, prin.
  Wild ES, 1910 S HIGHLANDS AVE 33870
    Patricia Landress, prin.
  Woodlawn ES, 718 FIELDER BLVD 33870
    Ellis Watson, prin.
  Other Schools – See Avon Park, Lake Placid

New Prospect Private School
  P O BOX 1418 33871

Seffner, Hillsborough Co., Pop. Code 3
  Hillsborough SD 29
  Supt. – See Tampa
  Lopez ES, 200 KINGSWAY RD N 33584
    Harris Carter, prin.
  McDonald ES, 501 PRUITT RD 33584
    Paul Edwards, prin.
  ES, 109 CACTUS RD 33584 – George Wagner, prin.

Seminole, Pinellas Co., Pop. Code 5
  Pinellas SD 52
  Supt. – See Clearwater
  Osceola MS, 9301 98TH ST 34647
    Dr. Robert Jackson, prin.
  MS, 8701 131ST ST 34646 – Charles Mock, prin.
  Orange Grove ES, 10300 65TH AVE 34642
    Charles Craig, prin.
  ES, 10950 74TH AVE 34642 – John Wuertz, prin.

Blessed Sacrament ES, 11501 66TH AVE 34642

Seville, Volusia Co.
  Volusia SD 64
  Supt. – See De Land
  ES, P O BOX 129 32090 – James McGinn, prin.

Shalimar, Okaloosa Co., Pop. Code 2
  Okaloosa SD 46
  Supt. – See Crestview
  Longwood ES, HOLLY AVE 32579
    Earl Childers, prin.
  ES, EGLIN PKWY 32579 – Philip Brogden, prin.

Silver Springs, Marion Co.
  Marion SD 42
  Supt. – See Ocala
  East Marion ES, P O BOX 928 32688
    Scott Hackmyer, prin.

Sneads, Jackson Co., Pop. Code 4
  Jackson SD 32
  Supt. – See Marianna
  ES, P O BOX 369 32460 – Virginia Blount, prin.

Sopchoppy, Wakulla Co., Pop. Code 2
  Wakulla SD 65
  Supt. – See Crawfordville
  ES, P O BOX 68 32358 – H. Mark Coyle, prin.

South Bay, Palm Beach Co., Pop. Code 5
  Palm Beach SD 50
  Supt. – See West Palm Beach
  Rosenwald ES, 1321 W PALM BEACH RD 33493
    Earlyne Harrell, prin.

South Daytona, Volusia Co., Pop. Code 6
  Volusia SD 64
  Supt. – See De Land
  ES, 600 ELIZABETH PL 32019
    Marlin Marcum, prin.

Warner Christian Academy
  1730 RIDGEWOOD AVE S 32019

South Miami, Dade Co., Pop. Code 7
  Dade SD 13
  Supt. – See Miami
  Ludham ES, 6639 SW 74TH ST 33143
    Donald Schwartz, prin.
  ES, 6800 SW 60TH ST 33143
    Lottie Downie, prin.

Southport, Bay Co.
  Bay SD 3
  Supt. – See Panama City
  ES, P O BOX 8000Q 32409 – Jerry Register, prin.

Sparr, Marion Co., Pop. Code 2
  Marion SD 42
  Supt. – See Ocala
  ES, P O BOX 539 32690 – Lamar Holder, prin.

Spring Hill, Hernando Co.
  Hernando SD 27
  Supt. – See Brooksville
  West Hernando MS
    9412 FOX CHAPEL LANE 34606
    Dennis McGeehan, prin.
  Floyd ES, 3139 DUMONT AVE 34609
    Janet Yungmann, prin.
  Pine Grove ES, 6000 ROBLE AVE 34608
    Michael Tellone, prin.
  ES, 6000 ROBLE AVE 34608
    Janet Dunleavy, prin.
  Westside ES, 5400 APPLEGATE DR 34606
    John Donato, prin.

  St. Theresa School, 1117 SUZANNE DR 34606

Starke, Bradford Co., Pop. Code 5
  Bradford SD 4
  Sch. Sys. Enr. Code 5
  Supt. – F. James Duncan
    582 N TEMPLE AVE 32091
  Bradford MS, 527 N ORANGE ST 32091
    John Mazzella, prin.
  Southside ES, 823 STANSBURY ST 32091
    Jesse J. Moore, prin.
  ES, 501 W WASHINGTON ST 32091
    Wayne McLeod, prin.
  Other Schools – See Brooker, Hampton, Lawtey

Steinhatchee, Dixie Co.
  Taylor SD 62
  Supt. – See Perry
  ES, P O BOX A 32359 – Joan Cooey, prin.

Stuart, Martin Co., Pop. Code 6
  Martin SD 43
  Sch. Sys. Enr. Code 7
  Supt. – V. James Navitsky, P O BOX 1049 34995
  Murray MS, 4400 SE MURRAY ST 34997
    Frank Brogan, prin.
  MS, 575 GEORGIA AVE 34994
    Shirley Granfield, prin.
  Parker ES, 1050 E 10TH ST 34996
    Bert Dubose, prin.
  Port Salerno ES, 4890 SE JACK ST 34997
    Marian Carpenter, prin.
  Other Schools – See Hobe Sound, Indiantown, Jensen Beach, Palm City

Redeemer Lutheran ES
  2450 SE OCEAN BLVD 34996
St. Joseph ES, 1200 E 10TH ST 34996
St. Michael's ES, 1300 E 10TH ST 34996

Sugar Loaf Key, Monroe Co.
  Monroe SD 44
  Supt. – See Key West
  Sugarloaf ES, RURAL ROUTE 02 33042
    (—), prin.

Summerfield, Marion Co.
  Marion SD 42
  Supt. – See Ocala
  Lake Weir MS, RURAL ROUTE 02 BOX 363 32691
    Jewett Springer, prin.

Sunrise, Broward Co., Pop. Code 8
  Broward County SD 6
  Supt. – See Fort Lauderdale
  Bair MS, 9100 NW 21ST MANOR 33322
    Kim Reid, prin.
  Banyan ES, 8800 NW 50TH ST 33351
    Brian Kohli, prin.
  Horizon ES, 2101 PINK ISLAND ROAD NW 33322
    Alonzetta Gibson, prin.
  Nob Hill ES, 2100 NW 104TH AVE 33322
    Joy Prescott, prin.
  Sandpiper ES, 5000 NW 94TH AVE 33351
    Cheri Zahn, prin.
  Village ES, 2100 NW 70TH AVE 33313
    Joanne Harrison, prin.

Tallahassee, Leon Co., Pop. Code 8
  Leon SD 37
  Sch. Sys. Enr. Code 8
  Supt. – Charles Couch
    2757 W PENSACOLA ST 32304
  Belle Vue MS, 2214 BELLE VUE WAY 32304
    Norman Ingram, prin.
  Cobb MS, 915 HILLCREST ST 32308
    Paul Green, prin.
  Fairview MS, 3415 ZILLAH ST 32301
    Kae Ingram, prin.

Griffin MS, 800 ALABAMA ST 32304
  Henry Murphy, prin.
Nims MS, 723 W ORANGE AVE 32304
  Dr. Nickie Beasley, prin.
Raa ES, 401 W THARPE ST 32303
  Marvin Henderson, prin.
Apalachee ES, 650 TROJAN TRL 32301
  Rachel Hammerly, prin.
Astoria Park ES, 2465 ATLAS RD 32303
  Alice Caswell, prin.
Bond ES, 2204 SAXON ST 32310
  Bill Johnson, prin.
Brevard ES, 2006 JACKSON BLUFF RD 32304
  Gloria Poole, prin.
Chaires ES, CHAIRES RD 32301
  Jeff Patterson, prin.
Ft. Braden ES, HCR 02 BOX 8224 32304
  Cleta Griffith, prin.
Gilchrist ES, 695 TIMBERLANE RD 32312
  Frank LaPorta, prin.
Hartsfield ES, 1414 CHOWKEEBIN NENE 32301
  Donald Chambers, prin.
Killearn Lakes ES, 8037 DEERLAKE E 32312
  Doris Jones, prin.
Moore ES, RURAL ROUTE 17 32308
  Shirley Eikeland, prin.
Oak Ridge ES, 4530 SHELFER RD 32310
  Georgia Greene, prin.
Pineview ES, 2230 LAKE BRADFORD RD 32310
  Ruth Hobbs, prin.
Riley ES, 1400 INDIANA ST 32304
  Zaheerah Shakir, prin.
Ruediger ES, 526 W 10TH AVE 32303
  Sam Alderman, prin.
Sabal Palm ES, 2813 RIDGEWAY ST 32310
  Hal Pitts, prin.
Sealey ES, 2815 ALLEN RD 32312
  Frank Voran, prin.
Springwood ES, 3801 FRED GEORGE RD 32303
  Doris Payne, prin.
Sullivan ES, 927 MICCOSUKEE RD 32308
  Nancy Duden, prin.
Wesson ES, 28013 S MERIDIAN ST 32301
  Nancy Russell, prin.
Other Schools – See Woodville

Lake Jackson Christian Academy
  3617 OLD BAINBRIDGE ROAD 32303
MacLay Day School
  3737 N MERIDIAN ROAD 32312
Holy Comforter Episcopal ES
  1500 MICCOSUKEE RD 32308
Trinity Catholic ES, 706 E BREVARD ST 32308

Tamarac, Broward Co., Pop. Code 8
  Broward County SD 6
  Supt. – See Fort Lauderdale
  ES, 7601 N UNIVERSITY DR 33321
    Patricia Rancati, prin.

St. Malachy ES, 7595 NW 61ST ST 33321

Tampa, Hillsborough Co., Pop. Code 10
  Hillsborough SD 29
  Sch. Sys. Enr. Code 9
  Supt. – Dr. Raymond Shelton
    P O BOX 3408 33601
  Alexander ES, 5602 N LOIS AVE 33614
    Elaine Diaz, prin.
  Anderson ES, 3910 W FAIR OAKS AVE 33611
    Dalia Jimenez, prin.
  Ballast Point ES
    2802 W BALLAST POINT BLVD 33611
    Linda Dortch, prin.
  Bay Crest ES, 4925 WEBB RD 33615
    Jennifer Kori, prin.
  Bellamy ES, 9720 WILSKY BLVD 33615
    B. Lamar Hammer, prin.
  Blake JHS, 1125 W SPRUCE ST 33607
    Calvin Bexley, prin.
  Broward ES, 400 W OSBORNE AVE 33603
    Beverly DeMott, prin.
  Bryan MS-Tampa
    2934 E HILLSBOROUGH AVE 33610
    O. Jack McMillan, prin.
  Cahoon ES, 2312 E YUKON ST 33604
    Beverly Parslow, prin.
  Carrollwood ES, 3516 MCFARLAND RD 33618
    Nancy Goldsmith, prin.
  Chiaramonte ES, 6001 S HIMES AVE 33611
    Beverly Weaver, prin.
  Citrus Park ES, 7700 GUNN HWY 33625
    Betty Alfano, prin.
  Clair-Mel ES, 1025 S 78TH ST 33619
    Rose-Ann Paar, prin.
  Claywell ES, 4500 NORTHDALE BLVD 33624
    Thomas Dessy, prin.
  Cleveland ES, 723 E HAMILTON AVE 33604
    Phyllis Lee, prin.
  Crestwood ES, 8110 N MANHATTAN AVE 33614
    Patsy Sissle, prin.
  DeSoto ES, 2618 CORRINE ST 33605
    Rose Chilura, prin.
  Dickenson ES, 4720 KELLY RD 33615
    Dennis Reed, prin.
  Dunbar MS, 1730 W UNION ST 33607
    Geraldine Smith, prin.
  Edison ES, 1607 E CURTIS ST 33610
    Sylvia Hornsby, prin.
  Egypt Lake ES, 6707 N GLEN AVE 33614
    Larry Moore, prin.
  Essrig ES, 13031 LYNN RD 33625
    Virginia Urbanek, prin.

Forest Hills ES, 10112 N OLA AVE 33612
 Ruby Wright, prin.
Foster ES, 2014 E DIANA ST 33610
 Kenneth Cathcart, prin.
Franklin JHS, 3915 E 21ST AVE 33605
 Anthony Satchel, prin.
Gorrie ES, 705 W DE LEON ST 33606
 Marilyn Wittner, prin.
Grady ES, 3910 W MORRISON AVE 33629
 Faye Pages, prin.
Graham ES
 2915 N MASSACHUSETTS AVE 33602
 James Pardo, prin.
Just MS, 1315 W SPRUCE ST 33607
 Lois Bowers, prin.
Kenly ES, 2909 N 66TH AVE 33619
 Shirley Trujillo, prin.
Lake Magdalene ES, 2002 PINE LAKE DR 33612
 Marian Peterson, prin.
Lanier ES, 4704 W MONTGOMERY AVE 33616
 Harry Schmidt, prin.
Lee MS, 305 E COLUMBUS DR 33602
 Michele Gregory, prin.
Lockhart MS, 1714 E LAKE AVE 33610
 Watts Sanderson, prin.
Lomax ES, 4207 N 26TH ST 33610
 Flossie Geathers, prin.
Mabry ES, 4201 W ESTRELLA ST 33629
 Myrna Robinson, prin.
Mendenhall ES, 5202 N MENDENHALL DR 33603
 Glenda Midili, prin.
Miles ES, 317 E 124TH AVE 33612
 J. Anthony Scolaro, prin.
Mitchell ES, 205 S BUNGALOW PARK AVE 33609
 Joseph Trumbach, prin.
Morgan Woods ES, 7001 ARMAND DR 33634
 Pearl Hojnacki, prin.
Mort ES, 1806 SKIPPER ROAD 33613
 Clarine Suarez, prin.
Northwest ES, 16438 HUTCHINSON RD 33625
 K. Lynn Wade, prin.
Oak Grove JHS, 6315 N ARMENIA AVE 33604
 Mary Padgett, prin.
Oak Park ES, 4916 E 10TH AVE 33605
 Jack Davis, prin.
Orange Grove MS, 3415 N 16TH ST 33605
 Nelson Luis, prin.
Palm River ES, 805 S MAYDELL DR 33619
 Millicent Davidson, prin.
Potter ES, 3224 E CAYUGA ST 33610
 Brenda Thompson, prin.
Progress Village ES, 8113 ZINNIA DR 33619
 Wilma Stone, prin.
Robles ES, 4405 E SLIGH AVE 33610
 Barbara Jefferson, prin.
Roland Park ES
 1510 N MANHATTAN AVE 33607
 Anthony Perrone, prin.
Roosevelt ES, 3205 S FERDINAND AVE 33629
 Richard Blandy, prin.
Seminole ES, 6201 N CENTRAL AVE 33604
 Ruth Ann Reynolds, prin.
Shaw ES, 11311 N 15TH ST 33612
 Helen Cathcart, prin.
Shore MS, 1908 E 2ND AVE 33605
 Olan Hill, prin.
Sligh JHS, 2011 E SLIGH AVE 33610
 Rudolph Ondrula, prin.
Sulphur Springs ES, 8412 N 13TH ST 33604
 Stephanie Moffitt, prin.
Tampa Bay Boulevard ES
 3111 W TAMPA BAY BLVD 33607
 Mary Lasris, prin.
Town and Country ES, 6025 HANLEY RD 33634
 Barbara Santana, prin.
Twin Lakes ES, 8507 N HABANA AVE 33614
 Mary Libroth, prin.
Washington JHS, 1407 ESTELLE ST 33605
 Barbara Harvey, prin.
West Shore ES, 7110 S WESTSHORE BLVD 33616
 Harriet Foundas, prin.
West Tampa ES, 2700 W CHERRY ST 33607
 Carl Barone, prin.
Williams ES, 4302 E ELLICOTT ST 33610
 Eloise Cabrera, prin.
Witter ES, 10801 N 22ND ST 33612
 Joann Shaw, prin.
Woodbridge ES, 8301 WOODBRIDGE BLVD 33615
 Richard Martinez, prin.
Young JHS, 1807 E BUFFALO AVE 33610
 Margaret Fisher, prin.
Other Schools — See Apollo Beach, Brandon, Dover,
 Gibsonton, Lithia, Lutz, Mac Dill AFB, Mango,
 Plant City, Riverview, Ruskin, Seffner, Temple
 Terrace, Thonotosassa, Valrico, Wimauma

Academy of the Holy Names
 3319 BAYSHORE BLVD 33629
Berkeley Prep School, 4811 KELLY ROAD 33615
Mary Help of Christians ES
 6400 E CHELSEA ST 33610
Temple Heights Christian School
 8406 N 46TH ST 33617
Academy of Holy Names ES
 3319 BAYSHORE BLVD 33629
Christ the King ES
 3809 W MORRISON AVE 33629
Incarnation Catholic ES, 5111 WEBB RD 33615
Most Holy Redeemer ES
 302 E LINEBAUGH AVE 33612
Sacred Heart ES, 3515 N FLORIDA AVE 33603
Seminole Presbyterian ES
 6101 N HABANA AVE 33614

St. Joseph Parish ES, 2200 N GOMEZ AVE 33607
St. Lawrence Parish ES
 5223 N HIMES AVE 33614
St. Mary's Episcopal ES
 2101 S HUBERT AVE 33629
St. Patrick Catholic ES
 4518 S MANHATTAN AVE 33611
St. Peter Claver ES, 1401 N GOVERNOR ST 33602
Villa Madonna School
 315 W COLUMBUS DR 33602

Tarpon Springs, Pinellas Co., Pop. Code 7
Pinellas SD 52
Supt. — See Clearwater
MS, 501 N FLORIDA AVE 34689
 Lawrence Goodbread, prin.
Sunset Hills ES, 1513 GULF RD 34689
 William Brewer, prin.
Tarpon Springs Fundamental ES
 400 E HARRISON ST 34689
 Marilyn Dennison, prin.
ES, 525 N DISSTON AVE 34689
 Harold Lane, prin.

Tavares, Lake Co., Pop. Code 5
Lake SD 35
Sch. Sys. Enr. Code 7
Supt. — Fred Garner
 210 W BURLEIGH BLVD 32778
MS, 1201 E IANTHE ST 32778 — Jerry Cox, prin.
ES, 520 E CLIFFORD ST 32778
 Robert Crawford, prin.
Other Schools — See Altoona, Clermont, Eustis,
 Fruitland Park, Groveland, Leesburg, Mascotte,
 Mount Dora, Umatilla

Tavernier, Monroe Co., Pop. Code 4
Monroe SD 44
Supt. — See Key West
Plantation Key ES, 100 LAKE RD 33070
 Sandi Bisceglia, prin.

Temple Terrace, Hillsborough Co., Pop. Code 7
Hillsborough SD 29
Supt. — See Tampa
Lewis ES, 6700 E WHITEWAY DR 33617
 Sonya Endicott, prin.
Riverhills ES, 405 S RIVERHILLS DR 33617
 Barbara English, prin.
ES, 124 FLOTTO AVE 33617 — Ann Huntley, prin.

Corpus Christi ES, 9715 N 56TH ST 33617

Thonotosassa, Hillsborough Co.
Hillsborough SD 29
Supt. — See Tampa
ES, 855 SKEW LEE RD 33592 — Louis Kota, prin.

Titusville, Brevard Co., Pop. Code 8
Brevard SD 5
Supt. — See Rockledge
Jackson MS, 1515 KNOX MCRAE DRIVE 32780
 Clifford Estes, prin.
Madison MS, 3375 DAIRY ROAD 32796
 Nathan Brown,Jr., prin.
Appolo ES, 3085 KNOX MCRAE DR 32780
 Dr. Barbara Row, prin.
Coquina ES, 850 KNOX MCRAE DR 32780
 Robert Jones, prin.
Imperial Estates ES, 5525 KATHY DR 32780
 Alice Graves, prin.
Oakpark ES, 3395 DAIRY RD 32796
 (—), prin.
Riverview ES, 3000 JOLLY ST 32780
 Willie Turner, prin.
South Lake ES, 3755 GARDEN ST 32796
 Frank Tomdale, prin.

St. Teresa Catholic School, P O BOX 1599 32781

Trenton, Gilchrist Co., Pop. Code 4
Gilchrist SD 21
Sch. Sys. Enr. Code 4
Supt. — Ray E. Thomas, P O BOX 67 32693
S, P O BOX 7 32693 — James Surrency, prin.
Other Schools — See Bell

Tyndall Air Base, Bay Co.
Bay SD 3
Supt. — See Panama City
Tyndall ES, TYNDALL A F B 32403
 John May, prin.

Umatilla, Lake Co., Pop. Code 4
Lake SD 35
Supt. — See Tavares
MS, 340 OAK AVE 32784 — Mickey Marks, prin.
ES, P O BOX B 32784 — David Tucker, prin.

Valparaiso, Okaloosa Co., Pop. Code 6
Okaloosa SD 46
Supt. — See Crestview
ES, 379 EDGE AVE 32580
 Robert McEachern, prin.

Valrico, Hillsborough Co.
Hillsborough SD 29
Supt. — See Tampa
Alafia ES, 3535 BRANDYBROOK DR 33594
 Grace Ippolito, prin.
Buckhorn ES, 1717 MILLER RD S 33594
 Evelyn Clites, prin.

Venice, Sarasota Co., Pop. Code 7
Sarasota SD 58
Supt. — See Sarasota

Venice Area MS, 1900 CENTER ROAD 34292
 Guy Bennett, prin.
Garden ES, 700 CENTER RD 34292
 Mark Cook, prin.
ES, 301 BAHAMA ST 34285 — Emile Quinn, prin.

Epiphany Catholic ES, 316 SARASOTA ST 34285

Vernon, Washington Co., Pop. Code 3
Washington SD 67
Supt. — See Chipley
MS, 210 JACKSON 32462 — Ruth McCray, prin.
ES 32462 — Hugh Balboni, prin.

Vero Beach, Indian River Co., Pop. Code 7
Indian River SD 31
Sch. Sys. Enr. Code 7
Supt. — James A. Burns, 1990 25TH ST 32960
Beachland ES, 3351 MOCKINGBIRD DR 32963
 Coyla Boob, prin.
Citrus ES, 2771 CITRUS RD 32962
 Celeste Rinehart, prin.
Dodgertown ES, 4350 43RD AVE 32967
 Bonnie Swanson, prin.
Glendale ES, 4840 8TH ST 32962
 Barry Sesack, prin.
Highlands ES, 500 20TH ST SW 32962
 Kathryn Wilson, prin.
Indian River Gifford MS, 4695 28TH AVE 32967
 Dr. Julius Teske, prin.
Indian River Gifford MS, 2726 45TH ST 32960
 Dr. Eddie Hudson, prin.
Osceola ES, 665 20TH ST 32960
 Pat Palmer, prin.
Rosewood ES, 3850 16TH ST 32960
 Roy Howard, prin.
Thompson ES, 1110 18TH AVE SW 32962
 Dale Klaus, prin.
ES, 1770 12TH ST 32960 — Godfrey Gipson, prin.
Other Schools — See Fellsmere, Sebastian

St. Edward's School, 246 S A1A 32963
St. Helen ES, 2050 VERO BEACH AVE 32960

Waldo, Alachua Co., Pop. Code 3
Alachua SD 1
Supt. — See Gainesville
Waldo Community ES, P O BOX 190 32694
 John Fielding, prin.

Warrington, Escambia Co., Pop. Code 7
Escambia SD 17
Supt. — See Pensacola
MS, 450 S OLD CORRY FIELD ROAD 32507
 Frank Willis, prin.
ES, 220 N NAVY BLVD 32507
 Marie Young, prin.

Redeemer Lutheran ES
 333 COMMERCE ST 32507

Wauchula, Hardee Co., Pop. Code 5
Hardee SD 25
Sch. Sys. Enr. Code 5
Supt. — Peggy Shackelford, P O BOX 1678 33873
Hardee JHS, 300 S FLORIDA AVE 33873
 Lee Burns, prin.
North Wauchula ES, N FLORIDA AVE 33873
 David Durastanti, prin.
MS, 400 S FLORIDA AVE 33873
 Mike Wilkinson, prin.
Other Schools — See Bowling Green, Zolfo Springs

Webster, Sumter Co., Pop. Code 3
Sumter SD 60
Supt. — See Bushnell
South Sumter MS
 RURAL ROUTE 02 BOX 994 33597
 Dr. Preston Morgan, prin.
ES, 300 S MARKET BLVD 33597
 Richard Shirley, prin.

Weirsdale, Marion Co.
Marion SD 42
Supt. — See Ocala
Stanton-Weirsdale ES, P O BOX 207 32695
 Bob Saunders, prin.

West Bay, Bay Co.
Bay SD 3
Supt. — See Panama City
ES, P O BOX 98 32407 — James Fuqua, prin.

West Palm Beach, Palm Beach Co., Pop. Code 8
Palm Beach SD 50
Sch. Sys. Enr. Code 8
Supt. — Thomas Mills
 3323 BELVEDERE ROAD 33406
Conniston JHS, 673 CONNISTON ROAD 33405
 Hugh Brady, prin.
Davis MS, 1560 KIRK ROAD 33406
 Wayne Nagy, prin.
Golfview JHS, 4260 W GATE AVE 33409
 R. Aiello, prin.
Roosevelt JHS, 1601 N TAMARIND AVE 33407
 Joseph Littles, prin.
Wellington Landings Community MS
 1100 AERO CLUB DR 33414
 Dr. Jo Reynolds, prin.
Belvedere ES, 3001 S LAKE AVE 33405
 Jamesena Marshall, prin.
Berkshire ES, 1060 KIRK RD 33406
 Margaret Brockmiller, prin.
Forest Hill ES, 5555 PURDY LN 33415
 Kathleen Gustafson, prin.

Meadow Park ES
956 FLORIDA MANGO RD   33406
Dr. James Pingrey, prin.
Melaleuca ES, 5759 W GUN CLUB RD   33415
Kenneth Tose, prin.
Northboro ES, 400 40TH ST   33407
Charles Shaw, prin.
Northmore ES, 4111 N TERRACE DR   33407
Kathryn Ryberg, prin.
Palmetto ES, 835 PALMETTO ST   33405
Samuel Cameron, prin.
Palmview ES, 800 11TH ST   33401
Ulysses Kinsey, prin.
Roosevelt ES, 1220 15TH ST   33401
Geneva Price, prin.
South Olive ES, 7101 S OLIVE AVE   33405
Dr. Kenneth Swain, prin.
Southboro ES, 524 OGSTON ST   33405
Dr. Joanne Kaiser, prin.
Wellington Community ES
1300 PADDOCK DR   33414
Francis Spooner, prin.
West Gate ES, 1545 LOXAHATCHEE DR   33409
Bruce Costanzo, prin.
Westward ES, 1101 GOLF AVE   33401
(—), prin.
Wynnebrook ES, 1167 DREXEL RD   33417
Allen Carnahan, prin.
Other Schools – See Belle Glade, Boca Raton, Boynton
Beach, Canal Point, Delray Beach, Greenacres City,
Jupiter, Lake Park, Lake Worth, Lantana,
Loxahatchee, North Palm Beach, Pahokee, Palm
Beach, Palm Beach Gardens, Palm Springs, Riviera
Beach, Royal Palm Beach, South Bay

Berean Christian School
8350 OKEECHOBEE BLVD   33411
Kings Academy, 4215 CHERRY ROAD   33409
Rosarian Academy, 807 N FLAGLER DRIVE   33401
Summit Christian School
4900 SUMMIT BLVD   33415
Holy Name of Jesus ES
345 S MILITARY TRL   33415
St. Ann Catholic ES, 324 N OLIVE AVE   33401
St. Juliana ES, 326 PINE TER   33405
Wee Wisdom Montessori ES
1957 S FLAGLER DR   33401
Wellington Christian ES
1000 WELLINGTON TRCE   33414

Westville, Holmes Co., Pop. Code 2
Holmes SD 30
Supt. – See Bonifay
Prosperity ES, RURAL ROUTE 03 BOX 437   32464
Woodrow Vaughan, prin.

Wewahitchka, Gulf Co., Pop. Code 4
Gulf SD 23
Supt. – See Port Saint Joe
ES, P O BOX 160   32465 – Jerry Kelley, prin.

Whitehouse, Duval Co.
Duval SD 16
Supt. – See Jacksonville
ES, 11160 GENERAL AVE   32220
James Rodgers, prin.

White Springs, Hamilton Co., Pop. Code 3
Hamilton SD 24
Supt. – See Jasper
South Hamilton ES, P O BOX B   32096
John Bullard, prin.

Wildwood, Sumter Co., Pop. Code 5
Sumter SD 60
Supt. – See Bushnell
MS, P O BOX 998   32785 – Rudy Baxter, prin.

North Sumter IS, 300 HUEY ST   32785
Josephine Strong, prin.
North Sumter PS, 104 N WARFIELD AVE   32785
Martha Ann Andrews, prin.

Williston, Levy Co., Pop. Code 4
Levy SD 38
Supt. – See Bronson
MS, 1345 NE 3RD AVE   32696
Harvey Markham, prin.
Bullock ES, 130 SW 3RD ST   32696
J. Kent Welborn, prin.

Wilton Manors, Broward Co., Pop. Code 7
Broward County SD 6
Supt. – See Fort Lauderdale
ES, 2401 NE 3RD AVE   33305
Linda Marable, prin.

Wimauma, Hillsborough Co.
Hillsborough SD 29
Supt. – See Tampa
ES, 5709 HICKMAN ST   33598 – Beny Peretz, prin.

Windermere, Orange Co., Pop. Code 4
Orange SD 48
Supt. – See Orlando
ES, 11125 PARK AVE   32786
Deborah Manuel, prin.

Winter Garden, Orange Co., Pop. Code 6
Orange SD 48
Supt. – See Orlando
Lakeview MS, 1200 W BAY ST   32787
Charlene Lyons, prin.
Dillard Street ES, 310 N DILLARD ST   32787
Elizabeth Rohrer, prin.
Maxey ES, 1100 E MAPLE ST   32787
Ted Gregory, prin.
Tildenville ES
RURAL ROUTE 02 BOX 128-D   32787
Richard Bouch, prin.

Calvary Baptist Christian School
631 S DILLARD ST   32787

Winter Haven, Polk Co., Pop. Code 7
Polk SD 53
Supt. – See Bartow
Brigham ES, 6TH & AVENUE C SE   33880
Lela Keith, prin.
Elbert ES, 205 15TH ST NE   33881
Richard Chapman, prin.
Garden Grove ES
4599 CYPRESS GARDENS RD SE   33884
Richard Dobler, prin.
Garner ES, 2500 HAVENDALE BLVD NW   33881
Charle Selph, prin.
Inwood ES, 2200 AVENUE G NW   33880
Martha Brantley, prin.
Jewett MS
2250 8TH ST NE FLRNC VL STA   33881
Alfred Hays, prin.
Jewett JHS, 601 AVE T NE   33881
Roosevelt Smith, prin.
Lake Shipp ES, 250 CAMELLIA DR SW   33880
(—), prin.
Snively ES, 1004 SNIVELY AVE   33880
Sandra Hellman, prin.
Wahneta ES, 4TH ST E WAHNETA   33880
Sallye Mccullough, prin.

Haven Christian Academy
2105 KING ROAD SW   33880
Grace Lutheran ES, 320 BATES AVE SE   33880
St. Joseph ES, 535 AVENUE M NW   33881

Winter Park, Orange Co., Pop. Code 7
Orange SD 48
Supt. – See Orlando
Glenridge MS, 800 GLENRIDGE WAY   32789
Charles Weidinger, prin.
Aloma ES, 2949 SCARLET RD   32792
Mary Hodges, prin.
Brookshire ES, 400 GREENE DR   32792
Nancy Livesay, prin.
Killarney ES, 2401 WELLINGTON BLVD   32789
Rob McNabb, prin.
Lakemont ES, 901 N LAKEMONT AVE   32792
John Harbilas, prin.

Seminole SD 59
Supt. – See Sanford
Eastbrook ES, 5525 TANGERINE AVE   32792
Mary Jane Armstrong, prin.

St. Margaret Mary ES, 142 E SWOOPE AVE   32789

Winter Springs, Seminole Co., Pop. Code 4
Seminole SD 59
Supt. – See Sanford
Keeth ES, 600 TUSKAWILLA ROAD   32708
David Sawyer, prin.
ES, 670 W HIGHWAY 434   32708
Ernest Prater, prin.

Woodville, Leon Co.
Leon SD 37
Supt. – See Tallahassee
ES, P O BOX 600   32362 – Georgia Greene, prin.

Yankeetown, Levy Co., Pop. Code 3
Levy SD 38
Supt. – See Bronson
ES, P O BOX 39   32698 – David Stone, prin.

Youngstown, Bay Co.
Bay SD 3
Supt. – See Panama City
Waller ES, P O BOX 190   32466
Thomas Marshall, prin.

Yulee, Nassau Co., Pop. Code 3
Nassau SD 45
Supt. – See Fernandina Beach
JHS, P O BOX 68   32097 – Marvin Davis, prin.
MS, P O BOX 57   32097 – Carolyn Edwards, prin.
PS, P O BOX 48   32097 – Robert Springer, prin.

Nassau Christian Academy
RURAL ROUTE 02 BOX 705 A   32097

Zellwood, Orange Co.
Orange SD 48
Supt. – See Orlando
ES, P O BOX 248   32798 – Ed Collinsworth, prin.

Zephyrhills, Pasco Co., Pop. Code 6
Pasco SD 51
Supt. – See Land O'Lakes
Stewart MS, 1007 10TH AVE   34248
Bruce Baldwin, prin.
Quail Hollow ES
200 QUAIL HOLLOW BLVD   34249
Ginny Yanson, prin.
West Zephyrhills ES, 502 14TH AVE W   34248
Jeanette Lovelace, prin.
Woodland ES, 801 HENRY DR   34248
Randall Belcher, prin.

Zolfo Springs, Hardee Co., Pop. Code 4
Hardee SD 25
Supt. – See Wauchula
Zolfo ES, SCHOOL HOUSE ROAD   33890
Monda Farmer, prin.

GEORGIA

STATE DEPARTMENT OF EDUCATION
2066 Twin Towers East, Atlanta 30334
(404) 656-2800

State Superintendent of Schools	Werner Rogers
Associate Superintendent Administrative Services	H. F. Johnson
Associate Superintendent Business/Education Partnerships	Ellis Bateman
Associate Superintendent Department Management	Bill Gambill
Associate Superintendent Evaluation & Personnel Development	Paul Vail
Associate Superintendent Instructional Programs	Peyton Williams
Associate Superintendent Special Services	Josephine Martin

STATE BOARD OF EDUCATION
James Smith, *Chairperson*   2066 Twin Towers East, Atlanta   30334

COMMITTEE ON POSTSECONDARY EDUCATION
Vacancy, *Director*   2 Martin Luther King Dr. #812, Atlanta   30334

PUBLIC, PRIVATE, AND PAROCHIAL ELEMENTARY SCHOOLS

Abbeville, Wilcox Co., Pop. Code 3
Wilcox County SD
Sch. Sys. Enr. Code 4
Supt. – Larry Gibbs   31001
ES   31001 – Alton Gibbs, prin.
Other Schools – See Pitts, Rochelle

Acworth, Cobb Co., Pop. Code 5
Cherokee County SD
Supt. – See Canton
Oak Grove ES, 6118 WOODSTOCK ROAD   30101
Don Hamrick, prin.

Cobb County SD
Supt. – See Marietta
ES, 4496 DIXIE AVE   30101 – Albert Price, prin.
Baker ES, 2361 BAKER ROAD   30101
Lynda Gruehn, prin.

Harvest Christian School
1573 ALABAMA ROAD   30101

Adairsville, Bartow Co., Pop. Code 4
Bartow County SD
Supt. – See Cartersville
ES, P O BOX 948   30103 – Terry Drew, prin.

Adel, Cook Co., Pop. Code 6
Cook County SD
Sch. Sys. Enr. Code 5
Supt. – Dr. Edward C. Leichner
1109 N PARRISH AVE   31620
Cook MS, 310 N M L KING   31620 – L. Hunt, prin.
ES, 216 E 8TH ST   31620 – Laura Hill, prin.
Other Schools – See Lenox, Sparks

Adrian, Emanuel Co., Pop. Code 3
Emanuel County SD
Supt. – See Swainsboro
ES, P O BOX 247   31002 – Dennis Whitfield, prin.

Ailey, Montgomery Co., Pop. Code 3
Montgomery County SD
Supt. – See Mount Vernon
Montgomery County MS   30410 – James Days, prin.

Alamo, Wheeler Co., Pop. Code 3
Wheeler County SD
Sch. Sys. Enr. Code 4
Supt. – William Cook, P O BOX 427   30411
Wheeler County PS, P O BOX 609   30411
Hannah Kent, prin.
Other Schools – See Glenwood

Alapaha, Berrien Co., Pop. Code 3
Berrien County SD
Supt. – See Nashville
ES, P O BOX 5   31622 – Dona Fields, prin.

Albany, Dougherty Co., Pop. Code 8
Dougherty County SD
Sch. Sys. Enr. Code 7
Supt. – Dr. William Gardner, P O BOX 1470   31702
MS, 1000 N JEFFERSON ST   31701
Jerry Clark, prin.
Dougherty MS, 1800 MASSEY DR   31705
Charles Farrell, prin.
Highland MS, 1001 HIGHLAND AVE   31708
Ted Horton, prin.

King MS, 2235 KING DRIVE   31701
Herman Phillips, prin.
Merry Acres MS, 1601 FLORENCE DR   31707
Lennis Price, prin.
Radium Springs MS
2600 RADIUM SPRINGS DR   31705
Vickie Gordy, prin.
Southside MS, 1615 NEWTON ROAD   31701
Ozell Kelley, prin.
Coachman Park ES, 1700 S MADISON ST   31701
Obzeine Shorter, prin.
Flintside ES, 2600 S JACKSON ST   31701
Stella Pete, prin.
Isabella ES, 300 S CASON ST   31705
Annette Davis, prin.
Jackson Heights MS, 1305 E 2ND AVE   31705
Ike McKinnie, prin.
King MS, 1200 M L KING JR DR   31701
Jennye Newsome, prin.
Lake Park ES, 605 MEADOWLARK DR   31707
Darlene Adams, prin.
Lincoln Fundamental ES, 700 CORN AVE   31701
JoAnne Taylor, prin.
Magnolia ES, 1700 SAMFORD DR   31707
Charles Sheppard, prin.
McIntosh MS, 518 SOCIETY AVE   31701
Lawrence Medlin, prin.
Mock Road ES, 2237 CUTTS DR   31705
James Ramsey, prin.
Morningside ES, 120 SUNSET LN   31705
Elizabeth Wolfe, prin.
Northside ES, 901 14TH AVE   31701
Dr. Bill Bates, prin.
Palmyra ES, 1225 FOUTH AVE   31707
LeAnna Walton, prin.
Radium Springs ES, 2400 ROXANNA RD   31705
Jan Henningfield, prin.
Sherwood Acres ES
2200 BARNESDALE WAY   31707
H. Henderson, prin.
Sylvandale ES, 1520 CORDELL LN   31705
Thomas Etheridge, prin.
Sylvester Road MS, 2600 TRENTON LN   31705
Theodore Cutts, prin.
Turner ES, 2001 LEONARD AVE   31705
Stephen Feit, prin.
West Town ES, 113 UNIVERSITY AVE   31707
Michael Manning, prin.

Byne Memorial Baptist Church School
313 SOCIETY AVE   31708
Deerfield-Windsor Academy
2301 STUART AVE   31707
Riverview Academy, RURAL ROUTE 05   31708
Sherwood Baptist School
2200 STUART AVE   31707
South Georgia Christian School
1731 BEATTIE RD   31707
St. Teresa School, 417 EDGEWOOD LN   31707

Alma, Bacon Co., Pop. Code 5
Bacon County SD
Sch. Sys. Enr. Code 4
Supt. – R. Johnson, 601 N PIERCE ST   31510
Bacon County MS, 16TH ST   31510
Timothy Warnock, prin.

Bacon County ES, 108 W 8TH ST   31510
Aubrey Lee, prin.

Alpharetta, Fulton Co., Pop. Code 5
Forsyth County SD
Supt. – See Cumming
Midway ES, 4805 HIGHWAY 9 N   30201
Dennis Whittle, prin.

Fulton County SD
Supt. – See Atlanta
Haynes Bridge MS
10665 HAYNES BRIDGE ROAD   30201
Gayle Giles, prin.
Holcomb Bridge MS
2700 HOLCOMB BRIDGE ROAD   30201
Janet Hopping, prin.
ES, 192 MAYFIELD ST   30201 – Doris Couch, prin.
Barnwell ES, 9425 BARNWELL RD   30201
Dr. Jane Pulling, prin.
Dolvin ES, 10495 JONES BRIDGE RD   30201
Ann Kingrea, prin.
Kimball Bridge ES
154 KIMBALL BRIDGE RD   30201
Carolyn Meeks, prin.
Northwestern ES
12760 BIRMINGHAM HWY   30201
Wilhelmina Largin, prin.

Ambrose, Coffee Co., Pop. Code 2
Coffee County SD
Supt. – See Douglas
ES, P O BOX 60   31512 – Geneva Justice, prin.

Americus, Sumter Co., Pop. Code 7
Americus ISD
Sch. Sys. Enr. Code 5
Supt. – Dr. Ronnie Williams, P O BOX 847   31709
Staley MS, 915 N LEE ST   31709
Clyde McGrady, prin.
Cherokee ES, 300 CHEROKEE ST   31709
Robin Lowrey, prin.
Cobb MS, 2000 VALLEY DR   31709
Vickie Hayes, prin.
Eastview ES, 802 ASHBY ST   31709
Betty Harris, prin.

Sumter County SD
Sch. Sys. Enr. Code 4
Supt. – Robin Johnson, P O BOX 967   31709
Sumter County ES
1982 BUMPHEAD ROAD   31709
Pat McCullough, prin.

Brooklyn Heights Christian School
1602 WASHINGTON ST   31709
Southland Academy, P O BOX 1127   31709

Appling, Columbia Co.
Columbia County SD
Sch. Sys. Enr. Code 7
Supt. – Tucker Vaughn, P O BOX 10   30802
North Columbia ES
RURAL ROUTE 01 BOX 10   30802
Amy Wright, prin.
Other Schools – See Evans, Grovetown, Harlem, Martinez

Arlington, Calhoun Co., Pop. Code 4
Calhoun County SD
Supt. – See Morgan
MS, P O BOX 556 31713 – Fred Oliver, prin.
Calhoun County ES, P O BOX T 31713
William Sanders, prin.

Ashburn, Turner Co., Pop. Code 5
Turner County SD
Sch. Sys. Enr. Code 4
Supt. – W. G. Hardin,Jr.
213 N CLEVELAND ST 31714
Turner County JHS
820 W WASHINGTON AVE 31714
Wayne Baxter, prin.
Turner County ES at Ashburn
210 GILMORE ST 31714 – Eli Reinhardt, prin.
Other Schools – See Sycamore

Athens, Clarke Co., Pop. Code 8
Clarke County SD
Sch. Sys. Enr. Code 2
Supt. – Dr. Carol Purvis, P O BOX 1708 30603
Burney-Harris-Lyons MS
440 DEARING EXT 30606 – Barbara Mathis, prin.
Clarke MS, 1235 BAXTER ST 30606
Nancy Hart, prin.
Hilsman MS, 870 GAINES SCHOOL ROAD 30605
Pat Cliffon, prin.
Alps Road ES, 200 ALPS RD 30606
Dr. Joan Humphries, prin.
Barnett Shoals ES
3220 BARNETT SHOALS RD 30605
Sherry Malone, prin.
Barrow ES, 100 PINECREST DR 30605
Lola Finn, prin.
Chase Street ES, 757 N CHASE ST 30601
Harold Horton, prin.
Fowler Drive ES, 400 FOWLER DR 30601
Dr. Sharon Denero, prin.
Gaines ES, 280 GAINES SCHOOL RD 30605
Dr. Maxine Easom, prin.
Oglethorpe Avenue ES
1150 OGLETHORPE AVE 30606
Dr. Robert Bluett, prin.
Timothy Road ES, 1900 TIMOTHY RD 30606
Tom Davis, prin.
Whitehead Road ES, 500 WHITEHEAD RD 30606
June Baldwin, prin.
Other Schools – See Winterville

Jackson County SD
Supt. – See Jefferson
South Jackson ES, RURAL ROUTE 02 30607
Marcia Tallent, prin.

Athens Academy, P O BOX 6548 30604
Athens Christian School, 1270 HWY 29 N 30601
Prince Avenue Baptist Christian School
595 PRINCE AVE 30601
St. Joseph's Catholic School
134 PRINCE AVE 30610

Atlanta, Fulton Co., Pop. Code 10
Atlanta ISD
Sch. Sys. Enr. Code 8
Supt. – J. Harris, 210 PRYOR ST SW 30303
Bunche MS, 1925 NISKEY LAKE ROAD SW 30331
Dr. Alphonso Jones, prin.
Coan MS, 1550 BOULEVARD DRIVE NE 30317
Dr. Willie Dancy, prin.
East Atlanta MS, 1820 MARY DELL DR SE 30316
Barbara Robinson, prin.
Inman MS, 774 VIRGINIA AVE NE 30306
Betty Strickland, prin.
Kennedy MS, 225 CHESTNUT ST NW 30314
Benjamin Peterson, prin.
King MS, 582 CONNALLY ST SE 30312
Leviticus Roberts, prin.
Long MS, 3200 LATONA DR SW 30354
Alger Coleman, prin.
Parks MS, 1090 WINDSOR ST SW 30310
Rosa Hadley, prin.
Price MS, 1670 CAPITOL AVE SE 30315
Robert Hall, prin.
Southwest MS, 3116 MAYS PLACE SW 30311
Dr. John Blackshear, prin.
Sutton MS
4360 POWERS FERRY ROAD NW 30327
David York, prin.
Sylvan Hills MS, 1461 SYLVAN RD SW 30310
Archie Wilson, prin.
Walden MS, 320 IRWIN ST NE 30312
Robert Morrisson, prin.
Adamsville ES, 286 WILSON MILL RD SW 30331
Alfred Ellis, prin.
Anderson Park ES
2050 TIGER FLOWERS DR NW 30314
Dr. Charles Fannings, prin.
Arkwright ES, 1261 LOCKWOOD DR SW 30311
Rebecca Jackson, prin.
Beecher Hills ES
2257 BOLLINGBROOK DR SW 30311
Dr. Henry Harris, prin.
Benteen ES, 200 CASSANOVA ST SE 30315
Eunice Robinson, prin.
Bethune ES, 220 NORTHSIDE DR NW 30314
Ercell McIver, prin.
Blalock ES, 1445 MAYNARD RD NW 30331
Dr. Robert Lowe, prin.
Boyd ES, 1891 JOHNSON RD NW 30318
Annie Neely, prin.
Brandon ES, 2741 HOWELL MILL RD NW 30327
Doris John, prin.

Brewer ES, 2352 BAGWELL DR SW 30315
William Brinkley, prin.
Burgess ES, 480 CLIFTON ST SE 30316
Samuel Bacote, prin.
Campbell ES, 21 THIRKIELD AVE SW 30315
Wardell Sims, prin.
Capitol View ES, 1442 STEWART AVE SW 30310
Dr. M. Norman, prin.
Carey ES, 1157 SIXTH ST NW 30318
Dr. David Blount, prin.
Carter ES, 80 ASHBY ST NW 30314
Charlotte Johnson, prin.
Cascade ES, 2326 VENETIAN DR SW 30311
Ozzie Quarterman, prin.
Cleveland ES, 81 CLEVELAND AVE SW 30315
Darlene Glover, prin.
Collier Heights ES, 3050 COLLIER DR NW 30318
Rosco Twiggs, prin.
Connally ES, 1654 S ALVARADO TER SW 30311
Doris Kemp, prin.
Continental Colony ES
3181 HOGAN RD SW 30331 – Ann Jones, prin.
Cook ES, 211 MEMORIAL DR SE 30312
Sidney Blackstone, prin.
Dobbs ES, 1965 LEWIS RD SE 30315
Dr. Paula Snowden, prin.
Drew ES, 409 E LAKE BLVD SE 30317
James Doanes, prin.
Dunbar ES, 403 RICHARDSON ST SW 30312
Marjorie Gosier, prin.
East Lake ES
2440 COTTAGE GROVE AVE SE 30317
Dr. Jacquelyn Ponder, prin.
English Avenue ES, 627 ENGLISH AVE NW 30318
Fred Hammonds, prin.
Fain ES, 2751 PEYTON RD NW 30318
Dr. Bortah Walton, Jr., prin.
Fickett ES, 3935 RUX RD SW 30331
L'Tanya Sloan, prin.
Fowler Street ES, 595 FOWLER ST NW 30313
Gwendolyn Mayfield, prin.
Garden Hills ES, 285 SHERIDAN DR NE 30305
Dr. Peggy Geren, prin.
Gideons ES, 897 WELCH ST SW 30310
Armstead Salters, prin.
Gordon, 1205 METROPOLITAN AVE SE 30316
Gene Chandler, prin.
Grove Park ES, 20 EVELYN WAY NW 30318
Sylvia Jones, prin.
Guice ES, 1485 WOODLAND AVE SE 30316
Barbara Culp, prin.
Harris ES, 1444 LUCILE AVE SW 30310
Carolyn Jackson, prin.
Harwell Road ES, 631 HARWELL RD NW 30318
Harvenia Hill, prin.
Herndon ES, 1075 SIMPSON RD NW 30314
Dr. Vincent Murray, prin.
Hill ES, 3844 CAMPBELLTON RD SW 30331
Margaret Gardner, prin.
Hill ES, 386 PINE ST NE 30308
Dr. Paula Calhoun, prin.
Hope ES, 112 BOULEVARD NE 30312
Wilma Blanding, prin.
Howell ES, 399 MACEDONIA RD SE 30354
Alfred Scott, prin.
Hubert ES, 1043 MEMORIAL DR SE 30316
Vivien Stocks, prin.
Humphries ES, 3029 HUMPHRIES DR SE 30354
Dr. Narvie Puls, prin.
Hutchinson ES, 650 CLEVELAND AVE SW 30315
Dr. Obadiah Jordan,Jr., prin.
Jackson ES, 1325 MOUNT PARAN RD NW 30327
Dr. Helen Branch, prin.
Jones ES, 1040 FAIR ST SW 30314
Alfonso Jessie,Jr., prin.
Kimberly ES, 3090 MCMURRAY DR SW 30311
Effie Turner, prin.
Kirkwood ES, 138 KIRKWOOD RD NE 30317
Jessie Lanier, prin.
Lakewood ES, 335 SAWTELL AVE SE 30315
Bruce Blake, prin.
Lin ES, 586 CANDLER PARK DR NE 30307
Barbara Naylor, prin.
McGill ES, 760 MARTIN ST SE 30315
Josephine Jackson, prin.
Miles ES, 4215 BAKERS FERRY RD SW 30331
Donella Byrd, prin.
Mitchell ES, 2845 M MITCHELL DR NW 30327
Joseph Pearson, prin.
Morningside ES
1053 E ROCK SPRINGS RD NE 30306
Michael Cooper, prin.
Oglethorpe ES, 601 BECKWITH ST SW 30314
Dr. Edwina Hill-Miles, prin.
Perkerson ES, 2895 LAKEWOOD AVE SW 30315
Joan Polite, prin.
Peterson ES, 1757 MARY DELL DR SE 30316
Raymond Harris, prin.
Peyton Forest ES, 301 PEYTON RD SW 30311
Deanna Davis, prin.
Pitts ES, 2210 PERRY BLVD NW 30318
William Harding, prin.
Ragsdale ES, 1114 AVON AVE SW 30310
Robert Sellers, prin.
Rivers ES
8 PEACHTREE BATTLE AVE NW 30305
Ann Burch, prin.
Rusk ES, 433 PEEPLES ST SW 30310
John Aldridge, prin.
Scott ES, 1752 HOLLYWOOD RD NW 30318
Dr. Ruth Pace, prin.
Slater ES, 1320 PRYOR RD SW 30315
Wayne Jack, prin.

Slaton ES, 688 GRANT ST SE 30315
William Sheffield, prin.
Smith ES, 370 OLD IVY RD NE 30342
Charles Pepe, prin.
Stanton ES, 1625 M L KING JR DR NW 30314
Bobby Huff, prin.
Stanton ES, 970 MARTIN ST SE 30315
Roland Yates, prin.
Sylvan Hills ES, 1757 MELROSE DR SW 30310
Reba Treon, prin.
Thomasville Heights ES
1820 HENRY THOMAS DR SE 30315
John Fouch, prin.
Toomer ES, 65 ROGERS ST NE 30317
Dr. Nellie Adams, prin.
Towns ES, 760 BOLTON RD NW 30331
Dr. Betty Clark, prin.
Venetian Hills ES, 1910 VENETIAN DR SW 30311
Cynthia May, prin.
Waters ES, 660 MCWILLIAMS RD SE 30315
James Taylor, prin.
West Atlanta ES, 1335 KIMBERLY RD SW 30331
Dr. Clifton Tinsley, prin.
West ES, 820 ESSIE AVE SE 30316
Veleria Henson, prin.
West Manor ES, 570 LYNHURST DR SW 30311
Bettye Shelling, prin.
White ES, 1890 DETROIT AVE NW 30314
Dr. Jacquelyn Daniel, prin.
Whitefoord ES, 35 WHITEFOORD AVE SE 30317
Betty Blasingame, prin.
Williams ES, 1065 WILKES CIR NW 30318
Dr. E. Norman, prin.
Woodson ES, 1605 BANKHEAD AVE NW 30318
Margaret Jacobs, prin.
Wright ES, 350 AUTUMN LN SW 30310
Norma Dawson, prin.
Other Schools – See Hapeville

DeKalb County SD
Supt. – See Decatur
Ashford Park ES
2968 CRAVENRIDGE DR NE 30319
C. Hall III, prin.
Briar Vista ES, 1131 BRIAR VISTA TER NE 30324
Forrest Stevens, prin.
Clifton ES, 3132 CLIFTON CHURCH RD SE 30316
William Diggs, prin.
Fernbank ES, 157 HEATON PARK DR NE 30307
Lloyd Shivers, prin.
Gresham Park ES, 1848 VICKI LN SE 30316
Larry Kimes, prin.
Hawthorne ES, 2535 CALADIUM DR NE 30345
Gary Durham, prin.
Henderson Mill ES
2408 HENDERSON MILL RD NE 30345
Lillian Cantrell, prin.
Kittredge Magnet MS
2383 N DRUID HILLS RD NE 30329
Steven Dunlap, prin.
Meadowview ES, 1879 WEE-KIRK RD SE 30316
Dr. Roosevelt Daniels, prin.
Montclair ES, 1680 CLAIRMONT PL NE 30329
G. Williams, prin.
Montgomery ES
3995 ASHFORD-DUNWOODY RD NE 30319
Crawford Lewis, prin.
Nancy Creek ES
1663 E NANCY CREEK DR NE 30319
Henry Hicks, prin.
Oak Grove ES, 1857 OAK GROVE RD NE 30345
Barbara Miller, prin.
Sagamore Hills ES
1865 ALDERBROOK RD NE 30345
Judith Rice, prin.
Sky Haven ES, 1372 SKY HAVEN RD SE 30316
George Moss, prin.
Terry Mill ES, 797 FAYETTEVILLE RD SE 30316
Shirley Reams, prin.
Woodward ES, 3034 CURTIS DR NE 30319
Dr. Lamar Schell, prin.

Fulton County SD
Sch. Sys. Enr. Code 8
Supt. – Dr. James Fox,Jr.
786 CLEVELAND AVE SW 30315
Ridgeview MS, 5340 TRIMBLE ROAD NE 30342
Dr. Hannah Martin, prin.
Sandy Springs MS
227 SANDY SPRINGS PLACE NE 30328
Dr. Mary Chandler, prin.
Heards Ferry ES
1050 HEARDS FERRY RD NW 30328
Amanda Dunn, prin.
High Point ES, 520 GREENLAND RD NE 30342
Michael Rossario, prin.
Sandtown ES
5320 CAMPBELLTON RD SW 30331
Frances Reeves, prin.
Spalding Drive ES, 130 SPALDING DR NE 30328
Cheryl Bogrow, prin.
Utoy Springs ES, 4001 DANFORTH RD SW 30331
Jean George, prin.
Woodland ES, 1130 SPALDING DR 30350
Larry Land, prin.
Other Schools – See Alpharetta, College Park, East
Point, Fairburn, Hapeville, Palmetto, Roswell,
Union City

Berean Academy
230 WESTVIEW PLACE SW 30314
DeKalb Christian Academy
1985 LA VISTA ROAD NE 30329
Galloway School, 215 WEST ROAD 30342

Howard School
1246 PONCE DE LEON AVE NE 30306
Lovett School
4075 PACES FERRY ROAD NW 30327
New School
6955 BRANDON MILL ROAD NW 30328
Pace Academy
966 W PACES FERRY ROAD NW 30327
Paideia School
1509 PONCE DE LEON AVE NE 30307
Westminister School
1424 W PACES FERRY ROAD NW 30327
Christ the King School
46 PEACHTREE WAY NE 30305
First Montessori School
5750 LONG ISLAND DR NW 30327
Florence Jackson Academy
1581 FAIRBURN RD SW 30331
Harry Epstein School/Atlanta
600 PEACHTREE BATTLE AV 350 30327
Hebrew Academy of Atlanta
5200 NORTHLAND DR 30342
Holy Innocents Episcopal School
805 MOUNT VERNON HWY NW 30327
Immaculate Heart of Mary School
2855 BRIARCLIFF RD NE 30329
International Prep Institute
1102 CASCADE AVE SW 30311
Mt. Vernon Presbyterian School
471 MOUNT VERNON HWY NE 30328
Our Lady of Lourdes School
29 BOULEVARD NE 30312
Our Lady of the Assumption School
1460 HEARST DR NE 30319
Romar Academy, 4560 TELL RD SW 30331
St. Anthony's Catholic School
951 GORDON ST SW 30310
St. Jude the Apostle School
7171 GLENRIDGE DR NE 30328
St. Paul of the Cross School
551 HARWELL RD NW 30318
Suzuki International Learning Ctr.
3201 CAINS HILL PL NW 30305
The Heiskell School
3260 NORTHSIDE DR NW 30305
Trinity School, 3254 NORTHSIDE PKY NW 30327
Village of St. Joseph School
2969 BUTNER RD SW 30331
Wesleyan Day School
86 MOUNT VERNON HWY NE 30328

Attapulgus, Decatur Co., Pop. Code 3
Decatur County SD
Supt. – See Bainbridge
Williams ES 31715 – James Austin,Jr., prin.

Auburn, Barrow Co., Pop. Code 3
Barrow County SD
Supt. – See Winder
ES, P O BOX 1029 30203 – Terry Dover, prin.

Augusta, Richmond Co., Pop. Code 8
Richmond County SD
Sch. Sys. Enr. Code 8
Supt. – Dr. John Strelec, 2083 HECKLE ST 30904
East Augusta MS, 320 KENTUCKY AVE 30901
Lee Beard, prin.
Langford MS, 3019 WALTON WAY 30909
David Smith, prin.
Murphey MS
2610 MILLEDGEVILLE ROAD 30904
Winnette Bradley, prin.
Sego MS, 3420 JULIA AVE 30906
Charles Byrd,Jr., prin.
Tubman MS, 1740 WALTON WAY 30904
Tracy Williams,Jr., prin.
Tutt MS, 495 BOY SCOUT ROAD 30909
William Watson, prin.
Barton Chapel Road ES
2329 BARTON CHAPEL RD 30906
Dr. Audrey Wood, prin.
Bayvale ES, 3309 MILLEDGEVILLE RD 30909
Baxton Garland, prin.
Bungalow Road ES, 2216 BUNGALOW RD 30906
Frances Register, prin.
Copeland ES, 1440 JACKSON RD 30909
Eddie Robertson, prin.
Craig ES, 400 HALE ST 30901 – Betty Tutt, prin.
Forest Hills ES, 3015 WALTON WAY 30909
Gerald Baygents, prin.
Garrett ES, 1100 EISENHOWER DR 30904
Sally Boulineau, prin.
Glenn Hills ES, 2838 GLENN HILLS DR 30906
Maxine Hammond, prin.
Hains MS, 1820 WINDSOR SPRING RD 30906
Nathan Dunn, prin.
Hornsby ES, 105 LANEY WALKER BLVD 30901
Thelma Williams, prin.
Houghton MS, 333 GREENE ST 30901
Dr. Wilson Rice, prin.
Jenkins ES, 101 DAN BOWLES RD 30901
Sylvester Brown, prin.
Lake Forest ES, 3140 LAKE FOREST DR 30909
Shirley Ledbetter, prin.
Lamar ES, 970 BAKER AVE 30904
Horace Lamback, prin.
Meadowbrook ES, 3630 GOLDFINCH DR 30906
Dr. Jerry Walters, prin.
Merry ES, 415 BOY SCOUT RD 30909
Harold Johnston, prin.
Milledge ES, 510 EVE ST 30904
Flonita Lawrence, prin.
Monte Sano ES, 2164 RICHMOND AVE 30904
Bertha Sutton, prin.

National Hills ES, 1215 NORTHWOOD RD 30909
William Pardue, prin.
Reynolds ES, RURAL ROUTE 02 BOX 299 30909
Teresa Vaiden, prin.
Rollins ES, 2160 MURA DR 30906
George Turner, prin.
Southside ES, 3310 OLD LOUISVILLE RD 30906
William Doss, prin.
Terrace Manor ES, 3110 TATE RD 30906
Ernest James, prin.
Walker Traditional ES
1301 WRIGHTSBORO RD 30901
Jimmy Boozer, prin.
Warren Road ES, 311 WARREN RD 30907
Peter Paige, prin.
Wheeless Road ES, 2530 WHEELESS RD 30906
John Black, prin.
White MS, 800 15TH ST 30901
Willie Jarman, prin.
Wilkinson Gardens ES
1918 TUBMAN HOME RD 30906
Barbara Williams, prin.
Windsor Spring Road ES
2534 WINDSOR SPRINGS RD 30906
Travis Brown, prin.
Other Schools – See Blythe, Gracewood, Hephzibah

Augusta Christian Academy
1930 TUBMAN HOME ROAD 30906
Augusta Christian School
313 BASTON ROAD 30907
One Way Christian School
4229 FRONTAGE ROAD 30909
Southgate Baptist School
2226 PEACH ORCHARD ROAD 30906
Alleluia Community School
2819 PEACH ORCHARD RD 30906
Curtis Baptist ES, 1326 BROAD ST 30910
Episcopal Day School
2248 WALTON WAY 30904
Hillcrest Baptist School
3045 DEANS BRIDGE RD 30906
Immaculate Conception School
1016 LANEY WALKER BLVD 30901
St. Mary's on the Hill School
1220 MONTE SANO AVE 30904
Temple Baptist School
967 BENNOCK MILL RD 30906
Wee Wisdom School
3423 PEACH ORCHARD RD 30906
Westminster Day School
3067 WHEELER RD 30909

Austell, Cobb Co., Pop. Code 5
Cobb County SD
Supt. – See Marietta
Garrett MS
5235 AUSTELL-PWDR SPRNGS RD 30001
Larry Cooper, prin.
ES, 5600 MULBERRY ST 30001
Jane Montague, prin.
Clarkdale ES, 4455 WESLEY DR 30001
David Sims, prin.

Avondale Estates, De Kalb Co., Pop. Code 4
DeKalb County SD
Supt. – See Decatur
Avondale ES, 10 LAKESHORE DR 30002
Kay Stringer, prin.

Forrest Hills Christian School
150 N CLARENDON AVE 30002

Bainbridge, Decatur Co., Pop. Code 7
Decatur County SD
Sch. Sys. Enr. Code 6
Supt. – David Mosely, 100 WEST ST 31717
Hutto JHS, 1201 PLANTER ST 31717
Saint Thomas, prin.
MS, 1417 DOTHAN RD 31717 – Tal Johnson, prin.
Elcan-King ES, 725 E LOUISE ST 31717
Freida Dunlap, prin.
Johnson ES, 1947 S WEST ST 31717
Dr. Martha O'Howell, prin.
Jones-Wheat ES, 1400 E BROUGHTON ST 31717
Charles Fuller, prin.
West Bainbridge ES, 507 MARTIN ST 31717
Clyde Smart, prin.
Other Schools – See Attapulgus, Climax

Baldwin, Banks Co., Pop. Code 4
Habersham County SD
Supt. – See Clarkesville
ES 30511 – J. Durham, prin.

Ball Ground, Cherokee Co., Pop. Code 3
Cherokee County SD
Supt. – See Canton
ES, P O BOX 127 30107 – Lory Hill, prin.

Barnesville, Lamar Co., Pop. Code 5
Lamar County SD
Sch. Sys. Enr. Code 4
Supt. – James Jenkins, 204 GORDON ROAD 30204
PS, 133 FORSYTH ST 30204 – Willie Miles, prin.
Other Schools – See Milner

Barnesville Academy, 64 ACADEMY DRIVE 30204

Barwick, Brooks Co., Pop. Code 2
Brooks County SD
Supt. – See Quitman
ES, P O BOX 68 31720 – William McCoy, prin.

Baxley, Appling Co., Pop. Code 5
Appling County SD
Sch. Sys. Enr. Code 5
Supt. – James Twiggs
RURAL ROUTE 07 BOX 36 31513
Appling County JHS, E ALLEN ST 31513
James Allen, prin.
Altamaha ES, RURAL ROUTE 01 BOX 1220 31513
Clennie Branch, prin.
Appling County MS
RURAL ROUTE 07 BOX 250 31513
G. Herndon, prin.
Appling County PS
RURAL ROUTE 07 BOX 255 31513
Sheila Tillman, prin.
Other Schools – See Surrency

Bellville, Evans Co., Pop. Code 2

Pinewood Christian Academy, P O BOX 7 30414

Bethlehem, Barrow Co., Pop. Code 2
Barrow County SD
Supt. – See Winder
ES, P O BOX 85 30620 – Randy Howell, prin.

Blackshear, Pierce Co., Pop. Code 5
Pierce County SD
Sch. Sys. Enr. Code 5
Supt. – Edwin Pope, P O BOX 349 31516
Grady Street ES
RURAL ROUTE 01 BOX 503 31516
Joyce Turner, prin.
Ware Street MS, 623 SYCAMORE ST 31516
Darryl Rabbitt, prin.
Other Schools – See Patterson

Blairsville, Union Co., Pop. Code 2
Union County SD
Sch. Sys. Enr. Code 4
Supt. – Earl Odom, SCHOOL ST 30512
Union County MS
RURAL ROUTE 02 BOX 2000 30512
Thomas Stephens, prin.
Union County ES
RURAL ROUTE 02 BOX 3000 30512
Jim Colwell, prin.
Other Schools – See Suches

Blakely, Early Co., Pop. Code 6
Early County SD
Sch. Sys. Enr. Code 5
Supt. – Ray Knight, 503 COLUMBIA ROAD 31723
Early County MS, 413 COLUMBIA RD 31723
J. Harris, prin.
Early County ES, 649 HOWELL ST 31723
Bob Pace, prin.

Bloomingdale, Chatham Co., Pop. Code 4
Chatham County SD
Supt. – See Savannah
ES 31302 – Amelia Poppell, prin.

Blue Ridge, Fannin Co., Pop. Code 4
Fannin County SD
Sch. Sys. Enr. Code 5
Supt. – Gene Crawford, P O BOX 606 30513
ES 30513 – Teresa Colwell, prin.
Other Schools – See Epworth, Mc Caysville, Mineral
Bluff, Morganton

Blythe, Richmond Co., Pop. Code 2
Richmond County SD
Supt. – See Augusta
ES, P O BOX C 30805 – Franklin Boulineau, prin.

Bonaire, Houston Co.
Houston County SD
Supt. – See Perry
ES, P O BOX 40 31005 – David Carpenter, prin.

Bowdon, Carroll Co., Pop. Code 4
Carroll County SD
Supt. – See Carrollton
MS, 233 KENT AVE 30108 – Jerry Crawford, prin.
PS, 225 E COLLEGE ST 30108
John Malcolm, prin.

Bowersville, Hart Co., Pop. Code 2
Hart County SD
Supt. – See Hartwell
Air Line ES, RURAL ROUTE 01 30516
Nancy Clark, prin.

Bowman, Elbert Co., Pop. Code 3
Elbert County SD
Supt. – See Elberton
ES, P O BOX 158 30624 – James Creason, prin.

Braselton, Jackson Co., Pop. Code 2
Jackson County SD
Supt. – See Jefferson
Jackson County ES, RURAL ROUTE 01 30517
Louis Brummett, prin.

Bremen, Haralson Co., Pop. Code 5
Bremen ISD
Sch. Sys. Enr. Code 4
Supt. – T. Murphy McManus
504 LAUREL ST 30110
MS, 504 GEORGIA AVE 30110
James Harris, prin.
Jones ES, LAKEVIEW DR 30110 – Gary Hall, prin.

Brooklet, Bulloch Co., Pop. Code 4
Bulloch County SD
Supt. – See Statesboro
ES, P O BOX 308 30415 – Doris Minick, prin.

Stilson ES, P O BOX 18 30415 – Dianne Bath, prin.

Brooks, Fayette Co., Pop. Code 2
Fayette County SD
Supt. – See Fayetteville
ES, P O BOX 1 30205 – Wayne Stone, prin.

Broxton, Coffee Co., Pop. Code 4
Coffee County SD
Supt. – See Douglas
S, RURAL ROUTE 02 BOX BHS 31519
Billy Cliett, prin.

Brunswick, Glynn Co., Pop. Code 7
Glynn County SD
Sch. Sys. Enr. Code 7
Supt. – Kermit Keenum, P O BOX 1677 31521
Glynn MS, 909 GEORGE ST 31520
Pam Lewis, prin.
Macon MS, 3885 ALTAMA AVE 31523
Dawne Hudson, prin.
Risley MS, 2900 ALBANY ST 31523
Murray Miller, prin.
Altama ES, 5505 ALTAMA AVE 31520
F. Atkinson, prin.
Ballard ES, 169 OLD JESUP RD 31523
Kenneth Jones, prin.
Burroughs-Molette ES, 1900 LEE ST 31520
Don Johnson, prin.
Glyndale ES, 711 OLD JESUP RD 31520
Mariellen Morris, prin.
Goodyear ES, 3001 GLYNN AVE 31520
G. Davis, prin.
Greer ES, 3400 NORWICH ST 31520
Bailey Walker, prin.
Risley ES, 1800 ALBANY ST 31520
Lynn Krauss, prin.
Other Schools – See Saint Simmons Island

Brunswick Christian Academy
RURAL ROUTE 02 BOX 1 31520
Christian Renewal School
4265 NORWICH ST 31520
St. Francis Xavier School, 1121 UNION ST 31520

Buchanan, Haralson Co.
Haralson County SD
Sch. Sys. Enr. Code 5
Supt. – Bob Downey, P O BOX 508 30113
MS 30113 – Joe Jones, prin.
ES 30113 – Frank Hutcheson, prin.
Other Schools – See Tallapoosa, Waco

Buena Vista, Marion Co., Pop. Code 4
Marion County SD
Sch. Sys. Enr. Code 4
Supt. – Herman Long, P O BOX 391 31803
Marion County ES, P O BOX 16 31803
Bob Dennis, prin.

Buford, Gwinnett Co., Pop. Code 6
Buford ISD
Sch. Sys. Enr. Code 4
Supt. – Beauty Baldwin, 181 BONA ROAD 30518
ES, 615 HILL ST 30518 – Joyce Hooper, prin.
MS, 601 HILL PLACE 30518 – Dale Barnes, prin.

Gwinnett County SD
Supt. – See Lawrenceville
Lanier MS, 918 BUFORD HIGHWAY 30518
Charles Crawford, prin.
Harmony ES, 3946 S BOGAN RD 30518
James Fredrick, prin.
Sugar Hill ES, 1160 LEVEL CREEK RD 30518
Scott Pryor, prin.

Butler, Taylor Co., Pop. Code 4
Taylor County SD
Sch. Sys. Enr. Code 4
Supt. – Norman Carter, P O BOX 1937 31006
Taylor County ES, P O BOX 428 31006
Matthew Knowlton, prin.

Byron, Peach Co., Pop. Code 4
Peach County SD
Supt. – See Fort Valley
ES 31088 – Carl Martin, prin.

Cairo, Grady Co., Pop. Code 6
Grady County SD
Sch. Sys. Enr. Code 5
Supt. – Cecil McDonald, P O BOX 300 31728
Washington MS, 1277 BOOKERHILL BLVD 31728
Larry Rawlins, prin.
Eastside ES, 1201 20TH ST NE 31728
Dr. Rosemary Adams, prin.
Northside ES, 985 1ST ST NW 31728
David Coley, prin.
Southside ES, 491 3RD ST SE 31728
Ed Gravenstein, prin.
Other Schools – See Pelham, Whigham

Calhoun, Gordon Co., Pop. Code 6
Calhoun ISD
Sch. Sys. Enr. Code 4
Supt. – J. Kenneth Smallwood
P O BOX 785 30701
MS, RIVER ST 30701 – Brenda Erwin, prin.
Eastside ES, BARRETT ROAD 30701
Freida Jenkins, prin.

Gordon County SD
Sch. Sys. Enr. Code 5
Supt. – Malachi Carnes, P O BOX 127 30701
Red Bud S, RURAL ROUTE 03 30701
Walter Walraven, prin.

Belwood ES, 590 BELWOOD ROAD SE 30701
Michael DeVitt, prin.
Sonoraville ES
7414 FAIRMOUNT HWY SE 30701
Beverly Swancy, prin.
Other Schools – See Fairmount, Plainville, Resaca

Camilla, Mitchell Co., Pop. Code 5
Mitchell County SD
Sch. Sys. Enr. Code 5
Supt. – Bobby Tabb, P O BOX 588 31730
Mitchell County MS, 108 S HARNEY ST 31730
Isreal Eady, prin.
Mitchell County ES
550 MARTIN L KING JR ROAD 31730
Hugh Inman, prin.

Westwood Academy, 255 FULLER ST 31730

Canon, Franklin Co., Pop. Code 3
Hart County SD
Supt. – See Hartwell
Eagle Grove ES, RURAL ROUTE 01 30520
Willard Morris, prin.

Canton, Cherokee Co., Pop. Code 5
Cherokee County SD
Sch. Sys. Enr. Code 7
Supt. – Marguerite Cline, P O BOX 769 30114
Rusk MS, RURAL ROUTE 02 30114
Dr. Joe Blackwell, prin.
Teasley MS, RURAL ROUTE 06 30114
Randy Martin, prin.
Buffington ES, RURAL ROUTE 10 BOX 17 30114
William Jones, prin.
ES, 551 MARIETTA HWY 30114
Jack Weaver, prin.
Clayton ES, RURAL ROUTE 03 30114
Lawrence Fitts, prin.
Free Home ES, RURAL ROUTE 01 30114
Darrell Brock, prin.
Hickory Flat ES, RURAL ROUTE 02 30114
Allen Browning, prin.
Macedonia ES, RURAL ROUTE 05 30114
Kenny Morris, prin.
Tippens ES, 8 GLENWOOD STREET 30114
Patrick Cates, prin.
Other Schools – See Acworth, Ball Ground, Holly
Springs, Waleska, Woodstock

Carnesville, Franklin Co., Pop. Code 3
Franklin County SD
Sch. Sys. Enr. Code 5
Supt. – Travis Moon, P O BOX 98 30521
Franklin County JHS, P O BOX 544 30521
Ken Hendrix, prin.
ES, P O BOX 39 30521 – Thomas Bridges, prin.
Other Schools – See Lavonia, Royston

Carrollton, Carroll Co., Pop. Code 7
Carroll County SD
Sch. Sys. Enr. Code 6
Supt. – Timothy Wheeler
164 INDEPENDENCE DR 30117
Central MS, 633 STRIPLING CHAPEL RD 30117
Anthony Wilkins, prin.
Central PS, 175 PRIMARY SCHOOL RD 30117
Alan Krieger, prin.
Sand Hill ES, 45 SANDHILL SCHOOL RD 30117
Helen Hearn, prin.
Other Schools – See Bowdon, Mount Zion, Roopville,
Temple, Villa Rica, Whitesburg

Carrollton ISD
Sch. Sys. Enr. Code 5
Supt. – Tom Upchurch, 1 TROJAN DRIVE 30117
JHS, 510 STADIUM DR 30117
Ernest McClendon, prin.
Alabama Street MS, 423 ALABAMA ST 30117
Dr. G. Dixon, prin.
College Street ES, 423 COLLEGE ST 30117
Waymon Reeves, prin.
Maple Street ES, 601 MAPLE ST 30117
H. McCright, prin.

Oak Mountain Academy
1575 S HIGHWAY 16 30117

Cartersville, Bartow Co., Pop. Code 6
Bartow County SD
Sch. Sys. Enr. Code 6
Supt. – Raiford Cantrell, P O BOX 569 30120
Cloverleaf ES, P O BOX 564 30120
Bobby McMillan, prin.
Hamilton Crossing ES
116 HAMILTON CROSSING RD NW 30120
Davis Nelson, prin.
Mission Road ES, 1100 MISSION RD SW 30120
Ralph Lowe, prin.
Other Schools – See Adairsville, Cassville, Emerson,
Kingston, Rydal, Taylorsville, White

Cartersville ISD
Sch. Sys. Enr. Code 5
Supt. – Dr. Buford C. Arnold
310 OLD MILL ROAD 30120
MS, 315 ETOWAH DRIVE 30120
Barry Hester, prin.
ES, 315 ETOWAH DR 30120 – Doug Harris, prin.

Cassville, Bartow Co.
Bartow County SD
Supt. – See Cartersville
Cass MS, U S HWY 41 N 30123
Howard Bowman, prin.

Cataula, Harris Co.
Harris County SD
Supt. – See Hamilton
ES, P O BOX 273 31804 – (—), prin.

Cave Spring, Floyd Co., Pop. Code 3
Floyd County SD
Supt. – See Rome
ES, 13 ROME ST 30124 – Thomas Dempsey, prin.

Cedartown, Polk Co., Pop. Code 6
Polk County SD
Sch. Sys. Enr. Code 6
Supt. – E. Burch, P O BOX 128 30125
Cedar Hill MS, P O BOX 66 30125
James Mayben, prin.
Purks MS, 230 WEST AVE 30125
Clark Montgomery, prin.
Cherokee ES, 191 EVERGREEN LN 30125
David Warner, prin.
Westside ES, 51 FRANK LOTT DR 30125
Eddie Starnes, prin.
Other Schools – See Rockmart

Centerville, Houston Co., Pop. Code 5
Houston County SD
Supt. – See Perry
ES, 450 N HOUSTON LAKE BLVD 31028
W. Bassett, prin.

Chamblee, De Kalb Co., Pop. Code 6
DeKalb County SD
Supt. – See Decatur
Dresden ES, 2449 DRESDEN DR NE 30341
Jim Williams, prin.
Huntley Hills ES, 2112 SEAMAN CIR 30341
Carolyn Barkley, prin.

Chatsworth, Murray Co., Pop. Code 5
Murray County SD
Sch. Sys. Enr. Code 5
Supt. – Dr. Lamar Adams, P O BOX 68 30705
Murray MS, 700 OLD ELLIJAY RD 30705
Julian Coffey, prin.
ES, MARKET ST 30705 – Douglas Meyer, prin.
Northwest ES, HWY 225 N 30705
Larry Loughridge, prin.
Other Schools – See Eton, Spring Place

Chauncey, Dodge Co., Pop. Code 2
Dodge County SD
Supt. – See Eastman
ES, P O BOX 78 31011 – Mimi Dennis, prin.

Chester, Dodge Co., Pop. Code 2
Dodge County SD
Supt. – See Eastman
ES, P O BOX 98 31012 – Leola Moore, prin.

Chestnut Mountain, Hall Co.
Hall County SD
Supt. – See Gainesville
ES, P O BOX 7247 30502 – Wayne Colston, prin.

Chickamauga, Walker Co., Pop. Code 4
Chickamauga ISD
Sch. Sys. Enr. Code 4
Supt. – Leon Golden, 105 LEE CIRCLE 30707
ES, 210 CRESCENT AVE 30707
Nancy Van Prooyen, prin.

Walker County SD
Supt. – See La Fayette
Osburn ES, RURAL ROUTE 02 30707
Ryland Donald, prin.
Pond Springs ES, RURAL ROUTE 02 30707
Doyle Mills, prin.

Chula, Tift Co., Pop. Code 4

Tiftarea Academy, P O BOX 10 31733

Clarkesville, Habersham Co., Pop. Code 4
Habersham County SD
Sch. Sys. Enr. Code 5
Supt. – Lonnie Burns, P O BOX 467 30523
ES 30523 – Jimmy Black, prin.
Fairview ES, RURAL ROUTE 01 30523
Anna Ramey, prin.
Woodville ES, RURAL ROUTE 02 30523
Sandra Ridlehoover, prin.
Other Schools – See Baldwin, Cornelia, Demorest,
Mount Airy

Central Heights Christian School
P O BOX 252 30523

Clarkston, De Kalb Co., Pop. Code 2
DeKalb County SD
Supt. – See Decatur
Indian Creek ES, 724 N INDIAN CREEK DR 30021
Miles Williard, prin.
Jolly ES, 1070 OTELLO AVE 30021
Charles Fowler, prin.

Claxton, Evans Co., Pop. Code 5
Evans County SD
Sch. Sys. Enr. Code 4
Supt. – L. H. Griner, P O BOX 826 30417
ES, 4 N COLLEGE ST 30417 – Joyce Nesmith, prin.
MS, P O BOX 686 30417 – Neal Hammack, prin.

Clayton, Rabun Co., Pop. Code 4
Rabun County SD
Sch. Sys. Enr. Code 5
Supt. – J. L. Roach, P O BOX 468 30525
ES, P O BOX 1188 30525 – Albert Green, Jr., prin.
Other Schools – See Rabun Gap, Tiger

Cleveland, White Co., Pop. Code 4
White County SD
Sch. Sys. Enr. Code 4
Supt. – Albert Taylor, P O BOX 295   30528
White County MS, P O BOX 1039   30528
W. Jenkins,Jr., prin.
Nix PS, MERRITT ST, HWY 115 W   30528
June Parks, prin.
White County MS
RURAL ROUTE 05 BOX 5041   30528
Alice Fitzgerald, prin.

Climax, Decatur Co., Pop. Code 2
Decatur County SD
Supt. – See Bainbridge
ES, P O BOX 9   31734 – Duane Driggars, prin.

Cochran, Bleckley Co., Pop. Code 6
Bleckley County SD
Sch. Sys. Enr. Code 4
Supt. – F. Wimberly, P O BOX 516   31014
Bleckley County MS, RURAL ROUTE 03   31014
Ben Dykes, prin.
Bleckley ES, PETER ST   31014
Algie Jones,Jr., prin.

Cohutta, Whitfield Co., Pop. Code 2
Whitfield County SD
Supt. – See Dalton
ES   30710 – Howard Curtis, prin.

Colbert, Madison Co., Pop. Code 3
Madison County SD
Supt. – See Danielsville
ES   30628 – E. Hill,Jr., prin.

College Park, Fulton Co., Pop. Code 7
Clayton County SD
Supt. – See Jonesboro
North Clayton MS
5517 W FAYETTEVILLE ROAD   30349
Ralph Cooper, prin.
Northcutt ES, 5451 W FAYETTEVILLE RD   30349
Eddie White, prin.
West Clayton ES, 5580 RIVERDALE RD   30349
Ralph Matthews, prin.

Fulton County SD
Supt. – See Atlanta
Camp Creek MS
4345 WELCOME ALL ROAD SW   30349
James Abrams, prin.
McNair MS, 2800 BURDETTE RD   30349
Jessie Pottsdamer, prin.
Cliftondale ES, 6399 BUTNER RD   30349
Dr. Marna Barnard, prin.
College Park ES, 2075 PRICETON AVE   30337
Gary Field, prin.
Laurel Hills ES, 2825 CARRIAGE LN   30349
C. Libby, prin.
Lee ES, 4600 SCARBOROUGH RD   30349
Marie Washburn, prin.
Lewis ES, 6201 CONNELL RD   30349
Randee Nagler, prin.
Longino ES, 2001 WALKER AVE   30337
Sarah Lindsey, prin.
Mitchell ES, 2480 PAUL D WEST DR   30337
Locie Walthall, prin.
Nolan ES, 2725 CREEL RD   30349
Weldon Davis, prin.
Stonewall ES, 5545 STONEWALL TELL RD   30349
Nancy Said, prin.
The Meadows ES
5270 NORTHFIELD BLVD   30349
Helen Hall, prin.
Young ES, 1503 E TEMPLE AVE   30337
Hattie Jones, prin.

Woodward Academy, P O BOX 87190   30337
Old National Christian School
2601 FLAT SHOALS ROAD   30349

Collins, Tattnall Co., Pop. Code 3
Tattnal County SD
Supt. – See Reidsville
ES, RURAL ROUTE 02 BOX 1   30421
J. Lewis, prin.

Colquitt, Miller Co., Pop. Code 4
Miller County SD
Sch. Sys. Enr. Code 4
Supt. – Walter Daniels, P O BOX 188   31737
Miller County JHS   31737 – Raymond Grimes, prin.
Miller County ES   31737 – Niza Davis, prin.

Columbus, Muscogee Co., Pop. Code 9
Muscogee County SD
Sch. Sys. Enr. Code 8
Supt. – Dr. B. A. Nail
1200 BRADLEY DRIVE   31906
Arnold JHS, 2011 51ST ST   31904
C. Roberts,Jr., prin.
Daniel JHS, 1042 45TH ST   31904
Joseph Saulsbury, prin.
Eddy JHS, 2100 S LUMPKIN ROAD   31903
Joseph Gosha, prin.
Fort JHS, 2900 FLOYD ROAD   31907
Paul Jones, prin.
Marshall JHS, 1830 SHEPHERD DRIVE   31906
Dr. Morris Clarke, prin.
Richards JHS, 2892 EDGEWOOD ROAD   31906
William Arrington, prin.
Rothschild JHS, 1136 HUNT AVE   31907
Dr. James Hudson, prin.
Allen ES, 5201 23RD AVE   31904
James Snead, prin.

Beallwood ES, 1125 ALEXANDER ST   31904
Bertha McKay, prin.
Benning Hills ES, 61 MUNSON DR   31903
Mary Ryles, prin.
Bibb City ES, 96 40TH ST   31904
Wallace Huey, prin.
Blanchard ES, 3512 WEEMS RD   31909
David Shoemaker, prin.
Carver ES, 3042 8TH ST   31906
James Woods, prin.
Clubview ES, 2836 EDGEWOOD RD   31906
Ann Helms, prin.
Cusseta ES, 4200 CUSSETA RD   31903
Donald Caldwell, prin.
David ES, 5801 ARMOUR RD   31909
Thomas Hutcherson, prin.
Davis ES, 1822 SHEPHERD DR   31906
Fuller Heard, prin.
Dawson ES, 180 NORTHSTAR DR   31907
Clemon Deramus, prin.
Dimon ES, 480 DOGWOOD DR   31907
Jack Hendrix, prin.
Double Churches ES
1213 DOUBLE CHURCHES RD   31904
Charles Hidle, prin.
Eastway ES, 4601 BUENA VISTA RD   31907
Sidney Crews,Jr., prin.
Edgewood ES, 3835 FOREST RD   31907
Debra Mendoza, prin.
Forrest Road ES, 6400 FOREST RD   31907
Sarah Garrett, prin.
Fox ES, 3720 5TH AVE   31904 – Guy Sims, prin.
Gentian ES, 4201 PRIMROSE RD   31907
M. Richardson, prin.
Georgetown ES, 954 HIGH LN   31907
Dr. Eric Person, prin.
Johnson ES, 3700 WOODLAWN AVE   31904
Paul Grimes, prin.
Key ES, 2520 BROADMOOR DR   31903
Dr. Carol Hutcheson, prin.
Muscogee ES, 3900 BAKER PLAZA DR   31903
Karon Greyer, prin.
Reese Road ES, 3100 REESE RD   31907
James Motos, prin.
Rigdon Road ES, 1282 RIGDON RD   31906
Veronis Hall, prin.
River Road ES, 516 HEATH DR   31904
Tommy Bassett, prin.
Rose Hill ES, 435 21ST ST   31904
William Watson, prin.
South Columbus ES, 1964 TORCH HILL RD   31903
William Poovey, prin.
St. Elmo ES, 2101 18TH AVE   31901
James Hayes, prin.
St. Mary's ES, 4408 SAINT MARYS RD   31907
Dr. Thomas Moffett, prin.
Thirtieth Avenue ES, 151 30TH AVE   31903
Margaret Ingersoll, prin.
Waddell ES, 6101 MILLER RD   31907
Eugene Craig, prin.
Waverly Terrace ES, 2701 11TH AVE   31904
Sam Gregg, prin.
Wesley Heights ES, 1801 AMBER DR   31907
Glenn Wallace, prin.
Winterfield ES, 3025 DAWSON ST   31903
T. Redfearn, prin.
Wood ES, 1125 15TH ST   31901 – Esto Smith, prin.
Wynnton ES, 2303 WYNNTON RD   31906
Elizabeth Russell, prin.
Other Schools – See Midland

Brookstone School
440 BRADLEY PARK DRIVE   31904
Christian Heritage School
3564 FORREST ROAD   31907
Grace Christian School, 2915 14TH AVE   31904
Briarcrest School, 7300 LIVINGSTON DR   31909
Calvary Christian School, 7556 MOON RD   31909
Our Lady of Lourdes School
1973 TORCH HILL RD   31903
St. Anne's School, 3550 TRINITY DR   31907

Comer, Madison Co., Pop. Code 3
Madison County SD
Supt. – See Danielsville
ES   30629 – Robert Almond, prin.

Commerce, Jackson Co., Pop. Code 5
Commerce ISD
Sch. Sys. Enr. Code 4
Supt. – Doc Elliot, UNIVERSITY DRIVE   30529
MS, LAKEVIEW DR   30529 – Walker Davis, prin.
ES, MINISH DR   30529 – Don Canady, prin.

Conley, Clayton Co.
Clayton County SD
Supt. – See Jonesboro
Anderson ES, 4199 OLD ROCK CUT RD   30027
Bobby Brown, prin.

Conyers, Rockdale Co., Pop. Code 6
Rockdale County SD
Sch. Sys. Enr. Code 6
Supt. – Dr. John Phillips,Jr.
954 N MAIN ST NW   30207
MS, 335 SIGMAN ROAD NW   30207
William Silvey, prin.
Edwards MS, 2400 STANTON ROAD SE   30208
Dr. Kathy Garber, prin.
Barksdale ES, 596 OGLESBY BRIDGE RD SE   30208
Patricia DeVane, prin.
Flat Shoals ES, 1455 FLAT SHOALS RD SE   30208
Charles Price, prin.
Hicks ES, 930 ROWLAND RD NE   30207
Rose Arant, prin.

Hightower Trail ES, 2510 HWY 138   30208
Susan Brinson, prin.
Honey Creek ES, 700 HONEY CREEK RD SE   30208
Katherine Lawrence, prin.
House ES, 8134 LOGANVILLE HWY   30207
Joseph Weil,Jr., prin.
Pine Street ES, 960 PINE ST NE   30207
Stephen Elrod, prin.
Sims ES, 1821 WALKER RD   30208
Lowell Biddy, prin.

Philadelphia Christian School
2360 OLD COVINGTON HWY SW   30207

Cordele, Crisp Co., Pop. Code 7
Crisp County SD
Sch. Sys. Enr. Code 5
Supt. – Charles Bess, P O BOX 729   31015
Clark MS   31015 – Randy Ford, prin.
Blackshear Trail ES   31015 – Gail Nesbitt, prin.
Pate ES   31015 – Connie Peeples, prin.
Southwestern MS   31015 – Greg Hunt, prin.

Crisp Academy, RURAL ROUTE 03   31015

Cornelia, Habersham Co., Pop. Code 5
Habersham County SD
Supt. – See Clarkesville
ES   30531 – Grady Brooks, prin.

Covington, Newton Co., Pop. Code 7
Newton County SD
Sch. Sys. Enr. Code 6
Supt. – Richard C. Schneider
3187 NEWTON DRIVE NE   30209
Cousins MS, 8134 GEIGER ST NW   30209
Wayne Mullins, prin.
Sharp MS, 3135 NEWTON DR   30209
Thomas Glanton, prin.
East Newton ES, 2286 DIXIE RD   30209
Trina Russell, prin.
Fairview ES, 3325 FAIRVIEW RD   30209
Bruce Sliger, prin.
Ficquett ES, 2207 WILLIAMS ST NE   30209
Louise Adams, prin.
Heard-Mixon ES, 1410 HWY 36   30209
Nancy Guerrero, prin.
Livingston ES, 3657 HIGHWAY 81 S   30209
David O'Brien, prin.
Porterdale ES, 45 RAM DR   30209
T. Hendrix, prin.
Other Schools – See Mansfield, Oxford

Tabernacle Christian School, P O BOX 710   30209

Crawfordville, Taliaferro Co., Pop. Code 3
Taliaferro County SD
Sch. Sys. Enr. Code 2
Supt. – Lola Williams
RURAL ROUTE 02 BOX 154   30631
Taliaferro County ES
RURAL ROUTE 02 BOX 154   30631
Marvin Chatman, prin.

Cumming, Forsyth Co., Pop. Code 4
Forsyth County SD
Sch. Sys. Enr. Code 6
Supt. – Clarence Lambert, 101 SCHOOL ST   30130
Big Creek ES, 1984 PEACHTREE PKWY   30130
Don Williams, prin.
Coal Mountain ES
RURAL ROUTE 16 BOX 211   30130
Steve Benson, prin.
ES, 136 ELM ST   30130 – Ina Fossett, prin.
Mashburn ES, RURAL ROUTE 08 BOX 1640   30130
Peggy Walker, prin.
Sawnee ES, RURAL ROUTE 06 BOX 70   30130
Douglas Frederick, prin.
Other Schools – See Alpharetta, Gainesville

Cusseta, Chattahoochee Co., Pop. Code 4
Chattahoochee County SD
Sch. Sys. Enr. Code 2
Supt. – Ronnie Burgamy, P O BOX 188   31805
Chattahoochee County ES, P O BOX 249   31805
Leonard McGuire, prin.

Cuthbert, Randolph Co., Pop. Code 5
Randolph County SD
Sch. Sys. Enr. Code 4
Supt. – Margaret Hunt, 309 N WEBSTER ST   31740
Randolph ES   31740 – Pam Keadle, prin.
Randolph MS   31740 – Walter Dawkins, prin.

Dacula, Gwinnett Co., Pop. Code 4
Gwinnett County SD
Supt. – See Lawrenceville
MS, 192 DACULA ROAD   30211
Betty Keene, prin.
ES, 192 DACULA RD   30211 – Olivia Hodges, prin.

Dahlonega, Lumpkin Co., Pop. Code 5
Lumpkin County SD
Sch. Sys. Enr. Code 4
Supt. – Donald Kidd
101 MOUNTAIN VIEW DR   30533
Lumpkin County MS, P O BOX 187   30533
Thomas Johnson, prin.
Lumpkin County ES
300 SCHOOL HILL RD NE   30533
DeWey Moye, prin.

Dallas, Paulding Co., Pop. Code 4
Paulding County SD
Sch. Sys. Enr. Code 6
Supt. – Allene Magill, 522 HARDEE ST   30132

Jones JHS, 100 SCHOOL ST 30132
  Sammy McClure, prin.
Abney ES, 1635 DALLAS-ACWORTH RD 30132
  Ray Loftin, prin.
ES, 520 HARDEE ST 30132 – Connie Dugan, prin.
Matthews MS, 335 ACADEMY DR 30132
  Bob Watson, prin.
Other Schools – See Hiram, Rockmart, Temple, Villa
Rica

Dalton, Whitfield Co., Pop. Code 7
Dalton ISD
Sch. Sys. Enr. Code 5
Supt. – Frank Thomason, P O BOX 1408 30722
JHS, 408 W CRAWFORD ST 30720
  Don Amonett, prin.
Brookwood ES, 501 CENTRAL AVE 30720
  Debbie Baxter, prin.
City Park MS, 515 S PENTZ ST 30720
  Belva Barnhardt, prin.
Fort Hill MS, 104 N GREEN ST 30721
  David Perry, prin.
Morris Street ES, 803 E MORRIS ST 30721
  Edna Massengill, prin.
Roan ES, 1116 ROAN ST 30721
  Sheila Evans, prin.
Westwood ES, 708 TRAMMELL ST 30720
  Thomas Bartley, prin.

Whitfield County SD
Sch. Sys. Enr. Code 6
Supt. – Dr. J. Robert Cagle, P O BOX 2167 30722
Eastbrook MS, 700 HILL RD 30720
  Ray Sharpe, prin.
North Whitfield MS, 3264 CLEVELAND RD 30720
  K. Hillard, prin.
Valley Point MS, 3796 S DIXIE ROAD 30720
  Norma Gordon, prin.
Antioch ES, 1819 RIVERBEND RD 30721
  Jerry Davis, prin.
Dawnville ES, 1380 DAWNVILLE RD NE 30721
  Phyllis Conn, prin.
Dug Gap ES, 2032 DUG GAP RD 30720
  Dr. Donella Lowery, prin.
East Side ES, 2818 AIRPORT RD 30721
  Charles Allen, prin.
Pleasant Grove ES
  2725 CLEVELAND ROAD 30721
  Dr. James Bates, prin.
Valley Point ES, 3798 S DIXIE RD 30721
  Jerry Watkins, prin.
Varnell ES, 3256 CLEVELAND RD 30721
  Hugh McArthur, prin.
Other Schools – See Cohutta, Rocky Face, Tunnel Hill

Pathway Christian School, P O BOX 4299 30721

Damascus, Early Co., Pop. Code 2

Southwest Georgia Academy, P O BOX 99 31741

Danielsville, Madison Co., Pop. Code 2
Madison County SD
Sch. Sys. Enr. Code 5
Supt. – Jim Perkins
  ROYSTON ROAD HWY 29 30633
Madison Co. MS 30633 – Robert Harrison, prin.
ES 30633 – Robert Perry, prin.
Other Schools – See Colbert, Comer, Ila

Danville, Twiggs Co., Pop. Code 3
Twiggs County SD
Supt. – See Jeffersonville
ES 31017 – Margaret Davis, prin.

Darien, McIntosh Co., Pop. Code 4
McIntosh County SD
Sch. Sys. Enr. Code 4
Supt. – Ralph Huff, P O BOX 495 31305
Eulonia PS, P O BOX 517 31305
  Carole Ploeger, prin.
Todd-Grant MS, P O BOX 456 31305
  Evella Brown, prin.

Dawson, Terrell Co., Pop. Code 6
Terrell County SD
Sch. Sys. Enr. Code 4
Supt. – Richard C. Barry, P O BOX 151 31742
Terrell JHS, 480 PECAN ST NE 31742
  Rob Aaron, prin.
Carver MS, 761 1ST AVE SE 31742
  Mary Bolton, prin.
Cooper PS, P O BOX 636 31742
  Allie Jenkins, prin.

Terrell Academy, P O BOX 132 31742

Dawsonville, Dawson Co., Pop. Code 2
Dawson County SD
Sch. Sys. Enr. Code 4
Supt. – Randall Townley, P O BOX 280 30534
Dawson County MS, P O BOX 688 30534
  Stan Worley, prin.
Dawson County ES, P O BOX 360 30534
  Nicky Gilleland, prin.
Robinson MS, PERIMETER RD 30534
  Randell Kent, prin.

Dearing, McDuffie Co., Pop. Code 3
McDuffie County SD
Supt. – See Thomson
ES, P O BOX 7 30808 – Darrell Wells, prin.

Decatur, De Kalb Co., Pop. Code 7
DeKalb County SD
Sch. Sys. Enr. Code 8
Supt. – Dr. Robert R. Freeman
  3770 N DECATUR ROAD 30032
Alexander ES, 3414 MEMORIAL DR 30032
  Sandra Walker, prin.
Atherton ES, 1674 ATHERTON DR 30035
  Paul Warner, prin.
Briarlake ES, 3590 LAVISTA ROAD 30033
  James Harbuck, prin.
Canby Lane ES, 4150 GREEN HAWK TRL 30035
  Mary Budgett, prin.
Chapel Hill ES, 3536 RADCLIFF BLVD 30034
  Dr. Edward Bouie, Jr., prin.
Columbia ES
  3230 COLUMBIA WOODS DR 30032
  Ronald Sims, prin.
Fairington ES, 5505 PHILIP BRADLEY DR 30038
  Donna Asbell, prin.
Flat Shoals ES, 3226 FLAT SHOALS RD 30034
  Dorothy Brown, prin.
Forrest Hills ES, 923 FORREST BLVD 30030
  Dr. Frank Duncan, prin.
Glen Haven ES, 1402 AUSTIN DR 30032
  Odell Caldwell, prin.
Kelley Lake ES, 2590 KELLEY LAKE RD 30032
  Virginia Willis, prin.
Knollwood ES, 3039 SANTA MONICA DR 30032
  Jake Hardin, prin.
Laurel Ridge ES, 1215 BALSAM DR 30033
  Samuel Dyess, Jr., prin.
Mathis ES, 3505 BORING RD 30034
  Barbara Dover, prin.
McLendon ES, 3169 HOLLYWOOD DR 30033
  Harvey Clark, prin.
Medlock ES, 2418 WOOD TRAIL LN 30033
  Gil Aldridge, prin.
Midway ES, 3318 MIDWAY RD 30032
  Agnes McGregor, prin.
Peachcrest ES, 1530 JOY LN 30032
  Margaret Hollinshed, prin.
Rainbow ES, 2801 KELLY CHAPEL RD 30034
  Sarah West, prin.
Snapfinger ES, 1365 SNAPFINGER RD 30032
  Charles Maxwell, prin.
Steele ES, 2162 SECOND AVE 30032
  Clara Bates, prin.
Tilson ES, 2100 BIXLER CIR 30032
  Davis Cooper, prin.
Toney ES, 2701 OAKLAND TER 30032
  Clarence Montgomery, prin.
Wadsworth ES, 2084 GREEN FORREST DR 30032
  Clarence Callaway, prin.
Other Schools – See Atlanta, Avondale Estates,
Chamblee, Clarkston, Doraville, Dunwoody,
Ellenwood, Lithonia, Redan, Stone Mountain,
Tucker

Decatur ISD
Sch. Sys. Enr. Code 5
Supt. – Dr. Don Griffith
  320 N MCDONOUGH ST 30030
Renfroe MS, 220 W COLLEGE AVE 30030
  Patricia McElroy, prin.
Clairemont ES, 155 ERIE AVE 30030
  Judy Greene, prin.
College Heights ES
  917 S MCDONOUGH ST 30030
  Henry Brown, prin.
Fifth Avenue ES, 101 FIFTH AVE 30030
  Julian Relf, prin.
Glenwood ES, 440 E PONCE DE LEON AVE 30030
  Marie Matthews, prin.
Oakhurst ES, 175 MEAD RD 30030
  Karen Davenport, prin.
Westchester ES, 758 SCOTT BLVD 30030
  Cheryl Kuebler, prin.
Winnona Park ES, 510 AVERY ST 30030
  Karen Eldridge, prin.

Mt. Carmel Christian School
  3250 RAINBOW DRIVE 30034
A Child's Campus, 2780 FLAT SHOALS RD 30034
Becker Adventist School
  3567 COVINGTON HWY 30032
Chapel Hill Harvest School
  4650 FLAT SHOALS ROADY 30034
Green Pastures Christian Academy
  P O BOX 1286 30031
Rainbow Park Baptist School
  2941 COLUMBIA DR 30034
SS Peter and Paul School, 2560 TILSON RD 30032
St. Thomas More Catholic School
  630 W PONCE DE LEON AVE 30030

Demorest, Habersham Co., Pop. Code 4
Habersham County SD
Supt. – See Clarkesville
ES 30535 – James Perry, prin.

Dixie, Brooks Co., Pop. Code 2
Brooks County SD
Supt. – See Quitman
Simmon Hill ES
  RURAL ROUTE 01 BOX 216 31629
  George Lewis, prin.

Westbrook School, P O BOX 100 31629

Doerun, Colquitt Co., Pop. Code 4
Colquitt County SD
Supt. – See Moultrie
ES, P O BOX 188 31744
  Verna Hollingsworth, prin.

Donalsonville, Seminole Co., Pop. Code 5
Seminole County SD
Sch. Sys. Enr. Code 4
Supt. – Jesse McLeod, P O BOX 188 31745
Seminole County MS 31745
  Douglas Spivey, prin.
Seminole County PS 31745 – Curtis Dumas, prin.

Doraville, De Kalb Co., Pop. Code 6
DeKalb County SD
Supt. – See Decatur
Evansdale ES, 2914 EVANS WOOD DR 30340
  Rita Klee, prin.
Hightower ES, 4236 TILLY MILL RD 30360
  John Bellamy, prin.
Oakcliff ES, 3150 WILLOW OAK WAY 30340
  Marion Miller, prin.
Pleasantdale ES, 3695 N LAKE DR 30340
  James Chivers, prin.
Reynolds ES, 3498 PINE ST 30340
  Charlie Iddins, prin.

Buford Highway Christian School
  6690 BUFORD HWY NE 30340

Douglas, Coffee Co., Pop. Code 7
Coffee County SD
Sch. Sys. Enr. Code 6
Supt. – Dahl McDermitt, P O BOX 959 31533
Coffee JHS, P O BOX 999 31533
  Oscar Street, prin.
Eastside ES, P O BOX 1227 31533
  Leo Brooks, prin.
Satilla ES, RURAL ROUTE 03 BOX 340-B 31533
  L. Harrell, prin.
Westside ES, 311 WESTSIDE DR 31533
  Ray Kight, Jr., prin.
Other Schools – See Ambrose, Broxton, Nicholls, West
Green

Citizens Christian Academy, P O BOX 1064 31533

Douglasville, Douglas Co., Pop. Code 6
Douglas County SD
Sch. Sys. Enr. Code 7
Supt. – Kathryn Shehane, P O BOX 1077 30133
Chapel Hill MS, 3989 CHAPEL HILL ROAD 30135
  Vernon Hagen, prin.
Chestnut Log MS, 2544 POPE RD 30135
  Jesse Bitterman, prin.
Fairplay MS, 8311 HWY 166 30135
  Leon Frost, prin.
Stewart MS, 8138 MALONE ST 30134
  Jim Steele, prin.
Arbor Station ES, 9999 PARKWAY S 30135
  Samuel Land, prin.
Arp ES, 4841 HIGHWAY 5 30135
  Dr. Fran Karanovich, prin.
Beulah ES, 1150 BURNT HICKORY RD 30134
  Jane Sanders, prin.
Burnett MS, 8277 CONNALLY DR 30134
  Earl McCall, prin.
Chapel Hill ES, 3989 CHAPEL HILL RD 30135
  Dr. Virginia Slate, prin.
Dorsett Shoals ES
  5866 DOREST SHOALS RD 30135
  Dennis Swanger, prin.
Eastside ES, 8266 CONNALLY DR 30134
  Mary Mauney, prin.
Factory Shoals ES, 3046 FAIRBURN RD 30135
  Bobbie Morelock, prin.
Mt. Carmel ES, 2356 FAIRBURN RD 30135
  Harold Maier, prin.
South Douglas ES, 8299 HIGHWAY 166 30135
  Brenda Singleton, prin.
Other Schools – See Lithia Springs, Winston

Kings Way Christian School
  6456 KINGSWAY 30135

Dry Branch, Twiggs Co.
Twiggs County SD
Supt. – See Jeffersonville
ES 31020 – Timothy Grimes, prin.

Dublin, Laurens Co., Pop. Code 7
Dublin ISD
Sch. Sys. Enr. Code 5
Supt. – W. J. Rochelle, 1951 HILLCREST DR 31021
Central Dublin JHS, CALHOUN ST 31021
  Ernest Wade, prin.
Hillcrest ES 31021 – Shellie Stroman, prin.
Johnson Street ES 31021 – Dolores Byrne, prin.
Moore Street ES 31021 – Catherine Wooddy, prin.
Saxon Heights ES, SMITH ST 31021
  Lois Stroman, prin.

Laurens County SD
Sch. Sys. Enr. Code 5
Supt. – J. Warren, Jr., 2128 COURT SQ STA 31021
West Laurens JHS, RURAL ROUTE 05 31021
  Steve Kyzer, prin.
East Laurens MS, RURAL ROUTE 02 31021
  Woodrow Billups, prin.
East Laurens PS, RURAL ROUTE 06 31021
  Larry Waldrep, prin.
Southwest Laurens ES, RURAL ROUTE 05 31021
  Carolyn Watson, prin.
Other Schools – See Dudley

Trinity Christian HS, P O BOX 356 31040

Dudley, Laurens Co., Pop. Code 2
Laurens County SD
Supt. – See Dublin

Northwest Laurens MS, RURAL ROUTE 01   31022
  Rachel Branch, prin.
Northwest Laurens PS   31022
  Rachel Branch, prin.

Duluth, Gwinnett Co., Pop. Code 5
Gwinnett County SD
Supt. – See Lawrenceville
MS, 3057 S PEACHTREE ST   30136
  Jim Stephens, prin.
Berkeley Lake ES
  4300 BERKELEY LAKE RD   30136
  Shirley Davis-Chapman, prin.
Harris ES, 3123 CLAIRBORNE DR   30136
  Judy Sullivan, prin.

Dunwoody, Fulton Co., Pop. Code 2
DeKalb County SD
Supt. – See Decatur
Austin ES, 5435 ROBERTS DR   30338
  Mary Reid, prin.
Chesnut ES, 4576 N PEACHTREE RD   30338
  Dr. Juanesta Johnson, prin.
Kingsley ES, 2051 BRENDON DR   30338
  Carol Reams, prin.
Vanderlyn ES, 1877 VANDERLYN DR   30338
  Sam Harman, prin.

Eastanollee, Stephens Co., Pop. Code 2
Stephens County SD
Supt. – See Toccoa
Stephens County MS   30538 – James Bellamy, prin.
ES, RURAL ROUTE 01 BOX 40   30538
  Robert Stowe, prin.

Eastman, Dodge Co., Pop. Code 6
Dodge County SD
Sch. Sys. Enr. Code 5
Supt. – C. Williams, P O BOX 647   31023
MS, RURAL ROUTE 03   31023
  Waymon McCrannie, prin.
Dodge ES, RURAL ROUTE 06 BOX 332   31023
  Bobby Griffin, prin.
ES, 701 COLLEGE ST   31023 – David Jones, prin.
Other Schools – See Chauncey, Chester, Rhine

East Point, Fulton Co., Pop. Code 8
Fulton County SD
Supt. – See Atlanta
West MS, 2376 HEADLAND DRIVE   30344
  Hugh Wingo, prin.
Woodland MS, 2816 BRIARWOOD BLVD   30344
  Henry Porter, prin.
Brookview ES, 3250 HAMMARSKJOLD DR   30344
  James Cleveland, prin.
Central Park ES, 2715 CHENEY ST   30344
  Helen Stark, prin.
Dodson Drive ES, 2581 DODSON DR   30344
  Ronald Lane, prin.
Mt. Olive ES, 3353 MOUNT OLIVE RD   30344
  Dr. Thomas Kosslow, prin.
Oak Knoll ES, 2626 HOGAN RD   30344
  Jane Wright, prin.
Parklane ES, 2809 BLOUNT ST   30344
  James Stacy, prin.
Quillian-East Point ES
  1286 E WASHINGTON ST   30344
  Arthur Marshall, prin.
Smith ES, 3291 PENNSYLVANIA ST   30344
  Deborah Bent, prin.
Wells ES, 2148 NEWNAN AVE   30344
  Vicki Beck, prin.

Colonial Hills Christian HS
  2134 NEWNAN AVE   30344
Christ Lutheran School
  2719 DE LOWE DRIVE   30344
Pathway Christian School
  1706 WASHINGTON AVE   30344

Eatonton, Putnam Co., Pop. Code 5
Putnam County SD
Sch. Sys. Enr. Code 4
Supt. – Wm. Dabbs, P O BOX 31   31024
Putnam County MS
  314 S WASHINGTON AVE   31024
  Fabian Fain, prin.
Butler-Baker ES, ALICE WALKER DR   31024
  Robert O'Steen, prin.

Gatewood School, P O BOX 469   31024

Elberton, Elbert Co., Pop. Code 6
Elbert County SD
Sch. Sys. Enr. Code 5
Supt. – Charles Dixon, 50 LAUREL DRIVE   30635
Elbert County MS, 45 FOREST AVE   30635
  C. Munumer, prin.
Beaverdam ES
  739 NEW RUCKERSVILLE RD   30635
  Phillip Hart, prin.
Blackwell ES, 373 CAMPBELL ST   30635
  Ann Gunter, prin.
MS, 390 MILL ST   30635
  William Hunnicutt, prin.
Falling Creek ES
  1050 WASHINGTON HWY   30635
  Wallace Edwards, prin.
Other Schools – See Bowman

Ellaville, Schley Co., Pop. Code 4
Schley County SD
Sch. Sys. Enr. Code 2
Supt. – Samuel Wade, P O BOX 66   31806
Schley County ES, P O BOX 606   31806
  William Johnson, prin.

Ellenwood, Clayton Co.
Clayton County SD
Supt. – See Jonesboro
East Clayton ES, 2750 ELLENWOOD RD   30049
  Betty Brittian, prin.

DeKalb County SD
Supt. – See Decatur
Cedar Grove ES, 2330 RIVER RD   30049
  Betty Smart, prin.

Faith Christian Academy
  4851 RIVER ROAD   30049

Ellijay, Gilmer Co., Pop. Code 4
Gilmer County SD
Sch. Sys. Enr. Code 4
Supt. – Homer Hefner
  5 WEST SIDE SQUARE ST   30540
MS, 250 LIBRARY ST   30540
  Maxine Edwards, prin.
MS, P O BOX 1058   30540 – Fred Keith, prin.
PS, 500 LIBRARY ST   30540 – Ben Arp, prin.
Oakland ES, RURAL ROUTE 02 BOX 84A   30540
  Ilo Bossen, prin.

Emerson, Bartow Co., Pop. Code 4
Bartow County SD
Supt. – See Cartersville
ES, P O BOX 132   30137 – Dot Frasier-Hall, prin.

Epworth, Fannin Co.
Fannin County SD
Supt. – See Blue Ridge
ES   30541 – Mike Ballew, prin.

Eton, Murray Co., Pop. Code 2
Murray County SD
Supt. – See Chatsworth
ES   30724 – James Turner, prin.

Evans, Columbia Co., Pop. Code 4
Columbia County SD
Supt. – See Appling
MS, P O BOX 129   30809 – J. Wilcher, prin.
Bel Air ES, BEL AIR ROAD   30809
  Janice Blackledge, prin.
Blue Ridge ES, 550 BLUE RIDGE DR   30809
  Ann Abbott, prin.
ES, RURAL ROUTE 03 BOX 156   30809
  Joe Jolley, prin.

Arlington School, 4500 RIDGE ROAD   30213

Fairmount, Gordon Co., Pop. Code 3
Gordon County SD
Supt. – See Calhoun
S   30139 – John Penland, prin.

Fargo, Clinch Co.
Clinch County SD
Supt. – See Homerville
ES, P O BOX 158   31631 – Alphin Griffis, prin.

Fayetteville, Fayette Co., Pop. Code 5
Fayette County SD
Sch. Sys. Enr. Code 6
Supt. – Trigg Dalrymple
  210 STONEWALL AVE   30214
Fayette County JHS, BROOKER AVE   30214
  Harry Sweatman, prin.
East Fayette ES, 245 BOOKER AVE   30214
  Dr. Bob Martin, prin.
MS, 440 HOOD AVE   30214 – Jean Allen, prin.
Hood Avenue ES, 490 HOOD AVE   30214
  Pam Riddle, prin.
North Fayette ES, 609 KENWOOD RD   30214
  Edward Pollard, prin.
Other Schools – See Brooks, Peachtree City, Tyrone

Fayette Christian Academy
  280 LONGVIEW ROAD   30214
Counterpane School, P O BOX 898   30214

Fitzgerald, Ben Hill Co., Pop. Code 7
Ben Hill County SD
Sch. Sys. Enr. Code 4
Supt. – Louis E. Harper, COURTHOUSE   31750
Ben Hill County ES, RURAL ROUTE 03   31750
  Sylvia Bryant, prin.

Fitzgerald ISD
Sch. Sys. Enr. Code 4
Supt. – Warren Alexander, P O BOX 1047   31750
ES, 401 W ALTAMAHA ST   31750
  John Renfroe, prin.
JHS, W PALM ST   31750 – Wardell Herring, prin.

Flintstone, Walker Co.
Walker County SD
Supt. – See La Fayette
Chattanooga Valley ES, RURAL ROUTE 01   30725
  Dane Ward, prin.

Flowery Branch, Hall Co., Pop. Code 3
Hall County SD
Supt. – See Gainesville

ES, 5544 RADFORD RD   30542
  Lyn Harmon, prin.

Folkston, Charlton Co., Pop. Code 4
Charlton County SD
Sch. Sys. Enr. Code 4
Supt. – Charles Warnock, 500 S 3RD ST   31537
MS, 810 N 3RD ST   31537 – A. Lawrence, prin.
Bethune ES, RURAL ROUTE 03 BOX 170C   31537
  Steve McQueen, prin.
Other Schools – See Saint George

Forest Park, Clayton Co., Pop. Code 7
Clayton County SD
Supt. – See Jonesboro
Ash Street ES, 5277 ASH ST   30050
  Scotty Anderson, prin.
Edmonds ES, 4495 SIMPSON RD   30050
  Bill McAdams, prin.
Fountain JHS, 5212 WEST ST   30050
  Russell Kirklnd, prin.
Hendrix Drive ES, 4475 HENDRIX DR   30050
  Don Campbell, prin.
Huie ES, 1260 ROCKCUT RD   30050
  Ken Barnes, prin.

Forest Park Christian School
  5881 PHILLIPS DRIVE   30050

Forsyth, Monroe Co., Pop. Code 5
Monroe County SD
Sch. Sys. Enr. Code 5
Supt. – Charles E. Dumas, P O BOX 1308   31029
Monroe County MS, BROOKLYN AVE   31029
  Cecil Porter, prin.
Hubbard ES   31029 – William Querry,Jr., prin.

Monroe Academy, P O BOX 4   31029

Fort Gaines, Clay Co., Pop. Code 4
Clay County SD
Sch. Sys. Enr. Code 2
Supt. – Wright Wilkins, P O BOX 219   31751
Clay County ES   31751 – George Hartley, prin.

Fort Oglethorpe, Catoosa Co., Pop. Code 6
Catoosa County SD
Supt. – See Ringgold
Battlefield ES, 1101 BATTLEFIELD PKY   30742
  Patrick McMillen, prin.
ES, 600 BARNHARDT CIR   30742
  Sharon McMahan, prin.

Fortson, Muscogee Co.
Harris County SD
Supt. – See Hamilton
Mountain Hill ES
  RURAL ROUTE 01 BOX 318   31808
  Garnett Ray,Jr., prin.

Fort Valley, Peach Co., Pop. Code 6
Peach County SD
Sch. Sys. Enr. Code 5
Supt. – B. J. McClendon, P O BOX 1120   31030
MS, TULIP DR   31030 – Terry Cheek, prin.
Hunt ES, 700 SPRUCE ST   31030
  Carolyn Sampson, prin.
Other Schools – See Byron

Franklin, Heard Co., Pop. Code 3
Heard County SD
Sch. Sys. Enr. Code 4
Supt. – Benjamin Hyatt, P O BOX 99   30217
Centralhatchee ES, RURAL ROUTE 02   30217
  Tommy Chambers, prin.
Heard County ES   30217 – W. Lipham, prin.
Other Schools – See Roopville

Funston, Colquitt Co., Pop. Code 2
Colquitt County SD
Supt. – See Moultrie
ES, P O BOX 40   31753 – Scott Michie, prin.

Gainesville, Hall Co., Pop. Code 7
Forsyth County SD
Supt. – See Cumming
Chestatee ES, RURAL ROUTE 01 BOX 1411   30506
  Ann Sefzik, prin.

Gainesville ISD
Sch. Sys. Enr. Code 5
Supt. – Dr. Gary Smith
  850 WOODSMILL ROAD   30501
MS, 715 WOODSMILL ROAD   30501
  Charles McDonald, prin.
Enota ES, 1000 ENOTA AVE NE   30505
  Shirley Whitaker, prin.
Fair Street MS, 695 FAIR ST   30505
  Dr. John Davis, prin.

Hall County SD
Sch. Sys. Enr. Code 7
Supt. – Dr. Douglas Winters, 300 GREEN ST   30501
East Hall MS, 4120 E HALL RD   30505
  Gary Stewart, prin.
Jones ES, 50 SIXTH ST   30501
  Gerald Davidson, prin.
Lanier ES, RURAL ROUTE 12 BOX 500   30505
  Ben Fouts, prin.
Lyman Hall ES, 2150 MEMORIAL PARK RD   30505
  Crandall Autry, prin.
McEver ES, 3265 MONTGOMERY DR   30505
  Phil Carpenter, prin.
Myers ES, 2676 CANDLER RD   30501
  Louell Roper, prin.
North Hall MS, 4956 RILLA RD   30505
  Michael Greavu, prin.

Riverbend ES, 1742 CLEVELAND RD 30505
  Robert Ables, prin.
Sardis ES, 2805 SARDIS RD 30506
  Martha Fritchley, prin.
South Hall MS
  3515 POPLAR SPRINGS ROAD 30505
  Charles McKinney, prin.
Tadmore ES, 3278 GILLSVILLE HWY 30501
  Fern Patterson, prin.
Wauka Mountain ES, RURAL ROUTE 06 30505
  John Corley, prin.
White Sulphur ES
  2480 OLD CORNELIA HWY 30501
  Jerry Smith, prin.
Other Schools – See Chestnut Mountain, Flowery
  Branch, Lula, Oakwood

Lakeview Academy, 796 LAKEVIEW DRIVE 30501
Marantha Christian Academy
  1745 SKELTON RD 30501

Garden City, Chatham Co., Pop. Code 6
Chatham County SD
Supt. – See Savannah
Mercer MS, 201 ROMMEL AVE 31408
  Virginia Deloach, prin.
Sprague ES, 50 BYCK AVE 31408
  Bertha Tuten, prin.

Gay, Meriwether Co., Pop. Code 2
Meriwether County SD
Supt. – See Greenville
McCrary ES, RURAL ROUTE 01 BOX 173C 30218
  J. Daniel, prin.

Georgetown, Quitman Co., Pop. Code 3
Quitman County SD
Sch. Sys. Enr. Code 2
Supt. – James Gary,Jr., P O BOX 248 31754
Quitman County ES 31754 – Vince Turpin, prin.

Gibson, Glascock Co., Pop. Code 3
Glascock County SD
Sch. Sys. Enr. Code 3
Supt. – Andy Chalker, P O BOX 205 30810
Glascock County Cons. S, P O BOX 205 30810
  Barry Durden, prin.

Glennville, Tattnall Co., Pop. Code 5
Tattnal County SD
Supt. – See Reidsville
MS, P O BOX 624 30427 – Jim Poole, prin.
Seckinger PS, 525 PINE ST 30427
  Sylvester Ashford, prin.

Glenville Christian Academy, P O BOX 706 30427

Glenwood, Wheeler Co., Pop. Code 3
Wheeler County SD
Supt. – See Alamo
Wheeler County MS, P O BOX 308 30428
  Dane Butler, prin.

Gracewood, Richmond Co.
Richmond County SD
Supt. – See Augusta
ES, P O BOX 296 30812 – Harriet Roney, prin.

Grantville, Coweta Co., Pop. Code 4
Coweta County SD
Supt. – See Newnan
Grantville Brown ES
  99 BROWN SCHOOL DR 30220
  Ruth Mealor, prin.

Gray, Jones Co., Pop. Code 4
Jones County SD
Sch. Sys. Enr. Code 5
Supt. – L. Jordan, P O BOX 517 31032
Califf MS, CALIFF ST 31032 – Lani Schewe, prin.
ES, P O BOX 1389 31032 – Gretchen Bess, prin.
Other Schools – See Macon

Jonesco Academy, P O BOX 775 31032

Grayson, Gwinnett Co., Pop. Code 2
Gwinnett County SD
Supt. – See Lawrenceville
ES, 460 HIGHWAY 84 30221 – Herb Burrell, prin.

Graysville, Catoosa Co., Pop. Code 2
Catoosa County SD
Supt. – See Ringgold
ES 30726 – Beth Kellerhals, prin.

Greensboro, Greene Co., Pop. Code 5
Greene County SD
Sch. Sys. Enr. Code 4
Supt. – Edward Corry,Jr., P O BOX 209 30642
Corry MS, P O BOX 410 30642
  William Breeding, prin.
PS, P O BOX 390 30642 – Phillip Brock, prin.
Other Schools – See Union Point

Greenville, Meriwether Co., Pop. Code 4
Meriwether County SD
Sch. Sys. Enr. Code 5
Supt. – Lee Forehand, N COURT SQ 30222
ES, P O BOX G 30222 – Willie Anderson, prin.
Other Schools – See Gay, Luthersville, Manchester,
  Warm Springs, Woodbury

Griffin, Spalding Co., Pop. Code 7
Spalding County SD
Sch. Sys. Enr. Code 7
Supt. – Dr. Charles H. Green, P O BOX N 30224
Flynt Street MS, 1551 FLYNT ST 30223
  John Goodrum, prin.

Kelsey Avenue MS, KELSEY AVE 30223
  Michael McLemore, prin.
Taylor Street MS, 234 E TAYLOR ST 30223
  Tom Ison, prin.
Anne Street ES, 802 ANNE ST 30223
  Hobart Davenport, prin.
Atkinson ES, 307 ATKINSON DR 30223
  Frank Touchstone, prin.
Beaverbrook ES, 251 BIRDIE RD 30223
  Dr. Margaret Thrasher, prin.
Crescent Road ES, 201 CRESCENT RD 30223
  Dr. Helen Bornhauser, prin.
East Griffin ES, HIGH FALLS ROAD 30223
  Marian Dunn, prin.
Fourth Ward MS, 320 S 15TH ST 30223
  William Matchett, prin.
Jackson Road ES, 1233 JACKSON RD 30223
  Larry White, prin.
Moore ES, 201 CABIN CREEK DR 30223
  Dr. William Nesbit, prin.
North Side ES, 502 NORTH HILL ST 30223
  Dorothy Sampson, prin.
Orrs ES, SPALDING DR 30223 – Robert Nix, prin.
Third Ward ES, TILNEY AVE 30223
  Millie Childs, prin.
West Griffin ES, 814 EXPERIMENT ST 30223
  Joe Akin, prin.

Griffin Chrstn Academy
  1141 ATLANTA ROAD 30223

Grovetown, Columbia Co., Pop. Code 5
Columbia County SD
Supt. – See Appling
Columbia MS, 600 COLUMBIA ROAD 30813
  Gloria Hamilton, prin.
ES, P O BOX 640 30813 – Wayne Hardy, prin.

Guyton, Effingham Co., Pop. Code 3
Effingham County SD
Supt. – See Springfield
ES, P O BOX 9 31312 – H. Beacham, prin.
Marlow ES, RURAL ROUTE 01 BOX 72 31312
  Naomi Dasher, prin.
South Effingham ES
  RURAL ROUTE 01 BOX 430D 31312
  Harris Hinely,Jr., prin.

Hahira, Lowndes Co., Pop. Code 4
Lowndes County SD
Supt. – See Valdosta
MS, P O BOX 902 31632 – Ann Rodgers, prin.
ES, P O BOX 901 31632 – Lyndal Webb, prin.

Hamilton, Harris Co., Pop. Code 3
Harris County SD
Sch. Sys. Enr. Code 5
Supt. – Richard Carlisle, P O BOX 388 31811
Harris County MS, P O BOX 408 31811
  Arnold Jackson, prin.
Park ES, P O BOX 428 31811
  Rebecca Carlisle, prin.
Other Schools – See Cataula, Fortson, Waverly Hall

Hampton, Henry Co., Pop. Code 4
Clayton County SD
Supt. – See Jonesboro
Kemp ES, 10990 FOLSUM RD 30228
  Wilton Marchman, prin.

Henry County SD
Supt. – See Mc Donough
ES, 6 CENTRAL AVE 30228
  Sheila Binkney, prin.

Hapeville, Fulton Co., Pop. Code 6
Atlanta ISD
Supt. – See Atlanta
Blair Village ES, 370 BLAIR VILLA DR 30354
  Brenda Kilgore-DuBose, prin.

Fulton County SD
Supt. – See Atlanta
North Avenue ES, 689 NORTH AVE 30354
  Elizabeth Craig, prin.
Wells ES, 554 PARKWAY DR 30354
  Hazel Scraggs, prin.

St. John Evangelist School
  240 ARNOLD ST 30354

Harlem, Columbia Co., Pop. Code 4
Columbia County SD
Supt. – See Appling
MS, P O BOX 729 30814 – John Eckenroth, prin.
North Harlem ES, P O BOX 669 30814
  Joan Ashley, prin.

Hartsfield, Colquitt Co.
Colquitt County SD
Supt. – See Moultrie
Hamilton ES, RURAL ROUTE 01 31756
  R. Coleman, prin.

Hartwell, Hart Co., Pop. Code 5
Hart County SD
Sch. Sys. Enr. Code 5
Supt. – Vernon Edwards, P O BOX 696 30643
Hart County JHS, 410 RICHARDSON ST 30643
  Billy Shiflet, prin.
Hart ES, RURAL ROUTE 03 30643
  Billy Wood, prin.
ES, COLLEGE AVE 30643 – L. Harris, prin.
Mt. Olivet ES, RURAL ROUTE 04 30643
  Roy Morgan, prin.
Other Schools – See Bowersville, Canon

Hawkinsville, Pulaski Co., Pop. Code 5
Pulaski County SD
Sch. Sys. Enr. Code 4
Supt. – Robert Gentry, MCCORMICK AVE 31036
Pulaski County MS, WARREN ST 31036
  Tony Portivent, prin.
Pulaski County ES, BROAD ST 31036
  Kay Dawson, prin.

Baker Academy, P O BOX 449 31036

Hazlehurst, Jeff Davis Co., Pop. Code 5
Jeff Davis County SD
Sch. Sys. Enr. Code 5
Supt. – Gayle Wooten, P O BOX 571 31539
Davis JHS, P O BOX 1080 31539
  G. Herrington,Jr., prin.
Davis ES, P O BOX 511 31539 – Lula Perry, prin.
Davis MS, P O BOX 625 31539 – T. Padgett, prin.

Hephzibah, Richmond Co., Pop. Code 4
Richmond County SD
Supt. – See Augusta
MS, P O BOX 248 30815 – David Smith, prin.
Morgan Road MS, 2751 TOBACCO ROAD 30815
  Vivian Pennamon, prin.
Graham ES, P O BOX 158 30815
  Jason Jarrard, prin.
MS, P O BOX 248 30815 – Paul Hauser, prin.
Jamestown ES, 3637 HIERS BLVD 30815
  Yvonne Shaw, prin.

Hiawassee, Towns Co., Pop. Code 2
Towns County SD
Sch. Sys. Enr. Code 3
Supt. – Bill Kendall, P O BOX 386 30546
Towns County Comprehensive S
  P O BOX 327 30546 – Roy Barrett, prin.

Hinesville, Liberty Co., Pop. Code 7
Liberty County SD
Sch. Sys. Enr. Code 6
Supt. – Edgar Edwards, P O BOX 70 31313
MS, 307 E WASHINGTON ST 31313
  Charles Richardson, prin.
Bacon ES, 101 DEEN ST 31313
  Dorothy Cottom, prin.
Gwinnett ES, TAYLOR ROAD 31313
  William Tomberlin, prin.
Hall ES, RURAL ROUTE 03 BOX 289 31313
  Barbara Christmas, prin.
Martin ES, 1000 JOSEPH MARTIN DR 31313
  LaFayne May, prin.
Other Schools – See Midway

Hiram, Paulding Co., Pop. Code 3
Paulding County SD
Supt. – See Dallas
Ritch MS, RURAL ROUTE 01 BOX 2808 B 30141
  Don Rauscher, prin.
ES, SEABOARD AVE 30141 – John Pezold, prin.
McGarity ES
  8311 RAKESTRAW MILL ROAD 30141
  Yvonne Welch, prin.

Hoboken, Brantley Co., Pop. Code 3
Brantley County SD
Supt. – See Nahunta
ES, P O BOX 98 31542 – James Ferguson, prin.

Hogansville, Troup Co., Pop. Code 5
Hogansville ISD
Sch. Sys. Enr. Code 3
Supt. – Eugene Crocker, 103 E MAIN ST 30230
Crocker PS, 407 CHURCH ST 30230
  James Korytoski, prin.
MS, P O BOX 628 30230 – Sidney Wilson, prin.

Holly Springs, Cherokee Co., Pop. Code 3
Cherokee County SD
Supt. – See Canton
ES, P O BOX 611 30142 – Robert Wofford, prin.

Homer, Banks Co., Pop. Code 3
Banks County SD
Sch. Sys. Enr. Code 4
Supt. – Dock Sisk, P O BOX 1657 30547
Banks County MS, P O BOX 1717 30547
  David Dye, prin.
Banks County PS, P O BOX 197 30547
  Bobby LeWallen, prin.

Homerville, Clinch Co., Pop. Code 5
Clinch County SD
Sch. Sys. Enr. Code 4
Supt. – Dr. Tommy Lee, 101 COLLEGE ST 31634
Clinch MS, P O BOX 435 31634
  Sterling Newton, prin.
ES, P O BOX 415 31634 – Clayton Cross, prin.
Other Schools – See Fargo

Ila, Madison Co., Pop. Code 2
Madison County SD
Supt. – See Danielsville
ES 30647 – Linda Halloman, prin.

Irwinton, Wilkinson Co., Pop. Code 3
Wilkinson County SD
Sch. Sys. Enr. Code 4
Supt. – H. A. Mills, P O BOX 206 31042
Wilkinson County MS, P O BOX 193 31042
  Willie Scott, prin.
Wilkinson County MS, P O BOX 181 31042
  Kathy Culpepper, prin.
Other Schools – See Mc Intyre

Jackson, Butts Co., Pop. Code 5
Butts County SD
Sch. Sys. Enr. Code 5
Supt. – Loy Hutcheson
181 N MULBERRY ST 30233
Henderson JHS, 820 N MULBERRY ST 30233
George Tate, prin.
Henderson MS, 774 N MULBERRY ST 30233
Angelyn Hearn, prin.
PS, 218 WOODLAND WAY 30233
Laura Lester, prin.

Jasper, Pickens Co., Pop. Code 4
Pickens County SD
Sch. Sys. Enr. Code 4
Supt. – Don Enis, 211 N MAIN ST 30143
Pickens Co. MS, 950 REFUGE RD 30143
G. Little, prin.
ES 30143 – Ron Carlan, prin.
Other Schools – See Tate

Jefferson, Jackson Co., Pop. Code 4
Jackson County SD
Sch. Sys. Enr. Code 5
Supt. – Russell Cook, P O BOX 279 30549
Other Schools – See Athens, Braselton, Maysville,
Nicholson, Talmo

Jefferson ISD
Sch. Sys. Enr. Code 4
Supt. – Dr. Donald Rooks, P O BOX 507 30549
ES 30549 – Patricia Lance, prin.

Jeffersonville, Twiggs Co., Pop. Code 4
Twiggs County SD
Sch. Sys. Enr. Code 4
Supt. – C. W. Keily, I-16 & GA 96 31044
ES 31044 – Hosezell Blash, prin.
Other Schools – See Danville, Dry Branch

Twiggs Academy, Inc.
RURAL ROUTE 01 BOX 4637 31044

Jesup, Wayne Co., Pop. Code 6
Wayne County SD
Sch. Sys. Enr. Code 5
Supt. – Jerry Jones, 555 SUNSET BLVD 31545
Wayne County JHS, 1425 W ORANGE ST 31545
Donald Westberry, prin.
ES, 642 E PLUM ST 31545 – Tom Freeman, prin.
MS, 710 W PLUM ST 31545 – David Norris, prin.
Ritch ES, 420 CEDAR ST 31545
Earl Richardson, prin.
Other Schools – See Odum, Screven

Jonesboro, Clayton Co., Pop. Code 5
Clayton County SD
Sch. Sys. Enr. Code 7
Supt. – Joe Lovin, 120 SMITH ST 30236
Arnold ES, 216 STOCKBRIDGE RD 30236
Don Wilson, prin.
Brown ES, 9771 POSTON RD 30236
Charles Hale, prin.
Kilpatrick ES, 7534 TARA RD 30236
Bill Livingston, prin.
Lee Street ES, 178 LEE ST 30236
Bill Bibby, prin.
Mt. Zion ES, 2984 MOUNT ZION RD 30236
George McLeod, prin.
North Jonesboro ES, 1098 5TH AVE 30236
Marty Whiteman, prin.
Suder ES, 1400 LAKE JODECO RD 30236
Roy Pierce, prin.
Swint ES, 500 HIGHWAY 138 W 30236
Bobby Ball, prin.
Other Schools – See College Park, Conley, Ellenwood,
Forest Park, Hampton, Lake City, Morrow, Riverdale

Mt. Zion Christian Academy
7102 MOUNT ZION BLVD 30236

Kennesaw, Cobb Co., Pop. Code 6
Cobb County SD
Supt. – See Marietta
Awtrey MS, 3601 NOWLIN ROAD 30144
William Hamilton, prin.
Pine Mountain MS
2720 MINE MOUNT CIRCLE 30144
Henry Nettles, prin.
Big Shanty ES, 1600 BEN KING RD 30144
Robert Corry, prin.
ES, 6997 KEENE ST 30144 – David Butts, prin.
Lewis ES, 4179 JIM OWENS RD 30144
Jesse Bookhardt, prin.

Shiloh Hills Christian HS
75 HAWKINS STORE ROAD 30144

Kingsland, Camden Co., Pop. Code 4
Camden County SD
Sch. Sys. Enr. Code 5
Supt. – Gene Brewer, P O BOX 1329 31548
Camden MS, 1300 MIDDLE SCHOOL RD 31548
Gary Blount, prin.
Clark MS, 1300 MIDDLE SCHOOL RD 31548
Noel Carroll, prin.
ES, P O BOX 707 31548 – Edith Simpson, prin.
Other Schools – See Saint Marys, Woodbine

Kingston, Bartow Co., Pop. Code 3
Bartow County SD
Supt. – See Cartersville
ES, 90 MAIN ST NW 30145 – Brad Paulk, prin.

Kite, Johnson Co., Pop. Code 2
Johnson County SD
Supt. – See Wrightsville
ES, HWY 57 31049 – Talmadge Riner, prin.

La Fayette, Walker Co., Pop. Code 6
Walker County SD
Sch. Sys. Enr. Code 7
Supt. – Lanny Benson, P O BOX 29 30728
JHS, HWY 27 N 30728 – David Brothers, prin.
Armuchee Valley ES, RURAL ROUTE 03 30728
Ron Peck, prin.
Center Post ES, P O BOX 807 30728
Ralph Keith, prin.
Fortune ES, 600 CRANE ST 30728
Susan Wells, prin.
Naomi ES, RURAL ROUTE 03 30728
James Smith, prin.
North LaFayette ES, 610 DUKE ST N 30728
Lloyd Cochran, prin.
West LaFayette ES, COLERAIN ST 30728
Phillip Shelton, prin.
Other Schools – See Chickamauga, Flintstone, Rock
Spring, Rossville

La Grange, Troup Co., Pop. Code 7
La Grange ISD
Sch. Sys. Enr. Code 5
Supt. – Dr. Cal Adamson, 201 MAIN ST 30240
La Grange Boys JHS, 1001 E DEPOT ST 30240
Oliver Greene, prin.
West Side Girls JHS, 301 FORREST AVE 30240
Alice Norris, prin.
Dawson MS, 208 N DAWSON ST 30240
Ellen Partridge, prin.
East Side PS, 1001 E DEPOT ST 30240
Nancy Stevens, prin.
Hollis Hand ES, 641 COUNTRY CLUB RD 30240
Janet Bohannon, prin.
South Side PS, 115 E CANNON ST 30240
Betty Alexander, prin.
Weathersbee MS, 1200 FORREST AVE 30240
Ted Alford, prin.

Troup County SD
Sch. Sys. Enr. Code 5
Supt. – B. Wallace, 800 DALLIS ST 30240
Lees Crossing MS, 80 N KNIGHT DR 30240
Bette Whitley, prin.
Whitesville Road MS
1920 WHITESVILLE ROAD 30240
Thomas Whatley, prin.
Hillcrest ES, 3116 NEW FRANKLIN RD 30240
Freeman Mills, prin.
Long Cane ES, 238 LONG CANE RD 30240
William Hamilton, prin.
Mountville ES, 4117 GREENVILLE RD 30240
Bobby Brooks, prin.
Rosemont ES, 4679 HAMILTON RD 30240
John Thrower, prin.
Other Schools – See West Point

La Grange Academy, 1501 VERNON ST 30240
Oakside Christian School
1921 HAMILTON ROAD 30240

Lake City, Clayton Co., Pop. Code 5
Clayton County SD
Supt. – See Jonesboro
ES, 5354 PHILLIPS DR 30260 – Carl James, prin.

Lake City Christian School
5405 JONESBORO ROAD 30260

Lakeland, Lanier Co., Pop. Code 5
Lanier County SD
Sch. Sys. Enr. Code 4
Supt. – L. Raymond Moore, P O BOX 158 31635
Lanier County MS, P O BOX 26 31635
Robert Rice, prin.
Lanier County PS, P O BOX 186 31635
Cynthia Rice, prin.

Lake Park, Lowndes Co., Pop. Code 2
Lowndes County SD
Supt. – See Valdosta
ES, P O BOX B 31636 – Virginia Prince, prin.

Lavonia, Franklin Co., Pop. Code 4
Franklin County SD
Supt. – See Carnesville
ES 30553 – Arthur Outz, prin.

Lawrenceville, Gwinnett Co., Pop. Code 6
Gwinnett County SD
Sch. Sys. Enr. Code 8
Supt. – Dr. A. C. Crews
52 GWINNETT DRIVE 30245
Five Forks MS, 3250 RIVER ROAD 30245
Dr. Mike O'Neal, prin.
MS, 723 HI HOPE RD NE 30245 – Joan Akin, prin.
Richards MS, 600 HUSTON RD 30245
John Ford, prin.
Sweetwater MS, 3500 CRUSE RD 30245
Virginia Crowley, prin.
Benefield ES, 970 MCELVANEY LN 30244
Ann Adams, prin.
Bethesda ES, 525 BETHESDA SCHOOL RD 30244
Connie Greenman, prin.
Cedar Hill ES, 550 HUSTON RD 30245
Hugh May, prin.
Dyer ES, 713 HI HOPE RD 30243
Larry Smith, prin.
Gwin Oaks ES, 400 GWIN OAKS DR SW 30244
Dr. Beverly Dryden, prin.

ES, 122 GWINNETT DR SW 30245
Freddie Williams, prin.
McKendree ES, 650 LAKES PKWY 30243
Cindy Antrim, prin.
Other Schools – See Buford, Dacula, Duluth, Grayson,
Lilburn, Lithonia, Norcross, Snellville, Suwanee

Leesburg, Lee Co., Pop. Code 4
Lee County SD
Sch. Sys. Enr. Code 5
Supt. – Robert A. Clay, P O BOX 236 31763
Lee County MS
RURAL ROUTE 04 BOX 385 31763
Dr. E. Mike Davis, prin.
Lee County MS, P O BOX 146 31763
Ernest Reece, prin.
Lee County PS, P O BOX 9 31763
Opal Cannon, prin.

Lenox, Cook Co., Pop. Code 3
Berrien County SD
Supt. – See Nashville
Northwest ES, RURAL ROUTE 01 31637
James Hunt, prin.

Cook County SD
Supt. – See Adel
ES, HWY 41 N 31637 – Carl Duren, prin.

Lexington, Oglethorpe Co., Pop. Code 2
Oglethorpe County SD
Sch. Sys. Enr. Code 4
Supt. – Tom Y. Harris, P O BOX 190 30648
Oglethorpe County MS, RURAL ROUTE 01 30648
Nancy Fuller, prin.
Oglethorpe Co. ES, COMER ROAD 30648
Dr. Clyde Maxwell, prin.

Lilburn, Gwinnett Co., Pop. Code 5
Gwinnett County SD
Supt. – See Lawrenceville
MS, 4994 LAWRENCEVILLE HWY NW 30247
Mike Grzeskiewicz, prin.
Trickum MS, 948 COLE ROAD SW 30247
Michael Moody, prin.
Arcado ES, 5150 ARCADO RD SW 30247
Jean Murphy, prin.
Camp Creek ES, 958 COLE RD SW 30247
Lynne Horton, prin.
Head ES, 1801 HEWATT ROAD 30247
Betty Robinson, prin.
Hopkins ES, 1315 DICKENS RD NW 30247
Judy Graham, prin.
Knight ES, 401 N RIVER RD SW 30247
Dr. Burrelle Meeks, prin.
ES, 531 MCDANIEL ST NW 30247
Barbara Lunsford, prin.
Minor ES, 4129 SHADY DR NW 30247
John Tippins, prin.
Mountain Park ES, 1500 POUNDS RD SW 30247
Nelda Heatherley, prin.

Hawthorne Christian School, P O BOX 1485 30226
Killian Hill Christian School, P O BOX 1455 30226
St. John Neumann Reg. Catholic School
801 TOM SMITH ROAD 30247

Lincolnton, Lincoln Co., Pop. Code 4
Lincoln County SD
Sch. Sys. Enr. Code 4
Supt. – G. R. Edmunds, P O BOX 39 30817
Lincoln County ES, P O BOX 549 30817
Albert Redford III, prin.

Lindale, Floyd Co., Pop. Code 5
Floyd County SD
Supt. – See Rome
Pepperell MS, 200 HUGHES DAIRY ROAD 30147
Jerry Gatlin, prin.
Pepperell ES, 1 DRAGON DR 30147
Brenda Brannon, prin.

Lithia Springs, Douglas Co.
Douglas County SD
Supt. – See Douglasville
Turner MS, 7101 JUNIOR HIGH DRIVE 30057
John Bakelaar, prin.
ES, 6946 FLORENCE DR 30057
Cecelia Stracener, prin.
Winn ES, 3536 BANKHEAD HWY 30057
Steve Bailey, prin.

Lithonia, De Kalb Co., Pop. Code 5
DeKalb County SD
Supt. – See Decatur
Candler ES, 6775 S GODDARD RD 30038
James Robinson, prin.
Rock Chapel ES, 1130 ROCK CHAPEL RD 30058
Archie Brown, prin.
Stoneview ES, 2629 HUBER ST 30058
William McKinley, prin.

Gwinnett County SD
Supt. – See Lawrenceville
Shiloh MS, 4285 SHILOH ROAD 30058
Valerie Clark, prin.
Annistown ES, 3150 SPAIN RD 30058
Dr. Joy Marsee, prin.

Lizella, Bibb Co.
Bibb County SD
Supt. – See Macon
Redding ES, 8062 EISENHOWER PKY 31052
Gary Yetter, prin.

Locust Grove, Henry Co., Pop. Code 4
Henry County SD
Supt. – See Mc Donough
ES, 1727 GRIFFIN ROAD 30248
William Shearer, Jr., prin.

Loganville, Walton Co., Pop. Code 4
Walton County SD
Supt. – See Monroe
MS, P O BOX 394 30249 – John Seigler, prin.
PS, P O BOX 383 30249 – Randy Bradberry, prin.

Louisville, Jefferson Co., Pop. Code 5
Jefferson County SD
Sch. Sys. Enr. Code 5
Supt. – Kenneth Kelly, P O BOX 449 30434
Louisville Academy ES, P O BOX 405 30434
Issiah Thomas, prin.
Other Schools – See Wadley, Wrens

Thomas Jefferson Academy, P O BOX 523 30434

Ludowici, Long Co., Pop. Code 4
Long County SD
Sch. Sys. Enr. Code 3
Supt. – Joseph Murray, P O BOX 428 31316
Walker ES, P O BOX 729 31316
Dempsy Golden, prin.

Lula, Banks Co., Pop. Code 3
Hall County SD
Supt. – See Gainesville
ES, P O BOX 506 30554 – Jerry Lee, prin.

Lumber City, Telfair Co., Pop. Code 4
Telfair County SD
Supt. – See Mc Rae
ES, P O BOX 8 31549 – Steeny Banks, prin.

Ocmulgee Academy
RURAL ROUTE 01 BOX 20 31549

Lumpkin, Stewart Co., Pop. Code 4
Stewart County SD
Sch. Sys. Enr. Code 4
Supt. – B. W. Mayo, P O BOX 547 31815
ES, P O BOX 37 31815 – Jean Armour, prin.
Other Schools – See Richland

Luthersville, Meriwether Co., Pop. Code 3
Meriwether County SD
Supt. – See Greenville
ES, P O BOX 160 30251 – Charlie Glanton, prin.

Lyerly, Chattooga Co., Pop. Code 2
Chattooga County SD
Supt. – See Summerville
ES, CHURCH ST 30730 – Dale Willingham, prin.

Lyons, Toombs Co., Pop. Code 5
Toombs County SD
Sch. Sys. Enr. Code 4
Supt. – Johnnie Sikes, 118 NW BROAD ST 30436
JHS, P O BOX 151 30436 – Sam Jones, prin.
ES, P O BOX 307 30436 – J. Collins, prin.
Toombs Central ES, RURAL ROUTE 05 30436
Kendall Brantley, prin.

Toombs Christian School, P O BOX 277 30436

Mableton, Cobb Co., Pop. Code 3
Cobb County SD
Supt. – See Marietta
Floyd MS, 4803 FLOYD ROAD 30059
Don Sawicki, prin.
Lindley MS, BUCKNER ROAD 30059
J. Roberts, prin.
Clay ES, 730 BOGGS RD 30059
William Cobb, prin.
Harmony-Leland ES, 5891 DODGEN RD 30059
Frank Hair, prin.
ES, 5220 CHURCH ST 30059
Susan Brasfield, prin.
Riverside ES, 461 S GORDON RD 30059
Mary Ann Albrecht, prin.
Sky View ES, 5805 DUNN RD 30059
Dick Thorne, prin.

Macon, Bibb Co., Pop. Code 9
Bibb County SD
Sch. Sys. Enr. Code 8
Supt. – Dr. Thomas E. Hagler
P O BOX 6157 31213
Appling MS, 1210 SHURLING DR 31211
Weyman Ryals, prin.
Ballard MS, 1780 ANTHONY ROAD 31204
Anita Robinson, prin.
McEvoy MS, 1751 WILLIAMSON RD 31206
Charles Sheftall, prin.
Miller MS, 2421 MONTPELIER AVE 31204
Harry Trawick, prin.
Alexndr II Magnet ES, 1156 COLLEGE ST 31201
Vivian Pennington, prin.
Barden ES, 2521 ANDERSON DR 31206
Nancy Pinaud, prin.
Bellevue ES, 4090 NAPIER AVE 31204
Freddie Stewart, prin.
Bernd ES, 4160 OCMULGEE EAST BLVD 31201
Robert Sanders, prin.
Bruce ES, 3660 HOUSTON AVE 31206
H. Edwards, prin.
Burdell ES, 972 FT HILL ST 31201
Vivian Hatcher, prin.
Burghard ES, 6020 BLOOMFIELD RD 31206
Stanley Messer, prin.
Burke ES, 2051 SECOND ST 31201
Horace Black, prin.

Clisby Magnet ES, 2260 VINEVILLE AVE 31204
Dr. Karen Konke, prin.
Danforth PS, 1301 SHURLING DR 31211
Karen Shockley, prin.
Hamilton ES, 1870 PIO NONO AVE 31204
Myrtice Johnson, prin.
Hartley ES, 2230 ANTHONY RD 31204
Marion McCarthy, prin.
Heard ES, 6515 HOUSTON RD 31206
Gloria McSwain, prin.
Hunt Magnet ES, 990 SHURLING DR 31211
Richard Burnes, prin.
Ingram/Pye ES, 855 ANTHONY RD 31204
Ed McDowell, prin.
Jones ES, 2350 ALANDALE DR 31211
Ella Carter, prin.
King MS, 1307 SHURLING DR 31211
Morris Seltzer, prin.
Lane ES, 990 NEWPORT RD 31210
Dr. Tina Singleton, prin.
Morgan ES, 4901 FAUBUS AVE 31204
Sharron Bourland, prin.
Porter ES, 5802 SCHOOL RD 31206
Andrew Young, prin.
Rice ES, 3750 JESSIE RICE ST 31206
Word Train, prin.
Riley ES, 3522 GREENBRIAR RD 31204
Louis Tompkins, prin.
Springdale ES, 4965 NORTHSIDE DR 31210
Jim Littlefield, prin.
Stephens ES, 3321 NAPIER AVE 31204
Linda Harris, prin.
Taylor ES, 2976 CRESTLINE DR 31204
Peggy Moody, prin.
Tinsley ES, 709 PIERCE AVE 31204
Jan Cowles, prin.
Union ES, 4831 MAMIE CARTER DR 31210
B. Jordan, prin.
Weir ES, 1180 ROCKY CREEK RD 31206
Claxton Walker, prin.
Williams ES, 325 PURSLEY ST 31201
Burney Lester, prin.
Winship ES, 2560 BEECH AVE 31204
Willie Durham, prin.
Other Schools – See Lizella

Jones County SD
Supt. – See Gray
Wells ES, P O BOX 100 31207
Robert Bragg, prin.

Central Fellowship Christian Academy
8460 HAWKINSVILLE ROAD 31206
Chapel Hill Christian Academy
4500 JORDAN LAKE ROAD 31206
Cross Keys Christian Academy
8736 SGODA ROAD 31201
First Presbyterian Day School
5671 CALVIN DRIVE 31210
Gilead Christian Academy
1931 ROCKY CREEK RD 31206
Stratford Academy, 6010 PEAKE ROAD 31297
Tatnell Square Academy
760 LAKE CREST DRIVE 31210
Windsor Academy, 4150 MONES ROAD 31206
Progressive Christian Academy
2290 SECOND ST 31206
St. Joseph School, 905 HIGH ST 31201
St. Peter Claver ES, 133 WARD ST 31204

Madison, Morgan Co., Pop. Code 5
Morgan County SD
Sch. Sys. Enr. Code 5
Supt. – James Hagin, Jr., RURAL ROUTE 02 30650
Morgan County MS, 920 PEARL ST 30650
Alfred Murray, prin.
Morgan County PS, 993 EAST AVE 30650
Dr. Wayne Myers, prin.

Manchester, Meriwether Co., Pop. Code 5
Meriwether County SD
Supt. – See Greenville
MS, E BOUNDARY 31816 – A. Randolf, prin.
ES, PERRY ST 31816 – Ed Barnes, prin.

Manor, Ware Co.
Ware County SD
Supt. – See Waycross
ES, P O BOX 7 31550 – L. Barber, prin.

Mansfield, Newton Co., Pop. Code 2
Newton County SD
Supt. – See Covington
ES 30255 – Phil Buchen, prin.

Marietta, Cobb Co., Pop. Code 8
Cobb County SD
Sch. Sys. Enr. Code 8
Supt. – Dr. Thomas Tocco, P O BOX 1088 30061
Daniell MS, 2900 SCOTT ROAD 30066
James Wilson, prin.
Dickerson MS, 855 WOODLAWN DRIVE 30067
Carole Kell, prin.
Dodgen MS, 1725 BILL MURDOCK ROAD 30062
Tony Melton, prin.
East Cobb MS, 380 HOLT ROAD 30067
Sharon Patterson, prin.
Mabry MS, 2700 JIMS ROAD 30066
Melba Fugitt, prin.
McCleskey MS, 4080 MAYBREEZE ROAD 30066
Steve Shelton, prin.
Pope MS, 3001 HEMBREE ROAD NE 30062
Kelly Henson, prin.
Simpson MS, 3340 TRICKUM ROAD 30066
Tony Melton, prin.

Addison ES, 3055 EBENEZER ROAD 30066
Carolyn Jurick, prin.
Bells Ferry ES, 2600 BELLS FERRY RD 30066
Charles Burrell, prin.
Birney ES
775 SMYRNA-POWDR SPRGS ROAD 30060
Gertrude Engelhardt, prin.
Blackwell ES, 3470 CANTON RD 30066
David McKenna, prin.
Brumby ES, 1306 POWERS FERRY RD 30067
Tom Mathis, prin.
Davis ES, 2433 JAMERSON RD 30066
Sandra Davis, prin.
Due West ES, RURAL ROUTE 04 30064
Jerry Pevey, prin.
East Side ES, 3850 ROSWELL RD 30062
Mary Widener, prin.
East Valley ES, 2570 LOWER ROSWELL RD 30067
Cynthia Stephens, prin.
Fair Oaks ES, 407 BARBER RD 30060
Jack McLeod, prin.
Garrison Mill ES
4111 WESLEY CHAPEL RD 30062
Patricia Mingledorff, prin.
Hollydale ES, 2901 BAYBERRY DR 30060
Peyton McQuary, prin.
Keheley ES, 1935 KEMP RD 30066
Dr. Bonnie Bell, prin.
Kincaid ES, 1410 KINCAID RD 30066
Mary Anderson, prin.
LaBelle ES, 230 CRESSON DR 30060
Doyle Crum, prin.
Milford ES, 2390 AUSTELL RD 30060
Mike Anderson, prin.
Mt. Bethel ES, 1210 JOHNSON FERRY RD 30068
Robin Pennock, prin.
Mountain View ES
3448 SANDY PLAINS RD 30066
Nancy Hoffman, prin.
Murdock ES, 2320 MURDOCK RD 30062
W. Robertson, prin.
Powers Ferry ES, 1845 POWERS FERRY RD 30067
Bill Hood, prin.
Rocky Mount ES
2400 ROCKY MOUNTAIN RD 30066
Bill Scott, prin.
Sedalia Park ES
2230 LOWER ROSWELL RD 30068
Ollie Grant, prin.
Sope Creek ES, 3320 PAPER MILL RD 30067
Ethel Kopkin, prin.
Tritt ES, 4435 POST OAK-TRITT RD 30062
Sandra Snipes, prin.
Other Schools – See Acworth, Austell, Kennesaw,
Mableton, Powder Springs, Smyrna

Marietta ISD
Sch. Sys. Enr. Code 5
Supt. – Dr. Roy D. Nichols, Jr.
P O BOX 1265 30061
JHS, 340 AVIATION ROAD 30060
Lucian Harris, prin.
Allgood MS, 461 ALLGOOD RD 30060
Dr. Paul Smith, prin.
Burruss ES, 325 MANNING RD 30064
Jerry Locke, prin.
Hickory Hills ES, 500 REDWOOD DR SW 30064
Jane Riley, prin.
Lockheed ES, 250 HOWARD ST 30060
Betty Schleicher, prin.
Park Street ES, 105 PARK ST 30060
Dr. Mary Jo Brubaker, prin.
Pine Forest ES, 311 AVIATION RD 30060
Fred Oliver, prin.
West Side ES, 344 POLK ST 30064
Reid Brown, prin.

Cobb County Christian School
545 LORENE DR 30060
Joseph Walker School
700 ALLGOOD ROAD 30062
Eastside Baptist Christian ES
2450 LOWER ROSWELL RD 30068
Faith Christian Lutheran School
2111 LOWER ROSWELL RD 30068
Mt. Paran Christian School
1700 ALLGOOD RD 30062
St. Joseph Catholic School, 81 LACY ST 30060
Wood Acres Country Day School
1772 JOHNSON FERRY RD 30062

Marshallville, Macon Co., Pop. Code 4
Macon County SD
Supt. – See Oglethorpe
Richardson ES, P O BOX 203 31057
Raymond Baker, prin.

Martinez, Richmond Co.
Columbia County SD
Supt. – See Appling
ES, 213 FLOWING WELLS RD 30907
Charles Horton, prin.
South Columbia ES, 325 MCCORMICK RD 30907
Linda Schrenko, prin.
Westmont ES, OAKLEY PIRKLE RD 30907
Brenda Jones, prin.

Augusta Country Day School
265 FLOWING WELLS RD 30907

Maysville, Jackson Co., Pop. Code 3
Jackson County SD
Supt. – See Jefferson
ES, RURAL ROUTE 02 30558
Anderson Byers, prin.

Mc Caysville, Fannin Co., Pop. Code 4
Fannin County SD
Supt. – See Blue Ridge
ES 30555 – Bill Howard, prin.

Mc Donough, Henry Co., Pop. Code 5
Henry County SD
Sch. Sys. Enr. Code 6
Supt. – F. T. Strickland
   396 E TOMLINSON ST 30253
Henry County JHS, G W LEMON DR 30253
   Brad James, prin.
Henderson ES, 354 N OLA RD 30253
   Dr. Marinelle Simpson, prin.
ES, 330 E TOMLINSON ST 30253
   Arch Brown, prin.
MS, 33 N CEDAR ST 30253 – Solomon Barge, prin.
Other Schools – See Hampton, Locust Grove,
   Stockbridge

Meadow Creek Academy, P O BOX 657 30253

Mc Intyre, Wilkinson Co., Pop. Code 2
Wilkinson County SD
Supt. – See Irwinton
Wilkinson County PS
   RURAL ROUTE 01 BOX 96 31054
   Dr. Robert James, prin.

Mc Rae, Telfair Co., Pop. Code 5
Telfair County SD
Sch. Sys. Enr. Code 4
Supt. – June Bradfield
   210B E PARSONAGE ST 31055
Central MS, CENTRAL AVE 31055
   Ted Morrison, prin.
McRae-Helena PS, P O BOX 369 31055
   Jennifer Singleton, prin.
Workmore ES, RURAL ROUTE 02 31055
   Carnell Wilson, prin.
Other Schools – See Lumber City

Meigs, Thomas Co., Pop. Code 4

Ravenwood Academy, S MARSHALL ST 31765

Menlo, Chattooga Co., Pop. Code 3
Chattooga County SD
Supt. – See Summerville
ES, ALPINE ROAD 30731 – E. Thompson, prin.

Metter, Candler Co., Pop. Code 5
Candler County SD
Sch. Sys. Enr. Code 4
Supt. – James Wilcox, P O BOX 536 30439
MS, P O BOX 27 30439 – William George, prin.
PS, 210 SOUTH COLLEGE 30439
   Ronnie Sikes, prin.

Midland, Muscogee Co.
Muscogee County SD
Supt. – See Columbus
Mathews ES, 7533 LYNCH RD 31820
   Joseph Ryan, prin.

Midway, Liberty Co., Pop. Code 2
Liberty County SD
Supt. – See Hinesville
Liberty County ES, P O BOX 689 31320
   Matilda Brown, prin.

Milledgeville, Baldwin Co., Pop. Code 7
Baldwin County SD
Sch. Sys. Enr. Code 6
Supt. – Dr. Dave Brotherton, P O BOX 1188 31061
Boddie MS, 1340 ORCHARD HILL ROAD 31061
   Harold Watson,Jr., prin.
Carver MS, 435 E WALTON ST 31061
   Sammy Hall, prin.
Davis ES, 1300 ORCHARD HILL ROAD 31061
   Naomi Brannon, prin.
Midway ES, 1745 IRWINTON RD 31061
   James Kauffmann, prin.
Northside ES, 1811 EATONTON ROAD 31061
   Zelma Ray, prin.
Southside ES, 200 SOUTHSIDE DR SE 31061
   Druey West, prin.
West End ES, 130 S IRWIN ST 31061
   Lucious Baldwin, prin.

John Milledge Academy
   197 LOG CABIN ROAD NE 31061

Millen, Jenkins Co., Pop. Code 5
Jenkins County SD
Sch. Sys. Enr. Code 4
Supt. – L. Batten, P O BOX 660 30442
Jenkins County MS
   RURAL ROUTE 05 BOX 630 30442
   David Adams, prin.
Jenkins County MS
   RURAL ROUTE 05 BOX 630 30442
   James Henry, prin.
Jenkins County PS
   100 W CLEVELAND AVE 30442
   Hayward Cordy, prin.

Milner, Lamar Co., Pop. Code 2
Lamar County SD
Supt. – See Barnesville
MS, P O BOX 98 30257 – Linda Akins, prin.

Mineral Bluff, Fannin Co., Pop. Code 2
Fannin County SD
Supt. – See Blue Ridge
ES 30559 – Billy Nichols, prin.

Monroe, Walton Co., Pop. Code 6
Walton County SD
Sch. Sys. Enr. Code 6
Supt. – Dr. Kenneth Cloud, 115 OAK ST 30655
Carver JHS, 500 BOOTH ST 30655
   Bob Jacobs, prin.
MS, 209 BOLD SPRINGS AVE 30655
   Tommy Richardson, prin.
PS, 109 BLAINE ST 30655
   Jacqueline McClendon, prin.
Walker Park ES, RURAL ROUTE 03 30655
   Anita Doster, prin.
Other Schools – See Loganville

Walton Academy, P O BOX 1026 30655

Montezuma, Macon Co., Pop. Code 5
Macon County SD
Supt. – See Oglethorpe
Douglass ES, P O BOX 471 31063
   Jasper Drew, prin.
Macon County MS, 324 ENGRAM ST 31063
   Thomas Emly, prin.

Southland Academy Branch
   MARSHALLVILLE HIGHWAY 31063

Monticello, Jasper Co., Pop. Code 4
Jasper County SD
Sch. Sys. Enr. Code 4
Supt. – L. H. Paschal, 126 COURTHOUSE 30164
Washington Park ES, 4 STAR ST 31064
   Andrew Thompson, prin.

Piedmont Academy, P O BOX 231 31064

Moreland, Coweta Co., Pop. Code 2
Coweta County SD
Supt. – See Newnan
ES, 11 SCHOOL ST 30259 – Beverly Yeager, prin.

Morgan, Calhoun Co., Pop. Code 2
Calhoun County SD
Sch. Sys. Enr. Code 5
Supt. – Bobby Paul, P O BOX 38 31766
Other Schools – See Arlington

Morganton, Fannin Co., Pop. Code 2
Fannin County SD
Supt. – See Blue Ridge
ES 30560 – Jack Mchan, prin.

Morrow, Clayton Co., Pop. Code 5
Clayton County SD
Supt. – See Jonesboro
Haynie ES, 1169 MORROW RD 30260
   Ben Lee, prin.
Lake Harbin ES, 2201 LAKE HARBIN RD 30260
   Bill McGarrah, prin.
ES, 6115 REYNOLDS RD 30260
   David Head, prin.
Tara ES, 937 MORROW IND BLVD 30260
   Dr. Jim Knight, prin.

Clayton Christian School
   4900 REYNOLDS ROAD 30260

Morven, Brooks Co., Pop. Code 2
Brooks County SD
Supt. – See Quitman
MS, P O BOX 158 31638 – J. Storie, prin.
PS, P O BOX 158 31638 – Duwayne Lewis, prin.

Moultrie, Colquitt Co., Pop. Code 7
Colquitt County SD
Sch. Sys. Enr. Code 6
Supt. – T. W. Wommack, P O BOX 1806 31776
Cox ES, 12TH ST SE 31768 – Brady Brock, prin.
Gray MS, 812 11TH AVE NW 31768
   Beauford Hicks, prin.
Odom ES, RURAL ROUTE 05 BOX 571K 31768
   Kermit Ary, prin.
Okapilco ES, RURAL ROUTE 03 31768
   Edward Turner, prin.
Stringfellow ES, 200 5TH AVE SW 31768
   Steve Godwin, prin.
Sunset ES, RURAL ROUTE 06 31768
   Jimmy Taylor, prin.
Wright ES, 2ND ST SE 31768 – Ed Willis, prin.
Other Schools – See Doerun, Funston, Hartsfield,
   Norman Park

Pineland School, 710 28TH AVE SE 31768

Mount Airy, Habersham Co., Pop. Code 3
Habersham County SD
Supt. – See Clarkesville
Hazel Grove ES, RURAL ROUTE 01 30563
   Eli Dunagan, prin.

Mount Vernon, Montgomery Co., Pop. Code 4
Montgomery County SD
Sch. Sys. Enr. Code 4
Supt. – J. P. Poole, P O BOX 315 30445
Other Schools – See Ailey

Mount Zion, Carroll Co., Pop. Code 2
Carroll County SD
Supt. – See Carrollton
ES, P O BOX 686 30150 – Donald Nixon, prin.

Nahunta, Brantley Co., Pop. Code 3
Brantley County SD
Sch. Sys. Enr. Code 4
Supt. – James S. Thornton, P O BOX 613 31553
ES, P O BOX 128 31553 – Gerald Thrift, prin.
Other Schools – See Hoboken

Nashville, Berrien Co., Pop. Code 5
Berrien County SD
Sch. Sys. Enr. Code 5
Supt. – Howard L. Smith, P O BOX 625 31639
MS, 305 N ANN ST 31639 – D. Connell, prin.
ES, P O BOX 366 31639 – Peggy Kent, prin.
Other Schools – See Alapaha, Lenox, Ray City

Newnan, Coweta Co., Pop. Code 7
Coweta County SD
Sch. Sys. Enr. Code 6
Supt. – Dr. Robert E. Lee, P O BOX 280 30264
Central MS, 160 MCINTOSH ST 30263
   Eddie Lovett, prin.
Evans MS, EVANS DR 30263 – Jerry Davis, prin.
Arnco-Sargent ES, 2449 HIGHWAY 16 W 30263
   Charles Byrd, prin.
Atkinson ES, 14 NIMMONS ST 30263
   Charles Wright, prin.
Elm Street ES, 46 ELM ST 30263
   Joeann Hanson, prin.
Fairmount ES, FAIRMOUNT DR 30263
   Hattie Dunn, prin.
Hill ES, SUNSET LN 30263
   Douglass Gower, prin.
Northside ES, 720 COUNTRY CLUB RD 30263
   James Spear, prin.
Western A ES, 1730 WELCOME RD 30263
   Earl Coulter, prin.
Western B ES, 106 WESTSIDE SCHOOL RD 30263
   Jeannette Teagle, prin.
White Oak ES, 770 LORA SMITH RD 30263
   John Sides, prin.
Other Schools – See Grantville, Moreland, Senoia

Heritage School, 2093 HIGHWAY 29 N 30263
Newnan Christian School, 1608 HWY 29 N 30264

Newton, Baker Co., Pop. Code 3
Baker County SD
Sch. Sys. Enr. Code 2
Supt. – Grady C. Etheredge, P O BOX 40 31770
Baker County ES, P O BOX 250 31770
   Thomas Rogers, prin.

Nicholls, Coffee Co., Pop. Code 4
Coffee County SD
Supt. – See Douglas
S, P O BOX 386 31554 – Jerry Yancey, prin.

Nicholson, Jackson Co., Pop. Code 2
Jackson County SD
Supt. – See Jefferson
Benton ES, RURAL ROUTE 01 BOX 69 30565
   Dr. Lois Settles, prin.

Norcross, Gwinnett Co., Pop. Code 5
Gwinnett County SD
Supt. – See Lawrenceville
Pinckneyville MS
   5440 W JONES BRIDGE ROAD 30092
   Judith Rogers, prin.
Summerour MS, 585 MITCHELL ROAD 30071
   Ron Pennington, prin.
Beaver Ridge ES, 1978 BEAVER RUIN RD 30071
   Becky Hopcraft, prin.
ES, 150 HUNT ST 30071 – Jan Hall, prin.
Peachtree ES, 5995 CROOKED CREEK RD 30092
   Deanna Fraker, prin.
Rockbridge ES
   6066 ROCKBRIDGE SCHOOL RD 30093
   Maureen Deloach, prin.

Greater Atlanta Christian School
   1575 INDIAN TRAIL ROAD 30093

Norman Park, Colquitt Co., Pop. Code 3
Colquitt County SD
Supt. – See Moultrie
ES, P O BOX B 31771 – C. Chafin, prin.

Oakwood, Hall Co., Pop. Code 3
Hall County SD
Supt. – See Gainesville
ES, 4500 ALLEN ST 30566 – Douglas Bryant, prin.

Ocilla, Irwin Co., Pop. Code 5
Irwin County SD
Sch. Sys. Enr. Code 4
Supt. – R. Gentry, P O BOX 225 31774
Irwin County JHS, P O BOX 106 31774
   Mary Anne Wilcox, prin.
Irwin County ES
   RURAL ROUTE 01 BOX 55 31774
   Bobby Griffin, prin.

Odum, Wayne Co., Pop. Code 2
Wayne County SD
Supt. – See Jesup
ES, P O BOX 8 31555 – Wayne Flowers, prin.

Oglethorpe, Macon Co., Pop. Code 4
Macon County SD
Sch. Sys. Enr. Code 5
Supt. – J. L. Fokes,Sr., P O BOX 488 31068
Macon County JHS, P O BOX 487 31068
   Annis Goddard, prin.
Macon County PS, P O BOX 515 31068
   DeLores Felder, prin.
Other Schools – See Marshallville, Montezuma

Omega, Tift Co., Pop. Code 3
Tift County SD
Supt. – See Tifton
ES, P O BOX 68 31775 – Ronald Fritz, prin.

Oxford, Newton Co., Pop. Code 4
Newton County SD
Supt. – See Covington
Palmer Stone ES 30267 – James Wardlow, prin.

Palmetto, Fulton Co., Pop. Code 4
Fulton County SD
Supt. – See Atlanta
ES, 253 FAYETTEVILLE RD 30268
Jemmie Willingham, prin.
Riley ES, 90 TURNER AVE 30268
Charles McClure, prin.

Patterson, Pierce Co., Pop. Code 3
Pierce County SD
Supt. – See Blackshear
ES, P O BOX 6 31557 – Joy Williams, prin.

Pavo, Thomas Co., Pop. Code 3
Thomas County SD
Supt. – See Thomasville
ES, P O BOX 188 31778 – Glenn Hobby, prin.

Peachtree City, Fayette Co., Pop. Code 6
Fayette County SD
Supt. – See Fayetteville
Booth JHS, 250 PEACHTREE PARKWAY 30269
Sara Goza, prin.
Huddleston MS, 200 MCINTOSH TRL 30269
John Decotis, prin.
Oak Grove ES, 101 CROSSTOWN RD 30269
Kathy Corley, prin.
ES, 201 WISDOM ROAD 30269 – Larry Teal, prin.

Pearson, Atkinson Co., Pop. Code 4
Atkinson County SD
Sch. Sys. Enr. Code 4
Supt. – Edwin Davis, P O BOX 608 31642
Atkinson County JHS, P O BOX 839 31642
Jeff Kirkland, prin.
ES, P O BOX 578 31642 – Tom Morris, prin.
Other Schools – See Willacoochee

Pelham, Mitchell Co., Pop. Code 5
Grady County SD
Supt. – See Cairo
Shiver ES, RURAL ROUTE 02 31779
Tommy Pharis, prin.

Pelham ISD
Sch. Sys. Enr. Code 4
Supt. – Chester Shelnutt
203 MATHEWSON AVE SW 31779
ES 31779 – Herbert Houston, prin.

Pembroke, Bryan Co., Pop. Code 4
Bryan County SD
Sch. Sys. Enr. Code 4
Supt. – Dr. Sallie Brewer, P O BOX 768 31321
Bryan County MS, P O BOX 997 31321
Debbie Hamm, prin.
Lanier ES, P O BOX 338 31321
Wynelle Purcell, prin.
Other Schools – See Richmond Hill

Perry, Houston Co., Pop. Code 6
Houston County SD
Sch. Sys. Enr. Code 7
Supt. – Matthew Arthur
1211 WASHINGTON ST 31069
MS, SUNSHINE AVE 31069
Bobby Pennington, prin.
Kings Chapel ES, RURAL ROUTE 01 31069
Kim Schoening, prin.
Morningside MS, MORNINGSIDE DR 31069
George Pope, prin.
ES, 906 SCHOOL ST 31069 – Mark Hurst, prin.
Tucker ES, 1200 TUCKER RD 31069
Paul Hartman, prin.
Other Schools – See Bonaire, Centerville, Warner
Robins

Westfield School, P O BOX 1241 31069

Pinehurst, De Kalb Co., Pop. Code 2

Fullington Academy, P O BOX B 31070

Pitts, Wilcox Co., Pop. Code 2
Wilcox County SD
Supt. – See Abbeville
ES 31072 – Roy Faircloth, prin.

Plainville, Gordon Co., Pop. Code 2
Gordon County SD
Supt. – See Calhoun
Swain ES, 2505 ROME ROAD SW 30733
Robert Cook, prin.

Pooler, Chatham Co., Pop. Code 5
Chatham County SD
Supt. – See Savannah
ES 31322 – Elaine Pandtle, prin.

Portal, Bulloch Co., Pop. Code 3
Bulloch County SD
Supt. – See Statesboro
Willow Hill MS
RURAL ROUTE 01 BOX 60 30450
Jerry Brown, prin.

Port Wentworth, Chatham Co., Pop. Code 5
Chatham County SD
Supt. – See Savannah
ES, 101 TURNBERRY ST 31407
Penny Maestretti, prin.

Powder Springs, Cobb Co., Pop. Code 5
Cobb County SD
Supt. – See Marietta
Tapp MS, 3900 MACEDONIA ROAD 30073
Mike Campbell, prin.
Compton ES, 3450 NEW MACLAND RD 30073
Betty Gray, prin.
ES, 4181 ATLANTA ST 30073
Charles Sanders, prin.
Still ES, 870 CASTEEL RD 30073
Gloria Jackson, prin.

Preston, Webster Co., Pop. Code 2
Webster County SD
Sch. Sys. Enr. Code 2
Supt. – Meredith Walker 31824
Webster County ES 31824 – J. Wiley, prin.

Quitman, Brooks Co., Pop. Code 5
Brooks County SD
Sch. Sys. Enr. Code 5
Supt. – John Horton, P O BOX 511 31643
MS, P O BOX 370 31643 – Robert Marshall, prin.
PS, P O BOX 271 31643 – Gracie Jefferson, prin.
Other Schools – See Barwick, Dixie, Morven

Rabun Gap, Rabun Co., Pop. Code 2
Rabun County SD
Supt. – See Clayton
ES, P O BOX 129 30568 – Dr. William Bailey, prin.

Ray City, Berrien Co., Pop. Code 3
Berrien County SD
Supt. – See Nashville
ES, 506 PAULINE ST 31645
Wynn Hancock, prin.

Redan, De Kalb Co.
DeKalb County SD
Supt. – See Decatur
ES, 1914 STONE MTN-LITHNIA RD 30074
Dr. James Bryant, prin.

Reidsville, Tattnall Co., Pop. Code 4
Tattnal County SD
Sch. Sys. Enr. Code 5
Supt. – Ben F. Sikes, P O BOX 157 30453
Tattnall ES, P O BOX 428 30453
R. Akins,Jr., prin.
Other Schools – See Collins, Glennville

Resaca, Gordon Co.
Gordon County SD
Supt. – See Calhoun
Tolbert ES
1435 HALL MEMORIAL ROAD NW 30735
Dene Land, prin.

Rhine, Dodge Co., Pop. Code 3
Dodge County SD
Supt. – See Eastman
ES, P O BOX 158 31077 – John Jones, prin.

Richland, Stewart Co., Pop. Code 4
Stewart County SD
Supt. – See Lumpkin
ES, P O BOX 399 31825 – John Morrison, prin.

Richmond Hill, Bryan Co., Pop. Code 4
Bryan County SD
Supt. – See Pembroke
ES, P O BOX 820 31324 – Mary Meeks, prin.

Rincon, Effingham Co., Pop. Code 4
Effingham County SD
Supt. – See Springfield
ES, RURAL ROUTE 03 BOX 155-A 31326
Walton Burns, prin.

Ringgold, Catoosa Co., Pop. Code 4
Catoosa County SD
Sch. Sys. Enr. Code 6
Supt. – Lee Sims, P O BOX 130 30736
JHS, 112 GYM ST 30736 – Dan Vest, prin.
Boynton ES, RURAL ROUTE 01 30736
Sharon Brock, prin.
ES, 101 SCHOOL ST 30736 – Carol Spurlock, prin.
Other Schools – See Fort Oglethorpe, Graysville,
Rossville, Tunnel Hill

Riverdale, Clayton Co., Pop. Code 6
Clayton County SD
Supt. – See Jonesboro
Church Street ES, 7013 CHURCH ST 30274
Fred Warren, prin.
Oliver ES, 1725 CHERYL LEIGH DR 30296
David Knowles, prin.
Pointe South ES, 631 FLINT RIVER RD SW 30274
Tommy Rayburn, prin.
ES, 6630 CAMP ST 30274 – Derrell Turner, prin.

Bible Baptist Christian School
91 VALLEY HILL ROAD 30274
Busey School/Woodward
8009 CARLTON RD 30296

Roberta, Crawford Co., Pop. Code 3
Crawford County SD
Sch. Sys. Enr. Code 4
Supt. – Elizabeth Scarborough
322 MANOR ST 31078
Crawford County MS, 348 CRUSSELLE ST 31078
Allison Manning, prin.
Crawford County ES, P O BOX 308 31078
Milton Bentley, prin.

Rochelle, Wilcox Co., Pop. Code 4
Wilcox County SD
Supt. – See Abbeville
ES 31079 – Charles Bloodsworth, prin.

Rockmart, Polk Co., Pop. Code 5
Paulding County SD
Supt. – See Dallas
Yorkville ES, RURAL ROUTE 03 30153
Ellen Kay, prin.

Polk County SD
Supt. – See Cedartown
Elm Street MS, MORGAN VALLEY RD 30153
Frank Irwin, prin.
Eastside ES, RURAL ROUTE 02 30153
William Paschal, prin.
Goodyear ES, 510 N PIEDMONT AVE 30153
Joe Maddox, prin.

Rock Spring, Walker Co., Pop. Code 2
Walker County SD
Supt. – See La Fayette
ES 30739 – Bennie Donahue, prin.

Rocky Face, Whitfield Co., Pop. Code 2
Whitfield County SD
Supt. – See Dalton
West Side MS, 580 LAFAYETTE ROAD 30740
Linda Gilpatrick, prin.
West Side ES, 1815 UTILITY RD 30740
Larry Gable, prin.

Rome, Floyd Co., Pop. Code 8
Floyd County SD
Sch. Sys. Enr. Code 6
Supt. – J. Terry Jenkins
181 RIVERSIDE PKWY NE 30161
Coosa MS, 5041 ALABAMA HIGHWAY SW 30161
Rob Puckett, prin.
Alto Park ES, 528 BURNETT FERRY RD SW 30161
Dennis Abney, prin.
Garden Lakes ES
2903 GARDEN LAKES BLVD 30161
Sherry Childs, prin.
Glenwood ES
75 GLENWOOD SCHOOL RD NE 30161
Lloyd Hinman, prin.
Johnson ES
1910 MORRISON CAMPGRND ROAD 30161
Michele Holmes, prin.
McHenry ES, 100 MCHENRY DR 30161
Ben Despern, prin.
Model ES, 3200 CALHOUN HWY NE 30161
John Henderson, prin.
Other Schools – See Cave Spring, Lindale, Silver Creek

Rome ISD
Sch. Sys. Enr. Code 5
Supt. – Dr. Jessie Laseter, 508 E 2ND ST 30161
East Rome JHS, 415 E 3RD AVE 30161
Harold Brock, prin.
West Rome JHS, 2508 REDMOND CIRCLE 30161
Dennis Chamberlain, prin.
Davie ES, 301 NIXON AVE 30161
Jackie Lynch, prin.
East Central ES, 1502 DEAN ST 30161
Polly Conger, prin.
Elm Street ES, 8 ELM ST 30161
Gayland Cooper, prin.
Main ES, 3 WATTERS ST 30161
Charlie Morrison, prin.
North Heights ES, 26 ATTEIRAM DR 30161
Peggy Patton, prin.
Southeast ES, 1400 CRANE ST 30161
Dr. Wayne Sanders, prin.
West Central ES, 402 LAVENDER DR 30161
James Proud, prin.
West End ES, 5 BROWN FOX DR 30161
Dr. Marcella Fowler, prin.

Darlington School
1014 CAVE SPRING ROAD SW 30161
St. Mary's Catholic School, 405 E 7TH ST 30161

Roopville, Carroll Co., Pop. Code 2
Carroll County SD
Supt. – See Carrollton
ES, 60 OLD CARROLLTON RD 30170
James Parmer, prin.

Heard County SD
Supt. – See Franklin
Ephesus ES, RURAL ROUTE 01 30170
Judy Miller, prin.

Rossville, Walker Co., Pop. Code 5
Catoosa County SD
Supt. – See Ringgold
Lakeview JHS, 1200 CROSS ST 30741
Mike Lusk, prin.
Cloud Springs ES, 910 FERNWOOD DR 30742
Phil Ledbetter, prin.
Westside ES, 1800 LAKEVIEW DR 30741
James Haddock, prin.

Walker County SD
Supt. – See La Fayette
Fairview ES, IVY AND JENKINS ROAD 30741
Wright Johnson, prin.
Happy Valley ES
HAPPY VALLEY AND SALEM RD 30741
Jerry Moody, prin.
Mountain View ES, 1012 GREEN HILL DR 30741
Robert Archer, prin.
North Rossville ES, 400 MCFARLAND AVE 30741
Ron James, prin.

South Rossville ES
  1400 MCFARLAND AVE   30741
  James Smith, prin.

Unity Christian School
  2010 MACK SMITH ROAD   30741

Roswell, Fulton Co., Pop. Code 7
  Fulton County SD
  Supt. – See Atlanta
  Crabapple MS, 10700 CRABAPPLE ROAD   30075
    Dr. Doris Robertson, prin.
  Jackson ES, 1400 MARTIN RD   30076
    Frances Buttolph, prin.
  Mimosa ES, 1550 WARSAW RD   30076
    Linda Markwell, prin.
  Mountain Park ES
    11895 MOUNTAIN PARK RD   30075
    Carolyn Clarke, prin.
  North Roswell ES, 275 WOODSTOCK RD   30075
    Martha Paris, prin.
  ES, 791 MIMOSA BLVD   30075
    Leonard Forti, prin.

High Meadows School, P O BOX 856   30077

Royston, Franklin Co., Pop. Code 4
  Franklin County SD
  Supt. – See Carnesville
  ES   30662 – Dan Terry, prin.

Rutledge, Morgan Co., Pop. Code 3

Rutledge Academy
  4031 DAVIS ACADEMY ROAD   30663

Rydal, Bartow Co.
  Bartow County SD
  Supt. – See Cartersville
  Pine Log ES, 3370 HIGHWAY 140   30171
    Gary Smith, prin.

Saint George, Charlton Co.
  Charlton County SD
  Supt. – See Folkston
  ES, RURAL ROUTE 01   31646 – Bill Bibby, prin.

Saint Marys, Camden Co., Pop. Code 5
  Camden County SD
  Supt. – See Kingsland
  Crooked River ES, 1820 SPUR 40   31558
    Sheila Hutchinson, prin.
  ES, 510 OSBORNE ST   31558
    Kenneth Williams, prin.

Saint Simmons Island, Glynn Co.
  Glynn County SD
  Supt. – See Brunswick
  ES, 805 OCEAN BLVD   31522 – Linda Lewis, prin.

Frederica Academy, 200 HAMILTON ROAD   31522

Sandersville, Washington Co., Pop. Code 6
  Washington County SD
  Sch. Sys. Enr. Code 5
  Supt. – E. Tarver Averett,Jr., P O BOX 716   31082
  Elder MS, P O BOX 816   31082
    Bern Anderson, prin.
  Elder PS, P O BOX 856   31082
    George Williams,Jr., prin.
  MS, 514 N HARRIS ST   31082
    James Hendricks, prin.
  Other Schools – See Tennille

Brentwood School, P O BOX 955   31082

Sardis, Burke Co., Pop. Code 4
  Burke County SD
  Supt. – See Waynesboro
  Cousins ES, RAILROAD AVE   30456
    Hubert Roberts, prin.
  S.G.A. MS, 604 BURKE ST   30456
    John MacDonald, prin.

Savannah, Chatham Co., Pop. Code 9
  Chatham County SD
  Sch. Sys. Enr. Code 8
  Supt. – Cecil Carter, 208 BULL ST   31401
  Bartlett MS
    207 E MONTGOMERY CROSSROADS   31406
    Joe Thomas, prin.
  Derenne MS, 3609 HOPKINS ST   31405
    Virginia Edwards, prin.
  Hubert MS, 768 GRANT ST   31401
    Patricia DeVoe, prin.
  Myers MS, 2316 BREVARD CIRCLE   31404
    Cheryl Clemens, prin.
  Scott MS, 402 MARKET ST   31408
    Beverly Oliver, prin.
  Shuman MS, 415 GOEBEL AVE   31404
    Roland James,Jr., prin.
  Wilder MS, 1300 E 66TH ST   31404
    Hazel Hutcheson, prin.
  Bartow ES, 1804 STRATFORD ST   31401
    Dora Myles, prin.
  Butler ES, 1909 CYNTHIA ST   31401
    Margaret Washington, prin.
  Ellis ES, 220 E 49TH ST   31405
    Anne Monaghan, prin.
  Gadsden ES, 919 MAY ST   31401
    Margaret Johnson, prin.
  Gould MS, 4910 PINELAND DR   31405
    Sarah Minchew, prin.
  Haven ES, 5111 DILLON AVE   31405
    Clevon Johnson, prin.

Haynes MS, 700 OAK ST   31408
  Dorothy Butler, prin.
Heard ES, 414 LEE BLVD   31405
  Carolus Daniel, prin.
Herty ES, 1835 SKIDAWAY RD   31404
  Delores Brown, prin.
Hesse ES, 9116 WHITFIELD AVE   31406
  Joel Formby, prin.
Hodge ES, 1101 W VICTORY DR   31405
  Ethel Gibbs, prin.
Howard ES, 115 WILMINGTON ISLAND RD   31410
  Pamela Stevenson, prin.
Isle of Hope ES, PARKERSBURG ROAD   31406
  Shirley Jordan, prin.
Largo-Tibet ES, 430 TIBET AVE   31406
  Martha Hayes, prin.
Low ES, 15 BLUE RIDGE AVE   31404
  Stephen Hefner, prin.
Pennsylvania Avenue ES
  PENNSYLVANIA AVE & ELGIN ST   31404
  Barbara Mobley, prin.
Pulaski ES, 5330 MONTGOMERY ST   31405
  Esther Britt, prin.
Riley ES, 1108 E ANDERSON ST   31404
  James Sheppard, prin.
Smith ES, 707 HASTINGS ST   31401
  Catherine Williams, prin.
Smith ES, 210 LAMARA DR   31405
  Marion Cheney, prin.
Spencer ES, BOUHAN & REIRDON STS   31404
  Marilyn Franklin, prin.
Thirty-Eighth Street ES, 315 W 38TH ST   31401
  Ernestine Hamilton, prin.
White Bluff ES, 9902 WHITE BLUFF RD   31406
  Dale King, prin.
Whitney ES, 2 LAURA AVE   31404
  Willie Pippens, prin.
Windsor Forest ES, 414 BRIARCLIFF CIR   31419
  Gretchen Reese, prin.
Other Schools – See Bloomingdale, Garden City,
  Pooler, Port Wentworth, Thunderbolt

Bible Baptist School
  4700 SKIDAWAY ROAD   31404
Calvary Baptist Day School
  4625 WATERS AVE   31404
Memorial Day School
  6500 HABERSHAM ST   31405
Pineland Christian School
  4906 PINELAND DR   31405
Savannah Christian School, P O BOX 2848   31498
Savannah Country Day School
  824 STILLWOOD ROAD   31406
St. Andrew's on the Marsh School
  P O BOX 30639   31410
Blessed Sacrament ES, 1003 E VICTORY DR   31405
Castle Heights Academy, 130 TIBET AVE   31406
Cathedral Day School, 324 ABERCORN ST   31401
Hancock Day School, 5526 SKIDAWAY RD   31406
Nativity of our Lord School
  7020 CONCORD RD   31410
Parent-Child Development School
  5000 JASMINE AVE   31404
Pathway School, 6600 HOWARD FOSS DR   31406
Ramah SDA Junior Academy
  3400 FLORANCE ST   31402
Sacred Heart School, 1709 BULL ST   31401
St. James Catholic School
  8412 WHITFIELD AVE   31406
St. Paul's Lutheran School, 10 W 31ST ST   31401

Screven, Wayne Co., Pop. Code 3
  Wayne County SD
  Supt. – See Jesup
  ES   31560 – Steve Harper, prin.

Senoia, Coweta Co., Pop. Code 3
  Coweta County SD
  Supt. – See Newnan
  East Coweta MS, 6291 E HWY 16   30276
    David Parrott, prin.
  Eastside ES, 1225 EASTSIDE SCHOOL RD   30276
    Winston Dowdell, prin.

Shellman, Randolph Co., Pop. Code 4

Randolph Southern School, P O BOX 287   31786

Siloam, Greene Co., Pop. Code 2

Nathaniel Green Academy, HWY 15   30665

Silver Creek, Floyd Co.
  Floyd County SD
  Supt. – See Rome
  Midway ES, 5 MIDWAY SCHOOL RD   30173
    Dr. Charles Elliott, prin.

Smyrna, Cobb Co., Pop. Code 7
  Cobb County SD
  Supt. – See Marietta
  Griffin MS, 4010 KING SPRINGS ROAD   30080
    Randy Allen, prin.
  Nash MS, 1101 WARD ST   30080
    Roy Livingston, prin.
  Argyle ES, 2420 SPRING ST   30080
    Don Porch, prin.
  Belmont Hills ES, 605 GLENDALE PL   30080
    Brian Roberts, prin.
  Brown ES, 3265 BROWN RD   30080
    Janice Repasky, prin.
  Fitzhugh Lee ES, 4400 ATLANTA RD   30080
    James Lavender, prin.
  King Springs ES, 1051 REED RD   30082
    Jim Ovbey, prin.

Norton Park ES, 3041 GRAY RD   30082
  Dr. Cheryl Hunt, prin.
Russell ES, 3290 S HURT ROAD   30080
  Trudy Sowar, prin.
Teasley ES, 3640 SPRINGHILL ROAD   30080
  Miriam Specht, prin.

Smyrna Christian Academy
  3269 OLD CONCORD ROAD   30082
First Baptist School, 1275 CHURCH ST   30080

Snellville, Gwinnett Co., Pop. Code 6
  Gwinnett County SD
  Supt. – See Lawrenceville
  MS, 3155 E PATE   30278 – R. Mullins, prin.
  Britt ES, 2503 SKYLAND DR   30278
    Gary Fairley, prin.
  Brookwood ES
    1330 HOLLY BROOK ROAD   30278
    Hal Beaver, prin.
  Centerville ES, 3600 SCENIC HWY NW   30278
    Marian Hicks, prin.
  Norton ES, 3050 CARSON RD   30278
    Dr. Wanda Warner, prin.

Social Circle, Walton Co., Pop. Code 5
  Social Circle ISD
  Sch. Sys. Enr. Code 3
  Supt. – Dr. John Burks, P O BOX 428   30279
  ES, 439 FAIRPLAY DR NE   30279
    Jeffery Welch, prin.

Soperton, Treutlen Co., Pop. Code 5
  Treutlen County SD
  Sch. Sys. Enr. Code 4
  Supt. – Gary Walden, 202 3RD ST   30457
  Treutlen MS, 611 COLLEGE ST   30457
    Joe Moore, prin.
  Treutlen PS, 201 RAILROAD AVE   30457
    Marion Shaw, prin.

Sparks, Cook Co., Pop. Code 4
  Cook County SD
  Supt. – See Adel
  MS, 402 GOODMAN ST   31647 – Tom Bryan, prin.

Sparta, Hancock Co., Pop. Code 4
  Hancock County SD
  Sch. Sys. Enr. Code 4
  Supt. – M. E. Lewis, P O BOX 488   31087
  Hancock Central MS, DYER DR   31087
    Ann Yancey, prin.
  Lewis ES, HWY 15   31087 – R. Warren, prin.
  Southwest ES, RURAL ROUTE 01 BOX 261   31087
    Annette Warren, prin.

John Hancock Academy, P O BOX E   31087

Springfield, Effingham Co., Pop. Code 4
  Effingham County SD
  Sch. Sys. Enr. Code 5
  Supt. – J. Michael Moore, P O BOX 346   31329
  Central JHS, RURAL ROUTE 01 BOX 175   31329
    Franklin Goldwire, prin.
  ES, P O BOX 367   31329 – Charles Duvall, prin.
  Other Schools – See Guyton, Rincon

Spring Place, Murray Co., Pop. Code 2
  Murray County SD
  Supt. – See Chatsworth
  ES, LEONARD BRIDGE ROAD   30705
    C. Dunn, prin.

Statenville, Echols Co., Pop. Code 3
  Echols County SD
  Sch. Sys. Enr. Code 3
  Supt. – J. L. Carter, P O BOX 207   31648
  Echols County S   31648 – Emory Corbett, prin.

Statesboro, Bulloch Co., Pop. Code 7
  Bulloch County SD
  Sch. Sys. Enr. Code 6
  Supt. – Dr. E. I. Wynn, P O BOX 877   30458
  James MS, 150 WILLIAMS ROAD   30458
    H. Tankersley,Jr., prin.
  Bryant MS, P O BOX 766   30458 – Jack Pye, prin.
  Lively ES, 204 DEBBIE DR   30458
    Billy Bice, prin.
  Nevils ES, RURAL ROUTE 06 BOX 225   30458
    Charles Stokes, prin.
  Northside MS, HWY 80 WEST   30458
    Morris Ward, prin.
  Pittman ES, LANDRUM BOX 8004   30458
    Johnny Tremble, prin.
  Zetterower ES, P O BOX 1037   30458
    Dennis Raith, prin.
  Other Schools – See Brooklet, Portal

Bulloch Academy
  RURAL ROUTE 05 BOX 3   30458

Statham, Barrow Co., Pop. Code 4
  Barrow County SD
  Supt. – See Winder
  ES, P O BOX 46   30666 – Vivian Arnold, prin.

Stillmore, Emanuel Co., Pop. Code 3

Emanuel Academy   30464

Stockbridge, Henry Co., Pop. Code 4
  Henry County SD
  Supt. – See Mc Donough
  JHS, 533 OLD CONYERS ROAD   30281
    Richard Schoen, prin.
  Fairview ES, 458 FAIRVIEW RD   30281
    Robert Swanson, prin.

Smith Barnes MS, 147 TYE ST 30281
  Fred Smith, prin.
ES, 4617 N HENRY BLVD 30281
  William Raulerson, prin.

Mt. Vernon Christian School
1738 FAIRVIEW ROAD 30281

Stone Mountain, De Kalb Co., Pop. Code 5
DeKalb County SD
Supt. – See Decatur
Stone Mountain II MS
  5265 MIMOSA DRIVE 30083 – Bill Edwards, prin.
Allgood ES, 659 ALLGOOD RD 30083
  George Kendrick, prin.
Dunaire ES, 651 S INDIAN CREEK DR 30083
  Joel Megginson, prin.
Hambrick ES, 1101 HAMBRICK RD 30083
  Dr. Henry Ayers, prin.
Mainstreet ES, 919 MARTIN RD 30088
  Dr. Eldridge Miller, prin.
Panola Way ES
  2170 PANOLA WAY COURT 30088
  C. Tuck, prin.
Rockbridge ES, 445 HALWICK WAY 30083
  Dr. James Pearce, prin.
Rowland ES, 1317 S INDIAN CREEK DR 30083
  Dr. Art Dexter, prin.
Smoke Rise ES, 1991 SILVER HILL RD 30087
  Ruth Fuiit, prin.
Stone Mill ES, 4900 SHEILA LN 30083
  John Jones, prin.
ES, 6720 MEMORIAL DR 30083
  Mike Gouge, prin.
Woodridge ES, 4120 CEDAR RIDGE TRL 30083
  Donald Gaddie, prin.

Stone Mountain Christian School
P O BOX 509 30086
Cornerstone Baptist School
1170 N HAIRSTON RD 30083

Suches, Union Co., Pop. Code 3
Union County SD
Supt. – See Blairsville
Woody Gap S, RURAL ROUTE 01 BOX 95 30572
  G. Burch, prin.

Summertown, Emanuel Co., Pop. Code 2
Emanuel County SD
Supt. – See Swainsboro
Summertown ES, P O BOX D 30466
  Nathaniel Billups, prin.

Summerville, Chattooga Co., Pop. Code 6
Chattooga County SD
Sch. Sys. Enr. Code 5
Supt. – Donald Hayes, P O BOX 30 30747
MS, HWY 100 30747 – David Jones, prin.
North Summerville MS, HIGHLAND AVE 30747
  Alma Lewis, prin.
Pennville ES, RURAL ROUTE 02 30747
  Billy Hayes, prin.
ES, 99 PENN AVE 30747 – Michael Poole, prin.
Other Schools – See Lyerly, Menlo

Surrency, Appling Co., Pop. Code 2
Appling County SD
Supt. – See Baxley
Fourth District ES, RURAL ROUTE 02 31563
  Robert Bryant, prin.

Suwanee, Gwinnett Co., Pop. Code 4
Gwinnett County SD
Supt. – See Lawrenceville
ES, 670 HIGHWAY 23 30174 – Don Graham, prin.

Swainsboro, Emanuel Co., Pop. Code 6
Emanuel County SD
Sch. Sys. Enr. Code 5
Supt. – Elizabeth Brown, P O BOX 98 30401
MS, 410 W CHURCH ST 30401 – Jim Snell, prin.
MS, 746 GUMLOG ROAD 30401
  James Harper, prin.
PS, WEST PINE ST 30401 – Ruth Maupin, prin.
Other Schools – See Adrian, Summertown, Twin City

Sycamore, Turner Co., Pop. Code 2
Turner County SD
Supt. – See Ashburn
Turner County ES at Sycamore
  LABELLE ST 31790 – Tommy Day, prin.

Sylvania, Screven Co., Pop. Code 5
Screven County SD
Sch. Sys. Enr. Code 5
Supt. – John Mills, P O BOX 1668 30467
Central MS, 501 PINE ST 30467
  Dr. Arthur Freeland, prin.
ES, 202 S ENNIS ST 30467
  Patricia Bazemore, prin.

Sylvester, Worth Co., Pop. Code 6
Worth County SD
Sch. Sys. Enr. Code 5
Supt. – James Whitfield, P O BOX 359 31791
Worth County MS, 504 E PRICE ST 31791
  Mance Daughtry, prin.
Deariso PS, 402 W KING ST 31791
  Lynda Cook, prin.
Holley MS, CARTER RD 31791
  Dr. Bruce Washington, prin.
PS, ELDRIDGE ST 31791 – Shirley Thomas, prin.

Worth Academy, P O BOX 428 31791

Talbotton, Talbot Co., Pop. Code 4
Talbot County SD
Sch. Sys. Enr. Code 4
Supt. – John R. Terry, P O BOX 515 31827
Central ES, P O BOX 428 31827
  Fred Clinkscales, prin.

Tallapoosa, Haralson Co., Pop. Code 5
Haralson County SD
Supt. – See Buchanan
West Haralson MS 30176 – Paul Dunn, prin.
ES 30176 – C. Brown, prin.

Talmo, Jackson Co., Pop. Code 4
Jackson County SD
Supt. – See Jefferson
North Jackson ES, RURAL ROUTE 01 30575
  Dr. Shannon Adams, prin.

Tate, Pickens Co.
Pickens County SD
Supt. – See Jasper
ES 30177 – Harold Hammontree, prin.

Taylorsville, Bartow Co., Pop. Code 2
Bartow County SD
Supt. – See Cartersville
ES, P O BOX 168 30178 – Isabel Bearden, prin.

Temple, Carroll Co., Pop. Code 4
Carroll County SD
Supt. – See Carrollton
Temple ES, 95 OTIS STREET 30179
  Kathleen Rogers, prin.

Paulding County SD
Supt. – See Dallas
Union ES, RURAL ROUTE 02 30179
  Wilson Freeman, prin.

Tennille, Washington Co., Pop. Code 4
Washington County SD
Supt. – See Sandersville
Crawford PS, P O BOX 127 31089
  Roy Wilcher, prin.
MS, P O BOX 67 31089 – Jim Waller, prin.

Thomaston, Upson Co., Pop. Code 7
Thomaston ISD
Sch. Sys. Enr. Code 4
Supt. – Wallace Rhodes, 311 CENTER ST S 30286
East Thomaston ES, P O BOX 872 30286
  Robert Walls, prin.
Lee JHS, P O BOX 872 30286
  Dr. Yancy Morris, prin.
North Thomaston PS, P O BOX 872 30286
  Claude Walton, prin.

Upson County SD
Sch. Sys. Enr. Code 5
Supt. – F. Lynn Bates, P O BOX 831 30286
Worthy MS, 300 ADAMS ST 30286
  Larry Woodruff, prin.
Upson ES, 172 ELEMENTARY DR 30286
  Jerry Helms, prin.

Thomasville, Thomas Co., Pop. Code 7
Thomas County SD
Sch. Sys. Enr. Code 5
Supt. – Dr. Terrel Solana, P O BOX 2300 31799
Magnolia-Chappelle JHS
  1600 MAGNOLIA ST 31792 – Earl Williams, prin.
Garrison-Pilcher ES, RURAL ROUTE 02 31792
  Gary Cullens, prin.
Other Schools – See Pavo

Thomasville ISD
Sch. Sys. Enr. Code 5
Supt. – Dr. Fred Dorminy, P O BOX 1999 31799
Douglas MS, FORREST S ST 31792
  Jay Wansley, prin.
Balfour ES, 201 CHATHAM DR 31792
  Sandra Wright, prin.
Harper ES, 110 BARTOW ST 31792
  Matthew Conyers, prin.
Jerger ES, 1006 S BROAD ST 31792
  Penny Dollar, prin.
MacIntyre Park MS, 117 GLENWOOD DR 31792
  Albert Copeland, prin.
Scott ES, 100 N HANSELL ST 31792
  Robin Gay, prin.

Brookwood Academy
  100 CARDINAL RIDGE ROAD 31792
Rose City Christian School
  RURAL ROUTE 06 31792

Thomson, McDuffie Co., Pop. Code 6
McDuffie County SD
Sch. Sys. Enr. Code 5
Supt. – Dr. William Barr, P O BOX 957 30824
Norris MS, 899 HARRISON RD 30824
  Roy Sapough, prin.
Maxwell ES, MOUNT PLEASANT ROAD 30824
  Mary Dunford, prin.
Pine Street MS, P O BOX 1075 30824
  John Hammond, prin.
ES, 409 GUILL ST 30824 – Gwen Rountree, prin.
Other Schools – See Dearing

Briarwood Academy, P O BOX 840 30824

Thunderbolt, Chatham Co., Pop. Code 4
Chatham County SD
Supt. – See Savannah
ES, 3313 LOUIS ST 31404 – Camille O'neill, prin.

Tifton, Tift Co., Pop. Code 7
Tift County SD
Sch. Sys. Enr. Code 6
Supt. – Frank King, P O BOX 389 31793
Bailey ES, 1430 NEWTON DR 31794
  O'Neal Bozeman, prin.
Clark ES, 506 W 12TH ST 31794
  Bobby Jenkins, prin.
Lastinger ES, 1210 LAKE DR 31794
  Albert Gibbs, prin.
Northside ES, 1815 CHESTNUT AVE 31794
  Sandra Withrow, prin.
Reddick MS, 404 M L KING DR 31794
  John Smith, prin.
Spencer ES, RURAL ROUTE 02 31794
  Charlotte Dechert, prin.
Wilson MS, 510 W 17TH ST 31794
  Billy Daniell, prin.
Other Schools – See Omega

Tiger, Rabun Co., Pop. Code 2
Rabun County SD
Supt. – See Clayton
South Rabun ES, P O BOX 68 30576
  Roger Nicholas, prin.

Toccoa, Stephens Co., Pop. Code 6
Stephens County SD
Sch. Sys. Enr. Code 5
Supt. – James M. Stephens
  RURAL ROUTE 01 BOX 75 30577
Big A ES, 127 BIG A SCHOOL RD 30577
  James Howard, prin.
Liberty ES, RURAL ROUTE 06 BOX 274 30577
  J. McFarlin, prin.
ES, 451 N POND ST 30577 – James Payne, prin.
Other Schools – See Eastanollee

Trenton, Dade Co., Pop. Code 4
Dade County SD
Sch. Sys. Enr. Code 4
Supt. – Charles Johnston, P O BOX 188 30752
Dade MS, RURAL ROUTE 03 BOX 94 30752
  Gayle Gallaher, prin.
Dade ES, RURAL ROUTE 03 BOX 93 30752
  Steven Ruff, prin.
Davis ES, STAR ROUTE BOX 373B 30752
  Herbert Jeansonne, prin.

Trion, Chattooga Co., Pop. Code 4
Trion ISD
Sch. Sys. Enr. Code 4
Supt. – Bill Kinzy, PARK AVE 30753
ES, PARK AVE 30753 – Larry Musick, prin.

Tucker, De Kalb Co., Pop. Code 7
DeKalb County SD
Supt. – See Decatur
Brockett ES, 1855 BROCKETT RD 30084
  Thomas Lankford, prin.
Idlewood ES, 1484 IDLEWOOD RD 30084
  E. Saye, prin.
Livsey ES, 4137 LIVSEY RD 30084
  Linda Chambers, prin.
Midvale ES, 3836 MIDVALE RD 30084
  Pam Bouie, prin.

Tunnel Hill, Whitfield Co., Pop. Code 3
Catoosa County SD
Supt. – See Ringgold
Tiger Creek ES, RURAL ROUTE 07 30755
  Janie Brown, prin.

Whitfield County SD
Supt. – See Dalton
ES, 203 E SCHOOL ST 30755
  Laverne Damron, prin.

Twin City, Emanuel Co., Pop. Code 4
Emanuel County SD
Supt. – See Swainsboro
PS, P O BOX 280 30471
  Crawford Von Johnson, prin.

Tybee Island, Chatham Co., Pop. Code 4

St. Michael's Catholic School
713 LOVELL AVE #746 31328

Tyrone, Fayette Co., Pop. Code 4
Fayette County SD
Supt. – See Fayetteville
ES, P O BOX 280 30290 – Jimmie Tollerson, prin.

Unadilla, Dooly Co., Pop. Code 4
Dooly County SD
Supt. – See Vienna
ES, P O BOX 198 31091 – Wendell Herndon, prin.

Union City, Fulton Co., Pop. Code 5
Fulton County SD
Supt. – See Atlanta
Gullatt ES, 6110 DODSON RD 30291
  Jeannette Williford, prin.
ES, 6280 BRYANT ST 30291 – Joanne Evans, prin.

Union Point, Greene Co., Pop. Code 4
Greene County SD
Supt. – See Greensboro
ES, P O BOX 317 30669 – Willie Chester, prin.

Valdosta, Lowndes Co., Pop. Code 8
Lowndes County SD
Sch. Sys. Enr. Code 6
Supt. – Willis G. Sears, P O BOX 1227 31698
Lowndes MS, 506 COPELAND ROAD 31601
  Fred Davis, prin.

Clyattville ES, P O BOX 132 31601
    Glenn Cater, prin.
Mathis ES, 1500 LANKFORD DR 31601
    Ralph Brown, prin.
Pine Grove MS
    RURAL ROUTE 08 BOX 165 31602
    Bernard Perry, prin.
Pine Grove PS, RURAL ROUTE 08 BOX 167 31602
    George Lord,Jr., prin.
Other Schools – See Hahira, Lake Park

Valdosta ISD
Sch. Sys. Enr. Code 6
Supt. – Walter Altman III, P O BOX 5407 31603
JHS, 110 BURTON AVE 31602
    Brenda Smith, prin.
Lomax-Pinevale ES
    930 OLD LAKE PARK ROAD 31601
    Sandra Allen, prin.
Mason ES, 1650 AZALEA DR 31602
    Roberta Wetherington, prin.
Nunn ES, 2201 N FORREST ST 31602
    Gary Mims, prin.
Sallas Mahone ES, 2401 N PATTERSON ST 31602
    Rick English, prin.
Southeast MS, 930 OLD STATENVILLE RD 31601
    Ulysses Mims, prin.
West Gordon MS, 813 W GORDON ST 31601
    David Babcock, prin.

Georgia Christian HS, RURAL ROUTE 02 31601
Lowndes Christian Academy
    P O BOX 3166 31603
Open Bible Christian HS
    3014 OAK ST EXT 31602
Vallwood School, 1903 GORNTO ROAD 31602
Morningside Christian School
    2604 BEMISS RD 31602
St. John Evangelist School
    800 GORNTO RD 31602

Vidalia, Toombs Co., Pop. Code 6
Vidalia ISD
Sch. Sys. Enr. Code 5
Supt. – T. P. Hutcheson
    200 E COLLEGE ST 30474
Dickerson PS, 800 NORTH ST E 30474
    Robert Warnock, prin.
Meadows MS, 205 WATERS DR 30474
    Michael Lupo, prin.
Trippe MS, 302 2ND ST W 30474
    Gloria Raber, prin.

Vienna, Dooly Co., Pop. Code 5
Dooly County SD
Sch. Sys. Enr. Code 5
Supt. – M. Hickerson, 202 COTTON ST 31092
ES, 216 9TH ST 31092 – Dr. Tom Collins, prin.
Other Schools – See Unadilla

Villa Rica, Carroll Co., Pop. Code 5
Carroll County SD
Supt. – See Carrollton
MS, 314 PEACHTREE ST 30180
    Randy Stapler, prin.
PS, 118 GLANTON ST 30180
    Bernice Brooks, prin.

Paulding County SD
Supt. – See Dallas
New Georgia ES, RURAL ROUTE 02 30180
    Barbara Cohran, prin.

Waco, Haralson Co., Pop. Code 2
Haralson County SD
Supt. – See Buchanan
ES 30182 – Harrell McDowell, prin.

Wadley, Jefferson Co., Pop. Code 4
Jefferson County SD
Supt. – See Louisville
Carver/Wadley ES, P O BOX 969 30477
    Vernon Hardy, prin.

Waleska, Cherokee Co., Pop. Code 2
Cherokee County SD
Supt. – See Canton
Moore ES, RURAL ROUTE 02 BOX 112 30183
    Charles Cox, prin.

Waresboro, Ware Co.
Ware County SD
Supt. – See Waycross
ES, P O BOX 40 31564 – Jack Hobbs, prin.

Warm Springs, Meriwether Co., Pop. Code 2
Meriwether County SD
Supt. – See Greenville
ES, COLUMBUS HWY 31830
    Connie Strickland, prin.

Warner Robins, Houston Co., Pop. Code 8
Houston County SD
Supt. – See Perry
Elberta ES, 304 ELBERTA RD 31093
    Mary Lou Dorough, prin.
Lindsey ES, 204 TABOR DR 31093
    Brevard Hunt, prin.
Miller ES, 101 PINE VALLEY DR 31088
    Thomas Lamberth, prin.

Parkwood ES, 503 PARKWOOD DR 31093
    Dennis Powell, prin.
Russell ES, 101 PATRIOT WAY 31088
    Billy Lee, prin.
Shirley Hills ES, 300 MARY LN 31088
    Charlie Harper, prin.
Thomas ES, 801 WATSON BLVD 31093
    Sharla Van Dyke, prin.
Watson ES, DOVER DR 31088
    Miriam Madison, prin.
Westside ES, N PLEASANT HILL ROAD 31093
    Gary Cook, prin.

Warner Robins Christian Academy
    2601 WATSON BLVD 31093
Sacred Heart School
    250 S DAVIS DR #1466 31088

Warrenton, Warren Co., Pop. Code 4
Warren County SD
Sch. Sys. Enr. Code 4
Supt. – Robert Warren, P O BOX 228 30828
Freeman ES, P O BOX 72 30828
    Talmadge Cook, prin.

Washington, Wilkes Co., Pop. Code 5
Wilkes County SD
Sch. Sys. Enr. Code 4
Supt. – Charles Prince, P O BOX 279 30673
Washington-Wilkes ES
    910 E ROBERT TOOMBS AVE 30673
    Laura Toburen, prin.
Washington-Wilkes MS, 109 EAST ST 30673
    Ben Willis, prin.

Wilkes Academy, P O BOX 769 30673

Watkinsville, Oconee Co., Pop. Code 4
Oconee County SD
Sch. Sys. Enr. Code 5
Supt. – S. H. Sanders, P O BOX 146 30677
Oconee County IS 30677 – Annette Short, prin.
Oconee County MS 30677 – Merle Gay, prin.
Oconee County PS 30677
    Dr. Austine Wallis, prin.

Waverly Hall, Harris Co., Pop. Code 3
Harris County SD
Supt. – See Hamilton
ES, P O BOX 38 31831 – L. Meadows,Jr., prin.

Waycross, Ware Co., Pop. Code 7
Ware County SD
Sch. Sys. Enr. Code 5
Supt. – Dr. Donald Dial, P O BOX 1789 31502
Ware County JHS, 1429 GORMAN ROAD 31501
    Tony Adams, prin.
Emerson Park ES
    RURAL ROUTE 03 BOX 51 31501
    Denton Dial, prin.
Memorial Drive ES
    RURAL ROUTE 06 BOX 52 31501
    James Taylor, prin.
Wacona ES, RURAL ROUTE 05 BOX 700 31501
    Richard Brantley, prin.
Other Schools – See Manor, Waresboro

Waycross ISD
Sch. Sys. Enr. Code 5
Supt. – Ted Walden, 1200 COLLEY ST 31501
Center JHS, 1301 BAILEY ST 31501
    Rubert Bussey, prin.
Alice Street ES, 1800 ALICE ST 31501
    Ken Fields, prin.
Crawford Street ES, 415 N CRAWFORD ST 31501
    Glenn Jones, prin.
McDonald Street ES, 1235 MCDONALD ST 31501
    Franklin Pinckney, prin.
Morton/Gilchrist ES, 701 MORTON AVE 31501
    Dan Miller, prin.
Williams Heights ES, 402 MAGNOLIA ST 31501
    Randy Jones, prin.

Southside Christian School
    301 BRUWEL ST 31501

Waynesboro, Burke Co., Pop. Code 6
Burke County SD
Sch. Sys. Enr. Code 5
Supt. – J. D. Smith, P O BOX 596 30830
Burke County MS, PARK DR 30830
    Jesse Gray, prin.
Blakeney MS, COLLEGE ST 30830
    Wilbert Roberts, prin.
ES, ACADEMY AVE 30830 – Calvin Gill, prin.
Other Schools – See Sardis

Burke Academy, P O BOX 350 30830
Burke Haven Christian School
    498 PARK DR 30830

West Green, Coffee Co.
Coffee County SD
Supt. – See Douglas
ES, P O BOX 190 31567 – Jimmy Roberts, prin.

Weston, Webster Co., Pop. Code 2

Greenfield Academy, HWY 41 S 31832

West Point, Troup Co., Pop. Code 5
Troup County SD
Supt. – See La Grange
ES, 1701 E 12TH ST 31833 – Mary Freeman, prin.

Whigham, Grady Co., Pop. Code 3
Grady County SD
Supt. – See Cairo
ES 31797 – Rex Powell, prin.

White, Bartow Co., Pop. Code 3
Bartow County SD
Supt. – See Cartersville
ES, P O BOX 38 30184 – Earl Crapps, prin.

Whitesburg, Carroll Co., Pop. Code 3
Carroll County SD
Supt. – See Carrollton
ES, 868 MAIN ST 30185 – Donald Tillman, prin.

Willacoochee, Atkinson Co., Pop. Code 4
Atkinson County SD
Supt. – See Pearson
ES, P O BOX 338 31650
    Vernon Marcoullier, prin.

Winder, Barrow Co., Pop. Code 6
Barrow County SD
Sch. Sys. Enr. Code 6
Supt. – Dr. Don Hight, P O BOX 767 30680
Russell MS, 211 W MIDLAND 30680
    Jerris Hayes, prin.
Winder-Barrow MS, P O BOX 767 30680
    R. Wimberly, prin.
County Line ES
    RURAL ROUTE 05 BOX 312 30680
    Montene Lewis, prin.
Holsenbeck ES
    RURAL ROUTE 04 BOX 262 30680
    Mike Lee, prin.
Kennedy ES, P O BOX 728 30680
    Ralph Pack, prin.
Other Schools – See Auburn, Bethlehem, Statham

Winder-Barrow Christian School
    RURAL ROUTE 01 BOX 262 30680

Winston, Douglas Co.
Douglas County SD
Supt. – See Douglasville
ES, 7465 HIGHWAY 78 30187
    Linda Lumpkin, prin.

Winterville, Clarke Co., Pop. Code 3
Clarke County SD
Supt. – See Athens
ES, 305 CHEROKEE RD 30683
    Thomas Brown, prin.

Woodbine, Camden Co., Pop. Code 3
Camden County SD
Supt. – See Kingsland
ES, P O BOX 528 31569 – Richard Wilson, prin.

Woodbury, Meriwether Co., Pop. Code 4
Meriwether County SD
Supt. – See Greenville
ES, RURAL ROUTE 02 BOX 165 30293
    Grover Reese, prin.

Flint River Academy, P O BOX 247 30293

Woodstock, Cherokee Co., Pop. Code 5
Cherokee County SD
Supt. – See Canton
Booth MS, RURAL ROUTE 03 30188
    Karen Allen, prin.
Boston ES, 105 OTHELLO DR 30188
    Janice Prather, prin.
Chapman ES, 6500 PUTNAM FORD DR 30188
    Phil Gramling, prin.
Johnston ES, 2031 E CHEROKEE DR 30188
    Darothea Kirkland, prin.
Little River ES, 3170 TRICKUM RD 30188
    Rick Ingram, prin.
ES, 210 N MAIN ST 30188 – Lewis Peters, prin.

Wrens, Jefferson Co., Pop. Code 4
Jefferson County SD
Supt. – See Louisville
ES, P O BOX 308 30833 – Wade Brooks, prin.

Wrightsville, Johnson Co., Pop. Code 5
Johnson County SD
Sch. Sys. Enr. Code 4
Supt. – Burton Dixon, P O BOX 110 31096
MS, DUBLIN HWY BOX 319 31096
    Curtis Dixon, prin.
PS, P O BOX 68 31096 – Nancy Colston, prin.
Other Schools – See Kite

Zebulon, Pike Co., Pop. Code 3
Pike County SD
Sch. Sys. Enr. Code 4
Supt. – Dr. James Turpin
    115 W JACKSON ST 30295
Pike County MS, P O BOX 405 30295
    F. Pitts, prin.
Pike County ES, P O BOX 407 30295
    Edna Miller, prin.

HAWAII

STATE DEPARTMENT OF EDUCATION
Queen Liliuokalani Building
P.O. Box 2360, Honolulu 96804
(808) 548-6911

Superintendent of Education	Charles Toguchi
Deputy Superintendent	Kengo Takata
Assistant Superintendent Business Services	Eugene Imai
Assistant Superintendent Instructional Services	Herman Aizawa
Assistant Superintendent Personnel Services	Donald Nugent

STATE BOARD OF EDUCATION
Francis McMillen, *Chairperson*   1390 Miller St. #405, Honolulu   96804

STATE POSTSECONDARY EDUCATION COMMISSION
Dr. Fujio Matsuda, *Executive Officer*   2444 Dole St., Honolulu   96822

PUBLIC, PRIVATE, AND PAROCHIAL ELEMENTARY SCHOOLS

Aiea, Honolulu Co., Pop. Code 7
Central Oahu SD
Supt. – See Wahiawa
IS, 99-600 KULAWEA ST 96701
Lester Chuck, prin.
ES, 99-370 MOANALUA ROAD 96701
Irene Okawaki, prin.
Pearl Ridge ES, 98-940 MOANALUA ROAD 96701
Edith Lee, prin.
Scott ES, 98-1230 MOANALUA ROAD 96701
Harold Look, prin.
Waimalu ES, 98-825 MOANALUA ROAD 96701
Robert Lee, prin.
Webling ES, 99-370 PAIHI ST 96701
George Kojima, prin.

Our Savior Lutheran School
98-1098 MOANALUA ROAD 96701
St. Elizabeth School
99-310 MOANALUA ROAD 96701

Captain Cook, Hawaii Co., Pop. Code 4
Hawaii SD
Supt. – See Hilo
Honaunau ES, RURAL ROUTE 01 BOX 425 96704
Charles Okino, prin.
Hookena ES, RURAL ROUTE 01 BOX 41 96704
Alvin Rho, prin.

Eleele, Kauai Co.
Kauai SD
Supt. – See Lihue
ES, P O BOX 38 96705 – David Cole, prin.

Ewa Beach, Honolulu Co., Pop. Code 6
Leeward Oahu SD
Supt. – See Waipahu
Ilima IS, 91884 FORT WEAVER ROAD 96706
John Aki, prin.
Barbers Point ES, BOXER ROAD 96706
William Cupit, prin.
ES, 91-740 PAPIPI ROAD 96706 – Ted Abear, prin.
Ewa ES, 91-1280 RENTON ROAD 96706
Merle Iwamasa, prin.
Iroquois Point ES, 5553 CORMORANT AVE 96706
Carlton Chang, prin.
Kaimiloa ES, 91-1028 KAUNOLU ST 96706
Howard Humphreys, prin.
Makakilo ES, 92-675 ANIPEAHI 96706
Michio Shishido, prin.
Mauka Lani ES, 92-1300 PANANA ST 96707
Kaylene Yee, prin.
Pohakea ES, 91-750 FT WEAVER ROAD 96706
Patricia Pedersen, prin.

Our Lady of Perpetual Help School
91-1010 NORTH ROAD 96706

Haiku, Maui Co.
Maui SD
Supt. – See Wailuku
ES, 105 PAUWELA ROAD 96708
Donald Kuwada, prin.

Haleiwa, Honolulu Co., Pop. Code 5
Central Oahu SD
Supt. – See Wahiawa
ES, 66-505 HALEIWA ROAD 96712
Takashi Matsuyama, prin.

Windward Oahu SD
Supt. – See Kaneohe
Sunset Beach ES
59-360 KAMEHAMEHA HIGHWAY 96712
Gilbert Chun, prin.

Sunset Beach Christian School
59-578 KAMEHAMEHA HWY 96712

Hana, Maui Co., Pop. Code 4
Maui SD
Supt. – See Wailuku
S, P O BOX 128 96713 – Patricia Eason, prin.
Keanae ES, P O BOX 128 96713
Patricia Eason, prin.

Hanalei, Kauai Co.
Kauai SD
Supt. – See Lihue
ES, P O BOX 46 96714 – Nichols Beck, prin.

Hauula, Honolulu Co., Pop. Code 4
Windward Oahu SD
Supt. – See Kaneohe
ES, 54-046 KAMEHAMEHA HIGHWAY 96717
Jean Izu, prin.

Hilo, Hawaii Co., Pop. Code 8
Hawaii SD
Sch. Sys. Enr. Code 7
Supt. – Alan Garson, P O BOX 4160 96720
IS, 587 WAIANUENUE AVE 96720
Miriam Agcaoili, prin.
Waiakea IS, 200 W PUAINAKO ST 96720
Gertrude Ebesu, prin.
Chiefess Kapiolani ES, 966 KILAUEA AVE 96720
George Miyashiro, prin.
DeSilva ES, 278 AINAKO AVE 96720
Edward Hayashi, prin.
Haaheo ES, 121 HAAHEO ROAD 96720
Stanley Golembeski, prin.
Hilo Union ES, 506 WAIANUENUE AVE 96720
Kosuke Tamashiro, prin.
Kaumana ES, 1710 KAUMANA DR 96720
Dr. John Masuhara, prin.
Keaukaha ES, 240 DESHA AVE 96720
Pat Seely, prin.
Waiakea ES, 180 W PUAINAKO ST 96720
Clifton Iwamoto, prin.
Waiakeawaena ES, 2420 KILAUEA AVE 96720
Dr. James Kurashige, prin.
Other Schools – See Captain Cook, Holualoa,
Honokaa, Kailua-Kona, Kamuela, Kapaau, Keaau,
Kealakekua, Laupahoehoe, Mountain View,
Naalehu, Paauilo, Pahala, Pahoa, Papaikou

St. Joseph ES, 999 ULULANI ST 96720

Holualoa, Hawaii Co., Pop. Code 3
Hawaii SD
Supt. – See Hilo
ES, P O BOX 345 96725 – Dan Yoshida, prin.

Honokaa, Hawaii Co., Pop. Code 4
Hawaii SD
Supt. – See Hilo
S, P O BOX 239 96727 – Jerry Sakamoto, prin.

Honolulu, Honolulu Co., Pop. Code 10
Central Oahu SD
Supt. – See Wahiawa

Aliamanu IS, 3271 SALT LAKE BLVD 96818
Gary Griffiths, prin.
Moanalua IS, 1289 MAHIOLE ST 96819
Melvin Seki, prin.
Aliamanu ES, 3265 SALT LAKE BLVD 96818
Wallace Higashi, prin.
Lt. Col. Hickam ES, MANZELMAN CIRCLE 96818
Lois Matsuda, prin.
Makalapa ES, 4435 SALT LAKE BLVD 96818
Marian Crislip, prin.
Moanalua ES, 1337 MALIOLE ST 96819
Shannon Ajifu, prin.
Mokulele ES, 1304 14TH ST 96818
Nancy Latham, prin.
Nimitz ES, 520 MAIN ST 96818
Dorothy Nakamura, prin.
Pearl Harbor ES, MOANALUA RIDGE 96818
Francis Oshiro, prin.
Pearl Harbor Kai ES, C AVE & CENTER DR 96818
Judith Saranchock, prin.
Red Hill ES, 1265 ALA KULA PLACE 96819
Richard Honda, prin.
Salt Lake ES, 1131 ALA LILIKOI ST 96818
Carmielita Minami, prin.
Shafter ES, FORT SHAFTER 96819
Ralph Ige, prin.

Honolulu SD
Sch. Sys. Enr. Code 8
Supt. – Margaret Oda, 4967 KILAUEA AVE 96816
Central IS, 1302 QUEEN EMMA ST 96813
Richard Anbe, prin.
Jarrett IS, 1903 PALOLO AVE 96816
Yoshiji Asami, prin.
Kaimuki IS, 631 18TH AVE 96816
Frank Fernandes, prin.
Kawananakoa IS, 49 FUNCHAL ST 96813
Charles Higgins, prin.
Niu Valley IS, 310 HALEMANUMAU ST 96821
Eric Heu, prin.
Stevenson IS, 1202 PROSPECT ST 96822
C. Stevens, prin.
Washington IS, 1633 S KING ST 96826
Marsha Alegre, prin.
Aina Haina ES, 801 W HIND DRIVE 96821
Randy Erskine, prin.
Ala Wai ES, 503 KAMOKU ST 96826
Eugene Shizuru, prin.
Aliiolani ES, 1240 7TH AVE 96816
Haroldeen Wakida, prin.
Hahaione ES, 595 PEPEEKEO ST 96825
Charles Shores, prin.
Hokulani ES, 2940 KAMAKINI ST 96816
Annette Chun-Ming, prin.
Jefferson ES, 324 KAPAHULU AVE 96815
Kiyoko Kagawa, prin.
Kaewai ES, 1929 KAM IV ROAD 96819
Stanley Morikawa, prin.
Kahala ES, 4559 KILAUEA AVE 96816
Susan Yoshinaka, prin.
Kalihi ES, 2471 KULA KOLEA DR 96819
Florentine Smith, prin.
Kalihi-Kai ES, 626 MCNEILL ST 96817
Richard Yogi, prin.
Kalihi-Uka ES, 2411 KALIHI ST 96819
Charles Oba, prin.
Kalihi-Waena ES, 1240 GULICK AVE 96819
Brian Mizuguchi, prin.
Kamiloiki ES, 7788 HAWAII KAI DR 96825
Ronald Spinney, prin.

Kapalama ES, 1601 N SCHOOL ST 96817
  Elvin Low, prin.
Kauluwela ES, 1486 AALA ST 96817
  Gwendolyn Lee, prin.
King Liholiho ES, 3430 MANUNALOA AVE 96816
  Benjamin Lopalio, prin.
King Lunalilo ES, 810 PUMEHANA ST 96826
  Betty Shishido, prin.
Koko Head ES
  189 LUNALILO HOME ROAD 96825
  Cicilia Lum, prin.
Lanakila ES, 717 N KUAKINI ST 96817
  Kathleen Mau, prin.
Linapuni ES, 1434 LINAPUNI ST 96819
  Suzanne Fonoti, prin.
Lincoln ES, 615 AUWAIOLIMU ST 96813
  Mamo Carreira, prin.
Maemae ES, 319 WYLLIE ST 96817
  Morris Kimoto, prin.
Manoa ES, 3155 MANOA ROAD 96822
  James Tomita, prin.
Mayor Fern ES, 1121 MIDDLE ST 96819
  Stanley Kau, prin.
Mayor Wilson ES, 4945 KILAUEA AVE 96816
  Elsie Hu, prin.
Noelani ES, 2655 WOODLAWN DR 96822
  Clayton Fujie, prin.
Nuuanu ES, 3055 PUIWA LANE 96817
  Barbara Nagaue, prin.
Palolo ES, 2106 10TH AVE 96816
  Peter Chun, prin.
Pauoa ES, 2300 PAUOA ROAD 96813
  Samuel Kaahanui, prin.
Prince Kuhio ES, 2759 S KING ST 96826
  Lauretta Gum, prin.
Princess Likelike ES, 1618 PALAMA ST 96817
  Theodore Nishijo, prin.
Princess Kaiulani ES, 783 N KING ST 96817
  Roland Lum, prin.
Puuhale ES, 345 PUUHALE ROAD 96819
  Helen Sanpei, prin.
Queen Kaahumanu ES, 1141 KINAU ST 96814
  Frank Sasaoka, prin.
Queen Liliuokalani ES
  3633 WAIALAE AVE 96816 – Arthur Wong, prin.
Royal ES, 1519 QUEEN EMMA ST 96813
  Winchell Lee, prin.
Waialae ES, 1045 19TH AVE 96816
  Melvin Furukawa, prin.
Waikiki ES, 3710 LEAHI AVE 96815
  Doris Choi, prin.
Wailupe Valley ES, 939 HIND LUKA DR 96821
  Lois Okino, prin.

Iolani School, 563 KAMOKU ST 96826
Kamehameha School
  KAPALAMA HEIGHTS 96817
Punahou School, 1601 PUNAHOU ST 96822
St. Andrew's Priory School
  224 QUEEN EMMA SQUARE 96813
Bingham Tract ES, 1232 ALEXANDER ST 96826
Cathedral School, 1728 NUUANU AVE 96817
Christian Academy, 930 LUNALILO ST 96822
Church of Holy Nativity School
  5286 KALANIANAOLE HWY 96821
Epiphany School, 1041 10TH AVE 96816
Hanahauoli School, 1922 MAKIKI ST 96822
Hawaii Baptist Academy, 21 BATES 96817
Hawaiian Mission ES, 1415 MAKIKI ST 96814
Holy Family School, 830 MAIN ST 96818
Holy Trinity School
  5919 KALANIANAOLE HWY 96821
Hongwanji Mission School
  1728 PALI HWY 96813
Honolulu Waldorf School, 350 ULUA ST 96821
Island Paradise Academy
  1238 WILHELMINA RISE 96816
Island Paradise School, 1506 PIIKOI ST 96822
Kaimuki Christian School
  1117 KOKO HEAD AVE 96816
Maryknoll, 1722 DOLE ST 96822
Navy Hale Keiki ES
  153 BOUGAINVILLE DRIVE 96818
Our Redeemer Lutheran School
  2428 WILDER AVE 96822
Sacred Hearts Academy
  3253 WAIALAE AVE 96816
Sacred Hearts Convent School
  21 BATES ST 96817
St. Anthony's School, 640 PUUHALE ROAD 96819
St. John the Baptist School
  2340 OMILO LANE 96819
St. Patrick School, 1124 7TH AVE 96816
St. Theresa School, 712 N SCHOOL ST 96817
Star of the Sea ES, 4469 MALIA ST 96821
Waolani-Judd School, 408 N JUDD ST 96817

Kaaawa, Honolulu Co., Pop. Code 3
  Windward Oahu SD
  Supt. – See Kaneohe
  ES, 51-296 KAMEHAMEHA HIGHWAY 96730
    Cynthia Chun, prin.

Kahuku, Honolulu Co., Pop. Code 3
  Windward Oahu SD
  Supt. – See Kaneohe
  S, P O BOX 308 96731 – Lea Albert, prin.
  Kahuku ES, P O BOX 3001 96731
    Frank Kalama, prin.

Kahului, Maui Co., Pop. Code 7
  Maui SD
  Supt. – See Wailuku
  ES, 410 HINA AVE 96732 – Howard Omura, prin.

Lihikai ES, 335 S PAPA AVE 96732
  Ralph Murakami, prin.

Christ the King School
  211 KAULAWAHINE ST 96732
Emmanuel ES, 520 W ONE STREET 96732

Kailua, Honolulu Co., Pop. Code 8
  Windward Oahu SD
  Supt. – See Kaneohe
  IS, 145 S KAINALU DRIVE 96734 – Lyla Hee, prin.
  Aikahi ES, 281 ILIHAU ST 96734
    Roberta Tokumaru, prin.
  Enchanted Lake ES, 770 KEOLU DR 96734
    Hiroshi Honma, prin.
  Kaelepulu ES, 530 KEOLU DR 96734
    Shirley Yamashiro, prin.
  ES, 315 KUULEI ROAD 96734
    Francine Fernandez, prin.
  Kainalu ES, 165 KAIHOLU ST 96734
    Annette Ogata, prin.
  Keolu ES, 1416 KEOLU DR 96734
    Mary Murakami, prin.
  Lanikai ES, 140 ALALA ROAD 96734
    Jacquelin Gordon, prin.
  Maunawili ES, 1465 ULUPII ST 96734
    Judith Wicker, prin.
  Mokapu ES, 1193 MOKAPU BLVD 96734
    Carol Ching, prin.

Le Jardin Academy, 1110 A KAILUA ROAD 96734
St. John Vianney School
  940 KEOLU DRIVE 96734

Kailua-Kona, Hawaii Co.
  Hawaii SD
  Supt. – See Hilo
  Kealakehe IS, 74 5090 KEALAKAA ST 96740
    Brian Nakashima, prin.
  Kahakai ES
    76-147 ROYAL POINCIANA DR 96740
    Claire Yoshida, prin.
  Kealakehe ES, 74-5119 KEALAKAA ST 96740
    Ed Okada, prin.

Kalaheo, Kauai Co., Pop. Code 4
  Kauai SD
  Supt. – See Lihue
  ES, P O BOX 427 96741 – Robert Town, prin.

Holy Cross School, P O BOX 488 96741

Kamuela, Hawaii Co., Pop. Code 3
  Hawaii SD
  Supt. – See Hilo
  Waimea ES, P O BOX 339 96743
    Patricia Bergin, prin.

Hawaii Prep Academy Low & MS
  P O BOX 428 96743

Kaneohe, Honolulu Co., Pop. Code 8
  Windward Oahu SD
  Sch. Sys. Enr. Code 7
  Supt. – Sakae Loo
    46169 KAMEHAMEHA HWY 96744
  King IS
    46-155 KAMEHAMEHA HIGHWAY 96744
    Jane Sugimoto, prin.
  Ahuimanu ES, 47-470 HUI AEKO PL 96744
    Gladys Inada, prin.
  Heeia ES, 46-202 HAIKU ROAD 96744
    Francine Honda, prin.
  Kahaluu ES, 47-280 WAIHEE ROAD 96744
    Bruce Shimomoto, prin.
  ES, 45-495 KAMEHAMEHA HIGHWAY 96744
    Lenore Higa, prin.
  Kapunahala ES, 45-828 ANOI ROAD 96744
    Ruby Hiraishi, prin.
  Parker ES, 45-259 WAIKALUA ROAD 96744
    Naomi Matsuzaki, prin.
  Puohala ES, 45-233 KULAULI ST 96744
    Lois Mui, prin.
  Waiahole ES
    48-215 WAIAHOLE VALLEY ROAD 96744
    Raymond Sugai, prin.
  Other Schools – See Haleiwa, Hauula, Kaaawa,
    Kahuku, Kailua, Laie, Waimanalo

St. Ann School, 46-125 HAIKU ROAD 96744
St. Anthony ES, 148 MAKAWAO ST 96734
St. Mark Lutheran School
  45-725 KAMEHAMEHA HWY 96744

Kapaa, Kauai Co., Pop. Code 5
  Kauai SD
  Supt. – See Lihue
  ES, 4886 KAWAIHAU ROAD 96746
    Roy Shimamoto, prin.

St. Catherine School
  5021 KAWAIHAU ROAD 96746

Kapaau, Hawaii Co., Pop. Code 2
  Hawaii SD
  Supt. – See Hilo
  Kohala S, P O BOX 279 96755
    Albert Gaddis, prin.

Kaunakakai, Maui Co.
  Maui SD
  Supt. – See Wailuku
  ES, P O BOX 6 96748 – Edward Kahiwamura, prin.
  Kilohana ES, HCR 96748 – Stephen Petro, prin.

Keaau, Hawaii Co., Pop. Code 3
  Hawaii SD
  Supt. – See Hilo
  ES, P O BOX 128 96749 – Nanette Hiraoka, prin.

Kealakekua, Hawaii Co., Pop. Code 3
  Hawaii SD
  Supt. – See Hilo
  Konawaena ES, P O BOX 728 96750
    Ed Murai, prin.

Kekaha, Kauai Co., Pop. Code 4
  Kauai SD
  Supt. – See Lihue
  ES, P O BOX 580 96752 – Jon Derby, prin.

St. Theresa School, P O BOX 277 96752

Kihei, Maui Co., Pop. Code 3
  Maui SD
  Supt. – See Wailuku
  Lokelani IS, 250 E LIPOA ST 96753
    Andrea Kaumeheiwa, prin.
  ES, 250 E LIPOA ST 96753
    Andrea Kaumeheiwa, prin.

Kilauea, Kauai Co., Pop. Code 3
  Kauai SD
  Supt. – See Lihue
  ES, P O BOX 37 96754 – Darryl Goo, prin.

Koloa, Kauai Co., Pop. Code 4
  Kauai SD
  Supt. – See Lihue
  ES, RURAL ROUTE 01 BOX 57 96756
    Dora Hong, prin.

Kualapuu, Maui Co.
  Maui SD
  Supt. – See Wailuku
  ES, P O BOX 260 96757
    Randolph Kobayashi, prin.

Kula, Maui Co.
  Maui SD
  Supt. – See Wailuku
  ES, P O BOX 299 96790 – Edwin Ichiriu, prin.

Haleakala School
  RURAL ROUTE 02 BOX 790 96790

Lahaina, Maui Co., Pop. Code 7
  Maui SD
  Supt. – See Wailuku
  IS, 871 LAHAINALUNA ROAD 96761
    Beverly Stanich, prin.
  King Kamehameha III ES, 611 FRONT ST 96761
    H. Williams, prin.
  Nahienaena ES, 816 NIHEU ST 96761
    H. Williams, prin.

Sacred Hearts School, 239 DICKENSON ST 96761

Laie, Honolulu Co., Pop. Code 5
  Windward Oahu SD
  Supt. – See Kaneohe
  ES, 55-109 KULANUI ST 96762
    Gilbert Hatter, prin.

Lanai City, Maui Co., Pop. Code 4
  Maui SD
  Supt. – See Wailuku
  Lanai S, P O BOX 757 96763
    Howard Sakamoto, prin.

Laupahoehoe, Hawaii Co., Pop. Code 2
  Hawaii SD
  Supt. – See Hilo
  S, P O BOX 189 96764 – Randal Tanaka, prin.

Lawai, Kauai Co.

Kauai Adventist School
  2-4035 KAUMALII HWY #A 96765

Lihue, Kauai Co., Pop. Code 5
  Kauai SD
  Sch. Sys. Enr. Code 6
  Supt. – Shirley Akita, 3060 EIWA ST 96766
  Wilcox ES, 4319 HARDY ST 96766
    Ernest Dela Cruz, prin.
  Other Schools – See Eleele, Hanalei, Kalaheo, Kapaa,
    Kekaha, Kilauea, Koloa, Makaweli, Waimea

Immaculate Conception School
  3343 KANAKOLU ST 96766

Makawao, Maui Co., Pop. Code 4
  Maui SD
  Supt. – See Wailuku
  Kalama IS, 120 MAKANI ROAD 96768
    David Keala, prin.
  ES, 3542 BALDWIN AVE 96768
    Donald Karimoto, prin.

St. Joseph School, 57 DOMINICAN LANE 96768

Makaweli, Kauai Co.
  Kauai SD
  Supt. – See Lihue
  Niihau ES, NIIHAU 96769
    Lulubelle Kelley, prin.

Maunaloa, Maui Co., Pop. Code 3
  Maui SD
  Supt. – See Wailuku
  ES, P O BOX 128 96770 – Ronald Kula, prin.

Mililani Town, Honolulu Co., Pop. Code 4
Central Oahu SD
Supt. – See Wahiawa
Kipapa ES, 95-075 KIPAPA DR 96789
  Ralph Watanabe, prin.
Miliani-Uka ES, 94-380 KUAHELANI AVE 96789
  Betty Mow, prin.
Mililani-Waena ES, 95-502 KIPAPA DR 96789
  Gervacio Buenconsejo, prin.

King's Schs., 94294 ANANIA DR 96789

Mountain View, Hawaii Co.
Hawaii SD
Supt. – See Hilo
ES, P O BOX 9 96771 – Muriel Hughes, prin.

Naalehu, Hawaii Co., Pop. Code 4
Hawaii SD
Supt. – See Hilo
ES, P O BOX A 96772 – Karen Mitsuyoshi, prin.

Paauilo, Hawaii Co.
Hawaii SD
Supt. – See Hilo
ES, P O BOX 329 96776 – Clarence Mills, prin.

Pahala, Hawaii Co., Pop. Code 4
Hawaii SD
Supt. – See Hilo
Ka'u S, P O BOX 100 96777 – Annette Fujii, prin.

Pahoa, Hawaii Co., Pop. Code 3
Hawaii SD
Supt. – See Hilo
S, P O BOX 3 96778 – Winston Towata, prin.

Paia, Maui Co.
Maui SD
Supt. – See Wailuku
ES, P O BOX 697 96779 – Larry Libres, prin.

Todd Memorial Christian School
  P O BOX 729 96779

Papaikou, Hawaii Co., Pop. Code 4
Hawaii SD
Supt. – See Hilo
Kalanianaole ES, P O BOX 28 96781
  Roy Katayama, prin.

Pearl City, Honolulu Co., Pop. Code 7
Leeward Oahu SD
Supt. – See Waipahu
Highlands IS, 1460 HOOLAULEA ST 96782
  Rhoda Hirokawa, prin.
Lehua ES, 791 LEHUA AVE 96782
  Karen McCloskey, prin.
Manana ES, 1147 KUMANO ST 96782
  Candace Koga, prin.
Momilani ES, 2130 HOOKIEKIE ST 96782
  Bert Yamamoto, prin.
Palisades ES, 2306 AUHUHU ST 96782
  Samuel Oshio, prin.
ES, 1090 WAIMANO HOME ROAD 96782
  Jane Himeda, prin.

Pearl City Highlands ES
  1419 WAIMANO HOME ROAD 96782
  Patricia Hamamoto, prin.
Waiau ES, 98-450 HOOKANIKE ST 96782
  Diana Oshiro, prin.

Children's House, Inc.
  1840 KOMO MAI DRIVE 96782
Our Lady of Good Counsel School
  1530 HOOLANA ST 96782

Pukalani, Maui Co., Pop. Code 4
Maui SD
Supt. – See Wailuku
ES, 2945 IOLANI ST 96768
  Osamu Kawakami, prin.

Wahiawa, Honolulu Co., Pop. Code 8
Central Oahu SD
Sch. Sys. Enr. Code 8
Supt. – Liberato Viduya
  1136 CALIFORNIA AVE 96786
IS, 275 ROSE ST 96786 – Robert Golden, prin.
Wheeler IS, 2 WHEELER AFB 96786
  Daniel Lau, prin.
Hale Kula ES, WAIANAE & AYERS AVES 96786
  Arlene Shigemasa, prin.
Helemano ES, 1001 IHIIHI AVE 96786
  Dennis Kato, prin.
Iliahi ES, 2035 CALIFORNIA AVE 96786
  Jane Serikaku, prin.
Kaala ES, 130 CALIFORNIA AVE 96786
  Jane Wakukawa, prin.
Solomon ES, 1 SCHOFIELD BARRACKS 96786
  Bjarne Kaer, prin.
ES, 1402 GLEN AVE 96786
  George Nakasone, prin.
Wheeler ES, WHEELER A F BASE 96854
  Phyllis Shipman, prin.
Other Schools – See Aiea, Haleiwa, Honolulu,
  Mililani Town, Waialua

Our Lady of Sorrows School
  1403 CALIFORNIA AVE 96786
Trinity Lutheran School
  1611 CALIFORNIA AVE 96786

Waialua, Honolulu Co., Pop. Code 6
Central Oahu SD
Supt. – See Wahiawa
ES, 67-020 WAIALUA BEACH ROAD 96791
  Sharon Nakagawa, prin.

St. Michael's School, 67-340 HAONA ST 96791

Waianae, Honolulu Co., Pop. Code 5
Leeward Oahu SD
Supt. – See Waipahu
IS, 85-626 FARRINGTON HIGHWAY 96792
  Hubert Murakawa, prin.
Leihoku ES, 86-285 LEIHOKU ST 96792
  Frances Matsuoka, prin.
Maili ES, 87-360 KULAAUPUNI ST 96792
  Eleanor Fujioka, prin.
Makaha ES, 84-760 LAHAINA ST 96792
  Hazel Sumile, prin.

Nanaikapono ES
  89-195 FARRINGTON HIGHWAY 96792
  Clara Burrows, prin.
Nanakuli ES, 89-778 HALEAKALA AVE 96792
  Edward Kawamoto, prin.
ES, 85-220 MCARTHUR ST 96792
  Roger Bellinger, prin.

Maili Christian School
  87-138 GILIPAKE ST 96792

Wailuku, Maui Co., Pop. Code 7
Maui SD
Sch. Sys. Enr. Code 7
Supt. – Lokelani Lindsey, P O BOX 1070 96793
Iao IS, 1910 KAOHU ST 96793
  Dr. Elizabeth Ayson, prin.
Waihee ES, RURAL ROUTE 01 BOX 122 96793
  Lawrence Joyo, prin.
ES, 355 S HIGH ST 96793 – Yeiko Arakaki, prin.
Other Schools – See Haiku, Hana, Kahului,
  Kaunakakai, Kihei, Kualapuu, Kula, Lahaina, Lanai
  City, Makawao, Maunaloa, Paia, Pukalani

St. Anthony ES, 1627 MILL ST 96793

Waimanalo, Honolulu Co., Pop. Code 4
Windward Oahu SD
Supt. – See Kaneohe
Pope ES, 41-133 HULI ST 96795
  Louise Wolcott, prin.
ES, 41-1330 KALANIANAOLE HWY 96795
  Marian Holokai, prin.

Waimea, Kauai Co., Pop. Code 4
Kauai SD
Supt. – See Lihue
Waimea Canyon ES, P O BOX 518 96796
  Clifton Bailey, prin.

Waipahu, Honolulu Co., Pop. Code 8
Leeward Oahu SD
Sch. Sys. Enr. Code 8
Supt. – Edward Nakano
  94-366 PUPUPANI ST 96797
IS, 94-455 FARRINGTON HIGHWAY 96797
  Glenn Tatsuno, prin.
August Ahrens ES, 94-1170 WAIPAHU ST 96797
  Arthur Ouye, prin.
Honowai ES, 94-600 HONOWAI ST 96797
  Roy Kimura, prin.
Kanoelani ES, 94-1091 OLI LOOP 96797
  Walter Luke, prin.
ES, 94-465 WAIPAHU ST 96797
  William Wong, prin.
Other Schools – See Ewa Beach, Pearl City, Waianae

Lanakilia Baptist School
  94-1250 WAIPAHU ST 96797
St. Joseph School
  94-651 FARRINGTON HWY 96797

IDAHO

STATE DEPARTMENT OF EDUCATION
Len B. Jordan Office Building
650 W. State St., Boise 83720
(208) 334-3300

State Superintendent of Public Instruction — Jerry Evans
Deputy State Superintendent — August Hein
Associate Superintendent Finance & Administration — Robert Dutton
Associate Superintendent State-Federal Instructional Services — Darrell Loosle

STATE BOARD OF EDUCATION
Rayburn Barton, *Executive Director* — Len B. Jordan Bldg. #307, Boise 83720

BOARD OF REGENTS
Vacancy, *Executive Director* — 650 W. State St. #307, Boise 83720

PUBLIC, PRIVATE, AND PAROCHIAL ELEMENTARY SCHOOLS

Aberdeen, Bingham Co., Pop. Code 4
Aberdeen SD 58
Sch. Sys. Enr. Code 3
Supt. – John Murdoch, P O BOX 610 83210
ES, FOURTH & LINCOLN 83210
  Donald Dempster, prin.

Acequia, Minidoka Co., Pop. Code 1
Minidoka County JSD 331
Supt. – See Rupert
ES, RURAL ROUTE 04 BOX 160 83350
  Goldie McClure, prin.

Albion, Cassia Co., Pop. Code 2
Cassia County JSD 151
Supt. – See Burley
ES 83311 – Shirley Clark, prin.

Almo, Cassia Co.
Cassia County JSD 151
Supt. – See Burley
ES 83312 – Janice Aragon, prin.

American Falls, Power Co., Pop. Code 5
American Falls JSD 381
Sch. Sys. Enr. Code 4
Supt. – Sheldon Kovarsky
  827 FORT HALL AVE 83211
Thomas MS, 400 MADISON ST 83211
  George McOmber, prin.
Hillcrest ES, 100 BENNETT ST 83211
  Ronald Bolinger, prin.

Arbon, Power Co.
Arbon ESD 383
Sch. Sys. Enr. Code 1
Supt. – (—)
  4405 ARBON VALLEY HWY 83212
ES, 4405 ARBON VALLEY HWY 83212
  Barbara Robinson, prin.

Arco, Butte Co., Pop. Code 4
Arco JSD 111
Sch. Sys. Enr. Code 3
Supt. – Michael Ford, 120 S WATER ST 83213
ES, P O BOX 675 83213 – Robert Howard, prin.
Other Schools – See Butte, Howe

Arimo, Bannock Co., Pop. Code 2
Marsh Valley JSD 21
Sch. Sys. Enr. Code 4
Supt. – Dr. Gordon Loosle, P O BOX 180 83214
Marsh Valley MS, P O BOX 157 83214
  Ron Jolley, prin.
Other Schools – See Downey, Inkom, Lava Hot
  Springs, McCammon

Ashton, Fremont Co., Pop. Code 4
Freemont County JSD 215
Supt. – See Saint Anthony
ES, P O BOX 630 83420 – Jack Boggetti, prin.

Athol, Kootenai Co., Pop. Code 2
Lakeland SD 272
Supt. – See Rathdrum
ES, P O BOX H 83801 – Jack Derting, prin.

Atlanta, Elmore Co., Pop. Code 2
Mountain Home SD 193
Supt. – See Mountain Home
ES 83601 – Patricia Inama, prin.

Avery, Shoshone Co., Pop. Code 2
Avery SD 394
Sch. Sys. Enr. Code 1
Supt. – Robert Leonard, P O BOX 77 83802

ES 83802 – Robert Leonard, prin.
Other Schools – See Calder, Clarkia

Bancroft, Caribou Co., Pop. Code 3
North Gem SD 149
Sch. Sys. Enr. Code 2
Supt. – Elzo White, P O BOX 70 83217
North Gem ES, 111 W 4TH S 83217
  Phil Campbell, prin.

Bellevue, Blaine Co., Pop. Code 4
Blaine County SD 61
Supt. – See Hailey
PS, P O BOX 390 83313 – Claude Ballard, prin.

Blackfoot, Bingham Co., Pop. Code 7
Blackfoot SD 55
Sch. Sys. Enr. Code 5
Supt. – Daniel Schartz, 440 W JUDICIAL ST 83221
Mountain View MS
  RURAL ROUTE 03 BOX 429 83221
  Ron Reese, prin.
Elmwood ES, 155 E FRANCIS ST 83221
  (—), prin.
Groveland ES, 165 N 370 W RD 83221
  Martin Wallace, prin.
Shilling ES, 50 S SHILLING AVE 83221
  Barbara Duncan, prin.
Stalker ES, 991 W CENTER ST 83221
  Dewane Wren, prin.
Stoddard ES, 460 YORK DRIVE 83221
  Jylene Morgan, prin.
Wapello ES, N 195 E 350 N 83221
  Chris Gardner, prin.
Other Schools – See Fort Hall

Snake River SD 52
Sch. Sys. Enr. Code 4
Supt. – Blair Wilding
  RURAL ROUTE 02 BOX 249 83221
Snake River JHS, RURAL ROUTE 05 83221
  Brian Jolley, prin.
Riverside ES, 16 S 700 W RD 83221
  Candis Donicht, prin.
Rockford ES, 1152 W HIGHWAY 39 83221
  Theo Perkes, prin.
Snake River MS, 1060 W 110 S RD 83221
  Gerald Heath, prin.
Other Schools – See Moreland, Pingree

Bliss, Gooding Co., Pop. Code 2
Bliss JSD 234
Sch. Sys. Enr. Code 2
Supt. – Wendell Anderson, E MAIN 83314
S, E MAIN 83314 – Wendell Anderson, prin.

Boise, Ada Co., Pop. Code 9
ISD of Boise City 1
Sch. Sys. Enr. Code 7
Supt. – Dr. B. C. Parker, 1207 W FORT ST 83702
Adams ES, 1725 WARM SPRINGS AVE 83712
  Tim Neil, prin.
Amity ES, 10000 W AMITY ROAD 83709
  Robert Deakins, prin.
Campus ES, 2100 UNIVERSITY DR 83706
  Robert Beaver, prin.
Cole ES, 7415 FAIRVIEW AVE 83704
  LeLace Gregory, prin.
Collister ES, 4425 CATALPA DR 83703
  Bruce Herron, prin.
Franklin ES, 5007 FRANKLIN ROAD 83705
  Dr. Jim Saad, prin.
Garfield ES, 1914 BROADWAY AVE 83706
  Jim Reed, prin.

Hawthorne ES, 2401 TARGEE ST 83705
  Mike Cunningham, prin.
Highlands ES, 3434 BOGUS BASIN ROAD 83702
  Pete Bailey, prin.
Hillcrest ES, 2045 S POND ST 83705
  Roger Hanshew, prin.
Jackson ES, 334 S COLE ROAD 83709
  Duane Roberts, prin.
Jefferson ES, 200 S LATAH ST 83705
  Joan Craven, prin.
Koelsch ES, 2015 N CURTIS ROAD 83706
  Carol Coate, prin.
Liberty ES, 1740 BERGESON ST 83706
  Arvin Spofford, prin.
Longfellow ES, 1511 N 9TH ST 83702
  Christina Olson, prin.
Lowell ES, 1507 N 28TH ST 83703
  Judy Bogle, prin.
Madison ES, 2215 MADISON AVE 83702
  Tim Neil, prin.
Maple Grove ES
  2800 S MAPLE GROVE ROAD 83709
  Hylon Plumb, prin.
McKinley ES, 6400 OVERLAND ROAD 83709
  Leona Burkett, prin.
Monroe ES, 3615 CASSIA ST 83705
  Darrel Burbank, prin.
Mountain View ES, 3500 CABARTON LN 83704
  Dr. David Brandt, prin.
Owyhee ES, 3434 PASADENA DR 83705
  Al Blacklock, prin.
Pierce Park ES, 5015 PIERCE PARK LN 83703
  Shirley Ewing, prin.
Roosevelt ES, 908 E JEFFERSON ST 83712
  Richard Bogle, prin.
Taft ES, 3722 ANDERSON ST 83703
  Joan Rusk, prin.
Valley View ES, 3555 N MILWAUKEE ST 83704
  Daniel Burns, prin.
Washington ES, 1607 N 15TH ST 83702
  Dick Lagerstrom, prin.
Whitney ES, 1609 S OWYHEE ST 83705
  Dr. Tom Morley, prin.
Whittier ES, 301 N 29TH ST 83702
  Sharron Jarvis, prin.

Meridian JSD 2
Supt. – See Meridian
Lake Hazel MS, 11625 LA GRANGE ST 83709
  Lee Mitchell, prin.
Frontier ES, 11851 MUSKET DRIVE 83704
  Douglas Rutan, prin.
Joplin ES, 12081 DE MEYER ST 83704
  Linda Clark, prin.
Lake Hazel ES, 11711 LAKE HAZEL ROAD 83709
  John Mikkelson, prin.
McMillan ES, 10901 MCMILLAN ROAD 83704
  Christine DeSilvia, prin.
Ridgewood ES, 7075 S FIVE MILE ROAD 83709
  Kenton Travis, prin.
Silver Sage ES, 7700 SNOHOMISH ST 83709
  Sharon North, prin.
Summerwind ES, 3675 JULLION ST 83704
  Paul Loree, prin.

Maranatha Christian Schools
  12000 FAIRVIEW AVE 83704
Cole-Christian School, 8775 USTICK RD 83704
Sacred Heart School, 3901 CASSIA ST 83705
St. Joseph's School, 825 W FORT ST 83702
St. Mark's School, 7503 NORTHVIEW ST 83704
St. Mary's School, 2628 W STATE ST 83702

Bonners Ferry, Boundary Co., Pop. Code 4
Boundary County SD 101
Sch. Sys. Enr. Code 4
Supt. – Robert Singleton, P O BOX 899   83805
Mt. Hall ES, HCR 60 BOX 66A   83805
    Gerald Thomas, prin.
Northside ES, HCR 61 BOX 80   83805
    Robert Singleton, prin.
Valley View ES
    RURAL ROUTE 01 BOX 340Z   83805
    Dan Meeker, prin.
Other Schools – See Moyie Springs, Naples

Bovill, Latah Co., Pop. Code 2
Whitepine SD 284
Supt. – See Troy
ES, P O BOX 686   83806 – Paul Eck, prin.

Bruneau, Owyhee Co., Pop. Code 1
Bruneau-Grand View JSD 365
Supt. – See Grand View
ES, P O BOX 158   83604 – Nova Hatch, prin.

Buhl, Twin Falls Co., Pop. Code 5
Buhl JSD 412
Sch. Sys. Enr. Code 4
Supt. – Eugene Pyles, 216 7TH AVE N   83316
JHS, 216 7TH AVE N   83316 – Dennis Osman, prin.
Popplewell ES, 200 6TH AVE N   83316
    Lawrence Larue, prin.

Clover Trinity Lutheran School
    RURAL ROUTE 01   83316

Burley, Cassia Co., Pop. Code 6
Cassia County JSD 151
Sch. Sys. Enr. Code 6
Supt. – Norman Hurst, 237 E 19TH ST   83318
Dworchak ES, 19TH & OVERLAND AVE   83318
    Darrell Hatfield, prin.
Mountain View IS, 333 W 27TH ST   83318
    Harold Blauer, prin.
Overland ES, 830 OVERLAND AVE   83318
    Kevin Bushman, prin.
Southwest ES, 401 W 21ST ST   83318
    Gary Masoner, prin.
Other Schools – See Albion, Almo, Declo, Malta, Oakley

Butte, Butte Co., Pop. Code 1
Arco JSD 111
Supt. – See Arco
Butte County MS, 250 S WATER ST   83213
    Michael Ford, prin.

Calder, Shoshone Co.
Avery SD 394
Supt. – See Avery
ES   83808 – (—), prin.

Caldwell, Canyon Co., Pop. Code 7
Caldwell SD 132
Sch. Sys. Enr. Code 5
Supt. – Darrel A. Deide
    1101 CLEVELAND BLVD   83605
Lincoln PS, 1200 GRANT ST   83605
    Dr. Richard Mack, prin.
Van Buren PS, 516 N 11TH AVE   83605
    Keitha Hahn, prin.
Washington IS, 1600 FILLMORE ST   83605
    Dennis Keogh, prin.
Wilson MS, 10TH AVE & LINDEN ST   83605
    George Grant, prin.

Vallivue SD 139
Sch. Sys. Enr. Code 4
Supt. – Dr. Roy Rummier
    RURAL ROUTE 08 BOX 474   83605
Vallivue JHS, RURAL ROUTE 08 BOX 474   83605
    James Robison, prin.
West ES, RURAL ROUTE 06 BOX 130   83605
    Earnie Lewis, prin.
Other Schools – See Nampa

Caldwell SDA ES, 2317 WISCONSIN AVE   83605

Cambridge, Washington Co., Pop. Code 2
Cambridge JSD 432
Sch. Sys. Enr. Code 2
Supt. – Richard Peters, P O BOX 38   83610
ES, P O BOX 38   83610 – Gerald Van Order, prin.

Carey, Blaine Co., Pop. Code 2
Blaine County SD 61
Supt. – See Hailey
S, P O BOX 8   83320 – Robert Bash, prin.

Cascade, Valley Co., Pop. Code 3
Cascade SD 422
Sch. Sys. Enr. Code 2
Supt. – Eugene J. Novotny, P O BOX 291   83611
ES, P O BOX 291   83611 – Eugene Novotny, prin.

Castleford, Twin Falls Co., Pop. Code 1
Castleford JSD 417
Sch. Sys. Enr. Code 2
Supt. – Ronald Erickson, 222 W MAIN   83321
ES, 224 W MAIN   83321 – Kelly Murphey, prin.

Cataldo, Kootenai Co.
Kellogg JSD 391
Supt. – See Kellogg
Canyon ES, CATALDO ROAD   83810
    Sherron Rewoldt, prin.

Challis, Custer Co., Pop. Code 3
Challis JSD 181
Sch. Sys. Enr. Code 3
Supt. – Robert Lisonbee, P O BOX 304   83226
ES, P O BOX 304   83226 – Robert Lisonbee, prin.
Other Schools – See Clayton, May, Stanley

Clark Fork, Bonner Co., Pop. Code 2
Bonner County SD 82
Supt. – See Sandpoint
Hope ES, P O BOX 266   83811
    Mark Berryhill, prin.

Clarkia, Shoshone Co.
Avery SD 394
Supt. – See Avery
ES   83812 – (—), prin.

Clayton, Custer Co., Pop. Code 1
Challis JSD 181
Supt. – See Challis
PS, P O BOX 586   83227
    Vivienne Kinsfather, prin.

Clifton, Franklin Co., Pop. Code 2
West Side JSD 202
Supt. – See Dayton
ES, 50 NORTH 1ST WEST   83228
    Reed Ripplinger, prin.

Cocolalla, Bonner Co.
Bonner County SD 82
Supt. – See Sandpoint
Southside ES, P O BOX 94   83813
    Steve Johnson, prin.

Coeur D'Alene, Kootenai Co., Pop. Code 7
Coeur D'Alene SD 271
Sch. Sys. Enr. Code 6
Supt. – Merlin Ludwig, 311 N 10TH ST   83814
Canfield MS, E 1800 DALTON AVE   83814
    Judy Drake, prin.
Lakes MS, 15TH & HASTING AVE   83814
    John Brumley, prin.
Borah ES, 632 E BORAH AVE   83814
    Dan Hicks, prin.
Bryan ES, 802 E HARRISON AVE   83814
    Robert Olson, prin.
Dalton Gardens ES
    6335 N MOUNT CARROLL ST   83814
    Karen Coppess, prin.
Harding ES, 15TH & INDIANA AVE   83814
    Jay Glover, prin.
Ramsey ES, W 1351 KATHLEEN AVE   83814
    Warren Bakes, prin.
Sorensen ES, 9TH & COEUR D'ALENE AVE   83814
    Linda Glover, prin.
Winton ES, 920 W LACROSSE AVE   83814
    Keith Jones, prin.
Other Schools – See Hayden Lake

Cottonwood, Idaho Co., Pop. Code 3
Cottonwood JSD 242
Sch. Sys. Enr. Code 2
Supt. – Tim Bruce, P O BOX 158   83522
Prairie MS, P O BOX 158   83522
    Milton Baerlocher, prin.
Prairie ES, P O BOX 158   83522
    Maryclare Kelly, prin.

Council, Adams Co., Pop. Code 3
Council SD 13
Sch. Sys. Enr. Code 2
Supt. – Keith Trappett, P O BOX 468   83612
ES, P O BOX 468   83612 – Joy Hummer, prin.

Craigmont, Lewis Co., Pop. Code 3
Highland JSD 305
Sch. Sys. Enr. Code 2
Supt. – James L. McPherson, P O BOX 127   83523
Highland ES, P O BOX 127   83523
    James McPherson, prin.

Culdesac, Nez Perce Co., Pop. Code 2
Culdesac JSD 342
Sch. Sys. Enr. Code 2
Supt. – Larry Manly, P O BOX 106   83524
S, P O BOX 106   83524 – Alan Felgenhauer, prin.

Dayton, Franklin Co., Pop. Code 2
West Side JSD 202
Sch. Sys. Enr. Code 3
Supt. – Melvin Beutler, P O BOX 89   83232
ES, P O BOX 89   83232 – Bruce Winward, prin.
Other Schools – See Clifton

Declo, Cassia Co., Pop. Code 2
Cassia County JSD 151
Supt. – See Burley
ES, 120 E MAIN   83323 – Wayne Bagwell, prin.

Dietrich, Lincoln Co., Pop. Code 2
Dietrich SD 314
Sch. Sys. Enr. Code 2
Supt. – Wayne Perron, P O BOX 428   83324
S, P O BOX 428   83324 – Wayne Perron, prin.

Donnelly, Valley Co., Pop. Code 2
McCall-Donnelly SD 421
Supt. – See McCall
McCall-Donnelly JHS, P O BOX 369   83615
    Bradley Royse, prin.

Downey, Bannock Co., Pop. Code 3
Marsh Valley JSD 21
Supt. – See Arimo
ES, P O BOX 290   83234
    Christine Levesque, prin.

Driggs, Teton Co., Pop. Code 3
Teton County SD 401
Supt. – See Tetonia
Teton MS, 211 HOWARD AVE   83422
    Craig Kunz, prin.

Dubois, Clark Co., Pop. Code 2
Clark County SD 161
Sch. Sys. Enr. Code 2
Supt. – Dr. Larry Wilson, P O BOX 237   83423
Ross ES, P O BOX 237   83423
    Dr. Larry Wilson, prin.

Eagle, Ada Co., Pop. Code 5
Meridian JSD 2
Supt. – See Meridian
ES, 475 N EAGLE RD   83616
    Mark VanSkiver, prin.
Eagle Hills ES, 650 RANCH DRIVE   83616
    Nancy Amell, prin.

Eden, Jerome Co., Pop. Code 2
Valley SD 262
Supt. – See Hazelton
PS   83325 – Bryce Sorenson, prin.

Elk City, Idaho Co., Pop. Code 2
Grangeville JSD 241
Supt. – See Grangeville
ES   83525 – Evelyn Butler, prin.

Elk River, Clearwater Co., Pop. Code 2
Elk River SD 172
Sch. Sys. Enr. Code 1
Supt. – Ron Tisdall, P O BOX 187   83827
Elk River Public S, P O BOX 187   83827
    Ray Ireland, prin.

Emmett, Gem Co., Pop. Code 5
Emmett JSD 221
Sch. Sys. Enr. Code 4
Supt. – Russel Harrach, 601 E 3RD ST   83617
MS, 301 E 4TH ST   83617 – Steve Mills, prin.
Brick ES, 498 W IDAHO BLVD   83617
    Judyth McConnel, prin.
Butte View ES, 400 S PINE ST   83617
    Ralph Donaldson, prin.
Hanna IS, 3600 HANNA AVE   83617
    Dorine Eisenbarth, prin.
Other Schools – See Letha, Ola, Sweet

Fairfield, Camas Co., Pop. Code 2
Camas County SD 121
Sch. Sys. Enr. Code 2
Supt. – Harold Stroud, P O BOX 117   83327
Camas County ES, P O BOX 377   83327
    Jack Altemose, prin.

Fernwood, Benewah Co., Pop. Code 2
St. Maries JSD 41
Supt. – See Saint Maries
Up River ES, P O BOX 249   83830
    Douglas Strong, prin.

Filer, Twin Falls Co., Pop. Code 4
Filer SD 413
Sch. Sys. Enr. Code 4
Supt. – Dave Teater, P O BOX X   83328
MS, P O BOX H   83328 – Victor Koshuta, prin.
ES, P O BOX U   83328 – Beverly Loranger, prin.
Other Schools – See Twin Falls

Firth, Bingham Co., Pop. Code 2
Firth SD 59
Sch. Sys. Enr. Code 2
Supt. – Dr. Bert Nixon, P O BOX 68   83236
Harding Gibbs JHS, P O BOX 247   83236
    Bert Nixon, prin.
Johnson ES, P O BOX 158   83236
    Robert Hanson, prin.

Fort Hall, Bannock Co., Pop. Code 3
Blackfoot SD 55
Supt. – See Blackfoot
ES, P O BOX 429   83203 – George Dunbar, prin.

Fruitland, Payette Co., Pop. Code 4
Fruitland SD 373
Sch. Sys. Enr. Code 4
Supt. – Ben L. Kerfoot, P O BOX 387   83619
JHS, P O BOX 387   83619 – Myron J. Little, prin.
ES, P O BOX 387   83619 – Joseph Wozniak, prin.

Garden Valley, Boise Co., Pop. Code 2
Garden Valley SD 71
Sch. Sys. Enr. Code 2
Supt. – Clark Gardner   83622
ES   83622 – Clark Gardner, prin.
Lowman ES   83622 – Roy Bryant, prin.

Genesee, Latah Co., Pop. Code 3
Genesee JSD 282
Sch. Sys. Enr. Code 2
Supt. – Tom Jentges, P O BOX 98   83832
ES, P O BOX 98   83832 – Tom Jentges, prin.

Geneva, Bear Lake Co.
Bear Lake County SD 33
Supt. – See Montpelier
ES   83238 – Jane Taylor, prin.

Georgetown, Bear Lake Co., Pop. Code 3
Bear Lake County SD 33
Supt. – See Montpelier
ES   83239 – Grant Messerly, prin.

Glenns Ferry, Elmore Co., Pop. Code 4
Glenns Ferry JSD 192
Sch. Sys. Enr. Code 3
Supt. – Robert Fontaine, P O BOX 850   83623
ES, P O BOX 850   83623 – John Taggart, prin.

Gooding, Gooding Co., Pop. Code 5
Gooding JSD 231
Sch. Sys. Enr. Code 4
Supt. – James Cobble, 507 IDAHO STREET   83330
Frahm JHS, 830 MAIN ST   83330
  Richard Thompson, prin.
Gibbons ES, 906 MAIN ST   83330
  Robin Winslow, prin.

Grace, Caribou Co., Pop. Code 4
Grace JSD 148
Sch. Sys. Enr. Code 3
Supt. – G. Millward, P O BOX 328   83241
JHS, 710 S MAIN ST   83241 – Barbara Lloyd, prin.
ES, 117 WEST 4TH S   83241
  Gene Millward, prin.
Other Schools – See Thatcher

Grand View, Owyhee Co., Pop. Code 2
Bruneau-Grand View JSD 365
Sch. Sys. Enr. Code 3
Supt. – Ralph Hatch, P O BOX 310   83624
ES, P O BOX 39   83624 – Nova Hatch, prin.
Other Schools – See Bruneau

Grangeville, Idaho Co., Pop. Code 5
Grangeville JSD 241
Sch. Sys. Enr. Code 4
Supt. – Al Arnzen, P O BOX 430   83530
ES, 400 IDAHO ST   83530 – Ken Pollworth, prin.
Other Schools – See Elk City, Kooskia, Riggins, White
  Bird

Greenleaf, Canyon Co., Pop. Code 3

Greenleaf Friends Academy, P O BOX 368   83626

Hagerman, Gooding Co., Pop. Code 3
Hagerman JSD 233
Sch. Sys. Enr. Code 2
Supt. – Kenneth Black, P O BOX 236   83332
ES, LAKE ST   83332 – Kenneth Black, prin.

Hailey, Blaine Co., Pop. Code 4
Blaine County SD 61
Sch. Sys. Enr. Code 4
Supt. – David W. Noonan, P O BOX 1008   83333
MS, P O BOX 1240   83333 – Ellen Morrical, prin.
Other Schools – See Bellevue, Carey, Ketchum

Hamer, Jefferson Co., Pop. Code 1
West Jefferson SD 253
Supt. – See Terreton
ES, P O BOX 1010   83425
  Thomas Williams,Jr., prin.

Hansen, Twin Falls Co., Pop. Code 4
Hansen SD 415
Sch. Sys. Enr. Code 2
Supt. – Richard Smith, P O BOX 151   83334
JHS, P O BOX 151   83334 – Barry Espil, prin.
ES, 219 WALNUT W   83334
  Richard Evensen, prin.

Harrison, Kootenai Co., Pop. Code 2
Kootenai SD 274
Sch. Sys. Enr. Code 2
Supt. – Ronald Hill
  RURAL ROUTE 01 BOX 25   83833
ES, P O BOX 26   83833 – Ron Hill, prin.

Hayden Lake, Kootenai Co., Pop. Code 2
Coeur D'Alene SD 271
Supt. – See Coeur D'Alene
ES, HWY 95   83835 – David Groth, prin.

Hazelton, Jerome Co., Pop. Code 2
Valley SD 262
Sch. Sys. Enr. Code 3
Supt. – Arlyn Bodily, RURAL ROUTE 01   83335
IS   83335 – Bryce Sorensen, prin.
Other Schools – See Eden

Heyburn, Minidoka Co., Pop. Code 5
Minidoka County JSD 331
Supt. – See Rupert
ES, P O BOX 117   83336 – John Jenkins, prin.

Homedale, Owyhee Co., Pop. Code 4
Homedale JSD 370
Sch. Sys. Enr. Code 3
Supt. – Edward Marshall, P O BOX 187   83628
JHS, P O BOX 187   83628 – Nolan Taggart, prin.
Lincoln IS, P O BOX 187   83628
  Herbert Fritzley, prin.
Washington PS, P O BOX 187   83628
  Herbert Fritzley, prin.

Horseshoe Bend, Boise Co., Pop. Code 3
Horseshoe Bend ESD 73
Sch. Sys. Enr. Code 2
Supt. – Robert Kesler, P O BOX 116   83629
ES, P O BOX 116   83629 – Robert Kesler, prin.

Howe, Butte Co.
Arco JSD 111
Supt. – See Arco
ES   83244 – Lori Arnold, prin.

Idaho City, Boise Co., Pop. Code 2
Basin ESD 72
Sch. Sys. Enr. Code 2
Supt. – Kenneth Ross, P O BOX 128   83631

Basin ES, P O BOX 128   83631
  Kenneth Ross, prin.

Idaho Falls, Bonneville Co., Pop. Code 8
Bonneville JSD 93
Sch. Sys. Enr. Code 6
Supt. – Dr. Richard Goodworth
  RURAL ROUTE 01 BOX 400   83401
Ammon IS, 2900 CENTRAL AVE   83406
  (—), prin.
Cloverdale ES, 3939 GREENWILLOW LN   83406
  James Bird, prin.
Fairview ES, 989 E 97 N   83401 – (—), prin.
Falls Valley ES, 455 VIRLOW ST   83401
  Dr. Bruce Roberts, prin.
Hillview ES, 3075 TETON STS   83401
  Farrell Pilkington, prin.
Lincoln ES, 3175 E LINCOLN RD   83401
  Richard Black, prin.
Tiebreaker ES, 3100 FIRST ST   83401
  McKay Guthrie, prin.
Ucon ES, RURAL ROUTE 08 BOX 72A   83401
  Stephen Palaniuk, prin.
Other Schools – See Iona

Idaho Falls SD 91
Sch. Sys. Enr. Code 6
Supt. – Jerry Jacobson
  690 JOHN ADAMS PARKWAY   83401
Boyes ES, 1875 BRENTWOOD DR   83402
  Dick Wagner, prin.
Bunker ES, 1385 E 16TH ST   83404
  Shirley Stephenson, prin.
Bush ES, 380 W ANDERSON ST   83402
  Dennis Griffeth, prin.
Edgemont Gardens ES
  1240 AZALEA ROAD   83401 – Bruce Schultz,
  prin.
Emerson ES, 335 5TH ST   83401 – Ann Albin, prin.
Erickson ES, 850 CLEVELAND ST   83401
  Dave Schjeldahl, prin.
Hawthorne ES, 1520 S BOULEVARD ST   83402
  Denice Nelson, prin.
Linden Park ES, 1305 9TH ST   83404
  Sandy Johnson, prin.
Longfellow ES, 2500 S HIGBEE ST   83401
  Maureen McFadden, prin.
Osgood ES, RURAL ROUTE 05 BOX 270   83402
  Connie Stoneberg, prin.
Temple View ES, 1500 SCORPIUS ST   83401
  Marvin Quinton, prin.
Westside ES, 2680 NEWMAN DR   83402
  Craig Ashton, prin.

Holy Rosary School, 161 9TH ST   83404
Hope Lutheran School, 2071 12TH ST   83404

Inkom, Bannock Co., Pop. Code 3
Marsh Valley JSD 21
Supt. – See Arimo
ES, P O BOX D   83245 – David Wheat, prin.

Iona, Bonneville Co., Pop. Code 4
Bonneville JSD 93
Supt. – See Idaho Falls
ES, P O BOX 310   83427 – Paul Sewell, prin.

Irwin, Bonneville Co., Pop. Code 2
Swan Valley ESD 92
Sch. Sys. Enr. Code 1
Supt. – (—), P O BOX 208   83428
Swan Valley ES   83428 – Douglas Jordan, prin.

Jerome, Jerome Co., Pop. Code 6
Jerome JSD 261
Sch. Sys. Enr. Code 5
Supt. – Richard Kugler, 107 3RD AVE W   83338
JHS, 116 3RD AVE W   83338
  Craig Ainswurth, prin.
Central IS, 311 N LINCOLN AVE   83338
  Betty Hyder, prin.
Jefferson PS, 600 N FILLMORE ST   83338
  Lavar Buttars, prin.
Washington PS, 500 S LINCOLN AVE   83338
  Ann Reynolds, prin.

Juliaetta, Latah Co., Pop. Code 3
Kendrick SD 283
Supt. – See Kendrick
ES, P O BOX 459   83535 – Marlene Meyer, prin.

Kamiah, Lewis Co., Pop. Code 4
Kamiah JSD 304
Sch. Sys. Enr. Code 3
Supt. – Herm Yates, P O BOX 877   83536
ES, P O BOX 458   83536 – Gary Miller, prin.

Kellogg, Shoshone Co., Pop. Code 5
Kellogg JSD 391
Sch. Sys. Enr. Code 4
Supt. – Larry Curry, 800 BUNKER AVE   83837
MS, 800 BUNKER AVE   83837
  Gregory Godwin, prin.
Sunnyside ES, 101 W RIVERSIDE AVE   83837
  Ann Breeden, prin.
Other Schools – See Cataldo, Pinehurst

Kendrick, Latah Co., Pop. Code 2
Kendrick SD 283
Sch. Sys. Enr. Code 2
Supt. – Dr. L. Eldon Taylor
  RURAL ROUTE 02 BOX 6   83537
Other Schools – See Juliaetta

Ketchum, Blaine Co., Pop. Code 4
Blaine County SD 61
Supt. – See Hailey

Hemingway ES, P O BOX 298   83340
  John Dominick, prin.

Kimberly, Twin Falls Co., Pop. Code 4
Kimberly SD 414
Sch. Sys. Enr. Code 3
Supt. – Dr. Richard Bauscher, P O BOX 0   83341
ES, P O BOX O   83341 – Mary Charlton, prin.

Kooskia, Idaho Co., Pop. Code 3
Grangeville JSD 241
Supt. – See Grangeville
Clearwater Valley ES   83539
  Raymond Bloom, prin.

Kuna, Ada Co., Pop. Code 4
Kuna JSD 3
Sch. Sys. Enr. Code 4
Supt. – C. Eric Dorsey, 208 S SCHOOL AVE   83634
JHS, RURAL ROUTE 03   83634
  Steven Snider, prin.
Hubbard ES, 311 PORTER ROAD   83634
  Nancy Martin, prin.
Kuna Indian Creek ES, 911 W 4TH ST   83634
  Richard Evensen, prin.
Ross MS, 610 N SCHOOL AVE   83634
  Karen Blacklock, prin.

Lapwai, Nez Perce Co., Pop. Code 4
Lapwai SD 341
Sch. Sys. Enr. Code 3
Supt. – Robert J. Sobotta, P O BOX 247   83540
ES, AGENCY LOOP WEST   83540
  Robert Debuhr, prin.
Other Schools – See Lenore

Lava Hot Springs, Bannock Co., Pop. Code 2
Marsh Valley JSD 21
Supt. – See Arimo
Lava ES, 213 W FIFE   83246 – Verl Hawes, prin.

Leadore, Lemhi Co., Pop. Code 2
South Lemhi SD 292
Sch. Sys. Enr. Code 2
Supt. – Gregory Cox, P O BOX 119   83464
S, P O BOX 119   83464 – Gregory Cox, prin.
Other Schools – See Tendoy

Lenore, Nez Perce Co.
Lapwai SD 341
Supt. – See Lapwai
ES   83541 – Marie Jessup, prin.

Orofino JSD 171
Supt. – See Orofino
Cavendish Teakean ES
  MIDDLE ROAD RT 1   83541 – (—), prin.

Letha, Gem Co.
Emmett JSD 221
Supt. – See Emmett
PS   83636 – Sheila Stickler, prin.

Lewiston, Nez Perce Co., Pop. Code 6
Lewiston ISD 1
Sch. Sys. Enr. Code 5
Supt. – Dr. Glen Morgan, 3317 12TH ST   83501
Camelot ES, 1903 GRELLE AVE   83501
  Lenard Vaughn, prin.
Centennial ES, 815 BURRELL AVE   83501
  Esther Thorpe, prin.
McGhee ES, 636 WARNER AVE   83501
  Rodney Storey, prin.
McSorley ES, 2020 15TH ST   83501
  Joy Rapp, prin.
Orchards ES, 3429 12TH ST   83501
  Doug Armitage, prin.
Webster ES, 1409 8TH ST   83501
  David Laird, prin.
Whitman ES, 1840 9TH AVE   83501
  Michael Hill, prin.

Tammany ESD 343
Sch. Sys. Enr. Code 2
Supt. – (—)
  6800 TAMMANY CREEK ROAD   83501
Tammany ES
  6800 TAMMANY CREEK ROAD   83501
  Robert Farris, prin.

St. Stanislaus School, 641 5TH AVE   83501
Valley Christian School
  3215 ECHO HILLS DRIVE   83501

McCall, Valley Co., Pop. Code 4
McCall-Donnelly SD 421
Sch. Sys. Enr. Code 4
Supt. – Everett Howard, P O BOX 967   83638
McCall-Donnelly ES, P O BOX 967   83638
  John Wall, prin.
Other Schools – See Donnelly, Yellow Pine

McCammon, Bannock Co., Pop. Code 3
Marsh Valley JSD 21
Supt. – See Arimo
Mountain View ES, P O BOX 67   83250
  Gary Brown, prin.

Mackay, Custer Co., Pop. Code 3
MacKay JSD 182
Sch. Sys. Enr. Code 2
Supt. – R. Palmer, P O BOX 208   83251
ES, 530 E SPRUCE ST   83251 – R. Palemer, prin.

Malad City, Oneida Co., Pop. Code 4
Oneida County SD 351
Sch. Sys. Enr. Code 3
Supt. – Howard May, 250 W 400 N   83252

Malad ES, 250 W 4TH N ST 83252
  Lynn Schow, prin.
  Other Schools – See Stone

Malta, Cassia Co., Pop. Code 2
  Cassia County JSD 151
  Supt. – See Burley
  ES 83342 – Glendon Jones, prin.

Marsing, Owyhee Co., Pop. Code 3
  Marsing JSD 363
  Sch. Sys. Enr. Code 3
  Supt. – Joe Whitten, P O BOX 340 83639
  IS, P O BOX 340 83639 – Ron Hutter, prin.
  PS, P O BOX 340 83639 – Ron Hutter, prin.

May, Lemhi Co.
  Challis JSD 181
  Supt. – See Challis
  Patterson ES, P O BOX 2100 83253
  Paulette Hadden, prin.

Melba, Canyon Co., Pop. Code 2
  Melba JSD 136
  Sch. Sys. Enr. Code 3
  Supt. – Norman D. Winters, P O BOX 185 83641
  MS, 213 N CARRIE REX 83641
  Scott Freeby, prin.

Menan, Jefferson Co., Pop. Code 3
  Jefferson County JSD 251
  Supt. – See Rigby
  Midway ES, 635 NORTH 3500 EAST 83434
  Kent Durst, prin.
  Midway MS, RURAL ROUTE 01 83434
  Greg Barrett, prin.

Meridian, Ada Co., Pop. Code 6
  Meridian JSD 2
  Sch. Sys. Enr. Code 7
  Supt. – Dr. Norman Hallett
  911 MERIDIAN ST 83642
  MS, 1507 W 8TH ST 83642 – Bev Bradford, prin.
  Scott MS, 3400 E MCMILLAN ROAD 83642
  James Hoyle, prin.
  Linder ES, 1825 CHATEAU DR 83642
  Phyllis Schroeder, prin.
  McPherson ES, 1050 E AMITY ROAD 83642
  David McFaddan, prin.
  ES, 49 W STATE AVE 83642 – Susan Liehe, prin.
  Ustick ES, 4535 USTICK ROAD 83642
  (–), prin.
  Other Schools – See Boise, Eagle, Star

Middleton, Canyon Co., Pop. Code 4
  Middleton SD 134
  Sch. Sys. Enr. Code 4
  Supt. – James Garrett, P O BOX 368 83644
  MS, P O BOX 160 83644 – Allen Lake, prin.
  Middleton Heights MS, 611 N HIGHLAND 83644
  Louise Nagel, prin.
  PS, 115 W MAIN ST 83644 – Kristine Keller, prin.

Midvale, Washington Co., Pop. Code 2
  Midvale SD 433
  Sch. Sys. Enr. Code 2
  Supt. – Jim Kantola, BRIDGE & SCHOOL ST 83645
  ES, BRIDGE & SCHOOL ST 83645
  Jim Kantola, prin.

Montpelier, Bear Lake Co., Pop. Code 5
  Bear Lake County SD 33
  Sch. Sys. Enr. Code 4
  Supt. – Lyle Loosle, 697 JACKSON ST 83254
  Bear Lake MS, 633 WASHINGTON ST 83254
  Ron Echols, prin.
  Winters ES, 535 CLAY ST 83254 – (–), prin.
  Other Schools – See Geneva, Georgetown, Paris

Moreland, Bingham Co., Pop. Code 2
  Snake River SD 52
  Supt. – See Blackfoot
  ES, P O BOX B 83256 – Mary Mortensen, prin.

Moscow, Latah Co., Pop. Code 7
  Moscow SD 281
  Sch. Sys. Enr. Code 5
  Supt. – Dr. Alethia Fasolino, P O BOX 8459 83843
  McDonald ES, P O BOX 8459 83843
  Dale Golis, prin.
  Russell ES, P O BOX 8459 83843
  Mary Jo Martin, prin.
  West Park ES, P O BOX 8459 83843
  Marilyn Howard, prin.
  Whitmore ES, P O BOX 8459 83843
  Dr. James Christiansen, prin.

  St. Mary's School, 412 N HOWARD ST 83843

Mountain Home, Elmore Co., Pop. Code 6
  Mountain Home SD 193
  Sch. Sys. Enr. Code 5
  Supt. – Harry Light, P O BOX 890 83647
  East ES, 775 N 10TH E ST 83647
  Tim McMurtrey, prin.
  Mountain Home AFB IS, 200 MAIN ST 83648
  Elizabeth Bermensolo, prin.
  Mountain Home AFB PS, 100 MAIN ST 83648
  Mary Neely, prin.
  North ES, 290 E 12TH N ST 83647
  George Donaldson, prin.
  Pine ES, C/O ROCKY BAR STAGE 83647
  Lois Swope, prin.
  West ES, 415 W 2ND N ST 83647
  Otis Eastman, prin.
  Other Schools – See Atlanta

Prairie ESD 191
  Sch. Sys. Enr. Code 1
  Supt. – (–), P O BOX 56 83647
  Prairie ES, P O BOX 56 83647
  Patricia Rose, prin.

Moyie Springs, Boundary Co., Pop. Code 2
  Boundary County SD 101
  Supt. – See Bonners Ferry
  Evergreen ES, HWY 2 83845
  Gerald Thomas, prin.

Mullan, Shoshone Co., Pop. Code 4
  Mullan SD 392
  Sch. Sys. Enr. Code 2
  Supt. – R. M. Donohue, P O BOX 71 83846
  ES, P O BOX 71 83846 – Robert Donohue, prin.

Murtaugh, Twin Falls Co., Pop. Code 2
  Murtaugh JSD 418
  Sch. Sys. Enr. Code 2
  Supt. – Frederick Diaz-Granados
  P O BOX 117 83344
  MS, P O BOX 117 83344 – Herald Jardine, prin.
  ES, P O BOX 117 83344 – James Espe, prin.

Nampa, Canyon Co., Pop. Code 8
  Nampa SD 131
  Sch. Sys. Enr. Code 6
  Supt. – Dr. Stephenson Youngerman
  619 S CANYON ST 83651
  Centennial ES, 522 MASON LN 83651
  William Deakins, prin.
  Central MS, 1415 5TH ST S 83651
  John Montgomery, prin.
  Eastside ES, 145 22ND AVE S 83651
  Myrlene Allred, prin.
  Greenhurst ES, 5423 E GREENHURST 83651
  Myrlene Allred, prin.
  Lakeview IS, 1220 5TH ST N 83651
  Ricardo Cedillo, prin.
  Lincoln ES, 212 S CANYON ST 83651
  Byron Yankey, prin.
  Parkview PS, 609 15TH AVE N 83651
  Ricardo Cedillo, prin.
  Roosevelt ES, 1215 12TH AVE S 83651
  William Montgomery, prin.
  Scism ES, ROUTE 7 BOX 7130 83651
  Mike Bierman, prin.
  Sunny Ridge ES
  RRUAL ROUTE 04 BOX 4146 83651
  Mike Bierman, prin.

Vallivue SD 139
  Supt. – See Caldwell
  East IS, USTIC & NORTHSIDE ROAD 83651
  Gregory Scheele, prin.
  Midway PS, RURAL ROUTE 5 BOX 5192 83651
  Gary Folwell, prin.

  Nampa Christian Schools, P O BOX G 83653
  St. Paul's School, 1515 8TH ST S 83651
  Zion Lutheran ES, 1012 12TH AVE RD 83651

Naples, Boundary Co.
  Boundary County SD 101
  Supt. – See Bonners Ferry
  ES, P O BOX 134 83847 – Robert Singleton, prin.

New Meadows, Adams Co., Pop. Code 3
  Meadows Valley SD 11
  Sch. Sys. Enr. Code 2
  Supt. – Will Spalding, P O BOX F 83654
  Meadows Valley ES, P O BOX F 83654
  Will Spalding, prin.

New Plymouth, Payette Co., Pop. Code 4
  New Plymouth SD 372
  Sch. Sys. Enr. Code 3
  Supt. – Jerry Currin, P O BOX 388 83655
  ES, P O BOX 388 83655 – Nadine Horton, prin.

Nezperce, Lewis Co., Pop. Code 3
  Nezperce JSD 302
  Sch. Sys. Enr. Code 2
  Supt. – Dr. Donald Darling, P O BOX 278 83543
  ES, P O BOX 279 83543 – Cindy Albers, prin.

Notus, Canyon Co., Pop. Code 2
  Notus SD 135
  Sch. Sys. Enr. Code 2
  Supt. – Warren Taylor, P O BOX 256 83656
  ES, P O BOX 256 83656 – Warren Taylor, prin.

Oakley, Cassia Co., Pop. Code 3
  Cassia County JSD 151
  Supt. – See Burley
  ES 83346 – Laurell Adams, prin.

Ola, Gem Co.
  Emmett JSD 221
  Supt. – See Emmett
  ES 83657 – Mary Beal, prin.

Old Town, Bonner Co., Pop. Code 2
  Bonner County SD 82
  Supt. – See Sandpoint
  Idaho Hill ES, RURAL ROUTE 02 BOX 266 83822
  Bill Boyd, prin.

Orofino, Clearwater Co., Pop. Code 5
  Orofino JSD 171
  Sch. Sys. Enr. Code 4
  Supt. – Albert Vaughn, P O BOX 789 83544
  JHS, 429 MICHIGAN 83544 – Eugene Hobbs, prin.
  ES, 100 MICHIGAN BOX 1941 83544
  David Wright, prin.
  Other Schools – See Lenore, Peck, Pierce, Weippe

Osburn, Shoshone Co., Pop. Code 4
  Wallace SD 393
  Supt. – See Wallace
  ES, P O BOX 1008 83849 – Kathleen Kuntz, prin.

Paris, Bear Lake Co., Pop. Code 3
  Bear Lake County SD 33
  Supt. – See Montpelier
  ES, P O BOX 300 83261 – Gary Mitchell, prin.

Parma, Canyon Co., Pop. Code 4
  Parma SD 137
  Sch. Sys. Enr. Code 3
  Supt. – Dr. Philip Reiter, P O BOX 246 83660
  JHS, P O BOX 246 83660 – Dominic Iaderosa, prin.
  ES, P O BOX 246 83660 – Rhea Zaldain, prin.
  Roswell MS, P O BOX 246 83660
  Dominic Iaderosa, prin.

Paul, Minidoka Co., Pop. Code 3
  Minidoka County JSD 331
  Supt. – See Rupert
  ES, P O BOX 7 83347 – Frank Peterson, prin.

Payette, Payette Co., Pop. Code 6
  Payette JSD 371
  Sch. Sys. Enr. Code 4
  Supt. – Richard Dillon, P O BOX 349 83661
  MS, 1215 CENTER AVE 83661
  Willie Sullivan, prin.
  Eastside ES, 1315 CENTER AVE 83661
  David Nuttycombe, prin.
  Westside MS, 609 N 5TH ST 83661
  Sheryl Belknap, prin.

Peck, Nez Perce Co., Pop. Code 2
  Orofino JSD 171
  Supt. – See Orofino
  ES, P O BOX 48 83545 – (–), prin.

Pierce, Clearwater Co., Pop. Code 4
  Orofino JSD 171
  Supt. – See Orofino
  MS, WHISPERING PINES DRIVE 83546
  Richard Anthony, prin.
  Peirce ES, WHISPERING PINES DR 83546
  Richard Anthony, prin.

Pinehurst, Shoshone Co., Pop. Code 4
  Kellogg JSD 391
  Supt. – See Kellogg
  ES, P O BOX 97 83850 – Ronald Boothe, prin.

Pingree, Bingham Co.
  Snake River SD 52
  Supt. – See Blackfoot
  ES, P O BOX 113 83262 – Theo Perkes, prin.

Plummer, Benewah Co., Pop. Code 3
  Western Benewah SD 42
  Sch. Sys. Enr. Code 2
  Supt. – Harold Walker, P O BOX 130 83851
  ES, P O BOX 130 83851 – Judy Drevlow, prin.

Pocatello, Bannock Co., Pop. Code 8
  Pocatello SD 25
  Sch. Sys. Enr. Code 7
  Supt. – Dr. David Peck, P O BOX 1390 83204
  Bonneville ES, 320 N 8TH ST 83201
  Marjean Waford, prin.
  Chubbuck ES, 5045 HAWTHORNE ROAD 83202
  Marcia Bielby, prin.
  Edahow ES, 2020 POCATELLO CRK ROAD 83201
  Helen Whitmore, prin.
  Ellis ES, 11888 N WHITAKER ROAD 83202
  Roger Wheeler, prin.
  Gate City ES, 2288 HISKEY ST 83201
  Grant Olson, prin.
  Greenacres ES, HYDE AVE & OAK ST 83201
  Derold Bates, prin.
  Indian Hills MS, BANNOCK & CHEYENNE 83204
  Rita Shail, prin.
  Jefferson ES, 1455 GWEN DR 83204
  Joan Bowman, prin.
  Lewis & Clark ES, 800 GRACE DR 83201
  Evelyn Robinson, prin.
  Lincoln ES, 330 OAKWOOD DRIVE 83204
  John Leasure, prin.
  Roosevelt ES, 240 E MAPLE ST 83201
  Lila Johnson, prin.
  Syringa ES, VEDA ST & GRIFFITH ROAD 83201
  John Redd, prin.
  Tendoy ES, 957 E ALAMEDA ROAD 83201
  Judy Thomas, prin.
  Tyhee ES, TYHEE ROAD 83202
  George Mickelsen, prin.
  Washington ES, 226 S 10TH AVE 83201
  Dr. Byron Christensen, prin.
  Wilcox ES, 427 LARK LN 83201
  James Liday, prin.

  Grace Lutheran School
  1250 PERSHING AVE 83201
  St. Anthony's School, 524 N 7TH AVE 83201

Post Falls, Kootenai Co., Pop. Code 6
  Post Falls SD 273
  Sch. Sys. Enr. Code 5
  Supt. – Kathryn Canfield-Davis, P O BOX 40 83854
  JHS, P O BOX 40 83854 – William Ramich, prin.
  Ponderosa ES, P O BOX 40 83854
  Robert Sloyka, prin.
  Post ES, P O BOX 40 83854
  Marylu Ann Arndt, prin.
  Seltice ES, P O BOX 40 83854
  Pamela Francis, prin.

Potlatch, Latah Co., Pop. Code 3
Potlatch SD 285
Sch. Sys. Enr. Code 3
Supt. – Donald Armstrong, P O BOX 518   83855
ES, P O BOX 518   83855 – Timothy Knowles, prin.

Preston, Franklin Co., Pop. Code 5
Preston JSD 201
Sch. Sys. Enr. Code 4
Supt. – Dr. Orson L. Bowler
   120 E 2ND & SOUTH ST   83263
Jefferson JHS, 1ST E & 1ST S STS   83263
   John W. Palmer, prin.
Oakwood ES, 525 S 4TH ST   83263
   Dr. Jerry Waddoups, prin.

Priest River, Bonner Co., Pop. Code 4
Bonner County SD 82
Supt. – See Sandpoint
JHS, P O BOX 519   83856 – Thomas Keough, prin.
Priest Lake ES, RURAL ROUTE 05 BOX 150   83856
   Gary Go, prin.
ES, P O BOX 489   83856 – Charles Maines, prin.

Rathdrum, Kootenai Co., Pop. Code 4
Lakeland SD 272
Sch. Sys. Enr. Code 4
Supt. – Robert Jones, P O BOX 39   83858
Brown ES, P O BOX 10   83858
   Deborah Long, prin.
Rathdrum MS, P O BOX 70   83858
   Dan Melick, prin.
Other Schools – See Athol, Spirit Lake

Rexburg, Madison Co., Pop. Code 7
Madison SD 321
Sch. Sys. Enr. Code 5
Supt. – Edward Hill, 290 N 1ST EAST ST   83440
Adams ES, 110 N 2ND E ST   83440
   Neta Brown, prin.
Archer ES, 7833 S 200 W ROAD   83440
   Scott Shirley, prin.
Burton ES, 1764 N 4000 W RD   83440
   Steve Baldwin, prin.
Hibbard ES, 2413 N 3000 W RD   83440
   Steve Baldwin, prin.
Kennedy ES, 60 S 5TH W ST   83440
   Marjorie Whatcott, prin.
Lincoln ES, 358 E 2ND S ST   83440
   Jeffery Hawkes, prin.
Lyman ES, 2786 W 5200 S RD   83440
   Ben Lindsay, prin.
Washington MS, 110 W MAIN ST   83440
   Alan Dunn, prin.

Richfield, Lincoln Co., Pop. Code 2
Richfield SD 316
Sch. Sys. Enr. Code 2
Supt. – Neuman Matson, P O BOX E   83349
ES, P O BOX E   83349 – Neuman Matson, prin.

Rigby, Jefferson Co., Pop. Code 5
Jefferson County JSD 251
Sch. Sys. Enr. Code 5
Supt. – Elwood Wilson, 201 IDAHO AVE   83442
Harwood ES, 200 W 3RD N ST   83442
   Thomas Wakefield, prin.
Kinghorn PS, 219 N 1ST W ST   83442
   Lynn McKinlay, prin.
Other Schools – See Menan, Roberts

Riggins, Idaho Co., Pop. Code 3
Grangeville JSD 241
Supt. – See Grangeville
ES, US HWY 95   83549 – Marvin Anderson, prin.

Ririe, Jefferson Co., Pop. Code 3
Ririe JSD 252
Sch. Sys. Enr. Code 3
Supt. – T. L. Johnson, P O BOX 508   83443
ES, P O BOX 528   83443 – Thales Johnson, prin.

Roberts, Jefferson Co., Pop. Code 2
Jefferson County JSD 251
Supt. – See Rigby
ES, P O BOX 249   83444 – William Mercer, prin.
MS, P O BOX 256   83444 – William Mercer, prin.

Rockland, Power Co., Pop. Code 2
Rockland SD 382
Sch. Sys. Enr. Code 2
Supt. – Cloyd Barker, P O BOX 119   83271
S, P O BOX 119   83271 – Cloyd Barker, prin.

Rogerson, Twin Falls Co.
Three Creek JESD 416
Sch. Sys. Enr. Code 1
Supt. – (—)   83302
Three Creek ES   83302 – (—), prin.

Rupert, Minidoka Co., Pop. Code 6
Minidoka County JSD 331
Sch. Sys. Enr. Code 6
Supt. – Gene Snapp, 633 FREMONT ST   83350
Big Valley MS, 202 18TH ST   83350
   Judith Nielsen, prin.
Memorial PS, P O BOX 495   83350
   Garth Baker, prin.
Pershing PS, P O BOX 453   83350
   Lewis Roberts, prin.
Other Schools – See Acequia, Heyburn, Paul

St. Nicholas School, 800 F ST   83350

Sagle, Bonner Co.
Bonner County SD 82
Supt. – See Sandpoint
ES, P O BOX 140   83860 – Richard Williams, prin.

Saint Anthony, Fremont Co., Pop. Code 5
Freemont County JSD 215
Sch. Sys. Enr. Code 5
Supt. – M. Duane Handy
   147 N 2ND WEST ST   83445
South Fremont JHS, 226 W 3RD NORTH ST   83445
   Sam Christiansen, prin.
Central MS, 425 N 3RD W ST   83445
   Jerald Gee, prin.
Lincoln PS, 825 S 4TH W ST   83445
   Gail Blanchard, prin.
Parker Egin ES, RURAL ROUTE 02   83445
   Chester Peterson, prin.
Other Schools – See Ashton, Teton

Saint Maries, Benewah Co., Pop. Code 5
St. Maries JSD 41
Sch. Sys. Enr. Code 4
Supt. – Gary Barton
   1315 W JEFFERSON AVE   83861
MS, 1315 W JEFFERSON AVE   83861
   Ken Tams, prin.
Heyburn ES, 1405 MAIN AVE   83861
   Janet Bartenhagen, prin.
Other Schools – See Fernwood

Salmon, Lemhi Co., Pop. Code 5
Salmon SD 291
Sch. Sys. Enr. Code 4
Supt. – James Smith, P O BOX 790   83467
MS, P O BOX 790   83467 – George Artemis, prin.
Brooklyn IS, P O BOX 790   83467
   Melvin Skeen, prin.
Salmon Pioneer PS, P O BOX 790   83467
   Melvin Skeen, prin.

Sandpoint, Bonner Co., Pop. Code 5
Bonner County SD 82
Sch. Sys. Enr. Code 6
Supt. – Edward Humble, P O BOX 1390   83864
Stidwell JHS, 1624 W SPRUCE STREET   83864
   Ron Hopkins, prin.
Farmin ES, 1000 N DIVISION AVE   83864
   Donald Moore, prin.
Lake Street MS, 102 EUCLID   83864
   Leni Hassell, prin.
Northside ES
   9300 COLBURN CULVER ROAD   83864
   Mark Berryhill, prin.
Washington ES, 420 S BOYER AVE   83864
   Leni Hassell, prin.
Other Schools – See Clark Fork, Cocolalla, Old Town, Priest River, Sagle

Sandpoint Jr. Academy SDA, 2255 PINE ST   83864

Shelley, Bingham Co., Pop. Code 5
Shelley JSD 60
Sch. Sys. Enr. Code 4
Supt. – Dr. Steve Toy, 545 SEMINARY AVE   83274
Goodsell PS, 185 W CENTER ST   83274
   Michael Call, prin.
Stuart MS, 475 W CENTER ST   83274
   E. Wolfley, prin.

Shoshone, Lincoln Co., Pop. Code 4
Shoshone JSD 312
Sch. Sys. Enr. Code 2
Supt. – Wayne Waddoups, P O BOX 2D   83352
Lincoln ES, P O BOX 2D   83352
   Wayne Waddoups, prin.

Soda Springs, Caribou Co., Pop. Code 5
Soda Springs JSD 150
Sch. Sys. Enr. Code 4
Supt. – Lawrence Rigby, P O BOX 947   83276
JHS, 250 E 2ND SOUTH ST   83276
   Randall Davis, prin.
Hooper Avenue IS, 95 E HOOPER AVE   83276
   Bruce Hoggan, prin.
Thirkill PS, 60 E 4TH S ST   83276
   Bruce Hoggan, prin.
Other Schools – See Wayan

Spirit Lake, Kootenai Co., Pop. Code 1
Lakeland SD 272
Supt. – See Rathdrum
ES, P O BOX 189   83869 – Jack Derting, prin.

Stanley, Custer Co., Pop. Code 1
Challis SD 181
Supt. – See Challis
ES, P O BOX 77   83278 – Maryellen McCartin, prin.

Star, Ada Co.
Meridian JSD 2
Supt. – See Meridian
ES   83669 – Barbara Pease, prin.

Stone, Oneida Co.
Oneida County SD 351
Supt. – See Malad City
ES   83280 – Phil Gillies, prin.

Sugar City, Madison Co., Pop. Code 4
Sugar-Salem JSD 322
Sch. Sys. Enr. Code 4
Supt. – Michael Bishop, 102 N PARK AVE   83448
Kershaw IS, 1100 N 3RD   83448
   Stephen Gee, prin.
Central ES, P O BOX 239   83448
   Mervin Howard, prin.

Sweet, Gem Co.
Emmett JSD 221
Supt. – See Emmett

Sweet Montour ES, P O BOX 2654   83670
   Mary Anne Glodowski, prin.

Tendoy, Lemhi Co.
South Lemhi SD 292
Supt. – See Leadore
ES   83468 – Gregory Cox, prin.

Terreton, Jefferson Co.
West Jefferson SD 253
Sch. Sys. Enr. Code 3
Supt. – Melvin Hansen, HCR 63   BOX 1000   83450
ES, P O BOX 1020   83450 – John Condie, prin.
Other Schools – See Hamer

Teton, Fremont Co., Pop. Code 3
Freemont County JSD 215
Supt. – See Saint Anthony
ES, 126 W MAIN   83451 – Chester Peterson, prin.

Tetonia, Teton Co., Pop. Code 2
Teton County SD 401
Sch. Sys. Enr. Code 3
Supt. – Cless Olney, P O BOX 128   83452
ES, P O BOX 128   83452 – Selar Marcum, prin.
Other Schools – See Driggs, Victor

Thatcher, Caribou Co.
Grace JSD 148
Supt. – See Grace
ES   83283 – Blair Findlay, prin.

Troy, Latah Co., Pop. Code 3
Whitepine SD 284
Sch. Sys. Enr. Code 3
Supt. – Roger Swanson, P O BOX 278   83871
ES, P O BOX 280   83871 – Karen Nelson, prin.
Other Schools – See Bovill

Twin Falls, Twin Falls Co., Pop. Code 8
Filer SD 413
Supt. – See Filer
Hollister ES, RURAL ROUTE 01 BOX 4508   83301
   Arleigh Dodson, prin.

Twin Falls SD 411
Sch. Sys. Enr. Code 6
Supt. – Carl Snow, 201 MAIN AVE W   83301
Bickel ES, 607 2ND AVE E   83301
   Gordon Armstrong, prin.
Harrison ES, 600 HARRISON ST   83301
   Steven Wills, prin.
Lincoln ES, 238 7TH ST N   83301
   Ted Popplewell, prin.
Morningside ES, 701 MORNINGSIDE DR   83301
   Dennis Sonius, prin.
Perrine ES, 452 CASWELL AVE W   83301
   Lillie Brown, prin.
Sawtooth ES, 1771 STADIUM BLVD   83301
   Randy Rutledge, prin.

Immanuel Lutheran School
   2055 FILER AVE E   83301
St. Edward's School, 139 6TH AVE E   83301

Victor, Teton Co., Pop. Code 2
Teton County SD 401
Supt. – See Tetonia
ES, P O BOX 169   83455 – Selar Marcum, prin.

Wallace, Shoshone Co., Pop. Code 4
Wallace SD 393
Sch. Sys. Enr. Code 3
Supt. – Frank Bertino, P O BOX 500   83873
MS, P O BOX 500   83873 – Howard Reasor, prin.
Other Schools – See Osburn

Wayan, Bonneville Co.
Soda Springs JSD 150
Supt. – See Soda Springs
Grays Lake ES   83285 – (—), prin.

Weippe, Clearwater Co., Pop. Code 3
Orofino JSD 171
Supt. – See Orofino
MS, P O BOX 208   83553 – Dale Durkee, prin.
ES, P O BOX 208   83553 – Dale Durkee, prin.

Weiser, Washington Co., Pop. Code 5
Weiser SD 431
Sch. Sys. Enr. Code 4
Supt. – Tom Falash, 925 PIONEER ROAD   83672
JHS, 320 E GALLOWAY ST   83672
   Larry Goto, prin.
Park IS, 758 E PARK ST   83672
   Cynda Campbell, prin.
Pioneer PS, 624 PIONEER ROAD   83672
   George Morris, prin.

Wendell, Gooding Co., Pop. Code 4
Wendell SD 232
Sch. Sys. Enr. Code 3
Supt. – George Crawford, P O BOX 307   83355
ES, P O BOX 366   83355 – Gary Thomasson, prin.

White Bird, Idaho Co., Pop. Code 2
Grangeville JSD 241
Supt. – See Grangeville
PS, MAIN ST   83554 – Mary Newby, prin.

Wilder, Canyon Co., Pop. Code 4
Wilder SD 133
Sch. Sys. Enr. Code 3
Supt. – Bedford Boston, P O BOX 488   83676
Holmes ES, P O BO X488   83676
   Carol Culver, prin.

Worley, Kootenai Co., Pop. Code 2
 Worley SD 275
 Sch. Sys. Enr. Code 2
 Supt. – Burton Lenker, P O BOX 98 83876
 ES, P O BOX 82 83876 – Burton Lenker, prin.

Yellow Pine, Valley Co.
 McCall-Donnelly SD 421
 Supt. – See McCall
 ES 83677 – John Wall, prin.

ILLINOIS

STATE DEPARTMENT OF EDUCATION
100 N. 1st St., Springfield 62777
(217) 782-2221

Superintendent of Education	C. Robert Leininger
Executive Deputy Superintendent	Sally Pancrazio
Executive Assistant/Chief of Staff	Gordon Brown
Associate Superintendent Educational Programs	Dorothy Magett
Associate Superintendent Finance & Support Service	Michael Belletire

ILLINOIS STATE BOARD OF EDUCATION
Donald F. Muirheid, *Chairperson*   100 N. First St., Springfield   62777

ILLINOIS BOARD OF HIGHER EDUCATION
James M. Furman, *Executive Director*   500 Reisch Building, Springfield   62701

REGIONAL SUPERINTENDENTS OF SCHOOLS

Adams-Pike Region, James Steinman, Supt.
 237 N 6TH STREET, Quincy 62301
Alexander/Johnson/Massac/Pulaski/Union, Jerry Johnson, Supt.
 2000 WASHINGTON AVE, Cairo 62914
Bond/Effingham/Fayette Region, James Staff, Supt.
 COURTHOUSE, Vandalia 62471
Boone/Winnebago Region, Richard Fairgrieves, Supt.
 400 WEST STATE #712, Rockford 61101
Brown/Cass/Schuyler Region, Gene Ralston, Supt.
 121 E 2ND STREET, Beardstown 62618
Bureau Region, C. W. Hamilton, Supt.
 COURTHOUSE, Princeton 61356
Calhoun/Greene/Jersey Region, David Mills, Supt.
 P O BOX 409, Jerseyville 62052
Carroll/JoDaviess Region, John B. Lang, Supt.
 330 N BENCH ST, Galena 61036
Champaign/Ford Region, Charles Sutton, Supt.
 P O BOX 919, Rantoul 61806
Christian/Montgomery Region, Thomas Rigdon, Supt.
 P O BOX 456, Taylorville 62568
Clark/Coles/Cmbrlnd/Edgr/Moultrie/Shelby, Rose Shepherd, Supt.
 P O BOX 340, Charleston 61920
Clay/Jasper Richland Region, Sam White, Supt.
 COURTHOUSE, Olney 62450
Clinton/Washington Region, Larry Wolfe, Supt.
 COURTHOUSE ANNEX, Carlyle 62231
Cook Region, Richard Martwick, Supt.
 33 W GRAND AVE, Chicago 60610
Crawford/Lawrence Region, Roger Lewis, Supt.
 P O BOX 866, Lawrenceville 62439
DeKalb Region, Thomas Weber, Supt.
 2301 SYCAMORE ROAD, De Kalb 60115
Dewitt/McLean Region, Donald Robinson, Supt.
 P O BOX 3125, Bloomington 61702
Douglas/Piatt Region, C. Edmundson, Supt.
 P O BOX 10A, Atwood 61913
Dupage Region, Berardo Desimone, Supt.
 421 N COUNTY FARM ROAD, Wheaton 60187

Edwards/Wabash/Wayne/White Region, Kermit Braddock, Supt.
 P O BOX 277, Fairfield 62837
Franklin Region, Elvis Nolen, Supt.
 P O BOX 415, Benton 62812
Fulton Region, Gary Grzanich, Supt.
 P O BOX 307, Lewistown 61542
Gallatin/Hardin/Pope/Saline Region, John Wilson, Supt.
 112 N GUM ST, Harrisburg 62946
Grundy/Kendall Region, Richard Krase, Supt.
 COURTHOUSE ROOM 29, Harrisburg 60450
Hamilton/Jefferson Region, P. E. Cross, Supt.
 COURTHOUSE, Mount Vernon 62864
Hancock/McDonough Region, Donald Simpkins, Supt.
 P O BOX 556, Macomb 61455
Henderson/Mercer/Warren Region, Clyde Farwell, Supt.
 200 W BROADWAY AVE, Monmouth 61462
Henry/Stark Region, Ronald Hewitt, Supt.
 P O BOX 5, Cambridge 61238
Iroquois Region, Donald Deany, Supt.
 COURTHOUSE ROOM 100, Watseka 60970
Jackson/Perry Region, Donald Brewer, Supt.
 COURTHOUSE, Murphysboro 62966
Kane Region, Douglas Hoeft, Supt.
 719 BATAVIA AVE, Geneva 60134
Kankakee Region, Alan Lemon, Supt.
 470 E MERCHANT ST, Kankakee 60901
Knox Region, Raymond Franson, Supt.
 P O BOX 430, Galesburg 61402
Lake Region, Sybil Yastrow, Supt.
 18 N COUNTY ST #A-904, Waukegan 60085
LaSalle Region, William Novotney, Supt.
 119 W MADISON ST, Ottawa 61350
Lee Region, Thomas Coffey, Supt.
 OLD COURTHOUSE, Dixon 61021
Livingston Region, Wayne Blunier, Supt.
 310 E TORRANCE AVE, Pontiac 61764
Logan/Mason/Menard Region, G. Janet, Supt.
 LOGAN CO COURTHOUSE, Lincoln 62656

Macon Region, David Cooprider, Supt.
 2240 E GEDDES AVE, Decatur 62526
Macoupin Region, Russell Massinelli, Supt.
 P O BOX 475, Carlinville 62626
Madison Region, Harold Briggs, Supt.
 P O BOX 600, Edwardsville 62025
Marion Region, Sam Nall, Supt.
 200 E SCHWARTZ ST, Salem 62881
Marshall/Putnam/Woodford Region, Iner Anderson, Supt.
 P O BOX 249, Lacon 61540
McHenry Region, Leslie Helleman, Supt.
 2200 N SEMINARY AVE, Woodstock 60098
Monroe/Randolph Region, James M. Carpenter, Supt.
 146 W MARKET ST, Red Bud 62278
Morgan/Scott Region, Paul Keller, Supt.
 COURTHOUSE, Jacksonville 62650
Ogle Region, Charles Hays, Supt.
 P O BOX 196, Oregon 61061
Peoria Region, Gerald Brookhart, Supt.
 CO COURTHOUSE ROOM 501, Peoria 61602
Rock Island Region, John Conlon, Supt.
 1504 3RD AVE, Rock Island 61201
St. Clair Region, Martha O'Malley, Supt.
 10 PUBLIC SQUARE, Belleville 62220
Sangamon Region, Harold Vose, Supt.
 CO BUILDING ROOM 208, Springfield 62701
Stephenson Region, Marvin Maaske, Supt.
 15 N GALENA AVE, Freeport 61032
Tazewell Region, Solie Myers, Supt.
 P O BOX 699, Pekin 61555
Vermilion Region, Richard Weller, Supt.
 RURAL ROUTE 01 BOX 12D, Danville 61832
Whiteside Region, Gary Steinert, Supt.
 COURTHOUSE, Morrison 61270
Will Region, Raymond Gornik, Supt.
 14 W JEFFERSON ST, Joliet 60431
Williamson Region, David Hindman, Supt.
 CO COURTHOUSE, Marion 62959

PUBLIC, PRIVATE, AND PAROCHIAL ELEMENTARY SCHOOLS

Abingdon, Knox Co., Pop. Code 5
 Abingdon CUSD 217
 Sch. Sys. Enr. Code 4
 Supt. – Billy M. Taylor, 201 W LOWER ST 61410
 JHS, 202 W SNYDER ST 61410
  Donald Smith, prin.
 Hedding ES, 401 W LATIMER ST 61410
  Morris Moore, prin.

Addison, Du Page Co., Pop. Code 8
 Addison SD 4
 Sch. Sys. Enr. Code 5
 Supt. – Dr. Larry Weck
  222 N KENNEDY DRIVE 60101
 Indian Trail JHS, 222 N KENNEDY DRIVE 60101
  Douglas McFarland, prin.
 Army Trail ES, 346 ARMY TRAIL 60101
  Dean Denicolo, prin.

 Fullerton ES, 400 S MICHIGAN AVE 60101
  Joseph Patricelli, prin.
 Lake Park ES, 330 W LAKE PARK DR 60101
  John Young, prin.
 Lincoln ES, 720 N LINCOLN AVE 60101
  George Shannon, prin.
 Stone ES, 1404 W STONE AVE 60101
  James Frontier, prin.
 Wesley ES, 1111 W WESTWOOD TRL 60101
  Thomas Romano, prin.

 Lutherbrook Childrens School
  343 W LAKE STREET 60101
 St. Joseph School, 401 E PALMER AVE 60101
 St. Paul Lutheran School
  105 W ARMY TRAIL BLVD 60101
 St. Philip the Apostle School
  1233 W HOLTZ AVE 60101

Akin, Franklin Co.
 Akin CCSD 91
 Sch. Sys. Enr. Code 2
 Supt. – John Metzger, P O BOX 1 62805
 Akin Community Consolidated ES
  P O BOX 1 62805 – Dr. John Metzger, prin.

Albany, Whiteside Co., Pop. Code 4
 River Bend CUSD 2
 Supt. – See Fulton
 ES, P O BOX 405 61230 – Bob Bradley, prin.

Albers, Clinton Co., Pop. Code 3
 Albers SD 63
 Sch. Sys. Enr. Code 2
 Supt. – Bernard J. Fuehne
  BROADWAY & HENDRICKS 62215

ES, BROADWAY & HENDRICKS　62215
　Bernard Fuehne, prin.

Damiansville SD 62
Sch. Sys. Enr. Code 2
Supt. – Bernard Fuehne, RURAL ROUTE 01　62215
Damiansville ES, RURAL ROUTE 01　62215
　Ben Fuehne, prin.

Albion, Edwards Co., Pop. Code 4
Edwards Co. CUSD 1
Sch. Sys. Enr. Code 4
Supt. – Dr. Richard Peltonen
　106 W MAIN ST　62806
Edwards County S, 361 W MAIN ST　62806
　Marilyn Yokel, prin.
Other Schools – See West Salem

Aledo, Mercer Co., Pop. Code 5
Aledo CUSD 201
Sch. Sys. Enr. Code 4
Supt. – Dr. N. Kendall Pottorff
　401 SW 2ND AVE　61231
North Side MS, 200 N COLLEGE AVE　61231
　Glen Braden, prin.
Apollo ES, SW 8TH AVE & 9TH ST　61231
　Victor Johnson, prin.

Alexander, Morgan Co.
Franklin CUSD 1
Supt. – See Franklin
ES, P O BOX 101　62601 – Paula Roscetti, prin.

Alexis, Warren Co., Pop. Code 4
Alexis CUSD 400
Sch. Sys. Enr. Code 2
Supt. – John Elder, P O BOX 278　61412
JHS, HOLLOWAY ST　61412 – John Elder, prin.
ES, P O BOX 299　61412 – Gerald Goodman, prin.

Algonquin, McHenry Co., Pop. Code 6
Dundee CUSD 300
Supt. – See Dundee
MS, 500 LONGWOOD DRIVE　60102
　Darrel Westerbeck, prin.
Eastview ES, 451 E CHICAGO ST　60102
　P. Carlton Rice, prin.
Lake In The Hills ES, 519 WILLOW ST　60102
　Helen Moore, prin.
Neubert ES, 1100 HUNTINGTON DR　60102
　Donna Schuring, prin.

St. John Lutheran School
　300 JEFFERSON ST　60102
St. Margaret Mary School
　3 S HUBBARD ST　60102

Alhambra, Madison Co., Pop. Code 3
Highland CUSD 5
Supt. – See Highland
ES, JEFFERSON AVE　62001 – Verna Abert, prin.

Allendale, Wabash Co., Pop. Code 3
Allendale CCSD 17
Sch. Sys. Enr. Code 2
Supt. – Grover Burkett, 3RD & MAIN　62410
ES, P O BOX 128　62410 – Linda Graves, prin.

Alma, Marion Co., Pop. Code 2
Kinmundy Alma CUSD 301
Supt. – See Kinmundy
Kinmundy-Alma JHS　62801
　Theodore Phillips, prin.

Alorton, St. Clair Co., Pop. Code 4
East St. Louis SD 189
Supt. – See East Saint Louis
Grahmann MS, 4400 GRAND ST　62207
　Elitor Wallace, prin.

Alpha, Henry Co., Pop. Code 3
Alwood CUSD 225
Supt. – See Woodhull
Alwood ES, P O BOX 67　61413
　William Griffin, prin.

Alsip, Cook Co., Pop. Code 7
Alsip-Hazelgreen-Oaklawn SD 126
Supt. – See Worth
Prairie JHS, 11910 S KOSTNER AVE　60658
　Harold Hansen, prin.
Lane ES, 4600 W 123RD ST　60658
　Jerry Vrshek, prin.
Stony Creek ES, 11700 S KOLIN AVE　60658
　George Kernwein, prin.

Atwood Heights SD 125
Supt. – See Oak Lawn
Hamlin Upper MS, 12150 S HAMLIN AVE　60658
　Samuel Rizzo, prin.

Altamont, Effingham Co., Pop. Code 4
Altamont CUSD 10
Sch. Sys. Enr. Code 3
Supt. – Bernard F. May, 7 S EWING ST　62411
ES, 407 S EDWARDS ST　62411
　Charles Miller, prin.

Altamont Lutheran School
　7 S EDWARDS ST　62411

Alton, Madison Co., Pop. Code 8
Alton CUSD 11
Sch. Sys. Enr. Code 6
Supt. – Dr. David VanWinkle
　1854 E BROADWAY　62002
East MS, 1035 WASHINGTON AVE　62002
　James Clark, prin.

West MS, 1513 STATE ST　62002
　David Elson, prin.
Smith MS, 2400 HENRY ST　62002
　Edward Hightower, prin.
Irving ES, 1020 STATE ST　62002
　Robert Ray, prin.
Jefferson ES, 2603 N RODGERS AVE　62002
　Duane Mossman, prin.
Lovejoy MS, 1043 TREMONT ST　62002
　H. Brent Schindewolf, prin.
Mann MS, 2708 EDWARDS ST　62002
　Ronald Fedorchak, prin.
McKinley MS, 121 W ELM ST　62002
　R. Joseph Ducey, prin.
Twain ES, 907 MILTON RD　62002
　Richard Condrey, prin.
Other Schools — See Godfrey

Mississippi Valley Christian School
　2009 SEMINARY ST　62002
SS Peter & Paul School, 801 STATE ST　62002
St. Mary's School, 536 E 3RD ST　62002
St. Matthew School, 1015 MILTON RD　62002

Altona, Knox Co., Pop. Code 3
ROWVA CUSD 208
Supt. – See Oneida
ES　61414 – William Ault, prin.

Amboy, Lee Co., Pop. Code 4
Amboy CUSD 272
Sch. Sys. Enr. Code 4
Supt. – Dr. George Steffen
　METCALF & HAWLEY STS　61310
JHS, 140 APPLETON AVE　61310
　Richard Bumba, prin.
Amboy Central ES, 30 E PROVOST ST　61310
　Dennis Weidman, prin.

Andalusia, Rock Island Co., Pop. Code 4
Rockridge CUSD 300
Supt. – See Taylor Ridge
ES, P O BOX 910　61232 – Clayton Naylor, prin.

Anna, Union Co., Pop. Code 6
Anna CUSD 37
Sch. Sys. Enr. Code 3
Supt. – Dr. Ben Cauble. 301 S GREEN ST　62906
JHS, 301 S GREEN ST　62906
　Duane Hileman, prin.
Davie MS, 300 FREEMAN ST　62906
　Ronald Cross, prin.
Lincoln ES, 108 WARREN ST　62906
　Relis Oliver, prin.

Annawan, Henry Co., Pop. Code 3
Annawan CUSD 226
Sch. Sys. Enr. Code 2
Supt. – Ronald Tuisl, 501 W SOUTH ST　61234
ES, 503 W SOUTH ST　61234
　Rodney Miller, prin.

Antioch, Lake Co., Pop. Code 5
Antioch CCSD 34
Sch. Sys. Enr. Code 4
Supt. – Dr. Donald E. Skidmore
　850 HIGHVIEW DRIVE　60002
Antioch Upper MS, 800 HIGHVIEW DRIVE　60002
　William Herbst, prin.
ES, 817 MAIN ST　60002 – Harlan Ware, prin.
Oakland ES, 22018 W GRASS LAKE RD　60002
　Walter Soderman, prin.
Petty ES, 850 HIGHVIEW DR　60002
　Paul Hain, prin.

Emmons SD 33
Sch. Sys. Enr. Code 2
Supt. – Jill Ballock
　24226 W BEACH GROVE ROAD　60002
Emmons ES, 24226 W BEACH GROVE RD　60002
　Jill Ballock, prin.

Grass Lake SD 36
Sch. Sys. Enr. Code 2
Supt. – Anthony Przeklasa
　26177 W GRASS LAKE ROAD　60002
Grass Lake ES, 26177 W GRASS LAKE RD　60002
　Raymond Liss, prin.

St. Peter School, 900 SAINT PETER ST　60002

Apple River, Jo Daviess Co., Pop. Code 2
Warren CUSD 205
Supt. – See Warren
MS　61001 – Roger Teuscher, prin.

Arcola, Douglas Co., Pop. Code 5
Arcola CUSD 306
Sch. Sys. Enr. Code 3
Supt. – Millard Goben
　351 W WASHINGTON ST　61910
ES, 351 W WASHINGTON ST　61910
　Alice Meador, prin.

Argenta, Macon Co., Pop. Code 3
Argenta-Oreana CUSD 01
Sch. Sys. Enr. Code 4
Supt. – Dr. Donald Magee, 500 N MAIN ST　62501
New Argenta MS, 500 N MAIN ST　62501
　Judy Brown, prin.
Old Argenta ES, 275 KENWOOD　62501
　Ary Anderson, prin.
Other Schools – See Oreana

Argo, Cook Co., Pop. Code 6
Summit SD 104
Supt. – See Summit

Graves JHS, 60TH ST & 74TH AVE　60501
　Thomas Dixey, prin.

Arlington, Bureau Co., Pop. Code 2
LaMoille CUSD 303
Supt. – See La Moille
ES　61312 – Cynthia Shevokas, prin.

Arlington Heights, Cook Co., Pop. Code 8
Aptakisic-Tripp CCSD 102
Supt. – See Prairie View
Aptakisic JHS
　2550 N ARLINGTON HTS ROAD　60004
　William Parker, prin.

Arlington Heights. SD 25
Sch. Sys. Enr. Code 5
Supt. – Donald Strong, 301 W SOUTH ST　60005
South JHS, 314 S HIGHLAND AVE　60005
　Kenneth Swanson, prin.
Thomas JHS, 303 E THOMAS AVE　60004
　Richard Hanke, prin.
Berkley ES, 2501 N CHESTNUT AVE　60004
　John Bennett, prin.
Dryden ES, 722 S DRYDEN PL　60005
　Ernest DeLabruere, prin.
Greenbrier ES, 2330 VERDE DR　60004
　James Hall, prin.
Ivy Hill ES, 2211 N BURKE DR　60004
　Maureen Hager, prin.
Olive ES, 303 E OLIVE ST　60004
　Mary Stitt, prin.
Patton ES, 1616 N PATTON AVE　60004
　Dr. Dorothy Weber, prin.
Westgate ES, 1211 W GROVE ST　60005
　Dr. Emily Alford, prin.
Windsor ES, 1315 E MINER ST　60004
　Priscilla Kirkpatrick, prin.

Community Consolidated SD 59
Sch. Sys. Enr. Code 6
Supt. – James Fay
　2123 S ARLINGTON HTS ROAD　60005
Low ES, 1530 S HIGHLAND AVE　60005
　Anton Waser, prin.
Other Schools – See Des Plaines, Elk Grove Village,
　Mount Prospect

Wheeling CCSD 21
Supt. – See Wheeling
Poe ES, 2800 N HIGHLAND AVE　60004
　Donald Werneske, prin.
Riley ES, 1209 E BURR OAK DR　60004
　Dr. Ferne Garrett, prin.

Our Lady of the Wayside School
　432 S MITCHELL AVE　60005
St. James School
　821 N ARLINGTON HEIGHTS RD　60004
St. Peter Lutheran School, 111 W OLIVE ST　60004

Armstrong, Vermilion Co., Pop. Code 2
Armstrong-Ellis CSD 61
Sch. Sys. Enr. Code 2
Supt. – James DeYoung, P O BOX 7　61812
Armstrong-Ellis ES, P O BOX 7　61812
　James Deyoung, prin.

Aroma Park, Kankakee Co., Pop. Code 3
Kankakee SD 111
Supt. – See Kankakee
ES, P O BOX 239　60910 – Willa White, prin.

Arrowsmith, McLean Co., Pop. Code 2
Saybrook-Arrowsmith CUSD 11
Supt. – See Saybrook
Saybrook-Arrowsmith ES, ULMER ST　61722
　Dr. Donald Raycraft, prin.

Arthur, Moultrie Co., Pop. Code 4
Arthur CUSD 305
Sch. Sys. Enr. Code 3
Supt. – Allen Froman
　301 E COLUMBIA DRIVE　61911
JHS, 301 E COLUMBIA DRIVE　61911
　Edgar Coller, prin.
ES, 126 E LINCOLN ST　61911 – Harold Bell, prin.

Ashkum, Iroquois Co., Pop. Code 3
Central CUSD 4
Supt. – See Clifton
ES, P O BOX 158　60911 – James Rankin, prin.

Ashland, Cass Co., Pop. Code 4
Ashland CUSD 212
Sch. Sys. Enr. Code 2
Supt. – Harold Showalter, P O BOX P　62612
JHS, P O BOX P　62612 – Don Parsons, prin.
ES, P O BOX 260　62612 – Michael Donnan, prin.

Ashley, Washington Co., Pop. Code 3
Ashley CCSD 15
Sch. Sys. Enr. Code 2
Supt. – Robert L. Aaron, P O BOX 315　62808
Ashley Community Consolidated ES
　P O BOX 315　62808 – Robert Aaron, prin.

Ashmore, Coles Co., Pop. Code 3
Charleston CUSD 1
Supt. – See Charleston
ES, P O BOX 218　61912 – Jean Walters, prin.

Ashton, Lee Co., Pop. Code 4
Ashton CUSD 275
Sch. Sys. Enr. Code 2
Supt. – Gregory Sawka, P O BOX 329　61006
MS, WESTERN AVE　61006
　Robert Cicciarelli, prin.

ES, P O BOX 329 61006 – Robert Cicciarelli, prin.

Assumption, Christian Co., Pop. Code 4
Assumption CUSD 9
Sch. Sys. Enr. Code 2
Supt. – Randolph Tinder
    105 N COLLEGE ST 62510
JHS, 404 COLEGROVE ST 62510
    Connie Jansen, prin.
Bond ES, 105 N COLLEGE ST 62510
    Randolph Tinder, prin.

Astoria, Fulton Co., Pop. Code 4
Astoria CUSD 1
Sch. Sys. Enr. Code 3
Supt. – Greg LaPlante, P O BOX 487 61501
JHS, P O BOX 487 61501 – Alan Hawkins, prin.
ES, JEFFERSON ST BOX 487 61501
    Gregory LaPlante, prin.

Athens, Menard Co., Pop. Code 4
Athens CUSD 213
Sch. Sys. Enr. Code 3
Supt. – William DePratt
    RURAL ROUTE 01 BOX 11 62613
ES, E JACKSON ST 62613 – J. Curt Benanti, prin.
Fancy Prairie ES, RURAL ROUTE 01 62613
    Ronald Schwabe, prin.
Other Schools – See Cantrall

Atkinson, Henry Co., Pop. Code 4
Geneseo CUSD 228
Supt. – See Geneseo
ES, 109 N STATE STREET 61235
    Don Dolieslager, prin.

Atlanta, Logan Co., Pop. Code 4
Olympia CUSD 16
Supt. – See Stanford
ES, RURAL ROUTE 01 BOX 29A 61723
    R. Lynn Camel, prin.

Atwood, Piatt Co., Pop. Code 4
Atwood-Hammond CUSD 39
Sch. Sys. Enr. Code 2
Supt. – James Morgan, P O BOX 429 61913
Atwood-Hammond ES, 316 N ILLINOIS ST 61913
    (—), prin.

Auburn, Sangamon Co., Pop. Code 5
Auburn CUSD 10
Sch. Sys. Enr. Code 3
Supt. – Dr. James Doglio, 606 W NORTH 3T 62615
JHS, 606 W NORTH ST 62615
    Anton Cerveny, prin.
ES, N 5TH ST 62615 – Edward Lewis, prin.

Augusta, Hancock Co., Pop. Code 3
Southeastern CUSD 337
Sch. Sys. Enr. Code 2
Supt. – Terry Robertson, P O BOX 236 62311
Other Schools – See Bowen

Aurora, Kane Co., Pop. Code 8
Aurora East Unit SD 131
Sch. Sys. Enr. Code 6
Supt. – Dr. Charles Ponquinette
    417 FIFTH ST 60505
Simmons JHS, 1130 SHEFFER ROAD 60505
    Melvin Guider, prin.
Waldo JHS, 56 JACKSON ST 60505
    Bruce Weirich, prin.
Allen ES, 700 S FARNSWORTH AVE 60505
    Jerry Sondgeroth, prin.
Bardwell ES, 550 S LINCOLN AVE 60505
    Jack Pool, prin.
Beaupre ES, 954 E BENION ST 60505
    Sandra Dressler, prin.
Brady ES, 600 COLUMBIA ST 60505
    Verland Brown, prin.
Dieterich ES, 1141 JACKSON ST 60505
    Gwendolyn Miller, prin.
Gates ES, 800 SEVENTH AVE 60505
    Thomas Kircher, prin.
Hermes ES, 1000 JUNGLES AVE 60505
    Mary White, prin.
Johnson ES, LIBERTY ST ROAD 60504
    Thomas Hartman, prin.
Oak Park ES, 1200 FRONT ST 60505
    Donna Thurow, prin.
O'Donnell ES, 1640 RECKINGER RD 60505
    Alan Neitzel, prin.
Other Schools – See Montgomery

Aurora West Unit SD 129
Sch. Sys. Enr. Code 6
Supt. – Dr. Gary Jewel, 80 S RIVER ST 60506
Jefferson MS, 1151 PLUM ST 60506
    Dr. Robert Lathrop, prin.
Washington MS, 123 WINIFRED ROAD 60506
    Rose Pinnick, prin.
Freeman ES, 153 S RANDALL RD 60506
    Richard Johnson, prin.
Greenman ES, 729 W GALENA BLVD 60506
    Douglas Zolper, prin.
Hall ES, 2001 HEATHER DR 60506
    James Toynton, prin.
Hill ES, 724 PENNSYLVANIA AVE 60506
    Steve Sibon, prin.
Lincoln ES, 641 S LAKE ST 60506
    C. Alan Randall, prin.
McCleery ES, 1002 W ILLINOIS AVE 60506
    Maureen Granger, prin.
Smith ES, 1332 ROBINWOOD DR 60506
    Margaret Kratzer, prin.
Other Schools – See Montgomery, North Aurora

Indian Prairie CUSD 204
Supt. – See Naperville
Georgetown ES, 995 LONG GROVE DR 60504
    Gregory Anerino, prin.

Annunciation of B V M School
    1840 CHURCH RD 60504
Emmanuel Lutheran School
    551 FOURTH AVE 60505
Holy Angels School, 720 KENSINGTON PL 60506
Our Lady of Good Counsel School
    601 TALMA ST 60505
Sacred Heart School, 755 FULTON ST 60505
St. Joseph School, 706 HIGH ST 60505
St. Nicholas-M. Schumacher School
    312 HIGH ST 60505
St. Paul Lutheran School
    550 SECOND AVE 60505
St. Peter School, 915 SARD AVE 60506
St. Rita of Cascia School
    770 OLD INDIAN TRL 60506
St. Therese School
    255 N FARNSWORTH AVE 60505

Aviston, Clinton Co., Pop. Code 3
Aviston SD 21
Sch. Sys. Enr. Code 2
Supt. – Leon Luber, 198 S SPRING ST 62216
ES, 198 S SPRING ST 62216 – Leon Luber, prin.

Avon, Fulton Co., Pop. Code 4
Avon CUSD 176
Sch. Sys. Enr. Code 2
Supt. – John Mowery, 301 E CLINTON 61415
JHS, WOOD ST 61415 – John Alden, prin.
ES, 400 WOOD ST 61415 – John Alden, prin.

Barrington, Lake Co., Pop. Code 6
Barrington CUSD 220
Sch. Sys. Enr. Code 6
Supt. – Dr. Clyde Slocum, 310 JAMES ST 60010
MS, 215 EASTERN AVE 60010
    Don Thompson, prin.
Countryside ES, 205 W COUNTY LINE RD 60010
    Jean Mason, prin.
Grove Avenue ES, 900 S GROVE AVE 60010
    Cynthia Kalogeropoulos, prin.
Hough Street ES, 310 S HOUGH ST 60010
    Marie Plozay, prin.
Lines ES, 217 EASTERN AVE 60010
    (—), prin.
North Barrington ES, 310 N HIGHWAY 59 60010
    Robert Key, prin.
Roslyn Road ES, 224 ROSLYN RD 60010
    Frank Cole, prin.
Other Schools – See Carpentersville

St. Anne ES, 312 CHESTNUT ST 60010

Barry, Pike Co., Pop. Code 4
Barry CUSD 1
Sch. Sys. Enr. Code 2
Supt. – C. Michael Kovachevich
    401 MCDONOUGH ST 62312
JHS, 401 MCDONOUGH ST 62312
    Kenneth Fagan, prin.
ES, 406 MCDONOUGH ST 62312
    Kenneth Fagan, prin.

Barstow, Rock Island Co.
Carbon Cliff-Barstow SD 36
Supt. – See Carbon Cliff
Aldrin JHS, P O BOX 140 61236
    Harold Roggendorf, prin.

Bartelso, Clinton Co., Pop. Code 2
Bartelso SD 57
Sch. Sys. Enr. Code 2
Supt. – Don Kilpatrick
    50 WASHINGTON ST 62218
ES, S WASHINGTON ST 62218
    Don Kilpatrick, prin.

Bartlett, Cook Co., Pop. Code 7
Elgin Unit SD 46
Supt. – See Elgin
ES, 111 NORTH AVE 60103 – Jon Mink, prin.
Eastview ES, 321 N OAK AVE 60103
    Donnie Berry, prin.

Bartonville, Peoria Co., Pop. Code 6
Bartonville SD 66
Sch. Sys. Enr. Code 2
Supt. – John Hlavach, 6000 SW ADAMS 61607
ES, 6000 SW ADAMS ST 61607
    William Tear, prin.

Monroe SD 70
Sch. Sys. Enr. Code 3
Supt. – William Tear, 5137 W CISNA ROAD 61607
Monroe ES, 5137 W CISNA RD 61607
    Thomas Kahn, prin.

Oak Grove SD 68
Sch. Sys. Enr. Code 3
Supt. – Richard L. Wagner
    4812 W PFEIFFER ROAD 61607
Oak Grove West JHS
    6018 W LANCASTER ST 61607
    Stephen W. Heath, prin.
Oak Grove East ES
    4812 W PFEIFFER ROAD 61607
    Richard Wagner, prin.

Batavia, Kane Co., Pop. Code 7
Batavia Unit SD 101
Sch. Sys. Enr. Code 5
Supt. – Dr. Edward Cave, 12 W WILSON ST 60510
JHS, 10 S BATAVIA AVE 60510
    Sam R. Rotolo, prin.
Gustafson ES, 905 CARLISLE RD 60510
    Alan McCloud, prin.
McWayne ES, 328 W WILSON ST 60510
    Mary Jaeger, prin.
Nelson ES, WILLIAM WOOD LANE 60510
    Laurence Dibblee, prin.
Storm ES, 305 N VAN NORIWICK 60510
    Nancy Smith, prin.
White ES, 800 N PRAIRIE ST 60510
    Albert Burnell, prin.

Bath, Mason Co., Pop. Code 2
Balyki CUSD 125
Sch. Sys. Enr. Code 2
Supt. – Thomas Long, P O BOX 1860 62617
Balyki JHS, P O BOX 1860 62617
    Gerald Johnson, prin.
ES, P O BOX 186 62617 – Dale Osing, prin.
Other Schools – See Kilbourne

Beardstown, Cass Co., Pop. Code 6
Beardstown CUSD 15
Sch. Sys. Enr. Code 4
Supt. – Wayne Johnson
    515 WASHINGTON 62618
JHS, 200 E 15TH ST 62618 – Mary Castro, prin.
Brick ES, RURAL ROUTE 01 BOX 60 62618
    Doris Edwards, prin.
Gard ES, 400 E 15TH ST 62618
    Laurence Foley, prin.
Washington ES, 515 CANAL ST 62618
    Doris Edwards, prin.

Beason, Logan Co.
Beason CCSD 17
Sch. Sys. Enr. Code 1
Supt. – Dean Baker, P O BOX 68 62512
ES, P O BOX 68 62512 – Dean Baker, prin.

Beckemeyer, Clinton Co., Pop. Code 4
Breese SD 12
Supt. – See Breese
MS, LOUIS ST 62219 – David Timmermann, prin.

St. Anthony School, 2ND AND MADDUX 62219

Bedford Park, Cook Co., Pop. Code 3
Summit SD 104
Supt. – See Summit
Walker ES, 7735 W 66TH PL 60501
    Samuel Santora, prin.

Beecher, Will Co., Pop. Code 4
Beecher CUSD 200U
Sch. Sys. Enr. Code 3
Supt. – Jack Keller, 538 MILLER ST 60401
ES, 629 PENFIELD 60401 – Richard Preston, prin.

Zion Lutheran School, 540 OAK PARK AVE 60401

Beecher City, Effingham Co., Pop. Code 2
Beecher City CUSD 20
Sch. Sys. Enr. Code 2
Supt. – Joseph Stokes, P O BOX 98 62414
MS, P O BOX 97 62414 – Doug Heiden, prin.
Other Schools – See Shumway

Belle Rive, Jefferson Co., Pop. Code 2
Opdyke-Belle-Rive CCSD 5
Sch. Sys. Enr. Code 2
Supt. – Fred Edwards, P O BOX 128 62810
PS, P O BOX 128 62810 – Bill Lathrop, prin.
Other Schools – See Opdyke

Belleville, St. Clair Co., Pop. Code 8
Belle Valley SD 119
Sch. Sys. Enr. Code 4
Supt. – Ralph Cox, 100 ANDORA DRIVE 62221
Belle Valley MS South
    1901 MASCOUTAH ROAD 62221
    Robert Buscher, prin.
Belle Valley ES North, 100 ANDORA DR 62221
    Lonnie Smith, prin.

Belleville SD 118
Sch. Sys. Enr. Code 5
Supt. – Ronald Riegel, 105 WEST A ST 62220
Central JHS, 200 S ILLINOIS ST 62220
    Thomas Mentzer, prin.
West JHS, 820 ROYAL HEIGHTS ROAD 62223
    Bill Porzukowiak, prin.
Douglas ES, 125 CARLYLE AVE 62220
    Ferd Kaufman, prin.
Franklin ES, 301 N 2ND ST 62220
    Joan Kirchoff, prin.
Jefferson ES, 1400 N CHARLES ST 62221
    James Rosborg, prin.
Lincoln ES, 820 ROYAL HEIGHTS RD 62223
    Joan Kirchoff, prin.
Primary Enrichment ES, 105 W A ST 62220
    Mary Johnson, prin.
Raab ES, 1120 UNION AVE 62220
    Janice Dorris, prin.
Roosevelt ES, 700 W CLEVELAND AVE 62220
    Janice Dorris, prin.
Union ES, 20 S 27TH ST 62223
    Frank Wokcik, Jr., prin.
Washington ES, 400 S CHARLES ST 62220
    Ferd Kaufman, prin.

Harmony Emge SD 175
Sch. Sys. Enr. Code 3
Supt. – Carl Shannon
  7401 WESTCHESTER DRIVE   62223
Emge JHS, 7401 WESTCHESTER DRIVE   62223
  Marvin McKellips, prin.
Ellis ES, 250 ILLINI DR   62223
  James Meyer, prin.

High Mount SD 116
Sch. Sys. Enr. Code 2
Supt. – Dr. Richard Adams
  1721 BOUL AVE   62220
High Mount ES, 1721 BOUL AVE   62220
  Dr. Richard Adams, prin.

Pontiac-West Holliday SD 105
Supt. – See Fairview Heights
Holliday ES, 400 JOSEPH DR   62221
  Denise Cox, prin.

Signal Hill SD 181
Sch. Sys. Enr. Code 2
Supt. – Darrel Hardt
  40 SIGNAL HILL PLACE   62223
Signal Hill ES, 40 SIGNAL HILL PL   62223
  Darrel Hardt, prin.

Whiteside SD 115
Sch. Sys. Enr. Code 3
Supt. – Dr. Raymond Mack
  2028 LEBANON AVE   62221
Whiteside ES, 2028 LEBANON AVE   62221
  Robert Wessel, prin.

Wolf Branch SD 113
Sch. Sys. Enr. Code 2
Supt. – Dr. James Smith
  125 HUNTWOOD ROAD   62221
Wolf Branch ES, 125 HUNTWOOD RD   62221
  Dr. Thomas Jewett, prin.
  _____

Blessed Sacrament School
  8809 W MAIN ST   62223
Queen of Peace School, 5923 N BELT W   62223
St. Augustine Canterbury School
  1900 W BELLE ST   62223
St. Henry School, 5303 W MAIN ST   62223
St. Mary School, 1722 W MAIN ST   62223
St. Peter Cathedral School, 200 S 2ND ST   62220
St. Teresa School, 1108 LEBANON AVE   62221
Zion Lutheran School
  1810 MCCLINTOCK ST   62221

Bellflower, McLean Co., Pop. Code 2
Blue Ridge CUSD 18
Supt. – See Farmer City
ES, STATE & CENTER STS   61724
  Sharon Johnson, prin.

Bellmont, Wabash Co., Pop. Code 2
Wabash CUSD 348
Supt. – See Mount Carmel
ES, POST OFFICE   62811 – Bill Priest, prin.

Bellwood, Cook Co., Pop. Code 7
Bellwood SD 88
Supt. – See Stone Park
Roosevelt JHS, 25TH AVE & OAK ST   60104
  Dr. Vinston Birdin, prin.
Lincoln MS, LINDEN & JACKSON   60104
  Dr. Ronald Boyd, prin.
Lincoln PS, 3519 WILCOX AVE   60104
  Dr. Ronald Boyd, prin.
Mckinley ES, 3317 BUTTERFIELD RD   60104
  Rosemarie Nicholes, prin.
Roosevelt ES, 27TH AVENUE AND OAK ST   60104
  Ronald Dunlap, prin.
Wilson ES, 1136 S 24TH AVE   60104
  Dr. Bertha Winingham, prin.

Berkeley SD 87
Supt. – See Berkeley
Jefferson ES, 225 46TH AVE   60104
  Dean Rutan, prin.
  _____

St. Simeon School, 501 BELLWOOD AVE   60104

Belvidere, Boone Co., Pop. Code 7
Belvidere CUSD 100
Sch. Sys. Enr. Code 5
Supt. – Frank Evans, 1201 5TH AVE   61008
MS, 520 PEARL ST   61008 – Lewis Emry, prin.
Lincoln ES, 505 N MAIN ST   61008
  Gene Chamberlain, prin.
Logan ES, 620 LOGAN AVE   61008
  Mickey Brei, prin.
Perry ES, 633 W PERRY ST   61008
  Steven Lennon, prin.
Washington ES, 1031 5TH AVE   61008
  Marvin Schuster, prin.
Other Schools – See Caledonia, Garden Prairie
  _____

Immanuel Lutheran School, 1225 E 2ND ST   61008
St. James School, 320 LOGAN AVE   61008

Bement, Piatt Co., Pop. Code 4
Bement CUSD 5
Sch. Sys. Enr. Code 3
Supt. – Greg Zollman
  201 S CHAMPAIGN ST   61813
MS, 201 S CHAMPAIGN ST   61813
  Joyce Kaufman, prin.
ES, 201 S CHAMPAIGN ST   61918
  Joyce Kaufman, prin.

Benld, Macoupin Co., Pop. Code 4
Gillespie CUSD 7
Supt. – See Gillespie
JHS, 100 E DORSEY ST   62009
  Louis Polovich, prin.
ES, 100 E DORSEY ST   62009
  Louis Polovich, prin.

Bensenville, Du Page Co., Pop. Code 7
Bensenville SD 2
Sch. Sys. Enr. Code 4
Supt. – Dr. James R. Coad, 119 E GREEN ST   60106
Blackhawk JHS, 250 S CHURCH ROAD   60106
  Loren May, prin.
Chippewa MS, 322 S YORK RD   60106
  Robert Barr, prin.
Johnson ES, 252 S RIDGEWOOD DR   60106
  N. Eugene Leggett, prin.
Mohawk ES, 917 W HILLSIDE DR   60106
  George Peternel, prin.
Tioga ES, 212 W MEMORIAL RD   60106
  Judith Zito, prin.
  _____

St. Charles Borromeo School
  145 E GRAND AVE   60106
Zion Lutheran School, 865 S CHURCH RD   60106

Benson, Woodford Co., Pop. Code 2
Roanoke-Benson CUSD 60
Supt. – See Roanoke
Roanoke-Benson JHS, 139 REITER ST   61516
  Randy Dunn, prin.

Benton, Franklin Co., Pop. Code 6
Benton CCSD 47
Sch. Sys. Enr. Code 4
Supt. – Allan Patton, 308 E CHURCH ST   62812
Benton MS, 1000 FORREST ST   62812
  Harl Lewis, prin.
Grant ES, 1007 N MCLEANSBORO ST   62812
  Jeannine Smith, prin.
Lincoln ES, 325 W 4TH ST   62812
  Keith Ing, prin.
Logan PS, 230 E CHURCH ST   62812
  Gene Alexander, prin.
Washington ES, 201 S BROWNING ST   62812
  Keith Ing, prin.

Berkeley, Cook Co., Pop. Code 6
Berkeley SD 87
Sch. Sys. Enr. Code 4
Supt. – Dr. Neil Winebrenner
  5400 SAINT CHARLES ROAD   60163
MacArthur MS, 1310 S WOLF ROAD   60162
  Joe Palermo, prin.
Sunnyside ES, 5412 ST CHARLES RD   60163
  Richard Riley, prin.
Other Schools – See Bellwood, Northlake

Berwyn, Cook Co., Pop. Code 8
Berwyn North SD 98
Sch. Sys. Enr. Code 4
Supt. – R. F. Smith, 1427 OAK PARK AVE   60402
Lincoln JHS, 6432 16TH ST   60402
  Dr. Gail Duke, prin.
General Custer ES, 1427 OAK PARK AVE   60402
  Lawrence Holstlaw, prin.
Havlicek ES, 6401 15TH ST   60402
  Richard Korzen, prin.
Jefferson ES, 7035 16TH ST   60402
  Donald Wenhart, prin.

Berwyn South SD 100
Sch. Sys. Enr. Code 4
Supt. – Dr. Gary M. Smit
  3105 CLINTON AVE   60402
Emerson ES, 3105 CLINTON AVE   60402
  Mary Kitzberger, prin.
Hiawatha ES, 6539 26TH ST   60402
  James McElwee, prin.
Irving ES, 3501 CLINTON AVE   60402
  Charles Gardner, prin.
Komensky ES, 2515 CUYLER AVE   60402
  Diane Pikcunas, prin.
Pershing ES, 6537 37TH ST   60402
  James Bala, prin.
  _____

St. Leonard School, 3322 CLARENCE AVE   60402
St. Mary of Celle School
  1448 WESLEY AVE   60402
St. Odilo School, 6617 23RD ST   60402
St. Pius X School, 4311 GROVE AVE   60402

Bethalto, Madison Co., Pop. Code 6
Bethalto CUSD 8
Sch. Sys. Enr. Code 5
Supt. – Lewis Hauser, 322 E CENTRAL ST   62010
Trimpe JHS, 910 2ND ST   62010
  Robert Cleveland, prin.
Bethalto East ES, MILLS & ALBERS   62010
  Neil Claussen, prin.
Bethalto West ES, 101 SCHOOL ST   62010
  Barbara Thompson, prin.
Other Schools – See Cottage Hills, Moro
  _____

Our Lady of Peace School
  618 N PRAIRIE ST   62010
Zion Lutheran School, 625 CHURCH DR   62010

Bethany, Moultri Co., Pop. Code 4
Bethany CUSD 301
Sch. Sys. Enr. Code 3
Supt. – R. Don Miller, P O BOX 97   61914
JHS, P O BOX 97   61914 – Robert Doan, prin.
ES, 319 N WASHINGTON   61914
  Marilyn Bayley, prin.

Biggsville, Henderson Co., Pop. Code 2
Union CUSD 115
Supt. – See Gladstone
ES, POST OFFICE   61418 – Donald Daily, prin.

Big Rock, Kane Co., Pop. Code 4
Hinkley-Big Rock CUSD 429
Supt. – See Hinckley
ES, P O BOX 197   60511 – Roy Dittmann, prin.

Bismarck, Vermilion Co., Pop. Code 2
Bismarck CUSD 1
Sch. Sys. Enr. Code 3
Supt. – Timothy Musgrave, P O BOX 157   61814
Bismarck-Henning JHS, P O BOX 157   61814
  Earl Lindsey, prin.
MS, P O BOX 155   61814
  Donald Cunningham, prin.
Other Schools – See Henning

Blackstone, Livingston Co.
Sunbury CCSD 431
Sch. Sys. Enr. Code 1
Supt. – Patricia Guyon, RURAL ROUTE 01   61313
Sunbury Community Consolidated ES
  RURAL ROUTE 01   61313 – Patricia Guyon, prin.

Bloomingdale, Du Page Co., Pop. Code 7
Bloomingdale SD 13
Sch. Sys. Enr. Code 4
Supt. – Dr. Jerome Gordon
  181 S BLOOMINGDALE ROAD   60108
Westfield JHS, 149 FAIRFIELD WAY   60108
  Charles Swangren, prin.
Central ES, 112 DAY ST   60108
  John Markgraf, prin.
Dujardin ES, 166 S EUCLID AVE   60108
  Dr. Janice Cernock, prin.

Community Consolidated SD 93
Supt. – See Carol Stream
Stratford JHS, BOX 251 BUTTERFIELD   60108
  Larry Fox, prin.

Marquardt SD 15
Supt. – See Glendale Heights
Winnebago ES, 195 GREENWAY DR   60108
  Mark Wagener, prin.
  _____

St. Isadore School
  431 W ARMY TRAIL ROAD   60108

Bloomington, McLean Co., Pop. Code 8
Bloomington SD 87
Sch. Sys. Enr. Code 6
Supt. – Dr. Leonard Roberts, P O BOX 249   61702
JHS, 510 E WASHINGTON ST   61701
  Walter Kistenfeger, prin.
Bent ES, 904 N ROOSEVELT STREET   61701
  Dr. Earl Dickson, prin.
Centennial ES, 901 N COLTON AVE   61701
  Dr. Vincent McClean, prin.
Irving ES, 602 W JACKSON ST   61701
  Richard Laleman, prin.
Lincoln ES, 1206 S LEE ST   61701
  Dr. Vincent McClean, prin.
Oakland ES, 1605 E OAKLAND AVE   61701
  Glen Newton, prin.
Sheridan ES, 1403 W WALNUT ST   61701
  Donald Melican, prin.
Stevenson ES, 2106 ARROWHEAD DR   61704
  Dr. Richard White, prin.
Washington ES, 1201 E WASHINGTON ST   61701
  Robert Bryant, prin.

Normal CUSD 5
Supt. – See Normal
Brigham ES, RURAL ROUTE 13 BOX 594   61704
  Ronald Hofbauer, prin.
  _____

Holy Trinity School
  705 N ROOSEVELT AVE   61701
St. Clare School, 1909 E LINCOLN ST   61701
St. Mary School, 603 W JACKSON ST   61701
Trinity Lutheran School
  701 S MADISON ST   61701

Blue Island, Cook Co., Pop. Code 7
Blue Island SD 130
Sch. Sys. Enr. Code 5
Supt. – Dr. Karl Plank
  12300 GREENWOOD AVE   60406
Kerr MS, 12320 GREENWOOD AVE   60406
  Dr. Henry Dannenberg, prin.
Greenbriar ES, 12015 S MAPLE AVE   60406
  Joyce Eddy, prin.
Greenwood ES, 12418 HIGHLAND AVE   60406
  Maude Davis, prin.
Kerr IS, 12320 S GREENWOOD   60406
  John Hoekstra, prin.
Lincoln ES, 2140 BROADWAY ST   60406
  Barbara Mackey, prin.
Mann ES, 2975 W BROADWAY   60406
  Dr. Wilma Rutherford, prin.
Revere MS, 12331 GREGORY ST   60406
  Joyce Eddy, prin.
Whittier ES, 13043 MAPLE AVE   60406
  Rocco Marelli, prin.
Other Schools – See Crestwood

West Harvey-Dixmoor SD 147
Supt. – See Harvey
Garfield ES, 138TH & CHATHAM   60406
  Mary Arnold, prin.
  _____

First Lutheran School, GROVE & ANN STS   60407
St. Benedict School, 2324 NEW ST   60406

St. Isadore School, 12731 WOOD ST   60406

Blue Mound, Macon Co., Pop. Code 4
Blue Mound-Boody CUSD 10
Sch. Sys. Enr. Code 3
Supt. – Jerry Hoffman, P O BOX 238   62513
ES, P O BOX 325   62513 – James Edwards, prin.

Bluffs, Scott Co., Pop. Code 3
Scott-Morgan CUSD 2
Sch. Sys. Enr. Code 2
Supt. – Robert G. Rogers
   100 W ROCKWOOD ST   62621
JHS, 100 W ROCKWOOD ST   62621
   Nyle Waters, prin.
ES, 100 W ROCKWOOD ST   62621
   Nyle Waters, prin.

Bluford, Jefferson Co., Pop. Code 3
Bluford CCSD 114
Sch. Sys. Enr. Code 2
Supt. – William Suddarth, 6TH & PIERCE   62814
ES, SIXTH & PRICE ST   62814
   William Suddarth, prin.

Farrington CCSD 99
Sch. Sys. Enr. Code 1
Supt. – David Stewart, RURAL ROUTE 01   62814
Farrington ES, RURAL ROUTE 01   62814
   David Stewart, prin.

Bolingbrook, Will Co., Pop. Code 8
Valley View CUSD 365U
Supt. – See Romeoville
Addams MS, 905 LILY CACHE LANE   60439
   Kenneth Kalina, prin.
Humphrey MS, 777 FALCONRIDGE WAY   60439
   Gary Catalani, prin.
Ward MS, 200 RECREATION DRIVE   60439
   Michael Damler, prin.
Brook View ES, 520 GARY DR   60439
   John Tibbott, prin.
Independence ES, 230 ORCHARD DR   60439
   Edward Carli, prin.
McGee ES, 179 COMMONWEALTH DR   60439
   Michael Silver, prin.
North View ES, 151 E BRIARCLIFF RD   60439
   William Zielke, prin.
Oak View ES, 150 N SCHMIDT RD   60439
   Dr. Elizabeth Prusaitis, prin.
Salk ES, 500 KING ARTHUR WAY   60439
   Gary Woolwine, prin.
Wood View ES, 197 WINSTON DR   60439
   Dorothy Senese, prin.

Bonfield, Kankakee Co., Pop. Code 2
Herscher CUSD 2
Supt. – See Herscher
ES, P O BOX 96   60913 – William Davison, prin.

Bourbonnais, Kankakee Co., Pop. Code 7
Bourbonnais SD 53
Sch. Sys. Enr. Code 4
Supt. – Ron Goodall
   281 JOHN CASEY DRIVE   60914
JHS, 200 JOHN CASEY DRIVE   60914
   Richard Campbell, prin.
Frost ES, 160 W RIVER ST   60914
   Paul Shellenberger, prin.
Levasseur ES, 601 BETHEL DR   60914
   Pamela Gean, prin.
Shabbona ES, 321 N CONVENT ST   60914
   Tom Patton, prin.
Shepard MS, 325 N CONVENT ST   60914
   James Dezwaan, prin.

St. George CCSD 258
Sch. Sys. Enr. Code 2
Supt. – Stephen Harman
   RURAL ROUTE 01 BOX 103   60914
St. George ES, RURAL ROUTE 01 BOX 103   60914
   Stephen Harman, prin.

Maternity B V M School
   324 E MARSILE ST   60914

Bowen, Hancock Co., Pop. Code 3
Southeastern CUSD 337
Supt. – See Augusta
Southeastern JHS, P O BOX 247   62316
   Terry Robertson, prin.
Southeastern ES, P O BOX 247   62316
   Terry Robertson, prin.

Braceville, Grundy Co., Pop. Code 3
Braceville SD 75
Sch. Sys. Enr. Code 2
Supt. – Ted Struck, P O BOX 178   60407
ES, P O BOX 178   60407 – Ted Struck, prin.

Bradford, Stark Co., Pop. Code 3
Bradford CUSD 1
Sch. Sys. Enr. Code 2
Supt. – Dr. John Connelly, 115 HIGH ST   61421
ES, 345 SILVER ST   61421
   Dr. John Connelly, prin.

Bradley, Kankakee Co., Pop. Code 7
Bradley SD 61
Sch. Sys. Enr. Code 4
Supt. – L. Trumble, 200 STATE ST   60915
Bradley Central MS, 235 N MICHIGAN AVE   60915
   Larry Macari, prin.
Bradley East ES, 610 LIBERTY ST   60915
   Willard Dewitt, prin.
Bradley West ES, 200 STATE ST   60915
   William Bos, prin.

St. Joseph School, 24 N CENTER ST   60915

Braidwood, Will Co., Pop. Code 5
Reed Custer CUSD 2550U
Sch. Sys. Enr. Code 4
Supt. – A. Hendricks, 255 COMET DRIVE   60408
Reed-Custer JHS, 134 S SCHOOL ST   60408
   Thomas Greene, prin.
Braidwood ES, 162 S SCHOOL ST   60408
   Myrna McCarthy, prin.
Other Schools – See Custer Park, Essex

Breese, Clinton Co., Pop. Code 5
Breese SD 12
Sch. Sys. Enr. Code 2
Supt. – Jerry Williams, 1100 N 7TH ST   62230
ES, 1100 N 7TH ST   62230 – Jerry Williams, prin.
Other Schools – See Beckemeyer

St. Rose SD 141-5
Sch. Sys. Enr. Code 2
Supt. – Philip Phillips
   RURAL ROUTE 01 BOX 63   62230
St. Rose ES, RURAL ROUTE 01 BOX 63   62230
   Philip Phillips, prin.

St. Augustine School, 260 S MAIN ST   62230
St. Dominic School, 295 N CLINTON ST   62230

Bridgeport, Lawrence Co., Pop. Code 4
Red Hill CUSD 10
Sch. Sys. Enr. Code 4
Supt. – Gary Glosser, 1250 JUDY AVE   62417
ES, N MAIN STREET   62417
   Lenn Jamerson, prin.
Seed ES, 749 CHURCH ST   62417
   Lenn Jamerson, prin.
Other Schools – See Sumner

Bridgeview, Cook Co., Pop. Code 7
Indian Springs SD 109
Supt. – See Justice
ES, 7800 THOMAS AVE   60455 – Ruth Bill, prin.
Lyle SD 76TH ST   60455
   William Klein, prin.

Ridgeland SD 122
Supt. – See Oak Lawn
Lieb ES, 9101 PEMBROKE LN   60455
   Walter Pleviak, prin.

Brighton, Jersey Co., Pop. Code 2
Piasa CUSD 9
Supt. – See Piasa
Brighton MS North, BUNKER HILL ROAD   62012
   J. Darrell Molen, prin.
Brighton West ES, MAPLE ST BOX 728   62012
   J. Darrell Molen, prin.

Brimfield, Peoria Co., Pop. Code 3
Brimfield CUSD 309
Sch. Sys. Enr. Code 3
Supt. – Bill Hunter, P O BOX 236   61517
ES, P O BOX 426   61517 – James Griner, prin.

Bristol, Kendall Co., Pop. Code 6
Yorkville CUSD 115
Supt. – See Yorkville
ES, P O BOX 177   60512 – Dinah Simmen, prin.

Broadlands, Champaign Co., Pop. Code 2
ABL CUSD 6
Sch. Sys. Enr. Code 2
Supt. – Robert Chinn, P O BOX 62   61816
Abl ES, P O BOX 62   61816 – Robert Chinn, prin.
Other Schools – See Longview

Broadview, Cook Co., Pop. Code 6
Lindop SD 92
Sch. Sys. Enr. Code 2
Supt. – Joseph Matula, 2400 S 18TH AVE   60153
Lindop ES, 2400 S 18TH AVE   60153
   Stephen Latman, prin.

Maywood-Melrose Park-Broadview SD
Supt. – See Maywood
Roosevelt ES, 1927 S 15TH AVE   60153
   Alonzo Hughes, prin.

Broadwell, Logan Co., Pop. Code 2
Broadwell CCSD 68
Sch. Sys. Enr. Code 1
Supt. – Carl Sartwell, 108 OAK   62623
Broadwell Community Consolidated ES
   108 OAK   62623 – Carl Sartwell, prin.

Brookfield, Cook Co., Pop. Code 7
Brookfield SD 95
Sch. Sys. Enr. Code 3
Supt. – Herbert Hageman
   3524 MAPLE AVE   60513
Gross MS, 3525 MAPLE AVE   60513
   James Quilty, prin.
Other Schools – See La Grange Park

La Grange SD 102
Supt. – See La Grange Park
Congress Park ES
   RAYMOND AND SHIELDS   60513
   Shirley Fields, prin.

Lyons SD 103
Supt. – See Lyons
Lincoln ES, GROVE AND SHIELDS AVE   60513
   Peter Zika, prin.

Riverside SD 96
Supt. – See Riverside

Hollywood ES, 3423 HOLLYWOOD AVE   60513
   Bernardine Chimis, prin.

St. Barbara School, 8900 WINDEMERE AVE   60513
St. Paul Lutheran School
   9035 GRANT AVE   60513

Brookport, Massac Co., Pop. Code 4
Massac Unit SD 1
Supt. – See Metropolis
ES, 4TH & CROCKETT ST   62910
   Jeff Richey, prin.
Unity ES, RURAL ROUTE 01   62910
   Steve Kettler, prin.

Browning, Schuyler Co., Pop. Code 2
Schuyler Co. CUSD 1
Supt. – See Rushville
ES   62624 – Michael Lane, prin.

Brownstown, Fayette Co., Pop. Code 3
Brownstown CUSD 201
Sch. Sys. Enr. Code 2
Supt. – Robert Isaacs, P O BOX 255   62418
JHS, P O BOX 255   62418
   Betty-Jeanne Jones, prin.
ES, RURAL ROUTE 02 BOX 255   62418
   Edith Garrett, prin.

Brussels, Calhoun Co., Pop. Code 2
Brussels CUSD 42
Sch. Sys. Enr. Code 1
Supt. – Michael Barry, P O BOX 128   62013
Brussels-Richwood ES, P O BOX 128   62013
   Michael Barry, prin.

Buckley, Iroquois Co., Pop. Code 3
Buckley-Loda CUSD 8
Sch. Sys. Enr. Code 2
Supt. – Dr. Thomas Vaughn, LINCOLN ST   60918
Other Schools – See Loda

St. John Lutheran School, 206 E MAIN   60918

Buda, Bureau Co., Pop. Code 3
Western CUSD 306
Supt. – See Sheffield
Western JHS, STEWART ST   61314
   Merle Horwedel, prin.

Buffalo, Sangamon Co., Pop. Code 3
Tri-City Cusd 1
Sch. Sys. Enr. Code 3
Supt. – Henry Gartner, P O BOX 287   62515
Tri-City JHS, P O BOX 287   62515
   William R. Hardin, prin.
Tri-City ES, P O BOX 287   62515
   Larry Scott, prin.

Buffalo Grove, Cook Co., Pop. Code 7
Aptakisic-Tripp CCSD 102
Supt. – See Prairie View
Pritchett ES, 200 HORATIO BLVD   60089
   Dr. Joan Hochschild, prin.

Kildeer Countryside SD 96
Sch. Sys. Enr. Code 4
Supt. – Dr. David Willard
   135 N ARLINGTON HTS RD #105   60089
Twin Groves MS, 1072 IVY HALL LN   60089
   Peter Keegan, prin.
Prairie ES, 1930 BRANDWYN LANE   60089
   Alice Gruenberg, prin.
Willow Grove ES, 777 CHECKER DR   60089
   Veronica Patt, prin.
Other Schools – See Long Grove

Wheeling CCSD 21
Supt. – See Wheeling
Cooper JHS, 1050 W PLUM GROVE ROAD   60089
   Wendy Billington, prin.
Kilmer ES, 655 GOLFVIEW TER   60089
   Dr. Richard Boos, prin.
Longfellow ES
   501 N ARLINGTON HEIGHTS RD   60089
   Robert White, prin.

St. Mary School
   50 N BUFFALO GROVE ROAD   60090

Buncombe, Johnson Co., Pop. Code 2
Buncombe Consolidated SD 43
Sch. Sys. Enr. Code 2
Supt. – Lindell Croft, P O BOX 40   62912
Buncombe Consolidated ES, P O BOX 40   62912
   Dewaine Prater, prin.

Lick Creek CCSD 16
Sch. Sys. Enr. Code 2
Supt. – Ed Bridewell
   RURAL ROUTE 01 BOX 135   62912
Lick Creek ES, RURAL ROUTE 01 BOX 135   62912
   Ed Bridewell, prin.

Bunker Hill, Macoupin Co., Pop. Code 4
Bunker Hill Cusd 8
Sch. Sys. Enr. Code 3
Supt. – Anthony Prochaska, P O BOX Y   62014
Meissner MS, P O BOX Y   62014
   Harold Wilkinson, prin.
Wolf Ridge Educational MS, P O BOX Y   62014
   Harold Wilkinson, prin.

Burbank, Cook Co., Pop. Code 8
Burbank SD 111
Sch. Sys. Enr. Code 5
Supt. – James Bokenkamp
   7600 CENTRAL AVE   60459

ES, 83RD & LINDER   60459
  Richard Zarzycki, prin.
Byrd ES, 83RD & LAVERGNE   60459
  John Young, prin.
Fry ES, 78TH & MOBILE AVE   60459
  Clyde Senters, prin.
Kennedy ES, 77TH & CENTRAL AVE   60459
  James Rabbitt, prin.
Maddock ES, 83RD ST & SAYRE AVE   60459
  Richard Carter, prin.
McCord Elementary School
  8500 NASHVILLE AVE   60459 – Lois Walery, prin.
Tobin ES, 85TH & NARRAGANSETT   60459
  John Lonosky, prin.

St. Albert the Great School, 5535 STATE RD   60459

Bureau, Bureau Co., Pop. Code 2
Leepertown CCSD 175
Sch. Sys. Enr. Code 1
Supt. – Kim Leonard, P O BOX 1036   61315
Leepertown ES, P O BOX 1036   61315
  Kim Leonard, prin.

Burlington, Kane Co., Pop. Code 2
Central CUSD 301
Sch. Sys. Enr. Code 4
Supt. – Dr. Thomas Fegley, P O BOX 396   60109
Central JHS, P O BOX 396   60109
  Robert Warski, prin.
ES, P O BOX 395   60109 – Randall Moncelle, prin.
Other Schools – See Maple Park, Plato Center

Burnham, Cook Co., Pop. Code 5
Burnham SD 154-5
Sch. Sys. Enr. Code 2
Supt. – John Frattick
  13945 S GREEN BAY AVE   60633
ES, 13945 S GREEN BAY AVE   60633
  Paul Conley, prin.

Burr Ridge, Du Page Co., Pop. Code 5
Gower SD 62
Sch. Sys. Enr. Code 3
Supt. – Dr. Edward Vanmeir
  7941 S MADISON ST   60521
Gower MS, 7941 S MADISON ST   60521
  Douglas Freehauf, prin.
Other Schools – See Willowbrook

Hinsdale CCSD 181
Supt. – See Hinsdale
Elm ES, 15 W 201 60TH ST   60521
  Dale Devine, prin.

Pallisades CCSD 180
Sch. Sys. Enr. Code 2
Supt. – Dr. Drew Starsiak, 15W451 91ST ST   60521
Palisades MS, 15 W 451 91ST ST   60521
  Jane Thompson, prin.
Other Schools – See Hinsdale

Bushnell, McDonough Co., Pop. Code 5
Bushnell-Prairie City CUSD 170
Sch. Sys. Enr. Code 4
Supt. – F. Lynn Hartweger
  845 WALNUT ST   61422
Bushnell-Prairie City JHS, 847 WALNUT ST   61422
  Raymond Krey,Jr., prin.
Bushnell-Prairie City ES, 345 E HESS ST   61422
  Steven Russell, prin.

Byron, Ogle Co., Pop. Code 4
Byron CUSD 226
Sch. Sys. Enr. Code 3
Supt. – William Young, P O BOX K   61010
MS, TOWER ROAD   61010 – Frank Conry, prin.
Morgan ES, TOWER ROAD   61010
  Glen Dallman, prin.

Cahokia, St. Clair Co., Pop. Code 7
Cahokia CUSD 187
Sch. Sys. Enr. Code 5
Supt. – Elmer Kirchoff
  1700 JEROME LANE   62206
Wirth JHS, 1900 MOUSETTE LANE   62206
  David Midkiff, prin.
Huffman ES, 600 ST ROBERT DR   62206
  Tom Kowalski, prin.
Maplewood ES, 600 JEROME LN   62206
  Jerry Dunlap, prin.
Morris ES, 1500 ANDREWS DR   62206
  Lora Jones, prin.
Penniman ES, 300 ANNUNCIATION CT   62206
  Linda Lang, prin.
Other Schools – See East Saint Louis

Holy Family School, 116 E 1ST ST   62206
St. Catherine LaBoure School
  1820 JEROME LN   62206

Cairo, Alexander Co., Pop. Code 6
Cairo Unit SD 1
Sch. Sys. Enr. Code 4
Supt. – W. E. Armstrong, 303 34TH ST   62914
JHS, 2403 WALNUT ST   62914
  Lonnie Henderson, prin.
Bennett MS, 434 18TH ST & WALNUT   62914
  Roimonds Zvirbulis, prin.
Emerson ES, 3101 ELM ST   62914
  Inez Donnigan, prin.

St. Joseph School, 2008 WALNUT ST   62914

Caledonia, Boone Co., Pop. Code 4
Belvidere CUSD 100
Supt. – See Belvidere

ES, 2311 RANDOLPH   61011
  James Anderson, prin.

Calumet City, Cook Co., Pop. Code 8
Calumet City SD 155
Sch. Sys. Enr. Code 3
Supt. – Dr. James Rajchel
  MEMORIAL & SUPERIOR   60409
Wentworth JHS, 528 SUPERIOR AVE   60409
  Gregory O'Rourke, prin.
Wentworth ES, MEMORIAL & SUPERIOR   60409
  Gregory O'Rourke, prin.
Wilson ES, MEMORIAL & WENTWORTH   60409
  Edward McNamara, prin.

Calumet Public SD 132
Sch. Sys. Enr. Code 4
Supt. – Milton George
  1440 W VERMONT AVE   60643
Other Schools – See Chicago

Dolton SD 149
Supt. – See Dolton
Dirkson MS, 1650 MICHIGAN CITY ROAD   60409
  Raymond Wielgos, prin.
Sibley ES, 1550 SIBLEY BLVD   60409
  Alan Jentzen, prin.

Hoover-Schrum Memorial SD 157
Sch. Sys. Enr. Code 3
Supt. – Dr. Robert Schneider
  165TH & GORDON AVE   60409
Schrum Memorial MS
  165TH & GORDON AVE   60409
  Robert Graves, prin.
Schrum Memorial JHS, 150 GORDON AVE   60409
  Robert Graves, prin.
Hoover MS, 161ST & SUPERIOR AVE   60409
  Raymond Scahill, prin.
Hoover West ES, 161ST & SUPERIOR AVE   60409
  Raymond Scahill, prin.

Lincoln ESD 156
Sch. Sys. Enr. Code 3
Supt. – John Frattick, 410 157TH ST   60409
Lincoln ES, 410-157TH ST   60409
  Margaret Longo, prin.

Our Lady of Knock School, 497 163RD ST   60409
St. Andrew the Apostle School
  331-155TH PLACE   60409
St. Viator School, 548 PRICE ST   60409

Cambria, Williamson Co., Pop. Code 4
Carterville CUSD 5
Supt. – See Carterville
ES, P O BOX 98   62915 – Robert Dawson, prin.

Cambridge, Henry Co., Pop. Code 4
Cambridge CUSD 227
Sch. Sys. Enr. Code 3
Supt. – William Schehl, 300 S WEST ST   61238
JHS, 300 S WEST ST   61238 – Dan Caras, prin.
Cambridge Comm. ES, 312 S WEST ST   61238
  Wilbur Wigant, prin.

Campbell Hill, Jackson Co., Pop. Code 2
Trico CUSD 176
Sch. Sys. Enr. Code 4
Supt. – James H. Davis, P O BOX 121   62916
Trico JHS, P O BOX 121   62916
  Clarence Schorn, prin.
Trico ES, P O BOX 144   62916 – Joe O'Dell, prin.

Camp Point, Adams Co., Pop. Code 4
Camp Point CUSD 3
Sch. Sys. Enr. Code 3
Supt. – R. A. Scheiter   62320
Central MS, RURAL ROUTE 01   62320
  Robert Bergman, prin.
Central ES   62320 – Wilfred Flesner, prin.

Canton, Fulton Co., Pop. Code 7
Canton Union SD 66
Sch. Sys. Enr. Code 5
Supt. – Paul Vonderhaar
  20 W WALNUT ST   61520
Ingersoll JHS, 1605 E ASH ST   61520
  Phillip Murphy, prin.
Eastview ES, 1490 E MYRTLE ST   61520
  Thomas Hammond, prin.
Lincoln ES, 20 LINCOLN RD   61520
  Mike Fahrenbacher, prin.
Westview ES, RURAL ROUTE 02   61520
  Ben Bishop, prin.

Cantrall, Sangamon Co., Pop. Code 2
Athens CUSD 213
Supt. – See Athens
ES, POST OFFICE   62625 – J. Curt Benanti, prin.

Capron, Boone Co., Pop. Code 3
North Boone CUSD 200
Supt. – See Poplar Grove
ES   61012 – Richard Smelter, prin.

Carbon Cliff, Rock Island Co., Pop. Code 4
Carbon Cliff-Barstow SD 36
Sch. Sys. Enr. Code 2
Supt. – Harold Roggendorf, P O BOX 10-A   61239
Apollo ES, P O BOX 280   61239
  Bonnie Nelson, prin.
Other Schools – See Barstow

Carbondale, Jackson Co., Pop. Code 8
Carbondale ESD 95
Sch. Sys. Enr. Code 4
Supt. – Larry Jacober, P O BOX 968   62903

Lincoln JHS, 501 S WASHINGTON ST   62901
  Ross Franklin, prin.
Glendale ES, RURAL ROUTE 07   62901
  John Wilkins, prin.
Lewis ES, 801 S LEWIS LN   62901
  Carroll Nelson, prin.
Parrish ES, 121 N PARRISH LN   62901
  Gaylin Fligor, prin.
Thomas ES, 1025 N WALL ST   62901
  Mary Dillard, prin.
Winkler ES, 1218 W FREEMAN ST   62901
  Marylou Goodman, prin.

Giant City CCSD 130
Sch. Sys. Enr. Code 2
Supt. – Manul Goins, RURAL ROUTE 01   62901
Giant City ES, RURAL ROUTE 01   62901
  Dr. Manul Goins, prin.

Unity Point CCSD 140
Sch. Sys. Enr. Code 3
Supt. – Gene Broombaugh
  RURAL ROUTE 01 BOX 199   62901
Unity Point ES, RURAL ROUTE 01   62901
  James Siebert, prin.

Carlinville, Macoupin Co., Pop. Code 6
Carlinville CUSD 1
Sch. Sys. Enr. Code 4
Supt. – James Bottrell, 812 W MAIN ST   62626
JHS, 829 W MAIN ST   62626
  Richard Nicholson, prin.
North ES, 506 N HIGH   62626
  Christine Brinkley, prin.
South ES, 218 S BROAD ST   62626
  Christine Brinkley, prin.
West ES, 450 W BUCHANAN ST   62626
  Sue Fischer, prin.

Carlock, McLean Co., Pop. Code 2
Normal CUSD 5
Supt. – See Normal
ES, P O BOX 165   61725 – Teresa Smith, prin.

Carlyle, Clinton Co., Pop. Code 5
Carlyle CUSD 1
Sch. Sys. Enr. Code 4
Supt. – Robert H. Evans
  RURAL ROUTE 127 N   62231
ES, 951 6TH ST   62231 – Bill Kolmer, prin.
St. Mary's Public ES
  LIVINGSTON & ROUTE 127   62231
  Don Rahm, prin.

Carmi, White Co., Pop. Code 6
Carmi-White Co. CUSD 5
Sch. Sys. Enr. Code 4
Supt. – Robert Kidd, 301 W MAIN ST   62821
MS, 201 W MAIN ST   62821 – David Johnson, prin.
Big Prairie ES, RURAL ROUTE 01 BOX 237   62821
  Lowell Smith, prin.
Jefferson ES, 701 4TH ST   62821
  Dale Medlin, prin.
Lincoln ES, 113 S TENTH ST   62821
  Frank Barbre, prin.
Other Schools – See Crossville

Carol Stream, Du Page Co., Pop. Code 7
Benjamin SD 25
Supt. – See West Chicago
Evergreen ES, 1041 EVERGREEN DR   60188
  James Ask, prin.

Community Consolidated SD 93
Sch. Sys. Enr. Code 4
Supt. – John Dibuono, P O BOX 88093   60188
ES, 422 SIOUX LN   60188 – Philip Kemp, prin.
De Shane ES, 475 CHIPPEWA TRL   60188
  Noel Kalis, prin.
Stream MS, 283 EL PASO LANE   60188
  Larry Fox, prin.
Western Trails ES, 860 IDAHO ST   60188
  Arthur Mesch, prin.
Other Schools – See Bloomingdale, Hanover Park

Carpentersville, Kane Co., Pop. Code 7
Barrington CUSD 220
Supt. – See Barrington
Sunny Hill ES, 2500 HELM ROAD   60110
  Ronald Brandt, prin.
Woodland ES, 770 NAVAJO DR   60110
  Herb Price, prin.

Dundee CUSD 300
Supt. – See Dundee
MS, 100 CLEVELAND AVE   60110
  Leigh Gilbert, prin.
Golfview ES, 124 GOLFVIEW LN   60110
  Richard Rayka, prin.
Lakewood ES, 1651 RAVINE LN   60110
  George Strombom, prin.
Meadowdale ES, 14 ASH ST   60110
  Craig Sunstedt, prin.
Parkview ES, 122 CARPENTER BLVD   60110
  Bernadette Alber, prin.
Perry ES, 251 AMARILLO DR   60110
  Russell Ballard, prin.

Carrier Mills, Saline Co., Pop. Code 4
Carrier Mills-Stonefort CUSD 2
Sch. Sys. Enr. Code 3
Supt. – William Hull, RURAL ROUTE 45   62917
ES, E WASHINGTON   62917
  Joseph Rodocker, prin.

Carrollton, Greene Co., Pop. Code 5
Carrollton CUSD 1
Sch. Sys. Enr. Code 3
Supt. – Dr. William W. Riley, 950 3RD ST 62016
ES, S 4TH ST 62016 – Bill Schimpf, prin.

St. John's School, 3RD & LOCUST STS 62016

Carterville, Williamson Co., Pop. Code 5
Carterville CUSD 5
Sch. Sys. Enr. Code 4
Supt. – Dr. Robert Mees
　　306 VIRGINIA AVE 02910
JHS, 116 SCHOOL ST 62918
　　Thomas Armstrong, prin.
ES, 116 SCHOOL ST 62918 – Anna Duncan, prin.
ES, RURAL ROUTE 03 BOX 240 62918
　　Jean Ellen Reynolds, prin.
Other Schools – See Cambria

Carthage, Hancock Co., Pop. Code 5
Hancock Central CUSD 338
Sch. Sys. Enr. Code 3
Supt. – Thomas J. Phelps 62321
Hancock Central JHS
　　BUCHANAN & WASHINGTON 62321
　　James Hamilton, prin.
Hancock MS
　　RUCHANAN & WASHINGTON 62321
　　(—), prin.
Union Douglas ES, RURAL ROUTE 01 62321
　　John Hurwitz, prin.

Cary, McHenry Co., Pop. Code 6
Cary CCSD 26
Sch. Sys. Enr. Code 4
Supt. – Richard Fluck, 15 S SECOND ST 60013
JHS, 233 E ORIOLE TRAIL 60013
　　Robert Lipinski, prin.
Briargate ES, 100 S WULFF ST 60013
　　Eligio Marcheschi, prin.
Maplewood ES, 422 KRENZ AVE 60013
　　James Waschbusch, prin.
Oak Knoll ES, 409 1ST ST 60013
　　John Sanders, prin.

SS Peter & Paul School, 416 1ST ST 60013

Casey, Clark Co., Pop. Code 5
Casey-Westfield CUSD 4C
Sch. Sys. Enr. Code 4
Supt. – James R. Koss, P O BOX C 62420
Casey-Westfield JHS, 306 E EDGAR AVE 62420
　　Richard Yandell, prin.
Monroe ES, 301 E MONROE AVE 62420
　　John Shoot, prin.
Roosevelt MS, 401 E MAIN ST 62420
　　John Shoot, prin.
Other Schools – See Westfield

Caseyville, St. Clair Co., Pop. Code 5
Collinsville CUSD 10
Supt. – See Collinsville
ES, 433 S 2ND ST 62232 – Ann Moss, prin.
Hollywood Heights ES, 6 OAKLAND DR 62232
　　Dr. Fred Bloss, prin.

East St. Louis SD 189
Supt. – See East Saint Louis
Bluff View Park ES, 8100 BUNKUM RD 62232
　　Levi Dozier, prin.

St. Stephen School, 111 S 2ND ST 62232

Catlin, Vermilion Co., Pop. Code 4
Catlin CUSD 5
Sch. Sys. Enr. Code 3
Supt. – Joseph D. Stutsman, P O BOX 323 C 61817
ES, P O BOX 323 B 61817 – Robert Shafer, prin.

Cedar Point, La Salle Co., Pop. Code 2
John Kennedy CCSD 129
Sch. Sys. Enr. Code 1
Supt. – C. Ray Watson, P O BOX 43 61316
Kennedy ES, POST OFFICE 61316
　　C. Ray Watson, prin.

Centralia, Marion Co., Pop. Code 7
Central City SD 133
Sch. Sys. Enr. Code 2
Supt. – (—), 129 DOUGLAS ST 62801
Central City ES, 129 DOUGLAS ST 62801
　　(—), prin.

Centralia SD 135
Sch. Sys. Enr. Code 4
Supt. – Dr. Roger Jensen, 400 S ELM ST 62801
JHS, 900 S PINE ST 62801 – Donald Bretsch, prin.
Bronson ES, 226 CHICAGO AVE 62801
　　Kenneth Spicer, prin.
Field ES, 1100 S LOCUST ST 62801
　　Clara Rouse, prin.
Irving ES, 200 S PINE ST 62801
　　Clara Rouse, prin.
Jordan ES, 161 EAST ST 62801
　　Kenneth Spicer, prin.
Lincoln MS, 501 N ELM ST 62801
　　Donald Rightnowar, prin.
Schiller ES, 800 W 4TH ST 62801
　　Donald Rightnowar, prin.

Grand Prairie CCSD 6
Sch. Sys. Enr. Code 2
Supt. – Mark Scheurich
　　RURAL ROUTE 05 BOX 202 62801

Grand Prairie ES
　　RURAL ROUTE 05 BOX 202 62801
　　Mark Scheurich, prin.

North Wamac SD 186
Sch. Sys. Enr. Code 2
Supt. – Allan McCarthy, 1500 CASE ST 62801
North Wamac ES, 1500 CASE ST 62801
　　Allan McCarthy, prin.

Raccoon CSD 1
Sch. Sys. Enr. Code 1
Supt. – Lillian Phillips, RURAL ROUTE 01 62801
Raccoon Consolidated ES
　　RURAL ROUTE 01 62801 – Roger Campbell, prin.

Willow Grove SD 46
Sch. Sys. Enr. Code 2
Supt. – Howard Lambert, 815 W 7TH ST 62801
Willow Grove ES, 815 W 7TH ST 62801
　　Howard Lambert, prin.

St. Mary School, 424 E BROADWAY 62801
Trinity Lutheran School
　　203 S PLEASANT ST 62801

Centreville, St Clair Co., Pop. Code 6
East St. Louis SD 189
Supt. – See East Saint Louis
Kennedy ES, 700 RIDGE AVE 62203
　　Bessie Peabody, prin.

Cerro Gordo, Piatt Co., Pop. Code 4
Cerro Gordo CUSD 100
Sch. Sys. Enr. Code 3
Supt. – Wayne Ingalls, P O BOX 98 61818
JHS, 300 E DURFEE 61818 – Keith Ashcraft, prin.
ES, P O BOX 98 61818 – Keith Ashcraft, prin.

Chadwick, Carroll Co., Pop. Code 3
Chadwick CUSD 399
Sch. Sys. Enr. Code 2
Supt. – Howard Kennedy, P O BOX 15 61014
ES, P O BOX 15 61014 – Nina Fritz, prin.

Champaign, Champaign Co., Pop. Code 8
Champaign CUSD 4
Sch. Sys. Enr. Code 6
Supt. – Dr. Timothy Hyland, 703 S NEW ST 61820
Champaign MS at Columbia
　　1102 N NEIL ST 61820 – Michael Cain, prin.
Edison MS, 306 W GREEN ST 61820
　　John Harland, prin.
Jefferson MS, 1115 S CRESCENT DRIVE 61821
　　Gary Niehaus, prin.
Bottenfield ES, 1801 S PROSPECT AVE 61820
　　Dr. Marcia Hull, prin.
Busey ES, 1605 W KIRBY AVE 61821
　　Doris Jones, prin.
Franklin ES, 817 N HARRIS AVE 61820
　　Jim Casey, prin.
Garden Hills ES, 2001 GARDEN HILLS DR 61821
　　Michael Hough, Jr., prin.
Howard ES, 1117 W PARK AVE 61821
　　Margaret Stillwell, prin.
Kenwood ES, 1001 STRATFORD DR 61821
　　John McGinnis, prin.
Robeson ES, 2501 SOUTHMOOR DR 61821
　　Thomas Pickett, prin.
Washington ES, 606 E GROVE ST 61820
　　Hester Suggs, prin.
Westview ES, 703 S RUSSELL ST 61821
　　William Freeman, prin.

Holy Cross School, 410 W WHITE ST 61820
St. John Lutheran School, 509 S MATTES 61821
St. Matthew School
　　1307 LINCOLNSHIRE DR 61821

Chandlerville, Cass Co., Pop. Code 3
Chandlerville CUSD 62
Sch. Sys. Enr. Code 2
Supt. – Ray Morelli, P O BOX 369 62627
ES, P O BOX 369 62627 – Ray Morelli, prin.

Channahon, Will Co., Pop. Code 5
Channahon SD 17
Sch. Sys. Enr. Code 3
Supt. – Richard Dombrowski
　　1210 SUNSET DRIVE 60410
JHS, CHANNAHON-MINOOKA ROAD 60410
　　Tom Lesniak, prin.
Galloway ES, 1201 SUNSET DR 60410
　　Joan Ferguson, prin.

Charleston, Coles Co., Pop. Code 7
Charleston CUSD 1
Sch. Sys. Enr. Code 5
Supt. – Dr. William E. Hill
　　410 W POLK AVE 61920
JHS, 910 SMITH DRIVE 61920
　　John A. Dively, prin.
Jefferson ES, 801 JEFFERSON AVE 61920
　　Jim Louthan, prin.
Lincoln ES, 4 W MADISON AVE 61920
　　Patricia Tucker-Ladd, prin.
Twain ES, 1021 13TH ST 61920
　　Patricia Tucker-Ladd, prin.
Sandburg ES, 1924 REYNOLDS DR 61920
　　Dr. Joann Bock, prin.
Other Schools – See Ashmore, Lerna

Chatham, Sangamon Co., Pop. Code 6
Ball Chatham CUSD 5
Sch. Sys. Enr. Code 4
Supt. – Donald Kauerauf, 500 S PINE ST 62629

Glenwood JHS
　　RURAL ROUTE 01 BOX 193 62629
　　Rick Taylor, prin.
Ball ES, RURAL ROUTE 01 62629
　　G. Jackson, prin.
ES, 525 S COLLEGE ST 62629
　　William Bird, prin.

Chatsworth, Livingston Co., Pop. Code 4
Prairie Central CUSD 8
Supt. – See Forrest
ES, P O BOX 60921 – Joseph Delaney, prin.

Chebanse, Iroquois Co., Pop. Code 4
Central CUSD 4
Supt. – See Clifton
ES, P O BOX 8 60922 – Nancie Alexander, prin.

Zion Lutheran School
　　RURAL ROUTE 01 BOX 14 60922

Chenoa, McLean Co., Pop. Code 4
Chenoa CUSD 9
Sch. Sys. Enr. Code 3
Supt. – Alfred Smith, 202 S 3RD AVE 61726
ES, S SECOND AVE 61726 – Thomas Krones, prin.

Cherry, Bureau Co., Pop. Code 3
Cherry SD 92
Sch. Sys. Enr. Code 1
Supt. – Richard Mariani, 314 S MAIN 61317
ES, 314 S MAIN ST 61317 – Richard Mariani, prin.

Cherry Valley, Winnebago Co., Pop. Code 3
Rockford SD 205
Supt. – See Rockford
ES, 619 W STATE ST 61016 – John Johnson, prin.

Chester, Randolph Co., Pop. Code 6
Chester CUSD 139
Sch. Sys. Enr. Code 3
Supt. – Harold Diebolt
　　1901 SWANWICK ST 62233
ES, 650 OPDYKE ST 62233 – Dana Thornton, prin.

St. John Lutheran School
　　302 W HOLMES ST 62233
St. Mary's School, 835 SWANWICK ST 62233

Chicago, Cook Co., Pop. Code 12
Calumet Public SD 132
Supt. – See Calumet City
Calumet MS, 1440 W VERMONT AVE 60643
　　Bernard Jumbeck, prin.
Burr Oak ES, 1440 W 125TH ST 60643
　　Dr. Matthew Racich, prin.
Calumet K-1 PS, 1301 W VERMONT AVE 60643
　　Bernard Jumbeck, prin.

Central Stickney SD 110
Sch. Sys. Enr. Code 2
Supt. – Dr. James Nelson
　　50TH ST & S LONG AVE 60638
Sahs ES, 50TH ST & S LONG AVE 60638
　　Dr. James Nelson, prin.

Cicero SD 99
Supt. – See Cicero
Roosevelt ES, 15TH ST AND 50TH AVE 60657
　　E. Aksamit, prin.

City of Chicago SD 299
Sch. Sys. Enr. Code 8
Supt. – Dr. Manford Byrd, Jr.
　　1819 W PERSHING ROAD 60609
Arai MS, 900 W WILSON AVE 60640
　　Nathan Lofton, Jr., prin.
Black Magnet ES, 9101 S EUCLID AVE 60617
　　Dr. Patricia McGlinn, prin.
Burns MS, 2514 S CENTRAL PARK AVE 60623
　　Donald Kriz, prin.
Carver MS, 801 E 133RD ST 60627
　　Joseph Kazmierczak, prin.
Clark MS, 5101 W HARRISON ST 60644
　　Clara Holton, prin.
Cooper Upper Cycle JHS
　　1645 W 18TH PLACE 60608
　　Dr. Mary Mikros, prin.
Doolittle IS, 535 E 35TH ST 60616
　　Elisha Walker, prin.
Douglass MS, 543 N WALLER AVE 60644
　　Alvin Lubov, prin.
Dyett MS, 555 E 51ST ST 60615
　　Alvin Boyd, prin.
Hope Community Academy
　　5515 S LOWE AVE 60621 – Joseph Lee, prin.
McCosh MS, 6543 S CHAMPLAIN AVE 60637
　　Ronald Robinson, prin.
Medill IS, 1326 W 14TH PL 60608
　　Dr. James Malles, prin.
Morton Upper Cycle JHS, 431 N TROY ST 60612
　　Elmer Newell, prin.
Piccolo MS, 1040 N KEELER AVE 60651
　　Dr. Thomas Stewart, prin.
Saucedo Magnet MS, 2850 W 24TH BLVD 60623
　　Karen Morris, prin.
Schiller MS, 640 W SCOTT ST 60610
　　Doris Barnes, prin.
Von Steuben Upper Cycle JHS
　　5039 N KIMBALL AVE 60625
　　William Schertler, prin.
Warren MS, 9239 S JEFFERY AVE 60617
　　Dian Cooper, prin.
Wirth Experimental JHS
　　4959 S BLACKSTONE AVE 60615
　　Elizabeth Jochner, prin.

Woodson North MS, 4414 S EVANS AVE   60653
  William Taylor, prin.
Abbott ES, 3630 S WELLS ST   60609
  Michael Jacobson, prin.
Addams ES, 10810 S AVENUE H   60617
  Alice Keane, prin.
Agassiz ES, 2851 N SEMINARY AVE   60657
  Robert Guercio, prin.
Alcott ES, 2625 N ORCHARD ST   60614
  Seymour Rabens, prin.
Aldridge ES, 630 E 131ST ST   60627
  George Pazell, prin.
Altgeld ES, 1340 W 71ST ST   60636
  Julian Kanner, prin.
Andersen ES, 1148 N HONORE ST   60622
  Marie Iska, prin.
Anthony ES Branch Of Burnham
  9800 S TORRENCE AVE   60617
  Regina Koehl, prin.
Armour ES, 950 W 33RD PL   60608
  Oriano Nomellini, prin.
Armstrong ES-Branch
  5221 W CONGRESS PKY   60644
  Benjamin Terry, prin.
Armstrong MS, 5345 W CONGRESS PKY   60644
  Benjamin Terry, prin.
Armstrong ES, 2111 W ESTES AVE   60645
  Arline Hersh, prin.
Attucks ES, 3813 S DEARBORN ST   60609
  Marcella Davis, prin.
Audubon ES, 3500 N HOYNE AVE   60618
  Juris Graudins, prin.
Avalon Park ES, 8045 S KENWOOD AVE   60619
  Charles McCabe Jr., prin.
Avondale ES, 2945 N SAWYER AVE   60618
  Renetta Jarka, prin.
Banneker ES, 6656 S NORMAL BLVD   60621
  Rufus Brown, prin.
Barnard ES, 10354 S CHARLES ST   60643
  Muriel Vonalbade, prin.
Barry ES, 2828 N KILBOURN AVE   60641
  John Duffey, prin.
Barton ES, 7650 S WOLCOTT AVE   60620
  Marian Eugene, prin.
Bass ES, 6554 S MAY ST   60621
  Marcella Gillie, prin.
Bateman ES, 4214 N RICHMOND ST   60618
  Manuel Sanchez, prin.
Beale ES, 6006 S PEORIA ST   60621
  Lillian Nicholson, prin.
Beasley Academic Center
  5255 S STATE ST   60609
  William McNerney, prin.
Beaubien ES, 5025 N LARAMIE AVE   60630
  Dr. Thomas Plain, prin.
Beethoven ES, 25 W 47TH ST   60609
  Grace Dawson, prin.
Beidler ES, 3151 W WALNUT ST   60612
  Ernest Billups, prin.
Belding ES, 4257 N TRIPP AVE   60641
  Thomas Walter, prin.
Bell ES, 3730 N OAKLEY AVE   60618
  Leo Priebe, prin.
Bennett ES, 10115 S PRAIRIE AVE   60628
  John McCormick, prin.
Bethune ES, 3030 W ARTHINGTON ST   60612
  Dr. Warren Franczyk, prin.
Black Magnet ES Branch
  7133 S COLES AVE   60649
  Patricia McGlinn, prin.
Blaine ES, 1420 W GRACE ST   60613
  Dr. Karl Siewers, prin.
Bond ES, 7050 S MAY ST   60621
  Donald Prather, prin.
Bontemps ES, 1240 W 58TH ST   60636
  Kathryn Milner, prin.
Boone ES, 6710 N WASHTENAW AVE   60645
  Anastasia Graven, prin.
Bradwell ES, 7736 S BURNHAM AVE   60649
  Camille Roby, prin.
Brenan ES, 11411 S EGGLESTON AVE   60628
  George Scripp, prin.
Brenneman ES, 4251 N CLARENDON AVE   60613
  William Haran, prin.
Brentano ES, 2723 N FAIRFIELD AVE   60647
  Dr. Patricia Kubistal, prin.
Bridge ES, 3800 N NEW ENGLAND AVE   60634
  Ann Bannor, prin.
Bright ES, 10740 S CALHOUN AVE   60617
  Barbara Gallagher, prin.
Brown ES, 54 N HERMITAGE AVE   60612
  Dr. Shjayle Gerstein, prin.
Brownell ES, 6741 S MICHIGAN AVE   60637
  Ruth Williams, prin.
Bryn Mawr ES, 7355 S JEFFERY BLVD   60649
  Joseph Lavizzo, Jr., prin.
Budlong ES, 2701 W FOSTER AVE   60625
  Becky Orphan, prin.
Bunche ES, 6515 S ASHLAND AVE   60636
  Patrick Kenny, prin.
Burbank ES, 2035 N MOBILE AVE   60639
  Hiram Byoyls, prin.
Burke ES, 5356 S DR M L KING DR   60615
  June Chenelle, prin.
Burley ES, 1630 W BARRY AVE   60657
  Barbara Gordon, prin.
Burnham ES, 1903 E 96TH ST   60617
  Regina Koehl, prin.
Burnside Scholastic ES, 650 E 91ST PL   60619
  Elaine Shannon, prin.
Burr ES, 1621 W WABANSIA AVE   60622
  Scott Rzechula, prin.
Burroughs ES, 3542 S WASHTENAW AVE   60632
  Anthony Pasko, prin.

Byford ES, 5600 W IOWA ST   60651
  Leroy Boyce, prin.
Byrd Community ES, 363 W HILL ST   60610
  Janis Todd, prin.
Byrn Mawr ES-Branch
  7401 S CHAPPEL AVE   60649
  Joseph Lavizzo Jr., prin.
Byrne ES, 5329 S OAK PARK AVE   60638
  Dr. Randy Wortman, prin.
Caldwell ES, 8546 S CREGIER AVE   60617
  Genevieve Massey, prin.
Calhoun North ES, 2833 W ADAMS ST   60612
  Richard Portee, prin.
Cameron ES, 1234 N MONTICELLO AVE   60651
  Thomas Culhane, prin.
Canty ES, 3740 N PANAMA AVE   60634
  Michael Striegl, prin.
Cardenas ES, 2345 S MILLARD AVE   60623
  Dolores Fitzgerald, prin.
Carnegie ES, 1414 E 61ST PL   60637
  Mary Timlin, prin.
Carpenter ES, 1250 W ERIE ST   60622
  Walter Kazmier, prin.
Carroll ES, 2929 W 83RD ST   60652
  Mae Simon, prin.
Carter ES, 5740 S MICHIGAN AVE   60637
  Rita Mitchell, prin.
Carver PS, 901 E 133RD PL   60627
  Alma Jones, prin.
Cassell ES, 11314 S SPAULDING AVE   60655
  Ruth Muth, prin.
Cather ES, 2908 W WASHINGTON BLVD   60612
  Jerome Tunney, prin.
Chalmers ES, 2745 W ROOSEVELT RD   60608
  Donald Kimball, prin.
Chappell ES, 5145 N LEAVITT ST   60625
  (—), prin.
Chase ES, 2021 N POINT ST   60647
  Martin Ellin, prin.
Chopin ES, 2450 W RICE ST   60622
  Dolores Engelskirchen, prin.
Clark ES-Branch Of Key
  1045 S MONITOR AVE   60644
  Louise Perez, prin.
Clay ES, 13231 S BURLEY AVE   60633
  Walter Leyden, prin.
Cleveland ES, 3121 W BYRON ST   60618
  Robert Donald, prin.
Clinton ES, 6110 N FAIRFIELD AVE   60659
  Robert Gallagher, prin.
Clissold ES, 2350 W 110TH PL   60643
  Donald Bayer, prin.
Coles ES, 8440 S PHILLIPS AVE   60617
  Theresa Parker, prin.
Colman ES, 4655 S DEARBORN ST   60609
  Harry Donahoo, Jr., prin.
Columbus ES, 1003 N LEAVITT ST   60622
  Joseph Edmonds, prin.
Cook ES, 8150 S BISHOP ST   60620
  George Eddings, prin.
Coonley ES, 4046 N LEAVITT ST   60618
  Charles Pace, prin.
Cooper Upper Cycle ES, 1645 W 18TH PL   60608
  Dr. Mary Mikros, prin.
Copernicus ES, 6010 S THROOP ST   60636
  Dr. Edward Bennett, prin.
Corkery ES, 2510 S KILDARE AVE   60623
  Shelby Grant, prin.
Crown Community ES
  2128 S SAINT LOUIS AVE   60623
  Terrance Murphy, prin.
Cuffe ES, 1540 W 84TH ST   60620
  William Cox Jr., prin.
Cullen ES, 10650 S EBERHART AVE   60628
  Ruby Anderson, prin.
Curtis ES, 11445 S STATE ST   60628
  Osanna Nesper, prin.
Darwin ES, 3116 W BELDEN AVE   60647
  John Paton, prin.
Davis ES, 3014 W 39TH PL   60632
  David Gardner, prin.
Dawes ES, 3810 W 81ST PL   60652 – (—), prin.
De Priest ES, 140 S CENTRAL AVE   60644
  Ruth Knight, prin.
Decatur Classical ES
  7030 N SACRAMENTO AVE   60645
  Anastasia Graven, prin.
Deland ES, 3937 W WILCOX ST   60624
  Bernard Tanenbaum, prin.
Deneen ES, 7240 S WABASH AVE   60619
  Harold Moody, prin.
Dett ES, 2306 W MAYPOLE AVE   60612
  Dr. Donald Feinstein, prin.
Dever ES, 3436 N OSCEOLA AVE   60634
  Grace Stagno, prin.
Dewey ES, 5415 S UNION AVE   60609
  Robert Kellberg, prin.
Diego Community Academy
  1313 N CLAREMONT AVE   60622
  Lawrence McDougald, prin.
Dirksen ES, 8601 W FOSTER AVE   60656
  Alvin Bass, prin.
Disney Magnet ES, 4140 N MARINE DR   60613
  John Bean, prin.
Dixon ES, 8306 S SAINT LAWRENCE AVE   60619
  Joan Crisler, prin.
Dodge ES, 2651 W WASHINGTON BLVD   60612
  John Nichols, prin.
Donoghue Child Parent Center
  707 E 37TH ST   60653 – Marion Joplin, prin.
Donoghue ES, 707 E 37TH ST   60653
  Marion Joplin, prin.
Doolittle PS, 521 E 35TH ST   60616
  Henry Coretz, prin.

Dore ES, 6108 S NATOMA AVE   60638
  Dr. Joseph Lineman, prin.
Douglas Community ES
  3200 S CALUMET AVE   60616
  Rebecca Henderson, prin.
Drake ES, 2722 S M L KING DR   60616
  Lena Gaines, prin.
Drummond ES, 1845 W CORTLAND ST   60622
  Dudley Nee, prin.
Dubois ES, 330 E 133RD ST   60627
  Joyce Johnson, prin.
Dulles ES, 6311 S CALUMET AVE   60637
  Melvyn Cornelius, prin.
Dumas ES, 6650 S ELLIS AVE   60637
  Sylvia Peters, prin.
Dunne ES, 10845 S UNION AVE   60628
  Dr. Early Nichols, prin.
Dvorak ES, 3615 W 16TH ST   60623
  Stanley Smart, prin.
Earhart ES Branch of Hoyne
  1710 E 93RD ST   60617 – Joyce Kempf, prin.
Earle ES, 6121 S HERMITAGE AVE   60636
  Scott Feaman, prin.
Eberhart ES, 3400 W 65TH PL   60629
  Joyce Kempf, prin.
Ebinger ES, 7350 W PRATT AVE   60631
  Dr. Frances Pietch, prin.
Edgebrook ES, 6525 N HIAWATHA AVE   60646
  Dr. Diane Maciejewski, prin.
Edison ES, 6220 N OLCOTT AVE   60631
  Joseph Catanzaro, prin.
Edwards ES, 4815 S KARLOV AVE   60632
  Dr. William Murawski, prin.
Einstein ES, 3830 S COTTAGE GROVE AVE   60653
  Sander Postol, prin.
Ellington Branch ES, 241 N CENTRAL AVE   60644
  Vernon Robinson, prin.
Ellington ES, 224 N CENTRAL AVE   60644
  Vernon Robinson, prin.
Emmet ES, 5500 W MADISON ST   60644
  Carol Reardon, prin.
Ericson ES, 3600 W FIFTH AVE   60624
  Edith Edington, prin.
Esmond ES, 1865 W MONTVALE AVE   60643
  Earl Fornaciari, prin.
Everett ES, 3419 S BELL AVE   60608
  Anthony Pasko, prin.
Evers ES, 9811 S LOWE AVE   60628
  Emmerine Clarkston, prin.
Falconer ES, 3020 N LAMON AVE   60641
  Julian Lewit, prin.
Faraday ES, 3250 W MONROE ST   60624
  Edward Hegarty, prin.
Farnsworth ES, 5414 N LINDER AVE   60630
  Dr. Catherine Wells, prin.
Farren ES, 5055 S STATE ST   60609
  William Auksi, prin.
Fermi ES, 1415 E 70TH ST   60637
  Cora Smith, prin.
Fernwood ES, 10041 S UNION AVE   60628
  George Turk, prin.
Field ES, 7019 N ASHLAND AVE   60626
  Florence Paskind, prin.
Fiske ES, 6145 S INGLESIDE AVE   60637
  Clarice Jackson, prin.
Fleming ES Branch of Grimes
  4918 W 64TH ST   60638 – Joyce Seidel, prin.
Fort Dearborn ES, 9025 S THROOP ST   60620
  Edwin Scott, prin.
Foster Park ES, 8530 S WOOD ST   60620
  Robert Nelson, prin.
Franklin Magnet ES
  225 W EVERGREEN AVE   60610
  Alice Maresh, prin.
Frazier ES, 4027 W GRENSHAW ST   60624
  Lynn Stinnette, prin.
Fuller ES, 4214 S SAINT LAWRENCE AVE   60653
  Cozette Epps-Buckney, prin.
Fulton ES-Branch
  1800 W GARFIELD BLVD   60609
  John Jones, prin.
Fulton ES, 5300 S HERMITAGE AVE   60609
  John Jones, prin.
Funston ES, 2010 N CENTRAL PARK AVE   60647
  Sally Acker, prin.
Gale Community ES, 1631 W JONQUIL TER   60626
  Edis Snyder, prin.
Gallistel Language ES, 10347 S EWING AVE   60617
  Hulon Johnson, prin.
Garvey ES, 10309 S MORGAN ST   60643
  Eleanor Temple, prin.
Garvy ES, 5225 N OAK PARK AVE   60656
  Joseph Catanzaro, prin.
Gary ES, 3740 W 31ST ST   60623
  Robert Doyle, prin.
Gershwin ES, 6206 S RACINE AVE   60636
  Frank Moscowitz, prin.
Gillespie ES, 9301 S STATE ST   60619
  Thelma Merchant, prin.
Gladstone ES, 1231 S DAMEN AVE   60608
  Estella Faulk, prin.
Goethe ES, 2236 N ROCKWELL ST   60647
  Jean Walker, prin.
Goldblatt ES, 4257 W ADAMS ST   60624
  Phedonia Johnson, prin.
Goldsmith ES Branch of Burnham
  10211 S CRANDON AVE   60617
  Dr. James Bernerd, prin.
Gompers ES, 12302 S STATE ST   60628
  Dr. Blondean Day, prin.
Goodlow Magnet ES, 2040 W 62ND ST   60636
  James Gubbins, prin.
Goudy ES, 5120 N WINTHROP AVE   60640
  Dr. Thomas McDonald, prin.

Graham ES, 4436 S UNION AVE 60609
  Mary Ryan, prin.
Grant ES, 145 S CAMPBELL AVE 60612
  Donald Moran, prin.
Gray ES, 3730 N LARAMIE AVE 60641
  Stuart Gold, prin.
Greeley ES, 832 W SHERIDAN RD 60613
  Ronald Cestar, prin.
Green ES, 1150 W 96TH ST 60643
  Vera Green, prin.
Greene ES, 3537 S PAULINA ST 60609
  John Daly Jr., prin.
Gregory ES, 3715 W POLK ST 60624
  Sherye Garmony, prin.
Gresham ES, 8510 S GREEN ST 60620
  Shirley Pittman, prin.
Grimes ES, 5450 W 64TH PL 60638
  Joyce Seidel, prin.
Grissom ES, 12810 S ESCANABA AVE 60633
  Walter Leyden, prin.
Guggenheim ES, 7141 S MORGAN ST 60621
  Michael Alexander, prin.
Gunsaulus Scholastic Academy
  4420 S SACRAMENTO AVE 60632
  Jane Weldon, prin.
Haines ES, 247 W 23 PLACE 60607
  Edmond Walsh, prin.
Hale ES, 6140 S MELVINA AVE 60638
  Dr. Joseph Lineman, prin.
Hamilton ES, 1650 W CORNELIA AVE 60657
  Mila Strasburg, prin.
Hamline ES, 4747 S BISHOP ST 60609
  Dr. Walter Bjork, prin.
Hammond ES, 2819 W 21ST PL 60623
  Catherine Glynn, prin.
Hanson Park ES, 5411 W FULLERTON AVE 60639
  Dr. Frank Depaul, prin.
Harte ES, 1556 E 56TH ST 60637
  Daniel O'Neill, prin.
Hartigan ES, 8 W ROOT ST 60609
  James Graves, Jr., prin.
Harvard ES, 7525 S HARVARD AVE 60620
  Alma Heck, prin.
Haugan ES, 4540 N HAMLIN AVE 60625
  Marcellus Stamps, Jr., prin.
Hawthorne Scholastic ES
  3319 N CLIFTON AVE 60657 – June Dudeck, prin.
Hay Community Academy
  1018 N LARAMIE AVE 60651
  Edward Kwasigroch, prin.
Hay Community Academy Branch
  849 N LEAMINGTON AVE 60651
  Edward Kwasigroch, prin.
Hayt ES, 1518 W GRANVILLE AVE 60660
  Shigesaio Murad, prin.
Healy ES, 3010 S PARNELL AVE 60616
  Beverly Tunney, prin.
Hearst ES, 4640 S LAMON AVE 60638
  Esther Krane, prin.
Hedges Branch-East
  5017 S HERMITAGE AVE 60609
  Paul Mandel, prin.
Hedges Branch-West ES
  3815 N KEDVALE AVE 60641
  Paul Mandel, prin.
Hedges ES, 4735 S WINCHESTER AVE 60609
  Paul Mandel, prin.
Hefferan ES, 4409 W WILCOX ST 60624
  William Earwaker, prin.
Henderson ES, 5650 S WOLCOTT AVE 60636
  Edward Tobin, prin.
Hendricks ES, 4316 S PRINCETON AVE 60609
  Grace Dawson, prin.
Henry ES, 4250 N SAINT LOUIS AVE 60618
  Frederick Barth, prin.
Henson ES, 1326 S AVERS AVE 60623
  Dr. Joseph Gehrman, prin.
Herbert ES, 32131 W MONROE ST 60612
  William Rankin, prin.
Herzl ES, 3711 W DOUGLAS BLVD 60623
  John McGovern, prin.
Hibbard ES, 3244 W AINSLIE AVE 60625
  Helen Marcyan, prin.
Higgins Community ES
  11710 S MORGAN ST 60643
  William Meade, prin.
Hinton ES, 644 W 71 ST 60621
  Lewis Webster, prin.
Hitch ES, 1104 W 31ST 60608
  Patricia Hoffman, prin.
Holden ES, 1104 W 31ST ST 60608
  Terri Katsulis, prin.
Holmes ES, 955 W GARFIELD BLVD 60621
  Richard Bradley, prin.
Howe ES, 720 N LOREL AVE 60644
  Dr. Dorothy Petak, prin.
Howland ES, 1616 S SPAULDING AVE 60623
  Anita Moore, prin.
Hoyne ES, 8905 S CRANDON AVE 60617
  Patrick Harrigan, prin.
Hughes ES, 4247 W 15TH ST 60623
  Harold London, prin.
Hughes Langston ES, 226 W 104TH ST 60628
  (—), prin.
Hurley ES, 3849 W 69TH PL 60629
  Marjorie Joy, prin.
Inter-American Magnet ES
  919 W BARRY AVE 60657 – Eva Helwing, prin.
Irving ES, 2140 W LEXINGTON ST 60612
  Eleanor Brazier, prin.
Irving Park ES, 3815 N KEDVALE AVE 60641
  Noreen Nagle, prin.
Jackson ES, 917 W 88TH ST 60620
  Jack Cooper, prin.

Jackson Language ES
  820 S CARPENTER ST 60607
  Vicki Gunther, prin.
Jahn ES, 3149 N WOLCOTT AVE 60657
  Edwin Uhlig, prin.
Jamieson ES, 5650 N MOZART ST 60659
  Elizabeth Brayton, prin.
Jefferson ES, 1522 W FILLMORE ST 60607
  Harold Miller, prin.
Jenner ES, 1009 N CLEVELAND AVE 60610
  Doris Barnes, prin.
Jensen Scholastic ES
  3030 W HARRISON ST 60612
  Wayne Hoffman, prin.
Jessie Owens Comm. Academy
  12450 S STATE ST 60628
  Vincent Castrogiovanni, prin.
Johnson ES, 1420 S ALBANY AVE 60623
  Herschel Rader, prin.
Joplin ES, 7931 S HONORE ST 60620
  Daniel Curley, prin.
Jungman Branch MS, 1652 S ALLPORT ST 60608
  (—), prin.
Jungman MS, 1746 S MILLER ST 60608
  (—), prin.
Kanoon Magnet ES, 2233 S KEDZIE AVE 60623
  Belkis Santos, prin.
Keller Magnet ES, 3020 W 108TH ST 60655
  Ruth Muth, prin.
Kellogg ES, 9241 S LEAVITT ST 60620
  Jeanne Junker, prin.
Kershaw ES, 6450 S LOWE AVE 60621
  Laura Hill, prin.
Key ES, 517 N PARKSIDE AVE 60644
  Louise Perez, prin.
Kilmer ES, 6700 N GREENVIEW AVE 60626
  Albert Orenstein, prin.
King ES, 740 S CAMPBELL AVE 60612
  Dolores Eder, prin.
Kinzie ES, 5625 S MOBILE AVE 60638
  James Burke, prin.
Kipling ES, 9351 S LOWE AVE 60620
  Marie Sloyan, prin.
Kohn ES, 10414 S STATE ST 60628
  Dr. Peter Zansitis, Jr., prin.
Komensky ES, 2001 S THROOP ST 60608
  Ralph Warner, prin.
Kosciuszko ES, 1424 N CLEAVER ST 60622
  James Bailey, prin.
Kozminski Community ES, 936 E 54TH ST 60615
  Allen Travis, prin.
La Salle Language ES, 1734 N ORLEANS ST 60614
  Amy Narea, prin.
LaFayette ES, 2714 W AUGUSTA BLVD 60622
  (—), prin.
Lathrop ES, 1440 S CHRISTIANA AVE 60623
  Georgia Hudson, prin.
Lawndale Community ES
  3500 W DOUGLAS BLVD 60623
  Bobby Roper, prin.
Lee ES, 6448 S TRIPP AVE 60629
  Majorie Joy, prin.
LeMoyne ES, 851 W WAVELAND AVE 60613
  John Fewkes, prin.
Lewis ES, 1431 N LEAMINGTON AVE 60651
  Norma Wilkins, prin.
Libby ES, 5300 S LOOMIS ST 60609
  Matthew Bonds, prin.
Lincoln ES, 615 W KEMPER PL 60614
  George May, prin.
Linne ES, 3221 N SACRAMENTO AVE 60618
  Judith Baker, prin.
Lloyd ES, 2103 N LAMON AVE 60639
  Edward Paetsch, prin.
Locke ES, 2845 N NEWCASTLE AVE 60634
  Myrtle Burton, prin.
Lovett ES, 6333 W BLOOMINGDALE AVE 60639
  Brenda Harter, prin.
Lowell ES, 3320 W HIRSCH ST 60651
  Margoann Brown, prin.
Luella ES, 9928 S CRANDON AVE 60617
  Dr. James Bernero, prin.
Lyon ES, 2941 N MCVICKER AVE 60634
  Kenneth Deiml, prin.
Madison ES, 7433 S DORCHESTER AVE 60619
  Clarence Holland, prin.
Manierre ES, 1420 N HUDSON AVE 60610
  Marlene Szymanski, prin.
Mann ES, 8050 S CHAPPEL AVE 60617
  Harold Whitfield, prin.
Marconi Community ES
  230 N KOLMAR AVE 60624 – Eugene Kaide, prin.
Marquette ES, 6550 S RICHMOND ST 60629
  Dorothy Hogan, prin.
Marsh ES, 9810 S EXCHANGE AVE 60617
  Clara Spaulding, prin.
Mason ES, 4217 W 18TH ST 60623
  Noel Leveaux, prin.
May ES, 512 S LAVERGNE AVCE 60644
  Eddie Thomas, Jr., prin.
Mayer ES, 2250 N CLIFTON AVE 60614
  John Garvey, prin.
Mayo ES, 249 E 37TH ST 60653 – Ida Cross, prin.
McClellan ES, 3527 S WALLACE ST 60609
  Geraldine Johnson, prin.
McCorkle ES, 4421 S STATE ST 60609
  Dorothea Avant, prin.
McCormick Branch ES, 2832 W 24TH BLVD 60623
  James Crowe, prin.
McCormick ES, 2712 S SAWYER AVE 60623
  James Crowe, prin.
McCutcheon ES, 4865 N SHERIDAN RD 60640
  Edward Ploog, prin.

McCutcheon ES-Branch
  4850 N KENMORE AVE 60640
  Edward Ploog, prin.
McDade Classical ES
  8801 S INDIANA AVE 60619
  Linus O'Connell, prin.
McDowell ES-Branch of Caldwell
  1419 E 89TH ST 60619 – Genevieve Massey, prin.
McKay ES, 6901 S FAIRFIELD AVE 60629
  Daniel Zelazek, prin.
McPherson ES, 4728 N WOLCOTT AVE 60640
  Camille Chase, prin.
Modill PS, 1301 W 14TH ST 60608
  Doris Scott, prin.
Melody ES, 412 S KEELER AVE 60624
  Jewel Koch, prin.
Metcalfe Magnet ES
  12339 S NORMAL AVE 60628
  Barbara Valerious, prin.
Mitchell ES, 2233 W OHIO ST 60612
  Deanna Rattner, prin.
Mollison ES, 4415 S DR M L KING DR 60653
  Barbara Eason, prin.
Monroe ES, 3651 W SCHUBERT AVE 60647
  Efrain Orduz, prin.
Moos ES, 1711 N CALIFORNIA AVE 60647
  Dr. Alice Peters, prin.
Morgan ES, 8407 S KERFOOT AVE 60620
  Robert Weitzel, prin.
Morrill ES, 6011 S ROCKWELL ST 60629
  James Lilek, prin.
Morse ES, 620 N SAWYER AVE 60624
  Robert Nesper, prin.
Mt. Greenwood ES, 10-841 S HOMAN AVE 60655
  Dr. William McGowan, prin.
Mt. Vernon ES, 10540 S MORGAN ST 60643
  Benjamin Furman, Jr., prin.
Mozart ES, 2200 N HAMLIN AVE 60647
  Charlotte Projansky, prin.
Mulligan ES, 1855 N SHEFFIELD AVE 60614
  Alice Maresh, prin.
Murphy ES, 3539 W GRACE ST 60618
  Harold Zimmerman, prin.
Murray Language ES
  5335 S KENWOOD AVE 60615
  Virginia Vaske, prin.
Nansen ES, 12607 S UNION AVE 60628
  William Moore, prin.
Nash ES, 4837 W ERIE ST 60644
  Richard Kerr, prin.
Nell ES, 8555 S MICHIGAN AVE 60619
  Dr. Charles Keenan, prin.
Nettlehorst ES, 3252 N BROADWAY ST 60657
  Peggy Lubin, prin.
Newberry Magnet ES, 700 W WILLOW ST 60614
  Mary Ransford, prin.
Nightingale ES, 5250 S ROCKWELL ST 60632
  Thomas Kernan, prin.
Ninos Heroes Magnet ES
  8344 S COMMERCIAL AVE 60617
  Grace Beavers, prin.
Nixon ES, 2121 N KEELER AVE 60639
  Elizabeth Evan, prin.
Nobel ES, 4127 W HIRSCH ST 60651
  Theodore Besser, prin.
Norwood Park ES, 5900 N NINA AVE 60631
  Peter Hastings, prin.
Ogden ES, 24 W WALTON ST 60610
  Roberta Vandivier, prin.
Oglesby ES, 7646 S GREEN ST 60620
  Lillie White, prin.
O'Keeffe ES, 6940 S MERRILL AVE 60649
  Timothy Knop, prin.
Onahan ES, 6634 W RAVEN ST 60631
  Peter Hastings, prin.
Oriole Park ES, 5424 N OKETO AVE 60656
  Robert Bures, prin.
Otis ES, 525 N ARMOUR ST 60622
  James Cosme, prin.
O'Toole ES, 6550 S SEELEY AVE 60636
  Mary McDonnell Hornung, prin.
Overton Child-Parent Center
  4935 S INDIANA AVE 60615 – (—), prin.
Owen Scholastic ES
  8247 S CHRISTIANA AVE 60652
  Leo Ellis, Jr., prin.
Paderewski ES, 2221 S LAWNDALE AVE 60623
  Orlando Orpen, prin.
Palmer ES, 5051 N KENNETH AVE 60630
  Mary Spillane-Barth, prin.
Park Manor ES, 7037 S RHODES AVE 60637
  Diane Dyer, prin.
Parker Community ES
  6800 S STEWART AVE 60621
  Leona Collins, prin.
Parkman ES, 245 W 51ST ST 60609
  Rolland Hinton, prin.
Parkside Community ES
  6938 S EAST END AVE 60649
  Alvin Miller, prin.
Pasteur ES, 5825 S KOSTNER AVE 60629
  Dr. William Murawski, prin.
Peabody ES, 1444 W AUGUSTA BLVD 60622
  Michael Bailen, prin.
Peck ES, 3826 W 58TH ST 60629
  Alice Harper, prin.
Penn ES, 1616 S AVERS AVE 60623
  Philip Ragan, prin.
Perry ES, 9130 S UNIVERSITY 60619
  Albert Foster, Jr., prin.
Pershing Magnet ES
  3113 S RHODES AVEY 60616
  Maude Lightfoot, prin.

Peterson ES, 5510 N CHRISTIANA AVE 60625
  Therese McMahamon, prin.
Piccolo ES, 1040 N KEELER AVE 60651
  Dr. James Stewart, prin.
Pickard ES, 2301 W 21ST PL 60608
  Sylvia Asllami, prin.
Pierce ES, 1423 W BRYN MAWR AVE 60660
  Janice Rosales, prin.
Pilsen Community ES, 1420 W 17TH ST 60608
  William Levin, prin.
Pirie ES, 650 E 85TH ST 60619
  Gladys Adams, prin.
Plamondon ES, 1525 S WASHTENAW AVE 60608
  Guadalupe Hamersma, prin.
Poe Classical ES, 10538 S LANGLEY AVE 60628
  Joyce Johnson, prin.
Pope ES, 1852 S ALBANY AVE 60623
  (—), prin.
Portage Park ES, 5330 W BERTEAU AVE 60641
  Mary Kelly-Dowd, prin.
Powell ES, 7530 S SOUTH SHORE DR 60649
  Earl Sanders, prin.
Prescott ES, 1632 W WRIGHTWOOD AVE 60614
  Hugh Levoy, prin.
Price ES, 4351 S DREXEL BLVD 60653
  Hugh McCartan, prin.
Pritzker ES, 2009 W SCHILLER ST 60622
  Gweneth Henslee, prin.
Prussing ES, 4650 N MENARD AVE 60630
  Robert Bures, prin.
Pulaski ES, 2230 W MCLEAN AVE 60647
  Samuel Vickery, prin.
Pullman ES, 11311 S FORRESTVILLE AVE 60628
  Norman Kremen, prin.
Randolph Magnet ES, 7316 S HOYNE AVE 60636
  Dr. Charlene Schroeder, prin.
Raster Branch ES, 6723 S WOOD ST 60636
  George Swain Jr., prin.
Raster ES, 4936 S HERMITAGE AVE 60609
  Earl Jeffrey, prin.
Ravenswood ES, 4332 N PAULINA ST 60613
  Roberta Chapman, prin.
Ray ES, 5631 S KIMBARK AVE 60637
  Sara Spurlark, prin.
Raymond ES, 3663 S WABASH AVE 60653
  Richard Wnek, prin.
Reavis ES, 834 E 50TH ST 60615
  Birdie Miller, prin.
Reed ES, 6350 S STEWART AVE 60621
  Richard Niedvares, prin.
Reilly ES, 3650 W SCHOOL ST 60618
  Rosemary Culverwell, prin.
Reinberg ES, 3425 N MAJOR AVE 60634
  Fred Rosen, prin.
Revere ES, 1010 E 72ND ST 60619
  Dean Gustafson, prin.
Riis ES, 1018 S LYTLE ST 60607
  Theodore Hagansee, prin.
Robinson ES-Branch of Oakenwald North
  4155 S LAKE PARK AVE 60653 – (—), prin.
Rogers ES, 7345 N WASHTENAW AVE 60645
  Robert Stardzuk, prin.
Rosenwald ES Branch of Carroll
  2541 W 80TH ST 60652 – Mae Simon, prin.
Ross ES, 6059 S WABASH AVE 60637
  Josephine Logan Woods, prin.
Ruggles ES, 7831 S PRAIRIE AVE 60619
  Dr. Nicholas Kushia, prin.
Ryder ES, 8716 S WALLACE ST 60620
  V. Jerome O'Neill, prin.
Ryerson ES, 646 N LAWNDALE AVE 60624
  Donald Schmitt, prin.
Sabin Magnet ES, 2216 W HIRSCH ST 60622
  Lourdes Monteagudo, prin.
Sauganash ES, 6040 N KILPATRICK AVE 60646
  Sarah Schwarcz, prin.
Sawyer ES, 5248 S SAWYER AVE 60632
  Ellen Reiter, prin.
Sayre Language ES
  1850 N NEWLAND AVE 60635
  Rose Marici, prin.
Sbarbaro ES, 8505 S INGLESIDE AVE 60619
  Matthew McDowell, Jr., prin.
Scammon ES, 4201 W HENDERSON ST 60641
  William Whelan, prin.
Scanlan ES, 11725 S PERRY AVE 60628
  Loesther Foley, prin.
Schmid ES, 9755 S GREENWOOD AVE 60628
  Linus O'Connell, prin.
Schneider ES, 2957 N HOYNE AVE 60618
  Margaret Cooper, prin.
Schubert ES, 2727 N LONG AVE 60639
  Cynthia Wnek, prin.
Seward ES, 4600 S HERMITAGE AVE 60609
  Christine Speiser, prin.
Sexton ES, 6020 S LANGLEY AVE 60637
  Chauncey Bertha, prin.
Shakespeare ES, 1119 E 46TH ST 60653
  Arline Hersh, prin.
Shedd ES-Branch Of Bennett
  200 E 99TH ST 60628 – John McCormick, prin.
Sheridan ES, 9000 S EXCHANGE AVE 60617
  Robert McNamara, prin.
Sheridan Magnet ES, 533 W 27TH ST 60616
  Beverly Tunney, prin.
Sherman ES, 1000 W 52ND ST 60609
  Peggy Jackson, prin.
Sherwood ES, 245 W 57TH ST 60621
  Shirley Dukes, prin.
Shields ES, 4250 S ROCKWELL ST 60632
  Robert Church, Jr., prin.
Shoesmith ES, 1330 E 50TH ST 60615
  Clare Dubrock, prin.

Shoop ES, 1460 W 112TH ST 60643
  James Blackman, prin.
Skinner Classical ES, 111 S THROOP ST 60607
  William Connery, prin.
Smith ES, 744 E 103RD ST 60628
  Frederick Sears, prin.
Smyser ES, 4310 N MELVINA AVE 60634
  Brenda Heffner, prin.
Smyth ES, 1059 W 13TH ST 60608
  George Swain, Jr., prin.
Solomon ES, 6206 N HAMLIN AVE 60659
  Sarah Schwarcz, prin.
Spencer ES, 214 N LAVERGNE AVE 60644
  D. Dandridge-Alexander, prin.
Spry ES, 2400 S MARSHALL BLVD 60623
  Benedict Natzke, Jr., prin.
Stagg ES, 7424 S MORGAN ST 60621
  Mary Kirby, prin.
Stevenson ES, 8010 S KOSTNER AVE 60652
  James Cunningham, prin.
Stewart ES, 4525 N KENMORE ST 60640
  Dr. Patricia Ryan, prin.
Stockton ES, 4420 N BEACON ST 60640
  Dr. Carl Lieberman, prin.
Stone Scholastic ES, 6239 N LEAVITT ST 60659
  Ian Campbell, prin.
Stowe ES, 3444 W WABANSIA AVE 60647
  Juanita Quinones, prin.
Suder ES, 2022 W WASHINGTON BLVD 60612
  Brenda Daigre, prin.
South Loop Branch, 1950 S FEDERAL ST 60616
  (—), prin.
Sullivan ES, 8255 S HOUSTON AVE 60617
  Rose Koperniak, prin.
Sumner ES, 4320 N FIFTH AVE 60624
  Donna Wilson-Williams, prin.
Sutherland ES, 10015 S LEAVITT ST 60643
  John Frantz, prin.
Swift ES, 5900 N WINTHROP AVE 60660
  Seymour Miller, prin.
Talcott ES, 1840 W OHIO ST 60622
  Marcella Richman, prin.
Tanner ES, 7350 S EVANS AVE 60619
  Robert McCabe, prin.
Taylor ES, 9912 S AVENUE H 60617
  Sally Culhane, prin.
Terrell ES, 5410 S STATE ST 60609
  Reva Hairston, prin.
Thorp ES, 8914 S BUFFALO AVE 60617
  Sheldon Rosen, prin.
Thorp Scholastic Academy
  6024 W WARWICK AVE 60634
  Dr. Arthur Fumarold, prin.
Tilton ES, 223 N KEELER AVE 60624
  Jesse O'Moore, prin.
Tonti ES, 5815 S HOMAN AVE 60629
  (—), prin.
Trumbull ES, 5200 N ASHLAND AVE 60640
  Merle Davis, prin.
Truth ES, 1443 N OGDEN AVE 60610
  Elouise Cantrell, prin.
Turner-Drew Language Academy
  9300 S PRINCETON AVE 60620 – (—), prin.
Twain ES, 5131 W LINDER AVE 60638
  Thomas Keating, prin.
Van Vlissingen ES, 137 W 108TH PL 60628
  Jacqueline Carothers, prin.
Vanderpoel Magnet ES
  9510 S PROSPECT AVE 60643
  E. Robert Olson, prin.
Volta ES, 4950 N AVERS AVE 60625
  Naomi Nickerson, prin.
Von Humboldt ES, 2620 W HIRSCH ST 60622
  Edwin Tyska, prin.
Wacker ES, 9746 S MORGAN ST 60643
  Charles Tauchman, prin.
Wadsworth ES, 6434 S UNIVERSITY AVE 60637
  (—), prin.
Walsh ES, 2015 S PEORIA ST 60608
  Dr. Ronald Clayton, prin.
Ward ES, 2701 S SHIELDS AVE 60616
  Dr. Daniel Breen, prin.
Ward ES, 410 N MONTICELLO AVE 60624
  Janice Choll, prin.
Washington ES, 3611 E 114TH ST 60617
  Dr. Patricia Doherty, prin.
Waters ES, 4540 N CAMPBELL AVE 60625
  Edward Scott, prin.
Webster ES, 4055 W ARTHINGTON ST 60624
  James Sanders, prin.
Wentworth ES, 6950 S SANGAMON ST 60621
  John Jackson, prin.
Wescott ES, 8023 S NORMAL AVE 60620
  Dr. Joan Wright, prin.
West Pullman ES, 11941 S PARNELL AVE 60628
  Elihu Blanks, prin.
West Pullman ES-White Branch
  1136 W 122ND ST 60643 – Elihu Blanks, prin.
Whistler ES, 11533 S ADA ST 60643
  Marcus Ahmed, prin.
Whitney ES, 2815 S KOMENSKY AVE 60623
  Leonard Dominguez, prin.
Whittier Branch ES, 1818 S PAULINA ST 60608
  Ralph Guajardo, prin.
Whittier ES, 1900 W 23 ST 60608
  Raphael Guajardo, prin.
Wildwood ES, 6950 N HIAWATHA AVE 60646
  Dr. Diane Maciejewski, prin.
Williams ES, 2710 S DEARBORN ST 60616
  Floyd Banks, prin.
Woodson South ES, 4444 S EVANS AVE 60653
  Jacquelynne Gilmore, prin.
Wright ES, 627 N HARDING AVE 60624
  Roberta Kalb, prin.

Yale ES, 7025 S PRINCETON AVE 60621
  Millicent Tolbert, prin.
Yates ES, 1839 N RICHMOND ST 60647
  Burton Hirsch, prin.
Young ES, 1434 N PARKSIDE AVE 60651
  Michael Kroll, prin.

Norridge SD 80
Supt. – See Norridge
Giles ES, 4251 N ORIOLE AVE 60634
  Ralph Gebert, prin.
Leigh ES, 8151 W LAWRENCE AVE 60656
  Rocco Montemurro, prin.

Pennoyer SD 79
Supt. – See Norridge
Pennoyer ES, 5200 N CUMBERLAND AVE 60656
  Dr. Deno Fenili, prin.

Francis Parker School
  330 W WEBSTER AVE 60614
Harvard School, 4731 S ELLIS AVE 60615
Latin School of Chicago
  59 W NORTH BLVD 60610
Morgan Park Academy, 2153 W 111TH ST 60643
Shiloh Academy, 7008 S MICHIGAN AVE 60637
University of Chicago Lab School
  1362 E 59TH ST 60637
Akiba Southside Day School
  5200 S HYDE PARK BLVD 60615
All Sts.-St. Anthony School
  512 W 28TH PL 60616
Ancona School Society
  4770 S DORCHESTER AVE 60615
Annunciata School, 3750 E 112TH ST 60617
Anshe Emet Day School
  3760 N PINE GROVE AVE 60613
Ashburn Lutheran School, 3345 W 83RD ST 60652
Assumption B V M School
  12238 S PARNELL AVE 60628
Bais Yaakov Hebrew Boys School
  6122 N CALIFORNIA AVE 60659
Bais Yaakov Hebrew Girl School
  2447 W GRANVILLE AVE 60659
Bethel ES, 1410 N SPRINGFIELD STREET 60651
Bethel Evang. Lutheran School
  3910 W HIRSCH ST 60651
Bethesda Lutheran School
  6803 N CAMPBELL AVE 60645
Bethlehem Lutheran School
  3715 E 103RD ST 60617
Blessed Agnes School
  2643 S CENTRAL PARK AVE 60623
Blessed Sacrament School
  2130 S CENTRAL PARK AVE 60623
Bridgeport Catholic Academy-South
  3700 S LOWE AVE 60609
Christ Lutheran School
  5335 W LE MOYNE ST 60651
Christ The King School
  9240 S HOYNE AVE 60620
Corpus Christi School, 4910 S KING DR 60615
Divine Savior School
  7750 W MONTROSE AVE 60634
Engelwood Catholic St. Raphael School
  6020 S LAFLIN ST 60636
Epiphany School, 4223 W 25TH ST 60623
Five Holy Martyrs School
  4325 S RICHMOND ST 60632
Gloria Dei Lutheran School
  5259 S MAJOR AVE 60638
Golgotha Lutheran School
  1850 W MARQUETTE RD 60636
Good Shepherd School, 2733 S KOLIN AVE 60623
Grace Lutheran School
  2725 N LARAMIE AVE 60639
Grace Lutheran School
  4106 W 28TH STREET 60623
Hardey Prep School, 6250 N SHERIDAN RD 60660
Holy Angels School
  545 E OAKWOOD BLVD 60653
Holy Cross School
  6547 S MARYLAND AVE 60637
Holy Family School, 1029 S MAY ST 60607
Holy Innocents School
  1447 W SUPERIOR ST 60622
Holy Name Cathredal School
  751 N STATE ST 60610
Holy Name of Mary School
  1425 W 112TH ST 60643
Holy Trinity School, 1900 W TAYLOR ST 60612
Hope Lutheran School
  6416 W WASHTENAW AVE 60629
Immaculate Conception School
  4420 S FAIRFIELD AVE 60632
Immaculate Conception School
  7263 W TALCOTT AVE 60631
Immaculate Heart of Mary
  3820 N SPAULDING AVE 60618
Jesus Our Brother School
  8401 S SAGINAW AVE 60617
Jevohah Lutheran School
  3740 W BELDEN AVE 60647
Little Flower School, 1821 W 80TH ST 60620
Maternity BVM School
  1537 N LAWNDALE 60651
Messiah Lutheran School
  6200 W PATTERSON AVE 60634
Most Holy Redeemer School
  9536 S MILLARD AVE 60642
Mt. Carmel Academy of Lakeview
  720 W BELMONT AVE 60657
Nativity B V M School
  6820 S WASHTENAW AVE 60629

Nazareth Lutheran School
  5950 S SPAULDING AVE   60629
Near North Montessorri School
  1010 W CHICAGO AVE   60622
Notre Dame School
  1338 W FLOURNOY ST   60607
Our Lady Gate of Heaven School
  2230 E 99TH ST   60617
Our Lady Help of Christians School
  847 N LEAMINGTON AVE   60651
Our Lady Lourdes School
  4637 N ASHLAND AVE   60640
Our Lady Lourdes School
  1449 S KEELER AVE   60623
Our Lady of Charity School
  3620 S 57TH CT   60650
Our Lady of Good Counsel School
  3540 S HERMITAGE AVE   60609
Our Lady of Grace School
  2448 N RIDGEWAY   60647
Our Lady of Guadalupe School
  9050 S BURLEY AVE   60617
Our Lady of Mercy School
  4416 N TROY AVE   60626
Our Lady of Peace School
  7847 S JEFFERY AVE   60649
Our Lady of Pompeii School
  1220 W LEXINGTON ST   60607
Our Lady of Ransom School
  8300 N GREENWOOD AVE   60648
Our Lady of Sorrows School
  3141 W JACKSON BLVD   60612
Our Lady of Victory School
  4434 N LARAMIE AVE   60630
Our Lady of Vilna School, 2337 W 23RD PL   60608
Our Lady of the Angels School
  3814 W IOWA ST   60651
Our Lady of the Gardens School
  13300 S LANGLEY AVE   60627
Our Lady of the Snows School
  4810 S LEAMINGTON AVE   60638
Our Lady of the Westside School
  3900 W LEXINGTON ST   60624
Our Savior Lutheran School
  7151 W CORNELIA AVE   60634
Our Savior Lutheran School
  6035 N NORTHCOTT AVE   60631
Peace Lutheran School
  4307 S MOZART ST   60632
Pilgrim Lutheran School
  4300 N WINCHESTER AVE   60613
Prince of Peace Lutheran School
  4913 W MEDILL AVE   60639
Providence of God School
  1814 S UNION AVE   60616
Queen of Angels School
  4520 N WESTERN AVE   60625
Queen of Apostles School
  14419 S ATLANTIC AVE   60627
Queen of Martyrs School
  3550 W 103RD ST   60655
Queen of Saints School
  6230 N LEMONT AVE   60646
Queen of the Universe School
  7130 S HAMLIN AVE   60629
Resurrection Lutheran School
  9349 S WENTWORTH AVE   60620
Resurrection School
  5072 W JACKSON BLVD   60644
Roseland Christian School
  314 W 108TH ST   60628
SS Joseph & Anne School
  2744 W PERSHING RD   60632
SS Peter & Paul School
  3737 S PAULINA ST   60609
SS Stanislaus and Boniface School
  1255 N NOBLE ST   60622
Sacred Heart School
  4637 S WOLCOTT AVE   60609
Sacred Heart School, 7007 S MAY ST   60621
Sacred Heart School, 2906 E 96TH ST   60617
Santa Lucia School, 3017 S WELLS ST   60616
Santa Maria Addolorata School
  1337 W OHIO ST   60622
Seven Holy Founders School
  12440 S ADA ST   60643
Ss Peter & Paul School
  12255 S EMERALD AVE   60628
St. Adrian School
  7014 S WASHTENAW AVE   60629
St. Ailbe School, 9037 S HARPER AVE   60619
St. Alphonsus School
  1439 W WELLINGTON AVE   60657
St. Ambrose School, 1014 E 47TH ST   60653
St. Andrew School, 1710 W ADDISON ST   60613
St. Angela School
  1332 N MASSASOIT AVE   60651
St. Ann Grade School, 2211 W 18TH PL   60608
St. Anselm School, 6042 S INDIANA AVE   60637
St. Anthony School, 11530 S PRAIRIE AVE   60628
St. Augustine School, 5019 S LAFLIN ST   60609
St. Barbara School, 2867 S THROOP ST   60608
St. Barnabas School
  10121 S LONGWOOD DR   60643
St. Bartholomew School
  4041 W PATTERSON AVE   60641
St. Basil School, 1824 W GARFIELD BLVD   60609
St. Bede the Venerable School
  4440 W 83RD ST   60652
St. Benedict School, 3920 N LEAVITT ST   60618
St. Bernadette School
  9311 S FRANCISCO AVE   60642
St. Bonaventure School
  1651 W DIVERSEY PKY   60614

St. Bride School, 7765 S COLES AVE   60649
St. Bruno School, 4839 S HARDING AVE   60632
St. Cajetan School, 2447 W 112TH ST   60655
St. Callistus School, 2187 W BOWLER ST   60612
St. Camillus School
  5434 S LOCKWOOD AVE   60638
St. Casimir Grade School
  3047 W CERMAK RD   60623
St. Catherine of Genoa School
  11756 S LOWE AVE   60628
St. Celestine School, 3017 N 77TH AVE   60635
St. Charles Lwanga School, 220 W 45TH PL   60609
St. Christina School, 3332 W 110TH ST   60655
St. Clare of Montefalco School
  5450 S TALMAN AVE   60632
St. Clement School, 2524 N ORCHARD ST   60614
St. Clotilde School, 321 E 84TH ST   60619
St. Columba School, 3340 E 134TH ST   60633
St. Columbanus School
  7120 S CALUMET AVE   60619
St. Constance School, 5841 W STRONG ST   60630
St. Cornelius School, 5252 N LONG AVE   60630
St. Cyril Carmelite School
  6358 S BLACKSTONE AVE   60637
St. Daniel the Phophet School
  5337 S NATOMA AVE   60638
St. Denis School
  8300 S SAINT LOUIS AVE   60652
St. Dorothy School
  7740 S EBERHART AVE   60619
St. Edward School
  4343 W SUNNYSIDE AVE   60630
St. Elizabeth School, 4052 S WABASH AVE   60653
St. Ethelreda School, 8734 S PAULINA ST   60620
St. Eugene School, 7930 W FOSTER AVE   60656
St. Felicitas School, 1501 E 83RD PL   60619
St. Ferdinand School, 3131 N MASON AVE   60634
St. Fidelis School
  1405 N WASHTENAW AVE   60622
St. Florian School
  13110 S BALTIMORE AVE   60633
St. Francis Borgia School
  3535 S PANAMA AVE   60634
St. Francis De Paula School
  7825 S ELLIS AVE   60619
St. Francis De Sales School
  10200 S AVENUE J   60617
St. Francis Xavier School
  2845 W BARRY AVE   60618
St. Francis of Assisi School
  4424 W WALTON ST   60651
St. Gabriel School, 4500 S WALLACE ST   60609
St. Gall School, 5515 S SAWYER AVE   60629
St. Genevieve School
  4846 W MONTANA ST   60639
St. George School, 9536 S EWING AVE   60617
St. Gertrude School
  6214 N GLENWOOD AVE   60660
St. Gregory School
  1643 W BRYN MAWR AVE   60660
St. Hedwig School
  2219 N HAMILTON AVE   60647
St. Helen School, 2347 W AUGUSTA BLVD   60622
St. Helena of the Cross School
  10115 S PARNELL AVE   60628
St. Henry School, 6325 N HOYNE AVE   60659
St. Hilary School, 5614 N FAIRFIELD AVE   60659
St. Hyacinth School
  3640 W WOLFRAM ST   60618
St. Ignatius School, 1300 W LOYOLA AVE   60626
St. Isaac Jogues School, 8101 W GOLF RD   60648
St. Ita School, 5525 N MAGNOLIA AVE   60640
St. James Lutheran School
  2046 N FREMONT ST   60614
St. James School, 2920 S WABASH AVE   60616
St. James School, 2456 N MANGO AVE   60639
St. Jane De Chantal School
  5201 S MCVICKER AVE   60638
St. Jerome School, 2801 S PRINCETON AVE   60616
St. Jerome School, 1706 W MORSE AVE   60626
St. Joachim School, 9035 S LANGLEY AVE   60619
St. John Berchmans School
  2509 W LOGAN BLVD   60647
St. John Bosco School
  2245 N MCVICKER AVE   60639
St. John Brebeuf School
  8301 N HARLEM AVE   60648
St. John De La Salle School
  10216 S VERNON AVE   60628
St. John Fisher School
  10200 S WASHTENAW AVE   60642
St. John Lutheran School
  4939 W MONTROSE AVE   60641
St. John of God School
  5130 S ELIZABETH ST   60609
St. Josaphat School
  2245 N SOUTHPORT AVE   60614
St. Joseph School, 4818 S PAULINA ST   60609
St. Joseph School, 1065 N ORLEANS ST   60610
St. Juliana School, 7400 W TOUHY AVE   60648
St. Justin Martyr School
  7033 S HONORE ST   60636
St. Kilian School, 8748 S ABERDEEN ST   60620
St. Ladislaus School
  3330 N LOCKWOOD AVE   60641
St. Laurence School, 1349 E 72ND ST   60619
St. Leo the Great ES
  7746 S EMERALD AVE   60620
St. Ludmilla School, 2414 S ALBANY AVE   60623
St. Luke Lutheran School
  1500 W BELMONT AVE   60657
St. Malachy School
  2252 W WASHINGTON BLVD   60612

St. Margaret Mary School
  7318 N OAKLEY AVE   60645
St. Margaret of Scotland School
  9833 S THROOP ST   60643
St. Mark School, 2510 W CORTEZ ST   60622
St. Mark the Evangelist School
  11816 S INDIANA   60628
St. Martin School, 5838 S PRINCETON AVE   60621
St. Mary School, 313 E 137TH ST   60627
St. Mary of the Angels School
  1810 N HERMITAGE AVE   60622
St. Mary of the Lake School
  1026 W BUENA AVE   60613
St. Mary of the Sea School
  6424 S KENNETH AVE   60629
St. Mary of the Woods School
  7033 N MOSELLE AVE   60646
St. Matthias School
  4910 N CLAREMONT AVE   60625
St. Maurice School, 3625 S HOYNE AVE   60609
St. Michael School, 1949 W 48TH ST   60609
St. Michael School
  8235 S SOUTH SHORE DR   60617
St. Michael School, 2315 W 24TH PL   60608
St. Monica School
  5115 N MONT CLARE AVE   60656
St. Nicholas Cathedral School
  2200 W RICE ST   60622
St. Nicholas of Tolentine School
  3731 W 62ND ST   60629
St. Pancratius School, 2940 W 40TH PL   60632
St. Pascal School
  6143 W IRVING PARK RD   60634
St. Paul Lutheran School
  846 N MENARD AVE   60651
St. Paul Lutheran School, 233 E 138TH ST   60627
St. Paul Lutheran School
  5650 N CANFIELD AVE   60631
St. Paul-Our Lady of Vilna School
  2114 W 22ND PLACE   60608
St. Peter Canisius School
  5035 W NORTH AVE   60639
St. Philip Lutheran School
  2500 W BRYN MAWR AVE   60659
St. Philip Neri School, 2110 E 72ND ST   60649
St. Philomena School
  4131 W CORTLAND ST   60639
St. Pius V School, 1919 S ASHLAND AVE   60608
St. Priscilla School, 7001 W ADDISON ST   60634
St. Procopius School, 1625 S ALLPORT ST   60608
St. Rene Goupil School
  6340 S NEW ENGLAND AVE   60638
St. Richard School, 5025 S KENNETH AVE   60632
St. Rita School, 6201 S FAIRFIELD AVE   60629
St. Robert Bellarmine School
  6036 W EASTWOOD AVE   60630
St. Roman School, 2651 W 23RD ST   60608
St. Rosalie School
  6740 W MONTROSE AVE   60634
St. Sabina School, 7801 S THROOP ST   60620
St. Sebastian School
  810 W WELLINGTON AVE   60657
St. Simon the Apostle School
  5135 S CALIFORNIA AVE   60632
St. Stanislaus B & M School
  2218 N LOREL AVE   60639
St. Stephen School, 1846 W 22ND PL   60608
St. Sylvester School, 3027 W PALMER ST   60647
St. Symphorosa School
  6125 S AUSTIN AVE   60638
St. Tarcissus School
  6040 W ARDMORE AVE   60646
St. Teresa School, 1940 N KENMORE AVE   60614
St. Thaddeus School
  9540 S HARVARD AVE   60628
St. Thecla School
  6323 N NEWCASTLE AVE   60631
St. Therese School, 247 W 23RD ST   60616
St. Thomas Aquinas School
  116 N LECLAIRE AVE   60644
St. Thomas More School
  8130 S CALIFORNIA AVE   60652
St. Thomas of Canterbury School
  4827 N KENMORE AVE   60640
St. Thomas the Apostle School
  5467 W WOODLAWN AVE   60615
St. Timothy School
  6330 N WASHTENAW AVE   60659
St. Turibius School, 4125 W 56TH PL   60629
St. Veronica School, 3318 N WHIPPLE ST   60618
St. Viator School, 4140 W ADDISON ST   60641
St. Walter School, 11741 S WESTERN AVE   60643
St. Wenceslaus School
  3435 N LALWNDALE AVE   60618
St. William School, 2559 N SAYRE AVE   60635
Tabor Lutheran School
  3542 W SUNNYSIDE AVE   60625
Timothy Lutheran School, 1700 W 83RD ST   60620
Transfiguration School
  5044 N ROCKWELL ST   60625
Visitation School, 900 W GARFIELD BLVD   60609
Zion Lutheran School
  10858 S M L KING DR   60628

Chicago Heights, Cook Co., Pop. Code 8
  Chicago Heights SD 170
  Sch. Sys. Enr. Code 5
  Supt. – Richard Felicetti
    1611 ABERDEEN ST   60411
  Garfield ES, 23RD NEAR WALLACE ST   60411
    Micaleen Vasilj, prin.
  Gavin ES, 280 E 12TH ST   60411
    Yvonne Robinson, prin.

Greenbriar ES, 101 W GREENBRIAR AVE   60411
    Patricia Hanto, prin.
Jefferson ES, UNION AVE & 11TH ST   60411
    Dorothy Furnace, prin.
Kennedy ES, 10TH & DIVISION STS   60411
    Patricia Leoni, prin.
Lincoln ES, CENTER AVE NEAR 15TH   60411
    Yvonne Robinson, prin.
Roosevelt ES, 14TH ST & SUNNYSIDE   60411
    Joseph Wachel, prin.
Washington-McKinley ES
    16TH PLACE & SCHOOL ST   60411
    Donald Aprati, prin.
Wilson ES, 16TH PLACE & WILSON AVE   60411
    Joseph Wachel, prin.
Other Schools – See South Chicago Heights

Flossmoor SD 161
Supt. – See Flossmoor
Serena Hills ES, 255 PLEASANT DR   60411
    James Glunz, prin.

Park Forest SD 163
Supt. – See Park Forest
Beacon Hill ES, 401 CONCORD DR   60411
    Fred Segner, prin.

Mt. Carmel School, 334 E 21ST ST   60411
St. Agnes Consolidated School
    1501 CHICAGO RD   60411
St. James School, 22410 TORRENCE AVE   60411
St. Kieran School, 724 195TH ST   60411
St. Paul Lutheran School
    330 W HIGHLAND DR   60411

Chicago Ridge, Cook Co., Pop. Code 7
Chicago Ridge SD 127-5
Sch. Sys. Enr. Code 4
Supt. – Dr. John E. Johnson
    10835 LOMBARD AVE   60415
Finley JHS, 10835 LOMBARD AVE   60415
    Louis Desmet, prin.
Ridge Central ES, 10800 LYMAN AVE   60415
    Matthew Accomando, prin.
Ridge Lawn ES, 5757 105TH ST   60415
    Diane North, prin.

Our Lady of the Ridge School
    10859 RIDGELAND AVE   60415

Chillicothe, Peoria Co., Pop. Code 6
Illinois Valley Central Unit SD 321
Sch. Sys. Enr. Code 4
Supt. – James Thornton, P O BOX 298   61523
JHS, 914 W TRUITT   61523 – Richard Greene, prin.
South ES, 616 W HICKORY ST   61523
    Gary McNaught, prin.
Other Schools – See Mossville, Rome

St. Edward School, 1221 N FIFTH ST   61523

Chrisman, Edgar Co., Pop. Code 4
Edgar Co. CUSD 6
Sch. Sys. Enr. Code 2
Supt. – Dr. Donald Walker, P O BOX 477   61924
ES, P O BOX 447   61924 – Roger Lawson, prin.

Christopher, Franklin Co., Pop. Code 5
Christopher SD 34
Sch. Sys. Enr. Code 3
Supt. – Walter Montgomery
    501 S SNIDER ST   62822
ES, 501 S SNIDER ST   62822 – (—), prin.

Cicero, Cook Co., Pop. Code 8
Cicero SD 99
Sch. Sys. Enr. Code 6
Supt. – Dr. John Hayes, 5110 W 24TH ST   60650
Burnham ES, 1630 S 59TH AVE   60650
    Dennis Socha, prin.
ES, 2324 S 49TH AVE   60650 – C. Pluister, prin.
Columbus ES, 3100 S 54TH AVE   60650
    George Beranek, prin.
Drexel ES, 5407 W 36TH ST   60650
    Thomas Hegner, prin.
Goodwin ES, 2625 S AUSTIN BLVD   60650
    A. Bruce MacDougall, prin.
Lincoln ES, 3545 S 61ST AVE   60650
    Anthony Scariano, prin.
Mckinley ES, 5900 W 14TH ST   60650
    Bette Jungels, prin.
Sherlock ES, 5347 W 22ND PL   60650
    Bette Jungels, prin.
Warren Park MS, 1225 S 60TH CT   60650
    Pierce McCabe, prin.
Wilson ES, 2310 S 57TH AVE   60650
    Miles Soumar, prin.
Woodbine ES, 3003 S 50TH CT   60650
    Raymond Michaels, prin.
Other Schools – See Chicago

Mary Queen of Heaven School
    5300 W 24TH ST   60650
Our Lady of the Mount School
    2400 S 61ST AVE   60650
St. Anthony School, 1510 S 49TH CT   60650
St. Dionysius School, 2831 S 49TH AVE   60650
St. Frances of Rome School
    1401 S AUSTIN BLVD   60650
St. Mary of Czestochowa School
    3009 S 49TH AVE   60650

Cisne, Wayne Co., Pop. Code 3
North Wayne CUSD 200
Sch. Sys. Enr. Code 3
Supt. – Victor Buehler, P O BOX 235   62823

MS, P O BOX 69   62823 – Joyce Carson, prin.
Other Schools – See Johnsonville, Mount Erie

Wayne City CUSD 100
Supt. – See Wayne City
Berry ES, RURAL ROUTE 02   62823
    Sharon White, prin.

Cissna Park, Iroquois Co., Pop. Code 3
Cissna Park CUSD 6
Sch. Sys. Enr. Code 2
Supt. – Dr. Daniel Heinold, P O BOX 7   60924
JHS, P O BOX 7   60924 – Jeffrey Holmes, prin.
ES, P O BOX 1   60924 – Dr. Daniel Heinhold, prin.

Claremont, Richland Co., Pop. Code 2
East Richland CUSD 1
Supt. – See Olney
ES, P O BOX 68   62421 – Bernard Edwards, prin.

Clarendon Hills, Du Page Co., Pop. Code 6
Hinsdale CCSD 181
Supt. – See Hinsdale
Prospect ES, 130 N PROSPECT AVE   60514
    Dr. Cheryl Kopecky, prin.
Walker ES, 120 WALKER AVE   60514
    Catherine Chesta, prin.

Maercker SD 60
Sch. Sys. Enr. Code 3
Supt. – Dr. David Lundeen
    5800 HOLMES AVE   60514
Westview Hills MS, 630 65TH ST   60514
    Greg Ostrowski, prin.
Holmes ES, 5800 HOLMES AVE   60514
    Fred Mundinger, prin.
Other Schools – See Westmont

Notre Dame School, 66 NORFOLK AVE   60514

Clay City, Clay Co., Pop. Code 4
Clay City CUSD 10
Sch. Sys. Enr. Code 3
Supt. – Kern Doerner, P O BOX 542   62824
ES, 511 S ILLINOIS BOX 545   62824
    Cecil Cochran, prin.

Clifton, Iroquois Co., Pop. Code 4
Central CUSD 4
Sch. Sys. Enr. Code 4
Supt. – Richard Bukowski, P O BOX 637   60927
Nash JHS, P O BOX 486   60927
    Arlyn Rabideau, prin.
MS, P O BOX 6   60927 – Robert Vondrak, prin.
Other Schools – See Ashkum, Chebanse

Clinton, De Witt Co., Pop. Code 6
Clinton CUSD 15
Sch. Sys. Enr. Code 4
Supt. – Gary G. Archey
    115 W JOHNSON ST   61727
JHS, 401 N CENTER ST   61727
    James E. Trent, prin.
Douglas ES, 905 E MAIN ST   61727
    Thomas Dougherty, prin.
Lincoln MS, 407 S JACKSON ST   61727
    Richard Green, prin.
Washington ES, 411 N MULBERRY ST   61727
    Phillip Bolser, prin.
Webster MS, 612 N GEORGE ST   61727
    Enoch Nunnery, prin.

Coal City, Grundy Co., Pop. Code 5
Coal City CUSD 1
Sch. Sys. Enr. Code 4
Supt. – Jerry Arthur, 655 W DIVISION ST   60416
MS, 305 E DIVISION ST   60416
    Terrence Sorensen, prin.
ES, 300 N BROADWAY ST   60416
    Gary Snyder, prin.

Coal Valley, Rock Island Co., Pop. Code 5
Moline Unit SD 40
Supt. – See Moline
Bicentennial ES, 1004 1ST ST   61240
    G. Lentz, prin.

Cobden, Union Co., Pop. Code 3
Cobden Unit SD 17
Sch. Sys. Enr. Code 3
Supt. – Robert Schluter, P O BOX 158   62920
JHS, P O BOX 158   62920 – Robert Schluter, prin.
ES, P O BOX 158   62920 – Oran Lamer, prin.

Coffeen, Montgomery Co., Pop. Code 3
Hillsboro CUSD 3
Supt. – See Hillsboro
ES, P O BOX 62017 – Lamoine Reeves, prin.

Colchester, McDonough Co., Pop. Code 4
Colchester CUSD 180
Sch. Sys. Enr. Code 3
Supt. – McClelland Knight, P O BOX 357   62326
JHS, P O BOX 357   62326 – Dan Patterson, prin.
ES, P O BOX 261   62326 – Perry Lotz, prin.

Colfax, McLean Co., Pop. Code 3
Octavia CUSD 8
Sch. Sys. Enr. Code 2
Supt. – Eugene Jontry, P O BOX 100   61728
Octavia JHS, 202 E WOOD   61728
    Steve Johnson, prin.
Octavia ES, P O BOX 90   61728
    Robert Baughman, prin.

Collinsville, Madison Co., Pop. Code 7
Collinsville CUSD 10
Sch. Sys. Enr. Code 6
Supt. – John A. Renfro, 201 W CLAY ST   62234
North JHS, 1841 VANDALIA ST   62234
    Joseph Giglotto, prin.
Dorris ES, 500 PENNSYLVANIA ST   62234
    Yvonne Mossman, prin.
Jefferson ES, BOSKYDELLS   62234
    Gene Augustin, prin.
Kreitner ES, 9000 COLLEGE ST   62234
    Richard Lickfield, prin.
Lincoln ES, CAMELOT DR   62234
    Dennis Craft, prin.
Summit ES, 408 WILLOUGHBY LN   62234
    Dennis Craft, prin.
Twin Echo ES, 1937 S MORRISON AVE   62234
    Gene Augustin, prin.
Webster ES, 108 W CHURCH ST   62234
    Edward Wentz, prin.
Other Schools – See Caseyville, Maryville

Good Shepherd ES, 1300 BELTLINE ROAD   62234
Holy Cross Lutheran School
    S AND SEMINARY STS   62234
SS Peter & Paul School
    210 N MORRISON AVE   62234
St. John Neumann School, 142 WILMA DR   62234

Colona, Henry Co., Pop. Code 4
Colona SD 190
Sch. Sys. Enr. Code 2
Supt. – Dan Wright, 700 FIRST ST   61241
ES, 700 1ST ST   61241 – Michael Ryan, prin.

Columbia, Monroe Co., Pop. Code 5
Columbia CUSD 4
Sch. Sys. Enr. Code 3
Supt. – William Mygatt, 113 S RAPP AVE   62236
JHS, 113 S RAPP AVE   62236
    William J. McDannold, prin.
ES, 113 S RAPP AVE   62236
    William McDannold, prin.

Immaculate Conception School
    321 S METTER AVE   62236

Concord, Morgan Co., Pop. Code 2
Triopia CUSD 27
Sch. Sys. Enr. Code 2
Supt. – Michael Alexander
    RURAL ROUTE 01 BOX 141A   62631
Triopia ES, RURAL ROUTE 01 BOX 141-B   62631
    Steve McCarty, prin.

Congerville, Woodford Co., Pop. Code 2
Eureka CUSD 140
Supt. – See Eureka
ES, P O BOX 68   61729 – Patrick Grisham, prin.

Cornell, Livingston Co., Pop. Code 3
Cornell CCSD 426
Sch. Sys. Enr. Code 2
Supt. – Martha Angulo, P O BOX 217   61319
ES, P O BOX 217   61319 – Martha Angulo, prin.

Cottage Hills, Madison Co.
Bethalto CUSD 8
Supt. – See Bethalto
ES, 46 LENORA ST   62018
    Walter Ahlemeyer, prin.
Forest Homes ES, 950 14TH ST   62018
    Ron Lawson, prin.

Coulterville, Randolph Co., Pop. Code 4
Coulterville Unit SD 1
Sch. Sys. Enr. Code 2
Supt. – Ronald Mazander, P O BOX 386   62237
JHS, P O BOX 386   62237 – Les Oyler, prin.
ES, P O BOX 386   62237 – Les Oyler, prin.

Country Club Hills, Cook Co., Pop. Code 7
Country Club Hills SD 160
Sch. Sys. Enr. Code 4
Supt. – Edward L. Chartraw
    4411 185TH ST   60477
Southwood JHS, 18536 LEE ST   60477
    Roger Johnston, prin.
Meadowview ES, 4701 179TH ST   60477
    Judith Vostal, prin.
Southwood ES, 4600 187TH ST   60477
    Raymond Owens, prin.
Sykuta MS, 4301 180TH ST   60477
    Pauline Payette, prin.

Prairie Hills ESD 144
Supt. – See Hazel Crest
Nob Hill ES, 3701 168TH ST   60477
    Mark Vanclay, prin.

Countryside, Cook Co., Pop. Code 6
La Grange SD 105
Supt. – See La Grange
Ideal ES, 9901 E 58TH ST   60525
    Linda Fausch, prin.

Cowden, Shelby Co., Pop. Code 3
Cowden-Herrick ECCD 11
Sch. Sys. Enr. Code 2
Supt. – William Hill, P O BOX 188   62422
ES, P O BOX 188   62422 – John Vanvoorhis, prin.
Other Schools – See Herrick

Creal Springs, Williamson Co., Pop. Code 3
Marion CUSD 2
Supt. – See Marion
ES, POST OFFICE   62922 – Guy Peterson, prin.

Crescent City, Iroquois Co., Pop. Code 3
Crescent CITY CCSD 275
Sch. Sys. Enr. Code 2
Supt. – Russel White, P O BOX 190 60928
City C. C. ES, P O BOX 190 60928
Russell White, prin.

Crest Hill, Will Co., Pop. Code 6
Chaney-Monge SD 88
Sch. Sys. Enr. Code 3
Supt. – Bruce Lane, 400 ELSIE AVE 60435
Chaney-Monge JHS, 400 ELSIE AVE 60435
Bruce Lane, prin.
Chaney-Monge ES, 400 ELSIE AVE 60435
Bruce Lane, prin.

Richland SD 88A
Supt. – See Joliet
Richland ES, 1919 CATON FARM RD 60435
Ralph Haldorson, prin.

Creston, Ogle Co., Pop. Code 3
Creston CCSD 161
Sch. Sys. Enr. Code 2
Supt. – Adrian Pourchot, P O BOX 37 60113
ES, 202 W SOUTH ST #37 60113
Adrian Pourchot, prin.

Crestwood, Cook Co., Pop. Code 7
Blue Island SD 130
Supt. – See Blue Island
Hale MS, 5220 135TH ST 60445
Dr. Willie Mack, prin.
Hale IS, 5312 135TH ST 60445
Barry Ekman, prin.
Hale PS, 5324 135TH ST 60445
Edward Pitlik, prin.

Crete, Will Co., Pop. Code 6
Crete-Monee CUSD 201U
Sch. Sys. Enr. Code 5
Supt. – Jack Slaybaugh
1742 DIXIE HIGHWAY 60417
Balmoral ES, 701 MONEE RD 60417
Lugh Dixon, prin.
ES, 435 NORTH ST 60417 – Gale Guyer, prin.
Other Schools – See Monee, Park Forest, University Park

Creve Coeur, Tazewell Co., Pop. Code 6
Creve Coeur SD 76
Sch. Sys. Enr. Code 3
Supt. – Phillip Hardy
400 N HIGHLAND ST 61611
Parkview JHS, 800 GROVELAND ST 61611
Don Bockler, prin.
Homewood Heights ES, 107 RIVERVIEW DR 61611
Theodore Bradshaw, prin.
Lasalle ES, 300 N HIGHLAND ST 61611
Phillip Hardy, prin.

Crossville, White Co., Pop. Code 3
Carmi-White Co. CUSD 5
Supt. – See Carmi
ES, N STATE STREET 62827
Steven Martin, prin.

Crystal Lake, McHenry Co., Pop. Code 7
Crystal Lake CCSD 47
Sch. Sys. Enr. Code 5
Supt. – Richard Bernotas, 174 N OAK ST 60014
Lundahl JHS, 570 NASH ROAD 60014
Paul L. Rieger, prin.
North JHS, 170 N OAK ST 60014
Dennis Rasmussen, prin.
Canterbury ES, 875 CANTERBURY LN 60014
Lloyd Mueller, prin.
Coventry ES, 820 DARLINGTON LN 60014
Martin Anderson, prin.
Husman ES, 131 W PADDOCK ST 60014
Larry Vander Meade, prin.
North ES, 500 W WOODSTOCK ST 60014
Harold Wajrowski, prin.
South ES, 601 GOLF RD 60014
William Fetzner, prin.
West ES, 100 BRIARWOOD DR 60014
Kenneth Thelander, prin.

Prairie Grove CCSD 46
Sch. Sys. Enr. Code 3
Supt. – Dr. William Roy, 3223 ROUTE 176 60014
Prairie Grove ES, 3223 ROUTE 176 60014
Robert Nesladek, prin.

Immanuel Lutheran School
174 MCHENRY AVE 60014
St. Thomas the Apostle School
265 KING ST 60014

Cuba, Fulton Co., Pop. Code 4
Fulton County CUSD 3
Sch. Sys. Enr. Code 3
Supt. – David Ford, 669 E MAIN ST 61427
JHS, 652 E MAIN ST 61427
Charles Fleming, prin.
ES, 616 E POLK ST 61427 – Charles Barber, prin.
Other Schools – See Smithfield

Custer Park, Will Co.
Reed Custer CUSD 2550U
Supt. – See Braidwood
Custer Park ES
RURAL ROUTE 01 BOX 360 60418
Kenneth Wise, prin.

Cypress, Johnson Co., Pop. Code 2
Cypress SD 64
Sch. Sys. Enr. Code 2
Supt. – Lindell Croft, P O BOX 146 62923
ES, P O BOX 146 62923 – Lindell Croft, prin.

Dahlgren, Hamilton Co., Pop. Code 3
Hamilton Co. CUSD 10
Supt. – See Mc Leansboro
ES, 5TH & DALE STS 62828 – Debbie Owen, prin.

Dakota, Stephenson Co., Pop. Code 3
Dakota CUSD 201
Sch. Sys. Enr. Code 3
Supt. – Gary Schurz, P O BOX 128 61018
JHS, P O BOX 128 61018 – David Ziesmer, prin.
MS, P O BOX 128 61018 – Steven Panoske, prin.
PS, P O BOX 128 61018 – Steven Panoske, prin.

Dale, Hamilton Co.
Hamilton Co. CUSD 10
Supt. – See Mc Leansboro
ES, P O BOX 136 62829 – Karen Combs, prin.

Dallas City, Hancock Co., Pop. Code 4
Dallas City CUSD 336
Sch. Sys. Enr. Code 3
Supt. – Robert R. Clifton, 203 E 4TH ST 62330
ES, RURAL ROUTE 02 62330
Carroll Hickenbottom, prin.

Dalton City, Moultrie Co., Pop. Code 3
Mt. Zion CUSD 3
Supt. – See Mount Zion
ES, P O BOX 13 61925 – Barbara Backs, prin.

Dalzell, Bureau Co., Pop. Code 3
Dalzell SD 98
Sch. Sys. Enr. Code 2
Supt. – Linda Gustafson, P O BOX 200 61320
ES, P O BOX 200 61320 – Linda Gustafson, prin.

Danforth, Iroquois Co., Pop. Code 3
Iroquois West CUSD 10
Supt. – See Gilman
Iroquois West ES, 101 LOCUST 60930
Glen Phillips, prin.

Danvers, McLean Co., Pop. Code 3
Olympia CUSD 16
Supt. – See Stanford
ES, 205 N STATE 61732 – Fred Shears, prin.

Danville, Vermilion Co., Pop. Code 8
Community Unit SD 76
Supt. – See Fithian
Newton MS, RURAL ROUTE 01 BOX 226A 61832
James Trask, prin.
Diamond ES, 1701 BATESTOWN RD 61832
Thomas Burke, prin.

Danville CCSD 118
Sch. Sys. Enr. Code 6
Supt. – Dr. Donald Pennington
516 N JACKSON ST 61832
North Ridge MS, 1619 N JACKSON ST 61832
Phillip Smith, prin.
South View MS, 133 E 9TH ST 61832
Larry Roderick, prin.
Cannon ES, 1202 E MAIN ST 61832
David Carrell, prin.
Daniel ES, 1525 GEORGETOWN RD 61832
William Keller, prin.
Douglas ES, 500 FLORIDA ST 61832
Gary Rogers, prin.
East Park ES, 930 COLFAX DRIVE 61832
Mark Denman, prin.
Edison ES, 2101 N VERMILION ST 61832
David Guiliani, prin.
Garfield ES, 88 N GILBERT ST 61832
David Stimac, prin.
Liberty ES, 20 E LIBERTY LN 61832
George Vrentas, prin.
Meade Park ES, 200 S KANSAS AVE 61832
Ronald Davis, prin.
Northeast ES, 1330 E ENGLISH ST 61832
Barbara Hood-Winland, prin.

Holy Family School, 502 E MAIN ST 61832
Interparish Lutheran School
1930 N BOWMAN AVE 61832
St. Paul School, 1307 N WALNUT ST 61832

Darien, Du Page Co., Pop. Code 7
Cass SD 63
Sch. Sys. Enr. Code 3
Supt. – Robert Leli, 8502 BAILEY ROAD 60559
Cass JHS, 8502 BAILEY ROAD 60559
Harry Bohn, prin.
Concord ES, 1019 CONCORD PL 60559
Carole Pyle, prin.

Darien SD 61
Sch. Sys. Enr. Code 4
Supt. – John Nothacker, 7414 S CASS AVE 60559
Eisenhower JHS, 1410 75TH ST 60559
Joseph Pederson, prin.
Delay ES, 6801 S WILMETTE ST 60559
Charles Gray, prin.
Fairview ES, 7301 FAIRVIEW AVE 60559
Bernadette Everhart, prin.
Lace ES, 7414 S CASS AVE 60559
Daniel Tufo, prin.
Marion Hills ES, 133 PLAINFIELD RD 60559
Michael Gormley, prin.

Decatur, Macon Co., Pop. Code 8
Decatur SD 61
Sch. Sys. Enr. Code 7
Supt. – Walt Warfield
101 W CERRO GORDO ST 62523
Jefferson MS, 4735 E CANTRELL ST 62521
Robert Hantel, prin.
Mound MS, 3789 N WATER ST 62526
David Geibel, prin.
Roosevelt MS, 701 W GRAND AVE 62522
Don Diller, prin.
Adams ES, 300 MEADOW TERRACE PL 62521
Priscilla Palmer, prin.
Baum ES, 801 S LAKE RIDGE AVE 62521
Robert Patterson, prin.
Brush College ES
575 N BRUSH COLLEGE RD 62521
Janet Woodby, prin.
Coppenbarger ES, 1500 E CONDIT ST 62521
Alana Kirk, prin.
Dennis ES, 1499 W MAIN ST 62521
William Cogan, prin.
Durfee ES, 12222 E GRAND 62521
Carl Wilkey, prin.
Enterprise ES, 2115 S TAYLOR RD 62521
Lloyd Moma, prin.
Franklin ES, 2440 N SUMMIT AVE 62526
Walter Grant, prin.
French ES, 520 W WOOD ST 62522
Constance Ground, prin.
Garfield ES, 1000 W GRAND AVE 62522
Frank Lee, prin.
Harris ES, 620 E GARFIELD AVE 62526
Sandra Walker, prin.
Johns Hill Magnet ES, 1025 E JOHNS AVE 62521
Susan Henseler, prin.
Muffley ES, 88 S COUNTRY CLUB RD 62521
Robert Byrkit, prin.
Oak Grove ES, 2160 W CENTER ST 62526
Karen Paulson, prin.
Parsons ES, 3591 N MACARTHUR RD 62526
Leonard Long, prin.
Pershing ES, 2912 N UNIVERSITY AVE 62526
Patricia Scheiderer, prin.
South Shores ES
2500 S FRANKLIN STREET RD 62521
Katherine Lindsay, prin.
Southeast ES, 1900 E CLEVELAND AVE 62521
Anne Noland, prin.
Spencer ES, 3420 E GARFIELD AVE 62526
Janico Kuhila, prin.
Stevenson ES, 3900 N NEELY AVE 62526
Leo LaFauce, prin.
Washington ES, 400 S MAFFIT ST 62521
Barry Buttz, prin.

Mt. Zion CUSD 3
Supt. – See Mount Zion
Salem ES, 2610 SALEM SCHOOL RD 62521
Barbara Backs, prin.

Lutheran MS, 340 W WOOD ST 62522
Holy Family School
2400 S FRANKLIN STREET RD 62521
Lutheran ES, 340 W WOOD STREET 62522
Our Lady of Lourdes School
3950 LOURDES DR 62526
St. James School, 249 S WEBSTER ST 62521
St. Patrick School, 412 N JACKSON ST 62523
St. Thomas the Apostle School
2170 N EDWARD ST 62526

Deer Creek, Tazewell Co.
Deer Creek-Mackinaw CUSD 701
Supt. – See Mackinaw
ES, P O BOX 68 61733 – R. Thomas Avery, prin.

Deerfield, Lake Co., Pop. Code 7
Bannockburn SD 106
Sch. Sys. Enr. Code 2
Supt. – Dr. Lester Lavine
2165 TELEGRAPH ROAD 60015
Bannockburn ES, 2165 TELEGRAPH RD 60015
Dr. Lester Lavine, prin.

Deerfield SD 109
Sch. Sys. Enr. Code 4
Supt. – Dr. Charles J. Caruso
517 DEERFIELD ROAD 60015
Shepard JHS, 440 GROVE AVE 60015
Dante Divirgilio, prin.
Wilmot JHS, 1801 MONTGOMERY ROAD 60015
Alvin Cohen, prin.
Kipling ES, 700 KIPLING PL 60015
Kenneth Nilsen, prin.
South Park ES, 1421 HACKBERRY RD 60015
Earl Hartman, prin.
Walden ES, 630 ESSEX CT 60015
Harry Grover, prin.
Wilmot ES, 795 WILMOT RD 60015
Dale Roeing, prin.

Holy Cross School, 720 ELDER LN 60015

Deer Grove, Whiteside Co., Pop. Code 1
Tampico CUSD 4
Supt. – See Tampico
Hahanaman MS, P O BOX 68 61243
James Hochstatter, prin.

De Kalb, De Kalb Co., Pop. Code 8
DeKalb CUSD 428
Sch. Sys. Enr. Code 5
Supt. – Dr. Jack Deere, 145 FISK AVE 60115

Huntley MS, 821 S 7TH ST 60115
Del Brouwer, prin.
Rosette MS, 650 N 1ST ST 60115
George Pfister, prin.
Chesebro ES, 9TH ST & GARDEN 60115
Larry Fullerton, prin.
Jefferson ES, 211 MCCORMICK DR 60115
Dr. Robert Healey, prin.
Lincoln ES, SO SECOND & SUNSET 60115
James Keeney, prin.
Littlejohn ES, N 12TH & SCHOOL 60115
Ruth Kahl, prin.
Tyler ES, 1015 ALDEN CIRCLE 60115
James Keeney, prin.

St. Mary School, 320 FISK AVE 60115

De Land, Piatt Co., Pop. Code 3
Deland-Weldon CUSD 57
Sch. Sys. Enr. Code 2
Supt. – Robert L. Bowen, RURAL ROUTE 01 61839
Other Schools – See Weldon

Delavan, Tazewell Co., Pop. Code 4
Delavan CUSD 703
Sch. Sys. Enr. Code 3
Supt. – Richard Dutton, 907 LOCUST ST 61734
JHS, 907 LOCUST ST 61734 – Robert Shanks, prin.
ES, P O BOX 577 61734 – Bryan Hieser, prin.

Depue, Bureau Co., Pop. Code 4
DePue Unit SD 103
Sch. Sys. Enr. Code 2
Supt. – Ronald Fagan, 204 PLEASANT ST 61322
ES, 204 PLEASANT ST 61322
Robert Button, prin.

De Soto, Jackson Co., Pop. Code 4
DeSoto CCSD 86
Sch. Sys. Enr. Code 2
Supt. – Wade Hudgens
406 E WASHINGTON ST 62924
ES, 406 E WASHINGTON ST 62924
Wade Hudgens, prin.

Des Plaines, Cook Co., Pop. Code 8
Community Consolidated SD 59
Supt. – See Arlington Heights
Friendship JHS, 550 ELIZABETH LANE 60018
Walter Hamann, prin.
Brentwood ES, 260 DULLES RD 60016
Patricia Clifford, prin.
Devonsire ES, 1401 PENNSYLVANIA ST 60018
Russel Haak, prin.

Des Plaines CCSD 62
Sch. Sys. Enr. Code 5
Supt. – Paul Jung
777 E ALGONQUIN ROAD 60016
Algonquin JHS, 767 E ALGONQUIN ROAD 60016
Raymond Gunn, prin.
Chippewa JHS, 123 N EIGHT AVE 60016
James Hoffman, prin.
Iroquois JHS, 1836 E TOUHY AVE 60018
Jay Matthiesen, prin.
Central ES, 1526 THACKER ST 60016
Robert Kaszniak, prin.
Cumberland ES, 700 E GOLF RD 60016
Ronald Wuczynski, prin.
Forest ES, 1375 S 5TH AVE 60018
Phyllis Johnson, prin.
North ES, 1789 RAND RD 60016
Mari Cleary, prin.
Orchard Place ES, 2727 MAPLE ST 60018
Joy Kadlecik, prin.
Plainfield ES, 1850 PLAINFIELD DR 60018
John Pacay, prin.
South ES, 1535 EVERETT AVE 60018
William Walter, prin.
Terrace ES, 735 S WESTGATE RD 60016
Philip Dilallo, prin.

East Maine SD 63
Sch. Sys. Enr. Code 5
Supt. – Dr. Eldon Gleichman
10150 DEE ROAD 60016
Stevenson ES, 9000 CAPITOL DR 60016
Dr. Stewart Liechti, prin.
Twain ES, 9401 HAMLIN AVE 60016
Raymond Kuper, prin.
Other Schools – See Glenview, Niles

Immanuel Lutheran School, 832 LEE ST 60016
St. Mary School, 795 CENTER ST 60016
St. Stephen Protomartyr School
1880 S ASH ST 60018
St. Zachary School
567 W ALGONQUIN RD 60016

Dieterich, Effingham Co., Pop. Code 3
Dieterich CUSD 30
Sch. Sys. Enr. Code 2
Supt. – Clifford Jones, CHURCH & PINE 62424
JHS, P O BOX 187 62424 – Bill McClain, prin.
ES, P O BOX 187 62424
Stanley Struckmeyer, prin.

Teutopolis CUSD 50
Supt. – See Teutopolis
Bishop Creek ES, RURAL ROUTE 02 62424
Pat Green, prin.

Divernon, Sangamon Co., Pop. Code 4
Divernon CUSD 13
Sch. Sys. Enr. Code 2
Supt. – Thomas Veihman, P O BOX B 62530
ES, P O BOX B 62530 – Thomas Veihman, prin.

Dix, Jefferson Co., Pop. Code 2
Rome CCSD 2
Sch. Sys. Enr. Code 2
Supt. – Duane Bryant, 233 W SOUTH ST 62830
Rome Comm. Cons. ES, 233 W SOUTH ST 62830
Duane Bryant, prin.

Dixmoor, Cook Co., Pop. Code 5
West Harvey-Dixmoor SD 147
Supt. – See Harvey
King ES, 14400 SEELEY AVE 60426
Essie Harris, prin.
Lincoln ES, 141ST & HONORE 60426
Mary Arnold, prin.

Dixon, Lee Co., Pop. Code 7
Dixon Unit SD 170
Sch. Sys. Enr. Code 5
Supt. – Dr. Larry Roth
415 S HENNEPIN AVE 61021
Madison MS, 620 DIVISION ST 61021
Robert Wasson, prin.
Jefferson ES, 800 4TH AVE 61021
Christine Millenacker, prin.
Lincoln ES, 501 S LINCOLN AVE 61021
Larry Taylor, prin.
Washington ES, 703 E MORGAN ST 61021
Charles Malone, prin.

St. Anne School, 1112 BRINTON AVE 61021
St. Mary's School, 704 PEORIA AVE 61021

Dolton, Cook Co., Pop. Code 7
Dolton SD 148
Sch. Sys. Enr. Code 4
Supt. – Mark Van Clay
14151 LINCOLN AVE 60419
Lincoln JHS, 14151 LINCOLN AVE 60419
Michael Stritch, prin.
Roosevelt JHS, 146TH & LASALLE 60419
M. Zuiker, prin.
Franklin ES, 14701 CHICAGO RD 60419
Dorothia Fitzgerald, prin.
Lincoln ES, 14151 LINCOLN AVE 60419
Michael Stritch, prin.
Roosevelt ES, 146TH ST & LASALLE 60419
Carmon Labianca, prin.
Other Schools – See Riverdale

Dolton SD 149
Sch. Sys. Enr. Code 4
Supt. – James Medlock
15141 DORCHESTER AVE 60419
Berger-Vandenberg ES
14833 AVALON AVE 60419
Dr. Kenneth Jandes, prin.
Diekman ES, 15121 DORCHESTER AVE 60419
Dr. James Cunneen, prin.
Other Schools – See Calumet City

Dongola, Union Co., Pop. Code 3
Dongola Unit SD 66
Sch. Sys. Enr. Code 2
Supt. – Maurice Wilhoit
RURAL ROUTE 01 BOX DIST 62926
JHS, RURAL ROUTE 01 62926 – John Hill, prin.
ES, RURAL ROUTE 01 62926 – John Hill, prin.

Donovan, Iroquois Co., Pop. Code 2
Donovan CUSD 3
Sch. Sys. Enr. Code 2
Supt. – Stephen Shuda, P O BOX 186 60931
ES, RURAL ROUTE 01 60931
Charles Jackson, prin.

Dow, Jersey Co.
Jerseyville CUSD 100
Supt. – See Jerseyville
ES, RURAL ROUTE 01 62022 – Paul Brown, prin.

Downers Grove, Du Page Co., Pop. Code 8
Center Cass SD 66
Sch. Sys. Enr. Code 5
Supt. – Richard Motuelle
300 MANNING ROAD 60516
Lakeview JHS, 701 PLAINFIELD ROAD 60516
William Ward, prin.
Center Cass ES 60516 – Loren Tiede, prin.
Ide ES, 300 MANNING RD 60516
Frank Weber, prin.

Downers Grove SD 58
Sch. Sys. Enr. Code 5
Supt. – Dr. Jeffrey Weaver, 1860 63RD ST 60516
Herrick JHS, 4335 MIDDAUGH AVE 60515
(—), prin.
O'Neill JHS, 635 59TH ST 60516
Daniel Mahaffey, prin.
Belle Aire ES, 3935 BELLEAIRE DR 60515
James Swade, prin.
El Sierra ES, 6835 FAIRMOUNT AVE 60516
Robert Gullborg, prin.
Fairmount ES, 6036 BLODGETT AVE 60516
Ronald Hale, prin.
Highland ES, 3935 HIGHLAND AVE 60515
Marybeth Webeler, prin.
Hillcrest ES, 1435 JEFFERSON AVE 60516
Dr. Donald Del Bene, prin.
Indian Trail ES, 6235 STONEWALL AVE 60516
Paul Mikulcik, prin.
Kingsley ES, 1335 NORFOLK ST 60516
Jane Webster, prin.
Lester ES, 235 LINCOLN ST 60515
Fred Haber, prin.
Pierce-Downer ES, 1436 GRANT ST 60515
Norman Crandus, prin.

Whittier ES, 536 HILL ST 60515
Susan Borowiak, prin.

Puffer-Hefty SD 69
Sch. Sys. Enr. Code 2
Supt. – Wilmot Walker
2220 HADDOW AVE 60515
Puffer-Hefty ES, 2220 HADDOW AVE 60515
Kenneth Johannson, prin.

Marquette Manor Baptist Academy
333 75TH ST 60516
Avery Coonley School, 1400 MAPLE AVE 60515
St. Joseph School, 4824 HIGHLAND AVE 60515
St. Mary School, 445 PRAIRIE AVE 60515
St. Scholastica School, 7720 JANES AVE 60517

Downs, McLean Co., Pop. Code 3
Le Roy CUSD 2
Supt. – See Le Roy
Leroy ES, 805 N BARNETT ST 61752
Michael Company, prin.

Tri-Valley CUSD 3
Sch. Sys. Enr. Code 3
Supt. – Louie Boward
410 E WASHINGTON 61736
Tri-Valley JHS, 503 E WASHINGTON 61736
Dennis Moll, prin.
Tri-Valley ES, 409 E WASHINGTON 61736
John Balke, prin.

Dundee, Kane Co., Pop. Code 5
Dundee CUSD 300
Sch. Sys. Enr. Code 7
Supt. – Dr. Joseph Scime, 405 N 6TH ST 60118
MS, 37 W 450 ROUTE 72 60118
Dick Chamberlain, prin.
Dundee Highlands ES, 407 S 5TH ST 60118
Stephen Renne, prin.
Sleepyhollow ES, 898 GLEN OAK DR 60118
Sandra Tillery, prin.
Other Schools – See Algonquin, Carpentersville,
Hampshire

Immanuel Lutheran School
407 JOHNSON ST 60118
St. Catherine of Siena School
ROUTES 72 & 31 60118

Dunfermline, Fulton Co., Pop. Code 2
Dunfermline SD 88
Sch. Sys. Enr. Code 1
Supt. – Michael Brown, P O BOX 40 61524
ES, P O BOX 30 61524 – Mike Brown, prin.

Dunlap, Peoria Co., Pop. Code 3
Dunlap CUSD 323
Sch. Sys. Enr. Code 4
Supt. – Dr. William Collier
12610 N ALLEN ROAD 61525
Pioneer JHS, P O BOX 248 61525
S. Patrick Cassady, prin.
Banner ES, 12610 N ALLEN RD 61525
Harvey Varness, prin.
ES, 301 S FIRST 61525 – Dan Roberts, prin.
Other Schools – See Peoria

Dupo, St. Clair Co., Pop. Code 5
Dupo CUSD 196
Sch. Sys. Enr. Code 4
Supt. – Patrick H. Mudd, 600 LOUISA AVE 62239
JHS, 600 LOUISA AVE 62239
William Reynolds, prin.
ES, 400 LOUISA AVE 62239 – Georgia Horn, prin.
Hough ES, 2008 N MAIN ST 62239
Ed Brashear, prin.
Other Schools – See East Carondelet

Du Quoin, Perry Co., Pop. Code 6
Duquoin CUSD 300
Sch. Sys. Enr. Code 4
Supt. – Freddie Banks, 120 E SPRING ST 62832
Ward MS, 120 E SPRING ST 62832
Dr. Freddie Banks Jr., prin.
Lincoln ES, 306 W PARK ST 62832
Rosa Plunkett, prin.
McKinley ES, 302 W REED ST 62832
Emma Williams, prin.
Wheatley ES, 602 E FRANKLIN ST 62832
Linda Davis, prin.
Other Schools – See Tamaroa

Sacred Heart School, 110 W MAIN ST 62832

Durand, Winnebago Co., Pop. Code 4
Durand CUSD 322
Sch. Sys. Enr. Code 3
Supt. – Frank Miller, P O BOX 398 61024
JHS, P O BOX 398 61024 – Louis Tangorra, prin.
ES, P O BOX 398 61024 – (—), prin.

Dwight, Livingston Co., Pop. Code 5
Dwight Common SD 232
Sch. Sys. Enr. Code 3
Supt. – Larry Copes, 801 S COLUMBIA ST 60420
Dwight Common ES, 801 S COLUMBIA ST 60420
Larry Frye, prin.

Goodfarm CCSD 35C
Sch. Sys. Enr. Code 1
Supt. – Tim Hall, RURAL ROUTE 01 60420
Goodfarm Com. Cons. ES
RURAL ROUTE 01 60420 – Tim Hall, prin.

Earlville, La Salle Co., Pop. Code 4
Community Unit SD 2
Supt. – See Serena
Harding ES, RURAL ROUTE 02 60518
Michael Schneider, prin.

Earlville CUSD 9
Sch. Sys. Enr. Code 2
Supt. – Avery L. Wilson, P O BOX 539 60518
ES, P O BOX 539 60518 – Avery Wilson, prin.

East Alton, Madison Co., Pop. Code 6
East Alton SD 13
Sch. Sys. Enr. Code 4
Supt. – Michael Gray
180 E SAINT LOUIS AVE 62024
JHS, 1000 3RD ST 62024 – Gale Brown, prin.
Blair ES, 300 WASHINGTON AVE 62024
Paul Hellrung, prin.
Eastwood ES, 1030 3RD ST 62024
Ronald Malone, prin.
Lincoln ES, 163 N SHAMROCK 62024
Betty Cole, prin.
Washington ES, 180 E ST LOUIS AVE 62024
George Franke, prin.

Roxana CUSD 1
Supt. – See Roxana
Rosewood ES, 435 W ROSEDALE DR 62024
Marilyn Law, prin.

St. Kevin School, 4 ST KEVINS DR 62024

East Carondelet, St. Clair Co., Pop. Code 3
Dupo CUSD 196
Supt. – See Dupo
ES, POST OFFICE 62240 – Ed Brashear, prin.

East Chicago Heights, Cook Co., Pop. Code 6
East Chicago Heights SD 169
Sch. Sys. Enr. Code 4
Supt. – Dr. Constance Shorter
910 WOODLAWN AVE 60411
Cottage Grove MS
1400 COTTAGE GROVE AVE 60411
Mac Byrom, prin.
Evers ES, 1101 E 10TH ST 60411
Autry Arbor, prin.
Phillips MS, 1401 E 13TH PL 60411
Brenda Jones, prin.

East Dubuque, Jo Daviess Co., Pop. Code 4
East Dubuque Unit SD 119
Sch. Sys. Enr. Code 3
Supt. – Donald Kussmaul
200 PARKLANE DRIVE 61025
ES, HIGHWAY 35 61025
A. John Peseiski II, prin.

St. Mary's School, 701 ROUTE 35 N 61025

East Galesburg, Knox Co., Pop. Code 3
Knoxville CUSD 202
Supt. – See Knoxville
Marquith ES, MAIN ST 61430 – Bob Johnson, prin.

East Hazel Crest, Cook Co., Pop. Code 4
Hazel Crest SD 152-5
Supt. – See Hazel Crest
Lincoln ES, 173RD & THROOP 60429
Raymond Penn, prin.

East Moline, Rock Island Co., Pop. Code 7
East Moline SD 37
Sch. Sys. Enr. Code 5
Supt. – Garry Rudish, 836 17TH AVE 61244
Glenview JHS, 3210 7TH ST 61244
Robert Bailey, prin.
Hillcrest ES, 451 22ND AVE 61244
Sheila Wildermuth, prin.
Ridgewood ES, 3000 7TH ST 61244
Robert Nixon, prin.
Wells ES, 490 42ND AVE 61244
Curtis Behrends, prin.
Other Schools – See Silvis

St. Anne School, 602 17TH AVE 61244
St. Mary's School, 1925 13TH ST 61244

Easton, Mason Co., Pop. Code 2
Easton CUSD 121
Sch. Sys. Enr. Code 2
Supt. – Dr. Ronald Guenther, P O BOX 8 62633
JHS, P O BOX 8 62633 – Beverly Lafrance, prin.
ES, P O BOX 8 62633 – Beverly Lafrance, prin.

East Peoria, Tazewell Co., Pop. Code 7
East Peoria SD 86
Sch. Sys. Enr. Code 4
Supt. – Robert Becker
601 E WASHINGTON ST 61611
Central JHS, 601 E WASHINGTON ST 61611
John Knight, prin.
Armstrong-Oakview ES
1848 HIGHVIEW RD 61611 – Marvin Bohls, prin.
Bolin ES, 428 ARNOLD RD 61611
Ronald Dwyer, prin.
Glendale ES, 1000 BLOOMINGTON RD 61611
Michael Burdette, prin.
Lincoln ES, 801 SPRINGFIELD RD 61611
Michael Risen, prin.
Pleasant Hill ES, 304 S PLEASANT HILL 61611
Harold Fogelmark, prin.
Shute ES, 300 BRIARBROOK DR 61611
Dale Hovey, prin.
Wilson ES, 300 OAKWOOD AVE 61611
Sue Hurd, prin.

Riverview CCSD 2
Sch. Sys. Enr. Code 2
Supt. – Edwin Adam, RURAL ROUTE 08 61611
Riverview ES, RURAL ROUTE 08 61611
Peter Mellen, prin.

Robein SD 85
Sch. Sys. Enr. Code 2
Supt. – Gerald Stemas, 200 CAMPUS AVE 61611
Robein ES, 200 CAMPUS AVE 61611
Gerald Stemas, prin.

Sacre Coeur School, 601 RUSCHE LN 61611

East Saint Louis, St. Clair Co., Pop. Code 8
Cahokia CUSD 187
Supt. – See Cahokia
Centerville ES, 3429 CAMP JACKSON RD 62206
Roger Kohlman, prin.
Lalumier MS, 6702 BOND AVE 62207
Amanda Lewis, prin.

East St. Louis SD 189
Sch. Sys. Enr. Code 7
Supt. – Leroy Ducksworth, 1005 STATE ST 62201
Clark JHS, 3310 STATE ST 62205
Fonzy Coleman, prin.
Hughes-Quinn JHS, 1100 E BROADWAY 62201
Wendell Mitchell, prin.
King JHS, 70TH & RIDGE 62203
Leroy Howell, prin.
Lansdowne JHS, 3939 CASEYVILLE AVE 62204
John Morgan, prin.
Rock JHS, 10TH & OHIO AVE 62201
Stanley Campbell, prin.
Alta Sita ES, 2601 BOND AVE 62207
Dr. Garland Hawkins, prin.
Attucks ES, 2600 KANSAS AVE 62205
Dr. Garland Hawkins, prin.
Brown ES, 4901 GEORGE ST 62207
Walter Haire, prin.
Cannady ES, 1500 LAKE AVE 62205
Jesse Elverton, prin.
Davis ES, 725 N 15TH ST 62205
Richard Brooks, prin.
Dunbar ES, 1900 TUDOR AVE 62207
Elliott McKinney, prin.
Edgemont ES, 8601 WASHINGTON ST 62203
Lasalle Johnson, prin.
Garfield-Carver ES, 1024 N 2ND ST 62201
Charles Smith, prin.
Golden Garden ES, 327 PFIEFFER RD 62205
Walter Haire, prin.
Harding ES, 731 N 74TH ST 62203
Levi Dozier, prin.
Hawthorne ES, 1600 N 40TH ST 62204
Joseph Lewis, prin.
Jackson ES, 1798 COLLEGE AVE 62205
James Croom, prin.
Jefferson ES, 1800 N 25TH ST 62204
Scott Randolph, prin.
Lily-Freeman ES, 1236 E BROADWAY 62201
Charles Tigue, prin.
Lucas ES, 1620 RUSSELL AVE 62207
Thelma Starks, prin.
Manners ES, 1915 N 55TH ST 62204
Shirley Reid, prin.
McHenry ES, 2700 SUMMIT AVE 62205
Frederick Birth, prin.
Monroe ES, 1620 M L KING DR 62205
Eldora Adkins, prin.
Morrison ES, 630 N 59TH ST 62203
Mary Wrenn, prin.
Park Annex ES, 525 N 25TH ST 62205
Charles Smith, prin.
Robinson ES, 1435 MARKET AVE 62201
Eldora Adkins, prin.
Washington ES, 1100 PIGGOTT AVE 62201
Thelma Starks, prin.
Wilson ES, 4817 HALLOWS AVE 62204
Bennie Donald, prin.
Other Schools – See Alorton, Caseyville, Centreville

Holy Rosary School, 2727 N 43RD ST 62201
St. Joseph School
1501 MARTIN L KING DR 62205
St. Martin of Tours School
58TH & WARREN AVE 62204
St. Patrick School, 33RD AND SUMMIT 62205
St. Philip School, 8213 CHURCH LN 62203

Edgewood, Effingham Co., Pop. Code 3
Effingham CUSD 40
Supt. – See Effingham
MS 62426 – Walter Lebegue, prin.

Edinburg, Christian Co., Pop. Code 4
Edinburg CUSD 4
Sch. Sys. Enr. Code 2
Supt. – Charles Bartimus
RURAL ROUTE 01 BOX 5 62531
JHS, RURAL ROUTE 01 BOX 5 62531
Deborah Hapli, prin.
ES, RURAL ROUTE 01 BOX 5 62531
Deborah Hapli, prin.

Edwards, Peoria Co.

St. Mary School, P O BOX 56 61528

Edwardsville, Madison Co., Pop. Code 7
Edwardsville CUSD 7
Sch. Sys. Enr. Code 5
Supt. – Allen McCowan, 708 ST LOUIS ST 62025
JHS, SAINT LOUIS ROAD 62025 – Ron Goff, prin.

Coluumbus ES, 315 N KANSAS ST 62025
John Novotny, prin.
LeClaire ES, 801 FRANKLIN AVE 62025
Gary Ragan, prin.
Nelson ES, 1225 W HIGH ST 62025
Janet Rose, prin.
Other Schools – See Glen Carbon, Hamel, Moro

St. Boniface School, 128 N BUCHANAN ST 62025
Trinity Lutheran School, 600 WATER ST 62025

Effingham, Effingham Co., Pop. Code 7
Effingham CUSD 40
Sch. Sys. Enr. Code 5
Supt. – Robert Hickman
1000 W GROVE AVE 62401
Central ES, RURAL ROUTE 01 BOX 9 62401
Michael Schmitz, prin.
East Side ES, 215 N 1ST ST 62401
Mary Day, prin.
Funkhouser ES, RURAL ROUTE 04 62401
Chris Long, prin.
South Side ES, 211 W DOUGLAS AVE 62401
Chris Long, prin.
West Side ES, 900 W EDGAR AVE 62401
David Durr, prin.
Other Schools – See Edgewood, Mason

Teutopolis CUSD 50
Supt. – See Teutopolis
Green Creek ES, RURAL ROUTE 03 62401
(—), prin.

Sacred Heart School, 405 S BANKER ST 62401
St. Anthony Grade School, 412 N 3RD ST 62401

Eldorado, Saline Co., Pop. Code 6
Eldorado CUSD 4
Sch. Sys. Enr. Code 4
Supt. – Gary Siebert
1040 WASHINGTON ST 62930
JHS, 1907 1ST ST 62930 – Glenn Dexter, prin.
ES, RURAL ROUTE 01 62930
Steven Nelson, prin.

Elgin, Kane Co., Pop. Code 8
Elgin Unit SD 46
Sch. Sys. Enr. Code 8
Supt. – Dr. Richard Wiggall
4 S GIFFORD ST 60120
Abbott MS, 949 VAN ST 60123
James Entwistle, prin.
Ellis MS, 225 S LIBERTY ST 60120
James Feuerborn, prin.
Kimball MS, 451 N MCLEAN BLVD 60123
David Covey, prin.
Larsen MS, 665 DUNDEE AVE 60120
Ronald O'Neal, prin.
Century Oaks ES, 1235 BRAEBURN DR 60123
Dr. Harold Henrikson, prin.
Channing Memorial ES
63 S CHANNING ST 60120 – Clark White, prin.
Coleman ES, 1220 DUNDEE AVE 60120
(—), prin.
Garfield ES, 420 MAY ST 60120 – Ann Jones, prin.
Gifford ES, 240 S CLIFTON AVE 60123
Harvey Eisner, prin.
Grant ES, 265 N JACKSON ST 60123
Ruth Miller, prin.
Highland ES, 1221 W HIGHLAND AVE 60123
John Larson, prin.
Hillcrest ES, 80 AIRLITE ST 60123
Gretchen Ludwig, prin.
Huff ES, 801 HASTINGS ST 60120
Luis Cabrera, prin.
Illinois Park ES, 1350 WING ST 60123
Catherine Dunphy, prin.
Lords Park ES, 323 WAVERLY DR 60120
(—), prin.
Lowrie ES, 264 OAK ST 60123
Thomas Dahlfors, prin.
McKinley ES, 258 LOVELL ST 60120
(—), prin.
Sheridan ES, 510 FRANKLIN BLVD 60120
Elaine King, prin.
Washington ES, 819 W CHICAGO ST 60123
Gregory Schneider, prin.
Other Schools – See Bartlett, Hanover Park, South Elgin, Streamwood, Wayne

Elgin Academy, 350 PARK ST 60120
Chicago Junior School, 1600 DUNDEE AVE 60120
Good Shepherd Lutheran School
111 VAN ST 60120
St. John's Lutheran School
109 N SPRING ST 60120
St. Joseph School, 274 DIVISION ST 60120
St. Laurence School, 572 STANDISH ST 60123
St. Mary School, 103 S GILFORD ST 60120
St. Thomas More School
1625 W HIGHLAND AVE 60123

Elizabeth, Jo Daviess Co., Pop. Code 3
River Ridge CUSD 210
Sch. Sys. Enr. Code 3
Supt. – James Burgett, P O BOX J 61028
ES, P O BOX J 61028 – Steven Pennock, prin.
Other Schools – See Hanover

Elizabethtown, Hardin Co., Pop. Code 2
Hardin Co. CUSD 1
Sch. Sys. Enr. Code 4
Supt. – Neal S. Cole, P O BOX 218 62931
Hardin Co. JHS, RURAL ROUTE 02 62931
Steve Karraker, prin.

Hardin County ES, RURAL ROUTE 02 62931
  Wendell Robinson, prin.

Elk Grove Village, Cook Co., Pop. Code 8
Community Consolidated SD 59
Supt. – See Arlington Heights
Grove JHS, 777 W ELK GROVE BLVD 60007
  Dr. Phillip Thornton, prin.
Byrd ES, 265 WELLINGTON AVE 60007
  Nancy Fritz, prin.
Clearmont ES, 280 CLEARMONT DR 60007
  Anthony Mostardo, prin.
Rupley ES, 305 E OAKTON ST 60007
  Dale Wilke, prin.
Salt Creek ES, 65 KENNEDY BLVD 60007
  Robert Koehnke, prin.

Schaumburg CCSD 54
Supt. – See Schaumburg
Mead JHS, 1765 BIESTERFIELD ROAD 60007
  Kenneth Ciosek, prin.
Link ES, 900 GLENN TRL 60007
  Judith Shipka, prin.
Stevenson ES, 1414 ARMSTRONG LN 60007
  Donald Litchfield, prin.

Queen of the Rosary School
  680 ELK GROVE BLVD 60007

Elkhart, Logan Co., Pop. Code 2
Mt. Pulaski CUSD 23
Supt. – See Mount Pulaski
ES, P O BOX 217 62634 – Donald Hawkins, prin.

Elkville, Jackson Co., Pop. Code 3
Elverado CUSD 196
Sch. Sys. Enr. Code 3
Supt. – William Valerius, 114 S 8TH ST 62932
ES, 114 S 8TH ST 62932 – William Valerius, prin.
Other Schools – See Vergennes

Ellis Grove, Randolph Co., Pop. Code 2
Sparta CUSD 140
Supt. – See Sparta
Central ES, RURAL ROUTE 01 62241
  Michael Reeves, prin.

Elmhurst, Du Page Co., Pop. Code 8
Elmhurst SD 205
Sch. Sys. Enr. Code 6
Supt. – Dr. Russell Thiems
  145 ARTHUR ST 60126
Bryan JHS, 111 W BUTTERFIELD ROAD 60126
  Richard Stahl, prin.
Churchville JHS, 155 VICTORY PARKWAY 60126
  Dennis Hatt, prin.
Sandburg JHS
  345 E SAINT CHARLES ROAD 60126
  Mary Ann Ross, prin.
Edison ES, FAIR & HUNTINGTON 60126
  Barbara Habschmidt, prin.
Emerson ES, 400 N WEST AVE 60126
  Daniel Wachholz, prin.
Field ES, 295 EMROY ST 60126
  Dr Milton Honel, prin.
Fischer ES, WILSON & VICTORY PARK 60126
  George Jacobs, prin.
Hawthorne ES, 145 ARTHUR ST 60126
  Peter Graber, prin.
Jackson ES, 925 SWAIN ST 60126
  Dr. Ramona McNeese, prin.
Jefferson ES, 360 E CRESCENT ST 60126
  Tad Ryan, prin.
Lincoln ES, 565 FAIRFIELD ST 60126
  Linda Kime, prin.

Salt Creek SD 48
Supt. – See Villa Park
Salt Creek ES, 980 RIVERSIDE DR 60126
  John Carpenter, prin.

Timothy Christian JHS
  188 W BUTTERFIELD RD 60126
Immaculate Conception School
  132 ARTHUR ST 60126
Immanuel Lutheran School, 148 E 3RD ST 60126
Timothy Christian School
  188 W BUTTERFIELD RD 60126
Visitation School, 851 S YORK RD 60126

Elmwood, Peoria Co., Pop. Code 4
Elmwood CUSD 322
Sch. Sys. Enr. Code 3
Supt. – Michael Duffy, 301 W BUTTERNUT 61529
JHS, 301 W BUTTERNUT 61529
  John Capasso, prin.
ES, 201 S ALTHEA 61529 – Jeffrey Nelson, prin.

Elmwood Park, Cook Co., Pop. Code 7
Elmwood Park CUSD 401
Sch. Sys. Enr. Code 4
Supt. – Larry Beckley
  8201 W FULLERTON AVE 60635
Elm ES, 7607 W CORTLAND ST 60635
  John Corwin, prin.
Elmwood ES, 2319 N 76TH AVE 60635
  William Schmidt, prin.
Mills ES, 2824 N 76TH AVE 60635
  Sharon Kaczmarek, prin.

El Paso, Woodford Co., Pop. Code 5
El Paso CUSD 375
Sch. Sys. Enr. Code 3
Supt. – James Miller, P O BOX 115 61738
Centennial MS, 5TH & ELM 61738
  Donald Juricka, prin.

Jefferson Park ES, 250 W 3RD ST 61738
  George Boyd, prin.

Elwood, Will Co., Pop. Code 3
Elwood CCSD 203
Sch. Sys. Enr. Code 2
Supt. – Ron Pazanin
  NORTH CHICAGO AVE 60421
Elwood Community Consolidated ES
  N CHICAGO AVE 60421 – Ronald Pazanin, prin.

Emden, Logan Co., Pop. Code 3
Hartsburg-Emden CUSD 21
Supt. – See Hartsburg
MS, P O BOX 62635 – Douglas Horner, prin.

Energy, Williamson Co., Pop. Code 4
Herrin CUSD 4
Supt. – See Herrin
ES, ROUTE 148 62933 – Louis Schwarn, prin.

Enfield, White Co., Pop. Code 3
Norris City-Omaha-Enfield CUSD 3
Supt. – See Norris City
ES, US 45 NORTH 62835 – Norman Fechtig, prin.

Eola, Du Page Co.
Indian Prairie CUSD 204
Supt. – See Naperville
Indian Plains ES, 5 S 700 EOLA RD 60519
  Frederick Lacher, prin.

Equality, Gallatin Co., Pop. Code 3
Gallatin CUSD 7
Supt. – See Shawneetown
ES, P O BOX 8 62934 – Michael Phelps, prin.

Erie, Whiteside Co., Pop. Code 4
Erie CUSD 1
Sch. Sys. Enr. Code 3
Supt. – Earle Mailand
  RURAL ROUTE 02 BOX 86 61250
MS, 508 5TH AVE 61250 – Leslie O'Melia, prin.
ES, 6TH ST & 6TH AVE 61250 – Ronald Vail, prin.
Other Schools – See Fenton

Esmond, De Kalb Co.
Eswood CCSD 269
Supt. – See Lindenwood
ES, P O BOX 99 60129 – Gerald Olson, prin.

Essex, Kankakee Co., Pop. Code 2
Reed Custer CUSD 2550U
Supt. – See Braidwood
Essex ES, POST OFFICE 60935
  Edgar Gaskill, prin.

Eureka, Woodford Co., Pop. Code 5
Eureka CUSD 140
Sch. Sys. Enr. Code 4
Supt. – Ronald McIntire
  200 W CRUGER AVE 61530
MS, 2005 S MAIN ST 61530
  James D. Kelly, prin.
Davenport ES, 301 S MAIN ST 61530
  Wayne Logsdon, prin.
Other Schools – See Congerville, Goodfield

Evanston, Cook Co., Pop. Code 8
Evanston CCSD 65
Sch. Sys. Enr. Code 6
Supt. – Joseph Pollack, 1314 RIDGE AVE 60201
Chute MS, 1400 OAKTON ST 60202
  Edward C. Pate, prin.
Haven MS, 2417 PRAIRIE AVE 60201
  Lorraine Morton, prin.
Nichols MS, 800 GREENLEAF ST 60202
  Carmen Marcy, prin.
Dawes ES, 440 DODGE AVE 60202
  Frank Miralgio, prin.
Dewey ES, 1551 WESLEY AVE 60201
  Michael Martin, prin.
King Jr. Lab Experimental ES
  2424 LAKE ST 60201 – Corrine Schumacher, prin.
Lincoln ES, 910 FOREST AVE 60202
  Warren Cherry, prin.
Lincolnwood ES, 2600 COLFAX ST 60201
  Alan Nieman, prin.
Oakton ES, 436 RIDGE AVE 60202
  Clara Pate, prin.
Orrington ES, 2636 ORRINGTON AVE 60201
  Jo Ann Wilkin, prin.
Washington ES, 914 ASHLAND AVE 60202
  Annette Grubman, prin.
Willard ES, 2700 HURD AVE 60201
  Walter Schiller, prin.
Other Schools – See Skokie

Roycemore School, 640 LINCOLN ST 60201
St. Athansius School, 2510 ASHLAND AVE 60201
Pope John XXIII School
  1120 WASHINGTON ST 60202

Evansville, Randolph Co., Pop. Code 3
Sparta CUSD 140
Supt. – See Sparta
MS, TAYLOR ST 62242 – Michael Reeves, prin.

Evergreen Park, Cook Co., Pop. Code 7
Evergreen Park ESD 124
Sch. Sys. Enr. Code 4
Supt. – Dr. Thomas W. Eson
  9400 S SAWYER AVE 60642
Central JHS, 95TH ST & SAWYER AVE 60642
  Earl Canfield, prin.
Northeast ES, 91ST & CALIFORNIA 60642
  Darrell Trotter, prin.

Northwest ES, 92ND & MILLARD 60642
  Thomas Ivano, prin.
Southeast ES, 98TH ST & FRANCISCO 60642
  Rita Welsh, prin.
Southwest ES, 99TH & CENTRAL PARK 60642
  James Cross, prin.

Ewing, Franklin Co., Pop. Code 2
Ewing Northern CCSD 115
Sch. Sys. Enr. Code 2
Supt. – Ron McCormick, P O BOX 525 62836
Ewing-Northern ES, P O BOX 525 62836
  Walter Montgomery, prin.

Fairbury, Livingston Co., Pop. Code 5
Prairie Central CUSD 8
Supt. – See Forrest
Westview ES, 600 S 1ST ST 61739
  Anthony Menke, prin.

Fairfield, Wayne Co., Pop. Code 6
Fairfield SD 112
Sch. Sys. Enr. Code 3
Supt. – William Phillips
  200 W CENTER ST 62837
Center Street MS, 200 W CENTER ST 62837
  Michael Simpson, prin.
North Side ES, 806 N 1ST ST 62837
  William Phillips, prin.

Jasper CCSD 17
Sch. Sys. Enr. Code 2
Supt. – Billie Hubbell, RURAL ROUTE 03 62837
Jasper ES, RURAL ROUTE 03 62837
  Billie Hubbell, prin.

Merriam CCSD 19
Sch. Sys. Enr. Code 2
Supt. – David Hock, RURAL ROUTE 02 62837
Merriam ES, RURAL ROUTE 02 62837
  David Hock, prin.

New Hope CCSD 6
Sch. Sys. Enr. Code 2
Supt. – Gerald Taylor, RURAL ROUTE 04 62837
New Hope ES, RURAL ROUTE 04 62837
  Fred Kieslar, prin.

Fairview Heights, St. Clair Co., Pop. Code 7
Grant CCSD 110
Sch. Sys. Enr. Code 3
Supt. – Kenneth Perkins
  10110 LINCOLN TRAIL 62208
Grant JHS, 10110 LINCOLN TRAIL 62208
  Carl Buehler, prin.
Illini ES, 21 CIRCLE DR 62208 – (—), prin.

Pontiac-West Holliday SD 105
Sch. Sys. Enr. Code 3
Supt. – Denise Cox, 400 ASHLAND PLACE 62208
Pontiac JHS, 400 ASHLAND PLACE 62208
  Bill Fulk, prin.
Other Schools – See Belleville

Our Lady of the Assumption School
  9940 BUNKUM RD 62208
St. Albert the Great School
  15 LINCOLN HWY 62208

Farina, Fayette Co., Pop. Code 3
LaGrove CUSD 206
Sch. Sys. Enr. Code 2
Supt. – Joseph E. Ross, P O BOX 250 62838
Lagrove ES, P O BOX 250 62838
  Lindell Roberts, prin.

Farmer City, De Witt Co., Pop. Code 4
Blue Ridge CUSD 18
Sch. Sys. Enr. Code 3
Supt. – Don Albracht, 398 N JOHN ST 61842
Franklin ES, 408 E HIGH ST 61842
  Charles Williams, prin.
Schneider MS, 309 N JOHN ST 61842
  Charles Williams, prin.
Other Schools – See Bellflower, Mansfield

Farmersville, Montgomery Co., Pop. Code 3
Panhandle CUSD 2
Supt. – See Raymond
ES, P O BOX 158 62533 – Howard Hartke, prin.

Farmington, Fulton Co., Pop. Code 5
Farmington Central CUSD 265
Supt. – See Trivoli
Chapman JHS, 322 E FORT ST 61531
  John Patterson, prin.
Harris ES, 362 W FORT ST 61531
  John Patterson, prin.

Fenton, Whiteside Co., Pop. Code 3
Erie CUSD 1
Supt. – See Erie
ES, RURAL ROUTE 61251 – Ronald Vail, prin.

Fieldon, Jersey Co., Pop. Code 2
Jerseyville CUSD 100
Supt. – See Jerseyville
ES 62031 – Charles Berlman, prin.

Findlay, Shelby Co., Pop. Code 3
Findlay CUSD 2
Sch. Sys. Enr. Code 2
Supt. – Ron Nash, 501 W DIVISION 62534
JHS, 501 W DIVISION 62534
  Larry Bradford, prin.
ES, 206 N MAIN ST 62534 – Ron Hash, prin.

Fisher, Champaign Co., Pop. Code 4
Fisher CUSD 1
Sch. Sys. Enr. Code 3
Supt. – Richard Taylor, P O BOX 568 61843
ES, 100 E SCHOOL ST 61843
    Richard Taylor, prin.

Fithian, Vermilion Co., Pop. Code 3
Community Unit SD 76
Sch. Sys. Enr. Code 4
Supt. – Dr. James Ellis
    RURAL ROUTE 02 BOX 52A 61844
ES, P O BOX 98 61844 – Michael Metzen, prin.
Other Schools – See Danville, Oakwood

Flanagan, Livingston Co., Pop. Code 3
Flanagan CUSD 4
Sch. Sys. Enr. Code 2
Supt. – William Braksick, P O BOX 367 61740
ES 61740 – William Braksick, prin.

Flora, Clay Co., Pop. Code 6
Flora CUSD 35
Sch. Sys. Enr. Code 4
Supt. – Floyd Henson, 509 S LOCUST ST 62839
JHS, RURAL ROUTE 01 BOX 188 62839
    Charles Martin, prin.
Lincoln MS, RURAL ROUTE 02 62839
    Mart Haycock, prin.
McEndree ES, 200 N OLIVE RD 62839
    Larry Rinehart, prin.
Washington ES, 114 E WASHINGTON 62839
    Charles Martin, prin.
Other Schools – See Xenia

Flossmoor, Cook Co., Pop. Code 6
Flossmoor SD 161
Sch. Sys. Enr. Code 4
Supt. – Dr. L. Thomas Moore
    2810 SCHOOL ST 60422
Parker JHS, 2810 SCHOOL ST 60422
    Richard Wilson, prin.
Flossmoor Hills ES, 3721 BEECH ST 60422
    Patricia Wolsko, prin.
Heather Hill ES, 1439 LAWRENCE CRESC 60422
    Joan Bertram, prin.
Western Avenue ES, 940 WESTERN AVE 60422
    Lary Bolt, prin.
Other Schools – See Chicago Heights

Infant Jesus of Prague School
    1101 DOUGLAS AVE 60422

Forest Park, Cook Co., Pop. Code 7
Forest Park SD 91
Sch. Sys. Enr. Code 3
Supt. – Joseph Scolire, 939 BELOIT AVE 60130
MS, 925 BELOIT AVE 60130 – John Ericksen, prin.
Garfield ES, HANNAH & JACKSON 60130
    Edward Phillips, prin.
Grant-White ES, CIRCLE & RANDOLPH 60130
    Edward Phillips, prin.
Ross ES, 13TH & MARENGO AVE 60130
    Robert Priest, prin.
Stevenson ES, 925 BELOIT AVE 60130
    Robert Priest, prin.

St. Bernardine School, 815 ELGIN AVE 60130
St. John Lutheran School, 305 CIRCLE AVE 60130

Forrest, Livingston Co., Pop. Code 4
Prairie Central CUSD 8
Sch. Sys. Enr. Code 4
Supt. – Dr. Calvin Jackson
    312 N CENTER ST 61741
Prairie Central JHS, 312 N CENTER ST 61741
    Leeon Carrico, prin.
Meadowbrook ES, 450 N BACH ST 61741
    Joseph Delaney, prin.
Other Schools – See Chatsworth, Fairbury

Forreston, Ogle Co., Pop. Code 4
Forrestville Valley CUSD 221
Sch. Sys. Enr. Code 3
Supt. – T. M. Gapinski, P O BOX 665 61030
ES, P O BOX 665 61030 – Romaine Capps, prin.
German Valley ES, P O BOX 665 61030
    Romaine Capps, prin.

Forsyth, Macon Co., Pop. Code 4
Maroa-Forsyth CUSD 2
Supt. – See Maroa
ES, P O BOX 30 62535 – Robert Ritter, prin.

Fox Lake, Lake Co., Pop. Code 6
Fox Lake Grade SD 114
Sch. Sys. Enr. Code 3
Supt. – Ralph Stanton, 17 FOREST AVE 60020
Shady Lane Building ES
    101 HAWTHORNE LN 60020
    Bill Steichmann, prin.
Forest Building ES, 17 FOREST AVE 60020
    Ralph Stanton, prin.

Fox River Grove, McHenry Co., Pop. Code 5
Fox River Grove CSD 3
Sch. Sys. Enr. Code 2
Supt. – Robert Stanger
    975 ALGONQUIN ROAD 60021
Orchard Street MS, 401 ORCHARD ST 60021
    Kathleen Kuhr, prin.
Algonquin Road ES, 975 ALGONQUIN RD 60021
    Robert Stanger, prin.

Frankfort, Will Co., Pop. Code 5
Frankfort CCSD 157C
Sch. Sys. Enr. Code 3
Supt. – Leroy Olson, 110 OREGON ST 60423
JHS, P O BOX 22 60423 – John Loecke, prin.
Chelsea ES, 601 WILLOW ST 60423
    Dennis Nielsen, prin.
Hickory Creek MS
    RURAL ROUTE 01 BOX 22A 60423
    John White, prin.

Peotone CUSD 207U
Supt. – See Peotone
Green Garden ES
    RURAL ROUTE 02 BOX 197 60423
    Hal Paddock, prin.

Summit Hill SD 161
Sch. Sys. Enr. Code 4
Supt. – Julian Rogus, RURAL ROUTE 03 60423
Summit Hill JHS, 354 ROSEWOOD DRIVE 60423
    John Peterson, prin.
Frankfort Square ES
    399 KINGSTON DRIVE 60423
    Karen Prudik, prin.
Indian Trail ES, 100 FRANKFORT SQUARE 60423
    Steve Pieritz, prin.
Other Schools – See Mokena

Franklin, Morgan Co., Pop. Code 3
Franklin CUSD 1
Sch. Sys. Enr. Code 2
Supt. – Fred Roberts, 110 STATE ST 62638
JHS, 110 STATE ST 62638 – Ross Myers, prin.
Franklin East ES, P O BOX 188 62638
    Paula Roscetti, prin.
Other Schools – See Alexander

Franklin Grove, Lee Co., Pop. Code 3
Lee Center CUSD 271
Supt. – See Paw Paw
ES, P O BOX 205 61031 – Bennett Dillon, prin.

Franklin Park, Cook Co., Pop. Code 7
Franklin Park SD 84
Sch. Sys. Enr. Code 3
Supt. – Lawrence W. Passow
    9750 W FULLERTON AVE 60131
Hester JHS, 2836 GUSTAVE ST 60131
    Robert Bradley, prin.
North ES, 9500 GAGE ST 60131
    Helen Wegrzyn, prin.
South ES, 9750 FULLERTON AVE 60131
    Thomas O'brien, prin.
West ES, 2838 CALWAGNER AVE 60131
    Richard Hrejsa, prin.

Mannheim SD 83
Sch. Sys. Enr. Code 4
Supt. – Dr. John F. Ludolph
    10401 GRAND AVE 60131
Other Schools – See Melrose Park, Northlake

St. Gertrude School, 9617 SCHILLER BLVD 60131

Freeburg, St. Clair Co., Pop. Code 5
Freeburg CCSD 70
Sch. Sys. Enr. Code 3
Supt. – Dr. Clarence Haege
    408 S BELLEVILLE ST 62243
ES, 408 S BELLEVILLE ST 62243
    Lawrence Meggs, prin.

St. Joseph School, 2 N ALTON ST 62243

Freeport, Stephenson Co., Pop. Code 8
Freeport SD 145
Sch. Sys. Enr. Code 5
Supt. – Dr. Ted Wetekamp
    1205 S CHICAGO AVE 61032
JHS, W EMPIRE ST 61032 – Scott Wiley, prin.
Blackhawk ES, 1401 S BLACKHAWK AVE 61032
    John Maaske, prin.
Center ES, 718 E ILLINOIS ST 61032
    Thomas Nesmith, prin.
Empire ES, 1401 W EMPIRE ST 61032
    Patricia Burke, prin.
Lincoln-Douglas ES, 1700 W LAUREL ST 61032
    Terry Anderson, prin.
Sandburg Upper MS, 1717 W EBY ST 61032
    James Argo, prin.
Taylor Park ES, 806 E STEPHENSON ST 61032
    Ann Stevens, prin.

Immanuel Lutheran School
    1964 W PEARL CITY RD 61032
St. Joseph ES, 202 W PLEASANT ST 61032

Fulton, Whiteside Co., Pop. Code 5
River Bend CUSD 2
Sch. Sys. Enr. Code 4
Supt. – Kent Hammer, 415 12TH ST 61252
JHS, 415 12TH ST 61252 – Ben Ray, prin.
ES, 13TH ST & 7TH AVE 61252 – Ben Ray, prin.
Other Schools – See Albany

Gages Lake, Lake Co., Pop. Code 4
Woodland CCSD 50
Sch. Sys. Enr. Code 4
Supt. – Marlin Meyer
    17368 W GAGES LAKE ROAD 60030
Woodland JHS
    17371 W GAGES LAKE ROAD 60030
    Donald Bradley, prin.
Woodland ES, 17368 W GAGES LAKE RD 60030
    Fred Becker, prin.

Woodland IS, 17261 W GAGES LAKE RD 60030
    J. Eiduke, prin.

Galatia, Saline Co., Pop. Code 4
Galatia CUSD 1
Sch. Sys. Enr. Code 2
Supt. – Linda Blackman
    RURAL ROUTE 01 BOX SD 62935
JHS, RURAL ROUTE 01 62935
    Jim Stunson, prin.
ES, P O BOX 97 62935 – Dr. Linda Blackman, prin.

Galena, Jo Daviess Co., Pop. Code 5
Galena Unit SD 120
Sch. Sys. Enr. Code 4
Supt. – Dale Nabors, 1300 N FRANKLIN ST 61036
MS, 1200 FRANKLIN ST 61036
    Dale Henze, prin.
PS, HIGHWAY 20 W 61036
    Harvey Witzenburg, prin.

Galesburg, Knox Co., Pop. Code 8
Galesburg CUSD 205
Sch. Sys. Enr. Code 6
Supt. – Dr. William Abel, P O BOX 1206 61402
Churchill JHS, 905 MAPLE AVE 61401
    Larry Kreeb, prin.
Lombard JHS, 1220 E KNOX ST 61401
    Patrick Callahan, prin.
Gale ES, 1131 W DAYTON ST 61401
    Lorraine Seggelke, prin.
King ES, 1018 S FARNHAM ST 61401
    Marlowe Cowley, prin.
Lincoln ES, 932 HARRISON ST 61401
    Pamela Kershaw, prin.
Nielson ES, 547 N FARNHAM ST 61401
    Shirley Weese, prin.
Steele ES, 1480 W MAIN ST 61401
    Maury Lyon, prin.
Willard ES, 495 E FREMONT ST 61401
    Elizabeth Rinehart, prin.

Costa Catholic School, 2726 COSTA DR 61401

Galva, Henry Co., Pop. Code 5
Galva CUSD 224
Sch. Sys. Enr. Code 3
Supt. – William Owens, MORGAN ROAD 61434
MS, MORGAN ROAD & NW 3RD 61434
    William Gregory, prin.
White ES, NW FOURTH AVE 61434
    Roy Saatkamp, prin.

Garden Prairie, Boone Co.
Belvidere CUSD 100
Supt. – See Belvidere
Kishwaukee ES
    7133 GARDEN PRAIRIE RD 61038
    Denver Foltz, prin.

Gardner, Grundy Co., Pop. Code 4
Gardner CCSD 72C
Sch. Sys. Enr. Code 2
Supt. – Paul Knight, ELM ST 60424
ES, ELM ST 60424 – Paul Knight Sr., prin.

Geff, Wayne Co.
Geff CCSD 14
Sch. Sys. Enr. Code 2
Supt. – Herman Ahlfield, P O BOX 68 62842
ES, LAFAYETTE ST 62842 – Richard Adair, prin.

Geneseo, Henry Co., Pop. Code 6
Geneseo CUSD 228
Sch. Sys. Enr. Code 5
Supt. – Dr. Fred Benson
    209 S COLLEGE AVE 61254
JHS, 115 W PEARL ST 61254
    Richard Kulupka, prin.
Millikin ES, 5 CONGRESS ST 61254
    Terry Blackert, prin.
Northside ES, 415 N RUSSELL AVE 61254
    James Lodico, prin.
Southwest ES, 715 S CENTER ST 61254
    William Menendez, prin.
Other Schools – See Atkinson

St. Malachy School, 208 E PARK ST 61254

Geneva, Kane Co., Pop. Code 6
Geneva CUSD 304
Sch. Sys. Enr. Code 4
Supt. – Dr. Donald Marcotte
    638 LOGAN AVE 60134
Coultrap MS, 1113 PEYTON ST 60134
    Max M. Minnich, prin.
Fourth ES, 227 N 4TH ST 60134
    John Schrader, prin.
Harrison Street ES, 201 N HARRISON ST 60134
    Ronald Anderson, prin.
Western Avenue ES, 1500 WESTERN AVE 60134
    Thomas Watrobka, prin.

St. Peter School, 1881 KANEVILLE RD 60134

Genoa, De Kalb Co., Pop. Code 5
Genoa-Kingston CUSD 424
Sch. Sys. Enr. Code 4
Supt. – Sherwood Dees, 941 W MAIN ST 60135
MS, 602 E HILL ST 60135 – Kevin Holland, prin.
Davenport ES, 123 W 1ST ST 60135
    Gary Gathman, prin.
Other Schools – See Kingston

Georgetown, Vermilion Co., Pop. Code 5
Georgetown-Ridge Farm CUSD 4
Sch. Sys. Enr. Code 5
Supt. – Derry Behm, 400 W WEST ST 61846
Miller JHS, 414 W WEST ST 61846
Rex Avery, prin.
Frazier MS, 902 N MAIN ST 61846
Donald Strohl, prin.
Pine Crest ES, 505 KENNEDY DR 61846
Donald Strohl, prin.
Other Schools – See Ridge Farm

Germantown, Clinton Co., Pop. Code 4
Germantown SD 60
Sch. Sys. Enr. Code 2
Supt. – Dennis Hollenkamp
401 WALNUT ST 62245
ES, 401 WALNUT ST 62245
Dennis Hollenkamp, prin.

Gibson City, Ford Co., Pop. Code 5
Gibson City CUSD 1
Sch. Sys. Enr. Code 2
Supt. – Dr. Richard Berg, 217 E 17TH ST 60936
JHS, P O BOX 272 60936 – James McCarthy, prin.
ES, 902 N CHURCH ST 60936
James McClard, prin.

Gifford, Champaign Co., Pop. Code 3
Gifford CCSD 188
Sch. Sys. Enr. Code 2
Supt. – Albert Shepherd, P O BOX 7 61847
ES, P O BOX 70 61847 – Albert Shepherd, prin.

Gillespie, Macoupin Co., Pop. Code 5
Gillespie CUSD 7
Sch. Sys. Enr. Code 4
Supt. – Richard Wilson, 510 W ELM ST 62033
MS, 412 OREGON ST 62033
Stephen Majzel, prin.
Maple Street ES, 109 E MAPLE ST 62033
Stephen Majzel, prin.
Other Schools – See Benld

Gilman, Iroquois Co., Pop. Code 4
Iroquois West CUSD 10
Sch. Sys. Enr. Code 3
Supt. – Frank Meyer, 529 E 2ND ST 60938
Iroquois West ES, 215 E 2ND ST 60938
Glen Phillips, prin.
Other Schools – See Danforth, Onarga

Girard, Macoupin Co., Pop. Code 4
Girard CUSD 3
Sch. Sys. Enr. Code 3
Supt. – Richard Well, 525 N 3RD ST 62640
ES, THIRD & NORTH 62640
Elmer Humphrey, prin.

Gladstone, Henderson Co., Pop. Code 2
Union CUSD 115
Sch. Sys. Enr. Code 3
Supt. – Larry Crim, P O BOX 547 61437
Tri-Valley MS 61437 – Henry Bonner, prin.
ES, POST OFFICE 61437 – Henry Bonner, prin.
Other Schools – See Biggsville, Oquawka

Glasford, Peoria Co., Pop. Code 4
Illini Bluffs CUSD 327
Sch. Sys. Enr. Code 4
Supt. – Marvin A. Strube
RURAL ROUTE 01 61533
MS, 212 N SAYLOR ST 61533
Lawrence Geltmaker, prin.
Lancaster West ES, RURAL ROUTE 01 61533
Lawrence Geltmaker, prin.
Other Schools – See Hanna City, Mapleton, Peoria

Glen Carbon, Madison Co., Pop. Code 6
Edwardsville CUSD 7
Supt. – See Edwardsville
ES, RURAL ROUTE 01 BIRGER AVE 62034
Jane Westerhold, prin.

Glencoe, Cook Co., Pop. Code 6
Glencoe SD 35
Sch. Sys. Enr. Code 3
Supt. – Richard Olson
620 GREENWOOD AVE 60022
Glencoe Central JHS
620 GREENWOOD AVE 60022
Thomas Amos, prin.
Central IS, 620 GREENWOOD AVE 60022
Nelson Armour, prin.
South ES, 266 LINDEN AVE 60022
Barbara Unikel, prin.

Glendale Heights, Du Page Co., Pop. Code 7
Marquardt SD 15
Sch. Sys. Enr. Code 4
Supt. – Dr. Lawrence Golden
1890 GLEN ELLYN ROAD 60139
Marquardt MS, 1912 GLEN ELLYN ROAD 60139
James Sayers, prin.
Black Hawk ES, 2101 GLADSTONE DR 60139
Michael Zivic, prin.
Hall ES, 1447 WAYNE AVE 60139
Maryanne Friend, prin.
Reskin ES, 1555 ARDMORE AVE 60139
David Beard, prin.
Other Schools – See Bloomingdale

Queen Bee SD 16
Sch. Sys. Enr. Code 4
Supt. – James White
1560 BLOOMINGDALE ROAD 60139

Glenside JHS
1560 BLOOMINGDALE ROAD 60139
Dr. Jacqueline Wolff, prin.
Americana ES, 1629 PRESIDENT ST 60139
William Snyder, prin.
Glen Hill ES
2N220 BLOOMINGDALE ROAD 60139
John Karras, prin.
Pheasant Ridge ES, 43 E STEVENSON DR 60139
William Huska, prin.
Queen Bee ES, 2N655 BLOOMINGDALE 60139
Gale Wiedman, prin.

St. Matthew School, 1555 GLEN ELLYN RD 60139

Glen Ellyn, Du Page Co., Pop. Code 7
Glen Ellyn CCSD 89
Sch. Sys. Enr. Code 4
Supt. – Dr. Paul Zaccarine
799 ROOSEVELT ROAD 60137
Glen Crest JHS, 725 SHEEHAN AVE 60137
Calvin Roesner, prin.
Arbor View ES, 22 W 430 IRONWOOD DR 60137
J. Kevin Diehl, prin.
Park View ES, 250 S PARK BLVD 60137
Glenn Rogers, prin.
Westfield ES, 2 S 125 MAYFIELD LANE 60137
John Proctor, prin.
Other Schools – See Wheaton

Glen Ellyn SD 41
Sch. Sys. Enr. Code 4
Supt. – Dr. Arthur Jones, 793 N MAIN ST 60137
Hadley JHS, 240 HAWTHORNE ST 60137
Kenneth Stellon, prin.
Churchill ES, 240 GENEVA RD 60137
Howard Decamp, prin.
Forest Glen ES, 561 ELM ST 60137
James Crabtree, prin.
Franklin ES, 350 BRYANT AVE 60137
Douglas Craig, prin.
Lincoln ES, 380 GREENFIELD AVE 60137
Joan Witherbee, prin.

St. James the Apostle School
490 S PARK BLVD 60137
St. Petronille School, 456 HILLSIDE AVE 60137

Glenview, Cook Co., Pop. Code 8
Avoca SD 37
Supt. – See Wilmette
Avoca West ES, 235 BEECH DR 60025
Carol Rak, prin.

East Maine SD 63
Supt. – See Des Plaines
Washington ES, 2710 GOLF RD 60025
Patricia Johnson, prin.

Glenview CCSD 34
Sch. Sys. Enr. Code 5
Supt. – Dr. W. J. Attea
1401 GREENWOOD ROAD 60025
Springman JHS, 2701 CENTRAL ROAD 60025
Dr. Thomas Kersten, prin.
Glen Grove MS, 3900 GLENVIEW RD 60025
Irene Diedrich, prin.
Henking ES, 2941 LINNEMAN ST 60025
Thomas Powers, prin.
Hoffman MS, 2000 HARRISON ST 60025
J. Weir, prin.
Lyon ES, 1335 WAUKEGAN RD 60025
Henry Gmitro, prin.
Pleasant Ridge MS
1730 SUNSET RIDGE RD 60025
Richard Palumbo, prin.
Westbrook ES, 1333 GREENWOOD RD 60025
Ronald Glovetski, prin.

Northbrook/Glenview SD 30
Supt. – See Northbrook
Willowbrook ES
2500 HAPPY HOLLOW RD 60025
Robert Olson, prin.

West Northfield SD 31
Supt. – See Northbrook
Winkelman ES, 1919 LANDWEHR RD 60025
Marilyn Helberg, prin.

Immanuel Lutheran School
1850 CHESTNUT AVE 60025
Our Lady of Perpetual Help School
1123 CHURCH ST 60025
St. Catherine Laboure School
3425 THORNWOOD AVE 60025

Glenwood, Cook Co., Pop. Code 7
Brookwood SD 167
Sch. Sys. Enr. Code 4
Supt. – Kenneth Peterson
201 E GLENWOOD DYER ROAD 60425
Brookwood JHS
GLENWOOD-LANSING ROAD 60425
Stephen Racz, prin.
Brookwood IS
GLENWOOD-LANSING ROAD 60425
Terry Anderson, prin.
Hickory Bend ES, 600 E 191ST PL 60425
George Rau, prin.
Longwood ES, LONGWOOD DRIVE 60425
Margot Schlenker, prin.

Godfrey, Madison Co., Pop. Code 4
Alton CUSD 11
Supt. – See Alton

North MS, 5600 GODFREY ROAD 62035
Thomas Gunning, prin.
Brown MS, 1613 W DELMAR AVE 62035
Jerry Montague, prin.
ES, 6008 GODFREY RD 62035
Dorothy Adams, prin.
Lewis and Clark ES, 6800 HUMBERT RD 62035
C. Richard Propes, prin.

Faith Lutheran School, P O BOX 126 62035
St. Ambrose School
820 HOMER ADAMS PARKWAY 62035

Golconda, Pope Co., Pop. Code 3
Pope Co. CUSD 1
Sch. Sys. Enr. Code 3
Supt. – Herman Adkerson, P O BOX 397 62938
Pope County ES
RURAL ROUTE 02 BOX 20B 62938
R. Henard, prin.

Goodfield, Woodford Co., Pop. Code 2
Eureka CUSD 140
Supt. – See Eureka
ES 61742 – Patrick Grisham, prin.

Good Hope, McDonough Co., Pop. Code 2
Northwest CUSD 175
Supt. – See Sciota
Northwestern ES 61438 – Barbara Shrode, prin.

Goreville, Johnson Co., Pop. Code 3
Goreville CUSD 1
Sch. Sys. Enr. Code 2
Supt. – Gary Vaughn, P O BOX 210 62939
ES, P O BOX 210 62939 – Bob Webb, prin.

Gorham, Jackson Co., Pop. Code 2
Miss Valley CUSD 166
Sch. Sys. Enr. Code 2
Supt. – F. Dee Wiley 62940
S 62940 – Robert Crain, prin.
ES, P O BOX 62940 – F. Wiley, prin.

Grafton, Jersey Co., Pop. Code 4
Jerseyville CUSD 100
Supt. – See Jerseyville
ES 62037 – Paul Brown, prin.

Grand Chain, Pulaski Co., Pop. Code 2
Century CUSD 100
Supt. – See Ullin
Century ES, P O BOX 107 62941
Robert Cross, prin.

Grand Ridge, La Salle Co., Pop. Code 3
Grand Ridge CCSD 95
Sch. Sys. Enr. Code 2
Supt. – Wally Marquardt, 400 W MAIN ST 61325
ES, 400 W MAIN ST 61325
Wally Marquardt, prin.

Grand Tower, Jackson Co., Pop. Code 3
Shawnee CUSD 84
Supt. – See Wolf Lake
Shawnee ES North, P O BOX 128 62942
Robert Davie, prin.

Granite City, Madison Co., Pop. Code 8
Granite City CUSD 9
Sch. Sys. Enr. Code 6
Supt. – Gilbert Walmsley, 1947 ADAMS ST 62040
Coolidge JHS, 3231 MANEOKI ROAD 62040
James Jeffries, prin.
Grigsby JHS, 3801 OLD CARGILL ROAD 62040
Fred Schuman, prin.
Frohardt ES, 2040 JOHNSON RD 62040
Donald Kopp, prin.
Marshall ES, 2700 MARSHALL AVE 62040
Goni Michaeloff, prin.
Maryville ES, 4651 MARYVILLE RD 62040
Arthur Menendez, prin.
Mitchell ES, 316 E CHAIN OF ROCKS RD 62040
Alfred Wilson, prin.
Niedringhaus ES, 29TH AND STATE 62040
Joan Harris, prin.
Parkview ES, 3200 MARYVILLE RD 62040
Nancy Marti, prin.
Prather ES, 2300 W 25TH ST 62040
(—), prin.
Webster ES, 25TH & KATE STS 62040
Helen Schmisseur, prin.
Wilson ES, 2400 WILSON AVE 62040
Ellen Voyles, prin.

St. Elizabeth School, 2300 PONTOON RD 62040
Holy Family School, 1900 ST CLAIR AVE 62040

Grant Park, Kankakee Co., Pop. Code 4
Grant Park CUSD 6
Sch. Sys. Enr. Code 3
Supt. – Dr. Edward Butler
421 W HAMBLETON ST 60940
ES, 421 W TAYLOR ST 60940
George Swanson, prin.

Granville, Putnam Co., Pop. Code 4
Putnam County CUSD 535
Sch. Sys. Enr. Code 3
Supt. – Fred Ruck, P O BOX 607 61326
Putnam County ES-Hopkins Building
400 E SILVERSPOON 61326
William Ellena, prin.
Other Schools – See Hennepin, Mc Nabb

Graymont, Livingston Co.
Rooks Creek CCSD 425
Sch. Sys. Enr. Code 1
Supt. – Richard Hackl, P O BOX 55 61743
ES, P O BOX 55 61743 – Richard Hackl, prin.

Grayslake, Lake Co., Pop. Code 6
Grayslake CCSD 46
Sch. Sys. Enr. Code 2
Supt. – David Duffy, 440 BARRON BLVD 60030
JHS, 440 BARRON BLVD 60030
  Charles Davis, prin.
Lakeview ES, 275 S LAKE ST 60030
  James Miller, prin.
Woodview ES, 340 ALLEGHANY 60030
  Jim Miller, prin.
Other Schools – See Lake Villa

St. Gilbert School, 231 E BELVIDERE RD 60030

Grayville, White Co., Pop. Code 4
Grayville CUSD 1
Sch. Sys. Enr. Code 2
Supt. – Dr. Robert A. Clancy
  728 W NORTH ST 62844
JHS, 728 W NORTH ST 62844
  Jim O'Donley, prin.
Wells ES, 704 W NORTH ST 62844
  Jim O'Donley, prin.

Great Lakes, Lake Co.
North Chicago SD 64
Supt. – See North Chicago
Forrestal ES, WASHINGTON ST 60088
  Kathleen Ellis, prin.

Greenfield, Greene Co., Pop. Code 4
Greenfield CUSD 10
Sch. Sys. Enr. Code 3
Supt. – Charles Barber, 311 MULBERRY ST 62044
ES, 115 PRAIRIE ST 62044 – Marilyn Kreher, prin.

Green Valley, Tazewell Co., Pop. Code 3
Green Valley CCSD 695
Sch. Sys. Enr. Code 2
Supt. – James Oltman, P O BOX 224 61534
ES, 121 N CHURCH ST 61534
  James Oltman, prin.

Greenview, Menard Co., Pop. Code 3
Greenview CUSD 200
Sch. Sys. Enr. Code 2
Supt. – Robert Turk, P O BOX C 62642
JHS, P O BOX C 62642 – Terry Phillips, prin.
ES, P O BOX C 62642 – Clarence Thayer, Jr., prin.

Greenville, Bond Co., Pop. Code 6
Bond County CUSD 2
Sch. Sys. Enr. Code 4
Supt. – Dr. Philip Pogue, 1008 N HENA ST 62246
JHS, 513 E BEAUMONT AVE 62246
  Hugh Westbrook, prin.
ES, 800 N DEWEY 62246 – Jim Kessinger, prin.
Other Schools – See Pocahontas, Sorento

Gridley, McLean Co., Pop. Code 4
Gridley CUSD 10
Sch. Sys. Enr. Code 2
Supt. – Gene Cwick, P O BOX 958 61744
JHS, P O BOX 958 61744 – John Marr, prin.
ES, P O BOX 958 61744 – John Marr, prin.

Griggsville, Pike Co., Pop. Code 4
Griggsville CUSD 4
Sch. Sys. Enr. Code 2
Supt. – Delbert L. Camp
  STANFORD & LIBERTY 62340
JHS, STANFORD & LIBERTY 62340
  Thomas Leahy, prin.
ES, STANFORD & LIBERTY 62340
  Thomas Leahy, prin.

Gurnee, Lake Co., Pop. Code 6
Gurnee SD 56
Sch. Sys. Enr. Code 4
Supt. – Wayne Schurter
  900 KILBOURNE ROAD 60031
Viking JHS, 4460 GRAND AVE 60031
  Douglas Schultze, prin.
MS, 940 KILBOURNE RD 60031
  Fred Nielsen, prin.
Other Schools – See Waukegan

Hamel, Madison Co., Pop. Code 3
Edwardsville CUSD 7
Supt. – See Edwardsville
ES, P O BOX 157 62046 – Lee Kovarik, prin.

Hamilton, Hancock Co., Pop. Code 5
Hamilton CCSD 328
Sch. Sys. Enr. Code 3
Supt. – Dr. W. Viniard, 210 N 10TH ST 62341
MS, 270 N 10TH ST 62341
  Diane Van Fleet, prin.
ES, 250 S 9TH ST 62341 – Edith Ewing, prin.

Hampshire, Kane Co., Pop. Code 4
Dundee CUSD 300
Supt. – See Dundee
MS, 560 STATE ST 60140 – Carl Brooks, prin.
ES, 321 TERWILLIGER AVE 60140
  Gary Wright, prin.

St. Charles Borromeo School
  288 E JEFFERSON 60140

Hampton, Rock Island Co., Pop. Code 4
Hampton SD 29
Sch. Sys. Enr. Code 2
Supt. – Goodman Bradley, 206 5TH ST 61256
ES, 206 5TH ST 61256 – Goodman Bradley, prin.

Hanna City, Peoria Co., Pop. Code 4
Farmington Central CUSD 265
Supt. – See Trivoli
Logan City MS, RURAL ROUTE 01 61536
  Philip McAlearney, prin.
ES, POST OFFICE 61536
  Philip McAlearney, prin.

Illini Bluffs CUSD 327
Supt. – See Glasford
Westwood ES, RURAL ROUTE 01 61536
  Bradford Janzen, prin.

Hanover, Jo Daviess Co., Pop. Code 4
River Ridge CUSD 210
Supt. – See Elizabeth
River Ridge MS, P O BOX 25 61041
  Steven Pennock, prin.
ES, P O BOX 25 61041 – Steven Pennock, prin.

Hanover Park, Cook Co., Pop. Code 8
Community Consolidated SD 93
Supt. – See Carol Stream
Johnson ES, 1380 NAUTILUS LN 60103
  Mary Harden, prin.

Elgin Unit SD 46
Supt. – See Elgin
Horizon ES, 1701 GREENBROOK BLVD 60103
  Dr. Richard Carlson, prin.
Laurel Hill ES, 1750 LAUREL AVE 60103
  Alice Ericksen, prin.
Ontarioville ES, ELM & CENTER STS 60103
  Richard Pijanowski, prin.
Parkwood ES, 2150 LAUREL AVE 60103
  William Ristow, prin.

Keeneyville SD 20
Supt. – See Roselle
Spring Wood JHS
  5540 E ARLINGTON DRIVE 60103
  Charles Crissey, prin.
Greenbrook ES, 5208 ARLINGTON CIR 60103
  Paul Zaander, prin.

Schaumburg CCSD 54
Supt. – See Schaumburg
Einstein ES, 1100 LAURIE LN 60103
  Marvin Husby, prin.
Fox ES, 1035 PARKVIEW DR 60103
  James Binder, prin.
Hanover Highlands ES, 1451 CYPRESS AVE 60103
  Patricia McConnell, prin.

Hardin, Calhoun Co., Pop. Code 4
Calhoun CUSD 40
Sch. Sys. Enr. Code 3
Supt. – James A. Ringhausen, P O BOX 387 62047
ES, P O BOX 387 62047 – Terry Strauch, prin.
Other Schools – See Kampsville

St. Norbert School, 401 VINEYARD ST 62047

Harrisburg, Saline Co., Pop. Code 6
Harrisburg CUSD 3
Sch. Sys. Enr. Code 4
Supt. – Dennis Carpenter, 40 S MAIN ST 62946
Malan JHS, 124 S WEBSTER ST 62946
  William McNew, prin.
East Side ES, 315 E CHURCH ST 62946
  Jack Yates, prin.
West Side ES, 411 W LINCOLN ST 62946
  Richard Vinyard, prin.

Harristown, Macon Co., Pop. Code 4
Niantic-Harristown CUSD 6
Supt. – See Niantic
Niantic-Harristown ES
  315 S MERIDIAN ST 62537
  Lawrence Turner, prin.

Hartford, Madison Co., Pop. Code 4
Wood River-Hartford ESD 15
Supt. – See Wood River
ES, 110 W 2ND ST 62048 – Michael Cox, prin.

Hartsburg, Logan Co., Pop. Code 2
Hartsburg-Emden CUSD 21
Sch. Sys. Enr. Code 2
Supt. – Dr. Douglas Horner
  400 W FRONT ST 62643
Other Schools – See Emden

Harvard, McHenry Co., Pop. Code 6
Harvard CUSD 50
Sch. Sys. Enr. Code 4
Supt. – Richard Crosby
  1101 N JEFFERSON ST 60033
JHS, 1301 GARFIELD ST 60033
  Stanley Goldsmith, prin.
Central ES, DIVISION & DIGGINS 60033
  Darlene Hoeft, prin.
Jefferson MS, 1200 N JEFFERSON ST 60033
  William Courtright, prin.
Washington ES, 305 S HUTCHINSON ST 60033
  Kathleen Steichmann, prin.

St. Joseph School, 201 N DIVISION ST 60033

Harvey, Cook Co., Pop. Code 8
Harvey SD 152
Sch. Sys. Enr. Code 5
Supt. – Charles Bowen
  15147 MYRTLE AVE 60426
Brooks JHS, 14741 WALLACE AVE 60426
  Betty Owens, prin.
Bryant ES, MAIN & 147TH ST 60426
  Glen Honsbruch, prin.
Emerson ES, PAGE AVE & 158TH ST 60426
  Rotha Patterson, prin.
Field ES, WALLACE AVE & 147TH 60426
  Jerry Jordan, prin.
Holmes ES, CARSE & 160TH ST 60426
  Phillip Skubal, prin.
Lowell-Longfellow ES
  15636 LEXINGTON AVE 60426
  Herman Bluford, prin.
Riley ES, LINCOLN AVE & 160TH 60426
  Sophia Taylor, prin.
Sandburg ES, 145TH & MYRTLE 60426
  Anna Kreske, prin.
Whittier ES, LOOMIS AVE & 152ND 60426
  Leroy Coleman, prin.

South Holland SD 151
Supt. – See South Holland
Taft ES, 16300 UNION AVE 60426
  Sharon Hamilton, prin.

West Harvey-Dixmoor SD 147
Sch. Sys. Enr. Code 4
Supt. – Samuel Rhone
  155TH PLACE & HOYNE 60426
Parks JHS, 14700 ROBEY AVE 60426
  Winston Johnson, prin.
Kich ES, 155TH PLACE & HOYNE 60426
  William Colbert, Sr., prin.
Washington ES, 153RD AND LINCOLN AVE 60426
  Ronald Kimmons, prin.
Other Schools – See Blue Island, Dixmoor

Mary of Nazareth School
  15726 UNION AVE 60426

Harwood Heights, Cook Co., Pop. Code 6
Union Ridge SD 86
Sch. Sys. Enr. Code 2
Supt. – Denis Curran
  4600 N OAK PARK AVE 60656
Union Ridge ES, 4600 N OAK PARK AVE 60656
  Denis Curran, prin.

Havana, Mason Co., Pop. Code 5
Havana CUSD 126
Sch. Sys. Enr. Code 4
Supt. – Dr. Jack Wagoner
  500 S MCKINLEY ST 62644
JHS, 700 E LAUREL AVE 62644
  Wesley Wilson, prin.
New Central ES, 215 N PEARL ST 62644
  Loren Kennedy, prin.

Hazel Crest, Cook Co., Pop. Code 7
Hazel Crest SD 152-5
Sch. Sys. Enr. Code 4
Supt. – Dorothy Williams Boyd
  1910 170TH ST 60429
Warren Palm MS
  170TH & DIXIE HIGHWAY 60429
  Jeanette Shivers, prin.
Woodland MS, 169TH & WESTERN AVE 60429
  John Finn, prin.
Other Schools – See East Hazel Crest, Markham

Prairie Hills ESD 144
Sch. Sys. Enr. Code 4
Supt. – Dr. Jack D. Felger, P O BOX 233 60429
Chateaux ES, 3600 CHAMBORD LN 60429
  Sharon Okleshen, prin.
Highlands ES, 3420 LAUREL LN 60429
  Earl Rowe, prin.
Other Schools – See Country Club Hills, Markham,
  Oak Forest

St. Anne School, 16801 DIXIE HWY 60429

Hebron, McHenry Co., Pop. Code 3
Alden Hebron SD 19
Sch. Sys. Enr. Code 2
Supt. – Roger Damrow, 9604 ILLINOIS ST 60034
Alden-Hebron JHS, 9604 ILLINOIS ST 60034
  Gary Calsyn, prin.
Alden-Hebron ES, 11915 PRICE RD 60034
  Roger Damrow, prin.

Hennepin, Putnam Co., Pop. Code 3
Putnam County CUSD 535
Supt. – See Granville
Putnam County ES-Hennepin
  RURAL ROUTE 01 61327 – William Ellena, prin.

Henning, Vermilion Co., Pop. Code 2
Bismarck CUSD 1
Supt. – See Bismarck
ES, P O BOX 68 61848 – Earl Lindsey, prin.

Henry, Marshall Co., Pop. Code 5
Henry CCSD 35
Sch. Sys. Enr. Code 3
Supt. – Rick Stoecker, RICHARD ST 61537
Henry Community-Consolidated ES
  201 RICHARD ST 61537 – David Stauffacher, prin.

Herrick, Shelby Co., Pop. Code 2
Cowden-Herrick ECCD 11
Supt. – See Cowden

ES, P O BOX 97   62431 – John Vanvoorhis, prin.

Herrin, Williamson Co., Pop. Code 7
Herrin CUSD 4
Sch. Sys. Enr. Code 4
Supt. – Dr. William Clarida, 700 N 10TH ST   62948
Lincoln ES, 500 N 10TH ST   62948
   Dale Taylor, prin.
North Side ES, 601 N 17TH ST   62948
   Helen Hamilton, prin.
South Side ES, 700 S 14TH ST   62948
   Richard Henley, prin.
West Side ES, 320 S 22ND ST   62948
   Monte Franklin, prin.
Other Schools – See Energy, Hurst

Our Lady of Mt. Carmel School
   300 W MONROE ST   62948

Herscher, Kankakee Co., Pop. Code 4
Herscher CUSD 2
Sch. Sys. Enr. Code 4
Supt. – Dr. Lawrence Jacobsen
   501 MAIN ST N   60941
ES, 501 N MAIN ST   60941 – Donald Johnson, prin.
Other Schools – See Bonfield, Kankakee, Reddick

Heyworth, McLean Co., Pop. Code 4
Heyworth CUSD 4
Sch. Sys. Enr. Code 3
Supt. – Roger Little, 308 W CLEVELAND   61745
ES, 101 JOSELYN   61745 – William Kennedy, prin.
Other Schools – See Shirley

Hickory Hills, Cook Co., Pop. Code 7
North Palos SD 117
Sch. Sys. Enr. Code 4
Supt. – Dr. Tom P. Kostes, 9045 88TH AVE   60457
Conrady JHS, 97TH & ROBERTS ROAD   60457
   Ronald Kanzulak, prin.
Dorn ES, 7840 W 92ND ST   60457
   Raymond Venezio, prin.
Glen Oaks ES, 9045 S 88TH AVE   60457
   Joseph Dubec, prin.
Other Schools – See Palos Hills

Hidalgo, Jasper Co., Pop. Code 2
Jasper Co. CUSD 1
Supt. – See Newton
ES   62432 – J. Patrick Stanley, prin.
Rose Hill ES, RURAL ROUTE 01 BOX 62   62432
   J. Patrick Stanley, prin.

Highland, Madison Co., Pop. Code 6
Highland CUSD 5
Sch. Sys. Enr. Code 4
Supt. – Robert Freeman
   1800 LINDENTHAL ST   62249
JHS, 1600 LINDENTHAL ST   62249
   Roger Kesner, prin.
Grantfork ES, RURAL ROUTE 01 BOX 155   62249
   Neil Wyatt, prin.
ES, 1800 LINDENTHAL ST   62249
   Daniel Grandame, prin.
IS, 1600 LINDENTHAL ST   62249
   Roger Kesner, prin.
Other Schools – See Alhambra, New Douglas

St. Paul ES, 1416 MAIN ST   62249

Highland Park, Lake Co., Pop. Code 8
Highland Park SD 107
Sch. Sys. Enr. Code 1
Supt. – Darrell Lund, 2075 ST JOHNS AVE   60035
Elm Place MS, 2031 SHERIDAN RD   60035
   Peter Roknich, prin.
Indian Trail ES, 2075 ST JOHNS AVE   60035
   Dr. Alan Simon, prin.

Highland Park SD 108
Sch. Sys. Enr. Code 4
Supt. – Dr. Gerald R. Williams
   530 RED OAK LANE   60035
Edgewood Mid. HS
   920 EDGEWOOD ROAD   60035
   Dr. Gregory Mullen, prin.
Braiside ES, 150 PIERCE RD   60035
   Anne Powell, prin.
Lincoln ES, 711 W LINCOLN AVE   60035
   Sally Glenn, prin.
Ravinia ES, 763 DEAN AVE   60035
   Barb Habschmidt, prin.
Red Oak ES, 530 RED OAK LN   60035
   Robert Deen, prin.
Sherwood ES, 1900 STRATFORD RD   60035
   Paul Zavagno, prin.

Highwood Highland Park SD 111
Supt. – See Highwood
Northwood JHS, 945 NORTH AVE   60035
   (—), prin.
Thomas ES, 2939 SUMMIT AVE   60035
   Dr. Robert Wilhite, prin.

Highwood, Lake Co., Pop. Code 6
Highwood Highland Park SD 111
Sch. Sys. Enr. Code 4
Supt. – Karl Fivek, 240 PRAIRIE AVE   60040
Oak Terrace ES, 240 PRAIRIE AVE   60040
   John Ourth, prin.
Other Schools – See Highland Park

St. James School, 140 NORTH AVE   60040

Hillsboro, Montgomery Co., Pop. Code 5
Hillsboro CUSD 3
Sch. Sys. Enr. Code 4
Supt. – Les Dollinger
   1311 VANDALIA ROAD   62049
JHS, 909 ROUNTREE ST   62049
   Mike Gaither, prin.
Beckemeyer ES, 1035 SEYMOUR AVE   62049
   Earl Meier, prin.
Other Schools – See Coffeen

Hillside, Cook Co., Pop. Code 6
Hillside SD 93
Sch. Sys. Enr. Code 2
Supt. – Dr. Donald Van Devander
   4804 HARRISON ST   60162
ES, 4804 HARRISON ST   60162
   William Hart, prin.

Immanuel Lutheran School
   2329 S WOLF RD   60162
St. Domitilla School, 605 N HILLSIDE AVE   60162

Hinckley, De Kalb Co., Pop. Code 4
Hinkley-Big Rock CUSD 429
Sch. Sys. Enr. Code 3
Supt. – Roland Thompson, P O BOX 1217   60520
ES, P O BOX 1277   60520 – Richard Sjolund, prin.
Other Schools – See Big Rock

Hinsdale, Du Page Co., Pop. Code 7
Hinsdale CCSD 181
Sch. Sys. Enr. Code 4
Supt. – Dr. R. W. Simcox
   200 55TH & GRANT ST   60521
JHS, 100 S GARFIELD AVE   60521
   James Voris, prin.
Lane ES, 500 N ELM ST   60521
   Salvo Marks, prin.
Madison ES, 611 S MADISON ST   60521
   Linda Murphy, prin.
Monroe ES, 210 N MADISON ST   60521
   Barbara Sirotin, prin.
Oak ES, 950 S OAK ST   60521
   Mary Madden, prin.
Other Schools – See Burr Ridge, Clarendon Hills

Pallisades CCSD 180
Supt. – See Burr Ridge
Jeans ES, 16 W 631 91ST ST   60521
   Bridget Stillo, prin.

St. Isaac Jogues School, 421 S CLAY ST   60521
Trinity Lutheran School
   11500 GERMAN CHURCH RD   60521
Zion Lutheran School, 125 S VINE ST   60521

Hodgkins, Cook Co., Pop. Code 4
La Grange SD 105
Supt. – See La Grange
ES, 6516 KANE AVE   60525 – Paul Vorwick, prin.

Hoffman, Clinton Co., Pop. Code 2

Trinity Lutheran School, P O BOX 147   62250

Hoffman Estates, Cook Co., Pop. Code 8
Palatine CCSD 15
Supt. – See Palatine
Jefferson ES, 3805 WINSTON DR   60195
   Alan Hopkins, prin.

Schaumburg CCSD 54
Supt. – See Schaumburg
Eisenhower JHS, 800 HASSELL ROAD   60195
   Robert Hanlon, prin.
Armstrong ES, 1320 KINGSDALE RD   60194
   Bernard Osterberger, prin.
Fairfiew ES, 375 ARIZONA BLVD   60194
   Marilyn Halliday, prin.
Lakeview ES, 615 LAKEVIEW LN   60194
   Pamela Samson, prin.
McArthur ES, 1800 CHIPPENDALE RD   60195
   Roy Johnson, prin.
Muir ES, 1973 KENSINGTON LN   60195
   Kathleen Polach, prin.

Homer, Champaign Co., Pop. Code 4
Homer CCSD 208
Sch. Sys. Enr. Code 2
Supt. – Donald Mulch, 512 W 1ST ST   61849
JHS, 512 W 1ST ST   61849 – (—), prin.
ES, 512 W 1ST ST   61849 – Donald Mulch, prin.

Hometown, Cook Co., Pop. Code 6
Oak Lawn-Hometown SD 123
Supt. – See Oak Lawn
ES, DUFFY & KILDARE   60456
   Charles Hayes, prin.

Homewood, Cook Co., Pop. Code 7
Homewood SD 153
Sch. Sys. Enr. Code 4
Supt. – H. James Mahan
   18211 ABERDEEN ST   60430
Hart JHS, 18211 ABERDEEN ST   60430
   Richard Dervin, prin.
Churchill ES, 190TH AND CENTER AVE   60430
   Neil Chance, prin.
Willow ES, 1804 WILLOW RD   60430
   Donald Christo, prin.

St. Joseph School, 17949 DIXIE HWY   60430

Hoopeston, Vermilion Co., Pop. Code 6
Hoopeston CUSD 11
Sch. Sys. Enr. Code 4
Supt. – Dale Miller, 615 E ORANGE ST   60942
Greer MS, 609 W MAIN ST   60942
   Chalmers Flint, prin.
Honeywell ES, 600 HONEYWELL AVE   60942
   Dennis Catron, prin.
Maple ES, 500 S FOURTH   60942
   Dennis Catron, prin.

Hopedale, Tazewell Co., Pop. Code 3
Olympia CUSD 16
Supt. – See Stanford
ES, P O BOX 297   61747 – William Thomas, prin.

Hopkins Park, Kankakee Co.
Pembroke CCSD 259
Sch. Sys. Enr. Code 3
Supt. – Billy Mitchell, P O BOX AA   60944
Smith MS, P O BOX AG   60944
   Robert Turner, prin.
Busch ES, P O BOX AF   60944
   Freddie McClinton, prin.
Carver ES, 1 WHEELER ROAD   60944
   Barbara Howery, prin.

Hoyleton, Washington Co., Pop. Code 3
Hoyleton CCSD 29
Sch. Sys. Enr. Code 1
Supt. – Steven Launius
   RURAL ROUTE 01 BOX 15   62803
Hoyleton Consolidated ES
   RURAL ROUTE 01 BOX 15   62803
   Steven Launius, prin.

Trinity Lutheran School, P O BOX 57   62803

Hudson, McLean Co., Pop. Code 3
Normal CUSD 5
Supt. – See Normal
ES, P O BOX 147   61748
   J. Stephen Liebenow, prin.

Hull, Pike Co., Pop. Code 3
West Pike CUSD 2
Supt. – See Kinderhook
West Pike ES   62343 – Henry Walton, prin.

Humboldt, Coles Co., Pop. Code 2
Matoon CUSD 2
Supt. – See Mattoon
ES, P O BOX 37   61931 – Lester Edwards, prin.

Hume, Edgar Co., Pop. Code 2
Shiloh SD 2
Sch. Sys. Enr. Code 2
Supt. – Jay Stortzum
   RURAL ROUTE 01 BOX 100   61932
Shiloh ES, RURAL ROUTE 01   61932
   Alan Zuber, prin.

Huntley, McHenry Co., Pop. Code 4
Huntley Consolidated SD 158
Sch. Sys. Enr. Code 3
Supt. – Dr. Robert Bunt, 12015 MILL ST   60142
ES, 11302 S LINCOLN ST   60142
   Janice Kirkel, prin.

Hurst, Williamson Co., Pop. Code 3
Herrin CUSD 4
Supt. – See Herrin
ES, P O BOX 316   62949 – Terry Hughes, prin.

Hutsonville, Crawford Co., Pop. Code 3
Hutsonville CUSD 1
Sch. Sys. Enr. Code 2
Supt. – Gary D. Matteson, W CLOVER ST   62433
ES, W CLOVER ST   62433 – Kent Anderson, prin.

Illinois City, Rock Island Co.
Rockridge CUSD 300
Supt. – See Taylor Ridge
ES, 24017 122ND AVE W   61259
   Larry Hesch, prin.

Illiopolis, Sangamon Co., Pop. Code 4
Illiopolis CUSD 12
Sch. Sys. Enr. Code 2
Supt. – James Francis, P O BOX 240   62539
JHS, P O BOX 240   62539 – Ronald Kitchen, prin.
ES, P O BOX 240   62539 – Ronald Kitchen, prin.

Ina, Jefferson Co.
Ina CCSD 8
Sch. Sys. Enr. Code 2
Supt. – Clyde Hayes
   ELM & TAMAROA ROAD   62846
Ina Comm. Cons. ES
   ELM & TAMAROA ROAD   62846
   Clyde Hayes, prin.

Industry, McDonough Co., Pop. Code 3
Industry CUSD 165
Sch. Sys. Enr. Code 2
Supt. – Dr. Charles Waggoner, P O BOX 207   61440
ES, P O BOX 207   61440 – Roger Icenogle, prin.

Ingleside, Lake Co., Pop. Code 4
Big Hollow SD 38
Sch. Sys. Enr. Code 2
Supt. – Dr. James Egan
   34699 N HIGHWAY 12   60041
Big Hollow MS, 34643 N HIGHWAY 12   60041
   Gary Mical, prin.
Big Hollow ES, 34699 N HIGHWAY 12   60041
   Dr. James Egan, prin.

Gavin SD 37
Sch. Sys. Enr. Code 3
Supt. – Walter Sheets
  25775 W HIGHWAY 134   60041
Gavin South JHS, 25775 W HIGHWAY 134   60041
  Robert H. Bein, prin.
Gavin Central ES, 26016 W GRAND AVE   60041
  Charles Spillner, prin.
Other Schools – See Lake Villa

St. Bede School, 36399 N WILSON RD   60041

Irvington, Washington Co., Pop. Code 3
Irvington CCSD 11
Sch. Sys. Enr. Code 2
Supt. – Ralph McTall, P O BOX 213   62848
ES, P O BOX 130   62848 – Ralph McTall, prin.

Itasca, Du Page Co., Pop. Code 6
Itasca SD 10
Sch. Sys. Enr. Code 3
Supt. – Dr. Glennon Acksel
  400 E IRVING PARK ROAD   60143
Peacock JHS, 301 E NORTH ST   60143
  E. Anthony Degrazia, prin.
Franzen ES, 730 CATALPA AVE   60143
  Reinhard Nickisch, prin.
Washington ES, 301 E WASHINGTON ST   60143
  Dr. Marcia Deyoung, prin.

St. Luke Lutheran School, 410 S RUSH ST   60143
St. Peter School, 500 N CHERRY ST   60143

Iuka, Marion Co., Pop. Code 2
Iuka CCSD 7
Sch. Sys. Enr. Code 2
Supt. – Galen Dalton, P O BOX 68   62849
ES, P O BOX 68   62849 – Galen Dalton, prin.

Jacksonville, Morgan Co., Pop. Code 7
Jacksonville SD 117
Sch. Sys. Enr. Code 5
Supt. – Dr. Robert L. Crowe
  516 JORDAN ST   62650
Turner JHS, 664 LINCOLN AVE   62650
  Paul Belobrajdic, prin.
Eisenhower ES, 1901 W LAFAYETTE AVE   62650
  James Kiesow, prin.
Franklin ES, 352 FRANKLIN DR   62650
  Tom Smith, prin.
Graham ES, 747 W LAFAYETTE AVE   62650
  Helen Klosterman, prin.
Jefferson ES, 733 N CLAY ST   62650
  Lee Hovasse, prin.
Lincoln ES, 320 W INDEPENDENCE AVE   62650
  Neal Brawner, prin.
North Jacksonville ES, 704 N MAIN RD   62650
  Thomas Mussatto, prin.
South Jacksonville ES, 301 DEWEY DR   62650
  Martha Griffin, prin.
Washington ES, 524 S KOSCIUSKO   62650
  Leonard Bogle, prin.
Other Schools – See Murrayville

Our Savior School, 455 E STATE ST   62650
Salem Lutheran School
  222 E BEECHER AVE   62650

Jerseyville, Jersey Co., Pop. Code 6
Jerseyville CUSD 100
Sch. Sys. Enr. Code 5
Supt. – Maurice W. Jones
  119 E EXCHANGE ST   62052
Illini JHS, LIBERTY & COUNTY ROAD   62052
  Thomas Frazier, prin.
Delhi ES, 1901 DELHI RD   62052
  Thomas Metzger, prin.
Jerseyville East ES, 201 N GIDDINGS AVE   62052
  Edward Sheley, prin.
Jerseyville West ES
  1000 W CARPENTER ST   62052
  Thomas Metzger, prin.
Other Schools – See Dow, Fieldon, Grafton

Holy Ghost School
  309 N WASHINGTON ST   62052
St. Francis Xavier School, 412 S STATE ST   62052

Johnsonville, Wayne Co., Pop. Code 1
North Wayne CUSD 200
Supt. – See Cisne
ES, P O BOX A   62850 – Janice Meagher, prin.

Johnston City, Williamson Co., Pop. Code 5
Johnston City CUSD 1
Sch. Sys. Enr. Code 4
Supt. – John Parks, 1103 MONROE AVE   62951
Jefferson ES, 1200 GRAND AVE   62951
  Fred Duncan, prin.
Washington ES, 100-200 E 12TH ST   62951
  Joe Castrale, prin.
Other Schools – See Pittsburg

Joliet, Will Co., Pop. Code 8
Joliet SD 86
Sch. Sys. Enr. Code 6
Supt. – Mary Jayne Broncato
  420 N RAYNOR AVE   60435
Dirksen JHS, 203 S MIDLAND   60436
  Charles Kransberger, prin.
Gompers JHS, 1501 COPPERFIELD AVE   60432
  Robert Simmen, prin.
Hufford JHS, 1001 N LARKIN AVE   60435
  Sharon Marzuke, prin.
Washington JHS, 402 RICHARDS STREET   60435
  Eugene Toms, prin.

Culbertson ES
  1521 E WASHINGTON STREET   60433
  Charles Kollross, prin.
Cunningham ES, 500 MORAN STREET   60435
  Luvenia Taylor, prin.
Dirksen ES, 203 S MIDLAND   60436
  Charles Kransberger, prin.
Eisenhower ES, 406 BURKE STREET   60433
  Anna Jean Gleason, prin.
Farragut ES, 701 GLENWOOD AVE   60435
  Claire Heitman, prin.
Forest Park Individual Education ES
  1220 CALIFORNIA   60432 – James Poch, prin.
Jefferson ES, 2651 GLENWOOD AVE   60435
  Rosamond Flynn, prin.
Keith ES, 400 4TH AVE   60433 – Ruth Griffin, prin.
Kelly ES, 401 S JOLIET STREET   60436
  Carl Grigsby, prin.
Lincoln ES, 960 ROYCE STREET   60432
  Angelo Barney, prin.
Marsh ES, CASS & HERKIMER STS   60432
  Terence Ziesmer, prin.
Marshall ES, 319 HARWOOD STREET   60432
  Joan Morgan, prin.
Marycrest ES, 303 PURDUE CT   60436
  Joe Orlovich, prin.
Parks ES, 500 PARKS AVE   60432 – (—), prin.
Pershing ES, 251 N MIDLAND AVE   60435
  Edward Stefanich, prin.
Sandburg ES, 1100 LILAC LANE   60435
  Jennifer Johnson, prin.
Taft ES, 1125 OREGON AVE   60435
  Louise Coleman, prin.
Woodland ES, 701 THIRD AVE   60433
  William Ferguson, prin.

Laraway CCSD 70C
Sch. Sys. Enr. Code 2
Supt. – Dennis Broniecki
  RURAL ROUTE 03   60433
Laraway MS, 275 W LARAWAY RD   60436
  Kathleen Randolph, prin.
Oak Valley ES, 1705 RICHARDS ST   60433
  Lois Schaper, prin.

Plainfield SD 202
Supt. – See Plainfield
Crystal Lawns ES, 2544 CRYSTAL DR   60435
  Charles Anderson, prin.
Grand Prairie ES, 3100 CATON FARM RD   60435
  Howard Saar, prin.

Richland SD 88A
Sch. Sys. Enr. Code 2
Supt. – Ralph Haldorson
  1919 CATON FARM ROAD   60435
Other Schools – See Crest Hill

Rockdale SD 84
Sch. Sys. Enr. Code 2
Supt. – Dr. Robert Stahl
  715 MEADOW AVE   60436
Rockdale ES, 715 MEADOW AVE   60436
  John Liberatore, prin.

Troy CCSD 30 C
Supt. – See Shorewood
Troy Craughwell PS, BLACK & ESSINGTON   60435
  William Laken, prin.

Union SD 81
Sch. Sys. Enr. Code 2
Supt. – Gary Layton
  1661 CHERRY HILL RD   60433
Union ES, 1661 CHERRY HILL RD   60433
  Gary Layton, prin.

Holy Family School, 1205 N LARKIN AVE   60435
St. John Baptist School, 403 N HICKORY ST   60435
St. Joseph School, 409 SCOTT ST   60432
St. Jude School, 2204 MCDONOUGH ST   60436
St. Mary Magdalene School
  201 S BRIGGS ST   60433
St. Mary Nativity School
  700 N BROADWAY ST   60435
St. Patrick School, 110 WILLOW AVE   60436
St. Paul of the Apostle School
  120 WOODLAWN AVE   60435
St. Peter Lutheran School
  310 N BROADWAY   60435
St. Raymond School, 713 DOUGLAS ST   60435
St. Thaddeus School, 510 COLUMBIA ST   60432

Jonesboro, Union Co., Pop. Code 4
Jonesboro CCSD 43
Sch. Sys. Enr. Code 2
Supt. – Delmar Russell, 309 COOK AVE   62952
ES, P O BOX 69   62952 – Robert Johnson, prin.

Joppa, Massac Co., Pop. Code 3
Joppa-Maple Grove CUSD 38
Sch. Sys. Enr. Code 2
Supt. – Gene Mason, P O BOX 229   62953
Other Schools – See Metropolis

Joy, Mercer Co., Pop. Code 3
Westmer CUSD 203
Sch. Sys. Enr. Code 3
Supt. – William Heitman, N WASHINGTON   61260
Westmer JHS, P O BOX F   61260
  Kevin Crawford, prin.
Other Schools – See New Boston

Justice, Cook Co., Pop. Code 7
Indian Springs SD 109
Sch. Sys. Enr. Code 4
Supt. – Dr. Arvid E. Nelson
  80TH ST & 82ND AVE   60458
Wilkins JHS, 8001 S 82ND AVE   60458
  Charles Thier, prin.
Brodnicki ES, 8641 W 75TH ST   60458
  Leroy Kubinski, prin.
Dosher ES, 8000 S CORK AVE   60458
  Paul Roberts, prin.
Wilkins ES, 80TH ST & 82ND AVE   60458
  John Dove, prin.
Other Schools – See Bridgeview

Kampsville, Calhoun Co., Pop. Code 2
Calhoun CUSD 40
Supt. – See Hardin
ES, P O BOX 336   62053 – Terry Strauch, prin.

Kankakee, Kankakee Co., Pop. Code 8
Herscher CUSD 2
Supt. – See Herscher
Limestone ES
  RURAL ROUTE 04 BOX 242A   60901
  Clifford Saupe, prin.

Kankakee SD 111
Sch. Sys. Enr. Code 6
Supt. – Dr. Joseph A. Doglio
  240 WARREN AVE   60901
Edison ES, 1991 E MAPLE ST   60901
  Clyde Price, prin.
Kennedy MS, 1550 W CALISTA ST   60901
  Lawrence Wier, prin.
King MS, 1440 E COURT ST   60901
  Dr. Marven Jones, prin.
Lafayette ES, 396 N FIFTH AVE   60901
  Avis Huff, prin.
Montessori ES, 240 WARREN AVE   60901
  Willie Davis, prin.
Proegler MS, 710 N CHICAGO AVE   60901
  Dr. Donald Melancon, prin.
Steuben ES, 520 S WILDWOOD AVE   60901
  Roger Rainbolt, prin.
Taft ES, 1155 W HAWKINS ST   60901
  A. Allen Lawrence, prin.
Twain ES, 2250 E COURT ST   60901
  James Huff, prin.
Other Schools – See Aroma Park

Grace Baptist Academy
  2499 WALDRON ROAD   60901
St. Paul's Lutheran School
  240 S DEARBORN AVE   60901
St. Martin School, 907 S NINTH AVE   60901
St. Patrick School, 366 E HICKORY ST   60901
St. Paul Lutheran School
  240 S DEARBORN AVE   60901

Kansas, Edgar Co., Pop. Code 3
Kansas CUSD 3
Sch. Sys. Enr. Code 2
Supt. – Lawrence Hanner, FRONT ST   61933
S, FRONT ST   61933 – C. Humphrey, prin.
ES, FRONT ST   61933 – Charles Humphrey, prin.

Kasbeer, Bureau Co.
Kasbeer Cons. SD 23
Sch. Sys. Enr. Code 2
Supt. – John Josephsen, P O BOX 1   61328
Kasbeer Consolidated ES
  100 SCHOOL ST #1   61328 – John Josephsen, prin.

Kell, Marion Co., Pop. Code 2
Kell CCSD 2
Sch. Sys. Enr. Code 2
Supt. – Dan Griffin, P O BOX 128   62853
Kell Consolidated ES, P O BOX 128   62853
  Dan Griffin, prin.

Kempton, Ford Co., Pop. Code 2
Tri-Point CUSD 6-J
Sch. Sys. Enr. Code 2
Supt. – George Obradovich, P O BOX 128   60946
Tri Point ES, P O BOX 128   60946
  George Obradovich, prin.

Kenilworth, Cook Co., Pop. Code 5
Kenilworth SD 38
Sch. Sys. Enr. Code 2
Supt. – Dr. John Beckwith
  542 ABBOTSFORD ROAD   60043
Sears ES, 542 ABBOTSFORD RD   60043
  Dr. John Beckwith, prin.

Kewanee, Henry Co., Pop. Code 7
Kewanee CUSD 229
Sch. Sys. Enr. Code 4
Supt. – J. L. Golby, 210 LYLE ST   61443
Alexander ES, 1401 LAKE ST   61443
  Cecil Duffy, prin.
Central ES, 215 E CENTRAL BLVD   61443
  Kenneth Sullens, prin.
Irving ES, 609 W CENTRAL BLVD   61443
  Maurie Graff, prin.
Lyle ES, 920 N BURR ST   61443
  Marcia Gleeson, prin.

Wethersfield CUSD 230
Sch. Sys. Enr. Code 3
Supt. – Gary Harrison, 439 WILLARD ST   61443
Wethersfield ES, 439 WILLARD ST   61443
  Chester Ward, prin.

St. Paul Lutheran School, 109 S ELM ST   61443
Visitation School, 101 S LEXINGTON AVE   61443

Kilbourne, Mason Co., Pop. Code 2
Balyki CUSD 125
Supt. – See Bath
MS, P O BOX 257   62655 – Dale Osing, prin.

Kincaid, Christian Co., Pop. Code 4
South Fork SD 14
Sch. Sys. Enr. Code 3
Supt. – Arthur Hendricks, P O BOX N   62540
ES, P O BOX K   62540 – Robert Davis, prin.

Kinderhook, Pike Co., Pop. Code 2
West Pike CUSD 2
Sch. Sys. Enr. Code 2
Supt. – Robert Rigney, CHANEY AVE   62345
West Pike JHS, CHANEY AVE   62345
   Henry F. Walton, prin.
Other Schools – See Hull

Kings, Rochelle Co.
Kings CCSD 144
Sch. Sys. Enr. Code 2
Supt. – William Mattingly, P O BOX 278   61045
Kings Consolidated ES, P O BOX 278   61045
   William Mattingly, prin.

Kingston, De Kalb Co., Pop. Code 3
Genoa-Kingston CUSD 424
Supt. – See Genoa
MS, 100 SCHOOL STREET   60145
   Martha Jurkowski, prin.

Kinmundy, Marion Co., Pop. Code 3
Kinmundy Alma CUSD 301
Sch. Sys. Enr. Code 3
Supt. – Joseph Ross, S MADISON ST   62854
Kinmundy-Alma ES, LOUISVILLE ROAD   62854
   Thomas Turner, prin.
Other Schools – See Alma

Kirkland, De Kalb Co., Pop. Code 4
Hiawatha CUSD 426
Sch. Sys. Enr. Code 3
Supt. – Lawrence Zitkus, P O BOX 428   60146
Other Schools – See Sycamore

Knoxville, Knox Co., Pop. Code 5
Knoxville CUSD 202
Sch. Sys. Enr. Code 4
Supt. – Ronald Cope, 600 E MAIN ST   61448
JHS, 701 MILL ST   61448 – Douglas Trumble, prin.
Woolsey ES, 106 PLEASANT AVE   61448
   Richard Hoffman, prin.
Other Schools – See East Galesburg

Lacon, Marshall Co., Pop. Code 4
Mid County CUSD 4
Supt. – See Varna
ES, 206 N HIGH ST   61540
   Rolland Marshall, prin.

Ladd, Bureau Co., Pop. Code 4
Ladd CCSD 94
Sch. Sys. Enr. Code 2
Supt. – Al Auler, P O BOX 457   61329
Ladd Community Consolidated ES
   232 E CLEVELAND ST   61329 – Al Auler, prin.

La Grange, Cook Co., Pop. Code 7
La Grange Highlands SD 106
Sch. Sys. Enr. Code 3
Supt. – Dr. Elise Grimes
   1750 W PLAINFIELD ROAD   60525
Highlands MS, 1850 W PLAINFIELD ROAD   60525
   H. Arthur Grundke, prin.
Highlands ES, 5850 LAUREL AVE   60525
   Teresa Ballentine, prin.

La Grange SD 102
Supt. – See La Grange Park
Park JHS, 325 N PARK ROAD   60525
   James Battle, prin.
Cossitt Avenue ES, COSSITT & MADISON   60525
   Thomas Backe, prin.
Ogden Avenue ES, OGDEN & WAIOLA AVE   60525
   Dale Schaefer, prin.

La Grange SD 105
Sch. Sys. Enr. Code 3
Supt. – David Amsler, 1001 S SPRING AVE   60525
Gurrie JHS, 1001 S SPRING AVE   60525
   Paul Avery, prin.
Seventh Avenue ES, 701 7TH AVE   60525
   Richard Majka, prin.
Spring Avenue ES, 1001 S SPRING AVE   60525
   James Ewing, prin.
Other Schools – See Countryside, Hodgkins

Pleasantdale SD 107
Sch. Sys. Enr. Code 1
Supt. – Arnold Witt, 7450 WOLF ROAD   60525
Pleasantdale North MS, 7450 WOLF RD   60525
   William Bitautas, prin.
Pleasantdale South ES, 8100 SCHOOL ST   60525
   Joseph Majchrowicz, prin.

St. Cletus School, 700 W 55TH ST   60525
St. Francis Xavier School
   145 N WAIOLA AVE   60525
St. John Lutheran School, 505 S PARK RD   60525
St. Louise De Marillac School
   1125 HARRISON AVE   60525

La Grange Park, Cook Co., Pop. Code 7
Brookfield SD 95
Supt. – See Brookfield
Brook Park ES, 30TH & RAYMOND   60525
   William Puckett, prin.

La Grange SD 102
Sch. Sys. Enr. Code 3
Supt. – Allen Zak, 333 N PARK ROAD   60525
Forest Road ES
   FOREST ROAD & JACKSON   60525
   Kathleen Jack, prin.
Other Schools – See Brookfield, La Grange

La Harpe, Hancock Co., Pop. Code 4
La Harpe CUSD 335
Sch. Sys. Enr. Code 2
Supt. – Ronald Blakley, P O BOX 545   61450
JHS, P O BOX 545   61450 – Charles Apt, prin.
ES, P O BOX 545   61450 – Ronald Blakley, prin.

Lake Bluff, Lake Co., Pop. Code 5
Lake Bluff ESD 65
Sch. Sys. Enr. Code 3
Supt. – Dr. Edward Noyes
   121 E SHERIDAN PLACE   60044
JHS, 31 E SHERIDAN PLACE   60044
   William Petullo, prin.
Central ES, 350 W WASHINGTON AVE   60044
   Janet Nelson, prin.
West MS, 906 MUIR AVE   60044
   Ann Lawrence, prin.

Lake Forest, Lake Co., Pop. Code 7
Lake Forest SD 67
Sch. Sys. Enr. Code 4
Supt. – Dr. Allen J. Klingenberg
   95 W DEERPATH ROAD   60045
Deer Path JHS, 155 W DEERPATH ROAD   60045
   Gary Kreischer, prin.
Cherokee ES, 475 CHEROKEE RD   60045
   Linda Chase, prin.
Deer Path MS, 95 W DEERPATH RD   60045
   Rosemary Ferche, prin.
Everett ES, 1111 LAWRENCE AVE   60045
   Linda Vieth, prin.
Sheridan ES, 1360 N SHERIDAN RD   60045
   James Walton, prin.

Lincolnshire-Prairieview SD 103
Supt. – See Lincolnshire
Wright MS, 1370 RIVERWOODS ROAD   60045
   Scott Guziec, prin.

Rondout SD 72
Sch. Sys. Enr. Code 1
Supt. – David Broman
   28593 N BRADLEY ROAD   60045
Rondout ES, 28593 N BRADLEY RD   60045
   David Broman, prin.

Lake Forest Country Day School
   145 S GREEN BAY RD   60045
St. Mary School, 185 ILLINOIS ROAD   60045

Lake Villa, Lake Co., Pop. Code 4
Gavin SD 37
Supt. – See Ingleside
Gavin North IS, 37850 N HIGHWAY 59   60046
   Denise Nielsen-Hall, prin.

Grayslake CCSD 46
Supt. – See Grayslake
Avon Center ES, 35275 N HWY 83   60046
   Edna Smyth, prin.

Lake Villa CCSD 41
Sch. Sys. Enr. Code 4
Supt. – Dr. Peter J. Palombi
   304 E GRAND AVE   60046
IS, 133 MCKINLEY AVE   60046
   Glenn Camp, prin.
Pleviak MS, 304 E GRAND AVE   60046
   Thomas Scott, prin.
Other Schools – See Lindenhurst

Prince of Peace Lutheran School
   135 S MILWAUKEE AVE   60046

Lake Zurich, Lake Co., Pop. Code 6
Lake Zurich CUSD 95
Sch. Sys. Enr. Code 5
Supt. – Dr. Edward Cox, 66 CHURCH ST   60047
JHS, 100 CHURCH ST   60047
   James Johnson, prin.
Adams MS, 555 OLD MILL GROVE RD   60047
   Peter King, prin.
Paine ES, 50 MILLER RD   60047
   James Giordano, prin.
Whitney MS, 120 CHURCH ST   60047
   Karen Larsen, prin.
Other Schools – See Palatine

St. Francis De Sales School
   11 S BUESCHING RD   60047
St. Matthew Lutheran School
   24480 N OLD MCHENRY ROAD   60047

La Moille, Bureau Co., Pop. Code 3
LaMoille CUSD 303
Sch. Sys. Enr. Code 2
Supt. – Gerald Donahue   61330
Allen JHS   61330 – John Hohertz, prin.
Other Schools – See Arlington, Van Orin

Lanark, Carroll Co., Pop. Code 4
Eastland CUSD 308
Sch. Sys. Enr. Code 2
Supt. – R. Joel McFadden
   200 S SCHOOL ST   61046
Eastland ES, 200 S SCHOOL ST   61046
   John Rogers, prin.
Other Schools – See Shannon

Lansing, Cook Co., Pop. Code 8
Lansing SD 158
Sch. Sys. Enr. Code 4
Supt. – W. H. Simpson, 2721 RIDGE ROAD   60438
Memorial JHS, 2721 RIDGE ROAD   60438
   James Shrader, prin.
Coolidge ES, 17845 HENRY ST   60438
   Bernard Kelly, prin.
Oak Glen ES, 2101 182ND ST   60438
   John Mau, prin.
Reavis ES, 17121 ROY ST   60438
   C. James Facklam, prin.

Sunnybrook SD 171
Sch. Sys. Enr. Code 4
Supt. – Durward L. Schuetz
   19266 BURNHAM AVE   60438
Heritage Mid School
   19250 BURNHAM AVE   60438
   Dennis Soustek, prin.
Hale ES, 19055 BURNHAM AVE   60438
   Richard Larkins, prin.

Lansing Christian School
   3660 RANDOLPH ST   60438
St. Ann Grade School, 3014 RIDGE RD   60438
St. John Lutheran School
   18241 WENTWORTH AVE   60438
Trinity Lutheran School
   18144 GLEN TERRACE AVE   60438

La Salle, La Salle Co., Pop. Code 7
Dimmick CCSD 175
Sch. Sys. Enr. Code 2
Supt. – Dr. James Carrow
   RURAL ROUTE 01   61301
Dimmick Community Consolidated ES
   RURAL ROUTE 01   61301
   Dr. James Carrow, prin.

La Salle ESD 122
Sch. Sys. Enr. Code 3
Supt. – Dr. Harold Banser
   1165 S VINCENT'S   61301
Lincoln JHS, 1165 S VINCENT'S   61301
   Gerald Affelt, prin.
Jackson ES, 3456 E 6TH RD   61301
   Jean Feeney, prin.
Northwest MS, BUCKLIN & O'CONOR ST   61301
   Ronald Schuetz, prin.

La Salle Catholic School, 1055 6TH ST   61301
St. Patrick School, 653 4TH ST   61301

Lawrenceville, Lawrence Co., Pop. Code 6
Lawrence Co. CUSD 20
Sch. Sys. Enr. Code 4
Supt. – William Waggoner, 1802 W CEDAR   62439
Park View JHS, 1802 W CEDAR ST   62439
   Donn Hammer, prin.
Arlington ES, 1609 LEXINGTON AVE   62439
   Philip Alsman, prin.
Brookside ES, RURAL ROUTE 03 BOX 216   62439
   Everett Adams, prin.
Central ES, 1307 11TH ST   62439
   Randall Masterson, prin.
Lincoln ES, 1413 11TH ST   62439
   Thomas Harstad, prin.
Other Schools – See Saint Francisville

Leaf River, Ogle Co., Pop. Code 3
Leaf River CUSD 270
Sch. Sys. Enr. Code 2
Supt. – Edward Olds III, 3RD & MAIN ST   61047
JHS, 605 S MAIN ST   61047 – Dean Albright, prin.
ES, 605 S MAIN ST   61047 – Dean Albright, prin.

Lebanon, St. Clair Co., Pop. Code 5
Lebanon CUSD 9
Sch. Sys. Enr. Code 3
Supt. – Terrell Johnson
   102 W SCHUETZ ST   62254
ES, 102 W SCHUETZ ST   62254 – W. Malina, prin.
Other Schools – See Summerfield

Leland, La Salle Co., Pop. Code 3
Leland CUSD 1
Sch. Sys. Enr. Code 2
Supt. – John F. Scholfield, 370 N MAIN ST   60531
ES, 370 N MAIN   60531 – James Doolin, prin.

Lemont, Cook Co., Pop. Code 6
Bromberek SD 65
Sch. Sys. Enr. Code 2
Supt. – Jonathan Lamberson
   109TH & DAVEY ROAD   60439
Bromberek ES, RURAL ROUTE 07 BOX 109   60439
   Jonathan Lamberson, prin.

Lemont CCSD 113
Sch. Sys. Enr. Code 3
Supt. – C. Thomas Reiter, 1130 KIM PLACE   60439
Central MS, 410 MCCARTHY RD   60439
   Thomas Lenhardt, prin.
Oakwood ES, 1130 KIM PL   60439
   Ralph Wilhite, prin.

St. Patrick School, 205 CASS ST   60439
SS Cyril & Methodius School
   607 SOBIESKI ST   60439
St. Alphonsus School, STATE & LOGAN   60439
St. Dominic School
   420 BRIARCLIFF ROAD   60439

Lena, Stephenson Co., Pop. Code 4
Lena-Winslow CUSD 202
Sch. Sys. Enr. Code 3
Supt. – Dr. James Ludwick
517 FREMONT ST 61048
Lena-Winslow JHS, 517 FREMONT ST 61048
David Morrison, prin.
ES, 111 E MASON ST 61048 – Debra Beving, prin.
Other Schools – See Winslow

Lerna, Coles Co., Pop. Code 2
Charleston CUSD 1
Supt. – See Charleston
ES 62440 – Walter McKenzie, prin.

Le Roy, McLean Co., Pop. Code 5
Le Roy CUSD 2
Sch. Sys. Enr. Code 3
Supt. – Randy Crump, 600 E PINE ST 61752
JHS, 600 E PINE ST 61752 – James Dunnan, prin.
Other Schools – See Downs

Lewistown, Fulton Co., Pop. Code 5
Lewistown SD 141
Sch. Sys. Enr. Code 3
Supt. – Richard Ellinger, 315 S ILLINOIS ST 61542
Central MS, 401 E AVE L 61542
Stanley Leesman, prin.
McNally PS, 315 S ILLINOIS ST 61542
Richard Ellinger, prin.

Prichard Clark CESD 340
Sch. Sys. Enr. Code 1
Supt. – Bud Cozad
RURAL ROUTE 02 BOX 107 61542
Clark Cons. ES
RURAL ROUTE 02 BOX 107 61542
Bud Cozad, prin.

Lexington, McLean Co., Pop. Code 4
Lexington CUSD 7
Sch. Sys. Enr. Code 3
Supt. – Joe Underwood, P O BOX 67 61753
JHS, P O BOX 67 61753 – John Coffey, prin.
ES, P O BOX 67 61753 – John Coffey, prin.

Liberty, Adams Co., Pop. Code 3
Liberty CUSD 2
Sch. Sys. Enr. Code 3
Supt. – Hobson Bale, P O BOX 199 62347
ES, RURAL ROUTE 01 62347
Myron Mason, prin.

Libertyville, Lake Co., Pop. Code 7
Libertyville SD 70
Sch. Sys. Enr. Code 4
Supt. – Dr. Lawrence Baskin
310 W ROCKLAND ROAD 60048
Highland JHS, 310 W ROCKLAND ROAD 60048
Paul Kremaku, prin.
Adler Park ES, 1740 N MILWAUKEE 60048
Janet Brownlie, prin.
Butterfield ES I, 1441 LAKE ST 60048
Joe Wilson, prin.
Copeland Manor ES, 801 7TH AVE 60048
Michael Snow, prin.
Rockland ES, 160 W ROCKLAND RD 60048
Alana Mraz, prin.

Oak Grove SD 68
Sch. Sys. Enr. Code 2
Supt. – Patrick Patt, 1700 OPLAINE ROAD 60048
Oak Grove ES, 1700 OPLAINE RD 60048
Gale Minnice-Carlson, prin.

St. Joseph School, 221 PARK PL 60048

Lincoln, Logan Co., Pop. Code 7
Chester-East CCSD 61
Sch. Sys. Enr. Code 2
Supt. – Gordon Lanning, RURAL ROUTE 03 62656
Chester-East Lincoln ES, RURAL ROUTE 03 62656
Gordon Lanning, prin.

Lincoln ESD 27
Sch. Sys. Enr. Code 4
Supt. – Lester D. Plotner, 100 S MAPLE ST 62656
JHS, 108 BROADWAY ST 62656
Wilbur Williams, prin.
Adams ES, 1311 NICHOLSON RD 62656
Leonard Janet, prin.
Central ES, 101 8TH ST 62656
Leonard Janet, prin.
Jefferson ES, 710 5TH ST 62656 – Jerry Bales, prin.
Northwest ES, 506 11TH ST 62656
Jerry Bales, prin.
Washington-Monroe ES, 1002 PEKIN ST 62656
Marjorie Lowman, prin.

West Lincoln CCSD 72
Sch. Sys. Enr. Code 2
Supt. – Jon Odle, RURAL ROUTE 01 62656
West Lincoln Community Consolidated ES
RURAL ROUTE 01 62656 – Jon Odle, prin.

Carroll Catholic School, 111 4TH ST 62656
Zion Lutheran School
1600 WOODLAWN RD 62656

Lincolnshire, Lake Co., Pop. Code 5
Lincolnshire-Prairieview SD 103
Sch. Sys. Enr. Code 3
Supt. – Dr. Oscar Bedrosian
2425 RIVERWOODS ROAD 60015
Sprague ES, 2425 RIVERWOODS RD 60015
Richard Best, prin.
Other Schools – See Lake Forest

Lincolnwood, Cook Co., Pop. Code 7
Lincolnwood SD 74
Sch. Sys. Enr. Code 3
Supt. – John Cahill, 6950 E PRAIRIE ROAD 60645
Lincoln Hall MS, 6855 N CRAWFORD AVE 60646
Dr. Mary Lou Johns, prin.
Hall ES, 3925 W LUNT AVE 60645
Jacqueline Feare, prin.
Rutledge Hall ES
6850 N EAST PRAIRIE RD 60645
Dr. Gerald Hodel, prin.

Lindenhurst, Lake Co., Pop. Code 0
Lake Villa CCSD 41
Supt. – See Lake Villa
Hooper ES, 2400 E SAND LAKE RD 60046
Mathias Tabar, prin.

Lindenwood, Ogle Co.
Eswood CCSD 269
Sch. Sys. Enr. Code 2
Supt. – Gerald Olson, P O BOX 7 61049
MS, P O BOX 7 61049 – Gerald Olson, prin.
Other Schools – See Esmond

Lisle, Du Page Co., Pop. Code 7
Lisle CUSD 202
Sch. Sys. Enr. Code 4
Supt. – Richard Hogan, 5211 CENTER AVE 60532
JHS, 5207 CENTER AVE 60532
Roger Wanic, prin.
Scheiser ES, 5205 KINGSTON AVE 60532
Marion Widmoyer, prin.
Tate Woods ES, 1736 MIDDLETON AVE 60532
Theresa Sak, prin.

St. Joan of Arc School
4913 COLUMBIA AVE 60532

Litchfield, Montgomery Co., Pop. Code 6
Litchfield CUSD 12
Sch. Sys. Enr. Code 4
Supt. – William Cornman
1702 N STATE ST 62056
JHS, 1719 N STATE ST 62056
Don Williams, prin.
Colt ES, 615 E TYLER AVE 62056
Gary Zerrusen, prin.
Madison Park ES, 700 E PARK PL 62056
Jomarilyn Hartke, prin.
Russell ES, 700 N JEFFERSON ST 62056
John Denton, prin.
Sihler ES, 601 S STATE ST 62056
Maxine Nimmons, prin.

Zion Lutheran School, 1301 N STATE ST 62056

Livingston, Madison Co., Pop. Code 3
Livingston CCSD 4
Sch. Sys. Enr. Code 2
Supt. – Dr. Walter Bishop, P O BOX 599 62058
Graiff ES, P O BOX 399 62058
Wayne Brooke, prin.

Loami, Sangamon Co., Pop. Code 3
CUSD 16
Supt. – See New Berlin
ES, P O BOX 238 62661 – Alice Moss, prin.

Lockport, Will Co., Pop. Code 6
Fairmont SD 89
Sch. Sys. Enr. Code 3
Supt. – Dillard Harris
745 GREEN GARDEN PLACE 60441
Fairmont JHS, 735 GREEN GARDEN PLACE 60441
J. Witkowski, prin.
Fairmont ES, 745 GREEN GARDEN PLACE 60441
Dillard Harris, prin.

Homer CCSD 33C
Sch. Sys. Enr. Code 4
Supt. – Dr. Edward Karns
16025 N CEDAR ROAD 60441
Homer JHS, 15711 BELL RD 60441
Wm. Butler, prin.
Goodings Grove ES, 12914 W 143RD ST 60441
Glenda Brandsetter, prin.
Hadley PS, 15731 BELL ROAD 60441
Edwin Hamilton, prin.
Schilling MS, RURAL ROUTE 01 60441
Ernst Jolas, prin.

Milne-Kelvin Grove SD 91
Sch. Sys. Enr. Code 2
Supt. – A Carpentier, 808 ADAMS ST 60441
Kelvin Grove JHS, 808 ADAMS ST 60441
A. Carpentier, prin.
Milne Grove ES, 565 E 7TH ST 60441
Karin Evans, prin.

Taft SD 90
Sch. Sys. Enr. Code 2
Supt. – James D'Amico
1605 S WASHINGTON ST 60441
Taft ES, 1605 S WASHINGTON ST 60441
James D'Amico, prin.

Will County SD 92
Sch. Sys. Enr. Code 2
Supt. – John Tarter, 710 N STATE ST 60441
Ludwig MS, 710 N STATE ST 60441
William Barney, prin.
Walsh ES, 514 MACGREGOR RD 60441
Steven Kleinfeldt, prin.

St. Andrew School, 505 KINGSTON DR 60441
St. Denis School, 223 E 12TH ST 60441

St. Joseph School, 529 MADISON ST 60441

Loda, Iroquois Co., Pop. Code 2
Buckley-Loda CUSD 8
Supt. – See Buckley
Buckley-Loda ES 60948 – Noel Ross, prin.

Logan, Franklin Co.
Logan CCSD 110
Sch. Sys. Enr. Code 1
Supt. – Barry Kohl, P O BOX 62856
ES, P O BOX 7 62856 – Barry Kohl, prin.

Lombard, Du Page Co., Pop. Code 8
Lombard SD 44
Sch. Sys. Enr. Code 5
Supt. – Dr. Gordon Wendlandt
150 W MADISON ST 60148
JHS, 150 W MADISON ST 60148
Theodore Zimmerman, prin.
Butterfield ES, 2 S 500 GRAY AVE 60148
Sandra Truax, prin.
Green Valley ES, 331 W MADISON ST 60148
Harold Ellinghausen, prin.
Hammerschmidt ES
617 HAMMERSCHMIDT ST 60148
James Adams, prin.
Hoy ES, 820 S FINLEY RD 60148
Robert Burckle, prin.
Manor Hill ES, 1464 S MAIN ST 60148
Ronald Dayton, prin.
Park View ES, 341 N ELIZABETH ST 60148
Kim Perkins, prin.
Pleasant Lane ES, 401 N MAIN ST 60148
Roy Kauzlarich, prin.

Villa Park SD 45
Supt. – See Villa Park
Schafer ES, 700 E PLEASANT LN 60148
John Turner, prin.
Westmore ES, 340 S SCHOOL ST 60148
Judith Kaminski, prin.
York Center ES, 14TH AND SCHOOL STS 60148
Neal Doden, prin.

Christ the King School, 115 E 15TH ST 60148
Sacred Heart School, 322 W MAPLE ST 60148
St. John Lutheran School
215 S LINCOLN ST 60148
St. Pius X School, 601 S WESTMORE AVE 60148
Trinity Lutheran School
1008 E ROOSEVELT RD 60148

London Mills, Fulton Co., Pop. Code 3
Spoon River Valley CUSD 4
Sch. Sys. Enr. Code 3
Supt. – Ercil Little
RURAL ROUTE 01 BOX 55 61544
Spoon River Valley JHS
RURAL ROUTE 01 BOX 55 61544
Daniel Whitsitt, prin.
Spoon River Valley ES, RURAL ROUTE 61544
John Mangers, prin.

Long Grove, Lake Co., Pop. Code 4
Kildeer Countryside SD 96
Supt. – See Buffalo Grove
Kildeer Countryside ES
BOX 3100 RURAL ROUTE 60047
John Mason, prin.

Longview, Champaign Co., Pop. Code 2
ABL CUSD 6
Supt. – See Broadlands
ABL JHS, P O BOX 7 61852 – Arley Brown, prin.

Loraine, Adams Co., Pop. Code 2
Mendon CUSD 4
Supt. – See Mendon
ES 62349 – (—), prin.

Lostant, La Salle Co., Pop. Code 3
Lostant CCSD 25
Sch. Sys. Enr. Code 2
Supt. – David Liesse, P O BOX 205 61334
ES, P O BOX 205 61334 – Dale Adams, prin.

Louisville, Clay Co., Pop. Code 4
North Clay CUSD 25
Sch. Sys. Enr. Code 3
Supt. – Richard Seelman, P O BOX 220 62858
North Clay ES, P O BOX 279 62858
Ray Green, prin.
North Clay ES, P O BOX 279 62858
Ray Green, prin.

Lovejoy, St. Clair Co., Pop. Code 4
Brooklyn Unit SD 188
Sch. Sys. Enr. Code 2
Supt. – Carl Jason, Sr., 800 MADISON ST 62059
JHS, 800 MADISON ST 62059
Mary Reddick, prin.
ES, 800 MADISON ST 62059
Mary Reddick, prin.

Loves Park, Winnebago Co., Pop. Code 7
Harlem Unit SD 122
Supt. – See Rockford
ES, 344 GRAND AVE 61111 – James Kiefer, prin.
Windsor ES, 935 WINDSOR RD 61111
Jerry Primm, prin.

Lovington, Moultrie Co., Pop. Code 4
Lovington CUSD 303
Sch. Sys. Enr. Code 2
Supt. – Phillip Phillips, P O BOX 167 61937
ES, 330 S HIGH 61937 – Dale Farr, prin.

Ludlow, Champaign Co., Pop. Code 2
Ludlow CCSD 142
Sch. Sys. Enr. Code 2
Supt. – R. Scott Mayer, P O BOX 156 60949
ES, P O BOX 156 60949 – R. Scott Mayer, prin.

Lyndon, Whiteside Co., Pop. Code 3
Prophetstown-Lyndon CUSD 3
Supt. – See Prophetstown
MS, 501 6TH AVE W 61261 – Steve Stefani, prin.

Lynwood, Cook Co., Pop. Code 5
Sandridge SD 172
Sch. Sys. Enr. Code 2
Supt. – Richard Wangerow
RURAL ROUTE 01 BOX 91 60411
Sandridge ES, RURAL ROUTE 01 BOX 91 60411
Richard Wangerow, prin.

Lyons, Cook Co., Pop. Code 6
Lyons SD 103
Sch. Sys. Enr. Code 4
Supt. – Dennis Conti, 4100 JOLIET AVE 60534
Robinson ES, 4431 GAGE AVE 60534
Barbara Caracci, prin.
Washington ES, 4040 JOLIET AVE 60534
Paul Arvia, prin.
Other Schools – See Brookfield, Stickney

St. Hugh School, 43RD AND JOLIET AVE 60534

Mackinaw, Tazewell Co., Pop. Code 4
Deer Creek-Mackinaw CUSD 701
Sch. Sys. Enr. Code 3
Supt. – Virgil Jacobs, 401 E 5TH ST 61755
ES, 102 E FIFTH ST 61755 – Dallas Davis, prin.
Other Schools – See Deer Creek

Macomb, McDonough Co., Pop. Code 7
Macomb CUSD 185
Sch. Sys. Enr. Code 4
Supt. – Dr. Thomas Wolf
323 W WASHINGTON ST 61455
Edison JHS, 521 S PEARL ST 61455
Robert Meixner, prin.
Grant ES, 330 N MCARTHUR ST 61455
Sarah Sallee, prin.
Lincoln MS, 315 N BONHAM ST 61455
Paul Hayes, prin.
Logan MS, 520 E PIPER ST 61455 – (—), prin.
MacArthur ES, W GRAND ST 61455
Sidney Smay, prin.
Wilson ES, 424 W PIPER ST 61455
Sally Sallee, prin.

St. Paul's School, 322 W WASHINGTON ST 61455

Macon, Macon Co., Pop. Code 4
Macon CUSD 5
Sch. Sys. Enr. Code 3
Supt. – Roger Mitchell, 728 S WALL ST 62544
JHS, 666 S WALL ST 62544 – Lynn Curtis, prin.
ES, 245 N TOWSON 62544 – Philip Sargent, prin.

Madison, Madison Co., Pop. Code 6
Madison CUSD 12
Sch. Sys. Enr. Code 4
Supt. – Daniel Kostencki, 1707 4TH ST 62060
MS, 2101 MCCASLAND AVE 62060
Kenneth Perkins, prin.
Blair ES, COLLEGE & MEREDOCIA 62060
Bernard Long, prin.
Harris ES, 7TH & ALTON 62060
David Becherer, prin.

St. Mary's-St. Mark's School
10TH & LEE STS 62060

Mahomet, Champaign Co., Pop. Code 4
Mahomet-Seymour CUSD 3
Sch. Sys. Enr. Code 4
Supt. – F. Leon Rodgers, P O BOX 210 61853
Mahomet-Seymour JHS, P O BOX 220 61853
Robert Handlin, prin.
Lincoln Trails ES, 102 W STATE ST #200 61853
Leamon Jessup, prin.
Middletown MS, 101 N DIVISION ST 61853
Delbert Ryan, prin.
Sangamon ES, JEFFERSON & MAIN 61853
Lawrence Gnagey, prin.

Malden, Bureau Co., Pop. Code 2
Malden CCSD 84
Sch. Sys. Enr. Code 2
Supt. – Edwin Leeper, P O BOX 216 61337
ES, P O BOX 216 61337 – Edwin Leeper, prin.

Malta, De Kalb Co., Pop. Code 3
Malta CUSD 433
Sch. Sys. Enr. Code 2
Supt. – Guy Banicki, 507 N 3RD ST 60150
ES, 507 N 3RD ST 60150 – Guy Banicki, prin.

Manhattan, Will Co., Pop. Code 4
Manhattan SD 114
Sch. Sys. Enr. Code 2
Supt. – Glenn A. Hoffman
2ND & EASTERN AVE 60442
McDonald ES, 2ND & EASTERN AVE 60442
Howard Butters, prin.

Peotone CUSD 207U
Supt. – See Peotone
Wilton Center ES
RURAL ROUTE 01 BOX 43 60442
Richard Benson, prin.

St. Joseph School, W NORTH ST 60442

Manito, Mason Co., Pop. Code 4
Forman CUSD 124
Sch. Sys. Enr. Code 4
Supt. – John Lowey
1010 S WASHINGTON ST 61546
Forman JHS, 350 SOUTHMOORE ST 61546
Darrell Wilson, prin.
Forman ES, 350 SOUTHMOOR ST 61546
Dean Peyton, prin.

Spring Lake CCSD 606
Sch. Sys. Enr. Code 1
Supt. – James Malone
RURAL ROUTE 02 BOX 249 61546
Spring Lake ES
RURAL ROUTE 02 BOX 249 61546
James Malone, prin.

Manlius, Bureau Co., Pop. Code 2
Manlius CUSD 305
Sch. Sys. Enr. Code 2
Supt. – Dean Metz, P O BOX 247 61338
ES, W MAPLE ST 61338 – Robert Prusator, prin.

Mansfield, Piatt Co., Pop. Code 3
Blue Ridge CUSD 18
Supt. – See Farmer City
Blue Ridge JHS, 247 MCKINLEY ST 61854
Robert Hooker, prin.
ES, 250 MCKINLEY ST 61854
Robert Hooker, prin.

Manteno, Kankakee Co., Pop. Code 5
Manteno CUSD 5
Sch. Sys. Enr. Code 3
Supt. – William Dickson
250 N POPLAR AVE 60950
JHS, 250 N POPLAR AVE 60950
Lloyd Hulick, prin.
ES, 25 N MAPLE ST 60950
Robert Fennema, prin.

Maple Park, Kane Co., Pop. Code 3
Central CUSD 301
Supt. – See Burlington
Lily Lake ES, 5N720 ROUTE 47 60151
Michael Switzer, prin.

Kaneland CUSD 302
Sch. Sys. Enr. Code 4
Supt. – Dr. Ray Bandlow
RURAL ROUTE 01 60151
Kaneland JHS
RURAL ROUTE 01 BOX A-25 60151
Richard Anderson, prin.
Kaneland ES, 1N137 MEREDITH ROAD 60151
Walter Duy, prin.

Mapleton, Peoria Co., Pop. Code 2
Illini Bluffs CUSD 327
Supt. – See Glasford
ES, MAIN & VINE 61547 – Bradford Janzen, prin.

Marengo, McHenry Co., Pop. Code 5
Marengo-Union CCSD 165
Sch. Sys. Enr. Code 2
Supt. – Leslie Hellemann, S LOCUST ST 60152
Hawthorn ES, 1913 HAWTHORN RD 60152
Emil Williams, prin.
Locust ES, 541 LOCUST ST 60152
Donald Holtzee, prin.

Riley CCSD 18
Sch. Sys. Enr. Code 2
Supt. – Roy Asplund, 9406 RILEY ROAD 60152
Riley Community Consolidated ES
9406 RILEY RD 60152 – Roy Asplund, prin.

Zion Lutheran School
JACKSON AND PAGE STS 60152

Marine, Madison Co., Pop. Code 3
Triad CUSD 2
Supt. – See Saint Jacob
ES, W DIVISION ST 62061 – Michael Loftus, prin.

Marion, Williamson Co., Pop. Code 7
Crab Orchard CUSD 3
Sch. Sys. Enr. Code 2
Supt. – H. E. Stettler, RURAL ROUTE 02 62959
Crab Orchard ES, RURAL ROUTE 02 62959
Howard Stephens, prin.

Marion CUSD 2
Sch. Sys. Enr. Code 5
Supt. – Thomas Oates
1410 W HENDRICKSON ST 62959
JHS, 1501 W MAIN ST 62959
Herman Graves, prin.
Jefferson ES, 700 EAST BLVD 62959
Guy Peterson, prin.
Lincoln ES, 915 W CHESTNUT ST 62959
Wayne Whitehead, prin.
Longfellow ES, 1400 W HENDRICKSON ST 62959
John Ledbetter, prin.
Washington ES, 502 E MAIN ST 62959
Don Sullins, prin.
Other Schools – See Creal Springs

Marissa, St. Clair Co., Pop. Code 5
Marissa CUSD 40
Sch. Sys. Enr. Code 3
Supt. – Charles Slagley, 215 NORTH ST 62257
JHS, 300 SCHOOL VIEW DRIVE 62257
Michael Reeves, prin.

ES, 206 E FULTON ST 62257
William Quick, prin.

Markham, Cook Co., Pop. Code 7
Hazel Crest SD 152-5
Supt. – See Hazel Crest
Bunche ES, 165TH & PARK AVE 60426
Vallie Anderson, prin.

Prairie Hills ESD 144
Supt. – See Hazel Crest
Prairie-Hills JHS, 3035 W 153RD 60426
Kay Giles, prin.
Markham Park ES, 16239 LAWNDALE AVE 60426
Rebecca Nelson, prin.
Prairie-Hills PS, 3055 W 163RD ST 60426
Marguerite McKenzie, prin.

Maroa, Macon Co., Pop. Code 4
Maroa-Forsyth CUSD 2
Sch. Sys. Enr. Code 3
Supt. – Stephen Stenger, P O BOX 98 61756
Maroa-Forsyth JHS, P O BOX 98 61756
Leroy Mills, prin.
ES, P O BOX 38 61756 – Ronald Gossman, prin.
Other Schools – See Forsyth

Marseilles, La Salle Co., Pop. Code 5
Marseilles Unit SD 155
Sch. Sys. Enr. Code 3
Supt. – Greg LaPlante, 201 CHICAGO ST 61341
MS, CHICAGO & ILLINOIS STS 61341
Loris Lambert, prin.
McKinley ES, 521 E BLUFF ST 61341
Roberta Tapen, prin.
McKinley Annex ES, 501 E BLUFF STREET 61341
Roberta Tapen, prin.
Washington ES, 425 W BLUFF ST 61341
Roberta Tapen, prin.

Miller Twp. CCSD 210
Sch. Sys. Enr. Code 2
Supt. – George Hess
RURAL ROUTE 02 BOX 141 61341
Pope ES, RURAL ROUTE 02 BOX 141 61341
George Hess, prin.

Marshall, Clark Co., Pop. Code 5
Marshall CUSD 2C
Sch. Sys. Enr. Code 4
Supt. – Russel Ross, 503 PINE ST 62441
JHS, 806 N 6TH ST 62441
Robert Bondurant, prin.
North ES, 1006 N 6TH ST 62441
Dan Stephens, prin.
South ES, 805 S 6TH ST 62441
James Cooper, prin.

Martinsville, Clark Co., Pop. Code 4
Martinsville CUSD 3C
Sch. Sys. Enr. Code 2
Supt. – William Walters, P O BOX K 62442
JHS, W VINE ST 62442 – Fredrick Wheeler, prin.
ES, 410 E KENDALL ST 62442
Douglas Slover, prin.

Maryville, Madison Co., Pop. Code 4
Collinsville CUSD 10
Supt. – See Collinsville
Maryville West ES, W MAIN ST 62062
Shari Marshall, prin.

Mascoutah, St. Clair Co., Pop. Code 5
Mascoutah CUSD 19
Sch. Sys. Enr. Code 5
Supt. – Victor Van Dyne
720 W HARNETT ST 62258
JHS, 846 N 6TH ST 62258
Stephen Schwartz, prin.
Sixth Street ES, 533 N 6TH ST 62258
Walter Morio, Jr., prin.
Other Schools – See Scott A F B

Holy Childhood School, 215 N JOHN ST 62258

Mason, Effingham Co., Pop. Code 2
Effingham CUSD 40
Supt. – See Effingham
ES 62443 – Walter Lebegue, prin.

Mason City, Mason Co., Pop. Code 5
Mason City CUSD 123
Sch. Sys. Enr. Code 3
Supt. – Randolph Harhausen
208 N WEST ST 62664
JHS, 208 N WEST ST 62664
Randolph Harhausen, prin.
ES, 208 NORTH WEST AVE 62664
Randolph Harhausen, prin.

Matherville, Mercer Co., Pop. Code 3
Sherrard CUSD 200
Sch. Sys. Enr. Code 4
Supt. – Max Redmond, P O BOX 599 61263
ES, P O BOX 639 61263 – Richard Duty, prin.
Other Schools – See Milan, Sherrard, Viola

Matteson, Cook Co., Pop. Code 7
ESD 159
Sch. Sys. Enr. Code 4
Supt. – Donald Tesmond
6131 ALLEMONG DRIVE 60443
Sieden Prairie ES, 725 NOTRE DAME DR 60443
Cynthia Sedgwick, prin.
Woodgate ES, 101 CENTRAL AVE 60443
Timothy McCarthy, prin.
Yates ES, 6131 ALLEMONG DR 60443
Laverne Zell, prin.

Other Schools — See Richton Park

Matteson ESD 162
Sch. Sys. Enr. Code 4
Supt. – Jacob Schlenker, Jr.
21244 ILLINOIS ST   60443
Huth JHS, 3718 213TH PLACE   60443
Ernestine Foster, prin.
ES, 21245 MAIN ST   60443
Rocco D'Amelio, prin.
Other Schools — See Olympia Fields, Park Forest,
Richton Park

St. Laurence O'Toole School
214 GOVERNORS HWY   60443
Zion Lutheran School, 3850 216TH ST   60443

Mattoon, Coles Co., Pop. Code 7
Matoon CUSD 2
Sch. Sys. Enr. Code 5
Supt. – Earnest Smith, 100 N 22ND ST   61938
JHS, 1200 S 9TH ST   61938 – John Swick, prin.
Bennett ES, 205 S 32ND ST   61938
Durl Kruse, prin.
Columbian ES, 2709 MARION AVE   61938
Paul Yates, prin.
Franklin Annex ES, 1301 S 5TH ST   61938
G. Hanneken, prin.
Franklin ES, 1201 S 6TH ST   61938
G. D. Hanneken, prin.
Hawthorne ES, 2405 CHAMPAIGN AVE   61938
Tom Belcher, prin.
Lincoln ES, 1200 S 17TH ST   61938
Kathy Hanneken, prin.
Washington ES, 1200 SHELBY AVE   61938
Carolyn Kindrick, prin.
Other Schools — See Humboldt

St. Mary School, 2000 RICHMOND AVE   61938

Maywood, Cook Co., Pop. Code 8
Maywood-Melrose Park-Broadview SD
Sch. Sys. Enr. Code 1
Supt. – Raymond Slas, 1133 S 8TH AVE   60153
Emerson ES, 311 WASHINGTON BLVD   60153
Wanda Jordan, prin.
Garfield ES, 1514 S 9TH AVE   60153
Joyce Willis, prin.
Irving ES, 805 S 17TH AVE   60153
Dr. Thomas Kovalik, prin.
Lexington ES, 415 LEXINGTON ST   60153
Anitra McClothin, prin.
Lincoln ES, 811 CHICAGO AVE   60153
Francis Parisi, prin.
Van Buren ES, 1204 VAN BUREN ST   60153
Joyce Willis, prin.
Washington ES, 1111 WASHINGTON BLVD   60153
Earl Taylor, prin.
Other Schools — See Broadview, Melrose Park

Divine Infant Jesus School
1640 NEWCASTLE AVE   60153
Divine Providence School
2500 MAYFAIR AVE   60153
St. Eulalia School, 815 LEXINGTON ST   60153
St. James School, 611 MAPLE ST   60153

Mazon, Grundy Co., Pop. Code 3
Mazon-Verona-Kinsman CUSD 2
Sch. Sys. Enr. Code 3
Supt. – William Murray, P O BOX R   60444
Mazon-Verona-Kinsman JHS, P O BOX 289   60444
Gary Fechter, prin.
ES, 513 8TH ST BOX 289   60444
Gary Fechter, prin.
Other Schools — See Verona

Mc Clure, Alexander Co.
Shawnee CUSD 84
Supt. – See Wolf Lake
Shawnee ES South   62957 – Gene Vandeven, prin.

Mc Henry, McHenry Co., Pop. Code 7
Johnsburg CUSD 12
Sch. Sys. Enr. Code 4
Supt. – Robert Gough
21227 W CHURCH ST   60050
Johnsburg JHS, 2117 W CHURCH AVE   60050
Roger Kriewaldt, prin.
Bush ES, 2117 W CHURCH AVE   60050
Harold Thompson, prin.
Johnsburg MS, 2117 W CHURCH AVE   60050
Harold May, prin.
Ringwood ES, 2117 W CHURCH AVE   60050
Harold Thompson, prin.

Mc Henry CCSD 15
Sch. Sys. Enr. Code 5
Supt. – Dr. Robert Cassidy, 3926 MAIN ST   60050
JHS, 3711 W KANE AVE   60050 – Oscar Sola, prin.
Parkland JHS, 1802 N RINGWOOD ROAD   60050
James Blockinger, prin.
Edgebrook ES, 701 GREEN ST   60050
James LaShelle, prin.
Hilltop ES, 2615 W LINCOLN RD   60050
William Uhl, prin.
Landmark MS, 3614 WAUKEGAN RD   60050
John Nilles, prin.
Valley View ES, 6515 W ROUTE 120   60050
Susan Kostelny, prin.

Montini MS, 1405 N RICHMOND RD   60050
Montini PS, 3504 WASHINGTON ST   60050
St. John the Baptist School
2304 W CHURCH AVE   60050

Mc Lean, McLean Co., Pop. Code 3
Olympia CUSD 16
Supt. – See Stanford
McLean/Waynesville ES, P O BOX 326   61754
Kathryn Riddle, prin.

Mc Leansboro, Hamilton Co., Pop. Code 5
Hamilton Co. CUSD 10
Sch. Sys. Enr. Code 4
Supt. – Donald Roberts
109 N WASHINGTON ST   62859
Hamilton County JHS
501 E RANDOLPH ST   62859
Edgar Satterfield, prin.
Beaver Creek ES, RURAL ROUTE 03   62859
Debra Owen, prin.
East Side MS, 501 E RANDOLPH ST   62859
Penny Lee, prin.
West Side ES, 200 W MARKET ST   62859
Penny Lee, prin.
Other Schools — See Dahlgren, Dale

Mc Nabb, Putnam Co., Pop. Code 2
Putnam County CUSD 535
Supt. – See Granville
Putnam Co. JHS
RURAL ROUTE 01 BOX 15   61335
Gilbert Tonozzi, prin.

Media, Henderson Co., Pop. Code 3
Southern CUSD 120
Supt. – See Stronghurst
Southern JHS, P O BOX 758   61460
Leroy Hammond, prin.

Medinah, Du Page Co.
Medinah SD 11
Supt. – See Roselle
Medinah North ES, 7N330 MEDINAH RD   60157
Richard Dewitt, prin.

Medora, Macoupin Co., Pop. Code 3
Piasa CUSD 9
Supt. – See Piasa
ES, POST OFFICE   62063 – Bill Mills, prin.

Melrose Park, Cook Co., Pop. Code 7
Bellwood SD 88
Supt. – See Stone Park
Grant ES, 1300 N 34TH AVE   60160
Joseph Pater Sr., prin.

Mannheim SD 83
Supt. – See Franklin Park
Mannheim JHS, 2600 HYDE PARK AVE   60164
Shirley Lord, prin.

Maywood-Melrose Park-Broadview SD
Supt. – See Maywood
Addams ES, 910 DIVISION ST   60160
Willard Hansen, prin.
ES, 1715 W LAKE ST   60160
Mary De Ricco, prin.
Stevenson ES, 1630 20TH AVE   60160
Elden Stockey, prin.

Apostles Lutheran ES, 10430 MEDILL AVE   60164
Our Lady of Mt. Carmel School
1102 22ND AVE   60160
Sacred Heart School, 815 16TH AVE   60160
St. Charles Borromeo School
1635 N 37TH AVE   60160
St. Paul Lutheran School
1000 SUPERIOR ST   60160

Melvin, Ford Co., Pop. Code 3
Melvin Sibley CUSD 4
Supt. – See Sibley
Sibley JHS, 300 N CENTER ST   60952
Steven Fink, prin.

Mendon, Adams Co., Pop. Code 3
Mendon CUSD 4
Sch. Sys. Enr. Code 3
Supt. – Gerhard Jung, 380 COLLINS ST   62351
Unity MS, 380 COLLINS   62351
Ray Aubuchon, prin.
ES, 304 W WASHINGTON   62351
Dean Herring, prin.
Other Schools — See Loraine, Ursa

Mendota, La Salle Co., Pop. Code 6
Mendota CCSD 289
Sch. Sys. Enr. Code 4
Supt. – Michael Castiglia
1806 GUILES AVE   61342
Northbrook MS, 1804 GUILES AVE   61342
Ernest Egnstrom, prin.
Blackstone ES, 1308 WASHINGTON ST   61342
John Stuckey, prin.
Lincoln ES, 805 4TH AVE   61342
Steve Abel, prin.
Northbrook ES, 1804 GUTLES AVE   61342
John Stuckey, prin.

Holy Cross School, 1008 JEFFERSON ST   61342

Meredosia, Morgan Co., Pop. Code 4
Meredosia-Chambersburg CUSD 11
Sch. Sys. Enr. Code 2
Supt. – Jessie F. Morton, P O BOX 440   62665
Meredosia-Chambersburg JHS, P O BOX 440   62665
John Larimer, prin.
Meredosia-Chambersburg ES, P O BOX 440   62665
J. Fred Morton, prin.

Merrionette Park, Cook Co., Pop. Code 4
Atwood Heights SD 125
Supt. – See Oak Lawn
Meadow Lane IS
118TH & MEADOW LANE   60655
Frank Gregory, prin.

Metamora, Woodford Co., Pop. Code 4
Germantown Hills SD 69
Sch. Sys. Enr. Code 3
Supt. – Joe Stieglitz, 110 N FANDEL ROAD   61548
Germantown Hills JHS
200 S SCHMITT LANE   61548
J. Michael Dougherty, prin.
Germantown Hills ES, 110 N FANDEL RD   61548
Joseph Stieglitz, prin.

Metamora CCSD 1
Sch. Sys. Enr. Code 3
Supt. – Francis Frisk, 815 E CHATHAM   61548
ES, 815 E CHATHAM   61548 – Francis Rink, prin.

St. Mary School, 220 TAZEWELL ST   61548

Metropolis, Massac Co., Pop. Code 6
Joppa-Maple Grove CUSD 38
Supt. – See Joppa
Maple Grove ES, RURAL ROUTE 01   62960
Donald Smothers, prin.

Massac Unit 1
Sch. Sys. Enr. Code 4
Supt. – Don Smith, P O BOX 530   62960
JHS, 1004 CATHERINE ST   62960
Richard Trampe, prin.
Central ES, 103 W 11TH ST   62960
George Sharp, prin.
Clark ES, 619 E 5TH ST   62960
Reuben Bremer, prin.
Franklin ES, RURAL ROUTE 01   62960
James Haley, prin.
Jefferson ES, RURAL ROUTE 02   62960
Doris Vogt, prin.
MS, 718 CATHERINE ST   62960 – Dan Goins, prin.
Other Schools — See Brookport

Middletown, Logan Co., Pop. Code 3
New Holland-Middletown ESD 88
Supt. – See New Holland
New Holland-Middletown MS
P O BOX 187   62666 – James Gray, prin.
New Holland-Middletown ES, P O BOX 8   62666
James Gray, prin.

Midlothian, Cook Co., Pop. Code 7
Midlothian SD 143
Sch. Sys. Enr. Code 1
Supt. – Frank Thomson
14620 SPRINGFIELD AVE   60445
Central Park ES, 3621 151ST ST   60445
Joan Bleck, prin.
Kolmar ES, 4500 143RD ST   60445
Robert Steffen, prin.
Springfield ES, 14620 SPRINGFIELD AVE   60445
Sandra Boelcke, prin.

St. Christopher School, 14611 KEELER AVE   60445

Milan, Rock Island Co., Pop. Code 6
Rock Island SD 41
Supt. – See Rock Island
Eddy ES, 125 2ND AVE W   61264
Dr. Gary Ackerson, prin.
Jefferson ES, 1307 4TH ST W   61264
Dr. Gary Ackerson, prin.

Sherrard CUSD 200
Supt. – See Matherville
Coyne Center ES, 11310 16TH ST   61264
Richard Duty, prin.

Milford, Iroquois Co., Pop. Code 4
Bryce-Ash CCSD 284
Sch. Sys. Enr. Code 1
Supt. – Paul Burton
RURAL ROUTE 02 BOX 196   60953
Bryce-Ash Grove ES
RURAL ROUTE 02 BOX 196   60953
Paul Burton, prin.

Milford CCSD 280
Sch. Sys. Enr. Code 2
Supt. – Bill Hudgens, 100 S CHICAGO ST   60953
Milford Comm. ES, 100 S CHICAGO ST   60953
Bill Hudgens, prin.

St. Paul Lutheran School
RURAL ROUTE 02 BOX 120   60953

Mill Shoals, White Co., Pop. Code 2
Mill Shoals CCSD 18
Sch. Sys. Enr. Code 1
Supt. – Roger Heckler, P O BOX 506   62862
ES, P O BOX 506   62862 – Roger Heckler, prin.

Milledgeville, Carroll Co., Pop. Code 4
Milledgeville CUSD 312
Sch. Sys. Enr. Code 2
Supt. – Terry Bowers, P O BOX 609   61051
ES, P O BOX 609   61051 – Terry Bowers, prin.

Millstadt, St. Clair Co., Pop. Code 5
Millstadt CCSD 160
Sch. Sys. Enr. Code 3
Supt. – Dennis White, 211 W MILL ST   62260
ES, 211 W MILL ST   62260
Billy Lee Howell, prin.

St. James School, 412 W WASHINGTON ST 62260

Minonk, Woodford Co., Pop. Code 4
Minonk-Dana-Rutland CUSD 108
Sch. Sys. Enr. Code 3
Supt. – Gerald Christensen
  435 MAPLE AVE 61760
Minonk-Dana-Rutland JHS
  435 MAPLE AVE 61760 – John Finlen, prin.
Minonk-Dana-Rutland ES
  523 JOHNSON ST 61760
  Richard Dishinger, prin.

Minooka, Grundy Co., Pop. Code 4
Minooka CCSD 201
Sch. Sys. Enr. Code 3
Supt. – Dr. Thomas Allen, P O BOX 519 60447
JHS, P O BOX 519 60447 – Mary Flatness, prin.
ES, 400 COADY DR BOX 519 60447
  Clark Shiefen, prin.

Mokena, Will Co., Pop. Code 5
Mokena SD 159
Sch. Sys. Enr. Code 3
Supt. – Dr. Raymond J. Garritano
  11331 195TH ST 60448
JHS, 11331 195TH ST 60448 – Gene Morrall, prin.
ES, WILLOW CREST LN 60448
  Lois Haffner, prin.
Willowcrest MS, WILLOW CREST LN 60448
  Dale Fausch, prin.

Summit Hill SD 161
Supt. – See Frankfort
Arbury Hills ES, 19651 S BEECHNUT 60448
  David Middleton, prin.

St. Mary School, 195TH ST 60448

Moline, Rock Island Co., Pop. Code 8
Moline Unit SD 40
Sch. Sys. Enr. Code 6
Supt. – Richard Hennegan, 1619 11TH AVE 61265
Deere JHS, 2035 11TH ST 61265
  Burdette Ringquist, prin.
Wilson JHS, 1301 48TH ST 61265
  Clyde Storbeck, prin.
Butterworth ES, 4205 48TH ST 61265
  Ronald Anderson, prin.
Ericsson ES, 355 5TH AVE 61265
  Patricia Nelson, prin.
Franklin ES, 5312 11 AVE C 61265
  Rick Shannon, prin.
Garfield ES, 1518 25 AVE 61265
  Fred McGlaughlin, prin.
Hamilton ES, 700 32ND AVE 61265
  John McGaughy, prin.
Lincoln-Irving ES, 1015 16 AVE 61265
  George Thuenen, prin.
Logan ES, 1602 25TH ST 61265
  Mary Hood, prin.
Mann ES, RURAL ROUTE 01 BOX 115 61265
  Stephen Haines, prin.
Roosevelt ES, 3530 23RD AVE 61265
  Douglas Lewis, prin.
Washington ES, 1550 41ST ST 61265
  D. Jennings, prin.
Willard ES, 1616 16TH ST 61265
  Ada Cabaniss, prin.
Other Schools – See Coal Valley

Seton Catholic School-St. Marys
  420 10TH ST 61265
Seton Catholic School-Sacred Heart
  1611 14TH ST 61265

Momence, Kankakee Co., Pop. Code 5
Momence CUSD 1
Sch. Sys. Enr. Code 4
Supt. – Joseph Wakeley
  415 N DIXIE HIGHWAY 60954
JHS, 801 W 2ND ST 60954 – Kenneth Fox, prin.
Je-Neir ES, 1001 W 2ND ST 60954
  Michael Hickey, prin.
Range ES, 415 N DIXIE HIGHWAY 60954
  Thomas Brooks, prin.

St. Patrick Academy, 404 W SECOND ST 60954

Monee, Will Co., Pop. Code 3
Crete-Monee CUSD 201U
Supt. – See Crete
ES, 450 MAIN ST 60449 – Lyell Stark, prin.

Monmouth, Warren Co., Pop. Code 7
Monmouth Unit SD 38
Sch. Sys. Enr. Code 4
Supt. – Dr. Donald Jenkins, 325 S 11TH ST 61462
Central JHS, 401 E 2ND AVE 61462
  Gary Collins, prin.
Garfield ES, 321 E EUCLID AVE 61462
  Larry Cline, prin.
Harding ES, 245 E 9TH AVE 61462
  Marvin Leuschke, prin.
Lincoln ES, 329 S 11TH ST 61462
  Cynthia Waltershausen, prin.
Willits Es, 105 NORTH E ST 61462
  Larry Cline, prin.

Warren CUSD 222
Sch. Sys. Enr. Code 2
Supt. – William Rees, RURAL ROUTE 01 61462
Warren ES, RURAL ROUTE 01 61462
  William Rees, prin.

Yorkwood CUSD 225
Sch. Sys. Enr. Code 2
Supt. – James Wenstrom
  RURAL ROUTE 03 BOX SD 61462
Yorkwood JHS, RURAL ROUTE 03 61462
  Lyman Schar, prin.
Yorkwood ES, RURAL ROUTE 03 61462
  Joseph Fillman, prin.

Immaculate Conception School, 115 N B ST 61462

Monroe Center, Ogle Co.
Meridian CUSD 223
Supt. – See Stillman Valley
ES, P O BOX 188 61052 – Ken McMillin, prin.

Montgomery, Kendall Co., Pop. Code 5
Aurora East Unit SD 131
Supt. – See Aurora
Krug ES, 240 MELROSE AVE 60538
  Beverly Miller, prin.

Aurora West Unit SD 129
Supt. – See Aurora
Nicholson ES, 649 N MAIN ST 60538
  Stephen Wilson, prin.

Oswego CUSD 308
Supt. – See Oswego
Boulder Hill ES, 161 BOULDER HILL PASS 60538
  Jerald Tollefson, prin.
Long Beach ES, 67 LONG BEACH RD 60538
  Roberta Van Amburgh, prin.

Monticello, Piatt Co., Pop. Code 5
Monticello CUSD 25
Sch. Sys. Enr. Code 4
Supt. – Donald L. Pratt, 817 S CHARTER ST 61856
Washington MS, 100 W JEFFERSON ST 61856
  Gerry Eckerty, prin.
Lincoln ES, 700 N BUCHANAN ST 61856
  Martin Maguet, prin.
Other Schools – See White Heath

Montrose, Effingham Co., Pop. Code 2
Jasper Co. CUSD 1
Supt. – See Newton
Grove ES, RURAL ROUTE 01 62445
  John Miller, prin.

Moro, Madison Co., Pop. Code 4
Bethalto CUSD 8
Supt. – See Bethalto
Meadowbrook ES, ROOSEVELT DR 62067
  Robert Freidline, prin.

Edwardsville CUSD 7
Supt. – See Edwardsville
Midway ES, RURAL ROUTE 01 BOX 437 62067
  Lee Kovarik, prin.

Morris, Grundy Co., Pop. Code 6
Morris SD 54
Sch. Sys. Enr. Code 4
Supt. – Dr. Michael Wright
  519 FRANKLIN ST 60450
Shabbona MS, 725 SCHOOL ST 60450
  Bernard Keating, prin.
Center ES, 720 DIVISION ST 60450
  Steve Black, prin.
Franklin ES, 519 FRANKLIN ST 60450
  James Biros, prin.
Garfield ES, 120 W HIGH ST 60450
  James Biros, prin.

Nettle Creek CCSD 24 C
Sch. Sys. Enr. Code 1
Supt. – David Walle
  8820 N SCOTT SCHOOL ROAD 60450
Nettle Creek MS, 8820 SCOTT SCHOOL RD 60450
  David Walle, prin.
Erienna ES, 8820 SCOTT SCHOOL RD 60450
  Karen Breunig, prin.

Saratoga CCSD 60C
Sch. Sys. Enr. Code 2
Supt. – Ted Struck, 4040 DIVISION ST 60450
Saratoga ES, 4040 DIVISION ST 60450
  Anthony Raciti, prin.

Immaculate Conception School
  505 E NORTH ST 60450

Morrison, Whiteside Co., Pop. Code 5
Morrison CUSD 6
Sch. Sys. Enr. Code 4
Supt. – Elmer Perkins, 643 GENESEE AVE 61270
JHS, 305 E WINFIELD ST 61270
  Gordon Nelson, prin.
Northside ES, N GENESEE 61270
  James Prombo, prin.
Southside ES, 307 S MADISON ST 61270
  James Prombo, prin.

Morrisonville, Christian Co., Pop. Code 4
Morrisonville CUSD 1
Sch. Sys. Enr. Code 2
Supt. – Ralph Marshall, P O BOX 155 62546
JHS, P O BOX 155 62546 – Daniel Fuentes, prin.
ES, P O BOX 13 62546 – Ralph Marshall, prin.

Morton, Tazewell Co., Pop. Code 7
Morton CUSD 709
Sch. Sys. Enr. Code 5
Supt. – Wayne Sutter, 235 E JACKSON ST 61550
JHS, 225 E JACKSON ST 61550
  J. Michael Fuoss, prin.

Brown ES, 2550 N MORTON AVE 61550
  David Diemer, prin.
Grundy ES, 1100 S FOURTH AVE 61550
  David Diemer, prin.
Jefferson ES, 220 E JEFFERSON ST 61550
  Allan Larocco, prin.
Lincoln ES, 100 S NEBRASKA AVE 61550
  Jolyon Webb, prin.

Blesed Sacrament School
  223 E GREENWOOD ST 61550

Morton Grove, Cook Co., Pop. Code 7
Golf ESD 67
Sch. Sys. Enr. Code 3
Supt. – Dr. Harry Trumfio
  9401 WAUKEGAN ROAD 60053
Golf JHS, 9401 WAUKEGAN ROAD 60053
  Dr. Karen Uhren, prin.
Hynes ES, 9000 BELLEFORTE AVE 60053
  Roger Procise, prin.

Morton Grove SD 70
Sch. Sys. Enr. Code 3
Supt. – John Graham, 6200 LAKE ST 60053
Park View JHS, 6200 LAKE ST 60053
  Leslie Lange, prin.
Park View ES, 6200 LAKE ST 60053
  Andrew Socha, prin.

Skokie SD 69
Supt. – See Skokie
Edison MS, 8200 GROSS POINT RD 60053
  Rose Gordon, prin.

St. Martha School, 8535 GEORGIANA AVE 60053

Mossville, Peoria Co.
Illinois Valley Central Unit SD 321
Supt. – See Chillicothe
ES, P O BOX 178 61552 – Paul Sowers, prin.

Mounds, Pulaski Co., Pop. Code 4
Meridian CUSD 101
Sch. Sys. Enr. Code 4
Supt. – Dr. Samuel Harbin
  RURAL ROUTE 01 BOX 78A 62964
Meridian ES, RURAL ROUTE 01 BOX 78 62964
  Edward Britton, prin.

Mount Auburn, Christian Co., Pop. Code 3
Mt. Auburn CUSD 5
Sch. Sys. Enr. Code 2
Supt. – L. Tolliver, P O BOX 98 62547
ES, P O BOX 98 62547 – Robert Sample, prin.

Mount Carmel, Wabash Co., Pop. Code 6
Wabash CUSD 348
Sch. Sys. Enr. Code 4
Supt. – Larry Bradfield, 218 W 13TH ST 62863
North MS, 1300 N WALNUT 62863
  Glenn Decker, prin.
South ES, 715 W 3RD ST 62863 – Bill Priest, prin.
Other Schools – See Bellmont

St. Mary's School, 417 CHESTNUT ST 62863

Mount Carroll, Carroll Co., Pop. Code 4
Mt. Carroll CUSD 304
Sch. Sys. Enr. Code 3
Supt. – Wm. Daters, 300 S MAIN ST 61053
JHS, 300 S MAIN ST 61053 – John Kilpatrick, prin.
ES, 300 S MAIN ST 61053 – John Kilpatrick, prin.
MS, RURAL ROUTE 01 61053
  William Daters, prin.

Mount Erie, Wayne Co., Pop. Code 2
North Wayne CUSD 200
Supt. – See Cisne
ES, RURAL ROUTE 01 BOX 01 62466
  Janice Meagher, prin.

Mount Morris, Ogle Co., Pop. Code 5
Mt. Morris CUSD 261
Sch. Sys. Enr. Code 3
Supt. – Edward Olds III
  401 S FLETCHER ST 61054
JHS, 406 S SEMINARY ST 61054 – (—), prin.
ES, 401 S FLETCHER ST 61054
  Kathleen Williams, prin.

Mount Olive, Macoupin Co., Pop. Code 4
Mt. Olive CUSD 5
Sch. Sys. Enr. Code 3
Supt. – William Gullick, 804 W MAIN ST 62069
ES, 804 W MAIN ST 62069
  Robert Viehweg, prin.

Mount Prospect, Cook Co., Pop. Code 8
Community Consolidated SD 59
Supt. – See Arlington Heights
Holmes JHS, 1900 W LONNQUIST BLVD 60056
  Richard Jenness, prin.
Forest View ES, 1901 W ESTATES DR 60056
  Donald Heitzman, prin.
Frost ES, 1308 S CYPRESS DR 60056
  Albeon Waltman, prin.
Jay ES, 1835 W PHEASANT LN 60056
  Joan Gifford, prin.

Mt. Prospect SD 57
Sch. Sys. Enr. Code 4
Supt. – Dr. Earl Sutter, 701 W GREGORY ST 60056
Lincoln JHS, 700 W LINCOLN ST 60056
  Dr. Donald Driver, prin.
Fairview ES, 300 N FAIRVIEW ST 60056
  Frances Higley, prin.

Lions Park ES, 300 E COUNCIL TRL 60056
Robert Guthrie, prin.
Westbrook ES, 103 S BUSSE RD 60056
Robert Ferguson, prin.

River Trails SD 26
Sch. Sys. Enr. Code 4
Supt. – Dr. Thomas Rich
1900 E KENSINGTON ROAD 60056
River Trails JHS, 1000 N WOLF ROAD 60056
Eugene Kukla, prin.
Euclid ES, 1211 N WHEELING RD 60056
Donald Kellen, prin.
Indian Grove ES
1340 N BURNING BUSH LN 60056
Joseph Wawak, prin.

Wheeling CCSD 21
Supt. – See Wheeling
Frost ES, 1805 N ASPEN DR 60056
George Galvan, prin.

St. Emily School, 1400 E CENTRAL RD 60056
St. Paul Lutheran School, 18 S SCHOOL ST 60056
St. Raymond School
300 S ELMHURST AVE 60056

Mount Pulaski, Logan Co., Pop. Code 4
Mt. Pulaski CUSD 23
Sch. Sys. Enr. Code 3
Supt. – Robert Mueller, 119 N GARDEN ST 62548
ES, GARDEN & MORGAN 62548
Richard Zatteau, prin.
Other Schools – See Elkhart

Mount Sterling, Brown Co., Pop. Code 4
Brown Co. CUSD 1
Sch. Sys. Enr. Code 3
Supt. – Michael Napp, 214 E NORTH ST 62353
North MS, 501 NW CROSS ST 62353
George Castro, prin.
South ES, 300 S CAPITOL AVE 62353
George Castro, prin.
Other Schools – See Versailles

St. Mary School, 407 W NORTH ST 62353

Mount Vernon, Jefferson Co., Pop. Code 7
Bethel SD 82
Sch. Sys. Enr. Code 2
Supt. – Charles Thierry, RURAL ROUTE 01 62864
Bethel ES, RURAL ROUTE 01 62864
Charles Thierry, prin.

Dodds CCSD 7
Sch. Sys. Enr. Code 2
Supt. – William Cross, RURAL ROUTE 04 62864
Dodds ES, RURAL ROUTE 04 62864
William Cross, prin.

McClellan CCSD 12
Sch. Sys. Enr. Code 2
Supt. – David Thomas, RURAL ROUTE 03 62864
McClellan ES, RURAL ROUTE 03 62864
David Thomas, prin.

Mt. Vernon SD 80
Sch. Sys. Enr. Code 4
Supt. – Lawrence Loveall, P O BOX 767 62864
Casey JHS, 1829 BROADWAY ST 62864
Merlin Hodge, prin.
Buford ES, 623 S 34TH ST 62864
Anson Smith, prin.
Franklin ES, 500 HARRISON ST 62864
James Upchurch, prin.
Hall ES, 301 S 17TH ST 62864
Lon McHaney, prin.
Lincoln ES, 1700 OAKLAND AVE 62864
Carl Baker, prin.
Mann ES, 1901 PERKINS AVE 62864
Jerry Clemens, prin.

Summersville SD 79
Sch. Sys. Enr. Code 2
Supt. – Mickey Wright, RURAL ROUTE 07 62864
Summersville ES
RURAL ROUTE 07 BOX 35 62864
Mickey Wright, prin.

St. Mary's School, 1416 MAIN ST 62864

Mount Zion, Macon Co., Pop. Code 5
Mt. Zion CUSD 3
Sch. Sys. Enr. Code 7
Supt. – Kenneth Hendriksen, 455 ELM ST 62549
JHS, 305 S HENDERSON ST 62549
Junius Futrell, prin.
McGaughey ES, 1320 W MAIN ST 62549
Jan Sweet-Gregor, prin.
ES, 135 S HENDERSON ST 62549
Steve Milnor, prin.
IS, 725 W MAIN ST 62549
William Fancher, prin.
Other Schools – See Dalton City, Decatur

Moweaqua, Shelby Co., Pop. Code 4
Moweaqua CUSD 6A
Sch. Sys. Enr. Code 3
Supt. – Mark Gregory, 229 E PINE ST 62550
JHS, 229 E PINE ST 62550 – Carroll Scrogin, prin.
ES, 229 E PINE ST 62550 – Carroll Scrogin, prin.

Mulberry Grove, Bond Co., Pop. Code 3
Mulberry Grove CUSD 1
Sch. Sys. Enr. Code 2
Supt. – Paul Seymour
RURAL ROUTE 02 BOX 327 62262

JHS, RURAL ROUTE 02 BOX 327 62262
Bill Donaldson, prin.
ES, RURAL ROUTE 02 BOX 327 62262
Jimmie Rice, prin.

Mundelein, Lake Co., Pop. Code 7
Diamond Lake SD 76
Sch. Sys. Enr. Code 3
Supt. – Dr. Philip Simons
500 ACORN LANE 60060
West Oak MS, 500 ACORN LANE 60060
Donald Kroening, prin.
Diamond Lake ES
RURAL ROUTE 01 BOX 257 60060
Gary Clair, prin.

Fremont SD 79
Sch. Sys. Enr. Code 2
Supt. – Dr. Dennis Dunton
28855 N FREMONT CTR ROAD 60060
Fremont ES
28855 N FREMONT CENTER RD 60060
Kevin O'Connor, prin.

Mundelein ESD 75
Sch. Sys. Enr. Code 4
Supt. – Dr. Richard Lanaghan
200 W MAPLE AVE 60060
Sandburg JHS, 855 W HAWLEY ST 60060
A. Stealy, prin.
Jefferson MS, 330 N CALIFORNIA AVE 60060
Michael Polite, prin.
Mechanics Grove ES
1200 N MIDLOTHIAN RD 60060
Michael Polite, prin.
Washington ES, 122 S GARFIELD AVE 60060
Shirley Anderson, prin.

St. Mary School, 22277 W ERHART RD 60060
Santa Maria Del Popolo School
126 N LAKE ST 60060

Murphysboro, Jackson Co., Pop. Code 6
Murphysboro CUSD 186
Sch. Sys. Enr. Code 4
Supt. – Dr. Michael Mugge
819 WALNUT ST 62966
Carruthers MS, CANDY LANE 62966
Hal Killebrew, prin.
JHS, 2125 SPRUCE ST 62966
George Starkweather, prin.
Lincoln ES, 20TH & DEWEY STS 62966
Frank Puttman, prin.
Logan ES, N 14TH ST 62966
Finas Stiegman, prin.
McElvain ES, RURAL ROUTE 03 62966
Ronald Burdick, prin.

Immanuel Lutheran School, 1915 PINE ST 62966
St. Andrew School, 723 MULBERRY ST 62966

Murrayville, Morgan Co., Pop. Code 3
Jacksonville SD 117
Supt. – See Jacksonville
ES, MASTERS STREET 62668
Alan Bradish, prin.

Naperville, Du Page Co., Pop. Code 8
Indian Prairie CUSD 204
Sch. Sys. Enr. Code 5
Supt. – Dr. Thomas Scullen
30W026 ROUTE 34 60540
Hill JHS, 1325 BROOKDALE ROAD 60540
Michael Pederson, prin.
Gregory MS, 2621 SPRINGDALE 60565
Greg Fischer, prin.
Brookdale ES, 1200 REDFIELD RD 60540
Charles Seidel, prin.
Clow ES, 1301 SPRINGDALE CIR 60565
Carl Pinnow, prin.
Longwood ES, 30 240 BRUCE LANE 60540
R. Jan Rodgriguez, prin.
Other Schools – See Aurora, Eola, Plainfield

Naperville CUSD 203
Sch. Sys. Enr. Code 7
Supt. – Dr. James Clark
WEBSTER AND HILLSIDE 60566
Jefferson JHS, 1525 N LOOMIS ST 60540
Russell Bryan, prin.
Lincoln JHS, 1320 S OLYMPUS DRIVE 60565
Robert Raynett, prin.
Madison JHS
RIVER OAK DRIVE/FAIR OAK 60540
Jerry Virgo, prin.
Washington JHS, 201 N WASHINGTON ST 60540
Terry Crandall, prin.
Beebe ES, 110 E 11TH AVE 60540
Dwight Hollonbeck, prin.
Ellsworth ES, 145 N SLEIGHT ST 60540
Carol McGuff, prin.
Elmwood ES, 1024 MAGNOLIA LN 60540
Donald Barnickle, prin.
Highlands ES, 525 S BRAINARD ST 60540
Jack Hinterlong, prin.
Maplebrook ES, WARBLER AT BAILEY 60565
Mary Kiser, prin.
Mills Street ES, 1300 N MILL ST 60540
Larry Nelson, prin.
Naper ES, 39 S EAGLE ST 60540
Sharon Wall, prin.
Prairie ES, PRAIRIE AT CHARLES 60540
Lenore Johnson, prin.
Ranch View ES
RANCH VIEW AND AUBURN 60565
Kenneth Johnson, prin.

River Woods ES, RIVER WOODS & NAPER 60565
R. Rodgriguez, prin.
Scott ES, 500 WARWICK DR 60565
Robert Hillenbrand, prin.
Steeple Run ES, STEEPLE RUN & PKMDW 60540
Steven Ligman, prin.

Bethany Lutheran School
919 S WASHINGTON ST 60540
SS Peter & Paul School, 201 E FRANKLIN 60540
St. Raphael School, 1215 MODAFF RD 60540

Nashville, Washington Co., Pop. Code 5
Nashville CCSD 49
Sch. Sys. Enr. Code 2
Supt. – Thomas J. Dahncke
RURAL ROUTE 03 62263
MS, RURAL ROUTE 03 62263 – Don Miller, prin.
PS, RURAL ROUTE 03 62263 – Don Miller, prin.

St. Ann Grade School, 607 S MILL ST 62263
Trinity-St. John Lutheran School
603 W WALNUT ST 62263

Nauvoo, Hancock Co., Pop. Code 4
Nauvoo-Colusa CUSD 325
Sch. Sys. Enr. Code 2
Supt. – Kenneth Nudd, HIGHWAY 96 N 62354
Nauvoo-Colusa JHS, HIGHWAY 96 N 62354
Ronald Yockey, prin.
ES, 450 KNIGHT ST 62354 – Kenneth Nudd, prin.

Nelson, Lee Co., Pop. Code 2
Nelson Public SD 8
Sch. Sys. Enr. Code 1
Supt. – Gregory Lutyens, P O BOX 53 61058
ES, P O BOX 53 61058 – Gregory Lutyens, prin.

Neoga, Cumberland Co., Pop. Code 4
Neoga CUSD 3
Sch. Sys. Enr. Code 4
Supt. – Richard Green, P O BOX 280 62447
JHS, P O BOX 280 62447 – David Carpenter, prin.
MS, P O BOX 310 62447 – Robert Schwindt, prin.
Pioneer ES, P O BOX 1586 62447
Robert Schwindt, prin.

Neponset, Bureau Co., Pop. Code 3
Neponset CCSD 307
Sch. Sys. Enr. Code 2
Supt. – William White, 201 W MAIN 61345
ES, 201 W MAIN 61345 – William White, prin.

Newark, Kendall Co., Pop. Code 3
Lisbon CCSD 90
Sch. Sys. Enr. Code 2
Supt. – Barb Sloan
RURAL ROUTE 01 BOX 62 60541
Lisbon ES, RURAL ROUTE 01 BOX 62 60541
Barb Sloan, prin.

Newark CCSD 66
Sch. Sys. Enr. Code 2
Supt. – Rob Nelson, 339 CHICAGO ROAD 60541
ES, 339 CHICAGO ROAD 60541
Robert Nelson, prin.

New Athens, St. Clair Co., Pop. Code 4
New Athens CUSD 60
Sch. Sys. Enr. Code 4
Supt. – John Ingalls, 501 HANFT ST 62264
JHS, BELSHA & HANFT 62264
George Lawrence, prin.
ES, HANFT & BELSHA ST 62264
George Lawrence, prin.

New Baden, Clinton Co., Pop. Code 4
Wesclin CUSD 3
Supt. – See Trenton
ES, 700 MARILYN DR 62265 – Carl Bann, prin.
St. George ES, 317 E MAPLE ST 62265
Carl Bann, prin.

New Berlin, Sangamon Co., Pop. Code 3
CUSD 16
Sch. Sys. Enr. Code 3
Supt. – J. Gregory Reynolds, ELLIS ST 62670
JHS, ELLIS ST 62670 – J. Gregory Reynolds, prin.
ES, ELLIS ST 62670 – Alice Moss, prin.
Other Schools – See Loami

New Boston, Mercer Co., Pop. Code 3
Westmer CUSD 203
Supt. – See Joy
Westmer ES, POST OFFICE 61272
Janet McCaw, prin.

New Douglas, Madison Co., Pop. Code 2
Highland CUSD 5
Supt. – See Highland
ES, POST OFFICE 62074 – James Gallatin, prin.

New Holland, Logan Co., Pop. Code 2
New Holland-Middletown ESD 88
Sch. Sys. Enr. Code 2
Supt. – James Gray, P O BOX 8 62671
Other Schools – See Middletown

New Lenox, Will Co., Pop. Code 6
New Lenox SD 122
Sch. Sys. Enr. Code 4
Supt. – Alex Martino, 809 N CEDAR ROAD 60451
Oster-Oakview JHS, 809 N CEDAR ROAD 60451
Del Bitter, prin.
Bentley MS, 511 E ILLINOIS HWY 60451
Robert Gaines, prin.
Haines ES, 155 HAINES AVE 60451
Lee Fears, prin.

Haven ES, 102 S CEDAR RD   60451
   Keith Pain, prin.
Tyler ES, 501 E ILLINOIS HWY   60451
   Edward Tatro, prin.

St. Jude School, 240 2 2ND AVE   60451

Newman, Douglas Co., Pop. Code 4
Newman CUSD 303
Sch. Sys. Enr. Code 2
Supt. – Charles White, 101 S COFFIN   61942
ES, 101 S COFFIN ST   61942 – Charles White, prin.

Newton, Jasper Co., Pop. Code 5
Jasper Co. CUSD 1
Sch. Sys. Enr. Code 4
Supt. – James B. Taylor
   609 S LAFAYETTE ST   62448
Newton Central JHS, 100 MAXWELL ST   62448
   Jay Hart, prin.
ES, 100 MAXWELL ST   62448 – Jay Hart, prin.
Other Schools – See Hidalgo, Montrose, Sainte Marie,
   Wheeler, Willow Hill, Yale

St. Thomas School, 306 W JOURDAN ST   62448

Niantic, Macon Co., Pop. Code 3
Niantic-Harristown CUSD 6
Sch. Sys. Enr. Code 3
Supt. – Roger Neal, P O BOX 127   62551
Niantic-Harristown JHS, P O BOX 127   62551
   Ronald Jump, prin.
Other Schools – See Harristown

Niles, Cook Co., Pop. Code 8
East Maine SD 63
Supt. – See Des Plaines
Gemini JHS, 8955 N GREENWOOD AVE   60648
   Donald Huebner, prin.
Nelson ES, 8901 N OZANAM AVE   60648
   Robert Jablon, prin.

Niles ESD 71
Sch. Sys. Enr. Code 2
Supt. – Eugene Zalewski
   6935 W TOUHY AVE   60648
Culver MS, 6921 W OAKTON ST   60648
   (—), prin.
Niles ES-South, 6935 W TOUHY AVE   60648
   Glenn Grieshaber, prin.

St. John Lutheran School
   7429 MILWAUKEE AVE   60648

Noble, Richland Co., Pop. Code 3
West Richland CUSD 2
Sch. Sys. Enr. Code 3
Supt. – David Newell, 300 E NORTH AVE   62868
West Richland JHS, 300 E NORTH AVE   62868
   Harold Ash, prin.
West Richland ES, 101 LOCUST ST   62868
   Jerry Burnell, prin.

Nokomis, Montgomery Co., Pop. Code 5
Nokomis CUSD 22
Sch. Sys. Enr. Code 3
Supt. – Joe Murphy, P O BOX 40   62075
Nokomis South MS, P O BOX 28   62075
   Michael J. Guidish, prin.
North ES, P O BOX 10   62075 – James Rupert, prin.

Normal, McLean Co., Pop. Code 8
Board of Regents SD
Sch. Sys. Enr. Code 3
Supt. – Dennis Kelly, 500 W GREGORY   61761
Metcalf ES, ILL STATE UNIVERSITY   61761
   Robert Dean, prin.

Normal CUSD 5
Sch. Sys. Enr. Code 6
Supt. – Dr. Richard MacFeely, 700 HALE ST   61761
Fairview ES, 416 FAIRVIEW ST   61761
   Jim Ewen, prin.
Field ES, 412 E CYPRESS ST   61761
   Randall Lloyd, prin.
Glenn ES, 306 GLENN AVE   61761
   Daniel Schweers, prin.
Hoose ES, 600 GRANDVIEW DR   61761
   John Pye, prin.
Oakdale ES, 601 S ADELAIDE ST   61761
   G. Lawrence Daghe, prin.
Sugar Creek ES, 200 N TOWANDA AVE   61761
   Duane Askew, prin.
Other Schools – See Bloomington, Carlock, Hudson,
   Towanda

Calvary Baptist Academy, P O BOX 587   61761
Epiphany School, 1002 E COLLEGE AVE   61761

Norridge, Cook Co., Pop. Code 7
Norridge SD 80
Sch. Sys. Enr. Code 3
Supt. – Ralph Gebert, 4251 N ORIOLE AVE   60634
Other Schools – See Chicago

Pennoyer SD 79
Sch. Sys. Enr. Code 2
Supt. – Dr. Deno Fenili
   5200 N CUMBERLAND AVE   60656
Other Schools – See Chicago

Norris City, White Co., Pop. Code 4
Norris City-Omaha-Enfield CUSD 3
Sch. Sys. Enr. Code 3
Supt. – Frank Blackman, EAST ST   62869
Norris City-Omaha ES, POST OFFICE   62869
   Norman Fechtig, prin.

Other Schools – See Enfield

North Aurora, Kane Co., Pop. Code 6
Aurora West Unit SD 129
Supt. – See Aurora
Goodwin ES, 18 POPLAR ST   60542
   Sandra Bauer, prin.
Schneider ES, 304 BANBURY RD   60542
   Richard Phillips, prin.

Northbrook, Cook Co., Pop. Code 8
Northbrook ESD 27
Sch. Sys. Enr. Code 4
Supt. – Dr. James L. Rohrabaugh
   637 LANDWEHR RD   60062
Wood Oaks JHS, 1250 SANDERS ROAD   60062
   Edward Raley, prin.
Grove ES, 1000 PFINGSTEN RD   60062
   Richard Sager, prin.
Hickory Point ES, 500 LABURNAM DR   60062
   Curtis Johnson, prin.
Shabonee MS, 2929 SHABONEE TER   60062
   David Stueckemann, prin.

Northbrook SD 28
Sch. Sys. Enr. Code 4
Supt. – Dr. Homer O. Harvey
   1475 MAPLE AVE   60062
JHS, 1475 MAPLE AVE   60062 – Steven Lake, prin.
Greenbriar ES, 1225 GREENBRIAR LN   60062
   Kent Raffel, prin.
Meadowbrook ES, 1600 WALTERS AVE   60062
   Geraldine Durcany, prin.
Westmoor ES, 2500 CHERRY LN   60062
   Gustav Chron, prin.

Northbrook/Glenview SD 30
Sch. Sys. Enr. Code 4
Supt. – Dr. Theodore Kamatos
   2374 SHERMER ROAD   60062
Maple JHS, 2370 SHERMER ROAD   60062
   James Lumb, prin.
Wescott ES, 1820 WESTERN AVE   60062
   Judith Gonwa, prin.
Other Schools – See Glenview

West Northfield SD 31
Sch. Sys. Enr. Code 3
Supt. – Dr. Robert Luckett
   3131 TECHNY ROAD   60062
Field JHS, 2055 LANDWEHR ROAD   60062
   Philip Zarob, prin.
Other Schools – See Glenview

Sager Sol Schecter Day School, 350 LEE RD   60062
St. Norbert School, 1817 WALTERS AVE   60062

North Chicago, Lake Co., Pop. Code 8
North Chicago SD 64
Sch. Sys. Enr. Code 2
Supt. – Dr. Charles Thomas
   2000 LEWIS AVE   60064
Green Bay ES, 2100 GREENBAY RD   60064
   Lawrence Jelinek, prin.
Hart ES, 1110-18TH ST   60064 – Susan Zook, prin.
Katzenmaier ES, 1829 KENNEDY DR   60064
   Michael Penich Jr., prin.
Neal ES, LEWIS AVE & ARGONNE   60064
   Vernon Shelton, prin.
North ES, 12TH & ADAMS   60064
   Robert Whitehead, prin.
Novak-King ES, 15TH & KEMBLE   60064
   Curtis Dorlsey, prin.
South ES, 1812 MORROW AVE   60064
   V Patrick Goodwin, prin.
Yeager ES, MORROW AVE & LEWIS   60064
   Lucille Johnson, prin.
Other Schools – See Great Lakes

Holy Rosary School, 1333 VICTORIA AVE   60064
Lake Shore Catholic Academy-S-Camp
   1836 LINCOLN ST   60064

Northfield, Cook Co., Pop. Code 6
Sunset Ridge SD 29
Sch. Sys. Enr. Code 2
Supt. – Dr. Howard Bultinck
   525 SUNSET RIDGE ROAD   60093
Sunset Ridge MS, 525 SUNSET RIDGE RD   60093
   Dr. Howard Bultinck, prin.
Middlefork PS, 405 WAGNER RD   60093
   Mary Osborne, prin.

Northlake, Cook Co., Pop. Code 7
Berkeley SD 87
Supt. – See Berkeley
Northlake MS, 202 S LAKEWOOD AVE   60164
   Wayne Dopke, prin.
Riley ES, 123 S WOLF RD   60164
   Salvatore Ferrera, prin.
Whittier ES, 338 WHITEHALL DR   60164
   Ronald Paul, prin.

Mannheim SD 83
Supt. – See Franklin Park
Roy ES, 533 N ROY AVE   60164
   Donald Flaws, prin.
Scott ES, 2250 SCOTT ST   60164
   Dr. Frank Tavano, prin.
Westdale ES, 99 DIVERSEY AVE   60164
   Marilyn Finesilver, prin.

St. John Vianney School
   27 N LA VERGNE AVE   60164

North Riverside, Cook Co., Pop. Code 6
Komarek SD 94
Sch. Sys. Enr. Code 2
Supt. – Rob Madonia, 8940 W 24TH ST   60546
Komarek ES, 8940 W 24TH ST   60546
   Neil Pellicci, prin.

Oak Brook, Du Page Co., Pop. Code 6
Butler SD 53
Sch. Sys. Enr. Code 2
Supt. – Dr. Marguerite Bloch
   2801 YORK ROAD   60521
Butler JHS, 2801 YORK ROAD   60521
   Charles Bolton, prin.
Brook Forest ES, 60 REGENT DR   60521
   Robert Carlo, prin.

Oakdale, Washington Co., Pop. Code 1
Oakdale CCSD 1
Sch. Sys. Enr. Code 1
Supt. – James Sprengel, RURAL ROUTE 1   62268
Oakdale Community Consolidated ES
   RURAL ROUTE 01   62268 – James Sprengel, prin.

Oakford, Menard Co., Pop. Code 2
Porta CUSD 202
Supt. – See Petersburg
ES, E CENTER ST   62673 – Dean Kerr, prin.

Oak Forest, Cook Co., Pop. Code 8
Arbor Park SD 145
Sch. Sys. Enr. Code 4
Supt. – James Upchurch, 15901 FOREST ST   60452
Arbor Park MS, 15900 OAK AVE   60452
   Thomas Savick, prin.
Gingerwood ES, 16936 FOREST AVE   60452
   Michael Chinino, prin.
Scarlet Oak ES, 5731 ALBERT DR   60452
   Robert Bacon, prin.
Other Schools – See Tinley Park

Forest Ridge SD 142
Sch. Sys. Enr. Code 4
Supt. – Arthur T. Lange
   14950 LARAMIE AVE   60452
Laramie JHS, 14950 LARAMIE AVE   60452
   Geraldine Kerkstra, prin.
Foster ES, 5931 SCHOOL ST   60452
   John Keane, prin.
Hille ES, 6900 151ST ST   60452
   Robert Schuit, prin.
Ridge ES, 5151 149TH ST   60452
   Donald Clark, prin.

Prairie Hills ESD 144
Supt. – See Hazel Crest
Fieldcrest ES, 4100 WAGMAN ST   60452
   Roberto Garcia, prin.

Tinley Park Community SD 146
Supt. – See Tinley Park
Fierke ES, 6535 VICTORIA DR   60452
   Robert Gardner, prin.

St. Damian School, 5300 155TH ST   60452

Oakland, Coles Co., Pop. Code 4
Oakland CUSD 5
Sch. Sys. Enr. Code 2
Supt. – Ezra Smithson, LOGAN AVE   61943
Lake Crest ES, TEETER ST   61943
   Ezra Smithson, prin.

Oak Lawn, Cook Co., Pop. Code 8
Atwood Heights SD 125
Sch. Sys. Enr. Code 3
Supt. – Stephen Horvath, Jr.
   4300 108TH PLACE   60453
Lawn Manor PS, 4300 108TH PL   60453
   Frank Gregory, prin.
Other Schools – See Alsip, Merrionette Park

Oak Lawn-Hometown SD 123
Sch. Sys. Enr. Code 4
Supt. – Dr. Dirk Manson
   105TH & LOCKWOOD AVE   60453
McGugan JHS, 105TH & LOCKWOOD AVE   60453
   James Paziotopoulos, prin.
Covington ES, 9130 52ND AVE   60453
   Lorelle Cutforth, prin.
Hannum ES, 98TH & TRIPP AVE   60453
   Terrence Bopp, prin.
Kolmar Avenue ES, 10425 S KOLMAR AVE   60453
   Arlene Ronshausen, prin.
Sward ES, 9830 BRANDT AVE   60453
   Lee Stanton, prin.
Other Schools – See Hometown

Ridgeland SD 122
Sch. Sys. Enr. Code 4
Supt. – Robert L. Olcese, 6500 95TH ST   60453
Simmons JHS, 6450 95TH ST   60453
   Dan Burke, prin.
Columbus Manor ES, 9700 MAYFIELD AVE   60453
   Bernice Blazis, prin.
Dearborn Heights ES
   9620 NORMANDY AVE   60453
   Glenn Babbitt, prin.
Harnew ES, 9100 AUSTIN AVE   60453
   Frank Milkevitch, prin.
Other Schools – See Bridgeview

Chicago S.W. Christian School
   5665 101ST ST   60453
Our Lady of Loretto School
   9003 S KOSTNER AVE   60456

St. Catherine Alexandria School
10621 KEDVALE AVE 60453
St. Gerald School, 9320 55TH CT 60453
St. Germaine School, 9735 S KOLIN AVE 60453
St. Linus School, 10400 LAWLER AVE 60453
St. Louis De Montfort School
8840 RIDGELAND AVE 60453
St. Patricia School, 9000 S 86TH AVE 60457
St. Paul Lutheran School, 4660 94TH ST 60453

Oak Park, Cook Co., Pop. Code 8
Oak Park ESD 97
Sch. Sys. Enr. Code 5
Supt. – John Fagan, 970 MADISON ST 60302
Emerson JHS, 916 WASHINGTON BLVD 60302
Glada Vaughn, prin.
Julian JHS, 416 S RIDGELAND AVE 60302
Dr. Benjamin Williams, prin.
Beye ES, 230 ONTARIO ST 60302
Susan Gibson, prin.
Hatch ES, 1000 N RIDGELAND AVE 60302
Thomas O'Loughlin, prin.
Holmes ES, 508 N KENILWORTH AVE 60302
Douglas Hesbol, prin.
Irving ES, 1125 S CUYLER AVE 60304
Thomas Hull Jr., prin.
Lincoln ES, 1111 S GROVE AVE 60304
Carol Dudzik, prin.
Longfellow ES, 715 S HIGHLAND AVE 60304
Mary Costa, prin.
Mann ES, 921 N KENILWORTH AVE 60302
Kenneth Panczyk, prin.
Whittier ES, 715 N HARVEY AVE 60302
Paula O'Malley, prin.

Ascension School, 601 VAN BUREN ST 60304
SS Catherine Siena-Lucy School
27 WASHINGTON BLVD 60302
St. Edmund School, 200 S OAK PARK AVE 60302
St. Giles School, 1030 LINDEN AVE 60302

Oakwood, Vermilion Co., Pop. Code 4
Community Unit SD 76
Supt. – See Fithian
ES, OLMSTEAD ST 61858 – Michael Metzen, prin.

Oblong, Crawford Co., Pop. Code 4
Oblong CUSD 4
Sch. Sys. Enr. Code 3
Supt. – Art McCormick, 108 N RANGE ST 62449
ES, 600 W MAIN ST 62449 – Steven Bahney, prin.

Odell, Livingston Co., Pop. Code 4
Odell CCSD 435
Sch. Sys. Enr. Code 2
Supt. – William Koenecke, 203 N EAST ST 60460
ES, 203 N EAST ST 60460
Dr. William Koenecke, prin.

St. Paul School, 300 S WEST ST 60460

Odin, Marion Co., Pop. Code 4
Odin SD 122
Sch. Sys. Enr. Code 2
Supt. – Tom Smith, MERRITT ST 62870
ES, MERRITT ST BOX 188 62870
David Wilson, prin.

O'Fallon, St. Clair Co., Pop. Code 7
Central SD 104
Sch. Sys. Enr. Code 2
Supt. – Joseph Arthur
309 HARTMAN LANE 62269
Central ES, 309 HARTMAN LN 62269
Joseph Arthur, prin.

O'Fallon CCSD 90
Sch. Sys. Enr. Code 2
Supt. – Dr. Remo Castrale
600 S SMILEY ST 62269
Schaefer JHS, 505 S CHERRY ST 62269
Mamie Dittemore, prin.
Evans ES, 802 DARTMOUTH DR 62269
Kent Mandrell, prin.
Hinchcliffe ES, P O BOX 126 62269
Lyle Henkel, prin.
Kampmeyer ES, 707 N SMILEY ST 62269
Dr. Hazel Loucks, prin.

Shiloh Village SD 85
Sch. Sys. Enr. Code 2
Supt. – Donald Frailey, 125 E JULIE ST 62269
Shiloh Village ES, 125 E JULIE ST 62269
Donald Frailey, prin.

St. Clare School, 214 W 3RD ST 62269

Ogden, Champaign Co., Pop. Code 3
Ogden CCSD 212
Sch. Sys. Enr. Code 2
Supt. – James Sayers, P O BOX 99 61859
ES, P O BOX 99 61859 – James Sayers, prin.

Oglesby, Bureau Co., Pop. Code 5
Oglesby ESD 125
Sch. Sys. Enr. Code 2
Supt. – Dr. James Boyle
212 W WALNUT ST 61348
Washington MS, 212 W WALNUT ST 61348
Robert Meehan, prin.
Lincoln ES, BENNETT AVE 61348
Dr. James Boyle, prin.

Holy Family School, 336 ALICE AVE 61348

Ohio, Bureau Co., Pop. Code 3
Ohio CCSD 17
Sch. Sys. Enr. Code 2
Supt. – Frank Dagne
103-105 MEMORIAL ST 61349
Ohio Community Consolidated ES
103-105 MEMORIAL ST 61349
James Scherrer, prin.

Okawville, Washington Co., Pop. Code 4
West Washington Co. CUSD 10
Sch. Sys. Enr. Code 3
Supt. – Dan Jansen, P O BOX 46 62271
ES, 300 W ILLINOIS 62271
Charles Dunning, prin.
Other Schools – See Venedy

Immanuel Lutheran School
RURAL ROUTE 01 BOX 59 62271

Olney, Richland Co., Pop. Code 6
East Richland CUSD 1
Sch. Sys. Enr. Code 4
Supt. – Dr. Jerry Ritchey
1100-1200 E LAUREL ST 62450
East Richland MS, 1099 N VAN ST 62450
Gary Kallenbach, prin.
Central MS, 200 W ELM ST 62450
Ralph Wendling, prin.
Cherry Street ES, EAST CHERRY ST 62450
Dolores McNabb, prin.
North Silver Street ES, NORTH SILVER ST 62450
Pamela Feutz, prin.
Other Schools – See Claremont

St. Joseph School, 520 E CHESTNUT ST 62450

Olympia Fields, Cook Co., Pop. Code 5
Matteson ESD 162
Supt. – See Matteson
Arcadia ES, 20519 ARCADIAN DR 60461
Lois Lewis, prin.

Onarga, Iroquois Co., Pop. Code 4
Iroquois West CUSD 10
Supt. – See Gilman
Iroquois West MS, 303 N EVERGREEN ST 60955
Mary Decker, prin.

Oneida, Knox Co., Pop. Code 3
ROWVA CUSD 208
Sch. Sys. Enr. Code 3
Supt. – Vincent Laird, P O BOX 69 61467
ROWVA JHS, P O BOX 69 61467
Jerry Daniels, prin.
ES, P O BOX 69 61467 – Jerry Daniels, prin.
Other Schools – See Altona, Rio, Victoria, Wataga

Opdyke, Jefferson Co.
Opdyke-Belle-Rive CCSD 5
Supt. – See Belle Rive
MS, RURAL ROUTE 01 62872
Fred Edwards, prin.

Oquawka, Henderson Co., Pop. Code 4
Union CUSD 115
Supt. – See Gladstone
ES, POST OFFICE 61469 – Donald Daily, prin.

Orangeville, Stephenson Co., Pop. Code 3
Orangeville CUSD 203
Sch. Sys. Enr. Code 3
Supt. – George Carrick, P O BOX 218 61060
JHS, 210 S ORANGE ST 61060
W. B. Kested, prin.
ES, 310 S EAST ST 61060 – George Carrick, prin.

Oreana, Macon Co., Pop. Code 3
Argenta-Oreana CUSD 01
Supt. – See Argenta
Argenta-Oreana MS, 400 W SOUTH ST 62554
Steven Mitchell, prin.
ES, 400 W SOUTH ST 62554
Steven Mitchell, prin.
White ES, RURAL ROUTE 01 62554
Nancy Conway, prin.

Oregon, Ogle Co., Pop. Code 5
Oregon CUSD 220
Sch. Sys. Enr. Code 4
Supt. – Dr. Richard Lovelace, P O BOX 219 61061
Etnyre MS, 1200 JEFFERSON ST 61061
Michael Ryder, prin.
Jefferson ES, 1100 JEFFERSON ST 61061
Dr. Richard Lovelace, prin.

Orion, Henry Co., Pop. Code 4
Orion CUSD 223
Sch. Sys. Enr. Code 4
Supt. – Donald Frakes, 900 12TH ST 61273
MS, 802 12TH ST 61273 – Richard Brooks, prin.
Hanna ES, 900 14TH AVE 61273
Wendell Torrance, prin.

Orland Park, Cook Co., Pop. Code 7
Kirby SD 140
Supt. – See Tinley Park
Fernway Park ES, 16600 88TH AVE 60462
Dennis Gurney, prin.

Orland Park SD 135
Sch. Sys. Enr. Code 5
Supt. – Dr. Thomas Pauley, 9401 151ST ST 60462
JHS, 14855 WEST AVE 60462 – Peter Yuska, prin.
High Point MS, 14825 WEST AVE 60462
Charles Palaces, prin.
Jerling MS, 8851 151ST ST 60462
Bonnie Wilson, prin.

Liberty MS, 8801 151ST ST 60462
Bonnie Wilson, prin.
Orland Center ES
151ST ST AND 94TH AVE 60462
Robert Blain, prin.
ES, 9960 143RD ST 60462 – Lynn Bush, prin.
Prairie ES, 14200 82ND AVE 60462
James Callahan, prin.

Tinley Park Community SD 146
Supt. – See Tinley Park
Kruse ES, 7617 HEMLOCK DR 60462
Jane Ellison, prin.

St. Michael School, 14355 HIGHLAND AVE 60462

Oswego, Kendall Co., Pop. Code 5
Oswego CUSD 308
Sch. Sys. Enr. Code 5
Supt. – Dr. Terry Tamblyn, ROUTE 71 60543
Thompson JHS
BOULDER HILL PASS ROAD 60543
Frederick La Chance, prin.
Traughber JHS, FRANKLIN ST 60543
Gerner Anderson, prin.
East View ES, RURAL ROUTE 71 60543
Edward Kral, prin.
Other Schools – See Montgomery

Ottawa, La Salle Co., Pop. Code 7
Deer Park CCSD 82
Sch. Sys. Enr. Code 2
Supt. – Raymond Chaon, RURAL ROUTE 04 61350
Deer Park ES, RURAL ROUTE 04 61350
Raymond Chaon, prin.

Ottawa ESD 141
Sch. Sys. Enr. Code 4
Supt. – Dr. Ronald Marino
400 CLINTON ST 61350
Shephard JHS, 701 E MCKINLEY ROAD 61350
Charles Ruff, prin.
Central ES, 400 CLINTON ST 61350
Margaret Reagan, prin.
Jefferson ES, 1709 COLUMBUS ST 61350
Patsy Mahoney, prin.
Lincoln ES, 1105 W MADISON ST 61350
Michael Lyons, prin.
McKinley ES, 1320 STATE ST 61350
M. Peed, prin.

Rutland CCSD 230
Sch. Sys. Enr. Code 1
Supt. – Lawrence Sebby, RURAL ROUTE 03 61350
Rutland ES, RURAL ROUTE 03 61350
Lawrence Sebby, prin.

Wallace CCSD 195
Sch. Sys. Enr. Code 2
Supt. – David Hermann, RURAL ROUTE 02 61350
Wallace ES, RURAL ROUTE 02 61350
David Hermann, prin.

Waltham CCSD 185
Supt. – See Utica
Waltham ES, 721 HIAWATHA DR 61350
Steven Jeanblanc, prin.

St. Columba School, 1110 LA SALLE ST 61350
St. Patrick School, 801 W JEFFERSON ST 61350

Palatine, Cook Co., Pop. Code 8
Lake Zurich CUSD 95
Supt. – See Lake Zurich
Quentin ES, 21250 W SHIRLEY RD 60074
Dean Hanebuth, prin.

Palatine CCSD 15
Sch. Sys. Enr. Code 6
Supt. – Dr. John Conyers
505 N QUENTIN ROAD 60067
Sundling JHS, 1100 N SMITH ST 60067
Donald Stipe, prin.
Winston Park JHS, 900 E PALATINE ROAD 60067
John Myers, prin.
Addams ES, 1020 SAYLES DR 60067
Edward Nelson, prin.
Churchill ES, 120 BABCOCK DR 60067
Charles Atkison, prin.
Hunting Ridge ES, 1105 W ILLINOIS AVE 60067
Forrest Neilson, prin.
Jordan ES, 100 N HARRISON ST 60067
Kay Woelfel, prin.
Lake Louise ES, 500 JONATHAN DR 60067
Gene Shull, prin.
Lincoln ES, 1021 RIDGEWOOD LN 60067
Victoria Kiviranta, prin.
Paddock ES, 225 W WASHINGTON ST 60067
David Corbett, prin.
Pleasant Hill ES, 434 W ILLINOIS AVE 60067
Joanne Rooney, prin.
Sanborn ES, 101 N OAK ST 60067
Patricia Cassidy, prin.
Virginia Lake ES, 925 N ROHLWING RD 60067
Lee Erickson, prin.
Other Schools – See Hoffman Estates, Rolling
Meadows

Immanuel Lutheran School
160 N PLUM GROVE RD 60067
St. Theresa School, 445 N BENTON ST 60067
St. Thomas of Villanova School
1141 ANDERSON DR 60067

Palestine, Crawford Co., Pop. Code 4
Palestine CUSD 3
Sch. Sys. Enr. Code 3
Supt. – Darrell Brown
    101 W GRAND PRAIRIE ST 62451
Palestine ES, 102 N MAIN ST 62451
    Jean Chrostoski, prin.

Robinson C. U. Dist. 2
Supt. – See Robinson
Washington ES, 201 S MAIN ST 62451
    Judith Ehorn, prin.

Palmyra, Macoupin Co., Pop. Code 3
Northwestern CUSD 2
Sch. Sys. Enr. Code 2
Supt. – E. Kent Tuttle
    RURAL ROUTE 01 BOX 8A 62674
Northwestern JHS
    RURAL ROUTE 01 BOX 08 62674
    Larry Redfern, prin.
Northwestern ES
    RURAL ROUTE 01 BOX 8A 62674
    E. Kent Tuttle, prin.

Palos Heights, Cook Co., Pop. Code 7
Palos CCSD 118
Supt. – See Palos Park
Palos East ES, 7700 W 127TH ST 60463
    Dr. George Timson, prin.

Palos Heights SD 128
Sch. Sys. Enr. Code 3
Supt. – Dr. Edward T. Rancic
    6610 W HIGHLAND DRIVE 60463
Independence JHS
    6610 W HIGHLAND DRIVE 60463
    James Willms, prin.
Chippewa ES, 12425 S AUSTIN AVE 60463
    Lee Stamberg, prin.
Navajo Heights ES
    12401 S OAK PARK AVE 60463
    Marilyn Finnegan, prin.

Incarnation School, 5705 W 127TH ST 60463
St. Alexander School, 126TH & 71ST AVE 60463

Palos Hills, Cook Co., Pop. Code 7
North Palos SD 117
Supt. – See Hickory Hills
Oak Ridge ES, W 103RD ST & 88TH AVE 60465
    Arlene Diericks, prin.
Opalinski PS, 7845 W 103RD ST 60465
    Albert Bialik, prin.
Quin MS, 7825 W 103RD ST 60465
    Albert Bialik, prin.

Palos Park, Cook Co., Pop. Code 5
Palos CCSD 118
Sch. Sys. Enr. Code 4
Supt. – Dr. James Riebock
    8800 W 119TH ST 60464
Palos South JHS, 131ST ST & 82ND AVE 60464
    Dennis Jones, prin.
Palos West ES, 12700 S 104TH AVE 60464
    Patricia Shores, prin.
Other Schools – See Palos Heights

Pana, Christian Co., Pop. Code 6
Pana CUSD 8
Sch. Sys. Enr. Code 4
Supt. – Barry Heaton, 14 E MAIN ST 62557
JHS, 407 S POPLAR ST 62557
    James Dunseth, prin.
Lincoln ES, 614 E 2ND ST 62557
    Richard Nicholas, prin.
Washington ES, 200 S SHERMAN ST 62557
    David Abell, prin.

Sacred Heart School, 3 E 4TH ST 62557

Paris, Edgar Co., Pop. Code 6
Paris CUSD 4
Sch. Sys. Enr. Code 3
Supt. – Verne Bear, P O BOX 160 61944
Crestwood JHS, P O BOX 160 61944
    Alan Zuber, prin.
Crestwood ES, RURAL ROUTE 03 BOX 160 61944
    Alan Zuber, prin.

Paris-Union SD 95
Sch. Sys. Enr. Code 4
Supt. – Larry Leonard, 414 S MAIN ST 61944
Mayo MS, 300 3 WOOD ST 61944
    Joseph Creedon, prin.
Memorial ES, E NEWTON ST 61944
    Dr. Mary Cerra, prin.
Redmon ES, S CENTRAL 61944
    Larry Eveland, prin.
Vance ES, 800 N MAIN ST 61944
    Dr. Mary Cerra, prin.
Wenz ES, W WASHINGTON 61944
    Larry Eveland, prin.

St. Mary's School, 507 CONNELLY ST 61944

Park Forest, Cook Co., Pop. Code 8
Crete-Monee CUSD 201U
Supt. – See Crete
Talala ES, 430 TALALA ST 60466
    W. Stewart Edmunds, prin.

Matteson ESD 162
Supt. – See Matteson
Indiana MS, 165 INDIANA ST 60466
    Rosemarie Carroll, prin.

Park Forest SD 163
Sch. Sys. Enr. Code 4
Supt. – Dr. Wayne Schurter
    242 S ORCHARD DRIVE 60466
Forest Trail JHS, 215 WILSON ST 60466
    A. William Ton, prin.
Algonquin ES, 170 ALGONQUIN ST 60466
    Jacqueline Davis, prin.
Blackhawk ES, 130 BLACKHAWK DR 60466
    William Stelter, prin.
Dogwood ES, 99 DOGWOOD ST 60466
    Marilyn Tannebaum, prin.
Mohawk ES, 301 MOHAWK ST 60466
    Robert Hulka, prin.
Other Schools – See Chicago Heights

St. Mary's ES, 227 MONEE RD 60466

Park Ridge, Cook Co., Pop. Code 8
Park Ridge CCSD 64
Sch. Sys. Enr. Code 5
Supt. – Dr. Raymond Hendee
    164 S PROSPECT AVE 60068
Lincoln JHS, 200 S LINCOLN AVE 60068
    Thomas Marvin, prin.
Carpenter ES, 300 N HAMLIN AVE 60068
    Dr. Phyllis Long, prin.
Field ES, 707 WISNER ST 60068
    Roger Steele, prin.
Franklin ES, 2401 MANOR LN 60068
    Donald Franke, prin.
Roosevelt ES, 1001 S FAIRVIEW AVE 60068
    Dr. Robert Hale, prin.
Washington ES, 1500 STEWART AVE 60068
    Lloyd Paulson, prin.

Mary Seat of Wisdom School
    1352 S CUMBERLAND AVE 60068
St. Andrew's Lutheran School
    260 N NORTHWEST HWY 60068
St. Paul of the Cross School
    140 S NORTHWEST HWY 60068

Patoka, Marion Co., Pop. Code 3
Patoka CUSD 100
Sch. Sys. Enr. Code 2
Supt. – Neil Jolliff, RURAL ROUTE 01 62875
JHS, RURAL ROUTE 01 62875
    Robert Towler, prin.
ES, RURAL ROUTE 01 62875
    Robert Towler, prin.

Patterson, Greene Co., Pop. Code 3
North Greene CUSD 3
Supt. – See White Hall
ES, P O BOX 398 62078 – Charles Stone, prin.

Pawnee, Sangamon Co., Pop. Code 5
Pawnee CUSD 11
Sch. Sys. Enr. Code 3
Supt. – P. David Schmink, 810 N 4TH ST 62558
ES, 810 FOURTH ST 62558 – John Stahly, prin.

Paw Paw, Lee Co., Pop. Code 3
Lee Center CUSD 271
Sch. Sys. Enr. Code 3
Supt. – Sherwood Dees, P O BOX 508 61353
ES, P O BOX 327 61353 – Gene Carlson, prin.
Other Schools – See Franklin Grove

Paxton, Ford Co., Pop. Code 5
Paxton CUSD 2
Sch. Sys. Enr. Code 3
Supt. – Charles Wood, 580 E FRANKLIN ST 60957
JHS, 341 E CENTER ST 60957
    William McBride, prin.
Peterson ES, 580 E FRANKLIN ST 60957
    James Flaherty, prin.

Payson, Adams Co., Pop. Code 4
Payson CUSD 1
Sch. Sys. Enr. Code 3
Supt. – James W. Cox, 406 W STATE 62360
Seymour ES, 406 W STATE 62360
    Karin Mccully, prin.

Pearl City, Stephenson Co., Pop. Code 3
Pearl City CUSD 200
Sch. Sys. Enr. Code 3
Supt. – John Pyfer, P O BOX 239 61062
JHS, P O BOX 239 61062 – Richard Harris, prin.
ES, P O BOX 239 61062 – Richard Harris, prin.

Pecatonica, Winnebago Co., Pop. Code 4
Pecatonica CUSD 321
Sch. Sys. Enr. Code 3
Supt. – David Zundahl, P O BOX 419 61063
ES, P O BOX 419 61063 – Robert Barr, prin.

Pekin, Tazewell Co., Pop. Code 8
N. Pekin & Marquette Hgts. SD 102
Sch. Sys. Enr. Code 3
Supt. – J. Maloney, 51 YATES ROAD 61554
Georgetown MS, 51 YATES ROAD 61554
    Robin Houchin, prin.
Marquette ES, 100 JOLIET RD 61554
    Robert Carrescia, prin.
Rogers ES, 109 ROGERS RD 61554
    Kevin Curtin, prin.

Pekin SD 108
Sch. Sys. Enr. Code 5
Supt. – Dr. Jerry Parker
    501 WASHINGTON ST 61554
Broadmoor JHS, 501 MAYWOOD AVE 61554
    John Kline, prin.

Edison JHS, 1400 EARL ST 61554
    Kenneth Ruth, prin.
Dirksen ES, 501 MAYWOOD AVE 61554
    Michael Muren, prin.
Jefferson ES, 900 S CAPITOL ST 61554
    Nicholas Vespa, prin.
Smith ES, 1314 MATILDA ST 61554
    Bradley Everett, prin.
Starke ES, 1800 HIGHWOOD AVE 61554
    Jeffery Erickson, prin.
Sunset Hills ES, 1800 HIGHWOOD AVE 61554
    Richard Lee, prin.
Washington ES, 501 WASHINGTON ST 61554
    Russell Trowbridge, prin.
Willow ES, 1110 VEERMAN ST 61554
    John Emery, prin.
Wilson ES, 900 KOCH ST 61554
    James Bernier, prin.

Rankin SD 98
Sch. Sys. Enr. Code 2
Supt. – John Closen
    RURAL ROUTE 02 BOX 216 61554
Rankin ES, P O BOX 216 61555
    John Closen, prin.

Good Shepherd Lutheran School
    333 STATE 61554
St. Joseph School, 300 S 6TH ST 61554

Penfield, Champaign Co.
Penfield CCSD 224
Sch. Sys. Enr. Code 1
Supt. – Albert Shepherd, P O BOX 96 61862
ES, 314 BUSEY ST 61862 – Albert Shepherd, prin.

Peoria, Peoria Co., Pop. Code 9
Bellevue Public SD 152
Sch. Sys. Enr. Code 2
Supt. – Gerald Glore, Jr., 200 S MAIN ST 61604
Bellevue Public ES, 200 N MAIN ST 61604
    Gerald Glore Jr., prin.

Dunlap CUSD 323
Supt. – See Dunlap
Wilder-Waite ES
    RURAL ROUTE 02 BOX 232 61615
    Frank Hutt, prin.

Hollis CCSD 328
Sch. Sys. Enr. Code 2
Supt. – Theodore Goldberg
    5613 W TUSCARORA ROAD 61607
Hollis Consolidated ES
    5613 W TUSCARORA RD 61607
    Theodore Goldberg, prin.

Illini Bluffs CUSD 327
Supt. – See Glasford
Wheeler ES
    7023 W SCHOOL HOUSE LANE 61607
    Bradford Janzen, prin.

Limestone Walters CCSD 316
Sch. Sys. Enr. Code 2
Supt. – Vernon Balda
    8223 W SMITHVILLE ROAD 61607
Limestone Walters ES
    8223 W SMITHVILLE RD 61607
    James Tripp, prin.

Norwood ESD 63
Sch. Sys. Enr. Code 2
Supt. – James Thomas
    6521 W FARMINGTON ROAD 61604
Norwood ES, 6521 W FARMINGTON RD 61604
    James Thomas, prin.

Peoria SD 150
Sch. Sys. Enr. Code 7
Supt. – John Strand
    3202 N WISCONSIN AVE 61603
Bills MS, 6001 N FROSTWOOD PKY 61615
    Jerry Daugherity, prin.
Columbia MS, 2612 N BOOTZ AVE 61604
    Robert Baldwin, prin.
Coolidge MS, 2708 W ROHMANN AVE 61604
    John Daniliuk, prin.
Greeley MS, 919 NE JEFFERSON AVE 61603
    Gary Tindall, prin.
Lindbergh MS, 6327 N SHERIDAN RD 61614
    James Troy, prin.
Longfellow MS, 1606 NE PERRY AVE 61603
    Ronald Hayes, prin.
Loucks MS, 2503 N UNIVERSITY ST 61604
    William Leverett, prin.
Rolling Acres MS, 5617 N MERRIMAC AVE 61614
    Adrian Hinton, prin.
Roosevelt MS, 1704 W AIKEN AVE 61605
    Paul Phillips, prin.
Sterling MS, 2315 N STERLING AVE 61604
    Neil Wicker, prin.
Trewyn MS, 1419 S FOLKERS AVE 61605
    Charles Siebel, prin.
Von Steuben MS
    801 E FORREST HILL AVE 61603
    William Ricca, prin.
Washington MS, 3706 N GRAND BLVD 61614
    John Garrett, prin.
White MS, 304 E ILLINOIS ST 61603
    Joseph Bauwens, prin.
Blaine-Sumner ES, 919 S MATTHEW ST 61605
    Robert Sorensen, prin.
Charter Oak ES, 5221 W TIMBEREDGE DR 61615
    John Slater, prin.

Franklin ES, 807 W COLUMBIA TER 61606
  Brewster Johnson, prin.
Garfield ES, 1507 S LYDIA AVE 61605
  John Hoehne, prin.
Glen Oak ES, 809 E FRYE AVE 61603
  Dr. Maxine Wortham, prin.
Harrison ES, 2702 W KRAUSE AVE 61605
  Kenneth Hinton, prin.
Hines ES, 4603 N KNOXVILLE AVE 61614
  James Gustafson, prin.
Irving ES, 519 NE GLENDALE AVE 61603
  Wilbert Ruck, prin.
Jefferson ES, 918 W FLORENCE AVE 61604
  Gustave Bohlman, prin.
Kellar ES, 6414 MOUNT HAWLEY ROAD 61614
  Rolland Abel, prin.
Kingman ES, 3129 NE MADISON AVE 61603
  Gene Clayton, prin.
Lincoln ES, 839 W MOSS AVE 61606
  Dickson Young, prin.
Northmoor ES, 1819 W NORTHMOOR RD 61614
  Sam Richardson, prin.
Tyng ES, 2212 W ANN ST 61605
  Willie Cox, prin.
Whittier ES, 1619 W FREDONIA AVE 61606
  Dr. Joan Brune, prin.
Wilson ES, 1907 W FORREST HILL AVE 61604
  Donald Phares, prin.

Pleasant Hill SD 69
Sch. Sys. Enr. Code 2
Supt. – William Reising
  3717 W MALONE ST 61605
Pleasant Hill ES, 3717 W MALONE ST 61605
  William Reising, prin.

Pleasant Valley SD 62
Sch. Sys. Enr. Code 3
Supt. – Terry Deppert
  4607 W ELWOOD RD 61604
Pleasant Valley MS, 4623 W RED BUD DR 61604
  John Link, prin.
Pleasant Valley North ES
  4607 W ELWOOD RD 61604 – Terry Deppert,
  prin.

Christ Lutheran School
  1311 S FARADAY AVE 61605
Concordia Lutheran School
  2000 W GLEN AVE 61614
Father Sweeney School
  401 NE MADISON AVE #2FL 61603
Holy Family School
  2329 W RESERVOIR BLVD 61615
South Side Catholic Community School
  1406 W ANTOINETTE ST 61605
St. Bernard School, 510 E KANSAS ST 61603
St. Mark School, 711 N UNDERHILL ST 61606
St. Philomena School, 3216 N EMERY AVE 61604
St. Thomas School, 607 MONROE AVE 61614
St. Vincent De Paul School
  6001 N UNIVERSITY ST 61614

Peoria Heights, Peoria Co., Pop. Code 6
Peoria Hts. CUSD 325
Sch. Sys. Enr. Code 3
Supt. – Roger Bergia, 1316 E KELLY AVE 61614
Kelly Avenue ES, 1316 E KELLY AVE 61614
  Richard Frost, prin.
Monroe Avenue ES, 3725 N MONROE AVE 61614
  Gene Beltz, prin.

Peotone, Will Co., Pop. Code 5
Peotone CUSD 207U
Sch. Sys. Enr. Code 4
Supt. – Dr. Allen Hall
  WEST & WILSON STS 60468
JHS, WEST & WILSON STS 60468
  Richard Benson, prin.
ES, P O BOX 399 60468 – Hal Paddock, prin.
Other Schools – See Frankfort, Manhattan

Perry, Pike Co., Pop. Code 2
Perry SD 57
Sch. Sys. Enr. Code 2
Supt. – Robert Adams, P O BOX 98 62362
ES, P O BOX 98 62362 – James Mccain, prin.

Peru, La Salle Co., Pop. Code 7
Peru ESD 124
Sch. Sys. Enr. Code 3
Supt. – Dr. Harry Dunn, P O BOX 404 61354
Peru Washington JHS, 10TH & ROCK 61354
  James Dellinger, prin.
Northview ES, 1429 SHOOTING PARK RD 61354
  Joan Orcutt, prin.
Roosevelt ES, 2233 6TH ST 61354
  John Ranger, prin.

Peru Catholic School, 900 SCHUYLER ST 61354

Pesotum, Champaign Co., Pop. Code 3
Tolono CUSD 7
Supt. – See Tolono
ES, 101 S HICKORY ST #238 61863
  Joyce Broughton, prin.

Petersburg, Menard Co., Pop. Code 4
Porta CUSD 202
Sch. Sys. Enr. Code 4
Supt. – Dean Broughton, P O BOX 117 62675
Porta JHS, P O BOX 117 62675
  David Turner, prin.
ES, 514 W MONROE ST 62675 – John Peters, prin.
Porta MS, 7TH AND JACKSON ST 62675
  James Conklin, prin.

Other Schools – See Oakford, Tallula

Philo, Champaign Co., Pop. Code 3
Tolono CUSD 7
Supt. – See Tolono
ES 61864 – Dennis Overmyer, prin.

Phoenix, Cook Co., Pop. Code 5
South Holland SD 151
Supt. – See South Holland
Coolidge JHS, 15500 SEVENTH AVE 60426
  Jessica Buckner, prin.

Piasa, Macoupin Co.
Piasa CUSD 9
Sch. Sys. Enr. Code 4
Supt. – Donald Stuckey 62079
Southwestern JHS 62079 – Charles Keene, prin.
Other Schools – See Brighton, Medora, Shipman

Pinckneyville, Perry Co., Pop. Code 5
CCSD 204
Sch. Sys. Enr. Code 2
Supt. – Dan Hoeinghaus
  RURAL ROUTE 04 BOX 137 62274
Community Cons. ES
  RURAL ROUTE 04 BOX 137 62274
  (—), prin.

Pinckneyville SD 50
Sch. Sys. Enr. Code 3
Supt. – Dr. George Edwards
  301 W MULBERRY ST 62274
JHS, RURAL ROUTE 02 62274
  Lewis Schweizer, prin.
ES, 301 W MULBERRY ST 62274
  Dr. George Edwards, prin.

St. Bruno School, 210 N GORDON 62274

Piper City, Ford Co., Pop. Code 3
Ford Central CUSD 8
Supt. – See Thawville
Ford Central JHS, 519 S MARGARET ST 60959
  James Zambon, prin.

Pittsburg, Williamson Co., Pop. Code 3
Johnston City CUSD 1
Supt. – See Johnston City
Lincoln ES, RURAL ROUTE 01 62974
  James Lindsay, prin.

Pittsfield, Pike Co., Pop. Code 5
Pikeland CUSD 10
Sch. Sys. Enr. Code 4
Supt. – Richard Basden, P O BOX 515 62363
Pittsfield-Higbee MS, 380 W ADAMS ST 62363
  Lee Hoffman, prin.
Pittsfield East ES, N ILLINOIS 62363
  Rodger Hannel, prin.
Pittsfield South ES
  RURAL ROUTE 02 BOX 50 62363
  Rodger Hannel, prin.

Plainfield, Will Co., Pop. Code 5
Indian Prairie CUSD 204
Supt. – See Naperville
Wheatland ES, 24024 W 103RD ST 60544
  Janet Stevenson, prin.

Plainfield SD 202
Sch. Sys. Enr. Code 5
Supt. – Dr. Roland M. Smith
  601 W PLAZA DRIVE 60544
Indian Trail JHS, 1005 N EASTERN AVE 60544
  Jo Jean Morris, prin.
Central ES, 305 W LOCKPORT RD 60544
  Richard Schleeter, prin.
Other Schools – See Joliet

St. Mary School, 140 S FREDERICK AVE 60544

Plano, Kendall Co., Pop. Code 5
Plano CUSD 88
Sch. Sys. Enr. Code 4
Supt. – Dr. Donald Larson, 804 S HALE ST 60545
JHS, W ABE ST 60545 – Keith Peterson, prin.
Centennial ES, 800 S WEST ST 60545
  James Jensen, prin.
Miller ES, 904 N LEW ST 60545
  James Jensen, prin.

St. Mary School, 817 N CENTER AVE 60545

Plato Center, Kane Co.
Central CUSD 301
Supt. – See Burlington
ES, P O BOX 87 60170 – James Warner, prin.

Pleasant Hill, Pike Co., Pop. Code 4
Pleasant Hill CUSD 3
Sch. Sys. Enr. Code 2
Supt. – Gordon Sansom, P O BOX 207 62366
ES, P O BOX 207 62366 – Donald Peebles, prin.

Pleasant Plains, Sangamon Co., Pop. Code 3
Pleasant Plains CUSD 8
Sch. Sys. Enr. Code 3
Supt. – Alan Fox, P O BOX 247 62677
JHS, P O BOX 247 62677 – Alan Fox, prin.
Farmingdale ES, RURAL ROUTE 02 62677
  Dennis Beetzel, prin.
MS, P O BOX 158 62677 – Dennis Beetzel, prin.

Plymouth, Hancock Co., Pop. Code 3
Plymouth CCSD 319
Sch. Sys. Enr. Code 2
Supt. – Thomas Ulmer 62367

ES, P O BOX 249 62367 – Thomas Ulmer, prin.

Pocahontas, Bond Co., Pop. Code 3
Bond County CUSD 2
Supt. – See Greenville
ES 62275 – Charles Baum, prin.

Polo, Ogle Co., Pop. Code 5
Polo CUSD 222
Sch. Sys. Enr. Code 3
Supt. – Donald Hay, P O BOX 157 61064
Polo Aplington MS, 610 E MASON ST 61064
  Gerald Allison, prin.
Centennial ES, 308 S PLEASANT AVE #325 61064
  Arnold Diehl, prin.

Pontiac, Livingston Co., Pop. Code 7
Owego CCSD 434
Sch. Sys. Enr. Code 1
Supt. – Wanda Coyne, RURAL ROUTE 02 61764
Owego ES, RURAL ROUTE 02 61764
  Wanda Coyne, prin.

Pontiac CCSD 429
Sch. Sys. Enr. Code 4
Supt. – Dr. Wayne Krula
  117 W LIVINGSTON ST 61764
JHS, 600 N MORROW ST 61764
  Joseph McNary, prin.
Central ES, 117 W LIVINGTON ST 61764
  Jane Manning, prin.
Lincoln ES, 514 S MAIN ST 61764
  Don Linquist, prin.
Washington ES, MORROW AND HOWARD 61764
  Lyle Stine, prin.

Pontiac-Esmen CCSD 430
Sch. Sys. Enr. Code 1
Supt. – B. Smith, RURAL ROUTE 03 61764
Pontiac-Esmen ES, RURAL ROUTE 03 61764
  B. Smith, prin.

St. Mary's School, 414 N MAIN ST 61764

Poplar Grove, Boone Co., Pop. Code 3
North Boone CUSD 200
Sch. Sys. Enr. Code 3
Supt. – Gerald Buckler, P O BOX 10 61065
Manchester ES, 3501 BLAINE RD 61065
  Karen Severn, prin.
ES, 208 N STATE ST 61065 – (—), prin.
Other Schools – See Capron

Port Byron, Rock Island Co., Pop. Code 4
Riverdale CUSD 100
Sch. Sys. Enr. Code 4
Supt. – Dr. Dennis Rucker
  9624 256TH ST N 61275
Riverdale JHS, 9822 256TH ST N 61275
  Richard Robertson, prin.
Riverdale ES, 9424 256TH ST N 61275
  Gary Orr, prin.

Posen, Cook Co., Pop. Code 5
Posen-Robbins ESD 143-5
Sch. Sys. Enr. Code 4
Supt. – Dr. Richard Sinclair
  14545 CALIFORNIA AVE 60469
Gordon JHS, 14100 HARRISON AVE 60469
  Ronald Rutzky, prin.
ES, 14545 CALIFORNIA AVE 60469
  Charles Thompson, prin.
Ziebell ES, 149TH & ROCKWELL 60469
  George Walker, prin.
Other Schools – See Robbins

St. Stanislaus B & M School
  14418 MCKINLEY AVE 60469

Potomac, Vermilion Co., Pop. Code 3
Potomac CUSD 10
Sch. Sys. Enr. Code 2
Supt. – Ken Piggush
  RURAL ROUTE 01 BOX 335 61865
Potomac JHS, RURAL ROUTE 01 BOX 335 61865
  Neal Hoover, prin.
ES, RURAL ROUTE 01 BOX 335 61865
  Ken Piggush, prin.

Prairie Du Rchr, Randolph Co., Pop. Code 3
Prairie Du Rocher CCSD 134
Sch. Sys. Enr. Code 2
Supt. – Warren Buescher
  MIDDLE & CHARTRAND 62277
ES, MIDDLE & CHARTRAND 62277
  Dr. Wayne Reinking, prin.

Prairie View, Lake Co.
Aptakisic-Tripp CCSD 102
Sch. Sys. Enr. Code 4
Supt. – Dr. Glenn McGee
  21439 N WEILAND ROAD 60069
Tripp ES, 21439 N WEILAND RD 60069
  Robert Basofin, prin.
Other Schools – See Arlington Heights, Buffalo Grove

Hawthorn CCSD 73
Supt. – See Vernon Hills
Half Day MS, 239 OLD HALF DAY RD 60069
  Gary Zabilka, prin.

Princeton, Bureau Co., Pop. Code 6
Princeton ESD 115
Sch. Sys. Enr. Code 4
Supt. – Charles Zbrozek
  725 W PUTNAM ST 61356
Logan JHS, 302 W CENTRAL AVE 61356
  Judson Lusher, prin.

Douglas ES, 220 E LASALLE ST 61356
  Jean Stockham, prin.
Jefferson ES, P O BOX 280 61356
  Gary Patterson, prin.
Lincoln ES, 501 S EUCLID AVE 61356
  Eleanor Walker, prin.
Washington MS, 25 S MERCER ST 61356
  Jude Ney, prin.

St. Louis ES, 631 W PARK AVE 61356

Princeville, Peoria Co., Pop. Code 4
Princeville CUSD 326
Sch. Sys. Enr. Code 3
Supt. – W. G. Banks, 302 CORDIS AVE 61559
MS, 602 N TOWN AVE 61559
  Robert Dawson, prin.

Prophetstown, Whiteside Co., Pop. Code 4
Prophetstown-Lyndon CUSD 3
Sch. Sys. Enr. Code 3
Supt. – Leroy Hooks, 318 LINCOLN ST 61277
ES, 301 W 3RD ST 61277 – Steve Stefani, prin.
Other Schools – See Lyndon

Prospect Heights, Cook Co., Pop. Code 7
Prospect Heights SD 23
Sch. Sys. Enr. Code 4
Supt. – David Robert
  700 N SCHOENBECK ROAD 60070
Macarthur JHS
  700 N SCHOENBECK ROAD 60070
  Philip Arenstein, prin.
Eisenhower ES
  SCHOENBECK & MCDONALD 60070
  Robert Marshall, prin.
Ross ES, 700 N SCHOENBECK RD 60070
  Judie Lehman, prin.
Sullivan MS, 700 N SCHOENBECK RD 60070
  Donald Graham, prin.

St. Alphonsus Ligouri School
  411 N WHEELING RD 60070

Putnam, Putnam Co.
Senachwine CCSD 534
Sch. Sys. Enr. Code 1
Supt. – Eugene Pourchot
  RURAL ROUTE 01 BOX 1 61560
Senachwine ES, RURAL ROUTE 01 BOX 1 61560
  A. Eugene Pourchot, prin.

Quincy, Adams Co., Pop. Code 8
Quincy SD 172
Sch. Sys. Enr. Code 6
Supt. – Myrl Shireman, 1444 MAINE ST 62301
Adams ES, 2001 JEFFERSON ST 62301
  Paul Koscielski, prin.
Baldwin IS, 30TH & MAINE STS 62301
  Charles Akright, prin.
Dewey ES, 22ND & CHERRY STS 62301
  Patricia Rokusek, prin.
Ellington ES, 30TH AND LINDELL STS 62301
  William Fessler, prin.
Irving ES, 811 PAYSON AVE 62301
  Lynn Sprick, prin.
Monroe ES, 3211 PAYSON RD 62301
  Robert Moore, prin.
Washington ES, 8TH AND SYCAMORE 62301
  Rick Baldwin, prin.

St. Anthony School
  RURAL ROUTE 05 BOX 343 62301
St. Dominic School, 4100 COLUMBUS RD 62301
St. Francis Solanus School
  1720 COLLEGE AVE 62301
St. James Lutheran School
  1617 MADISON ST 62301
St. John the Baptist School
  1236 N 10TH ST 62301
St. Mary School, 1115 S 7TH ST 62301
St. Peter School, 2500 MAINE ST 62301

Ramsey, Fayette Co., Pop. Code 4
Ramsey CUSD 204
Sch. Sys. Enr. Code 3
Supt. – Richard Nelson, P O BOX 188 62080
ES, 610 W 6TH ST BOX 188 62080
  Lindell Martie, prin.

Rankin, Vermilion Co., Pop. Code 3
Rankin SD 8
Sch. Sys. Enr. Code 1
Supt. – Albert Liehr, 102 W 2ND ST 60960
ES, 102 W SECOND ST 60960
  Douglas Taylor, prin.

Ransom, La Salle Co., Pop. Code 2
Allen Twp. CCSD 65
Sch. Sys. Enr. Code 2
Supt. – Harold McKenzie, P O BOX 15 60470
Allen Twp. Community Consolidated ES
  P O BOX 15 60470 – Harold McKenzie, prin.

Rantoul, Champaign Co., Pop. Code 7
Rantoul CSD 137
Sch. Sys. Enr. Code 4
Supt. – David D. Glisson
  400 WABASH AVE 61866
Eater JHS, 400 E WABASH AVE 61866
  George Piland, prin.
Broadmeadow ES, SUNVIEW DRIVE 61866
  Stephen Murphy, prin.
Eastlawn ES, N MAPLEWOOD DRIVE 61866
  Terry Sheppard, prin.

Maplewood ES, EATER DRIVE 61866
  Lindell Hunt, prin.
Northview ES, N SHELDON ST 61866
  Larry Powell, prin.
Pleasant Acres ES, SHORT ST & HARPER 61866
  Nancy Clark, prin.

St. Malachy School, 348 E GROVE AVE 61866

Raymond, Montgomery Co., Pop. Code 3
Panhandle CUSD 2
Sch. Sys. Enr. Code 3
Supt. – Edward Allen, 317 E BROAD ST 62560
ES, P O BOX 80 62560 – Donald Bergdolt, prin.
Other Schools – See Farmersville

Red Bud, Randolph Co., Pop. Code 5
Red Bud CUSD 132
Sch. Sys. Enr. Code 4
Supt. – Eugene Holmes, 815 LOCUST ST 62278
ES, 200 FIELD DR 62278 – Ronald Hood, prin.

St. John Baptist School, 519 HAZEL ST 62278
St. John Lutheran School
  104 E SOUTH 6TH ST 62278

Reddick, Kankakee Co., Pop. Code 2
Herscher CUSD 2
Supt. – See Herscher
ES, MAIN ST 60961 – Dennis Pankey, prin.

Reynolds, Rock Island Co., Pop. Code 3
Rockridge CUSD 300
Supt. – See Taylor Ridge
MS, P O BOX 6 61279 – Stanley Kaiser, prin.

Richmond, McHenry Co., Pop. Code 4
Richmond CCSD 13
Sch. Sys. Enr. Code 2
Supt. – (—), P O BOX 505 60071
Richmond Consolidated ES
  5815 BROADWAY ST 60071 – (—), prin.

Richton Park, Cook Co., Pop. Code 6
ESD 159
Supt. – See Matteson
Armstrong ES, 5030 IMPERIAL DR 60471
  James Christ, prin.

Matteson ESD 162
Supt. – See Matteson
Sauk MS, 4435 S CHURCHILL DR 60471
  Larry Kindle, prin.

Ridge Farm, Vermilion Co., Pop. Code 4
Georgetown-Ridge Farm CUSD 4
Supt. – See Georgetown
ES, 12 N STATE ST 61870 – Kevin Tate, prin.

Ridgway, Gallatin Co., Pop. Code 4
Gallatin CUSD 7
Supt. – See Shawneetown
ES, VALTER ST 62979 – Ronald Culbreth, prin.
Shawneetown ES
  P O BOX J 130 E LOGAN ST 62979
  Andrew Hopsons, prin.

Rio, Knox Co., Pop. Code 2
ROWVA CUSD 208
Supt. – See Oneida
ES, POST OFFICE 61472 – Karen Larson, prin.

Riverdale, Cook Co., Pop. Code 7
Dolton SD 148
Supt. – See Dolton
Jefferson ES, 560 W 144TH ST 60627
  Ellen Tyrrell, prin.
Washington ES, 139TH & SCHOOL ST 60627
  Ellen Tyrrell, prin.

George Patton SD 133
Sch. Sys. Enr. Code 2
Supt. – William Small
  13700 S STEWART AVE 60627
Patton ES, 137 ST & STEWART AVE 60627
  Pamela Dukes, prin.

River Forest, Cook Co., Pop. Code 7
River Forest SD 90
Sch. Sys. Enr. Code 3
Supt. – Dr. Wayne Buchholz
  7776 LAKE ST 60305
Roosevelt JHS, 7560 OAK AVE 60305
  Daryl Unnasch, prin.
Lincoln ES, 511 PARK AVE 60305
  Betty Pruitt, prin.
Willard ES, 1250 ASHLAND AVE 60305
  Judy Lipshutz, prin.

Grace Lutheran School, 7300 DIVISION ST 60305
St. Luke School, 519 ASHLAND AVE 60305
St. Vincent Ferrer School
  1515 LATHROP AVE 60305

River Grove, Cook Co., Pop. Code 7
Rhodes SD 84-5
Sch. Sys. Enr. Code 2
Supt. – Dr. Edward McNally
  8931 W FULLERTON AVE 60171
Rhodes ES, 8931 W FULLERTON AVE 60171
  Steven Sievers, prin.

River Grove SD 85-5
Sch. Sys. Enr. Code 3
Supt. – Robert Vogt
  2650 N THATCHER AVE 60171
River Grove ES, 2650 N THATCHER AVE 60171
  John Jackson, prin.

Bethlehem Lutheran School
  2636 OAK STREET 60171
St. Cyprian School, 2561 N CLINTON ST 60171

Riverside, Cook Co., Pop. Code 6
Riverside SD 96
Sch. Sys. Enr. Code 3
Supt. – Robert Varga, 63 WOODSIDE ROAD 60546
Hauser JHS, 65 WOODSIDE ROAD 60546
  Johan Hille, prin.
Ames ES, 86 SOUTHCOTE RD 60546
  Bernardine Chimis, prin.
Blythe Park ES, 735 LEESLEY RD 60546
  Raymond Bronsteader, prin.
Central ES, 61 WOODSIDE RD 60546
  Raymond Bronsteader, prin.
Other Schools – See Brookfield

Mater Christi School, 2400 S 10TH AVE 60546
St. Mary School, 97 HERRICK RD 60546

Riverton, Sangamon Co., Pop. Code 5
Riverton CUSD 14
Sch. Sys. Enr. Code 4
Supt. – Don Parker, 1014 E LINCOLN ST 62561
MS, P O BOX 647 62561 – Charles Davis, prin.
ES, 7TH & JEFFERSON 62561
  James Roesch, prin.

Roanoke, Woodford Co., Pop. Code 4
Roanoke-Benson CUSD 60
Sch. Sys. Enr. Code 3
Supt. – John Crumrine, 208 W HIGH ST 61561
Sowers ES, 202 W HIGH ST 61561
  Sigrid Kurtyak, prin.
Other Schools – See Benson

Robbins, Cook Co., Pop. Code 6
Posen-Robbins ESD 143-5
Supt. – See Posen
Kellar JHS, 14125 S LYDIA AVE 60472
  Otto Bradford, prin.
Childs ES, 14123 S LYDIA AVE 60472
  Meralyn Johnson, prin.
Turner ES, 135TH & HAMLIN 60472
  Sarah Thompson, prin.

Robinson, Crawford Co., Pop. Code 1
Robinson C. U. Dist. 2
Sch. Sys. Enr. Code 4
Supt. – Howard Jackson, P O BOX 254 62454
Nuttall MS, 400 W RUSTIC ST 62454
  Ronald Biery, prin.
Lincoln MS, E POPLAR ST 62454
  Robert Brutcher, prin.
Other Schools – See Palestine

Rochelle, Ogle Co., Pop. Code 6
Rochelle CCSD 231
Sch. Sys. Enr. Code 4
Supt. – Dr. Joe Thiele, 444 N 8TH STREET 61068
JHS, 111 E SCHOOL ST 61068 – Kevin Zilm, prin.
Central ES, 444 N 8TH ST 61068
  Neil Swanson, prin.
Lincoln ES, 108 S MAIN ST 61068
  Kent Sabin, prin.
May ES, 1033 N 2ND STREET 61068
  Terry Ator, prin.
Tilton ES, 1050 N 9TH STREET 61068
  Arlyn Van Dyke, prin.

St. Paul Lutheran School, 1415 10TH AVE 61068

Rochester, Sangamon Co., Pop. Code 4
Rochester CUSD 3A
Sch. Sys. Enr. Code 4
Supt. – Jack Taylor, ROUTE 29 W 62563
JHS, ROUTE 29 W 62563
  Timothy Katzmark, prin.
ES, ROUTE 29 WEST 62563 – John Rigg, prin.
MS, ROUTE 29 WEST 62563 – John Rigg, prin.

Rock Falls, Whiteside Co., Pop. Code 7
East Coloma SD 12
Sch. Sys. Enr. Code 2
Supt. – Peter Ternetti, 1900 DIXON ROAD 61071
East Coloma ES, 1900 DIXON RD 61071
  Peter Ternetti, prin.

Montmorency CCSD 145
Sch. Sys. Enr. Code 2
Supt. – Leroy Hooks, 9415 HOOVER ROAD 61071
Montmorency ES, 9415 HOOVER ROAD 61071
  Richard Gartner, prin.

Riverdale SD 14
Sch. Sys. Enr. Code 2
Supt. – Walter Buchele
  3505 PROPHET ROAD 61071
Riverdale ES, 3505 PROPHET RD 61071
  Walter Buchele, prin.

Rock Falls SD 13
Sch. Sys. Enr. Code 4
Supt. – Jack Etnyre, 602 4TH AVE 61071
JHS, 1701 12TH AVE 61071 – Jeffrey Brown, prin.
Dillon ES, 1901 8TH AVE 61071
  Thomas Burrows, prin.
Merrill ES, 600 4TH AVE 61071
  Donald Stevens, prin.
Thome ES, 500 E 5TH ST 61071
  Jeffrey Hardy, prin.

St. Andrew's School, 701 11TH AVE 61071

Rockford, Winnebago Co., Pop. Code 9
Harlem Unit SD 122
Sch. Sys. Enr. Code 6
Supt. – Dr. Irving Miller, 8605 N 2ND ST 61111
Franklin JHS, 8615 N 2ND ST 61111
  John Hurley, prin.
Maple ES, 1405 MAPLE AVE 61111
  Daniel Newcomb, prin.
Marquette ES, 8500 VICTORY LN 61111
  Thomas Laughlin, prin.
Olson Park ES, 1414 MINAHAN DR 61111
  William Lewis, prin.
Ralston ES, 710 RALSTON RD 61111
  Vernon Awes, prin.
Rock Cut ES, 7944 FOREST HILLS RD 61111
  Jim Stephens, prin.
Other Schools – See Loves Park

Rockford SD 205
Sch. Sys. Enr. Code 8
Supt. – Millard Grell, 201 S MADISON ST 61108
Eisenhower MS
  3525 SPRING CREEK ROAD 61107
  Nate Martin, prin.
Flinn MS, 2525 OHIO PARKWAY 61108
  John Paulsgrove, prin.
Kennedy MS, 4664 N ROCKTON AVE 61103
  Donald Stocker, prin.
Lincoln MS, 1500 CHARLES ST 61108
  Michael Burkhard, prin.
Wilson MS, 520 N PIERPONT AVE 61103
  Jeannette Franklin, prin.
Barbour ES, 1116 MONTAGUE ST 61102
  James Anderson, prin.
Beyer ES, 333 15TH AVE 61104
  Jacqueline Mannery, prin.
Bloom ES, 2912 BRENDENWOOD RD 61107
  Cheryl Foltz, prin.
Brookview ES, 1750 MADRON RD 61107
  Karen Keller, prin.
Carlson ES, 4015 RIVER LN 61111
  Lynne Connelly, prin.
Church ES, 1411 BLAISDELL ST 61103
  Michael Pinter, prin.
Conklin ES, 3003 HALSTED RD 61103
  Donald Swanson, prin.
Dennis ES, 730 LINCOLN PARK BLVD 61102
  Vicki Jacobson, prin.
Ellis ES, 1520 ELM ST 61102
  Roberta Stiles, prin.
Froborg ES, 1555 20TH ST 61109
  Norma Sullivan, prin.
Garrison ES, 1105 N COURT ST 61103
  Linda Burkhard, prin.
Gregory ES, 4820 CAROL CT 61108
  Dennis Harezlak, prin.
Haight ES, 4704 N ROCKTON AVE 61103
  Nancy Porter, prin.
Hallstrom ES, 1300 17TH ST 61104
  Elmer Olson, prin.
Haskell ES, 515 MAPLE ST 61103
  Michael Griffith, prin.
Jackson ES, 315 SUMMIT ST 61107
  Curtis Slabaugh, prin.
Johnson ES, 3805 RURAL ST 61107
  Catherine Hall, prin.
Kiswaukee ES, 526 CATLIN ST 61104
  Thomas Mccullough, prin.
Lathrop ES, 2603 CLOVER AVE 61102
  Constance Tucker, prin.
King ES, 1306 S COURT ST 61102
  Paul Wixom, prin.
Mcintosh ES, 525 N PIERPONT AVE 61103
  Florence Cox, prin.
Nashold ES, 3303 20TH ST 61109
  Charlotte Akelaitis, prin.
Nelson ES, 623 15TH ST 61104
  Robert Jesse, prin.
New Milford ES
  2128 NEW MILFORD SCHOOL RD 61109
  Dan Carter, prin.
Riverdahl ES, 3520 KISHWAUKEE ST 61109
  Ed Ruef, prin.
Rock River ES, 2729 KISHWAUKEE ST 61109
  Dennis Johnson, prin.
Rolling Green ES, 3615 LOUISIANA RD 61108
  Fred Rogers, prin.
Spring Creek ES, 5222 SPRING CREEK RD 61111
  David Hawkinson, prin.
Stiles ES, 315 LA CLEDE AVE 61102
  Vicki Jacobson, prin.
Summerdale ES, 3320 GLENWOOD AVE 61103
  Sharon Clase, prin.
Swan Hillman ES
  3701 GREENDALE DRIVE 61109
  George Gibson, prin.
Thompson ES, 4949 MARION AVE 61108
  Michael Tronc, prin.
Vandercook ES, 5921 DARLENE DR 61109
  Jean Harezlak, prin.
Walker ES, 1520 POST AVE 61103
  Marjorie Price, prin.
Welsh ES, 2100 HUFFMAN BLVD 61103
  Randall Larson, prin.
West View Elementary School
  1720 HALSTED RD 61103 – Linda Burkhard, prin.
White Swan ES, 7550 MILL RD 61108
  John Johnson, prin.
Whitehead ES, 2325 OHIO PKY 61108
  Jean Harezlak, prin.
Other Schools – See Cherry Valley

Keith Country Day School
  1 JACOBY PLACE 61107

Concordia Lutheran School, 7424 N 2ND ST 61111
Holy Family School, 4407 HIGHCREST RD 61107
St. Bernadette School, 2300 BELL AVE 61103
St. Bridget School, 604 CLIFFORD AVE 61111
St. Edward School, 3020 11TH ST 61109
St. James School, 409 N 1ST ST 61107
St. Patrick School, 2605 SCHOOL ST 61103
St. Paul Lutheran School, 811 LOCUST ST 61103
St. Peters ES, 1321 N COURT ST 61103
St. Rita School, 6284 VALLEY KNOLL DR 61109

Rock Island, Rock Island Co., Pop. Code 8
Rock Island SD 41
Sch. Sys. Enr. Code 6
Supt. – Dr. Robert Willis, 541 21ST ST 61201
Edison JHS, 4141 9TH ST 61201
  Charles Dyson, prin.
Washington JHS, 3300 18TH AVE 61201
  Peter Nyman, prin.
Audubon ES, 2605 18TH AVE 61201
  James Davis, prin.
Denkmann ES, 2120 42ND AVE 61201
  Herbert Niemann, prin.
Field ES, 31ST AVE & 29TH ST 61201
  Kenneth Meyer, prin.
Grant ES, 621 12TH ST 61201
  Robert Hawthorne Ii, prin.
Hanson ES, 4000 9TH ST 61201
  Kenneth Meyer, prin.
Hawthorne-Irving ES, 1202 9TH AVE 61201
  Mary Meier, prin.
Lincoln ES, 2101 7TH AVE 61201
  Richard Loy, prin.
Longfellow ES, 4102 7TH AVE 61201
  Patricia Walkup, prin.
Ridgewood ES, 9607 14TH ST W 61201
  Jon Sedgwick, prin.
Willard ES, 2503 9TH ST 61201
  Judy Miller, prin.
Other Schools – See Milan

Immanuel Lutheran School, 3300 24TH ST 61201
Jordan Catholic School #1, 2825 5 1/2 AVE 61201
Jordan Catholic School #2
  2901 24TH ST #2 61201

Rockton, Winnebago Co., Pop. Code 4
Rockton SD 140
Sch. Sys. Enr. Code 3
Supt. – David Martin, 400 E CHAPEL ST 61072
Mack MS, 1050 E UNION ST 61072
  David Martin, prin.
ES, 400 E CHAPEL ST 61072 – Wes Morgan, prin.

Rolling Meadows, Cook Co., Pop. Code 7
Palatine CCSD 15
Supt. – See Palatine
Plum Grove JHS
  2600 PLUM GROVE ROAD 60008
  Richard Schmidt, prin.
Sandburg JHS, 2600 MARTIN LANE 60008
  E. Daniel Vucovich, prin.
Central Road ES, 3800 W CENTRAL RD 60008
  James Hess, prin.
Kimball Hill ES, 2905 MEADOW DR 60008
  Corbitte Henry, prin.
Willow Bend ES, 4700 BARKER AVE 60008
  Michael Zawacke, prin.

St. Colette School, 3900 PHEASANT DR 60008

Rome, Peoria Co.
Illinois Valley Central Unit SD 321
Supt. – See Chillicothe
ES, P O BOX 98 61562 – Gene Buckingham, prin.

Romeoville, Will Co., Pop. Code 7
Valley View CUSD 365U
Sch. Sys. Enr. Code 7
Supt. – Dr. Harry Hayes
  636 DALHART AVE 60441
West View MS, 530 BELMONT DRIVE 60441
  Earl Friend, prin.
Hill ES, 616 DALHART AVE 60441
  William Jenkins, prin.
King ES, 301 EATON AVE 60441
  James Crowl, prin.
Other Schools – See Bolingbrook

Roodhouse, Greene Co., Pop. Code 4
North Greene CUSD 3
Supt. – See White Hall
North Greene ES, NORTH ST 62082
  Robert Pinkerton, prin.

Roscoe, Winnebago Co., Pop. Code 4
Kinnikinnick CCSD
Sch. Sys. Enr. Code 2
Supt. – Robert Lauber, 5410 PINE LANE 61073
Kinnikinnick Comm. Cons. MS
  5410 PINE LN 61073 – Rod Sargeant, prin.
Ledgewood ES, 11685 SOUTHGATE ROAD 61073
  James Mcgarry, prin.

Roselle, Du Page Co., Pop. Code 7
Keeneyville SD 20
Sch. Sys. Enr. Code 4
Supt. – Dr. James Erickson
  6 N 632 GARY AVE 60172
Keeneyville ES, 6 N 632 GARY AVE 60172
  Michael Lyon, prin.
Waterbury MS, 355 RODENBURG RD 60172
  Michael Lyon, prin.
Other Schools – See Hanover Park

Medinah SD 11
Sch. Sys. Enr. Code 3
Supt. – L. Mitchell Bers
  700 E GRANVILLE AVE 60172
Medinah MS, 700 E GRANVILLE AVE 60172
  Richard Ganek, prin.
Medinah South ES
  22W-300 SUNNYSIDE ROAD 60157
  Gail Fahey, prin.
Other Schools – See Medinah

Roselle SD 12
Sch. Sys. Enr. Code 3
Supt. – Dr. Dennis O'Connell
  100 E WALNUT ST 60172
MS, 500 S PARK ST 60172 – Robert Wulffen, prin.
Spring Hills ES, 560 S PINECROFT AVE 60172
  Ann Meese, prin.

Schaumburg CCSD 54
Supt. – See Schaumburg
Nerge ES, 660 WOODFIELD TRAIL 60172
  Eugene Opalinski, prin.

St. John Lutheran School
  300 RODENBURG RD 60172
St. Walter School, 201 W MAPLE AVE 60172
Trinity Lutheran School, 405 RUSH ST 60172

Rosemont, Cook Co., Pop. Code 5
Rosemont ESD 78
Sch. Sys. Enr. Code 2
Supt. – Glen Gustafson, 6101 RUBY ST 60018
ES, 6101 RUBY ST 60018 – Dr. Mary Budzik, prin.

Roseville, Warren Co., Pop. Code 4
Roseville CUSD 200
Sch. Sys. Enr. Code 2
Supt. – William Hughes
  200 E GOSSETT ST 61473
ES, RURAL ROUTE 01 61473
  Paul Stevenson, prin.

Rossville, Vermilion Co., Pop. Code 4
Rossville-Alvin CUSD 7
Sch. Sys. Enr. Code 3
Supt. – Dennis Smith, 350 N CHICAGO ST 60963
Rossville-Alvin ES, 350 N CHICAGO ST 60963
  (—), prin.

Round Lake, Lake Co., Pop. Code 5
Round Lake Area SD 116
Sch. Sys. Enr. Code 6
Supt. – Clifton Houghton
  316 S ROSEDALE COURT 60073
Magee MS, 500 N CEDAR LAKE ROAD 60073
  Wilda Stanton, prin.
Ellis ES, 720 W CENTRAL PARK 60073
  James Menzer, prin.
Indian Hill ES, 1920 LOTUS DR 60073
  Mary Nemecek, prin.
Murphy ES, 220 GREENWOOD ST 60073
  Sheila St. Aubin, prin.
Round Lake Beach ES, 1421 ARDMORE DR 60073
  Michael Duax, prin.
Round Lake Village ES
  764 NIPPERSINK AVE 60073
  Barb Pergander, prin.

St. Joseph School, 118 LINCOLN AVE 60073

Roxana, Madison Co., Pop. Code 4
Roxana CUSD 1
Sch. Sys. Enr. Code 4
Supt. – Charles Conners
  401 CHAFFER AVE 62084
JHS, CHAFFER & THOMAS 62084
  James Ciccarelli, prin.
Central ES, 601 CHAFFER AVE 62084
  Darrell Waters, prin.
Other Schools – See East Alton, South Roxana

Royal, Champaign Co., Pop. Code 2
Prairieview CCSD 192
Sch. Sys. Enr. Code 2
Supt. – Richard Freehill, P O BOX 27 61871
MS, P O BOX 27 61871 – Richard Freehill, prin.
Other Schools – See Saint Joseph, Thomasboro

Rushville, Schuyler Co., Pop. Code 5
Schuyler Co. CUSD 1
Sch. Sys. Enr. Code 4
Supt. – Carroll Johnson
  215 W WASHINGTON ST 62681
JHS, 290 N MONROE 62681 – Lynn Painter, prin.
Washington ES, 100 BUCHANAN ST 62681
  Robert Heitz, prin.
Webster ES, 310 N MONROE 62681
  Robert Heitz, prin.
Other Schools – See Browning

Sadorus, Champaign Co., Pop. Code 2
Tolono CUSD 7
Supt. – See Tolono
ES, P O BOX 70 61872 – Joyce Broughton, prin.

Saint Anne, Kankakee Co., Pop. Code 4
St. Ann CCSD 256
Sch. Sys. Enr. Code 2
Supt. – Gael Kent, 333 S SAINT LOUIS AVE 60964
ES, 333 S SAINT LOUIS AVE 60964
  Wilbur Steele, prin.

Saint Charles, Kane Co., Pop. Code 7
St. Charles CUSD 303
Sch. Sys. Enr. Code 6
Supt. – Dr. Henry Bangser, P O BOX 188 60174

Haines JHS, 9TH & OAK ST 60174
  Raymond Hartman, prin.
Thompson JHS, 705 W MAIN ST 60174
  Robert Lindahl, prin.
Anderson MS, 35W071 VILLA MARIA RD 60174
  Linda Thompson, prin.
Davis ES, 7TH & HORNE STS 60174
  Ken Graham, prin.
Lincoln ES, 211 S 6TH AVE 60174 – (—), prin.
Little Woods ES, 5 N 466 ROUTE 25 60174
  Linda Thompson, prin.
Munhall ES, 1400 S 13TH AVE 60174
  Norman Huntley, prin.
Richmond ES, 12TH & OAK STS 60174
  Charles Bell, prin.
Wild Rose ES
  RED HAW LANE & THORNLY ST 60174
  Dr. Bonnie Wilkerson, prin.
Other Schools – See Wasco

St. Patrick ES, 5TH & STATE STS 60174

Saint David, Fulton Co., Pop. Code 3
St. David SD 87
  Sch. Sys. Enr. Code 1
  Supt. – Neil Williams, 100 COLLEGE AVE 61563
  ES, 100 COLLEGE AVE 61563
  Neil Williams, prin.

Saint Elmo, Fayette Co., Pop. Code 4
St. Elmo CUSD 202
  Sch. Sys. Enr. Code 3
  Supt. – William Phillips
    1200 N WALNUT ST 62458
  JHS, 300 W 12TH ST 62458
    Bruce Edwards, prin.
  ES, 519 W 2ND ST 62458 – Gary Hannagan, prin.

Sainte Marie, Jasper Co., Pop. Code 2
Jasper Co. CUSD 1
  Supt. – See Newton
  East JHS, P O BOX 157 62459 – Jack Adams, prin.
  Ste. Marie ES, P O BOX 157 62459
    Jack Adams, prin.

Saint Francisville, Lawrence Co., Pop. Code 4
Lawrence Co. CUSD 20
  Supt. – See Lawrenceville
  ES, ST JOHNS ST 62460 – Judith Phipps, prin.

Saint Jacob, Madison Co., Pop. Code 3
Triad CUSD 2
  Sch. Sys. Enr. Code 4
  Supt. – Robert Rogier, RURAL ROUTE 01 62281
  ES 62281 – Clark Crosier, prin.
  Other Schools – See Marine, Troy

Saint Joseph, Champaign Co., Pop. Code 4
Prairieview CCSD 192
  Supt. – See Royal
  Stanton Center PS, RURAL ROUTE 02 61873
    Lee Shores, prin.

St. Joseph CCSD 169
  Sch. Sys. Enr. Code 3
  Supt. – Gerald Meznarich, P O BOX M 61873
  JHS, P O BOX M 61873 – Randy Hird, prin.
  St. Joseph ES, 404 S 5TH ST BOX M 61873
    Gerald Meznarich, prin.

Saint Libory, St. Clair Co., Pop. Code 3
St. Libory CCSD 30
  Sch. Sys. Enr. Code 2
  Supt. – Dr. Raymond May, POST OFFICE 62282
  ES, POST OFFICE 62282 – Ruth May, prin.

Saint Peter, Fayette Co., Pop. Code 2

St. Peter Lutheran School
  RURAL ROUTE 01 BOX 70 62880

Salem, Marion Co., Pop. Code 6
Salem SD 111
  Sch. Sys. Enr. Code 4
  Supt. – Galen Brant, 315 S MAPLE ST 62881
  Salem Franklin Park JHS
    1325 N FRANKLIN ST 62881
    Barney Bruce, prin.
  Central ES, 315 S MAPLE 62881
    Galen Brant, prin.
  Hawthorn ES, 1300 HAWTHORN RD 62881
    Frank Brinkerhoff, prin.

Selmaville CCSD 10
  Sch. Sys. Enr. Code 2
  Supt. – Vernon Shook
    RURAL ROUTE 06 BOX 26 62881
  Selmaville South MS
    RURAL ROUTE 02 BOX 218 62881
    Earl Sullens, prin.
  Selmaville North ES
    RURAL ROUTE 06 BOX 26 62881
    Vernon Shook, prin.

St. Theresa of Avila School
  190 N OHIO AVE 62881

Sandoval, Marion Co., Pop. Code 4
Sandoval CUSD 501
  Sch. Sys. Enr. Code 3
  Supt. – Jim Beasley, P O BOX 68 62882
  JHS, P O BOX 68 62882 – Melvin Wood, prin.
  ES, P O BOX 308 62882 – Jace Telford, prin.

Sandwich, De Kalb Co., Pop. Code 5
Sandwich CUSD 430
  Sch. Sys. Enr. Code 4
  Supt. – Grant Bonner, 720 WELLS ST 60548
  Dummer JHS, 422 WELLS ST 60548
    Dean Van Horn, prin.
  Haskin MS, 720 WELLS ST 60548
    Andy Bertram, prin.
  Prairie View ES, 1201 CASTLE ST 60548
    Tom Dunlop, prin.
  Woodbury ES, 322 E 3RD ST 60548
    Walter Droppa, prin.

San Jose, Mason Co., Pop. Code 3
San Jose CUSD 122
  Sch. Sys. Enr. Code 2
  Supt. – Jimmy Rich, LINCOLN CIRCLE 62682
  ES, LINCOLN CIRCLE 62682 – Jimmy Rich, prin.

Sauk Village, Cook Co., Pop. Code 7
Community Consolidated SD 168
  Sch. Sys. Enr. Code 4
  Supt. – Willis Brown, 1825 215TH PLACE 60411
  Rickover JHS, 22151 TORRENCE AVE 60411
    Bernard Parlock, prin.
  Strassburg ES, 2002 E 223RD ST 60411
    George Kunkel, prin.
  Wagoner ES, 1831 215TH PL 60411
    Rita Schaap, prin.

Saunemin, Livingston Co., Pop. Code 2
Saunemin CCSD 438
  Sch. Sys. Enr. Code 2
  Supt. – James McNellis, P O BOX 195 61769
  ES, P O BOX 197 61769 – James McNellis, prin.

Savanna, Carroll Co., Pop. Code 5
Savanna CUSD 300
  Sch. Sys. Enr. Code 4
  Supt. – Dr. Max Pierson, 18 ADAMS ST 61074
  Lincoln ES, 414 3RD ST 61074
    Rex Kreuder, prin.

Saybrook, McLean Co., Pop. Code 3
Saybrook-Arrowsmith CUSD 11
  Sch. Sys. Enr. Code 2
  Supt. – Wayne Sutton, 201 W LOCUST 61770
  SayBrook-Arrowsmith JHS, 801 N MAIN ST 61770
    Leo Sherman, prin.
  Other Schools – See Arrowsmith

Scales Mound, Jo Daviess Co., Pop. Code 2
Scales Mound CUSD 211
  Sch. Sys. Enr. Code 2
  Supt. – Fred Sams, P O BOX 191 61075
  JHS, P O BOX 191 61075 – Wilson Ford, prin.
  ES, P O BOX 191 61075 – Wilson Ford, prin.

Schaumburg, Cook Co., Pop. Code 8
Schaumburg CCSD 54
  Sch. Sys. Enr. Code 7
  Supt. – Dr. William Kritzmire
    524 W SCHAUMBURG ROAD 60194
  Addams JHS
    700 S SPRINGINGSGUTH ROAD 60193
    William Litwitz, prin.
  Frost JHS, 320 W WISE ROAD 60193
    Marilyn Baier, prin.
  Aldrin ES, 617 BOXWOOD DR 60193
    Lee Cook, prin.
  Blackwell ES, 345 N WALNUT LN 60194
    Bernard Lucier, prin.
  Campanelli ES
    310 S SPRINGINGSGUTH RD 60193
    Terrence Baranowski, prin.
  Churchill ES, 1520 JONES RD 60195
    Daniel Farinosi, prin.
  Collins ES, 407 SUMMIT DR 60193
    Donald Stocker, prin.
  Dooley ES, 622 NORWOOD LN 60193
    William Shatkus, prin.
  Enders/Salk ES, 345 N SALEM DR 60194
    Roy Brodersen, prin.
  Hale ES, 1300 W WISE RD 60193
    Craig Gaska, prin.
  Hoover ES, 315 N SPRINGINGSGUTH RD 60194
    John Jones, prin.
  Other Schools – See Elk Grove Village, Hanover Park,
    Hoffman Estates, Roselle

St. Hubert School, 255 FLAGSTAFF LN 60194
St. Peter Lutheran School
  208 E SCHAUMBURG RD 60194

Schiller Park, Cook Co., Pop. Code 7
Schiller Park SD 81
  Sch. Sys. Enr. Code 3
  Supt. – Dr. M. Stramaglia
    4050 WAGNER ST 60176
  Lincoln JHS, 4050 WAGNER ST 60176
    Dr. R. Atkinson, prin.
  Kennedy ES, 3945 WEHRMAN AVE 60176
    Shirley Fitzpatrick, prin.
  Washington ES, 4835 MICHIGAN AVE 60176
    Mary Ann Sprafka, prin.

St. Beatrice School, 4141 ATLANTIC ST 60176
St. Maria Goretti School
  10050 IVANHOE AVE 60176

Sciota, McDonough Co., Pop. Code 1
Northwest CUSD 175
  Sch. Sys. Enr. Code 2
  Supt. – Charles Roth, P O BOX 2 61475
  Northwestern JHS, RURAL ROUTE 61475
    Robert Dickson, prin.

Other Schools – See Good Hope

Scott A F B, St. Clair Co.
Mascoutah CUSD 19
  Supt. – See Mascoutah
  Scott ES-North, SCOTT AFB 62225
    John Votrain, prin.
  Scott ES-South, SCOTT AFB 62225
    Henry Meinecke, prin.

Seneca, La Salle Co., Pop. Code 4
Seneca CCSD 170
  Sch. Sys. Enr. Code 2
  Supt. – David Yeck, 174 OAK ST 61360
  ES, 174 OAK ST 61360 – Larry Walker, prin.

Serena, La Salle Co., Pop. Code 2
Community Unit SD 2
  Sch. Sys. Enr. Code 3
  Supt. – Don Walker, P O BOX 107 60549
  ES, P O BOX 107 60549 – Lloyd Lange, prin.
  Other Schools – See Earlville, Sheridan

Sesser, Franklin Co., Pop. Code 4
Sesser-Valier CUSD 196
  Sch. Sys. Enr. Code 3
  Supt. – Farrell Flatt, P O BOX 465 62884
  Sesser-Valier JHS, P O BOX 465 62884
    Farrell Flatt, prin.
  Sesser-Valier ES
    RURAL ROUTE 01 BOX 465 62884
    Farrell Flatt, prin.

Seward, Winnebago Co.
Winnebago CUSD 323
  Supt. – See Winnebago
  ES, P O BOX 100 61077 – (—), prin.

Shabbona, De Kalb Co., Pop. Code 3
Shabbona CUSD 425
  Sch. Sys. Enr. Code 2
  Supt. – Len Harrington
    506 SHABBONA ROAD 60550
  ES, 301 CHEROKEE 60550 – James Hicks, prin.

Shannon, Carroll Co., Pop. Code 3
Eastland CUSD 308
  Supt. – See Lanark
  Eastland JHS, 7-11 W COOK BOX 46 61078
    John Rogers, prin.
  Eastland ES, 7-11 W COOK BOX 46 61078
    John Rogers, prin.

Shawneetown, Gallatin Co., Pop. Code 4
Gallatin CUSD 7
  Sch. Sys. Enr. Code 3
  Supt. – E. L. Felty, P O BOX J 62984
  Other Schools – See Equality, Ridgway

Sheffield, Bureau Co.
Western CUSD 306
  Sch. Sys. Enr. Code 2
  Supt. – Larry Marsh, EAST ST 61361
  Western ES, EAST ST 61361 – Larry Marsh, prin.
  Other Schools – See Buda

Shelbyville, Shelby Co., Pop. Code 6
Shelbyville CUSD 4
  Sch. Sys. Enr. Code 4
  Supt. – Ben Fletcher
    1001 W 6TH NORTH ST 62565
  Moulton MS, 1101 W NORTH 6TH ST 62565
    Robert Enkoff, prin.
  Main St. ES, 225 W MAIN ST 62565
    James Bliler, prin.
  Vine St. ES, 200 S VINE ST 62565
    James Bliler, prin.

Sheldon, Iroquois Co., Pop. Code 4
Sheldon CUSD 5
  Sch. Sys. Enr. Code 2
  Supt. – Thomas Rosene, 150 S RANDOLPH 60966
  ES, 150 S RANDOLPH 60966
    Thomas Rosene, prin.

Sheridan, La Salle Co., Pop. Code 3
Community Unit SD 2
  Supt. – See Serena
  ES, P O BOX 328 60551 – James Farson, prin.

Sherman, Sangamon Co., Pop. Code 4
Williamsville CUSD 15
  Supt. – See Williamsville
  ES, 313 SOUTH ST 62684
    Richard Thrasher, prin.

Sherrard, Mercer Co., Pop. Code 3
Sherrard CUSD 200
  Supt. – See Matherville
  JHS, 4701 176TH AVE 61281 – Harry Hunt, prin.
  ES, P O BOX 38 61281 – Stewart Klink, prin.

Shipman, Macoupin Co., Pop. Code 3
Piasa CUSD 9
  Supt. – See Piasa
  ES, POST OFFICE 62085 – Bill Mills, prin.

Shirland, Winnebago Co.
Shirland CCSD 134
  Sch. Sys. Enr. Code 2
  Supt. – Edward O'Brien, 8020 NORTH ST 61079
  Shirland Comm. Cons. ES, 8020 NORTH ST 61079
    Edward O'brien, prin.

Shirley, McLean Co.
Heyworth CUSD 4
  Supt. – See Heyworth
  Funk ES, RURAL ROUTE 01 61772
    Mike Lynch, prin.

Shobonier, Fayette Co.
Vandalia CUSD 203
Supt. – See Vandalia
ES 62885 – Eli Heffron, prin.

Shorewood, Will Co., Pop. Code 5
Troy CCSD 30 C
Sch. Sys. Enr. Code 4
Supt. – Clair Swan, 4000 SCHOOL ROAD 60436
Troy JHS, 4000 SCHOOL ROAD 60436
  William Sparlin, prin.
Troy Shorewood MS, SCHOOL ROAD 60436
  Thomas Staley, prin.
Other Schools – See Joliet

Shumway, Effingham Co., Pop. Code 2
Beecher City CUSD 20
Supt. – See Beecher City
ES, RURAL ROUTE 01 BOX 6 62461
  Doug Heiden, prin.

Sibley, Ford Co.
Melvin Sibley CUSD 4
Sch. Sys. Enr. Code 2
Supt. – Norman Kerans, P O BOX 157 61773
ES, P O BOX 157 61773 – Norman Kerans, prin.
Other Schools – See Melvin

Sidell, Vermilion Co., Pop. Code 3
Jamaica CUSD 12
Sch. Sys. Enr. Code 3
Supt. – Robert Yeazel, P O BOX 365 61876
Jamaica JHS, P O BOX 45 61876
  Jack Richardson, prin.
Jamaica ES, RURAL ROUTE 01 61876
  Jack Richardson, prin.

Sidney, Champaign Co., Pop. Code 3
Tolono CUSD 7
Supt. – See Tolono
ES, 216 E BYRON 61877 – Ed Phillips, prin.

Sigel, Shelby Co., Pop. Code 2
Teutopolis CUSD 50
Supt. – See Teutopolis
Lillyville ES, RURAL ROUTE 01 62462
  Dr. Richard Longbucco, prin.

St. Michael School, CHURCH ST 62462

Silvis, Rock Island Co., Pop. Code 6
East Moline SD 37
Supt. – See East Moline
Bowlesburg ES, 2221 10TH ST 61282
  Glen Anderson, prin.

Silvis SD 34
Sch. Sys. Enr. Code 3
Supt. – Ronald Smith, 1205 5TH AVE 61282
JHS, 1305 5TH AVE 61282 – Larry Brewer, prin.
Barr ES, 1305 5TH AVE 61282
  Rene Noppe, prin.

Skokie, Cook Co., Pop. Code 8
East Prairie SD 73
Sch. Sys. Enr. Code 2
Supt. – Ron Bearwald, 3907 DOBSON ST 60076
East Prairie ES, 3907 DOBSON ST 60076
  Robert Miller, prin.

Evanston CCSD 65
Supt. – See Evanston
Walker ES, 3601 CHURCH ST 60203
  Elmore Johnson, prin.

Skokie Fairview SD 72
Sch. Sys. Enr. Code 2
Supt. – Pamela Witt, 7040 LARAMIE AVE 60077
Fairview South MS, 7040 LARAMIE AVE 60077
  Thomas Williams, prin.

Skokie SD 68
Sch. Sys. Enr. Code 4
Supt. – Dr. Pierce Hoban
  9300 KENTON AVE 60076
Old Orchard JHS, 9310 KENTON AVE 60076
  Gerald Gregory, prin.
Devonshire ES, 9040 KOSTNER AVE 60076
  Dr. Lawrence Bizar, prin.
Highland ES, 9700 CRAWFORD AVE 60076
  Donna Joy, prin.
Stenson ES, 9201 LOCKWOOD AVE 60077
  Roger Skerrett, prin.

Skokie SD 69
Sch. Sys. Enr. Code 3
Supt. – Allan Maier, 5100 MADISON ST 60077
Lincoln JHS, 7839 LINCOLN AVE 60077
  James Metzinger, prin.
Madison ES, 5100 MADISON ST 60077
  Joan Thalmann, prin.
Other Schools – See Morton Grove

Skokie SD 73-5
Sch. Sys. Enr. Code 3
Supt. – Vickie Markavitch
  8000 E PRAIRIE ROAD 60076
McCracken MS, 8000 E PRAIRIE ROAD 60076
  John Becker, prin.
Middleton ES, 8300 ST LOUIS AVE 60076
  Jack Cantor, prin.

Arie Crown Hebrew Day School
  4600 MAIN ST 60076
Hillel Torah North Suburban School
  7120 LARAMIE AVE 60077
Solomon Schecter School
  9301 GROSS POINT RD 60076

St. Joan of Arc School
  9245 N LAWNDALE AVE 60203
St. Lambert School, 8141 KEDVALE AVE 60076
St. Paul Lutheran School, 5201 GALITZ ST 60077
St. Peter School, 8140 NILES CENTER RD 60077

Smithfield, Fulton Co., Pop. Code 2
Fulton County CUSD 3
Supt. – See Cuba
ES, POST OFFICE 61477 – Charles Barber, prin.

Smithton, St. Clair Co., Pop. Code 4
Smithton CCSD 130
Sch. Sys. Enr. Code 2
Supt. – William Zuehlke, P O BOX 218 62285
ES, P O BOX 218 62285 – William Zuehlke, prin.

St. John Baptist School
  JULIA & STOEGER STS 62285

Somonauk, De Kalb Co., Pop. Code 4
Somonauk CUSD 432
Sch. Sys. Enr. Code 3
Supt. – Emmett Dannenberg, P O BOX 278 60552
ES, 320 S MAPLE 60552 – James Wood, prin.

Sorento, Bond Co., Pop. Code 3
Bond County CUSD 2
Supt. – See Greenville
ES 62086 – Max Aten, prin.

South Beloit, Winnebago Co., Pop. Code 5
Prairie Hill CCSD 133
Sch. Sys. Enr. Code 2
Supt. – Roger Fenrick, RURAL ROUTE 02 61080
Prairie Hill ES, RURAL ROUTE 01 61080
  Roger Fenrick, prin.

South Beloit CUSD 320
Sch. Sys. Enr. Code 2
Supt. – Dennis Healy, 850 HAYES AVE 61080
Riverview MS, 306 MILLER ST 61080
  Kenneth Reidenbach, prin.
Clark ES, 464 OAK GROVE AVE 61080
  Suzanne Deesey, prin.

St. Peter School, 320 ELMWOOD AVE 61080

South Chicago Heights, Cook Co., Pop. Code 5
Chicago Heights SD 170
Supt. – See Chicago Heights
Grant ES, 27TH ST & MILLER AVE 60411
  John Anzelmo, prin.

Steger SD 194
Supt. – See Steger
Saukeiw ES, 3398 MILLER AVE 60411
  David Boger, prin.

South Elgin, Kane Co., Pop. Code 6
Elgin Unit SD 46
Supt. – See Elgin
Clinton ES, 770 MILL ST 60177
  David Wedemeyer, prin.
Willard ES, 370 W SPRING ST 60177
  Austin Ridenour, prin.

South Holland, Cook Co., Pop. Code 7
South Holland SD 150
Sch. Sys. Enr. Code 3
Supt. – Dr. Harry Agabedis
  170TH & COTTAGE GROVE AVE 60473
Mckinley JHS
  170TH & COTTAGE GROVE AVE 60473
  Donald Piersma, prin.
Greenwood ES, 168TH ST & GREENWOOD 60473
  Richard Kerber, prin.

South Holland SD 151
Sch. Sys. Enr. Code 4
Supt. – Dr. Janice Potter
  16001 MINERVA AVE 60473
Eisenhower ES, 16001 MINERVA AVE 60473
  James McGovern, prin.
Madison ES, 156TH & ORCHID DRIVE 60473
  John Madden, prin.
Other Schools – See Harvey, Phoenix

Holy Ghost School, 700 E 170TH ST 60473
St. Jude the Apostle School
  900 E 154TH ST 60473

South Pekin, Tazewell Co., Pop. Code 4
South Pekin SD 137
Sch. Sys. Enr. Code 4
Supt. – Robert Waller, 206 W MAIN ST 61564
ES, 206 W MAIN ST 61564 – Robert Waller, prin.

South Roxana, Madison Co., Pop. Code 4
Roxana CUSD 1
Supt. – See Roxana
ES, 400 MICHIGAN AVE 62087
  Dorothy Stickels, prin.

South Wilmington, Grundy Co., Pop. Code 3
South Wilmington CCSD 74
Sch. Sys. Enr. Code 2
Supt. – Arden Wills, 375 FIFTH AVE 60474
South Wilmington Cons. ES
  375 FIFTH AVE 60474 – Arden Wills, prin.

Sparland, Marshall Co., Pop. Code 3
Sparland CUSD 3
Sch. Sys. Enr. Code 2
Supt. – Stan Burcham
  RURAL ROUTE 01 BOX 43 61565
JHS, RURAL ROUTE 01 61565 – Mark Zotz, prin.
ES, RURAL ROUTE 01 61565 – Mark Zotz, prin.

Sparta, Randolph Co., Pop. Code 5
Sparta CUSD 140
Sch. Sys. Enr. Code 4
Supt. – Dr. Allan Brown
  123 W COLLEGE ST 62286
Sparta-Lincoln MS, 200 N ST LOUIS ST 62286
  Alison Bunte, prin.
PS, RURAL ROUTE 03 62286 – Betty Luthy, prin.
Other Schools – See Ellis Grove, Evansville, Tilden

Springfield, Sangamon Co., Pop. Code 8
Springfield SD 186
Sch. Sys. Enr. Code 7
Supt. – Dr. Donald J. Miedema
  1900 W MONROE ST 62704
Franklin MS, 1200 OUTER PARK DRIVE 62704
  Robert Leming, prin.
Grant MS, 1800 W MONROE ST 62704
  Elbert Betts, prin.
Washington MS, 2300 E JACKSON ST 62703
  Wayne Mendenhall, prin.
Addams ES, 10 BABIAK LN 62702
  Cheryl Benner, prin.
Black Hawk ES, 2500 S COLLEGE ST 62704
  Norman Cook, prin.
Butler ES, 1701 S MACARTHUR BLVD 62704
  Robert Hart, prin.
Dell ES, 850 W LAKE DR 62707
  Dr. Cora Benson, prin.
Dubois ES, 120 S LINCOLN AVE 62704
  Robert Goodhart, prin.
Enos ES, 524 W ELLIOTT AVE 62702
  (—), prin.
Fairview ES, 2200 E RIDGELY AVE 62702
  Dr. Laine Tadlock, prin.
Feitshans MS, 1101 S 15TH ST 62703
  A. Rudin, prin.
Harvard Park ES, 2501 S 11TH ST 62703
  Lon Scott, prin.
Hay-Edwards ES, 400 W LAWRENCE AVE 62704
  Frank Copi, prin.
Iles ES, 1700 S 15TH ST 62703
  Mary Anne Elson, prin.
Jefferson ES, 3001 S ALLIS ST 62703
  John Cavitt, prin.
Laketown ES, 1825 LEE ST 62703
  Dr. Charles Russell, prin.
Lincoln ES, 300 S 11TH ST 62703
  Phyllis Cheaney, prin.
Marsh ES, 1000 AVON DR 62704
  Dr. Diane Rutledge, prin.
Matheny ES, 2200 E JACKSON ST 62703
  Elizabeth Nelson, prin.
McClernand ES, 801 N 6TH ST 62702
  Barbara Lestikow, prin.
Pleasant Hill MS, 3040 E LINDEN AVE 62702
  Edna Shanklin, prin.
Ridgely ES, 2040 N 8TH ST 62702
  Cliff Hathaway, prin.
Sandburg ES, 2051 WABASH AVE 62704
  Hazel Broughton, prin.
Southern View ES, 3338 S 5TH ST 62703
  Dr. Judith Walsh, prin.
Wanless ES, 2120 RESEVOIR 62702
  Donald Augspurger, prin.
Wilcox ES, 2000 HASTINGS RD 62702
  Ray Clouser, prin.
Withrow ES, 1200 S POPE 62703
  Linda Rakers, prin.

Blessed Sacrament School
  748 W LAUREL ST 62704
Cathedral School, 815 S 6TH ST 62703
Christ the King School
  1920 BARBERRY DR 62703
Concordia Lutheran School
  2300 E WILSHIRE RD 62703
Immanuel Lutheran School
  2750 E SANGAMON AVE 62702
Little Flower School, 900 STEVENSON DR 62703
Our Savior Lutheran School
  2645 OLD JACKSONVILLE ROAD 62704
Sacred Heart Grade School
  1225 E LAWRENCE AVE 62703
St. Aloysius School
  2000 E SANGAMON AVE 62702
St. Cabrini School, 1024 N MILTON AVE 62702
St. Joseph School, 1344 N 5TH ST 62702
St. Patrick School, 1800 S GRAND AVE E 62703
Sy. Agnes School, 251 N AMOS AVE 62702
Trinity Lutheran School
  515 S MACARTHUR BLVD 62704

Spring Grove, McHenry Co., Pop. Code 3
Lotus SD 10
Sch. Sys. Enr. Code 2
Supt. – Arthur Smejkal
  29067 W GRASS LAKE ROAD 60081
Lotus ES, 29067 W GRASS LAKE RD 60081
  Arthur Smejkal, prin.

Spring Grove SD 11
Sch. Sys. Enr. Code 2
Supt. – Ronald Erdmann, P O BOX 158 60081
ES, 2018 MAIN STREET RD #158 60081
  Mary Davis, prin.

Spring Valley, Bureau Co., Pop. Code 6
Spring Valley CCSD 99
Sch. Sys. Enr. Code 3
Supt. – Charles Palia, 800 N RICHARDS ST 61362
Kennedy ES, 800 N RICHARDS ST 61362
  Steve Siska, prin.
Lincoln ES, 501 E ERIE ST 61362
  James Narczewski, prin.

Stanford, McLean Co., Pop. Code 3
Olympia CUSD 16
Sch. Sys. Enr. Code 4
Supt. – Dr. Jack Bowman
   RURAL ROUTE 01 BOX 150 61774
Olympia MS, RURAL ROUTE 01 BOX 150 61774
   Gary DeMoss, prin.
Minier-Arlington ES, P O BOX 461 61759
   Steven Schroeder, prin.
ES, P O BOX 236 61774 – Michael Noble, prin.
Other Schools – See Atlanta, Danvers, Hopedale, Mc
Lean

Staunton, Macoupin Co., Pop. Code 5
Staunton CUSD 6
Sch. Sys. Enr. Code 3
Supt. – Murlin A. Hawkins
   801 N DENEEN ST 62088
JHS, 801 N DENEEN ST 62088
   Mark Skertich, prin.
ES, 801 N DENEEN ST 62088
   Mark Skertich, prin.

St. Michael School, 419 E MAIN ST 62088
Zion Lutheran School, 220 W HENRY ST 62088

Steeleville, Randolph Co., Pop. Code 4
Steeleville CUSD 138
Sch. Sys. Enr. Code 3
Supt. – Donald Badgley, P O BOX 128 62288
ES, 609 S SPARTA ST 62288
   Donald Sanders, prin.

St. Mark Lutheran School, 504 N JAMES ST 62288

Steger, Cook Co., Pop. Code 6
Steger SD 194
Sch. Sys. Enr. Code 4
Supt. – Dr. Milton R. Whitten
   RICHTON ROAD & PARK AVE 60475
Central JHS, 19 W 33RD ST 60475
   Donald Moke, prin.
Eastview ES, 3411 HOPKINS ST 60475
   Robert Swanson, prin.
Parkview ES, 116 RICHTON RD 60475
   Frank Blazek, prin.
Other Schools – See South Chicago Heights

St. Liborius School, 3440 HALSTED BLVD 60475

Sterling, Whiteside Co., Pop. Code 7
Sterling CUSD 5
Sch. Sys. Enr. Code 5
Supt. – Dr. James A. Garnett, 1800 6TH AVE 61081
Challand JHS, 1700 6TH AVE 61081
   Robert Wolf, prin.
Franklin ES, 1510 E 25TH ST 61081
   Tom Marlin, prin.
Jefferson ES, 806 E LE FEVRE RD 61081
   Phil Hunsberger, prin.
Lincoln ES, 1501 E 6TH ST 61081
   Mark Thompson, prin.
Wallace ES, 506 W 4TH ST 61081 – (—), prin.
Washington ES, 815 W LE FEVRE RD 61081
   Luke Glowiak, prin.

St. Mary School, 6 W 6TH ST 61081

Steward, Lee Co., Pop. Code 2
Steward ESD 220
Sch. Sys. Enr. Code 2
Supt. – Ronald Rood, P O BOX 97 60553
ES, P O BOX 97 60553 – Ronald Rood, prin.

Stewardson, Shelby Co., Pop. Code 3
Stewardson-Strasburg CUSD 5A
Sch. Sys. Enr. Code 2
Supt. – Phillip S. Reasor, P O BOX 187 62463
Stewardson-Strasburg ES, P O BOX 187 62463
   Thomas Cox, prin.

Stickney, Cook Co., Pop. Code 6
Lyons SD 103
Supt. – See Lyons
Edison ES, 4100 SCOVILLE AVE 60402
   Larry Pinsky, prin.
Home ES, 4400 HOME AVE 60402
   James Rick, prin.

Stillman Valley, Ogle Co., Pop. Code 3
Meridian CUSD 223
Sch. Sys. Enr. Code 4
Supt. – David Miller, P O BOX 89 61084
Meridian JHS, 207 W MAIN ST 61084
   Jack Powell, prin.
Highland ES, 410 S HICKORY ST 61084
   Virgil Castelli Jr., prin.
Other Schools – See Monroe Center

Stockton, Jo Daviess Co., Pop. Code 4
Stockton CUSD 206
Sch. Sys. Enr. Code 3
Supt. – Robert Dunn, RUSH ST 61085
JHS, 500 N RUSH ST 61085
   Dr. Charles Snook, prin.
ES, 236 N PEARL ST 61085
   Dr. Darrel Fulton, prin.

Stone Park, Cook Co., Pop. Code 2
Bellwood SD 88
Sch. Sys. Enr. Code 5
Supt. – Dr. Joseph Payton
   1801 N 36TH AVE 60165
Other Schools – See Bellwood, Melrose Park

Stonington, Christian Co., Pop. Code 4
Stonington CUSD 7
Sch. Sys. Enr. Code 2
Supt. – John Mizell, 501 E NORTH ST 62567
JHS, 501 E NORTH ST 62567 – Stuart Chase, prin.
ES, 501 E NORTH ST 62567 – John Mizell, prin.

Streamwood, Kane Co., Pop. Code 7
Elgin Unit SD 46
Supt. – See Elgin
Canton MS, 1100 SUNSET CIRCLE 60107
   George Fornero, prin.
Tefft MS, IRVING PARK ROAD 60103
   Keith Sack, prin.
Glenbrook ES, 315 GARDEN CIR 60107
   Dr. J. Peter Lueck, prin.
Hanover Countryside ES
   6 S BARTLETT RD 60107 – John Schneck, prin.
Heritage ES, 507 ARNOLD AVE 60107
   William Peterson, prin.
Oakhill ES, 502 S OLTENDORF RD 60107
   Gloria Johnston, prin.
Ridge Circle ES, 420 RIDGE CIR 60107
   William White, prin.
Sunnydale ES, 716 SUNNYDALE BLVD 60107
   Susan Ford, prin.
Woodland Heights ES, 900 S PARK BLVD 60107
   George Vornero, prin.

St. John the Evangelist School
   513 PARKSIDE CIR 60107

Streator, La Salle Co., Pop. Code 7
Eagle ESD 43
Sch. Sys. Enr. Code 1
Supt. – Kenneth Pyszka, RURAL ROUTE 03 61364
Eagle ES, RURAL ROUTE 03 61364
   Kenneth Pyszka, prin.

Otter Creek ESD 56
Sch. Sys. Enr. Code 1
Supt. – Evelyn Hyatt, RURAL ROUTE 01 61364
Otter Creek ES, RURAL ROUTE 01 61364
   Evelyn Hyatt, prin.

Streator ESD 45
Sch. Sys. Enr. Code 4
Supt. – Richard M. Peters
   1520 N BLOOMINGTON ST 61364
Northlawn JHS, 202 E 1ST 61364
   Charles Irwin, prin.
Centennial ES, OAKLEY AVE 61364
   Dianne Haak, prin.
Kimes ES, 1207 READING ST 61364
   Edmund Studnicki, prin.
Oakland Park ES, 701 S STERLING ST 61364
   Jim Blalock, prin.
Sherman ES, 1206 E ELM ST 61364
   Michael Vaiaman, prin.

Streator Woodland CUSD 5
Sch. Sys. Enr. Code 3
Supt. – James Langan, RURAL ROUTE 02 61364
Woodland ES, RURAL ROUTE 02 61364
   Kathleen Taylor, prin.

St. Anthony's School, 410 S PARK ST 61364
St. Mary School, 405 BLOOMINGTON ST 61364
St. Stephen School, 807 LUNDY ST 61364

Stronghurst, Henderson Co., Pop. Code 3
Southern CUSD 120
Sch. Sys. Enr. Code 2
Supt. – Dr. Paul Cary, 116 S BROADWAY 61480
Southern ES, P O BOX 179 61480
   Richard Clifton, prin.
Other Schools – See Media

Sullivan, Moultrie Co., Pop. Code 5
Sullivan CUSD 300
Sch. Sys. Enr. Code 4
Supt. – Harold V. Edwards, 725 N MAIN ST 61951
MS, 725 N MAIN ST 61951 – John Prinz, prin.
Powers ES, 208 W JACKSON ST 61951
   Nancy Schaljo, prin.

Summerfield, St. Clair Co., Pop. Code 2
Lebanon CUSD 9
Supt. – See Lebanon
ES, P O BOX 213 62289 – Charles Kamm, prin.

Summit, Cook Co., Pop. Code 7
Summit SD 104
Sch. Sys. Enr. Code 4
Supt. – Kevin Cronin
   60TH ST & 74TH AVE 60501
Dr. Wharton ES, 7555 W 64TH ST 60501
   Azalee Elder, prin.
Graves ES, 60TH ST & 74TH AVE 60501
   Dennis Lewis, prin.
Walsh ES, 5640 S 75TH AVE 60501
   Edward Fee, prin.
Other Schools – See Argo, Bedford Park

St. Joseph School, 5641 S 73RD AVE 60501

Sumner, Lawrence Co., Pop. Code 4
Red Hill CUSD 10
Supt. – See Bridgeport
Petty ES, P O BOX 227 62466
   Dennis Kimmel, prin.
ES, 110 W LOCUST ST 62466
   Dennis Kimmel, prin.

Sycamore, De Kalb Co., Pop. Code 6
Hiawatha CUSD 426
Supt. – See Kirkland

Hiawatha ES, 245 W EXCHANGE ST 60178
   John Smith, prin.
Sycamore CUSD 427
Sch. Sys. Enr. Code 4
Supt. – Charles Norland
   245 W EXCHANGE ST 60178
JHS, 150 MAPLEWOOD DRIVE 60178
   Lewis Uhrich, prin.
North ES, BRICKVILLE RD 60178
   Helene Kraus, prin.
Southeast ES, 718 S LOCUST ST 60178
   Cheryl Nelson, prin.
West ES, 240 FAIR ST 60178
   David Hillmer, prin.

St. Mary School, 222 WATERMAN ST 60178

Table Grove, Fulton Co., Pop. Code 2
VIT CUSD 2
Sch. Sys. Enr. Code 3
Supt. – James Hermes
   RURAL ROUTE 01 BOX 06 61482
VIT JHS, RURAL ROUTE 01 BOX 06 61482
   Terry Hull, prin.
V I T ES, RURAL ROUTE 01 BOX 7 61482
   James Hermes, prin.

Tallula, Menard Co., Pop. Code 3
Porta CUSD 202
Supt. – See Petersburg
ES, N ELM ST 62688 – Dean Kerr, prin.

Tamaroa, Perry Co., Pop. Code 3
CCSD 211
Sch. Sys. Enr. Code 1
Supt. – Curtis Pierce
   RURAL ROUTE 03 BOX 8 62888
Comm. Cons. ES, RURAL ROUTE 03 BOX 8 62888
   Curtis Pierce, prin.

Duquoin CUSD 300
Supt. – See Du Quoin
Paradise Prairie ES
   RURAL ROUTE 01 BOX 75 62888
   Ann Schwengel, prin.

Tamaroa SD 5
Sch. Sys. Enr. Code 2
Supt. – Bobbie Swetland, P O BOX 175 62888
ES, P O BOX 175 62888 – Bobbie Swetland, prin.

Tamms, Alexander Co., Pop. Code 3
Egyptian CUSD 5
Sch. Sys. Enr. Code 3
Supt. – Dr. Leon Russell
   RURAL ROUTE 01 BOX SD 62988
Egyptian JHS, RURAL ROUTE 01 62988
   Kerry Baugher, prin.
Egyptian ES, RURAL ROUTE 01 62988
   Larry Naeger, prin.

Tampico, Whiteside Co., Pop. Code 3
Tampico CUSD 4
Sch. Sys. Enr. Code 2
Supt. – Larry Wilcoxen, P O BOX 188 61283
ES, 202 2ND ST 61283 – Larry Wilcoxen, prin.
Other Schools – See Deer Grove

Taylor Ridge, Rock Island Co.
Rockridge CUSD 300
Sch. Sys. Enr. Code 4
Supt. – Marrill Hughes
   14110 134TH AVE W 61284
Rockridge JHS, 14110 134TH AVE W 61284
   Dick Stoltz, prin.
ES, 13228 TURKEY HOLLOW RD 61284
   Stanley Kaiser, prin.
Other Schools – See Andalusia, Illinois City, Reynolds

Taylorville, Christian Co., Pop. Code 7
Taylorville CUSD 3
Sch. Sys. Enr. Code 5
Supt. – Dr. Verlin Bundy, 101 E ADAMS ST 62568
Memorial ES, 101 E ADAMS ST 62568
   William Harris, prin.
North ES, 805 N CHEROKEE ST 62568
   Roy Shoemaker, prin.
South ES, 1004 W PRAIRIE ST 62568
   David Hixenbaugh, prin.
West ES, N ELEVATOR 62568
   David Carlton, prin.

St. Mary's School, 422 S WASHINGTON ST 62568

Teutopolis, Effingham Co., Pop. Code 4
Teutopolis CUSD 50
Sch. Sys. Enr. Code 4
Supt. – Richard Longbucco, P O BOX 246 62467
ES, 309 E MAIN ST 62467 – James Hakman, prin.
Other Schools – See Dieterich, Effingham, Sigel

Texico, Jefferson Co.
Field CCSD 3
Sch. Sys. Enr. Code 2
Supt. – Donald Kelley, RURAL ROUTE 01 62889
Field ES, RURAL ROUTE 01 62889
   John Ashby, prin.

Thawville, Iroquois Co., Pop. Code 2
Ford Central CUSD 8
Sch. Sys. Enr. Code 2
Supt. – Joseph Trimmer, P O BOX 98 60968
Ford Central ES, P O BOX 98 60968
   Joseph Trimmer, prin.
Other Schools – See Piper City

Thomasboro, Champaign Co., Pop. Code 4
Prairieview CCSD 192
Supt. – See Royal
Flatville JHS, RURAL ROUTE 01   61878
    Lee Shores, prin.

Thomasboro CCSD 130
Sch. Sys. Enr. Code 2
Supt. – William Kurth, P O BOX 99   61878
ES, 201 N PHILLIPS BOX 99   61878
    William Kurth, prin.

Thompsonville, Franklin Co., Pop. Code 3
Thompsonville SD 62
Sch. Sys. Enr. Code 2
Supt. – O. Thompson
    302 W SHAWNEETOWN ROAD   62890
ES, 302 W SHAWNEETOWN ROAD   62890
    Karla Lee, prin.

Thomson, Carroll Co., Pop. Code 3
Thomson CCSD 301
Sch. Sys. Enr. Code 2
Supt. – Howard Kennedy, SOUTH ST   61285
ES, RURAL ROUTE 01 BOX 1   61285
    William Gengenbach, prin.

Thornton, Cook Co., Pop. Code 5
Thornton SD 154
Sch. Sys. Enr. Code 2
Supt. – Glen Littlefield
    200 N WOLCOTT ST   60476
Wolcott ES, 200 N WOLCOTT ST   60476
    Gae Mollin, prin.

Tilden, Randolph Co., Pop. Code 4
Sparta CUSD 140
Supt. – See Sparta
ES, SCHOOL ST   62292 – Karen McClintock, prin.

Tinley Park, Cook Co., Pop. Code 8
Arbor Park SD 145
Supt. – See Oak Forest
Kimberly Heights ES, 6141 KIMBERLY DR   60477
    Jane Foster, prin.

Kirby SD 140
Sch. Sys. Enr. Code 5
Supt. – Arnold Drzonek, P O BOX 98   60477
Grissom JHS, 17000 80TH AVE   60477
    Phillip Scully, prin.
Bannes ES, 16835 ODELL AVE   60477
    Robert Andersen, prin.
Keller ES, 7846 163RD ST   60477
    Marilyn Halpin, prin.
Kirby ES, 17300 OZARK AVE   60477
    Fred Schafer, prin.
McAuliffe ES, 8944 WL 174TH ST   60477
    John McCartney, prin.
Other Schools – See Orland Park

Tinley Park Community SD 146
Sch. Sys. Enr. Code 4
Supt. – Dr. Robert W. Procunier
    17316 OAK PARK AVE   60477
Central JHS, 17248 67TH AVE   60477
    Larry Anderson, prin.
Fulton ES, 6601 171ST ST   60477
    Carolyn Lane, prin.
Memorial ES, 6701 179TH ST   60477
    Dr. Bill Kinzer, prin.
Sandidge MS, 16600 66TH AVE   60477
    Susan Casey, prin.
Other Schools – See Oak Forest, Orland Park

St. Emeric School, 4300 180TH ST   60477
St. George School, 6700 176TH ST   60477
St. John Lutheran School, 4231 183RD ST   60477
Trinity Lutheran School, 6850 159TH ST   60477

Tiskilwa, Bureau Co., Pop. Code 3
Tiskilwa CUSD 300
Sch. Sys. Enr. Code 2
Supt. – Robert Prusator
    350 WASHINGTON ST   61368
ES, GALENA ST   61368 – Robert Prusator, prin.

Toledo, Cumberland Co., Pop. Code 4
Cumberland CUSD 77
Sch. Sys. Enr. Code 4
Supt. – Joseph Trimmer
    RURAL ROUTE 01 BOX 182   62468
Cumberland JHS
    RURAL ROUTE 01 BOX 182   62468
    Pat Smith, prin.
Cumberland ES
    RURAL ROUTE 01 BOX 182   62468
    (—), prin.

Tolono, Champaign Co., Pop. Code 4
Tolono CUSD 7
Sch. Sys. Enr. Code 4
Supt. – Leroy Durand, E WALNUT ST   61880
Unity JHS, P O BOX T   61880 – Ed Phillips, prin.
PS, BOURNE ST BOX R   61880
    Duane Walton, prin.
Other Schools – See Pesotum, Philo, Sadorus, Sidney

Toluca, Marshall Co., Pop. Code 4
Toluca CUSD 2
Sch. Sys. Enr. Code 2
Supt. – Michael Johnson, 306 N MAPLE ST   61369
JHS, 306 N MAPLE ST   61369
    Kenneth Baker, prin.
ES, 211 N WILLOW ST   61369
    Kenneth Baker, prin.

Tonica, La Salle Co., Pop. Code 3
Tonica CCSD 79
Sch. Sys. Enr. Code 2
Supt. – Clifford Arbogast, P O BOX 8   61370
ES, P O BOX 8   61370 – Terry Warren, prin.

Toulon, Stark Co., Pop. Code 4
Toulon-LaFayette CUSD 2
Sch. Sys. Enr. Code 2
Supt. – W. Turner, P O BOX 327   61483
Toulon-LaFayette JHS, RURAL ROUTE 01   61483
    A. Harland, prin.
Toulon-Lafayette ES, 402 S FRANKLIN   61483
    W. David Turner, prin.

Towanda, McLean Co., Pop. Code 3
Normal CUSD 5
Supt. – See Normal
ES, P O BOX 248   61776 – Carla Frinsko, prin.

Tower Hill, Shelby Co., Pop. Code 3
Tower Hill CCSD 10
Sch. Sys. Enr. Code 2
Supt. – Ouds Cheek
    BENTON & MICHIGAN   62571
ES, BENTON-MICHIGAN B 157   62571
    Donald Burton, prin.

Tremont, Tazewell Co., Pop. Code 4
Tremont CUSD 702
Sch. Sys. Enr. Code 3
Supt. – Brock Butts, 400 W PEARL ST   61568
JHS, 400 W PEARL ST   61568 – Rodger Page, prin.
ES, 50 JAMES ST   61568 – Robert Atwater, prin.

Trenton, Clinton Co., Pop. Code 5
Wesclin CUSD 3
Sch. Sys. Enr. Code 4
Supt. – Donald W. Jones, ROUTE 160 S   62293
Wesclin JHS, ROUTE 160 S   62293
    Paul Tockstein, prin.
St. Mary's ES, 313 S ADAMS ST   62293
    Gary Brink, prin.
ES, 308 N WASHINGTON ST   62293
    Gary Brink, prin.
Other Schools – See New Baden

Triumph, La Salle Co.
Ophir CCSD 235
Sch. Sys. Enr. Code 1
Supt. – Lynn Dewey, P O BOX 36   61371
Ophir ES, P O BOX 36   61371 – Lynn Dewey, prin.

Trivoli, Peoria Co.
Farmington Central CUSD 265
Sch. Sys. Enr. Code 4
Supt. – Larry Hippen, P O BOX 68   61569
Other Schools – See Farmington, Hanna City, Yates
City

Troy, Madison Co., Pop. Code 5
Triad CUSD 2
Supt. – See Saint Jacob
McCray-Dewey JHS, 201 N DEWEY ST   62294
    Terry C. Taake, prin.
Freeman ES, 201 STAUNTON RD   62294
    Marjorie Downey, prin.
Henning ES, 520 E HWY 40   62294
    William Hyten, prin.
Molden ES, 209 N DEWEY ST   62294
    William Hyten, prin.
Wakeland Center MS, 205 N DEWEY ST   62294
    Terry Taake, prin.

St. Pauls Lutheran ES
    112 N BORDER STREET   62294

Tunnel Hill, Johnson Co.
New Simpson Hill Consolidated SD 32
Sch. Sys. Enr. Code 2
Supt. – Dr. Terry Elms, P O BOX 142   62991
New Burnside Center MS, P O BOX 142   62991
    Robert Gorman, prin.
Tunnel Hill Center ES, P O BOX 142   62991
    Robert Gorman, prin.

Tuscola, Douglas Co., Pop. Code 5
Tuscola CUSD 301
Sch. Sys. Enr. Code 4
Supt. – James Voyles, 409 S PRAIRIE ST   61953
East Prairie JHS, 409 S PRAIRIE ST   61953
    William Sargent, prin.
North Ward ES, 400 E SALE ST   61953
    Darrell Sy, prin.

Ullin, Pulaski Co., Pop. Code 3
Century CUSD 100
Sch. Sys. Enr. Code 3
Supt. – Bob McIntosh
    RURAL ROUTE 01 BOX 41B   62992
Century JHS, RURAL ROUTE 01   62992
    Leon Shumaker, prin.
Other Schools – See Grand Chain

University Park, Will Co., Pop. Code 6
Crete-Monee CUSD 201U
Supt. – See Crete
Hickory ES, 1009 BLACKHAWK DR   60466
    Lorraine Watkins-Powers, prin.

Urbana, Champaign Co., Pop. Code 8
Urbana SD 116
Sch. Sys. Enr. Code 5
Supt. – Dr. Lee Grebner, P O BOX 3039   61801
King ES, 1008 FAIRVIEW AVE   61801
    David Adcock, prin.
Leal ES, 312 W OREGON ST   61801
    Richard Bodine, prin.

Paine ES, 1801 JAMES CHERRY DR   61801
    Richard Sturgeon, prin.
Prairie ES, 2102 E WASHINGTON ST   61801
    Dr. Gary Howrey, prin.
Washington ES, 1010 N BROADWAY AVE   61801
    Dr. Edward Cieniawski, prin.
Yankee Ridge ES, 2102 S ANDERSON ST   61801
    Mildred Ransom, prin.

Ursa, Adams Co., Pop. Code 2
Mendon CUSD 4
Supt. – See Mendon
Greenfield ES, RURAL ROUTE 01   62376
    Michael Herrington, prin.

Utica, La Salle Co.
Utica ESD 135
Sch. Sys. Enr. Code 2
Supt. – Fred Hoover, P O BOX 126   61373
ES, 248 W CANAL   61373 – Fred Hoover, prin.

Waltham CCSD 185
Sch. Sys. Enr. Code 2
Supt. – Edmund Wieczorek
    RURAL ROUTE 01   61373
Other Schools – See Ottawa

Valmeyer, Monroe Co., Pop. Code 3
Valmeyer CUSD 3
Sch. Sys. Enr. Code 2
Supt. – H. R. Baum, 603 W MAIN ST   62295
JHS, 603 W MAIN ST   62295
    Robert Heavner, prin.
ES, 603 W MAIN ST   62295 – H. Baum, prin.

Vandalia, Fayette Co., Pop. Code 6
Vandalia CUSD 203
Sch. Sys. Enr. Code 4
Supt. – Larry Bennett, 1109 N 8TH ST   62471
JHS, 8TH & FLETCHER STS   62471
    William Ladage, prin.
Jefferson ES, 1500 W JEFFERSON ST   62471
    Donald Holtcamp, prin.
Lincoln ES, 525 W LINCOLN ST   62471
    Rodney Deem, prin.
Washington ES, 301 S 8TH ST   62471
    Rodney Deem, prin.
Other Schools – See Shobonier

Van Orin, Bureau Co.
LaMoille CUSD 303
Supt. – See La Moille
ES   61374 – Dorothy Miller, prin.

Varna, Marshall Co., Pop. Code 2
Mid County CUSD 4
Sch. Sys. Enr. Code 3
Supt. – Arthur Urbanski, RURAL ROUTE 01   61375
Mid-County JHS, RURAL ROUTE 01   61375
    T. R. Bayler, prin.
ES, POST OFFICE   61375 – Rolland Marshall, prin.
Other Schools – See Lacon

Venedy, Washington Co.
West Washington Co. CUSD 10
Supt. – See Okawville
Johannisburg ES, P O BOX 45   62296
    Dennis Fancher, prin.

Venice, Madison Co., Pop. Code 5
Venice CUSD 3
Sch. Sys. Enr. Code 3
Supt. – Charles McCaskill
    700 BROADWAY   62090
ES, 700 BROADWAY   62090
    Seth Kirkpatrick, prin.

Vergennes, Jackson Co., Pop. Code 2
Elverado CUSD 196
Supt. – See Elkville
Elverado JHS, P O BOX 35   62994
    Dale Reach, prin.
ES, P O BOX 35   62994 – Dale Reach, prin.

Vernon Hills, Lake Co., Pop. Code 6
Hawthorn CCSD 73
Sch. Sys. Enr. Code 5
Supt. – Thomas Oakson
    201 HAWTHORN PARKWAY   60061
Hawthorn JHS
    201 HAWTHORN PARKWAY   60061
    Erwin Einhorn, prin.
Hawthorn IS, 810 ASPEN DR   60061
    Mick Hall, prin.
Hawthorn PS, 301 HAWTHORN PKY   60061
    Diane Betts, prin.
Hawthorn South ES, 430 ASPEN DR   60061
    Ruth Brockman, prin.
Other Schools – See Prairie View

Verona, Grundy Co., Pop. Code 2
Mazon-Verona-Kinsman CUSD 2
Supt. – See Mazon
ES, P O BOX 145   60479 – Gary Fechter, prin.

Versailles, Brown Co., Pop. Code 3
Brown CUSD 1
Supt. – See Mount Sterling
ES, P O BOX 79   62378 – (—), prin.

Victoria, Knox Co., Pop. Code 2
ROWVA CUSD 208
Supt. – See Oneida
ES, P O BOX 20   61485 – Donna Davis, prin.

Vienna, Johnson Co., Pop. Code 4
Vienna SD 55
Sch. Sys. Enr. Code 2
Supt. – D. Yandell, P O BOX 427   62995

ES, P O BOX 427   62995 – D. Ray Yandell, prin.

Villa Grove, Douglas Co., Pop. Code 5
Villa Grove CUSD 302
Sch. Sys. Enr. Code 3
Supt. – David Kuetemeyer
  700 N SYCAMORE ST   61956
JHS, 700 N SYCAMORE ST   61956
  Danny Powell, prin.
ES, 700 N SYCAMORE ST   61956
  Danny Powell, prin.

Villa Park, Du Page Co., Pop. Code 7
Salt Creek SD 48
Sch. Sys. Enr. Code 3
Supt. – John Belletini, 1110 S VILLA AVE   60181
Albright MS, 1110 S VILLA AVE   60181
  William E. Hermann, prin.
Swartz ES, 17W-160 16TH ST   60181
  John Carpenter, prin.
Other Schools – See Elmhurst

Villa Park SD 45
Sch. Sys. Enr. Code 5
Supt. – Barbara Devlin
  255 W VERMONT ST   60181
Jackson JHS, 301 W JACKSON ST   60181
  Donald Wegener, prin.
Jefferson JHS, 255 W VERMONT ST   60181
  David Vovpick, prin.
Ardmore ES, 225 S HARVARD AVE   60181
  Carol Hogfelt, prin.
North ES, 150 W SUNSET AVE   60181
  Dennis Gagnon, prin.
Other Schools – See Lombard

St. Alexander School, 136 S CORNELL AVE   60181

Viola, Mercer Co., Pop. Code 4
Sherrard CUSD 200
Supt. – See Matherville
Winola ES, P O BOX 347   61486
  Roger Birkhead, prin.

Virden, Macoupin Co., Pop. Code 5
Virden CUSD 4
Sch. Sys. Enr. Code 4
Supt. – James Kirbach, 231 W FORTUNE ST   62690
JHS, 231 W FORTUNE ST   62690
  David Bruna, prin.
ES, 231 W FORTUNE ST   62690 – John Hill, prin.

Virginia, Cass Co., Pop. Code 4
Virginia CUSD 64
Sch. Sys. Enr. Code 2
Supt. – Kenneth Cox, 651 S MORGAN ST   62691
JHS, 651 S MORGAN ST   62691
  Kenneth Cox, prin.
ES, 651 S MORGAN ST   62691
  Kenneth Cox, prin.

Wadsworth, Lake Co., Pop. Code 4
Millburn CCSD 24
Sch. Sys. Enr. Code 2
Supt. – Lee Smithey
  18550 MILLBURN ROAD   60083
Millburn C. C. ES, 18550 MILLBURN RD   60083
  Gary Cybul, prin.

St. Patrick School
  15020 WADSWORTH RD   60083

Walnut, Bureau Co., Pop. Code 4
Walnut CCSD 285
Sch. Sys. Enr. Code 2
Supt. – John Anderson, 323 S MAIN ST   61376
Walnut Community Consolidated ES
  323 S MAIN ST   61376 – John Anderson, prin.

Waltonville, Jefferson Co., Pop. Code 2
Waltonville CUSD 1
Sch. Sys. Enr. Code 2
Supt. – Jim Jenkins
  RURAL ROUTE 01 BOX 39   62894
ES   62894 – Don Neibel, prin.

Wapella, De Witt Co., Pop. Code 3
Wapella CUSD 5
Sch. Sys. Enr. Code 2
Supt. – W. Hedgcock, P O BOX 127   61777
JHS, P O BOX 127   61777 – Ricky Imig, prin.
ES, P O BOX 127   61777 – Charles Davenport, prin.

Warren, Jo Daviess Co., Pop. Code 4
Warren CUSD 205
Sch. Sys. Enr. Code 3
Supt. – Fred Sams, 109 MARY ST   61087
JHS, 311 WATER ST   61087 – James Nielsen, prin.
ES, 109 MARY ST   61087 – Roger Teuscher, prin.
Other Schools – See Apple River

Warrensburg, Macon Co., Pop. Code 4
Warrensburg-Latham CUSD 11
Sch. Sys. Enr. Code 4
Supt. – Ron Wisher, P O BOX 488   62573
Warrensburg-Latham MS, P O BOX 187   62573
  Craig Milligan, prin.
Warrensburg-Latham ES, P O BOX 187   62573
  Donald Swallow, prin.

Warrenville, Du Page Co., Pop. Code 6
Community Unit SD 200
Supt. – See Wheaton
Bower ES, 4 S 241 RIVER ROAD   60555
  Kevin Kane, prin.
Holmes ES, 3 S 241 WARREN AVE   60555
  Dr. Harold Street, prin.

St. Irene School, 3 S 601 WARREN AVE   60555

Warsaw, Hancock Co., Pop. Code 4
Warsaw CUSD 316
Sch. Sys. Enr. Code 3
Supt. – Dr. H. Borger, S 11TH ST   62379
ES, 220 UNDERWOOD ST   62379
  Jerry Baker, prin.

Wasco, Kane Co.
St. Charles CUSD 303
Supt. – See Saint Charles
ES, P O BOX 83   60183 – Robert Graham, prin.

Washburn, Woodford Co., Pop. Code 4
Lowpoint-Washburn CUSD 21
Sch. Sys. Enr. Code 3
Supt. – Richard Schuler
  508 E WALNUT ST   61570
Lowpoint-Washburn JHS
  508 E WALNUT ST   61570 – Bruce Williams, prin.
Lowpoint-Washburn ES, 701 N LYNN   61570
  Richard Schuler, prin.

Washington, Tazewell Co., Pop. Code 7
Central SD 51
Sch. Sys. Enr. Code 3
Supt. – Kenneth Holford, 307 EAGLE AVE   61571
Central ES, 307 EAGLE AVE   61571
  Kenneth Prater, prin.
Columbia ES, 314 SPRING CREEK ROAD   61571
  Kenneth Prater, prin.

District 50 Schools
Sch. Sys. Enr. Code 4
Supt. – James Funk, 304 E ALMOND DRIVE   61571
Beverly Manor JHS, SCHOOL ST   61571
  Gary Wynn, prin.
Beverly Manor ES, 100 SCHOOL ST   61571
  Ronald Carlock, prin.
Hensey ES, 304 E ALMOND DR   61571
  Lawrence Johnson, prin.

Pleasant View CSD 622
Sch. Sys. Enr. Code 1
Supt. – Georgine Austin
  RURAL ROUTE 02 BOX 34   61571
Pleasant View ES
  RURAL ROUTE 02 BOX 34   61571
  Mary Jo Parish, prin.

Washington SD 52
Sch. Sys. Enr. Code 1
Supt. – Ken Webb, 103 S SPRUCE ST   61571
ES, LINCOLN AND JACKSON   61571
  Kenneth Gisleson, prin.
ES, 105 S SPRUCE ST   61571
  Kenneth Webb, prin.

St. Patrick School, 100 HARVEY ST   61571

Wataga, Knox Co., Pop. Code 3
ROWVA CUSD 208
Supt. – See Oneida
ES, P O BOX 467   61488 – Laura Isele, prin.

Waterloo, Monroe Co., Pop. Code 5
Waterloo CUSD 5
Sch. Sys. Enr. Code 4
Supt. – Leo Hefner
  200 BELLEFONTAINE DRIVE   62298
JHS, 200 BELLEFONTAINE DRIVE   62298
  Edward Garden, prin.
Zahnow ES, 301 HAMACHER ST   62298
  Bill Saul, prin.

SS Peter & Paul School, 217 W 3RD ST   62298

Waterman, De Kalb Co., Pop. Code 3
Waterman CUSD 431
Sch. Sys. Enr. Code 2
Supt. – Charles McChesney, 425 S ELM ST   60556
JHS, 425 S ELM ST   60556
  Charles McChesney, prin.
ES, 220 N MAPLE   60556
  David Gudmunson, prin.

Watseka, Iroquois Co., Pop. Code 6
Iroquois Co. CUSD 9
Sch. Sys. Enr. Code 4
Supt. – Dr. Henry Boer, 109 S SECOND ST   60970
Raymond MS, W MULBERRY ST   60970
  Ron Schramm, prin.
Davis ES, 495 N FOURTH ST   60970
  John Dowling, prin.
Kendall ES, PORTER AVE   60970
  John Dowling, prin.
Other Schools – See Woodland

Wauconda, Lake Co., Pop. Code 6
Wauconda CUSD 118
Sch. Sys. Enr. Code 4
Supt. – Dr. Darrell Dick, 555 N MAIN ST   60084
JHS, 215 SLOCUM LAKE ROAD   60084
  Anthony Baade, prin.
Crown ES, 620 BONNER RD   60084
  Ed Hansen, prin.
Wauconda ES, 229 OSAGE ST   60084
  Craig Luxton, prin.

Transfiguration School, 316 W MILL ST   60084

Waukegan, Lake Co., Pop. Code 8
Gurnee SD 56
Supt. – See Gurnee

Spaulding ES, 3638 FLORIDA AVE   60087
  James Lienhardt, prin.
Waukegan CUSD 60
Sch. Sys. Enr. Code 7
Supt. – Dr. Jack Taylor
  1201 N SHERIDAN ROAD   60085
Benny JHS, 1401 MONTESANO ST   60087
  Robert Tabor, prin.
Jefferson JHS, 600 S LEWIS AVE   60085
  Danny Miller, prin.
Webster JHS, 930 NEW YORK ST   60085
  Robert Jones, prin.
Carman ES, 520 HELMHOLZ AVE   60085
  Isabelle Buckner, prin.
Clark ES, 601 BLANCHARD RD   60087
  Merle Holzman, prin.
Clearview ES, 1700 DELAWARE RD   60087
  Brian Ali, prin.
Cooke Magnet ES, 522 BELVIDERE RD   60085
  Bernice Gehrls, prin.
Glen Flora ES, 1110 CHESTNUT ST   60085
  Audrey Brown, prin.
Glenwood ES, 2808 TYLER AVE   60087
  Allan Mismash, prin.
Greenwood ES, 1919 NORTH AVE   60087
  Judith Lafferty, prin.
Hyde Park ES, 1525 HYDE PARK AVE   60085
  (—), prin.
Little Fort ES, 1775 BLANCHARD RD   60087
  John Pors, prin.
Lyon ES, 800 S ELMWOOD AVE   60085
  Olen Arrington Jr., prin.
McCall ES, 3215 N MCAREE RD   60087
  Charles Clement, prin.
North ES, 410 FRANKLIN ST   60085
  George Samuelian, prin.
Oakdale ES, 2230 N MCAREE RD   60087
  David Mackie, prin.
Washington ES, 110 S ORCHARD AVE   60085
  Barbara Prendergast, prin.
West ES, 1319 WASHINGTON ST   60085
  Neil Codell, prin.

Lake Shore Catholic Upper Grade
  510 10TH ST   60085
Immaculate Conception School
  510 GRAND AVE   60085
Lake Shore Catholic Academy-N-Camp
  515 S UTICA ST   60085
St. Anastasia School
  629 GLEN FLORA AVE   60085

Waverly, Morgan Co., Pop. Code 4
Waverly CUSD 6
Sch. Sys. Enr. Code 2
Supt. – Charles Rohn, 201 N MILLER ST   62692
ES, 201 N MILLER ST   62692
  John Marsaglia, prin.

Wayne, Du Page Co., Pop. Code 2
Elgin Unit SD 46
Supt. – See Elgin
ES, 5N443 SCHOOL ST   60184
  Dr. Sally Walker, prin.

Wayne City, Wayne Co., Pop. Code 4
Wayne City CUSD 100
Sch. Sys. Enr. Code 3
Supt. – Donald Sutton, P O BOX 476   62895
Oak Grove ES, RURAL ROUTE 01   62895
  Steve White, prin.
ES, P O BOX 536   62895 – Joe Draper, prin.
Other Schools – See Cisne

Weldon, De Witt Co., Pop. Code 3
Deland-Weldon CUSD 57
Supt. – See De Land
Deland-Weldon MS, RURAL ROUTE 01   61882
  John Baker, prin.
Deland-Weldon ES, RURAL ROUTE 01   61882
  John Baker, prin.

Wenona, Marshall Co., Pop. Code 4
Wenona CUSD 1
Sch. Sys. Enr. Code 2
Supt. – (—), P O BOX Z   61377
JHS, P O BOX 2   61377 – Lorin Stevens, prin.
ES, 102 W ELM BOX Z   61377 – Fred Sams, prin.

Westchester, Cook Co., Pop. Code 7
Westchester SD 92-5
Sch. Sys. Enr. Code 3
Supt. – Richard Crohn
  9981 CANTERBURY ST   60153
MS, 1620 NORFOLK AVE   60153 – L. Meyers, prin.
ES, 10900 CANTERBURY ST   60153
  A. Amato, prin.

West Chicago, Du Page Co., Pop. Code 7
Benjamin SD 25
Sch. Sys. Enr. Code 3
Supt. – Rob Sabitino
  28W250 SAINT CHARLES ROAD   60185
Benjamin ES, 28W-300 ST CHARLES RD   60185
  Richard Butterbaugh, prin.
Other Schools – See Carol Stream

McCauley SD 27
Sch. Sys. Enr. Code 1
Supt. – Daniel Olson
  ROOSEVELT ROAD ROUTE 38   60185
McAuley ES, ROOSEVELT RD RT 38   60185
  Daniel Olson, prin.

West Chicago SD 33
Sch. Sys. Enr. Code 4
Supt. – Dr. John E. Hennig
   312 E FOREST AVE 60185
JHS, 238 E HAZEL ST 60185 – David Burton, prin.
Gary ES, 130 E FOREST AVE 60185
   Linda Schielke, prin.
Indian Knoll ES, ON645 INDIAN KNOLL 60185
   Joseph Porto, prin.
Lincoln ES, 120 W GENEVA ST 60185
   Elaine Mcewan, prin.
Pioneer ES, 615 KENWOOD AVE 60185
   Phyllis O'Connell, prin.
Turner ES, 750 INGALTON AVE 60185
   George Capps, prin.

St. Mary School, 147 GARDEN ST 60185

Western Springs, Cook Co., Pop. Code 7
Western Springs SD 101
Sch. Sys. Enr. Code 4
Supt. – Dr. Donald E. Barnes
   4335 HOWARD AVE 60558
McClure JHS, 4225 WOLF ROAD 60558
   Dennis Lonstine, prin.
Field Park ES, 4335 HOWARD AVE 60558
   David Abhalter, prin.
Forest Hills ES, 5020 CENTRAL AVE 60558
   David Abhalter, prin.
Laidlaw ES, 4072 FOREST AVE 60558
   Catherine Nebel, prin.

St. John of the Cross School
   51ST ST AND WOLF RD 60558

Westfield, Clark Co., Pop. Code 3
Casey-Westfield CUSD 4C
Supt. – See Casey
ES, 410 S MADISON ST 62474 – John Shoot, prin.

West Frankfort, Franklin Co., Pop. Code 6
West Frankfort CUSD 168
Sch. Sys. Enr. Code 4
Supt. – Dr. Ronald Davis
   512 E SAINT LOUIS ST 62896
Central JHS, 1500 E 9TH ST 62896
   Gail Borton, prin.
Denning ES, 701 N COLUMBIA ST 62896
   Ronald Smith, prin.
Frankfort ES, P O BOX 434 62896
   Terry Warren, prin.

St. John Baptist School, 702 E POPLAR ST 62896

Westmont, Du Page Co., Pop. Code 7
Maercker SD 60
Supt. – See Clarendon Hills
Maercker MS, 5827 S CASS AVE 60559
   David Ivnik, prin.

Westmont CUSD 201
Sch. Sys. Enr. Code 4
Supt. – Dr. Donald Wold
   200 W LINDEN AVE 60559
JHS, 944 OAKWOOD DRIVE 60559
   Keith Becker, prin.
Manning ES, 200 N LINDEN ST 60559
   William Koubek, prin.
Miller ES, 125 W TRAUBE AVE 60559
   Ruth Hurley, prin.
South ES, 133 S GRANT ST 60559
   Marjorie Cich, prin.

Holy Trinity School, 25 E RICHMOND ST 60559
Our Lady of Peace School
   709 PLAINFIELD RD 60559

West Salem, Edwards Co., Pop. Code 4
Edwards Co. CUSD 1
Supt. – See Albion
ES, P O BOX 367 62476 – Linda Cavanaugh, prin.

Westville, Vermilion Co., Pop. Code 5
Westville CUSD 2
Sch. Sys. Enr. Code 4
Supt. – Larry Huber, 118 WASHINGTON ST 61883
JHS, 411 MOSES AVE 61883
   Dennis Watson, prin.
Giacoma ES, 200 S WALNUT ST 61883
   John Sabalaskey, prin.
Mc Millan MS, 2534 GEORGETOWN RD 61883
   James Cox, prin.

St. Mary's School, 215 N STATE ST 61883

Wheaton, Du Page Co., Pop. Code 8
Community Unit SD 200
Sch. Sys. Enr. Code 6
Supt. – Richard Short, 130 W PARK AVE 60187
Edison MS, 1125 S WHEATON AVE 60187
   Richard Rausch, prin.
Franklin MS, 211 E FRANKLIN ST 60187
   Dr. Robert Paolicchi, prin.
Wheaton-Warrenville MS
   1920 W WIESBROOK ROAD 60187
   Dr. Charles Miller, prin.
Emerson ES, 119 S WOODLAWN ST 60187
   Nona Stier, prin.
Hawthorne ES, 334 WAKEMAN AVE 60187
   Edward Dulaney, prin.
Lincoln ES, 630 DAWES AVE 60187
   David Schultz, prin.
Longfellow ES, 311 W SEMINARY AVE 60187
   Barbara Cobb, prin.
Lowell ES, 312 S PRESIDENT ST 60187
   Ben Heaton, prin.

Madison ES, 1620 MAYO AVE 60187
   Eugene Sikorski, prin.
Pleasant Hill ES, 26W212 GENEVA RD 60188
   Louise Lelivelt, prin.
Sandburg ES, 1345 JEWELL RD 60187
   Margaret Samples, prin.
Whittier ES, 218 W PARK AVE 60187
   Dr. Judith Crocker, prin.
Wiesbrook ES, 26W451 DURFEE RD 60187
   Dr. Mary Curley, prin.
Other Schools – See Warrenville

Glen Ellyn CCSD 89
Supt. – See Glen Ellyn
Briar Glen ES, 1800 BRIARCLIFFE BLVD 60187
   John Vanleirsburg, prin.

St. John Lutheran School
   125 E SEMINARY AVE 60187
St. Michael School, 314 W WILLOW 60187

Wheeler, Jasper Co., Pop. Code 2
Jasper Co. CUSD 1
Supt. – See Newton
West JHS, RURAL ROUTE 01 62479
   John Miller, prin.

Wheeling, Cook Co., Pop. Code 7
Wheeling CCSD 21
Sch. Sys. Enr. Code 6
Supt. – Bud Descarpentrie
   999 W DUNDEE ROAD 60089
Holmes JHS, 221 S WOLF ROAD 60090
   Avrum Poster, prin.
Field ES, 51 ST ARMANDS LN 60090
   Richard Klaslo, prin.
Tarkington ES, 310 SCOTT ST 60090
   Edward Searing, prin.
Twain ES, 515 E MERLE LN 60090
   Ralph Cook, prin.
Whitman ES, 133 WILLE AVE 60090
   Frances Voris, prin.
Other Schools – See Arlington Heights, Buffalo Grove,
   Mount Prospect

St. Joseph the Worker School
   171 W DUNDEE RD 60090

White Hall, Greene Co., Pop. Code 5
North Greene CUSD 3
Sch. Sys. Enr. Code 4
Supt. – James Whiteside
   528 N MAIN ST #SA 62092
ES, 119 E SHERMAN ST 62092
   Charles Stone, prin.
Other Schools – See Patterson, Roodhouse

White Heath, Piatt Co.
Monticello CUSD 25
Supt. – See Monticello
ES, P O BOX 300 61884 – Harold Kutz, prin.

Williamsfield, Knox Co., Pop. Code 3
Williamsfield CUSD 210
Sch. Sys. Enr. Code 2
Supt. – Dr. James H. Kutkat
   BOARD OF EDUC OFC 61489
MS, KENTUCKY AVE 61489 – John Bickell, prin.
ES, KENTUCKY AVE 61489
   Dr. James Kutkat, prin.

Williamsville, Sangamon Co., Pop. Code 3
Williamsville CUSD 15
Sch. Sys. Enr. Code 4
Supt. – Richard Hadfield, 500 S WALNUT 62693
JHS, 500 S WALNUT 62693 – Donald Hahn, prin.
MS, 500 S WALNUT 62693 – Donald Hahn, prin.
Other Schools – See Sherman

Willowbrook, Du Page Co., Pop. Code 5
Gower SD 62
Supt. – See Burr Ridge
Gower West ES
   7650 CLARENDON HILLS RD 60514
   Charles Moutvic, prin.

Willow Hill, Jasper Co., Pop. Code 2
Jasper Co. CUSD 1
Supt. – See Newton
ES, P O BOX 333 62480 – Sandra Ward, prin.

Willow Springs, Cook Co., Pop. Code 5
Willow Springs SD 108
Sch. Sys. Enr. Code 2
Supt. – Terrance Welke
   8345 ARCHER AVE 60480
ES, 8345 ARCHER AVE 60480
   William Eggebrecht, prin.

Wilmette, Cook Co., Pop. Code 8
Avoca SD 37
Sch. Sys. Enr. Code 2
Supt. – Dr. John Sloan
   2921 ILLINOIS ROAD 60091
Murphy MS, 2921 ILLINOIS RD 60091
   Larry Fleming, prin.
Other Schools – See Glenview

Wilmette SD 39
Sch. Sys. Enr. Code 4
Supt. – Dr. William Gussner
   615 LOCUST ROAD 60091
JHS, 620 LOCUST ROAD 60091
   William Melsheimer, prin.
Central ES, NINTH & CENTRAL 60091
   Paul Nilsen, prin.

Harper ES, DARTMOUTH & GREENWOOD 60091
   Barbara Savitt, prin.
McKenzie ES, CENTRAL & PRAIRIE 60091
   David Neustadt, prin.
Romona ES, 600 ROMONA RD 60091
   James Mattern, prin.

St. Francis Xavier School, 808 LINDEN AVE 60091

Wilmington, Will Co., Pop. Code 5
Wilmington CUSD 209U
Sch. Sys. Enr. Code 4
Supt. – Scott E. Flinn, 715 S JOLIET ST 60481
Stevens MS, 221 RYAN STREET 60481
   Stephen Willson, prin.
Booth Central ES
   201 N KANKAKEE STREET 60481
   Martha Nelson, prin.
Bruning ES, 1910 BRUNING DR 60481
   Paul Russert, prin.

St. Rose School, 626 S KANKAKEE ST 60481

Winchester, Scott Co., Pop. Code 4
Winchester CUSD 1
Sch. Sys. Enr. Code 3
Supt. – Rex Eddy, 25 S HILL ST 62694
ES, 283 S ELM ST 62694 – Tollie Evans, prin.

Windsor, Shelby Co., Pop. Code 4
Windsor CUSD 1
Sch. Sys. Enr. Code 2
Supt. – George Taubenheim
   1424 MINNESOTA AVE 61957
JHS, 1424 MINNESOTA AVE 61957
   Michael Weaver, prin.
ES, 808 WISCONSIN AVE 61957
   George Taubenheim, prin.

Winfield, Du Page Co., Pop. Code 5
Winfield SD 34
Sch. Sys. Enr. Code 2
Supt. – Robert T. Cobb, 0S150 PARK ST 60190
MS, 0S150 PARK ST 60190 – Joe McHaley, prin.
ES, 09150 WINFIELD RD 60190
   Joe McHaley, prin.

St. John Baptist School
   OS-259 CHURCH ST 60190

Winnebago, Winnebago Co., Pop. Code 4
Winnebago CUSD 323
Sch. Sys. Enr. Code 4
Supt. – Robert W. Colborn, P O BOX 98 61088
McNair MS, P O BOX 98 61088
   James Burns, prin.
Simon ES, P O BOX 517 61088 – (—), prin.
Other Schools – See Seward

Winnetka, Cook Co., Pop. Code 7
Winnetka SD 36
Sch. Sys. Enr. Code 4
Supt. – Dr. Donald S. Monroe
   1235 OAK ST 60093
Carleton-Washburne JHS
   515 HIBBARD ROAD 60093
   William Meuer, prin.
Crow Island ES, 1112 WILLOW RD 60093
   Elizabeth Hebert, prin.
Greeley ES, 275 FAIRVIEW AVE 60093
   Sandra Karaganis, prin.
Hubbard Woods ES, 1110 CHATFIELD RD 60093
   Richard Streedain, prin.

North Shore Country Day School
   310 GREEN BAY ROAD 60093
SS Faith Hope & Charity School
   180 RIDGE AVE 60093
Sacred Heart School, 1095 GAGE ST 60093
St. Philip the Apostle School
   1980 OLD WILLOW RD 60093

Winslow, Stephenson Co., Pop. Code 2
Lena-Winslow CUSD 202
Supt. – See Lena
ES, POST OFFICE 61089 – Debra Beving, prin.

Winthrop Harbor, Lake Co., Pop. Code 6
Winthrop Harbor SD 1
Sch. Sys. Enr. Code 3
Supt. – Dr. Kenneth Anton, 2309 9TH ST 60096
JHS, 2309 9TH ST 60096 – Richard Metzger, prin.
Spring Bluff ES, 628 COLLEGE AVE 60096
   Charles Shields Jr., prin.

Witt, Montgomery Co., Pop. Code 4
Witt Unit SD 66
Sch. Sys. Enr. Code 2
Supt. – Jerry Wesley, P O BOX 447 62094
JHS, P O BOX 447 62094 – Ernest Petray, prin.
MS, 220 N 3RD 62094 – Ernest Petray, prin.
ES, 220 N 3RD 62094 – Jerry Wesley, prin.

Wolf Lake, Union Co., Pop. Code 2
Shawnee CUSD 84
Sch. Sys. Enr. Code 3
Supt. – Wilmer Nall, P O BOX 128 62998
Shawnee JHS, P O BOX 128 62998
   John Phillippe, prin.
Other Schools – See Grand Tower, Mc Clure

Wonder Lake, McHenry Co.
Harrison SD 36
Sch. Sys. Enr. Code 2
Supt. – Charles Deany
   6809 MCCULLOM LAKE ROAD 60097

Harrison ES, 6809 MCCULLOM LAKE RD   60097
  Charles Deany, prin.

Wood Dale, Du Page Co., Pop. Code 7
Wood Dale SD 7
Sch. Sys. Enr. Code 4
Supt. – Michael Smoot
  543 N WOOD DALE ROAD   60191
JHS, 6N655 WOOD DALE ROAD   60191
  Lorenz Hartwig, prin.
Oakbrook ES, 170 S WOOD DALE RD   60191
  Frank Maisch, prin.
Westview ES, 200 N ADDISON RD   60191
  William Black, prin.

Holy Ghost School, 100 DIVISION ST   60191

Wood River, Madison Co., Pop. Code 7
Wood River-Hartford ESD 15
Sch. Sys. Enr. Code 3
Supt. – R. Whitlock, 501 E LORENA AVE   62095
Lewis-Clark JHS, 501 E LORENA AVE   62095
  Norman Bohnensteihl, prin.
Lewis-Clark ES, 501 E LORENA AVE   62095
  Richard Sanders, prin.
Other Schools – See Hartford

St. Bernard School, 4TH & ACTON STS   62095
St. Paul Lutheran School
  1327 VAUGHN RD   62095

Woodhull, Henry Co., Pop. Code 3
Alwood CUSD 225
Sch. Sys. Enr. Code 3
Supt. – H. Wayne French, P O BOX 428   61490
Other Schools – See Alpha

Woodland, Iroquois Co., Pop. Code 2
Iroquois Co. CUSD 9
Supt. – See Watseka
ES, P O BOX 188   60974 – Silas Light, prin.

Woodlawn, Jefferson Co., Pop. Code 2
Woodlawn CCSD 4
Sch. Sys. Enr. Code 2
Supt. – James Burnes, P O BOX 288   62898
ES, P O BOX 288   62898 – James Burnes, prin.

Woodridge, Du Page Co., Pop. Code 7
Woodridge SD 68
Sch. Sys. Enr. Code 2
Supt. – Edward Myracle
  2525 MITCHELL DR   60517
Jefferson JHS, 7200 JANES AVE   60517
  Richard Russell, prin.
Edgewood ES, 7900 WOODRIDGE DR   60517
  Sandra Duran, prin.
Goodrich ES, RT 53 & HOBSON ROAD   60517
  John Marshall, prin.
Meadowview ES, 2525 MITCHELL DR   60517
  Susan Goetzke, prin.
Sipley ES, 2811 CLARENDON LANE   60517
  Stanley Adolph, prin.
Willow Creek ES, 2901 JACKSON DR   60517
  Chris Gaylord, prin.
ES, LARCHWOOD & CRABTREE   60517
  Clement Campbell, prin.

Woodstock, McHenry Co., Pop. Code 7
Woodstock CUSD 200
Sch. Sys. Enr. Code 5
Supt. – Dr. Joseph Hentges
  501 W SOUTH ST   60098
Northwood JHS, 2121 N SEMINARY AVE   60098
  James Foley, prin.
Dean Street ES, 600 DEAN ST   60098
  Robert Bosman, prin.
Greenwood ES, 4618 GREENWOOD RD   60098
  William Schuette, prin.
Northwood ES, 2045 N SEMINARY AVE   60098
  Dr. Barbara Levandowski, prin.
Olson ES, 720 W JUDD ST   60098
  Gene Glover, prin.
Westwood ES, 14124 S STREET ROAD   60098
  Cheryl Rike, prin.

St. Mary School, 313 N TRYON ST   60098

Worth, Cook Co., Pop. Code 7
Alsip-Hazelgreen-Oaklawn SD 126
Sch. Sys. Enr. Code 3
Supt. – Dr. William D. Smith
  5201 W 115TH ST   60482
Hazelgreen ES, 11751 S LAWLER AVE   60482
  Donald Zickert, prin.
Other Schools – See Alsip

Worth SD 127
Sch. Sys. Enr. Code 3
Supt. – Dr. Rosemary Lucas
  111TH ST & OAK PARK   60482
JHS, 112TH & NEW ENGLAND   60482
  Joan Stoy, prin.
ES, 112TH ST & OAK PARK   60482
  Linda Whitaker, prin.
Worthwoods ES, 110TH & OKETO   60482
  Patricia Roach, prin.

Wyanet, Bureau Co., Pop. Code 4
Wyanet CCSD 126
Sch. Sys. Enr. Code 2
Supt. – Ralph Payne, FOURTH ST   61379
Wyanet Community Consolidated ES
  FOURTH ST   61379 – William Estes, prin.

Wyoming, Stark Co., Pop. Code 4
Valley CCSD 45
Sch. Sys. Enr. Code 1
Supt. – Dr. L. Fever
  RURAL ROUTE 01 BOX 78   61491
Valley ES, RURAL ROUTE 01 BOX 78   61491
  Dr. L. William Fever, prin.

Wyoming CCSD 27
Sch. Sys. Enr. Code 2
Supt. – William Wittmeyer
  300 VAN BUREN   61491
ES, 300 VAN BUREN   61491
  William Wittmeyer, prin.

Xenia, Clay Co., Pop. Code 2
Flora CUSD 35
Supt. – See Flora
ES, P O BOX 3   62899 – Mart Haycock, prin.

Yale, Jasper Co., Pop. Code 2
Jasper Co. CUSD 1
Supt. – See Newton
MS, P O BOX 8   62481 – Sandra Ward, prin.

Yates City, Knox Co., Pop. Code 3
Farmington Central CUSD 265
Supt. – See Trivoli
Yates ES, 100 AMES ST   61572
  Randy Welch, prin.

Yorkville, Kendall Co., Pop. Code 5
Yorkville CUSD 115
Sch. Sys. Enr. Code 4
Supt. – Dr. Jake Broncato, 106 ROUTE 126   60560
Circle Center JHS, 901 MILL ST   60560
  (—), prin.
Circle Center ES, 901 MILL ST   60560
  (—), prin.
Parkview MS, 201 W CENTER ST   60560
  Shirley Benson, prin.
ES, 201 W SOMONAUK ST   60560
  Doug Lia, prin.
Other Schools – See Bristol

Cross Evang. Lutheran School
  8535 ROUTE 47   60560

Zeigler, Franklin Co., Pop. Code 4
Zeigler-Royalton CUSD 188
Sch. Sys. Enr. Code 3
Supt. – George Connor, P O BOX 38   62999
Zeigler-Royalton JHS, P O BOX 87   62999
  (—), prin.
Ziegler-Royalton ES, P O BOX 87   62999
  (—), prin.

Zion, Lake Co., Pop. Code 7
Beach Park CCSD 3
Sch. Sys. Enr. Code 4
Supt. – Lewis Edwards
  11315 WADSWORTH ROAD   60099
Murphy JHS, 11315 WADSWORTH ROAD   60099
  Scott Murphy, prin.
Beach Park ES
  BEACH ROAD & LEWIS AVE   60099
  Donald Armstrong, prin.
Howe ES, 33RD & GREEN BAY ROAD   60099
  Cynthia Osgood, prin.
Newport ES, 41385 W 21ST ST   60099
  Douglas Edwards, prin.

Zion SD 6
Sch. Sys. Enr. Code 5
Supt. – Eugene Latz, 1716 27TH ST   60099
Central JHS, 1716 27TH ST   60099
  Jim Taylor, prin.
Beaulah Park ES, 1910 GILBOA AVE   60099
  Dallas Evans, prin.
East ES, 2913 ELIM AVE   60099
  Gerald Zoephel, prin.
Elmwood ES, 3025 EZRA AVE   60099
  Frank Walker, prin.
Shiloh Park ES, 2627 GABRIEL AVE   60099
  Roger Lemnus, prin.
West ES, 2412 JETHRO AVE   60099
  Robert Fink, prin.

Our Lady of Humility School
  10601 WADSWORTH RD   60099

INDIANA

STATE DEPARTMENT OF EDUCATION
100 N. Capitol St. #229, Indianapolis 46204
(317) 232-6610

Superintendent of Public Instruction	H. Dean Evans
Senior Officer Administration & Finanical Management	Steve Grimes
Senior Officer Community Relations & Special Populations	Marcella Taylor
Senior Officer Professional Development	Donald Moore
Senior Officer School Improvement & Performance	Phyllis Usher
Senior Officer School Assessment	William Strange

STATE BOARD OF EDUCATION
H. Dean Evans, *Chairperson*   229 State House, Indianapolis   46204

INDIANA HIGHER EDUCATION COMMISSION
Dr. Clyde Ingle, *Commissioner*   143 W. Market St., Indianapolis   46204

PUBLIC, PRIVATE, AND PAROCHIAL ELEMENTARY SCHOOLS

Acton, Marion Co.
Franklin Township Comm. SD
Supt. – See Indianapolis
ES, 8010 ACTON RD   46259 – Teresa Jackson, prin.

Akron, Fulton Co., Pop. Code 4
Tippecanoe Valley SD
Supt. – See Mentone
ES, P O BOX 8   46910 – Brett Boggs, prin.

Albany, Deleware Co., Pop. Code 5
Delaware Comm. SD
Supt. – See Muncie
ES, STATE AND CLEO STS   47320
   Steven Hall, prin.

Albion, Noble Co., Pop. Code 4
Central Noble Comm. SD
Sch. Sys. Enr. Code 4
Supt. – James Shrock, 200 E MAIN ST   46701
Central Noble MS, 401 E HIGHLAND ST   46701
   Joel Moore, prin.
ES, 202 COUGAR COURT   46701
   John Fitzpatrick, prin.
Other Schools – See Wolflake

Alexandria, Madison Co., Pop. Code 6
Alexandria Comm. SD
Sch. Sys. Enr. Code 5
Supt. – Bill Ringo, P O BOX 240   46001
MS, 308 W 11TH ST   46001 – Timothy Fihe, prin.
Cunningham ES
   RURAL ROUTE 04 BOX 56   46001
   James Wehsollek, prin.
Orestes ES, RURAL ROUTE 03 BOX 310-B   46001
   Richard Davis, prin.
Thurston ES, RURAL ROUTE 03 BOX 22   46001
   Robert McDaniel, prin.

St. Mary School, 818 W MADISON ST   46001

Amo, Hendricks Co., Pop. Code 2
Mill Creek Comm. SD
Supt. – See Clayton
Mill Creek West ES, P O BOX 128   46103
   Don Stinson, prin.

Anderson, Madison Co., Pop. Code 8
Anderson Comm. SD
Sch. Sys. Enr. Code 7
Supt. – Thomas Neat, 30 W 11TH ST   46016
East Side MS, 2300 LINDBERG ROAD   46012
   John Boyer, prin.
North Side MS, 1815 INDIANA AVE   46012
   John Dull, prin.
South Side MS, 101 W 29TH ST   46014
   Bruce King, prin.
College Corner ES
   RURAL ROUTE 02 BOX 425   46012
   Phillip Brown, prin.
Edgewood ES, 3525 WINDING WAY   46011
   Judith Goen, prin.
Forest Hills ES, 1600 HILLCREST AVE   46011
   Jerry Smith, prin.
Franklin ES, 2200 E 38TH ST   46013
   Nile Myers, prin.
Greenbriar ES, 2001 ASHBOURNE RD   46011
   Carolyn O'Neal, prin.
Killbuck ES, RURAL ROUTE 01 BOX 291A   46012
   Herb Pruett, prin.

Meadowbrook ES, 550 W 37TH ST   46013
   Robert Stinson, prin.
North Anderson ES, 112 E VINEYARD ST   46012
   William Bowman, prin.
Park Place ES, 802 E 5TH ST   46012
   Sylvia Lane, prin.
Robinson ES, 630 NICHOL AVE   46016
   J. Arms, prin.
Shadeland ES, 1525 W 14TH ST   46016
   Jodean Washington, prin.
Southview ES, 4500 MAIN ST   46013
   Paul Tunnell, prin.
Tenth Street ES, 3124 E 10TH ST   46012
   William Warmke, prin.
Twenty-Fifth Street ES, 3205 W 25TH ST   46011
   Darleen Westerfield, prin.
Twenty-Ninth Street ES, 119 W 29TH ST   46016
   Carolyn Johnson, prin.
Valley Grove ES
   RURAL ROUTE 07 BOX 248   46017
   Deborah Millikan, prin.
Westvale ES, 2200 W 22ND ST   46016
   Anna Lackey, prin.
Other Schools – See Chesterfield

West Central Comm. SD
Sch. Sys. Enr. Code 5
Supt. – Paul Davis
   RURAL ROUTE 09 BOX 126A   46011
Jackson Twp. ES
   RURAL ROUTE 06 BOX 428   46011
   Nancy Farley, prin.
Leach ES, RURAL ROUTE 05   46011
   Jon Trippeer, prin.
Other Schools – See Frankton, Lapel

St. Ambrose School, 2824 MORTON ST   46016
St. Mary's School, 1115 PEARL ST   46016

Andrews, Huntington Co., Pop. Code 4
Huntington Co. Comm. SD
Supt. – See Huntington
ES, P O BOX 428   46702 – Dan Rumple, prin.

Angola, Steuben Co., Pop. Code 6
Metro SD of Steuben Co.
Sch. Sys. Enr. Code 4
Supt. – Oren Skinner
   101 GROWTH PARKWAY   46703
MS, RURAL ROUTE 06 BOX 415   46703
   William Church, prin.
Carlin Park ES, 800 WILLIAMS ST   46703
   John Maurer, prin.
Hendry Park ES, 805 S WASHINGTON ST   46703
   June Fee, prin.
Other Schools – See Pleasant Lake

Arcadia, Hamilton Co., Pop. Code 4
Hamilton Heights SD
Sch. Sys. Enr. Code 4
Supt. – Wayne Kitch, P O BOX 469   46030
Hamilton Heights JHS
   RURAL ROUTE 02 BOX 12   46030
   Chris Walton, prin.
Hamilton Heights ES
   RURAL ROUTE 01 BOX 402A   46030
   Linda Castor, prin.

Arcola, Allen Co.
Northwest Allen Co. SD
Supt. – See Fort Wayne

ES, P O BOX 143   46704 – Raymond Hopper, prin.

Argos, Marshall Co., Pop. Code 4
Argos Comm. SD
Sch. Sys. Enr. Code 3
Supt. – William Rohl, 410 N 1ST ST   46501
Argos Community ES, 500 YEARICK ST   46501
   Ronald Leichty, prin.

Arlington, Rush Co.
Rushville Cons. SD
Supt. – See Rushville
ES, P O BOX 31   46104 – Dan Scholl, prin.

Ashley, De Kalb Co., Pop. Code 3
DeKalb Co. Central United SD
Supt. – See Auburn
ES, 500 S GONSER AVE   46705
   Bruce Hamilton, prin.

Attica, Fountain Co., Pop. Code 5
Attica Cons. SD
Sch. Sys. Enr. Code 4
Supt. – William Lake, 205 S COLLEGE ST   47918
ES, A500 E WASHINGTON   47918
   Harold Long, prin.

Atwood, Kosciusco Co.
Warsaw Comm. SD
Supt. – See Warsaw
ES, US 30 AND CO RD #128   46502
   Judy Mugg, prin.

Auburn, De Kalb Co., Pop. Code 6
DeKalb Co. Central United SD
Sch. Sys. Enr. Code 5
Supt. – James Watson, P O BOX 503   46706
East Auburn ES, 901 ECKHART AVE   46706
   Judy Brook, prin.
McIntosh ES, 800 S MAIN ST   46706
   David Wolff, prin.
McKenney-Harrison ES
   320 VAN AUKEN ST   46706 – Arthur Rahe, prin.
Other Schools – See Ashley, Corunna, Waterloo

La Porte Comm. SD
Supt. – See La Porte
McKenney-Harrison ES
   320 VAN AUKEN STREET   46706
   Arthur Rahe, prin.

Aurora, Dearborn Co., Pop. Code 5
South Dearborn Comm. SD
Sch. Sys. Enr. Code 5
Supt. – G. Platt, 408 GREEN BLVD   47001
MS, 404 GREEN BLVD   47001 – David Chalk, prin.
ES, 325 WASHINGTON ST   47001
   Arlin Hooker, prin.
Manchester ES, RURAL ROUTE 02   47001
   Ronald Jenks, prin.
Other Schools – See Dillsboro, Moores Hill

St. Mary School, 211 4TH ST   47001

Austin, Scott Co., Pop. Code 5
Scott Co. SD 1
Sch. Sys. Enr. Code 4
Supt. – Berley Goodin, P O BOX 9   47102
MS, 401 S HIGHWAY 31   47102 – Robert Fox, prin.
ES, 401 S HIGHWAY 31   47102
   Robert Anderson, prin.

Avilla, Noble Co., Pop. Code 4
East Noble SD
Supt. – See Kendallville
ES 46710 – William Hoppus, prin.

St. Mary's School, P O BOX 109   46710

Bainbridge, Putnam Co., Pop. Code 3
North Putnam Comm. SD
Sch. Sys. Enr. Code 4
Supt. – Thomas Rohr, P O BOX 169   46105
ES, P O BOX 239   46105 – Douglas Rose, prin.
Other Schools – See Roachdale, Russellville

Bargersville, Johnson Co., Pop. Code 4
Franklin Comm. SD
Supt. – See Franklin
Union ES, 3990 W DIVISION RD   46106
Robert Doles, prin.

Batesville, Ripley Co., Pop. Code 5
Batesville Comm. SD
Sch. Sys. Enr. Code 4
Supt. – Dr. James Freeland, P O BOX 121   47006
MS, 201 N MULBERRY ST   47006
Charles Birkholtz, prin.
Westwood ES, 707 COLUMBUS AVE   47006
Gayla Hegwood, prin.
Other Schools – See Oldenburg

St. Louis School, 17 E SAINT LOUIS PL   47006

Battle Ground, Tippecanoe Co., Pop. Code 3
Tippecanoe SD
Supt. – See Lafayette
MS   47920 – Harold May, prin.
ES   47920 – Ted Hunt, prin.

Bedford, Lawrence Co., Pop. Code 7
North Lawrence Comm. SD
Sch. Sys. Enr. Code 6
Supt. – James Peck, P O BOX 729   47421
JHS, 1501 N ST   47421 – Jim Pounds, prin.
Fayetteville ES
RURAL ROUTE 12 BOX 370   47421
Dale Underwood, prin.
Lincoln ES, 1014 F ST   47421
Richard Bohling, prin.
Needmore ES, RURAL ROUTE 14   47421
Ron Snapp, prin.
Parkview IS, 2024 16TH ST   47421
Philip Deckard, prin.
Parkview PS, 1701 S ST   47421 – Sari Little, prin.
Shawswick ES, RURAL ROUTE 13 BOX 592   47421
Michael Humphreys, prin.
Stalker ES, 1429 8TH ST   47421
Robert Stipp, prin.
Other Schools – See Heltonville, Oolitic, Springville

St. Vincent De Paul School, 1723 I ST   47421

Beech Grove, Marion Co., Pop. Code 7
Beech Grove CSD
Sch. Sys. Enr. Code 4
Supt. – Bradley Showalter, P O BOX 219   46107
MS, 1248 BUFFALO ST   46107
Samuel Merl, prin.
Central ES, 1000 MAIN ST   46107
Clayton Collins, prin.
South Grove MS, 851 S 9TH AVE   46107
Larry Williams, prin.

Holy Name School, 21 N 17TH AVE   46107

Berne, Adams Co., Pop. Code 5
South Adams SD
Sch. Sys. Enr. Code 4
Supt. – Doyle Lehman, 1000 PARKWAY ST   46711
ES, 605 W MAIN ST   46711 – Jerry Sprunger, prin.
Other Schools – See Geneva

Bicknell, Knox Co., Pop. Code 5
North Knox SD
Sch. Sys. Enr. Code 4
Supt. – Richard Althoff, RURAL ROUTE 01   47512
North Knox Central ES, 215 E 4TH ST   47512
Bradley Case, prin.
Other Schools – See Bruceville, Edwardsport

Birdseye, Dubois Co., Pop. Code 3
Southeast Dubois Co. SD
·Supt. – See Ferdinand
Pine Ridge ES, RURAL ROUTE 02 BOX 67   47513
Susan Brier, prin.

Bloomfield, Greene Co., Pop. Code 5
Bloomfield SD
Sch. Sys. Enr. Code 4
Supt. – Richard Richeson, P O BOX 226   47424
ES, P O BOX 226   47424 – Debra Desser, prin.

Eastern SD of Greene Co.
Sch. Sys. Enr. Code 4
Supt. – R. Dixon
RURAL ROUTE 04 BOX 623   47424
Eastern District ES
RURAL ROUTE 04 BOX 623   47424
Earlene Holland, prin.

Bloomington, Monroe Co., Pop. Code 8
Monroe Co. Comm. SD
Sch. Sys. Enr. Code 7
Supt. – Larry Rowedder
315 S NORTH DRIVE   47401
Batchelor MS, 900 W GORDON PIKE   47401
Dale Glenn, prin.

Tri-North MS, 3901 N KINSER PIKE   47401
Mike Walsh, prin.
Arlington Heights ES
800 W GOURLEY PIKE   47401
Tom Thompson, prin.
Binford MS, 600 S ROOSEVELT ST   47401
Betsy Walsh, prin.
Broadview ES, 705 W COOLIDGE DR   47401
Douglas Waltz, prin.
Childs ES, 2211 S HIGH ST   47401
Mary Sudbury, prin.
Clear Creek ES, 300 W CLEAR CREEK DR   47403
David Frye, prin.
Dyer ES, 1000 W 15TH ST   47404
William Hamilton, prin.
Fairview ES, 627 W 8TH ST   47404
Kathleen Rabold, prin.
Grandview ES, 3455 W STATE RD 45   47401
Janet Hohimer, prin.
Lakeview ES, 9090 STRAIN RIDGE RD   47401
Normand Horn, prin.
Marlin ES, 1655 E BETHEL LN   47408
Kathleen Kelley, prin.
Rogers ES, 2100 E 2ND ST   47401
David Bray, prin.
Templeton ES, 1400 S PARK AVE   47401
Jolinda Maiorino, prin.
University ES, 930 E STATE RD 46 BYP   47401
James Wade, prin.
Other Schools – See Unionville

St. Charles Borromeo School
2224 E 3RD ST   47401

Bluffton, Wells Co., Pop. Code 6
Metro SD of Bluffton-Harrison
Sch. Sys. Enr. Code 4
Supt. – Gary McMillen, 628 S BENNETT ST   46714
Bluffton-Harrison MS
1500 STOGDILL ROAD   46714 – Joe Ogden, prin.
Columbian ES, 1225 W WASHINGTON ST   46714
Thomas Gibson, prin.
East Side ES, 1100 E SPRING ST   46714
Edward Hanrahan, prin.

Northern Wells Comm. SD
Supt. – See Ossian
Lancaster Central ES, 3240E 300 NORTH   46714
Patty Felten, prin.

Boone Grove, Porter Co., Pop. Code 5
Porter Twp. SD
Supt. – See Hebron
ES, MAIN ST   46302 – Robert Theis, prin.

Boonville, Warrick Co., Pop. Code 6
Warrick Co. SD
Sch. Sys. Enr. Code 6
Supt. – Dr. James Gland, P O BOX 809   47601
JHS, 200 E GUM ST   47601 – Robert Lindley, prin.
Loge ES, 915 N 4TH ST   47601 – Keith Meyer, prin.
Oakdale ES, 802 S 8TH ST   47601
Jane Boultinghouse, prin.
Other Schools – See Chandler, Elberfeld, Lynnville,
Newburgh, Tennyson

Borden, Clark Co., Pop. Code 2
West Clark Comm. SD
Supt. – See Sellersburg
ES, P O BOX P   47106 – Wayne Hobbs, prin.
St. John ES, RURAL ROUTE 01   47106
Carol Messmer, prin.

Boswell, Benton Co., Pop. Code 3
Benton Comm. SD
Supt. – See Fowler
ES   47921 – Marilyn Mulligan, prin.

Bourbon, Marshall Co., Pop. Code 4
Triton SD
Sch. Sys. Enr. Code 4
Supt. – Rex Roth, 910 N HARRIS ST   46504
Triton ES, 806 N HARRIS ST   46504
Thomas Bowers, prin.

Brazil, Clay Co., Pop. Code 6
Clay Comm. SD
Supt. – See Knightsville
North Clay JHS, RURAL ROUTE 13   47834
Marvin Schopmeyer, prin.
East Side ES, 936 E NATIONAL AVE   47834
Denzil Adams, prin.
Forest Park ES, 800 S ALABAMA ST   47834
(—), prin.
Jackson Twp. ES
RURAL ROUTE 17 BOX 235   47834
Michael Mogan, prin.
Meridian Street ES, 410 N MERIDIAN ST   47834
Maurice Modesitt, prin.
Van Buren ES, RURAL ROUTE 13   47834
Annette Coakley, prin.

Bremen, Marshall Co., Pop. Code 5
Bremen Public SD
Sch. Sys. Enr. Code 4
Supt. – Larry Stinson, 512 W GRANT ST   46506
ES, 700 W SOUTH ST   46506
Lloyd Cabiness, prin.

St. Paul Lutheran School
605 SOUTH CENTER   46506

Bristol, Elkhart Co., Pop. Code 4
Elkhart Comm. SD
Supt. – See Elkhart
ES, 705 INDIANA ST   46507
Jerome Stajkowski, prin.

Middlebury Comm. SD
Supt. – See Middlebury
York ES, 13549 STATE RD 120   46507
Ronald Stump, prin.

Brook, Newton Co., Pop. Code 3
South Newton SD
Supt. – See Kentland
ES, 216 W WASHINGTON STREET   47922
Adrian Conrad, prin.

Brooklyn, Morgan Co., Pop. Code 3
Metro SD of Martinsville
Supt. – See Martinsville
ES, 251 N CHURCH ST   46111
Kenneth Addington, prin.

Brookston, White Co., Pop. Code 4
Frontier SD
Supt. – See Chalmers
Frontier ES, PRAIRIE & 8TH ST   47923
Mitchell Miller, prin.

Brookville, Franklin Co., Pop. Code 5
Franklin Co. Comm. SD
Sch. Sys. Enr. Code 5
Supt. – Donald Jobe, P O BOX 1   47012
JHS, P O BOX 1   47012 – Gary Frost, prin.
ES, RURAL ROUTE 04   47012
Ray Amrhein, prin.
Other Schools – See Cedar Grove, Laurel

Sunman-Dearborn Comm. SD
Supt. – See Sunman
Sunman-Dearborn MS
RURAL ROUTE 05 BOX 193-E   47012
Norman Griffith, prin.

St. Michael School, 145 WALLACE ST   47012

Brownsburg, Hendricks Co., Pop. Code 6
Brownsburg Comm. SD
Sch. Sys. Enr. Code 5
Supt. – Dr. Robert Herrold, 225 SCHOOL ST   46112
JHS, 320 STADIUM DRIVE   46112
Indalecio Ruiz, prin.
Brownsburg Harris ES, 725 S GREEN ST   46112
Philip Utterback, prin.
Lincoln ES, 310 S STADIUM DR   46112
Susan Grimes, prin.
White Lick ES, 1400 S ODELL ST   46112
Marjory Rickman, prin.

St. Malachy School, 330 N GREEN ST   46112

Brownstown, Jackson Co., Pop. Code 5
Brownstown Central Comm. SD
Sch. Sys. Enr. Code 4
Supt. – Robert Burton, 500 N ELM ST   47220
Brownstown Central MS
520 W WALNUT ST   47220 – Bill Day, prin.
ES, S JACKSON ST   47220 – Larry Raymer, prin.
Other Schools – See Freetown

Central Lutheran School, 415 N ELM ST   47220
Lutheran Central ES, 415 N ELM STREET   47220

Bruceville, Knox Co., Pop. Code 3
North Knox SD
Supt. – See Bicknell
North Knox West ES, RURAL ROUTE 01   47516
Roy Sloan, prin.

Bryant, Jay Co., Pop. Code 2
Jay SD
Supt. – See Portland
Bloomfield ES, RURAL ROUTE 02   47326
John Minch, prin.

Buffalo, White Co.
North White SD
Supt. – See Monon
ES, P O BOX 98   47925 – Tamarah Sherrard, prin.

Bunker Hill, Miami Co., Pop. Code 3
Maconaquah SD
Sch. Sys. Enr. Code 5
Supt. – Ronald Wilson
RURAL ROUTE 01 BOX 28-A   46914
Maconaquah MS, RURAL ROUTE 01   46914
Steven Walther, prin.
Maconaquah ES
RURAL ROUTE 01 BOX 28   46914
Dwight Stout, prin.
Other Schools – See Peru

Burket, Kosciusko Co., Pop. Code 2
Tippecanoe Valley SD
Supt. – See Mentone
ES, P O BOX 8   46508 – Oliver England, prin.

Burnettsville, White Co., Pop. Code 2
Twin Lakes SD
Supt. – See Monticello
Eastlawn ES, RURAL ROUTE 01   47926
Daryl Smith, prin.

Butler, De Kalb Co., Pop. Code 5
DeKalb Co. Eastern Comm. SD
Sch. Sys. Enr. Code 4
Supt. – Charles Hampel
300 W WASHINGTON ST   46721
ES, 503 E GREEN ST   46721 – Thomas Sekel, prin.
Other Schools – See Saint Joe

Cambridge City, Wayne Co., Pop. Code 4
Western Wayne SD
Sch. Sys. Enr. Code 4
Supt. – Lynn Sheets, P O BOX 109 47327
Central ES, 109 E MAIN ST 47327
David Gaddis, prin.
Other Schools – See Dublin, Milton, Pershing

Camby, Marion Co.
Mooresville Cons. SD
Supt. – See Mooresville
North Madison ES, 2732 HADLEY RD 46113
James Forester, prin.

Camden, Carroll Co., Pop. Code 3
Delphi Comm. SD
Supt. – See Delphi
ES, WATER ST 46917 – Terry Beach, prin.

Campbellsburg, Washington Co., Pop. Code 3
West Washington SD
Sch. Sys. Enr. Code 4
Supt. – Dan Roach, RURAL ROUTE 02 47108
West Washington ES, RURAL ROUTE 02 47108
James Newlin, prin.

Canaan, Jefferson Co.
Madison Cons. SD
Supt. – See Madison
ES, P O BOX 12 47224 – Alvin Sonner, prin.

Cannelton, Perry Co., Pop. Code 4
Cannelton CSD
Sch. Sys. Enr. Code 2
Supt. – Dale Lane, 3RD & TAYLOR STS 47520
ES, 6TH & TAYLOR STS 47520
William Bennett, prin.

Carlisle, Sullivan Co., Pop. Code 3
Southwest SD
Supt. – See Sullivan
ES, P O BOX 298 47838 – Don Slatton, prin.

Carmel, Hamilton Co., Pop. Code 7
Carmel-Clay SD
Sch. Sys. Enr. Code 6
Supt. – Robert Hartman, 5201 E 131ST ST 46032
ES, 101 4TH AVE SE 46032 – Rhonda Buzan, prin.
College Wood ES, 400 S GUILFORD RD 46032
James Moore, prin.
Forest Dale ES, 10721 W LAKESHORE DR 46032
William York, prin.
Mohawk Trails ES, 4242 E 126TH ST 46032
Don Setterlof, prin.
Woodbrook ES, 4311 E 116TH ST 46032
De Wayne Akin, prin.
Other Schools – See Indianapolis

Our Lady of Mt. Carmel School
1045 W 146TH ST 46032

Carthage, Rush Co., Pop. Code 3
Beard Memorial SD
Supt. – See Knightstown
ES, 1ST & HARRISON STS 46115
Donald Schlegel, prin.

Cayuga, Vermillion Co., Pop. Code 4
North Vermillion Comm. SD
Sch. Sys. Enr. Code 4
Supt. – P. James Renz
RURAL ROUTE 01 BOX 191 A 47928
ES 47928 – Michael Turner, prin.
Other Schools – See Newport, Perrysville

Cedar Grove, Franklin Co., Pop. Code 2
Franklin Co. Comm. SD
Supt. – See Brookville
Mt. Carmel ES
RURAL ROUTE 01 BOX 56A 47016
Debra Beiter, prin.

Cedar Lake, Lake Co., Pop. Code 6
Crown Point Comm. SD
Supt. – See Crown Point
MacArthur ES, 12900 FAIRBANKS ST 46303
Emert Graper, prin.

Hanover Comm. SD
Sch. Sys. Enr. Code 4
Supt. – See Robert Leturgez, P O BOX 645 46303
Ball ES, 13313 PARRISH AVE 46303
George Letz, prin.

Celestine, Dubois Co.
Northeast Dubois Co. SD
Supt. – See Dubois
ES 47521 – Sr. Dorothy Graf, prin.

Centerton, Morgan Co.
Metro SD of Martinsville
Supt. – See Martinsville
ES, HIGH ST 46116 – Joseph Summers, prin.

Centerville, Wayne Co., Pop. Code 4
Centerville-Abington Comm. SD
Sch. Sys. Enr. Code 4
Supt. – Don Kehoe, 115 W SOUTH ST 47330
JHS, 200-300 W SCHOOL ST 47330
Richard Bohlander, prin.
ES, 200-300 W SOUTH ST 47330
Ronald Helderman, prin.
Hamilton ES, ROUND BARN ROAD 47330
Donald McClurg, prin.

Central, Harrison Co.
South Harrison Comm. SD
Supt. – See Corydon
Heth-Washington ES 47110 – M. Moore, prin.

Chalmers, White Co., Pop. Code 3
Frontier SD
Sch. Sys. Enr. Code 3
Supt. – Norris Nierste, P O BOX 809 47929
Other Schools – See Brookston

Chandler, Warrick Co., Pop. Code 5
Warrick Co. SD
Supt. – See Boonville
ES, 491 S ILLINOIS ST 47610
Earl Pfettscher, prin.

Charlestown, Clark Co., Pop. Code 6
Greater Clark Co. SD
Supt. – See Jeffersonville
MS, 8804 HIGH JACKSON ROAD 47111
James Williams, prin.
Jennings MS, 603 MARKET ST 47111
Robert Stover, prin.
Pleasant Ridge ES, 601 MARKET ST 47111
Carolyn Saunders, prin.

St. Michael School, SAINT MICHAEL DR 47111

Charlottesville, Hancock Co., Pop. Code 2
Eastern Hancock Co. Comm. SD
Supt. – See Wilkinson
Eastern Hancock ES
COUNTY ROAD 1050E & 250N 46117
Terry Whitaker, prin.

Chesterfield, Madison Co., Pop. Code 5
Anderson Comm. SD
Supt. – See Anderson
ES, 17 ANDERSON RD 46017
L. Guenthensperger, prin.

Chesterton, Porter Co., Pop. Code 6
Duneland SD
Sch. Sys. Enr. Code 5
Supt. – Ken Payne, 700 W PORTER AVE 46304
Liberty MS, 50 W 900 N 46304 – Verne Ash, prin.
Westchester MS, 1050 S 5TH ST 46304
James Ton, prin.
Bailly ES, 800 S 5TH ST 46304
Narcine Shep, prin.
Brummit ES, 2500 INDIAN BOUNDRY RD 46304
Joe Bennett, prin.
Liberty ES, 50-1 WEST 900N 46304
William Neuffer, prin.
Other Schools – See Porter, Valparaiso

St. Patrick School, 640 N CALUMET RD 46304

Chrisney, Spencer Co., Pop. Code 3
North Spencer Co. SD
Supt. – See Dale
ES 47611 – Leroy Meyer, prin.

Churubusco, Whitley Co., Pop. Code 4
Smith-Green Comm. SD
Sch. Sys. Enr. Code 4
Supt. – Howard Hull, 200 W TULLEY ST 46723
ES, W TULLEY ST 46723
Randall Carpenter, prin.

Clarksville, Clark Co., Pop. Code 7
Clarksville Comm. SD
Sch. Sys. Enr. Code 4
Supt. – Bill Conley, 200 ETTELS LANE 47130
MS, 101 ETTELS LANE 47130 – J Pepper, prin.
Clark ES, 435 W STANSIFER AVE 47130
Dan Bullington, prin.
Greenacres ES, 700 N RANDOLPH AVE 47130
Ronald Decker, prin.

St. Anthony School
320 N SHERWOOD AVE 47130

Clay City, Clay Co., Pop. Code 3
Clay Comm. SD
Supt. – See Knightsville
ES, 601 LANKFORD ST 47841
Douglas Inman, prin.

Claypool, Kosciusko Co., Pop. Code 2
Warsaw Comm. SD
Supt. – See Warsaw
ES, RURAL ROUTE 02 BOX 1A 46510
Randy Polston, prin.

Clayton, Hendricks Co., Pop. Code 3
Mill Creek Comm. SD
Sch. Sys. Enr. Code 4
Supt. – A. Gold, P O BOX F 46118
Cascade JHS, P O BOX K 46118
Jack Livingston, prin.
Mill Creek East ES, P O BOX G 46118
Dr. Phillip Spears, prin.
Other Schools – See Amo

Clermont, Marion Co., Pop. Code 4
Metro SD of Wayne Twp.
Supt. – See Indianapolis
Robey ES, 8700 W 30TH ST 46234
Dr. Michael Barger, prin.

Clifford, Bartholomew Co., Pop. Code 2
Flat Rock-Hawcreek SD
Supt. – See Hope
Cross Cliff ES 47226 – Jerry Garrett, prin.

Clinton, Vermillion Co., Pop. Code 6
South Vermillion Comm. SD
Sch. Sys. Enr. Code 4
Supt. – Max Spaulding, 153 S 8TH ST 47842
South Vermillion MS, 358 MULBERRY ST 47842
Marie Spurr, prin.

Central ES, 205 S 8TH ST 47842
Donald Kemper, prin.
Pyle ES, RURAL ROUTE 01 47842
Douglas Orman, prin.
Van Duyn ES, RURAL ROUTE 03 47842
Jerry Shonk, prin.

Cloverdale, Putnam Co., Pop. Code 4
Cloverdale Comm. SD
Sch. Sys. Enr. Code 4
Supt. – John McKinney
RURAL ROUTE 03 BOX 1A 46120
ES, RURAL ROUTE 03 BOX 1A 46120
Leland McCammon, prin.

Columbia City, Whitley Co., Pop. Code 6
Columbia City SD
Sch. Sys. Enr. Code 3
Supt. – Ralph Bailey
400 N WHITLEY STREET 46725
Marshall MS, N WALNUT STREET 46725
Dan Mullett, prin.
Raber ES, E JACKSON STREET 46725
Dan Curless, prin.

Columbia Twp. SD
Sch. Sys. Enr. Code 2
Supt. – Joe Frederick, COURT HOUSE 46725
Columbia Township ES, RURAL ROUTE 01 46725
Allen Myers, prin.

Etna-Troy Twp. SD
Sch. Sys. Enr. Code 2
Supt. – Joe Frederick, COURT HOUSE 46725
Etna-Troy ES, RURAL ROUTE 06 46725
Tom Rethlake, prin.

Jefferson Twp. SD
Sch. Sys. Enr. Code 2
Supt. – Joe Frederick, COURT HOUSE 46725
Jefferson Center ES, RURAL ROUTE 05 46725
Steven Bloomfield, prin.

Thorncreek Twp. SD
Sch. Sys. Enr. Code 2
Supt. – Joe Frederick, COURT HOUSE 46725
Thorncreek Center ES, RURAL ROUTE 10 46725
Rebecca Barlow, prin.

Union Twp. SD
Sch. Sys. Enr. Code 2
Supt. – Joe Frederick, COURT HOUSE 46725
Union Township ES, RURAL ROUTE 09 46725
Robert Hoke, prin.

Washington Twp. SD
Sch. Sys. Enr. Code 2
Supt. – Joe Frederick, COURT HOUSE 46725
Washington Township ES
RURAL ROUTE 02 46725 – Robert Prout, prin.

Columbus, Bartholomew Co., Pop. Code 8
Bartholomew Cons. SD
Sch. Sys. Enr. Code 7
Supt. – Ralph Lieber, 2650 HOME AVE 47201
Central MS, 725 7TH ST 47201
Willis Hagan, prin.
Northside MS, 1400 27TH ST 47201
Gary McBride, prin.
Clifty Creek ES, 4625 E 50 N 47203
John Davis, prin.
Fodrea Community ES, 2775 ILLINOIS ST 47201
Dean Perry, prin.
Jefferson ES, 1209 SYCAMORE ST 47201
Sharon Wilson, prin.
Lincoln ES, 750 5TH ST 47201
Joel Metzler, prin.
Mt. Healthy ES
12150 SOUTH RURAL ROUTE 58 47201
Karen Garrity, prin.
Parkside ES, 1400 PARKSIDE DR 47203
Dr. Charles Dilk, prin.
Richards ES, 3311 FAIRLAWN DR 47203
Kevin Stockdell, prin.
Rockcreek ES, 13000 E 200 S 47203
Duane Horrall, prin.
Schmitt ES, 1057 27TH ST 47201
Sharon Owens, prin.
Smith ES, 4505 WAYCROSS DR 47203
Smith Snively, prin.
Southside ES, 1320 W 200 S 47201
Larry Harden, prin.
Other Schools – See Taylorsville

All Saints Catholic School, 1306 27TH ST 47201
St. Peter's Lutheran School, 819 5TH ST 47201
White Creek Lutheran School
16270 S 300 W 47201

Commiskey, Jennings Co.
Jennings Co. SD
Supt. – See North Vernon
Graham Creek ES, RURAL ROUTE 01 47227
Wayne Williams, prin.

Connersville, Fayette Co., Pop. Code 7
Fayette Co. SD
Sch. Sys. Enr. Code 6
Supt. – Gerald Knorr, 1401 SPARTAN DR 47331
Connersville North JHS
1900 N GRAND AVE 47331 – Henry Hilton, prin.
Alquina ES, RURAL ROUTE 04 47331
Charles Butler, prin.
Eastview ES, 401 S FOUNTAIN ST 47331
Coy Powell, prin.
Everton ES, RURAL ROUTE 05 47331
Thomas Whitaker, prin.

Fayette Central ES, RURAL ROUTE 02 47331
  Larry Gant, prin.
Frazee ES, 600 W 3RD ST 47331
  Martha Wiley, prin.
Grandview ES, 2659 N GRAND AVE 47331
  Robert Driggs, prin.
Maplewood ES, 1800 N EASTERN AVE 47331
  Ann Rose, prin.
Other Schools – See Glenwood

St. Gabriel School, 224 W 9TH ST 47331

Converse, Miami Co., Pop. Code 4
  Oak Hill United SD
  Sch. Sys. Enr. Code 4
  Supt. – William Carnes
    RURAL ROUTE 01 BOX 525 46919
  Oak Hill JHS, 7760 W DELPHI PIKE-27 46919
    Michael Costlow, prin.
  ES, P O BOX 486 46919 – Harold King, prin.
  Other Schools – See Swayzee, Sweetser

Cortland, Jackson Co.
  Seymour Comm. SD
  Supt. – See Seymour
  ES, P O BOX 8 47228 – John Kosco, prin.

Corunna, De Kalb Co., Pop. Code 2
  DeKalb Co. Central United SD
  Supt. – See Auburn
  Fairfield ES, 1291 COUNTY RD 12 46730
    Bruce Hamilton, prin.

Corydon, Harrison Co., Pop. Code 5
  South Harrison Comm. SD
  Sch. Sys. Enr. Code 5
  Supt. – Larry Carlson
    121 HIGH SCHOOL ROAD 47112
  MS, 602 E CHESTNUT ST 47112
    Ralph Baker, prin.
  ES, 125 BEECHMONT DR 47112
    Ronald Hostetler, prin.
  Other Schools – See Central, Elizabeth, New
    Middleton

St. Joseph School, 324 E HIGH ST 47112

Covington, Fountain Co., Pop. Code 5
  Covington Comm. SD
  Sch. Sys. Enr. Code 4
  Supt. – Nelson Miller, P O BOX 204 47932
  MS, 514 RAILROAD ST 47932 – John Lewis, prin.
  ES, P O BOX 194 47932 – Leroy Keeling, prin.

Crawfordsville, Montgomery Co., Pop. Code 7
  Crawfordsville Comm. SD
  Sch. Sys. Enr. Code 4
  Supt. – John Coomer, 1000 FAIRVIEW AVE 47933
  Tuttle MS, 612 ELM ST 47933 – Don Fine, prin.
  Beard ES, SPANN AVE & EAST COLLEGE 47933
    Janell Heidenreich, prin.
  Caleb ES, 808 W PIKE ST 47933
    Thomas Gourley, prin.
  Hoover ES, 1301 S ELM ST 47933
    Don Whitecotton, prin.
  Hose ES, 800 FAIRVIEW AVE 47933
    John Tidd, prin.
  Nicholson ES, 1010 LANE AVE 47933
    Thomas Gourley, prin.
  Wilson ES, 500 E JEFFERSON ST 47933
    Janell Heidenreich, prin.

  North Montgomery Comm. SD
  Supt. – See Linden
  Northridge MS, 25 W 575 N 47933
    Grenville Lefebvre, prin.
  Pleasant Hill ES
    RURAL ROUTE 04 BOX 291A 47933
    Randall Quimby, prin.
  Sommer ES, 3700 US 136 W 47933
    Jonathan Smith, prin.
  Sugar Creek ES
    RURAL ROUTE 05 BOX 108A 47933
    Ted Newell, prin.

  South Montgomery Comm. SD
  Supt. – See New Market
  Southmont JHS, RURAL ROUTE 02 47933
    Stephen House, prin.

Crothersville, Jackson Co., Pop. Code 4
  Crothersville Comm. SD
  Sch. Sys. Enr. Code 3
  Supt. – Dennis Brooks, 109 N PRESTON ST 47229
  ES, ELEMENTARY BLDG 47229
    Robert Spicer, prin.

Crown Point, Lake Co., Pop. Code 7
  Crown Point Comm. SD
  Sch. Sys. Enr. Code 5
  Supt. – Charles Skurka, 200 E NORTH ST 46307
  Taft JHS, 1000 S MAIN ST 46307
    David Sykes, prin.
  Ball ES, 720 W SUMMIT ST 46307
    Diana Smyser, prin.
  Eisenhower ES, 1450 S MAIN ST 46307
    Joan Orr, prin.
  Lake Street ES, 475 LAKE ST 46307
    William Bussel, prin.
  Robinson ES, WELLS & PETTIBONE 46307
    Ronald Bashia, prin.
  Whitfield ES, 13128 MONTGOMERY ST 46307
    Delos Keene, prin.
  Other Schools – See Cedar Lake

St. Mary School, 405 E JOLIET ST 46307

Trinity Lutheran School
  250 S INDIANA AVE 46307

Culver, Marshall Co., Pop. Code 4
  Culver Comm. SD
  Sch. Sys. Enr. Code 4
  Supt. – William Mills, 222 N OHIO ST 46511
  ES, 401 SCHOOL ST 46511 – Russell Hodges, prin.
  Other Schools – See Monterey

Dale, Spencer Co., Pop. Code 4
  North Spencer Co. SD
  Sch. Sys. Enr. Code 4
  Supt. – Thomas Brumett, P O BOX 316 47523
  Turnham Education ES
    DUNN AT LOCUST ST 47523
    Sharon Schaefer, prin.
  Other Schools – See Chrisney, Lamar, Saint Meinrad

Daleville, Delaware Co., Pop. Code 4
  Daleville Comm. SD
  Sch. Sys. Enr. Code 3
  Supt. – Robert Ferguson, P O BOX 525 47334
  ES, HIGH ST BOX 526 47334 – Tim Long, prin.

Danville, Hendricks Co., Pop. Code 5
  Danville Comm. SD
  Sch. Sys. Enr. Code 4
  Supt. – Bob Carnal, 400 URBAN ST 46122
  JHS, 49 N WAYNE ST 46122 – James Disney, prin.
  North ES, 398 URBAN ST 46122
    Kathryn Raasch, prin.
  South ES, 355 S WASHINGTON ST 46122
    Robert Boyd, prin.

Dayton, Tippecanoe Co.
  Tippecanoe SD
  Supt. – See Lafayette
  ES, P O BOX 187 47941 – Donald Timmons, prin.

Decatur, Adams Co., Pop. Code 6
  North Adams Comm. SD
  Sch. Sys. Enr. Code 4
  Supt. – Ken Springer, P O BOX 191 46733
  Bellmont JHS, 313 W JEFFERSON ST 46733
    Craig Anderson, prin.
  Monmouth ES, RURAL ROUTE 03 46733
    Kathleen Tunis, prin.
  Northwest ES, 1109 DAYTON ST 46733
    Neal Rich, prin.
  Southeast ES, 901 EVERHART DR 46733
    Gary Giessler, prin.

St. Joseph School, 127 N FOURTH ST 46733
St Peter-Immanuel School
  RURAL ROUTE 5 BOX 319 46733
Wyneken Memorial Lutheran School
  RURAL ROUTE 01 46733
Zion Lutheran School
  1022 W MONROE ST 46733

Decker, Knox Co., Pop. Code 2
  South Knox SD
  Supt. – See Monroe City
  ES, P O BOX 98 47524 – Alan Drew, prin.

Delphi, Carroll Co., Pop. Code 5
  Delphi Comm. SD
  Sch. Sys. Enr. Code 4
  Supt. – David Smith, 501 ARMORY ROAD 46923
  Delphi Community MS, 400 E MONROE ST 46923
    W. Jargstorf, prin.
  Hillcrest ES, VINE & WABASH 46923
    Steven Carroll, prin.
  Other Schools – See Camden

Demotte, Jasper Co., Pop. Code 5
  Kankakee Valley SD
  Supt. – See Wheatfield
  ES, P O BOX 340 46310 – Fred Rossmanith, prin.

DeMotte Christian School, P O BOX 430 46310

Denver, Miami Co., Pop. Code 3
  North Miami Comm. SD
  Sch. Sys. Enr. Code 4
  Supt. – Stephen Wise, P O BOX 218 46926
  North Miami ES
    RURAL ROUTE 01 BOX 138A 46926
    Donald Davis, prin.

Deputy, Jefferson Co.
  Madison Cons. SD
  Supt. – See Madison
  ES 47230 – Joyce Imel, prin.

Dillsboro, Dearborn Co., Pop. Code 4
  South Dearborn Comm. SD
  Supt. – See Aurora
  ES, W MAIN ST 47018 – Bill Lakes, prin.

Dublin, Wayne Co., Pop. Code 3
  Western Wayne SD
  Supt. – See Cambridge City
  ES 47335 – David Weston, prin.

Dubois, Dubois Co., Pop. Code 2
  Northeast Dubois Co. SD
  Sch. Sys. Enr. Code 4
  Supt. – Richard Kerby, P O BOX 158 47527
  MS, MAIN ST 47527 – Keith Wortinger, prin.
  ES, RURAL ROUTE 02 47527
    Sr. Mary Kinghorn, prin.
  Other Schools – See Celestine

Dugger, Sullivan Co., Pop. Code 4
  Northeast SD
  Supt. – See Hymera

ES, RURAL ROUTE 01 BOX 177 47848
  Jack Greenwood, prin.

Dunkirk, Jay Co., Pop. Code 5
  Jay SD
  Supt. – See Portland
  West Jay Co. JHS, 110 E HIGHLAND AVE 47336
    James Saunders, prin.
  Westlawn ES, 234 W PEARL ST 47336
    Wylie Sirk, prin.

Dupont, Jefferson Co., Pop. Code 2
  Madison Cons. SD
  Supt. – See Madison
  ES, P O BOX 400 47231 – James McDaniel, prin.

Dyer, Lake Co., Pop. Code 6
  Lake Central SD
  Supt. – See Saint John
  Kahler MS, 452 ELM ST 46311 – Jean Wease, prin.
  Bibich ES, 14600 81ST AVE 46311
    Anthony Arini, prin.
  Protsman ES, 1121 HARRISON AVE 46311
    Judith Beratis, prin.

St. Joseph School, 432 JOLIET ST 46311

East Chicago, Lake Co., Pop. Code 8
  East Chicago SD
  Sch. Sys. Enr. Code 6
  Supt. – Norman Comer
    210 E COLUMBUS DRIVE 46312
  Block JHS, 2700 CARDINAL DRIVE 46312
    Charles Carter, prin.
  West Side JHS, 4001 INDIANAPOLIS BLVD 46312
    Henry Gillis, prin.
  Field ES, 3551 BLOCK AVE 46312
    Kathryn Blachwell, prin.
  Franklin ES, 4215 ALDER ST 46312
    Rosemary Rucinski, prin.
  Gosch ES, 455 E 148TH ST 46312
    Maxine Cole, prin.
  Harrison ES, 4406 INDIANAPOLIS BLVD 46312
    Joseph Flores, prin.
  Lincoln ES, 2001 E 135TH ST 46312
    Wilma Vazquez, prin.
  McKinley ES, 4825 MAGOUN AVE 46312
    Raymond Halas, prin.
  Roxana Addition ES, 900 SHELL ST 46312
    Raymond Halas, prin.
  Washington ES, 1401 E 144TH ST 46312
    Eugene Mack, prin.

Holy Trinity School, 4742 CAREY ST 46312
Indiana Harbor Catholic School
  3916 PULASKI ST 46312
St. Mary's School, 816 W 144TH ST 46312
St. Stanislaus School
  4930 INDIANAPOLIS BLVD 46312

East Enterprise, Switzerland Co.
  Switzerland Co. SD
  Supt. – See Vevay
  Switzerland County ES, P O BOX 87 47019
    Roberta Cord, prin.

Eaton, Delaware Co., Pop. Code 4
  Delaware Comm. SD
  Supt. – See Muncie
  ES, NORTH EAST UNION ST 47338
    John Kelly, prin.

Edinburgh, Johnson Co., Pop. Code 5
  Edinburgh Comm. SD
  Sch. Sys. Enr. Code 4
  Supt. – Roberta Jackson, P O BOX 157 46124
  East Side ES, 810 E MAIN CROSS ST 46124
    James Gettinger, prin.

Edwardsport, Knox Co., Pop. Code 2
  North Knox SD
  Supt. – See Bicknell
  North Knox East ES 47528 – Rodney Perry, prin.

Elberfeld, Warrick Co., Pop. Code 3
  Warrick Co. SD
  Supt. – See Boonville
  ES, P O BOX 68 47613 – Vote Lindsey, prin.

Elizabeth, Harrison Co., Pop. Code 2
  South Harrison Comm. SD
  Supt. – See Corydon
  South Central ES, RURAL ROUTE 03 47117
    James Kendall, prin.

Elkhart, Elkhart Co., Pop. Code 8
  Baugo Comm. SD
  Sch. Sys. Enr. Code 4
  Supt. – Jerry Cook
    29125 COUNTY ROAD 22 46517
  Jimtown JHS, 58903 COUNTY ROAD 3 46517
    H. Thomas Hixon, prin.
  Holben ES, 30046 COUNTY RD 16 46516
    Robert Neilson, prin.
  Jimtown ES, 58901 COUNTY RD 3 46517
    Jerry Fawley, prin.

  Concord Comm. SD
  Sch. Sys. Enr. Code 5
  Supt. – Larry Shomber
    59040 MINUTEMAN WAY 46517
  Concord JHS, 24050 COUNTY ROAD 20 46517
    Roger Sweisberger, prin.
  Concord East Side ES
    57156 COUNTY RD 13 46516
    Frederick Miller, prin.

Concord Ox-Bow ES
23525 COUNTY RD 45 46516 – Kevin Caird, prin.
Concord South Side ES
23702 ARLENE AVE 46517 – Robert Frey, prin.
Concord West Side ES
230 W MISHAWAKA RD 46517
John Speicher, prin.

Elkhart Comm. SD
Sch. Sys. Enr. Code 7
Supt. – Frederick Bechtold
2720 CALIFORNIA ROAD 46514
Moran MS, 200 W LUSHER AVE 46517
Robert Ronk, prin.
North Side MS, 300 LAWRENCE 46514
G. Smith, prin.
West Side MS, 101 S NAPPANEE ST 46514
Vernon Paler, prin.
Beardsley ES, 1027 MCPHERSON ST 46514
Michael Ronzone, prin.
Beck ES, 818 MCDONALD ST 46516
Levar Johnson, prin.
Cleveland ES
53403 R-8 COUNTY ROAD 1 N 46514
Charles Walker, prin.
Daly ES, 1735 STRONG AVE 46514
Daniel Janicki, prin.
Eastwood ES
RURAL ROUTE 05 BOX 53215 46514
Delbert Detwiler, prin.
Feeser ES, 26665 COUNTY RD 4 46514
David Nicoson, prin.
Hawthorne ES, 501 W LUSHER AVE 46517
Bruce Klonowski, prin.
Monger ES, 1112 BISMARK AVE 46517
Robert Woods, prin.
Osolo ES, 24975 COUNTY ROAD 6E 46514
Yvonne Chapman, prin.
Pinewood ES, 23879 COUNTY RD 10 46514
Sara Boyland, prin.
Riverview ES, 2509 WOOD ST 46516
Grace Smith, prin.
Roosevelt ES, 215 E INDIANA AVE 46516
Irene Bohannon, prin.
Woodland ES, 54678 COUNTY RD 3 46514
Gary Stoltz, prin.
Other Schools – See Bristol

St. Thomas the Apostle School
1331 N MAIN ST 46514
St. Vincent De Paul School
1114 S MAIN ST 46516
Trinity Lutheran School
425 MASSACHUSETTS AVE 46514

Ellettsville, Monroe Co., Pop. Code 5
Richland-Bean Blossom Comm. SD
Sch. Sys. Enr. Code 5
Supt. – C. Ellis, EDGEWOOD DRIVE 47429
Edgewood JHS, P O BOX 277 47429
Phillip D. Rambo, prin.
ES, P O BOX 308 47429 – James Lundy, prin.
Other Schools – See Stinesville

Elnora, Daviess Co., Pop. Code 3
North Daviess Co. Comm. SD
Sch. Sys. Enr. Code 4
Supt. – Jess Harty, RURAL ROUTE 01 47529
ES, RURAL ROUTE 01 BOX 147X 47529
Loren Crane, prin.
Other Schools – See Odon, Plainville

Elwood, Madison Co., Pop. Code 7
Elwood Comm. SD
Sch. Sys. Enr. Code 4
Supt. – Richard Merritt
RURAL ROUTE 04 BOX 105 46036
MS, 1620 MAIN ST 46036 – Thomas Austin, prin.
Edgewood ES, 1600 N J ST 46036
Joe Barnett, prin.
Oakland ES, 2100 S P ST 46036
Robert Tippey, prin.

Madison-Grant United SD
Supt. – See Fairmount
Duckcreek-Boone ES, 1650 N 600 W 46036
Diana Williams, prin.

Eminence, Morgan Co., Pop. Code 2
Eminence Cons. SD
Sch. Sys. Enr. Code 2
Supt. – Ken Murray, P O BOX 105 46125
ES, HIGHWAY 42 N 46125 – Victoria Davis, prin.

English, Crawford Co., Pop. Code 3
Crawford Co. Comm. SD
Supt. – See Marengo
ES 47118 – Tom Doddridge, prin.

Evansville, Vanderburgh Co., Pop. Code 9
Evansville-Vanderburgh SD
Sch. Sys. Enr. Code 7
Supt. – Phil Schoffstall, 1 SE 9TH ST 47708
Evans MS, 837 TULIP AVE 47711
Donald Utley, prin.
Glenwood MS, 901 SWEETSER AVE 47713
Donald Marlow, prin.
Harwood MS, 3013 N FIRST AVE 47710
Robert Bain, prin.
Helfrich Park MS, 2603 W MARYLAND ST 47712
Mida Creekmur, prin.
McGary MS, 1535 JOYCE AVE 47715
William Miller, prin.
Oak Hill MS, 7700 OAK HILL ROAD 47711
Kenneth Wempe, prin.

Perry Heights MS, 5800 HOGUE ROAD 47712
Rob Kraft, prin.
Plaza Park MS, 7301 LINCOLN AVE 47715
Herbert Legrand, prin.
Thomkins MS, 1300 W MILL ROAD 47710
Robert Ahrens, prin.
Washington MS, 1801 WASHINGTON AVE 47714
Norman Van Winkle, prin.
Caze ES, 2013 S GREEN RIVER RD 47715
Dixie Christmas, prin.
Cedar Hall ES, 2100 N FULTON AVE 47710
Arnold Schmidt, prin.
Culver ES, 1301 JUDSON ST 47713
Norbert Woolley, prin.
Cynthia Heights ES
7225 CYNTHIANA ROAD 47712 – R. Ashby, prin.
Delaware ES, 700 N GARVIN ST 47711
Cateena Johnson, prin.
Dexter ES, 917 S DEXTER AVE 47714
Charles Kendall, prin.
Fairlawn ES, 2021 S ALVORD BLVD 47714
James Kerney, prin.
Harper ES, 21 S ALVORD BLVD 47714
Mattie Miller, prin.
Hebron ES, 4400 BELLEMEADE AVE 47715
H. McDonald, prin.
Highland ES, 6701 DARMSTADT RD 47710
Harold Gourley, prin.
Lincoln ES, 635 LINCOLN AVE 47713
Ronald Talley, prin.
Lodge ES, 2000 LODGE AVE 47714
Patricia Edwards, prin.
Roosa ES, 1230 E ILLINOIS ST 47711
E. Theriac, prin.
Scott ES, RURAL ROUTE 06 47711
Robert Forrester, prin.
Stockwell ES, 2501 N STOCKWELL RD 47715
Linda Danheiser, prin.
Stringtown ES, 4720 STRINGTOWN RD 47711
Martha Mays, prin.
Tekoppel ES, 111 N TEKOPPEL AVE 47712
Sandra Altheide, prin.
Vogel ES, 1500 OAK HILL RD 47711
Joy Yeager, prin.
Wertz ES, 1701 S RED BANK RD 47712
Patricia Stocks, prin.
West Terrace ES, 8000 W TERRACE DR 47712
Paul Farmer, prin.

Evansville Day School
3400 N GREEN RIVER ROAD 47715
Westside Catholic JHS
2031 W MICHIGAN ST 47712
Christ the King School
3101 BAYARD PARK DR 47714
Corpus Christi School, 5528 HOGUE RD 47712
Evansville Lutheran School
1000 W ILLINOIS ST 47710
Good Shepherd School
2301 N STOCKWELL RD 47715
Holy Redeemer School, 918 W MILL RD 47710
Holy Rosary School
1303 S GREEN RIVER RD 47715
Holy Spirit School, 1760 LODGE AVE 47714
Resurrection School
5301 NEW HARMONY RD 47712
St. Benedict School, 530 S HARLAN AVE 47714
St. Joseph School
RURAL ROUTE 04 BOX 469 47712
St. Theresa School, 700 HERNDON DR 47711
Trinity Lutheran School
1403 W BONNVIE NEW HRMY 47711
Westside Catholic IS
1620 GLENDALE AVE 47712
Westside Catholic PS, 2735 W FRANKLIN 47712

Fairbanks, Sullivan Co.
Northeast SD
Supt. – See Hymera
ES, RURAL ROUTE 01 47849
Mary Blackburn, prin.

Fairland, Shelby Co., Pop. Code 3
Northwestern Cons. SD
Sch. Sys. Enr. Code 4
Supt. – Ted Thompson
RURAL ROUTE 01 BOX 79Y 46126
Triton MS, P O BOX 219 46126
Robert McKinney, prin.
Triton ES, RURAL ROUTE 01 BOX 79Z 46126
Bert Miller, prin.

Fairmount, Grant Co., Pop. Code 5
Madison-Grant United SD
Sch. Sys. Enr. Code 4
Supt. – Robert Huff, 120 S MAIN ST 46928
Madison-Grant JHS, 11640 S 300 W 46928
Richard Hindman, prin.
Liberty ES, 8720 S 300 W 46928
Michael Rosen, prin.
Park ES, 500-600 S SYCAMORE 46928
Lora Spence, prin.
Other Schools – See Elwood, Summitville

Farmersburg, Sullivan Co., Pop. Code 4
Northeast SD
Supt. – See Hymera
ES, P O BOX A 47850 – Ronald Kamman, prin.

Ferdinand, Dubois Co., Pop. Code 4
Southeast Dubois Co. SD
Sch. Sys. Enr. Code 4
Supt. – Ronald Etienne, 244 W 13TH ST 47532
ES, RURAL ROUTE 03 BOX 375 47532
Lee Begle, prin.

Other Schools – See Birdseye, Saint Anthony

Fillmore, Putnam Co.
South Putnam Comm. SD
Supt. – See Greencastle
ES, P O BOX 125 46128 – Daniel Puckett, prin.

Fishers, Hamilton Co., Pop. Code 4
Hamilton Southeastern SD
Supt. – See Noblesville
ES, P O BOX 216 46038 – Randall Schoeff, prin.

Flora, Carroll Co., Pop. Code 4
Carroll Cons. SD
Sch. Sys. Enr. Code 4
Supt. – Marlin Creasy, 2 S 3RD ST 46929
Carroll ES, RURAL ROUTE 01 BOX 18 46929
Mary Snyder, prin.

Floyds Knobs, Floyd Co.
New Albany-Floyd Co. Cons. SD
Supt. – See New Albany
Lafayette ES, RURAL ROUTE 04 BOX 69 47119
Glenn Barnett, prin.
St. Mary of the Knobs ES
RURAL ROUTE 01 47119 – James Gohmann, prin.

Fort Branch, Gibson Co., Pop. Code 5
South Gibson SD
Sch. Sys. Enr. Code 4
Supt. – Michael Green, 204 W VINE ST 47648
Ft. Branch Community ES
800 S HILLCREST ST 47648
Richard Harder, prin.
Other Schools – See Haubstadt, Owensville

Holy Cross School, 202 S CHURCH ST 47648

Fortville, Hancock Co., Pop. Code 5
Mt. Vernon Community SD
Sch. Sys. Enr. Code 4
Supt. – Larry Yazel
RURAL ROUTE 01 BOX 284C 46040
Mt. Vernon MS
RURAL ROUTE 01 BOX 284C 46040
David Heller, prin.
Mt. Vernon ES
RURAL ROUTE 01 BOX 284E 46040
Jack McKinney, prin.
Other Schools – See Greenfield

Fort Wayne, Allen Co., Pop. Code 9
East Allen Co. SD
Supt. – See New Haven
Village Woods MS
2700 E MAPLEGROVE AVE 46806
Steven Stults, prin.
Southwick ES, 6500 WAYNE TRCE 46816
Daniel Spangler, prin.
Village ES, 4625 WERLING DR 46806
Audrey Sharpe, prin.

Fort Wayne Comm. SD
Sch. Sys. Enr. Code 8
Supt. – Bill Anthis, 1230 S CLINTON ST 46802
Blackhawk MS, 7200 E STATE BLVD 46815
Margaret Katter, prin.
Geyer MS, 420 E PAULDING ROAD 46816
Charles Hoffman, prin.
Jefferson MS, 5303 WHEELOCK ROAD 46815
Edward Innis, prin.
Kekionga MS, 2929 ENGLE ROAD 46809
Larry Johnson, prin.
Lakeside MS, 2100 LAKE AVE 46805
James Tallman, prin.
Lane MS, 4901 VANCE AVE 46815
Harry Riggs, prin.
Memorial Park MS, 2200 MAUMEE AVE 46803
Nick Karanovich, prin.
Miami MS, 8100 AMHERST DRIVE 46819
Charles Green, prin.
Northwood MS
1201 E WASHINGTON CTR ROAD 46825
Thomas Williams, prin.
Portage MS, 3521 TAYLOR ST 46802
Kenneth Howe, prin.
Shawnee MS, 1000 E COOK ROAD 46825
Thomas Duff, prin.
Abbett ES, 4325 SMITH ST 46806
Cornelia Shideler, prin.
Adams ES, 3000 NEW HAVEN AVE 46803
Joseph Pitzer, Jr., prin.
Arlington ES, 8118 SAINT JOE CENTER RD 46835
Marian Stover, prin.
Bloomingdale ES, 1300 ORCHARD ST 46808
Albert Bohnstedt, prin.
Brentwood ES, 3710 STAFFORD DR 46805
Robert Marshall, prin.
Bunche ES, 1111 GREENE ST 46803
Oscar Underwood, prin.
Croninger ES, 6700 TRIER RD 46815
John Steiner, prin.
Fairfield ES, 2825 FAIRFIELD AVE 46807
Darrel Schierling, prin.
Forest Park ES, 2004 ALABAMA AVE 46805
Ronald Wambach, prin.
Franke Park ES, 828 MILDRED AVE 46808
Jean Linville, prin.
Glenwood Park ES, 4501 VANCE AVE 46815
Ilene Hardisty, prin.
Haley ES, 2201 MAPLECREST RD 46815
Jerry White, prin.
Harris ES, 4501 THORNGATE DR 46835
Ralph Anderson, prin.
Harrison Hill ES, 339 N CORNELL CIR 46807
Roger Eichenauer, prin.

Holland ES, 7000 RED HAW DR 46825
  J. Michael Caywood, prin.
Indian Village ES, 3835 WENONAH LN 46809
  William Schroeder, prin.
Irwin ES, 3501 S ANTHONY BLVD 46806
  Mary Lowery, prin.
Lincoln ES, 1001 E COOK RD 46825
  Thomas Cook, prin.
Lindley ES, 2201 ARDMORE AVE 46802
  Thomas Smith, prin.
Maplewood ES, 2200 MAPLEWOOD RD 46819
  Arthur Myers, prin.
Nebraska ES, 1525 BOONE ST 46808
  Eugene Bruns, prin.
Northcrest ES, 5301 ARCHWOOD LN 46825
  Robert Connor, prin.
Pleasant Center ES
  2323 W PLEASANT CENTER RD 46819
  Sandra Shumaker, prin.
Price ES, 1901 W STATE BLVD 46808
  Donald Boness, prin.
Shambaugh ES, 5320 REBECCA AVE 46815
  Jerry Petrie, prin.
South Wayne ES, 810 COTTAGE AVE 46807
  Raymond Beights, prin.
Southern Heights ES, 950 E FAIRFAX AVE 46806
  Sharon Mukes, prin.
St. Joseph Central ES
  6341 SAINT JOE CENTER RD 46835
  Robert Stebbe, prin.
Study ES, 2414 BROOKLYN AVE 46802
  Charles Culp, prin.
Ward ES, 3501 WARSAW ST 46806
  Larry Duhamell, prin.
Washington Center ES
  1936 W WALLEN RD 46818
  Stephan Matthias, prin.
Washington ES
  1015 W WASHINGTON BLVD 46802
  W. Nathan Spicer, prin.
Waynedale ES, 7201 ELZEY ST 46809
  John Johnson, prin.
Weisser Park ES, 902 COLERICK ST 46806
  Steven Bollier, prin.
Young MS, 1026 E PONTIAC ST 46803
  Theodore Davis, prin.

Metro SD of Southwest Allen Co.
Sch. Sys. Enr. Code 5
Supt. – Dave Hales
  4510 HOMESTEAD ROAD 46804
Woodside MS, 4312 HOMESTEAD ROAD 46804
  Terry Hippensteel, prin.
Aboite MS, 5120 HOMESTEAD RD 46804
  John Flora, prin.
Haverhill ES, 4725 WEATHERSIDE RUN 46804
  James Joros, prin.
Indian Meadows ES
  4810 HOMESTEAD RD 46804 – Charles Hill, prin.
Other Schools – See Roanoke

Northwest Allen Co. SD
Sch. Sys. Enr. Code 4
Supt. – Pat Mark
  13119 COLDWATER ROAD 46825
Perry Hill ES, 13121 COLDWATER RD 46845
  Richard Vorick, prin.
Other Schools – See Arcola, Huntertown

Fort Wayne Christian School
  P O BOX 11120 46855
Bethlehem Suburb Lutheran School
  6318 W CALIFORNIA RD 46818
Bethlehem Trinity Lutheran School
  3705 S ANTHONY BLVD 46806
Concordia Lutheran Lower School
  4245 LAKE AVE 46815
Emmanuel St. Michael Lutheran School
  1123 UNION ST 46802
Emmaus Lutheran School
  2320 BROADWAY 46807
Holy Cross Lutheran School
  3425 CRESCENT AVE 46805
Precious Blood School
  1529 BARTHOLD ST 46808
Queen of Angels School
  1600 W STATE BLVD 46808
Sacred Heart School, 4643 GAYWOOD DR 46806
St. Charles Borromeo School
  3700 REED RD 46815
St. Henry School, 3029 E PAULDING RD 46816
St. John the Baptist School
  4500 FAIRFIELD AVE 46807
St. Joseph Hessen Cassel School
  11521 OLD US 27 S 46816
St. Joseph School, 2211 BROOKLYN AVE 46802
St. Jude School, 2110 PEMBERTON DR 46805
St. Patrick School, 220 W BUTLER ST 46802
St. Paul Lutheran School, 1125 BARR ST 46802
St. Peter Lutheran School
  7810 MAYSVILLE RD 46815
St. Therese School
  2222 LOWER HUNTINGTON RD 46819
St. Vincent De Paul School
  8753 AUBURN RD 46825
Trinity Lutheran School
  1636 SAINT MARYS AVE 46808
Unity Lutheran School
  5401 S CALHOUN ST 46807
Zion Lutheran School, 2313 HANNA ST 46803

Fountain City, Wayne Co., Pop. Code 3
Northeastern Wayne SD
Sch. Sys. Enr. Code 4
Supt. – Merle Bryan, P O BOX 406 47341
Northeastern ES
  RURAL ROUTE 01 BOX 23A 47341
  Jeanne Hoffman, prin.

Fowler, Benton Co., Pop. Code 4
Benton Comm. SD
Sch. Sys. Enr. Code 4
Supt. – Glenn Krueger, P O BOX 512 47944
ES, 301 E 2ND ST 47944 – Rex Russell, prin.
Other Schools – See Boswell, Otterbein, Oxford

Sacred Heart School
  605 N WASHINGTON AVE 47944

Francesville, Pulaski Co., Pop. Code 3
West Central SD
Sch. Sys. Enr. Code 3
Supt. – Roger Dickinson
  117 E MONTGOMERY ST 47946
West Central ES
  RURAL ROUTE 02 BOX 15E 47946
  Nancy White, prin.

Francisco, Gibson Co., Pop. Code 3
East Gibson SD
Supt. – See Oakland City
ES 47649 – Bart McCandless, prin.

Frankfort, Clinton Co., Pop. Code 7
Clinton Prairie SD
Sch. Sys. Enr. Code 4
Supt. – R. Spencer
  RURAL ROUTE 06 BOX 75 46041
Clinton Prairie ES
  RURAL ROUTE 05 BOX 307A 46041
  Thomas Borges, prin.

Frankfort Comm. SD
Sch. Sys. Enr. Code 5
Supt. – R. Ayres, 50 S MAISH ROAD 46041
MS, 329 N MAISH RD 46041 – Jim Platt, prin.
Kyger ES, 300 S 3RD ST 46041
  Nancy Walker, prin.
Lincoln ES, 751 GENTRY ST 46041
  Richard Gibson, prin.
Riley ES, 303 S WILLIAMS ST 46041
  Harry Moore, prin.
South Side ES, 1007 ALHAMBRA AVE 46041
  Glenda Frey, prin.
Woodside ES, 1100 W GREEN ST 46041
  Jerry Martin, prin.

Franklin, Johnson Co., Pop. Code 7
Clark-Pleasant Comm. SD
Supt. – See Whiteland
Clark ES, RURAL ROUTE 02 46131
  Anne West, prin.

Franklin Comm. SD
Sch. Sys. Enr. Code 5
Supt. – Sterling Haltom
  998 GRIZZLY CUB DRIVE 46131
Custer Baker MS, 101 W STATE ROAD 44 46131
  David Sever, prin.
Hopewell ES, RURAL ROUTE 01 46131
  Joyce Morris, prin.
Needham ES, RURAL ROUTE 04 46131
  Delbert Cragen, prin.
Northwood ES, 965 GRIZZLY CUB DR 46131
  Ray Jones, prin.
Webb ES, 1400 WEBB CT 46131
  Max Fitzpatrick, prin.
Other Schools – See Bargersville

Frankton, Madison Co., Pop. Code 4
West Central Comm. SD
Supt. – See Anderson
ES, 405 SIGLER ST 46044 – Linda Fox, prin.

Freetown, Jackson Co.
Brownstown Central Comm. SD
Supt. – See Brownstown
ES, COLUMBUS ROAD AND UN ST 47239
  Sidney Zabel, prin.

Fremont, Steuben Co., Pop. Code 4
Fremont Comm. SD
Sch. Sys. Enr. Code 3
Supt. – Barry Worl, P O BOX 665 46737
ES, P O BOX 625 46737 – Steven Cobb, prin.

French Lick, Orange Co., Pop. Code 4
Springs Valley Comm. SD
Sch. Sys. Enr. Code 3
Supt. – Dennis Weikert
  101 LARRY BIRD BLVD 47432
Springs Valley ES, 101 LARRY BIRD BLVD 47432
  James Cassidy, prin.

Fulton, Fulton Co., Pop. Code 2
Caston SD
Sch. Sys. Enr. Code 3
Supt. – David McKee, P O BOX 8 46931
Caston ES, P O BOX 128 46931
  Russell Phillips, prin.

Galveston, Cass Co., Pop. Code 4
Southeastern SD
Supt. – See Walton
ES, 401 S MAPLE ST 46932 – Mark Barker, prin.

Garrett, De Kalb Co., Pop. Code 5
Garrett-Keyser-Butler Comm. SD
Sch. Sys. Enr. Code 4
Supt. – Alan Middleton
  801 E HOUSTON ST 46738
Ober ES, 801 E HOUSTON ST 46738
  James Nixon, prin.

St. Joseph School, 301 W HOUSTON ST 46738

Gary, Lake Co., Pop. Code 9
Gary Comm. SD
Sch. Sys. Enr. Code 8
Supt. – Betty Mason, 620 E 10TH PLACE 46402
Bailly MS, 4621 GEORGIA ST 46409
  Van Hambrick, prin.
Beckman MS, 1430 W 23RD AVE 46407
  Donald Staten, prin.
Dunbar-Pulaski MS, 1867 GEORGIA ST 46407
  Eugenia Sacopulos, prin.
Edison MS, 5TH AVE & BURR ST 46406
  (—), prin.
Kennedy-King MS, 301 N PARKE ST 46403
  Joseph Winfrey, prin.
Tolleston MS, 2700 W 19TH AVE 46404
  Howard King, prin.
Aetna ES, 1327 ARIZONA ST 46403
  Maggie Carey, prin.
Ambridge ES, 370 RUTLEDGE ST 46404
  John Hill, prin.
Banneker ES, 1912 W 23RD AVE 46404
  Sylvia James, prin.
Bethune ES, 2367 E 21ST AVE 46407
  Sarah Givens, prin.
Beveridge ES, 1234 CLEVELAND ST 46404
  E. Albury, prin.
Brunswick ES, 5701 W 7TH AVE 46406
  Florine Gray, prin.
Carver ES, 2535 VIRGINIA ST 46407
  Willie Cook, prin.
Chase ES, 711 CHASE ST 46404
  Celeste Foster, prin.
Douglass ES, 2700 JACKSON ST 46407
  Archie Williams, prin.
Drew ES, 2065 MISSISSIPPI ST 46407
  Florine Lovelace, prin.
Duncan ES, 1110 W 21ST AVE 46407
  Thomas Kelley, prin.
Franklin ES, 600 E 35TH AVE 46409
  James Smith, prin.
Ivanhoe ES, 5700 W 15TH AVE 46406
  Welth Hutchinson, prin.
Jefferson ES, 601 JACKSON ST 46402
  Joseph Robertson, prin.
Kuny ES, 5050 VERMONT ST 46409
  Melvin McGill, prin.
Locke ES, 3757 W 21ST AVE 46404
  Byron Hubbard, prin.
Marquette ES, 6401 HEMLOCK AVE 46403
  Thurman Eldridge, prin.
Melton ES, 4581 FILLMORE ST 46408
  Pernella Landrum, prin.
Nobel ES, 8837 POTTAWATOMI TRL 46403
  Lucille Washington, prin.
Norton ES, 1356 HARRISON BLVD 46407
  Max Lynch, prin.
Pittman Square ES, 4948 DELAWARE ST 46409
  Juanita Evans, prin.
Pyle ES, 2545 W 19TH PL 46404
  Robert Thomas, prin.
Riley ES, 1301 E 43RD AVE 46409
  Joseph Spivey, prin.
Spaulding ES, 600 RHODE ISLAND ST 46402
  Carmen Cammaratha, prin.
Vohr ES, 1900 W 7TH AVE 46404
  Melinda White, prin.
Washington ES
  13TH AVENUE AND WRIGHT ST 46404
  Cordia Moore, prin.
Webster ES, 3710 PIERCE ST 46408
  Addie Goudeaux, prin.
Williams ES, 1320 E 19TH AVE 46407
  Vernon Smith, prin.

Lake Ridge SD
Sch. Sys. Enr. Code 5
Supt. – H. Abramson, 6111 W RIDGE ROAD 46408
Lake Ridge MS, 3601 W 41ST AVE 46408
  Peter Kokinda, prin.
Black Oak ES, 5400 W 29TH AVE 46406
  Frank Ballard, prin.
Grissom ES, 7201 W 25TH AVE 46406
  Alfred Govorchin, prin.
Hosford Park ES, 4735 ARTHUR ST 46408
  Anne Collins, prin.
Longfellow ES, 45TH & CALHOUN ST 46408
  Donald Peckenpaugh, prin.

Aquinas ES, 801 W 73RD AVE 46410
Blessed Sacrament School
  4101 GARFIELD ST 46408
Holy Angels Cathedral School
  975 W 6TH AVE 46402
Holy Trinity School, 425 W 12TH AVE 46407
St. Mark School, 511 W RIDGE RD 46408
St. Mary of the Lake School
  6070 MILLER AVE 46403

Gas City, Grant Co., Pop. Code 6
Mississinewa Comm. SD
Sch. Sys. Enr. Code 5
Supt. – Marcus Lane, 424 W MAIN ST 46933
Baskett MS, 125 N BROADWAY ST 46933
  Terry Talbott, prin.

East ES, 400 E SOUTH A ST 46933
Earl Hartzell, prin.
Northview ES, 725 E NORTH H ST 46933
Donald Curry, prin.
Other Schools – See Jonesboro

Gaston, Delaware Co., Pop. Code 4
Harrison-Washington Comm. SD
Sch. Sys. Enr. Code 4
Supt. – Walter Harrison, RURAL ROUTE 01 47342
Wes-Del MS, RURAL ROUTE 01 47342
William Bower, prin.
ES, P O BOX 308 47342 – Jon Hatcher, prin.
Harrison ES, RURAL ROUTE 01 47342
Thomas Mellish, prin.

Geneva, Adams Co., Pop. Code 4
South Adams SD
Supt. – See Berne
ES, 105 W LINE ST 46740 – William Morris, prin.

Georgetown, Floyd Co., Pop. Code 4
New Albany-Floyd Co. Cons. SD
Supt. – See New Albany
ES, P O BOX 128 47122 – David Merry, prin.

Glenwood, Fayette Co., Pop. Code 2
Fayette Co. SD
Supt. – See Connersville
Orange ES, RURAL ROUTE 01 46133
Charles Butler, prin.

Goodland, Newton Co., Pop. Code 4
South Newton SD
Supt. – See Kentland
ES, 124 BENTON STREET 47948
Jeff Neumann, prin.

Goshen, Elkhart Co., Pop. Code 7
Fairfield Comm. SD
Sch. Sys. Enr. Code 4
Supt. – Orville Bose
67315 COUNTY ROAD 31 46526
Other Schools – See Millersburg, New Paris

Goshen Comm. SD
Sch. Sys. Enr. Code 5
Supt. – Frank Algate, 721 E MADISON ST 46526
Towncrest JHS, 63682 COUNTY ROAD 21 46526
Darrell Johnson, prin.
Whiteman JHS, 501 LINCOLNWAY E 46526
Corally McCann, prin.
Chamberlain ES, 428 N 5TH ST 46526
Don Wysong, prin.
Chandler ES, 419 S 8TH ST 46526
Roberta Stutzman, prin.
Model ES, 412 GREENE ROAD 46526
B. Miller, prin.
Parkside ES, 1202 S 7TH ST 46526
Terry Yoder, prin.
Riverdale ES, 801 W WILKINSON ST 46526
Earlene Nofziger, prin.
Waterford ES
RURAL ROUTE 15 BOX 65560 46526
Gary Seymour, prin.
West Goshen ES, 215 DEWEY AVE 46526
Brad Pressler, prin.

Middlebury Comm. SD
Supt. – See Middlebury
Jefferson ES, 18565 COUNTY RD 20 46526
Gerald Wilson, prin.

Wa-Nee Comm. SD
Supt. – See Nappanee
Harrison ES, 64784 COUNTY RD 11 46526
Larry Nafziger, prin.

St. John the Evangelist School
117 W MONROE 46526

Gosport, Owen Co., Pop. Code 4
Spencer-Owen Comm. SD
Supt. – See Spencer
ES 47433 – Irene Brock, prin.

Granger, St. Joseph Co.
Penn-Harris-Madison SD
Supt. – See Mishawaka
Frank ES, 13111 ADAMS RD 46530
Robert Blake, prin.
Harris ES, 12400 BECKLEY ST 46530
Robert Blake, prin.

Graysville, Sullivan Co.
Southwest SD
Supt. – See Sullivan
ES, P O BOX 338 47852 – Keith Brashear, prin.

Greencastle, Putnam Co., Pop. Code 6
Greencastle Comm. SD
Sch. Sys. Enr. Code 4
Supt. – Gary Druckemiller, P O BOX 480 46135
MS, 110 S SPRING ST 46135 – Roy Boling, prin.
Jones ES, 209 W LIBERTY ST 46135
Alan Small, prin.
Northeast ES, 500 LINWOOD DR 46135
Michael Tzouanakis, prin.
Ridpath ES, 405 HOWARD ST 46135
Paul Luken, prin.

South Putnam Comm. SD
Sch. Sys. Enr. Code 4
Supt. – James Hammond
RURAL ROUTE 02 BOX 134 46135
Central ES, RURAL ROUTE 02 BOX 279 46135
Bruce Bernhardt, prin.
Other Schools – See Fillmore, Reelsville

Greenfield, Hancock Co., Pop. Code 7
Greenfield-Central Comm. SD
Sch. Sys. Enr. Code 5
Supt. – G. Essington, 1E W SOUTH ST 46140
JHS, 204 W PARK AVE 46140
John Coopman, prin.
Eden ES, RURAL ROUTE 05 46140
Philip John, prin.
Harris ES, 200 W PARK AVE 46140
D. Blue, prin.
Lincoln Park ES, N AND SCHOOL STS 46140
Robert Rodocker, prin.
Weston ES, 140 POLK ST 46140
Stephen Burt, prin.
Other Schools – See Maxwell

Mt. Vernon Community SD
Supt. – See Fortville
Mt. Comfort ES, 7667 W 38TH 46140
Phillip Davis, prin.

Southern Hancock Co. Comm. SD
Supt. – See New Palestine
Brandywine ES
RURAL ROUTE 04 BOX 232 46140
Bruce Miller, prin.

St. Michael School, 516 JEFFERSON BLVD 46140

Greensburg, Decatur Co., Pop. Code 6
Decatur Co. Comm. SD
Sch. Sys. Enr. Code 5
Supt. – Dr. Edward Kasamis
RURAL ROUTE 04 BOX 40 47240
North Decatur ES
RURAL ROUTE 01 BOX 95A 47240
Joyce Benge, prin.
South Decatur ES
RURAL ROUTE 05 BOX 246 47240
John Secor, prin.

Greensburg Comm. SD
Sch. Sys. Enr. Code 4
Supt. – Robert Frensemeier
504 E CENTRAL AVE 47240
Greensburg Community JHS
505 E CENTRAL AVE 47240
Richard Revalee, prin.
Billings ES, 310 W WASHINGTON ST 47240
Joyce Fulford, prin.
Jerman MS, 316 W WALNUT ST 47240
James Danner III, prin.
Rosenmund ES, 422 E CENTRAL AVE 47240
Roscoe Linville, prin.
Washington ES, 315 S SIRELAND ST 47240
Edward Daihl, prin.

St. Mary's School, 210 S EAST ST 47240

Greentown, Howard Co., Pop. Code 4
Eastern Howard Comm. SD
Sch. Sys. Enr. Code 4
Supt. – Lindan Hill, 220 S MERIDIAN ST 46936
Eastern ES, 301 S MERIDIAN ST 46936
Stephen Healy, prin.

Greenville, Floyd Co., Pop. Code 3
New Albany-Floyd Co. Cons. SD
Supt. – See New Albany
ES, P O BOX 158 47124 – Melvin Rahe, prin.

Greenwood, Johnson Co., Pop. Code 7
Center Grove Comm. SD
Sch. Sys. Enr. Code 6
Supt. – Lee Webb
2455 S MORGANTOWN ROAD 46142
Center Grove MS
4900 STONES XING ROAD 46142
James Halik, prin.
Center Grove ES
2455 S MORGANTOWN RD 46143
Roger Micnerski, prin.
Maple Grove ES
2911 S MORGANTOWN RD 46143
Nielen Busse, prin.
North Grove ES, 3280 W FAIRVIEW RD 46142
Robert Conlon, prin.
West Grove ES
5800 W SMITH VALLEY RD 46142
George Broyer, prin.

Greenwood Comm. SD
Sch. Sys. Enr. Code 5
Supt. – Donald Strobel, P O BOX 218 46142
MS, 523 S MADISON AVE 46142
Paul Velez, prin.
Greenwood Northeast ES
99 CRESTVIEW DR 46143 – Paul Adamson, prin.
Greenwood Southwest ES
619 W SMITH VALLEY RD 46142
Roger Kinsey, prin.
Isom Central ES, 50 E BROADWAY ST 46143
Arthur Board, prin.

Our Lady of Greenwood School
399 S MERIDIAN ST 46143

Griffith, Lake Co., Pop. Code 7
Griffith Public SD
Sch. Sys. Enr. Code 4
Supt. – Robert Kurtz, 132 N BROAD ST 46319
Beiriger ES, 600 N LILLIAN ST 46319
Stephen Bernath, prin.
Franklin ES, 201 N GRIFFITH BLVD 46319
Edward Skaggs, prin.

Ready ES, 1345 N BROAD ST 46319
Daniel McCain, prin.
Wadsworth ES, 600 N JAY ST 46319
Michael Buchko, prin.

St. Mary School, 525 N BROAD ST 46319

Guilford, Dearborn Co.
Sunman-Dearborn Comm. SD
Supt. – See Sunman
North Dearborn ES, RURAL ROUTE 01 47022
Chris Heller, prin.

Hagerstown, Wayne Co., Pop. Code 4
Nettle Creek SD
Sch. Sys. Enr. Code 4
Supt. – R. Howe
297 E NORTH MARKET ST 47346
ES, 299 N SYCAMORE ST 47346
Cas Downs, prin.

Hamilton, Steuben Co., Pop. Code 2
Hamilton Comm. SD
Sch. Sys. Enr. Code 3
Supt. – A. Gary Nordmann
RURAL ROUTE 01 BOX 207 46742
Hamilton Community ES
RURAL ROUTE 01 BOX 208 46742
Steven Keeslar, prin.

Hamlet, Starke Co., Pop. Code 3
Oregon-Davis SD
Sch. Sys. Enr. Code 3
Supt. – John Slusher, P O BOX 65 46532
Oregon-Davis ES
RURAL ROUTE 02 BOX 51 46532
Maureen Stafford, prin.

Hammond, Lake Co., Pop. Code 8
Hammond CSD
Sch. Sys. Enr. Code 7
Supt. – David Dickson
5935 HOHMAN AVE 46320
Scott MS, 3635 173RD ST 46323
John Tanke, prin.
Caldwell ES, 3105 173RD ST 46323
Ruth Mueller, prin.
Columbia ES, 1238 MICHIGAN ST 46320
Donald Robling, prin.
Edison ES, 7025 MADISON AVE 46324
John Mihalareas, prin.
Eggers ES, 5825 BLAINE AVE 46320
Jane Kendrick, prin.
Harding ES, 3211 165TH ST 46323
Jess Keltner, prin.
Irving ES, 4727 PINE AVE 46327
Bernard Smitka, prin.
Jefferson ES, 6940 NORTHCOTE AVE 46324
Matthew Gorsich, prin.
Kenwood ES, 6416 HOHMAN AVE 46324
Daniel Boits, prin.
Lafayette ES, 856 SIBLEY ST 46320
Bruce Garrison, prin.
Lincoln ES, 4221 TOWLE AVE 46327
Donald Turbin, prin.
Maywood ES, 6040 HOWARD AVE 46320
Milford Miller, prin.
Morton ES, 7006 MARSHALL AVE 46323
Ruth Tanner, prin.
Orchard Drive ES, 3640 ORCHARD DR 46323
Donald Broderick, prin.
Riley ES, 1245 RIVER DR 46324
Harold Lawrence, prin.
Spohn ES, 4925 SOHL AVE 46327
Michael Hriso, prin.
Wallace ES, 6235 JEFFERSON AVE 46324
Edward Brock, prin.
Wilson ES, 1317 173RD ST 46324
Ezekiel Barber, prin.
Other Schools – See Whiting

Highland Christian School, 3040 RIDGE RD 46321
Our Lady of Grace School
3025 HIGHWAY AVE 46322
Our Lady of Perpetual Help School
7128 ARIZONA AVE 46323
St. Casimir School, 4329 CAMERON AVE 46327
St. Catherine of Sienna School
6525 KENTUCKY AVE 46323
St. John Bosco School, 1231 171ST PL 46324

Hanover, Jefferson Co., Pop. Code 5
Southwestern Jefferson Co. Cons. SD
Sch. Sys. Enr. Code 4
Supt. – Patrick Leahey, P O BOX 45 47243
Southwestern ES, P O BOX 31 47243
Joyce Poling, prin.

Harlan, Allen Co.
East Allen Co. SD
Supt. – See New Haven
ES, 12616 SPENCERVILLE ROAD 46743
Marlin Bauer, prin.

Hartford City, Blackford Co., Pop. Code 6
Blackford Co. SD
Sch. Sys. Enr. Code 5
Supt. – Keith Powell, 1515 S MONROE ST 47348
JHS, 800 W VAN CLEVE ST 47348
Michael Parks, prin.
Jackson ES, 0064N-500E 47348
Clyde Lemen, prin.
Licking ES, 668 W 200 S 47348
Ann Ludwig, prin.
North Side ES, 400 E MCDONALD ST 47348
Clyde Lemen, prin.

Parkside MS, 700 W VAN CLEVE ST 47348
 Floyd Cline, prin.
Reed ES, 203 E CHESTNUT ST 47348
 Larry Crabtree, prin.
Southside ES, 1515 S MONROE ST 47348
 Larry Crabtree, prin.
Other Schools – See Montpelier

Haubstadt, Gibson Co., Pop. Code 4
South Gibson SD
Supt. – See Fort Branch
ES, WEST ST 47639 – Timothy Courtney, prin.
_____

Saints Peter & Paul School
 RURAL ROUTE 01 BOX 449 47639
St. Jame's School
 RURAL ROUTE 01 BOX 278-B 47639

Hayden, Jennings Co.
Jennings Co. SD
Supt. – See North Vernon
ES, US ROAD #50 47245 – Tom Judd, prin.

Hebron, Porter Co., Pop. Code 5
Boone Twp. SD
Supt. – See Valparaiso
ES, 307 S MAIN ST 46341 – Willis Allison, prin.

Porter Twp. SD
Sch. Sys. Enr. Code 4
Supt. – Dr. James Rice, 208 S 725 W 46341
Porter Lake ES, 208 S 725W 46341
 Cean Cartwright, prin.
Other Schools – See Boone Grove

Tri-Creek SD
Supt. – See Lowell
Center ES, 4702 E 173RD AVE 46341
 Douglas Wiseman, prin.

Heltonville, Lawrence Co.
North Lawrence Comm. SD
Supt. – See Bedford
ES 47436 – John Anderson, prin.

Henryville, Clark Co., Pop. Code 3
West Clark Comm. SD
Supt. – See Sellersburg
ES, 213 N FERGUSON ST 47126
 Ronald Lancioni, prin.

Highland, Lake Co., Pop. Code 8
Highland SD
Sch. Sys. Enr. Code 5
Supt. – Philip Cartwright
 9145 KENNEDY AVE 46322
JHS, 2941 41ST ST 46322 – Harvey Keim, prin.
Johnston ES, 2945 GRAND BLVD 46322
 Joseph Bandura, prin.
Merkley ES, 5TH & 42ND STS 46322
 Sandra Monzures, prin.
Southridge ES, 9221 JOHNSTON ST 46322
 William Davis, prin.
Warren ES, 2901 100TH ST 46322
 Sandra Monzures, prin.

Hoagland, Allen Co.
East Allen Co. SD
Supt. – See New Haven
ES, 12009 HOAGLAND RD 46745
 Gerald Hapke, prin.

Hobart, Lake Co., Pop. Code 7
City of Hobart SD
Sch. Sys. Enr. Code 5
Supt. – Dr. Raymond Golarz, 32 E 7TH ST 46342
MS, 705 E 4TH ST 46342 – Joanne Schafer, prin.
Earle ES, 400 N WILSON ST 46342
 George Plesac, prin.
Foreman ES, 301 E 10TH ST 46342
 Dr. Neil Vanderkolk, prin.
Liberty ES, 130 N LIBERTY ST 46342
 Richard Gross, prin.
Mundell ES, 52 N WISCONSIN ST 46342
 Rick Gadberry, prin.
Ridge View ES, 3333 W RIDGE RD 46342
 Stewart Mattix, prin.

Hobart Township Comm. SD
Sch. Sys. Enr. Code 4
Supt. – Peggy Chnupa, 3334 MICHIGAN ST 46342
River Forest JHS
 IND STREET & HUBER BLVD 46342
 John Edelmann, prin.
Meister ES, 33RD & JAY STS 46342
 Peter Svetcoff, prin.
River Forest ES, IND ST & HUBER BLVD 46342
 Judith Lee, prin.
Other Schools – See Lake Station

_____

St. Bridget School, 107 MAIN ST 46342
Trinity Lutheran School, 891 S LINDA ST 46342

Holland, Dubois Co., Pop. Code 3
Southwest Dubois Co. SD
Supt. – See Huntingburg
ES, STATE ROAD 161 47541
 Reuben Butke, prin.

Holton, Ripley Co., Pop. Code 2
South Ripley Comm. SD
Supt. – See Versailles
ES, P O BOX 98 47023 – Mark Collier, prin.

Hope, Bartholomew Co., Pop. Code 4
Flat Rock-Hawcreek SD
Sch. Sys. Enr. Code 4
Supt. – Glen Keller, P O BOX 34 47246

ES, P O BOX 93 47246 – (—), prin.
Other Schools – See Clifford

Howe, Lagrange Co., Pop. Code 2
Lakeland SD
Supt. – See Lagrange
Lima-Brighton ES, P O BOX 158 46746
 Thomas Smith, prin.

Huntertown, Allen Co., Pop. Code 4
Northwest Allen Co. SD
Supt. – See Fort Wayne
ES, P O BOX 8 46748 – Gilbert Baumgartner, prin.

Huntingburg, Dubois Co., Pop. Code 6
Southwest Dubois Co. SD
Sch. Sys. Enr. Code 4
Supt. – John Cochren, 511 1/2 E 4TH AVE 47542
Southridge MS, HWY 231 SOUTH 47542
 Larry Feldmeyer, prin.
Crestview ES, 4TH & ARJEM STS 47542
 Reuben Butke, prin.
Maple Park MS, 2ND AND JACKSON STS 47542
 Donald Stephens, prin.
Other Schools – See Holland

Huntington, Huntington Co., Pop. Code 7
Huntington Co. Comm. SD
Sch. Sys. Enr. Code 6
Supt. – Roger Schnepf
 1360 N WARREN ROAD 46750
Crestview JHS, 929 GUILFORD ST 46750
 Max McDowell, prin.
Riverview JHS, 465 WATERWORKS ROAD 46750
 Maurice Reed, prin.
Central ES, 600 N JEFFERSON ST 46750
 Gary Mast, prin.
Lancaster ES, 2932 W 300 S 46750
 Robert Trout, prin.
Lincoln ES, 943 SWAN ST 46750
 Dean Stephan, prin.
Mann ES, 500 WILLIAM ST 46750
 Daniel Bickel, prin.
Northwest ES, 4524 W 800 N 46750
 Fred Stricker, prin.
Other Schools – See Andrews, Roanoke, Warren

_____

St. Mary School, 960 WARREN ST 46750
St. Peter Lutheran School, 802 CHERRY ST 46750

Huron, Lawrence Co.
Mitchell Comm. SD
Supt. – See Mitchell
ES, P O BOX 248 47437 – Donald Bush, prin.

Hymera, Sullivan Co., Pop. Code 4
Northeast SD
Sch. Sys. Enr. Code 4
Supt. – Richard Walters, P O BOX C 47855
ES, P O BOX D 47855 – John Quick, prin.
Other Schools – See Dugger, Fairbanks, Farmersburg,
 Shelburn

Indianapolis, Marion Co., Pop. Code 11
Avon Comm. SD
Sch. Sys. Enr. Code 4
Supt. – Thomas Terry
 13013 ROCKVILLE ROAD 46234
Avon MS, 13013 ROCKVILLE ROAD 46234
 David Leach, prin.
Avon PS, 13013 ROCKVILLE RD 46234
 Jan Wright, prin.
Avon MS, 13013 ROCKVILLE RD 46234
 Lloyd Wenger, prin.

Carmel-Clay SD
Supt. – See Carmel
Orchard Park ES, 10475 SCHOOL PKY 46280
 Sherida Brower, prin.

Franklin Township Comm. SD
Sch. Sys. Enr. Code 5
Supt. – E.B. Carver
 6141 S FRANKLIN ROAD 46259
Franklin Twp. MS
 6019 S FRANKLIN ROAD 46259
 Leland Thompson, prin.
Arlington ES, 5814 S ARLINGTON AVE 46237
 Larry Renihan, prin.
Bunker Hill ES, 6620 SHELBYVILLE RD 46237
 Mark Harper, prin.
Wanamaker ES, 4150 S BAZIL AVE 46239
 James Roudebush, prin.
Other Schools – See Acton

Indianapolis SD
Sch. Sys. Enr. Code 8
Supt. – James Adams, 120 E WALNUT ST 46204
Crispus Attucks JHS, 1140 N WEST ST 46202
 Leon Reid, prin.
Donnan MS, 1202 E TROY AVE 46203
 Charles Robinson, prin.
Forest Manor JHS, 4501 E 32ND ST 46218
 Terry Ogle, prin.
Gambold MS, 3725 N KIEL AVE 46224
 Jack Hayes, prin.
Harshman MS, 1501 E 10TH ST 46201
 Leo Grissom, prin.
Marshall JHS, 10101 E 38TH ST 46236
 Carole Craig, prin.
Shortridge JHS, 3401 N MERIDIAN ST 46208
 Alfred Finnell, prin.
Sidener MS, 2424 KESSLER BLVD EAST 46220
 Juanita Hardiman, prin.
Arlington Woods ES 99, 5801 E 30TH ST 46218
 James Trinkle, prin.

Bell ES 60, 3330 N PENNSYLVANIA ST 46205
 Donald Coleman, prin.
Bellamy ES 102, 9501 E 36TH PL 46236
 Georgia Bowman, prin.
Bingham ES 84, 440 E 57TH ST 46220
 Kevin Gardner, prin.
Blaker ES 55, 1349 E 54TH ST 46220
 Jesse Lynch, prin.
Brandes ES 65, 4065 ASBURY ST 46227
 Diane Pillow, prin.
Brochhausen ES 88, 5801 E 16TH ST 46218
 Isiah Greene,Jr., prin.
Brookside ES 54, 3150 E 10TH ST 46201
 Gladys Reid, prin.
Brown ES 20
 1849 PLEASANT RUN PKW S DR 46203
 Clarence Sebree, prin.
Buck ES, 2701 DEVON AVE 46219
 James Ezell, prin.
Carver ES 87, 2411 INDIANAPOLIS AVE 46208
 Madeline Sweatman, prin.
Christian Park ES 82, 4700 ENGLISH AVE 46201
 Michael Poore, prin.
Coleman ES 110, 1740 3E 30TH ST 46218
 David Garrett, prin.
Diggs ES 42, 1002 W 25TH ST 46208
 Jacqueline Berry, prin.
Douglass ES 19, 2020 DAWSON ST 46203
 Olivia Gaither, prin.
Dye ES 27, 545 E 19TH ST 46202
 Minetta Richardson, prin.
Emerson ES 58, 321 N LINWOOD AVE 46201
 Richard Sturm, prin.
Evans ES 11, 3202 E 42ND ST 46205
 Mamie Thompson, prin.
Fairbanks ES 105, 8620 MONTERY RD 46226
 Marilyn Bradley, prin.
Farrington ES, 4326 PATRICIA STREET 46222
 Richard Owens, prin.
Fay ES 21, 2815 ENGLISH AVE 46201
 Alfreda Davis, prin.
Fisher ES 93, 7151 E 35TH ST 46226
 Helen Cross, prin.
Foster ES 67, 653 N SOMERSET AVE 46222
 John Airola, prin.
Frost ES 106, 5301 ROXBURY RD 46226
 Ruth Harris, prin.
Garfield ES 35, 2098 E RAYMOND ST 46203
 Judith Hall, prin.
Gilfoy ES 113, 4352 N MITTHOEFFER RD 46236
 Anne Falkner, prin.
Gregg ES 15, 2302 E MICHIGAN ST 46201
 Willard Litz, prin.
Harrison ES 2, 725 N NEW JERSEY ST 46202
 Marjorie Jackson, prin.
Hartmann ES 78, 3734 E VERMONT ST 46201
 Orrison Sharp, prin.
Hawthorne ES 50, 75 N BELLEVIEW PL 46222
 Carlie Cardwell, prin.
Hendricks ES 37, 2605 E 25TH ST 46218
 Helen Lewis, prin.
Hope ES 26, 1301 E 16TH ST 46202
 Paul Volk, prin.
Irving ES 14, 1229 E OHIO ST 46202
 David Harakas, prin.
Jennings ES 109, 6150 GATEWAY DR 46254
 Betty Chisley, prin.
Julian ES 57, 5435 E WASHINGTON ST 46219
 H. Stephens, prin.
Key ES 103, 3920 BAKER DR 46236
 Wayne Fairburn, prin.
Kilmer ES 69, 3421 N KEYSTONE AVE 46218
 Robert Lewis, prin.
Leach ES 68, 2107 N RILEY AVE 46218
 Mary Johnson, prin.
Lincoln ES 18, 1001 PALMER ST 46203
 Dorothy Crenshaw, prin.
Loomis ES 85, 338 S ARLINGTON AVE 46219
 William Wheatley, prin.
McClellan ES 91, 511 EVANSTON AVE 46205
 James Steckley, prin.
McFarland ES 112, 3200 E RAYMOND ST 46203
 Leland Stevenson, prin.
McKinley ES 39, 801 S STATE AVE 46203
 D. Bennett, prin.
Miller ES 114, 2251 SLOAN AVE 46203
 Betty McCarty, prin.
Morgan ES 86, 200 W 49TH ST 46208
 Jean Evan, prin.
Nicholson ES 96, 3651 N KIEL AVE 46224
 James Robinson, prin.
Nicholson ES 70, 510 E 46TH ST 46205
 Crystal Smith, prin.
Parker ES 56, 2353 COLUMBIA AVE 46205
 Joan Cooper, prin.
Parkview ES 81
 3092 BROOKSIDE PKY NORTH DR 46218
 Tom Carney, prin.
Penn ES 49, 1902 W MORRIS ST 46221
 Jane Ajabu, prin.
Potter ES 74, 1601 E 10TH ST 46201
 Rosena Johnson, prin.
Pyle ES 90, 3351 W 18TH ST 46222
 Anita Funches, prin.
Reiffel ES 31, 307 LINCOLN ST 46225
 Michael Shipman, prin.
Riley ES 43, 150 W 40TH ST 46208
 Rubie Crockett, prin.
Riverside ES 44, 2033 SUGAR GROVE AVE 46202
 Willis Oldham, prin.
Roberts ES, 1401 E 10TH STREET 46201
 Patricia Bolanos, prin.
Russell ES 48, 3445 CENTRAL AVE 46205
 Nancy Shipman, prin.

Skillen ES 34, 1410 WADE ST 46203
  Gary Pellico, prin.
Steele ES, 3698 DUBARRY ROAD 46226
  Alice Appel, prin.
Stowe ES 64, 2710 BETHEL AVE 46203
  Raeburn Rathbun, prin.
Tarkington ES 92, 6550 E 42ND ST 46226
  Richard Nuttall, prin.
Torrence ES 83, 5050 E 42ND ST 46226
  Doris Wills, prin.
Walker ES 89, 5950 E 23RD ST 46218
  Herbert Everett, prin.
Wallace ES 107, 3307 ASHWAY DR 46224
  Maurice Schankerman, prin.
Walsman ES, 1780 SLOAN AVE 46203
  Susan Robinson, prin.
Webster ES 46, 1702 W MILLER ST 46221
  Phyllis Imel, prin.
Wilde ES 79, 5002 W 34TH ST 46224
  Betty Beene, prin.
Woolen ES 45, 2301 N PARK AVE 46205
  Effie Ezzell, prin.

Metro SD of Decatur Twp.
Supt. – See West Newton
Decatur Twp. JHS
  5108 S HIGH SCHOOL ROAD 46241
  Walter Bourke, prin.
Decatur ES, 3935 W MOORESVILLE RD 46241
  Kathy Merl, prin.
Lynwood ES, 4640 SANTE FE DR 46241
  John Magers, prin.
Valley Mills ES, 5101 S HIGH SCHOOL RD 46241
  Carl Benson, prin.

Metro SD of Lawrence Twp.
Sch. Sys. Enr. Code 6
Supt. – Percy Clark, 7601 E 56TH ST 46226
Belzer MS, 7555 E 56TH ST 46226
  James Peterson, prin.
Craig MS, 6501 SUNNYSIDE ROAD 46236
  Fran Etheridge, prin.
Brook Park ES, 5259 DAVID ST 46226
  Ronald Barkes, prin.
Castle ES, 8502 E 82ND ST 46256
  Donald McHolland, prin.
Crestview ES, 7600 E 71ST ST 46256
  George Rupp, prin.
Harrison Hill ES, 7510 E 53RD ST 46226
  Wendell Norton, prin.
Indian Creek ES, 10833 E 56TH ST 46236
  Dr. Karen Gould, prin.
Oaklandon ES, 6702 OAKLANDON RD 46236
  Doris Downing, prin.
Skiles Test ES, 7001 JOHNSON RD 46220
  Judith Baker, prin.

Metro SD of Perry Twp.
Sch. Sys. Enr. Code 7
Supt. – Raymond L. Fatheree
  1130 E EPLER AVE 46227
Keystone MS, 5715 S KEYSTONE AVE 46227
  George Callon, prin.
Meridian MS, 8040 S MERIDIAN ST 46217
  Morris Beck, prin.
Southport MS, 6548 ORINOCO AVE 46227
  Haldon Cole, prin.
Burkhart ES, 5701 BRILL ST 46227
  Thomas Lakes, prin.
Bryan ES, 4355 E STOP ELEVEN RD 46237
  Stephen McGee, prin.
Glenns Valley ES
  8239 MORGANTOWN RD 46217
  Dennis Nichols, prin.
Homecroft ES, 1551 SOUTHVIEW DR 46227
  Thomas Wade, prin.
Lincoln ES, 5241 BREHOB RD 46217
  Roger Roembke, prin.
MacArthur ES, 454 E STOP ELEVEN RD 46227
  Stephen Craig, prin.
Young ES, 5740 MCFARLAND RD 46227
  Angie Artis, prin.
Other Schools – See Southport

Metro SD of Pike Twp.
Sch. Sys. Enr. Code 5
Supt. – Charles O. Jordan
  6901 ZIONSVILLE ROAD 46268
Guion Creek MS, 4401 W 52ND ST 46254
  M. Beth Copenhaver, prin.
Lincoln MS, 5555 W 71ST ST 46268
  John Maloy, prin.
Central ES, 6801 ZIONSVILLE RD 46268
  Thomas Little, prin.
College Park ES, 2811 BARNARD STREET 46268
  Edgar Harper, prin.
Eagle Creek ES, 6905 W 46TH ST 46254
  Nancy Carey, prin.
Eastbrook ES, 7839 NEW AUGUSTA RD 46268
  Dr. Linda Chapman, prin.
Guion Creek ES, 4301 W 52ND ST 46254
  Victoria Davis, prin.

Metro SD of Warren Twp.
Sch. Sys. Enr. Code 6
Supt. – Douglas Otto, 9301 E 18TH ST 46229
Brookview ES, 1401 N MITTHOEFFER RD 46229
  Marilyn Heavenridge, prin.
Eastridge ES, 10930 E 10TH ST 46229
  John Huston, prin.
Grassy Creek ES, 10330 PROSPECT ST 46239
  Leon Carter, prin.
Hawthorne ES, 8301 RAWLES AVE 46219
  Robert Mason, prin.

Heather Hills ES, 10502 E 21ST ST 46229
  Marilyn Cronan, prin.
Lakeside ES, 9601 E 21ST ST 46229
  Gerald Swisher, prin.
Lowell ES, 2150 S HUNTER RD 46239
  Michael Wallpe, prin.
Moorhead ES, 8400 E 10TH ST 46219
  James Craw, prin.
Pleasant Run ES, 1800 N FRANKLIN RD 46219
  Milton Bailey, prin.
Sunnyheights ES, 8931 E 30TH ST 46219
  Kathy Handy, prin.

Metro SD of Washington Twp.
Sch. Sys. Enr. Code 6
Supt. – Phillip McDaniel, 3801 E 79TH ST 46240
Eastwood MS, 4401 E 62ND ST 46220
  Gary Washburn, prin.
Northview MS, 8401 E WESTFIELD BLVD 46240
  Rudolph Wilson, prin.
Westlane MS, 1301 W 73RD ST 46260
  Steve Keith, prin.
Allisonville ES, 4900 E 79TH ST 46250
  Joseph Biddle, prin.
Crooked Creek ES
  2150 KESSLER BLVD WEST DR 46208
  Norman Foust, prin.
Greenbriar ES, 8201 DITCH RD 46260
  Anita Franklin, prin.
Harcourt ES, 7535 HARCOURT RD 46260
  Nathaniel Jones, prin.
Nora ES, 1000 E 91ST ST 46240
  Phyllis Russell, prin.
Spring Mill ES, 8250 SPRINGMILL RD 46260
  Jeannie Leininger, prin.
Strange ES, 3660 E 62ND ST 46220
  Ernest Copple, prin.

Metro SD of Wayne Twp.
Sch. Sys. Enr. Code 7
Supt. – Edward Bowes
  1220 S HIGH SCHOOL ROAD 46241
Chapel Glen ES, 701 LANSDOWNE RD 46234
  Donna Shultheis, prin.
Chapelwood ES
  1129 N GIRLS SCHOOL RD 46214
  Donald Masterson, prin.
Garden City ES, 4901 ROCKVILLE RD 46224
  Steven Stephanoff, prin.
Maplewood ES, 1643 DUNLAP AVE 46241
  Thomas Long, prin.
McClelland ES, 6740 W MORRIS ST 46241
  Carol Lindly, prin.
Rhoades ES, 502 S AUBURN ST 46241
  Gary Huddleston, prin.
Sanders ES, 4730 GADSEN ST 46241
  Bruce Haddix, prin.
Stout Field ES, 3820 W BRADBURY AVE 46241
  Donald Pirtle, prin.
Westlake ES, 271 N SIGSBEE ST 46214
  Gwendolyn Boyd, prin.
Other Schools – See Clermont

Park-Tudor School, 7200 N COLLEGE AVE 46240
All Saints Catholic School
  337 N WARMAN AVE 46222
Calvary Lutheran School, 6111 SHELBY ST 46227
Central Catholic School, 1115 E TABOR ST 46203
Christ the King School
  5858 CRITTENDEN AVE 46220
Emmaus Lutheran Memorial School
  1224 LAUREL ST 46203
Hebrew Academy, 6602 HOOVER RD 46260
Holy Angels School
  2822 NORTHWESTERN AVE 46208
Holy Cross Central School
  125 N ORIENTAL ST 46202
Holy Spirit School, 7241 E 10TH ST 46219
Immaculate Heart of Mary School
  317 E 57TH ST 46220
Nativity School, 3310 S MEADOW DR 46239
Our Lady of Lourdes School
  28 S DOWNEY AVE 46219
St. Andrew Apostle School
  4050 E 38TH ST 46218
St. Ann School, 2839 S MCCLURE ST 46241
St. Barnabas School, 8300 RAHKE RD 46217
St. Christopher School, 5375 W 16TH ST 46224
St. Gabriel School, 6000 W 34TH ST 46224
St. Joan of Arc School, 500 E 42ND ST 46205
St. John Lutheran School
  6630 SOUTHEASTERN AVE 46203
St. Jude School, 5375 MCFARLAND RD 46227
St. Lawrence School, 6950 E 46TH ST 46226
St. Luke School, 7650 N ILLINOIS ST 46260
St. Mark School, 541 E EDGEWOOD AVE 46227
St. Matthew School, 4100 E 56TH ST 46220
St. Michael School, 3352 W 30TH ST 46222
St. Monica School, 6131 N MICHIGAN RD 46208
St. Philip Neri School, 545 EASTERN AVE 46201
St. Pius X School, 7200 SARTO DR 46240
St. Richard Episcopal School
  3243 N MERIDIAN ST 46208
St. Rita School, 1800 N ARSENAL AVE 46218
St. Roch School, 3603 S MERIDIAN ST 46217
St. Simon the Apostle School
  8400 ROY RD 46219
St. Theresa Little Flower School
  1401 N BOSART AVE 46201
St. Thomas Aquinas School
  4600 N ILLINOIS ST 46208
Trinity Lutheran School, 8540 E 16TH ST 46219

Ireland, Dubois Co.
Greater Jasper Cons. SD
Supt. – See Jasper
ES, N GREEN ST 47545 – Joseph Koval, prin.

Jamestown, Boone Co., Pop. Code 3
Western Boone Co. Comm. SD
Supt. – See Thorntown
Granville Wells ES, RURAL ROUTE 02 46147
  Bill Carney, prin.

Jasonville, Greene Co., Pop. Code 4
Metro SD Shakamak
Sch. Sys. Enr. Code 3
Supt. – Donovan Wells
  RURAL ROUTE 02 BOX 42 47438
Shakamak ES, RURAL ROUTE 02 BOX 42 47438
  Sheila Donis, prin.

Jasper, Dubois Co., Pop. Code 6
Greater Jasper Cons. SD
Sch. Sys. Enr. Code 4
Supt. – Walter W. Stutz, P O BOX 191 47546
MS, 340 W 6TH ST 47546 – M. L. Martin, prin.
Fifth Street ES, W FIFTH ST 47546
  Jack Yaggi, prin.
Tenth Street ES, P O BOX 127 47546
  John Miller, prin.
Other Schools – See Ireland

Holy Family School, 990 E CHURCH AVE 47546
Precious Blood School, RURAL ROUTE 05 47546

Jeffersonville, Clark Co., Pop. Code 4
Greater Clark Co. SD
Sch. Sys. Enr. Code 7
Supt. – Justin Roberts
  2710 E HIGHWAY 62 47130
Parkview MS, 1600 BRIGMAN AVE 47130
  Michael Ehringer, prin.
River Valley MS
  2220 N W ALBANY-CHRIST 47130
  Dick Klemens, prin.
Eastlawn ES, 1613 E 8TH ST 47130
  Gil Newton, prin.
Ewing Lane ES, 420 EWING LN 47130
  Patty Mcnames, prin.
Jefferson ES, RURAL ROUTE 02 BOX 984 47130
  Paul Gibson, prin.
Maple ES, 429 DIVISION ST 47130
  James Falkenstein, prin.
McCulloch ES, 1317 TRIANGLE DR 47130
  Eugene Coomer, prin.
Northaven ES, 1907 OAK RIDGE DR 47130
  George Weber, prin.
Parkwood ES, 748 SPICEWOOD DR 47130
  Harold Robinson, prin.
Riverside ES, 17 LAUREL DR 47130
  Miriam Matthews, prin.
Rose Hill ES, 301 W MAPLE ST 47130
  Douglas Chinn, prin.
Spring Hill ES, 201 E 15TH ST 47130
  Robert Brewer, prin.
Utica ES, 605 OLD SALEM RD 47130
  David Hedge, prin.
Wilson ES, 2915 CHARLESTOWN-JEFF RD 47130
  Brenda Johnston, prin.
Other Schools – See Charlestown, New Washington

Sacred Heart School, 1842 E 8TH ST 47130

Jonesboro, Grant Co., Pop. Code 4
Mississinewa Comm. SD
Supt. – See Gas City
Knight ES, 1201 S WATER ST 46938
  T. Bryan, prin.
Westview ES, 709 W 6TH ST 46938
  William Allen, prin.

Kendallville, Noble Co., Pop. Code 6
East Noble SD
Sch. Sys. Enr. Code 5
Supt. – Richard Hamilton
  702 DOWLING ST 46755
Kendallville Central ES
  RILEY AND DIAMOND STS 46755
  Jerry Daniels, prin.
North Side ES, 302 HARDING ST 46755
  Donald Shaw, prin.
Wayne Center ES, RURAL ROUTE 01 46755
  James Tilghman, prin.
Other Schools – See Avilla, Laotto, Rome City

St. John Lutheran School, 301 S OAK ST 46755

Kennard, Henry Co., Pop. Code 2
Beard Memorial SD
Supt. – See Knightstown
ES, PLUMB AND VINE ST 47351
  Larry Carmony, prin.

Kentland, Newton Co., Pop. Code 4
South Newton SD
Sch. Sys. Enr. Code 3
Supt. – William Riggs, 110 N 3RD ST 47951
ES, N 4TH ST 47951 – J. Carter, prin.
Other Schools – See Brook, Goodland

Kingsford Heights, La Porte Co., Pop. Code 4
La Porte Comm. SD
Supt. – See La Porte
ES, 460 EVANSTON RD 46346
  Patricia Bondeson, prin.

Knightstown, Henry Co., Pop. Code 4
Beard Memorial SD
Sch. Sys. Enr. Code 4
Supt. – William Freel, 340 N ADAMS ST 46148
Knightstown ES, P O BOX 239 46148
    Kenneth Allen, prin.
Other Schools – See Carthage, Kennard

Knightsville, Clay Co., Pop. Code 3
Clay Comm. SD
Sch. Sys. Enr. Code 5
Supt. – Roger Damerow, P O BOX 101 47857
Other Schools – See Brazil, Clay City, Staunton

Knox, Starke Co., Pop. Code 5
Knox Comm. SD
Sch. Sys. Enr. Code 4
Supt. – Harold Huff, 306 S PEARL ST 46534
Knox Community JHS, 901 S MAIN ST 46534
    Charles James, prin.
California ES, RURAL ROUTE 01 BOX 143 46534
    Betty Osterreicher, prin.
Palmer ES, 900 S MAIN ST 46534
    Mary Costello, prin.
Washington ES, RURAL ROUTE 03 46534
    Herbert McWhorter, prin.

Kokomo, Howard Co., Pop. Code 8
Kokomo-Center Twp. Cons. SD
Sch. Sys. Enr. Code 6
Supt. – Dr. Larry Horner, P O BOX 2188 46904
Bon Air ES, 2800 N APPERSON WAY 46901
    Harry McCool, prin.
Boulevard ES, 1901 WEST BLVD 46902
    John Kennedy, prin.
Columbian ES, 1234 N COURTLAND AVE 46901
    Thomas Power, prin.
Darrough Chapel ES, 900 S GOYER RD 46902
    Cynthia Dwyer, prin.
Haynes ES, 910 S COOPER ST 46901
    Warren Jeffers, prin.
Lafayette Park ES, 919 N KORBY ST 46901
    Theodore Schuck, prin.
Lincoln ES, 721 W JACKSON ST 46901
    Thomas Power, prin.
Maple Crest ES, 300 W LINCOLN RD 46902
    Edward Thomas, prin.
Petit Park ES, 901 W HAVENS ST 46901
    Robert Brooke, prin.
Sycamore ES, 1600 E SYCAMORE ST 46901
    Joe Mathias, prin.
Wallace ES, 2326 W JEFFERSON ST 46901
    Leslie Dumoulin, prin.
Washington ES, 1500 S WASHINGTON ST 46902
    Glenn Hobbs, prin.

Northwestern SD
Sch. Sys. Enr. Code 4
Supt. – Deborah Glass
    4154 WEST ROAD 350 NORTH 46901
Howard ES, 3526 NORTH ROAD 300 E 46901
    David Dewitte, prin.
Northwestern ES, 4223 W RD 350 N 46901
    Alan Jackson, prin.

Taylor Comm. SD
Sch. Sys. Enr. Code 4
Supt. – Damon Peigh
    3750 E CO ROAD 300 S 46902
Indian Heights ES, 5500 WEA DR 46902
    June Gist, prin.
Taylor ES, 3700 E COUNTY RD 300 S 46902
    George Laflin, prin.
_____

St. Joan of Arc School, 824 S PURDUM ST 46901
St. Patrick School
    1230 N ARMSTRONG ST 46901

Kouts, Porter Co., Pop. Code 4
Pleasant Twp. SD
Supt. – See Valparaiso
ES, 302 E COLLEGE ST BOX 348 46347
    Elmer Bechtel, prin.

La Crosse, La Porte Co., Pop. Code 3
Dewey Twp. SD
Supt. – See La Porte
S, P O BOX 360 46348 – James Biddle, prin.

Ladoga, Montgomery Co., Pop. Code 4
South Montgomery Comm. SD
Supt. – See New Market
ES, 418 E TAYLOR ST 47954
    Charles Coffman, prin.

Lafayette, Tippecanoe Co., Pop. Code 8
Lafayette SD
Sch. Sys. Enr. Code 6
Supt. – James Wagner, 2300 CASON ST 47904
Sunnyside MS, 2500 CASON ST 47904
    Leon Dickson, prin.
Tecumseh MS, S 18TH & TEAL ROAD 47905
    Dennis Cahill, prin.
Durgan ES, 1840 S 18TH ST 47905
    Charles Williamson, prin.
Edgelea ES, 2910 S 18TH ST 47905
    William Gerhart, prin.
Glen Acres ES, 3727 KIMBERLY DR 47905
    Thomas Hutchinson, prin.
Linnwood ES, 1415 BALL ST 47904
    Greg Schnepf, prin.
Miami ES, 2401 BECK LN 47905
    Donald Taylor, prin.
Miller ES, 700 S 4TH ST 47905
    David Williams, prin.

Murdock ES, 2100 CASON ST 47904
    Dianna Chalk, prin.
Oakland ES, 611 S 21ST ST 47905
    Douglas Kring, prin.
Vinton ES, 3101 ELMWOOD AVE 47904
    Pamela Frampton, prin.
Washington ES, 1100 ELIZABETH ST 47904
    Jerry Carter, prin.

Tippecanoe SD
Sch. Sys. Enr. Code 6
Supt. – Kenneth Koger, 21 ELSTON ROAD 47905
East Tipp MS, 7501 E 300 N 47905
    John Shoaf, prin.
Southwestern MS, 2100 W 800 S 47905
    John Christopher, prin.
Wainwright MS, 7501 E 700 S 47905
    Richard Watts, prin.
Cole ES, 6418 E 900 S 47905 – Vicki Kelley, prin.
Hershey ES, 7521 E 300 N 47905
    Gordon Bohs, prin.
Mayflower Mill ES, 200 E 500 S 47905
    David Notary, prin.
Mintonye ES, 200 W 800 S 47905
    John Price, prin.
Other Schools – See Battle Ground, Dayton, West
    Lafayette
_____

St. Boniface MS, 816 NORTH ST 47901
LaFayette Christian School, 525 N 26TH ST 47904
St. Jame's Lutheran School, 615 N 8TH ST 47901
St. Lawrence School, 1902 MEHARRY ST 47904
St. Mary Cathedral School, 1200 SOUTH ST 47901

La Fontaine, Wabash Co., Pop. Code 3
Metro SD of Wabash Co.
Supt. – See Wabash
ES, 207 N WABASH AVE 46940
    Tom Rigney, prin.

Lagrange, Lagrange Co., Pop. Code 4
Lakeland SD
Sch. Sys. Enr. Code 4
Supt. – William Smith, 200 CHERRY ST 46761
Lakeland JHS, RURAL ROUTE 05 46761
    Richard Knapp, prin.
Parkside ES, RURAL ROUTE 05 46761
    Ruth Jones, prin.
Other Schools – See Howe, Wolcottville

Prairie Heights Comm. SD
Sch. Sys. Enr. Code 4
Supt. – Robert Slavens
    RURAL ROUTE 02 BOX 602 46761
Prairie Heights MS
    RURAL ROUTE 02 BOX 604 46761
    Paul Thomas, prin.
Prairie Heights ES
    RURAL ROUTE 02 BOX 606 46761
    Gene Wake, prin.
Other Schools – See Wolcottville

Lake Station, Lake Co., Pop. Code 7
Hobart Township Comm. SD
Supt. – See Hobart
Evans ES, 2915 E 35TH AVE 46405
    Kevin Grindlay, prin.

Lake Station Comm. SD
Sch. Sys. Enr. Code 4
Supt. – K. Kayes, 2500 PIKE ST 46405
Edison JHS, 3304 PARKSIDE AVE 46405
    Helen Korpak, prin.
Bailey ES, 2100 UNION ST 46405
    Dale Griesel, prin.
Central ES, 2540 PIKE ST 46405
    Thomas Thurnes, prin.
Hamilton ES, 2900 LAKE ST 46405
    George Vondrak, prin.
Polk ES, 2460 VERMILLION ST 46405
    Dan Dehaven, prin.
_____

St. Francis Xavier School
    2453 PUTNAM ST 46405

Laketon, Wabash Co.
Manchester Comm. SD
Supt. – See North Manchester
ES, P O BOX 8 46943 – Jack Fisher, prin.

Lake Village, Newton Co.
North Newton SD
Supt. – See Morocco
ES 46349 – Steven Sharp, prin.

Lakeville, St. Joseph Co., Pop. Code 3
Union-North United SD
Sch. Sys. Enr. Code 4
Supt. – David Pruis, 215 S MICHIGAN ST 46536
Laville ES, 12645 TYLER RD 46536
    Paul Davis, prin.

Lamar, Spencer Co.
North Spencer Co. SD
Supt. – See Dale
Clay-Huff ES 47550 – Scott Stevens, prin.

Lanesville, Harrison Co., Pop. Code 3
Franklin Twp. SD
Sch. Sys. Enr. Code 3
Supt. – Carl Uesseler 47136
Franklin Twp. ES 47136 – Joyce Williams, prin.
St. Mary's ES 47136 – Joyce Williams, prin.
_____

St. John Lutheran School
    RURAL ROUTE 01 BOX 306 47136

Laotto, Noble Co.
East Noble SD
Supt. – See Kendallville
ES 46763 – William Lange, prin.

Lapel, Madison Co., Pop. Code 4
West Central Comm. SD
Supt. – See Anderson
ES, P O BOX 518 46051 – Jerry Kemerly, prin.

La Porte, La Porte Co., Pop. Code 7
Cass Twp. SD
Sch. Sys. Enr. Code 2
Supt. – Frederick John, 500 MONROE ST 46350
Other Schools – See Wanatah

Dewey Twp. SD
Sch. Sys. Enr. Code 2
Supt. – Fredrick John, 500 MONROE ST 46350
Other Schools – See La Crosse

La Porte Comm. SD
Sch. Sys. Enr. Code 6
Supt. – C. Steven Snider, 1921 A ST 46350
Boston MS, 1000 HARRISON ST 46350
    James Pantos, prin.
Kesling MS, 306 E 18TH ST 46350
    James Rubush, prin.
Crichfield ES, 336 W JOHNSON RD 46350
    Charles Crone, prin.
Hailmann ES, 1001 OHIO ST 46350
    Barbara Reidy, prin.
Handley ES, 408 TENTH ST 46350
    Stephen Bayer, prin.
Kingsbury ES, 802 W 400S 46350
    Patricia Steele, prin.
Lincoln ES, 402 HARRISON ST 46350
    Wendell Tarnow, prin.
Riley ES, 516 WELLER AVE 46350
    Richard Welch, prin.
Other Schools – See Auburn, Kingsford Heights, Mill
    Creek, Stillwell

New Durham Twp. SD
Sch. Sys. Enr. Code 3
Supt. – Fredrick John, 500 MONROE ST 46350
Other Schools – See Westville

New Prairie United SD
Supt. – See New Carlisle
Galena ES, 1933 E 800N 46350
    Russell Hochstetler, prin.
_____

St. John Lutheran School
    111 KINGSBURY AVE 46350
St. Joseph School, 101 C ST 46350

Laurel, Franklin Co., Pop. Code 3
Franklin Co. Comm. SD
Supt. – See Brookville
ES 47024 – Odell Calihan, prin.

Lawrenceburg, Dearborn Co., Pop. Code 5
Lawrenceburg Comm. SD
Sch. Sys. Enr. Code 4
Supt. – Ben Jennings, 477 LUDLOW ST 47025
Greendale MS, 200 TIGER BLVD 47025
    W. Kuebler, prin.
Central ES, 500 SHORT ST 47025
    Edward Gorman, prin.
_____

St. Lawrence School, 526 WALNUT ST 47025

Leavenworth, Crawford Co., Pop. Code 2
Crawford Co. Comm. SD
Supt. – See Marengo
ES, RURAL ROUTE 01 47137 – Terry Enlow, prin.

Lebanon, Boone Co., Pop. Code 7
Lebanon Comm. SD
Sch. Sys. Enr. Code 5
Supt. – David Hutton, 404 N MERIDIAN ST 46052
MS, 1800 N GRANT ST 46052
    Denny Hesler, prin.
Central ES, 515 E WILLIAMS ST 46052
    Ed Chambers, prin.
Harney ES, 1500 GARFIELD ST 46052
    Earl Slaughter, prin.
Stokes ES, 1005 S MERIDIAN ST 46052
    Jerry Bohannon, prin.
Worth ES, 3900 E 300 S 46052 – Gloria Earl, prin.

Leesburg, Kosciusko Co., Pop. Code 3
Warsaw Comm. SD
Supt. – See Warsaw
ES, P O BOX 247 46538 – Brent Widman, prin.

Leo, Allen Co., Pop. Code 3
East Allen Co. SD
Supt. – See New Haven
ES, 14815 WAYNE ST 46765 – Jerry Allred, prin.

Leopold, Perry Co., Pop. Code 3
Perry Central Comm. SD
Sch. Sys. Enr. Code 4
Supt. – John Kerekes 47551
Perry Central ES 47551 – Allen Krueger, prin.

Lewisville, Henry Co., Pop. Code 3
South Henry SD
Sch. Sys. Enr. Code 3
Supt. – Hal Jester, P O BOX 188 47352
Other Schools – See Spiceland, Straughn

Lexington, Scott Co.
Scott Co. SD 2
Supt. – See Scottsburg
ES, P O BOX 210 47138 – Merle Jackson, prin.

Liberty, Union Co., Pop. Code 4
Union Co. SD
Sch. Sys. Enr. Code 4
Supt. – Richard Amick, 107 S LAYMAN ST 47353
JHS, 402 E UNION ST 47353 – Carl Hylton, prin.
ES, 501 EATON ST 47353
  Kathryn Hennon, prin.

Ligonier, Noble Co., Pop. Code 5
West Noble SD
Sch. Sys. Enr. Code 4
Supt. – Bruce Hippensteel
  RURAL ROUTE 02 46767
West Noble MS, RURAL ROUTE 02 46767
  Robert Wechter, prin.
ES, 601 GRAND ST 46767 – Louise Hague, prin.
West Noble ES, RURAL ROUTE 02 46767
  Keenis Owens, prin.

Linden, Montgomery Co., Pop. Code 3
North Montgomery Comm. SD
Sch. Sys. Enr. Code 4
Supt. – James Tucker, 105 N MAIN 47955
Other Schools – See Crawfordsville

Linton, Greene Co., Pop. Code 6
Linton-Stockton SD
Sch. Sys. Enr. Code 4
Supt. – C. Glenn, 801 1ST ST NE 47441
Linton-Stockton JHS, 109 I ST NW 47441
  Daniel Phillips, prin.
Linton-Stockton ES
  RURAL ROUTE 02 BOX 161 47441
  Raymond Spencer, prin.

Lizton, Hendricks Co., Pop. Code 2
North West Hendricks SD
Sch. Sys. Enr. Code 4
Supt. – Larry Rambis, P O BOX 70 46149
Other Schools – See North Salem, Pittsboro

Logansport, Cass Co., Pop. Code 7
Logansport Comm. SD
Sch. Sys. Enr. Code 5
Supt. – Steve Kain, 2829 GEORGE ST 46947
Columbia MS, 1300 N 3RD ST 46947
  Michael Fiscel, prin.
Lincoln MS, 2901 USHER ST 46947
  James Hipsher, prin.
Columbia ES, 1301 PETER ST 46947
  Calvin Eltzroth, prin.
Fairview ES, 840 S CICOTT ST 46947
  William Moss, prin.
Franklin ES, 400 W MIAMI AVE 46947
  Noah Sheely, prin.
Tipton ES, 1529 WRIGHT ST 46947
  Dennis Richey, prin.
Webster ES, 2301 E MARKET ST 46947
  Stanley Smith, prin.

Stillwater Academy
  4343 GRAND PRIX DRIVE 46947
All Saints ES, 121 EDL RIVER AVE 46947

Loogootee, Martin Co., Pop. Code 5
Loogootee Comm. SD
Sch. Sys. Enr. Code 4
Supt. – Joe Woods, P O BOX 282 47553
JHS, 201 BROOKS AVE 47553
  Kenneth McIntosh, prin.
Loogootee East MS, CHURCH ST 47553
  Charles Lavely, prin.
Loogootee West ES, COSTELLO DR 47553
  John Spencer, prin.

Lowell, Lake Co., Pop. Code 6
Tri-Creek SD
Sch. Sys. Enr. Code 5
Supt. – J. Kuruzovich, 690 BURR ST 46356
MS, 200 W OAKLEY AVE 46356
  Robert Daley, prin.
Lake Prairie ES, 11601 W 181ST AVE 46356
  Stanley Hurst, prin.
Oak Hill ES, 195 W OAKLEY AVE 46356
  Jack Foss, prin.
Other Schools – See Hebron

St. Edward School, 210 S NICHOLS ST 46356

Lynn, Randolph Co., Pop. Code 4
Randolph Southern SD
Sch. Sys. Enr. Code 3
Supt. – Nyle Fox, P O BOX 385 47355
Randolph Southern ES, P O BOX 314 47355
  Eugene Hime, prin.

Lynnville, Warrick Co., Pop. Code 3
Warrick Co. SD
Supt. – See Boonville
ES, RURAL ROUTE 01 BOX 23C 47619
  Lowell McGlothlin, prin.

Lyons, Greene Co., Pop. Code 3
White River Valley SD
Supt. – See Worthington
L & M ES, RURAL ROUTE 01 BOX 70A 47443
  Kurt Lentz, prin.

Mackey, Gibson Co., Pop. Code 2
East Gibson SD
Supt. – See Oakland City
Barton Twp. ES, OLD STATE RD 57 47654
  Stanley Young, prin.

Madison, Jefferson Co., Pop. Code 7
Madison Cons. SD
Sch. Sys. Enr. Code 5
Supt. – Homer Lawson, P O BOX 445 47250
Anderson ES, 2407 MICHIGAN RD 47250
  N. Henderson, prin.
Eggleston ES, THIRD & EAST STS 47250
  Patrick Dryden, prin.
Middleton ES, 714 W MAIN ST 47250
  James Martin, prin.
Muncie ES, 800 LANIER DR 47250
  Larry Cummins, prin.
Rykers Ridge ES
  RURAL ROUTE 02 BOX 374A 47250
  Nancy Bear, prin.
Other Schools – See Canaan, Deputy, Dupont

Pope John XXIII School, 221 W STATE ST 47250

Manilla, Rush Co.
Rushville Cons. SD
Supt. – See Rushville
ES, P O BOX 81 46150 – Teresa Boyd, prin.

Marengo, Crawford Co., Pop. Code 3
Crawford Co. Comm. SD
Sch. Sys. Enr. Code 4
Supt. – Bayward Cole, P O BOX 366 47140
ES 47140 – Wendell Ford, prin.
Other Schools – See English, Leavenworth, Milltown,
Taswell

Marion, Grant Co., Pop. Code 8
Eastbrook Comm. SD
Sch. Sys. Enr. Code 4
Supt. – David Dick
  COUNTY ROAD 560 S 900 E 46953
Eastbrook JHS, 560 S 900 E 46953
  Mike Osha, prin.
Washington ES, 3031 E 450 N 46952
  John Clester, prin.
Other Schools – See Matthews, Upland, Van Buren

Marion Comm. SD
Sch. Sys. Enr. Code 4
Supt. – Mayer David, P O BOX 808 46952
Jones MS, 100 N PENNSYLVANIA ST 46952
  James McKinney, prin.
Justice MS, 720 N MILLER AVE 46952
  Michael Thorne, prin.
McCulloch MS, 3528 S WASHINGTON ST 46953
  James Gregory, prin.
Allen ES, 1115 E BRADFORD ST 46952
  Ed Hollingsworth, prin.
Center ES, 4415 S NEBRASKA ST 46953
  Gary McClure, prin.
Kendall ES, 2009 W KEM RD 46952
  John Stinger, prin.
Lincoln ES, 759 S LENFESTY AVE 46953
  Katherine Bobson, prin.
Riverview ES, 513 W BUCKINGHAM DR 46952
  Jerry McVicker, prin.
Slocum ES, 2909 S TORRENCE ST 46953
  June Gregory, prin.
Southeast ES, 3340 S LINCOLN BLVD 46953
  Robert Brunner, prin.

St. Paul School, 1009 W KEM RD 46952

Marshall, Parke Co., Pop. Code 2
Turkey Run Comm. SD
Sch. Sys. Enr. Code 3
Supt. – Dale Deplanty
  RURAL ROUTE 01 BOX 333 47859
Turkey Run ES
  RURAL ROUTE 01 BOX 333 47859
  Donald Baxter, prin.

Martinsville, Morgan Co., Pop. Code 7
Metro SD of Martinsville
Sch. Sys. Enr. Code 6
Supt. – James Auter, P O BOX 1416 46151
Martinsville East MS
  1459 E COLUMBUS ST 46151
  David Gordon, prin.
Martinsville West MS
  109 E GARFIELD AVE 46151
  Earl Williams, prin.
Central ES, 389 E JACKSON ST 46151
  David Satter, prin.
Green Twp. ES, 6275 MAPLE GROVE RD 46151
  Mel Ficklin, prin.
North ES, 60 E CUNNINGHAM ST 46151
  Becky Tidd, prin.
Poston Road ES, 139 E POSTON RD 46151
  Wayne Rosenbaum, prin.
Smith ES, 1359 E COLUMBUS ST 46151
  Louis Feagans, prin.
Other Schools – See Brooklyn, Centerton, Paragon

Mooresville Cons. SD
Supt. – See Mooresville
Waverly ES, 8525 WAVERLY RD 46151
  Donald Beck, prin.

Matthews, Grant Co., Pop. Code 3
Eastbrook Comm. SD
Supt. – See Marion
ES, P O BOX 7 46957 – Doris Crockett, prin.

Maxwell, Hancock Co.
Greenfield-Central Comm. SD
Supt. – See Greenfield
MS, STATE ROAD 9 46154
  Howard Mandel, prin.

Mays, Rush Co.
Rushville Cons. SD
Supt. – See Rushville
ES, P O BOX 85 46155 – Glenn Cunningham, prin.

Medora, Jackson Co., Pop. Code 3
Medora Comm. SD
Sch. Sys. Enr. Code 2
Supt. – Kenneth Kidd, P O BOX 248 47260
ES 47260 – Susan Kuzmie, prin.

Memphis, Clark Co.
West Clark Comm. SD
Supt. – See Sellersburg
ES, 14912 RAILROAD ST 47143
  Mary Matthews, prin.

Mentone, Kosciusko Co., Pop. Code 3
Tippecanoe Valley SD
Sch. Sys. Enr. Code 4
Supt. – Baxter Paige, P O BOX 338 46539
ES, YALE-JACKSON 46539 – Dan Kramer, prin.
Other Schools – See Akron, Burket

Merrillville, Lake Co., Pop. Code 8
Merrillville Comm. SD
Sch. Sys. Enr. Code 6
Supt. – Robert Schrenker
  6701 DELAWARE ST 46410
Pierce JHS, 199 E 70TH PLACE 46410
  Gerald Niemeyer, prin.
Fieler ES, 407 W 61ST AVE 46410
  Gary Sutton, prin.
Iddings ES, 7249 VAN BUREN ST 46410
  John Rosco, prin.
Miller ES, 5901 WAITE ST 46410
  Robert Tomb, prin.
Salk ES, 3301 W 77TH AVE 46410
  Cracia Reid, prin.
Wood ES, 7100 E 73RD AVE 46410
  Oscar Boswell Jr., prin.

Saints Peter & Paul School
  5861 HARRISON ST 46410

Michigan City, La Porte Co., Pop. Code 8
Michigan City Area SD
Sch. Sys. Enr. Code 6
Supt. – Alan Whitlow, 609 LAFAYETTE ST 46360
Barker JHS, 319 E BARKER ROAD 46360
  Dennis Martin, prin.
Krueger JHS, 2001 SPRINGLAND AVE 46360
  Kirk Rogers, prin.
Central ES, 301 E 8TH ST 46360
  Arlene Tarasick, prin.
Coolspring ES, 9121 W 300N 46360
  Bruce Leroy, prin.
Eastport ES, 1201 E MICHIGAN BLVD 46360
  Fred Wingert, prin.
Edgewood ES, 502 BOYD CIR 46360
  Wilbert Hedstrom, prin.
Joy ES, 1600 E COOLSPRING AVE 46360
  Thomas Hooper, prin.
Knapp ES, 321 BOLKA AVE 46360
  Dale Warren, prin.
Long Beach ES, STOP 24 LONG BEACH 46360
  Thomas Darman, prin.
Marsh ES, 401 E HOMER ST 46360
  Thomas Dombkowski, prin.
Mullen ES, 100 MANNY CT 46360
  Walter Zmuda, prin.
Niemann ES, 811 ROYAL RD 46360
  Dale Ferraro, prin.
Park ES, 222 MCCLELLAND AVE 46360
  Fred Laborn, prin.
Pine ES, RURAL ROUTE 02 46360
  Laura Harbart, prin.
Springfield ES, 3054 W 800N 46360
  Dan Firebaugh, prin.

Notre Dame School, 1000 MOORE ROAD 46360
Queen of All Saints School
  1715 E BARKER AVE 46360
St. Mary School, 312 W 10TH ST 46360
St. Paul Lutheran Day School
  818 FRANKLIN SQ 46360
St. Stanislaus School, 1506 FRANKLIN ST 46360

Michigantown, Clinton Co., Pop. Code 2
Clinton Central SD
Sch. Sys. Enr. Code 4
Supt. – Robert Brinson, P O BOX 178 46057
Clinton Central ES, P O BOX 238 46057
  Richard Swackhamer, prin.

Middlebury, Elkhart Co., Pop. Code 4
Middlebury Comm. SD
Sch. Sys. Enr. Code 4
Supt. – Rex Baker
  57853 NORTHRIDGE DRIVE 46540
Heritage MS, 57697 NORTHRIDGE DRIVE 2 46540
  Susan Weybright, prin.
ES, P O BOX 26 46540 – Melvin Yoder, prin.
Other Schools – See Bristol, Goshen

Middletown, Henry Co., Pop. Code 5
Shenendoah SD
Sch. Sys. Enr. Code 4
Supt. – Don Davenport, 108 S 5TH ST 47356
Shenandoah MS, RURAL ROUTE 01 47356
  Jerry Shreves, prin.
ES, 1130 LOCUST ST 47356 – David Gilbert, prin.
Other Schools – See Sulphur Springs

Milan, Ripley Co., Pop. Code 4
Milan Comm. SD
Sch. Sys. Enr. Code 4
Supt. – Richard Helton, P O BOX 278 47031
ES, P O BOX 337 47031 – Robert Collier, prin.

Milford, Kosciusko Co., Pop. Code 4
Wawasee Comm. SD
Supt. – See Syracuse
JHS, P O BOX 548 46542 – Russell Mikel, prin.
ES, P O BOX 548 46542 – Russell Mikel, prin.

Mill Creek, La Porte Co.
La Porte Comm. SD
Supt. – See La Porte
ES, COUNTY ROADS SOUTH & 875 E 46365
John Adams, prin.

Millersburg, Elkhart Co., Pop. Code 3
Fairfield Comm. SD
Supt. – See Goshen
ES, MAIN ST 46543 – Rhonda Knisely, prin.

Milltown, Crawford Co., Pop. Code 4
Crawford Co. Comm. SD
Supt. – See Marengo
ES 47145 – Terry Enlow, prin.

Milroy, Rush Co.
Rushville Cons. SD
Supt. – See Rushville
ES, N PLEASANT ST 46156
Phillip Mitchell, prin.

Milton, Wayne Co., Pop. Code 3
Western Wayne SD
Supt. – See Cambridge City
ES, STATE HIGHWAY 1 47357
William Hall, prin.

Mishawaka, St. Joseph Co., Pop. Code 5
City of Mishawaka SD
Sch. Sys. Enr. Code 6
Supt. – Richard Brainerd, 1402 S MAIN ST 46544
Young JHS, 1801 N MAIN ST 46545
Thomas Meyer, prin.
Battell ES, 715 E BROADWAY ST 46545
Daniel Wilson, prin.
Beiger ES, 1601 LINCOLN WAY E 46544
David Fisher, prin.
Emmons ES, 1206 S MAIN ST 46544
Terry Grass, prin.
Hums ES, 3208 HARRISON RD 46544
Donald Kominowski, prin.
Lasalle ES, 1511 MILBURN BLVD 46544
M. Novotny, prin.
North Side ES, 616 E MCKINLEY AVE 46545
Larry Weaver, prin.
Phillips ES, 702 W LAWRENCE ST 46545
Steven Van Bruaene, prin.
Twin Branch ES, 3810 LINCOLN WAY E 46544
Fred Stump, prin.

Penn-Harris-Madison SD
Sch. Sys. Enr. Code 6
Supt. – Dean Speicher
55900 BITTERSWEET ROAD 46545
Bittersweet ES, 55860 BITTERSWEET RD 46545
Richard Hahn, prin.
Disney ES, 54777 FILBERT RD 46545
James Hendress, prin.
Elm Road ES
RURAL ROUTE 01 BOX 59400 46544
Miriam Long, prin.
Rogers ES, 56219 CURRANT RD 46545
Leroy Heller, prin.
Other Schools – See Granger, Osceola, Wakarusa

South Bend Hebrew Day School
206 W 8TH ST 46544
St. Bavo School, 513 W 7TH ST 46544
St. Joseph School, 220 N 4TH ST 46544
St. Monica School, 223 W GROVE ST 46545

Mitchell, Lawrence Co., Pop. Code 5
Mitchell Comm. SD
Sch. Sys. Enr. Code 4
Supt. – James Oswalt
RURAL ROUTE 01 BOX 100 47446
JHS, 1010 W BISHOP BLVD 47446
James Terrell, prin.
Burris ES, RURAL ROUTE 01 BOX 94 47446
George Gentry, prin.
Hatfield ES, RURAL ROUTE 01 BOX 101 47446
George Gentry, prin.
Other Schools – See Huron

Modoc, Randolph Co., Pop. Code 2
Union SD
Sch. Sys. Enr. Code 3
Supt. – Darryl Stutts, RURAL ROUTE 01 47358
Union ES, RURAL ROUTE 01 47358
Terry Randall, prin.

Monon, White Co., Pop. Code 4
North White SD
Sch. Sys. Enr. Code 4
Supt. – John Heath, 322 N MARKET ST 47959
ES, RURAL ROUTE 01 47959
Mike Rennier, prin.
Other Schools – See Buffalo, Reynolds

Monroe, Adams Co., Pop. Code 3
Adams Central Comm. SD
Sch. Sys. Enr. Code 4
Supt. – Nancy Moller
222 W WASHINGTON ST 46772

Adams Central MS
222 W WASHINGTON ST 46772
Edwin Bryan, prin.
Adams Central ES
222 W WASHINGTON ST 46772
David Gorrell, prin.

Monroe City, Knox Co., Pop. Code 3
South Knox SD
Sch. Sys. Enr. Code 4
Supt. – William Case, P O BOX 388 47557
South Knox ES, P O BOX 38 47557
James Yochum, prin.
Other Schools – See Decker, Vincennes

Monroeville, Allen Co., Pop. Code 4
East Allen Co. SD
Supt. – See New Haven
ES, 401 MONROE ST 46773 – John Fries, prin.

St. John Lutheran Flatrock School
12912 FRANKE ROAD 46773

Monrovia, Morgan Co., Pop. Code 2
Monroe-Gregg SD
Sch. Sys. Enr. Code 4
Supt. – Brad Valentine, P O BOX 468 46157
Hall ES, RURAL ROUTE 01 BOX 57 46157
Bill Fisher, prin.
ES, P O BOX 468 46157 – Michael Finchum, prin.

Monterey, Pulaski Co., Pop. Code 2
Culver Comm. SD
Supt. – See Culver
ES, MAIN ST 46960 – Russell Hodges, prin.

Montezuma, Parke Co., Pop. Code 4
Southwest Parke Comm. SD
Sch. Sys. Enr. Code 4
Supt. – Alan Miller, RURAL ROUTE 01 47862
ES, STRAWBERRY ROAD 47862
J. Overberg, prin.
Other Schools – See Rosedale

Montgomery, Daviess Co., Pop. Code 2
Barr-Reeve Comm. SD
Sch. Sys. Enr. Code 3
Supt. – Merle Gould, P O BOX 97 47558
Bar Reeve IS, P O BOX 128 47558
J. Donahue, prin.
Bar Reeve PS, P O BOX 127 47558
J. Donahue, prin.

Monticello, White Co., Pop. Code 6
Twin Lakes SD
Sch. Sys. Enr. Code 5
Supt. – Rodney Rich, 565 S MAIN ST 47960
Roosevelt MS, 710 W HARRISON ST 47960
Patrick McTaggart, prin.
Meadowlawn ES, 715 W OHIO ST 47960
Robert Stockwell, prin.
Oaklawn ES, 402 E SOUTH ST 47960
Max Davis, prin.
Woodlawn ES, 300 BEACH DR 47960
Jerry Thacker, prin.
Other Schools – See Burnettsville

Montpelier, Blackford Co., Pop. Code 4
Blackford Co. SD
Supt. – See Hartford City
MS, 107 E MONROE ST 47359
Mitch Miller, prin.
ES, 337 S MAIN ST 47359 – Marietta Wolfe, prin.

Moores Hill, Dearborn Co., Pop. Code 3
South Dearborn Comm. SD
Supt. – See Aurora
ES, MAIN ST 47032 – Dan Rider, prin.

Mooresville, Morgan Co., Pop. Code 6
Mooresville Cons. SD
Sch. Sys. Enr. Code 5
Supt. – Albert Long, 320 N INDIANA ST 46158
Hadley JHS, 200 W CARLISLE ST 46158
James Patchet, prin.
Armstrong ES, 1000 ROAD 144 46158
Wallace Stewart, prin.
Newby Memorial ES, 240 N MONROE ST 46158
Curtis Freeman, prin.
Northwood ES, 630 N INDIANA ST 46158
Bill Colbert, prin.
Other Schools – See Camby, Martinsville

Morgantown, Morgan Co., Pop. Code 3
Brown Co. SD
Supt. – See Nashville
Helmsburg ES, RURAL ROUTE 03 BOX 273 46160
Kim Sechler, prin.

Morocco, Newton Co., Pop. Code 4
North Newton SD
Sch. Sys. Enr. Code 4
Supt. – Dan Blackketter, 30 E STATE ST 47963
ES, S LINCOLN ST 47963 – James Martin, prin.
Other Schools – See Lake Village, Roselawn

Morristown, Shelby Co., Pop. Code 3
Shelby Eastern SD
Supt. – See Shelbyville
ES, P O BOX 477 46161 – Diane Truster, prin.

Mount Summit, Henry Co., Pop. Code 2
Blue River Valley SD
Supt. – See New Castle
Blue River Valley ES, P O BOX 187 47361
Patricia Hughes, prin.

Mount Vernon, Posey Co., Pop. Code 6
Metro SD of Mt. Vernon
Sch. Sys. Enr. Code 5
Supt. – Melvin Levin, 1000 W 4TH ST 47620
JHS, 614 CANAL ST 47620
Jerry Funkhouser, prin.
Farmersville ES, RURAL ROUTE 03 47620
Mark Rice, prin.
Hedges Central ES, 716 LOCUST ST 47620
Edward Johnson, prin.
Mars ES, RURAL ROUTE 01 BOX 159A 47620
Jerry Putman, prin.
West ES, 1105 W 4TH ST 47620
Philip Ray, prin.

St. Matthew School, 401 MULBERRY ST 47620
St. Philip School, RURAL ROUTE 02 47620

Muncie, Delaware Co., Pop. Code 8
Burris Ball State SD
Sch. Sys. Enr. Code 3
Supt. – Kenneth Miller
2000 W UNIVERSITY AVE 47306
Ball State University S
2000 W UNIVERSITY AVE 47306
Kenneth Miller, prin.

Delaware Comm. SD
Sch. Sys. Enr. Code 5
Supt. – Thomas Fihe
RURAL ROUTE 03 BOX 48 47303
Delta MS, RURAL ROUTE 01 BOX 163 47303
Thomas Gourley, prin.
Desoto ES, RURAL ROUTE 13 47303
Douglas Stewart, prin.
Royerton ES, 1401 E ROYERTON RD 47303
M. Kile, prin.
Other Schools – See Albany, Eaton

Monroe Comm. SD
Sch. Sys. Enr. Code 3
Supt. – Darrell Martin
1000 W COUNTY ROAD 600 S 47302
Cowan ES, 100 W COUNTY RD 600 S 47302
Michael Garringer, prin.

Muncie Comm. SD
Sch. Sys. Enr. Code 7
Supt. – Donald Slauter
328 E WASHINGTON ST 47305
Northside MS, 2400 W BETHEL AVE 47304
Charles Childers, prin.
Wilson MS, 2000 S FRANKLIN ST 47302
Barb Phillips, prin.
Claypool ES, 3700 E WYSOR ST 47303
Dr. Homer Jackson, prin.
Garfield ES, 1600 S MADISON ST 47302
Rene Vanfleet, prin.
Grissom Memorial ES
3201 S MACEDONIA AVE 47302
Patricia Larue, prin.
Longfellow ES, 1900 E CENTENNIAL AVE 47303
Wendell Keesling, prin.
Mitchell ES, 2809 W PURDUE RD 47304
Darrell Gill, prin.
Mock ES, 3701 W GODMAN AVE 47304
Harold Roberts, prin.
North View ES, 807 W YALE AVE 47304
Robert Purtlebaugh, prin.
South View ES, 2100 S FRANKLIN ST 47302
Marion Black, prin.
Storer ES, 3211 W MANSFIELD DR 47304
John Arnold, prin.
Sutton ES, 3100 E MEMORIAL DR 47302
Michael Hirons, prin.
Washington-Carver Community ES
1000 E WASHINGTON ST 47305
Michael Ryan, prin.
West View ES, 3401 W GILBERT ST 47304
William Heath, prin.

St. Lawrence School, 301 S HACKLEY ST 47305
St. Mary School, 2401 W GILBERT ST 47303

Munster, Lake Co., Pop. Code 7
Town of Munster SD
Sch. Sys. Enr. Code 5
Supt. – Wallace Underwood
8616 COLUMBIA AVE 46321
Wright MS, 8650 COLUMBIA AVE 46321
Raymond Kley, prin.
Eads ES, 8001 HARRISON AVE 46321
Cleatus Aker, prin.
Elliott ES, 8718 WHITE OAK AVE 46321
R. White, prin.
Hammond ES, 1301 FRAN-LIN PKY 46321
Teresa Coulter, prin.

St. Paul Lutheran School
8601 HARRISON AVE 46321
St. Thomas More School
8501 CALUMET AVE 46321

Napoleon, Ripley Co., Pop. Code 2
Jac-Cen-Del Comm. SD
Supt. – See Osgood
ES, P O BOX 28 47034 – Michael Stephens, prin.

Nappanee, Elkhart Co., Pop. Code 5
Wa-Nee Comm. SD
Sch. Sys. Enr. Code 5
Supt. – Jerry Lelle, 104 S MAIN ST 46550
MS, E VAN BUREN ST 46550
George Roelandts, prin.
Nappanee Central ES, 107 E MARION ST 46550
Richard Strakowski, prin.

Nappannee South ES, 901 S MAIN ST   46550
  Richard Strakowski, prin.
Union Center ES, 69954 COUNTY RD 11   46550
  Larry Nafziger, prin.
Other Schools – See Goshen, Wakarusa

Nashville, Brown Co., Pop. Code 3
Brown Co. SD
Sch. Sys. Enr. Code 4
Supt. – Carol Walker, P O BOX 38   47448
Brown County JHS, P O BOX 755   47448
  Vincent Rozzi, prin.
ES, P O BOX 157   47448 – J. Hamblin, prin.
Van Buren ES, RURAL ROUTE 02 BOX 126   47448
  Diana Igo, prin.
Other Schools – See Morgantown, Nineveh

New Albany, Floyd Co., Pop. Code 8
New Albany-Floyd Co. Cons. SD
Sch. Sys. Enr. Code 7
Supt. – Dr. Tracy Dust, P O BOX 1087   47150
Emery ES, 1111 PEARL ST   47150
  Maxwell White, prin.
Fairmont ES, FAIRMONT & ABBIEDELL   47150
  Denver McFadden, prin.
Galena ES, RURAL ROUTE 02 BOX 445   47150
  Norman Perkins, prin.
Grant Line ES, 4811 GRANT LINE RD   47150
  Raymond Bruce, prin.
Green Valley ES, 2230 GREEN VALLEY RD   47150
  Gene Miller, prin.
Jones ES, 600 E 11TH ST   47150
  Leland Lang, prin.
Mt Tabor ES, 800 MOUNT TABOR RD   47150
  William Chilton, prin.
Pine View ES, 2524 CORYDON PIKE   47150
  Ralph Dooley, prin.
Reisz ES, 1613 E SPRING ST   47150
  Raymond Polly, prin.
Silver Street ES, 2023 EKIN AVE   47150
  William Stoops, prin.
Slate Run ES, 1452 SLATE RUN RD   47150
  Ronald Schad, prin.
Other Schools – See Floyds Knobs, Georgetown,
  Greenville

Graceland Christian School
  3600 KAMER MILLER ROAD   47150
Holy Family School, 217 W DAISY LN   47150
Our Lady of Perpetual Help School
  1752 SCHELLER LN   47150
St. Mary School, 420 E 8TH ST   47150

Newburgh, Warrick Co., Pop. Code 5
Warrick Co. SD
Supt. – See Boonville
Castle JHS, P O BOX 98   47630 – Joe Loge, prin.
Castle ES, P O BOX 339   47629
  Kenneth Kreke, prin.
ES, 306 STATE ST   47630 – Richard Reid, prin.
Sharon ES, 7300 SHARON RD   47630
  Paul Ramey, prin.
Yankeetown ES, 7422 S YANKEETOWN RD   47630
  Guy Stephens, prin.

St. John the Baptist School, 725 FRAME RD   47630

New Carlisle, St. Joseph Co., Pop. Code 4
New Prairie United SD
Sch. Sys. Enr. Code 4
Supt. – David Myers, 5329 N 700 E   46552
New Prairie JHS, 5331 N 700 E   46552
  Gregory Wilson, prin.
Hudson Lake ES, RURAL ROUTE 03   46552
  Richard Jones, prin.
Olive Twp. ES, BRAY & BEN ST   46552
  Doris Gamble, prin.
Other Schools – See La Porte, Rolling Prairie

New Castle, Henry Co., Pop. Code 7
Blue River Valley SD
Sch. Sys. Enr. Code 4
Supt. – Gerald Shelton
  RURAL ROUTE 05 BOX 143-A   47362
Other Schools – See Mount Summit

New Castle Comm. SD
Sch. Sys. Enr. Code 5
Supt. – Philip Borders, 522 ELLIOTT AVE   47362
Eastwood ES, 806 S 22ND ST   47362
  Hershel Denney, prin.
Greenstreet ES, 329 S 5TH ST   47362
  Robert Showalter, prin.
Parker ES, 1819 ROOSEVELT AVE   47362
  Robert Wiles, prin.
Parkview MS B7, 1407 WALNUT ST   47362
  Herbert Bunch, prin.
Riley ES, 1201 RILEY RD   47362
  Charlie Popplewell, prin.
Sunnyside ES, 2601 S 14TH ST   47362
  Linda Kinnett, prin.
Westwood ES, RURAL ROUTE 06 BOX 37   47362
  Robert Veach, prin.
Wright ES, 1950 WASHINGTON ST   47362
  D. Fitzgerald, prin.

New Harmony, Posey Co., Pop. Code 3
New Harmony Town & Twp. Cons. SD
Sch. Sys. Enr. Code 2
Supt. – B. McCuiston, P O BOX 396   47631
S, P O BOX 396   47631 – Paul Mikus, prin.

New Haven, Allen Co., Pop. Code 6
East Allen Co. SD
Sch. Sys. Enr. Code 6
Supt. – Michael Benway, 1240 US 30 E   46774

MS, 900 PROSPECT AVE   46774
  David Jones, prin.
Highland Terrace ES, 1445 BERWICK LN   46774
  Darwin Markley, prin.
Meadowbrook ES, 1065 WOODMERE DR   46774
  Karen Fletcher, prin.
ES, 800 HOMESTEAD DR   46774
  Steven Sprunger, prin.
Other Schools – See Fort Wayne, Harlan, Hoagland,
  Leo, Monroeville, Woodburn

Central Lutheran School, 1400 ELM ST   46774
St. John the Baptist School, 204 RUFUS ST   46774

New Market, Montgomery Co., Pop. Code 3
South Montgomery Comm. SD
Sch. Sys. Enr. Code 4
Supt. – Rob Tandy, P O BOX 8   47965
ES   47965 – James Zielinski, prin.
Other Schools – See Crawfordsville, Ladoga, New
  Ross, Waveland

New Middletown, Harrison Co., Pop. Code 2
South Harrison Comm. SD
Supt. – See Corydon
ES   47160 – James Wolfe, prin.

New Palestine, Hancock Co., Pop. Code 3
Southern Hancock Co. Comm. SD
Sch. Sys. Enr. Code 4
Supt. – Gene Pruitt, P O BOX 508   46163
Doe Creek MS, P O BOX 388   46163
  Lawrence Garton, prin.
ES, P O BOX 448   46163 – Donald Dawson, prin.
Other Schools – See Greenfield

Zion Lutheran School
  RURAL ROUTE 01 BOX 443   46163

New Paris, Elkhart Co.
Fairfield Comm. SD
Supt. – See Goshen
ES, 68080 DIVISION ST   46553
  Conrad Neff, prin.

Newport, Vermillion Co., Pop. Code 3
North Vermillion Comm. SD
Supt. – See Cayuga
ES   47966 – William Smith, prin.

New Ross, Montgomery Co., Pop. Code 2
South Montgomery Comm. SD
Supt. – See New Market
Walnut ES, RURAL ROUTE 01   47968
  Keith Airey, prin.

New Washington, Clark Co., Pop. Code 2
Greater Clark Co. SD
Supt. – See Jeffersonville
ES, P O BOX 130   47162 – Bill Holbrook, prin.

Nineveh, Johnson Co.
Brown Co. SD
Supt. – See Nashville
Sprunica ES, RURAL ROUTE 01 BOX 316A   46164
  Sheila Oliver, prin.

Noblesville, Hamilton Co., Pop. Code 7
Hamilton Southeastern SD
Sch. Sys. Enr. Code 4
Supt. – Charles Leonard
  RURAL ROUTE 05 BOX 280A   46060
Hamilton Southeastern MS
  RURAL ROUTE 05 BOX 280   46060
  Roger Norris, prin.
Cumberland Road ES
  RURAL ROUTE 05 BOX 280B   46060
  Stephen Foster, prin.
Durbin ES, 18000 DURBIN RD   46060
  Thomas Heller, prin.
Fall Creek ES, RURAL ROUTE 04 BOX 228   46060
  Jerril Staley, prin.
Other Schools – See Fishers

Noblesville SD
Sch. Sys. Enr. Code 5
Supt. – Loren Williams, 1775 FIELD DRIVE   46060
JHS, 1625 FIELD DRIVE   46060
  Lynn Lehman, prin.
Conner ES, 1700 CONNER ST   46060
  John Land, prin.
Forest Hill ES, 470 LAKEVIEW DR   46060
  Jeffrey Sherrill, prin.
Hinkle Creek ES, 595 S HARBOUR DR   46060
  Phillip Harrold, prin.
North ES, A440 NORTH 10TH   46060
  Victor Harber, prin.
Stony Creek ES, 1350 GREENFIELD AVE   46060
  Robert Harvey, prin.

North Judson, Starke Co., Pop. Code 4
North Judson-San Pierre SD
Sch. Sys. Enr. Code 4
Supt. – Dr. Stephen Timler
  902 W TALMER   46366
JHS, 302 KELLER AVE   46366
  Jerome Jernas, prin.
Liberty ES, 809 W TALMER AVE   46366
  Judith Weitgenant, prin.
Other Schools – See San Pierre

St. Peter Lutheran School, HIGHWAY 10 W   46366

North Liberty, St. Joseph Co., Pop. Code 4
John Glenn SD
Supt. – See Walkerton

ES, 400 HIGH SCHOOL ROAD   46554
  Brent Kaufman, prin.

North Manchester, Wabash Co., Pop. Code 6
Manchester Comm. SD
Sch. Sys. Enr. Code 4
Supt. – John Eckert, 404 W 9TH ST   46962
Manchester JHS, 404 W 9TH ST   46962
  Dan Risk, prin.
Chester ES, RURAL ROUTE 01 BOX 301   46962
  Scott Turney, prin.
Maple Park ES, 107 S BUFFALO ST   46962
  Tom Hess, prin.
Marshall ES, 603 BOND ST   46962
  Dan Sharp, prin.
Other Schools – See Laketon

North Salem, Hendricks Co., Pop. Code 3
North West Hendricks SD
Supt. – See Lizton
ES, P O BOX 69   46165 – Kenneth Carter, prin.

North Vernon, Jennings Co., Pop. Code 6
Jennings Co. SD
Sch. Sys. Enr. Code 5
Supt. – John Ellis, 34 MAIN ST   47265
JHS, WEBSTER & JENNINGS   47265
  Roger Dean, prin.
Brush Creek ES
  RURAL ROUTE 01 BOX 103   47265
  James Conner, prin.
ES, HIGHWAY 50 W   47265 – Connie Gatke, prin.
Other Schools – See Commiskey, Hayden, Scipio

St. Mary School, 209 WASHINGTON ST   47265

North Webster, Kosciusko Co., Pop. Code 3
Wawasee Comm. SD
Supt. – See Syracuse
JHS, P O BOX 338   46555 – Richard Long, prin.
ES, P O BOX 358   46555 – Richard Long, prin.

Oakland City, Gibson Co., Pop. Code 2
East Gibson SD
Sch. Sys. Enr. Code 4
Supt. – Everett Potts, 943 S FRANKLIN ST   47660
ES, S FRANKLIN ST   47660 – Roger Benson, prin.
Other Schools – See Francisco, Mackey

Odon, Daviess Co., Pop. Code 4
North Daviess Co. Comm. SD
Supt. – See Elnora
ES, 201-205 S JOHN ST   47562
  Kenneth Hudson, prin.
Raglesville ES, RURAL ROUTE 01   47562
  Kenneth Hudson, prin.

Oldenburg, Franklin Co., Pop. Code 3
Batesville Comm. SD
Supt. – See Batesville
ES   47036 – Kathleen Placke, prin.

Oolitic, Lawrence Co., Pop. Code 4
North Lawrence Comm. SD
Supt. – See Bedford
Dollens/Oolitic ES, 903 HOOSIER AVE   47451
  Mark Turner, prin.

Orleans, Orange Co., Pop. Code 4
Orleans Comm. SD
Sch. Sys. Enr. Code 3
Supt. – Leonard Vaught
  RURAL ROUTE 02 BOX 2   47452
ES, RURAL ROUTE 01 BOX 326   47452
  Marion Chapman, prin.

Osceola, St. Joseph Co., Pop. Code 4
Penn-Harris-Madison SD
Supt. – See Mishawaka
Moran ES, 57055 BEECH RD   46561
  Herbert Sloan, prin.

Osgood, Ripley Co., Pop. Code 4
Jac-Cen-Del Comm. SD
Sch. Sys. Enr. Code 3
Supt. – Stephen Gookins
  RURAL ROUTE 03 BOX 28   47037
ES, E RIPLEY ST   47037 – Raymond Coffey, prin.
Other Schools – See Napoleon

Ossian, Wells Co., Pop. Code 4
Northern Wells Comm. SD
Sch. Sys. Enr. Code 4
Supt. – Michael Sailsbery, P O BOX 386   46777
Norwell MS, 1100 E US 224   46777
  Ed Ritter, prin.
ES, 213 S JEFFERSON ST   46777
  Lonnie Buuck, prin.
Other Schools – See Bluffton

Bethlehem Lutheran School, 7545 N 650 E   46777

Otterbein, Benton Co., Pop. Code 4
Benton Comm. SD
Supt. – See Fowler
ES, OXFORD ST   47970 – Mark Pearl, prin.

Otwell, Pike Co.
Pike Co. SD
Supt. – See Petersburg
ES, P O BOX 38   47564 – Helen Fulcher, prin.

Owensville, Gibson Co., Pop. Code 4
South Gibson SD
Supt. – See Fort Branch
ES, 410 S MILL ST   47665 – Cornelius Epple, prin.

Oxford, Benton Co., Pop. Code 4
Benton Comm. SD
Supt. – See Fowler
ES, 555 N 5TH ST   47971 – Wayne Smith, prin.

Palmyra, Harrison Co., Pop. Code 3
North Harrison Comm. SD
Supt. – See Ramsey
Morgan ES   47164 – Von Marshall, prin.

Paoli, Orange Co., Pop. Code 5
Paoli Comm. SD
Sch. Sys. Enr. Code 4
Supt. – Alva Sibbitt, 501 S ELM ST   47454
Throop ES, 301 S ELM ST   47454
Warner Michener, prin.

Paragon, Morgan Co., Pop. Code 3
Metro SD of Martinsville
Supt. – See Martinsville
ES, P O BOX 27   46166 – Robert Blackketter, prin.

Parker City, Randolph Co., Pop. Code 4
Monroe Central SD
Sch. Sys. Enr. Code 4
Supt. – Michael Shonk, RURAL ROUTE 01   47368
Monroe Central ES, RURAL ROUTE 01   47368
Larry Hall, prin.

Patricksburg, Owen Co.
Spencer-Owen Comm. SD
Supt. – See Spencer
ES   47455 – Suzanne Tyler, prin.

Pekin, Washington Co., Pop. Code 3
East Washington SD
Sch. Sys. Enr. Code 4
Supt. – H. Butler, P O BOX 37   47165
East Washington ES
RURAL ROUTE 02 BOX E4   47165
Kenneth Weller, prin.

Pendleton, Madison Co., Pop. Code 4
South Madison Comm. SD
Sch. Sys. Enr. Code 5
Supt. – Charles Mock, 201 S EAST ST   46064
MS, 301 S EAST ST   46064 – Terry Auker, prin.
East ES, RURAL ROUTE 03 BOX 500   46064
Nancy Phenis, prin.
Pendleton South ES, 327 S EAST ST   46064
Karl Keller, prin.

Pennville, Jay Co., Pop. Code 3
Jay SD
Supt. – See Portland
ES, P O BOX 245   47369 – Randall Rains, prin.

Perrysville, Vermillion Co., Pop. Code 3
North Vermillion Comm. SD
Supt. – See Cayuga
Highland ES   47974 – Michael Bosc, prin.

Pershing, Wayne Co.
Western Wayne SD
Supt. – See Cambridge City
ES   47370 – David Gaddis, prin.

Peru, Miami Co., Pop. Code 7
Maconaquah SD
Supt. – See Bunker Hill
Pipe Creek ES, RURAL ROUTE 05 BOX 286   46970
Jerry Miller, prin.
Randall ES, RURAL ROUTE 05 BOX 246   46970
Robert Fulton, prin.

Peru Comm. SD
Sch. Sys. Enr. Code 5
Supt. – Larry Williams
2 1/2 N BROADWAY ST   46970
JHS, 30 DANIEL ST   46970 – (—), prin.
Central ES, 81 W 7TH ST   46970
David Hahn, prin.
Elmwood ES, 515 N WAYNE ST   46970
Joanne Werling, prin.
Holman ES, 425 W MAIN ST   46970
(—), prin.
Lincoln ES, 25 S BENTON ST   46970
Steve Gough, prin.
South Peru ES, PARK DRIVE   46970
Chris Newhouse, prin.

St. Charles School, 80 W 5TH ST   46970
St. John's Lutheran School, 181 W MAIN ST   46970

Petersburg, Pike Co., Pop. Code 5
Pike Co. SD
Sch. Sys. Enr. Code 4
Supt. – Howard Briscoe, 211 S 12TH ST   47567
ES, MAPLE ST   47567 – Steve Meadors, prin.
Other Schools – See Otwell, Winslow

Pierceton, Kosciusko Co., Pop. Code 4
Whitko Comm. SD
Sch. Sys. Enr. Code 4
Supt. – Dr. Kenneth Blad, P O BOX 114   46562
MS, P O BOX 94   46562 – Alan Frank, prin.
ES, P O BOX 94   46562 – Mark Stock, prin.
Other Schools – See South Whitley

Pine Village, Warren Co., Pop. Code 2
Metro SD of Warren Co.
Supt. – See Williamsport
ES, RURAL ROUTE 01   47975
Gretchen Leuenberger, prin.

Pittsboro, Hendricks Co., Pop. Code 3
North West Hendricks SD
Supt. – See Lizton
ES, P O BOX 279   46167 – Leslie Hassfurder, prin.

Plainfield, Hendricks Co., Pop. Code 6
Plainfield Comm. SD
Sch. Sys. Enr. Code 5
Supt. – Milo Eiche
985 LONGFELLOW DRIVE   46168
Brentwood ES, 1630 OLIVER AVE   46168
James Madden, prin.
Central ES, 110 WABASH ST   46168
Michael Underwood, prin.
Van Buren ES, 233 SHAW ST   46168
Sherry Carver, prin.

Plainville, Daviess Co., Pop. Code 3
North Daviess Co. Comm. SD
Supt. – See Elnora
ES, P O BOX 9   47568 – Loren Crane, prin.

Pleasant Lake, Steuben Co.
Metro SD of Steuben Co.
Supt. – See Angola
ES, P O BOX 69   46779 – Michael Christ, prin.

Plymouth, Marshall Co., Pop. Code 6
Plymouth Comm. SD
Sch. Sys. Enr. Code 5
Supt. – Danny Bates, 701 BERKLEY ST   46563
Lincoln JHS, 220 N LIBERTY ST   46563
Earl Richter, prin.
Jefferson ES, 401 KLINGER ST   46563
Jack Davis, prin.
Washington ES, 1500 LAKE AVE   46563
Charles Ray, Jr., prin.
Webster ES, 1101 S MICHIGAN ST   46563
Michael Pettibone, prin.
West ES, 9971 RURAL ROUTE 17   46563
Dean Rager, prin.

St. Michael School, 612 N CENTER ST   46563

Poneto, Wells Co., Pop. Code 2
Southern Wells Comm. SD
Sch. Sys. Enr. Code 3
Supt. – William Payne, RURAL ROUTE 01   46781
Southern Wells ES, 9120S S 300 W   46781
Robert Williams, prin.

Portage, Porter Co., Pop. Code 8
Portage Twp. SD
Sch. Sys. Enr. Code 6
Supt. – Donald Bivens
5894 CENTRAL AVE   46368
Fegely MS, 5384 STONE AVE   46368
Terrance Levenda, prin.
Willowcreek MS, 5962 CENTRAL AVE   46368
Gerald Dixon, prin.
Aylesworth ES, 5910 CENTRAL AVE   46368
Ken Ingram, prin.
Central ES, 2825 RUSSELL ST   46368
Lane Prescott, prin.
Crisman ES, 6161 OLD PORTER RD   46368
Linda Kuss, prin.
Jones ES, 2374 MCCOOL RD   46368
Terry Miller, prin.
Kyle ES, 2701 HAMSTROM RD   46368
Aris Psimos, prin.
Myers ES, 3100 WILLOWDALE RD   46368
Paul Swenson, prin.
Other Schools – See Valparaiso

Nativity ES, 2929 WILLOWCREEK RD   46368

Porter, Clark Co., Pop. Code 5
Duneland SD
Supt. – See Chesterton
Yost ES, SHERMAN & BEAM STS   46304
Ken Miller, prin.

Portland, Jay Co., Pop. Code 6
Jay SD
Sch. Sys. Enr. Code 5
Supt. – George Gilbert, 200 S WAYNE ST   47371
East Jay County JHS, 227 E WATER ST   47371
Larry May, prin.
East ES, 705 E TALLMAN ST   47371
C. Newman, prin.
General Shanks ES, 414 E FLORAL AVE   47371
Sidney Austin, prin.
Haynes ES, 800 HIGH ST   47371
Dan Hoffman, prin.
Other Schools – See Bryant, Dunkirk, Pennville, Redkey

Poseyville, Posey Co., Pop. Code 4
Metro SD of North Posey Co.
Sch. Sys. Enr. Code 4
Supt. – B. Brenton, P O BOX 277   47633
North Posey JHS, RURAL ROUTE 01   47633
Kevin Sergesketter, prin.
North ES, P O BOX 129   47633 – Robert Hunt, prin.
Other Schools – See Wadesville

Princeton, Gibson Co., Pop. Code 6
North Gibson SD
Sch. Sys. Enr. Code 4
Supt. – E. Swan, RURAL ROUTE 04   47670
Princeton Community MS, 410 STATE ST   47670
Charles Smith, prin.
Baldwin Heights ES, RURAL ROUTE 01   47670
Irie Horrall, prin.
Brumfield ES, RURAL ROUTE 03 BOX 225   47670
James Kolb, prin.
Lowell ES, WATER & WEST STS   47670
James Mason, prin.

St. Joseph School, 427 S STORMONT ST   47670

Ramsey, Harrison Co.
North Harrison Comm. SD
Sch. Sys. Enr. Code 4
Supt. – Roger Williams, P O BOX 8   47166
North Harrison MS   47166 – Jon Howerton, prin.
North Harrison ES   47166 – Thomas Smith, prin.
Other Schools – See Palmyra

Redkey, Jay Co., Pop. Code 4
Jay SD
Supt. – See Portland
ES, P O BOX 6   47373 – Jay Milhollin, prin.

Reelsville, Putnam Co.
South Putnam Comm. SD
Supt. – See Greencastle
Reelsville ES, RURAL ROUTE 01   46171
Robert Neier, prin.

Remington, Jasper Co., Pop. Code 4
Tri-County SD
Supt. – See Wolcott
ES, P O BOX 95   47977 – Karel Peck, prin.

Rensselaer, Jasper Co., Pop. Code 5
Rensselaer Central SD
Sch. Sys. Enr. Code 4
Supt. – Roberta Dinsmore, P O BOX 69   47978
MS, 1106 LEOPOLD ST   47978
Gordon Lewis, prin.
Monnett ES, 605 GROVE ST   47978
C. Ockermann, prin.
Van Rensselaer ES
E WASH & MELVILLE ST   47978
Thomas Effinger, prin.

St. Augustine School, 310 N MCKINLEY   47978

Reynolds, White Co., Pop. Code 3
North White SD
Supt. – See Monon
ES, GENERAL DELIVERY   47980
Tamarah Sherrard, prin.

Richland, Spencer Co.
South Spencer Co. SD
Supt. – See Rockport
Luce ES, RURAL ROUTE 01   47634
William Brauns, prin.

Richmond, Wayne Co., Pop. Code 8
Richmond Comm. SD
Sch. Sys. Enr. Code 6
Supt. – Richard Morrison
300 WHITEWATER BLVD   47374
Hibberd MS, 900 S L ST   47374
Sandra Hillman, prin.
Pleasant View MS
1820 PLEASANT VIEW ROAD   47374
James Isaacs, prin.
Test MS, 33 S 22ND ST   47374 – Don Warner, prin.
Worth MS, 222 N W 7TH ST   47374
Bill Upchurch, prin.
Baxter ES, 315 NW 3RD ST   47374
Robert Molnar, prin.
Charles ES, 2400 REEVESTON RD   47374
Ray Lewis, prin.
Crestdale ES, 701 CRESTDALE DR   47374
Stephen Price, prin.
Fairview ES, 60 NW L ST   47374
Robert Molnar, prin.
Garrison ES, 4138 NIEWOEHNER RD   47374
Phil Stafford, prin.
Highland Heights ES, 1751 E CHESTER RD   47374
Phil Bolser, prin.
Parkview ES, 131 NW 8TH ST   47374
Van Shank, prin.
Richardson ES, 1215 S J ST   47374
John Bender, prin.
Starr ES, 301 N 19TH ST   47374 – John Prall, prin.
Vaile ES, 301 S 13TH ST   47374
Nancy Mulick, prin.
Westview ES, 1717 SW A ST   47374
Van Shank, prin.

Elizabeth Ann Seton Catholic School West
801 W MAIN ST   47374
Elizabeth Ann Seton Catholic School East
720 N A ST   47374

Ridgeville, Randolph Co., Pop. Code 3
Randolph Central SD
Supt. – See Winchester
Deerfield ES, RURAL ROUTE 02 BOX 276A   47380
John Clodfelder, prin.

Riley, Vigo Co., Pop. Code 2
Vigo Co. SD
Supt. – See Terre Haute
ES, P O BOX 127   47871 – David Fuller, prin.

Rising Sun, Ohio Co., Pop. Code 4
Rising Sun-Ohio Co. Comm. SD
Sch. Sys. Enr. Code 3
Supt. – John Roeder, 210 S HENRIETTA ST   47040
Ohio County ES, 436 S MULBERRY ST   47040
Otis Noe, prin.

Roachdale, Putnam Co., Pop. Code 3
North Putnam Comm. SD
Supt. – See Bainbridge
ES, P O BOX 309   46172 – Warren Rush, prin.

Roanoke, Huntington Co., Pop. Code 3
Huntington Co. Comm. SD
Supt. – See Huntington
ES, 423 W VINE ST   46783 – Paul Roth, prin.

Metro SD of Southwest Allen Co.
Supt. – See Fort Wayne
Lafayette Central ES, RURAL ROUTE 01 46783
    Steven Cobb.

Rochester, Fulton Co., Pop. Code 6
Rochester Comm. SD
Sch. Sys. Enr. Code 4
Supt. – R. Poffenbarger, P O BOX 108 46975
Rochester Community MS, P O BOX 108 46975
    Richard Cole, prin.
Columbia ES, ELM & 15TH STS 46975
    Sherri Gow, prin.
Riddle ES, THIRD & CLAY STS 46975
    James Barkman, prin.

Rockport, Spencer Co., Pop. Code 5
South Spencer Co. SD
Sch. Sys. Enr. Code 4
Supt. – L. Fred Ayer, S 5TH ST 47635
South Spencer MS, S 5TH ST 47635
    Richard Hedrick, prin.
Rockport-Ohio ES, 6TH AND WALNUT 47635
    James Howard, prin.
Other Schools – See Richland

St. Bernard School, 547 ELM ST 47635

Rockville, Parke Co., Pop. Code 5
Rockville Comm. SD
Sch. Sys. Enr. Code 3
Supt. – Larry Gambaiani, 506 N BEADLE ST 47872
ES, 406 ELM ST 47872 – Roy Butts, prin.

Rolling Prairie, La Porte Co.
New Prairie United SD
Supt. – See New Carlisle
ES, P O BOX 38 46371 – Deborah Post, prin.

Rome City, Noble Co., Pop. Code 4
East Noble SD
Supt. – See Kendallville
ES 46784 – Nancy Flint, prin.

Rosedale, Parke Co., Pop. Code 3
Southwest Parke Comm. SD
Supt. – See Montezuma
ES, E CENTRAL 47874 – Adrienne Gideon, prin.

Roselawn, Newton Co.
North Newton SD
Supt. – See Morocco
Lincoln ES 46372 – Dan Brock, prin.

Rossville, Clinton Co., Pop. Code 4
Rossville Cons. SD
Sch. Sys. Enr. Code 3
Supt. – Charles Whitlock 46065
ES 46065 – Kenneth Cushman, prin.

Royal Center, Cass Co., Pop. Code 3
Pioneer Regional SD
Sch. Sys. Enr. Code 4
Supt. – Charles Pettit, 115 S CHICAGO ST 46978
Pioneer ES, P O BOX 8 46978
    Kevin Emsweller, prin.

Rushville, Rush Co., Pop. Code 6
Rushville Cons. SD
Sch. Sys. Enr. Code 5
Supt. – D. Smith, 8TH & JACKSON ST 46173
Rush JHS, 1600 N PARK ROAD 46173
    Jerry Fox, prin.
New Salem ES, RURAL ROUTE 01 46173
    Rockman Alspaugh, prin.
ES, WEST 16TH ST 46173 – Gerald Mohr, prin.
Other Schools – See Arlington, Manilla, Mays, Milroy

St. Mary School-Rushville
    503 N PERKINS ST 46173

Russiaville, Howard Co., Pop. Code 3
Western SD
Sch. Sys. Enr. Code 4
Supt. – James Smith, 600 W 250 S 46979
Western IS, 600 WEST 250 S 46979
    Joyce Dahlquist, prin.
Western MS, 600 W 250 S 46979
    Ronald Colby, prin.
Western PS, 600 WEST 250 S 46979
    Roy Nehl, prin.

Russellville, Putnam Co., Pop. Code 2
North Putnam Comm. SD
Supt. – See Bainbridge
ES, P O BOX 205 46175 – Sheila Smith, prin.

Saint Anthony, Dubois Co.
Southeast Dubois Co. SD
Supt. – See Ferdinand
St. Anthony ES, STATE ROAD 64 47575
    Stephen Scott, prin.

Saint Joe, De Kalb Co., Pop. Code 3
DeKalb Co. Eastern Comm. SD
Supt. – See Butler
Riverdale ES, P O BOX 172 46785
    Jeffrey Stephens, prin.

Saint John, Lake Co., Pop. Code 5
Lake Central SD
Sch. Sys. Enr. Code 6
Supt. – Thomas Roman, 8260 WICKER AVE 46373
Kolling ES, 8801 WICKER AVE 46373
    Nancy Sanasack, prin.
Other Schools – See Dyer, Schererville

St. John Evangelist School
    9400 WICKER AVE 46373

Saint Meinrad, Spencer Co., Pop. Code 3
North Spencer Co. SD
Supt. – See Dale
ES 47577 – James Freihaut, prin.

Salem, Washington Co., Pop. Code 6
Salem Comm SD
Sch. Sys. Enr. Code 4
Supt. – Morris Rosenbaum
    N HARRISON ST 47167
MS, 300 N WATER ST 47167 – Charles Hunt, prin.
Shrum ES, N SHELBY ST 47167
    Clifford Kinney, prin.

San Pierre, Starke Co.
North Judson-San Pierre SD
Supt. – See North Judson
ES, P O BOX 6 46374 – Frank Szynalski, prin.

Schererville, Lake Co., Pop. Code 7
Lake Central SD
Supt. – See Saint John
Grimmer MS, 222 W 77TH AVE 46375
    Ken Miller, prin.
Homan ES, 210 E JOLIET ST 46375
    G. Kellogg, prin.
Peifer ES, 1824 CLINE AVE 46375
    Richard Baer, prin.
Watson ES, 333 W 77TH AVE 46375
    David Andrews, prin.

St. Michael School, 16 W WILHELM ST 46375

Scipio, Jennings Co.
Jennings Co. SD
Supt. – See North Vernon
ES, P O BOX 126 47273 – James Reynolds, prin.

Scottsburg, Scott Co., Pop. Code 6
Scott Co. SD 2
Sch. Sys. Enr. Code 5
Supt. – Gerald McCullum
    375 E MCCLAIN AVE 47170
JHS, 145 S 3RD ST 47170 – James Hough, prin.
Johnson ES, RURAL ROUTE 04 47170
    Mark Douglas, prin.
ES, 49 N HYLAND ST 47170
    Marvin Carter, prin.
Vienna-Finley ES, RURAL ROUTE 06 47170
    Dale Hobbs, prin.
Other Schools – See Lexington

Sellersburg, Clark Co., Pop. Code 5
West Clark Comm. SD
Sch. Sys. Enr. Code 5
Supt. – H. Miller, 601 RENZ AVE 47172
Silver Creek JHS, 495 N INDIANA AVE 47172
    Reid Bailey, prin.
MS, 206 N NEW ALBANY AVE 47172
    Ronald Fidler, prin.
Stout ES, 503 N INDIANA AVE 47172
    David Losey, prin.
Other Schools – See Borden, Henryville, Memphis

St. Paul School, 105 SAINT PAUL ST 47172

Selma, Delaware Co., Pop. Code 4
Liberty-Perry Comm. SD
Sch. Sys. Enr. Code 4
Supt. – Joseph Wolfe, P O BOX 337 47383
MS, RURAL ROUTE 01 47383
    Donald Black, prin.
Perry ES, RURAL ROUTE 01 47383
    Robert Grove, prin.
ES, RURAL ROUTE 01 47383 – Tom Childs, prin.

Seymour, Jackson Co., Pop. Code 7
Seymour Comm. SD
Sch. Sys. Enr. Code 5
Supt. – Robert Mahan, 1638 S WALNUT ST 47274
MS, 920 N O'BRIEN ST 47274
    Timothy Lavery, prin.
Brown ES, 550 MILLER LN 47274
    Darrel Barnett, prin.
Emerson ES, W FIFTH & ELM STS 47274
    Gary Gilbert, prin.
Seymour-Jackson ES, S POPLAR ST 47274
    David Thompson, prin.
Seymour-Redding ES, 749 N EWING ST 47274
    Montie Prince, prin.
Other Schools – See Cortland

Immanuel Lutheran School
    520 S CHESTNUT ST 47274
St. Ambrose School, 301 S CHESTNUT ST 47274

Sharpsville, Tipton Co., Pop. Code 3
Northern Comm. Tipton Co. SD
Sch. Sys. Enr. Code 4
Supt. – Carl Henderson, RURAL ROUTE 02 46068
Tri Central ES, RURAL ROUTE 02 46068
    William Horner, prin.

Shelburn, Sullivan Co., Pop. Code 4
Northeast SD
Supt. – See Hymera
ES, 505 POPLAR STREET 47879
    Ronald Bush, prin.

Shelbyville, Shelby Co., Pop. Code 7
Shelby Eastern SD
Sch. Sys. Enr. Code 4
Supt. – Jerry Kent
    RURAL ROUTE 07 BOX 50 46176
Other Schools – See Morristown, Waldron

Shelbyville Central SD
Sch. Sys. Enr. Code 5
Supt. – William Couch
    54 W BROADWAY ST 46176
JHS, 315 SECOND ST 46176
    Elwood Thomas, prin.
Coulston ES, 121 KNIGHTSTOWN ROAD 46176
    Terry Barker, prin.
Hendricks ES, 415 W TAYLOR ST 46176
    Martin Carr, Jr., prin.
Loper ES, DRAKE DR 46176
    Denny Ramsey, prin.
Pearson ES, 115 COLESCOTT ST 46176
    Charles Craft, prin.

Southwestern Cons. Shelby Co. SD
Sch. Sys. Enr. Code 3
Supt. – Robert Wade
    RURAL ROUTE 4 BOX 245A 46176
Southwestern ES
    RURAL ROUTE 04 BOX 265A 46176
    Kevin Lester, prin.

St. Joseph School, 127 E BROADWAY ST 46176

Sheridan, Hamilton Co., Pop. Code 4
Marion-Adams SD
Sch. Sys. Enr. Code 4
Supt. – Wayne Long, 509 E FOURTH ST 46069
Adams ES, 509 E FOURTH ST 46069
    Patricia Brownlee, prin.
Marion ES, RURAL ROUTE 01 46069
    Patricia Brownlee, prin.

Shipshewana, Lagrange Co., Pop. Code 2
Westview SD
Supt. – See Topeka
Shipsewana-Scott ES, MIDDLEBURY ST 46565
    Phillip Self, prin.

Shoals, Martin Co., Pop. Code 3
Shoals Comm. SD
Sch. Sys. Enr. Code 3
Supt. – Mark Dartt, RURAL ROUTE 02 47581
Shoals Community ES, RURAL ROUTE 02 47581
    Mark Ransford, prin.

Silver Lake, Kosciusko Co., Pop. Code 3
Warsaw Comm. SD
Supt. – See Warsaw
ES, RURAL ROUTE 15 BOX 188 46982
    Eugene England, prin.

South Bend, St. Joseph Co., Pop. Code 9
South Bend Comm. SD
Sch. Sys. Enr. Code 7
Supt. – Monte Sriver, 635 S MAIN ST 46601
Clay MS, 52900 LILY ROAD 46637
    James Knight, prin.
Dickinson MS, 4404 ELWOOD AVE 46628
    Ron Johnson, prin.
Edison MS, 2701 EISENHOWER AVE 46615
    Daniel Morozowski, prin.
Jackson MS, 5001 MIAMI ST 46614
    Dennis Bodle, prin.
Navarre MS, 4702 FORD ST 46619
    Luther Dixon, prin.
Coquilliard ES, 1245 N SHERIDAN ST 46628
    Christie Isaacson, prin.
Darden ES, 18645 JANET DR 46637
    Anthony Germano, prin.
Eggleston ES, 19010 ADAMS RD 46637
    William Welling, prin.
Greene ES, 24702 ROOSEVELT RD 46614
    Michael Lindley, prin.
Harrison ES, 3302 W WESTERN AVE 46619
    Lee Porter, prin.
Hay ES, 19685 JOHNSON RD 46614
    Carolyn Higgins, prin.
Jefferson ES, 528 S EDDY ST 46617
    Mark Tulchinsky, prin.
Kennedy ES, 609 N OLIVE ST 46628
    Joseph Luten, prin.
Lafayette ES, 245 N LOMBARDY DR 46619
    (—), prin.
Lincoln ES, 1425 E CALVERT ST 46613
    Obera McDonald, prin.
Madison ES, 832 N LAFAYETTE BLVD 46601
    James Bishop, prin.
Marquette ES, 1905 COLLEGE ST 46628
    Myrtle Wilson, prin.
Marshall ES, 1433 BYRON DR 46614
    John Benjamin, prin.
McKinley ES, 228 N GREENLAWN AVE 46617
    Cyril Brooke, prin.
Monroe ES, 312 DONMOYER AVE 46614
    Archie Bradford, prin.
Muuessel ES, 1213 CALIFORNIA AVE 46628
    Dr. Virginia Calvin, prin.
Nuner ES, 2716 VINE ST 46615
    Stephen Kosanovich, prin.
Perley ES, 740 N EDDY ST 46617
    Sharon Hurt, prin.
Studebaker ES, 724 E DUBAIL ST 46613
    Jack Ruffner, prin.
Swanson Highlands ES, 17677 PARKER DR 46635
    Darwin Overpeck, prin.
Tarkington ES, 3414 HEPLER ST 46635
    (—), prin.

Warren ES, 55400 QUINCE RD 46619
Dave Court, prin.

Christ the King School
5273 US 31 BUSINESS 46637
Corpus Christi School
2817 CORPUS CHRISTI DR 46628
Holy Cross School, 1020 WILBER ST 46628
Holy Family School
56407 MAYFLOWER RD 46619
Our Lady of Hungary School
731 W CALVERT ST 46613
St. Adalbert School, 519 S OLIVE ST 46619
St. Anthony De Padua School
2310 E JEFFERSON BLVD 46615
St. John the Baptist School
3616 SAINT JOHNS WAY 46628
St. Joseph ES, 216 N HILL ST 46617
St. Jude School, 19657 HILDEBRAND ST 46614
St. Mary of Assumption School
3402 S LOCUST RD 46614
St. Matthew School, 1015 E DAYTON ST 46613
Stanley Clark School, 3123 MIAMI ST 46614

Southport, Marion Co., Pop. Code 4
Metro SD of Perry Twp.
Supt. – See Indianapolis
ES, 261 ANNISTON DR 46227 – Ned Loos, prin.
Winchester Village ES
1900 E STOP TWELVE RD 46227
Max Oldham, prin.

South Whitley, Whitley Co., Pop. Code 4
Whitko Comm. SD
Supt. – See Pierceton
MS, 407 W WAYNE ST 46787 – Mark Skiles, prin.
ES, 406 W WAYNE ST 46787
Marcia Ogden, prin.

Speedway, Marion Co., Pop. Code 7
Speedway City SD
Sch. Sys. Enr. Code 4
Supt. – N. Wagner, 5335 W 25TH ST 46224
JHS, 5151 W 14TH ST 46224 – Donald Ross, prin.
Allison ES 3, 5240 W 22ND ST 46224
Carl Kirkman, prin.
Fisher ES 1, 5151 W 14TH ST 46224
Donald Ross, prin.
Newby ES 2, 1849 N WHITCOMB AVE 46224
Glen Tuel, prin.
Wheeler ES 4, 5700 MEADOWOOD DR 46224
Julia Allen, prin.

Spencer, Owen Co., Pop. Code 5
Spencer-Owen Comm. SD
Sch. Sys. Enr. Code 5
Supt. – Gordon Wells, 205 E HILLSIDE AVE 47460
Owen Valley MS
RURAL ROUTE 04 BOX 12 47460
Beverly Moore, prin.
ES, 151 E HILLSIDE AVE 47460
Terry McDaniel, prin.
Other Schools – See Gosport, Patricksburg

Spiceland, Henry Co., Pop. Code 3
South Henry SD
Supt. – See Lewisville
ES, BROAD ST 47385 – Robert Malloy, prin.

Springville, Lawrence Co.
North Lawrence Comm. SD
Supt. – See Bedford
ES, P O BOX 61 47462 – Stephen Ray, prin.

Staunton, Clay Co., Pop. Code 3
Clay Comm. SD
Supt. – See Knightsville
ES 47881 – Rebecca Moore, prin.

Stillwell, La Porte Co.
La Porte Comm. SD
Supt. – See La Porte
ES, 0106 N STATE ROAD 104 46351
John Adams, prin.

Stinesville, Monroe Co., Pop. Code 2
Richland-Bean Blossom Comm. SD
Supt. – See Ellettsville
ES 47464 – James Stockton, prin.

Straughn, Henry Co., Pop. Code 2
South Henry SD
Supt. – See Lewisville
ES, RURAL ROUTE 01 47387
Robert Malloy, prin.

Sullivan, Sullivan Co., Pop. Code 5
Southwest SD
Sch. Sys. Enr. Code 4
Supt. – Reggie Laconi, 31 N COURT ST 47882
Central ES, 215 N COURT ST 47882
Lynn Blinzinger, prin.
Other Schools – See Carlisle, Graysville

Sulphur Springs, Henry Co., Pop. Code 2
Shenendoah SD
Supt. – See Middletown
ES, US ROAD #38 47388 – Joe Baker, prin.

Summitville, Madison Co., Pop. Code 4
Madison-Grant United SD
Supt. – See Fairmount
ES, E MILL ST 46070 – Robert Absher, prin.

Sunman, Ripley Co., Pop. Code 3
Sunman-Dearborn Comm. SD
Sch. Sys. Enr. Code 5
Supt. – John Armbruster, P O BOX 210 47041

ES, RURAL ROUTE 02 BOX 15 47041
David Jordan, prin.
Other Schools – See Brookville, Guilford

St. Nicholas School
RURAL ROUTE 01 BOX 270 47041

Swayzee, Grant Co., Pop. Code 4
Oak Hill United SD
Supt. – See Converse
ES, P O BOX 217 46986 – Charles Shroyer, prin.

Sweetser, Grant Co., Pop. Code 3
Oak Hill United SD
Supt. – See Converse
ES, P O BOX 230 46987 – Dennis Austin, prin.

Switz City, Greene Co., Pop. Code 2
White River Valley SD
Supt. – See Worthington
Central ES, P O BOX 147 47465
Sandra Headley, prin.

Syracuse, Kosciusko Co., Pop. Code 5
Wawasee Comm. SD
Sch. Sys. Enr. Code 5
Supt. – Roger Thorton
RURAL ROUTE 03 BOX 662A 46567
JHS, 201 E BROOKLYN ST 46567
John Naab, prin.
ES, 201 E BROOKLYN ST 46567
John Naab, prin.
Other Schools – See Milford, North Webster

Taswell, Crawford Co.
Crawford Co. Comm. SD
Supt. – See Marengo
Patoka ES, STATE ROUTE 64 47175
Tom Doddridge, prin.

Taylorsville, Bartholomew Co.
Bartholomew Cons. SD
Supt. – See Columbus
ES, P O BOX 277 47280 – Vera Brown, prin.

Tell City, Perry Co., Pop. Code 6
Tell City-Troy Twp. SD
Sch. Sys. Enr. Code 4
Supt. – Wm. Wilson, 1321 FULTON ST 47586
JHS, 3500 TELL STREET ROAD 47586
Michael Overmeyer, prin.
Newman ES, 821 10TH ST 47586
Charles May, prin.
St. Paul ES, 840 MAIN ST 47586
Ann Moore, prin.

Tennyson, Warrick Co., Pop. Code 2
Warrick Co. SD
Supt. – See Boonville
ES, 323 N MAIN 47637 – Carolyn Duffey, prin.

Terre Haute, Vigo Co., Pop. Code 8
Vigo Co. SD
Sch. Sys. Enr. Code 7
Supt. – Charles Clark
961 LAFAYETTE AVE 47804
Consolidated ES
RURAL ROUTE 11 BOX 48 47805
Patrick Sheehan, prin.
Crawford ES, 701 S FIFTH ST 47809
Pamela Hallock, prin.
Davis Park ES, 1800 POPLAR ST 47803
George Thompson, prin.
DeVaney ES, 1011 S BROWN AVE 47803
Wynona Batton, prin.
Deming ES, 1750 8TH AVE 47804
Joyce Snyder, prin.
Dixie Bee ES, 1377 E 77TH DR 47802
Patricia Fouty, prin.
Farrington Grove ES, 1826 S 6TH ST 47802
Daniel Tanoos, prin.
Fayette ES, RURAL ROUTE 12 BOX 103 47805
Guy Dillard, prin.
Franklin ES, 16TH AND ELM ST 47807
Robert Mardis, prin.
Fuqua ES, 1111 E WHEELER AVE 47802
Robert Thomas, prin.
Hoosier Prairie ES
RURAL ROUTE 22 BOX 2990 47802
Darrell Roundtree, prin.
Lost Creek ES, 6001 WABASH AVE 47803
Raymond Azar, prin.
Meadows ES, 55 S BROWN AVE 47803
Audrey Snyder, prin.
Ouabache ES, 501 MAPLE AVE 47804
Bert Nelson, prin.
Rio Grande ES
RURAL ROUTE 52 BOX 301A 47805
Rudolf Jacobsen, prin.
Sugar Grove ES, 2799 WALLACE AVE 47802
James Morris, prin.
Terre Town ES, 2121 BOSTON AVE 47805
Colleen Magnuson, prin.
Warren ES, 1300 N 25TH ST 47803
Sharon Pitts, prin.
University ES, 7TH AND CHESTNUT STS 47809
Gregory Ulm, prin.
Other Schools – See Riley, West Terre Haute

Father Gibault School
5901 DIXIE BEE ROAD 47802
Sacred Heart School
1330 LAFAYETTE AVE 47804
St. Patrick School, 449 S 19TH ST 47803

Thorntown, Boone Co., Pop. Code 4
Western Boone Co. Comm. SD
Sch. Sys. Enr. Code 4
Supt. – Harold Muncie
RURAL ROUTE 02 BOX 58 46071
ES, 200 W MILL ST 46071 – Gary Lanpher, prin.
Other Schools – See Jamestown

Tipton, Tipton Co., Pop. Code 6
Tipton Comm. SD
Sch. Sys. Enr. Code 4
Supt. – Dr. Max Glenn, 221 N MAIN ST 46072
MS, 817 MAIN ST 46072
Stephen VanHorn, prin.
Jefferson ES, JEFFERSON & 1ST ST 47072
Patricia Burden, prin.
Lincoln ES, 421 ASH ST 46072
Robert Gordon, prin.
Washington ES, 817 S MAIN ST 46072
David Lacy, prin.

Topeka, Lagrange Co., Pop. Code 3
Westview SD
Sch. Sys. Enr. Code 4
Supt. – Richard Wilson, RURAL ROUTE 01 46571
Honeyville ES, RURAL ROUTE 01 46571
Robert Hostler, prin.
ES, P O BOX 38 46571 – Robert Hostler, prin.
Other Schools – See Shipshewana

Trafalgar, Johnson Co., Pop. Code 2
Ninevah-Hensley-Jackson United SD
Sch. Sys. Enr. Code 4
Supt. – Norman Stockton, P O BOX 98 46181
Indian Creek MS
RURAL ROUTE 02 BOX 3M 46181
Joe Dehart, prin.
Indian Creek ES, P O BOX 68 46181
Donald Dehart, prin.

Union City, Randolph Co., Pop. Code 5
Randolph Eastern SD
Sch. Sys. Enr. Code 4
Supt. – Eugene Huddleston
907 N PLUM ST 47390
West Side MS, 310 N WALNUT ST 47390
Ken Ayers, prin.
North Side ES, 905 N PLUM ST 47390
Beverly Schemmer, prin.

Union Mills, La Porte Co., Pop. Code 2
South Central Comm. SD
Sch. Sys. Enr. Code 3
Supt. – David Geise, 9808 S 600 W 46382
South Central ES, 9808 S 600W 46382
J. Wengerd, prin.

Unionville, Monroe Co.
Monroe Co. Comm. SD
Supt. – See Bloomington
ES, 8144 E STATE RD 45 47468
David Marshall, prin.

Upland, Grant Co., Pop. Code 5
Eastbrook Comm. SD
Supt. – See Marion
ES, 712 S SECOND ST 46989
Doris Crockett, prin.

Valparaiso, Porter Co., Pop. Code 7
Boone Twp. SD
Sch. Sys. Enr. Code 3
Supt. – Stephen Hewlett
507 CAMPBELL ST 46383
Other Schools – See Hebron

Duneland SD
Supt. – See Chesterton
Jackson ES, 811N 400 E 46383
Dan Keilman, prin.

Morgan Twp. SD
Sch. Sys. Enr. Code 2
Supt. – H. Hewlett, 507 CAMPBELL ST 46383
Morgan Twp. S, 209 S STATE 49 ROAD 46383
Curtis Casbon, prin.

Pleasant Twp. SD
Sch. Sys. Enr. Code 3
Supt. – H. Hewlett, 507 CAMPBELL ST 46383
Other Schools – See Kouts

Portage Twp. SD
Supt. – See Portage
Saylor ES, 331 MIDWAY DR 46383
David Baker, prin.
South Haven ES, 395 MIDWAY DR 46383
Richard Knutson, prin.

Union Twp. SD
Sch. Sys. Enr. Code 4
Supt. – (—), 272 N 600 W 46383
Simatovich ES, 424 W 500N 46383
Mary Carr, prin.
Union Center ES, 272 N 600W 46383
Lucille Hand, prin.

Valparaiso Comm. SD
Sch. Sys. Enr. Code 5
Supt. – R. James Risk, 405 CAMPBELL ST 46383
Franklin MS, 605 CAMPBELL ST 46383
Glenn Gambel, prin.
Jefferson MS, 1600 ROOSEVELT ROAD 46383
Paul Knauff, prin.
Central ES, 305 FRANKLIN ST 46383
James Bedell, prin.
Cooks Corner ES, 358 BULLSEYE LAKE RD 46383
Lavern Turner, prin.

Hayes-Leonard ES
653 HAYES LEONARD RD 46383
Merlin Bray, prin.
Jefferson ES, 1700 ROOSEVELT RD 46383
Ron Vendl, prin.
Memorial ES, 1052 PARK & MILTON 46383
Leo Joint, prin.
Northview ES, 257 NORTHVIEW DR 46383
Enrico Frataccia, prin.
Parkview ES, 1405 WOOD ST 46383
Doug Hollar, prin.

Washington Twp. SD
Sch. Sys. Enr. Code 2
Supt. – H. Hewlett, 507 CAMPBELL ST 46383
Washington Twp. S, 383 E STATE ROAD 2 46383
Lonnie Steele, prin.

Immanuel Lutheran School
1700 MONTICELLO PARK DR 46383
St. Paul's School, 352 CHICAGO ST 46383

Van Buren, Grant Co., Pop. Code 3
Eastbrook Comm. SD
Supt. – See Marion
ES, P O BOX 451 46991 – John Clester, prin.

Veedersburg, Fountain Co., Pop. Code 4
Southeast Fountain SD
Sch. Sys. Enr. Code 4
Supt. – Gerald York
RURAL ROUTE 02 BOX 10A 47987
Southeast Fountain ES, RURAL ROUTE 02 47987
Robert Baker, prin.

Versailles, Ripley Co., Pop. Code 4
South Ripley Comm. SD
Sch. Sys. Enr. Code 4
Supt. – Stanley Nay, P O BOX 412 47042
ES, TYSON ST 47042 – Boaz Susnick, prin.
Other Schools – See Holton

Vevay, Switzerland Co., Pop. Code 4
Switzerland Co. SD
Sch. Sys. Enr. Code 4
Supt. – Chester Meisberger
305 W SEMINARY ST 47043
Jefferson-Craig ES
RURAL ROUTE 03 BOX 166A 47043
Jill Cord, prin.
Other Schools – See East Enterprise

Vincennes, Knox Co., Pop. Code 7
South Knox SD
Supt. – See Monroe City
South Knox MS, RURAL ROUTE 03 47591
William Amers, prin.

Vincennes Comm. SD
Sch. Sys. Enr. Code 5
Supt. – Wayne Ader, P O BOX 1267 47591
Clark JHS, 300 N 6TH ST 47591
Paul Couchenour, prin.
Franklin ES, 2600 WABASH AVE 47591
Arlene Meyer, prin.
Lasalle ES, S 7TH & BARNETT STS 47591
Patricia Klemeyer, prin.
Riley ES, UPPER 11TH & COLL AVE 47591
Gary Hackney, prin.
Tecumseh-Harrison ES, 2116 N 2ND ST 47591
William Hopper, prin.
Vigo ES, 15TH & MAIN STS 47591
William Ritterskamp, prin.
Washington ES, 2134 WASHINGTON AVE 47591
Thomas Nonte, prin.

Flaget ES, P O BOX 139 47591

Wabash, Wabash Co., Pop. Code 7
Metro SD of Wabash Co.
Sch. Sys. Enr. Code 5
Supt. – David Herbert, 282 N WABASH ST 46992
Metro North ES, RURAL ROUTE 01 46992
Donald Hammel, prin.
Sharp Creek ES, RURAL ROUTE 06 46992
Oren Guenin, prin.
Southwood ES, RURAL ROUTE 05 46992
Bill Arnold, prin.
Other Schools – See La Fontaine

Wabash CSD
Sch. Sys. Enr. Code 4
Supt. – Robert Myers, P O BOX 744 46992
MS, 150 COLERAIN STREET 46992
Rodrick Songer, prin.
Miami ES, 255 N MIAMI ST 46992
Diana Showalter, prin.
Mills ES, 1721 VERNON ST 46992
Robert Vanlandingham, prin.
Neighbours ES, 1545 N WABASH ST 46992
David Sodervick, prin.
West Ward ES, 277 N THORNE ST 46992
Diana Showalter, prin.

St. Bernard School, 191 N CASS ST 46992

Wadesville, Posey Co.
Metro SD of North Posey Co.
Supt. – See Poseyville
South Terrace ES, 8427 HAINES RD 47638
Don Thompson, prin.

St. Wendel School
4725 ST WENDEL-CYNTHIANA RD 47638

Wakarusa, Elkhart Co., Pop. Code 4
Penn-Harris-Madison SD
Supt. – See Mishawaka
Madison ES, 66030 DOGWOOD RD 46573
Cyril Cole, prin.

Wa-Nee Comm. SD
Supt. – See Nappanee
ES, 207 N ELKHART ST #367 46573
Carl Wesolek, prin.

Waldron, Shelby Co., Pop. Code 3
Shelby Eastern SD
Supt. – See Shelbyville
ES, P O BOX 38 46182 – Mark Kern, prin.

Walkerton, St. Joseph Co., Pop. Code 4
John Glenn SD
Sch. Sys. Enr. Code 4
Supt. – Roger Smith
506 ROOSEVELT ROAD 46574
Urey MS, 406 ADAMS ST 46574
Richard Reese, prin.
ES, 805 WASHINGTON ST 46574
Marilyn Lightfoot, prin.
Other Schools – See North Liberty

Walton, Cass Co., Pop. Code 4
Southeastern SD
Sch. Sys. Enr. Code 4
Supt. – Sam Wright, P O BOX 320 46994
Thompson ES, RURAL ROUTE 218 WEST 46994
Thomas Buchko, prin.
Other Schools – See Galveston

Wanatah, La Porte Co., Pop. Code 3
Cass Twp. SD
Supt. – See La Porte
Wanatah Public ES, P O BOX 248 46390
Paul Nye, prin.

Warren, Huntington Co., Pop. Code 4
Huntington Co. Comm. SD
Supt. – See Huntington
Salamonie ES, 1063E 900 S BOX 554 46792
Thomas Edington, prin.

Warsaw, Kosciusko Co., Pop. Code 7
Warsaw Comm. SD
Sch. Sys. Enr. Code 6
Supt. – Larry Crabb, P O BOX 288 46580
MS, 900 S UNION ST 46580 – Allen Myers, prin.
Lincoln ES, 203 N LINCOLN ST 46580
David Whaley, prin.
Madison ES, 201 N UNION ST 46580
Steven Hassinger, prin.
Washington ES, 423 KINCAIDE ST 46580
Edmund Anglin, prin.
Other Schools – See Atwood, Claypool, Leesburg,
Silver Lake, Winona Lake

Sacred Heart School, 135 N HARRISON ST 46580

Washington, Daviess Co., Pop. Code 7
Washington Comm. SD
Sch. Sys. Enr. Code 4
Supt. – Tom Miller, 301 E SOUTH ST 47501
JHS, 600 E WALNUT ST 47501 – W. Hatton, prin.
Dunn ES, RURAL ROUTE 01 47501
James Lindauer, prin.
Griffith ES, 803 E NATIONAL HWY 47501
Timothy Weaver, prin.
North ES, 60 NE 6TH ST 47501 – John Gray, prin.
Veale ES, RURAL ROUTE 04 47501
Art Neiswanger, prin.

Washington MS, 200 W MAIN ST 47501
Washington ES, 310 NE 2ND ST 47501

Waterloo, De Kalb Co., Pop. Code 4
DeKalb Co. Central United SD
Supt. – See Auburn
DeKalb MS, 3338 COUNTY ROAD 427 46793
Richard Barkman, prin.
ES, P O BOX 128 46793 – Dr. John Molin, prin.

Waveland, Montgomery Co., Pop. Code 3
South Montgomery Comm. SD
Supt. – See New Market
ES, 506 E GREEN ST 47989 – Gerald Shull, prin.

Westfield, Hamilton Co., Pop. Code 5
Westfield-Washington SD
Sch. Sys. Enr. Code 4
Supt. – Dr. Jeffrey Heier, 322 W MAIN ST 46074
MS, 328 W MAIN ST 46074 – Edwin Baker, prin.
Washington ES, 324 W MAIN ST 46074
Michael Shaver, prin.

West Lafayette, Tippecanoe Co., Pop. Code 7
Tippecanoe SD
Supt. – See Lafayette
Klondike MS, 3310 N 300 W 47906
Robert Foreman, prin.
Klondike ES, 3310 N 300 W 47906
Ardis Wipf, prin.

West Lafayette Comm. SD
Sch. Sys. Enr. Code 4
Supt. – Eric Casson, 1130 N SALISBURY ST 47906
JHS, 1200 N SALISBURY ST 47906
Anne Koivo, prin.
Burtsfield IS, SALISBURY & LINDBERGH 47906
Robert Foerster, prin.
Cumberland ES, 600 CUMBERLAND AVE 47906
Ronald Woods, prin.
Happy Hollow ES, 1200 N SALISBURY ST 47906
John Parente, prin.

West Lebanon, Warren Co., Pop. Code 3
Metro SD of Warren Co.
Supt. – See Williamsport
Warren Central ES, RURAL ROUTE 01 47991
David Poor, prin.

West Newton, Marion Co.
Metro SD of Decatur Twp.
Sch. Sys. Enr. Code 6
Supt. – Gerald Montgomery
7523 MOORESVILLE ROAD 46183
ES, 7529 MOORESVILLE RD 46183
Janet Larch, prin.
Other Schools – See Indianapolis

West Terre Haute, Vigo Co., Pop. Code 5
Vigo Co. SD
Supt. – See Terre Haute
West Vigo MS
RURAL ROUTE 15 BOX 194 47885
Dan Gossage, prin.
West Vigo ES, 500 W OLIVE ST 47885
David Lotter, prin.

Westville, La Porte Co., Pop. Code 5
New Durham Twp. SD
Supt. – See La Porte
ES, VALPARAISO ST 46391
Susan Schwartz, prin.

Wheatfield, Jasper Co., Pop. Code 3
Kankakee Valley SD
Sch. Sys. Enr. Code 5
Supt. – Iran Floyd, P O BOX 278 46392
Kankakee Valley MS
RURAL ROUTE 03 BOX 182 46392
Wayne Crawford, prin.
ES, P O BOX 158 46392 – Wayne Ryska, prin.
Other Schools – See Demotte

Whiteland, Johnson Co., Pop. Code 4
Clark-Pleasant Comm. SD
Sch. Sys. Enr. Code 4
Supt. – F. Patrick Garvey, 50 CENTER ST 46184
Clark Pleasant MS, 222 TRACY ST 46184
Robert Duke, prin.
Break-O-Day ES, 700 SAWMILL RD 46184
James Peterson, prin.
ES, 120 CENTER ST 46184
Robert Winslow, prin.
Other Schools – See Franklin

Whiting, Lake Co., Pop. Code 6
Hammond CSD
Supt. – See Hammond
Franklin ES, 1000 116TH ST 46394
Mark Biel, prin.

Whiting CSD
Sch. Sys. Enr. Code 3
Supt. – Gerald Novak, 1751 OLIVER ST 46394
Hale ES, 1433 119TH ST 46394
Marthann Hoffman, prin.

Sacred Heart School, 1723 LAPORTE AVE 46394
St. John the Baptist School
1844 LINCOLN AVE 46394

Wilkinson, Hancock Co., Pop. Code 2
Eastern Hancock Co. Comm. SD
Sch. Sys. Enr. Code 4
Supt. – Dennis Fox, P O BOX 38 46186
Other Schools – See Charlottesville

Williamsport, Warren Co., Pop. Code 4
Metro SD of Warren Co.
Sch. Sys. Enr. Code 4
Supt. – Roy Stroud, 101 N MONROE ST 47993
ES, 109 E MONROE ST 47993
George Taylor, prin.
Other Schools – See Pine Village, West Lebanon

Winamac, Pulaski Co., Pop. Code 4
Eastern Pulaski Comm. SD
Sch. Sys. Enr. Code 4
Supt. – Robert Klitzman
711 SCHOOL DRIVE 46996
Winamac Community MS
715 SCHOOL DRIVE 46996 – (—), prin.
Eastern Pulaski ES, 815 SCHOOL DR 46996
Susan Brash, prin.

Winchester, Randolph Co., Pop. Code 6
Randolph Central SD
Sch. Sys. Enr. Code 4
Supt. – Gary Keesling, 103 N EAST ST 47394
Driver MS, RURAL ROUTE 03 47394
Philip Wray, prin.
Baker ES, 625 S BROWN ST 47394
Eugene Richardson, prin.
Morton MS, 550 N RESIDENCE ST 47394
Eugene Richardson, prin.
Willard ES, 615 W SOUTH ST 47394
Chauncey Varner, prin.
Other Schools – See Ridgeville

Winona Lake, Kosciusko Co., Pop. Code 5
Warsaw Comm. SD
Supt. – See Warsaw
Jefferson ES, 100 SEMINARY DR 46590
Chris Gensinger, prin.

Winslow, Pike Co., Pop. Code 4
Pike Co. SD
Supt. – See Petersburg
ES, PORTER ST 47598 – Jay Lee, prin.

Wolcott, White Co., Pop. Code 3
Tri-County SD
Sch. Sys. Enr. Code 3
Supt. – Fred Minnick
RURAL ROUTE 02 BOX 73A 47995
ES, RURAL ROUTE 02 BOX 73B 47995
Karel Peck, prin.
Other Schools – See Remington

Wolcottville, Lagrange Co., Pop. Code 3
Lakeland SD
Supt. – See Lagrange
Wolcott Mills ES, P O BOX 308 46795
Richard White, prin.

Prairie Heights Comm. SD
Supt. – See Lagrange
Milford ES, RURAL ROUTE 01 46795
Edward Ludington, prin.

Wolflake, Noble Co.
Central Noble Comm. SD
Supt. – See Albion

ES, P O BOX 67 46796 – Lonnie Ladig, prin.

Woodburn, Allen Co., Pop. Code 4
East Allen Co. SD
Supt. – See New Haven
ES, RURAL ROUTE 01 46797
John Emerick, prin.

Woodburn Lutheran School, P O BOX 158 46797

Worthington, Greene Co., Pop. Code 4
White River Valley SD
Sch. Sys. Enr. Code 4
Supt. – Stephen Campbell
4 N WASHINGTON STREET 47471
Worthington-Jefferson ES
484 W MAIN STREET 47471 – Larry Catron, prin.
Other Schools – See Lyons, Switz City

Yorktown, Delaware Co., Pop. Code 5
Mt. Pleasant Twp. Comm. SD
Sch. Sys. Enr. Code 4
Supt. – Jerome Secttor, STATE ROAD 32 W 47396

MS 47396 – David Uptgraff, prin.
Pleasant View ES, 700 E SMITH ST 47396
Dr. Rosemary Hurst, prin.
MS, 700 E SMITH ST 47396 – Gary Crow, prin.

Zionsville, Boone Co., Pop. Code 5
Eagle-Union Comm. SD
Sch. Sys. Enr. Code 4
Supt. – Harold Sharpe, 690 BEECH ST 46077
MS, 900 WHITESTOWN ROAD 46077
John Johnson, prin.
Eagle ES, 350 N SIXTH ST 46077
John Hines, prin.
Pleasant View MS, 4800 S 975 E 46077
Charles Paddock, prin.
Union ES, RURAL ROUTE 32 BOX 9275 46077
Deborah Poole, prin.

IOWA

STATE DEPARTMENT OF PUBLIC INSTRUCTION
Grimes State Office Building
E. 14th & Grand Sts., Des Moines 50319
(515) 281-5294

Director of Education	William Lepley
Administrator Division of School Administrative Services	Ted Stilwill
Administrator Division of Instructional Services	Sue Donielson
Administrator Division of Vocational Rehabilitation Services	Jerry Starkweather
Administrator Planning, Evaluation & Information Services	Leland Tack

STATE BOARD OF EDUCATION
Karen Goodenow, *President*   Spirit Lake

STATE BOARD OF REGENTS
R. Wayne Richey, *Executive Secretary*   Lucas State Office Building, Des Moines   50319

AREA EDUCATION AGENCIES

Keystone AEA, Richard Hansen, Supt.
RURAL ROUTE 02 BOX 19, Elkader 52043
Northern Trails AEA, Dale Jensen, Supt.
P O BOX M, Clear Lake 50428
Lakeland AEA, Albert Wood, Supt.
P O BOX 38, Cylinder 50528
AEA 4, C. Irwin, Supt.
102 S MAIN AVE, Sioux Center 51250
Arrowhead AEA, Don Ambroson, Supt.
P O BOX 1399, Fort Dodge 50501

AEA 6, R. Ploeger, Supt.
210 S 12TH AVE, Marshalltown 50158
AEA 7, R. C. Dickinson, Supt.
3712 CEDAR HTS DR, Cedar Falls 50613
Mississippi Bend AEA, Glen Pelecky, Supt.
729 21ST ST, Bettendorf 52722
Grant Wood AEA, Ron Fielder, Supt.
4401 6TH ST SW, Cedar Rapids 52404
Heartland AEA, Bill Clark, Supt.
6500 CORPORATE DR, Johnston 50131

Western Hills AEA, Bruce Hopkins, Supt.
1520 MORNINGSIDE AVE, Sioux City 51106
Loess Hills AEA, James Blietz, Supt.
RURAL ROUTE 01 BOX 1109, Council Bluffs 51501
Green Valley AEA, Patrick Kelly, Supt.
GREEN VALLEY ROAD, Creston 50801
Southern Prairie AEA, D. G. Roseberry, Supt.
P O BOX 55, Ottumwa 52501
Great River AEA, Howard Sleight, Supt.
1200 UNIVERSITY, Burlington 52601

PUBLIC, PRIVATE, AND PAROCHIAL ELEMENTARY SCHOOLS

Ackley, Hardin Co., Pop. Code 4
Ackley-Geneva Comm. SD, AEA 6
Sch. Sys. Enr. Code 2
Supt. – Kirk Nelson, STATE ST 50601
ES, STATE ST 50601 – Wayne Slack, prin.

Adair, Guthrie Co., Pop. Code 3
Adair-Casey Comm. SD, AEA 11
Sch. Sys. Enr. Code 2
Supt. – Roger Myers
RURAL ROUTE 02 BOX 107 50002
Adair-Casey ES 50002 – Sig Wood, prin.

Adel, Dallas Co., Pop. Code 5
Adel-DeSoto Comm. SD, AEA 11
Sch. Sys. Enr. Code 4
Supt. – Tim Hoffman, 215 N 11TH ST 50003
Adel-De Soto MS, 215 N 11TH ST 50003
William Kimber, prin.
ES, 1608 GROVE ST 50003 – James Nelsen, prin.
Other Schools – See De Soto

Afton, Union Co., Pop. Code 3
East Union Comm. SD, AEA 14
Sch. Sys. Enr. Code 3
Supt. – Gerald Cowell 50830
ES 50830 – (—), prin.
Other Schools – See Arispe, Lorimor

Agency, Wapello Co., Pop. Code 3
Cardinal Comm. SD, AEA 15
Supt. – See Eldon
Cardinal MS 52530 – R. McClain, prin.

Ainsworth, Washington Co., Pop. Code 3
Highland Comm. SD, AEA 10
Sch. Sys. Enr. Code 3
Supt. – See Riverside
ES 52201 – Pat Gregory, prin.

Akron, Plymouth Co., Pop. Code 4
Akron Westfield Comm. SD, AEA 12
Sch. Sys. Enr. Code 3
Supt. – Charles Eskra, KERR DRIVE 51001
Akron Westfield MS, KERR DRIVE 51001
Joann Smith, prin.
Akron Westfield ES, KERR DR 51001
Joann Smith, prin.

Albert City, Buena Vista Co., Pop. Code 3
Albert City-Truesdale Comm. SD, AEA 5
Sch. Sys. Enr. Code 2
Supt. – Tom Behounek, P O BOX 98 50510
Albert City-Truesdale JHS, P O BOX 98 50510
Charles Woodworth, prin.
Albert City-Truesdale ES, P O BOX 98 50510
Tom Behounek, prin.

Albia, Monroe Co., Pop. Code 5
Albia Comm. SD, AEA 15
Sch. Sys. Enr. Code 4
Supt. – John Thomas, 120 BENTON AVE E 52531
MS, 222 N 2ND ST 52531 – Phillip Brock, prin.
Grant ES, S MAIN & 6TH AVE E 52531
John Palmer, prin.
Jefferson ES, 404 A AVE W 52531
Donna Hancock, prin.
Kendall ES, 623 WASHINGTON AVE E 52531
Donna Hancock, prin.
Other Schools – See Lovilia, Melrose

Alburnett, Linn Co., Pop. Code 2
Alburnett Comm. SD, AEA 10
Sch. Sys. Enr. Code 3
Supt. – Robert Rampulla 52202
ES 52202 – Roland Krouse, prin.
Other Schools – See Toddville

Alden, Hardin Co., Pop. Code 3
Alden Comm. SD, AEA 6
Sch. Sys. Enr. Code 2
Supt. – James Jess 50006
MS 50006 – Michael Niece, prin.
ES 50006 – Janice Jess, prin.

Algona, Kossuth Co., Pop. Code 6
Algona Comm. SD, AEA 3
Sch. Sys. Enr. Code 4
Supt. – Harold Prior, 220 N PHILLIPS ST 50511
Laing MS, NEBRASKA & HARLAN 50511
  Thomas Drake, prin.
Bryant ES, E NORTH & DODGE 50511
  John Lindeman, prin.
Godfrey ES, STATE AND MAIN 50511
  John Lindeman, prin.
Wallace ES, S PHILLIPS & KENNEDY 50511
  Bruce Ament, prin.

Seton ES, 807 E NORTH ST 50511

Alleman, Polk Co., Pop. Code 2
North Polk Comm. SD, AEA 11
Sch. Sys. Enr. Code 3
Supt. – George Cain 50007
Central ES 50007 – Thomas Jones, prin.
Other Schools – See Polk City

Allison, Butler Co., Pop. Code 4
Allison-Bristow Comm. SD, AEA 7
Sch. Sys. Enr. Code 2
Supt. – George Maurer, 513 BIRCH 50602
ES, 513 BIRCH 50602 – David Ghormley, prin.
MS, 513 BIRCH 50602 – David Ghormley, prin.

Alta, Buena Vista Co., Pop. Code 4
Alta Comm. SD, AEA 5
Sch. Sys. Enr. Code 3
Supt. – Alfred Greene, 101 W 5TH ST 51002
ES, 1009 S MAIN ST 51002
  Jerry Kleymann, prin.

Alton, Sioux Co., Pop. Code 3
Floyd Valley Comm. SD, AEA 4
Sch. Sys. Enr. Code 2
Supt. – Donald Adkins, 1108 5TH AVE 51003
Other Schools – See Hospers

Altoona, Polk Co., Pop. Code 6
Southeast Polk Comm. SD, AEA 11
Supt. – See Runnells
ES, 301 6TH ST SW 50009
  Charles Van Cleve, prin.
Centennial ES, 910 7TH AVE SE 50009
  Robert Larson, prin.

Ames, Story Co., Pop. Code 8
Ames Comm. SD, AEA 11
Sch. Sys. Enr. Code 5
Supt. – Ronald Rice, 120 S KELLOGG AVE 50010
MS, 321 STATE AVE 50010
  Donald Carlson, prin.
Crawford PS, 415 STANTON AVE 50010
  Leland Himan, prin.
Edwards ES, 3622 WOODLAND ST 50010
  Ronald Meals, prin.
Fellows ES, 1400 MCKINLEY DR 50010
  Glenn Connor, prin.
Meeker ES, 20TH & BURNETT AVE 50010
  Judith Haggard, prin.
Mitchell ES, 3521 JEWEL DR 50010
  Mary Sterling, prin.
Northwood ES, 601 28TH ST 50010
  Glenn Connor, prin.
Roosevelt ES, 921 9TH ST 50010
  Judith Haggard, prin.
Sawyer ES, 4316 ONTARIO ST 50010
  Ronald Meals, prin.

St. Cecilia School, 122 N OAK AVE 50010

Anamosa, Jones Co., Pop. Code 5
Anamosa Comm. SD, AEA 10
Sch. Sys. Enr. Code 4
Supt. – Marvin Boyer, S GARNAVILLO ST 52205
MS, S GARNAVILLO ST 52205
  Walter Fortney, prin.
Strawberry Hill ES, HAMILTON ST 52205
  Dale Hackett, prin.
Other Schools – See Martelle, Viola

St. Patrick School, N GARNAVILLO ST 52205

Andrew, Jackson Co., Pop. Code 2
Andrew Comm. SD, AEA 9
Sch. Sys. Enr. Code 2
Supt. – David Pappone, P O BOX 130 52030
ES 52030 – David Pappone, prin.

Anita, Cass Co., Pop. Code 4
Anita Comm. SD, AEA 13
Sch. Sys. Enr. Code 2
Supt. – Arvid Goettsche 50020
ES, 709 MCINTYRE DR 50020
  Dannie Crozier, prin.

Ankeny, Polk Co., Pop. Code 7
Ankeny Comm. SD, AEA 11
Sch. Sys. Enr. Code 5
Supt. – Ben Norman, 420 SW SCHOOL ST 50021
Parkview JHS, 105 SW PLEASANT ST 50021
  Bill Wilson, prin.
East ES, 710 S 3RD & TRI-LEIN DR 50021
  Randy McMahill, prin.
Neveln ES, 306 SW SCHOOL ST 50021
  Paula Lee, prin.
Northwest ES, 1200 W 1ST ST 50021
  Lloyd Nelson, prin.
Southeast ES, 1006 SE TRILEIN DR 50021
  Veronica Stalker, prin.
Terrace ES, 310 NW SCHOOL ST 50021
  Dennis Warren, prin.

Anthon, Woodbury Co., Pop. Code 3
Anthon-Oto Comm. SD, AEA 12
Sch. Sys. Enr. Code 2
Supt. – Dennis Johnson, 110 W DIVISION 51004
Anthon-Oto ES 51004 – Dennis Johnson, prin.

Aplington, Butler Co., Pop. Code 4
Aplington Comm. SD, AEA 7
Sch. Sys. Enr. Code 2
Supt. – Francis Schuelka, 210 10TH ST 50604
ES, 215 10TH ST 50604 – Franics Schuelka, prin.

Arcadia, Carroll Co., Pop. Code 2
AR-WE-VA Comm. SD, AEA 12
Supt. – See Westside
ES 51430 – Bob Gress, prin.

Holy Cross School 51430

Argyle, Lee Co.
Central Lee Comm. SD, AEA 16
Sch. Sys. Enr. Code 4
Supt. – Marjorie Wilhelm 52619
Central Lee JHS 52619 – Richard Denly, prin.
Other Schools – See Donnellson

Arispe, Union Co., Pop. Code 1
East Union Comm. SD, AEA 14
Supt. – See Afton
MS 50831 – (—), prin.

Armstrong, Emmet Co., Pop. Code 4
Armstrong-Ringsted Comm. SD, AEA 3
Sch. Sys. Enr. Code 3
Supt. – Donald Silvey 50514
Armstrong-Kingsted ES 50514
  Dennis Hoyer, prin.
Other Schools – See Ringsted

Arnolds Park, Dickinson Co., Pop. Code 4
Arnolds Park, Cons. SD, AEA 3
Sch. Sys. Enr. Code 6
Supt. – Marvin Anderson 51331
MS 51331 – George Morris, prin.

Arthur, Ida Co., Pop. Code 2
Odebolt-Arthur Comm. SD, AEA 5
Supt. – See Odebolt
Odebolt-Arthur MS 51431 – Rodger Miller, prin.

Atkins, Benton Co., Pop. Code 3
Benton Comm. SD, AEA 10
Supt. – See Van Horne
ES 52206 – Gary Holst, prin.

Atlantic, Cass Co., Pop. Code 6
Atlantic Comm. SD, AEA 13
Sch. Sys. Enr. Code 4
Supt. – Kenneth Fossen, 1100 LINN ST 50022
Schuler JHS, 1100 LINN ST 50022
  Dal Neary, prin.
Jackson ES, 8TH & CEDAR 50022
  Bernard Neary, prin.
Lincoln ES, 8TH & MAPLE 50022
  Bernard Neary, prin.
Washington ES, EAST 14TH ST 50022
  Gail Casey, prin.

Auburn, Sac Co., Pop. Code 2
Lake View-Auburn Comm. SD, AEA 5
Supt. – See Lake View
ES 51433 – Norma Wallace, prin.

Audubon, Audubon Co., Pop. Code 5
Audubon Comm. SD, AEA 11
Sch. Sys. Enr. Code 3
Supt. – Richard Paulsen, 3RD AVE 50025
ES, RURAL ROUTE 02 50025 – Jon Bintner, prin.
Other Schools – See Exira

Aurelia, Cherokee Co., Pop. Code 4
Aurelia Comm. SD, AEA 12
Sch. Sys. Enr. Code 3
Supt. – Marlin Lode, 3RD & ASH ST 51005
ES, 3RD & ASH ST 51005 – Richard Vogt, prin.
PS, 3RD & ASH ST 51005 – Marlin Lode, prin.

Avoca, Pottawattamie Co., Pop. Code 4
Avoha Comm. SD, AEA 13
Sch. Sys. Enr. Code 2
Supt. – Rodney Montang 51521
ES 51521 – Randy Achenbach, prin.

Badger, Webster Co., Pop. Code 3
Fort Dodge Comm. SD, AEA 5
Supt. – See Fort Dodge
ES, 328 HILL ST 50516 – Sondra Holmstrom, prin.

Bagley, Guthrie Co., Pop. Code 2
Yale-Jamaica-Bagley Comm. SD, AEA 11
Sch. Sys. Enr. Code 2
Supt. – Otto Faaborg, P O BOX 8 50026
MS, P O BOX 8 50026 – Otto Faaborg, prin.
Other Schools – See Yale

Bancroft, Kossuth Co., Pop. Code 4

St. John Grade School
  E CENTER & CLAY STS 50517

Barnum, Webster Co., Pop. Code 2
Northwest Webster Comm. SD, AEA 5
Sch. Sys. Enr. Code 2
Supt. – Warren Davison 50518
Northwest Webster ES 50501
  Warren Davison, prin.

Battle Creek, Ida Co., Pop. Code 3
Battle Creek Comm. SD, AEA 12
Sch. Sys. Enr. Code 2
Supt. – Bill Kruse
  RURAL ROUTE 02 BOX 22 51006
MS, RURAL ROUTE 02 BOX 22 51006
  James De Vore, prin.
ES 51006 – David Cass, prin.

Baxter, Jasper Co., Pop. Code 3
Baxter Comm. SD, AEA 11
Sch. Sys. Enr. Code 2
Supt. – Leland Morrison, P O BOX 189 50028
ES 50028 – Leland Morrison, prin.

Bayard, Guthrie Co., Pop. Code 3
Coon Rapids-Bayard Comm. SD,
Supt. – See Coon Rapids
Coon Rapids-Bayard MS 50029
  Terry Vitzthum, prin.

Bedford, Taylor Co., Pop. Code 4
Bedford Comm. SD, AEA 14
Sch. Sys. Enr. Code 3
Supt. – Deloy Bremer, 1103 ILLINOIS ST 50833
ES, 910 PENN ST 50833 – William Burns, prin.

Belle Plaine, Benton Co., Pop. Code 5
Belle Plaine Comm. SD, AEA 10
Sch. Sys. Enr. Code 3
Supt. – Richard Hobart, 16TH ST 52208
Lincoln JHS, 9TH AVE 52208
  Robert De Lacey, prin.
Central MS, 16TH ST 52208 – Rick Ironside, prin.
Longfellow ES, 7TH ST 52208
  Rick Ironside, prin.

Bellevue, Jackson Co., Pop. Code 4
Bellevue Comm. SD, AEA 9
Sch. Sys. Enr. Code 3
Supt. – C. Hammann
  RURAL ROUTE 01 BOX 67 52031
ES, 100 S 3RD ST 52031 – Virgil Murray, prin.

Bellevue Area Catholic School
  403 PARK ST 52031

Belmond, Wright Co., Pop. Code 5
Belmond Comm. SD, AEA 2
Sch. Sys. Enr. Code 3
Supt. – Thomas Williams
  411 10TH AVE NE 50421
Belmond Community MS, 611 4TH ST NE 50421
  James Kain, prin.
Ramsay ES, 503 4TH ST NE 50421
  James Kain, prin.

Bennett, Cedar Co., Pop. Code 2
Bennett Comm. SD, AEA 9
Sch. Sys. Enr. Code 2
Supt. – James White, P O BOX D 52721
ES, P O BOX D 52721 – James White, prin.

Bernard, Dubuque Co., Pop. Code 2
Western Dubuque Comm. SD, AEA 1
Supt. – See Farley
ES 52032 – Steve Rutz, prin.

Bettendorf, Scott Co., Pop. Code 8
Bettendorf Comm. SD, AEA 9
Sch. Sys. Enr. Code 5
Supt. – Rob Howard, 3311 CENTRAL AVE 52722
MS, 2030 MIDDLE ROAD 52722
  Wayne Cheramy, prin.
Armstrong ES, 800 23RD ST 52722
  Ronald Hovey, prin.
Hoover ES, 3223 S HAMPTON DR 52722
  Robert Pint, prin.
Jefferson ES, 610 HOLMES ST 52722
  Margaret Mackin, prin.
Norton ES, 4485 GREENBRIER DR 52722
  John Bregman, prin.
Twain ES, 1620 LINCOLN ROAD 52722
  Sue Weber, prin.
Wood ES, 1423 HILLSIDE DR 52722
  Edwin Waligora, prin.

St. Katherine/St. Mark School
  1821 SUNSET DRIVE 52722
Lourdes Memorial School
  1453 MISSISSIPPI BLVD 52722

Blairsburg, Hamilton Co., Pop. Code 2
Northeast Hamilton Comm. SD, AEA 5
Sch. Sys. Enr. Code 2
Supt. – Harvey Hindley 50034
Northeast Hamilton MS 50034
  David Strudthoff, prin.
Northeast Hamilton ES 50034
  Harvey Hindley, prin.

Blakesburg, Wapello Co., Pop. Code 2
Blakesburg Comm. SD, AEA 15
Sch. Sys. Enr. Code 2
Supt. – Thomas Crane 52536
ES 52536 – Chris Duree, prin.

Bloomfield, Davis Co., Pop. Code 5
Davis Co. Comm. SD, AEA 15
Sch. Sys. Enr. Code 4
Supt. – Dan Roe, 102 HIGH ST 52537
Middle MS, 500 E NORTH ST 52537
  Michael Bumgarner, prin.
ES, 200 W LOCUST ST 52537
  Steve Harding, prin.
Other Schools – See Pulaski

Blue Grass, Scott Co., Pop. Code 4
Davenport Comm. SD, AEA 9
Supt. – See Davenport
ES, 226 W SYCAMORE ST 52726
William Sandknop, prin.

Bode, Humboldt Co., Pop. Code 2
Twin Rivers Comm. SD, AEA 5
Sch. Sys. Enr. Code 2
Supt. – Gerald Scott, P O BOX 153 50519
Other Schools – See Livermore

Bonaparte, Van Buren Co., Pop. Code 2
Harmony Comm. SD, AEA 15
Supt. – See Farmington
Harmony ES, RURAL ROUTE 01 52620
Joseph Crozier, prin.

Bondurant, Polk Co., Pop. Code 4
Bondurrant-Farrar Comm. SD, AEA 11
Sch. Sys. Enr. Code 3
Supt. – Roger Ohde 50035
Anderson ES – Marvin Skinner, prin.
Other Schools – See Maxwell

Boone, Boone Co., Pop. Code 7
Boone Comm. SD, AEA 11
Sch. Sys. Enr. Code 4
Supt. – Donald Hansen
    621 CRAWFORD ST 50036
JHS, 621 CRAWFORD ST 50036
    Larry Harrington, prin.
Bryant MS, 511 CEDAR ST 50036
    Randy Braden, prin.
Franklin MS, 19TH & CRAWFORD 50036
    Daniel Gould, prin.
Garfield ES, 106 S WEBSTER ST 50036
    Daryl Boelman, prin.
Lincoln MS
    711 W MAMIE EISENHOWER AVE 50036
    Daryl Boelman, prin.
Lowell ES, 1420 BENTON ST 50036
    Daniel Gould, prin.
Page ES, 102 S BOONE ST 50036
    Randy Braden, prin.

United Comm. SD, AEA 11
Sch. Sys. Enr. Code 2
Supt. – Douglas Williams
    RURAL ROUTE 01 50036
United Community ES, RURAL ROUTE 01 50036
    Leonard Larsen, prin.

Sacred Heart School, 111 MARSHALL ST 50036
Trinity-St. Paul Lutheran School
    12TH & BOONE ST 50036

Boxholm, Boone Co., Pop. Code 2
Grand Comm. SD
Sch. Sys. Enr. Code 2
Supt. – Raymond Gaul 50040
ES 50040 – George Burrows, prin.

Boyden, Sioux Co., Pop. Code 3
Boyden-Hull Comm. SD, AEA 4
Supt. – See Hull
ES 51234 – Vincent Huls, prin.

Breda, Carroll Co.

Christ the King School, 304 N 2ND 51435

Bridgewater, Adair Co., Pop. Code 2
Bridgewater-Fontanelle Comm. SD, AEA 14
Supt. – See Fontanelle
Bridgewater-Fontanelle ES 50837
    Mary Wolfe, prin.

Britt, Hancock Co., Pop. Code 4
Britt Comm. SD, AEA 2
Sch. Sys. Enr. Code 3
Supt. – Ted Runyan, P O BOX 278 50423
ES, P O BOX 278 50423 – Hugh Carter, prin.

Bronson, Woodbury Co., Pop. Code 2
Lawton-Bronson Comm. SD, AEA 12
Supt. – See Lawton
ES 50554 – Patrick Girard, prin.

Brooklyn, Poweshiek Co., Pop. Code 4
Brooklyn-Guernsey-Malcom Comm. SD, AEA 6
Sch. Sys. Enr. Code 3
Supt. – Craig Cochran 52211
ES 52211 – Michele Barnes, prin.

Buffalo, Scott Co., Pop. Code 4
Davenport Comm. SD, AEA 9
Supt. – See Davenport
ES, 329 DODGE ST 52728
    William Thiessen, prin.

Buffalo Center, Winnebago Co., Pop. Code 4
Buffalo Center-Rake Comm. SD, AEA 2
Sch. Sys. Enr. Code 2
Supt. – Don West, P O BOX 510 50424
Buffalo Center-Rake ES, 111 3RD AVE NW 50424
    Don West, prin.

Burlington, Des Moines Co., Pop. Code 8
Burlington Comm. SD, AEA 16
Sch. Sys. Enr. Code 6
Supt. – James Mitchell, 1429 WEST AVE 52601
Madison MS, 2132 MADISON AVE 52601
    John Smull, prin.
Mann MS, 811 WHITE ST 52601
    James Wood, prin.
Oak Street MS, 903 OAK ST 52601
    Robert Cameron, prin.

Black Hawk ES, 2804 S 14TH ST 52601
    Jon Frischkorn, prin.
Corse ES, 711 S LEEBRICK ST 52601
    Larry Meyers, prin.
Grimes ES, 804 WALNUT ST 52601
    Dale Warner, prin.
North Hill ES, 825 N 8TH ST 52601
    Jesse Powell, prin.
Perkins ES, 1621 DODGE ST 52601
    Jon Frischkorn, prin.
Prospect Hill ES, 426 HARRISON AVE 52601
    Karen Nord, prin.
Salter MS, 705 MAPLE ST 52601
    Dale Warner, prin.
Sunnyside ES, 2040 SUNNYSIDE AVE 52601
    James Lens, prin.
Washington ES, 1910 AGENCY ST 52601
    Jack Lowther, prin.

Burlington Catholic School-St. Paul
    520 N 4TH ST 52601
St. John School, 712 DIVISION ST 52601

Burnside, Webster Co., Pop. Code 2
Central Webster Comm. SD, AEA 5
Sch. Sys. Enr. Code 2
Supt. – Allan Lyons 50521
ES 50521 – Richard Peterson, prin.

Burt, Kossuth Co., Pop. Code 3
Burt Comm. SD, AEA 3
Sch. Sys. Enr. Code 2
Supt. – Gene Fokken, 402 BUSH 50522
Burt/Sentral MS 50522 – David Kerkove, prin.
ES 50522 – Calvin Owens, prin.

Bussey, Marion Co., Pop. Code 3
Twin Cedars Comm. SD, AEA 11
Sch. Sys. Enr. Code 2
Supt. – D. Gilkerson, RURAL ROUTE 02 50044
Twin Cedars JHS 50044 – Norma Newhouse, prin.
Twin Cedars ES, RURAL ROUTE 02 50044
    Dan Thompson, prin.

Calamus, Clinton Co., Pop. Code 2
Calamus Comm. SD
Sch. Sys. Enr. Code 2
Supt. – Charles Freese 52729
ES 52729 – Everett Knudtson, prin.

Callender, Webster Co., Pop. Code 2
Prairie Comm. SD, AEA 5
Supt. – See Gowrie
ES 50523 – Dennis Tucker, prin.

Calmar, Winneshiek Co., Pop. Code 4
South Winneshiek Comm. SD, AEA 1
Sch. Sys. Enr. Code 3
Supt. – Russell Loven
    305 S WASHINGTON 52132
Other Schools – See Ossian

Calmar-Festina-Spillville School
    MARYVILLE ST 52132

Camanche, Clinton Co., Pop. Code 5
Camanche Comm. SD, AEA 9
Sch. Sys. Enr. Code 4
Supt. – Larry Dennis, 1400 9TH ST 52730
MS, 1400 9TH ST 52730 – Gary Cross, prin.
Northeast ES, 5TH AVE & 11TH PL 52730
    John Neville, prin.

Cambria, Wayne Co.
Wayne Comm. SD, AEA 15
Supt. – See Corydon
MS 50045 – D. Phillips, prin.

Cambridge, Story Co., Pop. Code 3
Ballard Comm. SD, AEA 11
Supt. – See Huxley
ES, 3RD ST 50046 – Daniel Lawler, prin.

Cantril, Van Buren Co., Pop. Code 2
Fox Valley Comm. SD, AEA 15
Sch. Sys. Enr. Code 2
Supt. – Cynthia Hollinger 52542
ES 52542 – Roger Davies, prin.
Other Schools – See Milton

Carlisle, Warren Co., Pop. Code 5
Carlisle Comm. SD, AEA 11
Sch. Sys. Enr. Code 4
Supt. – W. Turner, 430 SCHOOL ST 50047
ES, 430 SCHOOL ST 50047
    Ronald Pattison, prin.
Other Schools – See Hartford

Carroll, Carroll Co., Pop. Code 6
Carroll Comm. SD, AEA 11
Sch. Sys. Enr. Code 4
Supt. – Dale Proctor, 1026 N ADAMS ST 51401
MS, 1026 N ADAMS ST 51401
    John Kinley, prin.
ES, 18TH & GRANT ROAD 51401
    Terri Miller, prin.

Holy Spirit School, 201 S CLARK ST 51401
St. Lawrence School, 1519 NORTHWEST 51401

Carson, Pottawattamie Co., Pop. Code 3
Carson-Macedonia Comm. SD, AEA 13
Sch. Sys. Enr. Code 2
Supt. – Gary Funkhouser, P O BOX 218 51525
Other Schools – See Macedonia

Cascade, Dubuque Co., Pop. Code 4
Western Dubuque Comm. SD, AEA 1
Supt. – See Farley
ES 52033 – Steve Rutz, prin.

Aquin ES, 608 THIRD AVE NW 52033

Castana, Monona Co., Pop. Code 2
Maple Valley Comm. SD, AEA 12
Supt. – See Mapleton
MS 51010 – (—), prin.

Cedar Falls, Black Hawk Co., Pop. Code 8
Cedar Falls Comm. SD, AEA 7
Sch. Sys. Enr. Code 5
Supt. – James L. Robinson, 1002 W 1ST ST 50613
ES, 2417 RAINBOW DR 50613
    Susan Robinson, prin.
Hansen ES, 616 HOLMES DR 50613
    James Jackson, prin.
Lincoln ES, 7TH & FRANKLIN 50613
    John Focht, prin.
North Cedar ES, FERN AVE 50613
    Janice Ott, prin.
Orchard Hill ES, 3909 ROWND ST 50613
    Jariel Robinson, prin.
Southdale ES, 627 ORCHARD DR 50613
    Donald Ackman, prin.
Valley Park ES, 1026 E SEERLEY BLVD 50613
    Jariel Robinson, prin.

St. Patrick School, 615 WASHINGTON ST 50613

Cedar Rapids, Linn Co., Pop. Code 9
Cedar Rapids Comm. SD, AEA 10
Sch. Sys. Enr. Code 7
Supt. – Stephen Dueschner
    346 2ND AVE SW 52404
Franklin MS, 300 20TH ST NE 52402
    Thomas Van Deest, prin.
Harding MS, 4801 GOLF ST NE 52402
    Collin Williams, prin.
McKinley MS, 620 10TH ST SE 52403
    Frederick Maharry, prin.
Roosevelt MS, 300 13TH ST NW 52405
    Arnold Paulsen, prin.
Taft MS, 5200 E AVE NW 52405
    Eugene Whiteman, prin.
Wilson MS, 2301 J ST SW 52404
    John Christenson, prin.
Arthur ES, 2630 B AVE NE #B 52402
    Don Stonebraker, prin.
Cleveland ES, 2200 1ST AVE NW 52405
    John Hegarty, prin.
Coolidge ES, 6225 1ST AVE SW 52405
    William Brousard, prin.
Erskine ES, CLARK & 36TH ST SE 52403
    Robert Brighi, prin.
Garfield ES, 1201 MAPLEWOOD DR NE 52402
    Sidney Wallace, prin.
Grant Wood ES, 645 26TH ST SE 52403
    Sheila Billington, prin.
Harrison ES, 1310 11TH ST NW 52405
    Fred Steitzer, prin.
Hiawatha ES, 603 EMMONS ST 52233
    James O'Connor, prin.
Hoover ES, 4141 JOHNSTON AVE NW 52405
    Stuart Yager, prin.
Johnson ES, 355 18TH ST SE 52403
    Cynthia Monroe, prin.
Kenwood ES, 3700 E AVE NE 52402
    Glenn Oldorf, prin.
Madison ES, 1341 MOONSIDE DR NW 52405
    Mary Lehner, prin.
Pierce ES, 4343 MARILYN DR NE 52402
    Max Thompson, prin.
Polk ES, 1500 B AVE NE 52402
    Edward Rich, prin.
Taft ES, 441 WEST POST ROAD NW 52405
    Vernon Beasmore, prin.
Taylor ES, 720 7TH AVE SW 52404
    Michael Clover, prin.
Van Buren ES, 2525 29TH ST SW 52404
    Keith Moreland, prin.
Wilson ES, 254 OUTLOOK DR SW 52404
    Gregg Petersen, prin.
Wright ES, HOLLYWOOD NE & COUNCIL 52402
    Keith Wymore, prin.
Other Schools – See Hiawatha

College Comm. SD, AEA 10
Sch. Sys. Enr. Code 4
Supt. – William J. Bach, 401 76TH AVE SW 52401
Prairie ES, 401 76TH AVE SW 52401
    Robert Sherman, prin.
Prairie IS, 401 76TH AVE SW 52401
    David Brauhn, prin.
Prairie View ES, 401 76TH AVE SW 52401
    Marilyn Miller, prin.

All Saints School, 720 29TH ST SE 52403
St. Jude School, 50 EDGEWOOD ROAD NW 52405
St. Ludmila School, 215 21ST AVE SW 52404
St. Matthew School, 24TH ST & A AVE NE 52402
St. Patrick School, 509 A AVE NW 52405
St. Piux X School, 50TH & COUNCIL ST NE 52402
Trinity Lutheran School
    1361 7TH AVE SW 52404

Center Point, Linn Co., Pop. Code 4
Center Point Cons. SD, AEA 10
Sch. Sys. Enr. Code 3
Supt. – Richard Whitehead
    613 SUMMIT ST 52213
ES, 613 SUMMIT ST 52213 – Jane Fahey, prin.

Centerville, Appanoose Co., Pop. Code 6
Centerville Comm. SD, AEA 15
Sch. Sys. Enr. Code 4
Supt. – Jack Hoenshel, P O BOX 370 52544
Howar JHS, 11TH & TERRY 52544
Karpen Bruce, prin.
Central ES, DRAKE AVE 52544
Gordon Mosher, prin.
Garfield ES, WALSH & 17TH 52544
Gordon Mosher, prin.
Lakeview MS, WALSH & 17TH 52544
Forrest Buckallew, prin.
Lincoln ES, NORTH 10TH 52544
Gordon Mosher, prin.
Other Schools – See Cincinnati, Mystic

Central City, Linn Co., Pop. Code 4
Central City Comm. SD, AEA 10
Sch. Sys. Enr. Code 3
Supt. – William Newman, P O BOX 340 52214
MS, P O BOX 340 52214 – Kirk Ketelsen, prin.
ES, P O BOX 340 52214 – Kirk Ketelson, prin.

Chariton, Lucas Co., Pop. Code 5
Chariton Comm. SD, AEA 15
Sch. Sys. Enr. Code 4
Supt. – James Fields, 410 S 7TH ST 50049
MS, 501 N GRAND ST 50049
Richard Dawson, prin.
Columbus ES, LINDEN AVE & 12TH 50049
Loren Burkhalter, prin.
Van Allen ES, 12TH & ASHLAND 50049
Beatric Block, prin.
Other Schools – See Lucas, Williamson

Charles City, Floyd Co., Pop. Code 6
Charles City Comm. SD, AEA 2
Sch. Sys. Enr. Code 4
Supt. – Larry Beard, 500 N GRAND AVE 50616
Jefferson ES, 801 9TH ST 50616
Doug Bengtson, prin.
Lincoln ES, 510 F ST 50616
Adam Schreier, prin.
Washington ES, 1406 N GRAND AVE 50616
Leon Mulford, prin.

Immaculate Conception School
1203 CLARK ST 50616

Charter Oak, Crawford Co., Pop. Code 3
Charter Oak-Ute Comm. SD, AEA 12
Sch. Sys. Enr. Code 2
Supt. – D. L. Gries 51439
Charter Oak-Ute JHS 51439
Wade Bruggeman, prin.
Other Schools – See Ute

Chelsea, Tama Co., Pop. Code 2
South Tama Comm. SD, AEA 6
Supt. – See Tama
ES 52215 – John Foster, prin.

Cherokee, Cherokee Co., Pop. Code 6
Cherokee Comm. SD, AEA 12
Sch. Sys. Enr. Code 4
Supt. – Mick Starcevich, 207 N 2ND ST 51012
Wilson MS, 100 E WILLOW ST 51012
Larry Weede, prin.
Garfield ES, 515 W CEDAR ST 51012
David Deeonick, prin.
Roosevelt ES, 929 N ROOSEVELT AVE 51012
Lynn Schrier, prin.
Webster ES, 400 N ROOSEVELT AVE 51012
David Deedrick, prin.

Churdan, Greene Co., Pop. Code 3
Paton-Churdan Comm. SD, AEA 5
Sch. Sys. Enr. Code 2
Supt. – Oran Teut 50050
Other Schools – See Paton

Cincinnati, Appanoose Co., Pop. Code 3
Centerville Comm. SD, AEA 15
Supt. – See Centerville
ES 52549 – Gordon Mosher, prin.

Clarence, Cedar Co., Pop. Code 4
Clarence-Lowden Comm. SD, AEA 10
Sch. Sys. Enr. Code 2
Supt. – Donald Lamm, 416 5TH AVE 52216
Other Schools – See Lowden

Clarinda, Page Co., Pop. Code 6
Clarinda Comm. SD, AEA 13
Sch. Sys. Enr. Code 4
Supt. – Clarence Lippert, 114 E GARFIELD 51632
Garfield ES, 201 E DIVISION ST 51632
Arleen Vander Ploeg, prin.
Lincoln ES, 19TH & LINCOLN 51632
Leila De Pew, prin.
McKinley ES, NORTH 12TH 51632
Leila De Pew, prin.

Immanuel Lutheran School
RURAL ROUTE 01 BOX 61A 51632

Clarion, Wright Co.
Clarion Comm. SD, AEA 5
Sch. Sys. Enr. Code 3
Supt. – Byron Hofmeister, 3RD AVE NE 50525
MS, 3RD AVE NE 50525 – Kurt Wiethorn, prin.
ES, 3RD AVE NE 50525 – Kurt Wiethorn, prin.

Clarksville, Butler Co., Pop. Code 4
Clarksville Comm. SD, AEA 7
Sch. Sys. Enr. Code 2
Supt. – Kenneth Vance, P O BOX 60 50619

ES, P O BOX 689 50619 – Kenneth Vance, prin.

Clearfield, Taylor Co., Pop. Code 2
Clearfield Comm. SD, AEA 14
Sch. Sys. Enr. Code 2
Supt. – Keith Gillespie 50840
JHS 50840 – Keith Gillespie, prin.
ES 50840 – Keith Gillespie, prin.

Clear Lake, Cerro Gordo Co., Pop. Code 6
Clear Lake Comm. SD, AEA 2
Sch. Sys. Enr. Code 4
Supt. – Stephen Voelz, 125 N 20TH ST 50428
JHS, 1601 3RD AVE N 50428 – Joe Lambert, prin.
Central IS, 808 2ND AVE N 50428
Richard Hanson, prin.
Lincoln ES, 306 S 8TH ST 50428
Armand Oetken, prin.
Sunset View ES, 408 MARS HILL DR 50428
Armand Oetken, prin.

Cleghorn, Cherokee Co., Pop. Code 2
Meriden-Cleghorn Comm. SD, AEA 4
Sch. Sys. Enr. Code 2
Supt. – John Mitts 51014
Meriden-Cleghorn MS 51014 – Ken Williams, prin.
Other Schools – See Meriden

Clemons, Marshall Co., Pop. Code 2

Clemons Lutheran School
302 BEVIN STREET 50051

Clermont, Fayette Co., Pop. Code 3
Valley Comm. SD, AEA 1
Supt. – See Elgin
MS 52135 – John Stevens, prin.

Climbing Hill, Woodbury Co.
Woodbury Central Comm. SD, AEA 12
Supt. – See Moville
Woodbury Central MS 51015
Robert Jensen, prin.

Clinton, Clinton Co., Pop. Code 8
Clinton Comm. SD, AEA 9
Sch. Sys. Enr. Code 5
Supt. – Mary Garcia, 600 S 4TH ST 52732
Lyons MS, 2810 N 4TH ST 52732
James Moore, prin.
Washington MS, 751 2ND AVE S 52732
Thomas Streba, prin.
Buell ES, 216 31ST AVE N 52732
Jack Pringle, prin.
Harding ES, 1401 13TH AVE N 52732
Richard Shaw, prin.
Jefferson ES, 723 2ND AVE S 52732
Ronald Garrison, prin.
Longfellow ES, 1820 IOWA AVE 52732
Joyce Caprata, prin.
Mann ES, 20TH AVE N & 3RD ST 52732
Gary Herrity, prin.
Sabin ES, 1850 S BLUFF BLVD 52732
Donald Overland, prin.
Whittier ES, 100 N 13TH ST 52732
Peter Gluck, prin.

Northeast Comm. SD, AEA 9
Supt. – See Goose Lake
Elvira MS, RURAL ROUTE 01 52732
Wayne McLaughlin, prin.

Trinity Catholic MS, 806 S 5TH ST 52732
Trinity Catholic IS, 312 S 4TH ST 52732
Trinity Catholic PS, 234 4TH AVE N 52732

Coggon, Linn Co., Pop. Code 3
North Linn Comm. SD, AEA 10
Sch. Sys. Enr. Code 3
Supt. – Gary Pillman 52218
ES 52218 – John Mathre, prin.
Other Schools – See Troy Mills, Walker

Colesburg, Delaware Co., Pop. Code 2
Edgewood-Colesburg Comm. SD, AEA 1
Supt. – See Edgewood
Edgewood-Colesburg ES 52035
Chris Smith, prin.

Colfax, Jasper Co., Pop. Code 4
Colfax-Mingo Comm. SD, AEA 11
Sch. Sys. Enr. Code 3
Supt. – Leland Rankin, WEST BROADWAY 50054
Colfax-Mingo ES, WEST BROADWAY 50054
Larry Kruckenberg, prin.
Other Schools – See Mingo

College Springs, Page Co., Pop. Code 2
South Page Comm. SD, AEA 13
Sch. Sys. Enr. Code 2
Supt. – Randy Moffit, P O BOX 98 51637
ES 51637 – Randy Moffit, prin.

Collins, Story Co.
Collins-Maxwell Comm. SD, AEA 11
Supt. – See Maxwell
Collins-Maxwell MS 50055 – Mike Anthony, prin.

Colo, Story Co., Pop. Code 3
Colo Comm. SD, AEA 11
Sch. Sys. Enr. Code 2
Supt. – Elbert Sobotka, P O BOX 136 50056
ES, P O BOX 276 50056 – Keith Tadlock, prin.

Columbus Junction, Louisa Co., Pop. Code 4
Columbus Comm. SD, AEA 9
Sch. Sys. Enr. Code 3
Supt. – John Currie, 1004 COLTON ST 52738

JHS, 1004 COLTON ST 52738
John Della Vedova, prin.
ES, 1004 COLTON ST 52738
William Wilson, prin.
Other Schools – See Cotter

Conrad, Grundy Co., Pop. Code 4
Beaman-Conrad-Liscomb Comm. SD, AEA 6
Sch. Sys. Enr. Code 2
Supt. – Fran Morrow 50621
Beaman-Conrad-Liscomb ES 50621
Paul Eckerman, prin.

Coon Rapids, Carroll Co., Pop. Code 4
Coon Rapids-Bayard Comm. SD,
Sch. Sys. Enr. Code 3
Supt. – Marvin Judkins, 905 NORTH ST 50058
Coon Rapids-Bayard ES, P O BOX 297 50058
Jeffrey Peterson, prin.
Other Schools – See Bayard

Coralville, Johnson Co., Pop. Code 6
Iowa City Comm. SD, AEA 10
Supt. – See Iowa City
Northwest JHS, 1507 8TH ST 52241
(–), prin.
Central ES, 501 6TH ST 52241
Michael O'Leary, prin.
Kirkwood ES, 1401 9TH ST 52241 – (–), prin.

Corning, Adams Co., Pop. Code 4
Corning Comm. SD, AEA 14
Sch. Sys. Enr. Code 3
Supt. – Kenneth Mallas, 904 8TH ST 50841
JHS, 10TH & WASHINGTON 50841
Fred Shearer, prin.
ES, LOOMIS AVE & 10TH ST 50841
Richard Shellenberg, prin.

Correctionville, Woodbury Co., Pop. Code 3
Eastwood Comm. SD, AEA 12
Sch. Sys. Enr. Code 2
Supt. – Leonard Grasso 51016
Other Schools – See Cushing

Corwith, Hancock Co., Pop. Code 2
Corwith-Wesley Comm. SD, AEA 2
Sch. Sys. Enr. Code 2
Supt. – Ronald Okones 50430
Wesley ES, P O BOX 127 50430
Ronald Okones, prin.

Corydon, Wayne Co., Pop. Code 4
Wayne Comm. SD, AEA 15
Sch. Sys. Enr. Code 3
Supt. – C. L. Frizzell, P O BOX 308 50060
ES, P O BOX 308 50060 – Duane Klett, prin.
Other Schools – See Cambria

Cotter, Louisa Co.
Columbus Comm. SD, AEA 9
Supt. – See Columbus Junction
ES 52221 – William Wilson, prin.

Council Bluffs, Pottawattamie Co., Pop. Code 8
Council Bluffs Comm. SD, AEA 13
Sch. Sys. Enr. Code 6
Supt. – Richard Christie, 207 SCOTT ST 51501
Kirn JHS, 100 NORTH AVE 51501
Larry Dechant, prin.
Wilson JHS, 715 N 21ST ST 51501
Barbara Licklider, prin.
Bloomer ES, 210 S 7TH ST 51501
Douglas Smith, prin.
Carter Lake ES, 1105 REDICK BLVD 51510
Douglas Smith, prin.
Crescent ES 51526 – Jack Holder, prin.
Edison ES, 2218 3RD AVE 51501 – (–), prin.
Franklin ES, 3130 AVENUE C ST 51501
John Eller, prin.
Glendale ES, RURAL ROUTE 04 51501
Mary Dickerson, prin.
Gunn ES, 1735 N BROADWAY ST 51503
Jack Holder, prin.
Hoover ES, 1205 N BROADWAY ST 51503
Allen Kurland, prin.
Lewis & Clark ES, 1603 GRAND AVE 51503
Duane Wiechelman, prin.
Longfellow ES, 2011 S 10TH ST 51501
Robert Rossie, prin.
Pusey ES, 147 15TH AVE 51503
Mary Dickerson, prin.
Roosevelt ES, 517 N 17TH ST 51501
Daniel Fellows, prin.
Rue ES, 3326 6TH AVE 51501 – Diane Weitz, prin.
Walnut Grove ES, 2920 AVENUE J ST 51501
Norman Bush, prin.
Washington ES, 207 SCOTT ST 51503
Len Faraci, prin.

Lewis Central Comm. SD, AEA 13
Sch. Sys. Enr. Code 4
Supt. – Wayne Rand
1600 E S OMAHA BRIDGE ROAD 51501
Lewis Central MS, 2000 HIGHWAY 275 51501
Don Friday, prin.
Central ES, HIGHWAY 275 51501
Beverly Fletcher, prin.
Kreft ES, 3206 RENNER DR 51501
Ronald Kelley, prin.
Lakeview ES, PIUTE & WRIGHT ROAD 51501
Glenn McBurney, prin.

St. Albert's IS, 3330 4TH AVE 51501
St. Albert's PS, 2301 AVENUE B ST 51501

Crawfordsville, Washington Co., Pop. Code 2
Waco Comm. SD, AEA 16
Supt. – See Wayland
ES, P O BOX 158 52421 – Bobby Wise, prin.

Cresco, Howard Co., Pop. Code 5
Howard-Winneshiek Comm. SD, AEA 1
Sch. Sys. Enr. Code 4
Supt. – Donald Pettengill
  1000 SCHRODER DRIVE 52136
Crestwood JHS, 320 3RD AVE E 52136
  Robert Myers, prin.
ES, 315 3RD AVE E 52136 – Robert Myers, prin.
Other Schools – See Elma, Lime Springs, Ridgeway

Notre Dame ES, 221 2ND AVE E 52136

Creston, Union Co., Pop. Code 6
Creston Comm. SD, AEA 14
Sch. Sys. Enr. Code 4
Supt. – P. G. Grumley, 619 N MAPLE ST 50801
Franklin ES, 500 S OAK ST 50801
  Opal Gordon, prin.
Irving MS, 901 S ELM ST 50801
  Keith Langholz, prin.
Jefferson ES, 501 N CHERRY ST 50801
  Keith Langholz, prin.
Lincoln ES, 1001 W JEFFERSON ST 50801
  Opal Gordon, prin.

St. Malachy School, 403 W CLARK ST 50801

Cumberland, Cass Co., Pop. Code 2
C & M Comm. SD, AEA 13
Supt. – See Massena
C and M ES 50843 – Dannie Crozier, prin.

Cushing, Woodbury Co., Pop. Code 2
Eastwood Comm. SD, AEA 12
Supt. – See Correctionville
ES 51018 – Robert Cord, prin.

Dakota City, Humboldt Co., Pop. Code 4
Humboldt Comm. SD, AEA 5
Supt. – See Humboldt
Mease ES 50529 – Kay Kollmorgen, prin.

Dallas, Marion Co., Pop. Code 2
Melcher-Dallas Comm. SD, AEA 11
Sch. Sys. Enr. Code 2
Supt. – Craig Okerberg, P O BOX C 50062
ES 50062 – Fred Lange, prin.
Other Schools – See Melcher

Dallas Center, Dallas Co., Pop. Code 4
Dallas Center Grimes Comm. SD, AEA 11
Sch. Sys. Enr. Code 4
Supt. – Dr. Dennis Bishop, P O BOX 512 50063
ES, 802 15TH ST 50063 – Paul Jones, prin.
Other Schools – See Grimes

Danbury, Woodbury Co., Pop. Code 2
Maple Valley Comm. SD, AEA 12
Supt. – See Mapleton
Maple Valley JHS 51019 – Lawrence Nelson, prin.

Danville, Des Moines Co., Pop. Code 3
Danville Comm. SD, AEA 16
Sch. Sys. Enr. Code 3
Supt. – Ronald E. Bickford, 415 S MAIN ST 52623
ES 52623 – Ronald Bickford, prin.

Davenport, Scott Co., Pop. Code 9
Davenport Comm. SD, AEA 9
Sch. Sys. Enr. Code 7
Supt. – Peter Flynn, 1001 N HARRISON ST 52803
Adams ES, 3029 N DIVISION ST 52804
  Loren Stouffer, prin.
Buchanan ES, 4515 N FAIRMONT ST 52806
  Steve Johnson, prin.
Eisenhower ES, 2827 JERSEY RIDGE ROAD 52803
  Harold Moore, prin.
Fillmore ES, 7307 PACIFIC ST 52806
  James Dexter, prin.
Garfield ES, 902 E 29TH ST 52803
  Kenneth Krumwiede, prin.
Grant ES, 216 W HAYES ST 52803
  Morris Williams, prin.
Harrison ES, 1032 W 53RD ST 52806
  Patricia Robinson, prin.
Hayes ES, 622 S CONCORD ST 52802
  Fred Frazier, prin.
Hoover ES, 1002 SPRING ST 52803
  William Long, prin.
Jackson ES, 1307 WISCONSIN AVE 52804
  George Bleich, prin.
Jefferson ES, 1027 N MARQUETTE ST 52804
  Henry Caudle, prin.
Johnson ES, 1730 WILKES AVE 52804
  Roger Beier, prin.
Lincoln Fundamental ES, 318 E 7TH ST 52803
  Saul Herrera, prin.
Madison ES, 116 E LOCUST ST 52803
  Henry Krambeck, prin.
McKinley ES, 1716 KENWOOD AVE 52803
  Michael Lake, prin.
Monroe ES, 1926 W 4TH ST 52802
  Leon McDevitt, prin.
Perry ES, 5121 WAPELLO AVE 52802
  William Theissen, prin.
Roosevelt ES, 1220 MINNIE AVE 52802
  Fred Frazier, prin.
Washington ES, 1608 E LOCUST ST 52803
  William Long, prin.
Wilson ES, 2002 N CLARK ST 52804
  Verlyn Siglin, prin.
Other Schools – See Blue Grass, Buffalo, Walcott

Holy Family School
  1926 N MARQUETTE ST 52804
Holy Trinity Catholic School
  1116 W 6TH ST 52802
Kennedy School, 1627 W 42ND ST 52806
Sacred Heart School, 408 E 11TH ST 52803
St. Alphonsus School, 2626 BOIES AVE 52802
St. Paul the Apostle School
  1007 E RUSHOLME ST 52803
Trinity Lutheran School
  1122 W CENTRAL PARK AVE 52804

Dayton, Webster Co., Pop. Code 3
Dayton Comm. SD, AEA 5
Sch. Sys. Enr. Code 2
Supt. – Allan Lyons, P O BOX 26 50530
MS, P O BOX 26 50530 – Tony Tjaden, prin.
ES, P O BOX 26 50530 – Tony Tjaden, prin.

Decatur, Decatur Co., Pop. Code 2
Central Decatur Comm. SD, AEA 14
Supt. – See Leon
MS 50067 – Donald Forman, prin.

Decorah, Winneshiek Co., Pop. Code 6
Decorah Comm. SD, AEA 1
Sch. Sys. Enr. Code 4
Supt. – Francis Peterson, VERNON ST 52101
Cline ES, CLAIBORNE DR 52101
  Paul Knipe, prin.
East Side MS, 210 VERNON ST 52101
  Oliver Lybeck, prin.
West Side ES, IOWA AVE 52101
  Paul Knipe, prin.

North Wineshiek Comm. SD, AEA 1
Sch. Sys. Enr. Code 2
Supt. – Harold Isley, RURAL ROUTE 03 52101
North Winneshiek ES, RURAL ROUTE 03 52101
  John Weaver, prin.

St. Benedict School, 402 RURAL AVE 52101

Dedham, Carroll Co., Pop. Code 2

Dedham Willey School, 502 MAIN 51440

Deep River, Poweshiek Co., Pop. Code 2
Deep River-Millersburg Comm. SD, AEA 10
Supt. – See Millersburg
Deep River-Millersburg ES, EAST LOCUST 52222
  Corrine Tandy, prin.

Delhi, Delaware Co., Pop. Code 3
Maquoketa Valley Comm. SD, AEA 1
Sch. Sys. Enr. Code 3
Supt. – Robert Vittenger 52223
ES 52223 – Thomas Gatto, prin.
Other Schools – See Earlville, Hopkinton

Delmar, Clinton Co., Pop. Code 3
Delwood Comm. SD
Sch. Sys. Enr. Code 2
Supt. – John Lawrence 52037
ES 52037 – Steven Fuglsang, prin.

Denison, Crawford Co., Pop. Code 6
Denison Comm. SD, AEA 12
Sch. Sys. Enr. Code 4
Supt. – John Finnessy, 819 N 16TH ST 51442
MS, 1515 BROADWAY 51442 – Larry Bandy, prin.
ES, NORTH 20TH ST 51442 – Robert Meyer, prin.

St. Rose of Lima School, 1012 2ND AVE S 51442
Zion Lutheran School
  1003 W BROADWAY 51442

Denmark, Lee Co.
Fort Madison Comm. SD, AEA 16
Supt. – See Fort Madison
ES 52624 – Edward Bleeker, prin.

Denver, Bremer Co., Pop. Code 4
Denver Comm. SD, AEA 7
Sch. Sys. Enr. Code 3
Supt. – Robert Conway, P O BOX 384 50622
MS, P O BOX 384 50622
  Robert H. Ehrhardt, prin.
ES, 401 E FRANKLIN ST 50622
  Duane Boehmke, prin.

Des Moines, Polk Co., Pop. Code 9
Des Moines Comm. ISD, AEA 11
Sch. Sys. Enr. Code 8
Supt. – Gary Wegenke, 1800 GRAND AVE 50309
Brody JHS, 2501 PARK AVE 50321
  Richard Tuller, prin.
Callanan JHS, 3010 CENTER ST 50312
  Marian Ehlers, prin.
Goodrell JHS, 3300 E 29TH ST 50317
  William McCollaugh, prin.
Harding JHS, 203 E EUCLID AVE 50313
  Mike Loffredo, prin.
Hiatt JHS, 1214 E 15TH ST 50316
  Joan Roberts, prin.
Hoyt MS, 2700 E 42ND ST 50317
  Betty Hyde, prin.
McCombs JHS
  201 SW COUNTY LINE ROAD 50315
  John Barrett, prin.
Meredith JHS, 4827 MADISON AVE 50310
  Robert Wells, prin.
Merrill JHS, 5301 GRAND AVE 50312
  Lacey Spriggs, prin.
Weeks JHS, 901 SE PARK AVE 50315
  Wendell Miskimins, prin.

Adams ES, 3720 E 29TH ST 50317
  Joseph Turner, prin.
Brooks ES, 2124 DES MOINES ST 50317
  Judith Cunningham, prin.
Cattell ES, 1210 HULL AVE 50316
  Gay Ross, prin.
Cowles PS, 6401 COLLEGE AVE 50311
  Jack Gibbons, prin.
Douglas ES, 3800 E DOUGLAS AVE 50317
  Peg Floden, prin.
Edmunds ES, 1601 CROCKER ST 50314
  Frances Hawthorne, prin.
Findley ES, 3000 CAMBRIDGE ST 50313
  Mike Schaumburg, prin.
Garton ES, 2820 E 24TH ST 50317
  John Viviano, prin.
Granger ES, 101 E LEACH AVE 50315
  Jerry Mills, prin.
Greenwood ES, 316 37TH ST 50312
  Lois Smith, prin.
Hanawalt ES, 225 56TH ST 50312
  Helen Oliver, prin.
Hillis ES, 2401 56TH ST 50310
  Jack Gibbons, prin.
Howe ES, 2900 INDIANOLA ROAD 50315
  Wilbert Coleman, prin.
Hubbell ES, 800 42ND STOLA ROAD 50312
  Mary Chapman, prin.
Jackson ES, 3825 INDIANOLA ROAD 50320
  Bob Langbehn, prin.
Jefferson ES, 2425 WATROUS AVE 50321
  Kenneth Hook, prin.
King ES, 1849 FOREST AVE 50314
  Lawrence Streyfeller, prin.
Longfellow ES, 1101 E 6TH ST 50316
  Bobbretta Williams, prin.
Lovejoy ES, 801 SE KENYON AVE 50315
  Mel Kiner, prin.
Lucas ES, 1535 CAPITOL AVE 50316
  Sandra O'Brien, prin.
Madison ES, 806 HOFFMAN AVE 50316
  Val Near, prin.
Mann ES, 1001 AMOS AVE 50315
  Gary Sheldon, prin.
McKee ES, 2115 E 39TH ST 50317
  John Johnson, prin.
McKinley ES, 1610 SE 6TH ST 50315
  Dominic Bonanno, prin.
Mitchell ES, 111 PORTER AVE 50315
  Sandra Bell, prin.
Monroe ES, 2250 30TH ST 50310
  Barbara Sloan, prin.
Moore ES, 3725 52ND ST 50310
  Udell Cason, prin.
Moulton ES, 710 COLLEGE AVE 50314
  Sally Liechty, prin.
Oak Park ES, 3928 6TH AVE 50313
  Gloria McCrorey, prin.
Park Avenue ES, 3141 SW 9TH ST 50315
  Gene Stephany, prin.
Perkins MS, 4301 COLLEGE AVE 50311
  Lawrence Streyfeller, prin.
Phillips ES, 1701 LAY ST 50317
  Dorla Eisenlauer, prin.
Pleasant Hill ES, 4801 E OAKWOOD DR 50317
  Virginia Lawrence, prin.
Rice ES, 3001 BEAVER AVE 50310
  Barbara Sloan, prin.
Stowe ES, 1411 E 33RD ST 50317
  Keith Banwart, prin.
Studebaker ES, 300 COUNTY LINE ROAD 50320
  Linda Hansen, prin.
Wallace ES, 1404 E 13TH ST 50316
  Lester Rees, prin.
Watrous ES, 6430 SW 14TH ST 50315
  James Mitchell, prin.
Willard ES, 2941 DEAN AVE 50317
  James Graeber, prin.
Windsor ES, 5912 UNIVERSITY AVE 50311
  Marie Cardemone, prin.
Woodlawn ES
  4000 LOWER BEAVER ROAD 50310
  Don Shaw, prin.
Wright ES, 5001 SW 14TH ST 50315
  Gerald Clutts, prin.

Saydel Cons. SD, AEA 11
Sch. Sys. Enr. Code 4
Supt. – Ken Jensen, 5401 NW 2ND ST 50313
Woodside MS, 5810 NE 14TH ST 50313
  Lee McCarty, prin.
Cornell ES, 5817 NE 3RD ST 50313
  James Haigh, prin.
Norwoodville ES, NE 29TH & BROADWAY 50317
  Stanley Voss, prin.

Southeast Polk Comm. SD, AEA 11
Supt. – See Runnells
Delaware ES, 4401 NE 46TH ST 50317
  Faye Davis, prin.
Four Mile ES, 670 SE 68TH ST 50317
  Richard Tomlin, prin.

West Des Moines Comm. SD, AEA 11
Supt. – See West Des Moines
Indian Hills JHS
  9401 INDIAN HILLS DRIVE 50322
  Thomas Drake, prin.
Clive ES, 1600 73RD ST 50322 – Jim Mayse, prin.
Crestview ES, 8355 FRANKLIN AVE 50322
  Martha Davis, prin.

All Saints School, 3415 3RD ST 50313
Christ the King School, 701 WALL AVE 50315

Des Moines Christian School
 4801 FRANKLIN AVE 50310
Grandview Park Baptist ES
 1701 E 33RD ST 50317
Holy Family-St. John Center
 1913 UNIVERSITY AVE 50314
Holy Family School-Visitation Center
 1111 GARFIELD 50316
Holy Trinity School, 2922 BEAVER AVE 50310
Mt. Olive Lutheran School
 5625 FRANKLIN AVE 50310
St. Anthony School, 16 COLUMBUS AVE 50315
St. Augustin School, 4320 GRAND AVE 50312
St. Joseph ES, 2107 E 33RD ST 50317
St. Piux X School, 3601 66TH ST 50322
St. Theresa School
 1230 MERLE MAY ROAD 50311

De Soto, Dallas Co., Pop. Code 4
 Adel-DeSoto Comm. SD, AEA 11
 Supt. – See Adel
 MS, 317 SPRUCE ST 50069 – Jerry Hilton, prin.

De Witt, Clinton Co., Pop. Code 5
 Central Clinton Comm. SD, AEA 9
 Sch. Sys. Enr. Code 4
 Supt. – Joseph Drips, 924 3RD AVE E 52742
 Ekstrand ES, 1140 15TH ST 52742
  Robert Gillum, prin.
 Other Schools – See Grand Mound, Welton

 St. Joseph School, 417 6TH AVE 52742

Dexter, Dallas Co., Pop. Code 3
 Dexfield Comm. SD, AEA 11
 Supt. – See Redfield
 Dexfield MS 50070 – Robert Vellinga, prin.

Diagonal, Ringgold Co., Pop. Code 2
 Diagonal Comm. SD, AEA 14
 Sch. Sys. Enr. Code 2
 Supt. – Dennis Tassell, P O BOX D 50845
 ES, P O BOX D 50345 – Dennis Tassell, prin.

Dike, Grundy Co., Pop. Code 3
 Dike Comm. SD, AEA 7
 Sch. Sys. Enr. Code 3
 Supt. – Donald Gunderson, 220 MAIN ST 50624
 ES, 220 MAIN ST 50624
  Dudley Humphrey, prin.

Donahue, Scott Co., Pop. Code 2
 North Scott Comm. SD, AEA 9
 Supt. – See Eldridge
 Glenn ES 52746 – Joseph Ragona, prin.

Donnellson, Lee Co., Pop. Code 3
 Central Lee Comm. SD, AEA 16
 Supt. – See Argyle
 Central Lee ES, P O BOX 1356 52625
  B. Joan Palmer, prin.

Douds, Van Buren Co.
 Van Buren Comm. SD, AEA 15
 Supt. – See Keosauqua
 ES 52551 – Fred Parsons, prin.

Dow City, Crawford Co., Pop. Code 3
 Dow City-Arion Comm. SD, AEA 12
 Sch. Sys. Enr. Code 2
 Supt. – Jerry Mullins 51528
 ES 51528 – John Nielsen, prin.

Dows, Wright Co., Pop. Code 3
 Dows Comm. SD, AEA 5
 Sch. Sys. Enr. Code 3
 Supt. – Jerry McIntire 50071
 ES 50071 – Jerry McIntire, prin.

Dubuque, Dubuque Co., Pop. Code 8
 Dubuque Comm. SD, AEA 1
 Sch. Sys. Enr. Code 6
 Supt. – Howard D. Pigg
  2300 CHANEY ROAD 52001
 Jefferson JHS, 1105 ALTHAUSER AVE 52001
  Duane Frick, prin.
 Jones JHS, 1090 ALTA VISTA ST 52001
  Bret Johannsen, prin.
 Washington JHS, 51 N GRANDVIEW AVE 52001
  Arthur Roling, prin.
 Audubon ES, 605 LINCOLN AVE 52001
  Thomas Emrick, prin.
 Bryant ES, 1280 RUSH ST 52001
  Dean Halverson, prin.
 Eisenhower ES
  3170 SPRING VALLEY ROAD 52001
  Daniel Roush, prin.
 Fulton ES, 2540 CENTRAL AVE 52001
  Robert Lehman, prin.
 Hoover ES, 3259 ST ANNE DR 52001
  Deborah Otto, prin.
 Irving ES, 2520 PENNSLVANIA AVE 52001
  Ben Temple, prin.
 Kennedy ES, 2135 WOODLAND DR 52001
  Charles Reed, prin.
 Lincoln ES, 1101 W 5TH ST 52001
  Gene Potts, prin.
 Marshall ES, 1450 RHOMBERG AVE 52001
  Fred Smith, prin.
 Prescott ES, 1249 WHITE ST 52001
  Laura Margeson, prin.
 Sageville ES, RURAL ROUTE 01 52001
  Arthur Whalen, prin.
 Table Mound ES, 100 TOWER DR 52001
  Nancy Bradley, prin.

Downtown Catholic St. Mary-Patrick
 1600 WHITE ST 52001
Holy Ghost School, 2981 CENTRAL AVE 52001
Nativity School, 1001 ALTA VISTA ST 52001
Resurrection School, 4300 ASBURY ROAD 52001
Sacred Heart School, 2222 QUEEN ST 52001
St. Anthony School, 2190 ROSEDALE AVE 52001
St. Columbkilles School, 1198 RUSH ST 52001
St. Joseph School, KEY WEST DR 52001
St. Joseph School, 2105 ST JOSEPH ST 52001

Dumont, Butler Co., Pop. Code 3
 Dumont Comm. SD, AEA 2
 Sch. Sys. Enr. Code 2
 Supt. – Randall Clegg, P O BOX 425 50625
 MS 50625 – Randall Clegg, prin.
 ES 50625 – Randall Clegg, prin.

Dunkerton, Black Hawk Co., Pop. Code 3
 Dunkerton Comm. SD, AEA 7
 Sch. Sys. Enr. Code 2
 Supt. – Dan Janssen, 509 S CANFIELD ST 50626
 ES, 509 S CANFIELD ST 50626
  Roger Wilcox, prin.

Dunlap, Harrison Co., Pop. Code 4
 Dunlap Comm. SD, AEA 13
 Sch. Sys. Enr. Code 2
 Supt. – Jerry Mullins, 1102 IOWA AVE 51529
 ES, 1102 IOWA AVE 51529
  Robert Kirschbaum, prin.

Durant, Cedar Co., Pop. Code 4
 Durant Comm. SD, AEA 9
 Sch. Sys. Enr. Code 3
 Supt. – James Wagner, 408 7TH ST 52747
 MS, 408 7TH ST 52747 – Steve Callison, prin.
 ES, 408 7TH ST 52747 – Steven Callison, prin.

Dyersville, Dubuque Co., Pop. Code 5
 Western Dubuque Comm. SD, AEA 1
 Supt. – See Farley
 MS, KORTEN KAMP HALL 52040
  Tom Wickham, prin.
 ES, WARNING HALL 52040
  Tom Wickham, prin.

 St. Francis Xavier School, 203 2ND ST SW 52040

Dysart, Tama Co., Pop. Code 4
 Dysart-Geneseo Comm. SD, AEA 7
 Sch. Sys. Enr. Code 2
 Supt. – Robert Crouse, 505 WEST 52224
 Dysart-Geneseo MS, 505 WEST 52224
  Lorraine Tressler, prin.
 Dysart-Geneseo ES, 411 LINCOLN 52224
  Joseph Coffey, prin.

Eagle Grove, Wright Co., Pop. Code 5
 Eagle Grove Comm. SD, AEA 5
 Sch. Sys. Enr. Code 3
 Supt. – John Nicholls 50533
 Blue MS, NW 2ND & FORT 50533
  Mike Woodall, prin.
 Howland ES, 218 N JACKSON AVE 50533
  Richard Gibson, prin.
 Lincoln ES, 201 N WESTERN AVE 50533
  Richard Gibson, prin.

Earlham, Madison Co., Pop. Code 4
 Earlham Comm. SD, AEA 11
 Sch. Sys. Enr. Code 2
 Supt. – Paul Hopp 50072
 MS 50072 – Michael Teigland, prin.
 ES 50072 – Michael Teigland, prin.

Earling, Shelby Co., Pop. Code 3

 St. Joseph School, P O BOX 227 51530

Earlville, Delaware Co., Pop. Code 3
 Maquoketa Valley Comm. SD, AEA 1
 Supt. – See Delhi
 ES 52041 – Raymond Bley, prin.

Early, Sac Co., Pop. Code 3
 Crestland Comm. SD, AEA 5
 Sch. Sys. Enr. Code 2
 Supt. – Alan Meyer 50535
 Other Schools – See Nemaha

Eddyville, Wapello Co., Pop. Code 4
 Eddyville Comm. SD, AEA 15
 Sch. Sys. Enr. Code 3
 Supt. – Timothy Dose 52553
 ES 52553 – Emmett Cooney, prin.

Edgewood, Delaware Co., Pop. Code 3
 Edgewood-Colesburg Comm. SD, AEA 1
 Sch. Sys. Enr. Code 3
 Supt. – Richard Bachman 52042
 Other Schools – See Colesburg

Eldon, Wapello Co., Pop. Code 4
 Cardinal Comm. SD, AEA 15
 Sch. Sys. Enr. Code 3
 Supt. – Frederick Whipple 52554
 Cardinal ES, RURAL ROUTE 02 52554
  Ronald White, prin.
 Other Schools – See Agency

Eldora, Hardin Co., Pop. Code 5
 Eldora-New Providence Comm. SD, AEA 6
 Sch. Sys. Enr. Code 3
 Supt. – Ingvert Appel, 1102 10TH ST 50627
 Eldora-New Providence ES, 10TH ST 50627
  Larry Reed, prin.

Other Schools – See New Providence

Eldridge, Scott Co., Pop. Code 5
 North Scott Comm. SD, AEA 9
 Sch. Sys. Enr. Code 5
 Supt. – Pascal Deluca, 251 E IOWA ST 52748
 North Scott JHS, 502 S 5TH ST 52748
  Richard Thompson, prin.
 Armstrong ES, 212 S PARKVIEW DR 52748
  Dennis Albertson, prin.
 White ES, 121 S 5TH ST 52748
  David Fairweather, prin.
 Other Schools – See Donahue, Long Grove, Princeton

Elgin, Fayette Co., Pop. Code 3
 Valley Comm. SD, AEA 1
 Sch. Sys. Enr. Code 3
 Supt. – Neil Moritz 52141
 ES 52141 – John Stevens, prin.
 Other Schools – See Clermont

Elkader, Clayton Co., Pop. Code 4
 Central Comm. SD, AEA 1
 Sch. Sys. Enr. Code 3
 Supt. – Robert D. Buckner 52043
 ES, FIRST ST NW 52043
  William McHugh, Jr., prin.
 Other Schools – See Volga

Elk Horn, Shelby Co., Pop. Code 3
 Elk Horn-Kimballton Comm. SD, AEA 13
 Sch. Sys. Enr. Code 2
 Supt. – J. Allan Hjelle 51531
 Elk Horn-Kimballton ES 51531
  Neal Hadden, prin.

Elliott, Montgomery Co., Pop. Code 2
 Griswold Comm. SD, AEA 13
 Supt. – See Griswold
 ES 51532 – Jay Hoogeveen, prin.

Elma, Howard Co., Pop. Code 3
 Howard-Winneshiek Comm. SD, AEA 1
 Supt. – See Cresco
 ES 50628 – Irvin Myron, prin.

Emmetsburg, Palo Alto Co., Pop. Code 5
 Emmetsburg Comm. SD, AEA 3
 Sch. Sys. Enr. Code 3
 Supt. – Randy Flack, 16TH & GRAND ST 50536
 MS, 10TH & PALMER 50536 – Dean Newlon, prin.
 West ES, 6TH & CALL ST 50536
  Ronald Baack, prin.

 Emmetsburg Catholic School
  1903 BROADWAY ST 50536

Epworth, Dubuque Co., Pop. Code 4
 Western Dubuque Comm. SD, AEA 1
 Supt. – See Farley
 ES 52045 – Geraldine McCarthy, prin.

 Epworth-Peosta-Placid ES, 106 1ST ST SE 52045

Essex, Page Co., Pop. Code 4
 Essex Comm. SD, AEA 13
 Sch. Sys. Enr. Code 2
 Supt. – Russell E. Hilker, P O BOX 280 51638
 ES, P O BOX 299 51638 – Rosalee Kinnison, prin.

Estherville, Emmet Co., Pop. Code 6
 Estherville Comm. SD, AEA 3
 Sch. Sys. Enr. Code 4
 Supt. – William Hutchinson, 301 N 6TH ST 51334
 MS, 321 N 6TH ST 51334 – Allen Steen, prin.
 DeMoney ES, 109 S 17TH ST 51334
  Gordon Cornwall, prin.
 Lincoln ES, 815 12TH AVE N 51334
  Gordon Cornwall, prin.
 McKinley ES, 119 W 2ND AVE N 51334
  Gordon Cornwall, prin.

Evansdale, Black Hawk Co., Pop. Code 5
 Waterloo Comm. SD, AEA 7
 Supt. – See Waterloo
 Jewett ES, 600 COLLINS AVE 50707
  Kenneth Erickson, prin.

Everly, Clay Co., Pop. Code 2
 Everly Comm. SD, AEA 3
 Sch. Sys. Enr. Code 2
 Supt. – Richard Wede, P O BOX 218 51338
 MS, P O BOX 218 51338 – Harry Tatum, prin.
 ES, P O BOX 218 51338 – Richard Wede, prin.

Exira, Audubon Co., Pop. Code 3
 Audubon Comm. SD, AEA 11
 Supt. – See Audubon
 Audubon JHS, RURAL ROUTE 02 50076
  Jon Bintner, prin.

 Exira Comm. SD, AEA 11
 Sch. Sys. Enr. Code 2
 Supt. – Robert Templeton, SCHOOL ST 50076
 ES, P O BOX 335 50076 – Neal Hadden, prin.

Fairbank, Buchanan Co., Pop. Code 3
 Jesup Comm. SD, AEA 7
 Supt. – See Jesup
 Prairie Grove ES 50629 – Elwood Sapp, prin.
 Triumph ES 50629 – Elwood Sapp, prin.

 Wapsie Valley Comm. SD, AEA 7
 Sch. Sys. Enr. Code 3
 Supt. – David K. Owens
  RURAL ROUTE 02 BOX 58 50629
 ES 50629 – David Owens, prin.
 Rural ES 1 50629 – David Owens, prin.
 Rural ES 2 50629 – David Owens, prin.

Rural ES 3 50629 – David Owens, prin.
Rural ES 4 50629 – David Owens, prin.
Other Schools – See Oran, Readlyn

Fairfield, Jefferson Co., Pop. Code 6
Fairfield Comm. SD, AEA 15
Sch. Sys. Enr. Code 4
Supt. – John R. Kelley, E BROADWAY ST 52556
MS, 404 W FILLMORE ST 52556
Larry Gilpin, prin.
Lincoln ES, 4TH & STONE 52556
Joseph Carr, prin.
Pence ES, 1000 S 6TH ST 52556
Richard Unkrich, prin.
Washington ES, D & MADISON 52556
Dwain Dooley, prin.
Other Schools – See Libertyville, Lockridge

Maharishi School Age of Enlightment 52556

Farley, Dubuque Co., Pop. Code 4
Western Dubuque Comm. SD, AEA 1
Sch. Sys. Enr. Code 5
Supt. – Wayne F. Drexler, P O BOX 27 52046
ES 52046 – Mike Houselog, prin.
Other Schools – See Bernard, Cascade, Dyersville, Epworth

Farley-Bankston Catholic School
206 SECOND AVE SE 52046

Farmington, Van Buren Co., Pop. Code 3
Harmony Comm. SD, AEA 15
Sch. Sys. Enr. Code 3
Supt. – A. Whitlatch, RURAL ROUTE 01 52626
Harmony MS, RURAL ROUTE 02 52626
Joseph Crozier, prin.
Other Schools – See Bonaparte

Farnhamville, Calhoun Co., Pop. Code 2
Cedar Valley Comm. SD, AEA 5
Sch. Sys. Enr. Code 2
Supt. – Edward Shultz, RURAL ROUTE 01 50538
Cedar Valley MS, RURAL ROUTE 01 50538
Richard Wolter, prin.
Cedar Valley ES, RURAL ROUTE 01 50538
Edward Shultz, prin.

Farragut, Fremont Co., Pop. Code 3
Farragut Comm. SD, AEA 13
Sch. Sys. Enr. Code 2
Supt. – Leo Humphrey, P O BOX 36 51639
ES 51639 – Richard Ekwell, prin.

Fayette, Fayette Co., Pop. Code 4
North Fayette County Comm. SD, AEA 1
Supt. – See West Union
ES, 200 VOLGA 52142 – Richard Glidden, prin.

Fenton, Kossuth Co., Pop. Code 2
Sentral Comm. SD, AEA 3
Sch. Sys. Enr. Code 2
Supt. – Gene Fokken 50539
Sentral MS 50539 – E. Jon Tracy, prin.
Sentral ES 50531 – Ray Owens,Jr., prin.

Ferguson, Marshall Co., Pop. Code 2
LDF Comm. SD, AEA 6
Supt. – See Le Grand
ES 50078 – Charles Loerwald, prin.

Fonda, Pocahontas Co., Pop. Code 3
Fonda Comm. SD, AEA 5
Sch. Sys. Enr. Code 2
Supt. – Jack Kiser 50540
ES 50540 – Jack Kiser, prin.

Fontanelle, Adair Co., Pop. Code 3
Bridgewater-Fontanelle Comm. SD, AEA 14
Sch. Sys. Enr. Code 2
Supt. – Otis Chubick 50846
Other Schools – See Bridgewater

Forest City, Winnebago Co., Pop. Code 5
Forest City Comm. SD, AEA 2
Sch. Sys. Enr. Code 4
Supt. – Wayne Sesker, 810 W K ST 50436
MS, 810 W K ST 50436 – Lee Hinkley, prin.
ES, 1405 W I ST 50436 – Gary Kipling, prin.

Fort Dodge, Webster Co., Pop. Code 8
Fort Dodge Comm. SD, AEA 5
Sch. Sys. Enr. Code 5
Supt. – David Haggard, 330 1ST AVE N 50501
Fair Oaks MS, 416 S 10TH ST 50501
Darwin Hopkins, prin.
Phillips MS, 1015 5TH AVE N 50501
J. Wormsley, prin.
Arey ES, 104 S 17TH ST 50501 – E. Dick, prin.
Butler ES, 1012 S 19TH ST 50501
Jerry Spittal, prin.
Cooper ES, 1523 N 24TH ST 50501
Joanne Lyons, prin.
Duncombe ES, 615 N 16TH ST 50501
Bill McCullough, prin.
Feelhaver ES, 1300 14TH AVE N 50501
Linda Whiting, prin.
Hillcrest ES, 712 3RD ST NW 50501
Stephen Harbaugh, prin.
Riverside ES, 733 F ST 50501
Jeffrey Daniel, prin.
Other Schools – See Badger, Otho

Sacred Heart JHS, 214 S 13TH ST 50501
Corpus Christi School, 415 N 8TH ST 50501
Holy Rosary School, 2406 9TH 1/2 AVE S 50501

St. Paul's Lutheran School
1229 4TH AVE S 50501

Fort Madison, Lee Co., Pop. Code 7
Fort Madison Comm. SD, AEA 16
Sch. Sys. Enr. Code 5
Supt. – David Benson, 1930 AVENUE M 52627
JHS, 1801 AVE G 52627 – Gordon Roxberg, prin.
Jefferson MS, 2301 AVENUE G 52627
Timothy Rawley, prin.
Lincoln ES, 1326 AVENUE E 52627
Robert Carr, prin.
Richardson ES, 3301 AVENUE L 52627
Dennis Heth, prin.
Other Schools – See Denmark

Aquinas East School, 509 AVE F 52627
Aquinas West School, 509 AVE F 52627

Fredericksburg, Chickasaw Co., Pop. Code 4
Fredericksburg Comm. SD, AEA 1
Sch. Sys. Enr. Code 2
Supt. – Jerry Kjerguard, E MAIN 50630
ES, EAST HIGH ST 50630 – Jerry Kjergaard, prin.

Fremont, Mahaska Co., Pop. Code 3
Fremont Comm. SD, AEA 15
Sch. Sys. Enr. Code 2
Supt. – Randall McCaulley, P O BOX 68 52561
MS, P O BOX 68 52561 – Douglas Englent, prin.
ES, P O BOX 68 52561 – Douglas Englent, prin.

Galva, Ida Co., Pop. Code 2
Galva-Holstein Comm. SD, AEA 12
Supt. – See Holstein
Galva-Holstein MS 51020 – Dennis Ohde, prin.

Garnavillo, Clayton Co., Pop. Code 3
Garnavillo Comm. SD, AEA 1
Sch. Sys. Enr. Code 2
Supt. – Gary Stumberg, P O BOX 17 52049
ES, P O BOX 17 52049 – David Kuehl, prin.

Garner, Hancock Co., Pop. Code 5
Garner-Hayfield Comm. SD, AEA 2
Sch. Sys. Enr. Code 3
Supt. – Ben Halupnik, 605 W LYONS 50438
Garner-Hayfield JHS, 830 BUSH AVE 50438
Kevin Kopperud, prin.
ES, 1080 DIVISION ST 50438
Kevin Kopperud, prin.

Garwin, Tama Co., Pop. Code 3
Garwin Comm. SD, AEA 6
Sch. Sys. Enr. Code 2
Supt. – Richard Hessenius
RURAL ROUTE 01 BOX 81 50632
ES 50632 – Richard Hessenius, prin.

George, Lyon Co., Pop. Code 4
George Comm. SD, AEA 4
Sch. Sys. Enr. Code 2
Supt. – Dwight Schulz
500 E INDIANA AVE 51237
ES, 500 E INDIANA AVE 51237
Everett Jensen, prin.

Gilbert, Story Co., Pop. Code 3
Gilbert Comm. SD, AEA 11
Sch. Sys. Enr. Code 3
Supt. – Douglas Williams
103 MATHEWS DRIVE 50105
ES, 109 ROTHMOOR 50105 – David Ashby, prin.

Gilbertville, Black Hawk Co., Pop. Code 3

Gilbertville & Raymond Unit ES
311 16TH AVE 50634
Immaculate Conception St. Joseph School
311 16TH AVE 50634

Gillett Grove, Clay Co., Pop. Code 1
South Clay Comm. SD, AEA 3
Sch. Sys. Enr. Code 2
Supt. – Richard Moore 51341
South Clay ES 51341 – Richard Moore, prin.

Gilman, Marshall Co., Pop. Code 3
Semco Comm. SD, AEA 6
Sch. Sys. Enr. Code 2
Supt. – Elizabeth Silhanek 50106
Other Schools – See Laurel

Gilmore City, Humboldt Co., Pop. Code 3
Gilmore City-Bradgate Comm. SD, AEA 5
Sch. Sys. Enr. Code 2
Supt. – Richard Schreck 50541
ES 50541 – Richard Shreck, prin.

Gladbrook, Tama Co., Pop. Code 3
Gladbrook Comm. SD, AEA 6
Sch. Sys. Enr. Code 2
Supt. – Darwin Winke, P O BOX 370 50635
MS, P O BOX 370 50635 – Charles Earp, prin.
ES, P O BOX 370 50635 – Charles Earp, prin.

Glenwood, Mills Co., Pop. Code 6
Glenwood Comm. SD, AEA 13
Sch. Sys. Enr. Code 4
Supt. – David Scala, 116 S WALNUT ST 51534
JHS, 707 SHARP ST 51534 – David Stickrod, prin.
Northeast ES, 8TH & LINN 51534
Charles McGinnis, prin.
West ES, 707 SHARP ST 51534
Daniel Tuma, prin.

Glidden, Carroll Co., Pop. Code 4
Glidden-Ralston Comm. SD, AEA 11
Sch. Sys. Enr. Code 2
Supt. – Dale Johnson, P O BOX B 51443
Glidden-Ralston ES 51443 – Dale Johnson, prin.

Goldfield, Wright Co., Pop. Code 3
Goldfield Comm. SD
Sch. Sys. Enr. Code 2
Supt. – Byrun Hufmeister, P O BOX 158 50542
ES, P O BOX 158 50542 – Byron Hofmeister, prin.

Goose Lake, Clinton Co., Pop. Code 2
Northeast Comm. SD, AEA 9
Sch. Sys. Enr. Code 3
Supt. – Gordon Cook 52750
ES 52750 – Wayne McLaughlin, prin.
Other Schools – See Clinton

Gowrie, Webster Co., Pop. Code 4
Prairie Comm. SD, AEA 5
Sch. Sys. Enr. Code 3
Supt. – (—), 1005 RIDDLE ST 50543
Other Schools – See Callender

Graettinger, Palo Alto Co., Pop. Code 3
Graettinger Comm. SD, AEA 3
Sch. Sys. Enr. Code 2
Supt. – Randy Flack 51342
MS 51342 – James Towell, prin.
ES 51342 – Randy Flack, prin.

Grafton, Worth Co.
St. Ansgar Comm. SD, AEA 2
Supt. – See Saint Ansgar
MS 50440 – Leslie Turner, prin.

Grand Junction, Greene Co., Pop. Code 3
East Greene Comm. SD, AEA 5
Sch. Sys. Enr. Code 2
Supt. – Jack Anderson, P O BOX 186 50107
Other Schools – See Rippey

Grand Mound, Clinton Co., Pop. Code 3
Central Clinton Comm. SD, AEA 9
Supt. – See De Witt
ES 52751 – Leslie Huddley, prin.

Grand River, Decatur Co., Pop. Code 2
Grand Valley Comm. SD, AEA 14
Supt. – See Kellerton
ES 50108 – William Hullinger, prin.

Grandview, Louisa Co., Pop. Code 2
Louisa-Muscatine Comm. SD, AEA 9
Supt. – See Letts
MS 52752 – Robert Torrence, prin.

Granger, Dallas Co., Pop. Code 3
Woodward-Granger Comm. SD, AEA 11
Supt. – See Woodward
ES, 2200 STATE ST 50109
Vincent Verlengia, prin.

Assumption ES, 1904 SYCAMORE AVE 50109

Granville, Sioux Co., Pop. Code 2

Spalding ES, BROAD AND GARFIELD 51022

Greene, Butler Co., Pop. Code 4
Greene Comm. SD, AEA 2
Sch. Sys. Enr. Code 2
Supt. – Steve Ward, 208 N 4TH ST 50636
ES, 210 W SOUTH ST 50636
Joen Blanchfield, prin.

Greenfield, Adair Co., Pop. Code 4
Greenfield Comm. SD, AEA 14
Sch. Sys. Enr. Code 3
Supt. – Wm. Sandholm, P O BOX 119 50849
JHS, 410 NW 2ND ST 50849 – Carl Schwartz, prin.
ES, 324 NW 2ND ST 50849 – Carl Schwartz, prin.

Green Mountain, Marshall Co.
Green Mountain ISD
Sch. Sys. Enr. Code 2
Supt. – Richard Hessenius 50637
G-M-G MS 50637 – Mavis Gray, prin.
ES 50657 – Mavis Gray, prin.

Grimes, Polk Co., Pop. Code 4
Dallas Center Grimes Comm. SD, AEA 11
Supt. – See Dallas Center
JHS, P O BOX 218 50111 – Jerry Crosser, prin.
ES, 410 N MAIN ST 50111 – Paul Jones, prin.

Grinnell, Poweshiek Co., Pop. Code 6
Grinnell-Newburg Comm. SD, AEA 6
Sch. Sys. Enr. Code 4
Supt. – Clement Bodensteiner
927 4TH AVE 50112
MS, S EAST ST 50112 – Michael Fitzgerald, prin.
Bailey Park ES, 210 8TH AVE 50112
Gerald Hagen, prin.
ES, 818 HAMILTON AVE 50112
Douglas Cameron, prin.
Fairview ES, 1310 HOBART ST 50112
Gerald Hagen, prin.

Griswold, Cass Co., Pop. Code 4
Griswold Comm. SD, AEA 13
Sch. Sys. Enr. Code 3
Supt. – Steven Wehr, 110 MONTGOMERY 51535
Other Schools – See Elliott, Lewis

Grundy Center, Grundy Co., Pop. Code 5
Grundy Center Comm. SD, AEA 7
Sch. Sys. Enr. Code 3
Supt. – D. Mulford, 1301 12TH ST 50638
JHS, 1006 M AVE 50638 – Howard Hockert, prin.
Grundy Center Lower ES, 908 I AVE 50638
Roger Whitcome, prin.
Grundy Center MS, 1001 8TH ST 50638
Roger Whitcome, prin.

Gruver, Emmet Co., Pop. Code 2
Lincoln Central Comm. SD, AEA 3
Sch. Sys. Enr. Code 2
Supt. – John Graham, P O BOX 717 51344
Lincoln Central ES 51344 – John Graham, prin.

Guthrie Center, Guthrie Co., Pop. Code 4
Guthrie Center Comm. SD, AEA 11
Sch. Sys. Enr. Code 3
Supt. – Leonard Snyder, 700 STATE ST 50115
JHS, P O BOX 367 50115 – Richard Friedrich, prin.
ES, 700 STATE ST 50115 – Steve Smith, prin.

Guttenberg, Clayton Co., Pop. Code 4
Guttenberg Comm. SD, AEA 1
Sch. Sys. Enr. Code 3
Supt. – James Pasut
131 S RIVER PARK DRIVE 52052
ES, 131 S RIVER PARK DR 52052
Michael Harrold, prin.

St. Mary's School, 502 S 2ND ST 52052

Hamburg, Fremont Co., Pop. Code 4
Hamburg Comm. SD, AEA 13
Sch. Sys. Enr. Code 2
Supt. – Leo Humphrey, 105 E ST 51640
Simons ES, 309 S ST 51640
James Stephens,Jr., prin.

Hampton, Franklin Co., Pop. Code 5
Hampton Comm. SD, AEA 2
Sch. Sys. Enr. Code 4
Supt. – James Alexander, 420 1ST AVE NE 50441
MS, 420 1ST AVE NE 50441 – Neal Nelson, prin.
North Side ES, 114 11TH PL NE 50441
Lowell Lange, prin.
Park ES, 27 FIFTH ST 50441 – Lowell Lange, prin.
South Side ES, 507 4TH AVE SE 50441
Lowell Lange, prin.

Hanlontown, Worth Co., Pop. Code 2
North Central Comm. SD, AEA 2
Supt. – See Manly
ES 50644 – James Carter, prin.

Harlan, Shelby Co., Pop. Code 6
Harlan Comm. SD, AEA 13
Sch. Sys. Enr. Code 4
Supt. – Roy Baker, 2102 DURANT ST 51537
MS, 7TH & BALDWIN 51537 – Loyal Moore, prin.
Park ES, 10TH & TARKINGTON 51537
Mark Knoell, prin.
West Ridge ES, 19TH & VICTORIA 51537
Mike Morgan, prin.

St. Michael's School
2009 COLLEGE PLACE 51537

Harris, Osceola Co., Pop. Code 2
Harris-Lake Park Comm. SD, AEA 3
Supt. – See Lake Park
Harris-Lake Park ES 51545
Judith Brueggman, prin.

Hartford, Warren Co., Pop. Code 3
Carlisle Comm. SD, AEA 11
Supt. – See Carlisle
ES 50118 – Dennis Keeney, prin.

Hartley, O'Brien Co., Pop. Code 4
Hartley-Melvin Comm. SD, AEA 4
Sch. Sys. Enr. Code 3
Supt. – Kenton Schwiesow
600 3RD ST NW 51346
Hartley-Melvin ES, 240 1ST ST SE 51346
Peder Buck, prin.

Hastings, Mills Co., Pop. Code 2
Nishna Valley Comm. SD, AEA 13
Sch. Sys. Enr. Code 2
Supt. – Jerry Hoffman
RURAL ROUTE 01 BOX 80B 51540
Nishna Valley ES 51540 – Jerry Hoffman, prin.

Havelock, Pocahontas Co., Pop. Code 2
Havelock-Plover Comm. SD
Sch. Sys. Enr. Code 1
Supt. – Dennis Pierce 50546
ES 50546 – Lynn Moody, prin.

Hawarden, Sioux Co., Pop. Code 5
West Sioux Comm. SD, AEA 4
Sch. Sys. Enr. Code 3
Supt. – Gerald Bradley, 1300-1400 AVE P 51023
West Sioux MS, 1130 CENTRAL AVE 51023
Marlin Hansen, prin.
ES, 806 13TH ST 51023
Arvin Kitchenmaster, prin.
Other Schools – See Ireton

Hawkeye, Fayette Co., Pop. Code 3
North Fayette County Comm. SD, AEA 1
Supt. – See West Union
ES 52147 – Richard Glidden, prin.

Hedrick, Keokuk Co., Pop. Code 3
Hedrick Comm. SD, AEA 15
Sch. Sys. Enr. Code 2
Supt. – Roger Younkin Supt 52563
ES 52563 – Roger Younkin, prin.

Hiawatha, Linn Co., Pop. Code 5
Cedar Rapids Comm. SD, AEA 10
Supt. – See Cedar Rapids
Nixon ES, 200 NORTHWOOD DR 52233
Henry Small, prin.

Hills, Johnson Co., Pop. Code 3
Iowa City Comm. SD, AEA 10
Supt. – See Iowa City
ES, P O BOX 137 52235 – John Marshall, prin.

Hinton, Plymouth Co., Pop. Code 3
Hinton Comm. SD, AEA 12
Sch. Sys. Enr. Code 3
Supt. – Marvin Boehme 51024
MS 51024 – Earl Oleson, prin.
ES 51024 – Mary Heller, prin.

Holstein, Ida Co., Pop. Code 4
Galva-Holstein Comm. SD, AEA 12
Sch. Sys. Enr. Code 3
Supt. – Bill Kruse, 207 LUBECK ST 51025
Galva-Holstein ES, 207 LUBECK ST 51025
Harold Post, prin.
Other Schools – See Galva

Hopkinton, Delaware Co., Pop. Code 3
Maquoketa Valley Comm. SD, AEA 1
Supt. – See Delhi
Johnston ES 52237 – Raymond Bley, prin.

Hospers, Sioux Co., Pop. Code 3
Floyd Valley Comm. SD, AEA 4
Supt. – See Alton
ES 51238 – Donald Adkins, prin.

Houghton, Lee Co., Pop. Code 2

Marquette PS, P O BOX 134 52631

Hudson, Black Hawk Co., Pop. Code 4
Hudson Comm. SD, AEA 7
Sch. Sys. Enr. Code 3
Supt. – Marcus Haack
245 S WASHINGTON 50643
ES, 136 S WASHINGTON 50643
Dean Staack, prin.

Hull, Sioux Co., Pop. Code 4
Boyden-Hull Comm. SD, AEA 4
Sch. Sys. Enr. Code 3
Supt. – Craig Anderson, 801 1ST ST 51239
Other Schools – See Boyden

Hull Christian School, P O BOX 550 51239

Humboldt, Humboldt Co., Pop. Code 5
Humboldt Comm. SD, AEA 5
Sch. Sys. Enr. Code 4
Supt. – W. Carlson, 900 SUMNER AVE 50548
Taft ES, TAFT & 2ND AVE NORTH 50548
Lawrence Dorhout, prin.
Other Schools – See Dakota City

St. Mary School, 305 3RD AVE N 50548

Humeston, Wayne Co., Pop. Code 3
Mormon Trail Comm. SD, AEA 14
Sch. Sys. Enr. Code 2
Supt. – Richard Dexter 50123
ES 50123 – Sue Brock, prin.

Huxley, Story Co., Pop. Code 4
Ballard Comm. SD, AEA 11
Sch. Sys. Enr. Code 4
Supt. – Craig Scott, 315 N MAIN AVE 50124
Other Schools – See Cambridge, Kelley, Slater

Ida Grove, Ida Co., Pop. Code 4
Ida Grove Comm. SD, AEA 12
Sch. Sys. Enr. Code 3
Supt. – Dean Collopy 51445
MS, 301 MOOREHEAD ST 51445
Stanley Henderson, prin.
ES, 5TH & BARNES ST 51445
Stanley Henderson, prin.

Independence, Buchanan Co., Pop. Code 6
Independence Comm. SD, AEA 7
Sch. Sys. Enr. Code 4
Supt. – Stan Slessor, 1207 1ST ST W 50644
MS, 1301 1ST ST W 50644
Meredith Miller, prin.
East ES, 211 9TH AVE SE 50644
Terry O'Neil, prin.
West MS, 1103 1ST ST W 50644
Gene Oxley, prin.
Other Schools – See Rowley

Jesup Comm. SD, AEA 7
Supt. – See Jesup
Perry ES, RURAL ROUTE 04 50644
Elwood Sapp, prin.

St. John ES, 407 4TH AVE SE 50644

Indianola, Warren Co., Pop. Code 7
Indianola Comm. SD, AEA 11
Sch. Sys. Enr. Code 5
Supt. – Carol Seevers, 301 N BUXTON ST 50125
Emerson ES, 1109 E EUCLID AVE 50125
Lee Riemersma, prin.

Hawthorne ES, 203 E 2ND AVE 50125
Richard Stock, prin.
MS, 301 N BUXTON ST 50125 – Robert Gray, prin.
Irving ES, 500 W CLINTON AVE 50125
Richard Stock, prin.
Whittier ES, 1306 W SALEM AVE 50125
Lee Riemersma, prin.

Inwood, Lyon Co., Pop. Code 3
West Lyon Comm. SD, AEA 4
Sch. Sys. Enr. Code 3
Supt. – Frank Ashmore 51240
West Lyon JHS 51240 – James Van Steenwyk, prin.
West Lyon ES 51240 – Donald Nelson, prin.

Iowa City, Johnson Co., Pop. Code 8
Iowa City Comm. SD, AEA 10
Sch. Sys. Enr. Code 6
Supt. – David Cronin, 509 S DUBUQUE ST 52240
Southeast JHS, 2501 BRADFORD DRIVE 52240
Frank Ward, prin.
Bohumil Shimek ES, 1400 GRISSELL PL 52245
Thomas Holmes, prin.
Hoover ES, 2200 E COURT ST 52245
Guerin Thompson, prin.
Horn ES, 600 KOSER AVE 52246
Paul Davis, prin.
Lemme ES, 3100 E WASHINGTON ST 52245
Pam Ehly, prin.
Lincoln ES, 300 TEETERS COURT 52246
Christine Kolarik, prin.
Longfellow ES, 1130 SEYMOUR AVE 52240
Tim Grieves, prin.
Lucas ES, 830 SOUTHLAWN DR 52245
Sandra Lawrence, prin.
Mann ES, 521 N DODGE ST 52245
Robert Mata, prin.
Roosevelt ES, 724 W BENTON ST 52246
Nora Steinbrech, prin.
Twain ES, 1355 DE FOREST AVE 52240
James Thomas, prin.
Wood ES, 1930 LAKESIDE DR 52240
James Blank, prin.
Other Schools – See Coralville, Hills, North Liberty

Regina ES, 2120 ROCHESTER AVE 52245

Iowa Falls, Hardin Co., Pop. Code 6
Iowa Falls Comm. SD, AEA 6
Sch. Sys. Enr. Code 4
Supt. – D. Teigland, P O BOX 670 50126
Riverbend MS, RIVER ROAD 50126
Victor Amundson, prin.
North/Stodard ES, 710 NORTH ST 50126
Karl Behrends, prin.
West ES, 1510 WASHINGTON AVE 50126
Karl Behrends, prin.

Ireton, Sioux Co., Pop. Code 3
West Sioux Comm. SD, AEA 4
Supt. – See Hawarden
ES, P O BOX 248 51027
Arvin Kitchenmaster, prin.

Ireton Christian School, 104 5TH ST 50707

Irwin, Shelby Co., Pop. Code 2
Irwin Comm. SD, AEA 13
Sch. Sys. Enr. Code 2
Supt. – Dave Sextro 51446
MS 51446 – Joseph Graves, prin.
ES 51446 – Dave Sextro, prin.

Jackson Junction, Winneshiek Co., Pop. Code 1
Turkey Valley Comm. SD, AEA 1
Sch. Sys. Enr. Code 3
Supt. – Keith O'Connell 52150
Turkey Valley ES 52150 – James Darnall, prin.

Janesville, Bremer Co., Pop. Code 3
Janesville Cons. SD, AEA 7
Sch. Sys. Enr. Code 2
Supt. – Jeffry Sales, 505 BARRICK ROAD 50647
ES, 505 BARRICK ROAD 50646
David Piper, prin.

Jefferson, Greene Co., Pop. Code 5
Jefferson Comm. SD, AEA 5
Sch. Sys. Enr. Code 3
Supt. – Robert Schmidt, MADISON & ELM 50129
MS, 203 W HARRISON ST 50129
Thomas Yepsen, prin.
ES, ADAMS AND WILSON 50129
Fred Muth, prin.

Jesup, Buchanan Co., Pop. Code 4
Jesup Comm. SD, AEA 7
Sch. Sys. Enr. Code 3
Supt. – Michael Krumm, 531 PROSPECT ST 50648
ES, 531 PROSPECT ST 50648
Edwood Sapp, prin.
Other Schools – See Fairbank, Independence

St. Anthanasius School, 641 STEVENS ST 50648

Jewell, Hamilton Co., Pop. Code 4
South Hamilton Comm. SD, AEA 5
Sch. Sys. Enr. Code 3
Supt. – Richard Textor, P O BOX 100 50130
ES, P O BOX 38 50130 – Willis Welp, prin.

Johnston, Polk Co., Pop. Code 5
Johnston Comm. SD, AEA 11
Sch. Sys. Enr. Code 4
Supt. – L. Friestad, P O BOX 10 50131
MS, 5925 NW 62ND AVE 50131
Terry Cunconan, prin.

Lawson ES, P O BOX 10 50131
  Ronald Spurlin, prin.
Wallace ES, 6510 NW 62ND AVE 50131
  (—), prin.

Kalona, Washington Co., Pop. Code 4
  Mid-Prairie Comm. SD, AEA 10
  Supt. – See Wellman
  ES, 702 6TH ST 52247
    Richard Van Hoozer, prin.
  Washington Township ES, P O BOX 152 52247
    Richard Van Hoozer, prin.

Kanawha, Hancock Co., Pop. Code 3
  Kanawha Comm. SD, AEA 2
  Sch. Sys. Enr. Code 2
  Supt. – Ronald Okones 50447
  ES 50447 – Mark Lawler, prin.

Kellerton, Ringgold Co., Pop. Code 2
  Grand Valley Comm. SD, AEA 14
  Sch. Sys. Enr. Code 2
  Supt. – William Hullinger 50133
  Other Schools – See Grand River

Kelley, Story Co., Pop. Code 2
  Ballard Comm. SD, AEA 11
  Supt. – See Huxley
  ES, 1111 GRACE ST 50134 – Daniel Lawler, prin.

Kellogg, Jasper Co., Pop. Code 3
  Newton Comm. SD, AEA 11
  Supt. – See Newton
  ES 50135 – Armond Miller, prin.

Keokuk, Lee Co.
  Keokuk Comm. SD, AEA 16
  Sch. Sys. Enr. Code 5
  Supt. – W. Cameron, P O BOX 128 52632
  MS, 14TH & MAIN 52632 – Paul Gaylord, prin.
  Hawthorne ES, 2940 DECATUR ST 52632
    Oscar Davids, prin.
  Lincoln ES, 1402 S 7TH ST 52632
    Douglas Wilson, prin.
  Torrence ES, 17TH & FRANKLIN 52632
    Timothy Patterson, prin.
  Washington ES, 116 N 8TH ST 52632
    Timothy Patterson, prin.
  Wells-Carey ES, 9TH & TIMEA 52632
    Douglas Wilson, prin.

  St. Vincents School, 610 TIMEA ST 52632

Keosauqua, Van Buren Co., Pop. Code 4
  Van Buren Comm. SD, AEA 15
  Sch. Sys. Enr. Code 3
  Supt. – Ed Looney, P O BOX 250 52565
  Other Schools – See Douds, Stockport

Keota, Keokuk Co., Pop. Code 4
  Keota Comm. SD, AEA 15
  Sch. Sys. Enr. Code 2
  Supt. – Keith Sasseen 52248
  ES, NORTH ELLIS AVE 52248 – Tom Perry, prin.

Keswick, Keokuk Co., Pop. Code 2
  Tri-County Comm. SD, AEA 15
  Supt. – See Thornburg
  ES 50136 – Richard Corrick, prin.

Keystone, Benton Co., Pop. Code 3
  Benton Comm. SD, AEA 10
  Supt. – See Van Horne
  MS 52249 – Timothy Sanderson, prin.

Kingsley, Plymouth Co., Pop. Code 4
  Kingsley-Pierson Comm. SD, AEA 12
  Sch. Sys. Enr. Code 2
  Supt. – Robert Bahl, 90 VALLEY DRIVE 51028
  ES, 90 VALLEY DR 51028
    Stewart Goslinga, prin.
  Other Schools – See Pierson

Klemme, Hancock Co., Pop. Code 3
  Klemme Comm. SD, AEA 2
  Sch. Sys. Enr. Code 2
  Supt. – Thomas Williams 50449
  ES 50449 – Gary Schwartz, prin.

Knoxville, Marion Co., Pop. Code 6
  Knoxville Comm. SD, AEA 11
  Sch. Sys. Enr. Code 4
  Supt. – Daniel Smith, 108 S FREMONT ST 50138
  East Elementary School
    614 E WASHINGTON ST 50138 – (—), prin.
  MS, 306 SOUTH PARK LANE DR 50138
    Clyde Prichard, prin.
  Northstar ES, 407 W LARSON ST 50138
    James Brown, prin.

Lacona, Warren Co., Pop. Code 2
  Southeast Warren Comm. SD, AEA 11
  Supt. – See Liberty Center
  MS 50139 – Larry Dawson, prin.

Lake City, Calhoun Co., Pop. Code 4
  Lake City Comm. SD, AEA 5
  Sch. Sys. Enr. Code 3
  Supt. – Vernard Keerbs, 709 MAIN ST W 51449
  Lincoln ES, 510 E NORTH ST 51449
    Kevin Brummer, prin.

Lake Mills, Winnebago Co., Pop. Code 4
  Lake Mills Comm. SD, AEA 2
  Sch. Sys. Enr. Code 3
  Supt. – Dale Sorenson, 102 S 4TH AVE E 50450
  JHS, 102 S 4TH AVE E 50450 – James Bryant, prin.
  ES, 102 S 4TH AVE E 50450 – Donald Borey, prin.

Lake Park, Dickinson Co., Pop. Code 4
  Harris-Lake Park Comm. SD, AEA 3
  Sch. Sys. Enr. Code 2
  Supt. – Quentin Reifenrath 51347
  Other Schools – See Harris

Lake View, Sac Co., Pop. Code 4
  Lake View-Auburn Comm. SD, AEA 5
  Sch. Sys. Enr. Code 2
  Supt. – Kurt Kaiser, 801 JACKSON 51450
  Lake View-Auburn MS, P O BOX 1027 51450
    Norma Wallace, prin.
  ES, P O BOX 1027 51450 – Norma Wallace, prin.
  Other Schools – See Auburn

Lakota, Kossuth Co., Pop. Code 2
  Lakota Cons. SD
  Sch. Sys. Enr. Code 1
  Supt. – Richard Phillips 50451
  ES, P O BOX 44 50451 – Richard Phillips, prin.

Lamoni, Decatur Co., Pop. Code 5
  Lamoni Comm. SD, AEA 14
  Sch. Sys. Enr. Code 2
  Supt. – David Clinefelter
    202 N WALNUT ST 50140
  MS, 202 N WALNUT ST 50140
    Beverly Vitek, prin.
  ES, 202 N WALNUT ST 50140
    Beverly Vitek, prin.

Lamont, Buchanan Co., Pop. Code 3
  Starmont Comm. SD, AEA 1
  Supt. – See Strawberry Point
  ES, P O BOX 128 50650 – Larry Dougherty, prin.

Lansing, Allamakee Co., Pop. Code 4
  Eastern Allamakee Comm. SD, AEA 1
  Sch. Sys. Enr. Code 2
  Supt. – John Grampovnik 52151
  Mid. Sch 52151 – James Hanson, prin.
  Other Schools – See New Albin

La Porte City, Black Hawk Co., Pop. Code 4
  La Porte City Comm. SD, AEA 7
  Sch. Sys. Enr. Code 3
  Supt. – Ronald Crooks, 200 ADAMS ST 50651
  ES, 515 FILMORE ST 50651 – Arthur Finke, prin.

Latimer, Franklin Co., Pop. Code 2
  Cal Comm. SD, AEA 2
  Sch. Sys. Enr. Code 2
  Supt. – Richard Roach, P O BOX 459 50452
  Cal Community ES 50452
    Cynthia Martinek, prin.

Laurel, Marshall Co., Pop. Code 2
  Semco Comm. SD, AEA 6
  Supt. – See Gilman
  Semco ES 50141 – Charles Loerwald, prin.

Laurens, Pocahontas Co., Pop. Code 4
  Laurens-Marathon Comm. SD, AEA 5
  Sch. Sys. Enr. Code 3
  Supt. – Delmer Hofer, 300 W GARFIELD ST 50554
  Laurens-Marathon MS
    300 W GARFIELD ST 50554
    Rob Wolverton, prin.
  Laurens-Marathon ES, 300 W GARFIELD ST 50554
    Dan Braunschweig, prin.

Lawton, Woodbury Co., Pop. Code 2
  Lawton-Bronson Comm. SD, AEA 12
  Sch. Sys. Enr. Code 3
  Supt. – Hal Pruin, P O BOX 128 51030
  Other Schools – See Bronson

Le Grand, Marshall Co., Pop. Code 3
  LDF Comm. SD, AEA 6
  Sch. Sys. Enr. Code 3
  Supt. – Leroy Kivett, HIGHWAY 30 50142
  Other Schools – See Ferguson, Marshalltown

Leighton, Mahaska Co., Pop. Code 2
  Pella Comm. SD, AEA 11
  Supt. – See Pella
  ES 50143 – Merlyn Vander Leest, prin.

Le Mars, Plymouth Co., Pop. Code 6
  Le Mars Comm. SD, AEA 12
  Sch. Sys. Enr. Code 6
  Supt. – Roy Messerol'e, 921 3RD AVE SW 51031
  Clark ES, 201 2ND AVE NW 51031
    James Hess, prin.
  Franklin ES, 400 3RD AVE SE 51031
    James Hess, prin.
  Kluckhohn ES, 1338 CENTRAL AVE SE 51031
    David Horken, prin.
  Other Schools – See Merrill

  Gehlen Catholic School
    709 PLYMOUTH ST NE 51031

Lenox, Taylor Co., Pop. Code 4
  Lenox Comm. SD, AEA 14
  Sch. Sys. Enr. Code 2
  Supt. – Ralph Rogers, 600 S LOCUST ST 50851
  ES, 301 W MICHIGAN ST 50851
    Paul Parkhurst, prin.

Leon, Decatur Co., Pop. Code 4
  Central Decatur Comm. SD, AEA 14
  Sch. Sys. Enr. Code 3
  Supt. – Tom Spear, 606 N CHURCH ST 50144
  South ES, 201 SE 6TH 50144
    Donald Forman, prin.
  Other Schools – See Decatur

Letts, Louisa Co., Pop. Code 2
  Louisa-Mascatine Comm. SD, AEA 9
  Sch. Sys. Enr. Code 2
  Supt. – David Lau, RURAL ROUTE 02 52754
  ES 52754 – Robert Torrence, prin.
  Other Schools – See Grandview

Lewis, Cass Co., Pop. Code 2
  Griswold Comm. SD, AEA 13
  Supt. – See Griswold
  ES 51544 – Jay Hoogeveen, prin.

Liberty Center, Warren Co.
  Southeast Warren Comm. SD, AEA 11
  Sch. Sys. Enr. Code 3
  Supt. – Carl Reno 50145
  Other Schools – See Lacona, Milo

Libertyville, Jefferson Co., Pop. Code 2
  Fairfield Comm. SD, AEA 15
  Supt. – See Fairfield
  ES 52567 – Charles Shults, prin.

Lime Springs, Howard Co., Pop. Code 2
  Howard-Winneshiek Comm. SD, AEA 1
  Supt. – See Cresco
  ES 52155 – Irvin Myron, prin.

Linden, Dallas Co., Pop. Code 2
  Panora-Linden Comm. SD, AEA 11
  Supt. – See Panora
  Pandra-Linden ES 50146
    Timothy Fitzgerald, prin.

Lineville, Wayne Co., Pop. Code 2
  Lineville-Clio Comm. SD, AEA 15
  Sch. Sys. Enr. Code 1
  Supt. – R. Bethards 50147
  ES 50147 – Ron Bethards, prin.

Lisbon, Linn Co., Pop. Code 4
  Lisbon Comm. SD, AEA 10
  Sch. Sys. Enr. Code 2
  Supt. – John Messerli, 235 W SCHOOL 52253
  MS, P O BOX 217 52253 – George Karam, prin.
  ES 52253 – George Karam, prin.

Little Rock, Lyon Co., Pop. Code 2
  Little Rock Comm. SD, AEA 4
  Sch. Sys. Enr. Code 2
  Supt. – Dwight Schulz 51243
  ES 51243 – Wayne Hinrichs, prin.

Livermore, Humboldt Co., Pop. Code 2
  Twin Rivers Comm. SD, AEA 5
  Supt. – See Bode
  ES 50558 – Byron How, prin.

Lockridge, Jefferson Co., Pop. Code 2
  Fairfield Comm. SD, AEA 15
  Supt. – See Fairfield
  ES 52635 – Joseph Carr, prin.

Logan, Harrison Co., Pop. Code 4
  Logan-Magnolia Comm. SD, AEA 13
  Sch. Sys. Enr. Code 3
  Supt. – L. Eugene Evans, RURAL ROUTE 02 51546
  Logan-Magnolia ES, 130 W 4TH ST 51546
    Robert Kirschbaum, prin.

Lohrville, Calhoun Co., Pop. Code 3
  Lohrville Comm. SD, AEA 5
  Sch. Sys. Enr. Code 2
  Supt. – Richard Caldwell, P O BOX 276 51453
  MS, P O BOX 276 51453 – Art Pixler, prin.
  ES, P O BOX 276 51453 – Richard Caldwell, prin.

Lone Tree, Johnson Co., Pop. Code 4
  Lone Tree Comm. SD, AEA 10
  Sch. Sys. Enr. Code 2
  Supt. – Larry Shay, 303 S DEVOES ST 52755
  ES, 303 S DEVOES ST 52755 – Larry Shay, prin.

Long Grove, Scott Co., Pop. Code 3
  North Scott Comm. SD, AEA 9
  Supt. – See Eldridge
  Shepard ES, 211 PINE ST 52756
    Barry Lahann, prin.

Lorimor, Union Co., Pop. Code 2
  East Union Comm. SD, AEA 14
  Supt. – See Afton
  ES 50149 – (—), prin.

Lost Nation, Clinton Co., Pop. Code 3
  Lost Nation Comm. SD, AEA 9
  Sch. Sys. Enr. Code 2
  Supt. – Carl Whipple 52254
  MS 52254 – Paul Galer, prin.
  PS 52254 – Paul Galer, prin.

Lovilia, Monroe Co., Pop. Code 3
  Albia Comm. SD, AEA 15
  Supt. – See Albia
  ES 50150 – Donna Hancock, prin.

Lowden, Cedar Co., Pop. Code 3
  Clarence-Lowden Comm. SD, AEA 10
  Supt. – See Clarence
  Clarence-Lowden ES 52255
    Peggy Wainwright, prin.

Luana, Clayton Co., Pop. Code 2
  M-F-L Comm. SD, AEA 1
  Supt. – See Monona
  MS 52156 – Roger Swanson, prin.

Lucas, Lucas Co., Pop. Code 2
  Chariton Comm. SD, AEA 15
  Supt. – See Chariton

ES 50151 – Loren Burkhalter, prin.

Lu Verne, Kossuth Co., Pop. Code 2
Lu Verne Community SD
Sch. Sys. Enr. Code 2
Supt. – J. D. Simmons 50560
ES 50560 – J. D. Simmons, prin.

Luxemburg, Dubuque Co., Pop. Code 2

Richardville-Holy Cross School
P O BOX 138 52056

Lytton, Calhoun Co., Pop. Code 2
Lytton Comm. SD, AEA 5
Sch. Sys. Enr. Code 2
Supt. – Albert Carr 50561
ES 50561 – Gary Willett, prin.

Mc Callsburg, Story Co., Pop. Code 2
Nesco Comm. SD, AEA 11
Sch. Sys. Enr. Code 2
Supt. – Elbert Sobotka 50154
ES 50154 – Keith Tadlock, prin.
Other Schools – See Zearing

Macedonia, Pottawattamie Co., Pop. Code 2
Carson-Macedonia Comm. SD, AEA 13
Supt. – See Carson
ES 51549 – Myron Nourse, prin.

Mc Gregor, Clayton Co., Pop. Code 3
Mar-Mac Comm. SD, AEA 1
Sch. Sys. Enr. Code 2
Supt. – Dale Black 52157
Mar-Mac MS 52157 – Larry Cox, prin.
ES 52157 – Dale Black, prin.

Madrid, Boone Co., Pop. Code 4
Madrid Comm. SD, AEA 11
Sch. Sys. Enr. Code 3
Supt. – M. Romitti, HIGHWAY 17 N 50156
JHS, 213 W 1ST ST 50156 – Dean Flaws, prin.
ES, 213 W 1ST ST 50156 – Dean Flaws, prin.

Mallard, Palo Alto Co., Pop. Code 2
Mallard Comm. SD, AEA 3
Sch. Sys. Enr. Code 2
Supt. – Stephen Litts 50562
MS 50562 – Gary Schrage, prin.
ES 50562 – Bryce Gadbury, prin.

Malvern, Mills Co., Pop. Code 4
Malvern Comm. SD, AEA 13
Sch. Sys. Enr. Code 2
Supt. – Jim Matre, 409 E 10TH ST 51551
Chantry ES, 409 E 9TH ST 51551
  Barbara Kalleson, prin.

Manchester, Delaware Co., Pop. Code 5
West Delaware Co. Comm. AS, AEA 1
Sch. Sys. Enr. Code 4
Supt. – Steve Swanson, 601 NEW ST 52057
West Delaware MS, DOCTOR ST 52057
  Sidney Barrick, prin.
Lambert ES, 1001 DOCTOR ST 52057
  George Cabalka, prin.
Other Schools – See Ryan

St. Mary's School, 132 W BUTLER ST 52057

Manilla, Crawford Co., Pop. Code 4
Manilla Comm. SD, AEA 12
Sch. Sys. Enr. Code 2
Supt. – David Sextro 51454
MS 51454 – William Miller, prin.
PS 51454 – Michael Davis, prin.

Manly, Worth Co., Pop. Code 4
North Central Comm. SD, AEA 2
Sch. Sys. Enr. Code 3
Supt. – William Connell, 105 S EAST ST 50456
Other Schools – See Hanlontown, Plymouth

Manning, Carroll Co., Pop. Code 4
Manning Comm. SD, AEA 11
Sch. Sys. Enr. Code 2
Supt. – Wayne Curlile 51455
ES 51455 – Wayne Curlile, prin.

Manson, Calhoun Co., Pop. Code 4
Manson Comm. SD, AEA 5
Sch. Sys. Enr. Code 3
Supt. – Keith Hart, 1227 16TH ST 50563
ES, 1227 16TH ST 50563 – Gary Mays, prin.

Mapleton, Monona Co., Pop. Code 4
Maple Valley Comm. SD, AEA 12
Sch. Sys. Enr. Code 3
Supt. – D. Webner, 410 S 6TH ST 51034
ES, 410 S 6TH ST 51034 – Lawrence Nelson, prin.
Other Schools – See Castana, Danbury

Maquoketa, Jackson Co., Pop. Code 6
Maquoketa Comm. SD, AEA 9
Sch. Sys. Enr. Code 4
Supt. – Richard Drey, 607 W SUMMIT ST 52060
JHS, 200 E LOCUST ST 52060
  Lynn Disney, prin.
Briggs ES, WEST QUARRY 52060
  Douglas Schermer, prin.
Cardinal ES, PERSHING ROAD 52060
  Susanne Baty, prin.

Sacred Heart School, 302 EDDY PLACE 52060

Marble Rock, Floyd Co., Pop. Code 2
Rudd-Rockford-Marble Rock Comm. SD, AEA
Supt. – See Rockford

ES 50653 – Larry Hicok, prin.

Marcus, Cherokee Co., Pop. Code 4
Marcus Comm. SD, AEA 4
Sch. Sys. Enr. Code 2
Supt. – Jon Mitts, E FENTON ST 51035
ES, 305 N OAK 51035 – Kathryn Tillo, prin.

Marengo, Iowa Co., Pop. Code 4
Iowa Valley Comm. SD, AEA 10
Sch. Sys. Enr. Code 3
Supt. – E. Clayton Morlan
  359 E HILTON ST 52301
Iowa Valley ES, 151 E MAY ST 52301
  Terry Housman, prin.

Marion, Linn Co., Pop. Code 7
Linn-Mar Comm. SD, AEA 10
Sch. Sys. Enr. Code 5
Supt. – G. Easterday, 3333 10TH ST 52302
Linn-Mar JHS, 3333 10TH ST 52302
  John Corkery, prin.
Bowman Woods ES
  151 BOWMAN ROAD NE 52302
  Roger Messerly, prin.
Indian Creek ES, 3333 10TH ST 52302
  James Gard, prin.
Novak MS, 3333 10TH ST 52302
  James Brust, prin.
Wilkins ES, 2127 27TH ST 52302
  Karen Neilsen, prin.

Marion ISD, AEA 10
Sch. Sys. Enr. Code 4
Supt. – Harold Hulleman
  10TH AVE & 29TH ST 52302
Vernon MS, 1301 5TH AVE 52302
  William Cink, prin.
Emerson ES, 10TH AVE & 14TH ST 52302
  Larry Munson, prin.
Mentzer MS, 305 S 2ND ST 52302
  William Yeisley, prin.
Starry ES, 655 S 14TH ST 52302
  Arnold Benedict, prin.

St. Joseph School, 1430 14TH ST 52302

Marshalltown, Marshall Co., Pop. Code 8
LDF Comm. SD, AEA 6
Supt. – See Le Grand
Dunbar MS, RURAL ROUTE 02 50158
  Charles Loerwald, prin.

Marshalltown Comm. SD, AEA 6
Sch. Sys. Enr. Code 5
Supt. – Stephen Williams
  317 COLUMBUS DRIVE 50158
Anson ES, SOUTH 3RD AVE 50158
  Martin Swenson, prin.
Fisher ES, 2001 S 4TH ST 50158
  Patrick Kremer, prin.
Franklin ES, WEST MAIN & 14TH ST 50158
  Duane Meyer, prin.
Glick ES, SOUTH 3RD & LINN ST 50158
  Julia Messersmith, prin.
Hoglan ES, S 3RD AVE & S RIDGE ROAD 50158
  William Vana, prin.
Rogers ES, 406 SUMMIT ST 50158
  Thomas Renze, prin.
Woodbury ES, E MAIN ST & N 7TH AVE 50158
  Melvin Schuchmann, prin.

Martensdle-St. Mary's Comm. SD, AEA 11
Supt. – See Martensdale
Martensdale ES, P O BOX 186 50160
  Judith Jesse, prin.

Marshalltown Catholic School
10 W LINN ST 50158

Martelle, Jones Co., Pop. Code 2
Anamosa Comm. SD, AEA 10
Supt. – See Anamosa
ES 52305 – (—), prin.

Martensdale, Warren Co., Pop. Code 2
Martensdle-St. Mary's Comm. SD, AEA 11
Sch. Sys. Enr. Code 3
Supt. – Tom Scheldahl 50160
Other Schools – See Marshalltown

Mason City, Cerro Gordo Co., Pop. Code 8
Mason City Comm. SD, AEA 2
Sch. Sys. Enr. Code 5
Supt. – David Darnell
  1515 S PENNSYLVANIA AVE 50401
Adams MS, 29 S ILLINOIS AVE 50401
  Stephen Pottratz, prin.
Roosevelt MS, 303 15TH ST SE 50401
  Robert Boone, prin.
Harding ES, 1239 N RHODE ISLAND AVE 50401
  Vernon Bottorff, prin.
Hoover ES, 1123 8TH NW ST 50401
  Timothy Walrod, prin.
Jefferson ES, 1421 4TH ST SE 50401
  John Fritz, prin.
Madison ES, 2620 S JEFFERSON AVE 50401
  Keith Sersland, prin.
Roosevelt ES, 313 15TH ST SE 50401
  Tom Stevens, prin.
Washington ES, 710 N WASHINGTON AVE 50401
  Nancy Sweetman, prin.

Central Catholic ES, 320 5TH ST SE 50401

Massena, Cass Co., Pop. Code 3
C & M Comm. SD, AEA 13
Sch. Sys. Enr. Code 2
Supt. – Leroy Ortman 50853
Other Schools – See Cumberland

Maxwell, Story Co., Pop. Code 3
Bondurant-Farrar Comm. SD, AEA 11
Supt. – See Bondurant
Farrar MS 50161 – Marvin Skinner, prin.

Collins-Maxwell Comm. SD, AEA 11
Sch. Sys. Enr. Code 2
Supt. – Patrick Sullivan, P O BOX 207 50161
Collins-Maxwell ES 50161 – Patrick Sullivan, prin.
Other Schools – See Collins

Maynard, Fayette Co., Pop. Code 3
West Central Comm. SD, AEA 1
Sch. Sys. Enr. Code 2
Supt. – Onalee Baker Oakes 50655
ES 50655 – Onalee Oakes, prin.

Mechanicsville, Cedar Co., Pop. Code 4
Lincoln Comm. SD, AEA 10
Supt. – See Stanwood
Lincoln ES 52306 – Scott Clark, prin.

Mediapolis, Des Moines Co., Pop. Code 4
Mediapolis Comm. SD, AEA 16
Sch. Sys. Enr. Code 4
Supt. – Steve Waterman, 725 NORTHFIELD 52637
JHS 52637 – T. Coates, prin.
ES 52637 – James Tiedemann, prin.
Other Schools – See Yarmouth

Melcher, Marion Co., Pop. Code 3
Melcher-Dallas Comm. SD, AEA 11
Supt. – See Dallas
Melcher-Dallas JHS 50163 – Don Lang, prin.

Melrose, Monroe Co., Pop. Code 2
Albia Comm. SD, AEA 15
Supt. – See Albia
ES 52569 – John Palmer, prin.

Menlo, Guthrie Co., Pop. Code 2
Stuart-Menlo Comm. SD, AEA 11
Supt. – See Stuart
ES 50164 – Roger Perling, prin.

Meriden, Cherokee Co., Pop. Code 2
Meriden-Cleghorn Comm. SD, AEA 4
Supt. – See Cleghorn
ES 51037 – Kathy Tillo, prin.

Merrill, Plymouth Co., Pop. Code 3
Le Mars Comm. SD, AEA 12
Supt. – See Le Mars
Kissinger ES, 608 MAIN ST 51038
  David Horken, prin.

Middle, Iowa Co.
Amana Comm. SD, AEA 10
Sch. Sys. Enr. Code 2
Supt. – Robert Steele, BOX 70 52307
Amana MS 52307 – Mike Hooley, prin.
Lakeside ES 52307 – Mike Hooley, prin.

Miles, Jackson Co., Pop. Code 2
East Central Comm. SD, AEA 9
Sch. Sys. Enr. Code 3
Supt. – James House, P O BOX 367 52064
ES, P O BOX 267 52064 – Carl Keuter, prin.
Other Schools – See Sabula

Milford, Dickinson Co., Pop. Code 4
Okoboji Comm. SD, AEA 3
Sch. Sys. Enr. Code 3
Supt. – M. Anderson, P O BOX 147 51351
Okoboji MS, P O BOX 147 51351
  George Morris, prin.
Okoboji ES, P O BOX 147 51351
  Kenneth Carter, prin.

Millersburg, Iowa Co., Pop. Code 2
Deep River-Millersburg Comm. SD, AEA 10
Sch. Sys. Enr. Code 2
Supt. – Lewis Doty, 127 WASHINGTON ST 52308
Other Schools – See Deep River

Milo, Warren Co., Pop. Code 3
Southeast Warren Comm. SD, AEA 11
Supt. – See Liberty Center
ES 50166 – Larry Dawson, prin.

Milton, Van Buren Co., Pop. Code 3
Fox Valley Comm. SD, AEA 15
Supt. – See Cantril
Fox Valley MS 52570 – William Mertens, prin.

Minburn, Dallas Co., Pop. Code 2
Central Dallas Comm. SD, AEA 11
Sch. Sys. Enr. Code 2
Supt. – Jim Slade, P O BOX 186 50167
Central Dallas ES, P O BOX 186 50167
  Jim Slade, prin.

Minden, Pottawattamie Co., Pop. Code 2
Tri-Center Comm. SD, AEA 13
Supt. – See Neola
MS 51553 – Larry Hornbostel, prin.

Mingo, Jasper Co., Pop. Code 2
Colfax-Mingo Comm. SD, AEA 11
Supt. – See Colfax
Colfax-Mingo MS 50168 – Leland Rankin, prin.

Missouri Valley, Harrison Co., Pop. Code 5
Missouri Valley Comm. SD, AEA 13
Sch. Sys. Enr. Code 4
Supt. – Edwin Meyer, 711 E SUPERIOR ST   51555
MS, 711 E SUPERIOR ST   51555
  Frank Smith, prin.
Linn ES, LINN ST   51555 – Ferdy Mefford, prin.
PS, 109 E MICHIGAN ST   51555
  Ferdy Mefford, prin.

Mitchellville, Polk Co., Pop. Code 4
Southeast Polk Comm. SD, AEA 11
Supt. – See Runnells
ES, 308 ELM AVE NW   50169
  David Edwards, prin.

Modale, Harrison Co., Pop. Code 2
West Harrison Comm. SD, AEA 13
Supt. – See Mondamin
West Harrison South ES   51564 – H. Bolte, prin.

Mondamin, Harrison Co., Pop. Code 2
West Harrison Comm. SD, AEA 13
Sch. Sys. Enr. Code 2
Supt. – Larry Holland   51557
Other Schools – See Modale, Pisgah

Monona, Clayton Co., Pop. Code 4
M-F-L Comm. SD, AEA 1
Sch. Sys. Enr. Code 3
Supt. – Dale Black   52159
M-F-L JHS   52159 – Jay Pedersen, prin.
ES   52159 – Roger Swanson, prin.
Other Schools – See Luana

Monroe, Jasper Co., Pop. Code 4
Monroe Comm. SD, AEA 11
Sch. Sys. Enr. Code 3
Supt. – James Botts   50170
ES, 400 N JASPER   50170
  Michael Montgomery, prin.

Montezuma, Poweshiek Co., Pop. Code 4
Montezuma Comm. SD, AEA 6
Sch. Sys. Enr. Code 3
Supt. – Lewis Lundy   50171
ES   50171 – Tom Erickson, prin.

Monticello, Jones Co., Pop. Code 5
Monticello Comm. SD, AEA 10
Sch. Sys. Enr. Code 4
Supt. – David Lane, 615 N GILL ST   52310
MS, 217 S MAPLE ST   52310 – Daniel Lock, prin.
Carpenter MS, 615 N GILL ST   52310
  Craig Campbell, prin.
Shannon ES, 321 W SOUTH ST   52310
  Craig Campbell, prin.

Sacred Heart ES, 254 N SYCAMORE ST   52310

Montour, Tama Co., Pop. Code 2
South Tama Co. Comm. SD, AEA 6
Supt. – See Tama
ES   50173 – (—), prin.

Moorhead, Monona Co., Pop. Code 2
East Monona Comm. SD, AEA 12
Sch. Sys. Enr. Code 2
Supt. – Roger Friedrichsen   51558
East Monona ES   51558 – Roger Friedrichsen, prin.

Moravia, Appanoose Co., Pop. Code 3
Moravia Comm. SD, AEA 15
Sch. Sys. Enr. Code 2
Supt. – William Nielsen   52571
ES   52571 – Phyllis Fowler, prin.

Morning Sun, Louisa Co., Pop. Code 3
Morning Sun Comm. SD, AEA 16
Sch. Sys. Enr. Code 2
Supt. – Francis Davis   52640
ES, P O BOX 129   52640 – Francis Davis, prin.

Moulton, Appanoose Co., Pop. Code 3
Moulton-Udell Comm. SD, AEA 15
Sch. Sys. Enr. Code 2
Supt. – Marilyn Koehler, 305-309 E 8TH ST   52572
ES, P O BOX 84   52572 – Marilyn Koehler, prin.

Mount Ayr, Ringold Co., Pop. Code 4
Mount Ayr Comm. SD, AEA 14
Sch. Sys. Enr. Code 3
Supt. – Philip Burmeister
  1001 E COLUMBUS ST   50854
ES, 607 E JEFFERSON ST   50854
  Larry Giles, prin.

Mount Pleasant, Henry Co., Pop. Code 6
Mt. Pleasant Comm. SD, AEA 16
Sch. Sys. Enr. Code 4
Supt. – R. Goodwin, 801 E HENRY ST   52641
Harlan ES, ORANGE & MAIN ST   52641
  Richard McBeth, prin.
Lincoln ES, 501 S CORKHILL ST   52641
  Waldo Sutton, prin.
Manning ES, 603 S JACKSON ST   52641
  Donald Young, prin.
Pleasant Lawn ES, RURAL ROUTE 02   52641
  Donald Young, prin.
Saunders ES, 203 N WHITE ST   52641
  Richard McBeth, prin.
Van Allen MS, 801 E HENRY ST   52641
  Roger Williams, prin.
Other Schools – See Salem

Mount Vernon, Linn Co., Pop. Code 5
Mt. Vernon Comm. SD, AEA 10
Sch. Sys. Enr. Code 4
Supt. – Adrian Ringold
  525 PALISADES ROAD   52314
MS, A AVE & 1ST ST E   52314
  Thomas Lass, prin.
Washington ES, 600 5TH AVE S   52314
  Joseph Cullen, prin.

Moville, Woodbury Co., Pop. Code 4
Woodbury Central Comm. SD, AEA 12
Sch. Sys. Enr. Code 3
Supt. – Thomas Cooper   51039
ES   51039 – Dean Von Bergen, prin.
Other Schools – See Climbing Hill

Murray, Clarke Co., Pop. Code 3
Murray Comm. SD, AEA 14
Sch. Sys. Enr. Code 2
Supt. – Lynn Padellford, P O BOX 187   50174
ES, P O BOX 187   50174 – Lynn Padellford, prin.

Muscatine, Muscatine Co., Pop. Code 7
Muscatine Comm. SD, AEA 9
Sch. Sys. Enr. Code 6
Supt. – Thomas Wirtz, 1403 PARK AVE   52761
Central MS, 901 CEDAR ST   52761
  Marvin Koopman, prin.
West MS, 600 KINDLER ST   52761
  Paul Smith, prin.
Colorado ES, 149 COLORADO ST   52761
  Paul Brooks, prin.
Franklin ES, 210 TAYLOR ST   52761
  Robert Andresen, prin.
Garfield ES, 1409 WISCONSIN ST   52761
  Robert Andresen, prin.
Grant ES, 705 BARRY AVE   52761
  Polly Levine, prin.
Jefferson ES, 1000 MULBERRY AVE   52761
  Edwin Chamberlin, prin.
Madison ES, 1820 1ST AVE   52761
  Paul Brooks, prin.
McKinley ES, 621 KINDLER ST   52761
  Clyde Evans, prin.
Mulberry ES, 3211 MULBERRY AVE   52761
  Clyde Evans, prin.
Washington ES, 610 MAIDEN LANE   52761
  Jerry Lange, prin.

Hayes Catholic ES, 2407 CEDAR ST   52761

Mystic, Appanoose Co., Pop. Code 3
Centerville Comm. SD, AEA 15
Supt. – See Centerville
ES   52574 – Gordon Mosher, prin.

Nashua, Chickasaw Co., Pop. Code 4
Nashua Comm. SD, AEA 7
Sch. Sys. Enr. Code 3
Supt. – Linda Johanningmeier
  612 GREELEY ST   50658
ES, 621 PANAMA ST   50658
  Daniel Thomas, prin.

Nemaha, Sac Co., Pop. Code 2
Crestland Comm. SD, AEA 5
Supt. – See Early
ES   50567 – Phyllis Munster, prin.

Neola, Pottawattamie Co., Pop. Code 3
Tri-Center Comm. SD, AEA 13
Sch. Sys. Enr. Code 3
Supt. – Melvin Rogers
  RURAL ROUTE 02 BOX 217A   51559
Tri-Center ES
  RURAL ROUTE 02 BOX 217A   51559
  James Wright, prin.
Other Schools – See Minden

Nevada, Story Co., Pop. Code 6
Nevada Comm. SD, AEA 11
Sch. Sys. Enr. Code 4
Supt. – Kenneth Shaw, 901 9TH ST   50201
JHS, 901 9TH ST   50201 – James Walker, prin.
Central ES, NINTH ST & I AVE   50201
  Robert McIntire, prin.
Milford MS   50201 – James Walker, prin.

New Albin, Allamakee Co., Pop. Code 3
Eastern Allamakee Comm. SD, AEA 1
Supt. – See Lansing
ES   52160 – James Hanson, prin.

Newell, Buena Vista Co., Pop. Code 3
Newell-Providence Comm. SD, AEA 5
Sch. Sys. Enr. Code 2
Supt. – Merle Boerner   50568
Newell-Providence ES, CLARK ST   50568
  Merle Boerner, prin.

Newhall, Benton Co., Pop. Code 3

Central Lutheran School, P O BOX 190   52315

New Hampton, Chickasaw Co., Pop. Code 5
New Hampton Comm. SD, AEA 1
Sch. Sys. Enr. Code 4
Supt. – Robert Longmuir, 206 W MAIN ST   50659
MS, 206 W MAIN ST   50659 – Larry Plumb, prin.
ES, 206 W MAIN ST   50659 – Paul Mann, prin.

St. Joseph Community Catholic School
  216 N BROADWAY AVE   50659

New Hartford, Butler Co., Pop. Code 3
New Hartford Comm. SD, AEA 7
Sch. Sys. Enr. Code 2
Supt. – Virgil Goodrich, 508 BEAVER   50660
ES, 508 BEAVER   50660
  Roberta Bodensteiner, prin.

New London, Henry Co., Pop. Code 4
New London Comm. SD, AEA 16
Sch. Sys. Enr. Code 3
Supt. – K. Arrowsmith, WILSON ST   52645
Clark ES, WALNUT ST   52645
  Randal Nemitz, prin.

New Market, Taylor Co., Pop. Code 3
New Market Comm. SD, AEA 14
Sch. Sys. Enr. Code 2
Supt. – Dave Anctil, P O BOX 8   51646
ES, P O BOX 8   51646 – Dave Anctil, prin.

New Providence, Hardin Co., Pop. Code 2
Eldora-New Providence Comm. SD, AEA 6
Supt. – See Eldora
Eldora-New Providence MS, P O BOX 98   50206
  Russ Freeman, prin.

New Sharon, Mahaska Co., Pop. Code 4
North Mahaska Comm. SD, AEA 15
Sch. Sys. Enr. Code 2
Supt. – John Van Pelt   50207
North Mahaska ES   50207 – Larry Blinn, prin.

Newton, Jasper Co., Pop. Code 7
Newton Comm. SD, AEA 11
Sch. Sys. Enr. Code 5
Supt. – Philip Hintz, 807 S 6TH AVE W   50208
Berg JHS, 1900 N 5TH AVE E   50208
  David Gallaher, prin.
Aurora Heights ES, 310 E 23RD ST S   50208
  Duane Hovick, prin.
Berg ES, 1900 N 5TH AVE E   50208
  Don Black, prin.
Emerson Hough ES, 700 N 4TH AVE E   50208
  John Villotti, prin.
Jefferson ES
  LAMBS GROVE JEFFERSON DR   50208
  Mike Hogan, prin.
Lincoln ES, 701 S 4TH AVE E   50208
  Armond Miller, prin.
Wilson ES, 801 S 8TH AVE W   50208
  Ken Erpelding, prin.
Other Schools – See Kellogg

New Vienna, Dubuque Co., Pop. Code 2

Hennessy Catholic School, P O BOX 210   52065

New Virginia, Warren Co., Pop. Code 3
Interstate 35 Comm. SD, AEA 11
Supt. – See Truro
Interstate 35 JHS, P O BOX 98   50210
  Kenneth Johnson, prin.
ES   50210 – Kenneth Johnson, prin.

Nora Springs, Floyd Co., Pop. Code 4
Nora Springs-Rock Falls Comm. SD, AEA 2
Sch. Sys. Enr. Code 3
Supt. – Clark Dey, 509 N IOWA AVE   50458
ES, 509 N IOWA AVE   50458 – James Clark, prin.

North English, Iowa Co., Pop. Code 4
English Valleys Comm. SD, AEA 10
Sch. Sys. Enr. Code 2
Supt. – Patricia McClure   52316
English Valleys ES, WEST CLARK ST   52316
  Patricia McClure, prin.

North Liberty, Johnson Co., Pop. Code 4
Iowa City Comm. SD, AEA 10
Supt. – See Iowa City
Penn ES, P O BOX 9   52317
  Theresa Schoen, prin.

Northwood, Worth Co., Pop. Code 4
Northwood-Kensett Comm. SD, AEA 2
Sch. Sys. Enr. Code 3
Supt. – William Connell, 1210 1ST AVE N   50459
Northwood-Kensett MS, 103 11TH ST N   50459
  James Simmelink, prin.
ES, 103 11TH ST N   50459
  James Simmelink, prin.

Norwalk, Warren Co., Pop. Code 5
Norwalk Comm. SD, AEA 11
Sch. Sys. Enr. Code 4
Supt. – L. Johnson, 1201 NORTH AVE   50211
MS, 1412 NORTH AVE   50211
  Elaine Smith, prin.
East ES, 906 SCHOOL AVE   50211
  Ron Perkins, prin.
Lakewood ES, 9208 HAPPY HOLLOW DR   50211
  Thomas McLaughlin, prin.
West ES, 715 SCHOOL AVE   50211
  Ron Perkins, prin.

Norway, Benton Co., Pop. Code 3
Norway Comm. SD, AEA 10
Sch. Sys. Enr. Code 2
Supt. – Leland Wise   52318
ES   52318 – Gary Holst, prin.

Oakland, Pottawattamie Co., Pop. Code 4
Oakland Comm. SD, AEA 13
Sch. Sys. Enr. Code 2
Supt. – Gary Funkhouser
  501 OAKLAND AVE   51560
ES, 708 GLASS ST   51560
  Kenneth Finnegan, prin.

Ocheyedan, Osceola Co., Pop. Code 3
Sibley-Ocheyedan Comm. SD
Supt. – See Sibley
ES 51354 – Marion Brink, prin.

Odebolt, Sac Co., Pop. Code 4
Odebolt-Arthur Comm. SD, AEA 5
Sch. Sys. Enr. Code 3
Supt. – Carl Mattes, 600 MAPLE 51458
Odebolt-Arthur ES 51458
Theron Kirkpatrick, prin.
Other Schools – See Arthur

Oelwein, Fayette Co., Pop. Code 6
Oelwein Comm. SD, AEA 1
Sch. Sys. Enr. Code 4
Supt. – Eldon Pyle, 307 8TH AVE SE 50662
Harlan ES, 412 2ND AVE NW 50662
Dennis Rowse, prin.
Parkside ES, 301 6TH AVE SW 50662
Dennis Rowse, prin.
Wings Park ES, 111 8TH AVE NE 50662
Stephen Bradley, prin.

Sacred Heart ES, 401 1ST ST SW 50662

Ogden, Boone Co., Pop. Code 4
Ogden Comm. SD, AEA 11
Sch. Sys. Enr. Code 3
Supt. – Raymond Gaul, P O BOX 250 50212
North MS 50212 – Gary Paulsen, prin.
Howe ES 50212 – Bill Mullins, prin.

Olin, Jones Co., Pop. Code 3
Olin Cons. SD, AEA 10
Sch. Sys. Enr. Code 2
Supt. – Marvin Ryan, TRILBY ST 52320
ES 52320 – Marvin Ryan, prin.

Onawa, Monona Co., Pop. Code 5
West Monona Comm. SD, AEA 12
Sch. Sys. Enr. Code 3
Supt. – D. Southwick, 1314 15TH ST 51040
Central ES, 1100 10TH ST 51040
Richard Schlitter, prin.
Lark ES, 611 4TH ST 51040
Richard Schlitter, prin.

Onslow, Jones Co., Pop. Code 2
Midland Comm. SD, AEA 10
Supt. – See Wyoming
ES 52309 – Robert Baxter, prin.

Oran, Fayette Co., Pop. Code 3
Wapsie Valley Comm. SD, AEA 7
Supt. – See Fairbank
Wapsie Valley JHS 50664 – Robert Cue, prin.

Orange City, Sioux Co., Pop. Code 5
Maurice-Orange City Comm. SD, AEA 4
Sch. Sys. Enr. Code 3
Supt. – Rod Wilbeck, 615 8TH ST SE 51041
ES, 315 2ND ST SW 51041
Henry Van Aartsen, prin.

Orange City Christian School
604 3RD ST SW 51041

Orient, Adair Co., Pop. Code 2
Orient-Macksburg Comm. SD, AEA 14
Sch. Sys. Enr. Code 2
Supt. – Bill Cox 50858
ES 50858 – James Tussey, prin.

Osage, Mitchell Co., Pop. Code 5
Osage Comm. SD, AEA 2
Sch. Sys. Enr. Code 4
Supt. – Dean Meier
7TH ST & SAWYER DRIVE 50461
Lincoln ES, 515 CHASE ST 50461
Paul Bisgard, prin.
Washington ES, 314 S 7TH ST 50461
Paul Bisgard, prin.

Sacred Heart School, 218 S 12TH ST 50461

Osceola, Clarke Co., Pop. Code 5
Clarke Comm. SD, AEA 14
Sch. Sys. Enr. Code 4
Supt. – David Thomas, 800 N JACKSON ST 50213
East ES, 201 S KOSSUTH ST 50213
William Young, prin.
North MS, 300 N MAIN ST 50213
Howard Latham, prin.
Other Schools – See Weldon

Oskaloosa, Mahaska Co., Pop. Code 7
Oskaloosa Comm. SD, AEA 15
Sch. Sys. Enr. Code 4
Supt. – Harold Westra
E AVE E & N MARKET ST 52577
Garfield MS, 227 S M ST 52577
John Bowker, prin.
Grant ES, 715 B AVE E 52577 – Dale Malloy, prin.
Jefferson ES, FIFTH AVE WEST & S B ST 52577
John Bowker, prin.
Lincoln ES, 911 B AVE W 52577
Rod Blanchard, prin.
Webster ES, 508 S 7TH ST 52577
Robert McCaulley, prin.
Whittier ES, 604 N B ST 52577
Rod Blanchard, prin.

School for Christian Instruct
810 NORTH E ST 52577

Ossian, Winneshiek Co., Pop. Code 3
South Winneshiek Comm. SD, AEA 1
Supt. – See Calmar
South Winneshiek MS 52161 – Clark Goltz, prin.
South Winneshiek ES 52161 – Clark Goltz, prin.

DeSales ES, MAINE ST 52161

Otho, Webster Co.
Fort Dodge Comm. SD, AEA 5
Supt. – See Fort Dodge
ES 50569 – Carol Johannsen, prin.

Otley, Marion Co.
Pella Comm. SD, AEA 11
Supt. – See Pella
ES 50214 – Merlyn Vander Leest, prin.

Ottumwa, Wapello Co., Pop. Code 8
Ottumwa Comm. SD, AEA 15
Sch. Sys. Enr. Code 5
Supt. – Richard Geith, P O BOX 698 52501
Evans JHS, 812 CHESTER AVE 52501
Jim Barton, prin.
Agassiz ES, 608 E WILLIAMS ST 52501
Kevin Farmer, prin.
Douma ES, 307 W MARY ST 52501
Jerry Zesiger, prin.
Eisenhower ES, 2624 MARILYN ROAD 52501
Robert Snell, prin.
James ES, 1001 N BENTON ST 52501
Robert Snell, prin.
Lincoln ES, 458 N COURT ST 52501
Jess Terrell, prin.
Mann ES, 1523 N COURT ST 52501
Jess Terrell, prin.
Pickwick ES, 1306 W WILLIAMS ST 52501
Ron Roggentien, prin.
Wildwood ES, 438 MCKINLEY AVE 52501
Norlan Sapp, prin.
Wilson ES, 1102 E 4TH ST 52501
Dan Bitner, prin.

Seton Catholic ES, 117 E FOURTH ST 52501

Oxford, Johnson Co., Pop. Code 3
Clear Creek Comm. SD, AEA 10
Sch. Sys. Enr. Code 3
Supt. – Bob Steele 52322
Clear Creek MS, RURAL ROUTE 01 52322
Raymond Strobbe, prin.
Clear Creek ES, P O BOX 487 52322
Raymond Strobbe, prin.

Oxford Junction, Jones Co., Pop. Code 3
Oxford Junction Cons. SD, AEA 10
Sch. Sys. Enr. Code 2
Supt. – Dwaine Persels 52323
ES 52323 – Dwaine Persels, prin.

Packwood, Keokuk Co., Pop. Code 2
Pekin Comm. SD, AEA 15
Sch. Sys. Enr. Code 3
Supt. – James Rood 52580
Pekin ES 52580 – Sam Ritchie, prin.

Palmer, Pocahontas Co., Pop. Code 2
Palmer Cons. SD, AEA 5
Sch. Sys. Enr. Code 2
Supt. – Alden Skinner 50571
ES 50571 – Alden Skinner, prin.

Panama, Shelby Co., Pop. Code 2

St. Mary Regional School 51562

Panora, Guthrie Co., Pop. Code 4
Panora-Linden Comm. SD, AEA 11
Sch. Sys. Enr. Code 2
Supt. – Wm. Weddingfeld, P O BOX 39 50216
Panora-Linden MS 50216 – Louis McCrea, prin.
Other Schools – See Linden

Parkersburg, Butler Co., Pop. Code 4
Parkersburg Comm. SD, AEA 7
Sch. Sys. Enr. Code 3
Supt. – Virgil Goodrich 50665
ES 50665 – Lloyd Urbanek, prin.

Parnell, Iowa Co., Pop. Code 2
Williamsburg Comm. SD, AEA 10
Supt. – See Williamsburg
MS 52325 – Terry Curtis, prin.

Paton, Greene Co., Pop. Code 2
Paton-Churdan Comm. SD, AEA 5
Supt. – See Churdan
ES 50217 – Ron Fick, prin.

Paullina, O'Brien Co., Pop. Code 4
Paullina Comm. SD, AEA 4
Sch. Sys. Enr. Code 2
Supt. – Jerry McMullen, P O BOX 638 51046
JHS, P O BOX 638 51046 – Hans Sorensen, prin.
ES, P O BOX 638 51046 – Jerry McMullen, prin.

Zion-St. John Lutheran School
103 W BERTHA 51046

Pella, Marion Co., Pop. Code 6
Pella Comm. SD, AEA 11
Sch. Sys. Enr. Code 4
Supt. – Orville Dunkin
210 E UNIVERSITY ST 50219
MS, 612 E 13TH ST 50219 – Donald Roehr, prin.
Lincoln ES, 1102 BROADWAY ST 50219
Merlyn Vander Leest, prin.

Webster ES, 401 MAIN ST 50219
Rex Steddom, prin.
Other Schools – See Leighton, Otley

Pella Christian ES, 216 LIBERTY ST 50219

Perry, Dallas Co., Pop. Code 6
Perry Comm. SD, AEA 11
Sch. Sys. Enr. Code 4
Supt. – Richard Staver
3RD & WARFORD ST 50220
JHS, 10TH & WILLIS AVE 50220
Donald Flynn, prin.
Lincoln ES, 5TH & EVELYN 50220
William Salmon, prin.
Roosevelt MS, 8TH & WEST WILLIS 50220
John Schnicker, prin.
Webster ES, 3RD & NORTH 50220
John Schnicker, prin.

St. Patrick School, 1324 5TH ST 50220

Peterson, Clay Co., Pop. Code 2
Sioux Valley Comm. SD, AEA 3
Sch. Sys. Enr. Code 2
Supt. – R. Doherty 51047
ES 51047 – Raymond Doherty, prin.

Pierson, Woodbury Co., Pop. Code 2
Kingsley-Pierson Comm. SD, AEA 12
Supt. – See Kingsley
JHS 51048 – Stewart Goslinga, prin.
MS 51048 – Stewart Goslinga, prin.

Pisgah, Harrison Co., Pop. Code 2
West Harrison Comm. SD, AEA 13
Supt. – See Mondamin
West Harrison North ES 51564 – H. Bolte, prin.

Plainfield, Bremer Co., Pop. Code 2
Plainfield Comm. SD, AEA 7
Sch. Sys. Enr. Code 2
Supt. – Marty Lucas, P O BOX 38 50666
ES, P O BOX 38 50666 – Robert Murphy, prin.

Pleasant Valley, Scott Co., Pop. Code 3
Pleasant Valley Comm. SD, AEA 9
Sch. Sys. Enr. Code 5
Supt. – M. Parsons, P O BOX 332 52767
Black Hawk JHS, WISCONSIN ST 52767
Patricia Runyan, prin.
Bridgeview ES, P O BOX 332 52767
Raymond Anderegg, prin.
Cody ES, ARGO ROAD 52767
Norma Hofmann, prin.
ES, CROW CREEK ROAD 52767
Keith Osborn, prin.
Riverdale ES, HIGHWAY 67 52767
Larry Brown, prin.

Pleasantville Comm. SD, AEA 11
Supt. – See Pleasantville
East ES, 405 E MONROE 52767
Jan Haugen, prin.

Pleasantville, Marion Co., Pop. Code 4
Pleasantville Comm. SD, AEA 11
Sch. Sys. Enr. Code 3
Supt. – James Poole, 415 JONES 50225
North ES, 414 JONES 50225
Donna Hancock, prin.
Other Schools – See Pleasant Valley

Plymouth, Cerro Gordo Co., Pop. Code 2
North Central Comm. SD, AEA 2
Supt. – See Manly
ES 50464 – James Carter, prin.

Pocahontas, Pocahontas Co., Pop. Code 4
Pocahontas Comm. SD, AEA 5
Sch. Sys. Enr. Code 2
Supt. – D. Pierce, 201 1ST AVE SW 50574
JHS, 205 2ND AVE NW 50574
Grant Stimson, prin.
ES, 208 1ST AVE SW 50574 – Lynn Moody, prin.

Polk City, Polk Co., Pop. Code 4
North Polk Comm. SD, AEA 11
Supt. – See Alleman
West ES 50226 – Thomas Jones, prin.

Pomeroy, Calhoun Co., Pop. Code 3
Pomeroy Comm. SD, AEA 5
Sch. Sys. Enr. Code 2
Supt. – A. Sinek, 202 E HARRISON ST 50575
ES, 202 E HARRISON ST 50575 – Al Sinek, prin.

Postville, Allamakee Co., Pop. Code 4
Postville Comm. SD, AEA 1
Sch. Sys. Enr. Code 3
Supt. – Joseph Hrecz, 312 W POST 52162
Darling ES, 312 W POST 52162
Daryl Bachtell, prin.

Prairie City, Jasper Co., Pop. Code 4
Prairie City Comm. SD, AEA 11
Sch. Sys. Enr. Code 3
Supt. – James Botts
405 PLAINSMEN ROAD 50228
MS, 405 PLAINSMEN ROAD 50228
Robert Buyert, prin.
ES, 407 JEFFERSON 50228 – Mary Poulter, prin.

Prescott, Adams Co., Pop. Code 2
Prescott Comm. SD, AEA 14
Sch. Sys. Enr. Code 2
Supt. – Russell Mahaffey, P O BOX 1 50859
ES, P O BOX 1 50859 – Lana Bearder, prin.

Preston, Jackson Co., Pop. Code 4
Preston Comm. SD, AEA 9
Sch. Sys. Enr. Code 2
Supt. – Kim Kreinbring, P O BOX 10 52069
ES, 121 S MITCHELL 52069
David Hoffman, prin.

Primghar, O'Brien Co., Pop. Code 4
Primghar Comm. SD, AEA 4
Sch. Sys. Enr. Code 2
Supt. – Richard Partlow 51245
ES 51245 – Richard Partlow, prin.

Princeton, Scott Co., Pop. Code 3
North Scott Comm. SD, AEA 9
Supt. – See Eldridge
Grissom ES 52768 – John Lengenhan, prin.

Pulaski, Davis Co., Pop. Code 2
Davis Co. Comm. SD, AEA 15
Supt. – See Bloomfield
ES 52584 – Rebecca Birdsong, prin.

Quasqueton, Buchanan Co., Pop. Code 3
East Buchanan Comm. SD, AEA 7
Supt. – See Winthrop
East Buchanan South ES 52326
James Zimmerman, prin.

Radcliffe, Hardin Co., Pop. Code 3
Radcliffe Comm. SD, AEA 6
Sch. Sys. Enr. Code 2
Supt. – Larry Fudge 50230
Radcliffe/Hubbard ES 50230
Edmund Frangenberg, prin.

Readlyn, Bremer Co., Pop. Code 3
Wapsie Valley Comm. SD, AEA 7
Supt. – See Fairbank
ES 50668 – Robert Cue, prin.

Community Lutheran School, P O BOX 129 50668

Redfield, Dallas Co., Pop. Code 3
Dexfield Comm. SD, AEA 11
Sch. Sys. Enr. Code 2
Supt. – Larry Sarver 50233
ES 50233 – Robert Vellinga, prin.
Other Schools – See Dexter

Red Oak, Montgomery Co., Pop. Code 6
Red Oak Comm. SD, AEA 14
Sch. Sys. Enr. Code 4
Supt. – Al Adair, 408 COOLBAUGH ST 51566
Bancroft ES, 3RD & PROSPECT 51566
Dean Raabe, prin.
Inman ES, NORTH 8TH ST 51566
Fred Laughlin, prin.
Jefferson ES, SOUTH 3RD ST 51566
Fred Laughlin, prin.
Washington MS
BROADWAY & WASHINGTON 51566
Dean Raabe, prin.
Webster ES, BROAD & VALLEY 51566
Fred Laughlin, prin.

Reinbeck, Grundy Co., Pop. Code 4
Reinbeck Comm. SD, AEA 7
Sch. Sys. Enr. Code 2
Supt. – K. Stoakes, 600 BLACKHAWK ST 50669
ES 50669 – Kenneth Stoakes, prin.

Rembrandt, Buena Visa Co., Pop. Code 2
Sioux Rapids-Rembrandt Comm. SD, AEA 5
Supt. – See Sioux Rapids
Sioux Rapids-Rembrandt ES 50576
Mahlan Carothers, prin.

Remsen, Plymouth Co., Pop. Code 4
Remson-Union Comm. SD, AEA 12
Sch. Sys. Enr. Code 2
Supt. – Willis Hoff, 511 ROOSEVELT 51050
Remson-Union JHS, 511 ROOSEVELT ST 51050
D. Meneely, prin.
ES, 412 FULTON ST 51050
Berneta Dunham, prin.

St. Catherine-St. Mary School
321 FULTON ST 51050

Riceville, Howard Co., Pop. Code 3
Riceville Comm. SD, AEA 1
Sch. Sys. Enr. Code 3
Supt. – Norman Kolberg 50466
IS 50466 – Steve Harnack, prin.
ES 50466 – Steve Harnack, prin.

Ridgeway, Winneshiek Co., Pop. Code 2
Howard-Winneshiek Comm. SD, AEA 1
Supt. – See Cresco
ES 52165 – Irvin Myron, prin.

Ringsted, Emmet Co., Pop. Code 3
Armstrong-Ringsted Comm. SD, AEA 3
Supt. – See Armstrong
Armstrong-Ringsted MS 50578
Dennis Hoyer, prin.

Rippey, Greene Co., Pop. Code 2
East Greene Comm. SD, AEA 5
Supt. – See Grand Junction
ES 50235 – Richard Marks, prin.

Riverside, Washington Co., Pop. Code 3
Highland Comm. SD, AEA 10
Sch. Sys. Enr. Code 3
Supt. – Don Lewis 52327
Highland JHS 52327 – Don Lewis, prin.
ES 52327 – Pat Gregory, prin.

Other Schools – See Ainsworth

Rockford, Floyd Co., Pop. Code 4
Rudd-Rockford-Marble Rock Comm. SD, AEA
Sch. Sys. Enr. Code 3
Supt. – Lynn Hansen 50468
ES 50468 – Larry Hicok, prin.
Other Schools – See Marble Rock, Rudd

Rock Rapids, Lyon Co., Pop. Code 5
Central Lyon Comm. SD, AEA 4
Sch. Sys. Enr. Code 3
Supt. – Melvin Wishman
1105 STORY ST S 51246
Central Lyon MS, 1105 STORY ST S 51246
Lance Olson, prin.
Central Lyon ES, 1105 S STORY ST 51246
Lance Olson, prin.

Rock Valley, Sioux Co., Pop. Code 5
Rock Valley Comm. SD, AEA 4
Sch. Sys. Enr. Code 3
Supt. – N. R. Hulst, 1712 20TH AVE 51247
ES, 1910 15TH ST 51247
Jerry Starkweather, prin.

Netherlands Reformed Christian ES
RURAL ROUTE 01 BOX 269K 51247
Rock Valley Christian School
1405 17TH ST 51247

Rockwell, Cerro Gordo Co., Pop. Code 4
Rockwell-Swaledale Comm. SD, AEA 2
Sch. Sys. Enr. Code 2
Supt. – Larry Kauzlarich 50469
Rockwell-Swaledale ES 50469
Mary Ellen Crane, prin.

Rockwell City, Calhoun Co., Pop. Code 4
Rockwell City Comm. SD, AEA 5
Sch. Sys. Enr. Code 2
Supt. – Gene Panning
1000 TONAWANDA ST 50579
ES, 330 BROWER ST 50579
Richard Jensen, prin.

Rowley, Buchanan Co.
Independence Comm. SD, AEA 7
Supt. – See Independence
South ES 52329 – Gene Oxley, prin.

Roland, Story Co., Pop. Code 4
Roland-Story Comm. SD, AEA 11
Supt. – See Story City
Roland-Story ES, 900 HILLCREST DR 50236
Roger Bohning, prin.
Roland-Story ES, 220 MAIN ST 50236
David Hemphill, prin.

Rolfe, Pocahontas Co., Pop. Code 3
Rolfe Comm. SD, AEA 5
Sch. Sys. Enr. Code 2
Supt. – Richard Schreck 50581
MS 50581 – Fred Columbus, prin.
ES 50581 – Fred Columbus, prin.

Royal, Clay Co., Pop. Code 3
Clay Central Comm. SD, AEA 3
Sch. Sys. Enr. Code 2
Supt. – Charles Missman 51357
Clay Central JHS 51357 – Marlin Gustin, prin.
Clay Central ES 51357 – Marlin Gustin, prin.

Rudd, Floyd Co., Pop. Code 2
Rudd-Rockford-Marble Rock Comm. SD, AEA
Supt. – See Rockford
ES 50471 – Larry Hicok, prin.

Runnells, Polk Co., Pop. Code 4
Southeast Polk Comm. SD, AEA 11
Sch. Sys. Enr. Code 5
Supt. – Kenneth Sand
8379 NE UNIVERSITY AVE 50237
Southeast Polk JHS
8325 NE UNIVERSITY AVE 50237
Ray Svendson, prin.
ES, RURAL ROUTE 01 50237
Robert Sutton, prin.
Other Schools – See Altoona, Des Moines,
Mitchellville

Russell, Lucas Co., Pop. Code 3
Russell Comm. SD, AEA 15
Sch. Sys. Enr. Code 2
Supt. – Robert McCurdy, P O BOX 536 50238
ES, P O BOX 536 50238 – Robert McCurdy, prin.

Ruthven, Palo Alto Co., Pop. Code 3
Ruthven-Ayrshire Cons. SD, AEA 3
Sch. Sys. Enr. Code 2
Supt. – Jerry Golden 51358
Ruthven-Ayrshire ES 51358 – Jerry Golden, prin.

Ryan, Delaware Co., Pop. Code 2
West Delaware Co. Comm. AS, AEA 1
Supt. – See Manchester
ES 52330 – Wayne Sweet, prin.

Sabula, Jackson Co., Pop. Code 3
East Central Comm. SD, AEA 9
Supt. – See Miles
MS 52070 – Carl Kueter, prin.
ES 52070 – Carl Keuter, prin.

Sac City, Sac Co., Pop. Code 5
Sac Comm. SD, AEA 5
Sch. Sys. Enr. Code 3
Supt. – Albert Bemer, W MAIN ST 50583

Sac Community ES, S 16TH ST 50583
Lowell Samuelson, prin.

Saint Ansgar, Mitchell Co., Pop. Code 4
St. Ansgar Comm. SD, AEA 2
Sch. Sys. Enr. Code 3
Supt. – Norman Kolberg, P O BOX 599 50472
ES, 5TH & WASHINGTON 50472
Ronald Mueller, prin.
Other Schools – See Grafton

Saint Charles, Madison Co., Pop. Code 3
Interstate 35 Comm. SD, AEA 11
Supt. – See Truro
ES 50240 – Richard Gray, prin.

Saint Lucas, Fayette Co., Pop. Code 2

St. Lukes-St. John Consolidated School
P O BOX 127 52166

Salem, Henry Co., Pop. Code 2
Mt. Pleasant Comm. SD, AEA 16
Supt. – See Mount Pleasant
ES 52649 – Waldo Sutton, prin.

Sanborn, O'Brien Co., Pop. Code 4
Sanborn Comm. SD, AEA 4
Sch. Sys. Enr. Code 2
Supt. – Gerald Cummins 51248
JHS 51248 – W. Remme, prin.
ES 51248 – Gerald Cummins, prin.

Sanborn Christian School, P O BOX 546 51248

Schaller, Sac Co., Pop. Code 3
Schaller Comm. SD, AEA 5
Sch. Sys. Enr. Code 2
Supt. – Alan Meyer, 300 S BERWICK 51053
ES, 301 S HANOVER 51053
Phyllis Munster, prin.

Schleswig, Crawford Co., Pop. Code 3
Schleswig Comm. SD, AEA 12
Sch. Sys. Enr. Code 2
Supt. – John Selk, P O BOX 378 51461
ES, P O BOX 378 51461 – John Selk, prin.

Scranton, Greene Co., Pop. Code 3
Scranton Cons. SD
Sch. Sys. Enr. Code 2
Supt. – Robert Schmidt 51462
ES 51462 – Kenneth Morlan, prin.

Sergeant Bluff, Woodbury Co., Pop. Code 4
Sergeant Bluff-Luton Comm. SD, AEA 12
Sch. Sys. Enr. Code 4
Supt. – Charles Scott, P O BOX 97 51054
Sergeant Bluff-Luton MS, P O BOX 97 51054
Ron Brandl, prin.
Sergeant Bluff-Luton ES, P O BOX 97 51054
George Holland, prin.

Seymour, Wayne Co., Pop. Code 4
Seymour Comm. SD, AEA 15
Sch. Sys. Enr. Code 2
Supt. – Glee Guess 52590
ES 52590 – Glee Guess, prin.

Sheffield, Franklin Co., Pop. Code 4
Sheffield-Chapin Comm. SD, AEA 2
Sch. Sys. Enr. Code 2
Supt. – Clifford Cameron 50475
ES, 504 PARK 50475 – Charles Rabey, prin.

Shelby, Shelby Co., Pop. Code 3
Shelby Comm. SD, AEA 13
Sch. Sys. Enr. Code 2
Supt. – Rod Montang, 100 WESTERN AVE 51570
ES 51570 – Rod Montang, prin.

Sheldon, O'Brien Co., Pop. Code 6
Sheldon Comm. SD, AEA 4
Sch. Sys. Enr. Code 4
Supt. – Jerry Peterson, 1700 E 4TH ST 51201
MS, 727 6TH AVE 51201 – Jack Duffy, prin.
East ES, NORMAL COLLEGE AVE 51201
Jack Duffy, prin.

Sheldon Christian School, 1425 E 9TH ST 51201
St. Patrick School, 1020 4TH AVE 51201

Shell Rock, Butler Co., Pop. Code 4
Waverly-Shell Rock Comm. SD, AEA 7
Supt. – See Waverly
ES, 714 CHERRY ST 50670 – Richard Jensen, prin.

Shellsburg, Benton Co., Pop. Code 3
Shellsburg Comm. SD, AEA 10
Sch. Sys. Enr. Code 2
Supt. – Richard Whitehead 52332
ES, 203 COTTAGE ST 52332
Melida Krumm, prin.

Shenandoah, Page Co., Pop. Code 6
Shenandoah Comm. SD, AEA 13
Sch. Sys. Enr. Code 4
Supt. – Joseph Kirchoff
306 W NISHNA ROAD 51601
MS, CENTER & UNIVERSITY 51601
William Rabel, prin.
Broad Street ES, N BROAD ST 51601
Glen Adkins, prin.
Central ES, W CLARINDA AVE 51601
Glen Adkins, prin.
Logan ES, 306 W NISHNA ROAD 51601
Glen Adkins, prin.

Lowell Avenue ES, 1111 W LOWELL AVE   51601
  Glen Adkins, prin.

Sherrill, Dubuque Co., Pop. Code 2

Balltown-Sherrill Catholic Schs.
  RURAL ROUTE 02   52073

Sibley, Osceola Co.
Sibley-Ocheyedan Comm. SD
Sch. Sys. Enr. Code 3
Supt. – Michael Rogers, 120 11TH AVE NE   51249
Central MS, 120 11TH AVE NE   51249
  Michael Schafer, prin.
Franklin ES, 416 9TH AVE   51249
  Marion Brink, prin.
Other Schools – See Ocheyedan

Sidney, Fremont Co., Pop. Code 4
Sidney Comm. SD, AEA 13
Sch. Sys. Enr. Code 2
Supt. – Eugene Hess   51652
ES   51652 – Michael Manning, prin.

Sigourney, Keokuk Co., Pop. Code 4
Sigourney Comm. SD, AEA 15
Sch. Sys. Enr. Code 3
Supt. – Keith Sasseen, 107 W MARION ST   52591
MS, 408 E WASHINGTON ST   52591
  J. D. Miletich, prin.
Sigourney North ES, 218 W NORTH ST   52591
  Russell Parcell, prin.
Sigourney South ES
  205 E PLEASANT VALLEY   52591
  Russell Parcell, prin.

Sioux Center, Sioux Co., Pop. Code 5
Sioux Center Comm. SD, AEA 4
Sch. Sys. Enr. Code 3
Supt. – Lyle Kooiker, 550 9TH ST NE   51250
JHS, 550 9TH ST NE   51250 – Ken Wiersma, prin.
Kinsey ES, 4TH AVE & 10TH ST SE   51250
  Robert Mars, prin.

Sioux Center Christian School
  630 FIRST AVE SE   51250

Sioux City, Woodbury Co., Pop. Code 8
Sioux City Comm. SD, AEA 12
Sch. Sys. Enr. Code 7
Supt. – Thomas Brown, 1221 PIERCE ST   51105
Riverside S, 2303 RIVERSIDE BLVD   51109
  Norman Ashby, prin.
East MS, 1720 MORNINGSIDE AVE   51106
  Conrad Cameron, prin.
Hoover MS, 3601 COUNTRY CLUB BLVD   51104
  Raymond Burnight, prin.
West MS, 1121 W 5TH ST   51103
  Richard Bathurst, prin.
Wilson MS, 1010 IOWA ST   51105
  Gordon Hull, prin.
Bryant ES, 821 30TH ST   51104
  Michael Bartek, prin.
Clark ES, 4315 PERRYCREEK ROAD   51104
  Morris Graber, prin.
Crescent Park ES, 1114 W 27TH ST   51103
  Morris Graber, prin.
Emerson ES, 2410 W 1ST ST   51103
  Linda Madison, prin.
Everett ES, 1314 W 3RD ST   51103
  Rita Busch, prin.
Grant ES, 3001 18TH ST   51105
  Wilbur House, prin.
Hawthorne ES, 4405 CENTRAL ST   51108
  Marvin Rants, prin.
Hunt ES, 615 20TH ST   51104 – Leon Koster, prin.
Irving ES, 1022 JENNINGS ST   51105
  Duane Schubert, prin.
Joy ES, 3409 INDIANA AVE   51106
  Roger Godfrey, prin.
Leeds MS, 3919 JEFFERSON ST   51108
  George Finzen, prin.
Lincoln ES, 115 MIDVALE AVE   51104
  Duane Vandeberg, prin.
Longfellow ES, 1800 SIOUX TRAIL   51106
  Jean Carlson, prin.
McKinley ES, 200 PAXTON ST   51105
  Eugene Linkvis, prin.
Nodland ES, 5000 MAYHEW AVE   51106
  Veral Heller, prin.
Riverview ES, 2205 BRYAN ST   51109
  James Lyons, prin.
Roosevelt ES, 2015 W 6TH ST   51103
  Clarence Greene, prin.
Smith ES, 1623 REBECCA ST   51103
  Merlynn Cady, prin.
Sunnyside ES, 2700 S MAPLE ST   51106
  Warren Montgomery, prin.
Washington ES, 2550 S MARTHA ST   51106
  James Gaul, prin.
Whittier ES, 4820 4TH AVE   51106
  Leon Koster, prin.

Blessed Sacrament School
  3030 JACKSON ST   51104
Holy Family School, 700 W 6TH ST   51103
Holy Family School, 1000 DOUGLAS ST   51105
Holy Family School, 710 IOWA ST   51105
Immaculate Conception School
  3719 RIDGE AVE   51106
Sacred Heart School
  5010 MILITARY ROAD   51103
St. Michael School, 4105 HARRISON ST   51108
St. Pauls Lutheran School
  614 JENNINGS STREET   51105

Sioux Rapids, Buena Vista Co., Pop. Code 3
Sioux Rapids-Rembrandt Comm. SD, AEA 5
Sch. Sys. Enr. Code 2
Supt. – Robert Raymer, 505 ELM ST   50585
Sioux Rapids-Rembrandt MS, 505 ELM ST   50585
  Morris Johnson, prin.
Other Schools – See Rembrandt

Slater, Story Co., Pop. Code 4
Ballard Comm. SD, AEA 11
Supt. – See Huxley
ES, 505 LINN   50244 – Daniel Lawler, prin.

Sloan, Woodbury Co., Pop. Code 3
Westwood Comm. SD, AEA 12
Sch. Sys. Enr. Code 3
Supt. – D. N. Hoffman   51055
Westwood ES   51055 – Robert Jones, prin.

Solon, Johnson Co., Pop. Code 3
Solon Comm. SD, AEA 10
Sch. Sys. Enr. Code 3
Supt. – Kirk Rentschler, 403 S IOWA   52333
ES   50173 – Virginia Clark, prin.

Spencer, Clay Co., Pop. Code 7
Spencer Comm. SD, AEA 3
Sch. Sys. Enr. Code 4
Supt. – Joe Graff, 800 E 3RD ST   51301
MS, 104 E 4TH ST   51301 – Tom Conley, prin.
Fairview Park ES, E 16TH ST & 5TH AVE E   51301
  Millard De Gooyer, prin.
Jefferson ES, 411 E 10TH ST   51301
  Millard De Gooyer, prin.
Johnson ES, 724 W 9TH ST   51301
  George Whitworth, prin.
Lincoln ES, 312 W 4TH ST   51301
  George Kruger, prin.
Reynolds ES, 216 6TH AVE E   51301
  George Whitworth, prin.

Sacred Heart School
  600 SACRED HEART COURT   51301

Spirit Lake, Dickinson Co., Pop. Code 5
Spirit Lake Comm. SD, AEA 3
Sch. Sys. Enr. Code 4
Supt. – H. A. Overmann, P O BOX D   51360
JHS, 800 20TH ST   51360
  Harold Overmann, prin.
ES, 2800 HILL AVE   51360 – Dick Nervig, prin.

Springville, Linn Co., Pop. Code 4
Springville Comm. SD, AEA 10
Sch. Sys. Enr. Code 3
Supt. – Gary Biles   52336
ES   52336 – Stephen Auen, prin.

Stacyville, Mitchell Co., Pop. Code 3

Visitation ES   50476

Stanton, Montgomery Co., Pop. Code 3
Stanton Comm. SD, AEA 14
Sch. Sys. Enr. Code 2
Supt. – Judson Ashley   51573
ES   51573 – Judson Ashley, prin.

Stanwood, Cedar Co., Pop. Code 3
Lincoln Comm. SD, AEA 10
Sch. Sys. Enr. Code 3
Supt. – Donald Lamm, P O BOX 247   52337
Other Schools – See Mechanicsville

State Center, Marshall Co., Pop. Code 4
West Marshall Comm. SD, AEA 6
Sch. Sys. Enr. Code 3
Supt. – Jerry Nichols   50247
West Marshall MS   50247 – William Grimes, prin.
ES   50247 – William Grimes, prin.

Steamboat Rock, Hardin Co., Pop. Code 2
Steamboat Rock Comm. SD
Sch. Sys. Enr. Code 2
Supt. – Neil Okones   50672
ES, P O BOX 128   50672 – Robert Hutchcroft, prin.

Stockport, Van Buren Co., Pop. Code 2
Van Buren Comm. SD, AEA 15
Supt. – See Keosauqua
ES   52431 – Fred Parsons, prin.

Storm Lake, Buena Vista Co., Pop. Code 6
Storm Lake Comm. SD, AEA 5
Sch. Sys. Enr. Code 4
Supt. – (—), 419 LAKE AVE   50588
JHS, 310 CAYUGA ST   50588 – Ralph Welch, prin.
East ES, 930 E 5TH ST   50588 – Jack Kooker, prin.
North ES, 301 E 7TH ST   50588
  Edward Rude, prin.
South ES, 210 E 3RD ST   50588
  Edward Rude, prin.
West ES, 1001 W 6TH ST   50588
  Jack Kooker, prin.

St. Mary ES, 312 SENECA ST   50588

Story City, Story Co., Pop. Code 5
Roland-Story Comm. SD, AEA 11
Sch. Sys. Enr. Code 3
Supt. – Dale W. Henricks, 1009 STORY ST   50248
Other Schools – See Roland

Stratford, Hamilton Co., Pop. Code 3
Stratford Comm. SD
Sch. Sys. Enr. Code 2
Supt. – Wayne Larson   50249
ES   50249 – Wayne Larson, prin.

Strawberry Point, Clayton Co., Pop. Code 4
Starmont Comm. SD, AEA 1
Sch. Sys. Enr. Code 3
Supt. – Richard Johns, P O BOX 40   52076
Starmont ES, P O BOX 39   52076
  Dennis Coon, prin.
Other Schools – See Lamont

Stuart, Guthrie Co., Pop. Code 4
Stuart-Menlo Comm. SD, AEA 11
Sch. Sys. Enr. Code 3
Supt. – Larry Nulph, N 2ND & MAIN   50250
Stuart-Menlo MS   50250 – Mark Becker, prin.
Other Schools – See Menlo

Sully, Jasper Co., Pop. Code 3
Lynnville-Sully Comm. SD, AEA 11
Sch. Sys. Enr. Code 3
Supt. – Randall Betz   50251
Lynville-Sully MS   50251 – David Walkup, prin.
Lynnville-Sully ES   50251 – Robert Sward, prin.

Sully Christian School   50251

Sumner, Bremer Co., Pop. Code 4
Sumner Comm. SD, AEA 7
Sch. Sys. Enr. Code 3
Supt. – Don Miller, 300 W 4TH ST   50674
JHS, 300 W 4TH ST   50674 – Darwin Propes, prin.
Durant ES, 601 W 5TH ST   50674
  James Lahmann, prin.

Sutherland, O'Brien Co., Pop. Code 3
Sutherland Comm. SD, AEA 4
Sch. Sys. Enr. Code 2
Supt. – William Brandt   51058
ES   51058 – Lawrence Jaske, prin.

Swea City, Kossuth Co., Pop. Code 3
North Kossuth Comm. SD, AEA 3
Sch. Sys. Enr. Code 2
Supt. – Robert Pilcher   50590
North Kossuth MS   50590 – Sara Pinion, prin.
North Kossuth ES   50590 – Sara Pinion, prin.

Tabor, Fremont Co., Pop. Code 4
Fremont-Mills Comm. SD, AEA 13
Sch. Sys. Enr. Code 3
Supt. – Robert Abbott   51653
Fremont-Mills ES, P O BOX 310   51653
  Lowell Ranck, prin.

Tama, Tama Co., Pop. Code 5
South Tama Co. Comm. SD, AEA 6
Sch. Sys. Enr. Code 4
Supt. – James Austin, 1702 HARDING ST   52339
IS, 215 W 9TH ST   52339 – (—), prin.
PS, 806 STATE ST   52339 – John Foster, prin.
Other Schools – See Chelsea, Montour, Toledo

Templeton, Carroll Co., Pop. Code 2

Holy Trinity Parochial School   51463

Terril, Dickinson Co., Pop. Code 2
Terril Comm. SD, AEA 3
Sch. Sys. Enr. Code 2
Supt. – Rodger Ritchie   51364
ES   51364 – Rodger Ritchie, prin.

Thompson, Winnebago Co., Pop. Code 3
Thompson Comm. SD, AEA 2
Sch. Sys. Enr. Code 2
Supt. – C. R. Adams   50478
ES   50478 – Chuck Block, prin.

Thornburg, Keokuk Co., Pop. Code 2
Tri-County Comm. SD, AEA 15
Sch. Sys. Enr. Code 2
Supt. – Richard Corrick   50255
Tri-County JHS   50255 – Max Wolf, prin.
MS   50255 – Richard Corrick, prin.
Other Schools – See Keswick

Thornton, Cerro Gordo Co., Pop. Code 2
Meservey-Thornton Comm. SD, AEA 2
Sch. Sys. Enr. Code 2
Supt. – Leroy Scharnhorst   50479
Meservey-Thornton MS, 212 ELM   50479
  Leroy Scharnhorst, prin.
Meservey-Thornton ES   50479
  Leroy Scharnhorst, prin.

Tipton, Cedar Co., Pop. Code 5
Tipton Comm. SD, AEA 10
Sch. Sys. Enr. Code 3
Supt. – W. Diedrichsen, 400 E 6TH ST   52772
ES, 400 E 6TH ST   52772
  Richard Grimoskas, prin.

Titonka, Kossuth Co., Pop. Code 3
Titonka Cons. SD, AEA 3
Sch. Sys. Enr. Code 2
Supt. – Gene Fokken, P O BOX A-H   50480
ES, P O BOX 287T   50480 – Jeriene Sleper, prin.

Toddville, Linn Co.
Alburnett Comm. SD, AEA 10
Supt. – See Alburnett
ES   52341 – Roland Krouse, prin.

Toledo, Tama Co., Pop. Code 4
South Tama Co. Comm. SD, AEA 6
Supt. – See Tama
South Tama Co. MS, 201 S GREEN ST   52342
  Les Koch, prin.

Traer, Tama Co., Pop. Code 4
North Tama Co. Comm. SD, AEA 7
Sch. Sys. Enr. Code 3
Supt. – Gary Croskrey, 605 WALNUT ST 50675
ES, 605 WALNUT ST 50675
Stephen Foster, prin.

Treynor, Pottawattamie Co., Pop. Code 3
Treynor Comm. SD, AEA 13
Sch. Sys. Enr. Code 2
Supt. – L. L. Haack 51575
ES 51575 – Keith Lambertsen, prin.

Tripoli, Bremer Co., Pop. Code 4
Tripoli Comm. SD, AEA 7
Sch. Sys. Enr. Code 2
Supt. – Dale Kanack 50676
ES 50676 – Dale Kanack, prin.

Troy Mills, Linn Co.
North Linn Comm. SD, AEA 10
Supt. – See Coggon
North Linn JHS 52344 – Gary Pillman, prin.

Truro, Madison Co., Pop. Code 2
Interstate 35 Comm. SD, AEA 11
Sch. Sys. Enr. Code 3
Supt. – Don Brichacek, P O BOX 98 50257
Other Schools – See New Virginia, Saint Charles

Underwood, Pottawattamie Co., Pop. Code 2
Underwood Comm. SD, AEA 13
Sch. Sys. Enr. Code 3
Supt. – Robert Eastman, P O BOX 130 51576
JHS, P O BOX 130 51576 – (—), prin.
ES 51576 – Paul Charest, prin.

Union, Hardin Co., Pop. Code 3
Union-Whitten Comm. SD
Sch. Sys. Enr. Code 2
Supt. – John Arnett 50258
Union-Whitten ES 50258 – Diane Petty, prin.

Urbana, Benton Co., Pop. Code 3
Urbana Comm. SD, AEA 10
Sch. Sys. Enr. Code 2
Supt. – Richard Whitehead, P O BOX 246 52345
ES, P O BOX 246 52345 – (—), prin.

Urbandale, Polk Co., Pop. Code 7
Urbandale Comm. SD, AEA 11
Sch. Sys. Enr. Code 5
Supt. – John Cox, 7101 AIRLINE AVE 50322
MS, 7701 AURORA AVE 50322 – Steve Fey, prin.
Jensen ES, 6301 AURORA AVE 50322
Bruce Christensen, prin.
Karen Acres ES, 3500 74TH ST 50322
Bruce Christensen, prin.
Olmsted ES, 7110 PRAIRIE AVE 50322
Larry Jablonski, prin.
Rolling Green ES, 8100 AIRLINE AVE 50322
Harry Heiligenthal, prin.

Ute, Monona Co., Pop. Code 2
Charter Oak-Ute Comm. SD, AEA 12
Supt. – See Charter Oak
Charter Oak-Ute ES 51060 – Donald Gries, prin.

Vail, Crawford Co., Pop. Code 2
AR-WE-VA Comm. SD, AEA 12
Supt. – See Westside
ES 51465 – Bob Gress, prin.

Van Horne, Benton Co., Pop. Code 3
Benton Comm. SD, AEA 10
Sch. Sys. Enr. Code 4
Supt. – Leland Wise 52346
Benton Comm. MS 52346 – Gary Zittergruen, prin.
ES 52366 – Gary Zittergruen, prin.
Other Schools – See Atkins, Keystone

Van Meter, Dallas Co., Pop. Code 3
Van Meter Comm. SD, AEA 11
Sch. Sys. Enr. Code 2
Supt. – Phil Rink, P O BOX 257 50261
ES, 520 FIRST AVE 50261 – Philip Rink, prin.

Ventura, Cerro Gordo Co., Pop. Code 3
Ventura Comm. SD, AEA 2
Sch. Sys. Enr. Code 2
Supt. – G. B. Schichtl 50482
ES 50482 – Gary Schichtl, prin.

Victor, Iowa Co., Pop. Code 4
H-L-V Comm. SD, AEA 10
Sch. Sys. Enr. Code 2
Supt. – Wm. Lynch, P O BOX B 52347
H-L-V ES, P O BOX B 52347 – June Hand, prin.

Villisca, Montgomery Co., Pop. Code 4
Villisca Comm. SD, AEA 14
Sch. Sys. Enr. Code 2
Supt. – Robert Busch 50864
Enarson ES, CENTRAL AVE 50864
Robert Busch, prin.

Vinton, Benton Co., Pop. Code 6
Vinton Comm. SD, AEA 10
Sch. Sys. Enr. Code 4
Supt. – E. J. Hidlebaugh, 503 3RD AVE 52349
Tilford JHS, 308 E 13TH ST 52349
Ronald Bryan, prin.
East ES, 510 4TH AVE 52349
Joan Sainsbury, prin.
Lincoln MS, 503 3RD AVE 52349
Donna Lindsey, prin.
West ES, 516 W 9TH ST 52349
Ronald Baldwin, prin.

Viola, Linn Co.
Anamosa Comm. SD, AEA 10
Supt. – See Anamosa
ES 52350 – (—), prin.

Volga, Clayton Co., Pop. Code 2
Central Comm. SD, AEA 1
Supt. – See Elkader
MS 52077 – William McHugh, Jr., prin.

Walcott, Scott Co., Pop. Code 4
Davenport Comm. SD, AEA 9
Supt. – See Davenport
ES, 545 E JAMES ST 52773 – Dellmer Sly, prin.

Walker, Linn Co., Pop. Code 3
North Linn Comm. SD, AEA 10
Supt. – See Coggon
ES 52352 – John Mathre, prin.

Wall Lake, Sac Co., Pop. Code 3
Wall Lake Comm. SD, AEA 5
Sch. Sys. Enr. Code 2
Supt. – Leroy Fugitt, 206 BOYER ST 51466
ES 51466 – Leroy Fugitt, prin.

Walnut, Pottawattamie Co., Pop. Code 3
Walnut Comm. SD, AEA 13
Sch. Sys. Enr. Code 2
Supt. – Warren Winterhof 51577
ES 51577 – Warren Winterhof, prin.

Wapello, Louisa Co., Pop. Code 4
Wapello Comm. SD, AEA 16
Sch. Sys. Enr. Code 3
Supt. – Francis Davis, 445 N CEDAR ST 52653
JHS, CEDAR ST 52653 – Wm. Denning, prin.
ES, CEDAR ST 52653 – Larry Dossett, prin.

Washington, Washington Co., Pop. Code 6
Washington Comm. SD, AEA 10
Sch. Sys. Enr. Code 4
Supt. – Thomas Engler, P O BOX 926 52353
Lincoln MS, 606 S 4TH AVE 52353
John Sproule, prin.
Stewart ES, 821 N 4TH AVE 52353
Gary Murphy, prin.

St. James School, 616 W 2ND ST 52353

Washta, Cherokee Co.
Willow Comm. SD, AEA 12
Sch. Sys. Enr. Code 2
Supt. – Leonard Grasso 51061
Willow ES 51061 – Cheryl Spear, prin.

Waterloo, Black Hawk Co., Pop. Code 8
Waterloo Comm. SD, AEA 7
Sch. Sys. Enr. Code 7
Supt. – Donald Hanson
1516 WASHINGTON ST 50702
Central IS, 1350 KATOSKI DR 50701
Fred Stewart, prin.
Hoover IS, 630 HILLCREST ROAD 50701
Nancy Zimmerman, prin.
Logan IS, 1515 LOGAN AVE 50703
Donald Duggan, prin.
West IS, 1115 W 5TH ST 50702
Richard Brudevold, prin.
Black Hawk ES, 1700 DOWNING AVE 50701
Gary Murtinger, prin.
Edison ES, 800 ROCK ISLAND AVE 50701
Lucille Lee, prin.
Elk Run ES, MC COY ROAD 50707
Maurice Parker, prin.
Grant ES, 1223 MOBILE ST 50703
Carol Murtinger, prin.
Irving ES, 728 HAWTHORNE AVE 50702
Betty Cline, prin.
Kingsley ES, 201 SUNSET ROAD 50701
John Lesyshen, prin.
Kittrell ES, 1520 EASTON AVE 50702
Jack Hylton, prin.
Lincoln ES, PARKER & BURTON 50703
Jack Hanson, prin.
Longfellow ES, 416 LINCOLN ST 50703
James Martin, prin.
Lowell ES, 1628 WASHINGTON ST 50702
William Dodd, prin.
McKinstry ES, 1408 INDEPENDENCE AVE 50703
Robert Diller, prin.
Orange ES, 6028 KIMBALL AVE 50701
Arthur Trebon, prin.
Roosevelt ES, 200 E ARLINGTON ST 50703
Helen Walton, prin.
Other Schools – See Evansdale

Blessed Sacrament School
600 STEPHEN AVE 50701
Immanuel Lutheran School
130 WALNUT ST 50703
Sacred Heart School, 620 W 5TH ST 50702
St. Edward's School, 139 E MITCHELL AVE 50702
St. John-St. Nichols School
1729 MULBERRY ST 50703
St. Mary's School, 127 E PARKER ST 50703
Walnut Ridge Baptist Academy
1307 W RIDGEWAY AVE 50701

Waterville, Allamakee Co., Pop. Code 2
Allamakee Comm. SD, AEA 1
Supt. – See Waukon
ES 52170 – Kenneth West, prin.

Waukee, Dallas Co., Pop. Code 4
Waukee Comm. SD, AEA 11
Sch. Sys. Enr. Code 3
Supt. – Clair E. Eason 50263
MS, 4TH & LOCUST 50263 – James Nass, prin.
ES, 4TH & LOCUST 50263 – Jim Ford, prin.

Waukon, Allamakee Co., Pop. Code 5
Allamakee Comm. SD, AEA 1
Sch. Sys. Enr. Code 4
Supt. – Joe Schmitz, 1105 3RD AVE NW 52172
East Campus MS, 107 6TH ST NW 52172
Harry Lamphier, prin.
West Campus ES, 1005 3RD AVE N W 52172
Richard Moody, prin.
Other Schools – See Waterville

St. Patrick School, 200 2ND ST SW 52172

Waverly, Bremer Co., Pop. Code 6
Waverly-Shell Rock Comm. SD, AEA 7
Sch. Sys. Enr. Code 4
Supt. – Michael Book, 215 3RD ST NW 50677
Waverly-Shell Rock JHS, 215 3RD ST NW 50677
James McGrew, prin.
Carey ES, THIRD ST NW 50677
Nathan Frazee, prin.
Irving MS, 213 6TH ST SW 50677
Constance Schrupp, prin.
Southeast ES, 714 CHERRY ST 50677
Richard Jensen, prin.
West Cedar ES, FOURTEENTH ST NW 50677
Nathan Frazee, prin.
Other Schools – See Shell Rock

St. Paul's Lutheran School
112 2ND AVE NW 50677

Wayland, Henry Co., Pop. Code 3
Waco Comm. SD, AEA 16
Sch. Sys. Enr. Code 3
Supt. – Laverne Hueholt, MAIN ST 52654
Other Schools – See Crawfordsville

Webster City, Hamilton Co., Pop. Code 6
Webster City Comm. SD, AEA 5
Sch. Sys. Enr. Code 4
Supt. – William Garner, 304 PROSPECT ST 50595
Elm Park ES, 705 ELM ST 50595
Delma McLaughlin, prin.
Hilltop PS, 915 HIGH ST 50595
Delma McLaughlin, prin.
Lawn Hill ES, 825 BEACH AVE 50595
Delma McLaughlin, prin.
Lincoln MS, 1100 DES MOINES ST 50595
Delma McLaughlin, prin.
Pleasant View ES, 1901 WILLSON AVE 50595
Kenneth Harfst, prin.
Riverview ES, 705 ODELL ST 50595
Kenneth Harfst, prin.
Sunset Heights ES, 1101 BOONE ST 50595
Kenneth Harfst, prin.

St. Thomas Aquinas School
624 DUBUQUE ST 50595

Weldon, Decator Co., Pop. Code 2
Clarke Comm. SD, AEA 14
Supt. – See Osceola
ES 50264 – Joyce Mason, prin.

Wellman, Washington Co., Pop. Code 4
Mid-Prairie Comm. SD, AEA 10
Sch. Sys. Enr. Code 4
Supt. – Rose Dillard, HIGHWAY 22 52356
ES, 800 SIXTH AVE 52356 – Edwin Miller, prin.
Other Schools – See Kalona

Wellsburg, Grundy Co., Pop. Code 3
Wellsburg Comm. SD, AEA 6
Sch. Sys. Enr. Code 2
Supt. – Neil Okones, 609 S MONROE 50680
ES, 609 S MONROE 50680 – Neil Okones, prin.

Welton, Clinton Co., Pop. Code 2
Central Clinton Comm. SD, AEA 9
Supt. – See De Witt
ES 52774 – Leslie Huddley, prin.

West Bend, Palo Alto Co., Pop. Code 3
West Bend Comm. SD, AEA 3
Sch. Sys. Enr. Code 2
Supt. – Stephen Litts 50597
ES 50597 – Bryce Cadbury, prin.

St. Peter & Paul School, P O BOX 349 50597

West Branch, Cedar Co., Pop. Code 4
West Branch Comm. SD, AEA 10
Sch. Sys. Enr. Code 3
Supt. – James Behle, P O BOX 637 52358
MS, P O BOX 637 52358 – Jean Gerig, prin.
Hoover ES, P O BOX 637 52358 – Jean Gerig, prin.

West Burlington, Des Moines Co., Pop. Code 5
West Burlington ISD, AEA 16
Sch. Sys. Enr. Code 2
Supt. – James Huelskamp
408 VAN WEISS BLVD 52655
MS, 211 RAMSEY ST 52655
Robert Waymen, prin.
ES, 545 RAMSEY ST 52655
Robert Wayman, prin.

West Des Moines, Polk Co., Pop. Code 7
West Des Moines Comm. SD, AEA 11
Sch. Sys. Enr. Code 6
Supt. – D. L. Grabinski, 1101 5TH ST   50265
Stilwell JHS, 16TH & VINE   50265
  Les Aasheim, prin.
Clegg Park ES, 1020 8TH ST   50265
  Vernon Hart, prin.
Crossroads Park ES, 1050 50TH ST   50265
  Doyle Miller, prin.
Fair Meadows ES, 807 23RD ST   50265
  Beverly Roach, prin.
Mathes ES, 14TH & VINE   50265
  Eugene Meier, prin.
Phenix ES, 415 7TH ST   50265
  Debra Van Gorp, prin.
Western Hills ES, 600 39TH ST   50265
  Nancy Werner, prin.
Other Schools – See Des Moines

Sacred Heart School, 708 16TH ST   50265

West Liberty, Muscatine Co., Pop. Code 5
West Liberty Comm. SD, AEA 9
Sch. Sys. Enr. Code 4
Supt. – Lynn Richardson, 823 N ELM ST   52776
MS, 806 N MILLER ST   52776 – Dick Cornick, prin.
West ES, 111 W 7TH ST   52776
  Lewis Morrison, prin.

Westside, Crawford Co., Pop. Code 2
AR-WE-VA Comm. SD, AEA 12
Sch. Sys. Enr. Code 2
Supt. – Robert W. Neilsen   51467
Other Schools – See Arcadia, Vail

West Union, Fayette Co., Pop. Code 5
North Fayette County Comm. SD, AEA 1
Sch. Sys. Enr. Code 4
Supt. – Donald Mueller, 105 MAIN ST   52175
ES, 400 N PINE ST   52175 – Garry Kuhens, prin.
Other Schools – See Fayette, Hawkeye

Whiting, Monona Co., Pop. Code 3
Whiting Comm. SD, AEA 12
Sch. Sys. Enr. Code 2
Supt. – Dwight Pierson   51063
ES   51052 – Dwight Pierson, prin.

Whittemore, Kossuth Co., Pop. Code 3

St. Michael's ES, 701 3RD ST   50598

Williamsburg, Iowa Co., Pop. Code 4
Williamsburg Comm. SD, AEA 10
Sch. Sys. Enr. Code 3
Supt. – Dale Pierce, 810 W WALNUT   52361
ES, 501 HIGHLAND   52361 – Terry Curtis, prin.
Other Schools – See Parnell

Lutheran Inter-Parish School, 804 COURT   52361

Williamson, Lucas Co., Pop. Code 2
Chariton Comm. SD, AEA 15
Supt. – See Chariton
ES   50272 – Loren Burkhalter, prin.

Wilton, Muscatine Co., Pop. Code 5
Wilton Comm. SD, AEA 9
Sch. Sys. Enr. Code 3
Supt. – Philip Wainwright
  210 W WATE ST   52778
ES, 213 E 6TH ST   52778 – Susan Garton, prin.

Zion Lutheran School
  117 E PRAIRIE STREET   52778

Winfield, Henry Co., Pop. Code 4
Winfield-Mt. Union Comm. SD, AEA 16
Sch. Sys. Enr. Code 2
Supt. – John Roederer   52659
ES   52644 – David Christensen, prin.

Winterset, Madison Co., Pop. Code 5
Winterset Comm. SD, AEA 11
Sch. Sys. Enr. Code 4
Supt. – Kenneth J. Bassett
  302 W SOUTH ST   50273
MS, 110 W WASHINGTON ST   50273
  Molly Clark, prin.
ES, 404 S 2ND AVE   50273 – David Elgin, prin.

Winthrop, Buchanan Co., Pop. Code 3
East Buchanan Comm. SD, AEA 7
Sch. Sys. Enr. Code 3
Supt. – Wayne Burk   50682
East Buchanan JHS   50682 – Dale Barnhill, prin.

East Buchanan Central ES   50682
  James Zimmerman, prin.
Other Schools – See Quasqueton

Woden, Hancock Co., Pop. Code 4
Woden-Crystal Lake Comm. SD
Sch. Sys. Enr. Code 2
Supt. – Don West, P O BOX 135   50484
ES, P O BOX 135   50484 – (—), prin.

Woodbine, Harrison Co., Pop. Code 4
Woodbine Comm. SD, AEA 13
Sch. Sys. Enr. Code 3
Supt. – David F. Lynch, 501 WEARE ST   51579
ES, 5TH & WEARE   51579 – Phil Lubbers, prin.

Woodward, Dallas Co., Pop. Code 4
Woodward-Granger Comm. SD, AEA 11
Sch. Sys. Enr. Code 3
Supt. – D. E. Weeks, W 3RD ST   50276
ES, WEST 3RD ST   50276
  Vincent Verlengia, prin.
Other Schools – See Granger

Worthington, Dubuque Co., Pop. Code 2

St. Paul School   52078

Wyoming, Jones Co., Pop. Code 3
Midland Comm. SD, AEA 10
Sch. Sys. Enr. Code 2
Supt. – M. L. McDonald   52362
MS   52362 – Robert Baxter, prin.
Other Schools – See Onslow

Yale, Guthrie Co., Pop. Code 2
Yale-Jamaica-Bagley Comm. SD, AEA 11
Supt. – See Bagley
ES, P O BOX 306   50277 – Otto Faaborg, prin.

Yarmouth, Des Moines Co.
Mediapolis Comm. SD, AEA 16
Supt. – See Mediapolis
ES   52660 – James Tiedemann, prin.

Zearing, Story Co., Pop. Code 3
Nesco Comm. SD, AEA 11
Supt. – See Mc Callsburg
Nesco MS   50278 – Duane Newton, prin.

KANSAS

STATE DEPARTMENT OF EDUCATION
Kansas State Education Building
120 E. 10th St., Topeka 66612
(913) 296-3201

Commissioner of Education	Dr. Lee Droegemueller
Assistant Commissioner Educational Services	Dr. Sharon Freden
Deputy Commissioner Financial Services & Operations	Dale Dennis
Assistant Commissioner Community Colleges & Vocational Education	Ferman Marsh

STATE BOARD OF EDUCATION
Bill Musick, *Chairperson*   508 E. 2nd, Minneapolis   67467

STATE BOARD OF REGENTS
Stanley Koplik, *Executive Director*   400 S.W. 8th #609, Topeka   66603

PUBLIC, PRIVATE, AND PAROCHIAL ELEMENTARY SCHOOLS

Abilene, Dickinson Co., Pop. Code 6
Abilene USD 435
Sch. Sys. Enr. Code 4
Supt. – William Neuenwander
  1101 N MULBERRY ST   67410
Mid S, 500 NW 14TH ST   67410
  Stephen Groninga, prin.
Garfield ES, 300 NW 7TH ST   67410
  W. Goldsmith, prin.
Kennedy ES, 1501 N KUNEY ST   67410
  David Bond, prin.
McKinley ES, 112 N ROGERS ST   67410
  Robert Sorensen, prin.

Chapman USD 473
Supt. – See Chapman
Blue Ridge ES, RURAL ROUTE 05   67410
  Tony Frieze, prin.

Rural Center ES, RURAL ROUTE 02   67410
  Tony Frieze, prin.

St. Andrew's School, 301 S BUCKEYE AVE   67410

Admire, Lyon Co., Pop. Code 2
North Lyon Co. USD 251
Supt. – See Americus
ES   66830 – Dorothy Ricketts, prin.

Agra, Phillips Co., Pop. Code 2
Eastern Hts. USD 324
Sch. Sys. Enr. Code 2
Supt. – Earl McGee, P O BOX 38   67621
Other Schools – See Kirwin

Albert, Barton Co., Pop. Code 2
Otis-Bison USD 403
Sch. Sys. Enr. Code 2
Supt. – Ira Frank Randel
  RURAL ROUTE 01   67511
Other Schools – See Bison, Otis, Timken

Alden, Rice Co., Pop. Code 2
Sterling USD 376
Supt. – See Sterling
MS, P O BOX 128   67512 – Ron Claussen, prin.

Alma, Wabaunsee Co., Pop. Code 3
Mill Creek Valley USD 329
Sch. Sys. Enr. Code 3
Supt. – John Hetlinger, P O BOX 157   66401
ES   66401 – Lesa Frantz, prin.
Other Schools – See Maple Hill, Paxico

St. John Lutheran School, P O BOX 368   66401

Almena, Norton Co., Pop. Code 3
Northern Valley USD 212
Sch. Sys. Enr. Code 2
Supt. – LeeRoy Schuckman
512 W BRYANT   67622
ES   67622 – Dwight Vallin, prin.
Other Schools – See Long Island

Altamont, Labette Co., Pop. Code 4
Labette Co. USD 506
Sch. Sys. Enr. Code 4
Supt. – L. Curran, P O BOX 188   67330
ES, P O BOX 306   67330 – Jack Blackwell, prin.
Other Schools – See Bartlett, Edna, Mound Valley,
Parsons

Alta Vista, Wabaunsee Co., Pop. Code 2
Council Grove USD 417
Supt. – See Council Grove
ES   66834 – S. Elliott, prin.

Alton, Osborne Co., Pop. Code 2
Osborne Co. USD 392
Supt. – See Osborne
Alton-Osborne JHS   67623 – Larry Bernard, prin.

Altoona, Wilson Co., Pop. Code 3
Altoona-Midway USD 387
Supt. – See Buffalo
Altoona-Midway MS   66710
Frank Kennedy, prin.
ES   66710 – Frank Kennedy, prin.
Midway ES   66717 -- Owen Modeland, prin.

Americus, Lyon Co., Pop. Code 3
North Lyon Co. USD 251
Sch. Sys. Enr. Code 3
Supt. – Marvin Selby, P O BOX 186   66835
ES   66835 – Bob Commons, prin.
Other Schools – See Admire, Reading

Andale, Sedgwick Co., Pop. Code 3
Renwick USD 267
Sch. Sys. Enr. Code 4
Supt. – Richard Flores, P O BOX 68   67001
ES, P O BOX 58   67001 – Mike Young, prin.
Other Schools – See Colwich, Garden Plain, Mount
Hope

Andover, Butler Co., Pop. Code 5
Andover USD 385
Sch. Sys. Enr. Code 4
Supt. – Dr. Harry Austin, P O BOX 248   67002
MS, 1747 N ANDOVER ROAD   67002
Robert Palmer, prin.
ES, 1411 N MAIN   67002 – Robert Martin, prin.

Anthony, Harper Co., Pop. Code 5
Anthony-Harper USD 361
Sch. Sys. Enr. Code 4
Supt. – Dennis Versch
124 N JENNINGS AVE   67003
ES, 215 S SPRINGFIELD AVE   67003
Gary Gerber, prin.
Harper ES, 1317 WALNUT   67058
James Williams, prin.

Argonia, Sumner Co., Pop. Code 3
Argonia USD 359
Sch. Sys. Enr. Code 2
Supt. – William Muckenthaler, P O BOX 7   67004
ES   67004 – Harry Cline, prin.

Arkansas City, Cowley Co., Pop. Code 7
Arkansas City USD 470
Sch. Sys. Enr. Code 5
Supt. – Dr. Leonard Steinle
119 W WASHINGTON AVE   67005
MS, 400 E KANSAS AVE   67005
Blaine Babb, prin.
1 X L ES, RURAL ROUTE 04   67005
William Morgan, prin.
Adams ES, 1201 N 10TH ST   67005
William Morgan, prin.
C-4 ES, RURAL ROUTE 03   67005
Dwain Stewart, prin.
Jefferson ES, 131 E OSAGE AVE   67005
Guy Stamps, prin.
Lincoln ES, 301 E MADISON AVE   67005
Guy Stamps, prin.
Pershing ES, 1100 N 2ND ST   67005
Dwain Stewart, prin.
Roosevelt ES, 300 N B ST   67005
Mary Hooley, prin.
Willard ES, 201 N 4TH ST   67005
Mary Hooley, prin.

Sacred Heart ES, 312 S B ST   67005

Arlington, Reno Co., Pop. Code 3
Fairfield USD 310
Supt. – See Langdon
ES   67514 – Robert Hopkins, prin.

Arma, Crawford Co., Pop. Code 4
Northeast USD 246
Sch. Sys. Enr. Code 3
Supt. – Bill Biggs, P O BOX 669   66712
ES   66712 – Billy Billiard, prin.

Ashland, Clark Co., Pop. Code 4
Ashland USD 220
Sch. Sys. Enr. Code 2
Supt. – Dale Moody, P O BOX 187   67831
ES   67831 – Gilbert Park, prin.

Atchison, Atchison Co., Pop. Code 7
Atchison USD 409
Sch. Sys. Enr. Code 4
Supt. – Michael Pomarico
605 KANSAS AVE   66002
Central ES, 215 N 8TH ST   66002
Charles Gartenmayer, prin.
Franklin ES, 1326 KANSAS AVE   66002
Charles Gartenmayer, prin.
Martin East ES, 507 DIVISION ST   66002
Royal Shults, prin.
Martin West MS, 810 DIVISION ST   66002
Royal Shults, prin.
Washington ES, 508 R ST   66002 – Ivan Jones, prin.

Atchison Catholic ES, 201 DIVISION ST   66002
Trinity Lutheran ES, 609 N 8TH ST   66002

Atlanta, Crowley Co., Pop. Code 2
Central USD 462
Supt. – See Burden
Central ES   67008 – Joe Deweese, prin.

Attica, Harper Co., Pop. Code 3
Attica USD 511
Sch. Sys. Enr. Code 2
Supt. – James Wilson   67009
Puls ES   67009 – Dale Miller, prin.

Atwood, Rawlins Co., Pop. Code 4
Atwood USD 318
Sch. Sys. Enr. Code 2
Supt. – Dr. Theador Jones, 406 MAIN ST   67730
ES, 205 N 4TH   67730 – Michael Specht, prin.

Auburn, Shawnee Co., Pop. Code 3
Auburn-Washburn USD 437
Supt. – See Topeka
MS   66402 – Marcia Bone, prin.
ES   66402 – Virginia Ary, prin.
Pauline Central ES
6625 SW WESTVIEW ROAD   66619
Lewis Stookey, prin.

Augusta, Butler Co., Pop. Code 6
Augusta USD 402
Sch. Sys. Enr. Code 4
Supt. – Dr. Lyle Boyles, 301 W KELLY AVE   67010
MS, 1003 STATE ST   67010
Robert McCalla, prin.
Garfield ES, OSAGE & HIGH   67010
Terry Kidd, prin.
Lincoln ES, 1801 DEARBORN ST   67010
James Markos, prin.
Robinson ES, 1301 HELEN ST   67010
Mark Cleveland, prin.

Bluestem USD 205
Supt. – See Leon
Haverhill ES, RURAL ROUTE 02   67010
David Kohls, prin.

Axtell, Marshall Co., Pop. Code 2
Axtell USD 488
Sch. Sys. Enr. Code 2
Supt. – Demitry Evancho, P O BOX N   66403
ES   66403 – Don Day, prin.
Bern ES   66408 – Dallas Lee, prin.
Other Schools – See Summerfield

Baileyville, Nemaha Co., Pop. Code 2
Baileyville-St. Benedict USD 451
Sch. Sys. Enr. Code 2
Supt. – James Weixelman
301 NEMAHA ST   66404
Other Schools – See Seneca

Baldwin City, Douglas Co., Pop. Code 5
Baldwin City USD 348
Sch. Sys. Enr. Code 3
Supt. – Bert Hitchcock, P O BOX 67   66006
Baldwin MS, 8TH & CHAPEL   66006
Chryss Brunner, prin.
Baldwin ES, 8TH & CHAPEL   66006
Tom Mundinger, prin.
Marion Springs ES, RURAL ROUTE 01   66006
Gus Wegner, prin.
Vinland ES, RURAL ROUTE 03   66006
Gus Wegner, prin.

Barnes, Washington Co., Pop. Code 2
Barnes USD 223
Sch. Sys. Enr. Code 2
Supt. – Daryl Johnson, P O BOX 94   66933
Other Schools – See Hanover, Linn

Bartlett, Labette Co., Pop. Code 2
Labette Co. USD 506
Supt. – See Altamont
ES, P O BOX 4676   67332 – Robert Holtzman, prin.

Basehor, Leavenworth Co., Pop. Code 4
Basehor-Linwood USD 458
Sch. Sys. Enr. Code 4
Supt. – Charles Edmonds
2008 N 155TH ST   66007
ES, 15602 LEAVENWORTH ROAD   66007
Rich McDaneld, prin.
Other Schools – See Linwood

Baxter Springs, Cherokee Co., Pop. Code 5
Baxter Springs USD 508
Sch. Sys. Enr. Code 3
Supt. – James Harris
1520 CLEVELAND AVE   66713
MS, 1520 CLEVELAND AVE   66713
Gary Krokroskia, prin.

Central MS, 15TH & PARK   66713
Jack Shoemaker, prin.
Lincoln ES, 8TH & LINCOLN   66713
Robert Harper, prin.

Bazine, Ness Co., Pop. Code 2
Bazine USD 304
Sch. Sys. Enr. Code 2
Supt. – Jess Paul, P O BOX 218   67516
ES   67516 – Jess Paul, prin.

Beattie, Marhall Co., Pop. Code 2
Marysville USD 364
Supt. – See Marysville
ES   66406 – Robert Patterson, prin.
Lincoln ES, 405 N 4TH ST   66508
John Godfrey, prin.

Belle Plaine, Sumner Co., Pop. Code 4
Belle Plaine USD 357
Sch. Sys. Enr. Code 3
Supt. – W. Peterson, 719 N MAIN   67013
MS, 614 N MERCHANT   67013
Charles Bray, prin.
ES, 614 N MERCHANT   67013
Mary Bentley, prin.

Belleville, Republic Co., Pop. Code 5
Belleville USD 427
Sch. Sys. Enr. Code 3
Supt. – Dale Rawson, P O BOX 469   66935
West MS, P O BOX 469   66935 – Larry Cates, prin.
East ES, P O BOX 469   66935
Donald Westphal, prin.
Other Schools – See Munden

Beloit, Mitchell Co., Pop. Code 5
Beloit USD 273
Sch. Sys. Enr. Code 3
Supt. – John Bottom, P O BOX 547   67420
ES, 12TH & BELL   67420 – Ron Marozas, prin.

St. John's ES, 712 E MAIN ST   67420

Bennington, Ottawa Co., Pop. Code 3
Twin Valley USD 240
Sch. Sys. Enr. Code 2
Supt. – J. McClain, P O BOX 38   67422
ES   67422 – Bill Becker, prin.
Other Schools – See Tescott

Bentley, Sedgwick Co., Pop. Code 2
Halstead USD 440
Supt. – See Halstead
ES   67016 – Larry Hobbs, prin.

Benton, Butler Co., Pop. Code 3
Circle USD 375
Supt. – See Towanda
ES   67017 – Leslie Plunk, prin.

Berryton, Shawnee Co.
Shawnee Hts. USD 450
Supt. – See Tecumseh
ES, 2921 SE 69TH ST   66409
Howard Diacon, prin.

Big Bow, Johnson Co.
Stanton Co. USD 452
Supt. – See Johnson
ES   67832 – Larry Johnson, prin.

Bird City, Cheyenne Co., Pop. Code 3
Cheylin USD 103
Sch. Sys. Enr. Code 2
Supt. – Loyal Vincent, P O BOX 28   67731
Cheylin MS, P O BOX 107   67731
Keith Sanders, prin.
Other Schools – See McDonald

Bison, Rush Co., Pop. Code 2
Otis-Bison USD 403
Supt. – See Albert
Otis-Bison JHS   67520 – Jim Collins, prin.

Blue Mound, Linn Co., Pop. Code 2
Jayhawk USD 346
Supt. – See Mound City
ES   66010 – (—), prin.

Blue Rapids, Marshall Co., Pop. Code 4
Valley Hts. USD 498
Supt. – See Waterville
Valley Heights ES   66411 – Charles Steele, prin.

Bogue, Graham Co., Pop. Code 2
Hill City USD 281
Supt. – See Hill City
ES   67625 – Eugene Hamel, prin.

Bonner Springs, Wyandotte Co., Pop. Code 6
Bonner Springs USD 204
Sch. Sys. Enr. Code 4
Supt. – Timothy Rundus, P O BOX 435   66012
McDaneild ES, P O BOX 383   66012
Bryan Biles, prin.
Southwest MS, 212 S NECONI AVE   66012
Donald Bell, prin.
Other Schools – See Edwardsville

Sacred Heart ES, 216 ALLCUTT AVE   66012

Brewster, Thomas Co., Pop. Code 2
Brewster USD 314
Sch. Sys. Enr. Code 2
Supt. – Jean Lavid, P O BOX 220   67732
ES, P O BOX 220   67732 – Jean Lavid, prin.

Brookville, Saline Co., Pop. Code 2
Ell-Saline USD 307
Supt. – See Salina
Ell-Saline JHS 67425 – Bernard White, prin.
ES   67425 – Gaylene Youngberg, prin.

Bucklin, Ford Co., Pop. Code 3
Bucklin USD 459
Sch. Sys. Enr. Code 2
Supt. – Terry Marshall, P O BOX 8 67834
ES   67834 – John Jones, prin.

Bucyrus, Miami Co.
Louisburg USD 416
Supt. – See Louisburg
ES   66013 – Robert Austin, prin.

Buffalo, Wilson Co., Pop. Code 2
Altoona-Midway USD 387
Sch. Sys. Enr. Code 2
Supt. – James Jerome, RURAL ROUTE 01 66717
Other Schools – See Altoona

Buhler, Reno Co., Pop. Code 4
Buhler USD 313
Sch. Sys. Enr. Code 4
Supt. – Jack Parker, 122 N MAIN 67522
ES   67522 – John Geuy, prin.
Other Schools – See Hutchinson

Burden, Cowley Co., Pop. Code 3
Central USD 462
Sch. Sys. Enr. Code 2
Supt. – Dean McGrath, P O BOX 128 67019
Other Schools – See Atlanta, Grenola

Burdett, Pawnee Co., Pop. Code 2
Pawnee Heights USD 496
Supt. – See Rozel
Pawanee Heights West ES 67523
   John Bolan, prin.

Burlingame, Osage Co., Pop. Code 4
Burlingame USD 454
Sch. Sys. Enr. Code 2
Supt. – Steve Neely, 303 S DACOTAH ST 66413
Lincoln MS 66413 – Gary Schultz, prin.
Schuyler ES 66413 – Gary Schultz, prin.

Burlington, Coffey Co., Pop. Code 5
Burlington USD 244
Sch. Sys. Enr. Code 3
Supt. – Larry Clark, 219 N 3RD ST 66839
MS, 720 CROSS ST 66839 – Joseph Logan, prin.
PS, 7TH & NIAGARA 66839
   Dr. Fred LeMaster, prin.

Burns, Marion Co., Pop. Code 2
Peabody-Burns USD 398
Supt. – See Peabody
ES   66840 – Sue Anderson, prin.

Burr Oak, Jewell Co., Pop. Code 2
White Rock USD 104
Supt. – See Esbon
White Rock ES   66936 – Vern Minor, prin.

Burrton, Harvey Co., Pop. Code 3
Burrton USD 369
Sch. Sys. Enr. Code 2
Supt. – Emmett Hedges, P O BOX 356 67020
ES   67020 – Bernard Friesen, prin.

Caldwell, Sumner Co., Pop. Code 4
Caldwell USD 360
Sch. Sys. Enr. Code 2
Supt. – D. Monson, 21 N OSAGE ST 67022
ES   67022 – Terry McCloud, prin.

Caney, Montgomery Co., Pop. Code 4
Caney Valley USD 436
Sch. Sys. Enr. Code 3
Supt. – H. Howard, 109 W 4TH AVE 67333
Lincoln Memorial ES 67333
   Ted Holtzman, Jr., prin.

Canton, McPherson Co., Pop. Code 3
Canton-Galva USD 419
Sch. Sys. Enr. Code 2
Supt. – Donald Margreiter, P O BOX 317 67428
ES, P O BOX 275 67428 – Donald Margreiter, prin.
Other Schools – See Galva

Carbondale, Osage Co., Pop. Code 4
Santa Fe Trail USD 434
Sch. Sys. Enr. Code 4
Supt. – Dr. Clarence Hickman
   RURAL ROUTE 01 66414
ES 66414 – James Toburen, prin.
Other Schools – See Overbrook, Scranton

Cassoday, Butler Co., Pop. Code 2
Flinthills USD 492
Supt. – See Rosalia
ES   66842 – Carl Harvey, prin.

Catharine, Ellis Co.
Hays USD 489
Supt. – See Hays
ES   67627 – Ken Allen, prin.

Cawker City, Mitchell Co., Pop. Code 3
Waconda USD 272
Sch. Sys. Enr. Code 3
Supt. – Norman Baldwin, P O BOX 326 67430
ES   67430 – Dan Newman, prin.
Other Schools – See Downs, Glen Elder, Tipton

Cedar Vale, Chautauqua Co., Pop. Code 3
Cedar Vale USD 285
Sch. Sys. Enr. Code 2
Supt. – David Gailey, P O BOX 458 67024
ES   67025 – David Gailey, prin.

Centralia, Nemaha Co., Pop. Code 2
Vermillion USD 380
Supt. – See Vermillion
ES   66415 – David Zumbahlen, prin.

Chanute, Neosho Co., Pop. Code 7
Chanute USD 413
Sch. Sys. Enr. Code 4
Supt. – Dr. Marvin Johnson
   410 S EVERGREEN ST 66720
Alcott ES, 500 N FOREST ST 66720
   Harry Disbrow, prin.
Fairfield ES, RURAL ROUTE 03 66720
   Jim Catterson, prin.
Hutton ES, 600 S ASHBY ST 66720
   Harold Barnhart, prin.
Lincoln ES, MAIN & ALLEN 66720
   Jim Catterson, prin.
Murray Hill ES, 3RD & GARFIELD 66720
   Sam Carraway, prin.
Roosevelt ES, 1506 S EVERGREEN ST 66720
   Harry Disbrow, prin.

Chapman, Dickinson Co., Pop. Code 4
Chapman USD 473
Sch. Sys. Enr. Code 4
Supt. – Kenneth Root 67431
JHS   67431 – John Sanborn, prin.
ES   67431 – Gerald Dorsch, prin.
Other Schools – See Abilene, Enterprise, Talmage

Chase, Rice Co., Pop. Code 3
Chase USD 401
Sch. Sys. Enr. Code 2
Supt. – Bruce Ward, P O BOX 366 67524
ES, P O BOX 366 67524 – Bruce Ward, prin.
Other Schools – See Raymond

Cheney, Sedgwick Co., Pop. Code 4
Cheney USD 268
Sch. Sys. Enr. Code 3
Supt. – Don Wells, 100 W 6TH 67025
JHS, 100 W 6TH 67025 – James Wells, prin.
ES, 5TH & MARSHALL 67025
   Ralph Stutzman, prin.

Cherokee, Crawford Co., Pop. Code 3
Cherokee USD 247
Sch. Sys. Enr. Code 3
Supt. – Thomas Woolbright, P O BOX 277 66724
ES   66724 – Frank Crespino, prin.
Other Schools – See McCune, Weir, West Mineral

Cherryvale, Montgomery Co., Pop. Code 5
Cherryvale USD 447
Sch. Sys. Enr. Code 3
Supt. – Larry Thomas, 618 E 4TH ST 67335
MS, 4265 E 4TH 67335 – Gordon McBride, prin.
Lincoln Central ES, 401 E MAIN ST 67335
   Glenn Clarkson, prin.
McKinley ES, 600 W MAIN ST 67335
   Glenn Clarkson, prin.

Chetopa, Labette Co., Pop. Code 4
Chetopa USD 505
Sch. Sys. Enr. Code 2
Supt. – Douglas Dean
   RURAL ROUTE 01 BOX D-1 67336
ES, RURAL ROUTE 01 BOX D-1 67336
   Douglas Dean, prin.

Cimarron, Gray Co., Pop. Code 4
Cimarron-Ensign USD 102
Sch. Sys. Enr. Code 3
Supt. – Duane Rankin, P O BOX 209 67835
ES   67835 – Willy Penner, prin.
Other Schools – See Ensign

Claflin, Barton Co., Pop. Code 3
Claflin USD 354
Sch. Sys. Enr. Code 2
Supt. – R. Connell, P O BOX 346 67525
ES   67525 – Richard Connell, prin.

Clay Center, Clay Co., Pop. Code 5
Clay Center USD 379
Sch. Sys. Enr. Code 4
Supt. – Ross Knitter, P O BOX 97 67432
McKinley MS, 731 CRAWFORD ST 67432
   Francis Arpin, prin.
Lincoln ES, 1020 GRANT ST 67458
   Jack Wallace, prin.
Other Schools – See Garfield, Green, Longford,
   Morganville, Wakefield

Clayton, Norton Co., Pop. Code 2
Prairie Hts. USD 295
Supt. – See Jennings
ES   67629 – Wallace Severson, prin.

Clearwater, Sedgwick Co., Pop. Code 4
Clearwater USD 264
Sch. Sys. Enr. Code 3
Supt. – Dr. Gary Reynolds
   150 S PROSPECT 67026
MS, 140 S 4TH ST 67026 – Joe Pate, prin.
Clearwater Annex MS, 112 PROSPECT 67026
   Jim January, prin.
ES, 615 E ROSS 67026 – Jim January, prin.

Clifton, Washington Co., Pop. Code 2
Republican Valley USD 224
Sch. Sys. Enr. Code 2
Supt. – Mike Killian, P O BOX A 66937
MS, P O BOX B 66937 – Wayne Dunn, prin.
ES, P O BOX B 66937 – Wayne Dunn, prin.
Other Schools – See Clyde

Clyde, Cloud Co., Pop. Code 3
Republican Valley USD 224
Supt. – See Clifton
ES   66938 – Ed Wright, prin.

Coffeyville, Montgomery Co., Pop. Code 7
Coffeyville USD 445
Sch. Sys. Enr. Code 5
Supt. – Jack Reed, P O BOX 968 67337
Roosevelt MS, 1000 W 8TH ST 67337
   Joe Martin, prin.
Edgewood ES, 4TH & OHIO 67337
   Dr. James Sweeten, prin.
Garfield ES, 5TH & GRANT 67337
   Martha Landrith, prin.
Longfellow ES, 15TH & ELM 67337
   Delmar Curtis, prin.
Lowell ES, 9TH & CEDAR 67337
   Alfred Buffington, prin.
McKinley MS, 10TH & GILLIAM 67337
   Harold Thomas, prin.
Whittier ES, 3RD & WALNUT 67337
   Paul McCurtain, prin.
Other Schools – See Dearing

Holy Name ES, 406 WILLOW ST 67337

Colby, Thomas Co., Pop. Code 6
Colby USD 315
Sch. Sys. Enr. Code 4
Supt. – Dr. Jean Snell, 210 S RANGE AVE 67701
MS, 750 W 3RD ST 67701 – Francis Karlin, prin.
ES, 210 N GRANT AVE 67701
   Kirk Nielsen, prin.

Sacred Heart ES, 1150 W 6TH ST 67701

Coldwater, Comanche Co., Pop. Code 3
Comanche Co. USD 300
Sch. Sys. Enr. Code 2
Supt. – J. Chadwick, P O BOX 721 67029
ES   67029 – Sam Rawdon, prin.
Other Schools – See Protection

Colony, Anderson Co., Pop. Code 2
Crest USD 479
Supt. – See Kincaid
Crest West ES 66015 – Ron Thorson, prin.

Columbus, Cherokee Co., Pop. Code 5
Columbus USD 493
Sch. Sys. Enr. Code 4
Supt. – Larry Reynolds, P O BOX 21 66725
Central MS, 850 S HIGH SCHOOL ST 66725
   Galen Christiansen, prin.
Greenlawn ES, RURAL ROUTE 04 66725
   Paul Troop, prin.
Highland ES, 319 N HIGHSCHOOL AVE 66725
   Ray Golden, prin.
Park ES, GARFIELD AVE 66725
   Paul Troop, prin.
Other Schools – See Galena, Scammon

Colwich, Sedgwick Co., Pop. Code 3
Renwick USD 267
Supt. – See Andale
ES, P O BOX 248 67030 – Wallace Ungles, prin.
St. Mark's ES, P O BOX 84 67030
   James Aylward, prin.

Concordia, Cloud Co., Pop. Code 6
Concordia USD 333
Sch. Sys. Enr. Code 4
Supt. – Larry Nelson, 217 W 7TH ST 66901
Lincoln ES, 803 VALLEY 66901
   Kenneth Cannon, prin.
McKinley ES, 1105 KANSAS ST 66901
   Kenneth Cannon, prin.
MS, 1001 E 7TH 66901 – Raymond Stanton, prin.
Washington ES, 237 W 9TH 66901
   Raymond Stanton, prin.

Conway Springs, Sumner Co., Pop. Code 4
Conway Springs USD 356
Sch. Sys. Enr. Code 2
Supt. – R. Scraper, P O BOX 218 67031
Trueblood ES, P O BOX 218 67031
   Rick Weiss, prin.

St. Joseph ES, 218 N 5TH 67031

Copeland, Gray Co., Pop. Code 2
Copeland USD 476
Sch. Sys. Enr. Code 2
Supt. – Jerry Nordberg, P O BOX 156 67837
ES   67837 – Jerry Nordberg, prin.

Cottonwood Falls, Chase Co., Pop. Code 3
Chase Co. USD 284
Sch. Sys. Enr. Code 3
Supt. – Rudy Pouch, P O BOX 569 66845
ES   66845 – John Schierling, prin.
Other Schools – See Strong City

Council Grove, Morris Co., Pop. Code 4
Council Grove USD 417
Sch. Sys. Enr. Code 4
Supt. – Jim Selby, 17 WOOD ST 66846
ES, 706 E MAIN 66846 – Philip Mahan, prin.

Other Schools – See Alta Vista, Dwight, Wilsey

Courtland, Republic Co., Pop. Code 2
Pike Valley USD 426
Supt. – See Scandia
Pike Valley JHS, P O BOX 127   66939
  Stanley Estes, prin.
Pike Valley ES, P O BOX 127   66939
  Stanley Estes, prin.

Cuba, Republic Co., Pop. Code 2
Hillcrest USD 455
Sch. Sys. Enr. Code 2
Supt. – Robert Brock, P O BOX 167   66940
Hillcrest ES   66940 – Vernon Newman, prin.

Cummings, Atchison Co.
Atchison Co. Comm. USD 377
Supt. – See Effingham
JU 4 ES   66016 – Robin Schuckman, prin.

Cunningham, Kingman Co., Pop. Code 3
Cunningham USD 332
Sch. Sys. Enr. Code 2
Supt. – Melvin Ormiston, P O BOX 67   67035
ES   67035 – Steve Miller, prin.
Other Schools – See Zenda

Dearing, Montgomery Co., Pop. Code 2
Coffeyville USD 445
Supt. – See Coffeyville
ES   67340 – Robert Price, prin.

Deerfield, Kearny Co., Pop. Code 3
Deerfield USD 216
Sch. Sys. Enr. Code 2
Supt. – William Jones, P O BOX 274   67838
ES   67838 – Richard Caldwell, prin.

Delia, Jackson Co., Pop. Code 2
Kaw Valley USD 321
Supt. – See Saint Marys
ES   66418 – John Blackard, prin.

Delphos, Ottawa Co., Pop. Code 3
North Ottawa Co. USD 239
Supt. – See Minneapolis
ES   67436 – Gloria Scheetz, prin.

Denison, Jackson Co., Pop. Code 2
Holton USD 336
Supt. – See Holton
ES   66419 – Harold Hauck, prin.

Denton, Doniphan Co., Pop. Code 2
Midway USD 433
Sch. Sys. Enr. Code 2
Supt. – Robert Albers   66017
Midway ES   66017 – Robert Albers, prin.

Derby, Sedgwick Co., Pop. Code 6
Derby USD 260
Sch. Sys. Enr. Code 6
Supt. – Charles Hubbard
  120 E WASHINGTON ST   67037
MS, 715 E MADISON AVE   67037
  Eric Stiffler, prin.
Derby Hills ES, 2230 N WOODLAWN BLVD   67037
  Gregg Dunkelberger, prin.
El Paso ES, 900 E CRESTWAY ST   67037
  Tom Biggs, prin.
Pleasantview ES, 1101 N GEORGIE ST   67037
  Kevin Singer, prin.
Swaney ES, 501 ENGLISH ST   67037
  V. Honeycutt, prin.
Tanglewood ES, 830 RIDGECREST ROAD   67037
  Joseph Harrison, prin.
Other Schools – See Wichita

St. Mary's ES, 700 N DERBY AVE   67037

De Soto, Johnson Co., Pop. Code 4
De Soto USD 232
Sch. Sys. Enr. Code 4
Supt. – Dr. Harold Vestal, P O BOX 449   66018
Countryside IS, P O BOX 489   66018
  (—), prin.
ES, P O BOX 489   66018
  Dr. Marilyn Layman, prin.
Monticello ES, RURAL ROUTE 01   66018
  Carol Phillips, prin.
Woodsonia ES, RURAL ROUTE 01   66018
  (—), prin.

Dexter, Cowley Co., Pop. Code 2
Dexter USD 471
Sch. Sys. Enr. Code 2
Supt. – Max Logsdon, P O BOX 97   67038
ES, P O BOX 97   67038 – Max Logsdon, prin.

Dighton, Lane Co., Pop. Code 4
Dighton USD 482
Sch. Sys. Enr. Code 2
Supt. – Ron Musselwhite, P O BOX 878   67839
MS, 320 E JAMES   67839 – William Scott, prin.
Lincoln ES, 720 E LINCOLN   67839
  William Scott, prin.

Dodge City, Ford Co., Pop. Code 7
Dodge City USD 443
Sch. Sys. Enr. Code 5
Supt. – Dr. Richard Branstrator
  1000 2ND AVE   67801
Central ES, 1100 CENTRAL AVE   67801
  Kenneth Friend, prin.
Lincoln ES, 613 W CEDAR ST   67801
  Richard McVay, prin.

Miller ES, 1100 AVE G   67801
  Annette Aldape, prin.
Northwest ES, 2100 6TH AVE   67801
  Alan Cunningham, prin.
Richland Valley ES, RURAL ROUTE 03   67801
  Donna Ortiz, prin.
Sixth Grade Center S, 210 SOULE ST   67801
  Sharon Germes, prin.
Sunnyside ES, 511 SUNNYSIDE ST   67801
  Leland Kincaid, prin.
Wilroads Gardens ES   67801 – Donna Ortiz, prin.
Other Schools – See Wright

Sacred Heart Cathedral School
  905 CENTRAL AVE   67801

Dorrance, Russell Co., Pop. Code 2
Russell Co. USD 407
Supt. – See Russell
ES   67634 – Don Degenhardt, prin.

Douglass, Butler Co., Pop. Code 4
Douglass USD 396
Sch. Sys. Enr. Code 3
Supt. – M. Sisk, 320 S CHESTNUT   67039
ES   67039 – Robert Swigart, prin.

Dover, Shawnee Co.
Wabaunsee East USD 330
Supt. – See Eskridge
ES   66420 – Teresa Anderson, prin.

Downs, Osborne Co., Pop. Code 4
Waconda USD 272
Supt. – See Cawker City
ES   67437 – Steve Heide, prin.

Dwight, Morris Co., Pop. Code 2
Council Grove USD 417
Supt. – See Council Grove
ES   66849 – Eldon Moore, prin.

Easton, Leavenworth Co., Pop. Code 2
Easton USD 449
Sch. Sys. Enr. Code 3
Supt. – Don Simmons
  RURAL ROUTE 01 BOX 110   66020
Easton-Salt Creek MS   66020
  William Rogers, prin.
ES   66020 – Sarah McMillin, prin.
Other Schools – See Leavenworth

Edgerton, Johnson Co., Pop. Code 4
Gardner USD 231
Supt. – See Gardner
ES, P O BOX 256   66021 – Sharon Buffington, prin.

Edna, Labette Co., Pop. Code 3
Labette Co. USD 506
Supt. – See Altamont
ES, P O BOX 220   67342 – Henry Watson, prin.

Edwardsville, Wyandotte Co., Pop. Code 5
Bonner Springs USD 204
Supt. – See Bonner Springs
ES   66111 – John Mills, prin.

Effingham, Atchison Co., Pop. Code 3
Atchison Co. Comm. USD 377
Sch. Sys. Enr. Code 3
Supt. – Frank Maher, P O BOX 289   66023
MS   66023 – Monica Davenport, prin.
ES   66023 – Robin Schuckman, prin.
Other Schools – See Cummings, Lancaster, Muscotah

El Dorado, Butler Co., Pop. Code 7
Circle USD 375
Supt. – See Towanda
Oil Hill MS, 2700 W 6TH AVE   67042
  Elmer McDermeit, prin.
Vanora ES, RURAL ROUTE 01   67042
  Elmer McDermeit, prin.

El Dorado USD 490
Sch. Sys. Enr. Code 4
Supt. – Dr. Wynona Winn, P O BOX 311   67042
JHS, 500 W CENTRAL AVE   67042
  Bonnie Lynch, prin.
Grandview ES, 1300 LAWNDALE ST   67042
  Ferrel Nutley, prin.
Jefferson ES, 1216 W 3RD AVE   67042
  Randy Culbertson, prin.
Lincoln ES, 522 W 5TH AVE   67042
  Bernadette Spradling, prin.
Skelly ES, 1421 W TOWANDA AVE   67042
  Gary McEachern, prin.
Washington ES, 701 S ATCHISON ST   67042
  Gerald Haines, prin.

Elkhart, Morton Co., Pop. Code 4
Elkhart USD 218
Sch. Sys. Enr. Code 3
Supt. – Philip Johnston, P O BOX 999   67950
MS, P O BOX 999   67950 – G. Endicott, prin.
ES, P O BOX 778   67950 – Boyd McNabb, prin.

Ellinwood, Barton Co., Pop. Code 5
Ellinwood USD 355
Sch. Sys. Enr. Code 3
Supt. – Dr. Ronald Lantaff, P O BOX 368   67526
JHS, P O BOX 368   67526 – Don Caffee, prin.
ES, P O BOX 368   67526 – Joe Hickel, prin.

St. Joseph ES, 111 W 3RD ST   67526

Ellis, Ellis Co., Pop. Code 4
Ellis USD 388
Sch. Sys. Enr. Code 2
Supt. – Clair Beecher, P O BOX 26   67637
Washington ES, 1300 WASHINGTON ST   67637
  William Fritschen, prin.

St. Mary's ES, 603 MONROE ST   67637

Ellsworth, Ellsworth Co., Pop. Code 4
Ellsworth USD 327
Sch. Sys. Enr. Code 3
Supt. – Kent Garhart, P O BOX C   67439
ES, P O BOX 106   67439 – Donald Smischny, prin.
Other Schools – See Kanopolis

Elsmore, Allen Co., Pop. Code 2
Marmaton Valley USD 256
Supt. – See Moran
ES   66732 – Debbie Nilges, prin.

Elwood, Doniphan Co., Pop. Code 4
Elwood USD 486
Sch. Sys. Enr. Code 2
Supt. – Edwin Harbeston, P O BOX 368   66024
ES   66024 – Lee Woodrum, prin.

Emmett, Pottawatomie Co., Pop. Code 2
Kaw Valley USD 321
Supt. – See Saint Marys
ES   66422 – Wilbur Russell, prin.

Emporia, Lyon Co., Pop. Code 8
Emporia USD 253
Sch. Sys. Enr. Code 5
Supt. – Dr. Harold Hosey, P O BOX 1008   66801
Lowther-South MS, 216 W 6TH AVE   66801
  Wayne Bastin, prin.
Butcher Children ES
  1200 COMMERCIAL ST   66801
  Dr. Michael Kasnic, prin.
Herbert ES, 1700 W 7TH AVE   66801
  Gerald Duncan, prin.
Logan Avenue ES, 521 S EAST ST   66801
  Bill Warner, prin.
Lowther-North MS, 216 W 6TH AVE   66801
  Wayne Bastin, prin.
Maynard ES, 19 CONSTITUTION ST   66801
  Dr. Brian Frisch, prin.
Village ES, 2302 W 15TH AVE   66801
  Dr. Ed Gerhardt, prin.
Walnut ES, 801 GROVE AVE   66801
  Kanice Vidal, prin.
White ES, 902 EXCHANGE ST   66801
  Bradley Miller, prin.

Southern Lyon Co. USD 252
Supt. – See Hartford
Harmony Hill ES
  RURAL ROUTE 04   BOX 127   66801
  Michael Dougherty, prin.

Sacred Heart ES, 102 COTTONWOOD ST   66801

Ensign, Gray Co., Pop. Code 2
Cimarron-Ensign USD 102
Supt. – See Cimarron
ES   67841 – Virgil Nason, prin.

Enterprise, Dickinson Co., Pop. Code 3
Chapman USD 473
Supt. – See Chapman
ES   67441 – James Opat, prin.

Erie, Neosho Co., Pop. Code 4
Erie-St. Paul USD 101
Sch. Sys. Enr. Code 4
Supt. – Paul Bingle, P O BOX 37   66733
MS   66733 – Gary Snawder, prin.
ES, P O BOX 68   66733 – Ron Faircloth, prin.
Other Schools – See Galesburg, Saint Paul, Thayer

Esbon, Jewell Co., Pop. Code 2
White Rock USD 104
Sch. Sys. Enr. Code 2
Supt. – Dana Randel, P O BOX 38   66941
White Rock MS   66941 – Dana Randel, prin.
Other Schools – See Burr Oak

Eskridge, Wabaunsee Co., Pop. Code 3
Wabaunsee East USD 330
Sch. Sys. Enr. Code 3
Supt. – G. Anshutz, P O BOX 158   66423
ES   66423 – Sherry Gerner, prin.
Other Schools – See Dover, Harveyville

Eudora, Douglas Co., Pop. Code 5
Eudora USD 491
Sch. Sys. Enr. Code 3
Supt. – Dr. Dan Bloom, P O BOX 500   66025
JHS, P O BOX A   66025 – Charlie Watts, prin.
Nottingham ES, P O BOX K   66025
  Thomas Jerome.

Eureka, Greenwood Co., Pop. Code 5
Eureka USD 389
Sch. Sys. Enr. Code 3
Supt. – Leon Attebery, 106 W 6TH ST   67045
JHS, 214 N MULBERRY ST   67045
  Charles Schooler, prin.
Mulberry ES, 214 N MULBERRY ST   67045
  Stan Mitchell, prin.
Other Schools – See Toronto

Everest, Brown Co., Pop. Code 2
South Brown Co. USD 430
Supt. – See Horton
MS   66424 – James Kepple, prin.

Florence, Marion Co., Pop. Code 3
Marion USD 408
Supt. – See Marion
MS, 7TH & DOYLE ST 66851
  Doug Huxman, prin.

Fontana, Miami Co., Pop. Code 2
Prairie View USD 362
Supt. – See La Cygne
ES 66026 – Tom Likely, prin.

Fort Leavenworth, Leavenworth Co., Pop. Code 6
Ft. Leavenworth USD 207
Sch. Sys. Enr. Code 4
Supt. – Clyde Ransom 66027
Bradley ES 66027 – Raymond Hittle, prin.
Eisenhower ES 66027 – John Dickinson, prin.
MacArthur ES 66027 – Deborah Baeuchle, prin.

Fort Riley, Geary Co., Pop. Code 4
Junction City USD 475
Supt. – See Junction City
Custer Hill ES 66442 – Carlye Gilmore, prin.
ES 66442 – Hazel Swarts, prin.
Jefferson ES 66442 – Jim Weis, prin.
Morris Hill ES 66442 – Dr. Patricia Flanagan, prin.
Ware ES 66442 – Leland Sharpe, prin.

Fort Scott, Bourbon Co., Pop. Code 6
Ft. Scott USD 234
Sch. Sys. Enr. Code 4
Supt. – Fred Campbell,Jr., 5TH & MAIN STS 66701
MS, 412 S NATIONAL AVE 66701
  Bill Sailors, prin.
Scott ES, 10TH & EDDY 66701
  Dr. Richard Werling, prin.
Ware ES, 900 E 3RD ST 66701
  Duane Rector, prin.

St. Mary ES, 702 S EDDY ST 66701

Fowler, Meade Co., Pop. Code 3
Fowler USD 225
Sch. Sys. Enr. Code 2
Supt. – Lyman Hanson 67844
ES 67844 – Lyman Hansen, prin.

Frankfort, Marshall Co., Pop. Code 4
Vermillion USD 380
Supt. – See Vermillion
ES 66427 – Gene Davis, prin.

Fredonia, Wilson Co., Pop. Code 5
Fredonia USD 484
Sch. Sys. Enr. Code 3
Supt. – Max Wilson, P O BOX 539 66736
JHS, 203 N 8TH ST 66736
  J. Robert Graham, prin.
Lincoln MS, P O BOX 270 66736
  Michael Myers, prin.
Paulen PS, P O BOX 270 66736
  Charlotte Svaty, prin.

Friend, Finney Co.
Garden City USD 457
Supt. – See Garden City
ES 67845 – Adrienne Carrica, prin.

Frontenac, Crawford Co., Pop. Code 5
Frontenac USD 249
Sch. Sys. Enr. Code 2
Supt. – Joseph Smith
  201 S CRAWFORD ST 66762
Layden ES, 200 E LANYON ST 66762
  Gerald Falletti, prin.

Galena, Cherokee Co., Pop. Code 5
Columbus USD 493
Supt. – See Columbus
Spencer ES, RURAL ROUTE 01 66739
  Jim Sarwinski, prin.

Galena USD 499
Sch. Sys. Enr. Code 3
Supt. – James Christman, 704 S MAIN ST 66739
Liberty ES, 8TH & WATER 66739
  Marion Davies, prin.
Spring Grove ES, 19TH & GALENA 66739
  William Van Cleave, prin.

Galesburg, Neosho Co., Pop. Code 2
Erie-St. Paul USD 101
Supt. – See Erie
ES 66740 – Gayle Huff, prin.

Galva, McPherson Co., Pop. Code 3
Canton-Galva USD 419
Supt. – See Canton
Canton-Galva MS, P O BOX 96 67443
  Michael Engstrom, prin.
ES, P O BOX 96 67443 – Michael Engstrom, prin.

Garden City, Finney Co., Pop. Code 7
Garden City USD 457
Sch. Sys. Enr. Code 6
Supt. – Dr. Gerald Moseman
  201 BUFFALO JONES AVE 67846
Barker ES, IMPERIAL ROUTE 67846
  Patti Ansley, prin.
Brown ES, PINE & HUDSON 67846
  Patty Hutton, prin.
Garfield ES, 121 W WALNUT ST 67846
  Willis Pracht, prin.
Jones ES, 708 TAYLOR AVE 67846
  Manuel Maciel, prin.
Matthews ES, 111 JOHNSON 67846
  Bernard Killer, prin.

Ornelas ES, 3401 E SPRUCE ST 67846
  Dr. Robert Creamer, prin.
Pierceville-Plymell ES, SOUTH HCR 67846
  Merle Wiederstein, prin.
Scheuerman ES, 1901 W WILCOX ST 67846
  Ronald Brown, prin.
Walker ES, 805 W FAIR ST 67846
  Adrienne Carrica, prin.
Wilson ES, 1406 HARDING AVE 67846
  Teresa Weisz, prin.
Wilson ES, 1709 LABRADOR BLVD 67846
  Lorie Francis, prin.
Other Schools – See Friend, Ingalls

St. Dominic ES, 617 J C ST 67846
St. Mary ES, 503 SAINT JOHN ST 67846

Garden Plain, Sedgwick Co., Pop. Code 3
Renwick USD 267
Supt. – See Andale
ES 67050 – Sue Givens, prin.

Gardner, Johnson Co., Pop. Code 4
Gardner USD 231
Sch. Sys. Enr. Code 4
Supt. – Dr. Gary George, P O BOX 97 66030
Nike JHS, I-35 AT GARDNER-ANTIOCH RD 66030
  Gary Manford, prin.
ES, 218 E SHAWNEE ST 66030
  Lynn Firestone, prin.
Other Schools – See Edgerton

Garfield, Pawnee Co., Pop. Code 2
Clay Center USD 379
Supt. – See Clay Center
MS, 815 4TH ST 67432 – Tim McFarland, prin.

Ft. Larned USD 495
Supt. – See Larned
ES 67529 – Richard Carlton, prin.

Garnett, Anderson Co., Pop. Code 5
Garnett USD 365
Sch. Sys. Enr. Code 3
Supt. – Charles Mansfield, P O BOX 328 66032
Irving ES, 300 E 3RD AVE 66032
  Darwin Alexander, prin.
Longfellow ES, 424 W 6TH AVE 66032
  Larry Stewart, prin.
Other Schools – See Greeley, Welda, Westphalia

Holy Angels ES, 530 E 4TH AVE 66032

Gas, Allen Co., Pop. Code 3
Iola USD 257
Supt. – See Iola
Gas City MS 66742 – Richard Chase, prin.

Gaylord, Smith Co., Pop. Code 2
Smith Center USD 237
Supt. – See Smith Center
ES 67638 – Debra Edwards, prin.

Geneseo, Rice Co., Pop. Code 2
Little River USD 444
Supt. – See Little River
ES 67444 – Bill Ritcha, prin.

Girard, Crawford Co., Pop. Code 5
Girard USD 248
Sch. Sys. Enr. Code 4
Supt. – John Battitori
  401-415 N SUMMIT ST 66743
MS, 401 N SUMMIT ST 66743 – Gary Pernot, prin.
Haderlein ES 66743 – Gene Christy, prin.

Glasco, Cloud Co., Pop. Code 3
Southern Cloud Co. USD 334
Sch. Sys. Enr. Code 2
Supt. – Curtis Norris, P O BOX 427 67445
ES 67445 – Tom Lynch, prin.
Other Schools – See Miltonvale

Glen Elder, Mitchell Co., Pop. Code 2
Waconda USD 272
Supt. – See Cawker City
ES 67446 – Douglas Scholl, prin.

Goddard, Sedgwick Co., Pop. Code 4
Goddard USD 265
Sch. Sys. Enr. Code 4
Supt. – C. Vogelgesang, P O BOX 207 67052
IS 67052 – Mary McElroy, prin.
PS 67052 – Milton Matthews, prin.

Goessel, Marion Co., Pop. Code 2
Goessel USD 411
Sch. Sys. Enr. Code 2
Supt. – Robert Van Arsdale, P O BOX 6 67053
ES 67053 – Perry McCabe, prin.

Goodland, Sherman Co., Pop. Code 6
Goodland USD 352
Sch. Sys. Enr. Code 4
Supt. – Larry Jess, P O BOX 509 67735
Grant JHS, P O BOX 509 67735
  Bernard Tipp, prin.
Central ES, 1311 MAIN ST 67735
  Dale Burgess, prin.
North ES, 700 E 4TH ST 67735 – Paul Taylor, prin.
West ES, 912 W 12TH ST 67735
  William Pittman, prin.

Gorham, Russell Co., Pop. Code 2
Russell Co. USD 407
Supt. – See Russell
ES 67640 – Don Degenhardt, prin.

Grainfield, Gove Co., Pop. Code 2
Grainfield USD 292
Sch. Sys. Enr. Code 2
Supt. – Lonny Zwickle, P O BOX 165 67737
ES, P O BOX 174 67737 – Charles King, prin.
Other Schools – See Park

Grantville, Jefferson Co.
Perry USD 343
Supt. – See Perry
ES 66429 – Paula Kellogg, prin.

Great Bend, Barton Co., Pop. Code 7
Great Bend USD 428
Sch. Sys. Enr. Code 5
Supt. – Leo Lake, 2408 JEFFERSON ST 67530
Eisenhower ES, 1212 GARFIELD ST 67530
  Don Atkinson, prin.
Jefferson ES, 2716 24TH ST 67530
  Janice Strecker, prin.
Lincoln ES, 5630 BROADWAY ST 67530
  Laverne Lessor, prin.
Morrison ES, 18TH & JEFFERSON 67530
  Dr. Jack Bronson, prin.
Park ES, 1801 WILLIAMS ST 67530
  Mary Paul, prin.
Riley ES, 1515 10TH ST 67530 – Steve Wolf, prin.
Shady Grove ES, RURAL ROUTE 01 67530
  Don Atkinson, prin.
Washington ES, 2535 LAKIN AVE 67530
  Betty Dennis, prin.

St. Patrick ES, 4200 BROADWAY ST 67530
St. Rose of Lima ES, 1400 BAKER ST 67530

Greeley, Anderson Co., Pop. Code 2
Garnett USD 365
Supt. – See Garnett
ES 66033 – Ron VanSickle, prin.

Green, Clay Co., Pop. Code 2
Clay Center USD 379
Supt. – See Clay Center
ES 67447 – Ellen Rook, prin.

Greenleaf, Washington Co., Pop. Code 2
Washington USD 222
Supt. – See Washington
ES 66943 – Dr. Roger Baskerville, prin.

Greensburg, Kiowa Co., Pop. Code 4
Greensburg USD 422
Sch. Sys. Enr. Code 2
Supt. – Robert Mosier, 401 S OAK ST 67054
ES, 600 S MAIN ST 67054 – LeMeul Marsh, prin.

Grenola, Elk Co., Pop. Code 2
Central USD 462
Supt. – See Burden
Central ES 67346 – Joe Deweese, prin.

Gridley, Coffey Co., Pop. Code 2
Le Roy-Gridley USD 245
Supt. – See Le Roy
ES 66852 – James Ochs, prin.

Grinnell, Gove Co., Pop. Code 2
Grinnell USD 291
Sch. Sys. Enr. Code 2
Supt. – Emery Hart 67738
MS 67738 – Emery Hart, prin.
Angelus ES 67738 – Emery Hart, prin.

Gypsum, Saline Co., Pop. Code 2
Southeast of Saline USD 306
Sch. Sys. Enr. Code 3
Supt. – Raymond Salmon
  RURAL ROUTE 01 67448
Southeast of Saline ES, RURAL ROUTE 01 67448
  Leon Griffitts, prin.

Haddam, Washington Co., Pop. Code 2
North Central USD 221
Sch. Sys. Enr. Code 2
Supt. – Wayne Wilgers
  RURAL ROUTE 01 BOX 122 66944
North Central ES 66944 – Wayne Wilgers, prin.

Halstead, Harvey Co., Pop. Code 4
Halstead USD 440
Sch. Sys. Enr. Code 3
Supt. – Earl Guiot, 520 W 6TH ST 67056
ES 67056 – Carl Haetten, prin.
Other Schools – See Bentley

Hamilton, Greenwood Co., Pop. Code 2
Hamilton USD 390
Sch. Sys. Enr. Code 2
Supt. – Charles Schneider, P O BOX 129 66853
ES 66853 – Charles Schneider, prin.

Hanover, Washington Co., Pop. Code 3
Barnes USD 223
Supt. – See Barnes
ES 66945 – John Enos, prin.

Hanston, Hodgeman Co., Pop. Code 2
Hanston USD 228
Sch. Sys. Enr. Code 2
Supt. – Ralph Bradley, P O BOX 219 67849
ES, P O BOX 219 67849 – Ralph Bradley, prin.

Hardtner, Barber Co., Pop. Code 2
South Barber Co. USD 255
Supt. – See Kiowa
South Barber ES 67057 – Juanita Smith, prin.

Hartford, Lyon Co., Pop. Code 3
Southern Lyon Co. USD 252
Sch. Sys. Enr. Code 2
Supt. – Winferd Hamm, P O BOX 278 66854
Other Schools – See Emporia, Neosho Rapids, Olpe

Harveyville, Waubounsee Co., Pop. Code 2
Wabaunsee East USD 330
Supt. – See Eskridge
ES 66431 – Jerry Wenciker, prin.

Haven, Reno Co., Pop. Code 4
Haven USD 312
Sch. Sys. Enr. Code 4
Supt. – H. Voth, 308 E 4TH 67543
ES 67543 – Brian Boston, prin.
Yoder ES 67543 – Larry Phillips, prin.
Other Schools – See Hutchinson, Mount Hope,
Partridge

Havensville, Pottawatomie Co., Pop. Code 2
Onaga-Havensville-Wheaton USD 322
Supt. – See Onaga
ES 66432 – Darwin Olson, prin.

Haviland, Kiowa Co., Pop. Code 3
Haviland USD 474
Sch. Sys. Enr. Code 2
Supt. – Larry Wade, P O BOX 243 67059
ES, P O BOX 243 67059 – Ken Stanage, prin.

Hays, Ellis Co., Pop. Code 7
Hays USD 489
Sch. Sys. Enr. Code 5
Supt. – Fred Kaufman, 323 W 12TH ST 67601
Felton MS, 101 E 29TH ST 67601
Wilbur Roth, prin.
Kennedy MS, 1309 FORT ST 67601
Eric Harfmann, prin.
Jefferson ES, 1800 MILNER ST 67601
Gary LeCount, prin.
Lincoln ES, 1906 ASH ST 67601
Joyce Darnell, prin.
Munjor ES, MUNJOR ROUTE 67601
Francis Stremel, prin.
Roosevelt ES, 2000 MACARTHUR ROAD 67601
Dale Koerner, prin.
Washington ES, 305 MAIN ST 67601
Tanya Channell, prin.
Wilson ES, 101 E 28TH ST 67601
David Baisinger, prin.
Other Schools – See Catharine, Schoenchen

St. Joseph ES, 210 W 13TH ST 67601

Haysville, Sedgwick Co., Pop. Code 6
Haysville USD 261
Sch. Sys. Enr. Code 5
Supt. – Lynn Stevens, 1745 W GRAND AVE 67060
JHS, 900 W GRAND AVE 67060
G. Kirk Pope, prin.
Freeman MS, 1745 W GRAND AVE 67060
Mike Wolfe, prin.
Nelson ES, 245 N DELOS AVE 67060
Larry Tate, prin.
Rex ES, 110 W GRAND 67060
Richard Wasinger, prin.
Other Schools – See Wichita

Healy, Lane Co., Pop. Code 2
Healy USD 468
Sch. Sys. Enr. Code 2
Supt. – Raymond Parrott, 410 N MAIN 67850
Roosevelt ES 67850 – Raymond Parrott, prin.

Herington, Dickinson Co., Pop. Code 5
Herington USD 487
Sch. Sys. Enr. Code 3
Supt. – Thomas Vernon, 19 N BROADWAY 67449
MS, 2 S A ST 67449 – Bill Swendson, prin.
Herington Lower ES, 201 E HAWLEY ST 67449
Lawrence Killer, prin.

Herndon, Rawlins Co., Pop. Code 2
Herndon USD 317
Sch. Sys. Enr. Code 1
Supt. – Henry Potts 67739
ES 67739 – Henry Potts, prin.

Hesston, Harvey Co., Pop. Code 5
Hesston USD 460
Sch. Sys. Enr. Code 3
Supt. – Gary Price, P O BOX 2000 67062
MS, P O BOX 2000 67062
Kermit Gingerich, prin.
ES, P O BOX 2000 67062 – Roger Pfaff, prin.

Hiawatha, Brown Co., Pop. Code 5
Hiawatha USD 415
Sch. Sys. Enr. Code 4
Supt. – Dr. Milton Pippenger
600 OREGON ST 66434
ES, 6TH & MIAMI 66434 – Dwight Clum, prin.
Other Schools – See Robinson

Highland, Doniphan Co., Pop. Code 3
Highland USD 425
Sch. Sys. Enr. Code 2
Supt. – Jan Collins, P O BOX 8 66035
ES 66035 – Conrad Clary, prin.

Hill City, Graham Co., Pop. Code 4
Hill City USD 281
Sch. Sys. Enr. Code 3
Supt. – Thomas Heiman, P O BOX 309 67642
Longfellow MS, 203 N 2ND 67642
Curtis Orr, prin.
ES, 216 N 4TH AVE 67642 – Curtis Orr, prin.

Other Schools – See Bogue

Hillsboro, Marion Co., Pop. Code 5
Hillsboro-Durham-Lehigh USD 410
Sch. Sys. Enr. Code 3
Supt. – Dr. Robert Brown, 812 E A ST 67063
MS, GRAND & JEFFERSON 67063
Marilyn Jost, prin.
ES, 812 E A ST 67063 – Dr. Robert Brown, prin.

Hillsdale, Miami Co.
Paola USD 368
Supt. – See Paola
ES, P O BOX 98 66036 – Loretta Barnard, prin.

Hoisington, Barton Co., Pop. Code 5
Hoisington USD 431
Sch. Sys. Enr. Code 3
Supt. – Randall Evans, 106 N MAIN ST 67544
MS, 108 E 7TH ST 67544 – Dean Andereck, prin.
Lincoln MS, 515 N PINE ST 67544
Alan Charles, prin.
Roosevelt ES, 315 N VINE ST 67544
Roger Michaelis, prin.

St. John Evangelist School, 206 E 5TH ST 67544

Holcomb, Finney Co., Pop. Code 3
Holcomb USD 363
Sch. Sys. Enr. Code 3
Supt. – Loyd Milligan, P O BOX 8 67851
ES 67851 – Ken Spencer, prin.

Holton, Jackson Co., Pop. Code 5
Holton USD 336
Sch. Sys. Enr. Code 3
Supt. – C. L. Riley, 208 W 4TH 66436
JHS, 9TH & IOWA 66436 – Mark Wilson, prin.
Central MS, 4TH & NEW JERSEY 66436
Ted Sipe, prin.
Colorado ES, 5TH & COLORADO 66436
Ted Sipe, prin.
Other Schools – See Denison

Jackson Hts. USD 335
Sch. Sys. Enr. Code 2
Supt. – Robert Clark, RURAL ROUTE 03 66436
Jackson Heights ES, RURAL ROUTE 03 66436
Paul Moser, prin.

Holyrood, Ellsworth Co., Pop. Code 3
Lorraine USD 328
Supt. – See Lorraine
Quivira Heights MS 67450 – Kenneth Parks, prin.
Quivira Heights ES 67450 – Kenneth Parks, prin.

Hope, Dickinson Co., Pop. Code 2
Rural Vista USD 481
Sch. Sys. Enr. Code 2
Supt. – Bob McDaniel, P O BOX 217 67451
ES 67451 – Gregg Pennington, prin.
Other Schools – See White City

Horton, Brown Co., Pop. Code 4
South Brown Co. USD 430
Sch. Sys. Enr. Code 3
Supt. – Daryl Haegert, 114 W 8TH ST 66439
ES, 300 E 16TH ST 66439 – C. Bartak, prin.
Other Schools – See Everest

Howard, Elk Co., Pop. Code 3
West Elk USD 282
Sch. Sys. Enr. Code 2
Supt. – Charles Hill, P O BOX 607 67349
Other Schools – See Moline, Severy

Hoxie, Sheridan Co., Pop. Code 4
Hoxie USD 412
Sch. Sys. Enr. Code 3
Supt. – Archie Vernon, 724 MAIN 67740
ES 67740 – Charles Buechman, prin.

Hoyt, Jackson Co., Pop. Code 3
Mayetta USD 337
Supt. – See Mayetta
ES 66440 – John Rundle, prin.

Hudson, Stafford Co., Pop. Code 2
St. John USD 350
Supt. – See Saint John
MS 67545 – Jerry Paden, prin.

Hugoton, Stevens Co., Pop. Code 5
Hugoton USD 210
Sch. Sys. Enr. Code 3
Supt. – Dr. Nelson A. Bryant, 205 3 6TH ST 67951
MS, 115 W 11TH ST 67951 – Louise Jones, prin.
ES, 304 E 6TH ST 67951 – James Begley, prin.

Humboldt, Allen Co., Pop. Code 4
Humboldt USD 258
Sch. Sys. Enr. Code 3
Supt. – John E. Smith, 910 NEW YORK ST 66748
Zillah MS, RURAL ROUTE 01 BOX 92 66748
Warren Isaac, prin.
ES, 1100 CENTRAL ST 66748 – Larry Hart, prin.

Hutchinson, Reno Co., Pop. Code 8
Buhler USD 313
Supt. – See Buhler
Prairie Hills MS, 3200 LUCILLE DRIVE 67502
E. Williams, prin.
Obee ES, 4712 E 4TH 67501 – Janet Sims, prin.
Prosperity MS, 4601 N PLUM ST 67502
Mike Bryan, prin.
Union Valley ES, 30TH & HALSTEAD 67501
Douglas Murphy, prin.

Haven USD 312
Supt. – See Haven
Elreka ES, RURAL ROUTE 01 67501
Robert Snyder, prin.

Hutchinson USD 308
Sch. Sys. Enr. Code 5
Supt. – W. L. Hawver, P O BOX 1908 67504
Liberty MS, 200 W 14TH AVE 67501
Greg Sandstrom, prin.
Sherman MS, 210 E A 67501 – Lila Fritschen, prin.
Allen ES, 403 W 10TH AVE 67501
Jane Taylor, prin.
Avenue A ES, 111 S MADISON ST 67501
Annabeth Hind, prin.
Faris ES, 300 E 9TH 67501 – Tim Marshall, prin.
Graber ES, 1600 N CLEVELAND ST 67501
Richard Fritschen, prin.
Grandview ES, 1900 E 4TH AVE 67501
Norberta Perez, prin.
Lincoln ES, 315 E BIGGER ST 67501
Dennis Berndsen, prin.
McCandless ES, 700 N BAKER ST 67501
Trudy Swint, prin.
Morgan ES, 100 W 27TH AVE 67502
Frederick Bichet, prin.
Roosevelt ES, 1615 N ADAMS ST 67501
Patricia Lemmon, prin.
Wiley ES, 900 W 21ST AVE 67502
Janis Bair, prin.
Winans ES, 805 E B ST 67501
Loretta Miller, prin.

Nickerson USD 309
Supt. – See Nickerson
North Reno MS, 1616 WILSHIRE DR 67501
A. Disney, prin.
Mitchell ES, 2804 W 56TH 67502
A. Disney, prin.

Holy Cross ES
2633 INDEPENDENCE ROAD 67502
St. Teresa ES, 215 E 5TH AVE 67501

Independence, Montgomery Co., Pop. Code 7
Independence USD 446
Sch. Sys. Enr. Code 4
Supt. – Dr. Charles Mock, P O BOX 487 67301
MS, 300 W LOCUST ST 67301
Orlin Milner, prin.
Lincoln ES, 701 W LAUREL ST 67301
Thurman Cook, prin.
Riley ES, 1201 N 10TH ST 67301
Dale Payne, prin.
Washington ES, 300 E MYRTLE ST 67301
Rosemary Noel, prin.

St. Andrew School, 215 NORTH PARK 67301
Zion Lutheran ES, 301 S 11TH ST 67301

Ingalls, Gray Co., Pop. Code 2
Garden City USD 457
Supt. – See Garden City
Theoni ES 67846 – Willis Pracht, prin.

Ingalls USD 477
Sch. Sys. Enr. Code 2
Supt. – John O'Brien, P O BOX 99 67853
ES 67853 – John O'Brien, prin.

Inman, McPherson Co., Pop. Code 3
Inman USD 448
Sch. Sys. Enr. Code 2
Supt. – Dr. Richard Erickson, 119 S MAIN 67546
ES, 207 N MAPLE 67546 – Ralph Vogel, prin.

Iola, Allen Co., Pop. Code 6
Iola USD 257
Sch. Sys. Enr. Code 4
Supt. – Don Bain, 402 E JACKSON ST 66749
Jefferson ES, 300 S JEFFERSON ST 66749
Richard Sears, prin.
Lincoln ES, 700 N JEFFERSON ST 66749
Susan Lonergan, prin.
McKinley ES, 209 S KENTUCKY ST 66749
Ken McGuffin, prin.
Other Schools – See Gas, La Harpe

Jennings, Decatur Co., Pop. Code 2
Prairie Hts. USD 295
Sch. Sys. Enr. Code 2
Supt. – Wallace Severson, P O BOX 160 67643
MS 67643 – Wallace Severson, prin.
Other Schools – See Clayton

Jetmore, Hodgeman Co., Pop. Code 3
Jetmore USD 227
Sch. Sys. Enr. Code 2
Supt. – Donald McWhirt, P O BOX 217 67854
ES 67854 – Frederick Lindenmeyer, prin.

Jewell, Jewell Co., Pop. Code 3
Jewell USD 279
Sch. Sys. Enr. Code 2
Supt. – Donovan Williams 66949
ES 66949 – Larry Girard, prin.
Other Schools – See Randall

Johnson, Stanton Co., Pop. Code 4
Stanton Co. USD 452
Sch. Sys. Enr. Code 3
Supt. – Dr. Roger Pickerign, P O BOX 579 67855
MS 67855 – Jack LaFay, prin.
ES 67855 – Larry Johnson, prin.
Other Schools – See Big Bow, Manter

Junction City, Geary Co., Pop. Code 7
Junction City USD 475
Sch. Sys. Enr. Code 6
Supt. – Max Heim, P O BOX 370 66441
Eisenhower ES, 1625 SAINT MARYS ROAD 66441
　Joe Clouse, prin.
Franklin ES, 2ND & MADISON 66441
　Gordon Gulseth, prin.
Grandview ES, P O BOX 370 66441
　Nancy Hubbard, prin.
Lincoln ES, 300 N LINCOLN SCHOOL DR 66441
　Susan Kamphaus, prin.
Sheridan ES, 427 W ASH ST 66441
　Nancy Hubbard, prin.
Washington ES, 15TH & WASHINGTON 66441
　Robert Hellerud, prin.
Westwood ES, 16TH & EISENHOWER 66441
　Randall Harris, prin.
Other Schools – See Fort Riley, Milford

St. Xavier ES, 125 W 3RD ST 66441

Kanopolis, Ellsworth Co., Pop. Code 3
Ellsworth USD 327
Supt. – See Ellsworth
MS, P O BOX 37 67454
　Harold A. Muninger, prin.

Kansas City, Wyandotte Co., Pop. Code 9
Kansas City USD 500
Sch. Sys. Enr. Code 7
Supt. – Dr. David Lusk
　625 MINNESOTA AVE 66101
Argentine MS, 22ND & RUBY 66106
　Glenn Schoenfish, prin.
Arrowhead MS, 1715 N 82ND ST 66112
　James Tinsley, prin.
Central MS, 10TH & IVANDALE 66101
　Claudia Makin, prin.
Coronado MS, 1735 N 64TH TERRACE 66102
　Karl Baxley, prin.
Eisenhower MS, 2901 N 72ND ST 66109
　Stanley Jasinskas, prin.
Northwest MS, 18TH & HASKELL 66104
　Leslie Brown, prin.
Rosedale MS, 36TH & SPRINGFIELD 66103
　James Maier, prin.
West MS, 2600 N 44TH ST 66104
　Benton Harding, prin.
Banneker ES, 2026 N 4TH ST 66101
　Linda Daniel, prin.
Bethel ES, 7750 YECKER AVE 66109
　Doreen Ryabik, prin.
Central ES, 8TH & BARNETT 66101
　Barb Harpst, prin.
Chelsea ES, 25TH & WOOD 66104
　Mary Moore, prin.
Douglass ES, 9TH & WASHINGTON 66101
　Flora Anderson, prin.
Edison ES, 10TH & LOCUST 66103
　Wayne Winkler, prin.
Emerson ES, 1429 S 29TH ST 66106
　Ellen White, prin.
Fairfax ES, 3101 N 10TH ST 66104
　Jackie Gering, prin.
Fiske ES, 625 S VALLEY ST 66105
　Laura Swartz, prin.
Grant ES, 1510 N 4TH ST 66101
　Jean Henderson, prin.
Hawthorne ES, 11TH & WAVERLY 66104
　James White, prin.
Hazel Grove ES, 2401 N 67TH ST 66104
　Dora Currie, prin.
Huyck ES, 1530 N 83RD ST 66112
　Doreen Ryabik, prin.
Kennedy ES, 2600 N 72ND ST 66109
　Judy Webber, prin.
Lindbergh ES, 641 N 57TH ST 66102
　Nelda Kibby, prin.
McKinley ES, 611 N 14TH ST 66102
　Michael Stithem, prin.
Morse ES, BALTIMORE & MIAMI 66105
　Laura Swartz, prin.
Parker ES, 33RD & HASKELL 66104
　Jean Henderson, prin.
Pearson ES, 310 N 11TH ST 66102
　Arthur Newton, prin.
Prentis ES, 14TH & GIBBS 66103
　Wayne Winkler, prin.
Quindaro ES, 28TH & FARROW 66104
　Gloria Willis, prin.
Roosevelt ES, 36TH & WASHINGTON 66102
　Thomas Picklar, prin.
Rushton ES, 2605 W 43RD AVE 66103
　Betty Burgess, prin.
Silver City ES, 2515 LAWRENCE AVE 66106
　Ellen White, prin.
Stanley ES, 36TH & METROPOLITAN 66106
　Donna Hardy, prin.
Stony Point North ES
　8200 ELIZABETH AVE 66112 – Judy Walle, prin.
Stony Point South ES, 150 S 78TH ST 66111
　James Thornton, prin.
Twain ES, 23RD & MINNESOTA 66102
　Barb Harpst, prin.
Vance ES, 3650 N 67TH ST 66104
　Donald Hudlin, prin.
Ware ES, 4820 OAKLAND AVE 66102
　Fred Vaughan, prin.
Welborn ES, 5200 LEAVENWORTH ROAD 66104
　Judith Farmer, prin.
White Church ES, 2226 N 85TH ST 66109
　Steve Bock, prin.

White ES, 2600 N 43RD TERRACE 66104
　Beverly Hodges, prin.
Whittier ES, 10TH & GILMORE 66102
　Michael Stithem, prin.
Willard ES, 34TH & ORVILLE 66102
　Thomas Picklar, prin.

Piper USD 203
Sch. Sys. Enr. Code 3
Supt. – Dr. Ron E. Brown
　12036 LEAVENWORTH ROAD 66109
Piper West ES, 3130 N 122ND 66109
　Laurence Breedlove, prin.

Turner USD 202
Sch. Sys. Enr. Code 5
Supt. – Dr. Robert Hale, 1800 S 55TH ST 66106
Junction MS, 2540 JUNCTION ROAD 66106
　Allan Amos, prin.
Junction ES, 2570 S 42ND ST 66106
　Allan Amos, prin.
Morris ES, 7120 GIBBS ROAD 66106
　James Neihart, prin.
Oak Grove ES, 5340 OAK GROVE ROAD 66106
　Cecil Martin, prin.
Turner East MS, 831 S 55TH ST 66106
　James Biles, prin.
Turner West ES, 800 S 55TH ST 66106
　James Biles, prin.
Other Schools – See Muncie

All Saints Consolidated School
　809 VERMONT AVE 66101
Blessed Sacrament ES
　2215 PARALLEL AVE 66104
Cathedral of St. Peter School
　422 N 14TH ST 66102
Christ the King ES, 3027 N 54TH ST 66104
Grace Lutheran ES, 3333 WOOD AVE 66102
Holy Family ES, 515 OHIO AVE 66101
Holy Name ES, 1007 SOUTHWEST BLVD 66103
Our Lady of Unity ES, 1331 S 30TH ST 66106
St. John Baptist ES, 420 BARNETT AVE 66101
St. Patrick ES, 1066 N 94TH ST 66112

Kensington, Smith Co., Pop. Code 3
West Smith Co. USD 238
Sch. Sys. Enr. Code 2
Supt. – Bradley Killen, P O BOX 188 66951
West Smith County ES 66951
　Bradley Killen, prin.

Kincaid, Anderson Co., Pop. Code 2
Crest USD 479
Sch. Sys. Enr. Code 2
Supt. – Larry Wittmer, P O BOX 68 66039
Crest East MS 66039 – George Ferguson, prin.
Other Schools – See Colony

Kingman, Kingman Co., Pop. Code 5
Kingman USD 331
Sch. Sys. Enr. Code 4
Supt. – Lynn Smith, P O BOX 416 67068
ES, 607 SPRUCE ST 67068 – Theron Jones, prin.
Other Schools – See Murdock, Norwich

St. Patrick ES, 605 AVE D WEST 67068

Kinsley, Edwards Co., Pop. Code 4
Kinsley-Offerle USD 347
Sch. Sys. Enr. Code 2
Supt. – Lonn Poage, 110 E 1ST ST 67547
Southside ES, 605 E 8TH ST 67547
　Bill Inman, prin.
Other Schools – See Offerle

Kiowa, Barber Co., Pop. Code 4
South Barber Co. USD 255
Sch. Sys. Enr. Code 2
Supt. – Glen Piper, P O BOX 124 67070
South Barber MS, 913 MAIN ST 67070
　Wesley Rader, prin.
Other Schools – See Hardtner

Kirwin, Phillips Co., Pop. Code 2
Eastern Hts. USD 324
Supt. – See Agra
Eastern Heights ES 67644 – Earl McGee, prin.

Kismet, Seward Co., Pop. Code 2
Kismet-Plains USD 483
Supt. – See Plains
ES 67859 – Harold Jantzen, prin.

La Crosse, Rush Co., Pop. Code 4
La Crosse USD 395
Sch. Sys. Enr. Code 2
Supt. – Dr. Dennis Wilson, P O BOX 790 67548
McCracken MS 67556 – Melvin Barnett, prin.
LaCrosse West ES 67548 – James Doyle, prin.
Other Schools – See Rush Center

La Cygne, Linn Co., Pop. Code 4
Prairie View USD 362
Sch. Sys. Enr. Code 3
Supt. – Galen Kelly, RURAL ROUTE 02 66040
Prairie View JHS 66040 – Daniel Stwalley, prin.
Other Schools – See Fontana, Parker, Prairie View

La Harpe, Allen Co., Pop. Code 3
Iola USD 257
Supt. – See Iola
ES 66751 – Richard Chase, prin.

Lakin, Kearny Co., Pop. Code 4
Lakin USD 215
Sch. Sys. Enr. Code 3
Supt. – Ernest McClain, P O BOX 47 67860

MS, P O BOX 47 67860 – Vernon Dietz, prin.
ES, P O BOX 26 67860 – Lester Mouse, prin.

Lancaster, Atchison Co., Pop. Code 2
Atchison Co. Comm. USD 377
Supt. – See Effingham
ES 66041 – Robin Schuckman, prin.

Langdon, Reno Co., Pop. Code 1
Fairfield USD 310
Sch. Sys. Enr. Code 2
Supt. – Dan Thornton, P O BOX D 67549
Other Schools – See Arlington, Sylvia, Turon

Lansing, Leavenworth Co., Pop. Code 3
Lansing USD 469
Sch. Sys. Enr. Code 4
Supt. – Dean Weaver, 110 S MAIN ST 66043
ES, 210 MARY ST 66043 – Patrick Tate, prin.
IS, 108 S 2ND ST 66043 – Marietta Gray, prin.
Zoll ES, 200 MARY ST 66043
　Marietta Gray, prin.

Lawrence USD 497
Supt. – See Lawrence
Centennial ES, 2145 LOUISIANA ST 66046
　Robert Arevalo, prin.

Larned, Pawnee Co., Pop. Code 5
Ft. Larned USD 495
Sch. Sys. Enr. Code 4
Supt. – Dr. Dale Lucas, 120 E 6TH ST 67550
JHS, 11TH & SANTA FE 67550
　Tom Renshaw, prin.
Hillside ES, 5TH & STATE 67550
　Dorothy Arensman, prin.
Northside MS, 16TH & STATE 67550
　Dorothy Arensman, prin.
Phinney ES, 523 E 12TH ST 67550
　Ruth Heinrichs, prin.
Other Schools – See Garfield, Pawnee Rock

Sacred Heart ES, 1123 STATE ST 67550

Lawrence, Douglas Co., Pop. Code 8
Lawrence USD 497
Sch. Sys. Enr. Code 6
Supt. – Dr. Dan Neuenswander
　2017 LOUISIANA ST 66046
Cordley ES, 19TH & VERMONT 66044
　Janet Broers, prin.
Deerfield ES, 101 LAWRENCE AVE 66044
　Verlin Gilbert, prin.
East Heights ES, 15TH & HASKELL 66044
　Willie Amison, prin.
Grant ES, RURAL ROUTE 03 66044
　Dr. Gary Haworth, prin.
Hillcrest ES, 1045 HILLTOP DR 66044
　William Armstrong, prin.
India-Kaw Valley ES, 1701 E 23RD ST 66046
　Russell Brooks, prin.
Kennedy ES, 1605 DAVIS ROAD 66046
　Sandra Holloway, prin.
New York ES, 936 NEW YORK ST 66044
　Diane Miller, prin.
Pinckney ES, 810 W 6TH ST 66044
　Gary Freeman, prin.
Quail Run ES, 1130 INVERNESS DR 66044
　Linda Herbel, prin.
Riverside ES, LAKEVIEW COURT 66044
　Lauri Becker, prin.
Schwegler ES, 2201 OUSDAHL ROAD 66046
　Gary Stauffer, prin.
Sunset Hill ES, 901 SCHWARZ ROAD 66044
　Calvin Rice, prin.
Wakarusa Valley ES, RURAL ROUTE 05 66046
　Ernest Coleman, prin.
Woodlawn ES, 5TH & ELM 66044
　Dr. Gary Haworth, prin.
Other Schools – See Lansing

St. John's ES, 1208 KENTUCKY ST 66044

Leavenworth, Leavenworth Co., Pop. Code 8
Easton USD 449
Supt. – See Easton
Salt Creek Valley ES, RURAL ROUTE 04 66048
　Jim Weaver, prin.

Leavenworth USD 453
Sch. Sys. Enr. Code 5
Supt. – Dr. Michael Slusher
　4TH & SENECA 66048
Anthony ES, 2ND & EVERGREEN 66048
　Roy Parks, prin.
Brewer ES, 17TH & OSAGE 66048
　Frank Kukuk, prin.
Hartnett MS, 3RD & CONGRESS 66048
　Steve Weissenfluh, prin.
Lincoln MS, 5TH & DAKOTA 66048
　Larry Doll, prin.
Muncie ES, 449 MUNCIE ROAD 66048
　Sharon Goodwin, prin.
North Broadway ES
　N BROADWAY & KIOWA 66048
　Larry Doll, prin.
Third Avenue ES, 3RD & MARSHALL 66048
　Steve Weissenfluh, prin.
Wilson ES, GRAND & OLIVE 66048
　Craig Carter, prin.

St. Paul Lutheran School, 320 N 7TH ST 66048
Xavier ES, 522 KICKAPOO ST 66048

Leawood, Johnson Co., Pop. Code 7
Blue Valley USD 229
Supt. – See Stanley
MS, 2410 W 123RD ST 66209 – Jim Gill, prin.
Indian Valley ES, 11600 KNOX ST 66210
Ronald Meyer, prin.
ES, 2400 W 123RD ST 66209 – Doug Harris, prin.

Cure of Ars ES, 9403 MISSION ROAD 66206

Lebanon, Smith Co., Pop. Code 2
Smith Center USD 237
Supt. – See Smith Center
ES 66952 – Debra Edwards, prin.

Lebo, Coffey Co., Pop. Code 3
Lebo-Waverly USD 243
Supt. – See Waverly
ES 66856 – Gary Massey, prin.

Lecompton, Douglas Co., Pop. Code 3
Perry USD 343
Supt. – See Perry
ES 66050 – Dennis Yoder, prin.

Lenexa, Johnson Co., Pop. Code 7
Shawnee Mission USD 512
Supt. – See Shawnee Mission
Bonjour ES, 9400 PFLUMM ROAD 66215
Gene Johnson, prin.
Rosehill ES, 9801 ROSEHILL ROAD 66215
Juanita Mermoud, prin.
Shawanoe ES, 11230 W 75TH ST 66214
Frank Croskey, prin.

Holy Trinity ES, 13600 W 92ND ST 66215

Lenora, Norton Co., Pop. Code 2
West Solomon Valley USD 213
Sch. Sys. Enr. Code 2
Supt. – Donald Skipton, P O BOX 98 67645
ES 67645 – Donald Skipton, prin.

Leon, Butler Co., Pop. Code 3
Bluestem USD 205
Sch. Sys. Enr. Code 3
Supt. – L. Gerald Schuetz, P O BOX 8 67074
Bluestem JHS, RURAL ROUTE 02 67074
Ron Wrampe, prin.
ES, P O BOX 98 67074 – Don Bohannon, prin.
Other Schools – See Augusta

Leoti, Wichita Co., Pop. Code 4
Leoti USD 467
Sch. Sys. Enr. Code 3
Supt. – John Heim, P O BOX 967 67861
Wichita County MS, P O BOX 908 67861
Tom Williams, prin.
High Plains ES, RURAL ROUTE 01 67861
Joe Zitnik, prin.
Stewart ES, P O BOX 807 67861
Ronald Moyer, prin.
Other Schools – See Marienthal

Le Roy, Coffey Co., Pop. Code 3
Le Roy-Gridley USD 245
Sch. Sys. Enr. Code 2
Supt. – Dr. Harvey Watson, P O BOX 57 66857
ES 66857 – Dr. Harvey Watson, prin.
Other Schools – See Gridley

Lewis, Edwards Co., Pop. Code 3
Lewis USD 502
Sch. Sys. Enr. Code 2
Supt. – Gary Akers, P O BOX 97 67552
ES 67552 – Gary Akers, prin.

Liberal, Seward Co., Pop. Code 7
Liberal USD 480
Sch. Sys. Enr. Code 5
Supt. – Donald Hall, P O BOX 949 67901
South JHS, 950 S GRANT AVE 67901
Vernon Welch, prin.
West JHS, 6TH & WESTERN 67901
Walter Autem, prin.
Garfield ES, 516 W 1ST ST 67901 – Don Hill, prin.
Lincoln ES, 1002 W 11TH ST 67901
Raymond Attebery, prin.
MacArthur ES, 925 S HOLLY DR 67901
Bryce Slack, prin.
McDermott ES
439 S PENNSYLVANIA AVE 67901
Milton Hughes, prin.
McKinley ES, 700 W 7TH ST 67901
Beth Koehn, prin.
Southlawn ES, 836 S JORDAN AVE 67901
Curtis Beer, prin.
Washington ES, 840 N WASHINGTON AVE 67901
Emmitt Millhouse, prin.

St. Anthony ES, 15TH & CALHOUN 67901

Lincoln, Lincoln Co., Pop. Code 4
Lincoln USD 298
Sch. Sys. Enr. Code 2
Supt. – J. C. Stolfus, P O BOX 289 67455
ES 67455 – H. Collins, prin.

Lindsborg, McPherson Co., Pop. Code 5
Lindsborg USD 400
Sch. Sys. Enr. Code 3
Supt. – Irvin Myers, 126 S MAIN ST 67456
ES, 227 N WASHINGTON ST 67456
Kenneth Forsberg, prin.
Other Schools – See Marquette

Linn, Washington Co., Pop. Code 2
Barnes USD 223
Supt. – See Barnes
ES 66953 – Delbert Learned, prin.

Linwood, Leavenworth Co., Pop. Code 2
Basehor-Linwood USD 458
Supt. – See Basehor
MS, P O BOX 1 66052 – David Reese, prin.
ES, P O BOX 1 66052 – William Foust, prin.

Little River, Rice Co., Pop. Code 3
Little River USD 444
Sch. Sys. Enr. Code 2
Supt. – C. Thieszen, P O BOX 218 67457
ES 67457 – Glen Davis, prin.
Other Schools – See Geneseo, Windom

Logan, Phillips Co., Pop. Code 3
Logan USD 326
Sch. Sys. Enr. Code 2
Supt. – Earl Loyd, P O BOX 98 67646
ES, P O BOX 98 67646 – Earl Loyd, prin.

Longford, Clay Co., Pop. Code 2
Clay Center USD 379
Supt. – See Clay Center
ES 67458 – Tim McFarland, prin.

Long Island, Phillips Co., Pop. Code 2
Northern Valley USD 212
Supt. – See Almena
MS 67647 – Dwight Vallin, prin.

Longton, Elk Co., Pop. Code 2
Elk Valley USD 283
Sch. Sys. Enr. Code 2
Supt. – R. W. Olivier, P O BOX 87 67352
Elk Valley ES 67352 – Rodney Olivier, prin.

Lorraine, Ellsworth Co., Pop. Code 2
Lorraine USD 328
Sch. Sys. Enr. Code 2
Supt. – N. E. Linton, P O BOX 76 67459
Other Schools – See Holyrood, Wilson

Lost Springs, Marion Co., Pop. Code 1
Centre USD 397
Sch. Sys. Enr. Code 2
Supt. – Jerry Will, P O BOX 38 66859
Centre ES 66859 – Jerry Will, prin.

Louisburg, Miami Co., Pop. Code 4
Louisburg USD 416
Sch. Sys. Enr. Code 4
Supt. – J. T. Knox, P O BOX 550 66053
ES 66053 – Jack Turner, prin.
Circle Grove ES 66053 – Robert Austin, prin.
Other Schools – See Bucyrus

Luray, Russell Co., Pop. Code 2
Russell Co. USD 407
Supt. – See Russell
Luray-Lucas ES 67649 – Duane Jamison, prin.

Lyndon, Osage Co., Pop. Code 4
Lyndon USD 421
Sch. Sys. Enr. Code 2
Supt. – Tom Bishard, P O BOX X 66451
ES 66451 – Leo Heidebrecht, prin.

Lyons, Rice Co., Pop. Code 5
Lyons USD 405
Sch. Sys. Enr. Code 3
Supt. – Larry L. Frisbie, 510 EAST AVE S 67554
MS, 401 S DOUGLAS AVE 67554
Lee Danyluk, prin.
Central ES, 501 W LINCOLN ST 67554
Phillip Smyth, prin.
Park ES, 100 S WORKMAN ST 67554
Gerald Hornbaker, prin.
South ES, EAST TAYLOR 67554
Irma Johnson, prin.

McCune, Crawford Co., Pop. Code 3
Cherokee USD 247
Supt. – See Cherokee
ES 66753 – Max Newell, prin.

McDonald, Rawlins Co., Pop. Code 2
Cheylin USD 103
Supt. – See Bird City
Cheylin ES, P O BOX 96 67745
Keith Sanders, prin.

Macksville, Stafford Co., Pop. Code 3
Macksville USD 351
Sch. Sys. Enr. Code 2
Supt. – F. Denis Stanley, P O BOX 487 67557
ES, P O BOX 308 67557 – Tom Morris, prin.

McLouth, Jefferson Co., Pop. Code 3
McLouth USD 342
Sch. Sys. Enr. Code 3
Supt. – Jack Bittner, 217 SUMMIT 66054
JHS, 217 SUMMIT 66054 – Dennis Cox, prin.
ES, 217 SUMMIT 66054 – James Campbell, prin.

McPherson, McPherson Co., Pop. Code 7
McPherson USD 418
Sch. Sys. Enr. Code 4
Supt. – Jack Hobbs, 514 N MAIN ST 67460
MS, 700 E ELIZABETH ST 67460
Merry Wade, prin.
Lincoln ES, 900 N ASH ST 67460
Stephen Burkholder, prin.
Roosevelt ES, 800 S WALNUT ST 67460
Richard King, prin.

Washington ES, 128 N PARK ST 67460
David Bauer, prin.

Madison, Greenwood Co., Pop. Code 4
Madison Virgil USD 386
Sch. Sys. Enr. Code 2
Supt. – Kenneth Schnautz, P O BOX 398 66860
ES, P O BOX 398 66860 – Larry Campbell, prin.

Maize, Sedgwick Co., Pop. Code 4
Maize USD 266
Sch. Sys. Enr. Code 4
Supt. – Joe Hickey, 120 E ALBERT 67101
IS 67101 – Ken Rickard, prin.
MS 67101 – Mike Meier, prin.
Vermillion PS 67101 – Dennis Wright, prin.

Manhattan, Riley Co., Pop. Code 8
Manhattan USD 383
Sch. Sys. Enr. Code 6
Supt. – Dr. Hal Rowe, 2031 POYNTZ AVE 66502
MS, 10TH & POYNTZ 66502
Marvin Marsh, prin.
Arnold ES, 1435 HUDSON AVE 66502
Clark Reinke, prin.
Bluemont ES, 714 BLUEMONT AVE 66502
Henrietta Bock, prin.
Field ES, 1700 LEAVENWORTH ST 66502
Teresa Northern, prin.
Lee ES, 701 LEE ST 66502 – Connie Evans, prin.
Marlatt ES, 2715 HOBBS DR 66502
Raymond Woods, prin.
Northview ES, 300 GRIFFITH DR 66502
Dan Yunk, prin.
Roosevelt ES, 1401 HOUSTON ST 66502
James Singer, prin.
Wilson ES, 312 N JULIETTE AVE 66502
Darcy Rourk, prin.
Other Schools – See Ogden

Seven Dolors ES, 306 S JULIETTE AVE 66502

Mankato, Jewell Co., Pop. Code 4
Mankato USD 278
Sch. Sys. Enr. Code 2
Supt. – M. Boyles, P O BOX 308 66956
ES 66956 – Robert Crowell, prin.

Manter, Stanton Co., Pop. Code 2
Stanton Co. USD 452
Supt. – See Johnson
ES 67862 – Larry Johnson, prin.

Maple Hill, Wabaunsee Co., Pop. Code 2
Mill Creek Valley USD 329
Supt. – See Alma
ES 66507 – Larry Longhofer, prin.

Marienthal, Wichita Co.
Leoti USD 467
Supt. – See Leoti
ES 67863 – John Heim, prin.

Marion, Marion Co., Pop. Code 4
Marion USD 408
Sch. Sys. Enr. Code 3
Supt. – John Burke, 601 E MAIN ST 66861
Corby ES, 412 N 2ND ST 66861
John Burke, prin.
MS, 1400 E LAWRENCE ST 66861
Doug Huxman, prin.
Other Schools – See Florence

Marquette, McPherson Co., Pop. Code 3
Lindsborg USD 400
Supt. – See Lindsborg
ES, P O BOX 307 67464 – Gary Mayfield, prin.

Marysville, Marshall Co., Pop. Code 5
Marysville USD 364
Sch. Sys. Enr. Code 3
Supt. – William Oborny, 1011 WALNUT ST 66508
JHS, 1005 WALNUT ST 66508
Darrell Genereux, prin.
Industrial Arts ES, 1006 OAK ST 66508
Robert Patterson, prin.
Other Schools – See Beattie

St. Gregory's ES, 207 N 14TH ST 66508

Mayetta, Jackson Co., Pop. Code 2
Mayetta USD 337
Sch. Sys. Enr. Code 3
Supt. – F. Staker, P O BOX 117 66509
Royal Valley MS 66509 – Raymond Thomas, prin.
ES 66509 – Raymond Thomas, prin.
Other Schools – See Hoyt

Meade, Meade Co., Pop. Code 4
Meade USD 226
Sch. Sys. Enr. Code 2
Supt. – Dannie Clodfelter
407 SCHOOL ADDITION 67864
ES 67864 – Max Newby, prin.

Medicine Lodge, Barber Co., Pop. Code 4
Barber Co. North USD 254
Sch. Sys. Enr. Code 3
Supt. – Bernard Girard, P O BOX 288 67104
IS, 1ST & MAIN 67104 – Lloyd Sumner, prin.
PS, 320 N WALNUT ST 67104
Harold Wanger, prin.
Other Schools – See Sharon

Melvern, Osage Co., Pop. Code 2
Marais Des Cygnes Valley USD 456
Sch. Sys. Enr. Code 2
Supt. – Jim Irey, P O BOX 158 66510

Marais Des Cygnes ES 66510
  Lonnie Bratcher, prin.
  Other Schools – See Quenemo

Meriden, Jefferson Co., Pop. Code 3
  Jefferson West USD 340
  Sch. Sys. Enr. Code 3
  Supt. – Ronald D. Burgess, P O BOX 267 66512
  Jefferson West ES 66512 – Charles Ireland,Jr., prin.
  Other Schools – See Ozawkie

Milford, Geary Co., Pop. Code 2
  Junction City USD 475
  Supt. – See Junction City
  ES 66514 – Susan Kamphaus, prin.

Miltonvale, Cloud Co., Pop. Code 3
  Southern Cloud Co. USD 334
  Supt. – See Glasco
  ES 67466 – John Rauch, prin.

Minneapolis, Ottawa Co., Pop. Code 4
  North Ottawa Co. USD 239
  Sch. Sys. Enr. Code 3
  Supt. – Ron Clifton, PO BOX A 67467
  ES, 312 DELIA AVE 67467 – John Dyck, prin.
  Other Schools – See Delphos

Minneola, Clark Co., Pop. Code 3
  Minneola USD 219
  Sch. Sys. Enr. Code 2
  Supt. – Eddie L. Goble, P O BOX 157 67865
  ES 67865 – Tom Hudson, prin.

Mission, Johnson Co., Pop. Code 6
  Shawnee Mission USD 512
  Supt. – See Shawnee Mission
  Highlands ES, 6200 ROE AVE 66205
    Leon Dawson, prin.
  Rushton ES, 6001 W 52ND ST 66202
    Richard King, prin.

St. Pius X ES, 5500 WOODSON ROAD 66202

Moline, Elk Co., Pop. Code 3
  West Elk USD 282
  Supt. – See Howard
  ES 67353 – Marvin Francisco, prin.

Montezuma, Gray Co., Pop. Code 3
  Montezuma USD 371
  Sch. Sys. Enr. Code 2
  Supt. – George Smirl, P O BOX 355 67867
  ES 67867 – George Smirl, prin.

Monument, Logan Co., Pop. Code 2
  Oakley USD 274
  Supt. – See Oakley
  ES 67747 – E. Fricker, prin.

Moran, Allen Co., Pop. Code 3
  Marmaton Valley USD 256
  Sch. Sys. Enr. Code 2
  Supt. – Ernie Price
    RURAL ROUTE 01 BOX 35 66755
  ES 66755 – Ken McWhirter, prin.
  Other Schools – See Elsmore

Morganville, Clay Co., Pop. Code 2
  Clay Center USD 379
  Supt. – See Clay Center
  ES 67468 – Ellen Rook, prin.

Morland, Graham Co., Pop. Code 2
  West Graham-Morland USD 280
  Sch. Sys. Enr. Code 1
  Supt. – James Deines, P O BOX 226 67650
  ES 67650 – James Deines, prin.

Moscow, Stevens Co., Pop. Code 2
  Moscow USD 209
  Sch. Sys. Enr. Code 2
  Supt. – Donald Nelson, P O BOX 158 67952
  ES, P O BOX 158 67952 – Robert Briggs, prin.

Mound City, Linn Co., Pop. Code 3
  Jayhawk USD 346
  Sch. Sys. Enr. Code 3
  Supt. – Gary Wimmer 66056
  ES 66056 – Kenneth Otto, prin.
  Other Schools – See Blue Mound, Prescott

Moundridge, McPherson Co., Pop. Code 4
  Moundridge USD 423
  Sch. Sys. Enr. Code 2
  Supt. – Terry Schmidt, P O BOX K 67107
  MS, P O BOX 607 67107
    Lucinda Lombardo, prin.
  ES, P O BOX F 67107 – Mary Norton, prin.

Mound Valley, Labette Co., Pop. Code 2
  Labette Co. USD 506
  Supt. – See Altamont
  ES, P O BOX 170 67354 – Gerald Beaver, prin.

Mount Hope, Sedgwick Co., Pop. Code 3
  Haven USD 312
  Supt. – See Haven
  ES 67108 – Mike Fast, prin.

Renwick USD 267
  Supt. – See Andale
  St. Joe ES 67108 – Leroy Blasi, prin.

Mullinville, Kiowa Co., Pop. Code 2
  Mullinville USD 424
  Sch. Sys. Enr. Code 2
  Supt. – Glen Hughes, P O BOX 6 67109
  ES, P O BOX 6 67109 – Donna Hughes, prin.

Mulvane, Sedgwick Co., Pop. Code 5
  Mulvane USD 263
  Sch. Sys. Enr. Code 4
  Supt. – Dean Parks, P O BOX 129 67110
  MS, 430 E MAIN ST 67110 – Marcus Huslig, prin.
  Munson ES, 1007 WESTVIEW DR 67110
    Donald George, prin.

Muncie, Wyandotte Co.
  Turner USD 202
  Supt. – See Kansas City
  ES, 65TH & RIVERVIEW 66057
    James Saragusa, prin.

Munden, Republic Co., Pop. Code 2
  Belleville USD 427
  Supt. – See Belleville
  ES 66959 – Donald Westphal, prin.

Murdock, Kingman Co.
  Kingman USD 331
  Supt. – See Kingman
  ES 67111 – Wes Kaufman, prin.

Muscotah, Atchison Co., Pop. Code 2
  Atchison Co. Comm. USD 377
  Supt. – See Effingham
  ES 66058 – Robin Schuckman, prin.

Natoma, Osborne Co., Pop. Code 3
  Paradise USD 399
  Sch. Sys. Enr. Code 2
  Supt. – Paul Sellon, P O BOX 100 67651
  ES 67651 – Keith Higgins, prin.
  Other Schools – See Paradise

Neodesha, Wilson Co., Pop. Code 5
  Neodesha USD 461
  Sch. Sys. Enr. Code 3
  Supt. – Jerry Webster, 522 WISCONSIN ST 66757
  Heller ES, 415 N 8TH ST 66757
    Bob Henson, prin.
  North Lawn MS, 1400 N 8TH ST 66757
    Walter Beard, prin.

Neosho Rapids, Lyon Co., Pop. Code 2
  Southern Lyon Co. USD 252
  Supt. – See Hartford
  ES, P O BOX 38 66864 – Jack Mahan, prin.

Ness City, Ness Co., Pop. Code 4
  Ness City USD 303
  Sch. Sys. Enr. Code 2
  Supt. – Terry Karlin, 414 E CHESTNUT ST 67560
  ES 67560 – Anthony Deane, prin.

Newton, Harvey Co., Pop. Code 7
  Newton USD 373
  Sch. Sys. Enr. Code 5
  Supt. – Clark Whiting, P O BOX 307 67114
  Chisholm MS, 900 E 1ST ST 67114
    Ronald Walker, prin.
  Santa Fe MS, 130 W BROADWAY ST 67114
    Gordon Stineman, prin.
  Cooper ES, 816 OAK ST 67114
    Dianna Harper, prin.
  Lincoln ES, 406 W 6TH ST 67114
    John Kelly, prin.
  McKinley ES, 308 E 1ST ST 67114
    John Bevan, prin.
  Northridge ES, 1900 WINDSOR DR 67114
    Marlin Frey, prin.
  Roosevelt ES, 701 E BROADWAY ST 67114
    Dianna Harper, prin.
  South Breeze ES, 1020 OLD MAIN ST 67114
    John Bevan, prin.
  Sunset ES, 619 BOYD AVE 67114
    Evan Johnson, prin.
  Other Schools – See Walton

St. Mary's ES, 124 E 8TH ST 67114

Nickerson, Reno Co., Pop. Code 4
  Nickerson USD 309
  Sch. Sys. Enr. Code 4
  Supt. – Samuel Ulsaker, P O BOX 408 67561
  ES, P O BOX 348 67561 – Donald Eilerts, prin.
  South Hutchinson ES
    405 S POPLAR SH ST 67505
    Herman Diener, prin.
  Other Schools – See Hutchinson

Norton, Norton Co., Pop. Code 5
  Norton USD 211
  Sch. Sys. Enr. Code 3
  Supt. – Dr. Patrick Terry
    105 E WAVERLY ST 67654
  JHS, 706 JONES AVE 67654 – Greg Mann, prin.
  Eisenhower ES, 1100 EISENHOWER DRIVE 67654
    Rosalie Stull, prin.

Nortonville, Jefferson Co., Pop. Code 3
  Jefferson Co. North USD 339
  Supt. – See Winchester
  Jefferson County North MS, P O BOX 298 66060
    Linda Aldridge, prin.

Norwich, Kingman Co., Pop. Code 2
  Kingman USD 331
  Supt. – See Kingman
  ES 67118 – Fred Garten, prin.

Oakley, Logan Co., Pop. Code 4
  Oakley USD 274
  Sch. Sys. Enr. Code 3
  Supt. – Dr. Donald Marchant, 208 E 2ND 67748
  ES 67748 – E. Fricker, prin.
  Other Schools – See Monument

St. Joseph School, 725 FREEMAN AVE 67748

Oberlin, Decatur Co., Pop. Code 4
  Oberlin USD 294
  Sch. Sys. Enr. Code 3
  Supt. – Wayne Steinert
    131 E COMMERCIAL ST 67749
  ES, 201 W ASH ST 67749 – Darrell Jones, prin.

Offerle, Edwards Co., Pop. Code 2
  Kinsley-Offerle USD 347
  Supt. – See Kinsley
  MS, P O BOX 130 67563 – Bill Inman, prin.

Ogden, Riley Co., Pop. Code 4
  Manhattan USD 383
  Supt. – See Manhattan
  ES 66517 – Doyle Barnes, prin.

Olathe, Johnson Co., Pop. Code 8
  Blue Valley USD 229
  Supt. – See Stanley
  Morse ES, 15201 S HALSEY ST 66062
    Richard Lewis, prin.

  Olathe USD 233
  Sch. Sys. Enr. Code 7
  Supt. – Dr. M. L. Winters, P O BOX 2000 66061
  Black Bob ES, 14701 S BROUGHAM DR 66062
    Kenneth Roberts, prin.
  Briarwood ES, 14101 S BROUGHAM 66062
    Pamela Burrus, prin.
  Brougham ES, 15500 S BROUGHAM DR 66062
    Angela Grasso, prin.
  Central ES, 324 S WATER ST 66061
    Fred Fuqua, prin.
  Countryside ES, 15800 W 124TH TERRACE 66062
    Earl Martin, prin.
  Fairview ES, 600 N MARION ST 66061
    Ron Thompson, prin.
  Havencroft ES, 1700 E SHERIDAN ST 66062
    Orin Swift, prin.
  Heritage ES, 1500 E PAWNEE 66061
    Leon Brewer, prin.
  Indian Creek ES
    15800 INDIAN CREEK PKY 66062
    Donna Hemphill, prin.
  Meadow Lane ES, 21880 W 111TH 66061
    Mary McDonough, prin.
  Northview ES, 905 N WALKER ST 66061
    Anthony Pettijohn, prin.
  Prairie Center ES, 629 N PERSIMMON DR 66061
    Elaine Herrman, prin.
  Ridgeview ES, 1201 E ELM ST 66061
    Jim Thomas, prin.
  Rolling Ridge ES, 1500 W ELM TERRACE 66061
    Terry Croskey, prin.
  Scarborough ES, 2200 LINDENWOOD 66062
    Gerald Cox, prin.
  Tomahawk ES, 13820 S BROUGHAM DR 66062
    David Kearney, prin.
  Walnut Grove ES, 11800 S PFLUMM ROAD 66062
    David Brewer, prin.
  Washington ES, 1202 N RIDGEVIEW ST 66061
    Meldon Wesley, prin.
  Westview ES, WABASH & LEE 66061
    Ernie Claudel, prin.

Prince of Peace ES, 16000 W 143RD 66062
St. Paul ES, EDGEMERE & HONEYSUCKLE 66061

Olpe, Lyon Co., Pop. Code 2
  Southern Lyon Co. USD 252
  Supt. – See Hartford
  JHS, P O BOX 206 66865 – Mike Dougherty, prin.
  ES, P O BOX 206 66865
    Michael Dougherty, prin.

Olsburg, Pottawatomie Co., Pop. Code 2
  Blue Valley USD 384
  Supt. – See Randolph
  ES 66520 – Jim McCormick, prin.

Onaga, Pottawatomie Co., Pop. Code 2
  Onaga-Havensville-Wheaton USD 322
  Sch. Sys. Enr. Code 2
  Supt. – M. Dale Carlson, 310 LEONARD ST 66521
  ES 66521 – Gwen Poss, prin.
  Other Schools – See Havensville, Wheaton

Osage City, Osage Co., Pop. Code 5
  Osage City USD 420
  Sch. Sys. Enr. Code 3
  Supt. – Dr. Frank Colaw
    5TH & CALIFORNIA 66523
  ES 66523 – Brian Davies, prin.

Osawatomie, Miami Co., Pop. Code 5
  Osawatomie USD 367
  Sch. Sys. Enr. Code 4
  Supt. – Robert Hull
    12TH & TROJAN DRIVE 66064
  MS, 428 PACIFIC AVE 66064
    Douglas Tyrrell, prin.
  Osawatomie East ES, 5TH & BROWN 66064
    Robert Cook, prin.
  West ES, 10TH & PACIFIC 66064
    William Lewis, prin.

Osborne, Osborne Co., Pop. Code 4
  Osborne Co. USD 392
  Sch. Sys. Enr. Code 2
  Supt. – James Fraley, P O BOX 209 67473
  ES 67473 – Larry Bernard, prin.
  Other Schools – See Alton

Oskaloosa, Jefferson Co., Pop. Code 4
Oskaloosa USD 341
Sch. Sys. Enr. Code 3
Supt. – James White, P O BOX 345   66066
ES   66066 – Edward Albert, prin.

Oswego, Labette Co., Pop. Code 4
Oswego USD 504
Sch. Sys. Enr. Code 2
Supt. – Edwin Sink, P O BOX 129   67356
Eastside MS   67356 – Robert Harris, prin.
Neosho Heights ES   67356 – Robert Harris, prin.
Other Schools – See Parsons

Otis, Rush Co., Pop. Code 2
Otis-Bison USD 403
Supt. – See Albert
Otis-Bison IS   67565 – C. Richardson, prin.
Otis-Bison PS   67511 – C. Richardson, prin.

Ottawa, Franklin Co., Pop. Code 7
Ottawa USD 290
Sch. Sys. Enr. Code 4
Supt. – Don Duncan, 420 S MAIN ST   66067
JHS, S MAIN ST   66067 – Margaret Betterton, prin.
Eisenhower ES, 1404 ASH ST   66067
   Albert Keefer, prin.
Field ES, 720 TREMONT ST   66067
   Dorothy Snyder, prin.
Garfield ES, 12TH & COLLEGE   66067
   Bill Ratliff, prin.
Hawthorne ES, SOUTH POPLAR   66067
   (—), prin.
Lincoln ES, NORTH CEDAR   66067
   Marlin Kimball, prin.

Overbrook, Osage Co., Pop. Code 3
Santa Fe Trail USD 434
Supt. – See Carbondale
ES   66524 – George Hughes, prin.

Overland Park, Johnson Co., Pop. Code 8
Blue Valley USD 229
Supt. – See Stanley
Stanley ES, 15000 METCALF AVE   66223
   Connie Vilott, prin.
Valley Park ES, 12301 LAMAR AVE   66209
   Dr. John Anderson, prin.

Shawnee Mission USD 512
Supt. – See Shawnee Mission
Apache ES, 8910 GODDARD ST   66214
   Lee Miller, prin.
Arrowhead ES, 6601 SANTA FE DR   66202
   Rick Carter, prin.
Brookridge ES, 9920 LOWELL AVE   66212
   Connie Welsh, prin.
Carpenter ES, 9700 W 96TH ST   66212
   Bill Dowden, prin.
Cherokee ES, 8714 ANTIOCH RD   66212
   Betty Barton, prin.
Diemer ES, 9600 LAMAR AVE   66207
   Jim Owens, prin.
East Antioch ES, 7342 LOWELL AVE   66204
   Richard Selensky, prin.
Moody ES, 10101 ENGLAND ST   66212
   Susan Knight, prin.
Nall Hills ES, 102ND & HORNTON   66207
   Don Wyatt, prin.
ES, 8200 SANTA FE DR   66204
   Gerald Honn, prin.
Pawnee ES, 9501 W 91ST ST   66212
   Wolfgang Thiergart, prin.
Santa Fe Trail ES, 7100 LAMAR AVE   66204
   Richard Barrett, prin.
Tomahawk ES, 6301 W 78TH ST   66204
   Alma Lunn, prin.
Trailwood ES, 5101 W 95TH ST   66207
   Mary Horton, prin.

Hyman Brand Hebrew Academy
   5901 COLLEGE BLVD   66211
Brookridge Day School, 9555 HADLEY ST   66212
Holy Cross ES, 8101 W 95TH ST   66212
Holy Spirit ES, 11300 W 103RD ST   66214
Queen of the Holy Rosary ES
   6915 W 71ST ST   66204

Oxford, Sumner Co., Pop. Code 4
Oxford USD 358
Sch. Sys. Enr. Code 2
Supt. – A. O. George   67119
ES   66119 – George Curry, prin.

Ozawkie, Jefferson Co., Pop. Code 2
Jefferson West USD 340
Supt. – See Meriden
Jefferson West MS   66070
   Robert E. Overstreet, prin.

Palco, Rooks Co., Pop. Code 2
Palco USD 269
Sch. Sys. Enr. Code 2
Supt. – William Wilson, P O BOX 21   67657
Damar MS   67657 – Charles Stahl, prin.
ES   67657 – Charles Stahl, prin.

Paola, Miami Co., Pop. Code 5
Paola USD 368
Sch. Sys. Enr. Code 4
Supt. – Dr. W. R. Cleary, P O BOX 268   66071
MS, P O BOX 268   66071 – Olin McCool, prin.
North ES, 302 N OAK ST   66071
   Eileen Scroggie, prin.
Sunflower MS, 1401 E 303RD   66071
   Ken Emley, prin.
Other Schools – See Hillsdale

Holy Trinity ES, 801 E CHIPPEWA ST   66071

Paradise, Russell Co., Pop. Code 1
Paradise USD 399
Supt. – See Natoma
MS   67658 – Keith Higgins, prin.

Park, Gove Co., Pop. Code 2
Grainfield USD 292
Supt. – See Grainfield
ES   67751 – Charles King, prin.

Parker, Linn Co., Pop. Code 2
Prairie View USD 362
Supt. – See La Cygne
ES   66072 – John Ammel, prin.

Parsons, Labette Co., Pop. Code 7
Labette Co. USD 506
Supt. – See Altamont
Meadow View ES
   RURAL ROUTE 02 BOX 243   67357
   Rex Toomey, prin.

Oswego USD 504
Supt. – See Oswego
Service Valley ES, RURAL ROUTE 04   67357
   William Barnes, prin.

Parsons USD 503
Sch. Sys. Enr. Code 4
Supt. – Dr. Willis Heck, P O BOX 1056   67357
MS, 2719 MAIN ST   67357 – Rich Ney, prin.
Garfield ES, 300 S 14TH ST   67357
   Steven Frazell, prin.
Guthridge ES, 1020 S 31ST ST   67357
   John Ewbank, prin.
Lincoln ES, 18TH & DIRR   67357
   Timothy Fox, prin.
Washington ES, 2631 STEVENS AVE   67357
   John Benson, prin.

Parsons Catholic ES, 1831 STEVENS AVE   67357

Partridge, Reno Co., Pop. Code 2
Haven USD 312
Supt. – See Haven
ES   67566 – Rod Nikkel, prin.

Pawnee Rock, Barton Co., Pop. Code 2
Ft. Larned USD 495
Supt. – See Larned
JHS   67567 – Verl McKinney, prin.
ES   67567 – Lyle Parks, prin.

Paxico, Wabaunsee Co., Pop. Code 2
Mill Creek Valley USD 329
Supt. – See Alma
ES   66526 – Daniel Wagner, prin.

Peabody, Marion Co., Pop. Code 4
Peabody-Burns USD 398
Sch. Sys. Enr. Code 2
Supt. – John Glover, 506 ELM ST   66866
MS   66866 – Don Hague, prin.
Peabody ES   66866 – Sue Anderson, prin.
Other Schools – See Burns

Perry, Jefferson Co., Pop. Code 3
Perry USD 343
Sch. Sys. Enr. Code 3
Supt. – J. R. Shepherd, P O BOX 29   66073
MS   66073 – Eric Hyler, prin.
ES   66073 – Paula Kellogg, prin.
Williamstown ES   66073 – Dennis Yoder, prin.
Other Schools – See Grantville, Lecompton

Phillipsburg, Phillips Co., Pop. Code 5
Phillipsburg USD 325
Sch. Sys. Enr. Code 3
Supt. – Dorrell George, 240 S 7TH ST   67661
MS, 647 7TH ST   67661 – Dr. Jeff Anschutz, prin.
South ES, 300 NEBRASKA AVE   67661
   Virgil Nelson, prin.

Pittsburg, Crawford Co., Pop. Code 7
Pittsburg USD 250
Sch. Sys. Enr. Code 5
Supt. – Dr. Jerry Steele, 510 DEILL ST   66762
MS, 14TH & BROADWAY   66762 – Rob Heck, prin.
Field ES, 1009 E 6TH ST   66762
   Francis Smith, prin.
Lakeside ES, 709 S COLLEGE ST   66762
   Mary Remington, prin.
Lincoln ES, 1700 N LOCUST ST   66762
   Phil Carter, prin.
Nettels ES, 1912 HOMER ST   66762
   Donald Porter, prin.
Westside ES, 430 W 5TH ST   66762
   Harold Fisher, prin.

St. Mary ES, 213 E 9TH ST   66762

Plains, Seward Co., Pop. Code 3
Kismet-Plains USD 483
Sch. Sys. Enr. Code 3
Supt. – D. J. Miller, P O BOX 517   67869
ES   67859 – Weldon Allen, prin.
Other Schools – See Kismet

Plainville, Rooks Co., Pop. Code 4
Plainville USD 270
Sch. Sys. Enr. Code 3
Supt. – J. D. Brunnemer, 111 W MILL ST   67663
ES   67663 – Dwight Hemmerling, prin.

Sacred Heart ES, 300 N WASHINGTON ST   67663

Pleasanton, Linn Co., Pop. Code 4
Pleasanton USD 344
Sch. Sys. Enr. Code 2
Supt. – Jack Collins, P O BOX 450   66075
ES   66075 – Bernard Stine, prin.

Pomona, Franklin Co., Pop. Code 3
West Franklin USD 287
Sch. Sys. Enr. Code 3
Supt. – James Cain, P O BOX 38   66076
Appanoose ES   66076 – Fred Meyers, prin.
ES   66076 – Susan Myers, prin.
Other Schools – See Williamsburg

Potwin, Butler Co., Pop. Code 3
Remington-Whitewater USD 206
Supt. – See Whitewater
ES   67123 – Fay Fry, prin.

Prairie View, Phillips Co., Pop. Code 2
Prairie View USD 362
Supt. – See La Cygne
Lacygne ES   66040 – Frank Leone, prin.

Prairie Village, Johnson Co., Pop. Code 7
Shawnee Mission USD 512
Supt. – See Shawnee Mission
Belinder ES, 7230 BELINDER AVE   66208
   Betsy Degan, prin.
Briarwood ES, 5300 W 86TH ST   66207
   Helen Cohen, prin.
Corinth ES, 83RD & MISSION ROAD   66206
   Larry Campbell, prin.
Prairie ES, 6642 MISSION ROAD   66208
   Betty France, prin.
Somerset ES, 79TH & BELINDER   66206
   Cynthia Anderson, prin.

St. Ann ES, 7241 MISSION ROAD   66208

Pratt, Pratt Co., Pop. Code 6
Pratt USD 382
Sch. Sys. Enr. Code 4
Supt. – Howard E. Gray
   401 N NINNESCAH ST   67124
Liberty IS, 300 S LUKA   67124 – Rich McCall, prin.
Haskins ES, LAWRENCE & SCHOOL   67124
   Cleo Rucker, prin.
Southwest ES, 8TH & WASHINGTON   67124
   Carl Carlson, prin.

Skyline USD 438
Sch. Sys. Enr. Code 2
Supt. – A. Boland, RURAL ROUTE 02   67124
Skyline ES, RURAL ROUTE 02   67124
   John Dunn, prin.

Sacred Heart School, 330 NORTH OAK   67124

Prescott, Linn Co., Pop. Code 2
Jayhawk USD 346
Supt. – See Mound City
ES   66767 – (—), prin.

Pretty Prairie, Reno Co., Pop. Code 3
Pretty Prairie USD 311
Sch. Sys. Enr. Code 2
Supt. – Barton Goering, P O BOX 218   67570
MS   67570 – William Crosley, prin.
ES   67570 – Barton Goering, prin.

Protection, Comanche Co., Pop. Code 3
Comanche Co. USD 300
Supt. – See Coldwater
ES   67127 – John Garvie, prin.

Quenemo, Osage Co., Pop. Code 2
Marais Des Cygnes Valley USD 456
Supt. – See Melvern
Marais Des Cygnes MS   66528 – Lynn Thrall, prin.
Marais Des Cygnes ES   66528 – Lynn Thrall, prin.

Quinter, Gove Co., Pop. Code 3
Quinter USD 293
Sch. Sys. Enr. Code 2
Supt. – Larry Geil, P O BOX 429   67752
ES   67752 – Larry Geil, prin.

Randall, Jewell Co.
Jewell USD 279
Supt. – See Jewell
MS   66963 – Larry Girard, prin.

Randolph, Riley Co., Pop. Code 2
Blue Valley USD 384
Sch. Sys. Enr. Code 2
Supt. – Larry Phye, P O BOX 98   66554
MS   66554 – Larry Phye, prin.
Other Schools – See Olsburg

Ransom, Ness Co., Pop. Code 2
Smoky Hill USD 302
Sch. Sys. Enr. Code 2
Supt. – Ralph Kenworthy, P O BOX 248   67572
JHS, P O BOX 248   67572 – Mike Kastle, prin.
ES   67572 – Ralph Kenworthy, prin.

Raymond, Rice Co., Pop. Code 2
Chase USD 401
Supt. – See Chase
MS   67573 – Ralph Renfro, Jr., prin.

Reading, Lyon Co., Pop. Code 2
North Lyon Co. USD 251
Supt. – See Americus
ES   66868 – Loren Long, prin.

Rexford, Thomas Co., Pop. Code 2
Golden Plains USD 316
Supt. – See Selden
Golden Plains JHS 67753 – Michael Wilson, prin.

Richmond, Franklin Co., Pop. Code 3
Central Heights USD 288
Sch. Sys. Enr. Code 2
Supt. – Leo E. Laird, RURAL ROUTE 01 66080
Central Heights ES, RURAL ROUTE 01 66080
Charles Patry, prin.

Riley, Riley Co., Pop. Code 3
Riley Co. USD 378
Sch. Sys. Enr. Code 3
Supt. – Rob Winter, P O BOX 326 66531
ES 66531 – Lori Martin, prin.

Riverton, Cherokee Co., Pop. Code 2
Riverton USD 404
Sch. Sys. Enr. Code 3
Supt. – S. E. Woodrum, P O BOX D 66770
JHS, P O BOX D 66770 – Dewayne Treece, prin.
ES, P O BOX A 66770 – Monty Phipps, prin.

Robinson, Brown Co., Pop. Code 2
Hiawatha USD 415
Supt. – See Hiawatha
JHS 66532 – John Severin, prin.

Rolla, Morton Co., Pop. Code 2
Rolla USD 217
Sch. Sys. Enr. Code 2
Supt. – Walter Hays, P O BOX 167 67954
Dermot ES 67954 – Selola Lewis, prin.
ES, P O BOX 167 67954 – Mac Plummer, prin.

Rosalia, Butler Co., Pop. Code 3
Flinthills USD 492
Sch. Sys. Enr. Code 2
Supt. – John Watson, P O BOX 125 67132
Flinthills MS, 1 SCHOOL ST 67132
Carl Harvey, prin.
ES 67132 – Carl Harvey, prin.
Other Schools – See Cassoday

Rose Hill, Butler Co., Pop. Code 4
Rose Hill USD 394
Sch. Sys. Enr. Code 4
Supt. – Terry McGreevy
315 S ROSE HILL ROAD 67133
MS 67133 – Steve Wyckoff, prin.
ES 67133 – David Dunbar, prin.

Rossville, Shawnee Co., Pop. Code 4
Kaw Valley USD 321
Supt. – See Saint Marys
ES 66533 – Ron Napier, prin.

Rozel, Pawnee Co., Pop. Code 2
Pawnee Heights USD 496
Sch. Sys. Enr. Code 2
Supt. – Jim Barrett, P O BOX 98 67574
Other Schools – See Burdett

Rush Center, Rush Co., Pop. Code 2
La Crosse USD 395
Supt. – See La Crosse
ES 67575 – James Doyle, prin.

Russell, Russell Co., Pop. Code 6
Russell Co. USD 407
Sch. Sys. Enr. Code 4
Supt. – LeRoy Jaggers, 802 N MAIN ST 67665
Ruppenthal JHS, 400 N ELM ST 67665
Rick Riffel, prin.
Bickerdyke ES, 4TH & MAPLE 67665
John Farrell, prin.
Simpson ES, 1301 N MAIN ST 67665
Don Degenhardt, prin.
Other Schools – See Dorrance, Gorham, Luray

Sabetha, Nemaha Co., Pop. Code 4
Sabetha USD 441
Sch. Sys. Enr. Code 3
Supt. – Von C. Lauer, 107 OREGON ST 66534
MS, 1ST & MAIN 66534 – Terry L. Duntz, prin.
ES 66534 – Timothy Foist, prin.
Other Schools – See Wetmore

Saint Francis, Cheyenne Co., Pop. Code 4
St. Francis USD 297
Sch. Sys. Enr. Code 2
Supt. – Carl Werner, P O BOX 605 67756
ES 67756 – Larry Gabel, prin.

Saint George, Pottawatomie Co., Pop. Code 2
Westmoreland USD 323
Supt. – See Westmoreland
ES 66535 – Mary Stamey, prin.

Saint John, Stafford Co., Pop. Code 4
St. John USD 350
Sch. Sys. Enr. Code 2
Supt. – B. Parker, 406 N MONROE ST 67576
ES 67576 – Klon Mathews, prin.
Other Schools – See Hudson

Saint Marys, Pottawatomie Co., Pop. Code 4
Kaw Valley USD 321
Sch. Sys. Enr. Code 4
Supt. – George Brown, P O BOX 160 66536
ES 66536 – Delores Thomas, prin.
Other Schools – See Delia, Emmett, Rossville

Saint Paul, Neosho Co., Pop. Code 3
Erie-St. Paul USD 101
Supt. – See Erie
ES 66771 – Kenneth Rundle, prin.

Salina, Saline Co., Pop. Code 8
Ell-Saline USD 307
Sch. Sys. Enr. Code 2
Supt. – William Walz, RURAL ROUTE 02 67401
Happy Corner ES
RURAL ROUTE 02 BOX 69 67401
William Walz, prin.
Other Schools – See Brookville

Salina USD 305
Sch. Sys. Enr. Code 6
Supt. – Dr. Andy Tompkins, P O BOX 797 67402
Roosevelt Lincoln JHS, 8TH & MULBERRY 67401
Stan Lauer, prin.
South JHS, 100 E LESLIE AVE 67401
Clay Thompson, prin.
Bartlett ES, 300 S 9TH ST 67401
Lyle Johnson, prin.
Coronado ES, 518 E NEAL AVE 67401
Dr. Helen Hooper, prin.
Franklin ES, 830 S 9TH ST 67401
Garry Rowson, prin.
Gleniffer Hill ES, 1511 GYPSUM AVE 67401
Gail Konzem, prin.
Hageman ES, 409 W CLOUD ST 67401
Patricia Fells, prin.
Hawthorne ES, 715 N 9TH ST 67401
Lois Gay, prin.
Heusner ES, 425 E JEWELL AVE 67401
Ted Roberts, prin.
Kennedy ES, 700 JUPITER AVE 67401
Mary Ann Lay, prin.
Lowell ES, 1009 HIGHLAND 67401
Mary Lay, prin.
Meadowlark Ridge ES, 2200 GLEN AVE 67401
Jerry Baxa, prin.
Oakdale ES, 811 E IRON AVE 67401
Gail Konzem, prin.
Schilling ES, 3131 CANTERBURY DR 67401
Dwight Powell, prin.
Stewart ES, 2123 ROACH ST 67401
James Hughes, prin.
Sunset ES, 1510 W REPUBLIC AVE 67401
Jerry Dyck, prin.
Whittier ES, 711 CEDAR ST 67401
Irvin Albin, prin.

Sacred Heart Cathedral ES
406 W IRON AVE 67401
St. Mary's ES, 304 E CLOUD ST 67401

Satanta, Haskell Co., Pop. Code 4
Satanta USD 507
Sch. Sys. Enr. Code 2
Supt. – Dennis Thompson, P O BOX 279 67870
ES, P O BOX 129 67870 – Leonard Brock, prin.

Scammon, Cherokee Co., Pop. Code 3
Columbus USD 493
Supt. – See Columbus
ES 66773 – Jim Sarwinski, prin.

Scandia, Republic Co., Pop. Code 2
Pike Valley USD 426
Sch. Sys. Enr. Code 2
Supt. – Richard Ahlvers, P O BOX 291 66966
Other Schools – See Courtland

Schoenchen, Ellis Co., Pop. Code 2
Hays USD 489
Supt. – See Hays
ES 67667 – Ron Ream, prin.

Scott City, Scott Co., Pop. Code 5
Scott Co. USD 466
Sch. Sys. Enr. Code 4
Supt. – James Thompson, P O BOX 249 67871
MS, 9TH & ADA 67871 – Richard Barton, prin.
Beaver Flats ES 67871 – Joe Palmer, prin.
ES, 704 S COLLEGE ST 67871
Kenneth Long, prin.
Other Schools – See Shallow Water

Scranton, Osage Co., Pop. Code 3
Santa Fe Trail USD 434
Supt. – See Carbondale
ES 66537 – Steven Berg, prin.

Sedan, Chautauqua Co., Pop. Code 4
Chautauqua Co. USD 286
Sch. Sys. Enr. Code 2
Supt. – Clayton Williams, 416 E ELM ST 67361
ES 67361 – James Clark, prin.

Sedgwick, Harvey Co., Pop. Code 4
Sedgwick USD 439
Sch. Sys. Enr. Code 2
Supt. – W. Krase, P O BOX K 67135
ES 67135 – Ashley Anderson, prin.

Selden, Sheridan Co., Pop. Code 2
Golden Plains USD 316
Sch. Sys. Enr. Code 2
Supt. – Michael Wilson, P O BOX A 67757
Golden Plains ES, P O BOX 199 67757
Michael Wilson, prin.
Other Schools – See Rexford

Seneca, Nemaha Co., Pop. Code 4
Baileyville-St. Benedict USD 451
Supt. – See Baileyville
St. Benedict ES 66538 – Allen Pokorny, prin.

Nemaha Valley USD 442
Sch. Sys. Enr. Code 2
Supt. – L. Holaday, 318 MAIN ST 66538

Nemaha Valley JHS, 709 NEMAHA ST 66538
John Eppich, prin.
ES, 709 NEMAHA ST 66538 – John Eppich, prin.

Sts. Peter & Paul ES, 401 ELK ST 66538

Severy, Greenwood Co., Pop. Code 2
West Elk USD 282
Supt. – See Howard
ES 67137 – Thomas Eubank, prin.

Shallow Water, Scott Co.
Scott Co. USD 466
Supt. – See Scott City
ES 67872 – Joe Palmer, prin.

Sharon, Barber Co., Pop. Code 2
Barber Co. North USD 254
Supt. – See Medicine Lodge
ES 67138 – Melvin Coyle, prin.

Sharon Springs, Wallace Co., Pop. Code 3
Wallace Co. USD 241
Sch. Sys. Enr. Code 2
Supt. – Paul McNall, P O BOX 580 67758
ES 67758 – Daniel Van Laeys, prin.
Other Schools – See Wallace

Shawnee, Johnson Co., Pop. Code 8
Shawnee Mission USD 512
Supt. – See Shawnee Mission
Benninghoven ES, 6720 CAENEN ST 66216
Lloyd Trauer, prin.
Flint ES, 5705 FLINT ST 66203 – Jan Jones, prin.
Marsh ES, 5642 ROSEHILL ROAD 66216
John Dill, prin.
Nieman ES, 10917 W 67TH ST 66203
Kim Zier, prin.

Hope Lutheran ES, 6308 QUIVIRA ROAD 66216

Shawnee Mission, Johnson Co.
Blue Valley USD 229
Supt. – See Stanley
Oxford MS, 12500 SWITZER 66213
Robert Wilson, prin.
Oak Hill ES, 10200 W 124TH 66213
Russ Pieken, prin.
Tomahawk Ridge ES, 11902 LOWELL 66213
Mike Sportsman, prin.

Shawnee Mission USD 512
Sch. Sys. Enr. Code 8
Supt. – Dr. Raj Chopra
7325 ANTIOCH ROAD 66204
Antioch MS, 8200 W 81ST ST 66204
Larry Blair, prin.
Hocker Grove MS, 10400 JOHNSON DRIVE 66203
Charlotte Sands, prin.
Indian Hills MS, 6400 MISSION ROAD 66208
Glen Griepenstroh, prin.
Indian Woods MS, 9700 WOODSON DRIVE 66207
Larry Neelly, prin.
Mission Valley MS, 8500 MISSION ROAD 66206
Rob Welch, prin.
Trailridge MS, 7500 QUIVIRA ROAD 66216
Mary Fugate, prin.
Westridge MS, 9300 NIEMAN ROAD 66214
Rob Winter, prin.
Bluejacket ES, 11615 W 49TH TERRACE 66203
Marilyn Lawrenz, prin.
Brookwood ES, 103RD & WENONGA 66206
Yancy Whitworth, prin.
Comanche ES, 8200 GRANT ST 66204
Dorothy Rea, prin.
Crestview ES, 6101 CRAIG ST 66202
Leona Martin, prin.
Greenwood ES, 16000 W 65TH ST 66217
Kendall Stephenson, prin.
McAuliffe, 15600 W 83RD 66219
Joanne Grote, prin.
Merriam ES, 6100 MASTIN ST 66203
Wilbur Jones, prin.
Mill Creek ES, 13951 W 79TH ST 66215
Kenneth Cheves, prin.
Oak Park ES, 10000 NIEMAN ROAD 66214
Deborah Cheves, prin.
Roeland Park ES, 5527 JUNIPER DR 66205
Robert Benson, prin.
Roesland ES, 4900 PARISH 66205
Don Morris, prin.
South Park ES, 8715 W 49TH TERRACE 66203
Michael Windes, prin.
West Antioch ES, 7101 SWITZER ST 66203
Joann Lawrence, prin.
Westwood View ES, 2511 W 50TH 66205
Gary Proctor, prin.
Other Schools – See Lenexa, Mission, Overland Park,
Prairie Village, Shawnee

Midland SDA ES, 6915 MAURER ROAD 66217
St. Agnes ES, 5130 MISSION ROAD 66205
St. Joseph ES, 5901 FLINT ST 66203

Silver Lake, Shawnee Co., Pop. Code 4
Silver Lake USD 372
Sch. Sys. Enr. Code 2
Supt. – Michael Barricklow, P O BOX 39 66539
ES 66539 – William Ross, prin.

Smith Center, Smith Co., Pop. Code 4
Smith Center USD 237
Sch. Sys. Enr. Code 3
Supt. – D. Stockstill, P O BOX 329 66967
ES, P O BOX 329 66967 – John Wright, prin.
Other Schools – See Gaylord, Lebanon

Solomon, Dickinson Co., Pop. Code 4
Solomon USD 393
Sch. Sys. Enr. Code 2
Supt. – John McFarland, P O BOX 247 67480
ES 67480 – Joe Wiggins, prin.

South Haven, Sumner Co., Pop. Code 2
South Haven USD 509
Sch. Sys. Enr. Code 2
Supt. – Donald Devine, P O BOX 228 67140
ES 67140 – Donald DeVine, prin.

Spearville, Ford Co., Pop. Code 3
Spearville USD 381
Sch. Sys. Enr. Code 2
Supt. – Gordon King, P O BOX 338 67876
ES 67876 – Gordon King, prin.

Spring Hill, Johnson Co., Pop. Code 4
Spring Hill USD 230
Sch. Sys. Enr. Code 4
Supt. – Dr. Perry Perkins, P O BOX 346 66083
MS, P O BOX 388 66083 – Rob Bliss, prin.
Hilltop ES 66083 – Larry Meyer, prin.
ES 66083 – Stephen Thompson, prin.

Stafford, Stafford Co., Pop. Code 4
Stafford USD 349
Sch. Sys. Enr. Code 2
Supt. – R. Combs, P O BOX 400 67578
ES, P O BOX 400 67578 – R. Combs, prin.

Stanley, Johnson Co., Pop. Code 2
Blue Valley USD 229
Sch. Sys. Enr. Code 6
Supt. – Dr. J. C. Thompson, P O BOX 23095 66223
Blue Valley MS, 7500 W 149TH TER 66223
Dr. Richard Seipel, prin.
Other Schools – See Leawood, Olathe, Overland Park,
Shawnee Mission, Stilwell

Sterling, Rice Co., Pop. Code 4
Sterling USD 376
Sch. Sys. Enr. Code 3
Supt. – C. W. Deel, P O BOX 188 67579
ES, 308 E WASHINGTON ST 67579
Randy Roberts, prin.
Other Schools – See Alden

Stilwell, Johnson Co.
Blue Valley USD 229
Supt. – See Stanley
ES, 6410 W 199TH ST 66085
Joyce Flowers, prin.

Stockton, Rooks Co., Pop. Code 4
Stockton USD 271
Sch. Sys. Enr. Code 2
Supt. – Robert Wells, 211 MAIN ST 67669
ES, 201 N CYPRESS ST 67669
Francis Mahoney, prin.

Strong City, Chase Co., Pop. Code 3
Chase Co. USD 284
Supt. – See Cottonwood Falls
Chase County MS 66869 – Jerry Pittman, prin.
ES 66869 – John Schierling, prin.

Sublette, Haskell Co., Pop. Code 4
Sublette USD 374
Sch. Sys. Enr. Code 3
Supt. – Dr. G. L. Marshall, P O BOX 670 67877
ES, P O BOX 550 67877 – Russell Branden, prin.

Summerfield, Marshall Co., Pop. Code 2
Axtell USD 488
Supt. – See Axtell
ES 66541 – Demitry Evancho, prin.

Sylvan Grove, Lincoln Co., Pop. Code 2
Sylvan Grove USD 299
Sch. Sys. Enr. Code 2
Supt. – K. C. Jackson, P O BOX 308 67481
ES 67481 – Dale True, prin.

Sylvia, Reno Co., Pop. Code 2
Fairfield USD 310
Supt. – See Langdon
ES 67881 – John New, prin.

Syracuse, Hamilton Co., Pop. Code 4
Syracuse USD 494
Sch. Sys. Enr. Code 2
Supt. – Roy Piper, P O BOX 966 67878
ES 67878 – Stephen Pummel, prin.

Talmage, Dickson Co.
Chapman USD 473
Supt. – See Chapman
MS 67482 – Tony Frieze, prin.

Tecumseh, Shawnee Co., Pop. Code 6
Shawnee Hts. USD 450
Sch. Sys. Enr. Code 5
Supt. – Richard Allen
44TH & SHAWNEE HEIGHTS ROAD 66542
Shawnee Heights JHS
4141 SE SHAWNEE HTS ROAD 66542
Gerald Tilley, prin.
Tecumseh North ES
314 S E STANTON ROAD 66542
Dennis Hippe, prin.
Tecumseh South ES
3346 SE TECUMSEH ROAD 66542
David Bowman, prin.
Other Schools – See Berryton, Topeka

Tescott, Ottawa Co., Pop. Code 2
Twin Valley USD 240
Supt. – See Bennington
ES 67484 – Martin Helmer, prin.

Thayer, Neosho Co., Pop. Code 3
Erie-St. Paul USD 101
Supt. – See Erie
ES 66776 – Jim Clayton, prin.

Timken, Rush Co., Pop. Code 1
Otis-Bison USD 403
Supt. – See Albert
Otis-Bison PS 67582 – Bruce Kenyon, prin.

Tipton, Mitchell Co., Pop. Code 2
Waconda USD 272
Supt. – See Cawker City
ES 67485 – Larry Tonne, prin.

Tonganoxie, Leavenworth Co., Pop. Code 4
Tonganoxie USD 464
Sch. Sys. Enr. Code 4
Supt. – Dr. S. G. McClure, P O BOX 199 66086
ES, P O BOX 259 66086 – Colene DeHoff, prin.

Topeka, Shawnee Co., Pop. Code 9
Auburn-Washburn USD 437
Sch. Sys. Enr. Code 5
Supt. – Howard Shuler, 5928 SW 53RD ST 66610
Shideler MS
4948 SW WANAMAKER ROAD 66610
Robert McVicker, prin.
Indian Hills ES, 7445 W 29TH 66614
Victor Dyck, prin.
Wanamaker ES, 6804 SW 10TH AVE 66615
Charles Gant, prin.
Other Schools – See Auburn, Wakarusa

Seaman USD 345
Sch. Sys. Enr. Code 5
Supt. – Kent Hurn
1124 NW LYMAN ROAD 66608
East Indianola ES, 2000 NW FILLMORE ST 66608
Gordon Myers, prin.
Elmont ES, 6432 NW ELMONT ROAD 66618
Jane Anderson, prin.
Indian Creek ES
4303 NE INDIAN CREEK ROAD 66617
Gary Slimmer, prin.
Lyman ES, 2032 N KANSAS AVE 66608
Gary Groves, prin.
North Fairview ES, 1941 NE 39TH ST 66617
Larry Beam, prin.
Pleasant Hill ES, 5830 NW TOPEKA BLVD 66617
Larry Carr, prin.
Rochester ES
3421 NW ROCHESTER ROAD 66617
Sandra Adams, prin.
West Indianola ES
4201 NW BRICKYARD ROAD 66618
Dr. Michael Culp, prin.

Shawnee Hts. USD 450
Supt. – See Tecumseh
Shawnee Heights ES, 2410 SE BURTON ST 66605
Ed Pettit, prin.

Topeka USD 501
Sch. Sys. Enr. Code 7
Supt. – Gary Livingston, 624 W 24TH ST 66611
Chase MS, 2250 NE STATE ST 66616
Jack Strukel, prin.
Eisenhower MS
3305 SE MINNESOTA AVE 66605
James Carter, prin.
French MS, 5257 SW 33RD ST 66614
Wagner VanVlack, prin.
Jardine MS, 2600 SW 33RD ST 66611
Ralph Clark, prin.
Robinson MS, 1125 SW 14TH ST 66604
Judy Reiners, prin.
Avondale East ES
455 SE GOLF PARK BLVD 66605
Ted Walters, prin.
Avondale West ES
3229 SW WESTVIEW AVE 66611
Dr. Stan Wagstaff, prin.
Belvoir ES, 2401 SE 11TH ST 66607
Dean Martin, prin.
Bishop ES, 3601 W 32ST 66614
Pauline Muxlow, prin.
Crestview ES, 2200 SW EVENINGSIDE DR 66614
Nancy Hedstrom, prin.
Gage ES, 3028 SW 8TH AVE 66606
Gary Scoggin, prin.
Highland Park Central ES
2727 SE ILLINOIS AVE 66605
Richard Rauch, prin.
Highland Park North ES
1921 SE INDIANA AVE 66607
Dr. Terry Sandlin, prin.
Highland Park South ES, 1400 SE 34TH ST 66605
Woody Houseman, prin.
Hudson ES, 2400 SE HIGHLAND AVE 66605
Cynthia Gilbert, prin.
LaFayette ES, 420 SE CALIFORNIA AVE 66607
Duke Palmer, prin.
Linn ES, 200 E 40TH 66609 – Barbara Davis, prin.
Lowman Hill ES, 1101 SW GARFIELD AVE 66604
Virgil Funk, prin.
Lundgren ES, 1020 NE FOREST AVE 66616
Wilfred Dreiling, prin.
McCarter ES, 5512 W 18TH 66604
Paul Fink, prin.

McClure ES, 2529 CHELSEA DR 66614
Dr. Billy Horn, prin.
McEachron ES, 4433 SW 29TH TERRACE 66614
Claude Ritchie, prin.
Potwin ES, 208 ELMWOOD 66606
William Wagaman, prin.
Quincy ES, 1500 NE QUINCY ST 66608
Connie Skinner, prin.
Quinton Heights ES
2331 SW TOPEKA BLVD 66611
Abigail Calkin, prin.
Randolph ES, 1400 SW RANDOLPH AVE 66604
Bart Dever, prin.
Shaner ES, 1600 SW 34TH ST 66611
Win Tidwell, prin.
State Street ES, 500 NE SUMNER ST 66616
George Huckabee, prin.
Stout ES, 2303 SW COLLEGE AVE 66611
Karl Loomis, prin.
Sumner ES, 330 SW WESTERN AVE 66606
Dr. Betsy Jackson, prin.
Whitson ES, 1725 SW ARNOLD AVE 66604
Wes Peters, prin.

Assumption ES, 735 SW JACKSON ST 66603
Holy Name ES, 934 SW CLAY ST 66606
Most Pure Heart of Mary School
1750 SW STONE AVE 66604
Our Lady of Guadalupe School
210 NE BRANNER ST 66616
Sacred Heart ES, 1725 NE SEWARD AVE 66616
St. Matthew ES, 1000 SE 28TH ST 66605
Topeka Lutheran School Assn.
701 SW ROOSEVELT ST 66606

Toronto, Woodson Co., Pop. Code 2
Eureka USD 389
Supt. – See Eureka
ES, P O BOX 245 66777 – Melinda Hall, prin.

Towanda, Butler Co., Pop. Code 4
Circle USD 375
Sch. Sys. Enr. Code 4
Supt. – Dr. John Gahagan
EAST HIGHWAY 254 BOX 8 67144
ES 67144 – Nita McEachern, prin.
Other Schools – See Benton, El Dorado

Tribune, Greeley Co., Pop. Code 3
Greeley Co. USD 200
Sch. Sys. Enr. Code 2
Supt. – Herb Weissenfels, P O BOX 580 67879
Greeley County ES, P O BOX 580 67879
Marian Harper, prin.

Troy, Doniphan Co., Pop. Code 4
Troy USD 429
Sch. Sys. Enr. Code 2
Supt. – Stephen Joel, P O BOX 585 66087
ES 66087 – Donald Harter, prin.

Turon, Reno Co., Pop. Code 2
Fairfield USD 310
Supt. – See Langdon
ES 67583 – Patricia Thayer, prin.

Udall, Cowley Co., Pop. Code 3
Udall USD 463
Sch. Sys. Enr. Code 2
Supt. – Aubury Schultz 67146
ES 67146 – Larry Blevins, prin.

Ulysses, Grant Co., Pop. Code 5
Ulysses USD 214
Sch. Sys. Enr. Code 4
Supt. – Dr. Bruce Kienapfel
111 S BAUGHMAN ST 67880
Kepley JHS, 113 N COLORADO ST 67880
Theresa Davidson, prin.
Hickok ES, 810 N MISSOURI ST 67880
Kenneth Warner, prin.
Joyce MS, 111 S BAUGHMAN ST 67880
Irvin Levin, prin.
Red Rock ES, RURAL ROUTE 01 67880
Irvin Levin, prin.
Sullivan ES, 600 W NEBRASKA ST 67880
Bobby Welch, prin.

Uniontown, Bourbon Co., Pop. Code 2
Uniontown USD 235
Sch. Sys. Enr. Code 2
Supt. – James Lambert 66779
West Bourbon ES 66779 – Charles Shelton, prin.

Utica, Ness Co., Pop. Code 2
Nes Tre La Go USD 301
Sch. Sys. Enr. Code 1
Supt. – James Koftan, P O BOX 128 67584
ES, P O BOX 128 67584 – James Koftan, prin.

Valley Center, Sedgwick Co., Pop. Code 5
Valley Center USD 262
Sch. Sys. Enr. Code 4
Supt. – Dr. Wayne Clark, P O BOX 157 67147
JHS, 737 N MERIDIAN ST 67147
Donald Grover, prin.
Abilene ES, 530 N ABILENE AVE 67147
Albert Koster, prin.
West ES, 501 N WEST ST 67147
Wallace Hinkle, prin.

Valley Falls, Jefferson Co., Pop. Code 4
Valley Falls USD 338
Sch. Sys. Enr. Code 2
Supt. – Jerry Fuqua, 700 OAK ST 66088
ES 66088 – Randy Freeman, prin.

Vermillion, Marshall Co., Pop. Code 2
Vermillion USD 380
Sch. Sys. Enr. Code 2
Supt. – Nilwon Kraushaar 66544
Other Schools – See Centralia, Frankfort

Victoria, Ellis Co., Pop. Code 4
Victoria USD 432
Sch. Sys. Enr. Code 2
Supt. – Peter O'Brien, P O BOX 157 67671
ES, RURAL ROUTE 02 67671
Ferrill Standage, prin.

Wakarusa, Shawnee Co.
Auburn-Washburn USD 437
Supt. – See Topeka
Pauline South MS 66546 – Alvin Camblin, prin.

Wa Keeney, Trego Co., Pop. Code 4
Wa Keeney USD 208
Sch. Sys. Enr. Code 3
Supt. – Roy D. Keller, P O BOX 68 67672
ES 67672 – Godfrey Lang, prin.

Wakefield, Clay Co., Pop. Code 3
Clay Center USD 379
Supt. – See Clay Center
ES 67487 – Lynn Wait, prin.

Wallace, Wallace Co., Pop. Code 1
Wallace Co. USD 241
Supt. – See Sharon Springs
ES 67761 – Paul McNall, prin.

Walton, Harvey Co., Pop. Code 2
Newton USD 373
Supt. – See Newton
ES 67151 – John Kelly, prin.

Wamego, Pottawatomie Co., Pop. Code 5
Wamego USD 320
Sch. Sys. Enr. Code 4
Supt. – Dr. Norris Wika, P O BOX 26 66547
JHS, N LINCOLN 66547 – J. Harshbarger, prin.
Central ES, 7TH & POPLAR 66547
Janalee Fry, prin.
West MS, 1911 6TH ST 66547
Lloyd Snodgrass, prin.

Washington, Washington Co., Pop. Code 4
Washington USD 222
Sch. Sys. Enr. Code 2
Supt. – Dr. Roger Baskerville 66968
ES 66968 – Ronald Scott, prin.
Other Schools – See Greenleaf

Waterville, Marshall Co., Pop. Code 3
Valley Hts. USD 498
Sch. Sys. Enr. Code 2
Supt. – David Walters, P O BOX 89 66548
Valley Heights ES 66548 – Charles Steele, prin.
Other Schools – See Blue Rapids

Wathena, Doniphan Co., Pop. Code 4
Wathena USD 406
Sch. Sys. Enr. Code 2
Supt. – Richard Heaton, P O BOX 38 66090
ES 66090 – Kay Schultz, prin.

Waverly, Coffey Co., Pop. Code 3
Lebo-Waverly USD 243
Sch. Sys. Enr. Code 3
Supt. – Ted Vannocker, P O BOX 457 66871
ES 66871 – Anthony Houchin, prin.
Other Schools – See Lebo

Weir, Cherokee Co., Pop. Code 3
Cherokee USD 247
Supt. – See Cherokee
ES 66781 – Frank Crespino, prin.

Welda, Anderson Co., Pop. Code 2
Garnett USD 365
Supt. – See Garnett
Mt. Ida ES, RURAL ROUTE 66091
Paul Upshaw, prin.

Wellington, Sumner Co., Pop. Code 6
Wellington USD 353
Sch. Sys. Enr. Code 4
Supt. – Ronald Fagan, P O BOX 648 67152
Eisenhower ES, 924 N PLUM ST 67152
Carl Garnand, prin.
Kennedy ES, 501 N WOODLAWN ST 67152
James Chisham, prin.
Lincoln ES, 104 S F ST 67152 – Bill Horsch, prin.
Roosevelt MS, 201 N B ST 67152
Tom Palmer, prin.
Washington ES
1100 N WASHINGTON AVE 67152
Kendall Hay, prin.

Wellsville, Franklin Co., Pop. Code 4
Wellsville USD 289
Sch. Sys. Enr. Code 3
Supt. – Donald Martin, P O BOX 537 66092
ES 66092 – Bettye Coughenour, prin.

Weskan, Wallace Co., Pop. Code 2
Weskan USD 242
Sch. Sys. Enr. Code 2
Supt. – Allaire Homburg, P O BOX 155 67762
ES 67762 – Allaire Homburg, prin.

West Mineral, Cherokee Co., Pop. Code 2
Cherokee USD 247
Supt. – See Cherokee
ES 66782 – Max Newell, prin.

Westmoreland, Pottawatomie Co., Pop. Code 3
Westmoreland USD 323
Sch. Sys. Enr. Code 3
Supt. – Lewis R. Hitch, P O BOX 70 66549
ES 66549 – Larry Wilkerson, prin.
Other Schools – See Saint George

Westphalia, Anderson Co., Pop. Code 2
Garnett USD 365
Supt. – See Garnett
ES 66093 – Paul Upshaw, prin.

Wetmore, Nemaha Co., Pop. Code 2
Sabetha USD 441
Supt. – See Sabetha
ES 66550 – Russell DeVillier, prin.

Wheaton, Pottawatomie Co., Pop. Code 1
Onaga-Havensville-Wheaton USD 322
Supt. – See Onaga
ES 66551 – M. Carlson, prin.

White City, Morris Co., Pop. Code 3
Rural Vista USD 481
Supt. – See Hope
ES 66872 – C. Harris, prin.

Whitewater, Butler Co., Pop. Code 3
Remington-Whitewater USD 206
Sch. Sys. Enr. Code 2
Supt. – Mike Philpot, RURAL ROUTE 01 67154
ES 67154 – Herman Merritt, prin.
Other Schools – See Potwin

Wichita, Sedgwick Co., Pop. Code 10
Derby USD 260
Supt. – See Derby
Cooper ES, 4625 JUNIPER ST 67216
Deanna Rogers, prin.
Oaklawn ES, 5000 S CLIFTON AVE 67216
Dennis Williams, prin.
Wineteer ES, 8801 ENT DR 67210
Bert Moore, prin.

Haysville USD 261
Supt. – See Haysville
Oatville ES, 4335 S HOOVER ROAD 67215
Annette Rastellini, prin.

Wichita USD 259
Sch. Sys. Enr. Code 8
Supt. – Dr. Stuart Berger, 217 N WATER 67202
Allison JHS, 221 S SENECA ST 67213
James Sowers, prin.
Brooks JHS, 3802 E 27TH ST N 67220
Brenda Moore, prin.
Coleman JHS, 1544 N GOVERNEOUR ST 67206
Allen Hillen, prin.
Curtis JHS, 1031 S EDGEMOOR ST 67218
Charles McLean, prin.
Hadley JHS, 1101 DOUGHERTY ST 67212
Kathy Wilson, prin.
Hamilton MS, 1407 S BROADWAY 67211
James Haught, prin.
Jardine JHS, 3550 ROSS PARKWAY 67210
Evies Cranford, prin.
Mann MS, 1243 N MARKET 67214 – J. Muci, prin.
Marshall JHS, 1510 PAYNE ST 67203
Ralph Teran, prin.
Mayberry JHS, 207 S SHERIDAN ST 67213
Fred Spexarth, prin.
Mead JHS, 2601 E SKINNER ST 67211
Fred Hale, prin.
Pleasant Valley JHS, 2220 W 29TH ST N 67204
Marlene Brown, prin.
Robinson JHS, 328 N OLIVER ST 67208
Roel Quintanilla, prin.
Truesdell JHS, 2464 S GLENN ST 67217
Betty Lessard, prin.
Wilbur JHS, 340 N TYLER ROAD 67212
Dale Dunn, prin.
Adams ES, 1002 N OLIVER ST 67208
Robert Baker, prin.
Allen ES, 4814 MOUNT VERNON ROAD 67218
Darrel Doerksen, prin.
Anderson ES, 2945 VICTORIA ST 67216
Duane Ohlemeier, prin.
Arkansas Avenue ES
3361 ARKANSAS AVE 67204
Peggy Dokken, prin.
Beech ES, 1830 S CYPRESS ST 67207
Gloria McAfee, prin.
Benton ES, 338 S WOODCHUCK ST 67209
George Doerksen, prin.
Black ES, 1045 HIGH ST 67203
Robert Snell, prin.
Booth ES, 5920 E MOUNT VERNON ST 67218
Leicle Bostic, prin.
Buckner ES, 3530 E 27TH ST N 67220
N. Ray, prin.
Bryant ES, 4702 W 9TH ST N 67212
Glenda Richardson, prin.
Caldwell ES, 5528 E BOSTON ST 67218
Robert Coykendall, prin.
Carter ES, 4640 E 15TH ST N 67208
Daniel McAdam, prin.
Cessna ES, 2101 W 45TH ST S 67217
Stanley McGee, prin.
Chisholm ES, 2515 E OSIE ST 67211
Monroe Nikkel, prin.
Chisholm Trail ES, 6001 FORRESTER DR 67219
Byron Morris, prin.
Clark ES, 7000 COTTONWOOD ST 67207
Mary Breckenridge, prin.
Cleaveland ES, 3345 W 33RD ST S 67217
Harry Schmidt, prin.

Cloud ES, 1205 W 26TH ST 67204
Gerald Lewis, prin.
College Hill ES, 211 N CLIFTON AVE 67208
John Furan, prin.
Colvin ES, 2820 S ROOSEVELT ST 67210
Dr. Benjamin Mevey, prin.
Dodge ES, 4801 W 2ND ST N 67212
Cynthia Shaffer, prin.
Earhart Environment Complex ES
4401 ARKANSAS AVE 67204
Barbara McPherson, prin.
Emerson Open Alternative ES
2330 W 15TH ST N 67203 – Priscilla Salem, prin.
Enterprise ES, 3612 S SENECA ST 67217
Robert Macy, prin.
Field ES, 3612 S SENECA ST 67217
Curtis LaPorte, prin.
Franklin ES, 214 S ELIZABETH ST 67213
Dr. Asa Cleavinger, prin.
Funston ES, 4801 S HYDRAULIC ST 67216
Janet Jump, prin.
Gammon ES, 3240 N RUSHWOOD ST 67226
C. Silvertooth, prin.
Gammon-B ES, 4531 E 37TH N 67220
C. Silvertooth, prin.
Gardiner ES, 1926 IDA ST 67211
Leroy Rolfe, prin.
Griffith ES, 1802 S BLUFF ST 67218
Winston Brooks, prin.
Harris ES, 706 N ARMOUR ST 67206
Billy Breckenridge, prin.
Harry Street ES, 107 E HARRY ST 67211
Gloria Martin, prin.
Hyde ES, 210 N OLIVER ST 67208
Greta Parsons, prin.
Ingalls ES, 2316 E 10TH ST N 67214
Saundra Rutter, prin.
Irving ES, 1642 N MARKET ST 67214
Dr. Jean Williams, prin.
Isely Magnet MS, 2500 E 18TH ST N 67214
Karen Whittle, prin.
Isely Magnet-B ES, 1847 N CHAUTAUQUA 67214
Karen Whittle, prin.
Jefferson ES, 4615 E ORME ST 67218
Gloria Robb, prin.
Kellogg Traditional Alternative ES
1220 E KELLOGG DR 67211 – F. Seminoff, prin.
Kelly ES, 3143 S MILLWOOD ST 67217
H. Ediger, prin.
Kensler ES, 1030 WILBUR LANE 67212
Phillip Fullerton, prin.
Lawrence ES, 3440 MAPLE ST 67213
Charles Myers, prin.
Lincoln ES, 1210 S TOPEKA ST 67211
Eugene Young, prin.
Linwood ES, 1340 PATTIE ST 67211
Monroe Nikkel, prin.
Longfellow ES, 2116 S MAIN ST 67213
Billy Pickens, prin.
L'ouverture ES, 1539 OHIO ST 67214
Deborah Laudermilk, prin.
McCollom ES, 1201 WADDINGTON ST 67212
Mychael Willon, prin.
McCormick ES, 855 S MARTINSON ST 67213
Curtis LaPorte, prin.
McLean ES, 2277 MARIGOLD ST 67204
Anne Lassey, prin.
Minneha ES, 701 N WEBB ROAD 67206
Sonja Seemann, prin.
Mueller ES, 2821 E 24TH ST N 67219
Devin Stahl, prin.
O K ES, 1607 N WEST ST 67203 – C. Osborn, prin.
Park ES, 1025 N MAIN ST 67203
Phyllis Brady, prin.
Payne ES, 1601 S EDWARDS ST 67213
Willia Crawford, prin.
Peterson ES, 9710 W CENTRAL ST 67212
Dorothy Goodger, prin.
Pleasant Valley ES, 2000 W 29TH ST N 67204
Clifton Johnson, prin.
Price ES, 6123 E 11TH ST N 67208
Goldie Bowen, prin.
Riverside ES, 1001 PORTER ST 67203
Paul Spacil, prin.
Riverview ES, 5355 N SENECA ST 67204
Noah Welsch, prin.
Seltzer ES, 903 S 127TH ST E 67207
Diane Osborn, prin.
South Hillside ES, 2161 S HILLSIDE ST 67211
Winston Brooks, prin.
Sowers ES, 2400 WASSALL ST 67216
Leicle Bostic, prin.
Stanley ES, 1749 S MARTINSON ST 67213
Anita Allard, prin.
Stearman ES, 8103 E GILBERT ST 67207
Sharon Jones, prin.
Sunnyside ES, 3003 E KELLOGG DR 67211
Dr. Donovan Moore, prin.
Washington ES, 1600 E 3RD ST N 67214
J. Johnson, prin.
White ES, 5148 S KANSAS ST 67216
Beverly Harmon, prin.
Woodland ES, 1705 SALINA ST 67203
Paul Spacil, prin.
Woodman ES, 2500 HIRAM ST 67217
Dr. A. Lovette, prin.

Wichita Collegiate School
9115 E 13TH ST N 67206
All Saints ES, 3313 GRAND ST 67218
Bethel Life ES, 3777 S MERIDIAN ST 67217
Blessed Sacrament ES
3820 E DOUGLAS AVE 67208

Central Christian Academy
  2900 N ROCK ROAD   67226
Christ the King ES, 4501 MAPLE ST   67209
Christian Challenge ES
  249 N ATHENIAN ST   67203
Holy Cross Lutheran ES
  1018 N DELLROSE ST   67208
Holy Savior ES, 1432 N ERIE ST   67214
Independent ES, 8301 E DOUGLAS AVE   67207
School of the Magdalen
  6355 WILLOWBROOK ST   67218
St. Anne ES, 1121 REGAL ST   67217
St. Elizabeth Ann Seton School
  645 N 119TH ST W   67212
St. Francis of Assisi School
  853 N SOCORA ST   67212
St. Joseph ES, 139 S MILLWOOD ST   67213
St. Jude ES, 3030 AMIDON ST   67204
St. Margaret Mary ES, 2635 PATTIE ST   67216
St. Patrick ES, 2023 ARKANSAS AVE   67203
St. Peter Schulte ES, 135 PETER ST   67215
St. Thomas Aquinas School
  1215 N STRATFORD ST   67206

Williamsburg, Franklin Co., Pop. Code 2
  West Franklin USD 287
  Supt. – See Pomona
  ES   66095 – Pat Happer, prin.

Wilsey, Morris Co., Pop. Code 2
  Council Grove USD 417
  Supt. – See Council Grove
  ES   66873 – John Honas, prin.

Wilson, Ellsworth Co., Pop. Code 3
  Lorraine USD 328
  Supt. – See Lorraine
  MS, P O BOX 220   67490 – Larry Lysell, prin.
  ES   67490 – Robert King, prin.

Winchester, Jefferson Co., Pop. Code 3
  Jefferson Co. North USD 339
  Sch. Sys. Enr. Code 2
  Supt. – Robert Shanks, P O BOX Q   66097
  Jefferson County North ES, P O BOX Q   66097
    Linda Aldridge, prin.
  Other Schools – See Nortonville

Windom, Rice Co., Pop. Code 2
  Little River USD 444
  Supt. – See Little River
  MS   67491 – Harold Schrag, prin.

Winfield, Cowley Co., Pop. Code 7
  Winfield USD 465
  Sch. Sys. Enr. Code 4
  Supt. – William Medley
    920 MILLINGTON ST   67156
  MS, 400 E 9TH AVE   67156
    Dan Flummerfelt, prin.
  Country View ES, RURAL ROUTE 04   67156
    Kay Hogan, prin.
  Irving ES, 311 HARTER ST   67156
    Carmen Gonzales, prin.
  Lowell ES, 1411 LOOMIS ST   67156
    Larry Helzer, prin.

Pleasant Valley ES, RURAL ROUTE 03   67156
  Kay Hogan, prin.
South Vernon ES, RURAL ROUTE 02   67156
  Carmen Gonzales, prin.
Whittier ES, 1400 MOUND ST   67156
  Mark Richardson, prin.

Winona, Logan Co., Pop. Code 2
  Triplains USD 275
  Sch. Sys. Enr. Code 2
  Supt. – Roger Brenner, P O BOX 97   67764
  ES   67774 – Roger Brenner, prin.

Wright, Ford Co.
  Dodge City USD 443
  Supt. – See Dodge City
  ES   67882 – Sharon Germes, prin.

Yates Center, Woodson Co., Pop. Code 4
  Yates Center USD 366
  Sch. Sys. Enr. Code 3
  Supt. – Billy Norris, P O BOX 160   66783
  ES   66783 – Frank Van Bettega, prin.

Zenda, Kingman Co., Pop. Code 2
  Cunningham USD 332
  Supt. – See Cunningham
  ES   67159 – Stephen Hood, prin.

KENTUCKY

STATE DEPARTMENT OF EDUCATION
1725 Capitol Plaza Tower, Frankfort 40601
(502) 564-4770

Superintendent of Public Instruction	John Brock
Deputy Superintendent Administration	Arnold Guess
Deputy Superintendent Instruction	Betty Steffy
Deputy Superintendent Research & Planning	Dan Branham
Deputy Superintendent Vocational-Technical, Adult & Rehab Services	Charles Byers

STATE BOARD OF EDUCATION
Henry Pogue, *Chairperson*   1st Floor, Capitol Plaza Tower, Frankfort   40601

COUNCIL ON HIGHER EDUCATION
Gary Cox, *Executive Director*   1050 U.S. 127, S., Frankfort   40601

PUBLIC, PRIVATE, AND PAROCHIAL ELEMENTARY SCHOOLS

Adairville, Logan Co., Pop. Code 4
  Logan County SD
  Supt. – See Russellville
  MS, P O BOX 277   42202 – Marshall Kemp, prin.
  ES, P O BOX 277   42202 – Marshall Kemp, prin.

Albany, Clinton Co., Pop. Code 4
  Clinton County SD
  Sch. Sys. Enr. Code 4
  Supt. – James Carver, P O BOX 416   42602
  ES, BURKESVILLE RD   42602
    Jerry Branham, prin.
  Clinton County ES   42602 – Michael Owens, prin.
  Irwin MS, RURAL ROUTE 01   42602
    Jerome Grider, prin.

Alexandria, Campbell Co., Pop. Code 5
  Campbell County SD
  Sch. Sys. Enr. Code 5
  Supt. – Dan Sullivan, 101 ORCHARD LANE   41001
  Reiley MS, 4930 US 27   41001
    Franklin Watts, prin.
  ES, 51 ORCHARD LN   41001
    William Voelker, prin.
  Grants Lick ES, 170 W CLAY RDG RD   41001
    Bob Tuttle, prin.
  Other Schools – See California, Cold Spring, Highland
    Heights

  St. Mary School, 9 S JEFFERSON ST   41001

Allen, Floyd Co., Pop. Code 2
  Floyd County SD
  Supt. – See Prestonsburg
  ES, P O BOX 480   41601 – Daniel Branson, prin.

Alvaton, Warren Co.
  Warren County SD
  Supt. – See Bowling Green
  ES, 6350 OLD SCOTTSVILLE RD   42122
    Robert Morgan, prin.

Anchorage, Jefferson Co., Pop. Code 4
  Anchorage ISD
  Sch. Sys. Enr. Code 4
  Supt. – Dr. Robert Wynkoop
    11400 RIDGE ROAD   40223
  Anchorage MS, 11400 RIDGE RD   40223
    Margarite McCall, prin.
  ES, 11400 RIDGE RD   40223
    Margarite McCall, prin.

Annville, Jackson Co.
  Jackson County SD
  Supt. – See Mc Kee
  Moores Creek ES, P O BOX 140   40402
    Don Collett, prin.

Argillite, Greenup Co.
  Greenup County SD
  Supt. – See Greenup
  ES, HCR 61 BOX 670   41121
    Lawrence Popovich, prin.

Danleyton ES, HCR 61 BOX 855   41121
  Linda Moon, prin.

Arjay, Bell Co.
  Bell County SD
  Supt. – See Pineville
  ES   40902 – Bruce Thompson, prin.

Artemus, Knox Co.
  Knox County SD
  Supt. – See Barbourville
  ES, P O BOX 87   40903 – Corbett Hembree, prin.

Ary, Perry Co.
  Perry County SD
  Supt. – See Hazard
  Robinson ES   41712 – Yvon Allen, prin.

Ashcamp, Pike Co.
  Pike County SD
  Supt. – See Pikeville
  Sycamore ES, ASH CAMP   41512
    James Bartley, prin.

Ashland, Boyd Co., Pop. Code 8
  Ashland ISD
  Sch. Sys. Enr. Code 5
  Supt. – William Foutch
    1420 CENTRAL AVE   41101
  Verity MS, 2600 KANSAS ST   41101
    Herb Conley, prin.
  Crabbe ES, 17TH & CENTRAL   41101
    James Williams, prin.

Hager ES, BLACKBURN & ACKLEY 41101
  Judith Morris, prin.
Hatcher ES, HICKMAN ST 41101
  Linda Ferguson, prin.
Oakview ES, HIGH & BLACKBURN 41101
  Kay Gevedon, prin.
Poage ES, 3215 29TH ST 41101
  Clifton Salyers, prin.
Russell ES, 1100 RUSSELL ST 41101
  Clifton Salyers, prin.

Boyd County SD
Supt. – See Catlettsburg
Cannonburg ES
  12219 MIDLAND TRAIL RD 41101
  William Scott, prin.
Ironville ES, 904 W ROSE RD 41101
  Sammie Cox, prin.
Summit ES, 830 ST RT 716 41101
  Howard Wallace, prin.

Fairview ISD
Sch. Sys. Enr. Code 3
Supt. – Paul Reliford, 2127 MAIN ST W 41101
Pine Acres ES, 258 MCKNIGHT ST 41101
  George Cooke, prin.
Renfroe MS, 2100 MAIN ST WW 41101
  George Cooke, prin.

———————————

Holy Family ES, 932 WINCHESTER AVE 41101

Auburn, Logan Co., Pop. Code 4
Logan County SD
Supt. – See Russellville
MS, COLLEGE ST 42206 – Michael Hurt, prin.
Chandlers MS, RURAL ROUTE 02 42206
  James Thompson, prin.
ES, COLLEGE ST 42206 – Michael Hurt, prin.
Chandlers ES, RURAL ROUTE 02 42206
  James Thompson, prin.

Augusta, Bracken Co., Pop. Code 4
Augusta ISD
Sch. Sys. Enr. Code 2
Supt. – M. Wallace 41002
ES, 3RD & BRACKEN ST 41002
  Joseph Kelsch, prin.

Auxier, Floyd Co.
Floyd County SD
Supt. – See Prestonsburg
ES 41602 – Wayne Combs, prin.

Avawam, Perry Co.
Perry County SD
Supt. – See Hazard
Big Creek ES 41713 – Charles Campbell, prin.

Bagdad, Shelby Co.
Shelby County SD
Supt. – See Shelbyville
ES, P O BOX 68 40003 – David Sparrow, prin.

Bandana, Ballard Co
Ballard County SD
Supt. – See Barlow
ES, P O BOX 116 42022 – Edna Webb, prin.

Barbourville, Knox Co., Pop. Code 5
Barbourville ISD
Sch. Sys. Enr. Code 2
Supt. – James Davis, P O BOX 540 40906
ES, SCHOOL ST 40906 – Larry Warren, prin.

Knox County SD
Sch. Sys. Enr. Code 6
Supt. – J. Hampton, P O BOX 228 40906
Boone ES, HCR 81 BOX 532 40906
  Wilma Hinkle, prin.
Hampton ES, HCR 73 BOX 48 40906
  Quentin West, prin.
Lay ES 40906 – William Hamlin, prin.
Other Schools – See Artemus, Corbin, Dewitt, Flat
  Lick, Girdler, Gray

Bardstown, Nelson Co., Pop. Code 6
Bardstown ISD
Sch. Sys. Enr. Code 4
Supt. – Dr. Robert Smotherman
  308 N 5TH ST 40004
MS, 410 N 5TH ST 40004 – Gilbert Milburn, prin.
ES, 420 N FIFTH ST 40004
  Merrlylen Sparks, prin.

Nelson County SD
Sch. Sys. Enr. Code 5
Supt. – Victor Johnson, 114 S 3RD ST 40004
Old Kentucky Home MS, 221 E MUIR AVE 40004
  Bill Peterson, prin.
Foster Heights ES, 211 E MUIR AVE 40004
  Flora Clements, prin.
Other Schools – See Bloomfield, Boston, Chaplin,
  Coxs Creek, New Haven

———————————

St. Joseph School
  320 W STEPHEN FOSTER AVE 40004
St. Thomas School
  RURAL ROUTE 03 BOX 233 40004

Bardwell, Carlisle Co., Pop. Code 3
Carlisle County SD
Sch. Sys. Enr. Code 3
Supt. – Robert Watson, RURAL ROUTE 01 42023
Carlisle County MS, RURAL ROUTE 01 42023
  Joe Adams, prin.
Carlisle County ES, RURAL ROUTE 03 42023
  Joe Adams, prin.

Barlow, Ballard Co., Pop. Code 3
Ballard County SD
Sch. Sys. Enr. Code 4
Supt. – Bobby Buchanan
  RURAL ROUTE 01 42024
Ballard County MS, RURAL ROUTE 01 42024
  Jerry McGregor, prin.
ES, RURAL ROUTE 02 42024
  Donald Roberts, prin.
Other Schools – See Bandana, Kevil, La Center,
  Wickliffe

Battletown, Meade Co.
Meade County SD
Supt. – See Brandenburg
ES, HCR 40104 – James Scott, prin.

Baxter, Jefferson Co.
Harlan County SD
Supt. – See Harlan
Rosspoint ES, RURAL ROUTE 01 BOX 212 40806
  Linda White, prin.

Bear Branch, Leslie Co.
Leslie County SD
Supt. – See Hyden
Big Creek ES, HCR 35 BOX 520 41714
  Frank Baker, prin.

Beattyville, Lee Co., Pop. Code 4
Lee County SD
Sch. Sys. Enr. Code 4
Supt. – Glenn Wilson, BOX 668 41311
Lee County MS, P O BOX 547 41311
  Tom Cockerham, prin.
ES, P O BOX 638 41311 – Edith Pack, prin.
South Side ES, RURAL ROUTE 03 BOX 233 41311
  Rachel Stamper, prin.

Beaver Dam, Ohio Co., Pop. Code 5
Ohio County SD
Supt. – See Hartford
ES, HWY 62 42340 – Don Williams, prin.
Southern ES, RURAL ROUTE 04 BOX 170 42320
  Jerry Carpenter, prin.

Bedford, Trimble Co., Pop. Code 3
Trimble County SD
Sch. Sys. Enr. Code 4
Supt. – J. Sachleben, P O BOX 67 40006
Trimble County MS, P O BOX 215 40006
  Dale Vincent, prin.
ES, P O BOX 137 40006
  Sharon Kay Rowlett, prin.
Other Schools – See Milton

Beechmont, Muhlenberg Co.
Muhlenberg County SD
Supt. – See Greenville
Kirk ES 42323 – Bill Knight, prin.

Bellevue, Campbell Co., Pop. Code 6
Bellevue ISD
Sch. Sys. Enr. Code 3
Supt. – William Armstrong
  215 CENTER ST 41073
Grandview ES
  GRANDVIEW & FOOTE AVE 41073
  Raymond Spaulding, prin.

———————————

St. Michael ES, 347 TAYLOR AVE 41073

Belton, Muhlenberg Co.
Muhlenberg County SD
Supt. – See Greenville
Lake Malone ES, RURAL ROUTE 01 42324
  Joseph Wells, prin.

Benham, Harlan Co., Pop. Code 3
Harlan County SD
Supt. – See Harlan
ES, P O BOX 369 40807 – Gary Hensley, prin.

Benton, Marshall Co., Pop. Code 5
Marshall County SD
Sch. Sys. Enr. Code 5
Supt. – Kenneth Shadowen
  RURAL ROUTE 07 BOX 102 42025
South Marshall MS, RURAL ROUTE 01 42025
  Darrell Morgan, prin.
ES, 208 W 11TH ST 42025 – Don Cothran, prin.
Jonathon ES, RURAL ROUTE 05 42025
  Coy Garrett, prin.
Sharpe ES, RURAL ROUTE 06 42025
  Burneda Larimer, prin.
South Marshall ES, RURAL ROUTE 01 42025
  Russell Anderson, prin.
Other Schools – See Calvert City, Gilbertsville

Berea, Madison Co., Pop. Code 6
Berea ISD
Sch. Sys. Enr. Code 4
Supt. – Jimmy Wallace
  WALNUT MEADOW ROAD 40403
Berea Community ES
  WALNUT MEADOW RD 40430
  Margaret Ann Davis, prin.

Madison County SD
Supt. – See Richmond
Foley MS, 211 GLADES ROAD 40403
  Robert Harris, prin.
Kingston ES, RURAL ROUTE 01 BOX 170 40403
  Paul Baker, prin.
Silver Creek ES, RURAL ROUTE 05 40403
  Sylvia Powell, prin.

Bethel, Bath Co.
Bath County SD
Supt. – See Owingsville
ES 40306 – Wendell Moore, prin.

Bethelridge, Casey Co.
Casey County SD
Supt. – See Liberty
Garrett ES, RURAL ROUTE 01 42516
  Roger Durham, prin.

Betsy Layne, Floyd Co., Pop. Code 3
Floyd County SD
Supt. – See Prestonsburg
ES 41905 – Enoch Mitchell, prin.

Beverly, Clay Co.
Bell County SD
Supt. – See Pineville
Red Bird ES, HCR 69 BOX 710 40913
  Byron Perrine, prin.

Bevinsville, Floyd Co.
Floyd County SD
Supt. – See Prestonsburg
Osborne ES 41606 – Virginia Jamerson, prin.

Blaine, Lawrence Co., Pop. Code 2
Lawrence County SD
Supt. – See Louisa
ES, HCR 80 BOX 120 41124 – Joe Hewlett, prin.

Bledsoe, Harlan Co.
Harlan County SD
Supt. – See Harlan
Green Hills ES 40810 – Linda White, prin.

Bloomfield, Nelson Co., Pop. Code 3
Nelson County SD
Supt. – See Bardstown
MS 40008 – L. Cheek, prin.
Brown ES, P O BOX 248 40008 – Larry Cheek, prin.

Bonnieville, Hart Co., Pop. Code 2
Hart County SD
Supt. – See Munfordville
ES, P O BOX 89 42713 – Susan Mattingly, prin.

Booneville, Owsley Co., Pop. Code 2
Breathitt County SD
Supt. – See Jackson
Turner ES, RURAL ROUTE 01 BOX 131A 41314
  Arch Turner, prin.

Owsley County SD
Sch. Sys. Enr. Code 4
Supt. – E. Rasner, P O BOX 416 41314
Owsley County ES, P O BOX 660 41314
  Steve Turner, prin.

Boston, Nelson Co.
Nelson County SD
Supt. – See Bardstown
ES, P O BOX 38 40107 – Eddie Swain, prin.

Bowling Green, Warren Co., Pop. Code 8
Bowling Green ISD
Sch. Sys. Enr. Code 5
Supt. – Joel Brown, 224 E 12TH ST 42101
JHS, 1141 CENTER ST 42101 – John Napier, prin.
Bennett ES, BLOOMFIELD ST 42101
  Anna Senter, prin.
Cherry ES, 1001 LIBERTY WAY 42101
  Joseph Tinius, prin.
Curry ES, GLENLILY & DURBIN ST 42101
  Mike Cobb, prin.
Gray ES, WAKEFIELD DR 42101
  Mae Mefford, prin.
McGinnis ES, OLD MORGANTOWN RD 42101
  Jesse Kimbrough, prin.
McNeill ES, 1800 CREASON ST 42101
  Harold Dexter, prin.

Warren County SD
Sch. Sys. Enr. Code 6
Supt. – Robert Gover, 806 KENTON ST 42101
Drakes Creek MS, 704 CYPRESS WOOD 42101
  Monte Chance, prin.
Moss MS, 2565 RUSSELLVILLE RD 42101
  Marvin Burgess, prin.
Warren East MS, 7031 LOIUSVILLE RD 42101
  Harold Cowles, prin.
Bristow ES, 6151 LOUISVILLE RD 42101
  Betty Lou Smith, prin.
Cumberland Trace ES
  830 CUMBERLAND TRACE RD 42101
  Dr. Dennis Minix, prin.
Delafield ES, MAIN & JACKSON ST 42101
  Robert Hancock, prin.
Jones Jaggers ES, 325 UNIVERSITY BLVD 42101
  Dr. Connie Allen, prin.
Rich Pond ES, 530 RICHPOND RD 42101
  William Blankenbaker, prin.
Warren County ES, 1846 LOOP DR 42101
  William Franklin, prin.
Other Schools – See Alvaton, Oakland, Richardsville,
  Rockfield, Smiths Grove

———————————

Anchored Christian School
  1000 ROSELAWN WAY 42101
St. Joseph School, 416 CHURCH ST 42101

Brandenburg, Meade Co., Pop. Code 4
Meade County SD
Sch. Sys. Enr. Code 5
Supt. – Stuart Pepper, P O BOX 337 40108
Meade County MS, 814 OLD EKREN ROAD 40108
  Clayton Cornett, prin.

Allen MS, OLD STATE RD 40108
    Edwin Goodman, prin.
ES, 642 BLAND ST 40108 – Dianne Brady, prin.
Other Schools – See Battletown, Ekron, Muldraugh,
    Payneville, Vine Grove

St. John the Apostle School
    513 E BROADWAY 40108

Bremen, Muhlenberg Co., Pop. Code 2
Muhlenberg County SD
Supt. – See Greenville
ES 42325 – Ken Arbuckle, prin.

Brodhead, Rockcastle Co., Pop. Code 3
Rockcastle County SD
Supt. – See Mount Vernon
ES 40409 – Tom Payne, prin.

Bromley, Kenton Co., Pop. Code 3
Kenton County SD
Supt. – See Independence
ES, BOONE & HARRIS ST 41016
    Garrett Swain, prin.

Brooksville, Bracken Co., Pop. Code 3
Bracken County SD
Sch. Sys. Enr. Code 4
Supt. – Howard Hall,Jr., P O BOX 26 41004
Bracken County MS, GIBSON DR 41004
    Gary Clayton, prin.
Taylor ES, P O BOX 3C 41004 – Roy Machen, prin.

Brownsville, Edmonson Co., Pop. Code 3
Edmonson County SD
Sch. Sys. Enr. Code 4
Supt. – D. Webb, P O BOX 129 42210
Edmonson County MS, P O BOX 98 42210
    Gerald White, prin.
ES, 181 S MAIN ST 42210 – Darrell Cassady, prin.
Other Schools – See Sweeden

Buckhorn, Perry Co., Pop. Code 4
Perry County SD
Supt. – See Hazard
ES 41721 – Dennis Wooton, prin.

Buckner, Oldham Co.
Oldham County SD
Supt. – See La Grange
Oldham County MS, P O BOX 157 40010
    Joe McWilliams, prin.

Buffalo, Larue Co.
Larue County SD
Supt. – See Hodgenville
ES, P O BOX 8 42716 – C. Rice, prin.

Burdine, Letcher Co.
Jenkins ISD
Supt. – See Jenkins
ES, P O BOX 300 41517 – John Smith, prin.

Burgin, Mercer Co., Pop. Code 4
Burgin ISD
Sch. Sys. Enr. Code 2
Supt. – Charles Scott, P O BOX B 40310
ES, P O BOX B 40310 – Richard Carlton, prin.

Burkesville, Cumberland Co., Pop. Code 4
Cumberland County SD
Sch. Sys. Enr. Code 4
Supt. – Gary Lee, P O BOX 420 42717
Cumberland County MS, P O BOX 70 42717
    Jimmie Radford, prin.
Cumberland County ES, P O BOX 190 42717
    Michael Irby, prin.

Burlington, Boone Co.
Boone County SD
Supt. – See Florence
ES, P O BOX 188 41005 – Burlie King, prin.
Kelly ES, 6775 MCVILLE RD 41005
    Selma Siekman, prin.

Burna, Livingston Co., Pop. Code 2
Livingston County SD
Supt. – See Smithland
Livingston County MS, P O BOX 23 42028
    Elbert Wilson, prin.

Burnside, Pulaski Co., Pop. Code 3
Pulaski County SD
Supt. – See Somerset
ES 42519 – Collas Simpson, prin.

Busy, Perry Co.
Perry County SD
Supt. – See Hazard
Willard ES 41723 – Ruby Napier, prin.

Butler, Pendleton Co., Pop. Code 3
Pendleton County SD
Supt. – See Falmouth
Northern ES, RURAL ROUTE 01 41006
    Nellie Mitchell, prin.

Cadiz, Trigg Co., Pop. Code 4
Trigg County SD
Sch. Sys. Enr. Code 4
Supt. – John Randolph, P O BOX 31 42211
Trigg County MS, P O BOX 504-A 42211
    Jim Edwards, prin.
Trigg Co. ES, P O BOX 502A 42211
    Dr. Martha Davis, prin.

Calhoun, McLean Co., Pop. Code 4
McLean County SD
Sch. Sys. Enr. Code 4
Supt. – J. Anthony, RURAL ROUTE 01 42327
ES, P O BOX 130 42327 – William Melloy, prin.
Other Schools – See Island, Livermore, Sacramento

California, Campbell Co.
Campbell County SD
Supt. – See Alexandria
Jolly ES, RURAL ROUTE 02 BOX 3 41007
    Ann Painter, prin.

Calvert City, Marshall Co., Pop. Code 4
Marshall County SD
Supt. – See Benton
North Marshall MS, P O BOX 325 42029
    Donna Perry, prin.
ES, P O BOX 215 42029 – Ray Chumbler,Jr., prin.

Campbellsburg, Henry Co., Pop. Code 3
Henry County SD
Supt. – See New Castle
ES, P O BOX 280 40011 – Craig Kessler, prin.

Campbellsville, Taylor Co., Pop. Code 6
Campbellsville ISD
Sch. Sys. Enr. Code 4
Supt. – David Fryrear
    136 S COLUMBIA AVE 42718
MS, ROBERTS ROAD 42718 – Larry Ennis, prin.
ES, 230 W MAIN ST 42718 – Jack Keeney, prin.

Taylor County SD
Sch. Sys. Enr. Code 4
Supt. – Gary Seaborne
    1209 E BROADWAY ST 42718
Taylor County MS, SPURLINGTON ROAD 42718
    J. Richerson, prin.
Taylor County ES, 1100 LEBANON AVE 42718
    Maurice Mings, prin.
Other Schools – See Mannsville

Camp Dix, Lewis Co.
Lewis County SD
Supt. – See Vanceburg
Laurel ES, RURAL ROUTE 01 BOX 108 41127
    Sharon Bloomfield, prin.

Campton, Wolfe Co., Pop. Code 2
Wolfe County SD
Sch. Sys. Enr. Code 4
Supt. – Owen Collins, P O BOX 160 41301
ES 41301 – Douglas Nickell, prin.
Other Schools – See Hazel Green, Rogers

Caneyville, Grayson Co., Pop. Code 3
Grayson County SD
Supt. – See Leitchfield
ES, P O BOX 17 42721 – William Givan, prin.

Cannel City, Morgan Co.
Morgan County SD
Supt. – See West Liberty
ES 41408 – K. Risner, prin.

Carlisle, Nicholas Co., Pop. Code 4
Nicholas County SD
Sch. Sys. Enr. Code 4
Supt. – D. Elder, 395 W MAIN ST 40311
Nicholas County ES, 133 SCHOOL DR 40311
    Gerald Hammons, prin.

Carrollton, Carroll Co., Pop. Code 5
Carroll County SD
Sch. Sys. Enr. Code 4
Supt. – Harry Day, P O BOX 90 41008
Carroll County MS, 5TH & SEMINARY STS 41008
    John Scheper, prin.
Cartmell MS, 1708 HIGHLAND AVE 41008
    John Allen, prin.
Winn ES, 9TH & HAWKINS 41008
    Larry Morgan, prin.

Carter, Carter Co.
Carter County SD
Supt. – See Grayson
ES 41128 – John Ramey, prin.

Catlettsburg, Boyd Co., Pop. Code 5
Boyd County SD
Sch. Sys. Enr. Code 5
Supt. – Delmis Donta, P O BOX 522 41129
ES, 3380 COURT ST 41129 – Ronda Tamme, prin.
Durbin ES, 28410 US ROUTE 23 41129
    Danny Knipp, prin.
Edison ES, 5701 CATLETTS CRK 41129
    Ralph Phelps, prin.
Other Schools – See Ashland, Rush

Cave City, Barren Co., Pop. Code 4
Caverna ISD
Sch. Sys. Enr. Code 4
Supt. – Billy Bruce, P O BOX 428 42127
Caverna ES, RURAL ROUTE 03 42127
    Tommye Cagle, prin.

Cawood, Harlan Co.
Harlan County SD
Supt. – See Harlan
ES 40815 – Sharon Dean, prin.

Cecilia, Hardin Co., Pop. Code 5
Hardin County SD
Supt. – See Elizabethtown
Hardin Central JHS
    RURAL ROUTE 02 BOX 100 42724
    Cletus Coats, prin.

Howevalley ES, 8450 HARDINSBURG RD 42724
    Bill Hay, prin.

Centertown, Ohio Co., Pop. Code 2
Ohio County SD
Supt. – See Hartford
ES, 446 MOSEA ST 42328 – William Leach, prin.
Western ES, RURAL ROUTE 01 42328
    James Sympson, prin.

Central City, Muhlenberg Co., Pop. Code 6
Muhlenberg County SD
Supt. – See Greenville
ES, RURAL ROUTE 03 42330
    Wayne Divine, prin.

Chaplin, Nelson Co.
Nelson County SD
Supt. – See Bardstown
ES 40012 – Elaine Armstrong, prin.

Clarkson, Grayson Co., Pop. Code 3
Grayson County SD
Supt. – See Leitchfield
ES, P O BOX 98 42726 – Larry Lee, prin.

Clay, Webster Co., Pop. Code 4
Webster County SD
Supt. – See Dixon
ES, P O BOX 158 42404 – Thomas Franklin, prin.

Clay City, Powell Co., Pop. Code 4
Powell County SD
Supt. – See Stanton
ES, P O BOX 237 40312 – James Potts, prin.

Clayhole, Breathitt Co.
Breathitt County SD
Supt. – See Jackson
Caney Consolodated ES 41317
    Paul Caudill, prin.

Clearfield, Rowan Co.
Rowan County SD
Supt. – See Morehead
ES, P O BOX 151 40313 – Virginia Reynolds, prin.

Clinton, Hickman Co., Pop. Code 4
Hickman County SD
Sch. Sys. Enr. Code 3
Supt. – Voris Clark, RURAL ROUTE 02 42031
Hickman County ES, EAST CLAY ST 42031
    Danny Whitlock, prin.

Cloverport, Breckinridge Co., Pop. Code 4
Cloverport ISD
Sch. Sys. Enr. Code 2
Supt. – J. Scaggs, P O BOX 217 40111
Natcher ES, 101 4TH ST 40111
    William Snodgrass, prin.

Cold Spring, Campbell Co., Pop. Code 4
Campbell County SD
Supt. – See Alexandria
Cline MS, 20 E ALEXANDRIA PIKE 41076
    Robert Ihrig, prin.
ES, EAST ALEXANDRIA PIKE 41076
    Don Augsback, prin.

St. Joseph ES, 4011 ALEXANDRIA PIKE 41076

Columbia, Adair Co., Pop. Code 5
Adair County SD
Sch. Sys. Enr. Code 5
Supt. – Kermit Grider, GREENSBURG ST 42728
Adair MS, GREENSBURG ST 42728
    Richie Coomer, prin.
Casey ES, GREENSBURG ST 42728
    Perry Farris, prin.
Sheperd ES, RURAL ROUTE 03 BOX 70A 42728
    Terry Farris, prin.
Sparksville ES, RURAL ROUTE 02 BOX 602 42728
    Billy Rodgers, prin.
Other Schools – See Knifley

Combs, Perry Co.
Perry County SD
Supt. – See Hazard
ES, P O BOX 31 41729 – R. Barker, prin.

Coopersville, Wayne Co.
Wayne County SD
Supt. – See Monticello
Rocky Branch ES, HCR 574 BOX 27 42611
    Robert Abbott, prin.

Corbin, Whitley Co., Pop. Code 6
Corbin ISD
Sch. Sys. Enr. Code 4
Supt. – Louie Martin, 108 E CENTER ST 40701
MS, 700 S KENTUCKY AVE 40701
    Wendal Mitchell, prin.
Central ES, SEVENTH & STEELE STS 40701
    Donald Byrd, prin.
East Ward MS, 529 MASTER ST 40701
    Roger Marcum, prin.
South Ward ES, 404 17TH ST 40701
    George Grove, prin.

Knox County SD
Supt. – See Barbourville
Lynn Camp ES, BOURBOURVILLE HWY 40701
    Roy Mitchell, prin.

Laurel County SD
Supt. – See London
Felts ES, RURAL ROUTE 11 BOX 49 40701
    Doug Wells, prin.

Whitley County SD
Supt. – See Williamsburg
Oak Grove ES, RURAL ROUTE 08 BOX 440 40701
  Dewey Bradley, prin.

St. Camillus Academy, 709 E CENTER ST 40701

Corinth, Grant Co., Pop. Code 2
Grant County SD
Supt. – See Williamstown
ES, P O BOX 37 41010 – Robert True, prin.

Corydon, Henderson Co., Pop. Code 3
Henderson County SD
Supt. – See Henderson
ES, P O BOX 225 42406 – John Duckworth, prin.

Covington, Kenton Co., Pop. Code 8
Covington ISD
Sch. Sys. Enr. Code 6
Supt. – Dr. Donald Hunter, 25 E 7TH ST 41011
Carlisle ES, ROBBINS & HOLMAN 41011
  Michael Ellis, prin.
First District ES, 525 SCOTT ST 41011
  Paul Veldhams, prin.
Fourth District ES, 1516 SCOTT ST 41011
  William Shelton, prin.
Latonia ES, 40TH & HUNTINGTON 41015
  Jerry Lancaster, prin.
Ninth District ES, 28TH AND INDIANA 41015
  Gordon MacIntosh, prin.
Sixth District ES, 19TH AND MARYLAND 41014
  Shirley Schildmeyer, prin.
Swing ES, 19TH & JEFFERSON 41014
  Evelyn Eaton, prin.

Kenton County SD
Supt. – See Independence
Park Hills ES, 1030 OLD STATE RD 41011
  Margaret Hoffman, prin.
Ryland Heights ES, RURAL ROUTE 05 41015
  Garry Jackson, prin.
Taylor Mill ES, 5907 TAYLOR MILL RD 41015
  Lonnie Watts, prin.
Visalia ES, RURAL ROUTE 05 41015
  Cassandra Wright, prin.

Calvary Christian School
  5955 TAYLOR MILL RD 41015
Villa Madonna Academy
  2500 AMSTERDAM ROAD 41016
Holy Cross ES, 3617 CHURCH ST 41015
Mary Queen of Heaven School
  1130 DONALDSON RD 41018
Prince of Peace ES, 625 PIKE ST 41011
St. Agnes School
  1322 SLEEPY HOLLOW RD 41011
St. Anthony ES, GRAND & HOWARD AVE 41015
St. Augustine School
  19TH AND JEFFERSON AVE 41014
St. Benedict School, 336 E 16TH ST 41014
St. Henry School, 3825 DIXIE HWY 41018
St. Jospeh School, 2474 LORRAINE CT 41017
St. Pius X School, 348 DUDLEY PIKE 41017

Coxs Creek, Nelson Co.
Nelson County SD
Supt. – See Bardstown
ES 40013 – Kenneth Drake, prin.

St. Gregory School
  RURAL ROUTE 03 BOX 232 40013

Crab Orchard, Lincoln Co., Pop. Code 3
Lincoln County SD
Supt. – See Stanford
Broughtontown ES, RURAL ROUTE 01 40419
  Shelby Reynolds, prin.
ES, P O BOX 430 40419 – Royce Killen, prin.

Cranks, Harlan Co.
Harlan County SD
Supt. – See Harlan
ES 40820 – Sharon Dean, prin.

Crestwood, Oldham Co., Pop. Code 3
Oldham County SD
Supt. – See La Grange
South Oldham MS, P O BOX 451 40014
  Tim Jackson, prin.
Camden Station ES, 6401 W HWY 146 40014
  Joseph Jacovino, prin.
Centerfield ES, 4512 S HIGHWAY 393 40014
  Paul Upchurch, prin.
ES, 6500 W HIGHWAY 146 40014
  Rick McHargue, prin.

Crockett, Morgan Co.
Morgan County SD
Supt. – See West Liberty
ES 41413 – Paula Williams, prin.

Crofton, Christian Co., Pop. Code 3
Christian County SD
Supt. – See Hopkinsville
ES, P O BOX 216 42217 – John Pyle, prin.

Cubage, Bell Co.
Bell County SD
Supt. – See Pineville
ES 40822 – David Messer, prin.

Cub Run, Hart Co.
Hart County SD
Supt. – See Munfordville
ES 42729 – James McCoy, prin.

Cumberland, Harlan Co., Pop. Code 5
Harlan County SD
Supt. – See Harlan
ES, P O BOX 0 40823 – Charles Dunaway, prin.

Custer, Breckinridge Co.
Breckinridge County SD
Supt. – See Hardinsburg
ES 40115 – Harold Childers, prin.

Cynthiana, Harrison Co., Pop. Code 6
Harrison County SD
Sch. Sys. Enr. Code 5
Supt. – Dr. Wade Roby
  RURAL ROUTE 04 BOX 27 41031
Harrison County MS, 550 WEBSTER AVE 41031
  Robert Ogden, prin.
Eastside ES, RURAL ROUTE 02 41031
  Maurice McGlone, prin.
Northside ES, RURAL ROUTE 02 41031
  Ted Sullivan, prin.
Southside ES, WEBSTER AVE 41031
  Cynthia Hill, prin.
Westside ES, RURAL ROUTE 06 41031
  Richard Wills, prin.

St. Edward ES, 123 N WALNUT ST 41031

Dana, Floyd Co.
Floyd County SD
Supt. – See Prestonsburg
Prater ES 41615 – Gene Davis, prin.

Danville, Boyle Co., Pop. Code 7
Boyle County SD
Sch. Sys. Enr. Code 4
Supt. – Emajo Carlton, P O BOX 520 40422
Boyle County MS, RURAL ROUTE 01 40422
  Richard Jasper, prin.
Woodlawn ES, RURAL ROUTE 01 40422
  Charles Edwards, prin.
Other Schools – See Junction City, Perryville

Danville ISD
Sch. Sys. Enr. Code 4
Supt. – Justin Minnehan
  203 E LEXINGTON AVE 40423
Danville Bate MS, 470 STANFORD AVE 40422
  Jane Scarborough, prin.
Hogsett ES, WAVELAND AVE 40422
  Sandy Embree, prin.
Rogers ES, E MAIN ST 40422
  James Trachsel, prin.
Toliver ES, MAPLE AVE 40422
  James Atkins, prin.

Dawson Springs, Hopkins Co., Pop. Code 5
Dawson Springs ISD
Sch. Sys. Enr. Code 3
Supt. – John Ray, HICKORY & ELI STS 42408
ES, HICKORY AND ELI STS 42408
  Billy Outland, prin.

Hopkins County SD
Supt. – See Madisonville
Charleston MS
  RURAL ROUTE 01 BOX 184 42408
  Ben Finley, prin.
Dalton MS, RURAL ROUTE 01 42408
  Patrick Courtney, prin.
Charleston ES, RURAL ROUTE 01 BOX 184 42408
  Ben Finley, prin.
Dalton ES, RURAL ROUTE 01 42408
  Patrick Courtney, prin.

Dayton, Campbell Co., Pop. Code 6
Dayton ISD
Sch. Sys. Enr. Code 4
Supt. – Jack Moreland, 999 VINE ST 41074
Lincoln ES, 5TH & JACKSON STS 41074
  Harold Starnes, prin.

St. Bernard School
  FOURTH AND BERRY STS 41074

Debord, Martin Co.
Martin County SD
Supt. – See Inez
Venters Branch ES 41214 – Rosa Blackburn, prin.

Decoy, Knott Co.
Knott County SD
Supt. – See Hindman
ES 41321 – Ray Smith, prin.

Denniston, Menifee Co.
Menifee County SD
Supt. – See Frenchburg
Menifee County Botts ES, P O BOX 37 40316
  Kirk Peck, prin.

Dewitt, Knox Co.
Knox County SD
Supt. – See Barbourville
ES 40930 – Robert Messer,Jr., prin.

Dice, Perry Co.
Perry County SD
Supt. – See Hazard
Lost Creek ES, P O BOX 159 41736 – (—), prin.

Dixon, Webster Co., Pop. Code 3
Webster County SD
Sch. Sys. Enr. Code 5
Supt. – Nataniel Green, P O BOX 128 42409
ES, HWY 41A SOUTH 42409
  Terry Rakestraw, prin.
Other Schools – See Clay, Sebree, Slaughters

Dorton, Pike Co., Pop. Code 5
Pike County SD
Supt. – See Pikeville
ES 41520 – John Wallace, prin.

Drakesboro, Muhlenberg Co., Pop. Code 3
Muhlenberg County SD
Supt. – See Greenville
Drakesboro Consolidated ES, P O BOX 127 42337
  Randall Everly, prin.

Drift, Floyd Co.
Floyd County SD
Supt. – See Prestonsburg
ES 41619 – Bobbie Blackburn, prin.

Dry Ridge, Grant Co., Pop. Code 4
Grant County SD
Supt. – See Williamstown
Grant County MS, RURAL ROUTE 02 41035
  Joyce Doyle, prin.
Crittenden Mt. Zion ES, RURAL ROUTE 02 41035
  Dwight Raleigh, prin.
ES, RURAL ROUTE 01 41035
  Deborah Reed, prin.

Earlington, Hopkins Co., Pop. Code 4
Hopkins County SD
Supt. – See Madisonville
MS, 299 W THOMPSON ST 42410
  Donald Gamblin, prin.
ES, 299 W THOMPSON ST 42410
  Donald Gamblin, prin.

East Bernstadt, Laurel Co.
East Bernstadt ISD
Sch. Sys. Enr. Code 2
Supt. – Ernest Wiggins, P O BOX 128 40729
ES, P O BOX 128 40729 – Homer Radford,Jr., prin.

Laurel County SD
Supt. – See London
Hazel Green ES
  RURAL ROUTE 02 BOX 38 1/2 40729
  Bill Moore, prin.

Eastview, Hardin Co.
Hardin County SD
Supt. – See Elizabethtown
Western ES
  19688 SONORA HARDIN SPGS RD 42732
  A. Johnson, prin.

Eddyville, Lyon Co., Pop. Code 4
Lyon County SD
Sch. Sys. Enr. Code 3
Supt. – Tom Buchanan, P O BOX 674 42038
Lyon County MS, P O BOX 400 42038
  Buddy Nichols, prin.
Lyon County ES, P O BOX 430 42038
  Jimmie Cagle, prin.

Edmonton, Metcalfe Co., Pop. Code 4
Metcalfe County SD
Sch. Sys. Enr. Code 4
Supt. – Dr. Charles Roberts 42129
ES 42129 – Hurshel Toms, prin.
Other Schools – See Sulpher Well, Summer Shade

Ekron, Meade Co., Pop. Code 2
Meade County SD
Supt. – See Brandenburg
ES 40117 – William Garnett, prin.

Elizabethtown, Hardin Co., Pop. Code 7
Elizabethtown ISD
Sch. Sys. Enr. Code 4
Supt. – Dr. David Thompson, P O BOX 605 42701
Stone JHS, MORNINGSIDE DRIVE 42701
  Robert Hilton, prin.
Helmwood Heights ES, CARDINAL DR 42701
  Ray Vencill, prin.
Morningside ES, MORNINGSIDE DR 42701
  William Sorrell, prin.
Valley View ES, HAWKINS DR 42701
  Hade Durbin, prin.

Hardin County SD
Sch. Sys. Enr. Code 7
Supt. – Dr. Steve Towler, 110 S MAIN ST 42701
Burkhead ES, 521 CHARLEMAGNE BLVD 42701
  John Benton, prin.
Lincoln Trail ES, 3154 BARDSTOWN RD 42701
  Michael Byers, prin.
New Highland ES
  110 HIGHLAND SCHOOL RD 42701
  Dane Hicks, prin.
Other Schools – See Cecilia, Eastview, Radcliff,
  Rineyville, Sonora, Upton, Vine Grove, White Mills

St. James School, 114 N MILES ST 42701

Elkhorn City, Pike Co., Pop. Code 4
Pike County SD
Supt. – See Pikeville
ES, 553-55 RUSSELL ST 41522
  Joe Elswick, prin.

Elkton, Todd Co., Pop. Code 4
Todd County SD
Sch. Sys. Enr. Code 4
Supt. – Howard Gorrell, P O BOX 638 42220
Todd Co. MS, P O BOX 428 42220
  Waldo Wolfe, prin.
North Todd ES, GREENVILLE RD 42220
  Mac Harper, prin.
Other Schools – See Guthrie

Elliottville, Rowan Co.
Rowan County SD
Supt. – See Morehead
ES 40317 – Juanita Crawford, prin.

Eminence, Henry Co., Pop. Code 4
Eminence ISD
Sch. Sys. Enr. Code 3
Supt. – J. Edwards, P O BOX 146 40019
ES, P O BOX 146 40019 – David Baird, prin.

Emmalena, Knott Co.
Knott County SD
Supt. – See Hindman
ES 41740 – Juanita Combs, prin.

Eolia, Neon Co.
Letcher County SD
Supt. – See Whitesburg
Boggs ES, HWY 806 BOX S 40826
Ted Corder, prin.

Erlanger, Kenton Co., Pop. Code 7
Erlanger-Elsmere ISD
Sch. Sys. Enr. Code 4
Supt. – Harold Ensor, P O BOX 18399 41018
Tichenor MS, 305 BARTLETT 41018
Timothy Jones, prin.
Arnett ES, 3552 KIMBERLY DR 41018
Oliver Bryant, prin.
Howell ES, CENTRAL ROW 41018
Charles Perry, prin.
Lindeman ES, 558 ERLANGER RD 41018
Rodney Kincer, prin.
Miles ES, P O BOX 339 41018
David Whaley, prin.

Eubank, Pulaski Co., Pop. Code 2
Pulaski County SD
Supt. – See Somerset
ES 42567 – Paul Morris, prin.

Evarts, Harlan Co., Pop. Code 4
Harlan County SD
Supt. – See Harlan
ES, P O BOX 189 40828 – James Madden, prin.
Verda ES, P O BOX 190 40828 – Donald Fain, prin.

Ewing, Fleming Co.
Fleming County SD
Supt. – See Flemingsburg
ES, P O BOX 218 41039 – Linda Donovan, prin.

Ezel, Morgan Co.
Morgan County SD
Supt. – See West Liberty
ES 41425 – Bucky Ellis, prin.

Fairdale, Jefferson Co., Pop. Code 4
Jefferson County SD
Supt. – See Louisville
Coral Ridge ES, 10608 NATIONAL TURN 40118
Beverly Goodwin, prin.
ES, 10104 MITCHELL HILL RD 40118
Larry Harrison, prin.

St. Jerome ES, 901 FAIRDALE RD 40118

Falmouth, Pendleton Co., Pop. Code 4
Pendleton County SD
Sch. Sys. Enr. Code 4
Supt. – Clifford Wallace, RURAL ROUTE 05 41040
Pendleton County MS, 506 CHAPEL ST 41040
Herb Owen, prin.
Southern ES, WOODSON US 27 RD 41040
Thomas Henry, prin.
Other Schools – See Butler

Fancy Farm, Hickman Co.
Graves County SD
Supt. – See Mayfield
ES, P O BOX 96 42039 – Philip Forester, prin.

Farmers, Rowan Co.
Rowan County SD
Supt. – See Morehead
ES 40319 – Fred Ellington, prin.

Farmington, Graves Co.
Graves County SD
Supt. – See Mayfield
ES, P O BOX 8 42040 – Al Colley, prin.

Fedscreek, Pike Co.
Pike County SD
Supt. – See Pikeville
Rowe ES 41524 – Phylis Hunt, prin.

Fern Creek, Jefferson Co., Pop. Code 6
Jefferson County SD
Supt. – See Louisville
ES, 8703 FERNDALE RD 40291
Roger Conwell, Jr., prin.
Wheeler ES, 5410 CYNTHIA DR 40291
Charlene Bush, prin.

Flatgap, Johnson Co.
Johnson County SD
Supt. – See Paintsville
ES, HCR 85 BOX 381 41219
Larry Pennington, prin.

Flat Lick, Knox Co.
Knox County SD
Supt. – See Barbourville
ES, P O BOX 379 40935 – Charles Dixon, prin.

Flemingsburg, Fleming Co., Pop. Code 5
Fleming County SD
Sch. Sys. Enr. Code 4
Supt. – C. Brown, 211 W WATER 41041
Simons MS, 242 W WATER ST 41041
Wendell Johnson, prin.
ES 41041 – Claude Asbury, prin.
Other Schools – See Ewing, Hillsboro, Wallingford

Florence, Boone Co., Pop. Code 7
Boone County SD
Sch. Sys. Enr. Code 6
Supt. – Larry Ryle, 8330 US 42 41042
Jones MS, 8000 SPRUCE DRIVE 41042
Keen Johnson, prin.
Ockerman MS, 8300 US ROUTE 42 41042
Melvyn Carroll, prin.
ES, 103 CENTER ST 41042 – Ralph Rush, prin.
Ockerman ES, 8250 US 42 41042
Lynda Sewak, prin.
Yealey ES, YEALEY DR 41042 – Paul Kroth, prin.
Other Schools – See Burlington, Hebron, Union

Heritage Academy ES, 7216 US 42 41042
St. Paul School, 7303 DIXIE HWY 41042

Fordsville, Ohio Co., Pop. Code 3
Ohio County SD
Supt. – See Hartford
ES, P O BOX 139 42343 – Leonard Ralph, prin.

Fort Campbell, Christian Co., Pop. Code 7

North MS, FORREST & GORGAS 42223
South MS, CHAFFEE ROAD & S CARO 42223

Fort Knox, Hardin Co., Pop. Code 8

MacDonald MS, BUILDING 7729 40121
Walker MS, 5549 CONROY ST 40121

Fort Mitchell, Kenton Co., Pop. Code 6
Beechwood ISD
Sch. Sys. Enr. Code 3
Supt. – Dr. Dennis Hockney
54 BEECHWOOD ROAD 41017
Beechwood ES, 54 BEECHWOOD RD 41017
Robert Hutton, prin.

Kenton County SD
Supt. – See Independence
Turkey Foot MS
3230 TURKEY FOOT ROAD 41017
Leslie Holbrook, prin.
Caywood ES, 25 SUMMIT DR 41017
John Mann, prin.
Crescent Springs ES
541 BUTTERMILK PIKE 41017
James Kiger, prin.
Hinsdale ES, 440 DUDLEY PIKE 41017
Rosa Weaver, prin.

Blessed Sacrament ES, 2407 DIXIE HWY 41017

Fort Thomas, Campbell Co., Pop. Code 7
Ft. Thomas ISD
Sch. Sys. Enr. Code 4
Supt. – Dr. Fred Williams
2356 MEMORIAL PARKWAY 41075
Johnson ES, 1180 N FT THOMAS AVE 41075
H. Beekley, prin.
Moyer ES, 219 HIGHLAND AVE 41075
Judith Poole, prin.
Woodfill ES, 1025 ALEXANDRIA PIKE 41075
Howard Fischer, prin.

St. Thomas ES, 428 S FT THOMAS AVE 41075

Fountain Run, Monroe Co., Pop. Code 2
Monroe County SD
Supt. – See Tompkinsville
ES 42133 – (—), prin.

Fourmile, Knox Co.
Bell County SD
Supt. – See Pineville
Lone Jack ES, P O BOX 98 40939
Marvis Hall, prin.

Frakes, Bell Co.
Bell County SD
Supt. – See Pineville
ES, P O BOX 201 40940 – Nevada Partin, prin.

Frankfort, Franklin Co., Pop. Code 8
Frankfort ISD
Sch. Sys. Enr. Code 3
Supt. – Albert Wall, 315 STEELE ST 40601
Second Street ES, W 2ND ST 40601
Ward Stauffer, prin.

Franklin County SD
Sch. Sys. Enr. Code 6
Supt. – Dr. F. Coogle, 916 E MAIN ST 40601
Bondurant MS
OLD HARRODSBURG ROAD 40601
Edward Speer, prin.
Elkhorn MS, 920 E MAIN ST 40601
David Simpson, prin.
Bald Knob ES, RURAL ROUTE 04 40601
Gary Stinnett, prin.
Bridgeport ES, RURAL ROUTE 02 40601
Roy McCall, prin.
Collins Lane ES, 1051 COLLINS LN 40601
Moner Kalla, prin.
Elkhorn ES, 928 E MAIN ST 40601
Allen Jackson, prin.

Hearn ES, LARALAN AVE 40601
John Vickers III, prin.
Peaks Mill ES, RURAL ROUTE 06 40601
Gary White, prin.

Good Shepherd School, 316 WAPPING ST 40601

Franklin, Simpson Co., Pop. Code 6
Simpson County SD
Sch. Sys. Enr. Code 5
Supt. – Charles Campbell, P O BOX 467 42134
Franklin Simpson MS, P O BOX 637 42134
Eddie Copas, prin.
ES, P O BOX 506 42134 – Marie Arney, prin.
Lincoln MS, P O BOX 429 42134
Billy Johnson, prin.
Simpson ES, P O BOX 409 42134
Lowell Hammers, prin.

Fredonia, Caldwell Co., Pop. Code 3
Caldwell County SD
Supt. – See Princeton
ES, P O BOX 177 42411 – Joycelyn Jones, prin.

Fredville, Magoffin Co.
Magoffin County SD
Supt. – See Salyersville
Arnett ES, SE LICKING RIVER RD 41430
Frank Smith, prin.

Freeburn, Pike Co.
Pike County SD
Supt. – See Pikeville
ES, P O BOX 170 41528 – Douglas Compton, prin.

Frenchburg, Menifee Co., Pop. Code 3
Menifee County SD
Sch. Sys. Enr. Code 4
Supt. – Richard Ratliff, P O BOX 118 40322
Menifee County ES, HCR 69 BOX 340 40322
James Trimble, prin.
Other Schools – See Denniston

Fulton, Fulton Co., Pop. Code 5
Fulton ISD
Sch. Sys. Enr. Code 3
Supt. – Larry Salmon, 311 MAIN ST 42041
Carr ES, W STATE LINE 42041
Pete Morgan, prin.

Gamaliel, Monroe Co., Pop. Code 2
Monroe County SD
Supt. – See Tompkinsville
MS 42140 – Kenneth Holbrook, prin.
ES 42140 – Kenneth Holbrook, prin.

Garrett, Floyd Co.
Floyd County SD
Supt. – See Prestonsburg
ES 41630 – Ralph Quinn, prin.

Garrison, Lewis Co.
Lewis County SD
Supt. – See Vanceburg
ES, P O BOX 547 41141
Mildred Richardson, prin.

Georgetown, Scott Co., Pop. Code 7
Scott County SD
Sch. Sys. Enr. Code 5
Supt. – Dr. John Herlihy, P O BOX 561 40324
MS, CLAY AVE 40324 – George Lusby, prin.
Scott County MS, RURAL ROUTE 03 40324
Patrick Lair, prin.
Eastern ES, RURAL ROUTE 01 40324
Barbara Cockrum, prin.
Garth ES, 501 S HAMILTON ST 40324
Donald Beaven, prin.
Great Crossing ES, 2168 FRANKFORT RD 40324
Danny Glass, prin.
Southern ES, 1200 FAIRFAX WAY 40324
Jack Wise, prin.
Other Schools – See Sadieville, Stamping Ground

Gilbertsville, Marshall Co.
Marshall County SD
Supt. – See Benton
ES 42044 – Jim Goheen, prin.

Girdler, Knox Co.
Knox County SD
Supt. – See Barbourville
ES 40943 – Michael Jones, prin.

Glasgow, Barren Co., Pop. Code 7
Barren County SD
Sch. Sys. Enr. Code 5
Supt. – Roy Withrow
202 W WASHINGTON ST 42141
Eastern ES, RURAL ROUTE 05 42141
W. Rock, prin.
Temple Hill ES, RURAL ROUTE 04 42141
James Lindsey, prin.
Other Schools – See Hiseville, Lucas, Park City

Glasgow ISD
Sch. Sys. Enr. Code 4
Supt. – Eldon Smith, P O BOX 239 42141
MS, 215 S LIBERTY ST 42141
Robert Reece, prin.
Bunche MS, 301 BUNCHE AVE 42141
John Westerfield, prin.
Happy Valley ES, HAPPY VALLEY RD 42141
Zeb Ricketts, prin.
South Green ES, S GREEN ST 42141
Jimmy Brown, prin.
Terry ES, 317 COLUMBIA AVE 42141
Stephen Mayhew, prin.

Glencoe, Gallatin Co., Pop. Code 2
Gallatin County SD
Supt. – See Warsaw
ES 41046 – Margery Minch, prin.

Goshen, Oldham Co.
Oldham County SD
Supt. – See La Grange
ES, P O BOX 116 40026 – Dalton Oak, prin.
Liberty ES, 8120 W HIGHWAY 42 40026
James Hill, prin.

Graham, Muhlenberg Co., Pop. Code 4
Muhlenberg County SD
Supt. – See Greenville
ES 42344 – Carl Sparks, prin.

Grahn, Carter Co.
Carter County SD
Supt. – See Grayson
ES, P O BOX 6 41142 – James Roe, prin.

Grand Rivers, Livingston Co., Pop. Code 2
Livingston County SD
Supt. – See Smithland
ES, P O BOX 157 42045 – Jack Monroe, prin.

Gray, Knox Co.
Knox County SD
Supt. – See Barbourville
ES, P O BOX 1 40734 – Luther Gaddis,Jr., prin.

Grays Knob, Harlan Co.
Harlan County SD
Supt. – See Harlan
Hall ES 40829 – Mitchell Barrett, prin.

Grayson, Carter Co., Pop. Code 5
Carter County SD
Sch. Sys. Enr. Code 6
Supt. – H. Holbrook, P O BOX 517 41143
Prichard ES, 401 E MAIN ST 41143
Roger McGlone, prin.
Other Schools – See Carter, Grahn, Hitchins, Lawton,
Olive Hill, Rush, Willard

Greensburg, Green Co., Pop. Code 4
Green County SD
Sch. Sys. Enr. Code 4
Supt. – M. Lowe, BOX 369 42743
Green County MS, P O BOX 369 42743
James Mills, prin.
ES, P O BOX 369 42743 – James Cowherd, prin.
Pierce ES, RURAL ROUTE 04 42743
Forrest Kelly, prin.
Other Schools – See Summersville

Greenup, Greenup Co., Pop. Code 4
Greenup County SD
Sch. Sys. Enr. Code 5
Supt. – R. Stephens, 3449 OLD DAM CT 41144
ES, 1621 MAIN ST 41144 – James Stuart, prin.
Greysbranch ES, 4311 OHIO RIVER RD 41144
Stephen Stephens, prin.
Lynn ES, RURAL ROUTE 01 BOX 563 41144
Larry Popovich, prin.
Warnock ES, HCR 63 BOX 694 41144
Roger Dillion, prin.
Other Schools – See Argillite, Oldtown, South
Portsmouth, Wurtland

Greenville, Muhlenberg Co., Pop. Code 5
Muhlenberg County SD
Sch. Sys. Enr. Code 5
Supt. – B. Topmiller,Jr., P O BOX 167 42345
ES, 120 COLLEGE ST 42345
Charles Summers, prin.
Longest ES, P O BOX 71 42345
Robert Reynolds, prin.
Other Schools – See Beechmont, Belton, Bremen,
Central City, Drakesboro, Graham

Grethel, Floyd Co.
Floyd County SD
Supt. – See Prestonsburg
Stumbo ES, P O BOX 100 41631
Gary Newman, prin.

Guthrie, Todd Co., Pop. Code 4
Todd County SD
Supt. – See Elkton
South Todd ES, CLARSVILLE RD 42234
Waldo Wolfe, prin.

Hagerhill, Johnson Co.
Johnson County SD
Supt. – See Paintsville
Porter ES, BOX 160 HCR 41222
Howard Wallen, prin.

Haldeman, Rowan Co.
Rowan County SD
Supt. – See Morehead
ES 40329 – Sandy Knipp, prin.

Hallie, Letcher Co.
Letcher County SD
Supt. – See Whitesburg
Campbells Branch ES 41821 – Shelby Watts, prin.

Hampton, Livingston Co.
Livingston County SD
Supt. – See Smithland
ES 42047 – Sarah Flatt, prin.

Hanson, Hopkins Co., Pop. Code 2
Hopkins County SD
Supt. – See Madisonville
ES 42413 – Bobby Higgins, prin.

Happy, Perry Co.
Perry County SD
Supt. – See Hazard
Combs ES, HWY 15 S 41712 – James Combs, prin.

Hardinsburg, Breckinridge Co., Pop. Code 4
Breckinridge County SD
Sch. Sys. Enr. Code 5
Supt. – Huston Dehaven
BRECKINRIDGE MANOR 40143
ES, RURAL ROUTE 01 40163 – Ints Kampars, prin.
Other Schools – See Custer, Irvington, Mc Daniels, Mc
Quady, Stephensport

St. Romuald ES, N MAIN ST 40143

Hardyville, Hart Co.
Hart County SD
Supt. – See Munfordville
Memorial ES, RURAL ROUTE 01 42746
Jerry Ralston, prin.

Harlan, Harlan Co., Pop. Code 5
Harlan County SD
Sch. Sys. Enr. Code 6
Supt. – Robert Shepherd, P O BOX C 40831
Guthrie ES, HCR 78 BOX 559 40831
Mitchell Barrett, prin.
Other Schools – See Baxter, Benham, Bledsoe,
Cawood, Cranks, Cumberland, Evarts, Grays Knob,
Holmes Mill, Kenvir, Loyall, Totz, Wallins Creek

Harlan ISD
Sch. Sys. Enr. Code 4
Supt. – Dr. William Wesley 40831
ES 40831 – Enoch Foutch, prin.

Holy Trinity ES, 2301 S US HWY 421 40831
Woodland Hills Christian School
P O BOX 975 40831

Harold, Floyd Co.
Floyd County SD
Supt. – See Prestonsburg
ES, P O BOX 130 41635 – David Hinchman, prin.

Harrodsburg, Mercer Co., Pop. Code 6
Harrodsburg ISD
Sch. Sys. Enr. Code 4
Supt. – Dale Kirk, E LEXINGTON ST 40330
MS, E LEXINGTON ST 40330 – Dean Ensey, prin.
Harlow ES, PERRYVILLE ST 40330
Robert Anderson, prin.

Mercer County SD
Sch. Sys. Enr. Code 4
Supt. – K. King, P O BOX 287 40330
Mercer County ES, 741 TAPP RD 40330
Michael Barnard, prin.

Hartford, Ohio Co., Pop. Code 5
Ohio County SD
Sch. Sys. Enr. Code 5
Supt. – R. Goff, P O BOX 67 42347
Ohio County MS, 1400 US HWY 231 S 42347
H. Davis, prin.
Alexander ES, 100 RENDER ST 42347
Larry Embry, prin.
Other Schools – See Beaver Dam, Centertown,
Fordsville, South Branch

Hawesville, Hancock Co., Pop. Code 4
Hancock County SD
Sch. Sys. Enr. Code 4
Supt. – Vickie Basham, P O BOX 159 42348
ES, P O BOX 428 42348 – William Buck, prin.
South Hancock ES
RURAL ROUTE 02 BOX 989 42348
Barbara Spindel, prin.
Other Schools – See Lewisport

Immaculate Conception School 42348

Hazard, Perry Co., Pop. Code 6
Hazard ISD
Sch. Sys. Enr. Code 4
Supt. – Roscoe Shackleford
325 BROADWAY ST 41701
Eversole MS, BROADWAY 41701
John Farler, prin.
Walkertown ES, 325 SCHOOL ST 41701
Don Collins, prin.

Knott County SD
Supt. – See Hindman
Cordia ES, RURAL ROUTE 02 BOX 265 41701
Bobby Smith, prin.

Perry County SD
Sch. Sys. Enr. Code 6
Supt. – K. Colwell, 800 HIGH ST 41701
Wooton ES, RURAL ROUTE 03 BOX 545C 41701
Alfred Collins, prin.
Other Schools – See Ary, Avawam, Buckhorn, Busy,
Combs, Dice, Happy, Jeff, Leatherwood, Saul, Viper

Hazel Green, Wolfe Co., Pop. Code 2
Wolfe County SD
Supt. – See Campton
Red River Valley ES 41332 – Earl May,Jr., prin.

Hebron, Boone Co., Pop. Code 4
Boone County SD
Supt. – See Florence
Goodridge ES, P O BOX 37 41048
Charles Massey, prin.

Immaculate Heart of Mary School
3970 LIMABURG RD 41048

Hellier, Pike Co.
Pike County SD
Supt. – See Pikeville
ES 41534 – Irene Spears, prin.

Helton, Harlan Co.
Leslie County SD
Supt. – See Hyden
Beech Fork ES 40840 – Wendell Wilson, prin.

Henderson, Henderson Co., Pop. Code 7
Henderson County SD
Sch. Sys. Enr. Code 6
Supt. – Dr. Gayle Ecton, 1805 SECOND ST 42420
Bend Gate ES, 920 BEND GATE RD 42420
Charles Mays, prin.
Cairo ES, RURAL ROUTE 02 BOX 390 42420
Claiborne Moore, prin.
Central ES, 851 CENTER ST 42420
Raymond Rhorer, prin.
East Heights ES, ZION RD 42420
Rodney Watkins, prin.
Hebbardsville ES, RURAL ROUTE 04 42420
Gary Rust, prin.
Jefferson ES, 315 JACKSON ST 42420
Brenda McCully, prin.
Niagara ES, RURAL ROUTE 03 42420
William Denton, prin.
Seventh Street ES, 328 SEVENTH ST 42420
Marion Hill, prin.
South Heights ES, 1200 WRIGHT ST 42420
William Womack, prin.
Other Schools – See Corydon, Robards, Smith Mills,
Spottsville

Holy Name ES, 628 SECOND ST 42420

Hendricks, Magoffin Co.
Magoffin County SD
Supt. – See Salyersville
Middle Fork ES, MIDDLE FORK RD 41441
Paul Rowe, prin.

Herndon, Christian Co.
Christian County SD
Supt. – See Hopkinsville
South Christian ES 42236 – James Jackson, prin.

Hickman, Fulton Co., Pop. Code 5
Fulton County SD
Sch. Sys. Enr. Code 4
Supt. – Charles Terrett, P O BOX 50 42050
Fulton County MS, MOSCOW AVE 42050
Charles Murphy, prin.
Fulton County ES, RURAL ROUTE 04 42050
Richard Wilkerson, prin.

Highland Heights, Campbell Co., Pop. Code 5
Campbell County SD
Supt. – See Alexandria
ES, MAIN AND RENSHAW 41076
Glennis Ramey, prin.

Hillsboro, Fleming Co.
Fleming County SD
Supt. – See Flemingsburg
ES, P O BOX 8 41049 – Forest Tackett, prin.

Hindman, Knott Co., Pop. Code 3
Knott County SD
Sch. Sys. Enr. Code 5
Supt. – R. Singleton, P O BOX 869 41822
ES 41822 – Cloys Thornsberry, prin.
Other Schools – See Decoy, Emmalena, Hazard,
Hueysville, Littcarr, Mousie, Pippa Passes, Topmost,
Vest

Hiseville, Barren Co., Pop. Code 2
Barren County SD
Supt. – See Glasgow
ES 42152 – Darrell Florence, prin.

Hisle, McKee Co.
Jackson County SD
Supt. – See Mc Kee
ES 40436 – Donna Rose, prin.

Hitchins, Carter Co.
Carter County SD
Supt. – See Grayson
ES, P O BOX 2 41146 – Steven McDavid, prin.

Hodgenville, Larue Co., Pop. Code 4
Larue County SD
Sch. Sys. Enr. Code 4
Supt. – Everett Sanders, P O BOX 39 42748
Larue County MS, RURAL ROUTE 01 42748
John Sullivan, prin.
ES, COLLEGE ST 42748 – Liane McDowell, prin.
Other Schools – See Buffalo, Magnolia

Holmes Mill, Harlan Co.
Harlan County SD
Supt. – See Harlan
ES, P O BOX 6 40843 – James Madden, prin.

Honaker, Floyd Co.
Floyd County SD
Supt. – See Prestonsburg
Spruce Pine ES 41639 – Mazie Tackett, prin.

Hopkinsville, Christian Co., Pop. Code 8
Christian County SD
Sch. Sys. Enr. Code 6
Supt. – Leon Roberts, P O BOX 609 42240

Christian County MS, 720 GLASS AVE   42240
    William McConnell, prin.
MS, 434 KOFFMAN DRIVE   42240
    Clyde Lile, prin.
Belmont ES, 814 BELMONT ST   42240
    B. Kelley, prin.
Highland ES, 141 HIGHLAND SCHOOL RD   42240
    Ruth White, prin.
Holiday ES, 3910 ANSSAU CIRCLE   42240
    Bob Eaker, prin.
Indian Hills ES, 313 BLANE DR   42240
    Linda Ledford, prin.
Lacy ES, 12015 GREENVILLE RD   42240
    Hurchel Myers, prin.
Millbrooke ES, 415 MILLBROOKE DR   42240
    Edward Holmes, prin.
Morningside ES, MORNINGSIDE DR   42240
    Mary DeBow, prin.
North Drive MS, 831 NORTH DR   42240
    Robert Roach, prin.
Sinking Fork ES, 8290 PRINCETON RD   42240
    Robert Durden, prin.
Other Schools – See Crofton, Herndon, Pembroke

University Heights Academy
    P O BOX 1070   42240
    SS. Peter & Paul ES, 902 E 9TH ST   42240

Horse Branch, Ohio Co.
Ohio County SD
Supt. – See Hartford
ES, RURAL ROUTE 01   42349
    Kenneth Autry, prin.

Horse Cave, Hart Co., Pop. Code 4
Hart County SD
Supt. – See Munfordville
LeGrande ES, RURAL ROUTE 03   42749
    Joanne Smith, prin.

Hoskinston, Leslie Co.
Leslie County SD
Supt. – See Hyden
Stinnett ES   40844 – Charles Hoskins, prin.

Hueysville, Floyd Co.
Knott County SD
Supt. – See Hindman
Upper Quicksand ES   41634
    Bradford Handshoe, prin.

Hulen, Bell Co.
Bell County SD
Supt. – See Pineville
Blackmont ES, RURAL ROUTE 01   40845
    Eddie Saylor, prin.

Hustonville, Lincoln Co.
Lincoln County SD
Supt. – See Stanford
ES, P O BOX 6   40437 – Larry Woods, prin.

Hyden, Leslie Co., Pop. Code 2
Leslie County SD
Sch. Sys. Enr. Code 5
Supt. – Richard Bowling, P O BOX 949   41749
ES, P O BOX 926   41749 – George Sizemore, prin.
Other Schools – See Bear Branch, Helton, Hoskinston,
    Wooton, Yeaddiss

Independence, Kenton Co., Pop. Code 6
Kenton County SD
Sch. Sys. Enr. Code 7
Supt. – Dr. John Forbeck
    5533 MADISON PIKE   41051
Twenhofel MS, 6955 TAYLOR MILL ROAD   41051
    Ronald Schneider, prin.
Beech Grove ES, 1029 BRISTOW RD   41051
    Clifford Perkins, prin.
Kenton ES, 5577 MADISON PIKE   41051
    Charles Miller, prin.
White Towers ES, 705 HARRIS RD   41051
    Larry Compton, prin.
Other Schools – See Bromley, Covington, Fort
    Mitchell, Latonia, Morning View

St. Cecilia School, 5309 MADISON PIKE   41051

Inez, Martin Co., Pop. Code 2
Martin County SD
Sch. Sys. Enr. Code 5
Supt. – Glenn Prichard, P O BOX 366   41224
ES   41224 – James Webb, prin.
ES, P O BOX 1308   41224 – Thomas Dials, prin.
Mouth/Turkey ES, HCR 69 BOX 1250   41224
    Carolyn Sumpter, prin.
Other Schools – See Debord, Job, Pilgrim, Tomahawk,
    Warfield

Ingram, Bell Co.
Bell County SD
Supt. – See Pineville
Buckeye ES, RURAL ROUTE 02 BOX 408   40955
    Lee Gambrel, prin.

Irvine, Estill Co., Pop. Code 5
Estill County SD
Sch. Sys. Enr. Code 5
Supt. – William Alexander, P O BOX 391   40336
Estill County MS, P O BOX 156   40336
    Stephen Garrett, prin.
Estill Springs MS, 314 MAIN   40336
    Robert Daniel, prin.
Hargett ES, P O BOX 279   40336
    Gary Taylor, prin.
ES, BROADWAY   40336 – Debra Stone, prin.

South Irvine ES, RURAL ROUTE 05   40336
    Danny Click, prin.
West Irvine ES
    RURAL ROUTE 05 BOX 215   40336
    William Beard, prin.
Other Schools – See Ravenna

Irvington, Breckinridge Co., Pop. Code 4
Breckinridge County SD
Supt. – See Hardinsburg
ES, RURAL ROUTE 02   40146 – Frank Reams, prin.

Island, McLean Co, Pop. Code 3
McLean County SD
Supt. – See Calhoun
ES, HWY 431   42350 – Eugene Bidwell, prin.

Isonville, Elliott Co.
Elliott County SD
Supt. – See Sandy Hook
ES   41149 – Charles Tussey, prin.

Jackhorn, Letcher Co.
Letcher County SD
Supt. – See Whitesburg
Hemphill ES, GENERAL DELIVERY   41825
    Ron Lester, prin.

Jackson, Breathitt Co., Pop. Code 5
Breathitt County SD
Sch. Sys. Enr. Code 5
Supt. – Alex Browning   41339
Sebastian MS, P O BOX 788   41339
    James Gabbard, prin.
L. B. J. ES, P O BOX 707   41339
    Edgar Raleigh, prin.
Other Schools – See Booneville, Clayhole, Lost Creek,
    Rousseau

Jackson ISD
Sch. Sys. Enr. Code 2
Supt. – Phyllis Williamson
    938 HIGHLAND AVE   41339
ES, 938 HIGHLAND AVE   41339
    Dwight Johnson, prin.

Mt. Carmel HS
    RURAL ROUTE 01   BOX 350   41339

Jamestown, Russell Co., Pop. Code 4
Russell County SD
Sch. Sys. Enr. Code 5
Supt. – S. Stephens, P O BOX 260   42629
ES, P O BOX 530   42629 – Danny Skaggs, prin.
Union Chapel ES
    RURAL ROUTE 03 BOX 227   42629
    Keith Blakey, prin.
Other Schools – See Russell Springs

Jeff, Perry Co., Pop. Code 2
Perry County SD
Supt. – See Hazard
Chavies ES   41751 – David Heath, prin.

Jeffersontown, Jefferson Co., Pop. Code 7
Jefferson County SD
Supt. – See Louisville
Tully ES, 3300 COLLEGE DRIVE   40299
    Carol Buddo, prin.

Jenkins, Letcher Co., Pop. Code 5
Jenkins ISD
Sch. Sys. Enr. Code 3
Supt. – Alex Eversole, P O BOX 74   41537
MS, P O BOX 552   41537 – Carson Slone, prin.
Other Schools – See Burdine, Mc Roberts

Job, Martin Co.
Martin County SD
Supt. – See Inez
Grassy ES, HCR 268 BOX 608   41225
    Janice Runyons, prin.

Junction City, Boyle Co., Pop. Code 4
Boyle County SD
Supt. – See Danville
ES, P O BOX 200   40440 – Jerry Leber, prin.

Keavy, Laurel Co.
Laurel County SD
Supt. – See London
ES   40737 – Ivan Wells, prin.

Kenvir, Harlan Co.
Harlan County SD
Supt. – See Harlan
Black Mountain ES   40847 – Donald Fain, prin.

Kevil, Ballard Co., Pop. Code 2
Ballard County SD
Supt. – See Barlow
ES, P O BOX 174   42053 – Haskell Sheeks, prin.

Kimper, Pike Co.
Pike County SD
Supt. – See Pikeville
ES, HCR 35 BOX 1938   41539
    Danny Patierno, prin.

Knifley, Adair Co
Adair County SD
Supt. – See Columbia
ES, RURAL ROUTE 01 BOX 50   42753
    Patty Collins, prin.

Kona, Letcher Co.
Letcher County SD
Supt. – See Whitesburg
Potter ES   41829 – William Webb, prin.

La Center, Ballard Co., Pop. Code 4
Ballard County SD
Supt. – See Barlow
ES, P O BOX 276   42056 – Rodney Steele, prin.

La Grange, Oldham Co., Pop. Code 5
Oldham County SD
Sch. Sys. Enr. Code 6
Supt. – R. Arvin, P O BOX 207   40031
ES, 500 W JEFFERSON ST   40031
    Don Craig, prin.
Other Schools – See Buckner, Crestwood, Goshen

Immaculate Conception School
    500 N 5TH ST   40031

Lancaster, Garrard Co., Pop. Code 5
Garrard County SD
Sch. Sys. Enr. Code 4
Supt. – Dr. John Thompson
    322 W MAPLE AVE   40444
Camp Robinson ES, RURAL ROUTE 04   40444
    Z. Lester, prin.
ES, 205 LEXINGTON ST   40444
    Delmer Warren, prin.
Other Schools – See Paint Lick

Langley, Floyd Co.
Floyd County SD
Supt. – See Prestonsburg
Maytown ES, P O BOX 220   41645
    Lorena Chaffin, prin.

Latonia, Kenton Co.
Kenton County SD
Supt. – See Independence
Woodland MS, OLD TAYLOR MILL RD   41015
    Don Deller, prin.

Lawrenceburg, Anderson Co., Pop. Code 6
Anderson County SD
Sch. Sys. Enr. Code 5
Supt. – Ronald Fentress, 103 N MAIN ST   40342
Anderson County MS, 126 N MAIN ST   40342
    Wayne King, prin.
Saffell Street ES, 210 SAFFELL ST   40342
    Max Workman, prin.
Ward MS, BROADWAY   40342
    Glenn Karsner, prin.
Western ES, 4188 BARDSTOWN RD   40342
    Melvin Stevens, prin.

Lawton, Carter Co.
Carter County SD
Supt. – See Grayson
ES   41153 – Larna Cotten, prin.

Leatherwood, Perry Co.
Perry County SD
Supt. – See Hazard
ES   41756 – Robert Lootens, prin.

Lebanon, Marion Co., Pop. Code 6
Marion County SD
Sch. Sys. Enr. Code 5
Supt. – Happy Osborne, 223 N SPALDING   40033
MS, 235 N SPALDING AVE   40033
    David Hogan, prin.
St. Charles MS, RURAL ROUTE 02   40033
    Herman Rowlett, prin.
Calvary ES, RURAL ROUTE 01 BOX 138   40033
    Diane Evans, prin.
Glasscock ES, RURAL ROUTE 03   40033
    R. Benningfield, prin.
ES, 420 W MAIN ST   40033
    Martha Gribbins, prin.
St. Charles ES, RURAL ROUTE 02   40033
    Judy Gaddie, prin.

St. Augustine School
    236 S SPALDING AVE   40033

Lebanon Junction, Bullitt Co., Pop. Code 4
Bullitt County SD
Supt. – See Shepherdsville
ES, RURAL ROUTE 01 BOX 74   40150
    Larry Belcher, prin.

St. Benedict School, 206 OAK ST   40150

Ledbetter, Livingston Co.
Livingston County SD
Supt. – See Smithland
ES, P O BOX A   42058 – Tom Counts, prin.

Leitchfield, Grayson Co., Pop. Code 5
Grayson County SD
Sch. Sys. Enr. Code 5
Supt. – Robert Boggs, P O BOX 256   42754
Grayson County MS, 726 MILL ST   42754
    James Purcell, prin.
Wilkey ES, 201 WALLACE AVE   42754
    Gerald Claypool, prin.
Other Schools – See Caneyville, Clarkson

St. Paul School
    RURAL ROUTE 01 BOX 329   42754

Letcher, Letcher Co.
Letcher County SD
Supt. – See Whitesburg
ES   41832 – Sherrill Slone, prin.

Lewisburg, Logan Co., Pop. Code 3
Logan County SD
Supt. – See Russellville
MS   42256 – Darrell Dooley, prin.

ES 42256 – Darrell Dooley, prin.

Lewisport, Hancock Co., Pop. Code 4
Hancock County SD
Supt. – See Hawesville
Hancock County MS, RURAL ROUTE 01 42351
George Fallin, prin.
ES, P O BOX D 42351 – Jerry Griffin, prin.

Lexington, Fayette Co., Pop. Code 9
Fayette County SD
Sch. Sys. Enr. Code 8
Supt. – Dr. Ronald Walton, 701 E MAIN ST 40502
Allen ES, 1901 APPOMATTOX RD 40504
David Fresh, prin.
Arlington ES, 928 N LIMESTONE ST 40505
Robin Fankhouser, prin.
Ashland ES, 195 N ASHLAND AVE 40502
George McKenzie, prin.
Athens ES
6270 ATHENS-WALNUT HILL RD 40515
Sarah Adams, prin.
Breckinridge ES
2101 SAINT MATHILDA DR 40502
Mary Williams, prin.
Cardinal Valley ES, 218 MANDALAY RD 40504
Ronald Beckett, prin.
Cassidy ES, 1125 TATES CREEK RD 40502
Dorothy Friend, prin.
Clays Mill ES, 2319 CLAYS MILL RD 40503
Barbara Albaugh, prin.
Deep Springs ES, 1919 BRYNELL DR 40505
Hazel Olinger, prin.
Dixie ES, 1940 EASTLAND PKY 40505
Linda Keller, prin.
Ewan ES, 350 HENRY CLAY BLVD 40502
James Hardin, prin.
Garden Springs ES
2151 GARDEN SPRINGS DR 40504
Gerald Cooper, prin.
Glendover ES, GLENDOVER RD 40503
Jana Fremd, prin.
Harrison ES, 161 BRUCE ST 40508
Vicki Moore, prin.
Johnson ES, 123 E SIXTH ST 40508
Patricia Michaux, prin.
Lansdowne ES, 336 REDDING RD 40502
Jane Gettler, prin.
Linlee ES, 2545 GEORGETOWN RD 40511
Marjorie Magedanz, prin.
Marks ES, 3277 PEPPERHILL RD 40502
A. Pope, prin.
Maxwell ES, 301 WOODLAND AVE 40508
J. Casey, prin.
Meadowthorpe ES, 1710 N FORBES RD 40511
Richard Day, prin.
Mill Creek ES, 3660 APPIAN WAY 40502
Edward Rudd, prin.
Northern ES, 340 ROOKWOOD PKY 40505
Gail Toye, prin.
Picadome ES, 1642 HARRODSBURG RD 40504
John McIntyre,Jr., prin.
Russell Cave ES, 3375 RUSSELL CAVE RD 40511
Della Burrus, prin.
Russell ES, 201 W FIFTH ST 40508
Valinda Livingston, prin.
Southern ES, 340 WILSON DOWNING RD 40503
Nawanna Fairchild, prin.
Squires ES, 3337 SQUIRES OAKS DR 40515
Stanley Jordan, prin.
Stonewall ES, 3215 CORNWALL DR 40503
Nancy West, prin.
Tates Creek ES, 1113 CENTRE PKY 40502
Stanton Simandle, prin.
Todd ES, PARKSIDE DR 40505
James McCaw, prin.
Washington ES, GEORGETOWN ST 40508
Katye Jenkins, prin.
Yates ES, NEW CIRCLE RD 40505
Ronald Eads, prin.

Lexington Christian School
940 HOLLY SPRINGS DRIVE 40504
New Covenant Academy
2700 TODDS ROAD 40509
Sayre School, 194 N LIMESTONE ST 40507
Academy ES, 3815 HARRODSBURG RD 40503
Christ the King School, 412 COCHRAN RD 40502
Community Montessori ES
166 CRESTWOOD DR 40503
Lexington School, 1050 LANE ALLEN RD 40504
Mary Queen of Holy Rosary School
2501 CLAYS MILL RD 40503
St. Peter School, 133 BARR ST 40507

Liberty, Casey Co., Pop. Code 4
Casey County SD
Sch. Sys. Enr. Code 5
Supt. – Wendell Emerson
RURAL ROUTE 01 BOX 21 42539
Casey Co. MS, RURAL ROUTE 04 42539
Steve Butcher, prin.
Douglas ES, RURAL ROUTE 01 42539
Marcus Wiles, prin.
Liberty ES, COLLEGE AVE 42539
Robert Anderson, prin.
Phillips ES, RURAL ROUTE 08 42539
Humphrey Elliott, prin.
Other Schools – See Bethelridge, Middleburg, Windsor

Lily, Laurel Co.
Laurel County SD
Supt. – See London
ES, RURAL ROUTE 02 BOX 25 40740
Jack Sears, prin.

Linefork, Letcher Co.
Letcher County SD
Supt. – See Whitesburg
Kingdom Come Settlement ES 41833
Sadie Caudill, prin.

Littcarr, Knott Co.
Knott County SD
Supt. – See Hindman
Carr Creek ES 41834 – Ellis Hall, prin.

Livermore, McLean Co., Pop. Code 4
McLean County SD
Supt. – See Calhoun
ES 42352 – Michael Heflin, prin.

Livingston, Rockcastle Co., Pop. Code 2
Rockcastle County SD
Supt. – See Mount Vernon
ES, MAIN ST 40445 – Robert Mink, prin.

London, Laurel Co., Pop. Code 5
Laurel County SD
Sch. Sys. Enr. Code 6
Supt. – Joe McKnight, 1715 S MAIN ST 40741
Bush ES, RURAL ROUTE 10 BOX 464 40741
Willard Bowling, prin.
Camp Ground ES
RURAL ROUTE 04 BOX 136 40741
Jim McKnight, prin.
Cold Hill ES, RURAL ROUTE 01 BOX 427 40741
Betty Blanschi, prin.
Colony ES, RURAL ROUTE 02 BOX 197 40741
Diana Lincks, prin.
Johnson ES, RURAL ROUTE 09 BOX 280 40741
Willa Mae Reams, prin.
ES, NORTH MAIN ST 40741 – Jack Binder, prin.
Sublimity ES, RURAL ROUTE 05 BOX 215 40741
David Young, prin.
Other Schools – See Corbin, East Bernstadt, Keavy,
Lily

London Christian Academy HS
1505 S MAIN ST 40741

Lookout, Pike Co.
Pike County SD
Supt. – See Pikeville
ES 41542 – Donald Coleman, prin.

Lost Creek, Breathitt Co.
Breathitt County SD
Supt. – See Jackson
Roberts ES 41348 – Roy Smith, prin.

Riverside Christian Training HS 41348

Louisa, Lawrence Co., Pop. Code 4
Lawrence County SD
Sch. Sys. Enr. Code 5
Supt. – Robert Prichard, P O BOX 607 41230
MS, P O BOX 567 41230 – William Sparks, prin.
Fallsburg ES, RURAL ROUTE 04 BOX 137A 41230
Richard Lyon, prin.
ES, BOONE ST 41230 – Phillip Allen, prin.
Other Schools – See Blaine

Louisville, Jefferson Co., Pop. Code 10
Bullitt County SD
Supt. – See Shepherdsville
Maryville ES, 4504 SUMMERS DR 40229
Mary Lou Smith, prin.
Overdale ES, 80 OVERDALE DR 40229
Patricia Foster, prin.

Jefferson County SD
Sch. Sys. Enr. Code 8
Supt. – Dr. Donald Ingwerson
P O BOX 34020 40232
Brown S, 546 S 1ST ST 40202
William Proctor, prin.
Barret MS, 2561 GRINSTEAD DRIVE 40206
Don Matlock, prin.
Bruce MS, 3307 E INDIAN TRL 40213
Mildretta Hinkle, prin.
Carrithers MS, 4320 BILLTOWN ROAD 40299
Lou Tsioropoulas, prin.
Conway MS, 6300 TERRY ROAD 40258
Dennis Boswell, prin.
Highland MS, 1700 NORRIS PLACE 40205
Ron Crutcher, prin.
Iroquois MS, 5650 SOUTHERN PARKWAY 40214
Bobby Zachery, prin.
Jefferson County Traditional MS
1418 MORTON AVE 40204 – James Taylor, prin.
Jefferson MS, 4401 RANGELAND ROAD 40219
John Hosbach, prin.
Johnson MS, 2509 WILSON AVE 40210
(—), prin.
Kammerer MS, 7315 WESBORO ROAD 40222
Nancy Weber, prin.
Knight MS, 9803 BLUE LICK ROAD 40229
Susan Freepartner, prin.
Lassiter MS, 8200 CANDLEWORTH DRIVE 40214
John Sizemore, prin.
Meyzeek MS, 828 S JACKSON ST 40203
Deborah Jo Baker, prin.
Myers MS, 2815 KLONDIKE LANE 40218
Larry McKeehan, prin.
Newburg MS, 5008 E INDIAN TRAIL 40218
Nancy Hottman, prin.
Noe MS, 121 W LEE ST 40208 – (—), prin.
Southern MS, 4530 BELLEVUE AVE 40215
Frances Jones, prin.
Western MS, 2201 W MAIN ST 40212
Jimmy Harris, prin.

Westport MS, 8100 WESTPORT ROAD 40222
James Stone, prin.
Williams MS, 2415 ROCKFORD LN 40216
Robert Butler, prin.
Atkinson ES, 2811 DUNCAN ST 40212
Emil Salman, prin.
Auburndale ES, 5749 NEW CUT RD 40214
Jerry Adams, prin.
Audubon Traditional ES, 1051 HESS LN 40217
Michael Murphy, prin.
Bates ES, 7601 BARDSTOWN RD 40291
Rita Johnson, prin.
Blake ES, 3801 BONAVENTURE BLVD 40219
Lynda Seitz, prin.
Bloom ES, 1627 LUCIA AVE 40204
Joseph Villanova, prin.
Blue Lick ES, 9801 BLUE LICK RD 40229
John Mayhall, prin.
Brandeis ES, 925 S 26TH STREET 40210
Cheryl Sivak, prin.
Breckinridge ES, 1128 E BROADWAY ST 40204
Elmo Martin, prin.
Byck ES, 2328 CEDAR ST 40212
Matt Benningfield, prin.
Camp Taylor ES, 1446 BELMAR DR 40213
William Perkins, prin.
Cane Run ES, 3951 CANE RUN RD 40211
Arthur Moody, prin.
Carter Traditional ES, 3628 VIRGINIA AVE 40211
Patsy Brisbon, prin.
Chenoweth ES, 3622 BROWNSBORO RD 40207
Maxie Johnson, prin.
Cochran ES, 1507 S 2ND ST 40208
Joanna Smith, prin.
Cochrane ES, 2511 TREGARON AVE 40299
Clarence Jones, prin.
Coleridge Taylor ES
1115 W CHESTNUT ST 40203
Rosemary Chambers, prin.
Crums Lane ES, 3212 CRUMS LN 40216
Marshall Trautwein, prin.
Dixie ES, 10201 CASALANDA DR 40272
Timothy Daly, prin.
Dunn ES, 2010 RUDY LN 40207
Judith Mullins, prin.
Engelhard ES, 1004 S 1ST ST 40203
Alma Davis, prin.
Field ES, GARDINER & SACRED HE 40206
Robert Spencer, prin.
Foster ES, 4020 GARLAND AVE 40211
Shelley Floyd, prin.
Franklin ES, 1800 ARLINGTON AVE 40206
Walter Logan, prin.
Frayser ES, 1230 LARCHMONT AVE 40215
Rebecca Harmon, prin.
Gilmore Lane ES, 1281 GILMORE LN 40213
Helen Ford, prin.
Goldsmith Lane ES, 3510 GOLDSMITH LN 40220
Nancy Reynolds, prin.
Greathouse Shryock Traditional ES
2700 BROWNS LN 40220 – Daniel Detwiler, prin.
Guthermuth ES, 1500 SANDERS LN 40216
Lewis Harp, prin.
Hartstern ES, 5200 MORNING SIDE WAY 40219
Billy Lacy, prin.
Hawthorne ES, 2301 CLARENDON AVE 40205
Patricia Lambert, prin.
Hazelwood ES, 1325 BLUEGRASS AVE 40215
Carolyn Hayes, prin.
Indian Trail ES, 3709 E INDIAN TRL 40213
Coreta Pratt, prin.
Jacob ES, 3670 WHEELER AVE 40215
Phyllis Connelly, prin.
Jeffersontown ES
3610 CEDARWOOD WAY 40299
Larry Foley, prin.
Johnsontown Road ES
7201 JOHNSONTOWN RD 40272
John Waldrop, prin.
Kennedy ES, 3807 YOUNG AVE 40211
Jacqueline Austin, prin.
Kenwood ES, 7420 JUSTAN AVE 40214
Gary Tatum, prin.
Kerrick ES, 2210 UPPER HUNTERS TRCE 40216
(—), prin.
King ES, 4325 VERMONT AVE 40211
Darrell Jarrett, prin.
Klondike Lane ES, 3807 KLONDIKE LN 40218
James Koshewa, prin.
Laukhuf ES, 5100 CAPEWOOD DR 40229
Donald White, prin.
Lincoln ES, 930 E MAIN ST 40206
Ronda Garrison, prin.
Lowe ES, 210 OXFORDSHIRE LN 40222
Laverne Billinger, prin.
Lowell ES, 4501 CRITTENDEN DR 40209
Martha Ann Long, prin.
Luhr ES, 6900 FEGENBUSH LN 40228
(—), prin.
Maupin ES, 1309 CATALPA ST 40211
Janice Walker, prin.
McFerran ES, 1515 CYPRESS ST 40210
Carol Miller, prin.
Millcreek ES, 3816 DIXIE HWY 40216
Faye Owens, prin.
Minors ES, 8510 MINORS LN 40219
Betsy Holton, prin.
Okolona ES, 7606 PRESTON HWY 40219
Clay Lykins, prin.
Portland ES, 3410 N WESTERN PKY 40212
(—), prin.
Price ES, 5001 GARDEN GREEN WAY 40218
Carletta Bell, prin.

Rangeland ES, 5001 RANGELAND RD 40219
  Maryanne Davis, prin.
Roosevelt ES, 1606 MAGAZINE ST 40203
  J. Back, prin.
Rutherford ES, 301 SOUTHLAND BLVD 40214
  Joseph Bishop, prin.
Semple ES, 724 DENMARK ST 40215
  Sharon Brown, prin.
Shacklette ES, 5310 MERCURY DR 40258
  Rosa Clack, prin.
Shelby ES, 930 MARY ST 40204
  Frederick Goeschel, prin.
Slaughter ES, 3805 FERN VALLEY RD 40219
  Mary Staten, prin.
Smyrna ES, 6401 OUTER LOOP 40228
  Phillip Locke, prin.
St. Matthew's ES, 601 BROWNS LN 40207
  Christina Bowling, prin.
Trunnel ES, 7609 ST ANDRES CHURCH 40214
  H. Yates, prin.
Watson Lane ES, 7201 WATSON LN 40272
  Rosemarie Young, prin.
Watterson ES, 3900 BRECKENRIDGE LN 40218
  Marlene Mitchell, prin.
Wellington ES, 4800 KAUFMAN LN 40216
  Edward Sullivan, prin.
Wheatley ES, 1107 S 17TH ST 40210
  C. Hydes, prin.
Wilder ES, 1913 HERR LN 40222
  Rosamary Bell, prin.
Wilkerson ES, 5601 JOHNSONTOWN RD 40272
  Von Powell, prin.
Wilt ES, 6700 PRICE LN 40229
  Sedalia Lomax, prin.
Young ES, 3526 MUHAMMAD ABI BLVD 40212
  (—), prin.
Other Schools – See Fairdale, Fern Creek,
  Jeffersontown, Lyndon, Middletown, Pleasure
  Ridge Park, Valley Station

Alliance Christian Academy
  3726 BARDSTOWN ROAD 40218
Christian Academy of Louisville
  3110 ROCK CREEK DRIVE 40207
Evangel Christian School
  5400 MINORS LANE 40219
Highview Baptist School
  7711 FEGENBUSH LANE 40228
Kentucky Country Day School
  4100 SPRINGDALE ROAD 40222
Landmark Christian Academy
  6502 JOHNSONTOWN ROAD 40272
Louisville Collegiate School
  2427 GLENMARY AVE 40204
Ninth & O Baptist Academy
  2921 TAYLOR BLVD 40208
Southwest Christian School
  10301 DEERING ROAD 40272
Walden School, P O BOX 6247 40206
St. Albert ES, 1301 TECHNY LN 40222
Ascension School, 4600 LYNNBROOK DR 40220
Chance ES,Inc., 4200 LIME KILN LN 40222
Christ the King ES, 724 S 44TH ST 40211
Community Catholic School
  2530 SLEVIN ST 40212
Guardian Angels School
  6010 PRESTON HWY 40219
Holy Family School
  3934 POPLAR LEVEL RD 40213
Holy Name School, 2917 SOUTHSIDE DR 40208
Holy Spirit School, 322 CANNONS LN 40206
Holy Trinity ES, 423 CHERRYWOOD RD 40207
Martin Luther Lutheran School
  1335 GARDINER LN 40213
Most Blessed Scrament School
  1128 BERRY BLVD 40215
Our Lady Consolation School
  10803 DEERING RD 40272
Our Lady of Lourdes School
  510 BRECKENRIDGE LN 40207
Our Lady of Mt. Carmel School
  7333 SOUTHSIDE DR 40214
Our Mother of Sorrows School
  770 EASTERN PRKY 40217
Resurrection School
  4605 POPLAR LEVEL RD 40213
SS. Simon & Jude School
  4333 HAZELWOOD AVE 40215
St. Agnes School, 1800 NEWBURG RD 40205
St. Athanasius School, 5915 OUTER LOOP 40219
St. Barnabas School, 3044 HIKES LN 40220
St. Bartholomew School
  2036 BUECHEL BANK RD 40218
St. Bernard School, 7501 TANGELO DR 40228
St. Clement School
  5437 JOHNSONTOWN RD 40272
St. Columba School, 221 S 36TH ST 40212
St. Denis School, 4209 CANE RUN RD 40216
St. Edward School, 9610 SUE HELEN DR 40299
St. Elizabeth of Hungary School
  1016 E BURNETT AVE 40217
St. Francis Assisi School
  1936 ALFRESCO PL 40205
St. Gabriel the Archangel School
  8419 HUDSON LN 40291
St. Helen School, 4007 DIXIE HWY 40216
St. Igantius Martyr School
  1818 RANGELAND RD 40219
St. James School, 1818 EDENSIDE AVE 40204
St. John Vianney School
  4841 SOUTHSIDE DR 40214
St. Joseph School
  1420 E WASHINGTON ST 40206

St. Lawrence School, 1927 LEWISTON DR 40216
St. Leonard School, 440 ZORN AVE 40206
St. Luke School, 4211 JIM HAWKINS DR 40229
St. Margaret Mary School
  7813 SHELBYVILLE RD 40222
St. Martha School, 2825 KLONDIKE LN 40218
St. Matthias ES, 2208 DIXIE HWY 40210
St. Paul School, 6901 DIXIE HWY 40258
St. Pius X School, 3525 GOLDSMITH LN 40220
St. Polycarp School, 7724 COLUMBINE DR 40258
St. Raphael School
  2131 LANCASHIRE AVE 40205
St. Rita School, 8709 PRESTON HWY 40219
St. Stephen Martyr School
  2931 PINDELL AVE 40217
St. Therese School, 1107 E KENTUCKY ST 40204
St. Thomas More School
  226 INVERNESS AVE 40214
St. Timothy School
  10300 LOWER RIVER RD 40272
West End Catholic School
  3308 CHAUNCEY AVE 40211

Lowes, Graves Co.
  Graves County SD
  Supt. – See Mayfield
  ES 42061 – Charles Ford, prin.

Loyall, Harlan Co., Pop. Code 4
  Harlan County SD
  Supt. – See Harlan
  ES 40854 – D. Gaw, prin.

Lucas, Barren Co.
  Barren County SD
  Supt. – See Glasgow
  Tracy ES 42156 – Glenn Flanders, prin.

Ludlow, Kenton Co., Pop. Code 5
  Ludlow ISD
  Sch. Sys. Enr. Code 3
  Supt. – Dr. Jon Draud, 524 OAK ST 41016
  Goetz ES, 524 OAK ST 41016
    Daniel Jones,Jr., prin.

Lyndon, Jefferson Co., Pop. Code 4
  Jefferson County SD
  Supt. – See Louisville
  Bowen ES, 1601 ROOSEVELT AVE 40242
    Sarah Harris, prin.
  Norton ES, 8101 BROWNSBORO RD 40241
    Deanna Tinsley, prin.
  Taylor ES, 9620 WESTPORT RD 40241
    Marvin Haller, prin.

Mother Good Counsel School
  8509 WESTPORT RD 40242

Mc Daniels, Breckinridge Co.
  Breckinridge County SD
  Supt. – See Hardinsburg
  Johnson ES, P O BOX 51 40152 – Ione Hines, prin.

Mc Dowell, Floyd Co., Pop. Code 3
  Floyd County SD
  Supt. – See Prestonsburg
  ES 41647 – Frank Pack, prin.

Maceo, Daviess Co.
  Daviess County SD
  Supt. – See Owensboro
  ES, 9733 HWY 60 42355 – William Morris, prin.

Mc Kee, Jackson Co., Pop. Code 3
  Jackson County SD
  Sch. Sys. Enr. Code 5
  Supt. – Henry Clay Harmon,Jr. 40447
  ES, P O BOX 429 40447 – Jerry Bond, prin.
  Other Schools – See Annville, Hisle, Sandgap, Tyner

Mc Kinney, Lincoln Co.
  Lincoln County SD
  Supt. – See Stanford
  ES 40448 – Thelma Moore, prin.

Mackville, Washington Co., Pop. Code 2
  Washington County SD
  Supt. – See Springfield
  ES, MAIN ST 40040 – Glenn Black, prin.

Mc Quady, Breckinridge Co.
  Breckinridge County SD
  Supt. – See Hardinsburg
  ES 40153 – Morris Carman, prin.

Mc Roberts, Letcher Co.
  Jenkins ISD
  Supt. – See Jenkins
  ES, P O BOX 500 41835 – David Ladd, prin.

Madisonville, Hopkins Co., Pop. Code 7
  Hopkins County SD
  Sch. Sys. Enr. Code 6
  Supt. – Dr. David Gover, 537 W ARCH ST 42431
  Browning Springs MS, SPRING ST 42431
    Paul Armstrong, prin.
  Anton ES, RURAL ROUTE 03 BOX 248 42431
    Floyd Brown, prin.
  Grapevine ES, HAYES AVE 42431
    Henrietta Buffington, prin.
  Hall Street ES, HALL ST 42431
    Robert Harrison, prin.
  Pride Avenue ES, PRIDE AVE 42431
    Jim Bearden, prin.
  Waddill Avenue ES, WADDILL AVE 42431
    Sam Aldridge, prin.
  West Broadway ES, 127 W BROADWAY ST 42431
    Macy Wheelock, prin.

Other Schools – See Dawson Springs, Earlington,
  Hanson, Mortons Gap, Nebo, Nortonville, Saint
  Charles, White Plains

Christ the King School, RURAL ROUTE 06 42431

Magnolia, Larue Co.
  Larue County SD
  Supt. – See Hodgenville
  ES 42757 – Deborah Atherton, prin.

Majestic, Pike Co.
  Pike County SD
  Supt. – See Pikeville
  Majestic Knox Creek ES 41547
    David Pinson, prin.

Manchester, Clay Co., Pop. Code 4
  Clay County SD
  Sch. Sys. Enr. Code 6
  Supt. – W. Sizemore, P O BOX 246 40962
  Burning Springs ES
    RURAL ROUTE 06 BOX 312 40962
    Norman Cornett, prin.
  Goose Rock ES
    RURAL ROUTE 07 BOX 200 40962
    James Morgan, prin.
  Hacker ES, RURAL ROUTE 08 BOX 463 40962
    Lee Sizemore, prin.
  Horse Creek ES, RURAL ROUTE 04 BOX 5 40962
    Jean Wagers, prin.
  Laurel Creek ES, RURAL ROUTE 02 40962
    Eddie Dobson, prin.
  ES, RURAL ROUTE 07 BOX 42 40962
    Charles White, prin.
  Paces Creek ES
    RURAL ROUTE 03 BOX 14B 40962
    Currie Smallwood, prin.
  Other Schools – See Oneida

Mannsville, Taylor Co.
  Taylor County SD
  Supt. – See Campbellsville
  ES, P O BOX 178 42758 – Norman Feese, prin.

Marion, Crittenden Co., Pop. Code 5
  Crittenden County SD
  Sch. Sys. Enr. Code 4
  Supt. – Dr. Dennis Lacy, P O BOX 362 42064
  Crittenden County MS, P O BOX 71 42064
    (—), prin.
  Crittenden County ES
    RURAL ROUTE 02 BOX 214 42064
    Sylvia Thurman, prin.
  Frances ES, RURAL ROUTE 10 42064
    (—), prin.
  Tolu ES, P O BOX 28 42064 – Bruce Moore, prin.

Martin, Floyd Co., Pop. Code 3
  Floyd County SD
  Supt. – See Prestonsburg
  ES 41649 – William Hughes, prin.

Mountain Christian Academy
  P O BOX 1120 41649

Mayfield, Graves Co., Pop. Code 7
  Graves County SD
  Sch. Sys. Enr. Code 5
  Supt. – Bobby Miller, 1007 CUBA ROAD 42066
  Cuba ES, RURAL ROUTE 01 42066
    James Baker, prin.
  Other Schools – See Fancy Farm, Farmington, Lowes,
    Sedalia, Symsonia, Wingo

Mayfield ISD
  Sch. Sys. Enr. Code 4
  Supt. – Don Sparks, 709 S 8TH ST 42066
  MS, S 7TH ST 42066 – James Almand, prin.
  Longfellow ES, 2 10TH ST 42066
    Elsie Jones, prin.
  Washington ES, BROADWAY 42066
    Clyde Crook, prin.

St. Joseph School, 112 S 14TH ST 42066

Maysville, Mason Co., Pop. Code 6
  Mason County SD
  Sch. Sys. Enr. Code 4
  Supt. – Felici Felice, P O BOX 97 41056
  Mason County MS, 420 CHENAULT DRIVE 41056
    Ronald Ishmael, prin.
  Staub ES, 387 CHENAULT DR 41056
    Charles Metcalfe, prin.

Maysville ISD
  Sch. Sys. Enr. Code 3
  Supt. – Robert Biddle, P O BOX 99 41056
  Jones ES, 1112 FOREST AVE 41056
    Dan Seithers, prin.

Melvin, Floyd Co.
  Floyd County SD
  Supt. – See Prestonsburg
  ES 41650 – Gleason Slone, prin.

Middleburg, Casey Co.
  Casey County SD
  Supt. – See Liberty
  ES 42541 – Dale Wilson, prin.

Middlesboro, Bell Co., Pop. Code 7
  Bell County SD
  Supt. – See Pineville
  Chapel ES, RURAL ROUTE 02 40965
    Larry Elliott, prin.

Yellow Creek Center ES
RURAL ROUTE 01 BOX 370 40965
Eugene Burnett, prin.

Middlesboro ISD
Sch. Sys. Enr. Code 4
Supt. – Dr. Dwight Henn, 220 N 20TH ST 40965
MS, 4004 CUMBERLAND AVE 40965
Larry Davis, prin.
IS, 4400 CUMBERLAND AVE 40965
Paul Spangler, prin.
PS, 16TH AND ASHBURY 40965
Gale Parke, prin.

Gateway Christian ES, P O BOX Z 40965

Middletown, Jefferson Co., Pop. Code 2
Bourbon County SD
Supt. – See Paris
North Middletown ES, COLLEGE ST N 40357
Harold Grooms, prin.

Jefferson County SD
Supt. – See Louisville
Crosby MS, 303 GATEHOUSE LANE 40243
Carolyn Harris, prin.
Hite ES, 12408 OLD SHELBYVILLE RD 40243
Phyllis Rees, prin.
ES, 218 N MADISON AVE 40243
George Ockerhausen, prin.

Midway, Woodford Co., Pop. Code 4
Woodford County SD
Supt. – See Versailles
ES, S WINTER ST 40347 – Paul Stahler, prin.

Millersburg, Bourbon Co., Pop. Code 3
Bourbon County SD
Supt. – See Paris
ES, P O BOX 397 40348 – David Jenks, prin.

Milton, Trimble Co., Pop. Code 3
Trimble County SD
Supt. – See Bedford
ES, P O BOX 75 40045 – Deborah Abbott, prin.

Monticello, Wayne Co., Pop. Code 6
Monticello ISD
Sch. Sys. Enr. Code 3
Supt. – Vernon Miniard, 135 CAVE ST 42633
ES, 135 CAVE ST 42633 – A. Edwards, prin.

Wayne County SD
Sch. Sys. Enr. Code 5
Supt. – C. Bates, P O BOX 441 42633
Wayne County MS, P O BOX 05 42633
Gary Upchurch, prin.
Powersburg ES, HCR 586 42633
Ralph Booher, prin.
Sinking Consolidated ES, HCR 572 42633
Jonell Ramsey, prin.
Wayne County ES 1, RURAL ROUTE 04 42633
Philip Catron, prin.
Wayne County MS 3
RURAL ROUTE 03 BOX 3 42633
Harold Turner, prin.
Other Schools – See Coopersville

Morehead, Rowan Co., Pop. Code 6
Rowan County SD
Sch. Sys. Enr. Code 5
Supt. – Kenneth Bland
118 UNIVERSITY BLVD 40351
Rowan County MS, W SUN ST 40351
Herbert Ramey, prin.
Hogge ES, RURAL ROUTE 02 40351
Wanda Conn, prin.
ES, W SUN ST 40351 – Gary Trent, prin.
Other Schools – See Clearfield, Elliottville, Farmers, Haldeman

Morganfield, Union Co., Pop. Code 5
Union County SD
Sch. Sys. Enr. Code 5
Supt. – Ray Hammers, 510 S MART ST 42437
Union Co. MS, RURAL ROUTE 04 42437
William Omen, prin.
ES, 505 S MART ST 42437 – Sam Smith, prin.
Other Schools – See Sturgis, Uniontown

St. Ann School, 304 S CHURCH ST 42437

Morgantown, Butler Co., Pop. Code 4
Butler County SD
Sch. Sys. Enr. Code 4
Supt. – Weymouth Martin,Jr., P O BOX 339 42261
Fifth District ES, RURAL ROUTE 02 42261
James Goff, prin.
Fourth District ES
RURAL ROUTE 04 BOX 660 42261
Raymond Burden, prin.
ES, P O BOX 337 42261 – James Beliles, prin.
Other Schools – See Rochester

Morning View, Kenton Co.
Kenton County SD
Supt. – See Independence
Piner ES, RURAL ROUTE 01 41063
Phillip Webb, prin.

Mortons Gap, Hopkins Co., Pop. Code 4
Hopkins County SD
Supt. – See Madisonville
MS, P O BOX 97 42440 – Bruce Slate, prin.
ES, P O BOX 129 42440 – Bruce Slate, prin.

Mount Olivet, Robertson Co., Pop. Code 2
Robertson County SD
Sch. Sys. Enr. Code 2
Supt. – John Willis Smith, P O BOX 108 41064
Deming ES 41064 – Dale Kleinjan, prin.

Mount Sterling, Montgomery Co., Pop. Code 6
Montgomery County SD
Sch. Sys. Enr. Code 5
Supt. – Robert Haynes, P O BOX 7277 40353
Montgomery County MS
3570 INDIAN MOUND DR 40353
Bill Morgan, prin.
Camargo ES, 4307 CAMARGO RD 40353
Charles Wills, prin.
Mapleton ES, 512 HOLT AVE 40353
Timothy Keenan, prin.
ES, 212 N MAYSVILLE ST 40353
Bobby Breeding, prin.

Mount Vernon, Rockcastle Co., Pop. Code 4
Rockcastle County SD
Sch. Sys. Enr. Code 5
Supt. – Bige Towery,Jr. 40456
ES, SCHOOL ST 40456 – John Hale, prin.
Roundstone ES, RURAL ROUTE 03 40456
William Parsons, prin.
Other Schools – See Brodhead, Livingston

Mount Washington, Bullitt Co., Pop. Code 5
Bullitt County SD
Supt. – See Shepherdsville
MS, WATER ST 40047 – Cecil Mattingly, prin.
Mt. Washington ES, HWY 44 40047
John Carnes, prin.
Old Mill ES, HWY 44E 40047
Helen Harrah, prin.

Mousie, Knott Co.
Knott County SD
Supt. – See Hindman
Jones Fork ES, P O BOX 129 41839
Harold Mosley, prin.

Muldraugh, Meade Co., Pop. Code 4
Meade County SD
Supt. – See Brandenburg
ES, P O BOX 306 40155 – Russell Hinkle, prin.

Munfordville, Hart Co., Pop. Code 4
Hart County SD
Sch. Sys. Enr. Code 4
Supt. – W. Strange 42765
ES 42765 – Wayland Johnston, prin.
Other Schools – See Bonnieville, Cub Run, Hardyville, Horse Cave

Murray, Calloway Co., Pop. Code 7
Calloway County SD
Sch. Sys. Enr. Code 5
Supt. – J. Rose, P O BOX 800 42071
Calloway County MS
2108A COLLEGE FARM ROAD 42071
Roy Cothran, prin.
East ES, RURAL ROUTE 06 42071
James Feltner, prin.
North ES, RURAL ROUTE 02 BOX 12-A3 42071
Ronnie Walker, prin.
Southwest ES, WISWELL RD 42071
Ray Dunn, prin.

Murray ISD
Sch. Sys. Enr. Code 4
Supt. – Robert Jeffrey, POPLAR AT 9TH 42071
MS, 801 MAIN ST 42071 – John Hina, prin.
ES, S 13TH ST 42071 – Willie Jackson, prin.

Nancy, Pulaski Co., Pop. Code 2
Pulaski County SD
Supt. – See Somerset
ES, 404A 42544 – Larry Compton, prin.

Nebo, Hopkins Co., Pop. Code 2
Hopkins County SD
Supt. – See Madisonville
MS 42441 – Euel Darnall, prin.
ES 42441 – Euel Darnall, prin.

Neon, Letcher Co.
Letcher County SD
Supt. – See Whitesburg
Fleming Neon ES, P O BOX 425 41840
Dannie Caudill, prin.

Nevisdale, Whitley Co.
Whitley County SD
Supt. – See Williamsburg
ES 40754 – Kenneth Rickett, prin.

New Castle, Henry Co., Pop. Code 3
Henry County SD
Sch. Sys. Enr. Code 4
Supt. – Robert Lumsden, P O BOX 377 40050
Henry County MS, P O BOX 267 40050
Stephen Dent, prin.
ES, P O BOX 297 40050 – Deania Hurst, prin.
Other Schools – See Campbellsburg, Pleasureville

New Haven, Nelson Co., Pop. Code 3
Nelson County SD
Supt. – See Bardstown
MS, HIGH ST 40051 – William Broaddus, prin.
ES, HIGH STREET 40051
William Broaddus, prin.

St. Catherine School, FIRST ST 40051

Newport, Campbell Co., Pop. Code 7
Newport ISD
Sch. Sys. Enr. Code 5
Supt. – Bernard Sandfoss, 301 E 8TH ST 41071
MS, 8TH & COLUMBIA STS 41071
Charles Griffith, prin.
Dean ES, 1360 GRAND AVE 41071
Mackie Turner, prin.
Fourth Street ES
4TH AND MONMOUTH STS 41071
Vikki Clemons, prin.
Owens ES, 11TH & YORK STS 41071
William Deegan, prin.

Holy Spirit ES, 840 WASHINGTON AVE 41071
St. Catherine of Siena School
23 ROSSFORD AVE 41075
St. Therese School
2516 ALEXANDRIA PIKE 41071

Nicholasville, Jessamine Co., Pop. Code 7
Jessamine County SD
Sch. Sys. Enr. Code 6
Supt. – Dr. Donald Martin, P O BOX 186 40356
Jessamine County MS, RURAL ROUTE 04 40356
John Brown, prin.
Brookside ES, 199 BROOKSIDE ST 40356
Carl Megee, prin.
ES, 5TH ST 40356 – Connie Aubrey, prin.
Warner ES, RURAL ROUTE 04 40356
Richard Williams, prin.
Other Schools – See Wilmore

Nortonville, Hopkins Co., Pop. Code 4
Hopkins County SD
Supt. – See Madisonville
MS, P O BOX 1610 42442 – Larry Yandell, prin.
ES, P O BOX 1610 42442 – Larry Yandell, prin.

Oakland, Warren Co., Pop. Code 2
Warren County SD
Supt. – See Bowling Green
ES, P O BOX 128 42159 – James Ross, prin.

Oil Springs, Johnson Co.
Johnson County SD
Supt. – See Paintsville
ES 41238 – Patricia Gambill, prin.

Oldtown, Greenup Co.
Greenup County SD
Supt. – See Greenup
ES, HCR 60 BOX 1270 41163 – Linda Moon, prin.

Olive Hill, Carter Co., Pop. Code 5
Carter County SD
Supt. – See Grayson
Hill ES, P O BOX 910 41164 – Phillip Barker, prin.
ES, P O BOX 540 41164 – Junior Poling, prin.
Upper Tygaht ES
RURAL ROUTE 04 BOX 440 41164
David Tabor, prin.

Olmstead, Logan Co.
Logan County SD
Supt. – See Russellville
MS 42265 – Mark Bennett, prin.
ES 42265 – Mark Bennett, prin.

Oneida, Clay Co., Pop. Code 3
Clay County SD
Supt. – See Manchester
Big Creek ES, RURAL ROUTE 01 BOX 163 40972
Victor Arnett, prin.
ES, RURAL ROUTE 01 BOX 2 40972
Roger Allen, prin.

Oneida Institute 40972

Owensboro, Daviess Co., Pop. Code 8
Daviess County SD
Sch. Sys. Enr. Code 6
Supt. – Ed Allen, P O BOX 1510 42302
Daviess County MS, 1415 E 4TH ST 42303
Mike Robinson, prin.
Fort Burns MS, RURAL ROUTE 03 42301
Robert Berry, prin.
Burns ES, 4513 GOETZ DR 42301
Nannette Parish, prin.
Country Heights ES, 4961 KY HWY 54 42302
Brenda Harmon, prin.
Highland ES, 2909 LEITCHFIELD RD 42303
Joe Johnson, prin.
Sorgho ES, 5620 KY HWY 56 42301
Gene Ferrell, prin.
Tamarack ES, 1733 TAMARACK RD 42301
Arthur Gray, prin.
Thruston ES, 5260 KY HWY 144 42301
Aubrey Pendley, prin.
West Louisville ES, 9661 KY HWY 56 42301
Ewing Rascoe, prin.
Other Schools – See Maceo, Philpot, Stanley, Utica, Whitesville

Owensboro ISD
Sch. Sys. Enr. Code 5
Supt. – Dr. Frank Yeager, P O BOX 746 42302
MS, 1300 BOOTH AVE 42301 – Fred Reeves, prin.
Cravens ES, 2741 W 5TH ST RD 42301
George Kyle, prin.
Estes ES, 1675 LEITCHFIELD RD 42303
John Blaney,Jr., prin.
Foust ES, 601 FOUST AVE 42301
Francis Watrous, prin.
Newton Parrish ES, 510 W BYERS AVE 42301
Robert Willis, prin.

Seven Hills ES, 2401 MCCONNELL AVE   42303
  Robert Willis, prin.
Sutton ES, 2060 LEWIS LN   42301
  Dwight Wilkinson, prin.

Good Shepherd Christian School
  P O BOX 1099   42302
Blessed Mother School, 525 E 23RD ST   42301
Cathedral School, 600 LOCUST ST   42301
Immaculate School, 2540 CHRISTIE PL   42301
Our Lady of Lourdes School
  4017 FREDERICA ST   42301
Precious Blood School, 3400 FENMORE ST   42301
St. Martin ES, 5900 KY 81   42301
St. Pius Tenth School
  3418 HARDINSBURG RD   42303

Owenton, Owen Co., Pop. Code 4
Owen County SD
  Sch. Sys. Enr. Code 4
  Supt. – Carl Banks
    RURAL ROUTE 04 BOX 51   40359
  Bowling MS, RURAL ROUTE 04   40359
    Jo Ella Wallace, prin.
  Owen Co. ES, RURAL ROUTE 04   40359
    Michael Ramsey, prin.

Owingsville, Bath Co., Pop. Code 4
Bath County SD
  Sch. Sys. Enr. Code 4
  Supt. – Darvin Estes, P O BOX 327   40360
  ES, MAIN ST   40360 – Leslie Christy, prin.
  Other Schools – See Bethel, Salt Lick

Paducah, McCracken Co., Pop. Code 8
McCracken County SD
  Sch. Sys. Enr. Code 6
  Supt. – Larry Harper, RURAL ROUTE 10   42001
  Lone Oak MS, 300 CUMBERLAND AVE   42001
    Cliff Owen, prin.
  Reidland MS, RURAL ROUTE 13 BOX 203   42003
    James Mitchell, prin.
  Concord ES, 5184 US HWY 60 W   42001
    Tommy Logan, prin.
  Farley ES, 1250 HUSBAND RD   42003
    Barbara Sturm, prin.
  Hendron Lone Oak ES
    2501 MARSHALL AVE   42001
    Edgar Doores, prin.
  Lone Oak ES, 301 CUMBERLAND AVE   42001
    Janet Shelton, prin.
  Reidland ES, 5741 BENTON RD   42003
    George Hanrahan, prin.
  Other Schools – See West Paducah

Paducah ISD
  Sch. Sys. Enr. Code 5
  Supt. – Lawrence Allen, P O BOX 2550   42002
  MS, 342 LONE OAK ROAD   42001
    Terry Waltman, prin.
  Clark ES, 3401 BUCKNER LN   42001
    Berton Chapman, prin.
  Cooper MS, 1350 S 6TH ST   42001
    Marnette Calloway, prin.
  McNabb ES, 21ST & PAEK AVE   42001
    Jessie Beasley, prin.
  Morgan ES, S 28TH ST   42001
    Frances Cooper, prin.
  Whiteside ES, 800 CALDWELL ST   42001
    Patricia Koch, prin.

St. John Evangelist School
  RURAL ROUTE 10 BOX 277   42001
St. Mary ES, 3230 BUCKNER LN   42001

Paint Lick, Garrard Co.
Garrard County SD
  Supt. – See Lancaster
  ES, RURAL ROUTE 02   40461 – Mary Davis, prin.

Paintsville, Johnson Co., Pop. Code 5
Johnson County SD
  Sch. Sys. Enr. Code 5
  Supt. – Frank Hamilton   41240
  Central ES, RURAL ROUTE 23 NORTH   41240
    Gerald Preston, prin.
  Other Schools – See Flatgap, Hagerhill, Oil Springs,
    Williamsport, Wittensville

Paintsville ISD
  Sch. Sys. Enr. Code 3
  Supt. – Leon Burchett, 2ND ST   41240
  MS, 260 2ND ST   41240 – Grayson Boyd, prin.
  ES, 248 2ND ST   41240 – Paul Williams, prin.

Our Lady of the Mountains School
  300 3RD ST   41240

Paris, Bourbon Co., Pop. Code 6
Bourbon County SD
  Sch. Sys. Enr. Code 4
  Supt. – William Birdwell
    3343 LEXINGTON ROAD   40361
  Bourbon County MS
    3343 LEXINGTON ROAD   40361
    Eugene Correll, prin.
  Bourbon Central ES, 367 BETHLEHEM RD   40361
    Jack Tucker,Jr., prin.
  Center Hill ES, 596 RUSSELL CAVE RD   40361
    Gary Brown, prin.
  Clintonville ES, 144 AUSTERLITZ RD   40361
    Curtis Rose, prin.
  Ruddles Mills ES, 1600 RUDDLES MILL RD   40361
    Lana Fryman, prin.
  Other Schools – See Middletown, Millersburg

Paris ISD
  Sch. Sys. Enr. Code 4
  Supt. – Ronald Chumbley, 301 W 7TH ST   40361
  Southside MS, 1481 S MAIN ST   40361
    Mark Crain, prin.
  ES, 2 7TH ST   40361 – Garey Jefferson, prin.

Park City, Barren Co., Pop. Code 3
Barren County SD
  Supt. – See Glasgow
  ES, P O BOX 247   42160 – Carroll Furlong, prin.
  Red Cross ES, RURAL ROUTE 01   42160
    Rita Berry, prin.

Parkers Lake, McCreary Co.
McCreary County SD
  Supt. – See Stearns
  Eagle ES, RURAL ROUTE 02 BOX 273   42634
    Glenn Taylor, prin.

Payneville, Meade Co.
Meade County SD
  Supt. – See Brandenburg
  Cross Road ES, P O BOX 213   40157
    Sister Marie McCarty, prin.
  ES, P O BOX 14   40157 – James Thompson, prin.

Pembroke, Christian Co., Pop. Code 3
Christian County SD
  Supt. – See Hopkinsville
  ES   42266 – Charles Duncan, prin.

Perryville, Boyle Co., Pop. Code 3
Boyle County SD
  Supt. – See Danville
  ES   40468 – David Randolph, prin.

Pewee Valley, Oldham Co., Pop. Code 3

St. Aloysius School
  212 MOUNT MERCY DR   40056

Phelps, Pike Co., Pop. Code 4
Pike County SD
  Supt. – See Pikeville
  ES, P O BOX 529   41553 – Buford Wolford, prin.

Philpot, Daviess Co
Daviess County SD
  Supt. – See Owensboro
  ES, KY HWY 54E   42366 – Charles Ross, prin.

Mary Carrico Memorial School
  RURAL ROUTE 01   42366

Phyllis, Pike Co.
Pike County SD
  Supt. – See Pikeville
  Grapevine ES   41554 – Danny Bevins, prin.

Pikeville, Pike Co., Pop. Code 5
Pike County SD
  Sch. Sys. Enr. Code 7
  Supt. – Charles Wright, P O BOX 3097   41501
  Johns Creek ES
    RURAL ROUTE O1 BOX 870   41501
    Ronald Thompson, prin.
  Millard ES, RURAL ROUTE 02 BOX 258   41501
    Blanche Branham, prin.
  Mullins ES, RURAL ROUTE 03 BOX 524   41501
    Jimmy Goodman, prin.
  Other Schools – See Ashcamp, Dorton, Elkhorn City,
    Fedscreek, Freeburn, Hellier, Kimper, Lookout,
    Majestic, Phelps, Phyllis, Pinsonfork, Ransom,
    Robinson Creek, Shelbiana, Sidney, South
    Williamson, Toler, Turkey Creek, Varney, Virgie

Pikeville ISD
  Sch. Sys. Enr. Code 4
  Supt. – John Waddell
    RURAL ROUTE 04 BOX 799   41501
  ES, 178 CHLOE RD   41501 – Chester Bailey, prin.

Pilgrim, Martin Co.
Martin County SD
  Supt. – See Inez
  Mouth/Pigeon Roost ES   41250
    Clifford Clark, prin.

Pine Knot, McCreary Co., Pop. Code 3
McCreary County SD
  Supt. – See Stearns
  MS, P O BOX 187   42635 – Ray Ball, prin.
  ES, P O BOX 157   42635 – June Lominae, prin.

Pineville, Bell Co., Pop. Code 5
Bell County SD
  Sch. Sys. Enr. Code 5
  Supt. – Ike Slusher,Jr., P O BOX 340   40977
  Harmony ES, RURAL ROUTE 01   40977
    Robert Howard, prin.
  Page ES, RURAL ROUTE 01 BOX 174   40977
    George Ingram, prin.
  Other Schools – See Arjay, Beverly, Cubage,
    Fourmile, Frakes, Hulen, Ingram, Middlesboro,
    Stoney Fork

Pineville ISD
  Sch. Sys. Enr. Code 3
  Supt. – Patrick Clore, 401 W VIRGINIA AVE   40977
  ES, 401 W VIRGINIA AVE   40977
    Thomas Kelemen, prin.

Pinsonfork, Pike Co.
Pike County SD
  Supt. – See Pikeville
  Runyon ES, RURAL ROUTE 01 BOX 2   41555
    Charles Williamson, prin.

Pippa Passes, Knott Co., Pop. Code 2
Knott County SD
  Supt. – See Hindman
  Caney Creek ES   41844 – Clyde King, prin.

Buchanan School   41844

Pleasant View, Whitley Co.
Whitley County SD
  Supt. – See Williamsburg
  ES, GENERAL DELIVERY   40769
    James Meadors, prin.

Pleasure Ridge Park, Jefferson Co., Pop. Code 7
Jefferson County SD
  Supt. – See Louisville
  Eisenhower ES, 5300 JESSAMINE LN   40258
    Albert Giancola, prin.
  Greenwood ES, 5801 GREENWOOD RD   40258
    Nancy Lovett, prin.
  Sanders ES, 8408 TERRY RD   40258
    Ima Johns, prin.

Pleasureville, Henry Co., Pop. Code 3
Henry County SD
  Supt. – See New Castle
  Eastern ES, RURAL ROUTE 02   40057
    Earl Holmes,Jr., prin.

Shelby County SD
  Supt. – See Shelbyville
  Cropper ES, P O BOX 51   40057
    Charlotte White, prin.

Prestonsburg, Floyd Co., Pop. Code 5
Floyd County SD
  Sch. Sys. Enr. Code 6
  Supt. – Ronald Hager, ARNOLD AVE   41653
  Clark ES, RURAL ROUTE 01 BOX 277B   41653
    Dempil Goble, prin.
  ES, COLLEGE LANE   41653
    Thomas Tackett, prin.
  Other Schools – See Allen, Auxier, Betsy Layne,
    Bevinsville, Dana, Drift, Garrett, Grethel, Harold,
    Honaker, Langley, Mc Dowell, Martin, Melvin,
    Wayland

Princeton, Caldwell Co., Pop. Code 6
Caldwell County SD
  Sch. Sys. Enr. Code 4
  Supt. – Joseph Clark, P O BOX 229   42445
  Caldwell County MS
    612 W WASHINGTON ST   42445
    David Franklin, prin.
  East Side ES, 100 N EAGLE ST   42445
    Charles Davis, prin.
  West Side ES, 201 SHORT ST   42445
    Franklin Anderson, prin.
  Other Schools – See Fredonia

Providence, Webster Co., Pop. Code 5
Providence ISD
  Sch. Sys. Enr. Code 5
  Supt. – Martha Wooten, 310 W MAIN ST   42450
  Broadway ES, 416 S BROADWAY ST   42450
    Jerry Fritz, prin.

Raceland, Greenup Co., Pop. Code 4
Raceland ISD
  Sch. Sys. Enr. Code 3
  Supt. – Charles Sammons, US 23   41169
  Campbell ES, US 23   41169 – Joe Weis, prin.
  Other Schools – See Worthington

Radcliff, Hardin Co., Pop. Code 7
Hardin County SD
  Supt. – See Elizabethtown
  Radcliff MS, 1145 S DIXIE BLVD   40160
    Dan McCamish, prin.
  Meadow View MS, 1255 W VINE ST   40160
    Faye Atcher, prin.
  Parkway ES, 1080 S LOGADON PKWY   40160
    Gary Cottrell, prin.

St. Christopher School, 1181 S WILSON RD   40160

Ransom, Pike Co.
Pike County SD
  Supt. – See Pikeville
  Blackberry ES, HCR 76 BOX 855   41558
    Francis Smith, prin.

Ravenna, Estill Co., Pop. Code 3
Estill County SD
  Supt. – See Irvine
  ES, 230 HUDSON DR   40472 – Robert Smith, prin.

Richardsville, Warren Co.
Warren County SD
  Supt. – See Bowling Green
  ES, HIGHWAY 263   42270 – Thomas Hunt, prin.

Richmond, Madison Co., Pop. Code 7
Madison County SD
  Sch. Sys. Enr. Code 5
  Supt. – Shannon Johnson, 707 N 2ND ST   40475
  Clark-Moores MS, RURAL ROUTE 03   40475
    Douglas Roberts, prin.
  Madison MS, 141 N 2ND ST   40475
    Hubert Broaddus, prin.
  Model Laboratory MS
    EASTERN KENTUCKY UNIVERSITY   40475
    (—), prin.
  Bellevue ES, BELLEVUE DR   40475
    Ray Read, prin.
  Boone ES, 710 N 2ND ST   40475
    Douglas Bowlin, prin.

Carson ES, 450 TATES CREEK RD 40475
   Carl Powell, prin.
Kirksville ES, 664 KIRKSVILLE RD 40475
   Edgar Adams, prin.
Mayfield MS, 321 BOND ST 40475
   Ray Read, prin.
Model Lab ES, EASTERN KY UNIVERSITY 40475
   (—), prin.
White Hall ES, 2176 LEXINGTON RD 40475
   Douglas Jackson, prin.
Other Schools — See Berea, Waco

St. Mark School, 614 W MAIN ST 40475

Rineyville, Hardin Co.
Hardin County SD
Supt. — See Elizabethtown
ES, P O BOX 48 40162 — Don Martin, prin.

Robards, Henderson Co.
Henderson County SD
Supt. — See Henderson
ES, P O BOX B 42452 — Robert Mitchell, prin.

Robinson Creek, Pike Co.
Pike County SD
Supt. — See Pikeville
ES 41560 — James Clay, prin.

Rochester, Butler Co., Pop. Code 2
Butler County SD
Supt. — See Morgantown
Third District ES, 240 H'VILLE/QUALITY 42273
   Wally Johnson, prin.

Rockfield, Warren Co.
Warren County SD
Supt. — See Bowling Green
ES, 7597 RUSSELLVILLE RD 42274
   Everett Leasor, prin.

Rockholds, Whitley Co.
Whitley County SD
Supt. — See Williamsburg
ES, P O BOX 28 40759 — Pete Yates, prin.

Rogers, Wolfe Co.
Wolfe County SD
Supt. — See Campton
ES 41365 — Kendall Clark, prin.

Rousseau, Breathitt Co.
Breathitt County SD
Supt. — See Jackson
ES 41366 — Bobby Sallee, prin.

Rush, Boyd Co.
Boyd County SD
Supt. — See Catlettsburg
Garner ES, 19231 STATE ROUTE 3 41168
   Larry Midkiff, prin.

Carter County SD
Supt. — See Grayson
Star ES, P O BOX 485 41168
   Terry Marshall, prin.

Russell, Greenup Co., Pop. Code 5
Russell ISD
Sch. Sys. Enr. Code 5
Supt. — Fred Madden, 409 BELFONTE ST 41169
MS, P O BOX S 41169 — Scott Grosse, prin.
Advance ES, P O BOX S 41169 — John Jones, prin.
Bellfonte ES, P O BOX S 41169
   Dorothy Lester, prin.
Central ES, P O BOX S 41169 — Nelson Allen, prin.
McDowell ES, P O BOX S 41169
   Bobby Crager, prin.

Russell Springs, Russell Co., Pop. Code 4
Russell County SD
Supt. — See Jamestown
ES, P O BOX J 42642 — Wilbur Barnes, prin.
Salem ES, RURAL ROUTE 04 BOX 255 42642
   Donald Miller, prin.

Russellville, Logan Co., Pop. Code 6
Logan County SD
Sch. Sys. Enr. Code 5
Supt. — H. Marksberry, P O BOX 417 42276
Other Schools — See Adairville, Auburn, Lewisburg,
   Olmstead

Russellville ISD
Sch. Sys. Enr. Code 4
Supt. — James Young,Jr.
   7TH AND SUMMER STS 42276
MS, 7TH AND SUMMER ST 42276
   Glen McGehee, prin.
Stevenson ES, HIGHWAY 431 N 42276
   Joseph Meguiar, prin.

Sacramento, McLean Co., Pop. Code 3
McLean County SD
Supt. — See Calhoun
ES 42372 — Joseph Hicklin, prin.

Sadieville, Scott Co., Pop. Code 2
Scott County SD
Supt. — See Georgetown
ES, COLLEGE AVE 40370 — Danny Bolling, prin.

Saint Charles, Hopkins Co., Pop. Code 2
Hopkins County SD
Supt. — See Madisonville
MS 42453 — Samuel Carneal, prin.
ES 42453 — Samuel Carneal, prin.

Salem, Livingston Co., Pop. Code 3
Livingston County SD
Supt. — See Smithland
ES, P O BOX 406 42078 — Henry Ramage, prin.

Salt Lick, Bath Co., Pop. Code 2
Bath County SD
Supt. — See Owingsville
ES 40371 — Lonnie Vice, prin.

Salyersville, Magoffin Co., Pop. Code 4
Magoffin County SD
Sch. Sys. Enr. Code 5
Supt. — Carter Whitaker, P O BOX 109 41465
Borders ES, 132 MINE FORK RD 41465
   Jerry Arnett, prin.
Hensley ES, HC RT 6 BOX 479 41465
   Owen Barnett, prin.
Salyer ES, 5781 ROYALTON RD 41465
   Eddie McFarland, prin.
ES, GARDNER TRAIL 41465 — Grover Arnett, prin.
Other Schools — See Fredville, Hendricks

Sandgap, Jackson Co.
Jackson County SD
Supt. — See Mc Kee
ES 40481 — James Harrison, prin.

Sandy Hook, Elliott Co., Pop. Code 3
Elliott County SD
Sch. Sys. Enr. Code 4
Supt. — E. Binion, P O BOX 767 41171
Lakeside ES, P O BOX 749 41171
   William Utchek, prin.
ES 41171 — Robert Kelly, prin.
Other Schools — See Isonville

Saul, Perry Co.
Perry County SD
Supt. — See Hazard
Lower Leatherwood ES 40981
   Glenna Hudson, prin.

Science Hill, Pulaski Co., Pop. Code 3
Science Hill ISD
Sch. Sys. Enr. Code 2
Supt. — Joe Burton, P O BOX 9 42553
ES, P O BOX 9 42553 — Ernest Debord, prin.

Scottsville, Allen Co., Pop. Code 5
Allen County SD
Sch. Sys. Enr. Code 4
Supt. — James Bazzell
   RURAL ROUTE 03 BOX 3A 42164
Allen County MS, 305 W CHERRY ST 42164
   Tommy Keen, prin.
Allen County ES, 307 W CHERRY ST 42164
   Gary Shelton, prin.
MS, N 6TH ST 42164 — Tommy Law, prin.
White Plaines ES, 188 FRANKLIN RD 42164
   Louella Spencer, prin.

Sebree, Webster Co., Pop. Code 4
Webster County SD
Supt. — See Dixon
ES, P O BOX 37 42455 — Leva Cottingham, prin.

Sedalia, Graves Co.
Graves County SD
Supt. — See Mayfield
ES 42079 — Jimmy Wiggins, prin.

Shelbiana, Pike Co.
Pike County SD
Supt. — See Pikeville
Greasy Creek ES
   RURAL ROUTE 01 BOX 95A 41562
   Justine Roberts, prin.

Shelbyville, Shelby Co., Pop. Code 6
Shelby County SD
Sch. Sys. Enr. Code 5
Supt. — Dr. Leon Mooneyhan, P O BOX 159 40065
Shelby County East MS
   RURAL ROUTE 07 BOX 336 40065
   (—), prin.
Shelby County West MS, 1155 MAIN ST 40065
   J. W. Roberts,Jr., prin.
Clay ES, RURAL ROUTE 03 BOX 484 40065
   David Sparrow, prin.
North Side MS, 821 COLLEGE ST 40065
   William Lancaster, prin.
South Side ES, 800 S 7TH ST 40065
   Robert Blair, prin.
Wright ES, 500 ROCKET LN 40065
   Norma Roberts, prin.
Other Schools — See Bagdad, Pleasureville,
   Simpsonville

Shepherdsville, Bullitt Co., Pop. Code 5
Bullitt County SD
Sch. Sys. Enr. Code 7
Supt. — Dr. Neyland Clark, P O BOX 97 40165
Bullitt Lick MS, 1080 W BLUELICK ROAD 40165
   Glenn Gray, prin.
Hebron MS, RURAL ROUTE 04 40165
   John Rowland, prin.
MS, P O BOX 368 40165 — Joe Mills, prin.
Brooks ES, RURAL ROUTE 04 40165
   Marvin Stewart, prin.
Cedar Grove ES, RURAL ROUTE 03 40165
   Joann Barr, prin.
Roby ES, STAR ROUTE 40165
   Ronald Murphy, prin.
Other Schools — See Lebanon Junction, Louisville,
   Mount Washington, West Point

St. Aloysius School, 1017 PLUM ST 40165

Sidney, Pike Co.
Pike County SD
Supt. — See Pikeville
Bevins ES 41564 — Gene Phillips, prin.

Siler, Whitley Co.
Whitley County SD
Supt. — See Williamsburg
Poplar Creek ES, P O BOX 427 40763
   Wesley Jones, prin.

Silver Grove, Campbell Co., Pop. Code 4
Silver Grove ISD
Sch. Sys. Enr. Code 2
Supt. — Michael King, 3RD ST 41085
ES, 3RD AND 4TH MILE PARK 41085
   Tim Barrow, prin.

Simpsonville, Shelby Co., Pop. Code 3
Shelby County SD
Supt. — See Shelbyville
ES, P O BOX 69 40067 — James Embree, prin.

Slaughters, Hopkins Co.
Webster County SD
Supt. — See Dixon
ES, P O BOX 68 42456 — Nevelyn Zachary, prin.

Smithland, Livingston Co.
Livingston County SD
Sch. Sys. Enr. Code 4
Supt. — Lee Jones, P O BOX 219 42081
ES, P O BOX 397 42081 — Jack Monroe, prin.
Other Schools — See Burna, Grand Rivers, Hampton,
   Ledbetter, Salem

Smith Mills, Henderson Co.
Henderson County SD
Supt. — See Henderson
ES, P O BOX 153 42457 — Elaine Neely, prin.

Smiths Grove, Warren Co., Pop. Code 3
Warren County SD
Supt. — See Bowling Green
North Warren ES, COLLEGE ST 42171
   David Eakles, prin.

Somerset, Pulaski Co., Pop. Code 7
Pulaski County SD
Sch. Sys. Enr. Code 6
Supt. — Bert Minton, P O BOX P 42501
Pulaski ES, 107 W UNIVERSITY DR 42501
   Donald Burris, prin.
Shopville ES, RURAL ROUTE 04 BOX 144 42501
   Philip Baker, prin.
Southern ES, 4030 ENTERPRISE DR 42501
   Bobby Overbey, prin.
White Lily ES
   RURAL ROUTE 07 BOX 202A 42501
   Christine Cothron, prin.
Woodstock ES, RURAL ROUTE 03 BOX 166 42501
   John Mayne, prin.
Other Schools — See Burnside, Eubank, Nancy

Somerset ISD
Sch. Sys. Enr. Code 4
Supt. — Conley Manning, COLLEGE ST 42501
Meece MS, 210 BARNETT ST 42501
   Bill Mauney, prin.
Hopkins ES, MAY ST 42501
   Bobby Sullivan, prin.
Memorial MS, LANGDON ST 42501
   William Adams, prin.

Sonora, Hardin Co., Pop. Code 2
Hardin County SD
Supt. — See Elizabethtown
ES 42776 — Carl Ford, prin.

Southgate, Campbell Co., Pop. Code 5
Southgate ISD
Sch. Sys. Enr. Code 2
Supt. — Raymond King
   BLATT & EVERGREEN 41071
ES, BLATT & EVERGREEN 41071
   Raymond King, prin.

South Portsmouth, Greenup Co.
Greenup County SD
Supt. — See Greenup
ES, P O BOX 507 41174 — John Younce, prin.

South Shore, Greenup Co.
Greenup County SD
Supt. — See Greenup
McKell MS, P O BOX 325 41175
   Sheila Reeder, prin.
McKell ES, P O BOX 325 41175
   Sheila Reeder, prin.
Sunshine ES, BOX 2303 HIGHWAY 7 41175
   Randy Shepherd, prin.

South Williamson, Pike Co., Pop. Code 6
Pike County SD
Supt. — See Pikeville
South Williamson ES, 411 CENTRAL AVE 41503
   Roy Cochrane, prin.

Spottsville, Henderson Co.
Henderson County SD
Supt. — See Henderson
ES, RURAL ROUTE 01 BOX 72A 42458
   Thomas Hurt, prin.

Springfield, Washington Co., Pop. Code 5
Washington County SD
Sch. Sys. Enr. Code 4
Supt. – Jack Waff, P O BOX 192   40069
Fredricktown ES, RURAL ROUTE 02   40069
   John Reinle, prin.
Washington County ES
   LINCOLN PARK RD   40069 – John Walker, prin.
Other Schools – See Mackville, Willisburg

   St. Dominic School, 309 W MAIN ST   40069

Stamping Ground, Scott Co., Pop. Code 3
Scott County SD
Supt. – See Georgetown
ES, MAIN ST   40379 – Gary Pruitt, prin.

Stanford, Lincoln Co., Pop. Code 5
Lincoln County SD
Sch. Sys. Enr. Code 5
Supt. – Joseph Blair, P O BOX 265   40484
ES, DANVILLE AVE   40484 – Ralph Roberts, prin.
Other Schools – See Crab Orchard, Hustonville, Mc
   Kinney, Waynesburg

Stanley, Daviess Co.
Daviess County SD
Supt. – See Owensboro
ES, US HIGHWAY 60 W   42375
   Billy Blaine, prin.

Stanton, Powell Co., Pop. Code 5
Powell County SD
Sch. Sys. Enr. Code 4
Supt. – Nelson White, P O BOX 5   40380
Powell County MS, RURAL ROUTE 01   40380
   Billy Rose, prin.
Bowen ES, RURAL ROUTE 01   40380
   Brenda White, prin.
ES, P O BOX 367   40380 – Juanita King, prin.
Other Schools – See Clay City

Stearns, McCreary Co., Pop. Code 6
McCreary County SD
Sch. Sys. Enr. Code 5
Supt. – Eddie Lowell Brown
   HCR 69 BOX 24   42647
Smithtown ES, P O BOX 367   42647
   Landon Sexton, prin.
ES, P O BOX 506   42647 – Don Douglas, prin.
Other Schools – See Parkers Lake, Pine Knot, Whitley
   City

Stephensport, Breckinridge Co.
Breckinridge County SD
Supt. – See Hardinsburg
Milner ES   40170 – Bernard Lewis, prin.

Stoney Fork, Bell Co.
Bell County SD
Supt. – See Pineville
Rightfork Center ES, HCR 86 BOX 1250   40988
   Gary Smith, prin.

Sturgis, Union Co., Pop. Code 4
Union County SD
Supt. – See Morganfield
ES, GRANT ST   42459 – John Belt, prin.

Sulpher Well, Metcalfe Co.
Metcalfe County SD
Supt. – See Edmonton
North Metcalfe ES   42129 – Byron Jeffries, prin.

Summer Shade, Metcalfe Co.
Metcalfe County SD
Supt. – See Edmonton
ES, 235 NOBOB ROAD   42166
   Elbert Hunley,Jr., prin.

Summersville, Green Co.
Green County SD
Supt. – See Greensburg
ES, P O BOX 67   42782 – Claudie Hancock, prin.

Sweeden, Edmonson Co.
Edmonson County SD
Supt. – See Brownsville
Kyrock ES, 5270 LEITCHFIELD RD   42285
   Johnny Vincent, prin.

Symsonia, Marshall Co.
Graves County SD
Supt. – See Mayfield
ES   42082 – Albert Gibson, prin.

Taylorsville, Spencer Co., Pop. Code 3
Spencer County SD
Sch. Sys. Enr. Code 4
Supt. – Dr. Bill Stout, P O BOX 158   40071
Spencer County ES, P O BOX 549   40071
   David Nedros, prin.

Toler, Pike Co.
Pike County SD
Supt. – See Pikeville
Varney ES   41569 – Billy Tussey, prin.

Tollesboro, Lewis Co., Pop. Code 3
Lewis County SD
Supt. – See Vanceburg
ES, P O BOX 81   41189 – John Ocull, prin.

Tomahawk, Martin Co.
Martin County SD
Supt. – See Inez
ES, P O BOX 140   41262 – Larry Fitzpatrick, prin.

Tompkinsville, Monroe Co., Pop. Code 5
Monroe County SD
Sch. Sys. Enr. Code 4
Supt. – James Graves, MAGNOLIA ST   42167
Carter ES, RURAL ROUTE 03   42167
   Jimmie Thompson, prin.
ES, CELIA RD   42167 – Samuel Carter, prin.
Other Schools – See Fountain Run, Gamaliel

Topmost, Knott Co.
Knott County SD
Supt. – See Hindman
Beaver Creek ES, HCR 80 BOX 8080   41862
   Walter Bentley, prin.

Totz, Harlan Co.
Harlan County SD
Supt. – See Harlan
ES   40870 – Gary Hensley, prin.

Turkey Creek, Pike Co.
Pike County SD
Supt. – See Pikeville
ES, P O BOX 419   41570 – Paul Tackett, prin.

Tyner, Jackson Co.
Jackson County SD
Supt. – See Mc Kee
ES   40486 – Fredrick McQueen, prin.

Union, Boone Co., Pop. Code 3
Boone County SD
Supt. – See Florence
New Haven ES, P O BOX 10854   41091
   Barry Hartman, prin.

Uniontown, Union Co., Pop. Code 4
Union County SD
Supt. – See Morganfield
ES, P O BOX 517   42461 – Philip Collings, prin.

Upton, Hardin Co., Pop. Code 3
Hardin County SD
Supt. – See Elizabethtown
ES, P O BOX 147   42784 – Gary Coffey, prin.

Utica, Daviess Co.
Daviess County SD
Supt. – See Owensboro
Masonville ES, 6500 U S 231   42376
   Kenny Baughn, prin.
ES, 231 KY 140W   42376 – Anita Newman, prin.

Valley Station, Jefferson Co., Pop. Code 7
Jefferson County SD
Supt. – See Louisville
Frost MS, 13700 SANDRAY BLVD   40272
   Joseph Vibbert, prin.
Stuart MS, 4603 VALLEY STATION ROAD   40272
   Gil Polston, prin.
Layne ES, 9831 EAST AVE   40272
   Winford Allen, prin.
Medora ES, 11801 DEERING RD   40272
   Judy Finn, prin.
Stonestreet ES, 10007 STONESTREET RD   40272
   Diann Gaines, prin.

   Beth Haven Christian School
      5515 JOHNSONTOWN ROAD   40272

Vanceburg, Lewis Co., Pop. Code 4
Lewis County SD
Sch. Sys. Enr. Code 5
Supt. – Michael Forman, P O BOX 158   41179
Lewis County Central ES, P O BOX 220   41179
   Fred Smith, prin.
Other Schools – See Camp Dix, Garrison, Tollesboro

Varney, Pike Co.
Pike County SD
Supt. – See Pikeville
Brushy ES, P O BOX 4078   41571
   Herman Smith, prin.

Verona, Boone Co.
Walton-Verona ISD
Supt. – See Walton
Walton-Verona ES, 15066 PORTER RD   41092
   Reed Tyler, prin.

Versailles, Woodford Co., Pop. Code 6
Woodford County SD
Sch. Sys. Enr. Code 5
Supt. – Dr. Jim Jackson, 131 MAPLE ST   40383
Woodford County MS, 130 MAPLE ST   40383
   Bill Grimes, prin.
Huntertown ES, HUNTERTOWN RD   40383
   Ernest Trosper, prin.
Mortonsville ES, RURAL ROUTE 03   40383
   Lois Hamm, prin.
Simmons ES, TYRONE PK   40383
   Tom McMillin, prin.
Other Schools – See Midway

   St. Leo School, 239 N MAIN ST   40383

Vest, Knott Co.
Knott County SD
Supt. – See Hindman
Beckham Combs ES   41772 – Vernon Smith, prin.

Vine Grove, Hardin Co., Pop. Code 5
Hardin County SD
Supt. – See Elizabethtown
Alton MS, 400 BROWN ST   40175
   Gary King, prin.
ES, 301 FIRST ST   40175 – Donald Lynch, prin.

Meade County SD
Supt. – See Brandenburg
Flaherty ES, RURAL ROUTE 02   40175
   Donald Hawkins, prin.

   St. Brigid School, 310 E MAIN ST   40175

Viper, Perry Co.
Perry County SD
Supt. – See Hazard
ES   41774 – James Boothe, prin.

Virgie, Pike Co., Pop. Code 2
Pike County SD
Supt. – See Pikeville
Johnson ES, HCR 83 BOX 196   41572
   Paul Goodman, prin.

Waco, Madison Co.
Madison County SD
Supt. – See Richmond
ES, HWY 52   40385 – Robert Azbill, prin.

Wallingford, Fleming Co.
Fleming County SD
Supt. – See Flemingsburg
Fox Valley ES, RURAL ROUTE 02   41093
   Eddie Ward, prin.

Wallins Creek, Harlan Co., Pop. Code 2
Harlan County SD
Supt. – See Harlan
Wallins ES, P O BOX 8   40873 – William Lee, prin.

Walton, Boone Co., Pop. Code 4
Walton-Verona ISD
Sch. Sys. Enr. Code 3
Supt. – Gary Munsie, P O BOX 167   41094
Other Schools – See Verona

   St. Joseph Academy, 48 NEEDMORE ST   41094

Warfield, Martin Co., Pop. Code 2
Martin County SD
Supt. – See Inez
MS   41267 – Randy Hughes, prin.
ES   41267 – Estella Horn, prin.

Warsaw, Gallatin Co., Pop. Code 4
Gallatin County SD
Sch. Sys. Enr. Code 3
Supt. – D. Griffith, 110 W MAIN   41095
Gallatin County ES, P O BOX 146   41095
   Ralph Edwards, prin.
Other Schools – See Glencoe

Wayland, Floyd Co., Pop. Code 3
Floyd County SD
Supt. – See Prestonsburg
ES, P O BOX 249   41666 – Gwen Harmon, prin.

Waynesburg, Lincoln Co.
Lincoln County SD
Supt. – See Stanford
Highland ES, RURAL ROUTE 01   40489
   Roger Meek, prin.
Kings Mountain ES, RURAL ROUTE 01   40489
   Lanny Hubbard, prin.
ES, RURAL ROUTE 01   40489 – Steve Dunn, prin.

West Liberty, Morgan Co., Pop. Code 4
Morgan County SD
Sch. Sys. Enr. Code 4
Supt. – James Earl Reed, P O BOX 489   41472
Morgan County MS   41472 – Olen Gamble, prin.
ES, RURAL ROUTE 01   41472 – Neil Hunley, prin.
Other Schools – See Cannel City, Crockett, Ezel,
   Wrigley

West Paducah, McCracken Co.
McCracken County SD
Supt. – See Paducah
Heath MS, RURAL ROUTE 01   42086
   Joe Chumbler, prin.
Heath ES, RURAL ROUTEL 01   42086
   Willie Blackwell, prin.

West Point, Hardin Co., Pop. Code 4
Bullitt County SD
Supt. – See Shepherdsville
Nichols ES, RURAL ROUTE 01   40177
   John Sullivan, prin.

   West Point ISD
   Sch. Sys. Enr. Code 2
   Supt. – David Stephens, P O BOX 367   40177
   ES, P O BOX 367   40177 – Larry Burke, prin.

White Mills, Hardin Co.
Hardin County SD
Supt. – See Elizabethtown
Lynnvale ES, WHITE MILLS RD   42788
   E. Thompson, prin.

White Plains, Hopkins Co., Pop. Code 3
Hopkins County SD
Supt. – See Madisonville
MS, E CHURCH ST   42464 – Samuel Larkin, prin.
ES, E CHURCH ST   42464 – Wayne Larkins, prin.

Whitesburg, Letcher Co., Pop. Code 4
Letcher County SD
Sch. Sys. Enr. Code 6
Supt. – Bernard Watts, BOX 788   41858
MS, PARK ST   41858 – Raymond Thomas, prin.
Bates ES, HCR 85 BOX 1080   41858
   Lawrence Hale, prin.
Cowan ES, P O BOX 2230   41858
   Billy Stamper, prin.

West Whitesburg ES, PARK ST 41858
  E. Collins, prin.
Other Schools – See Eolia, Hallie, Jackhorn, Kona,
  Letcher, Linefork, Neon

Whitesville, Daviess Co., Pop. Code 3
Daviess County SD
Supt. – See Owensboro
ES, P O BOX 27 42378 – Barry Beck, prin.

  St. Mary of the Woods School, P O BOX 14 42378

Whitley City, McCreary Co., Pop. Code 4
McCreary County SD
Supt. – See Stearns
MS, P O BOX 520 42653 – Ralph Nevels, prin.
ES, P O BOX 250 42653 – Crit King,Jr., prin.

Wickliffe, Ballard Co., Pop. Code 4
Ballard County SD
Supt. – See Barlow
ES, P O BOX 678 42087 – Chan Case, prin.

Willard, Carter Co.
Carter County SD
Supt. – See Grayson
ES, P O BOX 9 41181 – Johannah Lawson, prin.

Williamsburg, Whitley Co., Pop. Code 6
Whitley County SD
Sch. Sys. Enr. Code 5
Supt. – William Mayne, P O BOX 358 40769
Whitley County MS
  RURAL ROUTE 01 BOX 356 40769
  Terry Skinner, prin.
Boston ES, RURAL ROUTE 05 BOX 336 40769
  Glenn Steely, prin.
Liberty ES, HCR 88 BOX 528 40769
  Jerome Hill, prin.
Wofford ES, RURAL ROUTE 01 BOX 637 40769
  Don Grimes, prin.
Other Schools – See Corbin, Nevisdale, Pleasant
  View, Rockholds, Siler, Woodbine

Williamsburg ISD
Sch. Sys. Enr. Code 3
Supt. – Leonard McCoy, P O BOX 509 40769
ES, 1000 MAIN ST 40769 – Jack Foley, prin.

Williamsport, Johnson Co.
Johnson County SD
Supt. – See Paintsville
Meade Memorial ES, RURAL ROUTE 40 41271
  Jonah Belcher, prin.

Williamstown, Grant Co., Pop. Code 5
Grant County SD
Sch. Sys. Enr. Code 4
Supt. – O. Jones, P O BOX 369 41097
Mason ES, RURAL ROUTE 01 41097
  Robert True, prin.
Other Schools – See Corinth, Dry Ridge

Williamstown ISD
Sch. Sys. Enr. Code 3
Supt. – Bobby Chaney, 300 HELTON ST 41097
ES, P O BOX 220 41097 – (—), prin.

Willisburg, Washington Co., Pop. Code 2
Washington County SD
Supt. – See Springfield
ES, P O BOX 37 40078 – Ralph Harris, prin.

Wilmore, Jessamine Co., Pop. Code 5
Jessamine County SD
Supt. – See Nicholasville
ES, 300 N LEXINGTON AVE 40390
  C. Wilder, prin.

Winchester, Clark Co., Pop. Code 7
Clark County SD
Sch. Sys. Enr. Code 6
Supt. – Donald Pace
  1600 W LEXINGTON AVE 40391
Belmont MS, BURNS & BELMONT 40391
  Gene Mosley, prin.
Conkwright MS
  360 MOUNT STERLING ROAD 40391
  Robert Lee, prin.
Becknerville ES
  RURAL ROUTE 01 BOX 121 40391
  Kenneth Caudill, prin.
Bush ES, 250 N MAIN ST 40391
  Larry Tipton, prin.
Central ES, 330 MOUNT STERLING RD 40391
  Gerald Roades, prin.
Gross ES, 150 MARYLAND AVE 40391
  Frank Vermillion, prin.
McClure ES, 30 BECHNER ST 40391
  James Wells, prin.
Pilot View ES, RURAL ROUTE 05 BOX 164 40391
  Melvin Howard, prin.
Providence ES, RURAL ROUTE 04 BOX 122 40391
  Kenneth Caudill, prin.
Shearer ES, 244 E BROADWAY ST 40391
  Conard Young, prin.
Trapp ES, RURAL ROUTE 03 BOX 190 40391
  Melvin Howard, prin.

  St. Agatha Academy, 244 S MAIN ST 40391

Windsor, Russell Co.
Casey County SD
Supt. – See Liberty
Phelps ES 42565 – Virtreas Godbey, prin.

Wingo, Graves Co., Pop. Code 3
Graves County SD
Supt. – See Mayfield
ES 42088 – Donald Spicer, prin.

Wittensville, Johnson Co.
Johnson County SD
Supt. – See Paintsville
Castle Memorial ES
  RURAL ROUTE 276 BOX 915 41274
  Michael Barber, prin.

Woodbine, Knox Co.
Whitley County SD
Supt. – See Williamsburg
ES, P O BOX 218 40771 – Kenneth Harp, prin.

Wooton, Leslie Co.
Leslie County SD
Supt. – See Hyden
Muncy ES, P O BOX 140 41776
  Damon Huff, prin.

Worthington, Greenup Co., Pop. Code 4
Raceland ISD
Supt. – See Raceland
ES, WORTHINGTON ST 41183 – Joe Weis, prin.

Wrigley, Morgan Co.
Morgan County SD
Supt. – See West Liberty
ES 41477 – Arlie Smith, prin.

Wurtland, Greenup Co., Pop. Code 4
Greenup County SD
Supt. – See Greenup
ES, 611 EAST ST 41144 – Linna Craft, prin.

Yeaddiss, Leslie Co.
Leslie County SD
Supt. – See Hyden
Hayes Lewis ES 41777 – Glen Hendrix, prin.

LOUISIANA

STATE DEPARTMENT OF EDUCATION
P.O. Box 94064, Baton Rouge 70804
(504) 342-4411

Superintendent of Education	Wilmer Cody
Deputy Superintendent Education	Robert Schiller
Deputy Superintendent Management & Finance	Graig Luscombe
Associate Superintendent Research & Development	Vacant
Assistant Superintendent Edcuational Support Programs	Charles Allen
Assistant Superintendent Vocational Education	Don Wood
Assistant Superintendent Academic Programs	Leonard Haynes
Assistant Superintendent Special Education Services	Thomas Paulette

STATE BOARD OF EDUCATION
Em Tampke, *Executive Director*   P.O. Box 94064, Baton Rouge   70804

LOUISIANA BOARD OF REGENTS FOR HIGHER EDUCATION
Robert Bodet, *Chairperson*   150 Riverside Mall, Baton Rouge   70801

PUBLIC, PRIVATE, AND PAROCHIAL ELEMENTARY SCHOOLS

Abbeville, Vermilion Parish, Pop. Code 7
Vermilion Parish SD
Sch. Sys. Enr. Code 6
Supt. – Easton Herbert, P O BOX 520 70511
Williams MS, 1105 PRARIE AVE 70510
  Daniel Dartez, prin.
East Abbeville ES, 120 ODEA ST 70510
  Clifton Allemen, prin.

Eaton Park ES, 1503 SYLVESTER ST 70510
  Ebrar Reaux, prin.
Forked Island East Broussard ES
  RURAL ROUTE 01 BOX 1574 70510
  James Quirk, prin.
Herod ES, 1411 LAMPMAN 70510
  Robert Wilson, prin.

Meaux ES, RURAL ROUTE 04 BOX 1658 70510
  Charles Robichaux, prin.
Seventh Ward ES
  RURAL ROUTE 06 BOX 468 70510
  Daniel Huval, prin.
Other Schools – See Erath, Gueydan, Kaplan,
  Maurice, Rayne

Mt. Carmel ES, 405 PARK AVE 70510

Abita Springs, St. Tammany Parish, Pop. Code 4
St. Tammany Parish SD
Supt. – See Covington
ES, P O BOX 427 70420 – Carol Rogers, prin.

Albany, Livingston Parish, Pop. Code 3
Livingston Parish SD
Supt. – See Livingston
MS, P O BOX 1210 70711 – Janice Bernard, prin.
ES, P O BOX 970 70711 – Rhonda Robertson, prin.

Alexandria, Rapides Parish, Pop. Code 8
Rapides Parish SD
Sch. Sys. Enr. Code 7
Supt. – Allen Nichols, P O BOX 1230 71309
JHS, 122 MARYLAND AVE 71301 – K. Allen, prin.
Brame JHS, 4800 DAWN ST 71301
   Donald Holloway, prin.
Jones Street JHS, P O BOX 2030 71309
   Clifton Randall, prin.
Acadian 6th MS, 310 RICHMOND DRIVE 71302
   Mary Wilder, prin.
Brasher ES, 601 CLOVER LEAF BLVD 71303
   Dr. William Connella, prin.
Cherokee ES, 5700 PRESCOTT ROAD 71301
   Jacquelyn Sanders, prin.
Hall ES, P O BOX 121 71309
   Granvel Metoyer, prin.
Horseshoe Drive ES, 2905 HORSESHOE DR 71301
   M. Ford, prin.
Huddle ES, 505 TEXAS AVE 71301
   Morris Thomas, prin.
Lincoln Road PS, 4645 LINCOLN ROAD 71302
   Walter Hadnot, prin.
Lincoln Road Sixth MS, P O BOX 5423 71307
   Calvin Johnson, prin.
Martin Park ES, 4203 LISA ST 71302
   Paul Williams, prin.
North Bayou Rapides ES
   5500 ENGLAND DR 71303 – Ralph Mertens, prin.
Nachman ES, 4102 CASTLE ROAD 71303
   Kathleen Poole, prin.
Peabody Sixth MS, P O BOX 1747 71309
   Murrell Atwood, prin.
Poland ES, RURAL ROUTE 02 BOX 363 71302
   John Francis, prin.
Reed Avenue ES, P O BOX 1052 71309
   Julius Patrick,Jr., prin.
Rosenthal ES, 1951 MONROE ST 71301
   Amos Wesley, prin.
Ruby-Wise ES, KOLIN RURAL STATION 71301
   Henry Megison, prin.
Rugg ES, 1319 BUSH AVE 71301
   Elwood Dyess, prin.
South Alexandria Sixth MS
   1323 VANCE ST 71301 – Katie Smith, prin.
Other Schools – See Boyce, Buckeye, Elmer, Forest
   Hill, Glenmora, Lecompte, Pineville, Tioga

Alexandria Country Day School
   611 BAYOU RAPIDES ROAD 71303
England Air Force Base Dependent School
   HDQ 23RD COMBAT SUPPORT GRP 71311
Our Lady of Prompt Succor School
   420 TWENTY-FIRST ST 71301
St. Frances Cabrini School
   2215 E TEXAS AVE 71301
St. Rita Catholic School, P O BOX 7664 71306

Amelia, St. Mary Parish, Pop. Code 5
St. Mary Parish SD
Supt. – See Centerville
Aucoin ES, P O BOX 1040 70340
   Roland Verret, prin.

Amite, Tangipahoa Parish, Pop. Code 5
St. Helena Parish SD
Supt. – See Greensburg
Fifth Ward ES
   RURAL ROUTE 04 BOX 60A 70422
   Willie Johnson, prin.

Tangipahoa Parish SD
Sch. Sys. Enr. Code 7
Supt. – Sam Pigno, 313 E OAK ST 70422
West Side MS, 409 W OAK ST 70422
   Edwin Anderson, prin.
ES, 300 VERNON AVE 70422 – Sam Hyde, prin.
Other Schools – See Hammond, Independence,
   Kentwood, Loranger, Natalbany, Ponchatoula,
   Roseland, Tickfaw

Oak Forest Academy, 600 WALNUT ST 70422

Anacoco, Vernon Parish, Pop. Code 1
Vernon Parish SD
Supt. – See Leesville
ES, P O BOX 230 71403 – Don Stokes, prin.

Angie, Washington Parish, Pop. Code 2
Washington Parish SD
Supt. – See Franklinton
JHS 70426 – James Kennedy, prin.
Varnado ES, RURAL ROUTE 03 BOX 64 70426
   Gary Fornea, prin.
Wesley ES, P O BOX 161 70426
   Charles Penton, prin.

Arabi, St. Bernard Parish, Pop. Code 7
St. Bernard Parish SD
Supt. – See Chalmette

Arabi Park MS
   MEHLE & N ROCHEBLAVE AVE 70032
   Dr. Shirley Kneale, prin.
ES, 721 FRISCOVILLE AVE 70032
   Billie Ann Lopez, prin.
Carolyn Park PS, 100 LLAMA DRIVE 70032
   Katherine Thornton, prin.
St. Claude Heights ES, ALEXANDER AVE 70032
   Gayle Hunter, prin.

St. Louise De Marillac School
   1914 AYCOCK ST 70032
St. Robert Bellarmine School
   815 BADGER DR 70032

Arcadia, Bienville Parish, Pop. Code 5
Bienville Parish SD
Sch. Sys. Enr. Code 5
Supt. – Richard Pullig, P O BOX 418 71001
Crawford ES, 1700 DANIEL ST 71001
   Edward Mason, prin.
Other Schools – See Bienville, Castor, Gibsland,
   Ringgold, Saline

Arnaudville, St. Landry Parish, Pop. Code 4
St. Landry Parish SD
Supt. – See Opelousas
S, P O BOX 70 70512 – Lanny Moreau, prin.

Little Flower Catholic School, P O BOX 466 70512

Athens, Claiborne Parish, Pop. Code 2
Claiborne Parish SD
Supt. – See Homer
ES, P O BOX 128 71003 – Bertrand Heckel, prin.

Atlanta, Winn Parish, Pop. Code 2
Winn Parish SD
Supt. – See Winnfield
S, RURAL ROUTE 01 BOX 38 71404
   John Thompson, prin.

Avery Island, Iberia Parish, Pop. Code 3
Iberia Parish SD
Supt. – See New Iberia
ES, P O BOX 107 70513 – Catherine Segura, prin.

Baker, East Baton Rouge Parish, Pop. Code 7
East Baton Rouge Parish SD
Supt. – See Baton Rouge
MS, 5903 GROOM ROAD 70714
   Hilda Randall, prin.
Baker Heights ES, 3750 HARDING ST 70714
   Lucille Johnson, prin.
Bakerfield ES, 2550 SOUTH ST 70714
   Cornelia DeBessonet, prin.
Park Ridge ES, 5905 GROOM ROAD 70714
   Elwood Debessonet, prin.
White Hills ES, 5300 BENTLEY DRIVE 70714
   Victoria Meares, prin.

Central Private School
   12801 CENTERRA COURT 70714

Baldwin, St. Mary Parish, Pop. Code 5
St. Mary Parish SD
Supt. – See Centerville
ES, P O BOX 616 70514 – Leonard Sudduth, prin.
Hamilton MS, P O BOX 10 70514
   Albert Alexander, prin.

Basile, Evangeline Parish, Pop. Code 5
Evangeline Parish SD
Supt. – See Ville Platte
Stewart ES, P O BOX 338 70515
   Christine Bacon, prin.

Baskin, Franklin Parish, Pop. Code 2
Franklin Parish SD
Supt. – See Winnsboro
S, RURAL ROUTE 01 71219
   Charles Powers, prin.

Bastrop, Morehouse Parish, Pop. Code 7
Morehouse Parish SD
Sch. Sys. Enr. Code 6
Supt. – Dr. Jerry Atkins, P O BOX 872 71221
Adams ES, 704 KAMMELL ST 71220
   John Washington,Jr., prin.
MS, 715 S WASHINGTON ST 71220
   Billy Rabon, prin.
Beekman ES, RURAL ROUTE 03 71220
   Charles Peterson, prin.
Carver MS, 1510 ELM ST 71220
   Dorothy Olds, prin.
Cherry Ridge ES
   RURAL ROUTE 06 BOX 610 71220
   George Chain, prin.
East Side ES, 102 MCCREIGHT ST 71220
   Herbert Dawkins, prin.
Oak Hill ES, 630 COLLINSTON ROAD 71220
   Viva Murry, prin.
Pine Grove ES
   RURAL ROUTE 06 BOX 367 71220
   Mary Lou Herrington, prin.
South Side ES, 500 S VINE ST 71220
   Melvin Anderson, prin.
West Side ES, 909 LARCHE LANE 71220
   Sharon Mitcham, prin.
Other Schools – See Bonita, Collinston, Mer Rouge

Prairie View Academy
   RURAL ROUTE 07 BOX 126 71220
Cherry Ridge Christian School
   1001 CHERRY RIDGE ROAD 71220

Our Lady Help of Christians School
   1602 W MADISON AVE 71220
St. Joseph Catholic School
   217 HARRINGTON AVE 71220

Baton Rouge, East Baton Rouge Parish, Pop. Code 9
East Baton Rouge Parish SD
Sch. Sys. Enr. Code 8
Supt. – Dr. Bernard Weiss, P O BOX 2950 70821
Southern University Lab School
   P O BOX 9414 70813 – Annette Paul, prin.
University Lab School
   LOUISIANA STATE UNIVERSITY 70803
   James Fox, prin.
Broadmoor MS, 1225 SHARP ROAD 70815
   George Williams, prin.
Capitol MS, 4200 GUS YOUNG AVE 70802
   Charles Stevenson, prin.
Central MS, RURAL ROUTE 04 70818
   Shelton Watts, prin.
Crestworth MS, 10650 AVENUE F 70807
   Victor Baham, prin.
Glasgow MS, 1676 GLASGOW AVE 70808
   Daniel Landry, prin.
Glen Oaks MS, 5300 MONARCH AVE 70811
   Thomas Germany, prin.
Istrouma MS, 2500 ERIE ST 70805
   Kenneth Payne, prin.
Kenilworth MS, 7600 BOONE AVE 70808
   Gerald Scallan, prin.
McKinley MS, 1557 MCCALOP ST 70802
   Josie Williams, prin.
Park Forest MS, 3760 ALETHA DRIVE 70814
   Lois Sumrall, prin.
Prescott MS, 4055 PRESCOTT ROAD 70805
   Patricia Stephens, prin.
Scotlandville MS
   9147 ELMGROVE GARDEN DRIVE 70807
   Willie Phillips, prin.
Sherwood MS, 1020 MARLBROOK DRIVE 70815
   Darryl Morris, prin.
Southeast MS
   15000 S HARRELLS FERRY ROAD 70816
   Richard Day, prin.
Westdale MS, 5650 CLAYCUT ROAD 70806
   Patsy Smack, prin.
Audubon ES, 10730 GOODWOOD BLVD 70815
   Phyllis Crawford, prin.
Banks ES, 2400 72ND AVE 70807
   Donald Dixon, prin.
Beechwood MS, 2555 DESOTO DR 70807
   Geraldine Simms, prin.
Belfair ES, 4451 FAIRFIELDS AVE 70802
   Willard Chrisentery, prin.
Bernard Terrace ES, 241 EDISON ST 70806
   Claudia Daniel, prin.
Broadmoor ES, 9650 GOODWOOD BLVD 70815
   Frances England, prin.
Brookstown ES, 4375 E BROOKSTOWN DR 70805
   Jacklyn Porta, prin.
Brownfields ES, 11615 ELLEN DR 70811
   Jo Ann Leggett, prin.
Buchanan ES, 1222 E BUCHANAN ST 70802
   Bernadine Simmons, prin.
Cedarcrest-Southmoor ES
   10187 TWIN CEDARS ST 70816
   Linda Ydarraga, prin.
Claiborne ES, 4700 DENHAM ST 70805
   Phyllis Territo, prin.
Crestworth ES, 11200 AVENUE F 70807
   Corinne Maybuce, prin.
Dalton ES, 3605 ONTARIO ST 70805
   Alberta Jones, prin.
Delmont ES, 5300 DOUGLAS AVE 70805
   Dr. Emily Elliott, prin.
DuFrocq ES, 330 S 19TH ST 70806
   Barbara Parker, prin.
Eden Park ES
   1650 N ACADIAN THRUWAY E 70802
   Robert Jones, prin.
Forest Heights ES, 7447 SUMRALL DR 70812
   Cherry Boudreaux, prin.
Glen Oaks Park ES, 5656 LANIER DR 70812
   Geraldine Roberts, prin.
Goodwood ES, 6550 SEVEN OAKS AVE 70806
   Brenda Sterling, prin.
Greenbrier ES, 12203 CANTERBURY DR 70814
   Dr. Henry Denham,Jr., prin.
Greenville ES, 1645 N FOSTER DR 70806
   Leola Washington, prin.
Harding ES, 8600 ELM GROVE GARDEN 70807
   Katie Smith, prin.
Highland ES, 280 SUNSET BLVD 70808
   Melba Kinchen, prin.
Howell Park ES, 6125 WINBOURNE AVE 70805
   Dina Bumgarner, prin.
Jefferson Terrace ES
   9902 CAL ROADE AVE 70809
   Rudolph Rumfellow, prin.
Labelle Aire ES, 12255 TAMS DR 70815
   Dr. Elizabeth Walsh, prin.
Lanier ES, 4705 LANIER DR 70812
   Norma Dillon, prin.
Lasalle ES, 8000 LASALLE AVE 70806
   Syble Sartin, prin.
Magnolia Woods ES, 760 MAXINE DR 70808
   Lula Lejeune, prin.
Mayfair MS, 9880 HYACINTH AVE 70810
   Frederick McKee, prin.
Melrose ES, 1348 VALCOUR DR 70806
   Edward Broussard, prin.
Merrydale ES, 6700 RIO DR 70812
   Dr. Alvin Decuir, prin.

Nicholson ES, 1143 NORTH ST 70802
John Hooper, prin.
North Highlands ES, 3875 BYRON AVE 70805
Dianne Helire, prin.
Northdale ES, 1555 MADISON AVE 70802
Leroy Helire,Jr., prin.
Park ES, 2700 FUQUA ST 70802
Lora Patureau, prin.
Park Forest ES, 10717 ELAIN DR 70814
Ann Torregrossa, prin.
Parkview ES, 5660 PARK FOREST 70816
Allen Alonzo, prin.
Polk ES, 408 E POLK ST 70802
Cordelia Jones, prin.
Progress ES, 855 PROGRESS ROAD 70807
Udieth Dotson, prin.
Red Oaks ES, 10755 CLETUS DR 70815
Mary Jane Barksdale, prin.
Riveroaks ES, 950 FOUNTAINBLEAU DR 70819
Benny Webb,Jr., prin.
Ryan ES, 10337 ELM GROVE GARDEN 70807
Wilmer Jones, prin.
Sharon Hills ES, 6450 GUYNELL DR 70811
Linda Sorrell, prin.
Shenandoah ES
16555 APPOMATTOX AVE 70817
James Machen, prin.
South Boulevard Extended ES
802 MAYFLOWER ST 70802
Kathleen Craig, prin.
Tanglewood ES, 9353 RUSTLING OAKS DR 70818
Joan Schouest, prin.
Twin Oaks ES, 819 TRAMMELL DRIVE 70815
George Ann Brown, prin.
University Terrace ES
575 W ROOSEVELT ST 70802
Richard Capps, prin.
Villa Del Ray ES
9765 CUYHANGA PARKWAY 70815
Billy Stephens, prin.
Walnut Hills ES
2040 S ACADIAN THRUWAY 70808
Orlena McKenzie, prin.
Wedgewood ES, 2330 ASPENWOOD DR 70816
Sheridan Harris, prin.
Westdale ES, 2000 COLLEGE DR 70808
Travis Lartigue, prin.
Westminister ES, 8935 WESTMINISTER DR 70809
Joy McElveen, prin.
Wildwood ES, 444 HALFWAY TREE ROAD 70810
Virginia Worley, prin.
Winbourne ES, 4501 WINBOURNE AVE 70805
Barbara Brownfield, prin.
Other Schools – See Baker, Greenwell Springs, Pride, Zachary

Baton Rouge Prep School
12108 PARKMEADOW AVE 70816
Christian Life Academy
2037 QUAIL ROAD 70808
Cornerstone Academy, 1433 SHARP LANE 70815
Divine Guidance School, 3617 LANIER DR 70814
Parkview Baptist School
11795 JEFFERSON HIGHWAY 70816
Redemptorist Catholic ES
2305-A CHOCTAW DR 70805
Runnels School
17255 S HARRELL'S FERRY RD 70816
Starkey Academy, 10510 JOOR ROAD 70818
Baton Rouge Christian Academy
1357 SHARP ROAD 70815
Berean SDA School, P O BOX 1925 B 70821
Brownsfield Baptist Academy
11998 PLANK ROAD 70811
DePaul Catholic School
9150 BEREFORD DR 70809
Family Christian Academy
9119 WORLD MINISTRY AVE 70810
First Assembly Christian Academy
8850 GOODWOOD BLVD 70806
L'Ecole School, P O BOX 45212 70895
Lake Sherwood ES, 12158 COURSEY BLVD 70816
Millerville Academy
1615 MILLERVILLE ROAD 70816
Most Blessed Sacrament ES
8033 BARRINGER ROAD 70817
Our Lady of Mercy Catholic ES
400 MARQUETTE AVE 70806
Sacred Heart of Jesus School
2251 MAIN ST 70802
St. Aloysius Catholic School
2025 STUART AVE 70808
St. Francis Xavier School, 1150 S 12TH ST 70802
St. George Catholic School
7880 SIEGEN LANE 70809
St. Gerard Majella School
3655 SAINT GERARD AVE 70805
St. Isadaore Catholic School
RURAL ROUTE 07 BOX 182A 70807
St. James Episcopal Day School
445 CONVENTION ST 70802
St. Jean Vianney Catholic School
16266 S HARRELLS FERRY ROAD 70816
St. Jude ES, 9150 HIGHLAND ROAD 70810
St. Louis King of France ES
2311 N SHERWOOD FOREST DR 70815
St. Lukes Episcopal School
8833 GOODWOOD BLVD 70806
St. Pius X Catholic School
6380 HOOPER ROAD 70811
St. Thomas More School
11400 SHERBROOK DRIVE 70815

The Chapel School
11111 ROY EMERSON DRIVE 70810
Trinity Episcopal Day School
3552 MORNING GLORY AVE 70808
Victory Academy
3953 N FLANNERY ROAD 70814

Bayou Goula, Iberville Parish, Pop. Code 3
Iberville Parish SD
Supt. – See Plaquemine
ES, P O BOX 56 70716 – Marguerite Jones, prin.

Belcher, Caddo Parish, Pop. Code 2
Caddo Parish SD
Supt. – See Shreveport
Herndon Magnet ES, 11845 GAMM RD 71004
Elmer Washam, prin.

Bell City, Calcasieu Parish
Calcasieu Parish SD
Supt. – See Lake Charles
S, P O BOX 98 70630 – Roy Blanchette, prin.

Belle Chasse, Plaquemines Parish, Pop. Code 4
Plaquemines Parish SD
Sch. Sys. Enr. Code 6
Supt. – Irwin Rhodes, P O BOX 69 70037
MS, RURAL ROUTE 01 BOX 581AA 70037
Denis Rousselle, prin.
Other Schools – See Buras, Carlisle, Port Sulphur, Venice

Our Lady of Perpetual Help School
803 BELLE CHASSE HWY S 70037

Belle Rose, Assumption Parish, Pop. Code 3
Assumption Parish SD
Supt. – See Napoleonville
MS, P O BOX 245 70341
Harding Anderson, prin.
Belle Rose PS, P O BOX 245 70341
Diane Landry, prin.

Benton, Bossier Parish, Pop. Code 4
Bossier Parish SD
Sch. Sys. Enr. Code 7
Supt. – Douglas Peterson, P O BOX 2000 71006
ES, RURAL ROUTE 03 BOX 10 71006
Bobbie Joe Adams, prin.
Other Schools – See Bossier City, Elm Grove, Haughton, Plain Dealing, Princeton

Berwick, St. Mary Parish, Pop. Code 5
St. Mary Parish SD
Supt. – See Centerville
JHS, 3010 HIGHWAY 182 70342
Gary Matherne, prin.
ES, P O BOX 249 70342 – Stanley Beaubouef, prin.

Bienville, Bienville Parish, Pop. Code 2
Bienville Parish SD
Supt. – See Arcadia
S, P O BOX 106 71008 – Charles Hines, prin.

Blanchard, Caddo Parish, Pop. Code 4
Caddo Parish SD
Supt. – See Shreveport
ES, P O BOX 629 71009
Charles Gouthiere,Jr., prin.

Bogalusa, Washington Parish, Pop. Code 7
Bogalusa City SD
Sch. Sys. Enr. Code 5
Supt. – Gary Holcomb, P O BOX 310 70427
JHS, 1403 NORTH AVE 70427
James Raborn, prin.
Byrd Avenue ES, 1600 BYRD AVE 70427
Gladys Sampson, prin.
Columbia Street MS, 1020 COLUMBIA ST 70427
Sue Fortenberry, prin.
Denhamtown ES, 1101 AVENUE M 70427
Bertha Breland, prin.
Long Avenue MS, 1100 LONG AVE 70427
Willie Belle Harry, prin.
Northside ES, 517 MISSISSIPPI AVE 70427
Velma Moses, prin.
Pleasant Hill MS, 725 AVENUE C 70427
Theresa Keller, prin.
Superior Avenue ES, 625 SUPERIOR AVE 70427
Wannette Vaughn, prin.
Terrace MS, 510 DERBIGNEY ST 70427
Acy Hartfield, prin.

Annunciation Catholic School
511 AVENUE C 70427

Bonita, Morehouse Parish, Pop. Code 3
Morehouse Parish SD
Supt. – See Bastrop
ES, P O BOX 148 71223 – Dale Bishop, prin.

Bossier City, Bossier Parish, Pop. Code 8
Bossier Parish SD
Supt. – See Benton
Cope JHS, 4814 SHED ROAD 71111
Timothy Gilbert, prin.
Greenacres JHS, 2300 AIRLINE DRIVE 71111
D. Machen, prin.
Rusheon JHS, 2401 OLD MINDEN ROAD 71112
Wayne Earp, prin.
Apollo ES, 2400 VIKING DRIVE 71111
John Castore, prin.
Bellaire ES, 1310 BELLAIRE BLVD 71112
Jerry Fowler, prin.
Bossier ES, 322 COLLQUITT ST 71111
Bunny Langston, prin.

Butler MS, 541 DETROIT ST 71111
LeMuel Marshall, prin.
Central Park ES, CENTRAL PARK BLVD 71112
Darlene Pace, prin.
Curtis MS, RURAL ROUTE 01 BOX 414 71112
Sue Merritt, prin.
Kerr ES, 1700 AIRLINE DRIVE 71111
Susan Kirkland, prin.
Meadowview ES, 4312 SHED ROAD 71111
Patsy Rhodes, prin.
Plantation Park ES
2410 PLANTATION DRIVE 71111
Martha Christy, prin.
Stockwell Place ES, 5800 SHED ROAD 71111
Raymond Polson, prin.
Sun City ES, 4230 VAN DEEMAN ST 71112
Michael Russell, prin.
Waller ES, 1130 PATRICIA DRIVE 71112
Mary Lynn Owens, prin.

Christ the King Catholic School
1000 OGILVIE ST 71111

Bourg, Terrebone Parish, Pop. Code 3
Terrebonne Parish SD
Supt. – See Houma
ES, P O BOX 2165 70343 – Earl Bauddin, prin.

Boyce, Rapides Parish, Pop. Code 4
Rapides Parish SD
Supt. – See Alexandria
Northwood ES, P O BOX 66 71409
Walter Jones, prin.
ES, P O BOX 310 71409 – Walter Jones, prin.

Braithwaite, Plaquemines Parish

Lynn Oaks School, 1 LYNN OAKS DRIVE 70040
Promised Land Academy
RURAL ROUTE 01 BOX 109 70040

Branch, Acadia Parish
Acadia Parish SD
Supt. – See Crowley
ES, P O BOX 428 70516 – Dean Daigle, prin.

Breaux Bridge, St. Martin Parish, Pop. Code 6
St. Martin Parish SD
Supt. – See Saint Martinville
JHS, MAIN & MARTIN 70517 – John Beazley, prin.
MS, 702 W BRIDGE ST 70517 – Alvin Jones, prin.
PS, SAINT CHARLES ST 70517
Glenn Breaux, prin.
Teche MS, RURAL ROUTE 04 BOX 220 70517
Lulla Wiltz, prin.

St. Bernard Catholic School
251 E BRIDGE ST 70517

Broussard, Lafayette Parish, Pop. Code 5
Lafayette Parish SD
Supt. – See Lafayette
MS, 1325 S MORGAN AVE 70518
Gale Gates, prin.
Drexel ES, 409 SAINT JULIEN ST 70518
Sylvia Hudson, prin.

St. Cecilia Catholic School, P O BOX 706 70518

Brusly, West Baton Rouge Parish, Pop. Code 4
West Baton Rouge Parish SD
Supt. – See Port Allen
MS, 601 N KIRKLAND ST 70719
Jerry Lowe, prin.
Lukeville ES, P O BOX 218 70719
Melba Honey, prin.

Buckeye, Rapides Parish
Rapides Parish SD
Supt. – See Alexandria
Buckeye ES, GENERAL DELIVERY 71321
Murphy Belgard,Jr., prin.

Bunkie, Avoyelles Parish, Pop. Code 6
Avoyelles Parish SD
Supt. – See Marksville
MS, P O BOX 470 71322 – Leon Holts, prin.
ES, P O BOX 711 71322 – Lynn Fogleman, prin.

St. Anthony Catholic School
116 S KNOLL AVE 71322

Buras, Plaquemines Parish, Pop. Code 4
Plaquemines Parish SD
Supt. – See Belle Chasse
S, 700 HIGHWAY 23 S 70041
Stanley Gaudet, prin.
Buras MS, 3333 HWY 11 N 70041
Carmen Ingraham, prin.

Bush, St. Tammany Parish
St. Tammany Parish SD
Supt. – See Covington
Fifth Ward ES, HWY 21 70431 – Bruce Davis, prin.

Calhoun, Ouachita Parish, Pop. Code 2
Ouachita Parish SD
Supt. – See Monroe
Calhoun MS, P O BOX 30 71225
J. P. Mobley, prin.
Central ES, P O BOX 100 71225
Andy Jackson, prin.

Calvin, Winn Parish, Pop. Code 2
Winn Parish SD
Supt. – See Winnfield
S, P O BOX 80 71410 – Lanis Carpenter, prin.

Cameron, Cameron Parish, Pop. Code 3
Cameron Parish SD
Sch. Sys. Enr. Code 4
Supt. – Thomas McCall, P O BOX W   70631
Johnson Bayou S, JB ROUTE BOX 232   70631
  Howard Romero, prin.
ES, P O BOX 609   70631
  Clarence Vidrine,Jr., prin.
Other Schools – See Creole, Grand Chenier,
  Hackberry, Lake Charles

Campti, Natchitoches Parish, Pop. Code 4
Natchitoches Parish SD
Supt. – See Natchitoches
JHS, P O BOX 407   71411 – Samuel Jackson, prin.

Carencro, Lafayette Parish, Pop. Code 5
Lafayette Parish SD
Supt. – See Lafayette
MS, 4301 SAINT JOSEPH ST   70520
  William Butcher, prin.
Carencro Heights ES, 601 FARMER ROAD   70520
  Jane Miller, prin.

Carencro Catholic School
  200 W SAINT PETERS ST   70520

Carlisle, Plaquemines Parish
Plaquemines Parish SD
Supt. – See Belle Chasse
Phoenix S   70042 – John Barthelemy, prin.

Castor, Bienville Parish, Pop. Code 2
Bienville Parish SD
Supt. – See Arcadia
S, HWY 153   71016 – Laura Bell, prin.

Cecilia, St. Martin Parish, Pop. Code 3
St. Martin Parish SD
Supt. – See Saint Martinville
JHS, P O BOX 129   70521 – Antoine Kidder, prin.
PS, P O BOX 97   70521 – Charlene LeBlanc, prin.

Centerville, St. Mary Parish, Pop. Code 2
St. Mary Parish SD
Sch. Sys. Enr. Code 7
Supt. – Ronald Perry, P O BOX 170   70522
S, P O BOX 59   70521 – Robert McDonald, prin.
Other Schools – See Amelia, Baldwin, Berwick,
  Charenton, Franklin, Morgan City, Patterson

Chalmette, St. Bernard Parish, Pop. Code 7
St. Bernard Parish SD
Sch. Sys. Enr. Code 6
Supt. – Dr. Daniel Daste
  75 E CHALMETTE CIRCLE   70043
MS, 76 W CHALMETTE CIRCLE   70043
  Sam Boyd, prin.
LaCoste ES, 1101 E JUDGE PEREZ DR   70043
  Gwendolyn Guillory, prin.
Meraux ES, 200 E SAINT BERNARD HWY   70043
  Nora Harold, prin.
Rowley PS, 49 MADISON AVE   70043
  Dr. Elizabeth Lane, prin.
Other Schools – See Arabi, Meraux, Saint Bernard,
  Violet

Chalmette Christian Academy
  209 MAGNOLIA ST   70043
Our Lady of Prompt Succor School
  2305 FENELON ST   70043
St. Mark Catholic ES, 1625 MISSOURI ST   70043

Charenton, St. Mary Parish, Pop. Code 3
St. Mary Parish SD
Supt. – See Centerville
Hines ES, P O BOX 368   70523
  John Richard, prin.

Chataignier, Evangeline Parish, Pop. Code 2
Evangeline Parish SD
Supt. – See Ville Platte
Carver ES, P O BOX 219   70524
  Herman Malveaux, prin.

Chatham, Jackson Parish, Pop. Code 3
Jackson Parish SD
Supt. – See Jonesboro
Henderson ES
  RURAL ROUTE 01 BOX 153   71226
  Cleo Anders, prin.

Chauvin, Terrebonne Parish, Pop. Code 5
Terrebonne Parish SD
Supt. – See Houma
MS, RURAL ROUTE 01 BOX 331   70344
  Mark Trosclair, prin.
Boudreaux Canal ES, HCR BOX 360-BB   70344
  Robert Rankin, prin.
Little Caillou MS, HCR BOX 76A   70344
  Robert Rankin, prin.
Upper Little Caillou ES
  RURAL ROUTE 01 BOX 165   70344
  Edward Richard,Jr., prin.

Choudrant, Lincoln Parish, Pop. Code 3
Lincoln Parish SD
Supt. – See Ruston
S, P O BOX 220   71227 – Ronald Crawford, prin.

Church Point, Acadia Parish, Pop. Code 5
Acadia Parish SD
Supt. – See Crowley
MS, 340 W BRISCOE ROAD   70525
  Katherine Mouille', prin.
ES, 415 E LOUGARRE ST   70525
  Ronald Doguet, prin.

Richard ES, RURAL ROUTE 04 BOX 415   70525
  Sandra Doguet, prin.

Our Mother of Peace School
  218 N ROGERS ST   70525

Clinton, East Feliciana Parish, Pop. Code 4
East Feliciana Parish SD
Sch. Sys. Enr. Code 5
Supt. – Graydon Walker, P O BOX 397   70722
MS, RURAL ROUTE 02 BOX 12   70722
  James Sensley, prin.
Clinton ES, P O BOX 366   70722
  Beulah Robertson, prin.
Other Schools – See Jackson, Slaughter

Silliman Institute, P O BOX 946   70722

Cloutierville, Natchitoches Parish, Pop. Code 2
Natchitoches Parish SD
Supt. – See Natchitoches
Springhill ES, RURAL ROUTE 01 BOX 261   71416
  Dewey Page, prin.

Colfax, Grant Parish, Pop. Code 4
Grant Parish SD
Sch. Sys. Enr. Code 5
Supt. – Jack Smith, P O BOX 208   71417
ES, 301 3RD ST   71417 – Charles Simmons, prin.
Other Schools – See Dry Prong, Georgetown,
  Montgomery, Pollock, Verda

Collinston, Morehouse Parish, Pop. Code 2
Morehouse Parish SD
Supt. – See Bastrop
ES, P O BOX D   71229 – Jamie Jones, prin.

Columbia, Caldwell Parish, Pop. Code 3
Caldwell Parish SD
Sch. Sys. Enr. Code 4
Supt. – James Turner, P O BOX 1019   71418
Caldwell Parish JHS, RURAL ROUTE 02   71418
  Leon Basco, prin.
Central ES, P O BOX 868   71418
  Valda Parker, prin.
ES, P O BOX 248   71418 – Jerry Richardson, prin.
Other Schools – See Grayson, Kelly

Convent, St. James Parish
St. James Parish SD
Supt. – See Lutcher
Romeville ES, RURAL ROUTE 01 BOX 93   70723
  Janie Henderson, prin.

Converse, Sabine Parish, Pop. Code 2
Sabine Parish SD
Supt. – See Many
S, P O BOX 120   71419 – Norman Beason, prin.

Cottonport, Avoyelles Parish, Pop. Code 4
Avoyelles Parish SD
Supt. – See Marksville
ES, P O BOX 427   71327
  Roosevelt Joshua,Jr., prin.

St. Mary's Catholic School, P O BOX 309   71327

Coushatta, Red River Parish, Pop. Code 4
Natchitoches Parish SD
Supt. – See Natchitoches
Fairview-Alpha ES
  RURAL ROUTE 03 BOX 242   71019
  Janie Adams, prin.

Red River Parish SD
Sch. Sys. Enr. Code 4
Supt. – Maxie Kitchings, P O BOX 350   71019
Martin ES, RURAL ROUTE 02 BOX 2340   71019
  Ronnie Monroe, prin.
Springville JHS, P O BOX 466   71019
  Luther Myers, prin.
ES, P O BOX 668   71019 – Susan Taylor, prin.
Other Schools – See Hall Summit

Riverdale Academy
  RURAL ROUTE 01 BOX 99M   71019

Covington, St. Tammany Parish, Pop. Code 6
St. Tammany Parish SD
Sch. Sys. Enr. Code 8
Supt. – Terry Bankston, P O BOX 940   70434
ES, 325 S JACKSON ST   70433
  William Brady, prin.
Lee Road ES, LEE ROAD   70433
  Frank Sharp, prin.
Lyon ES, 1615 N FLORIDA ST   70433
  Troy Jackson, prin.
Pine View MS, 1115 W 28TH AVE   70433
  Cynthia Russell, prin.
Schoen MS, 300 N JEFFERSON   70433
  Lawton McKee, prin.
Other Schools – See Abita Springs, Bush, Folsom,
  Lacombe, Madisonville, Mandeville, Pearl River,
  Slidell

Northlake Christian School, P O BOX 1566   70434
Christ Episcopal School
  120 N NEW HAMPSHIRE ST   70433
River Forest Academy, P O BOX 1149   70434
St. Peter Catholic School
  228 E TEMPERANCE ST   70433

Creole, Cameron Parish
Cameron Parish SD
Supt. – See Cameron
South Cameron ES, P O BOX 60   70632
  Barry Richard, prin.

Crowley, Acadia Parish, Pop. Code 7
Acadia Parish SD
Sch. Sys. Enr. Code 7
Supt. – Bob Stringer, P O BOX 309   70527
JHS, 401 W NORTHERN AVE   70526
  Roderick Lafosse, prin.
MS, 820 W 15TH ST   70526
  Herschel McDonald,Jr., prin.
Ross ES, 2809 W HUTCHINSON   70526
  John Julian, prin.
South Crowley ES
  1102 S PARKERSON AVE   70526
  Kenneth Hoffpauir, prin.
Other Schools – See Branch, Church Point, Egan,
  Estherwood, Evangeline, Iota, Mermentau, Morse,
  Rayne

Redemptorist Catholic School
  606 S AVENUE NORTH   70526
St. Michael Catholic School
  805 E NORTHERN AVE   70526

Crowville, Franklin Parish
Franklin Parish SD
Supt. – See Winnsboro
S, P O BOX 128   71230 – Shelton Kavalir, prin.

Cut Off, Lafourche Parish, Pop. Code 4
Lafourche Parish SD
Supt. – See Thibodaux
ES, P O BOX 398   70345 – Rudy Guidroz, prin.

Delcambre, Iberia Parish, Pop. Code 4
Iberia Parish SD
Supt. – See New Iberia
ES, 706 W PERSHING ST   70528
  James Campbell, prin.

Delhi, Richland Parish, Pop. Code 5
Richland Parish SD
Supt. – See Rayville
JHS, 107 TOOMBS ST   71232
  Leonard Guine, prin.
PS, 610 MAIN ST   71232 – Milton Linder, prin.

Denham Springs, Livingston Parish, Pop. Code 6
Livingston Parish SD
Supt. – See Livingston
JHS, 340 RANGE AVE NE   70726
  Wade Smith, prin.
Southside JHS, P O BOX 907   70727
  Warren Curtis, prin.
ES, 306 N RANGE AVE   70726 – Earl Britton, prin.
Freshwater ES, 1025 COCKERHAM ROAD   70726
  Ann Carpenter, prin.
Northside ES, P O BOX 1045   70727
  Joie Hooks, prin.
Seventh Ward ES
  RURAL ROUTE 13 BOX 96   70726
  Randy Pope, prin.
Southside ES, 1129 S RANGE AVE   70726
  L. Harris, prin.
Vincent ES, P O BOX 1058   70727
  Patrick Harris, prin.

Abundant Life Christian Academy
  206 EDGEWOOD DR   70726

De Quincy, Calcasieu Parish, Pop. Code 5
Calcasieu Parish SD
Supt. – See Lake Charles
MS, 502 S GRAND AVE   70633
  James Burnham, prin.
ES, 304 MCNEESE ST   70633 – Ross Young, prin.

De Ridder, Beauregard Parish, Pop. Code 7
Beauregard Parish SD
Sch. Sys. Enr. Code 6
Supt. – Dr. F. Gary Brewer, P O BOX 938   70634
East Beauregard S
  RURAL ROUTE 02 BOX 61   70634
  L. Spears, prin.
JHS, 415 N FRUSHA DRIVE   70634
  Hayward Steele, prin.
Carver ES, 211 VERNON ST   70634
  Lee Blount,Jr., prin.
Hanchey ES, 611 N FRUSHA DRIVE   70634
  Nelda Lambert, prin.
Pine Wood MS, DRAGON DRIVE   70634
  Gus Martinez, prin.
Other Schools – See Fields, Longville, Merryville,
  Singer

Des Allemands, St. Charles
St. Charles Parish SD
Supt. – See Luling
ES, P O BOX A   70030 – Rodney Lafon, prin.

Destrehan, St. Charles Parish
St. Charles Parish SD
Supt. – See Luling
Hurst MS, P O BOX X   70047
  Ralph Wilderson, prin.

St. Charles Borromeo School, P O BOX 337   70047

Dodson, Winn Parish, Pop. Code 2
Winn Parish SD
Supt. – See Winnfield
S, P O BOX 97   71422 – Charles Fox, prin.

Donaldsonville, Ascension Parish, Pop. Code 6
Ascension Parish SD
Sch. Sys. Enr. Code 7
Supt. – Ralph Ricardo, P O BOX 189   70346
Lowery MS, P O BOX 311   70346
  Jesse Sanders, prin.

ES, P O BOX 150 70346 – Mary Chauff, prin.
West Ascension ES, P O BOX 493 70346
Trudye LeBlanc, prin.
Other Schools – See Geismar, Gonzales, Prairieville,
Saint Amant

Bayou Lafourche Academy
2199 S MOURET ROAD 70346
Ascension Catholic ES, 618 IBERVILLE ST 70346
Ascension Catholic IS
311 SAINT VINCENT ST 70346

Downsville, Union Parish, Pop. Code 2
Union Parish SD
Supt. – See Farmerville
S, P O BOX 8 71234 – J. Lazenby, prin.

Doyline, Webster Parish, Pop. Code 3
Webster Parish SD
Supt. – See Minden
Union ES, P O BOX 637 71023
Evvie Smith, prin.

Dry Prong, Grant Parish, Pop. Code 3
Grant Parish SD
Supt. – See Colfax
JHS, P O BOX 147 71423 – Jerrell Paige, prin.

Dubach, Lincoln Parish, Pop. Code 4
Lincoln Parish SD
Supt. – See Ruston
Hico ES, RURAL ROUTE 01 BOX 18 71235
James Pilgreen, prin.

Dubberly, Webster Parish, Pop. Code 2
Webster Parish SD
Supt. – See Minden
Central JHS, RURAL ROUTE 01 BOX 660 71024
Halvern Carodine, prin.
ES, P O BOX 18 71024 – Bill Huth, prin.

Duson, Lafayette Parish, Pop. Code 4
Lafayette Parish SD
Supt. – See Lafayette
Judice MS, 2645 S FIELDSPAN ROAD 70529
Robert Adamson, prin.
ES, P O BOX 7 70529 – Carl Dugas, prin.
Ridge ES, 2901 S FIELDSPAN ROAD 70529
Joyce Thomas, prin.

Edgard, St. John The Baptist Parish, Pop. Code 2
St. John The Baptist Parish SD
Supt. – See Reserve
West St. John ES, P O BOX 67 70049
Barbara Falgoust, prin.

Effie, Avoyelles Parish
Avoyelles Parish SD
Supt. – See Marksville
Lafargue ES, HCR 65 BOX 1 71331
Ronald Lemoine, prin.

Egan, Acadia Parish
Acadia Parish SD
Supt. – See Crowley
ES, P O BOX 158 70531 – Dr. Marietta James, prin.

Elizabeth, Allen Parish, Pop. Code 2
Allen Parish SD
Supt. – See Oberlin
S, P O BOX 580 70638 – Larry Crawford, prin.

Elmer, Rapides Parish
Rapides Parish SD
Supt. – See Alexandria
Oak Hill S 71424 – Joseph Rivers, prin.

Elm Grove, Bossier Parish, Pop. Code 2
Bossier Parish SD
Supt. – See Benton
JHS, P O BOX 108 71051 – Kenneth Kruithof, prin.

Elton, Jefferson Davis Parish, Pop. Code 4
Jefferson Davis Parish SD
Supt. – See Jennings
JHS, P O BOX 430 70532 – Raymond Segura, prin.

Enterprise, Catahoula Parish
Catahoula Parish SD
Supt. – See Jonesville
S, P O BOX 100 71425 – John Bartmess, prin.

Epps, West Carroll Parish, Pop. Code 3
West Carroll Parish SD
Supt. – See Oak Grove
S, P O BOX 277 71237 – Donald Gwin, prin.

Erath, Vermilion Parish, Pop. Code 4
Vermilion Parish SD
Supt. – See Abbeville
Henry S, RURAL ROUTE 01 BOX 182 70533
Joseph Hebert, prin.
MS, 808 S BROADWAY ST 70533
Donald Primeaux, prin.
Dozier ES, 415 W PRIMEAUX ST 70533
Teddy Broussard, prin.

Estherwood, Acadia Parish, Pop. Code 3
Acadia Parish SD
Supt. – See Crowley
ES, GENERAL DELIVERY 70534
Carl Lejeune, prin.

Eunice, St. Landry Parish, Pop. Code 7
St. Landry Parish SD
Supt. – See Opelousas
Central MS, P O BOX 987 70535
Gerald Hardy, prin.

East ES, 550 MATHILDA AVE 70535
George Soileau,Jr., prin.
ES, 451 S 9TH ST 70535 – William Gil, prin.
Glendale ES, 900 W DEAN AVE 70535
Eugenia Veillon, prin.
Highland ES, 1341 DUCK AVE 70535
Claude Moody,Jr., prin.

St. Edmunt School, 331 N 3RD ST 70535

Evangeline, Acadia Parish, Pop. Code 2
Acadia Parish SD
Supt. – See Crowley
ES 70537 – Milton Simar, prin.

Evans, Vernon Parish, Pop. Code 2
Vernon Parish SD
Supt. – See Leesville
S, P O BOX 67 70639 – Richard Schwartz, prin.

Farmerville, Union Parish, Pop. Code 5
Union Parish SD
Sch. Sys. Enr. Code 5
Supt. – Malvin Sistrunk, P O BOX 308 71241
MS, RURAL ROUTE 03 BOX 269 71241
Stephen Richardson, prin.
ES, 606 BERNICE ST 71241
Vivanae Daniels, prin.
Rocky Branch ES
RURAL ROUTE 02 BOX 314 71241
Patsy Terral, prin.
Other Schools – See Downsville, Lillie, Marion

Fenton, Jefferson Davis Parish, Pop. Code 2
Jefferson Davis Parish SD
Supt. – See Jennings
S, P O BOX 805 70640 – Alton Bass, prin.

Ferriday, Concordia Parish, Pop. Code 5
Concordia Parish SD
Supt. – See Vidalia
JHS, P O BOX 672 71334 – Mack Moore, prin.
Ferriday Lower ES, P O BOX 232 71334
Richard Alwood, prin.
Ferriday Upper MS, P O BOX 8 71334
Eddie Washington, prin.

Huntington School, 300 LYNWOOD ST 71334

Fields, Beauregard Parish
Beauregard Parish SD
Supt. – See De Ridder
Hyatt S 70641 – Maxine Eaves, prin.

Florien, Sabine Parish, Pop. Code 3
Sabine Parish SD
Supt. – See Many
ES, P O BOX 8 71429 – James Miller, prin.

Folsom, St. Tammany Parish, Pop. Code 2
St. Tammany Parish SD
Supt. – See Covington
ES, P O BOX D 70437 – Elwood Loyd, prin.

Forest, West Carroll Parish, Pop. Code 2
West Carroll Parish SD
Supt. – See Oak Grove
S, P O BOX 368 71242 – Larry Denmon, prin.

Forest Hill, Rapides Parish, Pop. Code 2
Rapides Parish SD
Supt. – See Alexandria
ES, P O BOX 10 71430 – Bonnie Lee, prin.

Forest Hill Academy, BLUE LAKE ROAD 71430

Fort Necessity, Franklin Parish
Franklin Parish SD
Supt. – See Winnsboro
S, HCR 62 BOX 1 71243 – Leo Thornhill, prin.

Fort Polk, Vernon Parish
Vernon Parish SD
Supt. – See Leesville
Polk ES, ENTRANCE ROAD 71459
Betty Morgan, prin.

Franklin, St. Mary Parish, Pop. Code 6
St. Mary Parish SD
Supt. – See Centerville
JHS, 525 MORRIS ST 70538
Gordon Casselman, prin.
Foster ES, 101 2ND ST 70538
Glenda Comeaux, prin.
Gibbs ES, HCR B BOX 198 70538
Janis Jones, prin.
Glencoe ES, HCR B BOX 224 70538
Murphy Pontiff, prin.
LaGrange MS
RURAL ROUTE 01 BOX 192 B 70538
Murphy Armelin, prin.
Willow Street ES, 1400 WILLOW ST 70538
Gary Snellgrove, prin.

St. John Catholic ES, 924 MAIN ST 70538

Franklinton, Washington Parish, Pop. Code 5
Washington Parish SD
Sch. Sys. Enr. Code 6
Supt. – Earle Brown, P O BOX 587 70438
JHS, 617 MAIN ST 70438 – Edward Logan, prin.
Enon ES, RURAL ROUTE 07 BOX 147 70438
Linda Crain, prin.
MS, 902 CLEVELAND ST 70438
Karen Spears, prin.
PS, 601 T W BARKER DR 70438
Eathel Lawson, prin.

Thomas ES, RURAL ROUTE 05 BOX 231 70438
Russell Jackson, prin.
Other Schools – See Angie, Mount Hermon

Bowling Green School, 700 VARRADO 70438

French Settlement, Livingston Parish, Pop. Code 3
Livingston Parish SD
Supt. – See Livingston
ES, 15810 LA HWY 16 70733
Geraldine Sziber, prin.

Galliano, Lafourche Parish, Pop. Code 4
Lafourche Parish SD
Supt. – See Thibodaux
ES, P O BOX 398 70354 – Alfred Lefort, prin.

Garyville, St. John The Baptist Parish, Pop. Code 4
St. John The Baptist Parish SD
Supt. – See Reserve
ES, P O BOX R 70051 – Hilton Mitchell,Jr., prin.
Sixth Ward MS, P O BOX M 70051
Herbert Smith, prin.

Geismar, Ascension Parish
Ascension Parish SD
Supt. – See Donaldsonville
Dutchtown ES
RURAL ROUTE 02 BOX 226 70734
Donald Songy, prin.

Georgetown, Grant Parish, Pop. Code 2
Grant Parish SD
Supt. – See Colfax
S, P O BOX 66 71432 – Tommy Brumley, prin.

Gibsland, Bienville Parish, Pop. Code 4
Bienville Parish SD
Supt. – See Arcadia
Gibsland-Coleman S, P O BOX 278 71028
John Thomas, prin.

Gibson, Terrebonne Parish
Terrebonne Parish SD
Supt. – See Houma
ES, P O BOX 880 70356 – Leslie Brunet, prin.
Greenwood MS
RURAL ROUTE 01 BOX 46 70356
Mack Terrebonne, prin.

Gilbert, Franklin Parish, Pop. Code 3
Franklin Parish SD
Supt. – See Winnsboro
S, P O BOX 900 71336 – Gary Barton, prin.

Glenmora, Rapides Parish, Pop. Code 4
Rapides Parish SD
Supt. – See Alexandria
Plainview S, P O BOX 1057 71433
J. Johnson, prin.
ES, P O BOX 1168 71433 – Don Grant, prin.

Golden Meadow, Lafourche Parish, Pop. Code 4
Lafourche Parish SD
Supt. – See Thibodaux
Golden Meadow Lower ES
2617 ALCIDE ST 70357 – Roland Cheramie, prin.
MS, 2201 N 3RD ST 70357
Curtis Boudreaux, prin.

Goldonna, Natchitoches Parish, Pop. Code 3
Natchitoches Parish SD
Supt. – See Natchitoches
ES, P O BOX 231 71031 – Samuel Perkins, prin.

Gonzales, Ascension Parish, Pop. Code 6
Ascension Parish SD
Supt. – See Donaldsonville
MS, 1502 W ORICE ROTH ST 70737
Willie Cushenberry, prin.
Carver PS, 518 W OAK ST 70737
Rosa Jackson, prin.
PS, 521 N BURNSIDE AVE 70737
Frank Bourgeois, prin.

St. Theresa of Avila School
212 E NEW RIVER ST 70737

Grambling, Lincoln Parish, Pop. Code 5
Lincoln Parish SD
Supt. – See Ruston
Grambling State University MS
407 CENTRAL 71245 – Dr. Leroy Simmons, prin.
Brown ES, 300 RALPH JONES DR 71245
A. Butler, prin.

Gramercy, St. James Parish, Pop. Code 5
St. James Parish SD
Supt. – See Lutcher
ES, P O BOX 70052 – Carol Bourgeois, prin.

Grand Cane, De Soto Parish, Pop. Code 2

Central School Corporation, P O BOX 71 71032

Grand Chenier, Cameron Parish, Pop. Code 4
Cameron Parish SD
Supt. – See Cameron
ES, RURAL ROUTE 01 70643
Benjamin Welch, prin.

Grand Coteau, St. Landry Parish, Pop. Code 4
St. Landry Parish SD
Supt. – See Opelousas
ES, P O BOX K 70541 – John Bobb,Jr., prin.

Academy of the Sacred Heart, P O BOX 310 70541
St. Ignatius Catholic School, P O BOX J 70541

Grand Isle, Jefferson Parish, Pop. Code 4
Jefferson Parish SD
Supt. – See Harvey
S, P O BOX 995   70358 – Ernie Knoblock, prin.

Grant, Allen Parish
Allen Parish SD
Supt. – See Oberlin
Fairview S, P O BOX 91 70644
   Charles Nevils, prin.

Grayson, Caldwell Parish, Pop. Code 3
Caldwell Parish SD
Supt. – See Columbia
ES, P O BOX 238 71435 – Loleta May, prin.

Greensburg, St. Helena Parish, Pop. Code 3
St. Helena Parish SD
Sch. Sys. Enr. Code 4
Supt. – Perry Spears, P O BOX 540 70441
St. Helena MS, RURAL ROUTE 02 BOX 31 70441
   Myrtie Wofford, prin.
PS, P O BOX 490 70441 – Malcolm Mizell, prin.
Other Schools – See Amite, Kentwood, Pine Grove

Greenwell Springs, East Baton Rouge Parish
East Baton Rouge Parish SD
Supt. – See Baton Rouge
Bellingrath Hills ES, RURAL ROUTE 01 70739
   Charles Wilkins, prin.

St. Alphonsus Cath School
   13940 GREENWELL SPRINGS RD 70739

Gretna, Jefferson Parish, Pop. Code 7
Jefferson Parish SD
Supt. – See Harvey
Boudreaux ES, 950 BEHRMAN HWY 70056
   Mary Ehret, prin.
Congetta Trippe ES
   2630 BELLE CHASSE HWY 70056
   Carol Braun, prin.
Cox ES, 2630 BELLE CHASSE HWY 70056
   D. Robichaux III, prin.
Douglass ES, 1400 HUEY P LONG AVE 70053
   Jesse Brasset,Jr., prin.
Hart ES, 2001 HANCOCK ST 70053
   Joan Weinberg, prin.
Johnson/Gretna Park ES
   1130 GRETNA BLVD 70053
   Betty Simmons, prin.
McDonogh #26 ES, 1200 JEFFERSON ST 70053
   Jeanine M. Chance, prin.
Solis ES, 2850 MOUNT LAUREL DR 70056
   Virginia Gaudet, prin.
Terrytown ES, 550 E FOREST LAWN DR 70056
   Pat Mendozza, prin.

Christ the King Catholic School
   2106 DEERFIELD ROAD 70056
Salem Lutheran School, 418 4TH ST 70053
St. Anthony Catholic School
   900 FRANKLIN AVE 70053
St. Cletus Catholic School
   3610 CLAIRE AVE 70053
St. Joseph Catholic School, 600 7TH ST 70053

Gueydan, Vermilion Parish, Pop. Code 4
Vermilion Parish SD
Supt. – See Abbeville
Owens ES, 203 13TH ST 70542
   Ned Robinson,Jr., prin.

St. Peter ES, 513 SIXTH ST 70510

Hackberry, Cameron Parish, Pop. Code 3
Cameron Parish SD
Supt. – See Cameron
S, MRH BOX 78 70645 – Pamela LaFleur, prin.

Hahnville, St. Charles Parish, Pop. Code 4
St. Charles Parish SD
Supt. – See Luling
Landry MS, RURAL ROUTE 01 BOX 108 70057
   William Picard, prin.
Carver MS, P O BOX 331 70057
   Joyce August, prin.

Hall Summit, Red River Parish, Pop. Code 2
Red River Parish SD
Supt. – See Coushatta
S, P O BOX 68 71034 – Charles Womack, prin.

Hammond, Tangipahoa Parish, Pop. Code 7
Tangipahoa Parish SD
Supt. – See Amite
JHS, 111 JACKSON ROAD 70401
   Edward Dillon, prin.
Hammond Eastside PS, 160 RIVER RD 70401
   Pat Heleniak, prin.
Hammond Eastside Upper ES
   158 RIVER ROAD 70401
   Burnadean Warren, prin.
Hammond Westside PS
   902 COLUMBUS DR 70401 – Linda Abels, prin.
Hammond Westside Upper ES
   902 COLUMBUS DR 70401 – Louis Joseph, prin.
Southeastern Louisiana University Lab ES
   P O BOX 832 70404 – Dr. Ray Humphrey, prin.

Holy Ghost Catholic School
   506 N MAGNOLIA ST 70401
Trafton Academy,Inc., P O BOX 2845 70404

Harahan, Jefferson Parish, Pop. Code 7
Jefferson Parish SD
Supt. – See Harvey

ES, 6723 JEFFERSON HWY 70123
   Pamela Edwards, prin.
Hazel Park/Knoff ES
   8809 JEFFERSON HWY 70123 – Jewel Lorio, prin.

St. Rita Catholic School, 194 RAVAN AVE 70123

Harrisonburg, Catahoula Parish, Pop. Code 3
Catahoula Parish SD
Supt. – See Jonesville
ES, GENERAL DELIVERY 71340
   Howard Cater, prin.

Harvey, Jefferson Parish, Pop. Code 6
Jefferson Parish SD
Sch. Sys. Enr. Code 8
Supt. – Dr. Russell Protti
   501 MANHATTAN BLVD 70058
Elm Grove ES, 1121 PAILET AVE 70058
   Prince Washington, prin.
Homedale ES, 500 MAPLE AVE 70058
   Phyllis Breaux, prin.
Pittman ES, 3800 13TH ST 70058
   Barbara Doles, prin.
Woodland West ES, 2143 MARS ST 70058
   Richard Ansson, prin.
Woodmere ES, 3720 DESTREHAN AVE 70058
   Joy Gregory, prin.
Other Schools – See Grand Isle, Gretna, Harahan,
   Jefferson, Kenner, Lafitte, Marrero, Metairie,
   Waggaman, Westwego

St. Rosalie Catholic School, 617 2ND AVE 70058

Haughton, Bossier Parish, Pop. Code 4
Bossier Parish SD
Supt. – See Benton
Platt MS, RURAL ROUTE 04 BOX 425 71037
   Henry Meachum, prin.
Rodes ES, RURAL ROUTE 04 BOX 425A 71037
   Roland Champagne,Jr., prin.

Haynesville, Claiborne Parish, Pop. Code 5
Claiborne Parish SD
Supt. – See Homer
JHS, 1000 FIRST ST E 71038
   Keith Alexander, prin.
ES, 500 FIRST EAST SOUTH ST 71038
   Betty Waldron, prin.

Claiborne Academy
   RURAL ROUTE 03 BOX 174 71038

Heflin, Webster Parish, Pop. Code 2
Webster Parish SD
Supt. – See Minden
ES, RURAL ROUTE 01 BOX 15 71039
   Van Gardner, prin.

Hicks, Vernon Parish
Vernon Parish SD
Supt. – See Leesville
S, GENERAL DELIVERY 71437
   Dale Hardwick, prin.

Hodge, Jackson Parish, Pop. Code 3
Jackson Parish SD
Supt. – See Jonesboro
MS, P O BOX 70 71247 – Mary Burnum, prin.
Union ES, P O BOX 580 71247
   William Decou, prin.

Holden, Livingston Parish
Livingston Parish SD
Supt. – See Livingston
S, GENERAL DELIVERY 70744
   Jeanette Fekete, prin.

Holly Ridge, Richland Parish, Pop. Code 1
Richland Parish SD
Supt. – See Rayville
ES, RURAL ROUTE 04 71248
   Doyle Hammons, prin.

Homer, Claiborne Parish, Pop. Code 5
Claiborne Parish SD
Sch. Sys. Enr. Code 5
Supt. – James Scriber, P O BOX 600 71040
JHS, 1009 PEARL ST 71040 – Cullen Jackson, prin.
ES, BONNER ST 71040 – Willadean Bless, prin.
Other Schools – See Athens, Haynesville, Lisbon,
   Summerfield

Hornbeck, Vernon Parish, Pop. Code 2
Vernon Parish SD
Supt. – See Leesville
S, P O BOX 9 71439 – Dempsey Haymon, prin.

Hosston, Caddo Parish, Pop. Code 2
Caddo Parish SD
Supt. – See Shreveport
ES, P O BOX 188 71043 – Roland Mason, prin.

Houma, Terrebonne Parish, Pop. Code 8
Lafourche Parish SD
Supt. – See Thibodaux
Bayou Blue ES, 1916 BAYOU BLUE RD 70364
   Alvin Hebert, prin.

Terrebonne Parish SD
Sch. Sys. Enr. Code 7
Supt. – Paul Fournier, P O BOX 5097 70361
Grand Caillou MS
   4077 GRAND CAILLOU ROAD 70363
   Danny Smith, prin.
Acadian ES, 1020 SAADI ST 70363
   Ulyse Louviere, prin.

Bayou Black ES, 4449 BAYOU BLACK DR 70360
   Betty Peltier, prin.
Broadmoor ES, 1010 BROADMOOR AVE 70364
   Robert George, prin.
Coteau-Bayou Blue ES
   2550 COTEAU ROAD 70364
   Malcolm DuPlantis, prin.
East Houma ES, 222 CONNELY ST 70363
   Charles Cherry, prin.
Elysian Fields MS, 700 HIBERNIA PLACE 70363
   Willard Guidry, prin.
Grand Caillou ES
   5141 GRAND CAILLOU ROAD 70363
   Danny Smith, prin.
Honduras ES, 810 GRAND CAILLOU ROAD 70363
   Eulice Sparks, prin.
Legion Park MS, 710 WILLIAMS AVE 70364
   Merle Hinchee, prin.
Lisa Park ES, 1900 WILLIE LOU AVE 70364
   Myron Chauvin, prin.
Mulberry ES
   450 OLD BAYOU DULARGE ROAD 70360
   Henry Babin,Jr., prin.
Oakshire ES, 3620 VICARI ST 70364
   Joy Broussard, prin.
Southdown ES, 400 SAINT CHARLES ST 70360
   Eual Phillips, prin.
Village East MS, 315 VILLAGE EAST BLVD 70363
   James Hutchinson, prin.
West Park ES, 155 WEST PARK AVE 70364
   Albert Martin, prin.
Other Schools – See Bourg, Chauvin, Gibson,
   Montegut, Schriever, Theriot

Maria Immocolata Catholic School
   324 ESTATE DR 70364
St. Bernadette Catholic School
   309 FUNDERBURK AVE 70364
St. Francis De Sales School, P O BOX 8034 70361
St. Gregory Barbarigo School, 441 6TH ST 70364
St. Matthews Episcopal School
   725 BELANGER ST 70360

Independence, Tangipahoa Parish, Pop. Code 4
Tangipahoa Parish SD
Supt. – See Amite
MS, P O BOX 97 70443 – Carol Knight, prin.
ES, P O BOX 190 70443 – Katie Simms, prin.

Mater Dolorosa Catholic School
   P O BOX 380 70443

Innis, Pointe Coupee Parish
Point Coupee Parish SD
Supt. – See New Roads
Upper Pointe Coupee ES, P O BOX 858 70747
   Virginia Monk, prin.

Iota, Acadia Parish, Pop. Code 4
Acadia Parish SD
Supt. – See Crowley
ES, P O BOX 910 70543 – Donald Amy, prin.

St. Francis Catholic School, P O BOX 870 70543

Iowa, Calcasieu Parish, Pop. Code 4
Calcasieu Parish SD
Supt. – See Lake Charles
Watson ES, P O BOX 687 70647
   Robert Monk, prin.

Jackson, East Feliciana Parish, Pop. Code 5
East Feliciana Parish SD
Supt. – See Clinton
MS, RURAL ROUTE 01 BOX 5560 70748
   Hattie Reed, prin.
ES, P O BOX 338 70748 – Shirley Cupit, prin.

Jeanerette, Iberia Parish, Pop. Code 6
Iberia Parish SD
Supt. – See New Iberia
MS, 694 PELLERIN ST 70544 – W. Viator, prin.
Canal Street PS, 800 CANAL ST 70544
   Gail Viator, prin.
Grand Marais ES
   RURAL ROUTE 01 BOX 163 70544
   Anita Wiseman, prin.
ES, 600 IRA ST 70544 – Hammond Johnson, prin.
Saint Charles Street ES
   1927 ST CHARLES ST 70544
   Michael Mouhot, prin.

St. Joseph School
   5207 OLD JEANERETTE RD 70544

Jefferson, Jefferson Parish, Pop. Code 7
Jefferson Parish SD
Supt. – See Harvey
ES, 375 VINET ST 70181 – Carolyn Sanders, prin.

St. Agnes Catholic School
   3410 JEFFERSON HWY 70121

Jena, La Salle Parish, Pop. Code 4
LaSalle Parish SD
Sch. Sys. Enr. Code 5
Supt. – Robert Coleman, P O BOX 90 71342
JHS, P O BOX 920 71342 – A. Kip Wall, prin.
Goodpine MS, RURAL ROUTE 01 BOX 496 71342
   Earl Brooks, prin.
ES, P O BOX 880 71342 – Mary Lou Welch, prin.
Nebo ES, HCR 60 BOX 192 71342
   Jim Deloach, prin.
Other Schools – See Olla, Trout, Tullos, Urania

Jennings, Jefferson Davis Parish, Pop. Code 7
Jefferson Davis Parish SD
Sch. Sys. Enr. Code 6
Supt. – W. Whitford, P O BOX 640 70546
Hathaway S, RURAL ROUTE 01 BOX 500 70546
  Carl Langley, prin.
Northside JHS, 208 SHANKLAND AVE 70546
  John Adams, prin.
Ward ES, P O BOX 1189 70546
  Robert Vincent, prin.
West End MS, 802 W JEFFERSON ST 70546
  Jimmy Spears, prin.
Other Schools – See Elton, Fenton, Lacassine, Lake
  Arthur, Roanoke, Welsh

Our Lady Immaculate School
  600 ROBERTS AVE 70546

Jonesboro, Jackson Parish, Pop. Code 6
Jackson Parish SD
Sch. Sys. Enr. Code 5
Supt. – John Tollett, P O BOX 705 71251
Weston S, RURAL ROUTE 01 71251
  James Staples, prin.
Jonesboro-Hodge JHS, 401 WAKER ROAD 71251
  Richard Tew, prin.
Southside ES, 2105 S POLK AVE 71251
  Dorothy Dorsey, prin.
Other Schools – See Chatham, Hodge, Quitman

Jonesville, Catahoula Parish, Pop. Code 5
Catahoula Parish SD
Sch. Sys. Enr. Code 5
Supt. – L. Keith Guice, P O BOX 308 71343
Central S, RURAL ROUTE B 71343
  Robert Smith, prin.
ES, 1219 CORA DR 71343 – Charlie Sanson, prin.
JHS, 802 STATE ST 71343 – Roy Mazique, prin.
Manifest ES, RURAL ROUTE 02 BOX 90 71343
  Ronald Lofton, prin.
Other Schools – See Enterprise, Harrisonburg, Sicily
  Island

Kaplan, Vermilion Parish, Pop. Code 6
Vermilion Parish SD
Supt. – See Abbeville
Pecan Island S, P O BOX 41 70548
  Roxwell Prejean, prin.
Rost MS, 112 W 6TH ST 70548
  Ken Broussard, prin.
ES, 608 ELEAZAR AVE 70548
  Rebecca LeMaire, prin.

Maltrait Memorial ES, 612 N HEBERT AVE 70548

Keithville, Caddo Parish, Pop. Code 1
Caddo Parish SD
Supt. – See Shreveport
Keithville ES, 12201 MANSFIELD ROAD 71047
  Mary Bethel, prin.

Grawood Christian School
  10420 GRAWOOD SCHOOL RD 71047

Kelly, Caldwell Parish
Caldwell Parish SD
Supt. – See Columbia
ES, P O BOX 130 71441
  Carolyn McDougald, prin.

Kenner, Jefferson Parish, Pop. Code 8
Jefferson Parish SD
Supt. – See Harvey
Barbre JHS, 1610 3RD ST 70062
  Otis Guichet, prin.
Roosevelt JHS, 3315 MAINE AVE 70065
  Peter Breithoff, prin.
Alexander ES, 600 W ESPLANADE AVE 70065
  Christine Cox, prin.
Audubon ES, 200 W LOYOLA DR 70065
  Marie Carroll, prin.
Chateau Estates ES, 4121 MEDOC DRIVE 70065
  Richard Nelson, prin.
Clancy ES, 8900 21ST ST 70062
  Lucinda Frutos, prin.
Greenlawn Terrace ES, 1500 38TH ST 70065
  Katherine Croft, prin.
Schneckenburger ES, 26 EARNEST AVE 70065
  Evelyn Paternostro, prin.
Washington ES, 606 CLAY ST 70062
  Evangeline Jones, prin.
Woods ES, 1037 31ST ST 70065
  Mamie Gardner, prin.

Our Lady of Perpetual Help School
  530 MINOR ST 70062
St. Elizabeth Ann Seton School
  4119 SAINT ELIZABETH DR 70065

Kentwood, Tangipahoa Parish, Pop. Code 5
St. Helena Parish SD
Supt. – See Greensburg
New Zion ES, RURAL ROUTE 01 BOX 109 70444
  Joseph Coleman, prin.

Tangipahoa Parish SD
Supt. – See Amite
Chesbrough ES
  RURAL ROUTE 04 BOX 577 70444
  Harold Smith, prin.
ES, P O BOX J 70444 – Fochia Wilson, prin.
Spring Creek ES
  RURAL ROUTE 02 BOX 44 70444
  Charles Schwartz, prin.

Kentwood Learning Center, 205 AVENUE A 70444

Kilbourne, West Carroll Parish, Pop. Code 2
West Carroll Parish SD
Supt. – See Oak Grove
S, P O BOX 98 71253 – Truman Smith, prin.

Kinder, Allen Parish, Pop. Code 5
Allen Parish SD
Supt. – See Oberlin
ES, P O BOX 610 70648 – Robert Cronan, prin.

Kraemer, Lafourche Parish, Pop. Code 2
Lafourche Parish SD
Supt. – See Thibodaux
Bayou Boeuf ES, KRAEMER POST OFFICE 70371
  Gerald Long, prin.

Krotz Springs, St. Landry Parish, Pop. Code 4
St. Landry Parish SD
Supt. – See Opelousas
ES, P O BOX 456 70750 – Cathy Soileau, prin.

Labadieville, Assumption Parish, Pop. Code 3
Assumption Parish SD
Supt. – See Napoleonville
MS, P O BOX 127 70372 – Gerald Boudreaux, prin.
PS, RURAL ROUTE 02 BOX 170 70372
  Mildred Sylvester, prin.

St. Philomena Catholic School
  110 CONVENT ST 70372

Labarre, Pointe Coupee Parish
Point Coupee Parish SD
Supt. – See New Roads
LaBarre ES, GENERAL DELIVERY 70751
  Lionel Haynes, prin.

Lacassine, Jefferson Davis Parish
Jefferson Davis Parish SD
Supt. – See Jennings
S, P O BOX E 70650 – John Juneau, prin.

Lacombe, St. Tammany Parish, Pop. Code 4
St. Tammany Parish SD
Supt. – See Covington
Bayou Lacombe JHS, P O BOX 787 70445
  John Slinker, prin.
Chahta-Ina ES, P O BOX 806 70445
  Israel Batiste, prin.

Lafayette, Lafayette Parish, Pop. Code 8
Lafayette Parish SD
Sch. Sys. Enr. Code 8
Supt. – Allen Meyers, P O BOX 2158 70502
Acadian MS, 4201 MOSS ST 70507
  J. Carrol Mouton, prin.
Alleman MS, 600 ROSELAWN BLVD 70503
  J. Harold Hollier, prin.
Breaux MS, 1400 S ORANGE ST 70501
  Elry Pradia, prin.
MS, 1301 W UNIVERSITY AVE 70506
  John Prejean, prin.
Martin MS, 401 BROADMOOR BLVD 70503
  Lester Duhon, prin.
Moss MS, 801 MUDD AVE 70501
  Preston Welcome, prin.
Boucher ES, 400 PATTERSON ST 70501
  Thomas Brown, prin.
Broadmoor ES, 609 BROADMOOR BLVD 70503
  Ellen Ventress, prin.
Evangeline ES
  610 E BUTCHER SWITCH ROAD 70507
  Catherine Andrus, prin.
Faulk ES, 711 E WILLOW ST 70501
  Dorothy Scott, prin.
James ES, 100 POYDRAS ST 70501
  L. Ventroy, prin.
Montgomery ES, 600 FOREMAN DR 70506
  Dina Schmersahl, prin.
Myrtle Place ES, 1100 MYRTLE PL 70506
  Cynthia Vige, prin.
Ossun ES, 400 JOE COMEAUX ROAD 70507
  Simon Stout, prin.
Plantation ES
  1801 KALISTE SALOOM ROAD 70508
  Marcus Denais, prin.
Prairie ES
  2910 AMBASSADOR CAFFERY PKY 70506
  Perry Dubose, prin.
St. Antoine MS, 111 S SAINT ANTOINE ST 70501
  Helen Magee, prin.
Truman ES, 200 CLARA ST 70501
  Edward Sam, prin.
Vermillion ES, 326 CAUTHIER ROAD 70501
  Theresa Davis, prin.
Woodvale ES, LEON DR 70503
  Katherine Landry, prin.
Other Schools – See Broussard, Carencro, Duson,
  Milton, Scott, Youngsville

Ascension Day School
  1030 JOHNSTON ST 70501
Cathedral-Carmel School
  848 SAINT JOHN ST 70501
Holy Family Catholic School
  518 HOPKINS ST 70501
Immaculate Heart of Mary School
  800 12TH ST 70501
Our Lady of Fatima ES, 705 BONIN ROAD 70508
St. Genevieve Catholic School
  201 ELIZABETH AVE 70501
Sts. Leo-Seton ES, 502 SAINT LEO ST 70501

Lafitte, Jefferson Parish, Pop. Code 4
Jefferson Parish SD
Supt. – See Harvey

ES, 235 CITY PARK DR 70067 – C. Bordelon, prin.

Lake Arthur, Jefferson Davis Parish, Pop. Code 5
Jefferson Davis Parish SD
Supt. – See Jennings
ES, P O BOX J 70549 – Roy Lapoint, prin.

Goretti School, 701 7TH ST 70549

Lake Charles, Calcasieu Parish, Pop. Code 8
Calcasieu Parish SD
Sch. Sys. Enr. Code 8
Supt. – Charles Oakley, 1724 KIRKMAN ST 70601
Molo MS, 2300 MEDORA ST 70601
  Edward McKinley, prin.
Moss Bluff MS
  RURAL ROUTE 09 BOX 125 70611
  Al Heimback, prin.
Oak Park MS, 2200 OAK PARK BLVD 70601
  Tom Ballard, prin.
Reynaud MS, 745 S SHATTUCK ST 70601
  Ivory Beloney, prin.
Welsh MS, 1500 W MCNEESE ST 70605
  John Garner, prin.
White JHS, 1000 E MCNEESE ST 70605
  William Stokes, prin.
Barbe ES, PENN & ERNEST STS 70601
  Dr. Jean Mancuso, prin.
Brentwood ES, 3825 BRENTWOOD ST 70605
  Charles Sullivan, prin.
Cherry Street ES, 300 N CHERRY ST 70601
  Melvin Guice, prin.
College Oaks ES, 3618 ERNEST ST 70605
  Perry Knox, prin.
Combre ES, 2115 FITZENRIETER ROAD 70601
  Joseph Guillory, prin.
Cooley Magnet ES, 2711 COMMON ST 70601
  Nelda Boese, prin.
Dolby ES, 817 JEFFERSON DR 70605
  John Moore, prin.
Eastwood ES, 2903 OPELOUSAS ST 70601
  Herman Metoyer, prin.
Fairview ES, ROUTE 14 BOX 2500 70605
  Annette Ballard, prin.
Gillis ES, P O BOX 12176 70612
  Troy Parsons, prin.
Henry Heights ES, 3600 LOUISIANA AVE 70605
  Gerald Simmons, prin.
Johnson ES, 1618 MILL STNA AVE 70601
  George Reado, prin.
Kaufman ES, 301 TEKEL RD 70605
  Lawrence Primeaux, prin.
Kennedy ES, 2001 RUSSELL ST 70601
  Julius Pearce, prin.
Moss Bluff ES, RURAL ROUTE 05 BOX 200 70611
  Clarence Etheridge, prin.
Nelson ES, 1001 BIG LAKE ROAD 70605
  Anthony Kravchuk, prin.
Oak Park ES, 2001 18TH ST 70601
  Leo Miller,Jr., prin.
Prien Lake ES, 3741 NELSON ROAD 70605
  E. Dyer, prin.
St. John ES, ROUTE 12 BOX 481 70605
  Opal Young, prin.
Watkins ES, 2501 7TH AVE 70601
  Robert Shelton, prin.
Watson ES, 1300 5TH ST 70605
  Leonard Broussard, prin.
Wilson ES, 1400 OPELOUSAS ST 70601
  Carl Ambrose, prin.
Other Schools – See Bell City, De Quincy, Iowa,
  Starks, Sulphur, Vinton, Westlake

Cameron Parish SD
Supt. – See Cameron
Grand Lake S
  RURAL ROUTE 02 BOX 360B 70605
  Pearl Leach, prin.

Bishop Noland Episcopal School
  715 KIRKMAN ST 70601
Immaculate Conception School
  1536 RYAN ST 70601
Immaculate Heart of Mary School
  500 N CHERRY ST 70601
Our Lady Queen of Heaven School
  3908 CREOLE ST 70605
Sacred Heart School, 1100 MILL ST 70601
St. Margaret Catholic School
  2510 ENTERPRISE BLVD 70601

Lakeland, Pointe Coupee Parish
Point Coupee Parish SD
Supt. – See New Roads
ES, GENERAL DELIVERY 70752
  Anthony Juge, prin.

Lake Providence, East Carroll Parish, Pop. Code 6
East Carroll Parish SD
Sch. Sys. Enr. Code 4
Supt. – Robert Williams, P O BOX 592 71254
Monticello S, RURAL ROUTE 01 BOX 314 71254
  Phil Jackson, prin.
Northside ES, 300 REGENOLD ST 71254
  Eugene Haley, prin.
Southside ES, P O BOX 128 71254
  Willie Lee Bell, prin.
Other Schools – See Transylvania

Briarfield Academy, RURAL ROUTE 02 71254
St. Patrick Catholic School
  300 SECOND ST 71254

LaPlace, St. John The Baptist Parish, Pop. Code 6
St. John The Baptist Parish SD
Supt. – See Reserve
ES, 393 GREENWOOD DR 70068
Andrew Cupit, prin.
Ory ES, 435 W 5TH ST 70068 – Nora Pierre, prin.
Woodland ES, P O BOX 1049 70069
Lowell Bacas, prin.

Ascension of Our Lord School
1809 GREENWOOD DR 70068
St. Joan of Arc Catholic School, 487 FIR ST 70068

Larose, Lafourche Parish, Pop. Code 5
Lafourche Parish SD
Supt. – See Thibodaux
Larose Lower ES, P O BOX 310 70373
Van Cheramie, prin.
MS, P O BOX AVENUE 70373 – Ray Bernard, prin.

Holy Rosary Catholic School, P O BOX 40 70373

Lawtell, St. Landry Parish, Pop. Code 3
St. Landry Parish SD
Supt. – See Opelousas
ES, P O BOX 218 70550 – Clifford Gauthier, prin.

Lecompte, Rapides Parish, Pop. Code 4
Rapides Parish SD
Supt. – See Alexandria
Raymond JHS, P O BOX 429 71346
Causby Watson, prin.

Leesville, Vernon Parish, Pop. Code 6
Vernon Parish SD
Sch. Sys. Enr. Code 7
Supt. – Sam Hinson, 201 BELVIEW ROAD 71446
JHS, MILLER AVE 71446 – Jackie Self, prin.
East Leesville ES, P O BOX 1550 71446
Faye Ellis, prin.
Pickering ES, RURAL ROUTE 02 71446
L. Midkiff, prin.
Vernon MS, 1410 NONA ST 71446
Fletcher Cheatham, prin.
West Leesville ES, 1200 ABE ALLEN DR 71446
Louis Massie, prin.
Other Schools – See Anacoco, Evans, Fort Polk,
Hicks, Hornbeck, Pitkin, Rosepine, Simpson

Leonville, St. Landry Parish, Pop. Code 4
St. Landry Parish SD
Supt. – See Opelousas
ES, P O BOX 38 70551 – Charles Chavis, prin.

Lillie, Union Parish, Pop. Code 2
Union Parish SD
Supt. – See Farmerville
Lillie MS, P O BOX 3 71256 – Vera Jackson, prin.

Lisbon, Claiborne Parish, Pop. Code 2
Claiborne Parish SD
Supt. – See Homer
Pineview S, HCR 18 BOX 1050 71048
Shirtee Evans, prin.

Livingston, Livingston Parish, Pop. Code 4
Livingston Parish SD
Sch. Sys. Enr. Code 7
Supt. – J. Rogers Pope, P O BOX 128 70754
Doyle ES, GENERAL DELIVERY 70754
Donna Bencaz, prin.
Frost ES, 19174 LA HIGHWAY 42 70754
H. Comish, prin.
Other Schools – See Albany, Denham Springs, French
Settlement, Holden, Maurepas, Springfield, Walker,
Watson

Lockport, Lafourche Parish, Pop. Code 4
Lafourche Parish SD
Supt. – See Thibodaux
Lockport Lower ES, 1421 CRESCENT AVE 70374
Richard Champagne, prin.
Lockport Upper MS, 201 SCHOOL ST 70374
Robert Adams, prin.

Holy Savior Catholic School
201 CHURCH ST 70374

Logansport, De Soto Parish, Pop. Code 4
De Soto Parish SD
Supt. – See Mansfield
Stanley S, RURAL ROUTE 01 BOX 371 71049
Roy Moton, prin.
Logansport-Rosenwald ES, P O BOX 579 71049
Kenneth Hendrickson, prin.

Longville, Beauregard Parish
Beauregard Parish SD
Supt. – See De Ridder
South Beauregard ES
RURAL ROUTE 01 BOX 49A 70652
Gary Ross, prin.

Loranger, Tangipahoa Parish
Tangipahoa Parish SD
Supt. – See Amite
MS, P O BOX 469 70446 – Burnell Stevens, prin.
PS, P O BOX 598 70446 – John Simmons,Jr., prin.

Loreauville, Iberia Parish, Pop. Code 3
Iberia Parish SD
Supt. – See New Iberia
ES, P O BOX 425 70552 – Earl Price,Sr., prin.

Luling, St. Charles Parish, Pop. Code 5
St. Charles Parish SD
Sch. Sys. Enr. Code 6
Supt. – Stanley Berard, P O BOX 46 70070

Lakewood MS, 124 E 3RD ST 70070
Keith Theriot, prin.
ES, 904 SUGARHOUSE ROAD 70070
Dr. Ray Matherne, prin.
Mimosa Park ES, 150 1ST ST 70070
Lloyd Vautrot, prin.
Other Schools – See Des Allemands, Destrehan,
Hahnville, Norco, Paradis, Saint Rose

Lutcher, St. James Parish, Pop. Code 5
St. James Parish SD
Sch. Sys. Enr. Code 5
Supt. – Karen Poirrier, P O BOX 338 70071
JHS, RURAL ROUTE 01 BOX 268 70071
Lawrence Gordon, prin.
ES, P O BOX P 70071 – Shirley Rodrigue, prin.
Other Schools – See Convent, Gramercy, Paulina,
Saint James, Vacherie

Madisonville, St. Tammany Parish, Pop. Code 3
St. Tammany Parish SD
Supt. – See Covington
ES, ROSENWALD ROAD 70447
Jean Emmert, prin.

Mamou, Evangeline Parish, Pop. Code 5
Evangeline Parish SD
Supt. – See Ville Platte
MS, 1205 4TH ST 70554 – Richard Sylvest, prin.
PS, 912 7TH ST 70554 – Rayford Fontenot, prin.

Mandeville, St. Tammany Parish, Pop. Code 6
St. Tammany Parish SD
Supt. – See Covington
JHS, 639 CARONDELET ST 70448
Rich Sylvest, prin.
ES, 519 MASSENA ST 70448 – Rose Vance, prin.
MS, 1620 LIVINGSTON ST 70448
Martin Simmons, prin.
Woodlake ES, 1620 LIVINGSTON ST 70448
Marian Arrowsmith, prin.

Our Lady of the Lake School
316 LAFITTE ST 70448

Mangham, Richland Parish, Pop. Code 3
Richland Parish SD
Supt. – See Rayville
JHS, P O BOX 428 71259
Bobby Joe Chapman, prin.
ES, P O BOX 388 71259 – Frances Hurst, prin.

Mansfield, De Soto Parish, Pop. Code 6
De Soto Parish SD
Sch. Sys. Enr. Code 6
Supt. – Dr. Daniel Rawls, P O BOX 631 71052
De Soto JHS, P O BOX 313 71052
Willie Guiton, prin.
Johnson MS, 1201 S WASHINGTON AVE 71052
Joe Palmer, prin.
ES, 100 JENKINS ST 71052 – Shirley Purvis, prin.
Other Schools – See Logansport, Pelican, Stonewall

Mansura, Avoyelles Parish, Pop. Code 4
Avoyelles Parish SD
Supt. – See Marksville
MS, SAINT JEAN & PORTERIE STS 71350
George Voinche, prin.

Many, Sabine Parish, Pop. Code 5
Sabine Parish SD
Sch. Sys. Enr. Code 5
Supt. – Larry Skinner, P O BOX 1153 71449
JHS, 850 HIGHLAND AVE 71449
Lyndon Chance, prin.
ES, 265 MIDDLE CREEK ROAD 71449
Bessie Lang, prin.
Other Schools – See Converse, Florien, Negreet,
Noble, Pleasant Hill, Zwolle

Maringouin, Iberville Parish, Pop. Code 4
Point Coupee Parish SD
Supt. – See New Roads
Valverda ES, RURAL ROUTE 01 BOX 1945 70757
Alex Palmer, prin.

Marion, Union Parish, Pop. Code 3
Union Parish SD
Supt. – See Farmerville
S, RURAL ROUTE 02 BOX 14D 71260
John Ellis, prin.
S, P O BOX 67 71260 – Lillie Davis, prin.

Marksville, Avoyelles Parish, Pop. Code 6
Avoyelles Parish SD
Sch. Sys. Enr. Code 6
Supt. – Burnell Lemoine
201 W TUNICA DRIVE 71351
MS, 401 ALLEN ST 71351 – Rufus Johnson, prin.
ES, 401 W WADDILL ST 71351
Howard Jeansonne, prin.
Other Schools – See Bunkie, Cottonport, Effie,
Mansura, Plaucheville, Simmesport

Marksville Catholic School, P O BOX 187 71351

Marrero, Jefferson Parish, Pop. Code 8
Jefferson Parish SD
Supt. – See Harvey
Ellender MS, 4501 E AMES BLVD 70072
Thomas Hebert, prin.
MS, 4100 7TH ST 70072 – Etta Liccardi, prin.
Truman JHS, 5417 EHRET ROAD 70072
Arthur Majorie, prin.
Ames ES, 500 PINE ST 70072
Phyllis Benoit, prin.

Estelle ES, P O BOX 938 70073
Jackie Boudreaux, prin.
Lincoln ES, 1429 AMES BLVD 70072
Lawrence Washington, prin.
Ruppel ES, 2820 MOUNT KENNEDY DR 70072
Sandra Wilson, prin.
Wall ES, 2001 BONNIE ANN DR 70072
Laura Toups, prin.

Westbank Cathedral Academy
7301 LAPAICO BLVD 70072
Concordia Lutheran School
6700 WESTBANK EXPY 70072
Immaculate Conception School
601 AVENUE C 70072
St. Joseph the Worker School, 440 PINE ST 70072
Visitation of Our Lady School
3520 AMES BLVD 70072

Marthaville, Natchitoches Parish
Natchitoches Parish SD
Supt. – See Natchitoches
ES, P O BOX 148 71450 – Bobby Birdwell, prin.

Maurepas, Livingston Parish
Livingston Parish SD
Supt. – See Livingston
S, P O BOX 39 70449 – Gerald Bantaa, prin.

Maurice, Vermilion Parish, Pop. Code 2
Vermilion Parish SD
Supt. – See Abbeville
ES, P O BOX 277 70555 – Cordell Dartez, prin.

Melrose, Natchitoches Parish
Natchitoches Parish SD
Supt. – See Natchitoches
St. Matthew JHS, HCR 66 BOX 1335 71452
Thurman Baptiste, prin.

Melville, St. Landry Parish, Pop. Code 4
St. Landry Parish SD
Supt. – See Opelousas
ES, P O BOX 485 71353 – Michael Nassif, prin.

Meraux, St. Bernard Parish, Pop. Code 5
St. Bernard Parish SD
Supt. – See Chalmette
Trist MS, LIONEL DRIVE 70075
Lee Dennis, prin.

Mermentau, Acadia Parish, Pop. Code 3
Acadia Parish SD
Supt. – See Crowley
ES, P O BOX 250 70556 – Melvyn Smith, prin.

Mer Rouge, Morehouse Parish, Pop. Code 3
Morehouse Parish SD
Supt. – See Bastrop
Mer Rouge ES Campus 2, P O BOX 164 71261
James Johnson, prin.

Merryville, Beauregard Parish, Pop. Code 4
Beauregard Parish SD
Supt. – See De Ridder
S, P O BOX B 70653 – H. Whitman, prin.

Metairie, Jefferson Parish, Pop. Code 9
Jefferson Parish SD
Supt. – See Harvey
Harris JHS, 911 ELISE AVE 70003
Ruth Autin, prin.
Haynes JHS, 1416 METAIRIE ROAD 70005
Julius Palone, prin.
Meisler JHS, 3700 CLEARY AVE 70002
Al Montgomery, prin.
Airline Park ES, 6201 CAMPHOR ST 70003
Bonnie Nelson, prin.
Birney ES, 4829 HASTINGS ST 70006
Milton Skorlich, prin.
Bissonet Plaza ES, 6818 KAWANEE AVE 70003
Barbara Cassara, prin.
Bridgedale ES, 808 ZINNIA AVE 70001
Janet Zelden, prin.
Dolhonde ES, 219 SEVERN AVE 70001
Joseph Moscona, prin.
Ellis ES, 801 BROCKENBRAUGH CT 70005
Pamela Milto, prin.
Green Park ES, 1409 N UPLAND AVE 70003
Ellen Hawkins, prin.
Hearst ES, 6208 WABASH ST 70001
Mary Ann Delaneuville, prin.
Keller ES, 5301 IRVING ST 70003
Gwen Bowman, prin.
Matas ES, 1101 ELISE AVE 70003
William Simpson III, prin.
ES, 201 METAIRIE ROAD 70005
Dr. Judy Allain, prin.
Riviere ES, 1564 LAKE AVE 70005
Mona Navarro, prin.
Westgate ES, 2504 MAINE AVE 70003
Carolyn Starita, prin.

Crescent City Baptist School
4828 UTICA ST 70006
Ecole Classique School
5236 GLENDALE ST 70006
First Assembly Academy
2001 AIRLINE HWY 70001
Metairie Park Country Day School
300 PARK ROAD 70005
Ridgewood Prepatatory School
201 PASADENA AVE 70001
St. Martin's Episcopal School
5309 AIRLINE HIGHWAY 70003
Atonement Lutheran ES
6205 VETERANS MEM BLVD 70003

Kehoe-France Day School, 720 ELISE AVE 70003
Memorial Baptist Christian School
5701 VETERANS MEMORIAL BLVD 70003
Our Lady of Divine Providence School
917 N ATLANTA ST 70003
St. Angela Merici School, 835 MELODY DR 70002
St. Ann Catholic School
4921 MEADOWDALE ST 70006
St. Benilde Catholic School
1801 DIVISION ST 70001
St. Catherine of Siena School
400 CODIFER BLVD 70005
St. Christopher Catholic School
3900 DERBIGNY ST 70001
St. Clement of Rome School
3978 W ESPLANADE AVE S 70002
St. Edward the Confessor School
4901 W METAIRIE AVE 70001
St. Francis Xavier School, 215 BETZ PLACE 70005
St. Lawrence the Martyr School
2505 MAINE AVE 70005
St. Louis King of France School
1600 LAKE AVE 70005
St. Mary Magdalen School
6425 W METAIRIE AVE 70003
St. Philip Neri Catholic School
6600 KAWANEE AVE 70003

Milton, Lafayette Parish
Lafayette Parish SD
Supt. – See Lafayette
ES, P O BOX 239 70558 – Daniel Lapointe, prin.

Minden, Webster Parish, Pop. Code 7
Webster Parish SD
Sch. Sys. Enr. Code 6
Supt. – Jerry Lott, P O BOX 520 71058
Webster JHS, P O BOX 857 71058
Len Harris, prin.
Harper ES, 618 GERMANTOWN ROAD 71055
Joe Windham, prin.
Jones ES, 620 DISTRICT DR 71055
Grover Lewis,Jr., prin.
Phillips MS, 811 DURWOOD DR 71055
James Smith, prin.
Richardson ES, 515 W TODD ST 71055
Dr. Christine Hunt, prin.
Stewart ES, 215 N MIDDLE LANDING RD 71055
Lonnie Simpson, prin.
Other Schools – See Doyline, Dubberly, Heflin,
Shongaloo, Springhill

Glenbrook School
COUNTRY CLUB CIRCLE 71055

Monroe, Ouachita Parish, Pop. Code 8
Monroe City SD
Sch. Sys. Enr. Code 7
Supt. – Dr. N. Stafford, P O BOX 4180 71212
Carroll JHS, P O BOX 4315 71212
Jimmy Jones, prin.
Jefferson JHS, 1009 PECAN ST 71202
Walter Collins, prin.
Lee JHS, 1600 N 19TH ST 71201
James Hammond, prin.
Benton ES, 3307 LEE AVE 71202
Margaret Copeland, prin.
Carver ES, 1700 ORANGE 71202
Calvin Jordan, prin.
Clark MS, 1202 BREARD ST 71201
Dorth Blade, prin.
Faulk ES, 2110 JACKSON ST 71202
Fred Cheeks, prin.
Hall ES, 1000 PLUM ST 71202
Glen Hammett, prin.
Humble ES, 3800 WESTMINSTER AVE 71201
Gary Jones, prin.
Jones ES, 3000 BERG JONES LANE 71202
John Beckwith, prin.
King MS, 3716 NUTLAND ROAD 71202
Emma Jones, prin.
Lexington ES, 1900 LEXINGTON BLVD 71201
Charles Rohner, prin.
Lincoln ES, 4200 ELM ST 71203
Roy Shelling, prin.
Ruffin ES, 1801 PARKVIEW DR 71202
Andrew Hill, prin.
Sherrouse ES, 300 SHERROUSE ST 71203
Patsy McDonald, prin.
Tucker ES, 405 STUBBS AVE 71201
Donald Robinson, prin.

Ouachita Parish SD
Sch. Sys. Enr. Code 7
Supt. – Dr. Lanny Johnson, P O BOX 1642 71212
Ouachita MS, 5500 BLANKS ST 71203
W. Middleton, prin.
Hayes ES, 22 OLD STERLINGTON ROAD 71203
Lynda Burns, prin.
Lakeshore ES, 550 BALBOA DR 71203
Kevin Welch, prin.
Robinson ES, 5101 BERG JONES LANE 71202
Theodore Brown,Jr., prin.
Shady Grove ES, 2304 TICHELI ROAD 71202
Jeanette Ramsey, prin.
Swayze ES, 2400 BERG JONES LANE 71202
Charles Johnson, prin.
Other Schools – See Calhoun, Sterlington, Swartz,
West Monroe

Ouachita Christian School
RURAL ROUTE 04 BOX 197-B 71203
River Oaks School, P O BOX 4804 71211
Grace Episcopal School, 1400 N 4TH ST 71201

Jesus the Good Shepherd School
900 GOOD SHEPHERD LANE 71201
Little Flower Academy, 600 S 16TH ST 71201
Our Lady of Fatima Catholic School
3202 FRANKLIN ST 71201

Montegut, Terrebonne Parish, Pop. Code 3
Terrebonne Parish SD
Supt. – See Houma
MS, RURAL ROUTE 01 BOX 138 70377
Louise Vice Adams, prin.
ES, RURAL ROUTE 01 BOX 144 70377
A. Cenac, prin.
Pointe Aux Chenes ES
RURAL ROUTE 01 BOX 46-A 70377
Steven Redmond, prin.

Monterey, Concordia Parish
Concordia Parish SD
Supt. – See Vidalia
S, P O BOX 127 71354 – Dr. Edgar Gibson, prin.

Montgomery, Grant Parish, Pop. Code 3
Grant Parish SD
Supt. – See Colfax
Montgomery-Gaines JHS, P O BOX 558 71454
Brian Hines, prin.

Mooringsport, Caddo Parish, Pop. Code 3
Caddo Parish SD
Supt. – See Shreveport
ES, P O BOX 428 71060
Margaret Buddecke, prin.

Moreauville, Avoyelles Parish, Pop. Code 3

Sacred Heart Catholic School, P O BOX 1 71355

Morgan City, St. Mary Parish, Pop. Code 7
Assumption Parish SD
Supt. – See Napoleonville
Bayou L'ourse PS, 216 LARK DRIVE 70380
Robert Crochet, prin.

St. Martin Parish SD
Supt. – See Saint Martinville
Stephensville ES
RURAL ROUTE 04 BOX 220-D 70380
Lucille Husband, prin.

St. Mary Parish SD
Supt. – See Centerville
JHS, 911 MARGUERITE ST 70380
John Weimer, prin.
Bayou Vista ES, 1301 DELMAR AVE 70380
Elizabeth DeVillier, prin.
Maitland ES, 1907 FEDERAL AVE 70380
P. Richie, prin.
Norman PS, 900 SPRUCE ST 70380
A. Streva, prin.
Shannon MS, 409 BRASHEAR AVE 70380
Howard Rogers, prin.
Wyandotte ES, 2 GLENWOOD ST 70380
Julius Hebert, prin.

Holy Cross Catholic School
2100 CEDAR ST 70380
Sacred Heart Catholic School, 318 3RD ST 70381

Morganza, Pointe Coupee Parish, Pop. Code 3
Point Coupee Parish SD
Supt. – See New Roads
ES, P O BOX 429 70759 – Sidney LaCoste, prin.

Morrow, St. Landry Parish
St. Landry Parish SD
Supt. – See Opelousas
ES, P O BOX 115 71356 – Leonard Armand, prin.

Morse, Acadia Parish, Pop. Code 3
Acadia Parish SD
Supt. – See Crowley
ES, P O BOX 247 70559 – Betty Thebodeaux, prin.

Mount Hermon, Washington Parish
Washington Parish SD
Supt. – See Franklinton
S, RURAL ROUTE 02 BOX 1 70450
Gary Fowler, prin.

Napoleonville, Assumption Parish, Pop. Code 3
Assumption Parish SD
Sch. Sys. Enr. Code 5
Supt. – Lynn Aysenne, P O BOX B 70390
MS, P O BOX 236 70390 – Billie Nweze, prin.
PS, P O BOX 536 70390 – Octavia Lewis, prin.
Other Schools – See Belle Rose, Labadieville, Morgan
City, Pierre Part

Natalbany, Tangipahoa Parish
Tangipahoa Parish SD
Supt. – See Amite
MS, P O BOX 9 70451 – Ted Cason, prin.
Midway ES, P O BOX 69 70451
Robert Elzy, prin.

Southeast Louisiana Christian School
P O BOX 219 70451

Natchitoches, Natchitoches Parish, Pop. Code 7
Natchitoches Parish SD
Sch. Sys. Enr. Code 6
Supt. – Mike Whitford, P O BOX 16 71458
JHS, 1621 WELCH ST 71457 – (—), prin.
N. S. U. Lab. MS
NORTHWESTERN STATE UNIV 71457
Jim Berry, prin.

East Natchitoches MS, 1001 E 5TH ST 71457
Joshua Hayes, prin.
North Natchitoches ES, 1500 GOLD ST 71457
Toni Bennett, prin.
N.S.U. Lab ES
NSU CAMPUS WARREN EAST BLDG 71457
Elwanda Murphy, prin.
Parks ES, 800 KOONCE ST 71457
John Winston, prin.
Weaver ES, 520 SAINT MAURICE LANE 71457
Martha Wynn, prin.
Other Schools – See Campti, Cloutierville, Coushatta,
Goldonna, Marthaville, Melrose, Provencal

St. Marys School, 1101 E 5TH ST 71457

Negreet, Sabine Parish
Sabine Parish SD
Supt. – See Many
S, P O BOX 14 71460 – Harold Ledford, prin.

Newellton, Tensas Parish, Pop. Code 4
Tensas Parish SD
Supt. – See Saint Joseph
Routhwood MS, P O BOX 646 71357
James Kelly, prin.

New Iberia, Iberia Parish, Pop. Code 8
Iberia Parish SD
Sch. Sys. Enr. Code 7
Supt. – Dave Cavalier
RURAL ROUTE B BOX 390 B 70560
Anderson MS, 1059 ANDERSON ST 70560
Herman James, prin.
MS, 415 CENTER ST 70560
Eugene Broussard, prin.
Bank Avenue MS, 500 BANK AVE 70560
Lloyd Boseman, prin.
Center Street ES, 1600 CENTER ST 70560
Diane Hearn, prin.
Coteau ES, RURAL ROUTE 05 BOX 326 70560
Deborah Viator, prin.
Dodson Street ES, 420 DODSON ST 70560
Sidney Leger, prin.
Hopkins Street ES, 1200 HOPKINS ST 70560
Marjorie Small, prin.
Johnston Street ES, 400 JOHNSTON ST 70560
Barbara Boudreaux, prin.
Lee Street PS
CORNER LEE AND PARK AVE 70560
Ronald Bienvenu, prin.
Live Oak ES, 809 W MAIN ST 70560
J. Mouton, prin.
Magnolia ES, 413 S LEWIS ST 70560
Michael Faulk, prin.
North Lewis ES, 604 N LEWIS ST 70560
Robert Benoit, prin.
North Street MS, 121 NORTH ST 70560
Patrick Leblanc, prin.
Park MS, 201 GILBERT DR 70560
Roger Hamilton, prin.
Peebles MS, RURAL ROUTE 04 BOX 407 70560
C. Harvison, prin.
Pesson Addition ES, 500 BROUSSARD ST 70560
Willie Jefferson, prin.
Other Schools – See Avery Island, Delcambre,
Jeanerette, Loreauville

Assembly Christian School
2402 E ADMIRAL DOYLE DR 70561
St. Edward Catholic School
720 PROVIDENCE ST 70560

New Orleans, Orleans Parish, Pop. Code 11
Orleans Parish SD
Sch. Sys. Enr. Code 8
Supt. – Everett Williams, 4100 TOURO ST 70122
Carver MS, 3019 HIGGINS BLVD 70126
Jean Demas, prin.
Green ES, 2319 VALENCE ST 70115
Darrell McConduit, prin.
Kohn MS, 4001 N ROMAN ST 70117
Juanita Boniface, prin.
Live Oak MS, 3128 CONSTANCE ST 70115
Armand Devezin, prin.
Livingston MS, 7301 DWYER ROAD 70126
Constance Yeaton, prin.
Peters MS, 425 S BROAD ST 70119
Delores Berquist, prin.
Williams MS, 5316 MICHOUD BLVD 70129
Marie Kaigler, prin.
Wright MS, 1426 NAPOLEON AVE 70115
Jimmie Teague, prin.
Abrams ES, 6519 VIRGILIAN ST 70126
Melvalee Pichon, prin.
Allen ES, 5625 LOYOLA AVE 70115
Ethel Nicholas, prin.
Audubon Montessori ES
428 BROADWAY ST 70118 – Jill Otis, prin.
Bauduit ES, 3649 LAUREL ST 70115
Victoria Dahmes, prin.
Behrman ES, 715 OPELOUSAS AVE 70114
Anthony Fisher, prin.
Benjamin ES, 4040 EAGLE ST 70118
Dr. Alfred Gourrier, prin.
Bienville ES, 1456 GARDENA DR 70122
Vidal Easton, prin.
Bradley ES, 2401 HUMANITY ST 70122
Dr. Anita Dumas, prin.
Chester ES, 3929 ERATO ST 70125
Velma Pryce, prin.
Claiborne ES, 4617 MIRABEAU AVE 70126
Donaldo Batiste, prin.
Coghill ES, 5500 PIETY DR 70126
Gail Lazard, prin.

Couvent ES, 2021 PAUGER ST   70116
  Mildred Weber, prin.
Craig ES, 1423 SAINT PHILIP ST   70116
  Wilfred Norris, prin.
Crocker ES, 2300 GENERAL TAYLOR ST   70115
  Cynthia Williams, prin.
Crossman ES, 4407 S CARROLLTON AVE   70119
  Anita Garcia, prin.
Danneel ES, 3411 BROADWAY ST   70125
  Rudolph Detiege, prin.
Davis ES, 7701 GRANT ST   70126
  Dr. Robert Nicaud, prin.
DeBore ES, 5100 CANNES ST   70129
  Louise Olsen, prin.
Dibert ES, 4217 ORLEANS AVE   70119
  Wiley Ates, prin.
Dunbar ES, 9330 FORSHEY ST   70118
  Alexander Brunfield,Jr., prin.
Dunn ES, 3601 DESIRE PARKWAY   70126
  Durell Williams, prin.
Edison ES, 1339 FORSTALL ST   70117
  Shan Williams, prin.
Edwards ES, 3039 HIGGINS BLVD   70126
  Helen Leslie, prin.
Eisenhower ES, 3700 TALL PINES DR   70131
  Vertilee Robinson, prin.
Fischer ES, 1801 WHITNEY AVE   70114
  Carol Lang, prin.
Fisk-Howard ES, 211 S LOPEZ ST   70119
  Hilda Young, prin.
Frantz ES, 3811 N GALVEZ ST   70117
  Troy Vincent, prin.
Gaudet ES, 12000 HAYNE BLVD   70128
  Dr. Maxine Pijeaux, prin.
Gayarre ES, 2515 N ROBERTSON ST   70117
  Roslyn Smith, prin.
Gentilly Terrace ES, 4720 PAINTERS ST   70122
  Dr. Juanita Schroeder, prin.
Gordon ES, 6101 CHATHAM DR   70122
  Brian Riedlinger, prin.
Guste ES, 2625 THALIA ST   70113
  Dr. Arthur Age, prin.
Habans ES, 3819 HERSCHEL ST   70114
  Virginia Valle, prin.
Hardin ES, 2401 SAINT MAURICE AVE   70117
  Doris Hicks, prin.
Harney ES, 2503 WILLOW ST   70113
  Lawrence Taylor,Jr., prin.
Harte ES, 5300 BERKLEY DR   70131
  Louis Berges, prin.
Henderson ES, 1912 WHITNEY AVE   70114
  Patricia Collins, prin.
Hoffman ES, 2622 S PRIEUR ST   70125
  Dr. John Harper, prin.
Hynes ES, 990 HARRISON AVE   70124
  Judee Morovich, prin.
Jackson ES, 1400 CAMP ST   70130
  Herman Johnston, prin.
Johnson ES, 1800 MONROE ST   70118
  Denise Lewis, prin.
Jones ES, 1901 N GALVEZ ST   70119
  Dr. Edward Washington, prin.
Lafayette ES, 2727 S CARROLLTON AVE   70118
  Ina Gex, prin.
Lafon-Audubon ES, 2601 7TH ST   70115
  Clarence Proctor, prin.
Laurel ES, 820 JACKSON AVE   70130
  Harold Johnson, prin.
Lawless ES, 2440 ANDRY ST   70117
  Patricia Arnold, prin.
Lee ES, 1607 S CARROLLTON AVE   70118
  Velta Simms, prin.
Lewis ES, 1116 JEFFERSON AVE   70115
  Dr. Walter Langs,Jr., prin.
Little Woods ES, 10200 CURRAN BLVD   70127
  Dr. Carl Kirst,Jr., prin.
Lockett ES, 3240 LAW ST   70117
  Wilbert Dunn, prin.
Lusher Alternative ES, 7315 WILLOW ST   70118
  Kathleen Riedlinger, prin.
McDonogh 15 ES, 721 SAINT PHILIP ST   70116
  Cynthia Morrell, prin.
McDonogh 19 ES
  5909 SAINT CLAUDE AVE   70117
  Edward Broussard, prin.
McDonogh 24 ES, 421 BURDETTE ST   70118
  Joseph Ridolfo, prin.
McDonogh 31 ES, 800 N RENDON ST   70119
  Clarence Becknell, prin.
McDonogh 32 ES, 800 DE ARMAS ST   70114
  Albert Carter,Jr., prin.
McDonogh 36 ES, 2101 FERRET ST   70113
  Jean Pepin, prin.
McDonogh 38 ES, 1307 DRYADES ST   70113
  Kathy Augustine, prin.
McDonogh 39 ES, 5800 SAINT ROCH AVE   70122
  James Waller, prin.
McDonogh 40 MS, 4348 REYNES ST   70126
  Audette Patterson, prin.
McDonogh 42 ES, 1651 N TONTI ST   70119
  Dr. Ara Dozier, prin.
McDonogh 7 ES, 1111 MILAN ST   70115
  Joseph Lofaso, prin.
Meyer ES, 2013 GENERAL MEYER AVE   70114
  Felix Bernard, prin.
Moton ES, 3000 ABUNDANCE ST   70126
  Ellenese Simms, prin.
Nelson ES, 1300 MILTON ST   70122
  Joseph Taylor,Jr., prin.
New Orleans Free ES, 3601 CAMP ST   70115
  Robert Ferris, prin.
Osborne ES, 6701 CURRAN BLVD   70126
  Preston Coppels, prin.

Palmer ES, 1339 CLOUET ST   70117
  (—), prin.
Phillips ES, 3800 CADILLAC ST   70122
  Vorice Waters, prin.
Rogers ES, 2327 SAINT PHILIP ST   70119
  Cynthia Williams, prin.
Rosenwald MS, 6501 BERKLEY DR   70131
  Gertrude Ivory, prin.
Schaumburg ES, 9940 SPRINGWOOD ST   70127
  Dr. Mildred Noto, prin.
Shaw ES, 2518 ARTS ST   70117
  Denise Cates, prin.
Sherwood Forest ES
  4801 MAID MARION DR   70128
  Pat Vulcano,Jr., prin.
Washington ES, 3819 SAINT CLAUDE AVE   70117
  Ethel Martin, prin.
Wheatley ES, 2300 DUMAINE ST   70119
  Marshall Grady, prin.
White ES, 3519 TRAFALGAR ST   70119
  Sandra Wilson, prin.
Wicker ES, 2011 BIENVILLE ST   70112
  (—), prin.
Williams ES
  3127 MARTIN L KING JR BLVD   70125
  Joseph Bradford,Jr., prin.
Wilson ES, 3617 GENERAL PERSHING ST   70125
  Winston Ricks, prin.

New Orleans Academy, 200 ACADEMY DR   70124
Carrollton Presbyterian School
  2032 S CARROLLTON AVE   70118
Carrollton Presbyterian School
  2032 S CARROLLTON AVE   70118
Ganus School, 6026 PARIS AVE   70122
Isadore Newman School
  1903 JEFFERSON AVE   70115
McGehee School, 2433 PRYTANIA ST   70130
Sacred Heart Academy
  4521 SAINT CHARLES AVE   70115
St. James Major School
  3774 GENTILLY BLVD   70122
Ursuline Academy, 2635 STATE ST   70118
Word of Faith School
  13123 I 10 E SERVICE ROAD   70128
All Saints Catholic School, 1415 TECHE ST   70114
Arden Cahill Academy
  1871 FARRAGUT ST   70114
Aurora Gardens Academy
  2200 HUDSON PLACE   70131
Christian Brothers Boys School
  P O BOX 19596   70179
Corpus Christi Catholic School
  2022 SAINT BERNARD AVE   70116
Ephesus Jr. Academy SDA, P O BOX 3155   70117
Epiphany Catholic School, 1949 DUELS ST   70119
Faith Lutheran School
  300 COLONIAL CLUB DR   70123
Holy Ghost Catholic School
  2035 TOLEDANO ST   70115
Holy Name of Jesus Catholic School
  6325 CROMWELL PLACE   70118
Holy Name of Mary Catholic School
  502 OLIVIER ST   70114
Holy Redeemer Catholic School
  1941 DAUPHINE ST   70116
Immaculate Heart of Mary School
  6360 PINES BLVD   70126
Our Lady Star of the Sea School
  1927 SAINT ROCH AVE   70117
Our Lady of Good Counsel School
  1215 LOUISIANA AVE   70115
Our Lady of Lourdes School, 2437 JENA ST   70115
Our Lady of the Rosary School
  1342 MOSS ST   70119
Our Savior Lutheran School
  6054 VERMILLION BLVD   70122
Prince of Peace Lutheran School
  9301 CHEF MENTEUR HWY   70127
Resurrection of Our Lord School
  4901 ROSALIA DR   70127
St. Alphonsus Catholic School
  2001 CONSTANCE ST   70130
St. Andrew the Apostle School
  3131 ETON ST   70131
St. Anthony of Padua School
  4601 CLEVELAND AVE   70119
St. Cecilia Catholic School
  4219 N RAMPART ST   70117
St. David Catholic School
  1230 LAMANCHE ST   70117
St. Dominic Catholic School
  6326 MEMPHIS ST   70124
St. Frances Cabrini School
  1500 PRENTISS AVE   70122
St. Francis of Assisi School, 611 STATE ST   70118
St. George's Episcopal School
  923 NAPOLEON AVE   70115
St. James Major ES, 3774 GENTILLY BLVD   70122
St. Joan of Arc Catholic School
  919 CAMBRONNE ST   70118
St. John Lutheran School, 3937 CANAL ST   70119
St. Julian Eymard School
  2727 LAWRENCE ST   70114
St. Leo the Great School
  1501 ABUNDANCE ST   70119
St. Louis Cathedral School
  820 DAUPHINE ST   70116
St. Mary of the Angels School
  2225 CONGRESS ST   70117
St. Monica Catholic School
  2323 S GALVEZ ST   70125

St. Paul the Apostle School
  6828 CHEF MENTEUR HWY   70126
St. Paul's Episcopal School
  6249 CANAL BLVD   70124
St. Paul-First English Lutheran School
  2624 BURGUNDY ST   70117
St. Peter Claver Catholic School
  1020 N PRIEUR ST   70116
St. Philip the Apostle School
  3333 CLOUET ST   70126
St. Pius X Catholic School
  6600 SPANISH FORT BLVD   70124
St. Raphael the Archangel School
  5601 ELYSIAN FIELDS AVE   70122
St. Raymond Catholic School
  3717 HAMBURG ST   70122
St. Rita Catholic School
  65 FONTAINBLEAU DR   70125
St. Stephen Catholic School
  4310 CHESTNUT ST   70115
Ursuline, 2635 STATE STREET   70118
Sts. Peter and Paul Catholic School
  2301 BURGUNDY ST   70117
The Learning Academy
  3121 LOUISIANA AVE PKY   70125
The Primary School
  7949 EDGELAKE COURT   70126
Trinity Episcopal School
  2111 CHESTNUT ST   70130
Washington Private School, 2310 JENA ST   70115

New Roads, Point Coupee Parish, Pop. Code 5
Point Coupee Parish SD
Sch. Sys. Enr. Code 5
Supt. – Michael Lucia, P O BOX 579   70760
Poydras ES, P O BOX 9   70760
  Marcia Pinsonat, prin.
Other Schools – See Innis, Labarre, Lakeland,
  Maringouin, Morganza

False River Academy
  201 MAJOR PARKWAY   70760
Catholic ES, 304 NAPOLEON ST   70760

Noble, Sabine Parish, Pop. Code 2
Sabine Parish SD
Supt. – See Many
S, RURAL ROUTE 01 BOX 774   71462
  Genevieve Morgan, prin.

Norco, St. Charles Parish, Pop. Code 5
St. Charles Parish SD
Supt. – See Luling
MS, 102 5TH ST   70079 – Margaret Anderson, prin.
PS, 149 APPLE ST   70079 – Sandra Oubre, prin.

Sacred Heart of Jesus School
  453 SPRUCE ST   70079

Oakdale, Allen Parish, Pop. Code 6
Allen Parish SD
Supt. – See Oberlin
JHS, 101 S 13TH ST   71463
  Nathan Benjamin, prin.
ES, 340 N LOOP   71463 – Leslie Smith, prin.

Oak Grove, West Carroll Parish, Pop. Code 4
West Carroll Parish SD
Sch. Sys. Enr. Code 4
Supt. – Billy Kay, P O BOX 220   71263
Oak Grove S, P O BOX H   71263
  Gene Gammill, prin.
Fiske Union ES, P O BOX U   71263
  Wayne Holley, prin.
Goodwill ES, RURAL ROUTE 03   71263
  Henry Butler, prin.
Other Schools – See Epps, Forest, Kilbourne, Pioneer

Oberlin, Allen Parish, Pop. Code 4
Allen Parish SD
Sch. Sys. Enr. Code 5
Supt. – Louis Jeans, P O BOX C   70655
ES, P O BOX E   70655 – Tommy Germany, prin.
Other Schools – See Elizabeth, Grant, Kinder,
  Oakdale, Reeves

Oil City, Caddo Parish, Pop. Code 4
Caddo Parish SD
Supt. – See Shreveport
ES, P O BOX 488   71061 – Ethel Haughton, prin.

Olla, La Salle Parish, Pop. Code 4
LaSalle Parish SD
Supt. – See Jena
Olla Standard ES, P O BOX 698   71465
  Elvin Allbritton, prin.

Opelousas, St. Landry Parish, Pop. Code 7
St. Landry Parish SD
Sch. Sys. Enr. Code 7
Supt. – Claude Oubre, P O BOX 310   70571
Plaisance S, RURAL ROUTE 04 BOX 362   70570
  Elgy Sam, prin.
Creswell ES, P O BOX 1316   70571
  Albert Taylor, prin.
Grolee ES, 1670 W GROLEE ST   70570
  Ervin Fontenot, prin.
North ES, P O BOX 885   70571 – Joe Mason, prin.
Northeast ES, P O BOX 771   70571
  Robert Morrison, prin.
Park Vista ES, P O BOX 752   70571
  Steve Vidrine, prin.
Southwest ES, 898 W FRANKLIN ST   70570
  Joseph Thomas, prin.
South Street ES, P O BOX 709   70570
  Mary Dupre, prin.

Other Schools – See Arnaudville, Eunice, Grand
Coteau, Krotz Springs, Lawtell, Leonville, Melville,
Morrow, Palmetto, Port Barre, Sunset, Washington

Amy B. Ware School
1421 GARLAND BELT ROAD 70570
Belmont Academy, P O BOX 1505 70571
Opelousas Catholic School
415 E PRUDHOMME LANE 70570

Paincourtville, Assumption Parish, Pop. Code 2

St. Elizabeth School, P O BOX M 70391

Palmetto, St. Landry Parish, Pop. Code 2
St. Landry Parish SD
Supt. – See Opelousas
ES, P O BOX 200 71358 – John LeBlanc, prin.

Paradis, St. Charles Parish, Pop. Code 3
St. Charles Parish SD
Supt. – See Luling
Martin MS, P O BOX 1468 70080
Juanita Haydel, prin.
Vial MS, P O BOX 1528 70080
John Walker, prin.

Patterson, St. Mary Parish, Pop. Code 5
St. Mary Parish SD
Supt. – See Centerville
JHS, P O BOX R 70392 – Robert Ayres, prin.
Watts ES, P O BOX 639 70392
Carey MacStaples, prin.

Paulina, St. James Parish
St. James Parish SD
Supt. – See Lutcher
ES, P O BOX 99 70763 – Julie Abreo, prin.

Chanel School, P O BOX 159 70763

Pearl River, St. Tammany Parish, Pop. Code 4
St. Tammany Parish SD
Supt. – See Covington
MS, P O BOX 250 70452 – John Downey, prin.
Riverside PS, 100 SULLIVAN DR 70452
William Rowley, prin.
Sixth Ward ES, HIGHWAY 41 70452
William McDermott, prin.

Pelican, De Soto Parish
De Soto Parish SD
Supt. – See Mansfield
All Saints-Pelican ES
RURAL ROUTE 01 BOX 48 71063
Gary Hunt, prin.

Pierre Part, Assumption Parish, Pop. Code 3
Assumption Parish SD
Supt. – See Napoleonville
MS, 3321 HIGHWAY 70 70339
Earl Martinez, prin.
PS, 3323 HWY 70 70339 – Carol Aucoin, prin.

Pine Grove, St. Helena Parish
St. Helena Parish SD
Supt. – See Greensburg
ES, P O BOX 728 70453 – Curtis Bishop, prin.

Pine Prairie, Evangeline Parish, Pop. Code 3
Evangeline Parish SD
Supt. – See Ville Platte
S, P O BOX 186 70576 – Terry Ardoin, prin.

Pineville, Rapides Parish, Pop. Code 7
Rapides Parish SD
Supt. – See Alexandria
JHS, 501 EDGEWOOD DRIVE 71360
Lemon Coleman, prin.
Ball ES, RURAL ROUTE 03 BOX 125 71360
Leroy Landry, prin.
Barron ES, 3655 HOLLOWAY ROAD 71360
James Stewart, prin.
Goff ES, 6900 SHREVEPORT HWY 71360
Lester Hilton,Jr., prin.
Moore ES, 207 GRIFFITH ST 71360
Henry Shorter, prin.
Paradise ES, 5010 MONROE HWY 71360
John Cotton, prin.
ES, 835 MAIN ST 71360 – Madeline Coby, prin.
Slocum ES, 901 CREPE MYRTLE ST 71360
Robert Wakefield, prin.
Tioga ES, 4310 PARDUE ROAD 71360
Tommy Lay, prin.

Pioneer, West Carroll Parish, Pop. Code 2
West Carroll Parish SD
Supt. – See Oak Grove
S, P O BOX 98 71266 – M. Albritton, prin.

Pitkin, Vernon Parish, Pop. Code 2
Vernon Parish SD
Supt. – See Leesville
S, P O BOX 307 70656 – Mike Perkins, prin.

Plain Dealing, Bossier Parish, Pop. Code 4
Bossier Parish SD
Supt. – See Benton
ES, P O BOX 386 71064 – Betty Rich, prin.
Rocky Mount ES
RURAL ROUTE 03 BOX 1828 71064
Parnell Jones, prin.

Plain Dealing Academy, P O BOX 176 71064

Plaquemine, Iberville Parish, Pop. Code 6
Iberville Parish SD
Sch. Sys. Enr. Code 6
Supt. – Wallace Davis, P O BOX 151 70765
Crescent JHS, RURAL ROUTE 04 BOX 690 70764
Obie Watts, prin.
JHS, 910 FERDINAND ST 70764
Frank Ferachi, prin.
Crescent Bend ES, P O BOX 454 70765
Thomas Bouvay, prin.
Gay ES, P O BOX 717 70765 – William Bujol, prin.
Iberville MS, 1430 IRON FARM ROAD 70764
Raymond Smith,Sr., prin.
ES, 600 PLAQUEMINE ST 70764
Mildred Blanchard, prin.
Other Schools – See Bayou Goula, Rosedale, Saint
Gabriel, White Castle

St. John Catholic ES, 1111 OSAGE AVE 70764

Plaucheville, Avoyelles Parish, Pop. Code 2
Avoyelles Parish SD
Supt. – See Marksville
ES, P O BOX 108 71362 – J. Best, prin.

St. Joseph School, P O BOX 38 71362

Pleasant Hill, Sabine Parish, Pop. Code 3
Sabine Parish SD
Supt. – See Many
Zwolle ES, P O BOX 548 71065 – David Hall, prin.

Pollock, Grant Parish
Grant Parish SD
Supt. – See Colfax
ES, P O BOX 68 71467 – George Davidson, prin.

Ponchatoula, Tangipahoa Parish, Pop. Code 6
Tangipahoa Parish SD
Supt. – See Amite
JHS, 315 E OAK ST 70454 – Rob Greer, prin.
Champ Cooper ES
RURAL ROUTE 02 BOX 223 70454
Clarence Zahn, prin.
Reeves ES, P O BOX 656 70454
Harry Viener, prin.
Tucker Memorial ES, 310 S 3RD ST 70454
(—), prin.
Vinyard MS, P O BOX 666 70454
James Perrin, prin.

St. Joseph Catholic School, 175 N 8TH ST 70454

Port Allen, West Baton Rouge Parish, Pop. Code 6
West Baton Rouge Parish SD
Sch. Sys. Enr. Code 5
Supt. – John Charleville
670 ROSEDALE ROAD 70767
DeVall MS, 11851 N RIVER ROAD 70767
Arnold Chauvin, prin.
MS, 610 ROSEDALE ROAD 70767
Anderson Johnson, prin.
Chamberlin ES, 6024 SECTION ROAD 70767
Clarence Beverly,Jr., prin.
Cohn ES, 805 N 14TH ST 70767
Lenora Leblanc, prin.
ES, 609 ROSEDALE RD 70767 – John Wyble, prin.
Other Schools – See Brusly

Holy Family School
335 N JEFFERSON AVE 70767

Port Barre, St. Landry Parish, Pop. Code 5
St. Landry Parish SD
Supt. – See Opelousas
ES, P O BOX 310 70577 – Westley Jones, prin.

Port Sulphur, Plaquemines Parish, Pop. Code 5
Plaquemines Parish SD
Supt. – See Belle Chasse
S, RURAL ROUTE 02 BOX 110 70083
Albert LaFrance, prin.

St. Jude Catholic School, P O BOX 36 70083

Prairieville, Ascension Parish
Ascension Parish SD
Supt. – See Donaldsonville
Galvez Mid. Sch., 42618 HWY 933 70769
Robert Clouatre, prin.
Galvez PS
16093 HENDERSON BAYOU ROAD 70769
Regina Thomas, prin.
ES, 16200 HIGHWAY 930 70769
Eartha Rayborn, prin.

Pride, East Baton Rouge Parish
East Baton Rouge Parish SD
Supt. – See Baton Rouge
Northeast ES, P O BOX C 70770
Frances Price, prin.

Princeton, Bossier Parish
Bossier Parish SD
Supt. – See Benton
JHS, P O BOX 118 71067
Ronald Gormanous, prin.

Provencal, Natchitoches Parish, Pop. Code 3
Natchitoches Parish SD
Supt. – See Natchitoches
ES, P O BOX 425 71468 – Jerry Wester, prin.

Quitman, Jackson Parish, Pop. Code 2
Jackson Parish SD
Supt. – See Jonesboro
S, P O BOX 38 71268 – Paul Walsworth, prin.

Raceland, Lafourche Parish, Pop. Code 5
Lafourche Parish SD
Supt. – See Thibodaux
Raceland Lower ES, P O BOX 529 70394
Francis Rodriguez, prin.
Raceland Upper MS, P O BOX 370 70394
Alden Foret, prin.

St. Hilary of Poitiers School
306 TWIN OAKS DRIVE 70394
St. Mary's School, P O BOX K 70394

Rayne, Acadia Parish, Pop. Code 6
Acadia Parish SD
Supt. – See Crowley
Armstrong MS, 700 WEST E ST 70578
Darrell Cart, prin.
Martin Petitjean ES, P O BOX 488 70578
Alfred Norman,Jr., prin.
Mire ES, RURAL ROUTE 03 BOX 126 70578
James Young, prin.
South Rayne MS, 101 E BRANCH ST 70578
Theresa LeBlanc, prin.
Vermilion Parish SD
Supt. – See Abbeville
Indian Bayou S
RURAL ROUTE 02 BOX 249 70578
Luther Suire, prin.

Rayne Catholic School, 407 S POLK ST 70578

Rayville, Richland Parish, Pop. Code 5
Richland Parish SD
Sch. Sys. Enr. Code 5
Supt. – Arlon Adams, P O BOX 599 71269
JHS, 700 SE PEARL ST 71269 – W. Moore, prin.
ES, SOUTH SULIA ST 71269
Bonnie Adams, prin.
Other Schools – See Delhi, Holly Ridge, Mangham,
Start

Riverfield Academy
RURAL ROUTE 02 BOX 1 71269

Reeves, Allen Parish, Pop. Code 2
Allen Parish SD
Supt. – See Oberlin
S, P O BOX 100 70658 – Larry Young, prin.

Reserve, St. John The Baptist Parish, Pop. Code 6
St. John The Baptist Parish SD
Sch. Sys. Enr. Code 6
Supt. – Dr. B. DeSpain, P O BOX AL 70084
Godchaux JHS, P O BOX AH 70084
Isiah Jones, prin.
East St. John MS, EAST 29TH ST 70084
Francis Donaldson, prin.
Godchaux PS, P O BOX AB 70084
Alex Nicholas, prin.
Reserve Rosenwald MS, P O BOX R 70084
Betty Brouillette, prin.
Other Schools – See Edgard, Garyville, LaPlace

Riverside School, P O BOX J 70084
Our Lady of Grace Catholic School
RURAL ROUTE 01 BOX 686 70084
St. Peter Catholic School
RURAL ROUTE 02 BOX 1050 70084

Ridgecrest, Concordia Parish, Pop. Code 3
Concordia Parish SD
Supt. – See Vidalia
ES, 200 CYPRESS ST 71334
Herschel Chelette, prin.

Ringgold, Bienville Parish, Pop. Code 4
Bienville Parish SD
Supt. – See Arcadia
ES, P O BOX 9 71068 – Odis Green, prin.

River Ridge, Jefferson Parish, Pop. Code 7

St. Matthew the Apostle School
10021 JEFFERSON HWY 70123

Roanoke, Jefferson Davis Parish
Jefferson Davis Parish SD
Supt. – See Jennings
Welsh-Roanoke JHS, P O BOX 622 70581
Richard Sockrider, prin.

Rosedale, Iberville Parish, Pop. Code 3
Iberville Parish SD
Supt. – See Plaquemine
Levy ES, HIGHWAY 76 70772
Myrtis Hawkins, prin.

Roseland, Tangipahoa Parish, Pop. Code 4
Tangipahoa Parish SD
Supt. – See Amite
ES, P O BOX B 70456 – Kara Whittington, prin.

Rosepine, Vernon Parish, Pop. Code 3
Vernon Parish SD
Supt. – See Leesville
ES, GENERAL DELIVERY 70659
Rufus Goins, prin.

Ruston, Lincoln Parish, Pop. Code 7
Lincoln Parish SD
Sch. Sys. Enr. Code 6
Supt. – Gerald Cobb
300 S FARMERVILLE ST 71270
JHS, LINCOLN PARISH #106 71270
Charles Scriber, prin.

Cypress Springs ES, 1004 SARATOGA ST 71270
Danny Bell, prin.
Glen View ES, 1601 BITTERSWEET AVE 71270
Jackson Thigpen, prin.
Hillcrest ES, NORTHWOOD TERRACE 71270
Ann Gilbert, prin.
Lewis MS, MITCHELL ST 71270
Willie Washington,Jr., prin.
Phillips Lab ES, P O BOX 10168 71272
Robert Hearn, prin.
ES, 200 N BERNARD ST 71270
Howard Whitlock, prin.
Other Schools – See Choudrant, Dubach, Grambling,
Simsboro

Cedar Creek School
2400 CEDAR CREEK DRIVE 71270

Saint Amant, Ascension Parish
Ascension Parish SD
Supt. – See Donaldsonville
Lake PS, 14185 HWY 431 70774
Percy Babin, prin.
ES, P O BOX 400 70774 – Eva Bourgeois, prin.

Saint Bernard, St. Bernard Parish, Pop. Code 2
St. Bernard Parish SD
Supt. – See Chalmette
Beauregard MS, SAINT BERNARD P O 70085
Kathy Boyd, prin.
Gauthier ES, 2204 BOBOLINK ST 70085
Faith Moran, prin.
Roy ES, RURAL ROUTE 01 BOX 376 70085
Lynn Gagnon, prin.

Saint Francisville, West Feliciana Parish, Pop. Code 4
West Feliciana Parish SD
Sch. Sys. Enr. Code 4
Supt. – Wendell Hall, P O BOX 1910 70775
Bains ES, P O BOX 1940 70713
Jessie Perkins,Jr., prin.
Other Schools – See Tunica

Saint Gabriel, Iberville Parish
Iberville Parish SD
Supt. – See Plaquemine
ES, GENERAL DELIVERY 70776
Melvin Craige, prin.

Saint James, St. James Parish, Pop. Code 2
St. James Parish SD
Supt. – See Lutcher
Fifth Ward ES
RURAL ROUTE 02 BOX 432 70086
James Florent, prin.

Saint Joseph, Tensas Parish, Pop. Code 4
Tensas Parish SD
Sch. Sys. Enr. Code 4
Supt. – Donald Pennington, P O BOX 318 71366
Tensas ES, P O BOX 468 71366
Sherry Keahey, prin.
Other Schools – See Newellton, Waterproof

Tensas Academy, P O BOX 287 71366

Saint Martinville, St. Martin Parish, Pop. Code 6
St. Martin Parish SD
Sch. Sys. Enr. Code 6
Supt. – Nolan Braud, P O BOX 859 70582
JHS, 1120 S COLLEGE ST 70582
Laura Turpeau, prin.
Catahoula ES
RURAL ROUTE 02 BOX 2550 70582
Georgie Blanchard, prin.
Parks MS, PARKS RURAL STATION 70582
Murphy Simon, prin.
Parks PS, PARKS RURAL STATION 70582
Glenda McGee, prin.
MS, 1004 S COLLEGE ST 70582
Nancy Dore, prin.
PS, 716 N MAIN ST 70582
Bonnie Brettrager, prin.
Other Schools – See Breaux Bridge, Cecilia, Morgan
City

Trinity Catholic School, P O BOX 438 70582

Saint Rose, St. Charles Parish
St. Charles Parish SD
Supt. – See Luling
MS, P O BOX 269 70087 – Sandra Scott, prin.
PS, P O BOX 188 70087 – Carol Palliser, prin.

Saline, Bienville Parish, Pop. Code 2
Bienville Parish SD
Supt. – See Arcadia
S, P O BOX 118 71070 – William Britt, prin.

Schriever, Terrebonne Parish, Pop. Code 2
Terrebonne Parish SD
Supt. – See Houma
Caldwell MS, HCR 02 BOX 600 70395
A. Martin, prin.
ES, 1018 HWY 24 70395 – Earl Clement, prin.

Scott, Layfayette Parish, Pop. Code 4
Lafayette Parish SD
Supt. – See Lafayette
MS, P O BOX 427 70583 – John Boudreaux, prin.
Judice ES, P O BOX 237 70583
Mary Kathleen Moss, prin.
Westside ES, P O BOX 428 70583
Mary Domingue, prin.

Shongaloo, Webster Parish, Pop. Code 3
Webster Parish SD
Supt. – See Minden
S, RURAL ROUTE 01 BOX 15 71072
Wayne Thrash, prin.

Shreveport, Caddo Parish, Pop. Code 9
Caddo Parish SD
Sch. Sys. Enr. Code 8
Supt. – Walter Lee, P O BOX 37000 71133
Bethune MS, 4331 HENRY ST 71109
Billie Alford, prin.
Bickham MS
6470 OLD MOORINGSPORT ROAD 71107
Kenneth Cochran, prin.
Broadmoor Lab MS, 441 ATLANTIC AVE 71105
W. Hearron, prin.
Caddo Parish Magnet MS
7635 CORNELIOUS LANE 71106
Lel McCullough, prin.
Clark MS, 351 HEARNE AVE 71103
Ecotry Fuller, prin.
Hollywood MS, 6310 CLIFT AVE 71106
Donald McLaurin, prin.
Linear MS, 2175 LINEAR ST 71107
Walter White, prin.
Linwood MS, 401 W 70TH ST 71106
Linda Cox, prin.
Midway MS, 3840 GREENWOOD ROAD 71109
Roosevelt Crosby, prin.
Ridgewood MS, 2001 RIDGEWOOD DRIVE 71118
Lonnie Dunn, prin.
Youree Drive MS, 6008 YOUREE DRIVE 71105
J. Reginald, prin.
Arthur Circle ES, 261 ARTHUR AVE 71105
Mary Manitzas, prin.
Atkins ES, 7611 SAINT VINCENT AVE 71106
William Jones, prin.
Barrett ES, 2600 BARRETT ST 71104
Melvin Ashley, prin.
Caddo Heights ES, 1702 CORBITT ST 71108
John Kerely,Jr., prin.
Central ES, 1627 WEINSTOCK ST 71103
Gloria Harrison, prin.
Cherokee Park ES
2010 E ALGONQUIN TRAIL 71107
Curtis White,Jr., prin.
Claiborne Fundamental ES
2345 CLAIBORNE AVE 71103
Sebron Deloach, prin.
Creswell ES, 2901 CRESWELL AVE 71104
Niccie Johnson, prin.
Eden Gardens Fundamental ES
626 EDEN BLVD 71106 – Martha Peal, prin.
Fairfield ES, 6215 FAIRFIELD AVE 71106
Bettye Phillips, prin.
Forest Hill ES, 2005 FRANCAIS DR 71118
Elizabeth Booty, prin.
Hendrix ES, 701 PIERRE AVE 71103
Marie Clark, prin.
Hillsdale ES, 3460 HUTCHINSON ST 71109
Joseph Carter, prin.
Ingersoll ES, 401 N HOLZMAN ST 71101
Mary Williams, prin.
Judson Fundamental ES, 3809 JUDSON ST 71109
Essie Holt, prin.
Lakeshore ES, 1807 SAN JACINTO ST 71109
Isaac Manuel,Jr, prin.
North Highlands ES, 885 POLEMAN ROAD 71107
Mary Ann Sweeters, prin.
Northside ES, 2000 NORTHSIDE DR 71107
Winnie Antoine, prin.
Oak Park ES, 4941 MCDANIEL DR 71109
Velma Howard, prin.
Pine Grove ES, 1800 CALDWELL ST 71107
Linda Henderson, prin.
Queensborough ES, 1105 LOUISIANA AVE 71101
Shirley Culbert, prin.
Riverside ES, 625 DIXIE GARDEN RD 71105
Edward Hudson, prin.
Shreve Island ES, 836 SEWANNE PLACE 71105
Kerry Laster, prin.
Smith ES, 3000 M L KING DR 71107
Priscilla Pullen, prin.
South Highlands Magnet ES, 831 ERIE ST 71106
Pamela Byrd, prin.
Southern Hills ES, 9075 KINGSTON ROAD 71118
Melvin McConnell, prin.
Steere ES, 4009 YOUREE DR 71105
Dan Waters, prin.
Stoner Hill Lab ES, 2127 HOPEWELL ST 71104
Judith Butcher, prin.
Summer Grove ES, 2955 REISOR ROAD 71118
Dr. Emily Rachal, prin.
Summerfield ES, 3131 ARDIS TAYLOR DR 71118
John Renfro, prin.
Sunset Acres ES, 6514 W CANAL BLVD 71108
Nancy Melroy, prin.
Timmons ES
1410 GREENWOOD MOORINGSPORT 71107
Martha Keith, prin.
Turner ES, 5904 W 70TH ST 71129
Dr. James Becken, prin.
University ES, 9900 SMITHERMAN DR 71115
James Sanders, prin.
West Shreveport ES, 2226 MURPHY ST 71103
Dr. Horace Maxile, prin.
Walnut Hill ES, RURAL ROUTE 02 BOX 85 71129
Albert Hardison, prin.
Werner Park ES, 2715 CORBITT ST 71108
Lloyd Parker, prin.
Westwood ES, 7325 JEWELLA AVE 71108
Lucille Becken, prin.

Other Schools – See Belcher, Blanchard, Hosston,
Keithville, Mooringsport, Oil City, Vivian

Baptist Christian Academy
3031 HOLLYWOOD AVE 71108
Calvary Baptist Academy
9333 LINWOOD AVE 71106
First Baptist Church School
OCKLEY AT HIGHLAND 71106
Southfield School
1100 SOUTHFIELD ROAD 71106
Trinity Heights Christian Academy
4800 OLD MOORINGSPORT ROAD 71107
First Baptist Church School
533 OCKLEY DRIVE 71106
Holy Rosary Catholic School, 1730 COX ST 71108
Our Lady Blessed Sacarment Academy
2932 MURPHY ST 71103
St. John Berchmans School
947 JORDAN ST 71101
St. Joseph Catholic School
1210 ANNISTON AVE 71105
St. Mark's Evangel School
908 RUTHERFORD ST 71104
St. Pius Tenth Catholic School
4300-A N MARKET ST 71107

Sicily Island, Catahoula Parish, Pop. Code 3
Catahoula Parish SD
Supt. – See Jonesville
Martin JHS, P O BOX 373 71368
Wilbert Gardner, prin.
ES, P O BOX 207 71368 – Nan Smith, prin.

Sikes, Winn Parish, Pop. Code 2
Winn Parish SD
Supt. – See Winnfield
S, P O BOX 10 71473 – Ronald Brazzell, prin.

Simmesport, Avoyelles Parish, Pop. Code 4
Avoyelles Parish SD
Supt. – See Marksville
Simmesport ES, S MAIN ST 71369
James Bordelon, prin.

Simpson, Vernon Parish, Pop. Code 3
Vernon Parish SD
Supt. – See Leesville
S, P O BOX 8 71474 – Jim Funderburk, prin.

Simsboro, Lincoln Parish, Pop. Code 3
Lincoln Parish SD
Supt. – See Ruston
S, P O BOX 118 71275 – Dr. David Gullatt, prin.

Singer, Beauregard Parish, Pop. Code 2
Beauregard Parish SD
Supt. – See De Ridder
S, P O BOX 398 70660 – Larue Cooley, prin.

Slaughter, East Feliciana Parish, Pop. Code 3
East Feliciana Parish SD
Supt. – See Clinton
ES, P O BOX 60 70777 – Larry Meares, prin.

Slidell, St. Tammany Parish, Pop. Code 8
St. Tammany Parish SD
Supt. – See Covington
Boyet JHS, 380 REBEL DRIVE 70461
R. Magee, prin.
St. Tammany JHS, 701 CLEVELAND AVE 70458
Victor Doucette, prin.
JHS, 333 PENNSYLVANIA AVE 70458
John Mire, prin.
Abney ES, P O BOX 849 70459
E. Dubuisson, prin.
Alton ES, P O BOX 748 70459
Anthony Alfred, prin.
Bayou Woods ES, 115 LIBERTY DR 70460
Dr. Edward Burow, prin.
Bonne Ecole ES, 900 RUE VERAND 70458
Port Evans, prin.
Brock ES, 259 BRAKEFIELD ST 70458
Melba Vander, prin.
Carolyn Park MS, ROUTE 15 BOX 466 70460
Phyllis Crow, prin.
Clearwood ES, 130 CLEARWOOD DR 70458
Dr. Jordan Brooks,Jr., prin.
Florida Avenue ES, P O BOX 1997 70459
Charles Sumrall, prin.
Honey Island PS, 600 S MILITARY ROAD 70460
Robert Williams, prin.
Little Oak ES, 250 REBEL DR 70461
Marilyn Faust, prin.

Our Lady of the Lourdes School
345 WESTCHESTER BLVD 70458
St. Margaret Mary School
1050 ROBERT ROAD 70458

Springfield, Livingston Parish, Pop. Code 2
Livingston Parish SD
Supt. – See Livingston
MS, P O BOX 279 70462 – Charles King, prin.
ES, P O BOX 8 70462 – George Stewart, prin.

Springhill, Webster Parish, Pop. Code 6
Webster Parish SD
Supt. – See Minden
JHS, 410 W CHURCH ST 71075
Henry Colvin, prin.
Brown MS, 804 4TH ST SW 71075
Jonathan Washington, prin.
Browning ES, 505 HERRINGTON DR 71075
Jerry Camp, prin.
Howell ES, P O BOX 716 71075 – Ted Souter, prin.

Starks, Calcasieu Parish, Pop. Code 3
Calcasieu Parish SD
Supt. – See Lake Charles
S, P O BOX 68 70661 – Roger Creel, prin.

Start, Richland Parish
Richland Parish SD
Supt. – See Rayville
ES 71279 – Larry Butler, prin.

Sterlington, Ouachita Parish, Pop. Code 4
Ouachita Parish SD
Supt. – See Monroe
Smith ES, P O BOX 646 71280
  Bobby Caldwell, prin.

Stonewall, De Soto Parish, Pop. Code 4
De Soto Parish SD
Supt. – See Mansfield
ES, P O BOX 260 71078 – Linda Binning, prin.

Sulphur, Calcasieu Parish, Pop. Code 7
Calcasieu Parish SD
Supt. – See Lake Charles
Leblanc/Drost MS, 1100 N CROCKER ST 70663
  Robert Hunter, prin.
Lewis MS, 1752 CYPRESS ST 70663
  Charles Hansen, prin.
Frasch ES, 540 S HUNTINGTON ST 70663
  Roderick Truax, prin.
Henning ES, 774 HENNING DR 70663
  Charles Ritchie, prin.
Key ES, 1201 E BURTON ST 70663
  Lewis Moss, prin.
Maplewood ES, 4401 MAPLEWOOD DRIVE 70663
  Betty Jo Sample, prin.
Perkins ES, 565 N CROCKER ST 70663
  Edwin Dawdy, prin.
Vincent ES, 16634 ARIZONA ST 70663
  William Hess, prin.

Our Lady's Catholic School
  1111 CYPRESS ST 70663

Summerfield, Claiborne Parish, Pop. Code 2
Claiborne Parish SD
Supt. – See Homer
S, P O BOX 158 71079 – William Kennedy, prin.

Sunset, St. Landry Parish, Pop. Code 4
St. Landry Parish SD
Supt. – See Opelousas
Cankton ES, 260 MAIN ST 70584
  John Daigle, prin.
ES, P O BOX C 70584 – Charles Malbrough, prin.

Swartz, Ouachita Parish
Ouachita Parish SD
Supt. – See Monroe
ES, P O BOX 8 71281 – Alice Morris, prin.

Tallulah, Madison Parish, Pop. Code 7
Madison Parish SD
Sch. Sys. Enr. Code 5
Supt. – Martin Verhagen, P O BOX 1620 71284
Thomastown S, RURAL ROUTE 02 BOX 90 71282
  Johnny Ford, prin.
McCall JHS, 900 W ASKEW ST 71282
  Adell Williams, prin.
ES, 1100 JOHNSON ST 71282
  Norman Powell, prin.
Wright ES, FISH AND UNIVERSITY STS 71282
  Ernestine Toney, prin.

Tallulah Academy-Delta Christian HS
  P O BOX 911 71284

Theriot, Terrebonne Parish
Terrebonne Parish SD
Supt. – See Houma
Dularge ES, THERIOT POST OFFICE 70397
  Henry Hebert, prin.
Dularge MS, THERIOT POST OFFICE 70397
  Willie Gaither, prin.

Thibodaux, Lafourche Parish, Pop. Code 7
Lafourche Parish SD
Sch. Sys. Enr. Code 7
Supt. – Arden Rogers, P O BOX 879 70302
Chackbay ES, 101 SCHOOL LANE 70301
  Maedra Clement, prin.
Lafargue ES, 700 PLANTATION ROAD 70301
  Oneil Andras, prin.
South Thibodaux MS
  IRIS ST & STADIUM DR 70301 – E. Ledet,Jr., prin.
St. Charles ES, HIGHWAY 1 BOX 1690 70301
  Roland Toups, prin.
Sixth Ward MS, HCR 02 BOX K-398A 70301
  Perry Rodrique, prin.
ES, 700 E 7TH ST 70301
  Dr. G. Marie Kinchen, prin.
Other Schools – See Cut Off, Galliano, Golden
  Meadow, Houma, Kraemer, Larose, Lockport,
  Raceland

St. Genevieve Catholic School
  807 BARBIER AVE 70301
St. Joseph Catholic School
  501 CARDINAL DR 70301

Tickfaw, Tangipahoa Parish, Pop. Code 3
Tangipahoa Parish SD
Supt. – See Amite
Nesom ES, P O BOX 280 70466
  Charles Kirkfield, prin.

Tioga, Rapides Parish, Pop. Code 2
Rapides Parish SD
Supt. – See Alexandria
JHS, P O BOX 638 71477 – Winston Welch, prin.

Transylvania, East Carroll Parish
East Carroll Parish SD
Supt. – See Lake Providence
ES, P O BOX 8 71286 – Charles Vining,Jr., prin.

Trout, La Salle Parish, Pop. Code 2
LaSalle Parish SD
Supt. – See Jena
Fellowship ES
  RURAL ROUTE 01 BOX 193 71371
  John Parker, prin.

Tullos, La Salle Parish, Pop. Code 3
LaSalle Parish SD
Supt. – See Jena
Lasalle JHS, P O BOX 7 71479 – Steve Long, prin.

Tunica, West Feliciana Parish
West Feliciana Parish SD
Supt. – See Saint Francisville
ES, GENERAL DELIVERY 70782
  Sidney Davis,Jr., prin.

Urania, La Salle Parish, Pop. Code 3
LaSalle Parish SD
Supt. – See Jena
ES, P O BOX 725 71480 – Joe Shaver, prin.

Vacherie, St. James Parish, Pop. Code 4
St. James Parish SD
Supt. – See Lutcher
St. James JHS, RURAL ROUTE 02 BOX 6M 70090
  Morris Mitchell, prin.
MS, RURAL ROUTE 01 BOX 965 70090
  David Granier, prin.
Sixth Ward ES, P O BOX 438 70090
  Ralph Plaisance, prin.
PS, RURAL ROUTE 01 BOX 800 70090
  Abraham Williams, prin.

Venice, Plaquemines Parish, Pop. Code 2
Plaquemines Parish SD
Supt. – See Belle Chasse
Boothville-Venice S, RURAL ROUTE 01 70091
  Allen Olson, prin.

Verda, Grant Parish
Grant Parish SD
Supt. – See Colfax
ES, GENERAL DELIVERY 71481
  Peggy Seward, prin.

Vidalia, Concordia Parish, Pop. Code 6
Concordia Parish SD
Sch. Sys. Enr. Code 6
Supt. – Harold Graham, P O BOX 950 71373
JHS, P O BOX 429 71373 – James Lee, prin.
Vidalia Lower ES, 300 N HICKORY ST 71373
  Gary Parnham, prin.
Vidalia Upper MS, 1 CONCOARDIA AVE 71373
  Warren Enterkin, prin.
Other Schools – See Ferriday, Monterey, Ridgecrest

Ville Platte, Evangeline Parish, Pop. Code 6
Evangeline Parish SD
Sch. Sys. Enr. Code 6
Supt. – Larry Broussard
  1101 TE MAMOU ROAD 70586
Vidrine S, RURAL ROUTE 05 BOX 200 70586
  Roland Smith, prin.
Heath ES, RURAL ROUTE 03 BOX 129 70586
  Shirley Tezeno, prin.
Stephens MS, P O BOX 557 70586
  Mark Latigue, prin.
Ville Platte Lower ES
  708 HIGH SCHOOL DR 70586
  Fredrick Soileau, prin.
Other Schools – See Basile, Chataignier, Mamou, Pine
  Prairie

Sacred Heart ES, 532 E MAIN ST 70586

Vinton, Calcasieu Parish, Pop. Code 5
Calcasieu Parish SD
Supt. – See Lake Charles
Vinton Northside MS, 900 HORRIDGE ST 70668
  Glyndel Ebarb, prin.
ES, 1610 HAMPTON ST 70668
  Henry Soileau, prin.

Violet, St. Bernard Parish
St. Bernard Parish SD
Supt. – See Chalmette
Borgnemouth ES, GENERAL DELIVERY 70092
  Lynn Gagnon, prin.
Millaudon MS
  6701 SAINT BERNARD HWY 70092
  Milton Boackle, prin.

Vivian, Caddo Parish, Pop. Code 5
Caddo Parish SD
Supt. – See Shreveport
ES, 100 W KENTUCKY AVE 71082
  William Jordan, prin.

Waggaman, Orleans Parish, Pop. Code 3
Jefferson Parish SD
Supt. – See Harvey
Cherbonnier ES, 700 DANDELION DR 70094
  Margie Zeno, prin.
Rillieux ES, 7121 RIVER ROAD 70094
  Cynthia Lassere, prin.

Walker, Livingston Parish, Pop. Code 5
Livingston Parish SD
Supt. – See Livingston
JHS, P O BOX 219 70785 – Paul Ledoux, prin.
Milton ES, P O BOX 187 70785
  Carolyn Spence, prin.
Walker PS, P O BOX 188 70785
  Carlton Ellis, prin.
Walker MS, P O BOX 250 70785
  Jerry Fletcher,Sr., prin.

Washington, St. Landry Parish, Pop. Code 4
St. Landry Parish SD
Supt. – See Opelousas
S, P O BOX 98 70589 – Jim Red, prin.
Grand Prairie ES, HCR BOX 149 70589
  Dillard DeVille, prin.

Waterproof, Tensas Parish, Pop. Code 4
Tensas Parish SD
Supt. – See Saint Joseph
Lisbon ES, P O BOX 158 71375
  Arthur Johnson, prin.

Watson, Livingston Parish
Livingston Parish SD
Supt. – See Livingston
Live Oak MS, P O BOX 147 70786 – (—), prin.
Live Oak ES, P O BOX 220 70786
  Patricia Davis, prin.

Welsh, Jefferson Davis Parish, Pop. Code 5
Jefferson Davis Parish SD
Supt. – See Jennings
ES, 222 E BOURGEOIS ST 70591
  Wilbert Gilbeaux, prin.

Westlake, Calcasieu Parish, Pop. Code 6
Calcasieu Parish SD
Supt. – See Lake Charles
Arnett MS, 400 SULPHUR AVE 70669
  B. Jardell, prin.
Mossville ES
  RURAL ROUTE 02 BOX 436-A 70669
  Lasalle Williams, prin.
Western Heights ES, 1100 ELIZABETH ST 70669
  Daniel Cupit, prin.
Westwood ES, 1900 WESTWOOD ROAD 70669
  Earnest Smith, prin.

West Monroe, Ouachita Parish, Pop. Code 7
Ouachita Parish SD
Supt. – See Monroe
Richardson MS, 910 THOMAS ROAD 71291
  Louis Pargoud, prin.
Riser JHS, 100 PRICE DRIVE 71291
  Linda Brian, prin.
MS, 1600 N 7TH ST 71291 – Ernest Reed, prin.
Boley ES, 2213 CYPRESS ST 71291
  Amy Dewees, prin.
Claiborne ES, HIGHWAY 80 WEST 71291
  Claude Smith, prin.
Crosley ES, 700 NATCHITOCHES ST 71291
  Thomas Perry, prin.
Drew ES, RURAL ROUTE 01 BOX 266 71291
  Barbara Dykes, prin.
Highland ES, WELLERMAN ROAD 71291
  Patricia Valentine, prin.
Kiroli ES, 600 KIROLI ROAD 71291
  Pearl Maxey, prin.
Lenwil ES, 112 ARRANT ROAD 71291
  Roy Simms, prin.
Mitchell ES, 400 MITCHELL LANE 71291
  Georgianna Webb, prin.
Pinecrest ES, RURAL ROUTE 06 BOX 242 71291
  Michael McCall, prin.
Ransom ES, 420 WHEELIS ST 71291
  Dr. Mary Tiller, prin.
Riser ES, 100 PRICE DR 71291
  Freddie Whitten, prin.
Woodlawn ES
  RURAL ROUTE 03 BOX 126-C 71291
  Betty Oxford, prin.

Ridgedale Academy
  122 RIDGEDALE ROAD 71294
St. Paschal Catholic School
  801 WILSON ST 71291

Westwego, Jefferson Parish, Pop. Code 7
Jefferson Parish SD
Supt. – See Harvey
Bridge City ES, 1805 BRIDGE CITY AVE 70094
  Phillip Ragozzino, prin.
Butler ES, 300 FOURTH ST 70094
  P. Billiot, prin.
Live Oak Manor ES
  ARCADIA & HALLE STS 70094
  Gloria Loumiet, prin.
Pitre ES, 1525 SPRUCE ST 70094
  Cindy Brown, prin.
Strehle ES, 178 MILLIE DR 70094
  Dr. Jackie Pizanno, prin.
ES, 537 AVE D 70094 – Claire Loch, prin.

Our Lady of Prompt Succor School
  531 AVE A 70094

White Castle, Iberville Parish, Pop. Code 4
Iberville Parish SD
Supt. – See Plaquemine
Dorseyville MS, P O BOX 370 70788
  John Bueche, prin.
Samstown ES, RURAL ROUTE 01 BOX 19 70788
  Irene Williams, prin.

Our Lady of Prompt Succor School
609 BOWIE ST 70788

Winnfield, Winn Parish, Pop. Code 6
Winn Parish SD
Sch. Sys. Enr. Code 5
Supt. – Derwood Duke, P O BOX 430 71483
MS, P O BOX 1140 71483 – Jefferson Hobdy, prin.
IS, 400 S SAINT JOHN ST 71483
Archie Chandler, prin.
PS, 401 S SAINT JOHN ST 71483 – J. Hobdy, prin.
Other Schools – See Atlanta, Calvin, Dodson, Sikes

Winnsboro, Franklin Parish, Pop. Code 6
Franklin Parish SD
Sch. Sys. Enr. Code 6
Supt. – Jacquelyn Shipp, P O BOX 349 71295
Ogden S, RURAL ROUTE 02 BOX 200 71295
Dorothy Brown, prin.
Ward III S, RURAL ROUTE 01 71295
Charles Harris, prin.

JHS, RURAL ROUTE 01 BOX 33   71295
Michael Caldwell, prin.
Winnsboro Lower ES, 1310 WARREN ST 71295
Arthur Rhodes III, prin.
Winnsboro Upper MS, 1306 WARREN ST 71295
Evelyn Dean, prin.
Other Schools – See Baskin, Crowville, Fort
Necessity, Gilbert, Wisner

Franklin Academy, 2110 LOOP ROAD 71295

Wisner, Franklin Parish, Pop. Code 4
Franklin Parish SD
Supt. – See Winnsboro
ES, P O BOX 220 71378 – Louis Johnson,Sr., prin.

Youngsville, Lafayette Parish, Pop. Code 4
Lafayette Parish SD
Supt. – See Lafayette
MS, P O BOX 1049 70592 – O. Guilliot, prin.
Lindon ES, P O BOX 29 70592
Leander Gray III, prin.

Zachary, East Baton Rouge Parish, Pop. Code 6
East Baton Rouge Parish SD
Supt. – See Baton Rouge
Northwestern MS, 5200 E CENTRAL AVE 70791
Ann Clark, prin.
Northwestern ES
ROLLINS AND POPE ROAD 70791
Donald Thomas, prin.
ES, 3775 HEMLOCK ST 70791
Ronald Daniel, prin.

Zwolle, Sabine Parish, Pop. Code 5
Sabine Parish SD
Supt. – See Many
IS, P O BOX 768 71486 – John Leslie, prin.

MAINE

DEPARTMENT OF EDUCATION & CULTURAL SERVICES
Education Building
State House Station #23, Augusta 04333
(207) 289-5800

Commissioner of Education	Eve Bither
Deputy Commissioner	Richard Card
Associate Commissioner Bureau of School Management	David Brown
Associate Commissioner Bureau of Instruction	William Richards
Associate Commissioner Bureau of Vocational Education	William Cassidy

STATE BOARD OF EDUCATION
Carol Wishcamper, *Chairperson*   Wolf's Neck Rd., Freeport 04032

POSTSECONDARY EDUCATION COMMISSION
Thomas Williams, *Chairperson*   State House Station #23, Augusta 04333

PUBLIC, PRIVATE, AND PAROCHIAL ELEMENTARY SCHOOLS

Abbot Village, Piscataquis Co., Pop. Code 3
SAD 4
Supt. – See Guilford
Abbot ES, P O BOX 90 04406 – David Pratt, prin.

Addison, Washington Co., Pop. Code 4
SAD 37
Supt. – See Harrington
Merritt ES 04606 – Clarence Reed, prin.

Albion, Kennebec Co., Pop. Code 4
SAD 49
Supt. – See Fairfield
ES, RURAL ROUTE 01 BOX 1398 04910
John Bacon, prin.

Alfred, York Co., Pop. Code 2
SAD 57
Supt. – See Waterboro
ES, P O BOX 579 04002 – Frank Tarazewich, prin.

Andover, Oxford Co., Pop. Code 2
SAD 44
Supt. – See Bethel
ES, P O BOX 70 04216 – Karen Robinson, prin.

Anson, Somerset Co., Pop. Code 3
SAD 59
Supt. – See Madison
Starks ES, RURAL ROUTE 01 BOX 510 04911
Noreen Beane, prin.

SAD 74
Supt. – See North Anson
Schenck ES, P O BOX 317 04911
Regina Campbell, prin.

Ashland, Aroostook Co., Pop. Code 4
SAD 32
Sch. Sys. Enr. Code 3
Supt. – W. Greg Botka, P O BOX 289 04732
Ashland Central ES, P O BOX Q 04732
Roger Marecaux, prin.

Athens, Somerset Co., Pop. Code 3
SAD 59
Supt. – See Madison
ES, P O BOX 265 04912 – Brian Bonneau, prin.

Auburn, Androscoggin Co., Pop. Code 7
Auburn SD
Sch. Sys. Enr. Code 5
Supt. – R. Loux, 23 HIGH ST 04210
MS, 610 COURT ST 04210 – Peter Selwood, prin.
East Auburn ES
RURAL ROUTE 03 BOX 874 04210
Charles Plummer, prin.
Fairview-Stevens Mills ES, MINOT AVE 04210
Donn Marcus, prin.
Great Falls IS, ACADEMY ST 04210
Barbara Eretzian, prin.
Lake Street ES, LAKE STREET 04210
Ronald Logan, prin.
Sherwood Heights ES, SHERWOOD DR 04210
Thomas Deschaine, prin.
Washburn ES, 35 LAKE AUBURN AVE 04210
Charles Plummer, prin.
Webster MS, 99 HAMPSHIRE ST 04210
Antoinette Davino, prin.
Wight ES, C/O LAKE ST SCHOOL 04210
Ronald Logan, prin.
Woodbury PS, MT AUBURN AVE 04210
Janet Williams, prin.

Augusta, Kennebec Co., Pop. Code 7
Augusta SD
Sch. Sys. Enr. Code 5
Supt. – W. Logan
RURAL ROUTE 02 BOX 1080 04330
Buker JHS, 22 ARMORY ST 04330
Michael Buckley, prin.
Hodgkins JHS, 17 MALTA ST 04330
Barbara Sinskie, prin.
Farrington ES, HOSPITAL STREET 04330
Peter Washburn, prin.
Gilbert ES, 1 SUNSET AVE 04330
Earl Mann, prin.

Hussey ES, 11 GEDNEY ST 04330
Gloria McGraw, prin.
Lincoln ES, JOHNSON STREET 04330
Richard Dyke, prin.

SAD 47
Supt. – See Oakland
Bean ES, RURAL ROUTE 03 BOX 500 04330
Joseph Mattos, prin.

Union SD 52
Supt. – See Winslow
Riverside ES, RURAL ROUTE 01 BOX 680 04330
Elizabeth Avery, prin.

Unorganized Territories SD
Sch. Sys. Enr. Code 2
Supt. – R Adams, STATION 23 04333
Other Schools – See Benedicta, Brookton, Caribou,
Dennysville, Kingman, Rockwood, Sinclair

St. Augustine ES, 24 WASHINGTON ST 04330
St. Mary's ES, 56 SEWALL ST 04330

Aurora, Hancock Co., Pop. Code 2
Airline Community SD
Supt. – See East Holden
Airline Community ES
GREAT POND ROAD 04408 – Karen Frye, prin.

Baileyville, Washington Co., Pop. Code 4
Union SD 107
Sch. Sys. Enr. Code 3
Supt. – R. Fifield, P O BOX 580 04694
Other Schools – See Princeton, Woodland

Bangor, Penobscot Co., Pop. Code 8
Bangor SD
Sch. Sys. Enr. Code 5
Supt. – J. Doughty, 73 HARLOW ST 04401
Fifth Street MS, 143 FIFTH ST 04401
William Grant, prin.
Garland Street MS, 304 GARLAND ST 04401
Stephen Bishop, prin.

Downeast ES, 100 MOOSEHEAD BLVD 04401
Dorothy Pratt, prin.
Fairmount MS, 58 THIRTEENTH ST 04401
Peter Prescott, prin.
Fourteenth Street PS, 224 14TH ST 04401
Christine MacGregor, prin.
Fruit Street PS, 175 FRUIT ST 04401
Daniel Lee, prin.
Lincoln ES, 45 FOREST AVE 04401
Deborah Belyea, prin.
Snow MS, 435 BROADWAY 04401
Joseph Morrison, prin.
Vine Street ES, 66 VINE ST 04401
Charles Thayer, prin.

Union SD 34
Sch. Sys. Enr. Code 4
Supt. – G. MacDonald
RURAL ROUTE 03 BOX 1208 04401
Glenburn ES, RURAL ROUTE 540 04401
Gregory Knight, prin.
Hermon ES, RURAL ROUTE 02 BOX 366 04401
Michael O'Brien, prin.

Union SD 87
Supt. – See Orono
Graham ES, 3 FLAGG ST 04401
Michael Cyr, prin.

St. John's ES, 166 STATE ST 04401
St. Mary's ES, 70 FIRST ST 04401

Bar Harbor, Hancock Co., Pop. Code 5
Union SD 98
Supt. – See Mount Desert
Conners/Emerson ES, EAGLE LAKE ROAD 04609
Peter Nagorniuk, prin.

Bar Mills, York Co., Pop. Code 2
SAD 6
Sch. Sys. Enr. Code 5
Supt. – R. Barker, P O BOX 38 04004
Libby ES, P O BOX 57 04004
Millicent Smith, prin.
Other Schools – See Hollis Center, Limerick, Sebago
Lake, Standish, Steep Falls, West Buxton

Bass Harbor, Hancock Co., Pop. Code 2
Union SD 98
Supt. – See Mount Desert
Tremont ES 04653 – Val Perkins, prin.

Bath, Sagadhoc Co., Pop. Code 7
Union SD 47
Sch. Sys. Enr. Code 5
Supt. – L. Hickey, 2 SHERIDAN ROAD 04530
Dike-Newell ES, WRIGHT DR 04530
Lorraine Redwine, prin.
Fisher-Mitchell ES, 597 HIGH ST 04530
Andree Tostevin, prin.
Huse Memorial ES, ANDREWS ROAD 04530
Charles Manchester, prin.
West Bath ES, NEW MEADOWS ROAD 04530
John McPhail,Jr., prin.
Other Schools – See Georgetown, Phippsburg,
Woolwich

Beals, Washington Co., Pop. Code 3
Union SD 103
Supt. – See Jonesport
ES, P O BOX 220 04611 – Leon Crowley, prin.

Belfast, Waldo Co., Pop. Code 6
SAD 34
Sch. Sys. Enr. Code 4
Supt. – S. Payne, P O BOX 363 04915
Crosby JHS, CHURCH ST 04915
Sarah Crosby, prin.
Anderson ES, 126 HIGH ST 04915
Susan Murphy, prin.
Drinkwater ES, RURAL ROUTE 01 04915
David Foster, prin.
East Belfast ES, SWAN LAKE AVE 04915
Susan Murphy, prin.
Nickerson ES, RURAL ROUTE 02 04915
Susan Murphy, prin.
Peirce ES, SCHOOL STREET 04915
Davis Foster, prin.
Robertson MS, SCHOOL STREET 04915
David Foster, prin.
Other Schools – See Searsmont

Belgrade, Kennebec Co., Pop. Code 4
SAD 47
Supt. – See Oakland
Belgrade Central ES, P O BOX 98 04917
Reno Deschaine, prin.

Benedicta, Aroostook Co., Pop. Code 2
Unorganized Territories SD
Supt. – See Augusta
ES 04733 – Joseph Costa, prin.

Berwick, York Co., Pop. Code 5
SAD 60
Supt. – See North Berwick
Noble JHS, P O BOX 693 03901
Jack Clements, prin.
ES, P O BOX 695 03901 – Lynette Plaisted, prin.

Bethel, Oxford Co., Pop. Code 4
SAD 44
Sch. Sys. Enr. Code 4
Supt. – D. Craig
RURAL ROUTE 01 BOX 1220 04217
Bisbee ES, P O BOX 210 04217
Nancy Davis, prin.

Crescent Park ES, P O BOX 210 04217
Nancy Davis, prin.
Other Schools – See Andover, Bryant Pond

Biddeford, York Co., Pop. Code 7
Arundel SD
Sch. Sys. Enr. Code 2
Supt. – D. Beal
RURAL ROUTE 04 BOX 566 04005
Day ES, RURAL ROUTE 04 BOX 566 04005
D. Beal, prin.

Biddeford SD
Sch. Sys. Enr. Code 5
Supt. – R. Hodge, 2 MAPLEWOOD AVE 04005
JHS, 189 ALFRED ST 04005
Suzanne Lukas, prin.
Emery ES, 83 BIRCH ST 04005
Jeffrey Hodgdon, prin.
Kennedy Memorial ES, WEST STREET 04005
John Narsiff, prin.

SAD 57
Supt. – See Waterboro
Cousens Memeorial ES, RURAL ROUTE 03 04005
Edward Newell,Jr., prin.

St. Andre ES, 39 SULLIVAN ST 04005
St. Joseph ES, 25 GRAHAM ST 04005
St. Mary's, 6 SAINT MARYS ST 04005

Bingham, Somerset Co., Pop. Code 4
Pleasant Ridge Unit SD
Sch. Sys. Enr. Code 1
Supt. – C. Barnes, P O BOX 139 04920
Longfellow ES, HCR BOX 35 04920
Ruth Austin, prin.

SAD 13
Sch. Sys. Enr. Code 2
Supt. – C. Barnes, P O BOX 139 04920
Caratunk MS, P O BOX 109 04920
Linda Hunnewell, prin.
Moscow ES, P O BOX 109 04920
Linda Hunnewell, prin.
Quimby MS, P O BOX 109 04920
Linda Hunnewell, prin.
Other Schools – See West Forks

Blue Hill, Hancock Co., Pop. Code 4
Union SD 93
Sch. Sys. Enr. Code 3
Supt. – K. Hall, P O BOX 630 04614
Blue Hill Consolodated ES, P O BOX 522 04614
Elizabeth Beardsley, prin.
Other Schools – See Brooksville, Castine, Penobscot

Boothbay Harbor, Lincoln Co., Pop. Code 4
Boothbay Harbor Community SD
Sch. Sys. Enr. Code 3
Supt. – D. Hopkins, 96 TOWNSEND AVE 04538
Boothbay Regional ES
156B TOWNSEND AVE 04538
Gloria Walter, prin.

Union SD 49
Sch. Sys. Enr. Code 2
Supt. – D. Hopkins, 96 TOWNSEND AVE 04538
Other Schools – See North Edgecomb, West Southport

Bowdoinham, Sagadahoc Co., Pop. Code 4
SAD 75
Supt. – See Topsham
Bowdoin Central ES
RURAL ROUTE 02 BOX 164 04008
Elizabeth Manchester, prin.
Bowdoinham Community ES
CEMETERY ROAD 04008 – R. Burns, prin.

Bradford, Penobscot Co., Pop. Code 3
SAD 64
Supt. – See East Corinth
ES, RURAL ROUTE 01 BOX 283 04410
Norma Trask, prin.

Bradley, Penobscot Co., Pop. Code 4
Union SD 90
Supt. – See Milford
Rand ES, P O BOX 64 04411 – Michael Cyr, prin.

Brewer, Penobscot Co., Pop. Code 6
Brewer SD
Sch. Sys. Enr. Code 4
Supt. – P. Jordan, 49 CAPRI ST 04412
MS, 5 SOMERSET ST 04412 – Robert Dyer, prin.
Capri Street ES, 49 CAPRI ST 04412
Islay Hedger, prin.
Pendelton Street ES, 88 PENDLETON ST 04412
Lester Young, prin.
State Street MS, 131 STATE ST 04412
Kerry Priest, prin.
Washington Street MS
100 WASHINGTON ST 04412 – Allan Snell, prin.

SAD 63
Supt. – See East Holden
Holden ES, RURAL ROUTE 01 BOX 1631 04412
Lester Butler, prin.

Bridgewater, Aroostook Co., Pop. Code 3
Bridgewater Unit SD
Sch. Sys. Enr. Code 1
Supt. – R. Hasenfus, P O BOX 205 04735
ES, P O BOX 205 04735 – Rhoda Collins, prin.

Bridgton, Cumberland Co., Pop. Code 5
SAD 61
Sch. Sys. Enr. Code 5
Supt. – J. Fontana, P O BOX 80 04009
Lake Region JHS
RURAL ROUTE 02 BOX 525 04009
Larry Thompson, prin.
ES, P O BOX 50 04009 – Jacqueline Kelly, prin.
Stevens Brook MS, P O BOX 50 04009
Jacqueline Kelly, prin.
Other Schools – See Casco, East Sebago, Naples

Brooklin, Hancock Co., Pop. Code 3
Union SD 76
Supt. – See Stonington
JHS, MAIN ST 04616 – Richard Welch, prin.
ES, MAIN STREET 04616 – Richard Welch, prin.

Brooks, Waldo Co., Pop. Code 3
SAD 3
Supt. – See Unity
Morse Memorial ES, SCHOOL STREET 04921
Sarah Crawford, prin.

Brooksville, Hancock Co., Pop. Code 3
Union SD 93
Supt. – See Blue Hill
ES, P O BOX 178 04617 – Dale Carter, prin.

Brookton, Washington Co.
Unorganized Territories SD
Supt. – See Augusta
ES 04413 – Joseph Costa, prin.

Brownfield, Oxford Co., Pop. Code 3
SAD 72
Supt. – See Fryeburg
Brownfield Consolidated MS, P O BOX 130 04010
Thomas Doughty, prin.

Brownville, Piscataquis Co., Pop. Code 4
SAD 41
Supt. – See Milo
ES, RURAL ROUTE 01 BOX 10B 04414
David Walker, prin.

Brunswick, Cumberland Co., Pop. Code 7
Brunswick SD
Sch. Sys. Enr. Code 5
Supt. – D. Douglas, 35 UNION ST 04011
JHS, BARROWS ST 04011
Michael Galarneau, prin.
Coffin ES, 35 UNION ST 04011
Gilbert Peterson, prin.
Hawthorn ES, 46 FEDERAL ST 04011
Gregory Scott, prin.
Jordan Acres ES, MERRYMEETING RD 04011
Barbara Kurz, prin.
Longfellow ES, 21 LONGFELLOW AVE 04011
Gregory Scott, prin.

SAD 75
Supt. – See Topsham
Harpswell Island ES
RURAL ROUTE 02 BOX 2066 04011
Frances Ambrose, prin.

St. John's Parish School, 39 PLEASANT ST 04011

Bryant Pond, Oxford Co.
SAD 44
Supt. – See Bethel
Woodstock ES, RURAL ROUTE 02 BOX 731 04219
David Murphy, prin.

Buckfield, Oxford Co., Pop. Code 4
SAD 39
Sch. Sys. Enr. Code 3
Supt. – S. Meyers
RURAL ROUTE 03 BOX 156 04220
Hartford-Sumner ES
RURAL ROUTE 02 BOX 840 04220
Dennis Carpentier, prin.

Bucksport, Hancock Co., Pop. Code 5
Bucksport SD
Sch. Sys. Enr. Code 4
Supt. – V. Crockett, P O BOX 1519 04416
JHS, 63 ELM ST 04416 – F. Phinney, prin.
Jewett MS, P O BOX 636 04416
Darrold Mitchell, prin.
Warren ES, P O BOX 310 04416
Rosemary Babcock, prin.

Union SD 91
Sch. Sys. Enr. Code 3
Supt. – M. Curtis, P O BOX V 04416
Other Schools – See Orland, Orrington

Burlington, Penobscot Co., Pop. Code 2
SAD 31
Supt. – See Howland
ES, MAIN STREET 04417 – James Winslow, prin.

Burnham, Waldo Co., Pop. Code 3
SAD 53
Supt. – See Pittsfield
Burnham Village ES, RURAL ROUTE 01 04922
Charles Phillips, prin.

Calais, Washington Co., Pop. Code 5
Maine Indian Education SD
Sch. Sys. Enr. Code 2
Supt. – J. Smith, P O BOX 412 04619
Other Schools – See Old Town, Perry, Princeton

Union SD 106
Sch. Sys. Enr. Code 4
Supt. – R. Marx, RIVER ROAD 04619

MS, 1 WASHINGTON ST   04619
  Ralph Shannon, prin.
ES, GARFIELD STREET   04619 – Jean Wood, prin.
Other Schools – See Robbinston, Woodland

Cambridge, Somerset Co., Pop. Code 2
SAD 4
Supt. – See Guilford
ES, RURAL ROUTE 01 BOX 2305   04923
  Brenda Post, prin.

Camden, Knox Co., Pop. Code 5
SAD 28
Sch. Sys. Enr. Code 4
Supt. – T. Marx, P O BOX 657   04843
Taylor MS, 34 KNOWLTON ST   04843
  Michael Weatherwax, prin.
Elm Street ES, P O BOX 657   04843
  Marvin Higgins, prin.
Other Schools – See Rockport

Union SD 69
Sch. Sys. Enr. Code 2
Supt. – T. Marx, P O BOX 657   04843
Other Schools – See Union

Canaan, Somerset Co., Pop. Code 4
SAD 54
Supt. – See Skowhegan
ES, P O BOX 128   04924 – Laura Salley, prin.

Canton, Oxford Co., Pop. Code 3
SAD 21
Supt. – See Dixfield
ES   04221 – Nelson Neil, prin.

Cape Elizabeth, Cumberland Co., Pop. Code 6
Cape Elizabeth SD
Sch. Sys. Enr. Code 4
Supt. – D. Pelletier, P O BOX 6267   04107
MS, 4 SCOTT DYER ROAD   04107
  Christopher Toy, prin.
Pond Cove Lunt ES, 12 SCOTT DYER RD   04107
  Daryl Pelletier, prin.

Caribou, Aroostook Co., Pop. Code 6
Caribou SD
Sch. Sys. Enr. Code 4
Supt. – G. Johnston, 348 MAIN ST   04736
MS, 21 GLENN ST   04736 – John Plourde, prin.
Hilltop ES, 11 MARSHALL AVE   04736
  Madeline Belanger, prin.
Teague Park ES, 59 GLENN ST   04736
  Thomas Folsom, prin.

Union SD 122
Sch. Sys. Enr. Code 2
Supt. – A. Benner
  RURAL ROUTE 03 BOX 122   04736
Woodland ES, RURAL ROUTE 01 BOX 83A   04736
  Philip Caverhill, prin.
Other Schools – See New Sweden, Stockholm

Unorganized Territories SD
Supt. – See Augusta
Connor Consolodated ES
  RURAL ROUTE 04   04736
  Steven Anderson, prin.

Carmel, Penobscot Co., Pop. Code 4
SAD 23
Sch. Sys. Enr. Code 2
Supt. – P. Whitney, P O BOX 142   04419
Caravel JHS, P O BOX 142   04419
  Harold Stewart, prin.
ES, P O BOX 148   04419 – Orrison Moody, prin.
Other Schools – See Levant

SAD 38
Sch. Sys. Enr. Code 2
Supt. – P. Whitney, P O BOX 142   04419
Other Schools – See Etna

Casco, Cumberland Co., Pop. Code 4
SAD 61
Supt. – See Bridgton
Casco Memorial ES, P O BOX 307   04015
  Bonnie Reidman, prin.
Crooked River MS
  RURAL ROUTE 01 BOX 432   04015
  Ralph Maines, prin.

Castine, Hancock Co., Pop. Code 4
Union SD 93
Supt. – See Blue Hill
Adams ES, P O BOX C-4   04421
  Theresa Stanton, prin.

Charleston, Penobscot Co., Pop. Code 4
SAD 68
Supt. – See Dover-Foxcroft
ES, P O BOX 29   04422 – Brian Barrett, prin.

Chebeague Island, Cumberland Co.
SAD 51
Supt. – See Cumberland Center
ES   04017 – Brian Albert, prin.

Cherryfield, Washington Co., Pop. Code 3
SAD 37
Supt. – See Harrington
ES, SCHOOL STREET   04622 – Ralph Beal, prin.

China, Kennebec Co., Pop. Code 5
Union SD 52
Supt. – See Winslow
ES, ROUTE 202   04926 – Prescott Verrill,Jr., prin.

Cliff Island, Cumberland Co.
Portland SD
Supt. – See Portland
ES, P O BOX 7   04019 – Paul Steele, prin.

Clinton, Kennebec Co., Pop. Code 5
SAD 49
Supt. – See Fairfield
ES, P O BOX 189   04927 – Robert Clukey, prin.

Columbia Falls, Washington Co., Pop. Code 3
SAD 37
Supt. – See Harrington
ES, POINT STREET   04623 – Brenda Ward, prin.

Coopers Mills, Lincoln Co.
Union SD 51
Supt. – See Gardiner
Somerville ES, RURAL ROUTE 01   04341
  Robert Holland, prin.

Corinna, Penobscot Co., Pop. Code 4
SAD 48
Supt. – See Newport
JHS, P O BOX 403   04928 – Douglas Doyon, prin.
Eastland ES, P O BOX 411   04928
  Douglas Doyon, prin.

Cornish, York Co., Pop. Code 4
SAD 55
Sch. Sys. Enr. Code 4
Supt. – J. Hoyt   04020
ES, SCHOOL STREET   04020
  Margaret Hoxie, prin.
South Hiram ES
  RURAL ROUTE 01 BOX 65   04020
  Sylvia Pease, prin.
Other Schools – See Hiram, Kezar Falls, West Baldwin

Cranberry Isles, Hancock Co.
Union SD 98
Supt. – See Mount Desert
Longfellow ES, P O BOX 59   04625
  Shannon Shannon, prin.

Cumberland Center, Cumberland Co., Pop. Code 6
SAD 51
Sch. Sys. Enr. Code 4
Supt. – J. Nye, P O BOX 6A   04021
Greely JHS, 303 MAIN ST   04021
  Thomas Joyce, prin.
North Yarmouth Memorial MS
  RURAL ROUTE 02   04021
  Stephen McAllister, prin.
Wilson ES, TUTTLE ROAD   04021
  Brian Albert, prin.
Other Schools – See Chebeague Island

Cutler, Washington Co., Pop. Code 3
SAD 77
Supt. – See Machias
ES, P O BOX 368   04626 – Robert Allen, prin.

Damariscotta, Lincoln Co., Pop. Code 4
Great Salt Bay Community SD
Sch. Sys. Enr. Code 2
Supt. – M. Harrison, P O BOX 907   04543
Great Salt Bay Community ES, P O BOX 937   04543
  Richard Marchi, prin.

Union SD 74
Sch. Sys. Enr. Code 3
Supt. – M. Harrison, P O BOX 907   04543
Other Schools – See Nobleboro, Pemaquid, South
  Bristol, Waldoboro

Danforth, Washington Co., Pop. Code 3
East Range Community SD
Sch. Sys. Enr. Code 1
Supt. – D. Wells   04424
Other Schools – See Topsfield

SAD 14
Sch. Sys. Enr. Code 2
Supt. – D. Wells   04424
East Grand S, P O BOX 218   04424
  Charles Pease, prin.

Union SD 108
Sch. Sys. Enr. Code 1
Supt. – D. Wells   04424
Other Schools – See Vanceboro

Deer Isle, Hancock Co., Pop. Code 4
Deer Isle-Stonington Comm. SD
Supt. – See Stonington
ES, P O BOX 27   04627 – Joseph Watson, prin.

Denmark, Oxford Co., Pop. Code 3
SAD 72
Supt. – See Fryeburg
Denmark Village ES, RURAL ROUTE 160   04022
  Thomas Doughty, prin.

Dennysville, Washington Co., Pop. Code 2
Unorganized Territories SD
Supt. – See Augusta
Edmunds Consolodated ES
  HARRISON ROAD   04628
  Howard McFadden, prin.

Dexter, Penobscot Co., Pop. Code 5
SAD 46
Sch. Sys. Enr. Code 4
Supt. – M. Keegan, 10 SPRING ST   04930
ES, 14 ABBOTT HILL RD   04930
  Gilbert Reynolds, prin.
Other Schools – See Exeter, Garland

Dixfield, Oxford Co., Pop. Code 4
SAD 21
Sch. Sys. Enr. Code 3
Supt. – C. Howes, 103 WELD ST   04224
Dirigo MS, SCHOOL ST   04224
  Timothy Kelly, prin.
ES, PARK STREET   04224 – Nelson Neil, prin.
Other Schools – See Canton

Dover-Foxcroft, Piscataquis Co., Pop. Code 5
SAD 41
Supt. – See Milo
Atkinson ES, RURAL ROUTE 03   04426
  Ann Chenery, prin.

SAD 68
Sch. Sys. Enr. Code 3
Supt. – R. Curtis, P O BOX 98   04426
Sedomocha JHS, 45 HARRISON AVE   04426
  John Spruce, prin.
Mayo Street MS, MAYO STREET   04426
  Fred Johnston, prin.
Morton Avenue ES, MORTON AVE   04426
  Fred Johnston, prin.
Other Schools – See Charleston, Monson

Dresden, Lincoln Co., Pop. Code 3
Union SD 48
Supt. – See Wiscasset
ES, RURAL ROUTE 01 BOX 330   04342
  Marsha Cottrell, prin.

Eagle Lake, Aroostook Co., Pop. Code 4
SAD 27
Supt. – See Fort Kent
ES, P O BOX 190   04739 – Wayne Wilbur, prin.

East Corinth, Penobscot Co.
SAD 64
Sch. Sys. Enr. Code 4
Supt. – L. Ney, P O BOX 179   04427
Central ES, P O BOX 19   04427
  Glenn Burleigh, prin.
Morison Memorial MS, P O BOX 7   04427
  Dale Pineo, prin.
Other Schools – See Bradford, Hudson, Kenduskeag,
  Stetson

East Holden, Hancock Co.
Airline Community SD
Sch. Sys. Enr. Code 1
Supt. – R. Ervin, P O BOX 1245   04429
Other Schools – See Aurora

Dedham Unit SD
Sch. Sys. Enr. Code 2
Supt. – R. Ervin, P O BOX 1245   04429
Dedham ES, RURAL ROUTE 02 BOX 330   04429
  Richard Norton, prin.

SAD 63
Sch. Sys. Enr. Code 3
Supt. – R. Ervin, P O BOX 1245   04429
Holbrook MS, P O BOX 1245   04429
  Ralph Russell, prin.
Eddington ES, RURAL ROUTE 01 BOX 707   04429
  Lester Butler, prin.
Other Schools – See Brewer

East Lebanon, York Co.
Acton SD
Sch. Sys. Enr. Code 2
Supt. – L. Tracy, HCR 01 BOX 528   04027
Acton ES, HCR 01 BOX 528   04027
  Lyonel Tracy, prin.

SAD 60
Supt. – See North Berwick
Lebanon MS, P O BOX 159   04027
  Eric Knowlton, prin.

East Machias, Washington Co., Pop. Code 4
SAD 77
Supt. – See Machias
Elm Street MS   04630 – John Gardner, prin.
Bucknam ES, RURAL ROUTE 69 BOX 167   04630
  Irene Faulkingham, prin.
Burns ES, P O BOX 194   04630 – Diane Grant, prin.

East Millinocket, Penobscot Co., Pop. Code 4
Union SD 113
Sch. Sys. Enr. Code 3
Supt. – R. Ryder, 33-41 NORTH ST   04430
Myrick ES, 6 1/2 BEECH ST   04430
  Thomas Jarvis, prin.
Other Schools – See Medway

Easton, Aroostook Co., Pop. Code 4
Easton SD
Sch. Sys. Enr. Code 2
Supt. – G. Clockedile, P O BOX 126   04740
ES, P O BOX 126   04740 – Gerald Clockedile, prin.

Eastport, Washington Co., Pop. Code 4
Union SD 104
Sch. Sys. Enr. Code 3
Supt. – E. Chmielewski, HIGH ST   04631
ES, 100 HIGH ST   04631 – Maureen Pottle, prin.
Other Schools – See Pembroke, Perry

East Sebago, Cumberland Co.
SAD 61
Supt. – See Bridgton
Sebago ES, RURAL ROUTE 114   04029
  Michael Foye, prin.

East Vassalboro, Kennebec Co.
Union SD 52
Supt. – See Winslow

ES 04935 – Michael Black, prin.

East Waterboro, York Co.
SAD 57
Supt. – See Waterboro
Waterboro ES, RURAL ROUTE 01 BOX 357 04030
  Mark Petersen, prin.

Eliot, York Co., Pop. Code 5
SAD 35
Sch. Sys. Enr. Code 4
Supt. – B. McGray, ROUTE 236 03903
ES, 132 STATE RD 03903 – Mark Bradbury, prin.
Other Schools – See South Berwick

Ellsworth, Hancock Co., Pop. Code 6
Ellsworth SD
Sch. Sys. Enr. Code 4
Supt. – V. Lacombe, P O BOX 669 04605
Moore MS, 99 STATE ST 04605
  Frederick Woodman, prin.
Knowlton ES, 142 STATE ST 04605
  Kenneth Riddell, prin.

SAD 26
Sch. Sys. Enr. Code 1
Supt. – J. Turcotte, P O BOX 829 04605
Other Schools – See Franklin

Union SD 92
Sch. Sys. Enr. Code 3
Supt. – J. Turcotte, P O BOX 829 04605
Beech Hill ES, RURAL ROUTE 04 04605
  Cathy Lewis, prin.
Lamoine Consolodated ES
  RURAL ROUTE 02 BOX 80 04605
  David Phaneuf, prin.
Trenton ES, RURAL ROUTE 01 04605
  Clayton Savage, prin.
Other Schools – See Hancock, Surry

Etna, Penobscot Co., Pop. Code 3
SAD 38
Supt. – See Carmel
Etna-Dixmont ES
  RURAL ROUTE 143 BOX 143 04434
  Lawrence Plaisted, prin.

Exeter, Penobscot Co., Pop. Code 3
SAD 46
Supt. – See Dexter
Exeter Consolodated MS, P O BOX 30 04435
  Roy Allen, prin.

Fairfield, Somerset Co., Pop. Code 6
SAD 49
Sch. Sys. Enr. Code 5
Supt. – E. Fabian, 9 SCHOOL ST 04937
Lawrence JHS, 7 SCHOOL ST 04937
  Robert Fairbrother, prin.
Fairfield PS, WESTERN AVE 04937
  Suanne Giorgetti, prin.
Lawrence MS, HIGH STREET 04937
  Eugene Morrison, prin.
South ES Complex
  HIGH & BURRILL STREETS 04937
  Suanne Giorgetti, prin.
Other Schools – See Albion, Clinton, Waterville

Falmouth, Cumberland Co., Pop. Code 6
Falmouth SD
Sch. Sys. Enr. Code 4
Supt. – T. Sharp, 74 LUNT ROAD 04105
MS, 52 WOODVILLE ROAD 04105
  Terrence Allen, prin.
Plummer-Motz ES, 192 MIDDLE RD 04105
  William Bagley, prin.

Farmington, Franklin Co., Pop. Code 6
SAD 9
Sch. Sys. Enr. Code 5
Supt. – L. Rutherford, P O BOX 471 04938
Ingalls MS, 28 HIGH ST 04938
  Thomas Taylor, prin.
Mallet ES, 1 QUEBEC ST 04938
  Gerald Libby, prin.
Other Schools – See New Sharon, Weld, Wilton

Fort Fairfield, Aroostook Co., Pop. Code 5
SAD 20
Sch. Sys. Enr. Code 3
Supt. – R. Doddy, P O BOX 212 04742
MS, 20 COLUMBIA ST 04742
  Jeannette Condon, prin.
Hacker ES, 40 COLUMBIA ST 04742
  Jeannette Condon, prin.
Jenkins Elementary School, 10 SCHOOL ST 04742
  Jeannette Condon, prin.

Fort Kent, Aroostook Co., Pop. Code 5
SAD 27
Sch. Sys. Enr. Code 4
Supt. – D. Waddell, 69 PLEASANT ST 04743
ES, 65 PLEASANT ST 04743
  Roland LaBrie, prin.
Other Schools – See Eagle Lake, Saint Francis, Soldier Pond

Frankfort, Waldo Co., Pop. Code 3
SAD 56
Supt. – See Searsport
ES, THIRD CLASS ROAD 04438
  Carl Bowen, prin.

Franklin, Hancock Co., Pop. Code 3
SAD 26
Supt. – See Ellsworth

Cave Hill ES, RURAL ROUTE 01 BOX 282 04634
  Audrey Fogg, prin.

Schoodic Community SD
Supt. – See Gouldsboro
Mountain View MS
  RURAL ROUTE 01 BOX 203 04634
  Charles Cashman, prin.
ES, P O BOX 121 04634 – Charles Cashman, prin.

Freeport, Cumberland Co., Pop. Code 6
Freeport SD
Sch. Sys. Enr. Code 4
Supt. – R. Lyman, 30 HOLBROOK ST 04032
MS, 12 HOWARD PL 04032 – Daniel Bigley, prin.
Morse Street ES, MORSE STREET 04032
  Judy Higbea, prin.
Other Schools – See South Freeport

Pine Tree Academy
  RURAL ROUTE 04 BOX 4260 04032

Frenchboro, Waldo Co.
Union SD 98
Supt. – See Mount Desert
ES 04635 – Mary Anne Pye, prin.

Friendship, Knox Co., Pop. Code 3
SAD 40
Supt. – See Waldoboro
Friendship Village ES, P O BOX 100 04547
  Elaine Nutter, prin.

Fryeburg, Oxford Co., Pop. Code 5
SAD 72
Sch. Sys. Enr. Code 3
Supt. – R. Ansley, 7 PORTLAND ST 04037
Snow MS, 7 PORTLAND ST 04037
  Barbara Neilly, prin.
Snow ES Annex, 7 PORTLAND ST 04037
  Barbara Neilly, prin.
Other Schools – See Brownfield, Denmark, Lovell, North Fryeburg

Gardiner, Kennebec Co., Pop. Code 6
SAD 11
Sch. Sys. Enr. Code 5
Supt. – M. Peacock, P O BOX 250 04345
Gardiner Regional JHS, COBBOSSEE AVE 04345
  Arthur Warren, prin.
Central Street ES, 46 CENTRAL STREET 04345
  Cheryle Clukey, prin.
Hamlin ES, 19 SCHOOL ST 04345
  Roger Linton, prin.
Pittston Consolodated ES
  RURAL ROUTE 04 BOX 6060 04345
  Roger Linton, prin.
Pray Street ES, 14 PRAY ST 04345
  Rohnie Dunn, prin.
Thompson ES
  RURAL ROUTE 03 BOX 1520 04345
  Cheryl Clukey, prin.
Woodman MS, 25 PLEASANT ST 04345
  Stephen Cottrell, prin.
Other Schools – See South Gardiner

SAD 16
Supt. – See Hallowell
Hall-Dale MS, SHELDON STREET 04345
  Gary Barrett, prin.

Union SD 51
Sch. Sys. Enr. Code 4
Supt. – H. Nye
  RURAL ROUTE 01 BOX 273B 04345
Chelsea ES, RURAL ROUTE 01 BOX 139 04345
  Brenda Chaisson, prin.
Other Schools – See Coopers Mills, Jefferson, North Whitefield, Palermo, Windsor

Garland, Penobscot Co., Pop. Code 3
SAD 46
Supt. – See Dexter
ES, P O BOX 68 04939 – Jane Little, prin.

Georgetown, Sagadahoc Co., Pop. Code 3
Union SD 47
Supt. – See Bath
Georgetown Central ES, BAY POINT ROAD 04548
  Charles Goodman, prin.

Gorham, Cumberland Co., Pop. Code 7
Gorham SD
Sch. Sys. Enr. Code 4
Supt. – G. Goldman, 270 MAIN ST 04038
Shaw JHS, 75 SOUTH ST 04038
  Richard Klain, prin.
Narragansett ES, 284 MAIN ST 04038
  Cynthia O'Shea, prin.
Village MS, 12 ROBIE ST 04038
  Gloria LeVeillee, prin.
White Rock ES
  RURAL ROUTE 02 BOX 353 04038
  Sanford Prince, prin.
Other Schools – See Windham

Gouldsboro, Hancock Co., Pop. Code 2
Schoodic Community SD
Sch. Sys. Enr. Code 2 ·
Supt. – K. Webster
  RURAL ROUTE 01 BOX 43 04607
Other Schools – See Franklin, West Sullivan

Union SD 96
Sch. Sys. Enr. Code 2
Supt. – K. Webster
  RURAL ROUTE 01 BOX 96 04607
ES, RURAL ROUTE 01 04607 – Carl Lusby, prin.

Other Schools – See Steuben, Winter Harbor

Grand Isle, Aroostook Co., Pop. Code 3
Grand Isle Unit SD
Sch. Sys. Enr. Code 1
Supt. – John Houghton, P O BOX 178 04746
ES, MAIN ST 04746 – John Houghton, prin.

Gray, Cumberland Co., Pop. Code 5
SAD 15
Sch. Sys. Enr. Code 4
Supt. – L. Bernard, P O BOX 178 04039
Gray-New Gloucester JHS
  10 LIBBY HILL ROAD 04039
  Philip McCormick, prin.
Russell ES, P O BOX 709 04039
  Donald O'Malley, prin.
Other Schools – See New Gloucester

Greene, Androscoggin Co.
SAD 52
Supt. – See Turner
Greene Central ES
  RURAL ROUTE 01 BOX 3405 04236
  Robert Wall, prin.

Greenville, Piscataquis Co., Pop. Code 4
Union SD 60
Sch. Sys. Enr. Code 2
Supt. – P. Harvey, P O BOX 547 04441
S, PRITHAM AVE 04441 – James Richards, prin.
Nickerson MS, P O BOX 547 04441
  James Richards, prin.
Other Schools – See Shirley Mills

Guilford, Piscataquis Co., Pop. Code 4
SAD 4
Sch. Sys. Enr. Code 4
Supt. – R. Poulin,Jr., P O BOX 228 04443
MS, P O BOX 88 04443 – Allyn Ward, prin.
ES, P O BOX 268 04443 – Joyce Miller, prin.
McKusick ES, P O BOX 268 04443
  Priscilla Carle, prin.
Other Schools – See Abbot Village, Cambridge, Sangerville, Wellington

Hallowell, Kennebec Co., Pop. Code 5
SAD 16
Sch. Sys. Enr. Code 3
Supt. – N. Lemieux, MIDDLE ST 04347
Hall-Dale JHS, WARREN ST 04347
  Barry Albert, prin.
Hall-Dale PS, LINCOLN STREET 04347
  Marcia Rohman, prin.
Other Schools – See Gardiner

Hampden, Penobscot Co., Pop. Code 6
SAD 22
Sch. Sys. Enr. Code 4
Supt. – C. Dubois, P O BOX 279 04444
Weatherbee MS, 22 MAIN ROAD N 04444
  William Cattelle, prin.
McGraw ES, 20 MAIN RD N 04444
  Willard Hillier, prin.
Newburgh ES
  RURAL ROUTE 01 BOX 1925 04444
  David Porter, prin.
Other Schools – See Winterport

Hancock, Hancock Co., Pop. Code 4
Union SD 92
Supt. – See Ellsworth
ES 04640 – S. Enman, prin.

Harmony, Somerset Co., Pop. Code 3
Harmony SD
Sch. Sys. Enr. Code 2
Supt. – P. Crosby, P O BOX 68 04942
ES, P O BOX 100 04942 – Philip Crosby, prin.

Harrington, Washington Co., Pop. Code 3
SAD 37
Sch. Sys. Enr. Code 4
Supt. – J. White, P O BOX 74 04643
ES, P O BOX 77 04643 – Ronald Looke, prin.
Other Schools – See Addison, Cherryfield, Columbia Falls, Milbridge

Harrison, Cumberland Co., Pop. Code 4
SAD 17
Supt. – See South Paris
Harrison Village ES, P O BOX 306 04040
  Judith Potter, prin.

Hartland, Somerset Co., Pop. Code 4
SAD 48
Supt. – See Newport
JHS, ACADEMY ST 04943 – Larry Pineo, prin.
Hartland Consolodated ES, ELM STREET 04943
  Larry Pineo, prin.

Hebron, Oxford Co., Pop. Code 3
SAD 17
Supt. – See South Paris
ES, P O BOX 115 04238 – Bruce Garrow, prin.

Hiram, Oxford Co., Pop. Code 4
SAD 55
Supt. – See Cornish
ES, MAIN STREET 04041 – Charles Pease, prin.

Hollis Center, York Co., Pop. Code 5
SAD 6
Supt. – See Bar Mills
Hollis Consolodated MS
  RURAL ROUTE 01 BOX 334 04042
  Millicent Smith, prin.
Hollis ES, RURAL ROUTE 01 BOX 333 04042
  Millicent Smith, prin.

Union SD 7
Supt. – See Saco
Dayton Consolodated ES
　RURAL ROUTE 02 BOX 402　04042
　Constance Lambert, prin.

Houlton, Aroostook Co., Pop. Code 6
SAD 29
Sch. Sys. Enr. Code 4
Supt. – W. McDonnell, P O BOX 190　04730
ES, 60 SOUTH ST　04730
　Robert Cowperthwaite, prin.
Lambert MS, 27 SCHOOL ST　04730
　Barbara Burton, prin.
Other Schools – See Monticello

SAD 70
Sch. Sys. Enr. Code 3
Supt. – T. Comeau, P O BOX 763　04730
Hodgdon ES, P O BOX 763　04730
　Joseph Dahl, prin.

St. Mary ES, 10 WATER ST　04730

Howland, Penobscot Co., Pop. Code 4
SAD 31
Sch. Sys. Enr. Code 3
Supt. – G. Wilbur　04448
Hichborn MS, CROSS ST　04448
　Jayne Branscombe, prin.
Ring Street ES, RING STREET　04448
　James Winslow, prin.
Other Schools – See Burlington, West Enfield

Hudson, Penobscot Co., Pop. Code 3
SAD 64
Supt. – See East Corinth
MS, P O BOX 66　04449 – Beatrice DuBois, prin.

Island Falls, Aroostook Co., Pop. Code 3
South Aroostook Community SD
Sch. Sys. Enr. Code 3
Supt. – W. Parsons
　RURAL ROUTE 01 BOX 104 A　04747
South Aroostook Community S
　RURAL ROUTE 01 BOX 104 A　04747
　D. Wiggin, prin.

Isle Au Haut, Hancock Co.
Isle Au Haut Unit SD
Supt. – See Stonington
Isle Au Haut Rural ES　04645 – Tanis Jason, prin.

Islesboro, Waldo Co., Pop. Code 3
Islesboro SD
Sch. Sys. Enr. Code 1
Supt. – William Dove, P O BOX 118　04848
Islesboro Central S, P O BOX 118　04848
　William Dove, prin.

Islesford, Hancock Co.
Union SD 98
Supt. – See Mount Desert
ES, P O BOX 8　04646 – Meredith Aase, prin.

Jackman, Somerset Co., Pop. Code 4
SAD 12
Sch. Sys. Enr. Code 2
Supt. – D. Higgins, P O BOX 239　04945
Forest Hills Consolidated S, P O BOX 239　04945
　Kermit Knowles, prin.

Jay, Franklin Co., Pop. Code 6
Jay SD
Sch. Sys. Enr. Code 4
Supt. – G. Hartley, 2 SCHOOL ST　04239
JHS, 3 SCHOOL ST　04239 – Carlton Faloon, prin.
ES, 5 SCHOOL ST　04239 – Claton Corriveau, prin.

Jefferson, Lincoln Co., Pop. Code 4
Union SD 51
Supt. – See Gardiner
Jefferson Village ES, P O BOX 907　04348
　George Cross, prin.

Jonesboro, Washington Co., Pop. Code 3
Union SD 102
Supt. – See Machias
ES　04648 – George Alley, prin.

Jonesport, Washington Co., Pop. Code 4
Union SD 103
Sch. Sys. Enr. Code 2
Supt. – B. Crowley, P O BOX 309　04649
ES, P O BOX 209　04649 – Charles Lakeman, prin.
Other Schools – See Beals

Kenduskeag, Penobscot Co., Pop. Code 4
SAD 64
Supt. – See East Corinth
ES, RURAL ROUTE 15　04450
　John Costello, prin.

Kennebunk, York Co., Pop. Code 6
SAD 57
Supt. – See Waterboro
Lyman MS, RURAL ROUTE 01　04043
　Edward Newell,Jr., prin.

SAD 71
Sch. Sys. Enr. Code 4
Supt. – L. Martin, 10 STORER ST　04043
JHS, SEA ROAD　04043 – Sandra Caldwell, prin.
Cousens ES, DAY STREET　04043
　Albert Meserve, prin.
Park Street MS, PARK STREET　04043
　Vicki Labrie, prin.
Other Schools – See Kennebunkport

Kennebunkport, York Co., Pop. Code 5
SAD 71
Supt. – See Kennebunk
Kennebunkport Consolidated ES
　RURAL ROUTE 01 BOX 661　04046
　Joan Carroll, prin.

Kents Hill, Kennebec Co., Pop. Code 2
SAD 36
Supt. – See Livermore Falls
Fayette Central ES
　RURAL ROUTE 01 BOX 1320　04349
　Jean Vautour, prin.

Kezar Falls, York Co.
SAD 55
Supt. – See Cornish
Morrill ES, RURAL ROUTE 02　04047
　Grace Gilpatrick, prin.

Kingfield, Franklin Co., Pop. Code 4
SAD 58
Sch. Sys. Enr. Code 4
Supt. – E. Pinkham
　RURAL ROUTE 01 BOX 1580　04947
ES, RURAL ROUTE 01 BOX 1500　04947
　Thomas Morrill, prin.
Other Schools – See Phillips, Stratton, Strong

Kingman, Penobscot Co., Pop. Code 2
Unorganized Territories SD
Supt. – See Augusta
ES　04451 – Joseph Costa, prin.

Kittery, York Co., Pop. Code 6
Kittery SD
Sch. Sys. Enr. Code 4
Supt. – P. Donahue, ROGERS ROAD　03904
Frisbee MS, 120 ROGERS ROAD　03904
　Anne Heisey, prin.
Mitchell ES, PEPPERRELL RD　03905
　Eleanor Dickens, prin.
Shapleigh ES, RURAL ROUTE 02 BOX 260　03904
　Beverly Johnson, prin.

Lagrange, Penobscot Co., Pop. Code 3
SAD 41
Cook ES　04453 – Ann Chenery, prin.

Lee, Penobscot Co., Pop. Code 3
SAD 30
Sch. Sys. Enr. Code 2
Supt. – H. Robinson, P O BOX 368　04455
Mt. Jefferson JHS, WINN ST　04455
　Mary Hinse, prin.
Ham ES, P O BOX 368　04455
　Karleen Proctor, prin.
Other Schools – See Springfield, Winn

Union SD 110
Sch. Sys. Enr. Code 1
Supt. – H. Robinson, P O BOX 368　04455
Other Schools – See Wytopitlock

Leeds, Androscoggin Co., Pop. Code 4
SAD 52
Supt. – See Turner
Leeds Central ES
　RURAL ROUTE 01 BOX 125　04263
　Henry Aliberti,Jr., prin.

Levant, Penobscot Co., Pop. Code 4
SAD 23
Supt. – See Carmel
Levant Consolidated ES, P O BOX 47　04456
　Suzanne Smith, prin.

Lewiston, Androscoggin Co., Pop. Code 8
Lewiston SD
Sch. Sys. Enr. Code 6
Supt. – R. Connors, 36 OAK ST　04240
JHS, 65 CENTRAL AVE　04240
　Charles Douglas, prin.
Farwell ES, 84-110 FARWELL STREET　04240
　Susan Martin, prin.
Martel ES, 880 LISBON ST　04240
　Joanne Lebel, prin.
McMahon ES, 151 N TEMPLE ST　04240
　Lynda Hood, prin.
Montello ES, 399 EAST AVE　04240
　Thomas Hood, prin.
Multi Purpose ES, 145 BIRCH ST　04240
　Carroll Scribner, prin.
Pettingill ES, 405 COLLEGE ST　04240
　John McDonald,Jr., prin.
Wallace ES, 388 MAIN ST　04240
　Richard Bernier, prin.

Holy Cross ES, 10 ST CROIX ST　04240
St. Joseph ES, 393 MAIN ST　04240
St. Peters ES, 250 BATES ST　04240

Liberty, Waldo Co., Pop. Code 3
SAD 3
Supt. – See Unity
Walker Memorial ES, P O BOX 117　04949
　Peter Weston, prin.

Limerick, York Co., Pop. Code 4
SAD 57
Supt. – See Waterboro
Line ES, RURAL ROUTE 02 BOX 665　04048
　Richard Harnett, prin.

SAD 6
Supt. – See Bar Mills

Emery ES, RURAL ROUTE 01 BOX 687　04048
　James Pillsbury, prin.

Limestone, Aroostook Co., Pop. Code 6
Caswell Unit SD
Sch. Sys. Enr. Code 1
Supt. – B. Ryder, VAN BUREN RD　04750
Caswell ES, VAN BUREN RD　04750
　Dawn Barnes, prin.

Limestone SD
Sch. Sys. Enr. Code 4
Supt. – B. Ryder, 275 MAIN ST　04750
Damon ES, CALIFORNIA RD LORING AFB　04750
　Geryaldine Penninger, prin.
ES, 71 HIGH ST　04750 – John Leggett, prin.

Lincoln, Penobscot Co., Pop. Code 6
SAD 67
Sch. Sys. Enr. Code 4
Supt. – C. Casey, P O BOX 250　04457
Mattanawcook JHS, 41 SCHOOL ST　04457
　Milledge McConnell, prin.
Burr ES, P O BOX 250　04457
　Alden McPike, prin.
Other Schools – See Mattawamkeag

Lincolnville, Waldo Co., Pop. Code 4
Lincolnville SD
Sch. Sys. Enr. Code 2
Supt. – W. Sternberg
　RURAL ROUTE 01 BOX 159　04849
Lincolnville Central ES
　RURAL ROUTE 01 BOX 159　04849
　Francis Merrow, prin.

Lisbon, Androscoggin Co., Pop. Code 4
Union SD 30
Supt. – See Lisbon Falls
ES, GARTLEY ROAD　04250 – Vance Keene, prin.

Lisbon Falls, Androscoggin Co., Pop. Code 5
Union SD 30
Sch. Sys. Enr. Code 4
Supt. – R. Ladner, P O BOX 38　04252
Sugg MS, MIDDLE SCHOOL ROAD RT 196　04252
　Sheila McAllister, prin.
Durham ES, RURAL ROUTE 02 BOX 1960　04252
　William Ziemer, prin.
Morse ES, 18 SCHOOL ST　04252
　Philip Higgins, prin.
Other Schools – See Lisbon

Litchfield, Kennebec Co., Pop. Code 4
Union SD 44
Supt. – See Sabattus
Libby-Tozier MS
　HCR ROUTE 01 BOX 1290　04350
　Scott Snedden, prin.
Litchfield Central ES, HCR #1 BOX 1290　04350
　Scott Snedden, prin.

Livermore Falls, Androscoggin Co., Pop. Code 5
SAD 36
Sch. Sys. Enr. Code 4
Supt. – J. Laux, P O BOX S　04254
MS, 25 CEDAR ST　04254 – Robert Miller, prin.
Livermore ES
　RURAL ROTUE 02 BOX 1990　04254
　Robert Millay, prin.
Livermore Falls MS, CEDAR STREET　04254
　Jeannine Backus, prin.
Livermore Falls PS, 20 BALDWIN ST　04254
　Meredith Dalessandro, prin.
Other Schools – See Kents Hill

Long Island, Cumberland Co.
Portland SD
Supt. – See Portland
ES, RURAL ROUTE 01 BOX 57　04050
　Paul Steele, prin.

Lovell, Oxford Co., Pop. Code 3
SAD 72
Supt. – See Fryeburg
New Suncook ES, P O BOX H　04051
　Gary MacDonald, prin.

Lubec, Washington Co., Pop. Code 4
SAD 19
Sch. Sys. Enr. Code 2
Supt. – O. Bridgham　04652
ES, SOUTH STREET　04652 – Patricia Godin, prin.

Machias, Washington Co., Pop. Code 4
SAD 77
Sch. Sys. Enr. Code 2
Supt. – E. Bouchard, 27 MAIN ST　04654
Other Schools – See Cutler, East Machias,
　Machiasport, Whiting

Union SD 102
Sch. Sys. Enr. Code 3
Supt. – W. Clark, LOWER MAIN ST　04654
Gaffney ES, 99 COURT ST　04654
　Barbara Poirier, prin.
Other Schools – See Jonesboro, Wesley

Machiasport, Washington Co., Pop. Code 4
SAD 77
Supt. – See Machias
Ft. O'Brien ES　04655 – Mitchell Look, prin.

Madawaska, Aroostook Co., Pop. Code 6
Madawaska SD
Sch. Sys. Enr. Code 4
Supt. – M. Labbe, 96 SAINT THOMAS ST　04756
Acadia MS, 282 E MAIN ST　04756
　Roger Dechene, prin.

Evangeline ES, 22 5TH AVE   04756
  Roger Dechene, prin.

Madison, Somerset Co., Pop. Code 5
SAD 59
Sch. Sys. Enr. Code 4
Supt. – R. Woodbury, 30 MAIN ST   04950
JHS, 189 MAIN ST   04950 – John Krasnavage, prin.
Main Street ES, 189 MAIN ST   04950
  Malcolm Watts,Jr., prin.
Old Point Avenue ES, 108 OLD POINT AVE   04950
  Carey Clement, prin.
Other Schools – See Anson, Athens

Manchester, Kennebec Co., Pop. Code 4
Union SD 42
Supt. – See Readfield
ES, P O BOX 217   04351 – James Burns,Jr., prin.

Mapleton, Aroostook Co., Pop. Code 4
SAD 1
Supt. – See Presque Isle
ES, RURAL ROUTE 01 BOX 50   04757
  David Rand, prin.

Mars Hill, Aroostook Co., Pop. Code 4
SAD 42
Sch. Sys. Enr. Code 2
Supt. – M. Eastman, P O BOX 1006   04758
Fort Street ES, P O BOX 509   04758
  Laurine York, prin.

Mattawamkeag, Penobscot Co., Pop. Code 3
SAD 67
Supt. – See Lincoln
Troutt ES, P O BOX 35   04459
  Harold Michaud, prin.

Mechanic Falls, Androscoggin Co., Pop. Code 5
Union SD 29
Sch. Sys. Enr. Code 4
Supt. – W. Terry III, P O BOX 129   04256
Elm Street ES, ELM STREET   04256
  Nathan Morris, prin.
Minot Consolodated ES, RURAL ROUTE 02   04256
  John Mullen,Jr., prin.
Other Schools – See Poland

Medway, Penobscat Co., Pop. Code 4
Union SD 113
Supt. – See East Millinocket
MS, P O BOX L   04460 – Roger Wallace, prin.
PS, P O BOX L   04460 – Roger Wallace, prin.

Mexico, Oxford Co., Pop. Code 5
SAD 43
Sch. Sys. Enr. Code 3
Supt. – C. Prentiss, 32 PARKER ST   04257
Meroby ES, 28 CROSS ST   04257
  Melvin Burnham, prin.

Milbridge, Washington Co., Pop. Code 4
SAD 37
Supt. – See Harrington
ES, WASHINGTON STREET   04658
  Wayne Willey, prin.

Milford, Penobscot Co., Pop. Code 4
Union SD 90
Sch. Sys. Enr. Code 3
Supt. – R. Unruh,Jr., 26 DAVENPORT ST   04461
Libby ES, P O BOX 529   04461
  Thomas Graves, prin.
Other Schools – See Bradley, Olamon, Old Town

Millinocket, Penobscot Co., Pop. Code 6
Millinocket SD
Sch. Sys. Enr. Code 4
Supt. – R. Pelletier   04462
MS, 275 KATAHDIN AVE   04462
  Bruce Ives, prin.
Aroostook Avenue ES, AROOSTOOK AVE   04462
  Charles Sanders, prin.
Granite Street ES, GRANITE STREET   04462
  David Dearing, prin.
Katahdin Avenue ES, KATAHDIN AVE   04462
  Charles Sanders, prin.

Milo, Piscataquis Co., Pop. Code 5
SAD 41
Sch. Sys. Enr. Code 4
Supt. – P. Harvey, 37 W MAIN ST   04463
Penquis Valley MS, 35 W MAIN ST   04463
  Francis Foss, prin.
ES, 19 BELMONT ST   04463 – Ann Chenery, prin.
Other Schools – See Brownville, Dover-Foxcroft,
  Lagrange

Monhegan, Lincoln Co.
Monhegan Unit SD
Supt. – See Rockland
Monhegan Island ES   04852
  Coleen Faulkingham, prin.

Monmouth, Kennebec Co., Pop. Code 5
Union SD 43
Supt. – See Richmond
Cottrell ES, RURAL ROUTE 01 BOX 38   04259
  Alfreda Fournier, prin.

Monroe, Waldo Co., Pop. Code 3
SAD 3
Supt. – See Unity
ES   04951 – Sarah Crawford, prin.

Monson, Piscataquis Co., Pop. Code 3
SAD 68
Supt. – See Dover-Foxcroft
ES, P O BOX 288   04464 – Betty Morrell, prin.

Monticello, Aroostook Co., Pop. Code 3
SAD 29
Supt. – See Houlton
Littleton ES, RURAL ROUTE 01 BOX 60   04760
  Patricia Chase, prin.
Wellington ES, P O BOX 11   04760
  Leslie Buswell, prin.

Mount Desert, Hancock Co., Pop. Code 4
SAD 76
Sch. Sys. Enr. Code 1
Supt. – R. McFalls   04660
Other Schools – See Swans Island

Union SD 98
Sch. Sys. Enr. Code 3
Supt. – R. McFalls   04660
Other Schools – See Bar Harbor, Bass Harbor,
  Cranberry Isles, Frenchboro, Islesford, Northeast
  Harbor, Southwest Harbor

Mount Vernon, Kennebec Co., Pop. Code 4
Union SD 42
Supt. – See Readfield
ES, RURAL ROUTE 01 BOX 3190   04352
  Barbara Doughty, prin.

Naples, Cumberland Co., Pop. Code 4
SAD 61
Supt. – See Bridgton
ES, P O BOX W   04055 – Bonnie Reidman, prin.

New Gloucester, Cumberland Co., Pop. Code 5
SAD 15
Supt. – See Gray
Memorial ES, RURAL ROUTE 231 BOX 131   04260
  Elizabeth Tracey, prin.

Newport, Penobscot Co., Pop. Code 5
SAD 48
Sch. Sys. Enr. Code 4
Supt. – R. Freve, P O BOX 128   04953
JHS, 100 ELM ST   04953 – Donald Hill, prin.
ES, 100 ELM ST   04953 – Donald Hill, prin.
Other Schools – See Corinna, Hartland, Palmyra,
  Saint Albans

New Sharon, Franklin Co., Pop. Code 3
SAD 9
Supt. – See Farmington
ES   04955 – Thomas Taylor, prin.

New Sweden, Aroostook Co., Pop. Code 3
Union SD 122
Supt. – See Caribou
ES, RURAL ROUTE 161   04762
  Helen Espling, prin.

Nobleboro, Lincoln Co., Pop. Code 4
Union SD 74
Supt. – See Damariscotta
Nobleboro Central ES, RURAL ROUTE 01   04555
  Wilder Hunt, prin.

Norridgewock, Somerset Co., Pop. Code 5
SAD 54
Supt. – See Skowhegan
Central ES, P O BOX 98   04957 – Ann Lynch, prin.
Mercer ES, RURAL ROUTE 02 BOX 2540   04957
  Helen Cole, prin.

North Anson, Somerset Co., Pop. Code 3
SAD 74
Sch. Sys. Enr. Code 3
Supt. – R. Hatch, P O BOX 159   04958
Embden ES, P O BOX 87   04958
  James Hodgkins, prin.
Emery ES, P O BOX 187   04958
  Judith Benson, prin.
Other Schools – See Anson, North New Portland,
  Solon

North Berwick, York Co., Pop. Code 5
SAD 60
Sch. Sys. Enr. Code 5
Supt. – P. Johnson, P O BOX 819   03906
ES, P O BOX 609   03906 – Katherine Garon, prin.
Other Schools – See Berwick, East Lebanon

Northeast Harbor, Hancock Co.
Union SD 98
Supt. – See Mount Desert
Mt. Desert ES, P O BOX 408   04662
  James Morin, prin.

North Edgecomb, Lincoln Co., Pop. Code 3
Union SD 49
Supt. – See Boothbay Harbor
Edgecomb Eddy ES, CROSS POINT ROAD   04556
  Lisa Bolster, prin.

North Fryeburg, Oxford Co.
SAD 72
Supt. – See Fryeburg
Adams ES, P O BOX 89   04058
  Gary MacDonald, prin.

North Haven, Knox Co., Pop. Code 2
SAD 7
Sch. Sys. Enr. Code 1
Supt. – Jerry White   04853
North Haven Community S, P O BOX 699   04853
  J. White, prin.

North New Portland, Somerset Co., Pop. Code 3
SAD 74
Supt. – See North Anson
Central ES, P O BOX 208   04961
  William Judkins, prin.

North Vassalboro, Kennebec Co.
Union SD 52
Supt. – See Winslow
Lord MS, MAPLE ST   04962 – Anne Fuller, prin.

North Whitefield, Lincoln Co., Pop. Code 4
Union SD 51
Supt. – See Gardiner
Whitefield ES, ROUTE 126   04353
  Isaac Dyer, prin.

Norway, Oxford Co., Pop. Code 5
SAD 17
Supt. – See South Paris
Rowe ES, 94 MAIN ST   04268 – Bruce Tyner, prin.

Oakland, Kennebec Co., Pop. Code 6
SAD 47
Sch. Sys. Enr. Code 4
Supt. – J. Albanese, P O BOX 158   04963
Williams JHS, P O BOX 67   04963
  Melvin Williams, prin.
Atwood-Tapley ES, HEATH STREET   04963
  William Sawtelle, prin.
Other Schools – See Augusta, Belgrade

Ogunquit, York Co., Pop. Code 4
Wells-Ogunquit Comm. SD
Supt. – See Wells
Ogunquit Village ES, P O BOX 2399   03907
  Robert Hasson,Jr., prin.

Olamon, Penobscot Co.
Union SD 90
Supt. – See Milford
Dunn ES   04467 – Paul Frost, prin.

Old Orchard Beach, York Co., Pop. Code 6
Old Orchard Beach SD
Sch. Sys. Enr. Code 4
Supt. – V. McGee, JAMESON HILL ROAD   04064
JHS, SACO AVE   04064 – Michael Pulsifer, prin.
Jameson ES, 6 JAMESON HILL RD   04064
  Pamela Mullen, prin.
Loranger Memorial MS
  4 JAMESON HILL RD   04064
  Judy Whitman, prin.

Old Town, Penobscot Co., Pop. Code 6
Maine Indian Education SD
Supt. – See Calais
Indian Island ES, P O BOX 566   04468
  Sr. Helen KcKeough, prin.

Old Town SD
Sch. Sys. Enr. Code 4
Supt. – J. Grady, 151 OAK ST   04468
Gray ES, 190 STILLWATER AVE   04468
  Larry Reynolds, prin.
Hunt MS, SOUTH BRUNSWICK STREET   04468
  John O'Connor, prin.
Jefferson Street ES, JEFFERSON STREET   04468
  Edward Haggerty, prin.
Other Schools – See Stillwater

Union SD 90
Supt. – See Milford
Alton ES, RURAL ROUTE 01 BOX 382B   04468
  Ralph Turner, prin.

Orland, Hancock Co., Pop. Code 4
Union SD 91
Supt. – See Bucksport
Orland Consolidated ES, P O BOX 9   04472
  Louise Biggie, prin.

Orono, Penobscot Co., Pop. Code 7
Union SD 87
Sch. Sys. Enr. Code 4
Supt. – R. Moreau, 18 GOODRICH DRIVE   04473
Adams ES, GOODRICH DRIVE   04473
  Robert Robinson, prin.
Other Schools – See Bangor

Orrington, Penobscot Co., Pop. Code 5
Union SD 91
Supt. – See Bucksport
Center Drive MS
  RURAL ROUTE 02 BOX 426   04474
  James White, prin.
North Orrington ES
  RURAL ROUTE 01 BOX 182   04474
  Carol MacRae, prin.

Owls Head, Knox Co., Pop. Code 4
SAD 5
Supt. – See Rockland
Owls Head Central MS, P O BOX 245   04854
  Craig Borgerson, prin.

Oxford, Oxford Co., Pop. Code 5
SAD 17
Supt. – See South Paris
Otisfield Central ES, P O BOX 199   04270
  Maurice Kautz, prin.
Perkins-Peaco ES, P O BOX 199   04270
  M. Kautz, prin.
Staples MS, P O BOX 199   04270
  Maurice Kautz, prin.

Palermo, Waldo Co., Pop. Code 3
Union SD 51
Supt. – See Gardiner
Palermo Consolodated ES
  RURAL ROUTE 03   04354 – Rosemary Foster, prin.

Palmyra, Somerset Co., Pop. Code 4
SAD 48
Supt. – See Newport

Palmyra Consolodated ES, P O BOX 5   04965
  Theodore Boyce, prin.

Patten, Penobscot Co., Pop. Code 4
  SAD 25
  Supt. – See Sherman Station
  Patten MS   04765 – Gregory Bagley, prin.
  Patten PS   04765 – Gregory Bagley, prin.

Peaks Island, Cumberland Co.
  Portland SD
  Supt. – See Portland
  ES, CHURCH STREET   04108 – Paul Steele, prin.

Pejepscot, Sagadhoc Co.
  SAD 75
  Supt. – See Topsham
  PS, GENERAL DELIVERY   04067
    Reginia Campbell, prin.

Pemaquid, Lincoln Co.
  Union SD 74
  Supt. – See Damariscotta
  Bristol Consolodated ES, HCR 62 BOX 200   04558
    Gordon Best,Jr., prin.

Pembroke, Washington Co., Pop. Code 3
  Union SD 104
  Supt. – See Eastport
  Charlotte ES, RFD   04666 – Peggy Lingley, prin.
  ES, RURAL ROUTE 01   04666 – Ralph Mahar, prin.

Penobscot, Hancock Co., Pop. Code 4
  Union SD 93
  Supt. – See Blue Hill
  ES, HCR 02 BOX 2   04476
    Donald Buckingham,Jr., prin.

Perry, Washington Co., Pop. Code 3
  Maine Indian Education SD
  Supt. – See Calais
  Rafferty ES   04667 – Sr. Maureen Wallace, prin.

  Union SD 104
  Supt. – See Eastport
  ES, ROUTE 1   04667 – Arlo Smith, prin.

Phillips, Franklin Co., Pop. Code 4
  SAD 58
  Supt. – See Kingfield
  ES, P O BOX 9   04966 – Kenneth Goodale, prin.

Phippsburg, Sagadahoc Co., Pop. Code 4
  Union SD 47
  Supt. – See Bath
  ES, CHR 04   04562 – Richard Hawkins, prin.

Pittsfield, Somerset Co., Pop. Code 5
  SAD 53
  Sch. Sys. Enr. Code 3
  Supt. – R. Shaw, 27 SCHOOL ST   04967
  Warsaw MS, 27 SCHOOL ST   04967
    Linda Leotsakos, prin.
  Manson Park ES, LANCEY STREET   04967
    Charles Phillips, prin.
  Vickery ES, 30 SCHOOL ST   04967
    Charles Phillips, prin.
  Other Schools – See Burnham

Poland, Androscoggin Co., Pop. Code 5
  Union SD 29
  Supt. – See Mechanic Falls
  Poland Community ES, HCR bOX 20   04273
    Donald McGlauflin, prin.

Portland, Cumberland Co., Pop. Code 8
  Portland SD
  Sch. Sys. Enr. Code 6
  Supt. – R. Hermes, 331 VERANDA ST   04103
  King MS, 92 DEERING AVE   04103
    Michael McCarthy, prin.
  Lincoln MS, 522 STEVENS AVE   04103
    Dana Allen, prin.
  Moore MS, 175 AUBURN ST   04103
    Charles Pressey, prin.
  Baxter ES, 150 OCEAN AVE   04103
    Marysue Morrison, prin.
  Clifford ES, 180 FALMOUTH ST   04102
    Marysue Morrison, prin.
  Hall ES, 23 ORONO RD   04102
    Frank Smith, prin.
  Jack ES, 414 EASTERN PROMENADE   04101
    Katherine Norris, prin.
  Longfellow ES, 432 STEVENS AVE   04103
    Alan Argondizza, prin.
  Lyseth ES, 175 AUBURN ST   04103
    Richard McGarvey, prin.
  Presumpscot PS, 69 PRESUMPSCOT ST   04103
    Carole Clark, prin.
  Reiche Community ES, 166 BRACKETT ST   04102
    Miriam Remar, prin.
  Riverton ES, 1600 FOREST AVE   04103
    Paul Steele, prin.
  Other Schools – See Cliff Island, Long Island, Peaks Island

Wayneflete School, 360 SPRING ST   04102
Breakwater School, 858 BRIGHTON AVE   04102
Cathedral ES of Portland, 14 LOCUST ST   04101
St. Joseph's ES, 695 STEVENS AVE   04103
St. Patrick ES, 1251 CONGRESS ST   04102

Pownal, Cumberland Co., Pop. Code 4
  SAD 62
  Sch. Sys. Enr. Code 2
  Supt. – J. Gale, ELMWOOD ROAD   04069
  ES, ELMWOOD ROAD   04069 – Jon Gale, prin.

Presque Isle, Aroostook Co., Pop. Code 7
  SAD 1
  Sch. Sys. Enr. Code 5
  Supt. – G. Johnson, P O BOX 1118   04769
  Cunningham Mid., 5 THIRD ST   04769
    Frank Hallett, prin.
  Skyway MS, SKYWAY INDUSTRIAL PARK   04769
    John Graves, prin.
  Gouldville ES, 44 PARK ST   04769
    Pamela Hallett, prin.
  Pine Street ES, 50 PINE ST   04769
    Lawrence Hunter, prin.
  Zippel ES, 5 THIRD ST   04769
    Richard Lyons, prin.
  Other Schools – See Mapleton, Westfield

Princeton, Washington Co., Pop. Code 3
  Maine Indian Education SD
  Supt. – See Calais
  Indian Township ES   04668
    Sr. Ellen Turner, prin.

  Union SD 107
  Supt. – See Baileyville
  ES, MAIN STREET   04668 – Barry Wheaton, prin.

Rangeley, Franklin Co., Pop. Code 4
  Union SD 37
  Sch. Sys. Enr. Code 2
  Supt. – K. Marks, P O BOX 97   04970
  Rangeley Lakes Regional S, P O BOX 97   04970
    Robert Welch, prin.
  Lincoln/Magalloway ES, P O BOX 97   04970
    Rose Hessmiller, prin.

Raymond, Cumberland Co., Pop. Code 4
  Raymond SD
  Sch. Sys. Enr. Code 2
  Supt. – David Bois,Jr., ROUTE 85   04071
  Jordan-Small ES
    RURAL ROUTE 01 BOX 271   04071
    David Bois,Jr., prin.

Readfield, Kennebec Co., Pop. Code 4
  Union SD 42
  Sch. Sys. Enr. Code 3
  Supt. – F. Bechard, P O BOX 87   04355
  ES, SOURTH ROAD   04355 – Forrest Yates, prin.
  Other Schools – See Manchester, Mount Vernon, Wayne

Richmond, Sagadahoc Co., Pop. Code 5
  Union SD 43
  Sch. Sys. Enr. Code 4
  Supt. – R. Spearin, P O BOX 190   04357
  MS, 118 MAIN ST   04357 – Douglas Reed, prin.
  Buker ES, 20 HIGH ST   04357
    William York, prin.
  Other Schools – See Monmouth

Robbinston, Washington Co., Pop. Code 2
  Union SD 106
  Supt. – See Calais
  Robbinston ES, RURAL ROUTE 01   04671
    Paul Johnson, prin.

Rockland, Knox Co., Pop. Code 6
  Monhegan Unit SD
  Sch. Sys. Enr. Code 1
  Supt. – P. Schwalbenberg, HCR 32 BOX 105   04841
  Other Schools – See Monhegan

  SAD 5
  Sch. Sys. Enr. Code 4
  Supt. – D. Fredericks, 5 GRACE ST #5   04841
  Rockland District JHS, 38 LINCOLN ST   04841
    Thomas Mellor, prin.
  McLain ES, 38 LINCOLN ST   04841
    Leonard Goeke,Jr., prin.
  North ES, BROADWAY   04841
    Corey Douglas, prin.
  South ES, BROADWAY & HOLMES ST   04841
    James Toomey, prin.
  Other Schools – See Owls Head, South Thomaston

  SAD 65
  Sch. Sys. Enr. Code 1
  Supt. – W. Sternberg, 5 GRACE ST   04841
  Matinicus ES, 40 GROVE ST   04841
    William Sternberg, prin.

Pen Bay ES, 1 WALDO AVE   04841

Rockport, Knox Co., Pop. Code 5
  SAD 28
  Supt. – See Camden
  ES, P O BOX 9   04856 – Marvin Higgins, prin.

Rockwood, Piscataquis Co.
  Unorganized Territories SD
  Supt. – See Augusta
  Blaine ES   04478 – Katherine Buzzell, prin.

Rumford, Oxford Co., Pop. Code 6
  Union SD 25
  Sch. Sys. Enr. Code 4
  Supt. – R. Spugnardi, 121 LINCOLN AVE   04276
  ES, LINCOLN AVE   04276 – Dexter Berry, prin.
  Virginia ES, FOREST AVE   04276
    Gertrude Downs, prin.

Sts. Athanasius and John ES
  138 FRANKLIN ST   04276

Sabattus, Androscoggin Co., Pop. Code 5
  Union SD 44
  Sch. Sys. Enr. Code 4
  Supt. – R. Pelletier, P O BOX 220   04280

ES, P O BOX 280   04280 – Betsy McElvein, prin.
Wales Central ES
  RURAL ROUTE 01 BOX 1800   04280
    Ann Dooling, prin.
Other Schools – See Litchfield

Saco, York Co., Pop. Code 7
  Union SD 7
  Sch. Sys. Enr. Code 4
  Supt. – H. Cushman, TASKER ST   04072
  MS, BUXTON ROAD   04072
    Larry Littlefield, prin.
  Burns MS, MIDDLE STREET   04072
    William Soucy, prin.
  Fairfield ES, PEPPERELL PARK   04072
    Elizabeth Foley, prin.
  Young ES, TASKER STREET   04072
    Evelyn Turner, prin.
  Other Schools – See Hollis Center

Notre Dame De Lords ES, 50 BEACH ST   04072

Saint Agatha, Aroostook Co., Pop. Code 4
  SAD 33
  Sch. Sys. Enr. Code 3
  Supt. – W. O'Connell, P O BOX 347   04772
  Other Schools – See Upper Frenchville

Saint Albans, Somerset Co., Pop. Code 4
  SAD 48
  Supt. – See Newport
  St. Albans Consolidated ES   04971
    Theodore Boyce, prin.

Saint Francis, Aroostook Co., Pop. Code 3
  SAD 10
  Sch. Sys. Enr. Code 2
  Supt. – P. Kelly
    RURAL ROUTE 01 BOX 146   04774
  Allagash Consolidated S
    RURAL ROUTE 01 BOX 146   04774
    Ralph Niemi, prin.

  SAD 27
  Supt. – See Fort Kent
  ES, GENERAL DELIVERY   04774
    William Pettengill, prin.

Sanford, York Co., Pop. Code 7
  Sanford SD
  Sch. Sys. Enr. Code 5
  Supt. – W. Grogan, 265 MAIN ST   04073
  JHS, 8 MAIN ST   04073 – D. Terracin, prin.
  Central ES, WENTWORTH STREET   04073
    Debora Bunn, prin.
  Edison ES, OXFORD STREET   04073
    Jean Smith, prin.
  Emerson ES, MAIN STREET   04073
    Patricia Matthews, prin.
  Lafayette ES, 43 BROOK ST   04073
    Thomas Cagne, prin.
  Sanford MS, 2 MAIN ST   04073
    Robert Powers, prin.
  Smith ES, RURAL ROUTE 02 BOX 300   04073
    Donald Gnecco, prin.
  Other Schools – See Springvale

St. Thomas ES, 69 NORTH AVE   04073

Sangerville, Piscataquis Co., Pop. Code 4
  SAD 4
  Supt. – See Guilford
  Fowler ES, P O BOX 247   04479
    Kathy Richard, prin.

Scarborough, Cumberland Co., Pop. Code 7
  Scarborough SD
  Sch. Sys. Enr. Code 4
  Supt. – S. Grover, P O BOX 370   04074
  Wentworth MS, GORHAM ROAD   04074
    Douglas Joy, prin.
  Bessey MS, RURAL ROUTE 01   04074
    Paul Bellavance, prin.
  Blue Point ES, PINE POINT RD   04074
    Paul Bellavance, prin.
  Eight Corners ES, MUSSEY RD   04074
    Paul Bellavance, prin.
  Pleasant Hill ES, HIGHLAND AVE   04074
    Paul Bellavance, prin.
  Wentworth IS, 10 GORHAM RD   04074
    Paul Bellavance, prin.

Searsmont, Waldo Co., Pop. Code 3
  SAD 34
  Supt. – See Belfast
  Belmont ES, P O BOX 58   04973
    Randall Curtis, prin.
  MS, P O BOX 58   04973 – Randall Curtis, prin.
  Weymouth ES, P O BOX 58   04973
    Randall Curtis, prin.

Searsport, Waldo Co., Pop. Code 4
  SAD 56
  Sch. Sys. Enr. Code 3
  Supt. – M. Cormier, P O BOX 467   04974
  Central ES, MORTLAND ROAD   04974
    Douglas Lockwood, prin.
  MS, MORTLAND ROAD   04974
    Douglas Lockwood, prin.
  Other Schools – See Frankfort, Stockton Sprngs

Sebago Lake, Cumberland Co., Pop. Code 3
  SAD 6
  Supt. – See Bar Mills
  Libby ES, P O BOX 177   04075
    Joyce Freeman, prin.

Sedgwick, Hancock Co., Pop. Code 3
Union SD 76
Supt. – See Stonington
Reach Road ES 04676 – Richard Welch, prin.
PS, MAIN STREET 04676 – Richard Welch, prin.

Sherman, Aroostook Co., Pop. Code 4
SAD 25
Supt. – See Sherman Station
ES, SHERMAN MILLS 04776 – John Johnson, prin.

Sherman Station, Penobscot Co., Pop. Code 2
SAD 25
Sch. Sys. Enr. Code 3
Supt. – C. Nightingale, P O BOX 20 04777
Katahdin JHS, P O BOX 10 04777
  Steven Greenlaw, prin.
Other Schools – See Patten, Sherman, Stacyville

Shirley Mills, Piscataquis Co., Pop. Code 2
Union SD 60
Supt. – See Greenville
Shirley ES 04485 – Charles Baker, prin.

Sinclair, Aroostook Co.
Unorganized Territories SD
Supt. – See Augusta
Therriault ES, RURAL ROUTE 162 BOX 62 04779
  Claudette Beaulieu, prin.

Skowhegan, Somerset Co., Pop. Code 6
SAD 54
Sch. Sys. Enr. Code 5
Supt. – L. Young, P O BOX 69 04976
Skowhegan Area MS, WILLOW ST 04976
  Jerome Lynch, prin.
Bloomfield ES, P O BOX 506 04976
  Elaine Miller, prin.
Cornville Consolidated ES
  RURAL ROUTE 01 BOX 2150 04976
  Debra Primmerman, prin.
North ES, REED STREET 04976
  Deborah Smith, prin.
Smith MS, HESELTON STREET 04976
  James McManus, prin.
Other Schools – See Canaan, Norridgewock,
  Smithfield

Smithfield, Somerset Pond Co., Pop. Code 3
SAD 54
Supt. – See Skowhegan
MS, P O BOX 69 04978 – Helen Cole, prin.

Soldier Pond, Aroostook Co.
SAD 27
Supt. – See Fort Kent
Wallagrass ES, CHURCH STREET 04781
  Violet Daigle, prin.

Solon, Somerset Co., Pop. Code 3
SAD 74
Supt. – See North Anson
ES, P O BOX 146 04979 – Mary Jones, prin.

South Berwick, York Co., Pop. Code 5
SAD 35
Supt. – See Eliot
Marshwood JHS, P O BOX 186 03908
  Walter Barrett, prin.
Central ES, 197 MAIN ST 03908
  Jill Appleby, prin.

Berwick Academy, ACADEMY ST 03908

South Bristol, Lincoln Co., Pop. Code 3
Union SD 74
Supt. – See Damariscotta
ES, P O BOX 370 04568 – Stephen Dixon, prin.

South Freeport, Cumberland Co.
Freeport SD
Supt. – See Freeport
Soule MS, P O OBX 150 04078
  Eugene Berg, prin.

South Gardiner, Kennebec Co.
SAD 11
Supt. – See Gardiner
ES, RIVER ROAD 04345 – Rohnie Dunn, prin.

South Harpswell, Cumberland Co.
SAD 75
Supt. – See Topsham
West Harpswell ES
  RURAL ROUTE 02 BOX 427 04079
  Regina Campbell, prin.

South Paris, Oxford Co., Pop. Code 4
SAD 17
Sch. Sys. Enr. Code 5
Supt. – N. Smith, 23 MARKET SQ 04281
Oxford Hills JHS, 100 PINE ST 04281
  Herbert Adams, prin.
Fox ES, EAST MAIN ST 04281
  Bruce Garrow, prin.
Other Schools – See Harrison, Hebron, Norway,
  Oxford, Waterford, West Paris

South Portland, Cumberland Co., Pop. Code 7
South Portland SD
Sch. Sys. Enr. Code 5
Supt. – R. MacDonald
  130 WESCOTT ROAD 04106
Mahoney MS, 240 OCEAN ST 04106
  Kenneth Murphy, prin.
Memorial MS, 120 WESCOTT RD 04106
  John Gailey, prin.

Brown ES, 37 HIGHLAND AVE 04106
  James Minott, prin.
Dyer ES, 52 ALFRED ST 04106
  Robert Paradis, prin.
Hamlin ES, 496 OCEAN ST 04106
  Katherine Germani, prin.
Kaler ES, 165 KELSEY ST 04106
  Douglas Caldwell, prin.
Redbank Village ES, MACARTHUR CIRCLE 04106
  Mary Marsh, prin.
Sawyer ES, 81 WESTBROOK ST 04106
  Jeanne Vickers, prin.
Skillin ES, 180 WESCOTT RD 04106
  Joyce Freeman, prin.
Small ES, 87 THOMPSON ST 04106
  Alan Hawkings, prin.

Great Portlnd Christian School
  1338 BROADWAY 04106
Holy Cross ES, 436 BROADWAY 04106

South Thomaston, Knox Co., Pop. Code 4
SAD 5
Supt. – See Rockland
Gilford Butler ES, P O BOX 146 04858
  Craig Borgerson, prin.

Southwest Harbor, Hancock Co.
Union SD 98
Supt. – See Mount Desert
Pemetic ES 04679 – David Pierce, prin.

South Windham, Cumberland Co., Pop. Code 4
Windham SD
Sch. Sys. Enr. Code 4
Supt. – J. Love, RURAL ROUTE 01 BOX 22 04082
Andrew ES, HIGH STREET 04082
  Susan Gendron, prin.
Other Schools – See Windham

Springfield, Penobscot Co., Pop. Code 2
SAD 30
Supt. – See Lee
Lombard MS, RURAL ROUTE 06 04487
  Wanda Mallett, prin.

Springvale, York Co., Pop. Code 5
SAD 57
Supt. – See Waterboro
Shapleigh Memorial ES, RURAL ROUTE 01 04083
  Richard Harnett, prin.

Sanford SD
Supt. – See Sanford
Lincoln ES, KING STREET 04083
  Sharon Remick, prin.
Springvale PS, OAK ST 04083
  Sheila Guiney, prin.

Stacyville, Penobscot Co., Pop. Code 3
SAD 25
Supt. – See Sherman Station
ES, SHERMAN STA 04782 – Gregory Cole, prin.

Standish, Cumberland Co., Pop. Code 6
SAD 6
Supt. – See Bar Mills
Jack ES, P O BOX 126 04084
  Joyce Freeman, prin.

Steep Falls, Cumberland Co.
SAD 6
Supt. – See Bar Mills
ES, P O BOX 781 04085 – James Pillsbury, prin.

Stetson, Penobscot Co., Pop. Code 3
SAD 64
Supt. – See East Corinth
ES, P O BOX 67 04488 – Donna Archer, prin.

Steuben, Washington Co., Pop. Code 3
Union SD 96
Supt. – See Gouldsboro
Lewis ES 04680 – Francis Boynton, prin.

Stillwater, Penobscot Co.
Old Town SD
Supt. – See Old Town
Sargent ES, 83 BENNOCH RD 04489
  Philip Avila, prin.

Stockholm, Aroostook Co., Pop. Code 2
Union SD 122
Supt. – See Caribou
ES, RURAL ROUTE 01 BOX 98 04783
  Denise Bossie, prin.

Stockton Sprngs, Waldo Co., Pop. Code 4
SAD 56
Supt. – See Searsport
ES, CHURCH STREET 04981 – Carl Bowen, prin.

Stonington, Hancock Co., Pop. Code 4
Deer Isle-Stonington Comm. SD
Sch. Sys. Enr. Code 3
Supt. – J. Lucarelli, P O BOX 98 04681
MS, P O BOX 7 04681 – Joseph Watson, prin.
Other Schools – See Deer Isle

Isle Au Haut Unit SD
Sch. Sys. Enr. Code 1
Supt. – J. Lucarelli, P O BOX 98 04681
Other Schools – See Isle Au Haut

Union SD 76
Sch. Sys. Enr. Code 2
Supt. – J. Lucarelli, P O BOX 98 04681
Other Schools – See Brooklin, Sedgwick

Stratton, Franklin Co., Pop. Code 2
SAD 58
Supt. – See Kingfield
ES, P O BOX 10 04982 – Sarah Boone, prin.

Strong, Franklin Co., Pop. Code 4
SAD 58
Supt. – See Kingfield
ES 04983 – Felecia Corson, prin.

Surry, Hancock Co., Pop. Code 3
Union SD 92
Supt. – See Ellsworth
ES, NORTH BEND ROAD 04684
  Warren Berkowitz, prin.

Swans Island, Hancock Co., Pop. Code 2
SAD 76
Supt. – See Mount Desert
Swans Island Consolodated ES
  P O BOX 128 04685 – Kim Colbeth, prin.

Tenants Harbor, Knox Co.
SAD 50
Supt. – See Thomaston
St. George ES, P O BOX 153 04860
  Michael Lafortune, prin.

Thomaston, Knox Co., Pop. Code 5
SAD 50
Sch. Sys. Enr. Code 3
Supt. – P. Luttrell, P O BOX 182 04861
MS, WATTS LANE 04861 – Terry Kenniston, prin.
Libby ES, VALLEY STREET 04861
  Elizabeth O'Brien, prin.
Other Schools – See Tenants Harbor, Warren

Thorndike, Waldo Co., Pop. Code 3
SAD 3
Supt. – See Unity
Mt. View JHS, RURAL ROUTE 02 BOX 180 04986
  Wayne Suomi, prin.
Mount View ES
  RURAL ROUTE 02 BOX 180 04986
  Peter Weston, prin.

Topsfield, Washington Co., Pop. Code 2
East Range Community SD
Supt. – See Danforth
East Range II ES
  RURAL ROUTE 06 BOX 55 04490
  Charles Noyes, prin.

Topsham, Sagadahoc Co., Pop. Code 6
SAD 75
Sch. Sys. Enr. Code 5
Supt. – R. Cartmill, 22 ELM ST 04086
Williams-Cone ES, 1 PERKINS ST EXT 04086
  Brenda Brown, prin.
Other Schools – See Bowdoinham, Brunswick,
  Pejepscot, South Harpswell

Troy, Waldo Co., Pop. Code 3
SAD 3
Supt. – See Unity
Troy Central ES 04987 – Dennis Volpe, prin.

Turner, Androscoggin Co., Pop. Code 5
SAD 52
Sch. Sys. Enr. Code 4
Supt. – S. Sawyer
  RURAL ROUTE 01 BOX 1220 04282
Tripp MS, RURAL ROUTE 01 BOX 1253 04282
  Richard Brouillette, prin.
ES, RURAL ROUTE 02 BOX 1252 04282
  Ronald Dunn, prin.
Other Schools – See Greene, Leeds

Union, Knox Co., Pop. Code 4
SAD 40
Supt. – See Waldoboro
Union/Gaul ES, ROUTE 131 04862
  Richard Crosman, prin.

Union SD 69
Supt. – See Camden
Appleton Village ES
  RURAL ROUTE 01 BOX 150 04862
  Carol Lariviere, prin.
Hope ES, RURAL ROUTE 02 BOX 171 04862
  Richard Hamel, prin.

Unity, Waldo Co., Pop. Code 4
SAD 3
Sch. Sys. Enr. Code 4
Supt. – W. Pagnano 04988
ES, SCHOOL STREET 04988 – Dennis Volpe, prin.
Other Schools – See Brooks, Liberty, Monroe,
  Thorndike, Troy

Upper Frenchville, Aroostook Co., Pop. Code 4
SAD 33
Supt. – See Saint Agatha
Levesque ES, P O BOX J 04784
  Fernande Desjardins, prin.

Van Buren, Aroostook Co., Pop. Code 5
SAD 24
Sch. Sys. Enr. Code 3
Supt. – W. Mowatt, 29 POPLAR ST #24 04785
Gateway ES, 20 WRIGHT ST 04785
  Clayton Belanger, prin.

Vanceboro, Washington Co., Pop. Code 2
Union SD 108
Supt. – See Danforth
ES, P O BOX D 04491 – Jeffrey Born, prin.

Vinalhaven, Knox Co., Pop. Code 4
SAD 8
Sch. Sys. Enr. Code 2
Supt. – Eugene Welentiechick   04863
Lincoln S, P O BOX R   04863
   Eugene Welentiechick, prin.

Waldoboro, Lincoln Co., Pop. Code 5
SAD 40
Sch. Sys. Enr. Code 4
Supt. – D. Gaul, P O BOX L   04572
Gray JHS, CHURCH ST   04572 – Barry Belyea, prin.
Miller ES, P O BOX C   04572 – James Morse, prin.
Other Schools – See Friendship, Union, Warren,
   Washington

Union SD 74
Supt. – See Damariscotta
Bremen ES, HCR 61 BOX 23   04572
   John Trainor, prin.

Warren, Knox Co., Pop. Code 5
SAD 40
Supt. – See Waldoboro
Rowe MS, P O BOX 344   04864
   Robert Hamalainen, prin.
PS, P O BOX 344   04864
   Robert Hamalainen, prin.

SAD 50
Supt. – See Thomaston
Cushing Consolodated ES
   RURAL ROUTE 02   04864
   Elizabeth O'Brien, prin.

Washburn, Aroostook Co., Pop. Code 4
SAD 45
Sch. Sys. Enr. Code 3
Supt. – D. Lyon, P O BOX 507   04786
Foster MS, P O BOX 278   04786
   Sheldon Lauritsen, prin.
ES, P O BOX 278   04786 – Sheldon Lauritsen, prin.

Washington, Knox Co., Pop. Code 3
SAD 40
Supt. – See Waldoboro
Prescott Memorial ES, RURAL ROUTE 01   04574
   Robert Koenig, prin.

Waterboro, York Co., Pop. Code 5
SAD 57
Sch. Sys. Enr. Code 5
Supt. – V. Gallucci   04087
Massabesic JHS, WEST ROAD   04087
   William Fisher, prin.
Other Schools – See Alfred, Biddeford, East
   Waterboro, Kennebunk, Limerick, Springvale

Waterford, Oxford Co., Pop. Code 3
SAD 17
Supt. – See South Paris
Waterford Memorial ES, VALLEY RD   04088
   Judith Potter, prin.

Waterville, Kennebec Co., Pop. Code 7
SAD 49
Supt. – See Fairfield
Benton ES, 62 OLD BENTON NECK RD   04901
   John Bacon, prin.

Waterville SD
Sch. Sys. Enr. Code 4
Supt. – A. Hall, PLEASANT ST   04901
JHS, 120 W RIVER ROAD   04901
   Russell Clukey, prin.
Brookside ES, DRUMMOND AVE   04901
   Lenora Murray, prin.
Pleasant Street MS, 25 PLEASANT ST   04901
   Michael Gallagher, prin.

Mt. Merici ES, 142 WESTERN AVE   04901

Wayne, Kennebec Co., Pop. Code 3
Union SD 42
Supt. – See Readfield
ES, RURAL ROUTE 01 BOX 30   04284
   Robert Hunter, prin.

Weld, Franklin Co., Pop. Code 2
SAD 9
Supt. – See Farmington
ES, P O BOX 38   04285 – Paul Gooch,Jr., prin.

Wellington, Piscataquis Co., Pop. Code 2
SAD 4
Supt. – See Guilford
ES, P O BOX 262   04990 – Laurie Nile, prin.

Wells, York Co., Pop. Code 3
Wells-Ogunquit Comm. SD
Sch. Sys. Enr. Code 4
Supt. – R. Kautz, P O BOX 578   04090
JHS, P O BOX 310   04090 – Robert Hasson, prin.
ES, P O BOX 429   04090 – Robert Hasson,Jr., prin.
Other Schools – See Ogunquit

Wesley, Washington Co., Pop. Code 2
Union SD 102
Supt. – See Machias
Wesley Corner ES, RURAL ROUTE 09   04654
   Diana O'Neal, prin.

West Baldwin, Cumberland Co.
SAD 55
Supt. – See Cornish
Baldwin Consolodated ES
   RURAL ROUTE BOX 4   04091
   Barbara Bouchard, prin.

Westbrook, Cumberland Co., Pop. Code 7
Westbrook SD
Sch. Sys. Enr. Code 5
Supt. – E. Connolly, 765 MAIN ST   04092
JHS, 426 BRIDGE ST   04092 – Spencer Hardy, prin.
Congin MS, 341 CUMBERLAND ST   04092
   Coleman Rogers, prin.
Oxford-Cumberland Canal MS
   GLENWOOD AVE   04092 – Robert Hall, prin.
Pride's Corner ES, BRIDGTON RD   04092
   Steven Harnois, prin.
Saccarappa ES, 110 HUNTRESS AVE   04092
   Deborah Peck, prin.

West Buxton, York Co., Pop. Code 2
SAD 6
Supt. – See Bar Mills
Bonny Eagle JHS
   RURAL ROUTE 01 BOX 430   04093
   James Pouravelis, prin.
Hanson MS, RURAL ROUTE 01 BOX 190   04093
   Paul Vincent, prin.
Jack Memorial ES
   RURAL ROUTE 01 BOX 288   04093
   Paul Vincent, prin.
Jewett ES, RURAL ROUTE 01 BOX 186   04093
   Paul Vincent, prin.

West Enfield, Penobscot Co., Pop. Code 2
SAD 31
Supt. – See Howland
Curtis ES, MAIN ST W   04493
   James Winslow, prin.

Westfield, Aroostook Co., Pop. Code 3
SAD 1
Supt. – See Presque Isle
ES, P O BOX B   04787 – Dawn Jandreau, prin.

West Forks, Somerset Co., Pop. Code 1
SAD 13
Supt. – See Bingham
Ball-Franklin ES, P O BOX 109   04985
   Linda Hunnewell, prin.

West Paris, Oxford Co., Pop. Code 4
SAD 17
Supt. – See South Paris
Gray-Legion Memorial ES, P O BOX 38   04289
   Bruce Garrow, prin.

West Peru, Oxford Co., Pop. Code 2
Peru SD
Sch. Sys. Enr. Code 2
Supt. – J. Backus, RURAL ROUTE BOX 80   04290
Peru ES, RURAL ROUTE BOX 80   04290
   John Backus, prin.

West Southport, Lincoln Co., Pop. Code 3
Union SD 49
Supt. – See Boothbay Harbor
Southport Central ES, P O BOX 279   04576
   Carl Olsen, prin.

West Sullivan, Hancock Co.
Schoodic Community SD
Supt. – See Gouldsboro
Sullivan ES, HCR   04689
   Charles Cashman,Jr., prin.

Whiting, Washington Co., Pop. Code 2
SAD 77
Supt. – See Machias
Whiting Village ES   04691 – Pauline Cates, prin.

Wilton, Franklin Co., Pop. Code 5
SAD 9
Supt. – See Farmington
Academy Hill MS, P O BOX S   04294
   Henry Veilleux, prin.
Cushing ES, P O BOX 548   04294
   Paul Gooch,Jr., prin.
PS, P O BOX 548   04294 – Paul Gooch,Jr., prin.

Windham, Cumberland Co., Pop. Code 7
Gorham SD
Supt. – See Gorham
Little Falls ES, 40 OAK ST   04062
   Gloria LeVeillee, prin.

Windham SD
Supt. – See South Windham

Allen ES, RURAL ROUTE 01   04062
   Susan Gendron, prin.
Arlington ES, 709 ROOSEVELT TRL   04062
   Susan Gendron, prin.
Manchester MS, RURAL ROUTE 02   04062
   Thomas Quinn, prin.

Windsor, Kennebec Co., Pop. Code 4
Union SD 51
Supt. – See Gardiner
ES, ROUTE 32   04363 – Daniel Joslyn, prin.

Winn, Penobscot Co., Pop. Code 3
SAD 30
Supt. – See Lee
Haynes MS   04495 – Kay Rollins, prin.

Winslow, Kennebec Co., Pop. Code 6
Union SD 52
Sch. Sys. Enr. Code 5
Supt. – L. Duff, 16 BENTON AVE #52   04901
Boston Avenue MS, BOSTON AVE   04901
   Richard Williams, prin.
Garand Street ES, 12 DANIELSON ST   04901
   Betty Turner, prin.
Halifax Street ES, 37 1/2 HALIFAX ST   04901
   Diane McGowan, prin.
St. John's Public MS, 36 GARAND ST   04901
   Steven Frank, prin.
Other Schools – See Augusta, China, East Vassalboro,
   North Vassalboro

St. John Catholic ES, 36 1/2 GARAND ST   04901

Winter Harbor, Hancock Co., Pop. Code 4
Union SD 96
Supt. – See Gouldsboro
ES, P O BOX 99   04693 – Dennis Perry, prin.

Winterport, Waldo Co., Pop. Code 5
SAD 22
Supt. – See Hampden
Smith ES, P O BOX 10   04496 – Keith Welch, prin.

Winthrop, Kennebec Co., Pop. Code 6
Winthrop SD
Sch. Sys. Enr. Code 4
Supt. – N. Megna, TOWN HALL LANE   04364
MS, CHARLES ST EXIT   04364 – Mark Flight, prin.
ES, HIGHLAND AVE   04364
   Marcia Bechard, prin.

Wiscasset, Lincoln Co., Pop. Code 5
Union SD 48
Sch. Sys. Enr. Code 4
Supt. – J. Ashe, P O BOX 430   04578
MS, P O BOX 348   04578 – Don Siviski, prin.
PS, P O BOX J   04578 – Jan Hoffman, prin.
Other Schools – See Dresden

Woodland, Washington Co., Pop. Code 4
Union SD 106
Supt. – See Calais
Alexander ES, P O BOX 1430   04694
   Mary Bouchard, prin.

Union SD 107
Supt. – See Baileyville
ES, 7 FOURTH AVE   04694 – Dwight Ferry, prin.

Woolwich, Sagadahoc Co., Pop. Code 4
Union SD 47
Supt. – See Bath
Woolwich Central ES, NEQUASSET ROAD   04579
   Paul Timberlake, prin.

Wytopitlock, Aroostook Co.
Union SD 110
Supt. – See Lee
ES   04497 – John Lemole, prin.

Yarmouth, Cumberland Co., Pop. Code 4
Yarmouth SD
Sch. Sys. Enr. Code 4
Supt. – F. Harrison, 8 PORTLAND ST   04096
Rowe ES, SCHOOL ST   04096
   Lawrence Frazier, prin.
Yarmouth IS, MCCARTNER STREET   04096
   Peter Cheney, prin.

York, York Co., Pop. Code 4
York SD
Sch. Sys. Enr. Code 4
Supt. – R. Barnes, 46 ORGANUG ROAD   03909
MS, 46 ORGANUG ROAD   03909
   Elton Knowles, prin.
ES, 122 YORK ST   03909 – L. Ingraham, prin.

MARYLAND

STATE DEPARTMENT OF EDUCATION
200 W. Baltimore St., Baltimore 21201
(301) 333-2000

State Superintendent of Schools	Joseph Schilling
Deputy Superintendent	Claude Kitchens
Assistant Deputy Superintendent Educational Development	Martha Fields
Assistant Deputy Superintendent Vocational Rehabilitation	Richard Batterton
Assistant Deputy Superintendent Educational Support	Richard Petre
Assistant Superintendent Administration & Finance	John Tritt
Assistant Superintendent Communications & Special Projects	Bonnie Copeland

STATE BOARD OF EDUCATION
Lawrence Shulman, *President*   Rockville   20850

MARYLAND HIGHER EDUCATION COMMISSION
J. Henry Butta, *Chairperson*   16 Francis St., Annapolis   21401

PUBLIC, PRIVATE, AND PAROCHIAL ELEMENTARY SCHOOLS

Aberdeen, Harford Co., Pop. Code 7
Harford County SD
Supt. – See Bel Air
MS, 111 MOUNT ROYAL AVE   21001
  Shirley Rose, prin.
Bakerfield ES, 36 BAKER ST   21001
  Lloyd Fry, prin.
Halls Cross Roads ES, 203 E BEL AIR AVE   21001
  Thomas McShane, prin.
Hillsdale ES, 810 EDMUND ST   21001
  Louis Seidel, prin.

St. Joan of Arc ES, 222 S LAW ST   21001

Abingdon, Harford Co.
Harford County SD
Supt. – See Bel Air
James ES, 1 LAURENTUM PKY   21009
  Richard Bishop, prin.
Paca/Old Post Road ES
  2706 PHILADELPHIA RD   21009
  Walter Mitchell, prin.

Accident, Garret Co., Pop. Code 2
Garrett County SD
Supt. – See Oakland
Northern MS, RURAL ROUTE 02 BOX 5   21520
  Wilda Massi, prin.
ES, P O BOX 260   21520 – Robert Wilson, prin.

Accokeek, Prince George's Co.
Prince Georges County SD
Supt. – See Upper Marlboro
Burroughs MS, 1400 BERRY ROAD   20607
  Bruce Katz, prin.
Ferguson ES, 14600 BERRY RD   20607
  John Dade, prin.

Adamstown, Frederick Co.
Frederick County SD
Supt. – See Frederick
Carroll Manor ES, 5624 ADAMSTOWN RD   21710
  Delmar Rippeon, prin.

Adelphi, Prince George's Co., Pop. Code 6
Prince Georges County SD
Supt. – See Upper Marlboro
Buck Lodge MS, 2611 BUCK LODGE ROAD   20783
  Rob Weimer, prin.
ES, 8820 RIGGS RD   20783 – David Jamison, prin.
Cherokee Lane ES, 9000 25TH AVE   20783
  Jack St. Clair, prin.

Annapolis, Anne Arundel Co., Pop. Code 8
Anne Arundel County SD
Sch. Sys. Enr. Code 8
Supt. – Larry Lorton, 2644 RIVA ROAD   21401
ES, 180 GREEN ST   21401 – Dixie Stack, prin.
Cape St. Claire ES, 931 BLUE RIDGE DR   21401
  Charles Bowers, prin.
Eastport ES, 420 FIFTH ST   21403
  Joseph Lo Cascio, prin.
Georgetown East ES, 111 DOGWOOD RD   21403
  Virginia Bradley, prin.
Germantown ES, 1411 CEDAR PARK RD   21401
  Peter Zimmer, prin.
Hillsmere ES
  3052 ARUNDEL ON THE BAY RD   21403
  Lambert Zaengle, prin.

Parole ES, 103 CHINQUAPIN ROUND RD   21401
  Preston Hebron, prin.
Rolling Knolls ES, 1996 VALLEY RD   21401
  Joyce Paga, prin.
Tyler Heights ES, 200 JANWALL CT   21403
  Oscar Kidd II, prin.
West Annapolis ES, 210 ANNAPOLIS ST   21401
  Barry Fader, prin.
Other Schools – See Arnold, Baltimore, Crownsville,
  Davidsonville, Deale, Edgewater, Fort George G.
  Meade, Gambrills, Glen Burnie, Hanover, Jessup,
  Laurel, Linthicum Heights, Lothian, Mayo,
  Millersville, Odenton, Pasadena, Severn, Severna
  Park, Shady Side, Tracys Landing

Annapolis Christian School
  RIDGELY AVE & WILSON ROAD   21403
Key School, 534 HILLSMERE DRIVE   21403
St. Mary ES, DUKE OF GLOUCESTER ST   21401

Arnold, Anne Arundel Co.
Anne Arundel County SD
Supt. – See Annapolis
Severn River JHS
  241 PENINSULA FARM ROAD   21012
  Don McClenahan, prin.
ES, 90 CHURCH RD   21012 – James Seamon, prin.
Belvedere ES, MAGO VISTA ROAD   21012
  Donald Smith, prin.
Broadneck ES, 470 SHORE ACRES RD   21012
  Phyllis Mentzell, prin.
Magothy River MS
  241 PENINSULA FARM ROAD   21012
  Ellen Tamlinson, prin.

Avenue, St. Mary's Co., Pop. Code 6

Holy Angels Sacred Heart ES   20609

Baldwin, Baltimore Co.
Baltimore County SD
Supt. – See Towson
Carroll Manor ES
  4434 CARROLL MANOR RD   21013
  Paul Murrell, prin.

Baltimore, Baltimore Co., Pop. Code 11
Anne Arundel County SD
Supt. – See Annapolis
Belle Grove ES, 4502 BELLE GROVE RD   21225
  Gloria Reid, prin.
Brooklyn Park ES, 200 14TH AVE   21225
  Michael Trippett, prin.
Park ES, 201 E 11TH AVE   21225
  Karlie Everett, prin.

Baltimore CSD
Sch. Sys. Enr. Code 9
Supt. – Richard Hunter, 3 E 25TH ST   21218
Canton MS, 801 S HIGHLAND AVE   21224
  Gary Thrift, prin.
Cherry Hill MS, 2700 SEAMON AVE   21225
  Arnette Brown, prin.
Chinquapin MS, 900 WOODBOURNE AVE   21212
  Willie Butler, prin.
Dunbar MS, 500 N CAROLINE ST   21205
  Frances Jolley, prin.
Fallstaff MS, 3801 FALLSTAFF ROAD   21215
  Gloria Pegram, prin.

Franklin MS, 1201 CAMBRIA ST   21225
  Don Knox, prin.
Garrison MS, 3910 BARRINGTON ROAD   21207
  Andrew Harvey, prin.
Greenspring MS, 4701 GREENSPRING AVE   21209
  Jennye Thomas, prin.
Hamilton MS, 5609 SEFTON AVE   21214
  Eugene Lawrence, prin.
Hampstead Hill JHS, 101 S ELLWOOD AVE   21224
  Preston Roney, prin.
Harlem Park MS, 1500 HARLEM AVE   21217
  Stanley Holmes, prin.
Lemmel MS, 2801 N DUKELAND ST   21216
  Gwendolyn Cooke, prin.
Lombard MS, 1500 E LOMBARD ST   21231
  Lillie Myers, prin.
Northeast MS, 5001 MORAVIA ROAD   21206
  Beverly Crisp, prin.
Pimlico MS, 3500 W NORTHERN PKWY   21215
  Gloria Richeson, prin.
Poole MS, 1300 W 36TH ST   21211
  Mary Silva, prin.
Southeast MS, 6820 FAIT AVE   21224
  John Mohamed, prin.
Washington MS, 1301 MCCULLOH ST   21217
  Ruth Bukatman, prin.
West Baltimore MS, 201 N BEND ROAD   21229
  Sheila Kolman, prin.
Winston MS, 1101 WINSTON AVE   21212
  Cecelia Chesno, prin.
Abbottston ES, 1300 GORSUCH AVE   21218
  Cornelius Johnson, prin.
Arlington ES, 3705 W ROGERS AVE   21215
  James Smith, prin.
Armistead Gardens ES
  5001-5061 E EAGER ST   21205 – Joe Wilson, prin.
Arundel ES, 2400 ROUND RD   21225
  Judith Dixon, prin.
Ashburton ES, 3935 HILTON RD   21215
  Robert Marino, prin.
Barclay ES, 2900 BARCLAY ST   21218
  Gertrude Williams, prin.
Bay-Brook ES, 4301 10TH ST   21225
  Sharman Rowe, prin.
Beechfield ES, 301 S BEECHFIELD AVE   21229
  Gloria Campbell, prin.
Belmont ES, 1406 N ELLAMONT ST   21216
  Helen Beverly, prin.
Bentalou ES, 220 N BENTALOU ST   21223
  Mary Ann Winterling, prin.
Brehms Lane ES, 3536 BREHMS LN   21213
  William Koutrelakos, prin.
Brent ES, 100 E 26TH ST   21218
  Lauretta Walden, prin.
Browne ES, 1000 N MONTFORD AVE   21205
  Dolores Spriggs, prin.
Callaway ES, 3701 FERNHILL AVE   21215
  Stanley Curtain, prin.
Carroll of Carrollton ES
  200 N CENTRAL AVE   21202 – Harold Eason, prin.
Carroll ES, 1327 WASHINGTON BLVD   21230
  Joyce Kavanagh, prin.
Carter ES, 820 E 43RD ST   21212
  Colyn Harrington, prin.
Cecil ES, 2000 CECIL AVE   21218
  Anna Coplin, prin.

Cherry Hill ES, 801 BRIDGEVIEW RD   21225
  William Howard, prin.
City Springs ES, 100 S CAROLINE ST   21231
  Matthew Riley, prin.
Coldstream Park ES
  1400 EXETER HALL AVE   21218
  Nora Cheek, prin.
Coleman ES, 2400 WINDSOR AVE   21216
  Addie Johnson, prin.
Collington Square ES
  1409 N COLLINGTON AVE   21213
  Francis Roberts, prin.
Cross Country ES
  6100 CROSS COUNTRY BLVD   21215
  Barb Lee, prin.
Curtis Bay ES, 4301 W BAY AVE   21225
  George Logue, prin.
Dickey Hill ES, 5025 DICKEY HILL RD   21207
  Joan Stevenson, prin.
Edgecombe Circle ES, 2835 VIRGINIA AVE   21215
  Mary Sollers, prin.
Edgewood ES, 1900 EDGEWOOD ST   21216
  Shirley Johnson, prin.
Eutaw-Marshburn ES, 1624 EUTAW PL   21217
  Louise Smith, prin.
Farring ES, 300 PONTIAC AVE   21225
  Shirley Zonker, prin.
Federal Hill ES, 1040 WILLIAM ST   21230
  Edith Harrison, prin.
Fort Worthington MS, 2701 E OLIVER ST   21213
  Peggy Madison, prin.
Frankford MS, 6001 FRANKFORD AVE   21206
  J. Stokes, prin.
Franklin Square MS
  1400 W LEXINGTON ST   21223
  Frank Whorley, prin.
Frederick ES, 2501 FREDERICK AVE   21223
  Ruth Brown, prin.
Furley ES, 4633 FURLEY AVE   21206
  Barb Myers, prin.
Gardenville ES, 5300 BELAIR RD   21206
  Carlyn Dawson, prin.
Garrett Heights ES, 2800 AILSA AVE   21214
  Billie Rinaldi, prin.
George Street ES, 601 BRUNE ST   21201
  Barbara Hill, prin.
Gilmor ES, 1311-1321 N GILMOR ST   21217
  Henry Wolpert, prin.
Glenmount ES, 6211 WALTHER AVE   21206
  Marylee Felton, prin.
Govans ES, 5801 YORK RD   21212
  Grace Hernandez, prin.
Graceland/O'Donnell ES
  6300 ODONNELL ST   21224 – Ruth Cowan, prin.
Grove Park ES, 5545 KENNISON AVE   21215
  Janet Cooper, prin.
Guilford ES, 4520 YORK RD   21218
  Patricia Talley, prin.
Gwynns Falls ES
  2700 GWYNNS FALLS PKY   21216
  Ernestine Dunston, prin.
Hamilton ES, 800 POPLAR GROVE ST   21216
  Tee Hamilton, prin.
Hamilton ES, 6101 OLD HARFORD RD   21214
  Frances Ellington, prin.
Hampden ES, 3608 CHESTNUT AVE   21211
  Shirley Rogers, prin.
Hampstead Hill ES, 500 S LINWOOD AVE   21224
  Shirley Curtain, prin.
Harford Heights ES, 1919 N BROADWAY   21213
  Mary Nicholsonne, prin.
Harlem Park ES, 1401 W LAFAYETTE AVE   21217
  Lauretta Reid, prin.
Harris ES, 1400 N CAROLINE ST   21213
  Alma Brown, prin.
Hayes ES, 601 N CENTRAL AVE   21202
  Pauline Bruce, prin.
Hazelwood ES, 4517 HAZELWOOD AVE   21206
  Gloria Streat, prin.
Henderson ES, 1101-1125 N WOLFE ST   21213
  Anne Larkins, prin.
Henson ES, 1600 N PAYSON ST   21217
  Leah Hasty, prin.
Highlandtown ES, 231-259 S EATON ST   21224
  Herman Polhein, prin.
Highlandtown ES, 3223 E PRATT ST   21224
  Mildred Waxman, prin.
Hilton ES, 3301 CARLISLE AVE   21216
  Brenda Sewell, prin.
Holabird ES, 1500 IMLA ST   21224
  Marion Garrett, prin.
Howard MS, 2011 LINDEN AVE   21217
  Karl Boone, prin.
Jefferson ES, 605 DRYDEN DR   21229
  Elaine Davis, prin.
Johnson ES, 100 E HEATH ST   21230
  Allen Kershman, prin.
Johnston Square ES, 1101 VALLEY ST   21202
  Roosevelt Hobbs, prin.
Kelson ES, 701 GOLD ST   21217
  Wyatt Coger, prin.
Kennedy/Ellington PS, 790 W NORTH AVE   21217
  Barb Grier, prin.
Key ES, 1425 E FORT AVE   21230
  David Benson, prin.
King ES, 3750 GREENSPRING AVE   21211
  Marlene Wise, prin.
Lafayette ES, 850 BRADDISH AVE   21216
  Iolas Drake, prin.
Lakewood ES, 2625 E FEDERAL ST   21213
  Virginia Johns, prin.
Langston Hughes ES, 5011 ARBUTUS AVE   21215
  Alice Thomas, prin.

Leith Walk ES, 1235 SHERWOOD AVE   21239
  Ernestine Lewis, prin.
Lexington Terrace ES
  732 W LEXINGTON ST   21201
  Delores Winston, prin.
Liberty ES, 3901 MAINE AVE   21207
  Elizabeth Craig, prin.
Lockerman-Bundy ES, 301 N PULASKI ST   21223
  Lana Powell, prin.
Lyndhurst ES, 621 WILDWOOD PKY   21229
  Linwood Roberts, prin.
Malcolm X ES, 2810 SHIRLEY AVE   21215
  Linda Chinnia, prin.
McHenry ES, 31 S SCHROEDER ST   21223
  Thomas Husted, prin.
Medfield Heights ES
  4300 BUCHANAN AVE   21211
  James Sasiadek, prin.
Monroe ES, 1634 GUILFORD AVE   21202
  Anne Roberts, prin.
Montebello ES, 2040 E 32ND ST   21218
  Janet DeSota, prin.
Moravia Park PS, 6201 FRANKFORD AVE   21206
  Ann Brooks, prin.
Morrell Park ES, 2601 TOLLEY ST   21230
  Goldye Sanders, prin.
Morse MS, 424-426 S PULASKI ST   21223
  Ronne Lippenholz, prin.
Mosher ES, 2400 W MOSHER ST   21216
  Gertrude Brooks, prin.
Mt. Royal ES, 121 MCMECHEN ST   21217
  Marguerite Walker, prin.
Mt. Washington ES, 1801 SULGRAVE AVE   21209
  Edna Greer, prin.
Nicholas ES, 201 E 21ST ST   21218
  Ardena Dixon, prin.
Northwood ES, 5201 LOCH RAVEN BLVD   21239
  Judson Wood, prin.
Paca ES, 200 N LAKEWOOD AVE   21224
  Agnes Hill, prin.
Park Heights ES, 4910 PARK HEIGHTS AVE   21215
  Carolyn Blackwell, prin.
Patapsco ES, 844 ROUNDVIEW RD   21225
  Shirley Vauls, prin.
Pimlico ES, 4849 PIMLICO RD   21215
  James Patterson, prin.
Pinderhughes ES, 1200 N FREMONT AVE   21217
  Ann Moore, prin.
Roach ES, 3434 OLD FREDERICK RD   21229
  Marion Simmons, prin.
Rodgers ES, 100 N CHESTER ST   21231
  Willie Grier,Jr., prin.
Rodman ES, 3510 W MULBERRY ST   21229
  James Walker, prin.
Rodwell ES, 3501 HILLSDALE RD   21207
  Earlene Cole, prin.
Rognel Heights ES, 4300 SIDEHILL RD   21229
  Stanley Hendricks, prin.
Roland Park ES, 5207 ROLAND AVE   21210
  Evelyn Beasley, prin.
Rosemont ES, 2777 PRESSTMAN ST   21216
  Norman Smith, prin.
Ruhrah ES, 701 RAPPOLLA ST   21224
  Beverly Ellinwood, prin.
Sinclair Lane ES, 3880 SINCLAIR LN   21213
  Constance Jeffries, prin.
Steuart Hill ES, 30 S GILMOR ST   21223
  A. Wheeler, prin.
Taylor ES, 507-577 W PRESTON ST   21201
  Jerome Williams, prin.
Templeton ES, 1200 PENNSYLVANIA AVE   21217
  Ellen Gonzales, prin.
Tench Tilghman ES
  600 N PATTERSON PARK AVE   21205
  Elizabeth Turner, prin.
Tubman ES, 1807 HARLEM AVE   21217
  Alexander Gates, prin.
Victory ES, 1440 CHESAPEAKE AVE   21226
  Sarah Dyce, prin.
Violetville ES, 1207 PINE HEIGHTS AVE   21229
  Elizabeth Lauter, prin.
Washington ES, 1001-1049 W SARATOGA   21223
  Sharon Van Dyke, prin.
Waverly ES, 3400 ELLERSLIE AVE   21218
  Louis Franz, prin.
Westport ES, 2401 NEVADA ST   21230
  Mildred Llewellyn, prin.
Westside ES, 2235 N FULTON AVE   21217
  Frances Parks, prin.
Windsor Hills ES, 4001 ALTO RD   21216
  Hattye Jackson, prin.
Wolfe ES, 245 S WOLFE ST   21231
  Laura Whitfield, prin.
Woodhome ES, 7300 MOYER AVE   21234
  Charles Burke, prin.
Woodson ES, 2501 SEABURY RD   21225
  Flora Johnson, prin.
Yorkwood ES, 5931 YORKWOOD RD   21239
  Marjorie Hunt, prin.

Baltimore County SD
Supt. – See Towson
Arbutus MS, 5525 SHELBOURNE ROAD   21227
  Julie Szymasek, prin.
Catonsville MS, 2301 EDMONDSON AVE   21228
  Alice Poole, prin.
Deep Creek MS, 1000 S MARLYN AVE   21221
  David Mollenkopf, prin.
Dumbarton MS, 300 DUMBARTON ROAD   21212
  Ron Sanders, prin.
Dundalk MS, 7400 DUNMANWAY   21222
  James Colbeck, prin.
Golden Ring MS, 6700 KENWOOD AVE   21237
  Ronald Boone, prin.

Holabird MS, 1701 DELVALE AVE   21222
  William Bevans, prin.
Johnnycake JHS
  6200 JOHNNYCAKE ROAD   21207
  Ralph Wood, prin.
Lansdowne MS, 2400 LANSDOWNE ROAD   21227
  Carl Jackson, prin.
Middle River MS
  800 MIDDLE RIVER ROAD   21220
  M. Conrad, prin.
Old Court MS, 4627 OLD COURT ROAD   21208
  Donald Snooderly, prin.
Parkville MS, 8711 AVONDALE ROAD   21234
  Richard Barranger, prin.
Perry Hall MS, 4300 EBENEZER ROAD   21236
  Alfred Marsilio, prin.
Pikesville MS, 7701 SEVEN MILE LANE   21208
  Elliot Merenbloom, prin.
Pine Grove MS
  9200 OLD HARFORD ROAD   21234
  John Jedlicka, prin.
Sparrows Point MS, 7400 N POINT ROAD   21219
  Lyle Patzkowsky, prin.
Stemmers Run MS
  201 STEMMERS RUN ROAD   21221
  Joan Powell, prin.
Stricker MS, 7855 TRAPPE ROAD   21222
  Stephen Ponzillo, prin.
Woodlawn MS, 3033 SAINT LUKES LANE   21207
  Charles Livingston, prin.
Arbutus ES, 1302 SULPHUR SPRING RD   21227
  Daniel March, prin.
Baltimore Highlands ES
  4200 ANNAPOLIS RD   21227
  William Beckwith, prin.
Bear Creek ES
  MELBOURNE & DEL HAVEN ROADS   21222
  Joan Burnett, prin.
Bedford ES, 7407 DORMAN DR   21208
  Linda Cook, prin.
Berkshire ES, 7431 POPLAR AVE   21224
  Donald Dailey, prin.
Carney ES, 3131 E JOPPA RD   21234
  John Anthony, prin.
Chadwick ES, 1918 WINDER RD   21207
  Emil Granitzki, prin.
Charlesmont ES, 7800 W COLLINGHAM DR   21222
  Dorothy Raff, prin.
Chase ES, 11701 EASTERN AVE   21220
  T. Hopewell, prin.
Chesapeake Terrace ES
  2112 LODGE FARM RD   21219
  Helen Wilson, prin.
Colgate ES, GOUGH AND 51ST STS   21224
  Harry Belsinger, prin.
Deep Creek ES, 1101 HOMBERG AVE   21221
  John Gross, prin.
Dundalk ES, 1 PLAYFIELD ST   21222
  Beverly Norwood, prin.
Edgemere ES, 7201 N POINT RD   21219
  Joanne Koehler, prin.
Edmondson Heights ES
  1600 LANGFORD RD   21207
  Geraldine Young, prin.
Elmwood ES, 531 DALE AVE   21206
  George Sparks,Jr., prin.
Featherbed Lane ES
  6700 RICHARDSON AVE   21207
  Charles Minor, prin.
Fort Garrison ES, 3310 WOODVALLEY DR   21208
  Ann Glazer, prin.
Fullerton ES, 4400 FULLERTON AVE   21236
  John Hutchinson, prin.
Glenmar ES, 9700 COMMUNITY DR   21220
  Richard McCall, prin.
Grange ES, 2000 CHURCH RD   21222
  Barbara Ellis, prin.
Gunpowder ES
  9540 HOLIDAY MANOR RD   21236
  Dawn Beck, prin.
Harford Hills ES, 8902 OLD HARFORD RD   21234
  John Elmore, prin.
Hawthorne ES, 125 KINGSTON RD   21220
  Patricia Moses, prin.
Hebbville ES, 3335 WASHINGTON AVE   21207
  Roberta Fishel, prin.
Hillcrest ES, 1500 FREDERICK RD   21228
  Hazel Mowery, prin.
Hillendale ES, 1111 HALSTEAD RD   21234
  John Wilson, prin.
Johnnycake ES, 5910 CRAIGMONT RD   21228
  John Tyson, prin.
Lansdowne ES, 2301 ALMA RD   21227
  Carl Bochau, prin.
Logan ES, 7601 DUNMANWAY   21222
  Kathleen East, prin.
Mars Estates ES, 1500 HOMBERG AVE   21221
  Michael Zajdel, prin.
Martin Boulevard ES, 1500 MARTIN BLVD   21220
  Karen Schafer, prin.
McCormick ES, 5101 HAZELWOOD AVE   21206
  R. Law, prin.
Middleborough ES, 313 WEST RD   21221
  Louis DiPietro, prin.
Middlesex ES
  BENNETT AND LANGLEY RD   21221
  Jean Gladden, prin.
Milbrook ES, 4300 CREST HEIGHTS RD   21215
  Judith Schwartz, prin.
Norwood ES, 1700 DELVALE AVE   21222
  Richard Fox, prin.
Oakleigh ES, 1840 WHITE OAK AVE   21234
  Joan Kozlovsky, prin.

Oliver Beach ES
  12912 CUNNING HILL COVE RD   21220
    Arline Ford, prin.
Orems ES, 711 HIGH VILLA RD   21221
    Carol Hilleary, prin.
Perry Hall ES, 9021 BELAIR RD   21236
    Charles Brawn, prin.
Pine Grove ES, 2701 SUMMIT AVE   21234
    George Hohl, prin.
Powhatan ES, 3300 KELOX RD   21207
    Barbara Bohl, prin.
Red House Run ES, 1717 WEYBURN RD   21237
    Rodney Obaker, prin.
Relay ES, 5885 SELFORD RD   21227
    Arthur Frotton, prin.
Riderwood ES, 1711 LANDRAKE RD   21204
    Donald Rollins, prin.
Riverview ES
    KESSLER AND HOLLNS FRY RD   21227
    G. Proudfoot, prin.
Rodgers Forge ES, 250 DUMBARTON RD   21212
    Joseph Watkins, prin.
Sandalwood ES, 900 S MARLYN AVE   21221
    Michael Citro, prin.
Sandy Plains ES, 8330 KAVANAGH RD   21222
    Harold Goodspeed, prin.
Scotts Branch ES, 8220 TAWNMOORE RD   21207
    Joan Brown, prin.
Seneca ES, 545 CARROLLWOOD RD   21220
    Betty Butcher, prin.
Shady Spring ES, 8868 GOLDENWOOD RD   21237
    Lubeth Cornell, prin.
Stoneleigh ES, 900 PEMBERTON RD   21212
    Doris Benner, prin.
Summit Park ES, 6920 DIANA RD   21209
    Betty Fischer, prin.
Sussex ES, 516 S WOODWARD DR   21221
    Nancy Hanna, prin.
Victory Villa ES, 500 COMPASS RD E   21220
    Beverly German, prin.
Villa Cresta ES, RADER AVE   21234
    H. Gehring, prin.
Westowne ES, 401 HARLEM LN   21228
    Barbara Gordon, prin.
Winand ES, 8301 SCOTTS LEVEL RD   21208
    James Joy, prin.
Winfield ES, 8300 CARLSON LN   21207
    Kim James, prin.
Woodbridge ES
    1410 PLEASANT VALLEY DR   21228
    Tony Byers, prin.
Woodmoor ES, 3200 ELBA DR   21207
    Rosalind Flaggs, prin.

Howard County SD
  Supt. – See Ellicott City
Elkridge ES, 6135 OLD WASHINGTON RD   21227
    Mary Jane Mitchell, prin.
––––––––––––
Boys Latin School of Maryland
  822 W LAKE AVE   21210
Bryn Mawr School, 109 W MELROSE AVE   21210
Father Kolbe MS, 1035 S KENWOOD AVE   21224
Fr. Hall MS, 2848 W LAFAYETTE AVE   21216
Friends School, 5114 N CHARLES ST   21210
Gilman School, 5407 ROLAND AVE   21210
Holy Spirit MS, 932 GORSUCH AVE   21218
Loyola MS, 500 CHESTNUT AVE   21204
Madonna ES, 3601 OLD FREDERICK ROAD   21229
Notre Dame Lower School
  815 HAMPTON LANE   21204
Our Lady of Pompei HS
  201 S CONKLING ST   21224
Queen of Peace MS
  814 N COLLINGTON AVE   21205
Roland Park Country School
  5204 ROLAND AVE   21210
Rosa Parks MS
  4406 LIBERTY HEIGHTS AVE   21207
Talmudical Academy of Baltimore
  4445 OLD COURT ROAD   21208
Ascension School, 4601 MAPLE AVE   21227
Beth Tfiloh ES, 3300 OLD COURT RD   21208
Bethlehem Christian ES
  4815 HAMILTON AVE   21206
Bishop Neumann ES, 3500 FOSTER AVE   21224
Calvary Christian ES
  2625 E NORTHERN PKY   21214
Calvert ES, 105 TUSCANY RD   21210
Cathedral Mary are Queen ES
  111 AMBERLY WAY   21210
Catholic Community ES
  BATTERY AVE/GITTINGS ST   21230
Community School Holy Spirit
  3710 ROLAND AVE   21211
Emmanuel Christian ES
  929 INGLESIDE AVE   21228
Father Hall ES, 1546 N FREMONT AVE   21217
Father Kolbe ES, 724 S ANN ST   21231
Holy Rosary ES, 420 S CHESTER ST   21231
Immaculate Conception ES
  112 WARE HAVE   21204
Immaculate Heart of Mary ES
  8501 LOCH RAVEN BLVD   21204
Immanuel Lutheran School
  LOCH RAVEN AND BLVDRE   21239
John Paul Regional ES
  6946 DOGWOOD RD   21207
Our Lady Queen of Peace ES
  10001 BIRD RIVER ROAD   21220
Our Lady Victory ES, 4416 WILKENS AVE   21229
Our Lady of Fatima ES, 6400 E PRATT ST   21224
Our Lady of Hope ES
  8003 N BOUNDARY RD   21222

Our Lady of Mt. Carmel ES
  1702 EASTERN AVE   21221
Pilgrim Lutheran School
  LIBERTY & LATHAM   21207
Rosa Parks ES, 3333 WINDSOR AVE   21216
Rosa Parks ES, 4506 PARK HEIGHTS AVE   21215
SS. James & John ES, 1012 SOMERSET ST   21202
Sacred Heart Mary ES
  6726 YOUNGSTOWN AVE   21222
Shrine of Little Flower ES
  2800 BRENDAN AVE   21213
Shrine of the Sacred Heart ES
  5800 SMITH AVE   21209
Solomon Schechter Day School
  8100 STEVENSON RD   21208
St. Agnes ES, 603 ST AGNES LN   21229
St. Alphonsus ES, 114 W SARATOGA ST   21201
St. Anthony ES, 4410 FRANKFORD AVE   21206
St. Augustine ES
  5990 OLD WASHINGTON RD   21227
St. Chas Borromeo ES, 110 SUDBROOK LN   21208
St. Clare ES, 716 MYRTH AVE   21221
St. Clement ES, 139 1ST AVE   21227
St. Clement ES, 1216 CHESACO AVE   21237
St. Dominic ES, 5302 HARFORD RD   21214
St. Elizabeth ES, 35 N LAKEWOOD AVE   21224
St. Frances of Assisi ES
  3617 HARFORD RD   21218
St. James Lutheran Day School
  8 W OVERLEA AVE   21206
St. Joseph ES-Fullerton, 8416 BELAIR RD   21236
St. Katherine School, 1201 N ROSE ST   21213
St. Luke's ES, 7517 N POINT RD   21219
St. Mark ES, 26 MELVIN AVE   21228
St. Mary ES, 403 MARKLAND AVE   21212
Shehan ES, 5407 LOCK RAVEN BLVD   21239
St. Michael the Archangel ES
  10 WILLOW AVE   21206
St. Paul Lutheran School
  2001 OLD FREDERICK RD   21228
St. Peters Lutheran School
  7910 BELAIR RD   21236
St. Pius X ES, 6432 YORK RD   21212
St. Rita ES, 2905 DUNLEER RD   21222
St. Rose of Lima ES, 410 JEFFREY ST   21225
St. Ursula ES, 8900 HARFORD RD   21234
St. William of York ES, 600 COOKS LN   21229

Barton, Allegany Co., Pop. Code 3
Allegany County SD
  Supt. – See Cumberland
ES   21521 – Nancy Robeson, prin.

Bel Air, Harford Co., Pop. Code 6
Harford County SD
  Sch. Sys. Enr. Code 8
  Supt. – Ray Keech, 45 E GORDON ST   21014
MS, 99 IDLEWILD ST   21014
    Matthew Plevyak, prin.
Southampton MS
  1201 MOORES MILL ROAD   21014
    Thomas Wimbrow, prin.
ES, 30 E LEE ST   21014 – Marlin Dellinger, prin.
Hickory ES, 2100 CONOWINGO RD   21014
    Patrick McCarty, prin.
Homestead/Wakefld ES, 800 S MAIN ST   21014
    Christopher Terry, prin.
Prospect Mill ES, 101 PROSPECT MILL RD   21014
    John Roschy, prin.
Other Schools – See Aberdeen, Abingdon,
  Churchville, Darlington, Edgewood, Fallston, Forest
  Hill, Havre De Grace, Jarrettsville, Joppa, Pylesville,
  Street, White Hall
––––––––––––
St. Margaret ES, 205 N HICKORY AVE   21014

Beltsville, Prince George's Co., Pop. Code 6
Prince Georges County SD
  Supt. – See Upper Marlboro
King MS, 4545 AMMENDALE ROAD   20705
    Bette Lewis, prin.
ES, 4300 WICOMICO AVE   20705
    William Veater, prin.
Calverton ES, 3400 BELTSVILLE RD   20705
    Joshua Parks, prin.
––––––––––––
St. Joseph ES, 11011 MONTGOMERY RD   20705

Berlin, Worcester Co., Pop. Code 4
Worcester County SD
  Supt. – See Newark
MS, FRANKLIN AVE   21811 – Jesse Lynch, prin.
Buckingham ES, BUCKINGHAM ROAD   21811
    Stuart Scott, prin.
––––––––––––
Worcester Country School
  SOUTH MAIN ST   21811

Bethesda, Montgomery Co., Pop. Code 8
Montgomery County SD
  Supt. – See Rockville
Pyle MS, 6311 WILSON LANE   20817
    Harvey Strine, prin.
Westland MS
  5501 MASSACHUSETTS AVE   20816
    Sarah Murkey, prin.
Ashburton ES, 6314 LONE OAK DR   20817
    J. Penn, prin.
Bannockburn ES, 6520 DALROY LN   20817
    Barbara Moore, prin.
ES, 5011 MOORLAND LN   20814
    Russell Gordon, prin.
Bradley Hills ES, 7000 RADNOR RD   20817
    William Porton, prin.

Burning Tree ES, 7900 BEECH TREE RD   20817
    Ken Snoots, prin.
Carderock Springs ES
  7401 PERSIMMON TREE LN   20817
    Rudolph White, prin.
Seven Locks ES, 9500 SEVEN LOCKS RD   20817
    William Snyder, prin.
Westbrook ES, 5110 ALLAN TER   20816
    Mary Allison, prin.
Wood Acres ES, 5800 CROMWELL DR   20816
    Kathleen Lasinski, prin.
Wyngate ES, 9300 WADSWORTH DR   20817
    Barbara Leister, prin.
––––––––––––
Stone Ridge Country Day School
  9101 ROCKVILLE PIKE   20814
Little Flower ES
  5601 MASSACHUSETTS AVE   20816
Little Flower School
  5601 MASSACHUSETTS AVE   20816
Mater Dei School, 9600 SEVEN LOCKS RD   20817
Norwood School, 8821 RIVER RD   20817
Our Lady of Lourdes ES, 7500 PEARL ST   20814
Sidwell Friends Lower School
  5100 EDGEMOOR LAND   20814
St. Bartholomew ES, 6900 RIVER RD   20817
St. Jane De Chantel ES
  9525 OLD GEORGETOWN RD   20814
The Woods Academy
  6801 GREENTREE RD   20817

Bladensburg, Prince George's Co., Pop. Code 6
Prince Georges County SD
  Supt. – See Upper Marlboro
ES, 5150 ANNAPOLIS RD   20710
    Francis Minni, prin.
Rogers Heights ES, 4301 58TH AVE   20710
    Susan DePlatchett, prin.

Bloomington, Garrett Co.
Garrett County SD
  Supt. – See Oakland
ES, P O BOX 208   21523 – Eleanor Sloan, prin.

Boonsboro, Washington Co., Pop. Code 4
Washington County SD
  Supt. – See Hagerstown
MS, 1 J H WADE DRIVE   21713
    Charles McElrath, prin.
ES, 5 CAMPUS AVE   21713
    Richard Reynolds, prin.
Greenbrier ES
  RURAL ROUTE 02 BOX 296-C   21713
    Frank Novinger, prin.

Bowie, Prince George's Co., Pop. Code 8
Prince Georges County SD
  Supt. – See Upper Marlboro
Tasker MS, 4901 COLLINGTON ROAD   20715
    Nancy McClelland, prin.
Heather Hills ES, 12605 HEMING LN   20716
    Patricia Brooks, prin.
High Bridge ES, 7011 HIGH BRIDGE RD   20715
    Barbara Smith, prin.
Kenilworth ES, 12520 KEMBRIDGE DR   20715
    John O'Donnell, prin.
Ogle ES, 4111 CHELMONT LN   20715
    Joseph Carr, prin.
Pointer Ridge ES, 1110 PARKINGTON LN   20716
    Rebecca Weeks, prin.
Rockledge ES, 7701 LAUREL BOWIE RD   20715
    Arlene Verge, prin.
Tulip Grove ES, 2909 TRAINOR LN   20715
    Patrick Logan, prin.
––––––––––––
Holy Trinity Day School
  13106 ANNAPOLIS RD   20715
St. Pius X ES, 14700 ANNAPOLIS RD   20715

Bradshaw, Baltimore Co., Pop. Code 3
––––––––––––
St. Stephen ES, 8028 BRADSHAW RD   21021

Brandywine, Prince George's Co., Pop. Code 6
Prince Georges County SD
  Supt. – See Upper Marlboro
Gwynn Park MS, 8000 DYSON ROAD   20613
    John Flynn, prin.
Baden ES, 13601 BADEN WESTWOOD RD   20613
    Robert Kessler, prin.
ES, 14101 BRANDYWINE RD   20613
    Benny Wolford, prin.

Brookeville, Montgomery Co., Pop. Code 2
Montgomery County SD
  Supt. – See Rockville
Greenwood ES, 3336 GOLD MINE RD   20833
    Sherene Webb, prin.

Brooklandville, Baltimore Co.
––––––––––––
Park School, OLD COURT ROAD   21022
St. Paul's School, 11152 FALLS ROAD   21022

Brunswick, Frederick Co., Pop. Code 5
Frederick County SD
  Supt. – See Frederick
MS, 101 CUMMINGS DRIVE   21716
    Hal Mosser, prin.
ES, 400 CENTRAL AVE   21716 – Ric Gerwig, prin.

Bryantown, Charles Co.
Charles County SD
  Supt. – See La Plata
Martin ES, ROUTE 232   20617
    Jane Hawkings, prin.

St. Mary ES   20617

Burtonsville, Montgomery Co., Pop. Code 4
Montgomery County SD
Supt. – See Rockville
Banneker MS, 14600 OLD COLUMBIA PIKE   20866
Donald Kress, prin.
ES, 15516 OLD COLUMBIA PIKE   20866
Dawn Marlin, prin.

Bushwood, St. Mary's Co.
St. Mary's County SD
Supt. – See Leonardtown
Bethune ES   20618 – Ardith Harle, prin.

Cambridge, Dorchester Co., Pop. Code 7
Dorchester County SD
Sch. Sys. Enr. Code 5
Supt. – William Potter, P O BOX 619   21613
Maces Lane MS, 1101 MACES LANE   21613
Donna Spedden, prin.
Maple ES, RURAL ROUTE 01 BOX 143   21613
Kenneth Gerlach, prin.
Sandy Hill ES, 1503 GLASGOW ST   21613
Howard Brown, prin.
Other Schools – See Church Creek, Hurlock,
Secretary, Vienna

Capitol Heights, Prince George's Co., Pop. Code 5
Prince Georges County SD
Supt. – See Upper Marlboro
Walker Mill MS, 800 KAREN BLVD   20743
Joan Brown, prin.
Bayne ES, 7010 WALKER MILL RD   20743
Joanne Benson, prin.
Bradbury Heights ES, 1401 GLACIER AVE   20743
Ronald Hillard, prin.
Brooks ES, 1301 BROOKE RD   20743
Margaret Williams, prin.
ES, 601 SUFFOLK AVE   20743
Thelma Butler, prin.
Carmody Hills ES, 401 JADELEAF AVE   20743
Marian Martin, prin.
Howard ES, 4400 SHELL ST   20743
Edith Massey, prin.
Lyndon Hill ES, 6181 CENTRAL AVE   20743
Michael Koss, prin.
Seat Pleasant ES, 6411 G ST   20743
Julia Wright, prin.

Cascade, Washington Co., Pop. Code 4
Washington County SD
Supt. – See Hagerstown
ES, RURAL ROUTE 01 BOX 48D   21719
Randall Schultz, prin.

Catonsville, Baltimore Co., Pop. Code 8
Baltimore County SD
Supt. – See Towson
ES, 615 FREDERICK RD   21228 – Mary Day, prin.

Cecilton, Cecil Co., Pop. Code 3
Cecil County SD
Supt. – See Elkton
ES, WEST MAIN ST   21913 – Eileen O'Neill, prin.

Centreville, Queen Anne's Co., Pop. Code 4
Queen Annes County SD
Sch. Sys. Enr. Code 6
Supt. – John Miller, P O BOX 110   21617
MS   21617 – Thaddeus Kalmanowicz, prin.
ES   21617 – Samuel Wilson, prin.
Other Schools – See Church Hill, Grasonville,
Stevensville, Sudlersville

Chaptico, St. Mary's Co.
St. Mary's County SD
Supt. – See Leonardtown
Dynard MS   20621 – Ardith Harle, prin.

Charlestown, Cecil Co., Pop. Code 3
Cecil County SD
Supt. – See Elkton
ES, 550 BALTIMORE ST   21914
Evelyn Jordan, prin.

Chesapeake Beach, Calvert Co., Pop. Code 4
Calvert County SD
Supt. – See Prince Frederick
Beach ES   20732 – Faith Ricketts, prin.

Chesapeake City, Cecil Co., Pop. Code 3
Cecil County SD
Supt. – See Elkton
ES, 214 THIRD ST   21915 – Wellington Ward, prin.

Chestertown, Kent Co., Pop. Code 5
Kent County SD
Sch. Sys. Enr. Code 4
Supt. – James Lupis, WASHINGTON AVE   21620
MS   21620 – L. Taylor, prin.
Garnett ES   21620 – William Alexander, prin.
Other Schools – See Galena, Millington, Rock Hall,
Worton

Kent School, WILKINS LANE   21620

Chevy Chase, Montgomery Co., Pop. Code 4
Montgomery County SD
Supt. – See Rockville
MS, 4015 ROSEMARY ST   20815
Gabriel Massaro, prin.
North Chevy Chase MS
3700 JONES BRIDGE RD   20815
Delores Baden, prin.
Rock Creek Forest ES, 8330 GRUBB RD   20815
Sandra Walker, prin.

Somerset ES, 5811 WARWICK PL   20815
Sally Veres, prin.

Childs, Cecil Co.

Mt. Aviat Academy, 399 CHILDS RD   21916

Church Creek, Dorchester Co., Pop. Code 2
Dorchester County SD
Supt. – See Cambridge
South Dorchester ES   21622 – Paula Beath, prin.

Church Hill, Queen Anne's Co., Pop. Code 2
Queen Annes County SD
Supt. – See Centreville
ES   21623 – Frederick Leadbetter, prin.

Churchville, Harford Co.
Harford County SD
Supt. – See Bel Air
ES, 2935 LEVEL RD   21028 – James Lewis III, prin.

Clarksburg, Montgomery Co., Pop. Code 3
Montgomery County SD
Supt. – See Rockville
ES, 13530 REDGRAVE PL   20871
Jack Roach, prin.

Clarksville, Howard Co., Pop. Code 8
Howard County SD
Supt. – See Ellicott City
MS, 6535 TROTTER ROAD   21029
James Evans, prin.
ES, 12041 MD ROUTE 108   21029
Philip Arbaugh, prin.

St. Louis ES, RURAL ROUTE 108 BOX 155   21029

Clear Spring, Washington Co., Pop. Code 2
Washington County SD
Supt. – See Hagerstown
MS, RURAL ROUTE 02   21722 – R. Wantz, prin.
ES   21722 – William Price, prin.
Fairview ES, DRAPER ROAD   21722
Gregory Wilkes, prin.

Clinton, Prince George's Co., Pop. Code 5
Prince Georges County SD
Supt. – See Upper Marlboro
Decatur MS, 8200 PINEWOOD DRIVE   20735
Clifford Stevens, prin.
Clinton Grove ES, 9420 TEMPLE HILL RD   20735
Karen Foster, prin.
Evans ES
6720 OLD ALXNDRA FERRY ROAD   20735
Joseph Crossman, prin.
Randall ES, 5410 KIRBY RD   20735
Sally Mack, prin.
Waldon Woods ES, 10301 THRIFT RD   20735
Michael Kovach, prin.

St. John the Evangelist ES
8912 OLD BRANCH AVE   20735
St. Mary ES, 13407 PISCATAWAY RD   20735

Cockeysville, Baltimore Co., Pop. Code 5
Baltimore County SD
Supt. – See Towson
MS, 10401 GREENSIDE DRIVE   21030
R. McCaslin, prin.
Padonia ES, 9834 GREENSIDE DR   21030
Dorothy Dorman, prin.
Warren ES, 900 BOSLEY RD   21030
G. Loeschke, prin.

St. Jospeh ES-Texas, 105 CHURCH LN   21030

College Park, Prince George's Co., Pop. Code 7
Prince Georges County SD
Supt. – See Upper Marlboro
Hollywood ES, 9811 49TH AVE   20740
Gail Naworal, prin.
Paint Branch ES, 5101 PIERCE AVE   20740
Linda Dudley, prin.

Holy Redeemer ES
49TH AVE & BERWYN ROAD   20740

Columbia, Howard Co., Pop. Code 6
Howard County SD
Supt. – See Ellicott City
Brown MS, 8700 CRADLEROCK WAY   21045
David Oaks, prin.
Harper's Choice MS
5450 BEAVERKILL ROAD   21044
Jesse Scharff, prin.
Oakland Mills MS
9540 KILIMANJARO ROAD   21045
Marchmont Girod, prin.
Wilde Lake MS, 10481 CROSS FOX LANE   21044
Jesse Smith, prin.
Atholton ES, 6700 SENECA DR   21046
Donald Hall, prin.
Bryant Woods ES, 5450 BLUE HERON LN   21044
Judith Bland, prin.
Clemens Crossing ES
10320 QUARTERSTAFF RD   21044
Shirley Via, prin.
Dasher Green ES
6700 CRADLEROCK WAY   21045
Bernard Taylor, prin.
Guilford ES, 7335 OAKLAND MILLS RD   21046
Donald Hoes, prin.
Jeffers Hill ES, 6000 TAMAR DR   21045
Fredrika Hill, prin.
Longfellow ES, 5470 HESPERUS DR   21044
Marianne Pfeiffer, prin.

Phelps Luck ES, 5370 OLDSTONE CT   21045
John Wineke, prin.
Running Brook ES
5215 W RUNNING BROOK RD   21044
Donald Setzer, prin.
Stevens Forest ES
6045 STEVENS FOREST RD   21045
James Pope, prin.
Swansfield ES, 5610 CEDAR LN   21044
Thomas Bruner, prin.
Talbott Springs ES, 9550 BASKET RING RD   21045
Thomas Brown, prin.
Thunder Hill ES, 9357 MELLENBROOK RD   21045
C. Yount, prin.
Waterloo ES, 5940 WATERLOO RD   21045
Madrianne Johnson, prin.

Brown Montessori School
9760 OWEN BROWN RD   21045

Conowingo, Cecil Co.
Cecil County SD
Supt. – See Elkton
ES, 471 ROWLANDSVILLE RD   21918
Carolyn Kirk, prin.

Cordova, Talbot Co.
Talbot County SD
Supt. – See Easton
ES   21625 – Gregory Thornton, prin.
Upper County ES   21625 – Gregory Thornton, prin.

Cresaptown, Allegany Co., Pop. Code 4
Allegany County SD
Supt. – See Cumberland
ES   21502 – Kathleen High, prin.

Crisfield, Somerset Co., Pop. Code 5
Somerset County SD
Supt. – See Princess Anne
ES   21817 – Allison Milbourne, prin.
Woodson MS   21817 – George Todd, prin.

Crownsville, Ann Arundel Co., Pop. Code 3
Anne Arundel County SD
Supt. – See Annapolis
South Shore ES, 1376 FAIRFIELD LOOP RD   21032
Charles Owens, prin.

Cumberland, Allegany Co., Pop. Code 8
Allegany County SD
Sch. Sys. Enr. Code 7
Supt. – Harold Winstanley, P O BOX 1724   21501
Braddock MS   21502 – Joseph Carter, prin.
Washington MS   21502 – Charles Smith, prin.
Bel Air ES, 14401 BARTON BLVD   21502
Robert McKenzie, prin.
Humbird ES, 120 MARY ST   21502
Willard Kitzmiller, prin.
Northeast ES, VALLEY ROAD   21502
Gary Stein, prin.
South Penn ES, 500 E SECOND ST   21502
Gary Llewellyn, prin.
West Side ES, 425 PACA ST   21502
John Festerman, prin.
Other Schools – See Barton, Cresaptown, Flintstone,
Frostburg, La Vale, Lonaconing, Mount Savage,
Oldtown, Westernport

St. John Neumann School
FAYETTE ST & SMALLWOOD   21502
St. Mary's ES, 300 E OLDTOWN RD   21502

Damascus, Montgomery Co., Pop. Code 5
Montgomery County SD
Supt. – See Rockville
Baker MS, 25400 OAK DRIVE   20872
Phillip Dean, prin.
Clearspring ES, 9930 MOYER RD   20872
Alan Thormeyer, prin.
ES, 10201 BETHESDA CHURCH RD   20872
Laura Hart, prin.

Darlington, Harford Co., Pop. Code 2
Harford County SD
Supt. – See Bel Air
ES, 1522 KIRK ROAD   21034 – Ann Ramsay, prin.

Davidsonville, Ann Arundel Co.
Anne Arundel County SD
Supt. – See Annapolis
ES, 962 W CENTRAL AVE   21035
Jeanne Paglee, prin.

Deale, Ann Arundel Co., Pop. Code 4
Anne Arundel County SD
Supt. – See Annapolis
ES, 795 MASONS BEACH RD   20751
Judith Strauff, prin.

Deal Island, Somerset Co., Pop. Code 2
Somerset County SD
Supt. – See Princess Anne
ES   21821 – Stanley Bozman, prin.

Delmar, Wicomico Co., Pop. Code 4
Wicomico County SD
Supt. – See Salisbury
ES   21875 – Barb Purnell, prin.

Denton, Caroline Co., Pop. Code 4
Caroline County SD
Sch. Sys. Enr. Code 5
Supt. – William Ecker, 112 MARKET ST   21629
Riverview MS, 207 LOCKERMAN ST   21629
Harry Martin, prin.
ES, RURAL ROUTE 02 BOX 7-C   21629
Charles Carey, prin.

Other Schools – See Federalsburg, Greensboro, Preston, Ridgely

Dickerson, Montgomery Co.
Montgomery County SD
Supt. – See Rockville
Monocacy ES, 18801 BARNESVILLE RD 20842
Phyllis Snelson, prin.

District Heights, Prince George's Co., Pop. Code 6
Prince Georges County SD
Supt. – See Upper Marlboro
Key MS, 2301 SCOTT KEY DRIVE 20747
Gordon Sampson, prin.
Berkshire ES, 6201 SURREY SQUARE LN 20747
Rita Robinson, prin.
Claggett ES, 2001 ADDISON RD S 20747
Roland Moore, prin.
Concord ES, 2004 CONCORD LN 20747
Joyce Dandridge, prin.
ES, 2200 COUNTY RD 20747 – Carrie Irby, prin.

Easton, Talbot Co., Pop. Code 6
Talbot County SD
Sch. Sys. Enr. Code 5
Supt. – John Fink, P O BOX 1029 21601
MS, OXFORD ROAD 21601 – Mary Reeser, prin.
Glenwood MS, GLENWOOD AVE 21601
Robert Tingle, prin.
Mt. Pleasant ES, MOUNT PLEASANT AVE 21601
Dorothy Johns, prin.
Other Schools – See Cordova, Saint Michaels, Tilghman, Trappe

SS. Peter and Paul School, 900 HIGH ST 21601
Country ES, 716 GOLDSBOROUGH ST 21601

Edgewater, Anne Arundel Co.
Anne Arundel County SD
Supt. – See Annapolis
Central MS, 221 E CENTRAL AVE 21037
Norbert Paga, prin.
Central ES, 130 STEPNEY LN 21037
Shirley Allen, prin.
ES, 121 WASHINGTON RD 21037
Nora Long, prin.

Edgewood, Harford Co., Pop. Code 6
Harford County SD
Supt. – See Bel Air
MS, 2411 WILLOUGHBY BEACH ROAD 21040
Robert Williams, prin.
Deerfield ES
2307 WILLOUGHBY BEACH RD 21040
Irvin Wilkinson, prin.
ES, 2000 CEDAR DR 21040
Hannah Randall, prin.

Elkton, Cecil Co., Pop. Code 6
Cecil County SD
Sch. Sys. Enr. Code 7
Supt. – Jerry Kunkle, BOOTH ST CTR 21921
Cherry Hill MS, 2535 SINGERLY ROAD 21921
John Abel, prin.
MS, 625 NORTH ST 21921
Leonard Lundberg, prin.
Cecil Manor ES, 971 ELK MILLS RD 21921
George Rumsey, prin.
Gilpin Manor ES, NEWARK AVE 21921
Sandra Anderson, prin.
Holly Hall ES, 260 WHITEHALL RD 21921
Dennis Catron, prin.
Kenmore ES, 2475 SINGERLY RD 21921
Helen Chapman, prin.
Leeds ES, 615 DEAVER RD 21921
Robert Harris, prin.
Thomson Estates ES, 203 THOMSON DR 21921
Peter Leyon, prin.
Other Schools – See Cecilton, Charlestown, Chesapeake City, Conowingo, North East, Perryville, Port Deposit, Rising Sun

Immaculate Conception ES, 455 BOW ST 21921

Ellicott City, Howard Co., Pop. Code 7
Howard County SD
Sch. Sys. Enr. Code 8
Supt. – Michael Hickey, 10910 ROUTE 108 21043
Dunloggin MS, 9129 NORTHFIELD ROAD 21043
Eugene Estes, prin.
Ellicott Mills MS
4445 MONTGOMERY ROAD 21043
Rose Levine, prin.
Patapsco MS, 8885 OLD FREDERICK ROAD 21043
Alice Haskins, prin.
Centennial Lane ES, 3825 CENTENNIAL LN 21043
James Mitchell, prin.
Northfield ES, 9125 NORTHFIELD RD 21043
Shirley Meighan, prin.
St. John's Lane ES, 2960 ST JOHNS LN 21043
Andrew Barshinger, prin.
Worthington ES, 4570 ROUND HILL RD 21043
Betty King, prin.
Other Schools – See Baltimore, Clarksville, Columbia, Glenwood, Jessup, Laurel, Lisbon, West Friendship

Our Lady of Perpetual Help ES
4801 ILCHESTER RD 21043
Ressurection ES, PAULSKIRK DR 21043
Trinity Lower ES, P O BOX 299 21043

Emmitsburg, Frederick Co., Pop. Code 4
Frederick County SD
Supt. – See Frederick
ES, 300 S SETON AVE 21727
Nancy Hendricks, prin.

Mother Seton ES, 100 CREAMERY RD 21727

Essex, Baltimore Co., Pop. Code 8
Baltimore County SD
Supt. – See Towson
ES, 100 MACE AVE 21221 – Thomas Ellis, prin.

Ewell, Somerset Co.
Somerset County SD
Supt. – See Princess Anne
ES 21824 – Karen Marshall, prin.

Fallston, Harford Co.
Harford County SD
Supt. – See Bel Air
Youths Benefit ES, 1901 FALLSTON RD 21047
James Dryden, prin.

Faulkner, Charles Co.
Charles County SD
Supt. – See La Plata
Higdon ES, RURAL ROUTE 02 BOX 207 20632
David Trudnak, prin.

Federalsburg, Caroline Co., Pop. Code 4
Caroline County SD
Supt. – See Denton
Richardson MS
RURAL ROUTE 02 BOX 348 21632
James Orr, prin.
ES, 302 S UNIVERSITY AVE 21632
Edward Cutler, prin.

Finksburg, Carroll Co.
Carroll County SD
Supt. – See Westminster
Sandymount ES
2222 OLD WESTMINSTER PIKE 21048
Dean Johnson, prin.

Flintstone, Allegany Co., Pop. Code 4
Allegany County SD
Supt. – See Cumberland
S 21530 – Theodore Kight, prin.

Forest Hill, Harford Co., Pop. Code 3
Harford County SD
Supt. – See Bel Air
ES, 2407 ROCKS RD 21050 – Francis Navin, prin.

Fort George G. Meade, Anne Arundel Co., Pop. Code 7
Anne Arundel County SD
Supt. – See Annapolis
MacArthur MS, 3033 ROCKENBACH ROAD 20755
John Kozora, prin.
Manor View ES, 2900 MACARTHUR RD 20755
Edwin Bokee, prin.
Meade Heights ES, 1300 REECE ROAD 20755
Esther White, prin.
Pershing Hill ES, 7600 29TH DIVISION RD 20755
Ralph McCann, prin.
West Meade ES, 7700 RAY ST 20755
Barb Mason, prin.

Fort Washington, Prince George's Co.
Prince Georges County SD
Supt. – See Upper Marlboro
Lord Baltimore MS
8700 ALLENTOWN ROAD 20744
Eugene Kidwell, prin.
Oxon Hill MS, 9570 FORT FOOTE ROAD 20744
Gerald Boarman, prin.
Apple Grove ES, 7400 BELLEFIELD AVE 20744
Charlene Ivy, prin.
Avalon ES, 7302 WEBSTER LN 20744
Ed Keafer, prin.
Dent ES, 2400 CORNING AVE 20744
John Gearrity, prin.
Fort Foote ES, 8300 OXON HILL RD 20744
Francis Murphy, prin.
Ft. Washington Forest ES
1300 FILLMORE RD 20744 – Beatrice Largay, prin.
Indian Queen ES, 9551 FORT FOOTE RD 20744
Margaret Ellinger, prin.
Potomac Landing ES
12500 FORT WASHINGTON RD 20744
Susan Miller, prin.
Rose Valley ES, 9800 JACQUELINE DR 20744
Russell Chestnut, prin.
Tayac ES, 8600 ALLENTOWN RD 20744
Kelly Randolph, prin.

Frederick, Frederick Co., Pop. Code 8
Frederick County SD
Sch. Sys. Enr. Code 8
Supt. – Noel Farmer, 115 E CHURCH ST 21701
Johnson MS, 1501 N MARKET ST 21701
Carolyn Kimberlin, prin.
Monocacy MS
8009 OPOSSUMTOWN PIKE 21701
Steven Arlen, prin.
West Frederick MS, 551 W PATRICK ST 21701
Michael Trout, prin.
East Frederick MS, 1350 E PATRICK ST 21701
Vicki Stultz, prin.
Hillcrest ES, 1285 HILLCREST DR 21701
Carol Young, prin.
Lewistown ES
11119 HESSONG BRIDGE RD 21701
Martha Grimes, prin.
Monocacy ES, 7421 HAYWARD ROAD 21701
Carolyn Strum, prin.
North Frederick ES, 1001 MOTTER AVE 21701
Kyle Pritts, prin.
Parkway ES, 300 CARROLL PKY 21701
Albertine Baker, prin.
South Frederick ES, 250 MADISON ST 21701
Emily Sines, prin.
Urbana ES, 3554 URBANA PIKE 21701
Robert Humphrey, prin.
Waverley ES, 201 WAVERLEY DR 21701
Colleen Garrett, prin.
Yellow Springs ES
8717 YELLOW SPRINGS RD 21701
H. Storm, prin.
Other Schools – See Adamstown, Brunswick, Emmitsburg, Jefferson, Keymar, Libertytown, Middletown, Monrovia, Myersville, New Market, Sabillasville, Smithsburg, Thurmont, Walkersville, Woodsboro

St. John the Evangelist ES, 114 E 2ND ST 21701
Visitation Academy, 200 E SECOND AVE 21701

Freeland, Baltimore Co.
Baltimore County SD
Supt. – See Towson
Prettyboy ES, 19810 MIDDLETOWN RD 21053
A. Rathbone, prin.

Friendsville, Garrett Co., Pop. Code 3
Garrett County SD
Supt. – See Oakland
ES, P O BOX 59 21531 – Jane Fox, prin.

Frostburg, Allegany Co., Pop. Code 6
Allegany County SD
Supt. – See Cumberland
Beall ES 21532 – Donna Komatz, prin.
Frost ES, SHAW ST 21532
Willard Cleavenger, prin.

Garrett County SD
Supt. – See Oakland
Route 40 ES, HCR 21532 – Patrick Delaney, prin.

St. Michael ES, 56 E MAIN ST 21532

Fruitland, Wicomico Co., Pop. Code 5
Wicomico County SD
Supt. – See Salisbury
IS, 208 N DIVISION ST 21826 – Robert Greer, prin.
PS, 301 N DIVISION ST 21826
Robert Greer, prin.

Gaithersburg, Montgomery Co., Pop. Code 8
Montgomery County SD
Supt. – See Rockville
Ridgeview IS, 12100 CHEYENNE ROAD 20878
Lewis Jones, prin.
Brown Station ES
801 QUINCE ORCHARD BLVD 20878
John Lewis, prin.
Darnestown ES, 15030 TURKEY FOOT RD 20878
Daniel Shaheen, prin.
Diamond ES, 4 MARQUIS DR 20878
Jennie Fleming, prin.
Dufief ES, 15001 DUFIEF DR 20878
Donald Jackson, prin.
Fields Road ES, 1 SCHOOL DR 20878
Gwendolyn Page, prin.
Flower Hill ES, 18425 FLOWER HILL WAY 20879
Marie Anderson, prin.
ES, 35 N SUMMIT AVE 20877
Karen Karch, prin.
Jones Lane ES, 15110 JONES LN 20878
Judith Levine, prin.
Rosemont ES, 16400 ALDEN AVE 20877
Mary Ann Britton, prin.
South Lake ES, 18201 CONTOUR RD 20877
James Griesi, prin.
Stedwick ES, 10631 STEDWICK RD 20879
Joan Lewis, prin.
Stone Mill ES
14323 STONEBRIDGE VIEW DR 20879
Arlie Kingery, prin.
Strawberry Knoll ES
18820 STRAWBERRY KNOLL RD 20879
William Wilhoyte, prin.
Summit Hall ES, 100 W DEER PARK DR 20877
Lois Bell, prin.
Travilah ES, 13801 DUFIEF MILL RD 20878
Judith Gaston, prin.
Washington Grove ES, 8712 OAKMONT ST 20877
Davisson Ayers, prin.
Watkins Mill ES
19001 WATKINS MILL RD 20879
Mable Smith, prin.
Whetstone ES, 19201 THOMAS FARM RD 20879
Stan Schaub, prin.
Woodfield ES, 24200 WOODFIELD RD 20879
Anne Bruce, prin.

St. Martin ES, 115 S FREDERICK AVE 20878

Galena, Kent Co., Pop. Code 2
Kent County SD
Supt. – See Chestertown
MS, 114 S MAIN ST 21635 – Thomas Groce, prin.

Gambrills, Anne Arundel Co., Pop. Code 2
Anne Arundel County SD
Supt. – See Annapolis
Four Seasons ES, 979 WAUGH CHAPEL RD 21054
Thomas Maxwell, prin.

Garrett Park, Montgomery Co., Pop. Code 4
Montgomery County SD
Supt. – See Rockville

ES, 4810 OXFORD ST 20896
Albert Bidwick, prin.

Holy Cross ES, 4900 STRATHMORE AVE 20896

Garrison, Baltimore Co., Pop. Code 3

Garrison Forest School
GARRISON FOREST ROAD 21055

Germantown, Montgomery Co.
Montgomery County SD
Supt. – See Rockville
King MS, 11700 NEELSVILLE CHURCH RD 20874
James Terrill, prin.
Cedar Grove ES, 24001 CEDAR GRV RD 20874
Mary O'Connell, prin.
Clopper Mill ES, 18501 CINNAMON DR 20874
J. Stevenson, prin.
Fox Chapel ES, 19315 CRAWFORD ROAD 20874
Richard Ervin,Jr., prin.
ES, 19110 GERMANTOWN RD 20874
David Vader, prin.
Lake Seneca ES, 13600 WANEGARDEN DR 20874
Elizabeth Morgan, prin.
McAuliffe ES, 12500 WISTERIA DR 20874
Eugene Haines, prin.
Waters Landing ES
13000 WATERS LANDING RD 20874
Stephen Bedi, prin.

Gibson Island, Anne Arundel Co.

Gibson Island Country School, P O BOX 92 21056

Glen Burnie, Anne Arundel Co., Pop. Code 8
Anne Arundel County SD
Supt. – See Annapolis
Corkran JHS, 7600 QUARTERFIELD ROAD 21061
Richard Kubatko, prin.
Cromwell ES, 1015 WELLHAM AVE NW 21061
Richard Chilipko, prin.
Ferndale ES, 105 PACKARD AVE 21061
Louis Thomas, prin.
Freetown ES, 7904 FREETOWN RD 21061
Martha Collison, prin.
Glen Burnie Park ES, 500 MARLBORO RD 21061
Jerry Christian, prin.
Glendale ES, 105 CARROLL RD 21061
Marvin Heptinstall, prin.
Hilltop ES, 6825 MELROSE AVE 21061
Harry Sharkey, prin.
Lee ES, 400 A STREET SW AT 4TH AVE 21061
Lauralee Whitmore, prin.
Marley ES, 201 MARLEY STATION RD 21061
Lorraise Brooks, prin.
North Glen ES
615 W FURNACE BRANCH RD 21061
Janet Anderson, prin.
Oakwood ES, 330 OAK MANOR DR 21061
Sharon Doyle, prin.
Point Pleasant ES, 1035 DUMBARTON RD 21061
Evelyn Reed, prin.
Rippling Woods ES, 530 NOLFIELD DR 21061
Roger Wilson, prin.
Solley ES, 7608 SOLLEY RD 21061
S. Walter, prin.
Southgate ES, 290 SHETLANDS LN 21061
Betty Lou Hayes, prin.
Woodside ES, 160 FUNKE RD 21061
Frank Rocco, prin.

Slade Regional Catholic ES
120 DORSEY RD 21061
St. Paul's Lutheran School
308 OAK MANOR DR 21061

Glenelg, Howard Co., Pop. Code 1

Glenelg Country School
FOLLY QUARTER ROAD 21737

Glenwood, Howard Co.
Howard County SD
Supt. – See Ellicott City
MS, 2680 ROUTE 97 21738 – Rob Childers, prin.
Bushy Park ES, 2670 ROUTE 97 21738
David MacPherson, prin.

Glyndon, Baltimore Co., Pop. Code 4

Sacred Heart ES, 63 SACRED HEART LANE 21071

Grantsville, Garrett Co., Pop. Code 2
Garrett County SD
Supt. – See Oakland
ES, 120 GRANT ST 21536
Matthew Stieringer, prin.
Yoder ES, RURAL ROUTE 01 BOX 175 21536
Carolyn Tice, prin.

Grasonville, Queen Anne's Co., Pop. Code 4
Queen Annes County SD
Supt. – See Centreville
ES 21638 – Samuel Wilson, prin.

Great Mills, St. Mary's Co.
St. Mary's County SD
Supt. – See Leonardtown
Greenview Knolls ES 20634 – John Hazuda, prin.

Little Flower School 20634

Greenbelt, Prince George's Co., Pop. Code 7
Prince Georges County SD
Supt. – See Upper Marlboro

MS, 8950 EDMONSTON ROAD 20770
Robert McKean, prin.
Greenbelt Center ES, 15 CRESCENT RD 20770
John Van Schoonhoven, prin.
Springhill Lake ES, 6060 SPRINGHILL DR 20770
Stanley Klein, prin.

St. Hughs ES, 145 CRESCENT RD 20770

Greensboro, Caroline Co., Pop. Code 4
Caroline County SD
Supt. – See Denton
ES, RURAL ROUTE 01 BOX 32 21639
David McCarthy, prin.

Hagerstown, Washington Co., Pop. Code 8
Washington County SD
Sch. Sys. Enr. Code 7
Supt. – Wayne Gersen, P O BOX 730 21741
Hicks MS, 1321 S POTOMAC ST 21740
James Conrad, prin.
Northern MS, 701 W NORTHERN AVE 21740
Deidre Shumaker, prin.
Western Heights MS, 1200 MARSHALL ST 21740
Edward Koogle, prin.
Bester ES, 30 MEMORIAL BLVD E 21740
Ken Mann, prin.
Conococheague ES
RURAL ROUTE 02 BOX 132 21740
Patricia Leonard, prin.
Doub ES, 1221 S POTOMAC ST 21740
Thomas Carnes, prin.
Fountain Rock ES
RURAL ROUTE 03 BOX 158-C 21740
Ron Ingram, prin.
Fountaindale ES, 901 W NORTHERN AVE 21740
James Young, prin.
Funkstown ES
RURAL ROUTE 09 BOX 236A 21740
Joanne Hilton, prin.
Lincolnshire ES, 1910 LINCOLNSHIRE RD 21740
Elinor McLeod, prin.
Old Forge ES, RURAL ROUTE 10 BOX 48 21740
Nancy Martin, prin.
Pangborn Boulevard ES
195 PANGBORN BLVD 21740 – Don Kendall,
prin.
Paramount ES, 1 E LONGMEADOW RD 21740
Ronald Phillips, prin.
Potomac Heights ES
301 E MAGNOLIA AVE 21740
BoAnn Kearns, prin.
Salem Avenue ES, 1323 SALEM AVE 21740
Vincent Spong, prin.
Winter Street ES, 59 WINTER ST 21740
Peggy Carroll, prin.
Other Schools – See Boonsboro, Cascade, Clear
Spring, Hancock, Knoxville, Maugansville,
Sharpsburg, Smithsburg, Williamsport

St. Mary ES, 218 W WASHINGTON ST 21740

Halethorpe, Baltimore Co., Pop. Code 8
Baltimore County SD
Supt. – See Towson
ES, 4300 MAPLE AVE 21227
June Boarman, prin.

Hampstead, Carroll Co., Pop. Code 4
Carroll County SD
Supt. – See Westminster
North Carroll MS, 2401 HANOVER PIKE 21074
Richard DeLong, prin.
ES, 3737 SHILOH RD 21074 – Larry Bair, prin.

Hancock, Washington Co., Pop. Code 4
Washington County SD
Supt. – See Hagerstown
ES 21750 – Edward Meyers, prin.

Hanover, Anne Arundel Co.
Anne Arundel County SD
Supt. – See Annapolis
Harman ES, 7660 RIDGE CHAPEL RD 21076
Lawrence Campbell, prin.

Havre De Grace, Harford Co., Pop. Code 7
Harford County SD
Supt. – See Bel Air
MS, 401 LEWIS LANE 21078 – R. Denton, prin.
ES, 700 S JUNIATA ST 21078
Joseph Deschak, prin.
Meadowvale ES, 910 GRACE VIEW DR 21078
Richard Hyson, prin.
Royce-Williams ES, 201 OAKINGTON RD 21078
Ellwood Quigg, prin.

Hebron, Wicomico Co., Pop. Code 3
Wicomico County SD
Supt. – See Salisbury
Westside IS 21830 – Ronald Willey, prin.

Helen, St. Mary's Co.
St. Mary's County SD
Supt. – See Leonardtown
Brent MS 20635 – Jacob Wright, prin.

Calverton School 20639
Mother Spalding ES 20635

Hollywood, St. Mary's Co.
St. Mary's County SD
Supt. – See Leonardtown
ES 20636 – Kathy Glaser, prin.

St. John ES, ST JOHN ROAD 20636

Huntingtown, Calvert Co.
Calvert County SD
Supt. – See Prince Frederick
ES 20639 – MaCarthur Jones, prin.

Hurlock, Dorchester Co., Pop. Code 4
Dorchester County SD
Supt. – See Cambridge
North Dorchester MS, RURAL ROUTE 02 21643
Gwen Handy, prin.
ES, CHARLES ST 21643 – William Batson, prin.

Hyattsville, Prince George's Co., Pop. Code 7
Prince Georges County SD
Supt. – See Upper Marlboro
MS, 6001 42ND AVE 20781 – Joseph Lupo, prin.
Orem MS, 5920 33RD AVE 20782
Toni Menchan, prin.
Cheverly Tuxedo ES
2300 BELLEVIEW AVE 20785
Dorothea Lembke, prin.
Chillum ES, 1420 CHILLUM RD 20782
Clara Scott, prin.
ES, 5311 43RD AVE 20781 – Emidio Cicolini, prin.
Langley Park/McCormick ES
8201 15TH AVE 20783 – Lee Meiners, prin.
Lewisdale ES, 2400 BANNING PL 20783
Catherine Hudson, prin.
Ridgecrest ES, 6120 RIGGS RD 20783
Margaret Cady, prin.
University Park ES, 4315 UNDERWOOD ST 20782
R. Powell, prin.
Woodridge ES, 5001 FLINTRIDGE DR 20784
Jack Pevenstein, prin.

Ascension Lutheran ES
7420 ARDMORE RD 20784
Concordia Lutheran ES
3705 LONGFELLOW ST 20782
St. Ambrose ES, 6310 JASON ST 20785
St. Jerome ES, 5207 42ND PL 20781
St. John the Baptist ES, 5704 SARGENT RD 20782
St. Mark's ES, 7501 ADELPHI RD 20783
St. Mary's ES, 7207 ANNAPOLIS RD 20784

Hydes, Baltimore Co.

St. John the Evangelist ES
13311 LONG GREEN PIKE 21082

Indian Head, Charles Co., Pop. Code 4
Charles County SD
Supt. – See La Plata
Henson MS, RURAL ROUTE 01 BOX 122 20640
Nancy Renfro, prin.
Smallwood MS, ROUTE 210 20640
Richetta Aker, prin.
ES, ROUTE 210 20640 – Ronald Ovens, prin.
Parks ES, RURAL ROUTE 01 BOX 113M 20640
Minnie Reynolds, prin.

Star of the Sea School
RURAL ROUTE 01 BOX 157 20640

Jarrettsville, Harford Co., Pop. Code 3
Harford County SD
Supt. – See Bel Air
ES, 3818 NORRISVILLE RD 21084
Deborah Heiberger, prin.

Jefferson, Frederick Co.
Frederick County SD
Supt. – See Frederick
Valley ES, 3519 JEFFERSON PIKE 21755
Philip Harper, prin.

Jessup, Anne Arundel Co., Pop. Code 3
Anne Arundel County SD
Supt. – See Annapolis
ES, 2900 JESSUP RD 20794
Shirley Moaney, prin.

Howard County SD
Supt. – See Ellicott City
Bollman Bridge ES
8200 SAVAGE-GUILFORD RD 20794
Carey Wright, prin.

Joppa, Harford Co., Pop. Code 6
Harford County SD
Supt. – See Bel Air
Magnolia MS, 299 FORT HOYLE ROAD 21085
Kenneth Gill, prin.
Joppatowne ES, 410 BARKSDALE RD 21085
J. Mills, prin.
Magnolia ES, 901 TRIMBLE RD 21085
John Potter, prin.
Riverside ES, 211 STILLMEADOW DR 21085
Beretta Goodwin, prin.

Kensington, Montgomery Co., Pop. Code 4
Montgomery County SD
Supt. – See Rockville
Kensington-Parkwood ES, 4710 SAUL RD 20895
Alan Stein, prin.
Rock View ES, 3901 DENFELD AVE 20895
Margery Auerbach, prin.

Holy Redeemer ES, 9715 SUMMIT AVE 20895
Newport Prep Schs.
11311 NEWPORT MILL ROAD 20895

Keymar, Carroll Co.
Frederick County SD
Supt. – See Frederick

New Midway ES
   12226 WOODSBORO PIKE   21757
   Don Cline, prin.

Kingsville, Baltimore Co., Pop. Code 3
   Baltimore County SD
   Supt. – See Towson
   ES, 7300 SUNSHINE AVE   21087
   Dale Orwig, prin.

   St. Paul Lutheran School
   12022 JERUSALEM RD   21087

Kitzmiller, Garrett Co.
   Garrett County SD
   Supt. – See Oakland
   ES, P O BOX 300   21538 – Brenda McCartney, prin.

Knoxville, Washington Co.
   Washington County SD
   Supt. – See Hagerstown
   Pleasant Valley ES, RURAL ROUTE 02   21758
   Raymond Barrett, prin.

Landover, Prince George's Co.
   Prince Georges County SD
   Supt. – See Upper Marlboro
   Kenmoor MS, 2500 KENMOOR DRIVE   20785
   John Robinson, prin.
   Ardmore ES, 9301 ARDMORE RD   20785
   Robert Estep, prin.
   Carroll ES, 1400 NALLEY TER   20785
   Walterene Brooks, prin.
   Columbia Park ES
   1901 KENT VILLAGE DR   20785
   Patricia Green, prin.
   Dodge Park ES, 3401 HUBBARD RD   20785
   John Webster, Jr., prin.
   Henson ES, 7910 SCOTT RD   20785
   Edward Clement, prin.
   Kenmoor ES, 3211 82ND AVE   20785
   Edward Johnson, prin.
   Oakcrest ES, 929 HILL RD   20785
   James Chase, prin.
   Pullen ES, 700 BRIGHTSEAT RD   20785
   Lois Hobbs, prin.

Landover Hills, Prince George's Co., Pop. Code 4
   Prince Georges County SD
   Supt. – See Upper Marlboro
   Cooper Lane ES, 3817 COOPER LN   20784
   Suzanne Wolff, prin.
   Glenridge ES, 7200 GALLATIN ST   20784
   Paul Bolig, prin.

Lanham-Seabrook, Prince George's Co.
   Prince Georges County SD
   Supt. – See Upper Marlboro
   Johnson MS, 5401 BARKER PLACE   20706
   R. Eschbacher, prin.
   Glenarden Woods ES
   7801 GLENARDEN PKY   20706
   Oretha Bridgwaters, prin.
   Magnolia ES, 8400 NIGHTINGALE DR   20706
   Laurie Carter, prin.
   McHenry ES, 8909 MCHENRY LN   20706
   Monroe Simms, prin.
   Reed ES, 9501 GREENBELT RD   20706
   Elizabeth Thomas, prin.

   St. Matthias Apostle ES
   9473 ANNAPOLIS RD   20706

La Plata, Charles Co., Pop. Code 4
   Charles County SD
   Sch. Sys. Enr. Code 7
   Supt. – John Bloom, P O BOX D   20646
   Somers MS, P O BOX A   20646
   Kenneth Rineaman, prin.
   Mitchell ES, P O BOX AB   20646
   Welford Bowling, prin.
   Other Schools – See Bryantown, Faulkner, Indian
   Head, Marbury, Nanjemoy, Newburg, Pomfret,
   Waldorf

   Archbishop Neale ES, HCR 01 BOX 1011   20646

Laurel, Prince George's Co., Pop. Code 7
   Anne Arundel County SD
   Supt. – See Annapolis
   Brock Bridge ES, 405 BROCK BRIDGE RD   20707
   James Preston, prin.
   Maryland City ES, 3359 CRUMPTON S   20707
   Marion Keenan, prin.

   Howard County SD
   Supt. – See Ellicott City
   Hammond MS, 8110 ALLADIN DRIVE   20707
   David Lovewell, prin.
   Hammond ES, 8110 ALADDIN DR   20707
   John Morningstar, prin.
   Whiskey Bottom Road ES
   9250 N LAUREL RD   20707 – John Vermette, prin.

   Prince Georges County SD
   Supt. – See Upper Marlboro
   Eisenhower MS
   13725 BRIARWOOD DRIVE   20708
   Brian Giersch, prin.
   Bond Mill ES, 16001 SHERWOOD AVE   20707
   Mary Jane Lusby, prin.
   Deerfield Run ES
   13000 LAUREL BOWIE RD   20708
   Michael Lapriola, prin.
   Harrison ES, 13200 LARCHDALE RD   20708
   William Diehl, prin.

ES, 5TH & MONTGOMERY STS   20707
   Kathleen James, prin.
   Montpelier ES, 9200 MUIRKIRK RD   20708
   Donald Forrester, prin.
   Oaklands ES, 13710 LAUREL BOWIE RD   20708
   Ralph Viggiano, prin.

   St. Mary of the Mills ES, EIGHTH STREET   20707

La Vale, Allegany Co.
   Allegany County SD
   Supt. – See Cumberland
   Cash Valley ES, CASH VALLEY ROAD   21502
   Beverly Mease, prin.
   Parkside ES, 50 PARKSIDE BLVD   21502
   Helen Warnick, prin.

Leonardtown, St. Mary's Co., Pop. Code 4
   St. Mary's County SD
   Sch. Sys. Enr. Code 7
   Supt. – William Burroughs, P O BOX 343   20650
   MS   20650 – George Kirby III, prin.
   ES   20650 – Robert Hmieleski, prin.
   Other Schools – See Bushwood, Chaptico, Great
   Mills, Helen, Hollywood, Lexington Park, Loveville,
   Mechanicsville, Park Hall, Ridge, Tall Timbers

   Father White ES, P O BOX 297   20650

Lexington Park, St. Mary's Co., Pop. Code 7
   St. Mary's County SD
   Supt. – See Leonardtown
   Esperanza MS   20653 – Lloyd Jenkins, prin.
   Spring Ridge MS   20653 – William Sluder, prin.
   Carver ES   20653 – Janice Walthour, prin.
   Knox ES   20653 – Charles Cuffley, prin.
   ES   20653 – M. Ohler, prin.
   Town Creek ES, 110 DENT DR   20653
   Herman Riffe, prin.

Libertytown, Frederick Co.
   Frederick County SD
   Supt. – See Frederick
   Liberty ES, 11820 LIBERTY RD   21762
   Howard Gilpin, prin.

Linthicum Heights, Anne Arundel Co., Pop. Code 7
   Anne Arundel County SD
   Supt. – See Annapolis
   Linthicum ES
   101 SCHOOL LN AT CAMP MEADE   21090
   Gregory Metrinko, prin.
   Overlook ES, 401 HAMPTON RD   21090
   Wayne Bark, prin.

   St. Philip Neri ES, 6401 S ORCHARD RD   21090

Lisbon, Howard Co.
   Howard County SD
   Supt. – See Ellicott City
   ES, 15901 FREDERICK RD   21765
   Kaye Cornmesser, prin.

Lonaconing, Allegany Co., Pop. Code 4
   Allegany County SD
   Supt. – See Cumberland
   Georges Creek ES, ROUTE 36   21539
   Robert Miller, prin.

Lothian, Anne Arundel Co., Pop. Code 3
   Anne Arundel County SD
   Supt. – See Annapolis
   Southern MS, RURAL ROUTE 02   20711
   Elizabeth Collinson, prin.
   ES, 5175 SOLOMONS ISLAND RD   20711
   Betty Moreland, prin.

Loveville, St. Mary's Co.
   St. Mary's County SD
   Supt. – See Leonardtown
   Banneker ES   20656 – Judy Williams, prin.

Lusby, Calvert Co.
   Calvert County SD
   Supt. – See Prince Frederick
   Southern MS   20657 – Edward Weiland, prin.
   Appeal ES   20657 – Theodore Haynie, prin.

Lutherville, Baltimore Co., Pop. Code 7
   Baltimore County SD
   Supt. – See Towson
   Ridgely MS, 121 E RIDGELY ROAD   21093
   P. Amberman, prin.
   Hampton ES, 1115 CHARMUTH RD   21093
   Richard Bradley, prin.

Manchester, Carroll Co., Pop. Code 4
   Carroll County SD
   Supt. – See Westminster
   ES, 100 YORK ST   21102 – Larry Tyree, prin.

Marbury, Charles Co., Pop. Code 2
   Charles County SD
   Supt. – See La Plata
   Gale-Bailey ES
   RURAL ROUTE 01 BOX 306   20658
   Keith Hettel, prin.

Mardela Springs, Wicomico Co., Pop. Code 2
   Wicomico County SD
   Supt. – See Salisbury
   Northwestern ES   21837 – Doretha Jones, prin.

Marion Station, Somerset Co.
   Somerset County SD
   Supt. – See Princess Anne
   ES   21838 – Marguerite Robinson, prin.

Maugansville, Washington Co., Pop. Code 4
   Washington County SD
   Supt. – See Hagerstown
   ES   21767 – Thomas Ingram, Jr., prin.

Mayo, Anne Arundel Co.
   Anne Arundel County SD
   Supt. – See Annapolis
   ES, 1152 MAYO RD   21106
   Victoria Waidner, prin.

Mechanicsville, St. Mary's Co.
   St. Mary's County SD
   Supt. – See Leonardtown
   Dent ES   20659 – Patricia Russavage, prin.
   ES   20659 – Rhodessa Milham, prin.
   Oakville ES   20659 – Regena Williams, prin.
   White Marsh ES   20659 – Jo Ann Barthelme, prin.

Middletown, Frederick Co., Pop. Code 4
   Frederick County SD
   Supt. – See Frederick
   MS, 100 HIGH ST   21769 – Michael Kline, prin.
   ES, 201 E GREEN ST   21769 – Roy Clever, prin.

Millersville, Anne Arundel Co., Pop. Code 2
   Anne Arundel County SD
   Supt. – See Annapolis
   Old Mill MS-North, 610 OLD MILL ROAD   21108
   Richard Schreiner, prin.
   Old Mill MS-South, 620 OLD MILL ROAD   21108
   Ed Holshey, prin.
   ES, 1601 MILLERSVILLE RD   21108
   Henry Shubert, prin.

Millington, Kent Co., Pop. Code 3
   Kent County SD
   Supt. – See Chestertown
   ES   21651 – L. Willis, prin.

Mitchellville, Prince George's Co.
   Prince Georges County SD
   Supt. – See Upper Marlboro
   Woodmore ES, 12500 WOODMORE RD   20716
   Beth Hadley, prin.

Monkton, Baltimore Co.
   Baltimore County SD
   Supt. – See Towson
   Hereford MS, 712 CORBETT ROAD   21111
   Lawrence Kimmel, prin.

Monrovia, Frederick Co.
   Frederick County SD
   Supt. – See Frederick
   Green Valley ES, 11501 FINGERBOARD RD   21770
   Jerome Strum, prin.
   Kemptown ES
   3456 KEMPTOWN CHURCH RD   21770
   Michelle Krantz, prin.

Mountain Lake Park, Garrett Co.
   Garrett County SD
   Supt. – See Oakland
   Loch Lynn ES, 302 ROANOKE AVE   21550
   Herbert Lambert, Jr., prin.

Mount Airy, Carroll Co., Pop. Code 4
   Carroll County SD
   Supt. – See Westminster
   MS, 102 WATERSVILLE ROAD   21771
   J. Devault, prin.
   ES, 405 N MAIN ST   21771 – Althea Miller, prin.

Mount Rainier, Prince George's Co., Pop. Code 6
   Prince Georges County SD
   Supt. – See Upper Marlboro
   ES, 4011 32ND ST   20712 – Philip Catania, prin.
   Stone ES, 4500 34TH ST   20712
   Charles Poole, prin.

Mount Savage, Allegany Co., Pop. Code 4
   Allegany County SD
   Supt. – See Cumberland
   S, RURAL ROUTE 01   21545
   Ronald Chapman, prin.

Myersville, Frederick Co., Pop. Code 2
   Frederick County SD
   Supt. – See Frederick
   ES   21773 – Gerald Degrange, prin.

Nanjemoy, Charles Co.
   Charles County SD
   Supt. – See La Plata
   Mt. Hope/Nanjemoy ES
   RURAL ROUTE 01 BOX 63   20662
   Nancy Roche, prin.

Newark, Worcester Co., Pop. Code 3
   Worcester County SD
   Sch. Sys. Enr. Code 6
   Supt. – Francis Ruffo
   RURAL ROUTE 01 BOX 110 A   21841
   Other Schools – See Berlin, Ocean City, Pocomoke
   City, Showell, Snow Hill

Newburg, Charles Co.
   Charles County SD
   Supt. – See La Plata
   Piccowaxen MS, RURAL ROUTE 01 BOX 6   20664
   Garth Bowling, prin.

New Carrollton, Prince George's Co., Pop. Code 7
   Prince Georges County SD
   Supt. – See Upper Marlboro
   Carroll MS, 6130 LAMONT DRIVE   20784
   Herman Schiemer, prin.

Carrollton ES, 8300 QUINTANA ST   20784
  Linda Cornfield, prin.
Frost ES, 6419 85TH AVE   20784
  Lynn Chadderdon, prin.
Lamont ES, 7101 GOOD LUCK RD   20784
  David Fischvogt, prin.

New Market, Frederick Co., Pop. Code 2
Frederick County SD
Supt. – See Frederick
MS, P O BOX 58   21774 – Paul Smith, prin.
ES, P O BOX 284   21774 – Thomas Shade, prin.

New Windsor, Carroll Co., Pop. Code 3
Carroll County SD
Supt. – See Westminster
MS   21776 – Jeffrey Kimble, prin.

North East, Cecil Co., Pop. Code 4
Cecil County SD
Supt. – See Elkton
MS, 300 E CECIL AVE   21901
  Douglas Dunston, prin.
Bay View ES, 910 N EAST RD   21901
  Anthony Ligatti, prin.
ES, 301 THOMAS AVE   21901 – Gary Lewis, prin.

Oakland, Garrett Co., Pop. Code 4
Garrett County SD
Sch. Sys. Enr. Code 6
Supt. – Jerome Ryscavage, P O BOX 313   21550
Southern MS, 903 BROADFORD ROAD   21550
  John Rickman, prin.
Broad Ford ES, 905 BROADFORD RD   21550
  Thomas Fowler, prin.
Crellin ES, HCR 02 BOX 98   21550
  Asa McCain,Jr., prin.
Dennett Road ES, 1217 DENNETT RD   21550
  Clark Sharpless, prin.
Red House ES, RURAL ROUTE 02 BOX 177   21550
  Gary Galloway, prin.
Swan Meadow ES
  RURAL ROUTE 02 BOX 117   21550
  Esther Yoder, prin.
Other Schools – See Accident, Bloomington,
  Friendsville, Frostburg, Grantsville, Kitzmiller,
  Mountain Lake Park

Ocean City, Worcester Co., Pop. Code 5
Worcester County SD
Supt. – See Newark
ES, RURAL ROUTE 01 BOX 262   21842
  Lenore Huffer, prin.

Odenton, Anne Arundel Co., Pop. Code 6
Anne Arundel County SD
Supt. – See Annapolis
Crofton ES, 1405 DUKE OF KENT   21114
  Virginia Pope, prin.
Crofton Woods ES, 1750 URBY DR   21114
  Peter Nicolini, prin.
ES, 1290 ODENTON RD   21113
  Barbara San Gabino, prin.
Waugh Chapel ES
  841 WAUGH CHAPEL RD   21113
  Robert Masters, prin.

Oldtown, Allegany Co., Pop. Code 4
Allegany County SD
Supt. – See Cumberland
S   21555 – Roger Flanagan, prin.

Olney, Montgomery Co., Pop. Code 5
Montgomery County SD
Supt. – See Rockville
Farquhar MS
  16915 BATCHELORS FOREST RD   20832
  Thomas Hickman, prin.
Belmont ES, 19528 OLNEY MILL RD   20832
  Barbara Frank, prin.
ES, 3401 QUEEN MARY DR   20832
  Karen Fulton, prin.

St. Peter School
  2900 OLNEY SANDY SPRING RD   20832

Owings, Calvert Co.
Calvert County SD
Supt. – See Prince Frederick
Northern MS   20736 – Earle Thorne, prin.
Mt. Harmony ES   20736 – Thomas Howie, prin.

Owings Mills, Baltimore Co., Pop. Code 6
Baltimore County SD
Supt. – See Towson
Deer Park ES, 9809 LYONS MILL RD   21117
  David Fry, prin.
ES, 10824 REISTERSTOWN RD   21117
  Shirley Bacon, prin.
Timber Grove ES, 701 ACADEMY AVE   21117
  Doris Ensminger, prin.

Bais Yaakov Girls School
  11111 PARK HGTS AVE   21117
McDonogh School, P O BOX 380   21117

Oxon Hill, Prince George's Co., Pop. Code 7
Prince Georges County SD
Supt. – See Upper Marlboro
Barnaby Manor ES, 2411 OWENS RD   20745
  Sharon Quarles, prin.
Flintstone ES, 800 COMANCHE DR   20745
  Dodson Burns,Jr., prin.
Forest Heights ES, 200 TALBERT DR   20745
  Howard Wright, prin.
Glassmanor ES, 1011 MARCY AVE   20745
  Howard Burnett, prin.

Owens Road ES, 1616 OWENS RD   20745
  Dorothy Giersch, prin.
ES, 7701 LIVINGSTON RD   20745
  Frances Collins, prin.
Valley View ES, 5500 DANBY AVE   20745
  Beatrice Sklarewitz, prin.

Park Hall, St. Mary's Co.
St. Mary's County SD
Supt. – See Leonardtown
ES   20667 – Janet Kellam, prin.

Parkton, Baltimore Co., Pop. Code 2
Baltimore County SD
Supt. – See Towson
Seventh District ES, 20300 YORK RD   21120
  Donald Wright, prin.

Parkville, Baltimore Co., Pop. Code 8
Baltimore County SD
Supt. – See Towson
White Oak ES, 8401 LEEFIELD RD   21234
  Donna Smither, prin.

Pasadena, Anne Arundel Co., Pop. Code 4
Anne Arundel County SD
Supt. – See Annapolis
Chesapeake Bay MS
  4804 MOUNTAIN ROAD   21122
  Thomas Evans, prin.
Bodkin ES, 8320 VENTNOR RD   21122
  Donald Kelly, prin.
Fort Smallwood ES
  1720 POPLAR RIDGE RD   21122
  Gladiola Savage, prin.
Fox MS, 7922 OUTING AVE   21122
  John Brown, prin.
High Point ES, 924 DUVALL HWY   21122
  Robert Kanach, prin.
Jacobsville ES, 3801 MOUNTAIN RD   21122
  Wayne Miller, prin.
Lake Shore ES, 4531 MOUNTAIN RD   21122
  Sheila Kendall, prin.
ES, 105 SPRUCE AVE   21122 – Max Muller, prin.
Riviera Beach ES, 8515 JENKINS RD   21122
  Louise Dejesu, prin.
Sunset ES, 8572 FORT SMALLWOOD RD   21122
  Shirley Phillips, prin.

St. Jane Frances School
  8513 SAINT JANE DR   21122

Perry Hall, Baltimore Co.
Baltimore County SD
Supt. – See Towson
Chapel Hill ES, 5200 E JOPPA RD   21128
  Lucien Peters,Jr., prin.

Perryville, Cecil Co., Pop. Code 4
Cecil County SD
Supt. – See Elkton
MS, AIKEN AVE   21903 – David Rudolph, prin.
ES, MARYLAND & MAYWOOD AVES   21903
  James Slaughter, prin.

Good Shepherd ES, 810 AIKEN AVE   21903

Pikesville, Baltimore Co., Pop. Code 4
Baltimore County SD
Supt. – See Towson
Wellwood ES, 2901 SMITH AVE   21208
  Frederick Ray, prin.

Pittsville, Wicomico Co., Pop. Code 3
Wicomico County SD
Supt. – See Salisbury
ES   21850 – W. Hammond, prin.

Pocomoke City, Worcester Co., Pop. Code 5
Worcester County SD
Supt. – See Newark
Pocomoke MS, 800 EIGHTH ST   21851
  Coleen Mister, prin.
Pocomoke ES
  RURAL ROUTE 02 BOX 196-A   21851
  Irene Hazel, prin.

Pomfret, Charles Co.
Charles County SD
Supt. – See La Plata
Craik ES, RURAL ROUTE 02 BOX 76   20675
  Vivian Belcher, prin.

Poolesville, Montgomery Co., Pop. Code 5
Montgomery County SD
Supt. – See Rockville
ES, 19565 FISHER AVE   20837
  Thelma Monk, prin.

Port Deposit, Cecil Co., Pop. Code 3
Cecil County SD
Supt. – See Elkton
Bainbridge ES, 41 PRESTON DR   21904
  Michael Schmook, prin.

Port Republic, Calvert Co.
Calvert County SD
Supt. – See Prince Frederick
Mutual ES   20676 – Robert Conway, prin.

Potomac, Montgomery Co., Pop. Code 4

Our Lady of Mercy ES
  9222 KENTSDALE DR   20854

Preston, Caroline Co., Pop. Code 2
Caroline County SD
Supt. – See Denton

ES, P O BOX 69   21655 – Larry Anders, prin.

Prince Frederick, Calvert Co., Pop. Code 6
Calvert County SD
Sch. Sys. Enr. Code 6
Supt. – Eugene Karol
  DARES BEACH ROAD   20678
Calvert MS, RURAL ROUTE 02   20678
  Patricia Young, prin.
Calvert ES   20678 – Mildred Wilson, prin.
Other Schools – See Chesapeake Beach, Huntingtown,
  Lusby, Owings, Port Republic, Sunderland

Princess Anne, Somerset Co., Pop. Code 4
Somerset County SD
Sch. Sys. Enr. Code 5
Supt. – H. DeWayne Whittington
  PRINCE WILLIAM ST   21853
Greenwood MS   21853 – Brenda Webster, prin.
Mt. Vernon ES, RURAL ROUTE 01   21853
  Frank O'Rourke, prin.
ES   21853 – Cheryl Richardson, prin.
Other Schools – See Crisfield, Deal Island, Ewell,
  Marion Station, Tylerton, Westover

Pylesville, Harford Co.
Harford County SD
Supt. – See Bel Air
North Harford MS, 213 PYLESVILLE ROAD   21132
  Harry Hinman, prin.
North Harford ES, 120 PYLESVILLE RD   21132
  Daniel Harner, prin.

Quantico, Wicomico Co.
Wicomico County SD
Supt. – See Salisbury
Westside PS   21856 – Ronald Willey, prin.

Randallstown, Baltimore Co., Pop. Code 7
Baltimore County SD
Supt. – See Towson
Deer Park MS, 9830 WINANDS ROAD   21133
  Thelma Stanley, prin.
Church Lane ES, 3820 FERNSIDE RD   21133
  Benson Maser, prin.
Hernwood ES, 9919 MARRIOTTSVILLE RD   21133
  Gary Hilleary, prin.
ES, 9013 LIBERTY RD   21133
  Stephen Mackert, prin.

Holy Family ES, 9535 LIBERTY RD   21133

Reisterstown, Baltimore Co., Pop. Code 7
Baltimore County SD
Supt. – See Towson
Franklin MS
  MAIN & COCKEYSMILL ROAD   21136
  Carroll Parker, prin.
Cedarmere ES, 17 NICODEMUS RD   21136
  Barbara Barr, prin.
Chatsworth ES, 222 NEW AVE   21136
  Suzanne Ockun, prin.
Franklin ES, 33 COCKEYSMILL RD   21136
  Mary Brauer, prin.
Glyndon ES, 445 GLYNDON DR   21136
  Celine Wachter, prin.
ES, 223 WALGROVE RD   21136
  Edward Schaffer, prin.

Ridge, St. Mary's Co.
St. Mary's County SD
Supt. – See Leonardtown
ES   20680 – Elfreda Mathis, prin.

St. Michael ES, ROUTE 235   20680

Ridgely, Caroline Co., Pop. Code 3
Caroline County SD
Supt. – See Denton
ES, RURAL ROUTE 01 BOX 22-M   21660
  Rosemary Thayer, prin.

Rising Sun, Cecil Co., Pop. Code 4
Cecil County SD
Supt. – See Elkton
Calvert ES, 79 BRICK MEETING HOUSE RD   21911
  Earle Miller, prin.
ES, 500 HOPEWELL RD   21911
  Carroll Ayres, prin.

Riverdale, Prince George's Co., Pop. Code 5
Prince Georges County SD
Supt. – See Upper Marlboro
Wirt MS, 62ND PL & TUCKERMAN ST   20782
  Ernest Caldwell, prin.
Beacon Heights ES, 6929 FURMAN PKY   20737
  Everett Gollihew, prin.
ES, 5006 RIVERDALE RD   20737
  Paula Poulis, prin.
Templeton ES, 6001 CARTERS LN   20737
  Milton Jews, prin.

St. Bernard's ES, 5811 RIVERDALE RD   20737

Rock Hall, Kent Co., Pop. Code 4
Kent County SD
Supt. – See Chestertown
MS, RURAL ROUTE 02   21661 – C. Hawkins, prin.
ES   21661 – Clarence Hawkins, prin.

Rockville, Montgomery Co., Pop. Code 8
Montgomery County SD
Sch. Sys. Enr. Code 8
Supt. – Harry Pitt
  850 HUNGERFORD DRIVE   20850
Frost MS, 9201 SCOTT DRIVE   20850
  Michael Glascoe, prin.

Redland MS
6505 MUNCASTER MILL ROAD   20855
Bonnie Fox, prin.
Tilden MS, 6300 TILDEN LANE   20852
Arch Webster, prin.
West MS, 651 FALLS ROAD   20850
Joseph Headman, prin.
Wood MS, 14615 BAUER DRIVE   20853
Jerome Lynch, prin.
Barnsley ES, 14516 NADINE DR   20853
William Beckman, prin.
Beall ES, 451 BEALL AVE   20850
Mariana Doores, prin.
Bells Mill ES, 8225 BELLS MILL RD   20854
Kathleen Holliday, prin.
Beverly Farms ES, 8501 POSTOAK RD   20854
Charles Ison, prin.
Brookhaven ES, 4610 RENN ST   20853
Malcolm Halliday, prin.
Candlewood ES, 7210 OSPREY DR   20855
Donald Graham, prin.
Cashell ES, 17101 CASHELL RD   20853
Mary Tannhauser, prin.
Cold Spring ES
9201 FALLS CHAPEL WAY   20854
Sharon Beischer, prin.
College Gardens ES, 1700 YALE PL   20850
Gerald Frick, prin.
Fallsmead ES, 180 GREENPLACE TER   20850
Jeffrey Pitt, prin.
Farmland ES, 7000 OLD GATE RD   20852
F. Bonner, prin.
Flower Valley ES, 4615 SUNFLOWER DR   20853
Jeremiah Sullivan, prin.
Lakewood ES, 2534 LINDLEY TER   20850
Judith Kenney, prin.
Laytonsville ES, 15101 BAUER DR   20853
Laura Turner, prin.
Luxmanor ES, 6201 TILDEN LN   20852
Beverly Hopkins, prin.
Maryvale ES, 1000 FIRST ST   20850
Gerald Johnson, prin.
Meadow Hall ES, 931 TWINBROOK PKY   20851
Francis Sweeney, prin.
Mill Creek Towne ES
17700 PARK MILL DR   20855
Horace Ashby, prin.
Potomac ES, 10311 RIVER RD   20854
Jonathan Jones, prin.
Ritchie Park ES, 1514 DUNSTER LN   20854
Robert Hudak, prin.
Rock Creek Valley ES, 5121 RUSSETT RD   20853
Robert Dornburg, prin.
Twinbrook ES, 5815 WAINWRIGHT AVE   20851
Darius Brown, prin.
Wayside ES, 10011 GLEN RD   20854
Matthew Tronzano, prin.
Wheaton Woods ES, 4510 FAROE PL   20853
Stephanie Jackson, prin.
Other Schools — See Bethesda, Brookeville,
Burtonsville, Chevy Chase, Clarksburg, Damascus,
Dickerson, Gaithersburg, Garrett Park, Germantown,
Kensington, Olney, Poolesville, Sandy Spring,
Silver Spring, Takoma Park

Smith Jewish Day School
1901 E JEFFERSON ST   20852
Christ Episcopal ES
109 S WASHINGTON ST   20850
Green Acres School, 11701 DANVILLE DR   20852
St. Elizabeth ES, 917 MONTROSE RD   20852
St. Jude ES, 4820 WALBRIDGE ST   20853
St. Mary ES, 600 VEIRS MILL RD   20852

Sabillasville, Frederick Co.
Frederick County SD
Supt. — See Frederick
ES, 16210-B SABILLASVILLE RD   21780
Wanda Severance, prin.

Saint Michaels, Talbot Co., Pop. Code 4
Talbot County SD
Supt. — See Easton
ES   21663 — Douglas Gibson, prin.

Salisbury, Wicomico Co., Pop. Code 7
Wicomico County SD
Sch. Sys. Enr. Code 7
Supt. — Evelyn Holman, P O BOX 1538   21801
Bennett MS, E COLLEGE AVE   21801
Edward Carey, prin.
Wicomico MS, 635 E MAIN ST   21801
William Evans, prin.
Beaver Run MS, OCEAN CITY ROAD   21801
James Fox, prin.
Chipman ES, LAKE STREET   21801
Jane Burke, prin.
East Salisbury MS, OCEAN CITY RD   21801
Barbara Twilley, prin.
Glen Avenue MS, GLEN AVE   21801
Judith Stein, prin.
North Salisbury MS, 201 UNION AVE   21801
Charles Bounds, prin.
Pemberton MS, PEMBERTON DR   21801
C. Bowmann, prin.
Pinehurst MS, PINEHURST AVE   21801
Joana Donovan, prin.
Prince Street MS, 400 PRINCE ST   21801
Charles Goslee, prin.
West Salisbury ES, WEST ROAD   21801
Lillie Giddens, prin.
Other Schools — See Delmar, Fruitland, Hebron,
Mardela Springs, Pittsville, Quantico, Willards

Christian School of Salisbury
PARKER ROAD   21801
Salisbury School, HOBBS RD   21801
St. Francs De Sales ES, 500 CAMDEN AVE   21801

Sandy Spring, Montgomery Co., Pop. Code 3
Montgomery County SD
Supt. — See Rockville
Sherwood ES
316 OLNEY SANDY SPRING RD   20860
Thomas Buck, prin.

Seabrook, Prince George's Co.
Prince Georges County SD
Supt. — See Upper Marlboro
Goddard MS, 9850 GOOD LUCK ROAD   20706
Karl Taschenberger, prin.
Gaywood ES, 6701 97TH AVE   20706
Walter Cuttler, prin.
ES, 6001 SEABROOK RD   20706
John Krouse, prin.

Secretary, Dorchester Co., Pop. Code 2
Dorchester County SD
Supt. — See Cambridge
Warwick ES   21664 — Frederic Hildenbrand, prin.

Severn, Anne Arundel Co.
Anne Arundel County SD
Supt. — See Annapolis
Quarterfield ES, 7967 QUARTERFIELD RD   21144
Diane Lenzi, prin.
Ridgeway ES, 1440 EVERGREEN RD   21144
Louis Kamm, prin.
ES, 838 REECE RD   21144 — M. Carpenter, prin.
Van Bokkelen ES, 1140 REECE RD   21144
Raymond Herbert, prin.

Severna Park, Anne Arundel Co., Pop. Code 7
Anne Arundel County SD
Supt. — See Annapolis
MS, 401 JUMPERS HOLE ROAD   21146
Victoria Hutchins, prin.
Benfield ES, 365 LYNWOOD DR   21146
Jane McNeel, prin.
Jones ES, 122 HOYLE LN   21146
Preston Hebron, prin.
McKinsey ES, 175 ARUNDEL BEACH RD   21146
Linda Unklesbee, prin.
Oak Hill ES, 34 TRUCK HOUSE RD   21146
Lewis Frey, prin.
ES, 6 RIGGS AVE   21146 — Anita Murray, prin.
Shipley's Choice ES   21146
Mary Ellen Street, prin.

St. John the Evangelist ES
660 RITCHIE HWY   21146

Shady Side, Anne Arundel Co., Pop. Code 4
Anne Arundel County SD
Supt. — See Annapolis
ES, 4859 ATWELL RD   20764 — Jeff Wagner, prin.

Sharpsburg, Allegany Co., Pop. Code 3
Washington County SD
Supt. — See Hagerstown
ES, RURAL ROUTE 01 BOX 27   21782
William Wells, prin.

Showell, Worcester Co.
Worcester County SD
Supt. — See Newark
ES, P O BOX 306   21862 — Wilda Stroh, prin.

Silver Spring, Montgomery Co., Pop. Code 8
Montgomery County SD
Supt. — See Rockville
Eastern MS, 300 UNIVERSITY BLVD E   20901
Margaret Egan, prin.
Lee MS, 11800 MONTICELLO AVE   20902
Robert Hatchel, prin.
Sligo MS, 1401 DENNIS AVE   20902
Dorothy Jackson, prin.
Takoma Park IS
6711 PINEY BRANCH ROAD   20910
Stephen Tarason, prin.
White Oak MS
12201 NEW HAMPSHIRE AVE   20904
John Schneider, prin.
Bel Pre ES, 13801 RIPPLING BROOK DR   20906
Aileen Craig, prin.
Broad Acres ES, 710 BEACON RD   20903
Tim Riggott, prin.
Cannon Road ES, 901 CANNON RD   20904
Ray Myrtle, prin.
Cresthaven ES, 1234 CRESTHAVEN DR   20903
Kennon Evans, prin.
East Silver Spring ES
631 SILVER SPRING AVE   20910
Geraldine Fowlkes, prin.
Fairland ES, 13313 OLD COLUMBIA PIKE   20904
Thomas Poore, prin.
Forest Knolls ES, 10830 EASTWOOD AVE   20901
Carolyn Starek, prin.
Galway ES, 12612 GALWAY DR   20904
John Ditomasso, prin.
Georgian Forest ES, 3100 REGINA DR   20906
Eric Mills, prin.
Glen Haven ES, 10900 INWOOD AVE   20902
Jevoner Adams, prin.
Glenallan ES, 12520 HEURICH RD   20902
Eoline Cary, prin.
Greencastle ES, 13611 ROBEY RD   20904
Meriam Flam, prin.

Harmony Hills ES, 13407 LYDIA ST   20906
Robin Weaver, prin.
Highland ES, 3100 MEDWAY ST   20902
Katherine Patterson, prin.
Highland View ES
9010 PROVIDENCE AVE   20901
Myra Abramovitz, prin.
Jackson Road ES, 900 JACKSON RD   20904
Ben Ellis, Jr., prin.
Kemp Mill ES, 411 SISSON ST   20902
Mary Melbourne, prin.
Montgomery Knolls ES, 807 DALEVIEW DR   20901
Pamela Prue, prin.
New Hampshire Estates ES
8720 CARROLL AVE   20903
Joanne Busalacchi, prin.
Oak View ES, 400 E WAYNE AVE   20901
William Baranick, prin.
Oakland Terrace ES
2720 PLYERS MILL RD   20902
Susan Marks, prin.
Page ES, 13400 TAMARACK RD   20904
Lester Birchall, prin.
Pine Crest ES, 201 WOODMOOR DR   20901
Jane McAuliffe, prin.
Rosemary Hills ES, 2111 PORTER RD   20910
Linda Weber, prin.
Stonegate ES, 14811 NOTLEY RD   20904
Kenneth Egloff, prin.
Strathmore ES, 3200 BEAVERWOOD LN   20906
Vera Torrence, prin.
Viers Mills ES, 11711 JOSEPH MILL RD   20906
John Burley, prin.
Weller Road ES, 3301 WELLER RD   20906
Drucille Stafford, prin.
Westover ES, 401 HAWKESBURY LN   20904
Marcia Wilson, prin.
Woodlin ES, 2101 LUZERNE AVE   20910
Emily Kesser, prin.

Hebrew Academy of Greater Washington
2010 LINDEN LANE   20910
Barrie Day ES, 13500 LAYHILL RD   20906
Calvery Lutheran ES, 9545 GEORGIA AVE   20910
Grace Episcopal Day School
9115 GEORGIA AVE   20910
Hebrew Day School-Montgomery
1401 ARCOLA AVE   20902
St. Andrew ES, 11602 KIMPT MILL RD   20902
St. Bernadettes ES
80 UNIVERSITY BLVD E   20901
St. Camillus ES
1500 SAINT CAMILLUS DR   20903
St. Catherine LaBoure ES
11811 CLARIDGE RD   20902
St. John the Baptist ES
12319 NEW HAMPSHIRE AVE   20904
St. John the Evangelist ES
10201 WOODLAND DR   20902
St. Michael's ES, 824 WAYNE AVE   20910
Washington Christian School
1820 FRANWALL AVE   20902

Smithsburg, Washington Co., Pop. Code 3
Frederick County SD
Supt. — See Frederick
Wolfsville ES, 12520 WOLFSVILLE RD   21783
Lynda Johnson, prin.

Washington County SD
Supt. — See Hagerstown
MS, 68 N MAIN ST   21783 — Roger Stenersen, prin.
ES, 67 N MAIN ST   21783 — Charles Fager, prin.

Snow Hill, Worcester Co., Pop. Code 4
Worcester County SD
Supt. — See Newark
MS, RURAL ROUTE 03 BOX 307   21863
Dan Richardson, prin.
ES, COULBOURNE LN   21863
Rick Lambertson, prin.

Solomons, Calvert Co., Pop. Code 2

Our Lady Star of Sea ES   20688

Southern MD Facility, Prince George's Co.
Prince Georges County SD
Supt. — See Upper Marlboro
Longfields ES, 3300 NEWKIRK AVE   20747
Dorsey Scofield, prin.
North Forestville ES, 2311 RITCHIE RD   20747
Michael Perich, prin.

Holy Family ES, 2200 CALLAWAY ST   20748
Mt. Calvary ES, 6704 MARLOBORO PIKE   20747
St. Columba ES, 7800 LIVINGSTON RD   20745
St. Ignatius ES, 2317 BRINKLEY RD   20744
St. Margaret ES, 410 ADDISON RD S   20743

Sparks, Baltimore Co.
Baltimore County SD
Supt. — See Towson
ES, 1000 SPARKS RD   21152
Wanda McKelvie, prin.

Stevensville, Queen Anne's Co.
Queen Annes County SD
Supt. — See Centreville
MS, RURAL ROUTE 03   21666
Dominick Romano, prin.
Kent Island ES   21666 — Joseph Ollock, prin.

Street, Harford Co.
Harford County SD
Supt. — See Bel Air

Dublin ES, 1527 WHITEFORD RD   21154
  Norval Carr, prin.

Sudlersville, Queen Anne's Co., Pop. Code 2
  Queen Annes County SD
  Supt. – See Centreville
  MS   21668 – Robert Jackson, prin.
  ES   21668 – Frederick Leadbetter, prin.

Suitland, Prince George's Co., Pop. Code 8
  Prince Georges County SD
  Supt. – See Upper Marlboro
  Jackson MS, 2500 REGENCY PKWY   20746
    James Proctor, prin.
  Beanes ES, 5108 DIANNA DR   20746
    Carolyn Howard, prin.
  Foulois ES, 4601 BEAUFORD RD   20746
    Anthony Randolph, prin.
  Morningside ES, 6900 AMES ST   20746
    Elsie Neely, prin.
  Poe ES, 2001 SHADYSIDE AVE   20746
    William Hussong III, prin.
  Princeton ES, 6101 BAXTER DR   20746
    Phyllis Dunan, prin.
  Shadyside ES, 4601 LACY AVE   20746
    Gloria Singleton, prin.
  Skyline ES, 6311 RANDOLPH RD   20746
    Ronald Etue, prin.

  St. Philip the Apostle School
    5414 HENDERSON WAY   20746

Sunderland, Calvert Co., Pop. Code 7
  Calvert County SD
  Supt. – See Prince Frederick
  ES   20689 – J. Williams, prin.

Sykesville, Carroll Co., Pop. Code 4
  Carroll County SD
  Supt. – See Westminster
  MS, 7301 SPRINGFIELD AVE   21784
    Donald Pyles, prin.
  Carrolltowne ES, 6542 RIDGE RD   21784
    Ronald Burinsky, prin.
  Eldersburg ES, 1021 JOHNSVILLE RD   21784
    Miriam Beck, prin.
  Freedom District ES, 5626 SYKESVILLE RD   21784
    Helen Metz, prin.
  Mechanicsville ES, 3838 SYKESVILLE RD   21784
    Robert Bonner, prin.

Takoma Park, Montgomery Co., Pop. Code 7
  Montgomery County SD
  Supt. – See Rockville
  Piney Branch MS, 7510 MAPLE AVE   20912
    Joseph Press, prin.
  Rolling Terrace ES, 705 BAYFIELD ST   20912
    Geraldine Meltz, prin.
  ES, 201 PHILADEPHIA AVE   20912
    Phinnize Brown, prin.

  Prince Georges County SD
  Supt. – See Upper Marlboro
  Carole Highlands ES, 1610 HANNON ST   20912
    Barbara Scott, prin.

  Andrews School, 117 ELM AVE   20912
  Our Lady of Sorrows ES, 1010 LARCH AVE   20912
  Sligo SDA School, 8300 CARROLL AVE   20912

Tall Timbers, St. Mary's Co.
  St. Mary's County SD
  Supt. – See Leonardtown
  Piney Point ES   20690 – Robert Abell, prin.

Taneytown, Carroll Co., Pop. Code 5
  Carroll County SD
  Supt. – See Westminster
  Northwest MS   21787 – Richard McPartland, prin.
  ES, UNIONTOWN RD   21787
    Larry McKinney, prin.

Temple Hills, Prince George's Co.
  Prince Georges County SD
  Supt. – See Upper Marlboro
  Shugart MS, 2000 CALLOWAY ST   20748
    Robert Weidner, prin.
  Stoddert MS, 2501 OLSON ST   20748
    Robert Robinson, prin.
  Taney MS, 4909 BRINKLEY ROAD   20748
    Regina Humaine, prin.
  Allenwood ES, 6300 HARLEY LN   20748
    Barbara Conley, prin.
  Chase ES, 5700 FISHER RD   20748
    Gerald Fondessy, prin.
  Green Valley ES, 2215 CHADWICK ST   20748
    James Quarles, prin.
  Hillcrest Heights ES, 4305 22ND PL   20748
    Jo Anne Thompson, prin.
  Middleton Valley ES, 4815 DALTON ST   20748
    Mary Jean Lawrence, prin.
  Overlook ES, 3298 CURTIS DR   20748
    Robert Griffin, prin.

Thurmont, Frederick Co., Pop. Code 5
  Frederick County SD
  Supt. – See Frederick
  MS, 408 E MAIN ST   21788 – Claire Kondig, prin.
  ES, 805 E MAIN ST   21788 – Retta Varkley, prin.

Tilghman, Talbot Co., Pop. Code 3
  Talbot County SD
  Supt. – See Easton
  ES   21671 – George Pringle, prin.

Timonium, Baltimore Co.
  Baltimore County SD
  Supt. – See Towson
  Lutherville/Timonium ES
    2001 EASTRIDGE RD   21093
    Frederick Brown, prin.
  Pinewood ES, 200 RICKSWOOD RD   21093
    Robert Stroble, prin.
  Pot Spring ES, 2410 SPRINGLAKE DR   21093
    Harold Slaughter, prin.

Towson, Baltimore Co., Pop. Code 8
  Baltimore County SD
  Sch. Sys. Enr. Code 8
  Supt. – Robert Dubel, 6901 N CHARLES ST   21204
  Loch Raven MS, 8101 LASALLE ROAD   21204
    William Jordan, prin.
  Pleasant Plains ES
    8300 PLEASANT PLAINS RD   21204
    Helen Kubik, prin.
  Other Schools – See Baldwin, Baltimore, Catonsville,
    Cockeysville, Essex, Freeland, Halethorpe,
    Kingsville, Lutherville, Monkton, Owings Mills,
    Parkton, Parkville, Perry Hall, Pikesville,
    Randallstown, Reisterstown, Sparks, Timonium,
    Upperco

Tracys Landing, Anne Arundel Co.
  Anne Arundel County SD
  Supt. – See Annapolis
  Traceys ES, 20 DEALE RD   20779
    Helen Cook, prin.

Trappe, Talbot Co., Pop. Code 3
  Talbot County SD
  Supt. – See Easton
  White Marsh ES   21673 – Denise Hershberger, prin.

Tylerton, Somerset Co.
  Somerset County SD
  Supt. – See Princess Anne
  ES   21866 – Alice Evans, prin.

Union Bridge, Carroll Co., Pop. Code 3
  Carroll County SD
  Supt. – See Westminster
  Wolfe ES   21791 – Gilaman Williar, prin.

Upperco, Carroll Co.
  Baltimore County SD
  Supt. – See Towson
  Fifth District ES, 3725 MT CARMEL RD   21155
    Frank Kaufmann, prin.

Upper Marlboro, Prince George's Co., Pop. Code 3
  Prince Georges County SD
  Sch. Sys. Enr. Code 9
  Supt. – John Murphy
    14201 SCHOOL LANE   20782
  Kettering MS, 65 HERRINGTON DRIVE   20772
    Eleanor White, prin.
  Madison MS, 7300 WOODYARD ROAD   20772
    Paul Lewis, prin.
  Arrowhead ES, 2300 SANDSBURY ROAD   20772
    G. Weslow, prin.
  Kettering ES, 11000 LAYTON ST   20772
    Lucy Marr, prin.
  Marlton ES, 8506 OLD COLONY DR S   20772
    C. Ridgely, prin.
  Mattaponi ES, 11701 DULEY STATION RD   20772
    Barbara Taylor, prin.
  Melwood ES, 7100 WOODYARD RD   20772
    George Yates, prin.
  Patuxent ES, 4410 BISHOPMILL DR   20772
    Clare Rozzell, prin.
  Williams ES, 9601 PRINCE PL   20772
    Patrick McGraw, prin.
  Other Schools – See Accokeek, Adelphi, Beltsville,
    Bladensburg, Bowie, Brandywine, Capitol Heights,
    Clinton, College Park, District Heights, Fort
    Washington, Greenbelt, Hyattsville, Landover,
    Landover Hills, Lanham-Seabrook, Laurel,
    Mitchellville, Mount Rainier, New Carrollton, Oxon
    Hill, Riverdale, Seabrook, Southern MD Facility,
    Suitland, Takoma Park, Temple Hills

  St. Mary of the Assumption ES
    4610 OLD LARGO ROAD   20772

Vienna, Dorchester Co., Pop. Code 2
  Dorchester County SD
  Supt. – See Cambridge
  ES   21869 – Barbara Murphy, prin.

Waldorf, Charles Co., Pop. Code 8
  Charles County SD
  Supt. – See La Plata
  Hanson MS, RURAL ROUTE 05 BOX 22D   20601
    J. Ronald Black, prin.
  Stoddert MS, SAINT CHARLES PKWY   20601
    William Wise, prin.
  Brown ES, UNIVERSITY AVE   20601
    Marvella McCall, prin.
  Daniel of St. Thomas Jenifer ES
    P O BOX 266   20604 – Alfred Richardson, prin.
  Malcolm ES, RURAL ROUTE 01 BOX 136   20601
    Gladys Camp, prin.
  Middleton ES, 1109 COPLEY AVE   20602
    Richard Barbone, prin.
  Mudd ES, STONE AVE   20601 – Eva Coffman, prin.
  Ryon ES, P O BOX 22B   20601
    Norma Delaney, prin.
  Turner ES, RURAL ROUTE 04 BOX 24   20601
    Adrienne Jennings, prin.

  St. Peter's ES, SAINT PETERS CHURCH RD   20601

Walkersville, Frederick Co., Pop. Code 4
  Frederick County SD
  Supt. – See Frederick
  MS, 55 FREDERICK ST   21793
    Bruce Brown, prin.
  ES, 83 FREDERICK ST   21793 – Larry Cassell, prin.

Westernport, Allegany Co., Pop. Code 5
  Allegany County SD
  Supt. – See Cumberland
  Bruce MS   21562 – David Malone, prin.
  ES   21562 – L. Blaine Watson, prin.

West Friendship, Howard Co., Pop. Code 2
  Howard County SD
  Supt. – See Ellicott City
  ES, 12500 FREDERICK ROAD   21794
    Leah Farmer, prin.

Westminster, Carroll Co., Pop. Code 6
  Carroll County SD
  Sch. Sys. Enr. Code 7
  Supt. – Edward Shilling, 55 N COURT ST   21157
  Westminster East MS, 100 LONGWELL AVE   21157
    D. Reck, prin.
  Westminster West MS, 60 MONROE ST   21157
    Harry Lambert, prin.
  Carroll ES, 3719 LITTLESTOWN PIKE   21157
    Pamela Ayers, prin.
  Moton ES, 1413 WASHINGTON RD   21157
    Curtis Schnorr, prin.
  Uniontown ES, 3455 UNIONTOWN RD   21157
    Mary Stong, prin.
  ES, 811 UNIONTOWN RD   21157
    Larry Thompson, prin.
  Winchester ES, CARROLL ST   21157
    Patricia Dorsey, prin.
  Winfield ES, 4401 SALEM BOTTOM RD   21157
    J. Mathias, prin.
  Other Schools – See Finksburg, Hampstead,
    Manchester, Mount Airy, New Windsor, Sykesville,
    Taneytown, Union Bridge

  St. John ES, 45 MONROE ST   21157

Westover, Somerset Co., Pop. Code 3
  Somerset County SD
  Supt. – See Princess Anne
  ES   21871 – Frank O'Rourke, prin.

White Hall, Harford Co.
  Harford County SD
  Supt. – See Bel Air
  Norrisville ES, 5302 NORRISVILLE RD   21161
    Stephen Hagenbuch, prin.

Willards, Wicomico Co., Pop. Code 3
  Wicomico County SD
  Supt. – See Salisbury
  ES   21874 – W. Hammond, prin.

Williamsport, Washington Co., Pop. Code 4
  Washington County SD
  Supt. – See Hagerstown
  Springfield MS, 305 E SUNSET AVE   21795
    Ralph Kline, prin.
  Hickory ES, RURAL ROUTE 02 BOX 139A   21795
    Joseph Byers, prin.
  ES, 1 N CLIFTON DR   21795
    Steven Bowers, prin.

Woodsboro, Frederick Co., Pop. Code 3
  Frederick County SD
  Supt. – See Frederick
  ES, 101 LIBERTY ROAD   21798 – Don Cline, prin.

Worton, Kent Co.
  Kent County SD
  Supt. – See Chestertown
  ES   21678 – Benjamin Hirsh, prin.

MASSACHUSETTS

PUBLIC, PRIVATE, AND PAROCHIAL ELEMENTARY SCHOOLS

Abington, Plymouth Co., Pop. Code 7
Abington SD
Sch. Sys. Enr. Code 4
Supt. – Chester Millett
   1071 WASHINGTON ST   02351
Frolio MS, 1071 WASHINGTON ST   02351
   Joseph Rosenthal, prin.
Center ES, THAXTER AVE   02351
   Joseph Eisenmann, prin.
North ES, ADAMS   02351 – Peter Giannards, prin.
Woodsdale ES, 128 CHESTNUT ST   02351
   Joseph Sergi, prin.

St. Bridget ES, 455 PLYMOUTH ST   02351

Acton, Middlesex Co., Pop. Code 7
Acton SD
Sch. Sys. Enr. Code 4
Supt. – Robert Kessler, 16 CHARTER ROAD   01720
Conant ES, 80 TAYLOR RD   01720
   Joan Little, prin.
Douglas ES, 21 ELM   01720 – M. Kaplowitz, prin.
Gates ES, 75 SPRUCE ST   01720
   James Palavras, prin.
McCarthy ES, CHARTER ROAD   01720
   Parker Damon, prin.

Acton-Boxborough SD
Sch. Sys. Enr. Code 4
Supt. – Robert Kessler, 16 CHARTER ROAD   01720
Grey Regional JHS, 16 CHARTER ROAD   01720
   Clifford Card, prin.

Boxborough SD
Sch. Sys. Enr. Code 2
Supt. – Norman Bossio
   MASSACHUSETTS AVE   01719
Blanchard Memorial ES
   MASSACHUSETTS AVE   01720
   Norman Bossio, prin.

Acushnet, Bristol Co., Pop. Code 6
Acushnet SD
Sch. Sys. Enr. Code 3
Supt. – John Souza, 130 MAIN ST   02743
Ford MS, 708 MIDDLE ROAD   02743
   John Tavares, prin.
ES, 800 MIDDLE RD   02743
   Christine Collins, prin.

St. Francis Xavier ES, 223 MAIN ST   02743

Adams, Berkshire Co., Pop. Code 7
Adams-Cheshire SD
Sch. Sys. Enr. Code 4
Supt. – William McLaren, 5 COLUMBIA ST   01220
Adams Memorial PS, COLUMBIA   01220
   Richard Moreau, prin.
Plunket IS, 14 COMMERCIAL ST   01220
   C. Love, prin.
Other Schools – See Cheshire

St. Stanislaus ES, 108 SUMMER ST   01220

Agawam, Hampden Co., Pop. Code 8
Agawam SD
Supt. – See Feeding Hills

MS, 68 MAIN ST   01001 – Ralph Zavarella, prin.
Clark ES, 65 OXFORD ST   01001
   Smith Rovelli, prin.
Phelps ES, 689 MAIN ST   01001
   William Miller, prin.

Allston, Suffolk Co.
Boston SD
Supt. – See Boston
Gardner ES, BRENTWOOD&ATHOL   02134
   Roland Doherty, prin.
Mann ES, 40 ARMINGTON ST   02134
   Gregory Toupouzis, prin.

St. Anthony ES, 57 HOLTON ST   02134

Amesbury, Essex Co., Pop. Code 7
Amesbury SD
Sch. Sys. Enr. Code 4
Supt. – Stephen Gerber, 15 SCHOOL ST   01913
MS, MAIN ST   01913 – Raymond Tiezzi, prin.
ES, 20 S HAMPTON RD   01913
   David Shaw, prin.
Cashman ES, FRIEND   01913 – Victor Atkins, prin.

Amherst, Hampshire Co., Pop. Code 8
Amherst SD
Sch. Sys. Enr. Code 4
Supt. – Donald Frizzle, 170 CHESTNUT ST   01002
Crocker Farm ES, 280 WEST ST   01002
   Justin O'Connor, prin.
Fort River ES, 70 S EAST ST   01002
   John Dalton, prin.
Wildwood ES, 71 STRONG ST   01002
   Nancy Morrison, prin.

Pelham SD
Sch. Sys. Enr. Code 1
Supt. – Donald Frizzle, CHESTNUT ST   01002
Pelham ES, AMHERST ROAD   01002
   Russel Vernon-Jones, prin.

The Common ES, P O BOX 52   01004

Andover, Essex Co., Pop. Code 8
Andover SD
Sch. Sys. Enr. Code 5
Supt. – K. Seifert, ANNS LANE   01810
Bancroft ES, BANCROFT   01810
   Iora Alexander, prin.
Sanborn ES, 84 LOVEJOY RD   01810
   Eileen Woods, prin.
South ES, WOBURN   01810 – Jade Reitman, prin.
West ES, 58 BEACON ST   01810
   John Coyle, prin.

St. Augustine ES, 26 CENTRAL ST   01810
The Pike ES Inc, SUNSET ROCK RD   01810

Arlington, Middlesex Co., Pop. Code 8
Arlington SD
Sch. Sys. Enr. Code 5
Supt. – Walter Devine, P O BOX 167   02174
Gibbs JHS, FOSTER ST   02174
   Paul Lamoureaux, prin.
Ottoson JHS, 63 ACTON ST   02174
   Edmund Mahoney, prin.

Bishop ES, 25 COLUMBIA RD   02174
   Joan Warren, prin.
Brackett ES, 66 EASTERN AVE   02174
   Vito Sammarco, prin.
Dallin ES, 185 FLORENCE AVE   02174
   Robert Lynch, prin.
Hardy ES, 52 LAKE ST   02174
   Barbara Long, prin.
Peirce ES, PARK AVE EXIT   02174
   Marilyn Flaherty, prin.
Stratton ES, 180 MOUNTAIN AVE   02174
   Bernard Walsh, prin.
Thompson ES, 60 N UNION ST   02174
   Michael McCabe, prin.

Ecole Bilingue ES, 17 IRVING ST   02174
St. Agnes ES, 51 MEDFORD ST   02174

Ashburnham, Worcester Co., Pop. Code 5
Ashburnham-Westminster SD
Sch. Sys. Enr. Code 4
Supt. – Raymond Glynn, P O BOX 724   01430
Other Schools – See South Ashburnham, Westminster

Ashby, Middlesex Co., Pop. Code 4
North Middlesex SD
Supt. – See Townsend
ES, MAIN   01431 – Marsha Guy, prin.

Ashfield, Franklin Co., Pop. Code 4
Ashfield-Plainfield Regional SD
Supt. – See Shelburne Falls
Sanderson Academy ES, BUCKLAND AVE   01330
   Martha Conani, prin.

Ashland, Middlesex Co., Pop. Code 6
Ashland SD
Sch. Sys. Enr. Code 4
Supt. – B. Ruthfield, 90 CONCORD ST   01721
Mindess MS, 90 CONCORD ST   01721
   Joseph Apicella, prin.
Warren ES, 73 FRUIT ST   01721
   Robert Heaton, prin.

Athol, Worcester Co., Pop. Code 7
Athol-Royalston SD
Sch. Sys. Enr. Code 4
Supt. – James Kelley, 584 MAIN ST   01331
JHS, 494 SCHOOL ST   01331
   Wilfred Gallagher, prin.
Bigelow ES, 129 ALLEN ST   01331
   William Colo, prin.
Pleasant Street ES, 1060 PLEASANT ST   01331
   Allen Hodgdon, prin.
Riverbend MS, 174 RIVERBEND ST   01331
   William Colo, prin.
Sanders Street ES, 314 SANDERS ST   01331
   Edward Hayne, prin.
Silver Lake ES, 245 SILVER LAKE ST   01331
   Martha Blackmer, prin.
Other Schools – See Royalston

Narragansett SD
Supt. – See Otter River
Phillipston Memorial ES
   RURAL ROUTE 01   01331
   Saverio Kaczmarczyk, prin.

Attleboro, Bristol Co., Pop. Code 8
Attleboro SD
Sch. Sys. Enr. Code 6
Supt. – Bartholomew O'Connor
  RATHBUN WILLARD DRIVE   02703
Brennan MS, 135 COUNTY ST   02703
  Edward McCarthy, prin.
Thatcher MS, JAMES ST   02703
  Charles Forester, prin.
Finberg ES, 1025 S MAIN ST   02703
  Roberta Bristow, prin.
Fine ES, 790 OAK HILL AVE   02730
  Dolores Fitzgerald, prin.
Studley ES, RATHBUN WILLARD DR   02703
  William O'Neil, prin.
Willet ES, 32 WATSON AVE   02703
  Mary Fishbeck, prin.
Other Schools – See South Attleboro

St. John Evangelist ES, 11 HODGES ST   02703

Auburn, Worcester Co., Pop. Code 7
Auburn SD
Sch. Sys. Enr. Code 4
Supt. – Joanne Newcombe, 5 WEST ST   01501
JHS, 10 SWANSON ROAD   01501
  W. Richard Granger, prin.
Bancroft MS, OXFORD & VINAL   01501
  Robert Graham, prin.
Bryn Mawr ES, 35 SWANSON RD   01501
  Gerald Poulin, prin.
Pakachoag MS, 110 PAKACHOAG ST   01501
  Rocco Morano, prin.
Stone ES, 10 CHURCH ST   01501
  Robert Morway, prin.

Auburndale, Suffolk Co.
Newton SD
Supt. – See Newtonville
Burr ES, 171 PINE ST   02166
  Barbara Carlson, prin.
Williams ES, 141 GROVE ST   02166
  Christopher Martes, prin.

Avon, Norfolk Co., Pop. Code 6
Avon SD
Sch. Sys. Enr. Code 3
Supt. – Joseph Rappa, BUCKLEY CENTER   02322
Crowley MS, FAGAN DRIVE   02322
  Jane Macdonald, prin.
Butler ES, PATRICK CLARK DR   02322
  Robert Adams, prin.

Ayer, Middlesex Co., Pop. Code 6
Ayer SD
Sch. Sys. Enr. Code 5
Supt. – R. Neville Markham
  141 WASHINGTON ST   01432
JHS, 141 WASHINGTON ST   01432
  Louise Gaskins, prin.
Ft. Devens ES, ANTIETAM   01433
  Gerald Millson, prin.
Hilltop ES, 119 WASHINGTON ST   01432
  Paul Farley, prin.
Page MS, WASHINGTON   01432
  Donald Scullane, prin.

Baldwinville, Worcester Co., Pop. Code 4
Narragansett SD
Supt. – See Otter River
ES, P O BOX 24   01436 – Rodney McDowell, prin.

Barre, Worcester Co., Pop. Code 5
Quabbin SD
Sch. Sys. Enr. Code 4
Supt. – Maureen Marshall, WEST ST   01005
Ruggles Lane MS, RUGGLES LN   01005
  John Cirelli, prin.
Other Schools – See Gilbertville, Hubbardston, New
  Braintree, Oakham, South Barre

Becket, Berkshire Co., Pop. Code 4
Central Berkshire SD
Supt. – See Dalton
Becket Consol ES, MAPLE   01223
  C. Sharron, prin.

Bedford, Middlesex Co., Pop. Code 7
Bedford SD
Sch. Sys. Enr. Code 4
Supt. – Joseph Buckley, 9 MUDGE WAY   01730
Glenn MS, 99 MCMAHON ROAD   01730
  Laurence Aronstein, prin.
Davis ES, DAVIS ROAD   01730
  Ronald Barbagallo, prin.
Lane ES, SWEETWATER AVE   01730
  Robert Hentz, prin.

Lincoln SD
Supt. – See Lincoln
Hanscom MS, HANSCOM A F B   01730
  Ronald Hadge, prin.
Hanscom PS, HANSCOM A F B   01730
  Sally Webber, prin.

Belchertown, Hampshire Co., Pop. Code 6
Belchertown SD
Sch. Sys. Enr. Code 4
Supt. – Robert Byard, S MAIN BOX 841   01007
Chestnut Hill Community MS
  59 STATE ST   01007 – Joe Giroux, prin.
Center ES, MAPLE   01007 – Lawrence Barrett, prin.
Cold Spring ES, SOUTH MAIN   01007
  Lawrence Barrett, prin.
Franklin ES, FRANKLIN   01007
  Lawrence Barrett, prin.

Bellingham, Norfolk Co., Pop. Code 7
Bellingham SD
Sch. Sys. Enr. Code 4
Supt. – Peter Vangel, 11 S MAIN ST   02019
Macy ES, MONIQUE DR   02019
  Annette Packard, prin.
South District ES, HARPIN   02019
  Joseph Dipietro, prin.
Stallbrook ES, 338 HARTFORD AVE   02019
  James Turner, prin.

Belmont, Middlesex Co., Pop. Code 8
Belmont SD
Sch. Sys. Enr. Code 5
Supt. – Peter Holland, 644 PLEASANT ST   02178
Chenery MS, 95 WASHINGTON ST   02178
  Marvin Shapiro, prin.
Brook ES, 97 WATERHOUSE RD   02178
  Loretta Warden, prin.
Burbank ES, 266 SCHOOL ST   02178
  Arthur Bush, prin.
Butler ES, 90 WHITE ST   02178
  Barbara Hunt, prin.
Wellington ES, 121 ORCHARD ST   02178
  Charles Crisafulli, prin.

Belmont Day ES, 55 DAY SCHOOL LN   02178

Berkley, Bristol Co., Pop. Code 5
Berkley SD
Supt. – See North Dighton
MS, BERKLEY COMMON   02780
  Edward G. Canuel, prin.
Canuel PS, NORTH MAIN   02780
  Edward Canuel, prin.

Berlin, Worcester Co., Pop. Code 4
Berlin SD
Supt. – See Boylston
Berlin Memorial ES, LINDEN   01503
  Linda Casaceli, prin.

Bernardston, Franklin Co., Pop. Code 4
Bernardston SD
Supt. – See Northfield
ES, SCHOOL ROAD   01337 – Margo Marvin, prin.

Beverly, Essex Co., Pop. Code 8
Beverly SD
Sch. Sys. Enr. Code 5
Supt. – Jean Perron, 4 COLON ST   01915
Briscoe MS, 7 SOHIER ROAD   01915
  John Lapsley, prin.
Memorial MS, 502 CABOT ST   01915
  Ken Stowe, prin.
Ayers/Ryal Side ES, WOODLAND AVE   01915
  David Disessa, prin.
Beadle ES, 415 RANTOUL ST   01915
  Edward McDonald, prin.
Centerville ES, 17 HULL ST   01915
  John Grillo, prin.
Cove ES, EINSENHOWER AVE   01915
  Peter Sarkunas, prin.
Edwards ES, 45 RANTOUL ST   01915
  Francesca Steele, prin.
Hannah ES, R41 BRIMBAL AVE   01915
  Norman Pfaff, prin.
McKay ES, 131 MCKAY ST   01915
  Judith Alexander, prin.
North Beverly ES, PUTNAM   01915
  Thomas Kokos, prin.

Shore Country Day ES, 545 CABOT ST   01915
St. John Evangelist ES, 111 NEW BALCH ST   01915
St. Mary ES, 15 CHAPMAN   01915
Urquhart ES, 74 HART ST   01915

Billerica, Middlesex Co., Pop. Code 8
Billerica SD
Sch. Sys. Enr. Code 6
Supt. – Robert Calabrese
  390 BOSTON ROAD   01821
Locke MS, 132 ALLEN ROAD   01821
  Rich Loranger, prin.
Marshall MS, 32 FLOYD ST   01821
  Stan Jekanoski, prin.
Ditson ES, 793 BOSTON RD   01821
  William Downing, prin.
Hajjar ES, ROGERS   01862 – Anthony Larosa, prin.
Kennedy ES, 26 KIMBROUGH RD   01821
  James Dumas, prin.
Parker ES, 52 RIVER ST   01821
  Richard Cogan, prin.
Vining ES, 121 LEXINGTON RD   01821
  Frank Callahan, prin.
Other Schools – See North Billerica

Blackstone, Worcester Co., Pop. Code 6
Blackstone-Millville SD
Sch. Sys. Enr. Code 4
Supt. – Thomas J. Cullen, LINCOLN ST   01504
Kennedy ES, LINCOLN   01504
  Robert Keefe, prin.
Maloney MS, MAIN   01504 – John Pilibosian, prin.
Other Schools – See Millville

Blandford, Hampden Co., Pop. Code 4
Gateway SD
Supt. – See Huntington
ES, RUSSELL ROAD   01008
  Cynthia Walowicz, prin.

Bolton, Worcester Co., Pop. Code 5
Bolton SD
Sch. Sys. Enr. Code 2
Supt. – Arthur Bettencourt, 692 MAIN ST   01740

Emerson ES, 692 MAIN ST   01740
  Alfred Rocci, prin.

Bondsville, Hampden Co., Pop. Code 4
Palmer SD
Supt. – See Palmer
ES, 61 MAIN   01009 – Ronald Laviolette, prin.

Boston, Suffolk Co., Pop. Code 11
Boston SD
Sch. Sys. Enr. Code 8
Supt. – Laval Wilson, 26 COURT ST   02108
Mackey MS, 90 WARREN AVE   02116
  Pamela Houlares, prin.
Blackstone ES, 380 SHAWMUT AVE   02118
  William Ubinas, prin.
Eliot ES, 16 CHARTER ST   02113
  Edmund Cardoni, prin.
Farragut ES, 10 FENWOOD RD   02115
  George Hermiston, prin.
Hurley ES, 70 WORCESTER ST   02118
  Nydia Mendez, prin.
Quincy ES, 885 WASHINGTON ST   02111
  Charles Gibbons, prin.
Other Schools – See Allston, Brighton, Brookline,
  Charlestown, Dorchester, East Boston, Grove Hall,
  Hyde Park, Jamaica Plain, Mattapan, Roslindale,
  Roxbury, South Boston, West Roxbury

Advent ES, 17 BRIMMER ST   02108
Cathedral ES, 595 HARRISON AVE   02118
St. John ES, 9 MOON ST   02113
St. John Evangelist ES, 122 RINDGE AVE   02140
St. Mary ES, 121 CRESCENT ST   02169

Bourne, Barnstable Co., Pop. Code 7
Bourne SD
Sch. Sys. Enr. Code 5
Supt. – John O'Brien, 36 SANDWICH ROAD   02532
Coady MS, 85 COTUIT ROAD   02532
  Paul Innis, prin.
Lyle MS, 5700 LEMAY AVE   02542
  William Wibel, prin.
Stone MS, 5400 LINDBERG AVE   02542
  Mary Fuller, prin.
Hoxie ES, RURAL ROUTE 01   02532
  Joseph Sullivan, prin.
Otis Memorial ES, 5500 CURTIS BLVD   02542
  Frederick Dunbury, prin.
Peebles ES, 70 TROWBRIDGE RD   02532
  Donald Morrissey, prin.

Boxford, Essex Co., Pop. Code 6
Boxford SD
Supt. – See Topsfield
Cole ES, MIDDLETON ROAD   01921
  Nancy Diamonti, prin.
Spofford Pond MS, SPOFFORD ROAD   01921
  Bernard Creeden, prin.

Boylston, Worcester Co., Pop. Code 5
Berlin SD
Sch. Sys. Enr. Code 2
Supt. – Donald Dupont, MAIN ST   01505
Other Schools – See Berlin

Boylston SD
Sch. Sys. Enr. Code 2
Supt. – Donald Dupont, MAIN ST   01505
ES, 200 SEWALL ST   01505
  Stephen Keating, prin.

Bradford, Essex Co.

Sacred Hearts ES, 31 S CHESTNUT ST   01835

Braintree, Norfolk Co., Pop. Code 8
Braintree SD
Sch. Sys. Enr. Code 5
Supt. – John Monbouquette
  482 WASHINGTON ST   02184
East MS, 305 RIVER ST   02184
  Kenneth W. Peters, prin.
South MS, 232 PEACH ST   02184
  Ed Arcikowski, prin.
Highlands ES, 144 WILDWOOD AVE   02184
  Raymond Willock, prin.
Lakeside ES, 99 LAKESIDE DR   02184
  Mary Flaherty, prin.
Liberty ES, 49 PROCTOR RD   02184
  Michael Malone, prin.
Monatiquot ES, 25 BROW AVE   02184
  Louise Moline, prin.
Morrison ES, 15 MAYFLOWER RD   02184
  Joseph De Sario, prin.
Ross ES, 20 HAYWARD   02184
  Elizabeth Baker, prin.

St. Francis Assisi ES
  850 WASHINGTON ST   02184

Brewster, Barnstable Co.
Brewster SD
Supt. – See Orleans
ES, P O BOX S   02631 – Richard Bridgwood, prin.

Bridgewater, Plymouth Co., Pop. Code 7
Bridgewater SD
Sch. Sys. Enr. Code 4
Supt. – Stephen Childs, 35 SOUTH ST   02324
Williams JHS, 200 SOUTH ST   02324
  Rob Blakeley, prin.
Burnell Laboratory ES, HOOPER ST   02324
  L. Traw, prin.
Hunt ES, 26 SCHOOL ST   02324
  Paul O'Brien, prin.

McElwain ES, 250 MAIN ST 02324
  Donald Delutis, prin.
Williams ES, 200 SOUTH 02324
  Bridget Boyle, prin.

Brighton, Suffolk Co.
Boston SD
Supt. – See Boston
Edison JHS, 60 GLENMONT ROAD 02135
  Domenic Amaro, prin.
Taft MS, 20 WARREN ST 02135
  Michael Fung, prin.
Garfield ES, 95 BEECHCROFT ST 02135
  Nicholas Diaguardi, prin.
Hamilton ES, 196 STRATHMORE RD 02135
  John Molloy, prin.
Winship ES, 54 DIGHTON ST 02135
  Gerald McGrath, prin.

St. Columbkille School, 25 ARLINGTON ST 02135
Our Lady Presentation ES, 3 TREMONT ST 02135

Brimfield, Hampden Co., Pop. Code 4
Brimfield SD
Supt. – See Sturbridge
ES, WALES ROAD 01010 – Brady Fisher, prin.

Brockton, Plymouth Co., Pop. Code 8
Brockton SD
Sch. Sys. Enr. Code 7
Supt. – Manthala George, 43 CRESCENT ST 02401
East JHS, 464 CENTER ST 02402
  Ed Cheromcha, prin.
North JHS, 108 OAK 02401
  Elizabeth O'Hearn, prin.
South JHS, 105 KEITH AVE 02401
  Rich Williams, prin.
West JHS, 271 WEST ST 02401
  Eugene Franciosi, prin.
Arnone ES, 175 WARREN AVE 02401
  Richard Flemming, prin.
Ashfield ES, 225 COE RD 02402
  Harold McDonald, prin.
Brookfield ES, JON DR 02402
  James O'Loughlin, prin.
Davis ES, 380 PLAIN ST 02402
  Gerald Shea, prin.
Downey ES, 55 ELECTRIC AVE 02402
  Robert Casey, prin.
Franklin ES, SAWTELL AVE 02402
  Frederic Stevens, prin.
Gilmore ES, 150 CLINTON ST 02402
  Richard Capone, prin.
Goddard ES, 20 UNION AVE 02401
  Frank Dunbar, prin.
Hancock ES, 125 PEARL ST 02401
  Leo Bergeron, prin.
Huntington ES, 1121 WARREN AVE 02401
  George Bezreh, prin.
Kennedy ES, 906 ASH ST 02401
  Paul Smiegal, prin.
Paine ES, 211 CRESCENT ST 02402
  Charles Crivellaro, prin.
Raymond ES, 125 OAK ST 02401
  John Scanlon, prin.
Whitman ES, GIFFORD 02401
  Robert Brennan, prin.
Winthrop ES, 478 N MAIN ST 02401
  David Cohen, prin.

New England Baptist Academy
  34 NILSSON ST 02401
Brockton Christian ES, 1367 MAIN ST 02401
Sacred Heart ES, 283 COURT ST 02402
St. Casimir ES, 26 SAINT CASIMIR AVE 02402
St. Edward ES, 631 N MAIN ST 02401

Brookfield, Worcester Co., Pop. Code 4
Brookfield SD
Supt. – See Sturbridge
ES, 1 CENTRAL 01506 – Linda Denault, prin.

Brookline, Norfolk Co., Pop. Code 8
Boston SD
Supt. – See Boston
Baldwin ES, 121 COREY RD 02146
  Charles James, prin.

Brookline SD
Sch. Sys. Enr. Code 6
Supt. – James Walsh
  333 WASHINGTON ST 02146
Devotion ES, 345 HARVARD ST 02146
  Gerald Kaplan, prin.
Driscoll ES, 64 WESTBOURNE TER 02146
  Carol Schraft, prin.
Lawrence ES, 27 FRANCIS ST 02146
  Nathan Purpel, prin.
Lincoln ES, 194 BOYLSTON ST 02146
  Pamela Capege, prin.
Pierce ES, 50 SCHOOL ST 02146
  Kristin Field, prin.
Runkle ES, 50 DRUCE ST 02146
  Martin Sleeper, prin.
Other Schools – See Chestnut Hill

Maimonides School, 34 PHILBRICK ROAD 02146
New England Hebrew Academy
  1845 COMMONWEALTH AVE 02146
Dexter ES, 20 NEWTON ST 02146
St. Mary of Assumption ES, 75 HARVARD 02146
The Park ES, 171 GODDARD AVE 02146

Burlington, Middlesex Co., Pop. Code 7
Burlington SD
Sch. Sys. Enr. Code 5
Supt. – Thomas Michael, 21 CENTER ST 01803
Simunds MS, WINN ST 01803
  Rich Connors, prin.
Fox Hill ES, FOX HILL ROAD 01803
  Gloria Lombard, prin.
Memorial ES, WINN 01803
  Ann McNammara, prin.
Pine Glen ES, WILMINGTON ROAD 01803
  Stephen Preston, Jr., prin.
Wildwood ES, FRANCIS WYMAN ROAD 01803
  Paul Cabral, prin.

Byfield, Essex Co.
Newbury SD
Sch. Sys. Enr. Code 3
Supt. – Gerald Kohn, P O BOX 56 01922
ES, LUNT 01922 – Richard Joy, prin.
Other Schools – See Newbury

Rowley SD
Sch. Sys. Enr. Code 2
Supt. – Gerald Kohn, P O BOX 56 01922
Other Schools – See Rowley

Salisbury SD
Sch. Sys. Enr. Code 3
Supt. – Gerald Kohn, P O BOX 36 01922
Other Schools – See Salisbury

Cambridge, Middlesex Co., Pop. Code 8
Cambridge SD
Supt. – See Cambridge C
Agassiz ES, 28 SACRAMENTO 02138
  Katherine Cox, prin.
Fitzgerald ES, 70 RINDGE AVE 02140
  Paul Mahoney, prin.
Fletcher ES, 89 ELM ST 02139
  Marilyn McGinn, prin.
Graham/Parks ES, 15 UPTON ST 02139
  Leonard Solo, Sr., prin.
Haggerty ES, 110 CUSHING ST 02138
  Katherine Synnott, prin.
Harrington ES, 850 CAMBRIDGE ST 02141
  Francis Foley, prin.
King ES, 100 PUTNAM AVE 02139
  John Caulfield, prin.
Longfellow ES, 359 BROADWAY 02139
  Margaret Carroll, prin.
Maynard ES, 225 WINDSOR ST 02139
  Raymond Dancy, prin.
Morse ES, 40 GRANITE ST 02139
  James Coady, prin.
Peabody ES, 44 LINNAEAN ST 02138
  Richard Calnan, prin.
Tobin ES, 197 VASSALL LN 02138
  Daniel Kelly, prin.

Buckingham Browne & Nichols HS
  GERRYS LANDING ROAD 02138
Blessed Sacrament ES, 12 CPL MOTERNAN 02139
Cambridge Friends ES, 5 CADBURY RD 02140
Fayerweather Street ES
  748 FAYERWEATHER 02138
Shady Hill ES, 178 COOLIDGE HL 02138
St. Peter ES, 96 CONCORD AVE 02138

Cambridge C, Middlesex Co.
Cambridge SD
Sch. Sys. Enr. Code 6
Supt. – Mary Lou Mcgrath
  159 THORNDIKE ST 02141
Kennedy MS, 158 SPRING ST 02141
  Mary Mroz, prin.
Other Schools – See Cambridge

Canton, Norfolk Co., Pop. Code 7
Canton SD
Sch. Sys. Enr. Code 5
Supt. – Peter Capernanos
  960 WASHINGTON ST 02021
Galvin MS, 55 PECUNIT ST 02021
  Charles Howard, prin.
Hansen ES, 25 PECUNIT ST 02021
  Lawrence Walsh, prin.
Kennedy ES, 100 DEDHAM ST 02021
  Judith Manthel, prin.
Luce ES, 45 INDEPENDENCE ST 02021
  Susan Rogers, prin.

St. John ES, 698 WASHINGTON ST 02021

Carlisle, Middlesex Co., Pop. Code 5
Carlisle SD
Sch. Sys. Enr. Code 3
Supt. – Matthew King, CHURCH ST 01741
ES, CHURCH 01741 – Richard Deppe, prin.

Carver, Plymouth Co., Pop. Code 6
Carver SD
Sch. Sys. Enr. Code 4
Supt. – Martin Hanley, MAIN ST 02330
ES, MAIN 02330 – Fred Morris, prin.

Centerville, Barnstable Co., Pop. Code 4
Barnstable SD
Supt. – See Hyannis
ES, 658 BAY LN 02632 – David Crosby, prin.

Charlemont, Franklin Co., Pop. Code 4
Hawlemont SD
Supt. – See Shelburne Falls
Hawlemont Regional ES, SCHOOL 01339
  Gwen Van Dorp, prin.

Charlestown, Suffolk Co.
Boston SD
Supt. – See Boston
Edwards MS, 28 WALKER ST 02129
  Greg Thomas, prin.
Harvard-Kent ES, 50 BUNKER HILL 02129
  Joanne McManus, prin.
Warren-Prescott ES, 50 SCHOOL ST 02129
  Marilyn Kiely, prin.

St. Catherine ES, 13 TUFTS ST 02129
St. Francis Desales ES
  340 BUNKER HILL ST 02129

Charlton, Worcester Co., Pop. Code 6
Dudley-Charlton Regional SD
Supt. – See Dudley
ES, BURLINGAME ROAD 01507
  Joseph Tripp, prin.
IS, MAIN 01507 – John Prouty, prin.
City Grade ES, ROUTE 20 01507
  Joseph Tripp, prin.

Chatham, Barnstable Co., Pop. Code 6
Chatham SD
Sch. Sys. Enr. Code 3
Supt. – Allen Brown
  127 OLD HARBOR ROAD 02633
ES, 702 MAIN ST 02633 – Richard Davis, prin.

Chelmsford, Middlesex Co., Pop. Code 8
Chelmsford SD
Sch. Sys. Enr. Code 6
Supt. – William Mullen
  75 GRANITEVILLE ROAD 01824
McCarthy MS, 250 NORTH ROAD 01824
  Robert Bennett, prin.
Byam ES, MAPLE ROAD 01824
  Richard Bergeron, prin.
South Row ES, 250 BOSTON RD 01824
  Richard Hentz, prin.
Westlands ES, 170 DALTON RD 01824
  Robert Noy, prin.
Other Schools – See North Chelmsford

Chelsea, Suffolk Co., Pop. Code 8
Chelsea SD
Sch. Sys. Enr. Code 5
Supt. – J. Herlihy, 208 CITY HALL 02150
Williams JHS, WALNUT ST 02150
  Anthony Digregorio, prin.
Burke ES, SPENCER AVE 02150
  John Andreadis, prin.
Prattville ES, WASHINGTON AVE 02150
  Richard Denning, prin.
Shurtleff ES, 76 CONGRESS AVE 02150
  Carol Murphy, prin.
Williams ES, WALNUT 02150
  Anthony Digregorio, prin.

Saint Rose School, 580 BROADWAY ST 02150
Assumption ES, 49 CLARK AVE 02150
St. Rose ES, 580 BROADWAY 02150
St. Stanislaus ES, 179 CHESTNUT ST 02150

Cheshire, Berkshire Co., Pop. Code 5
Adams-Cheshire SD
Supt. – See Adams
ES, CHURCH 01225 – Paul Sullivan, prin.

Chester, Berkshire Co.
Gateway SD
Supt. – See Huntington
ES, MAIN 01011 – Johanna McKenna, prin.

Chesterfield, Hampshire Co., Pop. Code 3
Chesterfield SD
Supt. – See Westhampton
Davenport ES, MAIN 01012
  Donald MacLeod, prin.

Chestnut Hill, Suffolk Co.
Brookline SD
Supt. – See Brookline
Baker ES, 205 BEVERLY RD 02167
  Thomas Cavanagh, prin.
Heath ES, 100 ELIOT ST 02167
  Ethel Sadowsky, prin.

Brimmer & May School
  69 MIDDLESEX ROAD 02167
Chestnut Hill ES, 428 HAMMOND ST 02167
Mt. Alvernia ES, 20 MANET RD 02167

Chicopee, Hampden Co., Pop. Code 8
Chicopee SD
Sch. Sys. Enr. Code 6
Supt. – Herbert Curry, 180 BROADWAY ST 01020
Bellamy MS, 314 PENDLETON AVE 01020
  Rita Rodden, prin.
Barry ES, LAGADIA 01020 – Peter Clarke, prin.
Belcher ES, 176 EAST ST 01013
  Joseph Kosiorek, prin.
Bowe ES, 115 HAMPDEN ST 01013
  Barbara Cove, prin.
Bowie ES, WESTOVER AFB 01022
  Norman Burgess, prin.
Chapin ES, 40 MEADOW ST 01013
  Evelyn Crevier, prin.
Lambert-Lavoie ES, 91 KENDALL ST 01020
  Eugene Krupa, prin.
Litwin ES, 10 MURPHY LN 01020
  Normand Girourd, prin.
Stefanik ES, 720 MEADOW ST 01013
  John Dowd, prin.

Streiber Memorial ES, TELEGRAPH AVE 01020
Francis Driscoll, prin.
_____

Assumption ES, 120 SPRINGFIELD ST 01013
Holy Name ES, 63 SOUTH ST 01013
Mt. Carmel ES, 35 MOUNT CARMEL AVE 01013
St. George ES, 33 MAPLE ST 01020
St. Joan of Arc ES, 587 GRATTAN ST 01020
St. Patrick's ES, 125 MONTGOMERY ST 01020
St. Stanislaus ES, 534 FRONT ST 01013

Chilmark, Dukes Co., Pop. Code 2
Chilmark SD
Supt. – See Vineyard Haven
Menemsha ES, P O BOX 639 02535
Mary Jacobson, prin.

Clinton, Worcester Co., Pop. Code 7
Clinton SD
Sch. Sys. Enr. Code 4
Supt. – Brendon J. Bailey, 100 CHURCH ST 01510
MS, 100 W BOYLSTON ST 01510
Francis Murphy, prin.
ES, 150 SCHOOL ST 01510 – Patrick Burke, prin.
_____

Our Lady Jasna Gora ES, 128 FRANKLIN ST 01510

Cohasset, Norfolk Co., Pop. Code 6
Cohasset SD
Sch. Sys. Enr. Code 4
Supt. – Stephen Hart, 143 POND ST 02025
Deer Hill MS, 206 SOHIER ST 02025
Kenneth Ekberg, prin.
Osgood ES, 35 RIPLEY RD 02025
John Creamer, prin.

Colrain, Franklin Co., Pop. Code 4
Buckland Colrain Shelburn SD
Supt. – See Shelburne Falls
Colrain Central ES, JACKSONVILLE ROAD 01340
David Rempell, prin.

Concord, Middlesex Co., Pop. Code 7
Concord SD
Sch. Sys. Enr. Code 4
Supt. – Thomas Scott, 120 MERIAM ROAD 01742
Concord Peabody MS
1231 OLD MARLBORO ROAD 01742
Thomas Scott, prin.
Concord Sanborn MS
835 OLD MARLBORO ROAD 01742
Thomas Scott, prin.
Alcott ES, LAUREL 01742
Philip Benincasa, prin.
Thoreau ES, 29 PRAIRIE ST 01742
Joe Griffith, prin.
Willard ES, 185 POWDER MILL RD 01742
Richard Ford, prin.
_____

Nashoba Brooks ES
200 STRAWBERRY HILL RD 01742

Conway, Franklin Co., Pop. Code 4
Conway SD
Supt. – See South Deerfield
ES, SCHOOL 01341 – Richard Dacey, prin.

Cotuit, Barnstable Co., Pop. Code 4
Barnstable SD
Supt. – See Hyannis
MS, 250 OLD OYSTER RD 02635
Jane Sheckells, prin.

Cummington, Hampshire Co., Pop. Code 3
Central Berkshire SD
Supt. – See Dalton
MS, MAIN ST 01026 – Jane Allen, prin.

Cuttyhunk, Dukes Co.
Goshold SD
Supt. – See North Dighton
ES, CUTTYHUNK IS 02713
Theresa Cronin, prin.

Dalton, Berkshire Co., Pop. Code 6
Central Berkshire SD
Sch. Sys. Enr. Code 4
Supt. – John Jangro, UNION BLOCK MAIN 01226
Nessacus MS, 120 FIRST ST 01226
Lee Brown, prin.
Craneville ES, 95 PARK AVE 01226
K. Koza, prin.
Other Schools – See Becket, Cummington, Hinsdale,
Windsor
_____

St. Agnes ES, 56 CARSON AVE 01226

Danvers, Essex Co., Pop. Code 7
Danvers SD
Sch. Sys. Enr. Code 5
Supt. – Calvin Cleveland, 64 CABOT RD 01923
Dunn JHS, 60 CABOT RD 01923
Paul Coleman, prin.
Great Oak ES, 76 PICKERING 01923
Robert Tivnan, prin.
Highlands ES, 190 HOBART ST 01923
Dorothea Gemallaro, prin.
Riverside ES, 95 LIBERTY ST 01923
Dorothea Gemallaro, prin.
Smith ES, 15 LOBAO DR 01923
Albert Robinson,Jr., prin.
Thorpe ES, AVON ROAD 01923
John McMath, prin.
_____

St. Mary Annunciation ES, 20 OTIS ST 01923

Dedham, Norfolk Co., Pop. Code 8
Dedham SD
Sch. Sys. Enr. Code 5
Supt. – Thomas Curran, 30 WHITING AVE 02026
MS, 86 WHITING AVE 02026
Michael Rafferty, prin.
Avery ES, 123 HIGH ST 02026
Regina Tierney, prin.
Greenlodge ES, 191 GREENLODGE ST 02026
Joanne Benton, prin.
Oakdale ES, 141 CEDAR ST 02026
Robert Irons, prin.
Riverdale ES, 143 NEEDHAM ST 02026
John Raffa, prin.
_____

Dedham Country Day ES
80 SANDY VALLEY RD 02026

Deerfield, Franklin Co., Pop. Code 5
Deerfield SD
Supt. – See South Deerfield
Old Deerfield ES, MEMORIAL 01342
Edward Trzcienski, prin.
_____

The Bement ES, P O BOX N 01342

Dennis Port, Barnstable Co., Pop. Code 4
Dennis-Yarmouth SD
Supt. – See South Yarmouth
Baker ES, P O BOX 85 02639
Donald Eldredge, prin.

Dighton, Bristol Co., Pop. Code 6
Dighton-Rehoboth SD
Supt. – See North Dighton
Dighton ES, 1250 SOMERSET AVE 02715
Paul Swett, prin.

Dorchester, Suffolk Co., Pop. Code 9
Boston SD
Supt. – See Boston
Cleveland MS, 11 CHARLES ST 02122
Bill Abbott, prin.
Holmes MS, 40 SCHOOL ST 02124
Edward Mabardi, prin.
King MS, 77 LAWRENCE AVE 02121
James Watson, prin.
McCormack MS, 315 MOUNT VERNON ST 02125
Robert Martin, prin.
Thompson MS, 100 MAXWELL ST 02124
Ron Spratling, prin.
Wilson MS, 18 CROFTLAND AVE 02124
Michael Anderson, prin.
Clap ES, 35 HARVEST ST 02125
Ralph D'Angelo, prin.
Dever ES, 325 MT VERNON ST 02125
Mary Sullivan, prin.
Dickerman ES, 206 MAGNOLIA ST 02121
Mildred Griffith, prin.
Endicott ES, 2 MCLELLAN ST 02121
Michael Berrigan, prin.
Everett ES, 71 PLEASANT ST 02125
Robert Glennon, prin.
Fifield ES, 25 DUNBAR AVE 02124
Daniel Walsh, prin.
Greenwood ES, 189 GLENWAY ST 02121
Leo Howard, prin.
Hernandez ES, 61 SCHOOL ST 02119
Margarita Muniz, prin.
Holland ES, 85 OLNEY ST 02121
Mary Daniels, prin.
Kenny ES, 19 OAKTON AVE 02122
William Hart, prin.
Lee ES, 155 TALBOT AVE 02124
Frances Kelley, prin.
Marshall ES, 35 WESTVILLE ST 02124
Louis Tobasky, prin.
Mather ES, MEETING HOUSE HILL 02122
William Connor, prin.
Murphy ES, 1 WORRELL ST 02122
John Hughes, prin.
O'Hearn ES, 1669 DORCHESTER AVE 02122
Gladys De Costa, prin.
Russell ES, 750 COLUMBIA RD 02125
Archie Walsh, prin.
Shaw ES, 429 NORFOLK ST 02124
John Bradley, prin.
Stone ES, 22 REGINA RD 02124
Ronald Bagley, prin.
Winthrop ES, 35 BROOKFORD ST 02125
Joseph Joyce, prin.
_____

St. Ambrose ES, 23 LEONARD ST 02122
St. Ann ES, 241 NEPONSET AVE 02122
St. Brendan ES, 29 RITA RD 02124
St. Gregory ES, 2214 DORCHESTER AVE 02124
St. Kevin ES, 516 COLUMBIA RD 02125
St. Margaret ES, 790 COLUMBIA RD 02125
St. Mark ES, 197 CENTRE ST 02124
St. Matthew ES, 29 STANTON ST 02124
St. Peter ES, 296 BOWDOIN ST 02122
St. William ES, 100 SAVIN HILL AVE 02125
Sister Clara Muhammed ES
150 MAGNOLIA 02121

Douglas, Worcester Co., Pop. Code 5
Douglas SD
Sch. Sys. Enr. Code 3
Supt. – Robin Leveillee, DEPOT 01516
Other Schools – See East Douglas

Dover, Norfolk Co., Pop. Code 5
Dover SD
Sch. Sys. Enr. Code 2
Supt. – Robert Couture, 137 FARM ST 02030

Caryl MS, 4 SPRINGDALE AVE 02030
Renee Rubin, prin.
Chickering ES, CROSS 02030 – Renee Rubin, prin.

Dover-Sherborn SD
Sch. Sys. Enr. Code 3
Supt. – Rob Couture, 137 FARM ST 02030
Dover-Sherborn Regional JHS
137 FARM ST 02030 – John Moore, prin.

Sherborn SD
Sch. Sys. Enr. Code 2
Supt. – Robert Couture, 137 FARM ST 02030
Other Schools – See Sherborn
_____

Charles River ES, 56 CENTRE ST 02030

Dracut, Middlesex Co., Pop. Code 7
Dracut SD
Sch. Sys. Enr. Code 5
Supt. – Christos Daoulas
2063 LAKEVIEW AVE 01826
Englesby JHS, 1580 LAKEVIEW AVE 01826
John C. Langland, prin.
Campbell ES, 1021 MFTHUEN 01826
Ethel Goulakos, prin.
ES, 1560 LAKEVIEW AVE 01826
William Pagones, prin.
Greenmont Avenue ES
37 GREENMONT AVE 01826
Janet Mulligan, prin.
Parker Avenue ES, 77 PARKER AVE 01826
Constance Desjardins, prin.

Dudley, Worcester Co., Pop. Code 6
Dudley-Charlton Regional SD
Sch. Sys. Enr. Code 5
Supt. – John F. Canavan, P O BOX 97 01570
ES, WEST MAIN 01570 – Gregory Sullivan, prin.
IS, SCHOOL 01570 – Joseph Christopher, prin.
Mason Road ES, MASON ROAD 01570
Gregory Sullivan, prin.
Other Schools – See Charlton

Dunstable, Middlesex Co., Pop. Code 4
Groton-Dunstable SD
Supt. – See Groton
Swallow/Union ES
SWALLOW UNION BLDGS 01827
Roger Pedjoe, prin.

Duxbury, Plymouth Co., Pop. Code 7
Duxbury SD
Sch. Sys. Enr. Code 5
Supt. – Donald Kennedy
130 SAINT GEORGES ST 02332
IS, 130 SAINT GEORGES ST 02332
Lawrence Hojlo, prin.
Alden ES, ALDEN 02332 – Charles Elliott,Jr., prin.
Chandler ES, 93 CHANDLER ST 02332
Richard Menice, prin.

East Boston, Suffolk Co.
Boston SD
Supt. – See Boston
Barnes MS, 127 MARION ST 02128
James Corscadden, prin.
Adams ES, 165 WEBSTER ST 02128
William Wright, prin.
Alighieri ES, 37 GROVE 02128 – John Gillis, prin.
Bradley ES, 110 PEACHVIEW ROAD 02128
F. Lyons, prin.
Guild ES, 5 ASHLEY ST 02128
John Vozella, prin.
Kennedy ES, 343 SARATOGA ST 02128
Libby Chui, prin.
McKay ES, 122 COTTAGE ST 02128
Dean Yarborough, prin.
O'Donnell ES, 33 TRENTON ST 02128
John Prince, prin.
Otis ES, 218 MARION ST 02128
Philip Matthews, prin.
_____

East Boston Central Catholic ES
69 LONDON 02128
St. Lazarus ES, 67 ASHLEY ST 02128
St. Mary Star of Sea ES, 58 MOORE ST 02128

East Bridgewater, Plymouth Co., Pop. Code 6
East Bridgewater SD
Sch. Sys. Enr. Code 4
Supt. – Gordon Mitchell
11 PLYMOUTH ST 02333
MS, 435 CENTRAL ST 02333 – John Collins, prin.
Central ES, 107 CENTRAL ST 02333
George Frye, prin.

East Brookfield, Worcester Co., Pop. Code 4
Spencer-East Brookfield SD
Supt. – See Spencer
Lashway JHS, SCHOOL ST 01515
Eileen Prizio, prin.
Memorial ES, CONNIE MACK DR 01515
Eileen Prizio, prin.

East Douglas, Worcester Co., Pop. Code 4
Douglas SD
Supt. – See Douglas
ES, GLEASON COURT 01516
Zaven Dagirmanjian, prin.

East Falmouth, Barnstable Co., Pop. Code 5
Falmouth SD
Sch. Sys. Enr. Code 5
Supt. – Robert Antonucci
340 TEATICKET HIGHWAY 02536

ES, DAVISVILLE ROAD 02536
Barb Francis, prin.
Other Schools – See Falmouth, North Falmouth,
Teaticket

East Freetown, Bristol Co., Pop. Code 5
Freetown SD
Sch. Sys. Enr. Code 3
Supt. – Nancy Sullivan
43 BULLOCK ROAD 02717
Freetown ES, 43 BULLOCK RD 02717
August Pereira,Jr., prin.

Freetown-Lakeville SD
Sch. Sys. Enr. Code 4
Supt. – Nancy Sullivan
43 BULLOCK ROAD 02717
Austin MS, 99 E HOWLAND ROAD 02717
Karl Smith, prin.

Lakeville SD
Sch. Sys. Enr. Code 3
Supt. – Nancy Sullivan
43 BULLOCK ROAD 02717
Other Schools – See Lakeville

Eastham, Barnstable Co., Pop. Code 5
Eastham SD
Supt. – See Orleans
ES, RURAL ROUTE 01 BOX 486 02642
Daniel Shay, prin.

Easthampton, Hampshire Co., Pop. Code 7
Easthampton SD
Sch. Sys. Enr. Code 4
Supt. – Randall Collins, 130 MAIN ST 01027
White Brook MS, 200 PARK ST 01027
Terry Trask, prin.
Center ES, 9 SCHOOL ST 01027
Clinton Burt, prin.
Maple ES, 7 CHAPEL ST 01027
Richard Guistina, prin.
Parsons ES, 48 PARSONS ST 01027
Clinton Burt, prin.

Westhampton SD
Supt. – See Westhampton
Westhampton Center ES
RURAL ROUTE 01 BOX 359 01027
D. MacLeod, prin.

Notre Dame Immaculate Conception ES
35 PLEASANT ST 01027

East Longmeadow, Hampden Co., Pop. Code 7
East Longmeadow SD
Sch. Sys. Enr. Code 4
Supt. – John Drinkwater, 180 MAPLE ST 01028
Birchland Park MS, 50 HANWARD HILL 01028
Richard Cunningham, prin.
Mapleshade ES, 175 MAPLESHADE AVE 01028
Frederick Lafayette, prin.
Meadow Brook ES, 607 PARKER ST 01028
Angelo Correale,Jr., prin.
Mountain View ES, 77 HAMPDEN RD 01028
Frederick Lafayette, prin.

New Life Baptist Academy
317 WESTWOOD AVE 01028

East Pepperell, Middlesex Co.
North Middlesex SD
Supt. – See Townsend
Varnum Brook MS, HOLLIS ST 01437
Ben Augello, prin.

East Taunton, Bristol Co.
Taunton SD
Supt. – See Taunton
Martin ES, 141 CASWELL ST 02718
Donald Cleary, prin.

East Templeton, Worcester Co., Pop. Code 3
Narragansett SD
Supt. – See Otter River
MS, P O BOX 299 01438 – Kenneth Vaidulas, prin.

East Walpole, Norfolk Co., Pop. Code 5
Walpole SD
Supt. – See Walpole
Bird MS, 141 WASHINGTON ST 02032
Suzanne Gillam, prin.
Old Post Road ES, OLD POST ROAD 02032
Harold Varney, prin.

East Wareham, Plymouth Co., Pop. Code 3
Wareham SD
Supt. – See Wareham
ES, DEPOT 02538 – Peter Coville, prin.

East Weymouth, Suffolk Co.
Weymouth SD
Supt. – See Weymouth
East JHS, 89 MIDDLE ST 02189
Howard Gilmore, prin.

Edgartown, Dukes Co., Pop. Code 4
Edartown SD
Supt. – See Vineyard Haven
ES, WEST TISBURY ROAD 02539
Edward Jerome, prin.

Essex, Suffolk Co., Pop. Code 4
Essex SD
Sch. Sys. Enr. Code 2
Supt. – Mark Kaufman, STORY ST 01929
ES, 12 STORY ST 01929 – Michael Jacobson, prin.

Everett, Middlesex Co., Pop. Code 8
Everett SD
Sch. Sys. Enr. Code 5
Supt. – Frederick Gibson, 121 VINE ST 02149
Parlin JHS, 587 BROADWAY 02149
Richard Mangerian, prin.
Centre ES, 337 BROADWAY 02149
Maria Nigro, prin.
Devens ES, CHURCH 02149
Anthony Russo, prin.
Hale ES, 80 GLENDALE 02149
Robert Sansone, prin.
Hamilton ES, 28 NICHOLS ST 02149
Henry Schlegal,Jr., prin.
Lafayette ES, SHUTE 02149
John Andreucci, prin.
Lewis ES, FLOYD 02149 – Paul Camello, prin.
Mann ES, 45 PROSPECT ST 02149
William McCarron, prin.
Webster ES, 26 DARTMOUTH ST 02149
Edward Murray, prin.

Immaculate Conception ES
51 SUMMER ST 02149
Our Lady of Grace ES, 190 NICHOLS ST 02149
St. Anthony ES, 54 OAKES ST 02149

Fairhaven, Bristol Co., Pop. Code 7
Fairhaven SD
Sch. Sys. Enr. Code 4
Supt. – Ronald Hoekstra
128 WASHINGTON ST 02719
Hastings JHS, 30 SCHOOL ST 02719
John Losert, prin.
East Fairhaven ES, 2 NEW BOSTON RD 02719
Bernard Roderick, prin.
Oxford ES, 347 MAIN ST 02719
Jenny Xifaras, prin.
Rogers ES, 100 PLEASANT ST 02719
Paul Doherty, prin.
Wood ES, 60 SCONTICUT NECK RD 02719
Victor Brunette, prin.

St. Joseph ES, SPRING AND DELAND 02719

Fall River, Bristol Co., Pop. Code 8
Fall River SD
Sch. Sys. Enr. Code 7
Supt. – John Correiro, 417 ROCK ST 02720
Kuss MS, 289 ROCK ST 02720
Angelo Stavros, prin.
Lord MS, 615 TUCKER ST 02721
George Howayeck, prin.
Morton MS, 376 PRESIDENT AVE 02720
Stephen Nawrocki, prin.
Talbot MS, 124 MELROSE ST 02723
Albert Attar, prin.
Belisle ES, 40 CLARKSON ST 02724
Harvey Lescault, prin.
Borden ES, 45 MORGAN ST 02721
Edward Mcguinness, prin.
Borden ES, 1400 PRESIDENT AVE 02720
Henry Dussault, prin.
Brayton Avenue ES, 425 BRAYTON AVE 02721
Roger Assad, prin.
Carroll ES, 117 HOOD ST 02720
Clorinda Ventura, prin.
Connell ES, 650 PLYMOUTH AVE 02721
Leonard Aguiar, prin.
Coughlin ES, 1975 PLEASANT ST 02723
George Rhoads, prin.
Davol ES, 112 FLINT ST 02723
John Pontes, prin.
Doran Annex ES, 403 DIVISION ST 02721
M. Almeida, prin.
Doran ES, 101 FOUNTAIN ST 02721
Tobias Monte, prin.
Dubuque ES, 330 OAK GROVE AVE 02723
Manuel Narciso, prin.
Fowler ES, 286 SPRAGUE ST 02724
Alice Souza, prin.
Greene ES, 409 CAMBRIDGE ST 02721
David Dunn, prin.
Healy ES, 726 HICKS ST 02724
Anne Joerres, prin.
Highland ES, 1151 ROBESON ST 02720
Raymond Powers, prin.
Laurel Lake ES, 152 ORSWELL ST 02724
Ed Foley, prin.
Letourneau ES, 323 ANTHONY ST 02721
Roland Boulay, prin.
Lincoln ES, 439 PINE ST 02720
Margaret LaFleur, prin.
Osborn Street ES, 160 OSBORN ST 02724
Susan Whalon, prin.
Silvia ES, 128 HARTWELL ST 02721
Barton Pauls, prin.
Slade ES, 200 LEWIS ST 02724
Ronald Cote, prin.
Small ES, 140 LONDON ST 02723
Frederick McDonald, prin.
Tansey ES, 711 RAY ST 02720
Daniel Kelly, prin.
Watson ES, 935 EASTERN AVE 02723
Frank Grimes, prin.
Westall ES, 276 MAPLE ST 02720
M. Fernandes, prin.
Wiley ES, 2585 N MAIN ST 02720
Marie Beckett, prin.
Wixon ES, 263 HAMLET ST 02724
Elizabeth O'Neill, prin.

Christian Fall River ES
484 HIGHLAND AVE 02720

Domincan Academy ES, 37 PARK ST 02721
Espirito Santo ES, 2 EVERETT ST 02723
Holy Name ES, 850 PEARCE ST 02720
Notre Dame ES, 34 SAINT JOSEPH ST 02723
Ss. Peter Paul ES, 240 DOVER ST 02721
St. Anne ES, 240 FOREST ST 02721
St. Jean Baptiste ES, LAMPHOR ST 02721
St. Michael ES, 189 ESSEX ST 02720
St. Stanislaus ES, P O BOX 217 02724

Falmouth, Barnstable Co., Pop. Code 7
Falmouth SD
Supt. – See East Falmouth
Lawrence MS, 113 LAKEVIEW AVE 02540
Howard Campbell, prin.
Morse Pond MS, 323 JONES RD 02540
Diane Hoppensteadt, prin.
Mullen-Hall ES, 130 KATHERINE BATES 02540
Michael Ward, prin.

Small World ES, 42 GIFFORD ST 02540

Feeding Hills, Hampden Co., Pop. Code 6
Agawam SD
Sch. Sys. Enr. Code 5
Supt. – James Bruno
1305 SPRINGFIELD ST 01030
Granger ES, 31 S WESTFIELD ST 01030
James Loomis,Jr., prin.
Other Schools – See Agawam

Fitchburg, Worcester Co., Pop. Code 8
Fitchburg SD
Sch. Sys. Enr. Code 5
Supt. – Philip Fallon, 1047 MAIN ST 01420
Brown JHS, 62 ACADEMY ST 01420
Ernest Hunter, prin.
Memorial MS, 615 ROLLSTONE ST 01420
Peter Stephens, prin.
Crocker ES, 333 CROCKER DR 01420
Donald Cummings, prin.
McKay Campus ES, RINDGE ROAD 01420
Mildred Vinskey, prin.
Reingold ES, 70 REINGOLD AVE 01420
Paul Benoit, prin.
South Fitchburg ES, 1011 WATER ST 01420
Thomas Lamey, prin.
South Street ES, 366 SOUTH ST 01420
Thomas Lamey, prin.

Applewild ES, 120 PROSPECT ST 01420
St. Anthony ES, 123 SALEM ST 01420
St. Bernard ES, 254 SUMMER ST 01420
St. Joseph ES, 35 COLUMBUS ST 01420

Florence, Northampton Co.
Northampton SD
Supt. – See Northampton
Kennedy JHS, 30 BRIDGE ROAD 01060
Richard Carnes, prin.
Finn ES, RYAN ROAD 01060 – W. Crowther, prin.
ES, 198 PINE ST 01060 – Alice Eastman, prin.

Foxboro, Norfolk Co., Pop. Code 7
Foxboro SD
Sch. Sys. Enr. Code 5
Supt. – Dean Toepfer
CARPENTER & SOUTH 02035
Ahern MS, MECHANIC ST 02035
Calvin Meeker, prin.
Burrell ES, MORSE 02035
Myrna Kesselman, prin.
Taylor ES, SOUTH 02035
George Bedrosian, prin.

Framingham, Middlesex Co., Pop. Code 8
Framingham SD
Sch. Sys. Enr. Code 6
Supt. – Rigas Rigopoulos, 454 WATER ST 01701
Farley ES, 115 FLAGG DRIVE 01701
J. Michael Dineen, prin.
Walsh MS, BROOK ST 01701
James Halliday, prin.
Barbieri ES, 190 DUDLEY RD 01701
Peter Dittami, prin.
Brophy ES, 575 PLEASANT ST 01701
Thomas Foley, prin.
Dunning ES, FROST 01701 – Nancy Grew, prin.
Hemenway ES, WATER 01701
Thomas Coburn, prin.
Juniper Hill ES, UPPER JOCLYN AVE 01701
Gloria Aspesi, prin.
McCarthy ES, FLAGG DR 01701
Edward Convery, prin.
Potter Road ES, POTTER ROAD 01701
William Matthews, prin.
Stapleton ES, ELM 01701 – Carol Getchell, prin.
Wilson ES, LELAND 01701
Richard Kennedy, prin.

St. Bridget ES, 832 WORCESTER RD 01701
St. Tarcisius ES, 560 WAVERLY ST 01701

Franklin, Norfolk Co., Pop. Code 7
Franklin SD
Sch. Sys. Enr. Code 5
Supt. – John Doherty, OAK ST 02038
Mann MS, 218 OAK ST 02038
Richard Palermc, prin.
Kennedy Memorial ES, POND 02038
Michael Konosky, prin.
Oak Street ES, OAK 02038 – Davida Fox, prin.
Thayer ES, 137 W CENTRAL ST 02038
Anne Bergen, prin.

Gardner, Worcester Co., Pop. Code 7
Gardner SD
Sch. Sys. Enr. Code 4
Supt. – Lawrence Cornell, 130 ELM ST 01440
JHS, 62 WATERFORD ST 01440
Joseph Bishop, prin.
Elm Street ES, 130 ELM ST 01440
Reino Sandberg, prin.
Prospect ES, 75 E BROADWAY ST 01440
Patricia Grenier, prin.
Waterford Street ES, 62 WATERFORD ST 01440
Joseph Bishop, Jr., prin.

Our Lady Holy Rosary ES, 99 NICHOLS ST 01440
Sacred Heart ES, 100 CENTRAL ST 01440

Georgetown, Essex Co., Pop. Code 6
Georgetown SD
Sch. Sys. Enr. Code 4
Supt. – Robert Sinabaldi, 1 LIBRARY ST 01833
Penn Brook MS, 68 ELM ST 01833
Ronald Kacherian, prin.
Perley ES, 51 NORTH ST 01833
Karla Schloss, prin.

Gilbertville, Worcester Co., Pop. Code 4
Quabbin SD
Supt. – See Barre
Hardwick ES, MAIN 01031 – Richard Bray, prin.

Gloucester, Essex Co., Pop. Code 8
Gloucester SD
Sch. Sys. Enr. Code 5
Supt. – Alphonse Swekla
99 BLACKBURN CIRCLE 01930
Beeman Memorial ES, 100 CHERRY ST 01930
Alfred Wolfe, prin.
East Gloucester ES, 20 DAVIS ST 01930
Vincent Cafasso, prin.
Fuller MS, 99 BLACKBURN CIR 01930
Shirley Coen, prin.
Veterans Memorial ES, 11 WEBSTER ST 01930
Vincent Cafasso, prin.
West Parish ES, 35 CONCORD ST 01930
Robert Penta, prin.

St. Ann ES, 70 PLEASANT ST 01930
St. Mel Day ES, FARRINGTON AVE 01930

Goshen, Hampshire Co., Pop. Code 3
Goshen SD
Supt. – See Westhampton
Center ES, RTE 9 01032 – D. MacLeod, prin.

Grafton, Worcester Co., Pop. Code 7
Grafton SD
Sch. Sys. Enr. Code 4
Supt. – William Compton
3 CENTRAL SQUARE 01519
MS, 82 NORTH ST 01519 – John Gorman, prin.
Other Schools – See North Grafton, South Grafton

Granby, Hampshire Co., Pop. Code 6
Granby SD
Sch. Sys. Enr. Code 3
Supt. – W. William Berglas
ALDRICH HALL 01033
East Meadow MS, EAST STATE 01033
James Pietras, prin.
West Street ES, WEST 01033 – James Pietras, prin.

Granville, Hampden Co.
Granville SD
Supt. – See Southwick
Granville Village ES, MAPLE 01034
James Yvon, prin.

Great Barrington, Berkshire Co., Pop. Code 6
Berkshire Hills SD
Supt. – See Stockbridge
Searles MS, 79 BRIDGE ST 01230
John Spencer, prin.
Bryant ES, 16 SCHOOL ST 01230
Joanne Flynn, prin.

Rudolph Steiner School
RURAL ROUTE 01 BOX 378 01230

Greenfield, Franklin Co., Pop. Code 7
Greenfield SD
Sch. Sys. Enr. Code 4
Supt. – Ilene Turock, 64 NORTH ST 01301
MS, 195 FEDERAL ST 01301 – John Byron, prin.
Davis Street ES, DAVIS 01301
Alfred Sommer, prin.
Federal Street North MS, 125 FEDERAL ST 01301
Paula Wilder, prin.
Federal Street South ES, 125 FEDERAL ST 01301
Paula Wilder, prin.
Four Corners ES, FERRANTE AVE 01301
Mary Clarkson, prin.
Green River ES, MERIDIAN 01301
Alfred Sommer, prin.
North Parish ES, PLACE TER 01301
Mary Clarkson, prin.

Leyden SD
Supt. – See Northfield
Leyden ES, BRATTLEBORO ROAD 01301
Pearl Rhodes, prin.

Greenfield Center ES, P O BOX 1024 01302
Holy Trinity ES, 10 BEACON ST 01301

Groton, Middlesex Co., Pop. Code 6
Groton-Dunstable SD
Sch. Sys. Enr. Code 4
Supt. – John Barranco, MAIN ST 01450
Prescott MS, MAIN 01450 – Edward Roberts, prin.
Roche ES, NORTH MAIN 01450
Marie Witham, prin.
Other Schools – See Dunstable, West Groton

Country Day Holy Union ES, 1 MAIN ST 01450

Grove Hall, Suffolk Co.
Boston SD
Supt. – See Boston
Trotter ES, 135 HUMOLDT AVE 02121
Barbara Jackson, prin.

Groveland, Essex Co., Pop. Code 6
Groveland SD
Supt. – See West Newbury
Bagnall ES, 253 SCHOOL ST 01834
Marie Witham, prin.

Hadley, Hampshire Co., Pop. Code 5
Hadley SD
Sch. Sys. Enr. Code 3
Supt. – Richard Sullivan, 49 RUSSELL ST 01035
Hooker ES, MIDDLE 01035 – Charles Hangs, prin.
Russell MS, RUSSELL 01035
Charles Hangs, prin.

Halifax, Plymouth Co., Pop. Code 6
Halifax SD
Supt. – See Kingston
ES, 464 PLYMOUTH ST 02338
Walter Malone, prin.

Hampden, Hampden Co., Pop. Code 10
Hampden SD
Sch. Sys. Enr. Code 3
Supt. – Maurice Heffernan
85 WILBRAHAM ROAD 01036
Burgess IS, 85 WILBRAHAM ROAD 01036
Benedetto Pallotta, prin.
Green Meadows ES, 38 NORTH RD 01036
John Farrell, prin.

Hancock, Berkshire Co., Pop. Code 3
Hancock SD
Supt. – See Lanesboro
ES, RTE 43 01237 – Stephen Dallmeyer, prin.

Hanover, Plymouth Co., Pop. Code 7
Hanover SD
Sch. Sys. Enr. Code 4
Supt. – Robert Fox, 848 MAIN ST 02339
JHS, 45 WHITING ST 02339 – Philip O'Neil, prin.
Cedar ES, 265 CEDAR ST 02339
Richard Erickson, prin.
Center ES, 65 SILVER ST 02339
Joseph Rull, prin.
Sylvester MS, 495 HANOVER ST 02339
Joseph Rull, prin.

Hanson, Plymouth Co., Pop. Code 6
Hanson SD
Sch. Sys. Enr. Code 4
Supt. – Carl Batchelder, SCHOOL ST 02341
Indian Head MS, 750 INDIAN HEAD ST 02341
Carroll Gagnon, prin.
Maquan ES, 50 SCHOOL ST 02341
Richard Skinner, prin.

Harvard, Worcester Co., Pop. Code 7
Harvard SD
Sch. Sys. Enr. Code 3
Supt. – Florence Seldin, P O BOX 273 01451
ES, MASS AVE 01451 – Richard Ingmanson, prin.

Harwich, Barnstable Co., Pop. Code 6
Harwich SD
Sch. Sys. Enr. Code 4
Supt. – Charles Ferris, SOUTH ST 02645
ES, SOUTH 02645 – Paul Koulouris, prin.

Hatfield, Hampshire Co., Pop. Code 5
Hatfield SD
Sch. Sys. Enr. Code 3
Supt. – Francis Gougeon, 34 SCHOOL ST 01038
ES, 33 MAIN ST 01038 – Linda Driscoll, prin.

Haverhill, Essex Co., Pop. Code 8
Haverhill SD
Sch. Sys. Enr. Code 6
Supt. – Thomas Fowler-Finn
4 SUMMER ST 01830
Consentino MS, 685 WASHINGTON ST 01830
Daniel Harrington, prin.
Hunking MS, WINCHESTER 01830
Thomas Behan, prin.
Nettle MS, 150 BOARDMAN ST 01830
Frederick Noone, prin.
Whittier MS, 256 CONCORD ST 01830
Raymond Rosatone, prin.
Bartlett ES, 551 WASHINGTON ST 01832
Daniel Harrington, prin.
Cogswell ES, 351 S MAIN ST 01835
Thomas Behan, prin.
Crowell ES, 26 BELMONT AVE 01830
Frederick Noone, prin.
Fox ES, 75 ELM ST 01830
Frederick Noone, prin.
Greenleaf ES, 58 CHADWICK ST 01835
Thomas Behan, prin.
Saint James ES, 415 PRIMROSE ST 01830
Ronald Selvaggio, prin.

Tilton ES, 70 GROVE 01830
Ronald Selvaggio, prin.
Walnut Square ES, MAIN 01830
Raymond Rosatone, prin.
Wood ES, 25 S SPRING ST 01835
Thomas Behan, prin.

St. Joseph ES, 56 OAK TER 01832

Hingham, Plymouth Co., Pop. Code 7
Hingham SD
Sch. Sys. Enr. Code 5
Supt. – Lewis Ernst, 14 MAIN ST 02043
Foster ES, 55 DOWNER AVE 02043
Mary Schlansker, prin.
Plymouth River ES, 200 HIGH ST 02043
Roger Lamoureux, prin.
South ES, 831 MAIN ST 02043
Judith Monahan, prin.

Derby Academy, 56 BURDITT AVE 02043
St. Paul ES, 18 FEARING RD 02043

Hinsdale, Berkshire Co., Pop. Code 4
Central Berkshire SD
Supt. – See Dalton
Kittredge ES, MAPLE 01235 – R. Murray, prin.

Holbrook, Norfolk Co., Pop. Code 7
Holbrook SD
Sch. Sys. Enr. Code 4
Supt. – John Spillane, 227 PLYMOUTH ST 02343
Kennedy ES, 339 PLYMOUTH ST 02343
A. Anderson, prin.
South ES, 719 S FRANKLIN ST 02343
Joseph Cirigliano, prin.

St. Joseph ES, 143 S FRANKLIN ST 02343

Holden, Worcester Co., Pop. Code 7
Holden SD
Sch. Sys. Enr. Code 4
Supt. – Robert Conn, 1128 MAIN ST 01520
Mountview MS, 270 SHREWSBURY ST 01520
Russell Palmer, prin.
Chaffins ES, 11 HOLDEN ST 01520
John Couture, prin.
Dawson ES, 155 SALISBURY ST 01520
Jaqueline Walsh, prin.
Rice ES, 48 PHILLIPS RD 01520
C. Howland, prin.
Other Schools – See Jefferson

Paxton SD
Sch. Sys. Enr. Code 2
Supt. – Robert Conn, 1128 MAIN ST 01520
Other Schools – See Paxton

Princeton SD
Sch. Sys. Enr. Code 2
Supt. – Robert Conn, 1128 MAIN ST 01520
Other Schools – See Princeton

Rutland SD
Sch. Sys. Enr. Code 3
Supt. – Robert Conn, 1128 MAIN ST 01520
Other Schools – See Rutland

Sterling SD
Sch. Sys. Enr. Code 3
Supt. – Robert Conn, 1128 MAIN ST 01520
Other Schools – See Sterling

Holliston, Middlesex Co., Pop. Code 7
Holliston SD
Sch. Sys. Enr. Code 5
Supt. – Savino Placentino, LINDEN ST 01746
Flagg-Adams MS, WOODLAND 01746
Marie Franson, prin.
Andrews ES, SCHOOL 01746
James Palladino, prin.
High School ES Annex, HOLLIS 01746
Paul Franson, prin.
Miller ES, WOODLAND 01746
Paul Franson, prin.
Wilder PS, PAKER 01746 – Jim Palladino, prin.

Holyoke, Hampden Co., Pop. Code 8
Holyoke SD
Sch. Sys. Enr. Code 6
Supt. – George Counter, 98 SUFFOLK ST 01040
Donahue MS, WHITTING FARMS ROAD 01040
Mary McGinnis, prin.
Highland ES, 84 LINCOLN ST 01040
Donald Gasiorowski, prin.
Kelly MS, 216 WEST ST 01040
Alphonse Laudato, prin.
Kirtland ES, 298 SARGEANT ST 01040
Jeanne Sarkis, prin.
Lawrence MS, 156 CABOT ST 01040
Edward O'Malley, prin.
McMahon ES, 75 KANE RD 01040
Jane Kane, prin.
Metcalf ES, 2019 NORTHAMPTON ST 01040
Alexander Borelli, prin.
Morgan ES, 596 S BRIDGE ST 01040
Daniel Doherty, prin.
Sullivan MS, 400 JARVIS AVE 01040
John Clark, prin.

Blessed Sacrament ES, 21 WESTFIELD RD 01040
First Lutheran ES
1810 NORTHAMPTON ST 01040
Mater Dolcrosa ES, 25 MAPLE ST 01040
Our Lady of Perpetual Help ES
261 CHESTNUT ST 01040

Hopedale, Worcester Co., Pop. Code 5
Hopedale SD
Sch. Sys. Enr. Code 3
Supt. – Donald Hayes, 25 ADIN ST 01747
Memorial ES, ADIN 01747 – Roger Morell, prin.
Park Street ES, PARK 01747 – Roger Morell, prin.

Hopkinton, Middlesex Co., Pop. Code 6
Hopkinton SD
Sch. Sys. Enr. Code 4
Supt. – William Hosmer, HAYDEN ROWE 01748
Center ES, 11 ASH ST 01748 – Thomas Argir, prin.
Elmwood MS, ELM 01748 – Thomas Argir, prin.

Housatonic, Berkshire Co.
Berkshire Hills SD
Supt. – See Stockbridge
ES, PLEASANT 01236 – Joanne Flynn, prin.

Hubbardston, Worcester Co., Pop. Code 4
Quabbin SD
Supt. – See Barre
Hubbardston Center ES, MAIN 01452
Joan Paula, prin.

Hudson, Middlesex Co., Pop. Code 7
Hudson SD
Sch. Sys. Enr. Code 4
Supt. – Peter Toohey, 155 APSLEY ST 01749
Kennedy MS, 201 MANNING ST 01749
David Quinn, prin.
Cox Street ES, COX 01749 – W. Maguire, prin.
Farley ES, COTTAGE 01749 – James Boyd, prin.
Forest Avenue ES, FOREST AVE 01749
George Calnan, prin.

St. Michael ES, 18 HIGH ST 01749

Hull, Plymouth Co., Pop. Code 6
Hull SD
Sch. Sys. Enr. Code 4
Supt. – Claire Sheff, 81 CENTRAL AVE 02045
Memorial MS, 81 CENTRAL AVE 02045
Walter Secatore, prin.
Jacobs ES, 180 HARBORVIEW RD 02045
James Curtis, prin.

Huntington, Hampshire Co., Pop. Code 4
Gateway SD
Sch. Sys. Enr. Code 4
Supt. – Lawrence Holland
LITTLEVILLE ROAD 01050
Gateway Regional MS, LITTLEVILLE ROAD 01050
James Lutat, prin.
Murrayfield ES, EAST MAIN 01050
Johanna McKenna, prin.
Other Schools – See Blandford, Chester, Russell,
Worthington

Hyannis, Barnstable Co., Pop. Code 6
Barnstable SD
Sch. Sys. Enr. Code 6
Supt. – Edward Tynan, 230 SOUTH ST 02601
Barnstable MS, 895 FALMOUTH ROAD 02601
Terence Russell, prin.
Barnstable Grade 6 MS
HIGH SCHOOL ROAD 02601
Charles Lindberg, prin.
ES, 165 BEARSES WAY 02601
Alfred Menesale, prin.
Hyannis West ES, 549 W MAIN ST 02601
John Berry, Jr., prin.
Other Schools – See Centerville, Cotuit, Marstons
Mills, Osterville, West Barnstable

Hyde Park, Suffolk Co.
Boston SD
Supt. – See Boston
Rogers MS, 15 EVERETT ST 02136
John Daniels, prin.
Channing ES, 35 SUNNYSIDE ST 02136
James Mulroy, prin.
Greenwood ES, 612 METROPOLITAN AVE 02136
Paul Donovan, prin.
Grew ES, 40 GORDON AVE 02136
Amanda Amis, prin.
Roosevelt ES, 95 NEEDHAM RD 02136
Timothy Galvin, prin.

Hyde Park Academy, 14 EVERETT ST 02136
Kennedy Memorial ES, 17 HALE ST 02136
Most Precious Blood ES
1286 HYDE PARK AVE 02136
St. Anne ES, 20 COMO RD 02136

Indian Orchard, Hampden Co.
Springfield SD
Supt. – See Springfield
ES, 95 MILTON 01151 – Ann Dryden, prin.

Immaculate Conception ES
34 KOPERNICK ST 01151
St. Matthew ES, 90 BERKSHIRE ST 01151

Ipswich, Essex Co., Pop. Code 7
Ipswich SD
Sch. Sys. Enr. Code 4
Supt. – Richard Thompson
1 LORD SQUARE 01938
MS, 23 GREEN ST 01938 – Ronald Landman, prin.
Doyon Memorial ES, 210 LINEBROOK RD 01938
Kenneth Cooper, prin.
Winthrop ES, 63 CENTRAL ST 01938
M. Vanderbogart, prin.

Jamaica Plain, Suffolk Co., Pop. Code 7
Boston SD
Supt. – See Boston
Curley MS, 493 CENTRE ST 02130
Valerie Lowe, prin.
Agassiz ES, 20 CHILD ST 02130
Alfredo Nunez, prin.
Curley ES, PERSHING RD 02130
George Guptill, prin.
Fuller ES, 25 GLEN RD 02130
Robert McLaughlin, prin.
Hennigan ES, 200 HEATH ST 02130
Eleanor Perry, prin.
Kennedy ES, 7 BOLSTER ST 02130
Donald De Grandis, prin.
Manning ES, 130 LOUDERS LN 02130
James Daly, prin.
Parkman ES, 25 WALK HILL ST 02130
Beatrice Wyatt, prin.

Blessed Sacrament ES, 35 CREIGHTON ST 02130
Our Lady Lourdes ES, 54 BROOKSIDE AVE 02130
Parkside ES, 215 FOREST HILLS ST 02130
St. Andrew ES, 86 WACHUSETT ST 02130

Jefferson, Worcester Co.
Holden SD
Supt. – See Holden
MS, 1745 MAIN ST 01522 – John Benoit, prin.

Kingston, Plymouth Co., Pop. Code 6
Halifax SD
Sch. Sys. Enr. Code 3
Supt. – Paul Squarcia, PEMBROKE ST 02364
Other Schools – See Halifax

Kingston SD
Sch. Sys. Enr. Code 3
Supt. – Paul Squarcia, 130 PEMBROKE ST 02364
ES, 150 MAIN ST 02364 – John Bastoni, prin.

Pembroke SD
Sch. Sys. Enr. Code 4
Supt. – Paul Squarcia, 130 PEMBROKE ST 02364
Other Schools – See Pembroke

Plympton SD
Sch. Sys. Enr. Code 2
Supt. – Paul Squarcia, 130 PEMBROKE ST 02364
Other Schools – See Plympton

Silver Lake SD
Sch. Sys. Enr. Code 5
Supt. – Paul Squarcia, 120 PEMBROKE ST 02364
Other Schools – See Pembroke

Sacred Heart ES, P O BOX 10 02364

Lakeville, Plymouth Co., Pop. Code 6
Lakeville SD
Supt. – See East Freetown
Assawompset ES, 232 MAIN ST 02347
Thomas Venice, prin.

Lancaster, Worcester Co., Pop. Code 3
Lancaster SD
Sch. Sys. Enr. Code 3
Supt. – Frank Mitchell
39 HARVARD ROAD 01523
MS, HOLLYWOOD DRIVE 01523
Larry Tata, prin.
Memorial ES, 39 HARVARD ROAD 01523
Frank Mitchell, prin.

Lanesboro, Berkshire Co., Pop. Code 5
Hancock SD
Sch. Sys. Enr. Code 1
Supt. – George St. Pierre, SUMMER ST 01237
Other Schools – See Hancock

Lanesboro SD
Sch. Sys. Enr. Code 2
Supt. – George St. Pierre, 188 SUMMER 01237
ES, 188 SUMMER ST 01237
Thomas Gillooly, prin.

Richmond SD
Sch. Sys. Enr. Code 2
Supt. – George St. Pierre, 188 SUMMER ST 01237
Other Schools – See Richmond

Lawrence, Essex Co., Pop. Code 8
Lawrence SD
Sch. Sys. Enr. Code 7
Supt. – James Scully, 58 LAWRENCE ST 01840
Kane JHS, 141 OSGOOD ST 01843
Juan Rodriguez, prin.
Oliver JHS, 183 HAVERHILL ST 01840
Norah McCarthy, prin.
Arlington ES, 150 ADLER 01841
William Carey III, prin.
Breen ES, 114 OSGOOD ST 01843
Elizabeth Murphy, prin.
Bruce MS, 135 BUTLER ST 01841
Joseph Twomey, Jr., prin.
Donovan ES, 50 CROSS ST 01841
Barbara Dillon, prin.
Frost ES, 33 HAMLET ST 01843
John Benjamin, prin.
Hennessey ES, 122 HANCOCK ST 01841
Alyce Merlino, prin.
Lawlor ES, 41 LEXINGTON ST 01841
Kathleen Borys, prin.
Leahy ES, 100 ERVING AVE 01841
Donna Grassis, prin.
Leonard MS, ALLEN 01841
Maria Narganes, prin.

Rollins ES, 451 HOWARD ST 01841
Claire Kennedy, prin.
Salem Street ES, 149 SALEM ST 01843
John Wilson, prin.
Tarbox ES, 59 ALDER 01841
Rosemarie Diresta, prin.
Wetherbee ES, 75 NEWTON ST 01843
Denise McCarthy, prin.

Holy Rosary ES, 100 SUMMER ST 01840
Holy Trinity ES, 31 TRINITY ST 01841
Sacred Heart ES, 22 GROTON ST 01843
St. Anne ES, 400 HAVERHILL ST 01840
St. Augustine ES, 526 LOWELL ST 01841
St. Mary ES, 301 HAVERHILL ST 01840
St. Patrick ES, 100 PARKER ST 01843

Lee, Berkshire Co., Pop. Code 6
Lee SD
Sch. Sys. Enr. Code 3
Supt. – Henry Zukauski, CROSSWAYS 01238
ES, 122 HIGH ST 01238 – Raymond Kavey, prin.

Otis SD
Sch. Sys. Enr. Code 2
Supt. – Henry Zukowski, CROSSWAYS 01238
Other Schools – See Otis

St. Mary ES, 111 ORCHARD ST 01238

Leeds, Hampshire Co.
Northampton SD
Supt. – See Northampton
ES, FLORENCE 01053 – Kathleen Sheehan, prin.

Leicester, Worcester Co., Pop. Code 6
Leicester SD
Sch. Sys. Enr. Code 4
Supt. – Don Rutter, 1078 MAIN ST 01524
Leicester Memorial MS, 400 PLEASANT ST 01524
Robert Prince, prin.
Leicester Center MS, WASHBURN SQ 01524
Jeanne King, prin.
PS, 210 PAXTON ST 01524
Bernard Clifford, prin.

Lenox, Berkshire Co., Pop. Code 6
Lenox SD
Sch. Sys. Enr. Code 3
Supt. – Roland Miller, 6 WALKER ST 01240
Cameron MS, 109 HOUSATONIC ST 01240
Robert Vaughan, prin.
Morris ES, 61 WEST ST 01240
Robert Vaughan, prin.

Stevens Christians School, 40 KEMBLE ST 01240
Berkshire Country Day ES, P O BOX 867 01240

Leominster, Worcester Co., Pop. Code 8
Leominster SD
Sch. Sys. Enr. Code 5
Supt. – Louis Amadio, 122 GRANITE ST 01453
Gallaher JHS, 24 CHURCH ST 01453
Geno Salvatelli, prin.
Appleseed ES, 845 MAIN ST 01453
Robert Salvatelli, prin.
Fall Brook ES, DECICCO DR 01453
Casto Migliozzi, prin.
Northwest ES, STEARNS AVE 01453
Donald Bracani, prin.
Priest Street ES, 115 PRIEST ST 01453
Donald Bracani, prin.
Southeast ES, VISCOLOID AVE 01453
Joseph DeCarolis, prin.

Julie Country Day ES, 365 LINDELL AVE 01453
St. Ann ES, 199 LANCASTER ST 01453
St. Leo ES, 118 MAIN ST 01453

Leverett, Franklin Co., Pop. Code 4
Leverett SD
Supt. – See Millers Falls
ES, MONTAGUE ROAD 01054
Leslie Edinson, prin.

Lexington, Middlesex Co., Pop. Code 8
Lexington SD
Sch. Sys. Enr. Code 5
Supt. – Philip Geiger
1557 MASSACHUSETTS AVE 02173
Clarke JHS, STEPMAN ROAD 02173
John Hibbard, prin.
Diamond JHS, 99 HANCOCK ST 02173
Eugene Sullivan, prin.
Bowman ES, 9 PHILIP RD 02173
David Horton, prin.
Bridge ES, 55 MIDDLEBY RD 02173
Ellen DeFantis, prin.
Estabrook ES, 117 GROVE ST 02173
William Terris, prin.
Fiske ES, 34A COLONY RD 02173
Edward Jacobus, prin.
Harrington ES, 146 MAPLE ST 02173
Paul Foley, prin.

Waldorf ES, 739 MASSACHUSETTS AVE 02173

Lincoln, Middlesex Co., Pop. Code 6
Lincoln SD
Sch. Sys. Enr. Code 4
Supt. – Gregory Ciardi, BALLFIELD ROAD 01773
Brooks MS, BALLFIELD ROAD 01773
Russell Tornrose, prin.
Hartwell ES, BALLFIELD ROAD 01773
Diane Nockles, prin.
Other Schools – See Bedford

Littleton, Middlesex Co., Pop. Code 6
Littleton SD
Sch. Sys. Enr. Code 4
Supt. – Vincent Franco, SHATTUK ST 01460
MS, RUSSELL 01460 – John O'Neil, prin.
Shaker Lane ES, SHAKER LN 01460
  Arthur Covell, prin.

Longmeadow, Hampden Co., Pop. Code 7
Longmeadow SD
Sch. Sys. Enr. Code 5
Supt. – Thomas McGarry
  811 LONGMEADOW ST 01106
Glenbrook MS, 195 AVONDALE ROAD 01106
  Robert Mumford, prin.
Williams MS, 410 WILLIAMS ST 01106
  Donald Fuller, prin.
Blueberry Hill ES
  275 BLUEBERRY HILL RD 01106
  Howard Hoyt,Jr.,prin.
Center ES, 837 LONGMEADOW ST 01106
  Carl Tripp, prin.
Wolf Swamp Road ES
  62 WOLF SWAMP RD 01106 – John Ciesluk, prin.

St. Mary ES, BLISS ROAD 01106

Lowell, Middlesex Co., Pop. Code 8
Lowell SD
Sch. Sys. Enr. Code 7
Supt. – Henry Mroz, 89 APPLETON ST 01852
Butler JHS, 864 GORHAM ST 01852
  Harry Kouloheras, prin.
Daley JHS, 150 FLEMING ST 01851
  Joseph Hogan, prin.
Moody JHS, 158 ROGERS ST 01852
  James Sullivan, prin.
Robinson MS, 110 JUNE ST 01850
  Donald Gagnon, prin.
Ames Street ES, 30 AMES ST 01852
  Betty Laytes, prin.
McDoungh Arts ES, DUGAN HALL 01854
  J. Downing, prin.
Bartlett ES, 79 WANNALANCIT ST 01854
  Lisa Bryant, prin.
McDoungh City ES, 43 FRENCH 01854
  Nanzetta Merriman, prin.
Colburn MS, 122 LAWRENCE ST 01852
  Betty Laytes, prin.
Green ES, 408 MERRIMACK ST 01854
  Roger Landry, prin.
Greenhalge ES, 149 ENNELL ST 01850
  Frederick Gallagher, prin.
LeBlanc ES, 58 SYCAMORE ST 01852
  Pauline Gallagher, prin.
Lincoln ES, 300 CHELMSFORD ST 01851
  Judith Rizzo, prin.
McAvinnue ES, 117 MAMMOTH RD 01854
  Leonard Flynn, prin.
Molloy ES, 125 SMITH ST 01851
  Leo Parent, prin.
Moore Street ES, 122 ANDREWS ST 01852
  Mary Smith, prin.
Morey ES, 114 PINE ST 01851
  John Abraham, prin.
O'Connell MS, 21 CARTER 01852
  Mary Smith, prin.
Pawtucketville Memorial ES
  WEST MEADOW ROAD 01854
  Hubert McQuade, prin.
Pine Street ES, 341 PINE ST 01851
  Patricia Brophy, prin.
Pyne MS, BOYLSTON 01852
  Francis Georges, prin.
Reilly ES, 115 DOUGLAS RD 01852
  Francis Moriarty, prin.
Rogers ES, 43 HIGHLAND ST 01852
  Richard Noonan, prin.
Shaughnessy ES, 1170 GORHAM ST 01852
  Linda Lee, prin.
Varnum ES, 115 6TH ST 01850
  Miriam Smith, prin.
Washington ES, 795 WILDER ST 01851
  Jeanne Green, prin.

Franco American ES, 357 PAWTUCKET ST 01854
Hellenic American ES, 41 BROADWAY ST 01854
Immaculate Conception ES
  218 E MERRIMACK ST 01852
Sacred Heart ES, 122 ANDREWS ST 01852
St. Joseph ES, 517 MOODY ST 01854
St. Louis ES, 77 BOISVERT ST 01850
St. Margaret ES, 486 STEVENS ST 01851
St. Michael ES, 15 6TH ST 01850
St. Patrick ES, 311 ADAMS ST 01854
St. Stanislaus ES, 475 VARNUM AVE 01854
Ste. Jeanne D'arc ES
  68 DRACUT ST #DARC 01854

Ludlow, Hampden Co., Pop. Code 7
Ludlow SD
Sch. Sys. Enr. Code 5
Supt. – James Tierney, 63 CHESTNUT ST 01056
Baird MS, 109 SPORTSMANS ROAD 01056
  Robert Smith, prin.
Chapin ES, 766 CHAPIN ST 01056
  Henry Casagrande, prin.
East Street ES, 508 EAST ST 01056
  Robert Glen, prin.
Veterans Park ES, 486 CHAPIN ST 01056
  Catherine Cauthier, prin.

St. John Baptist ES, 207 HUBBARD ST 01056

Lunenburg, Worcester Co., Pop. Code 6
Lunenburg SD
Sch. Sys. Enr. Code 4
Supt. – Concetta Verge
  1033 MASSACHUSETTS AVE 01462
Turkey Hill MS, 129 NORTHFIELD ROAD 01462
  Jean Killeen, prin.
Passios ES, 1025 MASS AVE 01462
  William McSheeny, prin.

Lynn, Essex Co., Pop. Code 8
Lynn SD
Sch. Sys. Enr. Code 7
Supt. – Robert Geradi, 42 FRANKLIN ST 01902
Breed JHS, 900 O'CALLAGHAN 01905
  James Daley, prin.
Eastern JHS, 19 PORTER ST 01902
  Andrew Fila, prin.
Pickering JHS, 70 CONOMO AVE 01904
  William McGuinness, prin.
Aborn ES, 409 EASTERN AVE 01902
  Thomas Fogarty, prin.
Brickett ES, 123 LEWIS ST 01902
  Cynthia McForlane, prin.
Callahan ES, 165 OCALLAGHAN WAY 01905
  Robert Powers, prin.
Cobbet ES, 40 FRANKLIN ST 01902
  Christy Ofilos, prin.
Connery ES, 50 ELM ST 01905
  William Cleary,Jr., prin.
Drewicz ES, 34 HOOD ST 01905
  Laurence Dawson, prin.
Ford ES, 49 HOLLINGSWORTH ST 01902
  John Reynolds, prin.
Harrington ES, 21 DEXTER ST 01902
  Edward Turmenne, prin.
Hood ES, 24 OAKWOOD AVE 01902
  Vincent Spirito, prin.
Ingalls ES, 1 COLLINS STREET TER 01902
  Edward Ray,Jr., prin.
Lincoln ES, 115 GARDINER ST 01905
  Robert Thomson, prin.
Lynn Woods ES, 31 TREVETT AVE 01904
  Robert Bailey, prin.
Sewell-Anderson ES, 25 ONTARIO ST 01905
  Shirley Foy, prin.
Shoemaker ES, 26 REGINA RD 01904
  Lillian McCarthy, prin.
Sisson ES, 58 CONOMO AVE 01904
  James Mazareas, prin.
Tracy ES, 35 WALNUT 01905 – Victor Tseki, prin.
Washington Community ES
  58 BLOSSOM ST 01902 – Martin Healey, prin.

North Shore Christian ES, 26 URBAN ST 01904
St. Jean Baptiste ES, 25 ENDICOTT ST 01902
St. Pius V ES, 28 BOWLER ST 01904

Lynnfield, Essex Co., Pop. Code 7
Lynnfield SD
Sch. Sys. Enr. Code 4
Supt. – Sally Dias, 505 MAIN ST 01940
MS, 505 MAIN ST 01940 – Kevin Plodzik, prin.
Huckleberry Hill ES, 5 KNOLL RD 01940
  John Crist IV, prin.
Summer Street ES, SUMMER 01940
  Nancy Santeusanio, prin.

Our Lady Assumption ES, 40 GROVE ST 01940

Malden, Middlesex Co., Pop. Code 8
Malden SD
Sch. Sys. Enr. Code 6
Supt. – George Holland, 77 SALEM ST 02148
Beebe JHS, 4901 PLEASANT ST 02148
  Camille Brandano, prin.
Browne JHS, 289 BROADWAY 02148
  Ron Dicesare, prin.
Lincoln JHS, 333 CROSS ST 02148
  Robert Lenehan, prin.
Belmont ES, 52 CROSS ST 02148
  Edward Kramer, prin.
Emerson ES, HIGHLAND AVE 02148
  Patricia Downing, prin.
Forestdale ES, SYLVAN 02148
  Stepehn Feldstein, prin.
Glenwood ES, 145 GLENWOOD ST 02148
  Donald Brunelli, prin.
Holmes ES, 257 MOUNTAIN AVE 02148
  Letty Russo, prin.
Lincoln ES, 333 CROSS ST 02148
  Peter Magner, prin.
Linden ES, WESCOTT 02148
  Nicholas Cattogio, prin.
Maplewood ES, 2 LAUREL ST 02148
  John Maccario, prin.

Cheverus ES, 30 IRVING ST 02148
Immaculate Conception ES
  306 HIGHLAND AVE 02148

Manchester, Essex Co., Pop. Code 6
Manchester SD
Sch. Sys. Enr. Code 3
Supt. – Paul Lengieza, LINCOLN ST 01944
Memorial ES, LINCOLN 01944
  Laurence Aiello, prin.

Brookwood ES, P O BOX 1429 01944

Mansfield, Bristol Co., Pop. Code 7
Mansfield SD
Sch. Sys. Enr. Code 4
Supt. – John Moran, P O BOX 428 02048

Quarters MS, EAST ST 02048
  Robert Cronin, prin.
Green ES, DEAN 02048 – Joseph Rosenberg, prin.
Park Row ES, PARK ROW 02048
  Joseph Rosenberg, prin.
Robinson ES, EAST 02048 – Charles Cormier, prin.

Marblehead, Essex Co., Pop. Code 7
Marblehead SD
Sch. Sys. Enr. Code 4
Supt. – James Kent, 2 HUMPHREY ST 01945
MS, 85 VILLAGE ST 01945 – D. Fuerst, prin.
Bell ES, 40 BALDWIN RD 01945
  Robert Farrell, prin.
Coffin ES, TURNER ROAD 01945
  Terrence Boylan, prin.
Eveleth ES, BROOK ROAD 01945
  Douglas Weinstock, prin.
Gerry ES, ELM 01945 – Terrence Boylan, prin.
Glover ES, 9 MAPLE 01945
  Douglas Weinstock, prin.

Cohen Hillel Academy, 6 COMMUNITY RD 01945
Tower ES, 61 WEST ST 01945

Marion, Plymouth Co., Pop. Code 5
Marion SD
Supt. – See Mattapoisett
Sippican ES, 16 SPRING ST 02738
  Roseli Weiss, prin.

Marlborough, Middlesex Co., Pop. Code 8
Marlborough SD
Sch. Sys. Enr. Code 5
Supt. – David Flynn, BOLTON ST 01752
MS, 41 UNION ST 01752 – William Downey, prin.
Bigelow ES, 51 ORCHARD ST 01752
  John Polymeros, prin.
Jaworek ES, 444 HOSMER ST 01752
  John Hanley, prin.
Kane ES, FARM ROAD 01752 – Susan Pikor, prin.
Mildreth ES, SAWIN 01752
  Robert Gardner, prin.
Richer ES, FOLEY ROAD 01752
  Frank Hess, prin.

Immaculate Conception ES
  13 WASHINGTON CT 01752

Marshfield, Plymouth Co., Pop. Code 7
Marshfield SD
Sch. Sys. Enr. Code 5
Supt. – Dan Bresnahan, S RIVER ST 02050
Martinson JHS, 275 FOREST ST 02050
  Richard Burgess, prin.
Eames Way ES, 165 EAMES WAY 02050
  Joan Mcquiston, prin.
Furnace Brook MS, 532 FURNACE ST 02050
  Daniel Kehoe, prin.
South River ES, MATCH 02050
  Richard DeVitt, prin.
Webster ES, 1456 OCEAN ST 02050
  Peter Noyes, prin.
Winslow ES, 60 REGIS RD 02050
  Frederick Hubbard, prin.

Marstons Mills, Barnstable Co.
Barnstable SD
Supt. – See Hyannis
ES, MAIN 02648 – Jane Sheckells, prin.

Mashpee, Barnstable Co., Pop. Code 5
Mashbee SD
Sch. Sys. Enr. Code 3
Supt. – Lincoln Demoura
  OLD BARNSTABLE ROAD 02649
Middle ES, OLD BARNSTABLE ROAD 02649
  Charles Liberty, prin.

Mattapan, Suffolk Co.
Boston SD
Supt. – See Boston
Lewenberg MS, 20 OUTLOOK ROAD 02126
  Thomas O'Neil, prin.
Chittick ES, 154 RUSKINDALE RD 02126
  Rita Manning, prin.
Mattahunt ES, 100 HEBRON ST 02126
  Nancy Dickerson, prin.
Taylor ES, 1060 MORTON ST 02126
  Marjorie Powell, prin.

Berea ES, 800 MORTON ST 02126
St. Angela ES, 120 BARSON 02126

Mattapoisett, Plymouth Co., Pop. Code 6
Marion SD
Sch. Sys. Enr. Code 2
Supt. – Joan Walsh, 135 MARION ROAD 02739
Other Schools – See Marion

Mattapoisett SD
Sch. Sys. Enr. Code 2
Supt. – Joan Walsh, 135 MARION ROAD 02739
Center ES, BARSTOW 02739
  Katherine Kozicki, prin.
Old Hammondtown MS, SHAW 02739
  William Reed, prin.

Old Rochester SD
Sch. Sys. Enr. Code 3
Supt. – Joan Walsh, 135 MARION ROAD 02739
Old Rochester Regional JHS
  MARION ROAD 02739 – Robert Gardner, prin.

Rochester SD
Sch. Sys. Enr. Code 2
Supt. – Joan Walsh, 135 MARION ROAD 02739

Other Schools – See Rochester

Maynard, Middlesex Co., Pop. Code 6
Maynard SD
Sch. Sys. Enr. Code 4
Supt. – Eileen Ahearn, MAIN ST 01754
Fowler JHS, 67 SUMMER ST 01754
  Richard Morse, prin.
Green Meadow ES, 143 GREAT RD 01754
  Frank Hill, prin.
Roosevelt ES, NASON 01754
  Francis Manzelli, prin.

St. Bridget ES, 1 PERCIVAL ST 01754

Medfield, Norfolk Co., Pop. Code 7
Medfield SD
Sch. Sys. Enr. Code 4
Supt. – Thomas Reis, 7 DALE ST 02052
MS, 88 SOUTH ST 02052 – Robert White, prin.
Dale Street MS, 45 ADAMS ST 02052
  Frank Hoffman, prin.
Wheelock ES, 17 ELM ST 02052
  Richard Fitzpatrick, prin.

Medford, Middlesex Co., Pop. Code 8
Medford SD
Sch. Sys. Enr. Code 6
Supt. – Raymond Murano
  489 WINTHROP ST 02155
Roberts JHS, 35 COURT ST 02155
  M. Hickey, prin.
Brooks/Hobbs Magnet ES, 25 AUBURN ST 02155
  Shirley Kountze, prin.
Columbus ES, 37 HICKS AVE 02155
  Rosemary Nicholson, prin.
Dame ES, 80 GEORGE ST 02155
  Ann Kenneally, prin.
Davenport ES, 25 HORNE AVE 02155
  Nancy LeBlanc, prin.
Forest Park ES, 225 GOVERNORS AVE 02155
  Marie Rizzo, prin.
Franklin ES, 69 CENTRAL AVE 02155
  Marie Rizzo, prin.
Gleason ES, 160 PLAYSTEAD RD 02155
  Rosemary Nicholson, prin.
Kennedy/Lincoln ES, 215 HARVARD ST 02155
  Arthur Swanson, prin.
Osgood ES, 101 FOURTH ST 02155
  J. Donovan, prin.
Swan ES, 75 PARK 02155
  Charles Martin,Jr., prin.

St. Francis Assisi ES, 1 ST CLARE RD 02155
St. Joseph ES, 132 HIGH ST 02155

Medway, Norfolk Co., Pop. Code 6
Medway SD
Sch. Sys. Enr. Code 4
Supt. – John Gawrys, 45 HOLLISTON ST 02053
Burke ES, LEGION AVE 02053
  Judith Kenney, prin.
North ES, LOVERING 02053
  John McGovern, prin.

Melrose, Middlesex Co., Pop. Code 8
Melrose SD
Sch. Sys. Enr. Code 5
Supt. – David Driscoll, 235 W FOSTER ST 02176
Beebe ES, 263 W FOSTER ST 02176
  Robert Brown, prin.
Franklin ES, 16 FRANKLIN ST 02176
  Kathleen Buckley, prin.
Hoover ES, GLENDOWER ROAD 02176
  Lois McCarthy, prin.
Lincoln ES, 80 W WYOMING AVE 02176
  Robert Fancy, prin.
Mann ES, DAMON AVE 02176
  Kathleen Buckley, prin.
Ripley ES, 94 LEBANON ST 02176
  Lois McCarthy, prin.
Roosevelt ES, 253 VINTON ST 02176
  Joseph Bateman, prin.
Winthrop ES, 162 FIRST ST 02176
  Gerald Carmody, prin.

St. Mary Annunciation ES, 4 MYRTLE ST 02176

Mendon, Worcester Co., Pop. Code 5
Mendon-Upton SD
Supt. – See Upton
Miscoe Hill MS, P O BOX 7 01756
  William Milligan, prin.
Clough ES, P O BOX 7 01756 – Edward Soter, prin.

Merrimac, Essex Co., Pop. Code 5
Merrimac SD
Supt. – See West Newbury
Donaghue MS, 10 UNION STREET EXT 01860
  Annette Autiello, prin.
Sweetsir ES, CHURCH 01860
  Annette Autiello, prin.

Methuen, Essex Co., Pop. Code 8
Methuen SD
Sch. Sys. Enr. Code 6
Supt. – Paul Zdanowicz, 160 MERRIMACK 01844
Timony Memorial MS
  45 PLEASANT VIEW ST 01844
  John Rimas, prin.
Tenney MS, 75 PLEASANT ST 01844
  James Smith, prin.
Ashford ES, 30 ASHFORD ST 01844
  Richard Heinz, prin.
Barker ES, 129 HAVERHILL ST 01844
  John Spina, prin.

Central ES, 250 LAWRENCE ST 01844
  Paula Sline, prin.
Howe ES, 11 HAMPSTEAD ST 01844
  David Webb, prin.
Marsh ES, 311 PELHAM ST 01844
  Ruth Higgins, prin.
Oakland ES, 125 OAKLAND AVE 01844
  Melvin Ferris, prin.
Pleasant Valley ES
  180 PLEASANT VALLEY ST 01844
  C. Stritch, prin.

Our Lady Mt. Carmel ES, 82 UNION ST 01844
St. Monica ES, 212 LAWRENCE ST 01844

Middleboro, Plymouth Co., Pop. Code 7
Middleboro SD
Sch. Sys. Enr. Code 5
Supt. – Lincoln Lynch, 1 NICKERSON AVE 02346
Memorial JHS, 219 N MAIN ST 02346
  Alan Lindsay, prin.
Burkland IS, 41 MAYFLOWER AVE 02346
  Robert DeSrosiers, prin.
Mayflower ES, 31 MAYFLOWER AVE 02346
  Louis Rizzo, prin.
Pratt Free ES, 85 PLYMOUTH ST 02346
  Franklin James, prin.
Rock ES, 99 MILLER ST 02346 – Louis Rizzo, prin.
School Street ES, 6 SCHOOL ST 02346
  Jeffrey Stevens, prin.
South Middleboro ES, 1701 WAREHAM 02346
  Louis Rizzo, prin.
Union Street ES, 41 UNION ST 02346
  Jeffrey Stevens, prin.
West Side ES, 13 W END AVE 02346
  Franklin James, prin.

Middleton, Essex Co., Pop. Code 5
Middleton SD
Sch. Sys. Enr. Code 2
Supt. – Francis Fitzgerald, 26 CENTRAL ST 01949
Howe-Manning ES, 26 CENTRAL ST 01949
  John Buckley, prin.

Milford, Worcester Co., Pop. Code 7
Milford SD
Sch. Sys. Enr. Code 5
Supt. – Thomas Cimino
  31 W FOUNTAIN ST 01757
Milford MS-East, 66 SCHOOL ST 01757
  Thomas Davoren, prin.
Brookside MS, CONGRESS ST 01757
  Francis Anderson, prin.
Memorial ES, WALNUT 01757 – Leo Fantini, prin.
Milford MS-West, 66 SCHOOL ST 01757
  Michael Brita, prin.
Woodland ES, NORTH VINE 01757
  John Shaughnessy, prin.

Milford Catholic ES, 11 E MAIN ST 01757

Millbury, Worcester Co., Pop. Code 7
Millbury SD
Sch. Sys. Enr. Code 4
Supt. – Alfred Sylvia, 12 MARTIN ST 01527
Elmwood Street ES, 40 ELMWOOD ST 01527
  Kelton Johnson, prin.
Shaw Memorial MS, 58 ELMWOOD ST 01527
  Francis Rogers, prin.

Assumption ES, 21 GROVE ST 01527

Millers Falls, Franklin Co., Pop. Code 4
Erving SD
Sch. Sys. Enr. Code 2
Supt. – Leonard Lubinsky, PLEASANT ST 01349
Erving ES, 50 NORTHFIELD RD 01349
  Kenneth Chapman, prin.

Leverett SD
Sch. Sys. Enr. Code 2
Supt. – Leonard Lubinsky, PLEASANT ST 01349
Other Schools – See Leverett

New Salem-Wendell SD
Sch. Sys. Enr. Code 2
Supt. – Leonard Lubinsky, PLEASANT ST 01349
Other Schools – See Orange

Shutesbury SD
Sch. Sys. Enr. Code 2
Supt. – Leonard Lubinsky, PLEASANT 01349
Other Schools – See Shutesbury

Millis, Norfolk Co., Pop. Code 6
Millis SD
Sch. Sys. Enr. Code 4
Supt. – Vahan Khachadoorian
  247 PLAIN ST 02054
MS, 247 PLAIN ST 02054 – William McIvor, prin.
Brown ES, PARK RD 02054 – Jane Walker, prin.
Memorial MS, 900 MAIN ST 02054
  Thomas Deffley, prin.

Millville, Worcester Co., Pop. Code 4
Blackstone-Millville SD
Supt. – See Blackstone
Longfellow ES, CENTRAL 01529
  Everett Campbell, prin.

Milton, Norfolk Co., Pop. Code 8
Milton SD
Sch. Sys. Enr. Code 5
Supt. – Frank Giuliano
  44 EDGE HILL ROAD 02186
Pierce MS, 25 GILE ROAD 02186
  Cornelius McIntire, prin.

Collicot ES, 75 EDGE HILL RD 02186
  William Griffin, prin.
Cunningham ES, 44 EDGE HILL RD 02186
  Mary Schofield, prin.
Glover ES, 255 CANTON AVE 02186
  Robert Connolly, prin.
Tucker ES, 187 BLUE HILLS PKY 02186
  Frank Guarino,Jr., prin.

Milton Academy, 170 CENTRE ST 02186
St. Agatha ES, 440 ADAMS ST 02186
St. Mary Hills ES, 250 BROOK RD 02186
Thacher Montessori ES, 44 EDGE HILL RD 02186

Monroe Bridge, Franklin Co.
Monroe SD
Supt. – See North Adams
Monroe ES, MONROE BRG 01350
  Sandra Goodermote, prin.

Monson, Hampden Co., Pop. Code 6
Monson SD
Sch. Sys. Enr. Code 4
Supt. – V. Carbone, 20 STATE ST 01057
Hiflside ES, 29 THOMPSON ST 01057
  Hugh Graham, prin.
Main Street MS, 110 MAIN ST 01057
  Hugh Graham, prin.

Montague, Franklin Co., Pop. Code 6
Gill-Montague SD
Supt. – See Turners Falls
Great Falls MS, TURNPIKE ROAD 01351
  Robert Kumin, prin.
Montague Center ES, SCHOOL 01351
  Anna Garbriel, prin.

Nahant, Essex Co., Pop. Code 5
Nahant SD
Sch. Sys. Enr. Code 2
Supt. – Helen Novack, CASTLE ROAD 01908
Johnson ES, 290 CASTLE RD 01908
  Patsy Bucca, prin.

Nantucket, Nantucket Co., Pop. Code 6
Nantucket SD
Sch. Sys. Enr. Code 3
Supt. – John O'Neil, 2 ATLANTIC AVE 02554
Peirce MS, 8 ATLANTIC AVE 02554
  G. Michael Welch, prin.
ES, 6 ATLANTIC AVE 02554 – John O'Neill, prin.

Natick, Middlesex Co., Pop. Code 8
Natick SD
Sch. Sys. Enr. Code 5
Supt. – Joseph Keefe, 13 E CENTRAL ST 01760
Kennedy MS, 165 MILL ST 01760
  William Donovan, prin.
Wilson MS, 24 RUTLEDGE ROAD 01760
  John McKenna, prin.
Bennett-Hemenway ES
  18 E EVERGREEN RD 01760 – Julius Winer, prin.
Brown ES, HARTFORD 01760
  John Crisafulli, prin.
Cole ES, BODEN LN 01760 – Robert Ferrari, prin.
Johnson ES, SOUTH MAIN 01760
  Keith Cassedy, prin.
Lilja ES, BACON AT OAK 01760
  Walter Vaughan, prin.
Memorial ES, ELIOT 01760
  Joseph Ailinger, prin.

Needham, Norfolk Co., Pop. Code 8
Needham SD
Sch. Sys. Enr. Code 5
Supt. – Fred Tirrell, 1330 HIGHLAND AVE 02192
Pollard MS, 200 HARRIS AVE 02192
  Fred Preston, prin.
Broadmeadow ES
  120 BROADMEADOW RD 02192
  Walter Power, prin.
High Rock ES, 77 FERNDALE RD 02192
  Paulina Robinson, prin.
Mitchell ES, 187 BROOKLINE ST 02192
  James Cain, prin.
Other Schools – See Needham Heights

St. Joseph ES, 90 PICKERING ST 02192

Needham Heights, Suffolk Co.
Needham SD
Supt. – See Needham
Eliot ES, 135 WELLESLEY AVE 02194
  William O'Neil, prin.
Hillside ES, 28 GLEN GARY RD 02194
  Miriam Kronish, prin.

New Bedford, Bristol Co., Pop. Code 8
New Bedford SD
Sch. Sys. Enr. Code 7
Supt. – C. Nanopoulos, 445 COUNTY ST 02740
Keith JHS, 70 HATHAWAY BLVD 02740
  W. Markey, prin.
Normandin JHS, 240 TARKILN HILL ROAD 02745
  John Viveiros, prin.
Roosevelt JHS, 120 DENNIS ST 02744
  Alwyn Griffith, prin.
Ashley ES, 122 POCHAMBEAU 02745
  Stasia Gorczca, prin.
Brooks ES, 212 NEMASKET 02740
  Roberta Rivet, prin.
Campbell ES, PHILLIPS ROAD 02745
  Maric Jardin, prin.
Carney Academy ES, 247 ELM ST 02740
  Herbert Waters, prin.

Congdon ES, 50 HEMLOCK ST   02740
 Anthony Freitas, prin.
DeValles ES, 120 KATHERINE ST   02744
 Leonard Roche, prin.
Dunbar ES, 338 DARTMOUTH ST   02740
 Mary Worden, prin.
Gomes ES, 286 S SECOND ST   02740
 M. Kaharl, prin.
Hannigan ES, 33 EMERY ST   02744
 Arthur Dutra, prin.
Hathaway ES, 256 COURT ST   02740
 Mary Walsh, prin.
Hayden/McFadden ES
 361 CEDAR GROVE ST   02746 – E. Weaver, prin.
Kampton ES, 135 SHAWMUT AVE   02740
 Ellen Shepherd, prin.
Lincoln ES, 445 ASHLEY BLVD   02745
 Joanne Mello, prin.
Mt. Pleasant ES
 261 MOUNT PLEASANT ST   02746
 John Kilgour, prin.
Ottiwell ES, 26 DIMAN ST   02746
 Anne Hopp, prin.
Parker ES, 705 COUNTY ST   02740
 Ellery Sherman, prin.
Phillips Avenue ES, 249 PHILLIPS AVE   02746
 James Welch, prin.
Pulaski ES, 1097 BRALEY RD   02745
 Lawrence Gibbs, prin.
Rodman ES, 497 HILL   02740 – Carol Smola, prin.
Swift ES, 2203 ACUSHNET AVE   02740
 James McQuade, prin.
Taylor ES, 620 BROCK AVE   02744 – J. Mello, prin.
Winslow ES, 561 ALLEN ST   02740
 Anne Asekoff, prin.

Holy Family Holy Name ES
 91 SUMMER ST   02740
Our Lady Mt. Carmel ES, 103 CRAPO ST   02744
St. Anthony ES, 106 BULLARD ST   02746
St. James St. John ES
 180 ORCHARD STREET   02740
St. Joseph ES, 35 KEARSARGE ST   02745
St. Mary ES, 115 ILLINOIS ST   02745

New Braintree, Worcester Co., Pop. Code 3
Quabbin SD
Supt. – See Barre
ES, UTLEY ROAD   01531
 Kathleen Fitzgibbons, prin.

Newbury, Essex Co., Pop. Code 5
Newbury SD
Supt. – See Byfield
ES, 63 HANOVER   01950 – Richard Joy, prin.
Woodbridge ES, GRAHAM AVE   01950
 Richard Joy, prin.

Newburyport, Essex Co., Pop. Code 7
Newburyport SD
Sch. Sys. Enr. Code 4
Supt. – Francis Bresnahan, 70 LOW ST   01950
Nock MS, 70 LOW ST   01950 – Eugene Case, prin.
Belleville ES, 333 HIGH ST   01950
 Harold Ingalls, prin.
Brown ES, MILK   01950 – Gurney Arnold, prin.
Kelley ES, 149 HIGH ST   01950
 Martin Fortune, prin.

Immaculate Conception ES
 1 WASHINGTON ST   01950

Newton, Middlesex Co., Pop. Code 8
Newton SD
Supt. – See Newtonville
Lincoln-Eliot ES, 191 PEARL ST   02158
 Cameron Larson, prin.
Underwood ES, 101 VERNON ST   02158
 Carmella Nadeau, prin.

Jackson ES, 200 JACKSON RD   02158
Newton Catholic ES, 25 LENGLEN RD   02158

Newton Center, Middlesex Co., Pop. Code 7
Newton SD
Supt. – See Newtonville
Brown JHS, 125 MEADOWBROOK ROAD   02159
 Judith Neville, prin.
Bowen ES, 280 CYPRESS ST   02159
 Jerrold Katz, prin.
Mason-Rice ES, 149 PLEASANT ST   02159
 Clara Hicks, prin.
Memorial Spaulding ES
 250 BROOKLINE ST   02159
 Kevin Andrews, prin.
Ward ES, 10 DOLPHIN RD   02159
 Samuel Turner, prin.

Solomon Schehter Day ES, 60 STEIN CIR   02159

Newton Highlands, Middlesex Co.
Newton SD
Supt. – See Newtonville
Countryside ES, 191 DEDHAM ST   02161
 Vincent Simone, prin.

Newtonville, Suffolk Co., Pop. Code 7
Newton SD
Sch. Sys. Enr. Code 6
Supt. – Irwin Blumer, 100 WALNUT ST   02160
Day JHS, 21 MINOT PLACE   02160
 Edward Fraktman, prin.
Cabot ES, 229 CABOT ST   02160
 Joseph Gattuso, prin.

Mann ES, 687 WATERTOWN ST   02160
 Kenneth Gatto, prin.
Other Schools – See Auburndale, Newton, Newton
 Center, Newton Highlands, Waban, West Newton

Norfolk, Norfolk Co., Pop. Code 6
King Philip SD
Supt. – See Wrentham
King Philip Regional MS North, 18 KING ST   02056
 Ron Marino, prin.

Norfolk SD
Sch. Sys. Enr. Code 3
Supt. – Thomas Delmonaco
 70 BOARDMAN ST   02056
Centennial ES, 70 BOARDMAN ST   02056
 Leland Miller, prin.
Freeman ES, 70 BOARDMAN ST   02056
 Leland Miller, prin.

North Adams, Berkshire Co., Pop. Code 7
Clarksburg SD
Sch. Sys. Enr. Code 2
Supt. – Joseph Joseph, RURAL ROUTE 02   01247
Clarksburg ES, RURAL ROUTE 01   01247
 Marguerite Myers, prin.

Florida SD
Sch. Sys. Enr. Code 1
Supt. – Joseph Joseph, RURAL ROUTE 02   01247
Abbott Memorial ES, CONTI DR   01247
 Frederick Bozek, prin.

Monroe SD
Sch. Sys. Enr. Code 1
Supt. – Joseph Joseph, RURAL ROUTE 02   01247
Other Schools – See Monroe Bridge

North Adams SD
Sch. Sys. Enr. Code 4
Supt. – Robert Maroni, 191 E MAIN ST   01247
MS, 171 E MAIN ST   01247
 Edward Lamarre, prin.
Greylock ES, 100 PHELPS AVE   01247
 Stephen Boisvert, prin.
Johnson ES, 31 SCHOOL ST   01247
 Carol Colantuono, prin.
Sullivan ES, KEMP AVE   01247
 Stephen Smachetti, prin.

Savoy SD
Sch. Sys. Enr. Code 1
Supt. – Joseph Joseph, RURAL ROUTE 02   01247
Other Schools – See Savoy

Northampton, Hampshire Co., Pop. Code 8
Northampton SD
Sch. Sys. Enr. Code 5
Supt. – Karen Conklin, 212 MAIN ST   01060
Bridge Street ES, 2 PARSONS ST   01060
 Gerald Bouthilette, prin.
Jackson Street ES, 120 JACKSON ST   01060
 Betsy Vaundell, prin.
South Street ES, 141 SOUTH ST   01060
 Gerald Bouthilette, prin.
Other Schools – See Florence, Leeds

Smith College Campus ES
 SMITH COLLEGE   01063

North Andover, Essex Co., Pop. Code 7
North Andover SD
Sch. Sys. Enr. Code 5
Supt. – George Blaisdell
 111 PHILIPS BROOK ROAD   01845
MS, 495 MAIN ST   01845 – Richard Neal, prin.
Atkinson ES, 111 PHILLIPS BRKS RD   01845
 Albert Goebel,Jr., prin.
Franklin ES, 1 CYPRESS TER   01845
 Charles Wiseman, prin.
Kittredge ES, 601 MAIN ST   01845
 John Deady, prin.
Thomson ES, 266 WAVERLY RD   01845
 John Nelson,Jr., prin.

Fellowship Bible School
 525 TURNPIKE ST   01845
St. Michael ES, 80 MAPLE AVE   01845

North Attleboro, Bristol Co., Pop. Code 7
North Attleboro SD
Sch. Sys. Enr. Code 5
Supt. – William Kelly
 45 S WASHINGTON ST   02760
JHS, 45 S WASHINGTON ST   02760
 Henry McDeed, prin.
Allen Avenue ES, ALLEN AVE   02760
 John Sienko, prin.
Amvet Boulevard ES, AMVET BLVD   02760
 Bowen Dieterle, prin.
Falls ES, JACKSON   02760 – Joseph Ambers, prin.
Martin ES, LANDRY AVE   02760
 Anthony Battista, prin.
Roosevelt Avenue ES, ROOSEVELT AVE   02760
 Victor Ventura, prin.
School Street ES, 25 SCHOOL ST   02760
 Joseph Ambers, prin.

St. Mary Sacred Heart ES
 57 RICHARDS AVE   02760

North Billerica, Middlesex Co., Pop. Code 6
Billerica SD
Supt. – See Billerica
Dutile ES, TREBLE COVE ROAD   01862
 Elizabeth McCarthy, prin.

Northborough, Worcester Co., Pop. Code 7
Northborough SD
Sch. Sys. Enr. Code 4
Supt. – Dennis Disalvo, 75 BARTLETT ST   01532
MS, 145 LINCOLN ST   01532
 Joseph Capallo, prin.
Lincoln Street ES, 76 LINCOLN ST   01532
 Ellen Cunniff, prin.
Peaslee ES, 31 MAPLE ST   01532
 Daniel Corcoran,Jr., prin.
Proctor ES, 26 JEFFERSON RD   01532
 Louis Anastas, prin.

Southborough SD
Sch. Sys. Enr. Code 3
Supt. – Dennis Disalvo, 75 BARTLETT ST   01532
Other Schools – See Southborough

Oxford Academy, HOWARD   01532

North Brookfield, Worcester Co., Pop. Code 5
North Brookfield SD
Sch. Sys. Enr. Code 3
Supt. – William Leach
 10 NEW SCHOOL DRIVE   01535
ES, 10 NEW SCHOOL DR   01535
 Lucia Provo, prin.

North Chelmsford, Middlesex Co., Pop. Code 6
Chelmsford SD
Supt. – See Chelmsford
Harrington ES, 120 RICHARDSON RD   01863
 Evelyn Desmarais, prin.
Parker MS, 75 GRANITEVILLE RD   01863
 James Doyle, prin.

North Dartmouth, Bristol Co., Pop. Code 6
Dartmouth SD
Supt. – See South Dartmouth
Dartmouth MS, 529 HAWTHORN ST   02747
 Douglas Pfeninger, prin.
Gidley ES, 1390 TUCKER RD   02747
 Michael Muffs, prin.
Potter ES, 185 CROSS RD   02747
 John Fletcher, prin.

Friends Academy, 1088 TUCKER RD   02747

North Dighton, Bristol Co., Pop. Code 4
Berkley SD
Sch. Sys. Enr. Code 3
Supt. – Russel Latham, HORTON   02764
Other Schools – See Berkley

Dighton-Rehoboth SD
Sch. Sys. Enr. Code 5
Supt. – Joseph Harrington
 155 R HORTON ST   02764
Dighton JHS, 1059 SOMERSET AVE   02764
 Paul Swett, prin.
Other Schools – See Dighton, Rehoboth

Goshold SD
Sch. Sys. Enr. Code 1
Supt. – Russel Latham, HORTON ST   02764
Other Schools – See Cuttyhunk

North Easton, Bristol Co., Pop. Code 6
Easton SD
Sch. Sys. Enr. Code 5
Supt. – George Lane, P O BOX 359   02375
Easton MS, 184 LINCOLN ST   02356
 Andrew Miller, prin.
Moreau Hall ES, 360 WASHINGTON ST   02356
 Sarah Gallahue, prin.
ES, 125 MAIN ST   02356 – Frank Sahl, prin.
Parkview ES, 50 SPOONER ST   02356
 Judith Frederick, prin.
Other Schools – See South Easton

North Falmouth, Barnstable Co., Pop. Code 4
Falmouth SD
Supt. – See East Falmouth
ES, P O BOX 367   02556 – Joseph Leary, prin.

Northfield, Franklin Co., Pop. Code 4
Bernardston SD
Sch. Sys. Enr. Code 2
Supt. – Kevin Courtney, ROUTE 10   01360
Other Schools – See Bernardston

Leyden SD
Sch. Sys. Enr. Code 1
Supt. – Kevin Courtney, RURAL ROUTE 10   01360
Other Schools – See Greenfield

Northfield SD
Sch. Sys. Enr. Code 2
Supt. – Kevin Courtney, ROUTE 10   01360
ES, MAIN   01360 – Joan Benneyan, prin.

Warwick SD
Sch. Sys. Enr. Code 1
Supt. – Kevin Courtney, ROUTE 10   01360
Other Schools – See Orange

North Grafton, Worcester Co., Pop. Code 5
Grafton SD
Supt. – See Grafton
ES, 44 WATERVILLE ST   01536
 Frank Moffat, prin.

North Quincy, Norfolk Co.
Quincy SD
Supt. – See Quincy
Montclair ES, 8 BELMONT ST   02171
 Leon Gould, prin.

Parker ES, 148 BILLINGS RD 02171
Daniel Malvesta, prin.
Squantum ES, 50 HUCKINS AVE 02171
Ruth Haggerty, prin.

Sacred Heart ES, 340 HANCOCK ST 02171

North Reading, Middlesex Co., Pop. Code 7
North Reading SD
Sch. Sys. Enr. Code 4
Supt. – Francis O'Donoghue
SHERMAN ROAD 01864
Batchelder ES, PEABODY 01864
Neal Sanders, prin.
Hood ES, MAYERHILL 01864 – Paul Perry, prin.
Little ES, 9 BARBERRY RD 01864
Ruth Jarvis, prin.

North Uxbridge, Worcester Co., Pop. Code 4
Uxbridge SD
Supt. – See Uxbridge
Blanchard ES, HARTFORD AVE 01538
Wallis Darnley, prin.

North Weymouth, Norfolk Co.
Weymouth SD
Supt. – See Weymouth
Johnson ES, 70 PEARL ST 02191
John Connell, prin.
Wessagusset ES, 75 PILGRIM RD 02191
Michael Merten, prin.

St. Jerome ES, 598 BRIDGE ST 02191

Norton, Bristol Co., Pop. Code 7
Norton SD
Sch. Sys. Enr. Code 4
Supt. – Maurice Splaine, 64 W MAIN ST 02766
MS, 64 W MAIN ST 02766 – Stanley Koss, prin.
Nourse ES, 38 PLAIN ST 02766 – K. Smith, prin.
Solmonese ES, 315 W MAIN ST 02766
Mary Brown, prin.

New Testament School
1 NEW TAUNTON AVE 02766

Norwell, Plymouth Co., Pop. Code 6
Norwell SD
Sch. Sys. Enr. Code 4
Supt. – Robert Bunnell, 322 MAIN ST 02061
JHS, 334 MAIN ST 02061 – Henry Goldman, prin.
Cole ES, 81 HIGH ST 02061 – W. Kaetzer, prin.
Sparrell ES, 322 MAIN ST 02061
Paula Delaney, prin.
Vinal ES, 102 OLD OAKEN BUCKET RD 02061
John Croley, prin.

Norwood, Norfolk Co., Pop. Code 8
Norwood SD
Sch. Sys. Enr. Code 5
Supt. – James Savage
100 WESTOVER PARKWAY 02062
Balch ES, WASHINGTON 02062
Andrew Ciarletta, prin.
Callahan ES, GARFIELD AVE 02062
John Manahan, prin.
Cleveland ES, NICHOLS 02062
William Kenny, prin.
Oldman ES, 165 PROSPECT ST 02062
Richard Talanian, prin.
Prescott ES, 66 RICHLAND RD 02062
Alan Wonson, prin.

St. Catherine of Siena School
249 NAHATAN ST 02062

Oak Bluffs, Dukes Co., Pop. Code 4
Oak Bluffs SD
Supt. – See Vineyard Haven
ES, P O BOX 1325 02557 – Robert Abbey, prin.

Oakham, Worcester Co., Pop. Code 3
Quabbin SD
Supt. – See Barre
Oakham Center ES, COLDBROOK ROAD 01068
Duncan Stewart, prin.

Onset, Plymouth Co., Pop. Code 4
Wareham SD
Supt. – See Wareham
Hammond ES, HIGHLAND AVE 02558
Philip Dyer, prin.

Orange, Franklin Co., Pop. Code 6
New Salem-Wendell SD
Supt. – See Millers Falls
Swift River ES, WENDELL RD 01364
Leonard Strauss, prin.

Orange SD
Sch. Sys. Enr. Code 3
Supt. – David Bramhall, 94 S MAIN ST 01364
Butterfield MS, 94 S MAIN ST 01364
Robert Gaudet, prin.
Dexter Park ES, 1 DEXTER ST EXT 01364
Peter Farrell, Jr., prin.

Warwick SD
Supt. – See Northfield
Warwick Center ES, ROUTE 78 01364
Wallace McCloud, prin.

Orleans, Barnstable Co., Pop. Code 4
Brewster SD
Sch. Sys. Enr. Code 2
Supt. – Robert Neely
78 ELDREDGE PARKWAY 02653

Other Schools – See Brewster
Eastham SD
Sch. Sys. Enr. Code 2
Supt. – Robert Neely
78 ELEREDGE PARKWAY RT 02 02653
Other Schools – See Eastham
Nauset SD
Sch. Sys. Enr. Code 4
Supt. – Robert Neely, 78 ELDREDGE PKY 02653
Nauset Regional MS, 64 ROUTE 28 02653
Brian Atkins, prin.
Orleans SD
Sch. Sys. Enr. Code 2
Supt. – Robert Neely
78 ELDRIDGE PKWY RT 02 02653
ES, 44 ELDRIDGE PARK WAY 02653
Lester Albee, prin.
Wellfleet SD
Sch. Sys. Enr. Code 2
Supt. – Robert Neely
78 ELDREDGE PKWY RT 02 02653
Other Schools – See Wellfleet

Osterville, Barnstable Co.
Barnstable SD
Supt. – See Hyannis
Osterville Bay MS, WEST BAY ROAD 02655
Bernard Powers, prin.
ES, 350 BUMPS RIVER RD 02655
Bernard Powers, prin.

Cape Cod Academy, P O BOX 469 02655

Otis, Berkshire Co., Pop. Code 3
Otis SD
Supt. – See Lee
Otis Consolidated ES, MAIN 01253
Maria Moulthrop, prin.

Otter River, Worcester Co.
Narragansett SD
Sch. Sys. Enr. Code 4
Supt. – Willard Chiasson, 133 S MAIN ST 01436
Other Schools – See Athol, Baldwinville, East
Templeton, Templeton

Oxford, Worcester Co., Pop. Code 7
Oxford SD
Sch. Sys. Enr. Code 4
Supt. – Francis G. Driscoll
5 SIGOURNEY ST 01540
Barton ES, 25 DEPOT RD 01540
Edward Connolly, prin.
Chaffee ES, 10 CLOVER ST 01540
Joan Comeau, prin.
Joslin MS, MAIN 01540 – Garry Degermajian, prin.
MS, 351 MAIN ST 01540 – Stan Sedor, prin.

Palmer, Hampden Co., Pop. Code 7
Palmer SD
Sch. Sys. Enr. Code 4
Supt. – James Pasquill, 24 CONVERSE ST 01069
Park Street ES, 83 PARK ST 01069
George Nicholas, prin.
Quabaug ES, 671 N MAIN ST 01069
Ronald LaViolette, prin.
Thorndike Street ES, 2 PARK ST 01069
Ronald LaViolette, prin.
Other Schools – See Bondsville, Thorndike, Three
Rivers

Paxton, Worcester Co., Pop. Code 5
Paxton SD
Supt. – See Holden
Paxton Center ES, WEST 01612
Charles Gruszka, prin.

Peabody, Essex Co., Pop. Code 8
Peabody SD
Sch. Sys. Enr. Code 6
Supt. – James Buckley, 3 KING ST 01960
Higgins MS, 71 KING ST 01960
John Murtagh, prin.
Brown ES, 200 LYNN ST 01960
Louis Surman, prin.
Burke ES, BIRCH 01960 – Phyllis Rantz, prin.
Carroll ES, NORTHEND 01960
Robert Manning, prin.
Center ES, 18 IRVING ST 01960
Timothy Roche, prin.
Kiley Bros. Memorial ES, 21 JOHNSON 01960
John Murtagh, prin.
South Memorial ES, MAPLE ST EXT 01960
John Birmingham, Jr., prin.
Welch ES, 3 SWAMPSCOTT AVE 01960
William Callahan, prin.
West Memorial ES, BOW 01960
Eugene Staid, prin.

St. John Baptist ES, 19 CHESTNUT ST 01960

Pembroke, Plymouth Co., Pop. Code 7
Pembroke SD
Supt. – See Kingston
Bryantville ES, 30 GURNEY DR 02359
Edwin Borsari, prin.
Hobomock ES, 81 LEARNING LN 02359
Alan Pullman, prin.
North Pembroke ES, 72 PILGRIM RD 02359
J. Fleming, prin.

Silver Lake SD
Supt. – See Kingston

Silver Lake Regional JHS, 559 SCHOOL ST 02359
William Pepper, prin.

Pepperell, Middlesex Co., Pop. Code 6
North Middlesex SD
Supt. – See Townsend
Fitzpatrick ES, MAIN 01463
William Smith, prin.

Petersham, Worcester Co., Pop. Code 4
Petersham SD
Sch. Sys. Enr. Code 1
Supt. – Eileen Perkins, SPRING ST 01366
Petersham Center ES, SPRING 01366
Nancy Ayer, prin.

Pittsfield, Berkshire Co., Pop. Code 8
Pittsfield SD
Sch. Sys. Enr. Code 6
Supt. – Robert Lafrankie, 269 FIRST ST 01201
Herberg MS, 501 POMEROY AVE 01201
Charles Katsounakis, prin.
Reid MS, 950 NORTH ST 01201
Douglas McNally, prin.
Allendale ES, 180 CONNECTICUT AVE 01201
Edward Basinski, prin.
Crosby ES, 517 WEST ST 01201
Eugene O'Brien, prin.
Egremont ES, 84 EGREMONT AVE 01201
Gary Clarkson, prin.
Highland ES, 86 BROOKS AVE 01201
George Farley, prin.
Morningside Community ES
100 BURBANK ST 01201 – James Tynan, prin.
Stearns ES, 75 LEBANON AVE 01201
Linda Porter, prin.
West Side Community ES, WEST UNION 01201
Frank Kelley, prin.
Williams ES, 50 BUSHEY RD 01201
Ann Kuhn, prin.

Notre Dame MS, 41 MELVILLE ST 01201
Sacred Heart ES, 1 MEADOW LN 01201

Plainville, Bristol Co., Pop. Code 5
Plainville SD
Sch. Sys. Enr. Code 3
Supt. – Francis Cinelli, 68 MESSENGER ST 02762
Jackson ES, 69 MESSENGER ST 02762
Francis Cinelli, prin.
Wood MS, 200 SOUTH ST 02762
Francis Cinelli, prin.

Plymouth, Plymouth Co., Pop. Code 8
Plymouth SD
Sch. Sys. Enr. Code 5
Supt. – Bernard Sidman, LINCOLN 02360
Cold Spring ES, ALDEN 02360
Roger Sawyer, prin.
Federal Furnace ES
FEDERAL FURNACE ROAD 02360
Anne Stempleski, prin.
Hedge ES, STANDISH AVE 02360
Marcel Richard, prin.
Indian Brook ES, RURAL ROUTE 08 02360
Joann Sikorsky, prin.
Manomet ES, RURAL ROUTE 01 02360
Martin Koempel, prin.
Morton MS, LINCOLN 02360 – Fred Sarke, prin.
South ES, RURAL ROUTE 06 02360
James Delphin, prin.
West ES
RURAL RTE 80 PLYMPTON ROAD 02360
Robert Cummings, prin.

Plympton, Plymouth Co., Pop. Code 4
Plympton SD
Supt. – See Kingston
Dennett ES, 80 CRESCENT ST 02367
Fred Scully, prin.

Princeton, Worcester Co., Pop. Code 4
Princeton SD
Supt. – See Holden
Princeton Center MS, BOYLSTON AVE 01541
Judith Hunt, prin.
Prince ES, STERLING ROAD 01541
Judith Hunt, prin.

Provincetown, Barnstable Co., Pop. Code 5
Provincetown SD
Sch. Sys. Enr. Code 2
Supt. – Robert Barbarisi, 12 WINSLOW ST 02657
ES, MAYFLOWER LN 02657 – Elliot Tocci, prin.

Truro SD
Sch. Sys. Enr. Code 2
Supt. – Frederick Bardsley, PRINCE ST 02657
Other Schools – See Truro

Quincy, Norfolk Co., Pop. Code 8
Quincy SD
Sch. Sys. Enr. Code 8
Supt. – Robert Ricci, 70 CODDINGTON ST 02169
Atlantic MS, 86 HOLLIS AVE 02171
Thomas Hall, prin.
Broad Meadows MS, 50 CALVIN ROAD 02169
Thomas Hall, prin.
Central MS, 1012 HANCOCK ST 02169
Louis Dimartinis, prin.
Quincy Point MS, EDWARDS AVE 02169
Jean MaClean, prin.
Sterling MS, 444 GRANITE ST 02169
Joseph Long, prin.
Atherton Hough ES, 1084 SEA ST 02169
Edward Baccari, prin.

Furnace Brook ES
 701 FURNACE BROOK PKY 02169
  Charles Bernazzani, prin.
Lincoln-Hancock ES, 300 GRANITE ST 02169
 Dennis Carini, prin.
Merrymount ES, 4 AGAWAM RD 02169
 Gerald Gowen, prin.
Snug Harbor ES, 333 PALMER ST 02169
 Morrie Hibbard, prin.
Webster ES, LANCASTER 02169
 Jean MacLean, prin.
Other Schools – See North Quincy

St. Joseph ES, 22 PRAY ST 02169

Randolph, Norfolk Co., Pop. Code 8
Randolph SD
Sch. Sys. Enr. Code 5
Supt. – John Zoino, 40-42 HIGHLAND AVE 02368
Kennedy JHS, 100 HURLEY DRIVE 02368
 Paul Hannigan, prin.
Devine ES, 29 OLD ST 02368
 John Murphy,Jr., prin.
Donovan ES, 125 REED ST 02368
 Jane Hyman, prin.
Lyons ES, VESEY ROAD 02368
 Francis Dudero, prin.
Young ES, LOU COURTNEY DR 02368
 Joseph Burke, prin.

Raynham, Bristol Co., Pop. Code 6
Raynham SD
Sch. Sys. Enr. Code 4
Supt. – Eileen Williams, 687 PLEASANT ST 02767
Laliberte JHS, PLEASANT 02767
 Alan Jaffe, prin.
Merrill MS, 687 PLEASANT ST 02767
 William Bruno, prin.
North ES, 53 BAKER RD 02767
 Nancy Flynn, prin.
South ES, SOUTH 02767 – Dorothy Newton, prin.
Sullivan ES, 558 S MAIN ST 02767
 Robert Smith, prin.

Reading, Middlesex Co., Pop. Code 7
Reading SD
Sch. Sys. Enr. Code 5
Supt. – Robert Munnelly, 34 GOULD ST 01867
Coolidge MS, 89 BIRCH MEADOW DRIVE 01867
 Albert Lahood, prin.
Parker MS, 45 TEMPLE ST 01867
 John Delaney, prin.
Barrows ES, 16 EDGEMONT AVE 01867
 Charles Papandreou, prin.
Birch Meadow ES, 27 A B LORD DR 01867
 Richard Davidson, prin.
Eaton ES, 365 SUMMER AVE 01867
 Donald Farnham, prin.
Killam ES, 333 CHARLES ST 01867
 Paul Guerrette, prin.

Rehoboth, Bristol Co., Pop. Code 6
Dighton-Rehoboth SD
Supt. – See North Dighton
Beckwith MS, 330 WINTHROP ST 02769
 Francis Lussier, prin.
Palmer River/Anawan ES, WINTHROP 02769
 Alfred St.John, prin.

Revere, Suffolk Co., Pop. Code 8
Revere SD
Sch. Sys. Enr. Code 5
Supt. – William J. Hill, 101 SCHOOL ST 02151
Beachmont ES, 15 EVERARD AVE 02151
 Marie Connors, prin.
Garfield ES, 168 GARFIELD AVE 02151
 William Wayman, prin.
Lincoln ES, 68 TUCKERMAN ST 02151
 Rocco Malfitano, prin.
McKinley ES, 65 YEAMANS ST 02151
 Fred McDonough,Jr., prin.
ES, 395 REVERE ST 02151 – Peter Sarno, prin.
Whelan Memorial ES, 107 NEWHALL ST 02151
 Katherine Romano, prin.

Immaculate Conception ES
 127 WINTHROP AVE 02151

Richmond, Berkshire Co., Pop. Code 4
Richmond SD
Supt. – See Lanesboro
Richmond Consolated ES, ROUTE 41 01254
 Norman Najimy, prin.

Rochester, Plymouth Co., Pop. Code 5
Rochester SD
Supt. – See Mattapoisett
Rochester Memorial ES, 16 PINE ST 02770
 Charles Elofson, prin.

Rockland, Plymouth Co., Pop. Code 7
Rockland SD
Sch. Sys. Enr. Code 5
Supt. – John W. Rogers, 394 UNION ST 02370
JHS, 100 TAUNTON AVE 02370
 Robert Levine, prin.
Esten ES, 733 SUMMER ST 02370
 Gerald Kohn, prin.
Jefferson ES, 34 JAMES 02370
 Anne Nigrosh, prin.
Memorial Park ES, 204 REED ST 02370
 Marilyn Donovan, prin.

Holy Family ES, 6 DEL PRETE AVE 02370

Rockport, Essex Co., Pop. Code 6
Rockport SD
Sch. Sys. Enr. Code 3
Supt. – Carl Knowlton, 4 BROADWAY 01966
Community MS, 16 JERDENS LANE 01966
 Reno Nastasi, prin.
Intermediate Unit MS
 4 BROADWAY #ELEM 01966
 Dorothy Flynn, prin.
Pigeon Cove PS, STORY 01966 – Selma Bell, prin.
Tarr ES, SCHOOL & BROADWAY 01966
 Nancy Grillo, prin.

Roslindale, Suffolk Co.
Boston SD
Supt. – See Boston
Irving MS, 114 CUMMINS HIGHWAY 02131
 R Maloney, prin.
Bates ES, 426 BEECH ST 02131
 Cathrine James, prin.
Conley ES, 450 POPLAR ST 02131
 Daniel Kearns, prin.
Haley ES, 570 AMERICAN LEGION HWY 02131
 Robert Berry, prin.
Longfellow ES, 885 SOUTH ST 02131
 Gerald Hill, prin.
Mozart ES, 236 BEECH ST 02131
 Lloyd Leake, prin.
Philbrick ES, 40 PHILBRICK ST 02131
 John Fisher, prin.
Sumner ES, 15 BASTILE 02131
 Robert Donahue, prin.

Sacred Heart ES, 1035 CANTERBURY ST 02131

Rowe, Berkshire Co.
Rowe SD
Supt. – See Shelburne Falls
ES, POND ROAD 01367 – Paul Swen, prin.

Rowley, Essex Co., Pop. Code 5
Rowley SD
Supt. – See Byfield
Pine Grove ES, MAIN 01969 – Susan King, prin.

Roxbury, Suffolk Co.
Boston SD
Supt. – See Boston
Dearborn MS, 35 GREENVILLE ST 02119
 Charles Ray, prin.
Lewis MS, 131 WALNUT AVE 02119
 William Stevens, prin.
Roosevelt MS, 61 SCHOOL ST 02119
 Tom Deveney, prin.
Timilty MS, 205 ROXBURY ST 02119
 Mary O'Neil, prin.
Wheatley MS, 20 KEARSARGE AVE 02119
 Eugene Ellis, prin.
Ellis ES, 302 WALNUT AVE 02119
 Florence Hadley, prin.
Emerson ES, 6 SHIRLEY ST 02119
 Cassandra Merrilles, prin.
Hale ES, 51 CEDAR 02119
 Pasquale Lochiatto, prin.
Higginson ES, 160 HARRISHOF ST 02119
 Leo Conway, prin.
Mason ES, 150 NORFOLK AVE 02119
 Philip Marino, prin.
Mendell ES, 164 SCHOOL ST 02119
 Patrick McDonough, prin.
Tobin ES, 40 SMITH 02119 – Janet Short, prin.

Our Lady Perpetual Help ES
 94 ST ALPHONSUS ST 02120
St. Francis Desales ES, P O BOX 337 02120
St. Joseph ES, 18 HULBERT ST 02119
St. Patrick ES, 131 MT PLEASANT AVE 02119

Royalston, Worcester Co.
Athol-Royalston SD
Supt. – See Athol
Raymond ES, MAIN 01368 – Anne Donovan, prin.
South Royalston MS, PLEASANT 01368
 Alan Genovese, prin.

Russell, Hampden Co.
Gateway SD
Supt. – See Huntington
ES, HIGHLAND AVE 01071
 Cynthia Walowicz, prin.

Rutland, Worcester Co., Pop. Code 5
Rutland SD
Supt. – See Holden
Naquag ES, 285 MAIN ST 01543
 Charles Varjian, prin.

Salem, Essex Co., Pop. Code 8
Salem SD
Sch. Sys. Enr. Code 5
Supt. – Ed Curtin, 29 HIGHLAND AVE 01970
Salem MS East, 211 LAFAYETTE ST 01970
 Charles Chaurette, prin.
Salem MS West, 29 HIGHLAND AVE 01970
 Joan Donoghue, prin.
Bates ES, LIBERTY HILL AVE 01970
 Peter Doyle, prin.
Bentley ES, 23 MEMORIAL DR 01970
 Lawrence Callahan, prin.
Carlton ES, 10 SKERRY ST 01970
 Charles Walsh, prin.
Mann Laboratory ES, 19 LORING AVE 01970
 Keven Dwyer, prin.
Witchcraft Heights ES, 1 FREDERICK ST 01970
 Edward Zielinski, prin.

St. Joseph ES, 20 HARBOR ST 01970

Salisbury, Essex Co.
Salisbury SD
Supt. – See Byfield
Memorial ES, 22 MAPLE ST 01952
 Marie Corcoran, prin.

Sandisfield, Berkshire Co.
Sandisfield SD
Supt. – See Southwick
ES, RURAL ROUTE 57 01255 – Eugene Drost, prin.

Sandwich, Barnstable Co., Pop. Code 6
Sandwich SD
Sch. Sys. Enr. Code 5
Supt. – Joseph F. Nicholson, P O BOX 646 02563
ES, BEALE AVE 02563 – James Dolan, prin.

Saugus, Essex Co., Pop. Code 8
Saugus SD
Sch. Sys. Enr. Code 5
Supt. – William Doyle, 25 MAIN ST 01906
Ballard ES, RICHARD 01906
 William Vitagliano, prin.
Evans ES, EAST DENVER 01906 – Earl Ellis, prin.
Lynnhurst ES, ELM 01906 – Michael Tanen, prin.
Oaklandvale ES, 266 MAIN ST 01906
 William Vitagliano, prin.
Veterans Memorial ES, HURD AVE 01906
 Victor Leone, prin.
Waybright ES, TALBOT 01906 – Earl Ellis, prin.

Savoy, Berkshire Co.
Savoy SD
Supt. – See North Adams
ES, CHAPEL ROAD 01256 – Daniel Wilk, prin.

Scituate, Plymouth Co., Pop. Code 7
Scituate SD
Sch. Sys. Enr. Code 5
Supt. – John P. Kulevich
 606 CUSHING HIGHWAY 02066
Gates IS, 327 FIRST PARISH ROAD 02066
 J Gibbons, prin.
Cushing ES, 1 ABERDEEN DR 02066
 Jacqueline White, prin.
Hatherly ES, 72 ANN VINAL RD 02066
 Guido Risi, prin.
Wampatuck ES, 266 TILDEN RD 02066
 Louis Von Kahle, prin.

Seekonk, Bristol Co., Pop. Code 7
Seekonk SD
Sch. Sys. Enr. Code 4
Supt. – George McLaughlin, 1 SCHOOL ST 02771
IS, 660 NEWMAN AVE 02771
 Gerald Kaveny, prin.
Aitken ES, NEWMAN AVE 02771
 John Kraskouskas, prin.
Martin ES, COLE 02771 – John Searles, prin.
North ES, NORTH 02771 – Stephen Dunn, prin.

Sharon, Norfolk Co., Pop. Code 7
Sharon SD
Sch. Sys. Enr. Code 5
Supt. – John F. Maloney, 1 SCHOOL ST 02067
JHS, 75 MOUNTAIN ST 02067
 Robert Stromberg, prin.
Cottage Street ES, 30 COTTAGE ST 02067
 Joseph Bruno, prin.
East ES, 45 WILSHIRE DR 02067
 Judith Freedberg, prin.
Heights ES, 454 S MAIN ST 02067
 Leona Flaxer, prin.

Sheffield, Berkshire Co., Pop. Code 5
Southern Berkshire SD
Sch. Sys. Enr. Code 3
Supt. – Thomas Consolati, P O BOX 339 01257
New Marlborough Central ES, P O BOX 326 01257
 Paul Langer, prin.
Sheffield Center ES, P O BOX 326 01257
 Paul Langer, prin.
South Egremont ES, P O BOX 326 01257
 Paul Langer, prin.

Shelburne Falls, Franklin Co., Pop. Code 4
Ashfield-Plainfield Regional SD
Sch. Sys. Enr. Code 2
Supt. – Bruce Willard, ASHFIELD HCR 01370
Other Schools – See Ashfield

Buckland Colrain Shelburn SD
Sch. Sys. Enr. Code 3
Supt. – Bruce Willard, ASHFIELD HCR 01370
Buckland-Shelburne Regional ES
 75 MECHANIC ST 01370 – Russell Jones, prin.
Other Schools – See Colrain

Hawlemont SD
Sch. Sys. Enr. Code 2
Supt. – Bruce Willard, ASHFIELD HCR 01370
Other Schools – See Charlemont

Rowe SD
Sch. Sys. Enr. Code 1
Supt. – Bruce Williard, ASHFIELD HCR 01370
Other Schools – See Rowe

Sherborn, Middlesex Co.
Sherborn SD
Supt. – See Dover
Pine Hill ES, PINE HILL LN 01770
 Robert Luther, prin.

Shirley, Middlesex Co.
Shirley SD
Sch. Sys. Enr. Code 2
Supt. – Burton Coffman
  LANCASTER ROAD 01464
White ES, LANCASTER ROAD 01464
  Burton Cofman, prin.

Shrewsbury, Worcester Co., Pop. Code 7
Shrewsbury SD
Sch. Sys. Enr. Code 5
Supt. – John P. Collins, 100 MAPLE AVE 01545
Coolidge ES, 15 MAY ST 01545
  Arthur Bergeron, prin.
Paton ES, GRAFTON 01545 – Gail Bisceglia, prin.
MS, 30 SHERWOOD AVE 01545
  Preston Shaw, prin.
Spring Street ES, SPRING ST 01545
  Peter Zona, prin.

St. Mary ES, 16 SUMMER ST 01545

Shutesbury, Franklin Co.
Shutesbury SD
Supt. – See Millers Falls
ES, W PELHAM RD 01072 – Leslie Edinson, prin.

Somerset, Bristol Co., Pop. Code 7
Somerset SD
Sch. Sys. Enr. Code 5
Supt. – Thomas J. Daley
  WOOD & COUNTY STS 02725
North MS, WHETSTONE HILL ROAD 02726
  Walter Palmer, prin.
South MS, 1141 BRAYTON AVE 02726
  Harry Donahue, prin.
Chace Street ES, CHACE 02726
  Robert Murphy, prin.
Pottersville ES, 101 WOOD ST 02726
  Betty Calise, prin.
South ES, 700 READ ST 02726
  Juliann Kerrigan, prin.
Village ES, HIGH 02726 – Lucia Gagnon, prin.
Wilbur ES, BRAYTON POINT ROAD 02725
  Robert Laing, prin.

Somerville, Middlesex Co., Pop. Code 8
Somerville SD
Sch. Sys. Enr. Code 6
Supt. – John Davis, 81 HIGHLAND AVE 02143
Brown ES, 201 WILLOW AVE 02144
  William McDonald, prin.
Conwell ES, 1 CAPEN COURT 02144
  John O'Meara, prin.
Cummings ES, 93 SCHOOL ST 02143
  John McDonald, prin.
East Somerville Community ES
  115 PEARL ST 02145 – David Johnston, prin.
Healey ES, 5 MEACHAM ST 02145
  James Papadonis, prin.
Kennedy ES, 85 ELM 02144 – John Russell, prin.
Lincoln Park Community ES
  290 WASHINGTON ST 02143
  Robert Sorabella, prin.
Powder House Community ES
  1060 BROADWAY 02144
  Cornelius McGreal, prin.
Winter Hill Community ES
  115 SYCAMORE ST 02145 – M. Hart, prin.

Little Flower ES, 17 FRANKLIN 02145
St. Ann ES, 50 THURSTON ST 02145
St. Anthony ES, 480 SOMERVILLE AVE 02143
St. Catherine Genda ES, 194 SUMMER ST 02143
St. Joseph ES, 15 WEBSTER AVE 02143
St. Polycarp ES, 8 BUTLER DR 02145

Southampton, Hampshire Co.
Southampton SD
Supt. – See Westhampton
Larrabee ES, COLLEGE HWY 01073
  Margaret Regan, prin.
Norris MS, POMEROY MEADOW ROAD 01073
  Margaret Regan, prin.

South Ashburnham, Worcester Co., Pop. Code 4
Ashburnham-Westminster SD
Supt. – See Ashburnham
Briggs ES, WILLIAMS ROAD 01466
  Steven Gould, prin.

South Attleboro, Bristol Co.
Attleboro SD
Supt. – See Attleboro
Coelho MS, 75 BROWN ST 02703
  Charles Cokonis, prin.
Roberts ES, 80 ROY AVE 02703
  William Skitt, prin.

Dayspring Christian ES
  1052 NEWPORT AVE 02703

South Barre, Worcester Co.
Quabbin SD
Supt. – See Barre
Langley ES, PEACH 01074 – John Cirelli, prin.

Southborough, Worcester Co., Pop. Code 6
Southborough SD
Supt. – See Northborough
Woodward MS, CORDAVILLE ROAD 01772
  P. Trottier, prin.
Finn ES, RICHARDS ROAD 01772
  Edward Valinski, prin.
Neary MS, 53 PARKERVILLE RD 01772
  Robert Rosenblatt, prin.

Fay ES, 48 MAIN ST 01772

South Boston, Suffolk Co.
Boston SD
Supt. – See Boston
Gavin MS, 2156 DORCHESTER ST 02127
  Joseph Lee, prin.
Condon ES, 200 D ST 02127
  Cornelius Cronin, prin.
Perkins ES, 50 BURKE ST 02127
  William O'Connell, prin.
Perry ES, 745 E 7TH ST 02127
  Sally Gorham, prin.
Tynan ES, 650 E FOURTH ST 02127
  Virginia Duseau, prin.

Gate of Heaven ES, 609 E FOURTH ST 02127
St. Augustine ES, 209 E ST 02127
St. Brigid ES, 866 E BROADWAY 02127
St. Mary ES, 52 BOSTON ST 02127
St. Peter ES, 518 E 6TH ST 02127

Southbridge, Worcester Co., Pop. Code 7
Holland SD
Supt. – See Sturbridge
Holland ES, RURAL ROUTE 2 01550
  Ruth Wade, prin.

Southbridge SD
Sch. Sys. Enr. Code 5
Supt. – Arnold Lanni, P O BOX 665 01550
Wells JHS, 82 MARCY ST 01550
  Don Cesarini, prin.
Charlton Street ES, 220 CHARLTON ST 01550
  David O'Brien, prin.
Eastford Road ES, 120 EASTFORD RD 01550
  C. Montigny, prin.
West Street ES, 156 WEST ST 01550
  Joann Austin, prin.

South Dartmouth, Bristol Co., Pop. Code 6
Dartmouth SD
Sch. Sys. Enr. Code 5
Supt. – Richard Warren, 8 BUSH ST 02748
Cushman ES, 746 DARTMOUTH ST 02748
  Victor Ladetto, prin.
Demello ES, 654 DARTMOUTH ST 02748
  Edmund Tavares, prin.
Other Schools – See North Dartmouth

South Deerfield, Franklin Co., Pop. Code 4
Conway SD
Sch. Sys. Enr. Code 2
Supt. – Richard Plimpton, 311 N MAIN ST 01373
Other Schools – See Conway

Deerfield SD
Sch. Sys. Enr. Code 2
Supt. – Richard Plimpton, 311 N MAIN ST 01373
ES, 60 CONWAY ST 01373
  Edward Trzcienski, prin.
Other Schools – See Deerfield

Sunderland SD
Sch. Sys. Enr. Code 2
Supt. – Richard Plimpton, 311 N MAIN ST 01373
Other Schools – See Sunderland

Whately SD
Sch. Sys. Enr. Code 2
Supt. – Richard Plimpton, 311 N MAIN ST 01373
Other Schools – See Whately

South Dennis, Barnstable Co., Pop. Code 4
Dennis-Yarmouth SD
Supt. – See South Yarmouth
Wixon MS, RURAL ROUTE 134 02660
  William Griffith, prin.

South Easton, Bristol Co.
Easton SD
Supt. – See North Easton
Center ES, DEPOT 02375 – Neil Mosman, prin.

South Grafton, Worcester Co.
Grafton SD
Supt. – See Grafton
ES, 188 MAIN ST 01560 – Anthony Cipro,Jr., prin.

South Hadley, Hampshire Co., Pop. Code 7
South Hadley SD
Sch. Sys. Enr. Code 4
Supt. – Chester Towne, 116 MAIN ST 01075
MS, 100 MOSIER ST 01075
  Richard Guerrera, prin.
Mosier MS, 101 MOSIER ST 01075
  Anita Page, prin.
Plains ES, 267 GRANBY RD 01075
  Edgar Noel, prin.

South Hamilton, Essex Co., Pop. Code 5
Hamilton-Wenham SD
Sch. Sys. Enr. Code 4
Supt. – Patricia Alger, 775 BAY ROAD 01982
Cutler ES, 237 ASBURY ST 01982
  Janice Yelland, prin.
Winthrop ES, 325 BAY RD 01982
  Glenn Rogers, prin.
Other Schools – See Wenham

South Lancaster, Worcester Co., Pop. Code 5

South Lancaster Academy
  GEORGE HILL ROAD 01561

South Weymouth, Suffolk Co.
Weymouth SD
Supt. – See Weymouth
Fulton ES, 245 POND ST 02190
  Donald Brightman, prin.
Nash ES, 1003 FRONT ST 02190
  Otis McCorkle, prin.
Talbot ES, 277 RALPH TALBOT ST 02190
  Robert Driscoll, prin.
Union Street ES, 400 UNION ST 02190
  Paul Kearney, prin.

St. Francis Xavier ES, 236 PLEASANT ST 02190

Southwick, Hampden Co., Pop. Code 6
Granville SD
Sch. Sys. Enr. Code 2
Supt. – Louis Josselyn
  63 FEEDING HILLS ROAD 01077
Other Schools – See Granville

Sandisfield SD
Sch. Sys. Enr. Code 1
Supt. – Louis Josselyn
  63 FEEDING HILLS ROAD 01077
Other Schools – See Sandisfield

Southwick-Tolland SD
Sch. Sys. Enr. Code 4
Supt. – Louis S. Josselyn
  63 FEEDING HILLS ROAD 01077
Powder Mill ES, 94 POWDER MILL ROAD 01077
  Robert Spear, prin.
Woodland ES, 80 POWDER MILL RD 01077
  Louis Crawford, prin.

South Yarmouth, Barnstable Co., Pop. Code 6
Dennis-Yarmouth SD
Sch. Sys. Enr. Code 5
Supt. – Michael McCaffray
  296 STATION AVE 02664
Simpkins MS, MAIN 02664 – Nancy Melia, prin.
ES, OFF ROUTH 28 02664
  Laurence MacArthur, prin.
Other Schools – See Dennis Port, South Dennis, West
  Yarmouth

Trinity Cape Cod ES, 10 CARTER RD 02664

Spencer, Worcester Co., Pop. Code 7
Spencer-East Brookfield SD
Sch. Sys. Enr. Code 4
Supt. – Phillip Devaux, 302 MAIN ST 01562
Prouty JHS, 195 MAIN ST 01562
  John Begley, prin.
Grove Street ES, GROVE 01562
  Virginia Westwell, prin.
Lake Street ES, LAKE 01562
  Michael Daniels, prin.
Maple Street MS, 68 MAPLE ST 01562
  David Police, prin.
Pleasant Street ES, 56 PLEASANT ST 01562
  Marie McDevitt, prin.
West Main Street ES, WEST MAIN 01562
  Wayne Jyringi, prin.
Other Schools – See East Brookfield

Springfield, Hampden Co., Pop. Code 9
Springfield SD
Sch. Sys. Enr. Code 7
Supt. – Thomas Donahoe, P O BOX 1410 01102
Armory Street MS, 426 ARMORY ST 01104
  James Moriarty, prin.
Balliet ES, 111 SEYMOUR AVE 01109
  Georgianna Marshall, prin.
Beal ES, 285 TIFFANY ST 01108
  Michael Glickman, prin.
Bowles ES, 24 BOWLES PARK 01104
  Sanda Vella, prin.
Brightwood ES, 471 PLAINFIELD ST 01107
  Bruno Marsili, prin.
Brookings MS, 367 HANCOCK ST 01105
  Maryanne Herron, prin.
Brunton ES, 1801 PARKER ST 01128
  Diantha Ferrier, prin.
DeBerry ES, 670 UNION ST 01109
  Barbara Jefferson, prin.
Dorman ES, 20 LYDIA ST 01109
  Ann Smyth, prin.
Ells ES, 319 CORTLAND ST 01109
  Raymond Lynch, prin.
Freedman MS, 90 CHEROKEE DR 01109
  Beverly Brown, prin.
Glenwood ES, 50 MORISON TER 01104
  Robert Kellther, prin.
Glickman ES, 120 ASHLAND AVE 01119
  Charles O'Leary, prin.
Harris ES, 58 HARTFORD TER 01118
  Claire Crean, prin.
Homer Street ES, 43 HOMER ST 01109
  Theodore LeVine, prin.
Howard Street ES, 59 HOWARD ST 01105
  Alfred Zanetti, prin.
Kensington Avenue ES
  31 KENSINGTON AVE 01108
  Jeffrey Sullivan, prin.
Liberty ES, 962 CAREW ST 01104
  Michael Fioretti, prin.
Lincoln ES, 732 CHESTNUT ST 01107
  John O'Malley, prin.
Lynch ES, 315 N BRANCH PKY 01119
  James Shea, prin.
Memorial ES, 190 SURREY RD 01118
  Nina Tabb, prin.

New North Community MS
    200 BIRNIE AVE   01107 – Mary Dryden, prin.
Pottenger ES, 1435 CAREW ST   01104
    Judith Kennedy, prin.
Sixteen Acres ES, 50 EMPRESS CT   01129
    Mary Walsh, prin.
Sumner Avenue ES, 45 SUMNER AVE   01108
    Carol Castigan, prin.
Talmadge ES, 1395 ALLEN ST   01118
    Hardin Stewart, prin.
Warner MS, 493 PARKER ST   01129
    Marcia Spaulding, prin.
Washington MS, 141 WASHINGTON ST   01108
    John Murphy,Jr., prin.
White ES, 300 WHITE ST   01108
    John Fitzgerald, prin.
Other Schools – See Indian Orchard

Pioneer Valley Christian School
    965 PLUMTREE ROAD   01119
Holy Cross ES, 153 EDDYWOOD ST   01118
Holy Name ES, 37 ALDERMAN ST   01108
Mt. Carmel ES, 36 MARGARET ST   01105
Our Lady Sacred Heart ES
    52 ROSEWELL ST   01109
Our Lady of Hope ES, 474 ARMORY ST   01104
Sacred Heart ES, 27 EVERETT ST   01104
Springfield Christian ES, 627 STATE ST   01109
St. Joseph ES, 1239 COLUMBUS AVE   01105

Sterling, Worcester Co.
Sterling SD
Supt. – See Holden
Butterick ES, MAIN   01564 – Zeven Santoian, prin.
Chocksett ES, BOUTELLE ROAD   01565
    Zaven Santoian, prin.
Houghton ES, 32 BOUTELLE RD   01564
    Zaven Santoian, prin.

Stockbridge, Berkshire Co., Pop. Code 4
Berkshire Hills SD
Sch. Sys. Enr. Code 4
Supt. – Edward Sakal
    BERKSHIRE HILLS REG   01262
Stockbridge Plain ES, MAIN   01262
    Thomas Meade, prin.
Other Schools – See Great Barrington, Housatonic,
    West Stockbridge

Stoneham, Middlesex Co., Pop. Code 7
Stoneham SD
Sch. Sys. Enr. Code 5
Supt. – William Hoyt, 149 FRANKLIN ST   02180
JHS, 101 CENTRAL ST   02180
    William Orman, prin.
Central ES, 25 WILLIAM ST   02180
    John Grillo, prin.
Colonial Park ES, AVALON ROAD   02180
    John Grillo, prin.
North ES, COLLINCOTE   02180
    Arthur Duffy, prin.
Robin Hood ES, MAGNOLIA TER   02180
    Robert Grant, prin.
South ES, SUMMER ST   02180
    Arthur Duffy, prin.

St. Patrick ES, 20 PLEASANT ST   02180

Stoughton, Norfolk Co., Pop. Code 8
Stoughton SD
Sch. Sys. Enr. Code 5
Supt. – John G. Murray, 232 PEARL ST   02072
JHS, 211 CUSHING ST   02072 – R. O'Donnell, prin.
Chemung Hill ES, 1800 CENTRAL ST   02072
    Helen Hansen, prin.
Gibbons ES, 235 MORTON ST   02072
    John Griffin, prin.
Jones ES, 31 PIERCE ST   02072
    James Bryant, prin.
North ES, 131 PINE ST   02072
    Joseph Dawe,Jr., prin.
South ES, 171 ASH ST   02072 – David Fisher, prin.
West ES, 1322 CENTRAL ST   02072
    Richard Wilkins, prin.

Stow, Middlesex Co., Pop. Code 6
Stow SD
Sch. Sys. Enr. Code 3
Supt. – Arthur Bettencourt
    403 GREAT ROAD   01775
Hale MS, HARTLEY ROAD   01775
    Gary Oakes, prin.
Center MS, 403 GREAT RD   01775
    Ethel Furst, prin.
Pompositticut ES, 511 GREAT RD   01775
    Ethel Furst, prin.

Sturbridge, Worcester Co., Pop. Code 6
Brimfield SD
Sch. Sys. Enr. Code 2
Supt. – Roland Wilson
    BROOKFIELD ROAD   01566
Other Schools – See Brimfield

Brookfield SD
Sch. Sys. Enr. Code 2
Supt. – Roland Wilson
    BROOKFIELD ROAD   01566
Other Schools – See Brookfield

Holland SD
Sch. Sys. Enr. Code 2
Supt. – Roland Wilson
    BROOKFIELD ROAD   01566
Other Schools – See Southbridge

Sturbridge SD
Sch. Sys. Enr. Code 3
Supt. – Roland Wilson
    BROOKFIELD ROAD   01566
Burgess ES, P O BOX 27   01566
    John Snelgrove, prin.

Wales SD
Sch. Sys. Enr. Code 2
Supt. – Roland Wilson
    BROOKFIELD ROAD   01566
Other Schools – See Wales

Sudbury, Middlesex Co., Pop. Code 7
Sudbury SD
Sch. Sys. Enr. Code 4
Supt. – David Jackson
    472 CONCORD ROAD   01776
Curtis MS, 22 PRATTS MILL ROAD   01776
    Joan McKenna, prin.
Haynes ES, 169 HAYNES RD   01776
    Chet Delani, prin.
Noyes ES, 280 OLD SUDBURY RD   01776
    Paul Pelletier, prin.

Sunderland, Franklin Co.
Sunderland SD
Supt. – See South Deerfield
ES, SCHOOL ST   01375 – Marshall Aronstam, prin.

Sutton, Worcester Co., Pop. Code 6
Sutton SD
Sch. Sys. Enr. Code 4
Supt. – Gordon Spence, BOSTON ROAD   01527
MS, 10 MEMORIAL DRIVE   01527
    Edward F. Grant, prin.
ES, BOSTON ROAD   01527 – Beverly Brown, prin.

Swampscott, Essex Co., Pop. Code 7
Swampscott SD
Sch. Sys. Enr. Code 4
Supt. – Richard Chrystal, 207 FOREST AVE   01907
JHS, 71 GREENWOOD AVE   01907
    Michael Connolly, prin.
Clarke ES, NORFOLK AVE   01907
    Leon Marden,Jr., prin.
Hadley ES, 24 REDINGTON ST   01907
    Leon Marden,Jr., prin.
Machon ES, 35 BURPEE RD   01907
    Norry Lessard, prin.
Stanley ES, 10 WHITMAN RD   01907
    Norry Lessard, prin.

Swansea, Bristol Co., Pop. Code 7
Swansea SD
Sch. Sys. Enr. Code 5
Supt. – John E. McCarthy
    1 GARDNER NECK ROAD   02777
Case JHS, 195 MAIN ST   02777
    Ken Sheehan, prin.
Bark Street ES, STEVENS ROAD   02777
    M. Zagorski, prin.
Brown ES, GARDNERS NECK ROAD   02777
    Elgin Boyce,Jr., prin.
Gardner ES, 10 CHURCH ST   02777
    Robert Couture, prin.
Luther ES, 100 PEARSE RD   02777
    Roger Pontes, prin.
Mason-Barney ES
    OLD PROVIDENCE ROAD   02777
    M. Zagorski, prin.
St. Louis De France MS
    66 BUFFINGTON ST   02777 – M. Zagorski, prin.

Taunton, Bristol Co., Pop. Code 8
Taunton SD
Sch. Sys. Enr. Code 6
Supt. – Gerald Croteau, 50 WILLIAMS ST   02780
Cohannet MS, 120A COHANNET ST   02780
    Richard Faulkner, prin.
Mulcahey MS, 28 CLIFFORD ST   02780
    Gerald Puccini, prin.
Parker MS, 50 WILLIAMS ST   02780
    Edmund Teixeira, prin.
Bennett ES, 41 N WALKER ST   02780
    Armand DeSrosters,Jr., prin.
Galligan ES, 15 SHERIDAN ST   02780
    Edward Pietnik, prin.
Hopewell ES, 16 MONROE   02780
    Edward Castle,Sr., prin.
Leddy ES, 36 SECOND   02780
    Mildred Braga, prin.
Leonard ES, 354 W BRITANNIA ST   02780
    George Ferreira, prin.
Maxham ES, 141 OAK   02780
    Bruce Buttermore, prin.
Pole ES, 110 COUNTY ST   02780
    James Lincoln, prin.
Walker ES, 145 BERKLEY ST   02780
    Arthur Travers, prin.
Other Schools – See East Taunton

Taunton Catholic MS, 61 SUMMER ST   02780
Our Lady of Lourdes ES, 52 FIRST ST   02780
St. Mary PS, 106 WASHINGTON ST   02780

Teaticket, Barnstable Co.
Falmouth SD
Supt. – See East Falmouth
ES, 45 MARAVISTA AVENUE EXT   02536
    Raymond Kenney, prin.

Templeton, Worcester Co.
Narragansett SD
Supt. – See Otter River

Templeton Center ES, P O BOX C   01468
    Kenneth Vaidulas, prin.

Tewksbury, Middlesex Co., Pop. Code 7
Tewksbury SD
Sch. Sys. Enr. Code 5
Supt. – John W. Wynn, 1469 ANDOVER ST   01876
JHS, 10 VICTOR DRIVE   01876
    Richard Griffin, prin.
Dewing ES, 1469 ANDOVER ST   01876
    John Weir, prin.
Heath-Brook ES, 165 SHAWSHEEN ST   01876
    Antonio Terenzi, prin.
North Street ES, 133 NORTH ST   01876
    William Tsimtsos, prin.
Trahan ES, SALEM RD   01876
    Edward Pelletier, prin.

Thorndike, Hampden Co.
Palmer SD
Supt. – See Palmer
ES, 23 MAIN   01079 – George Nicholas, prin.

Three Rivers, Hampden Co.
Palmer SD
Supt. – See Palmer
ES, 6 FRONT ST   01080 – George Nicholas, prin.

Topsfield, Essex Co., Pop. Code 6
Boxford SD
Sch. Sys. Enr. Code 3
Supt. – Joseph Connelly, 60 MAIN ST   01983
Other Schools – See Boxford

Topsfield SD
Sch. Sys. Enr. Code 2
Supt. – Joseph Connelly, 60 MAIN ST   01983
Proctor MS, 60 MAIN ST   01983
    William Leccese, prin.
Steward ES, 261 PERKINS ROW   01983
    Eva Paddock, prin.

Townsend, Middlesex Co., Pop. Code 6
North Middlesex SD
Sch. Sys. Enr. Code 5
Supt. – Daniel Cabral, P O BOX 482   01469
Hawthorne Brook MS, BROOKLINE ROAD   01469
    James McCormick, prin.
Spaulding Memorial ES, 1 WHITCOMB   01469
    Anthony Luzzetti, prin.
Other Schools – See Ashby, East Pepperell, Pepperell

Truro, Barnstable Co.
Truro SD
Supt. – See Provincetown
Truro Central ES, RURAL ROUTE 06   02666
    Martin Coyle, prin.

Turners Falls, Franklin Co., Pop. Code 5
Gill-Montague SD
Sch. Sys. Enr. Code 4
Supt. – D. R. Morrison, CROCKER AVE   01376
Gill ES, BOYLE ROAD   01376
    Beatrice Blain, prin.
Hillcrest Street ES, 12 GRISWOLD ST   01376
    John Collins, prin.
Sheffield MS, 41 CROCKER AVE   01376
    Joseph Ruscioaro, prin.
Other Schools – See Montague

Tyngsborough, Middlesex Co., Pop. Code 6
Tyngsborough SD
Sch. Sys. Enr. Code 4
Supt. – David Hawkins
    250 MIDDLESEX ROAD   01879
Lakeview MS, 135 COBURN RD   01879
    Thomas Saad, prin.
Winslow ES, 250 MIDDLESEX RD   01879
    Thomas Saad, prin.

Academy of Notre Dame
    180 MIDDLESEX ROAD   01879

Upton, Worcester Co., Pop. Code 5
Mendon-Upton SD
Sch. Sys. Enr. Code 4
Supt. – Dave Crisafulli, P O BOX 176   01568
Memorial ES, MAIN & FISKE   01568
    Edward Soter, prin.
Other Schools – See Mendon

Uxbridge, Worcester Co., Pop. Code 6
Uxbridge SD
Sch. Sys. Enr. Code 4
Supt. – Michael Ronan, CAPRON ST   01569
Whitin IS, GRANITE   01569
    Mary Dickerson, prin.
Taft ES, GRANITE   01569 – Wallis Darnley, prin.
Other Schools – See North Uxbridge

Our Lady of the Valley ES, 71 MENDON ST   01569

Vineyard Haven, Dukes Co., Pop. Code 4
Chilmark SD
Sch. Sys. Enr. Code 1
Supt. – Francis Pachico, P O BOX 639   02568
Other Schools – See Chilmark

Edartown SD
Sch. Sys. Enr. Code 2
Supt. – Francis Pachico, P O BOX 639   02568
Other Schools – See Edgartown

Oak Bluffs SD
Sch. Sys. Enr. Code 2
Supt. – Francis Pachico, P O BOX 639   02568
Other Schools – See Oak Bluffs

Tisbury SD
Sch. Sys. Enr. Code 2
Supt. – Francis Pachico, P O BOX 639   02568
Tisbury ES, P O BOX 878   02568
  Alan Campbell, prin.

West Tisbury SD
Sch. Sys. Enr. Code 2
Supt. – Francis Pachico, P O BOX 639   02568
Other Schools – See West Tisbury

Waban, Suffolk Co.
Newton SD
Supt. – See Newtonville
Angier ES, 1697 BEACON ST   02168
  Ruth Chapman, prin.
Zervas ES, 30 BEETHOVEN AVE   02168
  Sarah Williams, prin.

Wakefield, Middlesex Co., Pop. Code 7
Wakefield SD
Sch. Sys. Enr. Code 5
Supt. – Stephen F. Maio, 525 MAIN ST   01880
JHS, 525 MAIN ST   01880 – John Sardella, prin.
Atwell Central ES, 485 MAIN ST   01880
  Margaret McGrath, prin.
Dolbeare ES, 340 LOWELL ST   01880
  Charles Greene, prin.
Doyle ES, 11 PAUL AVE   01880
  George Weldon, prin.
Franklin ES, 100 NAHANT ST   01880
  Ron Eckel, prin.
Greenwood ES, 1030 MAIN ST   01880
  Nat Finklestein, prin.
Hurd ES, 26 CORDIS ST   01880 – Ron Eckel, prin.
Montrose ES, 531 LOWELL ST   01880
  Charles Greene, prin.
Walton ES, 40 WESTERN AVE   01880
  George Weldon, prin.
West Ward ES, 39 PROSPECT ST   01880
  George Weldon, prin.

St. Joseph ES, 15 GOULD ST   01880

Wales, Hampden Co.
Wales SD
Supt. – See Sturbridge
ES, MAIN   01081 – Leland Miller, prin.

Walpole, Norfolk Co., Pop. Code 7
Walpole SD
Sch. Sys. Enr. Code 5
Supt. – Don Burghess, SCHOOL   02081
Johnson MS, ROBBINS ROAD   02081
  Richard Sullivan, prin.
Fisher ES, GOULD   02081 – Harold Leblanc, prin.
Other Schools – See East Walpole

Blessed Sacrament ES, 808 EAST ST   02081

Waltham, Middlesex Co., Pop. Code 8
Waltham SD
Sch. Sys. Enr. Code 6
Supt. – John J. Daddona, 488 MAIN ST   02254
Central MS, 55 SCHOOL ST   02154
  Sidney Smith, prin.
Kennedy MS, 655 LEXINGTON ST   02154
  G. MacArthur, prin.
South MS, 520 MOODY ST   02154
  Paul Connolly, prin.
Banks ES, 948 MAIN ST   02154
  Sally Maloney, prin.
Bright ES, 260 GROVE ST   02154
  James Callahan, prin.
Fitch ES, 14 ASH ST   02154
  Suzanne McIvor, prin.
Fitzgerald ES, 140 BEAL RD   02154
  Leo Hill, prin.
MacArthur ES, 494 LINCOLN ST   02154
  John Cronin, prin.
Northeast ES, PUTNEY LN   02154
  Eugene Terrenzi, prin.
Plympton ES, 20 FARNSWORTH AVE   02154
  A. Suflit, prin.
Whittemore ES, 30 PARMENTER RD   02154
  Patricia Fitzgerald, prin.

Our Lady Comforter Afflict ES
  920 TRAPELO RD   02154
St. Jude ES, 175 MAIN ST   02154

Ware, Hampshire Co., Pop. Code 6
Ware SD
Sch. Sys. Enr. Code 4
Supt. – Augustus Pesce, OFF GOULD ROAD   01082
JHS, 68 CHURCH ST   01082
  David W. Carlson, prin.
ES, OFF GOULD ROAD   01082
  Carolyn Streeter, prin.

St. Mary ES, 60 SOUTH ST   01082

Wareham, Plymouth Co., Pop. Code 7
Wareham SD
Sch. Sys. Enr. Code 5
Supt. – Edwin Denton, 54 MARION ROAD   02571
IS, 121R MARION ROAD   02571
  Frederico Medina,Jr., prin.
Decas ES, 760 MAIN ST   02571
  Leo Peduzzi, prin.
Minot Forest ES, MINOT AVE   02571
  Peter Coville, prin.
Other Schools – See East Wareham, Onset, West
  Wareham

Warren, Worcester Co., Pop. Code 5
Warren SD
Sch. Sys. Enr. Code 2
Supt. – William Haggerty, HIGH ST   01083
ES, HIGH   01083 – G. Wells, prin.

Watertown, Middlesex Co., Pop. Code 8
Watertown SD
Sch. Sys. Enr. Code 5
Supt. – Daniel G. O'Connor
  30 COMMON ST   02172
Cunniff ES, 246 WARREN ST   02172
  John Degnan, prin.
Hosmer/East ES, CONCORD ROAD   02172
  Joseph Carroll, prin.
Lowell ES, ORCHARD   02172
  William Corbett, prin.
Phillips ES, 30 COMMON ST   02172
  Jack Chinian, prin.
West Marshall ES, WAVERLEY AVE   02172
  John Burns, prin.

Agbu Armenian ES, 465 MT AUBURN ST   02172
St. Patrick ES, 20 CHURCH HILL LN   02172

Wayland, Middlesex Co., Pop. Code 7
Wayland SD
Sch. Sys. Enr. Code 4
Supt. – William G. Zimmerman
  41 COCHITUATE ROAD   01778
JHS, 201 MAIN ST   01778 – Richard Schaye, prin.
Claypit Hill ES, CLAYPIT HILL ROAD   01778
  Chester Zwonik, prin.
Happy Hollow ES, 63 PEQUCT ROAD   01778
  John Talbot, prin.

Webster, Worcester Co., Pop. Code 7
Webster SD
Sch. Sys. Enr. Code 4
Supt. – Jeremiah Moriarity, P O BOX 430   01570
Park Avenue ES, PARK AVE   01570
  Chester Makowiecki, prin.
MS, NEGUS   01570 – Michael Nalewajk, prin.

St. Anne ES, DAY ST   01570
St. Joseph ES, 53 WHITCOMB ST   01570
St. Louis ES, 40 NEGUS ST   01570

Wellesley, Norfolk Co., Pop. Code 8
Wellesley SD
Sch. Sys. Enr. Code 5
Supt. – Carla Delitis, 12 SEWARD ROAD   02181
MS, 50 KINGSBURY ST   02181
  David Hardy, prin.
Bates ES, 116 ELMWOOD RD   02181
  Richard Talbot, prin.
Fiske ES, 45 HASTINGS ST   02181
  Edward Schofield, prin.
Hardy ES, 293 WESTON RD   02181
  Charles Bennett, prin.
Hunnenwell ES, 28 CAMERON   02181
  Leo Lamontange, prin.
Schofield ES, 27 CEDAR   02181
  Richard Meister, prin.
Upham ES, 35 WYNNEWOOD RD   02181
  Charles Coyle, prin.

St. Paul ES, 10 ATWOOD ST   02181
Tenacre Country Day ES, 78 BENVENUE ST   02181

Wellesley Hills, Suffolk Co.

St. John Evangelist ES, 9 LEDYARD ST   02181

Wellfleet, Barnstable Co.
Wellfleet SD
Supt. – See Orleans
ES, P O BOX L   02667 – Stefan Vogel, prin.

Wenham, Essex Co., Pop. Code 5
Hamilton-Wenham SD
Supt. – See South Hamilton
Buker MS, 11 SCHOOL ST   01984
  Steve Driscoll, prin.

West Barnstable, Barnstable Co., Pop. Code 2
Barnstable SD
Supt. – See Hyannis
ES, ROUTE 6A   02668 – Jerry Guy, prin.

Westborough, Worcester Co., Pop. Code 7
Westborough SD
Sch. Sys. Enr. Code 4
Supt. – Eileen Gress, 16 PHILLIPS ST   01581
JHS, 20 FISHER ST   01581 – Richard Dymek, prin.
Armstrong MS, WEST   01581
  Edward Sullivan, prin.
Fales ES, ELI WHITNEY   01581
  Charles Fournier, prin.
Hastings ES, 111 E MAIN ST   01581
  Raymond Scherdell, prin.

West Boylston, Worcester Co., Pop. Code 6
West Boylston SD
Sch. Sys. Enr. Code 3
Supt. – Leo Sullivan, 125 CRESCENT ST   01583
Edwards ES, CRESENT   01583
  John Freeman, prin.

West Bridgewater, Plymouth Co., Pop. Code 6
West Bridgewater SD
Sch. Sys. Enr. Code 4
Supt. – Ronald Gerhart, 65 N MAIN ST   02379
Howard MS, 70 HOWARD ST   02379
  William Jones, prin.
MacDonald ES, 164 N ELM ST   02379
  William Jones, prin.

West Brookfield, Worcester Co.
West Brookfield SD
Sch. Sys. Enr. Code 2
Supt. – William Haggerty, N MAIN ST   01585
ES, NORTH MAIN   01585 – Edward Malvey, prin.

Westfield, Hampden Co., Pop. Code 8
Westfield SD
Sch. Sys. Enr. Code 6
Supt. – William Allard, 22 ASHLEY ST   01085
MS, 30 W SILVER ST   01085 – Rein Rix, prin.
Franklin Avenue ES, 22 FRANKLIN AVE   01085
  Thomas Drummey, prin.
Gibbs ES, 50 W SILVER ST   01085
  Norma White, prin.
Highland ES, 34 WESTERN AVE   01085
  Laurence Brady, prin.
Juniper Park ES, WESTERN AVE   01085
  Thomas McManus,Jr., prin.
Moseley ES, 9 DARTMOUTH ST   01085
  David Noonan, prin.
Prospect Hill ES, 33 MONTGOMERY ST   01085
  Donald Swanson, prin.
Smith Avenue MS, 69 SMITH AVE   01085
  Edward Smith, prin.
Southampton Road ES
  330 SOUTHAMPTON RD   01085
  Leslie Withrell, prin.

Holy Trinity ES, 331 ELM ST   01085
St. Mary ES, 37 BARTLETT ST   01085

Westford, Middlesex Co., Pop. Code 7
Westford SD
Sch. Sys. Enr. Code 5
Supt. – John Crisafulli
  35 TOWN FARM ROAD   01886
Abbott MS, DEPOT   01886 – James Hunt, prin.
Day MS, E PRESCOTT   01886 – John D'auria, prin.
Cameron ES, PLEASANT   01886
  Margery Clark, prin.
Frost ES, 73 MAIN ST   01886
  Margery Clark, prin.
Nabnasset ES, PLAIN ROAD   01886
  Henry Leyland, prin.
Robinson ES, ROBINSON & CONCORD   01886
  Kenneth Debenedictis, prin.

West Groton, Middlesex Co.
Groton-Dunstable SD
Supt. – See Groton
Tarbell ES, P O BOX 276   01472
  Edward Roberts, prin.

Westhampton, Hampshire Co., Pop. Code 4
Chesterfield SD
Sch. Sys. Enr. Code 2
Supt. – Richard Dragon, STAGE ROAD   01027
Other Schools – See Chesterfield

Goshen SD
Sch. Sys. Enr. Code 1
Supt. – Richard Dragon, STAGE ROAD   01027
Other Schools – See Goshen

Southampton SD
Sch. Sys. Enr. Code 2
Supt. – Richard Dragon, 19 STAGE ROAD   01027
Other Schools – See Southampton

Westhampton SD
Sch. Sys. Enr. Code 2
Supt. – Richard Dragon, STAGE ROAD   01027
Other Schools – See Easthampton

Williamsburg SD
Sch. Sys. Enr. Code 2
Supt. – Richard Dragon, STAGE ROAD   01027
Dunphy ES, MAIN   01096 – Dorothy Ladd, prin.
Other Schools – See Williamsburg

West Lynn, Essex Co.

Sacred Heart ES, 100 ROBINSON ST   01905

West Medford, Suffolk Co.

St. Raphael ES, 516 HIGH ST   02155

Westminster, Worcester Co.
Ashburnham-Westminster SD
Supt. – See Ashburnham
ES, ACADEMY ST   01473 – Joseph Difabio, prin.

West Newbury, Essex Co., Pop. Code 5
Groveland SD
Sch. Sys. Enr. Code 2
Supt. – Thomas Jenkins, MAIN ST   01985
Other Schools – See Groveland

Merrimac SD
Sch. Sys. Enr. Code 2
Supt. – Thomas Jenkins, MAIN ST   01985
Other Schools – See Merrimac

West Newbury SD
Sch. Sys. Enr. Code 2
Supt. – Thomas Jenkins, MAIN ST   01985
Page ES, 694 MAIN ST   01985
  Carol Kendrick, prin.

West Newton, Middlesex Co.
Newton SD
Supt. – See Newtonville
Franklin ES, 126 DERBY ST   02165
  Granville Harris, prin.
Peirce ES, 170 TEMPLE ST   02165
  Pam Mason, prin.

Fessenden ES, 250 WALTHAM ST   02165

Weston, Middlesex Co., Pop. Code 7
Weston SD
Sch. Sys. Enr. Code 4
Supt. – Meredith Jones, 89 WELLESLEY ST   02193
MS, 456 WELLESLEY ST   02193
    Ronald Harris, prin.
Country ES, 10 ALPHABET LN   02193
    Marie Tegeler, prin.
Woodland MS, 12 ALPHABET LN   02193
    Jeremiah Kellett, prin.

Meadowbrook ES, 10 FARM RD   02193

Westport, Bristol Co., Pop. Code 7
Westport SD
Sch. Sys. Enr. Code 4
Supt. – Patrick Soccoroso, 856 MAIN ROAD   02790
MS, 400 OLD COUNTY ROAD   02790
    John Mello, prin.
Macomber ES, 154 GIFFORD RD   02790
    John Defusco, prin.
ES, 380 OLD COUNTY RD   02790
    Robert Smith, prin.

St. George ES
    AMERICAN LEGION HWY RT 177   02790

West Roxbury, Suffolk Co.
Boston SD
Supt. – See Boston
Shaw MS, 20 MOUNT VERNON ST   02132
    Cornelius Keohane, prin.
Beethoven ES, 5125 WASHINGTON ST   02132
    William Glennon, prin.
Kilmer ES, 36 BAKER   02132
    Marguerite McCauley, prin.
Ohrenberger ES, 175 W BOUNDARY RD   02132
    Mary Connolly, prin.

Holy Name ES, 535 W ROXBURY PKY   02132
Parkway Academy, VFW PARKWAY   02132
St. Theresa ES, 40 SAINT THERESA AVE   02132

West Somerville, Middlesex Co.

St. Clements ES, 589 BOSTON AVE   02144

West Springfield, Hampden Co., Pop. Code 8
West Springfield SD
Sch. Sys. Enr. Code 5
Supt. – William O'Shea, 26 CENTRAL ST   01089
JHS, 115 SOUTHWORTH ST   01089
    Richard Berte, prin.
Cowing ES, 160 PARK ST   01089
    James Bampos, prin.
Fausey ES, 784 AMOSTOWN RD   01089
    Joan Tapor, prin.
Memorial ES, 201 NORMAN ST   01089
    Martha Tighe, prin.
Mittineague ES, SECOND   01089
    Joan Sheehan, prin.
Tatham ES, 61 LAUREL RD   01089
    James Doyle, prin.

St. Thomas Apostle ES, 75 PINE ST   01089

West Stockbridge, Berkshire Co.
Berkshire Hills SD
Supt. – See Stockbridge
Village ES, ALBANY ROAD   01266
    Thomas Meade, prin.

West Tisbury, Dukes Co.
West Tisbury SD
Supt. – See Vineyard Haven
ES, OLD COUNTY RD   02575
    Irwin Freedman, prin.

West Wareham, Plymouth Co.
Wareham SD
Supt. – See Wareham
ES, MAIN   02576 – Leo Peduzzi, prin.

Westwood, Norfolk Co., Pop. Code 7
Westwood SD
Sch. Sys. Enr. Code 4
Supt. – Robert Monson, 660 HIGH ST   02090
Thurston JHS, 850 HIGH ST   02090
    James Russell, prin.
Downey MS, DOWNEY   02090
    Arthur Gearty, prin.
Hanlon ES, 790 GAY ST   02090
    Steven Silvestri, prin.
Jones ES, MARTHA JONES ROAD   02090
    Joanne Hadalski, prin.
Sheehan MS, 549 POND ST   02090
    David Lowry, prin.

West Yarmouth, Barnstable Co., Pop. Code 5
Dennis-Yarmouth SD
Supt. – See South Yarmouth
Mattacheese MS
    HIGGINS CROWELL ROAD   02673
    Charles Orloff, prin.
Small ES, 384 HIGGENS CROWELL RD   02673
    James Clarke,Jr., prin.

Weymouth, Norfolk Co., Pop. Code 8
Weymouth SD
Sch. Sys. Enr. Code 6
Supt. – Leon Farrin III, 650 MIDDLE ST   02189
South JHS, 280 PLEASANT ST   02190
    John Cotter, prin.

Academy Avenue ES, 94 ACADEMY AVE   02189
    John Byrant, prin.
Hunt ES, 45 BROAD ST   02188
    William Hughes, prin.
Pingree ES, 1250 COMMERCIAL ST   02189
    Joseph Spallino, prin.
Seach ES, 770 MIDDLE ST   02188
    Charles Aubut, prin.
Other Schools – See East Weymouth, North
    Weymouth, South Weymouth

First Baptist Christian ES, 40 WEST   02188
Sacred Heart ES, 75 COMMERCIAL ST   02188

Whately, Franklin Co.
Whately SD
Supt. – See South Deerfield
ES, DEPOT ROAD   01093 – Donald Skroski, prin.

Whitinsville, Worcester Co., Pop. Code 6
Northbridge SD
Sch. Sys. Enr. Code 4
Supt. – Harry Simonian, 87 LINWOOD AVE   01588
Balmer MS, 21 CRESCENT ST   01588
    Robert Wood, prin.
Northbridge PS, CROSS   01588
    Dwain Robbins, prin.

Whitinsville Christian School
    279 LINWOOD AVE   01588

Whitman, Plymouth Co., Pop. Code 7
Whitman SD
Sch. Sys. Enr. Code 4
Supt. – John Pini, 39 WHITMAN AVE   02382
MS, 77 CORTHELL AVE   02382
    Middleton McGoodwin, prin.
Conley ES, FOREST   02382 – Agnes Pierce, prin.
Holt ES, ESSEX   02382 – Thomas Evans, prin.
Park Avenue ES, PARK AVE   02382
    Mary Fitzpatrick, prin.
Regal Street ES, REGAL   02382
    Mary Fitzpatrick, prin.

Wilbraham, Hampden Co., Pop. Code 7
Wilbraham SD
Sch. Sys. Enr. Code 4
Supt. – J. Halloran, 621 MAIN ST   01095
MS, 269 STONY HILL ROAD   01095
    Richard Ullery, prin.
Memorial Trans ES, MAIN   01095
    Robert Lash, prin.
Soule Road ES, SOULE ROAD   01095
    Alan Rubin, prin.

Williamsburg, Hampshire Co., Pop. Code 4
Williamsburg SD
Supt. – See Westhampton
James ES, MAIN   01096 – Dorothy Ladd, prin.

Williamstown, Berkshire Co., Pop. Code 6
Williamstown SD
Sch. Sys. Enr. Code 3
Supt. – Paul Jennings, 96 SCHOOL ST   01267
ES, 60 SCHOOL ST   01267 – Howard Smith, prin.

Pine Cobble ES, 1095 MAIN ST   01267

Wilmington, Middlesex Co., Pop. Code 7
Wilmington SD
Sch. Sys. Enr. Code 5
Supt. – Robert Horan, 159 CHURCH ST   01887
North IS, SALEM ST   01887 – Mary Roy, prin.
West IS, 20 CARTER LANE   01887
    James Jordan, prin.
Shawsheen ES, 300 SHAWSHEEN AVE   01887
    Robert Coffill, prin.
Wildwood ES, 184 WILDWOOD ST   01887
    Michael Tironoff, prin.
Woburn Street ES, WOBURN   01887
    Dolores Silva, prin.

Abundant Life Christian ES
    17 BOUTWELL ST   01887

Winchendon, Worcester Co., Pop. Code 6
Winchendon SD
Sch. Sys. Enr. Code 4
Supt. – Richard Dillon, P O BOX 275   01475
MS, 28 MURDOCK AVE   01475
    Andrew Paciulli, prin.
Memorial ES, 32 ELMWOOD RD   01475
    Thomas Kane, prin.

Winchester, Middlesex Co., Pop. Code 7
Winchester SD
Sch. Sys. Enr. Code 5
Supt. – Charles Mitsakos
    154 HORN POND BRK ROAD   01890
McCall JHS, 458 MAIN   01890
    Evander French,Jr., prin.
Ambrose ES, 27 HIGH ST   01890
    George Flynn, prin.
Lincoln ES, 161 MYSTIC VAL PKWY   01890
    Susan Villani, prin.
Lynch ES, 10 BRANTWOOD RD   01890
    Andrew Allan, prin.
Muraco ES, 61 IRVING ST   01890
    Richard Young, prin.
Vinson-Owen ES, 75 JOHNSON RD   01890
    Suzanne McGee, prin.

Agape Christian Academy, 263 MAIN ST   01890
Bartlett ES, 40 SAMOSET RD   01890
St. Mary ES, 162 WASHINGTON ST   01890

Windsor, Berkshire Co.
Central Berkshire SD
Supt. – See Dalton
Crane Community ES, ROUTE 9   01270
    Jane Allen, prin.

Winthrop, Suffolk Co., Pop. Code 7
Winthrop SD
Sch. Sys. Enr. Code 4
Supt. – Joseph Laino, 721 MAIN ST   02176
MS, PAULINE ST   02176 – Thomas A. Nee, prin.
Dalrymple ES, GROVERS AVE   02152
    Richard Grillo, prin.
Willis ES, HERMON   02152
    Arthur Cummings, prin.

St. John Evangelist ES, 30 OCEAN VIEW ST   02152

Woburn, Middlesex Co., Pop. Code 8
Woburn SD
Sch. Sys. Enr. Code 5
Supt. – Paul Andrews, 990 MAIN ST   01801
Altavesta ES, 990 MAIN ST   01801
    F. Mooney,Jr., prin.
Clapp ES, MUDSON/ARLINGTON ROAD   01801
    Alyce Henchey, prin.
Goodyear ES, ORANGE ST   01801
    Edward Callahan, prin.
Hurld ES, BEDFORD ROAD   01801
    Francis McCall, prin.
Linscott-Rumford ES, 86 ELM ST   01801
    Katherine McKillop, prin.
Reeves ES, 240 LEXINGTON ST   01801
    George Gibbons, prin.
Shamrock ES, EASTERN AVE   01801
    Thomas McDonough, prin.
White ES, BOW   01801 – Robert Cronin, prin.
Wyman ES, MAIN/EATON AVE   01801
    Richard Hassett, prin.

St. Charles ES, 8 MYRTLE ST   01801

Wollaston, Suffolk Co.

St. Ann ES, 1 ST ANNS RD   02170

Worcester, Worcester Co., Pop. Code 9
Worcester SD
Sch. Sys. Enr. Code 7
Supt. – John Durkin, 20 IRVING ST   01609
Burncoat MS, 135 BURNCOAT ST   01606
    James Garvey, prin.
Forest MS, 495 GROVE ST   01605
    William Monroe, prin.
Sullivan MS, 14 RICHARDS ST   01603
    Bernard McManus, prin.
Worcester East MS, 420 GRAFTON ST   01604
    Charles Burock, prin.
Adams Street ES, 28 ADAMS ST   01604
    Shirley Saffy, prin.
Belmont Street Community ES
    170 BELMONT ST   01605 – John Monfredo, prin.
Burncoat Street ES, 526 BURNCOAT ST   01606
    Thomas Durkin, prin.
Canterbury ES, 129 CANTERBURY   01602
    Peter Trainor, prin.
Chandler Community ES
    114 CHANDLER ST   01609 – Irene Adamaitis, prin.
Chandler Magnet ES, 525 CHANDLER ST   01602
    John McGinn, prin.
Clark Street Community ES, 280 CLARK ST   01606
    Joan Merrill, prin.
Columbus Park ES, 75 LOVELL   01603
    Janice Johnson, prin.
Dartmouth Street ES, 13 DARTMOUTH ST   01604
    George Maloney, prin.
Downing Street ES, 92 DOWNING ST   01610
    Frank Sepuka, prin.
Elm Park Community ES
    23 N ASHLAND ST   01609 – John O'Leary, prin.
Flagg Street ES, 115 FLAGG ST   01602
    Judy Finkel, prin.
Freeland Street ES, 12 FREELAND   01603
    Judith Roy, prin.
Gage Street ES, 51 GAGE ST   01605
    Donald Shea, prin.
Gates Lane ES, 1238 MAIN ST   01603
    Anthony Caputo, prin.
Grafton Street ES, 311 GRAFTON ST   01604
    Claire Anger, prin.
Granite Street ES, 120 GRANITE ST   01604
    Stanley Wolosz, prin.
Greendale ES, 130 LEEDS ST   01606
    John O'Brien, prin.
Harlow Street ES, 15 HARLOW ST   01605
    David Braley, prin.
Heard Street ES, 200 HEARD ST   01603
    Russell Carroll, prin.
Lake View ES, 133 COBURN AVE   01604
    Robert Mullins, prin.
Lincoln Street ES, 549 LINCOLN ST   01605
    Lawrence Faron, prin.
May Street ES, 265 MAY ST   01602
    Paul Murray, prin.
McGrath ES, 51 CHADWICK   01605
    Charles Baniukiewicz, prin.
Midland Street ES, 18 MIDLAND ST   01602
    William Bombard, prin.
Mill Swan ES, 337 MILL ST   01602
    Francis Trainor, prin.
Millbury Street ES, 389 MILLBURY ST   01610
    Thomas Lynch, prin.
Nelson Place ES, 35 NELSON PL   01605
    William Pingeton, prin.

New Ludlow ES, 1407A MAIN ST   01603
  Raymond Cavanaugh, prin.
Norrback Avenue ES, 44 MALDEN   01606
  Joan Lucey, prin.
Quinsigamond ES, 832 MILLBURY ST   01607
  James Rawdon, prin.
Rice Square ES, 76 MASSASOIT RD   01604
  James Moran, prin.
Roosevelt ES, 1006 GRAFTON ST   01604
  James Murphy, prin.
St. Nicholas Avenue ES
  315 SAINT NICHOLAS AVE   01606
  Francis Scales, prin.
Tatnuck ES, 1083 PLEASANT ST   01602
  Venise Withstandley, prin.
Thorndyke Road ES, 30 THORNDYKE RD   01606
  Carol Shilinsky, prin.
Union Hill ES, 1 CHAPIN ST   01604
  James Mooney, prin.

Vernon Hill ES, 211 PROVIDENCE ST   01607
  Gerald Daley, prin.
Wawecus Road ES, 20 WAWECUS RD   01605
  Robert Hill, prin.
West Tatnuck ES, 300 MOWER ST   01602
  Alexander Radzik, prin.
Woodland Street Community ES
  93 WOODLAND ST   01610 – Robert Sullivan, prin.

Bancroft School, 110 SHORE DRIVE   01605
St. Mary's School, 50 RICHLAND ST   01610
Our Lady Angels ES, 1220 MAIN ST   01603
St. Stephen ES, 355 GRAFTON ST   01604
Venerini Academy, 23 EDWARD ST   01605
Worchester Central Catholic ES
  865 MAIN ST   01610
Yeshiva Hebrew Day Academy
  22 NEWTON AVE   01602

Worthington, Hampshire Co.
Gateway SD
  Supt. – See Huntington
  Conwell ES, HUNTINGTON ROAD   01098
    Johanna McKenna, prin.

Wrentham, Norfolk Co., Pop. Code 3
King Philip SD
  Sch. Sys. Enr. Code 4
  Supt. – William J. Costa, 201 FRANKLIN ST   02093
  Other Schools – See Norfolk

Wrentham SD
  Sch. Sys. Enr. Code 3
  Supt. – Robert O'Connell, 97 TAUNTON ST   02093
  Delaney ES, TAUNTON   02093
    Albert Gibbons, prin.
  Roderick MS, TAUNTON   02093
    Albert Gibbons, prin.
  Vogel ES, TAUNTON   02093
    Albert Gibbons, prin.

MICHIGAN

STATE DEPARTMENT OF EDUCATION
Ottawa Street Office Building
P.O. Box 30008, Lansing 48902
(517) 373-3324

Superintendent of Public Instruction	Donald Bemis
Deputy Superintendent	Barbara Markle
Associate Superintendent Planning & School Management	James Phelps
Associate Superintendent Educational Services	Teressa Staten
Associate Superintendent Postsecondary Education	Gary Hawks
Associate Superintendent Finance, Legislation & Personnel	Thomas Wagamon
Associate Superintendent Rehabilitation & Disability	Ivan Cotman

STATE BOARD OF EDUCATION
Barbara Roberts, *President*   P.O. Box 30008, Lansing   48909

HIGHER EDUCATION MANAGEMENT SERVICES
Ronald Root, *Director*   P.O. Box 30009, Lansing   48909

INTERMEDIATE SCHOOL DISTRICTS

Allegan County ISD, James Pavelka, Supt.
  310 THOMAS ST, Allegan   49010
Alpena/Montmorency/Alcona ISD, Jack Carpenter, Supt.
  1619 M-32 HIGHWAY, Alpena   49707
Barry ISD, John Fehsenfeld, Supt.
  202 S BRAODWAY ST, Hastings   49058
Bay/Arenac ISD, Thor Petersen, Supt.
  4228 TWO MILE ROAD, Bay City   48706
Berrien ISD, Jerry Reimann, Supt.
  711 SAINT JOSEPH AVE, Berrien Springs   49103
Branch ISD, William Tracy, Supt.
  P O BOX 509, Coldwater   49036
Calhoun ISD, Warren Fudge, Supt.
  17111 G DRIVE NORTH, Marshall   49068
Cass Lewis Cass ISD, Gary Waterkamp, Supt.
  61682 DAILEY RD, Cassopolis   49031
Charlevoix/Emmet ISD, James Shepard, Supt.
  P O BOX 318, Charlevoix   49720
Cheboygan/Otsego/Presque Isle ISD, Gerald Hanson, Supt.
  6065 LEARNING LANE, Indian River   49749
Chippewa/Luce/Mackinac ISD, Ed Jarvie, Supt.
  P O BOX 883, Sault Sainte Marie   49783
Clare/Gladwin ISD, G. Zubulake, Supt.
  4041 E MANNSIDING ROAD, Clare   48617
Clinton County ISD, Larry Schwartzkopf, Supt.
  4179 S US-27, Saint Johns   48879
COOR ISD, Peter Holley, Supt.
  11051 NORTH CUT ROAD, Roscommon   48653
Copper Country ISD, William Mannisto, Supt.
  302 FRONT ST, Hancock   49930
Delta/Schoolcraft ISD, Raymond Johnson, Supt.
  2525 3RD AVE S, Escanaba   49829
Dickinson/Iron ISD, Richard Jacobsen, Supt.
  800 CRYSTAL LAKE BLVD, Iron Mountain   49801
Eaton ISD, Stephen Hayden, Supt.
  1790 PACKARD HIGHWAY, Charlotte   48813
Genesee ISD, David Spathelf, Supt.
  2413 W MAPLE AVE, Flint   48507

Gogebic/Ontonagon ISD, Waino Korpela, Supt.
  P O BOX 218, Bergland   49910
Grnd Trvrs/Antrm/Bnzie/Kalksk/Lenlau ISD, Richard Asiala, Supt.
  2325 GARFIELD ROAD N, Traverse City   49684
Gratiot/Isabella ISD, Daniel Mahoney, Supt.
  1131 CENTER ST E, Ithaca   48847
Hillsdale ISD, David Steel, Supt.
  3471 BECK ROAD, Hillsdale   49242
Huron ISD, F. McBride, Supt.
  711 E SOPER ROAD, Bad Axe   48413
Ingham ISD, Donald Shebuski, Supt.
  2630 W HOWELL ROAD, Mason   48854
Ionia County ISD, Thomas Ferguson, Supt.
  2190 HARWOOD ROAD, Ionia   48846
Iosco ISD, Robert Elliott, Supt.
  686 AULERICH ST, East Tawas   48730
Jackson ISD, Gerald Kratz, Supt.
  67800 BROWNS LAKE ROAD, Jackson   49204
Kalamazoo Valley ISD, Paul Wollam, Supt.
  1819 E MILHAM ROAD, Kalamazoo   49002
Kent ISD, George Woons, Supt.
  2960 KNAPP ST NE, Grand Rapids   49505
Lapeer County ISD, Robert Cook, Supt.
  1996 W OREGON ST, Lapeer   48446
Lenawee ISD, William Ross, Supt.
  4107 N ADRIAN HIGHWAY, Adrian   49221
Livingston ISD, Paul Lehto, Supt.
  1425 W GRAND RIVER AVE, Howell   48843
Macomb ISD, Joseph Nicita, Supt.
  44001 GARFIELD ROAD, Mount Clemens   48044
Manistee ISD, Robert Tilmann, Supt.
  722 PARKDALE AVE, Manistee   49660
Marquette Alger ISD, Louis Myefski, Supt.
  427 W COLLEGE AVE, Marquette   49855
Mason/Lake ISD, Scott Russell, Supt.
  2130 W US 10, Ludington   49431
Mecosta/Osceloa ISD, Roger Dixon, Supt.
  P O BOX 1137, Big Rapids   49307

Menominee County ISD, Ronald Peltier, Supt.
  952 FIRST ST, Menominee   49858
Midland ISD, Harry Moulton, Supt.
  3917 JEFFERSON, Midland   48640
Monroe County ISD, William Morris, Supt.
  1101 RAISINVILLE ROAD S, Monroe   48161
Montcalm Area ISD, William Seiter, Supt.
  P O BOX 367, Stanton   48888
Muskegon Area ISD, Hugh Tyler, Supt.
  630 HARVEY ST, Muskegon   49442
Newaygo ISD, Richard Hogancamp, Supt.
  1035 JAMES ST, White Cloud   49349
Oakland ISD, William Keane, Supt.
  2100 PONTIAC LAKE ROAD, Pontiac   48054
Oceana ISD, Lawrence Stancliff, Supt.
  P O BOX 151, Hart   49420
Ottawa Area ISD, Roger Troupe, Supt.
  13565 PORT SHELDON ST, Holland   49423
Saginaw ISD, Jonathon Schelke, Supt.
  6235 GRATIOT ROAD, Saginaw   48603
St. Clair ISD, John Mader, Supt.
  P O BOX 5001, Port Huron   48061
St. Joseph ISD, James Clark, Supt.
  P O BOX 187, Centreville   49032
Sanilac ISD, Frederick Cady, Supt.
  46 N JACKSON ST, Sandusky   48471
Shiawassee ISD, Patrick Gilbert, Supt.
  Corunna   48817
Tuscola ISD, Bruce Dunn, Supt.
  1385 CLEAVER ROAD, Caro   48723
Van Buren ISD, Henry Gudith, Supt.
  701 S PAW PAW ST, Lawrence   49064
Washtenaw ISD, Michael Emlaw, Supt.
  P O BOX 1406, Ann Arbor   48106
Wayne ISD, William Simmons, Supt.
  P O BOX 807, Wayne   48184
Wexford/Missaukee ISD, William Penny, Supt.
  9905 13 MILE RD, Cadillac   49601

PUBLIC, PRIVATE, AND PAROCHIAL ELEMENTARY SCHOOLS

Acme, Grand Traverse Co., Pop. Code 5
Traverse City Area SD
Supt. – See Traverse City
Vos ES, 3277 SHORE RD   49610
  Meg Oberlin, prin.

Ada, Kent Co., Pop. Code 6

Ada Christian ES
  7192 BRADFIELD AVE SE   49301
St. Patrick ES, 4333 PARNELL AVE NE   49301

Addison, Lenawee Co., Pop. Code 3
Addison Comm. SD
Sch. Sys. Enr. Code 4
Supt. – Jeffrey Kersh
  219 COMSTOCK ROAD   49220
MS, 219 COMSTOCK ROAD   49220
  Bradley Hamilton, prin.
ES, 115 COMSTOCK ST   49220
  Robert Tebo, prin.

Adrian, Lenawee Co., Pop. Code 7
Adrian SD
Sch. Sys. Enr. Code 6
Supt. – James Leary, 159 E MAUMEE ST   49221
Drager MS, 340 E CHURCH ST   49221
  David Mowrey, prin.
Springbrook JHS, 615 SPRINGBROOK AVE   49221
  Robert Ritz, prin.
Alexander ES, 520 CHERRY ST   49221
  E. Benes, prin.
Comstock ES, 801 E MAUMEE ST   49221
  Lindle Cochran, prin.
Garfield ES, 239 CROSS ST   49221
  Donald Rose, prin.
Lincoln ES, 158 S SCOTT ST   49221
  Norman Chervo, prin.
McKinley ES, 726 ELM ST   49221
  Charles Brown, prin.
Michener ES, 104 DAWES AVE   49221
  Joanne Perez, prin.
Prairie ES, 2568 AIRPORT HWY   49221
  William Krohn, prin.

Madison SD
Sch. Sys. Enr. Code 3
Supt. – James Hartley
  3498 TREAT HIGHWAY   49221
Madison ES, 3498 TREAT HWY   49221
  W. Faulkner, prin.

Tecumseh SD
Supt. – See Tecumseh
Sutton ES, 2780 SUTTON RD   49221
  Thomas Sura, prin.

St. Joseph Academy
  1257 E SIENA HEIGHTS DR   49221

Alanson, Emmet Co., Pop. Code 3
Littlefield SD
Sch. Sys. Enr. Code 3
Supt. – Graydon Blank, 7400 NORTH ST   49706
Littlefield ES, 7400 NORTH ST   49709
  L. Grubaugh, prin.

Alba, Antrim Co., Pop. Code 2
Alba SD
Sch. Sys. Enr. Code 2
Supt. – Shari Hogue, 5935 ELM ST   49611
HS, 5935 ELM ST   49611 – Shari Hogue, prin.

Albion, Calhoun Co., Pop. Code 7
Albion SD
Sch. Sys. Enr. Code 4
Supt. – Albert Meloy
  401 E MICHIGAN AVE   49224
Caldwell ES, 1100 N BERRIEN ST   49224
  R. Campbell, prin.
Crowell ES, 1418 COOPER ST   49224
  Nancy Roush, prin.
Harrington ES, 100 S CLARK ST   49224
  Sylvia Lawhorn, prin.
Gardner ES, 401 E MICHIGAN AVE   49224
  James Behling, prin.

St. John ES, 1020 IRWIN AVE   49224

Algonac, St. Clair Co., Pop. Code 5
Algonac Comm. SD
Sch. Sys. Enr. Code 5
Supt. – Joseph Caimi
  1215 WASHINGTON ST   48001
Algonquin JHS, 9185 MARSH ROAD   48001
  William Foster, prin.
ES, 1300 ST CLAIR BLVD   48001
  John Streit, prin.
Pte. Tremble ES, 9541 PHELPS RD   48001
  William Walker, prin.
Other Schools – See Fair Haven, Harsens Island

St. Catherine of Alexandria
  1106 ST CLAIR BLVD   48001

Allegan, Allegan Co., Pop. Code 5
Allegan SD
Sch. Sys. Enr. Code 5
Supt. – Douglas McCall, 550 5TH ST   49010
Dawson ES, 125 ELM ST   49010
  John Swartz, prin.
North Ward ES, 440 RIVER ST   49010
  Jerry Evans, prin.

Pine Trails ES, 2950 CENTER ST   49010
  Debbie Michaels, prin.
West Ward ES, 630 VERNON ST   49010
  Sue Seely, prin.

Allendale, Ottawa Co., Pop. Code 6
Allendale SD
Sch. Sys. Enr. Code 4
Supt. – David Annis
  6561 LAKE MICHIGAN DRIVE   49401
ES, 6561 LAKE MICHIGAN DR   49401
  H. Jay Reenders, prin.

Allendale Christian ES
  6448 LAKE MICHIGAN DR   49401

Allen Park, Wayne Co., Pop. Code 8
Allen Park SD
Sch. Sys. Enr. Code 5
Supt. – Thomas Riutta
  19001 CHAMPAIGN ST   48101
MS, 8401 VINE ST   48101 – R. Wilkinson, prin.
Arno ES, 7500 FOX   48101 – Glenn Petersen, prin.
Lindemann ES, 9201 CARTER ST   48101
  J. Bianlowicz, prin.

Melvindale-Northern Allen Park SD
Supt. – See Melvindale
Mead ES, 4700 QUANDT ST   48101
  Bette Church, prin.

St. Frances Cabrini School
  15311 WICK ROAD   48101

Alma, Gratiot Co., Pop. Code 6
Alma SD
Sch. Sys. Enr. Code 5
Supt. – Wm. McKinstry, 1500 PINE AVE   48801
MS, 312 DOWNIE ST E   48801
  Howard Rittenger, prin.
Highland ES, 312 DOWNIE ST   48801
  Andrew Booth, prin.
Hillcrest ES, 515 E ELIZABETH ST   48801
  Chris Adams, prin.
Pine Avenue ES, 1065 PINE AVE   48801
  Kaye Mentley, prin.

St. Mary School, 220 DOWNIE   48801

Almont, Lapeer Co., Pop. Code 4
Almont Comm. SD
Sch. Sys. Enr. Code 4
Supt. – John Carlson, 401 CHURCH ST   48003
ES, 401 CHURCH ST   48003
  Frank Bacholzky, prin.

Alpena, Alpena Co., Pop. Code 7
Alpena SD
Sch. Sys. Enr. Code 6
Supt. – Robert Verdun
  2373 GORDON ROAD   49707
Thunder Bay JHS, 400 S 2ND AVE   49707
  Lois Brinkman, prin.
Besser ES, 355 WILSON ST   49707
  Marilyn Frank, prin.
Hinks ES, US 23 NORTH   49707
  Roger Witherbee, prin.
Lincoln ES, 309 W LAKE ST   49707
  Leona Wisniewski, prin.
Maple Ridge ES, 7065 DIETZ RD   49707
  Daniel Gouin, prin.
Sunset ES, 1421 HOBBS DR   49707
  Delbert Beyer, prin.
White ES, 201 N RIPLEY BLVD   49707
  Jerry Annis, prin.
Other Schools – See Herron, Hubbard Lake, Lachine,
  Ossineke

Immanuel ES, 355 WILSON ST   49707
St. Anne ES, 205 S 9TH ST   49707
St. Mary ES, 500 N 2ND AVE   49707

Alto, Kent Co.
Caledonia Comm. SD
Supt. – See Caledonia
Kettle Lake ES, 8451 GARBOW DR   49302
  Jeff Worman, prin.

Lowell Area SD
Supt. – See Lowell
ES, 6150 BANCROFT AVE   49302
  Jim White, prin.

Amasa, Iron Co.
Chippewa Hills SD
Supt. – See Remus
Weidman ES, N SCHOOL RD   49903
  Shirley Howard, prin.

Anchorville, St. Clair Co.

Our Lady of Immaculate Conception
  7043 CHURCH RD   48004

Ann Arbor, Washtenaw Co., Pop. Code 9
Ann Arbor SD
Sch. Sys. Enr. Code 7
Supt. – Richard Benjamin
  2555 STATE ST S   48104
Abbot ES, 2670 SEQUOIA PKY   48103
  Jean Baker, prin.
Allen ES, 2560 TOWNER BLVD   48104
  B. Springfield, prin.

Angell ES, 1608 UNIVERSITY AVE S   48104
  Nanette Gill, prin.
Bach ES, 600 JEFFERSON ST W   48103
  Joann Okey, prin.
Bryant ES, 2150 SANTA ROSA DR   48108
  Rick O'Neil, prin.
Burns Park ES, 1414 WELLS ST   48104
  Joan Burke, prin.
Carpenter ES, 4250 CENTRAL BLVD   48108
  Giannine Perigo, prin.
Dicken ES, 2135 RUNNYMEDE BLVD   48103
  William Morgan, prin.
Eberwhite ES, 800 SOULE BLVD   48103
  Anita Parks, prin.
Haisley ES, 825 DUNCAN ST   48103
  Glenn Munro, prin.
King ES, 3800 WALDENWOOD DR   48105
  Frank Tarzia, prin.
Lawton ES, 2250 SEVENTH ST S   48103
  W. Montibeller, prin.
Logan ES, 2685 TRAVER RD   48105
  Robert Carr, prin.
Mack ES, 920 MILLER AVE   48103
  Lamar Whitemore, prin.
Mitchell ES, 3550 PITTSVIEW DR   48108
  Betty Schaffner, prin.
Northside ES, 912 BARTON DR   48105
  Patty DeYoung, prin.
Pattengill MS, 2100 CRESTLAND ST   48104
  Gae Fitch, prin.
Pittsfield ES, 2543 PITTSFIELD BLVD   48104
  Pat Chapman, prin.
Thurston ES, 2300 PRAIRIE ST   48105
  Jeannette Jackson, prin.
Wines ES, 1701 NEWPORT RD   48103
  Burton Lamkin, prin.

St. Francis of Assisi ES
  2270 STADIUM BLVD E   48104
St. Paul ES, 495 EARHART RD   48105
St. Thomas ES, 540 ELIZABETH ST   48104

Armada, Macomb Co., Pop. Code 4
Armada Area SD
Sch. Sys. Enr. Code 4
Supt. – Dr. Elliott Burns
  23550 CENTER ROAD   48005
MS, 23550 CENTER ROAD   48005
  John Niska, prin.
ES, 74500 BURK   48005 – Chester Bauer, prin.

Ashley, Gratiot Co., Pop. Code 3
Ashley Comm. SD
Sch. Sys. Enr. Code 2
Supt. – James H. Seals, 104 N NEW ST   48806
ES, 104 NEW ST   48806 – Carl Wayer, prin.

Athens, Calhoun Co., Pop. Code 3
Athens Area SD
Sch. Sys. Enr. Code 3
Supt. – Dale Dittmer, 300 E HOLCOMB ST   49011
MS, 515 E WILLIAMS ST   49011
  Gar Underwood, prin.
Other Schools – See East Leroy

Atlanta, Montmorency Co., Pop. Code 3
Atlanta Comm. SD
Sch. Sys. Enr. Code 3
Supt. – James J. Wynes, P O BOX 407   49709
ES, P O BOX 407   49709 – Tarry Deo, prin.

Atlantic Mine, Houghton Co.
Stanton Twp. SD
Sch. Sys. Enr. Code 2
Supt. – Jeffery Kangas
  RURAL ROUTE 01 BOX 128   49905
Holman ES, RURAL ROUTE 01 BOX 128   49905
  Jeffery Kangas, prin.

Attica, Lapeer Co., Pop. Code 5
Lapeer Comm. SD
Supt. – See Lapeer
ES, 80 N LAKE PLEASANT RD   48412
  Dora Bianchini, prin.

Auburn, Bay Co., Pop. Code 4
Bay City SD
Supt. – See Bay City
Western MS, 500 W MIDLAND ROAD   48611
  Linda Martin, prin.
Adams ES, 1601 GARFIELD RD   48611
  Leo Borrello, prin.
ES, 301 E MIDLAND RD   48611
  R. Mrozinski, prin.
Forest ES, 2169 W MIDLAND RD   48611
  R. Mrozinski, prin.

Auburn Area Catholic ES
  114 W MIDLAND RD   48611
Grace ES, 303 RUTH ST   48611
Zion ES, 1557 SEIDLER RD   48611

Auburn Hills, Oakland Co., Pop. Code 5
Avondale SD
Sch. Sys. Enr. Code 5
Supt. – William H. Saville
  2950 WAUKEGAN ST   48057
Auburn ES, 2900 WAUKEGAN ST   48057
  Ann Wydoven, prin.
Graham ES, 2450 OLD SALEM RD   48057
  Kanelo Kastran, prin.
Other Schools – See Rochester

Au Gres, Arenac Co., Pop. Code 3
Au Gres-Sims SD
Sch. Sys. Enr. Code 3
Supt. – Leonard Tyler, P O BOX 129 48703
Au Gres-Sims ES, 310 S COURT ST 48703
Robert Matkin, prin.

Augusta, Kalamazoo Co., Pop. Code 3
Galesburg-Augusta Comm. SD
Supt. – See Galesburg
MS, 750 W VAN BUREN ST 49012
James VanZandt, prin.
MS, 600 W MICHIGAN AVE 49012
David Linton, prin.

Bad Axe, Huron Co., Pop. Code 5
Bad Axe SD
Sch. Sys. Enr. Code 4
Supt. – K. W. Pietscher
760 S VAN DYKE ROAD 48413
MS, 407 E WOODWORTH ST 48413
Wayne Brady, prin.
MS, 404 CEMETERY RD 48413
John Moore, prin.
Greene ES, 309 N OUTER DR 48413
Karen Morison, prin.

Baldwin, Lake Co., Pop. Code 3
Baldwin Comm. SD
Sch. Sys. Enr. Code 3
Supt. – Stanley Chase, 525 W 4TH ST 49304
ES, 525 4TH ST 49304 – A. Nichols, prin.
Nelson ES, 25 SPRING ST 49304
A. Nichols, prin.
Other Schools – See Idlewild

Bangor, Van Buren Co., Pop. Code 4
Bangor SD
Sch. Sys. Enr. Code 4
Supt. – Thomas McDougall
801 W ARLINGTON ST 49013
ES, 20 N WALNUT ST 49013
Wesley Boughner, prin.
MS, 801 W ARLINGTON ST 49013
Gary Kimble, prin.

Baraga, Baraga Co., Pop. Code 4
Baraga Area SD
Sch. Sys. Enr. Code 3
Supt. – K. R. Hammerberg, LYONS ST 49908
La Tendresse PS, LYONS ST 49908
Gary Albring, prin.
Other Schools – See Pelkie

Bark River, Delta Co.
Escanaba Area SD
Supt. – See Escanaba
Ford River ES, 4341 K RD 49807
Terry Hampton, prin.

Barryton, Mecosta Co., Pop. Code 2
Chippewa Hills SD
Supt. – See Remus
ES, 19701 30TH AVE 49305 – Joyce Shull, prin.

Bath, Clinton Co., Pop. Code 3
Bath Comm. SD
Sch. Sys. Enr. Code 4
Supt. – James Garner
13789 WEBSTER ROAD 48808
MS, 13675 WEBSTER ROAD 48808
Jack Brown, prin.
ES, P O BOX 139 48808 – James Hixson, prin.

Battle Creek, Calhoun Co., Pop. Code 8
Battle Creek SD
Sch. Sys. Enr. Code 6
Supt. – R. Bruce Sellers
3 VAN BUREN ST W 49017
Springfield MS, 1023 AVENUE A 49015
Norman Barea, prin.
Coburn ES, 39 FAIRHOME AVE 49015
Donald Miller, prin.
Dudley ES, 208 ROOSEVELT AVE W 49017
Leon Buford, prin.
Franklin ES, 20 NEWARK AVE 49017
Richard Sass, prin.
Fremont ES, 113 EMMETT ST E 49017
Joyce Bluhm, prin.
Kellogg ES, 306 CHAMPION ST 49017
Gloria Robertson, prin.
Lamora Park ES, 65 WOODLAWN AVE N 49017
Arthur Curtis, prin.
Level Park ES, 3515 MICHIGAN AVE W 49017
Frederick Klein, prin.
Lincoln ES, 636 VAN BUREN ST W 49017
Arnold Stucky, prin.
McKinley ES, 400 CAPITAL AVE NE 49017
Mary Callahan, prin.
Post ES, 340 CLIFF ST 49017 – M. Skidmore, prin.
Roosevelt ES, 485 CAPITAL AVE SW 49015
Margery Fields, prin.
Urbandale ES, 125 BEDFORD RD N 49017
K. Schimmelpfenneg, prin.
Valley View ES, 960 AVENUE A 49015
James McNutt, prin.
Verona ES, 825 CAPITAL AVE NE 49017
David Sauder, prin.
Washington ES, 450 WASHINGTON AVE N 49017
Cornelius Vonk, prin.
Wilson ES, 71 BLANCHE ST 49015
Thomas Stout, prin.

Harper Creek Comm. SD
Sch. Sys. Enr. Code 4
Supt. – C. Glen Walter, 7290 B DRIVE N 49017

Harper Creek JHS, 7254 B DRIVE N 49017
Michael Ott, prin.
Beadle ES, 8175 C DR N 49017
Douglas Bower, prin.
Sonoma ES, 4640 B DR S 49017
John Peruzze, prin.
Wattles ES, 132 WATTLES RD S 49017
Carroll Hughes, prin.

Lakeview SD
Sch. Sys. Enr. Code 5
Supt. – Paul Williams, 15 ARBOR ST 49015
Lakeview JHS, 20 WOODROW AVE S 49015
Paul Doersam, prin.
Minges Brook ES, LINCOLN HILLS DR 49015
Robert Wright, prin.
Prairieview ES, 1765 IROQUOIS ST 49015
Betty Hagberg, prin.
Riverside ES, 650 RIVERSIDE DR 49015
Rose Ferguson, prin.
Westlake ES, 1184 24TH ST S 49015
Dr. Dennis Guiser, prin.

Pennfield SD
Sch. Sys. Enr. Code 4
Supt. – Harold Creekmur, 8587 Q DRIVE N 49017
Dunlap MS, 8565 Q DRIVE N 49017
Don Richards, prin.
Central MS, 8587 Q DR N 49017
Edward Tersteeg, prin.
North PS, 8587 Q DR N 49017 – Jean Parker, prin.
Purdy PS, 8785 Q DR N 49017 – Jean Parker, prin.

Battle Creek Academy, 480 PARKWAY DR 49017
St. Philip Catholic Central School
20 CHERRY ST 49017
Battle Creek Chrstian ES
1035 WAGNER DR 49017
St. Joseph ES, 47 23RD ST N 49015

Bay City, Bay Co., Pop. Code 8
Bangor Twp. SD
Sch. Sys. Enr. Code 5
Supt. – William Mester III
3520 OLD KAWKAWLIN ROAD 48706
Bangor JHS, 3281 KIESEL ROAD 48706
Joyce Zeneberg, prin.
Central ES, 208 STATE PARK DR 48706
Miriam Sweigart, prin.
Lincoln ES, 2771 N EUCLID AVE 48706
B. Scheerhorn, prin.
North ES, 504 REVILO RD 48706
B. Scheerhorn, prin.
West ES, 3175 E WILDER RD 48706
Lynn Bollman, prin.

Bay City SD
Sch. Sys. Enr. Code 7
Supt. – Dale Martin, 910 N WALNUT ST 48706
Kolb MS, 305 W CRUMP ST 48706
Dale Dunham, prin.
Washington MS, 1821 MCKINLEY 48706
Vern Julian, prin.
Dolsen PS, 201 WOODSIDE LN 48708
Mary Boettger, prin.
Hampton ES, 1908 W YOUNGS DITCH RD 48708
Pete Mayo, prin.
Lincoln ES, 820 S LINCOLN ST 48708
Clement Kaye, prin.
Jefferson ES, 201 WOODSIDE LN 48708
Clem Kaye, prin.
Lindsay ES, 607 LASALLE ST 48706
Leon Katzinger, prin.
MacGregor ES, 1012 FREMONT ST 48708
T. Rodridguez, prin.
Mackensen ES, 5535 DENNIS DR 48706
Leo Borrello, prin.
McAlear-Saeden ES, 2300 E MIDLAND RD 48706
Mary Jo Kellogg, prin.
McKinley ES 48706 – (—), prin.
Reigel ES, 1805 RAYMOND ST 48706
Steven Anderson, prin.
Whittier ES 48706 – (—), prin.
Woodside MS, 201 WOODSIDE LN 48708
Mary Boetger, prin.
Other Schools – See Auburn

Faith ES, 3033 E WILDER RD 48706
Holy Trinity ES, 1004 S WENONA ST 48706
Immanuel ES, N LINCOLN & 10TH STS 48706
Notre Dame Academy, 1110 STATE ST 48706
St. Hyancinth ES, 2307 S MONROE ST 48708
St. James ES, 715 14TH ST 48708
St. John Lutheran School
1664 AMELITH ROAD 48706
St. Joseph ES, 1111 N SHERMAN ST 48708
St. Paul ES, 6094 W S SAGINAW 48706
St. Stanislaus ES, 900 S GRANT ST 48708
Trinity Lutheran School, 20 E SALZBURG 48706
Zion ES, 1707 S KIESEL ST 48706

Bear Lake, Manistee Co., Pop. Code 2
Bear Lake SD
Sch. Sys. Enr. Code 2
Supt. – James Brady, P O BOX 188 49614
ES, P O BOX 188 49614 – Robert Carlon, prin.

Beaverton, Gladwin Co., Pop. Code 4
Beaverton Rural SD
Sch. Sys. Enr. Code 4
Supt. – Thomas Randle, 3330 M-18 48612
JHS, 106 TONKIN ROAD 48612
W. Ashcroft, prin.
ES, 127 TONKIN ST 48612 – Ronald Roggow, prin.
MS, 44 S ROSS ST 48612 – Duane Whitman, prin.

Belding, Ionia Co., Pop. Code 6
Belding Area SD
Sch. Sys. Enr. Code 4
Supt. – Bert Emerson, 321 WILSON ST 48809
MS, 410 IONIA ST 48809 – Ronald Hughes, prin.
Ellis ES, 100 S ELLIS AVE 48809
Sandra Townsend, prin.
Hallpark ES, 520 HALL ST 48809
Charles Barker, prin.
Orchard Hills ES, 1975 ORCHARD ST 48809
Marjorie Byrnes, prin.

Bellaire, Antrim Co., Pop. Code 4
Bellaire SD
Sch. Sys. Enr. Code 3
Supt. – Larry Blackmer
204 W FOREST HOME AVE 49615
ES, 204 W FOREST HOME 49615
K. Szcodronski, prin.

Belleville, Wayne Co., Pop. Code 5
Lincoln Cons. SD
Supt. – See Ypsilanti
Hoffman MS, 50700 WILLOW ROAD 48111
Michael Bewley, prin.

VanBuren SD
Sch. Sys. Enr. Code 6
Supt. – Elvin Peets, 555 COLUMBIA AVE W 48111
North MS, 47097 MCBRIDE AVE 48111
William Sparrow, prin.
South MS, 45201 OWEN ST 48111
J. Richendollar, prin.
Edgemont ES, 125 EDGEMONT ST S 48111
Jonathan Hale, prin.
Elwell ES, 17601 ELWELL RD 48111
David Larabell, prin.
Haggerty ES, 13770 HAGGERTY RD 48111
William Chizmar, prin.
Savage ES, 42975 SAVAGE RD 48111
Clyde Stapleton, prin.
Tyler ES, 42200 TYLER RD 48111
Donald Priest, prin.
Other Schools – See Ypsilanti

St. Anthony ES, 373 COLUMBIA AVE W 48111

Bellevue, Eaton Co., Pop. Code 4
Bellevue Comm. SD
Sch. Sys. Enr. Code 4
Supt. – Richard Kelly
904 W CAPITAL AVE 49021
MS, 904 W CAPITAL AVE 49021
Joan Cipcic, prin.
ES, 201 WEST ST 49021 – Bernard Geyer, prin.

Hastings Area SD
Supt. – See Hastings
Pleasantview ES, 3754 LACEY RD 49021
Jo Stebbins, prin.

Belmont, Kent Co.
Rockford SD
Supt. – See Rockford
ES, 6097 BELMONT AVE NE 49306
Dr. Ty Wessell, prin.

Assumption ES, 6391 BELMONT AVE NE 49306

Benton Harbor, Berrien Co., Pop. Code 7
Benton Harbor Area SD
Sch. Sys. Enr. Code 6
Supt. – James Rutter, P O BOX 1107 49022
Fair Plain JHS, 120 E NAPIER AVE 49022
Kenneth Overley, prin.
King 8th Court MS, 750 E BRITAIN AVE 49022
George McGinnis, prin.
McCord 7th Court, 465 S MCCORD ST 49022
John Brown, prin.
Bard ES, 1200 E MAIN ST 49022
Greta Hines, prin.
Britain ES, 209 E BRITAIN AVE 49022
Donald Whitaker, prin.
Fair Plain East ES, 1995 UNION ST 49022
Renee Williams, prin.
Fair Plain Northeast ES, 400 LYNCH AVE 49022
Ralph Catania, prin.
Fair Plain West MS, 1901 FAIRPLAIN AVE 49022
Ralph Catania, prin.
Hull ES, 1716 TERRITORIAL RD 49022
Russell Tynes, prin.
Johnson ES, 3270 TERRITORIAL RD 49022
Janet Crump, prin.
Martindale MS, 2199 LAUREL DR 49022
Greta Hines, prin.
Morton ES, 267 N HULL AVE 49022
Erma Mitchell, prin.
Sorter MS, 1421 PIPESTONE RD 49022
Ann Kennedy, prin.
Sterne Brunson ES, 1131 COLUMBUS AVE 49022
Joyce Jones, prin.
Stump ES, 1651 NICKERSON AVE 49022
Jerry Farwell, prin.

Lake Michigan Catholic ES, 589 PEARL ST 49022

Benzonia, Benzie Co., Pop. Code 2
Benzie County Central SD
Sch. Sys. Enr. Code 4
Supt. – Robert Eisenlohr
9222 HOMESTEAD ROAD 49616
Crystal Lake ES, 7048 SEVERENCE ST 49616
Peter Moss, prin.
Other Schools – See Honor, Thompsonville

Berkley, Oakland Co., Pop. Code 7
Berkley SD
Sch. Sys. Enr. Code 5
Supt. – Robert Maxfield, 3127 BACON AVE　48072
Anderson MS, 3205 CATALPA DRIVE　48072
　Janet Chanoine, prin.
Angell ES, 3849 BEVERLY BLVD　48072
　Joan Janowsky, prin.
Pattengill ES, 3540 MORRISON　48072
　Barbara Potter, prin.
Rogers ES, 2265 HAMILTON AVE　48072
　R. Steadman, prin.
Other Schools – See Huntington Woods, Oak Park

Our Lady of Lasalette ES
　2219 COOLIDGE HWY　48072

Berrien Springs, Berrien Co., Pop. Code 4
Berrien Springs SD
Sch. Sys. Enr. Code 4
Supt. – Tedd Morris, 1 SYLVESTER AVE　49103
MS, P O BOX 130　49103 – Richard Bartz, prin.
Mars ES, ONE SYLVESTER AVE　49103
　Gerald Jennings, prin.
Sylvester MS, ONE SYLVESTER AVE　49103
　Thomas Topash, prin.

Berrien Springs SDA ES, P O BOX 230　49103
Trinity Lutheran School
　9123 S GEORGE STREET　49103

Bessemer, Gogebic Co., Pop. Code 5
Bessemer CSD
Sch. Sys. Enr. Code 3
Supt. – Clarence J. Hoeft, 102 E LEAD ST　49911
Washington ES, SELLAR ST　49911
　Clarence Hoeft, prin.

St. Sebastion ES, 305 E IRON ST　49911

Big Bay, Marquette Co.
Powell Twp. SD
Sch. Sys. Enr. Code 1
Supt. – William Lake, P O BOX 150　49808
Powell Twp. ES, P O BOX 150　49808
　William Lake, prin.

Big Rapids, Mecosta Co., Pop. Code 7
Big Rapids SD
Sch. Sys. Enr. Code 4
Supt. – John Jeffery, 500 WARREN AVE N　49307
MS, 215 STATE ST N　49307
　Thomas Owczarski, prin.
Brookside ES, 210 ESCOTT ST　49307
　Barbara Borth, prin.
Eastwood ES, 410 N 3RD AVE　49307
　David Borth, prin.
Hillcrest ES, 501 BRIDGE ST W　49307
　David Johnson, prin.
Riverview ES, 509 WILLOW AVE　49307
　Jeanette Fleury, prin.

St. Peter ES, 408 BELLEVUE ST W　49307

Birch Run, Saginaw Co., Pop. Code 4
Birch Run Area SD
Sch. Sys. Enr. Code 4
Supt. – Bart Jenniches, 12400 CHURCH ST　48415
MS, 8225 MAIN ST　48415 – Doug Rowley, prin.
North ES, 12400 CHURCH ST　48415
　Ron Helmer, prin.

Birmingham, Oakland Co., Pop. Code 7
Birmingham SD
Sch. Sys. Enr. Code 6
Supt. – Roger Garvelink
　550 W MERRILL ST　48009
Berkshire MS, 21707 W 14 MILE ROAD　48010
　Ronald Miller, prin.
Covington MS, 1525 COVINGTON ROAD　48010
　William Blackwell, prin.
Derby MS, 1300 DERBY ROAD　48008
　Helene Mills, prin.
West Maple MS, 6275 INKSTER ROAD　48010
　William Fredo, prin.
Beverly ES, 18305 BEVERLY RD　48009
　William Foust, prin.
Bingham Farms ES
　23400 W THIRTEEN MILE RD　48010
　Robert Jones, prin.
Greenfield ES, 31200 FAIRFAX AVE　48009
　Donald Tobe, prin.
Meadowlake ES, 7100 LINDENMERE　48010
　Robert Voss, prin.
Midvale ES, 2121 MIDVALE ST　48009
　Helen Burz, prin.
Pierce ES, 1829 PIERCE ST　48009
　Richard Durda, prin.
Quarton ES, 771 CHESTERFIELD AVE　48009
　J. Hammond-Mattews, prin.
Other Schools – See Bloomfield Hills, Pontiac, Troy

Detroit Country Day School
　22305 W THIRTEEN MILE RD　48010
Saa Beth Jacob School for Girls
　3605 BELLVINE TRAIL　48010
Holy Name ES, 680 HARMON ST　48009
Our Lady Queen of Martyrs ES
　32460 PIERCE ST　48009
Our Shepard ES, 1658 E LINCOLN ST　48009
St. Regis ES, 3691 LINCOLN DR　48010

Blissfield, Lenawee Co., Pop. Code 5
Blissfield Comm. SD
Sch. Sys. Enr. Code 4
Supt. – Larry C. Wilson, 630 S LANE ST　49228
MS, 1305 BEAMER ROAD　49228
　Paul Palka, prin.
South ES, 640 S LANE ST　49228
　Harold Schankin, prin.

Bloomfield Hills, Oakland Co., Pop. Code 5
Birmingham SD
Supt. – See Birmingham
Harlan ES, 3595 N ADAMS RD　48013
　Cass Miller, prin.

Bloomfield Hills SD
Sch. Sys. Enr. Code 6
Supt. – W. Robert Docking
　4175 ANDOVER ROAD　48013
MS, 4200 QUARTON ROAD　48013
　G. Grossnickle, prin.
East Hills MS, 2800 KENSINGTON ROAD　48013
　Donald Kevern, prin.
Conant ES, 4100 QUARTON RD　48013
　Joan Evans, prin.
Eastover ES, 1101 WESTVIEW RD　48013
　A. Crockett, prin.
Hickory Grove ES, 2800 LAHSER RD　48013
　Jim Felix, prin.
Way ES, 765 W LONG LAKE RD　48013
　Jill McConkey, prin.
Other Schools – See Orchard Lake, West Bloomfield

Academy of the Sacred Heart
　1250 KENSINGTON ROAD　48013
Cranbrook School, P O BOX 801　48013
Brookside ES, P O BOX 801　48303
Roeper City Country ES
　2190 N WOODWARD AVE　48013
St. Hugo of Hills ES, P O BOX 349　48303

Bloomingdale, Van Buren Co., Pop. Code 3
Bloomingdale SD
Sch. Sys. Enr. Code 4
Supt. – Thomas Hoke, P O BOX 217　49026
ES, P O BOX 217　49026 – James Scholley, prin.
Grand Junction ES, P O BOX 217　49026
　Garyle Voss, prin.
Pullman ES, P O BOX 217　49026
　Garyle Voss, prin.

Boone, Wexford Co.
Cadillac Area SD
Supt. – See Cadillac
Forest View ES, RURAL ROUTE 01　49618
　Gary Williams, prin.

Boyne City, Charlevoix Co., Pop. Code 5
Boyne City SD
Sch. Sys. Enr. Code 4
Supt. – Robert Nakoneczny, P O BOX 289　49712
MS, S PARK ST　49712 – Stephen Smith, prin.
ES, 930 BROCKWAY ST　49712
　Edwin Snyder, prin.

Boyne Falls, Charlevoix Co., Pop. Code 2
Boyne Falls SD
Sch. Sys. Enr. Code 2
Supt. – Charles Smith, 2329 CENTER ST　49713
S, 2329 CENTER ST　49713
　Michael Wallace, prin.

Breckenridge, Gratiot Co., Pop. Code 4
Breckenridge Comm. SD
Sch. Sys. Enr. Code 4
Supt. – Dennis Hagey, 700 WRIGHT ST　48615
East ES, P O BOX 217　48615 – Keith Shearer, prin.
West MS, P O BOX 217　48615
　M. Clingenpeel, prin.

Brethren, Manistee Co., Pop. Code 3
Kaleva-Norman-Dickson SD
Sch. Sys. Enr. Code 3
Supt. – Leonard Grams
　4350 HIGH BRIDGE ROAD　49619
Other Schools – See Kaleva, Wellston

Bridgeport, Saginaw Co., Pop. Code 7
Spaulding Comm. SD
Sch. Sys. Enr. Code 5
Supt. – Gene Karrow, 3878 SHERMAN ST　48722
Schluckebier ES, 4200 BROWN ST　48722
　Bernard Spencer, prin.
Schrah ES, 4221 BROWN ST　48722
　Michael Tate, prin.
White ES, 3500 SOUTHFIELD DR　48722
　Robert Scherzer, prin.
Other Schools – See Saginaw

Bridgman, Berrian Co., Pop. Code 4
Bridgman SD
Sch. Sys. Enr. Code 3
Supt. – Tom Smusz, 9964 GAST ROAD　49106
Reed MS, 10254 CALIFORNIA　49106
　Allen Skibbe, prin.
ES, 3891 LAKE ST　49106 – James Sullivan, prin.

Immanuel Lutheran School
　9650 N CHURCH ST　49106

Brighton, Livingston Co., Pop. Code 5
Brighton Area SD
Sch. Sys. Enr. Code 6
Supt. – Dennis McMahon
　4740 BAUER ROAD　48116
Maltby MS, 4740 BAUER ROAD　48116
　Rae McCall, prin.

Scranton MS, 125 CHURCH ST S　48116
　Ken Hamman, prin.
Hawkins ES, 8900 LEE RD　48116
　Baiba Jensen, prin.
Hornung ES, 4680 BAUER RD　48116
　Dave Pruneau, prin.
Lindbom ES, 1010 STATE ST　48116
　Arnie Huber, prin.
Spencer ES, 10639 SPENCER RD　48116
　Carol Owoc, prin.

St. Patrick ES, 710 RICKETT RD　48116

Brimley, Chippewa Co., Pop. Code 2
Brimley Area SD
Sch. Sys. Enr. Code 3
Supt. – Jacob Helms, P O BOX 156　49715
ES, P O BOX 156　49715 – Frances Robbins, prin.

Britton, Lenawee Co., Pop. Code 3
Britton-Macon Area SD
Sch. Sys. Enr. Code 2
Supt. – John Gasidlo, 210 COLLEGE AVE　49229
Britton Macon S, 201 COLLEGE AVE　49229
　John McEwan, prin.

Bronson, Branch Co., Pop. Code 4
Bronson Comm. SD
Sch. Sys. Enr. Code 4
Supt. – James Thrall, 450 E GRANT ST　49028
Anderson ES, 546 E CHICAGO ST　49028
　Chris Chopper, prin.
Chicago Street MS, 501 E CHICAGO ST　49028
　Chris Chopper, prin.
Ryan ES, 461 RUDD ST　49028
　Chris Chopper, prin.

St. Mary's Assumption ES, 204 ALBERS RD　49028

Brooklyn, Jackson Co., Pop. Code 4
Columbia SD
Sch. Sys. Enr. Code 4
Supt. – Gary Allen, 300 SCHOOL ST　49230
Columbia MS, 321 SCHOOL ST　49230
　Patricia Sampler, prin.
ES, 320 SCHOOL ST　49230 – Paul Graham, prin.
Miller ES, 130 JACKSON ST　49230
　D. Desmarais, prin.

Brown City, Sanilac Co., Pop. Code 4
Brown City Comm. SD
Sch. Sys. Enr. Code 4
Supt. – Dennis Sidebottom, 4290 2ND ST　48416
ES, 4334 SECOND ST　48416 – Joseph Furst, prin.

Buchanan, Berrien Co., Pop. Code 6
Buchanan Comm. SD
Sch. Sys. Enr. Code 4
Supt. – Allen Schau, 401 W CHICAGO ST　49107
MS, 610 W 4TH ST　49107 – Richard Proud, prin.
Moccasin ES, MOCCASIN AVE　49107
　Mark Nixon, prin.
Ottawa ES, OTTAWA AVE　49107
　Karin Falkenstein, prin.
Stark ES, CLAREMONT ST　49107
　David Casey, prin.

Buckley, Wexford Co., Pop. Code 2
Buckley Comm. SD
Sch. Sys. Enr. Code 2
Supt. – Paul Storm, P O BOX 38　49620
S, P O BOX 38　49620 – Lawrence Davis, prin.

Burr Oak, St. Joseph Co., Pop. Code 3
Burr Oak Comm. SD
Sch. Sys. Enr. Code 2
Supt. – Ronald Chapman, P O BOX 337　49030
S, P O BOX 337　49030 – Robert Peters, prin.

Burt, Saginaw Co.
Chesaning Un. SD
Supt. – See Chesaning
Albee ES, 11540 BUECHE RD　48417
　Jeff Murdoch, prin.

Burton, Genesee Co., Pop. Code 8
Atherton Comm. SD
Supt. – See Flint
Van Y ES, 2400 CLARICE AVE　48519
　James Brian, prin.

Bendle SD
Supt. – See Flint
Friel ES, 4469 GREENLEY ST　48529
　J. Dwight Robb, prin.
Griffith ES, 3420 COLUMBINE AVE　48529
　John Krish, prin.
South ES, 4341 LARKIN DR　48529
　John Krish, prin.
West ES, 4020 CERDAN DR　48529
　J. Dwight Robb, prin.

Bentley Comm. SD
Supt. – See Flint
Barhitte ES, 6080 ROBERTA ST　48509
　Susan Hobson, prin.

Carman-Ainsworth SD
Supt. – See Flint
Dillon ES, 1197 E SCHUMACHER AVE　48529
　Arnold Griffin, prin.

Holy Redeemer ES
　G 3468 GRAND TRAVERSE S　48529

Byron, Shiawassee Co., Pop. Code 3
Byron Area SD
Sch. Sys. Enr. Code 4
Supt. – Ronald Fencil, 312 W MAPLE AVE 48418
MS, 312 W MAPLE AVE 48418 – Paul Fox, prin.
ES, 401 E MAPLE AVE 48418
George Eaton, prin.

Byron Center, Kent Co., Pop. Code 3
Byron Center SD
Sch. Sys. Enr. Code 4
Supt. – Ronald Houle
8543 BYRON CENTER AVE SW 49315
MS, 8542 BYRON CENTER AVE SW 49315
Thomas Jeltes, prin.
Blain ES, 240 84TH ST SE 49315
Steven Parker, prin.
Brown ES, 8064 BYRON CTR AVE 49315
Wayne Rietberg, prin.
Marshall ES, 1756 64TH ST SW 49315
Steven Parker, prin.
Northwest ES, 6636 HOMRICH AVE SW 49315
Philip Swainston, prin.
Rider ES, 9930 BURLINGAME AVE SW 49315
Steven Parker, prin.

Byron Center Christian ES
8840 BYRON CENTER AVE SW 49315
Holy Family ES, 2455 146TH AVE SW 49315

Cadillac, Wexford Co., Pop. Code 7
Cadillac Area SD
Sch. Sys. Enr. Code 5
Supt. – Fred Carroll, 115 SOUTH ST 49601
MS, 500 CHESTNUT ST 49601
Maynard Thompson, prin.
Franklin ES, 505 LESTER ST 49601
G. Rosingana, prin.
Kenwood ES, 1700 CHESTNUT ST 49601
Ronald Vaughan, prin.
Lincoln ES, 125 AYER ST 49601
Sue Westhauser, prin.
McKinley ES, 601 E NORTH ST 49601
Edmund Host, prin.
Other Schools – See Boone

St. Ann ES, 711 OAK ST 49601

Caledonia, Kent Co., Pop. Code 3
Caledonia Comm. SD
Sch. Sys. Enr. Code 4
Supt. – Robert Myers, 203 MAIN ST 49316
MS, 203 JOHNSON ST 49316 – Marie Kelley, prin.
ES, 9770 DUNCAN LAKE RD 49316
Jeanne Glowicki, prin.
Dutton ES, 3820 68TH 49316 – Jerry Phillips, prin.
Other Schools – See Alto

Dutton Christian ES
6980 HANNA LAKE RD 49316

Calumet, Houghton Co., Pop. Code 4
Calumet-Laurium & Keweenaw SD
Sch. Sys. Enr. Code 4
Supt. – Robert Shea, 102 CALUMET AVE 49913
Washington MS, CALUMET AVE 49913
Robert Hager, prin.
Morrison ES, SEVENTH ST 49913
Donald Karvonen, prin.
Other Schools – See Mohawk

Camden, Hillsdale Co., Pop. Code 2
Camden-Frontier SD
Sch. Sys. Enr. Code 3
Supt. – Lee Ward
4971 W MONTGOMERY ROAD 49232
ES, 4971 W MONTGOMERY RD 49232
Barb Vallieu, prin.

Canton, Wayne Co.
Plymouth-Canton Comm. SD
Supt. – See Plymouth
Eriksson ES, 1275 HAGGERTY RD N 48187
Judith Ireson, prin.
Field ES, 1000 HAGGERTY RD S 48188
Larry Miller, prin.
Gallimore ES, 8375 SHELDON RD N 48187
Joyce Deren, prin.
Hoben ES, 44680 SALTZ 48187
W. Pearson, prin.
Hulsing ES, 8055 FLEET ST 48187
Cheryl Clason, prin.
Miller ES, 43721 HANFORD RD 48187
S. Barresi, prin.

Wayne-Westland Comm. SD
Supt. – See Westland
Walker ES, 39932 MICHIGAN AVE 48188
Larry Williams, prin.

Capac, St. Clair Co., Pop. Code 4
Capac Comm. SD
Sch. Sys. Enr. Code 4
Supt. – James Sundermann
403 N GLASSFORD ST 48014
ES, 351 W KEMPF CT 48014
Susan Strickler, prin.
MS, 201 N NEEPER ST 48014
Ramona Brown, prin.

Carleton, Monroe Co., Pop. Code 5
Airport Comm. SD
Sch. Sys. Enr. Code 5
Supt. – James Orwin, 12610 HARRIS ROAD 48117
Wagar MS, 11270 GRAFTON ROAD 48117
Gerald Bieniek, prin.

Eyler ES, 1335 CARLETON ST RCKWD RD 48117
Hinde Socol, prin.
Sterling MS, 160 FESSNER RD 48117
Paul Ensch, prin.
Other Schools – See Newport, South Rockwood

St. Patrick ES, 2970 W LABO ST 48117

Carney, Menominee Co.
Carney-Nadeau SD
Sch. Sys. Enr. Code 2
Supt. – L. R. Pieropon 49812
Carney-Nadeau S, P O BOX 68 49812
Ronald Solberg, prin.

Caro, Tuscola Co., Pop. Code 5
Caro Comm. SD
Sch. Sys. Enr. Code 4
Supt. – Thomas Lanway
301 N HOOPER ST 48723
MS, 301 N HOOPER ST 48723
Robert DeBoer, prin.
McComb MS, 303 N HOOPER ST 48723
Reid Ruggles, prin.
Shall ES, 325 E FRANK ST 48723
Sally Dittman, prin.

Carrollton, Saginaw Co., Pop. Code 6
Carrollton SD
Sch. Sys. Enr. Code 4
Supt. – Paul Novak, P O BOX 517 48724
Other Schools – See Saginaw

Carson City, Montcalm Co., Pop. Code 4
Carson City-Crystal Area SD
Sch. Sys. Enr. Code 4
Supt. – John Smith, 338 GRATIOT ST N 48811
ES, 338 GRATIOT ST N 48811
D. Sutherland, prin.
Hubbardston ES, 305 RUSSELL 48845
W. Steere, prin.
Other Schools – See Crystal

Carsonville, Sanilac Co., Pop. Code 3
Carsonville-Port Sanilac SD
Sch. Sys. Enr. Code 3
Supt. – Don S. Mueller
100 N GOETZE AT M-46 48419
ES, 4115 E CHANLER 48419 – J. Sutherland, prin.

Caseville, Huron Co., Pop. Code 3
Caseville SD
Sch. Sys. Enr. Code 2
Supt. – James Stahl, 6609 VINE ST 48725
ES, 6609 VINE ST 48725 – Janet Watts, prin.

Cass City, Tuscola Co., Pop. Code 4
Cass City SD
Sch. Sys. Enr. Code 4
Supt. – Kenneth Micklash
4868 SEEGER RD 48726
MS, 4690 SEEGER ST 48726
Donald Schelke, prin.
Campbell ES, 6627 ROSE ST 48726
David Lovejoy, prin.
Other Schools – See Decker, Deford

Cassopolis, Cass Co., Pop. Code 4
Cassopolis SD
Sch. Sys. Enr. Code 4
Supt. – (—), P O BOX 98 49031
Adams MS, EAST STATE ST 49031
Ed Vander West, prin.
Squires ES, CENTER ST 49031
Barbara Bahner, prin.

Cedar Lake, Montcalm Co., Pop. Code 3

Cedar Lake 7 Day ES
7195 ACADEMY ROAD 48812

Cedar Springs, Kent Co., Pop. Code 5
Cedar Springs SD
Sch. Sys. Enr. Code 4
Supt. – James A. Tackmann
204 E MUSKEGON 49319
MS, 204 E MUSKEGON 49319 – (—), prin.
Beach ES, 204 E MUSKEGON 49319
Daniel Davis, prin.
Hilltop MS, 204 E MUSKEGON 49319
Nyla Rypma, prin.

Cedarville, Mackinac Co., Pop. Code 3
Les Cheneaux Comm. SD
Sch. Sys. Enr. Code 2
Supt. – Kenneth Drenth, P O BOX 366 49719
ES, P O BOX 366 49719 – Thomas Wilson, prin.

Center Line, Macomb Co., Pop. Code 6
Centerline SD
Sch. Sys. Enr. Code 5
Supt. – Terry Follbaum
6775 E 10 MILE ROAD 48015
Wolfe MS, 8640 MCKINLEY ST 48015
Charles Hatch, prin.
Miller ES, 23855 LAWRENCE AVE 48015
E. Winterfield, prin.
Other Schools – See Warren

St. Clement School, 8155 RITTER ST 48015

Central Lake, Antrim Co., Pop. Code 3
Central Lake SD
Sch. Sys. Enr. Code 2
Supt. – C. L. Blamer, P O BOX 128 49622
ES, P O BOX 128 49622 – William Coaster, prin.

Centreville, St. Joseph Co., Pop. Code 4
Centreville SD
Sch. Sys. Enr. Code 3
Supt. – Ronald Mrozinski, 190 HOGAN ST 49032
MS, 190 HOGAN ST 49032 – (—), prin.
ES, 190 HOGAN ST 49032 – Allen Parfitt, prin.

Champion, Marquette Co., Pop. Code 2
Nice Comm. SD
Supt. – See Ishpeming
ES, P O BOX 66 49814 – Ronald Kulie, prin.

Charlevoix, Charlevoix Co., Pop. Code 5
Charlevoix SD
Sch. Sys. Enr. Code 4
Supt. – Gordon W. VanWieren
208 W CLINTON ST 49720
MS, 230 DIVISION ST 49720
Dennis Van Guilder, prin.
ES, 230 DIVISION ST 49720 – Vane Smith, prin.

Charlotte, Eaton Co., Pop. Code 6
Charlotte SD
Sch. Sys. Enr. Code 5
Supt. – Elwood Larsen, 378 STATE ST 48813
MS, 301 HORATIO ST 48813
Walter Honshell, prin.
Galewood ES, 512 E LOVETT ST 48813
Richard Larson, prin.
Parkview ES, 301 E KALAMO HWY 48813
C. Grundstrom, prin.
Washington ES, 525 HIGH ST 48813
Jane Nelson, prin.
Weymouth ES, 346 STATE ST 48813
Ed Yoder, prin.

St. Mary ES, 905 SAINT MARYS BLVD 48813

Chassell, Houghton Co., Pop. Code 4
Chassell Twp. SD
Sch. Sys. Enr. Code 2
Supt. – Edward Huls, P O BOX 40 49916
S, P O BOX 40 49916 – Daniel Scow, prin.

Cheboygan, Cheboygan Co., Pop. Code 6
Cheboygan Area SD
Sch. Sys. Enr. Code 4
Supt. – William Schewe, P O BOX 100 49721
MS, 504 DIVISION ST 49721
Thomas Cavanaugh, prin.
Black River ES, 2732 ORCHARD BEACH RD 49721
Floyd Stowe, prin.
East ES, 440 GARFIELD AVE 49721
Marilyn Florek, prin.
Inverness ES, 7461 N STRAITS HWY 49721
Todd Roberson, prin.
West ES, 512 PINE ST 49721
Paul Borowicz, prin.

Bishop Baraga School, 421 E STATE ST 49721

Chelsea, Washtenaw Co., Pop. Code 5
Chelsea SD
Sch. Sys. Enr. Code 4
Supt. – Joseph Piasecki
500 WASHINGTON ST 48118
Beach MS, MAYER DRIVE 48118
D. Stielstra, prin.
North ES, MCKINLEY ST 48118
William Wescott, prin.
South ES, PIERCE ST 48118
Robert Benedict, prin.

Chesaning, Saginaw Co., Pop. Code 5
Chesaning Un. SD
Sch. Sys. Enr. Code 5
Supt. – Robert Rhode, 820 S LINE ST 48616
MS, 431 N 4TH ST 48616 – Duane Ferry, prin.
Big Rock ES, 920 E BROAD ST 48616
Jan Krause, prin.
Line Street ES, 820 S LINE ST 48616
Richard Coon, prin.
Other Schools – See Burt, Oakley

Our Lady of Perpetual Help School
802 LOCKWOOD 48616

Clare, Clare Co., Pop. Code 5
Clare SD
Sch. Sys. Enr. Code 4
Supt. – Walter Schwarz
305 E WHEATON AVE 48617
MS, 209 E STATE ST 48617
Gregory McMillan, prin.
PS, 105 E WHEATON AVE 48617
John Leppanen, prin.

Clarkston, Oakland Co., Pop. Code 3
Clarkston Comm. SD
Sch. Sys. Enr. Code 6
Supt. – Gary Haner
6389 CLARKSTON ROAD 48016
Andersonville ES
10350 ANDERSONVILLE RD 48016
Sharon Devereaux, prin.
Bailey Lake ES, 8051 PINE KNOB RD 48016
Doris Mousseau, prin.
ES, 6595 WALDON RD 48016
William Potvin, prin.
North Sashabaw ES, 5290 MAYBEE RD 48016
John Hayden, prin.
Pine Knob ES, 6020 SASHABAW RD 48016
George White, prin.

Clawson, Oakland Co., Pop. Code 7
Clawson SD
Sch. Sys. Enr. Code 4
Supt. – William Price, 626 PHILLIPS AVE   48017
MS, 150 JOHN M AVE   48017
    Burton Schultz, prin.
Kenwood ES, 240 NAHMA AVE   48017
    Alan McClelland, prin.
Schalm ES, 940 N SELFRIDGE BLVD   48017
    C. Ruttledge, prin.

Guardian Angels ES
    521 E FOURTEEN MILE RD   48017

Clayton, Lenawee Co., Pop. Code 2
Hudson Area SD
Supt. – See Hudson
Hudson MS, PEARL ST   49235
    James DuVall, prin.

Climax, Kalamazoo Co., Pop. Code 3
Climax-Scotts Comm. SD
Sch. Sys. Enr. Code 3
Supt. – Ronald Parker, 372 S MAIN   49034
Climax-Scotts MS, 372 S MAIN   49034
    M. Kreutziger, prin.
Other Schools – See Scotts

Clinton, Lenawee Co., Pop. Code 4
Clinton Comm. SD
Sch. Sys. Enr. Code 4
Supt. – George Sargeant
    341 E MICHIGAN AVE   49236
MS, FRANKLIN ST   49236 – Gordon Clark, prin.
ES, 200 E FRANKLIN ST   49236 – David Pray, prin.

Clio, Genesee Co., Pop. Code 5
Clio Area SD
Sch. Sys. Enr. Code 5
Supt. – Albert Butler, 430 N MILL ST   48420
Carter MS, 300 UPLAND DRIVE   48420
    Marjorie Dahle, prin.
Edgerton ES, 11218 LINDEN RD   48420
    Ralph Linley, prin.
Garner ES, 10271 CLIO RD   48420
    Fay Latture, prin.
Lacure ES, 12167 N LEWIS RD   48420
    B. Fairweather, prin.

Coldwater, Branch Co., Pop. Code 6
Coldwater Comm. SD
Sch. Sys. Enr. Code 5
Supt. – Richard Fitzgerald
    500 W CHICAGO ST   49036
Legg MS, 175 GREEN ST   49036
    Mitchell Zaleski, prin.
Edison ES, 255 N CLAY ST   49036
    Jane Kuckel, prin.
Girard ES, 100 CENTER ST   49036
    Sharon Franz, prin.
Jefferson ES, 15 VANS AVE   49036
    Donald Reppert, prin.
Lakeland ES, 519 OTIS RD   49036
    Joseph Theines, prin.
Lincoln ES, 70 TIBBITS ST   49036
    Lary Cameron, prin.
Washington ES, 71 MORSE ST   49036
    J. Rebentisch, prin.

Coleman, Midland Co., Pop. Code 4
Coleman Comm. SD
Sch. Sys. Enr. Code 4
Supt. – Michael Smith, P O BOX W   48618
ES, P O BOX W   48618 – Richard Latta, prin.

Coloma, Berrien Co., Pop. Code 4
Coloma Comm. SD
Sch. Sys. Enr. Code 4
Supt. – Clifford Tallman, P O BOX 550   49038
ES, 262 N WEST ST   49038 – Dan Stack, prin.
North MS, 274 NW   49038 – Ilse Erickson, prin.
South MS, 274 A NW   49038 – Ilse Erickson, prin.
Washington ES, 6463 BECHT RD E   49038
    Joyce Tutton, prin.

Colon, St. Joseph Co., Pop. Code 4
Colon Comm. SD
Sch. Sys. Enr. Code 3
Supt. – (—), 400 DALLAS ST   49040
ES, 300 STATE ST   49040 – Marcia Griffin, prin.
Other Schools – See Leonidas

Columbiaville, Lapeer Co., Pop. Code 3
Lakeville Comm. SD
Supt. – See Otisville
ES, 4775 PINE ST   48421 – Jerry Swenor, prin.

Comstock, Kalamazoo Co., Pop. Code 7
Comstock SD
Sch. Sys. Enr. Code 5
Supt. – Robert Hamet
    5196 COMSTOCK AVE   49041
Northeast MS, 1423 N ST   49041 – Tim Fox, prin.
East ES, 175 HUNT ST   49041
    Aurelia Spengler, prin.
Green Meadow ES, 6171 E MINN AVE   49041
    Ceville Hinman, prin.
Gull Road ES, 3010 GULL RD   49041
    Larry Lindeman, prin.
North ES, 3100 N 26TH   49041
    William Buhro, prin.

Comstock Park, Kent Co., Pop. Code 4
Comstock Park SD
Sch. Sys. Enr. Code 4
Supt. – James Van Dyk
    7200 PINE ISLAND DRIVE   49321

Greenridge ES, 3841 OAKRIDGE AVE   49321
    Richard Zoodsma, prin.
Stoney Creek MS, 200 LANTERN DR   49321
    Byron Chitwood, prin.

Holy Trinity ES, 1304 ALPINE CHURCH RD   49321

Concord, Jackson Co., Pop. Code 3
Concord Comm. SD
Sch. Sys. Enr. Code 3
Supt. – Albert Widner, 405 S MAIN ST   49237
MS, 405 S MAIN ST   49237
    Marvelle Vannest, prin.
ES, 405 S MAIN ST   49237 – H. Dulmage, prin.

Conklin, Ottawa Co.

St. Joseph ES, EIGHTH AVE   49403

Constantine, St. Joseph Co., Pop. Code 4
Constantine SD
Sch. Sys. Enr. Code 4
Supt. – Dr. Ben Smith, 260 W 6TH ST   49042
MS, 750 CANARIS ST   49042 – Rod Begaman, prin.
Eastside ES, 935 WHITE PIGEON RD   49042
    Anna Johansen, prin.
Riverside MS, 600 W 6TH ST   49042
    Susan Bell, prin.

Cooks, Schoolcraft Co.
Big Bay de Noc SD
Sch. Sys. Enr. Code 2
Supt. – George Babladelis   49817
Big Bay de Noc S   49817 – (—), prin.

Coopersville, Ottawa Co., Pop. Code 5
Coopersville Area SD
Sch. Sys. Enr. Code 4
Supt. – Robert Fortin, 198 EAST ST   49404
MS, 198 EAST ST   49404 – Ross Conran, prin.
ES, 198 EAST ST   49404 – Leone Appell, prin.
Lamont ES   49404 – (—), prin.

Cornell, Delta Co.
Escanaba Area SD
Supt. – See Escanaba
ES, 9789 COUNTY ROAD   49818
    Nancy Schirmer, prin.

Corunna, Shiawassee Co., Pop. Code 5
Corunna SD
Sch. Sys. Enr. Code 4
Supt. – Duane Ash, 106 SHIAWASSEE ST S   48817
MS, COMSTOCK ST   48817
    Richard Ziegler, prin.
Meyer ES, 100 HASTINGS ST   48817
    D. Hulliberger, prin.
Peacock ES, 505 E MCARTHUR ST   48817
    Joseph Scott, prin.
Reed ES, 201 E WASHINGTON   48476
    Mark Miller, prin.

Covert, Van Buren Co., Pop. Code 5
Covert SD
Sch. Sys. Enr. Code 3
Supt. – A. Hawkins, P O BOX 55   49043
MS, 35323 M-140 HIGHWAY   49043
    Bernard Abrams, prin.
ES, 35323 M-140 HWY   49043
    Esther Lawson, prin.

Croswell, Sanilac Co., Pop. Code 4
Croswell-Lexington SD
Sch. Sys. Enr. Code 4
Supt. – Gary Davis, 15 S HOWARD AVE   48422
Cros-Lex MS, 5318 PECK ROAD   48422
    john Ferda, prin.
Frostick ES, 57 HOWARD   48422
    Ralph Roberts, prin.
Geiger MS, 27 HOWARD   48422
    Lewis Hurley, prin.
Meyer ES, 7201 LAKE ST   48450
    Joyce Judge, prin.

Crystal, Montcalm Co.
Carson City-Crystal Area SD
Supt. – See Carson City
ES, 217 PARK   48818 – Thomas Hain, prin.

Crystal Falls, Iron Co., Pop. Code 4
Forest Park SD
Sch. Sys. Enr. Code 3
Supt. – Clifford Luft
    801 FOREST PARKWAY   49920
Forest Park MS, 801 FOREST PARKWAY   49920
    E. Dzvibinski, prin.
Forest Park ES, 801 FOREST PKY   49920
    M. Stankenwicz, prin.

Curtis, Mackinac Co.
Tahquamenon Area SD
Supt. – See Newberry
ES   49820 – Alan Bitely, prin.

Custer, Mason Co., Pop. Code 2
Mason County Eastern SD
Sch. Sys. Enr. Code 3
Supt. – Michael Oakes, 18 S MAIN ST   49405
Mason County Eastern ES, 18 S MAIN ST   49405
    J. Jackoviak, prin.

Dafter, Chippewa Co.
Sault Sainte Marie Area SD
Supt. – See Sault Sainte Marie
Bruce ES, RURAL ROUTE 01   49724
    Richard Beacom, prin.

Daggett, Menominee Co., Pop. Code 2
Stephenson Area SD
Supt. – See Stephenson
ES   49821 – Ron Nelson, prin.

Dansville, Ingham Co., Pop. Code 2
Agricultural SD
Sch. Sys. Enr. Code 3
Supt. – C. Dean Atkins, 1264 ADAMS ST   48819
MS, 1264 ADAMS ST   48819 – Roger Pollok, prin.
ES, 1264 ADAMS ST   48819 – Larry Cook, prin.

Davisburg, Oakland Co.
Holly Area SD
Supt. – See Holly
ES, 12003 DAVISBURG RD   48019
    Steven Gaynor, prin.

Davison, Genesee Co., Pop. Code 6
Davison Comm. SD
Sch. Sys. Enr. Code 5
Supt. – R. C. Amble, 615 E CLARK ST   48423
JHS, 600 S DAYTON ST   48423
    Patrick Suriano, prin.
Central ES, 600 S STATE RD   48423
    Ronald Adam, prin.
Gates ES, G-2359 S IRISH RD   48423
    Ronald Wright, prin.
Hill ES, 404 ALOHA ST   48423 – Kay Forys, prin.
Siple ES, 9286 E COLDWATER RD   48423
    Carolyn Garnsey, prin.

Dearborn, Wayne Co., Pop. Code 8
Dearborn SD
Sch. Sys. Enr. Code 7
Supt. – Thomas McLennan, 4824 LOIS ST   48126
Bryant MS, 460 N VERNON ST   48128
    Karl Stuef, prin.
Lowery MS   48126 – (—), prin.
Smith MS, 23851 YALE ST   48124
    Daniel Kurmas, prin.
Stout MS, 18500 OAKWOOD BLVD   48124
    Ronald Doherty, prin.
Woodworth MS   48126 – (—), prin.
Duvall ES, 22561 BEECH ST   48124
    Allan Mcdonald, prin.
Ford ES, 16140 DRISCOLL ST   48126
    John Dutton, prin.
Ford ES, 5645 CHASE RD   48126
    Dr. J. Boatwright, prin.
Haigh ES, 601 N SILVERY LN   48128
    C. George, prin.
Howard ES, 1611 N YORK ST   48128
    Mary Ann Zammit, prin.
Howe ES, 18000 OAKWOOD BLVD   48124
    Lawrence Miller, prin.
Lindbergh ES, 500 N WAVERLY ST   48128
    Richard Fasing, prin.
Long ES, 3100 WESTWOOD ST   48124
    George Monroe, prin.
Lowery ES, 6601 JONATHAN ST   48126
    Charles Stanton, prin.
Maples ES, 6801 MEAD ST   48126
    Jack Samples, prin.
McDonald ES, 10151 DIVERSEY ST   48126
    Eugene Brusco, prin.
Nowlin ES, 23600 PENN ST   48124
    T. Biesiadecki, prin.
Oakman ES, 7545 CHASE RD   48126
    Ray Martin, prin.
Salina ES, 2623 SALINA ST   48120
    Gary Wolter, prin.
Snow ES, 2000 CULVER ST   48124
    James Hardie, prin.
Whitmore-Bolles ES, 21501 WHITMORE ST   48124
    Bernard Boyle, prin.
Woodworth ES, 4951 TERNES ST   48126
    Merrill Thomas, prin.
Other Schools – See Dearborn Heights

Westwood Comm. SD
Supt. – See Inkster
Thorne PS, 25251 ANNAPOLIS ST   48125
    Robert Camaiani, prin.

Atonement Lutheran School, 6961 MEAD   48126
Dearborn Christian ES
    21360 DONALDSON ST   48124
Divine Child ES, 25111 HOLLANDER   48128
Emmanuel ES, 22425 MORLEY AVE   48124
Guardian ES, 24544 CHERRY HILL ST   48124
Sacred Heart ES, 22513 GARRISON ST   48124
St. Alphonsus ES, 7230 SCHAEFER RD   48126
St. Barbara ES, 5277 CALHOUN ST   48126

Dearborn Heights, Wayne Co., Pop. Code 8
Crestwood School SD
Sch. Sys. Enr. Code 5
Supt. – David Tylor
    1501 BEECH DALY ROAD N   48127
Riverside MS, 25900 W WARREN AVE   48127
    Jack Miller, prin.
Highview ES, 25225 RICHARDSON   48127
    Hazel Durham, prin.
Hillcrest ES, 7500 VERNON ST N   48127
    Marilyn Shields, prin.
Kinloch ES, 1501 KINLOCH ST   48127
    R. Boatwright, prin.

Dearborn Heights SD
Sch. Sys. Enr. Code 4
Supt. – Dr. Paul Stamatakis
    20629 ANNAPOLIS ST   48125
Best JHS, 22201 POWERS AVE   48125
    Charles Davies, prin.

Bedford ES, 4650 CROISSANT ST 48125
  Louis Winek, prin.
Pardee ES, 4650 PARDEE AVE 48125
  Marvin olkowski, prin.
Polk ES, 4651 POLK ST 48125
  Remo Porchia, prin.

Dearborn SD
Supt. – See Dearborn
River Oaks ES, 20755 ANN ARBOR TRL 48127
  David Reid, prin.

Taylor SD
Supt. – See Taylor
Federal ES, 27280 POWERS 48127
  James Johnson, prin.

Wayne-Westland Comm. SD
Supt. – See Westland
Fisher ES, 244 JOHN DALY ST N 48127
  Larry Waynick, prin.

Westwood Comm. SD
Supt. – See Inkster
Allen MS, 25720 PENN ST 48125
  Kate Calhoun, prin.

Our Lady of Grace ES, 23713 JOY RD 48127
St. Albert the Great ES, 4671 PARKER ST 48125
St. Anselm ES, 17700 W OUTER DR 48127
St. John the Baptist ES, 26104 ETON AVE 48125
St. Linus ES, 6466 EVANGELINE ST N 48127
St. Mel ES, 7506 INKSTER RD N 48127
St. Sabina ES, 8147 ARNOLD ST 48127
St. Sebastian ES, 20700 COLGATE ST 48125

Decatur, Van Buren Co., Pop. Code 4
Decatur SD
Sch. Sys. Enr. Code 4
Supt. – Gerald Page, 110 CEDAR ST 49045
Bergen MS, 312 SCHOOL ST 49045
  Lloyd Dow, prin.
Davis ES, 409 N PHELPS ST 49045
  Douglas Olsen, prin.

Decker, Sanilac Co.
Cass City SD
Supt. – See Cass City
Evergreen ES, 5421 SHABBONA RD 48426
  Dorland Kuntz, prin.

Deckerville, Sanilac Co., Pop. Code 3
Deckerville Comm. SD
Sch. Sys. Enr. Code 3
Supt. – Ozzie Parks, 2633 BLACK RIVER ST 48427
ES, 2633 BLACK RIVER ST 48427
  James Popilek, prin.

Deerfield, Lenawee Co., Pop. Code 3
Deerfield SD
Sch. Sys. Enr. Code 2
Supt. – Paul Ellinger
  252 DEERFIELD ROAD 49238
ES, 2512 DEERFIELD RD 49238 – Pat Gabriel, prin.

Deford, Tuscola Co.
Cass City SD
Supt. – See Cass City
ES, 6010 E DECKERVILLE RD 48729
  Betty Murphy, prin.

Delton, Barry Co., Pop. Code 2
Delton Kellogg SD
Sch. Sys. Enr. Code 4
Supt. – John Sanders, 327 N GROVE ST 49046
Delton Kellogg MS, 327 N GROVE ST 49046
  Gregory Pratt, prin.
Delton Kellogg PS, 327 N GROVE ST 49046
  Marilynn Baker, prin.

De Tour Village, Chippewa Co., Pop. Code 2
De Tour Village Area SD
Sch. Sys. Enr. Code 2
Supt. – Jay Van Hoven, 202 S DIVISION ST 49725
S, P O BOX 68 49725 – Richard Roan, prin.
Drummond Island ES 49726 – (—), prin.

Detroit, Wayne Co., Pop. Code 12
Detroit SD
Sch. Sys. Enr. Code 9
Supt. – Arthur Jefferson
  5057 WOODWARD AVE 48202
Angell MS, 8323 HOLMUR ST 48204
  Oscar Session, prin.
Ann Arbor Trail MS, 7635 CHATHAM 48239
  Helen Carter, prin.
Area E Magnet MS 48202 – (—), prin.
Barbour MS, 4209 SENECA ST 48214
  Randall Moody, prin.
Boynton MS, 12800 VISGER ST 48217
  Vernon Nimocks, prin.
Brooks MS, 16101 W CHICAGO ST 48228
  Joseph Gilchrist, prin.
Burbank MS, 15600 STATE FAIR ST E 48205
  (—), prin.
Burroughs MS, 8950 SAINT CYRIL 48213
  Cleon Gilliam, prin.
Butzel MS, 2301 VAN DYKE ST 48214
  Napoleon Jordan, prin.
Cadillac MS, 15125 SCHOOLCRAFT ST 48227
  Barbara Dent, prin.
Cleveland MS, 13322 CONANT ST 48212
  William Washington, prin.
Clippert MS, 4725 MARTIN ST 48210
  Richard Reading, prin.
Coffey MS, 17210 CAMBRIDGE AVE 48235
  Marvin Davis, prin.

Columbus MS, 18025 BROCK ST 48205
  Raymond Hughes, prin.
Condon MS, 1314 GRAND BLVD W 48208
  William Snyder, prin.
Drew MS, 9600 WYOMING ST 48204
  James Lee, prin.
Durfee MS, 2470 COLLINGWOOD 48206
  Alvin Hill, prin.
Earhart MS, 1000 SCOTTEN ST 48209
  Theodore Sims, prin.
Emerson MS 48202 – (—), prin.
Farwell MS, 19955 FENELON ST 48234
  Maurice Wilson, prin.
Fisher MS, 10125 KING RICHARD ST 48224
  Thomas Washington, prin.
Foch MS, 2962 FAIRVIEW ST 48214
  Helen Clowney, prin.
Guest MS, 10825 FENKELL ST 48238
  William Moner, prin.
Hally MS, 2586 GROVE ST 48221
  James Bateman, prin.
Hamilton MS, 14223 SOUTHAMPTON ST 48213
  Walter Banks, prin.
Hutchins MS
  8820 WOODROW WILSON ST 48206
  Peter Van Lowe, prin.
Jackson MS, 4180 MARLBOROUGH ST 48215
  David White, prin.
Joy MS, 4611 FAIRVIEW ST 48214
  John Jones, prin.
Knudsen JHS, 2600 LELAND ST 48207
  James Foster, prin.
Lessenger MS, 8401 TRINITY ST 48228
  (—), prin.
Longfellow MS, 13141 ROSA PARKS BLVD 48238
  Bernard Dent, prin.
Ludington MS
  19355 EDINBOROUGH ROAD 48219
  Edward Williams, prin.
McMichael MS, 6050 LINWOOD ST 48208
  Wardell Gilliam, prin.
Miller MS, 2322 DUBOIS ST 48207
  Leonard Douglas, prin.
Munger MS, 5525 MARTIN ST 48210
  Roscoe McKnight, prin.
Noble JHS, 8646 FULLERTON ST 48238
  Raleigh Robinson, prin.
Nolan MS, 1150 LANTZ ST E 48203
  George Busch, prin.
Pelham MS, 2001 MYRTLE ST 48208
  Lewis Jeffries, prin.
Richard JHS, 13840 LAPPIN ST 48205
  Alma Greer, prin.
Robinson MS, 13000 ESSEX AVE 48215
  Charles L. Washington, prin.
Rosa Parks MS, 8030 OUTER DRIVE E 48213
  R. Demeulemeester, prin.
Ruddiman MS, 7350 SOUTHFIELD FWY 48228
  Camille Jones, prin.
Sherrard MS, 8300 CAMERON ST 48211
  Tommy Diggs, prin.
Taft MS, 19501 BERG ROAD 48219
  John Harris, prin.
Tappan JHS, 11775 AMERICAN ST 48204
  Herbert Williams, prin.
Von Steuben MS, 12300 LINNHURST ST 48205
  John Jones, prin.
Webber MS, 4700 TIREMAN ST 48204
  Mackie Bradford, prin.
Wilson MS, 7735 LANE ST 48209
  Joseph Wytrwal, prin.
Winship MS, 14717 CURTIS ST 48235
  Tom Barton, prin.
Winterhalter MS
  12121 BROADSTREET AVE 48204
  Herman Carroll, prin.
Young MS, 2757 MACOMB ST 48207
  Bernice Waddles, prin.
Angell PS, 8858 PETOSKEY AVE 48204
  Yvonne Walker, prin.
Atkinson ES, 4900 HILDALE ST E 48234
  Pealy Samples, prin.
Bagley ES, 8100 CURTIS ST 48221
  James Smith, prin.
Barton ES, 8530 JOY RD 48204
  Spencer Carpenter, prin.
Bates Academy ES 48202 – (—), prin.
Beard ES, 840 WATERMAN ST 48209
  Joe Mahan, prin.
Bell ES, 7600 GOETHE ST 48214
  William Luxmore, prin.
Bellevue ES, 1501 CANTON ST 48207
  Maxine Mills, prin.
Bennett ES, 2111 MULLANE ST 48209
  Manuel Nunez, prin.
Berry ES, 6600 BENSON ST 48207
  Thomas Schulte, prin.
Bethune PS, 13001 FENKELL ST 48227
  Willa Murphy, prin.
Biddle ES, 4601 SEEBALDT ST 48204
  Bev Mitchell, prin.
Birney ES, 4055 RICHTON ST 48204
  Johnnie Boyer, prin.
Bow ES, 19801 PREVOST ST 48235
  E. Graves, prin.
Brady ES, 2920 JOY RD 48206
  Harold Burton, prin.
Breitmeyer ES, 8210 CAMERON ST 48211
  Bradley Crosby, prin.
Brewer ES 48202 – (—), prin.
Bunche ES, 2601 ELLERY ST 48207
  Donald Kendrick, prin.
Burns ES, 14350 TERRY ST 48227
  Norma Graves, prin.

Burt ES, 20710 PILGRIM ST 48223
  Robert Edwards, prin.
Burton International ES 48202 – (—), prin.
Campbell ES, 2301 E ALEXANDRIA 48207
  Lavona Davis, prin.
Carleton ES, 11724 CASINO ST 48224
  William Dine, prin.
Carstens ES, 2592 COPLIN ST 48215
  Paul Buechler, prin.
Carver ES, 18701 PAUL ST 48228
  Robert Solari, prin.
Chandler ES, 9227 CHAPIN ST 48213
  Sharon Staff, prin.
Chaney ES, 2750 SELDEN ST 48208
  Barbara Lester, prin.
Chrysler ES, 1445 LAFAYETTE ST E 48207
  Linda Ford, prin.
Clark ES, 15755 BREMEN ST 48224
  Edith Gaillard, prin.
Clinton ES, 8145 CHALFONTE ST 48238
  (—), prin.
Columbian PS, 4700 VINEWOOD ST 48208
  Hattie Brown, prin.
Cooke ES, 18800 PURITAN ST 48223
  George Miller, prin.
Coolidge ES, 16501 ELMIRA ST 48227
  William Whiteside, prin.
Cooper ES, 6836 GEORGIA ST 48211
  Jane Johnson, prin.
Courtis ES, 8100 DAVISON W 48238
  Vernett Smith, prin.
Courville ES, 18040 SAINT AUBIN ST 48234
  Alvin Bell, prin.
Couzens ES, 3550 JOHN C LODGE FWY 48201
  Janette Cox, prin.
Crary ES, 16164 ASBURY PARK 48235
  Ascar Hobson, prin.
Custer ES, 15531 LINWOOD ST 48238
  Ozell Dupree, prin.
Davison ES, 2800 DAVISON ST E 48212
  Donald Corbin, prin.
Detroit Open ES 48202 – (—), prin.
Dixon ES, 195900 TIREMAN 48228
  Robert Kolnowski, prin.
Dossin ES, 16660 GLENDALE ST 48227
  Richard Allen, prin.
Doty ES, 10225 THIRD ST 48202
  Gloria Williams, prin.
Dow ES, 19900 MCINTYRE ST 48219
  (—), prin.
Duffield ES, 2715 MACOMB ST 48207
  Thomas Mason, prin.
Edison ES, 17045 GRAND RIVER AVE 48227
  Mary Gene Sturkey, prin.
Edmonson ES, 1300 CANFIELD ST W 48201
  Richard Harrison, prin.
Ellis ES, 5611 RICH ST 48210
  Joseph Jakubiec, prin.
Emerson ES, 18240 HUNTINGTON 48219
  (—), prin.
Fairbanks ES, 8000 JOHN C LODGE FWY 48202
  Amelia Powell, prin.
Ferry ES, 2920 PALMER ST E 48211
  Paul Kulhanjian, prin.
Fitzgerald ES, 8145 PURITAN ST 48238
  Joel Hackett, prin.
Fleming ES, 18501 WALTHAM ST 48205
  Dolores Trotter, prin.
Ford ES, 14735 ORANGELAWN ST 48227
  Jerome Thweatt, prin.
Fox PS, 17300 FARGO ST 48235
  Argie Harris, prin.
Gardner ES, 6528 MANSFIELD ST 48228
  John Papajohn, prin.
Glazer ES, 2001 LA BELLE ST 48238
  Robert Everson, prin.
Gompers ES, 20601 DAVISON ST W 48223
  Evangelis Lucas, prin.
Goodale ES, 9835 DICKERSON ST 48213
  John Hoye, prin.
Grant ES, 7479 STOCKTON ST 48234
  Janice Cowan, prin.
Grayling ES, 744 ADELINE ST 48203
  Delano Esselman, prin.
Greenfield Park ES, 17501 BRUSH ST 48203
  Bruce Bolton, prin.
Greenfield Union ES, 420 7 MILE RD W 48203
  Carolyn Anderson, prin.
Guyton ES, 355 PHILIP ST 48215
  Robert Bitter, prin.
Hampton ES, 3901 MARGARETA ST 48221
  Chrystal Tibbs, prin.
Hanneman ES, 6420 MCGRAW ST 48210
  Henry Wallace,Jr., prin.
Hanstein ES, 4290 MARSEILLES ST 48224
  Donald Bohlinger, prin.
Harding ES, 14450 BURT RD 48223
  Leo Hauer, prin.
Harms ES, 2400 CENTRAL ST 48209
  James Taylor, prin.
Healy ES, 12901 BEAVERLAND ST 48223
  Beverly Gibson, prin.
Herman ES, 16400 TIREMAN ST 48228
  Marcella Verdun, prin.
Higgins ES, 9200 OLIVET ST 48209
  Audrea Callway, prin.
Holcomb ES, 18100 BENTLER ST 48219
  Morton Bates, prin.
Holmes ES, 8950 CRANE ST 48213
  Bernard Tinsley, prin.
Holmes ES, 4833 OGDEN ST 48210
  Gerald Ernatt, prin.
Hosmer ES, 4365 NEWPORT ST 48215
  Richard White, prin.

Houghten ES, 16745 LAMPHERE ST 48219
　Mary Clement, prin.
Howe ES, 10430 CHARLEVOIX ST 48214
　Georgia Staples, prin.
Hubert ES, 14825 LAMPHERE ST 48223
　Varee Rhode-Crews, prin.
Hutchinson ES, 5221 MONTCLAIR ST 48213
　Walter Hall, prin.
Ilene ES, 15770 JAMES COUZENS FWY 48238
　(—), prin.
Ives ES, 1147 PHILIP ST 48215
　Eleanor Harrison, prin.
Jamieson ES, 2900 PHILADELPHIA ST W 48206
　Etheldria Varner, prin.
Jeffries ES, 12120 LEONARD ST 48217
　Benny McGough, prin.
Jones ES, 12120 LEONARD ST 48217
　Herbert Lewis, prin.
Joyce ES, 8411 SYLVESTER ST 48214
　Leslie Brown,Jr., prin.
Keidan ES, 4441 COLLINGWOOD ST 48204
　John Auckland, prin.
Keith ES, 10800 CANFIELD ST E 48214
　Melody Martin, prin.
King ES, 16800 CHEYENNE 48235
　Vivian Hughes, prin.
Kosciusko ES, 20220 TIREMAN ST 48228
　Diane Fleming, prin.
Krolik ES, 10101 CANFIELD ST E 48214
　Shirley Rhoades, prin.
Larned ES, 23700 CLARITA ST 48219
　Harvey Hambrick, prin.
Law ES, 19490 CARRIE ST 48234
　Charles Phillips, prin.
Lilibridge ES, 11131 KERCHEVAL ST 48214
　(—), prin.
Lodge ES, 24325 BENNETT ST 48219
　Theresa Lorino, prin.
Logan ES, 3811 CICOTTE ST 48210
　Jack Forster, prin.
Loving ES, 1000 LYNN ST 48211
　Sally Tisdell, prin.
Lynch Annex ES, 8085 DOYLE ST 48234
　Lavata Jones, prin.
Lynch ES, 7601 PALMETTO ST 48234
　Taletha Kennedy, prin.
MacCulloch ES, 13120 WILDEMERE ST 48238
　Dolores Snorton, prin.
MacDowell ES, 4201 OUTER DR W 48221
　Doris Ray, prin.
Macomb ES, 12021 EVANSTON ST 48213
　Alice Smith, prin.
Mann ES, 19625 ELMIRA ST 48228
　Emmit Polk, prin.
Marquette ES, 6145 CANYON ST 48236
　Ruth Randall, prin.
Marsh ES, 18600 WADSWORTH ST 48228
　Eileen Rodak, prin.
Marshall ES, 1255 STATE FAIR E 48203
　Joan Nagrant, prin.
Mason ES, 19635 MITCHELL ST 48234
　Robert Turner, prin.
Maybury ES, 4410 PORTER ST 48209
　Alice Fogarty, prin.
McColl ES, 20550 CATHREDRAL 48228
　John Butkiewicz, prin.
McFarlane ES, 8900 CHEYENNE ST 48228
　Gladys Scott, prin.
McGraw ES, 3500 MCGRAW ST 48208
　Charles Gordon, prin.
McGregor ES, 16206 EDMORE DR 48205
　John Hoye, prin.
McKenny ES, 20833 PEMBROKE AVE 48219
　John Roberts, prin.
McKinstry ES, 1981 MCKINSTRY ST 48209
　Kirk Walker, prin.
McLean ES, 9540 BRAMELL 48239
　Jesse Nimmons, prin.
McMillan ES, 615 S WEST END 48209
　Joyce Gallant, prin.
Monnier ES, 13600 WARD ST 48227
　Omelia Shaw, prin.
Neinas ES, 6021 MCMILLAN ST 48209
　Kate Civil, prin.
Newberry ES, 4045 29TH ST 48210
　Wilhelmina Quick, prin.
Newton ES, 16411 CURTIS ST 48235
　Sylvester Lockett, prin.
Nichols ES, 3020 BURNS ST 48214
　Paul Aviews, prin.
Owen ES, 3033 15TH ST 48216 – (—), prin.
Parker ES, 12744 ELMIRA ST 48227
　Katie Smith, prin.
Parkman ES, 15000 MACKENZIE ST 48228
　Henry Jolley, prin.
Pasteur ES, 19811 STOEPEL ST 48221
　John Malone, prin.
Pattengill ES, 8411 NORTHFIELD ST 48204
　Jonathan Redditt, prin.
Peck ES, 1600 LAWRENCE ST 48206
　Clifford Watson, prin.
Pitcher ES, 19779 STAHELIN AVE 48219
　Marjia Lee Cole, prin.
Priest ES, 7840 WAGNER ST 48210
　Brenda Clavon, prin.
Pulaski ES, 19725 STRASBURG ST 48205
　Samuel Berenbaum, prin.
Robinson ES, 12700 GROVER ST 48205
　Helen Martellock, prin.
Roosevelt ES, 11526 LINDWOOD 48206
　Justine Lofton, prin.
Rose ES, 5830 FIELD ST 48213
　Shirley Summers, prin.

Sampson ES, 6075 BEGOLE ST 48210
　Nell Scribner, prin.
Sanders ES, 8700 BYRON ST 48202
　Thomas Washington, prin.
Schulze ES, 10700 SANTA MARIA ST 48221
　Mount Allen, prin.
Scripps ES, 2100 HURLBUT ST 48214
　William Batchelor, prin.
Sherrill ES, 7300 GARDEN ST 48204
　Lillian Covington, prin.
Spain ES, 3700 BEAUBIEN ST 48201
　Charles Rozman, prin.
Stark ES, 12611 AVONDALE ST 48215
　Alva Robinson, prin.
Stellwagen ES, 11450 OUTER DR E 48224
　Charles Smith, prin.
Stephens ES, 6006 SENECA ST 48213
　Austerine Hambrick, prin.
Stewart ES, 12701 14TH ST 48238
　Althea Masterson, prin.
Thirkell ES, 7724 14TH ST 48206
　W. Gloria Middlebrook, prin.
Trix ES, 13700 BRINGARD DR 48205
　Susan Kozemko, prin.
Turner PS, 14900 PARKSIDE ST 48238
　Willie Leavelle, prin.
Twain ES, 12001 GLEASON ST 48217
　Reynolds Saddler, prin.
Van Zile ES, 2915 OUTER DR E 48234
　Elsie Dade, prin.
Vandenberg ES, 15000 TROJAN ST 48235
　Viola Miller, prin.
Vernor ES, 13726 PEMBROKE AVE 48235
　June Green Rivers, prin.
Vernor PS, 13735 7 MILE RD W 48235
　Argyle Wade, prin.
Vetal ES, 14200 WESTWOOD ST 48223
　Raymond Ernatt, prin.
Wayne ES, 10633 COURVILLE ST 48224
　Ernest Buechler, prin.
Weatherby ES, 20500 WADSWORTH ST 48228
　Oscar Abbott, prin.
Webster ES, 1450 25TH ST 48216
　Frank Lozano, prin.
White ES, 5161 CHARLES ST 48212
　John Harris, prin.
Wilkins ES, 12400 NASHVILLE ST 48205
　Annie Hubbard, prin.
Williams ES, 3700 GARFIELD ST 48207
　(—), prin.
Winship ES 48202 – (—), prin.
Woodward ES, 2900 WREFORD ST 48208
　Fred Greene, prin.
Yost ES, 16161 WINSTON ST 48219
　Anthony Byk, prin.
Young ES, 15771 HUBBELL ST 48227
　Phyllis White, prin.

Grosse Pointe SD
Supt. – See Grosse Pointe
Poupard ES, 20655 LENNON ST 48225
　James Cooper, prin.

Pinconning Area SD
Supt. – See Pinconning
ES, 517 W CENTER RD 48634
　Gloria Musiel, prin.

Redford Union SD
Sch. Sys. Enr. Code 6
Supt. – Kenneth Erickson
　18499 BEECH-DALY ROAD 48240
Hilbert MS, 26440 PURITAN 48239
　Brian Motter, prin.
Other Schools – See Redford

South Redford SD
Sch. Sys. Enr. Code 5
Supt. – Jan W. Jacobs
　26141 SCHOOLCRAFT 48239
Other Schools – See Redford

Friends School In Detroit
　1100 SAINT AUBIN ST 48207
St. Hedwig HS, 5680 KONKEL ST 48210
St. Vincent ES, 2020 14TH ST 48216
Assumption Grotto ES
　13780 GRATIOT AVE 48205
Berea ES, 7047 TIREMAN ST 48204
Bethany ES, 11475 OUTER DR E 48224
Christ the King ES, 16800 TRINITY ST 48219
Detroit Urban ES, 8091 OHIO ST 48204
East Bethlehem ES, 3510 OUTER DR E 48234
Eastside Vicariate ES
　4230 MCDOUGALL ST 48207
Evergreen Lutheran School
　8680 EVERGREEN ROAD 48228
Gesu ES, 17139 OAK DR 48221
Greenfield Peace ES, 7000 OUTER DR W 48235
Holy Cross ES, 14213 WHITCOMB ST 48227
Holy Redeemer ES, 1711 JUNCTION ST 48209
Holy Trinity ES, 1221 LABROSSE ST 48226
Immaculate Heart of Mary ES
　19940 MANSFIELD ST 48235
Mt. Calvary ES, 17100 CHALMERS ST 48205
Our Lady Help of Christians ES
　12555 MCDOUGALL ST 48212
Our Lady Queen of Angels ES
　4100 MARTIN ST 48210
Our Lady Queen of Heaven ES
　8230 ROLYAT ST 48234
Our Lady of Good Counsel ES
　17201 ANNOTT ST 48205
Our Lady of Loretto ES, 17175 OLYMPIA 48240
Our Saviour ES, 12844 ELMDALE 48213

Peace ES, 15760 WARREN AVE E 48224
Presentation ES, 19780 MEYERS RD 48235
Redford Lutheran School
　22159 GRAND RIVER AVE 48219
SS Peter & Paul ES, 7625 WESTWOOD ST 48228
St. Agatha ES, 19800 BEECH-DALY RD 48240
St. Ambrose ES, 1091 ALTER RD 48215
St. Anne ES, 200 FOURTH 48634
St. Bartholomew ES, 20001 WEXFORD ST 48234
St. Brendan ES, 11406 MORANG DR 48224
St. Brigid ES, 8735 SCHOOLCRAFT ST 48238
St. Casimir ES, 3361 23RD ST 48208
St. Cecilia ES, 6327 BURLINGAME ST 48204
St. Christine ES, 15320 LAMPHERE ST 48223
St. Christopher ES, 7800 WOODMONT AVE 48228
St. Cunegunda ES, 5874 ST LAWRENCE ST 48210
St. David ES, 8105 OUTER DR E 48213
St. Francis D'Assisi School
　5806 BUCHANAN ST 48210
St. Gemma ES, 13550 VIRGIL ST 48223
St. Gerard ES, 1990 EVERGREEN 48219
St. Hedwig ES, 5680 KONKEL ST 48210
St. Hilary ES, 23749 ELMIRA 48239
St. Hyacinth ES, 5240 MCDOUGALL ST 48211
St. John Bosco ES, 12170 BEECH-DALY RD 48239
St. John ES, 4950 OAKMAN BLVD 48204
St. Jude ES, 15865 7 MILE RD E 48205
St. Juliana ES, 14301 LONGVIEW ST 48213
St. Leo ES, 4851 14TH ST 48208
St. Mary of Redford ES
　14751 MANSFIELD ST 48227
St. Matthew ES, 5970 AUDUBON RD 48224
St. Phillip ES, 2884 GRAND BLVD E 48202
St. Raymond ES, 20045 JOANN ST 48205
St. Robert Bellarmine ES
　27201 W CHICAGO 48239
St. Scholastica ES
　17351 SOUTHFIELD FWY 48235
St. Stephen ES, 4330 CENTRAL ST 48210
St. Stephen ES, 1235 LAWNDALE ST 48209
St. Suzanne ES, 19321 W CHICAGO ST 48228
St. Theresa-Visitation ES, 4317 BLAINE ST 48204
St. Thomas Aquinas ES, 5845 AUBURN ST 48228
St. Timothy ES, 19400 EVERGREEN RD 48219
St. Valentine ES, 25800 DOW 48239
Transfiguration ES, 13301 MOUND RD 48212
Zion ES, 4305 MILITARY ST 48210
Zurstadt ES, 17200 BOSWORTH 48219

De Witt, Clinton Co., Pop. Code 5
De Witt SD
Sch. Sys. Enr. Code 4
Supt. – Terre Davis, 608 WILSON ST 48820
MS, SHAVEY ROAD 48820 – Earl Roseberry, prin.
Fuerstenau MS, 205 W WASHINGTON 48120
　M. Kay Hannah, prin.
Scott PS, 804 WILSON 48820 – J. Rundborg, prin.

Dexter, Washtenaw Co., Pop. Code 4
Dexter Comm. SD
Sch. Sys. Enr. Code 4
Supt. – John Hansen, 2615 BAKER ROAD 48130
Wylie MS, 3060 KENSINGTON ST 48130
　David Mills, prin.
Bates ES, 2704 BAKER RD 48130
　Caroline Sapsford, prin.
Copeland ES, 7714 DEXTER ANN ARBOR 48130
　Caroline Sapsford, prin.

Dollar Bay, Houghton Co., Pop. Code 3
Osceola Twp. SD
Sch. Sys. Enr. Code 2
Supt. – Harvey Filppula, P O BOX 371 49922
Davis ES 49922 – (—), prin.
MS, P O BOX 371 49922 – Harvey Filppula, prin.

Dorr, Allegan Co.
Hopkins SD
Supt. – See Hopkins
Sycamore PS, 2243 142ND AVE 49323
　William Howard, prin.

Wayland Un. SD
Supt. – See Wayland
ES, 4159 18TH ST 49323 – J. Wallington, prin.

St. Stanislaus ES, RURAL ROUTE 02 49323

Douglas, Allegan Co., Pop. Code 3
Saugatuck SD
Sch. Sys. Enr. Code 3
Supt. – Terry Brooks, 201 RANDOLPH ST 49406
ES, 261 RANDOLPH ST 49406 – J. Doane, prin.

Dowagiac, Cass Co., Pop. Code 6
Dowagiac Un. SD
Sch. Sys. Enr. Code 5
Supt. – Roger Dixon, 206 MAIN ST 49047
Central MS, 520 MAIN ST 49047
　D. Ebersole, prin.
Hamilton MS, 614 SPRUCE ST 49047
　Peggy Stowers, prin.
Gage PS, 301 OAK ST 49047
　Ronald O'Brien, prin.
Kincheloe PS, RURAL ROUTE 03 49047
　David Strikar, prin.
Lincoln PS, 405 E DIVISION ST 49047
　Ronald O'Brien, prin.
McKinley PS, 307 FIRST AVE 49047
　Dr. M. Douglas, prin.
Sister Lakes PS, M-152 49047
　Tom Lenhard, prin.

Drayton Plains, Oakland Co., Pop. Code 7
Waterford SD
Supt. – See Waterford

Cooley ES, 2000 HIGHFIELD RD 48020
  E. Pierre, prin.
Grayson ES, 3800 W WALTON BLVD 48020
  Douglas Lee, prin.
Manley ES, 2989 VAN ZANDT RD 48020
  Marilynn Wendt, prin.

St. Stephen ES, 3795 SASHABAW RD 48020

Dryden, Lapeer Co., Pop. Code 3
Dryden Comm. SD
Sch. Sys. Enr. Code 3
Supt. – Craig Gerard
  3866 ROCHESTER ROAD 48428
ES, 3835 N MILL RD 48428 – Sharon Billiau, prin.

Dundee, Monroe Co.
Dundee Comm. SD
Sch. Sys. Enr. Code 4
Supt. – David J. Bonnette
  420 YPSILANTI ST 48131
MS, 420 YPSILANTI ST 48131
  Shirley Tennant, prin.
ES, 420 YPSILANTI ST 48131
  Robert Rachor, prin.

Durand, Schiwassee Co., Pop. Code 5
Durand Area SD
Sch. Sys. Enr. Code 5
Supt. – Patrick Murphy
  310 N SAGINAW ST 48429
Lucas MS, 100 SYCAMORE ST 48429
  Barbara Hoevel, prin.
Bills ES, 251 W PRIOR ROAD 48414
  J. Standridge, prin.
Kerr ES, 9591 MONROE RD 48429
  M. Jean Sloan, prin.
Knight ES, 890 N OAK ST 48429
  Norman Abdella, prin.
Neal ES, 931 W MAIN ST 48429
  Roger Zick, prin.

East Detroit, Macomb Co., Pop. Code 8
East Detroit SD
Sch. Sys. Enr. Code 6
Supt. – John Gardiner
  19200 STEPHENS DRIVE 48021
Bellview ES, 15800 BELL AVE 48021
  Sharon Eccles, prin.
Crescentwood ES
  14500 CRESCENTWOOD AVE 48021
  Linda Johnson, prin.
Forest Park ES, 18361 FOREST AVE 48021
  Gerald Pagano, prin.
Kantner ES, 17363 TOEPFER DR 48021
  Roy Shehab, prin.
Pleasantview ES, 16501 TOEPFER DR 48021
  Dave Oleary, prin.
Woodland ES, 23750 DAVID AVE 48021
  Ray Rickert, prin.
Other Schools – See Warren

St. Peter ES, 23000 GRATIOT AVE 48021
St. Thomas ES, 23801 KELLY RD 48021
St. Veronica ES, 21450 UNIVERSAL AVE 48021

East Jordan, Charlevoix Co., Pop. Code 4
East Jordan SD
Sch. Sys. Enr. Code 4
Supt. – Jack Meeder, 401 WILLIAMS ST 49727
ES, 304 FOURTH ST 49727 – Gary Albring, prin.

East Lansing, Ingham Co., Pop. Code 8
East Lansing SD
Sch. Sys. Enr. Code 5
Supt. – William Mitchell
  509 BURCHAM DRIVE 48823
Hannah MS, 819 ABBOTT ROAD 48823
  Tony Egnatuk, prin.
MacDonald MS, 1601 BURCHAM DRIVE 48823
  Sal Di Franco, prin.
Donley ES, 2962 E LAKE LANSING RD 48823
  S. Claycomb, prin.
Glencairn ES, 939 N HARRISON RD 48823
  B. MacDonald, prin.
Marble ES, 729 N HAGADORN RD 48823
  Craig Marsh, prin.
Pinecrest ES, 1811 PINECREST DR 48823
  Robert Ulrich, prin.
Red Cedar ES, SEVER DR 48823
  William Lee, prin.
Spartan Village ES, 1460 MIDDLEVALE RD 48823
  Dr. Jessie Fry, prin.
Whitehills ES, 621 PEBBLEBROOK LN 48823
  S. McClintock, prin.

St. Thomas Aquinas ES, 915 ALTON RD 48823

East Leroy, Calhoun Co.
Athens Area SD
Supt. – See Athens
Leroy ES, 4320 K DR S 49051
  Gar Underwood, prin.

East Tawas, Iosco Co., Pop. Code 5
East Tawas Area SD
Sch. Sys. Enr. Code 4
Supt. – David Conzelmann
  325 NEWMAN ST 48730
ES, 325 NEWMAN ST 48730
  Herman Rollin, prin.
Tawas City MS, 825 SECOND ST 48763
  Herman Rollin, prin.
Other Schools – See Tawas City

Eaton Rapids, Eaton Co., Pop. Code 5
Eaton Rapids SD
Sch. Sys. Enr. Code 5
Supt. – Michael Rocca, 501 KING ST 48827
MS, 301 GREYHOUND DRIVE 48827
  Timothy Culver, prin.
Northwestern ES, 400 DEXTER RD 48827
  C. Hoffman, prin.
Southeastern ES, 300 GREYHOUND DR 48827
  Donald Lockwood, prin.
Union Street ES, 501 UNION ST 48827
  R. Williams, prin.

Eau Claire, Berrien Co., Pop. Code 3
Eau Claire SD
Sch. Sys. Enr. Code 3
Supt. – Glenn Bachman, 6300 E MAIN ST 49111
Lybrook ES, W MAIN ST 49111
  Madeline Kukla, prin.
Lybrook MS, W MAIN ST 49111
  Greg Chisek, prin.

Eben Junction, Alger Co., Pop. Code 2
Superior Central SD
Sch. Sys. Enr. Code 2
Supt. – Gerald Lasak, P O BOX 148 49825
Eben ES, P O BOX 148 49825 – M. Wanska, prin.

Ecorse, Wayne Co., Pop. Code 7
Ecorse SD
Sch. Sys. Enr. Code 4
Supt. – Richard Manning
  27385 OUTER DRIVE W 48229
Kennedy MS, 27225 OUTER DRIVE W 48229
  James Lovely, prin.
Bunch ES, 503 HYACINTHE ST 48229
  Lois West, prin.
School Three MS, 4530 SIXTH ST 48220
  Ralph Block, prin.
School Two ES, 44 JOSEPHINE ST W 48229
  Henry Isopi, prin.

Edmore, Montcalm Co., Pop. Code 4
Montabella Comm. SD
Sch. Sys. Enr. Code 4
Supt. – Jon Whan, 300 W MAIN 48829
Montabella MS, 300 W MAIN 48829
  Ronald Farrell, prin.
Blanchard ES, 410 PINE ST 49310
  Ron Patton, prin.
Webb ES, 200 GREENFIELD ST 48829
  Rick Rivas, prin.

Edwardsburg, Cass Co., Pop. Code 4
Edwardsburg SD
Sch. Sys. Enr. Code 4
Supt. – James Olin, 69410 SECTION ST 49112
JHS, 69410 SECTION ST 49112
  S. Ostrander, prin.
Eagle Lake MS, 69410 SECTION ST 49112
  James Culver, prin.
ES, 69410 SECTION ST 49112 – C. Wall, prin.

Elk Rapids, Antrim Co., Pop. Code 4
Elk Rapids SD
Sch. Sys. Enr. Code 4
Supt. – Elmer F. Peterman, 707 E 3RD 49629
Cherryland MS, 707 E 3RD 49629
  Robert Schwenter, prin.
Lakeland PS, 620 BUCKLEY 49629
  Nancy Muhlig, prin.

Ellsworth, Antrim Co., Pop. Code 2
Ellsworth Comm. SD
Sch. Sys. Enr. Code 2
Supt. – Dale McCarty, P O BOX 68 49729
S, P O BOX 68 49729 – Marvin Ruis, prin.

Elmira, Antrim Co.
Gaylord Comm. SD
Supt. – See Gaylord
ES 49730 – Donna Polus, prin.

Elsie, Clinton Co., Pop. Code 4
Ovid-Elsie Area SD
Sch. Sys. Enr. Code 4
Supt. – David J. Porrell
  8989 E COLONY ROAD 48831
MS, P O BOX 429 48831 – Joseph Thering, prin.
Knight ES, P O BOX 429 48831
  Frank Colavecchi, prin.
Other Schools – See Ovid

Emmett, St. Clair Co., Pop. Code 2
Yale SD
Supt. – See Yale
ES, 3300 KINNEY RD 48022 – Betty Clement, prin.

Engadine, Mackinac Co.
Engadine Cons. SD
Sch. Sys. Enr. Code 2
Supt. – R. Leveille
  RURAL ROUTE 01 BOX 1 49827
ES, RURAL ROUTE 01 BOX 1 49827
  Larry Wyse, prin.

Erie, Monroe Co., Pop. Code 5
Mason Cons. SD
Sch. Sys. Enr. Code 4
Supt. – R. W. Kackmeister
  2400 LAKESIDE ROAD 48133
Mason MS, 2400 LAKESIDE ROAD 48133
  James Seiber, prin.
Central ES, 2400 LAKESIDE RD 48133
  Howard Irwin, prin.
Luna Pier ES, ELMHURST DR 48133
  M. Gaffney, prin.

St. Joseph School, 2238 MANHATTAN 48133

Escanaba, Delta Co., Pop. Code 7
Escanaba Area SD
Sch. Sys. Enr. Code 5
Supt. – Thomas Vitito, 111 N 5TH ST 49829
MS, 1500 LUDINGTON ST 49829
  Erwood Slade, prin.
Franklin ES, 612 2ND AVE S 49829
  Ken Myllyla, prin.
Jefferson ES, 1905 S 21ST ST 49829
  Ken Myllyla, prin.
Lemmer ES, 700 S 20TH ST 49829
  Louis Diedrich, prin.
Soo Hill ES, 5219 18TH RD 49829
  James Aird, prin.
Washington ES, 215 N 15TH ST 49829
  Robert Koski, prin.
Webster ES, 1209 N 19TH ST 49829
  Robert Koski, prin.
Other Schools – See Bark River, Cornell, Wells

Holy Name Central ES, 409 S 22ND ST 49829

Essexville, Bay Co., Pop. Code 5
Hampton SD
Sch. Sys. Enr. Code 4
Supt. – Robert J. Winters, 303 PINE ST 48732
Cramer JHS, 313 PINE ST 48732
  Brian Malcho, prin.
Bush ES, 800 NEBOBISH RD 48732
  Janice Miller, prin.
Hughes ES, 805 LANGSTAFF ST 48732
  Barbara Shaw, prin.
Verellen ES, 612 W BORTON RD 48732
  Charles Brown, prin.

St. John ES, 619 MAIN ST 48732

Evart, Osceola Co., Pop. Code 4
Evart SD
Sch. Sys. Enr. Code 4
Supt. – Joseph Curtin, 515 N CEDAR ST 49631
ES, 515 N CEDAR ST 49631
  Dwight Cooper, prin.

Ewen, Ontonagon Co., Pop. Code 2
Trout Creek SD
Sch. Sys. Enr. Code 2
Supt. – Ray Rigoni, P O BOX 218 49925
Bergland ES, P O BOX 127 49925
  Kenneth Genisot, prin.
Trout Creek ES, P O BOX 134 49925
  Donald Olson, prin.

Fairgrove, Tuscola Co., Pop. Code 3
Akron-Fairgrove SD
Sch. Sys. Enr. Code 3
Supt. – Donald Lillrose, 1933 LIBERTY ST 48733
Akron MS, 4355 LYNN ST 48701
  D. Lillrose, prin.
ES, 1933 LIBERTY ST 48733 – Irene Aymer, prin.

Fair Haven, St. Clair Co.
Algonac Comm. SD
Supt. – See Algonac
ES, 8361 BROADBRIDGE RD 48023
  William Walker, prin.

Fairview, Oscoda Co., Pop. Code 2
Fairview Area SD
Sch. Sys. Enr. Code 2
Supt. – Donald P. Harrington 48621
Fairview ES 48621 – Genevieve Troyer, prin.

Farmington, Oakland Co., Pop. Code 7
Farmington SD
Sch. Sys. Enr. Code 7
Supt. – Graham Lewis
  32500 SHIAWASSEE ST 48024
Dunckel MS, 32800 TWELVE MILE RD 48018
  Donald Keen, prin.
East MS, 25000 MIDDLEBELT ROAD 48018
  William Martin, prin.
Power MS, 34740 RHONSWOOD ST 48024
  Robert Brown, prin.
Warner MS, 30303 W 14 MILE ROAD 48018
  Walter Scoble, prin.
Beechview ES, 26840 WESTMEATH 48018
  Wallace Prince, prin.
Flanders ES, 32600 FLANDERS ST 48024
  Frank Delewsky, prin.
Forest ES, 34545 OLD TIMBER RD 48331
  W. Jablonski, prin.
Gill ES, 21195 GILL 48024 – Michael Duff, prin.
Grace ES, 29040 SHIAWASSEE ST 48024
  Richard Close, prin.
Highmeadow ES, 30175 HIGH 48018
  Jan Colliton, prin.
Kenbrook ES, 32130 BONNETHILL 48018
  Carolyn Plsek, prin.
Larkshire ES, 23800 TUCK RD 48024
  J. Lanigan, prin.
Longacre ES, 34850 ARUNDEL ST 48024
  Mildred Bennett, prin.
Wood Creek ES, 28400 HARWICH DR 48018
  Barbara Novatis, prin.
Woodale ES, 28600 PEPPERMILL RD 48331
  David Coffin, prin.
Other Schools – See Pontiac

Our Lady of Sorrows ES
  23619 POWERS RD 48024
St. Fabian ES, 32170 W TWELVE MILE RD 48018
St. Paul ES, 20815 MIDDLEBELT RD 48024

Thomas P. Beahan ES, 23971 POWERS RD   48024

Farwell, Clare Co., Pop. Code 3
Farwell Area SD
Sch. Sys. Enr. Code 4
Supt. – Thomas Pelon, 399 MICHIGAN ST   48622
MS, 399 MICHIGAN ST   48622
    Kenneth Richardson, prin.
ES, 268 E OHIO ST   48622 – Dale Lewis, prin.

Fennville, Allegan Co., Pop. Code 3
Fennville SD
Sch. Sys. Enr. Code 4
Supt. – Alexander Galligan
    N ELIZABETH ST   49408
Michen Upper MS, 507 N MAPLE   49408
    Gerald Howard, prin.
Michen Lower ES, 507 N MAPLE   49408
    D. Coffindaffer, prin.

Fenton, Genesee Co., Pop. Code 6
Fenton Area SD
Sch. Sys. Enr. Code 5
Supt. – Roland Marmion
    3100 OWEN ROAD   48430
MS, 404 W ELLEN ST   48430 – Neil McPhee, prin.
North Road ES, 525 NORTH RD   48430
    Annette Walker, prin.
State Road ES, 1161 STATE ST   48430
    J. Blakey, prin.
Tomek-Eastern ES, 600 4TH ST   48430
    Carole Levens, prin.

Lake Fenton Comm. SD
Sch. Sys. Enr. Code 4
Supt. – Gerald Laskey
    11425 TORREY ROAD   48430
Torrey Hills MS, 12410 TORREY ROAD   48430
    James Allen, prin.
West Shore ES, 3076 LAHRING RD   48430
    Steve Bingham, prin.

St. John ES, 514 LINCOLN ST   48430

Ferndale, Oakland Co., Pop. Code 8
Ferndale SD
Sch. Sys. Enr. Code 5
Supt. – W. G. Coyne
    725 PINECREST DRIVE   48220
Coolidge MS, 2521 BERMUDA ST   48220
    Eric Langer, prin.
Grant ES, 21131 GARDENLANE   48220
    Z. Hollifield, prin.
Harding ES, 2920 BURDETTE ST   48220
    Peggy McGarry, prin.
Roosevelt ES, 2610 PINECREST DR   48220
    Jeanne McIntyre, prin.
Taft ES, 427 ALLEN ST   48220
    Stewart Dilly, prin.
Washington ES, 1201 LIVERNOIS ST   48220
    Debbra Lang, prin.
Wilson ES, 1244 PAXTON ST   48220
    Robert Corsini, prin.
Other Schools – See Oak Park

Hazel Park SD
Supt. – See Hazel Park
Webb JHS, 2100 WOODWARD HTS   48220
    Elsa Takacs, prin.
Clark ES, 2500 MARTIN RD   48220
    Michael Barlow, prin.
Edison ES, 1700 SHEVLIN ST   48220
    Charles Cox, prin.

Ferrysburg, Ottawa Co., Pop. Code 4
Grand Haven SD
Supt. – See Grand Haven
ES, 17290 ROOSEVELT RD   49409
    Carol Breen, prin.
Lake Hills MS, 18181 DOGWOOD DR   49409
    Roger Smart, prin.

Fife Lake, Grand Traverse Co.
Forest Area Comm. SD
Sch. Sys. Enr. Code 3
Supt. – Jim Tekiele, 100 SHIPPY ROAD   49633
MS   49633 – Dawn Decker, prin.
Other Schools – See South Boardman

Flat Rock, Wayne Co., Pop. Code 6
Flat Rock Comm. SD
Sch. Sys. Enr. Code 4
Supt. – Michael Witucki, P O BOX 158   48134
Simpson MS, 24900 MEADOWS DRIVE   48124
    Lloyd Drummonds, prin.
Barnes MS, 24925 MEADOWS ST   48134
    Jeffery Moorehead, prin.
Bobcean ES, 28300 EVERGREEN ST   48134
    Teresa Mathews, prin.

Woodhaven SD
Sch. Sys. Enr. Code 5
Supt. – Roy Bassett
    24975 VAN HORN ROAD   48134
Weginka ES, 23925 ARSENAL RD   48134
    Dr. Mitchell, prin.
Other Schools – See Trenton, Woodhaven, Wyandotte

Flint, Genesee Co., Pop. Code 9
Atherton Comm. SD
Sch. Sys. Enr. Code 4
Supt. – Alvin Du Bois
    3354 S GENESEE ROAD   48519
Atherton MS, 3354 S GENESEE ROAD   48519
    Bernard Romain, prin.
Other Schools – See Burton

Beecher Comm. SD
Sch. Sys. Enr. Code 5
Supt. – Ira A. Rutherford III
    1020 W COLDWATER ROAD   48505
Summit MS, G-5159 SUMMIT ST   48505
    J. Shelley, prin.
Buell ES, 5126 DETROIT ST   48505
    Donald Evans, prin.
Harrow ES, 5464 HORTAN   48505
    Donald Ricks, prin.
Other Schools – See Mount Morris

Bendle SD
Sch. Sys. Enr. Code 4
Supt. – Kenneth E. Gempel
    2283 E SCOTTWOOD AVE   48529
Other Schools – See Burton

Bentley Comm. SD
Sch. Sys. Enr. Code 4
Supt. – W. H. Young
    1223 S BELSAY ROAD   48509
Bentley MS, 1180 N BELSAY ROAD   48509
    Harold Neizke, prin.
Other Schools – See Burton

Carman-Ainsworth SD
Sch. Sys. Enr. Code 6
Supt. – Zane H. Stein, G-3475 W COURT ST   48504
Carman Park ES, 3375 VAN CAMPEN RD   48507
    Daniel Cypher, prin.
Dye ES, 1174 GRAHAM   48532
    Maryann Raske, prin.
Randels ES, 6022 BROBECK ST   48532
    Dale Wolfe, prin.
Woodland ES, G-3493 BEVERIDGE RD   48532
    Fred Kienitz, prin.
Other Schools – See Burton, Swartz Creek

Flint SD
Sch. Sys. Enr. Code 8
Supt. – Nathel Burtley
    923 E KEARSLEY ST   48503
Holmes MS, 6602 OXLEY DRIVE   48504
    George Hurley, prin.
Longfellow MS, 1255 N CHEVROLET AVE   48504
    James Davidson, prin.
McKinley MS, 4501 CAMDEN AVE   48507
    Robert Himelhoch, prin.
Whittier MS, 701 CRAPO ST   48503
    John Zupko, prin.
Anderson ES, G-3248 MACKIN RD   48504
    Sandra Pillow, prin.
Brownell ES, 6302 OXLEY DR   48504
    Curtis Speights, prin.
Bunche ES, 4121 DETROIT ST   48505
    Willa Hawkins, prin.
Carpenter Road ES, 6901 N WEBSTER RD   48505
    Charles Atwater, prin.
Civic Park ES, 1402 W DAYTON ST   48504
    Ralph Larsen, prin.
Cody ES, 3201 FENTON RD   48507
    Michael Tuohy, prin.
Cook ES, 500 WELCH BLVD   48503
    David Caswell, prin.
Coolidge ES, 3615 VAN BUREN ST   48503
    James Bracy, prin.
Dewey ES, 4119 N SAGINAW ST   48505
    James Cleaves, prin.
Dort ES, 2025 N SAGINAW ST   48505
    Doris Horton, prin.
Doyle/Ryder ES, 1040 N SAGINAW ST   48503
    Harold Major, prin.
Durant Tuuri Mott ES, 1518 W 3RD AVE   48504
    Etta Dotson, prin.
Eisenhower ES, 1235 PERSHING ST   48503
    Jack Hudson, prin.
Freeman ES, 4001 OGEMA AVE   48507
    Louis Scieszka, prin.
Garfield ES, 301 E MCCLELLAN ST   48505
    M. Latimer, prin.
Gundry ES, 6031 DUPONT ST   48505
    Rawlan Lillard, prin.
Homedale ES, 1501 DAVISON RD   48506
    L. Caine-Smith, prin.
Johnson ES, 5323 WESTERN RD   48506
    Ronald Schmitz, prin.
King ES, 520 W RANKIN ST   48505
    B. Ducket, prin.
Manley ES, 3002 FARLEY ST   48507
    Tyree Walker, prin.
Martin ES, 6502 STAFFORD PL   48505
    James Robinson, prin.
Merrill ES, 1501 W MOORE ST   48504
    Max Calhoun, prin.
Neithercut ES, 2010 CRESTBROOK LN   48507
    Harry Bigelow, prin.
Pierce ES, 1101 W VERNON DR   48503
    Joy Carter, prin.
Pierson ES, 300 E MOTT AVE   48505
    Howard Staisil, prin.
Potter ES, 2500 N AVERILL AVE   48506
    Sandra Epps, prin.
Scott ES, 1602 S AVERILL AVE   48503
    Robert Welch, prin.
Sobey ES, 3701 N AVERILL AVE   48506
    David Beavers, prin.
Stewart ES, 1950 BURR BLVD   48503
    Robert Simmons, prin.
Summerfield ES, 1360 MILBOURNE AVE   48504
    James Schulte, prin.
Washington ES, 1400 N VERNON AVE   48506
    Daryl Foster, prin.
Wilkins ES, 121 E YORK AVE   48505
    John McCoy, prin.

Williams ES, 3501 MINNESOTA AVE   48506
    Dorothy Hitts, prin.

Kearsley Comm. SD
Sch. Sys. Enr. Code 5
Supt. – Thomas Jones
    4396 UNDERHILL DRIVE   48506
Armstrong MS, 6161 HOPKINS ROAD   48506
    William Westhauser, prin.
Buffey ES, 4235 CROSBY RD   48506
    David Angus, prin.
Dowdall ES, 3333 SHILLELAGH DR   48506
    William Spear, prin.
Fiedler ES, 6317 NIGHTINGALE DR   48506
    Nancy Stuart, prin.

Westwood Heights SD
Sch. Sys. Enr. Code 4
Supt. – James Mitchell
    3207 FINNEY COURT   48504
Hamady MS, G-3223 W CARPENTER ROAD   48504
    Ronald Williams, prin.
Westwood ES, 3400 N JENNINGS RD   48504
    Ervin Delsman, prin.

Donovan-Mayotte ES, 2319 BAGLEY ST   48504
Dukette Catholic ES, 530 W PIERSON RD   48505
Holy Rosary ES, 5191 RICHFIELD RD   48506
St. Mary ES, 2500 N FRANKLIN AVE   48506
St. Paul ES, 402 S BALLENGER HWY   48532
St. Pius ES, X-G-3139 HOGARTH AVE   48504

Flushing, Genesee Co., Pop. Code 6
Flushing Comm. SD
Sch. Sys. Enr. Code 5
Supt. – William Tunnlcliff
    522 N MCKINLEY ROAD   48433
MS, 409 CHAMBERLAIN ST   48433
    Earnest Jones, prin.
Central ES, 525 COUTANT ST   48433
    Richard Pero, prin.
Elms ES, 6125 N ELMS RD   48433
    Keith Burba, prin.
Seymour ES, 3088 N SEYMOUR RD   48433
    John Springer, prin.
Springview ES, 2033 SPRINGVIEW   48433
    Kip Hogan, prin.

St. Robert ES, 214 E HENRY ST   48433

Fowler, Clinton Co., Pop. Code 2
Fowler SD
Sch. Sys. Enr. Code 3
Supt. – Mary Ann Chartrand, P O BOX 308   48835
Waldron ES, 11214 W KENT ST   48835
    R. McDermed, prin.

Most Holy Trinity ES, 11144 W KENT ST   48835

Fowlerville, Livingston Co., Pop. Code 4
Fowlerville Comm. SD
Sch. Sys. Enr. Code 4
Supt. – Fred Kessler, 450 HIBBARD ST N   48836
Munn MS, 440 HIBBARD ST N   48836
    Thomas Tannar, prin.
Smith ES, 440 N HIBBARD ST   48836
    John Snow, prin.

Frankenmuth, Saginaw Co., Pop. Code 5
Frankenmuth SD
Sch. Sys. Enr. Code 4
Supt. – J. B. McEwen, 941 E GENESEE ST   48734
Rittmueller MS, 965 E GENESEE ST   48734
    D. Michael Wescott, prin.
List ES, 805 E GENESEE ST   48734
    D. Wescott, prin.

St. Lorenz ES, 140 CHURCHGROVE RD   48734

Frankfort, Benzie Co., Pop. Code 4
Frankfort Area SD
Sch. Sys. Enr. Code 3
Supt. – Thomas Gorang
    613 LEELANAU AVE   49635
Frankfort ES, 613 LEELANAU AVE   49635
    Robert McCall, prin.

Fraser, Macomb Co., Pop. Code 7
Fraser SD
Sch. Sys. Enr. Code 5
Supt. – Gary Matsche
    33466 GARFIELD ROAD   48026
Richards MS, 33500 GARFIELD ROAD   48026
    R. Brunzell, prin.
Edison ES, 17470 SEWEL ST   48026
    Rex Balch, prin.
Eisenhower ES, 31275 EVENINGSIDE DR   48026
    Thomas Jager, prin.
Emerson ES, 32151 DANNA ST   48026
    James Bernardo, prin.
Salk ES, 17601 FIFTEEN MILE RD   48026
    G. Raszkowski, prin.
Other Schools – See Mount Clemens, Roseville

St. John ES, 16339 E 14 MILE RD   48026

Frederic, Crawford Co.
Crawford AuSable SD
Supt. – See Grayling
ES, MAINSTTE ST   49733 – David Hawkins, prin.

Freeland, Saginaw Co., Pop. Code 3
Freeland Comm. SD
Sch. Sys. Enr. Code 4
Supt. – Thomas Orr, 710 POWLEY DRIVE   48623
ES, 710 POWLEY DR   48623 – Lloyd Lewis, prin.

Free Soil, Mason Co., Pop. Code 2
Free Soil Comm. SD
Sch. Sys. Enr. Code 2
Supt. – Stephen Lites, 8699 N DEMOCRAT 49411
S, 8699 N DEMOCRAT 49411 – (—), prin.

Fremont, Newaygo Co., Pop. Code 5
Fremont SD
Sch. Sys. Enr. Code 4
Supt. – Bradley Hansen, 220 PINE ST W 49412
MS, 500 WOODROW ST W 49412
   James Hieftje, prin.
Cedar Street ES, 350 W CEDAR 49412
   James Peters, prin.
Daisey Brook MS, 502 N DIVISION AVE 49412
   Jody Byland, prin.
Pine Street ES, 450 E PINE ST 49412
   James Peters, prin.

Fremont Christian ES, 208 HILLCREST DR 49412

Fruitport, Muskegon Co., Pop. Code 4
Fruitport Comm. SD
Sch. Sys. Enr. Code 5
Supt. – Dan Bird, 305 PONTALUNA ROAD 49415
MS, 305 PONTALUNA ROAD 49415
   Gordon Mol, prin.
Edgewood ES, 305 PONTALUNA 49415
   Dale Levandoski, prin.
Other Schools – See Muskegon

Gagetown, Tuscola Co., Pop. Code 2
Owendale-Gagetown Area SD
Supt. – See Owendale
ES, 6475 4TH 48735 – William Britt, prin.

Galesburg, Kalamazoo Co., Pop. Code 4
Galesburg-Augusta Comm. SD
Sch. Sys. Enr. Code 4
Supt. – J. H. Wagar, P O BOX 308 49053
ES, 225 BLAKE BLVD 49053 – B. Kleinhans, prin.
Other Schools – See Augusta

Galien, Berrien Co., Pop. Code 3
Galien Twp. SD
Sch. Sys. Enr. Code 3
Supt. – D. Allan Disbrow, P O BOX 38 49113
Wolford ES, SOUTHEASTERN AVE 49113
   Anne Goodenough, prin.

Garden City, Wayne Co., Pop. Code 8
Garden City SD
Sch. Sys. Enr. Code 6
Supt. – Michael Wilmot
   1333 RADCLIFF ST 48135
Douglas ES, 6400 HARTEL ST 48135
   J. Perttunen, prin.
Farmington ES, 33411 MARQUETTE ST 48135
   Harold Estelle, prin.
Lathers ES, 28351 MARQUETTE ST 48135
   F. Wettlaufer, prin.
Memorial ES, 30001 MARQUETTE ST 48135
   Richard Enos, prin.
Ruff ES, 30300 MAPLEWOOD ST 48135
   Judith Patrick, prin.

St. Dunstan ES, 1615 BELTON ST 48135
St. Raphael ES, 31500 BEECHWOOD ST 48135

Gaylord, Otsego Co., Pop. Code 5
Gaylord Comm. SD
Sch. Sys. Enr. Code 5
Supt. – R. Mason Buckingham
   615 S ELM AVE 49735
MS, 600 E FIFTH ST 49735 – David Schopp, prin.
North Ohio ES, 912 N OHIO AVE 49735
   Dennis O'Brien, prin.
South Maple ES, 557 S MAPLE AVE 49735
   Ed Sandri, prin.
Other Schools – See Elmira

St. Mary ES, 321 N OTSEGO AVE 49735
St. Mary ES, 310 W MITCHELL 49735

Genesee, Genesee Co., Pop. Code 8
Genesee SD
Sch. Sys. Enr. Code 3
Supt. – Mark Hilt, 7347 N GENESEE ROAD 48437
Haas ES, 7347 N GENESEE RD 48437
   Kenneth Foyder, prin.

Gladstone, Delta Co., Pop. Code 5
Gladstone Area SD
Sch. Sys. Enr. Code 4
Supt. – Wayne E. Bucholz, 400 10TH ST S 49837
MS, 200 7TH ST S 49837 – Michael Oxford, prin.
Cameron ES, 803 29TH ST 49837
   Wayne Christoff, prin.
Flat Rock ES
   3920 COUNTY 416 20TH RD #TH 49837
   Gerald Hampton, prin.
Jones ES, 400 S 10TH ST 49837
   David Bukala, prin.

Gladwin, Gladwin Co., Pop. Code 4
Gladwin Comm. SD
Sch. Sys. Enr. Code 4
Supt. – Allen C. Fennell
   103 N BOWERY ST 48624
MS, 780 W 1ST ST 48624 – Bruce Lyon, prin.
ES, 900 N BOWERY AVE 48624
   Gary Longcore, prin.
MS, 780 W FIRST STREET 48624
   Ronald Watt, prin.

Sacred Heart School
   330 N SILVERLEAF ST 48624

Glennie, Alcona Co.
Oscoda Area SD
Supt. – See Oscoda
ES, BAMFIELD RD 48737 – William Martin, prin.

Gobles, Van Buren Co., Pop. Code 3
Gobles SD
Sch. Sys. Enr. Code 4
Supt. – Anthony Topoleski, P O BOX 01 49055
ES, 409 N STATE ST 49055 – Diane Holmes, prin.

Goodrich, Genesee Co., Pop. Code 3
Goodrich Area SD
Sch. Sys. Enr. Code 4
Supt. – Raymond Green, 7489 SENECA ST 48438
MS, 8029 S GALE ROAD 48438
   Jerry Lawrason, prin.
Reid ES, 7501 SENECA ST 48438
   Robert McNally, prin.

Grand Blanc, Genesee Co., Pop. Code 6
Grand Blanc Comm. SD
Sch. Sys. Enr. Code 6
Supt. – David Fultz, 11920 S SAGINAW ST 48439
MS, 5288 TODD ST 48439 – John Johnson, prin.
Brendel ES, 223 BUSH ST 48439
   Terry Patterson, prin.
Indian Hill ES, 11240 WOODBRIDGE DR 48439
   D. Baldwin, prin.
McGrath ES, 5288 TODD ST 48439
   Roger Swaim, prin.
Myers ES, 6985 SUN VALLEY 48439
   Thomas Shpakow, prin.

Valley School, 5290 LEROY ST 48439
Holy Family ES, 215 BUSH ST 48439

Grand Haven, Ottawa Co., Pop. Code 7
Grand Haven SD
Sch. Sys. Enr. Code 6
Supt. – J. S. Zapytowski
   1415 S BEECHTREE ST 49417
Central ES, 106 S 6TH ST 49417
   Jean McCabe, prin.
Ferry ES, 1050 PENNOYER 49417
   Vonda Walma, prin.
Griffin ES, 1700 S GRIFFIN ST 49417
   Dan Scanlan, prin.
Peach Plains ES, 15849 COMSTOCK ST 49417
   Melinda Eidson, prin.
Robinson ES, 11600 120TH AVE 49417
   Robert Swart, prin.
Rosy Mound ES, 14016 LAKESHORE 49417
   Henry Wezeman, prin.
White ES, 1400 WISCONSIN AVE 49417
   Steven Groters, prin.
Other Schools – See Ferrysburg

Grand Haven Christian ES, 1102 GRANT ST 49417
St. John Lutheran School
   525 TAYLOR STREET 49417

Grand Ledge, Eaton Co., Pop. Code 6
Grand Ledge SD
Sch. Sys. Enr. Code 5
Supt. – Larry Spencer, 952 JENNE 48837
Beagle MS, 600 SOUTH ST W 48837
   Richard Jones, prin.
Hayes MS, 12620 NIXON ROAD 48837
   Mark Christman, prin.
Greenwood ES, 310 GREENWOOD ST 48837
   R. Johnson, prin.
Hayes ES, 12620 NIXON RD 48837
   William Thorson, prin.
Holbrook ES, 615 JONES ST 48837
   Carol Bickenbach, prin.
Neff ES, 950 JENNE ST 48837
   Nancy Meddaugh, prin.
Wacousta ES, 9135 HERBISON RD 48837
   Richard Hill, prin.
Other Schools – See Lansing, Mulliken

St. Michael ES, 325 EDWARDS ST 48837

Grand Marais, Alger Co., Pop. Code 2
Burt Twp. SD
Sch. Sys. Enr. Code 1
Supt. – William Christensen, P O BOX 296 49839
Burt Twp S, P O BOX 296 49839 – (—), prin.

Grand Rapids, Kent Co., Pop. Code 9
East Grand Rapids SD
Sch. Sys. Enr. Code 4
Supt. – James Morse, 2915 HALL ST SE 49506
East Grand Rapids MS
   2425 LAKE DRIVE SE 49506 – James Ogilvie, prin.
Breton Downs ES, 2500 BOSTON ST SE 49506
   Steven Estes, prin.
Lakeside ES, 2325 HALL ST SE 49506
   Paul Claesson, prin.
Wealthy ES, 2018 WEALTHY ST SE 49506
   Ruth Rowe, prin.

Forest Hills SD
Sch. Sys. Enr. Code 6
Supt. – Dr. J. Michael Washburn
   6590 CASCADE ROAD SE 49506
Central MS, 5810 ADA DRIVE SE 49506
   Bruce Vorce, prin.
Northern Hills MS, 3775 LEONARD ST NE 49506
   Larry Curtis, prin.

Ada ES, 731 ADA DR SE 49506
   Marion Robinson, prin.
Collins ES, 4368 HEATHER LN SE 49506
   Larry Mathews, prin.
Orchard View ES
   2770 LEFFINGWELL AVE NE 49505
   Craig Mears, prin.
Pine Ridge ES, 3250 REDFORD DR SE 49506
   Peter Dion, prin.
Thornapple ES
   6932 BRIDGEWATER DR SE 49506
   Donald Bruckman, prin.

Grand Rapids SD
Sch. Sys. Enr. Code 8
Supt. – Patrick Sandro
   143 BOSTWICK AVE NE 49503
Burton MS, 2133 BUCHANAN AVE SW 49507
   John Crozier, prin.
Iroquois MS, 1050 IROQUOIS SE 49506
   Pam Clinkscales, prin.
Northeast MS, 1400 FULLER AVE NE 49505
   Joe Grandy, prin.
Riverside MS, 265 ELEANOR ST NE 49505
   Don Bultman, prin.
Westwood MS
   1525 MOUNT MERCY DRIVE NW 49504
   Mary Beth Parker, prin.
Aberdeen ES, 928 ABERDEEN ST NE 49505
   Al Couch, prin.
Alexander ES, 1010 ALEXANDER ST SE 49507
   Mildred Willis, prin.
Alger ES, 921 ALGER ST SE 49507
   Bonnie Piller, prin.
Beckwith ES, 2405 LEONARD ST NE 49505
   Michael Meyer, prin.
Brookside ES, 2505 MADISON AVE SE 49507
   Michael Stearns, prin.
Buchanan ES, 1775 BUCHANAN AVE SW 49507
   Raul Ysasi, prin.
Burton ES, 2133 BUCHANAN AVE SW 49507
   Robert Cichewicz, prin.
Campau ES, 50 ANTOINE ST SW 49507
   James Swanlund, prin.
Coit ES, 419 COIT AVE NE 49503
   Peter Chan, prin.
Covell ES, 1417 COVELL AVE NW 49504
   David Downer, prin.
Dickinson ES, 448 DICKINSON ST SE 49507
   Sally Joseph, prin.
East Leonard ES, 410 BARNETT ST NE 49503
   Richard Rinck, prin.
Eastern ES, 758 EASTERN AVE NE 49503
   Ken Kelly, prin.
Fountain ES, 159 COLLEGE AVE NE 49503
   M. Paskewicz, prin.
Franklin ES, 801 OAKLAND AVE SW 49503
   Marie Smith, prin.
Hall ES, 703 SHAMROCK ST SW 49509
   Michelle Ghareeb, prin.
Harrison Park ES, 1440 DAVIS AVE NW 49504
   C. Firlik, prin.
Henry ES, 419 HENRY AVE SE 49503
   Watson Phillips, prin.
Hillcrest ES, 1415 LYON ST NE 49503
   Cheryl King, prin.
Huff ES, 2288 BALL AVE NE 49505
   Jason Kuipers, prin.
Jefferson ES, 1356 JEFFERSON AVE SE 49507
   Earline Brown, prin.
Ken-O-Sha Park ES
   1353 VAN AUKEN ST SE 49508
   Sally Hale, prin.
Kent Hills ES, 1445 EMERALD AVE NE 49505
   E. Rowlands, prin.
Madison Park ES, 851 MADISON AVE SE 49507
   Pearl Randolph, prin.
Mulick Park ES, 1761 ROSEWOOD AVE SE 49506
   M. Mackinnon, prin.
North Park ES, 3375 CHENEY AVE NE 49505
   W. Kirkwood, prin.
Oakdale ES, 944 EVERGREEN ST SE 49507
   C. Chamberlain, prin.
Ottawa Hills ES, 1515 FISK RD SE 49506
   Mary Jo Birks, prin.
Palmer ES, 309 PALMER ST NE 49505
   Janet Jones, prin.
Riverside ES, 2420 COLT NE 49505
   D. Berghorst, prin.
Shawmut Hills ES, 2550 BURRITT ST NW 49504
   A. Nystrom, prin.
Shawnee Park ES
   2036 N CHESANING DR SE 49506
   A. Turner, prin.
Sheldon SEAC ES, 1010 SHELDON SE 49503
   E. Webley, prin.
Sherwood Park ES
   3859 CHAMBERLAIN AVE SE 49508
   Ralph Styles, prin.
Sibley ES, 947 SIBLEY ST NW 49504
   J. Pakalnis, prin.
Sigsbee ES, 1250 SIGSBEE ST SE 49506
   Lola Davis, prin.
Stocking ES, 863 7TH ST NW 49504
   Kevin O'Neill, prin.
Straight PS, 850 CHATHAM ST NW 49504
   Norma Berry, prin.
West Leonard ES, 1351 LEONARD ST NW 49504
   Gerard Altena, prin.

Grandville SD
Supt. – See Grandville

Cummings ES
4261 SCHOOLCRAFT ST SW 49504
Marcia Kaye, prin.

Kelloggsville SD
Sch. Sys. Enr. Code 4
Supt. – Richard Laninga, 242 52ND ST SE 49508
Kelloggsville JHS, 23 JEAN ST SW 49508
Rein Dukk, prin.
East ES, 242 52ND ST SE 49508
James Sypniewski, prin.
Northwest ES, 977 44TH ST SW 49509
Milton Homolka, prin.
Southeast ES, 240 52ND ST SE 49508
Milton Homolka, prin.
West ES, 4555 MAGNOLIA AVE SW 49508
Dwight Peceny, prin.

Kenowa Hills SD
Sch. Sys. Enr. Code 4
Supt. – Phillip O'Connell
2325 4 MILE ROAD 49504
Walker JHS, 4252 3 MILE ROAD NW 49504
Eugene De Wys, prin.
Alpine ES, 4730 BAUMHOFF NW 49521
Thomas DeJonge, prin.
Fairview ES, 2396 HILLSIDE DR NW 49504
Richard Doyle, prin.
Zinser ES, 1234 KINNEY AVE NW 49504
Monte Czuhai, prin.
Other Schools – See Marne

Kentwood SD
Sch. Sys. Enr. Code 6
Supt. – John Jeltes, 5820 EASTERN AVE SE 49508
Bowen ES, 4483 KALAMAZOO AVE SE 49508
Michael Miles, prin.
Brookwood ES
5485 KALAMAZOO AVE SE 49508
Joseph Baal, prin.
Glenwood ES, 912 SILVERLEAF ST SE 49508
Jerry Sherman, prin.
Hamilton ES, 3303 BRETON RD SE 49508
W. Mauchmar, prin.
Meadowlawn ES, 4939 BURGIS AVE SE 49508
Robert Dudley, prin.
Southwood ES, 630 66TH ST SE 49508
Rosemary Ervine, prin.
Townline ES, 100 60TH ST SE 49508
Joseph Iciek, prin.
Other Schools – See Kentwood

Northview SD
Sch. Sys. Enr. Code 5
Supt. – Paul C. Lemin
4365 HUNSBERGER AVE NE 49505
Hills & Dales MS, 4400 AMBROSE AVE NE 49505
Phillip Helzer, prin.
East Oakview ES
3940 SUBURBAN SHORES DR NE 49505
James Downs, prin.
Highlands MS, 4645 CHANDY DRIVE NE 49505
Terry Smith, prin.
North Oakview ES, 4300 COSTA AVE NE 49505
Timothy Purkey, prin.
West Oakview ES
3880 STUYVESANT AVE NE 49505
C. O'Connor, prin.

Tri-Unity Christian School
2104 44TH STREET 49509
Blessed Sacrament ES
2233 DIAMOND AVE NE 49505
Creston Mayfield Christian ES
1031 PAGE ST NE 49505
Cutlerville Christian ES
6746 CUTLER PARK DR SW 49508
Holy Name ES, 1650 GODFREY AVE SW 49509
Holy Spirit ES
2222 LAKE MICHIGAN DR NW 49504
Immaculate Heart of Mary-Plymouth ES 49506
Immanuel & James ES
338 DIVISION AVE N 49503
Martin Luther ES, 1916 RIDGEWOOD SE 49506
Marywood Academy ES
2025 FULTON ST E 49503
Millbrook Christian ES
3662 POINSETTIA AVE SE 49508
Oakdale Christian ES, 1050 FISK AVE SE 49507
Potters House ES
810 VAN RAALTE DR SW 49509
SS Peter & Paul ES
1433 HAMILTON AVE NW 49504
Sacred Heart ES, 140 VALLEY AVE SW 49504
Seymour Christian ES
2550 EASTERN AVE SE 49507
St. Adalbert ES, 640 5TH ST NW 49504
St. Alphonsus ES, 228 CARRIER ST NE 49505
St. Andrew ES, 302 SHELDON BLVD SE 49503
St. Anthony ES, 2510 RICHMOND ST NW 49504
St. Francis Xavier ES, 240 BROWN ST SE 49507
St. Isidore ES, 625 SPRING AVE NE 49503
St. James ES, 750 1ST ST NW 49504
St. John Vianney ES
4101 CLYDE PARK AVE SW 49509
St. Jude ES, 1110 4 MILE RD NE 49505
St. Mary ES, 515 TURNER AVE NW 49504
St. Paul ES, 2750 BURTON ST SE 49506
St. Stephen ES, 640 GLADSTONE DR SE 49506
St. Thomas ES, 1429 WILCOX PARK DR SE 49506
Sylvan Christian ES, 1630 GRIGGS ST SE 49506
West Side Christian ES
955 WESTEND AVE NW 49504

Grandville, Kent Co., Pop. Code 7
Grandville SD
Sch. Sys. Enr. Code 5
Supt. – Brian Callaghan
3131 BARRETT AVE 49418
MS, 3100 OTTAWA AVE 49418 – R. Smith, prin.
Central ES, 4052 PRAIRIE ST SW 49418
Richard Doyle, prin.
East ES, 3413 30TH ST SW 49418
James Tamminga, prin.
South ES, 3650 NAVAHO ST SW 49418
Neil Gottleber, prin.
West ES, 4027 38TH ST SW 49418
Robert Bradford, prin.
Other Schools – See Grand Rapids

Grandville Christian ES
3934 WILSON AVE SW 49418

Grant, Newaygo Co., Pop. Code 3
Grant SD
Sch. Sys. Enr. Code 4
Supt. – Cleland Methner, 331 STATE 49327
JHS, 156 STATE 49327 – Michael Ostyn, prin.
MS, 160 STATE 49327 – Duane Jones, prin.
PS, 12085 ELDER AVE 49327
Ronald Wardie, prin.

Grass Lake, Jackson Co., Pop. Code 3
Grass Lake Comm. SD
Sch. Sys. Enr. Code 3
Supt. – George Erickson, 899 S UNION ST 49240
Long ES, 829 S UNION ST 49240
Robert Tefft, prin.

Grayling, Crawford Co., Pop. Code 4
Crawford AuSable SD
Sch. Sys. Enr. Code 4
Supt. – Kent Reynolds
403 MICHIGAN AVE 49738
MS, 500 SPRUCE ST 49738 – Dale Nicholas, prin.
ES, 1000 MICHIGAN AVE 49738
Melvind Nunn, prin.
Other Schools – See Frederic

Greenville, Montcalm Co., Pop. Code 6
Greenville SD
Sch. Sys. Enr. Code 5
Supt. – Elmer Russell, 516 W CASS ST 48838
MS, 1321 CHASE ROAD 48838
Richard Laurent, prin.
Baldwin Heights ES, 821 W OAK ST 48838
John Meyer, prin.
Cedar Chest ES, 622 S CEDAR ST 48838
Carl Barberi, prin.
Lincoln Heights ES
12420 LINCOLN LAKE RD 48838
Howard Schantz, prin.
Walnut Hills ES, 712 N WALNUT ST 48838
Michael Devereaux, prin.

St. Charles ES, 502 S FRANKLIN ST 48838

Gregory, Livingston Co.
Stockbridge Comm. SD
Supt. – See Stockbridge
Howlett ES, 126 WEBB RD 48137
Lucy Stieber, prin.

Grosse Ile, Wayne Co., Pop. Code 6
Grosse Ile Twp. SD
Sch. Sys. Enr. Code 4
Supt. – Edward V. Sarkisian
23270 E RIVER ROAD 48138
MS, 23270 E RIVER ROAD 48138
Gerald Tecmire, prin.
East River ES, 23276 E RIVER RD 48138
Bernard Curtis, prin.
Meridan MS, 26700 MERIDIAN RD 48138
David McCulloch, prin.
Parke Lane MS, 21610 PARKE LN 48138
Diane Sanford, prin.

Grosse Pointe, Wayne Co., Pop. Code 6
Grosse Pointe SD
Sch. Sys. Enr. Code 6
Supt. – John Whritner
389 SAINT CLAIR ST 48230
Brownell MS, 260 CHALFONTE ST 48236
Don Messing, prin.
Parcells MS, 20600 MACK ST 48236
W. Christofferson, prin.
Pierce MS, 15430 KERCHEVAL ST 48230
Susan Klein, prin.
Defer ES, 15425 KERCHEVAL ST 48230
Robert Shover, prin.
Ferry ES, 748 ROSLYN RD 48236
Rena DeRidder, prin.
Kerby ES, 285 KERBY RD 48236
Leo Warras, prin.
Maire ES, 740 CADIEUX RD 48230
Jay Flowers, prin.
Mason ES, 1640 VERNIER RD 48236
William Mestdagh, prin.
Monteith ES, 1275 COOK RD 48236
J. Kubista, prin.
Richard ES, 176 MCKINLEY AVE 48236
Jack McMahon, prin.
Trombly ES, 820 BEACONSFIELD AVE 48230
Sheila Joyce, prin.
Other Schools – See Detroit

Our Lady Star of the Sea School
467 FAIRFORD ROAD 48236

University Liggett School
1045 COOK ROAD 48236
Grosse Pointe Academy
171 LAKE SHORE RD 48236
St. Clare of Montefalco ES
16231 CHARLEVOIX ST 48230
St. Paul ES, 170 GROSSE POINTE BLVD 48236

Gwinn, Marquette Co., Pop. Code 4
Gwinn Area SD
Sch. Sys. Enr. Code 5
Supt. – Dr. Charles Osborn 49841
MS 49841 – James Ghiardi, prin.
Gilbert ES, IRON ST 49843 – Ruth Spade, prin.
McDonald ES, K I SAWYER AFB 49843
Raymond Hjelt, prin.
Sawyer ES, K I SAWYER AFB 49843
June Shaw, prin.
Other Schools – See Skandia

Hadley, Lapeer Co.
Lapeer Comm. SD
Supt. – See Lapeer
ES, 4525 PRATT RD 48440 – Cindy Bond, prin.

Hale, Isoco Co., Pop. Code 2
Hale Area SD
Sch. Sys. Enr. Code 3
Supt. – John Gunnell, P O BOX 38 48739
ES, P O BOX 38 48739 – Dena Milks, prin.

Hamburg, Livingston Co., Pop. Code 7
Pinckney Comm. SD
Supt. – See Pinckney
ES, 7474 WASHINGTON ST 48139
Pam Olech, prin.

Hamilton, Allegan Co., Pop. Code 3
Hamilton Comm. SD
Sch. Sys. Enr. Code 4
Supt. – John Graves, 4815 136TH AVE 49419
Bentheim ES, 4057 38TH ST 49419
Rich Hoving, prin.
ES, 3472 M-40 49419 – Ron Hillegonds, prin.
Other Schools – See Holland

Hamtramck, Wayne Co., Pop. Code 7
Hamtramck SD
Sch. Sys. Enr. Code 5
Supt. – John Radwanski, P O BOX 12012 48212
Kosciuszko MS, 2333 BURGER ST 48212
E. Malczewski, prin.
Dickinson ES, 3385 NORWALK ST 48212
J. Waszelewski, prin.
Holbrook ES, 2361 ALICE ST 48212
T. Niczay, prin.

St. Florian School, 2622 FLORIAN ST 48212
Our Lady Queen of Apostles ES
11420 CONANT ST 48212
St. Ladislaus ES, 2650 CANIFF ST 48212

Hancock, Houghton Co., Pop. Code 6
Hancock SD
Sch. Sys. Enr. Code 4
Supt. – G. Barkell, 417 QUINCY ST 49930
Rippley MS, ROYCE RD 49930
Doug Middleton, prin.
Ryan ES, MICHIGAN ST 49930
Ed Longenecker, prin.
Wright ES, N LINCOLN DR 49930
Mary Stadius, prin.

Hanover, Jackson Co., Pop. Code 2
Hanover-Horton SD
Sch. Sys. Enr. Code 4
Supt. – (—), 101 FAIRVIEW 49241
ES, 10000 MOSCOW RD 49241
Anthony Foster, prin.
Other Schools – See Horton

Harbor Beach, Huron Co., Pop. Code 4
Harbor Beach Comm. SD
Sch. Sys. Enr. Code 3
Supt. – David Micinski, 402 S 5TH ST 48441
MS, 402 S 5TH ST 48441 – (—), prin.
Ramsey-Robertson ES, 650 TRESCOTT ST 48441
Timothy Vagts, prin.

Our Lady of Lake Huron ES, 222 COURT ST 48441

Harbor Springs, Emmet Co., Pop. Code 4
Harbor Springs SD
Sch. Sys. Enr. Code 3
Supt. – Jerome Allore, 327 E BLUFF DRIVE 49740
MS, 327 E BLUFF DR 49740 – James Wood, prin.
Shay ES, 174 E LAKE RD 49740
Thomas Richards, prin.

Harper Woods, Wayne Co., Pop. Code 7
Harper Woods SD
Sch. Sys. Enr. Code 3
Supt. – Arthur Toth
20225 BEACONSFIELD ST 48225
Beacon ES, 19475 BEACONSFIELD ST 48225
E. Winters, prin.
Tyrone MS, 19525 TYRONE ST 48225
E. Tomaka, prin.

Our Lady Queen of Peace ES
21101 BOURNEMOUTH ST 48225
St. Peter ES, 19800 ANITA ST 48225

Harris, Menominee Co., Pop. Code 4
Bark River-Harris SD
Sch. Sys. Enr. Code 3
Supt. – Gerald Ritenburgh 49845

Bark-River-Harris ES 49845
  Lawrence Wanic, prin.

Harrison, Clare Co., Pop. Code 4
Harrison Comm. SD
Sch. Sys. Enr. Code 4
Supt. – Donald Richards, 224 S MAIN ST 48625
MS, 224 S MAIN ST 48625
  Joseph Ashcroft, prin.
Amble ES, 8725 E ARNOLD LAKE RD 48625
  Edward Kerr,Jr., prin.
Hillside ES, 201 S FOURTH ST 48625
  John Tobey, prin.
Larson ES, 455 SPRUCE ST 48625
  Daniel Paulin, prin.

Harsens Island, St. Clair Co.
Algonac Comm. SD
Supt. – See Algonac
ES, 2669 COLUMBINE ST 48028
  John Streit, prin.

Hart, Oceana Co., Pop. Code 4
Hart SD
Sch. Sys. Enr. Code 4
Supt. – Patrick Gaudard, 300 JOHNSON ST 49420
MS, 300 JOHNSON ST 49420
  Lawrence DeAugustine, prin.
Elbridge ES, RURAL ROUTE 03 49420
  Jane Thocher, prin.
Spitler ES, 300 JOHNSON ST 49420
  D. McClennan, prin.
Other Schools – See Mears

Hartford, Van Buren Co., Pop. Code 4
Hartford SD
Sch. Sys. Enr. Code 4
Supt. – Robert Pobuda, P O BOX 158 49057
MS, P O BOX 158 49057 – James McQueen, prin.
Red Arrow ES, P O BOX 158 49057
  John Busch, prin.
Woodside ES, P O BOX 158 49057
  Mary McDonnell, prin.

Hartland, Livingston Co., Pop. Code 6
Hartland Cons. SD
Sch. Sys. Enr. Code 5
Supt. – Gary Wright, P O BOX 128 48029
Farms MS, P O BOX 128 48029
  Pete Caroselli, prin.
Lakes ES, P O BOX 128 48029 – B. Paxton, prin.
Round ES, P O BOX 128 48029
  Mike Kehoe, prin.
Village ES, P O BOX 128 48029
  A. Behrmann, prin.

Child of Christ Lutheran School
  3375 FENTON ROAD 48029

Haslett, Ingham Co., Pop. Code 5
Haslett SD
Sch. Sys. Enr. Code 4
Supt. – Jeremy M. Hughes
  1590 FRANKLIN ST 48840
MS, 1535 FRANKLIN ST 48840
  J. Etheridge, prin.
Murphy MS, 1875 LAKE LANSING RD 48840
  Thomas Lepo, prin.
Ralya MS, 5645 SCHOOL ST 48840
  Patricia Walton, prin.
Wilkshire ES, 5750 ACADEMIC WAY 48840
  Roy Doonan, prin.

Perry SD
Supt. – See Perry
Corcoran ES, 13248 WOODBURY RD 48840
  Lynne Harned, prin.

Hastings, Barry Co., Pop. Code 6
Hastings Area SD
Sch. Sys. Enr. Code 5
Supt. – Carl Schoessel, 232 W GRAND ST 49058
MS, 232 W GRAND ST 49058 – Jerry Horan, prin.
Central ES, 509 S BROADWAY ST 49058
  David Arnold, prin.
Northeastern ES, 519 E GRANT ST 49058
  David Styf, prin.
Southeastern ES, 1300 S EAST ST 49058
  Chris Warren, prin.
Other Schools – See Bellevue

St. Rose of Lima ES, 707 S JEFFERSON ST 49058

Hazel Park, Oakland Co., Pop. Code 7
Hazel Park SD
Sch. Sys. Enr. Code 6
Supt. – James Gibson, 23136 HUGHES AVE 48030
Beecher JHS, 22750 HIGHLAND AVE 48030
  Leonard Sak, prin.
Ford Community ES, 1620 E ELZA AVE 48030
  Victor Mayo, prin.
Hoover ES, 23720 HOOVER AVE 48030
  Rebecca Sullivan, prin.
Longfellow ES, 570 E MAPLEDALE AVE 48030
  William Kumpula, prin.
Roosevelt ES, 24131 S CHRYSLER DR 48030
  Larry Park, prin.
United Oaks ES, 1015 E HARRY AVE 48030
  Deana Whitehead, prin.
Webster ES, 431 W JARVIS AVE 48030
  Robert Marra, prin.
Other Schools – See Ferndale

St. Mary Magdalen ES
  99 E WOODWARD HEIGHTS BLVD 48030

Hemlock, Saginaw Co., Pop. Code 3
Hemlock SD
Sch. Sys. Enr. Code 4
Supt. – Lawrence Gariglio
  1095 N HEMLOCK ROAD 48626
MS, 525 N MAPLE ST 48626 – Reginald Rye, prin.
ES, 200 WILSON 48626 – Reginald Rye, prin.
Ling ES, 835 N PINE ST 48626
  Reginald Rye, prin.

St. Peter ES, 2400 N RAUCHOLZ RD 48626

Hermansville, Menominee Co., Pop. Code 3
North Central Area SD
Supt. – See Powers
Powers-Spalding-Hermansville ES 49847
  Hazel James, prin.

Herron, Alpena Co.
Alpena SD
Supt. – See Alpena
Wilson ES, 4999 HERRON RD 49744
  Delbert Beyer, prin.

Hersey, Osceola Co., Pop. Code 2
Reed City SD
Supt. – See Reed City
ES, P O BOX 68 49639 – Dan Garfalo, prin.

Hesperia, Oceana Co., Pop. Code 3
Hesperia Comm. SD
Sch. Sys. Enr. Code 4
Supt. – Max Kessler, 96 S DIVISION 49421
ES, 96 DIVISION ST 49421 – Ron Pickard, prin.

Hickory Corners, Barry Co.
Gull Lake Comm. SD
Supt. – See Richland
Gull Lake MS, 9500 40TH 49060
  Steven Smyth, prin.
Kellogg ES, 9594 40TH ST 49060
  Sandra Feuerstein, prin.

Highland, Oakland Co., Pop. Code 7
Huron Valley SD
Supt. – See Milford
Highland MS, 305 JOHN 48031
  James Lancaster, prin.
Spring Mills ES, 3150 HARVEY LAKE RD 48031
  Mary Berkfield, prin.

Highland Park, Wayne Co., Pop. Code 8
Highland Park SD
Sch. Sys. Enr. Code 5
Supt. – Eldon Martin, 20 BARTLETT ST 48203
Barger ES, 45 BUENA VISTA ST E 48203
  Fletcher Miller, prin.
Bright Ct. ES, 13321 HAMILTON AVE 48203
  Glen Homan, prin.
Cortland ES, 138 CORTLAND ST 48203
  Mabel Kenyon, prin.
Ferris ES, 60 CORTLAND ST 48203
  Charles Russell, prin.
Ford ES, 131 PILGRIM ST 48203
  Carl Pettway, prin.
Liberty ES, 16535 JOSLYN ST 48203
  B. Esselman, prin.

St. Benedict ES, 53 CANDLER ST 48203

Hillman, Montmorency Co., Pop. Code 2
Hillman Comm. SD
Sch. Sys. Enr. Code 3
Supt. – Tom Mateer, 245 3RD ST 49746
ES, 245 THIRD ST 49746 – David Werner, prin.

Hillsdale, Hillsdale Co., Pop. Code 6
Hillsdale Comm. SD
Sch. Sys. Enr. Code 4
Supt. – Richard Lane, 30 S NORWOOD AVE 49242
Davis MS, 30 N WEST ST 49242
  Chris Butler, prin.
Bailey ES, 59 S MANNING ST 49242
  D. Krzyaniak, prin.
Gier ES, 175 SPRING ST 49242
  Scott Siakel, prin.
Mauck ES, 113 E FAYETTE ST 49242
  Marty Ryan, prin.

Holland, Ottawa Co., Pop. Code 7
Hamilton Comm. SD
Supt. – See Hamilton
Blue Star ES, A3846 58TH 49423
  Wendell Rooks, prin.
Sandyview ES, A-4317 46TH ST 49423
  Larry Westrate, prin.

Holland SD
Sch. Sys. Enr. Code 6
Supt. – Ronald Rolph, 633 APPLE AVE 49423
Fell MS, 372 S RIVER AVE 49423
  Steve Farrar, prin.
Harrington ES, 1623 W 32ND ST 49423
  Archie Bell, prin.
Holland Heights ES, 856 E 12TH ST 49423
  D. Van Haitsma, prin.
MS, 500 W 24TH ST 49423 – Jim Zeedyk, prin.
Jefferson ES, 282 W 30TH ST 49423
  Richard Rust, prin.
Lakeview ES, 752 LUGERS RD 49423
  S. Dangremong, prin.
Lincoln ES, 257 COLUMBIA AVE 49423
  Jack Lowe, prin.
Longfellow ES, 36 E 24TH ST 49423
  C. Vanden Berg, prin.
Maplewood ES, 925 CENTRAL AVE 49423
  Lee Ten Brink, prin.

Van Raalte ES, 461 VAN RAALTE AVE 49423
  Carmen Hannah, prin.
Washington ES, 158 W 11TH ST 49423
  Steve Binder, prin.

West Ottawa SD
Sch. Sys. Enr. Code 5
Supt. – Charles Muncatchy
  294 W LAKEWOOD BLVD 49423
West Ottawa MS, 3700 140TH AVE 49423
  Gary Hodgson, prin.
Glerum ES, 342 W LAKEWOOD BLVD 49424
  Kathy Brown, prin.
Lakewood ES, 2134 W LAKEWOOD BLVD 49424
  William Kangas, prin.
North Holland ES
  11946 NEW HOLLAND ST 49424
  Joann Mulder, prin.
Pine Creek ES, 583 RILEY ST 49424
  Robert Hunt, prin.
Waukazoo MS, 1294 W LAKEWOOD BLVD 49424
  Kathy Brown, prin.
Woodside ES, 2519 N DIVISION AVE 49424
  John Skoglund, prin.
Other Schools – See West Olive

Holland Christian ES, 850 OTTAWA AVE 49423
Maplewood Christian ES, 913 PINE AVE 49423
Rose Park Christian ES
  556 BUTTERNUT DR 49424
South Olive Christian ES
  6230 N 120TH AVE 49424
St. Francis DeSales ES, 183 W 13TH ST 49423

Holly, Oakland Co., Pop. Code 5
Holly Area SD
Sch. Sys. Enr. Code 5
Supt. – Wayne Peters, 111 COLLEGE ST 48442
ES, 801 E MAPLE ST 48442 – D. Bradsher, prin.
Patterson ES, 3231 GRANGE HALL RD 48442
  Don Frownfelter, prin.
Other Schools – See Davisburg

Holt, Ingham Co., Pop. Code 6
Holt SD
Sch. Sys. Enr. Code 5
Supt. – Mark Maksimowicz
  4610 SPAHR ST 48842
Dimondale ES, 300 WALNUT ST 48821
  K. Thibaudeau, prin.
Elliott ES, 4200 BOND AVE 48842
  Ramona Berkey, prin.
Hope MS, 2020 PARK LANE 48842
  Gary Smith, prin.
Midway ES, 4552 SPAHR ST 48842
  D. Rumminger, prin.
Sycamore ES, 4429 SYCAMORE ST 48842
  Francine Minnick, prin.
Wilcox ES, 1650 LAURELWOOD DR 48842
  Ken Gibson, prin.

Holton, Muskegon Co., Pop. Code 4
Holton SD
Sch. Sys. Enr. Code 4
Supt. – Ruth McKenzie
  8897 HOLTON-DUCK LK ROAD 49425
MS, 8897 HOLTON-DUCK LAKE ROAD 49425
  L. Bartolameolli, prin.
ES, 8897 HOLTON DUCK LAKE RD 49425
  Albert Shaheen, prin.

Homer, Calhoun Co., Pop. Code 4
Homer Comm. SD
Sch. Sys. Enr. Code 4
Supt. – Lee Robinson, 403 S HILLSDALE ST 49245
MS, 403 S HILLSDALE ST 49245
  Kim Kramer, prin.
Fletcher ES, FULTON ST 49245
  Philip Duff, prin.

Honor, Benzie Co., Pop. Code 2
Benzie County Central SD
Supt. – See Benzonia
Platte River ES, 11434 MAIN 49640
  Amy Jones, prin.

Hope, Midland Co.
Meridian SD
Supt. – See Sanford
Hillside ES, 59 W BAKER RD 48628
  Linda Kirker, prin.

Hopkins, Allegan Co., Pop. Code 3
Hopkins SD
Sch. Sys. Enr. Code 4
Supt. – W. Craig Misner, 400 CLARK ST 49328
ES, 400 CLARK ST 49328 – Daniel Bushouse, prin.
Other Schools – See Dorr

Horton, Jackson Co., Pop. Code 2
Hanover-Horton SD
Supt. – See Hanover
Hanover-Horton MS
  10000 MOSCOW ROAD 49246
  Terry Catron, prin.
ES, 237 FARVIEW ST 49246
  Anthony Foster, prin.

Houghton, Houghton Co., Pop. Code 6
Portage Twp. SD
Sch. Sys. Enr. Code 4
Supt. – Dennis Harbour 49931
Portage ES, 203 JACKER ST 49931
  Gerald Sipola, prin.

Houghton Lake, Roscommon Co., Pop. Code 4
Houghton Lake Comm. SD
Sch. Sys. Enr. Code 4
Supt. – John P. Walkley
  6001 W HOUGHTON LAKE DRIVE 48629
MS, P O BOX 68 48629 – James E. French, prin.
Collins ES, 4451 E HOUGHTON LAKE DR 48629
  C. Pedersen, prin.
Merritt ES, MERRITT RD 49667
  C. Pedersen, prin.
Prudenville MS, 604 SULLIVAN 48651
  Kenneth Roberts, prin.

Howard City, Montcalm Co., Pop. Code 4
Tri County Area SD
Sch. Sys. Enr. Code 4
Supt. – Jerry Wabeke, 208 EDGERTON 49329
Tri County MS, 412 EDGERTON 49329
  Susan Wanner, prin.
MacNaughton ES, 415 CEDAR 49329
  Judy Kakonis, prin.
Other Schools – See Sand Lake

Howell, Livingston Co., Pop. Code 6
Howell SD
Sch. Sys. Enr. Code 6
Supt. – Charles Manuel
  415 N BARNARD ST 48843
Highlander Way MS
  511 HIGHLANDER WAY N 48843
  Donald Watson, prin.
McPherson MS
  1400 GRAND RIVER AVE W 48843
  G. Douglas Paige, prin.
Latson ES, 1201 S LATSON RD 48843
  Charles Kraegel, prin.
Northwest ES, 1233 BOWER ST 48843
  Fred Dobbs, prin.
Southeast ES, 861 E SIBLEY ST 48843
  John Clay, prin.
Southwest ES, 915 GAY ST 48843
  William Harvey, prin.

St. Joseph ES, 425 E WASHINGTON ST 48843

Hubbard Lake, Alpena Co.
Alpena SD
Supt. – See Alpena
ES, 6891 NICHOLSON HILL 49747
  Jane Guyott, prin.

Hudson, Lenawee Co., Pop. Code 5
Hudson Area SD
Sch. Sys. Enr. Code 4
Supt. – John G. Meredith
  746 N MAPLE GROVE AVE 49247
Lincoln ES, 746 B MAPLE GROVE 49247
  J. Reamsnyder, prin.
Other Schools – See Clayton

Sacred Heart ES, 300 S MARKET ST 49247

Hudsonville, Ottawa Co.
Hudsonville SD
Sch. Sys. Enr. Code 4
Supt. – Wayne Petroelje, 5037 32ND AVE 49426
MS, 5535 SCHOOL AVE 49426
  Jack Van Eden, prin.
Alward ES, 3811 PORT SHELDON ST 49426
  C. Sikkema, prin.
Bauer ES, 8136 48TH AVE 49426
  C. Sikkema, prin.
Forest Grove ES, 1645 32ND AVE 49426
  Justin Gebben, prin.
Park ES, 5525 PARK AVE 49426
  C. Sikkema, prin.
South ES, 3400 ALLEN ST 49426
  Justin Gebben, prin.
Other Schools – See Jamestown

Hudsonville Christian ES, 3435 OAK ST 49426

Huntington Woods, Oakland Co., Pop. Code 6
Berkley SD
Supt. – See Berkley
Burton ES, 26315 SCOTIA RD 48070
  Donald Lazarus, prin.

Ida, Monroe Co., Pop. Code 5
Ida SD
Sch. Sys. Enr. Code 4
Supt. – H. Gabehart, 3145 PRAIRIE 48140
MS, 3143 PRAIRIE 48140 – Sheldon Wiens, prin.
ES, 7900 IDA 48140 – W. Cunningham, prin.

Idlewild, Lake Co.
Baldwin Comm. SD
Supt. – See Baldwin
Yates MS, 5125 NELSON ROAD 49642
  M. Jazzar, prin.

Imlay City, Lapeer Co., Pop. Code 4
Imlay Comm. SD
Sch. Sys. Enr. Code 4
Supt. – Robert Regan
  634 W BORLAND ROAD 48444
Borland MS, 500 W BORLAND RD 48444
  T. Roekle, prin.
Weston ES, 275 WESTON ST 48444
  Mary Ruddy, prin.

Indian River, Cheboygan Co., Pop. Code 3
Inland Lakes SD
Sch. Sys. Enr. Code 3
Supt. – Thomas Makela
  5243 STRAITS HIGHWAY 49749

Inland Lakes ES, 5243 STRAITS HWY 49749
  Ronald Berg, prin.

Inkster, Wayne Co., Pop. Code 8
Inkster SD
Sch. Sys. Enr. Code 4
Supt. – Garnett L. Hegeman,Jr.
  29115 CARLYSLE ST 48141
Blanchette MS, 29193 BEECH ST 48141
  S. Mosley, prin.
Baylor ES, 288865 CARLYSLE 48141
  E. Ames, prin.
Meek ES, 29807 PARKWOOD ST 48141
  R. Brewis, prin.
Woodson ES, 29665 PINE ST 48141
  Daniel Brown, prin.

Wayne-Westland Comm. SD
Supt. – See Westland
Hicks ES, 100 HELEN ST 48141
  Peter Lawrie, prin.

Westwood Comm. SD
Sch. Sys. Enr. Code 4
Supt. – Equilla F. Bradford
  25912 ANNAPOLIS ST 48141
Daly ES, 25824 MICHIGAN AVE 48141
  Mary Lloyd, prin.
Thorne MS, 25251 ANNAPOLIS 48125
  Grace Peapples, prin.
Other Schools – See Dearborn, Dearborn Heights

Peterson-Warren Academy
  4000 SYLVIA ST 48141

Interlochen, Leelanau Co.
Traverse City Area SD
Supt. – See Traverse City
ES 49643 – Ted Jamison, prin.

Ionia, Ionia Co., Pop. Code 6
Ionia SD
Sch. Sys. Enr. Code 5
Supt. – Robert Hagerty, 433 UNION ST 48846
Emerson JHS, 645 HACKETT ST 48846
  Dan Evans, prin.
Boyce ES, 3550 STATE RD N 48846
  Dave Hess, prin.
Jefferson ES, 420 JEFFERSON ST N 48846
  Jim Lawther, prin.
Rather ES, 380 E TUTTLE RD 48846
  Jim Lewis, prin.
Twin River ES, 435 CENTER ST 48846
  Charles Seguna, prin.

St. John Lutheran School
  617 N JEFFERSON ST 48846
SS Peter & Paul ES, 317 BALDIE ST 48846

Iron Mountain, Dickinson Co., Pop. Code 6
Iron Mt. SD
Sch. Sys. Enr. Code 4
Supt. – Richard H. Allen, P O BOX 280 49801
Central MS, W HUGHITT ST 49801
  Richard Debelak, prin.
Central ES, WEST HUGHITT 49801
  Richard Debelak, prin.
East ES, EAST E ST 49801 – Marvin Harry, prin.

North Dickinson County SD
Sch. Sys. Enr. Code 3
Supt. – Thomas Rossler, HCR 1 49801
North Dickinson S, RURAL ROUTE 01 49801
  Michael Loy, prin.

Dickinson Area ES, 406 W B ST 49801

Iron River, Iron Co., Pop. Code 4
West Iron County SD
Supt. – See Stambaugh
Bates ES, 3257 E US 2 49935
  Sylvia Hronkin, prin.

Ironwood, Gogebic Co., Pop. Code 6
Ironwood Area SD
Sch. Sys. Enr. Code 4
Supt. – Wm. Hyry, 634-46 E AYER ST 49938
Newport ES, BUNDY ST 49938
  Robert Vaara, prin.
Norrie ES, BALSAM ST 49938
  Bruce Belmas, prin.
Sleight ES, ARCH ST 49938 – Carol Gertz, prin.

Ironwood Catholic ES, 126 ARCH ST 49938

Ishpeming, Marquette Co., Pop. Code 6
Ishpeming SD
Sch. Sys. Enr. Code 4
Supt. – Richard Hendra, 321 E DIVISION ST 49849
Phelps MS, N 3RD ST 49849
  Edwin Sansom, prin.
Birchview ES, 663 POPLAR ST 49849
  Richard Ross, prin.
Central ES, 324 E PEARL ST 49849
  Richard Ross, prin.

Nice Comm. SD
Sch. Sys. Enr. Code 4
Supt. – Francis Rilesing
  300 S WESTWOOD DRIVE 49849
Ely ES, P O BOX 163 49849 – John Pontti, prin.
North Lake ES, 905 SCHOOL ST 49849
  John Pontti, prin.
Other Schools – See Champion, National Mine

Ithaca, Gratiot Co., Pop. Code 5
Ithaca SD
Sch. Sys. Enr. Code 4
Supt. – Kenneth Federspiel, 530 UNION ST 48847
MS, 710 N UNION STREET 48847
  Lyle Thomas, prin.
North ES, 201 E ARCADA ST 48847
  N. Cain, prin.
South ES, 400 WEBSTER ST 48847
  William Upton, prin.

Jackson, Jackson Co., Pop. Code 8
East Jackson SD
Sch. Sys. Enr. Code 4
Supt. – Bruce Van Eyck
  1404 N SUTTON ROAD 49202
East Jackson MS, 4340 WALZ ROAD 49201
  Mary Ann Kessler, prin.
Memorial ES, 345 N DETTMAN RD 49202
  Stepen Lewis, prin.
Robinson ES, 5400 SEYMOUR RD 49201
  David Bosio, prin.

Jackson SD
Sch. Sys. Enr. Code 6
Supt. – William Pearson
  1400 W MONROE ST 49202
Allen ES, 803 E PEARL ST 49201
  Linda Brian, prin.
Bennett ES, 820 BENNETT ST 49202
  R. Niedzielski, prin.
Cascades ES, 1200 S WISNER ST 49203
  Farris Coppage, prin.
Dibble ES, 3450 KIBBY RD 49203
  Barbara Glover, prin.
Frost ES, 1226 S WISNER ST 49203
  Marvin Goad, prin.
Hunt ES, 1145 N BROWN ST 49202
  Lawrence Green, prin.
McCulloch ES, 710 NEW YORK ST 49203
  L. Rockquemore, prin.
Northeast ES, 1024 FLEMING AVE 49202
  David Reinhart, prin.
Wilson ES, 310 W MORRELL ST 49203
  Beverly Walters, prin.

Northwest SD
Sch. Sys. Enr. Code 5
Supt. – Robert Halle
  4000 VAN HORN ROAD 49201
Northwest MS, 6700 RIVES JCT ROAD 49201
  Bill Fitch, prin.
Northwest MS, 3757 LANSING AVE 49202
  Bob Badertscher, prin.
Parnall ES, 3737 LANSING AVE 49202
  Warren Dexter, prin.

Vandercook Lake SD
Sch. Sys. Enr. Code 4
Supt. – Burdette W. Andrews
  1000 E GOLF AVE 49203
McDevitt MS, 800 E MCDEVITT AVE 49203
  Frances Sweet, prin.
Townsend ES, 1005 FLOYD AVE 49203
  Marsha Bowers, prin.

Jackson Catholic ES, 915 COOPER ST 49202
Queens ES, 811 S WISNER ST 49203
St. John ES, 405 E NORTH ST 49202
St. Joseph ES, 717 N WATERLOO ST 49202
St. Mary ES, 120 E WESLEY AVE 49201
Trinity ES, 4900 MCCAIN RD 49201

Jamestown, Ottawa Co., Pop. Code 6
Hudsonville SD
Supt. – See Hudsonville
ES, 3291 LINCOLN ST 49427
  Justin Gebben, prin.

Jenison, Ottawa Co., Pop. Code 7
Jenison SD
Sch. Sys. Enr. Code 5
Supt. – David Dresslar, 8375 20TH AVE 49428
MS, 8295 20TH AVE 49428
  Richard Wagemaker, prin.
Bauerwood ES, 1443 BAUER RD 49428
  W. Bonzelaar, prin.
Bursley ES, 1195 PORT SHELDON ST 49428
  Jon Baker, prin.
Maplewood ES, 800 CONNIE ST 49428
  Jean Marlowe, prin.
Pinewood ES, 2405 CHIPPEWA ST 49428
  Donald Buning, prin.
Rosewood ES, 2370 TYLER ST 49428
  Ross Dehaan, prin.
Sandy Hill ES, 1990 BALDWIN ST 49428
  Mary Tracey, prin.

Jenison Christian Lower ES
  7700 GREENFIELD AVE 49428

Johannesburg, Otsego Co., Pop. Code 2
Johannesburg-Lewiston SD
Sch. Sys. Enr. Code 3
Supt. – Raymond A. Hyek, 10854 M-32 49751
ES, 10854 M 32 49751 – Carol Holley, prin.
Lewiston ES, MONTMORENCY ST 49756
  Sandra Stanley, prin.

Jonesville, Hillsdale Co., Pop. Code 4
Jonesville Comm. SD
Sch. Sys. Enr. Code 4
Supt. – John Collins, 440 ADRIAN ST 49250
Williams ES, 440 ADRIAN ST 49250
  Donald Weise, prin.

Kalamazoo, Kalamazoo Co., Pop. Code 8
Kalamazoo SD
Sch. Sys. Enr. Code 7
Supt. – Frank Rapley, 1200 HOWARD ST 49008
Hillside JHS, 1941 ALAMO AVE 49007
  Dorothy Young, prin.
Milwood JHS, 2916 KONKLE ST 49001
  Dale Steeby, prin.
South JHS, 922 W MAPLE ST 49008
  (—), prin.
Arcadia ES, 932 BOSWELL LN 49007
  Gary Cramer, prin.
Chime ES, 6750 CHIME ST 49009
  Dana Van't Zelfde, prin.
Edison MS, 924 RUSSELL ST 49001
  Hank Harper, prin.
Greenwood ES, 3501 MORELAND ST 49001
  Darrell Clay, prin.
Indian Prairie ES, GRAND PRAIRIE ROAD 49007
  Diane Misner, prin.
King MS, 1100 NICHOLS RD 49007
  P. Coles-Chalmers, prin.
Lakewood ES, 3122 LAKE ST 49001
  Sandra Howe, prin.
Lincoln MS, 912 N BURDICK ST 49007
  Linda Comer, prin.
Milwood ES, 3400 LOVERS LN 49001
  Carl Czuchna, prin.
Northeastern ES, 2433 GERTRUDE ST 49001
  Christie Enstrom, prin.
Northglade ES, 1914 COBB AVE 49007
  Richard Grushon, prin.
Oakwood ES, 3410 LAIRD AVE 49008
  Sharon Lockett, prin.
Parkwood/Upjohn ES, 23321 S PARK 49001
  Grace Stevens, prin.
Spring Valley ES, 3530 MT OLIVET RD 49004
  Ruth Hartman, prin.
Washington ES, 1919 PORTAGE ST 49001
  John Brown, prin.
Winchell ES, 2316 WINCHELL AVE 49008
  Bob Jennings, prin.
Woods Lake ES, 3215 OAKLAND DR 49008
  Shirley Gregory, prin.
Woodward MS, 606 STUART AVE 49007
  Ken McDonald, prin.

Parchment SD
Supt. – See Parchment
Northwood ES, 4031 GEORGE ST 49007
  Larry Seaver, prin.

Plainwell Comm. SD
Supt. – See Plainwell
Cooper ES, 7559 N 14TH ST 49007
  Clark Volz, prin.

Portage SD
Sch. Sys. Enr. Code 6
Supt. – James Rikkers
  8111 S WESTNEDGE AVE 49002
Central MS, 8035 S WESTNEDGE AVE 49002
  Richard Tyler, prin.
North MS, 5808 OREGON AVE 49002
  Peter Marsiglia, prin.
West MS, 7145 COOLEY DRIVE 49002
  John Schreur, prin.
Other Schools – See Portage

East Christian ES, 5196 COMSTOCK AVE 49001
North Christian ES, 1340 COBB AVE 49007
South Christian ES
  3333 S WESTNEDGE AVE 49008
St. Augustine ES, 600 W MICHIGAN AVE 49007
St. Joseph ES, 930 LAKE ST 49001
St. Mary ES, 929 CHARLOTTE AVE 49001
St. Monica ES, 530 W KILGORE RD 49008

Kaleva, Manistee Co., Pop. Code 2
Kaleva-Norman-Dickson SD
Supt. – See Brethren
ES, 9208 KAUKO ST 49645
  Robert Grostick, prin.

Kalkaska, Kalkaska Co., Pop. Code 4
Kalkaska SD
Sch. Sys. Enr. Code 4
Supt. – Robert Fein, P O BOX 580 49646
MS, 1700 W KALKASKA ROAD 49646
  Alfred DeOtte, prin.
Birch Street MS, 309 N BIRCH ST 49646
  (—), prin.
Cherry Street ES, N CHERRY ST 49646
  Anna Strang, prin.
Other Schools – See Rapid City

Kawkawlin, Bay Co., Pop. Code 6

St. Valentine ES, 1010 9 MILE RD 48631

Kent City, Kent Co., Pop. Code 3
Kent City Comm. SD
Sch. Sys. Enr. Code 4
Supt. – C. Gary Carlson, 341 N MAIN ST 49330
Main ES, 29 COLLEGE ST 49330
  Rebecca Moore, prin.
Upper ES, 35 W MUSKEGON ST 49330
  Russell Ainslie, prin.

Kentwood, Kent Co., Pop. Code 8
Kentwood SD
Supt. – See Grand Rapids
Crestwood MS, 2674 44TH ST SE 49508
  James Van Der Laan, prin.
Valleywood MS, 1110 50TH ST SE 49508
  Richard Dunn, prin.

Kinde, Huron Co., Pop. Code 3
North Huron SD
Sch. Sys. Enr. Code 3
Supt. – William Mayes, 21 MAIN ROAD 48445
North Huron MS, 8321 N VAN DYKE 48445
  Richard Fawcett, prin.
North Huron ES, 69 MICHIGAN ST 48445
  Carl Dickinson, prin.

Kingsford, Dickinson Co., Pop. Code 6
Breitung Twp. SD
Sch. Sys. Enr. Code 4
Supt. – William Howes, 440 HEMLOCK ST 49801
MS, HAMILTON AVE 49801
  Bruce Osterberg, prin.
Garden Village ES, CHESTNUT ST 49801
  David Corlett, prin.
Roosevelt ES, HEMLOCK ST 49801
  David Corlett, prin.
Westwood ES, WESTWOOD ST 49801
  James Verley, prin.
Other Schools – See Quinnesec

Kingsley, Grand Traverse Co., Pop. Code 3
Kingsley Area SD
Sch. Sys. Enr. Code 3
Supt. – Jerry Inman, 403 BLAIR ST 49649
ES, 403 BLAIR ST 49649 – Joel Donaldson, prin.

St. Mary ES, 2912 W KINGSLEY RD 49649

Kingston, Tuscola Co., Pop. Code 2
Kingston Comm. SD
Sch. Sys. Enr. Code 3
Supt. – Jerry Laycock, 5790 STATE ST 48741
ES, 3644 ROSS ST 48741 – James Franklin, prin.

Lachine, Alpena Co.
Alpena SD
Supt. – See Alpena
Long Rapids ES, 12595 LONG RAPIDS RD 49753
  Daniel Gouin, prin.

Laingsburg, Shiawassee Co., Pop. Code 4
Lainsburg Comm. SD
Sch. Sys. Enr. Code 4
Supt. – Halsted Beatty
  320 E GRAND RIVER RD 48848
MS, 117 PROSPECT ST 48848
  Gregory Kingdon, prin.
ES, 115 PROSPECT ST 48848 – Larry Larson, prin.

Lake City, Missaukee Co., Pop. Code 3
Lake City Area SD
Sch. Sys. Enr. Code 4
Supt. – Harold Burkholder, RUSSELL ST 49651
MS, RUSSELL ST 49651 – Charles Elmquist, prin.
ES, RUSSELL ST 49651 – Roger Moore, prin.

Lake Leelanau, Leelanau Co.

St. Mary School
  310 SAINT MARY SCHOOL 49653

Lake Linden, Houghton Co., Pop. Code 4
Lake Linden-Hubbell SD
Sch. Sys. Enr. Code 3
Supt. – Henry VerBerkmoes
  601 CALUMET ST 49945
ES, 700 CALUMET ST 49945 – D. Londo, prin.

Lake Odessa, Ionia Co., Pop. Code 4
Lakewood SD
Sch. Sys. Enr. Code 5
Supt. – William Eckstrom, 824 3RD AVE 48849
MS, 824 3RD AVE 48849 – W. Storey, prin.
Clarksville ES, FRONT ST 48815
  Dan Wallace, prin.
East MS, 824 THIRD AVE 48849 – W. Storey, prin.
West ES, 812 WASHING BLVD 48849
  Milli Haug, prin.
Other Schools – See Sunfield, Woodland

Lake Orion, Oakland Co., Pop. Code 5
Lake Orion Comm. SD
Sch. Sys. Enr. Code 5
Supt. – Fred Snow, 315 N LAPEER ST 48035
MS, 2509 WALDON ROAD 48035
  Richard Bouton, prin.
Pine Tree ES, 590 PINETREE ST 48035
  Linda Purvis, prin.
Sims ES, 465 E JACKSON ST 48035
  Lee Umpstead, prin.
Stadium Drive ES, 244 STADIUM DR 48035
  James Theunick, prin.
Webber ES, 3191 W CLARKSTON RD 48035
  Rose Edwards, prin.
Other Schools – See Pontiac

St. Joseph ES, 703 N LAPEER RD 48035

Lakeview, Montcalm Co., Pop. Code 4
Lakeview Comm. SD
Sch. Sys. Enr. Code 4
Supt. – Carl Hartman
  9800 YOUNGMAN ROAD 48850
MS, 4999 WASHINGTON ST 48850
  Robert Iran, prin.
ES, SHERMAN AVE 48850 – George Goulet, prin.
Other Schools – See Trufant

Lambertville, Monroe Co.
Bedford SD
Supt. – See Temperance
Douglas ES, 6875 DOUGLAS RD 48144
  Alfred Price, prin.

L'Anse, Baraga Co., Pop. Code 4
L'Anse Twp. SD
Sch. Sys. Enr. Code 3
Supt. – Karl Gipp, 201 N 4TH ST 49946
MS, 201 N 4TH ST 49946 – James Mattson, prin.
Sullivan ES, 201 N 4TH ST 49946
  Karl Gipp, prin.
Other Schools – See Pelkie

Sacred Heart ES, 325 BARAGA AVE 49946

Lansing, Ingham Co., Pop. Code 9
Grand Ledge SD
Supt. – See Grand Ledge
Delta Center ES, 305 S CANAL RD 48917
  Judith Alford, prin.

Lansing SD
Sch. Sys. Enr. Code 7
Supt. – Richard Halik
  519 W KALAMAZOO ST 48933
Gardner MS, 333 DAHLIA DRIVE 48910
  Robert Hecksel, prin.
Otto MS, 500 E THOMAS ST 48906
  Walker Beverly, prin.
Pattengill MS, 1017 JEROME ST 48912
  S. Rodriguez, prin.
Rich MS, 2800 HAMPDEN DRIVE 48910
  Cordell Henderson, prin.
Allen ES, 1614 E KALAMAZOO ST 48912
  R. SantaAna, prin.
Attwood ES, 915 ATTWOOD DR 48911
  Bob Rutledge, prin.
Averill ES, 3201 AVERILL CT 48911
  Bruce Rochowicak, prin.
Bingham ES, 121 BINGHAM ST 48912
  J. Urso, prin.
Cavanaugh ES, 300 W CAVANAUGH RD 48910
  Sam Sinicropi, prin.
Cumberland ES, 2801 CUMBERLAND RD 48906
  Rita Blair, prin.
Elmhurst ES, 2400 PATTENGILL AVE 48910
  J. Hengstebeck, prin.
Fairview ES, 815 N FAIRVIEW AVE 48912
  Ricardo Briones, prin.
Forest View ES, 3119 STONELEIGH DR 48910
  E. Turpin, prin.
Franks ES, 2924 NEWARK AVE 48911
  Eunice DeMyers, prin.
Gier Park ES, 401 E GIER ST 48906
  M. Burkholder, prin.
Grand River ES, 1107 E GRAND RIVER AVE 48906
  James Kaiser, prin.
Gunnisonville ES, 1454 E CLARK RD 48906
  Ruthie McIntyre, prin.
Kendon ES, 827 KENDON DR 48910
  M. Wheeler-Thomas, prin.
Lewton ES, 2000 LEWTON PL 48911
  Dennis Semrau, prin.
Lyons ES, 2901 LYONS AVE 48910
  Tom Mattson, prin.
Maple Grove ES, 6031 S LOGAN ST 48911
  Diana Rouse, prin.
Maplewood ES, 2216 S CEDAR ST 48910
  James Swift, prin.
Moores Park ES, 316 MOORES RIVER DR 48910
  Joe Sanchez, prin.
Mt. Hope ES, 1215 E MOUNT HOPE AVE 48910
  Barbara LeFurge, prin.
North ES, 333 E MILLER RD 48911
  M. Richardson, prin.
Northwestern ES, 2908 ANDREW AVE 48906
  Jack Keyes, prin.
Pleasantview ES
  4501 PLEASANT GROVE RD 48910
  Aggie Lipscomb, prin.
Post Oak ES, 2320 POST OAK LN 48912
  Mary McGuire, prin.
Reo ES, 1221 REO CT 48910 – D. Anderson, prin.
Riddle ES, 221 HURON ST 48915
  Steve Hecker, prin.
Sheridan Road ES, 3701 N CEDAR ST 48906
  Ruby Helton, prin.
Verlinden ES, 609 N VERLINDEN AVE 48915
  Ronald Moore, prin.
Wainwright ES, 4200 WAINWRIGHT AVE 48911
  David Cross, prin.
Walnut ES, 1012 N WALNUT ST 48906
  Jim Davis, prin.
Wexford ES, 5217 WEXFORD RD 48911
  Fred Whiting, prin.
Willow ES, 1012 W WILLOW ST 48915
  Robert Gann, prin.
Woodcreek ES, 4000 WOODCREEK LN 48911
  David Henderson, prin.

Waverly SD
Sch. Sys. Enr. Code 5
Supt. – Jon Reynolds, 515 SNOW ROAD 48917
Waverly MS, 620 SNOW ROAD 48917
  R. Soderman, prin.
Colt ES, 4344 W MICHIGAN AVE 48917
  Stanley Bump, prin.
Elmwood ES, 1533 ELMWOOD RD 48917
  A. Rowe, prin.
Winans ES, 5601 W MICHIGAN AVE 48917
  Daniel Pappas, prin.
Windmere View ES, 1500 BOYNTON DR 48917
  Ralph Chapman, prin.

Holy Cross ES, 1514 W SAGINAW ST 48915
Immaculate Heart ES, 3830 ROSEMONT ST 48910
Our Saviour ES, 1601 W HOLMES RD 48910
Resurrection ES, 1521 E MICHIGAN AVE 48912

St. Gerard ES, 4433 W WILLOW RD   48917
St. Therese ES, 2620 TURNER ST   48906

Lapeer, Lapeer Co., Pop. Code 6
Lapeer Comm. SD
Sch. Sys. Enr. Code 6
Supt. – Jack McCauley
   1025 W NEPESSING ST   48446
White MS, 201 JEFFERSON ST   48446
  David Dagley, prin.
Zemmer MS, 1920 W OREGON ST   48446
  Harold Harding, prin.
Elba ES, 300 N ELBA RD   48446 – Dave Roe, prin.
Irwin ES, 250 2ND ST   48446
  Irma Gelhousen, prin.
Lynch ES, 2035 ROOD LAKE RD   48446
  James Whitlock, prin.
Maple Grove ES, 2020 IMLAY CITY RD   48446
  James Jessop, prin.
Mayfield ES, 302 PLUM CREEK RD   48446
  Sandra Bradburn, prin.
Schickler ES, 2020 W OREGON ST   48446
  Jon Nugent, prin.
Seaton ES, 5065 COLDWATER RD   48446
  L. Hourtienne, prin.
Turrill ES, 785 S ELM ST   48446
  Fred Olive, prin.
Other Schools – See Attica, Hadley, Metamora

Bishop Kelley ES, 926 W NEPESSING ST   48446

Lathrup Village, Oakland Co., Pop. Code 5
Southfield SD
Supt. – See Southfield
Birney MS, 27225 EVERGREEN ROAD   48076
  Rick Kurche, prin.

Lawrence, Van Buren Co., Pop. Code 3
Lawrence SD
Sch. Sys. Enr. Code 3
Supt. – Richard Stoll
  650 W SAINT JOSEPH ST   49064
ES, 648 W ST JOSEPH ST   49064
  Bill Markovich, prin.

Lawton, Van Buren Co., Pop. Code 4
Lawton Comm. SD
Sch. Sys. Enr. Code 4
Supt. – Daniel Lukich, P O BOX 430   49065
MS, P O BOX 430   49065 – D. Pratley, prin.
ES, P O BOX 430   49065 – Betty Knapp, prin.

Leland, Leelanau Co., Pop. Code 4
Leland SD
Sch. Sys. Enr. Code 2
Supt. – Michael Kenney, PEARL ST   49654
S, PEARL ST   49654 – Michael Hartigan, prin.

Leonard, Oakland Co., Pop. Code 2
Oxford Area SD
Supt. – See Oxford
Leonard ES, 335 ELMWOOD   48038
  John Voorheis, prin.

Romeo Comm. SD
Supt. – See Romeo
Hamilton-Parsons ES
  69875 DEQUINDRE RD   48038
  Julia Markham, prin.

Leonidas, St Joseph Co.
Colon Comm. SD
Supt. – See Colon
ES   49066 – Richard Cordes, prin.

Le Roy, Oseola Co., Pop. Code 2
Pine River Area SD
Sch. Sys. Enr. Code 4
Supt. – Lee Sandy
  5425 N PINE RIVER ROAD   49655
Pine River MS, 6375 N PINE RIVER   49655
  Ted Raven, prin.
ES, 408 GILBERT   49655 – James Cooper, prin.
Luther ES, 924 STATE ST   49656
  Steven Parker, prin.
Other Schools – See Tustin

Leslie, Ingham Co., Pop. Code 4
Leslie SD
Sch. Sys. Enr. Code 4
Supt. – Tom Dove, 432 N MAIN ST   49251
MS, 112 WOODWORTH ST   49251
  Donald Vickers, prin.
ES, 212 PENNSYLVANIA ST   49251
  Joy Finley, prin.

Lincoln, Alcona Co., Pop. Code 2
Alcona Comm. SD
Sch. Sys. Enr. Code 4
Supt. – John Cook
  330 TRAVERSE BAY ROAD   48742
Alcona ES, 181 N BARLOW RD   48742
  Robert Kennedy, prin.

Lincoln Park, Wayne Co., Pop. Code 8
Lincoln Park SD
Sch. Sys. Enr. Code 6
Supt. – Dr. Douglas Knight
  1545 SOUTHFIELD ROAD   48146
Carr ES, 3901 FERRIS AVE   48146
  Marianne Dioyk, prin.
Foote ES, 3529 ABBOTT AVE   48146
  Sharen Roulo, prin.
Hoover ES, 3750 HOWARD ST   48146
  Pat Cavanaugh, prin.
Horger ES, 1959 HORGER ST   48146
  Jack Popescu, prin.

Keppen ES, 661 MILL ST   48146
  Fred Howard, prin.
LaFayette ES, 1360 LAFAYETTE BLVD   48146
  Ray Genman, prin.
LeBlanc ES, 3804 HAZEL AVE   48146
  Thomas Henson, prin.
Mixter ES, 3301 ELECTRIC AVE   48146
  Carol Picklo, prin.
Paun ES, 2821 BAILEY AVE   48146
  Robert Redden, prin.
Raupp ES, 1351 ETHEL AVE   48146
  Gerald Farkas, prin.

Calvary ES, 3320 ELECTRIC AVE   48146
Christ the Good Shepard ES
  1590 RIVERBANK ST   48146

Linden, Genessee Co., Pop. Code 4
Linden Comm. SD
Sch. Sys. Enr. Code 4
Supt. – Robert Hahn, 202 N BRIDGE ST   48451
MS, 325 STAN EATON DRIVE   48451
  Keenan Simpson, prin.
Central ES, 7199 W SILVER LAKE RD   48451
  Larry Dobbs, prin.
ES, 400 N BRIDGE ST   48451 – D. Thompson, prin.

Litchfield, Hillsdale Co., Pop. Code 4
Litchfield Comm. SD
Sch. Sys. Enr. Code 3
Supt. – James Avery, P O BOX 207   49252
ES, P O BOX 207   49252 – James Honey, prin.

Livonia, Wayne Co., Pop. Code 9
Clarenceville SD
Sch. Sys. Enr. Code 4
Supt. – Michael Shibler
  20210 MIDDLEBELT ROAD   48152
Clarenceville MS
  20210 MIDDLEBELT ROAD   48152
  Daniel Kelly, prin.
Botsford ES, 19515 LATHERS ST   48152
  Jesse Baker, prin.
Grandview ES, 19814 LOUISE ST   48152
  David Kamish, prin.

Livonia SD
Sch. Sys. Enr. Code 7
Supt. – James Carli
  15125 FARMINGTON ROAD   48154
Emerson MS, 29100 W CHICAGO ST   48150
  Michael Fenshel, prin.
Frost MS, 14041 STARK ROAD   48154
  Herb Hutchison, prin.
Holmes MS, 16200 NEWBURGH ROAD   48154
  Richard Haertel, prin.
Riley MS, 1555 HENRY RUFF ROAD   48154
  John Kuenzel, prin.
Adams ES, 28201 LYNDON ST   48154
  C. Lamont, prin.
Buchanan ES, 16400 HUBBARD ST   48154
  Ronald Van Horn, prin.
Cass ES, 34633 MUNGER ST   48154
  Harriet Shogan, prin.
Cleveland ES, 28030 CATHEDRAL ST   48150
  Gloria Parrello, prin.
Coolidge ES, 30500 CURTIS ST   48152
  Willis Brauer, prin.
Garfield ES, 10218 ARTHUR ST   48150
  Karen Winters, prin.
Grant ES, 9300 HUBBARD ST   48150
  Kent Gage, prin.
Hoover ES, 15900 LEVAN RD   48154
  Richard Burnham, prin.
Hull ES, 34715 LYNDON ST   48154
  Richard Braun, prin.
Johnson ES, 36651 ANN ARBOR TRL   48150
  Donald Harris, prin.
Kennedy ES, 14201 HUBBARD ST   48154
  Joanne Hughes, prin.
Marshall ES, 33901 CURTIS ST   48152
  Nancy Allen, prin.
McKinley ES, 9101 HILLCREST ST   48150
  Jan Van Poperin, prin.
Randolph ES, 14470 NORMAN ST   48154
  James Lauer, prin.
Roosevelt ES, 30200 LYNDON ST   48154
  Bonnie Schweitzer, prin.
Taylor ES, 36611 CURTIS ST   48152
  Donald Clark, prin.
Tyler ES, 32401 PEMBROKE ST   48152
  John Daniel, prin.
Washington ES, 9449 HIX RD   48150
  Patricia Laarman, prin.
Other Schools – See Westland

St. Edith ES, 15089 NEWBURGH RD   48154
St. Genevieve ES, 28933 JAMISON ST   48154
St. Michael ES, 11499 FAIRFIELD ST   48150

Lowell, Kent Co., Pop. Code 5
Lowell Area SD
Sch. Sys. Enr. Code 5
Supt. – Fritz Esch, 12685 FOREMAN ST   49331
MS, 12675 FOREMAN ST   49331
  Dave Burdette, prin.
Bushnell ES, 700 ELIZABETH ST   49331
  Bill Kirby, prin.
Runciman ES, 300 HIGH ST   49331
  Louis Dudeck, prin.
Other Schools – See Alto

St. Mary ES, 322 AMITY ST   49331

Ludington, Mason Co., Pop. Code 6
Ludington Area SD
Sch. Sys. Enr. Code 5
Supt. – Dr. James Ford
  809 E TINKHAM AVE   49431
DeJonge MS, 706 E TINKHAM AVE   49431
  G. Morawski, prin.
Foster ES, 505 E FOSTER ST   49431
  Norbert Mengot, prin.
Franklin ES, 721 ANDERSON ST   49431
  Michal Brody, prin.
Lakeview ES, 502 W HAIGHT ST   49431
  David Pierce, prin.
Pere Marquette ES, 1115 S MADISON ST   49431
  Norbert Mengot, prin.
South Hamlin ES, 6498 W DECKER RD   49431
  David Pierce, prin.
Summit ES, 4966 W LATTIN RD   49449
  Michal Brody, prin.

Ludington Area Catholic ES
  700 E BRYANT RD   49431

Mackinac Island, Mackinac Co., Pop. Code 2
Mackinac Island SD
Sch. Sys. Enr. Code 1
Supt. – Bruce Wolck, P O BOX 340   49757
S, P O BOX 340   49757 – Bruce Wolck, prin.

Mackinaw City, Cheboygan Co., Pop. Code 2
Mackinaw City SD
Sch. Sys. Enr. Code 2
Supt. – Michael Bootz
  609 W CENTRAL AVE   49701
ES, 609 W CENTRAL   49701
  Leonard Oliver, prin.

Madison Heights, Oakland Co., Pop. Code 8
Lamphere SD
Sch. Sys. Enr. Code 4
Supt. – James McCann
  31201 DORCHESTER AVE   48071
Page MS, 29353 TAWAS ST   48071
  John Gatz, prin.
Edmonson ES, 621 E KATHERINE AVE   48071
  Rosemary Athoff, prin.
Hiller ES, 400 E LA SALLE AVE   48071
  Curtis Benham, prin.
Lessenger ES, 30150 CAMPBELL RD   48071
  Sherrie Jones, prin.
Simonds ES, 30000 ROSE ST   48071
  Denise Jenkins, prin.

Madison SD
Sch. Sys. Enr. Code 5
Supt. – Jack Myers, 25421 ALGER ST   48071
Wilkinson MS, 26524 JOHN ROAD   48071
  Dell Weitzel, prin.
Edison ES, 27321 HAMPDEN ST   48071
  Paul Lipson, prin.
Halfman ES, 25601 COUZENS AVE   48071
  William McCann, prin.
Schoenhals ES, 27107 HALES ST   48071
  R. Sikorsky, prin.

St. Vincent Ferrer ES
  1075 E GARDENIA AVE   48071

Mancelona, Antrim Co., Pop. Code 4
Mancelona SD
Sch. Sys. Enr. Code 3
Supt. – William Briggs
  112 SAINT JOHNS ST   49659
MS, 209 MICHIGAN AVE   49659
  John Fichtner, prin.
ES, 231 W LIMITS   49659 – Paul Miller, prin.

Manchester, Washtenaw Co., Pop. Code 4
Manchester Comm. SD
Sch. Sys. Enr. Code 4
Supt. – Ronald Niedzwiecki, 710 MAIN   48158
Ackerson MS, 410 CITY ROAD   48158
  Brian Shick, prin.
Klager ES, 405 ANN ARBOR HILL RD   48158
  Yvonne Henry, prin.

Manistee, Manistee Co., Pop. Code 6
Manistee Area SD
Sch. Sys. Enr. Code 4
Supt. – John Kucnzli, 550 MAPLE ST   49660
MS, 550 MAPLE ST   49660 – Suzette Lee, prin.
Central ES, 515 BRYANT AVE   49660
  Leroy Libby, prin.
North MS, 610 PARKDALE AVE E   49660
  Jim Sibley, prin.
South ES, 1309 MADISON RD   49660
  Jack Anderson, prin.

Manistee Catholic ES, 1500 US 31 S   49660
Trinity Lutheran School, 420 OAK STREET   49660

Manistique, Schoolcraft Co., Pop. Code 5
Manistique Area SD
Sch. Sys. Enr. Code 4
Supt. – Herb Harroun, CEDAR & MAIN STS   49854
MS, CEDAR AND MAIN STS   49854
  Michael Jarski, prin.
Fairview ES, RIVER RD   49854
  Linda Levine, prin.
Hiawatha ES, RURAL ROUTE 01   49854
  Jeanne Hermes, prin.
Lakeside ES, OAK ST   49854
  Michael Flynn, prin.
Lincoln ES, DEER ST   49854
  Kenneth Zellar, prin.

St. Francis De Sales ES, 220 LAKE ST 49854

Manton, Wexford Co., Pop. Code 4
Manton Cons. SD
Sch. Sys. Enr. Code 3
Supt. – Lyle Spalding, 105 5TH ST 49663
ES, P O BOX 280 49663 – Jerry Sinkel, prin.

Maple City, Leelanau Co., Pop. Code 2
Glen Lake Comm. SD
Sch. Sys. Enr. Code 3
Supt. – James Gillette, RURAL ROUTE 02 49664
Glen Lake MS 49664 – (—), prin.
Glen Lake ES, RURAL ROUTE 02 49664
Zita Shipman, prin.

Marcellus, Cass Co., Pop. Code 4
Marcellus Comm. SD
Sch. Sys. Enr. Code 3
Supt. – Thomas Lamb, P O BOX 48 49067
MS, P O BOX 48 49067 – Michael Johnson, prin.
ES, P O BOX 48 49067 – Margaret Husa, prin.

Marenisco, Gogebic Co., Pop. Code 3
Marenisco SD
Sch. Sys. Enr. Code 2
Supt. – Don Parline, P O BOX 188 49947
ES 49947 – Otto Bufe, prin.

Marine City, St. Clair Co., Pop. Code 5
East China SD
Sch. Sys. Enr. Code 5
Supt. – Jon Schuster, 1585 MEISNER ROAD 48039
Belle River ES, 1601 CHARTIER RD 48039
Delbert Krueger, prin.
Palms ES, 6101 PALMS RD 48039
Elizabeth Harvey, prin.
Washington ES, 403 N MARY ST 48039
Virginia Kyro, prin.
Other Schools – See Saint Clair

Holy Cross School, 660 S WATER ST 48039

Marion, Osceola Co., Pop. Code 3
Marion SD
Sch. Sys. Enr. Code 3
Supt. – J. G. Schwartz, 510 W MAIN 49665
ES, 510 W MAIN ST 49665
R. D. McLean, Jr., prin.

Marlette, Sanilac Co., Pop. Code 4
Marlette Comm. SD
Sch. Sys. Enr. Code 4
Supt. – Donald Kanicki, 3051 MOORE ST 48453
MS, 6230 EUCLID ST 48453 – Jon Moore, prin.
McDonald ES, 3197 STERLING ST 48453
Nick Miu, prin.

Marne, Ottawa Co.
Kenowa Hills SD
Supt. – See Grand Rapids
Marne ES, 14141 STATE ST 49435
Richard Doyle, prin.

Marquette, Marquette Co., Pop. Code 7
Marquette SD
Sch. Sys. Enr. Code 5
Supt. – Thomas Gill, 1201 W FAIR AVE 49855
Bothwell MS, 1200 TIERNEY ST 49855
Robert Lantz, prin.
Fisher ES, 143 FISHER ST 49855
Esther Johnson, prin.
Parkview ES, 320 E HEWITT AVE 49855
John Arenz, prin.
Sandy Knoll ES, 401 N 6TH ST 49855
George Ruuska, prin.
Silver Creek ES, 219 SILVER CREEK RD 49855
Sam Oslund, prin.
Vandenboom ES, 2000 ERIE AVE 49855
Ken Martin, prin.
Whitman ES, 1400 NORWAY AVE 49855
Judy Hanson, prin.

Bishop Baraga ES, 500 S 4TH ST 49855
St. Michael ES, 414 W COLLEGE AVE 49855

Marshall, Calhoun Co., Pop. Code 6
Mar Lee SD
Sch. Sys. Enr. Code 2
Supt. – William Le Tarte, 21236 H DRIVE N 49068
Mar Lee ES, 21236 H DR N 49068 – (—), prin.

Marshall SD
Sch. Sys. Enr. Code 4
Supt. – Louis Giannunzio, 100 E GREEN ST 49068
MS, 100 E GREEN ST 49068
Dennis Osborne, prin.
Gordon PS, 400 N GORDON ST 49068
William Church, prin.
Hughes PS, 103 W HUGHES ST 49068
John Marsh, prin.
Madison MS, 100 E GREEN 49068
Lorna Giant, prin.
Shearman PS, 624 W MANSION ST 49068
Ione Candit, prin.

Martin, Allegan Co., Pop. Code 2
Martin SD
Sch. Sys. Enr. Code 3
Supt. – David Peden, 1619 UNIVERSITY 49070
Brandon ES, UNIVERSITY & TEMPLETON 49070
Ruth Rowe, prin.

Marysville, St. Clair Co., Pop. Code 6
Marysville SD
Sch. Sys. Enr. Code 4
Supt. – Charles Andrews
1111 DELAWARE AVE 48040
MS, 400 STADIUM DRIVE 48040
Keith Mino, prin.
Gardens ES, 905 SIXTEENTH ST 48040
Kenneth Oates, prin.
Washington ES, 905 SIXTEENTH ST 48040
F. Black, prin.

Mason, Ingham Co., Pop. Code 6
Mason SD
Sch. Sys. Enr. Code 5
Supt. – Glenn Doran, 118 OAK ST W 48854
MS, 235 TEMPLE ST 48854 – John Borgert, prin.
Alaiedon ES, 1723 OKEMOS RD 48854
Dwight Sinila, prin.
Cedar ES, 400 S CEDAR ST 48854
O. Creaser, prin.
North Aurelius ES, 115 AURELIUS RD 48854
Gary Peraino, prin.
Steele ES, 531 STEELE ST 48854
James Tobe, prin.

Mass City, Ontonagon Co.
Ontonagon Area SD
Supt. – See Ontonagon
Mass ES 49948 – James Ollila, prin.

Mattawan, Van Buren Co., Pop. Code 4
Mattawan Cons. SD
Sch. Sys. Enr. Code 4
Supt. – J. Weeldreyer, 370 MURRAY ST 49071
MS, 370 MURRAY ST 49071
William McNulty, prin.
ES, 56720 MURRAY ST 49071
Sharon Otto, prin.

Mayville, Tuscola Co., Pop. Code 3
Mayville Comm. SD
Sch. Sys. Enr. Code 4
Supt. – Lawrence Geiger, 6015 FULTON ST 48744
MS, 6210 FULTON ST 48744
Douglas Foote, prin.
ES, 104 ORCHARD 48744 – Robert Turak, prin.

Mc Bain, Missaukee Co., Pop. Code 3
McBain Rural Agr. SD
Sch. Sys. Enr. Code 3
Supt. – Howard Napp, 107 E MAPLE ST 49657
ES, 107 E MAPLE ST 49657 – John Chopard, prin.

Northern Michigan Christian HS 49657

Mears, Oceana Co.
Hart SD
Supt. – See Hart
Golden ES 49436 – Jane Thocher, prin.

Mecosta, Mecosta Co., Pop. Code 2
Chippewa Hills SD
Supt. – See Remus
ES, 555 W MAIN 49332 – Harry Howard, prin.

Melvindale, Wayne Co., Pop. Code 7
Melvindale-Northern Allen Park SD
Sch. Sys. Enr. Code 4
Supt. – E. James Rynearson
18530 PROSPECT ST 48122
Strong MS, 3303 OAKWOOD BLVD 48122
William Fluharty, prin.
Evans ES, 17415 ROBERT ST 48122
Donald Weber, prin.
Palmer ES, 19001 PALMER ST 48122
Sally Wilson, prin.
Other Schools – See Allen Park

St. Mary Magdalen ES, 19635 WOOD ST 48122

Memphis, St. Clair Co., Pop. Code 2
Memphis Comm. SD
Sch. Sys. Enr. Code 3
Supt. – George Jacob
34110 BORDMAN ROAD 48041
MS, 34165 BORDMAN ROAD 48041
Kenneth Reygaert, prin.
ES, 34100 BORDMAN RD 48041
James Rhodes, prin.

Mendon, St. Joseph Co., Pop. Code 3
Mendon Comm. SD
Sch. Sys. Enr. Code 3
Supt. – David McNeill, 26393 KIRBY ROAD 49072
ES, 302 LANE ST 49072 – Lee Fassett, prin.

Menominee, Menominee Co., Pop. Code 7
Menominee Area SD
Sch. Sys. Enr. Code 4
Supt. – Randall Neelis
13TH ST AT 13TH AVE 49858
MS, 13TH ST AT 13TH AVE 49858
Wayne Anttile, prin.
Central ES, 2100 18TH AVE 49858
Sheryl Cadieu, prin.
Lincoln ES, 1700 26TH 49858
Carl Mattoon, prin.
Roosevelt ES, EIGHTH AVE 49858
Carl Mattoon, prin.

Catholic Central ES, 1406 10TH AVE 49858

Merrill, Saginaw Co., Pop. Code 3
Merrill Comm. SD
Sch. Sys. Enr. Code 4
Supt. – Bernie Stelter, P O BOX 488 48637

MS, 755 W ALICE ST 48637 – Keith Clark, prin.
ES, 325 W ALICE ST 48637
Connie O'Toole, prin.

Mesick, Wexford Co., Pop. Code 2
Mesick Cons. SD
Sch. Sys. Enr. Code 3
Supt. – George Hubbard, 210 MESICK AVE 49668
Jewett ES, P O BOX 275 49668
Ronald Ford, prin.

Metamora, Lapeer Co., Pop. Code 3
Lapeer Comm. SD
Supt. – See Lapeer
Murphy ES, 1100 PRATT RD 48455
Nyla McAlpine, prin.

Michigan Center, Jackson Co., Pop. Code 5
Michigan Center SD
Sch. Sys. Enr. Code 4
Supt. – Monte Anderson, 400 S STATE ST 49254
Arnold ES, 4064 PAGE AVE 49254
John Jimenez, prin.
Keicher ES, 137 BROAD ST 49254
Diane Dray, prin.

Lady of Fatima ES, 911 NAPOLEON RD 49254

Middleton, Gratiot Co., Pop. Code 3
Fulton SD
Sch. Sys. Enr. Code 3
Supt. – Fred Cunningham
8060 ELY HIGHWAY 48856
Fulton ES, 8060 ELY HWY 48856
William Breckenfeld, prin.

Middleville, Barry Co., Pop. Code 4
Thornapple Kellogg SD
Sch. Sys. Enr. Code 4
Supt. – Stephen Gorrett
3885 BENDER ROAD 49333
Thornapple Kellogg MS, 509 W MAIN 49333
Joseph Sanford, prin.
McFall PS, 509 W MAIN 49333
William Rich, prin.
Page ES, 3887 BENDER RD 49333
Tony McLain, prin.
West PS, 509 W MAIN ST 49333 – William Rich, prin.

Midland, Midland Co., Pop. Code 8
Bullock Creek SD
Sch. Sys. Enr. Code 4
Supt. – John Trumbell
1519 S BADOUR ROAD 48640
Bullock Creek MS, 644 S BADOUR ROAD 48640
Greg Climie, prin.
Bullock Creek ES, 1037 POSEYVILLE RD 48640
Rose Burleson, prin.
Floyd ES, 725 S EIGHT MILE RD 48640
Carl Spalding, prin.
Pine River ES, 1894 W PRAIRIE CREEK RD 48640
Rose Burleson, prin.

Midland SD
Sch. Sys. Enr. Code 6
Supt. – Arthur Frock
600 E CARPENTER ST 48640
Adams ES, 1005 ADAMS DR 48640
Frank Perry, prin.
Carpenter ES, 1407 W CARPENTER ST 48640
Gary Ohlrich, prin.
Chestnut Hill ES
3900 CHESTNUT HILL DR 48640
Garry Veit, prin.
Chippewassee ES, 919 SMITH ST 48640
David Powell, prin.
Cook ES, 5500 PERRINE RD 48640
J. Prewozniak, prin.
Eastlawn ES, 115 EASTLAWN DR 48640
Larry Serrell, prin.
Longview ES, 337 LEMKE ST 48640
M. Fryar, prin.
Mills ES, 3329 E BAKER RD 48640
Paula Jorge, prin.
Parkdale ES, 1609 EASTLAWN DR 48640
Norman Dahl, prin.
Plymouth ES, 1105 E SUGNET RD 48640
David Chapin, prin.
Siebert ES, 5700 SIEBERT ST 48640
Michael Frazee, prin.
Woodcrest ES, 5500 DRAKE ST 48640
John Glines, prin.

Midland Christian School
4417 W WACKERLY ROAD 48640
Blessed Sacrament ES, 3109 SWEDE RD 48640
St. Brigid ES, 130 W LARKIN 48640
St. John ES, 505 E CARPENTER ST 48640

Milan, Washtenaw Co., Pop. Code 5
Milan Area SD
Sch. Sys. Enr. Code 4
Supt. – Clayton Symons, 920 NORTH ST 48160
MS, 432 PLATT ST S 48160 – D. Pennington, prin.
Paddock ES, 707 MARVIN ST 48160
Kathryn May, prin.

Milford, Oakland Co., Pop. Code 6
Huron Valley SD
Sch. Sys. Enr. Code 6
Supt. – James Doyle
2390 N MILFORD ROAD 48042
Muir MS, 425 GEORGE ST 48042
Christine Hoben, prin.
White Lake MS, 1450 BOGIE LAKE ROAD 48042
Ed Jaworowicz, prin.

Apollo ES, 2029 S MILFORD RD　48042
　Larry Adams, prin.
Baker ES, 716 UNION ST　48042
　Frank Bateman, prin.
Brooks ES, 1000 HILL RD　48042 – Pat Parish, prin.
Duck Lake Center ES
　5061 S DUCK LAKE RD　48042
　Eldon Vanspybrook, prin.
Highland ES, 300 LIVINGSTON RD　48031
　Julie Sajo, prin.
Johnson ES, 515 GENERAL MOTORS RD　48042
　Sue Gumpper, prin.
Kurtz ES, 425 BURNS RD　48042
　Frank Bateman, prin.
Lakewood ES, 1500 BOGIE LAKE RD　48042
　Fred Forsythe, prin.
Oxbow ES, 100 OXBOW LAKE RD　48055
　Bill Rose, prin.
Other Schools – See Highland

Millersburg, Presque Isle Co., Pop. Code 2
　Onaway Area SD
　Supt. – See Onaway
　ES　49759 – D. Wickstrom, prin.

Millington, Tuscola Co., Pop. Code 4
　Millington Comm. SD
　Sch. Sys. Enr. Code 4
　Supt. – Rob Peterson
　　8655 GLEASON ROAD　48746
　MS, 8537 GLEASON ROAD　48746
　　Donald Zoller, prin.
　Glaza ES, 8655 GLEASON RD　48746
　　Dale Cleland, prin.
　Kirk IS, 8664 DEAN DR　48746 – (—), prin.

　St. Paul ES, 4941 CENTER ST　48746

Mio, Oscoda Co., Pop. Code 2
　Mio-AuSable SD
　Sch. Sys. Enr. Code 3
　Supt. – R. B. Rank, P O BOX 158　48647
　Mio Ausable ES, P O BOX 909　48647
　　Kayleen Hill, prin.

Mohawk, Keweenaw Co.
　Calumet-Laurium & Keweenaw SD
　Supt. – See Calumet
　Keweenaw ES, STANTON AVE　49950
　　Donald Karvonen, prin.

Moline, Allegan Co.
　Wayland Un. SD
　Supt. – See Wayland
　ES, 1148 FIRST ST　49335 – J. Wallington, prin.

　Moline Christian ES, 1253100 44TH AVE　49335

Monroe, Monroe Co., Pop. Code 7
　Jefferson SD
　Sch. Sys. Enr. Code 5
　Supt. – Jon Rhoades
　　5102 STONEY CREEK ROAD N　48161
　Jefferson MS, 5102 STONY CREEK ROAD N　48161
　　Charles Kennon, prin.
　Hurd ES, 1960 E HURD RD　48161
　　Barbara Pursley, prin.
　Sodt ES, 2888 NADEAU RD　48161
　　Allen Pearsall, prin.

　Monroe SD
　Sch. Sys. Enr. Code 6
　Supt. – William Chamberlain
　　1275 MACOMB ST N　48161
　Cantrick IS, 1008 RIVERVIEW ST　48161
　　Blaine Zimmerman, prin.
　Christiancy ES, 306 LINCOLN AVE　48161
　　Barry Martin, prin.
　Custer #1 IS, 5003 ALBAIN W #1　48161
　　Mary Kay Kosa, prin.
　Custer #2 ES, 5001 ALBAIN W #2　48161
　　Richard Kleinsmith, prin.
　Hollywood ES, 1135 RIVERVIEW ST　48161
　　Jane Karau, prin.
　Lincoln ES, 908 E 2ND ST　48161
　　Ronald Frank, prin.
　Manor ES, 1731 W LORAIN ST　48161
　　Robert Schultz, prin.
　Raisinville ES, 2300 N RAISINVILLE RD　48161
　　John Salisbury, prin.
　Riverside ES, 77 N ROESSLER ST　48161
　　Leslie Northrop, prin.
　South Monroe ES, 15488 EASTWOOD DR　48161
　　Terry Semones, prin.
　Waterloo ES, 1933 S CUSTER RD　48161
　　Verna Anible, prin.

　Holy Ghost Lutheran School
　　3563 HEISS ROAD　48161
　St. John ES, 521 S MONROE ST　48161
　St. Mary Parish ES, 151 N MONROE ST　48161
　St. Michael ES, 510 W FRONT　48161
　Trinity ES, 315 SCOTT ST　48161

Montague, Muskegon Co., Pop. Code 4
　Montague Area SD
　Sch. Sys. Enr. Code 4
　Supt. – Joe Winger, 4900 STANTON BLVD　49437
　N.B.C. MS, 4700 STANTON BLVD　49437
　　Gary Beaudoin, prin.
　Oehrli ES, 4859 KNUDSON ST　49437
　　Dale Schreuder, prin.

Montrose, Genesee Co., Pop. Code 4
　Montrose Comm. SD
　Sch. Sys. Enr. Code 4
　Supt. – Fraser Dean, 300 NANITA ST　48457
　Kuehn-Haven MS, 309 ROY ST　48457
　　Dan Cwayna, prin.
　Carter ES, 200 PARK ST　48457 – Carol Fox, prin.

Morenci, Lenawee Co., Pop. Code 4
　Morenci Area SD
　Sch. Sys. Enr. Code 4
　Supt. – Neal V. Singles, 500 PAGE ST　49256
　MS, CONGRESS ST　49256 – Ronald Morillat, prin.
　ES, LOCUST ST　49256 – Nancy Horstman, prin.

Morley, Mecosta Co., Pop. Code 3
　Morley-Stanwood Comm. SD
　Sch. Sys. Enr. Code 4
　Supt. – Philip Crouse
　　4808 NORTHLAND DRIVE　49336
　ES, 151 E 7TH ST　49336 – Randall Lapreze, prin.
　Other Schools – See Stanwood

Morrice, Shiawassee Co., Pop. Code 3
　Morrice Area SD
　Sch. Sys. Enr. Code 3
　Supt. – Dale Howard, 691 PURDY LANE　48857
　ES, 111 MASON ST　48857 – Zel Seidenburg, prin.

Mount Clemens, Macomb Co., Pop. Code 7
　Chippewa Valley SD
　Sch. Sys. Enr. Code 6
　Supt. – James Rivard, 19120 CASS AVE　48044
　Algonquin MS, 19159 BRIARWOOD LANE　48043
　　John Savel, prin.
　Wyandot MS, 39490 GARFIELD ROAD　48044
　　Michael Samulski, prin.
　Clinton Valley ES, 1260 MULBERRY ST　48043
　　G. Gangler/Brown, prin.
　Fox ES, 17500 MILLSTONE DR　48044
　　Richard Zaranek, prin.
　Huron ES, 15800 TERRA BELLA ST　48044
　　Robert Plough, prin.
　Miami ES, 41290 KENTVALE DR　48044
　　Dan Martini, prin.
　Ojibwa ES, 46950 HEYDENREICH RD　48044
　　J. Scott Burns, prin.
　Ottawa ES, 18601 MILLAR RD　48043
　　Kathryn Dugall, prin.
　Other Schools – See Utica

　Clintondale Comm. SD
　Sch. Sys. Enr. Code 5
　Supt. – Raymond Contesti
　　35100 LITTLE MACK AVE　48043
　Clintondale MS, 35300 LITTLE MACK AVE　48043
　　Sheila Apisa, prin.
　Little Mack ES, 34950 LITTLE MACK AVE　48043
　　R. Muldrow, prin.
　McGlinnen ES, 21415 SUNNYVIEW ST　48043
　　Eddie Salem, prin.
　Parker ES, 22055 QUINN RD　48043
　　(—), prin.
　Rainbow ES, 33749 WURFEL ST　48043
　　W. McPherson, prin.

　Fraser SD
　Supt. – See Fraser
　Disney ES, 36155 KELLY RD　48043
　　Robert Peterson, prin.

　L'Anse Creuse SD
　Sch. Sys. Enr. Code 6
　Supt. – Francis A. Higgins
　　36727 JEFFERSON AVE　48045
　L'Anse Creuse South MS
　　34641 JEFFERSON AVE　48045
　　Ron Johnson, prin.
　Atwood ES, 45690 NORTH AVE　48045
　　L. Fanning, prin.
　Chesterfield ES, 25925 23 MILE RD　48045
　　A. Kummerow, prin.
　Graham ES, 25555 CROCKER BLVD　48045
　　Wayne Wrona, prin.
　Green ES, 47260 SUGARBUSH RD　48045
　　Daniel Sapp, prin.
　Lobbestael ES, 38495 PRENTISS ST　48045
　　J. Cambridge, prin.
　South River ES, 27733 S RIVER RD　48045
　　Pat Rabenburg, prin.
　Tenniswood ES, 23450 GLENWOOD ST　48043
　　Joe Carkenord, prin.
　Yacks ES, 34700 UNION LAKE RD　48045
　　Gerald Starkey, prin.

　Mount Clemens Comm. SD
　Sch. Sys. Enr. Code 5
　Supt. – Blanche Fraser, 167 CASS AVE　48043
　MS, 11 GRAND　48043 – Arthur Stone, prin.
　Macomb ES, 11 GRAND AVE　48043
　　Nelson Jackson, prin.
　Seminole ES, 1500 MULBERRY ST　48043
　　Warren Opel, prin.
　Washington ES, 196 N ROSE ST　48043
　　Lyn Hart, prin.

　Immanuel ES, 47120 ROMEO PLANK RD　48044
　St. Luke ES, 21400 S NUNNELEY RD　48043
　St. Mary ES, 98 NEW ST　48043
　St. Peter ES, 17051 24 MILE RD　48044
　St. Thecla ES, 20762 S NUNNELEY RD　48043
　Trinity ES, 38900 HARPER AVE　48043

Mount Morris, Genesee Co., Pop. Code 5
　Beecher Comm. SD
　Supt. – See Flint

　Dolan MS, 6255 NEFF ROAD　48458
　　DeWain Molter, prin.
　Dailey ES, 6236 NEFF RD　48458
　　David Steel, prin.

　Mount Morris Cons. SD
　Sch. Sys. Enr. Code 5
　Supt. – David Lawrence
　　12356 WALTER ST　48458
　MS, 12356 WALTER ST　48458 – Karyn Ford, prin.
　Central IS, 1000 GENESEE ST　48458
　　Kenneth Konesny, prin.
　Montague ES, 344 MORRIS ST　48458
　　Peggy O'Keefe, prin.
　Moore ES, 1201 WISNER ST　48458
　　Richard Murray, prin.
　Pinehurst ES, 1013 PINEHURST BLVD　48458
　　Burton Jones, prin.

　St. Mary ES, 11208 N SAGINAW ST　48458

Mount Pleasant, Isabella Co., Pop. Code 7
　Beal City SD
　Sch. Sys. Enr. Code 3
　Supt. – Carl Mayes, 3117 ELIAS ROAD　48858
　Beal City ES, 3117 ELIAS RD　48858
　　Sally White, prin.

　Mount Pleasant SD
　Sch. Sys. Enr. Code 5
　Supt. – Robert Janson
　　201 S UNIVERSITY AVE　48858
　West MS, 401 S BRADLEY ROAD　48858
　　Ted Jennings, prin.
　Fancher ES, 801 S KINNEY AVE　48858
　　Robert Decker, prin.
　Ganiard ES, 101 S ADAMS ST　48858
　　Tom Crawford, prin.
　McGuire ES, CROSSLANES & ISABELLA　48458
　　Richard Stokes, prin.
　Pullen ES, 251 S BROWN ST　48858
　　Kathleen Howell, prin.
　Rosebush ES, 3771 N MISSION　48458
　　Michael Linsday, prin.
　Vowles ES, 3800 S WATSON　48458
　　William Walters, prin.

　Sacred Heart Academy
　　200 S FRANKLIN ST　48858
　St. Joseph the Worker-Beal ES
　　2121 N WINN RD　48858

Mulliken, Eaton Co., Pop. Code 3
　Grand Ledge SD
　Supt. – See Grand Ledge
　ES, 400 CHARLOTTE ST　48861
　　William Thorson, prin.

Munising, Alger Co., Pop. Code 5
　Munising SD
　Sch. Sys. Enr. Code 4
　Supt. – George Truckey, P O BOX 70　49862
　Mather MS, P O BOX 70　49862
　　Steve Cromwell, prin.
　Central ES, CHOCOLAY ST　49862
　　Beth Vezzetti, prin.

Munith, Jackson Co.
　Stockbridge Comm. SD
　Supt. – See Stockbridge
　Katz ES, 11120 MUSBACH RD　49259
　　Robert Roberts, prin.

Muskegon, Muskegon Co., Pop. Code 8
　Fruitport Comm. SD
　Supt. – See Fruitport
　Beach ES, 2741 HTS RAVENNA　49444
　　Norm Heerema, prin.
　Shettler ES, 2187 SHETTLER RD　49444
　　David Kolberg, prin.

　Mona Shores SD
　Sch. Sys. Enr. Code 5
　Supt. – Gerard E. Keidel
　　3374 MCCRACKEN ST　49441
　Mona Shores MS, 1700 WOODSIDE ROAD　49441
　　Richard Jelier, prin.
　Campbell ES, 1355 GREENWICH　49441
　　R. Vanderscheer, prin.
　Hile ES, 891 HILE RD　49441
　　Thomas Powers, prin.
　Lincoln Park ES, 2951 LEON ST　49441
　　Tresea Goff, prin.
　Porter ES, 961 PORTER RD　49441
　　R. Nyenhuis, prin.

　Muskegon SD
　Sch. Sys. Enr. Code 6
　Supt. – James Agee, 349 WEBSTER AVE W　49440
　Angell ES, 571 E APPLE AVE　49442
　　Billy Scott, prin.
　Bluffton ES, 1875 WATERWORKS RD　49441
　　Paul Dehorn, prin.
　Glenside ES, 1213 W HACKLEY AVE　49441
　　Donald Roelofs, prin.
　Marquette ES, 480 BENNETT ST　49442
　　Susan Meston, prin.
　McLaughlin ES, 125 CATHERINE AVE　49442
　　Ann Schimke, prin.
　Moon ES, 1826 HOYT ST　49442
　　Daniel Poort, prin.
　Nelson ES, 550 W GRAND AVE　49441
　　Diana Groters, prin.
　Nims ES, 1161 W SOUTHERN AVE　49441
　　J. Vanderwall, prin.

Oakview ES, 1420 MADISON ST 49442
James McClain, prin.
Phillips ES, 349 W WEBSTER 49444
L. Humphreys, prin.

Oakridge SD
Sch. Sys. Enr. Code 4
Supt. – Edwin Bredeweg
481 WOLF LAKE ROAD S 49442
Oakridge MS, 481 WOLF LAKE ROAD S 49442
Rob Goryl, prin.
Carr ES, 1051 CARR RD 49442
Thomas Pastoor, prin.
Wolf Lake ES, 5290 BRYN MAWR PL 49442
James Morris, prin.

Orchard View SD
Sch. Sys. Enr. Code 4
Supt. – Gary Sarut
2310 MARQUETTE AVE 49442
Orchard View MS, 35 S SHERIDAN DRIVE 49442
P. Engblade, prin.
Jolman ES, 2389 E LAKETON AVE 49442
William Closz, prin.
Orchard View ES, 1074 SHONAT ST 49442
Gerald Walter, prin.

Reeths-Puffer SD
Supt. – See North Muskegon
Central MS, 1807 W GILES 49445
Thomas Hornik, prin.
Duck Creek ES, 4600 GIBSON RD 49445
Paul Hoppa, prin.
McMillan ES, 2885 HYDE PARK RD 49445
Paul Hoppa, prin.
Pennsylvania ES
2500 PENNSYLVANIA AVE 49445
Paul Hoppa, prin.
Reeths Puffer ES, 1500 N GETTY ST 49445
Gerald Brichan, prin.
Twin Lake ES, 1807 W GILES RD 49445
Frank Lundell, prin.

Muskegon Christian ES
1220 EASTGATE ST 49442
Our Lady of Grace ES, 495 S GETTY ST 49442
Our Redeemer ES, 1128 ROBERTS ST 49442
St. Francis DeSales ES
2947 MCCRACKEN ST 49441
St. Michael ES, 215 W DALE AVE 49441
Trinity ES, 1501 WOODSIDE 49441

Muskegon Heights, Muskegon Co., Pop. Code 7
Muskegon Heights SD
Sch. Sys. Enr. Code 5
Supt. – John Syndor, 2603 LEAHY ST 49444
MS, 2600 PECK ST 49444 – Nathan Allen, prin.
Edgewood ES, 3028 HOWDEN ST 49444
Janice Walker, prin.
Glendale ES, JEFFERSON AVE 49444
T. Beukiecz, prin.
King ES, BARNEY AVE 49444
Joseph Ward, prin.
Loftis ES 49444 – (—), prin.
Lindbergh ES, BARNEY AVE 49444
Alexander Davis, prin.
Roosevelt ES, SUMMIT AVE 49444
Sandra Earley, prin.

Sacred Heart ES, 2913 HOYT ST 49444

Napoleon, Jackson Co., Pop. Code 6
Napoleon Comm. SD
Sch. Sys. Enr. Code 4
Supt. – Robert Hard, 212 EAST AVE 49261
JHS, 204 WEST AVE 49261 – Jack Louden, prin.
Ezra ES, 220 WEST AVE 49261
Cynthia Duby, prin.

Nashville, Barry Co., Pop. Code 4
Maple Valley SD
Supt. – See Vermontville
Kellogg ES, QUEEN ST 49073
Nancy Potter, prin.

National Mine, Marquette Co.
Nice Comm. SD
Supt. – See Ishpeming
ES, P O BOX B 49865 – Maxine Mine, prin.

Negaunee, Marquette Co., Pop. Code 6
Negaunee SD
Sch. Sys. Enr. Code 4
Supt. – Don Mourand, 101 S PIONEER AVE 49866
MS, CASE ST 49866 – R. Trebilcock, prin.
Lakeview ES, 200 CROIX ST 49866
Werner Peterson, prin.
Other Schools – See Palmer

Newaygo, Newaygo Co., Pop. Code 4
Newaygo SD
Sch. Sys. Enr. Code 4
Supt. – Ralph Burde, 360 S MILL ST 49337
MS, 25 PARK ST 49337 – John Strahl, prin.
Wilsie ES, 140 MAIN ST 49337 – Jack Long, prin.

New Baltimore, Macomb Co., Pop. Code 6
Anchor Bay SD
Sch. Sys. Enr. Code 5
Supt. – E. Bruce, 52801 ASHLEY ST 48047
Anchor Bay JHS, 52801 ASHLEY ST 48047
Steven Lutz, prin.
Anchor Bay ES, 52347 ASHLEY ST 48047
Dianne Pellerin, prin.
Anchor Bay MS, 51880 WASHINGTON ST 48047
Lana Callihan, prin.

Naldrett ES, 47800 SUGARBUSH RD 48047
Linda Lang, prin.
Schmidt ES, 33700 HOOKER RD 48047
James Huset, prin.
Sugarbush ES, 48400 SUGARBUSH RD 48047
Pamara Babcock, prin.

Newberry, Luce Co., Pop. Code 4
Tahquamenon Area SD
Sch. Sys. Enr. Code 4
Supt. – F. Lamb, 700 NEWBERRY AVE 49868
MS, 700 NEWBERRY AVE 49868
William Peltier, prin.
ES, 700 NEWBERRY AVE 49868
Ralph Crosslin, prin.
Other Schools – See Curtis

New Boston, Wayne Co., Pop. Code 4
Huron SD
Sch. Sys. Enr. Code 4
Supt. – Gary Jackson
32044 HURON RIVER DRIVE 48164
Renton JHS, 31578 HURON RIVER DRIVE 48164
William Balwinski, prin.
Brown ES, 25485 MIDDLEBELT RD 48164
Gary Holtan, prin.
Miller ES, 18955 HANNAN RD 48164
William Miller, prin.

St. John ES, 28320 WALTZ RD 48164
St. Stephen ES, 18800 HURON RIVER DR 48164

New Buffalo, Berrien Co., Pop. Code 5
New Buffalo Area SD
Sch. Sys. Enr. Code 3
Supt. – Elmer Gough, 222 W DETROIT ST 49117
ES, W DETROIT ST 49117 – Robert Heit, prin.

St. Mary of the Lake ES
704 W MERCHANT ST 49117

New Era, Oceana Co., Pop. Code 2
Shelby SD
Supt. – See Shelby
ES, HILLCREST DR 49445 – Todd Kraai, prin.

New Haven, Macomb Co., Pop. Code 4
New Haven Comm. SD
Sch. Sys. Enr. Code 4
Supt. – Dr. Irwin Sutter, 30375 CLARK ST 48048
MS, 30375 CLARK ST 48048
Thomas Winkel, prin.
Siefert ES, 24255 26 MILE RD 48048
Thomas Winkel, prin.

New Lothrop, Shiawassee Co., Pop. Code 3
New Lothrop Area SD
Sch. Sys. Enr. Code 3
Supt. – Craig Younkman
9285 EASTON ROAD 48460
ES, 9435 BEECH ST 48460 – Robert Arnold, prin.

Newport, Monroe Co.
Airport Comm. SD
Supt. – See Carleton
Niedermeier ES, 8400 S NEWPORT RD 48166
Karen Budan, prin.

St. Charles ES, 8125 SWAN CREEK RD 48166

New Troy, Berrien Co.
River Valley SD
Supt. – See Three Oaks
ES, 13430 CALIFORNIA 49119
N. Richardson, prin.

Niles, Berrien Co., Pop. Code 7
Brandywine SD
Sch. Sys. Enr. Code 4
Supt. – John Carlson, 1700 BELL ROAD 49120
Brandywine ES, 2428 S 13TH ST 49120
Melba Ross, prin.

Niles Comm. SD
Sch. Sys. Enr. Code 5
Supt. – John Huffman, 111 SPRUCE ST 49120
Lardner MS, 801 N 17TH ST 49120
Sherwood Quick, prin.
Ballard ES, 1601 CHICAGO RD 49120
John Ostrowski, prin.
Eastside ES, 315 N 14TH ST 49120
Ronald Pletcher, prin.
Ellis ES, 2740 MANNIX ST 49120
Ronald Pletcher, prin.
Howard MS, 2788 MANNIX ST 49120
B. Garrard, prin.
Oak Manor ES, TYLER ST 49120
Frank Nowak, prin.

St. Mary ES, 217 S LINCOLN AVE 49120

North Adams, Hillsdale Co., Pop. Code 3
North Adams-Jerome SD
Sch. Sys. Enr. Code 3
Supt. – Woodrow Hall
451 KNOWLES ROAD 49262
North Adams-Jerome ES, 110 S HILLSDALE 49262
Ronald Boone, prin.

North Branch, Lapeer Co., Pop. Code 3
North Branch Area SD
Sch. Sys. Enr. Code 4
Supt. – D. A. Gleeson, 6600 BRUSH ST 48461
Fox JHS, 6570 BRUSH ST 48461
Larry Lambert, prin.
ES, 3960 BANKER ST 48421
R. Van Haaften, prin.

Sweet ES, 473 BARNES LAKE RD 48421
Al Piwinski, prin.

North Muskegon, Muskegon Co., Pop. Code 5
North Muskegon SD
Sch. Sys. Enr. Code 3
Supt. – Barbara Gowell, 1600 MILLS AVE 49445
ES, 1600 MILLS AVE 49445 – Phil Rogers, prin.

Reeths-Puffer SD
Sch. Sys. Enr. Code 5
Supt. – Peter Wharton, 991 GILES ROAD W 49445
Other Schools – See Muskegon

Northport, Leelanau Co., Pop. Code 3
Northport SD
Sch. Sys. Enr. Code 2
Supt. – Lloyd C. Freeman, 104 WING ST 49670
S, 104 WING ST 49670 – Lori Finnerty, prin.

North Street, St. Clair Co.
Port Huron Area SD
Supt. – See Port Huron
Ft. Gratiot MS, 3895 KEEWAHDIN ROAD 48049
James Dunn, prin.

Northville, Wayne Co., Pop. Code 5
Northville SD
Sch. Sys. Enr. Code 5
Supt. – George Bell, 501 MAIN ST W 48167
Meads Mill MS, 16700 FRANKLIN ROAD 48167
David Longridge, prin.
Amerman ES, 847 CENTER ST N 48167
Milton Jacobi, prin.
Silver Springs ES
19801 SILVER SPRINGS DR 48167
Ken Pawlowski, prin.
Winchester ES, 16141 WINCHESTER DR 48167
Kathy Morhous, prin.

Our Lady of Victory ES, 133 ORCHARD DR 48167
St. Paul ES, 201 ELM ST 48167

Norway, Dickinson Co., Pop. Code 5
Norway-Vulcan Area SD
Sch. Sys. Enr. Code 3
Supt. – James Maples, P O BOX 157 49870
Vulcan MS, P O BOX 158 49870
M. Tomasoski, prin.
ES, P O BOX 159 49870 – Scott McClure, prin.

Holy Spirit ES, 201 SAGINAW ST 49870

Novi, Oakland Co., Pop. Code 7
Novi Comm. SD
Sch. Sys. Enr. Code 5
Supt. – Robert J. Piwko, 25575 TAFT ROAD 48050
MS, 25299 TAFT ROAD 48050
Charles Nanas, prin.
Novi MS, 25549 TAFT RD 48050
Joseph Imrick, prin.
Novi Woods ES, 25195 TAFT RD 48050
Roy Williams, prin.
Orchard Hills ES, 41900 QUINCE ST 48050
Paul Leplae, prin.
Village Oaks ES, 23333 WILLOWBROOK 48050
David Brown, prin.

Oakley, Saginaw Co., Pop. Code 2
Chesaning Un. SD
Supt. – See Chesaning
Brady ES, 17295 S HEMLOCK RD 48649
Richard Coon, prin.

Oak Park, Wayne Co., Pop. Code 8
Berkley SD
Supt. – See Berkley
Norup MS, 14450 MANHATTAN ST 48237
Steve Frank, prin.
Avery ES, 14700 LINCOLN ST 48237
Cecelia Wiar, prin.

Ferndale SD
Supt. – See Ferndale
Best MS, 24220 ROSEWOOD ST 48237
Lawrence Sophiea, prin.
Jackson ES, 23561 ROSEWOOD ST 48237
Nanette Brown, prin.
Jefferson ES, 22011 REPUBLIC ST 48237
Jerry Wiese, prin.

Oak Park SD
Sch. Sys. Enr. Code 5
Supt. – Leonard Demak
13900 GRANZON ST 48237
Roosevelt MS, 23261 SCOTIA ST 48237
Richard Kyro, prin.
Einstein ES, 14001 NORTHEND AVE 48237
Eric Follo, prin.
Key ES, 23401 MORTON 48237
Avon McDaniel, prin.
Lessenger ES, 12901 ALBANY ST 48237
J. E. Cervenak, prin.
Pepper ES, 23400 CHURCH ST 48237
Darlene Russell, prin.

Okemos, Ingham Co., Pop. Code 6
Okemos SD
Sch. Sys. Enr. Code 5
Supt. – Dan Wertz, 4406 OKEMOS ROAD 48864
Kinawa MS, KINAWA DRIVE 48864
Thomas Tweedy, prin.
Central MS, 4406 OKEMOS RD 48864
Richard Njus, prin.
Cornell ES, 4371 CORNELL RD 48864
Thomas Belloili, prin.

Edgewood ES, 1826 OSAGE DR   48864
  Marcia Boznango, prin.
Wardcliff ES, 515 WARDCLIFF DR   48864
  Jeff Richburg, prin.

Olivet, Eaton Co., Pop. Code 4
Olivet Comm. SD
Sch. Sys. Enr. Code 4
Supt. – Thomas Pridgeon, 255 FIRST   49076
MS, 255 FIRST   49076 – Lois Shepard, prin.
ES, 4425 W BUTTEFIELD   49076
  Marilyn Weeks, prin.

Onaway, Presque Isle Co., Pop. Code 4
Onaway Area SD
Sch. Sys. Enr. Code 4
Supt. – James Hall, 4475 S M-33   49765
ES, 4475 S N-33 HWY   49765 – D. Wickstrom, prin.
Other Schools – See Millersburg

Onekama, Manistee Co., Pop. Code 3
Onekama Cons. SD
Sch. Sys. Enr. Code 3
Supt. – Kenneth Heikkinen, 5016 MAIN ST   49675
Arcadia ES, 3586 GLOVERS LAKE   49613
  Beth McCarthy, prin.
ES, 5016 MAIN ST   49675 – Beth McCarthy, prin.

Onsted, Lenawee Co., Pop. Code 3
Onsted Comm. SD
Sch. Sys. Enr. Code 4
Supt. – E. Deuel, W 2ND ST   49265
MS, SLEE ROAD   49265 – Michael Horning, prin.
ES, SLEE RD   49265 – Kathleen Roumel, prin.

Ontonagon, Ontonagon Co., Pop. Code 4
Ontonagon Area SD
Sch. Sys. Enr. Code 3
Supt. – Louis J. Gregory
  301 GREENLAND ROAD   49953
ES, 301 GREENLAND   49953 – James Ollila, prin.
Other Schools – See Mass City, Rockland

Orchard Lake, Oakland Co., Pop. Code 4
Bloomfield Hills SD
Supt. – See Bloomfield Hills
West Hills MS, 2601 LONE PINE ROAD   48033
  Beverly Stone, prin.

Our Lady of Refuge ES, P O BOX 5039   48033

Ortonville, Oakland Co., Pop. Code 4
Brandon SD
Sch. Sys. Enr. Code 5
Supt. – Richard Wilson
  1025 S ORTONVILLE ROAD   48462
Brandon MS, 209 VARSITY DRIVE   48462
  Donald Patrick, prin.
Belle Ann ES, 155 E GLASS RD   48462
  Mark Rodak, prin.
Burt ES, 209 VARSITY DR   48462
  S. Stanton, prin.
Harvey-Swanson ES, 209 VARSITY DR   48462
  Helen Clemetsen, prin.

Oscoda, Iosco Co., Pop. Code 7
Oscoda Area SD
Sch. Sys. Enr. Code 5
Supt. – Robert D. Hodges
  3550 RIVER ROAD   48750
Richardson JHS, 3630 RIVER ROAD   48750
  Peter Hervey, prin.
Cedar Lake ES, 4950 CEDAR LAKE RD   48750
  Wayne Schultz, prin.
ES, 110 PEARL ST N   48750 – Duane London, prin.
River Road MS, 3510 E SIDE RIVER   48750
  William Martin, prin.
Other Schools – See Glennie

Ossineke, Alpena Co.
Alpena SD
Supt. – See Alpena
Sanborn ES, US 23 SOUTH   49766
  Jane Guyott, prin.

Otisville, Genesee Co., Pop. Code 3
Lakeville Comm. SD
Sch. Sys. Enr. Code 5
Supt. – Leonard Shafley
  11107 WASHBURN ROAD   48463
Lakeville MS
  11107 WASHBURN ROAD #G   48463
  Frans Luoma, prin.
ES, 131 WOODWARD   48421 – R. Gutshall, prin.
Otter Lake ES, 6313 HART LAKE   48421
  Ford Longendyke, prin.
Southwest ES, 8254 GALE RD   48463
  Ed Stone, prin.
Other Schools – See Columbiaville

Otsego, Allegan Co., Pop. Code 5
Otsego SD
Sch. Sys. Enr. Code 4
Supt. – John Kingsnorth
  313 W ALLEGAN ST   49078
MS, 538 WASHINGTON ST   49078
  John Leland, prin.
Allegan ES, 313 ALLEGAN ST   49078
  G. Klaeren, prin.
Dix ES, 503 DIX ST   49078 – Robert Grill, prin.

St. Margaret ES, 736 S FARMER ST   49078

Ottawa Lake, Monroe Co., Pop. Code 2
Whiteford SD
Sch. Sys. Enr. Code 3
Supt. – Gerald Wing
  6655 CONSEAR ROAD   49267
Whiteford ES, 6655 CONSEAR RD   49267
  Bill Williams, prin.

Ovid, Clinton Co., Pop. Code 4
Ovid-Elsie Area SD
Supt. – See Elsie
MS, P O BOX 77   48866 – Lyle Howard, prin.
Leonard MS, 520 MABBIT RD   48866
  Larry Lloyd, prin.
North PS, 615 N MAIN ST   48866
  Ellen Maleck, prin.

Owendale, Huron Co., Pop. Code 2
Owendale-Gagetown Area SD
Sch. Sys. Enr. Code 3
Supt. – Harley Kirby, 7166 MAIN ST   48754
Other Schools – See Gagetown

Owosso, Shiawassee Co., Pop. Code 7
Owosso SD
Sch. Sys. Enr. Code 5
Supt. – David Bowman, 1405 W NORTH ST   48867
MS, 219 N WATER ST   48867 – Jack Raffaelli, prin.
Bentley ES, 1375 W NORTH ST   48867
  Carroll Johnson, prin.
Bryant ES, 925 HAMPTON ST   48867
  William Aue, prin.
Central ES, 600 W OLIVER ST   48867
  Brian Delbridge, prin.
Emerson ES, 515 E OLIVER ST   48867
  Linda Phaneuf, prin.
Roosevelt ES, 201 N BROOKS ST   48867
  Carroll Johnson, prin.
Washington ES, 645 ALGER ST   48867
  Clark Hill, prin.

St. Joseph School, 811 E OLIVER ST   48867
St. Paul ES, 718 W MAIN   48667

Oxford, Oakland Co., Pop. Code 5
Oxford Area SD
Sch. Sys. Enr. Code 5
Supt. – Mark Orchard, 105 PONTIAC ROAD   48051
MS, 1400 LAKEVILLE ROAD   48051
  Paul Gerhardt, prin.
Axford ES, 74 MECHANIC ST   48051
  Dean Best, prin.
Clear Lake ES, 2085 DRAHNER   48051
  Ellen DeLater, prin.
Other Schools – See Leonard

Kingsbury ES, 500 HOSNER RD   48051

Painesdale, Houghton Co., Pop. Code 3
Adams Twp. SD
Sch. Sys. Enr. Code 2
Supt. – Patrick Rozich, GOODELL ST   49955
Other Schools – See South Range

Palmer, Marquette Co.
Negaunee SD
Supt. – See Negaunee
Pineview ES, SMITH ST   49871
  David Gleason, prin.

Palo, Ionia Co.
Palo Comm. SD
Sch. Sys. Enr. Code 2
Supt. – Rosemary Reams, 8315 MILL ST   48870
ES, 8315 MILL ST   48870 – Rosemary Reams, prin.

Paradise, Chippewa Co., Pop. Code 2
Whitefish Twp. SD
Sch. Sys. Enr. Code 1
Supt. – Keith Krahnke, P O BOX 58   49768
Whitefish S, P O BOX 58   49768
  Keith Krahnke, prin.

Parchment, Kalamazoo Co., Pop. Code 4
Parchment SD
Sch. Sys. Enr. Code 4
Supt. – Dr. Timothy Jenney
  520 N ORIENT AVE   49004
MS, 307 N RIVERVIEW DRIVE   49004
  Brian Opria, prin.
Central ES, 520 N ORIENT AVE   49004
  Joan Mason, prin.
North ES, 5535 KEYES DR   49004
  M. O'Connor, prin.
Other Schools – See Kalamazoo

Parma, Jackson Co., Pop. Code 3
Western SD
Sch. Sys. Enr. Code 4
Supt. – Robert Bass
  1400 S DEARING ROAD   49269
Western MS, 1400 S DEARING ROAD   49269
  Blaine Goodrich, prin.
ES, 385 ELIZABETH ST   49269
  Margaret Tietjen, prin.
Other Schools – See Spring Arbor

Paw Paw, Van Buren Co., Pop. Code 5
Paw Paw SD
Sch. Sys. Enr. Code 4
Supt. – Darrell Crose, 119 S JOHNSON ST   49079
Michigan Avenue MS
  600 W MICHIGAN AVE   49079
  Richard Drury, prin.
Black River ES, 512 W NORTH ST   49079
  C. W. Wilson, prin.

Cedar Street ES, 555 CEDAR ST   49079
  Robert Hansen, prin.
Community Education ES
  313 W MICHIGAN AVE   49079 – Dean Wells, prin.

St. Mary ES, 508 E PAW PAW ST   49079

Peck, Sanilac Co., Pop. Code 3
Peck Comm. SD
Sch. Sys. Enr. Code 3
Supt. – James Bedford, 222 E LAPEER ST   48466
MS, 222 E LAPEER ST   48466
  J. Humerickhouse, prin.
ES, 222 E LAPEER ST   48466
  Kenneth Maher, prin.

Pelkie, Baraga Co.
Baraga Area SD
Supt. – See Baraga
ES   49958 – Jerry Paakola, prin.

L'Anse Twp. SD
Supt. – See L'Anse
Laird ES, P O BOX 159   49958 – Karl Gipp, prin.

Pellston, Emmet Co., Pop. Code 3
Pellston SD
Sch. Sys. Enr. Code 3
Supt. – Hugh Smyth, ZIPT ST   49769
ES, ZIPF ST   49769 – Donna Bazzler, prin.

Pentwater, Oceans Co., Pop. Code 4
Pentwater SD
Sch. Sys. Enr. Code 2
Supt. – John Ward, 600 E PARK ST   49449
ES, 600 E PARK ST   49449
  Douglas Busman, prin.

Perry, Shiawassee Co., Pop. Code 4
Perry SD
Sch. Sys. Enr. Code 4
Supt. – Jacklyn Hurd
  2775 BRITTON ROAD   48872
MS, 2885 BRITTON ROAD   48872
  Donald Vernon, prin.
ES, 401 N WATKINS   48872 – Karen Milton, prin.
Shaftsburg ES, 7380 W BEARD RD   48872
  Lynn Harned, prin.
Other Schools – See Haslett

Petersburg, Monroe Co., Pop. Code 4
Summerfield SD
Sch. Sys. Enr. Code 3
Supt. – Russell Hoogendoorn, P O BOX 8   49270
Summerfield ES, 232 E ELM ST   49270
  William Ryan, prin.

Petoskey, Emmet Co., Pop. Code 6
Petoskey SD
Sch. Sys. Enr. Code 4
Supt. – Franklin Ronan, 1130 HOWARD ST   49770
MS, 601 HOWARD ST   49770 – Carl Moser, prin.
Lincoln ES, 616 CONNABLE AVE   49770
  John McFall, prin.
Ottawa ES, 871 KALAMAZOO AVE   49770
  T. Van Deventer, prin.
Sheridan ES, 1415 HOWARD ST   49770
  John McFall, prin.

St. Francis Xavier ES, 414 MICHIGAN ST   49770

Pewamo, Ionia Co., Pop. Code 2
Pewamo-Westphalia SD
Sch. Sys. Enr. Code 3
Supt. – Michael Folk, RURAL ROUTE 01   48873
Pewamo-Westphalia JHS
  RURAL ROUTE 01   48873 – Dennis Toth, prin.
Pewamo-Westphalia ES, E MAIN ST   48873
  Dennis Toth, prin.

St. Joseph School, 160 EAST ST   48873

Pickford, Chippewa Co., Pop. Code 4
Pickford SD
Sch. Sys. Enr. Code 2
Supt. – Peter Injasoulian, P O BOX 278   49774
ES, P O BOX 278   49774 – Mary Howell, prin.

Pigeon, Huron Co., Pop. Code 4
Elkton-Pigeon-Bayport SD
Sch. Sys. Enr. Code 4
Supt. – Robert Drury, 6136 PIGEON ROAD   48755
Laker MS, 6136 PIGEON ROAD   48755
  Craig Douglas, prin.
Bay Port ES, 9853 POPLAR ST   48720
  Fred Joles, prin.
Elkton ES, 176 N MAIN ST   48731
  Ben Phillips, prin.
ES, 7332 PAUL RD   48755 – Fred Joles, prin.

Pinckney, Livingston Co., Pop. Code 4
Pinckney Comm. SD
Sch. Sys. Enr. Code 5
Supt. – Ted Culver, P O BOX 9   48169
MS, 2150 E M-36   48169 – Dave Smokerar, prin.
Country ES, P O BOX 590   48169
  Barb Reams, prin.
ES, 935 W M-36   48169 – R. McCloskey, prin.
Other Schools – See Hamburg

St. Mary ES, 550 E HAMBURG ST   48169

Pinconning, Bay Co., Pop. Code 4
Pinconning Area SD
Sch. Sys. Enr. Code 5
Supt. – Donald Dryden, 210 N LIBBY ST   48650

Central ES, 605 W FIFTH ST 48650
  Gerald Swallow, prin.
Garfield-Fraser ES, 1412 GARFIELD 48650
  Gloria Musiel, prin.
Mt. Forest ES, 4197 11 MILE ROAD 48650
  Ruth Toth, prin.
Other Schools – See Detroit

St. Michael ES, 310 E SECOND ST 48650

Pittsford, Hillsdale Co., Pop. Code 4
Pittsford Area SD
Sch. Sys. Enr. Code 3
Supt. – Max Baxter, 311 HAMILTON ST 49271
ES, 3111 HAMILTON ST 49271
  Ralph Crume, prin.

Plainwell, Allegan Co., Pop. Code 5
Plainwell Comm. SD
Sch. Sys. Enr. Code 5
Supt. – David Jones, 600 SCHOOL DR 49080
MS, 720 BRIGHAM ST 49080
  David Prentice, prin.
Gilkey ES, 707 S WOODHAMS ST 49080
  Sandra Hale, prin.
Starr ES, 601 SCHOOL DR 49080 – Carl Ill, prin.
Other Schools – See Kalamazoo

Plymouth, Wayne Co., Pop. Code 6
Plymouth-Canton Comm. SD
Sch. Sys. Enr. Code 7
Supt. – John M. Hoben, 454 HARVEY ST S 48170
Central MS, 650 CHURCH ST 48170
  Patricia Moore, prin.
East MS, 1042 MILL ST S 48170
  T. Workman, prin.
Allen ES, 11100 HAGGERTY RD N 48170
  James Burt, prin.
Bird ES, 220 SHELDON RD S 48170
  B. Marshall, prin.
Farrand ES, 41400 GREENBRIAR LN 48170
  Carrol Nichols, prin.
Fiegel ES, 39750 JOY RD 48170
  Barbara Young, prin.
Isbister ES, 9300 CANTON CTR ROAD 48170
  G. Belvitch, prin.
Smith ES, 1298 MCKINLEY ST 48170
  George Dodson, prin.
Other Schools – See Canton, Westland

Our Lady of Good Counsel ES
  1151 WILLIAM ST 48170

Pontiac, Oakland Co., Pop. Code 8
Birmingham SD
Supt. – See Birmingham
Walnut Lake ES, 2075 WALNUT LAKE RD 48033
  Carol Johnson, prin.

Farmington SD
Supt. – See Farmington
Eagle ES, 29410 W FOURTEEN MILE RD 48322
  Frank Kasun, prin.

Lake Orion Comm. SD
Supt. – See Lake Orion
Carpenter ES, 2290 FLINTEIDGE 48055
  Harold Rescoe, prin.

Pontiac SD
Sch. Sys. Enr. Code 7
Supt. – LaBarbara Gragg
  350 WIDE TRACK DRIVE E 48058
Jefferson JHS, 600 MOTOR ST 48053
  Jimmy Randolph, prin.
Kennedy JHS, 1700 BALDWIN AVE 48055
  Paul Gehman, prin.
Lincoln JHS, 131 HILLSIDE DRIVE 48058
  Jo Nebeker, prin.
Madison JHS, 1275 N PERRY ST 48058
  Verne Mannt, prin.
Washington JHS, 710 MENOMINEE ROAD 48053
  Leroy Williams, prin.
Alcott ES, 460 W KENNETT RD 48055
  Donald Robbins, prin.
Bagley ES, 320 BAGLEY ST 48053
  Zee Rabb, prin.
Bethune ES, 154 LAKE ST 48053
  Barry Rubin, prin.
Crofoot ES, 250 W PIKE ST 48053
  Janet Atkins, prin.
Emerson ES, 859 EMERSON AVE 48058
  Martin Peterson, prin.
Franklin ES, 661 FRANKLIN RD 48053
  Larry Beamer, prin.
Frost ES, 723 COTTAGE ST 48058
  Vivian Terry, prin.
Herrington ES, 541 BAY ST 48057
  Ellen Quarles, prin.
Lebaron ES, 1033 BARKELL ST 48055
  Alicia Coppola, prin.
Longfellow ES, 31 N ASTOR ST 48058
  Brian Castle, prin.
Owen ES, 43 E COLUMBIA AVE 48055
  John Colbert, prin.
Rogers ES, 2600 DEXTER RD 48057
  H. Childress, prin.
Twain ES, 729 LINDA VISTA DR 48058
  G. Sanders, prin.
Webster ES, 640 W HURON ST 48053
  Burton Apple, prin.
Whitfield ES, 2000 ORCHARD LAKE RD 48053
  Don Ostrander, prin.
Whitman ES, 125 E MONTCALM ST 48058
  D. Macquarrie, prin.

WHRC-East ES, 60 PARKHURST ST 48058
  Isabel Sabin, prin.
WHRC-North ES, 60 PARKHURST ST 48058
  Tommaleta Hughes, prin.

Walled Lake Cons. SD
Supt. – See Walled Lake
Maple ES, 7389 W MAPLE RD 48322
  Marcia Scarr, prin.
Twin Beach ES, 7149 OAKLEY PARK 48033
  Alec Bender, prin.

Waterford SD
Supt. – See Waterford
Adams ES, 3810 CLINTONVILLE RD 48055
  Barbara Ruelle, prin.
Beaumont ES, 6532 ELIZABETH LAKE RD 48054
  Janet Strong, prin.
Burt ES, 581 S WINDING DR 48054
  George McGrath, prin.
Crescent Lake ES, 5449 CRESCENT RD 48054
  Pat Knudsen, prin.
Donelson ES, 1200 W HURON ST 48054
  Alice Purves, prin.
Four Towns ES, 6370 COOLEY LAKE RD 48054
  Colleen Gardiner, prin.
Haviland ES, 5305 CASS ELIZABETH RD 48054
  Robert Elliott, prin.
Leggett ES, 3621 PONTIAC LAKE RD 48054
  R. Hutchinson, prin.
Lutes ES, 5195 PONTIAC LAKE RD 48054
  L. Grossnickle, prin.
Riverside ES, 5280 FARM RD 48054
  James Dieck, prin.
Sandburg ES, 1355 MERRY RD 48054
  Shawn Ruch, prin.

West Bloomfield SD
Supt. – See West Bloomfield
Ealy ES, 5475 W MAPLE RD 48322
  J. Pendergrass, prin.

St. Benedict ES, 60 S LYNN ST 48053

Portage, Kalamazoo Co., Pop. Code 8
Portage SD
Supt. – See Kalamazoo
Amberly ES, 6637 AMBERLY ST 49002
  James Garlick, prin.
Angling ES, 5340 ANGLING RD 49008
  Leonard Holmes, prin.
Central ES, 8422 S WESTNEDGE AVE 49002
  Charles Whitmore, prin.
Haverhill ES, 6633 HAVERHILL 49002
  Richard Kienbaum, prin.
Lake Center ES, 10011 PORTAGE ROAD 49002
  Mary Stafford, prin.
Waylee ES, 8106 WAYLEE ST 49002
  Frances Winegar, prin.
Woodland ES, 1401 WOODLAND DR 49002
  Robert Downing, prin.

Port Hope, Huron Co., Pop. Code 2
Port Hope Comm. SD
Sch. Sys. Enr. Code 2
Supt. – James Hunter
  7940 PORTLAND AVE 48468
S, 7940 PORTLAND AVE 48468
  William Murphy, prin.

Port Huron, St. Clair Co., Pop. Code 8
Port Huron Area SD
Sch. Sys. Enr. Code 7
Supt. – Larry Moeller
  2720 RIVERSIDE DRIVE 48060
Central MS, 200 32ND ST 48060
  Frank Haynes, prin.
Chippewa MS, 2800 CHIPPEWA TRAIL 48060
  Andrew Pochodylo, prin.
Holland Woods MS, 1617 HOLLAND AVE 48060
  Robert Barber, prin.
Cleveland ES, 2801 VANNESS ST 48060
  Yvonne Malachi, prin.
Crull ES, 2615 HANCOCK ST 48060
  Dorothy Feick, prin.
Edison ES, 3559 POLLINA AVE 48060
  Sally Gregg, prin.
Garfield ES, 1221 GARFIELD ST 48060
  C. Catalina, prin.
Harrison ES, 55 FIFTEENTH ST 48060
  Joann Monaghan, prin.
Indian Woods ES, 4975 W WATER ST 48060
  Gail Hunwick, prin.
Keewahdin ES, 4801 LAKESHORE RD 48060
  Jack Peters, prin.
Kimball ES, 5801 GRISWOLD RD 48060
  Gerald Weaver, prin.
Lakeport ES, 3835 FRANKLIN ST 48060
  David Butcher, prin.
Michigamme ES, 2855 MICHIGAN RD 48060
  Raymond Ellis, prin.
Roosevelt ES, 1112 TWENTIETH ST 48060
  Brian Winters, prin.
Sparlingville ES, 1963 ALLEN RD 48060
  Bernard Pelc, prin.
Wilson ES, 834 CHESTNUT ST 48060
  David Smith, prin.
Other Schools – See North Street

St. Edward on the Lake ES
  6995 LAKE SHORE DR 48060
St. Joseph ES, 1403 SEVENTH ST 48060
St. Mary ES, 1429 BALLENTINE ST 48060
Trinity ES, 1517 TENTH 48060

Portland, Ionia Co., Pop. Code 5
Portland SD
Sch. Sys. Enr. Code 4
Supt. – John Clarey, 883 CROSS ST 48875
MS, 306 BRUSH ST 48875 – William Adams, prin.
Oakwood ES, 500 OAK ST 48875
  L. Blumenshine, prin.
Westwood ES, 883 CROSS ST 48875
  Joel Wildrom, prin.

St. Patrick School, WEST & CENTER STS 48875

Posen, Presque Isle Co., Pop. Code 2
Posen Cons. SD
Sch. Sys. Enr. Code 2
Supt. – Michael Murch
  10575 MICHIGAN AVE 49776
ES, 10575 MICHIGAN AVE 49776
  Michael Murch, prin.

St. Casimir ES, P O BOX 217 49776

Potterville, Eaton Co., Pop. Code 4
Potterville SD
Sch. Sys. Enr. Code 3
Supt. – William Heath, 420 N HIGH ST 48876
ES, 420 HIGH ST 48876 – G. Schneider, prin.

Powers, Menominee Co., Pop. Code 2
North Central Area SD
Sch. Sys. Enr. Code 3
Supt. – Kenneth Groh 49874
North Central JHS 49874 – (—), prin.
Other Schools – See Hermansville

Prescott, Ogemaw Co., Pop. Code 2
Whittemore-Prescott Area SD
Supt. – See Whittemore
ES 48756 – Arnold Engster, prin.

Quincy, Branch Co., Pop. Code 4
Quincy Comm. SD
Sch. Sys. Enr. Code 4
Supt. – Rich Tait, 41 E JEFFERSON ST 49082
MS, 41 E JEFFERSON ST 49082
  Henry Longhini, prin.
Jennings ES, FULTON ST 49082
  John Worth, prin.

Quinnesec, Dickinson Co.
Breitung Twp. SD
Supt. – See Kingsford
ES 49876 – James Verley, prin.

Rapid City, Kalkaska Co.
Kalkaska SD
Supt. – See Kalkaska
ES 49676 – Marne Homberg, prin.

Rapid River, Delta Co., Pop. Code 3
Rapid River SD
Sch. Sys. Enr. Code 3
Supt. – John Males, P O BOX 68 49878
Bay De Noc ES 49878 – David Salminen, prin.

Ravenna, Muskegon Co., Pop. Code 3
Ravenna SD
Sch. Sys. Enr. Code 4
Supt. – David Lightfoot
  12322 STAFFORD ST 49451
MS, 2766 S RAVENNA ROAD 49451
  Charles Ash, prin.
ES, 3480 THOMAS ST 49451
  B. Vander Vilet, prin.

Reading, Hillsdale Co., Pop. Code 4
Reading Comm. SD
Sch. Sys. Enr. Code 3
Supt. – Bruce Kefgen, 233 STRONG AVE 49274
Reynolds ES, 221 STRONG 49274
  Don Richardson, prin.

Redford, Wayne Co.
Redford Union SD
Supt. – See Detroit
Beck ES, 27100 BENNETT 48240
  C. Kaselemis, prin.
Bulman ES, 15996 DELAWARE AVE 48239
  Hugh Laird, prin.
Keeler ES, 17715 BRADY 48240
  Patrick Lowney, prin.
MacGowan ES, 18255 KINLOCH 48240
  Diane Bert, prin.
Roosevelt ES, 15100 AUBREY 48239
  Earl Wuestnick, prin.
Stuckey ES, 26000 FARGO 48240
  James Morse, prin.

South Redford SD
Supt. – See Detroit
Pierce MS, 25600 ORANGELAWN 48239
  Lorraine Yadach, prin.
Addams ES, 14025 BERWYN 48239
  Kenneth Lentz, prin.
Fisher ES, 10000 CROSLEY 48239
  Mary Brun, prin.
Jefferson ES, 26555 WESTFIELD 48239
  Mary Brun, prin.
Vandenberg ES, 24901 CATHEDRAL 48239
  Nina Robins, prin.

Hosanna-Tabor ES, 9600 LEVERNE 48239

Reed City, Osceola Co., Pop. Code 4
Reed City SD
Sch. Sys. Enr. Code 4
Supt. – Dennis Rosen, 320 SEARS ST S 49677

Norman ES, 338 W LINCOLN AVE 49677
  Larry Johnson, prin.
Phillips MS, 829 S CHESTNUT ST 49677
  D. Jarzabkowski, prin.
MS, 238 LINCOLN ST W 49677
  D. Jarzabkowski, prin.
Other Schools – See Hersey

Trinity ES, 139 W CHURCH AVE 49677

Reese, Tuscola Co., Pop. Code 4
Reese SD
Sch. Sys. Enr. Code 4
Supt. – Charles H. Twork, 9535 CENTER ST 48757
MS, 9590 SAGINAW ST 48757
  Rodney Green, prin.
ES, 9535 CENTER ST 48757
  Katherine Zuzula, prin.

St. Elizabeth ES, 9970 CENTER ST 48757
Trinity ES, 1935 RHODES ST 48757

Remus, Mecosta Co., Pop. Code 2
Chippewa Hills SD
Sch. Sys. Enr. Code 4
Supt. – G. Lowery, 3226 ARTHUR ROAD 49340
MS, 350 E WHEATLAND 49340
  Darryl Soper, prin.
Other Schools – See Amasa, Barryton, Mecosta

St. Michael ES, 50TH AVE 49340

Republic, Marquette Co., Pop. Code 4
Republic-Michigamme SD
Sch. Sys. Enr. Code 2
Supt. – Grant Berggren, RURAL ROUTE 01 49879
Republic-Michigamme ES
  RURAL ROUTE 01 49879 – Dr. Berggren,Jr., prin.

Richland, Kalamazoo Co., Pop. Code 2
Gull Lake Comm. SD
Sch. Sys. Enr. Code 4
Supt. – Thomas Ryan, 11775 EAST D AVE 49083
Bedford ES, 351 HUTCHINSON ROAD 49020
  Ronald Miller, prin.
ES, 9360 M-89INSON ROAD 49083
  R. Schinderle, prin.
IS, RURAL ROUTE 01 BOX 8884 49083
  Dave Witt, prin.
Other Schools – See Hickory Corners

Richmond, McComb Co., Pop. Code 5
Richmond Comm. SD
Sch. Sys. Enr. Code 4
Supt. – Douglas Benit, 68931 N MAIN ST 48062
MS, RURAL ROUTE 01 BOX 35250 48062
  Garry Rumbaugh, prin.
Lee ES, 68399 S FOREST AVE 48062
  James Chopp, prin.

St. Augustine ES, 67901 HOWARD ST 48062
St. Peter ES, 37601 31 MILE RD 48062

Richville, Tuscola Co.

St. Michael ES, 9444 W SAGINAW 48758

River Rouge, Wayne Co., Pop. Code 7
River Rouge SD
Sch. Sys. Enr. Code 4
Supt. – William McCollum
  1411 COOLIDGE HIGHWAY 48218
Dunn ES, 163 BURKE ST 48218
  James Duffy, prin.
Sabbath ES, 340 FRAZIER ST 48218
  B. Benford, prin.
Visger ES, 1121 JEFFERSON AVE W 48218
  Joseph Corio, prin.
White ES, 550 EATON ST 48218
  William Holmes, prin.

Riverview, Wayne Co., Pop. Code 7
Riverview Comm. SD
Sch. Sys. Enr. Code 4
Supt. – Michael Krigelski
  13425 COLVIN ST 48192
Seitz MS, 17800 KENNEBEC ST 48192
  George Svitchan, prin.
Huntington ES, 17752 KENNEBEC ST 48192
  Bud McCourt, prin.
Memorial ES, 13425 COLVIN ST 48192
  Ernie Mayoros, prin.

St. Cyprian ES
  13249 PENNSYLVANIA AVE 48192

Rochester, Oakland Co., Pop. Code 6
Avondale SD
Supt. – See Auburn Hills
Avondale MS, 1435 W AUBURN ROAD 48309
  Gerald Hanley, prin.
Stiles ES, 3976 S LIVERNOIS RD 48063
  Maurice Anderson, prin.

Rochester Comm. SD
Sch. Sys. Enr. Code 7
Supt. – John Schultz, 4TH & WILCOX 48063
Reuther JHS, 1430 E AUBURN ROAD 48063
  Greg Owens, prin.
Van Hoosen JHS, 1339 S ADAMS ROAD 48063
  Jerry Freeman, prin.
West JHS, 500 OLD PERCH ROAD 48063
  Tresa Zumsteg, prin.
Baldwin ES, 4325 BANNISTER 48063
  Thomas Mikula, prin.

Brewster ES, 1535 BREWSTER RD 48064
  Mel Blahm, prin.
Brooklands ES, 480 E AUBURN RD 48063
  David Hurst, prin.
Hamlin ES, 270 HAMLIN 48063
  Gary Cornish, prin.
Hugger ES, 5050 SHELDON 48064
  Jane Paulton, prin.
Long Meadow ES, 450 ALLSTON 48063
  Janine Kateff, prin.
McGregor ES, 1101 1ST ST 48063
  Carmen Zeigler, prin.
Meadow Brook ES, 2350 MUNSTER RD 48309
  Sandra Feeley, prin.
North Hill ES, 1385 MAHAFFEY AVE 48063
  Donald Pell, prin.
University Hills ES, 1600 CROYDON RD 48309
  Robert Belk, prin.

Utica Comm. SD
Supt. – See Utica
Switzer ES, 53200 SHELBY RD 48064
  Dennis Cusack, prin.

Holy Family Regional ES
  1234 INGLEWOOD AVE 48063
St. John ES, 1011 W UNIVERSITY DR 48063

Rock, Delta Co., Pop. Code 2
Mid-Peninsula SD
Sch. Sys. Enr. Code 2
Supt. – Gene DeKeyser, P O BOX 188 49880
Mid-Peninsula S, P O BOX 188 49880
  Harvey Hoyum, prin.

Rockford, Kent Co., Pop. Code 5
Rockford SD
Sch. Sys. Enr. Code 5
Supt. – J. T. Raymer, 235 COURTLAND ST 49341
MS, 4500 KROES ST NE 49341
  Jack McMurphy, prin.
Cannonsburg ES, 4894 STURGIS 49341
  Sharon Bennett, prin.
Crestwood ES, 6340 COURTLAND DR NE 49341
  Dennis Schultz, prin.
Lakes ES, 6849 YOUNG AVE NE 49341
  Tom Kruithoff, prin.
Parkside ES, 156 LEWIS ST 49341
  Mike Micele, prin.
River Valley MS, 350 N MAIN ST 49341
  Jim Dolan, prin.
Valley View ES, 405 SUMMIT AVE NE 49341
  Dee Duzan, prin.
Other Schools – See Belmont

Our Lady of Consolation School
  4865 11 MILE RD NE 49351

Rockland, Ontonagon Co.
Ontonagon Area SD
Supt. – See Ontonagon
ES 49960 – James Ollila, prin.

Rockwood, Wayne Co., Pop. Code 5
Gilbraltar SD
Sch. Sys. Enr. Code 5
Supt. – Jerome Pavlov
  33494 JEFFERSON W 48173
Schumate MS, 30550 JEFFERSON W 48173
  Paul Turner, prin.
Chapman ES, 31500 OLMSTEAD RD 48173
  Richard Light, prin.
Parsons ES, 14473 M GILBRALTER 48173
  G. Barley, prin.
Weiss ES, 26632 RESUME 48183
  Rose Crane, prin.
Other Schools – See Trenton

St. Mary ES, 32447 CHURCH ST 48173

Rogers City, Presque Isle Co., Pop. Code 5
Rogers City Area SD
Sch. Sys. Enr. Code 3
Supt. – Delmar Conley, 251 W HURON AVE 49779
ES, 532 W ERIE ST 49779 – Marion Lamb, prin.

St. Ignatius ES, 545 S 3RD ST 49779
St. John ES, 145 N 5TH ST 49779

Romeo, McComb Co., Pop. Code 5
Romeo Comm. SD
Sch. Sys. Enr. Code 5
Supt. – George Harrison, 316 N MAIN ST 48065
Indian Hills ES, 8401 29 MILE ROAD 48094
  Myron Grabske, prin.
Moore ES, 209 DICKENSON ST 48065
  William Stidman, prin.
Washington ES, 48230 VAN DYKE 48094
  Judith Garrett, prin.
Other Schools – See Leonard

Romulus, Wayne Co., Pop. Code 7
Romulus Comm. SD
Sch. Sys. Enr. Code 5
Supt. – Wm. Bedell, 36540 GRANT ST 48174
JHS, 37300 WICK ROAD 48174
  J. Meriweather, prin.
Barth ES, 38207 BARTH ST 48174
  William Smith, prin.
Cory ES, 35200 SMITH RD 48174
  Peter Silver, prin.
Hale Creek ES, 16200 HARRISON AVE 48174
  A. McPharlin, prin.
Hayti ES, 30155 BEVERLY RD 48174
  Charles Shamey, prin.

Merriman ES, 15303 MERRIMAN RD 48174
  Daniel Murray, prin.
Wick ES, 36900 WICK RD 48174
  Nick Tottis, prin.

St. Aloysius School, 37200 NEVILLE ROAD 48174

Roscommon, Roscommon Co., Pop. Code 3
Gerrish-Higgins SD
Sch. Sys. Enr. Code 4
Supt. – Donald Mick, 814 LAKE ST 48653
MS, 606 LAKE ST 48653 – J Carter, prin.
ES, 175 W SUNSET DR 48653
  J. Pinsoneault, prin.
Other Schools – See Saint Helen

Roseville, Macomb Co., Pop. Code 8
Fraser SD
Supt. – See Fraser
Dooley ES, 16170 CANBERRA ST 48066
  Linda Lewis, prin.
Twain ES, 30601 CALAHAN RD 48066
  Louis Slater, prin.

Roseville Comm. SD
Sch. Sys. Enr. Code 6
Supt. – John Kment
  18175 E ELEVEN MILE ROAD 48066
Eastland MS, 18700 FRANK ST 48066
  Harry Uhlianuk, prin.
Guest MS, 16221 FRAZHO ROAD 48066
  J. Bresciami, prin.
Alumni ES, 29725 JOHN J ST 48066
  Anthony Maksym, prin.
Arbor ES, 19140 MEIER ST 48066
  Donald Culich, prin.
Dort ES, 16225 DORT ST 48066 – Jack Bock, prin.
Eastland ES, 2033 WASHINGTON 48066
  Vito Conti, prin.
Fountain ES, 16850 WELLINGTON AVE 48066
  Martha O'Kray, prin.
Huron Park ES, 18530 MARQUETTE ST 48066
  Roberta Fanti, prin.
Kaiser ES, 16700 WILDWOOD ST 48066
  Sue Enke, prin.
Lincoln ES, 16435 CHESTNUT ST 48066
  Olive Neelands, prin.
Patton ES, 18851 MCKINNON ST 48066
  Ron MacIntyre, prin.
Pierce ES, 18800 MELVIN ST 48066
  Donald Culich, prin.

Bethlehem ES, 29675 GRATIOT AVE 48066
Holy Innocents ES, 26000 RIDGEMONT ST 48066
St. Angela ES, 25275 CHIPPENDALE ST 48066

Royal Oak, Oakland Co., Pop. Code 8
Royal Oak SD
Sch. Sys. Enr. Code 6
Supt. – Lawrence Nichols
  1123 LEXINGTON BLVD 48073
Addams MS, 2222 W WEBSTER ROAD 48073
  Jennifer Jackson, prin.
Churchill MS, 707 GIRARD AVE 48073
  Martha Mullkoff, prin.
Keller MS, 1505 CAMPBELL ROAD 48067
  James Hunter, prin.
Adams ES, 2200 W WEBSTER RD 48073
  B. Schipper, prin.
Franklin ES, 1121 MOHAWK AVE 48067
  Richard Wood, prin.
Lincoln ES, 1901 E 11 MILE RD 48067
  B. Heater, prin.
Lockman ES, 1426 BELLAIRE AVE 48067
  Jerry Waldrop, prin.
Longfellow ES, 303 MAXWELL AVE 48067
  Phyllis Hertler, prin.
Northwood ES, 926 W TWELVE MILE RD 48073
  Nina Keener, prin.
Oak Ridge ES, 506 E 13 MILE RD 48073
  Rita Walker, prin.
Oakland ES, 2415 BROCKTON AVE 48067
  Estelle Bloom, prin.
Parker ES, 3704 W THIRTEEN MILE RD 48072
  Karen Blacklaw, prin.
Starr ES, 3412 DEVON RD 48073
  Judith Breseman, prin.
Twain ES, 4600 N CAMPBELL RD 48073
  Norma Hammond, prin.
Upton ES, 4400 MANDALAY AVE 48073
  James Penrod, prin.
Whittier ES, 815 E FARNUM AVE 48067
  Kay Cornell, prin.

Shrine of the Little Flower ES
  2108 W 12 MILE 48067
St. Dennis ES, 1415 N STEPHENSON HWY 48071
St. Mary ES, 628 S LAFAYETTE AVE 48067
St. Paul ES, 508 S WILLIAMS ST 48067

Rudyard, Chippewa Co., Pop. Code 4
Rudyard Area SD
Sch. Sys. Enr. Code 3
Supt. – G. Bosshart, 2ND & WILLIAM 49780
Turner-Howson ES, FOURTH ST 49780
  Donald Wallis, prin.

Saginaw, Saginaw Co., Pop. Code 8
Buena Vista SD
Sch. Sys. Enr. Code 4
Supt. – Dr. T. Wallace, P O BOX 4829 48605
Ricker MS, 1925 S OUTER DRIVE 48601
  Osborne Burks, prin.
Brunkow MS, 3000 S 24TH ST 48601
  Kenneth Waters, prin.

Claytor MS, 3200 PERKINS ST 48601
 Lloyd Bishop, prin.
Doerr ES, 3270 PERKINS ST 48601
 L. Weathersby, prin.
Koeltzow MS, 5173 LODGE ST 48601
 Oena McCray, prin.

Carrollton SD
Supt. – See Carrollton
Carrollton ES, 3211 CARLA DR 48604
 H. Ellsworth, prin.

Saginaw SD
Sch. Sys. Enr. Code 7
Supt. – F. B. Gibbs, 550 MILLARD ST 48607
Baille ES, 1124 FINDLEY ST 48601
 Louis Skipper, prin.
Coulter ES, 1450 BRIDGTON RD 48601
 Lynne George, prin.
Emerson ES, 1422 MERRILL ST 48601
 Carol Johnson, prin.
Fuerbringer ES, 2138 N CAROLINA ST 48602
 Charles Shelley, prin.
Haley ES, 3240 LIVINGSTON DR 48601
 Richard Luczak, prin.
Handley ES, 3021 COURT ST 48602
 Irene Hensinger, prin.
Heavenrich ES, 2435 PERKINS ST 48601
 Lawrence Wells, prin.
Herig ES, 1905 HOUGHTON AVE 48602
 Delores Moreland, prin.
Houghton ES, 1604 JOHNSON ST 48601
 Zoretta Davis, prin.
Jerome ES, 1501 S HARRISON ST 48602
 Donald Franz, prin.
Jones ES, 1602 CHERRY ST 48601
 Lucille Chaffer, prin.
Kempton ES, 3040 DAVENPORT AVE 48602
 Gerry Garcia, prin.
Longfellow ES, 1314 BROWN ST 48601
 Ernest Burnell, prin.
Longstreet ES, 504 CARROLL ST 48607
 J. Rousseau, prin.
Loomis ES, 2000 LOOMIS ST 48601
 Albert Zackrie, prin.
Merrill Park ES, 1800 GROUT ST 48602
 Zeph Phillips, prin.
Miller ES, 2020 BROCKWAY ST 48602
 James Wallace, prin.
Moore ES, 700 COURT ST 48602
 Della Smith, prin.
Morley ES, 2601 LAPEER AVE 48601
 Charles McNair, prin.
Rouse ES, 435 RANDOLPH ST 48601
 Patricia Clark, prin.
Salina ES, 3505 BUNDY ST 48601
 Carl Maple, prin.
Stone ES, 1006 STATE ST 48602
 Frances Carter, prin.
Webber ES, 2000 MORRIS ST 48601
 Jane Olivarez, prin.
Zilwaukee ES, 500 JOHNSON ST 48604
 James Sweeting, prin.

Saginaw Twp. Comm. SD
Sch. Sys. Enr. Code 6
Supt. – Wayne Vasher
 3465 N CENTER ROAD 48603
White Pine MS, 505 N CENTER 48603
 Kay Packwood, prin.
Arrowwood ES, P O BOX 6278RD 48608
 Dale Klein, prin.
Hemmeter ES, 1890 HEMMETER RD 48603
 C. Wierda, prin.
Plainfield ES, 2775 SHATTUCK RD 48603
 H. Harrington, prin.
Sherwood ES, 3870 SHATTUCK 48603
 Robert Finn, prin.
Weiss ES, 4645 WEISS ST 48603
 William Matson, prin.
Westdale ES, 705 S CENTER RD 48603
 Ben Webb, prin.

Spaulding Comm. SD
Supt. – See Bridgeport
Kaufmann ES, 1944 IOWA ST 48722
 William Case, prin.

Swan Valley SD
Sch. Sys. Enr. Code 4
Supt. – Richard Syrek, 8380 OHERN ROAD 48603
Shields MS, 8400 OHERN ROAD 48603
 Ed Brosofski, prin.
Havens ES, 457 VAN WORMER RD 48603
 Mary Lou Ederer, prin.
Shields ES, 6900 STROEBEL RD 48603
 Dennis Miner, prin.

Bethlehem ES, 2777 HERMANSAU RD 48604
Francis F. Reh Academy, 2201 OWEN 48601
Good Shepherd Lutheran School
 5335 BROCKWAY ROAD 48603
Holy Cross ES, 600 COURT ST 48602
Immanuel Lutheran School
 8210 HOLLAND ROAD 48601
Peace ES, 3427 ADAMS AVE 48602
SS Peter & Paul ES
 4735 W MICHIGAN AVE 48603
St. Helen ES, 2415 N CHARLES ST 48602
St. Josaphat ES, 479 SHATTUCK RD 48604
St. Stephen ES, 1315 SUTTON ST 48602
St. Thomas Aquinas ES
 2136 BERBEROVICH DR 48603

Saint Charles, Saginaw Co., Pop. Code 4
St. Charles Comm. SD
Sch. Sys. Enr. Code 4
Supt. – James Slick, 891 W WALNUT ST 48655
Thurston ES, 893 W WALNUT ST 48655
 Ernest Gendron, prin.
Miller ES, 302 FULTON ST 48655
 Dale Dekarske, prin.
Patterson ES, 801 W WALNUT ST 48655
 Terry Fuller, prin.

Saint Clair, St. Clair Co., Pop. Code 5
East China SD
Supt. – See Marine City
Eddy ES, 301 N NINTH ST 48079
 Ed Skowneski, prin.
Gearing ES, 200 CARNEY DR 48079
 Ronald Limberg, prin.
Pine River ES, 3575 KING RD 48079
 Martin Good, prin.

St. Mary ES, 811 ORCHARD ST 48079

Saint Clair Shores, Macomb Co., Pop. Code 8
Lake Shores SD
Sch. Sys. Enr. Code 5
Supt. – John Beleutz, 30401 TAYLOR ST 48082
Kennedy MS, 23101 MASONIC BLVD 48082
 Bert Sterling, prin.
Masonic Heights ES
 22100 MASONIC BLVD 48082
 Fred Woodstock, prin.
Rodgers ES, 21601 LANSE ST 48081
 Robert Olzem, prin.
Violet ES, 22022 VIOLET ST 48082
 H. Suminski, prin.

Lakeview SD
Sch. Sys. Enr. Code 5
Supt. – Joseph Giamalua
 20300 STATLER ST 48081
Jefferson MS, 27900 ROCKWOOD ST 48081
 Dr. Joseph Nurek, prin.
Ardmore ES, 27001 GREATER MACK AVE 48081
 Darlene Sulad, prin.
Greenwood ES, 27900 JOAN ST 48081
 Jean Campbell, prin.
Harmon ES, 24800 HARMON ST 48080
 Cindy Allison, prin.
Princeton ES, 20300 STATLER ST 48081
 M. Nowakowski, prin.

South Lake SD
Sch. Sys. Enr. Code 4
Supt. – Joseph White
 23700 GREATER MACK AVE 48080
South Lake MS, 21621 CALIFORNIA ST 48080
 Richard Gates, prin.
Avalon ES, 2000 AVALON 48080
 David Myers, prin.
Elmwood ES, 22700 CALIFORNIA ST 48080
 Norman Brady, prin.
Pare ES, 23500 PARE ST 48080
 Lois McKay, prin.

St. Germaine ES, 28250 ROCKWOOD ST 48081
St. Isaac Jogues ES, 21100 MADISON ST 48081
St. Joan of Arc ES, 22415 OVERLAKE ST 48080

Saint Helen, Roscommon Co.
Gerrish-Higgins SD
Supt. – See Roscommon
ES, 1350 N ST HELEN RD 48656
 Martin Meier, prin.

Saint Ignace, Mackinac Co., Pop. Code 5
Moran Twp. SD
Sch. Sys. Enr. Code 2
Supt. – Ronald Mitchell
 300 GROS CAP ROAD 49781
Gros Cap ES, 300 ROS CAP ROAD 49781
 Ronald Mitchell, prin.

St. Ignace Area SD
Sch. Sys. Enr. Code 3
Supt. – Jerry Gallagher, 840 PORTAGE ST 49781
Bertrand MS, BERTRAND ST 49781
 Mike Lehto, prin.
Evergreen Shore MS, 100 ST CLAIR TRL 49781
 Mike Lehto, prin.
McCann ES, 399 MCCANN ST 49781
 Mike Lehto, prin.

St. John's SD
Supt. – See Saint Johns
East Essex ES, LOWE & N LOWE 48879
 H. Freeman, prin.

Saint James, Charlevoix Co., Pop. Code 2
Beaver Island Comm. SD
Sch. Sys. Enr. Code 1
Supt. – James Shepard, MERCER BLVD 49782
Beaver Island S 49782 – K. McNamara, prin.

Saint Johns, Clinton Co., Pop. Code 6
St. John's SD
Sch. Sys. Enr. Code 5
Supt. – Stephen Bakita, P O BOX 230 48879
Wilson MS, 101 W CASS ST 48879
 Robert Kudwa, prin.
East Olive ES, 2583 GREEN RD 48879
 Ricki Dean, prin.
Eureka ES, 7550 N WELLING RD 48879
 H. Freeman, prin.
Perrin-Palmer ES, 611 N LANSING ST 48879
 John Arehart, prin.

Riley ES, 5935 E PRATT RD 48879
 Arline Rullman, prin.
Swegles ES, 401 S SWEGLES ST 48879
 John Arehart, prin.
Other Schools – See Saint Ignace

St. Joseph ES, 201 E CASS ST 48879

Saint Joseph, Berrien Co., Pop. Code 6
St. Joseph SD
Sch. Sys. Enr. Code 4
Supt. – Fred Richardson, 2214 S STATE ST 49085
Upton MS, 800 MAIDEN LANE 49085
 Charlotte Wenham, prin.
Brown ES, GARDEN LAND 49085
 John Jarpe, prin.
Clark ES, 515 E GLENLORD RD 49085
 David Ratajik, prin.
Lincoln ES, 1102 ORCHARD AVE 49085
 Anthony Belski, prin.

Trinity ES, 613 COURT ST 49085

Saint Louis, Gratiot Co., Pop. Code 5
St. Louis SD
Sch. Sys. Enr. Code 4
Supt. – Tom Kowalski, 113 E SAGINAW ST 48880
Nurnberger ES, 312 UNION ST 48880
 Linda Johnson, prin.
Knause ES, 1 & K STS 48880 – John Raab, prin.
Nikkara ES, 301 W STATE ST 48880
 Don Pavlik, prin.
Westgate ES, 840 CHEESEMAN RD 48880
 Don Pavlik, prin.

Salem, Wayne Co.
South Lyon Comm. SD
Supt. – See South Lyon
ES, 7806 SALEM RD 48175 – Thomas Judit, prin.

Saline, Washtenaw Co., Pop. Code 6
Saline Area SD
Sch. Sys. Enr. Code 5
Supt. – Maurice Conn
 7190 N MAPLE ROAD 48176
MS, 7265 N ANN ARBOR ST 48176
 Joseph Schwartz, prin.
Houghton ES, 555 MILLS RD 48176
 Ross Vandercook, prin.
Jensen MS, 203 RISDON DR 48176
 Jerry Henry, prin.

Sand Creek, Lenawee Co.
Sand Creek Comm. SD
Sch. Sys. Enr. Code 3
Supt. – Don M. Harlan
 6850 SAND CREEK HIGHWAY 49279
McGregor ES, 6850 SAND CREEK HWY 49279
 Eric Sullivan, prin.

Sand Lake, Kent Co., Pop. Code 2
Tri County Area SD
Supt. – See Howard City
ES, 7TH ST 49443 – Carl Hoitenga, prin.

Sandusky, Sanilac Co., Pop. Code 4
Sandusky Comm. SD
Sch. Sys. Enr. Code 4
Supt. – James Nolan
 395 S SANDUSKY ROAD 48471
MS, 76 LEXINGTON ST 48471 – Tim Lentz, prin.
Maple Valley ES, 138 MAPLE VALLEY ST 48471
 David Mortimer, prin.

Sanford, Midland Co., Pop. Code 3
Meridian SD
Sch. Sys. Enr. Code 4
Supt. – Richard Johnson, 3361 M-30 ROAD 48657
Meridian MS, 3475 M-30 ROAD 48657
 Michael Rickey, prin.
Meridian ES, 3353 N M-30 RD 48657
 Bruce Knight, prin.
Perkins ES, 3139 N M-30 RD 48657
 Bruce Knight, prin.
ES, 2534 W RIVER RD 48657 – Linda Kirker, prin.
Other Schools – See Hope

Saranac, Ionia Co., Pop. Code 4
Saranac Comm. SD
Sch. Sys. Enr. Code 4
Supt. – (—), 150 PLEASANT ST 48881
MS, 28 VOSPER ST 48881 – Roger Klunder, prin.
Harker ES 48881 – Bruce Chadwick, prin.
MS, 150 PLEASANT 48881 – D. Benjamien, prin.

Sault Sainte Marie, Chippewa Co., Pop. Code 7
Sault Sainte Marie Area SD
Sch. Sys. Enr. Code 5
Supt. – Johann Ingold, 400 W SPRUCE ST 49783
MS, 1 EDUCATIONAL PLAZA 49783
 David Gonyeau, prin.
Jefferson ES, CEDAR ST 49783
 Lila Malmborg, prin.
Lincoln ES, 701 E 5TH AVE 49783
 Ben Jones, prin.
McKinley ES, 2023 W 4TH AVE 49783
 Verlin Kusler, prin.
Soo ES, PICKFORD ROAD 49783
 Colleen McNeal, prin.
Washington ES, 1200 RYAN AVE 49783
 Nick Oshelski, prin.
Other Schools – See Dafter

Sawyer, Berrien Co.
River Valley SD
Supt. – See Three Oaks

Chikaming ES, 13742 THREE OAKS   49125
  R. Schroeder, prin.

Trinity Lutheran School, P O BOX 23   49125

Schoolcraft, Kalamazoo Co., Pop. Code 4
Schoolcraft Comm. SD
Sch. Sys. Enr. Code 3
Supt. – L. C. Warfield, P O BOX 278   49087
MS, P O BOX 278   49087 – John Blakely, prin.
ES, P O BOX 278   49087 – Matt Hanichen, prin.

Scotts, Kalamazoo Co.
Climax-Scotts Comm. SD
Supt. – See Climax
Climax-Scotts ES, 11250 Q R AVE E   49088
  Robert Tipton, prin.

Vicksburg Comm. SD
Supt. – See Vicksburg
Tobey ES, 8551 E LONG LAKE DR   49088
  James Shaw, prin.

Scottville, Mason Co., Pop. Code 4
Mason County Central SD
Sch. Sys. Enr. Code 4
Supt. – Rob Redmond
  300 BROADWAY ST W   49454
Mason County Central MS
  300 BERYL ST W   49454
  Edward Malkowski, prin.
Riverton ES   49454 – (—), prin.
ES, 201 W MAPLE AVE   49454 – Gary Papke, prin.
Victory ES   49454 – (—), prin.

Sebewaing, Huron Co., Pop. Code 4
Unionville-Sebewaing Area SD
Sch. Sys. Enr. Code 3
Supt. – William D. Dodge, 628 E MAIN ST   48759
Unionville-Sebewaing MS, 628 E MAIN ST   48759
  Victor Reister, prin.
Unionville ES, 2926 CHURCH ST   48759
  Timothy Edwards, prin.

Immanuel ES, 612 E BAY ST   48759

Shelby, Oceana Co., Pop. Code 4
Shelby SD
Sch. Sys. Enr. Code 4
Supt. – John Van Duinen, 155 6TH ST E   49455
MS, 5TH ST   49455 – Duane Shugart, prin.
Benona ES, 2750 40TH AVE S   49455
  Ruth Sullivan, prin.
Read ES, 155 6TH ST   49455
  Clifford Seybert, prin.
Other Schools – See New Era

Shepherd, Isabella Co., Pop. Code 4
Shepherd SD
Sch. Sys. Enr. Code 4
Supt. – Hugh Riley, 238 S CHIPPEWA ST   48883
MS, 100 E HALL ST   48883
  Thomas Shepard, prin.
ES, MAPLE ST   48883 – Robert Pries, prin.
Other Schools – See Winn

Skandia, Marquette Co.
Gwinn Area SD
Supt. – See Gwinn
ES   49885 – (—), prin.

South Boardman, Kalkaska Co.
Forest Area Comm. SD
Supt. – See Fife Lake
ES   49680 – Dawn Decker, prin.

Southfield, Oakland Co., Pop. Code 8
Southfield SD
Sch. Sys. Enr. Code 6
Supt. – Carl Hassel, 24661 LAHSER ROAD   48034
Levey MS, 25300 W 9 MILE ROAD   48034
  Charles Foster, prin.
Thompson MS, 16300 LINCOLN DRIVE   48076
  Michael Horn, prin.
Adler ES, 19100 FILMORE ST   48075
  M. Alexander, prin.
Brace Lederle ES, 18575 W NINE MILE RD   48075
  Bobbie Hentrel, prin.
Eisenhower ES, 24500 LARKINS ST   48034
  Patricia Scott, prin.
Kennedy ES, 16229 MT VERNON ST   48075
  G. Kubasiewicz, prin.
Leonhard ES, 20900 INDEPENDENCE DR   48076
  Carol Pyke, prin.
MacArthur ES, 24501 FREDRICK ST   48034
  Claire Garlick, prin.
McIntyre ES, 19600 SARATOGA BLVD   48076
  Phyllis Burton, prin.
Schoenhals ES, 16500 LINCOLN DR   48076
  B. Mansfield, prin.
Stevenson ES, 27777 LAHSER DR   48076
  Gary Quitquit, prin.
Vandenberg ES, 16100 EDWARDS AVE   48076
  Dick Cadarette, prin.
Other Schools – See Lathrup Village

Akiva Hebrew Day School
  27700 SOUTHFIELD ROAD   48076
St. Bede ES, 18300 W TWELVE MILE RD   48076
St. Michael ES, 25175 CODE RD   48034

Southgate, Wayne Co., Pop. Code 8
Southgate Comm. SD
Sch. Sys. Enr. Code 5
Supt. – Paul Jones, 13100 BURNS ST   48195
Gerisch MS, 12601 MCCANN ST   48195
  Michael Kell, prin.

Davidson ES, 13940 LEROY ST   48195
  James Egler, prin.
Fordine ES, 14775 FORDLINE ST   48195
  Ilene Devine, prin.
Grogan ES, 13300 BURNS ST   48195
  Eugene Moralli, prin.
North Pointe ES, 18635 BOWIE ST   48195
  James Candela, prin.
Shelters ES, 12600 FORDLINE ST   48195
  H. Wallschlager, prin.

Christ the King ES, 15600 TRENTON RD   48195
St. Pius, 14141 PEARL ST   48195

South Haven, Van Buren Co., Pop. Code 6
South Haven SD
Sch. Sys. Enr. Code 5
Supt. – Stephen Kelly, 554 GREEN ST   49090
Central MS, 500 BROADWAY ST   49090
  Larry Lethorn, prin.
Hartman ES, 335 HUBBARD ST   49090
  Donald Miller, prin.
Indiana ES, 615 INDIANA AVE   49090
  Donald Miller, prin.
Lincoln ES, 500 ELKENBURG ST   49090
  William French, prin.
Maple Grove ES, 72399 12TH AVE   49090
  Donald Miller, prin.

St. Basil ES, 94 SUPERIOR ST   49090

South Lyon, Oakland Co., Pop. Code 6
South Lyon Comm. SD
Sch. Sys. Enr. Code 5
Supt. – Wayne Case, 235 W LIBERTY ST W   48178
Centennial MS, 62500 9 MILE ROAD   48178
  Glen Croyden, prin.
Bartlett ES, 350 SCHOOL ST   48178
  Walter Herrala, prin.
Dolsen ES, 56775 RICE   48165 – John Sprys, prin.
Sayre ES, 23000 VALERIE ST   48178
  Sharon Hardy, prin.
Other Schools – See Salem

South Range, Houghton Co., Pop. Code 3
Adams Twp. SD
Supt. – See Painesdale
ES   49963 – Albert Anderson, prin.

South Rockwood, Monroe Co., Pop. Code 4
Airport Comm. SD
Supt. – See Carleton
Ritter ES
  5650 CARLETON ROCKWOOD RD   48179
  Richard Booth, prin.

Sparta, Kent Co., Pop. Code 5
Sparta Area SD
Sch. Sys. Enr. Code 5
Supt. – Michael Weiler
  10200 SPARTA AVE   49345
Sparta JHS, 565 MAPLE ST   49345
  Gary Griffin, prin.
Central ES, 200 ALMA ST   49345
  Patrick Smith, prin.
White ES, 1655 12 MILE ROAD NW   49345
  Mary Spencer, prin.

Spring Arbor, Jackson Co., Pop. Code 6
Western SD
Supt. – See Parma
Bean ES, 3201 NOBLE RD   49283
  Dena Dardzinski, prin.
Warner ES, 118 STAR ST   49283
  David Collins, prin.

Spring Lake, Ottawa Co., Pop. Code 5
Spring Lake SD
Sch. Sys. Enr. Code 4
Supt. – Duane Moore, 345 HAMMOND ST   49456
Holmes ES, 345 HAMMOND ST   49456
  Roger Vigland, prin.
Jeffers ES, 345 HAMMOND ST   49456
  Roger Susterich, prin.

St. Mary ES, 421 E EXCHANGE ST   49456

Springport, Jackson Co., Pop. Code 3
Springport SD
Sch. Sys. Enr. Code 4
Supt. – Ron Jones, P O BOX 100   49284
ES, P O BOX 100   49284 – R. Brelinski, prin.

Stambaugh, Iron Co., Pop. Code 4
West Iron County SD
Sch. Sys. Enr. Code 4
Supt. – Scott Peterson, P O BOX 580   49964
St. Agnes ES   49935 – Sylvia Hronkin, prin.
MS, WASHINGTON AVE   49964
  Don Sartorelli, prin.
Other Schools – See Iron River

Standish, Arenac Co., Pop. Code 4
Standish-Sterling Comm. SD
Sch. Sys. Enr. Code 4
Supt. – Claude Inch, 3789 WYATT ROAD   48658
Standish-Sterling MS, 3789 WYATT ROAD   48658
  J. Sommerfield, prin.
ES, 583 E CEDAR ST   48658
  Wendy Genella, prin.
Sterling ES, 338 W STATE   48659
  Roger Anderson, prin.

Stanton, Montcalm Co., Pop. Code 4
Central Montcalm SD
Sch. Sys. Enr. Code 4
Supt. – Robert Spencer
  1480 SHERIDAN ROAD SW   48888
Central MS, 1480 SHERIDAN ROAD SW   48888
  Kathy Brockdorf, prin.
Sheridan ES, P O BOX 282   48884
  Janis Pearl, prin.
ES, 710 N STATE ST   48888 – Steven Strait, prin.

Stanwood, Mecosta Co., Pop. Code 2
Morley-Stanwood Comm. SD
Supt. – See Morley
ES, 156 FRONT ST   49346 – Randall LaPreze, prin.

Stephenson, Menominee Co., Pop. Code 3
Stephenson Area SD
Sch. Sys. Enr. Code 4
Supt. – Charles Kalhoefer   49887
MS   49887 – (—), prin.
ES   49887 – Daisymae Mayer, prin.
Other Schools – See Daggett, Wallace

Sterling Heights, Macomb Co., Pop. Code 9
Utica Comm. SD
Supt. – See Utica
Burr ES, 41460 RYAN RD   48310
  Martin Kasiska, prin.
Dekeyser ES, 39600 ATKINSON DR   48078
  Cheryl Snell, prin.
Dresden ES, 11400 DELVIN DR   48078
  David Deview, prin.
Graebner ES, 41875 SAAL RD   48078
  George Tibor, prin.
Harvey ES, 41700 MONTROY DR   48078
  Elaine Morris, prin.
Havel ES, 41855 SCHOENHERR RD   48078
  R. Koenigsknecht, prin.
Kidd ES, 38397 GLADSTONE DR   48077
  Kathy Branch, prin.

St. Paul ES, 42681 HAYES RD   48078

Stevensville, Berrien Co., Pop. Code 4
Lakeshore SD
Sch. Sys. Enr. Code 5
Supt. – Ned Curtis, 5771 CLEVELAND AVE   49127
Lakeshore MS, 1459 W JOHN BEERS ROAD   49127
  John Woods, prin.
Hollywood ES, 143 W JOHN BEERS RD   49127
  Leslie Collins, prin.
Roosevelt ES, 5550 DENNIS ST   49127
  Charles Reed, prin.
Stewart ES, 2750 ORCHARD LN   49127
  Donald Frank, prin.

Christ ES, 4333 CLEVELAND AVE   49127

Stockbridge, Ingham Co., Pop. Code 4
Stockbridge Comm. SD
Sch. Sys. Enr. Code 4
Supt. – Donald Pobuda, 305 W ELIZABETH   49285
MS, 499 W ELIZABETH   49285
  Robert Boyd, prin.
Smith ES, MILLS ST   49285 – Donald Porter, prin.
Other Schools – See Gregory, Munith

Sturgis, St. Joseph Co., Pop. Code 6
Nottawa Comm. SD
Sch. Sys. Enr. Code 2
Supt. – (—), 26438 M-86   49091
Nottawa ES, 26438 M-86   49091
  Gary Seeley, prin.

Sturgis SD
Sch. Sys. Enr. Code 5
Supt. – Lawrence McConnell
  216 VINEWOOD AVE   49091
MS, 107 WEST ST   49091 – Thomas Revitte, prin.
Arden Park ES, ILENE ST   49091
  Jack Arbanas, prin.
Congress ES, 421 E CONGRESS ST   49091
  Roy Pearson, prin.
Fawn River ES, CARLS ROAD   49091
  Roy Pearson, prin.
Jerolene ES, JEROLENE ST   49091
  Viola Schuler, prin.
Park ES, 603 W NEUMAN ST   49091
  Jack Arbanas, prin.
Wall ES, E LAFAYETTE   49091 – K. Arend, prin.
Wenzel ES, 403 S PARK ST   49091
  Jack Arbanas, prin.

Holy Angels ES, 402 S NOTTAWA ST   49091
Trinity Lutheran School
  406 S LAKEVIEW AVE   49091

Sunfield, Eaton Co., Pop. Code 3
Lakewood SD
Supt. – See Lake Odessa
ES, 380 SCHOOL ST   48890 – Keith Heide, prin.

Suttons Bay, Leelanau Co., Pop. Code 3
Suttons Bay SD
Sch. Sys. Enr. Code 3
Supt. – Robert MacEachran, P O BOX 367   49682
ES, P O BOX 367   49682 – Stephen Alguire, prin.

Swartz Creek, Genesee Co., Pop. Code 6
Carman-Ainsworth SD
Supt. – See Flint
Rankin ES, G-3459 MUNDY   48473
  Robert Asher, prin.

Swartz Creek Comm. SD
Sch. Sys. Enr. Code 5
Supt. – Charles Townsend
   8354 CAPPY LANE 48473
Crapo MS, 8197 MILLER ROAD 48473
   Sharon Fouts, prin.
Dieck ES, 2239 VAN VLEET RD 48473
   Louie Medlin, prin.
Elms Road ES, 3259 ELMS RD 48473
   David Kittell, prin.
Gaines ES, 300 E LANSING 48436
   Andrew Cook, prin.
Morrish ES, 5055 MAPLE AVE 48473
   Martha Price, prin.
Syring ES, 5300 OAKVIEW DR 48473
   Frank Rehanek, prin.

St. Mary ES, 4413 MORRISH RD 48473

Tawas City, Iosco Co., Pop. Code 4
East Tawas Area SD
Supt. – See East Tawas
Tawas MS, 255 E HEMLOCK ROAD 48763
   Jerry Youngs, prin.

Taylor, Wayne Co., Pop. Code 8
Taylor SD
Sch. Sys. Enr. Code 7
Supt. – Jerry Montecillo
   23033 NORTHLINE ST 48180
Brake JHS, 13500 PINE ST 48180
   A. Sebastian, prin.
Hoover JHS, 27101 BEVERLY ST 48180
   R. Clements, prin.
West JHS, 10575 WILLIAMS ST 48180
   Kenneth Nelson, prin.
Eureka Heights ES, 25125 EUREKA RD 48180
   Steve Creutz, prin.
Eurekadale ES, 14616 DUNCAN ST 48180
   Dennis Joyce, prin.
Fischer ES, 8882 BEECH DALY RD 48180
   Jim Lofft, prin.
Holland ES, 10201 HOLLAND ST 48180
   John Daniels, prin.
Johnson ES, 20701 WOHLFEIL ST 48180
   Jim Schultz, prin.
Kinyon ES, 10455 MONROE BLVD 48180
   Gerald Smith, prin.
McDowell ES, 22929 BREST ST 48180
   Richard Kunzi, prin.
Moody ES, 8280 HIPP ST 48180
   Richard Prunty, prin.
Myers ES, 16201 LAUREN ST 48180
   Pat Leiby, prin.
Racho ES, 20955 NORTHLINE ST 48180
   Robert Adamczyk, prin.
Randall ES, 8699 ROBERT ST 48180
   Karen Luecke, prin.
Taylor Parks ES, 20614 PINECREST ST 48180
   Joan Gebhardt, prin.
Treadwell ES, 6375 INKSTER ST 48180
   D. Hopgood, prin.
Wareing ES, 24800 HAYES ST 48180
   Gloria McGarvey, prin.
Other Schools – See Dearborn Heights

St. Alfred ES, 9540 TELEGRAPH RD 48180
St. Cyril of Jerusalem ES
   6451 JACKSON ST 48180
St. John ES, 13115 TELEGRAPH RD 48180
St. Pascal ES, 8070 ROOSEVELT ST 48180

Tecumseh, Lenawee Co., Pop. Code 6
Tecumseh SD
Sch. Sys. Enr. Code 5
Supt. – Gene Cooley
   304 W CHICAGO BLVD 49286
MS, 212 N OTTAWA ST 49286
   Gary Lovett, prin.
Herrick Park ES, 600 HERRICK PARK DR 49286
   Lois Fleming, prin.
Patterson ES, 401 N VAN BUREN ST 49286
   Cynthia Opelt, prin.
Ridgeway ES, E MONROE ROAD 49286
   Lois Fleming, prin.
Tecumseh Acres ES, 600 S ADRIAN ST 49286
   Ben Thomas, prin.
Tipton ES, 41 N ADRIAN HWY 49286
   Thomas Sura, prin.
Other Schools – See Adrian

Tekonsha, Calhoun Co., Pop. Code 3
Tekonsha SD
Sch. Sys. Enr. Code 2
Supt. – Roger Carlson, 245 S ELM ST 49092
MS, 245 S ELM ST 49092 – M. Clark, prin.
Perrine ES, 327 CATHERINE ST 49092
   M. Clark, prin.

Temperance, Monroe Co., Pop. Code 4
Bedford SD
Sch. Sys. Enr. Code 5
Supt. – Herbert Moyer
   1575 W TEMPERANCE ROAD 48182
Jackman ES, 8008 JACKMAN RD 48182
   Duane Tucker, prin.
Smith ES, 1135 SMITH RD 48182
   George Cowdrey, prin.
Other Schools – See Lambertville

St. Anthony ES, 4607 M-151 RD W 48182

Thompsonville, Benzie Co., Pop. Code 2
Benzie County Central SD
Supt. – See Benzonia

Betzie Valley ES, M-115 49683 – Peter Moss, prin.

Three Oaks, Berrien Co., Pop. Code 4
River Valley SD
Sch. Sys. Enr. Code 4
Supt. – Charles Williams
   RURAL ROUTE 02 BOX 330 49128
River Valley MS
   RURAL ROUTE 02 BOX 330 49128
   James White, prin.
ES, 100 OAK ST 49128 – Peter Petros, prin.
Other Schools – See New Troy, Sawyer

Three Rivers, St. Joseph Co., Pop. Code 6
Three Rivers Comm. SD
Sch. Sys. Enr. Code 5
Supt. – Ronald P. Reece
   207 E MICHIGAN AVE 49093
MS, 1101 JEFFERSON ST 49093
   Louis Seman, prin.
Andrews ES, 200 S DOUGLAS AVE 49093
   Larry Miller, prin.
Barrows ES, 416 WASHINGTON ST 49093
   Michael Bosma, prin.
Hoppin ES, 415 N MAIN ST 49093
   Sue Ellen Potts, prin.
Norton ES, 59692 A L JONES 49093
   James Wetherbee, prin.
Park Community ES, 53806 WILBUR RD 49093
   Sylvia Hill, prin.

Immaculate Conception ES, 308 S MAIN ST 49093

Traverse City, Grand Traverse Co., Pop. Code 7
Traverse City Area SD
Sch. Sys. Enr. Code 6
Supt. – V. L. Oxender, P O BOX 32 49685
Central ES, 301 7TH ST 49684
   David Millross, prin.
Cherry Knoll ES, THREE MILE ROAD 49684
   David Beattie, prin.
East Bay ES, THREE MILE ROAD 49684
   Larry Dobler, prin.
Eastern ES, 1600 EASTERN AVE 49684
   Nancy Fieldman, prin.
Long Lake ES, 7738 N LONG LAKE RD 49684
   Charles Chase, prin.
Loomis ES, 1009 S OAK ST 49684
   Dave Dean, prin.
Norris ES, 10763 CHERRY BEND RD 49684
   Kathy Stratton, prin.
Oak Park ES, 301 S GARFIELD AVE 49684
   Megan Oberlin, prin.
Old Mission ES, 2735 ISLAND VIEW RD 49684
   James Linsell, prin.
Sabin ES, 2075 CASS RD 49684 – L. Rhoads, prin.
Silver Lake ES 49684 – George Sarns, prin.
Traverse Heights ES, 933 ROSE ST 49684
   Karen Schmidt, prin.
Willow Hill ES, 1250 HILL ST 49684
   Keith Forton, prin.
Other Schools – See Acme, Interlochen

Immaculate Conception ES, 218 VINE ST 49684
St. Francis ES, 130 E 10TH ST 49684
Trinity ES, 13TH & MAPLE 49684

Trenton, Wayne Co., Pop. Code 7
Gilbraltar SD
Supt. – See Rockwood
Hunter ES, 21320 ROCHE ST 48183
   James Vollmar, prin.

Trenton SD
Sch. Sys. Enr. Code 5
Supt. – Neil E. Van Riper
   2603 CHARLTON ROAD 48183
Monguagon MS, 4000 MARIAN DRIVE 48183
   Bill Miller, prin.
Anderson ES, 2600 HARRISON AVE 48183
   John Chapman, prin.
Hedke ES, 3201 MARIAN DR 48183
   Clifton Mace, prin.
Owen ES, 2271 GRANGE RD 48183
   Patricia Wagner, prin.
Taylor ES, 3700 BENSON ST 48183
   William Wilson, prin.

Woodhaven SD
Supt. – See Flat Rock
Henry MS, 24825 HALL ROAD 48183
   Herbert Kehrl, prin.
Bates ES, 22811 GUDITH ST 48183
   Robert Pizzuti, prin.
Yake ES, 16400 CARTER ST 48183
   Dr. Palazzolo, prin.

St. Joseph ES, 2675 3RD ST 48183

Troy, Oakland Co., Pop. Code 8
Birmingham SD
Supt. – See Birmingham
Pembroke ES, 955 ETON RD 48084
   Carol Schraeger, prin.

Troy SD
Sch. Sys. Enr. Code 7
Supt. – Dr. David Spencer
   4400 LIVERNOIS ROAD 48098
Baker MS, 1291 TORPEY DRIVE 48084
   John Acton, prin.
Boulan Park MS
   3570 NORTHFIELD PARKWAY 48084
   Anteinette Burke, prin.
Larson MS, 2222 E LONG LAKE ROAD 48098
   Leon Klein, prin.

Smith MS, 5835 DONALDSON AVE 48098
   Stuart Redpath, prin.
Barnard ES, 3601 FORGE DR 48083
   C. Hettenbach, prin.
Bemis ES, 3571 NORTHFIELD PKY 48084
   Kenneth Lahti, prin.
Costello ES, 1333 HAMMAN DR 48098
   Gary Wood, prin.
Hamilton ES, 5625 NORTHFIELD PKY 48098
   Thomas Andres, prin.
Hill ES, 4600 FORSYTH AVE 48098
   Kathy Davisson, prin.
Leonard ES, 4401 TALLMAN DR 48098
   J. Yashinsky, prin.
Martell ES, 5666 LIVERNOIS RD 48098
   Thomas Clippert, prin.
Morse ES, 475 CHERRY ST 48083
   Janet Gutowski, prin.
Schroeder ES, 3541 JACK DR 48084
   P. MacCarato, prin.
Troy Union ES, 1340 E SQ LK 48098
   Ronald O'Hara, prin.
Wass ES, 2340 WILLARD DR 48098
   D. Vanden Berghe, prin.
Wattles ES, 3555 ELLENBORO ST 48083
   Lennie Wells, prin.

Warren Cons. SD
Supt. – See Warren
Susick ES, 2200 CASTLETON DR 48083
   Sharon Prince, prin.

Trufant, Montcalm Co.
Lakeview Comm. SD
Supt. – See Lakeview
ES, 239 FIRST ST 49347 – George Goulet, prin.

Tustin, Osceola Co., Pop. Code 2
Pine River Area SD
Supt. – See Le Roy
ES, 107 BREMER ST 49688 – Daryl Morr, prin.

Twining, Arenac Co., Pop. Code 2
Arenac Eastern SD
Sch. Sys. Enr. Code 3
Supt. – Loren L. Wycoff, 200 SMALLEY ST 48766
Arenac Eastern ES, 200 SMALLEY 48766
   Loren Wycoff, prin.

Ubly, Huron Co., Pop. Code 3
Ubly Comm. SD
Sch. Sys. Enr. Code 3
Supt. – David Landeryou, 2020 UNION ST 48475
ES, 2020 UNION ST 48475
   Kenneth Sweeney, prin.

Union City, Branch Co., Pop. Code 4
Union City Comm. SD
Sch. Sys. Enr. Code 4
Supt. – William Tebbe
   430 SAINT JOSEPH ST 49094
MS, 435 SAINT JOSEPH ST 49094
   Eugene Pensari, prin.
Sherwood ES 49094 – (—), prin.
ES, WALNUT LN 49094 – Fred Davenport, prin.

Union Lake, Oakland Co., Pop. Code 6
Walled Lake Cons. SD
Supt. – See Walled Lake
Smart MS, 8500 COMMERCE ROAD 48085
   Lawrence Barlow, prin.
Commerce ES, 520 FARR ST 48085
   Barbara Garbutt, prin.
Keith ES, 2800 KEITH RD 48085
   Andrew Dale, prin.

Waterford SD
Supt. – See Waterford
Houghton ES, 8080 ELIZABETH LAKE RD 48085
   Dawn Davis, prin.

St. Patrick ES, 9040 HUTCHINS ST 48085

Unionville, Tuscola Co., Pop. Code 3

St. Paul Lutheran School, 6335 CENTER 48767

Utica, Macomb Co., Pop. Code 6
Chippewa Valley SD
Supt. – See Mount Clemens
Iroquois MS, 48301 ROMEO PLANK ROAD 48087
   Ron Haas, prin.
Mohawk ES, 48101 ROMEO PLANK 48087
   K. Madeleine, prin.

Utica Comm. SD
Sch. Sys. Enr. Code 7
Supt. – Richard LaBaere
   51040 SHELBY ROAD 48087
Collins ES, 12900 GRAND HAVEN DR 48077
   Donald Santilli, prin.
Crissman ES, 53550 WOLF DR 48087
   P. Schroeder, prin.
Ebeling ES, 15970 HAVERHILL DR 48087
   Lynn Robinson, prin.
Flickinger ES, 45400 VANKER AVE 48087
   Sheryl Swanson, prin.
Magahay ES, 44700 OLEANDER DR 48078
   Carolyn Smith, prin.
Messmore ES 48087 – (—), prin.
Monfort ES, 6700 MONTGOMERY DR 48087
   Joanne Teague, prin.
Oakbrook ES, 1260 GREENWAY 48077
   Paul Yelensky, prin.
Plumbrook ES, 39660 SPALDING DR 48078
   Joanne Simon, prin.

Roberts ES, 2400 BELL VIEW DR   48087
    V. Constand, prin.
Schuchard ES, 2900 HOLLY DR   48310
    Joe Jeannette, prin.
Schwarzkoff ES
    8401 CONSTITUTION BLVD   48078
    Paul Rand, prin.
Sterlin ES, 12500 19 MILE ROAD   48078
    Audrey St. John, prin.
Walsh ES, 38901 DODGE PARK RD   48077
    R. Wattersworth, prin.
West Utica ES, 5415 W UTICA RD   48087
    Robert O'Brien, prin.
Wiley ES, 47240 SHELBY RD   48087
    Randall Eckhardt, prin.
Other Schools – See Rochester, Sterling Heights

Warren Cons. SD
Supt. – See Warren
Angus ES, 3180 HEIN DR   48310
    Robert McGhee, prin.
Black ES, 14100 HERITAGE RD   48077
    Robert Cracknell, prin.
Fillmore ES, 8655 IRVING RD   48077
    Ronald Bulgarelli, prin.
Haitema ES, 11870 ELDORADO DR   48077
    Harry Bearse, prin.
Harwood ES, 4900 SOUTHLAWN DR   48310
    Martin Faulman, prin.
Hatherly ES, 35201 DAVISON ST   48310
    R. Crampton, prin.
Holden ES, 37565 CALKA DR   48310
    Leonard Piwko, prin.
Jefferson ES, 37555 CAROL DR   48310
    Douglas Haesler, prin.
North ES, 5400 MEADOWVIEW ST   48310
    Jerry Smigell, prin.
Thorpe ES, 36095 ENGLISH DR   48310
    Elsie Vargo, prin.
Willow Woods ES, 11001 DANIEL DR   48077
    William Block, prin.

Peace ES, 6580 TWENTY FOUR MILE RD   48087
St. Lawrence ES, 44429 UTICA RD   48087
Trinity ES, 45091 DESHON ST   48087

Vanderbilt, Otsego Co., Pop. Code 3
Vanderbilt Area SD
Sch. Sys. Enr. Code 2
Supt. – Robert Hansen, 947 DONOVAN ST   49795
S, 947 DONOVAN ST   49795
    Richard Diebold, prin.

Vassar, Tuscola Co., Pop. Code 5
Vassar SD
Sch. Sys. Enr. Code 4
Supt. – William Chinery, 220 ATHLETIC ST   48768
MS, 220 ATHLETIC ST   48768
    Tom Frampton, prin.
Central ES, 220 ATHLETIC ST   48768
    Tom Matuszewski, prin.
Townsend North ES, 220 ATHLETIC ST   48768
    Randy Middlin, prin.

Vermontville, Eaton Co., Pop. Code 3
Maple Valley SD
Sch. Sys. Enr. Code 4
Supt. – Carroll J. Wolff
    11090 NASHVILLE HWY   49096
Fuller ES, SCHOOL ST   49073
    Nancy Potter, prin.
Maplewood ES, 170 SEMINARY ST   49096
    David Doozan, prin.
Other Schools – See Nashville

Vestaburg, Montcalm Co., Pop. Code 2
Vestaburg Comm. SD
Sch. Sys. Enr. Code 3
Supt. – George Showers   48891
ES   48891 – Kary Kanitz, prin.

Vicksburg, Kalamazoo Co., Pop. Code 4
Vicksburg Comm. SD
Sch. Sys. Enr. Code 4
Supt. – Larry Cole, 301 S KALAMAZOO ST   49097
East Prairie MS, E PRAIRIE ST   49097
    Charles Glaes, prin.
Indian Lake ES, 11901 S 30TH ST   49097
    Patricia Bird, prin.
Sunset Lake ES, 201 N LVD   49097
    C. Babcock-Conant, prin.
Other Schools – See Scotts

Wakefield, Gogebic Co., Pop. Code 5
Wakefield Twp. SD
Sch. Sys. Enr. Code 3
Supt. – Richard King, 715 PUTNAM ST   49968
Central ES, 1401 PUTNAM ST   49968
    Richard King, prin.

Waldron, Hillsdale Co., Pop. Code 3
Waldron Area SD
Sch. Sys. Enr. Code 2
Supt. – Dewey R. Schramm
    1338 WALDRON ROAD   49288
ES, 1338 WALDRON ROAD   49288
    Dewey Schramm, prin.

Walkerville, Oceana Co., Pop. Code 2
Walkerville Rural Comm. SD
Sch. Sys. Enr. Code 2
Supt. – J. P. Ryan, FRANKLIN ST   49459
ES, FRANKLIN ST   49459 – D. Barnhouse, prin.

Wallace, Menominee Co.
Stephenson Area SD
Supt. – See Stephenson

Mellen ES 49893 – John Hoijer, prin.

Walled Lake, Oakland Co., Pop. Code 5
Walled Lake Cons. SD
Sch. Sys. Enr. Code 6
Supt. – James Geisler
    695 W PONTIAC TRAIL   48088
MS, 615 N PONTIAC TRAIL   48088
    R. Roy Danley, prin.
Decker ES, 1655 DECKER RD   48088
    M. Biziorek, prin.
Dublin ES, 9620 SANDYSIDE   48085
    Spencer Rush, prin.
Glengary ES, 3070 WOODBURY ST   48088
    Lois Ryan, prin.
Loon Lake ES, 2151 LOON LAKE ROAD   48088
    Susan Winder, prin.
Oakley Park ES, 2015 E OAKLEY PARK RD   48088
    Sylvia Whitmer, prin.
ES, 1055 W WEST MAPLE RD   48088
    Miriam Weberman, prin.
Other Schools – See Pontiac, Union Lake, Wixom

St. Matthew ES, 2040 S COMMERCE RD   48088
St. William ES, 125 OFLAHERTY ST   48088

Warren, Macomb Co., Pop. Code 9
Centerline SD
Supt. – See Center Line
Crothers ES, 27401 CAMPBELL AVE   48093
    Donald Wilcox, prin.
Peck ES, 11300 ENGLEMAN RD   48089
    Ray Allison, prin.
Roose ES, 25310 MASCH AVE   48091
    M. Corcoran, prin.

East Detroit SD
Supt. – See East Detroit
Roosevelt ES, 14200 STEPHENS RD   48089
    Steve Lopiccola, prin.
Warrendale ES, 14170 COUWLIER AVE   48089
    Carole Zielke, prin.

Fitzgerald SD
Sch. Sys. Enr. Code 5
Supt. – Anthony Galati
    23200 RYAN ROAD   48091
Chatterton MS, 23200 RYAN ROAD   48091
    Joy Holman, prin.
Mound Park ES, 23200 RYAN RD   48091
    Jerry Udell, prin.
Schofield ES, 23200 RYAN RD   48091
    Jerome Roeske, prin.
Westview ES, 23200 RYAN RD   48091
    Richard Fedelem, prin.

Van Dyke SD
Sch. Sys. Enr. Code 5
Supt. – Michael Dyke
    22100 FEDERAL AVE   48089
Carlson ES, 12355 MRUK AVE   48089
    Carole Marsiglio, prin.
Harding ES, 2230 PETERS   48089
    C. Kowalczyk, prin.
Kennedy ES, 11333 KALTZ AVE   48089
    Gene Winowski, prin.
Lincoln ES, 8465 STUDEBAKER AVE   48089
    David Cooper, prin.
Little ES, 23500 MACARTHUR BLVD   48089
    K. Sowinski, prin.
McKinley ES, 13173 TOEPFER RD   48089
    Stan Kubicki, prin.
Thompson ES, 11370 HUPP AVE   48089
    Helen MacGregor, prin.
Washington ES
    11400 CONTINENTAL AVE   48089
    M. Winterfield, prin.

Warren Cons. SD
Sch. Sys. Enr. Code 7
Supt. – George DePillo
    31300 ANITA DRIVE   48093
Cromie ES, 29797 GILBERT DR   48093
    Don Modrycki, prin.
Green Acres ES, 4655 HOMES   48092
    Raymond Brown, prin.
Lean ES, 2825 GIRARD DR   48092
    Gene Mignacca, prin.
Siersma ES, 3100 DONNA AVE   48091
    James Callaghan, prin.
Warner ES, 2791 KOPER   48310
    William Frazier, prin.
Wilde ES, 32343 BUNERT RD   48093
    Helen Nienhaus, prin.
Wilkerson ES, 12100 MASONIC BLVD   48093
    John Walker, prin.
Other Schools – See Troy, Utica

Warren Woods SD
Sch. Sys. Enr. Code 5
Supt. – Thomas Dobbs
    27100 SCHOENHERR ROAD   48093
Warren Woods MS, 13400 E 12 MILE ROAD   48093
    Alfred Cardinali, prin.
Briarwood ES, 14100 LEISURE DR   48093
    C. Brunn, prin.
Pinewood ES, 14411 BADE DR   48093
    Alice Johnson, prin.
Westwood ES, 11999 MARTIN RD   48093
    Gerald Hagerman, prin.

Immaculate Conception ES
    29500 WESTBROOK AVE   48092
Peace ES, 11701 E TWELVE MILE RD   48093
St. Anne ES, 5920 ARDEN AVE   48092
Trinity ES, 8130 CHAPP   48089

Waterford, Oakland Co., Pop. Code 8
Waterford SD
Sch. Sys. Enr. Code 7
Supt. – Alton Cowan
    6020 PONTIAC LAKE ROAD   48095
Schoolcraft ES, 6400 MACEDAY DR   48095
    Marylou Simmons, prin.
Waterford Village ES, 4241 STEFFIN RD   48095
    Michael Killian, prin.
Other Schools – See Drayton Plains, Pontiac, Union Lake

Our Lady of the Lakes ES, 5501 DIXIE HWY   48095

Watersmeet, Gogebic Co., Pop. Code 4
Watersmeet Twp. SD
Sch. Sys. Enr. Code 2
Supt. – J. Vestich, P O BOX 217   49969
S, P O BOX 217   49969 – Parnell Basanese, prin.

Watervliet, Berrien Co., Pop. Code 4
Watervliet SD
Sch. Sys. Enr. Code 4
Supt. – A. Bruce Watson
    450 E RED ARROW HIGHWAY   49098
JHS, 450 E RED ARROW HWY   49098
    Don Wilson, prin.
North ES, BALDWIN AVE   49098
    David Coffeen, prin.
South ES, LUCINDA LN   49098
    Darlene Dongvillo, prin.

St. Joseph ES, 200 W DIVISION   49098

Wayland, Allegan Co., Pop. Code 4
Wayland Un. SD
Sch. Sys. Enr. Code 4
Supt. – R. Brenner, 870 135TH AVE   49348
MS, 201 PINE ST   49348 – R. Marutz, prin.
Baker ES, 507 W SYCAMORE ST   49348
    Edgar Torkko, prin.
Steeby ES, 435 E SUPERIOR ST   49348
    Holly Lear, prin.
Other Schools – See Dorr, Moline

Wayne, Wayne Co., Pop. Code 7
Wayne-Westland Comm. SD
Supt. – See Westland
Franklin MS, 33555 ANNAPOLIS ST   48184
    Leo Schuster, prin.
Hoover ES, 5400 4TH ST   48184
    Don Chastain, prin.
Monroe ES, 5021 BIDDLE ST   48184
    Frank LaSota, prin.
Roosevelt McGrath ES, 36075 CURRIER ST   48184
    Suzanne McBride, prin.
Taft Galloway ES, 4035 GLORIA ST   48184
    Eugene Barnyak, prin.
Vandenberg ES, 32101 STELLWAGEN ST   48184
    David Gracy, prin.

St. Mary ES, 34516 MICHIGAN   48184
St. Michael ES, 3003 HANNAN RD   48184

Webberville, Ingham Co., Pop. Code 4
Webberville Comm. SD
Sch. Sys. Enr. Code 3
Supt. – Edward Schultz
    313 E GRAND RIVER AVE   48892
ES, 202 N MAIN ST   48892 – Gene Englerth, prin.

Wells, Delta Co.
Escanaba Area SD
Supt. – See Escanaba
ES, 5775 MAIN ST   49894 – James Aird, prin.

Wellston, Manistee Co.
Kaleva-Norman-Dickson SD
Supt. – See Brethren
ES, 17345 6TH ST   49689 – Mark Sharp, prin.

West Bloomfield, Oakland Co., Pop. Code 8
Bloomfield Hills SD
Supt. – See Bloomfield Hills
Lone Pine ES, 3100 W LONG LAKE RD   48033
    Marge Thomas, prin.
Pine Lake ES, 3333 W LONG LAKE RD   48033
    Donald Wilson, prin.

West Bloomfield SD
Sch. Sys. Enr. Code 5
Supt. – Seymour Gretchko
    3250 COMMERCE ROAD   48033
Abbott MS, 3380 ORCHARD LAKE ROAD   48033
    Teri Giannetti, prin.
Orchard Lake MS
    6000 ORCHARD LAKE ROAD   48322
    Esther Peterson, prin.
Doherty ES, 3575 WALNUT LAKE RD   48033
    John Hoye, prin.
Green ES, 4500 WALNUT LAKE RD   48033
    Katherine Sheiko, prin.
Roosevelt ES, 2065 CASS LK ROAD   48033
    Cheryl Flammer, prin.
Scotch ES, 5810 COMMERCE RD   48033
    Carl Childress, prin.
Other Schools – See Pontiac

West Branch, Ogemaw Co., Pop. Code 4
Rose City Area SD
Sch. Sys. Enr. Code 4
Supt. – James Zubulake
    960 S M-33 HIGHWAY   48661
Surline MS, 147 STATE ST   48661 – Peg Diss, prin.
Rose City ES, P O BOX 407   48661
    G. Harrington, prin.

Surline ES, 147 STATE ST 48661
 Michael Pugh, prin.

St. Joseph ES, 961 W HOUGHTON AVE 48661

Westland, Wayne Co., Pop. Code 8
 Livonia SD
 Supt. – See Livonia
 Cooper ES, 28611 ANN ARBOR TRL 48185
  Doreen Reid, prin.
 Hayes ES, 30600 LOUISE ST 48185
  Gerald Nehs, prin.
 Nankin Mills ES, 8100 HUBBARD ST N 48185
  Paul Derwich, prin.

 Plymouth-Canton Comm. SD
 Supt. – See Plymouth
 Lowell MS, 8400 HIX ROAD N 48185
  Patricia Patton, prin.

 Wayne-Westland Comm. SD
 Sch. Sys. Enr. Code 7
 Supt. – Dennis O'Neill
  36745 MARQUETTE ST 48185
 Adams MS, 33475 PALMER ROAD 48185
  Ronald Stratton, prin.
 Marshall MS, 35100 BAYVIEW ST 48185
  Walt Durant, prin.
 Stevenson ES, 38501 PALMER ROAD 48185
  Dennis Connolly, prin.
 Edison ES, 34505 HUNTER ST 48185
  B. Laporte, prin.
 Elliott ES, 30800 BENNINGTON ST 48185
  Jose Muller, prin.
 Graham ES, 1255 JOHN HIX ST S 48185
  S. Dietrich, prin.
 Hamilton ES, 1031 SCHUMAN ST S 48185
  Noah Baxter, prin.
 Jefferson ES, 32150 DORSEY ST 48185
  Donald Brooks, prin.
 Kettering ES, 1200 HUBBARD ST S 48185
  Warner Frazer, prin.
 Lincoln ES, 33800 GRAND TRAVERSE ST 48185
  James Jennings, prin.
 Madison ES, 1075 CARLSON ST S 48185
  H. Buerk, prin.
 Patchin ES, 6420 NEWBURGH RD N 48185
  Don Massey, prin.
 Schweitzer ES, 2601 TREADWELL ST 48185
  K. Obsniuk-Taylor, prin.
 Stottlemyer ES, 34801 MARQUETTE ST 48185
  Sue Johnson, prin.
 Titus ES, 300 HENRY RUFF ST S 48185
  John Harrison, prin.
 Wildwood ES, 500 WILDWOOD ST N 48185
  John Martin, prin.
 Other Schools – See Canton, Dearborn Heights,
  Inkster, Wayne

St. Damian ES, 29891 JOY RD 48185
St. Matthew ES, 5885 VENOY RD N 48185

West Olive, Ottawa Co.
 West Ottawa SD
 Supt. – See Holland
 Sheldon Woods MS, 15950 BLAIR ST 49460
  Joann Mulder, prin.

Westphalia, Clinton Co., Pop. Code 3

St. Mary ES, 209 N WESTPHALIA 48894

White Cloud, Newaygo Co., Pop. Code 4
 White Cloud SD
 Sch. Sys. Enr. Code 4
 Supt. – Herbert Milks, 555 W WILCOX AVE 49349
 Jones ES, 640 PINE HILL ST 49349
  Tim Rossler, prin.

Whitehall, Muskegon Co., Pop. Code 5
 Whitehall SD
 Sch. Sys. Enr. Code 4
 Supt. – Michael Bozym, 813 SLOCUM ST E 49461
 MS, 813 SLOCUM ST E 49461
  Donald Wood, prin.
 ES, 813 E SLOCUM ST 49461
  Charles Bourdon, prin.

White Pigeon, St. Joseph Co., Pop. Code 4
 White Pigeon Comm. SD
 Sch. Sys. Enr. Code 4
 Supt. – Dale Kimball, 410 E PRAIRIE AVE 49099
 Mottville MS, 105-160 THOMAS ROAD 49099
  Sharon Cummings, prin.
 Baldwin ES, 14701 W US 12 49099
  Sharon Cummings, prin.
 Central ES, 211 233 E HOTCHIN ST 49099
  William Magill, prin.

White Pine, Ontonagon Co., Pop. Code 4
 White Pine SD
 Sch. Sys. Enr. Code 2
 Supt. – Benjamin Leiker, P O BOX 307 49971
 S, P O BOX 307 49971 – Dave Koski, prin.

Whitmore Lake, Washtenaw Co., Pop. Code 5
 Whitmore Lake SD
 Sch. Sys. Enr. Code 3
 Supt. – Howard Oesterling
  8845 WHITMORE LAKE ROAD 48189

Spencer ES, 8821 MAIN 48189
 W. Schongalla, prin.
MS 48189 – (—), prin.

Whittemore, Iosco Co., Pop. Code 2
 Whittemore-Prescott Area SD
 Sch. Sys. Enr. Code 4
 Supt. – Larry Allen, P O BOX 188 48770
 ES 48770 – Gene Gillette, prin.
 Other Schools – See Prescott

Williamston, Ingham Co., Pop. Code 5
 Williamston Comm. SD
 Sch. Sys. Enr. Code 4
 Supt. – Emmett W. Lippe
  418 HIGHLAND ST 48895
 MS, 201 SCHOOL ST 48895 – Dale Cutler, prin.
 ES, 416 HIGHLAND ST 48895 – Chris Jencka, prin.

Winn, Isabella Co.
 Shepherd SD
 Supt. – See Shepherd
 ES 48896 – Mary Weber, prin.

Wixom, Oakland Co., Pop. Code 6
 Walled Lake Cons. SD
 Supt. – See Walled Lake
 ES, 301 N WIXOM RD 48096 – C. Pappas, prin.

Wolverine, Cheboygan Co., Pop. Code 2
 Wolverine Comm. SD
 Sch. Sys. Enr. Code 2
 Supt. – Paul Keene, 120 SCHOLES ST 49799
 ES, 5993 SHOLES ST 49799 – Paul Keene, prin.

Woodhaven, Wayne Co., Pop. Code 7
 Woodhaven SD
 Supt. – See Flat Rock
 Erving ES, 24175 HALL RD 48183
  Milan Knezovich, prin.

Woodland, Barry Co., Pop. Code 4
 Lakewood SD
 Supt. – See Lake Odessa
 MS, 223 BROADWAY ST W 48897
  Dan Royer, prin.
 ES, 233 BROADWAY ST W 48897
  Dan Royer, prin.

Wyandotte, Wayne Co., Pop. Code 8
 Woodhaven SD
 Supt. – See Flat Rock
 Gudith ES, 22700 SIBLEY RD 48192
  K. Kosowski, prin.

 Wyandotte SD
 Sch. Sys. Enr. Code 5
 Supt. – Michael Williams, 639 OAK ST 48192
 Wilson MS, 1275 15TH ST 48192
  Alfred DeFran, prin.
 Garfield ES, 340 SUPERIOR BLVD 48192
  G. Coscarelly, prin.
 Jefferson ES, 1515 15TH ST 48192
  George Gouth, prin.
 Lincoln ES, 4460 EIGHTEENTH 48192
  D. Kellerman, prin.
 Madison ES, 2101 GROVE ST 48192
  Cheri Kodrich, prin.
 McKinley ES, 640 PLUM ST 48192
  Donald Noble, prin.
 Monroe ES, 1501 GROVE ST 48192
  William Strait, prin.
 Taft ES, 891 GODDARD ST 48192
  A. Christensen, prin.
 Washington ES, 1440 SUPERIOR BLVD 48192
  Robert Riedel, prin.

Our Lady of Mt. Carmel School
 2609 10TH ST 48192
St. Stanislaus Kostka ES, 250 ANTOINE ST 48192
Trinity ES, 466 OAK ST 48192
Wyandotte Catholic Consolidated ES
 FOURTH & MAPLE 48192

Wyoming, Kent Co., Pop. Code 8
 Godfrey-Lee SD
 Sch. Sys. Enr. Code 3
 Supt. – Michael Ryan, 1335 LEE ST SW 49509
 Godfrey ES, 1920 GODFREY AVE SW 49509
  Frank D'Amico, prin.
 Lee ES, 1355 LEE ST SW 49509
  M. McClenathan, prin.

 Godwin Heights SD
 Sch. Sys. Enr. Code 4
 Supt. – Kenneth L. Carlson, 15 36TH ST SW 49508
 North ES, 161 34TH ST SW 49508
  Gloria Lewis, prin.
 South ES, 28 BELLEVUE ST SE 49508
  Michael Maloney, prin.
 West ES, 3546 CLYDE PARK AVE SW 49509
  Linda Gantos, prin.

 Wyoming SD
 Sch. Sys. Enr. Code 5
 Supt. – David Bailey
  3575 GLADIOLA AVE SW 49509
 Jackson Park MS, 1331 33RD ST SW 49509
  Jerry Thorton, prin.
 Newhall MS, 1840 38TH ST SW 49509
  Judith McCabe, prin.

East ES, 1585 36TH ST SW 49509
 T. Pilczuk, prin.
Gladiola ES, 3500 GLADIOLA AVE SW 49509
 W. Chassee, prin.
Oriole Park ES, 1420 40TH ST SW 49509
 Stephen Barnard, prin.
Parkview ES, 2075 LEE ST SW 49509
 L. O'Brien, prin.
Pinery Park ES
 2550 ROGERS LANE AVE SW 49509
 James Poll, prin.
Rogers Lane ES
 2929 ROGERS LANE AVE SW 49509
 William Dyke, prin.
Taft ES, 2700 TAFT AVE SW 49509
 A. Vanderwoude, prin.
West ES, 3600 BYRON CENTER AVE SW 49509
 Judith Barron, prin.

Yale, St. Clair Co., Pop. Code 4
 Yale SD
 Sch. Sys. Enr. Code 4
 Supt. – David Zuhlke, 198 SCHOOL DRIVE 48097
 Yale MS, 103 W MECHANIC ST 48097
  Ralph Darin, prin.
 Avoca ES, 8751 WILLOW ST 48022
  Betty Clement, prin.
 ES, 200 SCHOOL DR 48097 – C. Hershberger, prin.
 Other Schools – See Emmett

Ypsilanti, Washtenaw Co., Pop. Code 7
 Lincoln Cons. SD
 Sch. Sys. Enr. Code 5
 Supt. – Donald Chalker
  7425 WILLIS ROAD 48197
 Early ES, 8850 WHITTAKER RD 48197
  Donald Sprague, prin.
 Later ES, 8970 WHITTAKER RD 48197
  Mary Bowman, prin.
 Middle ES, 8888 WHITTAKER RD 48197
  Kathy Geddis, prin.
 Other Schools – See Belleville

 VanBuren SD
 Supt. – See Belleville
 Rawsonville ES, 3110 GROVE ST S 48198
  Theresa Green, prin.

 Willow Run Comm. SD
 Sch. Sys. Enr. Code 5
 Supt. – Youssef Yomtoob
  2171 MICHIGAN AVE E 48197
 Edmondson MS, 1800 FOREST AVE E 48197
  Norma Williams, prin.
 Cheney ES, 1500 STAMFORD RD 48198
  Mel Anglin, prin.
 Ford ES, 2440 CLARK RD E 48198
  G. Weatherspoon, prin.
 Holmes ES, 1255 HOLMES RD 48198
  Ruth Moorman, prin.
 Kaiser ES, 670 ONANDAGO ST 48198
  Laura Chew, prin.
 Kettering ES, 1633 KNOWLES ST 48198
  Vivian Lyte, prin.
 Thurston ES, 181 OREGON ST 48198
  Franci Moorman, prin.

 Ypsilanti SD
 Sch. Sys. Enr. Code 6
 Supt. – James Hawkins
  1885 PACKARD ROAD 48197
 Adams ES, 503 OAK ST 48198
  Maude Forbes, prin.
 Ardis ES, 2100 ELLSWORTH RD 48197
  S. Thompson, prin.
 Chapelle ES, 111 WALLACE BLVD S 48197
  Pat Derossett, prin.
 Erickson ES, 1427 LEVONA ST 48198
  (—), prin.
 Estabrook ES, 1555 CROSS ST W 48197
  H. Peper, prin.
 Fletcher ES, 1055 CORNELL RD 48197
  William Madsen, prin.
 George ES, 1076 ECORSE RD 48198
  Carla Heyn, prin.

St. Alexis ES, 1705 FOREST AVE E 48198

Zeeland, Ottawa Co., Pop. Code 5
 Zeeland SD
 Sch. Sys. Enr. Code 4
 Supt. – K. J. Harper, P O BOX 110 49464
 MS, 179 W ROOSEVELT AVE 49464
  Jae Shobbrook, prin.
 Lincoln ES, 60 E LINCOLN AVE 49464
  Arnold Yonker, prin.
 New Groningen ES, 10542 CHICAGO DR 49464
  James Schoettle, prin.
 Roosevelt ES, 175 W ROOSEVELT AVE 49464
  R. Vanderzwagg, prin.

Borculo Christian ES, 6830 96TH AVE 49464
Zeeland Christian ES
 334 W CENTRAL AVE 49464

MINNESOTA

STATE DEPARTMENT OF EDUCATION
712 Capitol Square Building
550 Cedar St., St. Paul 55101
(612) 296-6104

Commissioner of Education	Ruth Randall
Deputy Commissioner	Robert Wedl
Assistant Commissioner Management Effectiveness	Dan Skoog
Assistant Commissioner Instructional Effectiveness	James Sauter
Assistant Commissioner Development & Partnership Effectiveness	Nan Skelton

STATE BOARD OF EDUCATION
Ted Suss, *Administrator*   Lake Park   56554

HIGHER EDUCATION COORDINATING BOARD
Vacancy, *Executive Director*   550 Cedar Street #400, St. Paul   55101

PUBLIC, PRIVATE, AND PAROCHIAL ELEMENTARY SCHOOLS

Ada, Norman Co., Pop. Code 4
Ada SD
Sch. Sys. Enr. Code 3
Supt. – Thomas Hanson, 105 4TH AVE E   56510
ES, 209 6TH ST W   56510 – Ollen Church, prin.

Adams, Mower Co., Pop. Code 3
Southland SD
Sch. Sys. Enr. Code 3
Supt. – Larry Tompkins   55909
Other Schools – See Elkton, Rose Creek

Sacred Heart ES, 10 S 5TH ST   55909

Adrian, Nobles Co., Pop. Code 4
Adrian SD
Sch. Sys. Enr. Code 3
Supt. – Donald A. Jensen, P O BOX 40   56110
ES, P O BOX 40   56110 – Larry Noble, prin.

Aitkin, Aitkin Co., Pop. Code 4
Aitkin SD
Sch. Sys. Enr. Code 4
Supt. – Edward Anderson, 306 2ND ST NW   56431
Rippleside ES, 225 2ND AVE SW   56431
   James Pitt, prin.
Other Schools – See Palisade

Akeley, Hubbard Co., Pop. Code 2
Akeley SD
Sch. Sys. Enr. Code 2
Supt. – Michael Kulig, P O BOX 129   56433
ES, P O BOX 129   56433 – Michael Kulig, prin.

Albany, Stearns Co., Pop. Code 4
Albany SD
Sch. Sys. Enr. Code 4
Supt. – Ron Rollins, 140 3RD ST   56307
JHS, 140 3RD ST   56307 – Charles Griffith, prin.
ES, P O BOX 330   56307 – Louis Czarnowski, prin.
Farming ES, P O BOX 330   56307
   William Hakes, prin.
Other Schools – See Avon

Holy Family ES, P O BOX 674   56307

Albert Lea, Freeborn Co., Pop. Code 7
Albert Lea SD
Sch. Sys. Enr. Code 5
Supt. – Roger Norsted
   211 W RICHWAY DRIVE   56007
Southwest JHS, 901 S HIGHWAY 69   56007
   Terrance Moriarty, prin.
Brookside MS, 211 W RICHWAY DR   56007
   Stephan Lund, prin.
Halverson ES, 707 E 10TH ST   56007
   Paul Anderson, prin.
Hawthorne ES, 1000 E HAWTHORNE ST   56007
   Harlan Bang, prin.
Lakeview ES, 902 ABBOTT ST   56007
   David Paschka, prin.
Sibley ES, 1501 W FRONT ST   56007
   David Prescott, prin.

Albertville, Wright Co., Pop. Code 3
St. Michael-Albertville SD
Supt. – See Saint Michael
St. Michael-Albertville ES
   5386 MAIN AVE NE   55301 – Bernard Burke, prin.

Alborn, St. Louis Co., Pop. Code 2
St. Louis County SD
Supt. – See Virginia

ES   55702 – Robert Larson, prin.

Alden, Freeborn Co., Pop. Code 3
Alden SD
Sch. Sys. Enr. Code 2
Supt. – Stan Ries, P O BOX 99   56009
Alden-Conger ES, P O BOX 99   56009
   Lynette Russ, prin.

Alexandria, Douglas Co., Pop. Code 6
Alexandria SD
Sch. Sys. Enr. Code 5
Supt. – George Cassell, P O BOX 308   56308
Lincoln ES, 11TH & LARK ST   56308
   David Strand, prin.
Washington ES, 6TH & JEFFERSON ST   56308
   Paul Olinger, prin.
Other Schools – See Carlos, Garfield, Miltona

St. Mary's ES, 5TH AND HAWTHORNE   56308
Zion Lutheran ES, 310 LAKE ST   56308

Alvarado, Marshall Co., Pop. Code 2
Alvarado SD
Sch. Sys. Enr. Code 2
Supt. – Vern Pfeifer, P O BOX 816   56710
ES, P O BOX 816   56710 – Darryl Larson, prin.

Amboy, Blue Earth Co., Pop. Code 3
Amboy-Good Thunder SD
Sch. Sys. Enr. Code 2
Supt. – Patricia Mohn, P O BOX 70   56010
Amboy-Good Thunder/Mapleton JHS
   P O BOX 96   56010 – Patricia Mohn, prin.
Other Schools – See Good Thunder

Andover, Anoka Co., Pop. Code 6
Anoka SD
Supt. – See Coon Rapids
ES, 1490 HANSON BLVD NW   55304
   William Gallagher, prin.
Crooked Lake ES
   2939 BUNKER LAKE BLVD NW   55304
   Wallace Johnson, prin.

Annandale, Wright Co., Pop. Code 4
Annandale SD
Sch. Sys. Enr. Code 4
Supt. – Verle Conner, P O BOX 190   55302
Bendix ES, P O BOX 190   55302
   Arlen Johnson, prin.

Anoka, Anoka Co., Pop. Code 7
Anoka SD
Supt. – See Coon Rapids
Franklin ES, 215 MAIN ST W   55303
   Lorelli Byrne, prin.
Lincoln ES, 540 SOUTH ST   55303
   Ronald Rude, prin.
McKinley ES, 1740 CONSTANCE BLVD NE   55304
   Beth Mackey, prin.
Sandburg MS, 1902 WND AVE   55303
   Ronald Mitchell, prin.
Washington ES, 2171 6TH AVE   55303
   Jean Kincanon, prin.
Wilson ES, 1025 SUNNY LN   55303
   Robert Strand, prin.

Meadow Creek Christian School
   2937 BUNKER LAKE BLVD NW   55304
St. Stephen ES, 506 JACKSON ST   55303

Appleton, Swift Co., Pop. Code 4
Appleton SD
Sch. Sys. Enr. Code 3
Supt. – William Eggers, 128 S HERING ST   56208
ES, SEDQUIST ST   56208 – Roche Martin, prin.

Apple Valley, Dakota Co., Pop. Code 7
Rosemount-Apple Valley-Eagan SD
Supt. – See Rosemount
Scott Highlands MS
   14011 PILOT KNOB ROAD   55124
   Rich Barnes, prin.
Valley MS, 900 GARDEN VIEW DRIVE   55124
   Pat Sullivan, prin.

Argyle, Marshall Co., Pop. Code 3
Argyle SD
Sch. Sys. Enr. Code 2
Supt. – Victor D. Sletten, P O BOX 279   56713
ES, P O BOX 279   56713 – Jack Mohabir, prin.

Arlington, Sibley Co., Pop. Code 4
Arlington SD
Sch. Sys. Enr. Code 3
Supt. – George Maca, P O BOX 1000   55307
ES, P O BOX 1000   55307 – Zelora Lentz, prin.
Green Isle ES, P O BOX 1000   55307
   Zelora Lentz, prin.

Ashby, Grant Co., Pop. Code 2
Ashby SD
Sch. Sys. Enr. Code 2
Supt. – Raymond Dahlen, P O BOX C   56309
ES, P O BOX C   56309 – Raymond Dahlen, prin.

Askov, Pine Co., Pop. Code 2
Askov SD
Sch. Sys. Enr. Code 2
Supt. – Michael Hruby, P O BOX 158   55704
Other Schools – See Bruno

Atwater, Kandiyohi Co., Pop. Code 4
Atwater SD
Sch. Sys. Enr. Code 3
Supt. – John Tritabaugh   56209
ES   56209 – John Tritabaugh, prin.

Audubon, Becker Co., Pop. Code 2
Audubon SD
Sch. Sys. Enr. Code 2
Supt. – Ronald Bratlie, P O BOX 38   56511
ES, P O BOX 338   56511 – Richard Hanson, prin.

Aurora, St. Louis Co., Pop. Code 5
Aurora SD
Sch. Sys. Enr. Code 3
Supt. – Donald Langan, 601 N 1ST ST W   55705
Boase ES, 601 N 1ST ST W   55705 – (—), prin.

Austin, Mower Co., Pop. Code 7
Austin SD
Sch. Sys. Enr. Code 5
Supt. – William Nachatilo
   202 4TH AVE NE   55912
MS, 1700 4TH AVE SE   55912 – N. Hanson, prin.
Banfield ES, 301 17TH ST SW   55912
   Luther Meyer, prin.
Neveln ES, 1918 E OAKLAND AVE   55912
   John Pare, prin.
Shaw ES, 705 4TH AVE SW   55912
   Lewis Aase, prin.
Summer ES, 805 8TH AVE NW   55912
   Norman Hecimovich, prin.

Queen of Angels ES, 912 1ST AVE NE 55912
St. Augustine-Edward ES
511 4TH AVE NW 55912

Avon, Stearns Co., Pop. Code 3
Albany SD
Supt. – See Albany
ES 56310 – William Hakes, prin.

Babbitt, St. Louis Co., Pop. Code 4
Babbit SD
Sch. Sys. Enr. Code 3
Supt. – Norman Chaffee, 2 SOUTH DRIVE 55706
ES, SOUTH DR 55706 – Marvin Schubbe, prin.

Backus, Cass Co., Pop. Code 2
Backus SD
Sch. Sys. Enr. Code 2
Supt. – Daniel Froemming, P O BOX 47 56435
ES, P O BOX 47 56435 – William Makinen, prin.

Badger, Roseau Co., Pop. Code 2
Badger SD
Sch. Sys. Enr. Code 2
Supt. – Keith Kapphahn, P O BOX 68 56714
ES, P O BOX 68 56714 – Paul Neimark, prin.

Bagley, Clearwater Co., Pop. Code 4
Bagley SD
Sch. Sys. Enr. Code 4
Supt. – A. Toriseva, 308 N BAGLEY AVE 56621
ES, 308 N BAGLEY AVE 56621
Charles Johnson, prin.
Other Schools – See Shevlin

Balaton, Lyon Co., Pop. Code 3
Balaton SD
Sch. Sys. Enr. Code 2
Supt. – L. Domagala, 330 3RD ST 56115
ES, 330 3RD ST 56115 – Roland Dobberstein, prin.

Barnesville, Clay Co., Pop. Code 4
Barnesville SD
Sch. Sys. Enr. Code 3
Supt. – Edward Thompson, P O BOX 189 56514
ES, P O BOX 189 56514 – Glenn Filipi, prin.

Barnum, Carlton Co., Pop. Code 2
Barnum SD
Sch. Sys. Enr. Code 3
Supt. – Robert Sarff, P O BOX 227 55707
ES, P O BOX 227 55707 – John Braun, prin.

Barrett, Grant Co., Pop. Code 2
Barrett SD
Supt. – See Elbow Lake
ES, P O BOX 278 56311 – Roger Toso, prin.

Battle Lake, Otter Tail Co., Pop. Code 3
Battle Lake SD
Sch. Sys. Enr. Code 2
Supt. – John Widvey, P O BOX 1280 56515
ES, P O BOX 1280 56515 – Richard Dreyer, prin.

Baudette, Lake of the Woods Co., Pop. Code 4
Lake of the Woods SD
Sch. Sys. Enr. Code 3
Supt. – Al Edwards, P O BOX 310 56623
ES, P O BOX 310 56623 – Al Edwards, prin.

Baxter, Crow Wing Co., Pop. Code 5

Lake Region Christian School
2110 FAIRVIEW ROAD N 56401

Bayport, Washington Co., Pop. Code 5
Stillwater SD
Supt. – See Stillwater
ES, 309 4TH ST N 55003 – David Graham, prin.

Beardsley, Big Stone Co., Pop. Code 2
Beardsley SD
Sch. Sys. Enr. Code 2
Supt. – Roger Cook 56211
ES 56211 – Del Stein, prin.

Beaver Creek, Rock Co., Pop. Code 2
Hills-Beaver Creek SD
Supt. – See Hills
Hills-Beaver Creek ES, P O BOX 49 56116
Merlin Klein, prin.

Becker, Sherburne Co., Pop. Code 3
Becker SD
Sch. Sys. Enr. Code 3
Supt. – Jim Mantzke, 700 HANCOCK ST 55308
ES, 700 HANCOCK ST 55308
Louis Husmann, prin.

Belgrade, Stearns Co., Pop. Code 3
Belgrade-Elrosa SD
Sch. Sys. Enr. Code 3
Supt. – D. R. Swenson, P O BOX 339 56312
Belgrade-Elrosa ES 56312 – Stanley Sievert, prin.

Belle Plaine, Scott Co., Pop. Code 5
Belle Plaine SD
Sch. Sys. Enr. Code 3
Supt. – Thomas Lubovich
220 S MARKET ST 56011
ES, 330 S MARKET ST 56011 – Earl Gransee, prin.

Bellingham, Lac Qui Parle Co., Pop. Code 2
Bellingham SD
Sch. Sys. Enr. Code 2
Supt. – Ray Seiler, P O BOX 367 56212
ES, P O BOX 6155 56212 – Stan Krogsrud, prin.

Belview, Redwood Co., Pop. Code 2
Belview SD
Sch. Sys. Enr. Code 2
Supt. – C. A. Peterson, P O BOX 08 56214
ES, P O BOX 8 56214 – Carl Peterson, prin.

Bemidji, Beltrami Co., Pop. Code 7
Bemidji SD
Sch. Sys. Enr. Code 5
Supt. – Philip Bain, 201 15TH ST NW 56601
MS, 16TH ST 56601 – Fred Sanford, prin.
Bunyan ES, 1705 HIWHWAY 2W 56601
Bruce Anderson, prin.
Central ES, 8TH & BELTRAMI 56601
Ken Litzau, prin.
Deer Lake ES, RURAL ROUTE 07 56601
Patricia Welte, prin.
Lincoln ES, 410 LINCOLN AVE SE 56601
Ron Bouchie, prin.
May ES, 201 15TH ST NW 56601
Richard Sauer, prin.
Northern ES, RURAL ROUTE 01 56601
James Lahti, prin.
Smith ES, 18TH & AMERICA AVE 56601
P. Anderson, prin.
Solway ES, 201 15TH ST 56601
Patricia Welte, prin.

St. Phillips ES, 620 BELTRAMI AVE NW 56601

Benson, Swift Co., Pop. Code 5
Benson SD
Sch. Sys. Enr. Code 4
Supt. – Les Potas, 1400 MONTANA AVE 56215
Northside ES, 1800 NEVADA AVE 56215
Gale Skold, prin.
Southside ES, 300 14TH ST S 56215
Gale Skold, prin.

St. Francis Xavier ES, 501 12TH ST N 56215

Bertha, Todd Co., Pop. Code 3
Bertha-Hewitt SD
Sch. Sys. Enr. Code 3
Supt. – Earl Mathison 56437
ES 56437 – John Holle, prin.

Bigfork, Itasca Co., Pop. Code 2
Grand Rapids SD
Supt. – See Grand Rapids
ES 56628 – Frank Anselmo, prin.

Big Lake, Sherburne Co., Pop. Code 4
Big Lake SD
Sch. Sys. Enr. Code 4
Supt. – Laverne Lageson 55309
ES 55309 – Roland Olson, prin.

Birchdale, Koochiching Co.
South Koochiching SD
Supt. – See Northome
Indus ES, RURAL ROUTE 03 BOX 301C 56629
Leland Hayes, prin.

Bird Island, Renville Co., Pop. Code 4
Bird Island SD
Sch. Sys. Enr. Code 2
Supt. – Virgil Green, 110 S 9TH ST 55310
ES, 110 S 9TH ST 55310 – Virgil Green, prin.

St. Mary's ES, 140 S 10TH ST 55310

Biwabik, St. Louis Co., Pop. Code 4
Biwabik SD
Sch. Sys. Enr. Code 3
Supt. – Donald Langan, P O BOX 669 55708
Bray ES, P O BOX 669 55708
Michael Zupetz, prin.

Blackduck, Beltrami Co., Pop. Code 3
Blackduck SD
Sch. Sys. Enr. Code 3
Supt. – G. J. Kjellberg 56630
ES 56630 – Terrance Sorquist, prin.

Blaine, Anoka Co., Pop. Code 8
Anoka SD
Supt. – See Coon Rapids
Jefferson ES, 11331 JEFFERSON ST NE 55434
Kenneth Kunshler, prin.
Johnsville ES, 991 125TH AVE NE 55434
Harlan Danner, prin.
Madison ES, 650 TE4RRITORIAL ROAD NE 55434
Judith McKay, prin.
University ES, 9901 UNIVERSITY AVE NE 55433
Paul Tinquist, prin.

Centennial SD
Supt. – See Circle Pines
Westwood JHS, 711 91ST AVE NE 55434
(—), prin.

Spring Lake Park SD
Supt. – See Spring Lake Park
Westwood JHS, 711 91ST AVE NE 55434
Glenn Martin, prin.
Westwood ES, 701 91ST AVE NE 55434
Gerald Maeckelbergh, prin.

Blomkest, Kandiyohi Co., Pop. Code 2
Willmar SD
Supt. – See Willmar
ES 56216 – Paul Olberg, prin.

Blooming Prairie, Steele Co., Pop. Code 4
Blooming Prairie SD
Sch. Sys. Enr. Code 3
Supt. – Darwin Bostic, 202 4TH AVE NW 55917

ES, 110 1ST ST NW 55917 – James Thorn, prin.

Bloomington, Hennepin Co., Pop. Code 8
Bloomington SD
Sch. Sys. Enr. Code 7
Supt. – L. Anderson, 8900 PORTLAND AVE 55420
Olson JHS, 4551 W 102ND ST 55437
Roger Hahn, prin.
Indian Mounds ES, 9801 11TH AVE S 55437
Clarence Von Eschen, prin.
Normandale Hills ES, 9501 TOLEDO AVE S 55437
David Pansch, prin.
Oak Grove ES, 1301 W 104TH ST 55431
James Hotchkiss, prin.
Oak Grove IS, 1300 W 106TH ST 55431
Michael Santoro, prin.
Olson ES, 4501 W 102ND ST 55437
Muriel Stevenson, prin.
Poplar Bridge ES, 8401 PALMER RD 55437
Eldon Flatten, prin.
Ridgeview ES, 9400 NESBITT ROAD 55420
Debra Fincham, prin.
Valley View ES, 351 E 88TH ST 55420
Fred Freese, prin.
Washburn ES, 8401 XERXES AVE S 55431
Gerald Carlson, prin.
Westwood ES, 3701 W 108TH ST 55431
Charles Bianchi, prin.

Bloomington Lutheran ES
10600 BLOOMINGTON FERRY RD 55438
Mount Hope-Redemption ES
927 E OLD SHAKOPEE RD 55420
Nativity of Mary ES
9901 E BLOOMINGTON FWY 55420

Blue Earth, Faribault Co., Pop. Code 5
Blue Earth SD
Sch. Sys. Enr. Code 4
Supt. – K. Queensland, 300 E 6TH ST 56013
ES, EAST 6TH ST 56013 – Roger Strom, prin.

East Chain SD
Sch. Sys. Enr. Code 2
Supt. – Richard McGuire
RURAL ROUTE 01 56013
East Chain ES, RURAL ROUTE 01 56013
Bruce Klaehn, prin.

Borup, Norman Co., Pop. Code 2
Borup SD
Sch. Sys. Enr. Code 2
Supt. – Kitty Krueger, P O BOX 08 56519
ES, P O BOX 8 56519 – (—), prin.

Bovey, Itasca Co., Pop. Code 3
Coleraine SD
Supt. – See Coleraine
Connor-Jasper MS, P O BOX 40 55709
Fred Trebnick, prin.
Murray ES, P O BOX 40 55709
Gerald Saylor, prin.

Grand Rapids SD
Supt. – See Grand Rapids
Balsam ES, RURAL ROUTE 02 55709
Donovan Zuehlke, prin.

Braham, Isanti Co., Pop. Code 4
Braham SD
Sch. Sys. Enr. Code 4
Supt. – Riley Hoheisel, P O BOX 488 55006
MS, P O BOX 448 55006 – Wayne Turnquist, prin.
Southview ES, P O BOX 484 55006
Wayne Turnquist, prin.

Brainerd, Crow Wing Co., Pop. Code 7
Brainerd SD
Sch. Sys. Enr. Code 6
Supt. – Robert Gross, 300 QUINCE ST 56401
Baxter ES, RURAL ROUTE 08 BOX 211 56401
Lance Smith, prin.
Garfield ES, 1120 10TH AVE NE 56401
Jane Fritscher, prin.
Harrison ES, 1515 OAK ST 56401
Thomas Rosenberger, prin.
Lincoln ES, 604 S 6TH ST 56401
Julie Bolton, prin.
Lowell ES, G S T & 3RD AVE 56401
Roger McHaney, prin.
Riverside ES, 220 NW 3RD ST 56401
Cathy Engler, prin.
Washington MS, 804 OAK ST 56401
Dennis Martin, prin.
Whittier ES, 604 N 7TH ST 56401
Jane Fritscher, prin.
Other Schools – See Nisswa

St. Francis of Assisi ES, 817 JUNIPER ST 56401

Brandon, Douglas Co., Pop. Code 2
Brandon SD
Sch. Sys. Enr. Code 2
Supt. – Ray Farwell, P O BOX 185 56315
ES, P O BOX 185 56315 – Pam Peterson, prin.

Breckenridge, Wilkin Co., Pop. Code 5
Breckenridge SD
Sch. Sys. Enr. Code 3
Supt. – Richard Link, 710 13TH ST N 56520
ES, 8TH ST N AND BEEDE AVE 56520
Jerome Mock, prin.

St. Mary ES, 210 4TH ST N 56520

Brewster, Nobles Co., Pop. Code 3
Brewster SD
Sch. Sys. Enr. Code 2
Supt. – George Loudenslager, P O BOX 309   56119
ES, P O BOX 309   56119
   Marcia Schumacher, prin.

Bricelyn, Faribault Co., Pop. Code 2
Bricelyn SD
Sch. Sys. Enr. Code 2
Supt. – Lowell Mohn, P O BOX 277   56014
ES, P O BOX 277   56014 – Robert Watt, prin.

Brooklyn Center, Hennepin Co., Pop. Code 8
Anoka SD
Supt. – See Coon Rapids
Evergreen Park ES, 7070 DUPONT AVE N   55430
   Kenneth Berg, prin.

Brooklyn Center SD
Sch. Sys. Enr. Code 4
Supt. – Douglas M. Rossi
   6500 HUMBOLDT AVE N   55430
Brown ES, 5900 HUMBOLDT AVE N   55430
   Grace Young, prin.

Osseo SD
Supt. – See Osseo
Garden City ES, 3501 65TH AVE N   55429
   Ron Luehmann, prin.
Orchard Lane ES, 6201 NOBLE AVE N   55429
   William Tessman, prin.
Willow Lane ES, 7020 PERRY AVE N   55429
   Deanna Leach, prin.

Robbinsdale SD
Supt. – See New Hope
Northport ES, 5421 BROOKLYN BLVD   55429
   Lowell Hammer, prin.

Brookdale Christian Center
   6030 XERXES AVE N   55430

Brooklyn Park, Hennepin Co., Pop. Code 8
Anoka SD
Supt. – See Coon Rapids
Monroe ES, 901 BROOKDALE DR   55444
   James Fennick, prin.
Riverview ES, 1400 93RD AVE N   55444
   Dale Hartje, prin.

Osseo SD
Supt. – See Osseo
Birch Grove ES, 4690 BROOKDALE DR   55443
   Carolyn Humphrey, prin.
Crest View ES, 8200 ZANE AVE N   55443
   Daniel Wilson, prin.
Edgewood ES, 6601 XYLON AVE N   55428
   Lois Nordling, prin.
Edinbrook ES, 8925 ZANE AVE   55443
   Judy Birmingham, prin.
Fair Oaks ES, 5600 65TH AVE N   55429
   Jeanne Bursheim, prin.
Palmer Lake ES
   7300 PALMER LAKE DR W   55443
   Harold Johnson, prin.
Zanewood ES, 7000 ZANE AVE N   55429
   Donald Johnson, prin.

Robbinsdale SD
Supt. – See New Hope
Lincoln ES, 6200 W BROADWAY AVE   55428
   Frank Dimberio, prin.

Brooten, Stearns Co., Pop. Code 3
Brooten SD
Sch. Sys. Enr. Code 2
Supt. – Terry Frazee, P O BOX 38   56316
ES, P O BOX 39   56316 – Robert Bogart, prin.

Browerville, Todd Co., Pop. Code 3
Browerville SD
Sch. Sys. Enr. Code 2
Supt. – Larry Werder, P O BOX 185   56438
ES, P O BOX 185   56438 – (—), prin.

Brownsdale, Mower Co., Pop. Code 3
Hayfield SD
Supt. – See Hayfield
ES   55918 – (—), prin.

Browns Valley, Traverse Co., Pop. Code 3
Browns Valley SD
Sch. Sys. Enr. Code 2
Supt. – Roger Cook, P O BOX N   56219
MS, P O BOX N   56219 – Del Stein, prin.

Brownton, Mcleod Co., Pop. Code 3
Brownton SD
Sch. Sys. Enr. Code 2
Supt. – David R. Klepel, 335 3RD AVE N   55312
ES, 335 3RD ST S   55312 – John Chrest, prin.

Bruno, Pine Co., Pop. Code 2
Askov SD
Supt. – See Askov
ES   55712 – Susan Abrahamson, prin.

Buckman, Morrison Co., Pop. Code 2

St. Michael ES, P O BOX 627   56317

Buffalo, Wright Co., Pop. Code 5
Buffalo SD
Sch. Sys. Enr. Code 5
Supt. – M. D. Miller, 214 1ST AVE NE   55313
JHS, 214 1ST AVE NE   55313 – Alan Frost, prin.
ES, NE 2ND AVE   55313
   Harold Trombley, Jr., prin.

PS, 708 8TH ST NE   55313 – Dean Skallerud, prin.
Montrose ES   55313 – Judy Coley, prin.
Other Schools – See Hanover

St. Francis Xavier ES, 210 1ST AVE NW   55313

Buffalo Lake, Renville Co., Pop. Code 3
Buffalo Lake SD
Sch. Sys. Enr. Code 2
Supt. – Roy Rud, P O BOX 278   55314
Buffalo Lake-Hector MS, P O BOX 278   55314
   Lyle Katzenmeyer, prin.
ES, P O BOX 278   55314 – Lyle Katzenmeyer, prin.

Burnsville, Dakota Co., Pop. Code 8
Burnsville SD
Sch. Sys. Enr. Code 6
Supt. – Sally Bell
   100 RIVER RIDGE COURT   55337
Byrne ES, 11608 RIVER HILLS DR   55337
   Ronald Cin, prin.
Neill ES, 13409 UPTON AVE S   55337
   Dennis Senne, prin.
Pond ES, 630 E 130TH ST   55337
   Deedee Carpenter, prin.
Sioux Trail ES, 2801 RIVER HILLS DR   55337
   Larry Brady, prin.
Sky Oaks ES, 100 E 134TH ST   55337
   Peter King, prin.
Vista View ES, 13109 COUNTY ROAD 5   55337
   Richard Halverson, prin.
Other Schools – See Eagan, Savage

Butterfield, Watonwan Co., Pop. Code 3
Butterfield SD
Sch. Sys. Enr. Code 2
Supt. – Larry Phillips, P O BOX 189   56120
ES, P O BOX 289   56120 – Larry Phillips, prin.

Byron, Olmstead Co., Pop. Code 4
Byron SD
Sch. Sys. Enr. Code 4
Supt. – R. E. Carlson, P O BOX 157   55920
ES, P O BOX 157   55920 – Gary Hanson, prin.

Caledonia, Houston Co., Pop. Code 5
Caledonia SD
Sch. Sys. Enr. Code 3
Supt. – M. Miller, W MAIN ST   55921
ES, W MAIN ST   55921 – Mary Adams, prin.

St. John's Ev. Lutheran ES
   720 N MARSHALL ST   55921
St. Mary ES, 308 E SOUTH ST   55921

Cambridge, Isanti Co., Pop. Code 5
Cambridge-Isanti SD
Sch. Sys. Enr. Code 5
Supt. – R. T. Hoheisel, 439 8TH AVE NW   55008
MS, 428 2ND AVE NW   55008
   Craig Paulson, prin.
ES, NORTH ELM   55008 – Charles Niles, prin.
Other Schools – See Isanti

Campbell, Wilkin Co., Pop. Code 2
Campbell-Tintah SD
Sch. Sys. Enr. Code 2
Supt. – Richard H. Link, P O BOX 08   56522
Campbell-Tintah ES   56522 – Delmar Voss, prin.

Canby, Yellow Medicine Co., Pop. Code 4
Canby SD
Sch. Sys. Enr. Code 3
Supt. – B. L. Ailts, 307 1ST ST W   56220
ES, 307 1ST ST W   56220 – (—), prin.

St. Peter ES, 410 RING AVE N   56220

Cannon Falls, Goodhue Co., Pop. Code 5
Cannon Falls SD
Sch. Sys. Enr. Code 4
Supt. – John Nefstead
   820 MINNESOTA ST E   55009
ES, 115 MINNESOTA ST W   55009
   Ivan Edel, prin.
Wastedo ES, RURAL ROUTE 01   55009
   Ivan Edel, prin.

Canton, Fillmore Co., Pop. Code 2
Mabel-Canton SD
Supt. – See Mabel
Mabel-Canton ES   55922 – Carl Aegler, prin.

Carlos, Douglas Co., Pop. Code 2
Alexandria SD
Supt. – See Alexandria
ES   56319 – Cortlan Krogstad, prin.

Carlton, Carlton Co., Pop. Code 3
Carlton SD
Sch. Sys. Enr. Code 3
Supt. – J. W. Schwartz, P O BOX 310   55718
South Terrace ES, 530 STINE DR   55718
   Richard Cook, prin.

Carver, Carver Co., Pop. Code 3
Chaska SD
Supt. – See Chaska
East Union ES, 156755 COUNTY ROAD 43   55315
   Richard Menzel, prin.

Cass Lake, Cass Co., Pop. Code 4
Cass Lake SD
Sch. Sys. Enr. Code 3
Supt. – Judee Crep, P O BOX 1   56633
ES, RURAL ROUTE 02 BOX 4   56633
   Pamela Olson, prin.

Bug-O-Day-Ge-Shig School
   RURAL ROUTE 03 BOX 100   56633

Cedar, Anoka Co.
St. Francis SD
Supt. – See Saint Francis
ES, 18900 CEDAR DR NW   55011
   Raymond Churack, prin.
East Bethel ES, 21210 POLK ST NE   55011
   Robert Brenden, prin.

Ceylon, Martin Co., Pop. Code 3
Ceylon SD
Sch. Sys. Enr. Code 2
Supt. – Russell Hoeffner, 301 W GRANT   56121
ES, 301 W GRANT   56121 – Leila Swenberg, prin.

Champlin, Hennepin Co., Pop. Code 6
Anoka SD
Supt. – See Coon Rapids
ES, 111 DEAN AVE W   55316
   Ronald Miller, prin.
Oxbow Creek ES, 6050 109TH AVE N   55316
   Myron Bursheim, prin.

Chandler, Murray Co., Pop. Code 2
Chandler-Lake Wilson SD
Sch. Sys. Enr. Code 2
Supt. – Robert Dell, P O BOX 98   56122
Other Schools – See Lake Wilson

Chanhassen, Carver Co., Pop. Code 6
Chaska SD
Supt. – See Chaska
ES, 7600 LAREDO DR   55317
   Lowell McMillen, prin.

St. Hubert ES, 306 W 78TH ST   55317

Chaska, Carver Co., Pop. Code 6
Chaska SD
Sch. Sys. Enr. Code 5
Supt. – Carol Ericson
   1700 N CHESTNUT ST   55318
MS, 1750 N CHESTNUT ST   55318
   Leonard Takkunen, prin.
ES, 1800 N CHESTNUT ST   55318
   Richard Ewert, prin.
Other Schools – See Carver, Chanhassen

Guardian Angels ES, 217 W 2ND ST   55318
St. Johns Lutheran ES, OAK & 4TH ST   55318

Chatfield, Olmsted Co., Pop. Code 4
Chatfield SD
Sch. Sys. Enr. Code 3
Supt. – J. Ronald Hennings   55923
Chosen Valley ES, 405 MAIN ST S   55923
   William Thomas, prin.

Chisago City, Chisago Co., Pop. Code 4
Chisago Lakes SD
Supt. – See Lindstrom
Lakeside MS, 10345 WYOMING AVE   55013
   Warren Retzlaff, prin.

Chisago Lakes Baptist Academy
   P O BOX 350   55013

Chisholm, St. Louis Co., Pop. Code 6
Chisholm SD
Sch. Sys. Enr. Code 4
Supt. – John Regan, 3RD AVE SW & 3RD ST   55719
Chisholm MS, 3RD AVE & 4TH ST SW   55719
   Robert Belluzzo, prin.
Vaughan ES, 10TH ST NE & 1ST AVE   55719
   Herbert Sellars, prin.

Chokio, Stevens Co., Pop. Code 3
Chokio-Alberta SD
Sch. Sys. Enr. Code 2
Supt. – Ronald Breuer, P O BOX 87   56221
Chokio-Alberta ES, P O BOX 87   56221
   Leona Classen, prin.

Circle Pines, Anoka Co., Pop. Code 5
Centennial SD
Sch. Sys. Enr. Code 5
Supt. – J. McClellan, 4707 NORTH ROAD   55014
Centennial MS, 4707 NORTH ROAD   55014
   F. Neumann, prin.
Centennial ES, 4707 NORTH RD   55014
   Roger Ogren, prin.
Golden Lake ES, 1 SCHOOL RD   55014
   Richard Larson, prin.
Other Schools – See Blaine, Hugo

Forest Lake SD
Supt. – See Forest Lake
Lino Lakes ES, 725 MAIN ST   55014
   Frank LaPatka, prin.

Clara City, Chippewa Co., Pop. Code 4
Clara City SD
Sch. Sys. Enr. Code 2
Supt. – Roger Rueckert, P O BOX 590   56222
ES, P O BOX 590   56222 – Roy Tutsch, prin.

Claremont, Dodge Co., Pop. Code 3
Claremont SD
Sch. Sys. Enr. Code 2
Supt. – Harold Huber, P O BOX C   55924
ES, P O BOX C   55924 – Tom Kramer, prin.

Clarissa, Todd Co., Pop. Code 3
Clarissa SD
Sch. Sys. Enr. Code 2
Supt. – Russell Martinson 56440
ES 56440 – Michael Martin, prin.

Clarkfield, Yellow Medicine Co., Pop. Code 4
Clarkfield SD
Sch. Sys. Enr. Code 2
Supt. – R. Kleven 56223
Hagg ES 56223 – Richard Petersen, prin.

Clearbrook, Clearwater Co., Pop. Code 3
Clearbrook SD
Sch. Sys. Enr. Code 2
Supt. – William Turk 56634
ES 56634 – George McReynolds, prin.

Clear Lake, Sherburne Co., Pop. Code 2
St. Cloud SD
Supt. – See Saint Cloud
Clearview ES, 5408 CLEARVIEW DR 55319
Roger Lydeen, prin.

Cleveland, Le Sueur Co., Pop. Code 3
Cleveland SD
Sch. Sys. Enr. Code 2
Supt. – D. Klundt, P O BOX 308 56017
ES, P O BOX 310 56017 – Melvin Goede, prin.

Climax, Polk Co., Pop. Code 2
Climax SD
Sch. Sys. Enr. Code 2
Supt. – Walt Aanenson, P O BOX 45 56523
ES, P O BOX 45 56523 – Roger Morken, prin.

Clinton, Big Stone Co., Pop. Code 3
Clinton SD
Sch. Sys. Enr. Code 2
Supt. – Bruce Grosland, P O BOX 361 56225
Clinton-Graceville ES, P O BOX 361 56225
Duwayne Discher, prin.

Cloquet, Carlton Co., Pop. Code 7
Cloquet SD
Sch. Sys. Enr. Code 4
Supt. – Russell Smith, 509 CARLTON AVE 55720
MS, 509 CARLTON AVE 55720
Robert Gerlach, prin.
Churchill ES, 615 JEFFERSON ST 55720
Gail Gilliland, prin.
Washington ES
12TH ST AND DODDRIDGE AVE 55720
Thomas Walsh, prin.

Our Lady of Sacred Heart, 401 AVENUE G 55720

Cohasset, Itasca Co.
Grand Rapids SD
Supt. – See Grand Rapids
ES 55721 – Robert Pecha, prin.

Cokato, Wright Co., Pop. Code 4
Dassel-Cokato SD
Sch. Sys. Enr. Code 4
Supt. – Ed Otto
HWY 12 & COUNTY ROAD 100 55321
ES 55321 – Mike Athmann, prin.
Other Schools – See Dassel

Cold Spring, Stearns Co., Pop. Code 4
Cold Spring SD
Sch. Sys. Enr. Code 4
Supt. – Patrick DeSutter 56320
ES, 533 MAIN ST 56320 – Jerome Sparby, prin.
Other Schools – See Richmond, Rockville

St. Boniface ES, 501 MAIN ST 56320

Coleraine, Itasca Co., Pop. Code 4
Coleraine SD
Sch. Sys. Enr. Code 4
Supt. – R. E. Maertens, P O BOX 195 55722
Vandyke ES, 300 COLE AVE 55722
Michael Domish, prin.
Other Schools – See Bovey, Marble

Columbia Heights, Anoka Co., Pop. Code 7
Columbia Heights SD
Sch. Sys. Enr. Code 5
Supt. – Tim Rummel, 1400 49TH AVE NE 55421
Central MS, 900 49TH AVE NE 55421
Janet Anderson, prin.
Highland ES, 1500 49TH AVE NE 55421
Quinton Larson, prin.
Valley View ES, 800 49TH AVE NE 55421
C. Kavolak, prin.
Other Schools – See Fridley

Immaculate Conception ES
4053 QUINCY ST NE 55421

Comfrey, Brown Co., Pop. Code 3
Comfrey SD
Sch. Sys. Enr. Code 2
Supt. – Irving Peterson, P O BOX 68 56019
ES, P O BOX 68 56019 – (—), prin.

Cook, St. Louis Co., Pop. Code 3
St. Louis County SD
Supt. – See Virginia
ES 55723 – R. Malmstrom, prin.

Coon Rapids, Anoka Co., Pop. Code 8
Anoka SD
Sch. Sys. Enr. Code 8
Supt. – Lewis Finch
11299 HANSON BLVD NW 55433

Adams ES, 943 89TH AVE NW 55433
Donald Rautio, prin.
Eisenhower ES
151 NORTHDALE BLVD NW 55433
Stanley Peichel, prin.
Hamilton ES, 1374 111TH AVE NW 55433
Marlys Tietz, prin.
Hoover ES, 2369 109TH AVE NW 55433
Barbara Berquist, prin.
Jacob ES, 1700 COON RAPIDS BLVD NW 55433
C. Burgess, prin.
Mississippi ES
10620 DIRECT RIVER DR NW 55433
Gerald Johnson, prin.
Morris Bye ES
11931 CROOKED LAKE BLVD NW 55433
Bonnie Martinson, prin.
Sand Creek ES, 12156 OLIVE ST NW 55433
James Tonn, prin.
Sorteberg ES, 11400 MAGNOLIA ST NW 55433
Vern Trandem, prin.
Other Schools – See Andover, Anoka, Blaine,
Brooklyn Center, Brooklyn Park, Champlin, Dayton,
Ramsey

Epiphany Education Center
11001 HANSON BLVD NW 55433

Cosmos, Meeker Co., Pop. Code 3
Cosmos SD
Sch. Sys. Enr. Code 2
Supt. – Tom Knoll, 320 N SATURN ST 56228
ES, 320 N SATURN ST 56228 – Tom Knoll, prin.

Cottage Grove, Washington Co., Pop. Code 7
South Washington County SD
Sch. Sys. Enr. Code 6
Supt. – Clark Kirkpatrick, 8040 80TH ST S 55016
Armstrong ES, 8855 INWOOD AVE S 55016
Wilson Ennis, prin.
Crestview ES, 7380 80TH ST S 55016
Curtis Grover, prin.
Hillside ES, 8177 HILLSIDE TRL S 55016
Roger Mathiesen, prin.
Pine Hill ES, 9015 HADLEY AVE S 55016
Phillip McMullen, prin.
Other Schools – See Newport, Saint Paul Park,
Woodbury

Rose of Sharon ES, 7421 80TH ST S 55016

Cotton, St. Louis Co.
St. Louis County SD
Supt. – See Virginia
ES 55724 – (—), prin.

Cottonwood, Lyon Co., Pop. Code 3
Cottonwood SD
Sch. Sys. Enr. Code 2
Supt. – R. M. Brynelson, P O BOX 107 56229
ES, P O BOX 107 56229 – Lowell Peterson, prin.

Courtland, Nicollet Co., Pop. Code 2

Immanuel Lutheran ES
RURAL ROUTE 01 BOX 40 56021

Cromwell, Carlton Co., Pop. Code 2
Cromwell SD
Sch. Sys. Enr. Code 2
Supt. – Herbert Hilinski 55726
Other Schools – See Wright

Crookston, Polk Co., Pop. Code 6
Crookston SD
Sch. Sys. Enr. Code 4
Supt. – Richard Larson, 415 JACKSON AVE 56716
Highland MS
N CENTRAL & BARRETT AVE 56716
Ray Dusek, prin.
Washington ES, 724 UNIVERSITY AVE 56716
Mary Jo Schmid, prin.

Cathedral ES, 702 SUMMIT AVE 56716

Crosby, Crow Wing Co., Pop. Code 4
Crosby SD
Sch. Sys. Enr. Code 4
Supt. – Warren Schmidt 56441
Other Schools – See Deer Wood, Emily

Crystal, Hennepin Co., Pop. Code 8
Robbinsdale SD
Supt. – See New Hope
Forest ES, 6800 47TH AVE N 55428
Robert Olsen, prin.
Neill ES, 6600 275H AVE N 55427
Adele Hellweg, prin.

St. Raphael ES, 7301 BASS LAKE RD 55428

Cyrus, Pope Co., Pop. Code 2
Cyrus SD
Sch. Sys. Enr. Code 2
Supt. – Frederick Switzer, P O BOX 39 56323
ES, P O BOX 39 56323 – Dorothy Jenum, prin.

Dakota, Winona Co., Pop. Code 2
Winona SD
Supt. – See Winona
ES, P O BOX 357 55925 – Judy Davis, prin.

St. John's Lutheran ES
RURAL ROUTE 01 BOX 152A 55925

Danube, Renville Co., Pop. Code 3
Danube SD
Sch. Sys. Enr. Code 2
Supt. – Ivan Eckstrom, P O BOX 157 56230
MS, P O BOX 157 56230
Marshall Thorstad, prin.

Dassel, Meeker Co., Pop. Code 4
Dassel-Cokato SD
Supt. – See Cokato
ES, FIRST & WILLIAMS 55325 – Craig Kay, prin.

Dawson, Lac Qui Parle Co., Pop. Code 4
Dawson SD
Sch. Sys. Enr. Code 3
Supt. – W. G. Johnson, P O BOX S 56232
ES, P O BOX 1018 56232 – Vernon Stevens, prin.

Dayton, Hennepin Co., Pop. Code 5
Anoka SD
Supt. – See Coon Rapids
ES, 12000 DIAMOND LAKE RD S 55327
Roger Dorn, prin.

Deer Creek, Otter Tail Co., Pop. Code 2
Deer Creek SD
Sch. Sys. Enr. Code 2
Supt. – James Techar, P O BOX 235 56527
ES, P O BOX 235 56527 – James Techar, prin.

Deer River, Itasca Co., Pop. Code 3
Deer River SD
Sch. Sys. Enr. Code 4
Supt. – Wallace Schoeb 56636
King ES 56636 – Gary Sorenson, prin.
Other Schools – See Talmoon

Deer Wood, Crow Wing Co., Pop. Code 3
Crosby SD
Supt. – See Crosby
ES 56444 – Roy Hamlin, prin.

Delano, Wright Co., Pop. Code 4
Delano SD
Sch. Sys. Enr. Code 4
Supt. – James Tool 55328
MS 55328 – Richard Rominski, prin.
ES, P O BOX 168 55328
Richard Katzenberger, prin.

St. Peter ES, 235 SECOND ST 55328

Delavan, Faribault Co., Pop. Code 2
Delavan SD
Sch. Sys. Enr. Code 2
Supt. – D. H. Berkland, P O BOX 125 56023
ES, P O BOX 125 56023 – Edward Jones, prin.

Dent, Otter Tail Co., Pop. Code 2
Perham SD
Supt. – See Perham
ES 56528 – Rex Kingsbury, prin.

Detroit Lakes, Becker Co., Pop. Code 6
Detroit Lakes SD
Sch. Sys. Enr. Code 5
Supt. – Robert Melick, 702 LAKE AVE 56501
Callaway ES 56501 – Roger Lee, prin.
Lincoln ES, 204 WILLOW ST E 56501
Eugene Johnson, prin.
Rossman ES, 1221 ROSSMAN AVE 56501
Charles Edwards, prin.
Washington ES, 314 WASHINGTON AVE 56501
Roger Lee, prin.

Holy Rosary ES, 1032 WASHINGTON AVE 56501

Dilworth, Clay Co., Pop. Code 5
Dilworth SD
Sch. Sys. Enr. Code 3
Supt. – Joseph Peterson, P O BOX 188 56529
ES, P O BOX 188 56529 – Janet Pladson, prin.

Dodge Center, Dodge Co., Pop. Code 4
Dodge Center SD
Sch. Sys. Enr. Code 3
Supt. – John Klein, P O BOX 40 55927
ES, P O BOX 40 55927
Diane Schwinghammer, prin.

Dover, Olmsted Co., Pop. Code 2
Dover-Eyota SD
Supt. – See Eyota
MS 55929 – Richard Oscarson, prin.

Duluth, St. Louis Co., Pop. Code 8
Duluth SD
Sch. Sys. Enr. Code 7
Supt. – Elliott Moeser
LAKE AVE & 2ND ST 55802
Birchwood ES, 1504 SWAN LAKE RD 55811
Mark Myles, prin.
Chester Park ES, 31 W COLLEGE ST 55812
Paul Osterlund, prin.
Cobb ES, 3917 WOODLAND AVE 55803
Thomas Salmela, prin.
Congdon Park ES, 3116 E SUPERIOR ST 55812
Eugene Voelk, prin.
Grant MS, 127 N 8TH AVE E 55805
Henry Pedersen, prin.
Homecroft ES, 1108 HOWARD GNESEN RD 55803
James Marinac, prin.
Kenwood ES, 1750 KENWOOD AVE 55811
Larry Johnson, prin.
Lakeside ES, 4628 PITT ST 55804
Mavis Whiteman, prin.
Lakewood ES, 2601 N TISCHER RD 55804
Larry Johnson, prin.

Lester Park ES, 315 N 54TH AVE E   55804
  Richard Colin, prin.
Lincoln ES, 2427 W 4TH ST   55806
  Terence Churchill, prin.
Lowell ES, 155 W CENTRAL ENTRANCE   55811
  Roy Meyer, prin.
MacArthur West ES, 727 N CENTRAL AVE   55807
  John Downs, prin.
Merritt ES, 510 N 40TH AVE W   55807
  Sharon Strum, prin.
Nettleton ES, 108 E 6TH ST   55805
  Peter Bergman, prin.
Piedmont ES, 2827 CHAMBERSBURG AVE   55811
  Sharon Strum, prin.
Stowe ES, 715 101ST AVE W   55808
  Robert Boyat, prin.
Washburn ES, 201 W SAINT ANDREWS ST   55803
  Roger Gordon, prin.

Hermantown SD
Sch. Sys. Enr. Code 4
Supt. – Donald Sandstrom
  4190 UGSTAD ROAD   55811
Hermantown MS, 4190 UGSTAD ROAD   55811
  Burleigh Rapp, prin.
Hermantown ES, 4190 UGSTAD RD   55811
  Dean Wolff, prin.

Lake Superior SD
Supt. – See Two Harbors
North Shore ES, 720 RYAN RD   55804
  Phillip Carlson, prin.

Proctor SD
Supt. – See Proctor
Bay View ES, 8708 VINLAND ST   55810
  Charles Martin, prin.
Munger ES, 3994 MUNGER SHAW RD   55810
  Dave Stark, prin.
Pike Lake ES, 3880 MARTIN RD   55811
  Robert Higgins, prin.

Beaver River Christian School
  589 FISH LAKE ROAD   55803
Holy Rosary ES, 2802 E 4TH ST   55812
St. John ES, 1 W CHISHOLM ST   55803
St. Michael ES, 4924 PITT ST   55804

Eagan, Dakota Co., Pop. Code 7
Burnsville SD
Supt. – See Burnsville
Rahn ES, 4424 SANDSTONE DR   55122
  Marilyn Kjorlien, prin.

West St. Paul SD
Supt. – See West Saint Paul
Pilot Knob ES, 1436 LONE OAK RD   55121
  Wallace Gehrig, prin.

Eagle Lake, Blue Earth Co., Pop. Code 4
Mankato SD
Supt. – See Mankato
ES, 500 LESUEUR AVE   56024
  Sharon Fitch, prin.

East Grand Forks, Polk Co., Pop. Code 6
East Grand Forks SD
Sch. Sys. Enr. Code 4
Supt. – John Roche, P O BOX 151   56721
Crestwood ES, P O BOX 51   56721
  Shirley Pearson, prin.
River Heights ES, P O BOX 151   56721
  Dale Taylor, prin.
Valley ES, P O BOX 151   56721
  Donal Nudell, prin.

Sacred Heart School, 126 3RD ST NW   56721

Echo, Yellow Medicine Co., Pop. Code 2
Echo SD
Sch. Sys. Enr. Code 2
Supt. – Dudley Gerber, P O BOX 246   56237
Echo-Wood Lake ES, P O BOX 246   56243
  (—), prin.

Eden Prairie, Hennepin Co., Pop. Code 7
Eden Prairie SD
Sch. Sys. Enr. Code 6
Supt. – Gerald McCoy
  8100 SCHOOL ROAD   55344
Central MS, 8025 SCHOOL ROAD   55344
  John Lyngdal, prin.
Eden Lake ES
  12000 ANDERSON LAKES PKWY   55344
  John Hallett, prin.
Forest Hills ES, 13708 HOLLY RD   55346
  Diane Vollmers, prin.
Prairie View ES, 17255 PETERBORG RD   55346
  Thomas Myers, prin.
Other Schools – See Edina

Eden Valley, Meeker Co., Pop. Code 3
Eden Valley SD
Sch. Sys. Enr. Code 3
Supt. – Charles Kyte, P O BOX 100   55329
ES, P O BOX 298   55329 – Hugh Skaja, prin.

Edgerton, Pipestone Co., Pop. Code 4
Edgerton SD
Sch. Sys. Enr. Code 2
Supt. – William Richter, P O BOX 307   56128
ES, P O BOX 28   56128 – Vince Hurley, prin.

Edgerton Christian ES, P O BOX 217   56128

Edina, Hennepin Co., Pop. Code 8
Eden Prairie SD
Supt. – See Eden Prairie
Cahill ES, 5505 DONCASTER LANE   55435
  Patricia Tidgewell, prin.

Edina SD
Sch. Sys. Enr. Code 6
Supt. – Raymond Smyth, 5555 W 70TH ST   55435
Concord ES, 5900 CONCORD AVE   55424
  Roger Peterson, prin.
Cornelia ES, 7000 CORNELIA DR   55435
  Robert Burnett, prin.
Countryside ES, 5701 BENTON AVE   55436
  Virgina Anderson, prin.
Creek Valley ES, 6401 GLEASON RD   55435
  John Moynihan, prin.

Marantha Christian Academy
  5701 NORMANDALE ROAD   55424
Our Lady of Grace ES, 5051 EDEN AVE   55436
St. Peter's Lutheran ES
  5421 FRANCE AVE S   55410
Woodale Montessori Academy
  5601 W 70TH ST   55435

Effie, Itasca Co., Pop. Code 2
Grand Rapids SD
Supt. – See Grand Rapids
MS, P O BOX 98   56639 – Frank Anselmo, prin.

Elbow Lake, Grant Co., Pop. Code 4
Barrett SD
Sch. Sys. Enr. Code 2
Supt. – Lee Warne, 411 FIRST SE   56531
Other Schools – See Barrett

Elbow Lake SD
Sch. Sys. Enr. Code 2
Supt. – Lee Warne, 411 1ST ST SE   56531
Lynne ES, 411 1ST ST SE   56531
  Roger Toso, prin.

Elgin, Wabasha Co., Pop. Code 3
Elgin-Millville SD
Sch. Sys. Enr. Code 3
Supt. – Richard Pederson, P O BOX D   55932
ES, P O BOX D   55932 – Ross Mattke, prin.

Elk River, Sherburne Co., Pop. Code 6
Elk River SD
Sch. Sys. Enr. Code 6
Supt. – David Flannery, 400 SCHOOL ST   55330
Handke ES, 1170 4TH ST   55330
  Dawn Moyer, prin.
Parker ES, 500 SCHOOL ST   55330
  Kenwood Carr, prin.
Other Schools – See Rogers, Zimmerman

Alliance Christian Academy
  829 SCHOOL ST   55330
St. Andrew ES, 428 IRVING AVE   55330
St. Johns Lutheran ES
  9243 VIKING BLVD NW   55330

Elkton, Mower Co., Pop. Code 2
Southland SD
Supt. – See Adams
Southland MS, P O BOX 85   55933
  C. Olsen, prin.

Ellendale, Steele Co., Pop. Code 3
Ellendale SD
Sch. Sys. Enr. Code 2
Supt. – Martin Avelsgaurd, P O BOX 428   56026
ES, P O BOX 428   56026 – (—), prin.

Ellsworth, Nobles Co., Pop. Code 3
Ellsworth SD
Sch. Sys. Enr. Code 2
Supt. – Rick McClure, P O BOX 8   56129
ES, P O BOX 8   56129 – Rick McClure, prin.

Elmore, Faribault Co., Pop. Code 3
Elmore SD
Sch. Sys. Enr. Code 2
Supt. – Melvin Hauge, P O BOX 98   56027
ES, P O BOX 32   56027 – Lois Fischer, prin.

Ely, St. Louis Co., Pop. Code 5
Ely SD
Sch. Sys. Enr. Code 3
Supt. – Terrence Merfeld
  600 E HARVEY ST   55731
Washington ES, 600 E HARVEY ST   55731
  Robert Jalonen, prin.

Emily, Crow Wing Co., Pop. Code 3
Crosby SD
Supt. – See Crosby
ES   56447 – Roy Hamlin, prin.

Emmons, Freeborn Co., Pop. Code 2
Emmons SD
Sch. Sys. Enr. Code 2
Supt. – Richard Briesath, P O BOX 13   56029
ES, P O BOX 13   56029 – (—), prin.

Erskine, Polk Co., Pop. Code 3
Erskine SD
Sch. Sys. Enr. Code 2
Supt. – James Christianson, P O BOX 209   56535
ES, P O BOX 279   56535 – Galen Clow, prin.

Esko, Carlton Co., Pop. Code 3
Esko SD
Sch. Sys. Enr. Code 3
Supt. – William Hoffman   55733

Winterquist ES   55733 – (—), prin.

Evansville, Douglas Co., Pop. Code 3
Evansville SD
Sch. Sys. Enr. Code 2
Supt. – John Retrum, 123 2ND AVE   56326
ES, 123 2ND AVE   56326 – Pam Peterson, prin.

Eveleth, St. Louis Co., Pop. Code 6
Eveleth SD
Sch. Sys. Enr. Code 4
Supt. – Michael Lang, 801 JONES ST   55734
Franklin ES, FAYAL AVE   55734
  Herb Schur, prin.

Excelsior, Hennepin Co., Pop. Code 5
Minnetonka SD
Sch. Sys. Enr. Code 6
Supt. – D. Draayer, 261 SCHOOL AVE   55331
ES, 441 OAK ST   55331 – Charles Andrews, prin.
Minnetonka IS, 6421 HAZELTINE BLVD   55331
  Terry Tofte, prin.
Minnewashta PS, 26350 SMITHTOWN RD   55331
  Lloyd Law, prin.
Other Schools – See Minnetonka, Wayzata

Chapel Hill Academy
  4584 VINE HILL ROAD   55331
St. John the Baptist ES, 638 MILL ST   55331

Eyota, Olmsted Co., Pop. Code 4
Dover-Eyota SD
Sch. Sys. Enr. Code 3
Supt. – Joan Wilcox, P O BOX 268   55934
ES, P O BOX 268   55934 – Richard Oscarson, prin.
Other Schools – See Dover

Fairfax, Renville Co., Pop. Code 4
Fairfax SD
Sch. Sys. Enr. Code 2
Supt. – Dale Captain, 300 SE 2ND ST   55332
G. F. W. MS, P O BOX 489   55332
  Dwight Davis, prin.

Fairmont, Martin Co., Pop. Code 7
Fairmont SD
Sch. Sys. Enr. Code 4
Supt. – Donald Ruble, 115 S PARK ST   56031
MS, 724 VICTORIA ST   56031
  Richard Truman, prin.
Budd ES, 1001 ALBION AVE   56031
  Robert Sexe, prin.
Lincoln ES, 1200 N PARK ST   56031
  Gary Bachmann, prin.

St. John Vianney ES, 911 S PRAIRIE AVE   56031
St. Paul's Lutheran ES, 201 OXFORD ST   56031

Faribault, Rice Co., Pop. Code 7
Faribault SD
Sch. Sys. Enr. Code 5
Supt. – Richard Berge, 2855 1ST AVE NW   55021
Garfield ES, 421 3RD AVE SW   55021
  Robert Anhorn, prin.
Jefferson ES, 922 HOME PL   55021
  Bonnie Flom, prin.
Lincoln ES, 510 LINCOLN AVE N   55021
  Elizabeth Bergen, prin.
McKinley ES, 930 4TH AVE NW   55021
  Robert Anhorn, prin.
Washington ES, 117 SHUMWAY AVE   55021
  Roland Burgdorf, prin.
Other Schools – See Nerstrand

Consolidated Catholic ES, 15 3RD AVE SW   55021
Trinity Lutheran ES, 526 4TH ST NW   55021

Farmington, Dakota Co., Pop. Code 5
Farmington SD
Sch. Sys. Enr. Code 4
Supt. – Robert Boeckman, 510 WALNUT ST   55024
MS, 510 WALNUT ST   55024
  Donald Meyers, prin.
Akin Road ES, 5231 195TH ST W   55024
  Douglas Henke, prin.
ES, 500 MAPLE ST   55024 – Jon Reid, prin.

Christian Life ES, 19012 BLAINE AVE   55024

Fergus Falls, Otter Tail Co., Pop. Code 7
Fergus Falls SD
Sch. Sys. Enr. Code 5
Supt. – Robert Block, 600 N FRIBERG AVE   56537
MS, 601 RANDOLPH AVE   56537
  James Langlie, prin.
Adams ES, 301 W BANCROFT AVE   56537
  Duane Kern, prin.
Cleveland ES, 919 NORTHERN AVE   56537
  Eugene Manning, prin.
McKinley ES, 724 W LAUREL AVE   56537
  Eugene Manning, prin.

Our Lady of Victory ES
  426 W CAVOUR AVE   56537

Fertile, Polk Co., Pop. Code 3
Fertile SD
Sch. Sys. Enr. Code 3
Supt. – W. Lindberg, HIGHWAY 32 S   56540
ES, HWY 32 S   56540 – June Erickson, prin.

Finlayson, Pine Co., Pop. Code 2
Finlayson SD
Sch. Sys. Enr. Code 2
Supt. – Stanley Sjodahl   55735
ES   55735 – Stanley Sjodahl, prin.

Fisher, Polk Co., Pop. Code 2
Fisher SD
Sch. Sys. Enr. Code 2
Supt. – L. Barsness, P O BOX 37 56723
ES, P O BOX 37 56723 – Lowell Barsness, prin.

Floodwood, St. Louis Co., Pop. Code 3
Floodwood SD
Sch. Sys. Enr. Code 2
Supt. – Stephen Anderson, P O BOX 287 55736
ES, P O BOX 287 55736 – Stephen Anderson, prin.

Foley, Benton Co., Pop. Code 4
Foley SD
Sch. Sys. Enr. Code 4
Supt. – Noel Schroeder, 520 DEWEY ST 56329
ES, P O BOX 457 56329 – Karl Berlin, prin.

St. John ES, 215 7TH AVE 56329

Forest Lake, Washington Co., Pop. Code 5
Forest Lake SD
Sch. Sys. Enr. Code 6
Supt. – Gerald Brynildson
    308 15TH ST SW 55025
Columbus ES, 17345 NOTRE DAME ST NE 55025
    Lawrence Carlson, prin.
ES, 408 4TH ST SW 55025 – Benjamin Clark, prin.
Forest View ES, 620 4TH ST SW 55025
    Gerald Lunde, prin.
Other Schools – See Circle Pines, Scandia, Wyoming

St. Peter ES, 1250 SOUTH SHORE DRIVE 55025

Fosston, Polk Co., Pop. Code 4
Fosston SD
Sch. Sys. Enr. Code 3
Supt. – Dale Wain, E HIGHWAY 2 56542
Magelssen ES, 700 1ST ST E 56542
    Gregory Bruce, prin.

Franklin, Renville Co., Pop. Code 1
Franklin SD
Sch. Sys. Enr. Code 2
Supt. – William Bjorklund, P O BOX 38 55333
Cedar Mountain ES, P O BOX 38 55333
    Robert Tews, prin.

Frazee, Becker Co., Pop. Code 4
Frazee SD
Sch. Sys. Enr. Code 4
Supt. – J. Lamont, P O BOX 186 56544
ES, P O BOX 186 56544 – Maynard Johnson, prin.

Freeborn, Freeborn Co., Pop. Code 2
Freeborn SD
Sch. Sys. Enr. Code 2
Supt. – Patrick Flanagan, P O BOX 155 56032
ES, P O BOX 155 56032 – Lynette Russ, prin.

Freeport, Stearns Co., Pop. Code 2

Sacred Heart ES, P O BOX 38 56331

Fridley, Anoka Co., Pop. Code 8
Columbia Heights SD
Supt. – See Columbia Heights
North Park ES, 5575 FILLMORE ST NE 55432
    Victor Coffman, prin.

Fridley SD
Sch. Sys. Enr. Code 5
Supt. – Dennis Rens
    6000 MOORE LAKE DRIVE W 55432
MS, 6100 MOORE LAKE DRIVE W 55432
    Margaret Leibfried, prin.
Hayes ES, 615 MISSISSIPPI ST NE 55432
    Earl Switzer, prin.
Stevenson ES, 6080 E RIVER RD 55432
    Jerry Reitter, prin.

Fulda, Murray Co., Pop. Code 4
Fulda SD
Sch. Sys. Enr. Code 3
Supt. – Paul Wandersee 56131
ES, 303 N LAFAYETTE AVE 56131
    Dwayne Westra, prin.

Garden City, Blue Earth Co., Pop. Code 3
Garden City SD
Sch. Sys. Enr. Code 2
Supt. – Eric Bartleson 56034
Wellcome Memorial MS, HIGHWAY 169 56034
    Jane Schuck, prin.
Other Schools – See Mankato, Vernon Center

Garfield, Douglas Co., Pop. Code 2
Alexandria SD
Supt. – See Alexandria
ES 56332 – Cortlan Krogstad, prin.

Gary, Norman Co., Pop. Code 2
Gary SD
Sch. Sys. Enr. Code 2
Supt. – Karl Schultz, P O BOX 47 56545
ES, P O BOX 47 56545 – (—), prin.

Gaylord, Sibley Co., Pop. Code 4
Gaylord SD
Sch. Sys. Enr. Code 3
Supt. – John Fredericksen, 500 COURT AVE 55334
ES, P O BOX 356 55334 – Nordy Nelson,Jr., prin.

Gibbon, Sibley Co., Pop. Code 3
Gibbon SD
Sch. Sys. Enr. Code 2
Supt. – Arnold Prince, 323 E 11TH ST 55335

G.F.W. ES, 323 E 11TH ST 55335
    John Chrest, prin.

Gilbert, St. Louis Co., Pop. Code 5
Gilbert SD
Sch. Sys. Enr. Code 3
Supt. – Michael Lang 55741
Shean ES, SUMMIT ST 55741
    Barbara Goblirsch, prin.

Glencoe, Mcleod Co., Pop. Code 5
Glencoe SD
Sch. Sys. Enr. Code 4
Supt. – John Noennig, 1621 16TH ST E 55336
MS, 1103 11TH ST E 55336
    Richard Wickmann, prin.
Baker ES, 405 16TH ST E 55336
    Vinton Zabel, prin.
Lincoln ES, 1621 16TH ST E 55336
    Vinton Zabel, prin.

First Ev. Lutheran ES, 1015 14TH ST E 55336
St. Pius X ES, 1103 10TH ST E 55336

Glenville, Freeborn Co., Pop. Code 3
Glenville SD
Sch. Sys. Enr. Code 2
Supt. – Richard Briesath, 230 5TH ST SE 56036
ES, 240 2ND AVE SW 56036
    Janice Fischer, prin.

Glenwood, Pope Co., Pop. Code 5
Glenwood SD
Sch. Sys. Enr. Code 4
Supt. – Ernest Janisch, 2ND AVE NE 56334
Central MS, NE 2ND AVE 56334
    Barry Janssen, prin.
Norgaard ES, 209 5TH ST SE 56334
    Barry Janssen, prin.

Glyndon, Clay Co., Pop. Code 3
Glyndon SD
Sch. Sys. Enr. Code 3
Supt. – Joseph Peterson 56547
ES 56547 – Norma Jerdee, prin.

Golden Valley, Hennepin Co., Pop. Code 7
Hopkins SD
Supt. – See Hopkins
Meadowbrook ES, 5430 GLENWOOD AVE 55422
    Marilyn Olson, prin.

Robbinsdale SD
Supt. – See New Hope
Noble ES, 2601 NOBLE AVE N 55422
    Will Zimmerman, prin.
Olson ES, 1751 KELLY DR 55427
    Will Zimmerman, prin.

Breck School, 123 OTTAWA AVE N 55422
Good Shepherd ES, 145 JERSEY AVE S 55426
St. Margaret Mary ES, 2225 ZENITH AVE N 55422

Gonvick, Clearwater Co., Pop. Code 2
Gonvick SD
Sch. Sys. Enr. Code 2
Supt. – Don Danielson 56644
ES 56644 – Dale Wain, prin.

Goodhue, Goodhue Co., Pop. Code 3
Goodhue SD
Sch. Sys. Enr. Code 3
Supt. – Jerry Jensen, 510 3RD AVE 55027
ES, 510 3RD AVE 55027
    Carol Lindenfelser, prin.

Goodridge, Pennington Co., Pop. Code 2
Goodridge SD
Sch. Sys. Enr. Code 2
Supt. – Salvinus Hoffert, P O BOX 195 56725
ES, P O BOX 195 56725
    Gordon Hendrickson, prin.

Good Thunder, Blue Earth Co., Pop. Code 3
Amboy-Good Thunder SD
Supt. – See Amboy
Amboy-Good Thunder ES 56037
    Rodney Joyal, prin.

Granada, Martin Co., Pop. Code 2
Granada-Huntley SD
Sch. Sys. Enr. Code 2
Supt. – Richard McGuire, P O BOX 17 56039
Granada-Huntley ES, P O BOX 17 56039
    Bruce Klaehn, prin.

Grand Marais, Cook Co., Pop. Code 4
Cook County SD
Sch. Sys. Enr. Code 3
Supt. – Warren Rolek, P O BOX F 55604
Grand Portage ES 55064 – Bert Chamberlain, prin.
Sawtooth Mountain ES 55604
    Bert Chamberlain, prin.
Other Schools – See Tofte

Grand Meadow, Mower Co., Pop. Code 3
Grand Meadow SD
Sch. Sys. Enr. Code 2
Supt. – Darold Yost, P O BOX 68 55936
ES, P O BOX 68 55936 – Donald Beach, prin.

Grand Rapids, Itasca Co., Pop. Code 6
Grand Rapids SD
Sch. Sys. Enr. Code 5
Supt. – Leon Touminen
    820 POKEGAMA AVE N 55744
Forest Lake ES, 7TH AVE W & 8TH ST 55744
    Robert Swedberg, prin.

Murphy ES, 403 NE 8TH ST 55744
    Susan Mattson, prin.
Riverview ES, 300 SE 4TH ST 55744
    Roy Johnson, prin.
Southwest ES, 7TH ST SW & 7TH AVE 55744
    William Gray, prin.
Other Schools – See Bigfork, Bovey, Cohasset, Effie,
    Squaw Lake, Togo, Warba

St. Joseph ES, 614 NW 2ND AVE 55744

Granite Falls, Yellow Medicine Co., Pop. Code 5
Granite Falls SD
Sch. Sys. Enr. Code 3
Supt. – C. Flack, 450 9TH AVE 56241
ES, 700 5TH ST 56241 – David Roufs, prin.

Greenbush, Roseau Co., Pop. Code 3
Greenbush SD
Sch. Sys. Enr. Code 2
Supt. – K. F. Kapphahn, P O BOX 70 56726
ES, P O BOX 70 56726 – Paul Nelmark, prin.

Grey Eagle, Todd Co., Pop. Code 2
Grey Eagle SD
Sch. Sys. Enr. Code 2
Supt. – Vern Bagstad 56336
ES 56336 – Harry Grammond, prin.

Grove City, Meeker Co., Pop. Code 3
Grove City SD
Sch. Sys. Enr. Code 2
Supt. – Glenn Bakeberg, P O BOX 278 56243
ES 56243 – Glenn Bakeberg, prin.

Grygla, Marshall Co., Pop. Code 2
Grygla SD
Sch. Sys. Enr. Code 2
Supt. – Salvinus Hoffert, P O BOX 18 56727
ES, P O BOX 18 56727 – Loren Lusignan, prin.

Hallock, Kittson Co., Pop. Code 4
Hallock SD
Sch. Sys. Enr. Code 2
Supt. – Jerry Scott, P O BOX 670 56728
ES, P O BOX 670 56728 – Dean Dahlin, prin.

Halstad, Norman Co., Pop. Code 3
Hendrum SD
Sch. Sys. Enr. Code 2
Supt. – Don Blaeser, P O BOX 328 56548
Norman County West ES 56548
    William Sprung, prin.

Hamburg, Carver Co., Pop. Code 2

Emmanuel Lutheran ES, 18155 CTY RD 50 55339

Hampton, Dakota Co., Pop. Code 2

St. Mathias School
    23335 NORTHFIELD BVDL 55031

Hancock, Stevens Co., Pop. Code 3
Hancock SD
Sch. Sys. Enr. Code 2
Supt. – Russell Larson, P O BOX 367 56244
ES, P O BOX 367 56244 – Dorothy Jenum, prin.

Hanover, Wright Co., Pop. Code 3
Buffalo SD
Supt. – See Buffalo
ES, P O BOX 427 55341 – Roger Esterbrooks, prin.

Hanska, Brown Co., Pop. Code 2
New Ulm SD
Supt. – See New Ulm
ES 56041 – E. Ferguson, prin.

Harmony, Fillmore Co., Pop. Code 4
Harmony SD
Sch. Sys. Enr. Code 2
Supt. – Gary Honken, 145 MAIN AVE S 55939
ES, 225 3RD AVE SW 55939
    Margaret McKernan, prin.

Hastings, Dakota Co., Pop. Code 7
Hastings SD
Sch. Sys. Enr. Code 5
Supt. – K. LaCroix, 9TH & VERMILLION ST 55033
MS, 9TH & VERMILLION ST 55033
    Leonard Schwartz, prin.
Cooper ES, 17TH & VERMILLION 55033
    Peggy Ritter, prin.
Kennedy ES, 10 & TYLER 55033
    Gary Evenson, prin.
Pinecrest ES, 975 12TH ST W 55033
    Corolyn Mortensen, prin.
Tilden ES, 4TH & RIVER 55033
    Earl Andersen, prin.

Hastings Parochial ES, 600 TYLER ST 55033

Hawley, Clay Co., Pop. Code 4
Hawley SD
Sch. Sys. Enr. Code 3
Supt. – Duane Rafteseth, P O BOX 608 56549
ES, P O BOX 608 56549 – Dale Skallerud, prin.

Hayfield, Dodge Co., Pop. Code 4
Hayfield SD
Sch. Sys. Enr. Code 3
Supt. – Richard Guevremont 55940
ES 55940 – Myron Meier, prin.
Other Schools – See Brownsdale

Hector, Renville Co., Pop. Code 4
Hector SD
Sch. Sys. Enr. Code 2
Supt. – Roy Rud, P O BOX 307 55342
ES, P O BOX 307 55342 – Lester Perry, prin.

Henderson, Sibley Co., Pop. Code 3
Henderson SD
Sch. Sys. Enr. Code 2
Supt. – R. Fossum, 107 8TH ST 56044
Hilltop ES, 107 8TH ST 56044
 Thomas Murphy, prin.

Hendricks, Lincoln Co., Pop. Code 3
Hendricks SD
Sch. Sys. Enr. Code 2
Supt. – Norris Oerter, 200 E LINCOLN 56136
ES, 200 E LINCOLN 56136 – Norris Oerter, prin.

Henning, Otter Tail Co., Pop. Code 3
Henning SD
Sch. Sys. Enr. Code 2
Supt. – Bruce Montplaiser, P O BOX 15 56551
ES 56551 – Cheryl Davidson, prin.

Herman, Grant Co., Pop. Code 3
Herman-Norcross SD
Sch. Sys. Enr. Code 2
Supt. – Wilbur Smith 56248
ES 56248 – Richard Kennedy, prin.

Heron Lake, Jackson Co., Pop. Code 3
Heron Lake-Okabena SD
Sch. Sys. Enr. Code 2
Supt. – Richard Orcutt, P O BOX 378 56137
Heron Lake-Okabena ES, P O BOX 378 56137
 Richard Orcutt, prin.

Hibbing, St. Louis Co., Pop. Code 7
Hibbing SD
Sch. Sys. Enr. Code 5
Supt. – Gary Norris, 8TH AVE E 21ST ST 55746
Lincoln JHS, 11TH AVE E & 23RD ST 55746
 William Lah, prin.
Cobb-Cook ES, 3RD AVE W & 32ND ST 55746
 Laverne Walters, prin.
Greenhaven ES, 37TH ST & 3RD AVE 55746
 John Drazenovich, prin.
Jefferson ES 55746 – Bruce Anspaugh, prin.
Washington ES, 12TH AVE & 21ST 55746
 Daniel Molesky, prin.

Assumption ES, 2310 7TH AVE E 55746
St. Leo ES, 218 E 39TH ST 55746

Hill City, Aitkin Co., Pop. Code 3
Hill City SD
Sch. Sys. Enr. Code 2
Supt. – Darrell Nelson, 500 IONE AVE 55748
ES, P O BOX 69 55748 – Dennis Perreault, prin.

Hills, Rock Co., Pop. Code 3
Hills-Beaver Creek SD
Sch. Sys. Enr. Code 2
Supt. – G. LeBoutillier, P O BOX 547 56138
Other Schools – See Beaver Creek

Hinckley, Pine Co., Pop. Code 3
Hinckley SD
Sch. Sys. Enr. Code 3
Supt. – O.W. Ostrand, P O BOX 308 55037
ES, P O BOX 308 55037 – Roberta Azar, prin.

Holdingford, Stearns Co., Pop. Code 3
Holdingford SD
Sch. Sys. Enr. Code 4
Supt. – R. Doucet, P O BOX 250 56340
ES, P O BOX 250 56340 – Walter Wilson, prin.

Hopkins, Hennepin Co., Pop. Code 7
Hopkins SD
Sch. Sys. Enr. Code 6
Supt. – Arthur Bruning
 1001 STATE HIGHWAY 7 55343
Curren ES, 1600 EXCELSIOR AVE W 55343
 Marjorie Richardson, prin.
Eisenhower ES, 1001 HWY 7 55343
 Charles Mykleby, prin.
Glen Lake ES, 4801 WOODRIDGE RD 55345
 Edward Ryshavy, prin.
Smith ES, 801 MINNETONKA MILLS RD 55343
 Gary Prest, prin.
Tanglen ES, 10901 HILLSIDE LN 55343
 James Childs, prin.
Other Schools – See Golden Valley, Minnetonka

Blake Lower ES, 110 BLAKE ROAD 55343
Blake MS, 110 BLAKE RD S 55343
Ireland ES, 1320 MAIN ST W 55343

Houston, Houston Co., Pop. Code 4
Houston SD
Sch. Sys. Enr. Code 3
Supt. – Robert Svihel, 306 W ELM 55943
ES, 310 S SHERMAN 55943
 Beatrice Van Loon, prin.

Winona SD
Supt. – See Winona
Ridgeway ES, RURAL ROUTE 01 55943
 Judy Davis, prin.

Howard Lake, Wright Co., Pop. Code 4
Howard Lake SD
Sch. Sys. Enr. Code 3
Supt. – Murl Kletscher, P O BOX 708 55349
ES, P O BOX 708 55349 – Curtis Levang, prin.

St. James Lutheran ES, 1000 6TH AVE 55349

Hugo, Anoka Co., Pop. Code 5
Centennial SD
Supt. – See Circle Pines
Centerville ES, 1721 WESTVIEW AVE 55038
 Daniel Kelley, prin.

Stillwater SD
Supt. – See Stillwater
Withrow ES, 10158 122ND ST 55038
 Ruth Ranum, prin.

White Bear Lake SD
Supt. – See White Bear Lake
ES, 14895 FRANCESCA AVE N 55038
 Shirley Trossen, prin.

Humboldt, Kittson Co., Pop. Code 2
Humboldt SD
Sch. Sys. Enr. Code 1
Supt. – Robert Haller, P O BOX 54 56731
ES, P O BOX 54 56731 – Julie Johnson, prin.

Hutchinson, Mcleod Co., Pop. Code 6
Hutchinson SD
Sch. Sys. Enr. Code 4
Supt. – Glenn Matejka, 30 GLEN ST N 55350
Hutchinson Park MS, 100 GLEN ST S 55350
 Carol Beaver, prin.
Hutchinson West PS, 875 SCHOOL ROAD 55350
 Larry Ladd, prin.

Our Savior's Lutheran ES, 800 BLUFF ST 55350
St. Anastasia ES, 400 LAKE ST 55350

International Falls, Koochiching Co., Pop. Code 6
International Falls SD
Sch. Sys. Enr. Code 4
Supt. – J. Roberts, 4TH ST & 6TH AVE 56649
Backus MS, 600 4TH ST 56649
 Thomas Worth, prin.
Falls MS 56649 – Manny Herzig, prin.
Holler ES 56649 – Lloyd Arveson, prin.

St. Thomas Aquinas ES, 810 5TH ST 56649

Inver Grove Heights, Dakota Co., Pop. Code 7
Inver Grove SD
Sch. Sys. Enr. Code 5
Supt. – Kirby Lehman
 9875 INVER GROVE TRAIL 55075
Hilltop ES, 3201 68TH ST E 55075
 Thomas Lowrie, prin.
Inver Grove ES, 4100 66TH ST E 55075
 James Laska, prin.
Salem Hills ES, 5899 BABCOCK TRL E 55075
 Deborah Distad, prin.
South Grove ES, 7650 CLAYTON AVE E 55075
 Thomas Barker, prin.

Iron, St. Louis Co., Pop. Code 2
St. Louis County SD
Supt. – See Virginia
Cherry ES, RURAL ROUTE 01 BOX 266 55751
 (—), prin.

Isanti, Isanti Co., Pop. Code 3
Cambridge-Isanti SD
Supt. – See Cambridge
MS, P O BOX 518 55040 – Fred Nolan, prin.
ES, RURAL ROUTE 03 BOX 519 55040
 Paul Tatting, prin.

Isle, Mille Lacs Co., Pop. Code 3
Isle SD
Sch. Sys. Enr. Code 2
Supt. – Thomas Hoppe, P O BOX 25 56342
ES, P O BOX 54 56342 – Thomas Magoris, prin.

Ivanhoe, Lincoln Co., Pop. Code 3
Ivanhoe SD
Sch. Sys. Enr. Code 2
Supt. – Dwayne Pecks, P O BOX 9 56142
ES, P O BOX 9 56142 – Vivian Larsen, prin.

Jackson, Jackson Co., Pop. Code 5
Jackson SD
Sch. Sys. Enr. Code 4
Supt. – Michael Kuntz, 1128 N HIGHWAY 56143
MS, 405 5TH ST 56143 – James Spencer, prin.
Riverside ES, PARK & SPRINGFIELD PKWY 56143
 David Dejong, prin.

Janesville, Waseca Co., Pop. Code 4
Janesville SD
Sch. Sys. Enr. Code 3
Supt. – D. J. Lochner, 110 E 3RD ST 56048
ES, 110 E MAIN ST 56048 – Jeffrey Miller, prin.

Trinity Lutheran ES, 501 S MAIN ST 56048

Jasper, Pipestone Co., Pop. Code 3
Jasper SD
Sch. Sys. Enr. Code 2
Supt. – Bill Richter 56144
ES 56144 – Vince Hurley, prin.

Jordan, Scott Co., Pop. Code 5
Jordan SD
Sch. Sys. Enr. Code 4
Supt. – George Young, 500 SUNSET DRIVE 55352
ES, 815 SUNSET DR 55352 – Joseph Benko, prin.

St. John the Baptist ES, 215 2ND ST E 55352

Kandiyohi, Kandiyohi Co., Pop. Code 2
Willmar SD
Supt. – See Willmar
ES 56251 – Kathleen Haug, prin.

Karlstad, Kittson Co., Pop. Code 3
Karlstad SD
Sch. Sys. Enr. Code 2
Supt. – Lowell Schwalbe, P O BOX 178 56732
ES, P O BOX 178 56732 – Dean Dahlen, prin.

Kasson, Dodge Co., Pop. Code 5
Kasson-Mantorville SD
Sch. Sys. Enr. Code 4
Supt. – S. Anderson, P O BOX 158 55944
ES, 101 3RD AVE NW 55944
 Joseph Hampl, prin.
Other Schools – See Mantorville

Keewatin, Itasca Co., Pop. Code 4
Nashwauk-Keewatin SD
Supt. – See Nashwauk
JHS 55753 – John Klarich, prin.

Kelliher, Beltrami Co., Pop. Code 2
Kelliher SD
Sch. Sys. Enr. Code 2
Supt. – Antoine Hoyt, P O BOX 147 56650
ES, P O BOX 259 56659 – Antoine Hoyt, prin.

Kellogg, Wabasha Co., Pop. Code 2
Wabasha SD
Supt. – See Wabasha
ES 55945 – Frederick Brown,Jr., prin.

Kennedy, Kittson Co., Pop. Code 2
Kennedy SD
Sch. Sys. Enr. Code 2
Supt. – John Evans, P O BOX 127 56733
ES, P O BOX 9 56733 – James Poissant, prin.

Kensington, Douglas Co., Pop. Code 2
Kensington SD
Sch. Sys. Enr. Code 2
Supt. – (—) 56343
Hoffman-Kensington ES 56343 – (—), prin.

Kenyon, Goodhue Co., Pop. Code 4
Kenyon SD
Sch. Sys. Enr. Code 3
Supt. – Arlen Johnson, 401 FOREST ST 55946
ES, 400 6TH ST 55946 – Dennis Monroe, prin.

Kerkhoven, Swift Co., Pop. Code 3
Kerkhoven Murdock-Sunburg SD
Sch. Sys. Enr. Code 3
Supt. – Gary Shaw 56252
Other Schools – See Murdock

Kimball, Stearns Co., Pop. Code 3
Kimball SD
Sch. Sys. Enr. Code 3
Supt. – Kenneth Helling, P O BOX 368 55353
ES, P O BOX 368 55353 – Gary Lagerstedt, prin.

La Crescent, Houston Co., Pop. Code 5
La Crescent SD
Sch. Sys. Enr. Code 4
Supt. – Donald Groth, 504 S OAK ST 55947
La Crescent-Hokah ES, 4TH AND OAK ST S 55947
 Gary Murray, prin.

Crucifixion ES, 420 S 2ND ST 55947

Lafayette, Nicollet Co., Pop. Code 3
New Ulm SD
Supt. – See New Ulm
ES 56054 – Harry Stock, prin.

Lake Benton, Lincoln Co., Pop. Code 3
Lake Benton SD
Sch. Sys. Enr. Code 2
Supt. – Dwayne Pecks, 101 GARFIELD ST 56149
ES, 101 GARFIELD ST 56149 – Dany Castor, prin.

Lake City, Wabasha Co., Pop. Code 5
Lake City SD
Sch. Sys. Enr. Code 4
Supt. – Willard Olson 55041
Bluff View ES, LAKEWOOD AVE 55041
 Thomas Clough, prin.

St. John's Lutheran ES
 516 CHESTNUT ST W 55041

Lake Crystal, Blue Earth Co., Pop. Code 4
Lake Crystal SD
Sch. Sys. Enr. Code 3
Supt. – Eric Bartleson, P O BOX F 56055
ES, P O BOX F 56055 – Bruce Melander, prin.

Lake Elmo, Washington Co., Pop. Code 6
Stillwater SD
Supt. – See Stillwater
ES, 11030 STILLWATER BLVD N 55042
 William Rhodenbaugh, prin.

Lakefield, Jackson Co., Pop. Code 4
Lakefield SD
Sch. Sys. Enr. Code 2
Supt. – R. Clifford Busch, P O BOX 338 56150
Pleasantville ES, P O BOX 754 56150
 Dennis Brown, prin.

Immanuel Lutheran ES, P O BOX 487 56150

Lakeland, Washington Co., Pop. Code 4
Stillwater SD
Supt. – See Stillwater

Afton-Lakeland ES
475 SAINT CROIX TRL S 55043
John Sybrant, prin.

Lake Park, Becker Co., Pop. Code 3
Lake Park SD
Sch. Sys. Enr. Code 2
Supt. – J. Halvorson, P O BOX 357 56554
ES, P O BOX 479 56554 – Richard Hanson, prin.

Lakeville, Dakota Co., Pop. Code 7
Lakeville SD
Sch. Sys. Enr. Code 5
Supt. – Carl Wahlstrom, 8670 210TH ST W 55044
Crystal Lake ES, 16250 IPAVA AVE 55044
Robert Indihar, prin.
Huddleston ES, 9569 175TH ST W 55044
Constance Miller, prin.
Kennedy ES, 21240 HOLYOKE AVE 55044
Anne Lyons, prin.
Orchard Lake ES, 16531 KLAMATH TRL 55044
Kathleen Basiago, prin.

All Saints ES, 20950 HOWLAND AVE W 55044

Lake Wilson, Murray Co., Pop. Code 2
Chandler-Lake Wilson SD
Supt. – See Chandler
Chandler-Lake Wilson ES, P O BOX 32 56151
Mary Mattson, prin.

Lamberton, Redwood Co., Pop. Code 4
Lamberton SD
Sch. Sys. Enr. Code 2
Supt. – Richard Gulbranson, P O BOX 278 56152
ES, P O BOX 278 56152 – (—), prin.

Lancaster, Kittson Co., Pop. Code 2
Lancaster SD
Sch. Sys. Enr. Code 2
Supt. – Philip Dyrod, P O BOX 217 56735
ES, P O BOX 217 56735 – Bradley Homstad, prin.

Lanesboro, Fillmore Co., Pop. Code 3
Lanesboro SD
Sch. Sys. Enr. Code 2
Supt. – Richard Lamon, 101 RIDGEVIEW 55949
ES, 101 RIDGEVIEW LN S 55949
James Blahnik, prin.

Laporte, Hubbard Co., Pop. Code 2
LaPorte SD
Sch. Sys. Enr. Code 2
Supt. – Dan Brooks, P O BOX 01 56461
ES, RURAL ROUTE 01 BOX 1 56461
Sharon Lembke, prin.

Le Center, Le Sueur Co., Pop. Code 4
Le Center SD
Sch. Sys. Enr. Code 3
Supt. – John Lowe, 150 TYRONE ST W 56057
ES, 160 MILL AVE 56057 – Von Jordahl, prin.

Le Roy, Mower Co., Pop. Code 3
Le Roy SD
Sch. Sys. Enr. Code 2
Supt. – D. L. Yost, P O BOX 1000 55951
ES, P O BOX N 55951 – Don Beach, prin.

Lester Prairie, Mcleod Co., Pop. Code 4
Lester Prairie SD
Sch. Sys. Enr. Code 2
Supt. – A. O'Neil
HICKORY ST & 2ND AVE N 55354
ES, HICKORY AVE & 2ND ST N 55354
Robert Niederkorn, prin.

Le Sueur, Le Sueur Co., Pop. Code 5
Le Sueur SD
Sch. Sys. Enr. Code 4
Supt. – J. Hayden, 901 FERRY ST 56058
Park ES, 115 5TH ST N 56058
Paul Schullo, prin.

St. Anne ES, 511 4TH ST N 56058

Lewiston, Winona Co., Pop. Code 4
Lewiston SD
Sch. Sys. Enr. Code 3
Supt. – M. Krenz, P O BOX 741 55952
Altura ES, P O BOX 741 55952
Sandra Grenell, prin.
ES, P O BOX 741 55952 – Sandra Grenell, prin.

Immanuel Lutheran ES
RURAL ROUTE 02 BOX 63 55952
St. John ES, P O BOX 8 55952

Lindstrom, Chisago Co., Pop. Code 4
Chisago Lakes SD
Sch. Sys. Enr. Code 4
Supt. – Darrold Williams
13750 LAKE BLVD 55045
Chisago Lakes MS, 13750 LAKE BLVD 55045
Christopher Swaggert, prin.
Chisago Lakes ES 55045 – Steven Bromberg, prin.
Other Schools – See Chisago City

Litchfield, Meeker Co., Pop. Code 6
Litchfield SD
Sch. Sys. Enr. Code 4
Supt. – Donn Hoffman
901 N GILMAN AVE 55355
Lake Ripley ES, 100 W PLEASURE DR 55355
Jack Ralston, prin.
Wagner MS, 307 E 6TH ST 55355 – Leo Plut, prin.

St. Philip ES, 225 E 3RD ST 55355

Little Falls, Morrison Co., Pop. Code 6
Little Falls SD
Sch. Sys. Enr. Code 5
Supt. – Kerry Jacobson, 1001 5TH AVE SE 56345
Community MS, 1000 1ST AVE NE 56345
Roger Nelson, prin.
Knight ES, 1000 1ST AVE NE 56345
Dan Bakke, prin.
Lincoln ES, 300 6TH ST SW 56345
James Sylvester, prin.
Lindbergh ES, BROADWAY & SE 9TH ST 56345
Karl Kieffer, prin.

Our Lady of Lourdes ES, 205 3RD ST NW 56345
St. Mary ES, 307 4TH ST SE 56345

Littlefork, Koochiching Co., Pop. Code 3
Littlefork-Big Falls SD
Sch. Sys. Enr. Code 2
Supt. – Terry Erholtz, P O BOX D 56653
ES, P O BOX 63 56653 – Terry Erholtz, prin.

Long Lake, Hennepin Co., Pop. Code 4
Orono SD
Sch. Sys. Enr. Code 4
Supt. – Thomas Mich
685 OLD CRYSTAL BAY ROAD 55356
Orono MS, 685 OLD CRYSTAL BAY ROAD 55356
Warren Nelson, prin.
Orono IS, 685 OLD CRYSTAL BAY ROAD 55356
Ronald Gilbert, prin.
Schumann ES, 765 OLD CRYSTAL BAY RD 55356
Marvel Bongart, prin.

Long Prairie, Todd Co., Pop. Code 5
Long Prairie SD
Sch. Sys. Enr. Code 4
Supt. – Donald Hansen, 205 2ND ST S 56347
ES, 205 2ND ST S 56347 – John Stefanich, prin.

St. Mary of Mount Carmel ES
425 CENTRAL AVE 56347
Trinity Lutheran School
610 SECOND AVE SE 56347

Longville, Cass Co., Pop. Code 2
Remer SD
Supt. – See Remer
ES, P O BOX 117 56655 – Michael Doro, prin.

Lonsdale, Rice Co., Pop. Code 4

Lonsdale Consolidated ES, P O BOX 10 55046

Loretto, Hennepin Co., Pop. Code 2

Sts. Peter & Paul ES, 150 RAILWAY ST 55357

Luverne, Rock Co., Pop. Code 5
Luverne SD
Sch. Sys. Enr. Code 4
Supt. – N. Miller, P O BOX 278 56156
ES, 109 E LUVERNE ST 56156
Edward Salzer, prin.

Lyle, Mower Co., Pop. Code 3
Lyle SD
Sch. Sys. Enr. Code 2
Supt. – O. Paul Trelstad, P O BOX 38 55953
ES, P O BOX 38 55953 – Carol Cole, prin.

Lynd, Lyon Co., Pop. Code 2
Lynd SD
Sch. Sys. Enr. Code 2
Supt. – John Gustafson, P O BOX 64 56157
ES 56157 – John Gustafson, prin.

Mabel, Fillmore Co., Pop. Code 3
Mabel-Canton SD
Sch. Sys. Enr. Code 2
Supt. – James Casterton
316 W FILLMORE AVE 55954
Other Schools – See Canton

Mc Gregor, Aitkin Co., Pop. Code 2
McGregor SD
Sch. Sys. Enr. Code 3
Supt. – Ronald Luoma, MAIN ST 55760
ES, P O BOX 160 55760 – Loren Sauter, prin.

McIntosh, Polk Co., Pop. Code 3
McIntosh SD
Sch. Sys. Enr. Code 2
Supt. – James Christianson 56556
ES 56556 – Galen Clow, prin.

Madelia, Watonwan Co., Pop. Code 4
Madelia SD
Sch. Sys. Enr. Code 3
Supt. – D. Antoine, 320 BUCK AVE SE 56062
ES, 121 MAIN ST E 56062
Howard Norgaard, prin.

St. Mary ES, 223 1ST ST NE 56062

Madison, Lac Qui Parle Co., Pop. Code 4
Madison SD
Sch. Sys. Enr. Code 3
Supt. – V. Likness, 316 4TH ST 56256
ES, 316 4TH ST 56256 – Robert Jette, prin.

Magnolia, Rock Co., Pop. Code 2
Magnolia SD
Sch. Sys. Enr. Code 2
Supt. – Janice Nutter, P O BOX 40 56158
ES, P O BOX 40 56158 – Janice Nuffer, prin.

Mahnomen, Mahnomen Co., Pop. Code 4
Mahnomen SD
Sch. Sys. Enr. Code 3
Supt. – Ralph Christofferson, P O BOX 319 56557
ES, P O BOX 319 56557 – James Grayden, prin.
Other Schools – See Naytahwaush

Mahtomedi, Washington Co., Pop. Code 5
Mahtomedi SD
Sch. Sys. Enr. Code 4
Supt. – Don Lifto, 814 MAHTOMEDI AVE 55115
MS, 1520 MAHTOMEDI AVE 55115
Russell Peterson, prin.
Anderson ES, 666 S WARNER RD 55115
Carole Fargo, prin.
Wildwood ES, 535 WARNER RD N 55115
David Noennig, prin.

St. Jude of the Lake ES
600 MAHTOMEDI AVE 55115

Mankato, Blue Earth Co., Pop. Code 8
Garden City SD
Supt. – See Garden City
Rapidan ES, RURAL ROUTE 01 BOX 619 56001
Nancy Kluck, prin.

Mankato SD
Sch. Sys. Enr. Code 6
Supt. – J. Schendinger, 1000 N BROAD ST 56001
Mankato East JHS, 2600 HOFFMAN ROAD 56001
Jack Sjostrom, prin.
Mankato West JHS, 51 PARK LANE 56001
David Dakken, prin.
Franklin ES, N 2ND AND LAFAYETTE STS 56001
Marvin Winslow, prin.
Hoover ES, 1524 HOOVER DR 56001
Darlene Janovy, prin.
Jefferson ES, 100 JAMES AVE 56001
Sharon Fitch, prin.
Kennedy ES, 2600 E MAIN ST 56001
Thomas Ommen, prin.
Roosevelt ES, W 6TH & OWATONNA STS 56001
Joel Botten, prin.
Washington ES, 1101 ANDERSON DR 56001
Judith Brandon, prin.
Other Schools – See Eagle Lake, North Mankato

Immanuel Lutheran School, 421 N 2ND ST 56001
St. Joseph/John ES
BLUE EARTH & HUBBEL ST 56001
Sts. Peter & Paul ES, 110 N 6TH ST 56001

Mantorville, Dodge Co., Pop. Code 3
Kasson-Mantorville SD
Supt. – See Kasson
MS, P O BOX 97 55955 – Robert Melin, prin.

Maple Grove, Hennepin Co., Pop. Code 7
Osseo SD
Supt. – See Osseo
Cedar Island ES, 6777 HEMLOCK LN 55369
Kathleen Townsend, prin.
Elm Creek ES, 9830 REVERE LN 55369
Robert Hein, prin.
Fernbrook ES, 9661 FERNBROOK LN 55369
Jim Hoogheem, prin.
Rice Lake ES, 13755 89TH AVE N 55369
Roger Hastings, prin.

Maple Lake, Wright Co., Pop. Code 4
Maple Lake SD
Sch. Sys. Enr. Code 3
Supt. – Kenneth Engel, P O BOX K 55358
ES, 133 MOLAND AVE 55358
Charles Anderson, prin.

St. Timothy ES, 215 STAR ST E BOX 281 55358

Maple Plain, Hennepin Co., Pop. Code 4

Woods Academy, 5050 INDEPENDENCE ST 55359
Woods Academy, 5050 INDEPENDENCE ST 55359

Mapleton, Blue Earth Co., Pop. Code 4
Mapleton SD
Sch. Sys. Enr. Code 3
Supt. – Richard Kuball, 101 6TH AVE NE 56065
ES, P O BOX 365 56065 – Rodney Joyal, prin.

Maplewood, Ramsey Co., Pop. Code 8
Roseville SD
Supt. – See Roseville
Edgerton ES, 1929 EDGERTON ST 55117
John Ahern, prin.

Marble, Itasca Co., Pop. Code 3
Coleraine SD
Supt. – See Coleraine
ES, P O BOX 98 55764 – Gerald Saylor, prin.

Marietta, Lac qui Parle Co., Pop. Code 2
Marietta-Nassau SD
Sch. Sys. Enr. Code 2
Supt. – Barbara Walks 56257
ES 56257 – Barbara Walks, prin.

Marine on Saint Croix, Washington Co., Pop. Code 3
Stillwater SD
Supt. – See Stillwater
Marine ES 55047 – Ruth Ranum, prin.

Marshall, Lyon Co., Pop. Code 7
Marshall SD
Sch. Sys. Enr. Code 4
Supt. – Jerald Huber, 401 SARATOGA ST E 56258
MS, 207 4TH ST N 56258 – Doug Kodet, prin.

East Side ES, E COLLEGE DR   56258
Bill Swope, prin.
West Side ES, W HWY 19   56258
Larry Berghuls, prin.

Holy Redeemer ES, 501 WHITNEY ST S   56258

Mayer, Carver Co., Pop. Code 2

Zion Lutheran ES, 209 BLUEJAY AVE   55360

Maynard, Chippewa Co., Pop. Code 2
Maynard SD
Sch. Sys. Enr. Code 2
Supt. – Joan Prince, P O BOX 276   56260
ES, P O BOX 276   56260 – Joan Prince, prin.

Mazeppa, Wabasha Co., Pop. Code 3
Mazeppa SD
Sch. Sys. Enr. Code 2
Supt. – James Neuman, P O BOX 100   55956
JHS, P O BOX 100   55956 – Dennis Larson, prin.
ES, 425 CHESTNUT ST   55956
Ron Zuccarelli, prin.

Meadowlands, St. Louis Co., Pop. Code 2
St. Louis County SD
Supt. – See Virginia
Toivola-Meadowlands ES   55765
Richard Tuominen, prin.

Medford, Steele Co., Pop. Code 3
Medford SD
Sch. Sys. Enr. Code 3
Supt. – William Kennedy, P O BOX 38   55049
ES, P O BOX 38   55049 – Cheryl Davidson, prin.

Melrose, Stearns Co., Pop. Code 4
Melrose SD
Sch. Sys. Enr. Code 4
Supt. – Don Anderson, 546 5TH AVE NE   56352
JHS, 111 CENTRAL AVE S   56352
Donald Andersen, prin.
ES, 9 W 2ND ST S   56352 – Francis Hughes, prin.
New Munich ES, 9 W 2ND ST S   56352
Francis Hughes, prin.

St. Mary School, 320 S FIFTH AVE SE   56352

Menahga, Wadena Co., Pop. Code 3
Menahga SD
Sch. Sys. Enr. Code 3
Supt. – Harvey Kraabel, P O BOX 160   56464
ES, P O BOX 160   56464 – Robert Bean, prin.

Mendota Heights, Dakota Co., Pop. Code 6
West St. Paul SD
Supt. – See West Saint Paul
Mendota PS, 1979 SUMMIT LANE   55118
Patrick Murray, prin.

Mentor, Polk Co., Pop. Code 2
Mentor SD
Sch. Sys. Enr. Code 1
Supt. – Howard Watts   56736
ES, P O BOX 68   56736 – Howard Watts, prin.

Middle River, Marshall Co., Pop. Code 2
Middle River SD
Sch. Sys. Enr. Code 2
Supt. – P. M. Dyrud, P O BOX 130   56737
ES, P O BOX 130   56737 – Charles Woolcock, prin.

Milaca, Mille Lacs Co., Pop. Code 4
Milaca SD
Sch. Sys. Enr. Code 4
Supt. – Terry Schmidt, 500 4TH ST SW   56353
MS, 135 3RD ST SE   56353
George Schramm, prin.
ES, 350 3RD AVE SW   56353 – Harold Kurth, prin.

Milan, Chippewa Co., Pop. Code 2
Milan SD
Sch. Sys. Enr. Code 2
Supt. – Donavon Odegard, P O BOX 180   56262
ES, P O BOX 180   56262 – (—), prin.

Milroy, Redwood Co., Pop. Code 2
Milroy SD
Sch. Sys. Enr. Code 2
Supt. – Leroy Domagala, P O BOX 10   56263
ES, P O BOX 180   56263
Roland Dobberstein, prin.

Miltona, Douglas Co., Pop. Code 2
Alexandria SD
Supt. – See Alexandria
ES, P O BOX 113   56354 – Cortlan Krogstad, prin.

Minneapolis, Hennepin Co., Pop. Code 10
Minneapolis SD
Sch. Sys. Enr. Code 8
Supt. – Robert Ferrera
807 BROADWAY ST NE   55413
Anthony JHS, 5757 IRVING AVE S   55419
Arthur Indelicato, prin.
Anwatin JHS, 256 UPTON AVE S   55405
Dawn Mennes, prin.
Folwell JHS, 3611 20TH AVE S   55407
Gerald Hickmann, prin.
Franklin JHS, 1501 ALDRICH AVE N   55411
Betty Jo Webb, prin.
Northeast JHS, 2955 NE HAYES ST   55418
James Rutherford, prin.
Sanford JHS, 3524 42ND AVE S   55406
Shelton Rucker, prin.
Andersen Contemporary MS
2727 10TH AVE S   55407 – Robert Monson, prin.

Andersen Open ES, 1098 ANDERSEN LN   55407
Harold Benson, prin.
Armatage ES, 2501 W 56TH ST   55410
Richard Anderson, prin.
Audubon ES, 4030 CHOWEN AVE S   55413
Eloise Nelson, prin.
Bancroft MS, 1315 E 38TH ST   55407
Anthony Deeb, prin.
Barton Open ES, 4237 COLFAX AVE S   55409
Barbara Bellair, prin.
Bethune ES, 919 EMERSON AVE N   55411
Lowery Johnson, prin.
Burroughs Fundamental ES
1501 W 50TH ST   55419 – James Smrekar, prin.
Cooper ES, 3239 44TH AVE S   55406
Sajjad Haider, prin.
Dowling ES, 3900 W RIVER PARKWAY   55406
Jeffery Raison, prin.
Ericsson ES, 4315 31ST AVE S   55406
Irvin Larson, prin.
Field MS, 4645 4TH AVE S   55409
Douglas Schuster, prin.
Fulton ES, 4912 VINCENT AVE S   55410
Ann Danahy, prin.
Hale ES, 1220 E 54TH ST   55417
Rebecca Yarlott, prin.
Hall ES .55432 – Carol Johnson, prin.
Hamilton ES, 4119 DUPONT AVE N   55412
Theresa Edwards, prin.
Hiawatha ES, 4201 42ND AVE S   55406
Herticena Self, prin.
Holland MS, 1534 6TH ST NE   55413
Joseph Purvis, prin.
Howe ES, 3733 43RD AVE S   55406
Arthur Lakoduk, prin.
Jefferson ES, 1200 W 26TH ST   55405
Mitchell Trockman, prin.
Keewaydin ES, 5209 30TH AVE S   55417
Gordon Frattum, prin.
Kenny ES, 5720 EMERSON AVE S   55419
Doris Zachary, prin.
Kenwood ES, 2013 PENN AVE S   55405
Patricia Barta, prin.
Lincoln Fundamental ES
2131 12TH AVE N   55413 – Art Johnson, prin.
Longfellow ES, 3017 E 31ST   55413
Mary Schepman, prin.
Loring ES, 2600 445TH AVE N   55412
Nancy Shaner, prin.
Lyndale MS, 3333 GRAND AVE   55408
Richard Anderson, prin.
Marcy Open ES, 1042 18TH AVE SE   55414
Sylvia Adams, prin.
Morris Park ES, 3810 E 56TH ST   55417
Paul Modell, prin.
North Star ES, 2410 GIRARD AVE N   55411
Maureen Bizinet, prin.
Northrop ES, 1611 E 46TH ST   55407
Theodore Pollard, prin.
Olson ES, 1751 KELLY DRIVE   55427
Yvonne Beseler, prin.
Putnam MS, 1616 BUCHANAN ST NE   55413
Eileen Baker, prin.
Seward ES, 2309 28TH AVE S   55406
Margaret Lincoln, prin.
Sheridan MS   55413 – Bruce Gall, prin.
Shingle Creek ES, 5034 OLIVER AVE N   55430
Kerry Felt, prin.
Tuttle ES, 1042 18TH AVE SE   55414
Sylvia Adams, prin.
Waite Park MS, 1800 34TH AVE NE   55418
Charles McConville, prin.
Webster Open ES, 425 5TH ST NE   55413
Henry Taxis, prin.
Wenonah ES, 5625 23RD AVE S   55417
Charles Gustafson, prin.
Wilder Contempory MS, 3328 ELLIOT AVE   55407
Henry Terrell, prin.
Wilder Fundamental ES, 3322 ELLIOT AVE   55407
Frederick Dietrich, prin.
Willard ES, 1615 QUEEN AVE N   55413
Kathleen Cahill, prin.

Osseo SD
Supt. – See Osseo
Park Brook ES, 7400 HAMPSHIRE AVE N   55428
Kevin Samsel, prin.
Winnetka ES, 7940 55TH AVE N   55428
John Nelson, prin.

Faith Academy, P O BOX 29542   55429
Bethany Academy
6820 AUTO CLUB ROAD   55438
Fourth Baptist Christian School
2105 FREMONT AVE N   55411
Heart of Earth Survival School
1209 4TH ST SE   55414
Minnehaha Academy, 3107-47TH AVE S   55406
Woodcrest Baptist Academy
6875 UNIVERSITY AVE NE   55432
Annunciation ES, 525 W 54TH ST   55419
Ascension ES, 1726 DUPONT AVE N   55411
Assumption ES
3RD AVENUE AND 77TH ST E   55423
Calvin Christian ES
4015 INGLEWOOD AVE S   55416
Christ the King ES, 3210 W 51ST ST   55410
Golden Years Montessori, 4100 W 42ND ST   55416
Holy Name ES, 1120 E 37TH ST   55407
Holy Rosary ES, 2430 18TH AVE S   55404
Immanuel Lutheran ES
2201 GIRARD AVE N   55411
Incarnation ES. 3800 PLEASANT AVE   55409
Lake Country ES, 3755 PLEASANT AVE   55409

Mount Calvery Lutheran ES
6541 16TH AVE S   55423
Northeast Regional-Holy Cross ES
1630 4TH ST NE   55413
Our Lady of Victory ES
5140 FREMONT AVE N   55430
Pilgrim Lutheran ES, 3901 1ST AVE S   55409
Powderhorn Christian ES
4500 CLINTON AVE   55409
Prince of Peace Lutheran ES
7700 MONROE ST NE   55432
Resurrection ES, 5435 11TH AVE S   55417
St. Albert the Great ES, 2840 33RD AVE S   55406
St. Alphonsus ES
7031 AND HALIFAX AVE N   55430
St. Anne ES, 2620 RUSSELL AVE N   55411
St. Austin ES, 4021 THOMAS AVE N   55412
St. Bridget ES, 3820 EMERSON AVE N   55412
St. Charles Borromeo ES
2727 STINSOR BLVD NE   55418
St. Helena's ES, 3200 E 44TH ST   55406
St. Kevin ES, 59TH ST E & 27TH AVE S   55417
St. Peter ES, 6720 NICOLLET AVE   55423
St. Richard ES, 7540 PENN AVE S   55423
St. Stephen ES, 2123 CLINTON AVE   55404
St. Thomas the Apostle ES
2900 W 44TH STAVE SOUTH   55410
Visitation ES, 4530 LYNDALE AVE S   55409

Minneota, Lyon Co., Pop. Code 4
Minneota SD
Sch. Sys. Enr. Code 3
Supt. – Gerhard Meidt, 504 N MONROE ST   56264
ES, 504 N MONROE ST   56264
Dwayne Strand, prin.

St. Edward ES, 4TH & WASHINGTON   56264

Minnesota Lake, Faribault Co., Pop. Code 3
Minnesota Lake SD
Sch. Sys. Enr. Code 2
Supt. – Donald Berkland, P O BOX 218   56068
ES, P O BOX 218   56068 – Donald Berkland, prin.

Minnetonka, Hennepin Co., Pop. Code 8
Hopkins SD
Supt. – See Hopkins
Gatewood ES, 14900 GATEWOOD DR   55345
David Nelson, prin.

Minnetonka SD
Supt. – See Excelsior
JHS, 17000 LAKE ST EXT   55345
John Hruby, prin.
Clear Springs ES, 5701 HIGHWAY 101   55345
Linda Saukkonen, prin.
Scenic Heights PS
5650 SCENIC HEIGHTS DR   55345
Lynn Street, prin.

Immaculate Heart of Mary ES
13505 EXCELSIOR BLVD   55345

Montevideo, Chippewa Co., Pop. Code 6
Montevideo SD
Sch. Sys. Enr. Code 4
Supt. – Eddy Nystrom, 3RD & EUREKA   56265
Central MS, 3RD & EUREKA   56265
Gary Radke, prin.
Ramsey ES, HAMILTON AVE & 5TH ST   56265
(—), prin.
Sanford ES, 412 S 13TH ST   56265
Kenneth Swanson, prin.

Montgomery, Le Sueur Co., Pop. Code 4
Montgomery SD
Sch. Sys. Enr. Code 4
Supt. – H. Kane, 101 2ND ST NE   56069
ES, 101 2ND ST NE   56069
Michael Mrachek, prin.

Holy Redeemer ES, 205 VINE AVE W   56069

Monticello, Wright Co., Pop. Code 5
Monticello SD
Sch. Sys. Enr. Code 4
Supt. – S. Johnson, P O BOX 897   55362
MS, P O BOX 897   55362 – K. Bensen, prin.
Pinewood ES, P O BOX 897   55362
K. Douglass, prin.

Moorhead, Clay Co., Pop. Code 8
Moorhead SD
Sch. Sys. Enr. Code 5
Supt. – B. Trochlil, 810 4TH AVE S   56560
Moorhead South MS, 11TH ST & 20TH AVE   56560
Richard Jones, prin.
Asp ES, 910 N 11TH ST   56560
Betty Myers, prin.
Edison ES, 12TH AVE & 14TH ST S   56560
Alvina Lillibridge, prin.
Probstfield ES, 2410 14TH ST S   56560
Howard Murray, prin.
Riverside-Lincoln ES
4TH ST & 14TH AVE S   56560
Donald Iverson, prin.
Washington ES, 901 14TH ST N   56560
Robert Olson, prin.

Park Christian ES, 300 17TH ST N   56560
St. Francis De Sales ES, 1330 8TH AVE N   56560
St. Joseph ES, 202 10TH ST S   56560

Moose Lake, Carlton Co., Pop. Code 4
Moose Lake SD
Sch. Sys. Enr. Code 3
Supt. – R. Buro, 413 BIRCH AVE 55767
ES, 413 BIRCH AVE 55767 – Edward Ganske, prin.

Mora, Kanabec Co., Pop. Code 5
Mora SD
Sch. Sys. Enr. Code 4
Supt. – Phillip Moye, 400 MAPLE AVE E 55051
Fairview ES, 707 MCLEAN ST 55051
  Cynthia Stoffel, prin.

Morgan, Redwood Co., Pop. Code 3

St. Michael ES, P O BOX 443 56266

Morris, Stevens Co., Pop. Code 6
Morris SD
Sch. Sys. Enr. Code 4
Supt. – Dennis Rettke
  201 S COLUMBIA AVE 56267
ES, 600 COLUMBIA AVE 56267
  Delores Wiese, prin.

St. Mary ES, 411 COLORADO AVE 56267

Morristown, Rice Co., Pop. Code 3
Morristown SD
Sch. Sys. Enr. Code 2
Supt. – (—), P O BOX 278 55052
ES, P O BOX 278 55052 – James Lehman, prin.

Morton, Renville Co., Pop. Code 3
Morton SD
Sch. Sys. Enr. Code 2
Supt. – Dale Hanke, P O BOX 68 56270
ES, P O BOX 68 56270 – Dale Hanke, prin.

Motley, Morrison Co., Pop. Code 2
Motley SD
Sch. Sys. Enr. Code 2
Supt. – H. Jones, P O BOX 268 56466
ES, P O BOX 268 56466 – Robert Koll, prin.

Mound, Hennepin Co., Pop. Code 6
Westonka SD
Sch. Sys. Enr. Code 5
Supt. – James Smith
  5600 LYNWOOD BLVD 55364
Grandview MS, 1881 COMMERCE BLVD 55364
  Mary Alexander, prin.
Hilltop ES, 5700 GAMEFARM RD E 55364
  Wayne Smith, prin.
Shirley Hills ES, 2450 WILSHIRE BLVD 55364
  P. Hyytinen, prin.

Our Lady of the Lake ES
  2411 COMMERCE BLVD 55364

Mounds View, Ramsey Co., Pop. Code 7
Mounds View SD
Supt. – See Roseville
Pike Lake ES, 2101 14TH ST NW 55112
  Ray Lucas, prin.
Pinewood ES, 5500 QUINCY ST 55112
  Pat Erlandson, prin.
Sunnyside ES, 2070 COUNTY ROAD H W 55112
  Penelope Howard, prin.

Northside Christian ES
  7910 RED OAK DR NE 55432

Mountain Iron, St. Louis Co., Pop. Code 5
Mountain Iron-Buhl SD
Sch. Sys. Enr. Code 3
Supt. – Robert Duncan 55768
Merritt ES 55768 – Leonard Kucera, prin.

Mountain Lake, Cottonwood Co., Pop. Code 4
Mountain Lake SD
Sch. Sys. Enr. Code 3
Supt. – Robert Olson, 450 12TH ST 56159
ES, 450 12TH ST 56159 – Duane Stoesz, prin.

Murdock, Swift Co., Pop. Code 2
Kerkhoven Murdock-Sunburg SD
Supt. – See Kerkhoven
ES 56271 – Charles Askegard, prin.

Nashwauk, Itasca Co., Pop. Code 4
Nashwauk-Keewatin SD
Sch. Sys. Enr. Code 3
Supt. – T. Brascugli, 400 2ND ST 55769
Keewatin ES 55769 – John Klarich, prin.
Other Schools – See Keewatin

Naytahwaush, Mahnomen Co.
Mahnomen SD
Supt. – See Mahnomen
ES 56566 – James Grayden, prin.

Nerstrand, Rice Co., Pop. Code 2
Faribault SD
Supt. – See Faribault
ES, P O BOX 156 55053 – Dennis Deanovic, prin.

Nett Lake, St. Louis Co., Pop. Code 2
Nett Lake SD
Sch. Sys. Enr. Code 1
Supt. – Dennis Angell 55772
ES 55772 – Dennis Angell, prin.

Nevis, Hubbard Co., Pop. Code 2
Nevis SD
Sch. Sys. Enr. Code 2
Supt. – Marlow Halbur, P O BOX 183 56467
ES, P O BOX 183 56467 – Marlowe Halbur, prin.

New Brighton, Ramsey Co., Pop. Code 7
Mounds View SD
Supt. – See Roseville
Highview JHS, 2300 7TH ST NW 55112
  Michael McGlinch, prin.
Bel Air ES, 1800 5TH ST NW 55112
  Gary Peterson, prin.

St. John the Baptist ES, 845 2ND AVE NW 55112

Newfolden, Marshall Co., Pop. Code 2
Newfolden SD
Sch. Sys. Enr. Code 2
Supt. – R. Gene Busch, P O BOX 277 56738
ES, P O BOX 277 56738 – James Hodny, prin.
Other Schools – See Viking

New Germany, Carver Co., Pop. Code 2

St. Mark / St. John Lutheran ES
  211 ADAMS AVE S 55367

New Hope, Hennepin Co., Pop. Code 7
Osseo SD
Supt. – See Osseo
Sunny Hollow ES
  8808 NMEDICINE LAKE ROAD 55427
  Paul Tesdahl, prin.

Robbinsdale SD
Sch. Sys. Enr. Code 7
Supt. – Donna Carter
  4148 WINNETKA AVE N 55427
Meadowlake ES, 8525 62ND AVE N 55428
  Warren Tabor, prin.
ES, 8301 47TH AVE N 55428
  Robert Ziegler, prin.
Sonnesyn ES, 3421 BOONE AVE N 55427
  Mary Hertogs, prin.
Other Schools – See Brooklyn Center, Brooklyn Park,
  Crystal, Golden Valley, Plymouth, Robbinsdale

New London, Kandiyohi Co., Pop. Code 3
New London-Spicer SD
Sch. Sys. Enr. Code 4
Supt. – Ken Hanson, P O BOX 287 56273
Prairie Woods ES
  RURAL ROUTE 03 BOX A 56273
  H. Christianson, prin.

Newport, Washington Co., Pop. Code 5
South Washington County SD
Supt. – See Cottage Grove
ES, 851 6TH AVE 55055 – Robert Miller, prin.

New Prague, Scott Co., Pop. Code 5
New Prague SD
Sch. Sys. Enr. Code 4
Supt. – Charles Kinn, 721 CENTRAL AVE N 56071
MS, 405 1ST AVE NW 56071 – Paul Flick, prin.
ES, 1200 COLUMBUS AVE N 56071
  Robert Gullickson, prin.

St. Wenceslaus ES, 227 MAIN ST E 56071

New Richland, Waseca Co., Pop. Code 4
New Richland SD
Sch. Sys. Enr. Code 3
Supt. – Richard Lorenz, P O BOX 427 56072
ES, P O BOX 427 56072 – Kenneth Meyers, prin.

New Ulm, Brown Co., Pop. Code 7
New Ulm SD
Sch. Sys. Enr. Code 5
Supt. – Patricia Hanauer, 400 S PAYNE ST 56073
Jefferson ES, 300 S PAYNE ST 56073
  Harry Stock, prin.
Washington ES, 910 14TH ST N 56073
  E. Ferguson, prin.
Other Schools – See Hanska, Lafayette

Holy Trinity ES, 515 N STATE ST 56073
St. Mary's ES, 519 S MINNESOTA ST 56073
St. Paul Lutheran ES, 126 S PAYNE ST 56073

New York Mills, Otter Tail Co., Pop. Code 3
New York Mills SD
Sch. Sys. Enr. Code 3
Supt. – Jerald Nesland, P O BOX 218 56567
ES, P O BOX 218 56567 – Michael Hart, prin.

Nicollet, Nicollet Co., Pop. Code 3
Nicollet SD
Sch. Sys. Enr. Code 2
Supt. – M. Hinckley, P O BOX 108 56074
ES, P O BOX 108 56074 – Tanya Schull, prin.

Trinity Lutheran ES, P O BOX 387 56074

Nisswa, Crow Wing Co., Pop. Code 4
Brainerd SD
Supt. – See Brainerd
ES, P O BOX 5 56468 – Robert Hurst, prin.

North Branch, Chisago Co., Pop. Code 4
North Branch SD
Sch. Sys. Enr. Code 4
Supt. – James Walker, 320 MAIN ST 55056
MS, 320 MAIN ST 55056 – Rodney Lofquist, prin.
ES, 320 MAIN ST 55056 – Mike Kirkeby, prin.

Northfield, Rice Co., Pop. Code 7
Northfield SD
Sch. Sys. Enr. Code 5
Supt. – (—), 301 UNION ST 55057
MS, 301 UNION ST 55057 – David Peterson, prin.
Greenvale Park ES, 700 LINCOLN PKY 55057
  Bonnie Flom, prin.

Sibley MS, CORNER AMES & MAPLE 55057
  Jan Dallenbach, prin.

St. Dominic ES, 215 SPRING ST N 55057

North Mankato, Nicollet Co., Pop. Code 6
Mankato SD
Supt. – See Mankato
Garfield ES, 320 GARFIELD AVE 56001
  Robert Maas, prin.
Monroe ES
  MONROE AVENUE AND CENTER ST 56001
  Margaret DeBoom, prin.

Holy Rosary ES, 546 GRANT AVE 56001

Northome, Koochiching Co., Pop. Code 2
South Koochiching SD
Sch. Sys. Enr. Code 2
Supt. – Ronald Schuster, P O BOX 465 56661
ES, P O BOX 465 56661 – Anthony Hoyt, prin.
Other Schools – See Birchdale

North Saint Paul, Ramsey Co., Pop. Code 7
North St. Paul-Maplewood SD
Supt. – See Saint Paul
Beaver Lake ES, 1060 STERLING AVE N 55109
  Janet Nuckles, prin.
Castle ES, 6675 50TH STREET N 55109
  Drieke Van Giffen, prin.
Cowern ES, 2131 MARGARET ST N 55109
  E. Bourassa, prin.
Richardson ES, 2615 1ST ST N 55109
  Dean Cousineau, prin.
Webster ES, 2170 7TH AVE E 55109
  Joe Wemette, prin.

St. Peter ES, 2620 MARGARET ST N 55109

Norwood, Carver Co., Pop. Code 4
Norwood SD
Sch. Sys. Enr. Code 3
Supt. – Howard Caldwell
  531 CENTRAL AVE 55368
Central ES, 531 CENTRAL AVE 55368
  Kevin Starr, prin.

Ogema, Becker Co., Pop. Code 2
Waubun SD
Supt. – See Waubun
ES 56569 – David Stone, prin.

Ogilvie, Kanabee Co., Pop. Code 2
Ogilvie SD
Sch. Sys. Enr. Code 3
Supt. – D. Gornowich, P O BOX 160 56358
ES, P O BOX 160 56358 – Dennis Johnson, prin.

Oklee, Red Lake Co., Pop. Code 3
Oklee SD
Sch. Sys. Enr. Code 2
Supt. – James Christianson 56742
ES 56742 – Marvin Bronken, prin.

Olivia, Renville Co., Pop. Code 5
Olivia SD
Sch. Sys. Enr. Code 3
Supt. – Marty Duncan, 701 9TH ST S 56277
ES, 701 9TH ST S 56277 – Jim McDowell, prin.

St. Aloysius ES, 1005 FAIRVIEW AVE W 56277

Onamia, Mille Lacs Co., Pop. Code 3
Onamia SD
Sch. Sys. Enr. Code 3
Supt. – Kent Baldry, P O BOX B 56359
ES, EVERGREEN LN 56359 – Sandy Nelson, prin.

Orr, St. Louis Co., Pop. Code 2
St. Louis County SD
Supt. – See Virginia
ES 55771 – Corrine Spector, prin.

Ortonville, Big Stone Co., Pop. Code 5
Ortonville SD
Sch. Sys. Enr. Code 3
Supt. – Burton Nypen, 200 6TH ST NW 56278
Knoll ES, P O BOX 247 56278
  Morris Tietjen, prin.

Osage, Becker Co., Pop. Code 3
Park Rapids SD
Supt. – See Park Rapids
ES 56470 – (—), prin.

Osakis, Douglas Co., Pop. Code 4
Osakis SD
Sch. Sys. Enr. Code 3
Supt. – L. Mackove, 14 OAK ST E 56360
ES, 14 OAK ST E 56360 – Jerry Hanson, prin.

Osseo, Hennepin Co., Pop. Code 5
Osseo SD
Sch. Sys. Enr. Code 7
Supt. – Marl Ramsey, 11200 93RD AVE N 55369
ES, 324 6TH AVE NE 55369
  Luanne Lemberg, prin.
Other Schools – See Brooklyn Center, Brooklyn Park,
  Maple Grove, Minneapolis, New Hope

St. John's Lutheran ES
  9141 HIGHWAY 101 55369
St. Vincent De Paul ES, 6Y00 1ST AVE NE 55369

Owatonna, Steele Co., Pop. Code 7
Owatonna SD
Sch. Sys. Enr. Code 5
Supt. – (—), 515 W BRIDGE ST 55060

JHS, 500 15TH ST NE 55060
Janell Salcedo, prin.
Lincoln ES, 747 HAVANA RD 55060
Diane Larson, prin.
McKinley ES, 423 14TH ST NE 55060
Elmer Reseland, prin.
Washington ES, 338 E MAIN ST 55060
Jerry Peters, prin.
Wilson ES, 325 MEADOW LN 55060
Dean Sanderson, prin.

Owatonna Christian School
265 26TH ST NE 55060
Marian-Saint Mary's ES, MARIAN DRIVE 55060

Palisade, Aitkin Co., Pop. Code 2
Aitkin SD
Supt. – See Aitkin
ES 56469 – James Pitt, prin.

Parkers Prairie, Otter Tail Co., Pop. Code 3
Parkers Prairie SD
Sch. Sys. Enr. Code 3
Supt. – Phillip Smith, P O BOX 46 56361
ES, P O BOX 46 56361 – Marvin Dahl, prin.

Park Rapids, Hubbard Co., Pop. Code 5
Park Rapids SD
Sch. Sys. Enr. Code 4
Supt. – Leslie Norman, P O BOX 591 56470
MS, 113 3RD ST 56470 – Otto Kamrud, prin.
Central ES, P O BOX 591 56470 – (—), prin.
White ES, P O BOX 591 56470 – (—), prin.
Other Schools – See Osage

Paynesville, Stearns Co., Pop. Code 4
Paynesville SD
Sch. Sys. Enr. Code 4
Supt. – Russell Laposky
795 W HIGHWAY 23 56362
MS, 100 W MILL ST 56362 – Michael Lund, prin.
ES, 100 W MILL ST 56362 – Gary Heineman, prin.

Pease, Mille Lacs Co., Pop. Code 2

Community Christian ES, P O BOX 68 56363

Pelican Rapids, Otter Tail Co., Pop. Code 4
Pelican Rapids SD
Sch. Sys. Enr. Code 4
Supt. – Keith Klein, P O BOX V 56572
ES, P O BOX V 56572 – Blace Schmidt, prin.

Pequot Lakes, Crow Wing Co., Pop. Code 3
Pequot Lakes SD
Sch. Sys. Enr. Code 3
Supt. – Vernon Dowty, P O BOX 368 56472
ES, P O BOX 368 56472 – James Oraskovich, prin.

Perham, Otter Tail Co., Pop. Code 4
Perham SD
Sch. Sys. Enr. Code 4
Supt. – (—), 200 5TH ST SE 56573
ES, 200 5TH ST SE 56573 – Rex Kingsbury, prin.
Other Schools – See Dent

St. Henry ES, 253 2ND ST SW 56573
St. Paul Lutheran ES, 560 2ND STREET SW 56573

Peterson, Fillmore Co., Pop. Code 2
Peterson SD
Sch. Sys. Enr. Code 2
Supt. – Kent Nelson, P O BOX 08 55962
ES, P O BOX 8 55962 – Bruce Blixt, prin.

Pierz, Morrison Co., Pop. Code 4
Pierz SD
Sch. Sys. Enr. Code 3
Supt. – R. Opp 56364
Harding ES, RURAL ROUTE 04 56364
Robert Hoffman, prin.

St. Joseph ES, EDWARD ST 56364

Pillager, Cass Co., Pop. Code 2
Pillager SD
Sch. Sys. Enr. Code 2
Supt. – Douglas Hamilton, P O BOX 38 56473
ES, P O BOX 38 55473 – Gregg Allen, prin.

Pine City, Pine Co., Pop. Code 4
Pine City SD
Sch. Sys. Enr. Code 4
Supt. – Joseph Hobson, 605 6TH ST 55063
ES, 700 2 6TH AVE 55063
Richard Houston, prin.

Pine Island, Goodhue Co., Pop. Code 4
Pine Island SD
Sch. Sys. Enr. Code 4
Supt. – Brian Grenell, P O BOX 398 55963
ES, P O BOX 398 55963 – Jay Youmans, prin.

Pine River, Cass Co., Pop. Code 3
Pine River SD
Sch. Sys. Enr. Code 3
Supt. – David Paulson 56474
ES 56474 – Victor Rinke, prin.

Pipestone, Pipestone Co., Pop. Code 5
Pipestone SD
Sch. Sys. Enr. Code 4
Supt. – William Burkholder, P O BOX 71 56164
MS, P O BOX 71 56164 – Robert Zorich, prin.
Brown ES, P O BOX 400 56164
Kenneth Stanek, prin.
Hill ES, 6TH AVE SW 56164
Kenneth Stanek, prin.

Plainview, Wabasha Co., Pop. Code 4
Plainview SD
Sch. Sys. Enr. Code 3
Supt. – James Schmitt, 500 W BROADWAY 55964
ES, 500 W BROADWAY 55964
Daniel Kelley, prin.

Immanuel Lutheran ES, 30 S WABASHA 55964

Plummer, Red Lake Co., Pop. Code 2
Plummer SD
Sch. Sys. Enr. Code 2
Supt. – Richard Lorenson 56748
ES 56748 – Richard Lorenson, prin.

Plymouth, Hennepin Co., Pop. Code 8
Robbinsdale SD
Supt. – See New Hope
Pilgrim Lane ES, 3725A PILGRIM LN N 55441
Wayne Rau, prin.
Zachary Lane ES, 4350 ZACHARY LANE 55442
Rhonda Smith, prin.

Wayzata SD
Supt. – See Wayzata
Birchview ES, 425 RANCHVIEW LN N 55447
Jimmy Libby, prin.
Greenwood ES, 3635 HIGHWAY 101 N 55446
Louis Benko, prin.
Oakwood ES, 17340 COUNTY ROAD 6 55447
Douglas Obrien,Jr., prin.
Sunset Hill ES, 13005 COUNTY ROAD 15 55441
Carol Bryant, prin.

Ponemah, Beltrami Co.
Redlake SD
Supt. – See Redlake
ES 56666 – (—), prin.

Ponsford, Becker Co.
Pine Point SD
Sch. Sys. Enr. Code 1
Supt. – Erma Vizenor, P O BOX 61 56575
Pine Point ES, P O BOX 61 56575
Erma Vizenor, prin.

Preston, Fillmore Co., Pop. Code 4
Preston-Fountain SD
Sch. Sys. Enr. Code 3
Supt. – Gerald Nelson, P O BOX 407 55965
ES, P O BOX 407 55965 – (—), prin.

Princeton, Mille Lacs Co., Pop. Code 5
Princeton SD
Sch. Sys. Enr. Code 5
Supt. – Waldo Larson, 606 3RD ST S 55371
JHS, 606 3RD ST S 55371 – J. Hoff, prin.
North MS, 1202 7TH AVE N 55371
Roland Benson, prin.
South ES, 805 8TH AVE S 55371
Daniel Anderson, prin.

Prinsburg, Kandiyohi Co., Pop. Code 3

Central Minnesota Christian School
P O BOX 98 56281

Prior Lake, Scott Co., Pop. Code 6
Prior Lake SD
Sch. Sys. Enr. Code 5
Supt. – C. Kruse, P O BOX 539 55372
MS, P O BOX 539 55372 – Paula Tetzloff, prin.
Five Hawks MS, P O BOX 539 55372
Ronald MacHacek, prin.
Westwood ES, P O BOX 539 55372
Darwin Fosse, prin.

St. Michael ES, 16280 DULUTH AVE 55372
St. Paul Lutheran School
5634 LUTHER DR SE 55372

Proctor, St. Louis Co., Pop. Code 5
Proctor SD
Sch. Sys. Enr. Code 4
Supt. – Vernon Eilola, 131 N 9TH AVE 55810
Jedlicka MS, 201 1ST AVE N 55810
Allen Larson, prin.
IS, 201 N 1ST AVE 55810 – Allen Larson, prin.
Other Schools – See Duluth, Saginaw

St. Rose School, 2 S 6TH AVE 55810

Ramsey, Anoka Co., Pop. Code 7
Anoka SD
Supt. – See Coon Rapids
ES, 15100 NOWTHEN BLVD 55303
Paul Reifenberger, prin.

Randolph, Dakota Co., Pop. Code 2
Randolph SD
Sch. Sys. Enr. Code 2
Supt. – Ronald James, P O BOX 38 55065
ES, P O BOX 38 55065 – Ronald James, prin.

Raymond, Kandiyohi Co., Pop. Code 3
Raymond SD
Sch. Sys. Enr. Code 2
Supt. – Roger Rueckert, 309 DAY ST 56282
ES, 309 DAY ST 56282 – (—), prin.

Redlake, Beltrami Co., Pop. Code 2
Redlake SD
Sch. Sys. Enr. Code 3
Supt. – Burel Block 56671
ES 56671 – Roger Schmidt, prin.
Other Schools – See Ponemah

St. Mary Mission ES
RURAL ROUTE 01 BOX 150 56671

Red Lake Falls, Red Lake Co., Pop. Code 4
Red Lake Falls SD
Sch. Sys. Enr. Code 3
Supt. – Robert Anderson, P O BOX 399 56750
Hughes ES, P O BOX 399 56750 – (—), prin.

St. Joseph ES, 112 EDWARD AVE BOX 215 56750

Red Wing, Goodhue Co., Pop. Code 7
Red Wing SD
Sch. Sys. Enr. Code 5
Supt. – Clayton Hovda, 525 EAST AVE 55066
Burnside ES, RURAL ROUTE 02 55066
Rodney Frantzen, prin.
Colvill PS, 269 E 5TH ST 55066 – John Quist, prin.
Hancock ES, 469 12TH ST 55066
John O'Reilly, prin.
Jefferson ES, BUCHANAN ST 55066
John O'Reilly, prin.
Sunnyside ES, MAPLE ST 55066
John Quist, prin.

St. Joseph ES, 7TH & NORTH PARK 55066

Redwood Falls, Redwood Co., Pop. Code 6
Redwood Falls SD
Sch. Sys. Enr. Code 4
Supt. – Gary Swenson, 4TH & LINCOLN 56283
Gray ES, 201 MCPHAIL DR 56283
Judy Klukas, prin.

Remer, Cass Co., Pop. Code 2
Remer SD
Sch. Sys. Enr. Code 3
Supt. – (—), P O BOX 37 56672
ES, RURAL ROUTE 01 BOX C 56672
Michael Doro, prin.
Other Schools – See Longville

Rice, Benton Co., Pop. Code 2
Sauk Rapids SD
Supt. – See Sauk Rapids
ES, P O BOX 25 56367 – Jerry Leese, prin.

Richfield, Hennepin Co., Pop. Code 8
Richfield SD
Sch. Sys. Enr. Code 5
Supt. – L. Larson, 7001 HARRIET AVE 55423
JHS, 7461 OLIVER AVE S 55423
Alden Stoesz, prin.
Centennial ES, 7315 BLOOMINGTON AVE 55423
Nolan Bjorge, prin.
IS, 7020 12TH AVE S 55423 – Gen Orr, prin.
Sheridan Hills ES, 6400 SHERIDAN AVE S 55423
Judy Anderson, prin.
Spartan ES, 7001 HARRIET AVE S 55423
Jeannie Ryan, prin.

Richmond, Stearns Co., Pop. Code 3
Cold Spring SD
Supt. – See Cold Spring
ES 56368 – Gary Haberman, prin.

Sts. Peter & Paul ES
111 CENTRAL AVE N BOX 184 56368

Robbinsdale, Hennepin Co., Pop. Code 7
Robbinsdale SD
Supt. – See New Hope
Lakeview ES, 4110 LAKE DRIVE AVE N 55422
Arnold Brown, prin.

Sacred Heart ES, 4050 HUBBARD AVE N 55422

Rochester, Olmsted Co., Pop. Code 8
Rochester SD
Sch. Sys. Enr. Code 7
Supt. – Vernon Johnson, 615 7TH ST SW 55902
Bamber Valley ES
2001 BAMBER VALLEY RD SW 55902
Waldo Tagatz, prin.
Bishop ES, 406 NW 36TH AVE 55902
Dean Albertson, prin.
Churchill ES, 2240 NE 7TH AVE 55902
Donald Valentine, prin.
Elton Hills ES, 1421 ELTON HILLS DR NW 55901
Kathryn Schultz, prin.
Folwell ES, 15TH AVE & SW 6TH ST 55902
Francis Robb, prin.
Franklin ES, 1801 9TH AVE SE 55904
Arthur DeWitz, prin.
Gage ES, 1300 40TH ST NW 55901
Mike Ladin, prin.
Hawthorne ES, 700 4TH AVE SE 55904
Loren Carlson, prin.
Holmes ES, 1100 E CENTER ST 55904
Robert Funk, prin.
Hoover MS, 369 ELTON HILLS DR NW 55901
David Malcomson, prin.
Jefferson ES, 1390 10TH AVE NE 55904
Robert Sande, prin.
Longfellow ES, 1615 MARION RD SE 55904
Kenneth Swenson, prin.
Mann ES, 1122 8TH AVE SE 55904
Charles Carstensen, prin.
Pinewood ES, 1900 PINEWOOD RD SE 55904
Vivien Johnson, prin.
Sunset Terrace ES, 1924 17 1/2 ST NW 55901
Wade Nelson, prin.
Washington ES, 1200 11TH AVE NW 55901
Roger Field, prin.

Rochester Central Lutheran ES
2619 9TH AVE NW 55901
St. Francis ES, 318 11TH AVE SE 55904
St. John ES, 5TH AVE & W CENTER 55901
St. Pius X ES, 1205 12TH AVE NW 55901

Rockford, Wright Co., Pop. Code 4
Rockford SD
Sch. Sys. Enr. Code 4
Supt. – Allen Moen, P O BOX 09 55373
IS, P O BOX 189 55373 – Harold Greseth, prin.
ES, P O BOX 69 55373 – Terry Stansfield, prin.

Rockville, Stearns Co., Pop. Code 3
Cold Spring SD
Supt. – See Cold Spring
ES, P O BOX 37 56369 – Gary Haberman, prin.

Rogers, Hennepin Co., Pop. Code 3
Elk River SD
Supt. – See Elk River
ES, 12521 MAIN ST 55374
Ronald Burland, prin.

Rollingstone, Winona Co., Pop. Code 3
Winona SD
Supt. – See Winona
ES 55969 – John Kaehler, prin.

Roseau, Roseau Co., Pop. Code 4
Roseau SD
Sch. Sys. Enr. Code 4
Supt. – Herbert Benz, 509 3RD ST NE 56751
Malung ES, HCR B 56751 – Gale Halvorson, prin.
ES, 509 3RD ST NE 56751 – Gale Halvorson, prin.
Other Schools – See Wannaska

Rose Creek, Mower Co., Pop. Code 2
Southland SD
Supt. – See Adams
Southland ES 55970 – Peter Grover, prin.

Rosemount, Dakota Co., Pop. Code 6
Rosemount-Apple Valley-Eagan SD
Sch. Sys. Enr. Code 7
Supt. – R. Rehwaldt
14445 DIAMOND PATH W 55068
MS, 3135 143RD ST W 55068
Dennis Pregler, prin.
Cedar Park ES, 14445 DIAMOND PATH W 55068
Marvin Skinner, prin.
Deerwood ES, 14445 DIAMOND PATH 55068
Thomas Schwartz, prin.
Diamond Path ES
14445 DIAMOND PATH W 55068
Julie Olson, prin.
Echo Park ES, 14445 DIAMOND PATH W 55068
Robert Keeton, prin.
Greenleaf ES, 14445 DIAMOND PATH W 55068
Thomas Crosgrove, prin.
Highland ES, 14445 DIAMOND PATH 55068
Duane Burns, prin.
Northview ES, 14445 DIAMOND PATH W 55068
Robert Ferguson, prin.
Parkview ES, 14445 DIAMOND PATH W 55068
Paul Baarson, prin.
ES, 14445 DIAMOND PATH W 55068
Lisa Hannon, prin.
Southview ES, 14445 DIAMOND PATH W 55068
Ann Kastler, prin.
Thomas Lake ES
14445 DIAMOND PATH W 55068
James LeVasseur, prin.
Westview ES, 14445 DIAMOND PATH 55068
Jerry Bertsch, prin.
Woodland ES, 14445 DIAMOND PATH 55068
Terry Langager, prin.
Other Schools – See Apple Valley

First Baptist School, P O BOX 89 55068
St. Joseph ES, 14355 S ROBERT TRL 55068

Roseville, Ramsey Co., Pop. Code 8
Mounds View SD
Sch. Sys. Enr. Code 7
Supt. – Burton Nygren
2959 HAMLINE AVE N 55113
Other Schools – See Mounds View, New Brighton,
Saint Paul, Shoreview

Roseville SD
Sch. Sys. Enr. Code 6
Supt. – Roger Worner
1251 COUNTY ROAD B2 W 55113
Brimhall ES, 1744 COUNTY ROAD B W 55113
P. Storti, prin.
Central Park ES
535 COUNTY ROAD B W #2 55113
William Mack, prin.
Falcon Heights ES, 1393 W GARDEN AVE 55113
Ellen Blank, prin.
Other Schools – See Maplewood, Saint Paul,
Shoreview

King of Kings Lutheran ES
2330 DALE ST N 55113
St. Rose of Lima ES, 2072 HAMLINE AVE N 55113

Rothsay, Wilkin Co., Pop. Code 2
Rothsay SD
Sch. Sys. Enr. Code 2
Supt. – Joseph Merseth, P O BOX 247 56579
ES, P O BOX 247 56579 – Joe Merseth, prin.

Royalton, Morrison Co., Pop. Code 3
Royalton SD
Sch. Sys. Enr. Code 3
Supt. – Don Wilke, P O BOX 5 56373
ES, P O BOX 5 56373 – Philipp Gurbada, prin.

Rush City, Chisago Co., Pop. Code 4
Rush City SD
Sch. Sys. Enr. Code 3
Supt. – Jon McBroom 55069
ES 55069 – Martha Ward, prin.

Rushford, Fillmore Co., Pop. Code 4
Rushford SD
Sch. Sys. Enr. Code 3
Supt. – D. Rislove, P O BOX 267 55971
ES, P O BOX 627 55971 – William Burwell, prin.

Russell, Lyon Co., Pop. Code 2
Russell SD
Sch. Sys. Enr. Code 2
Supt. – James Redfield 56169
MS 56169 – Jerry Fulton, prin.
ES 56189 – Arnold Naeve, prin.

Ruthton, Pipestone Co., Pop. Code 2
Ruthton SD
Sch. Sys. Enr. Code 2
Supt. – James Redfield, P O BOX B 56170
ES, P O BOX B 56170 – Arnold Naeve, prin.

Sacred Heart, Renville Co., Pop. Code 3
Sacred Heart SD
Sch. Sys. Enr. Code 2
Supt. – Ivan Eckstrom 56285
ES 56285 – B. Fostveat, prin.

Saginaw, St. Louis Co.
Proctor SD
Supt. – See Proctor
Caribou Lake ES, 4581 INDUSTRIAL RD 55779
Dave Stark, prin.

St. Louis County SD
Supt. – See Virginia
Albrook ES, 4601 HWY 33 N 55779
Robert Larson, prin.

Saint Anthony, Hennepin Co., Pop. Code 6
St Anthony-New Brighton SD
Sch. Sys. Enr. Code 3
Supt. – Crystal Meriwether
3303 33RD AVE NE 55418
MS, 3303 33RD AVE NE 55418
David Abrahamson, prin.
Wilshire Park ES, 3600 HIGHCREST RD NE 55418
David Abrahamson, prin.

Saint Charles, Winona Co., Pop. Code 4
St. Charles SD
Sch. Sys. Enr. Code 3
Supt. – Thomas Ames, HWY 14 E 55972
ES, 925 CHURCH AVE 55972
Allen Rasmussen, prin.

Saint Clair, Blue Earth Co., Pop. Code 3
St. Clair SD
Sch. Sys. Enr. Code 2
Supt. – Jerry Olson 56080
ES 56080 – James Buysse, prin.

Saint Cloud, Stearns Co., Pop. Code 8
St. Cloud SD
Sch. Sys. Enr. Code 7
Supt. – Ronald Jandura
628 ROOSEVELT ROAD 56301
Jefferson ES, 430 3RD AVE NE 56301
(—), prin.
Lincoln ES, 336 5TH AVE SE 56304
Lew Johnson, prin.
Madison ES, 2805 9TH ST N 56303
Jack Horton, prin.
North MS, 1212 N 29TH AVE 56301
Ray Pontinen, prin.
Roosevelt ES, 3RD ST & 30TH AVE N 56301
William Hasbrouck, prin.
South MS, 1120 15TH AVE S 56301
William Challeen, prin.
Washington ES, 820 8TH AVE S 56301
Sandy Darling, prin.
Westwood ES, 5800 RIDGEWOOD RD 56303
William Armstrong, prin.
Other Schools – See Clear Lake, Saint Joseph, Waite
Park

Holy Spirit ES, 1615 11TH AVE S 56301
St. Anthony ES, 2410 1ST ST NTH ST N 56301
St. Augustine ES, 428 2ND ST SE 56304
St. Mary Help of Christians ES
RURAL ROUTE 03 BOX 41 56301
St. Wendelin ES
22776 STATE HIGHWAY 15 56301
Sts. Peter & Paul ES
11TH AVENUE AND 12TH ST N 56303
SS Peter & Paul PS
30TH AVE & NINTH ST N 56303

Saint Francis, Anoka Co., Pop. Code 4
St. Francis SD
Sch. Sys. Enr. Code 4
Supt. – William Gaslin, P O BOX 128 55070
MS, P O BOX 128 55070 – Michael Wyatt, prin.
ES, 22919 SAINT FRANCIS BLVD NW 55070
Susan Anderson, prin.
Other Schools – See Cedar

Trinity Lutheran ES, P O BOX 700 55070

Saint James, Watonwan Co., Pop. Code 5
St. James SD
Sch. Sys. Enr. Code 4
Supt. – Walter Conway, 10TH AVE N 56081
ES, 1273 10TH AVE N 56081
James Andrzejek, prin.

Saint Joseph, Stearns Co., Pop. Code 5
St. Cloud SD
Supt. – See Saint Cloud
Kennedy ES, 1ST AVE SE 56375
Jerome Hayenga, prin.

St. Joseph Lab ES, P O BOX 488 56374

Saint Louis Park, Hennepin Co., Pop. Code 8
St. Louis Park SD
Sch. Sys. Enr. Code 5
Supt. – Carl Holmstrom, 6425 W 33RD ST 55426
JHS, 2025 TEXAS AVE S 55426 – Les Bork, prin.
Aquila ES, 8500 W 31ST ST 55426
David Dooley, prin.
Cedar Manor MS, 9400 CEDAR LAKE RD S 55426
Neil Sandberg, prin.
Hobart ES, 6500 W 26TH ST 55426
Patricia Joslin, prin.
Lindgren ES, 4801 W 41ST ST 55416
Harry Hoff, prin.

Groves Learning Center
3200 HIGHWAY 100 S 55416
Holy Family ES, 5925 W LAKE ST 55416
Medicine Lake Lutheran Academy
6300 WALKER ST 55416
Torah Academy, 2800 JOPPA AVE S 55416

Saint Michael, Wright Co., Pop. Code 4
St. Michael-Albertville SD
Sch. Sys. Enr. Code 4
Supt. – Mario DeMatteis 55376
MS, 60 CENTRAL AVE W 55376
Duane Christenson, prin.
Other Schools – See Albertville

St. Michael ES, 14 MAIN ST N 55376

Saint Paul, Ramsey Co., Pop. Code 10
Mounds View SD
Supt. – See Roseville
Island Lake ES, 3555 VICTORIA ST N 55126
Howard Hass, prin.
Valentine Hills ES
1770 COUNTY ROAD E W #2 55112
Lawrence Eickhoff, prin.

North St. Paul-Maplewood SD
Sch. Sys. Enr. Code 6
Supt. – Richard St. Germain
2055 LARPENTEUR AVE E 55109
Glenn MS, 1560 COUNTY ROAD B E 55109
Fulton Klinkerfues, prin.
Maplewood MS, 2410 HOLLOWAY ST E 55109
Mary Leary, prin.
Carver ES, 2680 UPPER AFTON RD 55119
Jerry Hauble, prin.
Eagle Point ES, 7850 15TH ST N 55119
Thomas Loven, prin.
Oakdale ES, 821 GLENBROOK AVE N 55119
Marvin Brown, prin.
Weaver ES, 2135 BIRMINGHAM ST 55109
Mary Schrankler, prin.
Other Schools – See North Saint Paul

Roseville SD
Supt. – See Roseville
Little Canada ES, 400 ELI RD 55117
David O'Connor, prin.

St. Paul SD
Sch. Sys. Enr. Code 8
Supt. – David Bennett, 360 COLBORNE ST 55102
Battle Creek MS, 2121 N PARK DRIVE 55119
Benjamin Zachary, prin.
Cleveland JHS, 1000 WALSH ST 55106
Luz Serrano, prin.
Hazel Park JHS, 1140 WHITE BEAR AVE N 55106
Donald Donsalla, prin.
Highland Park JHS, 975 SNELLING AVE S 55116
Nancy Nielsen, prin.
Humboldt JHS, 640 HUMBOLDT AVE 55107
John Ettlinger, prin.
Murray JHS, 2200 BUFORD AVE 55108
John McManus, prin.
Ramsey JHS, 1700 SUMMIT AVE 55105
Dorothy LeGault, prin.
Washington JHS, 1041 MARION ST 55117
Joan Sorensen, prin.
Ames ES, 1760 AMES PL 55106
Joan Rourke, prin.
Battle Creek ES, 60 RUTH ST S 55119
Gerald Madigan, prin.
Chelsea Heights ES, 1557 HURON ST 55108
Harlan Balken, prin.
Cherokee Heights MS, 694 CHARLTON ST 55107
Thomas Haas, prin.
Como Park ES, 780 WHEELOCK PKY W 55117
Ann Degree, prin.
Daytons Bluff ES, 262 BATES AVE 55106
William Shrankler, prin.
East Consolidated ES, 409 CASE AVE 55101
Carol Sorenson, prin.
Eastern Heights ES, 2001 MARGARET ST 55119
Allen Saunders, prin.
Franklin Magnet ES, 690 JACKSON ST 55101
Anne Rosten, prin.

Frost Lake Magnet ES, 1505 HOYT AVE E 55106
 Anna Erbes, prin.
Galtier Magnet MS, 1317 CHARLES AVE 55104
 Dennis St. Sauver, prin.
Groveland Park ES
 2045 SAINT CLAIR AVE 55105
 Charles Weldin, prin.
Hancock ES, 1599 ENGLEWOOD AVE 55104
 Joan Fehden, prin.
Hayden Heights ES, 1863 CLEAR AVE 55119
 Thomas Foster, prin.
Highland Park ES, 1700 SAUNDERS AVE 55116
 Shirley Kaiser, prin.
Highwood Hills ES, 2188 LONDIN LN 55119
 Elnora Battle, prin.
Hill Magnet ES, 998 SELBY AVE 55104
 Delores Henderson, prin.
Homecroft ES, 1845 SHERIDAN AVE 55116
 Dale Srigley, prin.
Jackson ES, 437 EDMUND AVE 55103
 Kathleen Anderson, prin.
Longfellow Magnet ES, 318 MOORE ST 55104
 Juanita Morgan, prin.
Mann ES, 2001 ELEANOR AVE 55116
 Gordon Cherveny, prin.
Maxfield Magnet ES, 380 VICTORIA ST N 55104
 Robert Miller, prin.
Mays Fundamental ES, 631 N ALBERT 55104
 John Bennett, prin.
Mississippi Magnet ES, 1575 LORIENT ST 55117
 Judy Brzinski, prin.
Monroe ES, 810 PALACE AVE 55102
 Eugene Galatowitsch, prin.
North End ES, 27 GERANIUM AVE E 55117
 Irene Jelacic, prin.
Parkway ES, 1363 BUSH AVE 55106
 Gloria Kumagai, prin.
Phalen Lake ES, 1089 CYPRESS ST 55106
 Donald Lieb, prin.
Prosperity Heights ES
 1305 PROSPERITY AVE 55106
 John Ashmead, prin.
Randolph Heights ES, 348 HAMLINE AVE S 55105
 Joyce Shelton, prin.
Roosevelt ES, 160 ISABEL ST E 55107
 Peter Grams, prin.
St. Anthony Park ES, 2180 KNAPP ST 55108
 Hope Lea, prin.
Sheridan ES, 525 WHITE BEAR AVE N 55106
 Maria Calderon, prin.
Webster Magnet ES, 707 HOLLY AVE 55104
 Joanne Ventura, prin.

West St. Paul SD
 Supt. – See West Saint Paul
 Somerset ES, 1355 DODD RD 55118
 Donald Moore, prin.

Christ Household of Faith
 355 MARSHALL AVE 55102
Convent of the Visitation School
 2475 DODD ROAD 55120
Mounds Park Academy
 2051 LARPENTEUR AVE E 55109
Red School House HS, 643 VIRGINIA ST 55103
St. Agnes School, 525 THOMAS AVE 55103
Blessed Sacrament ES, 1800 AMES AVE 55119
Central Lutheran ES
 775 LEXINGTON PKY N 55104
Corpus Christi ES, 2131 FAIRVIEW AVE N 55113
East St. Paul Lutheran ES
 674 JOHNSON PKY 55106
Faith Baptist Christian ES
 1360 MISSISSIPPI ST 55101
Gethsemane Lutheran ES
 2410 STILLWATER RD 55119
Highland Catholic ES
 2017 BOHLAND AVE 55116
Holy Childhood ES, 1435 MIDWAY PKY 55108
Holy Spirit ES, 2406 RANDOLPH AVE 55105
Immaculate Heart of Mary ES
 1550 SUMMIT AVE 55105
Maternity of Mary ES
 592 ARLINGTON AVE W 55117
Nativity ES, 1900 STANFORD AVE 55105
Presentation of the BVM ES
 1695 KENNARD ST 55109
Sacred Heart & St. John ES, 835 5TH ST E 55106
St. Andrew ES, 1028 VAN SLYKE AVE 55103
St. Bernard's ES, 1167 ALBEMARLE ST 55117
St. Casimir ES, 930 GERANIUM AVE E 55106
St. Columba ES, 1330 BLAIR AVE 55104
St. Francis De Sales ES, 426 OSCEOLA AVE 55102
St. James ES, 486 VIEW ST 55102
St. Jerome ES, 384 ROSELAWN AVE E 55117
St. John the Evangelist ES
 2621 MCMENEMY RD 55117
St. Luke ES, 1065 SUMMIT AVE 55105
St. Mark ES, 1983 DAYTON AVE 55104
St. Matthew ES, 497 HUMBOLDT AVE 55107
St. Pascal ES, 1770 3RD ST E 55106
St. Patrick ES, 471 MAGNOLIA AVE E 55101
St. Paul Academy-Summit
 1150 GOODRICH AVE 55105
Transfiguration ES, 953 FERNDALE AVE 55119
Trinity Lone Oak Lutheran ES
 2950 DODD ROAD 55121

Saint Paul Park, Washington Co., Pop. Code 5
 South Washington County SD
 Supt. – See Cottage Grove
 Oltman JHS, 1020 3RD ST 55071
 Lelia Redin, prin.

Pullman ES, 1260 SELBY AVE 55071
 Sigurd Jacobson, prin.

Saint Peter, Nicollet Co., Pop. Code 6
 St. Peter SD
 Sch. Sys. Enr. Code 4
 Supt. – Raymond Folstrom
 LINCOLN DRIVE 56082
 North ES, 815 9TH ST 56082
 William Dixon, prin.
 South ES, 1405 S 7TH ST 56082
 Michael Rogers, prin.

John Ireland ES, 618 S 5TH ST 56082

Sanborn, Redwood Co., Pop. Code 3
 Sanborn SD
 Sch. Sys. Enr. Code 2
 Supt. – Richard Gulbranson 56083
 Sanborn/Lamberton MS 56083 – (—), prin.
 ES 56083 – (—), prin.

Sandstone, Pine Co., Pop. Code 4
 Sandstone SD
 Sch. Sys. Enr. Code 3
 Supt. – Michael Hruby 55072
 ES, COURT AVE & 5TH ST 55072
 Harold Berg, prin.

Sartell, Stearns Co., Pop. Code 5
 Sartell SD
 Sch. Sys. Enr. Code 4
 Supt. – Duane Wrightson, P O BOX 328 56377
 St. Stephens ES, P O BOX 328 56377
 Gerald Bouchie, prin.
 ES, P O BOX 328 56377 – Gerald Bouchie, prin.
 IS, P O BOX 328 56377 – Michael Spanier, prin.

St. Francis Xavier ES, P O BOX F 56377

Sauk Centre, Stearns Co., Pop. Code 5
 Sauk Centre SD
 Sch. Sys. Enr. Code 4
 Supt. – P. Foster, 933 STATE ROAD 56378
 ES, 4TH & OAK 56378 – Harold Nelson, prin.

Holy Family ES, 231 SINCLAIR LEWIS AVE 56378

Sauk Rapids, Benton Co., Pop. Code 6
 Sauk Rapids SD
 Sch. Sys. Enr. Code 4
 Supt. – Jerry Hartley, 901 1ST ST S 56379
 Hillside MS, 30 4TH AVE S 56379
 John Clark, prin.
 Pleasant View ES, 1009 6TH AVE N 56379
 Lila Johnson, prin.
 Other Schools – See Rice

Sacred Heart ES, 324 3RD AVE S 56379
Trintiy Lutheran ES, 219 4TH ST N 56379

Savage, Scott Co., Pop. Code 5
 Burnsville SD
 Supt. – See Burnsville
 ES, 4819 W 126TH ST 55378 – Ralph Vessey, prin.

St. John the Baptist ES, 12508 LYNN AVE 55378

Scandia, Washington Co.
 Forest Lake SD
 Supt. – See Forest Lake
 ES, 14351 SCANDIA TRL N 55073
 Jack Reese, prin.

Sebeka, Wadena Co., Pop. Code 3
 Sebeka SD
 Sch. Sys. Enr. Code 3
 Supt. – Elman Becker 56477
 ES 56477 – (—), prin.

Shakopee, Scott Co., Pop. Code 6
 Shakopee SD
 Sch. Sys. Enr. Code 4
 Supt. – Gayden Carruth, 505 HOLMES ST S 55379
 Central ES, 132 E FIFTH ST 55379
 Richard Nordstrom, prin.
 Pearson ES, 917 DAKOTA ST S 55379
 Donna Harms, prin.
 Sweeney ES, 1001 ADAMS ST S 55379
 Donald Tarr, prin.

Shakopee Area Catholic ES
 305 SCOTT ST S 55379

Sherburn, Martin Co., Pop. Code 4
 Sherburn SD
 Sch. Sys. Enr. Code 2
 Supt. – Don Helmstetter, 16 W 5TH ST 56171
 ES, E 5TH ST BOX 578 56171 – (—), prin.

Shevlin, Beltrami Co., Pop. Code 2
 Bagley SD
 Supt. – See Bagley
 ES 56676 – James Martin, prin.

Shoreview, Ramsey Co., Pop. Code 7
 Mounds View SD
 Supt. – See Roseville
 Chippewa JHS, 5000 HODGSON ROAD 55126
 Eugene Young, prin.
 Chippewa ES, 5000 HODGSON ROAD 55126
 Judy Paetznick, prin.
 Snail Lake ES, 4550 HODGSON RD 55126
 Leonard Holmen, prin.
 Turtle Lake ES, 1141 COUNTY ROAD I W 55126
 Barb Bocian, prin.

Roseville SD
 Supt. – See Roseville
 Williams ES, 955 COUNTY ROAD D W 55126
 Sally Thomas, prin.

St. Odilia ES, 3495 VICTORIA ST N 55126

Silver Bay, Lake Co., Pop. Code 5
 Lake Superior SD
 Supt. – See Two Harbors
 MacDonald ES, EDISON BLVD 55614
 Edward Pocrnich, prin.

Silver Lake, McLeod Co., Pop. Code 3
 Silver Lake SD
 Sch. Sys. Enr. Code 2
 Supt. – David Shapley 55381
 ES 55381 – Margaret Waterhouse, prin.

Silver Lake Catholic ES, P O BOX 346 55381

Slayton, Murray Co., Pop. Code 4
 Slayton SD
 Sch. Sys. Enr. Code 3
 Supt. – Cornelius Smit, 2420 28TH ST 56172
 ES, 2640 FLEETWOOD ST 56172
 Kenneth Hatch, prin.

Sleepy Eye, Brown Co., Pop. Code 5
 Sleepy Eye SD
 Sch. Sys. Enr. Code 3
 Supt. – Harold Kirchgasler
 400 4TH AVE SW 56085
 ES, 400 4TH AVE SW 56085 – (—), prin.

St. Mary's ES, 104 SAINT MARYS ST NW 56085

Soudan, St. Louis Co.
 Tower-Soudan SD
 Supt. – See Tower
 Tower-Soudan ES, P O BOX 55 55782
 Jerome Rooney, prin.

South Saint Paul, Dakota Co., Pop. Code 7
 South St. Paul SD
 Sch. Sys. Enr. Code 5
 Supt. – David Metzen, 700 2ND ST N 55075
 Lincoln Center ES, 357 9TH AVE N 55075
 Wayne Otto, prin.
 Roosevelt ES, 535 5TH AVE S 55075
 Mary Morin, prin.
 Washington ES, 120 DALE ST E 55075
 Karen Ferguson, prin.

Holy Trinity School, 745 SIXTH AVE S 55075
St. John Vianney ES, 1815 BROMLEY AVE 55075

Springfield, Brown Co., Pop. Code 4
 Springfield SD
 Sch. Sys. Enr. Code 3
 Supt. – Ronald Madsen, 12 BURNS AVE 56087
 ES, 12 BURNS AVE 56087 – John Dezeeuw, prin.

St. Raphael ES, 20 W VA DUSEN 56087

Spring Grove, Houston Co., Pop. Code 4
 Spring Grove SD
 Sch. Sys. Enr. Code 2
 Supt. – James Busta, P O BOX 626 55974
 ES, P O BOX 626 55974 – Shirley Ohl, prin.

Spring Lake Park, Anoka Co., Pop. Code 6
 Spring Lake Park SD
 Sch. Sys. Enr. Code 5
 Supt. – Chris Huber, 8000 HIGHWAY 65 NE 55432
 Hall ES, 8089 ABLE ST NE 55432
 Robert Hakala, prin.
 Park Terrace ES, 8301 TERRACE RD NE 55432
 Robert Pluth, prin.
 Woodcrest ES, 880 OSBORNE RD NE 55432
 Gary Erickson, prin.
 Other Schools – See Blaine

Spring Valley, Filmore Co., Pop. Code 5
 Spring Valley SD
 Sch. Sys. Enr. Code 3
 Supt. – Walter Simonson, P O BOX 72 55975
 ES, P O BOX 72 55975 – John Zierdt, prin.

Squaw Lake, Itasca Co., Pop. Code 2
 Grand Rapids SD
 Supt. – See Grand Rapids
 ES 56681 – Darrell Sampson, prin.

Staples, Todd Co., Pop. Code 5
 Staples SD
 Sch. Sys. Enr. Code 4
 Supt. – John Nelson, 223 3RD AVE NE 56479
 Lincoln Model ES, DAKOTA AVE 56479
 Donald Droubie, prin.
 Northside ES, 4TH ST N 56479
 Steve Stansberry, prin.

Sacred Heart ES, 324 FOURTH ST N 56479

Starbuck, Pope Co., Pop. Code 4
 Starbuck SD
 Sch. Sys. Enr. Code 2
 Supt. – Ernest Janisch, 500 JOHN ST 56381
 ES 56381 – Jerome Flom, prin.

Stephen, Marshall Co., Pop. Code 3
 Stephen SD
 Sch. Sys. Enr. Code 2
 Supt. – J. Schindele, P O BOX 68 56757
 ES, P O BOX 68 56757 – Bruce Jensen, prin.

Stewart, McLeod Co., Pop. Code 3
Stewart SD
Sch. Sys. Enr. Code 2
Supt. – Ray Vikander 55385
ES 55385 – Jody Stoffels, prin.

Stewartville, Olmsted Co., Pop. Code 5
Stewartville SD
Sch. Sys. Enr. Code 4
Supt. – R. Jorstad, 500 4TH ST SW 55976
Bonner ES, 526 5TH AVE SE 55976
  Max Broadwater, prin.
Central ES, 301 2ND ST SW 55976
  David Ruzek, prin.

Stillwater, Washington Co., Pop. Code 7
Stillwater SD
Sch. Sys. Enr. Code 6
Supt. – David Wettergren
  1875 S GREELEY ST 55082
Lily Lake ES, 2003 WILLARD ST W 55082
  Allen Posthumus, prin.
Oak Park ES, 6355 OSMAN AVE N 55082
  Burnell Anderson, prin.
Stonebridge ES, 900 OWENS ST N 55082
  John Johnson, prin.
Other Schools – See Bayport, Hugo, Lake Elmo,
  Lakeland, Marine on Saint Croix

St. Croix Catholic ES, 621 3RD ST S 55082

Storden, Cottonwood Co., Pop. Code 2
Storden-Jeffers SD
Sch. Sys. Enr. Code 2
Supt. – Norman Johnson, P O BOX 68 56174
Stordan-Jeffers ES 56174 – Norman Johnson, prin.

Strandquist, Marshall Co., Pop. Code 2
Strandquist SD
Sch. Sys. Enr. Code 2
Supt. – P. M. Dyrud, P O BOX 06 56758
ES, P O BOX 6 56758 – John Sheehan, prin.

Swanville, Morrison Co., Pop. Code 2
Swanville SD
Sch. Sys. Enr. Code 2
Supt. – James Loecken, P O BOX 98 56382
ES, P O BOX 98 56382 – Mary Goplen, prin.

Talmoon, Itasca Co.
Deer River SD
Supt. – See Deer River
North ES, TALMOON RURAL STATION 56637
  Philip Harris, prin.

Taylors Falls, Chisago Co., Pop. Code 3
Taylors Falls SD
Sch. Sys. Enr. Code 2
Supt. – Sig Rimestad, 670 WEST ST 55084
ES, 670 WEST ST 55084 – (—), prin.

Thief River Falls, Pennington Co., Pop. Code 6
Thief River Falls SD
Sch. Sys. Enr. Code 4
Supt. – Leo Ruberto, P O BOX 160 56701
Franklin MS, 300 SPRUCE AVE S 56701
  Milton Hoff, prin.
Knox ES, 701 HUGHES ST 56701
  Glenn Espe, prin.
Northrop ES, 914 LABREE AVE N 56701
  William Desrocher, prin.
Twain ES, 1424 GULF ST E 56701
  Glenn Espe, prin.
Washington ES, ARNOLD AVE & 3RD ST 56701
  William Desrocher, prin.

St. Bernard ES, 117 KNIGHT AVE N 56701

Tofte, Cook Co.
Cook County SD
Supt. – See Grand Marais
Birch Grove ES 55615 – Bert Chamberlain, prin.

Togo, St. Louis Co.
Grand Rapids SD
Supt. – See Grand Rapids
ES 55788 – Donald Erven, prin.

Tower, St. Louis Co., Pop. Code 3
Tower-Soudan SD
Sch. Sys. Enr. Code 2
Supt. – Peter Jurkovich, P O BOX 469 55790
Other Schools – See Soudan

Tracy, Lyon Co., Pop. Code 4
Tracy SD
Sch. Sys. Enr. Code 3
Supt. – Harold Remme, 934 PINE ST 56175
ES, 700 4TH ST E 56175 – Terry Hermanson, prin.

Trimont, Martin Co., Pop. Code 3
Trimont SD
Sch. Sys. Enr. Code 2
Supt. – Don Helmstetter, P O BOX N 56176
ES, P O BOX N 56176 – Charles Rick, prin.

Truman, Martin Co., Pop. Code 4
Truman SD
Sch. Sys. Enr. Code 2
Supt. – Richard Newkirk, P O BOX 276 56088
ES, P O BOX 276 56088
  Lyle Hammerschmidt, prin.

Twin Valley, Norman Co., Pop. Code 3
Twin Valley SD
Sch. Sys. Enr. Code 2
Supt. – Karl Schulz 56584
ES 56584 – Arne Martinson, prin.

Two Harbors, Lake Co., Pop. Code 5
Lake Superior SD
Sch. Sys. Enr. Code 4
Supt. – Elmer Frahm, 405 4TH AVE 55616
Minnehaha MS, 421 7TH ST 55616
  Lyle Northey, prin.
Johnson ES, 515 10TH AVE 55616
  Robert Lackore, prin.
Other Schools – See Duluth, Silver Bay

Ulen, Clay Co., Pop. Code 3
Ulen-Hitterdal SD
Sch. Sys. Enr. Code 2
Supt. – Daryl Bragg 56585
Ulen-Hitterdal ES 56585 – Arla Dockter, prin.

Underwood, Otter Tail Co., Pop. Code 2
Underwood SD
Sch. Sys. Enr. Code 2
Supt. – Brad Madsen, 200 SOUTHERN AVE 56586
ES, SOUTHERN AVE 56586
  Berthold Kinzler, prin.

Upsala, Morrison Co., Pop. Code 2
Upsala SD
Sch. Sys. Enr. Code 2
Supt. – Russell Johnson 56384
ES 56384 – Stan Corey, prin.

Verdi, Lincoln Co., Pop. Code 2
Verdi SD
Sch. Sys. Enr. Code 1
Supt. – John Feuerstein, P O BOX 58 56179
ES, P O BOX 58 56179 – Danny Castor, prin.

Vermillion, Dakota Co., Pop. Code 2

St. John the Baptist School
  111 W MAIN ST 55085

Verndale, Wadena Co., Pop. Code 3
Verndale SD
Sch. Sys. Enr. Code 2
Supt. – James Madsen, P O BOX G 56481
ES, P O BOX G 56481 – Arlene Ferrian, prin.

Vernon Center, Blue Earth Co., Pop. Code 2
Garden City SD
Supt. – See Garden City
ES 56090 – Nancy Kluck, prin.

Viking, Marshall Co., Pop. Code 2
Newfolden SD
Supt. – See Newfolden
ES 56760 – James Hodny, prin.

Villard, Pope Co., Pop. Code 2
Villard SD
Sch. Sys. Enr. Code 2
Supt. – Ernest Janisch, P O BOX 66 56385
ES, P O BOX 66 56385 – Richard Ofstedal, prin.

Virginia, St. Louis Co., Pop. Code 7
St. Louis County SD
Sch. Sys. Enr. Code 5
Supt. – Daniel Mobilia, 731 3RD ST S 55792
Other Schools – See Alborn, Cook, Cotton, Iron,
  Meadowlands, Orr, Saginaw

Virginia SD
Sch. Sys. Enr. Code 4
Supt. – R. Krebsbach, TECH BUILDING 55792
Madison ES, WILLIAMS ADDITION 55792
  Gerald Saisa, prin.
Roosevelt MS, 55TH AVE & 3RD ST 55792
  Wallace Christianson, prin.

Marquette ES, 311 3RD ST S 55792

Wabasha, Wabasha Co., Pop. Code 4
Wabasha SD
Sch. Sys. Enr. Code 3
Supt. – John Mattison
  611 BROADWAY AVE 55981
MS, 611 BROADWAY AVE 55981
  Frederick Brown, prin.
IS, 611 BROADWAY AVE 55981
  Frederick Brown, Jr., prin.
Other Schools – See Kellogg

St. Felix ES, 130 3RD ST E 55981

Wabasso, Redwood Co., Pop. Code 3
Wabasso SD
Sch. Sys. Enr. Code 2
Supt. – (—), 1333 MAY ST 56293
ES 56293 – (—), prin.

St. Anne School, 1023 CEDAR 56293

Waconia, Carver Co., Pop. Code 5
Waconia SD
Sch. Sys. Enr. Code 4
Supt. – Allen Frazier, 24 S WALNUT ST 55387
Southview ES, 4TH AND MAPLE ST 55387
  Ric Dressen, prin.

St. Joseph ES, 31 E 1ST ST 55387
Trinity Lutheran ES, 601 E 2ND ST 55387

Wadena, Wadena Co., Pop. Code 5
Wadena SD
Sch. Sys. Enr. Code 4
Supt. – Larry Foley, P O BOX 151 56482
JHS, P O BOX 151 56482
  Durwood Amundson, prin.
ES, P O BOX 151 56482 – Jack Stouten, prin.

St. Ann's ES, 519 2ND ST SE 56482

Waite Park, Stearns Co., Pop. Code 5
St. Cloud SD
Supt. – See Saint Cloud
McKinley ES, 216 8TH AVE N 56387
  Bill Thurmond, prin.

St. Joseph ES, 108 6TH AVE N 56387

Waldorf, Waseca Co., Pop. Code 2
Waldorf-Pemberton SD
Sch. Sys. Enr. Code 2
Supt. – Robert Hoppe 56091
Pemberton ES, P O BOX 8 56091
  Aileen Voelz, prin.

Walker, Cass Co., Pop. Code 3
Walker SD
Sch. Sys. Enr. Code 3
Supt. – Boyd McLarty 56484
ES 56484 – Gerald Demars, prin.

Walnut Grove, Redwood Co., Pop. Code 3
Walnut Grove SD
Sch. Sys. Enr. Code 2
Supt. – Orlyn Wiemers 56180
ES 56180 – Orlyn Wiemers, prin.

Wanamingo, Goodhue Co., Pop. Code 3
Wanamingo SD
Sch. Sys. Enr. Code 2
Supt. – Donald Pressnall 55983
ES 55983 – Donald Pressnall, prin.

Wannaska, Roseau Co.
Roseau SD
Supt. – See Roseau
ES 56761 – Gale Halvorson, prin.

Warba, Itasca Co., Pop. Code 2
Grand Rapids SD
Supt. – See Grand Rapids
ES 55739 – Darrell Sampson, prin.

Warren, Marshall Co., Pop. Code 4
Warren SD
Sch. Sys. Enr. Code 3
Supt. – Gerald Dalzell, 224 BRIDGE AVE E 56762
ES, 224 E BRIDGE AVE 56762
  Ronald Leverington, prin.

Warroad, Roseau Co., Pop. Code 4
Warroad SD
Sch. Sys. Enr. Code 4
Supt. – John Reishus, P O BOX 130 56763
Angle Inlet ES, CEDAR AVE 56763
  Ronald Ditsch, prin.
ES, 510 CEDAR AVE 56763 – Ronald Ditsch, prin.

Waseca, Waseca Co., Pop. Code 6
Waseca SD
Sch. Sys. Enr. Code 4
Supt. – Francis Heinen, 501 E ELM AVE 56093
Central MS, 501 E ELM AVE 56093
  James O'Regan, prin.
Central ES, 501 ELM AVE E 56093
  Paul Skagerberg, prin.
Hartley ES, 605 7TH ST NE 56093
  Paul Skagerberg, prin.
Southside ES, 609 S STATE ST 56093
  G. Towers, prin.

Sacred Heart ES, 308 W ELM AVE 56093

Watertown, Carver Co., Pop. Code 4
Watertown-Mayer SD
Sch. Sys. Enr. Code 4
Supt. – G. Thompson, P O BOX 368 55388
Watertown-Mayer ES, P O BOX 368 55388
  David Sloneker, prin.

St. Peter / St. Paul Lutheran ES
  P O BOX 656 55388

Waterville, Le Sueur Co., Pop. Code 4
Waterville SD
Sch. Sys. Enr. Code 3
Supt. – B. Johnson, 500 PAQUIN ST E 56096
ES, 500 PAQUIN ST E 56096
  Edward Henderson, prin.

Watkins, Meeker Co., Pop. Code 3

St. Anthony ES, P O BOX 469 55389

Waubun, Mahnomen Co., Pop. Code 2
Waubun SD
Sch. Sys. Enr. Code 3
Supt. – John Vorachek, P O BOX 98 56589
ES, P O BOX 98 56589 – David Stone, prin.
Other Schools – See Ogema

Wayzata, Hennepin Co., Pop. Code 5
Minnetonka SD
Supt. – See Excelsior
Deephaven ES, 4452 VINE HILL RD 55391
  Bradley Board, prin.
Groveland ES
  3325 GROVELAND SCHOOL RD 55391
  Duane Udstuen, prin.

Wayzata SD
Sch. Sys. Enr. Code 6
Supt. – David Landswerk, P O BOX 660 55391
Widsten ES, 726 RICE ST E 55391
  John Weeks, prin.

Other Schools – See Plymouth

___

Holy Name ES, 155 COUNTY ROAD 24   55391
Redeemer Lutheran ES
 115 WAYZATA BLVD W   55391
St. Bartholomew ES, 645 RICE ST E   55391
St. Therese ES
 183125 MINNETONKA BLVD   55391

Welcome, Martin Co., Pop. Code 3
Welcome SD
Sch. Sys. Enr. Code 2
Supt. – Don Helmstetter 56181
ES 56181 – Randy Voth, prin.

Wells, Faribault Co., Pop. Code 5
Wells SD
Sch. Sys. Enr. Code 3
Supt. – G. A. Hansen, 250 SW 2ND AVE   56097
ES, 250 SW 2ND AVE 56097
 James Sergeant, prin.

___

St. Casmimir ES, 330 SW 2ND AVE 56097

Westbrook, Cottonwood Co., Pop. Code 3
Westbrook SD
Sch. Sys. Enr. Code 2
Supt. – Don Knutson, P O BOX 128 56183
ES, P O BOX 128 56183 – Jerald Goehring, prin.

West Concord, Dodge Co., Pop. Code 3
West Concord SD
Sch. Sys. Enr. Code 2
Supt. – K. J. Doty, P O BOX 38 55985
ES, 600 1ST ST 55985 – Kenneth Doty, prin.

West Saint Paul, Dakota Co., Pop. Code 7
West St. Paul SD
Sch. Sys. Enr. Code 5
Supt. – Bruce Anderson
 1897 DELAWARE AVE 55118
Grass JHS, 181 BUTLER AVE W 55118
 James Bauck, prin.
Garlough ES, 1740 CHARLTON ST 55118
 Gordon Nelson, prin.
Moreland ES, 217 MORELAND AVE W 55118
 Ellein McDaniel, prin.
Other Schools – See Eagan, Mendota Heights, Saint
 Paul

___

Emanuel Ev. Lutheran ES
 115 CRUSADER AVE W 55118
St. Joseph ES, 1138 SEMINOLE AVE 55118
St. Michael ES, 335 E HURLEY ST 55118

Wheaton, Traverse Co., Pop. Code 4
Wheaton SD
Sch. Sys. Enr. Code 3
Supt. – (—), 1700 3RD AVE S 56296
Pearson ES, 710 4TH AVE N 56296
 Joseph Kalla, prin.

White Bear Lake, Ramsey Co., Pop. Code 7
White Bear Lake SD
Sch. Sys. Enr. Code 6
Supt. – T. F. Cunio, 2399 CEDAR AVE 55110
Central JHS, 4857 BLOOM AVE 55110
 Rob Thompson, prin.
Bellaire ES, 2540 COUNTY ROAD F E 55110
 Linda House, prin.
Birch Lake ES, 1616 BIRCH LAKE AVE 55110
 Werner Tismer, prin.
Golfview ES, 2449 ORCHARD LN 55110
 Carl Funk, prin.
Lakeaires ES, 3963 VAN DYKE ST 55110
 Lois Erickson, prin.
Lincoln ES, 1960 6TH ST 55110
 Jack Dzubnar, prin.

Otter Lake ES, 1401 CO RD H2 55110
 Bob Rosenbaum, prin.
Parkview ES, 2530 SPRUCE PL 55110
 Kay Hoffman, prin.
Vadnais Heights ES
 3645 CENTERVILLE RD 55127
 Bob Lundberg, prin.
Willow Lane ES, 3375 WILLOW LANE 55110
 Jeanne Eisenbarth, prin.
Other Schools – See Hugo

___

St. Mary of the Lake ES
 4690 BALD EAGLE AVE 55110
St. Pius X ES, 3878 HIGHLAND AVE 55110

Willmar, Kandiyohi Co., Pop. Code 7
Willmar SD
Sch. Sys. Enr. Code 5
Supt. – Orlo Almlie, 611 W 5TH ST 56201
Garfield MS, 512 8TH ST SW 56201
 Al Boonstra, prin.
Jefferson ES, 1202 W MONOGALIA AVE 56201
 Alton Boonstra, prin.
Lafayette ES, 1112 LAKE AVE NW 56201
 Paul Olberg, prin.
Lincoln ES, 511 JULII ST 56201
 Kathleen Haug, prin.
Roosevelt ES, 1800 SW 19TH AVE 56201
 Elden Bartz, prin.
Washington ES, 325 WILLMAR AVE SW 56201
 Paul Olberg, prin.
Other Schools – See Blomkest, Kandiyohi

___

Community Christian ES
 1300 19TH AVE SW 56201

Willow River, Pine Co., Pop. Code 2
Willow River SD
Sch. Sys. Enr. Code 2
Supt. – Gregory Ohl, P O BOX 66 55795
ES, P O BOX 66 55795 – (—), prin.

Windom, Cottonwood Co., Pop. Code 5
Windom SD
Sch. Sys. Enr. Code 4
Supt. – Philip Ledermann, P O BOX C-177 56101
Highland ES, 74 10TH ST 56101
 Barry Ommen, prin.
Winfair ES, 1454 6TH AVE N 56101
 Thomas Farrell, prin.

Winnebago, Faribault Co., Pop. Code 4
Winnebago SD
Sch. Sys. Enr. Code 2
Supt. – Paul Ford, P O BOX 65 56098
ES, P O BOX 65 56098 – Jean Yeager, prin.

Winona, Winona Co., Pop. Code 8
Winona SD
Sch. Sys. Enr. Code 5
Supt. – Lee Brittmenham
 166 W BROADWAY ST 55987
Central ES, 317 MARKET ST 55987
 John Kaehler, prin.
Goodview ES, 5100 W 9TH ST 55987
 Richard Adank, prin.
Jefferson ES, 1268 W 5TH ST 55987
 David Mahlke, prin.
Madison ES, 515 W WABASHA ST 55987
 Donald Nutt, prin.
Washington ES, 365 MANKATO AVE 55987
 Robert Hogenson, prin.
Other Schools – See Dakota, Houston, Rollingstone

___

Cathedral School, 352 CENTER ST 55987
St. Martin's ES, 253 LIBERTY ST 55987
St. Mary ES, 1315 W BROADWAY ST 55987
St. Matthew's ES, 756 W WABASHA ST 55987
St. Stanislaus ES, 602 E 5TH ST 55987

Winona Area Catholic ES
 101 E WABASHA ST 55987

Winsted, McLeod Co., Pop. Code 4
Winsted SD
Sch. Sys. Enr. Code 2
Supt. – Murl Kletscher, 435 4 ST N 55395
ES, 431 4TH ST N 55395 – Murl Kletscher, prin.

___

Holy Trinity School, 110 WINSTED AVE W 55395

Woodbury, Washington Co., Pop. Code 7
South Washington County SD
Supt. – See Cottage Grove
Woodbury JHS, 2665 WOODLANE DR 55125
 (—), prin.
Woodbury MS, 1425 SCHOOL DR 55125
 Jim Louma, prin.
Royal Oaks ES, 7335 STEEPLEVIEW RD 55125
 Kenneth Kovatch, prin.
ES, 1251 SCHOOL DR 55125 – (—), prin.

Worthington, Nobles Co., Pop. Code 7
Worthington SD
Sch. Sys. Enr. Code 4
Supt. – Bruce Thomas, P O BOX 878 56187
Central ES, 1215 4TH AVE 56187
 Gary Brandt, prin.
West ES, 117 11TH AVE 56187
 John Johnson, prin.

___

St. Mary ES, 12TH ST & 8TH AVE 56187

Wrenshall, Carlton Co., Pop. Code 2
Wrenshall SD
Sch. Sys. Enr. Code 2
Supt. – E. Schulz, P O BOX 68 55797
ES, P O BOX 68 55797 – Dennis Nelson, prin.

Wright, Carlton Co., Pop. Code 2
Cromwell SD
Supt. – See Cromwell
ES 55798 – Allan Karki, prin.

Wykoff, Fillmore Co., Pop. Code 2
Wykoff SD
Sch. Sys. Enr. Code 2
Supt. – Michael Smith, P O BOX 96 55990
ES, P O BOX 96 55990 – Dianne Dodge, prin.

Wyoming, Anoka Co., Pop. Code 4
Forest Lake SD
Supt. – See Forest Lake
Linwood ES, 21900 TYPO CREEK DR NE 55092
 Harold Baland, prin.
ES, 5397 266TH ST 55092
 Michael Conway, prin.

Young America, Carver Co., Pop. Code 4

___

St. John's Lutheran ES
 RURAL ROUTE 01 BOX 122A 55397

Zimmerman, Sherburne Co., Pop. Code 4
Elk River SD
Supt. – See Elk River
ES, 25959 4TH STREET W 55398
 John Etnier, prin.

Zumbrota, Goodhue Co., Pop. Code 4
Zumbrota SD
Sch. Sys. Enr. Code 3
Supt. – J. Neuman, 705 MILL ST 55992
ES, 799 MILL ST 55992 – David Fleming, prin.

MISSISSIPPI

STATE DEPARTMENT OF EDUCATION
Sillers State Office Building
P.O. Box 771, Jackson 39205
(601) 359-3513

Superintendent of Education	Richard Boyd
Deputy Superintendent	Thomas Saterfiel
Associate Superintendent Administration & Finance	Judy Rhodes
Special Assistant Research, Planning, Policy & Development	Roy DeBerry
Special Assistant External Relations	Andrew Mullins, Jr.
Associate Superintendent Vocational-Technical Education	Elwyn Wheat
Associate Superintendent Programs	Walter Moore

STATE BOARD OF EDUCATION
Joe Ross, Jr., *Chairperson*   Vicksburg

PUBLIC, PRIVATE, AND PAROCHIAL ELEMENTARY SCHOOLS

Aberdeen, Monroe Co., Pop. Code 6
Aberdeen SSD
Sch. Sys. Enr. Code 4
Supt. – John Curlee, P O BOX 607 39730
Shivers JHS, P O BOX 607 39730
  Preston Belle, prin.
ES, P O BOX 607 39730 – Jannette Peugh, prin.
MS, P O BOX 607 39730 – R. Grimes, prin.
Vine Street ES, P O BOX 607 39730
  Terry Cox, prin.
Other Schools – See Prairie

Monroe County SD
Sch. Sys. Enr. Code 5
Supt. – J. Hathcock, P O BOX 847 39730
Other Schools – See Amory, Becker, Greenwood
  Springs, Hamilton, Smithville

Ackerman, Choctaw Co., Pop. Code 4
Choctaw County SD
Sch. Sys. Enr. Code 4
Supt. – Ty Cobb, P O BOX 398 39735
ES, P O BOX 310 39735 – Terry Stacy, prin.
Other Schools – See French Camp, Weir

Agricola, George Co.
George County SD
Supt. – See Lucedale
ES, P O BOX 12 39452 – Timothy Havard, prin.

Amory, Monroe Co., Pop. Code 6
Amory SSD
Sch. Sys. Enr. Code 4
Supt. – Dr. Holace Morris
HIGHWAY 25 N & CRUMP BLVD 38821
MS, P O BOX 426 38821 – Travis Beard, prin.
ES, CONCORD DR 38821 – Bill Miley, prin.
Amory West ES, 111TH ST 38821 – J. Lewis, prin.

Monroe County SD
Supt. – See Aberdeen
Hatley Attendance Center
  RURAL ROUTE 03 38821 – J. Parham, prin.

Anguilla, Sharkey Co., Pop. Code 3
Anguilla SD
Sch. Sys. Enr. Code 3
Supt. – James Nicholson, 101 HOLLAND ST 38721
ES, P O BOX 296 38721 – Thomas Wicks, prin.

Arcola, Washington Co., Pop. Code 3
Hollandale Cons. SD
Supt. – See Hollandale
Chambers ES, P O BOX 366 38722
  Mary Kellum, prin.

Ashland, Benton Co., Pop. Code 3
Benton County SD
Sch. Sys. Enr. Code 4
Supt. – Thomas Doyle, P O BOX 247 38603
MS, RURAL ROUTE 02 BOX 19 38603
  Walter Tucker, prin.
ES, P O BOX 187 38603 – Palmer Givhan, prin.
Other Schools – See Hickory Flat

Avon, Washington Co.
Western Line Cons. SD
Sch. Sys. Enr. Code 4
Supt. – Dave Dunaway, P O BOX 319 38723
Riverside Attendance Center, P O BOX 339 38723
  Linda Dick, prin.
Other Schools – See Glen Allan, Greenville

Baldwyn, Prentiss Co., Pop. Code 5
Baldwyn SSD
Sch. Sys. Enr. Code 4
Supt. – George Ayers, 512 HIGHWAY 45 N 38824
MS, 57 S JONES 38824 – William Chambers, prin.
ES, 452 HIGHWAY 45 N 38824
  Fred Wilson, prin.

Bassfield, Jefferson Davis Co., Pop. Code 2
Jefferson Davis County SD
Supt. – See Prentiss
ES, P O BOX 8 39421 – W. Graves, prin.

Batesville, Panola Co., Pop. Code 5
South Panola Cons. SD
Sch. Sys. Enr. Code 5
Supt. – David Cole, 209 BOOTHE ST 38606
JHS, HIGHWAY 51 N 38606
  Robert Chapman, prin.
ES, 110 COLLEGE ST 38606 – John Farris, prin.
IS, 200 COLLEGE ST 38606 – Robert Hyde, prin.
Other Schools – See Pope

Bay Saint Louis, Hancock Co., Pop. Code 6
Bay St. Louis-Waveland SD
Sch. Sys. Enr. Code 4
Supt. – Dr. Roger Oge
  750 BLUE MEADOW ROAD 39520
Bay JHS, ULMAN AVE 39520
  Woods Alliston, prin.
North Bay ES, DUNBAR AVE 39520
  Rodney Fisher, prin.
Other Schools – See Waveland

Hancock County SD
Sch. Sys. Enr. Code 5
Supt. – Terrell Randolph, P O BOX 269 39520
Other Schools – See Lakeshore, Pass Christian,
  Pearlington

Bay St. Louis Catholic ES
  301 S SECOND ST 39520

Bay Springs, Jasper Co., Pop. Code 4
West Jasper Cons. SD
Sch. Sys. Enr. Code 4
Supt. – Charles Lyle, P O BOX 610 39422
MS, P O BOX 587 39422 – Rex Keeton, prin.
ES, P O BOX 927 39422 – Lois McBrayer, prin.
Other Schools – See Stringer

Beaumont, Perry Co., Pop. Code 4
Perry County SD
Supt. – See New Augusta
ES, RURAL ROUTE 01 BOX 8 39423
  Nancy Tice, prin.

Becker, Monroe Co.
Monroe County SD
Supt. – See Aberdeen
ES, HWY 25 S 38825 – Sam Willis, prin.

Belmont, Tishomingo Co., Pop. Code 4
Tishomingo County SD
Supt. – See Iuka
Belmont Attendance Center, P O BOX 250 38827
  John Moore, prin.

Belzoni, Humphreys Co., Pop. Code 5
Humphreys County SD
Sch. Sys. Enr. Code 5
Supt. – Lonnie Haynes, P O BOX 678 39038
Humphreys County JHS, P O BOX 678 39038
  Tommy Johnson, prin.

Humphreys County PS, P O BOX 678 39038
  W. Smith, Jr., prin.
Humphreys County MS, P O BOX 678 39038
  B. Stewart, prin.

Benoit, Bolivar Co., Pop. Code 2
Bolivar County Cons. SD 2
Sch. Sys. Enr. Code 2
Supt. – Willie Grissom, P O BOX 188 38725
Nugent Center ES, HWY 1 S 38725
  Bertha Rodgers, prin.

Bentonia, Yazoo Co., Pop. Code 3
Yazoo County SD
Supt. – See Yazoo City
Gibbs ES, RURAL ROUTE 01 BOX 229 39040
  Donald Shaffer, prin.

Biloxi, Harrison Co., Pop. Code 8
Biloxi SSD
Sch. Sys. Enr. Code 6
Supt. – Tom Burnham, P O BOX 168 39533
Michel MS, RYAN AVE 39530 – Susan Hunt, prin.
Nichols MS, 950 BELLMAN ST 39530
  Derbert Dilworth, prin.
Beauvoir ES, DEWEY LAWRENCE ROAD 39531
  Nolan Broussard, prin.
Davis ES, 834 SAINT MARY BLVD 39531
  Glendon Johnson, prin.
Du Kate ES, 502 E HOWARD AVE 39530
  Paul Tisdale, prin.
Gorenflo ES, 921 LAMEUSE ST 39530
  Terri Leavitt, prin.
Howard II ES, 1501 E HOWARD AVE 39530
  Beryl Dupont, prin.
Lopez ES, 300 SAINT JOHN AVE 39530
  Iris Brantley, prin.
Popps Ferry ES, 600 NELSON ROAD 39531
  Percy Howard, prin.
Other Schools – See Handsboro

Harrison County SD
Supt. – See Gulfport
d'Iberville MS, 225 CHURCH AVE 39532
  Tom Moore, prin.
D'Iberville ES, RURAL ROUTE 05 BOX 57 39532
  Bill Herrlich, prin.
Woolmarket ES
  RURAL ROUTE 01 BOX 718 39532
  James Lindsay, prin.

Jackson County SD
Supt. – See Pascagoula
St. Martin Attendance Center
  16300 LEMOYNE BLVD 39532 – Joe Barlow, prin.

Nativity B V M School
  1028 E BEACH BLVD 39530
Our Lady of Fatima School, 3800 PASS RD 39531
Sacred Heart School
  10482 LEMOYNE BLVD 39532

Blue Mountain, Tippah Co., Pop. Code 3
South Tippah Cons. SD
Supt. – See Ripley
ES, P O BOX 97 38610 – Larry Robbins, prin.

Blue Springs, Union Co., Pop. Code 2
Union County SD
Supt. – See New Albany
East Union Attendance Center
  RURAL ROUTE 03 38828 – Sidney Priest, prin.

Bogue Chitto, Lincoln Co., Pop. Code 2
Lincoln County SD
Supt. – See Brookhaven
Bogue Chitto Attendance Center
HIGHWAY 51   39629 – Stanton Long, prin.

Bolton, Hinds Co., Pop. Code 3
Hinds County SD
Supt. – See Raymond
ES, P O BOX 247   39041 – Joseph Brown, prin.

Booneville, Prentiss Co., Pop. Code 6
Booneville SSD
Sch. Sys. Enr. Code 4
Supt. – R. Griffin, P O BOX 387   38829
Anderson PS, 111 ANDERSON ST   38829
Lee Stewart, prin.
MS, 100 GEORGE E ALLEN DR   38829
Howard Long, prin.

Prentiss County SD
Sch. Sys. Enr. Code 5
Supt. – Lex Cain, P O BOX 179   38829
Jumpertown Attendance Center
RURAL ROUTE 03   38829 – Frank Henry, prin.
Thrasher Attendance Center
RURAL ROUTE 01   38829 – Jack Robinson, prin.
Hills Chapel ES
RURAL ROUTE 05 BOX 138   38829
Bernel Smith, prin.
Other Schools – See Marietta, Wheeler

Boyle, Bolivar Co.
Cleveland SD
Supt. – See Cleveland
Bell ES, P O BOX 368   38730 – Jurist Green, prin.

Brandon, Rankin Co., Pop. Code 6
Rankin County SD
Sch. Sys. Enr. Code 7
Supt. – Dr. Michael Vinson, P O BOX 1359   39042
MS, 200 SCHOOL ROAD   39042
Wilson Taylor, prin.
ES, 125 OVERBY ST   39042 – Elinor Comfort, prin.
Northwest ES, 500 VINE DR   39042
Jerry Compton, prin.
Pisgah ES, 2120 HIGHWAY 471   39042
Floydist Martin, prin.
Stevens ES, 206 S COLLEGE ST   39042
Ruth Watkins, prin.
Other Schools – See Florence, Pelahatchie, Puckett,
Richland

Brookhaven, Lincoln Co., Pop. Code 7
Brookhaven SSD
Sch. Sys. Enr. Code 5
Supt. – George Brumfield, P O BOX 540   39601
ES, P O BOX 922   39601 – Rita Rich, prin.
Lipsey MS, P O BOX 712   39601
Thomas Fauver, prin.
Martin ES, P O BOX 378   39601
Pamela Fearn, prin.
Mullins MS, 711 S HAMILTON ST   39601
James Tillman, prin.

Lawrence County SD
Supt. – See Monticello
Monticello ES, P O BOX 339   39601
Celeste Ward, prin.

Lincoln County SD
Sch. Sys. Enr. Code 5
Supt. – Harold Smith, P O BOX 826   39601
Enterprise Attendance Center
RURAL ROUTE 04   39601 – Billy Britt, prin.
Star Attendance Center
RURAL ROUTE 03 BOX 486   39601
Robert Allen, prin.
West Lincoln Attendance Center
RURAL ROUTE 05   39601 – Wayne Myers, prin.
Other Schools – See Bogue Chitto

Brooklyn, Forrest Co., Pop. Code 2
Forrest County SD
Supt. – See Hattiesburg
South Forrest ES
RURAL ROUTE 01 BOX 301   39425
Ronald Dyal, prin.

Brooksville, Noxubee Co., Pop. Code 4
Noxubee County SD
Supt. – See Macon
Wilson ES, P O BOX E   39739
Rev. Arthur Townsend, prin.

Bruce, Calhoun Co., Pop. Code 4
Calhoun County SD
Supt. – See Pittsboro
MS, P O BOX 248   38915 – W. Murphree, prin.
ES, P O BOX 248   38915 – Mike Young, prin.

Buckatunna, Wayne Co., Pop. Code 2
Wayne County SD
Supt. – See Waynesboro
ES, P O BOX 90   39322 – Sandra Waller, prin.

Burnsville, Tishomingo Co., Pop. Code 3
Tishomingo County SD
Supt. – See Iuka
Burnsville Attendance Center, P O BOX A   38833
Charles Skinner, prin.

Byhalia, Marshall Co., Pop. Code 3
Marshall County SD
Supt. – See Holly Springs
Henry ES, P O BOX 429   38611
Alva Gipson, prin.

Caledonia, Lowndes Co., Pop. Code 2
Lowndes County SD
Supt. – See Columbus
MS, 100 ACADEMY STREET   39740
(—), prin.
ES, 100 ACADEMY STREET   39740
Roger Hill, prin.

Calhoun City, Calhoun Co., Pop. Code 4
Calhoun County SD
Supt. – See Pittsboro
MS, P O BOX 559   38916 – Dale Hays, prin.
ES, P O BOX 559   38916 – Roger Hudson, prin.

Camden, Madison Co., Pop. Code 3
Madison County SD
Supt. – See Canton
Jackson Attendance Center, P O BOX 8   39045
George Cole, prin.

Sacred Heart Missions School
RURAL ROUTE 02 BOX 14   39045

Canton, Madison Co., Pop. Code 7
Canton SSD
Sch. Sys. Enr. Code 5
Supt. – Joe Galloway, 403 LINCOLN ST   39046
ES, S HARGON ST   39046
Richard MacNealy, prin.
McNeal ES, 364 OWEN ST   39046
Alice Scott, prin.
Nichols MS, 434 TROLIO ST   39046
George Harris, prin.

Madison County SD
Sch. Sys. Enr. Code 5
Supt. – C. Melvin Ray
RURAL ROUTE 01   BOX 47-A   39046
Branson ES, RURAL ROUTE 04 BOX 120-A   39046
George Gilreath, prin.
Other Schools – See Camden, Flora, Madison,
Ridgeland

Holy Child Jesus School, 315 GARRETT ST   39046

Carriere, Pearl River Co., Pop. Code 2
Pearl River County SD
Supt. – See Poplarville
Pearl River Central ES, P O BOX 238   39426
Charles Powell, prin.

Carrollton, Carroll Co., Pop. Code 2
Carroll County SD
Sch. Sys. Enr. Code 4
Supt. – James Alford, LEXINGTON ST   38917
Other Schools – See North Carrollton, Vaiden

Carthage, Leake Co., Pop. Code 5
Leake County SD
Sch. Sys. Enr. Code 5
Supt. – Joe Kea, P O BOX 478   39051
Edinburg Attendance Center
RURAL ROUTE 08   39051 – John McKinney, prin.
Thomastown Attendance Center
RURAL ROUTE 02 BOX 345   39051
Shelton Wilder, prin.
JHS, 801 PRESLEY ROAD   39051
Bobby Boone, prin.
ES, VANBUREN ST   39051 – Ray McGee, prin.
Other Schools – See Walnut Grove

Centreville, Wilkinson Co., Pop. Code 4
Wilkinson County SD
Supt. – See Woodville
Finch ES, P O BOX 130   39631
Willard Chrisentery, prin.

Charleston, Tallahatchie Co., Pop. Code 5
East Tallahatchie Cons. SD
Sch. Sys. Enr. Code 4
Supt. – Clyde Robinson, P O BOX 310   38921
MS, P O BOX 310   38921 – David Alford, prin.
ES, P O BOX 310   38921 – Elaine Venable, prin.
Charleston IS, P O BOX 310   38921
David Hargett, prin.

Clara, Wayne Co., Pop. Code 2
Wayne County SD
Supt. – See Waynesboro
Clara Attendance Center, P O BOX 90   39324
Jerry Nobles, prin.

Clarksdale, Coahoma Co., Pop. Code 7
Clarksdale SSD
Sch. Sys. Enr. Code 5
Supt. – Dr. Robert Ellard, P O BOX 1088   38614
Hall ES, P O BOX 1088   38614
Mertha Jackson, prin.
Heidelberg ES, P O BOX 1088   38614
Shirley Williams, prin.
Kirkpatrick ES, P O BOX 1088   38614
Dave Jennings, prin.
Myrtle Hall ES, P O BOX 1088   38614
Tim Burrel, prin.
Oliver ES, P O BOX 1088   38614
Jimmie Pittman, prin.
Riverton IS, P O BOX 1088   38614
John Starling, prin.
Riverton PS, P O BOX 1088   38614
Leonard Henderson, prin.
Washington ES, P O BOX 1088   38614
Louis Jackson, prin.

Coahoma County SD
Sch. Sys. Enr. Code 5
Supt. – Sherard Shaw, P O BOX 820   38614

Coahoma County JHS, LEE DRIVE   38614
Robert Willis, prin.
Roundaway ES
RURAL ROUTE 02 BOX 151   38614
Paul Johnson, prin.
Sherard ES, RURAL ROUTE 03 BOX 162   38614
Larry Jackson, prin.
Other Schools – See Friars Point, Jonestown, Lyon

Immaculate Conception School
520 RITCHIE AVE   38614
St. Elizabeth School, 107 CLARK ST   38614

Cleveland, Bolivar Co., Pop. Code 7
Cleveland SD
Sch. Sys. Enr. Code 5
Supt. – James Langin, 305 MERRITT DRIVE   38732
Eastwood JHS, 715 N PEARMAN ROAD   38732
General Burton, prin.
Cypress Park ES, 725 N PEARMAN RD   38732
James Wardlow, prin.
Nailor ES, CROSS ST   38732
James Williams, prin.
Parks ES, TERRACE ROAD   38732
Jerry Kitchings, prin.
Pearman ES, 420 ROBINSON DR   38732
Tommy Waldrup, prin.
Other Schools – See Boyle

Clinton, Hinds Co., Pop. Code 7
Clinton SSD
Sch. Sys. Enr. Code 6
Supt. – Dr. Virgil Belue, P O BOX 300   39056
JHS, 401 COLLEGE ST   39056
Danny Pepper, prin.
Clinton Park ES, 911 OLD VICKSBURG RD   39056
Valerie Wiggins, prin.
Eastside MS, 201 EASTHAVEN DR   39056
Virginia Maugh, prin.
Lovett MS, 2002 W NORTHSIDE DR   39056
Dr. Limmie Flowers, prin.
Northside ES, 1111 OLD VICKSBURG RD   39056
Shelly Quick, prin.

Coffeeville, Yalobusha Co., Pop. Code 4
Coffeeville Cons. SD
Sch. Sys. Enr. Code 3
Supt. – Dr. Trois Hill, 627 OKLAHOMA ST   38922
ES, 211 TILLATOBA ST   38922 – Sue Clifton, prin.
Other Schools – See Oakland

Coldwater, Tate Co., Pop. Code 4
Tate County SD
Supt. – See Senatobia
ES, P O BOX F   38618 – Allan Amburn, prin.
East Tate ES, RURAL ROUTE 02 BOX 488   38618
Woodrow Williams, prin.

Collins, Covington Co., Pop. Code 4
Covington County SD
Sch. Sys. Enr. Code 5
Supt. – Ronald Graves, P O BOX 1269   39428
ES, P O BOX 160   39428 – Herman Campbell, prin.
Hopewell ES, RURAL ROUTE 04   39428
Irvin Keys, prin.
Other Schools – See Mount Olive, Seminary

Collinsville, Lauderdale Co., Pop. Code 2
Lauderdale County SD
Supt. – See Meridian
West Lauderdale JHS
RURAL ROUTE 03   BOX 525   39325
Elaine Richardson, prin.
West Lauderdale ES
RURAL ROUTE 03 BOX 525   39325
Marvin Richardson, prin.

Columbia, Marion Co., Pop. Code 6
Columbia SD
Sch. Sys. Enr. Code 4
Supt. – Dr. Milton Walker, P O BOX 271   39429
Jefferson MS, 1200 PEACE ST   39429
Dr. Jerry Sharp, prin.
MS, 401 MARY ST   39429 – Donald Hales, prin.
PS, 501 DALE ST   39429 – Glenda Shivers, prin.
PS, 913 WEST AVE   39429 – Gayle Knight, prin.

Marion County SD
Sch. Sys. Enr. Code 5
Supt. – Dr. Thomas Blakeney
COURTHOUSE SQUARE   39429
East Marion Attendance Center
RURAL ROUTE 05   BOX 496   39429
Carnell Lewis, prin.
Other Schools – See Foxworth

Columbus, Lowndes Co., Pop. Code 8
Columbus Municipal SD
Sch. Sys. Enr. Code 6
Supt. – Thomas Cooley, P O BOX 1308   39701
Brandon ES, 2630 MCARTHUR DR   39701
Gerald Scallions, prin.
Coleman MS, 723 22ND ST S   39701
Otis Payton, prin.
Fairview ES, 225 AIRLINE RD   39702
Gladys Cash, prin.
Franklin Academy ES, 501 3RD AVE N   39701
Robert Sanford, prin.
Hughes MS, 1820 23RD ST N   39701
Marshall Wicks, prin.
Hunt MS, 924 20TH ST N   39701
Johnny Johnson, prin.
Mitchell MS, 1315 15TH ST S   39701
George Brooks, prin.
Sale ES, 520 WARPATH RD   39702
Rebecca Taylor, prin.

Stokes Beard ES, 424 24TH ST N   39701
  Dixie Butler, prin.
Union Academy ES, 1425 10TH AVE N   39701
  Otis Barry, prin.
Other Schools – See Columbus A F B

Lowndes County SD
Sch. Sys. Enr. Code 5
Supt. – Troy Holder, 505 2ND AVE N   39701
New Hope MS, RURAL ROUTE 06 BOX 1   39702
  Donnie Goss, prin.
New Hope ES, RURAL ROUTE 06 BOX 11   39702
  Sammy Townsend, prin.
Plum Grove ES
  RURAL ROUTE 01 BOX 105   39701
  Mary Woodrick, prin.
West Lowndes ES
  RURAL ROUTE 03 BOX 355   39701
  Fred Young, prin.
Other Schools – See Caledonia, Crawford

St. Mary's School, 223 N BROWDER ST   39702

Columbus A F B, Lowndes Co.
Columbus Municipal SD
Supt. – See Columbus
Cook JHS, 2217 7TH STREET N   39701
  A. Eaves, prin.

Como, Panola Co., Pop. Code 4
North Panola Consolidated SD
Supt. – See Sardis
ES, P O BOX 70   38619 – Eugene Trammell, prin.

Corinth, Alcorn Co., Pop. Code 7
Alcorn County SD
Sch. Sys. Enr. Code 5
Supt. – Tony Parker, P O BOX 1419   38834
Biggersbille ES
  RURAL ROUTE 04 BOX 349   38834
  Joe Duncan, prin.
Other Schools – See Glen, Kossuth, Rienzi, Walnut

Corinth SSD
Sch. Sys. Enr. Code 4
Supt. – Dr. O. Gann, 1101 CRUISE ST   38834
East Corinth ES, 3RD & MEEKS ST   38834
  Myra Caruth, prin.
South Corinth MS, SCALE ST   38834
  Edwin Davis, prin.
West Corinth ES, WENASOGA ROAD   38834
  Esther Timmons, prin.

Crawford, Lowndes Co., Pop. Code 2
Lowndes County SD
Supt. – See Columbus
ES, GENERAL DELIVERY   39743 – A. Beal, prin.

Oktibbeha County SD
Supt. – See Starkville
Moor Attendance Center
  RURAL ROUTE 01   39743 – Charles Davis, prin.

Crenshaw, Panola Co., Pop. Code 4
North Panola Consolidated SD
Supt. – See Sardis
ES, P O BOX 250   38621 – W. Franklin, prin.

Crowder, Panola Co., Pop. Code 3
Quitman County SD
Supt. – See Marks
ES, P O BOX 68   38622 – Leroy Matthews, Jr., prin.

Crystal Springs, Copiah Co., Pop. Code 5
Copiah County SD
Supt. – See Hazlehurst
MS, P O BOX 520   39059 – Carl Stokes, prin.

Decatur, Newton Co., Pop. Code 4
Newton County SD
Sch. Sys. Enr. Code 4
Supt. – Ken Pouncey, P O BOX 97   39327
Boler ES, P O BOX 249   39327
  Jeanette Thrash, prin.
Other Schools – See Hickory, Little Rock

De Kalb, Kemper Co., Pop. Code 4
Kemper County SSD
Sch. Sys. Enr. Code 4
Supt. – Wayne Killebrew, P O BOX 219   39328
West Kemper ES, P O BOX 250   39328
  Callie Robinson, prin.
Other Schools – See Scooba

Drew, Sunflower Co., Pop. Code 5
Drew SSD
Sch. Sys. Enr. Code 4
Supt. – W. Terry, 117 W SHAW AVE   38737
Hunter MS, P O BOX 287   38737
  Robert Hunter, prin.
James ES, 400 S BOULEVARD   38737
  Jo Freeman, prin.

Duck Hill, Montgomery Co., Pop. Code 3
Montgomery County SD
Supt. – See Winona
ES, P O BOX 428   38925 – J. Morgan, prin.

Duncan, Bolivar Co., Pop. Code 3
Bolivar County Cons. SD 3
Supt. – See Shelby
Brooks ES, P O BOX 168   38740
  Casper Hall, prin.

Durant, Holmes Co., Pop. Code 5
Durant SSD
Sch. Sys. Enr. Code 3
Supt. – Curtis Burrell, P O BOX 429   39063

Durant Attendance Center, HIGHWAY 51 S   39063
  Kermit Hutchins, prin.

Holmes County SD
Supt. – See Lexington
Sullivan Attendance Center
  HIGHWAY 51 S   39063 – John McGee, prin.

Ecru, Pontotoc Co., Pop. Code 3
Pontotoc County SD
Supt. – See Pontotoc
North Pontotoc Attendance Center
  RURAL ROUTE 01 BOX 252D   38841
  Larry Godfrey, prin.

Edwards, Hinds Co., Pop. Code 4
Hinds County SD
Supt. – See Raymond
ES, P O BOX 167   39066
  Booker Ducksworth, prin.

Ellisville, Jones Co., Pop. Code 5
Jones County SD
Sch. Sys. Enr. Code 6
Supt. – Jay Mason
  RURAL ROUTE 04 BOX 642A   39437
Ellisville PS, DEASON AT DEVALL   39437
  Steve Thrash, prin.
Ellisville MS, DEASON AT DEVALL   39437
  LaTrelle Touchstone, prin.
Other Schools – See Laurel, Moselle, Sandersville,
  Soso

Enterprise, Clarke Co., Pop. Code 3
Enterprise Cons. SD
Sch. Sys. Enr. Code 3
Supt. – Michael Taylor, P O BOX A   39330
ES, P O BOX 247   39330 – Ernest Smallwood, prin.

Eupora, Webster Co., Pop. Code 4
Webster County SD
Supt. – See Walthall
MS, 406 W FOX AVE   39744 – William Reed, prin.
ES, 406 W FOX AVE   39744
  Thomas Patterson, prin.

Falkner, Tippah Co., Pop. Code 2
North Tippah SD
Supt. – See Tiplersville
ES, P O BOX 146   38629 – Betty McMillin, prin.

Fayette, Jefferson Co., Pop. Code 4
Jefferson County SD
Sch. Sys. Enr. Code 4
Supt. – Daniel Smith, P O BOX 157   39069
Jefferson County JHS, P O BOX 2785   39069
  Seth Ballard, prin.
Jefferson County ES
  RURAL ROUTE 02 BOX 35C   39069
  William Billups, prin.

Flora, Madison Co., Pop. Code 4
Madison County SD
Supt. – See Canton
East Flora Attendance Center, P O BOX J   39071
  Thomas Nutter, prin.
ES, P O BOX 159   39071 – Hubert Smith, prin.

Florence, Rankin Co., Pop. Code 4
Rankin County SD
Supt. – See Brandon
McLaurin Attendance Center
  RURAL ROUTE 01 BOX 412   39073
  Terry Brister, prin.
MS, P O BOX 159   39073 – Fulton Rushing, prin.
ES, P O BOX 189   39073 – Nancy Ranager, prin.

Forest, Scott Co., Pop. Code 6
Forest Municipal SD
Sch. Sys. Enr. Code 4
Supt. – Richard Hill, 511 CLEVELAND ST   39074
Hawkins MS, 803 E OAK ST   39074
  James Harper, prin.
ES, 511 CLEVELAND ST   39074
  Sammye Webb, prin.

Scott County SD
Sch. Sys. Enr. Code 5
Supt. – James Johnson, COURTHOUSE   39074
Scott Central Attendance Center
  RURAL ROUTE 05 BOX 124   39074
  Thomas Woodfin, prin.
Other Schools – See Lake, Morton, Sebastopol

Foxworth, Marion Co., Pop. Code 3
Marion County SD
Supt. – See Columbia
West Marion PS, P O BOX 6   39483
  Jean Hahn, prin.

French Camp, Choctaw Co., Pop. Code 2
Choctaw County SD
Supt. – See Ackerman
ES, RURAL ROUTE 01   39745
  Rebekah Rogers, prin.

Friars Point, Coahoma Co., Pop. Code 4
Coahoma County SD
Supt. – See Clarksdale
ES, P O BOX 68   38631 – James Shelby, Jr., prin.

Fulton, Itawamba Co., Pop. Code 5
Itawamba County SD
Sch. Sys. Enr. Code 5
Supt. – F. Wiygul, 201 W MAIN ST   38843
Dorsey ES, RURAL ROUTE 05   38843
  Jerry Dulaney, prin.
ES, 605 S CUMMINGS605   38843
  Russell Loden, prin.

Other Schools – See Golden, Mantachie, Tremont

Gautier, Jackson Co., Pop. Code 4
Pascagoula SSD
Supt. – See Pascagoula
College Park ES, 2617 LADNIER RD   39553
  Susan McLaurin, prin.
ES, 2420 OLD SPANISH TRL   39553
  Joanne Wavra, prin.
Singing River ES, 4601 VANCLEAVE RD   39553
  Mary Jean Deakle, prin.

Glen, Alcorn Co.
Alcorn County SD
Supt. – See Corinth
Alcorn Central ES
  RURAL ROUTE 02 BOX 300   38846
  Paul Vandiver, prin.
Glendale ES, P O BOX 69   38846
  Robert Strickland, prin.

Glen Allan, Washington Co.
Western Line Cons. SD
Supt. – See Avon
Glen Allan ES, P O BOX 209   38744
  Wanda Dees, prin.

Glendora, Tallahatchie Co., Pop. Code 2
West Tallahatchie Cons. SD
Supt. – See Webb
Black Bayou ES, P O BOX 190   38928
  Elbert Burten, prin.

Gloster, Amite Co., Pop. Code 4
Amite County SD
Supt. – See Liberty
ES, P O BOX 220   39638 – Jo Ann Kaelin, prin.

Golden, Itawamba Co., Pop. Code 2
Itawamba County SD
Supt. – See Fulton
Fairview ES, RURAL ROUTE 01   38847
  Lonnie Senter, prin.

Goodman, Holmes Co., Pop. Code 4
Holmes County SD
Supt. – See Lexington
Goodman-Pickens ES
  RURAL ROUTE 01 BOX 23A   39079
  James Cain, prin.

Greenville, Washington Co., Pop. Code 8
Greenville SSD
Sch. Sys. Enr. Code 6
Supt. – Dr. Nolan Vickers, P O BOX 749   38702
Coleman JHS, 400 HIGHWAY 1 N   38701
  Sammie Felton, prin.
Solomon MS, 556 BOWMAN BLVD   38701
  Pat Caldwell, prin.
Akin ES, 361 BOWAN BLVD   38701
  Dr. Oneita Keith, prin.
Armstrong ES, 528 REDBUG   38701
  Hurtice Howard, prin.
Boyd ES, 1021 S COLORADO ST   38703
  Finley Edwards, prin.
Darling ES, 242 BROADWAY   38701
  Ira Dorsett, Jr., prin.
Fulwiler ES, 699 DUBLIN ST   38703
  Chris Gelenter, prin.
Manning ES, 430 HIGHWAY 1 N   38701
  Malindo Durastanti, prin.
McBride ES, 438 N POPLAR ST   38701
  Mary Singleton, prin.
Stern ES, 522 MCALLISTER ST   38701
  Carolyn Kurts, prin.
Trigg ES, 3304 LINCOLN DR   38703
  Robert Stevens, prin.
Webb ES, 600 S HARVEY ST   38701
  Thomas Williams, prin.
Weddington ES, 668 SAMPSON RD   38701
  Helen Moore, prin.

Western Line Cons. SD
Supt. – See Avon
O'Bannon Attendance Center
  P O BOX 5816   38704 – H. Remond, prin.

Our Lady of Lourdes School
  1600 E REED ROAD   38701

Greenwood, Leflore Co., Pop. Code 7
Greenwood SSD
Sch. Sys. Enr. Code 5
Supt. – Lester Beason, P O BOX 1497   38930
Davis MS, 400 COTTON STREET   38930
  Robert Sims, prin.
Threadgill MS, 1001 BROAD STREET   38930
  Wallace Smith, prin.
Bankston ES, 1200 GRAND BLVD   38930
  W. Williamson, prin.
Davis ES, 400 COTTON ST   38930
  Doris Banks, prin.
Dickerson ES, 100 E STONE ST   38930
  Vivian Redmond, prin.
Williams ES, 1300 CARROLLTON AVE   38930
  Jackie Harpole, prin.

Leflore County SD
Sch. Sys. Enr. Code 5
Supt. – Glenn Norwood, P O BOX 544   38930
East ES, MEADOWBROOK ROAD   38930
  Jackie Adams, prin.
Elzy ES, RURAL ROUTE 04 BOX 40   38930
  Clavis Thornton, prin.
Rising Sun ES, HWY 49 S   38930
  Willie Hall, prin.
Other Schools – See Itta Bena, Minter City

St. Francis School, HWY 82   38930

Greenwood Springs, Monroe Co.
Monroe County SD
Supt. – See Aberdeen
ES   38848 – Van Pearson, prin.

Grenada, Grenada Co., Pop. Code 7
Grenada SSD
Sch. Sys. Enr. Code 5
Supt. – Buddy Pender, P O BOX 878   38901
JHS, JONES ROAD   38901
    Margret Monteith Davis, prin.
Dotson ES, TELEGRAPH ST   38901
    Robert Wade, prin.
Horn MS, 423 S LINE ST   38901
    James Saxon, prin.
Tie Plant ES, RURAL ROUTE 04   38901
    Paul Portera, prin.
Wilson ES, TELEGRAPH ST   38901
    Sam Carollo, prin.

Gulfport, Harrison Co., Pop. Code 8
Gulfport SSD
Sch. Sys. Enr. Code 6
Supt. – Dr. W. Ray Strebeck, P O BOX 220   39502
28th Street ES, 2810 34TH AVE   39501
    Carolyn Rushing, prin.
Anniston Avenue ES
    2314 JONES MS STATION   39501
    Marilyn Holquist, prin.
Bayou View ES, 4898 WASHINGTON AVE   39507
    Nolena Stephens, prin.
Central ES, 1043 PASS RD   39501
    Linda Kremer, prin.
East Ward ES, 1525 THORNTON AVE   39501
    Ronnie Barnes, prin.
Gaston Point ES, 1501 MILLS AVE   39501
    Willie Carter, prin.
Pass Road ES, 37 PASS RD   39507
    Jean Nation, prin.
West ES, 1231 44TH AVE   39501
    Philip Terrell, prin.

Harrison County SD
Sch. Sys. Enr. Code 7
Supt. – Henry Arledge, P O BOX 1090   39502
North Gulfport MS, 4715 ILLINOIS AVE   39501
    C. Luckett, prin.
Bel Aire ES, RURAL ROUTE 04 BOX 1   39503
    Christine Skinner, prin.
Harrison Central ES
    RURAL ROUTE 11 BOX 3   39503
    Barney Hill, prin.
Lizana ES, RURAL ROUTE 02 BOX 264   39503
    Dawson Curtis, prin.
Lyman ES, RURAL ROUTE 03 BOX 225   39503
    Loretta Marks, prin.
Orange Grove MS
    RURAL ROUTE 11 BOX 465   39503
    Jack Clark, prin.
Other Schools – See Biloxi, Pass Christian, Saucier

St. James School, 603 W AVE   39507
St. John ES, 2415 17TH ST   39501

Gunnison, Bolivar Co., Pop. Code 3
West Bolivar SD
Supt. – See Rosedale
Woods ES, P O BOX 93   38746
    Alvin Collins, prin.

Guntown, Lee Co., Pop. Code 2
Lee County SD
Supt. – See Tupelo
ES, P O BOX 8   38849 – J. Hill, prin.

Hamilton, Monroe Co., Pop. Code 2
Monroe County SD
Supt. – See Aberdeen
Hamilton Attendance Center   39746
    Dale Beasley, prin.

Handsboro, Harrison Co.
Biloxi SSD
Supt. – See Biloxi
Fernwood MS, 2329 PASS ROAD   39501
    Ronnie Farris, prin.

Hattiesburg, Forrest Co., Pop. Code 8
Forrest County SD
Sch. Sys. Enr. Code 5
Supt. – Walter Cartier, 607 N MAIN ST   39401
Dixie ES, RURAL ROUTE 09 BOX 1810   39401
    Linda Steele, prin.
North Forrest ES
    RURAL ROUTE 01 BOX 709   39401
    Lavon Pierce, prin.
Rawls Springs ES
    RURAL ROUTE 15 BOX 984   39402
    Faye Riley, prin.
Travillion ES, 316 TRAVILLION ST   39401
    Ervin Carr, prin.
Other Schools – See Brooklyn

Hattiesburg SSD
Sch. Sys. Enr. Code 6
Supt. – Gordon Walker, P O BOX 1569   39401
Bethune MS, 610 DUMAS AVE   39401
    Della Jones, prin.
Burney MS, IDA ST   39401 – Darleen Dale, prin.
Christian MS, 2207 W 7TH ST   39401
    Norris Clark, prin.
Jones ES, LOULA ST   39401
    Tom Blackwell, prin.

Thames ES, 2900 JAMESTOWN RD   39402
    Durward Rushton, prin.
Woodley ES, 2006 OFERRELL ST   39401
    Jeanette Dickens, prin.

Lamar County SD
Supt. – See Purvis
Oak Grove MS, RURAL ROUTE 04   39402
    Phil Harrison, prin.
Oak Grove ES, RURAL ROUTE 04   39402
    Judy Bookout, prin.

Petal SSD
Supt. – See Petal
Petal ES, RURAL ROUTE 08 BOX 1560   39401
    Ione Bond, prin.

Sacred Heart School, 608 SOUTHERN AVE   39401

Hazlehurst, Copiah Co., Pop. Code 5
Copiah County SD
Sch. Sys. Enr. Code 5
Supt. – Dale Sullivan, P O BOX 550   39083
Other Schools – See Crystal Springs, Wesson

Hazlehurst SSD
Sch. Sys. Enr. Code 4
Supt. – George French, 119 E FROST ST   39083
MS, 101 S HALEY ST   39083 – Lynn Beall, prin.
PS, 431 MONTICELLO ST   39083
    Marvin Minor, prin.

Heidelberg, Jaspar Co., Pop. Code 4
East Jasper SD
Sch. Sys. Enr. Code 4
Supt. – Napoleon Leverette, Jr., P O BOX N   39439
South Side ES, P O BOX 0   39439
    Robert Boone, prin.

Hernando, De Soto Co., Pop. Code 5
DeSoto County SD
Sch. Sys. Enr. Code 7
Supt. – Albert Broadway
    655 HOLLY SPRINGS ST NE   38632
MS, 893 OAK GROVE ROAD   38632
    Jerry Couch, prin.
ES, 631 RILEY ST   38632 – Dawne Blazevich, prin.
Other Schools – See Horn Lake, Olive Branch,
    Southhaven, Walls

Hickory, Newton Co., Pop. Code 3
Newton County SD
Supt. – See Decatur
Harris ES, P O BOX 158   39332
    Vickie Beckham, prin.

Hickory Flat, Benton Co., Pop. Code 2
Benton County SD
Supt. – See Ashland
S, P O BOX 99   38633 – Ollice Massengill, prin.

Hollandale, Washington Co., Pop. Code 5
Hollandale Cons. SD
Sch. Sys. Enr. Code 4
Supt. – Howard Sanders, P O BOX 128   38748
Simmons ES, P O BOX 366   38748
    Robert Woodruff, prin.
Other Schools – See Arcola

Holly Bluff, Yazoo Co.
Holly Bluff Cons. SD
Sch. Sys. Enr. Code 2
Supt. – Jack Nicholson, P O BOX 128   39088
Holly Bluff Line Attendance Center
    P O BOX 188   39088 – Jackie Nicholson, prin.

Holly Springs, Marshall Co., Pop. Code 6
Holly Springs SD
Sch. Sys. Enr. Code 4
Supt. – Dr. Fenton Peters
    165 N WALTHALL ST   38635
IS, 210 W VALLEY AVE   38635 – Judy Smith, prin.
PS, S MAURY ST   38635 – Willis Baston, prin.

Marshall County SD
Sch. Sys. Enr. Code 5
Supt. – Lawrence Autry, P O BOX 38   38635
Byers Attendance Center
    RURAL ROUTE 02 BOX 199   38635
    Homer Byers, prin.
Galena ES, RURAL ROUTE 05 BOX 216A   38635
    Brenda Anderson, prin.
Other Schools – See Byhalia, Potts Camp

Horn Lake, De Soto Co., Pop. Code 5
DeSoto County SD
Supt. – See Hernando
MS, 6870 CENTER ST E   38637
    Peggy Slaughter, prin.
ES, 6341 RIDGEWOOD RD   38637
    Dorothy Ann Smith, prin.

Houlka, Chickasaw Co., Pop. Code 3
Chickasaw County SD
Sch. Sys. Enr. Code 3
Supt. – Raymond Paden, P O BOX 480   38850
S   38850 – William Cotten, prin.

Houston, Chickasaw Co., Pop. Code 5
Houston SSD
Sch. Sys. Enr. Code 4
Supt. – C. Stevenson, P O BOX 351   38851
MS, P O BOX 192   38851 – Warren Cousin, prin.
ES, 123 S STARKVILLE ST   38851
    J. Dyson, Jr., prin.

Hurley, Jackson Co., Pop. Code 2
Jackson County SD
Supt. – See Pascagoula

East Central Attendance Center, P O BOX 13   39555
    Rucks Robinson, prin.

Indianola, Sunflower Co., Pop. Code 6
Indianola SSD
Sch. Sys. Enr. Code 5
Supt. – Robert Merritt, HIGHWAY 82 E   38751
Carver ES, P O BOX 943   38751
    Willie Farmer, prin.
Carver MS, P O BOX 944   38751
    Bobby Rushing, prin.
Lockard ES, 302 N COLLEGE AVE   38751
    Paul Jaudon, prin.

Sunflower County SD
Sch. Sys. Enr. Code 5
Supt. – Herbert Hargett, P O BOX 70   38751
Other Schools – See Inverness, Moorhead, Sunflower

Inverness, Sunflower Co., Pop. Code 4
Sunflower County SD
Supt. – See Indianola
ES, P O BOX 241   38753 – J. Pitts, prin.

Itta Bena, Leflore Co., Pop. Code 5
Leflore County SD
Supt. – See Greenwood
Leflore County Attendance Center
    P O BOX 564   38941 – Cedell Pulley, prin.
Rogers ES, P O BOX 345   38941
    Frank Harris, prin.

Iuka, Tishomingo Co., Pop. Code 5
Iuka SSD
Sch. Sys. Enr. Code 4
Supt. – Dr. Jerry Clay Stone
    507 W QUITMAN ROAD   38852
ES, OLD WHITEHOUSE ROAD   38852
    Charles Evans, prin.

Tishomingo County SD
Sch. Sys. Enr. Code 4
Supt. – Larry Green, 1008 HIGHWAY 25 S   38852
Other Schools – See Belmont, Burnsville, Tishomingo

Jackson, Hinds Co., Pop. Code 9
Hinds County SD
Supt. – See Raymond
Gary Road ES, RURAL ROUTE 05   39212
    Patsy Mayo, prin.

Jackson SSD
Sch. Sys. Enr. Code 8
Supt. – Dr. Robert Fortenberry
    P O BOX 2338   39225
Alternative ES, 750 N CONGRESS STREET   39202
    Brenda Thompson, prin.
Baker ES, 300 E SANTA CLAIR ST   39212
    Barbara Hogan, prin.
Barr ES, 1593 W CAPITOL ST   39203
    Lester Richmond, prin.
Boyd ES, 4521 BROADMEADOW DR   39206
    Dr. Billie Ainsworth, prin.
Bradley ES, 2601 IVANHOE AVE   39213
    Inez Johnson, prin.
Brown ES, 146 E ASH ST   39202
    Edward King, prin.
Casey ES, 2101 LAKE CIR   39211
    Donna Noblitt, prin.
Clausell ES, 3330 HARLEY ST   39209
    Etta Smith, prin.
Dawson ES, 4215 SUNSET DR   39213
    Jesse Stegall, prin.
French ES, 311 JOEL AVE   39209
    James Thorne, prin.
Galloway ES, 186 IDLEWILD ST   39203
    Gerilyn Thomas, prin.
Green ES, 610 FOREST AVE   39206
    Alfred Terry, prin.
Hopkins ES, 170 JOHN HOPKINS AVE   39209
    Ollie Gentry, prin.
Isable ES, 1716 ISABLE ST   39204
    Dr. Bettie McKinley, prin.
Johnson ES, 1339 OAKPARK DR   39213
    Edward Johnson, prin.
Key ES, 699 W MCDOWELL RD   39204
    David Sessums, prin.
Lake ES, 472 MOUNT VERNON AVE   39209
    Vera Grace, prin.
Lee ES, 330 JUDY ST   39212
    James Robertson, prin.
Lester ES, 2350 OAKHURST ST   39211
    Vivian Usry, prin.
Marshall ES, 2909 OAK FOREST DR   39212
    Peggy Brewer, prin.
McLeod ES, 1616 SANDLEWOOD PL   39211
    Archie King, prin.
Morrison ES, 1224 EMINENCE ROW   39213
    Loie Jones, prin.
North Jackson ES, 650 LAKE DR   39206
    Dr. Jether Clay, prin.
Oak Forest ES, 1831 SMALLWOOD DR   39212
    Jack Rice, prin.
Poindexter ES, 1017 ROBINSON ST   39203
    Geraldine Bowie, prin.
Power ES, 1120 RIVERSIDE DR   39202
    Bennie Richard, prin.
Raines ES, 156 N FLAG CHAPEL RD   39209
    Rosalind Hambrick, prin.
Smith ES, 3900 PARKWAY AVE   39213
    Norman Rhymes, prin.
Spann ES, 1615 BRECON DR   39211
    Betty Faulkner, prin.
Sykes ES, 3555 SIMPSON ST   39212
    Betty Vickers, prin.

Timberlawn ES, 1980 N SIWELL RD 39209
  Olin Lewis,Jr., prin.
Van Winkle ES, 1655 WHITING RD 39209
  Shirley MacNealy, prin.
Walton ES, 3200 BAILEY AVE 39213
  Elton Greer, prin.
Watkins ES, 3915 WATKINS DR 39206
  Sylvester Griffin, prin.
Whitfield ES, 1020 HUNTER ST 39204
  Kisiah Nolan, prin.
Wilkins ES, 1970 CASTLE HILL DR 39204
  Edward Lord, prin.
Woodville Heights ES
  2930 W MCDOWELL RD 39204
  Cheryl Moore, prin.

St. Andrew's Episcopal School
  4120 OLD CANTON ROAD 39216
Christ the King School
  1217 HATTIESBURG ST 39209
Holy Family School, 820 FOREST AVE 39206
St. Mary School, 665 CLAIBORNE AVE 39209
St. Richard School, 1240 LYNWOOD DR 39206
St. Therese School, 309 W MCDOWELL RD 39204

Jonestown, Coahoma Co., Pop. Code 4
Coahoma County SD
Supt. – See Clarksdale
ES, P O BOX 26 38639 – Rubye Humphries, prin.
Jonestown MS, P O BOX 289 38639
  W. Jones, prin.

Kilmichael, Montgomery Co., Pop. Code 3
Montgomery County SD
Supt. – See Winona
ES, P O BOX 248 39747 – Jerry Boggan, prin.

Kosciusko, Attala Co., Pop. Code 6
Attala County SD
Sch. Sys. Enr. Code 4
Supt. – James Foster 39090
Other Schools – See Mc Cool, Sallis

Kosciusko SSD
Sch. Sys. Enr. Code 4
Supt. – A. McBeath, 206 S HUNTINGTON 39090
PS, P O BOX 678 39090 – Charles Prewett, prin.
ES, P O BOX 678 39090 – Robert Simpson, prin.
MS, P O BOX 678 39090 – Larry Stevens, prin.

Kossuth, Alcorn Co., Pop. Code 2
Alcorn County SD
Supt. – See Corinth
ES, RURAL ROUTE 05 38834 – Ray Allen, prin.

Lake, Scott Co., Pop. Code 2
Scott County SD
Supt. – See Forest
Lake Attendance Center, RURAL ROUTE 01 39092
  Huey Stone, prin.

Lakeshore, Hancock Co.
Hancock County SD
Supt. – See Bay Saint Louis
Gulfview ES, P O BOX 480 39558
  Donald North, prin.

Lambert, Quitman Co., Pop. Code 4
Quitman County SD
Supt. – See Marks
Southside ES, P O BOX 175 38643
  C. Gaston, prin.

Laurel, Jones Co., Pop. Code 7
Jones County SD
Supt. – See Ellisville
Calhoun ES, RURAL ROUTE 11 BOX 458 39440
  Billy Moss, prin.
Glade ES, RURAL ROUTE 04 BOX 92 39440
  John Simpson, prin.
Myrick ES, RURAL ROUTE 04 BOX 90 39440
  Thomas Parker, prin.
Powers ES, RURAL ROUTE 02 BOX 821 39440
  Lynn Lyons, prin.
Shady Grove ES
  RURAL ROUTE 03 BOX 164 39440
  Sue Meadows, prin.
Sharon ES, RURAL ROUTE 12 BOX 280 39440
  Annelle Holifield, prin.

Laurel SSD
Sch. Sys. Enr. Code 5
Supt. – David Sheppard, P O BOX 288 39441
JHS, 1125 N 5TH AVE 39440 – Joe Watson, prin.
Davis MS
  1305 MARTIN LUTHER KING DR 39440
  David Lewis, prin.
Gardiner MS, 303 W 8TH ST 39440
  Kent Headrick, prin.
Lamar ES, 400 W 15TH ST 39440
  Alice Tigert, prin.
Mason ES, 2026 BAY SPRINGS ROAD 39440
  Bobby Stevens, prin.
Oak Park MS, 114 TYLER ST 39440
  William Gully, prin.
Stainton ES, 795 S 19TH AVE 39440
  George Partlow, prin.

Immaculate Conception School
  833 W 6TH ST 39440

Leakesville, Greene Co., Pop. Code 4
Greene County SD
Sch. Sys. Enr. Code 4
Supt. – Joe James, P O BOX 466 39451
JHS, P O BOX 1479 39451 – Roger McLeod, prin.
ES, P O BOX 1299 39451 – Barbara McCalla, prin.

Other Schools – See Mc Lain, Richton, State Line

Leland, Washington Co., Pop. Code 6
Leland Cons. SD
Sch. Sys. Enr. Code 4
Supt. – Michael Sistrunk, P O BOX 151 38756
MS, 200 MILIAM ST 38756 – Johnny Tucker, prin.
ES, P O BOX 151 38756 – Edna Scott, prin.
MS, P O BOX 151 38756 – Beverlyn Pepper, prin.

Lexington, Holmes Co., Pop. Code 5
Holmes County SD
Sch. Sys. Enr. Code 5
Supt. – William Dean, P O BOX B 39095
McClain MS, P O BOX 270 39095
  Bennie Montgomery, prin.
ES, P O BOX K 39095 – Robert Lewis, prin.
Other Schools – See Durant, Goodman, Tchula

Liberty, Amite Co., Pop. Code 3
Amite County SD
Sch. Sys. Enr. Code 3
Supt. – Maurice Foreman, P O BOX 378 39645
ES, P O BOX 308 39645 – William Sharp, prin.
Other Schools – See Gloster

Little Rock, Newton Co., Pop. Code 1
Newton County SD
Supt. – See Decatur
Hubbard Attendance Center
  RURAL ROUTE 01 BOX 108 39337
  Roy Adams, prin.

Long Beach, Harrison Co., Pop. Code 6
Long Beach SSD
Sch. Sys. Enr. Code 6
Supt. – Dr. Bob Ferguson, QUARLES ST 39560
MS, CLEVELAND AVE 39560
  Marlin Ladner, prin.
Harper-McCaughan ES, JEFF DAVIS AVE 39560
  Donald Logan, prin.
Quarles ES, COMMISSION ROAD 39560
  Patsy Oakes, prin.
Reeves ES, SAINT AUGUSTINE DR 39560
  Dr. Dorothy Lott, prin.

St. Thomas School, 712 E BEACH BLVD 39560

Louisville, Winston Co., Pop. Code 6
Louisville Municipal SD
Sch. Sys. Enr. Code 5
Supt. – Dr. T. Fred Perkins, 200 IVY AVE 39339
Waiya Attendance Center
  RURAL ROUTE 07 BOX 233 39339
  James Gregory, prin.
MS, 508 CAMILE ST 39339 – Tommy Wylie, prin.
PS, 301 N COLUMBUS AVE 39339
  W. Rigdon, prin.
IS, 300 N COLUMBUS AVE 39339
  Robert Brown, prin.
Other Schools – See Noxapater

Lucedale, George Co., Pop. Code 4
George County SD
Sch. Sys. Enr. Code 5
Supt. – Steve Pugh, 100 E MAIN ST 39452
MS, CB 3309 39472 – Richard Fleming, prin.
Central ES, RURAL ROUTE 03 39452
  Clyde Dungan, prin.
ES, 200 W CHURCH ST 39452
  Joanna Brown, prin.
Rocky Creek ES, RURAL ROUTE 04 39452
  R. Renfroe, prin.
Other Schools – See Agricola

Lumberton, Lamar Co., Pop. Code 4
Lamar County SD
Supt. – See Purvis
Baxterville ES, RURAL ROUTE 05 BOX 64 39455
  Markel Knight, prin.

Lumberton SD
Sch. Sys. Enr. Code 3
Supt. – Carl Hancock, P O BOX 551 39455
ES 39455 – Dr. Patricia Ward, prin.

Lyon, Coahoma Co., Pop. Code 3
Coahoma County SD
Supt. – See Clarksdale
ES, P O BOX 407 38645 – Charles Ball,Jr., prin.

Maben, Oktibbeha Co., Pop. Code 3
Oktibbeha County SD
Supt. – See Starkville
Wicks ES, P O BOX 518 39750
  Nancy Henderson, prin.

Mc Comb, Pike Co., Pop. Code 7
McComb SSD
Sch. Sys. Enr. Code 5
Supt. – Dr. David Powe, P O BOX 868 39648
Kennedy ES, 207 S MYRTLE ST 39648
  Emily Burris, prin.
MS, 1000 ELMWOOD ST 39648
  Frank Chappell, prin.
Otken ES, 401 MONTANA AVE 39648
  Hazel Thompson, prin.
Other Schools – See Summit

Mc Cool, Attala Co., Pop. Code 2
Attala County SD
Supt. – See Kosciusko
Greenlee ES, RURAL ROUTE 03 39108
  James Morgan, prin.

Mc Lain, Greene Co., Pop. Code 3
Greene County SD
Supt. – See Leakesville

ES, P O BOX 39 39456 – W. Freeman, prin.

Mc Neill, Pearl River Co.
Pearl River County SD
Supt. – See Poplarville
Pearl River Central MS, P O BOX 430 39457
  Randell Breeland, prin.

Macon, Noxubee Co., Pop. Code 4
Noxubee County SD
Sch. Sys. Enr. Code 4
Supt. – Albert Williams, P O BOX 540 39341
Noxubee County JHS, P O BOX 129 39341
  Velma Jenkins, prin.
Noxubee County ES, P O BOX 391 39341
  Lorene Cannon, prin.
Other Schools – See Brooksville, Shuqualak

Madison, Madison Co., Pop. Code 4
Madison County SD
Supt. – See Canton
Scott MS, P O BOX 339 39130 – Mike Kent, prin.

Magee, Simpson Co., Pop. Code 5
Simpson County SD
Supt. – See Mendenhall
JHS, 501 E CHOCTAW ST 39111
  Ernest Jaynes, prin.
ES, RURAL ROUTE 04 BOX 5A 39111
  Edward Buck, prin.

Magnolia, Pike Co., Pop. Code 4
South Pike Cons. SD
Sch. Sys. Enr. Code 5
Supt. – Dr. Lauren Lanier, 250 W BAY ST 39652
Gordon ES, 1147 N CLARK AVE 39652
  Melvin Harris, prin.
ES, 275 W MYRTLE ST 39652
  John Williams, prin.
Other Schools – See Osyka

Mantachie, Itawamba Co., Pop. Code 3
Itawamba County SD
Supt. – See Fulton
Mantachie Attendance Center, P O BOX 38 38855
  Charles Barton, prin.

Marietta, Prentiss Co., Pop. Code 2
Prentiss County SD
Supt. – See Booneville
ES, P O BOX 10 38856 – David Bolen, prin.

Marks, Quitman Co., Pop. Code 4
Quitman County SD
Sch. Sys. Enr. Code 4
Supt. – S. Wright, P O BOX E 38646
Westside ES, P O BOX 290 38646
  Hubert Foster, prin.
Other Schools – See Crowder, Lambert, Sledge

Mathiston, Webster Co., Pop. Code 3
Webster County SD
Supt. – See Walthall
East Webster ES, P O BOX G 39752
  Mary Cole, prin.

Meadville, Franklin Co., Pop. Code 2
Franklin County SD
Sch. Sys. Enr. Code 4
Supt. – Larry Jones, P O BOX 605 39653
Franklin JHS, P O BOX 666 39653
  Lona Brown, prin.
Franklin PS, RURAL ROUTE 01 BOX 15 39653
  Pat Reed, prin.
Franklin MS, RURAL ROUTE 01 BOX 15 39653
  Tyree Thompson, prin.

Mendenhall, Simpson Co., Pop. Code 5
Simpson County SD
Sch. Sys. Enr. Code 5
Supt. – Cliff Reed, P O BOX 218 39114
JHS, P O BOX 218 39114 – Douglas Herbert, prin.
ES, P O BOX 218 39114 – Betty Floyd, prin.
Other Schools – See Magee, Pinola

Meridian, Lauderdale Co., Pop. Code 8
Lauderdale County SD
Sch. Sys. Enr. Code 6
Supt. – Randy Hodges, P O BOX 5498 39302
Northeast JHS, RURAL ROUTE 08 BOX 75 39305
  Richard Kelly, prin.
Southeast JHS
  RURAL ROUTE 07 BOX 477 39301
  Jerry Coleman, prin.
Clarkdale ES, RURAL ROUTE 01 BOX 417 39301
  Ann Schroeder, prin.
Northeast ES, RURAL ROUTE 04 BOX 317 39305
  Kathy Purvis, prin.
Southeast ES, RURAL ROUTE 07 BOX 477 39301
  Hildred Allgood, prin.
Other Schools – See Collinsville

Meridian SD
Sch. Sys. Enr. Code 6
Supt. – Larry Drawdy, P O BOX 31 39302
Carver MS, 900 44TH AVE 39305
  Robert Markham, prin.
Crestwood ES, 301 22ND AVENUE HTS 39301
  Carol Matfey, prin.
Magnolia MS, 1350 24TH ST 39301
  Idora White, prin.
Marion Park ES, 2815 25TH ST 39301
  Dr. Larry Van Dyke, prin.
Oakland Heights ES, 601 59TH AVE 39305
  Sherry Morgan, prin.
Parkview ES, 1225 26TH ST 39305
  Kathy Robinson, prin.

Poplar Springs ES, 4101 27TH AVE   39305
  Sylvia Autry, prin.
West End ES, 3930 14TH ST   39305
  Lavon Reed, prin.
West Hills ES, 4100 32ND ST   39305
  Emma Atkinson, prin.
Witherspoons ES, 1516 12TH AVE   39301
  Reola Daniels, prin.

St. Patrick School, 2700 DAVIS ST   39301

Minter City, Leflore Co.
  Leflore County SD
  Supt. – See Greenwood
  Fleming ES, RURAL ROUTE 02 BOX 1A   38944
    Charles Parham, prin.

Mize, Smith Co., Pop. Code 2
  Smith County SD
  Supt. – See Raleigh
  Mize Attendance Center, P O BOX 187   39116
    Ramon Johnston, prin.

Monticello, Lawrence Co., Pop. Code 4
  Lawrence County SD
  Sch. Sys. Enr. Code 5
  Supt. – Henry Russell, P O BOX 338   39654
  Topeka-Tilton ES
    RURAL ROUTE 02 BOX 89   39654
    J. Thomas Layton, prin.
  Other Schools – See Brookhaven, Newhebron

Montpelier, Clay Co.
  Clay County SD
  Supt. – See West Point
  West Clay County ES, P O BOX 77   39754
    Ethel Whisler, prin.

Mooreville, Lee Co.
  Lee County SD
  Supt. – See Tupelo
  Mooreville Attendance Center
    RURAL ROUTE 01   38857 – John Dye, prin.

Moorhead, Sunflower Co., Pop. Code 4
  Sunflower County SD
  Supt. – See Indianola
  MS, 908 WASHINGTON ST   38761
    Earnest Brown, prin.
  East Moorhead ES, 610 ELM ST   38761
    Sarah Thomas, prin.

Morton, Scott Co., Pop. Code 5
  Scott County SD
  Supt. – See Forest
  JHS, P O BOX L   39117 – Percy Parker, prin.
  ES, P O BOX L   39117 – Joanne Stevens, prin.

Moselle, Jones Co.
  Jones County SD
  Supt. – See Ellisville
  ES   39459 – R. Smith, prin.

Moss Point, Jackson Co., Pop. Code 7
  Moss Point SSD
  Sch. Sys. Enr. Code 6
  Supt. – Dr. C. Cronin, P O BOX 727   39563
  Eastpark ES, P O BOX 727   39563
    Mary Alfred, prin.
  Escatawpa ES, P O BOX 727   39563
    W. Brown, prin.
  Hyatt ES, P O BOX 727   39563
    Willie Williams, prin.
  Kreole ES, P O BOX 727   39563
    George Pickett, prin.
  Orange Lake ES, P O BOX 727   39563
    William Barkley, prin.
  West ES, P O BOX 727   39563 – Sara Hardin, prin.

Mound Bayou, Bolivar Co., Pop. Code 5
  Mound Bayou SD
  Sch. Sys. Enr. Code 4
  Supt. – Arthur Holmes, P O BOX 30   38762
  Montgomery ES, P O BOX 30   38762
    Legora Mitchell, prin.

St. Gabriel School, MCGINNIS ROAD   38762

Mount Olive, Covington Co., Pop. Code 3
  Covington County SD
  Supt. – See Collins
  Mt. Olive Attendance Center, P O BOX 509   39119
    Lavohn Moss, prin.

Myrtle, Union Co., Pop. Code 2
  Union County SD
  Supt. – See New Albany
  Myrtle Attendance Center, P O BOX 40   38650
    Paul Nolan, prin.
  West Union Attendance Center
    RURAL ROUTE 01   38650 – Ronald Scott, prin.

Natchez, Adams Co., Pop. Code 7
  Natchez SSD
  Sch. Sys. Enr. Code 6
  Supt. – M. Buckley, P O BOX 1188   39120
  Martin MS, 64 HOMOCHITTO ST   39120
    Robert Owens, prin.
  McLaurin MS, PRENTISS DRIVE   39120
    Rufus Carlock, prin.
  Morgantown MS
    101 COTTAGE HOME DRIVE   39120
    Michael Halford, prin.
  Thompson MS, 1038 N UNION ST   39120
    Wilson Bandord, prin.
  Carpenter ES, 802 N UNION ST   39120
    Priscilla Brown, prin.

Martin ES, 64 HOMOCHITTO ST   39120
  Robert Owens, prin.
McLaurin ES, PRENTISS DR   39120
  Freddie Seab, prin.
Morgantown ES, 101 COTTAGE HOME DR   39120
  Kate Cole, prin.
Northside ES, 1445 WATKINS ST   39120
  Joe Frazier, prin.
Prince ES, 2 PRINCE ST   39120
  Henry Smith, prin.
West ES, PROVIDENCE ROAD   39120
  Lillie Hoskin, prin.

Cathedral Unit School, P O BOX 1187   39120
Trinity Episcopal Day School
  RURAL ROUTE 01 BOX 482   39120
Holy Family School, 8 ORANGE AVE   39120

Nettleton, Monroe Co., Pop. Code 4
  Nettleton Line Cons. SD
  Sch. Sys. Enr. Code 4
  Supt. – Larry Williams, P O BOX 409   38858
  JHS, P O BOX 409   38858
    Cornelious Armstrong, prin.
  Nettleton PS, P O BOX 409   38858
    Melvin Malone, prin.
  Nettleton MS, P O BOX 409   38858
    Boyce Grayson, prin.

New Albany, Union Co., Pop. Code 6
  New Albany SSD
  Sch. Sys. Enr. Code 4
  Supt. – Dr. J. Bryson, P O BOX 771   38652
  MS, 400 APPLE ST   38652 – Wade Ivy, prin.
  Ford ES, 507 OAK ST   38652
    Thomas Wallace, prin.
  Thompson ES, CLEVELAND ST   38652
    Jamie Bramlitt, prin.

  Union County SD
  Sch. Sys. Enr. Code 4
  Supt. – Sam Dowdy, P O BOX 939   38652
  Ingomar Attendance Center
    RURAL ROUTE 01   38652 – John Weeden, prin.
  Other Schools – See Blue Springs, Myrtle

New Augusta, Perry Co., Pop. Code 3
  Perry County SD
  Sch. Sys. Enr. Code 4
  Supt. – Joel Powell, P O BOX 137   39462
  ES, P O BOX 197   39462 – Patricia Jones, prin.
  Other Schools – See Beaumont, Petal

Newhebron, Lawrence Co., Pop. Code 2
  Lawrence County SD
  Supt. – See Monticello
  ES, P O BOX 239   39140 – John Flynt, prin.

Newton, Newton Co., Pop. Code 5
  Newton Municipal SD
  Sch. Sys. Enr. Code 4
  Supt. – James Nelson, P O BOX 150   39345
  ES, 301 W TATUM ST   39345 – Sara May, prin.

Nicholson, Pearl River Co.
  Picayune SD
  Supt. – See Picayune
  ES, NICHOLSON ST   39463
    Dorothy Ladner, prin.

North Carrollton, Carroll Co., Pop. Code 3
  Carroll County SD
  Supt. – See Carrollton
  Marshall ES, MARSHALL RD   38947
    Stanley Flowers, prin.

Noxapater, Winston Co., Pop. Code 3
  Louisville Municipal SD
  Supt. – See Louisville
  Noxapater Attendance Center, ALICE ST   39346
    Buck Kennedy, prin.

Oakland, Yalobusha Co., Pop. Code 3
  Coffeeville Cons. SD
  Supt. – See Coffeeville
  ES, RURAL ROUTE 01 BOX 178   38948
    Clinton Jenkins, prin.

Ocean Springs, Jackson Co., Pop. Code 7
  Ocean Springs SSD
  Sch. Sys. Enr. Code 5
  Supt. – Allen Curry, P O BOX 7002   39564
  East ES, P O BOX 7002   39564 – Lynda Lee, prin.
  Magnolia Park ES, P O BOX 7002   39564
    Julie Wade, prin.
  Northeast Taconi MS, P O BOX 7002   39564
    Margaret Brenke, prin.
  Pecan Park ES, P O BOX 7002   39564
    William Rhinehart, prin.

St. Alphonsus School, 504 JACKSON AVE   39564

Okolona, Chickasaw Co., Pop. Code 5
  Okolona SSD
  Sch. Sys. Enr. Code 4
  Supt. – James Anderson, WINTER ST   38860
  JHS, WINTER ST   38860 – Nellie Adams, prin.
  ES, 411 W MAIN ST   38860 – Barbara Iles, prin.

Olive Branch, De Soto Co., Pop. Code 4
  DeSoto County SD
  Supt. – See Hernando
  MS, 8631 PIDGEON ROOST ROAD   38654
    Kenneth Reid, prin.
  ES, 9549 E PIDGEON ROOSE ROAD   38654
    LeMoyne Brigance, prin.

Osyka, Pike Co., Pop. Code 3
  South Pike Cons. SD
  Supt. – See Magnolia
  ES   39657 – Eleanor Theriot, prin.

Oxford, Lafayette Co., Pop. Code 6
  Lafayette County SD
  Sch. Sys. Enr. Code 4
  Supt. – J. Nelson, P O BOX 110   38655
  Lafayette ES, RURAL ROUTE 01   38655
    Nancy Metts, prin.

  Oxford SSD
  Sch. Sys. Enr. Code 5
  Supt. – Dr. Bob McCord
    224 BRAMLETT BLVD   38655
  JHS, 409 WASHINGTON AVE   38655
    D. Sanders, prin.
  Bramlett ES, 222 BRAMLETT BLVD   38655
    Dr. Carole Dye, prin.
  MS, 1637 HIGHWAY 30 E   38655
    Dr. Ivy Lovelady, prin.

Pascagoula, Jackson Co., Pop. Code 8
  Jackson County SD
  Sch. Sys. Enr. Code 6
  Supt. – Jimmy Smithie
    3103 MAGNOLIA ST   39567
  Other Schools – See Biloxi, Hurley, Vancleave

  Pascagoula SSD
  Sch. Sys. Enr. Code 6
  Supt. – Dr. Dwight Shelton, P O BOX 250   39568
  Arlington Heights ES, 3511 LOUISE ST   39567
    Nadine Carmichael, prin.
  Beach ES, 633 MARKET ST   39567
    Shirley Hunter, prin.
  Central ES, 100 DUPONT AVE   39567
    Rhenette Blake, prin.
  Cherokee ES, 4102 SCOVEL AVE   39567
    Thomas Ulm, prin.
  Eastlawn ES, 2611 INGALLS AVE   39567
    James Grissom, prin.
  Fair ES, 420 FAIR ST   39567
    Patricia Williams, prin.
  Jackson ES, 3203 LANIER AVE   39567
    Douglas Belk, prin.
  Lake ES, 4503 WILLOW ST   39567
    Arnold Tillman, prin.
  South ES, 2203 BUENA VISTA ST   39567
    Miriam Garrett, prin.
  Other Schools – See Gautier

Our Lady of Victories ES, 520 WATTS AVE   39567
Sacred Heart ES, P O BOX 2194   39567
St. Peter School, 1703 TELEPHONE RD   39567

Pass Christian, Harrison Co., Pop. Code 6
  Hancock County SD
  Supt. – See Bay Saint Louis
  Hancock North Central ES
    RURAL ROUTE 01   39571 – Kim Stasny, prin.

  Harrison County SD
  Supt. – See Gulfport
  Pineville ES, RURAL ROUTE 02   39571
    Pat Cunningham, prin.

  Pass Christian SSD
  Sch. Sys. Enr. Code 4
  Supt. – Leroy Lizana, 710 W NORTH ST   39571
  MS, 315 CLARK ST   39571 – John Deem, prin.
  Delisle ES, RURAL ROUTE 03 BOX 120   39571
    Kaye Rendfrey, prin.
  ES, 703 W NORTH ST   39571
    Sharon Lembright, prin.

St. Paul Interparochial School
  151 E SCENIC DR   39571

Pearl, Rankin Co., Pop. Code 7
  Pearl SD
  Sch. Sys. Enr. Code 5
  Supt. – Dr. William Dodson, P O BOX 5750   39208
  JHS, 200 MARY ANN DRIVE   39208
    David Daves, prin.
  Northside ES, P O BOX 5750   39208
    Clayton James, prin.
  MS, P O BOX 5750   39208 – Mary Price, prin.
  Pearl PS, P O BOX 5750   39208 – John Morris, prin.

Pearlington, Hancock Co.
  Hancock County SD
  Supt. – See Bay Saint Louis
  Murphy ES, GEN DELIVERY HIGHWAY 6   39572
    Clementine Williams, prin.

Pelahatchie, Rankin Co., Pop. Code 4
  Rankin County SD
  Supt. – See Brandon
  ES, P O BOX 599   39145 – Mae Green, prin.

Perkinston, Stone Co., Pop. Code 2
  Stone County SD
  Supt. – See Wiggins
  ES, P O BOX 6   39573 – Billy Ray Young, prin.

Petal, Forrest Co., Pop. Code 6
  Perry County SD
  Supt. – See New Augusta
  Runnelstown ES
    RURAL ROUTE 08 BOX 1030   39465
    Donald Reagan, prin.

  Petal SSD
  Sch. Sys. Enr. Code 5
  Supt. – Mike Walters, P O BOX 523   39465

JHS, CENTRAL AVE 39456
  Charles Blackwell, prin.
Smith MS, 400 HILLCREST LOOP 39465
  Janet Thornton, prin.
Other Schools – See Hattiesburg

Philadelphia, Neshoba Co., Pop. Code 6
Neshoba County SD
Sch. Sys. Enr. Code 4
Supt. – V. Manning, P O BOX 338 39350
Neshoba Central ES
  1002 SAINT FRANCIS DR 39350
  John Alford, prin.

Philadelphia SD
Sch. Sys. Enr. Code 4
Supt. – Therrell Myers, 248 BYRD AVE 39350
ES, 406 STRIBLING ST 39350 – Mack Alford, prin.

Picayune, Pearl River Co., Pop. Code 7
Picayune SD
Sch. Sys. Enr. Code 5
Supt. – Robert White
  706 GOODYEAR BLVD 39466
JHS, 702 GOODYEAR BLVD 39466
  Jack Rivers, prin.
Roseland Park ES, 1600 GILCREASE AVE 39466
  Jane Ann Handley, prin.
South Side ES, 400 BEECH ST 39466
  Velva Effler, prin.
West Side ES, 111 KIRKWOOD ST 39466
  Joyce Thompson, prin.
Other Schools – See Nicholson

Pinola, Simpson Co.
Simpson County SD
Supt. – See Mendenhall
West Union ES, RURAL ROUTE 01 BOX 85 39149
  Randall Neely, prin.

Pittsboro, Calhoun Co., Pop. Code 2
Calhoun County SD
Sch. Sys. Enr. Code 5
Supt. – Thomas Suggs, P O BOX 58 38951
Other Schools – See Bruce, Calhoun City, Vardaman

Plantersville, Lee Co.
Lee County SD
Supt. – See Tupelo
ES, P O BOX 129 38862 – M. Griffin, prin.

Pontotoc, Pontotoc Co., Pop. Code 5
Pontotoc CSD
Sch. Sys. Enr. Code 4
Supt. – Dr. Charles Harrison, P O BOX 150 38863
JHS, P O BOX 150 38863 – Conwell Duke, prin.
Cox MS, P O BOX 150 38863
  Rhonda Partridge, prin.
ES, P O BOX 150 38863 – Shelby McCullar, prin.

Pontotoc County SD
Sch. Sys. Enr. Code 5
Supt. – Hugh Turner
  285 HWY 15 BYPASS S 38863
South Pontotoc Attendance Center
  RURAL ROUTE 05 38863 – Gerald Hegan, prin.
Other Schools – See Ecru

Pope, Panola Co., Pop. Code 2
South Panola Cons. SD
Supt. – See Batesville
ES, HWY 51 38658 – James Broome, prin.

Poplarville, Pearl River Co., Pop. Code 5
Pearl River County SD
Sch. Sys. Enr. Code 4
Supt. – Adrian Lumpkin, 109 W PEARL ST 39470
Other Schools – See Carriere, Mc Neill

Poplarville SSD
Sch. Sys. Enr. Code 4
Supt. – Larry Tynes, 1301 S MAIN ST 39470
Poplarville PS, 209 W CHURCH ST 39470
  Ethel Lott, prin.
Poplarville MS, 701 E BEER ST 39470
  Gylde Fitzpatrick, prin.

Port Gibson, Claiborne Co., Pop. Code 4
Claiborne County SD
Sch. Sys. Enr. Code 4
Supt. – F. White, P O BOX 337 39150
Richardson ES, P O BOX 340 39150
  Horace Wicks, prin.

Potts Camp, Marshall Co., Pop. Code 3
Marshall County SD
Supt. – See Holly Springs
Reid PS, P O BOX 697 38659 – Donnal Ash, prin.

Prairie, Monroe Co.
Aberdeen SSD
Supt. – See Aberdeen
MS, P O BOX 607 39756
  Winfield Cunningham, prin.

Prentiss, Jefferson Davis Co., Pop. Code 4
Jefferson Davis County SD
Sch. Sys. Enr. Code 5
Supt. – Macon Holliman, P O BOX 1197 39474
JHS, P O BOX 1228 39474 – Willie Oatis, prin.
ES, P O BOX 1408 39474 – Thomas Booth, prin.
Prentiss MS, P O BOX 1348 39474
  Marion Fortenberry, prin.
Other Schools – See Bassfield

Puckett, Rankin Co., Pop. Code 2
Rankin County SD
Supt. – See Brandon

Puckett Attendance Center, P O BOX 40 39151
  Thad Haskin, prin.

Purvis, Lamar Co., Pop. Code 4
Lamar County SD
Sch. Sys. Enr. Code 6
Supt. – Emil Pav, P O BOX 609 39475
ES, P O BOX 267 39475 – Sue Jackson, prin.
Other Schools – See Hattiesburg, Lumberton, Sumrall

Quitman, Clarke Co., Pop. Code 5
Quitman Cons. SD
Sch. Sys. Enr. Code 5
Supt. – R. Hinton, 312 E FRANKLIN ST 39355
Quitman Consolidated JHS
  SHIRLEY DRIVE 39355 – Charles McClure, prin.
Quitman Consolidated ES
  312 E FRANKLIN ST 39355 – B. Barton, prin.
Quitman Consolidated MS, N HIGHWAY 45 39355
  Carolyn Smith, prin.

Raleigh, Smith Co., Pop. Code 3
Smith County SD
Sch. Sys. Enr. Code 5
Supt. – C. Boyles, P O BOX 308 39153
JHS, P O BOX 580 39153 – Clyde Garner, prin.
ES, P O BOX 188 39153 – Carolyn Stuart, prin.
Other Schools – See Mize, Taylorsville

Raymond, Hinds Co., Pop. Code 4
Hinds County SD
Sch. Sys. Enr. Code 6
Supt. – Roger McDaniel, P O BOX 100 39154
Carver ES, P O BOX 47 39154
  Dr. Edward Wiggins, prin.
Other Schools – See Bolton, Edwards, Jackson, Terry, Utica

Redwood, Warren Co.
Vicksburg Warren SD
Supt. – See Vicksburg
ES, P O BOX 98 39156 – Sara Hill, prin.

Richland, Rankin Co., Pop. Code 5
Rankin County SD
Supt. – See Brandon
PS, 1202 HIGHWAY 49 S 39218
  Susan Monsour, prin.
IS, 1202 HWY 49 S 39218 – Barry Male, prin.

Richton, Perry Co., Pop. Code 4
Greene County SD
Supt. – See Leakesville
Sand Hill ES, RURAL ROUTE 04 BOX 115 39476
  Lavon Freeman, prin.

Richton SSD
Sch. Sys. Enr. Code 4
Supt. – Dr. Lewis Holloway, P O BOX 568 39476
ES, P O BOX 568 39476 – Martha Moser, prin.

Ridgeland, Madison Co., Pop. Code 6
Madison County SD
Supt. – See Canton
ES, P O BOX 807 39158 – Ann Smith, prin.

Rienzi, Alcorn Co., Pop. Code 2
Alcorn County SD
Supt. – See Corinth
ES, RURAL ROUTE 02 BOX 8 38865
  Len Curlee, prin.

Ripley, Tippah Co., Pop. Code 5
South Tippah Cons. SD
Sch. Sys. Enr. Code 5
Supt. – J. Harris, P O BOX 439 38663
MS, 770 S CLAYTON ST 38663
  Troy Holliday, prin.
Pine Grove ES, RURAL ROUTE 02 38663
  William Witt, prin.
ES, 702 TERRY ST 38663 – E. Cummings, prin.
Other Schools – See Blue Mountain

Rolling Fork, Sharkey Co., Pop. Code 5
Sharkey-Issaquena Line Cons. SD
Sch. Sys. Enr. Code 4
Supt. – Ryan Grayson, 600 PARKWAY AVE 39159
ES, 600 PARKWAY AVE 39159
  Ethel Brown, prin.

Rosedale, Bolivar Co., Pop. Code 5
West Bolivar SD
Sch. Sys. Enr. Code 4
Supt. – Jordan Goins, P O BOX 189 38769
ES, P O BOX 880 38769 – Shirley Griffin, prin.
West Bolivar ES, P O BOX 429 38769
  James Wilson, prin.
Other Schools – See Gunnison

Sallis, Attala Co., Pop. Code 2
Attala County SD
Supt. – See Kosciusko
Long Creek ES 39160 – Maudie Benton, prin.

Sandersville, Jones Co., Pop. Code 3
Jones County SD
Supt. – See Ellisville
ES 39477 – Mary Ann Stevens, prin.

Sarah, Panola Co.
Tate County SD
Supt. – See Senatobia
Strayhorn ES, RURAL ROUTE 01 BOX 98 38665
  Lee Darnell, prin.

Sardis, Panola Co., Pop. Code 4
North Panola Consolidated SD
Sch. Sys. Enr. Code 4
Supt. – James Harris, P O BOX 334 38666

Green Hill ES, P O BOX 220 38666
  Jerry Hentz, prin.
Other Schools – See Como, Crenshaw

Satartia, Yazoo Co., Pop. Code 1
Yazoo County SD
Supt. – See Yazoo City
ES, P O BOX 39 39162 – Ike Anderson, prin.

Saucier, Harrison Co.
Harrison County SD
Supt. – See Gulfport
ES, P O BOX 8 39574 – Eugene Ladner, prin.

Scooba, Kemper Co., Pop. Code 3
Kemper County SSD
Supt. – See De Kalb
East Kemper ES, P O BOX 156 39358
  Annie Ramsey, prin.

Sebastopol, Scott Co., Pop. Code 2
Scott County SD
Supt. – See Forest
Sebastopol Attendance Center, P O BOX 86 39359
  Larry Carroll, prin.

Seminary, Covington Co., Pop. Code 2
Covington County SD
Supt. – See Collins
Seminary Attendance Center, P O BOX 34 39479
  Billy Ray Smith, prin.

Senatobia, Tate Co., Pop. Code 6
Senatobia SSD
Sch. Sys. Enr. Code 4
Supt. – Michael Waldrop, 304 W TATE ST 38668
ES, 403 W GILMORE ST 38668 – Jesse Jones, prin.
MS, 303 COLLEGE ST 38668 – Phil Mote, prin.

Tate County SD
Sch. Sys. Enr. Code 5
Supt. – Greg Freeman, P O BOX 667 38668
Other Schools – See Coldwater, Sarah

Shannon, Lee Co., Pop. Code 3
Lee County SD
Supt. – See Tupelo
ES, P O BOX 7 38868 – Valarie Jaynes, prin.

Shaw, Bolivar Co., Pop. Code 4
Shaw SD
Sch. Sys. Enr. Code 3
Supt. – Rueben Watson, P O BOX 489 38773
McEvans ES, P O BOX 529 38773
  Gail Towers, prin.

Shelby, Bolivar Co., Pop. Code 5
Bolivar County Cons. SD 3
Sch. Sys. Enr. Code 4
Supt. – Jimmy Langdon, P O BOX 28 38774
ES, P O BOX 28 38774 – Wade Russell, prin.
Other Schools – See Duncan

Shuqualak, Noxubee Co., Pop. Code 3
Noxubee County SD
Supt. – See Macon
Reed ES, RURAL ROUTE 01 BOX 114A 39361
  Julia Jefferson, prin.

Sledge, Quitman Co., Pop. Code 3
Quitman County SD
Supt. – See Marks
Falcon ES, P O BOX 65 38670 – H. Williams, prin.

Smithville, Monroe Co., Pop. Code 3
Monroe County SD
Supt. – See Aberdeen
Smithville Attendance Center 38870
  William Stevens, prin.

Soso, Jones Co., Pop. Code 2
Jones County SD
Supt. – See Ellisville
ES 39480 – James Walters, prin.

Southhaven, De Soto Co., Pop. Code 6
DeSoto County SD
Supt. – See Hernando
Greenbrook ES, 730 RASCO ROAD 38671
  Barbara James, prin.
ES, 8274 CLAIBORNE DR 38671
  Charles Alexander, prin.
Sullivan ES, 7985 SOUTHAVEN CIR W 38671
  Patricia Hefley, prin.

Starkville, Oktibbeha Co., Pop. Code 7
Oktibbeha County SD
Sch. Sys. Enr. Code 4
Supt. – Walter Conley
  105 N WASHINGTON ST 39759
Alexander Attendance Center
  RURAL ROUTE 06 BOX 118 39759
  Floyd Wade, prin.
Other Schools – See Crawford, Maben, Sturgis

Starkville SD
Sch. Sys. Enr. Code 5
Supt. – Charles Thompson, HWY 25 S 39759
Armstrong JHS, MCKEE ST 39759
  Glenn McGee, prin.
Emerson ES, HWY 25 S 39759
  Robbie Jones, prin.
Henderson IS, HIGHWAY 82 W 39759
  Joyce Polk, prin.
Overstreet ES, S JACKSON ST 39759
  Janet Henderson, prin.
Ward ES, HWY 82 W 39759 – Bob Smith, prin.

State Line, Greene Co., Pop. Code 2
Greene County SD
Supt. – See Leakesville
State Line ES, P O BOX 70   39362
David Dearman, prin.

Stringer, Jasper Co., Pop. Code 2
West Jasper Cons. SD
Supt. – See Bay Springs
Stringer Attendance Center, P O BOX 68   39481
Gerald Grayson, prin.

Sturgis, Oktibbeha Co., Pop. Code 2
Oktibbeha County SD
Supt. – See Starkville
Sturgis Attendance Center
RURAL ROUTE 01 BOX 257   39769
Ronnie Ware, prin.

Summit, Pike Co., Pop. Code 3
McComb SSD
Supt. – See Mc Comb
ES, 501 BALDWIN ST   39648 – J. Robertson, prin.

North Pike Cons. SD
Sch. Sys. Enr. Code 4
Supt. – Dr. James Jones, RURAL ROUTE 04   39666
North Pike MS, RURAL ROUTE 01   39666
Lee Brewer, prin.
North Pike ES, RURAL ROUTE 04 BOX 11D   39666
Robert Thompson, prin.

Sumner, Tallahatchie Co., Pop. Code 2
West Tallahatchie Cons. SD
Supt. – See Webb
West District MS, P O BOX 188   38957
Jeff King, prin.
ES, P O BOX 276   38957 – Carolyn Murphey, prin.

Sumrall, Lamar Co., Pop. Code 4
Lamar County SD
Supt. – See Purvis
MS, P O BOX 187   39482 – Janice Shivers, prin.
ES, P O BOX 187   39482 – Ellie Jo Rich, prin.

Sunflower, Sunflower Co., Pop. Code 4
Sunflower County SD
Supt. – See Indianola
East Sunflower ES, 804 CLAIBORNE ST   38778
Willie McDaniel, prin.

Taylorsville, Smith Co., Pop. Code 4
Smith County SD
Supt. – See Raleigh
ES, P O BOX 8   39168 – Janet Rogers, prin.

Tchula, Holmes Co., Pop. Code 4
Holmes County SD
Supt. – See Lexington
Marshall Attendance Center
HIGHWAY 12 E   39169 – Horace Glover, prin.
Marshall ES, P O BOX 307   39169
Willie Stewart, prin.
Mileston ES, RURAL ROUTE 02 BOX 173   39169
Sarah Davis, prin.

Terry, Hinds Co., Pop. Code 3
Hinds County SD
Supt. – See Raymond
Perryman ES, P O BOX 129   39170
Perceta Tuggle, prin.

Tiplersville, Tippah Co.
North Tippah SD
Sch. Sys. Enr. Code 4
Supt. – Billy Stroupe, P O BOX 65   38674
Other Schools – See Falkner, Walnut

Tishomingo, Tishomingo Co., Pop. Code 2
Tishomingo County SD
Supt. – See Iuka
Tishomingo Attendance Center, P O BOX 90   38873
Danny McClung, prin.

Tremont, Itawamba Co., Pop. Code 2
Itawamba County SD
Supt. – See Fulton
Tremont Attendance Center, P O BOX 9   38876
Jerry Kuykendall, prin.

Tunica, Tunica Co., Pop. Code 4
Tunica County SD
Sch. Sys. Enr. Code 4
Supt. – G. Henderson, P O BOX 758   38676
JHS, P O BOX 967   38676 – Woodrow Clark, prin.
Tunica/Rosa Fort ES, P O BOX 997   38676
James Bullock, prin.

Tupelo, Lee Co., Pop. Code 7
Lee County SD
Sch. Sys. Enr. Code 6
Supt. – Cecil Weeks, P O BOX 832   38802
Other Schools – See Guntown, Mooreville,
Plantersville, Shannon, Verona

Tupelo SSD
Sch. Sys. Enr. Code 6
Supt. – Richard Thompson, P O BOX 557   38802
Milam JHS, 720 W JEFFERSON ST   38801
Robert Thompson, prin.
Church Street ES, 445 N CHURCH ST   38801
Martha Cheney, prin.
Green Street MS, 1402 N GREEN ST   38801
Nathaniel Stone, prin.
Joyner ES, 1201 JOYNER ST   38801
John Cother, prin.
Lawhon ES, 140 LAKE ST   38801
Dale Dobbs, prin.

Pierce Street ES, 108 PIERCE ST   38801
Paul Pate, prin.
Rankin ES, 1908 FORREST ST   38801
Glenda Murphree, prin.
Thomas Street ES, 901 S THOMAS ST   38801
Martha Weatherford, prin.

Tutwiler, Tallahatchie Co., Pop. Code 4
West Tallahatchie Cons. SD
Supt. – See Webb
Hopson Bayou ES, P O BOX 157   38963
Ruth Lewis, prin.

Tylertown, Walthall Co., Pop. Code 4
Walthall County SD
Sch. Sys. Enr. Code 5
Supt. – (—), P O BOX 348   39667
Dexter Attendance Center
RURAL ROUTE 02 BOX 234   39667
G. Breeland, prin.
Salem Attendance Center
RURAL ROUTE 01 BOX 257   39667
Charles Boyd, prin.
IS, 705 BROAD ST   39667
Amos Newman, Jr., prin.
PS, 813 BALL AVE   39667
Norman Hammon, prin.

Union, Newton Co., Pop. Code 4
Union SSD
Sch. Sys. Enr. Code 3
Supt. – J. Searcy, 101 FOREST ST   39365
Union Attendance Center, 101 FOREST ST   39365
Jerry Jones, prin.

Utica, Hinds Co., Pop. Code 3
Hinds County SD
Supt. – See Raymond
Mixon ES, P O BOX E   39175 – Bobbie Davis, prin.

Vaiden, Carroll Co., Pop. Code 3
Carroll County SD
Supt. – See Carrollton
Hathorn ES, HWY 51   39176
Willie Thomas,Jr., prin.

Vancleave, Jackson Co.
Jackson County SD
Supt. – See Pascagoula
Vancleave Attendance Center
12424 HWY 57   39564 – Charles Brown, prin.

Vardaman, Calhoun Co., Pop. Code 4
Calhoun County SD
Supt. – See Pittsboro
ES, P O BOX 267   38878 – John Flippin, prin.

Vaughan, Yazoo Co.
Yazoo County SD
Supt. – See Yazoo City
Linwood ES, RURAL ROUTE 01 BOX 345   39179
A. Brent, prin.

Verona, Lee Co., Pop. Code 4
Lee County SD
Supt. – See Tupelo
ES, P O BOX 579   38879 – Sidney Cooley, prin.

Vicksburg, Warren Co., Pop. Code 8
Vicksburg Warren SD
Sch. Sys. Enr. Code 7
Supt. – Edward Gilley, P O BOX 1058   39180
Warren Central JHS, 1703 HIGHWAY 27   39180
Peter Pikul, prin.
Bovina ES, RURAL ROUTE 13   39180
Donald Maxwell, prin.
Bowmare Avenue ES, 912 BOWMAR AVE   39180
Robert Reddix, prin.
Culkin ES, RURAL ROUTE 11   39180
Jack Grogan, prin.
Grove Street ES, 1315 GROVE ST   39180
Donnell Ellis, prin.
Halls Ferry ES, 3341 HALLS FERRY RD   39180
Linda Herrod, prin.
Jett ES, 4232 WARRENTON RD   39180
Rick Tillotson, prin.
South Park ES, 1024 GOODRUM ROAD   39180
Patricia Segrest, prin.
MS, 3701 DRUMMOND ST   39180
Guyla Gould, prin.
Warrenton ES, 809 BELVA DRIVE   39180
Ron Harvey, prin.
Other Schools – See Redwood

St. Francis Xavier ES, 1021 CRAWFORD ST   39180

Walls, De Soto Co.
DeSoto County SD
Supt. – See Hernando
ES, 6131 DELTA VIEW RD   38680
Jean Nunnally, prin.

Sacred Heart School, P O BOX 96   38680

Walnut, Tippah Co., Pop. Code 3
Alcorn County SD
Supt. – See Corinth
Union Center ES
RURAL ROUTE 03 BOX 305   38683
Linda Brooks, prin.

North Tippah SD
Supt. – See Tiplersville
Chalybeate ES, P O BOX 35   38683
Douglas Jackson, prin.
ES, P O BOX 230   38683 – Troy Shaw, prin.

Walnut Grove, Leake Co., Pop. Code 2
Leake County SD
Supt. – See Carthage
South Leake ES, RURAL ROUTE 02   39189
Tony Martin, prin.

Walthall, Webster Co., Pop. Code 2
Webster County SD
Sch. Sys. Enr. Code 4
Supt. – Jimmy Powell, P O BOX 14   39771
Other Schools – See Eupora, Mathiston

Water Valley, Yalobusha Co., Pop. Code 5
Water Valley Cons. SD
Sch. Sys. Enr. Code 4
Supt. – Keny Goodwin, P O BOX 647   38965
ES, P O BOX 608   38965 – Sammy Hidgon, prin.

Waveland, Hancock Co., Pop. Code 5
Bay St. Louis-Waveland SD
Supt. – See Bay Saint Louis
ES, 1025 SAINT JOSEPH ST   39576
James Baldree, prin.

St. Clare School, 234 S BEACH BLVD   39576

Waynesboro, Wayne Co., Pop. Code 6
Wayne County SD
Sch. Sys. Enr. Code 5
Supt. – Dewey McKee, 609 AZALEA   39367
Beat Four Attendance Center
RURAL ROUTE 01 BOX 489   39367
Robert Lilly, prin.
JHS, 155 WAYNE ST   39367
Taylor Mayfield, prin.
ES, P O BOX 560   39367 – Mary Ezell, prin.
Other Schools – See Buckatunna, Clara

Webb, Tallahatchie Co., Pop. Code 3
West Tallahatchie Cons. SD
Sch. Sys. Enr. Code 4
Supt. – Charles George, P O BOX 126   38966
Other Schools – See Glendora, Sumner, Tutwiler

Weir, Choctaw Co., Pop. Code 3
Choctaw County SD
Supt. – See Ackerman
ES, P O BOX 98   39772
Tommye Ruth Kelley, prin.

Wesson, Copiah Co., Pop. Code 4
Copiah County SD
Supt. – See Hazlehurst
Wesson Attendance Center, 532 GROVE ST   39191
Larry Williams, prin.

West Point, Clay Co., Pop. Code 6
Clay County SD
Sch. Sys. Enr. Code 3
Supt. – Mary Joe Washington, P O BOX 759   39773
Other Schools – See Montpelier

West Point SSD
Sch. Sys. Enr. Code 5
Supt. – Dr. Thomas Lott, P O BOX 656   39773
Central MS, P O BOX 166   39773
Randy Hamblin, prin.
East Side ES, 813 E BROAD ST   39773
Lucille Crump, prin.
South Side ES, P O BOX 523   39773
Ruby Smith, prin.

Wheeler, Prentiss Co., Pop. Code 2
Prentiss County SD
Supt. – See Booneville
Wheeler Attendance Center, P O BOX 98   38880
Dennis Worley, prin.

Wiggins, Stone Co., Pop. Code 5
Stone County SD
Sch. Sys. Enr. Code 4
Supt. – Virgel Fulcher, 214 CRITZ ST   39577
Stone JHS, P O BOX 220   39577
Mary Garvin, prin.
Stone ES, HWY 26 E   39577 – Denna Hatten, prin.
Other Schools – See Perkinston

Winona, Montgomery Co., Pop. Code 6
Montgomery County SD
Sch. Sys. Enr. Code 4
Supt. – Joe Moore, P O BOX 687   38967
Other Schools – See Duck Hill, Kilmichael

Winona SSD
Sch. Sys. Enr. Code 4
Supt. – Dr. J. Tom Dulin
311 FAIRGROUND ST   38967
ES, 400 HIGHWAY 51 N   38967 – Ted Shook, prin.

Woodville, Wilkinson Co., Pop. Code 4
Wilkinson County SD
Sch. Sys. Enr. Code 4
Supt. – Charles Johnson, P O BOX 785   39669
Wilkinson County ES, P O BOX 1197   39669
Mildred McGhee, prin.
Other Schools – See Centreville

Yazoo City, Yazoo Co., Pop. Code 7
Yazoo City SSD
Sch. Sys. Enr. Code 5
Supt. – Leslie Johnson, P O BOX 127   39194
JHS, 516 E CANAL ST   39194
Marcus Dilworth, prin.
Ellis ES, 1318 GRAND AVE   39194
Ruby Stampley, prin.
Webster ES, 622 E FOURTH ST   39194
Beverly Frank, prin.

Woolfolk MS, 201 E FIFTH ST 39194
  Janet Forrester, prin.

Yazoo County SD
  Sch. Sys. Enr. Code 4
  Supt. – Margie Vaughan, P O BOX 988 39194
  Other Schools – See Bentonia, Satartia, Vaughan

MISSOURI

STATE DEPARTMENT OF EDUCATION
P.O. Box 480, Jefferson City 65102
(314) 751-4446

Commissioner of Education	Robert Bartman
Deputy Commissioner	Joel Denney
Assistant Commisioner Administration	Terrance Stewart
Assistant Commissioner Vocational & Adult Education	Frank Drake
Assistant Commissioner Instruction	Otis Baker
Assistant Commissioner Special Education	John Allan
Assistant Commissioner Urban & Teacher Education	L. Celestine Ferguson
Assistant Commissioner Vocational Rehabilitation	Don Gann

STATE BOARD OF EDUCATION
Roseann Bentley, *President*   P.O. Box 480, Jefferson City   65102

MISSOURI DEPARTMENT OF HIGHER EDUCATION
Dr. Shaila Aery, *Commissioner*   101 Adams, Jefferson City   65101

PUBLIC, PRIVATE, AND PAROCHIAL ELEMENTARY SCHOOLS

Adrian, Bates Co., Pop. Code 4
  Adrian RSD 3
  Sch. Sys. Enr. Code 3
  Supt. – Victor Kretzschmar, P O BOX 98 64720
  ES 64720 – Wallace Hendrickson, prin.

Advance, Stoddard Co., Pop. Code 4
  Advance RSD 4
  Sch. Sys. Enr. Code 3
  Supt. – W. T. Bradshaw, P O BOX 195 63730
  ES 63730 – Loy Moore Jr., prin.

Albany, Gentry Co., Pop. Code 4
  Albany RSD 3
  Sch. Sys. Enr. Code 3
  Supt. – Larry Price, 101 W JEFFERSON 64402
  George ES, 202 S EAST ST 64402
    Betty Weigand, prin.

Alexandria, Clark Co., Pop. Code 2
  Clark County RSD 1
  Supt. – See Kahoka
  Running Fox ES
    RURAL ROUTE 01 BOX 170 63430
    Richard Tuttle, prin.

Alma, Lafayette Co., Pop. Code 2
  Lafayette Co. RSD 10
  Sch. Sys. Enr. Code 3
  Supt. – Greg Prather 64001
  Other Schools – See Waverly

  Trinity Lutheran School, P O BOX 56 64001

Altenburg, Perry Co., Pop. Code 2
  Altenburg ESD
  Sch. Sys. Enr. Code 1
  Supt. – (—), P O BOX 127 63732
  ES 63732 – Richard Hoffman, prin.

Alton, Oregon Co., Pop. Code 3
  Alton RSD 9
  Sch. Sys. Enr. Code 3
  Supt. – Billy Smith
    RURAL ROUTE 02 BOX 64A1 65606
  ES, RURAL ROUTE 02 BOX 64A2 65606
    Wendell Williams, prin.

Amazonia, Andrew Co., Pop. Code 2
  Savannah RSD 3
  Supt. – See Savannah
  ES 64421 – Margaret Mcelduff, prin.

Amoret, Bates Co., Pop. Code 2
  Miami RSD 1
  Sch. Sys. Enr. Code 2
  Supt. – Lonnie Clair, RURAL ROUTE 01 64722
  Other Schools – See Miami

Anderson, McDonald Co., Pop. Code 4
  McDonald County RSD 1
  Sch. Sys. Enr. Code 4
  Supt. – Dr. Jack Allman, P O BOX 378 64831
  ES, P O BOX 373 64831 – Dan Rickett, prin.
  Other Schools – See Jane, Noel, Pineville, Rocky
    Comfort, South West City

Annapolis, Iron Co., Pop. Code 2
  South Iron RSD 1
  Sch. Sys. Enr. Code 2
  Supt. – John S. Wood, P O BOX 218 63620
  South Iron County ES 63620
    Marshall Lewis, prin.

Appleton City, St. Clair Co., Pop. Code 4
  Appleton City RSD 2
  Sch. Sys. Enr. Code 2
  Supt. – Mike Stevenson, P O BOX 126 64724
  ES 64724 – Terry Fisher, prin.

  Hudson RSD 9
  Sch. Sys. Enr. Code 1
  Supt. – (—), RURAL ROUTE 03 64724
  Hudson ES 64724 – Esther Breon, prin.

Archie, Cass Co., Pop. Code 3
  Cass County RSD 5
  Sch. Sys. Enr. Code 3
  Supt. – William Gordon, P O BOX 106 64725
  ES 64725 – Toni Hubbard, prin.

Argyle, Osage Co., Pop. Code 2
  Osage County RSD 3
  Supt. – See Westphalia
  ES 65001 – Wanda Hartsock, prin.

Arnold, Jefferson Co., Pop. Code 7
  Fox Cons. SD 6
  Sch. Sys. Enr. Code 6
  Supt. – Dr Charles Hudson
    745 JEFFCO BLVD 63010
  Fox ES 63010 – James Chellew, prin.
  Meremec Heights ES
    RURAL ROUTE 02 BOX 304B 63010
    Raymond Hodge, prin.
  Rockport Heights ES, 3871 JEFFCO BLVD 63010
    Louis Wright, prin.
  Sherwood ES, 1769 MISSOURI STATE RD 63010
    Alice Martin, prin.
  Other Schools – See Imperial

  Immaculate Conception School
    2316 CHURCH RD 63010
  St. David PS, 2322 TENBROOK RD 63010
  St. John's Lutheran School
    3511 JEFFCO BLVD 63010

Asbury, Jasper Co., Pop. Code 2
  Carl Junction RSD 1
  Supt. – See Carl Junction
  ES 64832 – Jeannette Verbryck, prin.

Ash Grove, Greene Co., Pop. Code 4
  Ash Grove RSD 4
  Sch. Sys. Enr. Code 3
  Supt. – B. B. McDonald, P O BOX 218 65604
  ES 65604 – Carolyn Murray, prin.
  Other Schools – See Bois D'arc

Ashland, Boone Co., Pop. Code 4
  Southern Boone County RSD 1
  Sch. Sys. Enr. Code 3
  Supt. – Dr. D. R. Burnett, P O BOX 168 65010
  ES, 303 S MAIN ST 65010 – David Decker, prin.

Atlanta, Macon Co., Pop. Code 2
  Atlanta Cons. SD 3
  Sch. Sys. Enr. Code 2
  Supt. – Ronald Martin, P O BOX 367 63530
  ES 63530 – John Ahern, prin.

Augusta, St. Charles Co., Pop. Code 2
  Washington SD
  Supt. – See Washington
  ES 63332 – Paul Suchland, prin.

Aurora, Lawrence Co., Pop. Code 6
  Aurora RSD 8
  Sch. Sys. Enr. Code 4
  Supt. – Lawrence McGovern
    W END LOCUST ST 65605
  Robinson MS, LINCOLN AVE 65605
    Larry Ewing, prin.
  Lowell ES, 5 W DELTA ST 65605
    Charles Flotz, prin.

  Jenkins ESD 35
  Sch. Sys. Enr. Code 1
  Supt. – (—), RURAL ROUTE 03 BOX 4 65605
  ES 65605 – Charles Moore, prin.

Auxvasse, Callaway Co., Pop. Code 3
  North Callaway County RSD 1
  Supt. – See Kingdom City
  ES, P O BOX 8 65231 – Robert Cannell, prin.

Ava, Douglas Co., Pop. Code 5
  Ava RSD 1
  Sch. Sys. Enr. Code 4
  Supt. – Tom Nichols, P O BOX 338 65608
  JHS 65608 – J. Holobaugh, prin.
  ES 65608 – Lena Pierce, prin.

Plainview RSD 8
Sch. Sys. Enr. Code 1
Supt. – (—)
    RUERAL ROUTE 03 BOX 145 65608
Plainview ES 65608 – Marjorie Voyles, prin.

Avilla, Jasper Co., Pop. Code 2
Avilla RSD 13
Sch. Sys. Enr. Code 2
Supt. – (—), P O BOX 7 64833
ES 64833 – Danny Friend, prin.

Bakersfield, Ozark Co., Pop. Code 2
Bakersfield RSD 4
Sch. Sys. Enr. Code 2
Supt. – Edison Nowlin, P O BOX 38 65609
ES 65609 – Mack Davis, prin.

Ballwin, St. Louis Co., Pop. Code 7
Parkway Cons. SD 2
Sch. Sys. Enr. Code 7
Supt. – See Chesterfield
Claymont ES, 405 COUNTRY CLUB DR 63011
    Aaron Oberman, prin.
Hanna Woods ES, 720 HANNA RD 63021
    Carol Osterloh, prin.
Sorrento Springs ES, 390 TUMULTY DR 63021
    John Morris, prin.
Wren Hollow ES, 655 WREN AVE 63021
    Verlin Dunker, prin.

Rockwood RSD 6
Supt. – See Eureka
ES, 400 JEFFERSON AVE 63021
    Charles Mercer, prin.
Westridge ES, 908 CRESTLAND DR 63011
    C. Terry Baum, prin.
Woerther ES, 314 NEW BALLWIN RD 63021
    Ralph Blevins Jr., prin.

Christ Prince Of Peace School
    417 WEIDMAN RD 63011
Holy Infant School, 627 DENNISON DR 63021
St. Clare of Assisi School
    1020 W CLAYTON RD 63011
St. John's Lutheran School
    15808 MANCHESTER ROAD 63011
St. Joseph School Manchester
    555 SAINT JOSEPH LANE 63011

Baring, Knox Co., Pop. Code 2
Bible Grove RSD 5
Sch. Sys. Enr. Code 1
Supt. – (—), RURAL ROUTE 01 63531
Bible Grove MS 63531 – Colleen Vreeland, prin.

Barnard, Nodaway Co., Pop. Code 2
South Nodaway County RSD 4
Sch. Sys. Enr. Code 2
Supt. – Warren Denney, P O BOX 7 64423
Other Schools – See Guilford

Belgrade, Washington Co., Pop. Code 3
Valley RSD 6
Supt. – See Caledonia
ES 63622 – Leonard Zanatta, prin.

Bell City, Stoddard Co., Pop. Code 3
Bell City RSD 2
Sch. Sys. Enr. Code 2
Supt. – R. L. McCormick, P O BOX 147 63735
ES 63735 – David Pierson, prin.

Belle, Maries Co., Pop. Code 4
Maries County RSD 2
Sch. Sys. Enr. Code 3
Supt. – Harold McCoy, P O BOX AC 65013
Bland JHS, P O BOX E 65013 – Dwane Smith, prin.
ES 65013 – Bernetta Williams, prin.
Bland ES, P O BOX E 65013
    Charles Thomas, prin.

Belleview, Iron Co., Pop. Code 4
Belleview RSD 3
Sch. Sys. Enr. Code 2
Supt. – Dr. Ray Puckett, HWY 32 & 21 63623
ES 63623 – Dr. Ray Puckett, prin.

Bellflower, Montgomery Co., Pop. Code 2
Montgomery County RSD 2
Supt. – See Montgomery City
ES 63333 – Nancy Foust, prin.

Belton, Cass Co., Pop. Code 7
Belton SD 124
Sch. Sys. Enr. Code 4
Supt. – Gordon Sunderland
    315 COLBERN ST 64012
Cambridge ES, CAMBRIDGE & S SCOTT 64012
    Judy Rush, prin.
Gladden ES
    WESTOVER ROAD & AIRWAY LANE 64012
    Greg Smith, prin.
Hillcrest ES
    HILLCREFEST ROAD & NORTH AVE 64012
    David Leone, prin.

Benton, Scott Co., Pop. Code 3
Kelso Cons. SD 7
Sch. Sys. Enr. Code 2
Supt. – (—)
    RURAL ROUTE 01 BOX 539 63736
Kelso ES 63736 – Richard Eggimann, prin.

Scott County RSD 4
Sch. Sys. Enr. Code 3
Supt. – Dr. Jerry Waddle, P O BOX 98 63736
Kelly ES 63736 – Mildred Mason, prin.

St. Denis School, ROUTE ONE 63736

Berger, Franklin Co., Pop. Code 2
Gasconade County RSD 1
Supt. – See Hermann
ES 63014 – Robert Delaney, prin.

Berkeley, St. Louis Co., Pop. Code 7
Ferguson-Florissant RSD 2
Supt. – See Florissant
MS, 8300 FROST AVE 63134 – Lee Ferguson, prin.
Airport ES, 8249 AIRPORT RD 63134
    Carolyn Neal, prin.
Holman ES, 8811 HAROLD DR 63134
    Stephanie Lane, prin.

St. William School
    9330 STANSBERRY AVE 63134

Bernie, Stoddard Co., Pop. Code 4
Bernie RSD 13
Sch. Sys. Enr. Code 3
Supt. – P. T. Dawson, P O BOX C 63822
ES 63822 – Stanley Smee, prin.

Bethany, Harrison Co., Pop. Code 5
South Harrison RSD 2
Sch. Sys. Enr. Code 3
Supt. – Dr. Robert Taylor, P O BOX 445 64424
ES, 22ND & BEEKMAN 64424
    Marilyn Henry, prin.
Other Schools – See New Hampton

Bevier, Macon Co., Pop. Code 3
Bevier Cons. SD 4
Sch. Sys. Enr. Code 2
Supt. – Joan Cox, 400 BLOOMINGTON ST 63532
ES 63532 – Joan Cox, prin.

Billings, Christian Co., Pop. Code 3
Billings RSD 4
Sch. Sys. Enr. Code 2
Supt. – Ronald Talley, RURAL ROUTE 01 65610
ES 65610 – William Sweet, prin.

Birch Tree, Shannon Co., Pop. Code 3
Mountain View-Birch Tree RSD 3
Supt. – See Mountain View
ES, RURAL ROUTE 02 65438
    Wilbert Shockley, prin.

Bismarck, St. Francois Co., Pop. Code 4
Bismarck RSD 5
Sch. Sys. Enr. Code 3
Supt. – Thomas G. Campbell, P O BOX 257 63624
ES 63624 – Richard Jones, prin.

Blackwater, Cooper Co., Pop. Code 2
Blackwater RSD 2
Sch. Sys. Enr. Code 2
Supt. – (—), P O BOX 117 65322
ES 65322 – Richard Harrison, prin.

Bloomfield, Stoddard Co., Pop. Code 4
Bloomfield RSD 14
Sch. Sys. Enr. Code 3
Supt. – John Shock, P O BOX 4 63825
ES 63825 – Stanley Durham, prin.

Bloomsdale, Ste. Genevieve Co., Pop. Code 2
St. Genevieve County RSD 2
Supt. – See Sainte Genevieve
ES, HCR 02 BOX 42 63627
    Terence McDaniel, prin.

St. Agnes School, SAINT AGNES DRIVE 63627

Blue Eye, Stone Co., Pop. Code 1
Blue Eye RSD 5
Sch. Sys. Enr. Code 2
Supt. – Speedy Branstetter, P O BOX 38 65611
ES 65611 – Roger Butler, prin.

Blue Springs, Jackson Co., Pop. Code 8
Blue Springs RSD 4
Sch. Sys. Enr. Code 6
Supt. – Dr. Charles McGraw
    1801 W VESPER ST 64015
Bryant ES
    1101 SUNNYSIDE SCHOOL ROAD 64015
    Gerald Snider, prin.
Cordill-Mason ES
    4001 CHRISTIANSEN DR 64015
    Floyd Dunaway, prin.
Hall-McCarter MS, 1609 VALLEY VIEW RD 64015
    Alan Masten, prin.
Lewis ES, 717 PARK RD 64015
    Dr. Carole Gran, prin.
Nowlin ES, 1605 VALLEY VIEW ROAD 64015
    Bradley Barnhart, prin.
Smith ES, 1609 CLARK RD 64015
    Clarence Miller, prin.
Ultican ES, 19TH & MAIN 64015
    Joy Conrad, prin.
Walker ES
    201 N SUNNYSIDE SCHOOL RD 64015
    Ernest Graham, prin.
Young ES, 505 E SHAMROCK LN 64015
    Linda Johnson, prin.
Other Schools – See Independence

St. John Lalande School
    801 W R D MIZE RD 64015

Bois D'arc, Green Co.
Ash Grove RSD 4
Supt. – See Ash Grove

ES 65612 – Betty Squibb, prin.

Bolckow, Andrew Co., Pop. Code 2
North Andrew County RSD 6
Supt. – See Rosendale
North Andrew County ES 64427
    Darell Hawley, prin.

Bolivar, Polk Co., Pop. Code 6
Bolivar RSD 1
Sch. Sys. Enr. Code 4
Supt. – Richard Trout, 604 W JACKSON ST 65613
MS 65613 – Stephen Skinner, prin.
Leonard ES, 706 LEONARD PL 65613
    Joyce Creemer, prin.

Bonne Terre, St. Francois Co., Pop. Code 5
North St. Francois County RSD 1
Sch. Sys. Enr. Code 5
Supt. – Dr. Gary Cain, OLD HIGHWAY 67 N 63628
North St. Francois County JHS
    114 N ALLEN ST 63628 – Kenneth Owen, prin.
North County ES, ALLEN & BENHAM 63628
    Terry Gibbons, prin.
Other Schools – See Desloge

Boonville, Cooper Co., Pop. Code 6
Boonville RSD 1
Sch. Sys. Enr. Code 4
Supt. – Greg Gettings, 700 MAIN ST 65233
Elliott MS 65233 – Donald Schupp, prin.
Barton MS, LOCUST ST 65233
    Joann Rhoades, prin.
Central ES, 901 6TH ST 65233
    Joann Rhoades, prin.

SS Peter & Paul School, 502 7TH ST 65233

Bosworth, Carroll Co., Pop. Code 2
Bosworth RSD 5
Sch. Sys. Enr. Code 2
Supt. – Terry Rinehart 64623
ES 64623 – Cheryl Sanders, prin.

Bourbon, Crawford Co., Pop. Code 4
Crawford County RSD 1
Sch. Sys. Enr. Code 3
Supt. – Merlin Shelton, P O BOX 40 65441
Crawford County MS, P O BOX 40 65441
    John Snider, prin.
Crawford County ES 65441 – John Snider, prin.

Bowling Green, Pike Co., Pop. Code 5
Bowling Green RSD 1
Sch. Sys. Enr. Code 4
Supt. – Bob Kirkpatrick 63334
JHS, 1000 W CENTENNIAL AVE 63334
    Dwane Rees, prin.
ES, HIGHWAY 61 S 63334
    R. Louise Mason, prin.
Other Schools – See Curryville, Frankford

St. Clement School, RURAL ROUTE 03 63334

Bradleyville, Taney Co., Pop. Code 1
Bradleyville RSD 1
Sch. Sys. Enr. Code 2
Supt. – Russell Hunt 65614
ES 65614 – Nona Norwine, prin.

Branson, Taney Co., Pop. Code 5
Branson RSD 4
Sch. Sys. Enr. Code 3
Supt. – Dr. Lee J. Orth, 500 S 5TH ST 65616
JHS, N HWY 65 65616 – Roger Newell, prin.
IS, SIXTH & COLLEGE 65616 – Larry Fritz, prin.
ES, SIXTH & BROWN 65616 – Gary Booher, prin.

Brashear, Adair Co., Pop. Code 2
Adair County RSD 2
Sch. Sys. Enr. Code 2
Supt. – Ted Green 63533
Adair County ES 63533 – Jeanne Mayfield, prin.

Braymer, Caldwell Co., Pop. Code 3
Braymer Cons. SD 4
Sch. Sys. Enr. Code 2
Supt. – Lonnie Daugherty, 1 BOBCAT AVE 64624
ES 64622 – Dave Jones, prin.

Breckenridge, Caldwell Co., Pop. Code 3
Breckenridge RSD 1
Sch. Sys. Enr. Code 2
Supt. – Harvey Chauvin, P O BOX 175 64625
ES 64625 – Gary Henry, prin.

Brentwood, St. Louis Co., Pop. Code 6
Brentwood SD
Sch. Sys. Enr. Code 3
Supt. – Dr. Raymond Bentz
    1775 PARKRIDGE AVE 63144
McGrath ES, 2350 ST CLAIR AVE 63144
    K. Douglas Cormack, prin.
Twain ES, 8636 LITZSINGER RD 63144
    Dr. Cameron Pulliam, prin.

Bridgeton, St. Louis Co., Pop. Code 7
Pattonville RSD 3
Supt. – See Maryland Heights
Bridgeway ES, 11635 OAKBURY CT 63044
    Kenneth Black, prin.
Carrollton ES, 3936 CELBURNE LN 63044
    Dr. Deborah Hines, prin.
Carrollton Oaks ES, 4385 HOLMFORD DR 63044
    Geroge Pathenos, prin.

Bronaugh, Vernon Co., Pop. Code 2
Bronaugh RSD 7
Sch. Sys. Enr. Code 2
Supt. – Jerry Sparks, 527 E 6TH ST 64728
ES 64728 – Robert McLean, prin.

Brookfield, Linn Co., Pop. Code 6
Brookfield RSD 3
Sch. Sys. Enr. Code 4
Supt. – Ted Davis, 200 LINN ST 64628
MS, RURAL ROUTE 03 64628 – Gary Ewing, prin.
ES, RURAL ROUTE 03 64628 – Gary Haag, prin.

Broseley, Butler Co., Pop. Code 2
Twin Rivers RSD 10
Sch. Sys. Enr. Code 4
Supt. – Dr. M. Riggins 63932
Other Schools – See Fisk, Qulin

Brunswick, Chariton Co., Pop. Code 4
Brunswick RSD 2
Sch. Sys. Enr. Code 2
Supt. – Owen Worstell
    RURAL ROUTE 01 BOX 450 65236
ES, 705 FILMORE ST 65236 – Michael Bain, prin.

Bucklin, Linn Co., Pop. Code 3
Bucklin RSD 2
Sch. Sys. Enr. Code 2
Supt. – Billy Lewis
    RURAL ROUTE 01 BOX 6F 64631
ES 64631 – Verna Monk, prin.

Buckner, Jackson Co.
Fort Osage RSD 1
Supt. – See Independence
ES 64016 – Richard Thompson, prin.

Buffalo, Dallas Co., Pop. Code 4
Dallas County RSD 1
Sch. Sys. Enr. Code 4
Supt. – Paul Darnell, P O BOX 800 65622
JHS, P O BOX 800 65622 – John Dull, prin.
Mallory ES 65622 – Pruitt Miller, prin.
Other Schools – See Long Lane

Bunceton, Cooper Co., Pop. Code 2
Cooper County RSD 4
Sch. Sys. Enr. Code 2
Supt. – Elvin Farguhar, P O BOX 184 65237
Cooper ES 65237 – Ronald Garber, prin.

Bunker, Reynolds Co., Pop. Code 3
Bunker RSD 3
Sch. Sys. Enr. Code 2
Supt. – Gary Grant, P O BOX 115 63629
ES 63629 – H. Darrell Hathcoat, prin.

Burfordville, Cape Girardeau Co.
Jackson RSD 2
Supt. – See Jackson
Attendance Ctr. 63739 – Melody Hagans, prin.

Burlington Junction, Nodaway Co., Pop. Code 3
West Nodaway RSD 1
Sch. Sys. Enr. Code 2
Supt. – David Grubb, P O BOX 229 64428
Other Schools – See Clearmont

Butler, Bates Co., Pop. Code 5
Ballard RSD 2
Sch. Sys. Enr. Code 1
Supt. – Derrall Beasley
    RURAL ROUTE 01 BOX 145 64730
ES 64730 – Mary Ann Bath, prin.

Butler RSD 5
Sch. Sys. Enr. Code 4
Supt. – Gary Crabtree, 420 S FULTON ST 64730
ES 64730 – Bill Kell, prin.

Cabool, Texas Co., Pop. Code 4
Cabool RSD 4
Sch. Sys. Enr. Code 2
Supt. – Kenneth Holloway 65689
MS, 1025 ROGERS ST 65689 – Robert Fields, prin.
ES, GARST ST 65689 – Paul Thompson, prin.

Cadet, Washington Co.
Kingston ESD K-14
Sch. Sys. Enr. Code 2
Supt. – (—), P O BOX 501 63630
Other Schools – See Kingston

St. Joachim School
    RURAL ROUTE 01 BOX 231 63630

Cainsville, Harrison Co., Pop. Code 2
Cainsville RSD 1
Sch. Sys. Enr. Code 2
Supt. – Dennis McCullough, P O BOX 10 64632
ES 64632 – Debbie Sherer, prin.

Cairo, Randolph Co., Pop. Code 2
Northeast Randolph County RSD 4
Sch. Sys. Enr. Code 2
Supt. – Edward Musgrove, P O BOX 145 65239
ES 65239 – Marge Gibson, prin.

Caledonia, Washington Co., Pop. Code 2
Valley RSD 6
Sch. Sys. Enr. Code 3
Supt. – George Boyd 63631
ES 63631 – Leonard Zanatta, prin.
Other Schools – See Belgrade

Calhoun, Henry Co., Pop. Code 2
Calhoun RSD 8
Sch. Sys. Enr. Code 2
Supt. – Leonard Filla, P O BOX 7 65323
ES 65323 – Yale Turnham, prin.

California, Moniteau Co., Pop. Code 5
Montieau County RSD 1
Sch. Sys. Enr. Code 4
Supt. – Dr. Larry Fletcher 65018
Moniteau County ES 65018 – Stephen Saak, prin.

Callao, Macon Co., Pop. Code 2
Callao Cons. SD 8
Sch. Sys. Enr. Code 1
Supt. – (—), P O BOX A 63534
ES 63534 – Patricia Henley, prin.

Camden Point, Platte Co., Pop. Code 2
North Platte County RSD 1
Supt. – See Dearborn
ES 64018 – Louis Buntin, prin.

Camdenton, Camden Co., Pop. Code 4
Camdenton RSD 3
Sch. Sys. Enr. Code 5
Supt. – Dr. John Bearden, P O BOX 1409 65020
ES 65020 – Curtis Lloyd, prin.
Other Schools – See Osage Beach, Sunrise Beach

Cameron, Clinton Co., Pop. Code 5
Cameron RSD 1
Sch. Sys. Enr. Code 4
Supt. – Darrel Walker
    1022 S CHESTNUT ST 64429
Cameron Middle MS, 116 W 4TH ST 64429
    Jerry Fischer, prin.
Parkview ES, 602 S HARRIS ST 64429
    Randall Relford, prin.

Campbell, Dunklin Co., Pop. Code 4
Campbell RSD 2
Sch. Sys. Enr. Code 3
Supt. – Dr. Jack Lincoln 63933
ES 63933 – Carol Blanton, prin.

Canton, Lewis Co., Pop. Code 4
Canton RSD 5
Sch. Sys. Enr. Code 3
Supt. – William Ray, 200 S 4TH ST 63435
ES 63435 – Ann Parker, prin.

Cape Girardeau, Cape Girardeau Co., Pop. Code 8
Cape Girardeau SD 63
Sch. Sys. Enr. Code 5
Supt. – Dr. Arthur Turner, 61 N CLARK ST 63701
Franklin ES, 215 N LOUISIANA ST 63701
    Ron Haggard, prin.
Greene ES, 1000 RANNEY AVE 63701
    Samuel Jarrell, prin.
Hawthorn ES, 2860 HOPPER RD 63701
    Charles Clippard, prin.
Jefferson ES, 520 MINNESOTA ST 63701
    Gary Kralemann, prin.
Schrader ES, 1360 RANDOL AVE 63701
    Roy Glass, prin.
Schultz MS, 101 S PACIFIC ST 63701
    Dr. Carolyn Vandeven, prin.
Washington ES, 621 N FOUNTAIN ST 63701
    Richard Bollwerk, prin.

Nell Holcomb RSD 4
Sch. Sys. Enr. Code 2
Supt. – (—), RURAL ROUTE 01 63701
Holcomb ES 63701 – Dr. Wallace Barrows, prin.

St. Marys School, 210 S SPRIGG ST 63701
St. Vincent De Paul School
    1919 RITTER DR 63701
Trinity Lutheran School, 55 N PACIFIC ST 63701

Cardwell, Dunklin Co., Pop. Code 3
Southland Cons. SD 9
Sch. Sys. Enr. Code 3
Supt. – Michael Back, P O BOX 47 63829
Southland ES 63829 – J B Gibbins, prin.

Carl Junction, Jasper Co., Pop. Code 5
Carl Junction RSD 1
Sch. Sys. Enr. Code 4
Supt. – Dr. Jerry B. Stark, P O BOX 4 64834
JHS 64834 – R. Moorehouse, prin.
Intermediate ES 64834 – Pamela Babbitt, prin.
PS 64834 – Carolyn Porter, prin.
Other Schools – See Asbury

Carrollton, Carroll Co., Pop. Code 5
Carrollton RSD 7
Sch. Sys. Enr. Code 4
Supt. – Irwin R. Thomas, E 9TH ST 64633
Adams-Dieterich ES, 306 N JEFFERSON ST 64633
    Wallace Stiles, prin.
Root MS, 221 S MAIN ST 64633
    Larry Flakne, prin.

Carterville, Jasper Co., Pop. Code 4
Webb City RSD 7
Supt. – See Webb City
ES 64835 – Larry McKenzie, prin.

Carthage, Jasper Co., Pop. Code 7
Carthage RSD 9
Sch. Sys. Enr. Code 5
Supt. – Dr. C. E. Johnson, 714 S MAIN ST 64836
Columbian ES, 1015 W MACON ST 64836
    Mervin Hight, prin.
Fairview ES, 1201 E FAIRVIEW AVE 64836
    Howard Smith, prin.

Field ES, 613 E CHESTNUT ST 64836
    Thomas Bewick, prin.
Hawthorne ES, 811 W CENTRAL AVE 64836
    Charles Paden, prin.
Pleasant Valley ES
    RURAL ROUTE 06 BOX 113 64836
    Marvin Messick, prin.
Twain ES, 1435 S MAIN ST 64836
    Dennis Conrow, prin.

Caruthersville, Pemiscot Co., Pop. Code 6
Caruthersville SD 18
Sch. Sys. Enr. Code 4
Supt. – C. S. Hutchinson, 1711 WARD AVE 63830
JHS, 18TH & ADAMS ST 63830
    James L. Moore, prin.
Southside ES, 16TH & WARD 63830
    Diane Sayre, prin.
Westside ES, 900 WASHINGTON AVE 63830
    Randy Gillespie, prin.

Pemiscot County RSD 3
Sch. Sys. Enr. Code 2
Supt. – (—)
    RURAL ROUTE 01 BOX 291 63830
Unit One ES 63830 – John Sellars, prin.

Cassville, Barry Co., Pop. Code 4
Cassville RSD 4
Sch. Sys. Enr. Code 4
Supt. – D. R. Bailey, 14TH & MAIN 65625
MS 65625 – Wayne Brower, prin.
ES 65625 – Martha Dunnam, prin.

Catawissa, Franklin Co.
Meramec Valley RSD 3
Supt. – See Pacific
Nike ES 63015 – Richard Smith, prin.

Cedarcreek, Taney Co.
Cedarcreek RSD 8
Sch. Sys. Enr. Code 1
Supt. – (—) 65627
ES 65627 – Donald Peebles, prin.

Cedar Hill, Jefferson Co., Pop. Code 2
Northwest RSD 1
Supt. – See House Springs
MS 63016 – Gerald Glidewell, prin.

Center, Ralls Co., Pop. Code 3
Ralls County RSD 2
Sch. Sys. Enr. Code 4
Supt. – Gary Schroer, P O BOX 26 63436
ES, W HAWKINS 63436 – William Daly, prin.
Other Schools – See New London, Perry

Centerview, Johnson Co., Pop. Code 2
Johnson County RSD 7
Sch. Sys. Enr. Code 2
Supt. – Ray V. Patrick
    RURAL ROUTE 02 BOX 94 64019
ES, P O BOX 175 64019 – Randy Sheriff, prin.
Other Schools – See Warrensburg

Centerville, Reynolds Co.
Centerville RSD 1
Sch. Sys. Enr. Code 1
Supt. – (—), P O BOX 99 63633
ES 63633 – John Caldwell, prin.

Centralia, Boone Co., Pop. Code 5
Centralia RSD 6
Sch. Sys. Enr. Code 4
Supt. – Thomas Quinn
    635 S JEFFERSON ST 65240
Boren MS, 110 N JEFFERSON ST 65240
    Dick Perkins, prin.
Chance ES, 510 S ROLLINS ST 65240
    Judy Musgraves, prin.

Chadwick, Christian Co., Pop. Code 2
Chadwick RSD 1
Sch. Sys. Enr. Code 2
Supt. – David Ellsworth 65629
ES 65629 – Joseph Mease, prin.

Chaffee, Scott Co., Pop. Code 5
Chaffee RSD 2
Sch. Sys. Enr. Code 3
Supt. – Dr. J. D. Payne, 109 N 5TH ST 63740
ES, 408 ELLIOTT AVE 63740
    Omer Creech Jr., prin.

St. Ambrose School, THIRD & ELLIOTT 63740

Chamois, Osage Co., Pop. Code 3
Osage County RSD 1
Sch. Sys. Enr. Code 2
Supt. – Vernon L. Altom
    RURAL ROUTE BOX 8A 65024
Osage County ES 65024 – N. Lee Shearer, prin.

Charleston, Mississippi Co., Pop. Code 6
Charleston RSD 1
Sch. Sys. Enr. Code 4
Supt. – Bill Bacchus, P O BOX 39 63834
JHS, MAIN ST 63834 – Kevin Miller, prin.
Hearnes ES, PLANT ROAD 63834
    Richard Wells, prin.
Simpson ES, E TOM BROWN 63834
    Richard Wells, prin.

Chesterfield, St. Louis Co., Pop. Code 3
Parkway Cons. SD 2
Sch. Sys. Enr. Code 7
Supt. – Leonard Burns
    455 N WOODS MILL ROAD 63017

Central JHS, 471 N WOODS MILL ROAD   63017
  William Myer, prin.
West JHS, 2312 BAXTER ROAD   63017
  Sam Sciortino, prin.
Green Trails ES, 170 PORTICO DR   63017
  Douglas Underwood, prin.
Highcroft Ridge ES, 15380 HIGHCROFT DR   63017
  Richard Overfelt, prin.
River Bend ES, 224 RIVER VALLEY DR   63017
  Jill Behan, prin.
Shenandoah Valley ES
  15399 APPALACHIAN TRL   63017
  Francis Brown, prin.
Other Schools – See Ballwin, Creve Coeur,
  Manchester, Maryland Heights, Saint Louis

Rockwood RSD 6
Supt. – See Eureka
ES, 17700 WILD HORSE CREEK RD   63017
  Wayne Byington, prin.

Ascension School, 238 SANTA MARIA DR   63017
Chesterfield Day School, 1100 WHITE RD   63017
Incarnate Word School, 13416 OLIVE BLVD   63017
Linda Vista Montessori School
  KEHRS MILL & STRECKER   63017

Chilhowee, Johnson Co., Pop. Code 2
Chilhowee RSD 4
Sch. Sys. Enr. Code 2
Supt. – E. Schoppenhorst, P O BOX 98   64733
ES   64733 – Robert Osgood, prin.

Shawnee SD 3
Sch. Sys. Enr. Code 1
Supt. – (—), RURAL ROUTE 01   64733
Shawnee ES   64733 – Sandy Hutchinson, prin.

Chillicothe, Livingston Co., Pop. Code 6
Chillicothe RSD 2
Sch. Sys. Enr. Code 4
Supt. – Dr. J. E. Eden, P O BOX 530   64601
JHS, 1529 CALHOUN ST   64601
  Ronald O'Dell, prin.
Central MS, 321 ELM ST   64601
  Donald Dupy, prin.
Dewey ES, 905 DICKINSON ST   64601
  Allen Stephens, prin.
Field ES, 1100 OAK ST   64601
  Donald Dupy, prin.

Bishop Hogan Memorial School
  KENNEDY AVE & VINE   64601

Chula, Livingston Co.
Livingston County RSD 3
Sch. Sys. Enr. Code 1
Supt. – (—), P O BOX 40   64635
Livingston County ES   64635
  Betty Jean Moore, prin.

Clarence, Shelby Co., Pop. Code 4
Shelby County RSD 4
Supt. – See Shelbina
ES, 206 N SHELBY   63437 – Wendell Ware, prin.

Clark, Randolph Co., Pop. Code 2
Clark RSD 6
Sch. Sys. Enr. Code 1
Supt. – (—), P O BOX 98   65243
ES   65243 – Jim Christal, prin.

Clarksburg, Moniteau Co., Pop. Code 2
Clarksburg Cons. SD 2
Sch. Sys. Enr. Code 2
Supt. – (—), P O BOX 143   65025
ES   65025 – William Smith, prin.

Clarksville, Pike Co., Pop. Code 3
Pike County RSD 3
Sch. Sys. Enr. Code 3
Supt. – Dr. Earl MacGreen, P O BOX 218   63336
Clopton ES   63336 – Dallas Singer, prin.

Clarkton, Dunklin Co., Pop. Code 4
Clarkton Cons. SD 4
Sch. Sys. Enr. Code 2
Supt. – Richard Reynolds, P O BOX 637   63837
ES   63837 – David Todd, prin.

Clayton, St. Louis Co., Pop. Code 7
Clayton SD
Sch. Sys. Enr. Code 4
Supt. – Dr. Earl W. Hobbs
  7530 MARYLAND AVE   63105
Wydown JHS, 6500 WYDOWN BLVD   63105
  Jere Hochman, prin.
Captain ES, 6345 NORTHWOOD AVE   63105
  Barbara Kohm, prin.
Glenbridge ES, 7447 WELLINGTON WAY   63105
  Phyllis Stoecklein, prin.
Meramec ES, 400 S MERAMEC AVE   63105
  Dr. Ruth Mach, prin.

Clearmont, Nodaway Co., Pop. Code 2
West Nodaway RSD 1
Supt. – See Burlington Junction
ES   64431 – Sharon Shain, prin.

Cleveland, Cass Co., Pop. Code 2
Midway RSD 1
Sch. Sys. Enr. Code 3
Supt. – Janice Larson, HIGHWAY 02   64734
Other Schools – See Midway

Clever, Christian Co., Pop. Code 3
Clever RSD 5
Sch. Sys. Enr. Code 2
Supt. – Larry Hale, P O BOX 128   65631
ES   65631 – Dean Meadows, prin.

Clifton Hill, Randolph Co., Pop. Code 2
Westran RSD 1
Supt. – See Huntsville
Westran MS   65244 – Richard Ray, prin.

Climax Springs, Camden Co., Pop. Code 1
Climax Springs RSD 4
Sch. Sys. Enr. Code 2
Supt. – Dr. Nila Tritt
  RURAL ROUTE 01 BOX 239   65324
ES, RURAL ROUTE 01 BOX 239   65324
  Patricia Middleton, prin.

Clinton, Henry Co., Pop. Code 6
Clinton SD
Sch. Sys. Enr. Code 4
Supt. – Dr. Gary Deskins, 510 W ALLEN ST   64735
MS, 2 8TH ST   64735 – Gladden Dye, prin.
Jefferson Park ES, ORCHARD & FRANKLIN   64735
  Richard Glasford, prin.
Southeast ES, 809 S 8TH ST   64735
  Michael Gantt, prin.

Davis RSD 12
Sch. Sys. Enr. Code 1
Supt. – (—), RURAL ROUTE 04   64735
Davis ES   64735 – Carla Crump, prin.

Leesville RSD 9
Sch. Sys. Enr. Code 1
Supt. – (—)
  RURAL ROUTE 03 BOX 126   64735
ES   64735 – William Harris, prin.

Coffey, Daviess Co., Pop. Code 2
Coffey RSD 1
Sch. Sys. Enr. Code 1
Supt. – (—), P O BOX 139   64636
ES   64636 – G. A. Iddings, prin.

Cole Camp, Benton Co., Pop. Code 4
Cole Camp RSD 1
Sch. Sys. Enr. Code 3
Supt. – David Probst   65325
ES   65325 – Linda Ricker, prin.

Lutheran ES, 204 BUTTERFIELD TR   65325

Collins, St. Clair Co., Pop. Code 2
Weaubleau RSD 3
Supt. – See Weaubleau
Weaubleau ES   64738 – Joyce Stewart, prin.

Columbia, Boone Co., Pop. Code 8
Columbia SD 93
Sch. Sys. Enr. Code 7
Supt. – Dr. R. Thompson
  1818 W WORLEY ST   65203
Benton ES, 1410 HINKSON AVE   65201
  John Fussner, prin.
Blue Ridge ES, 2801 LEEWAY DR   65202
  David Brunda, prin.
Cedar Ridge ES, RURAL ROUTE 13   65201
  Donna Dodge, prin.
Fairview ES, 909 S FAIRVIEW RD   65203
  Dr. James Wells, prin.
Field ES, 1010 RANGE LINE ST   65201
  Bob Lincoln, prin.
Grant ES, 10 E BROADWAY   65203
  Margaret Niemeyer, prin.
Lee ES, 1208 LOCUST ST   65201
  Dr. Ronald Schlimme, prin.
Midway Heights ES
  RURAL ROUTE 05 BOX 86   65202
  Dr. Elizabeth Schmitz, prin.
New Haven ES, 3301 NEW HAVEN AVE   65201
  L. Gene Nichols, prin.
Parkade ES, 111 PARKADE BLVD   65202
  Larry Jones, prin.
Ridgeway ES, 107 SEXTON ROAD   65203
  Dr. O. V. Wheeler, prin.
Rock Bridge ES, RURAL ROUTE 04   65203
  Michael Schooley, prin.
Russell Boulevard ES, 1800 W ROLLINS RD   65203
  Charles Deming, prin.
Shepard Boulevard ES
  2616 SHEPARD BLVD   65201
  James Delbert, prin.
Two Mile Prairie ES, RURAL ROUTE 06   65202
  Clay Austin, prin.
West Boulevard ES, 319 WEST BLVD N   65203
  Anne Forgy, prin.

Columbia Catholic School
  817 BERNADETTE DR   65203

Conception Junction, Nodaway Co., Pop. Code 2
Jefferson Cons. SD 123
Sch. Sys. Enr. Code 2
Supt. – David Cross, P O BOX 30   64434
Jefferson ES   64434 – Debra Runde, prin.

Concordia, Lafayette Co., Pop. Code 4
Concordia RSD 2
Sch. Sys. Enr. Code 2
Supt. – Phillip C. Dorth, 117 W 11TH ST   64020
ES, 802 GORDON   64020 – Jerry Basye, prin.

St. Paul's Lutheran School, 407 MAIN ST   64020

Conway, Laclede Co., Pop. Code 3
Laclede County RSD 1
Sch. Sys. Enr. Code 3
Supt. – Dr. Larry Ament, HIGHWAY J   65632
Ezard ES   65632 – Bob Ikerd, prin.

Cooter, Pemiscot Co., Pop. Code 2
Cooter RSD 4
Sch. Sys. Enr. Code 2
Supt. – Floyd Wilson, P O BOX 218   63839
ES   63839 – Jerry Hatley, prin.

Cosby, Andrew Co., Pop. Code 2
Avenue City RSD 4
Sch. Sys. Enr. Code 1
Supt. – (—), RURAL ROUTE 01   64436
Avenue City ES   64436 – Gene Fite, prin.

Cottleville, St. Charles Co., Pop. Code 2

St. Joseph School, MOTHERHEAD RD   63338

Cowgill, Caldwell Co., Pop. Code 2
Cowgill RSD 4
Sch. Sys. Enr. Code 1
Supt. – (—), P O BOX 39   64637
ES   64637 – Barbara Creason, prin.

Craig, Holt Co., Pop. Code 2
Craig RSD 3
Sch. Sys. Enr. Code 2
Supt. – J. W. Stone   64437
ES   64437 – Pam Kent, prin.

Crane, Stone Co., Pop. Code 4
Crane RSD 3
Sch. Sys. Enr. Code 3
Supt. – Dr. Calvin Baker, P O BOX E   65633
ES   65633 – Tyler Laney, prin.

Creighton, Cass Co., Pop. Code 2
Sherwood-Cass RSD 8
Sch. Sys. Enr. Code 3
Supt. – Donald Lovland, P O BOX 98   64739
Sherwood Cass ES   64739 – David Logan, prin.

Creve Coeur, St. Louis Co., Pop. Code 7
Parkway Cons. SD 2
Supt. – See Chesterfield
East JHS, 181 COEUR DEVILLE DRIVE   63141
  Bonnie Reid, prin.
Bellerive ES, 666 RUE DE FLEUR DR   63141
  Kenneth Russell, prin.
Mason Ridge ES, 715 S MASON RD   63141
  George Ramsey, prin.

Crocker, Pulaski Co., Pop. Code 3
Pulaski County RSD 2
Sch. Sys. Enr. Code 3
Supt. – Terry Reed, P O BOX 488   65452
Pulaski County ES   65452 – Chester Dye, prin.

Crystal City, Jefferson Co., Pop. Code 5
Crystal City SD 47
Sch. Sys. Enr. Code 3
Supt. – James Maze, 1100 MISSISSIPPI AVE   63019
ES, 600 MISSISSIPPI AVE   63019
  Harrell Kirkland, prin.

Cuba, Crawford Co., Pop. Code 4
Crawford County RSD 2
Sch. Sys. Enr. Code 4
Supt. – Dr. Larry Clark, 208 ELM AVE   65453
JHS, 208 ELM AVE   65453 – Larry Hutchcraft, prin.
Crawford County ES   65453
  Michael Coulter, prin.

Curryville, Pike Co., Pop. Code 2
Bowling Green RSD 1
Supt. – See Bowling Green
ES   63339 – Paul Young, prin.

Dadeville, Dade Co., Pop. Code 2
Dadeville RSD 2
Sch. Sys. Enr. Code 2
Supt. – Henry McBride, P O BOX 188   65635
ES   65635 – Roger Hall, prin.

Dearborn, Platte Co., Pop. Code 3
North Platte County RSD 1
Sch. Sys. Enr. Code 3
Supt. – Mike Newell, P O BOX 68   64439
Other Schools – See Camden Point, Edgerton

Deepwater, Henry Co., Pop. Code 2
Lakeland RSD 3
Sch. Sys. Enr. Code 3
Supt. – Norman Long, RURAL ROUTE 02   64740
Other Schools – See Lowry City

Deering, Pemiscot Co., Pop. Code 2
Pemiscot County Cons. SD 7
Sch. Sys. Enr. Code 2
Supt. – George Byers, P O BOX 297   63840
ES   63840 – Larry Hogan, prin.

De Kalb, Buchanan Co., Pop. Code 2
Buchanan County RSD 4
Sch. Sys. Enr. Code 2
Supt. – Robert Couldry, P O BOX 48   64440
Other Schools – See Rushville

Delta, Cape Girardeau Co., Pop. Code 3
Delta RSD 5
Sch. Sys. Enr. Code 2
Supt. – Doyle Wood, P O BOX 787   63744
ES   63744 – Patsy Dooley, prin.

Desloge, St. Francois Co., Pop. Code 5
North St. Francois County RSD 1
Supt. – See Bonne Terre
Cantwell MS, 801 E ELM ST 63601
  Robert Steels, prin.
Central ES, 100 N 3RD ST 63601
  Robert Steels, prin.

De Soto, Jefferson Co., Pop. Code 6
Desoto SD 73
Sch. Sys. Enr. Code 5
Supt. – Fred Bradley, 221 S 3RD ST 63020
JHS, 815 AMVETS DRIVE 63020
  Jerry L. Owen, prin.
Athena ES, RURAL ROUTE 01 BOX 148 63020
  Lloyd Agers, prin.
Vineland ES, 650 VINELAND ROAD 63020
  James Hawkins, prin.

Sunrise RSD 9
Sch. Sys. Enr. Code 2
Supt. – Kenneth Gibbs, RURAL ROUTE 03 63020
Sunrise ES 63020 – James Jamieson, prin.

St. Rose of Lima School, 523 S 4TH ST 63020

Dexter, Stoddard Co., Pop. Code 6
Dexter RSD 11
Sch. Sys. Enr. Code 4
Supt. – Dr. Sam McGowen, P O BOX 279 63841
MS, 1299 BROWN PILOT LANE 63841
  Mitchell Holifield, prin.
Central MS, MARKET & ELM ST 63841
  Ray Dowdy, prin.
Southwest ES
  ONE MILE ROAD & GRANT ST 63841
  Russell Hedrick, prin.

Diamond, Newton Co., Pop. Code 3
Diamond RSD 4
Sch. Sys. Enr. Code 3
Supt. – Willis Cagle, S MAIN 64840
ES 64840 – Steve Cohv, prin.

Dixon, Pulaski Co., Pop. Code 4
Dixon RSD 1
Sch. Sys. Enr. Code 4
Supt. – John Brummel, P O BOX A 65459
MS, HIGHWAY 28 E 65459 – Chris Hunt, prin.
ES, N PINE & W SIXTH 65459
  Neil Mossman, prin.

Doniphan, Ripley Co., Pop. Code 4
Doniphan RSD 1
Sch. Sys. Enr. Code 4
Supt. – Dr. Eugene Croarkin 63935
JHS 63935 – Charles V. Smith, prin.
ES 63935 – Bertram Wright, prin.

Ripley County RSD 4
Sch. Sys. Enr. Code 2
Supt. – (—), RURAL ROUTE 07 BOX 37 63935
Lone Star ES 63935 – Marden Hueter, prin.
Ripley County ES 63935 – Marden Hueter, prin.

Dora, Ozark Co., Pop. Code 1
Dora RSD 3
Sch. Sys. Enr. Code 2
Supt. – Roy Manion 65637
ES 65637 – Don Hamby, prin.

Drexel, Cass Co., Pop. Code 3
Drexel RSD 4
Sch. Sys. Enr. Code 2
Supt. – R. L. Larson, P O BOX 397 64742
ES 64742 – Phillip Denney, prin.

Duenweg, Jasper Co., Pop. Code 3
Joplin RSD 8
Supt. – See Joplin
ES 64841 – Dean Booher, prin.

Eagleville, Harrison Co., Pop. Code 2
North Harrison County RSD 3
Sch. Sys. Enr. Code 2
Supt. – Dennis Williams 64442
North Harrison ES 64442 – Jack Braby, prin.

East Lynne, Cass Co., Pop. Code 2
East Lynne ESD 40
Sch. Sys. Enr. Code 2
Supt. – (—), P O BOX 108 64743
ES 64743 – Renee Sagaser, prin.

Easton, Buchanan Co., Pop. Code 2
East Buchanan County Cons. SD 1
Supt. – See Gower
MS 64443 – Gary Summers, prin.

East Prairie, Mississippi Co., Pop. Code 5
East Prairie RSD 2
Sch. Sys. Enr. Code 4
Supt. – Jared Williams, 304 E WALNUT ST 63845
Webb JHS 63845 – Larry Young, prin.
Doyle ES 63845 – Carl Cox Jr., prin.
Martin MS 63845 – Ernest Feyler, prin.

Edgar Springs, Phelps Co., Pop. Code 2
Phelps County RSD 3
Sch. Sys. Enr. Code 2
Supt. – Bob Rensch
  RURAL ROUTE 03 BOX 175 65462
Phelps County ES 65462 – Bob Rensch, prin.

Edgerton, Platte Co., Pop. Code 3
North Platte County RSD 1
Supt. – See Dearborn
MS 64444 – Ron Ressler, prin.

Edina, Knox Co., Pop. Code 4
Knox County RSD 1
Sch. Sys. Enr. Code 3
Supt. – David Bethel
  RURAL ROUTE 03 BOX 59 63537
Baring ES, P O BOX 1 63537 – Neita Collins, prin.
ES, P O BOX 237 63537 – Neita Collins, prin.
Other Schools – See Hurdland, Novelty

Edwards, Benton Co.
Warsaw RSD 9
Supt. – See Warsaw
South ES, HCR 30 65326 – Janet Osborn, prin.

Eldon, Miller Co., Pop. Code 5
Eldon RSD 1
Sch. Sys. Enr. Code 4
Supt. – Walter Mooney, 110 S OAK ST 65026
JHS, RURAL ROUTE 02 65026
  Roger McCreery, prin.
South ES, S MAPLE 65026 – Philip Jones, prin.

El Dorado Springs, Cedar Co., Pop. Code 5
El Dorado Springs RSD 2
Sch. Sys. Enr. Code 4
Supt. – Dr. Ronald Cope, P O BOX 191 64744
South ES, P O BOX 191 64744 – Sam Christy, prin.

Ellington, Reynolds Co., Pop. Code 4
Southern Reynolds County RSD 2
Sch. Sys. Enr. Code 3
Supt. – Jerry Milligan 63638
Southern Reynolds County ES 63638
  James Hughes, prin.

Ellisville, St. Louis Co., Pop. Code 6
Rockwood RSD 6
Supt. – See Eureka
ES, 1425 FROESEL DR 63011
  Harryette Baker, prin.
Ellisville Intermediate MS
  265 OLD STATE RD 63021 – Mary Riedel, prin.
Green Pines ES, 16543 GREEN PINES DR 63011
  Dr. John Scatizzi, prin.

Ellsinore, Carter Co., Pop. Code 2
East Carter County RSD 2
Sch. Sys. Enr. Code 3
Supt. – Joe Knodell 63937
ES 63937 – Carroll Cookson, prin.
Other Schools – See Grandin

Elmer, Macon Co., Pop. Code 2
Elmer Cons. SD 1
Sch. Sys. Enr. Code 1
Supt. – (—) 63538
ES 63538 – Jaqueline Eitel, prin.

Elsberry, Lincoln Co., Pop. Code 4
Elsberry RSD 2
Sch. Sys. Enr. Code 3
Supt. – Winston Bailey
  SANDERSON & BROADWAY 63343
Cannon ES, SANDERSON & WELCH 63343
  James Watkins, prin.

Elvins, St. Francois Co., Pop. Code 4
Central RSD 3
Supt. – See Flat River
West ES, 403 W FITE ST 63601 – Lee Webb, prin.

Eminence, Shannon Co., Pop. Code 3
Eminence RSD 1
Sch. Sys. Enr. Code 2
Supt. – S. W. Ennis 65466
ES 65466 – James Chilton, prin.

Essex, Stoddard Co., Pop. Code 3
Richland RSD 1
Sch. Sys. Enr. Code 3
Supt. – J. G. Lawrence 63846
Other Schools – See Richland

Esther, St. Francois Co., Pop. Code 4
Central RSD 3
Supt. – See Flat River
Central JHS, 8TH & COLUMBIA 63601
  Dennis Norris, prin.

Eugene, Cole Co., Pop. Code 2
Cole County RSD 5
Sch. Sys. Enr. Code 3
Supt. – Gregory Wilson, P O BOX 78 65032
Cole ES, HWY 17 65032 – Mary Herst, prin.

Eureka, St. Louis Co., Pop. Code 5
Rockwood RSD 6
Sch. Sys. Enr. Code 7
Supt. – Dr. William Foster
  111 E NORTH ST 63025
ES, RURAL ROUTE 02 BOX 4 63025
  George Fritts, prin.
Geggie ES, 600 BALD HILL RD 63025
  Dr. Dan Schlegel, prin.
Other Schools – See Ballwin, Chesterfield, Ellisville,
  Fenton, Grover

Sacred Heart School, 330 E 4TH ST 63025

Everton, Dade Co., Pop. Code 2
Everton RSD 3
Sch. Sys. Enr. Code 2
Supt. – Hershel Bledsoe, P O BOX 107 65646
ES 65646 – Lyman Welch, prin.

Ewing, Lewis Co., Pop. Code 2
Lewis County Cons. SD 1
Sch. Sys. Enr. Code 4
Supt. – William Cornett, P O BOX 366 63440

ES 63440 – Beth Hansmeier, prin.
Other Schools – See La Grange

Excelsior Springs, Clay Co., Pop. Code 7
Excelsior Springs SD 40
Sch. Sys. Enr. Code 5
Supt. – Arthur Kurth, P O BOX 248 64024
Lewis MS, 501 LEAVENWORTH ST 64024
  H. Woolsey, prin.
Elkhorn ES, RURAL ROUTE 02 64024
  Clarence Schneider, prin.
Isley ES, 111 ASH ST 64024
  Clarence Schneider, prin.
Westview ES
  JESSE JAMES & WORNALL ROAD 64024
  Gail Doerr, prin.
Wyman ES, 108 DUNBAR AVE 64024
  Peggy Tharpe, prin.

Exeter, Barry Co., Pop. Code 3
Exeter RSD 2
Sch. Sys. Enr. Code 2
Supt. – Marvin Spragg
  FRONT & LOCUST ST 65647
ES 65647 – Jerry Caywood, prin.

Fairfax, Atchison Co., Pop. Code 3
Fairfax RSD 3
Sch. Sys. Enr. Code 2
Supt. – James Ruse, P O BOX 96 64446
ES 64446 – Martin Sweatman, prin.

Fair Grove, Greene Co., Pop. Code 3
Fairgrove RSD 10
Sch. Sys. Enr. Code 3
Supt. – Gary Yarber
  RURAL ROUTE 03 BOX 32 65648
Fair Grove MS 65648 – Dean Crayton, prin.
ES 65648 – Don Frese, prin.

Fair Play, Polk Co., Pop. Code 2
Fair Play RSD 2
Sch. Sys. Enr. Code 2
Supt. – Gary Boggs 65649
ES 65649 – Jay Ensor, prin.

Falcon, Laclede Co.
Competition Cons. SD 2
Sch. Sys. Enr. Code 1
Supt. – (—) 65470
Competition ES 65470 – Cynthia Day, prin.

Gasconade Cons. SD 4
Sch. Sys. Enr. Code 2
Supt. – (—) 65470
Gasconade ES 65470 – Donald Sexton, prin.

Farmington, St. Francois Co., Pop. Code 6
Farmington RSD 7
Sch. Sys. Enr. Code 5
Supt. – Dr. Robert Webb
  1022 SAINT GENEVIEVE AVE 63640
JHS, 506 S FLEMING 63640
  Jack Richardson, prin.
Jefferson ES, 9 SUMMIT DR 63640
  Cindy Presnell, prin.
Truman ES, 209 N COLLEGE 63640
  Terry Walton, prin.
Washington-Franklin ES
  409 WASHINGTON ST 63640
  David Cramp, prin.

Libertyville Cons. SD 2
Sch. Sys. Enr. Code 1
Supt. – (—), P O BOX 985 63640
Libertyville ES 63640 – Debbie Easley, prin.

St. Joseph School, 17 N LONG ST 63640
St. Paul's Lutheran School
  COLUMBIA AND CARLETON STS 63640

Farrar, Perry Co.

Salem Lutheran School 63746

Faucett, Buchanan Co., Pop. Code 2
Mid-Buchanan County RSD 5
Sch. Sys. Enr. Code 3
Supt. – Dr. Gary Bell 64448
Mid-Buchanan County ES 64448
  Paul Karlin, prin.

Fayette, Howard Co., Pop. Code 5
Fayette RSD 3
Sch. Sys. Enr. Code 3
Supt. – Bill J. Akers, LUCKY ST 65248
Daly ES 65248 – Dr. Gale Hairston, prin.

Fenton, St. Louis Co., Pop. Code 4
Rockwood RSD 6
Supt. – See Eureka
Bowles ES, 501 BOWLES AVE 63026
  William Dunn, prin.
Kellison ES, 1626 HAWKINS RD 63026
  Richard Pennycuick, prin.
Stanton ES, 1430 FLORA DEL DR 63026
  Jerome Woodson, prin.

Our Savior Lutheran School
  900 NEWSMINER MILL ROAD 63026
St. Paul School, 465 N HNIGHWAY 141 63026

Ferguson, St. Louis Co., Pop. Code 7
Ferguson-Florissant RSD 2
Supt. – See Florissant
MS, 701 JANUARY AVE 63135 – Daryl Hall, prin.
Central ES, 201 WESLEY AVE 63135
  Donald Saali, prin.

Griffith ES, 200 DAY DR   63135
  Lowell Lilly, prin.
Hamilton ES, 401 POWELL AVE   63135
  John Sexauer, prin.
Walnut Grove ES, 1248 N FLORISSANT RD   63135
  Samuel McCauley, prin.

Good Shepherd School, 1050 SMITH AVE   63135
SS John & James School
  150 N ELIZABETH AVE   63135
Zion Lutheran School, 123 CARSON RD   63135

Festus, Jefferson Co., Pop. Code 6
Festus RSD 6
Sch. Sys. Enr. Code 4
Supt. – Robert L. Tucker
  1515 MID-MEADOW LANE   63028
JHS, 1717 W MAIN ST   63028
  John Richeson, prin.
ES, 1500 MIDMEADOW LN   63028
  Martine Boyer, prin.

Jefferson County RSD 8
Sch. Sys. Enr. Code 2
Supt. – Randall J. Boyer, RURAL ROUTE 04   63028
Jefferson Upper MS   63028 – Diana Vittetoe, prin.
Jefferson Lower ES   63028 – Gary Dunbar, prin.

Our Lady School, 1599 ST MARYS LN   63028
Sacred Heart School, 201 BRIERTON LN   63028

Fillmore, Andrew Co., Pop. Code 2
Fillmore Cons. SD 1
Sch. Sys. Enr. Code 2
Supt. – Hugh Boswell   64449
ES   64449 – Sally Wermelskirchen, prin.

Fisk, Butler Co., Pop. Code 2
Twin Rivers RSD 10
Supt. – See Broseley
ES   63940 – James Woeltje, prin.

Flat River, St. Francois Co., Pop. Code 5
Central RSD 3
Sch. Sys. Enr. Code 4
Supt. – Orville Adams, 200 HIGH ST   63601
Central ES, 900 SAINT FRANCOIS AVE   63601
  Charles Bequette, prin.
Other Schools – See Elvins, Esther

West St. Francis County RSD 4
Supt. – See Leadwood
West County ES, RTE 33   BOX 322   63601
  William Kroeger, prin.

Florissant, St. Louis Co., Pop. Code 8
Ferguson-Florissant RSD 2
Sch. Sys. Enr. Code 4
Supt. – Dr. Dan Keck
  1005 WATERFORD DRIVE   63033
Cross Keys MS, 14205 COUGAR DRIVE   63033
  Dr. Dolores Graham, prin.
Combs ES, 300 ST JEAN ST   63031
  Jo Ann Jasin, prin.
Commons Lane ES, 2700 DERHAKE RD   63033
  Phillys Russell, prin.
Duchesne ES, 100 S FLORISSANT RD   63031
  Robert Cowles, prin.
Halls Ferry ES
  13585 NEW HALLS FERRY RD   63033
  Barbara Davis, prin.
Parker Road ES, 2800 PARKER RD   63033
  James Weaver, prin.
Robinwood ES, 955 DERHAKE RD   63033
  Robert Bartlett, prin.
Wedgewood ES
  14275 NEW HALLS FERRY RD   63033
  Dr. James Sallade, prin.
Other Schools – See Berkeley, Ferguson, Saint Louis

Hazelwood SD
Sch. Sys. Enr. Code 7
Supt. – Dr. Francis Huss
  15955 NEW HALLS FERRY ROAD   63031
Hazelwood JHS
  1605 SHACKELFORD ROAD   63031
  Dr. J. Dougherty, prin.
Brown ES, 3325 CHICORY CR LANE   63031
  John Gruender, prin.
Cold Water ES, 1105 WIETHAUPT RD   63031
  Charles Woods, prin.
Jamestown ES
  13750 OLD JAMESTOWN RD   63033
  Barbara Scotchmer, prin.
Jana ES, 405 JANA LN   63031 – Ronald Jones, prin.
Jury ES, 11950 OLD HALLS FERRY RD   63033
  Garry Waters, prin.
Lawson ES, 1830 CHARBONIER RD   63031
  Junette Gist, prin.
Lusher ES, 2015 MULLANPHY RD   63031
  Stephen Tighe, prin.
McCurdy ES, 975 LINDSAY LN   63031
  Anthony Fazio, prin.
Townsend ES, 6645 PARKER RD   63033
  Harold McNeal, prin.
Walker ES, 1250 HUMES LN   63031
  Edward Preston, prin.
Other Schools – See Hazelwood, Saint Louis

Atonement Lutheran School
  1285 N NEW FLORISSANT RD   63031
North American Martyrs School
  1350 S LAFAYETTE ST   63031
Our Lady of Fatima School
  4500 WASHINGTON ST   63033
Sacred Heart School, 703 N JEFFERSON ST   63031

Salem Lutheran School, 5190 PARKER RD   63033
St. Angela Merici School, 3860 N HWY 67   63034
St. Dismas School, 1220 PADDOCK DR   63033
St. Ferdinand School
  1735 CHARBONIER RD   63031
St. Sabina School, 1625 SWALLOW LN   63031
St. Thomas Apostle School
  3500 ST CATHERINE ST   63033
Transfiguration School
  12555 PARTRIDGE RUN DR   63033

Fordland, Webster Co., Pop. Code 3
Fordland RSD 3
Sch. Sys. Enr. Code 3
Supt. – Robert Wallace, P O BOX 118   65652
ES   65652 – Danny Neal, prin.

Forsyth, Taney Co., Pop. Code 4
Forsyth RSD 3
Sch. Sys. Enr. Code 3
Supt. – Maynard Wallace   65653
ES   65653 – Nadine Horner, prin.

Fort Leonard Wood, Pulaski Co., Pop. Code 8
Waynesville RSD 6
Supt. – See Waynesville
Wood MS   65473 – Jack King, prin.
Partridge ES   65473 – David Hunt, prin.
Pershing ES   65473 – David Lawson, prin.
Pick ES   65473 – Ralph Laughlin, prin.
Thayer ES   65473 – Anita Clarkston, prin.
Williams ES   65473 – Lisa Schwandt, prin.

Frankford, Pike Co., Pop. Code 2
Bowling Green RSD 1
Supt. – See Bowling Green
ES   63441 – Paul Young, prin.

Fredericktown, Madison Co., Pop. Code 5
Fredericktown RSD 6
Sch. Sys. Enr. Code 4
Supt. – Dr. G. Hamilton, HIGHWAY 72 E   63645
JHS, 501 S MAPLE ST   63645 – Perry Kegley, prin.
ES, HIGH ST   63645 – Kelly Burlison, prin.
Other Schools – See Millcreek

Freistatt, Lawrence Co., Pop. Code 2

Trinity Lutheran School, 218 N MAIN ST   65654

Fremont, Carter Co., Pop. Code 2
Van Buren RSD 1
Supt. – See Van Buren
MS, P O BOX 37   63941 – Judith Oakley, prin.

Frohna, Perry Co., Pop. Code 2

Concordia Lutheran School
  RURAL ROUTE 01 BOX 213   63748

Fulton, Callaway Co., Pop. Code 7
Fulton SD 58
Sch. Sys. Enr. Code 4
Supt. – Dr. Dennis Lea, 207 E 5TH ST   65251
Bartley ES, 604 HWY 54 S   65251
  Robert Tate, prin.
Bush ES, 908 WOOD ST   65251
  Terry Poindexter, prin.
Center MS, 808 CENTER ST   65251
  Robert Hogan, prin.
McIntire ES, 706 HICKMAN AVE   65251
  Robert Hogan, prin.

Gainesville, Ozark Co., Pop. Code 3
Gainesville RSD 5
Sch. Sys. Enr. Code 3
Supt. – John Ault, BULLDOG DRIVE   65655
ES, P O BOX 236   65655 – Ida Mae Huse, prin.

Galena, Stone Co., Pop. Code 2
Galena RSD 2
Sch. Sys. Enr. Code 2
Supt. – Dr. David Edge   65656
Galena-Abesville ES   65656
  Olen Leon Allen, prin.

Gallatin, Daviess Co., Pop. Code 4
Gallatin RSD 5
Sch. Sys. Enr. Code 3
Supt. – C. G. Baker, 602 S OLIVE ST   64640
Searcy ES   64640 – Roger Vanatta, prin.

Galt, Grundy Co., Pop. Code 2
Grundy County RSD 5
Sch. Sys. Enr. Code 2
Supt. – Harry Wheeler, P O BOX 6   64641
Other Schools – See Humphreys

Gatewood, Ripley Co., Pop. Code 2
Ripley County RSD 3
Sch. Sys. Enr. Code 2
Supt. – (—), RURAL ROUTE 06 BOX 98   63942
Ripley County ES   63942 – Kenneth Hunt, prin.

Gerald, Franklin Co., Pop. Code 3
Owensville RSD 2
Supt. – See Owensville
ES, HWY 50   63037 – Bill Depriest, prin.

Gideon, New Madrid Co., Pop. Code 4
Gideon SD 37
Sch. Sys. Enr. Code 3
Supt. – James Evans, P O BOX 227   63848
ES   63848 – Jamie Holiman, prin.

Gilliam, Saline Co., Pop. Code 2
Gilliam Cons. SD 4
Sch. Sys. Enr. Code 1
Supt. – (—), P O BOX 8   65330

ES   65330 – Jean Dowell, prin.

Gilman City, Harrison Co., Pop. Code 2
Gilman City RSD 4
Sch. Sys. Enr. Code 2
Supt. – Carl McDaniel, P O BOX 45   64642
ES   64642 – Carl McDaniel, prin.

Glasgow, Howard Co., Pop. Code 4
Howard County RSD 2
Sch. Sys. Enr. Code 3
Supt. – Dr. Arch Gordanier
  860 RANDOLPH ST   65254
Howard County ES   65254 – Charles McCue, prin.

St. Marys School, 503 3RD ST   65254

Glendale, St. Louis Co., Pop. Code 6
Kirkwood RSD 7
Supt. – See Kirkwood
North Glendale ES
  765 N SAPPINGTON RD   63122
  Thomas Waltz, prin.

Golden City, Barton Co., Pop. Code 3
Golden City RSD 3
Sch. Sys. Enr. Code 2
Supt. – G. B. Kaufman, P O BOX 248   64748
ES   64748 – Susan Whittle, prin.

Goodman, McDonald Co., Pop. Code 4
Neosho RSD 5
Supt. – See Neosho
ES   64843 – Carol Squibb, prin.

Gordonville, Cape Girardeau Co., Pop. Code 2
Jackson RSD 2
Supt. – See Jackson
Attendance Ctr.   63752 – Bessie Buck, prin.

Gorin, Scotland Co.
Gorin RSD 3
Sch. Sys. Enr. Code 1
Supt. – (—), P O BOX 98   63543
ES   63543 – Mary Jo Jepson, prin.

Gower, Buchanan Co., Pop. Code 4
East Buchanan County Cons. SD 1
Sch. Sys. Enr. Code 3
Supt. – Roger Adamson, 100 SMITH ST   64454
East Buchanan County ES   64454
  Paul Miller, prin.
Other Schools – See Easton

Grain Valley, Jackson Co., Pop. Code 4
Grain Valley RSD 5
Sch. Sys. Enr. Code 3
Supt. – David Hackett, 714 MAIN ST   64029
MS   64029 – Judith Doolin, prin.
Matthews ES   64029 – Richard Loman, prin.

Granby, Newton Co., Pop. Code 4
East Newton County RSD 6
Sch. Sys. Enr. Code 4
Supt. – Dr. Robert Conn   64844
ES   64844 – Gary Copeland, prin.
Other Schools – See Stella

Grandin, Carter Co., Pop. Code 2
East Carter County RSD 2
Supt. – See Ellsinore
East Carter County JHS   63943 – Alan Greer, prin.
ES   63943 – Alan Greer, prin.

Grandview, Jackson Co., Pop. Code 7
Grandview Cons. SD 4
Sch. Sys. Enr. Code 5
Supt. – Dr. Tony Stansberry, 724 MAIN ST   64030
Belvidere ES, 15200 WHITE AVE   64030
  Fred Price, prin.
Butcher-Greene ES, 5302 E 140TH ST   64030
  Ronald Hale, prin.
Conn-West ES, 1100 HIGH GROVE RD   64030
  Carole Kennedy, prin.
High Grove ES, 2500 HIGH GROVE ROAD   64030
  Jack Noble, prin.
Meadowmere ES, 7010 E 136TH ST   64030
  Marvin Wippich, prin.
Other Schools – See Kansas City

Grant City, Worth Co., Pop. Code 4
Worth County RSD 3
Sch. Sys. Enr. Code 3
Supt. – Dr. Gary Bennerotte, EAST AVE   64456
Worth County ES   64456 – Rose Findley, prin.

Green City, Sullivan Co., Pop. Code 3
Green City RSD 1
Sch. Sys. Enr. Code 2
Supt. – John Kelso   63545
ES   63545 – Charles Neighbors, prin.

Greenfield, Dade Co., Pop. Code 4
Greenfield RSD 4
Sch. Sys. Enr. Code 3
Supt. – Dennis Cooper, 410 W COLLEGE ST   65661
ES, 409 N MONTGOMERY ST   65661
  Jim Dykens, prin.

Green Ridge, Pettis Co., Pop. Code 2
Greenridge RSD 8
Sch. Sys. Enr. Code 2
Supt. – James Lewis, P O BOX 38   65332
ES   65332 – Robert Stone, prin.

Greenville, Wayne Co., Pop. Code 2
Greenville RSD 2
Sch. Sys. Enr. Code 3
Supt. – James Webber   63944

ES 63944 – Shirley Schweitzer, prin.
Other Schools – See Williamsville

Greenwood, Jackson Co., Pop. Code 4
Lee's Summit RSD 7
Supt. – See Lee's Summit
ES, 805 W MAIN ST 64034 – Charles Key, prin.

Grover, St. Louis Co.
Rockwood RSD 6
Supt. – See Eureka
Pond ES, 17200 MANCHESTER RD 63040
Clare Ann Maguire, prin.

Grovespring, Wright Co.
Hartville RSD 2
Supt. – See Hartville
ES 65662 – (—), prin.

Guilford, Nodaway Co., Pop. Code 1
South Nodaway County RSD 4
Supt. – See Barnard
South Nodaway ES, 418 E SECOND 64457
Carole Edmonds, prin.

Hale, Carroll Co., Pop. Code 3
Hale RSD 1
Sch. Sys. Enr. Code 2
Supt. – George Fischer, P O BOX 248 64643
ES 64643 – Connie Singleton, prin.

Half Way, Polk Co., Pop. Code 2
Halfway RSD 3
Sch. Sys. Enr. Code 2
Supt. – Larry King 65663
ES 65663 – Faye Peters, prin.

Hallsville, Boone Co., Pop. Code 2
Boone County RSD 4
Sch. Sys. Enr. Code 3
Supt. – Ralph Powell, RURAL ROUTE 01 65255
Boone County MS 65255
Constance McCallum, prin.
Boone ES 65255 – Terry Frazee, prin.

Halltown, Lawrence Co., Pop. Code 2
Miller RSD 2
Supt. – See Miller
East ES 65664 – Gerald Edwards, prin.

Hamilton, Caldwell Co., Pop. Code 4
Hamilton RSD 2
Sch. Sys. Enr. Code 3
Supt. – Dr. Thomas Trail, P O BOX 128 64644
JHS 64644 – Bill Mayers, prin.
ES 64644 – Ervin Ratliff, prin.

New York RSD 9
Sch. Sys. Enr. Code 1
Supt. – (—)
RURAL ROUTE 01 BOX 107 64644
ES 64644 – Mary Finch, prin.

Hannibal, Marion Co., Pop. Code 7
Hannibal SD 60
Sch. Sys. Enr. Code 5
Supt. – Dr. J. Chris Straub
4650 MCMASTERS AVE 63401
Central MS, 906 CENTER ST 63401
Larry Roberts, prin.
Field ES, 1405 PEARL ST 63401
Lawrence Degitz, prin.
Oakwood ES, 3716 MARKET ST 63401
Randy Speer, prin.
Pettibone ES, 600 NORTH ST 63401
Larry Roberts, prin.
Stowell ES, 700 FULTON AVE 63401
Ronald Mack, prin.
Twain ES, 2714 BIRD ST 63401
Julia Sharpe, prin.

Hannibal Catholic School
1113 BROADWAY 63401
St. John's Lutheran School, 1317 LYON ST 63401

Hardin, Ray Co., Pop. Code 3
Hardin-Central Cons. SD 2
Sch. Sys. Enr. Code 2
Supt. – Rick Edwards, P O BOX 548 64035
Hardin-Central ES 64035 – Nancy Barry, prin.

Harrisburg, Boone Co., Pop. Code 2
Harrisburg RSD 8
Sch. Sys. Enr. Code 2
Supt. – Ivan L. Phillips 65246
ES 65256 – Johnny Isaacs, prin.

Harrisonville, Cass Co., Pop. Code 6
Harrisonville RSD 9
Sch. Sys. Enr. Code 4
Supt. – Dr. Gerald Cook
402 EASTWOOD ROAD 64701
JHS, 601 S HIGHLAND DRIVE 64701
J. R. Hodge, prin.
Central ES, 501 S HIGHLAND DR 64701
Sandra Goforth, prin.
McEowen MS, 1901 S HALSEY 64701
Wayne Donnelson, prin.

Hartville, Wright Co., Pop. Code 3
Hartville RSD 2
Sch. Sys. Enr. Code 3
Supt. – Bob Dryer, P O BOX F 65667
ES 65667 – Harold McCoy, prin.
Other Schools – See Grovespring

Harviell, Butler Co.
Neelyville RSD 4
Supt. – See Neelyville

Hillview ES, RURAL ROUTE 01 BOX 40 63945
Lee Johnson, prin.

Hawk Point, Lincoln Co., Pop. Code 2
Troy RSD 3
Supt. – See Troy
ES 63349 – Linda Hopkins, prin.

Hayti, Pemiscot Co., Pop. Code 5
Hayti RSD 2
Sch. Sys. Enr. Code 4
Supt. – Dr. Thomas Stanford, 500 N 4TH ST 63851
MS, 209 N CEDAR ST 63851
Wilburn Simmons, prin.
Mathis ES, 103 THIRD ST 63851
James Hartsfield, prin.
Wallace MS, 600 S 4TH ST 63851
Renna Hatley, prin.

Hazelwood, St. Louis Co., Pop. Code 7
Hazelwood SD
Supt. – See Florissant
Armstrong ES, 6255 HOWDERSHELL RD 63042
James French, prin.
Garrett ES, 1400 VILLE ROSA LN 63042
Opalene Mullen, prin.
McNair ES, 585 COACHWAY LN 63042
Dr. Dorothy Ricketts, prin.
Russell ES, 7350 HOWDERSHELL RD 63042
Robert Mudrovic, prin.

Pattonville RSD 3
Supt. – See Maryland Heights
Rose Acres ES, 2905 ROSE ACRES LN 63043
Brent Underwood, prin.

St. Bartholomew School, 8390 LATTY AVE 63042
St. Blaise School, 3120 PARKWOOD LN 63043
St. Lawrence the Martyr School
4329 DUPAGE AVE 63044
St. Martin De Porres School
631 UNDERCLIFF DR 63042
St. Marys School, 4601 LONG RD 63044

Helena, Andrew Co.
Savannah RSD 3
Supt. – See Savannah
ES 64459 – Kennie Jo Deshon, prin.

Herculaneum, Jefferson Co., Pop. Code 4
Dunklin RSD 5
Sch. Sys. Enr. Code 4
Supt. – Shelton Smith, P O BOX 306 63048
Senn-Thomas MS, 204 MAIN ST 63048
James Chandler, prin.
Taylor ES, 440 JOACHIM AVE 63048
Alberta Smart, prin.
Other Schools – See Pevely

Hermann, Gasconade Co., Pop. Code 5
Gasconade County RSD 1
Sch. Sys. Enr. Code 4
Supt. – Chris Arand, HIGHWAY 100 W 65041
MS, WASHINGTON ST 65041
Margaret Roberts, prin.
ES, 328 W 7TH ST 65041 – Lois Hoerstkamp, prin.
Swiss ES, RURAL ROUTE 01 65041
Le Roy Nolting, prin.
Other Schools – See Berger

St. George School, 133 W 4TH ST 65041

Hermitage, Hickory Co., Pop. Code 2
Hermitage RSD 4
Sch. Sys. Enr. Code 2
Supt. – Ted Redhair, P O BOX 327 65668
ES 65668 – Barbara McCaslin, prin.

Higbee, Randolph Co., Pop. Code 3
Higbee RSD 8
Sch. Sys. Enr. Code 2
Supt. – James Farmer, P O BOX 128 65257
ES 65257 – Ralph Spurrier, prin.

Higginsville, Lafayette Co., Pop. Code 5
Lafayette County Cons. SD 1
Sch. Sys. Enr. Code 3
Supt. – Dr. Gary Evans, P O BOX 230 64037
Lafayette County JHS
31ST & HIGHWAY BLVD 64037
Jim Perrine, prin.
Emerson ES, 116 E 17TH ST 64037
Patricia Schumacher, prin.
Grandview MS, 31ST ST & PEACH 64037
Patricia Schumacher, prin.

Immanuel Lutheran School, 15TH & LIPPER 64037

Highlandville, Christian Co.
Spokane RSD 7
Supt. – See Spokane
ES 65669 – Wayne France, prin.

High Point, Moniteau Co.
High Point RSD 3
Sch. Sys. Enr. Code 1
Supt. – (—), GENERAL DELIVERY 65042
ES 65042 – William Dicus, prin.

High Ridge, Jefferson Co.

St. Anthony School
3005 HIGH RIDGE BLVD 63049

Hillsboro, Jefferson Co., Pop. Code 4
Grandview RSD 2
Sch. Sys. Enr. Code 3
Supt. – Dr. R. Kristofferson
1140 HIGHWAY C 63050
Grandview ES 63050 – Rebecca Faber, prin.

Hillsboro RSD 3
Sch. Sys. Enr. Code 5
Supt. – L. Chaney, P O BOX 500 63050
Hillsboro Upper S 63050 – Michael Page, prin.
ES, 13 HAWK DR 63050 – David Kingsland, prin.
Hillsboro Middle MS, 10486 HWY 21 63050
Donald Fitzgerald, prin.

Holcomb, Dunklin Co., Pop. Code 3
Holcomb RSD 3
Sch. Sys. Enr. Code 2
Supt. – Randall Winston, P O BOX 187 63852
ES 63852 – Richard Rickman, prin.

Holden, Johnson Co., Pop. Code 4
Holden RSD 3
Sch. Sys. Enr. Code 4
Supt. – Robert V. Hoffman
900 MARKET ST 64040
MS, 902 MARKET ST 64040 – Bob Cossin, prin.
South ES, 1901 MARKET ST 64040
Robyn Sisk, prin.

Holliday, Monroe Co., Pop. Code 2
Holliday Cons. SD 2
Sch. Sys. Enr. Code 1
Supt. – (—) 65258
ES 65258 – Anna Kinder, prin.

Hollister, Taney Co., Pop. Code 4
Hollister RSD 5
Sch. Sys. Enr. Code 3
Supt. – Darrell E. Boyer, P O BOX 208 65672
ES, P O BOX 208 65672 – Paula Sprouse, prin.

Holt, Clay Co., Pop. Code 2
Kearney RSD 1
Supt. – See Kearney
ES 64048 – Sammye Guenther, prin.

Holts Summit, Callaway Co., Pop. Code 5
Jefferson City SD
Supt. – See Jefferson City
Callaway Hills ES
RURAL ROUTE 01 BOX 79A 65043
Jack Morse, prin.
North ES 65043 – Marcus Kollmeyer, prin.

Hopkins, Nodaway Co., Pop. Code 3
North Nodaway County RSD 6
Sch. Sys. Enr. Code 2
Supt. – Ina Claire Lister, P O BOX 256 64461
Other Schools – See Pickering

Hornersville, Dunklin Co., Pop. Code 3
Senath Cons. SD 8
Supt. – See Senath
MS 63855 – Barth Larsen, prin.

House Springs, Jefferson Co., Pop. Code 2
Northwest RSD 1
Sch. Sys. Enr. Code 6
Supt. – Dr. John Gibson, P O BOX 500 63051
MS, P O BOX 500 63051 – Melvin Maharrey, prin.
North Jefferson MS, P O BOX 500 63051
Dr. Robert D. Maharrey, prin.
High Ridge ES 63051 – Dr. Robert Prywitch, prin.
ES 63051 – Gary Stephens, prin.
Maple Grove ES 63051 – Kenneth Dillner, prin.
Murphy ES 63051 – Helen Conway, prin.
Woods ES 63051 – Carl Altrogge, prin.
Other Schools – See Cedar Hill

Our Lady Queen of Peace School
4675 NOTRE DAME DR 63051

Houston, Texas Co., Pop. Code 4
Houston RSD
Sch. Sys. Enr. Code 4
Supt. – Dr. Ronald D. Griffin
423 W PINE ST 65483
JHS 65483 – Dennis Powell, prin.
ES 65483 – Kevin Tedlock, prin.

Houstonia, Pettis Co., Pop. Code 2
Pettis County RSD 5
Supt. – See Hughesville
Northwest ES, P O BOX 58 65333
Kevin Holbert, prin.

Hughesville, Pettis Co., Pop. Code 2
Pettis County RSD 5
Sch. Sys. Enr. Code 2
Supt. – Eldon Kreisel, P O BOX 36 65334
Other Schools – See Houstonia

Humansville, Polk Co., Pop. Code 3
Humansville RSD 4
Sch. Sys. Enr. Code 2
Supt. – James Kerns, P O BOX 307 65674
ES 65674 – Maggie Kelley, prin.

Hume, Bates Co., Pop. Code 2
Hume RSD 8
Sch. Sys. Enr. Code 2
Supt. – Elaine Brame, P O BOX 402 64752
ES 64752 – Elaine Brame, prin.

Humphreys, Sullivan Co., Pop. Code 2
Grundy County RSD 5
Supt. – See Galt

Grundy County ES 64646
Kathleen Lindquist, prin.

Huntsville, Randolph Co., Pop. Code 4
Westran RSD 1
Sch. Sys. Enr. Code 3
Supt. – John Berlekamp, 2100 DEPOT 65259
Westran ES 65259 – Thomas Jaeger, prin.
Other Schools – See Clifton Hill

Hurdland, Knox Co., Pop. Code 2
Knox County RSD 1
Supt. – See Edina
ES, P O BOX 126 63547 – Neita Collins, prin.

Hurley, Stone Co., Pop. Code 2
Hurley RSD 1
Sch. Sys. Enr. Code 2
Supt. – Don Gardner, P O BOX 248 65675
ES 65675 – Allyn Mathews, prin.

Iberia, Miller Co., Pop. Code 3
Iberia RSD 5
Sch. Sys. Enr. Code 3
Supt. – Larry Ewing, P O BOX 156 65486
ES 65486 – Norman Devore, prin.

Imperial, Jefferson Co.
Fox Cons. SD 6
Supt. – See Arnold
Antonia ES, 3901 M HWY 63052
Dr. Ivan Davenport, prin.
Hamrick ES, 4525 FOUR RIDGE RD 63052
Glyn Gilman, prin.
Seckman ES, 2824 SECKMAN RD 63052
Dr. Donald Corbin, prin.

Windsor Cons. SD 1
Sch. Sys. Enr. Code 4
Supt. – Leslie Duncan, 6208 HIGHWAY 61 63052
Windsor Cons. MS 63052 – Jim White, prin.
Freer ES, MONTICELLO AT HANOVER 63012
Kenneth Bouzek, prin.
Windsor ES 63052 – Richard Butchart, prin.

St. John School, 4525 HWY 21 63052

Independence, Jackson Co., Pop. Code 9
Blue Springs RSD 4
Supt. – See Blue Springs
Yates ES, 3600 DAVIDSON ST 64055
Dr. Voy Spears Jr., prin.

Fort Osage RSD 1
Sch. Sys. Enr. Code 6
Supt. – Dr. Victor Gragg
RURAL ROUTE 02 BOX 928 64050
Blue Hills ES
24 HWY & BLUE MILLS ROAD 64058
Arthur Butler, prin.
Cler-Mont ES, 19009 SUSQUEHANNA RDG 64056
Anna Margaret McGuire, prin.
Courtney ES, RURAL ROUTE 01 BOX 126 64050
Carol Marcks, prin.
Elm Grove ES, 18000 KENTUCKY RD 64058
Loy Williams, prin.
Sixth Grade Attendance Ctr.
RURAL ROUTE 02 BOX 98 64050
James Spurlock, prin.
Other Schools – See Buckner

Independence SD 30
Sch. Sys. Enr. Code 7
Supt. – Dr. Robert L. Henley
1231 WINDSOR ST 64055
Bridger JHS, 2110 SPECK ROAD 64050
William Norton, prin.
Palmer JHS, 218 N PLEASANT ST 64050
Jerry Moore, prin.
Benton ES, 429 S LESLIE ST 64050
Floyd Hastings Jr., prin.
Blackburn ES, 17302 R D MIZE RD 64057
Roger Myers, prin.
Bryant ES, 827 W COLLEGE ST 64050
Beverly Serig, prin.
Glendale ES, 2611 LEES SUMMIT ROAD 64050
Donald Ross, prin.
Luff ES, 37TH TERRACE AND DELAWARE 64055
Thomas Tracey, prin.
Mill Creek ES, 2601 N LIBERTY ST 64050
Lora Reed, prin.
Ott ES, 1525 N NOLAND RD 64050
Jerry Williams, prin.
Proctor ES, 1403 W LINDEN AVE 64052
Henri Goettel, prin.
Randall ES, 509 JENNINGS ST 64056
G. W. Gelven, prin.
Santa Fe Trails ES, 1301 WINDSOR ST 64055
Beatrice Agee, prin.
Southern ES, 4300 PHELPS RD 64055
Robert McDonald, prin.
Spring Branch ES, 20404 E TRUMAN RD 64056
Merlyn Grubb, prin.
Sycamore Hills ES, 15208 E 39TH ST 64055
Alfred Vaniten, prin.

Kansas City SD 33
Supt. – See Kansas City
Nowlin MS, 2800 S HARDY AVE 64052
Rich Norris, prin.
Fairmount ES Magnet, 120 N CEDAR ST 64053
Kenneth Labrie, prin.
Korte MS Magnet, 2437-45 S HARDY 64052
Cynthia Kupka, prin.
Mt. Washington ES Magnet
570 S EVANSTON ST 64053 – Jancie Cade, prin.

North Rock Creek ES Magnet
2425 S HARDY AVE 64052 – Cynthia Kupka, prin.
Pitcher ES, 9701 E 35TH ST 64052
Dean Lewis, prin.
Sugar Creek ES Magnet, 11424 GILL ST 64054
Marjorie Collier, prin.
Three Trails ES, 11801 E 32ND ST 64052
Brenda Powell, prin.

Holy Family School, 18400 SALISBURY ST 64056
Messiah Lutheran School, 613 S MAIN ST 64050
Nativity School, 10021 E 36TH TER 64052
St. Ann School, 217 S CEDAR ST 64053

Ironton, Iron Co., Pop. Code 4
Arcadia Valley RSD 2
Sch. Sys. Enr. Code 4
Supt. – J. D. Maguffee, 750 W PARK DRIVE 63650
Arcadia Valley MS, 550 W PARK DRIVE 63650
David Stevens, prin.
Arcadia Valley ES, 700 W PARK DR 63650
Terry Adams, prin.

Jackson, Cape Girardeau Co., Pop. Code 6
Jackson RSD 2
Sch. Sys. Enr. Code 5
Supt. – Dr. Frank Wiley
221 S OKLAHOMA ST 63755
Central ES, W MADISON ST 63755
Joseph Crain, prin.
Jackson Annex ES, JEFFERSON ST 63755
Joseph Crain, prin.
North ES, FRUITLAND 63755 – Dan Stover, prin.
West Lane MS, W LANE 63755 – Lloyd Law, prin.
Other Schools – See Burfordville, Gordonville, Millersville

Immaculate Conception School
308 S HOPE ST 63755
St. Paul's Lutheran School
211 S RUSSELL ST 63755

Jameson, Daviess Co., Pop. Code 2
Jameson RSD 3
Sch. Sys. Enr. Code 1
Supt. – Robert Dowis 64647
ES 64647 – Leta Wheeler, prin.

Jamesport, Daviess Co., Pop. Code 3
Tri-County RSD 7
Sch. Sys. Enr. Code 2
Supt. – Joe Dyke, P O BOX 224 64648
Tri-County ES 64648 – Joe Dyke, prin.

Jamestown, Moniteau Co., Pop. Code 2
Moniteau County Cons. SD 1
Sch. Sys. Enr. Code 2
Supt. – Dr. Ronald Brandly 65046
Moniteau County ES 65046
Dolores Stegner, prin.

Jane, McDonald Co.
McDonald County RSD 1
Supt. – See Anderson
White Rock ES 64846 – Robert McCulley, prin.

Jasper, Jasper Co., Pop. Code 4
Jasper RSD 5
Sch. Sys. Enr. Code 3
Supt. – Bob G. Arnold
RURAL ROUTE 03 BOX 20 64755
ES 64833 – John Metz, prin.

Jefferson City, Cole Co., Pop. Code 8
Cole County RSD 2
Sch. Sys. Enr. Code 3
Supt. – Dan Doerhoff, RURAL ROUTE 06 65101
Blair Oaks ES 65101 – Glenda Tucker, prin.
Other Schools – See Saint Thomas

Jefferson City SD
Sch. Sys. Enr. Code 6
Supt. – Dr. Larry Folkins
315 E DUNKLIN ST 65101
Simonsen JHS, 501 E MILLER ST 65101
Dr. Sarah Spalding, prin.
Belair ES, 701 BELAIR DRIVE 65101
Richard Naumann, prin.
Cedar Hill ES, 1510 VIETH DR 65109
Don Reed, prin.
East ES, 1229 E MCCARTY ST 65101
Vivian Whitney, prin.
Gordon ES, 1101 JACKSON ST 65101
Wayne Wheeler, prin.
Jefferson MS, 214 E MILLER ST 65101
R. Fern Ward, prin.
Lawson ES, 1105 FAIRGROUNDS RD 65109
Kenneth Chapman, prin.
Moreau Heights ES, 1410 HOUGH PARK ST 65101
Duane Schleuter, prin.
South ES, 707 LINDEN DR 65109
Thomas Bultmann, prin.
Southwest ES, 812 ST MARYS BLVD 65109
Joyce Kaiser, prin.
West ES, 100 DIX RD 65109 – Marion Webb, prin.
Other Schools – See Holts Summit

Immaculate Conception School
1208 E MCCARTY ST 65101
St. Francis Xavier School
RURAL ROUTE 03 65101
St. Joseph School, 2303 W MAIN ST 65109
St. Martin School, RURAL ROUTE 01 65109
St. Peter School, 314 W HIGH ST 65101
St. Stanislaus School, RURAL ROUTE 06 65101

Trinity Lutheran School, 803 SWIFTS HWY 65109

Jennings, St. Louis Co., Pop. Code 7
Jennings SD
Sch. Sys. Enr. Code 4
Supt. – Dr. W. Bell, 8866 COZENS AVE 63136
JHS, 8831 COZENS AVE 63136
David Winkler, prin.
Fairview ES, 7047 EMMA AVE 63136
Cecil Holloway, prin.
Northview ES, 8920 COZENS AVE 63136
Gary Gore, prin.
Woodland ES, 8420 SUNBURY AVE 63136
James Scott, prin.

Jonesburg, Montgomery Co., Pop. Code 3
Montgomery County RSD 2
Supt. – See Montgomery City
Jonesburg ES 63351 – James Beattie, prin.

Joplin, Jasper Co., Pop. Code 8
Joplin RSD 8
Sch. Sys. Enr. Code 6
Supt. – Dr. Jack Israel, P O BOX 128 64802
Columbia ES, F & SERGEANT 64801
Curtis Squire, prin.
Duquesne ES, 13TH & DUQUESNE ROAD 64801
Dean Booher, prin.
Eastmorland ES, 12TH & HIGHVIEW 64801
Clarence Jones, prin.
Emerson ES, 19TH & PENNSYLVANIA 64801
Ronald Howard, prin.
Floyd ES, 2201 W 24TH ST 64804
Charles Bunnell, prin.
Irving ES, 26TH & WALL 64801
Truman Dearing, prin.
Jefferson ES, SECOND AND MCKINLEY 64801
Doris Conyers, prin.
McKinley ES, SIXTH & HIGHLAND 64801
John Williams, prin.
Norman ES, 28TH & NEW HAMPSHIRE 64801
Dr. Charles Spradling, prin.
North MS, FIRST & GRAY 64801
Alden Drouin, prin.
Royal Heights ES, 2100 ROLLA ST 64801
Pamela Sells, prin.
South MS, 22ND & WALL 64802
Ted Clowers, prin.
Stapleton ES, 41ST & MAIN 64801
Stephen Jones, prin.
West Central ES, SEVENTH & GRAY 64801
Rick Cook, prin.
Other Schools – See Duenweg

St. Mary's Grade School, 25TH & BYERS 64801
St. Peters School, 802 BYERS 64801

Kahoka, Clark Co., Pop. Code 4
Clark County RSD 1
Sch. Sys. Enr. Code 4
Supt. – Ray Church, 427 W CHESTNUT ST 63445
Black Hawk ES, 712 W CHESTNUT ST 63445
Lee Lemmon, prin.
Other Schools – See Alexandria

Kansas City, Jackson Co., Pop. Code 10
Center SD 58
Sch. Sys. Enr. Code 5
Supt. – Dr. Walter L. Swanson
8701 HOLMES ST 64131
Center JHS, 326 E 103RD ST 64114
Ben Neal, prin.
Boone ES, 8817 WORNALL RD 64114
Jane Ball, prin.
Center ES, 85TH & PASEO 64131
Connie Vilott, prin.
Indian Creek ES, 9801 GRAND AVE 64114
Archie Sinclair, prin.
Red Bridge ES, 10781 OAK ST 64114
Ron Hoffman, prin.

Grandview Cons. SD 4
Supt. – See Grandview
Martin City ES, 201 E 133RD ST 64145
Allie Grace, prin.

Hickman Mills Cons. SD 1
Sch. Sys. Enr. Code 6
Supt. – Dr. Kirby Hall
9000 OLD SANTA FE ROAD 64138
Ervin JHS, 10530 GREENWOOD ROAD 64134
W. E. Katz, prin.
Smith-Hale JHS, 8925 LONGVIEW ROAD 64134
Larry Ham, prin.
Burke ES, 111TH & BENNINGTON 64134
William Patrick, prin.
Dobbs ES, 9400 EASTERN AVE 64138
Virginia Brown, prin.
Ingels ES, 11600 FOOD LN 64134
Dr. Orville Emanuel, prin.
Santa Fe ES, 8908 OLD SANTA FE RD 64138
Kevin Roberts, prin.
Spofford Home ES, 9700 GRANDVIEW RD 64137
Patricia Connor, prin.
Symington ES, 8650 RUSKIN WAY 64134
Dr. Pamela Henker, prin.
Truman ES, 9601 JAMES A REED RD 64134
Jack Colbern, prin.
Warford ES, 11400 CLEVELAND AVE 64137
Charles Brown, prin.

Kansas City SD 33
Sch. Sys. Enr. Code 8
Supt. – Dr. George Garcia, 1211 MCGEE ST 64106

Bingham Magnet MS
  7618 WYANDOTTE ST 64114
  Robert Russell, prin.
Central Magnet MS
  3611 E LINWOOD BLVD 64128
  William Rowan, prin.
King JHS, 4201 INDIANA AVE 64130
  Dr. Jerry Allen, prin.
Northeast MS, 4904 INDEPENDENCE AVE 64124
  Dr. Will McCarther, prin.
Southeast MS, 6410 SWOPE PARKWAY 64132
  Gloria Hall, prin.
Westport MS, 3845 MCGEE ST 64111
  Dr. William Love, prin.
Askew ES, 2630 TOPPING AVE 64129
  Bill Toms, prin.
Attucks ES, 1818 E 19TH ST 64127
  Pauline Foster, prin.
Bancroft ES, 4300 TRACY AVE 64110
  Frances Wholf, prin.
Blenheim ES, 2411 E 70TH TER 64132
  Gloria Jenkins, prin.
Border Star ES, 6321 WORNALL RD 64113
  Jessie Kirksey, prin.
Bryant ES, 319 WESTOVER RD 64113
  Donna Fay Burch, prin.
Chick ES, 4101 E 53RD ST 64130 – Ida Love, prin.
Cook ES Magnet, 7302 PENNSYLVANIA ST 64114
  Dr. Edythe Darton, prin.
Franklin ES Magnet, 3400 HIGHLAND AVE 64109
  Jessie Mae Carpenter, prin.
Garfield ES, 421 WABASH AVE 64124
  Collins Drake, prin.
Graceland ES, 2803 E 51ST ST 64130
  James Wade, prin.
Greenwood ES, 3711 E 27TH ST 64127
  John Duncan, prin.
Hartman ES Magnet, 8111 OAK ST 64114
  Elinor Etterling, prin.
Holmes ES, 3004 BENTON BLVD 64128
  Eddie Lane Jr., prin.
James ES, 5810 SCARRITT AVE 64123
  Delores Maxwell, prin.
Knotts ES, 3711 JACKSON 64128
  Rupert Bullard, prin.
Kumpf ES, 4423 OLIVE ST 64130
  Everlyn Williams, prin.
Ladd ES, 3640 BENTON BLVD 64128
  George Hatter, prin.
Lincoln Magnet MS, 4610 E 24TH ST 64127
  F. E. Rogers, prin.
Longan ES Magnet, 3421 CHERRY ST 64109
  Juana Hishaw, prin.
Longfellow ES, 2830 HOLMES ST 64109
  Meredith Milford, prin.
Manchester ES, 6839 E TRUMAN RD 64126
  Earnestine Matthews, prin.
Marlborough MS Magnet, 1300 E 75TH ST 64131
  Dr. Geral Moeller, prin.
McCoy ES, 1524 WHITE AVE 64126
  Elizabeth Overbey, prin.
Melcher ES, 3958 CHELSEA AVE 64130
  Dr. Deborah Thomas, prin.
Merservey ES, 4210 E 45TH ST 64130
  Carole Ladd, prin.
MS of Arts, 8201 HOLMES ST 64131
  Thomas Tews, prin.
Moore ES Magnet, 4510 E LINWOOD BLVD 64128
  Josephine Hurtado, prin.
Pershing ES, 5915 PARK AVE 64130
  Jo Ann Cooper, prin.
Phillips ES, 1619 E 24TH TER 64108
  Herman Gant Jr., prin.
Pinkerton ES, 6409 AGNES AVE 64132
  Marie Grant, prin.
Richardson ES, 3515 PARK AVE 64109
  Dr. Billy Groom, prin.
Scarritt ES, 3509 ANDERSON AVE 64123
  James Strong, prin.
Swinney ES Magnet, 6903 OAK 64113
  Phyllis Washington, prin.
Switzer ES, 1829 MADISON AVE 64108
  Jane Walker, prin.
Thacher ES, 5008 INDEPENDENCE AVE 64124
  Hargest Shumate, prin.
Troost ES, 5914 FOREST AVE 64110
  John Rivette, prin.
Volker ES Magnet, 3715 WYOMING ST 64111
  Rayna Levine, prin.
Weeks ES, 4201 INDIANA AVE 64130
  Della Guess, prin.
West Rock Creek ES, 8820 E 27TH ST 64129
  Mai Gray, prin.
Wheatley ES, 2415 AGNES AVE 64127
  Dr. Aileen Shine, prin.
Whittier ES, 1012 BALES AVE 64127
  Odell Roberts, prin.
Willard ES, 5015 GARFIELD AVE 64130
  Conrad Miner, prin.
Woodland ES, 711 WOODLAND AVE 64106
  Nathan Crookshank, prin.
Other Schools – See Independence

North Kansas City SD 74
Supt. – See North Kansas City
Chapel Hill ES, 3320 NE 67TH TER 64119
  Dr. Phyllis Budesheim, prin.
Chouteau ES, 3701 N JACKSON AVE 64117
  Holly Johansen, prin.
Clardy MS, 8100 N TROOST AVE 64118
  John Cook, prin.
Davidson ES, 5100 N HIGHLAND AVE 64118
  Thomas Hostetler, prin.

Gashland ES, 500 NE 83RD ST 64118
  Anna Toler, prin.
Gracemor ES, 5125 N SYCAMORE AVE 64119
  Lewis Gowin, prin.
Lakewood ES, 4624 N NORTON AVE 64117
  Michael Miller, prin.
Linden West ES, 7400 N MAIN ST 64118
  Eugene Wright, prin.
Maplewood ES, 6400 NE 52ND ST 64119
  Dr. Thomas Foraker, prin.
Meadowbrook ES, 6301 N MICHIGAN AVE 64118
  Dr. Wendell Holeman, prin.
Oakwood Manor ES, 5900 N FLORA AVE 64118
  Phyllis Gehrke, prin.
Ravenwood ES, 5020 NE 58TH ST 64119
  Sidney Keltner, prin.
Topping ES, 4433 N TOPPING AVE 64117
  Donald Davison, prin.
West Englewood ES
  1506 NW ENGLEWOOD RD 64118
  Eliceo Nunez Jr., prin.
Winnwood ES, 4601 NE 44TH TER 64117
  L. Mark Grant, prin.

Park Hill RSD 5
Sch. Sys. Enr. Code 6
Supt. – Dr. Merlin Ludwig
  7703 NW BARRY ROAD 64153
Park Hill JHS, 6501 NW 72ND ST 64151
  Thomas Lindahl, prin.
Chinn ES, 7100 N CHATHAM AVE 64151
  Judy Winfrey, prin.
Line Creek ES, 5801 NW WAUKOMIS DR 64151
  James Foutes, prin.
Renner ES, 7401 NW BARRY RD 64153
  Leslie Short Jr., prin.
Southeast ES, 5704 N NORTHWOOD RD 64151
  Michelle Jones, prin.
Union Chapel ES, 7100 N BETHEL AVE 64152
  Galen Hoff, prin.
Other Schools – See Parkville

Platte County RSD 3
Supt. – See Platte City
Barry IS, 2001 NW 87 TERRACE 64154
  Raymond Mahowski, prin.
East Platte ES, 123RD & NW SKYVIEW 64164
  Gregg McPherson, prin.

Raytown Cons. SD 2
Supt. – See Raytown
Pittman Hills MS, 4900 PITTMAN ROAD 64133
  N. D. Brooks, prin.
Eastwood Hills ES, 5290 SYCAMORE AVE 64129
  Dr. Barbara Martin, prin.
Fleetridge ES, 13001 E 55TH ST 64133
  William Barnes, prin.
Norfleet ES, 6140 NORFLEET RD 64133
  Marilyn Perry, prin.
Robinson ES, 6707 WOODSON RD 64133
  Harlan Larison, prin.
Southwood ES, 8015 RAYTOWN RD 64138
  Willene Hinken, prin.
Spring Valley ES, 8838 E 83RD ST 64138
  Michael Mulvihill, prin.
Westridge ES, 8500 E 77TH ST 64138
  David Coffman, prin.

Barstow School, 11511 STATE LINE ROAD 64114
Pembroke Country Day School
  5121 STATE LINE ST 64112
Calvary Lutheran School, 7500 OAK ST 64114
Christ The King School, 425 W 85TH ST 64114
Father Benedict Justice School
  2800 E LINWOOD BLVD 64128
Guardian Angels School, 4232 MERCIER ST 64111
Holy Cross Lutheran School
  2003 NE ENGLEWOOD RD 64118
Holy Cross School, 121 N QUINCY AVE 64123
Notre Dame De Sion School
  3823 LOCUST ST 64109
Our Lady of Americas School
  2310 MADISON AVE 64108
Our Lady of Lourdes School
  8812 GREGORY BLVD 64133
Our Lady of Peace School
  10526 GRANDVIEW RD 64137
Redemptorist School
  211 W LINWOOD BLVD 64111
St. Augustine School, 1818 E 79TH ST 64132
St. Bernadette School, 9020 E 51ST TER 64133
St. Charles Borromeo School
  804 NE SHADY LANE DR 64118
St. Elizabeth School, 14 W 75TH ST 64114
St. Francis Xavier School
  5220 TROOST AVE 64110
St. Gabriel School
  4737 N CLEVELAND AVE 64117
St. John Francis Regis School
  8941 JAMES A REED RD 64138
St. John Tri School, 548 BROOKLYN AVE 64124
St. Joseph School, 1524 PASEO BLVD 64108
St. Martin De Porres School
  5840 SWOPE PKY 64130
St. Patrick School, 1401 NE 42ND TER 64116
St. Peter School, 6400 CHARLOTTE ST 64131
St. Stephen Academy
  1001 BENNINGTON AVE 64126
St. Therese School, 5809 MICHIGAN AVE 64130
St. Therese School, 7277 NW HIGHWAY 9 64152
St. Thomas More School
  11800 HOLMES ST 64131
Visitation School, 5134 BALTIMORE AVE 64112

Kearney, Clay Co., Pop. Code 4
  Kearney RSD 1
  Sch. Sys. Enr. Code 4
  Supt. – Dr. Mark Yehle, P O BOX 108 64060
  MS, P O BOX 197 64060 – Karl Morrow, prin.
  ES, 902 S JEFFERSON 64060
    Richard Whitford, prin.
  Other Schools – See Holt

Kelso, Scott Co., Pop. Code 2

  St. Augustine School, P O BOX 20 63758

Kennett, Dunklin Co., Pop. Code 7
  Kennett SD 39
  Sch. Sys. Enr. Code 4
  Supt. – Dr. John C. McMullan 63857
  North JHS, 510 COLLEGE AVE 63857
    Joseph Brooks, prin.
  Masterson ES, 1600 ELY RD 63857
    Robert McCuiston, prin.
  South MS, 920 KENNETT ST 63857
    Harold Ferguson, prin.

Keytesville, Chariton Co., Pop. Code 3
  Keytesville RSD 3
  Sch. Sys. Enr. Code 2
  Supt. – Francis Moran
    RURAL ROUTE 01 BOX 55 65261
  ES, 705 FILMORE 65261 – Lonnie Jackson, prin.

Kimmswick, Jefferson Co., Pop. Code 2

  St. Joseph School, FIFTH ST 63053

King City, Gentry Co., Pop. Code 4
  King City RSD 1
  Sch. Sys. Enr. Code 2
  Supt. – Terry Karr, P O BOX 188 64463
  ES 64463 – Sharon Adams, prin.

Kingdom City, Callaway Co., Pop. Code 2
  North Callaway County RSD 1
  Sch. Sys. Enr. Code 4
  Supt. – Dr. Thomas Gerling, P O BOX 9 65262
  Hatton McCredie ES, RURAL ROUTE 01 65262
    Joe Crane, prin.
  Other Schools – See Auxvasse, Williamsburg

Kingston, Caldwell Co., Pop. Code 2
  Kingston ESD 42
  Sch. Sys. Enr. Code 1
  Supt. – (—), P O BOX 98 64650
  ES 64650 – Jack Pullen, prin.

  Kingston ESD K-14
  Supt. – See Cadet
  Cruise ES 63630 – Emory Oliver, prin.

Kingsville, Johnson Co., Pop. Code 2
  Kingsville RSD 1
  Sch. Sys. Enr. Code 2
  Supt. – Dean Schnakenberg 64061
  ES 64061 – Ruth Hammond, prin.

Kirbyville, Taney Co.
  Kirbyville RSD 6
  Sch. Sys. Enr. Code 2
  Supt. – (—), P O BOX 378 65679
  ES 65679 – A. Dean Dunn, prin.

Kirksville, Adair Co., Pop. Code 7
  Kirksville RSD 3
  Sch. Sys. Enr. Code 5
  Supt. – Dr. Kenneth Southard
    401 E MCPHERSON ST 63501
  Kirksville Upper MS, E NORMAL 63501
    Dr. Raymond Miller, prin.
  Benton ES, FIRST & PATTERSON 63501
    Bill Harrison, prin.
  Greenwood ES, E NORMAL 63501
    Bill Harrison, prin.
  Washington ES, E HARRISON 63501
    Bill Harrison, prin.
  Willard ES
    COTTONWOOD & CENTENNIAL 63501
    Bill Harrison, prin.

  Mary Immaculate School
    712 E WASHINGTON ST 63501

Kirkwood, St. Louis Co., Pop. Code 8
  Kirkwood RSD 7
  Sch. Sys. Enr. Code 5
  Supt. – Dr. Thomas Keating
    11289 MANCHESTER ROAD 63122
  Nipher MS, 700 S KIRKWOOD ROAD 63122
    Dan Edwards, prin.
  North Kirkwood MS
    11287 MANCHESTER ROAD 63122
    James Cockrell, prin.
  Keysor ES, 725 N GEYER RD 63122
    Virginia Sapp, prin.
  Robinson ES, 803 COUCH AVE 63122
    Max Loudenslager, prin.
  Tillman ES, 230 QUAN AVE 63122
    Gilbert Brown, prin.
  Westchester ES, 1416 WOODGATE DR 63122
    Cheryl Hartle, prin.
  Other Schools – See Glendale

  Christ Community ES, 110 W WOODBINE 63122

Knob Lick, St. Francois Co.
  Knob Lick Cons. SD 1
  Sch. Sys. Enr. Code 1
  Supt. – (—), GENERAL DELIVERY 63651

ES 63651 – Nancy Mahan, prin.

Knob Noster, Johnson Co., Pop. Code 4
Knob Noster RSD 8
Sch. Sys. Enr. Code 4
Supt. – Dr. Earl Finley, 211 E WIMER ST 65336
MS, 211 E WIMER ST 65336
Minter Ringen, prin.
ES, 405 E WIMER ST 65336 – Daniel Lowry, prin.
Other Schools – See Whiteman AFB

Koshkonong, Oregon Co., Pop. Code 2
Oregon-Howell RSD 3
Sch. Sys. Enr. Code 2
Supt. – Mike McAdams 65692
Oregon-Howell ES 65692 – Ron Taylor, prin.

Labadie, Franklin Co.
Washington SD
Supt. – See Washington
ES, RURAL ROUTE 01 BOX 135A 63055
Pamela Mirley, prin.

Laddonia, Audrain Co., Pop. Code 3
Community RSD 6
Sch. Sys. Enr. Code 3
Supt. – T. O. Spessard, RURAL ROUTE 01 63352
Community ES 63352 – Caryn Giarratano, prin.

La Grange, Lewis Co., Pop. Code 4
Lewis County Cons. SD 1
Supt. – See Ewing
ES 63448 – Beth Hansmeirer, prin.

Lake Ozark, Miller Co., Pop. Code 2
School of the Osage RSD 2
Sch. Sys. Enr. Code 4
Supt. – Dr. Dalton Ham, P O BOX 197 65049
School of the Osage MS 65049
Joshua McGowin, prin.
Mills ES 65049 – Lyle Sybert, prin.

Lamar, Barton Co., Pop. Code 5
Lamar RSD 1
Sch. Sys. Enr. Code 4
Supt. – Wayne Cook, P O BOX 428 64759
MS 64759 – John Garton, prin.
ES, P O BOX 428 64759 – Jan Vangilder, prin.

La Monte, Pettis Co., Pop. Code 4
La Monte RSD 4
Sch. Sys. Enr. Code 2
Supt. – Mark Mitchell, P O BOX 218 65337
ES 65337 – Janet Heimsoth, prin.

Pettis County RSD 1
Sch. Sys. Enr. Code 1
Supt. – (—), RURAL ROUTE 02 65337
Pettis County ES
RURAL ROUTE 02 BOX 171 65337
Mary Edwards, prin.

La Plata, Macon Co., Pop. Code 4
La Plata RSD 2
Sch. Sys. Enr. Code 2
Supt. – Dick Phillips, 101 N OWENSBY ST 63549
ES, 402 E MOORE ST 63549 – John Williams, prin.

Laquey, Pulaski Co.
Laquey RSD 5
Sch. Sys. Enr. Code 3
Supt. – Dale Passmore, P O BOX 130 65534
ES, P O BOX 130 65534 – Ron McElfresh, prin.

Laredo, Grundy Co., Pop. Code 2
Laredo SD 7
Sch. Sys. Enr. Code 2
Supt. – (—), P O BOX C 64652
ES 64652 – Ivan Worley, prin.

Latham, Moniteau Co.
Moniteau County RSD 5
Sch. Sys. Enr. Code 2
Supt. – (—), SCHOOL ROAD 65050
Moniteau County ES 65050 – Sandra Potts, prin.

Lathrop, Clinton Co., Pop. Code 4
Lathrop RSD 2
Sch. Sys. Enr. Code 3
Supt. – Remel S. Grey 64465
ES 64465 – Gerald Snodgrass, prin.

Lawson, Ray Co., Pop. Code 4
Lawson RSD 14
Sch. Sys. Enr. Code 4
Supt. – R. O. Gill, P O BOX 157 64062
Central MS, E 4TH ST 64062
Edward Duncan, prin.
Southeast ES, RURAL ROUTE 02 BOX 156 64062
Nora Hutcheson, prin.
Southwest ES, P O BOX 156 64062
Nora Hutcheson, prin.

Leadwood, St. Francois Co., Pop. Code 4
West St. Francis County RSD 4
Sch. Sys. Enr. Code 3
Supt. – Dr. Claude Lynch, 1124 MAIN ST 63653
Other Schools – See Flat River

Lebanon, Laclede Co., Pop. Code 6
Laclede County Cons. SD 5
Sch. Sys. Enr. Code 2
Supt. – (—), RURAL ROUTE 02 65536
Barber ES 65536 – Bill Wheeler, prin.

Lebanon RSD 3
Sch. Sys. Enr. Code 5
Supt. – Dr. Vic Slaughter
321 S JEFFERSON AVE 65536

Boswell ES, MILLCREEK ROAD 65536
James Renner, prin.
Donnelly ES, BRICE ROAD 65536
Lowell Richardson, prin.
Hillcrest ES, HOOVER AVE 65536
Michael Lawson, prin.
Maplecrest ES, MAPLE DR 65536
Scott Huddleston, prin.

Lee's Summit, Jackson Co., Pop. Code 8
Lee's Summit RSD 7
Sch. Sys. Enr. Code 6
Supt. – Stanley Magady, 6700 MILLER 64063
Pleasant Lea JHS, 630 W PURCELL ROAD 64063
Dennis Smith, prin.
Hazel Grove ES
50 HWY & COLBORN ROAD 64063
Patricia Hardy, prin.
ES, SECOND & GREEN STS 64063
Shirley McGuire, prin.
Mason ES, COLBORN ROAD RTE 04 64063
Douglas Johnson, prin.
Meadow Lane ES
1421 NE INDEPENDENCE AVE 64063
Harold Woods, prin.
Pleasant Lea ES, 700 SW PERSELS RD 64081
Kay Baker, prin.
Prairie View ES, 501 SE TODD GEORGE RD 64063
David Helmuth, prin.
Westview ES, 200 NW WARD RD 64063
Ken Rimmer, prin.
Other Schools – See Greenwood

Our Lady of Presentation School
150 NW MURRAY RD 64081

Leeton, Johnson Co., Pop. Code 3
Leeton RSD 10
Sch. Sys. Enr. Code 2
Supt. – Leon Cunningham 64761
ES 64761 – Sue Tyler, prin.

Leopold, Bollinger Co.
Leopold RSD 3
Sch. Sys. Enr. Code 1
Supt. – Robert Turner 63760
ES 63760 – Angela Carlisle, prin.

Lesterville, Reynolds Co., Pop. Code 3
Lesterville RSD 2
Sch. Sys. Enr. Code 2
Supt. – Dr. Dale Houck, P O BOX 120 63654
ES 63654 – Virginia Walker, prin.

Lexington, Lafayette Co., Pop. Code 6
Lexington RSD 5
Sch. Sys. Enr. Code 4
Supt. – Dr. C. Hutton, 100 S 13TH ST 64067
MS, 16TH & MAIN 64067 – Barbara Kitchell, prin.
Bell ES, 400 S 20TH ST 64067
Kirby Roach, prin.

Liberal, Barton Co., Pop. Code 3
Liberal RSD 2
Sch. Sys. Enr. Code 2
Supt. – Dr. Garold Barney, P O BOX 38 64762
ES 64762 – R. Gail Newman, prin.

Liberty, Clay Co., Pop. Code 7
Liberty SD 53
Sch. Sys. Enr. Code 5
Supt. – Dr. Ron Anderson, 14 S MAIN ST 64068
Doniphan ES, S 10 HWY & CLAY 64068
Rose Mary Gardner, prin.
Franklin ES, 201 W MILL ST 64068
Dr. Barbara Wippich, prin.
Lewis & Clark ES, 1407 NASHUA ROAD 64068
Bruce Gorze, prin.
Manor Hill ES, SKYLINE DRIVE & MEADE 64068
Penny Smith, prin.
Ridgeview ES, HILLCREST & THORNTON 64068
Maureen Poulin, prin.

St. James School, 309 S STEWART RD 64068

Licking, Texas Co., Pop. Code 4
Licking RSD 8
Sch. Sys. Enr. Code 3
Supt. – Russell Ford, P O BOX 179 65542
ES 65542 – David Barnes, prin.

Lilbourn, New Madrid Co., Pop. Code 4
New Madrid County RSD 1
Supt. – See New Madrid
ES, LEWIS AVE 63862 – Franklin Hicks, prin.

Lincoln, Benton Co., Pop. Code 3
Lincoln RSD 2
Sch. Sys. Enr. Code 3
Supt. – D. E. Brodersen 65338
ES 65338 – Marlin Hammond, prin.

Linn, Osage Co., Pop. Code 4
Osage County RSD 2
Sch. Sys. Enr. Code 3
Supt. – William Page, RURAL ROUTE 01 65051
Osage County MS 65051 – Jerry Cooper, prin.
Osage County ES 65051 – Jerry Cooper, prin.

St. George School, P O BOX 10 65051

Lockwood, Dade Co., Pop. Code 3
Lockwood RSD 1
Sch. Sys. Enr. Code 2
Supt. – Hurchel Sears, P O BOX W 65682
ES 65682 – William Malone, prin.

Lonedell, Franklin Co.
Lonedell RSD 14
Sch. Sys. Enr. Code 2
Supt. – (—), HIGHWAY FF 63060
ES 63060 – Vernon Wagoner, prin.

Lone Jack, Jackson Co., Pop. Code 2
Lone Jack Cons. SD 6
Sch. Sys. Enr. Code 2
Supt. – William Carter, P O BOX 40 64070
ES 64070 – Evelyn Evans, prin.

Long Lane, Dallas Co.
Dallas County RSD 1
Supt. – See Buffalo
ES 65590 – Barbara Randall, prin.

Loose Creek, Osage Co.

Immaculate Conception School, P O BOX 8 65054

Louisiana, Pike Co., Pop. Code 5
Boncl RSD 10
Sch. Sys. Enr. Code 1
Supt. – (—)
RURAL ROUTE 01 BOX 143 63353
Boncl ES 63353 – Raymond Davenport, prin.

Louisiana RSD 2
Sch. Sys. Enr. Code 3
Supt. – Dr. William Wilcox
515 JACKSON ST 63353
MS 63353 – Betty Dolbeare, prin.
PS, 500 WELLS LANE 63353 – Eileen Smith, prin.
Meriwether ES, 110 FRANKFORD ST 63353
Eileen Smith, prin.

Lowry City, St. Clair Co., Pop. Code 3
Lakeland RSD 3
Supt. – See Deepwater
Lakeland ES 64763 – Ruby Jackson, prin.

Lucerne, Putnam Co., Pop. Code 2
Putnam County RSD 1
Supt. – See Unionville
West ES, RURAL ROUTE 02 BOX 94 64655
John Maulsby, prin.

Ludlow, Livingston Co., Pop. Code 2
Southwest Livingston County RSD 1
Sch. Sys. Enr. Code 2
Supt. – Franklin E. Schottel
RURAL ROUTE 01 BOX 68 64656
Southwest Livingston County ES 64656
Robert Houchens, prin.

Luray, Clark Co., Pop. Code 2
Luray SD 33
Sch. Sys. Enr. Code 1
Supt. – (—) 63453
ES 63453 – Dean Hunziker, prin.

Lutesville, Bollinger Co., Pop. Code 3
Woodland RSD 4
Sch. Sys. Enr. Code 3
Supt. – Ron Wene, HIGHWAY 34 W 63762
Marble Hill ES 63762 – Dan Sitze, prin.
Woodland MS 63762 – Dan Sitze, prin.

Macks Creek, Camden Co., Pop. Code 2
Macks Creek RSD 5
Sch. Sys. Enr. Code 2
Supt. – William Jones, ROUTE N 65786
ES 65786 – Marie White, prin.

Macon, Macon Co., Pop. Code 6
Macon County RSD 1
Sch. Sys. Enr. Code 4
Supt. – J. King
MISSOURI ST & HIGHWAY 63 63552
MS 63552 – Robert A. Wyatt, prin.
Macon County ES 63552 – Bobby Grimshaw, prin.

Madison, Monroe Co., Pop. Code 3
Madison Cons. SD 3
Sch. Sys. Enr. Code 2
Supt. – Dr. Paul Franklin, P O BOX 123 65263
ES, 309 THOMAS ST 65263 – Ed Clem, prin.

Middle Grove Cons. SD 1
Sch. Sys. Enr. Code 1
Supt. – (—), RURAL ROUTE 01 65263
Middle Grove ES 65263 – Cindy Giovanini, prin.

Maitland, Holt Co., Pop. Code 2
Nodaway-Holt RSD 7
Sch. Sys. Enr. Code 2
Supt. – Don Neidt, 410 HICKORY 64466
Elem. (5-8) 64466 – Danny Johnson, prin.
Other Schools – See Skidmore

Malden, Dunklin Co., Pop. Code 6
Malden RSD 1
Sch. Sys. Enr. Code 4
Supt. – Carl Townsend, P O BOX 296 63863
Beckwith MS, BECKWITH ST 63863
D. Summers, prin.
Central ES, SMITH ST 63863
Susan Crumby, prin.

Malta Bend, Saline Co., Pop. Code 2
Malta Bend RSD 5
Sch. Sys. Enr. Code 2
Supt. – Larry Flanagan, P O BOX 10 65339
ES 65339 – Kay Best, prin.

Manchester, St. Louis Co., Pop. Code 6
Parkway Cons. SD 2
Supt. – See Chesterfield

South JHS, 760 WOODS MILL ROAD 63011
  Victoria Francis, prin.
Barretts ES
  CARMAN & DGHRTY FRY ROADS 63011
  Alvina Warner, prin.
Carman Trails ES, 555 S WEIDMAN RD 63021
  Bob Underwood, prin.
Henry ES, 700 HENRY RD 63011
  Richard Hakala, prin.
Pierremont ES, 1215 DAUPHINE LN 63011
  Charles Hoppe, prin.

Mansfield, Wright Co., Pop. Code 4
Mansfield RSD 4
Sch. Sys. Enr. Code 3
Supt. – Robert Perry, P O BOX 107 65704
Wilder ES, P O BOX 379 65704
  David Brouse, prin.

Maplewood, St. Louis Co., Pop. Code 7
Maplewood-Richmond Heights SD
Sch. Sys. Enr. Code 4
Supt. – Jerry Elliott Jr.
  7539 MANCHESTER AVE 63143
Bruce ES, 3431 CAMBRIDGE AVE 63143
  Bonnie Paulsmeyer, prin.
Valley ES, 2801 OAKLAND AVE 63143
  Mark Engelhardt, prin.
Other Schools – See Richmond Heights

Marceline, Linn Co., Pop. Code 5
Marceline RSD 5
Sch. Sys. Enr. Code 3
Supt. – W. Scott Taveau
  314 E SANTA FE ST 64658
Disney ES, 420 E CALIFORNIA 64658
  Richard Skinner, prin.

Marionville, Lawrence Co., Pop. Code 4
Marionville RSD 9
Sch. Sys. Enr. Code 3
Supt. – Ron Bilyeu, P O BOX J 65705
ES 65705 – Jacqualine Mais, prin.

Marquand, Madison Co., Pop. Code 2
Marquand RSD 6
Sch. Sys. Enr. Code 2
Supt. – Gerald Deardorff 63655
ES 63655 – Pamela Moyers, prin.

Marshall, Saline Co., Pop. Code 7
Hardeman RSD 10
Supt. – See Napton
Hardeman ES 65340 – Jeanie Gordon, prin.

Marshall SD
Sch. Sys. Enr. Code 4
Supt. – Dr. Alvin R. Lowe
  468 S JEFFERSON AVE 65340
Bueker MS, 565 S ODELL AVE 65340
  Spencer Fricke, prin.
Benton ES, 467 S ELLSWORTH AVE 65340
  Donald Garst, prin.
Eastwood ES, 313 E EASTWOOD ST 65340
  Joseph Mitchell, prin.
Northwest ES, 411 N BENTON AVE 65340
  Joseph Mitchell, prin.
Southeast ES, 215 E MITCHELL ST 65340
  Donald Garst, prin.

St. Peter School, 369 S ENGLISH AVE 65340

Marshfield, Webster Co., Pop. Code 5
Marshfield RSD 1
Sch. Sys. Enr. Code 4
Supt. – Jack Howard, P O BOX B 65706
JHS, MARSHFIELD CENTER 65706
  Audie Dehart, prin.
ES 65706 – Charles Moody, prin.
Marshfield Upper MS 65706
  Paul Van Giesen, prin.

Marthasville, Warren Co., Pop. Code 3
Washington SD
Supt. – See Washington
ES, RURAL ROUTE 03 BOX 458 63357
  Paul Suchland, prin.

St. Vincent School
  RURAL ROUTE 02 BOX 542 63357

Maryland Heights, St. Louis Co., Pop. Code 6
Parkway Cons. SD 2
Supt. – See Chesterfield
McKelvey ES, 1751 MCKELVEY RD 63043
  Michael Cerutti, prin.

Pattonville RSD 3
Sch. Sys. Enr. Code 6
Supt. – Roger Clough, 115 HARDING AVE 63043
Pattonville Hts. MS, 195 FEE FEE ROAD 63043
  Dr. Bernard Epstein, prin.
Parkwood ES, 3199 PARKWOOD LN 63043
  Michael Spector, prin.
Remington Traditional ES, 102 FEE FEE RD 63043
  David Latimer, prin.
Other Schools – See Bridgeton, Hazelwood, Saint
  Ann, Saint Louis

Maryville, Nodaway Co., Pop. Code 6
Maryville RSD 2
Sch. Sys. Enr. Code 4
Supt. – Dr. R. Tullberg, 1ST & VINE STS 64468
Washington MS 64468 – Glen Jonagan, prin.
Field ES, 418 E 2ND ST 64468 – Dana Sharp, prin.

St. Gregory Barbarigo School
  315 S DAVIS ST 64468

Matthews, New Madrid Co., Pop. Code 3
New Madrid County RSD 1
Supt. – See New Madrid
ES 63867 – Roy Hon, prin.

Maysville, DeKalb Co., Pop. Code 4
Maysville RSD 1
Sch. Sys. Enr. Code 3
Supt. – Doyle Denbow, 601 W MAIN 64469
ES 64469 – Kyle Walker, prin.

Mayview, Lafayette Co., Pop. Code 2
Odessa RSD 7
Supt. – See Odessa
ES 64071 – Larry Hol, prin.

Meadville, Linn Co., Pop. Code 2
Meadville RSD 4
Sch. Sys. Enr. Code 2
Supt. – Kenneth Dudley
  101 W CRANDALL 64659
ES 64659 – Velma Trentham, prin.

Memphis, Scotland Co., Pop. Code 4
Scotland County RSD 1
Sch. Sys. Enr. Code 3
Supt. – Dr. Robert Glasford, P O BOX 337 63555
North MS, RURAL ROUTE 03 63555
  Robert Moore, prin.
East ES, 326 E JEFFERSON ST 63555
  Robert Moore, prin.

Mendon, Chariton Co., Pop. Code 2
Northwestern RSD 1
Sch. Sys. Enr. Code 2
Supt. – Frank Darling, P O BOX 43 64660
Northwestern ES 64660 – David Michael, prin.

Mercer, Mercer Co., Pop. Code 2
North Mercer County RSD 3
Sch. Sys. Enr. Code 2
Supt. – William Casey, P O BOX 648 64661
North Mercer County ES 64661
  William Casey, prin.

Meta, Osage Co., Pop. Code 2
Osage County RSD 3
Supt. – See Westphalia
ES 65058 – Wanda Hartsock, prin.

Metz, Vernon Co., Pop. Code 2
Metz RSD 2
Sch. Sys. Enr. Code 1
Supt. – (—) 64765
ES 64765 – James Tipling, prin.

Mexico, Audrain Co., Pop. Code 7
Mexico SD 59
Sch. Sys. Enr. Code 5
Supt. – Dr. Ed Ferguson
  920 S JEFFERSON ST 65265
JHS, 1200 W BOULEVARD ST 65265
  Glenn Wheeler, prin.
Field ES, 704 W BOULEVARD ST 65265
  Melanie Richter, prin.
Hawthorne ES, 1250 W CURTIS ST 65265
  Dr. Roy Moeller, prin.
McMillan ES, 1101 E ANDERSON ST 65265
  Edward Larson, prin.

St. Brendan School, 620 S CLARK ST 65265

Miami, Saline Co., Pop. Code 2
Miami RSD 1
Sch. Sys. Enr. Code 1
Supt. – (—), RURAL ROUTE 01 65344
ES 65344 – Julie Germann, prin.

Miami RSD 1
Supt. – See Amoret
ES 64722 – Wanda Burns, prin.

Middletown, Montgomery Co., Pop. Code 2
Wellsville-Middletown RSD 1
Supt. – See Wellsville
ES 63359 – Jeff Carter, prin.

Midway, Newton Co., Pop. Code 2
Midway RSD 1
Supt. – See Cleveland
ES 64734 – Patricia Shade, prin.

Milan, Sullivan Co., Pop. Code 4
Milan Cons. SD 2
Sch. Sys. Enr. Code 3
Supt. – Clinton Southerland 63556
ES 63556 – David Stephenson, prin.

Millcreek, Madison Co.
Fredericktown RSD 1
Supt. – See Fredericktown
East Madison ES, HCR ROUTE 01 BOX 34 63858
  Kenneth Blanton, prin.
ES, RURAL ROUTE 01 63645
  Kenneth Blanton, prin.

Miller, Lawrence Co., Pop. Code 3
Miller RSD 2
Sch. Sys. Enr. Code 3
Supt. – James Young, HIGHWAY 39 65707
Central ES 65707 – Gerald Edwards, prin.
West ES 65707 – Gerald Edwards, prin.
Other Schools – See Halltown

Millersville, Cape Girardeau Co.
Jackson RSD 2
Supt. – See Jackson
Attendance Ctr. 63766 – Norman Thompson, prin.

Mineral Point, Washington Co., Pop. Code 2
Potosi RSD 3
Supt. – See Potosi
ES, P O BOX H 63660 – Jim Sherrill, prin.

Missouri City, Clay Co., Pop. Code 2
Missouri City ESD 56
Sch. Sys. Enr. Code 1
Supt. – (—), P O BOX 397 64072
ES 64072 – Jay Jackson, prin.

Moberly, Randolph Co., Pop. Code 7
Moberly SD
Sch. Sys. Enr. Code 5
Supt. – Dr. Paul Ricker, 101 JOHNSON ST 65270
JHS 65270 – Lynn Yocum, prin.
Bradley MS, 500 JOHNSON ST 65270
  George Rogers, prin.
East Park ES, 200 PORTER ST 65270
  Ronald Self, prin.
North Park ES, 909 PORTER ST 65270
  Norman Oehrle, prin.
South Park ES, 701 S 4TH ST 65270
  Pamela Williams, prin.
West Park ES, 1121 MYRA ST 65270
  Dave Harris, prin.

St. Pius X School, 210 S WILLIAMS ST 65270

Mokane, Callaway Co., Pop. Code 2
South Callaway County RSD 2
Sch. Sys. Enr. Code 3
Supt. – Ono Monachino 65059
South Callaway County MS 65059
  Stephen Walkenbach, prin.
South Callaway ES 65059 – Glen Scheer, prin.

Monett, Barry Co., Pop. Code 6
Monett RSD 1
Sch. Sys. Enr. Code 4
Supt. – Dr. Thomas Kurucz
  800 E SCOTT ST 65708
ES, 400 LINDEN AVE 65708
  Roberta Osterloh, prin.

Monroe City, Monroe Co., Pop. Code 5
Monroe City RSD 3
Sch. Sys. Enr. Code 3
Supt. – William Miles, HWY 24 & 36 E 63456
JHS, 420 N WASHINGTON ST 63456
  Anthony Yates, prin.
ES, 420 N WASHINGTON ST 63456
  Richard Hodits, prin.

Holy Rosary School, 620 S MAIN ST 63456

Montgomery City, Montgomery Co., Pop. Code 4
Montgomery County RSD 2
Sch. Sys. Enr. Code 4
Supt. – Orlo Shroyer 63361
MS, HIGHWAY 19 S 63361 – Bryan Knowles, prin.
ES, 817 N HARPER ST 63361
  Linda Prichard, prin.
Other Schools – See Bellflower, Jonesburg, New
  Florence

Montrose, Henry Co., Pop. Code 2
Montrose RSD 14
Sch. Sys. Enr. Code 2
Supt. – John Warmbrodt, P O BOX 68 64770
ES 64770 – Mary Lou Vandergriff, prin.

Morehouse, New Madrid Co., Pop. Code 4
Sikeston RSD 6
Supt. – See Sikeston
ES, P O BOX 48 63868 – Charles Reaves, prin.

Morrisville, Polk Co., Pop. Code 2
Marion C. Early RSD 5
Sch. Sys. Enr. Code 3
Supt. – Gene Rice, P O BOX 96 65710
Early ES 65710 – Tammy Condren, prin.

Moscow Mills, Lincoln Co., Pop. Code 2
Troy RSD 3
Supt. – See Troy
Brown ES 63362 – Clarence South, prin.
ES 63362 – Dale Kelley, prin.

Mound City, Holt Co., Pop. Code 4
Holt County RSD 2
Sch. Sys. Enr. Code 2
Supt. – Bill View, P O BOX 147 64470
Holt County ES 64470 – Cheri Patterson, prin.

Mountain Grove, Wright Co., Pop. Code 5
Manes RSD 5
Sch. Sys. Enr. Code 1
Supt. – (—), HCR BOX 160A 65711
Manes ES 65711 – Rauna Benson, prin.

Mountain Grove RSD 3
Sch. Sys. Enr. Code 4
Supt. – David Burns, P O BOX 806 65711
ES, 320 E 9TH ST 65711 – Ron Lehr, prin.

Mountain View, Howell Co., Pop. Code 4
Mountain View-Birch Tree RSD 3
Sch. Sys. Enr. Code 4
Supt. – G. A. Adams, P O BOX 464 65548
ES, 213 E 3RD 65548 – Mary Borman, prin.
Other Schools – See Birch Tree

Mount Vernon, Lawrence Co., Pop. Code 5
Mt. Vernon RSD 5
Sch. Sys. Enr. Code 4
Supt. – Dr. Johnny Fite
    SLOAN & LANDRUM STS 65712
ES, E BLAZE ROAD 65712 – Don Townsend, prin.

Myrtle, Oregon Co., Pop. Code 3
Couch RSD 1
Sch. Sys. Enr. Code 2
Supt. – Dr. Eugene Oakley
    RURAL ROUTE 01 65778
Couth ES 65778 – Rolla Fraley Jr., prin.

Napton, Saline Co.
Hardeman RSD 10
Sch. Sys. Enr. Code 1
Supt. – (—), RURAL ROUTE 01 65340
Other Schools – See Marshall

Naylor, Ripley Co., Pop. Code 3
Naylor RSD 2
Sch. Sys. Enr. Code 2
Supt. – Lloyd Mondy 63953
ES 63953 – J. C. Morrow, prin.

Neelyville, Butler Co., Pop. Code 2
Neelyville RSD 4
Sch. Sys. Enr. Code 3
Supt. – John Green, P O BOX 8 63954
ES 63954 – Lee Johnson, prin.
Other Schools – See Harviell

Neosho, Newton Co., Pop. Code 6
Neosho RSD 5
Sch. Sys. Enr. Code 5
Supt. – Dr. Gordon Warren
    511 S NEOSHO BLVD 64850
JHS 64850 – Guy Stephens, prin.
Benton ES, E PARK ST 64850
    Coralee Freund, prin.
Central ES, W HICKORY ST 64850
    Fern Johnson, prin.
Field ES, N HIGH ST 64850 – Dallas Kelly, prin.
Intermediate ES, 330 S WOOD ST 64850
    Ken Barnes, prin.
South ES, 1111 WORNALL ST 64850
    Robert Allen, prin.
Other Schools – See Goodman

Westview Cons. SD 6
Sch. Sys. Enr. Code 2
Supt. – (—)
    RURAL ROUTE 03 BOX 343 64850
Westview ES 64850 – Bob Wilson, prin.

Nevada, Vernon Co., Pop. Code 6
Nevada RSD 5
Sch. Sys. Enr. Code 4
Supt. – John Carmichael
    800 W HICKORY ST 64772
MS, 900 N OLIVE ST 64772
    Manley Jackson, prin.
Benton ES, 500 E VERNON ST 64772
    James Rhea, prin.
Bryan ES, 500 W LEE ST 64772
    James Rhea, prin.
Franklin ES, 200 S SPRING ST 64772
    James Rhea, prin.

New Bloomfield, Callaway Co., Pop. Code 3
Callaway County RSD 3
Sch. Sys. Enr. Code 3
Supt. – Dr. Joe Phillips, P O BOX 188 65063
Callaway County ES 65063 – Angela Shilt, prin.

Newburg, Phelps Co., Pop. Code 3
Newburg RSD 2
Sch. Sys. Enr. Code 3
Supt. – Dr. John Enloe 65550
ES 65550 – Dorothy Book, prin.

New Cambria, Macon Co., Pop. Code 2
Macon County RSD 4
Sch. Sys. Enr. Code 2
Supt. – George Carter 63558
Macon County ES 63558 – Kenneth Kelso, prin.

New Florence, Montgomery Co., Pop. Code 3
Montgomery County RSD 2
Supt. – See Montgomery City
ES 63363 – James Beattie, prin.

New Franklin, Howard Co., Pop. Code 4
New Franklin RSD 1
Sch. Sys. Enr. Code 2
Supt. – Richard Royston
    412 W BROADWAY 65274
ES 65274 – Vickie Robb, prin.

New Hampton, Harrison Co., Pop. Code 2
South Harrison RSD 2
Supt. – See Bethany
ES 64471 – Marilyn Henry, prin.

New Haven, Franklin Co., Pop. Code 4
Franklin County RSD 2
Sch. Sys. Enr. Code 2
Supt. – (—)
    RURAL ROUTE 02 BOX 207 63068
Franklin County ES 63068 – Alby Rohlfing, prin.

New Haven SD
Sch. Sys. Enr. Code 2
Supt. – Colin Moran, P O BOX 17 63068
New Haven Upper MS, 100 PARK DRIVE 63068
    David Menke, prin.
ES, 205 ELTON AVE 63068 – David Menke, prin.

Washington SD
Supt. – See Washington
Campbellton ES, RURAL ROUTE 63068
    Kenneth Menke, prin.

New London, Ralls Co., Pop. Code 4
Ralls County RSD 2
Supt. – See Center
ES, 1200 S MAIN 63459 – Kayrl Silvey, prin.

New Madrid, New Madrid Co., Pop. Code 5
New Madrid County RSD 1
Sch. Sys. Enr. Code 5
Supt. – Ray Melton, P O BOX 66 63869
ES, HWY 61 N 63869 – Agnes Harrington, prin.
Other Schools – See Lilbourn, Matthews, Parma

Newtown, Sullivan Co., Pop. Code 2
Newtown-Harris RSD 3
Sch. Sys. Enr. Code 2
Supt. – Phyllis Jones 64667
Newtown-Harris ES 64667 – Nancy Tucker, prin.

Niangua, Webster Co., Pop. Code 2
Niangua RSD 5
Sch. Sys. Enr. Code 2
Supt. – Tom McGuire, P O BOX 77 65713
ES 65713 – Nancy Brake, prin.

Nixa, Christian Co., Pop. Code 5
Nixa RSD 2
Sch. Sys. Enr. Code 4
Supt. – Hal Johnson, 205 NORTH ST 65714
MS, 301 S MAIN ST 65714
    Mark Sellenriek, prin.
East ES, 312 N MARKET ST 65714
    John Thomas, prin.
Espy MS, 220 GREGG ROAD 65714
    Al Michel, prin.

Noel, McDonald Co., Pop. Code 4
McDonald County RSD 1
Supt. – See Anderson
ES 64854 – Rocky Macy, prin.

Norborne, Carroll Co., Pop. Code 3
Norborne RSD 8
Sch. Sys. Enr. Code 2
Supt. – Robert Lobb, P O BOX 92 64668
Norborne ES, EAST 5TH ST 64668
    Larry Clinefelter, prin.

North Kansas City, Clay Co., Pop. Code 5
North Kansas City SD 74
Sch. Sys. Enr. Code 6
Supt. – Dr. S. Eugene Denisar
    2000 NE 46TH ST 64116
Antioch MS, 2100 NE 65TH ST 64118
    Sue Thompson, prin.
Eastgate MS, 4700 NE PARVIN ROAD 64117
    Dwayne Glass, prin.
Maple Park MS
    5300 N BENNINGTON AVE 64119
    M. Donald Horton, prin.
New Mark MS, 515 NE 106TH ST 64155
    John Hagan, prin.
Briarcliff ES, 4100 N BRIARCLIFF RD 64116
    L. Charlene Armitage, prin.
Crestview ES, 4327 N HOLMES ST 64116
    Gayle Hurst, prin.
Nashua ES, 114TH & N MCGEE ROUTE 20 64118
    Marjorie Gutelius, prin.
Other Schools – See Kansas City

Norwood, Wright Co., Pop. Code 2
Norwood RSD 1
Sch. Sys. Enr. Code 2
Supt. – Leon Pendergrass, P O BOX 37 65717
ES 65717 – Clayton Vance, prin.

Skyline RSD 2
Sch. Sys. Enr. Code 2
Supt. – (—), RURAL ROUTE 02 65717
Skyline ES 65717 – Martha McAdams, prin.

Novelty, Knox Co., Pop. Code 2
Knox County RSD 1
Supt. – See Edina
ES, P O BOX 107 63460 – Neita Collins, prin.

Novinger, Adair Co., Pop. Code 3
Adair County RSD 1
Sch. Sys. Enr. Code 2
Supt. – Robert Wallace 63559
Adair County ES 63559 – Collen Allen, prin.

Oak Grove, Jackson Co., Pop. Code 5
Oak Grove RSD 6
Sch. Sys. Enr. Code 4
Supt. – Dr. Ed Mills, 500 E 12TH ST 64075
MS 64075 – Joseph Wiggins, prin.
ES 64075 – Paul Maple, prin.

Oak Ridge, Cape Girardeau Co., Pop. Code 2
Oak Ridge RSD 6
Sch. Sys. Enr. Code 2
Supt. – Mike Johnson, P O BOX 10 63769
ES 63769 – Darryl Sauer, prin.

Odessa, Lafayette Co., Pop. Code 5
Odessa RSD 7
Sch. Sys. Enr. Code 4
Supt. – Dr. Bert Kimble, 701 S 3RD ST 64076
JHS, 310 S 1ST ST 64076 – Bob Wilson, prin.
McQuerry ES, 607 S 3RD ST 64076
    Charles Robison, prin.
Other Schools – See Mayview

O'Fallon, St. Charles Co., Pop. Code 6
Ft. Zumwalt RSD 2
Sch. Sys. Enr. Code 6
Supt. – Bernard Dubray, 110 VIRGIL ST 63366
North MS, 210 VIRGIL ST 63366
    Larry Lusch, prin.
Dardenne ES, 2621 HWY K 63366
    Peggy Barratt, prin.
Forest Park MS, 501 SUNFLOWER LN 63366
    Gerald Beatty, prin.
Mount Hope ES, 1099 HWY P 63366
    George Baner, prin.
Mudd ES, 610 PRINCE RUPPERT DR 63366
    Pamela Arnold, prin.
Other Schools – See Saint Peters

Assumption School, 203 W 3RD ST 63366
Immaculate Conception School
    2089 HANLEY ROAD 63366
St. Paul School-St. Paul, 1235 CHURCH RD 63366

Old Monroe, Lincoln Co., Pop. Code 2

Immaculate Conception School
    RURAL ROUTE 01 BOX 202 63369

Oran, Scott Co., Pop. Code 4
Oran RSD 3
Sch. Sys. Enr. Code 2
Supt. – Arnold Bell, P O BOX 250 63771
ES 63771 – Barbara Tyler, prin.

Guardian Angel School, 610 CHURCH 63771

Oregon, Holt Co., Pop. Code 3
South Holt County RSD 1
Sch. Sys. Enr. Code 2
Supt. – George Munro, P O BOX 257 64473
South Holt County ES 64473
    Melvon Anderson, prin.

Orrick, Ray Co., Pop. Code 3
Orrick RSD 11
Sch. Sys. Enr. Code 2
Supt. – D. Roberts, P O BOX 37 64077
ES 64077 – Dennis Brown, prin.

Osage Beach, Camden Co., Pop. Code 4
Camdenton RSD 3
Supt. – See Camdenton
ES 65065 – Mary Jo Newman, prin.

Osborn, DeKalb Co., Pop. Code 2
Osborn RSD 0
Sch. Sys. Enr. Code 2
Supt. – Gaylon Whitmer
    RURAL ROUTE 01 BOX 01 64474
ES 64474 – Chalice Jeffries, prin.

Osceola, St. Clair Co., Pop. Code 3
Osceola SD
Sch. Sys. Enr. Code 3
Supt. – Gary Hieronymus, P O BOX 347 64776
ES 64776 – Jeanie Naylor, prin.

Otterville, Cooper Co., Pop. Code 2
Otterville RSD 6
Sch. Sys. Enr. Code 2
Supt. – Larry Hagedorn, P O BOX 177 65348
ES 65348 – Linda Fry, prin.

Overland, St. Louis Co., Pop. Code 7
Normandy SD
Supt. – See Saint Louis
Washington ES, 1730 N HANLEY RD 63114
    Richard Kreitner, prin.

Ritenour SD
Sch. Sys. Enr. Code 6
Supt. – Dr. John DeArman
    2420 WOODSON ROAD 63114
MS, 8740 FOREST AVE 63114 – John Breen, prin.
Iveland ES, 1836 DYER AVE 63114
    Wesley Deprow, prin.
Marion ES, 2634 SIMS AVE 63114
    Judith Donohue, prin.
Marvin ES, 3520 WOODSON RD 63114
    Jack Williams, prin.
Wyland ES, 2200 BROWN RD 63114
    Dr. Barry Weston, prin.
Other Schools – See Saint Ann, Woodson Terrace

Owensville, Gasconade Co., Pop. Code 4
Owensville RSD 2
Sch. Sys. Enr. Code 4
Supt. – Ronald Hendricks, P O BOX 536 65066
ES, 208 W MONROE AVE 65066
    Brad Borcherding, prin.
Other Schools – See Gerald, Rosebud

Ozark, Christian Co., Pop. Code 5
Ozark RSD 6
Sch. Sys. Enr. Code 4
Supt. – Richard Bartow, P O BOX 166 65721
JHS 65721 – Leo Snelling, prin.
East ES 65721 – Guy Young, prin.
North MS 65721 – David Dawson, prin.

Pacific, Franklin Co., Pop. Code 5
Meramec Valley RSD 3
Sch. Sys. Enr. Code 5
Supt. – Dr. Howard Neeley
    126 N PAYNE ST 63069
JHS, 913 W UNION ST 63069
    Robert Thomas, prin.
Pacific Upper MS, 413 UNION 63069
    Harold Dunn, prin.

Truman ES, 101 UDE ST 63069
Donna Freter, prin.
Zitzman ES, PAYNE ST 63069
Bill Musgraves, prin.
Other Schools – See Catawissa, Robertsville, Villa
Ridge

St. Bridget School, 223 W UNION ST 63069

Palmyra, Marion Co., Pop. Code 5
Palmyra RSD 1
Sch. Sys. Enr. Code 4
Supt. – Paul James 63461
MS, W LINE ST 63461 – Christine Crawford, prin.
ES 63461 – Don McCain, prin.

Zion Lutheran School, 120 S SPRING ST 63461

Paris, Monroe Co., Pop. Code 4
Paris RSD 2
Sch. Sys. Enr. Code 3
Supt. – Larry Twellman
RURAL ROUTE 02 BOX 7 65275
IS, 112 S MAIN ST 65275 – Joe Branham, prin.
ES, 725 CLEVELAND ST 65275
Paul Allgood, prin.

Parkville, Platte Co., Pop. Code 4
Park Hill RSD 5
Supt. – See Kansas City
Graden ES, 8804 NW HIGHWAY 45 64152
Jeanette Hoy, prin.

Parma, New Madrid Co., Pop. Code 4
New Madrid County RSD 1
Supt. – See New Madrid
ES 63870 – Ralph Barnwell Jr., prin.

Parnell, Nodaway Co., Pop. Code 2
Northeast Nodaway County RSD 5
Supt. – See Ravenwood
ES 64475 – Bryon Miller Jr., prin.

Patton, Bollinger Co., Pop. Code 2
Meadow Heights RSD 2
Sch. Sys. Enr. Code 3
Supt. – Dan Tallent, P O BOX 2100 63662
Meadow Heights ES 63662 – Phillip Lewis, prin.

Pattonsburg, Daviess Co., Pop. Code 3
Pattonsburg RSD 1
Sch. Sys. Enr. Code 2
Supt. – William Walker, P O BOX 248 64670
ES 64670 – Margaret Kemp, prin.

Peace Valley, Howell Co.
Peace Valley Cons. SD 2
Sch. Sys. Enr. Code 1
Supt. – (—), GENERAL DELIVERY 65788
ES 65788 – Glen Tilson, prin.

Peculiar, Cass Co., Pop. Code 4
Raymore-Peculiar RSD 2
Sch. Sys. Enr. Code 4
Supt. – John Dean, P O BOX 366 64078
Raymore-Peculiar JHS, P O BOX 185 64078
Gene Vinson, prin.
ES 64078 – Dr. Michael Sportsman, prin.
Other Schools – See Raymore

Perry, Ralls Co., Pop. Code 3
Ralls County RSD 2
Supt. – See Center
ES, MADISON ST 63462 – D. Rhea Williams, prin.

Perryville, Perry Co., Pop. Code 6
Perry County SD 32
Sch. Sys. Enr. Code 4
Supt. – Dr. Larry Ackley
COLLEGE & EDWARD STS 63775
JHS, 326 COLLEGE ST 63775
Charles Penberthy, prin.
ES, 326 COLLEGE ST 63775 – Troy Wood, prin.

Immanuel Lutheran School
225 W SOUTH ST 63775
SS Vincent & Boniface School
1021 W SAINT JOSEPH ST 63775

Pevely, Jefferson Co., Pop. Code 5
Dunklin RSD 5
Supt. – See Herculaneum
ES, P O BOX 327 63070 – Thomas Dempsey, prin.

Philadelphia, Marion Co., Pop. Code 2
Marion County RSD 2
Sch. Sys. Enr. Code 2
Supt. – Randy Spratt, P O BOX 100 63463
Marion County ES 63463 – Robert Fohey, prin.

Pickering, Nodaway Co., Pop. Code 2
North Nodaway County RSD 6
Supt. – See Hopkins
ES, P O BOX 35 64476 – Terry Buholt, prin.

Piedmont, Wayne Co., Pop. Code 4
Clearwater RSD 1
Sch. Sys. Enr. Code 4
Supt. – Lloyd Phillips
RURAL ROUTE 01 BOX 1A 63957
Clearwater ES, 825 N MAIN ST 63957
Edwin Thompson, prin.

Pierce City, Lawrence Co., Pop. Code 4
Pierce City RSD 6
Sch. Sys. Enr. Code 3
Supt. – Charles Cudney, P O BOX E 65723

Central ES, GIBBS AVE 65723
Sammy Hudson, prin.

St. Marys School, FRONT & ELM ST 65723

Pilot Grove, Cooper Co., Pop. Code 3
Cooper County Cons. SD 4
Sch. Sys. Enr. Code 2
Supt. – Dr. Richard Mandell, P O BOX 145 65276
Cooper County ES 65276 – Marcia Eilers, prin.

Pineville, McDonald Co., Pop. Code 3
McDonald County RSD 1
Supt. – See Anderson
ES 64856 – Robert McCulley, prin.

Plato, Texas Co., Pop. Code 2
Plato RSD 5
Sch. Sys. Enr. Code 3
Supt. – Dr. Don Carriker 65552
ES, P O BOX A 65552
Charles Vanzyverden, prin.

Platte City, Platte Co., Pop. Code 4
Platte County RSD 3
Sch. Sys. Enr. Code 4
Supt. – Dr. Patricia Karasiewicz
P O BOX 387 64079
MS 64079 – T. Hart, prin.
Platte City Annex MS 64079
Ronald Harmon, prin.
ES 64079 – Ronald Harmon, prin.
Other Schools – See Kansas City

Plattsburg, Clinton Co., Pop. Code 4
Plattsburg RSD 3
Sch. Sys. Enr. Code 3
Supt. – Dr. James Raulsten
800 W FROST ST 64477
Ellis ES 64477 – Paul Huey, prin.

Pleasant Hill, Cass Co., Pop. Code 5
Pleasant Hill RSD 3
Sch. Sys. Enr. Code 4
Supt. – Mitchel Hanna
301 N MCKISSOCK ST 64080
MS 64080 – Robert Baldwin, prin.
PS 64080 – David Adamczyk, prin.

Pleasant Hope, Polk Co., Pop. Code 2
Pleasant Hope RSD 6
Sch. Sys. Enr. Code 3
Supt. – Donald Dittman, P O BOX 387 65725
ES 65725 – Rosa Routh, prin.

Polo, Caldwell Co., Pop. Code 3
Mirabile Cons. SD 1
Sch. Sys. Enr. Code 1
Supt. – (—), RURAL ROUTE 02 64671
Mirabile ES 64671 – Caroline Harris, prin.

Polo RSD 7
Sch. Sys. Enr. Code 2
Supt. – Kenneth Schaeffer, P O BOX 87 64671
ES 64671 – Michael Dejoode, prin.

Poplar Bluff, Butler Co., Pop. Code 7
Poplar Bluff RSD 1
Sch. Sys. Enr. Code 6
Supt. – Dr. Robert Moulton, P O BOX 47 63901
JHS, LESTER ST & HIGHWAY 67 N 63901
F. Wilkinson, prin.
Field ES 63901 – Robert Pumphrey, prin.
Kennedy ES, LINDSAY ST 63901
Betty Henson, prin.
Kinyon ES, 910 VINE ST 63901 – James King, prin.
Lake Road ES, RURAL ROUTE 03 BOX 277 63901
James King, prin.
O'Neal ES, 2300 BAUGH LANE 63901
David Henslee, prin.
Oak Grove ES, RURAL ROUTE 06 BOX 283 63901
Mildred Bryant, prin.
Twain MS, MAIN ST 63901 – Betty Henson, prin.

Sacred Heart School, 8TH & VINE STS 63901

Portageville, New Madrid Co., Pop. Code 5
North Pemiscot County RSD 1
Supt. – See Wardell
Ross Central MS, RURAL ROUTE 02 63873
Kery Henke, prin.

Portageville SD
Sch. Sys. Enr. Code 5
Supt. – John Thomas, 904 KING AVE 63873
MS 63873 – Marigene Gans, prin.
Central ES 63873 – Sandra Mudd, prin.

Potosi, Washington Co., Pop. Code 5
Potosi RSD 3
Sch. Sys. Enr. Code 5
Supt. – Jesse Jarvis, 306 S LEAD ST 63664
Evans MS, 303 S LEAD ST 63664
Gary Schack, prin.
ES, RURAL ROUTE 01 63664 – Jim Sherrill, prin.
Other Schools – See Mineral Point

Prairie Home, Cooper Co., Pop. Code 2
Prairie Home RSD 5
Sch. Sys. Enr. Code 2
Supt. – Ronald Wagner, P O BOX 105 65068
ES 65068 – Robert McKee, prin.

Princeton, Mercer Co., Pop. Code 4
Princeton RSD 5
Sch. Sys. Enr. Code 2
Supt. – Dr. Roger Dorson 64673
ES 64673 – Teri Baskett, prin.

Purdin, Linn Co., Pop. Code 2
Linn County RSD 1
Sch. Sys. Enr. Code 2
Supt. – Eldon Tietsort, P O BOX 130 64674
Linn ES 64674 – Timothy Gutzmer, prin.

Purdy, Barry Co., Pop. Code 3
Purdy RSD 2
Sch. Sys. Enr. Code 2
Supt. – Sheldon Buxton, P O BOX 248 65734
ES 65734 – Nola Nickols, prin.

Puxico, Stoddard Co., Pop. Code 3
Puxico RSD 8
Sch. Sys. Enr. Code 3
Supt. – James Wilthong, P O BOX 37 63960
ES 63960 – Jerry Robison, prin.

Queen City, Schuyler Co., Pop. Code 3
Schuyler County RSD 1
Sch. Sys. Enr. Code 3
Supt. – Dr. James Dishman, P O BOX 338 63561
MS 63561 – Linda Berry, prin.
Schuyler County ES 63561 – Linda Berry, prin.

Qulin, Butler Co., Pop. Code 3
Twin Rivers RSD 10
Supt. – See Broseley
ES 63961 – Dennis Whitlow, prin.

Ravenwood, Nodaway Co., Pop. Code 2
Northeast Nodaway County RSD 5
Sch. Sys. Enr. Code 2
Supt. – Jerry Archer 64479
Other Schools – See Parnell

Raymondville, Texas Co., Pop. Code 2
Raymondville RSD 7
Sch. Sys. Enr. Code 2
Supt. – (—), P O BOX 107 65555
ES 65555 – Phillip Palmerg, prin.

Raymore, Cass Co., Pop. Code 5
Raymore-Peculiar RSD 2
Supt. – See Peculiar
ES, P O BOX 430 64083 – Mary Ann Benner, prin.

Raytown, Jackson Co., Pop. Code 8
Raytown Cons. SD 2
Sch. Sys. Enr. Code 6
Supt. – Dr. Robert Atkin
10500 E 60TH TERRACE 64133
South MS, 8401 E 83RD ST 64138
Larry Taylor, prin.
Blue Ridge ES, 6410 BLUE RIDGE BLVD 64133
Ralph Williams, prin.
Laurel Hills ES, 5401 LANE AVE 64133
William Brown, prin.
Northwood ES, 4400 STERLING AVE 64133
Judith Estes, prin.
Other Schools – See Kansas City

Reeds Spring, Stone Co., Pop. Code 2
Reeds Spring RSD 4
Sch. Sys. Enr. Code 4
Supt. – John Williams, P O BOX 185 65737
JHS, P O BOX 268 65737 – James Holt, prin.
ES, P O BOX 129 65737 – Darwin Strohm, prin.

Renick, Randolph Co., Pop. Code 2
Renick RSD 5
Sch. Sys. Enr. Code 2
Supt. – Ira H. Cunningham, P O BOX 37 65278
ES 65278 – Ira Cunningham, prin.

Republic, Greene Co., Pop. Code 5
Republic RSD 3
Sch. Sys. Enr. Code 4
Supt. – Dr. Allan Crader
518 N HAMPTON AVE 65738
MS, 518 N HAMPTON AVE 65738
Larry Carter, prin.
ES I, 234 E ANDERSON ST 65738
Bobby Hollis, prin.
ES II, 235 E ANDERSON ST 65738
Bobby Hollis, prin.

Revere, Clark Co., Pop. Code 2
Revere Cons. SD 3
Sch. Sys. Enr. Code 2
Supt. – Jim Walling, P O BOX 300 63465
ES 63465 – Alan Marshall, prin.

Rich Hill, Bates Co., Pop. Code 4
Rich Hill RSD 4
Sch. Sys. Enr. Code 2
Supt. – Jesse Teel, 110 W OLIVE ST 64779
Poplar ES, 110 W OLIVE 64779
Linda Price, prin.

Richland, Pulaski Co., Pop. Code 4
Pulaski County RSD 4
Sch. Sys. Enr. Code 3
Supt. – John Roam, LSR BOX 4A 65556
Pulaski County ES 65556 – Kyle Stephenson, prin.

Richland RSD 1
Supt. – See Essex
ES 63846 – Clyde Allen Dixon, prin.

Richmond, Ray Co., Pop. Code 6
Richmond RSD 16
Sch. Sys. Enr. Code 4
Supt. – Dr. Joyce Dana, 118 E NORTH 64085
MS, COLLEGE & SUMMIT STS 64085
Pete Muenks, prin.
Woodson/Dear ES, 655 E MAIN ST 64085
Jan Jorgensen, prin.

Richmond Heights, St. Louis Co., Pop. Code 7
Maplewood-Richmond Heights SD
Supt. – See Maplewood
Chaney ES, 1800 PRINCETON PL 63117
Ronald McCracken, prin.
West Richmond ES, 1313 BOLAND PL 63117
Robert Moore, prin.

Richwoods, Washington Co., Pop. Code 4
Washington County RSD 7
Sch. Sys. Enr. Code 2
Supt. – (—), HCR BOX A45 63071
ES 63071 – Dr. Robert Sifford, prin.

Ridgeway, Harrison Co., Pop. Code 3
Ridgeway RSD 5
Sch. Sys. Enr. Code 2
Supt. – Harold Flint, P O BOX 179-A 64481
ES 64481 – Elizabeth Brooks, prin.

Risco, New Madrid Co., Pop. Code 2
Risco RSD 2
Sch. Sys. Enr. Code 2
Supt. – Robert Shaw, P O BOX 17 63874
ES, P O BOX 18 63874 – Michael Walker, prin.

Robertsville, Franklin Co.
Greene County RSD 8
Supt. – See Rogersville
MS, P O BOX 100 65742 – Floyd Hurst, prin.

Meramec Valley RSD 3
Supt. – See Pacific
ES 63072 – Richard Smith, prin.

Rock Port, Atchison Co., Pop. Code 4
Rock Port RSD 2
Sch. Sys. Enr. Code 3
Supt. – Roger Blakely
600 S NEBRASKA ST 64482
ES, 600 S NEBRASKA ST 64482
M. Steve Scamman, prin.

Rocky Comfort, McDonald Co.
McDonald County RSD 1
Supt. – See Anderson
ES 64861 – Carl Nichols Jr., prin.

Rogersville, Greene Co., Pop. Code 3
Greene County RSD 8
Sch. Sys. Enr. Code 4
Supt. – Danny Houser
RURAL ROUTE 04 BOX 251 65742
Greene County ES
RURAL ROUTE 02 BOX 88 65742
Alan Harville, prin.
Other Schools – See Robertsville

Rolla, Phelps Co., Pop. Code 7
Rolla SD 31
Sch. Sys. Enr. Code 5
Supt. – Dr. D. Kent King, 6TH & MAIN STS 65401
MS, 1111 SOEST RD 65401 – Jerry Giger, prin.
Truman ES, 1001 E 18TH ST 65401
Dr. Marilyn Stewart, prin.
Twain ES, 681 SALEM AVE 65401
Harry Kiefer, prin.
Wyman ES, 402 LANNING LN 65401
Donald Brown, prin.

St. Patrick School, 19 SAINT PATRICK LN 65401

Roscoe, St. Clair Co., Pop. Code 1
Roscoe Cons. SD 1
Sch. Sys. Enr. Code 2
Supt. – (—), MAIN ST 64781
ES 64781 – V. F. King, prin.

Rosebud, Gasconade Co., Pop. Code 2
Owensville RSD 2
Supt. – See Owensville
Rosebud Sixth Grade Ctr. 63091
Bill Depriest, prin.

Rosendale, Andrew Co., Pop. Code 2
North Andrew County RSD 6
Sch. Sys. Enr. Code 2
Supt. – R. Thomas Howard 64483
Other Schools – See Bolckow

Rueter, Taney Co.
Mark Twain RSD 8
Sch. Sys. Enr. Code 1
Supt. – (—), GENERAL DELIVERY 65744
Twain ES 65744 – E. J. Fowler, prin.

Rushville, Platte Co., Pop. Code 2
Buchanan County RSD 4
Supt. – See De Kalb
ES 64484 – Janice Parson, prin.

Russellville, Cole Co., Pop. Code 3
Cole County RSD 1
Sch. Sys. Enr. Code 3
Supt. – Barry Hoskins 65074
Cole ES 65074 – Jay Acock, prin.

Rutledge, Scotland Co., Pop. Code 2
Rutledge RSD 3
Sch. Sys. Enr. Code 1
Supt. – (—), P O BOX 13 63563
ES 63563 – Mary Wurtzberger, prin.

Saint Ann, St. Louis Co., Pop. Code 7
Pattonville RSD 3
Supt. – See Maryland Heights
Holman MS
11055 ST CHARLES ROCK ROAD 63074
John Pohl, prin.

Briar Crest ES, 2900 ADIE RD 63074
David Knes, prin.

Ritenour SD
Supt. – See Overland
Hoech MS, 3312 ASHBY ROAD 63074
Robert Ayres, prin.
Buder ES, 10350 BALTIMORE AVE 63074
John Antonio, prin.

Hope Lutheran School
3721 ST BRIDGET LN 63074
St. Gregory School, 3400 ST GREGORY LN 63074
St. Kevin School, 10901 ST HENRY LN 63074

Saint Charles, St. Charles Co., Pop. Code 8
Francis Howell RSD 3
Sch. Sys. Enr. Code 7
Supt. – Dr. Roger Russell
RURAL ROUTE 02 63303
Barnwell JHS, 1035 JUNG STATION ROAD 63303
Wayne Gronefeld, prin.
Hollenbach JHS
4555 CENTRAL SCHOOL ROAD 63303
Edwin Mossop, prin.
Becky-David ES, 1155 JUNGS STATION RD 63303
Leslie Palmer, prin.
Castlio ES, 1020 DINGLEDINE RD 63303
H. E. Wilfong, prin.
Central ES, 4525 CENTRAL SCHOOL RD 63303
Albert Cozzoni, prin.
Henderson ES, 2501 HACKMANN RD 63303
Joan McCarthy, prin.
Weldon Spring ES, 6325 S HWY 94 63303
Jim Grimes, prin.
Other Schools – See Saint Peters, Wentzville

St. Charles County RSD 5
Sch. Sys. Enr. Code 4
Supt. – Gary Van Meter
RURAL ROUTE 01 BOX 204 63301
Orchard Farm MS 63301 – Allen Hollrah, prin.
Orchard Farm ES
RURAL ROUTE 01 BOX 204 63301
Chris Chapman, prin.
Other Schools – See West Alton

St. Charles RSD 6
Sch. Sys. Enr. Code 6
Supt. – Dr. A. Deppe, 1916 ELM ST 63301
Hardin MS, 1950 ELM ST 63301
John Maxwell, prin.
Jefferson MS, 2660 ZUMBEHL ROAD 63301
Virginia Beaver, prin.
Benton ES, 400 N 6TH ST 63301
Donna Nack, prin.
Blackhurst ES, 2000 ELM ST 63301
Victor Thomas, prin.
Coverdell ES
RANDOLPH & CONCORDIA STS 63301
Mike Kersey, prin.
Harris ES, 1025 COUNTRY CLUB RD 63303
O. R. Keihne, prin.
Lincoln ES, 625 S 6TH ST 63301
O. Ercell Hodges, prin.
Monroe ES, 2670 ZUMBEHL RD 63301
Mike Johnson, prin.
Null ES, 435 YALE BLVD 63301
G. Hayden Owens, prin.

Academy Of The Sacred Heart
619 N 2ND ST 63301
Immanuel Lutheran School
SEVENTH & MADISON STS 63301
SS Elizabeth Seton-Robert School
1 SETON CT 63303
SS Joachim & Ann School
4110 MCCLAY RD 63303
St. Charles Borromeo School
431 DECATUR ST 63301
St. Cletus School, 2721 ZUMBEHL RD 63301
St. Peter ES, 333 S SECOND ST 63301
Zion Lutheran School, 3866 S OLD HWY 94 63303

Saint Clair, Franklin Co., Pop. Code 5
Anaconda ESD 87
Sch. Sys. Enr. Code 1
Supt. – (—)
RURAL ROUTE 02 BOX 46 63077
Anaconda ES 63077 – John Wagner, prin.

St. Clair RSD 13
Sch. Sys. Enr. Code 4
Supt. – R. Edwards, 905 BARDOT ST 63077
Murray MS 63077 – Joan Maxwell, prin.
ES 63077 – Stanley Zaremba, prin.

Saint Elizabeth, Miller Co., Pop. Code 2
St. Elizabeth RSD 4
Sch. Sys. Enr. Code 2
Supt. – Richard Nagel, P O BOX 68 65075
ES 65075 – Carl Hibdon, prin.

Sainte Genevieve, St. Genevieve Co., Pop. Code 5
Coffman RSD 5
Sch. Sys. Enr. Code 1
Supt. – (—), HCR 01 63670
Coffman ES 63670 – Paula Brashers, prin.

St. Genevieve County RSD 2
Sch. Sys. Enr. Code 4
Supt. – Thomas Kiehne
725 WASHINGTON ST 63670
JHS 63670 – Earl Wilson, prin.
ES 63670 – Bobby Webb, prin.
Other Schools – See Bloomsdale

St. Genevieve School, 49 DUBOURG PL 63670

Saint James, Phelps Co., Pop. Code 5
St. James RSD 1
Sch. Sys. Enr. Code 4
Supt. – Dr. Ron Fitch, 101 E SCIOTO ST 65559
James ES, 314 S JEFFERSON ST 65559
Loretta Keeney, prin.

Saint Joseph, Buchanan Co., Pop. Code 8
Savannah RSD 3
Supt. – See Savannah
Glenn ES, RURAL ROUTE 03 64505
Don Lawrence, prin.

St. Joseph SD
Sch. Sys. Enr. Code 7
Supt. – Dr. Randy Dewar
10TH & FELIX STS 64501
Bode MS, 720 N NOYES BLVD 64506
Dr. Vincent Paolillo, prin.
Robidoux MS, 4212 SAINT JOSEPH AVE 64505
Kenneth Quick, prin.
Spring Garden MS, 5802 S 22ND ST 64503
Robert Clemens, prin.
Truman MS, 3227 OLIVE ST #45 64507
Rex Geary, prin.
Edison ES, 515 N 22ND ST 64501
Nancy Mooney, prin.
Ellison ES, RURAL ROUTE 01 64507
Dr. Gerry Smith, prin.
Field ES, 2602 GENE FIELD RD 64506
Michael Flowers, prin.
Hall ES, 2509 DUNCAN ST 64507
Leo Blakey, prin.
Hawthorne ES, 3312 BECK RD 64506
Donald Parker, prin.
Hosea ES, 6401 GORDON AVE 64504
Donald Weston, prin.
Humboldt ES, 1604 N 2ND ST 64505
Nancy Murphy, prin.
Hyde ES, 509 THOMPSON AVE 64504
Joyce Johnson, prin.
Lake Contrary ES, 1800 ALABAMA ST 64504
Robert McCartney, prin.
Lindbergh ES
ST JOE AVE MONROE-CONCORD 64505
Ann Gerhardt, prin.
Neely ES, 1909 S 12TH ST 64503
Doyle Farmer, prin.
Noyes ES, 2596 DELAWARE ST 64506
Mary Ann Sadler, prin.
Parkway ES, 2900 DUNCAN ST 64507
Daniel Heckman, prin.
Pershing ES, 2610 BLACKWELL RD 64505
Marietta McLaughlin, prin.
Pickett ES, 3923 PICKETT RD 64503
Walter Hanabury, prin.
Skaith ES, 4701 SCHOOLSIDE LN 64503
Molly Ann Kelley, prin.
Twain ES, 31ST & NOYES 64507
Helen Richards, prin.
Webster ES, 1121 N 18TH ST 64501
Robert Blair, prin.

St. Francis Xavier School, 2614 SENECA ST 64507
St. James School, 120 MICHIGAN AVE 64504
St. Joseph Cathedral School
518 N 11TH ST 64501
St. Patrick School, 1813 S 12TH ST 64503

Saint Louis, St. Louis Co., Pop. Code 10
Affton SD 101
Sch. Sys. Enr. Code 4
Supt. – Dr. Gary Benedict
8701 MACKENZIE ROAD 63123
MacKenzie MS, 7550 MACKENZIE ROAD 63123
John Kosash, prin.
Gotsch MS, 8348 S LACLEDE STATION RD 63123
Pamela Sylvara, prin.
Messnier ES, 6930 WEBER RD 63123
Robert Mengersen, prin.

Bayless SD
Sch. Sys. Enr. Code 4
Supt. – Dr. Allan Ellis, 4530 WEBER ROAD 63123
Bayless MS 63123 – James Knackstedt, prin.
Bayless ES, 4530 WEBER RD 63123
Betty Poore, prin.

Ferguson-Florissant RSD 2
Supt. – See Florissant
Bermuda ES, 5835 BERMUDA AVE 63121
Dr. Peggy Dwyer, prin.
Cool Valley ES, 1351 S FLORISSANT RD 63121
Wayne Schiefelbein, prin.

Hancock Place SD
Sch. Sys. Enr. Code 4
Supt. – Dr. Roger Brodbeck, 275 W RIPA AVE 63125
Ward 1 ES, 9415 GENTRY AVE 63125
Robert Schnurman, prin.
Ward 2 ES, 8808 S GRAND AVE 63125
Paul Huff, prin.
Ward 3 ES, 243 W RIPA AVE 63125
Mary Lou Childers, prin.

Hazelwood SD
Supt. – See Florissant
Kirby JHS, 1865 DUNN ROAD 63138
Philip Shearrer, prin.
Grannemann ES, 2324 REDMAN RD 63136
Janet Maschoff, prin.
Keeven ES, 11230 OLD HLS FRY RD 63136
Dr. Brenda Youngblood, prin.

Larimore ES, 1025 TRAMPE AVE 63138
    Clinton Heil, prin.
Twillman ES, 11831 BELLEFONTAINE RD 63138
    Lynn Brown, prin.

Ladue SD
Sch. Sys. Enr. Code 5
Supt. – Dr. Charles McKenna
    9703 CONWAY ROAD 63124
Ladue JHS, 9701 CONWAY ROAD 63124
    Dr. Frank Fischel, prin.
Conway ES, 9900 CONWAY RD 63124
    Dr. Robert Bredin, prin.
Old Bonhomme ES
    9661 OLD BONHOMME RD 63132
    Wynn Miller, prin.
Reed ES, 9060 LADUE RD 63124
    Dr. Donald Flanagan, prin.
Spoede ES, 425 N SPOEDE RD 63141
    Richard Van Keuren, prin.

Lindbergh RSD 8
Sch. Sys. Enr. Code 6
Supt. – Dr. Gary K Wright
    4900 S LINBERGH BLVD 63126
Sperreng MS
    12211 TESSON FERRY ROAD 63128
    Victor Lenz Jr., prin.
Crestwood ES, 1020 S SAPPINGTON RD 63126
    Glenn Koehrer, prin.
Kennerly ES, 10025 KENNERLY RD 63128
    George Pachiva, prin.
Long ES, 9021 SAPPINGTON RD 63126
    Arthur Huskey, prin.
Sappington ES, 11011 GRAVOIS RD 63126
    Joan Fischer, prin.

Mehlville RSD 9
Sch. Sys. Enr. Code 6
Supt. – Dr. E. Burns
    3120 LEMAY FERRY ROAD 63125
Buerkle JHS, 623 BUCKLEY ROAD 63125
    Jack Jordan, prin.
Oakville JHS, 5950 TELEGRAPH ROAD 63129
    Laverne Buckner, prin.
Washington JHS, 5165 AMBS ROAD 63128
    Dr. B. W. Fulks, prin.
Beasley ES, 3131 KOCH RD 63125
    James Schibig, prin.
Bernard ES, 1054 FORDER RD 63129
    Dr. William Murphy, prin.
Bierbaum ES, 2050 UNION RD 63125
    Timothy Ricker, prin.
Blades ES, 5140 PATTERSON RD 63129
    Kenneth Haller, prin.
Forder ES, 623 W RIPA AVE 63125
    Deborah Decker, prin.
Oakville ES, 2911 YEAGER RD 63129
    James Muskopf, prin.
Point ES, 6790 TELEGRAPH RD 63129
    William Eydman, prin.
Trautwein ES, 5011 AMBS RD 63128
    Ruth Morris, prin.
Wohlwend ES, 5966 TELEGRAPH RD 63129
    William Black, prin.

Normandy SD
Sch. Sys. Enr. Code 6
Supt. – Dr. James Westbury
    7837 NATURAL BRIDGE ROAD 63121
Normandy JHS
    7855 NATURAL BRIDGE ROAD 63121
    Steven Huber, prin.
Bel Ridge MS, 8930 BOSTON AVE 63121
    Robert Brooks, prin.
Bel-Nor ES, 3101 NORDIC DR 63121
    Ruth Brown, prin.
Garfield ES, 6506 WRIGHT WAY 63121
    Jerome Greer, prin.
Harrison ES, 8129 ALBIN AVE 63114
    Glenda Adkins, prin.
Jefferson ES, 4315 CARDWELL DR 63121
    Harry Maier Jr., prin.
Lincoln ES, 6815 ROBBINS AVE 63133
    Celestine Knox, prin.
McKinley ES, 2100 LUCAS & HUNT RD 63121
    James McDonald, prin.
Pine Lawn ES, 2505 KIENLEN AVE 63121
    Thomas Zeitz, prin.
Other Schools – See Overland

Parkway Cons. SD 2
Supt. – See Chesterfield
Craig ES, 1492 CRAIG RD 63146
    Jaclyn Levy, prin.
Ross ES, 1150 ROSS AVE 63146
    Bonnie Maxey, prin.

Pattonville RSD 3
Supt. – See Maryland Heights
Willow Brook ES, 11022 SCHUETZ RD 63146
    William Pohlman, prin.

Riverview Gardens SD
Sch. Sys. Enr. Code 5
Supt. – Dr. Edwin J. Benton
    1370 NORTHUMBERLAND DRIVE 63137
Central, 9800 SCHOOLVIEW DRIVE 63137
    Dr. D. C. Sullivan, prin.
Danforth ES, 1111 ST CYR RD 63137
    Scott Scolle, prin.
Glasgow ES, 10560 RENFREW DR 63137
    Walter Van Pelt, prin.
Koch ES, 1910 EXUMA DR 63136
    Dr. Doris Stempniak, prin.

Lemasters ES, 1825 CRO3WN POINT DR 63136
    George Wilson, prin.
Lewis & Clark ES, 10242 PRINCE DR 63136
    Dr. James Earle, prin.
Meadows ES, 9801 EDGEFIELD DR 63136
    Dennis Dorsey, prin.

St. Louis City SD
Sch. Sys. Enr. Code 8
Supt. – Dr. Jerome Jones, 911 LOCUST ST 63101
Academic-Athletic Academy
    450 DES PERES AVE 63112 – Bart Collida, prin.
Blewett MS, 1927 CASS AVE 63106
    Sidney McNeal, prin.
Blow MS, 516 LOUGHBOROUGH AVE 63111
    Clarence Ward, prin.
Clinton MS, 1224 GRATTAN ST 63104
    Charles Shelton, prin.
Columbia MS, 3120 SAINT LOUIS AVE 63106
    Maurice Bell, prin.
Cook MS, 5935 HORTON PLACE 63112
    Robert Hudson, prin.
Dewey MS, 6746 CLAYTON AVE 63139
    William Bullerdick, prin.
Fanning MS, 3418 GRACE AVE 63116
    Fred Vasquez, prin.
Grant MS, 3009 PENNSYLVANIA AVE 63118
    Joann Perkins, prin.
Hickey MS, 3111 CORA AVE 63115
    Donald Hammonds, prin.
Humboldt Visual/Performing Art MS
    2516 S 9TH ST 63104 – David Bird, prin.
King MS, 1909 N KINGS HIGHWAY 63113
    Jimmie Billups, prin.
Langston MS, 5511 WABADA AVE 63112
    James Strughold, prin.
Long MS, 5028 MORGANFORD ROAD 63116
    David Eaton, prin.
Marquette MS, 4015 MCPHERSON AVE 63108
    Alice Roach, prin.
Mason MS, 6031 SOUTHWEST AVE 63139
    Doris Reece, prin.
Mullanphy MS, 4221 SHAW BLVD 63110
    Carolyn Eakin, prin.
Nottingham MS, 4165 DONOVAN AVE 63109
    Margaret Houlihan, prin.
Pruitt Military Academy, 1212 N 22ND ST 63106
    Maurice Grant, prin.
Simmons MS, 1033 WHITTIER ST 63113
    Charles White, prin.
Stevens MS, 1033 WHITTIER ST 63113
    Arthur Sharpe,Jr., prin.
Stowe MS, 5750 LOTUS AVE 63112
    Edgar Burnett, prin.
Turner MS, 2615 PENDLETON AVE 63113
    Arnold Martin, prin.
Webster MS, 2127 N 11TH ST 63106
    Jimmie Mahan, prin.
Williams MS
    3955 SAINT FERDINAND AVE 63113
    Acme Price, prin.
Yeatman MS, 4265 ATHLONE AVE 63115
    Chester Edmunds, prin.
Adams ES, 1311 TOWER GROVE AVE 63110
    William Tybura, prin.
Ames ES, 2900 HADLEY ST 63107
    Cleveland Young, prin.
Arlington ES, 1617 BURD AVE 63112
    Bernice Smith, prin.
Ashland ES & Branch
    3921 N NEWSTEAD AVE 63115
    Grover Johnson, prin.
Baden ES, 8724 HALLS FERRY RD 63147
    Jerome Buterin, prin.
Banneker ES, 2840 LUCAS AVE 63103
    Janice Mosby, prin.
Bryan Hill ES, 2128 GANO AVE 63107
    Louis McGowan Jr., prin.
Buder ES, 5319 LANSDOWNE AVE 63109
    Thomas Echols, prin.
Carr Lane ES, 1004 N JEFFERSON AVE 63106
    Robert Cloyd, prin.
Carver ES, 3325 BELL AVE 63106
    Olivia Malone, prin.
Clark ES, 1020 UNION BLVD 63113
    William Hardebeck, prin.
Clay ES, 3820 N 14TH ST 63107
    Francis Muehlheausler, prin.
Cole ES, 3935 ENRIGHT AVE 63108
    Leonard Evans, prin.
Cook Branch ES, 5890 ETZEL AVE 63112
    Warren Brunson, prin.
Cote Brilliante ES, 2616 CORA AVE 63113
    Donald Nabors, prin.
Cupples ES, 4908 COTE BRILLIANTE AVE 63113
    Thomas Stenger, prin.
Dunbar & Branch ES
    1415 N GARRISON AVE 63106
    Freddie Stevens, prin.
Eliot ES, 4242 GROVE ST 63107
    James Overton, prin.
Emerson ES, 5415 PAGE BLVD 63112
    William Busch II, prin.
Enright Class Jr. Academy
    5351 ENRIGHT AVE 63112 – Mary Purdy, prin.
Euclid Montessori ES, 1131 N EUCLID AVE 63113
    Lincoln Daniels, prin.
Farragut Branch 1 ES
    4130 LEXINGTON AVE #1 63115
    Donald Laddy, prin.
Farragut Branch 2 ES
    300 E PRAIRIE AVE #2 63107 – Gussie Fultz,
    prin.

Farragut ES, 4025 SULLIVAN AVE 63107
    Jimmie Irons, prin.
Field ES, 4466 OLIVE ST 63108
    Frederic Boyd, prin.
Ford MS & Branch, 1383 CLARA AVE 63112
    Doris Johnson, prin.
Froebel ES, 3709 NEBRASKA AVE 63118
    Richard Cadice, prin.
Garfield ES, 2612 WYOMING ST 63118
    Norman Brust, prin.
Gundlalch ES, 2931 ARLINGTON AVE 63120
    Gerald Declue, prin.
Hamilton Branch ES, 5859 CLEMENS AVE 63112
    Stanley Jordan, prin.
Hamilton ES, 5819 WESTMINSTER PL 63112
    John Bernard, prin.
Harrison ES, 4163 GREEN LEA PL 63115
    Herbert Turner, prin.
Hempstead Branch ES, 1435 LAUREL ST 63112
    Roger Twist, prin.
Hempstead ES, 5872 MINERVA AVE 63112
    Roger Twist, prin.
Henry ES, 1220 N 10TH ST 63106
    Eula Flowers, prin.
Herzog ES, 5831 PAMPLIN PL 63147
    Edmond Squires, prin.
Hodgen ES, 2748 HENRIETTA ST 63104
    Donald Dallas, prin.
Irving ES, 3829 N 25TH ST 63107
    Yetta Kilgore, prin.
Jackson ES, 1632 HOGAN ST 63106
    Mary Polk, prin.
Jefferson ES, 1301 HOGAN ST 63106
    Warren Benning, prin.
L'Ouverture MS, 3021 HICKORY ST 63104
    William Boyd, prin.
Laclede ES, 5821 KENNERLY AVE 63112
    Lonzola Buford, prin.
Lafayette ES, 815 ANN AVE 63104
    Gloria Abbington, prin.
Lexington ES, 5030 LEXINGTON AVE 63115
    Helen Young, prin.
Lowell ES, 1409 LINTON AVE 63107
    Lavaunt Maupin, prin.
Lyon Academic-Basic Instruction ES
    7417 VERMONT AVE 63111
    Richard Mirkay, prin.
Madison A.L.C.E. ES, 1118 S 7TH ST 63104
    David Learman, prin.
Mallinckrodt A.B.I. ES, 6020 PERNOD AVE 63139
    Emanuel Buren, prin.
Mann ES, 4047 JUNIATA ST 63116
    Katherine Vaughn, prin.
Marshall ES, 4342 ALDINE AVE 63113
    Earl Bonner, prin.
Meramec ES, 2745 MERAMEC ST 63118
    Paul Kuhn, prin.
Mitchell Branch ES, 5436 BARTMER AVE 63112
    Vivian Turner, prin.
Mitchell ES, 955 ARCADE AVE 63112
    Donald Smith, prin.
Oak Hill ES, 4300 MORGANFORD RD 63116
    Raymond Stahl, prin.
Peabody ES, 1224 S 14TH ST 63104
    L. C. Pollard Jr., prin.
Roe ES, 1921 PRATHER AVE 63139
    Michael Lewis, prin.
Scruggs ES, 4611 S GRAND BLVD 63111
    John Jackson, prin.
Scullin ES, 4160 N KINGSHIGHWAY BLVD 63115
    Robert Ward Jr., prin.
Shenandoah ES, 3412 SHENANDOAH AVE 63104
    Robert Jones, prin.
Shepard ES, 3450 WISCONSIN AVE 63118
    Savannah Young, prin.
Sherman ES, 3942 FLAD AVE 63110
    Juanita Doggett, prin.
Sigel ES, 2050 ALLEN AVE 63104
    Michael Miley, prin.
Stix I.L.C. ES, 226 S EUCLID AVE 63110
    Marian Cotter, prin.
Twain Branch ES, 5036 THELKA AVE 63115
    Jacquelyn Campbell, prin.
Twain ES, 5316 RUSKIN AVE 63115
    Bessie Mosley, prin.
Visual & Performing Arts Center ES
    5329 COLUMBIA AVE 63139
    Artie Whitmore, prin.
Wade I.G.E. ES
    2030 S VANDEVENTER AVE 63110
    Aaron Johnson, prin.
Walbridge ES, 5000 DAVISON AVE 63120
    James Ewing, prin.
Walnut Park ES, 5814 HEKLA AVE 63120
    Marion Knox, prin.
Waring A.B.I. ES, 25 S COMPTON AVE 63103
    August Hermann, prin.
Washington MS, 1130 N EUCLID AVE 63113
    Walter Glenn Jr., prin.
Wilkinson Foreign Language ES
    7212 ARSENAL ST 63143 – Ann Russek, prin.
Woerner I.G.E. ES, 6131 LEONA ST 63116
    Rejesta Perry, prin.
Woodward ES, 725 BELLERIVE BLVD 63111
    Everett Hughes, prin.
Wyman ES, 1547 S THERESA AVE 63104
    Lyle Eichborn, prin.

University City SD
Supt. – See University City
Boone ES, 1500 82ND BLVD 63132
    Jaunester Russell, prin.

Wellston SD
Sch. Sys. Enr. Code 4
Supt. – Dr. Ronald Stodghill
    6574 SAINT LOUIS AVE   63121
Bishop ES, 6310 WELLSMAR AVE   63133
    Daniel Hudson, prin.
Central ES, 6238 ELLA AVE   63133
    Delores Dalton, prin.

Academy of the Visitation
    3020 N BALLAS ROAD   63131
Christ Community Lutheran School
    110 W WOODBINE AVE   63122
Mary Institute, 101 N WARSON ROAD   63124
Principia School, 13201 CLAYTON ROAD   63131
All Souls School, 2543 HOOD AVE   63114
Ascension School Normandy
    3801 NELSON DR   63121
Assumption School, 4709 MATTIS RD   63128
Bethel Lutheran School
    7001 FORSYTH BLVD   63105
Bishop Healy School
    2727 N KINGSHIGHWAY BLVD   63113
Central Catholic Community School
    1106 N JEFFERSON AVE   63106
Central Christian School
    700 S HANLEY RD   63105
Central City Lutheran School
    515 PENDLETON AVE   63108
Christ The King School
    7324 BALSON AVE   63130
Concord Lutheran School
    1436 FERGUSON AVE   63133
Corpus Christi School, 2100 SWITZER AVE   63136
Covenant Christian School
    2143 N BALLAS RD   63131
De Porres School, 1327 ACADEMY AVE   63113
Epiphany of Our Lord School
    6576 SMILEY AVE   63139
Forsyth ES, 6235 WYDOWN BLVD   63105
Grace Chapel Lutheran School
    10015 LANCE DR   63137
Green Park Lutheran School
    4248 GREEN PARK RD   63125
Holy Cross Lutheran School
    3630 OHIO AVE   63118
Holy Cross School, 1018 BADEN AVE   63147
Holy Family School, 4130 WYOMING ST   63116
Holy Guardian Angels School
    1019 N 14TH ST   63104
Holy Innocents School, 4926 REBER PL   63139
Hope Lutheran School
    5320 BRANNON AVE   63109
Immaculate Heart of Mary School
    4070 BLOW ST   63116
Immanuel Lutheran School
    9733 OLIVE BLVD   63132
Immocolata School, 8910 CLAYTON RD   63117
Little Flower School, 1275 BOLAND PL   63117
Mary Queen of the Universe School
    4220 RIPA AVE   63125
Messiah Lutheran School
    2900 S GRAND BLVD   63118
Most Holy Trinity School
    1435 MALLINCKRODT ST   63107
Most Precious Blood School
    3701 UNION RD   63125
Mt. Providence Boys Boarding School
    8351 FLORISSANT RD   63121
Northside Catholic ES
    4324 MARGARETTA AVE   63115
Notre Dame ES, 2647 OHIO AVE   63118
Oakhill Elementary School
    777 N S SPOEDE RD   63131
Our Lady of Angels School
    8112 SCOTT ST   63140
Our Lady of Loretto School
    1650 REDMAN RD   63138
Our Lady of Mt. Carmel School
    8759 ANNETTA AVE   63147
Our Lady of Providence School
    8874 PARDEE RD   63123
Our Lady of Quadalupe School
    1115 S FLORISSANT RD   63121
Our Lady of Sorrows School
    5831 S KINGSHIGHWAY BLVD   63109
Our Lady of the Pillar School
    403 S LINDBERGH BLVD   63131
Our Lady-Good Counsel School
    1134 ST CYR RD   63137
Our Lady-Lourdes School
    7157 NORTHMOOR DR   63105
Our Lady-Perpetual Help School
    2017 LINTON AVE   63107
Our Lady-Presentation School
    8840 TUDOR AVE   63114
Our Redeemer Lutheran School
    9135 SHELLY AVE   63114
Queen of All Saints School
    6611 CHRISTOPHER   63129
Rabbi Epstein Hebrew Academy
    1138 N WARSON RD   63132
Resurrection School, 3880 MERAMEC ST   63116
River Roads Lutheran School
    8623 CHURCH RD   63147
Rohan Woods School, 1515 BENNETT AVE   63122
Rossman ES, 12660 CONWAY RD   63141
Salem Lutheran School
    5025 LAKEWOOD AVE   63123
Seven Holy Founders School
    6737 S ROCK HILL RD   63123
St. Aloysius Gonzaga School
    5628 N MAGNOLIA AVE   63139

St. Aloysius School, 12122 LARIMORE RD   63138
St. Ambrose School, 5110 WILSON AVE   63110
St. Andrew School
    317 HOFFMEISTER AVE   63125
St. Ann School
    7532 NATURAL BRIDGE RD   63121
St. Anthony of Padua School
    4235 S COMPTON AVE   63111
St. Bernadette School, 74 KEARNEY ST   63125
St. Boniface School, 7604 MICHIGAN AVE   63111
St. Catherine Laboure School
    9750 SAPPINGTON RD   63128
St. Catherine/Alexandria School
    10014 DIAMOND DR   63137
St. Cecilia School, 906 EICHELBERGER ST   63111
St. Clement School, 1508 BOPP RD   63131
St. Dominic Savio School
    7748 MACKENZIE RD   63123
St. Elizabeth of Hungary School
    1414 S SAPPINGTON RD   63126
St. Engelbert School, 4720 CARTER AVE   63115
St. Francis Xavier School
    3741 W PINE BLVD   63108
St. Francis of Assisi School
    4550 TELEGRAPH RD   63129
St. Gabriel the Archangel School
    4711 TAMM AVE   63109
St. Genevieve Dubois School
    1575 N WOODLAWN AVE   63122
St. George School, 4974 HEDGE ROAD   63123
St. Gherard Majella School
    2005 DOUGHERTY FERRY RD   63122
St. James the Greater School
    1360 TAMM AVE   63139
St. Jerome, 10257 ASHBROOK DR   63137
St. Joan of Arc School, 5821 PERNOD AVE   63139
St. John the Baptist School, 4170 DELOR ST   63116
St. John's Lutheran School
    3716 MORGANFORD RD   63116
St. Justin the Martyr School
    11914 EDDIE & PARK RD   63126
St. Louis Cathedral School
    4430 MARYLAND AVE   63108
St. Luke the Evangelist School
    1414 BELLEVUE AVE   63117
St. Lukes Lutheran School, 3415 TAFT AVE   63111
St. Margaret Mary Alacoque School
    4900 RINGER RD   63129
St. Margaret of Scotland School
    3964 CASTLEMAN AVE   63110
St. Martin of Tours School
    618 W PIPA AVE   63125
St. Mary Magdelen School
    8750 MAGDALEN AVE   63144
St. Mary Magdelen School
    4911 SUTHERLAND AVE   63109
St. Matthews Lutheran School
    5403 WREN AVE   63120
St. Matthias the Apostle School
    800 BUCKLEY RD   63125
St. Monica School, 12132 OLIVE BLVD   63141
St. Nicholas School, 1805 LUCAS AVE   63103
St. Paul Lutheran School
    1300 N BALLAS ROAD   63131
St. Peter School Kirkwood
    215 N CLAY AVE   63122
St. Pius V School, 3530 UTAH ST   63118
St. Pius X School, 355 SHEPLEY DR   63137
St. Raphael School, 6000 JAMIESON AVE   63109
St. Richard School, 11211 SCHUETZ RD   63146
St. Rita School, 1740 NORTH & SOUTH RD   63114
St. Roch School, 6040 WATERMAN BLVD   63112
St. Sebastian School, 1826 CHAMBERS RD   63136
St. Simon School, 11019 MUELLER RD   63123
St. Stephen School
    3929 WILMINGTON AVE   63116
St. Thomas More School
    3417 ST THOMAS MORE PL   63121
St. Thomas of Aquinas School
    4021 IOWA AVE   63118
St. Timothy School, 824 UNION RD   63123
The St. Michael School
    6345 WYDOWN & ELLENWOOD   63105
Trinity Lutheran School, 1809 S 8TH ST   63104
Washington School
    4474 BUTLER HILL ROAD   63128
Word of Life Lutheran School
    6535 EICHELBERGH ST   63109

Saint Peters, St. Charles Co., Pop. Code 7
Francis Howell RSD 3
Supt. – See Saint Charles
Fairmount ES, 1725 THOELE RD   63376
    Dr. Larry Smith, prin.

Ft. Zumwalt RSD 2
Supt. – See O'Fallon
South MS, 300 KNAUST ROAD   63376
    Lloyd Bailey, prin.
Hawthorn ES, 166 BOONE HILLS DR   63376
    Phyllis Wiig, prin.
Lewis & Clark MS, 460 MCMENAMY RD   63376
    Bill Mabrey, prin.
Progress South ES, 201 KNAUST RD   63376
    Judith Boyd, prin.
ES, 400 MCMENAMY RD   63376
    Walter Williams, prin.

All Saints School, 5 MCMENAMY RD   63376

Saint Thomas, Cole Co., Pop. Code 2
Cole County RSD 2
Supt. – See Jefferson City
ES   65076 – Glenda Tucker, prin.

Salem, Dent Co., Pop. Code 5
Dent-Phelps RSD 3
Sch. Sys. Enr. Code 2
Supt. – Gerald A. Pilz
    RURAL ROUTE 02 BOX 813   65560
Dent-Phelps ES   65560 – Roger Nash, prin.

Green Forest RSD 5
Sch. Sys. Enr. Code 2
Supt. – (—), RURAL ROUTE 05   65560
Green Forest ES   65560 – James Biggs, prin.

North Wood RSD 4
Sch. Sys. Enr. Code 2
Supt. – (—)
    RURAL ROUTE 04 BOX 111   65560
North Wood ES   65560 – Gary Gardner, prin.

Oak Hill RSD 1
Sch. Sys. Enr. Code 2
Supt. – (—)
    RURAL ROUTE 03 BOX 380   65560
Oak Hill ES   65560 – Steve Jones, prin.

Salem RSD 80
Sch. Sys. Enr. Code 4
Supt. – Ralph Parks, 1200 W 3RD ST   65560
Lynch ES, MAIN ST   65560 – Eric Mansfield, prin.
Salem Intermediate MS, 315 E 10TH ST   65560
    Dennis Twitchel, prin.

Salisbury, Chariton Co., Pop. Code 4
Salisbury RSD 4
Sch. Sys. Enr. Code 3
Supt. – R. Kelley Rogers, P O BOX B   65281
ES   65281 – John Gabbert, prin.

St. Joseph School, FRONT & WILLE   65281

Sarcoxie, Jasper Co., Pop. Code 4
Sarcoxie RSD 2
Sch. Sys. Enr. Code 3
Supt. – Ellis Sneed, P O BOX 310   64862
Wildwood ES   64862 – Norman Eldridge, prin.

Savannah, Andrew Co., Pop. Code 5
Savannah RSD 3
Sch. Sys. Enr. Code 4
Supt. – Dr. R. Fessler, P O BOX 151   64485
JHS, 701 W CHESTNUT ST   64485
    Donald Coulter, prin.
Cline ES, 808 W PRICE AVE   64485
    Wanda Sue Miller, prin.
Other Schools – See Amazonia, Helena, Saint Joseph

Schell City, Vernon Co., Pop. Code 2
Schell City RSD 1
Sch. Sys. Enr. Code 2
Supt. – Joe Stepp, P O BOX 68   64783
ES   64783 – Joe Stepp, prin.

Scott City, Scott Co., Pop. Code 5
Scott City RSD 1
Sch. Sys. Enr. Code 4
Supt. – Bob Brison, 3000 MAIN ST   63780
ES   63780 – Douglas Berry, prin.

Sedalia, Pettis Co., Pop. Code 7
Pettis County RSD 7
Sch. Sys. Enr. Code 1
Supt. – (—)
    RURAL ROUTE 03 BOX 117   65301
Pettis County ES   65301 – Donald Stratton, prin.

Sedalia SD 200
Sch. Sys. Enr. Code 5
Supt. – Howard Jones, 400 W 4TH ST   65301
MS, 2200 S INGRAM AVE   65301
    Robert Reavis, prin.
Hunt ES, SEVENTH & WARREN   65301
    Jiny Evans, prin.
Mann MS, 1100 W 16TH ST   65301
    A. L. Wilson, prin.
Striped College ES, RURAL ROUTE 06   65301
    John Eisenmenger, prin.
Washington ES, SIXTH AND ENGINEER   65301
    John Eisenmenger, prin.
Whittier MS, 907 E 16TH ST   65301
    Larry O'Neil, prin.

Sacred Heart School, 3RD & VERMONT   65301
St. Paul's Lutheran School
    701 S MASSACHUSETTS AVE   65301

Senath, Dunklin Co., Pop. Code 4
Senath Cons. SD 8
Sch. Sys. Enr. Code 3
Supt. – Lawayne Law, P O BOX G   63876
ES   63876 – Charles Horner, prin.
Other Schools – See Hornersville

Seneca, Newton Co., Pop. Code 4
Seneca RSD 7
Sch. Sys. Enr. Code 4
Supt. – Tom Fevurly, P O BOX 469   64865
MS, 911 ONEIDA ST   64865
    Claude D. Hobbs, prin.
ES, 1815 SAINT EUGENE ST   64865
    Glenn Camp, prin.

Seymour, Webster Co., Pop. Code 4
Seymour RSD 2
Sch. Sys. Enr. Code 3
Supt. – Floyd Blankenship, P O BOX 397   65746
ES   65746 – (—), prin.

Shelbina, Shelby Co., Pop. Code 4
Shelby County RSD 4
Sch. Sys. Enr. Code 3
Supt. – Timothy Dunaway
111 W COLLEGE AVE 63468
JHS, S CENTER 63468 – Ronald Smoot, prin.
ES 63468 – Gary Hawkins, prin.
Other Schools – See Clarence

Shelbyville, Shelby Co., Pop. Code 3
Shelby County Cons. SD 1
Sch. Sys. Enr. Code 2
Supt. – Michael Rustman 63469
North Shelby ES 63469 – Leon Shores, prin.

Sheldon, Vernon Co., Pop. Code 2
Sheldon RSD 8
Sch. Sys. Enr. Code 2
Supt. – Wayne Rumans, P O BOX 68 64784
ES 64784 – Wayne Rumans, prin.

Shell Knob, Barry Co.
Shell Knob ESD 78
Sch. Sys. Enr. Code 2
Supt. – (—), HIGHWAY 39 65747
ES 65747 – Billy Hadlow, prin.

Sikeston, Scott Co., Pop. Code 7
Scott County RSD 5
Sch. Sys. Enr. Code 3
Supt. – W. Ray Shoaf, RURAL ROUTE 01 63801
Scott Central ES 63801 – Gene Statler, prin.

Sikeston RSD 6
Sch. Sys. Enr. Code 5
Supt. – Robert Buchanan
1002 VIRGINIA ST 63801
JHS, 100 TWITTY DRIVE 63801
Harley Barnes, prin.
Hunter ES, 1002 VIRGINIA ST 63801
Richard Giles, prin.
Matthews ES, 1002 VIRGINIA ST 63801
Gerald Oliver, prin.
MS, 1002 VIRGINIA ST 63801
Larry Nickell, prin.
Southeast ES, 1002 VIRGINIA ST 63801
Allen Mays, prin.
Southwest ES, 1002 VIRGINIA ST 63801
Randal Greenlee, prin.
Other Schools – See Morehouse

Silex, Lincoln Co., Pop. Code 2
Silex RSD 1
Sch. Sys. Enr. Code 2
Supt. – Larry Beshears, P O BOX 46 63377
ES 63377 – Cyril Heintzelman, prin.

Skidmore, Nodaway Co., Pop. Code 2
Nodaway-Holt RSD 7
Supt. – See Maitland
ES 64487 – Marilyn Shamberger, prin.

Slater, Saline Co., Pop. Code 4
Orearville RSD 4
Sch. Sys. Enr. Code 1
Supt. – (—), RURAL ROUTE 02 65349
Orearville ES 65349 – Gene Neff, prin.

Slater SD
Sch. Sys. Enr. Code 3
Supt. – Darrel Lee, 515 ELM ST 65349
Alexander ES 65349 – (—), prin.

Smithton, Pettis Co., Pop. Code 3
Smithton RSD 6
Sch. Sys. Enr. Code 3
Supt. – Keith Robertson, P O BOX 97 65350
ES 65350 – Donald Zumsteg, prin.

Smithville, Clay Co., Pop. Code 4
Smithville RSD 2
Sch. Sys. Enr. Code 3
Supt. – David Leggard
645 S COMMERCIAL 64089
ES, 600 MAPLE ST 64089 – Ray Buckner, prin.

South West City, McDonald Co., Pop. Code 3
McDonald County RSD 1
Supt. – See Anderson
ES 64863 – Joe Harmon, prin.

Sparta, Christian Co., Pop. Code 3
Sparta RSD 3
Sch. Sys. Enr. Code 3
Supt. – Leroy Winkle, P O BOX 59 65753
ES 65753 – Glenn Dye, prin.

Spickard, Grundy Co., Pop. Code 2
Spickard RSD 2
Sch. Sys. Enr. Code 1
Supt. – (—)
RURAL ROUTE 01 BOX 140 64679
ES 64679 – Ruth Ann Shipps, prin.

Spokane, Christian Co., Pop. Code 1
Spokane RSD 7
Sch. Sys. Enr. Code 2
Supt. – Floyd Jarvis, HIGHWAY 160 65754
Other Schools – See Highlandville

Springfield, Greene Co., Pop. Code 9
Springfield RSD 12
Sch. Sys. Enr. Code 7
Supt. – Dr. Paul Hagerty
940 N JEFFERSON AVE 65802
Cherokee JHS, 420 E PLAINVIEW ROAD 65807
Dr. Charles Hawkins, prin.

Hickory Hills JHS
3429 E TRAFFICWAY ST 65802
Dr. Thomas Wyrick, prin.
Jarrett JHS, 840 S JEFFERSON AVE 65806
Julie Leeth, prin.
Pershing JHS, 2120 S VENTURA AVE 65804
Frank Wann, prin.
Pipkin JHS, 1215 N BOONVILLE AVE 65802
Robert Isreal, prin.
Pleasant View JHS
RURAL ROUTE 01 BOX 401 65803
Dr. Theodore Tabor, prin.
Reed JHS, 2000 N LYON AVE 65803
Dr. Lonnie Scott, prin.
Study JHS, 2343 W OLIVE ST 65802
Charles Nickel, prin.
Bingham ES, 2126 E CHERRY ST 65802
Dr. Lynne Moore, prin.
Bissett ES, 3014 W CALHOUN ST 65802
Roy Talent, prin.
Bowerman ES, 2148 N DOUGLAS AVE 65803
Bill Reed, prin.
Boyd ES, 1409 N WASHINGTON AVE 65802
Tom Snodgrass, prin.
Campbell ES, 506 S GRANT AVE 65806
Royce Haynes, prin.
Cherokee ES, 420 E PLAINVIEW RD 65807
Dr. Charles Hawkins, prin.
Cowden ES, 2927 S KIMBROUGH AVE 65807
Helen Harber, prin.
Delaware ES, 1505 S DELAWARE AVE 65804
Bill Williams, prin.
Disney ES, 4100 S FREMONT AVE 65804
Dr. Ron Wade, prin.
Doling ES, 1423 W ATLANTIC ST 65803
Dr. Gaylen Terrill, prin.
Fairbanks ES, 1126 N BROADWAY AVE 65802
Mary Hasty, prin.
Field ES, 2120 E BARATARIA ST 65804
Frieda Hornback, prin.
Fremont ES, 2814 N FREMONT AVE 65803
Sara Carter, prin.
Gray ES, 2102 W PLAINVIEW RD 65807
Dr. Robert Maggard, prin.
Hickory Hills ES, 3429 E TRAFFICWAY 65802
Dr. Thomas Wyrick, prin.
Holland ES, 2403 S HOLLAND AVE 65807
Donna Cox, prin.
Jeffries ES, 4051 S SCENIC AVE 65807
Susan Farr, prin.
Mann ES, 3745 S BROADWAY AVE 65807
Jane Hancock, prin.
McGregor ES, 1221 W MADISON ST 65806
Gina Clinkingbeard, prin.
Pepperdine ES, 1518 E DALE ST 65803
Daryl May, prin.
Pershing ES, 2120 S VENTURA AVE 65804
Frank Wann, prin.
Pittman ES, 2934 E BENNETT ST 65804
Joann Ryan, prin.
Pleasant View ES
RURAL ROUTE 01 BOX 401 65803
Dr. Theodore Tabor, prin.
Portland ES, 906 W PORTLAND ST 65807
Sondra Pearcy, prin.
Robberson ES, 1100 E KEARNEY ST 65803
Ramona Agruso, prin.
Rountree ES, 1333 E GRAND ST 65804
Dr. Phillip Harper, prin.
Sequiota ES, 3414 S MENTOR AVE 65804
Wesley Zongker, prin.
Shady Dell ES, 2757 E DIVISION ST 65803
Judy Harris, prin.
Sherwood ES, 1813 S SCENIC AVE 65807
Dr. Carol Ashton, prin.
Study ES, 2343 W OLIVE ST 65802
Charles Nickel, prin.
Sunshine ES, 421 E SUNSHINE ST 65807
Joyce Samsel, prin.
Tefft ES, 1418 E PYTHIAN ST 65802
Sharon Hardecke, prin.
Twain ES, 2352 S WEAVER AVE 65807
Sondra Hagerman, prin.
Watkins ES, 732 W TALMAGE ST 65803
Patricia Johnston, prin.
Weaver ES, 1461 N DOUGLAS AVE 65802
Maryann Wakefield, prin.
Weller MS, 1630 N WELLER AVE 65803
Sharon Hardecke, prin.
Westport ES, 415 S GOLDEN AVE 65802
Randy Galbraith, prin.
Wilder ES, 2526 S HILLSBORO AVE 65804
Granville Henderson, prin.
Williams ES, 2205 W KEARNEY ST 65803
Winston Burton, prin.
York ES, 2100 W NICHOLS ST 65802
Ruth Martin, prin.

Immaculate Conception School
3555A S FREMONT AVE 65804
St. Agnes School, 531 S JEFFERSON AVE 65806
St. Joseph School, 515 W SCOTT ST 65802

Stanberry, Gentry Co., Pop. Code 4
Gentry County RSD 2
Sch. Sys. Enr. Code 2
Supt. – G. Shineman, 610 N PARK ST 64489
Gentry County ES 64489 – Edward Brady, prin.

Steele, Pemiscot Co., Pop. Code 4
South Pemiscot County RSD 5
Sch. Sys. Enr. Code 3
Supt. – B. G. Lewis, 611 BEASLEY ROAD 63877

Central ES, 612 BEASLEY RD 63877
Stella Griffin, prin.
East MS 63877 – Billy Booth, prin.

Steelville, Crawford Co., Pop. Code 4
Steelville RSD 3
Sch. Sys. Enr. Code 3
Supt. – Paul Simmons, P O BOX 339 65565
MS 65565 – Arthur Cook, prin.
ES 65565 – Linda Tetley, prin.

Stella, Newton Co., Pop. Code 2
East Newton County RSD 6
Supt. – See Granby
Triway ES 64867 – W. Bud Kerley, prin.

Stet, Ray Co., Pop. Code 2
Stet RSD 15
Sch. Sys. Enr. Code 2
Supt. – Dale Wallace 64680
ES 64680 – Dale Wallace, prin.

Stewartsville, DeKalb Co., Pop. Code 3
Stewartsville Cons. SD 2
Sch. Sys. Enr. Code 2
Supt. – John Dunlap, P O BOX 150 64490
ES 64490 – John Bruce, prin.

Stockton, Cedar Co., Pop. Code 4
Stockton RSD 1
Sch. Sys. Enr. Code 2
Supt. – Dr. Raymond Scott, P O BOX 190 65785
ES 65788 – Darrol Jarvis, prin.

Stoutland, Camden Co., Pop. Code 2
Camden County RSD 2
Sch. Sys. Enr. Code 3
Supt. – Rex Dameron 65567
Camden County ES 65567 – Beverly Burd, prin.

Stover, Morgan Co., Pop. Code 4
Morgan County RSD 1
Sch. Sys. Enr. Code 3
Supt. – Jack Leatherman, P O BOX E 65078
Morgan County ES 65078 – Jim Tilly, prin.

Strafford, Greene Co., Pop. Code 4
Strafford RSD 6
Sch. Sys. Enr. Code 3
Supt. – James Tice, P O BOX 97 65757
ES 65757 – Lucille Cogdill, prin.

Strasburg, Cass Co., Pop. Code 2
Strasburg Cons. SD 3
Sch. Sys. Enr. Code 1
Supt. – (—), P O BOX 228 64090
ES 64090 – James Poisal, prin.

Sturgeon, Boone Co., Pop. Code 3
Sturgeon RSD 5
Sch. Sys. Enr. Code 2
Supt. – Franklin Curtis, P O BOX 248 65284
ES 65284 – Edward Morris, prin.

Success, Texas Co.
Success RSD 6
Sch. Sys. Enr. Code 2
Supt. – (—), HIGHWAY 17 65570
ES 65570 – Harold Means, prin.

Sullivan, Franklin Co., Pop. Code 6
Franklin County RSD 16
Sch. Sys. Enr. Code 1
Supt. – (—)
RURAL ROUTE 01 BOX 351 63080
Strain-Japan ES 63080 – Deanne Narsh, prin.

Spring Bluff RSD 15
Sch. Sys. Enr. Code 2
Supt. – (—)
RURAL ROUTE 02 BOX 286 63080
Spring Bluff ES 63080 – Michael Allison, prin.

Sullivan Cons. SD 2
Sch. Sys. Enr. Code 4
Supt. – Gary Keltner
WASHINGTON & CLARK 63080
MS, WASHINGTON & CLARK STS 63080
James Palmateer, prin.
ES, WASHINGTON & CLARK STS 63080
John Needham, prin.

St. Anthony School
101 W SPRINGFIELD ST 63080

Summersville, Texas Co., Pop. Code 3
Summersville RSD 2
Sch. Sys. Enr. Code 3
Supt. – Ben Griffin, P O BOX 198 65571
ES 65571 – Sherman Farrow, prin.

Sunrise Beach, Camden Co., Pop. Code 2
Camdenton RSD 3
Supt. – See Camdenton
Hurricane Deck ES 65079
Mary Ann Dejarnette, prin.

Swedeborg, Pulaski Co.
Swedeborg RSD 3
Sch. Sys. Enr. Code 1
Supt. – (—), P O BOX 33 65572
ES 65572 – Rodney Mitchell, prin.

Sweet Springs, Saline Co., Pop. Code 4
Sweet Springs RSD 7
Sch. Sys. Enr. Code 2
Supt. – Robert Schnieders 65351
ES, 105 MAIN 65351 – David Friel, prin.

Syracuse, Morgan Co., Pop. Code 2
Moniteau County RSD 6
Supt. – See Tipton
ES   65354 – Dennis Donley, prin.

Taneyville, Taney Co., Pop. Code 2
Taneyville RSD 2
Sch. Sys. Enr. Code 2
Supt. – (—)
   RURAL ROUTE 02 BOX 58   65759
ES   65759 – Lyle Rowland, prin.

Tarkio, Atchison Co., Pop. Code 4
Tarkio RSD 1
Sch. Sys. Enr. Code 3
Supt. – Robert Bruner, 312 S 11TH ST   64491
ES, 1210 PINE ST   64491 – John Wilcox, prin.

Thayer, Oregon Co., Pop. Code 4
Thayer RSD 2
Sch. Sys. Enr. Code 3
Supt. – William Wheeler, P O BOX 195   65791
ES, CHESTNUT & SIXTH STS   65791
   Tommie Masner, prin.

Theodosia, Ozark Co., Pop. Code 2
Lutie RSD 6
Sch. Sys. Enr. Code 2
Supt. – (—), HIGHWAY 160 E   65761
Lutie ES   65761 – Gary Arthaud, prin.

Thornfield, Ozark Co.
Thornfield RSD 1
Sch. Sys. Enr. Code 1
Supt. – (—), P O BOX 102   65762
ES   65762 – Carl Morgan, prin.

Tina, Carroll Co., Pop. Code 2
Tina-Avalon RSD 2
Sch. Sys. Enr. Code 2
Supt. – Merl E. O'Neal, HIGHWAY 65   64682
Tina-Avalon ES   64682 – David Garber, prin.

Tipton, Moniteau Co., Pop. Code 4
Moniteau County RSD 6
Sch. Sys. Enr. Code 3
Supt. – Sam Bayne   65081
ES   65081 – W. Lee Barnett, prin.
Other Schools – See Syracuse

St. Andrew School, 106 W COOPER   65081

Trenton, Grundy Co., Pop. Code 6
Pleasant View RSD 6
Sch. Sys. Enr. Code 1
Supt. – (—)
   RURAL ROUTE 03 BOX 156   64683
Pleasant View ES   64683 – Claude Eckert, prin.

Trenton RSD 9
Sch. Sys. Enr. Code 4
Supt. – Gary Howren, 1001 E 9TH ST   64683
Norton MS   64683 – Louise Johnson, prin.
Rissler ES, 801 W 4TH TER   64683
   Ardity Syfert, prin.

Troy, Lincoln Co., Pop. Code 5
Troy RSD 3
Sch. Sys. Enr. Code 4
Supt. – Dr. John Lawrence
   711 W COLLEGE ST   63379
JHS   63379 – Darrell Harvey, prin.
Other Schools – See Hawk Point, Moscow Mills

Sacred Heart School
   MAIN AND COLLEGE STS   63379

Tuscumbia, Miller Co., Pop. Code 2
Miller County RSD 3
Sch. Sys. Enr. Code 2
Supt. – Roy W. True   65082
Miller County ES   65082 – Michael Haines, prin.

Union, Franklin Co., Pop. Code 6
Union RSD 11
Sch. Sys. Enr. Code 4
Supt. – Dr. R. B. Payne, P O BOX 440   63084
Clark-Vitt JHS, CLARK-VITT SUBDIVISION   63084
   Paul Copeland, prin.
Beaufort ES, HWY 50   63084 – Rolland Sohn, prin.
Central ES, JEFFERSON AVE   63084
   Ronald Brune, prin.

Washington SD
Supt. – See Washington
Clearview ES, RURAL ROUTE 04 BOX 250   63084
   Kenneth Menke, prin.

Immaculate Conception School
   6 W STATE ST   63084

Union Star, DeKalb Co., Pop. Code 2
Union Star RSD 2
Sch. Sys. Enr. Code 2
Supt. – Sue Meyer, P O BOX 98   64494
ES   64494 – Sue Meyer, prin.

Unionville, Putnam Co., Pop. Code 4
Putnam County RSD 1
Sch. Sys. Enr. Code 3
Supt. – Marcus Hounsom
   RURAL ROUTE 03 BOX 15   63565
ES, 420 S 22ND ST   63565 – Ronald Hunt, prin.
Other Schools – See Lucerne

University City, St. Louis Co., Pop. Code 8
University City SD
Sch. Sys. Enr. Code 6
Supt. – Harold Dodge
   8346 DELCREST DRIVE   63124
Brittany Woods MS, 8125 GROBY ROAD   63130
   Deborah Holmes, prin.
Delmar-Harvard ES, 711 KINGSLAND AVE   63130
   David Ackerman, prin.
Flynn Park ES, 7220 WATERMAN AVE   63130
   Robert Oliveri, prin.
Hawthorne ES, 1351 N HANLEY RD   63130
   Jerry Young, prin.
Jackson Park ES, 7400 BALSON AVE   63130
   Gloria Davis, prin.
Pershing ES, 6761 BARTMER AVE   63130
   Billie Jacobs, prin.
Sixth Grade Ctr., 8136 GROBY RD   63130
   Arlene Antognoli, prin.
Other Schools – See Saint Louis

Urbana, Dallas Co., Pop. Code 2
Hickory County RSD 1
Sch. Sys. Enr. Code 3
Supt. – Dr. Ron Wilken   65767
Skyline ES, HWY 65   65767 – Craig Burger, prin.

Valley Park, St. Louis Co., Pop. Code 5
Valley Park SD
Sch. Sys. Enr. Code 3
Supt. – Dr. John J. Cleary
   356 MERAMEC STATION ROAD   63088
ES   63088 – Dr. Mary Wainscott, prin.

Sacred Heart School, 12 ANN AVE   63088

Van Buren, Carter Co., Pop. Code 3
Van Buren RSD 1
Sch. Sys. Enr. Code 3
Supt. – M. Dale Privett, P O BOX 550   63965
ES   63965 – Marie Nicholson, prin.
Other Schools – See Fremont

Vandalia, Audrain Co., Pop. Code 5
Van Far RSD 1
Sch. Sys. Enr. Code 4
Supt. – Ronald McSorley, HIGHWAY 54 W   63382
Van-Far ES, 500 N SCHOOL HOUSE RD   63382
   Steve Davisson, prin.

Verona, Lawrence Co., Pop. Code 3
Verona RSD 7
Sch. Sys. Enr. Code 2
Supt. – Dr. Harvey Walthall, P O BOX 98   65769
ES, 101 ELLA   65769 – Jack Purdom, prin.

Versailles, Morgan Co., Pop. Code 4
Morgan County RSD 2
Sch. Sys. Enr. Code 4
Supt. – Gary Dixon, HIGHWAY 52 W   65084
Morgan County ES, HWY 52 W   65084
   Linda Specie, prin.
South ES   65084 – Linda Specie, prin.

Viburnum, Iron Co., Pop. Code 3
Iron County Cons. SD 4
Sch. Sys. Enr. Code 3
Supt. – Jim Porter, P O BOX 368   65566
ES   65566 – Jerry Robnett, prin.

Vienna, Maries Co., Pop. Code 3
Maries County RSD 1
Sch. Sys. Enr. Code 3
Supt. – Bill Hodge   65582
Maries County ES   65582 – Cynthia Hollis, prin.

Villa Ridge, Franklin Co.
Meramec Valley RSD 3
Supt. – See Pacific
Coleman ES, RURAL ROUTE 01   63089
   David Kindel, prin.

St. John School
   RURAL ROUTE 01 BOX 243-   63089

Wakenda, Carroll Co., Pop. Code 1
Wakenda Cons. SD 2
Sch. Sys. Enr. Code 1
Supt. – (—), HIGHWAY B BOX 336   64687
ES   64687 – Jack Martin, prin.

Walker, Vernon Co., Pop. Code 2
Walker RSD 1
Sch. Sys. Enr. Code 2
Supt. – Michael Mendon   64790
ES   64790 – Merlin Johnson, prin.

Walnut Grove, Greene Co., Pop. Code 3
Walnut Grove RSD 5
Sch. Sys. Enr. Code 2
Supt. – Albert Erb, P O BOX 187   65770
ES   65770 – Patricia Hawk, prin.

Wardell, Pemiscot Co., Pop. Code 2
North Pemiscot County RSD 1
Sch. Sys. Enr. Code 3
Supt. – Edward Brogdon, P O BOX 38   63879
ES, 104 SCHOOL DR   63879 – Thomas Sadler, prin.
Other Schools – See Portageville

Warrensburg, Johnson Co., Pop. Code 7
Johnson County RSD 7
Supt. – See Centerview
Farmers ES, RURAL ROUTE 06 BOX 330   64093
   Charles Brock, prin.

Warrensburg RSD 6
Sch. Sys. Enr. Code 4
Supt. – Dr. Michael Jinks
   444 E MARKET ST   64093
MS, 105 S MAGUIRE ST   64093
   James Davis, prin.
Ridge View ES, 215 S RIDGE VIEW DR   64093
   Annette Erickson, prin.
South East ES, 415 E CLARK ST   64093
   Joyce Hunt, prin.
Warren MS, 105 S MAGUIRE ST   64093
   Dr. Carol Vacek, prin.

Warrenton, Warren Co., Pop. Code 5
Warren County RSD 3
Sch. Sys. Enr. Code 4
Supt. – Wendell Roehrs, 302 KUHL ST   63383
Boone ES   63383 – G. Dean Anders, prin.
Holstein ES   63383 – G. Dean Anders, prin.

Holy Rosary School
   716 E BOONESLICK RD   63383

Warsaw, Benton Co., Pop. Code 4
Benton County RSD 10
Sch. Sys. Enr. Code 1
Supt. – (—)
   RACKET HCR Z HIGHWAY   65355
Benton County ES   65355 – Janet Osborn, prin.

Warsaw RSD 9
Sch. Sys. Enr. Code 3
Supt. – John Boise, P O BOX 248   65355
North ES, P O BOX 307   65355 – Robert Lee, prin.
Other Schools – See Edwards

Washburn, Barry Co., Pop. Code 2
Southwest Barry County RSD 5
Sch. Sys. Enr. Code 3
Supt. – Paul Brink, P O BOX 297   65772
Southwest ES   65772 – James Sellers, prin.

Washington, Franklin Co., Pop. Code 6
Washington SD
Sch. Sys. Enr. Code 5
Supt. – Dr. D. L. Northington, P O BOX 357   63090
JHS, 401 E 14TH ST   63090 – James Perry, prin.
Fifth Street MS, 100 W 5TH ST   63090
   Pamela Mirley, prin.
South Point ES, P O BOX 551   63090
   Dr. Deborah Miles, prin.
Other Schools – See Augusta, Labadie, Marthasville,
   New Haven, Union

Immanuel Lutheran School, 214 W 5TH ST   63090
Our Lady of Lourdes School
   950 MADISON AVE   63090
St. Francis Borgia School, 225 CEDAR ST   63090
St. Gertrude School
   RURAL ROUTE 03 BOX 181   63090

Waverly, Lafayette Co., Pop. Code 3
Lafayette Co. RSD 10
Supt. – See Alma
Santa Fe ES   64096 – Kevin Begley, prin.

Waynesville, Pulaski Co., Pop. Code 5
Waynesville RSD 6
Sch. Sys. Enr. Code 6
Supt. – Dr. James Braden, 399 SCHOOL ST   65583
MS, 403 SCHOOL ST   65583
   Robert Slaughter, prin.
East MS, COUNTY ROAD F   65583
   Tommy Black, prin.
East PS, COUNTY ROAD F   65583
   Glenda Hendrix, prin.
Other Schools – See Fort Leonard Wood

Weaubleau, Hickory Co., Pop. Code 2
Weaubleau RSD 3
Sch. Sys. Enr. Code 2
Supt. – Leland Foster, P O BOX 198   65774
Other Schools – See Collins

Webb City, Jasper Co., Pop. Code 6
Webb City RSD 7
Sch. Sys. Enr. Code 5
Supt. – Dr. Ronald R. Barton
   411 N MADISON ST   64870
JHS, WASHINGTON & 1ST STS   64870
   Doyle Price, prin.
Alba ES, 411 N MADISON ST   64870
   Maxine Carlson, prin.
Field MS, 510 S ORONOGO ST   64870
   Ollie Patterson, prin.
Twain MS, W AYLOR AND COLLEGE   64870
   Donald Thurman, prin.
Webster ES, 700 N MAIN ST   64870
   Connie Godwin, prin.
Other Schools – See Carterville

Webster Groves, St. Louis Co., Pop. Code 7
Webster Groves SD
Sch. Sys. Enr. Code 5
Supt. – Dr. Max Wolfrum, 16 SELMA AVE   63119
Hixson JHS, 630 S ELM AVE   63119
   Dr. Paul Fredstrom, prin.
Avery ES, 909 N BOMPART AVE   63119
   John Miller, prin.
Bristol ES, 20 S GRAY AVE   63119
   William Tuckey, prin.
Clark ES, 9130 BIG BEND BLVD   63119
   Janice Finley, prin.
Computer ES, 701 N ROCK HILL RD   63119
   Dr. Donald Morrison, prin.
Edgar Road ES, 1131 EDGAR RD   63119
   Elaine Dearman, prin.

Hudson ES, 9825 HUDSON AVE 63119
David Skelton, prin.
Steger 6th Grade Ctr., 701 N ROCK HILL RD 63119
Dr. Donald Morrison, prin.

Annunciation School, 16 W GLENDALE RD 63119
Holy Redeemer School
341 E LOCKWOOD AVE 63119
Mary Queen of Peace School
680 W LOCKWOOD AVE 63119
St. Michael the Archangel School
7630 SUTHERLAND AVE 63119

Wellington, Lafayette Co., Pop. Code 3
Wellington-Napoleon RSD 9
Sch. Sys. Enr. Code 2
Supt. – Al Gilliam 64097
Wellington-Napoleon ES 64097
Cecil Flynn, prin.

Wellsville, Montgomery Co., Pop. Code 4
Wellsville-Middletown RSD 1
Sch. Sys. Enr. Code 3
Supt. – Ronald Harlan
BURLINGTON ROAD 63384
ES, 506 CLAY ST 63384 – Jeff Carter, prin.
Other Schools – See Middletown

Wentzville, St. Charles Co., Pop. Code 5
Francis Howell RSD 3
Supt. – See Saint Charles
Boone ES, 201 W HWY D 63385
Jim Grimes, prin.

Wentzville RSD 4
Sch. Sys. Enr. Code 5
Supt. – Dr. Larry Doyle, 1 CAMPUS DRIVE 63385
MS, 600 CAMPUS DRIVE 63385
Shirley Kaczmarski, prin.
Wentzville East MS, 601 CARR 63385
Charles James, prin.
Wentzville South ES, 1 E ACADEMY DR 63385
Pamela Stanfield, prin.
Wentzville West ES, 612 BLUMHOFF AVE 63385
Dr. Frank Thouvenot, prin.

Immanuel Lutheran School
317 W PEARCE BLVD 63385
St. Patrick School, 701 S CHURCH ST 63385

West Alton, St. Charles Co.
St. Charles County RSD 5
Supt. – See Saint Charles
ES, RURAL ROUTE 01 63386
Chris Chapman, prin.

Westboro, Atchison Co., Pop. Code 2
Westboro RSD 4
Sch. Sys. Enr. Code 1
Supt. – (—) 64498
ES 64498 – Jane Walter, prin.

Weston, Platte Co., Pop. Code 4
West Platte County RSD 2
Sch. Sys. Enr. Code 3
Supt. – Jimmie Dean
1105 WASHINGTON ST 64098
Central ES, 1025 WASHINGTON ST 64098
Larry Newman, prin.

Westphalia, Osage Co., Pop. Code 2
Osage County RSD 3
Sch. Sys. Enr. Code 3
Supt. – Dr. Donald Stieferman 65085

ES, P O BOX 37 65085 – Wanda Hartsock, prin.
Other Schools – See Argyle, Meta

St. Joseph School, P O BOX 205 65085

West Plains, Howell Co., Pop. Code 6
Fairview RSD 11
Sch. Sys. Enr. Code 2
Supt. – (—), POTTERSVILLE ROUTE 65775
Fairview ES 65775 – John Burkhead, prin.

Glenwood RSD 8
Sch. Sys. Enr. Code 2
Supt. – (—), ROUTE 17 BOX 141 65775
Glenwood ES 65775 – Robert Arnold, prin.

Howell Valley RSD 1
Sch. Sys. Enr. Code 2
Supt. – (—), ROVER ROUTE 65775
Howell Valley ES 65775 – Casus Baird, prin.

Junction Hill Cons. SD 12
Sch. Sys. Enr. Code 2
Supt. – (—), RURAL ROUTE 02 65775
Junction Hill ES 65775 – Lawrence Nevils, prin.

Richards RSD 5
Sch. Sys. Enr. Code 2
Supt. – (—)
RURAL ROUTE 04 BOX 500 65775
Richards ES 65775 – Rex Arnold, prin.

West Plains RSD 7
Sch. Sys. Enr. Code 4
Supt. – Wayne Lovan, 602 E OLDEN 65775
MS, OLDEN & DAVIDSON STS 65775
Davis Roush, prin.
Carmical ES, 613 W 1ST ST 65775
Edward Sholes, prin.
Foster ES, PAYDON & JACKSON STS 65775
Edward Sholes, prin.
Reese ES, GRACE & LOCUST STS 65775
Edward Sholes, prin.
South Fork ES, SOUTH FORK STATION 65775
Beverly Feller, prin.

Wheatland, Hickory Co., Pop. Code 2
Wheatland RSD 2
Sch. Sys. Enr. Code 2
Supt. – Donald Hotalling, P O BOX 68 65779
ES 65779 – Bob McCaslin, prin.

Wheaton, Barry Co., Pop. Code 3
Wheaton RSD 3
Sch. Sys. Enr. Code 2
Supt. – Dr. Rex Miller, P O BOX 249 64874
ES 64874 – Donald Cope, prin.

Wheeling, Livingston Co., Pop. Code 2
Wheeling RSD 4
Sch. Sys. Enr. Code 1
Supt. – Eldon Cowles, P O BOX 207 64688
ES 64688 – Betty Ireland, prin.

Whiteman AFB, Johnson Co.
Knob Noster RSD 8
Supt. – See Knob Noster
ES 65305 – Daniel Sevier, prin.

Willard, Greene Co., Pop. Code 4
Willard RSD 2
Sch. Sys. Enr. Code 4
Supt. – Jerry Bouse, P O BOX 98 65781
JHS, HIGHWAY AB 65781 – J. Millhouser, prin.

Willard North ES, SOUTH ON HWY AB 65781
Larry Chapman, prin.
Willard South ES 65781 – Les Hagemann, prin.

Williamsburg, Callaway Co.
North Callaway County RSD 1
Supt. – See Kingdom City
Williamsburg ES 63388 – Larry Nolte, prin.

Williamsville, Wayne Co., Pop. Code 2
Greenville RSD 2
Supt. – See Greenville
ES 63967 – Shirley Schwietzer, prin.

Willow Springs, Howell Co., Pop. Code 4
Willow Springs RSD 4
Sch. Sys. Enr. Code 4
Supt. – Terry Holder, 4TH & FERGUSON 65793
MS 65793 – Hubert Reaves, prin.
ES 65793 – Sam Carlson, prin.

Windsor, Henry Co., Pop. Code 5
Windsor RSD 1
Sch. Sys. Enr. Code 3
Supt. – Charles Snider, P O BOX 7 65360
ES, S MAIN 65360 – Jo Ann Lindsey, prin.

Winfield, Lincoln Co., Pop. Code 3
Winfield RSD 4
Sch. Sys. Enr. Code 4
Supt. – Lyle Laughman 63389
MS 63389 – Frank Barro, prin.
ES 63389 – Dee Gaddis, prin.

Winona, Shannon Co., Pop. Code 4
Winona RSD 3
Sch. Sys. Enr. Code 2
Supt. – Charles Green, P O BOX 248 65588
ES 65588 – Roy Greene, prin.

Winston, Daviess Co., Pop. Code 2
Winston RSD 6
Sch. Sys. Enr. Code 2
Supt. – Nylen Lewis 64689
ES 64689 – Delores Wyckoff, prin.

Woodson Terrace, St. Louis Co., Pop. Code 5
Ritenour SD
Supt. – See Overland
Kratz ES, 4301 EDMUNDSON RD 63134
Deb Hunsel, prin.

Wright City, Warren Co., Pop. Code 4
Wright City RSD 2
Sch. Sys. Enr. Code 3
Supt. – Maurice Overlander, P O BOX 198 63390
ES 63390 – Dr. Ron Hinrichs, prin.

Wyaconda, Clark Co., Pop. Code 2
Wyaconda Cons. SD 1
Sch. Sys. Enr. Code 2
Supt. – Dr. Michael Myers 63474
ES 63474 – Kathy Calvert, prin.

Zalma, Bollinger Co., Pop. Code 2
Zalma RSD 5
Sch. Sys. Enr. Code 2
Supt. – Wm. E. Pogue Jr. 63787
ES 63787 – David Templmire, prin.

MONTANA

OFFICE OF PUBLIC INSTRUCTION
Room 106, State Capitol, Helena 59620
(405) 449-3654

State Superintendent of Public Instruction	Nancy Keenan
Deputy Superintendent	Ray Shackelford
Assistant Superintendent Administrative Services	Francis Olson
Assistant Superintendent Curriculum Services	Gile Mitchell
Deputy Superintendent Education Services	Ray Shackelford

STATE BOARD OF EDUCATION
Ted Hazelbaker, *Chairperson*   P.O. Box 390, Dillon   59725

MONTANA BOARD OF REGENTS OF HIGHER EDUCATION
Dr. Carol Krause, *Commissioner*   33 S. Last Chance Gulch, Helena   59620

COUNTY SUPERINTENDENTS OF SCHOOLS

Beaverhead County, Patti Kipp, Supt.
P O BOX 351, Dillon 59725
Big Horn County, Roberta Snively, Supt.
P O BOX H, Hardin 59034
Blaine County, Carrol Elliot, Supt.
P O BOX 819, Chinook 59523
Broadwater County, Doris Hossfeld, Supt.
P O BOX 489, Townsend 59644
Carbon County, Penny Bourquin, Supt.
P O BOX 116, Red Lodge 59068
Carter County, Patricia Hanlan, Supt.
Ekalaka 59324
Cascade County, Tug Ikeda, Supt.
415 2ND AVE N, Great Falls 59401
Chouteau County, L. Stollfuss, Supt.
Fort Benton 59442
Custer County, Ellen Zook, Supt.
1010 MAIN ST, Miles City 59301
Daniels County, Howard Farver, Supt.
P O BOX 413, Scobey 59263
Dawson County, Jean Grow, Supt.
207 W BELL ST, Glendive 59644
Deer Lodge County, Carl Stetzner, Supt.
Anaconda 59711
Fallon County, Marlene Ferrell, Supt.
P O BOX 1117, Baker 59313
Fergus County, Shirley Barrick, Supt.
Lewistown 59457
Flathead County, Dorothy Laird, Supt.
723 5TH AVE E, Kalispell 59901
Gallatin County, M. Brown, Supt.
Bozeman 59715
Garfield County, Joann Stanton, Supt.
Jordan 59337
Glacier County, Daryl Omsberg, Supt.
Cut Bank 59427
Golden Valley County, S. Carpenter, Supt.
Ryegate 59074

Granite County, Julia Enman, Supt.
P O BOX 520, Philipsburg 59858
Hill County, Shirley Isbell, Supt.
300 4TH ST, Havre 59501
Jefferson County, Helen Williams, Supt.
Boulder 59632
Judith Basin County, Kathy Sessions, Supt.
Stanford 59479
Lake County, Glennadene Ferrell, Supt.
Polson 59860
Lewis & Clark County, Kay McKenna, Supt.
316 N PARK AVE, Helena 59601
Liberty County, Krystyna Cole, Supt.
Chester 59522
Lincoln County, Mary Hudspeth, Supt.
418 MINERAL AVE, Libby 59923
Madison County, Pat Miller, Supt.
P O BOX 247, Virginia City 59755
McCone County, Kay Wolff, Supt.
P O BOX 159, Circle 59215
Meagher County, Joseph Phillips, Supt.
White Sulphur Springs 59645
Mineral County, Billye Bricker, Supt.
Superior 59872
Missoula County, Rachel Vielleux, Supt.
301 W ALDER ST, Missoula 59802
Musselshell County, Margaret Reighard, Supt.
P O BOX 157, Roundup 59072
Park County, Billie Fleming, Supt.
Livingston 59047
Petroleum County, Robert Coffey, Supt.
Winnett 59087
Phillips County, Dolores Hughes, Supt.
Malta 59538
Pondera County, Andy Vandolah, Supt.
Conrad 59425
Powder River County, Charlotte Miller, Supt.
Broadus 59317

Powell County, Karl Roosa, Supt.
409 MISSOURI AVE, Deer Lodge 59722
Prairie County, Alice Pehl, Supt.
Terry 59349
Ravalli County, Greg Danelz, Supt.
P O BOX 5021, Hamilton 59840
Richland County, Joan Ritter, Supt.
Sidney 59270
Roosevelt County, Kathleen Tubman, Supt.
Wolf Point 59201
Rosebud County, Jean Nolan, Supt.
Forsyth 59327
Sanders County, Ted Kato, Supt.
P O BOX 698, Thompson Falls 59873
Sheridan County, Robert Smith, Supt.
Plentywood 59254
Silver Bow County, Fred Bull, Supt.
Butte 59701
Stillwater County, Carole Reynolds, Supt.
Columbus 59019
Sweet Grass County, Carol Schott, Supt.
P O BOX 220, Big Timber 59011
Teton County, Wilma Jensen, Supt.
P O BOX 610, Choteau 59422
Toole County, Louise Lorenzen, Supt.
Shelby 59474
Treasure County, Kathleen Thomas, Supt.
Hysham 59038
Valley County, Jan Allie, Supt.
P O BOX 631, Glasgow 59230
Wheatland County, Effie Winsky, Supt.
Harlowton 59036
Wibaux County, Patricia Zinda, Supt.
Wibaux 59353
Yellowstone County, Buzz Christianson, Supt.
P O BOX 35022, Billings 59101

PUBLIC, PRIVATE, AND PAROCHIAL ELEMENTARY SCHOOLS

Absarokee, Stillwater Co., Pop. Code 4
Absarokee HSD 52
Sch. Sys. Enr. Code 2
Supt. – G. Reynolds, P O BOX 407 59001
ES 59001 – Paul Jenkins, prin.

Alberton, Mineral Co., Pop. Code 2
Alberton HSD 2
Sch. Sys. Enr. Code 2
Supt. – Gary Weber, P O BOX 118 59820
ES 59820 – Gary Weber, prin.

Alder, Madison Co.
Alder Upper Ruby ESD 2
Sch. Sys. Enr. Code 1
Supt. – (—), P O BOX 110 59710
ES 59710 – Becky Flamm, prin.

Alzada, Carter Co.
Albion ESD 11
Sch. Sys. Enr. Code 1
Supt. – (—) 59311
Other Schools – See Hammond

Alzada ESD 56
Sch. Sys. Enr. Code 1
Supt. – (—), P O BOX 68 59311
ES 59311 – Jody Ludemann, prin.

Ridge ESD 22
Sch. Sys. Enr. Code 1
Supt. – (—) 59311

Ridge ES 59311 – Ronald Leafgreen, prin.

Anaconda, Deer Lodge Co., Pop. Code 7
Anaconda HSD 10
Sch. Sys. Enr. Code 2
Supt. – Mary Jo Oreskovich, P O BOX 1281 59711
JHS, 3RD & CHERRY 59711 – John Stergar, prin.
Dwyer IS, 1501 W PARK ST 59711
Edward Spiegle, prin.
Dwyer PS, 1601 TAMMANY ST 59711
Edward Spiegle, prin.
Lincoln ES, 506 CHESTNUT ST 59711
Stella Currie, prin.

Angela, Rosebud Co.
Rock Spring ESD 2
Sch. Sys. Enr. Code 1
Supt. – (—), P O BOX 170 59312
Rock Spring ES 59312 – Diane Lund, prin.

Sutherland Coulee ESD 18
Sch. Sys. Enr. Code 1
Supt. – (—), ROCK SPRINGS ROUTE 59312
Sutherland ES, P O BOX 173 59312
Connie Taylor, prin.
Tree Coulee ES, ROCK SPRINGS RT 59312
Alane Garneau, prin.

Arlee, Lake Co., Pop. Code 1
Arlee HSD JT & 8
Sch. Sys. Enr. Code 2
Supt. – Larry LaCounte, P O BOX 37 59821

JHS 59821 – Harold Brown, prin.
ES 59821 – Harold Brown, prin.

Ashland, Rosebud Co.
Ashland ESD 32J
Sch. Sys. Enr. Code 2
Supt. – (—), P O BOX 17 59003
ES 59003 – Dwight Gunnare, prin.

St. Labre Indian Catholic ES 59003

Augusta, Lewis and Clark Co., Pop. Code 3
Augusta HSD 45
Sch. Sys. Enr. Code 2
Supt. – Rick Ripley, P O BOX 307 59410
ES 59410 – Rick Ripley, prin.

Avon, Powell Co.
Avon ESD 29
Sch. Sys. Enr. Code 2
Supt. – (—), P O BOX 246 59713
ES 59728 – Deah Fryhover, prin.

Bainville, Roosevelt Co., Pop. Code 2
Bainville HSD 64D
Sch. Sys. Enr. Code 2
Supt. – Dale Sailer, P O BOX 188 59212
ES 59212 – Dale Sailer, prin.

Baker, Fallon Co., Pop. Code 4
Baker HSD 12
Sch. Sys. Enr. Code 3
Supt. – James Stanton, P O BOX 659 59313
JHS, P O BOX 816 59313 – Julia LaCross, prin.
Lincoln ES, 10 W CENTER AVE 59313
  Gordon Vanderpan, prin.
Longfellow MS, 115 S LINCOLN 59313
  Gordon Vanderpan, prin.
Washington ES, 115 E MONTANA 59313
  Gordon Vanderpan, prin.

Fertile Prairie ESD 50
Sch. Sys. Enr. Code 1
Supt. – (—), P O BOX 594 59313
Fertile Prairie ES 59313 – Lora Harms, prin.

Basin, Jefferson Co.
Basin ESD 5
Sch. Sys. Enr. Code 1
Supt. – (—), P O BOX 128 59631
ES, 119 N QUARTZ 59631 – Janice Hahn, prin.

Belfry, Carbon Co., Pop. Code 2
Belfry HSD 3
Sch. Sys. Enr. Code 2
Supt. – Gareld Willis, P O BOX 28 59008
ES 59008 – Gareld Willis, prin.

Belgrade, Gallatin Co., Pop. Code 4
Belgrade HSD 44
Sch. Sys. Enr. Code 4
Supt. – Harry Erickson, P O BOX 166 59714
JHS, P O BOX 166 59714 – Jerry Vanderpan, prin.
Quaw Heck ES, P O BOX 166 59714
  Fred Ranney, prin.

Pass Creek ESD 25
Sch. Sys. Enr. Code 1
Supt. – (—), 3747 PASS CREEK ROAD 59714
Pass Creek ES 59714 – Lois Hiebert, prin.

Springhill ESD 20
Sch. Sys. Enr. Code 1
Supt. – (—), 6020 SPRINGHILL ROAD 59714
Springhill ES 59714 – Linda Rice, prin.

Belle Creek, Powder River Co.
Belle Creek ESD 22
Sch. Sys. Enr. Code 1
Supt. – (—), P O BOX 69 59317
ES 59317 – Michael Rollings, prin.

Belt, Cascade Co., Pop. Code 3
Belt HSD D
Sch. Sys. Enr. Code 2
Supt. – Jan Cahill, P O BOX 197 59412
ES 59412 – Joseph Fontana, prin.

Biddle, Powder River Co.
Biddle ESD 6
Sch. Sys. Enr. Code 1
Supt. – (—) 59314
ES 59314 – Joan Reed, prin.

Bigfork, Flathead Co., Pop. Code 2
Bigfork HSD 38
Sch. Sys. Enr. Code 3
Supt. – Jean Hagan, P O BOX 188 59911
ES 59911 – Christopher Hagar, prin.

Swan River ESD 4
Sch. Sys. Enr. Code 2
Supt. – (—), 1205 SWAN HIGHWAY 59911
Swan River ES 59911 – Laurene Murphy, prin.

Big Sandy, Chouteau Co., Pop. Code 3
Big Sandy HSD 2
Sch. Sys. Enr. Code 2
Supt. – William Colter, P O BOX 570 59520
JHS 59520 – James Barsotti, prin.
Miley ES 59520 – William Colter, prin.

Warrick ESD 26
Sch. Sys. Enr. Code 1
Supt. – (—), WARRICK ROUTE 59520
Warrick ES 59520 – Vicki Parker, prin.

Big Timber, Sweet Grass Co., Pop. Code 4
Big Timber ESD 1
Sch. Sys. Enr. Code 2
Supt. – Gary Harkness, P O BOX 887 59011
ES, P O BOX 887 59011 – Gary Harkness, prin.

Bridge ESD 69
Sch. Sys. Enr. Code 1
Supt. – (—), P O BOX 535 59011
Bridge ES, HCR 89 BOX 4539 59011
  Julie Sanders, prin.

Billings, Yellowstone Co., Pop. Code 8
Billings HSD 2
Sch. Sys. Enr. Code 7
Supt. – Dr. Roger Eble, 101 10TH ST W 59102
Castle Rock JHS, 1441 GOVERNORS BLVD 59105
  Peggy Parker, prin.
James JHS, 1200 30TH ST W 59102
  Leo Wohler, prin.
Lewis & Clark JHS, 1315 LEWIS AVE 59102
  William Twilling, prin.
Riverside JHS, 3700 MADISON AVE 59101
  Jim Strecker, prin.
Alkaki Creek ES, 681 ALKALI CREEK RD 59105
  Fred Brinkman, prin.
Arrowhead ES, 2510 38TH ST W 59102
  Charles Lundgren, prin.
Beartooth ES, 1345 ELAINE ST 59105
  Billie Strissel, prin.

Bench ES, 505 MILTON RD 59105
  Sue McCunn, prin.
Big Sky ES, 3231 GRANGER AVE E 59102
  Keith Kohnke, prin.
Bitterroot ES, 1801 BENCH BLVD 59105
  Jo Swain, prin.
Boulder ES, 2202 32ND ST W 59102
  Ken Lane, prin.
Broadwater ES, 415 BROADWATER AVE 59101
  Cindy Holtz, prin.
Burlington ES, 2135 LEWIS AVE 59102
  Marvin Ehret, prin.
Central Heights ES, 120 LEXINGTON DR 59102
  Clayton Croff, prin.
Eagle Cliffs ES, 1260 MARIAS 59102
  Vivian Scoles, prin.
Garfield ES, 3212 1ST AVE S 59101
  Beverly Flaten, prin.
Highland ES, 729 PARKHILL DR 59102
  Kathy Olson, prin.
McKinley ES, 820 N 31ST ST 59101
  Lorraine Marsh, prin.
Meadowlark ES, 221 29TH ST W 59102
  George Nelson, prin.
Miles Avenue ES, 1601 MILES AVE 59102
  Gilbert Carrington, prin.
Newman ES, 605 S BILLINGS BLVD 59101
  Ed Jones, prin.
North Park ES, 615 N 19TH ST 59101
  Delton Christman, prin.
Orchard ES, 120 JACKSON ST 59101
  Rilla Hardgrove, prin.
Poly Drive ES, 2410 POLY DR 59102
  Bob Barone, prin.
Ponderosa ES, 4188 KING AVE E 59101
  Judith Evans, prin.
Rimrock ES, 2802 13TH ST W 59102
  Kay Gannon, prin.
Rose Park ES, 1812 19TH ST W 59102
  Ruth Tigges, prin.
Sandstone ES, 1440 NUTTER BLVD 59105
  Cheri Ring, prin.
Washington ES, 1441 GOVERNORS BLVD 59105
  David Munson, prin.

Blue Creek ESD 3
Sch. Sys. Enr. Code 1
Supt. – (—), 3652 BLUE CREEK ROAD 59101
Blue Creek ES 59101 – Maria Metzger, prin.

Canyon Creek ESD 4
Sch. Sys. Enr. Code 2
Supt. – (—), 3139 DUCK CREEK ROAD 59101
Canyon Creek ES 59101 – Fred Kimball, prin.

Elder Grove ESD 8
Sch. Sys. Enr. Code 2
Supt. – (—), 1532 S 64TH ST W 59106
Elder Grove ES 59106 – Ron Bender, prin.

Elysian ESD 23
Sch. Sys. Enr. Code 2
Supt. – (—), 6416 ELYSIAN ROAD 59101
Elysian ES 59101 – William Hope, prin.

Independent ESD 52
Sch. Sys. Enr. Code 2
Supt. – (—), RURAL ROUTE 11 59105
Independent ES 59105 – Lois Sindelar, prin.

Lockwood SD 26
Sch. Sys. Enr. Code 4
Supt. – Joe McCracken, RURAL ROUTE 02 59101
Lockwood JHS, HARDIN ROAD 59101
  Cameron Cronk, prin.
Lockwood IS, 1932 HIGHWAY 87 E 59101
  Michael Bowman, prin.
Lockwood PS, 1932 HIGHWAY 87 E 59101
  Darrell Rud, prin.

Morin ESD 17
Sch. Sys. Enr. Code 1
Supt. – (—), 8824 PRYOR ROAD 59101
Morin ES 59101 – Thora Dexter, prin.

Pioneer ESD 41
Sch. Sys. Enr. Code 1
Supt. – (—), 1937 DOVER ROAD 59105
Pioneer ES 59105 – Dale Ahrens, prin.

Fratt Memorial School, 205 N 32ND ST 59101
Holy Rosary School, 511 CUSTER AVE 59101
St. Pius X School
  1734 YELLOWSTONE AVE 59102
Trinity Lutheran School
  2802 BELVEDERE DR 59102

Birney, Rosebud Co.
Birney ESD 3
Sch. Sys. Enr. Code 1
Supt. – (—), P O BOX 521 59012
ES 59012 – Nancy Carson, prin.

Bloomfield, Dawson Co.
Bloomfield ESD 30
Sch. Sys. Enr. Code 1
Supt. – (—) 59315
ES 59315 – Linda Borntrager, prin.

Bonner, Missoula Co., Pop. Code 2
Bonner ESD 14
Sch. Sys. Enr. Code 2
Supt. – Jack Demmons, P O BOX 4 59836
ES 59823 – Larry Burlingame, prin.

Potomac ESD 11
Sch. Sys. Enr. Code 2
Supt. – (—), HCR ROUTE BOX 220 59823
Potomac ES 59823 – Gayle Everly, prin.

Boulder, Jefferson Co., Pop. Code 4
Boulder HSD 1
Sch. Sys. Enr. Code 2
Supt. – Richard Moe, P O BOX 176 59632
ES, 205 S WASHINGTON 59632
  Richard Moe, prin.

Box Elder, Hill Co., Pop. Code 2
Box Elder HSD G
Sch. Sys. Enr. Code 2
Supt. – John Lee, P O BOX 205 59521
ES 59521 – John Lee, prin.

Rocky Boy ESD 87J
Sch. Sys. Enr. Code 2
Supt. – (—), P O BOX 620 59521
Rocky Boy ES 59521 – Sandra Murie, prin.

Boyd, Carbon Co.
Boyd ESD 28
Sch. Sys. Enr. Code 1
Supt. – (—), P O BOX 204 59023
ES, P O BOX 298 59013 – Hazel McDowall, prin.

Bozeman, Gallatin Co., Pop. Code 7
Anderson ESD 41
Sch. Sys. Enr. Code 1
Supt. – (—), 9315 COUGAR DRIVE 59715
Anderson ES
  10040 COTTONWOOD ROAD 59715
  M. Vandenbos, prin.
Bozeman HSD 7
Sch. Sys. Enr. Code 5
Supt. – Dr. Keith Chambers, P O BOX 520 59771
Emerson ES, 111 S GRAND AVE 59715
  Nonnie Hughes, prin.
Hawthorne ES, 114 N ROUSE AVE 59715
  Art Hulett, prin.
Irving ES, 611 S 8TH AVE 59715
  Merry Fahrman, prin.
Longfellow ES, 516 S TRACY AVE 59715
  Mike Meagher, prin.
Whittier ES, 511 N 5TH AVE 59715
  Sally Richter, prin.
Wilson MS, 404 W MAIN ST 59715
  E. Mikkelson, prin.

Cottonwood ESD 22
Sch. Sys. Enr. Code 1
Supt. – (—)
  13233 COTTONWOOD ROAD 59715
Cottonwood ES 59715 – H. Reiser, prin.

Lamotte ESD 43
Sch. Sys. Enr. Code 1
Supt. – (—), 841 BEAR CANYON ROAD 59715
Lamotte ES 59715 – Janet Neault, prin.

Malmborg ESD 47
Sch. Sys. Enr. Code 1
Supt. – (—), 270 QUINN CREEK ROAD 59715
Malmorg ES 59715 – Jolene Baldwin, prin.

Monforton ESD 27
Sch. Sys. Enr. Code 2
Supt. – (—)
  6001 MONFORTON SCHOOL ROAD 59715
Monforton MS 59715 – Katherine Pattee, prin.
Monforton PS 59715 – Katherine Pattee, prin.

Mount Ellis Academy
  3641 BOZEMAN TRAIL ROAD 59715

Brady, Pondera Co., Pop. Code 2
Brady HSD 19
Sch. Sys. Enr. Code 2
Supt. – Kurt Hilyard, P O BOX 166 59416
ES 59416 – Kurt Hilyard, prin.

Knees ESD 59
Sch. Sys. Enr. Code 1
Supt. – (—), P O BOX 424 59416
Knees ES 59416 – Brenda Freeman, prin.

Bridger, Carbon Co., Pop. Code 3
Bridger HSD 2
Sch. Sys. Enr. Code 2
Supt. – Morris VanCampen
  429 W PARK AVE 59014
ES 59014 – Morris Vancampen, prin.

Broadus, Powder River Co., Pop. Code 3
Broadus HSD 79J
Sch. Sys. Enr. Code 2
Supt. – Duane Denny, P O BOX 489 59317
ES 59317 – Hal Hawley, prin.

Broadview, Yellowstone Co., Pop. Code 2
Broadview HSD 21-J
Sch. Sys. Enr. Code 2
Supt. – Dan Martin, P O BOX 106 59015
ES 59015 – Donald Widhalm, prin.

Brockton, Roosevelt Co., Pop. Code 2
Brockton HSD 55F
Sch. Sys. Enr. Code 2
Supt. – Dr. Ronald Allen, P O BOX 198 59213
Gilligan ES 59213 – Dr. Ronald Allen, prin.

Brockway, McCone Co.
Brockway ESD 84
Sch. Sys. Enr. Code 1
Supt. – (—), P O BOX 98 59214

ES   59214 – Judith Langemo, prin.

Browning, Glacier Co., Pop. Code 4
Browning HSD 9
Sch. Sys. Enr. Code 4
Supt. – Randy Johnson, P O BOX 610 59417
MS   59417 – Robert Parsons, prin.
Babb ES   59417 – June Tatsey, prin.
Bergan ES   59417 – June Tatsey, prin.
Big Sky ES   59417 – Carmen Marceau, prin.
Napi MS   59417 – Carmen Marceau, prin.
Starr ES   59417 – Sharon MaGee, prin.
Vina Chattin ES   59417 – Sharon MaGee, prin.
Other Schools – See Cut Bank

Brusett, Garfied Co.
Blackfoot ESD 32
Sch. Sys. Enr. Code 1
Supt. – (—), HCR ROUTE A 59318
Blackfoot ES   59318 – Lois Maxwell, prin.

Pine Grove ESD 19
Sch. Sys. Enr. Code 1
Supt. – (—), P O BOX 37 59318
Pine Grove ES   59318 – Elaine Savage, prin.

Busby, Big Horn Co., Pop. Code 2
Big Bend ESD 17K
Sch. Sys. Enr. Code 1
Supt. – (—), KIRBY ROUTE 59016
Big Bend ES   59016 – Terry Punt, prin.

Butte, Silver Bow Co., Pop. Code 8
Butte HSD 1
Sch. Sys. Enr. Code 6
Supt. – Dr. Peter Carparelli
  111 N MONTANA ST 59701
East MS, 2600 GRAND AVE 59701
  William Meagor, prin.
Emerson ES, 1919 GARRISON AVE 59701
  Tom Carter, prin.
Greeley ES, 2425 SILVER BOW BLVD 59701
  Charles Boyle, prin.
Hillcrest ES, 3100 CONTINENTAL DR 59701
  Lee Sundberg, prin.
Kennedy ES, HORNET & EMMETT 59701
  Daniel Rosa, prin.
Leary ES, 4 1/2 MILE VUE 59701
  Alice Vicevich, prin.
Longfellow ES, ROOSEVELT & WYNNE 59701
  Charles Wills, prin.
West ES, S EXCELSIOR & STEEL 59701
  Robert Kohn, prin.
Whittier ES, PRINCETON & SHERMAN 59701
  George Parrett, prin.

Central JHS, 400 W PARK ST 59701
Butte Central ES, 1100 DELAWARE 59701

Bynum, Teton Co.
Bynum ESD 12
Sch. Sys. Enr. Code 1
Supt. – (—) 59419
ES   59419 – Susan Luinstra, prin.

Canyon Creek, Lewis and Clark Co.
Trinity ESD 4
Sch. Sys. Enr. Code 1
Supt. – (—), P O BOX 523 59633
Trinity ES   59633 – Lynette Betlach, prin.

Cardwell, Jefferson Co.
Cardwell ESD 16-31
Sch. Sys. Enr. Code 1
Supt. – (—)
  RURAL ROUTE 01 BOX 2506 59721
ES   59721 – Donald Drivdahl, prin.

Carter, Chouteau Co.
Carter ESD 56
Sch. Sys. Enr. Code 1
Supt. – (—), P O BOX 159 59420
ES   59420 – Ruth Carlstrom, prin.

Cascade, Cascade Co., Pop. Code 3
Cascade HSD B
Sch. Sys. Enr. Code 2
Supt. – John Dallum
  W END CENTRAL AVE 59421
ES, P O BOX 307 59421 – Bruce Allen, prin.

Deep Creek ESD 95
Sch. Sys. Enr. Code 1
Supt. – (—), 2232 MILLEGAN ROAD 59421
Deep Creek ES   59421 – Emma Zurich, prin.

Charlo, Lake Co., Pop. Code 4
Charlo HSD 7-J
Sch. Sys. Enr. Code 2
Supt. – Steven Gaub, P O BOX 5 59824
MS   59824 – Joe Braach, prin.
ES   59824 – Steven Gaub, prin.

Chester, Liberty Co., Pop. Code 3
Chester HSD 33
Sch. Sys. Enr. Code 2
Supt. – James Foster, P O BOX 550 59522
ES   59522 – Violet Hills, prin.

Chinook, Blaine Co., Pop. Code 4
Bear Paw ESD 67
Sch. Sys. Enr. Code 1
Supt. – (—), ROUTE 71 BOX 16 59523
Ada ES, HCR 71 BOX 14B 59523
  Kethryn Ernst, prin.
Bear Paw ES, HCR 71 BOX 22 59523
  Delma Cabarett, prin.

Peoples ES, HCR 71 BOX 27 59523
  Catherine Dotson, prin.

Chinook HSD 10
Sch. Sys. Enr. Code 3
Supt. – Dan Haugen, P O BOX 1059 59523
Eastside MS, P O BOX 1059 59523
  Rita Surber, prin.
Meadowlark ES, 623 NEW YORK 59523
  Rita Surber, prin.

Cleveland Lone Tree ESD 14
Sch. Sys. Enr. Code 1
Supt. – (—), RT 70 BOX 70 59523
Cleveland ES, RURAL ROUTE 70 BOX 70 59523
  Joyce Olson, prin.
Other Schools – See Lloyd

Choteau, Teton Co., Pop. Code 4
Choteau HSD 1
Sch. Sys. Enr. Code 2
Supt. – E. Ketterling, P O BOX 857 59422
ES, P O BOX 400 59422 – Stanley Rathman, prin.

Circle, McCone Co., Pop. Code 3
Circle HSD 1
Sch. Sys. Enr. Code 2
Supt. – James Anderson, P O BOX 99 59215
Redwater MS 59215 – Donna Yarger, prin.
Bo Peep ES   59215 – Donna Yarger, prin.

Clancy, Jefferson Co.
Clancy ESD 1
Sch. Sys. Enr. Code 2
Supt. – Robert Brown, P O BOX 209 59634
ES, 6 N MAIN 59634 – Ann Ringling, prin.

Montana City ESD 27
Sch. Sys. Enr. Code 2
Supt. – Penny Koke, HCR ROUTE BOX 127 59634
Montana City ES   59634 – Penny Koke, prin.

Clinton, Missoula Co.
Clinton ESD 32
Sch. Sys. Enr. Code 2
Supt. – Ben Harrison, P O BOX 100 59825
ES   59825 – Ben Harrison, prin.

Clyde Park, Park Co., Pop. Code 2
Clyde Park HSD 2
Sch. Sys. Enr. Code 2
Supt. – Harold Barich, P O BOX AH 59018
ES   59018 – Ed Barich, prin.

Cohagen, Garfield Co.
Cohagen ESD 27
Sch. Sys. Enr. Code 1
Supt. – (—), P O BOX 327 59322
ES   59322 – Betty Sturtz, prin.

Colstrip, Rosebud Co., Pop. Code 2
Colstrip HSD 19
Sch. Sys. Enr. Code 4
Supt. – Harold Tokerud, P O BOX 127 59323
Brattin MS, 216 OLIVE DRIVE 59323
  Marilyn Colliflower, prin.
Isabel Bills ES, 520 POPLAR DR 59323
  Keith Chapman, prin.
Pine Butte PS, 2800 DURANGO DR 59323
  Linda Null, prin.

Columbia Falls, Flathead Co., Pop. Code 5
Columbia Falls HSD 6
Sch. Sys. Enr. Code 4
Supt. – Ryan Taylor, P O BOX 1259 59912
JHS, P O BOX 1259 59912 – Dennis Olson, prin.
Columbia Falls West Annex MS
  501 6TH AVE W 59912 – Robert Smith, prin.
Columbia Falls- Westview ES
  P O BOX 1259 59912 – Dave Dorn, prin.
PS, P O BOX 1259 59912 – Dave Dorn, prin.
Hungry Horse MS 59912 – Robert Smith, prin.
Martin City ES, P O BOX 1259 59912
  Robert Smith, prin.
Other Schools – See West Glacier

Deer Park ESD 2
Sch. Sys. Enr. Code 1
Supt. – (—), 2105 MIDDLE ROAD 59912
Deer Park ES 59912 – Daniel Danz, prin.

Columbus, Stillwater Co., Pop. Code 4
Columbus HSD 6
Sch. Sys. Enr. Code 2
Supt. – Conrad Robertson, P O BOX 899 59019
ES, 218 E 1ST AVE N 59019 – Todd Rowen, prin.

Conrad, Pondera Co., Pop. Code 5
Conrad HSD 10
Sch. Sys. Enr. Code 3
Supt. – Dennis Williams
  215 S MARYLAND ST 59425
Utterback MS, 213 S MARYLAND ST 59425
  Raymond Johnson, prin.
Meadowlark ES, 17 3RD AVE SW 59425
  Harley Ruff, prin.
Prairie View MS, 220 N WISCONSIN ST 59425
  Harley Ruff, prin.

Miami ESD 31
Sch. Sys. Enr. Code 1
Supt. – (—)
  RURAL ROUTE 03 BOX 448 59425
Miami MS, RURAL ROUTE 03 BOX 441 59425
  C. Molgaard, prin.

Corvallis, Ravalli Co., Pop. Code 2
Corvallis HSD 1
Sch. Sys. Enr. Code 3
Supt. – Donald Wetzel, P O BOX 133 59828
JHS   59828 – William Laurent, prin.
College Avenue ES 59828 – William Laurent, prin.
Thomas MS 59828 – William Laurent, prin.

Crow Agency, Big Horn Co., Pop. Code 3
Hardin HSD 1
Supt. – See Hardin
ES   59022 – Constance Pailliotet, prin.

Culbertson, Roosevelt Co., Pop. Code 3
Culbertson HSD 17C
Sch. Sys. Enr. Code 2
Supt. – Dr. Patrick Stuber, P O BOX 459 59218
ES, 423 1ST AVE W 59218 – Gene Dillman, prin.

Custer, Yellowstone Co., Pop. Code 2
Custer HSD 15
Sch. Sys. Enr. Code 2
Supt. – Linda Carter, P O BOX 68 59024
ES   59024 – Ron Scherry, prin.

Cut Bank, Glacier Co., Pop. Code 5
Browning HSD 9
Supt. – See Browning
Glendale ES   59427 – Carmen Marceau, prin.

Cut Bank HSD 15
Sch. Sys. Enr. Code 4
Supt. – T. Mattocks, 101 3RD AVE SE 59427
JHS, 101 4TH AVE SE 59427 – Dan Corcoran, prin.
Davis ES, 15 2ND AVE SE 59427
  Larry Morhardt, prin.
Jeffries MS, 115 2ND AVE NW 59427
  Marlene Zom, prin.

Seville ESD 64
Sch. Sys. Enr. Code 1
Supt. – (—), P O BOX 1255 59427
Seville ES, P O BOX 1255 59427
  Linda Cowell, prin.

Dagmar, Sheridan Co.
Hiawatha ESD 49
Sch. Sys. Enr. Code 1
Supt. – (—), P O BOX 278 59219
Hiawatha ES   59219 – Robert Olson, prin.

Darby, Ravalli Co., Pop. Code 3
Darby HSD 9
Sch. Sys. Enr. Code 3
Supt. – Dale Huhtanen, N MAIN 59829
JHS, N MAIN 59829 – Garry Gottfried, prin.
ES   59829 – Garry Gottfried, prin.

Decker, Big Horn Co.
Squirrel Creek ESD 1
Sch. Sys. Enr. Code 1
Supt. – (—) 59025
Squirrel Creek ES 59025 – Marilyn Thomas, prin.

Deer Lodge, Powell Co., Pop. Code 5
Deer Lodge ESD 1
Sch. Sys. Enr. Code 3
Supt. – Tom Cotton, P O BOX 630 59722
Duvall MS, 703 5TH ST 59722 – Pat Rogers, prin.
Granville Stuart MS, 703 5TH ST 59722
  Tom Cotton, prin.
Speer ES, 703 5TH ST 59722 – Tom Cotton, prin.

Denton, Fergus Co., Pop. Code 2
Denton HSD 84
Sch. Sys. Enr. Code 2
Supt. – Michael Smith, P O BOX 1084 59430
ES   59430 – Michael Smith, prin.

Dillon, Beaverhead Co., Pop. Code 5
Dillon ESD 10
Sch. Sys. Enr. Code 3
Supt. – George Delaney, 225 E REEDER ST 59725
Parkview JHS, 14 COTTOM DRIVE 59725
  Robert Lemelin, prin.
Innes ES, 225 E REEDER ST 59725
  Robert Lemelin, prin.
Parkview North MS, 14 COTTOM DR 59725
  Richard Jonasen, prin.

Grant ESD 7
Sch. Sys. Enr. Code 1
Supt. – (—), 11700 HIGHWAY 324 59725
Grant ES   59725 – Janet Spybrook, prin.

Divide, Silver Bow Co.
Divide ESD 4
Sch. Sys. Enr. Code 1
Supt. – (—), P O BOX 532 59727
ES   59727 – Maryann Smith, prin.

Dixon, Sanders Co.
Dixon ESD 9
Sch. Sys. Enr. Code 2
Supt. – (—), P O BOX 10 59831
ES   59831 – Keith Cable, prin.

Dodson, Phillips Co., Pop. Code 2
Dodson HSD C
Sch. Sys. Enr. Code 2
Supt. – Dr. Richard Shaffer, P O BOX 278 59524
ES   59524 – Dr Richard Shaffer, prin.

Hays-Lodge Pole HSD 50
Supt. – See Hays
Lodge Pole ES, LODGE POLE RT 59524
  Betty Campbell, prin.

Landusky ESD 7
Sch. Sys. Enr. Code 1
Supt. – (—), LANDUSKY ROUTE 59524
Landusky ES 59524 – Yvonne Kolczak, prin.

Drummond, Granite Co., Pop. Code 2
Drummond HSD 2
Sch. Sys. Enr. Code 2
Supt. – Walter Piippo, P O BOX 349 59832
ES 59832 – Alvan Bergman, prin.

Dupuyer, Pondera Co.
Dupuyer ESD 2
Sch. Sys. Enr. Code 1
Supt. – (—), P O BOX 287 59432
ES, P O BOX 287 59432 – Debra Grant, prin.

Dutton, Teton Co., Pop. Code 2
Dutton HSD 28
Sch. Sys. Enr. Code 1
Supt. – Rich Wilson, P O BOX 48 59433
ES 59433 – Sam Richter, prin.

East Glacier Park, Glacier Co., Pop. Code 2
East Glacier ESD 50
Sch. Sys. Enr. Code 1
Supt. – (—), P O BOX 70 59434
ES 59434 – Jim Syvertson, prin.

East Helena, Lewis and Clark Co., Pop. Code 4
East Helena ESD 9
Sch. Sys. Enr. Code 3
Supt. – Jim Koke, P O BOX H 59635
Radley ES, 226 E CLINTON 59635
  Lyle Eggum, prin.
Other Schools – See Helena

Edgar, Carbon Co.
Edgar ESD 33
Sch. Sys. Enr. Code 1
Supt. – (—), P O BOX 84 59026
ES 59026 – Terri Hodgson, prin.

Ekalaka, Carter Co., Pop. Code 3
Ekalaka ESD 15
Sch. Sys. Enr. Code 2
Supt. – (—), P O BOX 458 59324
ES 59324 – Charles Bostrom, prin.

Pine Hill Plainview ESD 14
Sch. Sys. Enr. Code 1
Supt. – (—), P O BOX 152 59324
Pine Hill ES 59324 – Elnor Knutson, prin.
Plainview ES 59324 – Karen Odell, prin.

Elliston, Powell Co.
Elliston ESD 27
Sch. Sys. Enr. Code 1
Supt. – (—), P O BOX 160 59728
ES, P O BOX 160 59728 – Susan Hillerman, prin.

Ennis, Madison Co., Pop. Code 3
Ennis HSD 52
Sch. Sys. Enr. Code 3
Supt. – Tom Warwick, P O BOX 517 59729
Madison Valley ES 59729 – Clair Rasmussen, prin.

Eureka, Lincoln Co., Pop. Code 4
Eureka ESD 13
Sch. Sys. Enr. Code 3
Supt. – Lou Mikkelson, P O BOX 2001 59917
ES 59917 – Fred Rainey, prin.

Fairfield, Teton Co., Pop. Code 3
Fairfield HSD 21
Sch. Sys. Enr. Code 2
Supt. – C. Kinna, P O BOX 99 59436
ES 59436 – Ward Fifield, prin.

Golden Ridge ESD 45
Sch. Sys. Enr. Code 1
Supt. – (—), RURAL ROUTE 02 59436
Golden Ridge ES 59436 – Charlotte Tacke, prin.

Greenfield ESD 75
Sch. Sys. Enr. Code 1
Supt. – (—), RURAL ROUTE 01 59436
Greenfield ES 59436 – Loren Sasser, prin.

Fairview, Richland Co., Pop. Code 4
Fairview HSD 3
Sch. Sys. Enr. Code 3
Supt. – Ken Avison, P O BOX 467 59221
ES 59221 – Gordon Gumke, prin.

Fallon, Prairie Co., Pop. Code 2
Fallon ESD 130
Sch. Sys. Enr. Code 1
Supt. – (—), P O BOX 56 59326
ES 59326 – P. Schilling, prin.

Fishtail, Stillwater Co.
Fishtail ESD 13
Sch. Sys. Enr. Code 1
Supt. – (—) 59028
ES 59028 – Kay Cannon, prin.

Flaxville, Daniels Co., Pop. Code 2
Flaxville HSD 3
Sch. Sys. Enr. Code 1
Supt. – Gene Berg, P O BOX 89 59222
ES, 400 1ST AVE 59222 – Gene Berg, prin.

Florence, Ravalli Co., Pop. Code 2
Florence-Carlton HSD 15-6
Sch. Sys. Enr. Code 3
Supt. – Rob Lukes
Florence-Carlton JHS 59833 – Bert Deglow, prin.
Florence Carlton ES 59833
  James Bruggeman, prin.

Floweree, Cascade Co.
Benton Lake ESD 99
Sch. Sys. Enr. Code 1
Supt. – (—), P O BOX 29 59440
Benton Lake ES 59440 – Marjorie Schuler, prin.

Forsyth, Rosebud Co., Pop. Code 5
Forsyth HSD 4
Sch. Sys. Enr. Code 3
Supt. – Dave Lloyd, P O BOX 319 59327
MS, 1850 CEDAR 59327 – Bruce Thomas, prin.
ES 59327 – Scott Schumacher, prin.

Fort Benton, Chouteau Co., Pop. Code 4
Ft. Benton HSD 1
Sch. Sys. Enr. Code 2
Supt. – Craig Brewington, P O BOX 399 59442
JHS, 1820 WASHINGTON 59442
  Craig Brewington, prin.
ES, 1406 FRANKLIN 59442 – James Gorder, prin.

Fortine, Lincoln Co.
Fortine ESD 14
Sch. Sys. Enr. Code 1
Supt. – (—), P O BOX 96 59918
ES, MEADOW CREEK ROAD 59918
  Joellyn Suchy, prin.

Fort Peck, Valley Co., Pop. Code 3
Fort Peck ESD 21
Sch. Sys. Enr. Code 1
Supt. – (—), P O BOX 188 59223
ES, N MISSOURI AVE 59223
  Virginia Rock, prin.

Frazer, Valley Co., Pop. Code 2
Frazer HSD 2B
Sch. Sys. Enr. Code 1
Supt. – Rob Heppner, P O BOX 488 59225
ES 59225 – Ken Bondy, prin.

Lustre ESD 23
Sch. Sys. Enr. Code 1
Supt. – (—), SR266 BOX 58 59225
Lustre ES 59225 – Joyce Wall, prin.

Frenchtown, Missoula Co., Pop. Code 5
Frenchtown HSD 40
Sch. Sys. Enr. Code 3
Supt. – Robert Banks, P O BOX 117 59834
ES 59834 – Norm Hagen, prin.

Froid, Roosevelt Co., Pop. Code 2
Froid HSD 65E
Sch. Sys. Enr. Code 2
Supt. – Rand Bradley, P O BOX 218 59226
ES 59226 – Rand Bradley, prin.

Fromberg, Carbon Co., Pop. Code 2
Fromberg HSD 6
Sch. Sys. Enr. Code 2
Supt. – Penny Nelson, P O BOX 188 59029
ES, 319 SCHOOL 59029 – Penny Nelson, prin.

Galata, Toole Co.
Galata ESD 10
Sch. Sys. Enr. Code 1
Supt. – (—), RURAL ROUTE 59444
Liberty ES 59444 – Becky Weinert, prin.

Galata ESD 21
Sch. Sys. Enr. Code 1
Supt. – (—), P O BOX 76 59444
ES 59444 – Virginia Hagen, prin.

Gallatin Gateway, Gallatin Co.
Gallatin Gateway ESD 35
Sch. Sys. Enr. Code 2
Supt. – (—), P O BOX 265 59730
ES 59730 – Janet Williams, prin.

Ophir ESD 72
Sch. Sys. Enr. Code 1
Supt. – (—)
  CANYON ROUTE BOX 178 59730
Ophir ES 59730 – (—), prin.

Gardiner, Park Co., Pop. Code 3
Gardiner HSD 4
Sch. Sys. Enr. Code 2
Supt. – Lynn Mavencamp, P O BOX 26 59030
ES 59030 – John Overstreet, prin.

Garrison, Powell Co.
Garrison ESD 20
Sch. Sys. Enr. Code 1
Supt. – (—), P O BOX 608 59731
ES 59731 – Cheryl George, prin.

Geraldine, Choteau Co., Pop. Code 2
Geraldine HSD 3
Sch. Sys. Enr. Code 2
Supt. – Ed Zabrocki, P O BOX 57 59446
ES 59446 – Ed Zabrocki, prin.

Geyser, Judith Basin Co., Pop. Code 3
Geyser HSD 58
Sch. Sys. Enr. Code 2
Supt. – Joel Voytoski, P O BOX 70 59447
ES 59447 – Joel Voytoski, prin.
Surprise Creek ES 59447 – Joel Voytoski, prin.

Gildford, Hill Co., Pop. Code 3
Gildford Colony ESD 89
Sch. Sys. Enr. Code 1
Supt. – (—), P O BOX 141 59525
Gildford Colony ES 59525 – Janice Delaney, prin.

K-G HSD H
Sch. Sys. Enr. Code 1
Supt. – Paul Preeshl, P O BOX 166 59525
Other Schools – See Kremlin

Glasgow, Valley Co., Pop. Code 5
Glasgow HSD 1-A
Sch. Sys. Enr. Code 4
Supt. – Gary Martin, P O BOX 28 59230
MS, P O BOX 28 59230 – Sidney Sulser, prin.
Irle ES, 825 8TH ST N 59230 – Dennis Idler, prin.
Southside MS, 435 7TH ST S 59230
  Gary Sauter, prin.

Glen, Beaverhead Co.
Reichle ESD 26
Sch. Sys. Enr. Code 1
Supt. – (—), P O BOX 5 59732
Reichle ES, P O BOX 5 59732 – (—), prin.

Glendive, Dawson Co., Pop. Code 6
Deer Creek ESD 3
Sch. Sys. Enr. Code 1
Supt. – (—), HCR 66 BOX 6393 59330
Deer Creek ES 59330 – Irene Fabian, prin.

Glendive ESD 1
Sch. Sys. Enr. Code 4
Supt. – (—), P O BOX 701 59330
Jefferson ES
  800 JEFFERSON SCHOOL ROAD 59330
  Reyneu Busch, prin.
Lincoln ES, 313 S NOWLAN AVE 59330
  William Kelly, prin.
Washington ES, 505 N MEADE AVE 59330
  Harry Darling, prin.

Upper Crackerbox/Amo ESD 10
Sch. Sys. Enr. Code 1
Supt. – (—), P O BOX 1185 59330
Upper Crackerbox ES, P O BOX 112 59330
  Kay Pisk, prin.

Gold Creek, Powell Co.
Gold Creek ESD 33
Sch. Sys. Enr. Code 1
Supt. – (—), P O BOX 26 59733
ES 59733 – Marilyn Wohlers, prin.

Grass Range, Fergus Co., Pop. Code 2
Ayers ESD 222
Sch. Sys. Enr. Code 1
Supt. – (—), P O BOX 111 59032
Ayers ES 59032 – Mary Finn, prin.

Grass Range HSD 27
Sch. Sys. Enr. Code 1
Supt. – Don Bidwell, P O BOX 47 59032
ES 59032 – Don Bidwell, prin.

Great Falls, Cascade Co., Pop. Code 8
Great Falls HSD A
Sch. Sys. Enr. Code 7
Supt. – Larry Williams, P O BOX 2428 59403
East JHS, 4040 CENTRAL AVE 59403
  Gordon Dahl, prin.
North JHS, 2601 8TH ST NE 59404
  Ted Snow, prin.
Chief Joseph ES, 5305 3RD AVE S 59405
  James Bergman, prin.
Lewis & Clark ES, 3800 1ST AVE S 59405
  Denise Conrad, prin.
Lincoln ES, 624 27TH ST S 59405
  Sherry Meadors, prin.
Longfellow ES, 1101 7TH AVE S 59405
  Willis Heupel, prin.
Loy ES, 501 57TH ST N 59405
  Kenwood Nordquist, prin.
Meadowlark ES, 2204 FOX FARM ROAD 59404
  Richard Marberg, prin.
Morningside ES, 4119 7TH AVE N 59405
  Robert Jewell, prin.
Mountain View ES, 3420 15TH AVE S 59405
  Mary Cosgrove, prin.
Riverview ES, 100 SMELTER AVE NW 59404
  Linus Yingst, prin.
Roosevelt ES, 2501 2ND AVE N 59401
  Leslie Duncan, prin.
Sacajawea ES, 630 SACAJAWEA DR 59404
  Bonita David, prin.
Sunnyside ES, 1800 19TH ST S 59405
  Marie Mastorovich, prin.
Valley View ES, 900 AVENUE A NW 59404
  Duane Dockter, prin.
West ES, 1205 1ST AVE NW 59404
  Robert McNees, prin.
Whittier ES, 305 8TH ST N 59401
  Dewey Swank, prin.

Holy Family School, 2820 CENTRAL AVE 59401
Our Lady of Lourdes School
  1305 5TH AVE S 59405

Greenough, Missoula Co.
Sunset ESD 30
Sch. Sys. Enr. Code 1
Supt. – (—), P O BOX 344 59836
Sunset ES 59836 – Michael Greene, prin.

Greycliff, Sweet Grass Co.
Greycliff ESD 16
Sch. Sys. Enr. Code 1
Supt. – (—), P O BOX 65 59033
ES 59033 – Judy Jacobi, prin.

Hall, Granite Co.
Hall ESD 8
Sch. Sys. Enr. Code 1
Supt. – (—) 59837
ES 59837 – Jacolyn Erfle, prin.

Hamilton, Ravalli Co., Pop. Code 5
Hamilton HSD 3
Sch. Sys. Enr. Code 4
Supt. – C. Johnson, P O BOX 980 59840
Westview JHS, 103 S 9TH ST 59840
  Webb Harrington, prin.
Daly ES 59840 – Greg Croff, prin.
Grantsdale ES 59840 – Webb Harrington, prin.
Washington ES 59840 – Gregg Croff, prin.

Hammond, Carter Co.
Albion ESD 11
Supt. – See Alzada
Albion ES 59332 – Noralla Thomas, prin.

Hammond Hawks Home ESD 1
Sch. Sys. Enr. Code 1
Supt. – (—), HCR RT 14 59332
ES 59332 – Coila Smith, prin.
Hawks Home ES 59332 – Marion Officer, prin.

Johnston ESD 8
Sch. Sys. Enr. Code 1
Supt. – (—), P O BOX 29 59332
Johnston ES 59332 – Betty Stafford, prin.

Hardin, Big Horn Co., Pop. Code 5
Community ESD 16
Sch. Sys. Enr. Code 1
Supt. – (—)
  RURAL ROUTE 01 BOX 1093 59034
Community ES
  RURAL ROUTE 01 BOX 1093 59034
  Eva Graves, prin.

Hardin HSD 1
Sch. Sys. Enr. Code 4
Supt. – Rodney Svee, 522 N CENTER AVE 59034
JHS, 611 5TH ST W 59034
  Charles Boughton, prin.
Fort Smith ES, 502 AVE C 59034
  Betty Kinney, prin.
IS, 631 5TH ST W 59034 – Keith Fletcher, prin.
PS, 314 3RD ST W 59034 – Keith Fletcher, prin.
Other Schools – See Crow Agency

Harlem, Blaine Co., Pop. Code 4
Harlem HSD 12
Sch. Sys. Enr. Code 3
Supt. – Roger Ranta, P O BOX 339 59526
ES, P O BOX 309 59526 – David McGuigan, prin.

North Harlem ESD 6
Sch. Sys. Enr. Code 1
Supt. – (—), P O BOX 489 59526
North Harlem Colony ES, 4 MI N 59526
  Laura Macann, prin.

Harlowton, Wheatland Co., Pop. Code 4
Harlowton HSD 16
Sch. Sys. Enr. Code 2
Supt. – Gary Scott, P O BOX 288 59036
Hillcrest ES, 500 8TH AVE NE 59036
  Clarene Dysart, prin.

Harrison, Madison Co., Pop. Code 3
Harrison HSD 23
Sch. Sys. Enr. Code 1
Supt. – Joe Brott, P O BOX 7 59735
ES 59735 – Joe Brott, prin.

Havre, Hill Co., Pop. Code 7
Cottonwood ESD 57
Sch. Sys. Enr. Code 1
Supt. – (—)
  RURAL ROUTE 01 BOX 22 59501
Cottonwood ES 59501 – Marilyn Granell, prin.

Davey ESD 12
Sch. Sys. Enr. Code 1
Supt. – (—), 718 1/2 5TH AVE 59501
Davey ES 59501 – L. MacFarlane, prin.

Havre HSD A
Sch. Sys. Enr. Code 4
Supt. – Robert Windel, P O BOX 7791 59501
JHS, 326 7TH ST 59501 – Pep Jewell, prin.
Devlin ES, 500 1ST AVE 59501
  William O'Donnell, prin.
Highland Park ES
  1207 WASHINGTON AVE 59501
  Leo Beardsley, prin.
Lincoln McKinley ES, 801 4TH ST 59501
  Jeff Pratt, prin.
Sunnyside ES, 601 14TH ST 59501
  Leo Beardsley, prin.

St. Jude Thaddeus School, 420 7TH AVE 59501

Hays, Blaine Co., Pop. Code 3
Hays-Lodge Pole HSD 50
Sch. Sys. Enr. Code 2
Supt. – Elmer Main, P O BOX 880 59527
ES 59527 – Betty Campbell, prin.
Other Schools – See Dodson

Heart Butte, Pondera Co.
Heart Butte ESD 1
Sch. Sys. Enr. Code 2
Supt. – (—) 59448
ES 59448 – Thomas Hoyer, prin.

Helena, Lewis and Clark Co., Pop. Code 7
East Helena ESD 9
Supt. – See East Helena
Eastgate ES, 4010 GRADESTAKE 59635
  Bob Gibson, prin.

Helena HSD 1
Sch. Sys. Enr. Code 6
Supt. – Jack Copps, P O BOX 5417 59604
Anderson MS, 1200 KNIGHT ST 59601
  Ken Stuker, prin.
MS, 1025 N RODNEY ST 59601
  Charles Strand, prin.
Anderson ES, 1200 KNIGHT ST 59601
  Tom Miller, prin.
Bjork ES, 1600 8TH AVE 59601
  Karen Sexton, prin.
Broadwater ES, 900 HOLLINS AVE 59601
  Bernard Hartman, prin.
Bryant ES, 1529 BOULDER AVE 59601
  Philip Mills, prin.
Central ES, 402 N WARREN ST 59601
  Marian Evenson, prin.
Darcy ES, 990 W LINCOLN ROAD 59601
  David Pepin, prin.
Four Georgians ES, 555 W CUSTER AVE 59601
  Warren Morehouse, prin.
Hawthorne ES, 430 MADISON AVE 59601
  Tom Miller, prin.
Jefferson ES, 1023 E BROADWAY ST 59601
  John Fero, prin.
Lincoln ES, 1325 POPLAR ST 59601
  Karen Sexton, prin.
Rossiter ES, 1497 SIERRA ROAD E 59601
  Robert Morris, prin.
Smith ES, 2320 5TH AVE 59601
  Mervin Finstad, prin.
Warren ES, 2690 YORK ROAD 59601
  James Wooley, prin.

Kessler ESD 2
Sch. Sys. Enr. Code 2
Supt. – (—), 2420 CHOTEAU ST 59601
Kessler ES 59601 – Keith Meyer, prin.

Helmville, Powell Co.
Helmville ESD 15
Sch. Sys. Enr. Code 1
Supt. – (—), P O BOX 68 59843
ES 59843 – Susan Graveley, prin.

Highwood, Chouteau Co., Pop. Code 2
Highwood HSD 4
Sch. Sys. Enr. Code 2
Supt. – Haydn Hedrick 59450
ES 59450 – Haydn Hedrick, prin.

Hilger, Fergus Co.
Hilger ESD 56
Sch. Sys. Enr. Code 1
Supt. – (—) 59451
ES 59451 – Sylvia Bingeman, prin.

Hinsdale, Valley Co., Pop. Code 3
Hinsdale HSD 7-C
Sch. Sys. Enr. Code 1
Supt. – Harry Knodel, P O BOX 398 59241
ES 59241 – Harold Knodel, prin.

Hobson, Judith Basin Co., Pop. Code 2
Hobson HSD 25
Sch. Sys. Enr. Code 2
Supt. – Jerry Thompson 59452
ES 59452 – Jerry Thompson, prin.

Hot Springs, Sanders Co., Pop. Code 3
Hot Springs HSD 14J
Sch. Sys. Enr. Code 2
Supt. – Gerald Sowden, P O BOX T 59845
ES 59845 – Joseph Erchul, prin.

Hysham, Treasure Co., Pop. Code 2
Hysham HSD 1
Sch. Sys. Enr. Code 2
Supt. – Patricia Price, P O BOX 272 59038
ES 59038 – Robert Miller, prin.

Ingomar, Rosebud Co.
Ingomar ESD 33
Sch. Sys. Enr. Code 1
Supt. – (—), P O BOX 88 59039
ES 59039 – Donald Hettinger, prin.

Ismay, Custer Co., Pop. Code 1
Cottonwood ESD 38
Sch. Sys. Enr. Code 1
Supt. – (—), BAKER HIGHWAY 59336
Cottonwood ES 59336 – Sherry Oster, prin.
Knowlton ES 59336 – Mary Lou Chatham, prin.

Whitney Creek ESD 42
Sch. Sys. Enr. Code 1
Supt. – (—)
  RURAL ROUTE 03 BOX 106 59336
Whitney Creek ES 59336 – Roberta Morgan, prin.

Jackson, Beaverhead Co.
Jackson ESD 24
Sch. Sys. Enr. Code 1
Supt. – (—), P O BOX 787 59736
ES, P O BOX 787 59736 – Anne Verbance, prin.

Joliet, Carbon Co., Pop. Code 3
Joliet HSD 7
Sch. Sys. Enr. Code 2
Supt. – Larry Blades, P O BOX G 59041
MS 59041 – Keith Obert, prin.
ES, P O BOX G 59041 – Larry Blades, prin.

Joplin, Liberty Co., Pop. Code 2
J-I HSD J
Sch. Sys. Enr. Code 2
Supt. – Bernard Rosling, P O BOX 227 59531
Joplin-Inverness JHS 59531
  Bernard Rosling, prin.
Joplin Inverness ES 59531 – Ken Monilaws, prin.

Jordan, Garfield Co., Pop. Code 2
Big Dry ESD 10
Sch. Sys. Enr. Code 1
Supt. – (—), P O BOX 160 59337
Big Dry ES 59337 – Rebecca Ripley, prin.

Cat Creek ESD 55
Sch. Sys. Enr. Code 1
Supt. – (—)
  RURAL ROUTE 02 BOX 14 59337
Cat Creek ES 59337 – Sheila Baker, prin.

Flat Creek ESD 56
Sch. Sys. Enr. Code 1
Supt. – (—), RURAL ROUTE 01 59337
Flat Creek ES 59337 – Eva Twitchell, prin.

Jordan ESD 1
Sch. Sys. Enr. Code 2
Supt. – (—), P O BOX 309 59337
ES 59337 – Steven Cascaden, prin.

Kester ESD 23
Sch. Sys. Enr. Code 1
Supt. – (—)
  RURAL ROUTE 02 BOX 11 59337
Kester ES 59337 – Charlotte Moran, prin.

Van Norman ESD 15
Sch. Sys. Enr. Code 1
Supt. – (—), P O BOX 237 59337
ES 59337 – Kari Heinsen, prin.

Judith Gap, Wheatland Co., Pop. Code 2
Judith Gap HSD 21J
Sch. Sys. Enr. Code 1
Supt. – Robert Korthuis, P O BOX 64 59453
ES, 306 4TH AVE 59453 – Robert Korthuis, prin.

Kalispell, Flathead Co., Pop. Code 7
Batavia ESD 26
Sch. Sys. Enr. Code 1
Supt. – (—), 2901 HIGHWAY 2 W 59901
Batavia ES 59901 – Harold Welling, prin.

Boorman ESD 39
Sch. Sys. Enr. Code 1
Supt. – (—), 600 BATAVIA LANE 59901
Boorman ES 59901 – Ron Edwards, prin.

Cayuse Prairie ESD 10
Sch. Sys. Enr. Code 2
Supt. – (—), 897 LAKE BLAINE ROAD 59901
Cayuse Prairie ES 59901 – John Babcock, prin.

Creston ESD 9
Sch. Sys. Enr. Code 1
Supt. – (—), 4495 MONTANA NO 35 59901
Creston ES 59901 – Barbara Walden, prin.

Evergreen SD 50
Sch. Sys. Enr. Code 3
Supt. – Robert Aumaugher
  18 W PHEASANT DRIVE 59901
Evergreen MS, 20 W EVERGREEN DRIVE 59901
  Ryan Swan, prin.
East Evergreen ES, 535 E PHEASANT DR 59901
  James Magness, prin.

Fair Mont Egan ESD 3
Sch. Sys. Enr. Code 1
Supt. – (—), 797 FAIRMONT ROAD 59901
Fair Mont Egan ES 59901 – Robert Benke, prin.

Helena Flats ESD 15
Sch. Sys. Enr. Code 2
Supt. – (—)
  1000 HELENA FLATS ROAD 59901
Helena Flats ES 59901 – Clinton Collins, prin.

Kalispell HSD 5
Sch. Sys. Enr. Code 5
Supt. – William Cooper, 233 1ST AVE E 59901
JHS, 135 NORTHWEST LN 59901
  Cathryn McDevitt, prin.
Linderman JHS, 3RD AVE E 59901
  Larry Schulz, prin.
Cornelus Hedges ES, 4TH AVE & 7TH ST E 59901
  Karla Jones, prin.
Edgerton ES, 1400 WHITEFISH STAGE 59901
  Rick Davis, prin.
Elrod ES, 3RD AVE & 4TH ST W 59901
  Russell Winters, prin.
Peterson ES, 2ND W & MERIDIAN 59901
  Steve Rasor, prin.
Russell ES, 2ND AVE WN 59901
  Mike Anderson, prin.

Mountain Brook ESD 62
Sch. Sys. Enr. Code 1
Supt. – (—), 2353 FOOTHILL ROAD 59901
Mountain Brook ES 59901 – Clara Tennant, prin.

West Valley ESD 1
Sch. Sys. Enr. Code 2
Supt. – (—)
  2290 FARM TO MARKET ROAD 59901
West Valley ES 59901 – Frank Dekort, prin.

St. Matthews School, 602 S MAIN ST 59901

Trinity Lutheran School
5TH AVE W N & CALIF ST 59901

Kevin, Toole Co., Pop. Code 2
Kevin ESD 8
Sch. Sys. Enr. Code 1
Supt. – (—), P O BOX 47 59454
ES 59454 – C. Peterschick, prin.

Kila, Flathead Co.
Kila ESD 20
Sch. Sys. Enr. Code 1
Supt. – (—), P O BOX 900 59920
ES, P O BOX 40 59920 – Berma Weatherly, prin.

Kinsey, Custer Co.
Kinsey ESD 63
Sch. Sys. Enr. Code 1
Supt. – (—) 59338
ES 59338 – Susan Kohn, prin.

Kremlin, Hill Co.
K-G HSD H
Supt. – See Gildford
K-G ES 59532 – Paul Preeshi, prin.

Lambert, Richland Co., Pop. Code 3
Lambert HSD 4
Sch. Sys. Enr. Code 2
Supt. – Jack Eggensperger, P O BOX 236 59243
ES 59243 – Jack Eggensperger, prin.

Lame Deer, Rosebud Co.
Lame Deer ESD 6
Sch. Sys. Enr. Code 2
Supt. – Raymond Mace, P O BOX 96 59043
JHS, P O BOX 96 59043 – Kent Cook, prin.
ES 59043 – Russell Pannoni, prin.

Laurel, Yellowstone Co., Pop. Code 6
Laurel HSD 7
Sch. Sys. Enr. Code 4
Supt. – Robert Singleton
410 COLORADO AVE 59044
MS, 410 COLORADO AVE 59044
Marvin Carter, prin.
Graff ES, 417 3 SIXTH 59044
Gordon Forster, prin.
South ES, 606 S 5TH ST 59044
Robert Western, prin.
West ES, 502 8TH AVE 59044
Robert Western, prin.

Lavina, Golden Valley Co., Pop. Code 2
Lavina HSD 2
Sch. Sys. Enr. Code 2
Supt. – David Konecny, P O BOX 146 59046
ES, 214 1ST E 59046 – David Konecny, prin.

Ledger, Pondera Co.
Nickol ESD 23
Sch. Sys. Enr. Code 1
Supt. – (—), HCR ROUTE BOX 25 59456
Nickol ES 59456 – Cynthia Fretheim, prin.

Lewistown, Fergus Co., Pop. Code 6
Brooks ESD 11
Sch. Sys. Enr. Code 1
Supt. – (—)
RURAL ROUTE 03 BOX 3091 59457
Brooks ES 59457 – Diana Albaugh, prin.

Cottonwood ESD 18
Sch. Sys. Enr. Code 1
Supt. – (—)
RURAL ROUTE 01 BOX 1836 59457
Cottonwood ES 59457 – Brenda Egge, prin.

Deerfield ESD 15
Sch. Sys. Enr. Code 1
Supt. – (—)
RURAL ROUTE 03 BOX 3138 59457
Deerfield ES, DEERFIELD COLONY 59457
Margaret Carr, prin.

King Colony ESD 40
Sch. Sys. Enr. Code 1
Supt. – (—)
RURAL ROUTE 02 BOX 2325 59457
King Colony ES
RURAL ROUTE 02 BOX 1143 59457
Lynn Whitmer, prin.

Lewistown HSD 1
Sch. Sys. Enr. Code 4
Supt. – Jim Turner, 215 7TH AVE S 59457
MS, 914 W MAIN ST 59457 – Dennis Bergo, prin.
Garfield ES, 415 E BOULEVARD ST 59457
John Moffatt, prin.
Highland Park ES, 1312 7TH AVE N 59457
L. Bowman, prin.
Lewis & Clark ES, 212 CRYSTAL DRIVE 59457
Patrick McGuire, prin.

Maiden ESD 3
Sch. Sys. Enr. Code 1
Supt. – (—)
RURAL ROUTE 03 BOX 27 59457
Maiden ES, MAIDEN ROAD 59457
Lynette Sallee, prin.

Spring Creek ESD 104
Sch. Sys. Enr. Code 1
Supt. – (—), P O BOX 1185 59457
Spring Creek Colony ES 59457 – Nancy Link, prin.

Libby, Lincoln Co., Pop. Code 5
Libby HSD 4
Sch. Sys. Enr. Code 4
Supt. – Paul Stebbins
111 E LINCOLN BLVD 59923
McGrade ES
899 FARM TO MARKET ROAD 59923
Gerald Dean, prin.
Plummer ES, 247 INDIAN HEAD ROAD 59923
George Gerard, prin.
Wood ES, 700 IDAHO AVE 59923
Susan Ennis, prin.

Lima, Beaverhead Co., Pop. Code 2
Lima HSD 12
Sch. Sys. Enr. Code 2
Supt. – Lance Mocabee, P O BOX AA 59739
ES, P O BOX AA 59739 – Lance Mocabee, prin.

Lincoln, Lewis and Clark Co., Pop. Code 4
Lincoln HSD 38
Sch. Sys. Enr. Code 2
Supt. – Richard Trerise, P O BOX 154 59639
ES 59639 – Richard Trerise, prin.

Lindsay, Dawson Co.
Lindsay ESD 36
Sch. Sys. Enr. Code 1
Supt. – (—), P O BOX B 59339
ES 59339 – Barbara Peterson, prin.

Livingston, Park Co., Pop. Code 6
Livingston HSD 1
Sch. Sys. Enr. Code 4
Supt. – Gaylord Lasher, 132 S B ST 59047
Lincoln JHS, B & LEWIS 59047
James Woodhull, prin.
East Side ES, 415 E LEWIS ST 59047
Stephen Jennings, prin.
Washington ES, 315 N 8TH ST 59047
Stephen Jennings, prin.
Winans ES, 1015 W CLARK ST 59047
Jim Huntzicker, prin.

Pine Creek ESD 19
Sch. Sys. Enr. Code 1
Supt. – (—)
RURAL ROUTE 38 BOX 2067 59047
Pine Creek ES 59047 – Ellie Raffety, prin.

Richland ESD 2
Sch. Sys. Enr. Code 1
Supt. – (—)
RURAL ROUTE 38 BOX 2259 59047
Richland ES 59047 – Wanda Melin, prin.

St. Mary's Catholic School
VIEW VISTA DR 59047

Lloyd, Blaine Co.
Cleveland Lone Tree ESD 14
Supt. – See Chinook
Lone Tree Bench ES
RURAL ROUTE 73 BOX 25 59535
Janice Hayworth, prin.

Cow Island Trail ESD 42
Sch. Sys. Enr. Code 1
Supt. – (—), P O BOX 12A 59535
Cow Island Trail ES 59535 – Ginger Lester, prin.

Lloyd ESD 24
Sch. Sys. Enr. Code 1
Supt. – (—), ROUTE 70 BOX 75 59535
ES 59523 – Glenda Butcher, prin.

Lodge Grass, Big Horn Co., Pop. Code 3
Lodge Grass HSD 2
Sch. Sys. Enr. Code 2
Supt. – Bert Corcoran, P O BOX AF 59050
Corral Creek ES, RURAL ROUTE 59050
Jerry Williamson, prin.
ES, 124 N GEORGE 59050 – Deanna Parisian, prin.

Lolo, Missoula Co., Pop. Code 5
Lolo ESD 7
Sch. Sys. Enr. Code 3
Supt. – (—), 13399 HIGHWAY 93 S 59847
JHS, 11395 HWY 93 S 59847 – (—), prin.
ES, 11395 HWY 93 S 59847 – (—), prin.

Woodman ESD 18
Sch. Sys. Enr. Code 1
Supt. – (—), LOLO CREEK ROAD 59847
Woodman ES 59847 – Karen Bakker, prin.

Loma, Chouteau Co.
Loma ESD 7
Sch. Sys. Enr. Code 1
Supt. – (—), P O BOX 202 59460
ES 59460 – Bonnie Boggs, prin.

Loring, Phillips Co.
Malta HSD A
Supt. – See Malta
Loring Colony ES 59537 – Cindy Christman, prin.

Luther, Carbon Co.
Luther ESD 10
Sch. Sys. Enr. Code 1
Supt. – (—) 59051
ES 59051 – Judy Cole, prin.

Mc Leod, Sweet Grass Co.
McLeod ESD 29
Sch. Sys. Enr. Code 1
Supt. – (—) 59052
ES 59052 – Connie Anderson, prin.

Malta, Phillips Co., Pop. Code 4
Malta HSD A
Sch. Sys. Enr. Code 3
Supt. – Robert Rust, P O BOX 670 59538
JHS, 219 S 5TH ST E 59538 – Scott King, prin.
ES, P O BOX LL 59538 – George Knudsen, prin.
Tallow Creek ES, SE OF MALTA 59538
Cath Steger, prin.
Other Schools – See Loring, Zortman

Second Creek ESD 6
Sch. Sys. Enr. Code 1
Supt. – (—), SECOND CREEK 59539
Second Creek ES 59538 – Jane Eberle, prin.

Sun Prairie ESD 8AA
Sch. Sys. Enr. Code 1
Supt. – (—), HCR ROUTE BOX 26 59538
Sun Prairie ES 59538 – Katy Thompson, prin.

St. Mary's School, P O BOX 70 59538

Manhattan, Gallatin Co., Pop. Code 3
Amsterdam ESD 75
Sch. Sys. Enr. Code 1
Supt. – (—), 6360 CAMP CREEK ROAD 59741
Amsterdam ES 59741 – Nancy Drusch, prin.

Logan ESD 1
Sch. Sys. Enr. Code 1
Supt. – (—), 140 1ST ST 59741
Logan ES 59741 – Sara Goulden, prin.

Manhattan HSD 3
Sch. Sys. Enr. Code 3
Supt. – Dale Moore, P O BOX 425 59741
ES, P O BOX 425 59741 – Ronald Zier, prin.

Marion, Flathead Co.
Marion ESD 54
Sch. Sys. Enr. Code 2
Supt. – (—), P O BOX 8 59925
ES 59925 – Roger Graham, prin.

Pleasant Valley ESD 27
Sch. Sys. Enr. Code 1
Supt. – (—)
7975 PLEASANT VALLEY ROAD 59925
Pleasant Valley ES 59925 – Aldon Schaefer, prin.

Martinsdale, Meagher Co.
Lennep ESD 4
Sch. Sys. Enr. Code 1
Supt. – (—), LENNEP ROUTE 59053
Lennep ES 59053 – B. Hereim, prin.

Medicine Lake, Sheridan Co., Pop. Code 2
Medicine Lake HSD 7
Sch. Sys. Enr. Code 2
Supt. – Calvin Moore, P O BOX 265 59247
ES 59247 – Thomas Prater, prin.

Melrose, Silver Bow Co.
Melrose ESD 5
Sch. Sys. Enr. Code 1
Supt. – (—), P O BOX 128 59743
ES 59743 – Marcy Busch, prin.

Melstone, Musselshell Co., Pop. Code 2
Melstone HSD 64-H
Sch. Sys. Enr. Code 2
Supt. – Robert Klein, P O BOX 97 59054
ES, 5 6TH AVE E 59054 – Robert Klein, prin.

Melville, Sweet Grass Co.
Melville ESD 5
Sch. Sys. Enr. Code 1
Supt. – (—) 59055
ES 59055 – Donna Swenumson, prin.

Miles City, Custer Co., Pop. Code 6
Garland ESD 11
Sch. Sys. Enr. Code 1
Supt. – (—), TONGUE RIVER STAGE 59301
Garland ES, TONGUE RIVER STAGE 59301
Mary Stark, prin.

Hockett Basin Spring ESD 16
Sch. Sys. Enr. Code 1
Supt. – (—), POWDERVILLE STAGE 59301
Hockett Basin ES, POWDERVILLE STAGE 59301
Debra Wildish, prin.
Spring Creek ES, POWDERVILLE STAGE 59301
Debra King, prin.

Kircher ESD 3
Sch. Sys. Enr. Code 1
Supt. – (—)
RURAL ROUTE 02 BOX 2352 59302
Kircher ES 59301 – Karen Murray, prin.

Miles City HSD 1
Sch. Sys. Enr. Code 4
Supt. – Robert Richards, 1604 MAIN ST 59301
Washington MS, 210 N 9TH ST 59301
Rick Powell, prin.
Garfield ES, 1015 MILWAUKEE ST 59301
Nolan Mikelson, prin.
Highland Park ES, 716 CALE AVE 59301
Donald Gundlach, prin.
Jefferson ES, 106 N STREVELL AVE 59301
Doug Ellingson, prin.
Lincoln ES, 210 S LAKE AVE 59301
Jack Nesbit, prin.
Roosevelt ES, 1608 N MERRIAM AVE 59301
Suzanne King, prin.

Moon Creek ESD 43
Sch. Sys. Enr. Code 1
Supt. – (—), TONGUE RIVER RT 59301
Moon Creek ES 59301 – Jeanie Parker, prin.

S H Foster Creek ESD 86
Sch. Sys. Enr. Code 1
Supt. – (—), TONGUE RIVER STAGE 59301
S H ES, TONGUE RIVER STAGE 59301
   Betty Miller, prin.

Sy ESD 83
Sch. Sys. Enr. Code 1
Supt. – (—), BROADUS STAGE 59301
S Y ES, BROADUS STAGE 59301
   Barbara Wilson, prin.

Trail Creek ESD 13
Sch. Sys. Enr. Code 1
Supt. – (—), P O BOX 1244 59301
Trail Creek ES, P O BOX 1244 59301
   Kem Wherley, prin.

Twin Buttes ESD 82
Sch. Sys. Enr. Code 1
Supt. – (—), CROW ROCK ROUTE 59302
Twin Buttes ES, CROW ROCK ROUTE 59301
   Laurie Tower, prin.

Sacred Heart ES, 519 N CENTER AVE 59301
Sacred Heart ES, 519 N MONTANA AVE 59301

Missoula, Missoula Co., Pop. Code 8
Desmet ESD 20
Sch. Sys. Enr. Code 1
Supt. – (—), 6355 PADRE LANE 59802
Desmet ES 59802 – Shirley Day, prin.

Hellgate SD 4
Sch. Sys. Enr. Code 3
Supt. – Don Waldron, 2385 FLYNN LANE 59802
Hellgate MS, 2385 FLYNN LANE 59802
   M. Walton, prin.
Hellgate ES 59802 – Bruce Whitehead, prin.

Missoula ESD 1
Sch. Sys. Enr. Code 6
Supt. – Jacob Block, 215 S 6TH ST W 59801
Meadow Hill JHS, 4210 S RESERVE ST 59803
   Gerald Ashmore, prin.
Porter JHS, 2510 W CENTRAL AVE 59801
   Jim Donovan, prin.
Rattlesnake JHS, PINEVIEW DRIVE 59801
   David Price, prin.
Roosevelt JHS, 503 EDITH ST 59801
   Thomas Brennan, prin.
Washington JHS, 645 W CENTRAL AVE 59801
   Mike Maxwell, prin.
Cold Springs ES, BRIGGS STREET 59801
   Ed Courtney, prin.
Dickinson ES, 310 CURTIS 59801
   Jim Denny, prin.
Franklin ES, 1901 S 10TH ST W 59801
   Palmer Scott, prin.
Hawthorne ES, 2835 S 3RD ST W 59801
   Darrel Peterson, prin.
Lewis & Clark ES, MARY AVE & PARK 59801
   Glenn Kozeluh, prin.
Lowell ES, 1200 SHERWOOD ST 59802
   Glenn Hoffman, prin.
Mt. Jumbo ES, 735 MICHIGAN AVE 59802
   Joe Stauduhar, prin.
Paxson ES, HIGGINS & EVANS 59801
   Judy Fenton, prin.
Prescott MS, HARRISON & ELM 59801
   Terry Wiedmer, prin.
Russell ES, 3216 S RUSSELL ST 59801
   John Alonzo, prin.
Willard ES, 901 S 6TH ST W 59801
   Steve Johnson, prin.

Target Range ESD 23
Sch. Sys. Enr. Code 2
Supt. – C. Beagle, 4095 SOUTH AVE W 59801
Target Range ES 59801 – Mark Thane, prin.

St. Joseph School, 430 W PINE ST 59802

Molt, Stillwater Co.
Molt ESD 12-12
Sch. Sys. Enr. Code 1
Supt. – (—), P O BOX 67 59057
ES 59057 – Joy Mallard, prin.

Moore, Fergus Co., Pop. Code 2
Moore HSD 44
Sch. Sys. Enr. Code 2
Supt. – R. Hughes, P O BOX I 59464
ES 59464 – Dorothy Schulze, prin.

Mosby, Petroleum Co.
Ross ESD 52
Sch. Sys. Enr. Code 1
Supt. – (—) 59058
Ross ES, 17 MILES N OF MOSBY 59058
   Kari Rinesmith, prin.

Musselshell, Musselshell Co.
Musselshell ESD 9
Sch. Sys. Enr. Code 1
Supt. – (—), P O BOX 198 59059
ES 59059 – Korinne Tande, prin.

Nashua, Valley Co., Pop. Code 2
Nashua HSD 13-E
Sch. Sys. Enr. Code 2
Supt. – Rob Barnes, P O BOX 167 59248
ES, 222 MABLE 59248 – Robert Barnes, prin.

Noxon, Sanders Co., Pop. Code 2
Noxon HSD 10
Sch. Sys. Enr. Code 2
Supt. – John Baule, P O BOX 1506 59853
ES 59853 – John Baule, prin.

Nye, Stillwater Co.
Nye ESD 31
Sch. Sys. Enr. Code 1
Supt. – (—)
   RURAL ROUTE 02 BOX 103 59061
ES 59061 – Jennie Ekwortzel, prin.

Opheim, Valley Co., Pop. Code 2
Opheim HSD 9-D
Sch. Sys. Enr. Code 2
Supt. – Robert Joscelyn, P O BOX 108 59250
ES 59250 – Robert Joscelyn, prin.

Otter, Powder River Co.
Bear Creek ESD 60
Sch. Sys. Enr. Code 1
Supt. – (—) 59062
Bear Creek ES 59062 – Gayla Wessels, prin.

Billup ESD 65
Sch. Sys. Enr. Code 1
Supt. – (—), RURAL ROUTE BOX 18 59062
Billup ES 59062 – Elizabeth Sollie, prin.

Outlook, Sheridan Co., Pop. Code 2
Outlook HSD 29
Sch. Sys. Enr. Code 1
Supt. – Clair Daniels, P O BOX 296 59252
ES 59252 – Jeff Arntson, prin.

Ovando, Powell Co.
Ovando ESD 11
Sch. Sys. Enr. Code 1
Supt. – (—) 59854
ES 59854 – Maureen Geary, prin.

Pablo, Lake Co.
Ronan HSD 30
Supt. – See Ronan
ES 59855 – Ida Lytton, prin.

Paradise, Sanders Co., Pop. Code 2
Paradise ESD 8
Sch. Sys. Enr. Code 1
Supt. – (—), P O BOX 126 59856
ES 59856 – James French, prin.

Park City, Stillwater Co., Pop. Code 4
Park City HSD 5
Sch. Sys. Enr. Code 2
Supt. – Ron Hatcher, P O BOX 278 59063
ES 59063 – Margit Thorndal, prin.

Peerless, Daniels Co., Pop. Code 2
Peerless HSD 2
Sch. Sys. Enr. Code 1
Supt. – Frank Loehding, P O BOX 475 59253
ES 59253 – Frank Loehding, prin.

Pendroy, Teton Co.
Pendroy ESD 61
Sch. Sys. Enr. Code 1
Supt. – (—), P O BOX 65 59467
ES 59467 – Jo Kann Bryant, prin.

Philipsburg, Granite Co., Pop. Code 4
Philipsburg HSD 1
Sch. Sys. Enr. Code 2
Supt. – Edward Longin, P O BOX 400 59858
ES, P O BOX 400 59858 – Elbert Luce, prin.

Plains, Sanders Co., Pop. Code 4
Camas Prairie ESD 11
Sch. Sys. Enr. Code 1
Supt. – (—), P O BOX 109 59859
Camas Prairie ES 59859 – Diane Alexander, prin.

Plains HSD 1
Sch. Sys. Enr. Code 3
Supt. – K. William Harvey, P O BOX 549 59859
MS, 200 W RAILROAD ST 59859
   Michael Thompson, prin.
ES, 412 RITTINOUR 59859 – K. Harvey, prin.

Plentywood, Sheridan Co., Pop. Code 4
Plentywood HSD 20
Sch. Sys. Enr. Code 3
Supt. – Doug Walsh, 100 E LAUREL AVE 59254
ES 59254 – Lowell Young, prin.

Plevna, Fallon Co., Pop. Code 2
Plevna HSD 55
Sch. Sys. Enr. Code 2
Supt. – George Baily, P O BOX 158 59344
ES 59344 – George Bailey, prin.

Polaris, Beaverhead Co.
Polaris ESD 21
Sch. Sys. Enr. Code 1
Supt. – (—), 3600 POLARIS ROAD 59725
ES, P O BOX 472 59746 – Kathleen Elser, prin.

Polson, Lake Co., Pop. Code 5
Polson HSD 23
Sch. Sys. Enr. Code 4
Supt. – Andrew Veis, 111 4TH AVE E 59860
MS 59860 – Darryl Dupuis, prin.
Cherry Valley ES 59860 – David Weld, prin.
Linderman MS 59860 – David Weld, prin.

Valley View ESD 35
Sch. Sys. Enr. Code 1
Supt. – (—), P O BOX 464 59860

Valley View ES
   RURAL ROUTE 01 BOX 152 59860
   Jonie Estell, prin.

Poplar, Roosevelt Co., Pop. Code 3
Poplar HSD 9B
Sch. Sys. Enr. Code 3
Supt. – Douglas Sullivan, P O BOX 458 59255
JHS, 400 4TH AVE W 59255 – Gary Greff, prin.
Mineral Bench ES 59255 – Donald Johnston, prin.
ES, 400 4TH AVE W 59255 – Gary Greff, prin.

Powderville, Custer Co.
Powderville ESD 2
Sch. Sys. Enr. Code 1
Supt. – (—) 59345
ES 59345 – Wilma Dodge, prin.

Power, Teton Co., Pop. Code 1
Power HSD 30
Sch. Sys. Enr. Code 2
Supt. – Larry Lehman, P O BOX 155 59468
ES 59468 – Larry Lehman, prin.

Pray, Park Co.
Arrowhead ESD 75
Sch. Sys. Enr. Code 1
Supt. – (—), P O BOX 37 59065
Arrowhead ES 59065 – Lewin Dover, prin.

Proctor, Lake Co.
Upper West Shore ESD 33
Sch. Sys. Enr. Code 1
Supt. – (—), P O BOX 155 59929
Dayton ES, UPPER WEST SHORE 59929
   Linda Gore, prin.

Pryor, Big Horn Co.
Pryor HSD 3
Sch. Sys. Enr. Code 2
Supt. – John Tietema, P O BOX 46 59066
ES, P O BOX 46 59066 – Dell Fritzier, prin.

St. Charles Indian Mission School
   P O BOX 108 59066

Ramsay, Siver Bow Co.
Ramsay ESD 3
Sch. Sys. Enr. Code 2
Supt. – (—), P O BOX 105 59748
ES 59748 – Rosemary Garvey, prin.

Rapelje, Stillwater Co., Pop. Code 1
Rapelje HSD 32
Sch. Sys. Enr. Code 1
Supt. – Leo Shepherd, P O BOX 104 59067
ES 59067 – Leo Shepherd, prin.

Raynesford, Judith Basin Co.
Raynesford ESD 49
Sch. Sys. Enr. Code 1
Supt. – (—), P O BOX 191 59469
ES 59469 – M. Anderson, prin.

Red Lodge, Carbon Co., Pop. Code 4
Jackson ESD 9
Sch. Sys. Enr. Code 1
Supt. – (—), P O BOX 784 59068
Jackson ES, RURAL ROUTE 02 BOX 3100 59068
   Margaret Sheehy, prin.

Red Lodge HSD 1
Sch. Sys. Enr. Code 2
Supt. – David Peters, P O BOX 1090 59068
Mountain View ES 59068 – Sherrie Martin, prin.
Roosevelt ES, 515 S BROADWAY 59068
   Sherrie Martin, prin.

Reedpoint, Stillwater Co., Pop. Code 2
Reedpoint HSD 9-9
Sch. Sys. Enr. Code 1
Supt. – Daryl Bertelsen, P O BOX 338 59069
ES 59069 – Daryl Bertelsen, prin.

Richey, Dawson Co., Pop. Code 2
Richey HSD 2
Sch. Sys. Enr. Code 2
Supt. – William Parker, P O BOX 16 59259
ES 59259 – William Parker, prin.

Ringling, Meagher Co.
Ringling ESD 34
Sch. Sys. Enr. Code 1
Supt. – (—), P O BOX 157 59642
ES 59642 – Elizabeth Brewer, prin.

Roberts, Carbon Co., Pop. Code 3
Roberts HSD 5
Sch. Sys. Enr. Code 3
Supt. – Ron Marshall, P O BOX 78 59013
ES, 106 MAPLE 59070 – Ron Marshall, prin.

Ronan, Lake Co., Pop. Code 4
Ronan HSD 30
Sch. Sys. Enr. Code 4
Supt. – Bob Halgren, P O BOX R 59864
JHS 59864 – Jim Gillhouse, prin.
Harvey ES 59855 – Terri O'Fallon, prin.
Other Schools – See Pablo

Rosebud, Rosebud Co., Pop. Code 5
Rosebud HSD 12
Sch. Sys. Enr. Code 2
Supt. – Dennis Fry, P O BOX 38 59347
ES 59347 – Martin Vennes, prin.

Roundup, Musselshell Co., Pop. Code 4
Roundup HSD 55-H
Sch. Sys. Enr. Code 3
Supt. – J. Jay Erdie, P O BOX 717 59072
MS, 6TH AVE & 5TH ST W 59072
Roger Brewer, prin.
Central ES, 600 1ST WEST 59072
Terry Loveland, prin.

Roy, Fergus Co., Pop. Code 2
Roy HSD 74
Sch. Sys. Enr. Code 2
Supt. – Ken Miller, P O BOX 9 59471
ES 59471 – Ken Miller, prin.

Rudyard, Hill Co., Pop. Code 3
Blue Sky HSD K
Sch. Sys. Enr. Code 2
Supt. – James Smith, P O BOX 129 59540
Blue Sky MS 59540 – James Smith, prin.
Blue Sky ES 59540 – James Smith, prin.

Ryegate, Golden Valley Co., Pop. Code 2
Ryegate HSD 1
Sch. Sys. Enr. Code 1
Supt. – Ron Bloomquist, P O BOX 127 59074
ES 59074 – Ronald Blomquist, prin.

Saco, Phillips Co., Pop. Code 2
Saco HSD B
Sch. Sys. Enr. Code 1
Supt. – Carl Knudsen, P O BOX 298 59261
ES 59261 – Carl Knudsen, prin.

Saint Ignatius, Lake Co., Pop. Code 3
St. Ignatius HSD 28
Sch. Sys. Enr. Code 3
Supt. – Harold McPherson, P O BOX 400 59865
ES, P O BOX 400 59865 – David Werdin, prin.

Saint Regis, Mineral Co., Pop. Code 2
St. Regis HSD 1
Sch. Sys. Enr. Code 2
Supt. – Ed White, P O BOX K 59866
ES 59866 – Ed White, prin.

Saltese, Mineral Co.
Saltese ESD 1
Sch. Sys. Enr. Code 1
Supt. – (—), P O BOX 3 59867
ES 59867 – Sally Coon, prin.

Sand Coulee, Cascade Co., Pop. Code 2
Sand Coulee HSD C
Sch. Sys. Enr. Code 2
Supt. – Jim Moulds 59472
Centerville ES 59472 – Kathy Moulds, prin.

Sand Springs, Garfield Co.
Benzien ESD 30
Sch. Sys. Enr. Code 1
Supt. – (—) 59077
Benzien ES 59077 – Barbara Koontz, prin.

Sand Springs ESD 42
Sch. Sys. Enr. Code 1
Supt. – (—) 59077
ES 59077 – Margaret Flint, prin.

Savage, Richland Co., Pop. Code 4
Savage HSD 2
Sch. Sys. Enr. Code 2
Supt. – John McNeil, P O BOX 127 59262
ES, 119 MESA NORTH 59262 – John McNeil, prin.

Scobey, Daniels Co., Pop. Code 4
Scobey HSD 1
Sch. Sys. Enr. Code 2
Supt. – Elbert Hatcher, P O BOX 10 59263
ES, P O BOX 10 59263 – Gary Germundson, prin.

Seeley Lake, Missoula Co., Pop. Code 4
Seeley Lake ESD 34
Sch. Sys. Enr. Code 2
Supt. – John Hebnes, P O BOX C 59868
ES 59868 – John Hebnes, prin.

Swan Valley ESD 33
Sch. Sys. Enr. Code 1
Supt. – (—), HCR ROUTE 59868
Swan Valley ES 59868 – Daniel White, prin.

Shawmut, Wheatland Co.
Shawmut ESD 20
Sch. Sys. Enr. Code 1
Supt. – (—), P O BOX 63 59078
ES 59078 – Atha Stagner, prin.

Shelby, Toole Co., Pop. Code 5
Shelby HSD 14
Sch. Sys. Enr. Code 3
Supt. – Dr. Dale Zorn, 141 6TH AVE N 59474
MS, 133 6TH AVE S 59474 – Charles Topley, prin.
Bitterroot ES, 622 N GRANITE AVE 59474
Ken Halverson, prin.
Meadowlark MS, 141 6TH AVE N 59474
Ken Halverson, prin.

Shepherd, Yellowstone Co., Pop. Code 5
Shepherd HSD 37
Sch. Sys. Enr. Code 3
Supt. – Calvin Spangler, P O BOX 08 59079
ES, 7842 SHEPHERD RD 59079
David Sharstrom, prin.

Sheridan, Madison Co., Pop. Code 3
Sheridan HSD 5
Sch. Sys. Enr. Code 2
Supt. – L. Kieckbusch, P O BOX 586 59749

ES 59749 – Brett Bassett, prin.

Sidney, Richland Co., Pop. Code 6
Brorson ESD 11
Sch. Sys. Enr. Code 1
Supt. – (—), GIRARD ROUTE 59270
Brorson ES 59270 – Linda Schieffer, prin.

Rau ESD 21
Sch. Sys. Enr. Code 1
Supt. – (—), SKAAR ROUTE BOX 4073 59270
Rau ES 59270 – Carolyn Koch, prin.

Sidney HSD 1
Sch. Sys. Enr. Code 4
Supt. – Jack Adkins, 121 5TH ST SW 59270
JHS, 415 S CENTRAL AVE 59270
Bill Nankivel, prin.
Central ES, 3RD AVE SE 59270
Charles Cummings, prin.
West Side ES, 405 11TH AVE SW 59270
C. Gabrielson, prin.

Simms, Cascade Co., Pop. Code 2
Simms HSD F
Sch. Sys. Enr. Code 2
Supt. – Fay Lesmeister, P O BOX 38 59477
Fort Shaw-Simms ES 59477 – Carl Roy, prin.

Somers, Flathead Co., Pop. Code 3
Somers ESD 29
Sch. Sys. Enr. Code 2
Supt. – (—), P O BOX 159 59932
ES 59932 – Wallace Vinnedge, prin.

Springdale, Park Co.
Springdale ESD 63-56
Sch. Sys. Enr. Code 1
Supt. – (—), P O BOX 102 59082
ES 59082 – Robin Lovec, prin.

Stanford, Judith Basin Co., Pop. Code 3
Stanford HSD 12
Sch. Sys. Enr. Code 2
Supt. – Larry Biere, P O BOX 506 59479
ES, P O BOX 506 59479 – Larry Biere, prin.

Stevensville, Ravalli Co., Pop. Code 4
Lone Rock ESD 13
Sch. Sys. Enr. Code 2
Supt. – James Palmer
994 THREE MILE CRK ROAD 59870
Lone Rock ES, 994 3-MILE CREEK ROAD 59870
Sheelia Miller, prin.

Stevensville HSD 2
Sch. Sys. Enr. Code 3
Supt. – Anthony Tognetti, 300 PARK ST 59870
JHS 59870 – Bruce Blahnik, prin.
MS 59870 – (—), prin.
ES 59870 – John Snyder, prin.

Sunburst, Toole Co., Pop. Code 2
Sunburst HSD 2
Sch. Sys. Enr. Code 2
Supt. – Alan Ryan, P O BOX 467 59482
ES 59482 – Gordon Puckett, prin.

Sun River, Cascade Co.
Sun River ESD 97
Sch. Sys. Enr. Code 2
Supt. – (—), P O BOX 1 59483
ES 59483 – Nellie Sherman, prin.

Superior, Mineral Co., Pop. Code 4
Superior HSD 3
Sch. Sys. Enr. Code 3
Supt. – William Donahue, P O BOX 400 59872
ES, 200 RIVER 59872 – John Brookins, prin.

Swan Lake, Flathead Co.
Swan Lake-Salmon Prairie ESD 73
Sch. Sys. Enr. Code 1
Supt. – (—) 59911
Salmon Prairie ES 59911 – Hazel Jones, prin.
ES 59911 – Nancy Potoczny, prin.

Terry, Prairie Co., Pop. Code 3
Terry HSD 5
Sch. Sys. Enr. Code 2
Supt. – Stanley Perkins, P O BOX 187 59349
ES, 215 EAST PARK 59349
Stanley Perkins, prin.

Thompson Falls, Sanders Co., Pop. Code 4
Thompson Falls HSD 2
Sch. Sys. Enr. Code 3
Supt. – G. Ostwald, P O BOX 129 59873
ES 59873 – Gary Morehouse, prin.

Three Forks, Gallatin Co., Pop. Code 4
Three Forks HSD J-24
Sch. Sys. Enr. Code 2
Supt. – Charles Ansley, P O BOX 616 59752
ES, 212 E NEAL 59752 – Jack Heebner, prin.

Toston, Broadwater Co.
Toston ESD 15
Sch. Sys. Enr. Code 1
Supt. – (—), P O BOX 27 59643
ES 59543 – Margaret Hogland, prin.

Townsend, Broadwater Co., Pop. Code 4
Townsend ESD 7
Sch. Sys. Enr. Code 2
Supt. – (—), P O BOX N 59644
Hazelton ES 59644 – Gerald Rodacker, prin.

Trego, Lincoln Co.
Trego ESD 53
Sch. Sys. Enr. Code 1
Supt. – (—), P O BOX 157 59934
ES 59934 – Donald Bulman, Jr., prin.

Yaak ESD 24
Supt. – See Troy
Yaak ES 59934 – Carol Patton, prin.

Trout Creek, Sanders Co.
Trout Creek ESD 6
Sch. Sys. Enr. Code 1
Supt. – (—)
RURAL ROUTE 03 BOX 141 59874
ES 59874 – Stephen Hendrick, prin.

Troy, Lincoln Co., Pop. Code 4
McCormick ESD 15
Sch. Sys. Enr. Code 1
Supt. – (—), HCR ROUTE 1 59935
McCormick ES 59935 – Bette Sanders, prin.

Sylvanite ESD 23
Sch. Sys. Enr. Code 1
Supt. – (—)
RURAL ROUTE 01 YAAK ROAD 59935
Sylvanite ES 59935 – Judy Chambers, prin.

Troy HSD 1
Sch. Sys. Enr. Code 3
Supt. – Richard Hill, P O BOX O 59935
Morrison ES 59935 – Bill Ackley, prin.

Yaak ESD 24
Sch. Sys. Enr. Code 1
Supt. – (—), RURAL ROUTE 01 59935
Other Schools – See Trego

Turner, Blaine Co., Pop. Code 2
Turner HSD 43
Sch. Sys. Enr. Code 2
Supt. – Dennis Maasjo, P O BOX 40 59542
ES 59542 – Dennis Maasjo, prin.

Twin Bridges, Madison Co., Pop. Code 2
Twin Bridges HSD 7
Sch. Sys. Enr. Code 2
Supt. – Kathleen Eaton, P O BOX AC 59754
ES 59754 – Douglas Denson, prin.

Twodot, Wheatland Co.
Two Dot ESD 15
Sch. Sys. Enr. Code 1
Supt. – (—) 59085
ES 59085 – Sue Davis, prin.

Ulm, Cascade Co., Pop. Code 2
Ulm ESD 85
Sch. Sys. Enr. Code 1
Supt. – (—), P O BOX 188 59485
ES 59485 – John Spurzem, prin.

Valier, Pondera Co., Pop. Code 3
Valier HSD 18
Sch. Sys. Enr. Code 2
Supt. – Richard Sirokman, P O BOX 528 59486
ES 59486 – Howard Hahn, prin.

Vaughn, Cascade Co., Pop. Code 2
Vaughn ESD 74
Sch. Sys. Enr. Code 2
Supt. – (—), P O BOX 279 59487
ES 59487 – Michael Button, prin.

Victor, Ravalli Co., Pop. Code 4
Victor HSD 7
Sch. Sys. Enr. Code 2
Supt. – Al McMilin, P O BOX 87 59875
ES 59875 – Lucy Lucas, prin.

Vida, McCone Co.
Southview ESD 85
Sch. Sys. Enr. Code 1
Supt. – (—)
RURAL ROUTE 02 BOX 39 59274
Southview ES 59274 – Darci Shane, prin.

Vida ESD 134
Sch. Sys. Enr. Code 1
Supt. – (—) 59274
ES 59274 – Faye Mischke, prin.

Volborg, Custer Co.
Horkan Creek ESD 94
Sch. Sys. Enr. Code 1
Supt. – (—) 59351
Horkan Creek ES 59351 – Stacey Tvedt, prin.

South Stacey ESD 90
Sch. Sys. Enr. Code 1
Supt. – (—) 59351
South Stacey ES 59351 – Zeda Dudley, prin.

Westby, Sheridan Co., Pop. Code 2
Westby HSD 3
Sch. Sys. Enr. Code 2
Supt. – Robert Otheim, P O BOX 108 59275
ES 59275 – Wayne Koterba, prin.

West Glacier, Flathead Co., Pop. Code 2
Columbia Falls HSD 6
Supt. – See Columbia Falls
ES, P O BOX 308 59936 – (—), prin.

West Glacier ESD 8
Sch. Sys. Enr. Code 1
Supt. – (—), P O BOX 308 59936
ES 59936 – Jackie Boshka, prin.

West Yellowstone, Gallatin Co., Pop. Code 3
West Yellowstone HSD 69
Sch. Sys. Enr. Code 2
Supt. – Donald Black, P O BOX 460 59758
ES, 121 MADISON 59758 – Donald Black, prin.

Whitefish, Flathead Co., Pop. Code 5
Olney -Bissell ESD 58
Sch. Sys. Enr. Code 1
Supt. – (—)
  5955 FARM TO MARKET ROAD 59937
Bissell ES, 5955 FARM TO MARKET RD 59937
  Philip Santee, prin.

Whitefish HSD 44
Sch. Sys. Enr. Code 4
Supt. – Ivan Hernandez, P O BOX 198 59937
Whitefish-Central JHS 59937 – Joe Malletta, prin.
Central 5-6 MS, 2ND & SPOKANE 59937
  Terry Nelson, prin.
Muldown ES, E 7TH ST 59937
  Roberta Barrett, prin.

Whitehall, Jefferson Co., Pop. Code 4
Whitehall HSD 2
Sch. Sys. Enr. Code 3
Supt. – Lyle Barringer, P O BOX 400 59759
JHS, 111 W YELLOWSTONE 59759
  Frank Magee, prin.
ES, 309 N DIVISION 59759 – Frank MaGee, prin.

White Sulphur Springs, Meagher Co., Pop. Code 4
White Sulphur Springs HSD 8
Sch. Sys. Enr. Code 2
Supt. – Frank Nelson, P O BOX C 59645
Martinsdale ES 59645 – Marsha Lindner, prin.
White Sulphur Springs ES
  405 CENTRAL AVE S 59645
  Marsha Lindner, prin.

Whitewater, Phillips Co., Pop. Code 3
Whitewater HSD D
Sch. Sys. Enr. Code 1
Supt. – Roger Britton, P O BOX 46 59544
ES 59544 – Roger Britton, prin.

Whitlash, Liberty Co.
Whitlash ESD 27
Sch. Sys. Enr. Code 1
Supt. – (—), P O BOX 91 59545
ES 59545 – Becky Weinert, prin.

Wibaux, Wibaux Co., Pop. Code 3
Wibaux HSD 6
Sch. Sys. Enr. Code 2
Supt. – Michael Nicosia, P O BOX 235 59353
ES, 400 W NOLAN AVE 59353
  Michael Nicosia, prin.

Willow Creek, Gallatin Co.
Willow Creek HSD 15
Sch. Sys. Enr. Code 1
Supt. – Russ Steinebach, P O BOX 198 59760
ES 59760 – Russ Steinebach, prin.

Wilsall, Park Co., Pop. Code 2
Wilsall HSD 3
Sch. Sys. Enr. Code 2
Supt. – Garret Franks, P O BOX 131 59086
ES 59086 – Garret Franks, prin.

Winifred, Fergus Co., Pop. Code 2
Winifred HSD 15
Sch. Sys. Enr. Code 2
Supt. – Carroll Lindsey 59489
ES 59489 – Carroll Lindsey, prin.

Winnett, Petroleum Co., Pop. Code 2
Winnett HSD 1
Sch. Sys. Enr. Code 2
Supt. – Dan Nelsen, P O BOX 167 59087
ES 59087 – Dan Nelsen, prin.

Wisdom, Beaverhead Co.
Wisdom ESD 16
Sch. Sys. Enr. Code 1
Supt. – (—), P O BOX 2 59761
ES, P O BOX 2 59761 – Gloria Reed, prin.

Wise River, Beaverhead Co.
Wise River ESD 11
Sch. Sys. Enr. Code 1
Supt. – (—) 59762
ES 59762 – Barbara Gneiting, prin.

Wolf Creek, Lewis and Clark Co.
Auchard Creek ESD 27
Sch. Sys. Enr. Code 1
Supt. – (—) 59648
Auchard Creek ES 59648 – Deborah Craven, prin.

Craig ESD 25
Sch. Sys. Enr. Code 1
Supt. – (—) 59648
Craig ES 59648 – Janice Dempsey, prin.

Wolf Creek ESD 13
Sch. Sys. Enr. Code 1
Supt. – (—), P O BOX 196 59648
ES 59648 – Leanne Wirth, prin.

Wolf Point, Roosevelt Co., Pop. Code 5
Frontier ESD 3
Sch. Sys. Enr. Code 2
Supt. – Milton Molsberry, P O BOX 3043 59201
Frontier ES 59201 – Milton Mosberry, prin.

Prairie Elk ESD 6
Sch. Sys. Enr. Code 1
Supt. – (—), P O BOX 4061 59201
Prairie Elk ES, P O BOX 4062 59201
  Estelle Maychrzak, prin.

Wolf Point HSD 45A
Sch. Sys. Enr. Code 4
Supt. – Rob Kinna, 213 6TH AVE S 59201
JHS, 213 6TH AVE S 59201
  William Gilman, prin.
North Side MS, 710 4TH AVE N 59201
  Tomas Anderson, prin.
South Side ES, 415 4TH AVE S 59201
  Richard Rossignol, prin.

Worden, Yellowstone Co., Pop. Code 2
Huntley Project HSD 24
Sch. Sys. Enr. Code 3
Supt. – Ramona Stout 59088
Huntley Project MS 59088
  Nickolas Schuering, prin.
Huntley Project ES 59088 – Lynda Drayson, prin.

Wyola, Big Horn Co.
Wyola SD 29
Sch. Sys. Enr. Code 1
Supt. – William LaForge, P O BOX 66 59089
JHS 59089 – William LaForge, prin.
ES 59089 – William Laforge, prin.

Zortman, Phillips Co.
Malta HSD A
Supt. – See Malta
ES 59538 – Mary Licht, prin.

Zurich, Blaine Co.
Zurich ESD 17
Sch. Sys. Enr. Code 1
Supt. – (—) 59547
ES 59547 – Pattie Ross, prin.

NEBRASKA

STATE DEPARTMENT OF EDUCATION
301 Centennial Mall South
P.O. Box 94987, Lincoln 68509
(402) 471-2367

Commissioner of Education	Joe Lutjeharms
Deputy Commissioner	Larry Vontz
Associate Commissioner Rehabilitation Services	Jason Andrew
Assistant Commissioner School Assistance & Support	Gerald Sughroue
Assistant Commissioner Vocational Education	Marge Harouff
Associate Commisioner State Schools	Jason Andrew

STATE BOARD OF EDUCATION
Max Larsen, *President* Lincoln

COORDINATING COMMISSION FOR POSTSECONDARY EDUCATION
Dr. William S. Fuller, *Executive Director* P.O. Box 95005, Lincoln 68509

COUNTY SUPERINTENDENTS OF SCHOOLS

Adams County, Glen Larsen, Supt.
  P O BOX 1088, Hastings 68901
Antelope County, Franklin Rempp, Supt.
  Neligh 68756
Arthur County, Frances Vasa, Supt.
  P O BOX 166, Arthur 69121
Banner County, Frank Madison, Supt.
  P O BOX 5, Harrisburg 69345
Blaine County, Gary Amen, Supt.
  P O BOX 98, Dunning 68833

Boone County, Lila Carter, Supt.
  222 S 4TH, Albion 68620
Box Butte County, Mary Jo Hoffman, Supt.
  5TH & BOX BUTTE, Alliance 69301
Boyd County, Linda Merchen, Supt.
  P O BOX 136, Butte 68722
Brown County, Audrey Wilson, Supt.
  148 W 4TH ST, Ainsworth 69210
Buffalo County, Alice Heckman, Supt.
  Kearney 68847

Burt County, Clinton Carr, Supt.
  111 N 13TH ST, Tekamah 68061
Butler County, Frank Parish, Supt.
  475 3RD ST, David City 68632
Cass County, H. Lancaster, Supt.
  Plattsmouth 68048
Cedar County, Ted Hillman, Supt.
  Hartington 68739
Chase County, Opal Fortcamp, Supt.
  P O BOX 548, Imperial 69033

Cherry County, Barbara Reed, Supt.
  P O BOX 118, Valentine 69201
Cheyenne County, William Kelley, Supt.
  P O BOX 77, Sidney 69162
Clay County, Sam Townsend, Supt.
  111 W FAIRFIELD ST, Clay Center 68933
Colfax County, Tom Narak, Supt.
  411 E 11TH ST, Schuyler 68661
Cuming County, Margaret Graves, Supt.
  West Point 68788
Custer County, Hayes McGraw, Supt.
  Broken Bow 68822
Dakota County, Mel Waldner, Supt.
  P O BOX 340, Homer 68030
Dawes County, Ida Holst, Supt.
  451 MAIN ST, Chadron 69337
Dawson County, Katherine Eliker, Supt.
  Lexington 68850
Deuel County, John Jones, Supt.
  P O BOX 608, Chappell 69129
Dixon County, Lionel Froseth, Supt.
  P O BOX 308, Ponca 68770
Dodge County, Cecil Walker, Supt.
  435 N PACK #105, Fremont 68025
Douglas County, Marvin Johnson, Supt.
  1819 FARNAM ST, Omaha 68183
Fillmore County, Jesse Graham, Supt.
  P O BOX 349, Geneva 68361
Franklin County, Aveline Howell, Supt.
  P O BOX 214, Franklin 68939
Frontier County, Ruby Kohler, Supt.
  P O BOX 39, Stockville 69042
Furnas County, Kurtis Bowden, Supt.
  Beaver City 68926
Gage County, Elvin Schultz, Supt.
  Beatrice 68310
Garden County, Corwin Arndt, Supt.
  P O BOX 488, Oshkosh 69154
Garfield County, Joyce Huffman, Supt.
  P O BOX 651, Burwell 68823
Gosper County, Rosemary Stagemeyer, Supt.
  P O BOX 125, Elwood 68937
Grant County, Barbara Rothwell, Supt.
  Hyannis 69350
Greeley County, James Beck, Supt.
  P O BOX 250, Greeley 68842
Hall County, Betty Saunders, Supt.
  114 E COURT ST, Grand Island 68801
Hamilton County, Russell Hoppner, Supt.
  Aurora 68818
Harlan County, Marilyn Shaffer, Supt.
  Alma 68920

Hayes County, Dewey Harouff, Supt.
  P O BOX 8, Hayes Center 69032
Hitchcock County, Mary Goodenberger, Supt.
  Trenton 69044
Holt County, Joseph Workman, Supt.
  O'Neill 68763
Hooker County, Robert Mandeville, Supt.
  P O BOX 127, Mullen 69152
Howard County, Douglas Ackles, Supt.
  P O BOX 268, Saint Paul 68873
Jefferson County, Dale Mooberry, Supt.
  Fairbury 68352
Johnson County, J. Stewart Catlett, Supt.
  P O BOX 687, Tecumseh 68450
Kearney County, Sarah Jepsen, Supt.
  P O BOX 105, Minden 68959
Keith County, Sidney Chase, Supt.
  P O BOX 269, Ogallala 69153
Keya Paha County, Donita Bammerlin, Supt.
  P O BOX 9, Springview 68778
Kimball County, Darryl Kile, Supt.
  301 S HOWARD ST, Kimball 69145
Knox County, Robert Jacobs, Supt.
  Center 68724
Lancaster County, William Workman, Supt.
  P O BOX 82889, Lincoln 68501
Lincoln County, Katy Varicak, Supt.
  North Platte 69101
Logan County, George Rogers, Supt.
  P O BOX 128, Stapleton 69163
Loup County, Christina Kochenash, Supt.
  P O BOX 170, Taylor 68879
Madison County, Douglas Jensen, Supt.
  P O BOX 210, Madison 68748
McPherson County, Karen Hunn, Supt.
  Tryon 69167
Merrick County, Gerald Carnes, Supt.
  Central City 68826
Morrill County, Hazel Varley, Supt.
  P O BOX 730, Bridgeport 69336
Nance County, Wayne Nicholls, Supt.
  P O BOX 70, Fullerton 68638
Nemaha County, Robert Smith, Supt.
  1824 N ST, Auburn 68305
Nuckolls County, William Classen, Supt.
  150 S MAIN, Nelson 68961
Otoe County, Ronald Wenninghoff, Supt.
  Nebraska City 68410
Pawnee County, Gary Beda, Supt.
  P O BOX 272, Pawnee City 68420
Perkins County, Lavonne Mrasek, Supt.
  P O BOX 236, Grant 69140

Phelps County, Emmett Gannon, Supt.
  715 5TH AVE, Holdrege 68949
Pierce County, Tilton Weber, Supt.
  P O BOX 85, Pierce 68767
Platte County, Lila Carter, Supt.
  2610 14TH ST, Columbus 68601
Polk County, Margaret Norton, Supt.
  P O BOX 275, Osceola 68651
Red Willow County, Lamoine Carmichael, Supt.
  P O BOX 875, Mc Cook 69001
Richardson County, Robert Smith, Supt.
  Falls City 68355
Rock County, Jane Peterson, Supt.
  Bassett 68714
Saline County, Eleanor Colvin, Supt.
  215 S COURT, Wilber 68465
Sarpy County, Lloyd Boilesen, Supt.
  1210 GOLDEN GATE DRIVE, Papillion 68046
Saunders County, Charles Runty, Supt.
  Wahoo 68066
Scotts Bluff County, Howard Backous, Supt.
  1825 10TH ST, Gering 69341
Seward County, Larry Bonner, Supt.
  P O BOX 10, Milford 68405
Sheridan County, Charles Smith, Supt.
  P O BOX 451, Rushville 69360
Sherman County, Eldon Kieborz, Supt.
  Loup City 68853
Sioux County, Grace Wilwand, Supt.
  P O BOX 115, Harrison 69346
Stanton County, Mary Timperley, Supt.
  P O BOX 498, Stanton 68779
Thayer County, Arlys Dill, Supt.
  220 N 4TH ST, Hebron 68370
Thomas County, William Raduenz, Supt.
  P O BOX 248, Thedford 69166
Thurston County, Ervin DeBoer, Supt.
  P O BOX 178, Pender 68047
Valley County, Eldon Kieborz, Supt.
  510 PEARL ST, Ord 68862
Washington County, James McDowell, Supt.
  Blair 68008
Wayne County, Glenn Wiseman, Supt.
  510 N PEARL ST, Wayne 68787
Webster County, Eunice Fritz, Supt.
  Red Cloud 68970
Wheeler County, John Ringlein, Supt.
  P O BOX 68, Bartlett 68622
York County, Paul Toms, Supt.
  611 PLATTE AVE, York 68467

PUBLIC, PRIVATE, AND PAROCHIAL ELEMENTARY SCHOOLS

Adams, Gage Co., Pop. Code 2
Adams SD
Sch. Sys. Enr. Code 2
Supt. – K. Nelson, P O BOX 107 68301
ES, P O BOX 107 68301 – Kenneth Nelson, prin.

Ainsworth, Brown Co., Pop. Code 4
Ainsworth SD
Sch. Sys. Enr. Code 2
Supt. – Gerald Ehlers, P O BOX 65 69210
ES, P O BOX 65 69210 – Thomas Hall, prin.

Albion, Boone Co., Pop. Code 4
Albion SD
Sch. Sys. Enr. Code 3
Supt. – Richard Stephens, 550 S FIFTH ST 68620
ES, 550 S FIFTH ST 68620 – Myron Synovec, prin.

St. Michaels School, 520 W CHURCH 68620

Allen, Dixon Co., Pop. Code 2
Allen SD
Sch. Sys. Enr. Code 2
Supt. – John Werner, P O BOX 190 68710
ES, P O BOX 190 68710 – (—), prin.

Alliance, Box Butte Co., Pop. Code 6
Alliance SD
Sch. Sys. Enr. Code 4
Supt. – Martin Peterson
  1450 BOX BUTTE AVE 69301
MS, 1112 LARAMIE AVE 69301
  Derald Morgan, prin.
Central ES, 715 BOX BUTTE AVE 69301
  Lowell Gaswick, prin.
Emerson ES, 8TH & BLACK HILL 69301
  Larry Butzine, prin.
Grandview ES, 615 GRAND AVE 69301
  Floyd Colwell, prin.

St. Agnes Academy, 1104 CHEYENNE AVE 69301

Alma, Harlan Co., Pop. Code 4
Alma SD
Sch. Sys. Enr. Code 2
Supt. – Eugene McCue, P O BOX 170 68920
ES, P O BOX 170 68920 – Paul Joseph, prin.
Alma ES at Republican City, P O BOX 170 68920
  Eugene McCue, prin.

Amherst, Buffalo Co., Pop. Code 2
Amherst SD
Sch. Sys. Enr. Code 2
Supt. – Elton Teter, P O BOX 8 68812
ES, P O BOX 8 68812 – Elton Teter, prin.

Ansley, Custer Co., Pop. Code 3
Ansley SD
Sch. Sys. Enr. Code 2
Supt. – Floyd Ruhl, P O BOX 370 68814

ES, P O BOX 370 68814 – Floyd Ruhl, prin.

Arapahoe, Furnas Co., Pop. Code 4
Arapahoe SD
Sch. Sys. Enr. Code 2
Supt. – George Robertson, P O BOX 466 68922
ES, P O BOX 466 68922 – Neva Kanost, prin.

Arcadia, Valley Co., Pop. Code 2
Arcadia SD
Sch. Sys. Enr. Code 2
Supt. – Charles Finley, P O BOX 248 68815
ES, P O BOX 248 68815 – Charles Finley, prin.

Arlington, Washington Co., Pop. Code 4
Arlington SD
Sch. Sys. Enr. Code 3
Supt. – Michael Marrymee, P O BOX K 68002
ES, P O BOX K 68002 – Laverne McKown, prin.

Arnold, Custer Co., Pop. Code 3
Arnold SD
Sch. Sys. Enr. Code 2
Supt. – Robert Reed 69120
ES 69120 – Robert Reed, prin.

Ashland, Saunders Co., Pop. Code 4
Ashland Greenwood SD
Sch. Sys. Enr. Code 3
Supt. – Craig Pease, 12TH & BOYD ST 68003
Ashland-Greenwood ES, 1200 BOYD ST 68003
  Thomas Sandberg, prin.

Ashton, Sherman Co., Pop. Code 2
Loup City SD
Supt. – See Loup City
ES at Ashton 68817 – Larry Hiatt, prin.

Atkinson, Holt Co., Pop. Code 4
Atkinson ESD
Sch. Sys. Enr. Code 2
Supt. – William Gall, P O BOX 370 68713
ES, P O BOX 370 68713 – William Gail, prin.

Auburn, Nemaha Co., Pop. Code 5
Auburn SD
Sch. Sys. Enr. Code 3
Supt. – Myron Ballain, 1406 22ND ST 68305
MS, 1713 J ST 68305 – Leo Dietrich, prin.
Calvert ES, 2103 O ST 68305
  Robert Robinson, prin.
Sheridan ES, 1110 M ST 68305
  Robert Robinson, prin.
Other Schools – See Peru

Aurora, Hamilton Co., Pop. Code 5
Aurora SD
Sch. Sys. Enr. Code 4
Supt. – Donald Burling, 3RD & L ST 68818
ES, 3RD & H ST 68818 – James Johnson, prin.

Axtell, Kearney Co., Pop. Code 3
Axtell Comm. SD
Sch. Sys. Enr. Code 2
Supt. – Samuel Bell, P O BOX 97 68924
ES, P O BOX 97 68924 – James Dimon, prin.

Bancroft, Cuming Co., Pop. Code 3
Bancroft-Rosalie SD
Sch. Sys. Enr. Code 2
Supt. – William Lewis, P O BOX 128 68004
Other Schools – See Rosalie

Bartlett, Wheeler Co., Pop. Code 2
Wheeler Central SD
Sch. Sys. Enr. Code 2
Supt. – John Ringlein, P O BOX 68 68622
Wheeler Central ES, P O BOX 68 68622
  John Ringlein, prin.

Bartley, Red Willow Co., Pop. Code 2
Bartley SD
Sch. Sys. Enr. Code 2
Supt. – Glen Troyer, P O BOX 187 69020
ES, P O BOX 187 69020 – Barbara Andrews, prin.

Bassett, Rock Co., Pop. Code 4
Bassett ESD
Sch. Sys. Enr. Code 2
Supt. – Robert Risler, P O BOX 407 68714
ES, P O BOX 407 68714 – Robert Rissier, prin.

Battle Creek, Madison Co., Pop. Code 3
Battle Creek SD
Sch. Sys. Enr. Code 2
Supt. – Delno Fuelberth, P O BOX 190 68715
ES, P O BOX 190 68715 – Beverly Bayne, prin.

St. Johns Lutheran ES, P O BOX 67 68715

Bayard, Morrill Co., Pop. Code 4
Bayard SD
Sch. Sys. Enr. Code 3
Supt. – Clayton Cundall, P O BOX 607 69334
ES, P O BOX 607 69334 – Lionel Wickard, prin.

Beatrice, Gage Co.
Beatrice SD
Sch. Sys. Enr. Code 4
Supt. – Robert Cothren, 213 N 5TH ST 68310
Cedar ES, 201 CEDAR ST 68310
  Loren Park, prin.
Lincoln ES, 500 N 19TH ST 68310
  Loren Park, prin.
Paddock Lane ES, 1300 N 14TH ST 68310
  Elizabeth Replogle, prin.
Stoddard ES, 400 S 7TH ST 68310
  Melvin Tekolste, prin.

St. Joseph ES, 420 N 6TH ST 68310
St. Pauls Lutheran ES, 930 PRAIRIE LN 68310

Beaver City, Furnas Co., Pop. Code 3
Beaver City SD
Sch. Sys. Enr. Code 2
Supt. – John Windhusen, P O BOX 130 68926
ES, P O BOX 130 68926 – John Windhusen, prin.

Beemer, Cuming Co., Pop. Code 3
Beemer SD
Sch. Sys. Enr. Code 2
Supt. – Ernest Heidt, P O BOX 176 68716
ES, P O BOX 176 68716 – Ernest Heidt, prin.

Bellevue, Sarpy Co., Pop. Code 7
Bellevue SD
Sch. Sys. Enr. Code 6
Supt. – Richard Triplett
    2009 FRANKLIN ST 68005
Avery ES, 2107 E AVERY RD 68005
    Rose Ann Trinkle, prin.
Barber ES, 1402 MAIN ST 68005 – (—), prin.
Belleaire ES, 1200 W MISSION AVE 68005
    George Hon, prin.
Betz ES, 27TH & VANBUREN ST 68005
    Doris Shoffner, prin.
Birchcrest ES
    HWY 131 & BIRCHCREST ROAD 68005
    Nicholas Blake, prin.
Central ES, 22ND AND MADISON ST 68005
    (—), prin.
Twin Ridge ES, 1400 SUNBURY DR 68005
    Ray Nesbitt, prin.
Wake Robin ES, 700 LINCOLN RD 68005
    Ronald Giller, prin.
Other Schools – See Omaha
_____

St. Bernadette ES, 7600 S 42ND ST 68005
St. Mary ES, 903 W MISSION AVE 68005

Benedict, York Co., Pop. Code 2
Benedict SD
Sch. Sys. Enr. Code 2
Supt. – Kenneth Brown, P O BOX 135 68316
ES, P O BOX 135 68316 – Rodney Oldenburg, prin.

Benkelman, Dundy Co., Pop. Code 4
Dundy County
Sch. Sys. Enr. Code 2
Supt. – Douglas Nollette, P O BOX 443 69021
ES, P O BOX 586 69021 – Dan Van Dyke, prin.
Other Schools – See Haigler

Bennet, Lancaster Co., Pop. Code 3
Palmyra SD
Supt. – See Palmyra
ES at Bennet, 50 DOGWOOD 68317
    George Conrad, prin.

Bennington, Douglas Co., Pop. Code 3
Bennington SD
Sch. Sys. Enr. Code 2
Supt. – Kenneth Rasmussen, P O BOX 98 68007
ES, P O BOX 265 68007 – Carol Fichter, prin.

Bertrand, Phelps Co., Pop. Code 3
Bertrand SD
Sch. Sys. Enr. Code 2
Supt. – Kendall Moseley, 503 SCHOOL ST 68927
ES, 503 SCHOOL ST 68927 – Carl Wells, prin.

Big Springs, Deuel Co., Pop. Code 3
Big Springs SD
Sch. Sys. Enr. Code 2
Supt. – Donald Osborn, P O BOX 457 69122
ES, P O BOX 457 69122
    Darrell Farnsworth, prin.

Bladen, Webster Co., Pop. Code 2
Silver Lake SD
Supt. – See Roseland
Silver Lake ES, P O BOX 127 68928
    Gale McDonald, prin.

Blair, Washington Co., Pop. Code 6
Blair Comm. SD
Sch. Sys. Enr. Code 4
Supt. – Gerald Otte, 140 S 16TH ST 68008
Blair Central MS, 16TH & COLFAX 68008
    Roger Petersen, prin.
Blair North ES, 14 PARK ST 68008
    Adrienne Lehl, prin.
Blair South ES, 16 BUTLER ST 68008
    Adrienne Lehl, prin.
Blair West ES, 23 WASHINGTON ST 68008
    Adrienne Lehl, prin.

Bloomfield, Knox Co., Pop. Code 4
Bloomfield SD
Sch. Sys. Enr. Code 2
Supt. – John Post, 311 E BENTON 68718
ES, 514 S MCNAMARA 68718
    Richard Kaiser, prin.

Blue Hill, Webster Co., Pop. Code 3
Blue Hill SD
Sch. Sys. Enr. Code 2
Supt. – Vaden Lane, P O BOX 217 68930
ES, P O BOX 155 68930 – James Duval, prin.

Blue Springs, Gage Co., Pop. Code 3
Southern SD 1
Supt. – See Wymore
Southern ES, 115 S 11TH ST 68318
    Ken Jujath, prin.

Bradshaw, York Co., Pop. Code 2
Bradshaw SD
Sch. Sys. Enr. Code 2
Supt. – Richard Berthold, P O BOX 98 68319

ES, P O BOX 98 68319 – Richard Berthold, prin.

Brady, Lincoln Co., Pop. Code 2
Brady SD
Sch. Sys. Enr. Code 2
Supt. – Lewis Shoff, P O BOX 68 69123
ES, P O BOX 68 69123 – Lewis Shoff, prin.

Brainard, Butler Co., Pop. Code 2
East Butler SD
Sch. Sys. Enr. Code 2
Supt. – Richard Dostal, P O BOX 36 68626
ES at Brainard, P O BOX 36 68626
    Richard Dostal, prin.
Other Schools – See Dwight

Brewster, Blaine Co., Pop. Code 1
Sandhills SD
Supt. – See Dunning
ES at Brewster, P O BOX 98 68821
    Gary Amen, prin.

Bridgeport, Morrill Co., Pop. Code 4
Bridgeport SD
Sch. Sys. Enr. Code 2
Supt. – James Putman, P O BOX 430 69336
ES, P O BOX 430 69336 – Myron Lembke, prin.

Brock, Nemaha Co., Pop. Code 2
Johnson-Brock SD
Supt. – See Johnson
ES at Brock 68320 – Edward Rastovski, prin.

Broken Bow, Custer Co., Pop. Code 5
Broken Bow SD
Sch. Sys. Enr. Code 3
Supt. – Donald Vanderheiden
    322 N 9TH AVE 68822
MS, 322 N 9TH AVE 68822 – Louis Stithem, prin.
Custer ES, 727 S 6TH AVE 68822
    Ross Ridenour, prin.
North Park ES, 1135 N H ST 68822
    Ross Ridenour, prin.

Brule, Keith Co., Pop. Code 2
Brule SD
Sch. Sys. Enr. Code 2
Supt. – John Frates
    RURAL ROUTE 01 BOX 09 69127
ES, RURAL ROUTE 01 BOX 9 69127
    (—), prin.

Bruning, Thayer Co., Pop. Code 2
Bruning SD
Sch. Sys. Enr. Code 2
Supt. – Wayne Koehler, P O BOX 70 68322
ES, P O BOX 70 68322 – Gary Cooper, prin.

Brunswick, Antelope Co., Pop. Code 2
Plainview SD
Supt. – See Plainview
ES at Brunswick 68720 – (—), prin.

Burwell, Garfield Co., Pop. Code 4
Burwell ESD
Sch. Sys. Enr. Code 2
Supt. – Joe Micanek, P O BOX 790 68823
ES, P O BOX 790 68823 – Joe Micanek, prin.

Butte, Boyd Co., Pop. Code 3
Butte SD
Sch. Sys. Enr. Code 2
Supt. – Bernard Straatmeyer, P O BOX 139 68722
ES, P O BOX 139 68722
    Benard Straatmeyer, prin.

Byron, Thayer Co., Pop. Code 2
Chester-Hubbell- Byron SD
Supt. – See Chester
ES at Byron, P O BOX 115 68325
    Kenneth Mahlin, prin.

Cairo, Hall Co., Pop. Code 3
Centura SD
Sch. Sys. Enr. Code 3
Supt. – Robert Norvell 68824
Centura ES 68824 – Steve Wilson, prin.

Callaway, Custer Co., Pop. Code 3
Callaway SD
Sch. Sys. Enr. Code 2
Supt. – James Grove, P O BOX 188 68825
ES, P O BOX 188 68825 – James Grove, prin.

Cambridge, Furnas Co., Pop. Code 4
Cambridge SD
Sch. Sys. Enr. Code 2
Supt. – James Tenopir, P O BOX 100 69022
ES, P O BOX 100 69022 – Robert Fuller, prin.

Campbell, Franklin Co., Pop. Code 2
Campbell SD
Sch. Sys. Enr. Code 2
Supt. – Luther Heller, P O BOX 218 68932
ES, P O BOX 218 68932 – (—), prin.

Carroll, Wayne Co., Pop. Code 2
Wayne SD
Supt. – See Wayne
ES 68787 – David Lutt, prin.

Cedar Bluffs, Saunders Co., Pop. Code 3
Cedar Bluffs SD
Sch. Sys. Enr. Code 2
Supt. – Lawrence McMann, P O BOX 66 68015
ES, P O BOX 66 68015 – Lawrence McMann, prin.

Cedar Rapids, Boone Co., Pop. Code 2
Cedar Rapids SD
Sch. Sys. Enr. Code 2
Supt. – Clifford Tegler, P O BOX M 68627
JHS, P O BOX M 68627 – (—), prin.
ES, P O BOX M 68627 – Clifford Tegler, prin.

Central City, Merrick Co., Pop. Code 5
Central City SD
Sch. Sys. Enr. Code 3
Supt. – Gerald Carnes, 1804 14TH AVE 68826
MS, 1804 14TH AVE 68826 – Gregg Wibbels, prin.
Central City North Ward ES
    1804 14TH AVE 68826 – James Davis, prin.
Central City South Ward ES
    1804 14TH AVE 68826 – James Davis, prin.

Ceresco, Saunders Co., Pop. Code 3
Raymond Central SD
Supt. – See Raymond
ES at Ceresco, P O BOX 10 68017
    Kristine Wolzen, prin.

Chadron, Dawes Co., Pop. Code 6
Chadron SD
Sch. Sys. Enr. Code 4
Supt. – Stephen Sexton, 7TH & ANN 69337
MS, 6TH & ANN 69337 – Henry Reitz, prin.
Chadron East Ward ES, 7TH & ANN 69337
    Donald Ross, prin.
Kenwood ES, W NORFOLK 69337
    Donald Ross, prin.

Chambers, Holt Co., Pop. Code 2
Chambers SD
Sch. Sys. Enr. Code 2
Supt. – Fred Boelter, P O BOX 218 68725
ES, P O BOX 218 68725 – Fred Boelter, prin.

Chappell SD
Supt. – See Chappell
Chappell ES, P O BOX 218 68725
    Darrell Lenz, prin.

Chappell, Deuel Co., Pop. Code 4
Chappell SD
Sch. Sys. Enr. Code 2
Supt. – John Jones, 3RD & WASHINGTON 69129
Other Schools – See Chambers

Chester, Thayer Co., Pop. Code 2
Chester-Hubbell- Byron SD
Sch. Sys. Enr. Code 2
Supt. – Kenneth Mahlin, P O BOX 337 68327
ES at Chester, P O BOX 337 68327
    Kenneth Mahlin, prin.
Other Schools – See Byron

Clarks, Merrick Co., Pop. Code 2
Clarks SD
Sch. Sys. Enr. Code 2
Supt. – Richard Ziegler, P O BOX 205 68628
ES, P O BOX 205 68628 – Richard Ziegler, prin.

Clarkson, Colfax Co., Pop. Code 3
Clarkson SD
Sch. Sys. Enr. Code 2
Supt. – David Rokusek, P O BOX G 68629
ES, P O BOX G 68629 – David Rokusek, prin.

Clay Center, Clay Co., Pop. Code 3
Clay Center SD
Sch. Sys. Enr. Code 2
Supt. – Sam Townsend, P O BOX 125 68933
ES, P O BOX 125 68933 – Timothy Hoffman, prin.

Clearwater, Antelope Co., Pop. Code 2
Clearwater SD
Sch. Sys. Enr. Code 2
Supt. – James Woodward, P O BOX 38 68726
ES, P O BOX 38 68726
    Alice Braunersreuther, prin.

Cody, Cherry Co., Pop. Code 2
Cody-Kilgore SD
Sch. Sys. Enr. Code 2
Supt. – Louis Hagan, P O BOX 216 69211
Other Schools – See Kilgore

Coleridge, Cedar Co., Pop. Code 3
Coleridge Comm. SD
Sch. Sys. Enr. Code 2
Supt. – W. Schnoor, P O BOX 37 68727
ES, P O BOX 37 68727 – William Schnoor, prin.

Columbus, Platte Co., Pop. Code 7
Columbus SD
Sch. Sys. Enr. Code 5
Supt. – Fred Bellum, 2508 27TH ST 68601
MS, 1661 25TH AVE 68601 – Gary Kruse, prin.
Columbus North Park ES, 2200 31ST ST 68601
    John Ernst, prin.
Columbus West Park ES, 4100 ADAMY ST 68601
    Patricia Beckenhauer, prin.
Emerson ES, 2059 24TH AVE 68601
    John Ernst, prin.
Field ES, 1610 9TH ST 68601 – Hugh Polson, prin.
Highland Park ES, 3418 15TH ST 68601
    Patricia Beckenhauer, prin.
Lost Creek ES, RURAL ROUTE 06 68601
    Donald Gronemeyer, prin.
Williams ES, 2316 9TH ST 68601
    Hugh Polson, prin.
Other Schools – See Duncan
_____

Immanuel Lutheran ES, 2520 28TH ST 68601
St. Anthony ES, 6TH ST 68601
St. Bonaventure ES, 1604 15TH ST 68601

St. Isadore ES, 3821 20TH ST   68601

Cook, Johnson Co., Pop. Code 2
Nemaha Valley SD
Sch. Sys. Enr. Code 2
Supt. – Gary Oxley, P O BOX 255   68329
Other Schools – See Talmage

Cozad, Dawson Co., Pop. Code 5
Cozad CSD
Sch. Sys. Enr. Code 3
Supt. – Rodney Koch, P O BOX 268   69130
MS, 815 AVE C   69130 – Randell Peck, prin.
Central ES, 808 AVENUE C   69130
　Allen Wright, prin.
Cozad East ES, 420 E 14TH ST   69130
　Allen Wright, prin.
Cozad North ES, 420 W 14TH ST   69130
　Allen Wright, prin.

Crawford, Dawes Co., Pop. Code 4
Crawford SD
Sch. Sys. Enr. Code 2
Supt. – Wayne Ferguson, P O BOX 543   69339
ES, P O BOX 543   69339 – Ann Garvin, prin.

Creighton, Knox Co., Pop. Code 4
Creighton SD
Sch. Sys. Enr. Code 2
Supt. – James Micek, 1609 REDICK AVE   68729
ES, P O BOX 87   68729 – Robert Rabe, prin.

Crete, Saline Co., Pop. Code 5
Crete SD
Sch. Sys. Enr. Code 4
Supt. – John Rogers, 920 LINDEN AVE   68333
ES, 920 LINDEN AVE   68333 – Robert Sykes, prin.

St. James ES, 515 E 14TH ST   68333

Crofton, Knox Co., Pop. Code 3
Crofton Comm. SD
Sch. Sys. Enr. Code 2
Supt. – Randall Anderson, P O BOX 229   68730
ES   68730 – John Bergonzi, prin.

St. Rose of Lima ES
　5TH & IOWA ST BOX 164   68730

Culbertson, Hitchcock Co., Pop. Code 3
Culbertson SD
Sch. Sys. Enr. Code 2
Supt. – Marvin Schleeman, P O BOX 128   69024
ES, P O BOX 138   69024 – Marvin Schleeman, prin.

Curtis, Frontier Co., Pop. Code 4
Medicine Valley SD
Sch. Sys. Enr. Code 2
Supt. – Jerry Neff, P O BOX 450   69025
Medicine Valley ES, P O BOX 65   69025
　Terry Storm, prin.

Dakota City, Dakota Co., Pop. Code 4
South Sioux City SD
Supt. – See South Sioux City
ES   68731 – Roger Winterlin, prin.

Dalton, Cheyenne Co., Pop. Code 2
Leyton SD
Sch. Sys. Enr. Code 2
Supt. – Donal Bartling, P O BOX 97   69131
Other Schools – See Gurley

Danbury, Red Willow Co., Pop. Code 2
Beaver Valley SD
Supt. – See Lebanon
ES at Danbury   69026 – Jolene Bartels, prin.

Davenport, Thayer Co., Pop. Code 2
Davenport Comm. SD
Sch. Sys. Enr. Code 2
Supt. – David Watters, P O BOX 190   68335
ES, P O BOX 190   68335 – Albert Anderson, prin.

David City, Butler Co., Pop. Code 5
David City SD
Sch. Sys. Enr. Code 2
Supt. – Douglas Townsend, 7TH & D STS   68632
ES, 750 D ST   68632 – Dolores Glock, prin.

St. Marys ES, 1026 N 5TH ST   68632

Dawson, Richardson Co., Pop. Code 2
Dawson-Verdon SD
Sch. Sys. Enr. Code 2
Supt. – Ray Blackburn, P O BOX 128   68337
ES at Dawson, P O BOX 138   68337
　Ray Blackburn, prin.

Daykin, Jefferson Co., Pop. Code 2
Meridian SD
Sch. Sys. Enr. Code 2
Supt. – Kenneth Babcock, P O BOX 68   68338
Meridian ES, P O BOX 68   68338
　Kenneth Babcock, prin.

Decatur, Burt Co., Pop. Code 3
Lyons-Decatur Northeast SD
Supt. – See Lyons
Northeast ES at Decatur, P O BOX 157   68020
　Teresa Morris, prin.

Deshler, Thayer Co., Pop. Code 3
Deshler SD
Sch. Sys. Enr. Code 2
Supt. – Larry Wilbeck, P O BOX 547   68340
ES   68340 – Mark Claussen, prin.

Deshler Lutheran ES, 509 E HEBRON   68340

De Witt, Saline Co., Pop. Code 3
Tri County SD
Sch. Sys. Enr. Code 3
Supt. – Marshall Adams
　RURAL ROUTE 01 BOX 164 A   68341
Tri County ES, RURAL ROUTE 01   68341
　Jerry Mangels, prin.

Diller, Jefferson Co., Pop. Code 2
Diller Comm. SD
Sch. Sys. Enr. Code 2
Supt. – Rolland Fenster, P O BOX 8   68342
ES, P O BOX 8   68342 – Rolland Fenster, prin.

Dix, Kimball Co., Pop. Code 2
Potter-Dix SD
Supt. – See Potter
Potter-Dix MS, P O BOX 125   69133
　Wilbur Brawner, prin.

Dodge, Dodge Co., Pop. Code 3
Dodge SD
Sch. Sys. Enr. Code 2
Supt. – Arnold Jakubowski, P O BOX 337   68633
ES, P O BOX 337   68633 – Joseph Reinert, prin.

St. Wenceslaus ES, LINDEN ST   68633

Doniphan, Hall Co., Pop. Code 3
Doniphan SD
Sch. Sys. Enr. Code 2
Supt. – Robert Broomfield, 3RD & PLUM   68832
ES, P O BOX D25   68832 – Gail Thompson, prin.

Dorchester, Saline Co., Pop. Code 3
Dorchester SD
Sch. Sys. Enr. Code 2
Supt. – Galen Johnson, P O BOX 7   68343
ES, P O BOX 7   68343 – Ronald Powers, prin.

Douglas, Otoe Co., Pop. Code 2
Douglas SD
Sch. Sys. Enr. Code 2
Supt. – Joseph Matrisciano, P O BOX 5   68344
ES, P O BOX 5   68344 – Linda Allen, prin.

Duncan, Platte Co., Pop. Code 2
Columbus SD
Supt. – See Columbus
ES at Duncan   68634 – Donald Gronemeyer, prin.

Dunning, Blaine Co., Pop. Code 2
Sandhills SD
Sch. Sys. Enr. Code 2
Supt. – Gary Amen, P O BOX 98   68833
Other Schools – See Brewster, Halsey

Dwight, Butler Co., Pop. Code 2
East Butler SD
Supt. – See Brainard
ES at Dwight, P O BOX 141   68635
　Richard Dostal, prin.

Eagle, Cass Co., Pop. Code 3
Waverly SD
Supt. – See Waverly
ES at Eagle, P O BOX 219   68347
　William Peterson, prin.

Edgar, Clay Co., Pop. Code 3
Sandy Creek SD
Supt. – See Fairfield
ES at Edgar   68935 – Glen Moorhead, prin.

Elba, Howard Co., Pop. Code 2
Elba SD
Sch. Sys. Enr. Code 2
Supt. – Archie Lind, P O BOX 100   68835
ES, P O BOX 100   68835
　Kayleen Lukasiewicz, prin.

Elgin, Antelope Co., Pop. Code 3
Elgin SD
Sch. Sys. Enr. Code 2
Supt. – Dwaine Uttecht, P O BOX 399   68636
ES, P O BOX 399   68636 – Dwaine Uttecht, prin.

St. Boniface ES, CHURCH ST BOX B   68636

Elkhorn, Douglas Co., Pop. Code 4
Elkhorn SD
Sch. Sys. Enr. Code 4
Supt. – Carl White, 502 GLENN   68022
MS, 500 HILLCREST ST   68022
　Thomas Furby, prin.
Hillrise ES, R00 HOPPER ST   68022
　Michaelene Meyer, prin.
Skyline ES, 400 S 210TH ST   68022
　Don Nordlund, prin.
Westridge ES, 500 N GREELEY ST   68022
　Roberta Hoy, prin.

Elm Creek, Buffalo Co., Pop. Code 3
Elm Creek SD
Sch. Sys. Enr. Code 2
Supt. – S. Sterling Troxel, P O BOX 490   68836
ES, P O BOX 490   68836 – Teresa Aten, prin.

Elmwood, Cass Co., Pop. Code 3
Elmwood SD
Sch. Sys. Enr. Code 2
Supt. – Wesley Shepard, P O BOX 100   68349
ES, P O BOX 100   68349 – Susan Cooperrider, prin.

Elsie, Perkins Co., Pop. Code 2
Wheatland SD
Supt. – See Madrid
Wheatland ES, P O BOX 79   69134 – (—), prin.

Elwood, Gosper Co., Pop. Code 3
Elwood SD
Sch. Sys. Enr. Code 2
Supt. – Conrad Huerta, P O BOX 107   68937
ES, P O BOX 107   68937 – Conrad Huerta, prin.

Emerson, Dakota Co., Pop. Code 3
Emerson-Hubbard SD
Sch. Sys. Enr. Code 2
Supt. – Rhonda Carstens, 401 3RD ST   68733
ES at Emerson, 401 3RD ST   68733
　Ruth Claeys, prin.
Other Schools – See Hubbard

Eustis, Frontier Co., Pop. Code 2
Eustis SD
Sch. Sys. Enr. Code 2
Supt. – Rodney Boss, P O BOX 9   69028
ES, P O BOX 9   69028 – Rodney Boss, prin.

Ewing, Holt Co., Pop. Code 3
Ewing SD
Sch. Sys. Enr. Code 2
Supt. – Tommy Hester, P O BOX 98   68735
ES, P O BOX 98   68735 – Tommy Hester, prin.

Exeter, Fillmore Co., Pop. Code 3
Exeter SD
Sch. Sys. Enr. Code 2
Supt. – Richard Becker, P O BOX 139   68351
ES, P O BOX 139   68351 – Charles Evans, prin.

Fairbury, Jefferson Co., Pop. Code 5
Fairbury SD
Sch. Sys. Enr. Code 2
Supt. – Mark Alderman, 1121 9TH ST   68352
Central ES, 8TH & F STS   68352
　Darrel Freitag, prin.
Fairbury East ES, 405 L ST   68352
　Darrel Freitag, prin.
Fairbury West ES, 1128 ELM ST   68352
　Darrel Freitag, prin.
Jefferson IS, 924 K ST   68352 – Darrel Freitag, prin.

Fairfield, Clay Co., Pop. Code 3
Sandy Creek SD
Sch. Sys. Enr. Code 2
Supt. – Lawrence Ramaekers, P O BOX 127   68938
ES at Fairfield, P O BOX 127   68938
　Glen Moorhead, prin.
Other Schools – See Edgar, Glenvil

Fairmont, Fillmore Co., Pop. Code 3
Fairmont SD
Sch. Sys. Enr. Code 2
Supt. – Donald Pieper, P O BOX 157   68354
ES, P O BOX 157   68354 – Donald Pieper, prin.

Falls City, Richardson Co., Pop. Code 6
Falls City SD
Sch. Sys. Enr. Code 3
Supt. – Donovan Betterman, 1522 LANE ST   68355
MS, 1415 MORTON   68355
　William Vossen, prin.
Falls City North ES, 25TH & STONE ST   68355
　Mary Kuester, prin.
Falls City South MS, 10TH & FULTON T   68355
　Mary Kuester, prin.

Sts. Peter & Paul ES, 807 E 19TH ST   68355

Farnam, Dawson Co., Pop. Code 2
Farnam SD
Sch. Sys. Enr. Code 2
Supt. – Larry Hermsmeyer, P O BOX 126   69029
ES, P O BOX 126   69029 – Larry Hermsmeyer, prin.

Filley, Gage Co., Pop. Code 2
Filley SD
Sch. Sys. Enr. Code 2
Supt. – William Tempelmeyer   68357
ES, P O BOX 87   68357
　William Tempelmeyer, prin.

Firth, Lancaster Co., Pop. Code 2
Norris SD 160
Sch. Sys. Enr. Code 4
Supt. – Dennis Nosal   68358
MS   68358 – Larry Grosshans, prin.
ES at Firth, RURAL ROUTE   68358
　David Moorhead, prin.

Fordyce, Cedar Co., Pop. Code 2

West Catholic ES, P O BOX 167   68736

Fort Calhoun, Washington Co., Pop. Code 3
Ft. Calhoun SD
Sch. Sys. Enr. Code 3
Supt. – Jerry Barabas, 1506 LINCOLN ST   68023
ES, 11TH & MONROE ST   68023
　Michael Hemen, prin.

Franklin, Franklin Co., Pop. Code 4
Franklin SD
Sch. Sys. Enr. Code 2
Supt. – Richard Kennedy
　1001 W HIGHWAY 136   68939
ES, 1001 W HIGHWAY 136   68939
　William Beck, prin.

Fremont, Dodge Co., Pop. Code 7
Fremont SD
Sch. Sys. Enr. Code 5
Supt. – James Buchanan, 957 N PIERCE ST   68025
Beebe ES, 957 N PIERCE   68025
　Selma Ganem, prin.

Clarkson ES, 1005 N CLARKSON ST   68025
  Larry Goodenough, prin.
Clarmar ES, 1865 E 19 ST   68025
  Robert Moeller, prin.
Davenport ES, 940 MICHAEL ST   68025
  Diane Johnson, prin.
Grant ES, 226 N GRANT ST   68025
  Michael Aerni, prin.
Howard ES, 240 N HOWARD ST   68025
  Harlan Spangler, prin.
Lincoln ES, 1350 RUTH AVE   68025
  Selma Ganem, prin.
Linden ES, 1205 N L ST   68025
  Velma Sims, prin.
Milliken Park ES, 2950 DALE ST   68025
  Lin Everett, prin.
Northside ES, 1830 N D ST   68025
  David Strong, prin.
Washington ES, 515 S BROAD ST   68025
  Diane Johnson, prin.

Trinity Lutheran ES, 1546 N LUTHER RD   68025

Friend, Saline Co., Pop. Code 4
Friend SD
Sch. Sys. Enr. Code 2
Supt. – Leo Stokes, 501 S MAIN ST   68359
ES, 501 S MAIN ST   68359 – Leroy Garrels, prin.

Fullerton, Nance Co., Pop. Code 4
Fullerton ESD
Sch. Sys. Enr. Code 2
Supt. – Gene Burton, P O BOX 520   68638
ES, P O BOX 520   68638 – Barbara Lucas, prin.

Garland, Seward Co., Pop. Code 2
Seward SD
Supt. – See Seward
ES at Garland   68360 – Janette Holtzen, prin.

Geneva, Fillmore Co., Pop. Code 4
Geneva North SD
Sch. Sys. Enr. Code 1
Supt. – Donald Best
  RURAL ROUTE 01 BOX 23A   68361
Geneva North MS, RURAL ROUTE 23A   68361
  Norma Knoche, prin.

Geneva SD
Sch. Sys. Enr. Code 3
Supt. – Kenneth Anderson, 1410 L ST   68361
ES, 215 N 17TH ST   68361 – Terry Snyder, prin.

Genoa, Nance Co., Pop. Code 4
Genoa SD
Sch. Sys. Enr. Code 3
Supt. – Ronald Pilgrim, P O BOX 465   68640
ES, P O BOX 465   68640 – Roger Adkins, prin.

Gering, Scotts Bluff Co., Pop. Code 6
Gering SD
Sch. Sys. Enr. Code 4
Supt. – William Lockwood, 800 Q ST   69341
Geil ES, 1600 D ST   69341 – Robert Hyland, prin.
Lincoln ES, 1701 13TH ST   69341
  Patricia Clark, prin.
McKinley ES, 1430 6TH ST   69341
  John Hardt, prin.
Northfield ES, FLATEN AVE   69341
  Richard Orr, prin.

Gibbon, Buffalo Co., Pop. Code 4
Gibbon SD
Sch. Sys. Enr. Code 3
Supt. – Kermit Belau, 2ND & COLLEGE   68840
ES, 2ND & COLLEGE   68840
  Steve Van Meter, prin.

Giltner, Hamilton Co., Pop. Code 2
Giltner SD
Sch. Sys. Enr. Code 2
Supt. – Donald Ferguson, P O BOX 157   68841
ES, P O BOX 157   68841 – Donald Ferguson, prin.

Glenvil, Clay Co., Pop. Code 2
Sandy Creek SD
Supt. – See Fairfield
ES at Glenville   68941 – Glen Moorhead, prin.

Goehner, Seward Co., Pop. Code 2
Seward SD
Supt. – See Seward
ES at Goehner   68364 – Janette Holtzen, prin.

Gordon, Sheridan Co., Pop. Code 4
Gordon ESD
Sch. Sys. Enr. Code 2
Supt. – William Reents, P O BOX 530   69343
ES, P O BOX 530   69343 – (—), prin.

Gothenburg, Dawson Co., Pop. Code 5
Gothenburg SD
Sch. Sys. Enr. Code 3
Supt. – Wayne Bell, 1415 AVE G   69138
ES, 1400 AVENUE G   69138
  Lawrence Debaere, prin.

Grand Island, Hall Co., Pop. Code 8
Grand Island SD
Sch. Sys. Enr. Code 6
Supt. – Larry Dlugosh, 615 N ELM ST   68801
Westridge MS, 1812 MANSFIELD ROAD   68803
  Michael Brasfield, prin.
Dodge ES, 641 S OAK ST   68801
  Elaine Deharde, prin.
Engleman ES, 4360 W CAPITAL AVE   68803
  Richard Daly, prin.

Gates ES, 2700 W LOUISE ST   68803
  Karl Hughes, prin.
Howard ES, 502 W 9TH ST   68801
  Bessie Frith, prin.
Jefferson ES, 1304 W 7TH ST   68801
  Michael Nichols, prin.
Knickrehm ES, 2013 N OAK ST   68801
  Betty Nelson, prin.
Lincoln ES, 910 E 8TH ST   68801
  Eugene Schneberger, prin.
Newell ES, 2700 W 13TH ST   68803
  Joseph Cook, prin.
Seedling Mile ES
  3208 E SEEDLING MILE RD   68801
  Kevin Riggert, prin.
Shoemaker ES, 4160 OLD POTASH HWY   68803
  Bill Mowinkel, prin.
Starr ES, 315 WYANDOTTE ST   68801
  Ralph Brostrom, prin.
Stolley Park ES
  1700 STOLLEY PARK ROAD   68801
  Stephen Gleason, prin.
Wasmer ES, 1613 W DIVISION ST   68801
  Nyla Alexander, prin.
West Lawn ES, 1804 STATE ST   68803
  Judith Campbell, prin.

Trinity Lutheran ES, 208 W 13TH ST   68801

Grant, Perkins Co., Pop. Code 4
Grant ESD
Sch. Sys. Enr. Code 2
Supt. – (—), P O BOX 809   69140
ES, P O BOX 809   69140 – Larry Tatum, prin.

Greeley, Greeley Co., Pop. Code 3
Greeley SD
Sch. Sys. Enr. Code 2
Supt. – Dean Cunningham, P O BOX 160   68842
ES, P O BOX 160   68842 – Dean Cunningham, prin.

Gresham, York Co., Pop. Code 2
Centennial SD
Supt. – See Utica
Centennial ES at Gresham   68367
  Kenneth Kinney, prin.
Centennial ES at Utica, P O BOX 187   68367
  Kenneth Kinney, prin.

Gretna, Sarpy Co., Pop. Code 4
Gretna SD
Sch. Sys. Enr. Code 3
Supt. – Gail Kopplin, 801 SOUTH ST   68028
ES, 801 SOUTH ST   68028 – Carolyn Eye, prin.

Guide Rock, Webster Co., Pop. Code 2
Guide Rock SD
Sch. Sys. Enr. Code 2
Supt. – David Kroger, P O BOX 128   68942
ES, P O BOX 128   68942 – David Kroger, prin.

Gurley, Cheyenne Co., Pop. Code 2
Leyton SD
Supt. – See Dalton
Leyton ES   69141 – Kirk Hughes, prin.

Haigler, Dundy Co., Pop. Code 2
Dundy County
Supt. – See Benkelman
ES, P O BOX 127   69030 – Dan Van Dyke, prin.

Halsey, Blaine Co., Pop. Code 2
Sandhills SD
Supt. – See Dunning
ES at Halsey, P O BOX 98   69142
  Gary Amen, prin.

Hampton, Hamilton Co., Pop. Code 2
Hampton SD
Sch. Sys. Enr. Code 2
Supt. – R. W. Hoppner, P O BOX 37   68843
ES, P O BOX 37   68843 – Gail Chapman, prin.

Harrisburg, Banner Co., Pop. Code 2
Banner County SD
Sch. Sys. Enr. Code 2
Supt. – Frank Madison, P O BOX 5   69345
Banner County ES, P O BOX 5   69345
  Frank Madison, prin.

Hartington, Cedar Co., Pop. Code 4
Hartington SD
Sch. Sys. Enr. Code 2
Supt. – Don Flakus
  BROADWAY & MADISON   68739
ES, BROADWAY & MADISON   68739
  Beverley Dodds, prin.

Holy Trinity ES   68739

Harvard, Clay Co., Pop. Code 4
Harvard SD
Sch. Sys. Enr. Code 2
Supt. – Roy Laue, P O BOX 100   68944
ES, P O BOX 100   68944 – Robert Stone, prin.

Hastings, Adams Co., Pop. Code 7
Hastings SD
Sch. Sys. Enr. Code 5
Supt. – Joseph Scalzo, P O BOX 489   68901
JHS, 505 N HASTINGS AVE   68901
  John H. Ewing, prin.
Alcott ES, 4TH & CEDAR   68901 – Gary Lake, prin.
Hawthorne ES, 2200 W 9TH ST   68901
  Edward O'Donnell, prin.
Lincoln ES, 720 FRANKLIN AVE   68901
  Jody Isernhagen, prin.

Longfellow ES, 828 N HASTINGS AVE   68901
  Kenneth Wiederspan, prin.
Morton ES, 8TH & BALTIMORE   68901
  John Nelson, prin.
Watson ES, 1720 CRANE AVE   68901
  Janet Hibbs, prin.

St. Michael ES, 314 S LINCOLN AVE   68901
Zion Lutheran ES, 601 S MARIAN RD   68901

Hayes Center, Hayes Co., Pop. Code 2
Hayes Center SD
Sch. Sys. Enr. Code 2
Supt. – Dewey Harouff, P O BOX 8   69032
ES, P O BOX 8   69032 – Gary Hastings, prin.

Hay Springs, Sheridan Co., Pop. Code 3
Hay Springs SD
Sch. Sys. Enr. Code 2
Supt. – Ronald G. Hiles, P O BOX 280   69347
ES, P O BOX 280   69347 – Cora Haberman, prin.

Hebron, Thayer Co., Pop. Code 4
Hebron SD
Sch. Sys. Enr. Code 2
Supt. – Donald Crowder, 10TH & EADS ST   68370
MS, 10TH & EADS   68370 – Thomas Kunkel, prin.
PS, 6TH & JEFFERSON   68370
  Thomas Kunkel, prin.

Hemingford, Box Butte Co., Pop. Code 4
Hemingford SD
Sch. Sys. Enr. Code 2
Supt. – Donald Hanks, P O BOX 217   69348
ES, P O BOX 217   69348 – Glen Kotschwar, prin.

Henderson, York Co., Pop. Code 4
Henderson SD
Sch. Sys. Enr. Code 2
Supt. – Norman Yoder, P O BOX 626   68371
ES, P O BOX 626   68371 – Henry Pauls, prin.

Herman, Washington Co., Pop. Code 2
Tekamah-Herman SD
Supt. – See Tekamah
ES at Herman   68029 – Richard Grandgenett, prin.

Hershey, Lincoln Co., Pop. Code 3
Hershey SD
Sch. Sys. Enr. Code 2
Supt. – Michael Cunning, P O BOX 188   69143
ES, P O BOX 188   69143 – David Rowe, prin.

Hildreth, Franklin Co., Pop. Code 2
Hildreth SD
Sch. Sys. Enr. Code 2
Supt. – Gary Fisher, P O BOX 157   68947
ES, P O BOX 157   68947 – Gary Fisher, prin.

Holbrook, Furnas Co., Pop. Code 2
Holbrook SD
Sch. Sys. Enr. Code 1
Supt. – Gerard Cotnoir, P O BOX 178   68948
ES, P O BOX 178   68948 – Gerard Cotnoir, prin.

Holdrege, Phelps Co., Pop. Code 6
Holdrege SD
Sch. Sys. Enr. Code 4
Supt. – D. Deriese, 315 EAST AVE   68949
MS, 315 EAST AVE   68949 – Richard Meyer, prin.
Franklin ES, 1015 SHERMAN ST   68949
  Lyle Walker, prin.
Lincoln ES, 516 LOGAN   68949
  Lyle Walker, prin.
Washington ES, 115 8TH AVE   68949
  Robert Haley, prin.

Homer, Dakota Co., Pop. Code 3
Homer Comm. SD
Sch. Sys. Enr. Code 2
Supt. – Mel Waldner, P O BOX 128   68030
ES, P O BOX 340   68030 – Mel Waldner, prin.

Hooper, Dodge Co., Pop. Code 3
Hooper ESD
Sch. Sys. Enr. Code 2
Supt. – Charles Griffith, P O BOX 446   68031
ES, P O BOX 446   68031 – Lucille Baum, prin.

Hordville, Hamilton Co., Pop. Code 2
Polk-Hordville SD
Supt. – See Polk
Polk-Hordville MS, P O BOX 45   68846
  Dennis Gray, prin.

Howells, Colfax Co., Pop. Code 3
Howells SD
Sch. Sys. Enr. Code 2
Supt. – A. Jakubowski, P O BOX 159   68641
JHS, P O BOX 159   68641
  Richard Hoelscher, prin.
ES, P O BOX 159   68641 – Joe Reinert, prin.

Howells Community Catholic School
  P O BOX 70   68641

Hubbard, Dakota Co., Pop. Code 2
Emerson-Hubbard SD
Supt. – See Emerson
ES at Hubbard   68741 – Ruth Claeys, prin.

Humboldt, Richardson Co., Pop. Code 4
Humboldt SD
Sch. Sys. Enr. Code 2
Supt. – D. L. Montgomery, P O BOX 278   68376
ES, P O BOX 278   68376 – Charlene Tomek, prin.

Humphrey, Platte Co., Pop. Code 3
Humphrey SD
Sch. Sys. Enr. Code 2
Supt. – Robert Heckathorn, P O BOX 278 68642
ES, P O BOX 278 68642 – Steven Robb, prin.

St. Francis ES, P O BOX 277 68642

Imperial, Chase Co., Pop. Code 4
Imperial ESD
Sch. Sys. Enr. Code 2
Supt. – Glen Beran, 1000 WELLINGTON 69033
ES, 723 BROADWAY 69033 – Thomas Hain, prin.

Indianola, Red Willow Co., Pop. Code 3
Republican Valley SD
Sch. Sys. Enr. Code 2
Supt. – John W. Symington
  RURAL ROUTE 01 69034
ES at Indianola 69034 – Sandra Hines, prin.

Johnson, Nemaha Co., Pop. Code 2
Johnson-Brock SD
Sch. Sys. Enr. Code 2
Supt. – Joe Anderson, P O BOX 186 68378
Other Schools – See Brock

Juniata, Adams Co., Pop. Code 3
Juniata ESD
Sch. Sys. Enr. Code 2
Supt. – (—), P O BOX 157 68955
ES, P O BOX 157 68955 – Michael Engel, prin.

Kearney, Buffalo Co., Pop. Code 7
Kearney SD
Sch. Sys. Enr. Code 5
Supt. – Gary Hammack, 310 W 24TH ST 68847
JHS, 915 W 35TH ST 68847 – Gerald Menke, prin.
Bryant ES, 1611 AVENUE C 68847
  Roger Nyffeler, prin.
Central ES, 300 W 24TH ST 68847
  Leonard McCarville, prin.
Emerson ES, 2705 AVENUE E 68847
  David Townsend, prin.
Kearney Northeast ES, 910 E 34TH ST 68847
  Melvin Johnson, prin.
Kenwood ES, 1511 5TH AVE 68847
  Tom Camp, prin.
Park ES, 3000 7TH AVE 68847
  Rodger Gage, prin.
Windy Hills ES, 4211 20TH AVE 68847
  Jerry Gloystein, prin.

Zion Lutheran ES, P O BOX 778 68848

Kenesaw, Adams Co., Pop. Code 3
Kenesaw SD
Sch. Sys. Enr. Code 2
Supt. – George Bauer, P O BOX 129 68956
ES, P O BOX 129 68956 – Donald Eberle, prin.

Kilgore, Cherry Co., Pop. Code 1
Cody-Kilgore SD
Supt. – See Cody
ES at Kilgoe, P O BOX 58 69216
  Betty Jean Peterson, prin.

Kimball, Kimball Co., Pop. Code 5
Kimball SD
Sch. Sys. Enr. Code 3
Supt. – Darryl Kile, 301 S HOWARD ST 69145
Kimball MS, 301 S HOWARD ST 69145
  Steven Pattison, prin.
Lynch MS, 301 S HOWARD ST 69145
  Steven Pattison, prin.
West ES, 301 S HOWARD ST 69145
  (—), prin.

Laurel, Cedar Co., Pop. Code 3
Laurel-Concord SD
Sch. Sys. Enr. Code 2
Supt. – William Gannon 68745
Laurel-Concord ES 68745 – Therese Logue, prin.

La Vista, Sarpy Co., Pop. Code 6
Papillion-La Vista SD
Sch. Sys. Enr. Code 6
Supt. – Roger Miller, 7552 S 84TH ST 68128
Hall ES, 7600 S 72ND ST 68128
  Bernard Gordon, prin.
La Vista West ES, 7821 TERRY AVE 68127
  Doris O'Connor, prin.
Parkview Heights ES, 7609 S 89TH ST 68128
  Robert Smith, prin.
Other Schools – See Omaha, Papillion

Lawrence, Nuckolls Co., Pop. Code 2
Lawrence SD
Sch. Sys. Enr. Code 2
Supt. – Dan Jantzen, P O BOX 128 68957
ES, P O BOX 128 68957 – Dan Jantzen, prin.

Lebanon, Red Willow Co., Pop. Code 2
Beaver Valley SD
Sch. Sys. Enr. Code 2
Supt. – Lloyd Howsden, P O BOX 157 69036
Other Schools – See Danbury, Wilsonville

Leigh, Colfax Co., Pop. Code 3
Leigh SD
Sch. Sys. Enr. Code 2
Supt. – Cecil Fields, P O BOX 98 68643
ES, P O BOX 98 68643 – Cecil Fields, prin.

Lewiston, Pawnee Co., Pop. Code 2
Lewiston SD
Sch. Sys. Enr. Code 2
Supt. – Glenn Heideman, P O BOX 74 68380

ES, P O BOX 13 68380 – Glenn Heideman, prin.

Lexington, Dawson Co., Pop. Code 6
Lexington SD
Sch. Sys. Enr. Code 4
Supt. – Randy Nelson
  1610 N WASHINGTON 68850
Bryan ES, 1003 N HARRISON ST 68850
  Wesley Reed, prin.
Morton ES, 505 S LINCOLN ST 68850
  Scott Dodson, prin.
Pershing ES, 1104 TYLER ST 68850
  Randy Gross, prin.
Sandoz ES, 1609 ERIE ST 68850
  Rodney Schainost, prin.

Lincoln, Lancaster Co., Pop. Code 9
Lincoln SD
Sch. Sys. Enr. Code 8
Supt. – Philip Schoo, 720 S 22ND ST 68510
Arnold ES, 5300 W KNIGHT DR 68524
  Jack Dodds, prin.
Beattie ES, 1901 CALVERT ST 68502
  Michelle Meier, prin.
Belmont ES, 3325 N 14TH ST 68521
  Cheryl Bayley, prin.
Brownell ES, 60TH & AYLESWORTH AVE 68505
  Donald Hobbs, prin.
Calvert ES, 3709 S 46TH ST 68506
  David Rutledge, prin.
Clinton ES, 1520 N 29TH ST 68503
  Donald Tewell, prin.
Dawes ES, 5130 COLFAX AVE 68504
  (—), prin.
Eastridge ES, 6245 L ST 68510
  Linda Douglas, prin.
Elliott ES, 225 S 25TH ST 68510
  Robert Bussman, prin.
Fredstrom ES, 5700 NW 10TH ST 68521
  Carole Matthes, prin.
Hartley ES, 730 N 33RD ST 68503
  Bonnie Spomer, prin.
Hawthorne ES, 300 S 48TH ST 68510
  Cecilia Hendrickson, prin.
Hill ES, 5230 TIPPERARY TRL 68512
  Ruthelen Sittler, prin.
Holmes ES, 5230 SUMNER ST 68506
  Delbert Emerson, prin.
Huntington ES, 4601 ADAMS ST 68504
  Geald Oehring, prin.
Kahoa ES, 7700 LEIGHTON AVE 68507
  Waldean Kuhns, prin.
Lake View ES, 300 CAPITOL BEACH BLVD 68528
  Daniel Navratil, prin.
McPhee ES, 820 S 15TH ST 68508
  John Zetterman, prin.
Meadow Lane ES, 7300 VINE ST 68505
  Thomas Guild, prin.
Morley ES, 68TH & MONTEREY 68506
  Gayle Hurlbert, prin.
Norwood Park ES, 4710 N 72ND ST 68507
  Barry Fritch, prin.
Park ES, 714 F ST 68508 – Marilyn Peterson, prin.
Pershing ES, 6402 JUDSON STY 68507
  Marlan Kaufman, prin.
Prescott ES, 1930 S 20TH ST 68502
  Barbara Jacobson, prin.
Pyrtle ES, 721 COTTONWOOD DR 68510
  Marlin Johnson, prin.
Randolph ES, 1024 S 37TH ST 68510
  Leslie Corr, prin.
Riley ES, 5021 ORCHARD ST 68504
  Carol Reed, prin.
Rousseau ES, 3701 S 33RD ST 68506
  Richard Spearman, prin.
Saratoga ES, 2215 S 13TH ST 68502
  Frederick Petersen, prin.
Sheridan ES, 3100 PLYMOUTH AVE 68502
  Maxine Sorensen, prin.
West Lincoln ES, 630 W DAWES AVE 68521
  Gerald Decker, prin.
Yankee Hill ES, 865 W BURNHAM ST 68522
  (—), prin.
Zeman ES, 4900 S 52ND ST 68516
  Dean Webb, prin.

Blessed Sacrament ES, 2500 S 17TH ST 68502
Calvary Lutheran ES, 1800 S 84TH ST 68506
Cathedral of Risen Christ ES
  3245 S 37TH ST 68506
Hyatt ES, 5240 CALVERT ST 68506
Lincoln Christian ES, 5801 S 84TH ST 68516
Living Word Christian ES, 2748 S 35TH 68503
Sacred Heart ES, 530 N 31ST ST 68503
St. Johns ES, 7601 VINE ST 68505
St. Josephs Catholic ES, 1940 N 77TH ST 68506
St. Marys ES, 1434 K ST 68508
St. Patricks ES, 6100 MORRILL AVE 68507
St. Teresa ES, 616 S 36TH ST 68510
Trinity Lutheran ES, 1200 N 56TH ST 68504

Lindsay, Platte Co., Pop. Code 2

Holy Family ES, P O BOX 158 68644

Litchfield, Sherman Co., Pop. Code 2
Litchfield SD
Sch. Sys. Enr. Code 2
Supt. – Eldon Epley, P O BOX 167 68852
ES, P O BOX 167 68852 – Eldon Epley, prin.

Lodgepole, Cheyenne Co., Pop. Code 2
Lodgepole SD
Sch. Sys. Enr. Code 2
Supt. – Dennis Mehlhaff, P O BOX 158 69149

ES, P O BOX 158 69149 – Robert Davis, prin.

Loomis, Phelps Co., Pop. Code 2
Loomis SD
Sch. Sys. Enr. Code 2
Supt. – Keith Fagot, P O BOX 250 68958
ES, P O BOX 250 68958 – Steven Smith, prin.

Louisville, Cass Co., Pop. Code 4
Louisville SD
Sch. Sys. Enr. Code 2
Supt. – G. Martin, P O BOX 489 68037
ES, P O BOX 489 68037 – Jim Flynn, prin.

Loup City, Sherman Co., Pop. Code 4
Loup City SD
Sch. Sys. Enr. Code 3
Supt. – Richard Yelkin, 109 N 7TH 68853
MS, 800 N 8TH 68853 – Larry Hiatt, prin.
ES, 630 N 7TH ST 68853 – Larry Hiatt, prin.
Other Schools – See Ashton

Lyman, Scotts Bluff Co., Pop. Code 3
Lyman SD
Sch. Sys. Enr. Code 2
Supt. – Thomas Whitmore, P O BOX 367 69352
ES, P O BOX 367 69352 – Thomas Whitmore, prin.

Lynch, Boyd Co., Pop. Code 2
Lynch SD
Sch. Sys. Enr. Code 2
Supt. – Dale Meritt 68746
ES 68746 – Dale Meritt, prin.

Lyons, Burt Co., Pop. Code 4
Lyons-Decatur Northeast SD
Sch. Sys. Enr. Code 2
Supt. – F. Forsberg, 5TH & CRYSTAL 68038
Northeast ES at Lyons, 5TH & CRYSTAL 68038
  Teresa Morris, prin.
Other Schools – See Decatur

Mc Cook, Red Willow Co., Pop. Code 6
McCook SD
Sch. Sys. Enr. Code 4
Supt. – Harold Bennett, 700 W 7TH ST 69001
Central ES, 604 W 1ST ST 69001
  Ronald Clark, prin.
East Ward ES, 500 E 5TH ST 69001
  Ron Clark, prin.
North Ward ES, 1500 W 3RD ST 69001
  Robert Ridenour, prin.
West Ward ES, 300 W 4TH ST 69001
  Robert Ridenour, prin.

St. Patricks ES, 401 E F ST 69001

Mc Cool Junction, York Co., Pop. Code 2
McCool Junction SD
Sch. Sys. Enr. Code 2
Supt. – Norman Bonde, S LOGAN ST 68401
ES, P O BOX 278 68401 – Norman Bonde, prin.

Macy, Thurston Co.
Macy SD
Sch. Sys. Enr. Code 2
Supt. – Scott Butterfield, P O BOX 68 68039
ES, P O BOX 68 68039 – Wanda Sornson, prin.

Madison, Madison Co., Pop. Code 4
Madison SD
Sch. Sys. Enr. Code 3
Supt. – Eugene Cerny, P O BOX A 68748
ES, P O XO 445 68748 – Gerald Bippes, prin.

Madrid, Perkins Co., Pop. Code 2
Wheatland SD
Sch. Sys. Enr. Code 2
Supt. – David Dawson, P O BOX 11D 69150
Other Schools – See Elsie

Malcolm, Lancaster Co., Pop. Code 2
Malcolm SD
Sch. Sys. Enr. Code 2
Supt. – Leland Knobel, P O BOX 198 68402
ES, P O BOX 198 68402 – Michael Johnson, prin.

Marquette, Hamilton Co., Pop. Code 2
Marquette SD
Sch. Sys. Enr. Code 2
Supt. – Chris Effken, P O BOX 100 68854
ES 68854 – Lee Rottman, prin.

Maxwell, Lincoln Co., Pop. Code 2
Maxwell SD
Sch. Sys. Enr. Code 2
Supt. – John Brown, P O BOX 188 69151
ES, P O BOX 188 69151 – Richard Heessel, prin.

Maywood, Frontier Co., Pop. Code 2
Maywood SD
Sch. Sys. Enr. Code 2
Supt. – Rodney Berryman, P O BOX 46 69038
ES, P O BOX 46 69038 – Rodney Berryman, prin.

Mead, Saunders Co., Pop. Code 3
Mead SD
Sch. Sys. Enr. Code 2
Supt. – William Metzger, 114 N VINE 68041
ES 68041 – Nancy Currie, prin.

Merna, Custer Co., Pop. Code 2
Anselmo-Merna SD
Sch. Sys. Enr. Code 2
Supt. – James Lofquist, P O BOX 68 68856
ES, P O BOX 68 68856 – Bobby Edelman, prin.

Milford, Seward Co., Pop. Code 4
Milford SD
Sch. Sys. Enr. Code 3
Supt. – Alan Katzberg, W 1ST ST 68405
ES, WEST 1ST ST 68405 – Rodney Bleich, prin.
Other Schools – See Pleasant Dale

Milligan, Fillmore Co., Pop. Code 2
Milligan SD
Sch. Sys. Enr. Code 2
Supt. – Charles Tonnies, P O BOX 188 68406
ES, P O BOX 188 68406 – Charles Tonnies, prin.

Minatare, Scotts Bluff Co., Pop. Code 3
Minatare SD
Sch. Sys. Enr. Code 2
Supt. – Norman Frerichs, P O BOX 425 69356
ES, P O BOX 425 69356 – Eddie Schultz, prin.

Minden, Kearney Co., Pop. Code 5
Minden SD
Sch. Sys. Enr. Code 3
Supt. – Richard Raecke, 520 W 3RD ST 68959
Jones MS, 520 W 3RD ST 68959
Charles Featherston, prin.
Minden East ES, 123 N MINDEN AVE 68959
Verl Nelson, prin.

Mitchell, Scotts Bluff Co., Pop. Code 4
Mitchell SD
Sch. Sys. Enr. Code 3
Supt. – Randall Zitterkopf, 1819 19TH AVE 69357
ES, 1439 13TH AVE 69357 – Frank Frailey, prin.

Monroe, Platte Co., Pop. Code 2
Monroe SD
Sch. Sys. Enr. Code 2
Supt. – Arthur Ferguson, P O BOX 106 68647
ES, P O BOX 156 68647 – Arthur Ferguson, prin.

Morrill, Scotts Bluff Co., Pop. Code 4
Morrill SD
Sch. Sys. Enr. Code 2
Supt. – Leigh Cull, P O BOX 486 69358
ES, P O BOX 486 69358 – Neal Custer, prin.

Mullen, Hooker Co., Pop. Code 3
Mullen SD
Sch. Sys. Enr. Code 2
Supt. – Robert Mandeville, P O BOX 127 69152
ES, P O BOX 89 69152 – Gary Tuton, prin.

Murdock, Cass Co., Pop. Code 2
Murdock SD
Sch. Sys. Enr. Code 2
Supt. – Kenneth Bowe 68407
ES 68407 – (—), prin.

Murray, Cass Co., Pop. Code 2
Conestoga SD
Sch. Sys. Enr. Code 3
Supt. – Rick Black, P O BOX 40 68409
Other Schools – See Nehawka

Naper, Boyd Co., Pop. Code 2
Naper SD
Sch. Sys. Enr. Code 1
Supt. – Leslie Weaver, P O BOX 168 68755
ES, P O BOX 168 68755 – John Broadbooks, prin.

Spencer-Naper SD
Supt. – See Spencer
Naper ES, P O BOX 168 68755 – Dale Reber, prin.

Nebraska City, Otoe Co., Pop. Code 6
Nebraska City SD
Sch. Sys. Enr. Code 4
Supt. – James Withee, 215 N 12TH ST 68410
Hayward ES, 306 S 14TH ST 68410
Lynn Friesen, prin.
Nebraska City Northside ES
12TH ST AND 12TH AVE 68410
Michael Redelfs, prin.

Lourdes Central School, 412 2ND AVE 68410

Nehawka, Cass Co., Pop. Code 2
Conestoga SD
Supt. – See Murray
Conestoga ES-Murray, P O BOX 187 68413
Karen Shields, prin.
Conestoga MS-Nehawka, P O BOX 187 68413
Karen Shields, prin.

Neligh, Antelope Co., Pop. Code 4
Neligh-Oakdale SD
Sch. Sys. Enr. Code 3
Supt. – Roger Macklem, P O BOX B 68756
MS, P O BOX 149 68756 – Terry Weber, prin.
ES at Neligh-Oakdale, P O BOX 149 68756
William Kuester, prin.

Nelson, Nuckolls Co., Pop. Code 3
Nelson SD
Sch. Sys. Enr. Code 2
Supt. – Oscar Mussman, P O BOX 368 68961
ES, P O BOX 368 68961 – Oscar Mussman, prin.

Newcastle, Dixon Co., Pop. Code 2
Newcastle SD
Sch. Sys. Enr. Code 2
Supt. – Ted Richard, P O BOX 187 68757
ES, P O BOX 187 68757 – Ted Richard, prin.

Newman Grove, Madison Co., Pop. Code 3
Newman Grove SD
Sch. Sys. Enr. Code 2
Supt. – Robert Behrens, P O BOX 370 68758
ES, P O BOX 370 68758 – Dennis Schmitz, prin.

Niobrara, Knox Co., Pop. Code 2
Niobrara SD
Sch. Sys. Enr. Code 2
Supt. – James Troshynski, P O BOX 310 68760
ES, P O BOX 310 68760 – James Troshynski, prin.

Santee SD
Sch. Sys. Enr. Code 2
Supt. – Robert Jacobs, RURAL ROUTE 02 68760
Santee ES, RURAL ROUTE 01 68760
Gordon Kitto, prin.

Norfolk, Madison Co., Pop. Code 7
Norfolk SD
Sch. Sys. Enr. Code 5
Supt. – James Merritt, P O BOX 139 68701
Bel Air ES, 1101 N 18TH ST 68701
Ivan Waggoner, prin.
Grant ES, 1106 PHILLIP AVE 68701
Tom Davis, prin.
Jefferson ES, 406 N COTTONWOOD ST 68701
Pamela Handke, prin.
Lincoln ES, 310 S 3RD ST 68701
Tom Davis, prin.
Northern Hills ES, 600 N 12TH ST 68701
Jack Prater, prin.
Washington ES, 1205 S 2ND ST 68701
Pamela Handke, prin.
Westside ES, 1703 PHILLIP AVE 68701
Jack Prater, prin.

Christ Lutheran ES, 511 S 5TH ST 68701
Sacred Heart ES, 201 S 6TH ST #1607 68701
St. Paul Lutheran ES, 1010 GEORGIA AVE 68701

North Bend, Dodge Co., Pop. Code 4
North Bend ESD
Sch. Sys. Enr. Code 2
Supt. – (—), P O BOX H 68649
ES, P O BOX H 68649 – Cecilia Hall, prin.

North Loup, Valley Co., Pop. Code 2
North Loup Scotia SD
Supt. – See Scotia
ES at North Loup, P O BOX 285 68859
Deborah Kluthe, prin.

North Platte, Lincoln Co., Pop. Code 7
North Platte SD
Sch. Sys. Enr. Code 5
Supt. – Douglas Christensen, P O BOX 1557 69103
Adams MS, 1200 MCDONALD ROAD 69101
Larry Roth, prin.
Madison MS, 14TH & MADISON ST 69101
Vernon Yanney, prin.
Buffalo ES, RURAL ROUTE 01 BOX 167 69101
Wallace Kucera, prin.
Cody ES, 2000 W 2ND ST 69101
Robert Rowe, prin.
Eisenhower ES, 3900 W A ST 69101
Michael McPherron, prin.
Jefferson ES, 700 E 3RD ST 69101
James Catterson, prin.
Lincoln ES, 200 W 9TH ST 69101
Brian Horst, prin.
McDonald ES, 601 MCDONALD RD 69101
James Hand, prin.
Osgood ES, S HWY 83 69101 – (—), prin.
Washington ES, 600 W 3RD ST 69101
Vikki Kershner, prin.

Mc Daid ES, P O BOX 970 69103
Our Redeemer Lutheran ES, 1421 E D ST 69101

Oakland, Burt Co., Pop. Code 4
Oakland Craig SD
Sch. Sys. Enr. Code 2
Supt. – Paul Heller, 309 N DAVIS AVE 68045
Oakland Craig JHS, 309 N DAVIS AVE 68045
Harold Hawkins, prin.
Oakland Craig ES, 400 N BREWSTER AVE 68045
Mark Ferg, prin.

Odell, Gage Co., Pop. Code 2
Odell SD
Sch. Sys. Enr. Code 2
Supt. – Milford Smith, P O BOX 188 68415
ES, P O BOX 188 68415 – Milford Smith, prin.

Ogallala, Keith Co., Pop. Code 6
Ogallala SD
Sch. Sys. Enr. Code 4
Supt. – Dr. John Brennan, 602 E G ST 69153
MS, 205 E 6TH ST 69153
Marlin Spellmeyer, prin.
Prairie View ES, 801 E O ST 69153
Jess Medina, prin.
Progress MS, 200 E 6TH ST 69153
Tearle List, prin.
West 5th ES, WEST 5TH & H ST 69153
Tearle List, prin.

St. Paul Lutheran ES, 312 W THIRD 69153

Omaha, Douglas Co., Pop. Code 10
Bellevue SD
Supt. – See Bellevue
Ft. Crook ES, 12501 S 25TH ST 68123
Roger Bickford, prin.
Lawrence ES, 13204 S 29TH ST 68123
Terry Lee, prin.
Lemay ES, PEASE & KENNEDY DR 68123
(—), prin.
Sarpy ES, 30TH & VANDENBERG AVE 68123
Jolene Heibel, prin.

Millard SD
Sch. Sys. Enr. Code 7
Supt. – Don Stroh, 1010 S 144TH ST 68154
Andersen MS, 15405 ADAMS ST 68137
Robert Lykke, prin.
Kiewit MS, 15650 HOWARD ST 68118
Bernard Vanis, prin.
Millard Central MS, 12801 L ST 68137
Michael Fjell, prin.
Millard North MS, 2828 S 139TH ST 68144
Gary Barta, prin.
Abbott ES, 1313 N 156TH 68154
Michael Tucker, prin.
Ackerman ES, 5110 S 156TH ST 68135
Barbara Winterburn, prin.
Bryan ES, 5010 S 144TH ST 68137
Jed Johnston, prin.
Cather ES, 3030 S 139TH ST 68144
Franklin Ellis, prin.
Cody ES, 3320 S 127TH ST 68144
Debra Mackie, prin.
Cottonwood ES, 615 PIEDMONT DR 68154
Janet Lemp, prin.
Disney ES, 5717 S 112TH ST 68137
Norma Pane, prin.
Hitchcock ES, 5809 S 104TH ST 68127
(—), prin.
Holling Heights ES, 6565 S 136TH ST 68137
Richard Pahls, prin.
Montclair ES, 2405 S 138TH ST 68144
Angelo Passarelli, prin.
Morton ES, 160TH & WOOD 68144
Harry Fleming, prin.
Neihardt ES, 15130 DREXEL ST 68137
Linda Kisler, prin.
Norris ES, 12424 WEIR ST 68137
Stanley Bluma, prin.
Oaks ES, 15228 SHIRLEY ST 68144
George Denkinger, prin.
Rockwell ES, 6370 S 140TH AVE 68137
Rex Rhodes, prin.
Sandoz ES, 5959 OAK HILLS DR 68137
Dick Spangler, prin.

Omaha SD
Sch. Sys. Enr. Code 8
Supt. – Norbert Schuerman
3902 DAVENPORT ST 68131
Beveridge JHS, 1616 S 120TH ST 68144
Anthony Lagreca, prin.
Bryan JHS, 8210 S 42ND ST 68147
Raymond Ramsey, prin.
Marrs JHS, 5619 S 19TH ST 68107
James Hubschman, prin.
McMillan JHS, 3802 REDICK AVE 68112
Norma Deeb, prin.
Monroe JHS, 5105 BEDFORD AVE 68104
James Vincent, prin.
Morton JHS, 4606 TERRACE DRIVE 68134
Roger Bridenbaugh, prin.
Adams ES, 3420 N 78TH ST 68134
Gerald Austin, prin.
Ashland Park ES, 4768 Q ST 68117
Raymond Perrigo, prin.
Bancroft ES, 2724 RIVERVIEW BLVD 68108
(—), prin.
Beals ES, 1720 S 48TH ST 68106
Cynthia Hardiman, prin.
Belvedere ES, 6224 N 37TH ST 68111
Cornelius Jackson, prin.
Benson West ES, 1312 ROBERTSON DR 68114
Edward Huff, prin.
Boyd ES, 8314 BOYD ST 68134
Gary Noerrlinger, prin.
Catlin ES, 12736 MARINDA ST 68144
Kay Mayberry, prin.
Central Park ES, 4914 N 42ND ST 68111
Claudia Watson, prin.
Chandler View ES, 7800 S 25TH ST 68147
David Peterson, prin.
Columbian ES, 330 S 127TH ST 68154
Marilynn Haig, prin.
Conestoga ES, 2115 BURDETTE ST 68110
Katie Dailey, prin.
Crestridge ES, 818 CRESTRIDGE RD 68154
Mary Ann Devaughn, prin.
Dodge ES, 3520 MAPLEWOOD BLVD 68134
Ramona Bartee, prin.
Druid Hill ES, 3030 SPAULDING ST 68111
Jeanne Rogers, prin.
Dundee ES, 310 N 51ST ST 68132
Virginia Bowers, prin.
Edison ES, 2303 N 97TH ST 68134
Joan Lopez, prin.
Field Club ES, 1711 S 36TH ST 68105
William Pullen, prin.
Florence ES, 7902 N 36TH ST 68112
Melvin Clancy, prin.
Fontenelle ES, 3905 N 52ND ST 68104
James Freeman, prin.
Franklin ES, 3506 FRANKLIN ST 68111
Linda Placzek, prin.
Gilder ES, 3705 CHANDLER RD 68147
Lorraine Giles, prin.
Harrison ES, 5304 HAMILTON ST 68132
David Schroeder, prin.
Hartman ES, 5530 N 66TH ST 68104
Janet Pinaire, prin.
Highland ES, 6313 S 27TH ST 68107
Vivian Roper, prin.
Indian Hill ES, 3902 DAVENPORT ST 68131
Kay Moore, prin.
Jefferson ES, 4065 VINTON ST 68105
Christie Fishbaugh, prin.

Joslyn ES, 11220 BLONDO ST 68164
  Sandra Pistone, prin.
Kellom ES, 1311 N 24TH ST 68102
  Joan Chapin, prin.
Kennedy ES, 2906 N 30TH ST 68111
  William Lutz, prin.
King PS, 3706 MAPLE ST 68111 – (—), prin.
King Science Centers
  3720 FLORENCE BLVD 68110 – (—), prin.
Lothrop ES, 3424 N 22ND ST 68110
  Warren Taylor, prin.
Lusa ES, 6905 N 28TH AVE 68112
  Richard Jorgensen, prin.
Marrs ES, 5619 S 19TH ST 68107
  James Hubschman, prin.
Masters ES, 5505 N 99TH ST 68134
  Donald Wohlers, prin.
Miller Park ES, 2758 ELLISON AVE 68111
  Duane Iwen, prin.
Mt. View ES, 5322 N 52ND ST 68104
  Sandra Hodges, prin.
Oak Valley ES, 3109 PEDERSEN DR 68144
  Norma Johnson, prin.
Pawnee ES, 7310 S 48TH ST 68157
  Betty Haskins, prin.
Pinewood ES, 6306 REDICK AVE 68152
  Stephen Maher, prin.
Ponca ES, 11300 N POST RD 68112
  Joann Haafke, prin.
Robbins ES, 4302 S 39TH AVE 68107
  Sandra McGee, prin.
Rosehill ES, 5605 CORBY ST 68104
  (—), prin.
Ryan ES, 1807 S 60TH ST 68106
  Jeanne Rogers, prin.
Saratoga ES, 2504 MEREDITH AVE 68111
  Kim Whitehouse, prin.
Sherman ES, 5618 N 14TH AVE 68110
  Hubert Carter, prin.
Spring Lake ES, 4215 S 20TH ST 68107
  Darline Blotzer, prin.
Springville ES, 7300 N 60TH ST 68152
  Phyllis Beam, prin.
Sunny Slope ES, 10828 OLD MAPLE RD 68164
  Lou Landholm, prin.
Wakonda ES, 4845 CURTIS AVE 68104
  Kevin Welsh, prin.
Walnut Hill ES, 4370 HAMILTON ST 68131
  Edwardene Armstrong, prin.
Washington ES, 5519 MAYBERRY AVE 68106
  Linda Krause, prin.
Western Hills ES, 6523 WESTERN AVE 68132
  Mercedes Bullard, prin.
Yates ES, 3260 DAVENPORT ST 68131
  William Brooks, prin.

Papillion-La Vista SD
Supt. – See La Vista
Anderson Grove ES, 11820 S 37TH ST 68123
  Mary Ella Pangle, prin.
Golden Hills ES, 2912 COFFEY AVE 68123
  Harlan Cook, prin.

Ralston SD
Supt. – See Ralston
Blumfield ES, 10310 MOCKINGBIRD DR 68127
  Jerry Rutherford, prin.
Meadows ES, 92ND & BERRY 68127
  Richard Bonham, prin.
Mockingbird ES, 93RD & Q ST 68127
  Howard Martin, prin.
Western ES, 6224 H ST 68117
  James Heater, prin.

South Sarpy SD 46
Supt. – See Springfield
La Platte ES, 16405 CLAY ST 68123
  Louis Dambrosia, prin.

Westside Comm. SD
Sch. Sys. Enr. Code 5
Supt. – James Tangdall, 909 S 76TH ST 68114
Westside MS, 8601 MARTHA ST 68124
  Leslie Sladek, prin.
Hillside ES, 75TH & WESTERN AVE 68114
  Paul Nelson, prin.
Loveland ES, 81ST AND PACIFIC ST 68127
  Robert Bruckner, prin.
Oakdale ES, 98TH & CENTER 68124
  Francis Carr, prin.
Paddock Road ES, 3535 PADDOCK RD 68124
  Carolyn Law, prin.
Prairie Lane ES, 114TH & HASCALL 68144
  Allan Inzerello, prin.
Rockbrook ES, 2514 S 108TH ST 68144
  Allan Inzerello, prin.
Sunset Hills ES, 94TH WALNUT 68124
  Francis Carr, prin.
Swanson ES, 86TH & HARNEY 68114
  Jacquelyn Estee, prin.
Underwood Hills ES, 90TH AND WESTERN 68114
  Jack Welch, prin.
Westgate ES, 78TH & HASCALL 68124
  Mary Drew, prin.

Bellevue Christian School, 1722 S 16TH ST 68108
Brownell Talbot School
  400 N HAPPY HOLLOW BLVD 68132
Holy Name School
  2909 FONTENELLE BLVD 68104
Assumption ES, 5602 S 22ND ST 68107
Blessed Sacrament ES, 6316 N 30TH ST 68111
Cardinal Spellman ES, 12210 S 36TH ST 68123
Catholic Southeast ES 1, 1333 S 10TH ST 68108
Catholic Southeast ES 2, 2326 S 14TH ST 68108

Christ the King ES, 831 S 88TH ST 68114
Holy Cross ES, 1502 S 48TH ST 68106
Holy Ghost ES, 5302 S 52ND ST 68117
Immaculate Conception ES
  2716 S 24TH ST 68108
Mary our Queen, 3405 S 119TH ST 68144
Our Lady of Lourdes ES, 2124 S 32ND AVE 68105
Sacred Heart ES, 2205 BINNEY ST 68110
St. Bernard ES, 3604 N 6TH ST 68104
St. Bernadette School, 7600 S 42ND ST 68147
St. Cecilia Cathedral ES, 3869 WEBSTER ST 68131
St. James-Seton ES
  9212 TOMAHAWK BLVD 68134
St. Joan of Arc ES, 7430 HASCALL ST 68124
St. Margaret Mary ES, 123 N 61ST ST 68132
St. Mary ES, 5215 S 36TH ST 68107
St. Paul Lutheran ES, 5016 GRAND AVE 68104
St. Peter ES, 2726 LEAVENWORTH ST 68105
St. Philip Neri ES, 8202 N 31ST ST 68112
St. Pius/St. Leo ES, 6905 BLONDO ST 68104
St. Richard ES, 4318 FORT ST 68111
St. Robert Bellermine ES
  11900 PACIFIC ST 68154
St. Stanislaus ES, 4501 S 41ST ST 68107
St. Thomas More ES, 3515 S 48TH AVE 68106
St. Wenceslaus School, 15353 PACIFIC ST 68154
Sts. Peter & Paul ES, 3619 X ST 68107
Temple Christian ES, 2702 N 61ST ST 68104
Zion Lutheran ES, 4001 Q STRRET 68107

O'Neill, Holt Co., Pop. Code 5
O'Neil SD
Sch. Sys. Enr. Code 3
Supt. – Richard Brommer, P O BOX 230 68763
ES, P O BOX 230 68763 – Denis Kaeding, prin.

St. Mary's ES, 3RD & BENTON 68763

Orchard, Antelope Co., Pop. Code 2
Orchard SD
Sch. Sys. Enr. Code 2
Supt. – J. Allen Schlueter, P O BOX 269 68764
ES, P O BOX 269 68764 – J. Schlueter, prin.

Ord, Valley Co., Pop. Code 5
Ord SD
Sch. Sys. Enr. Code 3
Supt. – William Gogan, 18TH & K STS 68862
ES, RURAL ROUTE 02 BOX 9 68862
  Thomas Wlaschin, prin.

St. Mary's School, 527 N 20TH ST 68862

Orleans, Harlan Co., Pop. Code 3
Orleans SD
Sch. Sys. Enr. Code 2
Supt. – Marvin Thomsen, P O BOX 477 68966
ES, P O BOX 477 68966 – David Brady, prin.

Osceola, Polk Co., Pop. Code 3
Osceola SD
Sch. Sys. Enr. Code 2
Supt. – Kenneth Sipes, P O BOX 175 68651
ES, P O BOX 175 68651 – Allen Brozovsky, prin.

Oshkosh, Garden Co., Pop. Code 4
Oshkosh ESD
Sch. Sys. Enr. Code 2
Supt. – Myron Jasnoch, P O BOX 200 69154
ES, P O BOX 200 69154 – Myron Jasnoch, prin.

Osmond, Pierce Co., Pop. Code 3
Osmond SD
Sch. Sys. Enr. Code 2
Supt. – James Walker, P O BOX 458 68765
ES, P O BOX 458 68765 – James Walker, prin.

Overton, Dawson Co., Pop. Code 3
Overton SD
Sch. Sys. Enr. Code 2
Supt. – Lyle Veal, P O BOX 310 68863
ES, P O BOX 310 68863 – William Patterson, prin.

Oxford, Furnas Co., Pop. Code 4
Oxford Comm. SD
Sch. Sys. Enr. Code 2
Supt. – Nathan Stineman, P O BOX 7 68967
ES, P O BOX 7 68967 – James Bathen, prin.

Palisade, Hitchcock Co., Pop. Code 2
Palisade SD
Sch. Sys. Enr. Code 2
Supt. – Stanley Kravig, P O BOX O 69040
ES, P O BOX O 69040 – Stanley Kravig, prin.

Palmer, Merrick Co., Pop. Code 2
Palmer SD
Sch. Sys. Enr. Code 2
Supt. – Richard Chochon, P O BOX 248 68864
ES, P O BOX 248 68864 – Richard Chochon, prin.

Palmyra, Otoe Co., Pop. Code 3
Palmyra SD
Sch. Sys. Enr. Code 2
Supt. – Gary Fritch, P O BOX 38 68418
Other Schools – See Bennet

Papillion, Sarpy Co., Pop. Code 6
Papillion-La Vista SD
Supt. – See La Vista
Carriage Hill ES, 400 CEDAR DALE RD 68046
  Donald Hooper, prin.
Hickory Hill ES, 1307 ROGERS DR 68128
  James Melonis, prin.
Tara Heights ES, 700 TARA RD 68046
  Richard Moore, prin.
Trumble Park ES, 500 VALLEY RD 68046
  Darlene Farrell, prin.

St. Columbkille ES, 224 E FIFTH ST 68046

Pawnee City, Pawnee Co., Pop. Code 4
Pawnee City SD
Sch. Sys. Enr. Code 2
Supt. – Larry Harnisch, P O BOX 393 68420
ES, P O BOX 393 68420 – L. Halley, prin.

Paxton, Keith Co., Pop. Code 3
Paxton Cons. SD
Sch. Sys. Enr. Code 2
Supt. – Glen Morgan, P O BOX 368 69155
ES, P O BOX 368 69155 – Glen Morgan, prin.

Pender, Thurston Co., Pop. Code 4
Pender SD
Sch. Sys. Enr. Code 2
Supt. – James Brazee, 609 WHITNEY 68047
ES, 609 WHITNEY ST 68047
  Carla Boeshart, prin.
Other Schools – See Thurston

Peru, Nemaha Co., Pop. Code 3
Auburn SD
Supt. – See Auburn
ES 68421 – Robert Robinson, prin.

Petersburg, Boone Co., Pop. Code 2
Petersburg SD
Sch. Sys. Enr. Code 2
Supt. – Richard Schlesselman, P O BOX 240 68652
ES, P O BOX 240 68652 – (—), prin.

Pierce, Pierce Co., Pop. Code 4
Pierce SD
Sch. Sys. Enr. Code 3
Supt. – Philip Fahlk, P O BOX 120 68767
ES, P O BOX 189 68767 – Michael Engel, prin.

Zion Lutheran ES, 520 E MAIN ST 68767

Pilger, Stanton Co., Pop. Code 2
Wisner-Pilger SD
Supt. – See Wisner
ES at Pilger 68768 – Carolyn Pint, prin.

Plainview, Pierce Co., Pop. Code 4
Plainview SD
Sch. Sys. Enr. Code 2
Supt. – Robert Mayer, 100 PILCHER AVE 68769
ES, 100 WOODLAND AVE 68769
  Gale Retzlaff, prin.
Other Schools – See Brunswick

Zion Lutheran ES, P O BOX 159 68769

Plattsmouth, Cass Co., Pop. Code 6
Plattsmouth SD
Sch. Sys. Enr. Code 4
Supt. – Jack Herweg, 2101 S 15TH ST 68048
MS, 8TH & MAIN 68048 – Dale Chesley, prin.
Central ES, 10TH & MAIN 68048
  Allan Pestel, prin.
Columbian ES, 6TH AVE 68048
  Allan Pestel, prin.
First Ward ES, 5TH & AVE D 68048
  Donna Lukash, prin.
Lincoln ES, LINCOLN & BRYANT 68048
  Donna Lukash, prin.

St. John the Baptist ES, 324 N 5TH ST 68048

Pleasant Dale, Seward Co., Pop. Code 2
Milford SD
Supt. – See Milford
ES 68423 – Rodney Bleich, prin.

Pleasanton, Buffalo Co., Pop. Code 2
Pleasanton SD
Sch. Sys. Enr. Code 2
Supt. – Larry Johnson, P O BOX 167 68866
ES, P O BOX 167 68866 – Larry Johnson, prin.

Polk, Polk Co., Pop. Code 2
Polk-Hordville SD
Sch. Sys. Enr. Code 2
Supt. – Dennis Gray, P O BOX 29 68654
ES, P O BOX 29 68654 – Dennis Gray, prin.
Other Schools – See Hordville

Ponca, Dixon Co., Pop. Code 4
Ponca SD
Sch. Sys. Enr. Code 2
Supt. – Lionel Froseth, P O BOX 610 68770
ES, P O BOX 610 68770 – Lionel Froseth, prin.

Potter, Cheyenne Co., Pop. Code 2
Potter-Dix SD
Sch. Sys. Enr. Code 2
Supt. – Virgil Combs, P O BOX P 69156
Potter-Dix ES, P O BOX P 69156
  Charles Bunner, prin.
Other Schools – See Dix

Prague, Saunders Co., Pop. Code 2
Prague SD
Sch. Sys. Enr. Code 2
Supt. – Robert Fyfe, P O BOX 98 68050
ES, P O BOX 98 68050 – Arlene Kracl, prin.

Ralston, Douglas Co., Pop. Code 6
Ralston SD
Sch. Sys. Enr. Code 5
Supt. – Kenneth Rippe, 8545 PARK DRIVE 68127
MS, 82ND & LAKEVIEW 68127
  Lonnie Bernth, prin.

Seymour ES, 79TH & SEYMOUR 68127
    Janice Branch, prin.
Wildewood ES, 81ST & RALSTON AVE 68127
    Donald Tuch, prin.
Other Schools – See Omaha

St. Gerald ES, 7857 LAKEVIEW ST 68127

Randolph, Cedar Co., Pop. Code 4
Randolph SD
Sch. Sys. Enr. Code 2
Supt. – N. Kluver, P O BOX 440 68771
ES, P O BOX 440 68771 – Gary Speer, prin.

Ravenna, Buffalo Co., Pop. Code 4
Ravenna SD
Supt. – Edwin Hollinger
    740 W CARTHAGE ST 68869
ES, 710 GRAND AVE 68869 – Mary Hoover, prin.

Raymond, Lancaster Co., Pop. Code 2
Raymond Central SD
Sch. Sys. Enr. Code 3
Supt. – Ron Karr, P O BOX 180A 68428
Other Schools – See Ceresco, Valparaiso

Red Cloud, Webster Co., Pop. Code 4
Red Cloud SD
Sch. Sys. Enr. Code 2
Supt. – Kenneth Anderson, P O BOX 488 68970
ES, P O BOX 488 68970 – Rick Michaelsen, prin.

Rising City, Butler Co., Pop. Code 2
Rising City SD
Sch. Sys. Enr. Code 2
Supt. – James Havelka, P O BOX 160 68658
ES, P O BOX 160 68658 – James Havelka, prin.

Rosalie, Thurston Co., Pop. Code 2
Bancroft-Rosalie SD
Supt. – See Bancroft
ES at Rosalie, P O BOX 225 68055
    William Lewis, prin.

Roseland, Adams Co., Pop. Code 2
Silver Lake SD
Sch. Sys. Enr. Code 2
Supt. – Gale McDonald, P O BOX 8 68973
Other Schools – See Bladen

Rushville, Sheridan Co., Pop. Code 4
Rushville SD
Sch. Sys. Enr. Code 2
Supt. – D. Jones, 310 SPRAGUE ST 69360
ES, 310 SPRAGUE ST 69360 – Paula Calkins, prin.

Saint Edward, Boone Co., Pop. Code 3
St. Edward SD
Sch. Sys. Enr. Code 2
Supt. – William Hellerich, P O BOX C 68660
ES, P O BOX C 68660 – William Hellerich, prin.

Saint Helena, Cedar Co., Pop. Code 2

East Catholic ES, P O BOX 59 68774

Saint Paul, Howard Co., Pop. Code 4
St. Paul SD
Sch. Sys. Enr. Code 3
Supt. – Douglas Ackles
    1305 HOWARD AVE 68873
ES, 1305 HOWARD AVE 68873
    Jolen Palmer, prin.

Sargent, Custer Co., Pop. Code 3
Sargent SD
Sch. Sys. Enr. Code 2
Supt. – James Berryman, P O BOX 366 68874
ES, P O BOX 366 68874 – (—), prin.

Schuyler, Colfax Co., Pop. Code 4
Schuyler ESD
Sch. Sys. Enr. Code 3
Supt. – Harlan Haile, 200 W 10TH ST 68661
Schuyler West Ward MS, 200 W 10TH ST 68661
    Harlan Hailey, prin.
Schuyler North Ward ES, 100 E 15TH ST 68661
    Harlan Hailey, prin.

Scotia, Greeley Co., Pop. Code 2
North Loup Scotia SD
Sch. Sys. Enr. Code 2
Supt. – Elmer Corbit, P O BOX 307 68875
Other Schools – See North Loup

Scottsbluff, Scotts Bluff Co., Pop. Code 7
Scottsbluff SD
Sch. Sys. Enr. Code 5
Supt. – James Brisson, 2601 BROADWAY 69361
Bluffs MS, 23RD & BROADWAY 69361
    Nicholas Marick, prin.
Lincoln Heights ES, 2212 AVENUE C 69361
    Virgil Baker, prin.
Longfellow ES, 2005 5TH AVE 69361
    Patricia Gritzfeld, prin.
Roosevelt ES, 1306 9TH AVE 69361
    Robert Ziegler, prin.
West Moor ES, 1722 AVENUE K 69361
    Robert Kihlthau, prin.

St. Agnes ES, 205 E 23RD ST 69361

Scribner, Dodge Co., Pop. Code 4
Scribner-Snyder SD
Sch. Sys. Enr. Code 2
Supt. – Dennis Wittmann, P O BOX L 68057
ES 68057 – Robert Stading, prin.

Snyder ES, P O BOX L 68057
    Robert Stading, prin.

Seward, Seward Co., Pop. Code 6
Seward SD
Sch. Sys. Enr. Code 4
Supt. – Marvin Shreve, 803 W SEWARD ST 68434
ES 68434 – Janette Holtzen, prin.
Other Schools – See Garland, Goehner, Staplehurst

St. John Lutheran ES
    877 N COLUMBIA AVE 68434

Shelby, Polk Co., Pop. Code 3
Shelby SD
Sch. Sys. Enr. Code 2
Supt. – R. Pesicka, P O BOX 218 68662
ES, P O BOX 218 68662 – Romaine Pesicka, prin.

Shelton, Buffalo Co., Pop. Code 4
Shelton SD
Sch. Sys. Enr. Code 2
Supt. – Don South, P O BOX 500 68876
ES, P O BOX 500 68876 – Ronald Hudson, prin.

Shickley, Fillmore Co., Pop. Code 2
Shickley SD
Sch. Sys. Enr. Code 2
Supt. – Edward Briscoe, P O BOX 137 68436
ES 68436 – (—), prin.

Sidney, Cheyenne Co., Pop. Code 6
Sidney SD
Sch. Sys. Enr. Code 4
Supt. – David Reichert, 1122 19TH AVE 69162
JHS, 1122 19TH AVE 69162
    Gerald Vanbuskirk, prin.
Central MS, 16TH & KING ST 69162
    William Rogers, prin.
North Ward ES, 434 16TH AVE 69162
    Lowell Hawks, prin.
South Ward ES, 12TH & TOLEDO 69162
    Lowell Hawks, prin.

Silver Creek, Merrick Co., Pop. Code 2
Silver Creek SD
Sch. Sys. Enr. Code 2
Supt. – Larry Meyer, P O BOX 247 68663
ES, P O BOX 247 68663 – Larry Meyer, prin.

South Sioux City, Dakota Co., Pop. Code 6
South Sioux City SD
Sch. Sys. Enr. Code 5
Supt. – Vandle Phillips, P O BOX 158 68776
Harney ES, 1201 B ST 68776
    William Tomicek, prin.
Lewis & Clark ES, 801 2ND AVE 68776
    Roger Winterlin, prin.
MS, 2116 A ST 68776 – Alvern Agrimson, prin.
Swett ES, 2300 C ST 68776
    William Tomicek, prin.
Other Schools – See Dakota City

St. Michael ES, 1315 1ST AVE 68776

Spalding, Greeley Co., Pop. Code 3
Spalding SD
Sch. Sys. Enr. Code 2
Supt. – Benje Hookstra, P O BOX 220 68665
ES, P O BOX 220 68665 – Benje Hookstra, prin.

Spalding Academy, P O BOX A 68665

Spencer, Boyd Co., Pop. Code 3
Spencer-Naper SD
Sch. Sys. Enr. Code 2
Supt. – Dale Reber, P O BOX 109 68777
ES, P O BOX 109 68777 – Dale Reber, prin.
Other Schools – See Naper

Springfield, Sarpy Co., Pop. Code 3
South Sarpy SD 46
Sch. Sys. Enr. Code 3
Supt. – Robert Diekmann, S 3RD 68059
Platteview Central JHS
    108TH & PLATTEVIEW ROAD 68059
    Gerald Ryan, prin.
ES, MAIN ST 68059 – Richard Hindalong, prin.
Westmont ES, RICHLAND DR & GLEN ST 68059
    Connie Baxter, prin.
Other Schools – See Omaha

Stanton, Stanton Co., Pop. Code 4
Stanton Comm. SD
Sch. Sys. Enr. Code 2
Supt. – Don Schmidt, P O BOX 857 68779
ES, P O BOX 749 68779 – Trudie Jansen, prin.

Staplehurst, Seward Co., Pop. Code 2
Seward SD
Supt. – See Seward
ES at Staplehurst 68439 – Janette Holtzen, prin.

Stapleton, Logan Co., Pop. Code 2
Stapleton SD
Sch. Sys. Enr. Code 2
Supt. – George Rogers, P O BOX 128 69163
ES, P O BOX 128 69163 – George Rogers, prin.

Stella, Richardson Co., Pop. Code 2
Southeast Cons. SD
Sch. Sys. Enr. Code 2
Supt. – Stephen Deger, P O BOX 73 68442
ES at Stella, P O BOX 73 68442
    Stephen Deger, prin.

Sterling, Johnson Co., Pop. Code 3
Sterling SD
Sch. Sys. Enr. Code 2
Supt. – Dennis Chipman, P O BOX 39 68443
ES, P O BOX 39 68443 – Dennis Chipman, prin.

Stratton, Hitchcock Co., Pop. Code 2
Stratton SD
Sch. Sys. Enr. Code 2
Supt. – Larry Schall, P O BOX 324 69043
ES, P O BOX 324 69043 – Larry Schall, prin.

Stromsburg, Polk Co., Pop. Code 4
Stromsburg SD
Sch. Sys. Enr. Code 2
Supt. – Donald Holmberg, P O BOX 525 68666
ES, P O BOX 525 68666 – Rodney Oldenburg, prin.

Stuart, Holt Co., Pop. Code 3
Stuart SD
Sch. Sys. Enr. Code 2
Supt. – Rodger Lenhard, P O BOX G 68780
ES, P O BOX G 68780 – Rodger Lenhard, prin.

Sumner, Dawson Co., Pop. Code 2
Sumner-Eddyville-Miller SD
Sch. Sys. Enr. Code 2
Supt. – Richard Hodge, P O BOX 126 68878
Sumner ES, P O BOX 126 68878
    Richard Hodge, prin.

Superior, Nuckolls Co., Pop. Code 5
Superior SD
Sch. Sys. Enr. Code 3
Supt. – Raymond Cox, W 8TH ST 68978
North Ward ES, 10TH & BLOOM 68978
    Larry Fuller, prin.
South Ward ES, 3RD & DAKOTA 68978
    Larry Fuller, prin.

Sutherland, Lincoln Co., Pop. Code 4
Sutherland SD
Sch. Sys. Enr. Code 2
Supt. – Michael Cunning, P O BOX 217 69165
ES, P O BOX 217 69165 – Lyn Johnson, prin.

Sutton, Clay Co., Pop. Code 4
Sutton SD
Sch. Sys. Enr. Code 2
Supt. – Ronald Wall, P O BOX 590 68979
ES, P O BOX 590 68979 – Dennis Isemhagen, prin.

Syracuse, Otoe Co., Pop. Code 4
Syracuse-Dunbar-Avoca SD
Sch. Sys. Enr. Code 3
Supt. – Edwin Johnson, 550 7TH ST 68446
ES at Syracuse, 550 7TH ST 68446
    Roger Witt, prin.

Table Rock, Pawnee Co., Pop. Code 2
Table Rock SD
Sch. Sys. Enr. Code 2
Supt. – Duane Stehlik, P O BOX F 68447
ES 68447 – Duane Stehlik, prin.

Talmage, Otoe Co., Pop. Code 2
Nemaha Valley SD
Supt. – See Cook
ES at Talmage 68448 – Gary Oxley, prin.

Taylor, Loup Co., Pop. Code 2
Loup County SD
Sch. Sys. Enr. Code 2
Supt. – Christina Kochenash, P O BOX 38 68879
Loup County ES, P O BOX 170 68879
    Christina Kochenash, prin.

Tecumseh, Johnson Co., Pop. Code 4
Tecumseh SD
Sch. Sys. Enr. Code 2
Supt. – Thomas Rother, P O BOX 338 68450
ES, P O BOX 338 68450 – Thomas Rother, prin.

Tekamah, Burt Co., Pop. Code 4
Tekamah-Herman SD
Sch. Sys. Enr. Code 3
Supt. – Raymond Chase, 112 N 13TH ST 68061
ES at Tekamah, 112 N 13TH ST 68061
    Richard Grandgenett, prin.
Other Schools – See Herman

Thurston, Thurston Co., Pop. Code 2
Pender SD
Supt. – See Pender
MS 68062 – Carla Boeshart, prin.

Tilden, Madison Co., Pop. Code 4
Elkhorn Valley SD
Sch. Sys. Enr. Code 2
Supt. – Frank Cummings, P O BOX 430 68781
Elkhorn Valley ES, 601 S MADISON 68781
    Frank Cummings, prin.

Trenton, Hitchcock Co., Pop. Code 3
Trenton SD
Sch. Sys. Enr. Code 2
Supt. – Kurt Harrison, P O BOX 368 69044
ES, P O BOX 368 69044 – Kurt Harrison, prin.

Trumbull, Clay Co., Pop. Code 2
Trumbull SD
Sch. Sys. Enr. Code 2
Supt. – Francis Shaughnessy, P O BOX 94 68980
ES, P O BOX 94 68980
    Francis Shaughnessy, prin.

Utica, Seward Co., Pop. Code 3
Centennial SD
Sch. Sys. Enr. Code 3
Supt. – Ronald Oswald, P O BOX 187 68456

Other Schools – See Gresham
_____

St. Paul Lutheran ES, P O BOX 67   68456

Valentine, Cherry Co., Pop. Code 5
Valentine ESD
Sch. Sys. Enr. Code 3
Supt. – Stephen Saum, 239 N WOOD ST   69201
MS, 239 N WOOD ST   69201
  Stephen Saum, prin.
ES, 239 N WOOD ST   69201
  Arthur Hudson, prin.

Valley, Douglas Co., Pop. Code 4
Valley SD
Sch. Sys. Enr. Code 3
Supt. – Gil Kettelhut, 401 S PINE ST   68064
MS, 401 S PINE   68064 – (—), prin.
ES, 401 S PINE ST   68064 – Robert Stiefel, prin.

Valparaiso, Saunders Co., Pop. Code 2
Raymond Central SD
Supt. – See Raymond
ES at Valparaiso, P O BOX 68   68065
  Kristine Wolzen, prin.

Venango, Perkins Co., Pop. Code 2
Venago SD
Sch. Sys. Enr. Code 1
Supt. – Alvin Christensen, P O BOX 37   69168
ES, P O BOX 37   69168 – (—), prin.

Verdigre, Knox Co., Pop. Code 3
Verdigre SD
Sch. Sys. Enr. Code 2
Supt. – William Troshynski   68783
ES   68783 – William Troshynski, prin.

Wahoo, Saunders Co., Pop. Code 5
Wahoo SD
Sch. Sys. Enr. Code 3
Supt. – Kent Mann, 2201 LOCUST ST   68066
MS, 2201 LOCUST ST   68066
  Cecil Tillman, prin.
West Ward ES, 743 LOCUST ST   68066
  Cecil Tillman, prin.
_____

St. Wenceslaus ES, 2ND & BEECH   68066

Wakefield, Dixon Co., Pop. Code 4
Wakefield SD
Sch. Sys. Enr. Code 2
Supt. – Derwin Hartman, P O BOX 98   68784
ES, P O BOX 98   68784 – Derwin Hartman, prin.

Wallace, Lincoln Co., Pop. Code 2
Wallace SD
Sch. Sys. Enr. Code 2
Supt. – Gene Haddix, P O BOX 197   69169
ES, P O BOX 197   69169 – Gene Haddix, prin.

Walthill, Thurston Co., Pop. Code 3
Walthill SD
Sch. Sys. Enr. Code 2
Supt. – Ervin Deboer, P O BOX 3C   68067
ES, P O BOX 3C   68067 – Joseph Colling, prin.

Waterloo, Douglas Co., Pop. Code 2
Waterloo SD
Sch. Sys. Enr. Code 2
Supt. – Thomas McMahon
  7TH & WASHINGTON   68069

ES, 7TH & WASHINGTON   68069
  Scott Clark, prin.

Wauneta, Chase Co., Pop. Code 3
Wauneta SD
Sch. Sys. Enr. Code 2
Supt. – Dennis Wentz, P O BOX 368   69045
ES, P O BOX 368   69045 – Dennis Wentz, prin.

Wausa, Knox Co., Pop. Code 3
Wausa SD
Sch. Sys. Enr. Code 2
Supt. – Robert Rogers, P O BOX 159   68786
ES, P O BOX 159   68786 – Robert Rogers, prin.

Waverly, Lancaster Co., Pop. Code 4
Waverly SD
Sch. Sys. Enr. Code 4
Supt. – James Ossian, P O BOX 426   68462
JHS, 14621 HEYWOOD ST   68462
  Kevin Peters, prin.
Hamlow ES, P O BOX 426   68462
  Tommy Hill, prin.
Other Schools – See Eagle

Wayne, Wayne Co., Pop. Code 6
Wayne SD
Sch. Sys. Enr. Code 3
Supt. – Francis Haun, 611 W 7TH ST   68787
MS, 312 DOUGLAS ST   68787
  Richard Metteer, prin.
Wayne West ES, 612 E 4TH ST   68787
  David Lutt, prin.
Other Schools – See Carroll

Weeping Water, Cass Co., Pop. Code 4
Weeping Water SD
Sch. Sys. Enr. Code 2
Supt. – Louis Eberhart, P O BOX 206   68463
ES, P O BOX 206   68463 – David Melick, prin.

Weston, Saunders Co., Pop. Code 2
_____

St. John School, P O BOX 10   68070

West Point, Cuming Co., Pop. Code 5
West Point SD
Sch. Sys. Enr. Code 3
Supt. – K. Echtenkamp, E WASHINGTON   68788
ES, 119 N COLFAX ST   68788
  Douglas Witte, prin.
_____

Guardian Angel ES, 408 E WALNUT ST   68788
St. Pauls Lutheran ES, 244 E WALNUT   68788

Wilber, Saline Co., Pop. Code 4
Wilber-Clatonia SD
Sch. Sys. Enr. Code 3
Supt. – Tucker Lillis, 9TH & FRANKLIN   68465
ES at Wilber, 500 W ELM   68465
  Thomas Reeser, prin.

Wilcox, Kearney Co., Pop. Code 2
Wilcox SD
Sch. Sys. Enr. Code 2
Supt. – Glen Lewis, P O BOX 190   68982
ES, P O BOX 190   68982 – Glen Lewis, prin.

Wilsonville, Furnas Co., Pop. Code 2
Beaver Valley SD
Supt. – See Lebanon
ES at Wilsonville, P O BOX 158   69046
  Ladonna Harrison, prin.

Winnebago, Thurston Co., Pop. Code 3
Winnebago SD
Sch. Sys. Enr. Code 2
Supt. – Gale Johnston, P O BOX KK   68071
ES, P O BOX KK   68071 – Kennith Wathen, prin.

Winside, Wayne Co., Pop. Code 2
Winside SD
Sch. Sys. Enr. Code 2
Supt. – Donavon Leighton, P O BOX 158   68790
ES, P O BOX 158   68790 – Donavon Leighton, prin.

Wisner, Cuming Co., Pop. Code 4
Wisner-Pilger SD
Sch. Sys. Enr. Code 2
Supt. – William Hakonson, P O BOX 580   68791
ES at Wisner, P O BOX 580   68791
  Carolyn Pint, prin.
Other Schools – See Pilger

Wolbach, Greeley Co., Pop. Code 2
Wolbach SD
Sch. Sys. Enr. Code 2
Supt. – John Bond, P O BOX 67   68882
ES, P O BOX 67   68882 – John Bond, prin.

Wood River, Hall Co., Pop. Code 4
Wood River ESD
Sch. Sys. Enr. Code 2
Supt. – Michael Kavanaugh, P O BOX 488   68883
ES, P O BOX 488   68883
  Michael Kavanaugh, prin.

Wymore, Gage Co., Pop. Code 4
Southern SD 1
Sch. Sys. Enr. Code 2
Supt. – Larry Humphrey, 115 S 11TH ST   68466
Other Schools – See Blue Springs

Wynot, Cedar Co., Pop. Code 2
Wynot SD
Sch. Sys. Enr. Code 2
Supt. – Tedsen Hillman, P O BOX 157   68792
ES, P O BOX 157   68792 – Tedsen Hellman, prin.

York, York Co., Pop. Code 6
York SD
Sch. Sys. Enr. Code 4
Supt. – Paul Toms, 611 PLATTE AVE   68467
MS, 12TH & EAST AVE   68467
  Richard Moses, prin.
Edison ES, 1822 IOWA AVE   68467
  Stuart Wiley, prin.
Lincoln ES, 515 YORK AVE   68467
  Linda Bolt, prin.
Willard ES, 510 BLACKBURN AVE   68467
  Ellwood Ziegler, prin.
_____

Emmanuel Lutheran ES, 9TH & BEAVER   68467
St. Josephs ES, 428 EAST AVE   68467

Yutan, Saunders Co., Pop. Code 3
Yutan SD
Sch. Sys. Enr. Code 2
Supt. – Nelson Hinkle, P O BOX C   68073
ES, P O BOX 502   68073 – Claudia Carter, prin.

NEVADA

STATE DEPARTMENT OF EDUCATION
Capitol Complex
400 W. King St., Carson City 89710
(700) 885-3100

Superintendent of Instruction	Eugene Paslov
Deputy Superintendent Administrative & Fiscal Services	Richard White
Deputy Superintendent Instructional, Research, Evaluative Services	Marcia Bandera

STATE BOARD OF EDUCATION
Marianne Logg, *President*   1021 E. Oakley Blvd., Las Vegas   89104

NEVADA COMMISSION ON POSTSECONDARY EDUCATION
John Griffin, *Administrator*   1000 E. Williams #102, Carson City   89710

PUBLIC, PRIVATE, AND PAROCHIAL ELEMENTARY SCHOOLS

Alamo, Lincoln Co., Pop. Code 4
Lincoln County SD
Supt. – See Panaca
Pahranagat Valley ES, P O BOX 178 89001
Helen Foremaster, prin.

Amargosa Valley, Nye Co.
Nye County SD
Supt. – See Tonopah
ES, HCR 15 BOX 4012 89020
Robert O'Brien, prin.

Austin, Lander Co., Pop. Code 2
Lander County SD
Supt. – See Battle Mountain
ES, P O BOX 160 89310
Wayne Montgomery, prin.

Baker, White Pine Co.
White Pine County SD
Supt. – See East Ely
MS 89311 – (—), prin.

Battle Mountain, Lander Co., Pop. Code 4
Lander County SD
Sch. Sys. Enr. Code 4
Supt. – Dr. Leon Hensley, P O BOX 1300 89820
JHS, P O BOX 1360 89820 – Steve Larsgaard, prin.
Black MS, P O BOX 1390 89820
Carl Hastings, prin.
Pierce ES, P O BOX 1390 89820
Carl Hastings, prin.
Other Schools – See Austin

Beatty, Nye Co., Pop. Code 5
Nye County SD
Supt. – See Tonopah
ES, P O BOX 368 89003 – Vera Metler, prin.

Beowawe, Elko Co.
Eureka County SD
Supt. – See Eureka
ES, P O BOX 598 89822 – (—), prin.

Blue Diamond, Clark Co., Pop. Code 2
Clark County SD
Supt. – See Las Vegas
ES 89004 – Robert Seals, prin.

Boulder City, Clark Co., Pop. Code 6
Clark County SD
Supt. – See Las Vegas
Garrett JHS, 1200 AVENUE G 89005
Dorrell Booth, prin.
Mitchell ES, 900 AVE B 89005
Donald Miller, prin.

Caliente, Lincoln Co., Pop. Code 3
Lincoln County SD
Supt. – See Panaca
ES, P O BOX 367 89008 – Berl Gordon, prin.

Carlin, Elko Co., Pop. Code 4
Elko County SD
Supt. – See Elko
ES, P O BOX 797 89822 – Kevin Melcher, prin.

Carson City, (Indep. City), Pop. Code 8
Carson City SD
Sch. Sys. Enr. Code 6
Supt. – Robert Scott, P O BOX 603 89702
Bordewich MS, W 2ND & THOMPSON 89701
Kirk Kinne, prin.
Bray ES, 710 W 4TH ST 89703 – Kirk Kinne, prin.
Corbett ES, 202 CORBETT ST 89706
David Vasick, prin.
Fremont ES, 700 E 5TH ST 89701
Dorothy Todd, prin.
Fritsch ES, 504 BATH ST 89703
David Aalbers, prin.
Gleason ES, 604 W MUSSER ST 89703
Kirk Kinne, prin.
Seeliger ES, 2800 S SALIMAN ROAD 89701
Elma Blaud, prin.

St. Teresa School, 567 S RICHMOND AVE 89703

Dayton, Lyon Co., Pop. Code 5
Lyon County SD
Supt. – See Yerington
ES, P O BOX 119 89403 – James Page, prin.

Denio, Humboldt Co.
Humboldt County SD
Supt. – See Winnemucca
ES 89404 – Erica Turner, prin.

Duckwater, White Pine Co.
Nye County SD
Supt. – See Tonopah
ES 89314 – (—), prin.

Dyer, Pershing Co.
Esmeralda County SD
Supt. – See Goldfield
ES, P O BOX 104 89010 – (—), prin.

East Ely, White Pine Co.
White Pine County SD
Sch. Sys. Enr. Code 4
Supt. – Dr. Jack Havertape, P O BOX 400 89315
White Pine County JHS, 11TH & K AVE 89315
Florindo Mariani, prin.
Mountain View ES, P O BOX 327 89315
Dean Stubbs, prin.
Other Schools – See Baker, Lund, Mc Gill

Sacred Heart School, 1080 AVE I 89301

Elko, Elko Co., Pop. Code 6
Elko County SD
Sch. Sys. Enr. Code 6
Supt. – Paul Billings, P O BOX 1012 89801
JHS, 777 COUNTRY CLUB DRIVE 89801
Glade Oberhansli, prin.
ES 2, 7TH & FIR STS 89801 – James Jund, prin.
Mountain View ES, 3300 ARGENT AVE 89801
Diane Hecht, prin.
Northside ES, 1645 SEWELL DR 89801
Richard Jennings, prin.
Southside ES, 501 LAMOILLE RD 89801
Donald Collins, prin.
Spring Creek ES, 7 E SPRING CREEK PKWY 89801
Royal Orser, prin.
Other Schools – See Carlin, Ely, Jackpot, Jarbidge,
Jiggs, Montello, Owyhee, Tuscarora, Wells,
Wendover

Ely, White Pine Co., Pop. Code 5
Elko County SD
Supt. – See Elko
Currie ES, CURRIE VIA ELY 89301
Duane Weight, prin.

Empire, Washoe Co., Pop. Code 2
Washoe County SD
Supt. – See Reno
Johnson ES 89405 – David Green, prin.

Eureka, Eureka Co., Pop. Code 3
Eureka County SD
Sch. Sys. Enr. Code 2
Supt. – Roy Casey, P O BOX 249 89316
ES, P O BOX 249 89316 – Rebecca Rowley, prin.
Other Schools – See Beowawe

Fallon, Churchill Co., Pop. Code 2
Churchill County SD
Sch. Sys. Enr. Code 5
Supt. – Elmo Dericco, 545 E RICHARDS ST 89406
Churchill County JHS, 650 S MAIN ST 89406
Gary Imelli, prin.
Best MS, 750 E WILLIAMS AVE 89406
Lonnie Moore, prin.
Northside ES, 340 VENTURACCI LANE 89406
Joyce Adams, prin.
West End ES, 280 S RUSSELL ST 89406
Kenneth Geis, prin.

Fernley, Lyon Co., Pop. Code 3
Lyon County SD
Supt. – See Yerington
IS, 450 HARDIE LANE 89408
Mary Goodman, prin.
ES, P O BOX 800 89408 – Ellen Rountree, prin.

Gabbs, Nye Co., Pop. Code 3
Nye County SD
Supt. – See Tonopah
ES, P O BOX 147 89409 – Ray Boyd, prin.

Gardnerville, Douglas Co., Pop. Code 3
Douglas County SD
Supt. – See Minden
Carson Valley MS, P O BOX 157 89410
Phil McKinnon, prin.
ES, P O BOX 157 89410 – Charles Condron, prin.
Meneley ES, P O BOX 157 89410
John Soderman, prin.
Scarselli ES, P O BOX 157 89410
Michael Robison, prin.

Goldfield, Esmeralda Co.
Esmeralda County SD
Sch. Sys. Enr. Code 2
Supt. – Harold Tokerud, P O BOX 546 89013
ES, P O BOX 546 89013 – (—), prin.
Other Schools – See Dyer, Silverpeak

Goodsprings, Clark Co.
Clark County SD
Supt. – See Las Vegas
ES 89019 – Robert Seals, prin.

Hawthorne, Mineral Co., Pop. Code 6
Mineral County SD
Sch. Sys. Enr. Code 4
Supt. – Arlo Funk, P O BOX 1540 89415
ES, P O BOX 1540 89415 – Granville Gage, prin.
Mina ES, P O BOX 1540 89415 – (—), prin.
Other Schools – See Schurz

Henderson, Clark Co., Pop. Code 7
Clark County SD
Supt. – See Las Vegas
Brown JHS, 307 CANNES ST 89015
Marlin Nielsen, prin.
Burkholder JHS, 355 W VAN WAGENEN ST 89015
Frank Lamping, prin.
Galloway ES, 701 TAMARAK DR 89015
Burke Gillies, prin.
Hinman ES, 450 MERLAYNE DR 89015
Susan Brand, prin.
Mack ES, 3170 LAUREL AVE 89014
Roger Gehring, prin.
McCaw ES, 57 LYNN LANE 89015
Carol Blount, prin.
McDoniel ES, 1821 FOX RIDGE DR 89015
Carolyn Reedom, prin.
Sewell ES, 700 E LAKE MEAD DR 89015
Maurice Flores, prin.

Taylor ES, 400 MCNEIL DR 89015
Donald Anderson, prin.

Imlay, Pershing Co.
Pershing County SD
Supt. – See Lovelock
ES, P O BOX 86 89418 – James Rowe, prin.

Incline Village, Washoe Co.
Washoe County SD
Supt. – See Reno
MS, 931 SOUTHWOOD BLVD 89450
David Mussatti, prin.
Incline ES, 771 SOUTHWOOD BLVD 89450
Lawrence Borino, prin.

Indian Springs, Clark Co., Pop. Code 3
Clark County SD
Supt. – See Las Vegas
ES 89018 – Arlen Simonson, prin.

Jackpot, Elko Co.
Elko County SD
Supt. – See Elko
ES, P O BOX 463 89825 – Gerald Pickner, prin.

Jarbidge, Elko Co.
Elko County SD
Supt. – See Elko
ES 89826 – Gerald Pickner, prin.

Jean, Clark Co.
Clark County SD
Supt. – See Las Vegas
Sandy Valley ES, HCR 70 BOX 111 89019
Robert Seals, prin.

Jiggs, Elko Co.
Elko County SD
Supt. – See Elko
Mound Valley ES, JIGGS STAR ROUTE 89827
Don Collins, prin.

Las Vegas, Clark Co., Pop. Code 9
Clark County SD
Sch. Sys. Enr. Code 9
Supt. – Dr. Robert Wentz
2832 E FLAMINGO ROAD 89121
Fremont JHS, 1100 E SAINT LOUIS AVE 89104
Stephen Augspurger, prin.
Garside JHS, 300 S TORREY PINES DRIVE 89107
Allen Coles, prin.
Martin JHS, 2800 STEWART AVE 89101
Steven McCoy, prin.
Robison JHS, 825 MARION DRIVE 89110
Wayne Tanaka, prin.
Woodbury JHS, 3875 E HARMON AVE 89121
Leroy Hurd, prin.
Adcock ES, 100 NEWCOMER ST 89107
Richard Masek, prin.
Beatty ES, 8685 HIDDEN PALMS PKWY 89123
Anecia Nelson, prin.
Beckley ES, 3223 GLENHURST DR 89121
Stuart Reid, prin.
Bell ES, 2900 WILMINGTON WAY 89102
Herbert Freeman, prin.
Booker MS, 2277 N HIGHLAND DR 89106
Alice Wisdom, prin.
Bracken ES, 1200 N 27TH ST 89101
Bernard Hamilton, prin.
Carson MS, 1735 N D ST 89106
Mary Richardson, prin.
Cox ES, 3855 TIMBERLAKE DR 89115
Noreen Hawley, prin.
Crestwood ES, 1300 PAULINE WAY 89104
Marsha Overton, prin.
Culley ES, 1200 N MALLARD ST 89108
Frances Johnson, prin.
Dearing ES, 3046 FERNDALE ST 89121
James Shipp, prin.
Decker ES, 3850 REDWOOD ST 89103
Roland Fagan, prin.
Deskin ES, 4550 N PIONEER WAY 89129
Thomas O'Roarke, prin.
Diskin ES, 4220 RAVENWOOD DR 89117
William Wallin, prin.
Dondero ES, 4450 RIDGEVILLE ST 89103
Kathryn Augspurger, prin.
Earl ES, 1463 MARION DR 89110
Beth Sylvester, prin.
Edwards ES, 4551 DIAMOND HEAD DR 89110
Dolores Kelly, prin.
Ferron ES, 4200 MOUNTAIN VISTA ST 89121
Margaret Cahoon, prin.
French ES, 3235 E HACIENDA AVE 89120
Lamar Terry, prin.
Fyfe ES, 4101 W BONANZA ROAD 89107
Doretta Morgan, prin.
Gragson ES, 555 N HONOLULU ST 89110
Fenton Tobler, prin.
Gray ES, 2825 S TORREY PINES DR 89102
Stella Helvie, prin.
Griffith ES, 324 E ESSEX DR 89107
Beverly Daly, prin.
Hancock ES, 1661 LINDELL ROAD 89102
Timothy Sands, prin.
Harmon ES, 5351 HILLSBORO LANE 89120
Bradley Reitz, prin.
Harris ES, 3620 S SANDHILL ROAD 89121
Robert Wondrash, prin.
Heard ES, 34 BAER DR 89115
Ryleen Hinkle, prin.
Hewetson ES, 701 N 20TH ST 89101
Gary Hafen, prin.

Hoggard MS, 950 N TONOPAH DR 89106
  Shirley Barber, prin.
Kim ES, 7600 PEACE WAY 89117
  Phyllis Carl, prin.
King ES, 2260 BETTY LANE 89115
  Eva Wolfe, prin.
Kelly MS, 1900 N J ST 89106 – Joan Gray, prin.
Lake ES, 2904 METRORO ST 89109
  Teddie Brewer, prin.
Long ES, 2000 S WALNUT ROAD 89104
  Ronald Gayoosh, prin.
Madison MS, 1030 J ST 89106
  Ronald Hawley, prin.
Manch ES, 4351 N LAMONT ST 89115
  Martha Tittle, prin.
McWilliams ES, 1315 HIAWATHA ROAD 89108
  Betty Hilts, prin.
Mountain View ES, 5436 KELL LANE 89115
  Allin Chandler, prin.
Mt. Charleston ES, P O BOX 275 89101
  Robert Seals, prin.
Paradise ES, 851 E TROPICANA AVE 89119
  Linda Kemp, prin.
Park ES, 931 FRANKLIN AVE 89104
  Alan Enomoto, prin.
Pittman ES, 6333 FARGO AVE 89107
  Keith Bryner, prin.
Red Rock ES, 408 UPLAND BLVD 89107
  William Evans, prin.
Reed ES, 2501 WINWOOD 89108
  Marjorie Conner, prin.
Ronnow ES, 1100 LENA ST 89101
  Hazel Sherman, prin.
Ronzone ES, 5701 STACEY AVE 89108
  Phoebe Spohn, prin.
Rowe ES, 4338 S BRUCE ST 89119
  Manuel Vega, prin.
Smith ES, 7101 PINEDALE AVE 89128
  Fredric Watson, prin.
Stanford ES, 5350 HARRIS AVE 89110
  Delloyd Hammond, prin.
Sunrise Acres ES, 2501 SUNRISE AVE 89101
  Andrew Martinez, prin.
Tate ES, 2450 LINCOLN RD 89115
  Elizabeth Duncombe, prin.
Thomas ES, 1560 CHROKEE LANE 89109
  Janice Bennington, prin.
Tobler ES, 6510 BUCKSKIN AVE 89108
  James Graff, prin.
Tomiyasu ES, 5445 ANNIE OAKLEY DR 89120
  Cornelius Baughn, prin.
Twin Lakes ES, 3300 RIVERSIDE DR 89108
  John Bass, prin.
Ullom ES, 4869 SUN VALLEY DR 89121
  Joyce Woodhouse, prin.
Vegas Verdes ES, 4000 EL PARQUE AVE 89102
  Carla Steinforth, prin.
Ward ES, 1555 E HACIENDA AVE 89119
  Norman Parker, prin.
Warren ES, 6451 BRANDYWINE WAY 89107
  Theron Goynes, prin.
Wasden ES, 2831 PALOMINO LANE 89107
  Susan Bernheisel, prin.
Wengert ES, 2001 WINTERWOOD BLVD 89122
  William Moore, prin.
Whitney ES, P O BOX 551 89125
  Robert Seals, prin.
Other Schools – See Blue Diamond, Boulder City,
  Goodsprings, Henderson, Indian Springs, Jean,
  Laughlin, Logandale, Mesquite, North Las Vegas,
  Searchlight

First Good Shepard Lutheran School
  301 S MARYLAND PKWY 89101
Our Lady of Las Vegas School
  3036 ALTA DR 89107
St. Anne School
  1813 S MARYLAND PKWY 89104
St. Francis De Sales School
  1111 MICHAEL WAY 89108
St. Joseph School
  13TH AND BRIDGER STS 89101
St. Viator School, 4246 S EASTERN AVE 89119

Laughlin, Clark Co.
  Clark County SD
  Supt. – See Las Vegas
  ES, 2750 NEEDLES HWY 89029
    Ellen Leavitt, prin.

Logandale, Clark Co.
  Clark County SD
  Supt. – See Las Vegas
  Bowler ES, 1425 WHIPPLE ROAD 89021
    Vee Wilson, prin.

Lovelock, Pershing Co., Pop. Code 4
  Pershing County SD
  Sch. Sys. Enr. Code 3
  Supt. – James Kiley, P O BOX 389 89419
  ES, P O BOX 621 89419 – James Rowe, prin.
  Other Schools – See Imlay

Lund, White Pine Co., Pop. Code 2
  White Pine County SD
  Supt. – See East Ely
  ES 89317 – Jolynn Maynard, prin.

Mc Dermitt, Humboldt Co., Pop. Code 4
  Humboldt County SD
  Supt. – See Winnemucca
  ES, P O BOX 98 89421 – Gerald Lugert, prin.

Mc Gill, White Pine Co., Pop. Code 4
  White Pine County SD
  Supt. – See East Ely
  ES, 25 AVENUE F 89318 – Virginia Terry, prin.

Mesquite, Clark Co., Pop. Code 3
  Clark County SD
  Supt. – See Las Vegas
  Virgin Valley ES 89024 – Kent Anderson, prin.

Minden, Douglas Co., Pop. Code 2
  Douglas County SD
  Sch. Sys. Enr. Code 5
  Supt. – Dr. F. Betts, P O BOX 1888 89423
  Jacks Valley ES, P O BOX 1888 89423
    Kirk Cunningham, prin.
  Other Schools – See Gardnerville, Zephyr Cove

Montello, Elko Co.
  Elko County SD
  Supt. – See Elko
  ES, P O BOX 93 89830 – Duane Weight, prin.

North Las Vegas, Clark Co., Pop. Code 8
  Clark County SD
  Supt. – See Las Vegas
  Bridger JHS, 2505 N BRUCE ST 89030
    Frank Dixon, prin.
  Smith JHS, 1301 E TONOPAH AVE 89030
    Kay Samolovitch, prin.
  Von Tobel JHS, 2436 N PECOS DRIVE 89030
    Larry Turner, prin.
  Cahlan ES, 2801 FT SUMPTER DR 89030
    Ruby Epps, prin.
  Craig ES, 2637 E GOWAN ROAD 89030
    David Smith, prin.
  Gilbert MS, 2101 W CARTIER AVE 89030
    John Ward, prin.
  Herron ES, 2421 KENNETH ROAD 89030
    Yolanda Arrington, prin.
  Lincoln ES, 3010 BERG ST 89030
    Dennis Petrell, prin.
  McCall ES, 800 CAREY AVE 89030
    Cecil Jackson, prin.
  Mackey MS, 2726 ENGLESTAD ST 89030
    Sylvia Springer, prin.
  Squires ES, 1312 E TONOPAH AVE 89030
    Nadine Nielsen, prin.
  Williams ES, 3000 E TONOPAH AVE 89030
    Ghita Shaw, prin.

Redeemer Lutheran ES
  1730 N PECOS ROAD 89115
St. Christopher School, 1840 N BRUCE ST 89030

Orovada, Humboldt Co.
  Humboldt County SD
  Supt. – See Winnemucca
  Kings River ES, P O BOX 134 89425
    James Porter, prin.
  ES, P O BOX 85 89425 – Joseph deArrieta, prin.

Owyhee, Elko Co., Pop. Code 2
  Elko County SD
  Supt. – See Elko
  ES, P O BOX 38 89832 – Harold Savage, prin.

Pahrump, Nye Co., Pop. Code 4
  Nye County SD
  Supt. – See Tonopah
  MS, P O BOX 610 89041 – John Sena, prin.
  IS, P O BOX 850 89041 – Don Worden, prin.
  PS, P O BOX 850 89041 – Ron Eason, prin.

Panaca, Lincoln Co., Pop. Code 3
  Lincoln County SD
  Sch. Sys. Enr. Code 3
  Supt. – Dr. Neldon Mathews, P O BOX 118 89042
  ES, P O BOX 307 89042 – Robert Beatty, prin.
  Other Schools – See Alamo, Caliente, Pioche

Paradise Valley, Clark Co.
  Humboldt County SD
  Supt. – See Winnemucca
  ES 89426 – Ann Miller, prin.

Pioche, Lincoln Co., Pop. Code 3
  Lincoln County SD
  Supt. – See Panaca
  ES, P O BOX 418 89043 – Charles Draper, prin.

Reno, Washoe Co., Pop. Code 9
  Washoe County SD
  Sch. Sys. Enr. Code 8
  Supt. – Dr. Marvin Moss, 425 E 9TH ST 89520
  Clayton MS, 1295 WYOMING AVE 89503
    William Campbell, prin.
  O'Brien MS, 10500 STEAD BLVD 89506
    Douglas Byington, prin.
  Pine MS, 4800 NEIL ROAD 89502
    Lewis Polizzi, prin.
  Swope MS, 901 KEELE DRIVE 89509
    Kenneth Vaughan, prin.
  Traner MS, 1700 CARVILLE DRIVE 89512
    Samuel Macias, prin.
  Vaughn MS, 1200 BRESSON AVE 89502
    Robert Kimbrough, prin.
  Anderson ES, 1055 BERRUM LANE 89509
    Vincent Ames, prin.
  Beck ES, 1900 SHARON WAY 89509
    Richard Marcucci, prin.
  Booth ES, 1450 STEWART ST 89502
    Mary Chambers, prin.
  Brown ES, 14101 OLD VIRGINIA ROAD 89511
    Dixie Bradshaw, prin.
  Cannan ES, 2450 CANNAN ST 89512
    Penny LeBranch, prin.

Corbett ES, 1901 VILLANOVA DR 89502
  Fred Harvey, prin.
Dodson ES, 4355 HOUSTON DR 89502
  Robert Trimble, prin.
Duncan ES, 1200 MONTELLO ST 89512
  Charlene Signala, prin.
Elmcrest ES, 855 MCDONALD DR 89503
  June Gronert, prin.
Gomes ES, 3870 LIMKIN ST 89506
  Craig Crow, prin.
Gomm ES, 4000 MAYBERRY DR 89509
  Jack Ricketts, prin.
Huffaker ES, 7495 S VIRGINIA ST 89511
  Margaret Lightner, prin.
Hunter Lake ES, 909 HUNTER LAKE DR 89509
  Michael Hawkes, prin.
Lemmon Valley ES, 255 W PATRICIAN DR 89506
  Fredrick Howell, prin.
Lenz ES, 2500 HOMELAND DR 89511
  Roberta Lawson, prin.
Loder ES, 600 APPLE ST 89502
  Russell McOmber, prin.
Mt. Rose ES, 915 LANDER ST 89509
  Lonnie Shields, prin.
Peavine ES, 1601 GRANDVIEW AVE 89503
  Judy Doctor, prin.
Pleasant Valley ES, 405 SURREY DR 89511
  Kenneth Grein, prin.
Sierra Vista ES, 2001 GETTO DR 89512
  Jerry Heitmann, prin.
Smithridge ES, 4801 NEIL ROAD 89502
  Robert Oliphant, prin.
Stead ES, STEAD BLVD 89506
  Francey Dennis, prin.
Towles ES, 2800 KINGS ROW 89503
  Roland Eaton, prin.
Veterans Memorial ES, 1200 LOCUST ST 89502
  Tony Limon, prin.
Warner ES, 3075 HEIGHTS DR 89503
  Barbara McLaury, prin.
Other Schools – See Empire, Incline Village, Sparks,
  Verdi, Wadsworth

Little Flower School, 1300 CASAZZA DR 89502
Our Lady of Snows School
  1125 LANDER ST 89509
St. Albert the Great School
  1255 SAINT ALBERTS ST 89503

Round Mountain, Nye Co.
  Nye County SD
  Supt. – See Tonopah
  ES, P O BOX 151 89045 – Rosemary O'Brien, prin.

Schurz, Mineral Co.
  Mineral County SD
  Supt. – See Hawthorne
  ES, P O BOX 219 89427 – Ihsan Qureshi, prin.

Searchlight, Clark Co.
  Clark County SD
  Supt. – See Las Vegas
  ES 89046 – Robert Seals, prin.

Silverpeak, Esmeralda Co.
  Esmeralda County SD
  Supt. – See Goldfield
  ES, P O BOX 170 89047 – (—), prin.

Silver Springs, Lyon Co., Pop. Code 2
  Lyon County SD
  Supt. – See Yerington
  ES, P O BOX 6000 89429 – Eleanor Holden, prin.

Smith, Lyon Co., Pop. Code 2
  Lyon County SD
  Supt. – See Yerington
  Smith Valley ES, P O BOX 30 89430
    Russell Colletta, prin.

Sparks, Washoe Co., Pop. Code 8
  Washoe County SD
  Supt. – See Reno
  Dilworth MS, 255 PRATER WAY 89431
    Jwood Raw, prin.
  MS, 2275 18TH ST 89431 – Gary Longson, prin.
  Diedrichsen ES, 1735 DEL ROSA WAY 89431
    Jesse Hall, Jr., prin.
  Drake ES, 2755 4TH ST 89431
    Donald Payton, prin.
  Dunn ES, 1135 O CALLAGHAN DR 89431
    Merrie Jo Savage, prin.
  Greenbrae ES, 4TH & O STS 89431
    John Mayer, prin.
  Juniper ES, 225 QUEENS WAY 89431
    Nancy Mertz, prin.
  Lincoln Park ES, 201 LINCOLN WAY 89431
    Stephen Kaylor, prin.
  Maxwell ES, 2300 N ROCK BLVD 89431
    Robert Huwe, prin.
  Mitchell ES, 1316 PRATER WAY 89431
    James Luttges, prin.
  Palmer ES, 5890 KLONDIKE DR 89433
    Greer Gladstone, prin.
  Risley ES, 1900 SULLIVAN LANE 89431
    Theodore Lokke, prin.
  Smith ES, 1925 F ST 89431
    Jackie Berrum, prin.
  Sun Valley ES, 5490 LEON DR 89433
    Lynel Cunningham, prin.
  Whitehead ES, 3570 WATERFALL DR 89431
    Ralph Cinfio, prin.

Tonopah, Nye Co., Pop. Code 5
  Nye County SD
  Sch. Sys. Enr. Code 5
  Supt. – Robert Ragar, P O BOX 113   89049
  Silver Rim ES, P O OBX 10677   89049
    Charles Keller, prin.
  ES, P O BOX 553   89049 – Selway Mulkey, prin.
  Other Schools – See Amargosa Valley, Beatty,
    Duckwater, Gabbs, Pahrump, Round Mountain

Tuscarora, Elko Co.
  Elko County SD
  Supt. – See Elko
  Independence Valley ES   89834
    Richard Jennings, prin.

Verdi, Washoe Co.
  Washoe County SD
  Supt. – See Reno
  ES   89439 – Harold Ferguson, prin.

Virginia City, Storey Co., Pop. Code 4
  Storey County SD
  Sch. Sys. Enr. Code 2
  Supt. – John Gamble, P O BOX C   89440
  Gallagher ES, SOUTH D ST   89440
    Kathy Peltier, prin.

Wadsworth, Washoe Co., Pop. Code 2
  Washoe County SD
  Supt. – See Reno
  Natchez ES   89442 – Richard Reeder, prin.

Wells, Elko Co., Pop. Code 4
  Elko County SD
  Supt. – See Elko
  O'Neil ES, ONEIL VIA WELLS   89835
    Gerald Pickner, prin.
  Ruby Valley ES, ARTHUR ROUTE   89835
    (—), prin.
  ES, P O BOX 338   89835 – Duane Weight, prin.

Wendover, Elko Co.
  Elko County SD
  Supt. – See Elko
  West Wendover ES, P O BOX 2400   89883
    Marcia McManus, prin.

Winnemucca, Humboldt Co., Pop. Code 5
  Humboldt County SD
  Sch. Sys. Enr. Code 4
  Supt. – Kenneth Lords, P O BOX 1070   89445
  JHS, 451 REINHART   89445 – Peter Stein, prin.
  Grass Valley ES, P O BOX 1070   89445
    Judith Thompson, prin.

  Jackson Mountain ES, HCR 336   89445
    Joseph deArrieta, prin.
  Leonard Creek ES, P O BOX 1010   89445
    Ken Lords, prin.
  Sonoma Heights ES, 1500 MELARKEY ST   89445
    James Porter, prin.
  ES, 522 LAY ST   89445 – Ann Miller, prin.
  Other Schools – See Denio, Mc Dermitt, Orovada,
    Paradise Valley

Yerington, Lyon Co., Pop. Code 4
  Lyon County SD
  Sch. Sys. Enr. Code 5
  Supt. – Dr. Barton Welsh
    25 E GOLDFIELD AVE   89447
  IS, 215 PEARL ST   89447 – John Prida, prin.
  ES, 112 CALIFORNIA ST   89447 – Susan Roe, prin.
  Other Schools – See Dayton, Fernley, Silver Springs,
    Smith

Zephyr Cove, Douglas Co.
  Douglas County SD
  Supt. – See Minden
  Kingsbury MS, P O BOX 648   89448
    Klaire Pirtle, prin.
  ES, P O BOX 7   89448 – Frank Bruno, prin.

NEW HAMPSHIRE

STATE DEPARTMENT OF EDUCATION
State Office Park South
101 Pleasant St., Concord 03301
(603) 271-3494

Commissioner of Education	John MacDonald
Deputy Commissioner	Charles Marston
Director Division of Instructional Services	Harry LaBranche
Director Division of Standards & Certification	Judith Fillion
Director Division of Vocational Rehabilitation	Bruce Archambault

STATE BOARD OF EDUCATION
R. Corbin, *Chairman*   Salem

POSTSECONDARY EDUCATION COMMISSION
Dr. James Brusselle, *Executive Director*   61 S. Spring St., Concord   03301

PUBLIC, PRIVATE, AND PAROCHIAL ELEMENTARY SCHOOLS

Acworth, Sullivan Co., Pop. Code 3
  School Administrative Unit 60
  Supt. – See Charlestown
  ES   03601 – Richard Neilsen, prin.

Allenstown, Merrimack Co., Pop. Code 5
  School Administrative Unit 53
  Supt. – See Suncook
  Dupont MS, SCHOOL STREET   03275
    Kathleen Sciarappa, prin.
  ES, 30 MAIN ST   03275 – Donna Blazon, prin.

Alstead, Cheshire Co., Pop. Code 4
  School Administrative Unit 60
  Supt. – See Charlestown
  Vilas MS, P O BOX 98   03602
    Richard Neilsen, prin.
  ES   03602 – Richard Neilsen, prin.

Alton, Belknap Co., Pop. Code 4
  School Administrative Unit 51
  Supt. – See Barnstead
  Alton Central S, SCHOOL ST   03809
    George Rogers, prin.

Amherst, Hillsborough Co., Pop. Code 6
  School Administrative Unit 39
  Sch. Sys. Enr. Code 4
  Supt. – Richard Lalley, P O BOX 849   03031
  MS, P O BOX 966   03031 – Paul Collins, prin.
  Clark ES, FOUNDRY STREET   03031
    Christina Trudo, prin.
  Wilkins ES, BOSTON POST ROAD   03031
    Herbert Oliver, prin.

Andover, Merrimack Co., Pop. Code 4
  School Administrative Unit 46
  Supt. – See Penacook
  ES   03216 – Richard Higgins,Jr., prin.

Antrim, Hillsboro Co., Pop. Code 4
  School Administrative Unit 47
  Supt. – See Peterborough
  MS, SUMMER ST   03440 – Robert Potter, prin.
  ES, SUMMER STREET   03440
    Richard Dalhaus, prin.

Ashland, Grafton Co., Pop. Code 4
  School Administrative Unit 2
  Supt. – See Meredith
  Ober ES, SCHOOL STREET   03217
    William Tirone, prin.

Atkinson, Rockingham Co., Pop. Code 5
  School Administrative Unit 55
  Supt. – See Plaistow
  Atkinson Academy, 17 ACADEMY AVE   03811
    Mary Gale, prin.

Hampstead Academy, 51 MAPLE AVE   03811

Auburn, Rockingham Co., Pop. Code 5
  School Administrative Unit 15
  Supt. – See Manchester
  Auburn Village ES, HOOKSET ROAD   03032
    Raymond Bourque, prin.

Barnstead, Belknap Co., Pop. Code 4
  School Administrative Unit 51
  Sch. Sys. Enr. Code 4
  Supt. – Andre Paquette, P O BOX 200   03225
  Other Schools – See Alton, Center Barnstead, Pittsfield

Barrington, Strafford Co., Pop. Code 5
  School Administrative Unit 44
  Supt. – See Farmington
  MS, HCR   03825 – John Freeman, prin.
  ES, ROUTE 09   03825 – Althea Sheaff, prin.

Bartlett, Carroll Co., Pop. Code 4
  School Administrative Unit 9
  Supt. – See North Conway
  ES, MAIN STREET   03812 – L. Rivers, prin.

Bath, Grafton Co., Pop. Code 3
  School Administrative Unit 23
  Supt. – See Woodsville
  Bath Village ES, ROUTE 302   03740
    Donald White, prin.

Bedford, Hillborough Co., Pop. Code 6
  School Administrative Unit 26
  Supt. – See Merrimack
  McKelvie MS, LIBERTY HILL ROAD   03102
    Arnold MacDonald, prin.
  Bedford Memorial ES
    33 OLD BEDFORD RD   03102 – Robert Cook, prin.
  Woodbury ES, COUNTRY ROAD   03102
    Robert Cook, prin.

Faith Christian Academy, 469 D W HWY S   03102

Belmont, Belknap Co., Pop. Code 5
  School Administrative Unit 46
  Supt. – See Penacook
  ES, RURAL ROUTE 140   03220
    Kenneth Williams, prin.

Bennington, Hillsborough Co., Pop. Code 3
  School Administrative Unit 47
  Supt. – See Peterborough
  Peirce ES, MAIN ST   03442 – Joan Schnare, prin.

Berlin, Coos Co., Pop. Code 7
  School Administrative Unit 3
  Sch. Sys. Enr. Code 4
  Supt. – Richard Steudle
    183 HILLSIDE AVE   03570
  MS, 200 STATE ST   03570 – Anthony Urban, prin.

Bartlett ES, 56 MOUNT FORIST ST   03570
  Beverly Dupont, prin.
Brown ES, 190 NORWAY ST   03570
  Corinne Cascadden, prin.
Marston ES, 270 WILLARD ST   03570
  Beverly Dupont, prin.

Berlin Regional Catholic School
  140 BLANCHARD ST   03570

Bethlehem, Grafton Co., Pop. Code 4
School Administrative Unit 35
Supt. – See Littleton
ES, MAIN STREET   03574
  Louis LaFasciano, prin.

Boscawen, Merrimack Co., Pop. Code 5
School Administrative Unit 46
Supt. – See Penacook
Main Street ES, MAIN STREET   03303
  Martin Feuerstein, prin.

Bow, Merrimack Co., Pop. Code 5
School Administrative Unit 19
Supt. – See Goffstown
ES, 20 BOW CENTER RD   03301
  Patricia McLean, prin.

Bradford, Merrimack Co., Pop. Code 4
School Administrative Unit 43
Supt. – See Newport
Kearsarge Regional ES
  OLD WARNER ROAD   03221
  Carlton Fitzgerald, prin.
Sutton Central ES, P O BOX 159   03221
  Richard Lizotte, prin.

Bristol, Grafton Co., Pop. Code 4
School Administrative Unit 4
Sch. Sys. Enr. Code 4
Supt. – George Corrette II, 16 SCHOOL ST   03222
Alexandria Village ES, RURAL ROUTE 01   03222
  William Lance, prin.
ES, 23 N MAIN ST   03222 – Karen Soule, prin.
Danbury ES, ROUTE 104   03222
  William Lance, prin.
Other Schools – See Hebron, New Hampton

Brookline, Hillsboro Co., Pop. Code 4
School Administrative Unit 41
Supt. – See Hollis
ES, MILFORD ROAD   03033
  Richard Maghakian, prin.

Campton, Grafton Co., Pop. Code 4
School Administrative Unit 48
Supt. – See Plymouth
ES   03223 – M. Hamel, prin.
Thornton Central ES, RURAL ROUTE 01   03223
  Timothy Tyler, prin.

Canaan, Grafton Co., Pop. Code 4
School Administrative Unit 62
Supt. – See Enfield
Indian River MS   03741 – Andrew Mellow, prin.
ES, P O BOX 18   03741 – George Janas, prin.

Candia, Rockingham Co., Pop. Code 5
School Administrative Unit 15
Supt. – See Manchester
Moore ES, DEERFIELD ROAD   03034
  Stephan Russell, prin.

Canterbury, Merrimack Co., Pop. Code 4
School Administrative Unit 46
Supt. – See Penacook
ES, BAPTIST ROAD   03224 – Mary Morrison, prin.

Center Barnstead, Belknap Co., Pop. Code 4
School Administrative Unit 51
Supt. – See Barnstead
Barnstead ES, MAPLE STREET   03225
  Barbara Halla, prin.

Center Conway, Carroll Co., Pop. Code 6
School Administrative Unit 9
Supt. – See North Conway
Pine Tree ES, MAIN STREET   03813
  Laura Jawitz, prin.

Center Ossipee, Carroll Co., Pop. Code 4
School Administrative Unit 49
Supt. – See Wolfeboro
Effingham ES, P O BOX 68   03814
  Kenneth Perry, prin.
Ossipee Central ES, P O BOX 68   03814
  Kenneth Perry, prin.

Center Sandwich, Carroll Co., Pop. Code 3
School Administrative Unit 2
Supt. – See Meredith
Sandwich Central ES, SQUAM LAKE ROAD   03227
  Jean Shlager, prin.

Center Strafford, Strafford Co.
School Administrative Unit 44
Supt. – See Farmington
Strafford ES, HCR 71 BOX 113   03815
  Richard Jenisch, prin.

Center Tuftonboro, Carroll Co.
School Administrative Unit 49
Supt. – See Wolfeboro
Tuftonboro Central ES, P O BOX 118   03816
  (—), prin.

Charlestown, Sullivan Co., Pop. Code 5
School Administrative Unit 60
Sch. Sys. Enr. Code 4
Supt. – Harry Westcott, P O BOX 600   03603
MS, S MAIN ST   03603 – Wayne Evans, prin.
PS, EAST STREET   03603 – Wayne Evans, prin.
Farwell ES   03603 – Wayne Evans, prin.
Other Schools – See Acworth, Alstead, Londgon,
  Marlow, Walpole

Chester, Rockingham Co., Pop. Code 4
School Administrative Unit 14
Supt. – See Epping
ES   03036 – Norman Dugas, prin.

Chesterfield, Cheshire Co., Pop. Code 5
School Administrative Unit 29
Supt. – See Keene
Chesterfield Central ES, ROUTE 63   03443
  Lawrence Seavey, prin.

Claremont, Sullivan Co., Pop. Code 7
School Administrative Unit 6
Sch. Sys. Enr. Code 5
Supt. – Karen Angello, 165 BROAD ST   03743
JHS, 10 SOUTH ST   03743
  Donald Gaudreau, prin.
Bluff ES, SUMMIT ROAD   03743 – Mary Bell, prin.
Disnard MS, HANOVER STREET   03743
  Barbara McKinnon, prin.
Maple Avenue ES, MAPLE AVE   03743
  Scott Bouranis, prin.
North Street ES, NORTH STREET   03743
  Alan Cutler, prin.
Way ES, MYRTLE STREET   03743
  Doris Adler, prin.
Other Schools – See Cornish Flat, Newport

St. Mary School, 18 CENTRAL ST   03743

Colebrook, Coos Co., Pop. Code 4
School Administrative Unit 7
Sch. Sys. Enr. Code 4
Supt. – Paul Allen, 10 BRIDGE ST   03576
MS, 166 MAIN ST   03576 – Stephen Leshane, prin.
PS, 166 MAIN ST   03576 – Stephen Leshane, prin.
Hollow ES, RURAL ROUTE 02 BOX 255   03576
  Nancy Rose, prin.
Other Schools – See Pittsburg, West Stewartstown

Concord, Merrimack Co., Pop. Code 8
School Administrative Unit 19
Supt. – See Goffstown
Dunbarton ES, RURAL ROUTE 02   03301
  William Zeller, prin.

School Administrative Unit 46
Supt. – See Penacook
Loudon ES, RURAL ROUTE 01 BOX 12   03301
  Christine Barry, prin.
Washington Street ES
  26 WASHINGTON ST   03303
  Beverly McAloon, prin.
Webster Central ES, RURAL ROUTE 05   03303
  George Radcliff, prin.

School Administrative Unit 53
Supt. – See Suncook
Pembroke Hill ES, 113 ROWE AVE   03301
  Eleanor Harriger, prin.

School Administrative Unit 8
Sch. Sys. Enr. Code 5
Supt. – Mark Beauvais, 16 RUMFORD ST   03301
Beaver Meadow ES
  40 SEWALLS FALLS RD   03301
  Rober Brooks, prin.
Broken Ground MS, 123 PORTSMOUTH ST   03301
  F. Davis, prin.
ES, 160 SOUTH ST   03301 – E. Tousignant, prin.
Dame ES, CANTERBURY ROAD   03301
  Edward Barnwell, prin.
Dewey ES, LIBERTY STREET   03301
  Clinton Cogswell, prin.
Eastman ES, 15 SHAWMUT ST   03301
  Edward Barnwell, prin.
Kimball MS, NORTH SPRING STREET   03301
  Clinton Cogswell, prin.
Rumford ES, MONROE STREET   03301
  Philip Paskowitz, prin.
Walker ES, NORTH STATE STREET   03301
  Rosemary Duggan, prin.

Concord Christian School, 20 N STATE ST   03301
St. John Regional School, 61 S STATE ST   03301

Contoocook, Merrimack Co.
School Administrative Unit 24
Supt. – See Henniker
Maple Street MS, RURAL ROUTE BOX 27A   03229
  Sandra Burney, prin.
Martin ES, RURAL ROUTE BOX 27A   03229
  Cathy Hamblett, prin.

Conway, Carroll Co., Pop. Code 6
School Administrative Unit 9
Supt. – See North Conway
ES, MAIN STREET   03818 – Lois Gould, prin.

Cornish Flat, Sullivan Co., Pop. Code 4
School Administrative Unit 6
Supt. – See Claremont
Cornish ES, RURAL ROUTE 02   03745
  Thomas Luce, prin.

Danville, Rockingham Co., Pop. Code 4
School Administrative Unit 55
Supt. – See Plaistow
ES, MAIN ST   03819 – Dorothy Boisvert, prin.

Deerfield, Rockingham Co., Pop. Code 4
School Administrative Unit 53
Supt. – See Suncook
White ES, DEERFIELD CTR ROUTE 07   03037
  Peter Sweet, prin.

Derry, Rockingham Co., Pop. Code 7
School Administrative Unit 10
Sch. Sys. Enr. Code 5
Supt. – David Brown, 25 S MAIN ST   03038
Hood Memorial JHS, 15 HOOD ROAD   03038
  James Stevenson, prin.
Derry Village ES, S MAIN STREET   03038
  Glenn Blanchard, prin.
East Derry Memorial ES, DUBEAU DRIVE   03038
  Peter Smyrl, prin.
Floyd ES, 37 HIGHLAND AVE   03038
  J. Jones, prin.
Grinnell ES, 20 LENOX RD   03038
  Kathleen Murphy, prin.
South Range ES, DRURY LANE   03038
  Angelo Panteli, prin.

Calvary Christian School, P O BOX 303   03038
St. Thomas Aquinas ES, P O BOX 427   03038

Dover, Strafford Co., Pop. Code 7
School Administrative Unit 11
Sch. Sys. Enr. Code 5
Supt. – Gerald Daley, MUNICIPAL BLDG   03820
JHS, 61 LOCUST ST   03820 – Gilbert Barclay, prin.
Garrison ES, 20 GARRISON RD   03820
  George Rivers, prin.
Horne Street ES, 74 HORNE ST   03820
  James McShane, Jr., prin.
Woodman Park ES, 20 TOWLE AVE   03820
  Cynthia Theodoras, prin.

Dover Catholic ES, 222 CENTRAL AVE   03820

Dublin, Cheshire Co., Pop. Code 4
School Administrative Unit 47
Supt. – See Peterborough
ES, MAIN ST   03444 – David Lasser, prin.

Dublin Christian Academy, PAGE ROAD   03444
Dublin School, P O BOX 77   03444

Durham, Strafford Co., Pop. Code 7
School Administrative Unit 5
Sch. Sys. Enr. Code 7
Supt. – John Powers, 36 COE DR   03824
Oyster River MS, 47 GARRISON AVE   03824
  Donald Wilson, prin.
Mast Way ES, RURAL ROUTE 01   03824
  John Lowy, prin.
Oyster River ES, 47 GARRISON AVE   03824
  Jean Robbins, prin.

East Kingston, Rockingham Co., Pop. Code 4
School Administrative Unit 16
Supt. – See Exeter
Browns Academy, DEPOT ROAD   03827
  Sally Bowen, prin.
ES, 5 ANDREWS LN   03827 – Sally Bowen, prin.

School Administrative Unit 21
Supt. – See Hampton
South Hampton Barnard ES
  RURAL ROUTE 02 BOX 257   03827
  A. Marinos, prin.

East Lempster, Sullivan Co.
School Administrative Unit 43
Supt. – See Newport
Goshen Lempster Coop ES   03606
  John Bonfiglio, prin.

Enfield, Grafton Co., Pop. Code 5
School Administrative Unit 62
Sch. Sys. Enr. Code 3
Supt. – John Carr, P O BOX 789   03748
ES, P O BOX 329   03748 – Charles Stone, prin.
Other Schools – See Canaan

Epping, Rockingham Co., Pop. Code 5
School Administrative Unit 14
Sch. Sys. Enr. Code 4
Supt. – H. Wilson Eaves
  ROURAL ROUTE 01 BOX 136   03042
ES, ACADEMY STREET   03042
  Andre Goyer, prin.
Other Schools – See Chester, Fremont

Epsom, Merrimack Co., Pop. Code 5
School Administrative Unit 53
Supt. – See Suncook
Epsom Central ES, BLACK HALL RD   03234
  Bruce Farr, prin.

Errol, Coos Co., Pop. Code 2
School Administrative Unit 20
Supt. – See Gorham
Errol Consolidated ES   03579 – Jean Ham, prin.

Exeter, Rockingham Co., Pop. Code 7
School Administrative Unit 16
Sch. Sys. Enr. Code 5
Supt. – William Clancy, 40 MAIN ST   03833
Exeter Area JHS, 30 LINDEN ST   03833
  Thomas Meehan, prin.

Kensington ES, RURAL ROUTE 02   03833
    Frank Scala, prin.
Lincoln Street ES, 25 LINCOLN ST   03833
    Paul Ford, prin.
Main Street MS, 40 MAIN ST   03833
    Steven Bailey, prin.
Swasey ES Brentwood, RURAL ROUTE 01   03833
    Margaret Griffin, prin.
Other Schools – See East Kingston, Newfields,
    Stratham

Farmington, Strafford Co., Pop. Code 5
School Administrative Unit 44
Sch. Sys. Enr. Code 5
Supt. – Barry Clough, P O BOX 18   03835
Other Schools – See Barrington, Center Strafford,
    Milton, Milton Mills, Northwood, Nottingham,
    Sanbornville

School Administrative Unit 61
Sch. Sys. Enr. Code 4
Supt. – James Bibbo   03835
Main Street MS, 41 S MAIN ST   03835
    William Patison III, prin.
Memorial Drive ES, 10 MEMORIAL DR   03835
    Caroline Butler, prin.

Fitzwilliam, Cheshire Co., Pop. Code 4
School Administrative Unit 38
Supt. – See Keene
Emerson ES   03447 – Norman Evans, prin.

Francestown, Hillsborough Co., Pop. Code 3
School Administrative Unit 47
Supt. – See Peterborough
ES, MAIN STREET   03043 – Laura Doell, prin.

Franconia, Grafton Co., Pop. Code 3
School Administrative Unit 35
Supt. – See Littleton
MS, MAIN STREET   03580 – Richard Smiles, prin.

Franklin, Merrimack Co., Pop. Code 6
School Administrative Unit 18
Sch. Sys. Enr. Code 4
Supt. – Paul Fillion, 119 CENTRAL ST   03235
Rowell ES, ROWELL DRIVE   03235
    Wilbur Roberge, prin.
Other Schools – See Hill, West Franklin

Sant Bani School, RURAL ROUTE 01   03235
St. Mary ES, ELKINS STREET   03235

Freedom, Carroll Co., Pop. Code 3
School Administrative Unit 9
Supt. – See North Conway
ES, LOON LAKE ROAD   03836
    William Nelson, prin.

Fremont, Rockingham Co., Pop. Code 4
School Administrative Unit 14
Supt. – See Epping
Ellis ES, MAIN STREET   03044
    Timothy Green, prin.

Gilford, Belknap Co., Pop. Code 5

Faith Christian Academy, P O BOX 7321   03246

Gilmanton Iron Works, Belknap Co., Pop. Code 3
School Administrative Unit 30
Supt. – See Laconia
Gilmanton ES
    RURAL ROUTE 01 BOX 1325   03837
    Thomas Brunelle, prin.

Gilsum, Cheshire Co., Pop. Code 3
School Administrative Unit 38
Supt. – See Keene
ES, P O BOX 38   03448 – David Mousette, prin.

Goffstown, Hillsboro Co., Pop. Code 7
School Administrative Unit 19
Sch. Sys. Enr. Code 5
Supt. – Timothy Gormley   03045
Goffstown Upper MS, PARKER ST   03045
    William Brendle, prin.
Maple Avenue ES, MAPLE AVE   03045
    Marc Boyd, prin.
Other Schools – See Bow, Concord, Manchester, New
    Boston

Villa Augustina Academy, MAST ROAD   03045

Gorham, Coos Co., Pop. Code 5
School Administrative Unit 20
Sch. Sys. Enr. Code 3
Supt. – Robert Bellavance, 113 MAIN ST   03581
Fenn ES, 113 MAIN ST   03581
    Reny Demers, prin.
Other Schools – See Errol, Milan

Grantham, Sullivan Co., Pop. Code 3
School Administrative Unit 32
Supt. – See Lebanon
Grantham Village ES   03753
    Peter Bonaccorsi, prin.

Greenfield, Hillsborough Co., Pop. Code 3
School Administrative Unit 47
Supt. – See Peterborough
ES, BENNINGTON ROAD   03047
    Jared Brown, prin.

Greenland, Rockingham Co., Pop. Code 4
School Administrative Unit 50
Supt. – See Rye

Greenland Central ES, 70 POST RD   03840
    Carl Wood, prin.

Greenville, Hillsborough Co., Pop. Code 4
School Administrative Unit 63
Supt. – See Wilton
ES, CHRUCH STREET   03048 – Paul Ralston, prin.
Mason ES   03048 – Paul Ralston, prin.

Groveton, Coos Co., Pop. Code 4
School Administrative Unit 58
Sch. Sys. Enr. Code 3
Supt. – Warren Bouchard, 8 PREBLE ST   03582
ES, 22 MAIN ST   03582 – Thomas Monahan, prin.
Stark Village ES, RURAL ROUTE   03582
    Virginia Mondor, prin.
Other Schools – See Stratford

Hampstead, Rockingham Co., Pop. Code 5
School Administrative Unit 55
Supt. – See Plaistow
MS, HEATH ROAD   03841 – Robert Little, prin.
Hampstead Central ES, EMERSON AVE   03841
    Kathleen Sciarappa, prin.

Hampton, Rockingham Co., Pop. Code 7
School Administrative Unit 21
Sch. Sys. Enr. Code 5
Supt. – Norman Katner, ALUMNI DRIVE   03842
Hampton Academy JHS
    29 ACADEMY AVE   03842 – Pamela Mazur, prin.
Hampton Centre ES
    WINNACUNNET ROAD   03842
    Nicholas Hardy, prin.
Marston ES, 36 HIGH ST   03842
    Nancy Andrews, prin.
Other Schools – See East Kingston, Hampton Falls,
    North Hampton, Seabrook

Sacred Heart ES, 289 LAFAYETTE RD   03842

Hampton Falls, Rockingham Co., Pop. Code 4
School Administrative Unit 21
Supt. – See Hampton
Akerman ES, EXETER ROAD   03844
    Carol Evans, prin.

Hancock, Hillsborough Co., Pop. Code 4
School Administrative Unit 47
Supt. – See Peterborough
ES, MAIN STREET   03449 – Anita Willard, prin.

Hanover, Grafton Co., Pop. Code 6
School Administrative Unit 22
Sch. Sys. Enr. Code 4
Supt. – Joseph Della Badia
    47 LEBANON ST   03755
Richmond MS, 35 LEBANON ST   03755
    Susan Finer, prin.
Ray ES, RESERVOIR ROAD   03755
    Loretta Murphy, prin.
Other Schools – See Lyme, Lyme Center, Orford

Haverhill, Grafton Co., Pop. Code 5
School Administrative Unit 23
Supt. – See Woodsville
Haverhill Academy JHS, COURT STREET   03765
    Gordon Flight, prin.
Morrill MS, RURAL ROUTE 10   03774
    Pamela Melanson, prin.

Hebron, Grafton Co., Pop. Code 2
School Administrative Unit 4
Supt. – See Bristol
Hebron Village ES, VILLAGE SQUARE   03241
    William Lance, prin.

Henniker, Merrimack Co., Pop. Code 5
School Administrative Unit 24
Sch. Sys. Enr. Code 4
Supt. – Cynthia Mowles, P O BOX 516   03242
Cogswell Memorial MS, P O BOX 585   03242
    Trudy Morris, prin.
ES, P O BOX 585   03242 – Trudy Morris, prin.
Other Schools – See Contoocook, Stoddard, Weare

Hill, Merrimack Co., Pop. Code 3
School Administrative Unit 18
Supt. – See Franklin
Blake ES, CRESCENT STREET   03243
    David Hurley, prin.

Hillsboro, Hillsboro Co., Pop. Code 5
School Administrative Unit 34
Sch. Sys. Enr. Code 5
Supt. – Ralph Minichiello, P O BOX 893   03244
Hillsboro-Deering MS, SCHOOL STREET   03244
    David Dube, prin.
Hillsboro-Deering ES, SCHOOL STREET   03244
    Thomas Listzwan, prin.
Other Schools – See Washington

Hinsdale, Cheshire Co., Pop. Code 5
School Administrative Unit 38
Supt. – See Keene
ES, BRATTLEBORO ROAD   03451
    David Sicard, prin.

Hollis, Hillsboro Co., Pop. Code 5
School Administrative Unit 41
Sch. Sys. Enr. Code 4
Supt. – Philip Dahlinger, P O BOX 1588   03049
JHS, POUND ROAD   03049
    Robert McGittigan, prin.
ES, SILVER LAKE ROAD   03049
    Margaret McAllister, prin.
Other Schools – See Brookline

Hooksett, Merrimack Co., Pop. Code 6
School Administrative Unit 15
Supt. – See Manchester
Hooksett-Memorial JHS
    DANIEL WEBSTER HWY   03106
    Robert Suprenant, prin.
Hooksett Village MS, 35 S MAIN ST   03106
    Frederick Reischer, prin.
Underhill ES, 48 MARTINS FERRY RD   03106
    Bernard Mason, prin.

Hudson, Hillsborough Co., Pop. Code 7
School Administrative Unit 27
Sch. Sys. Enr. Code 5
Supt. – Peter Dolloff, 1 MEMORIAL DR   03051
Hudson Memorial MS, 1 MEMORIAL DR   03051
    Barbara Stone, prin.
Litchfield MS, MCELWAIN DR   03051
    Martin Schlichter, prin.
Griffin Memorial ES
    229 CHARLES BANCROFT HWY   03051
    Linda Kemper, prin.
Library Street ES, 27 LIBRARY ST   03051
    Robert Keeser, prin.
Smith ES, SCHOOL STREET   03051
    James Cunneen, prin.
Webster ES, 3 LIBRARY ST   03051
    Robert Keeser, prin.

Bethel Christian ES, 272 LOWELL RD   03051
Presentation of Mary ES, 182 LOWELL RD   03051

Jackson, Carroll Co., Pop. Code 3
School Administrative Unit 9
Supt. – See North Conway
ES, MAIN STREET   03846 – N. Poon, prin.

Jaffrey, Cheshire Co., Pop. Code 5
School Administrative Unit 47
Supt. – See Peterborough
Jaffrey-Rindge MS, 109 STRATTON ROAD   03452
    Jane Bergeron, prin.
ES, 31 SCHOOL ST   03452 – Ruthanne Fyfe, prin.

St. Patrick ES, P O BOX 324   03452

Jefferson, Coos Co., Pop. Code 3
School Administrative Unit 36
Supt. – See Whitefield
ES, LIBERTY STREET   03583
    William Cozort, prin.

Keene, Cheshire Co., Pop. Code 7
School Administrative Unit 29
Sch. Sys. Enr. Code 5
Supt. – H. Charles Larracey, 34 WEST ST   03431
JHS, 17 WASHINGTON ST   03431
    James Day, prin.
Daniels ES, MAPLE AVE   03431 – E. King, prin.
Franklin ES, 217 WASHINGTON ST   03431
    Michael White, prin.
Fuller ES, 422 ELM ST   03431
    Joseph Cunningham, Jr., prin.
Symonds ES, 70 PARK AVE   03431
    Richard Cate, prin.
Wheelock ES, 24 ADAMS ST   03431
    George Bergeron, prin.
Other Schools – See Chesterfield, Marlborough,
    Munsonville, Westmoreland

School Administrative Unit 38
Sch. Sys. Enr. Code 5
Supt. – William Wheeler
    RURAL ROUTE 01 BOX 232B   03431
Mt. Caesar ES, RURAL ROUTE 01   03431
    Lilla Decoste, prin.
Sullivan Central ES
    NELSON STAR ROUTE   03431
    David Mousette, prin.
Surry ES   03431 – David Mousette, prin.
Wilcox ES, RURAL ROUTE 01   03431
    Lilla Decoste, prin.
Other Schools – See Fitzwilliam, Gilsum, Hinsdale,
    Troy, West Swanzey, Winchester

Monadnock Waldorf ES, 98 S LINCOLN ST   03431
St. Joseph Regional ES, P O BOX 625   03431

Kingston, Rockingham Co., Pop. Code 5
School Administrative Unit 17
Sch. Sys. Enr. Code 4
Supt. – Mark Joyce, P O BOX 87   03848
Bakie ES, MAIN STREET   03848
    Joyce Hughes, prin.
Other Schools – See Newton Junction

Laconia, Belknap Co., Pop. Code 7
School Administrative Unit 30
Sch. Sys. Enr. Code 5
Supt. – Frank Poole, P O BOX 309   03247
Memorial MS, 150 MCGRATH ST   03246
    Douglas Whittum, prin.
Elm Street ES, ELM STREET   03246
    Dawn Cameron, prin.
Gilford ES, 77 BELKNAP MTN RD   03246
    Michael Tocci, prin.
Pleasant Street ES, 336 PLEASANT ST   03246
    Irene Wright, prin.
Woodland Heights ES, 225 WINTER ST   03246
    John Woodward, prin.
Other Schools – See Gilmanton Iron Works

Christian Fellowship School
    RURAL ROUTE 03 BOX 50   03246
Holy Trinity Catholic ES, 50 CHURCH ST   03246

Lancaster, Coos Co.
School Administrative Unit 36
Supt. – See Whitefield
ES, SCHOOL STREET   03584
  William Cozort, prin.

Lebanon, Grafton Co., Pop. Code 7
School Administrative Unit 32
Sch. Sys. Enr. Code 5
Supt. – Paul Rice, P O BOX 488   03766
JHS, 75 BANK ST   03766 – Robert Proulx, prin.
Hanover Street MS, 193 HANOVER ST   03766
  Douglas Carver, prin.
Mt. Lebanon ES, 5 WHITE AVE   03784
  Geraldine Williams, prin.
Sacred Heart ES, 11 ELDRIDGE STREET   03766
  Mary Koen, prin.
School Street ES, 22 SCHOOL ST   03766
  Mary Koen, prin.
Seminary Hill MS, 20 SEMINARY HL   03784
  Martha Langill, prin.
Other Schools – See Grantham, Pittsfield

Lincoln, Grafton Co., Pop. Code 4
School Administrative Unit 23
Supt. – See Woodsville
Lin.-Wood S, P O BOX 97   03251
  Robert Braman, prin.

Lisbon, Grafton Co., Pop. Code 4
School Administrative Unit 35
Supt. – See Littleton
S, 24 HIGHLAND AVE   03585
  Glenn Stillings, prin.
Blue ES, 30 MAPLE TER   03585
  Paul Sanchirico, prin.

Littleton, Grafton Co., Pop. Code 6
School Administrative Unit 35
Sch. Sys. Enr. Code 4
Supt. – Timothy Woodward, 30 MAPLE ST   03561
Bronson JHS, HIGH ST   03561
  Howard Burgess, prin.
Lakeway ES, 120 UNION ST   03561
  Grant Harris, prin.
Other Schools – See Bethlehem, Franconia, Lisbon,
  Sugar Hill

Londgon, Coos Co.
School Administrative Unit 60
Supt. – See Charlestown
Porter ES   03603 – Richard Neilsen, prin.

Londonderry, Rockingham Co., Pop. Code 7
School Administrative Unit 12
Sch. Sys. Enr. Code 5
Supt. – Arthur Ouillette
  268 MAMMOTH ROAD   03053
JHS, 313 MAMMOTH ROAD   03053
  Nancy Meyers, prin.
North Londonderry ES, 19 SANBORN RD   03053
  Donald Jobin, prin.
South Londonderry ES, 88 SOUTH RD   03053
  James Gratton, prin.
Thornton ES, 275 MAMMOTH RD   03053
  Robert Shea, prin.

Lyme, Grafton Co., Pop. Code 4
School Administrative Unit 22
Supt. – See Hanover
MS   03768 – Scott Kalter, prin.

Lyme Center, Grafton Co.
School Administrative Unit 22
Supt. – See Hanover
ES   03769 – Scott Kalter, prin.

Lyndeborough, Hillsborough Co., Pop. Code 4
School Administrative Unit 63
Supt. – See Wilton
Lyndeborough Central ES, P O BOX 46   03082
  Gail Hiltz, prin.

Madison, Carroll Co., Pop. Code 4
School Administrative Unit 9
Supt. – See North Conway
ES, ROUTE 113   03849 – Deborah Karmozyn, prin.

Manchester, Hillsborough Co., Pop. Code 8
School Administrative Unit 15
Sch. Sys. Enr. Code 5
Supt. – David Cawley, RURAL ROUTE 07   03104
Other Schools – See Auburn, Candia, Hooksett

School Administrative Unit 19
Supt. – See Goffstown
Bartlett ES, 627 MAST RD   03102
  Leon Cote, prin.

School Administrative Unit 37
Sch. Sys. Enr. Code 7
Supt. – Eugene Ross, 196 BRIDGE ST   03104
Hillside JHS, 112 RESERVIOR AVE   03104
  G. Campbell, prin.
Parkside JHS, PARKSIDE AVE   03102
  Edward Wade, prin.
Southside JHS, 140 S JEWETT ST   03103
  David Messier, prin.
Bakersville ES, 20 ELM ST   03103
  Philip Egan, prin.
Beech Street ES, 333 BEECH ST   03103
  Nancy Tessier, prin.
Gossler Park ES, 99 SULLIVAN ST   03102
  Anastas Christo, prin.
Green Acres ES, 100 AURORE AVE   03103
  John Devine,Jr., prin.
Hallsville ES, 275 JEWETT ST   03103
  William Shea, prin.

Highland/Goffes Falls ES
  GOFFES FALLS ROAD   03103
  Joseph Forseze, prin.
Jewett ES, 130 S JEWETT ST   03103
  Jean Sweeney, prin.
McDonough ES, 550 LOWELL ST   03104
  Nancy Moreschi, prin.
Northwest ES, 300 YOUVILLE ST   03102
  Robert Duclos, prin.
Parker-Varney ES
  223 JAME POLLACK DRIVE   03102
  Thomas Clow, prin.
Smyth Road ES, 245 BRUCE RD   03104
  Edward Ganem, prin.
Webster ES, 2519 ELM ST   03104
  Roger Groleau, prin.
Weston ES, 1066 HANOVER ST   03104
  John Aylward, prin.
Wilson ES, 401 WILSON ST   03103
  Rita Georgeou, prin.

St. Joseph JHS, 460 PINE ST   03104
West Side Catholic Regional ES
  281 CARTIER ST   03102
St. Anthony ES, 148 BELMONT ST   03103
St. Casimir ES, 456 UNION ST   03103
St. Catherine ES, N AND RUSSELL STS   03104
St. Francis Assisi ES, 3223 BROWN AVE   03103
West Side Catholic ES, 103 WALKER ST   03102

Marlborough, Cheshire Co., Pop. Code 4
School Administrative Unit 29
Supt. – See Keene
ES, SCHOOL STREET   03455
  Sandra Whippie, prin.
Wells Memorial ES
  RURAL ROUTE 01 BOX 123   03455
  Dorothy Frazier, prin.

Marlow, Cheshire Co., Pop. Code 3
School Administrative Unit 60
Supt. – See Charlestown
Perkins ES   03456 – Richard Brewer, prin.

Meredith, Belknap Co., Pop. Code 5
School Administrative Unit 2
Sch. Sys. Enr. Code 4
Supt. – Gary Burton, MAIN ST   03253
Inter-Lakes ES, RURAL ROUTE 03 BOX 153   03253
  Jean Shlager, prin.
Lang Street ES, LANG STREET   03253
  Jean Shlager, prin.
Other Schools – See Ashland, Center Sandwich

Merrimack, Hillsborough Co., Pop. Code 7
School Administrative Unit 26
Sch. Sys. Enr. Code 6
Supt. – James O'Neil, 8 MCELWAIN ST   03054
Mastricola MS, 32 BABOOSIC LAKE ROAD   03054
  Kenneth Taylor, prin.
Mastricola ES, 7 SCHOOL ST   03054
  Nancy Winthrop, prin.
Reeds Ferry ES, 15 LYONS RD   03054
  Francis Hoell, prin.
Thorntons Ferry ES
  134 CAMP SARGENT RD   03054
  Leslie Carter, prin.
Other Schools – See Bedford

Grace Christian ES, P O BOX 11   03054

Milan, Coos Co., Pop. Code 4
School Administrative Unit 20
Supt. – See Gorham
Milan Village ES, RURAL ROUTE 01 BOX 5   03588
  Jacqueline Quintal, prin.

Milford, Hillsborough Co., Pop. Code 6
School Administrative Unit 40
Sch. Sys. Enr. Code 5
Supt. – Damon Russell, 100 ELM ST   03055
Milford Area MS, OSGOOD ROAD   03055
  James Stetson, prin.
Milford ES, ELM STREET   03055
  Maryann Pank, prin.
Other Schools – See Mount Vernon

Milton, Strafford Co., Pop. Code 4
School Administrative Unit 44
Supt. – See Farmington
ES, SCHOOL ST   03851 – Nancy Drew, prin.

Milton Mills, Strafford Co.
School Administrative Unit 44
Supt. – See Farmington
ES, SCHOOL STREET   03852 – Earl Peabody, prin.

Monroe, Grafton Co., Pop. Code 3
School Administrative Unit 23
Supt. – See Woodsville
Monroe Consolidated ES, ROUTE 135   03771
  Michael Vigue, prin.

Mount Vernon, Hillsborough Co., Pop. Code 4
School Administrative Unit 40
Supt. – See Milford
McCollom ES, MAIN STREET   03057
  Barbara Callaghan, prin.
Mont Vernon Village ES, HARWOOD ROAD   03057
  Barbara Callaghan, prin.

Moultonboro, Carroll Co., Pop. Code 4
School Administrative Unit 45
Sch. Sys. Enr. Code 2
Supt. – Kenneth Greenbaum, P O BOX 64   03254
Moultonborough Central ES, P O BOX 149   03254
  John True, prin.

Munsonville, Cheshire Co.
School Administrative Unit 29
Supt. – See Keene
ES   03457 – Virginia Falk, prin.

Nashua, Hillsborough Co., Pop. Code 6
School Administrative Unit 42
Sch. Sys. Enr. Code 7
Supt. – Berard Masse, P O BOX 687   03061
Amherst Street ES, 71 AMHERST ST   03060
  Joan Murphy, prin.
Bicentennial ES, 298 E DUNSTABLE RD   03062
  Charles Katsohis, prin.
Birch Hill ES, 19 BIRCH HILL DR   03063
  Robert Paul, prin.
Broad Street ES, 390 BROAD ST   03063
  Nicholas Kontinos, prin.
Charlotte Avenue ES, 48 CHARLOTTE AVE   03060
  William Pimley,Jr., prin.
Crisp ES, 50 ARLINGTON ST   03060
  Lon Woods, prin.
Fairgrounds ES, 37 BLANCHARD ST   03060
  Warren Toohig, prin.
Ledge Street ES, LEDGE STREET   03060
  William Manley, prin.
Main Dunstable ES, 20 WHITFORD RD   03062
  Peter Kageleiry, prin.
Mt. Pleasant ES, 10 MANCHESTER ST   03060
  Gloria Egan, prin.
New Searles ES, 39 SHADY LN   03062
  Thomas Huskie,Jr., prin.
Sunset Heights ES, 15 OSGOOD RD   03060
  Robert Bettencourt, prin.

Holy Infant ES, 3 CROWN ST   03060
Nashua Catholic Regional ES
  20 CUSHING AVE   03060

New Boston, Hillsborough Co., Pop. Code 4
School Administrative Unit 19
Supt. – See Goffstown
New Boston Central ES
  15 CENTRAL SCHOOL ROAD   03457
  Richard Matthews, prin.

New Castle, Rockingham Co., Pop. Code 3
School Administrative Unit 50
Supt. – See Rye
Trefethen ES   03854 – Elizabeth Gilman, prin.

New Durham, Strafford Co.
School Administrative Unit 49
Supt. – See Wolfeboro
ES, P O BOX 212   03855 – Marcy Mager, prin.

Newfields, Rockingham Co., Pop. Code 3
School Administrative Unit 16
Supt. – See Exeter
ES, P O BOX 206   03856 – Beth Stevens, prin.

New Hampton, Belknap Co., Pop. Code 4
School Administrative Unit 4
Supt. – See Bristol
New Hampton Community ES
  P O BOX 485   03256 – William Lance, prin.

New Ipswich, Hillsborough Co., Pop. Code 4
School Administrative Unit 63
Supt. – See Wilton
Appleton MS, P O BOX 274   03071
  Richard Annis, prin.
New Ipswich Central ES, TURNPIKE ROAD   03071
  Richard Annis, prin.

New London, Merrimack Co., Pop. Code 5
School Administrative Unit 43
Supt. – See Newport
Kearsarge Regional MS, 31A W MAIN ST   03257
  Thomas Poliseno, prin.
Kearsarge Regional ES, MAIN STREET   03257
  Richard Lizotte, prin.

Newmarket, Rockingham Co., Pop. Code 5
School Administrative Unit 31
Sch. Sys. Enr. Code 3
Supt. – Chadwick Chase   03857
ES, 243 S MAIN ST   03857
  Edward O'Connor, prin.

Newport, Sullivan Co., Pop. Code 6
School Administrative Unit 43
Sch. Sys. Enr. Code 5
Supt. – John Sokul, P O BOX 269   03773
Croydon Village ES, RURAL ROUTE 01   03773
  Charles Bretell,Jr., prin.
Richards ES, 21 SCHOOL ST   03773
  Peter Reynolds, prin.
Towle MS, 86 N MAIN ST   03773 – E. Hoke, prin.
Other Schools – See Bradford, East Lempster, New
  London, Sunapee, Warner

School Administrative Unit 6
Supt. – See Claremont
Unity ES, HCR BOX 85   03773
  Rodney Walker, prin.

Newton Junction, Rockingham Co., Pop. Code 5
School Administrative Unit 17
Supt. – See Kingston
Sanborn Regional MS, 31A W MAIN ST   03859
  Gardner Hurlburt, prin.
Sanborn Regional Memorial ES, MAIN ST   03859
  Paul Hanson, prin.

North Conway, Carroll Co., Pop. Code 4
School Administrative Unit 9
Sch. Sys. Enr. Code 4
Supt. – William Jutras, P O BOX 650   03860

Fuller ES, PINE STREET   03860
  Mark Zangari, prin.
  Other Schools – See Bartlett, Center Conway,
    Conway, Freedom, Jackson, Madison, Tamworth

North Hampton, Rockingham Co., Pop. Code 5
  School Administrative Unit 21
  Supt. – See Hampton
  ES, 201 ATLANTIC AVE   03862
    Gordon Quimby, prin.

Northwood, Rockingham Co., Pop. Code 4
  School Administrative Unit 44
  Supt. – See Farmington
  ES, NORTHWOOD ROAD   03261
    Ann Ringling, prin.

Nottingham, Rockingham Co., Pop. Code 4
  School Administrative Unit 44
  Supt. – See Farmington
  ES   03290 – Linda Parkin, prin.

Orford, Grafton Co., Pop. Code 3
  School Administrative Unit 22
  Supt. – See Hanover
  Orfordville ES   03777 – Patricia Davenport, prin.

Pelham, Hillsborough Co., Pop. Code 6
  School Administrative Unit 28
  Sch. Sys. Enr. Code 5
  Supt. – Raymond Raudonis
    RURAL ROUTE 05 BOX 2   03076
  Pelham Memorial MS, 59 MARSH ROAD   03076
    Dennis Goyette, prin.
  Sherburne ES, 14 MARSH RD   03076
    Dewayne Howell, prin.
  Other Schools – See Windham

    St. Patrick ES, RURAL ROUTE 03 BOX 11A   03076

Penacook, Merrimack Co., Pop. Code 5
  School Administrative Unit 46
  Sch. Sys. Enr. Code 5
  Supt. – Phillip Bell, 105 CENTER ST   03303
  Merrimack Valley MS, 14 ALLEN STREET   03303
    Kenneth Hemingway, prin.
  Summer Street ES, SUMMER STREET   03303
    Kent Hemingway,Jr., prin.
  Other Schools – See Andover, Belmont, Boscawen,
    Canterbury, Concord, Salisbury

Peterborough, Hillsborough Co., Pop. Code 5
  School Administrative Unit 47
  Sch. Sys. Enr. Code 4
  Supt. – Lawrence Bramblett, 106 RT 202 N   03458
  ES, 17 HIGH ST   03458 – Maurice Leflem, prin.
  Other Schools – See Antrim, Bennington, Dublin,
    Francestown, Greenfield, Hancock, Jaffrey,
    Pittsburg, Rindge, Temple

Piermont, Grafton Co., Pop. Code 3
  School Administrative Unit 23
  Supt. – See Woodsville
  Piermont Village ES
    DARTMOUTH HIGHWAY   03779
    Jane Pushee, prin.

Pittsburg, Coos Co., Pop. Code 3
  School Administrative Unit 47
  Supt. – See Peterborough
  MS, ROUTE 202 N   03458
    Norman Lapalme, prin.

  School Administrative Unit 7
  Supt. – See Colebrook
  S, RURAL ROUTE 01   03592
    Winston Young, prin.

Pittsfield, Merrimack Co., Pop. Code 5
  School Administrative Unit 32
  Supt. – See Lebanon
  ES, ONEIDA STREET   03263 – Joan Garipay, prin.

  School Administrative Unit 51
  Supt. – See Barnstead
  ES, 63 MAIN ST   03263
    Bernadette McLaughlin, prin.

  School Administrative Unit 53
  Supt. – See Suncook
  Chicester Central ES, PITTSFIELD ROAD   03263
    Stewart Armstrong, prin.

Plaistow, Rockingham Co., Pop. Code 6
  School Administrative Unit 55
  Sch. Sys. Enr. Code 5
  Supt. – Terrance Holmes
    30 GREENOUGH DR   03865
  Timberlane Regional JHS
    36 GREENOUGH ROAD   03865
    Judith DeShaies, prin.
  Pollard ES, 120 MAIN STREET   03865
    Joean Griffin, prin.
  Other Schools – See Atkinson, Danville, Hampstead,
    Sandown

Plymouth, Grafton Co., Pop. Code 6
  School Administrative Unit 48
  Sch. Sys. Enr. Code 4
  Supt. – Paul Dulac, 3 TAMARACK EXT DR   03264
  Holderness Central ES
    RURAL ROUTE 03 BOX 95   03264
    Michael Maroni, prin.
  ES, OLD WARD BRIDGE ROAD   03264
    James Kemmerer, prin.
  Other Schools – See Campton, Rumney, Waterville
    Valley, Wentworth

Calvary Christian School
  RURAL ROUTE 02 BOX 95   03264

Portsmouth, Rockingham Co., Pop. Code 8
  School Administrative Unit 52
  Sch. Sys. Enr. Code 5
  Supt. – Timothy Monahan
    50 CLOUGH DRIVE   03801
  JHS, 155 PARROTT AVE   03801
    John Stokel, prin.
  Brackett ES, 1 RYE ST   03801
    Ernest Guimond, prin.
  Dondero ES, 32 VAN BUREN AVE   03801
    Frederick Apt, prin.
  Little Harbour ES, 50 CLOUGH DR   03801
    Edmund Heffernan, prin.
  New Franklin ES, DENNETT STREET   03801
    Constance Carmody, prin.
  Sherburne ES, 35 SHERBURNE RD   03801
    Nancy O'Rourke, prin.
  Wentworth ES, 25 GRANITE ST   03801
    Joan Wood, prin.

Bethel Christian Academy
  200 CUTTS AVE EXT   03801
  Lady Isle ES, LITTLE HARBOR RD   03801
  St. Patrick ES, 125 AUSTIN ST   03801

Raymond, Rockingham Co., Pop. Code 6
  School Administrative Unit 33
  Sch. Sys. Enr. Code 6
  Supt. – James Carnrite, 37 EPPING ROAD   03077
  MS, 5 SCHOOL ST   03077 – Donna Borowick, prin.
  Lamprey River ES
    OLD MANCHESTER ROAD   03077
    Roderick Crepeau, prin.

Rindge, Cheshire Co., Pop. Code 4
  School Administrative Unit 47
  Supt. – See Peterborough
  Rindge Memorial ES, 30 SCHOOL ST   03461
    John Cornellier, prin.

Rochester, Strafford Co., Pop. Code 7
  School Administrative Unit 54
  Sch. Sys. Enr. Code 5
  Supt. – Raymond Yeagley, 62 S MAIN ST   03867
  Allen ES, GRANITE STREET   03867
    Michael Hopkins, prin.
  Chamberlain Street ES
    CHAMBERLAIN STREET   03867
    Sally Riley, prin.
  East Rochester Annex ES, 5 COCHECO AVE   03867
    Nancy Loud, prin.
  Gonic ES, RAILROAD AVE   03867
    Garrett Vander Els, prin.
  Maple Street ES, MAPLE STREET   03867
    Elaine Berry, prin.
  McCelland ES, BROCK STREET   03867
    Lynn Ritvo, prin.
  New East Rochester ES, 38 PORTLAND ST   03867
    Arlene Welch, prin.
  School Street ES, SCHOOL STREET   03867
    Contance Rice, prin.

  Rochester Catholic ES, 16 BRIDGE ST   03867

Rollinsford, Strafford Co., Pop. Code 4
  School Administrative Unit 56
  Supt. – See Somersworth
  ES, LOCUST ST   03869 – Douglas Griggs, prin.

Rumney, Grafton Co., Pop. Code 4
  School Administrative Unit 48
  Supt. – See Plymouth
  ES   03266 – Susan Rubel, prin.

Rye, Rockingham Co., Pop. Code 5
  School Administrative Unit 50
  Sch. Sys. Enr. Code 3
  Supt. – Daniel Durgin, P O BOX 560   03870
  JHS, 501 WASHINGTON ROAD   03870
    Joseph Korowski, prin.
  ES, 461 SAGAMORE RD   03870
    Ralph Leonard, prin.
  Other Schools – See Greenland, New Castle,
    Strawbery Banke

Salem, Rockingham Co., Pop. Code 7
  School Administrative Unit 57
  Sch. Sys. Enr. Code 5
  Supt. – Paul Johnson, 206 MAIN ST   03079
  Woodbury MS, 206 MAIN ST   03079
    John Moody, prin.
  Barron ES, 14 BUTLER ST   03079
    Richard O'Shaughnessy, prin.
  Fisk ES, 14 MAIN ST   03079 – Jane Batts, prin.
  Haigh MS, 24 SCHOOL ST   03079
    Susan Nelson, prin.
  Lancaster ES, 54 MILLVILLE ST   03079
    Robert Chute, prin.
  North Salem ES, 140 ZION HILL RD   03079
    Michael Delahanty, prin.
  Soule ES, 173 S POLICY ST   03079
    Homer Hamlin, prin.

Temple Christian School
  1 SANDHILL ROAD   03079
  St. Joseph Regional ES, 40 MAIN ST   03079

Salisbury, Merrimack Co., Pop. Code 3
  School Administrative Unit 46
  Supt. – See Penacook
  ES, WHITTEMORE ROAD   03268
    Irene Plourde, prin.

Sanbornton, Belknap Co., Pop. Code 4
  School Administrative Unit 59
  Supt. – See Tilton
  Sanbornton Central ES   03269
    Dorothy Kraft, prin.

Sanbornville, Carroll Co.
  School Administrative Unit 44
  Supt. – See Farmington
  Paul ES, RURAL ROUTE 01 BOX 100   03872
    Candace Brown, prin.
  Union ES, RURAL ROUTE 02 BOX 770   03872
    Candace Brown, prin.

Sandown, Rockingham Co., Pop. Code 4
  School Administrative Unit 55
  Supt. – See Plaistow
  ES, ROUTE 121A   03873 – Judith Pence, prin.

Seabrook, Rockingham Co., Pop. Code 6
  School Administrative Unit 21
  Supt. – See Hampton
  ES, WALTON ROAD   03874 – Louis Nardello, prin.

Somersworth, Strafford Co., Pop. Code 7
  School Administrative Unit 56
  Sch. Sys. Enr. Code 5
  Supt. – Nathan Greenberg, 414 HIGH ST   03878
  MS, 20 MEMORIAL DR   03878
    Daniel Moegelin, prin.
  Great Falls ES, 319 MAIN ST   03878
    Patricia Danforth, prin.
  Hilltop ES, 17 GRAND ST   03878 – (—), prin.
  Maple Wood ES, MAPLE WOOD DRIVE   03878
    Dennis Harrington, prin.
  Other Schools – See Rollinsford

Southeast New Hampshire Christian Acad.
  ROCKY HILL ROAD   03878

Stoddard, Cheshire Co., Pop. Code 2
  School Administrative Unit 24
  Supt. – See Henniker
  Faulker ES   03464 – Barbara Cutting, prin.

Stratford, Coos Co., Pop. Code 3
  School Administrative Unit 58
  Supt. – See Groveton
  Stratford S   03590 – John Graziano, prin.

Stratham, Rockingham Co., Pop. Code 5
  School Administrative Unit 16
  Supt. – See Exeter
  Stratham Memorial ES, BUNKER HILL AVE   03885
    Katherine Kramer, prin.

Strawbery Banke, Portsmouth Co.
  School Administrative Unit 50
  Supt. – See Rye
  Newington ES   03801 – Richard Michaels, prin.

Sugar Hill, Grafton Co., Pop. Code 2
  School Administrative Unit 35
  Supt. – See Littleton
  Carolina Crapo ES   03585 – Richard Smiles, prin.

Sunapee, Sullivan Co., Pop. Code 4
  School Administrative Unit 43
  Supt. – See Newport
  Sunapee Central ES, MYRTLE STREET   03782
    Donald Stowe, prin.

Suncook, Merrimack Co., Pop. Code 5
  School Administrative Unit 53
  Sch. Sys. Enr. Code 5
  Supt. – Paul Deminico, RURAL ROUTE 01   03275
  Pembroke MS, HIGH ST   03275
    Allen Zipke, prin.
  Other Schools – See Allenstown, Concord, Deerfield,
    Epsom, Pittsfield

Tamworth, Carroll Co., Pop. Code 4
  School Administrative Unit 9
  Supt. – See North Conway
  Brett ES, P O BOX 219   03886
    Anthony Simone, prin.

Temple, Hillsborough Co., Pop. Code 3
  School Administrative Unit 47
  Supt. – See Peterborough
  ES, GENERAL DELIVERY   03084
    Niki McGettigan, prin.

Tilton, Belknap Co., Pop. Code 5
  School Administrative Unit 59
  Sch. Sys. Enr. Code 4
  Supt. – Daniel Stockwell, 367 W MAIN ST   03276
  Winnisquam Regional MS, P O BOX 318   03276
    Larry Dicenzo, prin.
  Union Sanborn ES, P O BOX 212   03276
    Dorothy Kraft, prin.
  Other Schools – See Sanbornton

Troy, Cheshire Co., Pop. Code 4
  School Administrative Unit 38
  Supt. – See Keene
  ES, SCHOOL STREET   03465
    Norman Evans, prin.

Walpole, Cheshire Co., Pop. Code 5
  School Administrative Unit 60
  Supt. – See Charlestown
  MS, TURNPIKE ROAD   03608
    Martin Mahoney, prin.
  North Walpole MS   03608 – Wayne Evans, prin.
  PS   03608 – Martin Mahoney, prin.

Warner, Merrimack Co., Pop. Code 4
School Administrative Unit 43
Supt. – See Newport
Simonds ES, CHURCH STREET 03278
Carlton Fitzgerald, prin.

Warren, Grafton Co., Pop. Code 3
School Administrative Unit 23
Supt. – See Woodsville
Warren Village ES, MAIN STREET 03279
Arthur St. George, prin.

Washington, Sullivan Co., Pop. Code 2
School Administrative Unit 34
Supt. – See Hillsboro
Washington Center ES 03280
Richard Lathrop, prin.

Waterville Valley, Grafton Co.
School Administrative Unit 48
Supt. – See Plymouth
ES 03223 – Mary Seeger, prin.

Weare, Hillsboro Co., Pop. Code 5
School Administrative Unit 24
Supt. – See Henniker
ES, EAST STREET 03281 – Fred Roberts, prin.

Wentworth, Grafton Co., Pop. Code 3
School Administrative Unit 48
Supt. – See Plymouth
ES 03282 – Christine LaMontagne, prin.

West Franklin, Merrimack Co.
School Administrative Unit 18
Supt. – See Franklin
Smith ES, DANIEL WEBSTER DRIVE 03235
Deborah McNeish, prin.

Westmoreland, Cheshire Co.
School Administrative Unit 29
Supt. – See Keene
ES, GLEBE ROAD 03467 – Janice Lefebvre, prin.

West Stewartstown, Coos Co.
School Administrative Unit 7
Supt. – See Colebrook
West Side ES, WASHINGTON ST 03597
Norma Chenevert, prin.

West Swanzey, Cheshire Co.
School Administrative Unit 38
Supt. – See Keene
Cutler MS, P O BOX 629 03469 – David Bell, prin.

Whitefield, Coos Co., Pop. Code 4
School Administrative Unit 36
Sch. Sys. Enr. Code 4
Supt. – Edgar Melanson, 21 HIGHLAND ST 03598
Dalton ES, RURAL ROUTE 02 03598
Donald LaPlante, prin.
McIntrye ES, 14 HIGHLAND ST 03598
Donald LaPlante, prin.
Other Schools – See Jefferson, Lancaster

Wilton, Hillsboro Co., Pop. Code 5
School Administrative Unit 63
Sch. Sys. Enr. Code 4
Supt. – Richard Lates, P O BOX 479 03086
ES, TREMONT STREET 03086 – John Allen, prin.
Other Schools – See Greenville, Lyndeborough, New Ipswich

Pine Hill Waldorf ES, ABBOT HILL ROAD 03086

Winchester, Cheshire Co., Pop. Code 5
School Administrative Unit 38
Supt. – See Keene

ES, PARKER STREET 03470
Curtis Cardine, prin.

Windham, Rockingham Co., Pop. Code 6
School Administrative Unit 28
Supt. – See Pelham
MS, LOWELL ROAD 03087
Stephen Plocharczyk, prin.
Golden Brook ES, LOWELL ROAD 03087
James Flynn, prin.
Windham Center MS, LOWELL ROAD 03087
Stephen Plocharczyk, prin.

Wolfeboro, Carroll Co., Pop. Code 5
School Administrative Unit 49
Sch. Sys. Enr. Code 4
Supt. – Carl Hesse, HCR 01 03894
Kingswood Regional JHS, S MAIN ST 03894
Barbara Hatch, prin.
Carpenter ES, P O BOX 659 03894
Sumner Harris, prin.
Other Schools – See Center Ossipee, Center Tuftonboro, New Durham

Woodsville, Grafton Co., Pop. Code 4
School Administrative Unit 23
Sch. Sys. Enr. Code 4
Supt. – Douglas McDonald, COURT ST 03785
ES, PARK STREET 03785
Pamela Melanson, prin.
Other Schools – See Bath, Haverhill, Lincoln, Monroe, Piermont, Warren

NEW JERSEY

STATE DEPARTMENT OF EDUCATION
225 W. State St., CN 500, Trenton 08625
(609) 292-4469

Commissioner of Education	Dr. Saul Cooperman
Assistant Commissioner County & Regional Services	Dr. Walter McCarroll
Assistant Commissioner Educational Programs	Richard DiPatri
Assistant Commissioner Executive Services	Dr. Cummings Piatt
Assistant Commissioner Finance	Robert Swissler
Assistant Commissioner General Academic Education	Dr. Joel Bloom
Assistant Commissioner & State Librarian	Barbara Weaver
Assistant Commissioner Vocational Education	Lloyd Newbaker

STATE BOARD OF EDUCATION
John Klagholz, *President*   Seaside Park

DEPARTMENT OF HIGHER EDUCATION
T. Edward Hollander, *Chancellor*   225 W. State St., Trenton 08625

COUNTY SUPERINTENDENTS OF SCHOOLS

Atlantic County, Gustav Ruh, Supt.
1200 HARDING HWY W, Mays Landing 08330
Bergen County, M. Kelly, Supt.
327 E RIDGEWOOD AVE, Paramus 07652
Burlington County, W. George Batzel, Supt.
UNION & HIGHS STS, Mount Holly 08060
Camden County, Donald Beineman, Supt.
120 WARWICK ROAD, Stratford 08084
Cape May County, Patricia Horton, Supt.
CREST HAVEN ROAD, Cape May Court House 08210
Cumberland County, Stephen Kalopos, Supt.
19 LANDIS AVE, Bridgeton 08302
Essex County, Elena Scambio, Supt.
240 S HARRISON ST, East Orange 07018

Gloucester County, Peter Contini, Supt.
RURAL ROUTE 05 BOX 635, Williamstown 08094
Hudson County, Louis Acocella, Supt.
595 NEWARK AVE, Jersey City 07306
Hunterdon County, Gerald Savage, Supt.
1 E MAIN ST, Flemington 08822
Mercer County, Greta Shepard, Supt.
P O BOX 8068, Trenton 08650
Middlesex County, Virginia Brinson, Supt.
200 OLD MATAWAN ROAD, Old Bridge 08857
Monmouth County, Milton Hughes, Supt.
P O BOX 1264, Freehold 07728
Morris County, George Snow, Supt.
W HANOVER AVE, Morristown 07960

Ocean County, Joseph Zack, Supt.
212 WASHINGTON ST, Toms River 08753
Passaic County, Melindo Persi, Supt.
31 MC BRIDE AVE, Paterson 07501
Salem County, Willetta Mulhorn, Supt.
P O BOX 344, Woodstown 08098
Somerset County, Donald Vansant, Supt.
P O BOX 3000, Somerville 08876
Sussex County, Bernard Andrews, Supt.
18 CHURCH ST, Newton 07860
Union County, Vito Gagliardi, Supt.
300 NORTH AVE E, Westfield 07090
Warren County, William Mancuso, Supt.
413 2ND ST, Belvidere 07823

PUBLIC, PRIVATE, AND PAROCHIAL ELEMENTARY SCHOOLS

Absecon, Atlantic Co., Pop. Code 6
Absecon CSD
Sch. Sys. Enr. Code 3
Supt. – Walter Krug, WEBB ROAD 08201
Attales MS, WEBB ROAD 08201
Norman Hirschfeld, prin.

Marsh ES, NEW JERSEY AVE 08201
Charles Pancoast, prin.

Galloway Twp. SD
Sch. Sys. Enr. Code 4
Supt. – Don Dearborn
1 S MOSS MILL ROAD 08201

Rann MS, 8TH AVE 08201 – Gerald Toscano, prin.
Reeds Road ES, 101 S REED RD 08201
David Dunlevy, prin.
Other Schools – See Cologne, Egg Harbor City, Oceanville, Pomona

Allamuchy, Warren Co., Pop. Code 5
Allamuchy Twp. SD
Sch. Sys. Enr. Code 2
Supt. – Kenneth Gross, P O BOX J 07820
Allamuchy Twp. Consolidated ES
P O BOX J 07820 – Kenneth Gross, prin.

Allendale, Bergen Co., Pop. Code 6
Allendale SD
Sch. Sys. Enr. Code 3
Supt. – James Hagy, BROOKSIDE AVE 07401
Brookside MS, BROOKSIDE AVE 07401
Aileen Wilson, prin.
Hillside ES, HILLSIDE AVE 07401
H. Powderly, prin.

Allentown, Monmouth Co., Pop. Code 4
Upper Freehold Regional SD
Sch. Sys. Enr. Code 4
Supt. – Stephen Sokolow, 27 HIGH ST 08501
Upper Freehold Regional ES, HIGH ST 08501
Edward Coldren, prin.

Alloway, Salem Co., Pop. Code 5
Alloway Twp. SD
Sch. Sys. Enr. Code 2
Supt. – Jean Walsh, CEDAR ST 08001
Remster MS, CEDAR ST 08001 – Jean Walsh, prin.
Alloway Twp. ES, CEDAR ST 08001
Jean Walsh, prin.

Alpha, Warren Co., Pop. Code 5
Aplha SD
Sch. Sys. Enr. Code 2
Supt. – Dr. Sandra Moore
NORTH BOULEVARD 08865
Alpha Borough ES, 817 NORTH BLVD 08865
Dr. Sandra Moore, prin.

Alpine, Bergen Co., Pop. Code 4
Alpine SD
Sch. Sys. Enr. Code 2
Supt. – Mathew Glowski, HILLSIDE AVE 07620
ES, HILLSIDE AVE 07620
Dr. Matthew Glowski, prin.

Annadale, Hunterdon Co., Pop. Code 1
Clinton Twp. SD
Sch. Sys. Enr. Code 4
Supt. – Pat McGaheran, P O BOX 6 08801
Other Schools – See Clinton, Lebanon

Asbury, Hunterdon Co.
Bethlehem Twp. SD
Sch. Sys. Enr. Code 2
Supt. – Bernard O'Brien
160 W PORTAL ROAD 08802
Hoppock MS, RURAL ROUTE 02 BOX 160 08802
Dennis Murphy, prin.
Conley ES, RURAL ROUTE 01 08802
Bernard O'Brien, prin.

Asbury Park, Monmouth Co., Pop. Code 7
Asbury Park SD
Sch. Sys. Enr. Code 5
Supt. – R. Jannarone, 1506 PARK AVE 07712
Middle School MS, 1200 BANGS AVE 07712
Sidney Wells, prin.
Bangs Avenue ES, 1300 BANGS AVE 07712
Howard West, prin.
Bradley ES, THIRD & PINE ST 07712
Judith Owens, prin.

Ocean Twp. SD
Supt. – See Oakhurst
Wanamassa ES, BENDERMERE AVE 07712
Camille Tighe, prin.
Wayside ES, 733 BOWNE RD 07712
Douglas Deicke, prin.

Hillel Yeshiva ES, 1025 DEAL RD 07712
Our Lady of Mt. Carmel ES
PINE AND FIRST AVES 07712
St. Mary ES, 73 WICKAPECKO DR 07712

Atco, Camden Co., Pop. Code 4
Lower Camden County Regional HSD 1
Sch. Sys. Enr. Code 5
Supt. – Paul Winkler
200 COOPERS FOLLY ROAD 08004
Other Schools – See Lindenwold

Waterford Twp. SD
Sch. Sys. Enr. Code 4
Supt. – Richard Salimena
925 LINCOLN AVE 08004
ES, COOPER ROAD 08004 – Dorothy Moran, prin.
Richards ES, 925 LINCOLN AVE 08004
Charles Delcamp III, prin.
Other Schools – See Waterford Works

Assumption School, 127 COOPER RD 08004

Atlantic City, Atlantic Co., Pop. Code 8
Atlantic City SD
Sch. Sys. Enr. Code 6
Supt. – Paul Lacity, 1809 PACIFIC AVE 08401
Central JHS, 29 S OHIO AVE 08401
Joseph Laco, prin.
Brighton Avenue ES, 30 N BRIGHTON AVE 08401
Bruce Greenfield, prin.
Chelsea MS, 2523 ARTIC AVE 08401
Herbert Milan, prin.
Chelsea Heights ES, 4101 FILBERT AVE 08401
Stanley Waldman, prin.
Indiana Avenue ES, 117 N INDIANA AVE 08401
Avon Chapman, prin.

Massachusetts Avenue ES
1 S MASSACHUSETTS AVE 08401
Jose Rios, prin.
New Jersey Avenue ES
35 N NEW JERSEY AVE 08401
Marven Hill, prin.
Richmond Avenue ES
4115 VENTNOR AVE 08401
Sylvia Williams, prin.
Uptown ES Complex, 323 MADISON AVE 08401
William Steele, prin.
West Side ES Complex
1700 MARMORA AVE 08401 – Earl Brown, prin.

Our Lady Star of the Sea ES
15 N CALIFORNIA AVE 08401

Atlantic Highlands, Monmouth Co., Pop. Code 5
Atlantic Highlands SD
Sch. Sys. Enr. Code 2
Supt. – Martha Hammond, 140 FIRST AVE 07716
ES, 140 1ST AVE 07716 – Antoni Mrozinski, prin.

St. Agnes ES, 55 SOUTH AVE 07716

Audubon, Camden Co., Pop. Code 6
Audubon SD
Sch. Sys. Enr. Code 4
Supt. – John Palomano
350 EDGEWOOD AVE 08106
Haviland Avenue ES
240 S HAVILAND AVE 08106
Ronald Shenk, prin.
Mansion Avenue ES
EDGEWOOD AND PNES 08106
Terri Freed, prin.

Augusta, Sussex Co.
Lafayette Twp. SD
Sch. Sys. Enr. Code 2
Supt. – J. Thomas Morton
RURAL ROUTE 01 BOX 542 07822
Lafayette Twp. ES
RURAL ROUTE 01 BOX 542 07822
J. Morton, prin.

Avalon, Cape May Co., Pop. Code 4
Avalon SD
Sch. Sys. Enr. Code 1
Supt. – Ron Bonner, 3200 OCEAN DRIVE 08202
ES, 32ND & OCEAN DR 08202
Ronald Bonner, prin.

Avenel, Middlesex Co., Pop. Code 7
Woodbridge Twp. SD
Supt. – See Woodbridge
Avenel Street ES, 230 AVENEL ST 07001
Frederick Geoffroy, prin.
Woodbine Avenue ES, WOODBINE AVE 07001
Ernest Dubay, prin.

Avon By The Sea, Monmouth Co., Pop. Code 4
Avon Borough SD
Sch. Sys. Enr. Code 2
Supt. – John Gatta, LINCOLN & 5TH AVES 07717
Avon ES, 505 LINCOLN AVE 07717
John Gatta, prin.

Barnegat, Ocean Co.
Barnegat Twp. SD
Sch. Sys. Enr. Code 4
Supt. – Robert Horbelt, 25 BIRDSALL ST 08005
Collins ES, BARNEGAT BLVD 08005
Gary Ravaioli, prin.
Dunfee ES, BARNEGAT BLVD 08005
Joseph Donahue, prin.
Edwards ES, 25 BIRDSALL ST 08005
Roger Caruba, prin.

Barrington, Camden Co., Pop. Code 6
Barrington SD
Sch. Sys. Enr. Code 3
Supt. – Nelson Malony, SCHOOL LANE 08007
Woodland MS, SCHOOL LANE 08007
Jane Kirschling, prin.
Other Schools – See Haddonfield

St. Francis DeSales ES
134 W GLOUCESTER PIKE 08007

Basking Ridge, Somerset Co., Pop. Code 5
Benards Twp. SD
Sch. Sys. Enr. Code 4
Supt. – Adrienne Vogrin
PEACHTREE ROAD 07920
Annin ES, 70 QUINCY ROAD 07920
Joan Tonnarelli, prin.
Cedar Hill MS, PEACHTREE RD 07920
J. Joseph Kaufman, prin.
Oak Street ES, 70 W OAK ST 07920
Edward Sperduto, prin.
Other Schools – See Liberty Corner

St. James ES, 200 S FINLEY AVE 07920

Bay Head, Ocean Co., Pop. Code 4
Bay Head SD
Sch. Sys. Enr. Code 1
Supt. – J. Robert Mullan, GROVE ST 08742
ES, 145 GROVE ST 08742 – J. Mullan, prin.

Bayonne, Hudson Co., Pop. Code 8
Bayonne SD
Sch. Sys. Enr. Code 6
Supt. – James Murphy, 669 AVENUE 07002
Bailey ES 12, 75 W 10TH ST 07002
Robert Craig, prin.

Donohoe ES 4, EAST 5TH ST 07002
Patricia McGeehan, prin.
Harris ES 1, AVENUE C & 5TH ST 07002
Mary Meaney, prin.
Lincoln ES 5, PROSPECT AVE & 30TH ST 07002
Robert Dougherty, prin.
Mann ES 6, WEST 38TH ST 07002
Richard Malanowski, prin.
Roberson ES 7, 29 ANDREW ST 07002
Harold Strohoefer, prin.
Robinson ES 3, BLVD & 31ST ST 07002
Dr. Carol Grasz, prin.
Roosevelt ES 11, 131 W 23RD ST 07002
Joseph Kubacz, prin.
Vroom ES 2, 18 W 26TH ST 07002
Daniel Doyle, prin.
Washington ES 9, AVENUE B & 47TH ST 07002
James McNally, prin.
Wilson ES 10, AVENUE B & 57TH ST 07002
John Wanko, prin.

Our Lady Mt. Carmel ES, 25 E 22ND ST 07002
Our Lady Star of the Sea ES, 19 W 13TH ST 07002
Our Lady of the Assumption ES
101 W 23RD ST 07002
St. Andrew ES, FOURTH & BROADWAY 07002
St. Joseph ES, 311 AVENUE E 07002
St. Vincent De Paul School, 80 W 47TH ST 07002

Bayville, Ocean Co., Pop. Code 3
Berkeley Twp. SD
Sch. Sys. Enr. Code 4
Supt. – Robert Ciliento
57 CENTRAL PARKWAY 08721
ES, 356 ATLANTIC CITY BLVD 08721
Richard Koenig, prin.
Potter ES, 60 VEEDER LN 08721
Paul Polito, prin.
Worth ES, 57 CENTRAL PKY 08721
W. Steiner, Jr., prin.

Central Regional HSD
Sch. Sys. Enr. Code 4
Supt. – Ronald DeConde
FORREST HILLS PKWY 08721
Central Regional MS
FORREST HILLS PKWY 08721
James McConnell, prin.

Beach Haven, Ocean Co., Pop. Code 4
Beach Haven Borough SD
Sch. Sys. Enr. Code 2
Supt. – Dr. Howard Luper
BEACH AVE AT EIGHTH AVE 08008
ES, 8TH ST & BEACH AVE 08008
Dr. Howard Luper, prin.

Beachwood, Ocean Co., Pop. Code 6
Toms River Regional SD
Supt. – See Toms River
Beachwood ES, BERKLEY AVE 08722
Thomas Venskus, prin.

Bedminster, Somerset Co., Pop. Code 4
Bedminster Twp. SD
Sch. Sys. Enr. Code 2
Supt. – Norman Rosenfeld, P O BOX 25 07921
Bedminster Twp. ES, 350 MAIN ST 07921
Dr. Norman Rosenfeld, prin.

Belford, Monmouth Co., Pop. Code 6
Middletown Twp. SD
Supt. – See Middletown
Bayview ES, 300 LEONARDVILLE RD 07718
Irma Kelleher, prin.

Belle Mead, Somerset Co.
Hillsborough Twp. SD
Sch. Sys. Enr. Code 5
Supt. – Michael Carey, P O BOX 427 08502
Hillsborough ES, ROUTE 206 08502
Harold Blackstone, prin.
Woods Road ES, SOUTH WOODS ROAD 08502
Theodore Smith, prin.
Other Schools – See Neshanic Station, Somerville

Belleville, Essex Co., Pop. Code 8
Belleville SD
Sch. Sys. Enr. Code 5
Supt. – Michael Nardiello
190 CORTLANDT ST 07109
MS, 279 WASHINGTON AVE 07109
Mario DiMaggio, prin.
ES 10, 527 BELLEVILLE AVE 07109
Nicholas Petti, prin.
ES 3, 230 JORALEMON ST 07109
Austin MacArthur, prin.
ES 4, 30 MAGNOLIA ST 07109
George Nucera, prin.
ES 5, 149 ADELAIDE ST 07109
Archibald Gallombardo, prin.
ES 7, 20 PASSAIC AVE 07109
Marilyn Hawthorne, prin.
ES 8, 183 UNION AVE 07109 – Arthur Pico, prin.
ES 9, 309 RALPH ST 07109
Michael Harvey, prin.

St. Peter ES, 152 WILLIAM ST 07109

Bellmawr, Camden Co., Pop. Code 7
Bellmawr SD
Sch. Sys. Enr. Code 3
Supt. – Robert Wyatt, N BELL ROAD 08031
Bell Oaks MS, N BELL ROAD 08031
Tim Bell, prin.

Bellmawr Park ES, VICTORY DR 08031
  Orlando Saccomanno, prin.
Burke ES, S BLACK HORSE PIKE 08031
  Anthony DeFerro, prin.

Annunciation ES, 605 W BROWNING RD 08031

Belmar, Monmouth Co., Pop. Code 6
Belmar SD
Sch. Sys. Enr. Code 3
Supt. – Lester Richens, 1101 MAIN ST 07719
ES, 1101 MAIN ST 07719
  Dr. Lester Richens, prin.

St. Rose ES, 605 6TH AVE 07719

Belvidere, Warren Co., Pop. Code 4
Belvidere SD
Sch. Sys. Enr. Code 3
Supt. – Andrew Mark, OXFORD ST 07823
Oxford Street MS, 801 OXFORD ST 07823
  Angelo Izzo, prin.
Third Street ES, THIRD ST 07823
  Angelo Izzo, prin.

White Twp. SD
Sch. Sys. Enr. Code 2
Supt. – Joseph Sofhauser
  RURAL ROUTE 01 BOX 476 07823
White Twp. Consolodated ES
  RURAL ROUTE 01 BOX 476 07823
  Joseph Sofhauser, prin.

Bergenfield, Bergen Co., Pop. Code 8
Bergenfield SD
Sch. Sys. Enr. Code 5
Supt. – John Habeeb, 100 S PROSPECT AVE 07621
Brown MS, 130 S WASHINGTON AVE 07621 ·
  Joan Lipkowitz, prin.
Franklin ES, 50 N FRANKLIN AVE 07621
  Rosemary Lagamma, prin.
Hoover ES
  MURRAY HILL TER & SYLVAN AV 07621
  Edward Callison, prin.
Jefferson ES, 200 HICKORY AVE 07621
  George Handera, prin.
Lincoln ES, 191 HIGHVIEW AVE 07621
  James Mongon, prin.
Washington ES, SOUTH SUMMIT ST 07621
  Henry Wortche, prin.

St. John Evangelist ES, 17 BRADLEY AVE 07621

Berkeley Heights, Union Co., Pop. Code 7
Berkeley Heights SD
Sch. Sys. Enr. Code 4
Supt. – Earling Clausen
  345 PLAINFIELD AVE 07922
Columbia MS, 345 PLAINFIELD AVE 07922
  Joseph Ierardi, prin.
Hughes ES, 446 SNYDER AVE 07922
  Debra Pavignano, prin.
Mountain Park ES, 55 FAIRFAX DR 07922
  William Palmer, prin.
Woodruff ES, BRAIRWOOD DR W 07922
  John Muly, prin.

Berlin, Camden Co., Pop. Code 6
Berlin Borough SD
Sch. Sys. Enr. Code 3
Supt. – Paul Maggioncalda
  215 FRANKLIN AVE 08009
Berlin Community ES
  215 S FRANKLIN AVE 08009
  Carolyn Baechtle, prin.

Our Lady of Mt. Carmel ES
  11 N CEDAR AVE 08009

Bernardsville, Somerset Co., Pop. Code 6
Bernardsville Borough SD
Sch. Sys. Enr. Code 4
Supt. – William Librera, 25 OLCOTT AVE 07924
Bernardsville MS, SENEY DR 07924
  Pamela Beck, prin.
ES, 141 SENEY DRIVE 07924 – Dr. John Taylor, prin.

St. Elizabeth School, SENEY DRIVE 07924
The Gill Street Bernards School
  CLAREMONT ROAD 07924

Beverly, Burlington Co., Pop. Code 5
Beverly CSD
Sch. Sys. Enr. Code 2
Supt. – Dr. Glenn Gray
  PINE ST & BENTLEY AVE 08010
ES, PINE ST & BENTLEY AVE 08010
  Dr. Glenn Gray, prin.

Edgewater Park SD
Sch. Sys. Enr. Code 3
Supt. – Walt Dold, WASHINGTON AVE 08010
Ridgeway MS, 300 DELLANCO ROAD 08010
  Walt Bowyer, prin.
Magowan ES, CHERRIX AVE 08010
  Dr. Harlene Galen, prin.

St. Joseph ES, 805 WARREN ST 08010

Blackwood, Camden Co., Pop. Code 5
Gloucester Twp. SD
Sch. Sys. Enr. Code 6
Supt. – James Lilley, RURAL ROUTE 01 08012
Landing MS
  LTTL GLCSTR/CHEWS CLMNTN RD 08012
  Arthur Brown, prin.

Lewis MS, 1200 ERIAL ROAD 08012
  Joe Sweeney, prin.
ES, BLENHEIM-ERIAL ROAD 08012
  James Thompson, prin.
Chews ES, SOMERDALE ROAD 08012
  James Palmer, prin.
Gloucester Twp. ES
  270 S BLACK HORSE PIKE 08012
  Donald Ulrich, prin.
Loring-Flemming ES
  LITTLE GLOUCESTER RD 08012
  Andrew Kelly, prin.
Other Schools – See Glendora, Sicklerville

St. Agnes ES, 117 W CHURCH ST 08012
St. Jude ES, 420 S BLACK HORSE PIKE 08012

Blairstown, Warren Co., Pop. Code 5
Blairstown Twp. SD
Sch. Sys. Enr. Code 3
Supt. – Arthur Schaare, P O BOX E 07825
ES, P O BOX E 07825 – Arthur Schaare, prin.

Bloomfield, Essex Co., Pop. Code 8
Bloomfield Twp. SD
Sch. Sys. Enr. Code 5
Supt. – Robert Schiller, 155 BROAD ST 07003
Berkeley ES, 351 BLOOMFIELD AVE 07003
  John Downey, prin.
Brookdale ES, 1230 BROAD ST 07003
  Dr. John Autore, prin.
Carteret ES, 158 GROVE ST 07003
  Thomas Dowd, prin.
DeMarest ES, 465 BROUGHTON AVE 07003
  Edward Glickman, prin.
Fairview ES, 376 BERKELEY AVE 07003
  Robert Pellegrino, prin.
Franklin ES, 85 CURTIS ST 07003
  James Barton, prin.
Oak View ES, 150 GARRABRANT AVE 07003
  Leonard DeSiderio, prin.
Watsessing ES, 71 PROSPECT ST 07003
  Evelyn Peterson, prin.

Sacred Heart ES, 683 BLOOMFIELD AVE 07003
St. Thomas Apostle ES, 50 BYRD AVE 07003

Bloomingdale, Passaic Co., Pop. Code 6
Bloomingdale SD
Sch. Sys. Enr. Code 3
Supt. – John Siemsen, 31 CAPTOLENE AVE 07403
Bergen MS, 225 GLENWILD AVE 07403
  Alfred Alvine, prin.
Day ES, 225 RAFKIND RD 07403
  Margaret Reda, prin.
Donald ES, CAPTOLENE AVE 07403
  Patrick Urciuoli, prin.

Bloomsbury, Hunterdon Co., Pop. Code 3
Bloomsbury SD
Sch. Sys. Enr. Code 2
Supt. – Dale Briggs, MAIN ST 08804
Bloomsbury Borough ES, P O BOX 375 08804
  Dale Briggs, prin.

Pohatcong Twp. SD
Sch. Sys. Enr. Code 2
Supt. – Michael Frinzi
  RURAL ROUTE 01 BOX 167 08804
Glen MS, RURAL ROUTE 01 BOX 167 08804
  Michael Frinzi, prin.
Other Schools – See Phillipsburg

Bogota, Bergen Co., Pop. Code 6
Bogota SD
Sch. Sys. Enr. Code 4
Supt. – Salvatore Montagna, 1 LUTHIN PL 07603
Bixby ES, FISHER & CHESTNUT AVE 07603
  Robert Otnisky, prin.
Dewey ES, PALISADE AVE 07603
  Anthony LaSala, prin.
Steen ES, RIVER ROAD & WEST MAIN ST 07603
  Hugh Kerrigan, prin.

St. Joseph ES, 131 E FORT LEE RD 07603

Boonton, Morris Co., Pop. Code 6
Boonton SD
Sch. Sys. Enr. Code 4
Supt. – James Swalm, 434 LATHROP AVE 07005
Hill MS, 435 LATHROP AVE 07005
  Michael Renaldo, prin.
School Street ES, 724 BIRCH ST 07005
  Thomas Stephenson, prin.

Boonton Twp. SD
Sch. Sys. Enr. Code 2
Supt. – James Bolan
  RURAL ROUTE 03 BOX 510 07005
Rockaway Valley ES
  RURAL ROUTE 04 BOX 510 07005
  Steven Dhein, prin.

Our Lady of Mt. Carmel ES, 205 OAK ST 07005

Bordentown, Burlington Co., Pop. Code 5
Bordentown Regional SD
Sch. Sys. Enr. Code 4
Supt. – James Black, 87 CROSSWICKS ST 08505
McFarland JHS, 87 CROSSWICKS ST 08505
  Norine Gerepka, prin.
Barton ES, 100 CROSSWICKS ST 08505
  John Carson, prin.
Muschal ES, 323 WARD AVE 08505
  Linda Mohl, prin.

St. Mary ES, 30 ELIZABETH ST 08505

Bound Brook, Somerset Co., Pop. Code 6
Bound Brook SD
Sch. Sys. Enr. Code 4
Supt. – George Daniel, 133 W MAPLE AVE 08805
La Monte MS, WEST SECOND ST 08805
  Dr. Robert Riemer, prin.
Lafayette ES, 50 W HIGH ST 08805
  Constance Young, prin.
Smalley ES, CHERRY AVE 08805
  Robert Hirschman, prin.

St. Joseph ES, 120 E SECOND ST 08805
St. Mary ES, VOSSELLER AVE 08805

Bradley Beach, Monmouth Co., Pop. Code 5
Bradley Beach SD
Sch. Sys. Enr. Code 2
Supt. – Gavin DeCapua, 515 BRINLEY AVE 07720
ES, 515 BRINLEY AVE 07720
  Gavin DeCapua, prin.

Branchville, Sussex Co., Pop. Code 3
Frankford Twp. SD
Sch. Sys. Enr. Code 3
Supt. – John Ericson, P O BOX 430 07826
Frankford Twp. ES, P O BOX 430 07826
  Richard Gassmann, prin.

Brick, Ocean Co., Pop. Code 8
Brick Twp. SD
Sch. Sys. Enr. Code 6
Supt. – Louis Argona
  101 HENDRICKSON AVE 08724
Lake Riviera MS, 171 BEAVERSON BLVD 08723
  Harvey Lynch, prin.
Veterans Memorial MS, 41 HARRISON AVE 08724
  Philip Pagano, prin.
Drum Point Road ES, 41 DRUM POINT RD 08723
  Stanley Davis, prin.
Herbertsville ES, 2282 LANES MILL RD 08724
  Andrew DeBenedictis, prin.
Lanes Mill ES, 1891 LANES MILL RD 08724
  James Napier, prin.
Midstreams ES, 500 MIDSTREAMS RD 08724
  Rosemary Cunningham, prin.
Osbornville ES, 218 DRUM POINT RD 08723
  Joseph Eid, prin.
Veterans Memorial ES
  43 HENDRICKSON AVE 08724
  Nicholas Stavres, prin.
Young ES, 43 DRUM POINT RD 08723
  Raymond Benedict, prin.

St. Dominic ES, 250 OLD SQUAN RD 08724

Bridgeport, Gloucester Co.
Logan Twp. SD
Sch. Sys. Enr. Code 3
Supt. – Andrew Donnelly, P O BOX 202 08014
Logan Twp. ES, 113 MAIN ST 08014
  Mary Lamey, prin.
Other Schools – See Gibbstown

Bridgeton, Cumberland Co., Pop. Code 7
Bridgeton SD
Sch. Sys. Enr. Code 5
Supt. – Thomas Lane, P O BOX 657 08302
MS, BROAD ST W 08302 – Jerry Benfer, prin.
Buckshutem Road ES
  500 BUCKSHUTEM RD 08302
  Cora Thomas, prin.
Cherry Street ES, 1 CHERRY ST 08302
  J. Coyne, prin.
Indian Aveune ES, 375 INDIAN AVE 08302
  Catherine Angrabe, prin.
Quarter Mile Lane ES, QUARTER MILE LN 08302
  Joseph Furio, prin.
West Avenue ES, W AVENUE SCHOOL 08302
  Joseph Furio, prin.

Fairfield Twp. SD
Sch. Sys. Enr. Code 3
Supt. – Emory Kiess
  RURAL ROUTE 04 BOX 337 08302
Fairfield Twp. IS
  RURAL ROUTE 07 BOX 388 08302
  Dan Kortvelesy, prin.
Fairfield Twp. PS
  RURAL ROUTE 04 BOX 337 08302
  Dr. Cadmus Hull, prin.

Hopewell Twp. SD
Sch. Sys. Enr. Code 3
Supt. – Richard Gable
  65 BARRETT RUN ROAD 08302
Hopewell Twp. MS
  65 BARRETT RUN ROAD 08302
  James Sanders, prin.
Hopewell Crest ES
  RURAL ROUTE 01 BOX 36 08302
  Richard Gable, prin.

Stow Creek Twp. SD
Sch. Sys. Enr. Code 2
Supt. – Kenneth Gravatt
  RURAL ROUTE 03 BOX 223 08302
Stow Creek Twp. ES
  RURAL ROUTE 03 BOX 223 08302
  Kenneth Gravatt, prin.

Immaculate Conception ES
  PEARL AND MORTON STS 08302

Bridgewater, Somerset Co., Pop. Code 5
Bridgewater-Raritan Regional SD
  Sch. Sys. Enr. Code 6
  Supt. – Richard Horowitz, P O BOX 6030 08807
  Eisenhower MS, 791 EISENHOWER AVE 08807
    James DeCicco, prin.
  Hillside MS, 844 BROWN ROAD 08807
    Wilson Bethard, prin.
  Adamsville ES, UNION AVE 08807
    Dr. Roger Gaglione, prin.
  Crim ES, 1300 CRIM RD 08807
    Marie Simone, prin.
  Gardens ES, PINE ST 08807
    Edward Goetzmann, prin.
  Van Holten ES, 360 VAN HOLTEN RD 08807
    Ernest Shuba, prin.
  Other Schools – See Raritan

Brielle, Monmouth Co., Pop. Code 5
Brielle Borough SD
  Sch. Sys. Enr. Code 2
  Supt. – Gerard Russoniello
    605 UNION LANE 08730
  ES, 605 UNION LN 08730
    Gerard Russoniello, prin.

Brigantine, Atlantic Co., Pop. Code 6
Brigantine CSD
  Sch. Sys. Enr. Code 3
  Supt. – Lenore Farrah, 200 14TH ST S 08203
  Brigantine ES
    LAFAYETTE & EVANS BLVD 08203
    Donald Marrandino, prin.

Atlantic City Friends School
  115 38TH ST S 08203
St. Philip the Apostle ES
  42ND BRIGANTINE AVE 08203

Brooklawn, Camden Co., Pop. Code 4
Brooklawn SD
  Sch. Sys. Enr. Code 2
  Supt. – Douglas Howlett, HAAKON ROAD 08030
  Other Schools – See Gloucester City

Brookside, Morris Co.
Mendham Twp. SD
  Sch. Sys. Enr. Code 2
  Supt. – Donald Crane, W MAIN ST 07926
  Mendham Twp. MS
    16 WASHINGTON VALLEY ROAD 07926
    Elizabeth Shrader, prin.
  Mendham Twp. ES, WEST MAIN ST 07926
    Nancy Gamble, prin.

Browns Mills, Burlington Co., Pop. Code 6
Pemberton Twp. SD
  Sch. Sys. Enr. Code 6
  Supt. – Robert Moore, P O BOX 98 08015
  Haines MS, P O BOX 98 08015
    Vincent Fynan, prin.
  Newcomb MS, P O BOX 98 08015
    Dominick DiNunzio, prin.
  Brotherhood ES, P O BOX 98 08015
    J. Beebe, prin.
  Busansky ES, P O BOX 98 08015
    James Malvern, prin.
  Crichton ES, P O BOX 98 08015
    Gerald DeClementi, prin.
  Denbo ES, P O BOX 98 08015
    Anita Homola, prin.
  Ft. Dix ES, P O BOX 98 08015
    Elmer Brown, prin.
  Stackhouse ES, P O BOX 98 08015
    Edwin Moore, prin.
  Wylie ES, P O BOX 98 08015
    Joseph Poedubicky, prin.
  Other Schools – See Pemberton

Budd Lake, Morris Co., Pop. Code 5
Mount Olive Twp. SD
  Sch. Sys. Enr. Code 5
  Supt. – Chester Stephens, 89 ROUTE 46 07828
  Mt. Olive MS, 99 SUNSET DRIVE 07828
    Thomas Shuba, prin.
  Sandshore Road ES, SANDSHORE ROAD 07828
    John Abbott, prin.
  Tinc Road ES, TINC ROAD 07836
    Richard Wenner, prin.
  Other Schools – See Flanders

Buena, Atlantic Co., Pop. Code 5
Buena Regional SD
  Sch. Sys. Enr. Code 5
  Supt. – Charles Hawn, HARDING HWY 08310
  Milanesi ES, HARDING HWY 08310
    David Capizola, prin.
  Other Schools – See Landisville, Minotola,
    Williamstown

Burlington, Burlington Co., Pop. Code 7
Burlington CSD
  Sch. Sys. Enr. Code 4
  Supt. – C. Joseph Martin, 518 LOCUST AVE 08016
  Watts MS, 550 HIGH ST 08016
    William Rush, prin.
  Boudinot ES, PEARL & ELLIS ST 08016
    William McNamara, prin.
  Lawrence ES, BARCLAY ST 08016
    David Ballard, prin.
  Smith ES, 250 FARNER AVE 08016
    Robert Williams, prin.

Burlington Twp. SD
  Sch. Sys. Enr. Code 4
  Supt. – Walter Haworth, P O BOX 428 08016

Hopkins MS, JACKSONVILLE ROAD 08016
  Gerald Gares, prin.
Springside ES, 1508 MOUNT HOLLY RD 08016
  David Duffy, prin.
Young ES, NECK ROAD 08016
  David Duffy, prin.

St. Mary's Hall-Doane Academy
  RIVER BANK 08016
All Saints ES, 500 HIGH ST 08016
St. Paul ES, SIXTH & JAMES STS 08016

Butler, Morris Co., Pop. Code 6
Butler SD
  Sch. Sys. Enr. Code 4
  Supt. – Frank Stranzl, 38 BARTHOLDI AVE 07405
  MS, 34 PEARL PLACE 07405 – James Smith, prin.
  Decker ES, DECKER ROAD 07405
    John Rossi, prin.

Our Lady of the Magnificat ES
  2 MILLER RD 07405
St. Anthony of Padua ES
  63 BARTHOLDI AVE 07405

Caldwell, Essex Co., Pop. Code 6
Caldwell-West Caldwell SD
  Sch. Sys. Enr. Code 4
  Supt. – Edward McKeon, 30 PROSPECT ST 07006
  Cleveland MS, 36 ACADEMY ROAD 07006
    Joseph Jacangelo, prin.
  Jefferson ES, 85 PROSPECT ST 07006
    Stephen O'Donnell, prin.
  Lincoln ES, 18 CRANE ST 07006
    Frank Disessa, prin.
  Other Schools – See West Caldwell

Fairfield Twp. SD
  Supt. – See Fairfield
  Churchill ES, 107 FAIRFIELD RD 07006
    Frank Codispoti, prin.
  Stevenson ES, 15 KNOLL RD 07006
    Anthony Santucci, prin.

North Caldwell SD
  Supt. – See North Caldwell
  Grandview ES, 35 HAMILTON DR E 07006
    George Rhen, prin.

St. Aloysius ES, 235 BLOOMFIELD AVE 07006

Califon, Hunterdon Co., Pop. Code 4
Califon SD
  Sch. Sys. Enr. Code 2
  Supt. – Walter Miller
    RURAL ROUTE 03 BOX 325 07830
  Califon Borough ES
    RURAL ROUTE 03 BOX 325 07830
    Walter Miller, prin.

Lebanon Twp. SD
  Sch. Sys. Enr. Code 3
  Supt. – John Deibert
    RURAL ROUTE 02 BOX 295 07830
  Woodglen MS
    RURAL ROUTE 02 BOX 295 07830
    John Deibert, prin.
  Valley View ES
    RURAL ROUTE 02 BOX 295 07830
    Dr. Gerald Isaacson, prin.

Tewksbury Twp. SD
  Supt. – See Lebanon
  Old Turnpike MS, RURAL ROUTE 01 07830
    Richard Ireland, prin.

Camden, Camden Co., Pop. Code 8
Camden SD
  Sch. Sys. Enr. Code 7
  Supt. – Arnold Webster 08101
  East Camden MS, 3064 STEVENS ST 08105
    Richard Macrina, prin.
  Hatch MS, PARK BLVD 08103
    Mutter Bowman, prin.
  Morgan Village MS, S 10TH ST 08104
    Patricia Cook, prin.
  Pyne Poynt MS, 7TH & ERIE ST 08102
    Vernon Dover, prin.
  Veterans Memorial MS, 26TH & HAYES 08105
    Dorothy Wilson, prin.
  Bonsall ES, 1575 MOUNT EPHRAIM AVE 08104
    Dorothy Wyatt, prin.
  Broadway ES
    S BROADWAY & CLINTON ST 08103
    Carmen Morales, prin.
  Coopers Poynt ES, 3RD & STATE ST 08102
    Annie Rubin, prin.
  ES, 29TH & MICKLE ST 08105
    Annetta Braxton, prin.
  Davis ES, 34TH & CRAMER ST 08105
    Florence Gavin, prin.
  Dudley ES, 23RD & HIGH ST 08105
    Paul Buondonno, prin.
  Forest Hill ES
    PARK BLVD & WILDWOOD AVE 08103
    Anita Ricks, prin.
  Lanning Square ES, 5TH & BERKLEY ST 08103
    Elsa Suarez, prin.
  Lincoln PS, ROSE AVE & KAIGSHNS AVE 08103
    (—), prin.
  McGraw ES, DUDLEY & FREMONT ST 08105
    Lynn Johnson, prin.
  Mickle ES, 6TH & VAN HOOK STS 08104
    Charles Jones, prin.
  Northeast ES, 7TH & VINE ST 08102
    Frances Gibson, prin.

Parkside ES
  PRINCESS & WILDWOOD AVES 08103
  Phontella Ruff, prin.
Powell ES, 10TH & LINDEN STS 08105
  Charles Jones, prin.
Sharp ES, 32ND & HAYES AVE 08105
  Joseph Falco, prin.
Sumner ES, 8TH & JACKSON STS 08104
  Consuela McFadden, prin.
Washington ES, 27TH ST & RIVER AVE 08105
  Richard Kozieja, prin.
Whittier ES, 8TH & CHESTNUT ST 08103
  Malcolm Adler, prin.
Wiggins ES, 5TH & MOUNT VERNON ST 08103
  Paul Stephenson, prin.
Wilson ES, 9TH & FLORENCE STS 08104
  Michael Hailey, prin.
Yorkship ES, COLLINGS ROAD 08104
  Stanley Boyd, prin.

Haddon Twp. SD
  Sch. Sys. Enr. Code 4
  Supt. – John McGovern
    MACARTHUR BLVD & RHOADS AVE 08108
  Other Schools – See Collingswood, Haddonfield,
    Oaklyn

Pennsauken Twp. SD
  Supt. – See Pennsauken
  Burling ES, 3600 HARRIS AVE 08105
    Shirley Upchurch, prin.

Woodlynne Borough SD
  Supt. – See Woodlynne
  Woodlynne ES, FRONT & DELAWARE ST 08104
    (—), prin.

Center City Catholic School
  15 N SEVENTH ST 08102
Holy Name ES, 5TH AND VINE ST 08102
Holy Saviour ES
  CAMBRIDGE AND VA AVES 08108
Martin Luther Lutheran School
  TERRACE AVE & ROUTE 130 08109
Sacred Heart ES
  FOURTH AND JASPER STS 08104
St. Anthony of Padua ES, 2824 RIVER RD 08105
St. Bartholomew/Parkside ES
  1725 PARK BLVD 08103
St. Joan of Arc ES
  ALABAMA AND COLLINS RD 08104
St. John ES-Collingswood, 100 LEES AVE 08108
St. Joseph Pro Cathedral ES
  WESTFIELD AVE 08105
St. Peter ES-Merchantville
  51 W MAPLE AVE 08109
St. Stephen ES, 6300 BROWNING RD 08109
Transfiguration ES
  MAGILL AVENUE AND WHP 08107

Cape May, Cape May Co., Pop. Code 2
Cape May CSD
  Sch. Sys. Enr. Code 2
  Supt. – Elizabeth Dworsky
    921 LAFAYETTE ST 08204
  Cape May City ES, 921 LAFAYETTE ST 08204
    Elizabeth Dworsky, prin.

Lower Cap May Regional SD
  Sch. Sys. Enr. Code 4
  Supt. – Richard Strauss, 687 ROUTE 9 08204
  Teitelman MS, 687 ROUTE 9 08204
    Claude McAllister, prin.

Lower Twp. SD
  Sch. Sys. Enr. Code 4
  Supt. – Joseph Cirrinicione
    834 SEASHORE ROAD 08204
  Abrams PS, 714 TOWN BANK RD 08204
    Oliver West, prin.
  Lower Twp. Consolodated MS
    838 SEASHORE RD 08204 – Robert McDade, prin.
  Other Schools – See Villas

Our Lady Star of the Sea ES
  520 LAFAYETTE ST 08204

Cape May Court House, Cape May Co., Pop. Code 4
Middle Twp. SD
  Sch. Sys. Enr. Code 4
  Supt. – Theodore Johnson, 115 S MAIN ST 08210
  Middle Twp. MS, 300 E PACIFIC AVE 08210
    John Gibson, prin.
  Middle Twp. ES 1, BENNETT RD 08210
    Charlotte Harmon, prin.
  Middle Twp. MS 3, 211 S MAIN ST 08210
    Henry Kobik, prin.

Carlstadt, Bergen Co., Pop. Code 6
Carlstadt SD
  Sch. Sys. Enr. Code 2
  Supt. – Kenneth Gorab, 325 THIRD ST 07072
  Lincoln ES, 503 SIXTH ST 07072
    Kas Hryckiewicz, prin.
  Lindbergh ES, 550 WASHINGTON ST 07072
    Kas Hryckiewicz, prin.
  Washington ES, 325 THIRD ST 07072
    Frank LeGato, prin.

Carney's Point, Salem Co., Pop. Code 6
Penns Grove-Carneys Point SD
  Supt. – See Penns Grove
  Field Street ES, FIELD ST 08069
    Henry Newman, prin.

Carteret, Middlesex Co., Pop. Code 7
Carteret Borough SD
Sch. Sys. Enr. Code 5
Supt. – Robert O'Donnell, CARTERET AVE 07008
Hale MS, ROOSEVELT AVE 07008
  J. Terebetsky, prin.
Columbus ES, ROOSEVELT AVE 07008
  Charles Bartley, prin.
Lincoln ES, CARTERET AVE 07008
  Louis Panigrosso, prin.
Minue ES, POST BLVD 07008 – Ben Ruela, prin.
Washington ES, ROOSEVELT AVE 07008
  J. Terebetsky, prin.

Holy Family ES, 140 EMERSON ST 07008
St. Joseph ES, 865 ROOSEVELT AVE 07008

Cedar Brook, Camden Co.
Winslow Twp. SD
Supt. – See Hammonton
Winslow Twp. ES 2, FIRST AVE 08018
  George Stallings, prin.

Cedar Grove, Essex Co., Pop. Code 7
Cedar Grove Twp. SD
Sch. Sys. Enr. Code 4
Supt. – John DeCesare, 122 STEVENS AVE 07009
Memorial MS, RUGBY RD 07009
  John Dennis, prin.
North End ES, 122 STEVENS AVE 07009
  Kenneth Brino, prin.
Parks ES, 520 POMPTON AVE 07009
  Sam Peshkopia, prin.
Ridge Road ES, RIDGE ROAD 07009
  William O'Toole, prin.
South End ES, HARPER TER 07009
  Judith Merz, prin.

St. Catherine of Siena ES
  39 E BRADFORD AVE 07009

Cedar Knolls, Morris Co.
Hanover, Twp. SD
Sch. Sys. Enr. Code 4
Supt. – Salvatore Sansone
  125 RIDGEDALE AVE 07927
Other Schools – See Morris Plains, Whippany

Cedarville, Cumberland Co.
Lawrence Twp. SD
Sch. Sys. Enr. Code 2
Supt. – Charles McGlone, EAST AVENUE 08311
Powell ES, EAST AVE 08311
  Susan Leopold, prin.

Chatham, Morris Co., Pop. Code 6
Chathams SD
Sch. Sys. Enr. Code 4
Supt. – Steven Adamowski, 492 MAIN ST 07928
Lafayette MS, 221 LAFAYETTE AVE 07928
  Ralph Pesapane, prin.
MS, 21 LUM AVE 07928 – Michael Conte, prin.
Milton Avenue ES, 16 MILTON AVE 07928
  Everett Lanthier, prin.
Southern Boulevard ES
  192 SOUTHERN BLVD 07928
  Raymond Arciszewski, prin.
Washington Avenue ES
  WASHINGTON AVE 07928 – John Dimpel, prin.

St. Patrick ES, 45 CHATHAM ST 07928

Chatsworth, Burlington Co.
Woodland Twp. SD
Sch. Sys. Enr. Code 2
Supt. – Rob Backer, SECOND ST 08019
ES, P O BOX 477 08019 – Dr. Robert Backer, prin.

Cherry Hill, Camden Co., Pop. Code 8
Cherry Hill Twp. SD
Sch. Sys. Enr. Code 7
Supt. – Phillip Esbrandt, P O BOX 5015 08034
Beck JHS, CROPWELL ROAD 08003
  Giacamo Rosa, prin.
Carusi JHS, ROOSEVELT DRIVE 08002
  Maxwell Wald, prin.
Barton ES, RHODE ISLAND AVE 08034
  John Byrne, prin.
Cooper ES, 1960 GREENTREE RD 08003
  Lucious Harvey, prin.
Harte ES, QUEEN ANNE DR 08003
  Joseph Franco, prin.
Johnson ES, 500 KRESSON RD 08034
  Mark Miles, prin.
Kilmer ES, 2900 CHAPEL AVE W 08002
  Albert Ferraro, prin.
Kingston ES, KINGSTON RD 08034
  Charles Dalessandro, prin.
Knight ES, OLD CARRIAGE ROAD 08034
  Robert Bleakley, prin.
Mann ES, WALT WHITMAN BLVD 08003
  Irwin Berschler, prin.
Paine ES, 4001 CHURCH RD 08034
  Barry Adler, prin.
Sharp ES, 300 OLD ORCHARD RD 08003
  Edward McCauley, prin.
Stockton ES, 200 WEXFORD DR 08003
  John Morrow, prin.
Woodcrest ES
  ASTOR DR AND CRANFORD RD 08003
  Robert Burdette, prin.

Holy Rosary ES
  EVESHAM AVE & BURNT MI 08003

Queen of Heaven ES
  11 CONNECTICUT AVE 08002
St. Peter Celestine ES, 402 A N KINGS HWY 08034

Chester, Morris Co., Pop. Code 4
Chester Twp. SD
Sch. Sys. Enr. Code 3
Supt. – Thomas Butler, ROUTE 513 07930
Black River MS, ROUTE 513 07930
  Andrew Lindstedt, prin.
Bragg/Dickerson ES, ROUTE 24 07930
  Donald Markmann, prin.

Cinnaminson, Burlington Co., Pop. Code 7
Cinnaminson Twp. SD
Sch. Sys. Enr. Code 4
Supt. – Joseph Carol, P O BOX 224 08077
MS, N FORKLANDING ROAD 08077
  Harold Miller, prin.
New Albany ES, NEW ALBANY RD 08077
  John Haag, prin.
Rush ES, WYNWOOD DR 08077
  William McGrath, prin.

Clark, Union Co., Pop. Code 7
Clark Twp. SD
Sch. Sys. Enr. Code 4
Supt. – Paul Ortenzio, SCHINDLER ROAD 07066
Kumpf MS, 65 MILDRED TERR 07066
  David Hart, prin.
Hehnly ES, 621 RARITAN RD 07066
  Susan Miksza, prin.
Valley Road ES, 190 VALLEY RD 07066
  Philip Foster, prin.

St. Agnes ES, 342 MADISON HILL RD 07066
St. John Apostle ES
  VALLEY RD & RIDGEVIEW TR 07066

Clarksburg, Monmouth Co.
Millstone Twp. SD
Sch. Sys. Enr. Code 3
Supt. – Thomas Gannon
  MILLSTONE ROAD 08510
Millstone Twp. MS, MILLSTONE ROAD 08510
  Gerald Popkin, prin.
ES, STAGE COACH ROAD 08510
  Gerald Popkin, prin.

Clayton, Gloucester Co., Pop. Code 6
Clayton SD
Sch. Sys. Enr. Code 4
Supt. – Harold Kurtz
  ACADEMY ST & AURORA ROAD 08312
MS, CLINTON ST E 08312
  Harry Alexandrowic, prin.
ES, ACADEMY ST AND AURA RD 08312
  Herma Simmons, prin.

St. Catherine ES, 630 DELSEA DR N 08312

Clementon, Camden Co., Pop. Code 6
Clementon SD
Sch. Sys. Enr. Code 2
Supt. – William Sherman, AUDUBON AVE 08021
ES, AUDUBON AVE 08021 – William Graf, prin.

St. Edward's ES, 400 ERIAL RD 08021
St. Lawrence ES
  S AVENUE AND WHITE HORSE 08021

Cliffside Park, Bergen Co., Pop. Code 7
Cliffside Park SD
Sch. Sys. Enr. Code 4
Supt. – James Colagreco
  525 PALISADE AVE 07010
ES 3, PARK & PALISADE AVES 07010
  Thomas Enrico, prin.
ES 4, COLUMBIA AVE 07010
  William Halpin, prin.
ES 5, DAY AVE 07010 – Andrew Pyryt, prin.
ES S, OAKDENE AVE 07010
  Dr. Joseph Korten, prin.

Epiphany ES, 263 LAFAYETTE AVE 07010

Cliffwood, Monmouth Co., Pop. Code 5
Matawan-Aberdeen Regional SD
Supt. – See Matawan
Matawan Avenue MS
  447 MATAWAN AVE 07721 – Rob Tuccillo, prin.
ES, 422 CLIFFWOOD AVE 07721
  John Walsh, prin.

Cliffwood Beach, Monmouth Co., Pop. Code 6
Old Bridge Twp. SD
Supt. – See Matawan
Cooper ES, 10 BIRCHWOOD DR 07735
  (—), prin.

Clifton, Passaic Co., Pop. Code 8
Clifton SD
Sch. Sys. Enr. Code 6
Supt. – William Liess, P O BOX 2209 07015
Columbus MS, 350 PIAGET AVE 07011
  Severin Palyclowycz, prin.
Wilson MS, 1400 VAN HOUTEN AVE 07013
  William Hahn, prin.
Clifton City ES 1, 158 PARK SLOPE 07011
  Mary Piazza, prin.
Clifton City ES 11, 147 MERSELIS AVE 07011
  Joseph Greene, Jr., prin.
Clifton City ES 12, 165 CLIFTON AVE 07011
  Anthony Zarandona, prin.
Clifton City ES 13, 782 VAN HOUTEN AVE 07013
  Salvatore Anzaldi, prin.

Clifton City ES 14
  99 SAINT ANDREWS BLVD 07012
  Richard Hogel, prin.
Clifton City ES 15, 700 GREGORY AVE 07011
  Robert Valenti, prin.
Clifton City ES 16, 755 GROVE ST 07013
  Edward Buzinky, prin.
Clifton City ES 2, 1270 VAN HOUTEN AVE 07013
  Florence Cannizzo, prin.
Clifton City ES 3, 365 WASHINGTON AVE 07011
  Rita Cadorin, prin.
Clifton City ES 4, 194 W 2ND ST 07011
  Barbara Ahern, prin.
Clifton City ES 5, 136 VALLEY RD 07013
  Mildred Mastroberte, prin.
Clifton City ES 8, 41 OAK ST 07014
  John Baskinger, prin.
Clifton City ES 9, 25 BRIGHTON RD 07012
  Constance Pomposelli, prin.

SS. Cyril and Methodius ES, 40 CUTLER ST 07011
Sacred Heart ES, 43 CLIFTON AVE 07011
St. Andrew the Apostle ES
  410 MOUNT PROSPECT AVE 07011
St. Brendan ES, 154 E 1ST ST 07011
St. Clare ES, 39 ALLWOOD RD 07014
St. John Kanty ES, 37 SPEER AVE 07013
St. Paul ES, 1255 MAIN AVE 07011
St. Philip the Apostle ES, 797 VALLEY RD 07013

Clinton, Hunterdon Co., Pop. Code 4
Clinton Town SD
Sch. Sys. Enr. Code 2
Supt. – Brian Bolig, SCHOOL ST 08809
Clinton Town ES, SCHOOL ST 08809
  Brian Bolig, prin.

Clinton Twp. SD
Supt. – See Annadale
Mitchell/Spruce Run ES
  42 BELVIDERE AVE 08809 – Richard Byrnes, prin.

Closter, Bergen Co., Pop. Code 6
Closter SD
Sch. Sys. Enr. Code 3
Supt. – Jeff Feifer, 340 HOMANS AVE 07624
Village MS, 511 DURIE AVE 07624
  Allan Deroian, prin.
Hillside ES, 340 HOMANS AVE 07624
  Maureen Todd, prin.
Tenakill ES, 275 HIGH ST 07624
  Walter Pevny, prin.

St. Mary ES, 300 HIGH ST 07624

Collingswood, Camden Co., Pop. Code 7
Collingswood Borough SD
Sch. Sys. Enr. Code 4
Supt. – Adam Pfeffer, 200 LEES AVE 08108
JHS, ELDRIDGE AVE 08108
  Edward Kurkian, prin.
Garfield ES, HADDON & GARFIELD AVES 08108
  Wayne Cochrane, prin.
Newbie ES, BROWNING ROAD 08108
  Carl Rickershauser, Jr., prin.
Tatem ES, LINCOLN AVE 08108
  Edward McDonnell, prin.
Zane North ES, STOKES & LEES AVE 08108
  Wayne Cochrane, prin.
Other Schools – See Oaklyn

Haddon Twp. SD
Supt. – See Camden
Edison ES, CENTER & MELROSE AVE 08108
  Douglas Hamilton, prin.
Strawbridge ES
  STRAWBRIDGE & EMERALD AVE 08108
  Douglas Hamilton, prin.

Cologne, Atlantic Co.
Galloway Twp. SD
Supt. – See Absecon
ES, COLOGNE AVE 08213 – Nicholas Davis, prin.

Colonia, Middlesex Co., Pop. Code 7
Woodbridge Twp. SD
Supt. – See Woodbridge
MS, 100 DELAWARE AVE 07067
  Lamont Shaffer, prin.
Claremont Avenue ES, CLAREMONT AVE 07067
  Robert Zanzalari, prin.
Lynn Crest ES, FOOT OF IRA AVE 07067
  William Pohutsky, prin.
Oak Ridge Heights ES, INMAN AVE 07067
  Norlyne Cole, prin.
Pennsylvania Avenue ES
  PENNSYLVANIA AVE 07067
  Donald Whitaker, prin.

Colts Neck, Monmouth Co., Pop. Code 6
Colts Neck Twp. SD
Sch. Sys. Enr. Code 3
Supt. – Jamie Savedoff
  20 COUNTY ROAD E 07722
Cedar Drive MS, 73 CEDAR DRIVE 07722
  Kenneth Noland, prin.
Conover Road ES
  20 COUNTY ROAD 537 EAST 07722
  Shirley Anderson, prin.

Columbia, Warren Co.
Knowlton Twp. SD
Sch. Sys. Enr. Code 2
Supt. – Steven Roethke
  RURAL ROUTE 01 ROUTE 46 07832
Other Schools – See Delaware

Columbus, Burlington Co., Pop. Code 3
 Mansfield Twp. SD
 Sch. Sys. Enr. Code 2
 Supt. – John Hydock, LOCUST AVE   08022
 ES, LOCUST AVE   08022 – John Hydock, prin.

 Northern Burlington County Regional SD
 Sch. Sys. Enr. Code 4
 Supt. – Walt Rudder, RURAL ROUTE 01   08022
 Northern Burlington JHS
    RURAL ROUTE 01 BOX 284   08022
    Richard Bryfogle, prin.

Cranbury, Middlesex Co., Pop. Code 4
 Cranbury Twp. SD
 Sch. Sys. Enr. Code 2
 Supt. – Charles Argento, 23 N MAIN ST   08512
 ES, 23 N MAIN ST   08512 – Charles Argento, prin.

 Monroe Twp. SD
 Supt. – See Jamesburg
 Applegarth MS, APPLEGARTH ROAD   08512
    John Dorney, prin.

Cranford, Union Co., Pop. Code 7
 Cranford Twp. SD
 Sch. Sys. Enr. Code 5
 Supt. – Robert Paul, 132 THOMAS ST   07016
 Brookside Place ES, BROOKSIDE PL   07016
    Burton Mandell, prin.
 Hillside Avenue ES, HILLSIDE AVE   07016
    Irwin Figman, prin.
 Livingston MS, LIVINGSTON AVE   07016
    Dr. Francis Lucash, prin.
 Orange Avenue ES, ORANGE AVE   07016
    Fritz Brown, prin.
 Walnut Avenue ES, WALNUT AVE   07016
    Joan Melvin, prin.

 Solomon Schechter Day School   07016
 St. Michael School, 100 ALDEN ST   07016

Cresskill, Bergen Co., Pop. Code 6
 Cresskill SD
 Sch. Sys. Enr. Code 4
 Supt. – I. Roy Stern, 50 LINCOLN DRIVE   07626
 Bryan ES, BROOKSIDE AVE   07626
    John Sestanovich, prin.
 Merritt Memorial ES, 91 DOGWOOD LN   07626
    Joseph Donnelly, prin.

 St. Therese ES, 220 JEFFERSON AVE   07626

Crosswicks, Atlanta Co.
 Chesterfield Twp. SD
 Sch. Sys. Enr. Code 2
 Supt. – Joe Schienholz, P O BOX 352   08515
 Chesterfield ES, P O BOX 352   08515
    Joseph Schienholz, prin.

Dayton, Middlesex Co.
 South Brunswick Twp. SD
 Supt. – See Monmouth Junction
 MS, GEORGES ROAD   08810
    Martin Bernstein, prin.

Deal, Monmouth Co., Pop. Code 4
 Deal Borough SD
 Sch. Sys. Enr. Code 2
 Supt. – Dr. Anthony Moro,Jr.
    201 ROSELD AVE   07723
 ES, ROSELO AVE   07723
    Dr. Anthony Moro,Jr., prin.

Delair, Camden Co.
 Pennsauken Twp. SD
 Supt. – See Pennsauken
 ES, 530 ENGARD AVE   08110 – (—), prin.

Delanco, Burlington Co., Pop. Code 5
 Delanco Twp. SD
 Sch. Sys. Enr. Code 2
 Supt. – Joseph Miller, 411 WALNUT ST   08075
 Walnut Street MS, 411 WALNUT ST   08075
    Paul Winkie, prin.
 Burlington Avenue ES
    BURLINGTON AVE & LILAC LN   08075
    Michael Livengood, prin.

Delaware, Warren Co.
 Knowlton Twp. SD
 Supt. – See Columbia
 ES, P O BOX 152   07833 – Steven Roethke, prin.

Delran, Burlington Co., Pop. Code 7
 Delran Twp. SD
 Sch. Sys. Enr. Code 4
 Supt. – Joseph Chinnici
    1812 UNDERWOOD BLVD #5   08075
 MS, CHESTER AVE   08075
    Michael Gallucci, prin.
 Bell ES, CREEK ROAD   08075
    Donald Lucas, prin.
 Cambridge ES, 3RD & MAIN STS   08075
    Donald Lucas, prin.
 Millbridge ES, CONROW ROAD   08075
    Daniel Topolski, prin.

Demarest, Bergen Co., Pop. Code 5
 Demarst SD
 Sch. Sys. Enr. Code 2
 Supt. – Paul Saxton, 568 PIERMONT ROAD   07627
 MS, 568 PIERMONT ROAD   07627
    Dennis McDonald, prin.
 County Road ES, 130 COUNTY RD   07627
    George Petty, prin.

St. Joseph ES, PIERMONT ROAD   07627

Dennisville, Cape May Co.
 Dennis Twp. SD
 Sch. Sys. Enr. Code 3
 Supt. – Victor Gilson, ACADEMY ROAD   08214
 Dennis Twp. ES, ACADEMY RD   08214
    Victor Gilson, prin.

Denville, Morris Co., Pop. Code 7
 Denville Twp. SD
 Sch. Sys. Enr. Code 4
 Supt. – Dennis Clancy, P O BOX 880   07834
 Valleyview MS, DIAMOND SPRING ROAD   07834
    George Deamer, prin.
 Lakeview ES, COOPER ROAD   07834
    Florence Dvorin, prin.
 Riverview ES, SAINT MARYS PL   07834
    George Vanatta, prin.

St. Mary ES, U S ROUTE 46   07834

Deptford, Gloucester Co., Pop. Code 7
 Deptford Twp. SD
 Sch. Sys. Enr. Code 5
 Supt. – David Moyer
    2022 GOOD INTENT ROAD   08096
 Deptford Central ES, 200 DELSEA DR   08096
    John Benfer, prin.
 Good Intent ES, 1555 GOOD INTENT RD   08096
    Bruno Gattuso, prin.
 Lake Tract ES, ISZARD ROAD   08096
    Robert Morris, prin.
 Other Schools – See Wenonah, Westville

Dividing Creek, Cumberland Co.
 Downe Twp. SD
 Supt. – See Newport
 Downe Twp. PS, ROUTE 553   08315
    Mary Eber, prin.

Dorothy, Atlantic Co.
 Weymouth Twp. SD
 Sch. Sys. Enr. Code 2
 Supt. – Marshall Behr, P O BOX 231   08317
 Weymouth Twp. ES, P O BOX 231   08317
    Marshall Behr, prin.

Dover, Morris Co., Pop. Code 7
 Dover SD
 Sch. Sys. Enr. Code 4
 Supt. – Frank Poulos, 100 GRACE ST   07801
 Academy Street ES, 14 ACADEMY ST   07801
    John Duffy, prin.
 East Dover ES, 280 E MCFARLAN ST   07801
    Richard Kesin, prin.
 North Dover ES, 51 HIGHLAND AVE   07801
    Francis Debell, prin.

 Mine Hill Twp. SD
 Sch. Sys. Enr. Code 2
 Supt. – Dr. David Ottaviawo
    CANFIELD AVE MINE HILL   07801
 Other Schools – See Mine Hill

 Rockaway Twp. SD
 Supt. – See Rockaway
 Birchwood ES, ART ST   07801
    Sylvia Ziegler, prin.
 O'Brien ES, MINERAL SPRING DR   07801
    Angelo Curcio,Jr., prin.

Sacred Heart ES, 30 N ESSEX ST   07801

Dumont, Bergen Co., Pop. Code 7
 Dumont SD
 Sch. Sys. Enr. Code 4
 Supt. – Paul Corazza, 25 DEPEW ST   07628
 Grant ES, 100 GRANT AVE   07628
    James Gardner, prin.
 Honiss ES, 31 DEPEW ST   07628
    Dale Genberg, prin.
 Lincoln ES, 80 PROSPECT AVE   07628
    Martin Rittenberg, prin.
 Selzer ES, 435 PROSPECT AVE   07628
    James Kennedy, prin.

St. Mary ES, 21-31 NEW MILFORD AVE   07628

Dunellen, Middlesex Co., Pop. Code 6
 Dunellen SD
 Sch. Sys. Enr. Code 3
 Supt. – Gerald Stefanski
    434 DUNELLEN AVE   08812
 Faber MS, HIGH ST   08812 – Henry Wernoch, prin.
 Whittier ES
    NEW MARKET ROAD/WHITIER AVE   08812
    Charlie Outlaw, prin.

St. John the Evangelist ES, 329 FIRST ST   08812

East Brunswick, Middlesex Co., Pop. Code 8
 East Brunswick Twp. SD
 Sch. Sys. Enr. Code 6
 Supt. – Joe Sweeney, 22 MILLTOWN ROAD   08816
 Hammarskjold MS, 200 RUES LANE   08816
    Phillip Houser, prin.
 Bowne-Munro ES, 120 MAIN ST   08816
    Richard Gonier, prin.
 Brook ES, GAGE ROAD & SULLIVAN WAY   08816
    Gabriel Amatucci, prin.
 Central ES, 371 CRANBURY RD   08816
    Dr. Joann Susko, prin.
 Chittick ES, 5 FLAGLER ST   08816
    Michael Laraus, prin.

Frost ES, 65 FROST AVE   08816
    Kenneth Burnett, prin.
 Irwin ES, RACETRACK ROAD   08816
    Lucille Fisher, prin.
 Memorial ES, 14 INNES RD   08816
    Albert Zusman, prin.
 Warnsdorfer ES, 9 HARDENBURG LN   08816
    Robert Jandernal, prin.

 Schechter Day School, 511 RYDERS LN   08816
 St. Bartholomew ES, 470 RYDERS LN   08816

East Hanover, Morris Co., Pop. Code 6
 East Hanover Twp. SD
 Sch. Sys. Enr. Code 4
 Supt. – Pat Piegari, 20 SCHOOL AVE   07936
 MS, 477 RIDGEDALE AVE   07936
    Preston Pratola, prin.
 Central MS, 400 RIDGEDALE AVE   07936
    Larry Santos, prin.
 Smith ES, 27 GREEN DR   07936
    Kenneth Miscia, prin.

St. Rose of Lima ES, 316 RIDGEDALE AVE   07936

East Keansburg, Monmouth Co., Pop. Code 5
 Middletown Twp. SD
 Supt. – See Middletown
 ES, 235 OCEAN AVE   07734
    Frank Vaccarelli, prin.

East Newark, Hudson Co., Pop. Code 4
 East Newark SD
 Sch. Sys. Enr. Code 2
 Supt. – Adam Drapczuk
    501 NORTH THIRD ST   07029
 ES, 501-11 N THIRD ST   07029 – (—), prin.

East Orange, Essex Co., Pop. Code 8
 East Orange SD
 Sch. Sys. Enr. Code 7
 Supt. – T. Haig, 715 PARK AVE   07017
 Costley MS, 116 HAMILTON ST   07017
    Leonard Moore, prin.
 Davey MS, 161 ELMWOOD AVE   07018
    Laura Trimmings, prin.
 Healy MS, 116 HAMILTON ST   07017
    Judith Dandridge, prin.
 Truth MS, 116 HAMILTON ST   07017
    Brenda Veale, prin.
 Ashland ES, 450 PARK AVE   07017
    (—), prin.
 Columbian ES, 410 N GROVE ST   07017
    Patricia Fairbanks, prin.
 Elmwood ES, 181 ELMWOOD AVE   07018
    Charles Haynes, prin.
 Franklin ES, 215 DODD ST   07017
    Henry Hamilton, prin.
 Jackson Academy, 16 PROSPECT ST   07017
    Gladys Calhoun, prin.
 Kentopp ES, 1 GROVE PL   07017
    Peggy Grogan, prin.
 Lincoln ES, 120 CENTRAL AVE   07018
    Herman Hamlin, prin.
 Nassau ES, 330 CENTRAL AVE   07018
    Dr. Roosevelt Weaver, prin.
 Stockton MS, 98 GREENWOOD AVE   07017
    Dr. Donald Wilkinson, prin.
 Washington ES, 175 SANFORD ST   07018
    Thelma Gelfond, prin.

 Holy Name ES, 190 MIDLAND AVE   07017
 Our Lady All Souls ES, 199 4TH AVE   07017
 Our Lady Help Christian ES
    23 N CLINTON ST   07017
 Our Lady Most Blessed Sacrament ES
    117 ELMWOOD AVE   07018
 St. Joseph ES, 115 TELFORD ST   07018

East Rutherford, Bergen Co., Pop. Code 6
 East Rutherford SD
 Sch. Sys. Enr. Code 3
 Supt. – William Jones
    GROVE & UHLAND STS   07073
 Faust MS, GROVE & UHLAND STS   07073
    Ed Bednarz, prin.
 Franklin ES, 160 HUMBOLDT ST   07073
    Louis Ravettine, prin.
 Lincoln ES, VREELAND AVE   07073
    Louis Ravettine, prin.
 McKenzie ES, 135 CARLTON AVE   07073
    Louis Ravettine, prin.

St. Joesph ES, 20 HACKENSACK ST   07073

Eatontown, Monmouth Co., Pop. Code 7
 Eatontown SD
 Sch. Sys. Enr. Code 4
 Supt. – Anthony Palmisano, 215 BROAD ST   07724
 Memorial MS, 7 GRANT AVE   07724
    Ron Danielson, prin.
 Meadowbrook ES, WYCKOFF ROAD   07724
    Paul Desmond, prin.
 Vetter ES, 3 GRANT AVE   07724
    Anthony Iacopino, prin.
 Woodmere ES, 65 RALEIGH CT   07724
    John Addeo,Jr., prin.

Edgewater, Bergen Co., Pop. Code 5
 Edgewater SD
 Sch. Sys. Enr. Code 2
 Supt. – Ted Blumstein
    251 UNDERCLIFF AVE   07020
 Van Gelder ES, 251 UNDERCLIFF AVE   07020
    Dr. Ted Blumstein, prin.

Edison, Middlesex Co., Pop. Code 8
Edison Twp. SD
Sch. Sys. Enr. Code 7
Supt. – Charles Boyle
  100 MUNICIPAL BLVD 08817
Adams MS, NEW DOVER ROAD 08820
  Harry Olsen, prin.
Hoover MS, 180 JACKSON AVE 08837
  Don Robinson, prin.
Jefferson MS, DIVISION ST 08817
  William Bohn, prin.
Wilson MS, WOODROW WILSON DRIVE 08820
  Cedric Richardson, prin.
Franklin ES, WOODBRIDGE AVE 08820
  Dr. Genevieve Miller, prin.
King ES, TINGLEY LN & INMAN AVE 08820
  Joseph Krajkovich, prin.
Lincoln ES, 45 BROOKVILLE RD 08817
  Gerald Young, prin.
Lindeneau ES, BLOOSOM ST 08817
  Allen Puorro, prin.
Madison IS, NEW DOVER ROAD 08820
  Arthur Weinfeld, prin.
Madison PS, NEW DOVER ROAD 08820
  Bonnie McHolme, prin.
Marshall ES, CORNELL ST 08817
  Judith Luger, prin.
Menlo Park ES, MONROE AVE 08820
  Margaret Leusenring, prin.
Monroe ES, SHARP RD 08837
  Louis Mannello, prin.
Washington ES
  WINTHROP & CAMBRIDGE ROADS 08817
  Ross Capaccio, prin.
Woodbrook ES, ROBIN ROAD 08820
  John Ahern, prin.

Raymon Yeshiva ES, 2 HARRISON ST 08817
St. Helena ES, 920 GROVE AVE 08820
St. Matthew ES, SEYMOUR AVE 08817

Egg Harbor City, Atlantic Co., Pop. Code 5
Egg Harbor City SD
Sch. Sys. Enr. Code 2
Supt. – L. Rhine, 528 PHILADELPHIA AVE 08215
Rittenberg MS, 528 PHILADELPHIA AVE 08215
  Irving Marshall, prin.
Spragg ES, 601 BUFFALO AVE 08215
  Joan Steinberg, prin.

Galloway Twp. SD
Supt. – See Absecon
South Egg Harbor ES
  W BELLADONNA AVE 08215
  Nicholas Davis, prin.

Washington Twp. SD
Sch. Sys. Enr. Code 1
Supt. – Adrian McCauley
  RURAL ROUTE 02 BOX 145 08215
Green Bank ES
  RURAL ROUTE 02 BOX 145 08215
  (—), prin.

St. Nicholas ES, 525 CHICAGO AVE 08215

Elizabeth, Union Co., Pop. Code 9
Elizabeth SD
Sch. Sys. Enr. Code 7
Supt. – Michell Potempa, 500 N BROAD ST 07208
Battin Ctr. MS, 300 S BROAD ST 07202
  Cecilia Cosgrove, prin.
Cleveland MS, 432 FIRST AVE 07206
  Deborah Dixon, prin.
Hamilton MS, 310 CHERRY ST 07208
  Leonard Jasczak, prin.
Lafayette MS, 1065 JULIA ST 07201
  William Eason, prin.
Roosevelt MS, 605 BAYWAY AVE 07202
  Robert Fitzsimmons, prin.
Butler ES 23, 501 UNION AVE 07208
  Catherine Reilly, prin.
Columbus ES 15, 511 THIRD AVE 07202
  Rose Perone, prin.
Elmora ES 12, 638 MAGIE AVE 07208
  Joseph Caporaso, prin.
Franklin ES 13, 248 RIPLEY PL 07206
  Marvin Halem, prin.
Halloran MS 22, 447 RICHMOND ST 07202
  Michael Cohn, prin.
Lafayette ES 6, 1065 JULIA ST 07201
  William Eason, prin.
Lincoln ES 14, 50 GROVE ST 07202
  Daniel Manies, prin.
Madison/Monroe ES 16, 1091 NORTH AVE 07201
  (—), prin.
Marshall ES 20, 521 MAGNOLIA AVE 07206
  Thelma Hurd, prin.
Morris ES 18, 860 CROSS AVE 07208
  Antonio Gonzalez, prin.
Mravlag ES 21, 132 SHELLEY AVE 07208
  Thomas Ficarra, prin.
Peterstown ES 3, 700 SECOND AVE 07202
  Nicholas DeMarco, prin.
Roosevelt ES 17, 650 BAYWAY AVE 07202
  Robert Fitzsimmons, prin.
Scott ES 2, 125 MADISON AVE 07201
  Albert Hawkins, prin.
Washington ES 1, 250 BROADWAY 07206
  John Richardson, prin.
Wilson ES 19, 529 EDGAR RD 07202
  Frances Abitanta, prin.

Jewish Educational Boys Center
  330 ELMORA AVE 07208
Bender Memorial Academy
  416 LINDEN AVE 07202
Blessed Sacrament School
  1086 NORTH AVE 07201
Holy Rosary ES, 535 FIRST AVE 07206
Immaculate Conception ES
  417 UNION AVE 07208
SS. Peter and Paul ES
  220 MSGR KENEZIS PLACE 07206
St. Adalbert ES, 261 FULTON ST 07206
St. Anthony ES, 227 CENTER ST 07202
St. Catherine School, 1003 N BRAOD ST 07208
St. Genevieve ES, 209 PRINCETON RD 07208
St. Hedwig ES, 720 CLARKSON AVE 07202
St. Joseph the Carpenter ES
  140 E THIRD AVE 07203
St. Mary Assumption ES, 237 S BROAD ST 07202
St. Patrick ES, 227 COURT ST 07206
St. Vladimir ES, 425 GRIER AVE 07202

Elmer, Salem Co., Pop. Code 4
Elmer Borough SD
Sch. Sys. Enr. Code 2
Supt. – Dr. Stephen Berkowitz
  P O BOX 596 08318
ES, P O BOX 596 08318
  Dr. Stephen Berkowitz, prin.

Pittsgrove Twp. SD
Sch. Sys. Enr. Code 4
Supt. – John Daspro
  RURAL ROUTE 01 BOX 280 A 08318
Olivet MS, RURAL ROUTE 01 08318
  Dr. J. Frith,Jr., prin.
Other Schools – See Norma

Upper Pittsgrove Twp. SD
Supt. – See Monroeville
Daretown ES, RURAL ROUTE 03 BOX 131 08318
  Christina White, prin.

Elmwood Park, Bergen Co., Pop. Code 7
Elmwood Park SD
Sch. Sys. Enr. Code 4
Supt. – John Santini, 330 E 54TH ST 07407
Gantner Avenue ES, 52 ROOSEVELT AVE 07407
  Dr. Vito Farese, prin.
Gilbert Avenue ES, 151 GILBERT AVE 07407
  Samuel Bracigliano, prin.
Sixteenth Avenue ES
  16TH AVENUE SCHOOL 07407
  Alex Maccia, prin.

St. Leo's ES, 300 MARKET ST 07407

Elwood, Atlantic Co.
Mullica Twp. SD
Sch. Sys. Enr. Code 3
Supt. – Martin Ney, P O BOX 318 08217
Mullica Twp. MS, P O BOX 318 08217
  Mary Lou DeFrancisco, prin.
Mullica Twp. PS, P O BOX 318 08217
  Richard Goldberg, prin.

Emerson, Bergen Co., Pop. Code 6
Emerson SD
Sch. Sys. Enr. Code 3
Supt. – Serge Angiel, 182 MAIN ST 07630
Memorial ES, 1 HAINES AVE 07630
  Ann Wilks, prin.
Villano MS, 175 LINWOOD AVE 07630
  Ann Wilks, prin.

Assumption School, 29 JEFFERSON AVE 07630

Englewood, Bergen Co., Pop. Code 7
Englewood CSD
Sch. Sys. Enr. Code 4
Supt. – Larry Leverett, 12 TENAFLY ROAD 07631
Cleveland ES, 325 TENAFLY RD 07631
  Marlene Guess, prin.
Dismus MS, 325 TRYON AVE 07631
  Henry Pruitt, prin.
Lincoln Early ES, 51 E ENGLEWOOD AVE 07631
  Arlene Clinkscale, prin.

Englewood Cliffs SD
Sch. Sys. Enr. Code 2
Supt. – Nickolas Mamola
  143 CHARLOTTE PLACE 07632
Upper MS, 143 CHARLOTTE PLACE 07632
  Nicholas Mamola, prin.
Other Schools – See Englewood Clffs

Bede ES, 255 WALNUT ST 07631
Moriah Hebrew ES, 53 S WOODLAND ST 07631
Morrow ES, 435 LYDECKER ST 07631
St. Cecilia ES, 85 W DEMAREST AVE 07631

Englewood Clffs, Bergen Co., Pop. Code 6
Englewood Cliffs SD
Supt. – See Englewood
Northcliff ES, FLOYD ST 07632
  Harry Linder, prin.

Englishtown, Monmouth Co., Pop. Code 3
Manalapan-Englishtown Regional SD
Sch. Sys. Enr. Code 5
Supt. – Joseph Scozzari, 11 MAIN ST 07726
Pine Brook MS, 98 PEASE ROAD 07726
  Rob Hagler, prin.
Clark Mills ES, 34 GORDONS CORNER RD 07726
  Charles Boehm,Jr., prin.

Lafayette Mills MS, 66 MAXWELL LN 07726
  Michael Garreau, prin.
Milford Brook MS, 13 GLO BAR DR 07726
  Carmen Daccurso, prin.
Taylor Mills ES, 59 GORDONS CORNER RD 07726
  Ruth Jacobson, prin.

Essex Fells, Essex Co., Pop. Code 4
Essex Fells SD
Sch. Sys. Enr. Code 2
Supt. – Ronald Wolfe
  102 HAWTORNE ROAD 07021
ES, 120 HAWTHORNE RD 07021
  Harris Ransom, prin.

Estell Manor, Atlantic Co., Pop. Code 3
Estell Manor CSD
Sch. Sys. Enr. Code 2
Supt. – William Goodwin, P O BOX 122 08319
ES, P O BOX 9 08319 – William Goodwin, prin.

Fairfield, Essex Co., Pop. Code 6
Fairfield Twp. SD
Sch. Sys. Enr. Code 3
Supt. – Barry Spagnoli
  230 FAIRFIELD ROAD 07006
Other Schools – See Caldwell

Fair Haven, Monmouth Co., Pop. Code 6
Fair Haven Borough SD
Sch. Sys. Enr. Code 3
Supt. – Robert Chartier, HANCE ROAD 07701
Sickles ES, 25 WILLOW ST 07704
  Richard Warga, prin.

Fair Lawn, Bergen Co., Pop. Code 8
Fair Lawn SD
Sch. Sys. Enr. Code 5
Supt. – Melvin Klein, 35-01 MORIOT AVE 07410
Memorial MS, 1ST & LAMBERG ROAD 07410
  David Miller, prin.
Forrest ES, 10-00 HOPPER AVE 07410
  Dr. Seena Brown, prin.
Lyncrest ES, 9-04 MORLOT AVE 07410
  Vincent Sadowski, prin.
Milnes ES, 8-01 PHILIP ST 07410
  Linda Schoeppler, prin.
Radburn ES, 18-00 RADBURN RD 07410
  James Jones, prin.
Warren Point ES, 3007 BROADWAY 07410
  Maryann Smith, prin.
Westmoreland ES, PARMALEE AVE 07410
  Frank Jacene, prin.

St. Anne ES, 1-30 SUMMIT AVE 07410

Fairview, Bergen Co., Pop. Code 7
Fairview SD
Sch. Sys. Enr. Code 3
Supt. – Charles Margolin
  59 ANDERSON AVE 07022
English Neighborhood PS, HURLEY PL 07022
  Joseph Mule, prin.
ES 3, SCHOOL #3 CLIFF ST 07022
  Joseph Mule, prin.
Lincoln ES, ANDERSON & DEY AVES 07022
  Angela Penna, prin.

Our Lady Grace ES, 400 KAMENA ST 07022
St. John Baptist ES
  FOURTH & WALKER STS 07022

Farmingdale, Monmouth Co., Pop. Code 4
Farmingdale Borough SD
Sch. Sys. Enr. Code 2
Supt. – William Cahill, P O BOX 706 07727
ES, P O BOX 706 07727 – James Cleary, prin.

Howell Twp. SD
Supt. – See Howell
Ardena ES, RURAL ROUTE 01 07727
  Dr. Andrew Rinko, prin.
Griebling ES, HAVENS BRIDGE ROAD 07724
  Robert Camoosa, prin.

Flanders, Morris Co.
Mount Olive Twp. SD
Supt. – See Budd Lake
Mountain View MS, CLOVERHILL DR 07836
  William Wolgamuth, prin.
Mountain View North ES, CLOVERHILL DR 07836
  Janet Zymroz, prin.

Flemington, Hunterdon Co., Pop. Code 5
Flemington-Raritan Regional SD
Sch. Sys. Enr. Code 4
Supt. – R. Resnick, 31 BONNELL ST 08822
Reading-Fleming MS, 31 BONNELL ST 08822
  Alego Bartolacci, prin.
Hunter ES, DAYTON ROAD 08822
  James Gamble, prin.
Sheaf ES, BARLEY SHEAF ROAD 08822
  Robert Bartoletti, prin.

Florence, Burlington Co., Pop. Code 6
Florence Twp. SD
Sch. Sys. Enr. Code 4
Supt. – Bernard D'Emidio, CEDAR ST 08518
Duffy ES, 208 W SECOND ST 08518
  Betty Hughes, prin.
Other Schools – See Roebling

Florham Park, Morris Co., Pop. Code 6
Florham Park SD
Sch. Sys. Enr. Code 3
Supt. – William Muller
  BRIARWOOD ROAD 07932

Ridgedale MS, 75 RIDGEDALE AVE　07932
　Michael Rabasca, prin.
Briarwood MS, BRIARWOOD ROAD　07932
　John Wootton, prin.
Brooklake ES, 139 BROOKLAKE RD　07932
　David Stackhouse, prin.

Holy Family ES, LLOYD AVE　07932

Fords, Middlesex Co., Pop. Code 7
Woodbridge Twp. SD
Supt. – See Woodbridge
Fords MS, 100 FANNING ST　08863
　David Peterson, prin.
Ford Avenue ES, FORD AVE & MAIN ST　08863
　Gerald Karycki, prin.
Lafayette Estates ES, FORD AVE　08863
　Charlotte Sciarpelleti, prin.

Forked River, Ocean Co.
Lacey Twp. SD
Sch. Sys. Enr. Code 5
Supt. – C. Beers, P O BOX 191　08731
ES, 925 W LACEY RD #477　08731
　Robert Paladino, prin.
Other Schools – See Lanoka Harbor

Fort Lee, Bergen Co., Pop. Code 8
Ft. Lee SD
Sch. Sys. Enr. Code 4
Supt. – A. Sugarman, 255 WHITEMAN ST　07024
Cole MS, 467 STILLWELL AVE　07024
　Charles Lauricella, prin.
ES 1, HOYM AVE　07024
　Ernest Ritenhouse, prin.
ES 2, JONES ROAD　07024 – Margaret Baffa, prin.
ES 3, MYRTLE AVE　07024 – John Caputo, prin.
ES 4, 1193 ANDERSON AVE　07024
　Vincent Taffaro, prin.

Holy Trinity ES, THIRD STREET　07024
Madonna ES, 359 WHITEMAN ST　07024

Franklin, Sussex Co., Pop. Code 5
Franklin Borough SD
Sch. Sys. Enr. Code 3
Supt. – Dr. Pat Piegari, WASHINGTON AVE　07416
ES, WASHINGTON AVE　07416
　Hobart Burd, prin.

Hardyston Twp. SD
Sch. Sys. Enr. Code 3
Supt. – Anthony Norod, P O BOX 155　07416
Hardyston Twp. ES, 50 ROUTE 23　07416
　James Opiekun, prin.

Immaculate Conception ES, 75 CHURCH ST　07416

Franklin Lakes, Bergen Co., Pop. Code 6
Franklin Lakes SD
Sch. Sys. Enr. Code 3
Supt. – Ed Sullivan, 490 PULIS AVE　07417
Franklin Avenue MS, 799 FRANKLIN AVE　07417
　Joseph Klingler, prin.
Colonial Road ES, 749 COLONIAL RD　07417
　George Ruocco, prin.
High Mountain Road ES
　765 HIGH MOUNTAIN RD　07417
　Philip Fontana, prin.
Woodside Avenue ES, 305 WOODSIDE AVE　07417
　Roy Egatz, prin.

Most Blessed Sacrament ES
　785 FRANKLIN LAKES RD　07417

Franklin Park, Somerset Co.
Franklin Twp. SD
Supt. – See Somerset
MS, HILLVIEW & CENTRAL AVES　08823
　Charlotte Weisner, prin.

Franklinville, Gloucester Co., Pop. Code 3
Franklin Twp. SD
Sch. Sys. Enr. Code 4
Supt. – Bernard Weisser, P O BOX 98　08322
ES, COLES MILL ROAD　08322
　Thomas Griggs, prin.
Janvier ES, STANTON AVE　08322
　Thomas Griggs, prin.
Reutter MS, DELSEA DR　08322
　Anthony Ettore, prin.
Other Schools – See Malaga, Newfield

Freehold, Monmouth Co., Pop. Code 7
Freehold Borough SD
Sch. Sys. Enr. Code 3
Supt. – Steven Fazekas, 280 PARK AVE　07728
IS, 280 PARK AVE　07728 – Mark Chitwood, prin.
Freehold Learning Center
　30 DUTCH LANE RD　07728
　Patricia Zaborniak, prin.
Park Avenue Annex ES, 280 PARK AVE　07728
　Mark Chitwood, prin.

Freehold Twp. SD
Sch. Sys. Enr. Code 4
Supt. – David Cole
　237 STONEHURST BLVD　07728
Barkalow MS
　498 STILWELLS CORNER ROAD　07728
　Rob MacMillan, prin.
Eisenhower MS, 3 BURLINGTON ROAD　07728
　Joe Quirk, prin.
Applegate ES, SHERWOOD DR　07728
　M. Brennan, prin.

Burlington Road ES, 1 BURLINGTON RD　07728
　Joseph Catena, prin.
Donovan ES, 237 STONEHURST BLVD　07728
　Dr. Robert Colangelo, prin.
Errickson ES, ELTON-ADELPHIC ROAD　07728
　Robert Lerner, prin.
West Freehold ES, 384 W MAIN ST　07728
　Dr. Judith Jalovick, prin.

St. Rose of Lima ES, 51 LINCOLN PL　07728

Frenchtown, Hunterdon Co., Pop. Code 4
Frenchtown Borough SD
Sch. Sys. Enr. Code 2
Supt. – Bernard Ruekgauer
　902 HARRISON ST　08825
Thomas ES, 902 HARRISON ST　08825
　Bernard Ruekgauer, prin.

Kingwood Twp. SD
Sch. Sys. Enr. Code 2
Supt. – Edwin Smith
　RURAL ROUTE 01 BOX 364　08825
Kingwood Twp. ES
　RURAL ROUTE 01 BOX 364　08825
　Robert McCrea, prin.

Garfield, Bergen Co., Pop. Code 8
Garfield SD
Sch. Sys. Enr. Code 4
Supt. – Jerome Benigno
　125 OUTWATER LANE　07026
Columbus ES, CEDAR ST　07026
　Anthony Brackett, prin.
Irving ES, MADONNA PL　07026
　Edward Mucha, prin.
Jefferson ES, ALPINE ST　07026
　Peter DeFranco, prin.
Lincoln ES, PALISADE AVE　07026
　Thomas Cangialosi, prin.
Roosevelt ES, ROOSEVELT #7 LINCOLN PL　07026
　Nicholas Perrapato, prin.
Wilson ES, 205 OUTWATER LN　07026
　Stephen Geydoshek, prin.

Most Holy Name ES, 96 MARSELLUS PL　07026
Our Lady of Mt. Virgin ES
　200 MACARTHUR AVE　07026
Our Lady of Sorrows ES, 30 MADONNA PL　07026
St. Stanislauss Kostka ES, 210 LANZA AVE　07026

Garwood, Union Co., Pop. Code 5
Garwood SD
Sch. Sys. Enr. Code 2
Supt. – John Halak,Jr., EAST ST　07027
Lincoln/Franklin ES
　WALNUT ST & SECOND AVE　07027
　Joseph Troiano, prin.
Washington ES, 500 EAST ST　07027
　John Halak,Jr., prin.

Gibbsboro, Camden Co., Pop. Code 2
Gibbsboro SD
Sch. Sys. Enr. Code 2
Supt. – William Kiernan
　37 KIRKWOOD ROAD　08026
ES, 37 KIRKWOOD RD　08026
　William Kiernan, prin.

Gibbstown, Gloucester Co.
Greenwich Twp. SD
Sch. Sys. Enr. Code 3
Supt. – Robert Wooton, 421 BROAD ST　08027
Greenwich Twp. ES, 421 W BROAD ST　08027
　Nancy Cox, prin.

Logan Twp. SD
Supt. – See Bridgeport
Logan IS, SWEDESBORO ROAD　08027
　Fred Cuddy, prin.

Gillette, Morris Co., Pop. Code 4
Passaic Twp. SD
Supt. – See Stirling
ES, 759 VALLEY RD　07933 – Robert Mosey, prin.

Glassboro, Gloucester Co., Pop. Code 7
Elk Twp. SD
Sch. Sys. Enr. Code 2
Supt. – James Davis
　RURAL ROUTE 01 BOX 338　08028
Aura ES, P O BOX 338　08028 – James Davis, prin.

Glassboro SD
Sch. Sys. Enr. Code 4
Supt. – Nicholas Mitcho
　506 J BOWE MEMORIAL BLVD　08028
MS, 250 DELSEA DRIVE N　08028
　Robert Washburn, prin.
Academy Street ES, 40 ACADEMY ST N　08028
　Gloria Lisa, prin.
Bowe MS
　CARPENTER ST & NORWAY AVE　08028
　Robert Murphy, prin.
Rodgers Memorial ES
　YALE & DICKINSON ROADS　08028
　Dr. Ralph Hallenbeck, prin.

St. Bridget ES, HIGH ST W　08028

Glendora, Camden Co., Pop. Code 6
Gloucester Twp. SD
Supt. – See Blackwood
ES, STATION ROAD & HUNTINGTON　08029
　Dr. George Bigge,Jr., prin.

Glen Ridge, Essex Co., Pop. Code 6
Glen Ridge SD
Sch. Sys. Enr. Code 4
Supt. – Rose McCaffery
　235 RIDGEWOOD AVE　07028
MS, 235 RIDGEWOOD AVE　07028
　Joseph Del Guercio, prin.
Forrest Avenue ES, 287 FOREST AVE　07028
　Catherine Vogel, prin.
Linden Avenue ES, 205 LINDEN AVE　07028
　Catherine Vogel, prin.

Glen Rock, Bergen Co., Pop. Code 7
Glen Rock SD
Sch. Sys. Enr. Code 4
Supt. – Dario Valcarcel
　620 HARRISTOWN ROAD　07452
Byrd ES, 640 DOREMUS AVE　07452
　Harold Knapp, prin.
Central ES, 600 S MAPLE AVE　07452
　David Skinner, prin.
Coleman ES, 100 PINELYNN RD　07452
　Dr. Clifford Kreismer, prin.

St. Catherine ES, 180 RODNEY ST　07452

Gloucester City, Camden Co., Pop. Code 7
Brooklawn SD
Supt. – See Brooklawn
Costello ES, 207 HAAKON RD　08030
　Dr. Douglas Howlett, prin.

Gloucester City SD
Sch. Sys. Enr. Code 4
Supt. – James Hetherington
　520 CUMBERLAND ST　08030
Broadway ES, CUMBERLAND & JOY STS　08030
　Dorothy Yunghans, prin.
Brown Street ES
　CUMBERLAND & JOY STS　08030
　Dorothy Yunghans, prin.
Costello ES, CUMBERLAND & JOY STS　08030
　Martin O'Connor, prin.
Gloucester Heights MS
　CUMBERLAND & JOY STS　08030
　Dorothy Yunghans, prin.
Highland Park ES
　CUMBERLAND & JOY STS　08030
　Dorothy Yunghans, prin.

St. Mary ES, 115 S SUSSEX ST　08030

Great Meadows, Warren Co.
Indedependence Twp. SD
Sch. Sys. Enr. Code 2
Supt. – Michael Doney　07838
Independence Twp. Central ES
　RURAL ROUTE 01 BOX 3　07838
　Michael Doney, prin.

Liberty Twp. SD
Sch. Sys. Enr. Code 2
Supt. – Thomas Reilly
　RURAL ROUTE 01 BOX 302　07838
Liberty Twp. ES
　RURAL ROUTE 01 BOX 302　07838
　Thomas Reilly, prin.

Green Brook, Somerset Co., Pop. Code 5
Green Brook Twp. SD
Sch. Sys. Enr. Code 3
Supt. – John Kolchin, 132 JEFFERSON AVE　08812
Feldkirchner ES, 105 ANDREW ST　08812
　Rubin Feldstein, prin.

Greendell, Sussex Co.
Green Twp. SD
Sch. Sys. Enr. Code 2
Supt. – John Fox, P O BOX 14　07839
Green Hills MS, P O BOX 14　07839
　Richard Cramer, prin.
Green PS, P O BOX 14　07839
　Mary Boutsikaris, prin.

Greenwich, Cumberland Co.
Greenwich Twp. SD
Sch. Sys. Enr. Code 1
Supt. – Dr. Jay Dunigan, MAIN ST　08323
Goodwin ES, P O BOX 360　08323
　Jay Dunigan, prin.

Guttenberg, Hudson Co., Pop. Code 6
Guttenberg SD
Sch. Sys. Enr. Code 3
Supt. – Patrick Forenza, 301 69TH ST　07093
Klein ES, 301 69TH ST　07093
　Patrick Forenza, prin.

Hackensack, Bergen Co., Pop. Code 8
Hackensack SD
Sch. Sys. Enr. Code 5
Supt. – Anthony Marseglia, 335 STATE ST　07601
MS, 360 UNION ST　07601
　Joseph Montesano, prin.
Fairmount ES, FAIRMOUNT AVE　07601
　Ann Small, prin.
Hillers ES, LONGVIEW AVE　07601
　Bernard Kaminsky, prin.
Jackson Avenue ES, 405 JACKSON AVE　07601
　Anthony Jones, prin.
Parker ES, MAPLE HILL DR　07601
　Thelma Smith, prin.

Holy Trinity ES, 43 MAPLE AVE　07601
Immaculate Conception School
　386 HUDSON ST　07601
St. Francis ES, 100 S MAIN ST　07601

Hackettstown, Warren Co., Pop. Code 6
Hackettstown SD
Sch. Sys. Enr. Code 4
Supt. – J. Fitzgibbon
315 WASHINGTON ST   07840
MS, 500 WASHINGTON ST   07840
Matthew Pinkman, prin.
Hatchery Hill ES, FIFTH AVE   07840
Arthur Sheninger, prin.
Willow Grove Street ES
601 WILLOW GROVE ST   07840
John Sarcone, prin.

St. Mary of Assumption School
COOK AND LIBERTY STS   07840

Haddonfield, Camden Co., Pop. Code 7
Barrington SD
Supt. – See Barrington
Avon PS, MERCER DR   08033
Anthony Negro, prin.

Haddon Twp. SD
Supt. – See Camden
Stoy ES, BRIARWOOD AVE   08033
Robert Andrews, prin.
Van Sciver ES, VALLEY DR   08033
Dale Payne, prin.

Haddonfield Borough SD
Sch. Sys. Enr. Code 4
Supt. – Barry Ersek, 1 LINCOLN AVE   08033
MS, 1 LINCOLN AVE   08033 – John Caggiano, prin.
Central ES
LINCOLN AVE & CHESTNUT ST   08033
Dr. John Caggiano, prin.
Haddon ES, REDMAN AVE & PEYTON AVE   08033
Jean Horn, prin.
Tatem ES, GLOVER AVE   08033
Kenneth Florentine, prin.

Christ the King Regional School
164 HOPLINS AVE   08033
Haddonfield Friends ES, 47 HADDON AVE   08033

Haddon Heights, Camden Co., Pop. Code 6
Haddon Heights SD
Sch. Sys. Enr. Code 4
Supt. – Ken MacGregor, 300 2ND AVE   08035
MS, 2ND AVE & GARDEN ST   08035
William Neveling, prin.
Atlantic Avenue ES
ATLANTIC AVE & GREEN ST   08035
Lorraine Wilson, prin.
Glenview Avenue ES
GLENVIEW & SYCAMORE STS   08035
Philip Raimondo, prin.
Seventh Avenue ES
SEVENTH AVE & HIGH ST   08035
Linda Steenrod, prin.

St. Rose of Lima ES, 3RD AND KINGS HWY   08035

Hainesport, Burlington Co.
Hainesport Township SD
Sch. Sys. Enr. Code 2
Supt. – Thomas Reardon, 211 BROAD ST   08036
ES, 211 BROAD ST   08036 – Walter Keiss, prin.

Haledon, Passaic Co., Pop. Code 6
Haledon SD
Sch. Sys. Enr. Code 3
Supt. – Dr. D. Raymond Orsi
120 BARBOUR ST   07508
ES, 120 BARBOUR ST   07508
Michael Antolino, prin.

Hamburg, Sussex Co., Pop. Code 4
Hamburg Borough SD
Sch. Sys. Enr. Code 2
Supt. – Dr. James Kane, 30 LINWOOD AVE   07419
ES, 30 LINWOOD AVE   07419
Dr. James Kane, prin.

Hamilton Square, Mercer Co., Pop. Code 6
Hamilton Twp. SD
Supt. – See Trenton
Alexander ES, 20 ROBERT FROST DR   08690
Carol Chiacchio, prin.

Hammonton, Atlantic Co., Pop. Code 7
Folsom SD
Sch. Sys. Enr. Code 2
Supt. – Salvatore Todaro
RURAL ROUTE 06   BOX 529   08037
Folsom ES, RURAL ROUTE 06 BOX 529   08037
Salvatore Todaro, prin.

Hammonton Town SD
Sch. Sys. Enr. Code 4
Supt. – Warren Benedetto, P O BOX 631   08037
MS, CENTRAL AVE   08037
Nicholas DeRosa, prin.
ES, 601 4TH ST   08037 – Jeffrey Garrison, prin.

Winslow Twp. SD
Sch. Sys. Enr. Code 5
Supt. – Barry Galasso, P O BOX 213   08037
Winslow Twp. ES 1
WALNUT AVE & INSKIP ROAD   08037
Raymond Gibson, prin.
Other Schools – See Cedar Brook, Sicklerville

St. Joseph School, 133 N 3RD ST   08037

Hampton, Hunterdon Co., Pop. Code 4
Hampton Borough SD
Sch. Sys. Enr. Code 2
Supt. – Thomas Lubben, SOUTH ST   08827
Hampton Boro ES
RURAL ROUTE 02 BOX 48A   08827
Thomas Lubben, prin.

Union Twp. SD
Sch. Sys. Enr. Code 2
Supt. – William Clawson
BURAL ROUTE 01   BOX 231   08827
Union Twp. ES
RURAL ROUTE 01 BOX 231   08827
William Clawson, prin.

Harrington Park, Bergen Co., Pop. Code 5
Harrington Park SD
Sch. Sys. Enr. Code 3
Supt. – Carol Moldan, 191 HARRIOT AVE   07640
ES, 191 HARRIOT AVE   07640
Bruce deLyon, prin.

Our Lady Victories ES, 155 PARKWAY   07640

Harrison, Hudson Co., Pop. Code 7
Harrison SD
Sch. Sys. Enr. Code 4
Supt. – O. DiSalvo, 517 HAMILTON ST   07029
Washington MS, 223 HAMILTON ST   07029
Mary Lenehan, prin.
Lincoln ES 3, 15 S FOURTH ST   07029
Frederick Confessore, prin.

Holy Cross ES, 15 S FOURTH ST   07029

Harrisonville, Gloucester Co.
South Harrison Twp. SD
Sch. Sys. Enr. Code 2
Supt. – Thomas Murphy,Jr., P O BOX 112   08039
South Harrison ES, P O BOX 112   08039
Dr. Thomas Murphy,Jr., prin.

Hasbrouck Heights, Bergen Co., Pop. Code 7
Hasbrouck Heights SD
Sch. Sys. Enr. Code 4
Supt. – Paul Arilotta, 379 BOULEVARD   07604
Euclid ES, PASSAIC AVE   07604
Arthur Ranges, prin.
Lincoln ES, BURTON & PATERSON AVES   07604
Jack Palma, prin.

Corpus Christi ES, 215 KIPP AVE   07604

Haskell, Passaic Co.
Wanaque SD
Supt. – See Wanaque
ES, 973 RINGWOOD AVE   07420
Ernest Palestis, prin.

St. Francis of Assisi ES
FATHER HAYES DRIVE   07420

Haworth, Bergen Co., Pop. Code 5
Haworth SD
Sch. Sys. Enr. Code 2
Supt. – Alan Grossberg, 205 VALLEY ROAD   07641
ES, 205 VALLEY RD   07641
Dr. Ralph Robinson, prin.

Hawthorne, Passaic Co., Pop. Code 7
Hawthorne SD
Sch. Sys. Enr. Code 4
Supt. – Frank Chiofalo, 121 REA AVE   07506
Lincoln MS, 225 HAWTHORNE AVE   07506
Rob Masiello, prin.
Jefferson ES, GOFFLE HILL ROAD   07506
Joseph Vitale, prin.
Roosevelt ES, 30 ROOSEVELT AVE   07506
Robert Hausner, prin.
Washington ES, 152 MOHAWK AVE   07506
Dr. Gerard McDonnell, prin.

St. Anthony ES
270 DIAMOND BRIDGE AVE   07506

Hazlet, Monmouth Co., Pop. Code 7
Hazlet Twp. SD
Sch. Sys. Enr. Code 5
Supt. – Joe Dispenziere, 319 MIDDLE ROAD   07730
Beers Street MS, 610 BEERS ST   07730
Nicholas Sardone, prin.
Union Avenue MS, 1631 UNION AVE   07730
Andrew Provence, prin.
Cove Road ES, 8 CORE ROAD   07730
Anthony Bruno, prin.
Lillian Drive ES, 28 LILLIAN DR   07730
Austin Sherman, prin.
Middle Road ES, 305 MIDDLE RD   07730
Vincent McCue, prin.
Raritan Valley ES, 37 CRESCI BLVD   07730
Errol Bottani, prin.
Sycamore Drive ES, 37 SYCAMORE DR   07730
Carmine Marmo, prin.

Holy Family ES, HIGHWAY 36   07730

Hewitt, Passaic Co.
West Milford Twp. SD
Supt. – See West Milford
Uppr Greenwood Lake ES, 41 HENRY RD   07421
Albert Pecci, prin.

Our Lady Queen of Peace ES
1905 UNION VALLEY RD   07421

High Bridge, Hunterdon Co., Pop. Code 5
High Bridge Borough SD
Sch. Sys. Enr. Code 2
Supt. – Joseph Stuby, 50 THOMAS ST   08829
MS, 50 THOMAS ST   08829 – Ed Bilinsky, prin.
ES, 40 FAIRVIEW AVE   08829
Kelley Kissiah, prin.

Highland Park, Middlesex Co., Pop. Code 7
Highland Park SD
Sch. Sys. Enr. Code 4
Supt. – Carolyn Hartley
435 MANSFIELD ST   08904
Bartle MS, 405 MANSFIELD ST   08904
Ron Erikson, prin.
Irving ES, SOUTH ELEVENTH AVE   08904
Dr. Lawrence Snow, prin.

St. Paul ES, 502 RARITAN AVE   08904

Highlands, Monmouth Co., Pop. Code 6
Highlands Borough SD
Sch. Sys. Enr. Code 2
Supt. – Robert Zolkiewicz, NAVESINK AVE   07732
ES, NAVESINK AVE   07732
Robert Zolkiewicz, prin.

Our Lady of Perpetual Help ES
141 NAVESINK AVE   07732

Hightstown, Mercer Co., Pop. Code 5
East Windsor Regional SD
Sch. Sys. Enr. Code 5
Supt. – Edgar Thomas,Jr.
384 STOCKTON ST   08520
Kreps MS, 994 KENT LN   08520
William Setaro, prin.
Rogers MS, 386 STOCKTON ST   08520
Valerie Carlisle, prin.
Black ES, 608 STOCKTON ST   08520
Joseph Chibbaro, prin.
Drew ES, TWIN RIVERS DR N   08520
Charmaine Neve, prin.
McKnight ES, 386 TWIN RIVERS DR N   08520
Raymond Broach, prin.

Hillsdale, Bergen Co., Pop. Code 7
Hillsdale SD
Sch. Sys. Enr. Code 3
Supt. – Michael Gardullo
32 RUCKMAN ROAD   07642
Meadowbrook ES, PIERMONT AVE   07642
M. DePascale, prin.
Smith ES, 455 HILLSDALE AVE   07642
Joan Dubell, prin.
White ES, 120 MAGNOLIA AVE   07642
Ronald Sands, prin.

St. John Baptist ES, 462 HILLSDALE AVE   07642

Hillside, Union Co., Pop. Code 7
Hillside Twp. SD
Sch. Sys. Enr. Code 5
Supt. – Anthony Avella, 195 VIRGINIA ST   07205
Coolidge ES, 614 TILLMAN ST   07205
Barbara Washington, prin.
Krumbiegel ES, 145 HILLSIDE AVE   07205
John Kaszak, prin.
Hurden-Looker ES, 1261 LIBERTY AVE   07205
Frank Deo, prin.
Morris-Saybrook ES, 143 COE AVE   07205
Frederick Mele,Jr., prin.
Washington ES, 1530 LESLIE ST   07205
Martin Gulino, prin.

Christ the King School
397 COLUMBIA AVE   07205

Hoboken, Hudson Co., Pop. Code 8
Hoboken SD
Sch. Sys. Enr. Code 5
Supt. – Walter Fine, 1115 CLINTON ST   07030
Brandt ES, NINTH & GARDEN STS   07030
Frank Spano, prin.
Calabro ES 4, 524 PARK AVE   07030
Richard Delboccio, prin.
Connors Memorial ES 9
SECOND & MONROE STS   07030
Edwin DuRoy, prin.
DeMarest ES, FOURTH & GARDEN STS   07030
Dorothy Ziegler, prin.
Kealey ES 3, FIFTH & ADAMS ST   07030
Charles Tortorella, prin.
Wallace ES 6
ELEVENTH ST & WILLOW AVE   07030
Patrick Gagliardi, prin.

Mustard Seed ES, 61 NINTH ST   07030
Our Lady Grace ES
FIFTH ST & WILLOW AVE   07030
SS. Peter and Paul ES
410-16 HUDSON STREET   07030
St. Ann's ES, 555 SEVENTH ST   07030
St. Francis ES, 506 THIRD ST   07030
St. Joseph ES, 73 JACKSON ST   07030

Ho Ho Kus, Bergen Co., Pop. Code 1
Ho-Ho-Kus SD
Sch. Sys. Enr. Code 2
Supt. – Dr. John Woodbury, LLOYD ROAD   07423
ES, LLOYD ROAD   07423
Dr. John Woodbury, prin.

St. Luke's ES, 340 N FRANKLIN TPKE   07423

Holmdel, Monmouth Co., Pop. Code 6
Holmdel Twp. SD
Sch. Sys. Enr. Code 4
Supt. – Tim Brennan
4 CRAWFORD'S CORNER ROAD 07733
Satz MS, 24 CRAWFORDS CORNER ROAD 07733
Frank Corrado, prin.
Indian Hill MS, 735 HOLMDEL RD 07733
Paul Hart, prin.
Village ES, 67 MCCAMPBELL RD 07733
Christopher Blejwas, prin.

St. Benedict ES, 165 BETHANY RD 07733

Hopatcong, Sussex Co., Pop. Code 7
Hopatcong Borough SD
Sch. Sys. Enr. Code 5
Supt. – Wayne Threlkeld, P O BOX 1029 07843
MS, P O BOX 1029 07843 – Douglas Squier, prin.
Durban Avenue ES, P O BOX 1029 07843
Robert Buchan, prin.
Maxim ES, P O BOX 1029 07843
Dr. Dennis Pallozzi, prin.
Tulsa Trail ES, P O BOX 1029 07843
Joseph Memoli, prin.

Hope, Warren Co.
Hope Twp. SD
Sch. Sys. Enr. Code 2
Supt. – Edward Bilinsky, P O BOX 293 07844
Hope Twp. ES, P O BOX 293 07844
Edward Bilinsky, prin.

Hopewell, Mercer Co., Pop. Code 4
Hopewell Valley Regional SD
Supt. – See Pennington
ES, 29 PRINCETON AVE 08525 – J. Schilder, prin.

Howell, Monmouth Co., Pop. Code 8
Howell Twp. SD
Sch. Sys. Enr. Code 5
Supt. – Dr. William Pelaia, P O BOX 579 07731
Aldrich ES, 585 ALDUCH ROAD 07731
Walter Litowinsky, prin.
Land O Pines ES, WINDELER ROAD 07731
Richard Thompson, prin.
Newbury ES, NEWBURY ROAD 07731
Bernard Chetkin, prin.
Ramtown ES
RAMTOWN-GREENVILLE ROAD 07731
Joseph Torrone, prin.
Southard ES, KENT ROAD 07731
Diane Schmidt, prin.
Taunton ES, TAUNTON DR 07731
James Bruno, prin.
Other Schools – See Farmingdale

St. Veronica ES, 2301 HIGHWAY 9 07731

Irvington, Essex Co., Pop. Code 8
Irvington SD
Sch. Sys. Enr. Code 6
Supt. – A. Scardaville
1150 SPRINGFIELD AVE 07111
Myrtle Avenue MS, 255 MYRTLE AVE 07111
Guy Ferri, prin.
Augusta Street ES, 97 AUGUSTA ST 07111
Helen Solon, prin.
Berkeley Terrace ES, 803 GROVE ST 07111
Louis Vitale, prin.
Chancellor Avenue ES
844 CHANDLER AVE 07111
Donald Robertson, prin.
Florence Avenue ES
1324 SPRINGFIELD AVE 07111
Dr. Harry Donovan,Jr., prin.
Grove Street ES, 594 GROVE ST 07111
Frank Ross, prin.
Madison Avenue ES, 163 MANDUAN AVE 07111
Kenneth Rogers, prin.
Mt. Vernon Avenue ES
36 MT VERNON AVE 07111
Donald DeBenedett, prin.
Union Avenue ES, 427 UNION AVE 07111
Walter Rusak, prin.

Sacred Heart of Jesus ES
15 SMALLEY TER 07111
St. Leo ES, 121 MYRTLE AVE 07111
St. Paul the Apostle ES, 285 NESBIT TER 07111

Iselin, Middlesex Co., Pop. Code 7
Woodbridge Twp. SD
Supt. – See Woodbridge
MS, WOODRUFF ST 08830 – Ralph Coppola, prin.
Indiana Avenue ES, INDIANA AVE 08830
William Hillyer, prin.
Kennedy Park ES, GOODRICH ST 08830
Dr. Eugene Patten, prin.
Mascenik ES, BENJAMIN AVE 08830
Robert Mascenik, prin.

St. Cecelia ES, 45 WILUS WAY 08830

Island Heights, Ocean Co., Pop. Code 4
Island Heights SD
Sch. Sys. Enr. Code 2
Supt. – Robert Remppies
115 SUMMIT AVE 08732
ES, 115 SUMMIT AVE 08732
Robert Remppies, prin.

Jackson, Ocean Co., Pop. Code 8
Jackson Twp. SD
Sch. Sys. Enr. Code 6
Supt. – Dominic Cotugno
COVENTRY ROAD 08527
Goetz IS, PATTERSON ROAD 08527
Carol D'Zio, prin.
Holman ES, MATTHATTAN ROAD 08527
John Amabile, prin.
Johnson ES, LAASEN ROAD 08527
Frank Miri, prin.
Rosenauer ES, 25 CITADEL DR 08527
Edward Leonard, prin.
Switlik ES, RURAL ROUTE 04 BOX 65 08527
Frank White, prin.

Jamesburg, Middlesex Co., Pop. Code 5
Jamesburg SD
Sch. Sys. Enr. Code 2
Supt. – Anthony Nami, 17 AUGUSTA ST 08831
Breckwedel MS, 13 AUGUSTA ST 08831
Jean Sadenwater, prin.
Kennedy ES, 28 FRONT ST 08831
Vincent Cardile, prin.

Monroe Twp. SD
Sch. Sys. Enr. Code 5
Supt. – Richard Marasco
RURAL ROUTE 02 BOX 300 08831
Barclay Brook ES
JAMESBURG-ENGLISHTOWN ROAD 08831
Carol Schwalje, prin.
Other Schools – See Cranbury, Spotswood

Jersey City, Hudson Co., Pop. Code 9
Jersey CSD
Sch. Sys. Enr. Code 8
Supt. – Franklin Williams
346 CLAREMONT AVE 07305
Barnes ES 12, 91 ASTOR PL 07304
Wilbert Jones, prin.
Bradford ES 16, 96 SUSSEX ST 07302
Lynne Zoss, prin.
Brensinger ES 17, 128 DUNCAN AVE 07306
Carol Kaiser, prin.
Conwell ES 3, 70 BRIGHT ST 07302
Marcia Leff, prin.
Copernicus ES 25
3385 JOHN F KENNEDY BLVD 07307
Joseph Ward, prin.
Cordero ES 37, 158 ERIE ST 07302
Marvin Strynar, prin.
DeFuccio ES 39, 214 PLAINFIELD AVE 07306
Salvatore Schifano, prin.
ES 28, 139 HANCOCK AVE 07307
Charles Silver, prin.
ES 14, 153 UNION ST 07304 – John Nagy, prin.
ES 20, 160 DANFORTH AVE 07305
William Fischer, prin.
ES 22, 264 VAN HOME ST 07304
Gerard Dynes, prin.
ES 23, 143 ROMAINE AVE 07306
Jack Schneider, prin.
ES 24, 220 VIRGINIA AVE 07304
George Pankewicz, prin.
ES 27, 201 NORTH ST 07307
Alfred Zampella, prin.
ES 29, 123 CLAREMONT AVE 07305
Charles Smith, prin.
ES 33, 362 UNION ST 07304
Dr. Paul Rafalides, prin.
ES 34, 1830 JOHN F KENNEDY BLVD 07305
John Phillips, prin.
ES 5, 182 MERSELES ST 07302
Evelyn Johnson, prin.
ES 8, 96 FRANKLIN ST 07307
Charles Trefurt, prin.
Kennedy ES 9, 222 MERCER ST 07302
Gerard Russoniello, prin.
King ES 11, 886 BERGEN AVE 07306
Angela Bruno, prin.
Martin ES 41, 59 WILKINSON AVE 07305
Claudette Searchwell, prin.
Murray ES 38, 339 STEGMAN PKY 07305
Jack Koval, prin.
Nichols ES 42, 700 NEWARK AVE 07306
Helen Aiosa, prin.
Nolan ES 40, 88 GATES AVE 07305
Margaret Penney, prin.
Sullivan ES 30, 171 SEAVIEW AVE 07305
Barbara Sachs, prin.
Wakeman ES 6, 100 SAINT PAULS AVE 07306
Margaret Mullin, prin.
Young ES 15, 135 STEGMAN ST 07305
William Smith, prin.

Academy of St. Aloysius
2495 JOHN F KENNEDY BLVD 07304
Assumption-All Saints School
301 WHITON ST 07304
Holy Rosary ES, 189 BRUNSWICK ST 07302
Our Lady Czestochowa ES
YORK & HENDERSON STS 07302
Our Lady Mt. Carmel ES, 95 BROADWAY 07306
Our Lady Victories ES, 240 EGE AVE 07304
Our Lady of Mercy ES
250 BARTHOLDI AVE 07305
Sacred Heart ES, 183 BAYVIEW AVE 07305
St. Aedan ES, 41 TUERS AVE 07306
St. Aloysius ES, 721 W SIDE AVE 07306
St. Bridget ES, 197 MERCER ST 07302
St. John Baptist ES
3044 JOHN F KENNEDY BLVD 07306
St. Joseph ES, 509 PAVONIA AVE 07306

St. Mary ES, 209 3RD ST 07302
St. Nicholas ES, 118 FERRY ST 07307
St. Patrick ES, 509 BRAMHALL AVE 07304
St. Paul of Cross ES, 211 SHERMAN AVE 07307
St. Paul's ES, 193 OLD BERGEN RD 07305
St. Peter ES, 153 YORK ST 07302

Jobstown, Burlington Co.
Springfield Twp. SD
Sch. Sys. Enr. Code 2
Supt. – Christy Ball, JACKSONVILLE RD 08041
Springfield Twp. ES
JACKSONVILLE ROAD 08041 – Christy Ball, prin.

Keansburg, Monmouth Co., Pop. Code 7
Keansburg Borough SD
Sch. Sys. Enr. Code 4
Supt. – J. Caruso
140 PORT MONMOUTH ROAD 07734
Francis Place MS, 81 FRANCIS PLACE 07734
Annie Miele, prin.
Port Monmouth Road ES
140 PORT MONMOUTH RD 07734
Paul Quirk, prin.

St. Ann ES, 285 CARR AVE 07734
St. Catherine ES, 30 SHORE ACRES AVE 07734

Kearny, Hudson Co., Pop. Code 8
Kearny SD
Sch. Sys. Enr. Code 5
Supt. – John Onnembo, 336 DEVON ST 07032
Franklin ES, 100 DAVIS AVE 07032
A. Reto, prin.
Garfield ES, 360 BELGROVE DR 07032
John Chieco, prin.
Lincoln ES, 101 BEECH ST 07032
Gerald Lawless, prin.
Roosevelt ES, 733 KEARNY AVE 07032
Robert Wynne, prin.
Schuyler ES, 644 FOREST ST 07032
John McGeehan, prin.
Washington ES, 80 BELGROVE DR 07032
John Mastroean, prin.

Our Lady of Sorrows ES
60 KINGSLAND AVE 07032
Queen of Peace ES, 21 CHURCH PL 07032
Sacred Heart School for Boys
22 WILSON AVE 07032
St. Cecilia ES, 114 CHESTNUT ST 07032
St. Stephen ES, 131 MIDLAND AVE 07032

Kendall Park, Middlesex Co., Pop. Code 6
South Brunswick Twp. SD
Supt. – See Monmouth Junction
Brunswick Acres ES, 41 KORY DR 08824
Gwendolyn Grant, prin.
Cambridge ES, 35 CAMBRIDGE RD 08824
Edward Kahler, prin.
Constable ES, 29 CONSTABLE RD 08824
Dr. Judy Zimmerman, prin.
Greenbrook ES, 30 ROBERTS ST 08824
Stephanie Craib, prin.

St. Augustine School, 45 HENDERSON RD 08824

Kenilworth, Union Co., Pop. Code 6
Kenilworth SD
Sch. Sys. Enr. Code 3
Supt. – Anthony Richel, 426 BOULEVARD 07033
Harding ES, 426 BOULEVARD 07033
Frederick Rica, prin.

St. Theresas ES, 540 WASHINGTON AVE 07033

Keyport, Monmouth Co., Pop. Code 6
Keyport SD
Sch. Sys. Enr. Code 4
Supt. – Dwight Pfennig, 351 BROAD ST 07735
Central ES, 335 BROAD ST 07735
Norman Zweiacher, prin.

St. Jospeh ES, 376 MAPLE PL 07735

Kingston, Middlesex Co.
Franklin Twp. SD
Supt. – See Somerset
ES, LAUREL AVE 08528 – Charlotte Weisner, prin.

Kinnelon, Morris Co., Pop. Code 6
Kinnelon Borough SD
Sch. Sys. Enr. Code 4
Supt. – Ransler Hall, 115 KIEL AVE 07405
Miller MS, 15 KIEL AVE 07405
Joseph Palladino, prin.
Kiel ES, KIEL AVE 07405 – (—), prin.
Stonybrook MS, BOONTON AVE 07405
Robert Kramer, prin.

Kirkwood Voorhees, Camden Co.
Voorhees Twp. SD
Sch. Sys. Enr. Code 5
Supt. – Raymond Brosel,Jr.
HOLLY OAK & EVERSHAM ROAD 08043
Voorhees MS, HOLLY OAK DRIVE 08043
Samuel Citron, prin.
Osage ES, 128 CHEWS LANDING RD 08043
Kathleen Alexandrowicz, prin.
Other Schools – See Voorhees, West Berlin

Lafayette, Sussex Co., Pop. Code 4

Northwest Christian School
RURAL ROUTE 15 07848

Lake Hiawatha, Morris Co., Pop. Code 7
Parsippany-Troy Hills Twp. SD
Supt. – See Parsippany
Knollwood ES, GLENWOOD AVE 07034
Joseph Monahan, prin.

Lake Hopatcong, Morris Co., Pop. Code 4
Jefferson Twp. SD
Supt. – See Oak Ridge
Briggs ES, ESPANONG ROAD 07849
James Opeken, prin.
Consolidated ES
RURAL ROUTE 03 BOX 700 07849
Dr. John Scheri, prin.

Lakehurst, Ocean Co., Pop. Code 5
Lakehurst SD
Sch. Sys. Enr. Code 3
Supt. – Mary Johnson, 301 UNION AVE 08733
ES, 301 UNION AVE 08733 – Mary Johnson, prin.

Manchester Twp. SD
Supt. – See Whiting
Ridgeway MS, 2861 RIDGEWAY RD 08733
Dr. John Coppola, prin.

Lakewood, Ocean Co., Pop. Code 8
Lakewood Twp. SD
Sch. Sys. Enr. Code 6
Supt. – John Patrick, 100 LINDEN AVE 08701
MS, E 7TH & SOMERSET AVE 08701
Ed Liuck, prin.
Clarke ES, MANETTA AVE 08701
Joseph Kohn, prin.
Clifton Avenue ES, CLIFTON AVE 08701
Donald Shaw, prin.
Oak Street ES, OAK ST 08701
Joseph Attardi, prin.
Princeton Avenue MS
600 PRINCETON AVE 08701
Dr. Sheldon Boxer, prin.
Spruce Street ES, SPRUCE ST 08701
Dr. Gene Abel, prin.

Holy Family ES, 1141 E COUNTY LINE RD 08701
Lakewood Hebrew ES, 419 5TH ST 08701
St. Mary Academy, 250 FOREST AVE 08701

Lambertville, Hunterdon Co., Pop. Code 5
Lambertville SD
Sch. Sys. Enr. Code 2
Supt. – Dennis Murphy, 200 N MAIN ST 08530
ES, 200 N MAIN ST 08530 – Betty Zdep, prin.

West Amwell Twp. SD
Sch. Sys. Enr. Code 2
Supt. – Anthony DeCanzio
ROUTE 179 BOX 295 08530
West Amwell Twp. ES, 295 HIGHWAY 179 08530
Anthony DeCanzio, prin.

Landing, Morris Co.
Roxbury Twp. SD
Supt. – See Succasunna
Nixon ES, MT ARLINGTON BLVD 07850
Alice Petko, prin.

Landisville, Atlantic Co.
Buena Regional SD
Supt. – See Buena
Donini ES, GROVE ROAD 08326
Roland Kuhar, prin.

Our Lady of Victories ES, CENTRAL AVE 08326

Lanoka Harbor, Ocean Co.
Lacey Twp. SD
Supt. – See Forked River
Lacey Twp. MS, P O BOX 197 08734
Paul Berkowicz, prin.
ES, P O BOX 186 08734 – David Elliott, prin.

Laurel Springs, Camden Co., Pop. Code 4
Laurel Springs SD
Sch. Sys. Enr. Code 2
Supt. – Elaine Wallenburg
623 GRAND AVE 08021
ES, 623 GRAND AVE 08021
Elaine Wallenburg, prin.

Laurence Harbor, Middlesex Co., Pop. Code 5
Old Bridge Twp. SD
Supt. – See Matawan
Memorial ES, 11 ELY AVE 08879
Joseph Burke, prin.

Lavallette, Ocean Co., Pop. Code 4
LaVallette Borough SD
Sch. Sys. Enr. Code 2
Supt. – Erwest Donnelly
105 BROOKLYN AVE 08735
ES, 105 BROOKLYN AVE 08735
Ernest Donnelly, prin.

Lawnside, Camden Co., Pop. Code 5
Lawnside Borough SD
Sch. Sys. Enr. Code 2
Supt. – Nathan Reeves
426 CHARLESTON AVE E 08045
ES, 426 CHARLESTON AVE E 08045
Nathaniel Reeves, prin.

Lawrenceville, Mercer Co., Pop. Code 5
Lawrence Twp. SD
Sch. Sys. Enr. Code 5
Supt. – Barry Gleim
2565 PRINCETON AVE 08648

Lawrence MS, 2455 PRINCETON AVE 08648
Thomas Davidson, prin.
Franklin ES, 2939 PRINCETON PIKE 08648
Russell Stanley, prin.
Lawrence IS, 66 EGGERTS CROSSING RD 08648
William Buss, prin.
ES, 40 CRAVEN LN 08648
Dr. Richard Graja, prin.
Slackwood ES, 2060 PRINCETON AVE 08648
Dr. Walter Woolley, prin.

Layton, Sussex Co.
Sandyston-Walpack Twp. SD
Sch. Sys. Enr. Code 2
Supt. – Edward Ibsen, P O BOX 128 07851
Sandyston-Walpack ES, P O BOX 128 07851
Edward Ibsen, prin.

Lebanon, Hunterdon Co., Pop. Code 3
Clinton Twp. SD
Supt. – See Annadale
McGaheran MS, 78C ALLERTON ROAD 07830
John Sulliivan, prin.
Round Valley MS, RURAL ROUTE 04 08833
Anthony Pierro, prin.

Lebanon Borough SD
Sch. Sys. Enr. Code 1
Supt. – Walter Schaufele, 6 HIGH ST 08833
Lebanon Borough ES, 6 HIGH ST 08833
Walter Schaufele, prin.

Tewksbury Twp. SD
Sch. Sys. Enr. Code 2
Supt. – Horace Roland, RURAL ROUTE 04 08833
Sawmill ES, RURAL ROUTE 02 08833
James Miller, prin.
Other Schools – See Califon

Leesburg, Cumberland Co.
Maurice River Twp. SD
Supt. – See Port Elizabeth
ES, MAIN ST 08327 – Joan Petersen, prin.

Leonardo, Monmouth Co., Pop. Code 5
Middletown Twp. SD
Supt. – See Middletown
Bayshore MS, 36 LEONARDVILLE ROAD 07737
Elaine Tryjankowski, prin.
ES, 14 HOSFORD AVE 07737
Morris Radler, prin.

Leonia, Bergen Co., Pop. Code 6
Leonia SD
Sch. Sys. Enr. Code 4
Supt. – Frank Marlow, 500 BROAD AVE 07605
MS, 500 BROAD AVE 07605 – Don Kouba, prin.
Scott ES, HIGHLAND ST 07605
Fred Selsky, prin.

St. John Evangelist ES, 260 HARRISON ST 07605

Liberty Corner, Somerset Co.
Benards Twp. SD
Supt. – See Basking Ridge
ES, 61 CHURCH ST 07938
Shirley Zimmerman, prin.

Lincoln Park, Morris Co., Pop. Code 6
Lincoln Park Borough SD
Sch. Sys. Enr. Code 3
Supt. – Rob Vitacco, 19 STATION ROAD 07035
Chapel Hill MS, 31 CHAPEL HILL ROAD 07035
Joseph DiBrigida, prin.
Patania ES, 90 RYERSON RD 07035
Marilyn Castellano, prin.
Pine Brook ES, PINEBROOK RD 07035
Theodore Arnold, prin.

St. Jospeh ES, 200 COMLY RD 07035

Lincroft, Monmouth Co., Pop. Code 5
Middletown Twp. SD
Supt. – See Middletown
ES, 279 NEWMAN SPRINGS ROAD 07738
George Ahlers, prin.

St. Leo the Great ES
550 NEWMAN SPRINGS RD 07738

Linden, Union Co., Pop. Code 8
Linden SD
Sch. Sys. Enr. Code 5
Supt. – Thomas Long, 728 N WOOD AVE 07036
McManus MS, 300 EDGEWOOD ROAD 07036
Joseph Placa, prin.
Soehl MS, 300 E HENRY ST 07036
S. Kaplowitz, prin.
Linden City MS 1, 728 N WOOD AVE 07036
James Iozzi, prin.
Deerfield Terrace ES, DEERFIELD TER NO 9 07036
Jules LeBoff, prin.
Highland Avenue ES, HIGHLAND AVE 07036
Anthony Cataline, prin.
Linden City ES 2, 4005 S WOOD AVE 07036
Arthur Boyd, prin.
Linden City ES 4, DILL AVE 07036
Dolores Masio, prin.
Linden City ES 5, BOWER ST 07036
Alexis Jarose, prin.
Linden City ES 6, 19 E MORRIS AVE 07036
Michael Dimicele, prin.
Linden City ES 8, 500 W BLANCKE ST 07036
Joseph Roper, prin.

Winfield Twp. SD
Sch. Sys. Enr. Code 2
Supt. – Frank Bradshaw
GULF STREAM AVE 07036
Winfield Twp. ES, GULFSTREAM AVE 07036
Frank Bradshaw, prin.

St. Elizabeth ES, 170 HUSSA ST 07036
St. Theresa ES, CLINTON & LIBERTY STS 07036

Lindenwold, Camden Co., Pop. Code 7
Lindenwold Borough SD
Sch. Sys. Enr. Code 4
Supt. – Edward Zirpoli
1017 E LINDEN AVE 08021
ES 1, 2115 S WHITE HORSE PIKE 08021
John Schilling, prin.
ES 4, 840 E GIBBSBORO RD 08021
John Carey, prin.
ES 5, 580 CHEWS LANDING RD 08021
Herbert Johnson II, prin.

Lower Camden County Regional HSD 1
Supt. – See Atco
Overbrook Regional JHS
WHITE HORSE AVE 08021
Nicholas Guerere, prin.

Linwood, Atlantic Co., Pop. Code 6
Egg Harbor Twp. SD
Supt. – See Pleasantville
Bargaintown ES
RURAL ROUTE 02 BOX 259 08221
Thomas Cooke, prin.

Linwood CSD
Sch. Sys. Enr. Code 3
Supt. – Ralph Schiavo, 51 BELHAVEN AVE 08221
Belhaven Avenue MS, 51 BELHAVEN AVE 08221
Susan Evinski, prin.
Poplar Avenue ES, 398 W POPLAR AVE 08221
James Smith, prin.
Seaview ES, SEAVIEW SCHOOL 08221
James Smith, prin.

Little Falls, Passaic Co., Pop. Code 7
Little Falls Twp. SD
Sch. Sys. Enr. Code 3
Supt. – James Nash, 36 STEVENS AVE 07424
Little Falls MS 1, STEVENS AVE 07424
Raymond Mead, prin.
ES 2, LONGHILL ROAD 07424
Ada Ruffolo, prin.

Our Lady Holy Angels ES, 467 MAIN ST 07424

Little Ferry, Bergen Co., Pop. Code 6
Little Ferry SD
Sch. Sys. Enr. Code 3
Supt. – Stacy Holmes, 123 LIBERTY ST 07643
Memorial MS, 130 LIBERTY ST 07643
Carmen Holster, prin.
Washington ES, 123 LIBERTY ST 07643
James Campbell, prin.

Little Silver, Monmouth Co., Pop. Code 3
Little Silver Borough SD
Sch. Sys. Enr. Code 3
Supt. – Thomas Gallagher
LITTLE SILVER POINT ROAD 07739
Markham Place MS, 99 MARKHAM PL 07739
Thomas McKelvey, prin.
Point Road ES
LITTLE SILVER POINT ROAD 07739
Dorothy Baldwin, prin.

Livingston, Essex Co., Pop. Code 8
Livingston SD
Sch. Sys. Enr. Code 5
Supt. – Robert Kish, 11 FOXCROFT DR 07039
Heritage MS, 20 FOXCROFT DRIVE 07039
Arthur Saliceti, prin.
Mt. Pleasant MS, 11 BROADLAWN DRIVE 07039
Johnert Rowley, prin.
Collins ES, 67 MARTIN RD 07039
Dr. Frank Whiting, prin.
Harrison ES, 148 N LIVINGSTON AVE 07039
Walter Motz, prin.
Hillside ES, BELMONT DR 07039
Dennis Monaghan, prin.
Mt. Pleasant ES, 11 BROADLAWN DR 07039
Ralph Celebre, prin.
Riker Hill ES, 31 BLACKSTONE DR 07039
Eunice Grippaldi, prin.

St. Philomena Academy
388 S LIVINGSTON AVE 07039

Lodi, Bergen Co., Pop. Code 7
Lodi SD
Sch. Sys. Enr. Code 4
Supt. – Rob Polisse 07644
Jefferson MS, FIRST ST 07644
Gary Carabin, prin.
Columbus ES, 370 WESTERVELT PL 07644
Philip Patire, prin.
Hilltop ES, 200 WOODSIDE AVE 07644
Richard Albanese, prin.
Washington ES, 310 MAIN ST 07644
Rose DeBiasio, prin.
Wilson ES, 80 UNION ST 07644
Linda Masullo, prin.

St. Francis DeSales ES
30 ST JOSEPH BLVD 07644
St. Joseph ES, 46 SPRING ST 07644

Long Branch, Monmouth Co., Pop. Code 8
Long Branch SD
Sch. Sys. Enr. Code 5
Supt. – Herbert Korey, 6 W END CT   07740
MS, 364 INDIANA AVE   07740
   Joseph Ferraina, prin.
Anastasia MS, 318 MORRIS AVE   07740
   Regina Gill, prin.
Conrow ES, 335 LONG BRANCH AVE   07740
   Kenneth Dunn, prin.
Elberon ES, 240 PARK AVE   07740
   Carmina Villa, prin.
Garfield MS, 192 GARFIELD AVE   07740
   Ronald Mantley, prin.
Gregory ES, 157 SEVENTH AVE   07740
   Dr. Donald Donofrio, prin.
West End MS, 132 W END AVE   07740
   Victor Burke, prin.

Holy Trinity ES, 375 EXCHANGE PL   07740

Long Valley, Morris Co., Pop. Code 4
Washington Twp. SD
Sch. Sys. Enr. Code 4
Supt. – B. Cucinella, 402 W MILL ROAD   07853
MS, 51 W MILL ROAD   07853 – Kevin Walsh, prin.
Flocktown Road ES, 90 FLOCKTOWN RD   07853
   W. Mabey, prin.
Kossmann ES, 90 FLOCKTOWN RD   07853
   Nancy Evans, prin.
Old Farmers Road ES
   51 OLD FARMERS RD   07853
   Robert Brennan, prin.

Lumberton, Burlington Co.
Lumberton Twp. SD
Sch. Sys. Enr. Code 3
Supt. – Cornellius McGlynn   08048
Walther ES, P O BOX 8   08048 – John Baily, prin.

Lyndhurst, Bergen Co., Pop. Code 7
Lyndhurst SD
Sch. Sys. Enr. Code 4
Supt. – G. Travisano, 281 RIDGE ROAD   07071
Lincoln MS, 281 RIDGE ROAD   07071
   Patricia Sabatino, prin.
Columbus ES, 640 LAKE AVE   07071
   Patricia Sabatino, prin.
Franklin ES, 360 STUYVESANT AVE   07071
   Carl DeGisi, prin.
Jefferson ES, 336 LAKE AVE   07071
   James Corino, prin.
Roosevelt ES, 530 STUYVESANT AVE   07071
   Joseph Sferruzza, prin.
Washington ES, 709 RIDGE RD   07071
   Timothy Geary, prin.

Sacred Heart ES, 620 VALLEY BROOK AVE   07071
St. Michael's ES, 624 PAGE AVE   07071

Mc Guire A F B, Burlington Co.
North Hanover Twp. SD
Sch. Sys. Enr. Code 4
Supt. – Clinton Miller, WEST SCOTT ST   08641
Challenger ES, SCHOOLHOUSE ROAD   08641
   Helena Kosoff, prin.
Columbia ES, SCHOOLHOUSE ROAD   08641
   Catherine Harris, prin.
Discovery PS, SCHOOLHOUSR ROAD   08641
   Ronald Russell, prin.
Other Schools – See Wrightstown

Madison, Morris Co., Pop. Code 7
Madison SD
Sch. Sys. Enr. Code 4
Supt. – Lawrence Feinsod
   359 WOODLAND ROAD   07940
JHS, 285 MAIN ST   07940 – Florence Senyk, prin.
Central Avenue ES, 51 CENTRAL AVE   07940
   William Hedrick, prin.
Kings Road ES, KINGS ROAD   07940
   Herbert Pennoyer, prin.
Sabatini ES, 359 WOODLAND RD   07940
   Dr. Robert Newhouse, prin.

St. Vincent Martyr ES
   26 GREEN VILLAGE RD   07940

Magnolia, Camden Co., Pop. Code 5
Magnolia Borough SD
Sch. Sys. Enr. Code 2
Supt. – Donald Falato
   420 WARWICK ROAD N   08049
ES, 420 WARWICK RD N   08049
   Donald Falato, prin.

Mahwah, Bergen Co., Pop. Code 7
Mahwah SD
Sch. Sys. Enr. Code 4
Supt. – Barrent Henry, RIDGE ROAD   07430
Ramapo Ridge MS, RIDGE ROAD   07430
   Don Duin, prin.
Kilmer MS, RIDGE RD   07430 – Judith Mabie, prin.
Perry ES, EAST RAMAPO AVE   07430
   Samuel Bishop, prin.
Ross ES, 20 MALCOLM RD   07430
   Ruth Spangler, prin.
Washington ES, RIDGE ROAD   07430
   Robert Brown, prin.

Immaculate Heart of Mary ES
   51 ISLAND RD   07430

Malaga, Gloucester Co.
Franklin Twp. SD
Supt. – See Franklinville

ES, ROUTE 47 & ROUTE 40   08328
   Thomas Griggs, prin.

Manahawkin, Ocean Co., Pop. Code 4
Stafford Twp. SD
Sch. Sys. Enr. Code 4
Supt. – Dr. George Connelly
   1000 MCKINLEY AVE   08050
Stafford ES, 250 N MAIN ST   08050
   John Sgombick, prin.
Stafford IS, 1000 MCKINLEY AVE   08050
   Dr. Stephen Swett, prin.

Manasquan, Monmouth Co., Pop. Code 6
Manasquan SD
Sch. Sys. Enr. Code 4
Supt. – Carole Morris, 142 BROAD ST   08736
ES, 142 BROAD ST   08736 – Liana Lang, prin.

St. Denis ES, 119 VIRGINIA AVE   08736

Mantua, Gloucester Co.
Mantua Twp. SD
Supt. – See Sewell
Centre City ES, LANSING DR   08051
   John Cattell, prin.
Tomlin ES, MAIN ST   08051
   Robert Preziosi, prin.

Manville, Somerset Co., Pop. Code 7
Manville Borough SD
Sch. Sys. Enr. Code 4
Supt. – Francis Heelan
   1100 BROOKS BLVD   08835
Batcho IS, 99 N 13TH AVE   08835
   Roderick Powell, prin.
Weston ES, 600 NEWARK AVE   08835
   Phyllis Anthony, prin.

Christ the King School, 99 N 13TH AVE   08835
Sacred Heart ES, 136 S MAIN ST   08835

Maple Shade, Burlington Co., Pop. Code 7
Maple Shade Twp. SD
Sch. Sys. Enr. Code 4
Supt. – John Sherry
   FREDERICK & CLINTON AVE   08052
ES 4, NORTH FORKLANDING ROAD   08052
   Dr. Charles Simpson, prin.
Steinhauer MS, N FELLOWSHIP RD   08052
   Betty Poley, prin.
Wilkins ES, MILL ROAD   08052
   Richard Didio, prin.

Our Lady Perpetual Help ES
   MAIN ST AND FELLOWSHIP   08052

Maplewood, Essex Co., Pop. Code 7
South Orange-Maplewood SD
Sch. Sys. Enr. Code 5
Supt. – Michael Ross, 525 ACADEMY ST   07040
MS, 7 BURNETT ST   07040 – Benard Ryan, prin.
Boyden ES, 274 BOYDEN AVE   07040
   Ruth Joseph, prin.
Clinton ES, 27 BERKSHIRE RD   07040
   Austin Byrne, prin.
Jefferson MS, 518 RIDGEWOOD RD   07040
   Marjorie Freeman, prin.
Tuscan ES, 25 HARVARD AVE   07040
   Dr. Arlene Pincus, prin.
Other Schools – See South Orange

Immaculate Heart Mary ES
   276 PARKER AVE   07040
St. Jospeh ES, 240 FRANKLIN AVE   07040

Margate City, Atlantic Co., Pop. Code 6
Margate City SD
Sch. Sys. Enr. Code 3
Supt. – Dominick Potena
   GRANVILLE & WINCHESTER AVES   08402
Tighe MS, ESSEX & AMHERST AVE   08402
   William Mosca, prin.
Union Avenue ES
   UNION & WINCHESTER AVE   08402
   Frederick Needham, prin.

Blessed Sacrament School
   14 N JEROME AVE   08402
Hebrew Academy Atlantic City
   601 N JEROME AVE   08402

Marlboro, Monmouth Co., Pop. Code 7
Marlboro Twp. SD
Sch. Sys. Enr. Code 5
Supt. – Frank DeFino
   1980 TOWNSHIP DRIVE   07746
MS, 109 ROUTE 520 E   07746
   Harvey Abramson, prin.
Central ES, ROUTE 79   07746
   Carole Swantek, prin.
Dugan ES, TOPANEMUS RD   07746
   Thomas Ellsworth, prin.
Holmes ES, TENNENT ROAD   07746
   Nancy Letteney, prin.
ES, 100 SCHOOL RD W   07746
   William Keers,Jr., prin.
Robertsville ES, TENNENT ROAD   07746
   Stephen Shifrinson, prin.

Marlton, Burlington Co., Pop. Code 7
Evesham Twp. SD
Sch. Sys. Enr. Code 5
Supt. – Leroy Meland, 26 S MAPLE AVE   08053
MS, 4 TOMLINSON MILL ROAD   08053
   Raymond Alioto, prin.

Beeler ES, RADNOR & CALDWELL AVE   08053
   Dr. Lawrence Passarella, prin.
Evans ES, ROUTE 73   08053
   Norman Allison, prin.
Jaggard ES, 2 WESCOTT RD   08053 – (—), prin.
Van Zant ES, 270 CONESTOGA DR   08053
   John Kloos, prin.

St. Joan of Arc ES, EVANS ROAD   08053

Marmora, Cape May Co.
Upper Twp. SD
Supt. – See Tuckahoe
Upper Twp. ES, 50 OLD TUCKAHOE RD   08223
   Raymond Cavanaugh, prin.

Matawan, Monmouth Co., Pop. Code 6
Matawan-Aberdeen Regional SD
Sch. Sys. Enr. Code 5
Supt. – Kenneth Hall, 203 BROAD ST   07747
Lloyd Road ES, 401 LLOYD ROAD   07747
   Martin Dempsey, prin.
Ravine Drive ES, 170 RAVINE DR   07747
   Sumner Clarke,Jr., prin.
Strathmore ES, 282 CHURCH ST   07747
   Phyllis Shore, prin.
Other Schools – See Cliffwood

Old Bridge Twp. SD
Sch. Sys. Enr. Code 6
Supt. – Patrick Torre, ROUTE 516   07747
Cheesequake ES, 80 HIGHWAY 34   07747
   Thomas Korshalla, prin.
Other Schools – See Cliffwood Beach, Laurence
   Harbor, Old Bridge, Parlin

Mays Landing, Atlantic Co., Pop. Code 4
Egg Harbor Twp. SD
Supt. – See Pleasantville
Scullville ES, RURAL ROUTE 01   08330
   Louis Dellabarca, prin.

Hamilton Twp. SD
Sch. Sys. Enr. Code 4
Supt. – Carl Scheetz
   220 N FARRAGUT AVE   08330
Davies MS, VIENNA AVE & RTE 40   08330
   Philip Zupa, prin.
Duberson MS, 2ND & FARRAGUT AVE   08330
   Phillip Zuba, prin.
Shaner Memorial ES
   THIRD ST & FARRAGUT AVE   08330
   Leonard Slota, prin.

St. Vincent DePaul ES, 101 MAIN ST E   08330

Maywood, Bergen Co., Pop. Code 6
Maywood SD
Sch. Sys. Enr. Code 3
Supt. – Dr. Frank Moran, 764 GRANT AVE   07607
Maywood Avenue MS
   452 MAYWOOD AVE   07607 – James Bogne, prin.
Memorial ES, 764 GRANT AVE   07607
   John Buffington, prin.

Our Lady Queen of Peace ES
   404 MAYWOOD AVE   07607

Medford, Burlington Co., Pop. Code 7
Medford Township SD
Sch. Sys. Enr. Code 5
Supt. – Patrick Johnson, STOKES ROAD   08055
Medford Twp. Memorial MS, MILL ST   08055
   Rob Elder, prin.
Allen ES, ALLEN AVE   08055
   Gordon Learn, prin.
Cranberry Pines ES, 400 FAIRVIEW RD   08055
   Raymond Bleiweiss, prin.
Haines ES, STOKES RD   08055 – Gail Hanley, prin.
Taunton Forge ES, EVERGREEN TRL   08055
   Steven Levine, prin.

St. Mary of Lakes ES, ROUTE 70   08055

Medford Lakes, Burlington Co., Pop. Code 5
Medford Lakes Borough SD
Sch. Sys. Enr. Code 3
Supt. – Timothy Wade, NEETA TRAIL   08055
Neeta ES, NEETA TRL   08055
   Ronald Starrett, prin.
Nokomis ES, NOKOMIS TRL   08055
   Ronald Starrett, prin.

Mendham, Morris Co., Pop. Code 5
Mendham Borough SD
Sch. Sys. Enr. Code 2
Supt. – Eugene Bradford
   12 HILLTOP ROAD   07945
Mountain View MS, 100 DEAN ROAD   07945
   Richard Shuck, prin.
Hilltop ES, 12 HILLTOP RD   07945
   Edith Von, prin.

St. Joseph ES, 8 W MAIN ST   07945

Merchantville, Camden Co., Pop. Code 5
Merchantville SD
Sch. Sys. Enr. Code 2
Supt. – Ernest Barlow,Jr., 130 S CENTER ST   08109
ES, 130 S CENTRE ST   08109
   Roseann Cialella, prin.

Pennsauken Twp. SD
Supt. – See Pennsauken
Fine ES, 3800 GLADWYN AVE   08109
   John Funston, prin.

Franklin ES, IRVING AND COOPER AVE 08109
  Virgil Johnson, prin.
Roosevelt ES, 5526 WISTERIA AVE 08109
  John Funston, prin.

Metuchen, Middlesex Co., Pop. Code 7
Metuchen SD
Sch. Sys. Enr. Code 4
Supt. – Gennaro Lepre
  596 MIDDLESEX AVE 08840
Campbell ES, DURHAN AVE 08840
  Mark Heinze, prin.
Edgar ES, BRUNSWICK AVE 08840
  Edward Joyce, prin.
Moss ES, SIMPSON PL 08840 – Fred Cohen, prin.

Woodbridge Twp. SD
Supt. – See Woodbridge
Menlo Park Terrace ES
  MARYKNOLL ROAD 08840 – James Smelas, prin.

St. Francis Catholic ES, 528 MAIN ST 08840

Mickleton, Gloucester Co.
East Greenwich Twp. SD
Sch. Sys. Enr. Code 3
Supt. – Joseph Conroy, 7 QUAKER ROAD 08056
East Greenwich Twp. MS, 7 QUAKER RD 08056
  Douglas Villanova, prin.
ES, 535 KINGS HWY 08056
  Douglas Villanova, prin.
Other Schools – See Mount Royal

Middlesex, Middlesex Co., Pop. Code 7
Middlesex Borough SD
Sch. Sys. Enr. Code 4
Supt. – Ron Campbell, 50 KENNEDY DR 08846
Mauger MS, FISHER AVE 08846
  Thomas Grifa, prin.
Hazelwood ES, 800 HAZELWOOD AVE 08846
  Elvin Van, prin.
Parker ES, 150 S LINCOLN AVE 08846
  Dr. Phillip Sidotti, prin.
Watchung ES, FISHER AVE 08846
  Robert Conway, prin.

Our Lady of Mt. Virgin ES, DRAKE AVE 08846

Middletown, Monmouth Co., Pop. Code 8
Middletown Twp. SD
Sch. Sys. Enr. Code 7
Supt. – Guy Sconzo, 59 TINDALL ROAD 07748
Thompson MS
  1001 MIDDLETOWN-LINCROFT RD 07748
  Patrick Houston, prin.
Middletown Village ES, 145 KINGS HWY 07748
  Richard Stepura, prin.
New Monmouth ES
  121 NEW MONMOUTH RD 07748
  Lawson Hatfield, prin.
Nut Swamp ES
  MIDDLETOWN-LINCROFT ROAD 07748
  Frank Lineberry, prin.
Other Schools – See Belford, East Keansburg,
  Leonardo, Lincroft, Navesink, New Monmouth, Port
  Monmouth, Red Bank

St. Mary ES/New Monmouth
  538 CHURCH ST 07748

Midland Park, Bergen Co., Pop. Code 6
Midland Park SD
Sch. Sys. Enr. Code 4
Supt. – Roger McEnnis, 31 HIGHLAND AVE 07432
Highland Avenue ES, 31 HIGHLAND AVE 07432
  Frederick Triano,Jr., prin.

Midland Park Christian ES, 25 BALDIN DR 07432
Nativity ES, 321 PROSPECT ST 07432

Milford, Hunterdon Co., Pop. Code 4
Holland Twp. SD
Sch. Sys. Enr. Code 3
Supt. – Robert Soprano
  RURAL ROUTE 04 BOX 167 08848
Holland Twp. ES
  RURAL ROUTE 04 BOX 168 08848
  Gerald Moninghoff, prin.

Milford Borough SD
Sch. Sys. Enr. Code 2
Supt. – Dr. Carol Stevenson, P O BOX 223 08848
Milford Boro ES
  RURAL ROUTE 04 BOX 223 08848
  Joseph Dockry, prin.

Millburn, Essex Co., Pop. Code 7
Millburn Twp. SD
Sch. Sys. Enr. Code 4
Supt. – Paul Rossey, 434 MILLBURN AVE 07041
Wyoming ES, MYRTLE AVE & PINE ST 07041
  Martin Burne, prin.
Other Schools – See Short Hills

Millington, Morris Co., Pop. Code 4
Passaic Twp. SD
Supt. – See Stirling
ES, 91 NORTHFIELD RD 07946
  Robert Mosey, prin.

Milltown, Middlesex Co., Pop. Code 6
Milltown SD
Sch. Sys. Enr. Code 3
Supt. – Patrick Wilder, 134 N MAIN ST 08850
Kilmer MS, W CHURCH ST 08850
  Bertram Nussbaum, prin.

Parkview ES, VIOLET TER 08850
  Lawrence Paul, prin.

Our Lady Lourdes ES, 44 CLEVELAND AVE 08850

Millville, Cumberland Co., Pop. Code 7
Millville SD
Sch. Sys. Enr. Code 6
Supt. – Gene Stanley, P O BOX 1278 08332
Bacon ES, SOUTH 3RD ST 08332
  Roger Simpkins, prin.
Culver ES, 110 N 3RD ST 08332
  J. Miskelly, prin.
Holly Heights ES, 2509 E MAIN ST 08332
  Gary Stanker, prin.
Mt. Pleasant ES, 100 CARMEL RD 08332
  Jennifer Lookabaugh, prin.
Rieck Avenue ES, 339 RIECK AVE 08332
  Gus Garton, prin.
Wood ES, 700 ARCHER ST 08332
  Greg Merritt, prin.

St. Mary Magdalen ES, 7 W POWELL ST 08332

Mine Hill, Morris Co., Pop. Code 5
Mine Hill Twp. SD
Supt. – See Dover
Canfield Avenue ES, 42 CANFIELD AVE 07801
  Dr. Ronald Armengol, prin.

Minotola, Atlantic Co.
Buena Regional SD
Supt. – See Buena
Cleary MS, 1309 CENTRAL AVE 08341
  Joseph Capizola, prin.

Monmouth Beach, Monmouth Co., Pop. Code 5
Monmouth Beach SD
Sch. Sys. Enr. Code 2
Supt. – Joseph Persiponko
  HASTINGS PLACE 07750
ES, HASTINGS PL 07750
  Joseph Persiponko, prin.

Monmouth Junction, Middlesex Co., Pop. Code 3
South Brunswick Twp. SD
Sch. Sys. Enr. Code 5
Supt. – James Kimple, 4 EXECUTIVE DR 08852
Crossroads MS, GEORGES ROAD 08852
  Frederick Nadler, prin.
Deans ES, GEORGES ROAD 08852
  Martin Bernstein, prin.
ES, RIDGE ROAD 08852 – Nathan Levy, prin.
Other Schools – See Dayton, Kendall Park

Monroeville, Salem Co.
Upper Pittsgrove Twp. SD
Sch. Sys. Enr. Code 2
Supt. – William Randazzo
  RURAL ROUTE 02 BOX 63 08343
Upper Pittsgrove MS
  RURAL ROUTE 02 BOX 63 08343
  William Randazzo, prin.
MS, MAIN ST 08343 – Joann Mathers, prin.
Other Schools – See Elmer

Montague, Sussex Co.
Montague SD
Sch. Sys. Enr. Code 2
Supt. – Dr. Charles Lusto
  RURAL ROUTE 05 BOX 571 07827
Montague Twp. ES
  RURAL ROUTE 05 BOX 571 07827
  Dr. Charles Lusto, prin.

Montclair, Essex Co., Pop. Code 8
Montclair SD
Sch. Sys. Enr. Code 6
Supt. – Mary Lee Fitzgerald
  22 VALLEY ROAD 07042
Glenfield MS, 25 MAPLE AVE 07042
  Janet Tunstall, prin.
Mt. Hebron MS, 173 BELLEVUE AVE 07043
  Agnes Bulmer, prin.
Bradford ES, 87 MOUNT HEBRON RD 07043
  Loren James, prin.
Edgemont ES, 20 EDGEMONT RD 07042
  Stephen Rowe, prin.
Hillside MS, 54 ORANGE RD 07042
  Robert Rosado, prin.
Nishuane ES, 32 CEDAR AVE 07042
  Sandra Brown, prin.
Northeast ES, 603 GROVE ST 07043
  David Gidich, prin.
Watchung ES, 14 GARDEN ST 07042
  Barbara Strobert, prin.

Montclair-Kimberley Academy
  LLOYD ROAD 07042
Immaculate Conception ES
  17-19 MUNN STREET 07042
La Cordaire ES, 155 LORRAINE AVE 07043
St. Cassian ES, 190 LORRAINE AVE 07043

Montvale, Bergen Co., Pop. Code 6
Montvale SD
Sch. Sys. Enr. Code 3
Supt. – Richard Rice
  47 SPRING VALLEY ROAD 07645
Fieldstone MS, 47 SPRING VALLEY ROAD 07645
  Roy Montesano, prin.
Memorial ES, 53 W GRAND AVE 07645
  Allen Luster, prin.

Montville, Morris Co., Pop. Code 7
Montville Twp. SD
Supt. – See Pine Brook
Lazar MS, 123 CHANGEBRIDGE ROAD 07045
  Mario Cardinale, prin.
Mason ES, 5 SHAWNEE TRL 07045
  Marianne DiSpenziere, prin.

St. Pius X ES, 24 CHANGE BRIDGE ROAD 07045

Moonachie, Bergen Co., Pop. Code 5
Moonachie SD
Sch. Sys. Enr. Code 2
Supt. – Francis Raftery, 20 WEST PARK ST 07074
Other Schools – See Rutherford

Moorestown, Burlington Co., Pop. Code 7
Moorestown Twp. SD
Sch. Sys. Enr. Code 4
Supt. – Vito Germinario
  N STANWICK ROAD 08057
Allen MS, STANWICK ROAD 08057
  (—), prin.
Baker ES, NORTH STANWICK ROAD 08057
  Dr. Richard Bucko, prin.
Roberts ES, NORTH STANWICK ROAD 08057
  Paul Braungart, prin.
South Valley ES
  SOUTH STANWICK ROAD 08057
  Violet Thompson, prin.

Moorestown Friends School, PAGE LANE 08057
Our Lady Good Counsel ES, PROSPECT ST 08057

Morris Plains, Morris Co., Pop. Code 6
Hanover Twp. SD
Supt. – See Cedar Knolls
Mountview Road ES, 25 MOUNTVIEW RD 07950
  Dr. Joann Hino, prin.

Morris Plains SD
Sch. Sys. Enr. Code 3
Supt. – Thomas Jones
  500 SPEEDWELL AVE 07950
Borough MS, 500 SPEEDWELL AVE 07950
  Ed Paone, prin.
Community Park ES, 10 JIM FEAR DR 07950
  Edward Hade, prin.
Mountain Way ES, 205 MOUNTAIN WAY 07950
  Edward Hade, prin.

Parsippany-Troy Hills Twp. SD
Supt. – See Parsippany
Littleton ES, BROOKLAWN DR 07950
  Leo Murphy, prin.

St. Virgil ES, 238 SPEEDWELL AVE 07950

Morristown, Morris Co., Pop. Code 7
Morris SD
Sch. Sys. Enr. Code 5
Supt. – William McIvor
  27 NORMANDY PARKWAY 07960
Frelinghuysen MS, 200 W HANOVER AVE 07960
  William Wenrich, prin.
Hamilton MS, 24 MILLS ST 07960
  Anita Barber, prin.
Hillcrest ES, 160 HILLCREST AVE 07960
  Reginald Smith, prin.
Jefferson MS, JAMES ST 07960
  Robert Floyd, prin.
Sussex Avenue MS, SUSSEX AVE 07960
  Larry Koch, prin.
Vail ES, 125 SPEEDWELL AVE 07960
  Arlene Grafstein, prin.
Woodland Avenue ES, 51 JOHNSTON DR 07960
  Elizabeth Morrison, prin.

Assumption of the BVM School
  63 MACCULLOCH AVE 07960
Peck ES, 247 SOUTH ST 07960
St. Margaret ES, 10 COLUMBA ST 07960

Mountain Lakes, Morris Co., Pop. Code 5
Mountain Lakes SD
Sch. Sys. Enr. Code 4
Supt. – Douglas Lyons, 400 BOULEVARD 07046
Briarcliff MS, 93 BRIARCLIFF ROAD 07046
  James Bagli, prin.
Wildwood ES, GLEN ROAD 07046
  Peter Fland, prin.

Wilson School, 271 BLVD 07046

Mountainside, Westfield Co., Pop. Code 6
Mountainside SD
Sch. Sys. Enr. Code 2
Supt. – Leonard Baccaro, 1391 ROUTE 22 07092
Deerfield ES
  SCHOOL DR & CENTRAL AVE 07092
  James Johnson, prin.

Vail Deane School, WOODACRES DRIVE 07092
Our Lady Lourdes ES, 304 CENTRAL AVE 07092

Mount Arlington, Morris Co., Pop. Code 5
Mt. Arlington SD
Sch. Sys. Enr. Code 2
Supt. – John McIntyre, 235 HOWARD BLVD 07856
MS, 235 HOWARD BLVD 07856
  William Desmond, prin.
Decker ES, HOWARD BLVD 07856
  William Desmond, prin.

Our Lady of the Lake ES, 9 ROONEY RD 07856

Mount Ephraim, Camden Co., Pop. Code 5
Mt. Ephraim Borough SD
Sch. Sys. Enr. Code 2
Supt. – Richard Serfling
121 BLACK HORSE PIKE 08059
Kershaw MS, S BLACK HORSE PIKE 08059
Richard Serfling, prin.
Bray ES, BLACK HORSE PIKE 08059
Richard Serfling, prin.

Sacred Heart ES, 12 W BUCKINGHAM AVE 08059

Mount Holly, Burlington Co., Pop. Code 7
Eastampton Twp. SD
Sch. Sys. Enr. Code 2
Supt. – John Holcroft, RURAL ROUTE 01 08060
Eastampton MS, RURAL ROUTE 01 08060
John Holcroft, prin.
Eastampton ES, N PEMBERTON RD 08060
Peter Granaldi, prin.

Mt. Holly Twp. SD
Sch. Sys. Enr. Code 4
Supt. – John Mengel, 301 LEVIS DRIVE 08060
Holbein MS, 301 LEVIS DRIVE 08060
Karl Mehl, prin.
Brainerd ES, WOLLNER DR 08060
Carole Street, prin.
Folwell ES, JACKONVILLE ROAD 08060
Lawrence Donahue, prin.

Westampton Twp. SD
Sch. Sys. Enr. Code 3
Supt. – Dan Martin, RURAL ROUTE 01 08060
Westampton MS, RURAL ROUTE 01 08060
D. Harris, prin.
Holly Hills ES, OGDEN & LAMBERT DRS 08060
John Azzatori, prin.

Sacred Heart ES, 250 HIGH ST 08060

Mount Laurel, Burlington Co., Pop. Code 7
Mt. Laurel Twp. SD
Sch. Sys. Enr. Code 5
Supt. – James Anzide
100 MOUNT LAUREL ROAD 08054
Harrington MS
514 MOUNT LAUREL ROAD 08054
James Waskovich, prin.
Countryside ES, SCHOOLHOUSE LN 08054
Hattie Green, prin.
Fleetwood ES, FLEETWOOD AVE 08054
Charles Scheels, prin.
Hillside ES, RURAL ROUTE 01 08054
Michael Zorfass, prin.
Parkway ES, RAMBLEWOOD PKWY 08054
Kenneth Ruhland, prin.

Mount Royal, Gloucester Co.
East Greenwich Twp. SD
Supt. – See Mickleton
ES, 19 MANTUA RD 08061 – John Crumley, prin.

Mullica Hill, Gloucester Co., Pop. Code 2
Harrison Twp. SD
Sch. Sys. Enr. Code 2
Supt. – Thomas Summerill,Jr., ROUTE 45 08062
Harrison Twp. ES, ROUTE 45 08062
David Datz, prin.

Friends School, P O BOX 162 08062

National Park, Gloucester Co., Pop. Code 5
National Park Borough SD
Sch. Sys. Enr. Code 2
Supt. – Peter Oteri, 516 LAKEHURST AVE 08063
ES, 516 LAKEHURST AVE 08063
Raymond Bider, prin.

Navesink, Monmouth Co., Pop. Code 4
Middletown Twp. SD
Supt. – See Middletown
ES, MONMOUTH AVE 07752
Christopher Halpin, prin.

Neptune, Monmouth Co., Pop. Code 8
Neptune Twp. SD
Sch. Sys. Enr. Code 5
Supt. – (—), 2106 W BANGS AVE 07753
Gables ES, 220 BLACKWELL WAY 07753
Thomas Marshall, prin.
Green Grove ES, 909 GREEN GROVE RD 07753
Walter Bird, prin.
Ridge Avenue MS, RIDGE & HECK AVES 07753
Raymond Kuzava, prin.
Shark River Hills ES, 320 BRIGHTON AVE 07753
Henry Forest, prin.
Summerfield ES, 527 GREEN GROVE RD 07753
Joseph Santanello, prin.
Other Schools – See Ocean Grove

Holy Innocents ES
W BANGS AVE - HWY 33 07753

Neptune City, Monmouth Co., Pop. Code 6
Neptune CSD
Sch. Sys. Enr. Code 2
Supt. – Joseph Polinski
210 W SYLVANIA AVE 07753
Wilson ES, 210 W SYLVANIA AVE 07753
Robert Shafer II, prin.

Neshanic Station, Somerset Co.
Hillsborough Twp. SD
Supt. – See Belle Mead
Woodfern ES, WOODFERN ROAD 08853
Joseph Thompson, prin.

Netcong, Morris Co., Pop. Code 5
Netcong SD
Sch. Sys. Enr. Code 2
Supt. – Vincent Togno, 26 COLLEGE ROAD 07857
ES, 26 COLLEGE RD 07857
Leonard Goduto, prin.

St. Michael ES, 10 CHURCH ST 07857

Newark, Essex Co., Pop. Code 10
Newark SD
Sch. Sys. Enr. Code 8
Supt. – Eugene Campbell, 2 CEDAR ST 07102
Bergen Street MS, 695 BERGEN ST 07108
Frank Walters, prin.
Camden MS, 321 BERGEN ST 07103
Anzela Nelms, prin.
Chancellor Avenue MS
321 CHANCELLOR AVE 07112
Geneva Wardell, prin.
Maple Avenue MS, 33 MAPLE AVE 07112
Arthur Marano, prin.
Vailsburg MS, 31 13TH AVE 07103
(—), prin.
Abington Avenue ES, 209 ABINGTON AVE 07107
Walter Afflitto, prin.
Alexander Street ES, 43 ALEXANDER ST 07106
Arthur Hooper, prin.
Ann Street ES, 30 ANN ST 07105
Joseph Maccia, prin.
Avon Avenue ES, 219 AVON AVE 07108
Lillian Gibson, prin.
Belmont Runyon ES, 68 W RUNYON ST 07108
Roger Watson, prin.
Bragaw Avenue ES, 103 BRAGAW AVE 07112
Martha Washington, prin.
Broadway ES, 108 ORATON ST 07104
Gerald Samuels, prin.
Burnet Street ES, 28 BURNET ST 07102
James Malone, prin.
Camden Street ES, 299 CAMDEN ST 07103
Esther Elliott, prin.
Carver ES, 333 CLINTON PL 07112
June Lockett, prin.
Chancllr Avenue Annex ES
255 CHANCELLOR AVE 07112
Harold Jones, prin.
Clemente ES Mt. Pleasant
2 MT PLEASANT AVE 07104
Harry Morsch, prin.
Clemente ES, 257 SUMMER AVE 07104
Fidiberto Soto, prin.
Cleveland ES, 388 BERGEN ST 07103
Juanita Robinson, prin.
Clinton Avenue ES, 534 CLINTON AVE 07108
Zelma Collins, prin.
Dayton Street ES, 226 DAYTON ST 07114
Joseph Parlevecchio, prin.
Eighteenth Avenue ES, 229 18TH AVE 07108
Willie Young, prin.
Elliott Street ES, 721 SUMMER AVE 07104
Jorge Almedo, prin.
Fifteenth Avenue ES, 557 15TH AVE 07103
Wallace Green, prin.
First Avenue ES, 284 1ST AVE W 07107
Caesar Casale, prin.
Flagg ES, 150 3RD ST 07107 – Muriel Lovell, prin.
Fourteenth Avenue ES, 186 14TH AVE 07103
John Hansen, prin.
Franklin ES, 42 PARK AVE 07104
Benigno Santiago, prin.
Hawkins Street ES, 8 HAWKINS ST 07105
Albert Williams, prin.
Hawthorne Avenue ES
428 HAWTHORNE AVE 07112
Milton Zucker, prin.
Horton ES, 291 N 7TH ST 07107
Charles Simmons, prin.
King ES, 108 S 9TH ST 07107
Ernest Thompson, prin.
Lafayette Street Annex ES
212 LAFAYETTE ST 07105
Matthew Russomanno, prin.
Lafayette Street ES, 205 LAFAYETTE ST 07105
Matthew Russomanno, prin.
Lincoln ES, 87 RICHELIEU TER 07106
Ann Kagdis, prin.
Madison ES, 823 S 16TH ST 07108
Leroy Dasher, prin.
Maple Avenue Annex ES, 200 LYONS AVE 07112
James Fredericks, prin.
McKinley ES, 1 COLONNADE PL 07104
Louis Giordano, prin.
Miller Street ES, 47 MILLER ST 07114
Alice Dunston, prin.
Morton Street ES, 75 MORTON ST 07103
Moses Cobb, prin.
Mt. Vernon ES, 142 MT VERNON PL 07106
Gladys Jones, prin.
Newton Street ES, 150 NEWTON ST 07103
Willie Thomas, prin.
Oliver Street ES, 104 OLIVER ST 07105
Anthony Savoca, prin.
Peshine Avenue ES, 433 PESHINE AVE 07112
James Vasselli, prin.
Quitman Street ES, 21 QUITMAN ST 07103
Norman Dultz, prin.
Ridge Street Annex ES
381 WOODSIDE AVE 07104
Howard Caesar, prin.
Ridge Street ES, 735 RIDGE ST 07104
Howard Caesar, prin.
Roseville Avenue ES, 70 ROSEVILLE AVE 07103
Hattie Black, prin.

South Seventeenth Street ES
619 S 17TH ST 07103 – Lester Fusco, prin.
South Street ES, 151 SOUTH ST 07114
Leonor Outor, prin.
Speedway Avenue ES, 26 SPEEDWAY AVE 07106
Daniel Portella, prin.
Spencer ES, 66 MUHAMMAD ALI AVE 07108
Maude Patterson, prin.
Sussex Avenue Annex ES
310 SUSSEX AVE 07107 – Herbert Johnson, prin.
Sussex Avenue ES, 307 SUSSEX AVE 07107
Herbert Johnson, prin.
Thirteenth Avenue ES, 359 13TH AVE 07103
Bert Berry, prin.
Tubman ES, 504 S 10TH AVE 07103
Noah Marshall, prin.
Warren Street ES, 212 WARREN ST 07103
Blanche Bishop, prin.
Wilson Avenue ES, 19 WILSON AVE 07105
Robert D'Amico, prin.

Project Link Education Center
146 IRVINE TURNER BLVD 07103
Blessed Sacrament School
CLINTON AVENUE AND VAN NESS 07108
Ironbound ES, 142 JEFFERSON ST 07105
Our Lady Good Counsel ES
239 WOODSIDE AVE 07104
Queen Angels ES
44 IRVINE TURNER BLVD 07103
Sacred Heart ES, 24 HAZELWOOD AVE 07106
St. Ann ES, 370 S 7TH ST 07103
St. Benedict ES
KOMORN & NIAGARA STS 07105
St. Casimir ES, 366 E KINNEY ST 07105
St. Columba ES, 25 PENNSYLVANIA AVE 07114
St. Francis Xavier ES, 594 N 7TH ST 07107
St. John Baptist ES, 745 SANFORD AVE 07106
St. Lucy ES, 12 AMITY PL 07104
St. Mary ES, 520 HIGH ST 07102
St. Michael School, 182 BROADWAY 07104
St. Rocco ES, 21 ASHLAND ST 07103
St. Rose of Lima ES, 540 ORANGE ST 07107

New Brunswick, Middlesex Co., Pop. Code 8
New Brunswick SD
Sch. Sys. Enr. Code 5
Supt. – Ron Larkin, 24 BAYARD ST 08901
Lincoln ES, 66 BARTLETT ST 08901
Joseph Homoki, prin.
Livingston ES, 206 DELAVAN ST 08901
Fred Perone, prin.
McKinley ES, 35 VAN DYKE AVE 08901
Joyce McGee, prin.
Redshaw ES, 216 LIVINGSTON AVE 08901
Lawrence Falzone, prin.
Robeson Community ES
199 COMMERICAL AVE 08901
Maurice Williams, prin.
Roosevelt ES, 83 LIVINGSTON AVE 08901
George Buono, prin.
Stirling ES, 43 CARMAN ST 08901
Ronald Payne, prin.
Wilson ES, 133 TUNISON RD 08901
Robert Boyler, prin.

North Brunswick SD
Supt. – See North Brunswick
Adams ES, REDMOND ST 08902
Sylvester Paladino, prin.
Judd ES, ROOSEVELT AVE 08902
Charles King, prin.
Livinston Park ES
RIDGEWOOD & LIVINGSTON AVES 08902
Andrew Costello, prin.
Parsons ES, 899 HOLLYWOOD ST 08902
Patrick Neary, prin.

St. Ladislaus ES, 40 PLUM ST 08901
St. Mary Mt. Virgin ES, 192 SANDFORD ST 08901
St. Peter ES, 165 SOMERSET ST 08901

New Egypt, Ocean Co.
Plumsted Twp. SD
Sch. Sys. Enr. Code 3
Supt. – Gerald Woehr, 44 N MAIN ST 08533
ES, 44 N MAIN ST 08533 – Joanne Stolte, prin.

Newfield, Gloucester Co., Pop. Code 4
Franklin Twp. SD
Supt. – See Franklinville
Lake ES, LAKE ROAD 08344
Thomas Griggs, prin.
Main Road MS
MAIN ROAD & HARDING HWY 08344
Robert Weigelt, prin.

Newfield SD
Sch. Sys. Enr. Code 2
Supt. – Marie Grochowski
CATAWBA & MADISON AVES 08344
Edgarton Memorial ES
CATAWBA & MADISON AVES 08063
Marie Grochowski, prin.

St. Rose of Lima ES, CHURCH STREET 08344

New Gretna, Burlington Co.
Bass River Twp. SD
Sch. Sys. Enr. Code 2
Supt. – Lawrence DeFeo, P O BOX 75 08224
Bass River Twp. ES, P O BOX 304 08224
Dr. Lawrence DeFeo, prin.

New Milford, Bergen Co., Pop. Code 7
New Milford SD
Sch. Sys. Enr. Code 4
Supt. – Mario Volpe, 8 RIVER ROAD   07646
Berkley Street ES, 800 BERKLEY ST   07646
    Robert Piela, prin.
Gibbs ES, SUTTON PL   07646
    Thomas Hoban, prin.
MS, ROSLYN AVE   07646 – Rob Seifert, prin.

Ascension ES, 1092 CARNATION DR   07646

New Monmouth, Middlesex Co.
Middletown Twp. SD
Supt. -- See Middletown
Harmony ES
    HARMONY & MURPHY ROADS   07748
    John Deignan, prin.

Newport, Cumberland Co.
Downe Twp. SD
Sch. Sys. Enr. Code 2
Supt. – Joseph Webb, ROUTE 553   08345
Downe Twp. MS, ROUTE 553   08345
    Mary Eber, prin.
Other Schools – See Dividing Creek

New Providence, Union Co., Pop. Code 7
New Providence SD
Sch. Sys. Enr. Code 4
Supt. – Robert Lachenauer
    340 CENTRAL AVE   07974
Roberts ES, 80 JONES DR   07974
    Edward Schmidt, prin.
Salt Brook ES, 40 MAPLE ST   07974
    Edward Rolek, prin.

Our Lady of Peace ES, 99 SOUTH ST   07974

Newton, Sussex Co., Pop. Code 6
Andover Regional SD
Sch. Sys. Enr. Code 3
Supt. – Ed Oskamp
    RURAL ROUTE 01 BOX 40   07860
Burd MS, 219 NEWTON SPARTA ROAD   07860
    Joe Aidala, prin.
Long Pond ES, RURAL ROUTE 01 BOX 40   07860
    Carolyn Spurlock, prin.

Fredon Twp. SD
Sch. Sys. Enr. Code 2
Supt. – Richard Walter
    RURAL ROUTE 02 BOX 212   07860
Fredon Twp. ES
    RURAL ROUTE 02 BOX 212   07860
    Richard Walter, prin.

Frelinghuysen Twp. SD
Sch. Sys. Enr. Code 2
Supt. – William King
    RURAL ROUTE 07 BOX 610   07860
Frelinghuysen Twp. ES, P O BOX 610   07860
    William King, prin.

Hampton Twp. SD
Sch. Sys. Enr. Code 2
Supt. – Michael Chirichello
    RURAL ROUTE 04 BOX 192   07860
McKeown ES, RURAL ROUTE 04 BOX 192   07860
    Michael Chirichello, prin.

Newton SD
Sch. Sys. Enr. Code 4
Supt. – Harry Selover, 57 TRINITY ST   07860
Halsted Street MS, HALSTED ST   07860
    John Hannum, prin.
Merriam Avenue ES, 81 MERRIAM AVE   07860
    Roberta Watson, prin.

St. Joseph Regional ES
    JEFFERSON STREET   07860

New Vernon, Morris Co.
Harding Twp. SD
Sch. Sys. Enr. Code 2
Supt. – Dr. Carol Conger, P O BOX 248   07976
Harding Twp. ES, P O BOX 248   07976
    Peter Eisele, prin.

Norma, Salem Co.
Pittsgrove Twp. SD
Supt. – See Elmer
ES, GERSHAL AVE   08347
    Dr. Audrey Pettijohn, prin.

North Arlington, Bergen Co., Pop. Code 7
North Arlington SD
Sch. Sys. Enr. Code 4
Supt. – Anthony Blanco, 222 RIDGE ROAD   07032
Jefferson ES, 100 PROSPECT AVE   07032
    Jerilyn Caprio, prin.
Roosevelt ES, 43 WEBSTER ST   07032
    John Delaney, prin.
Washington ES, HIGH & BELTMORE ST   07032
    Claire Greene, prin.
Wilson ES, 44 ARGYLE PL   07032
    David Klein, prin.

North Bergen, Hudson Co., Pop. Code 8
North Bergen SD
Sch. Sys. Enr. Code 5
Supt. – Leo Gattoni, 7317 KENNEDY BLVD   07047
Franklin ES 3, 522 COLUMBIA AVE   07047
    Thomas Muir, prin.
Fulton ES 2, 7407 HUDSON AVE   07047
    Patrick Capotorto, prin.

Kennedy ES 7, 1210 11TH ST   07047
    Paschal Tennaro, prin.
Lincoln ES 5, 1206 63RD ST   07047
    Nicholas Sacco, prin.
Mann ES 9, 1215 83RD ST   07047
    Peter Clark, prin.
McKinley ES 10, 3110 LIBERTY AVE   07047
    Albert Matash, prin.

Sacred Heart ES, 9034 BARR PL   07047
St. John Neponucene ES, 7115 POLK ST   07047

North Brunswick, Middlesex Co., Pop. Code 7
North Brunswick SD
Sch. Sys. Enr. Code 5
Supt. – Ed Leppert, P O BOX 1807   08902
Linwood MS, LINWOOD PLACE   08902
    Vito D'Eufemia, prin.
Other Schools – See New Brunswick

North Caldwell, Essex Co., Pop. Code 6
North Caldwell SD
Sch. Sys. Enr. Code 2
Supt. – Dr. Sharon Clover
    35 HAMILTON DRIVE E   07006
Gould MS, HAMILTON DR EAST   07006
    John Venezia, prin.
Other Schools – See Caldwell

Northfield, Atlantic Co., Pop. Code 6
Northfield CSD
Sch. Sys. Enr. Code 3
Supt. – Don Adams, W MILL ROAD   08225
Mill Road MS, W MILL ROAD   08225
    Cliff Nusbaum, prin.
Kresge ES, OAK AVE   08225 – Gloria Mako, prin.
Mt. Vernon Avenue ES
    MOUNT VERNON AVE   08225
    Gloria Mako, prin.

North Haledon, Passaic Co., Pop. Code 6
North Haledon SD
Sch. Sys. Enr. Code 3
Supt. – Emalene Renna
    515 HIGH MOUNTAIN ROAD   07508
High Mountain MS
    515 HIGH MOUNTAIN ROAD   07508
    Emalene Renna, prin.
Memorial ES, 670 HIGH MOUNTAIN RD   07508
    Charles Ferraro, prin.

North Plainfield, Somerset Co., Pop. Code 7
North Plainfield SD
Sch. Sys. Enr. Code 4
Supt. – Frank Herting, 33 MOUNTAIN AVE   07060
East End ES, 170 ONEIDA AVE   07060
    Robert Axmann, prin.
Somerset ES, 303 SOMERSET ST   07060
    Mary Bair, prin.
Stony Brook ES, 269 GROVE ST   07060
    Mary Bair, prin.
West End ES, 447 GREEN BROOK ROAD   07063
    Peter Fagone, prin.

Northvale, Bergen Co., Pop. Code 6
Northvale SD
Sch. Sys. Enr. Code 2
Supt. – Robert McGuire
    441 TAPPAN ROAD   07647
Hale MS, PARIS AVE   07647
    Sheldon Levine, prin.
Jefferson ES, TAPPAN ROAD   07647
    Dr. Sheldon Levine, prin.

North Wildwood, Cape May Co., Pop. Code 5
North Wildwood CSD
Sch. Sys. Enr. Code 2
Supt. – Richard Veit
    13TH & ATLANTIC AVES   08260
Mace ES, 1201 ATLANTIC AVE   08260
    Richard Veit, prin.

Norwood, Bergen Co., Pop. Code 5
Norwood SD
Sch. Sys. Enr. Code 3
Supt. – Andrew Rose, 177 SUMMIT ST   07648
ES, 177 SUMMIT ST   07648
    Naomi Jankowski, prin.

Immaculate Conception School
    200 SUMMIT ST   07648

Nutley, Essex Co., Pop. Code 1
Nutley SD
Sch. Sys. Enr. Code 5
Supt. – James Fadule
    369 BLOOMFIELD AVE   07110
Franklin MS, 325 FRANKLIN AVE   07110
    Paul Primamore, prin.
Lincoln ES, 301 HARRISON ST   07110
    Alex Conrad, prin.
Radcliffe ES, 379 BLOOMFIELD AVE   07110
    Kathleen Serafino, prin.
Spring Garden ES
    59 S SPRING GARDEN AVE   07110
    Anthony Stivala, prin.
Washington ES, 155 WASHINGTON AVE   07110
    Rosemarie DiGeronimo, prin.
Yantacaw ES, 20 YANTACAW PL   07110
    John Walker, prin.

Holy Family ES, 25 BROOKLINE AVE   07110
St. Mary ES, 16 MONSIGNOR OWENS PL   07110

Oakhurst, Monmouth Co., Pop. Code 5
Ocean Twp. SD
Sch. Sys. Enr. Code 5
Supt. – Robert Mahon
    163 MONMOUTH ROAD   07755
Ocean Twp. ES, DOW AVE   07755
    Barbara Villapiano, prin.
Other Schools – See Asbury Park, Ocean

Oakland, Bergen Co., Pop. Code 7
Oakland SD
Sch. Sys. Enr. Code 4
Supt. – Lawrence Ksanznak
    315 RAMAPO VALLEY ROAD   07436
Valley MS, 71 OAK ST   07436
    Richard Heflich, prin.
Dogwood Hill ES, 25 DOGWOOD DR   07436
    Eugene Cassaleggio, prin.
Heights ES, 114 SEMINOLE AVE   07436
    William Bruterri, prin.
Manito ES, 111 MANITO AVE   07436
    Barbara Tillman, prin.

Our Lady of Perpetual Help ES
    FRANKLIN & PURDUE AVES   07436

Oaklyn, Camden Co., Pop. Code 5
Collingswood Borough SD
Supt. – See Collingswood
Sharp ES, MCGILL & COMLY AVES   08107
    Carl Rickershauser,Jr., prin.

Haddon Twp. SD
Supt. – See Camden
Jennings ES, CEDAR & JOHNSON AVES   08107
    Robert Andrews, prin.

Oaklyn Borough SD
Sch. Sys. Enr. Code 2
Supt. – William Thompson
    KENDALL BLVD   08107
ES, KENDALL BLVD   08107 – Henry Lindner, prin.

Oak Ridge, Morris Co., Pop. Code 2
Jefferson Twp. SD
Sch. Sys. Enr. Code 5
Supt. – Sheldon Rubin, RURAL ROUTE 04   07438
Jefferson Twp. MS
    RURAL ROUTE 02 BOX 141   07438
    John Markey, prin.
Cozy Lake MS, COZY LAKE ROAD   07438
    Andrew Long, prin.
Milton ES, RURAL ROUTE 04   07438
    Andrew Long, prin.
White Rock ES, WHITE ROCK BLVD   07438
    William Stanton, prin.
Other Schools – See Lake Hopatcong, Wharton

West Milford Twp. SD
Supt. – See West Milford
Paradise Knoll ES, 103 PARADISE RD   07438
    Robert Lilienkamp, prin.

Ocean, Monmouth Co., Pop. Code 7
Ocean Twp. SD
Supt. – See Oakhurst
Ocean Twp. IS, 1200 W PARK AVE   07712
    Donald Vineburg, prin.

Ocean City, Cape May Co., Pop. Code 7
Ocean City SD
Sch. Sys. Enr. Code 4
Supt. – Anthony Scalzo, 801 ASBURY AVE   08226
IS, 1801 BAY AVE   08226 – Lyle Alverson, prin.
PS, 6TH & WEWST AVE   08226
    Margaret Toner, prin.

St. Augustine ES, 1337 ASBURY AVE   08226

Ocean Gate, Ocean Co., Pop. Code 4
Ocean Gate SD
Sch. Sys. Enr. Code 2
Supt. – Richard Adams, P O BOX 287   08740
ES, W ARVERNE AVE   08740
    Richard Adams, prin.

Ocean Grove, Monmouth Co., Pop. Code 5
Neptune Twp. SD
Supt. – See Neptune
ES, 90 LAWRENCE AVE   07756
    Nicholas Napolitano, prin.

Oceanport, Monmouth Co., Pop. Code 6
Oceanport SD
Sch. Sys. Enr. Code 3
Supt. – Rob Price, MAPLE PLACE   07757
Maple Place MS, MAPLE PLACE   07757
    John Barron, prin.
Wolf Hill ES, WOLF HILL AVE   07757
    Richard Entwistle, prin.

Oceanville, Atlantic Co.
Galloway Twp. SD
Supt. – See Absecon
ES, NEW YORK RD   08231
    Dr. Edwin Wood, prin.

Ogdensburg, Sussex Co., Pop. Code 5
Ogdensburg Borough SD
Sch. Sys. Enr. Code 2
Supt. – Patricia Dolan   07439
ES, 100 MAIN ST   07439 – Patricia Dolan, prin.

Old Bridge, Middlesex Co., Pop. Code 8
Old Bridge Twp. SD
Supt. – See Matawan
Salk MS, RURAL ROUTE 02   08857
    Joseph Alvarez, prin.

Sandburg MS　08857 – Joseph Wydra, prin.
Carpenter ES, 1 PAR AVE　08857
　Theodore Marcin, prin.
Grissom ES, 1 SUNIS AVE　08857
　Nancy Soper, prin.
McDivitt ES, PHILLIPS DR　08857
　Dorothy Engebretson, prin.
Schirra ES, 1 AWN ST　08857 – Clyde Smith, prin.
Sheppard ES, 33 BUSHNELL RD　08857
　Manuel Martin, prin.
Southwood ES, 64 SOUTHWOOD DR　08857
　Edward Sherman, prin.
Voorhees ES, 30 MIDWAY RD　08857
　Thomas Ruggiero, prin.

St. Ambrose ES, 75 THROCKMORTON LN　08857
St. Thomas the Apostle ES
　333 HIGHWAY 18　08857

Old Tappan, Bergen Co., Pop. Code 5
Old Tappan SD
Sch. Sys. Enr. Code 2
Supt. – Raymond Albano, 1 SCHOOL ST　07675
DeWolf MS, 275 OLD TAPPAN ROAD　07675
　Robert Lynch, prin.
DeMarest ES, 1 SCHOOL ST　07675
　Raymond Albano, prin.

Oradell, Bergen Co., Pop. Code 6
Oradell SD
Sch. Sys. Enr. Code 3
Supt. – J. Conk, 350 PROSPECT AVE　07649
ES, 350 PROSPECT AVE　07649
　Anthony Bouvalides, prin.

St. Joseph ES, 305 ELM ST　07649

Orange, Essex Co., Pop. Code 8
Orange CSD
Sch. Sys. Enr. Code 5
Supt. – Woodrow Zaros, 369 MAIN ST　07050
MS, 400 CENTRAL AVE　07050 – Ed Valente, prin.
Central ES, 33 CLEVELAND ST　07050
　Imogene Johnson, prin.
Cleveland Street ES, 355 CLEVELAND ST　07050
　Frank Capella, prin.
Forest Street ES, Y51 FOREST ST　07050
　Edwin Valente, prin.
Heywood Avenue ES, 421 HEYWOOD AVE　07050
　Matthew Bocchino, prin.
Lincoln Avenue ES, Y16 LINCOLN AVE　07050
　Sandra Thomas, prin.
Oakwood Avenue ES, 135 OAKWOOD AVE　07050
　Rachel Alston, prin.
Park Avenue ES, 231 PARK AVE　07050
　James Sherman, prin.

Our Lady Mt. Carmel ES
　268 CAPUCHIN WAY　07050
Our Lady the Valley ES
　VALLEY-MCCHESNEY STS　07050
St. John's ES, 455 WHITE ST　07050

Oxford, Warren Co., Pop. Code 4
Oxford Twp. SD
Sch. Sys. Enr. Code 2
Supt. – Harry Tachovsky, KENT STREET　07863
Oxford Central ES, KENT ST　07863
　Harry Tachovsky, prin.

Palisades Park, Bergen Co., Pop. Code 7
Palisades Park SD
Sch. Sys. Enr. Code 4
Supt. – George Fasciano, 270 1ST ST　07650
Lindbergh ES, 401 GLEN AVE　07650
　Gerard DeRoberto, prin.

St. Michael's ES, 312 1ST ST　07650
St. Nicholas ES, 233 14TH ST　07650

Palmyra, Burlington Co., Pop. Code 6
Palmyra SD
Sch. Sys. Enr. Code 4
Supt. – Dan Mastrobuono
　700 CINNAMINSON AVE　08065
Charles Street MS, 100 CHARLES ST W　08065
　(—), prin.
Delaware Avenue ES, 301 DELAWARE AVE　08065
　(—), prin.
Other Schools – See Riverton

Paramus, Bergen Co., Pop. Code 8
Paramus SD
Sch. Sys. Enr. Code 5
Supt. – Harry Galinsky
　145 SPRING VALLEY ROAD N　07652
East Brook MS
　190 SPRING VALLEY ROAD N　07652
　Paul Maramaldi, prin.
West Brook MS, 550 ROOSEVELT BLVD　07652
　Arien Hartman, prin.
Memorial ES, 235 E MIDLAND AVE　07652
　Carmen Panebianco, prin.
Parkway ES, ORADELL AVE　07652
　Joseph Roma, prin.
Ridge Ranch ES, ROCKWOOD DR　07652
　Dr. Roger Bayersdorfer, prin.
Stony Lane ES, EAST RIDGEWOOD AVE　07652
　James Wollenberg, prin.

Our Lady of Visitation ES
　222 FARVIEW AVE N　07652
Yavneh Academy, 155 FARVIEW AVE　07652

Park Ridge, Bergen Co., Pop. Code 6
Park Ridge SD
Sch. Sys. Enr. Code 4
Supt. – Robert Balentine, 2 PARK AVE　07656
East Brook ES, 167 SIBBALD DR　07656
　John Annillo, prin.
West Ridge ES, 18 S FIRST ST　07656
　Laurence Hughes, prin.

Our Lady of Mercy ES, 25 FREMONT AVE　07656

Parlin, Middlesex Co.
Old Bridge Twp. SD
Supt. – See Matawan
Madison Park ES, 33 HARVARD RD　08859
　Francis Perino, prin.

Sayerville SD
Sch. Sys. Enr. Code 5
Supt. – Marie Parnell, 1 TAFT PL　08859
Sayerville MS, 800 WASHINGTON ROAD　08859
　Soren Thomsen, prin.
Arleth ES, 3198 WASHINGTON RD　08859
　John Singer, prin.
Eisenhower ES, 601 ERNSTON RD　08859
　Robert Decker, prin.
Truman ES, 1 TAFT PL　08859
　Everett Adams, prin.
Other Schools – See Sayreville

Parsippany, Morris Co., Pop. Code 6
Parsippany-Troy Hills Twp. SD
Sch. Sys. Enr. Code 6
Supt. – Ruth Krawitz, P O BOX 52　07054
Brooklawn JHS, 250 BEECHWOOD ROAD　07054
　Nicholas Steenstra, prin.
Central JHS, 1602 ROUTE 46　07054
　Angelo Guiliana, prin.
Eastlake ES, 40 EBA RD　07054
　Theodore Smith, prin.
Intervale ES, 60 PITT ROAD　07054
　Frank Brockman, prin.
Lake Parsippany ES, KINGSTON RD　07054
　Kenneth Werner, prin.
Northvail ES, 10 EILEEN CT　07054
　Maryjane Park, prin.
Rockaway Meadow ES, 160 EDWARDS RD　07054
　Lee Burns, prin.
Troy Hills ES, 509 S BEVERWYCK RD　07054
　James Mariani,Jr., prin.
Other Schools – See Lake Hiawatha, Morris Plains

St. Christopher ES, 1050 LITTLETON RD　07054
St. Peter the Apostle ES, 189 BALDWIN RD　07054

Passaic, Passaic Co., Pop. Code 8
Passaic CSD
Sch. Sys. Enr. Code 6
Supt. – Allison McCoy, 101 PASSAIC ST　07055
Lincoln MS, 300 LAFAYETTE AVE　07055
　Louis Freda, prin.
Franklin ES 3, 18 BELMONT PL　07055
　Mario Drago, prin.
Gero ES 9, 140 FIRST ST　07055
　David McLean, prin.
Grant ES 7, SUMMER ST & MYRTLE AVE　07055
　Venice Harvey, prin.
Jefferson ES 1
　BROADWAY & VAN HOUTEN AVE　07055
　Barbara Liptak, prin.
King ES 6, 85 HAMILTON AVE　07055
　Joseph Werling, prin.
Memorial ES 11, MADISON ST　07055
　Jean Burwell, prin.
ES 8, FORTH ST　07055 – Kenneth Kurnath, prin.
Roosevelt ES 10, HARRISON ST　07055
　Sydney Lockwood, prin.

Hillel Academy, 565 BROADWAY　07055
Holy Trinity ES, 209 HOPE AVE　07055
Our Lady of Mt. Carmel School
　7 SAINT FRANCIS WAY　07055
Passaic Catholic Regional ES
　212 MARKET ST　07055
St. Anthony of Padua ES, 40 TULIP ST　07055
St. Nicholas ES, 123 JEFFERSON ST　07055

Paterson, Passaic Co., Pop. Code 9
Paterson SD
Sch. Sys. Enr. Code 7
Supt. – Frank Napier,Jr., 33 CHURCH ST　07505
MS 4, 55 CLINTON ST　07522
　Carlisle Parker, prin.
Clemente ES, GRAHAM AVE　07502
　Nathaniel Oliver, prin.
Dale Avenue ES, 21 DALE AVE　07505
　Dorothy Rowe, prin.
Kilpatrick ES, SUMMER ST　07505
　Joseph Quagliero, prin.
King ES, EAST 28TH ST COR 20TH AVE　07513
　Irene Reynolds, prin.
Paterson City ES 2, MILL & PASSAIC STS　07501
　Gleen Lagatol, prin.
Paterson City ES 3, 448 MAIN ST　07501
　Audrey Favors, prin.
Paterson City ES 5, 430 TOTOWA AVE　07502
　Ronald Sherman, prin.
Paterson City ES 6
　CARROLL ST & HAMILTON AVE　07514
　Charles Lighty, prin.
Paterson City ES 7
　RAMSEY ST & DIXON AVE　07501
　Samuel Del Mauro, prin.
Paterson City ES 8, 35 CHADWICK ST　07503
　George Roberto, prin.

Paterson City ES 9
　GEORGE ST & GETTY AVE　07503
　Margaret Dalton, prin.
Paterson City ES 10, 48 MERCER ST　07524
　George Hirschberg, prin.
Paterson City ES 11, 350 MARKET ST　07501
　Norman Rosenblum, prin.
Paterson City ES 12, NORTH 2ND ST　07522
　Richard Engelhardt, prin.
Paterson City ES 13
　15TH ST COR EAST 22ND ST　07504
　Jerome Gibson, prin.
Paterson City ES 14, UNION AVE　07522
　Jerome Zisblatt, prin.
Paterson City ES 15
　98 OAK ST SANDY HILL PARK　07503
　Vreeland Williams, prin.
Paterson City ES 16, 11 22ND AVE　07513
　Anna DeMolli, prin.
Paterson City ES 17
　112 N 5TH ST COR JEFFERSON　07522
　Marie Engelhardt, prin.
Paterson City ES 18, EAST 18TH ST　07524
　Peter Wild, prin.
Paterson City ES 19, JAMES ST　07502
　Elizabeth Pisacreta, prin.
Paterson City ES 20, 500 E 37TH ST　07504
　James Bradshaw, prin.
Paterson City ES 21
　TENTH & MADISON AVE　07514
　Henry Focacci, prin.
Paterson City ES 24
　19TH AVE & EAST 22ND ST　07513
　Harold Simon, prin.
Paterson City ES 25, TRENTON AVE　07503
　Emilie Renna, prin.
Paterson City ES 26
　EAST 32ND ST & 11TH AVE　07514
　William Booth, prin.
Paterson City ES 27, 250 RICHMOND AVE　07502
　Anne Carrera, prin.
Paterson City ES 28
　COR TEMPLE ST/PRESIDNTAL AV　07522
　Mary Holmes, prin.
Weir ES, 152 COLLEGE BLVD　07505
　Willa Mae Taylor, prin.

Blessed Sacrament School, 277 6TH AVE　07524
Our Lady Lourdes ES, 186 BUTLER ST　07524
St. Anthony ES, 144 BEECH ST　07501
St. Bonaventure ES, 88 DANFORTH AVE　07501
St. George ES, 30 MICHIGAN AVE　07503
St. Gerard Majella ES, 10 CARRELTON DR　07522
St. John Cathedral ES, 190 OLIVER ST　07501
St. Joseph ES, 279 CARROLL ST　07501
St. Mary ES, 93 SHERMAN AVE　07502
St. Paul's School, 286 HALEDON AVE　07508
St. Stephen ES, 100 MARTIN ST　07501
St. Therese ES, 765 14TH AVE　07504
Treader ES, 1 MARKET ST　07501

Paulsboro, Gloucester Co., Pop. Code 6
Paulsboro SD
Sch. Sys. Enr. Code 4
Supt. – (—), 1211 N DELAWARE ST　08066
Billingsport ES
　5TH AND GREENWICH AVE　08066
　William Reed, prin.
Loudenslager ES, SWEDESBORO AVE　08066
　Robert Catando, prin.

St. John ES, MANTUA AVE　08066

Pedricktown, Salem Co., Pop. Code 3
Oldmans Twp. SD
Sch. Sys. Enr. Code 2
Supt. – Maurice Madden, P O BOX 208　08067
Oldmans MS, P O BOX 208　08067
　Maurice Madden, prin.
ES, P O BOX 208　08067 – Maurice Madden, prin.

Pemberton, Burlington Co., Pop. Code 4
Pemberton Borough SD
Sch. Sys. Enr. Code 2
Supt. – Peter Cliquennoi, 50 EARLY ST　08068
Pemberton Borough ES, 50 EARLY ST　08068
　John Flammer, prin.

Pemberton Twp. SD
Supt. – See Browns Mills
Emmons ES, SCRAPETOWN RD　08068
　George Young, prin.

Pennington, Mercer Co., Pop. Code 4
Hopewell Valley Regional SD
Sch. Sys. Enr. Code 4
Supt. – Ed Gola, 425 S MAIN ST　08534
Timberlane MS, TIMBERLANE DR　08534
　Peter Brennan, prin.
Toll Gate ES, 275 MAIN ST　08534
　Barbara Newbaker, prin.
Other Schools – See Hopewell, Titusville

Pennsauken, Camden Co., Pop. Code 8
Pennsauken Twp. SD
Sch. Sys. Enr. Code 5
Supt. – Howard Phifer
　HYLTON ROAD & REMINGTON AVE　08110
MS, 8201 PARK AVE　08110
　James Chapman, prin.
Carson ES, GARFIELD AVE　08105
　Shirley Upchurch, prin.
Central ES, 2300 MERCHANTVILLE AVE　08110
　(—), prin.

Longfellow ES, GROSS & FORREST AVE 08110
  Joseph Bruni, prin.
Other Schools – See Camden, Delair, Merchantville

St. Cecilia ES, 49TH & CAMDEN AVE 08110

Penns Grove, Salem Co., Pop. Code 6
Penns Grove-Carneys Point SD
Sch. Sys. Enr. Code 4
Supt. – Leonard Fitts
  113 W HARMONY ST 08069
MS, E MAPLE AVE 08069 – Paul Rufino, prin.
Carleton MS, E MAPLE AVE 08069
  Joseph Davenport, prin.
Lafayette-Pershing ES, SHELL RD 08069
  William Sorrels, prin.
Other Schools – See Carney's Point

St. James ES, BEACH AVE 08069

Pennsville, Salem Co., Pop. Code 7
Pennsville Twp. SD
Sch. Sys. Enr. Code 4
Supt. – Ron Capasso, 30 CHURCH ST 08070
MS, WILLIAM PENN AVE 08070
  Anthony Iatarola, prin.
Central Park ES, 1 OLIVER AVE 08070
  Sidney Riley, prin.
Penn Beach ES
  SALEM DR & KANSAS ROAD 08070
  Thomas Hartman, prin.
Valley Park ES, MAHONEY ROAD 08070
  Benjamin Curtis, prin.

Pequannock, Morris Co., Pop. Code 6
Pequannock Twp. SD
Supt. – See Pompton Plains
Gerace ES, 59 BOULEVARD 07440
  Mary Diver, prin.

Holy Spirit ES, 330 TURNPIKE 07440

Perth Amboy, Middlesex Co., Pop. Code 8
Perth Amboy SD
Sch. Sys. Enr. Code 6
Supt. – Frank Sinatra, 178 BARRACKS ST 08861
McGinnis MS, 271 STATE ST 08861
  Alvin Mattes, prin.
Shull MS, 380 HALL AVE 08861
  Robert Mantz, prin.
Ceres ES, 445 STATE ST 08861
  Renee Howard, prin.
Flynn ES, 850 CHAMBERLAIN AVE 08861
  Charles Bodo, prin.
Galvin ES, 514 NEVILLE ST 08861
  Armand Cannamela, prin.
ES 1, 274 STATE ST 08861 – William Kun, prin.
ES 10, 318 STOCKTON ST 08861
  Herbert Richardson, prin.
ES 5, 690 CORTLANDT ST 08861
  Rose Lopez, prin.
ES 7, 163 PATERSON ST 08861
  Julius Uribe, prin.

Holy Spirit ES
  BRACE AND CARLOCK AVE 08861
Holy Trinity ES, 264 LAWRIE ST 08861
Most Holy Rosary ES, 301 BARCLAY ST 08861
Our Lady Hungary ES, 680 CATHERINE ST 08861
Our Lady of Peace School, MABOY AVE 08863
Our Redeemer Lutheran ES
  28 4TH STREET 08863
Perth Amboy Catholic School, P O BOX 651 08862
St. Mary ES, 351 MECHANIC ST 08861
St. Stephen ES, 500 STATE ST 08861
Ukranian Assumption School
  MEREDITH & JACQUES STS 08861

Phillipsburg, Warren Co., Pop. Code 7
Harmony Twp. SD
Sch. Sys. Enr. Code 2
Supt. – Nicholas Matlaga
  2551 BELVIDERE ROAD 08865
Harmony Consol ES, 2551 BELVIDERE RD 08865
  Nicholas Matlaga, prin.

Lopatcong Twp. SD
Sch. Sys. Enr. Code 3
Supt. – Albert Purdy
  RURAL ROUTE 03 BOX 137 08865
Lopatcong ES, RURAL ROUTE 03 BOX 137 08865
  Albert Purdy, prin.

Phillipsburg SD
Sch. Sys. Enr. Code 5
Supt. – Anthony Piperata, 675 CORLIS AVE 08865
MS, 525 WARREN ST 08865
  Russell DiMarco, prin.
Andover Morris ES, 712 S MAIN ST 08865
  Salvatore Patti, prin.
Barber ES, 50 SARGENT AVE 08865
  John Consentino, prin.
Freeman ES, 120 FILLMORE ST 08865
  Joanne Wilkins, prin.
Green Street ES, 1000 GREEN ST 08865
  Gene Healey, prin.

Pohatcong Twp. SD
Supt. – See Bloomsbury
Shimer ES, 599 NEW BRUNSWICK AVE 08865
  Michael Frinzi, prin.

SS. Philip and James ES
  S MAIN & STOCKTON STS 08865

Pine Brook, Morris Co.
Montville Twp. SD
Sch. Sys. Enr. Code 5
Supt. – Robert Garawski
  39 WOODMONT ROAD 07058
Hilldale ES, 123 KONNER AVE 07058
  Kevin McGrath, prin.
Valley View ES, MONTGOMERY AVE 07058
  Allan Goldberg, prin.
Woodmont ES, WOODMONT ROAD 07058
  Mary Ann Smith, prin.
Other Schools – See Montville, Towaco

Pine Hill, Camden Co., Pop. Code 6
Pine Hill Borough SD
Sch. Sys. Enr. Code 3
Supt. – James Mundy, 15 E SEVENTH AVE 08021
Bean ES, 70 E 3RD AVE 08021
  Tommie Stringer, prin.
Glenn ES, 1005 TURNERVILLE RD 08021
  William Frank III, prin.

Piscataway, Middlesex Co., Pop. Code 8
Piscataway Twp. SD
Sch. Sys. Enr. Code 6
Supt. – Burt Edelchick
  WILLOW AVE & SCOTT ST 08854
Conackamack MS
  5001 WITHERSPOON ST 08854
  John Gardner, prin.
Quibbletown MS, WASHINGTON AVE 08854
  Ed McGarigle, prin.
Schor MS, 289 N RANDOLPHVILLE ROAD 08854
  Allerton Spence, prin.
Arbor MS, ROCK AVE 08854 – Lon Rankin, prin.
Eisenhower ES, 360 STELTON RD 08854
  Joseph Chapkoski, prin.
Fellowship Farm ES, 1515 STELTON RD 08854
  Edward Palushock, prin.
Grandview ES, 130 N RANDOLPHVILLE RD 08854
  Walter Wilkos, prin.
King ES, LUDLOW ST 08854
  Harvey Yonowitz, prin.
Randolphville MS, 1 SUTTIE AVE 08854
  Frances Bradshaw, prin.

Our Lady Fatima ES
  499 NEW MARKET RD 08854
St. Frances Cabrini ES, 2300 COOPER ST 08854

Pitman, Gloucester Co., Pop. Code 6
Pitman SD
Sch. Sys. Enr. Code 4
Supt. – William Horton, 400 HUDSON AVE 08071
Elwood Kindle ES, WASHINGTON AVE 08071
  Frances Manbeck, prin.
ES, 118 E HOLLY AVE 08071
  Thomas Agnew, prin.
Pitman Memorial ES, 400 HUDSON AVE 08071
  Lawrence Hayden, prin.
Walls ES, GRANT AVE 08071
  Barbara Shellenberger, prin.

Pittstown, Hunterdon Co.
Alexandria Twp. SD
Sch. Sys. Enr. Code 2
Supt. – John Ammon
  RURAL ROUTE 01 BOX 80 08867
Alexandria MS, RURAL ROUTE 01 BOX 80 08867
  Fred Ferrone, prin.
Wilson ES, RURAL ROUTE 02 BOX 90 08867
  Philip Simon, prin.

Plainfield, Union Co., Pop. Code 8
Plainfield SD
Sch. Sys. Enr. Code 6
Supt. – Annette Kearney
  504 MADISON AVE 07060
Hubbard MS, 661 W 8TH ST 07060
  L. Jengeleski, prin.
Maxson MS, 920 E 7TH ST 07062
  Angelo Mone, prin.
Barlow ES, FARRAGUT & FRONT STS 07060
  Jeannette Williams, prin.
Cedarbrook ES, 1049 CENTRAL AVE 07060
  Joyce Haynes, prin.
Clinton ES
  CLINTON AVE & W FOURTH ST 07063
  Gloria Williams, prin.
Cook ES, 739 LELAND AVE 07062
  Ernest Hobbie, prin.
Emerson ES, 305 EMERSON AVE 07062
  Dr. Jeanette Williams, prin.
Evergreen ES, 1033 EVERGREEN AVE 07060
  Dorothy Henry, prin.
Jefferson ES, 1200 MYRTLE AVE 07063
  Mary Gladden, prin.
Stillman ES, 201 W 4TH ST 07060
  Cynthia Archer, prin.
Washington ES, 427 DARROW AVE 07060
  Henry Thompson, prin.
Woodland ES, 730 CENTRAL ST 07062
  Dorothy Henry, prin.

Holy Family School, 365 EMERWON AVE 07062
St. Joseph ES, 101 WESTERVELT AVE 07060

Plainsboro, Middlesex Co.
West Windsor-Plainsboro Regional SD
Supt. – See Princeton Junction
West Winsor-Plainsboro MS
  GROVERS MILL ROAD 08536
  Arthur Downs, prin.
Wicoff ES, PRINCETON ROAD 08536
  Rose Miller, prin.

Pleasantville, Atlantic Co., Pop. Code 7
Egg Harbor Twp. SD
Sch. Sys. Enr. Code 5
Supt. – Fred Nickles, 210 NAPLES AVE 08232
Slaybaugh MS, OCEAN HEIGHTS AVE 08232
  Don Robertson, prin.
Cardiff ES, RURAL ROUTE 01 08232
  Thomas Cooke, prin.
Davenport MS, 500 SPRUCE AVE 08232
  Dennis Burd, prin.
Farmington ES, RURAL ROUTE 03 08232
  Thomas Cooke, prin.
McKee City ES, RURAL ROUTE 01 08232
  Thomas Cooke, prin.
Swift MS, OCEAN HEIGHTS AVE 08232
  Carmen Infante, prin.
Other Schools – See Linwood, Mays Landing

Pleasantville CSD
Sch. Sys. Enr. Code 4
Supt. – John Garrity, W DECATUR AVE 08232
Leeds Avenue ES, WEST LEEDS AVE 08232
  John Thomas, prin.
North Main Street ES, NORTH MAIN ST 08232
  Dr. Edna Hunter, prin.
South Main Street ES, 701 S MAIN ST 08232
  James Watkins, prin.
Washington Avenue ES
  3RD ST AND WASHINGTON AVE 08232
  Frank Parker, prin.

St. Peter School
  CHESTNUT & DECATUR AVE 08232

Point Pleasant, Ocean Co., Pop. Code 7
Point Pleasant Beach SD
Sch. Sys. Enr. Code 3
Supt. – F. Crawley, 309 COOKS ROAD 08742
Antrim ES, 301 NIBLICK ST 08742
  Betty Gallagher, prin.

Point Pleasant Borough SD
Sch. Sys. Enr. Code 5
Supt. – George Kane
  2100 PANTHER PATH 08742
Memorial MS, LAURA HERBERT DR 08742
  Roy Feldman, prin.
Bennett ES, 2000 RIVIERA PKY 08742
  John McHugh, prin.
Ocean Road ES, STATE HWY 88 08742
  Dr. Carl Perry, prin.

St. Peter ES, 415 ATLANTIC AVE 08742

Pomona, Atlantic Co.
Galloway Twp. SD
Supt. – See Absecon
ES, GENOA AVE 08240 – Thomas Niland, prin.

Assumption School
  1993 WHITE HORSE PIKE 08240

Pompton Lakes, Passaic Co., Pop. Code 7
Pompton Lakes SD
Sch. Sys. Enr. Code 4
Supt. – Jon Kopko, VAN AVE 07442
Lakeside MS, 316 LAKESIDE AVE 07442
  Vincent Iraggi, prin.
Lenox ES, 35 LENOX AVE 07442
  Charles Anzolut, prin.
Lincoln ES, 40 MILL ST 07442
  Louis Shadiack, prin.

St. Mary ES, 25 POMPTON AVE 07442

Pompton Plains, Morris Co., Pop. Code 6
Pequannock Twp. SD
Sch. Sys. Enr. Code 4
Supt. – Frank Kaplan, 538 TURNPIKE 07444
Pequannock Valley MS, 493 TURNPIKE 07444
  Leslie Conlon, prin.
Hillview ES, 206 BOULEVARD 07444
  Elaine Soloman, prin.
North Boulevard ES, 263 BOULEVARD 07444
  Evelyn Justesenr, prin.
Other Schools – See Pequannock

Netherlands Reformed Church ES
  164 JACKSONVILLE RD 07444

Port Elizabeth, Cumberland Co.
Maurice River Twp. SD
Sch. Sys. Enr. Code 2
Supt. – Albert Monillas
  SOUTH DELSEA DR 08348
Maurice River Twp. MS, P O BOX D 08348
  William Zipparo, prin.
Other Schools – See Leesburg

Port Monmouth, Monmouth Co., Pop. Code 5
Middletown Twp. SD
Supt. – See Middletown
Thorne MS, 70 MURPHY ROAD 07758
  Joseph Czarnecki, prin.
ES, HWY 36 & MAIN ST 07758
  William Golubinski, prin.

Port Murray, Warren Co.
Mansfield Twp. SD
Sch. Sys. Enr. Code 3
Supt. – Carol Burns 07865
Mansfield Twp. ES
  PORT MURRAY ROAD & ROUTE 57 07865
  Carol Burns, prin.

Port Norris, Cumberland Co.
Commercial Twp. SD
Sch. Sys. Enr. Code 3
Supt. – Barry Ballard, RURAL ROUTE 01 08349
MS, RURAL ROUTE 02 BOX 10A 08349
Michael Killeen, prin.
Haleyvlle-Maurctown ES
RURAL ROUTE 01 08349
Audrey Reynolds, prin.

Port Reading, Middlesex Co.
Woodbridge Twp. SD
Supt. – See Woodbridge
ES, 77 TURNER ST 07064 – Robert Hickey, prin.

Port Republic, Atlantic Co., Pop. Code 3
Port Republic SD
Sch. Sys. Enr. Code 2
Supt. – Howard Paynter, POMONA AVE 08241
ES, POMONA AVE 08241 – Howard Paynter, prin.

Princeton, Mercer Co., Pop. Code 7
Princeton Regional SD
Sch. Sys. Enr. Code 4
Supt. – Carol Choye, P O BOX 711 08540
Witherspoon MS, 217 WALNUT LANE 08540
William Johnson, prin.
Community Park ES
372 WITHERSPOON ST 08540 – (—), prin.
Littlebrook ES, 39 MAGNOLIA LANE 08540
Robert Ginsberg, prin.
Riverside ES, 58 RIVERSIDE DR 08540
William Cirullo, prin.

Princeton Day School, P O BOX 75 08544
Stuart Country Day School
2 STUART CLOSE 08540
Chapin ES, 4101 PRINCETON PIKE 08540
St. Paul ES, 218 NASSAU STREET 08542

Princeton Junction, Mercer Co., Pop. Code 4
West Windsor-Plainsboro Regional SD
Sch. Sys. Enr. Code 5
Supt. – Richard Willever, P O BOX 248 08550
Dutch Neck MS, VILLAGE ROAD E 08550
Katherine Gross, prin.
Hawk ES, CLARKSVILLE ROAD 08550
Donald Rizzo, prin.
Other Schools – See Plainsboro

Prospect Park, Pussaic Co., Pop. Code 6
Prospect Park SD
Sch. Sys. Enr. Code 2
Supt. – Thomas Vannatta, 94 BROWN AVE 07508
ES 1, 94 BROWN AVE 07508
Dr. James Barriale, prin.

Quakertown, Hunterdon Co.
Franklin Twp. SD
Sch. Sys. Enr. Code 2
Supt. – Linda Lubben, P O BOX 368 08868
Franklin Twp. ES, P O BOX 368 08868
Dorothy Apgar, prin.

Quinton, Salem Co.
Quinton Twp. SD
Sch. Sys. Enr. Code 2
Supt. – John Buyarski, P O BOX 365 08072
Quinton Twp. ES, P O BOX 365 08072
John Buyarski, prin.

Rahway, Union Co., Pop. Code 8
Rahway SD
Sch. Sys. Enr. Code 5
Supt. – Frank Brunette, 1200 KLINE PLACE 07065
IS, 1200 KLINE PLACE 07065
Ralph Manfredi, prin.
Cleveland ES, 486 E MILTON AVE 07065
Arthur Lundgren, prin.
Franklin ES, 1809 ST GEORGES AVE 07065
Frank Buglione, prin.
Madison ES, 944 MADISON AVE 07065
Edwin Dykes, prin.
Roosevelt ES, 811 ST GEORGES AVE 07065
Eugene Warga, prin.

St. John Vianney ES, 420 INMAN AVE 07067
St. Mary ES, 244 CENTRAL AVE 07065

Ramsey, Bergen Co., Pop. Code 7
Ramsey SD
Sch. Sys. Enr. Code 4
Supt. – Carol Conger, 266 E MAIN ST 07446
Smith MS, MONROE ST 07466
John Dispoto, prin.
Dater ES, 305 SCHOOL ST 07446
Daniel Warnaar, prin.
Hubbard ES, WYCKOFF AVE 07446
Lynn Mintz, prin.
Tisdale ES, ISLAND AVE 07446
Michael Gratale, prin.

St. Paul ES, 187 WYCKOFF AVE 07446

Randolph, Morris Co., Pop. Code 7
Randolph Twp. SD
Sch. Sys. Enr. Code 5
Supt. – Robert Gordon
SCHOOLHOUSE ROAD 07869
IS, 507 MILLBROOK AVE 07869
Milton Ortiz, prin.
Center Grove ES, SCHOOLHOUSE RD 07869
Edward Geueke, prin.
Fernbrook ES, 206 QUAKER CHURCH RD 07869
Ruth Dorney, prin.

Ironia ES, DOVER CHESTER ROAD 07869
James Hofman, prin.
Shongum ES, WEST HANOVER AVE 07869
Harold Krueger, prin.

Raritan, Somerset Co., Pop. Code 6
Bridgewater-Raritan Regional SD
Supt. – See Bridgewater
Kennedy ES, WOODMERE ST 08869
Marilyn Topcik, prin.

St. Ann ES, 29 SECOND AVE 08869

Readington, Hunterdon Co., Pop. Code 1
Readington Twp. SD
Sch. Sys. Enr. Code 4
Supt. – Feore Orecchio, P O BOX 2 08870
MS, P O BOX 2 08870 – Frank Rovinski, prin.
Other Schools – See Three Bridges, White House
Station

Red Bank, Monmouth Co., Pop. Code 7
Middletown Twp. SD
Supt. – See Middletown
Fairview ES, 60 COOPER RD 07701
Anthony Falvo, prin.
River Plaza ES, 155 HUBBARD AVE 07701
Diane Lenartowicz, prin.

Red Bank SD
Sch. Sys. Enr. Code 3
Supt. – William DiMaio, 76 BRANCH AVE 07701
MS, 101 HARDING ROAD 07701
Theodore Brown, prin.
PS, 222 RIVER ST 07701 – Wade Turnock, prin.

St. James ES, 30 PETERS PL 07701

Ridgefield, Bergen Co., Pop. Code 7
Ridgefield SD
Sch. Sys. Enr. Code 4
Supt. – Richard Sabella, 555 CHESTNUT ST 07657
Slocum/Skewes ES, PROSPECT AVE 07657
Lawrence Dunn, prin.

St. Matthew ES, 555 PROSPECT AVE 07657

Ridgefield Park, Bergen Co., Pop. Code 7
Ridgefield Park SD
Sch. Sys. Enr. Code 4
Supt. – Charles Juris, 98 CENTRAL AVE 07660
Grant ES, 104 HENRY ST 07660
Kenneth Monaco, prin.
Lincoln ES, 712 LINCOLN AVE 07660
John Ranone, prin.
Roosevelt ES, 508 TEANECK RD 07660
David Verducci, prin.

St. Francis of Assisi ES
110 MT VERNON ST 07660

Ridgewood, Bergen Co., Pop. Code 8
Ridgewood Village SD
Sch. Sys. Enr. Code 5
Supt. – Fred Stokley, 49 COTTAGE PL 07450
Franklin MS, 335 N VAN DIEN AVE 07450
Paul Folkemer, prin.
Washington MS, 155 WASHINGTON PL 07450
George Neville, prin.
Hawes ES, 531 STEVENS AVE 07450
Sharon Jacobs, prin.
Orchard ES, 230 DEMAREST ST 07450
Charles Abate, prin.
Ridge ES, 325 W RIDGEWOOD AVE 07450
William Ward, prin.
Somerville ES, 45 S PLEASANT AVE 07450
C. Titus, prin.
Travell ES, 340 BOGERT AVE 07450
Dr. Cynthia Yoder, prin.
Willard ES, 601 MORNINGSIDE RD 07450
Joseph Lamela, prin.

Our Lady Mt. Carmel ES, 56 PASSAIC ST 07450

Ringoes, Hunterdon Co.
East Amwell Twp. SD
Sch. Sys. Enr. Code 2
Supt. – Fred Ferrone 08551
East Amwell Twp. ES, P O BOX A 08551
Samuel Mendelson, prin.

Ringwood, Passaic Co., Pop. Code 7
Ringwood SD
Sch. Sys. Enr. Code 4
Supt. – R. Sellitti
121 CARLETONDALE ROAD 07456
Ryerson MS, 130 VALLEY ROAD 07456
David Paulus, prin.
Cooper ES, 54 ROGER CT 07456
John Mangan, prin.
Erskine ES, 88 ERSKINE RD 07456
Joseph Presutto, prin.
Hewitt ES, FLOATSBURG ROAD 07456
R. Shelby Henriquez, prin.

St. Catherine of Bologna ES
112 ERSKINE RD 07456

Riverdale, Morris Co., Pop. Code 5
Riverdale SD
Sch. Sys. Enr. Code 2
Supt. – Anthony De Norchia
52 NEWARKPOMPTON TPKE 07457
ES, 52 NEWARK POMPTON TPKE 07457
Anthony Denorchia, prin.

River Edge, Bergen Co., Pop. Code 7
River Edge SD
Sch. Sys. Enr. Code 3
Supt. – Dr. John Lavigne
410 BOGERT ROAD 07661
Cherry Hill ES, 410 BOGERT RD 07661
John Choka, prin.
Roosevelt ES, 711 SUMMIT AVE 07661
Lawrence Mendelowitz, prin.

St. Peter the Apostle ES, 431 FIFTH AVE 07661

Riverside, Burlington Co., Pop. Code 6
Riverside Twp. SD
Sch. Sys. Enr. Code 4
Supt. – Joseph T. Cancellieri
112 E WASHINGTON ST 08075
ES, 112 E WASHINGTON ST 08075
Jane Butler, prin.

St. Casimir ES, 500 NEW JERSEY AVE 08075
St. Peter ES, 101 MIDDLETON ST 08075

Riverton, Burlington Co., Pop. Code 5
Palmyra SD
Supt. – See Palmyra
Sacred Heart ES, FOURTH & LINDEN AVES 08077
(—), prin.
Riverton Borough SD
Sch. Sys. Enr. Code 2
Supt. – John Flammer
FIFTH & HOWARD ST 08077
ES, 5TH AND HOWARD STS 08077
David Bell, prin.

St. Charles Borromeo ES
2500 BRANCH PIKE 08077
Westfield Friends ES
MOORESTOWN RIVERTON RD 08077

River Vale, Bergen Co., Pop. Code 6
River Vale SD
Sch. Sys. Enr. Code 4
Supt. – Phillip Kahn
393 RIVERVALE ROAD 07675
Holdrum MS, 385 RIVERVALE ROAD 07675
Thomas A. Daly, prin.
Roberge ES, 617 WESTWOOD AVE 07675
William Janowski, prin.
Woodside ES, 801 RIVERVALE RD 07675
Allen Spatola, prin.

Robbinsville, Mercer Co.
Washington Twp. SD
Supt. – See Windsor
Sharon ES, 234 SHARON ROAD 08691
Daniel Donnelly, prin.

Rochelle Park, Bergen Co., Pop. Code 6
Rochelle Park SD
Sch. Sys. Enr. Code 2
Supt. – S. Adler, 300 ROCHELLE AVE 07662
Midland ES 1, 300 ROCHELLE AVE 07662
Patricia Doloughty, prin.

Rockaway, Morris Co., Pop. Code 6
Rockaway Borough SD
Sch. Sys. Enr. Code 2
Supt. – John Phillips, 103 E MAIN ST 07866
Jefferson MS, 95 E MAIN ST 07866
James Esposito, prin.
Lincoln ES, 37 KELLER AVE 07866
James Steen, prin.
Washington ES, ACADEMY ST 07866
James Steen, prin.

Rockaway Twp. SD
Sch. Sys. Enr. Code 4
Supt. – John Fanning, P O BOX 500 07866
Copeland MS, LAKESHORE DRIVE 07866
Stephen Gottlieb, prin.
Malone ES, 524 GREEN POND RD 07866
Irwin Fidel, prin.
Stony Brook ES, STONYBROOK RD 07866
Joseph Burne, prin.
Other Schools – See Dover, Wharton

Sacred Heart ES, 40 E MAIN ST 07866
St. Cecilia ES, 87 HALSEY AVE 07866

Roebling, Burlington Co.
Florence Twp. SD
Supt. – See Florence
ES 5, 1352 HORNBERGER AVE 08554
(—), prin.

Holy Assumption ES
1238 HORNBERGER AVE 08554

Roosevelt, Monmouth Co., Pop. Code 3
Roosevelt Borough SD
Sch. Sys. Enr. Code 1
Supt. – Arthur Martin, P O BOX 160 08555
ES, P O BOX 160 08555 – Arthur Martin, prin.

Roseland, Essex Co., Pop. Code 6
Roseland SD
Sch. Sys. Enr. Code 2
Supt. – Nicholas Corbo, PASSAIC AVE 07068
Noecker ES, 130 PASSAIC AVE 07068
Frank Codispoti, prin.

Our Lady Blessed Sacrament ES
28 LIVINGSTON AVE 07068

Roselle, Union Co., Pop. Code 7
Roselle Borough SD
Sch. Sys. Enr. Code 4
Supt. – Peter Carter, 710 LOCUST ST　07203
Harrison ES, 310 HARRISON AVE　07203
　Jacqueline McConnell, prin.
Lincoln ES, 1100 WARREN ST　07203
　Dorothy Mayner, prin.
Moore MS, 800 LOCUST ST　07203
　Robert Briski, prin.
Washington ES, 501 W FIFTH AVE　07203
　Michael Ulaki, prin.
Wilday MS, 400 BROOKLAWN AVE　07203
　George Sliwiak, prin.

Roselle Park, Union Co., Pop. Code 7
Roselle Park SD
Sch. Sys. Enr. Code 4
Supt. – Ernest Finizio, 320 LOCUST ST　07204
Aldene ES
　WEST WEBSTER & FAITOUTE AVE　07204
　Anthony Basto, prin.
Gordon ES, WEST GRANT AVE　07204
　James Banyas, prin.
MS, 57 W GRANT AVE　07204 – Roy Dragon, prin.
Sherman ES, 375 E GRANT AVE　07204
　Thomas Faria, prin.

Rosenhayn, Cumberland Co.
Deerfield Twp. SD
Sch. Sys. Enr. Code 2
Supt. – David Hitchner, MORTON AVE　08352
Deerfield ES, P O BOX 375　08352
　David Hitchner, prin.

Rumson, Monmouth Co., Pop. Code 6
Rumson SD
Sch. Sys. Enr. Code 3
Supt. – Eileen Stevens, 60 FORREST AVE　07760
Forrestdale MS, 60 FORREST AVE　07760
　Robert Comba, prin.
Deane-Porter ES, BLACKPOINT ROAD　07760
　Nina Noonan, prin.

Holy Cross ES, 40 RUMSON RD　07760
Rumson ES, 35 BELLEVUE AVE　07760

Runnemede, Camden Co., Pop. Code 6
Runnemede Borough SD
Sch. Sys. Enr. Code 3
Supt. – Ron Denafo, 3RD & WILLIAMS AVE　08078
Volz MS, 3RD & WILLIAMS AVE　08078
　Joe Koch, prin.
Bingham ES, FIRST & ORCHARD AVE　08078
　Herbert Lancaster, prin.
Downing ES, 3RD & CENTRAL AVES　08078
　Herbert Shinn,Jr., prin.

St. Teresa ES, EVESHAM ROAD　08078

Rutherford, Bergen Co., Pop. Code 7
Moonachie SD
Supt. – See Moonachie
Craig ES, 20 W PARK ST　07074
　Francis Raftery, prin.

Rutherford SD
Sch. Sys. Enr. Code 4
Supt. – Luke Sarsfield, 176 PARK AVE　07070
Lincoln ES 5, 414 MONTROSS AVE　07070
　Joseph Loffredo, prin.
Pierrepont ES, 70 E PIERREPORT AVE　07070
　Anna Amorelli, prin.
Sylvan ES, 109 SYLVAN ST　07070
　Joseph Loffredo, prin.
Union ES, 359 UNION AVE　07070
　Salvatore Brancato, prin.
Washington ES, 89 WOOD ST　07070
　Joseph Loffredo, prin.

Assumption School, 151 FIRST ST　07075
St. Mary ES, 72 CHESTNUT ST　07070

Saddle Brook, Bergen Co., Pop. Code 7
Saddle Brook Twp. SD
Sch. Sys. Enr. Code 4
Supt. – Albert Gorab, 355 MAYHILL ST　07662
Franklin ES, CALDWELL AVE　07662
　Elmer Modla, prin.
Long Memorial ES, FLORAL LN　07662
　Dorothy Gorman, prin.
Smith ES, CAMBRIDGE AVE　07662
　Harry Comiskey, prin.
Washington ES, MARKET ST　07662
　Elmer Modla, prin.

St. Philip Apostle ES
　492 SADDLE RIVER RAOD　07662

Saddle River, Bergen Co.
Saddle River SD
Sch. Sys. Enr. Code 2
Supt. – Robert Collins
　97 E ALLENDALE AVE　07458
Wandell ES, 97 E ALLENDALE RD　07458
　Robert Collins, prin.

Salem, Salem Co., Pop. Code 6
Elsinboro Twp. SD
Sch. Sys. Enr. Code 2
Supt. – Mark Durand
　RURAL ROUTE 03　BOX 125　08079
Elsinboro Twp. ES
　RURAL ROUTE 03 BOX 125　08079
　Mark Durand, prin.

Lower Alloways Creek Twp. SD
Sch. Sys. Enr. Code 2
Supt. – Gary Myers, 967 MAIN ST　08079
Lower Alloways Creek ES
　967 MAIN ST CANTON　08079 – Gary Myers, prin.

Mannington Twp. SD
Sch. Sys. Enr. Code 2
Supt. – Stephen Combs, RURAL ROUTE 02　08079
Mannington ES, RURAL ROUTE 01　08079
　Stephen Combs, prin.

Salem CSD
Sch. Sys. Enr. Code 4
Supt. – Richard Rhau, 223 E BROADWAY　08079
MS, NEW MARKET ST　08079 – J Brown, prin.
Fenwick ES, WALNUT & SMITH ST　08079
　Esther Lee, prin.

St. Mary ES, 31 OAK ST　08079

Sayreville, Middlesex Co., Pop. Code 8
Sayerville SD
Supt. – See Parlin
Wilson ES, 65 DANE ST　08872 – Roy Dill, prin.

Our Lady of Victories ES, 36 MAIN ST　08872
St. Kostka ES, 221 MACARTHUR AVE　08872

Scotch Plains, Union Co., Pop. Code 7
Scotch Plains-Fanwood Regional SD
Sch. Sys. Enr. Code 5
Supt. – Robert J. Howlett
　2630 PLAINFIELD AVE　07076
Park MS, PARK AVE　07076 – Chester Janusz, prin.
Terrill MS, 1301 TERRILL ROAD　07076
　John Foulks, prin.
Brunner ES, 721 WESTFIELD RD　07076
　Dr. Albert DeSousa, prin.
Coles ES, 16 KEVIN RD　07076 – Carl Kumpf, prin.
Evergreen ES, EVERGREEN AVE　07076
　Beverlee Kaminetzky, prin.
McGinn ES, TRENTON AVE　07076
　Robert Raths, prin.
ES 1, WILLOW AVE　07076 – James Cerasa, prin.

St. Bartholomew the Apostle ES
　2032 WESTFIELD AVE　07076

Seabrook, Cumberland Co., Pop. Code 4
Upper Deerfield Twp. SD
Sch. Sys. Enr. Code 3
Supt. – L. Morris, HIGHWAY 77　08302
Woodruff MS, HIGHWAY 77　08302
　Sherman DeMill, prin.
Moore MS, HIGHWAY 77　08302
　Henry Suizman, prin.
ES, HIGHWAY 77　08302 – Adelaide White, prin.

Sea Girt, Monmouth Co., Pop. Code 5
Sea Girt Borough SD
Sch. Sys. Enr. Code 2
Supt. – William Pentony, BELL PLACE　08750
ES, BELL PL　08750 – William Pentony, prin.

Wall Twp. SD
Supt. – See Wall
Old Mill ES, 2119 OLD MILL RD　08750
　Harry Baldwin, prin.

Sea Isle City, Cape May Co., Pop. Code 5
Sea Isle CSD
Sch. Sys. Enr. Code 2
Supt. – Frank Dougherty, 4500 PARK ROAD　08243
Sea Isle ES, 4500 PARK RD　08243
　Frank Dougherty, prin.

St. Joseph Regional ES
　44TH AND CENTRAL AVE　08243

Seaside Heights, Ocean Co., Pop. Code 4
Seaside Heights Borough SD
Sch. Sys. Enr. Code 2
Supt. – Edmund DeLeo, BAY BOULEVARD　08751
Boyd ES, 1200 BAY BLVD　08751
　Edmund DeLeo, prin.

Seaside Park, Ocean Co., Pop. Code 4
Seaside Park Borough SD
Sch. Sys. Enr. Code 2
Supt. – Clara Thomas
　CENTRAL & FOURTH AVES　08752
ES, FOURTH AND CENTRAL AVE　08752
　Clara Thomas, prin.

Secaucus, Hudson Co., Pop. Code 7
Secaucus SD
Sch. Sys. Enr. Code 4
Supt. – Constantino Scerbo, 685 FIFTH ST　07094
Clarendon ES 4, 685 FIFTH ST　07094
　Francis Dougherty, prin.
Huber Street ES 3
　PATERSON PLANK ROAD　07094
　Peggy Burke, prin.

Immaculate Conception ES
　760 POST PLAC　07094

Sergeantsville, Hunterdon Co.
Delaware Twp. SD
Sch. Sys. Enr. Code 3
Supt. – Thomas Smith　08557
Delaware Twp. MS, ROUTE 604　08557
　John Fox, prin.
Delaware Twp. ES 1, ROUTE 604　08557
　John Fox, prin.

Sewaren, Middlesex Co., Pop. Code 5
Woodbridge Twp. SD
Supt. – See Woodbridge
Glen Cove ES, OLD ROAD　07077 – (—), prin.

Sewell, Gloucester Co., Pop. Code 4
Mantua Twp. SD
Sch. Sys. Enr. Code 3
Supt. – David Porreca
　DR H SIMMERMAN ADMIN BLDG　08080
ES, MCANNALLY DR　08080 – James Bailey, prin.
Other Schools – See Mantua

Washington Twp. SD
Sch. Sys. Enr. Code 6
Supt. – Robert Terrill
　RURAL ROUTE 03　BOX 286　08080
Grenloch Terrace ES, RURAL ROUTE 03　08080
　Willard Downham, prin.
Hurffville MS, RURAL ROUTE 03　08080
　Vincent Cavalea, prin.
Wedgwood ES, RURAL ROUTE 01 BOX 364　08080
　David Rauenzahn, prin.
Other Schools – See Turnersville

Shiloh, Cumberland Co., Pop. Code 3
Shiloh SD
Sch. Sys. Enr. Code 1
Supt. – Robert Kinzel, MAIN STREET　08353
ES, P O BOX 189　08353 – Robert Kinzel, prin.

Ship Bottom, Ocean Co., Pop. Code 4
Long Beach Island SD
Sch. Sys. Enr. Code 2
Supt. – Blossom Nissman
　20TH AND CENTRAL ST　08008
Long Beach Island MS
　20TH & CENTRAL ST　08008
　Blossom Nissman, prin.
Other Schools – See Surf City

Short Hills, Essex Co.
Millburn Twp. SD
Supt. – See Millburn
Deerfield ES, TROY DR　07078 – Dr. G. Clark, prin.
Glenwood ES, 315 TAYLOR RD S　07078
　Dr. Jean Schmidt, prin.
Hartshorn ES, 400 HARTSHORN DR　07078
　Robert Laib, prin.

Pingry Short Hills ES
　50 COUNTRY DAY DR　07078
St. Rose of Lima ES, 52 SHORT HILLS AVE　07078

Shrewsbury, Monmouth Co., Pop. Code 5
Shrewsbury Borough SD
Sch. Sys. Enr. Code 2
Supt. – Dr. Wayne Cochrane
　20 OBRE PLACE　07701
ES, 20 OBRE PL　07702
　Dr. Wayne Cochrane, prin.

Sicklerville, Camden Co.
Gloucester Twp. SD
Supt. – See Blackwood
Erial ES 5, P O BOX 778　08081
　Raymond Lipstas, prin.
Lilley ES, 1275 WILLIAMSTOWN ROAD　08081
　Nancy Decker, prin.

Winslow Twp. SD
Supt. – See Hammonton
Winslow Twp. ES 3, SICKERVILLE ROAD　08081
　Leslie Carestio, prin.
Winslow Twp. ES 4, 541 WILBY RD　08081
　William Dennison, prin.

Skillman, Somerset Co., Pop. Code 5
Montgomery Twp. SD
Sch. Sys. Enr. Code 4
Supt. – Jamieson McKenzie, P O BOX 147B　08558
Montgomery MS, BURNT HILL RD　08558
　Arthur Firestone, prin.
Burnt Hill Road ES, 270 ORCHARD RD　08558
　Basil Smith, prin.
Orchard Road MS, 244 ORCHARD RD　08558
　Herbert Forder, prin.

Somerdale, Camden Co., Pop. Code 6
Somerdale Borough SD
Sch. Sys. Enr. Code 2
Supt. – Karen Springer
　301 W SOMERDALE ROAD　08083
ES 1, 301 W SOMERDALE RD　08083
　Dr. Karen Springer, prin.
Somerdale Park ES, 500 GRACE ST　08083
　Charles Wiemer, prin.

Our Lady Grace ES
　105 N WHITE HORSE PIKE　08083

Somerset, Somerset Co., Pop. Code 7
Franklin Twp. SD
Sch. Sys. Enr. Code 5
Supt. – Ronald Whyte, 1 RAILROAD AVE　08873
Smith MS, 1651 AMWELL ROAD　08873
　Carl Wade, prin.
Conerly Road MS, CONERLY ROAD　08873
　Dr. Jack Pirone, prin.
Elizabeth Avenue ES, ELIZABETH AVE　08873
　Dr. Ralph Conti, prin.
Hillcrest MS, 500 FRANKLIN BLVD　08873
　Linda Beyea, prin.
MacAfee ES, 53 MACAFEE RD　08873
　C. Delcasale,Jr., prin.

Pine Grove Manor ES
 HIGHLAND & PINE GROVE AVES 09973
 George Dixon, prin.
 Other Schools – See Franklin Park, Kingston

Rutgers Prep School, 1345 EASTON AVE 08873
St. Matthias ES
 170 JOHN F KENNEDY BLVD 08873

Somers Point, Atlantic Co., Pop. Code 7
 Somers Point SD
 Sch. Sys. Enr. Code 4
 Supt. – William Troehler
  JORDAN SCHOOL ROAD 08244
 Dawes Avenue ES, DAWES AVE 08244
  Jack Burg, prin.
 Jordan Road ES, 129 JORDAN RD 08244
  John Wise,Jr., prin.
 New York Avenue ES, NEW YORK AVE 08244
  Jack Burg, prin.

St. Joseph ES, 580 SHORE RD 08244

Somerville, Somerset Co., Pop. Code 7
 Branchburg Twp. SD
 Sch. Sys. Enr. Code 4
 Supt. – John Pastre
  140 CEDAR GROVE ROAD 08876
 Central MS, 220 BAIRD ROAD 08876
  George Resavy, prin.
 Old York ES, 580 OLD YORK RD 08876
  Joseph Capanna, prin.
 Stony Brook MS, 136 CEDAR GROVE RD 08876
  George Bunting, prin.

Hillsborough Twp. SD
 Supt. – See Belle Mead
 Hillsborough MS, 260 TRIANGLE ROAD 08876
  Jane Benner, prin.
 Sunnymead ES, 55 SUNNYMEAD RD 08876
  William Schwalenberg, prin.
 Triangle ES, 156 TRIANGLE RD 08876
  Alan Rosenlicht, prin.

Somerville SD
 Sch. Sys. Enr. Code 4
 Supt. – James Dwyer, 51 W CLIFF ST 08876
 MS, W CLIFF ST 08876 – Francis Spera, prin.
 Central MS, WEST HIGH ST 08876
  Philip Chalupa, prin.
 Van Derveer ES, 55 UNION AVE 08876
  Margaret Pavol, prin.

Immaculate Conception ES
 41 MOUNTAIN AVE 08876

South Amboy, Middlesex Co., Pop. Code 6
 South Amboy SD
 Sch. Sys. Enr. Code 3
 Supt. – John Olexa, 240 JOHN ST 08879
 MS, LINCOLN ST 08879 – George Mahoney, prin.
 ES, 249 JOHN ST 08879 – Joanne Frank, prin.

Sacred Heart ES, 229 CEDAR ST 08879
St. Mary ES, 301 SECOND ST 08879

South Bound Brook, Somerset Co., Pop. Code 5
 South Bound Brook SD
 Sch. Sys. Enr. Code 2
 Supt. – Fred Cooley, 125 MADISON ST 08880
 Brampton MS, 125 MADISON ST 08880
  Barney Fabbo, prin.
 Morris/Voorhees ES, 107 ELIZABETH ST 08880
  Joseph Verderami, prin.

South Hackensac, Bergen Co., Pop. Code 4
 South Hackensack SD
 Sch. Sys. Enr. Code 2
 Supt. – Stephen Marchese, DYER AVE 07606
 Memorial ES, DYER AVE 07606
  Stephen Marchese, prin.

South Orange, Essex Co., Pop. Code 7
 South Orange-Maplewood SD
 Supt. – See Maplewood
 MS, 70 N RIDGEWOOD ROAD 07079
  Joseph Duchesneau, prin.
 Marshall ES, 262 GROVE RD 07079
  Edmund Krause, prin.
 South Mountain ES
  444 W SOUTH ORANGE AVE 07079
  Nancy Murray, prin.

Our Lady of Sorrows ES, 172 ACADEMY ST 07079

South Plainfield, Middlesex Co., Pop. Code 7
 South Plainfield SD
 Sch. Sys. Enr. Code 5
 Supt. – Leonard Tobias
  2480 PLAINFIELD AVE 07080
 MS, 2201 PLAINFIELD AVE 07080
  James Dowden, prin.
 Franklin ES, 1000 FRANKLIN AVE 07080
  Thomas Lenahan, prin.
 Kennedy ES, 2900 NORWOOD AVE 07080
  Victor Porcelli, prin.
 Riley ES, MORRIS AVE 07080
  Anthony Sincavage, prin.
 Roosevelt ES, 130 JACKSON AVE 07080
  Mario Barbiere, prin.

Sacred Heart ES, SACRED HEART DRIVE 07080

South River, Middlesex Co., Pop. Code 7
 South River SD
 Sch. Sys. Enr. Code 4
 Supt. – Ernest Barberio, MONTGOMERY ST 08882
 MS, 20 THOMAS ST 08882 – Louis Gambo, prin.
 Campbell ES, 22 DAVID ST 08882
  Edward Kloskowski, prin.
 Willett ES, 34A CHARLES ST 08882
  Walter Boyler, prin.

Corpus Christi ES, 80 DAVID ST 08882
St. Mary ES, 22 HOLMES AVE 08882

Sparta, Sussex Co., Pop. Code 7
 Sparta Twp. SD
 Sch. Sys. Enr. Code 5
 Supt. – John Greed, 328 SPARTA AVE 07871
 JHS, 18 MOHAWK AVE 07871
  Herbert Libourel, prin.
 Morgan ES, 100 STANHOPE RD 07871
  Mildred Hanley, prin.
 Sparta Alpine ES, 151 ANDOVER RD 07871
  Charles Leach, prin.

Hilltop Montessori ES, 32 LAFAYETTE RD 07871
Reverend Brown Memorial School
 294 SPARTA AVE 07871

Spotswood, Middlesex Co., Pop. Code 6
 Monroe Twp. SD
 Supt. – See Jamesburg
 Mill Lake ES, MONMOUTH RD 08884
  Nancy Richmond, prin.
 Woodland MS, HARRISON AVE 08884
  Peter Shamy, prin.

Spotswood SD
 Sch. Sys. Enr. Code 4
 Supt. – Robert Byrne, 500 MAIN ST 08884
 Appleby ES, VLIET ST 08884 – John Orlick, prin.
 Schoenly ES, 80 KANE AVE 08884
  Carolyn Deacon, prin.

Immaculate Conception ES
 23 MANALAPAN RD 08884

Springfield, Union Co., Pop. Code 7
 Springfield Twp. SD
 Sch. Sys. Enr. Code 3
 Supt. – Gary Friedland, P O BOX 210 07081
 Gaudineer MS, 75 S SPRINGFIELD AVE 07081
  Kenneth Bernabe, prin.
 Caldwell ES, 36 CALDWELL PL 07081
  Dr. Robert Black,Jr., prin.
 Sandmeier ES, 666 S SPRINGFIELD AVE 07081
  Michael Antolino, prin.

St. James ES, 41 S SPRINGFIELD AVE 07081

Spring Lake, Monmouth Co., Pop. Code 5
 Spring Lake Heights Borough SD
 Supt. – See Spring Lake Heights
 Spring Lake Heights ES, 1110 HIGHWAY 71 07762
  William Smith, prin.

Spring Lake SD
 Sch. Sys. Enr. Code 2
 Supt. – Frank Apito, 411 TUTTLE AVE 07762
 Mountz ES, 411 TUTTLE AVE 07762
  Frank Apito, prin.

St. Catherine ES, 2ND AND SALEM AVES 07762

Spring Lake Heights, Monmouth Co., Pop. Code 6
 Spring Lake Heights Borough SD
 Sch. Sys. Enr. Code 2
 Supt. – William Smith, 1110 HIGHWAY 71 07762
 Other Schools – See Spring Lake

Stanhope, Sussex Co., Pop. Code 5
 Bryam Twp. SD
 Sch. Sys. Enr. Code 3
 Supt. – Dr. Edward Domanico
  12 MANSIFIELD DR 07874
 Byram Twp. IS, 12 MANEFURD DR 07874
  James Direnzo, prin.
 Byram Twp. Consolidated ES
  12 MANEFURD DR 07874
  Arthur Anderson, prin.

Stanhope Borough SD
 Sch. Sys. Enr. Code 2
 Supt. – John Ammon, VALLEY ROAD 07874
 Linden Avenue ES, LINDEN AVE 07874
  Robert Herman, prin.
 Valley Road MS, VALLEY ROAD 07874
  Robert Herman, prin.

Stewartsville, Warren Co.
 Greenwich Twp. SD
 Sch. Sys. Enr. Code 2
 Supt. – John Frey II, P O BOX 276C 08886
 MS, RURAL ROUTE 01 BOX 276-C 08886
  John Frey II, prin.
 Greenwich Twp. ES
  RURAL ROUTE 01 BOX 276-C 08886
  John Frey II, prin.

Stillwater, Sussex Co.
 Stillwater Twp. SD
 Sch. Sys. Enr. Code 2
 Supt. – Jacqueline Giordano, P O BOX 12 07875
 Stillwater Twp. ES, P O BOX 12 07875
  Jacqueline Giordano, prin.

Stirling, Morris Co.
 Passaic Twp. SD
 Sch. Sys. Enr. Code 3
 Supt. – Victor Schumacher, 331 ELM ST 07980
 Central MS, 90 CENTRAL AVE 07980
  Vito D'Alconzo, prin.
 Other Schools – See Gillette, Millington

St. Vincent De Paul ES, 249 BEBOUT AVE 07980

Stockton, Hunterdon Co., Pop. Code 3
 Stockton Borough SD
 Sch. Sys. Enr. Code 1
 Supt. – Marlene Leeb, P O BOX F 08559
 Stockton Boro ES, BOX F MAIN ST 08559
  Marlene Leeb, prin.

Stone Harbor, Cape May Co., Pop. Code 4
 Stone Harbor SD
 Sch. Sys. Enr. Code 1
 Supt. – R. Donald Wendorf
  93RD ST & 3RD AVE 08247
 ES, 93RD ST 08247 – R. Wendorf, prin.

Stratford, Camden Co., Pop. Code 6
 Stratford Borough SD
 Sch. Sys. Enr. Code 3
 Supt. – Gene Iannette
  317 PRINCETON AVE 08084
 Yellin MS, 111 WARWICK RD 08084
  Arnold Wiseman, prin.
 Parkview PS, PARKVIEW ROAD 08084
  James Dailey, prin.

St. Luke ES, 55 WARWICK RD 08084

Succasunna, Morris Co., Pop. Code 6
 Roxbury Twp. SD
 Sch. Sys. Enr. Code 4
 Supt. – Leonard Elovitz, 25 MEEKER ST 07876
 Eisenhower MS, 47 EYLAND AVE 07876
  Owen Toale, prin.
 Franklin ES, 8 MEEKER ST 07876
  John Moschella, prin.
 Jefferson ES, CORN HOLLOW ROAD 07876
  Angela Krass, prin.
 Kennedy ES, PLEASANT HILL ROAD 07876
  Thomas O'Brien, prin.
 Lincoln/Roosevelt MS, 38 N HILLSIDE AVE 07876
  Joseph Mascott, prin.
 Other Schools – See Landing

St. Therese ES, 135 MAIN ST 07876

Summit, Union Co., Pop. Code 7
 Summit CSD
 Sch. Sys. Enr. Code 4
 Supt. – Richard Fiander
  14 BEEKMAN TERRACE 07901
 MS, 272 MORRIS AVE 07901
  Don DeBanico, prin.
 Brayton ES, 89 TULIP ST 07901
  Theodore Stanik, prin.
 Franklin ES, 136 BLACKBURN RD 07901
  Grace Kingsbury, prin.
 Jefferson ES, 110 ASHWOOD AVE 07901
  Janice Matistic, prin.
 Lincoln ES, 52 WOODLAND AVE 07901
  Dr. Gerard Murphy, prin.
 Washington ES, 507 MORRIS AVE 07901
  Dr. Diane Grannon, prin.

Kent Place School, 42 NORWOOD AVE 07901
Oak Knoll School, 44 BLACKBURN ROAD 07901

Surf City, Ocean Co., Pop. Code 4
 Long Beach Island SD
 Supt. – See Ship Bottom
 Jacobsen ES
  BARNEGAT AVE & SOUTH 2ND ST 08008
  (—), prin.

Sussex, Sussex Co., Pop. Code 4
 Sussex-Wantage Regional SD
 Sch. Sys. Enr. Code 4
 Supt. – Rob Clark, 31 RYAN ROAD 07461
 MS, 31 RYAN ROAD 07461 – Cort Kuehm, prin.
 Lawrence ES, 31 RYAN RD 07461
  Charles Lorber, prin.
 Wantage MS, RURAL ROUTE 01 BOX 1345 07461
  Shirley Siragusa, prin.

Sussex Christian ES, 51 UNIONVILLE AVE 07461

Swedesboro, Gloucester Co., Pop. Code 4
 Swedesboro-Woolwich SD
 Sch. Sys. Enr. Code 2
 Supt. – James Sarruda
  815 KINGS HIGHWAY 08085
 Clifford ES, AUBURN AVE 08085
  Richard Fisher, prin.
 Hill ES, 815 KINGS HWY 08085
  Richard Fisher, prin.

St. Joseph ES, 225 KINGS HWY 08085

Teaneck, Bergen Co., Pop. Code 8
 Teaneck SD
 Sch. Sys. Enr. Code 5
 Supt. – Harold Morris, 1 MERRISON AVE 07666
 Franklin MS, 1315 TAFF ROAD 07666
  Frank Allen, prin.
 Jefferson MS, 655 TENECK ROAD 07666
  Neil Glazer, prin.
 Bryant ES, TRYSON AVE 07666
  Victor Klein, prin.

Hawthorne MS, 201 FYCKE LN   07666
  Charles Attanasio, prin.
Longfellow ES, 50 OAKDENE AVE   07666
  Eunice Pruitt, prin.
Lowell MS, 1025 LINCOLN PL   07666
  Patricia Cantelmo, prin.
Whittier MS, 495 W ENGLEWOOD AVE   07666
  Alfred Mitchell, prin.

***

Grace Lutheran ES, 1200 RIVER RD   07666
St. Anastasia ES, 1135 TEANECK RD   07666

Tenafly, Bergen Co., Pop. Code 7
Tenafly SD
Sch. Sys. Enr. Code 4
Supt. – Gerald DeGrow
  500 TENAFLY ROAD   07670
MS, 36 SUNSET LANE   07670
  Robert Weldon, prin.
MacKay ES, JEFFERSON AVE   07670
  Rosemary Weltman, prin.
Maugham ES, 137 MAGNOLIA AVE   07670
  Dr. Abby Bergman, prin.
Smith ES, DOWNEY DR   07670
  Dr. Ellen Pressman, prin.
Stillman ES, TENAFLY ROAD   07670
  Dr. William Greene, prin.

***

Our Lady of Mt. Carmel ES, 10 COUNTY RD   07670

Thorofare, Gloucester Co.
West Deptford Twp. SD
Supt. – See West Deptford
Red Bank PS, PHILADELPHIA AVE   08086
  George Holefelder, prin.

Three Bridges, Hunterdon Co.
Readington Twp. SD
Supt. – See Readington
ES, MAIN ST   08887 – Karl Najaka, prin.

Tinton Falls, Monmouth Co., Pop. Code 6
Tinton Falls SD
Sch. Sys. Enr. Code 4
Supt. – Larry Ashley, 658 TINTON AVE   07724
MS, 674 TINTON AVE   07724 – Don Johnson, prin.
Atchison ES, 961 SYCAMORE AVE   07724
  Lloyd Leschuk, prin.
Swimming River MS, 220 HANCE AVE   07724
  Richard Clement, prin.

Titusville, Mercer Co.
Hopewell Valley Regional SD
Supt. – See Pennington
Bear Tavern ES, BEAR TAVERN ROAD   08560
  Richard Scheetz, prin.

Toms River, Ocean Co., Pop. Code 6
Toms River Regional SD
Sch. Sys. Enr. Code 7
Supt. – A. Dietrich, 54 WASHINGTON ST   08753
Toms River IS-East, HOOPER AVE   08753
  John Fitzgerald, prin.
Toms River IS-West, INDIAN HEAD ROAD   08753
  Mark Regan, prin.
Cedar Grove ES, 54 WASHINGTON ST   08753
  Gerald Grasso, prin.
East Dover ES, 54 WASHINGTON ST   08753
  Frank Falcetta, prin.
Hooper Avenue ES, 54 WASHINGTON ST   08753
  Ronald Swierzbin, prin.
North Dover ES, 54 WASHINGTON ST   08753
  Marie Policare, prin.
Pine Beach ES, 54 WASHINGTON ST   08753
  Carolyn Adams, prin.
Silver Bay ES, 54 WASHINGTON ST   08753
  Joseph Pizza, prin.
South Toms River ES
  54 WASHINGTON ST   08753 – John Pallen, prin.
Walnut Street ES, 54 WASHINGTON ST   08753
  Terence Bevilacqua, prin.
Washington Street ES
  54 WASHINGTON ST   08753
  Mildred Mueller, prin.
West Dover ES, 54 WASHINGTON ST   08753
  Joseph Catalano, prin.
Other Schools – See Beachwood

***

St. Joseph ES, 711 HOOPER AVE   08753

Totowa, Passaic Co., Pop. Code 7
Totowa SD
Sch. Sys. Enr. Code 3
Supt. – Nat Giancola, 93 LINCOLN AVE   07512
Memorial MS, 294 TOTOWA ROAD   07512
  Richard Trenery, prin.
Washington Park ES, 10 CREWS ST   07512
  Pat Corrado, prin.

***

St. James ES, 400 TOTOWA RD   07512

Towaco, Morris Co.
Montville Twp. SD
Supt. – See Pine Brook
Cedar Hill ES, 46 PINE BROOK RD   07082
  Bruce Delyon, prin.

Trenton, Mercer Co., Pop. Code 8
Ewing Twp. SD
Sch. Sys. Enr. Code 5
Supt. – Dennis Kelly
  1331 LOWER FERRY ROAD   08618
Antheil ES, 339 EWINGVILLE RD   08638
  Ross Gray, prin.
Lanning ES, 1927 PENNINGTON RD   08618
  Mary Riordan, prin.

Lore ES, WESTWOOD DR   08628
  John Heater, prin.
Parkway ES, PARKWAY AVE   08618
  Ralph Rogers, prin.

Hamilton Twp. SD
Sch. Sys. Enr. Code 7
Supt. – Albert DeMartin, 90 PARK AVE   08690
Grice MS, 901 WHITE HORSE-MERC ROAD   08610
  Joan Sigafoos, prin.
Reynolds MS
  2145 YARDVILLE-HAMILTON SQ   08690
  Dominick Salvatini, prin.
Greenwood ES, 2069 GREENWOOD AVE   08609
  Diane Drangula, prin.
Kisthardt ES, 215 HARCOURT DR   08610
  Patricia Vincent, prin.
Klockner ES, 830 KLOCKNER RD   08619
  Allen Gravie, prin.
Kuser ES, 70 NEWKIRK AVE   08629
  Richard Klockner, prin.
Lalor ES, 25 BARNT-DEKLYN RD   08610
  Katherine Geller, prin.
Langtree ES, 2080 WHATLEY RD   08690
  Lois Moreton, prin.
McGalliard ES, 1600 ARENA DR   08610
  Leonard Contardo, prin.
Mercerville ES, 60 REGINA AVE   08619
  Gary Bender, prin.
Morgan ES, 38 STAMFORD RD   08619
  Dr. Richard Radice, prin.
Robinson ES, 495 GROPP AVE   08610
  Richard Pierson, prin.
Sayen ES, 3333 NOTTINGHAM WAY   08690
  Amelia Marini, prin.
Sunnybrae ES, 166 ELTON AVE   08620
  Nancy Warr, prin.
Union Heights/Morrison ES
  645 PAXSON AVE   08619 – Chris Branas, prin.
Wilson ES, 600 E PARK AVE   08610
  Gary Gray, prin.
Yardville ES, 450 ALLENTOWN RD   08620
  Frank Tanzini, prin.
Other Schools – See Hamilton Square, Yardville

Trenton SD
Sch. Sys. Enr. Code 7
Supt. – Crosby Copeland
  108 N CLINTON AVE   08609
Cadwalader ES, 501 EDGEWOOD AVE   08618
  Lone Hodges, prin.
Franklin ES, WILLIAM AND LIBERTY STS   08610
  Thomas Williams, prin.
Grant ES, N CLINTON AVE & PERRY ST   08609
  Everene Downing, prin.
Gregory ES, 520 RUTHERFORD AVE   08618
  Thelma Smith, prin.
Harrison ES
  GENESSE ST NEAR CHESTNT AVE   08611
  Dr. Darwin Williams, prin.
Hill ES, 1010 E STATE ST   08609
  Howard Colvin, prin.
Jefferson ES, 411 BRUNSWICK AVE   08638
  Paul Gmitter, prin.
Kilmer ES
  STUYVESANT AVE/WHITTLESY RD   08618
  Lawrence Dun, prin.
Monument ES, MONROE ST   08618
  (—), prin.
Mott ES, STOKELY AVE   08611
  Harry Barber, prin.
Munoz-Rivera ES
  NORTH MONTGOMERY ST   08618
  Nathaniel Jones, prin.
Parker ES, UNION ST   08611 – Ernest Hilton, prin.
Robbins ES, TYLER ST   08609
  Fred Prunetti, prin.
Robeson ES, CUYLER AVE   08629
  Henry Deliz, prin.
Stokes ES, 913 PARKSIDE AVE   08618
  Kenneth Moore, prin.
Washington ES, 301 EMORY AVE   08611
  William Applegate, prin.
Wilson ES, 175 GIRARD AVE   08638
  John McBride, prin.

***

Blessed Sacrament School
  720 BELLEVUE AVE   08618
Cathedral Grammar School
  CHANCERY LANE   08618
Holy Angels ES, 1701 S BROAD ST   08610
Holy Cross ES, GRAND AND ARCH STS   08611
Immaculate Conception ES
  520 CHESTNUT AVE   08611
Incarnation ES, 1555 PENNINGTON RD   08618
Our Lady Divine Sheperd ES
  42 PENNINGTON AVE   08618
Our Lady of Sorrows ES
  3816 E STATE ST EXT   08619
Sacred Heart ES, 333 S BROAD ST   08608
St. Ann ES, 34 ROSSA AVE   08648
St. Anthony ES, 530 S OLDEN AVE   08629
St. Gregory the Great ES
  4680 HOTTINGHAM WAY   08690
St. Hedwig ES, N OLDEN & INDIANA AVES   08638
St. James ES, 27 E PAUL AVE   08638
St. Joachim ES, 21-23 BAYARD STREET   08611
St. Mary-Assumption ES, 411 ADELINE ST   08611
St. Raphael ES, 151 GROPP AVE   08610
St. Stanislaus ES, SMITH & HOME AVE   08611
Villa Victoria Lower Academy
  376 W UPPER FERRY RD   08628

Tuckahoe, Cape May Co.
Upper Twp. SD
Sch. Sys. Enr. Code 4
Supt. – John Tredinnick, P O BOX 158   08250
Upper Twp. MS, P O BOX 158   08250
  William F. Carpenter, prin.
Other Schools – See Marmora

Tuckerton, Ocean Co., Pop. Code 4
Little Egg Harbor Twp. SD
Sch. Sys. Enr. Code 4
Supt. – George Mitchell, NORTH GREEN ST   08087
Little Egg Harbor ES, NORTH GREEN ST   08087
  George Mitchell, prin.

Tuckerton Borough SD
Sch. Sys. Enr. Code 2
Supt. – Michael Fogg, P O BOX 217   08087
ES, 201 MARINE ST   08087 – Michael Fogg, prin.

Turnersville, Camden Co.
Washington Twp. SD
Supt. – See Sewell
Bells ES, GREENTREE ROAD   08012
  Terry Vanzoren, prin.
Birches ES, WESTMINSTER BLVD   08012
  Margaret Zycinsky, prin.
Jefferson ES, ALDEBERAN & ALTAIR DRS   08012
  Joseph Indriso, prin.
Whitman ES, COACH RD & WHITMAR DR   08012
  W. Suter, prin.

Union, Union Co., Pop. Code 8
Union Twp. SD
Sch. Sys. Enr. Code 6
Supt. – James Caulfield, 2369 MORRIS AVE   07083
Battle Hill ES, 2654 KILLIAN PL   07083
  Martin Poltrock, prin.
Central Six-Jefferson MS, HILTON AVE   07083
  Vernell Wright, prin.
Connecticut Farms ES
  711 STUYVESANT AVE   07083
  Robert Petracco, prin.
Franklin ES, LINDY TER   07083
  Robert Jeranek, prin.
Hamilton ES, 1231 BURNET AVE   07083
  Arlene Schor, prin.
Livingston ES, 960 MIDLAND BLVD   07083
  Joseph Catino, prin.
Washington ES, WASHINGTON ST   07083
  Michael Bury, prin.

***

Holy Spirit ES, 984 SUBURBAN RD   07083
St. Michael ES, 1212 KELLY ST   07083

Union Beach, Monmouth Co., Pop. Code 6
Union Beach Borough SD
Sch. Sys. Enr. Code 3
Supt. – Donald Foley, FLORENCE AVE   07735
Memorial ES, 201 MORNINGSIDE AVE   07735
  Melvin Card, prin.

Union City, Hudson Co., Pop. Code 8
Union City SD
Sch. Sys. Enr. Code 6
Supt. – Richard Hanna
  3912 BERGENLINE AVE   07087
Edison ES, 507 WEST ST   07087
  Walter Zuccaro, prin.
Gilmore ES, 815 17TH ST   07087
  Robert Leppert, prin.
Hudson ES, 167 19TH ST   07087
  Frank Acinapura, prin.
Roosevelt ES, 4507 HUDSON AVE   07087
  Charles Dallago, prin.
Washington ES, 3905 NEW YORK AVE   07087
  Anthony Gregory, prin.
Waters ES, 2800 SUMMIT AVE   07087
  Stanley Sanger, prin.

***

Holy Rosary ES, 501 15TH ST   07087
St. Anthony ES, 700 CENTRAL AVE   07087
St. Augustine ES, 3920 NEW YORK AVE   07087
St. Francis Academy, 1601 CENTRAL AVE   07087
St. Michael ES, 1500 NEW YORK AVE   07087

Upper Saddle River, Bergen Co., Pop. Code 6
Upper Saddle River SD
Sch. Sys. Enr. Code 3
Supt. – T. Benson
  395 W SADDLE RIVER ROAD   07458
Cavallini MS, 395 W SADDLE RIVER ROAD   07458
  James Meisterich, prin.
Bogert ES, WEST SADDLE RIVER ROAD   07458
  Robert Franchino, prin.
Reynolds ES, WEST SADDLE RIVER ROAD   07458
  Morris Corn, prin.

Ventnor City, Atlantic Co., Pop. Code 7
Ventnor CSD
Sch. Sys. Enr. Code 3
Supt. – Dennis Kelly, LAFAYETTE AVE N   08406
MS, LAFAYETTE AVE N   08406
  Anthony DiCosola, prin.
Lafayette PS, NORTH LAFAYETTE AVE   08406
  William Gussie, prin.

***

St. James ES, 30 S PORTLAND AVE   08406

Vernon, Sussex Co., Pop. Code 7
Vernon Twp. SD
Sch. Sys. Enr. Code 5
Supt. – George Iannacone, P O BOX 296   07462
Glen Meadow MS, P O BOX 516   07462
  George Chintala, prin.

Lounsberry Hollow MS, P O BOX 219   07462
  John Paskey, prin.
Cedar Mountain ES, P O BOX 99   07462
  Fred Podorf, prin.
Rolling Hills ES, P O BOX 769   07462
  Mark Mongon, prin.
Walnut Ridge ES, P O BOX 190   07462
  Fred Pordorf, prin.

Verona, Essex Co., Pop. Code 7
Verona SD
Sch. Sys. Enr. Code 4
Supt. – John P. Pryor, 30 GOULD ST   07044
Whitehorne MS, 600 BLOOMFIELD AVE   07044
  Robert Palo, prin.
Brookdale Avenue ES, 14 BROOKDALE CT   07044
  Donald West, prin.
Brown ES, 125 GROVE AVE   07044
  Donald West, prin.
Forest Avenue ES, 118 FOREST AVE   07044
  Regina Klein, prin.
Laning Avenue ES, 18 LANNING RD   07044
  Regina Klein, prin.

Our Lady of the Lake ES
  MONTROSE/LAKESIDE AVES   07044

Villas, Cape May Co., Pop. Code 5
Lower Twp. SD
Supt. – See Cape May
Memorial ES, 2600 BAYSHORE RD   08251
  Peter Holt, prin.

St. Raymond ES, 25 E OCEAN AVE   08251

Vincentown, Burlington Co.
Shamong Twp. SD
Sch. Sys. Enr. Code 3
Supt. – Leo Rea, RURAL ROUTE 02   08088
Indian Mills ES
  256 MEDFORD INDIAN MILLS RD   08088
  Roger Wagner, prin.

Southampton Twp. SD
Sch. Sys. Enr. Code 3
Supt. – James Kerfoot, P O BOX 2186   08088
Southampton Twp. MS, PLEASANT ST   08088
  Raymond Marini, prin.
Southampton Twp. PS 1, PLEASANT ST   08088
  Richard Gigliotti, prin.

Tabernacle Twp. SD
Sch. Sys. Enr. Code 4
Supt. – Ken Olson, 132 NEW ROAD   08088
Tabernacle MS, 132 NEW ROAD   08088
  Roger Hladky, prin.
Tabernacle ES 1, 132 NEW RD   08088
  Betty Kishler, prin.
Tabernacle ES 2, 132 NEW RD   08088
  Betty Shine, prin.

Vineland, Cumberland Co., Pop. Code 8
Vineland SD
Sch. Sys. Enr. Code 6
Supt. – Carl Simmons, 625 PLUM ST   08360
D'Ippolito MS, 1578 N VALLEY AVE   08360
  Leslie Moser, prin.
Landis JHS, 61 W LANDIS AVE   08360
  James Brown, prin.
Memorial MS, 424 S MAIN ROAD   08360
  Thomas Baldosaro, prin.
Rossi MS, 2572 PALERMO AVE   08360
  Charles Schoendorf, prin.
Barse ES, 240 S ORCHARD RD   08360
  Pauline Petway, prin.
Cunningham ES, 315 S EAST AVE   08360
  Howard Jay, prin.
Durand ES, 371 W FOREST GROVE RD   08360
  William Maenner, prin.
Johnstone ES, 165 S BREWSTER RD   08360
  Edward Walsh, prin.
Leuchter ES, 519 N WEST AVE   08360
  Frank Lombardo, prin.
Mennies ES, GRANT AVE   08360
  Richard Prochaska, prin.
South Vineland PS, 2831 SE BOULEVARD   08360
  Howard Jay, prin.
Winslow ES, 1335 MAGNOLIA RD   08360
  Keith Figgs, prin.

Sacred Heart ES, 922 E LANDIS AVE   08360
St. Francis of Assisi ES
  23 W CHESTNUT AVE   08360
St. Mary ES, 8 S UNION ROAD   08360

Voorhees, Camden Co., Pop. Code 7
Voorhees Twp. SD
Supt. – See Kirkwood Voorhees
Kresson ES 3, SCHOOL LANE   08043
  John Palsha, prin.

Waldwick, Bergen Co., Pop. Code 7
Waldwick SD
Sch. Sys. Enr. Code 4
Supt. – Joseph Mas, 155 SUMMIT AVE   07463
Crescent ES, CRESCENT AVE   07463
  Dr. Sally Downham, prin.
Traphagen ES, 165 SUMMIT AVE   07463
  Peter Muir, prin.

Wall, Monmouth Co., Pop. Code 7
Wall Twp. SD
Sch. Sys. Enr. Code 5
Supt. – Mark Franceschini, P O BOX 1199   07719
IS, RURAL ROUTE 01   07719
  Douglas Bohrer, prin.

Allenwood ES, P O BOX 1199   07719
  John Gasparini, prin.
Central ES, 2007 ALLENWOOD RD   07719
  John Najar, prin.
West Belmar ES, 925 17TH AVE   07719
  Francis Groff, prin.
Other Schools – See Sea Girt

Wallington, Bergen Co., Pop. Code 7
Wallington SD
Sch. Sys. Enr. Code 3
Supt. – G. Natale, 30 PINE ST   07057
Gavlak ES, 106 KING ST   07057
  John Markey, prin.
Jefferson ES, 30 PINE ST   07057
  John Markey, prin.

Most Sacred Heart ES, 6 BOND ST   07057

Wanaque, Passaic Co., Pop. Code 7
Wanaque SD
Sch. Sys. Enr. Code 3
Supt. – Enrico Cipolaro
  547 RINGWOOD AVE   07465
ES, 1 1ST ST   07465 – Franklyn Edwards, prin.
Other Schools – See Haskell

Waretown, Ocean Co.
Ocean Twp. SD
Sch. Sys. Enr. Code 3
Supt. – E. Stephen Seeley
  WELLS MILL ROAD RT 532   08758
Priff MS, ROUTE 532 WELLS MILL ROAD   08758
  E. Seeley, prin.
ES, RAILROAD AVE   08758
  Donald Bochicchio, prin.

Warren, Somerset Co., Pop. Code 6
Warren Twp. SD
Sch. Sys. Enr. Code 4
Supt. – Angelo Tomaso
  114 STIRLING ROAD   07060
MS, 100 OLD STIRLING ROAD   07060
  Michael Hoffman, prin.
Central ES, 109 MT BETHEL RD   07060
  Dr. Michael Gallina, prin.
Mt. Horeb ES, 80 MT HOREB RD   07060
  Dr. Joseph Ciklamini, prin.

Woodbridge Twp. SD
Supt. – See Woodbridge
Jago ES, OLD RD   07077 – Albina D'Allessio, prin.

Washington, Warren Co., Pop. Code 6
Franklin Twp. SD
Sch. Sys. Enr. Code 2
Supt. – Joseph Damms,Jr.
  RURAL ROUTE 01 BOX 155A   07882
Franklin Twp. Consolidated ES
  RURAL ROUTE 01 BOX 155A   07882
  Joseph Damms, prin.

Washington Borough SD
Sch. Sys. Enr. Code 3
Supt. – Patrick O'Malley
  300 W STEWART ST   07882
Taylor Street ES, 16-24 TAYLOR ST   07882
  John Santo, prin.
Washington Memorial ES
  300 W STEWART ST   07882
  Patrick O'Malley, prin.

Washington SD
Sch. Sys. Enr. Code 3
Supt. – Barry Dornich, R D #3 BOX 9   07882
Brass Castle ES, RURAL ROUTE 04 BOX 56   07882
  Barry Dornich, prin.
Port Colden ES, RURAL ROUTE 03 BOX 9   07882
  Barry Dornich, prin.

Watchung, Somerset Co., Pop. Code 6
Watchung Borough SD
Sch. Sys. Enr. Code 2
Supt. – Patrick Parenty
  VALLEYVIEW ROAD   07060
Valley View MS, VALLEYVIEW ROAD   07060
  Marlene Marburg, prin.
Bayberry ES, 113 BAYBERRY LN   07060
  Walter Kasman, prin.

Waterford Works, Camden Co.
Chesilhurst Borough SD
Sch. Sys. Enr. Code 2
Supt. – Shirley Foster
  SIXTH & EDWARDS AVES   08089
Chesilhurst ES, 6TH AND EDWARD AVE   08089
  Shirley Foster, prin.

Waterford Twp. SD
Supt. – See Atco
Waterford MS
  825 OLD WHITE HORSE PIKE   08089
  Gary Dentino, prin.

Wayne, Passaic Co., Pop. Code 8
Wayne Twp. SD
Sch. Sys. Enr. Code 6
Supt. – Rob Winter, 50 NELLIS DR   07470
Schuyler-Colfax JHS
  1500 HAMBURG TPKE   07470
  Eugene Sudol, prin.
Washington MS, 68 LENOX ROAD   07470
  Americo Romeo, prin.
Carter ES, 531 ALPS RD   07470
  Walter Liggett, prin.
Dey ES, 55 WEBSTER DR   07470
  Benjamin Veal, prin.

Kennedy ES, 1310 RATZER RD   07470
  Martin Brennan, prin.
Lafayette ES, 100 LAAUWE AVE   07470
  Joseph Briere, prin.
Packanack ES, 190 OAKWOOD DR   07470
  Lawrence Tilli, prin.
Pines Lake ES, SCHOOL ROAD   07470
  Albert Zanetti, prin.
Ryerson ES, 30 MCCLELLAND AVE   07470
  Charles Hunziker, prin.
Terhune ES, 40 CYANAMID DR   07470
  Russell DeVries, prin.

Immaculate Heart of Mary ES
  580 RATZER RD   07470
Our Lady Consolation ES
  1799 HAMBURG TPKE   07470
Our Lady of the Valley ES, 620 VALLEY RD   07470

Weehawken, Hudson Co., Pop. Code 7
Weehawken Twp. SD
Sch. Sys. Enr. Code 4
Supt. – Bernard Karabin
  53 LIBERTY PLACE   07087
Roosevelt ES 5, 1 LOUISA PL   07087
  Arthur Palumbo, prin.
Webster ES 2, 2700 PALISADE AVE   07087
  Bernard Karabin, prin.
Wilson ES 4, HAUXHURST AVE   07087
  Howard Wolf, prin.

Wenonah, Gloucester Co., Pop. Code 4
Deptford Twp. SD
Supt. – See Deptford
Oak Valley ES
  COLLEGE & UNIVERSITY BLVDS   08090
  Albert Miller, prin.
Pine Acres ES, LYNNE & PURDUE AVES   08090
  Charles Buchert, prin.

Wenonah SD
Sch. Sys. Enr. Code 2
Supt. – John Herbst, 200 N CLINTON AVE   08090
ES, CLINTON & ELM AVES   08090
  John Herbst, prin.

West Berlin, Camden Co., Pop. Code 5
Berlin Twp. SD
Sch. Sys. Enr. Code 3
Supt. – Charles Caramanna
  231 GROVE AVE   08091
Eisenhower Memorial MS, 189 GROVE AVE   08091
  Robert Neidig, prin.
Kennedy Memorial ES, 229 GROVE AVE   08091
  Robert Neidig, prin.

Voorhees Twp. SD
Supt. – See Kirkwood Voorhees
Hamilton ES, 1 BOUNDRY LN   08091
  Louise Ward, prin.

West Caldwell, Essex Co., Pop. Code 7
Caldwell-West Caldwell SD
Supt. – See Caldwell
Washington ES, CENTRAL AVE   07006
  Dr. Daniel Gerardi, prin.

West Cape May, Cape May Co., Pop. Code 4
West Cape May SD
Sch. Sys. Enr. Code 1
Supt. – Lawrence Kelly, 301 MOORE ST   08204
ES, 301 MOORE ST   08204 – Lawrence Kelly, prin.

West Creek, Ocean Co.
Eagleswood Twp. SD
Sch. Sys. Enr. Code 2
Supt. – Franklin Mattarazzo
  RURAL ROUTE 09 BOX 355   08092
Eagleswood Twp. ES, P O BOX 355   08092
  Franklin Mattarazzo, prin.

West Deptford, Gloucester Co., Pop. Code 7
West Deptford Twp. SD
Sch. Sys. Enr. Code 5
Supt. – Charles McNally, GROVE ROAD   08066
MS, GROVE ROAD   08066 – Fred Gilfillin, prin.
Other Schools – See Thorofare, Woodbury

Westfield, Union Co., Pop. Code 8
Westfield SD
Sch. Sys. Enr. Code 5
Supt. – Mark Smith, 305 ELM ST   07090
Edison IS, 800 RAHWAY AVE   07090
  Samuel Hazell, prin.
Roosevelt IS, 301 CLARK ST   07090
  Eugene Voll, prin.
Franklin ES, 700 PROSPECT ST   07090
  Faith Divisek, prin.
Jefferson ES, 1200 BOULEVARD   07090
  Kelley Kissiah, prin.
McKinley ES, 500 FIRST ST   07090
  Edward Braynock, prin.
Tamaques ES, 641 WILLOW GROVE RD   07090
  David Tuller, prin.
Washington ES, 900 SAINT MARKS AVE   07090
  Kenneth Wark, prin.
Wilson ES, 301 LINDEN AVE   07090
  Margaret Scheck, prin.

Holy Trinity ES, 336 FIRST ST   07090
Redeemer Lutheran ES
  229 COWPERTHWAITE PL   07090

West Long Branch, Monmouth Co., Pop. Code 6
West Long Branch SD
Sch. Sys. Enr. Code 3
Supt. – Peter Sandilos, 135 LOCUST AVE   07764

Antonides MS, 135 LOCUST AVE 07764
  Betty McElmon, prin.
Wall Street ES, 200 WALL ST 07764
  Dr. Betty McElmon, prin.

St. Jerome ES, 250 WALL ST 07764

West Milford, Passaic Co., Pop. Code 7
West Milford Twp. SD
Sch. Sys. Enr. Code 5
Supt. – William Koy, 46 ARNOLD ROAD 07480
Macopin MS, 70 ARNOLD ROAD 07480
  James Woldow, prin.
Apshawa ES, 140 HIGH CREST DR 07480
  Dr. C. Gateman, prin.
Maple Road ES, 36 MAPLE RD 07480
  Robert Florian, prin.
Marshall Hill ES, 210 MARSHALL HILL RD 07480
  Daniel Mullen, prin.
Westbrook ES, 55 MASENGO POND ROAD 07480
  James Sarto, prin.
Other Schools – See Hewitt, Oak Ridge

St. Joseph ES, 454 GERMANTOWN RD 07480

West New York, Hudson Co., Pop. Code 8
West New York SD
Sch. Sys. Enr. Code 6
Supt. – C. Raparelli, 100 51ST ST 07093
Bain ES, 6200 BROADWAY 07093
  Donald Rocker, prin.
ES 1, 62 & POLK STS 07093
  Ernest Modarelli, prin.
ES 2, 5200 BROADWAY 07093
  Edward Langan, prin.
ES 3, 5401 POLK ST 07093
  Bernard Abbadessa, prin.
ES 4, 317-66TH ST 07093 – Mario Capozzi, prin.
ES 5, 5401 HUDSON AVE 07093
  Nicholas Andrycich, prin.

Our Lady Libera ES, 5800 KENNEDY BLVD 07093
St. Joseph of the Palisades ES
  6408 PALISADE AVE 07093

West Orange, Essex Co., Pop. Code 8
West Orange SD
Sch. Sys. Enr. Code 5
Supt. – James Donovan
  179 EAGLE ROCK AVE 07052
Edison JHS, 75 WILLIAM ST 07052
  Andrew Carola, prin.
Roosevelt JHS, 36 GILBERT PLACE 07052
  Roy Knapp, prin.
Gregory ES, 301 GREGORY AVE 07052
  Valerie DaSaro, prin.
Hazel Avenue ES, 45 HAZEL AVE 07052
  Frederick Eckhardt, prin.
Pleasantdale ES
  555 PLEASANT VALLEY WAY 07052
  Errol Scales, prin.
Redwood ES, 75 REDWOOD AVE 07052
  David Millstein, prin.
St. Cloud ES, 71 SHERIDAN AVE 07052
  Dr. Joseph Bruno, prin.
Washington ES, 289 MAIN ST 07052
  Marie DeMaio, prin.

Our Lady of Lourdes ES, 100 VALLEY WAY 07052
St. Joseph ES, 8 ST CLOUD PL 07052

West Paterson, Passaic Co., Pop. Code 7
West Paterson SD
Sch. Sys. Enr. Code 3
Supt. – Anthony De Pasquale
  665 MCBRIDE AVE 07424
Memorial MS, 15 MEMORIAL DRIVE 07424
  Alfred Baumann, prin.
Gilmore ES, 1075 MCBRIDE AVE 07424
  Matthew Doyle, prin.
Olbon ES, LINCOLN LN 07424
  John Whitehead, prin.
ES 1, 665 MCBRIDE AVE 07424
  Matthew Doyle, prin.

Westville, Gloucester Co., Pop. Code 5
Deptford Twp. SD
Supt. – See Deptford
Shady Lane ES, SHADY LN & PINE AVE 08093
  William Smith, prin.

Westville SD
Sch. Sys. Enr. Code 2
Supt. – Geraldine Covely
  BIRCH & HIGH STS 08093
Parkview ES, BIRCH & HIGH STS 08093
  Joyce Stumpo, prin.

Most Holy Redeemer ES
  RURAL ROUTE 01 BOX 596 08093
St. Matthew School, HESSIAN AVE 08093

Westwood, Bergen Co., Pop. Code 7
Westwood Reg. SD
Sch. Sys. Enr. Code 4
Supt. – Reno Zinzarella
  701 RIDGEWOOD ROAD 07675
Berkeley Avenue ES, 47 BERKELEY AVE 07675
  Thomas Olsen, prin.
Brookside ES, 20 LAKE DR 07675
  Dr. Margaret Mittricker, prin.
George ES, PALM ST 07675
  Stanley Freeman, prin.
Ketler ES, 23 3RD AVE 07675
  Willard Kobuskie, prin.

Washington ES, 1 SCHOOL ST 07675
  Daniel Frost, prin.

St. Andrew ES, 120 WASHINGTON AVE 07675
Zion Lutheran ES
  FIRST AVENUE AND ELM ST 07675

Wharton, Morris Co., Pop. Code 6
Jefferson Twp. SD
Supt. – See Oak Ridge
Stanlick ES
  E SHAWNEE TRL LAKE SHAWNEE 07885
  Dr. John Scheri, prin.

Rockaway Twp. SD
Supt. – See Rockaway
Dwyer ES, MT HOPE AVE 07855
  John Terranova, prin.

Wharton Borough SD
Sch. Sys. Enr. Code 3
Supt. – Richard Ruffer
  145 E CENTRAL AVE 07885
MacKinnon MS, 145 E CENTRAL AVE 07885
  J. Morton, prin.
Duffy ES, 137 E CENTRAL AVE 07885
  J. Morton, prin.

St. Mary ES, 345 S MAIN ST 07885

Whippany, Morris Co., Pop. Code 6
Hanover Twp. SD
Supt. – See Cedar Knolls
Memorial JHS, 57 HIGHLAND AVE 07981
  Harvey Altman, prin.
Bee Meadow ES, 120 REYNOLDS AVE 07981
  Patricia Parnow, prin.
Salem Drive ES, 100 SALEM DR N 07981
  Barbara Morris, prin.

Our Lady of Mercy ES, 90 WHIPPANY RD 07981

White House Station, Hunterdon Co.
Readington Twp. SD
Supt. – See Readington
Whitehouse ES, P O BOX 157 08889
  George Ihnat, prin.

Whiting, Ocean Co., Pop. Code 2
Manchester Twp. SD
Sch. Sys. Enr. Code 5
Supt. – Richard Saxer, 121 ROUTE 539 08759
ES, 412 MANCHESTER BLVD 08759
  Barbara Juliano, prin.
Other Schools – See Lakehurst

Wildwood, Cape May Co., Pop. Code 5
Wildwood Crest SD
Sch. Sys. Enr. Code 2
Supt. – Eugene Whelan, 6101 PACIFIC AVE 08260
Crest Memorial ES, 9100 PACIFIC AVE 08260
  (—), prin.

Wildwood SD
Sch. Sys. Enr. Code 4
Supt. – Arthur Motz, 4300 PACIFIC AVE 08260
Glenwood Avenue ES
  GLENWOOD AND NEW YORK AVE 08260
  Dennis Anderson, prin.

St. Ann ES, MAGNOLIA & PACIFIC 08260

Williamstown, Gloucester Co., Pop. Code 5
Buena Regional SD
Supt. – See Buena
Collings Lake ES, 700 CAINS MILL RD 08094
  Margaret Maggioncalda, prin.

Monroe Twp. SD
Sch. Sys. Enr. Code 5
Supt. – Robert La Porta, ACADEMY ST E 08094
Oak Knoll MS, 23 BODINE AVE 08094
  Max Bienstock, prin.
Radix ES, RADIX ROAD 08094
  Vincent Tarantino, prin.
Shishoff ES, 900 N MAIN ST 08094
  Robert Brittingham, prin.
Whitehall ES, WHITEHALL ROAD 08094
  John Muller, prin.

St. Mary ES, 32 CARROLL AVE 08094

Willingboro, Burlington Co., Pop. Code 8
Willingboro Twp. SD
Sch. Sys. Enr. Code 6
Supt. – Peter Romanoli, 100 SALEM ROAD 08046
Bookbinder ES, BROOKLAWN DR 08046
  Edward Novak, prin.
Country Club Ridge ES
  BEVERLY-RANCOCAS ROAD 08046
  (—), prin.
Garfield Park East ES, 150 EVERGREEN DR 08046
  Gerard Delprato, prin.
Garfield Park ES, GLEN OLDEN LN 08046
  Thomas Shurgalla, prin.
Hawthorne Park ES, HAMPSHIRE LN 08046
  James Semmel, prin.
King ES, 157 NORTHAMPTON DR 08046
  Dr. Herbert Druker, prin.
Millbrook Park ES, MIDDLEBURY LN 08046
  Ronald Webb, prin.
Pennypacker Park ES, 49 PINETREE LN 08046
  George Carlin, prin.
Stuart ES, 16 SUNSET RD 08046
  Sally Landrum, prin.
Twinhills Park ES, TWIN HILL DR 08046
  Dr. Emerson Smith, Jr., prin.

Corpus Christi ES, 59 S SUNSET RD 08046

Windsor, Mercer Co.
Washington Twp. SD
Sch. Sys. Enr. Code 2
Supt. – Madeline Redmond, P O BOX 387 08561
Other Schools – See Robbinsville

Woodbine, Cape May Co., Pop. Code 5
Woodbine SD
Sch. Sys. Enr. Code 2
Supt. – Edward Pettitt, WEBSTER ST 08270
ES, WEBSTER ST 08270 – Edward Pettitt, prin.

Woodbridge, Middlesex Co., Pop. Code 8
Woodbridge Twp. SD
Sch. Sys. Enr. Code 7
Supt. – Fred Buonocore, P O BOX 428 07095
Woodbridge MS, 525 BARRON AVE 07095
  Jeanette Bernstein, prin.
Mawbey Street ES, MAWBEY ST 07095
  Harold Zimms, prin.
Ross Street ES, ROSS ST 07095
  Lawrence Ryan, prin.
Other Schools – See Avenel, Colonia, Fords, Iselin,
  Metuchen, Port Reading, Sewaren, Warren

St. James ES, 341 AMBOY AVE 07095

Woodbury, Gloucester Co., Pop. Code 7
West Deptford Twp. SD
Supt. – See West Deptford
Oakview ES, DUBOIS AVE 08096
  Thomas Strandwitz, prin.

Woodbury Heights SD
Sch. Sys. Enr. Code 2
Supt. – Mary Smith, ACADEMY AVE 08897
Other Schools – See Woodbury Heights

Woodbury SD
Sch. Sys. Enr. Code 4
Supt. – Claudio Arrington, 25 N BROAD ST 08096
Evergreen Avenue ES
  160 N EVERGREEN AVE 08096
  Richard Shetler, prin.
Walnut Street ES, WALNUT ST 08096
  Richard Moyer, prin.
West End ES, JACKSON & QUEEN STS 08096
  Elizabeth Sferrazza, prin.

St. Patrick ES, COOPER AND GREEN AVES 08096

Woodbury Heights, Gloucester Co., Pop. Code 5
Woodbury Heights SD
Supt. – See Woodbury
ES, ACADEMY AVE 08097 – Mary Smith, prin.

St. Margaret ES, 3RD & BEECH AVE 08097

Woodcliff Lake, Bergen Co., Pop. Code 6
Woodcliff Lake SD
Sch. Sys. Enr. Code 3
Supt. – Gus Perna, 134 WOODCLIFF AVE 07675
Woodcliff Lake MS, 134 WOODCLIFF AVE 07675
  Albert Cornewal, prin.
Dorchester ES, WOODCLIFF AVE 07675
  H. Riccardo, prin.

Woodlynne, Camden Co., Pop. Code 5
Woodlynne Borough SD
Sch. Sys. Enr. Code 2
Supt. – (—), ELM AVE & FRONT ST 08107
Other Schools – See Camden

Wood-Ridge, Bergen Co., Pop. Code 6
Wood-Ridge SD
Sch. Sys. Enr. Code 3
Supt. – Robert Smith, 73 HACKENSACK ST 07075
MS, 540 WINDSOR ROAD 07075
  Nicholas Sardone, prin.
Doyle ES, 250 WOOD-RIDGE AVE 07075
  Dr. Nicholas Sardone, prin.

Woodstown, Salem Co., Pop. Code 5
Woodstown-Pilesgrove Regional SD
Sch. Sys. Enr. Code 4
Supt. – Ronald Udy, 135 EAST AVE 08098
MS, 15 LINCOLN AVE 08098
  William Stanwood, prin.
Shoemaker ES 08098 – Barbara Ohmott, prin.

Wrightstown, Burlington Co., Pop. Code 5
New Hanover Twp. SD
Sch. Sys. Enr. Code 2
Supt. – George Pratt, P O BOX 276 08562
New Hanover Twp. ES, P O BOX 276 08562
  George Pratt, prin.

North Hanover Twp. SD
Supt. – See Mc Guire A F B
Lamb ES, RURAL ROUTE 01 BOX 168-1 08562
  Robert Levee, prin.

Wyckoff, Bergen Co., Pop. Code 7
Wyckoff Twp. SD
Sch. Sys. Enr. Code 4
Supt. – Roger Clark, 241 MORSE AVE 07481
Eisenhower MS, 344 CALVIN COURT 07481
  Joseph Desiderio, prin.
Coolidge ES, 420 GRANDVIEW AVE 07481
  Richard Schucic, prin.
Lincoln ES, 325 MASON AVE 07481
  Herman Van Teyens, prin.
Sicomac ES, 356 SICOMAC AVE 07481
  Richard Weisiger, prin.

Washington ES, 270 WOODLAND AVE   07481
  Patricia Ernest, prin.
_____

St. Elizabeth ES, GREENWOOD AVE   07481
Wyckott Christian ES, 518 SICOMAS AVE   07481

Yardville, Mercer Co., Pop. Code 6
  Hamilton Twp. SD
  Supt. – See Trenton
  Yardville Heights ES, 3880 S BROAD ST   08620
    Russell Wilbert, prin.

NEW MEXICO

_____

STATE DEPARTMENT OF EDUCATION
State Department of Education Building
300 Don Gaspar, Santa Fe 87501
(505) 827-6635

Superintendent of Public Instruction	Alan D. Morgan
Associate Superintendent Instruction	Jeanne Knight
Associate Superintendent School Finance	Stan Rounds
Assistant Superintendent Instructional Support	Mary Beavis
Director Administrative Services	Tres Giron

STATE BOARD OF EDUCATION
Catherine Smith, *President*   P.O. Box 49, Mimbres   88049

COMMISSIONER ON HIGHER EDUCATION
Dewayne Matthews, *Executive Director*   1068 Cerrillos Rd., Santa Fe   87501

PUBLIC, PRIVATE, AND PAROCHIAL ELEMENTARY SCHOOLS

Abiquiu, Rio Arriba Co.
  Espanola AU
  Supt. – See Espanola
  ES   87510 – Melva Trujillo, prin.

Alamogordo, Otero Co., Pop. Code 7
  Alamogordo AU
  Sch. Sys. Enr. Code 6
  Supt. – C. Stockton, P O BOX 617   88311
  Chaparral JHS, 1401 COLLEGE AVE   88310
    Dave Nunez, prin.
  Buena Vista ES, 2600 19TH ST   88310
    Charles Montjoy, prin.
  Heights ES, 2410 10TH ST   88310
    Clarissa Johnson, prin.
  North ES, 1300 N FLORIDA AVE   88310
    Louis Gonzales, prin.
  Oregon ES, FIFTEENTH & OREGON   88310
    Florence Lucero, prin.
  Sacrmento ES, THIRD & ALASKA   88310
    Jim Money, prin.
  Sierra ES, 2211 PORTO RICO AVE   88310
    Bernice Bryant, prin.
  Timberon ES, P O BOX 617   88311
    Leslie Dendy, prin.
  Yucca ES, 310 DALE SCOTT AVE   88310
    Karen Couch, prin.
  Other Schools – See High Rolls Mountain Park,
    Holloman A F B, La Luz, Weed
_____

Hay ES, 708 HAWAII AVE   88310

Albuquerque, Bernalillo Co., Pop. Code 10
  Albuquerque AU
  Sch. Sys. Enr. Code 8
  Supt. – Jack Bobroff, P O BOX 27504   87125
  Adams MS, 5401 GLENRIO ROAD NW   87105
    Tom Miller, prin.
  Cleveland MS, 6910 NATALIE AVE NE   87110
    Richard Beattie, prin.
  Eisenhower MS, 11001 CAMERO ROAD NE   87111
    Francelle Grisham, prin.
  Garfield MS, 3501 6TH ST NW   87107
    Charles Tafoya, prin.
  Grant MS, 1111 EASTERDAY ST NE   87112
    Charles Barnard, prin.
  Harrison MS, 3912 ISLETA BLVD SW   87105
    J. Patrick Garcia, prin.
  Hayes MS, 1100 TEXAS ST NE   87110
    Sheldon McGuire, prin.
  Hoover MS, 12015 TIVOLI AVE NE   87111
    Don Wolfley, prin.
  Jackson MS
    10600 INDIAN SCHOOL ROAD NE   87112
    Yvonne Kauffman, prin.
  Jefferson MS, 712 GIRARD BLVD NE   87106
    Timothy Whalen, prin.
  Kennedy MS, 721 TOMASITA AVE NE   87123
    Helen Johnson, prin.

Lincoln MS, 2287 LEMA ROAD SE   87124
  Jim Leuder, prin.
Madison MS, 3501 MOON ST NE   87111
  Bob Polson, prin.
McKinley MS, 4500 COMANCHE ROAD NE   87110
  Eugene Johnson, prin.
Polk MS, 2220 RAYMAC ROAD SW   87105
  Ruth Armstrong, prin.
Pyle MS, 1820 VALDORA ROAD SW   87105
  Don Duran, prin.
Taft MS, 620 SCHULTE ROAD NW   87107
  W. Hannon, prin.
Taylor MS, 8200 GUADALUPE TRAIL NW   87114
  George Hudson, prin.
Truman MS, 9400 BENAVIDES ST SW   87105
  Bill Zamora, prin.
Van Buren MS, 700 LOUISIANA BLVD SE   87108
  Gene Golden, prin.
Washington MS, 1101 PARK AVE SW   87102
  Joseph Vigil, prin.
Wilson MS, 1138 CARDENAS DRIVE SE   87108
  H. Goff, prin.
Acoma ES
  11800 PRINCESS JEANNE AV NE   87112
  Margaret Blasi, prin.
Adobe Acres ES
  1724 CAMINO DEL VALLE SW   87105
  Jim Jones, prin.
Alameda ES, 412 CORRALES RD NW   87114
  Dale Melada, prin.
Alamosa ES, 6500 SUNSET GARDENS SW   87105
  Henrietta Sanchez, prin.
Alvarado ES, 1100 SOLOAR RD NW   87107
  Mary Ann Anderson, prin.
Apache ES, 12800 COPPER AVE NE   87123
  Pam Wylie, prin.
Armijo ES, 1440 GATEWOOD ROAD SW   87105
  Jose Trujillo, prin.
Arroyo Del Oso ES, 6504 HARPER DR NE   87109
  Jose Lobato, prin.
Atrisco ES, 1201 ATRISCO DR SW   87105
  Lavonne Winther, prin.
Baker ES, 12015 TIVOLI AVE NE   87111
  Betty Wendell, prin.
Bandelier ES, 3309 PERSHING AVE SE   87106
  Joe Groom, prin.
Barcelona ES
  2311 BARCELONA ROAD SW   87105
  Cecilia Sanchez, prin.
Bel Air ES, 4725 CANDELARIA ROAD NE   87110
  Doug Carmichael, prin.
Bellhaven ES
  8701 PRINCESS JEANNE AVE NE   87112
  Francis Salazar, prin.
Bent ES, 5700 HENDRIX ROAD NE   87110
  Marilyn Davenport, prin.
Binford ES, 1400 CORRIZ ST SW   87105
  Gary Atwood, prin.

Carson ES, 1921 BYRON ST SW   87105
  Larry Adkins, prin.
Chaparral ES, 6325 MILNE ROAD NW   87120
  Trancito Romero, prin.
Chavez ES, 2700 MOUNTAIN ROAD NW   87104
  Dennis Romero, prin.
Chavez ES, 7500 BARSTOW ST NE   87109
  Michael Brady, prin.
Chelwood ES
  12701 CONSTITUTION AVE NE   87112
  David Melvin, prin.
Cochiti ES, 3100 SAN ISIDRO DR NW   87107
  Elizabeth Reid, prin.
Collet Park ES, 2100 MORRIS ST NE   87112
  Rafael Carrillo, prin.
Comanche ES
  3505 PENNSYLVANIA ST NE   87110
  Steve Wilkes, prin.
Duranes ES, 2436 ZICKERT ROAD NW   87104
  Ruthie Owens, prin.
East San Jose ES, 2015 JOHN ST SE   87102
  Dorella Perea, prin.
Emerson ES, 620 GEORGIA ST SE   87108
  Elizabeth Lawrence, prin.
Eubank ES
  9717 INDIAN SCHOOL ROAD NE   87112
  Ausencio Romero, prin.
Field ES, 700 EDITH BLVD SE   87102
  Mary Ellen Gallegos, prin.
Gonzales ES, 900 ATLANTIC AVE SW   87102
  Dora Ortiz, prin.
Griegos ES, 4040 SAN ISIDRO NW   87107
  Eddie Lucero, prin.
Hawthorne ES
  420 GENERAL SOMRVELL ST NE   87123
  Elizabeth Everitt, prin.
Hodgin ES, 3801 MORNINGTON NE   87110
  Joe Quintana, prin.
Hughes ES, 5701 MOJAVE ST NW   87120
  Kathy Potter, prin.
Humphrey ES
  9801 ACADEMY HILLS DR NE   87111
  Arthur Romero, prin.
Inez ES, 1700 PENNSYLVANIA ST NE   87110
  Joan La Mourie, prin.
Jackson ES, 4720 CAIRO DR NE   87111
  Jim Franklin, prin.
Kirtland ES, 3530 GIBSON BLVD SE   87106
  Virgil Morgan, prin.
La Luz ES, 225 GRIEGOS ROAD NW   87107
  Al Griego, prin.
La Mesa ES, 7500 COPPER AVE NE   87108
  Vito Miera, prin.
Lavaland ES, 501 57TH ST NW   87105
  Patricia Wagner, prin.
Longfellow ES, 400 EDITH BLVD NE   87102
  Vita Saavedra, prin.
Los Padillas ES, 2525 PADILLAS ROAD SW   87105
  Robin Hazen, prin.

Lowell ES, 1700 SUNSHINE TERRACE SE 87106
  Mary Sanchez, prin.
MacArthur ES, 1100 MACARTHUR NW 87107
  Nancy Blackler, prin.
Matheson Park ES
  10809 LEXINGTON AVE NE 87112
  Ruben Mures, prin.
McCollum ES
  10900 SAN JACINTO BLVD NE 87112
  Gilbert Villarreal, prin.
Mission Avenue ES, 725 MISSION AVE NE 87107
  Eli Bercier, prin.
Mitchell ES, 10121 COMANCHE ROAD NE 87111
  Harold Forrester, prin.
Monte Vista ES
  3211 MONTE VISTA BLVD NE 87106
  Jacque Hooton, prin.
Montezuma ES, 1616 RICHMOND DR NE 87106
  Carl Weingartner, prin.
Mountain View ES, 5317 2ND ST SW 87102
  Robert Herrera, prin.
Navajo ES, 2936 HUGHES RD SW 87105
  Patricia Gilberto, prin.
Onate ES
  12415 BRENTWOOD HILLS BL NE 87112
  Sue Provonzie, prin.
Osuna ES, 4715 MOON ST NE 87111
  William Schafer, prin.
Pajarito ES, 5816 ISLETA BLVD SW 87105
  Beverly Gard, prin.
Ranchos ES, 7609 4TH ST NW 87107
  Frank Salazar, prin.
Rey ES, 1215 CERRILLOS ROAD SW 87105
  Charles Starkey, prin.
Ross ES, 6700 PALOMAS DR NE 87109
  Raquel Reedy, prin.
Sierra Vista ES
  10220 PASEO DEL NORTE NW 87114
  Allan Holmquist, prin.
Sombra Del Monte ES
  9110 SHOSHONE ROAD NE 87111
  Charles Lefkofsky, prin.
Tomasita ES, 701 TOMASITA AVE NE 87123
  Terry Toman, prin.
Twain ES, 6316 CONSTITUTION AVE NE 87110
  Pam Bakke, prin.
Valle Vista ES, 1700 MAE AVE SW 87105
  Richard Ulibarri, prin.
Whittier ES, 1110 QUINCY ST SE 87108
  Nell New, prin.
Zia ES, 440 JEFFERSON ST NE 87108
  Eloise Forrester, prin.
Zuni ES, 6300 CLAREMONT AVE NE 87110
  Elizabeth Paak, prin.
Other Schools – See Corrales, Kirtland A F B East, Rio
  Rancho, Sandia Park, Tijeras

Amritsar Academy
  1650 GABALDON ROAD NW 87104
Bella Vista Baptist Church
  5620 DOGWOOD TRAIL NE 87109
Evangel Temple Academy
  4501 MONTGOMERY BLVD NE 87109
Temple Baptist Academy
  1620 SAN PEDRO DRIVE NE 87110
Annunciation School, 2610 UTAH ST NE 87110
Crestview SDA School
  6000 OURAY ROAD NW 87120
Holy Ghost School, 6201 ROSS AVE SE 87108
Immanuel Evangelist Lutheran School
  300 GOLD AVE SE 87102
Manzano Day School
  1801 MENAUL BLVD NE 87107
Our Lady of Assumption School
  817 GUQYMAS PL NE 87108
Our Lady of Fatima School
  520 MORNINGSIDE DR NE 87108
Parkview Baptist School
  1404 LEAD AVE SE 87106
Queen of Heaven School
  5303 PHOENIX AVE NE 87110
San Felipe School, 2000 LOMAS BLVD NW 87104
St. Charles Borromeo School
  1801 HAZELDINE AVE SE 87106
St. Mary ES, 224 7TH ST NW 87102
St. Therese School
  311 SHROPSHIRE AVE NW 87107
Sunset Mesa ES, 3020 MORRIS ST NE 87111

Alcalde, Rio Arriba Co., Pop. Code 3
Espanola AU
Supt. – See Espanola
ES 87511 – Edward Alarid, prin.

Algodones, Sandoval Co.
Bernalillo AU
Supt. – See Bernalillo
ES 87001 – Sharon Alt, prin.
Santo Domingo ES, P O BOX 100 87001
  Mary C. De Baca, prin.

Amistad, Union Co.
Clayton AU
Supt. – See Clayton
ES 88410 – Florence Hall, prin.

Animas, Hildago Co., Pop. Code 2
Animas AU
Sch. Sys. Enr. Code 3
Supt. – Richard Clifton, P O BOX 85 88020
ES 88020 – Noel Smith, prin.

Anthony, Dona Ana Co., Pop. Code 4
Gadsden AU
Sch. Sys. Enr. Code 6
Supt. – Edmund Gaussoin, P O BOX 70 88021
ES, P O BOX AE 88021 – Trini Barreras, prin.
Chaparral ES, 300 E LISA DR 88021
  Joe Mora, prin.
La Union ES, RURAL ROUTE 01 BOX 534 88021
  Tom Jackson, prin.
Other Schools – See La Mesa, Mesquite, San Miguel,
  Sunland Park

St. Lukes Episcopal School
  RURAL ROUTE 01 BOX 628 88021

Anton Chico, Guadalupe Co.
Santa Rosa AU
Supt. – See Santa Rosa
ES 87711 – Nicacio Maestas, prin.

Arrey, Sierra Co.
Truth or Consequences AU
Supt. – See Truth or Consequences
ES 87930 – Dale Jensen, prin.

Artesia, Eddy Co., Pop. Code 7
Artesia AU
Sch. Sys. Enr. Code 5
Supt. – Taylor Stephenson
  1106 W QUAY AVE 88210
Abo ES, 1802 W CENTRE AVE 88210
  Jim Hickerson, prin.
Central ES, 405 S 6TH ST 88210
  Jo Ann Lobianco, prin.
Hermosa ES, 601 W HERMOSA DR 88210
  Jerry Vest, prin.
Roselawn ES, 600 N ROSELAWN AVE 88210
  Jesse McGary, prin.
Yucca ES, 900 N 13TH ST 88210
  Johnny Saiz, prin.
Zia IS, 1100 W BULLOCK AVE 88210
  Perry Andrews, prin.
Other Schools – See Hope

Aztec, San Juan Co., Pop. Code 6
Aztec AU
Sch. Sys. Enr. Code 5
Supt. – Ron Helland
  455 N LIGHT PLANT ROAD 87410
McCoy Avenue ES, 1007 MCCOY AVE 87410
  Riley Roland, prin.
Park Avenue MS, 507 PARK AVE 87410
  Jesse Russell, prin.
Rippey ES, RIO PECOS RD 87410
  Charline Gaston, prin.

Bayard, Grant Co., Pop. Code 5
Cobre AU
Sch. Sys. Enr. Code 6
Supt. – Benny Trujillo, P O BOX R 88023
Snell MS, HIGHWAY 180 88023
  Michael May, prin.
ES, 100 PARK 88023 – Elizabeth Willis, prin.
Other Schools – See Central, Hurley, San Lorenzo

Belen, Valencia Co., Pop. Code 6
Belen AU
Sch. Sys. Enr. Code 5
Supt. – Pete Torres, 520 N MAIN ST 87002
JHS, 400 S 4TH ST 87002 – Calliope Chamis, prin.
Central MS, PICARD AVE 87002
  William Ulibarri, prin.
Chavez ES, 520 N MAIN 87002
  Jeff Sullivan, prin.
Jaramillo ES, MARIPOSA PARK 87002
  Rudolph Chavez, prin.
Rio Grande ES, 520 N MAIN 87002
  Alfred Padilla, prin.
Sanchez ES, 520 N MAIN ST 87002
  Laura Gilbert, prin.

St. Mary School, TENTH & CHURCH STS 87002

Bernalillo, Sandoval Co., Pop. Code 5
Bernalillo AU
Sch. Sys. Enr. Code 5
Supt. – Jesse Gonzales, P O BOX 640 87004
MS 87004 – Thomas Aguilar, prin.
Carroll ES 87004 – Judy Casaus, prin.
Other Schools – See Algodones, Pena Blanca, Placitas,
  Santo Domingo Pueblo

Blanco, San Juan Co.
Bloomfield AU
Supt. – See Bloomfield
ES, P O BOX 478 87412 – Nancy Hughes, prin.

Bloomfield, San Juan Co., Pop. Code 5
Bloomfield AU
Sch. Sys. Enr. Code 5
Supt. – Jack Ward, 325 N BERGIN LANE 87413
Mesa Alta JHS, 329 N BERGIN LANE 87413
  Jim Conyers, prin.
Central ES, P O BOX 1809 87413
  Louis Rodriguez, prin.
Naaba Ani ES, P O BOX 3100 87413
  Meredith Bowers, prin.
Rio Vista MS, P O BOX 1779 87413
  Joe Rasor, prin.
Other Schools – See Blanco

Bluewater, Cibola Co., Pop. Code 2
Grants AU
Supt. – See Grants
ES 87005 – Steve Rosenthal, prin.

Canjilon, Rio Arriba Co.
Chama Valley AU
Supt. – See Tierra Amarilla
ES 87515 – Sandra Crane, prin.

Capitan, Lincoln Co., Pop. Code 3
Capitan AU
Sch. Sys. Enr. Code 3
Supt. – Dr. Scott Childress, P O BOX 278 88316
ES 88316 – Jerry Newsom, prin.

Carlsbad, Eddy Co., Pop. Code 8
Carlsbad AU
Sch. Sys. Enr. Code 6
Supt. – Dr. Roger Harrell
  408 N CANYON ST 88220
Alta Vista MS, 301 ALTA VISTA ST 88220
  Tom Quintela, prin.
Eddy ES, 700 W STEVENS ST 88220
  Rita London, prin.
Edison ES, 406 N ALAMEDA ST 88220
  John Redman, prin.
Eisenhower MS, 500 W CHURCH ST 88220
  Art Anaya, prin.
Hillcrest ES, 215 N 6TH ST 88220
  Abel Montoya, prin.
Monterrey ES, 1101 N NINTH ST 88220
  Jay Redman, prin.
Pate MS, 120 KIRCHER ST 88220
  Patrick Gaffney, prin.
Puckett ES, 2212 PRIMROSE ST 88220
  Ernestina Carrasco, prin.
Riverside ES, 1600 JOHNSON ST 88220
  Lee Richards, prin.
Smith ES, 505 ALTA VISTA ST 88220
  Forrest Dickerson, prin.
South Ridge ES, 2415 CARVER ST 88220
  Patrick Gaffney, prin.
Sunset ES, 923 WALTER ST 88220
  L. Brown, prin.

St. Edward School, 805 WALTER STREET 88220

Carrizozo, Lincoln Co., Pop. Code 4
Carrizozo AU
Sch. Sys. Enr. Code 2
Supt. – Dan Burnett, P O BOX 99 88301
MS 88301 – Mel Holland, prin.
ES 88301 – Mel Holland, prin.

Central, Grant Co., Pop. Code 4
Cobre AU
Supt. – See Bayard
ES, 600 PRESCOTT 88026
  Anthony Romero, prin.

Chama, Rio Arriba Co., Pop. Code 4
Chama Valley AU
Supt. – See Tierra Amarilla
ES, P O BOX 337 87520 – Ben Branch, prin.

Chimayo, Rio Arriba Co.
Espanola AU
Supt. – See Espanola
ES 87522 – Wilfred Martinez, prin.

Church Rock, McKinley Co.
Gallup-McKinley AU
Supt. – See Gallup
ES, P O BOX 14 87311 – Donald Mitchell, prin.

Cimarron, Colfax Co., Pop. Code 3
Cimarron AU
Sch. Sys. Enr. Code 2
Supt. – Thelma Coker, P O BOX 605 87714
ES, 320 W 9TH ST 87714 – Marla Gadry, prin.
Other Schools – See Eagle Nest

Clayton, Union Co., Pop. Code 5
Clayton AU
Sch. Sys. Enr. Code 3
Supt. – Claude Austin, 323 S 5TH ST 88415
JHS, 3RD & SPRUCE 88415 – Kathryn Huff, prin.
Alvis ES, 4TH & ASPEN ST 88415
  Toni Dabovich, prin.
Kiser MS, 16 S 2ND AVE 88415
  James Curry, prin.
Other Schools – See Amistad

Cliff, Grant Co., Pop. Code 2
Silver AU
Supt. – See Silver City
ES 88028 – Eloy Gonzales, prin.

Cloudcroft, Otero Co., Pop. Code 3
Cloudcroft AU
Sch. Sys. Enr. Code 2
Supt. – Vernson Asbill, P O BOX 198 88317
ES 88317 – Jay Dark, prin.

Clovis, Curry Co., Pop. Code 8
Clovis AU
Sch. Sys. Enr. Code 6
Supt. – Richard Purvis, 8TH & PILE STS 88101
Barry ES
  THORNTON & LLANO ESTACADO 88101
  Elaine Ory, prin.
Bella Vista ES, 200 JEFFERSON 88101
  Helen Guana, prin.
Bickley ES, 500 W 14TH ST 88101
  B. Pierce, prin.
Cameo ES, FIFTENNTH & CAMEO STS 88101
  Dale Paul, prin.
Highland ES, 100 E PLAINS AVE 88101
  Grace Jones, prin.
La Casita ES, FOURTH & DAVIS 88101
  Matthew Trujillo, prin.

Lincoln Jackson ES, 206 ALPHON ST 88101
  Delman Shirley, prin.
Lockwood ES, LOCKWOOD DR 88101
  Iris Cox, prin.
Parkview ES, 1100 E 13TH ST 88101
  Jerry Wallace, prin.
Ranchvale ES, RURAL ROUTE 02 88101
  Bill Pyle, prin.
Sandia ES, W MANANA & LORE 88101
  Jim Jacobs, prin.
Zia ES, 2400 NORRIS 88101 – Mel Mapes, prin.

Columbus, Luna Co., Pop. Code 2
Deming AU
Supt. – See Deming
ES, P O BOX 68 88029 – Carol Stevenson, prin.

Cordova, Rio Arriba Co., Pop. Code 3
Espanola AU
Supt. – See Espanola
Mountain View ES 87523 – Carol Ortiz, prin.

Corona, Lincoln Co., Pop. Code 2
Corona AU
Sch. Sys. Enr. Code 2
Supt. – Lucille King, P O BOX 258 88318
ES 88318 – Betty Ann Bell, prin.

Corrales, Sandoval Co.
Albuquerque AU
Supt. – See Albuquerque
ES 87048 – Roger Wright, prin.

Costilla, Sandoval Co.
Questa AU
Supt. – See Questa
ES, P O BOX 440 87524 – Diana Pacheco, prin.

Coyote, Rio Arriba Co.
Jemez Mountain AU
Supt. – See Gallina
ES 87012 – Emily Vigil, prin.

Crownpoint, McKinley Co., Pop. Code 3
Gallup-McKinley AU
Supt. – See Gallup
ES, P O BOX C 87313 – Edward Monaghan, prin.

Cuba, Sandoval Co., Pop. Code 3
Cuba AU
Sch. Sys. Enr. Code 3
Supt. – Joe Lopez, P O BOX 70 87013
MS 87013 – Edumenio Gurle, prin.
ES 87013 – Edumenio Gurle, prin.

Jemez Mountain AU
Supt. – See Gallina
Lybrook ES, HCR 4 87013 – Emily Vigil, prin.

Immaculate Conception School
  P O BOX 218 87013

Cubero, Cibola Co., Pop. Code 2
Grants AU
Supt. – See Grants
ES 87014 – Lee Burchfield, prin.

Datil, Catron Co.
Quemado AU
Supt. – See Quemado
ES 87821 – Mona McCrary, prin.

Deming, Luna Co., Pop. Code 6
Deming AU
Sch. Sys. Enr. Code 5
Supt. – Ray Swinney, 501 W FLORIDA ST 88030
JHS, 500 W ASH ST 88030 – Dale Buss, prin.
Bell ES, 1000 E MAPLE ST 88030
  Manuel Teran, prin.
Chaparral ES, 1400 E HOLLY ST 88030
  Dan Anderson, prin.
Martin ES, 315 E 1ST ST 88030
  Joe Chaires, prin.
Memorial ES, 1000 S 10TH ST 88030
  Melbourne Fewell, prin.
Smith ES, 310 W ELM ST 88030
  Cleveland Orr, prin.
Sunshine ES, RURAL ROUTE 01 BOX 125 88030
  Allan McNiece, prin.
Other Schools – See Columbus

Des Moines, Union Co., Pop. Code 2
Des Moines AU
Sch. Sys. Enr. Code 2
Supt. – Midge Graham, P O BOX 38 88418
ES 88418 – Midge Graham, prin.

Dexter, Chaves Co., Pop. Code 3
Dexter AU
Sch. Sys. Enr. Code 3
Supt. – Ena Soflin, P O BOX 159 88230
JHS 88230 – Jimmy Derrick, prin.
ES 88230 – Patricia Parsons, prin.

Dixon, Rio Arriba Co., Pop. Code 2
Espanola AU
Supt. – See Espanola
ES 87527 – Mercy Romero, prin.

Dora, Roosevelt Co., Pop. Code 2
Dora AU
Sch. Sys. Enr. Code 2
Supt. – Guy Luscombe, P O BOX 327 88115
ES 88115 – Guy Luscombe, prin.

Dulce, Rio Arriba Co., Pop. Code 3
Dulce AU
Sch. Sys. Enr. Code 3
Supt. – Joe Montano, P O BOX 547 87528

MS 87528 – Dulces Guardiola, prin.
ES 87528 – Levi Pesata, prin.

Eagle Nest, Colfax Co., Pop. Code 2
Cimarron AU
Supt. – See Cimarron
ES 87718 – Marla Gadry, prin.

Elida, Roosevelt Co., Pop. Code 2
Elida AU
Sch. Sys. Enr. Code 2
Supt. – T. Goodwin, P O BOX 8 88116
ES 88116 – Nancy Ward, prin.

El Pueblo, San Miguel Co.
Las Vegas West AU
Supt. – See Las Vegas
Valley ES 87560 – David Salazar, prin.

El Rito, Rio Arriba Co., Pop. Code 1
Mesa Vista AU
Sch. Sys. Enr. Code 2
Supt. – Vernon Jaramillo, P O BOX 6 87530
ES 87530 – Esperanza Gonzales, prin.
Other Schools – See Ojo Caliente, Tres Piedras

Espanola, Rio Arriba Co., Pop. Code 6
Espanola AU
Sch. Sys. Enr. Code 5
Supt. – Dr. Gilbert Duran, P O BOX 249 87532
JHS 87532 – Arthur Salazar, prin.
ES 87532 – Corrine Salazar, prin.
Sombrillo ES
  RURAL ROUTE 03 BOX 132-A 87532
  Ricky Vigil, prin.
Other Schools – See Abiquiu, Alcalde, Chimayo,
  Cordova, Dixon, Fairview, Hernandez, San Juan
  Pueblo, Velarde

McCurdy School, P O BOX 127 87532

Estancia, Torrance Co., Pop. Code 3
Estancia AU
Sch. Sys. Enr. Code 3
Supt. – Carolyn Renteria, P O BOX 668 87016
ES 87016 – Roy George, prin.

Eunice, Lea Co., Pop. Code 5
Eunice AU
Sch. Sys. Enr. Code 3
Supt. – Don Herron, P O BOX 128 88231
Caton JHS, P O BOX 129 88231 – Don Jones, prin.
Jordan ES 88231 – Gary Johnson, prin.

Fairacres, Dona Ana Co.
Las Cruces AU
Supt. – See Las Cruces
ES, 301 W AMADOR AVE 88005
  Harry Harrison, prin.

Fairview, Rio Arriba Co.
Espanola AU
Supt. – See Espanola
ES 87532 – Jimmy Martinez, prin.

Farmington, San Juan Co., Pop. Code 8
Farmington AU
Sch. Sys. Enr. Code 6
Supt. – Dr. James Miller, P O BOX 5850 87499
Animas ES, 1612 HUTTON ROAD 87401
  Joe Sweat, prin.
Apache ES, 700 W APACHE ST 87401
  Ed Sweat, prin.
Bluffview ES, 1204 CAMINA REAL 87401
  Dan Taylor, prin.
Country Club ES, 5300 FOOTHILLS DR 87401
  Ginger McLamore, prin.
Ladera Del Norte ES, 308 SAN MARCUS 87401
  Marka Riley, prin.
McCormick ES
  701 MCCORMICK SCHOOL RD 87401
  Joyce Roberts, prin.
McKinley ES, 1201 N BUTLER AVE 87401
  Don Tinnin, prin.
Mesa Verde ES, 3801 COLLEGE BLVD 87401
  Ellen Maki, prin.
Northeast ES, 1400 E 23RD ST 87401
  Annette Moorehead, prin.
Swinburne ES, 301 N COURT AVE 87401
  Harold Andrews, prin.

Sacred Heart School, 404 N ALLEN AVE 87401

Floyd, Roosevelt Co., Pop. Code 2
Floyd AU
Sch. Sys. Enr. Code 2
Supt. – Bob Posey, P O BOX 75 88118
ES 88118 – Elizabeth Posey, prin.

Fort Sumner, De Baca Co., Pop. Code 4
Ft. Sumner AU
Sch. Sys. Enr. Code 2
Supt. – Dan Clark, P O BOX 387 88119
ES 88119 – Rodney Litke, prin.

Fruitland, San Juan Co., Pop. Code 3
Central AU
Supt. – See Shiprock
Ojo Amarillo ES, P O OBX 768 87416
  Rosellen Tsosie, prin.

Gallina, Rio Arriba Co.
Jemez Mountain AU
Sch. Sys. Enr. Code 2
Supt. – Mary Robinson, P O BOX 121 87017
ES 87017 – Emily Vigil, prin.
Other Schools – See Coyote, Cuba, Lindrith

Gallup, McKinley Co., Pop. Code 7
Gallup-McKinley AU
Sch. Sys. Enr. Code 7
Supt. – Ramon Vigil, P O BOX 1318 87301
MS, 1001 S GRANDVIEW DRIVE 87301
  Paul Newton, prin.
Kennedy MS, 600 S BOARDMAN AVE 87301
  Andre Trottier, prin.
Indian Hills ES, 3604 CINIZA DR 87301
  Martyn Stowe, prin.
Jefferson ES, 300 MOLLICA DR 87301
  Karen Woods, prin.
Juan De Onate ES, 505 E VEGA DR 87301
  Lyle Petzoldt, prin.
Lincoln ES, 801 W HILL AVE 87301
  Louise Smith, prin.
Red Rock ES, 1305 REDROCK DR 87301
  Rudy Sautter, prin.
Roat ES, MARQUERITE ST 87301
  Robert Montano, prin.
Roosevelt ES, 400 E LOGAN AVE 87301
  Dee Miles, prin.
Tse Bonito ES, HCR 5 BOX 22 87301
  Daniel Wyant, prin.
Twin Lakes ES
  FARMINGTON STAR ROUTE 5 87301
  Paul Graves, prin.
Washington ES, 700 W WILSON AVE 87301
  Ernestine Sarabia, prin.
Other Schools – See Church Rock, Crownpoint,
  Navajo, Ramah, Smith Lake, Thoreau, Tohatchi

Cathedral Grade School, LOS LUNAS RD 87301
St. Francis of Assisi School
  215 W WILSON AVE 87301

Garfield, Dona Ana Co., Pop. Code 2
Hatch AU
Supt. – See Hatch
ES 87936 – Jim Tomlinson, prin.

Glenwood, Catron Co.
Reserve AU
Supt. – See Reserve
ES 88039 – Harold Sloan, prin.

Grady, Curry Co., Pop. Code 2
Grady AU
Sch. Sys. Enr. Code 2
Supt. – Artis Hinds, P O BOX 71 88120
ES 88120 – Artis Hinds, prin.

Grants, Valencia Co., Pop. Code 7
Grants AU
Sch. Sys. Enr. Code 5
Supt. – Arnold Maxwell, P O BOX 8 87020
Los Alamitos MS
  ELM DRIVE & MOUNT TAYLOR 87020
  David Jiron, prin.
Mesa View ES, 400 E WASHINGTON AVE 87020
  Christine Drangmeister, prin.
Mt. Taylor ES, DEL NORTE & JEMEZ 87020
  Jerry Morris, prin.
Other Schools – See Bluewater, Cubero, Milan, New
  Laguna, San Mateo, Seboyeta

Grant Academy, 500 JEFFERSON AVE 87020
Southwestern Christian HS, P O BOX 298 87020
St. Theresa of Avila School
  400 E HIGH AVE 87020

Hagerman, Chaves Co., Pop. Code 3
Hagerman AU
Sch. Sys. Enr. Code 2
Supt. – John Wilbanks, P O BOX B 88232
JHS 88232 – Eric Cress, prin.
ES 88232 – John Wilbanks, prin.

Hatch, Dona Ana Co., Pop. Code 4
Hatch AU
Sch. Sys. Enr. Code 4
Supt. – Cecil Davis, P O BOX 799 87937
Hatch Valley JHS, P O BOX 790 87937
  Judd Nordyke, prin.
Hatch Valley ES 87937
  Santiago Arredondo, prin.
Other Schools – See Garfield

Hernandez, Rio Arriba Co.
Espanola AU
Supt. – See Espanola
ES 87537 – Joe Fresquez, prin.

High Rolls Mountain Park, Otera Co., Pop. Code 3
Alamogordo AU
Supt. – See Alamogordo
High Rolls ES 88325 – Carol Jaramillo, prin.

Hobbs, Lea Co., Pop. Code 8
Hobbs AU
Sch. Sys. Enr. Code 6
Supt. – Dr. Edgar Willhelm, P O BOX 1040 88241
Broadmoor ES, 1500 N HOUSTON ST 88240
  Jon Cearley, prin.
College Lane ES, 2000 COLLEGE LANE 88240
  Connie Webb, prin.
Coronado ES, 2600 N BRAZOS AVE 88240
  Sandra Newell, prin.
Edison ES, 501 E GYPSY ST 88240
  Carolina Greene, prin.
Jefferson ES, 1200 W PARK ST 88240
  Jerry Thomas, prin.
Mills ES, 200 W COPPER AVE 88240
  James Manes, prin.
Rogers ES, 300 E CLINTON ST 88240
  Roberta Thomas, prin.

Sanger ES, 2020 N ACOMA DR 88240
  Nancy Havink, prin.
Southern Heights ES, 101 E TEXAS ST 88240
  Karol Rupard, prin.
Stone ES, 1015 E CALLE S ST 88240
  Bobby Caton, prin.
Taylor ES, 1700 E YESO DR 88240
  Don Swift, prin.

St. Helena School, 110 E BENDER BLVD 88240

Holloman A F B, Otero Co.
  Alamogordo AU
  Supt. – See Alamogordo
  MS, P O BOX 1149 88330 – Susan Jim, prin.
  Holloman IS, P O BOX 1209 88330
    Gilbert Candelaria, prin.
  Holloman PS, P O BOX 1209 88330
    Kate Asbill, prin.

Holman, Mora Co., Pop. Code 2
  Mora AU
  Supt. – See Mora
  ES 87723 – Consuelo Cruz, prin.

Hondo, Lincoln Co.
  Hondo Valley AU
  Sch. Sys. Enr. Code 2
  Supt. – Maria Fuentes-Leas, P O BOX 55 88336
  ES 88336 – Maria Fuentes-Leas, prin.

Hope, Eddy Co., Pop. Code 2
  Artesia AU
  Supt. – See Artesia
  Penasco ES, HCR 1 88250 – Joel Pate, prin.

House, Quay Co., Pop. Code 2
  House SD
  Sch. Sys. Enr. Code 1
  Supt. – Michael Davis, P O BOX 673 88121
  ES 88121 – Michael Davis, prin.

Hurley, Grant Co., Pop. Code 4
  Cobre AU
  Supt. – See Bayard
  ES 88043 – Evangeline Herrera, prin.

Jal, Lea Co., Pop. Code 5
  Jal AU
  Sch. Sys. Enr. Code 3
  Supt. – Guan Miller, P O BOX 1386 88252
  ES, 301 W MINNESOTA AVE 88252
    David Randall, prin.

Jemez Pueblo, Sandoval Co., Pop. Code 4
  Jemez Springs AU
  Sch. Sys. Enr. Code 3
  Supt. – O. Meador
    CANYON ROUTE BOX 4A 87024
  Jemez Valley ES 87024 – Michael Garcia, prin.

San Diego Mission School, P O BOX 66 87024

Kirtland, San Juan Co., Pop. Code 3
  Central AU
  Supt. – See Shiprock
  MS, P O BOX 147 87417
    Robert Breckenridge, prin.
  Bond ES, P O BOX 98 87417
    Raymond Horvath, prin.
  ES, 30 ROAD 6446 84714 – Don Hornbecker, prin.
  Wilson MS, P O OBX 146 87417
    Bob Howerton, prin.

Kirtland A F B East, Bernalillo Co.
  Albuquerque AU
  Supt. – See Albuquerque
  Sandia Base ES 87115 – Marcella Jones, prin.
  Wherry ES 87116 – Patricia Hart, prin.

Lake Arthur, Chaves Co., Pop. Code 2
  Lake Arthur AU
  Sch. Sys. Enr. Code 2
  Supt. – Timothy Raftery, P O BOX 98 88253
  ES 88253 – Timothy Raftery, prin.

La Luz, Otero Co., Pop. Code 3
  Alamogordo AU
  Supt. – See Alamogordo
  ES 88337 – Ed Wilson, prin.

La Mesa, Dona Ana Co., Pop. Code 3
  Gadsden AU
  Supt. – See Anthony
  ES, P O BOX 67 88044 – Agueda Mora, prin.

Las Cruces, Dona Ana Co., Pop. Code 8
  Las Cruces AU
  Sch. Sys. Enr. Code 7
  Supt. – Harold Floyd
    301 W AMADOR AVE 88005
  Alameda ES, 1325 N ALAMEDA BLVD 88005
    Milton Shelton, prin.
  Central ES, 150 N ALAMEDA BLVD 88005
    Betty Dirk, prin.
  Conlee ES, 1701 BOSTON DR 88005
    John Stablein, prin.
  Dona Ana ES, 400 E DONA ANA SCH RD 88005
    Robert Aragon, prin.
  East Picacho ES, 4450 N HIGHWAY 85 88005
    Mary Garcia, prin.
  Hermosa Heights ES, 1655 E AMADOR AVE 88001
    Ramona Gonzales, prin.
  Highland ES, 3355 HWY 70 E 88001
    Jerry Melder, prin.
  Hillrise ES, 1400 CURNETT DR 88001
    Kathleen Easterling, prin.

Jornada ES, 3400 ELKS ROAD 88005
  Martha Wolfinger, prin.
Loma Heights ES, 1600 MADRID RD 88001
  Sharon Meier, prin.
MacArthur ES, 655 N 4TH ST 88005
  Vincent Rivera, prin.
University Hills ES, 2005 S LOCUST ST 88001
  Irene Willey, prin.
Valley View ES, 915 CALIFORNIA AVE 88001
  Martha Cole, prin.
Washington ES, 755 E CHESTNUT ST 88001
  Ernest Banegas, prin.
Other Schools – See Fairacres, Mesilla Park, White
  Sands Missile Range

Holy Cross ES, 1331 N MIRANDA ST 88005
Immaculate Heart of Mary School
  865 E IDAHO AVE 88001

Las Vegas, San Miguel Co., Pop. Code 7
  Las Vegas City AU
  Sch. Sys. Enr. Code 4
  Supt. – Dr. Jose Perea, 901 DOUGLAS AVE 87701
  Memorial MS, OLD NATIONAL ROAD 87701
    Arthur Garcia, prin.
  Henry ES, 1104 3RD ST 87701
    Nick Kavanaugh, prin.
  Legion Park ES, LEGION DRIVE 87701
    Lucille Stanfield, prin.
  Mora Avenue ES, MORA AVE 87701
    Cipriano Aguilar, prin.
  Sierra Vista ES, 475 LEGION DR 87701
    Alfredo Baca, prin.
  Other Schools – See Sapello

  Las Vegas West AU
  Sch. Sys. Enr. Code 4
  Supt. – Jose Lopez, 179 BRIDGE ST 87701
  West Las Vegas MS, 1310 S GONZALES ST 87701
    Ray Collins, prin.
  Armijo ES, PORTER ST 87701
    Rudy Castellano, prin.
  Conchas Dam ES 87701 – Susan Gabbert, prin.
  North Public ES, SANTA FE ST 87701
    Rudy Castellano, prin.
  Olo Sorrows ES, 1725 NEW MEXICO AVE 87701
    Henry Trujillo, prin.
  Union ES, 521 UNION ST 87701
    Henry Trujillo, prin.
  Other Schools – See El Pueblo, Trementina

Lindrith, Rio Arriba Co.
  Jemez Mountain AU
  Supt. – See Gallina
  ES 87029 – Emily Vigil, prin.

Logan, Quay Co., Pop. Code 3
  Logan AU
  Sch. Sys. Enr. Code 2
  Supt. – Bill Flowers, P O BOX 67 88426
  ES 88426 – Jim Harper, prin.

Lordsburg, Hidalgo Co., Pop. Code 5
  Lordsburg AU
  Sch. Sys. Enr. Code 3
  Supt. – Phillip DeFoor, 501 W 4TH ST 88045
  Dugan-Tarango MS, 1352 HARDIN DRIVE 88045
    Fred La Marca, prin.
  Central MS, 207 HIGH ST 88045
    Howard Brunje, prin.
  Southside ES, 200 E 9TH ST 88405
    Howard Brunje, prin.
  Traylor ES, 500 OWNBY ST 88045
    Howard Brunje, prin.

Los Alamos, Los Alamos Co., Pop. Code 7
  Los Alamos AU
  Sch. Sys. Enr. Code 5
  Supt. – David Barbosa, P O BOX 90 87544
  MS, 2101 CUMBRES DRIVE 87544
    Donald Holliway, prin.
  Aspen ES, 2182 33RD ST 87544
    Cheryl Pongratz, prin.
  Barranca Mesa ES
    57 LOMA DEL ESCOLAR ST 87544
    Dennis Paluczyk, prin.
  Mountain ES, 2280 NORTH RD 87544
    Mary Betta, prin.
  Other Schools – See White Rock

Los Lunas, Valencia Co., Pop. Code 5
  Los Lunas AU
  Sch. Sys. Enr. Code 6
  Supt. – Hugh Prather, P O BOX 1300 87031
  MS, 220 LUNA AVE SE 87021
    Erlinda Martinez, prin.
  Bosque Farms ES 87031 – June Wolfe, prin.
  Fernandez IS 87031 – Dan Garrison, prin.
  Gabaldon ES 87031 – Mary Jo Roch, prin.
  Gallegos ES, 26 SUN VALLEY 87031
    Maribelle Ogilvie, prin.
  Parish ES 87031 – Jesus Sedillos, prin.
  Peralta ES 87031 – Yolanda Denny, prin.

Loving, Eddy Co., Pop. Code 4
  Loving AU
  Sch. Sys. Enr. Code 2
  Supt. – David Chavez, P O BOX 98 88256
  ES, 610 CEDAR 88256 – Raul Sanchez, prin.

Lovington, Lea Co., Pop. Code 6
  Lovington AU
  Sch. Sys. Enr. Code 5
  Supt. – Ross Black, P O BOX 1537 88260
  Alexander ES, 1400 S 6TH ST 88260
    Lecil Richards, prin.

Jefferson ES, 300 W JEFFERSON AVE 88260
  Ray Wright, prin.
Lea ES, 1100 W BIRCH AVE 88260
  John Nance, prin.
Llano ES, 1000 S 1ST ST 88260
  Tom Robinett, prin.
Taylor MS, 700 S 11TH ST 88260
  William King, prin.
Yarbro ES, 700 W JEFFERSON AVE 88260
  H. Rickerson, prin.

Magdalena, Socorro Co., Pop. Code 4
  Magdalena AU
  Sch. Sys. Enr. Code 2
  Supt. – Ruben Cordova, P O BOX 24 87825
  MS 87825 – J. Travelstead, prin.
  Magdalena ES 87825 – J. Travelstead, prin.

Maxwell, Colfax Co., Pop. Code 2
  Maxwell AU
  Sch. Sys. Enr. Code 2
  Supt. – Wilfred Lackey, P O BOX 275 87728
  ES 87728 – Leroy Quintana, prin.

Melrose, Curry Co., Pop. Code 3
  Melrose AU
  Sch. Sys. Enr. Code 2
  Supt. – Franklin McKay, P O BOX 275 88124
  ES, 100 E MISSOURI 88124 – Bruce Hegwer, prin.

Mescalero, Otero Co., Pop. Code 3
  Tularosa AU
  Supt. – See Tularosa
  ES 88340 – Ronald Bateman, prin.

Mesilla Park, Dona Ana Co.
  Las Cruces AU
  Supt. – See Las Cruces
  Mesilla ES, CALLE DEL SUR 88047
    Robert Sanchez, prin.
  ES, 955 W UNION AVE 88047 – Joe Sipko, prin.

Mesquite, Dona Ana Co., Pop. Code 2
  Gadsden AU
  Supt. – See Anthony
  ES, P O BOX 320 88048 – Ray Saucedo, prin.

Milan, Cibola Co., Pop. Code 5
  Grants AU
  Supt. – See Grants
  ES, 404 SAND 87020 – Ronald Roth, prin.

Mora, Mora Co., Pop. Code 3
  Mora AU
  Sch. Sys. Enr. Code 3
  Supt. – Leonard Aragon, P O BOX 179 87732
  ES 87732 – Arturo Romero, prin.
  Other Schools – See Holman

Moriarty, Torrance Co., Pop. Code 4
  Moriarty AU
  Sch. Sys. Enr. Code 4
  Supt. – Joe Chavez, P O BOX 20 87035
  MS, P O BOX 20 87035 – Virginia Dugan, prin.
  Edgewood ES 87035 – James Satterfield, prin.
  ES 87035 – Earl Glenn, prin.
  Mountainview ES 87035 – Freddie Cardenas, prin.

Mosquero, Harding Co., Pop. Code 2
  Mosquero AU
  Sch. Sys. Enr. Code 2
  Supt. – George York, P O BOX 258 87733
  ES 87733 – Frank Maestas, prin.

Mountainair, Torrance Co., Pop. Code 4
  Mountainair AU
  Sch. Sys. Enr. Code 2
  Supt. – James Hayes, P O BOX 456 87036
  ES 87036 – Dr. Jack Snyder, prin.

Navajo, Gallup Co., Pop. Code 3
  Gallup-McKinley AU
  Supt. – See Gallup
  ES, P O BOX 12 87328 – Kristina Merritt, prin.

Newcomb, San Juan Co.
  Central AU
  Supt. – See Shiprock
  ES, P O BOX 7963 87455 – Juan Juarez, prin.

New Laguna, Cibola Co.
  Grants AU
  Supt. – See Grants
  Laguna-Acoma MS, P O BOX 76 87038
    Kilino Marquez, prin.

Ojo Caliente, Taos Co., Pop. Code 2
  Mesa Vista AU
  Supt. – See El Rito
  ES, P O BOX 1037 87549 – Joe Gurule, prin.

Pecos, San Miguel Co., Pop. Code 3
  Pecos AU
  Sch. Sys. Enr. Code 3
  Supt. – Leo Varela, P O BOX 1 87552
  ES 87552 – Ben Esquibel, prin.

Pena Blanca, Sandoval Co., Pop. Code 2
  Bernalillo AU
  Supt. – See Bernalillo
  Cochiti ES 87041 – Margaret Garza, prin.

Penasco, Taos Co., Pop. Code 2
  Penasco AU
  Sch. Sys. Enr. Code 3
  Supt. – Felix Duran, P O BOX 318 87553
  ES 87553 – Jose Griego, prin.

Placitas, Sandoval Co., Pop. Code 2
Bernalillo AU
Supt. – See Bernalillo
ES 87043 – Linda Williams, prin.

Polvadera, Socorro Co.
Socorro AU
Supt. – See Socorro
Midway ES 87828 – Dolores Griego, prin.

Portales, Roosevelt Co., Pop. Code 6
Portales AU
Sch. Sys. Enr. Code 5
Supt. – Dr. Howard Overby, P O BOX 779 88130
JHS, 300 E 5TH ST 88130 – David Jenkins, prin.
Brown ES, 520 W 5TH ST 88130
  Brian Arnold, prin.
James MS, 701 W 18TH ST 88130
  David Brooks, prin.
Lindsey MS, 1216 W IVY ST 88130
  Trina Valdez, prin.
Steiner ES, 525 S CHICAGO AVE 88130
  Larry Cantwell, prin.

Quemado, Catron Co., Pop. Code 2
Quemado AU
Sch. Sys. Enr. Code 2
Supt. – Lewis Stratton, P O BOX 128 87829
ES 87829 – Tim McCoy, prin.
Other Schools – See Datil

Questa, Taos Co., Pop. Code 3
Questa AU
Sch. Sys. Enr. Code 3
Supt. – Juan Aragon, P O BOX 440 87556
MS 87556 – Steve Archuleta, prin.
Cerro ES 87556 – Reynn Gonzales, prin.
MS 87556 – Steve Archuleta, prin.
Red River ES, P O BOX 440 87556
  Ann Crombie, prin.
Other Schools – See Costilla

Ramah, Cibola Co.
Gallup-McKinley AU
Supt. – See Gallup
ES, P O BOX 54 87321 – Joseph Collins, prin.

Ranchos De Taos, Taos Co., Pop. Code 4

San Fransico De Asisi School, P O BOX 463 87557

Raton, Colfax Co., Pop. Code 6
Raton AU
Sch. Sys. Enr. Code 4
Supt. – Aubrey McGowen, P O BOX 940 87740
MS, 500 S 3RD ST 87740 – Bill Naccarato, prin.
Columbian ES, 700 N 2ND ST 87740
  Harvey Green, prin.
Kearny MS, 800 S 3RD ST 87740
  Paul Malano, prin.
Longfellow ES, 700 E 4TH ST 87740
  Jerry Robbins, prin.

Raton Catholic School, 401 S 4TH ST 87740

Rehoboth, McKinley Co.

Rehoboth Christian HS, P O BOX 41 87322

Reserve, Catron Co., Pop. Code 2
Reserve AU
Sch. Sys. Enr. Code 2
Supt. – Harold Sloan, P O BOX 347 87830
ES 87830 – Harold Sloan, prin.
Other Schools – See Glenwood

Rio Rancho, Bernalillo Co., Pop. Code 5
Albuquerque AU
Supt. – See Albuquerque
King ES, 1301 27TH SE 87124
  Geraldine Harge, prin.
Puesta Del Sol ES, 1100 HOOD AVE SE 87125
  Israel Juarez, prin.
ES, 4601 PEPE ORTIZ ROAD SE 87124
  Roy Phillips, prin.

Roswell, Chaves Co., Pop. Code 8
Roswell AU
Sch. Sys. Enr. Code 6
Supt. – Dr. Milton Negus, P O BOX 1437 88202
Berrendo MS, RURAL ROUTE 04 BOX 579 88201
  E. Edward Phillips III, prin.
Mesa MS, 1601 E BLAND ST 88201
  Eloy Padilla, prin.
Mt. View MS, MR 273-A 88201
  Dan Gomez, prin.
Sierra MS, 615 S SYCAMORE AVE 88201
  Paul Babek, prin.
Berrendo ES, RURAL ROUTE 01 BOX 226B 88201
  Louis McDonald, prin.
Chisum ES, 2301 S VIRGINIA AVE 88201
  Grace Romero, prin.
Del Norte ES, 2701 N GARDEN AVE 88201
  William Greene, prin.
East Grand Plain ES
  RURAL ROUTE 02 BOX 79C 88201
  Gene Burke, prin.
Edgewood ES, 701 N GARDEN AVE 88201
  Omar Barragan, prin.
El Capitan ES, 2807 W BLAND ST 88201
  Jay Sherrard, prin.
Flora Vista ES, 1208 E BLAND ST 88201
  David Gomez, prin.
Military Heights ES
  1900 N MICHIGAN AVE 88201
  Terry Pierce, prin.

Missouri Avenue ES, 700 S MISSOURI AVE 88201
  Duane Evans, prin.
Monterrey ES, 910 W GAYLE ST 88201
  Dianne Doan, prin.
Parkview ES, 1700 W ALAMEDA ST 88201
  Allen Cloud, prin.
Pecos ES, 600 E HOBBS ST 88201
  Moises Campos, prin.
Sunset ES, M R #167 88201 – Peggy Brewer, prin.
Valley View ES
  1400 S WASHINGTON AVE 88201
  Jane Pemberton, prin.
Washington ES, 400 N WASHINGTON AVE 88201
  Bill Rapp, prin.

Central Christian School
  1200 W ALAMEDA ST 88201

Roy, Harding Co., Pop. Code 2
Roy AU
Sch. Sys. Enr. Code 2
Supt. – Mason Costin, P O BOX 96 87743
ES 87743 – Mason Costin, prin.

Ruidoso, Lincoln Co., Pop. Code 5
Ruidoso AU
Sch. Sys. Enr. Code 4
Supt. – Sid Miller, P O BOX 430 88345
Mid S, 100 REESE DR 88345
  Mike Gladden, prin.
Nob Hill ES, NOB HILL DR 88345
  Roger Sowder, prin.
White Mountain ES, 100 WHITE MT RD 88345
  Frank Cannella, prin.
White Mountain IS, 200 WHITE MT RD 88345
  Don Weems, prin.

San Antonio, Socorro Co., Pop. Code 2
Socorro AU
Supt. – See Socorro
ES 87832 – Joseph Garcia, prin.

Sandia Park, Bernaillo Co.
Albuquerque AU
Supt. – See Albuquerque
San Antonito ES, P O BOX 1170 87047
  Don Lange, prin.

San Fidel, Cibolo Co.

St. Joseph ES, P O BOX 37 87049

San Jon, Quay Co., Pop. Code 2
San Jon AU
Sch. Sys. Enr. Code 2
Supt. – William Coker, P O BOX 5 88434
ES 88434 – William Coker, prin.

San Juan Pueblo, Rio Arriba Co., Pop. Code 3
Espanola AU
Supt. – See Espanola
San Juan ES 87566 – Mary Gallegos, prin.

San Lorenzo, Grant Co.
Cobre AU
Supt. – See Bayard
ES 88057 – Arcencio Chavez, prin.

San Mateo, Cibola Co.
Grants AU
Supt. – See Grants
ES 87050 – Leroy Maes, prin.

San Miguel, Dona Ana Co.
Gadsden AU
Supt. – See Anthony
ES, GENERAL DELIVERY 88058
  Russell Phipps, prin.

San Rafael, Cibola Co., Pop. Code 3
Grants AU
Supt. – See Grants
ES 87051 – Danny Sedillos, prin.

Santa Cruz, Santa Fe Co., Pop. Code 3

Holy Cross School, P O BOX 1137 87567

Santa Fe, Santa Fe Co., Pop. Code 8
Pojoaque Valley AU
Sch. Sys. Enr. Code 4
Supt. – A. Casey Martinez, P O BOX 3468 87501
Pojoaque ES 87532 – Priscilla Montague, prin.

Santa Fe AU
Sch. Sys. Enr. Code 7
Supt. – Edward Ortiz, 610 ALTA VISTA ST 87501
Alameda JHS, 400 MADERA ST 87501
  Frank Montoya, prin.
Capshaw JHS, ZIA ROAD 87501
  Stephen Dilg, prin.
DeVargas JHS, LLANO ROAD 87501
  Rexie Baca, prin.
Acequia Madre ES, ACEQUIA MADRE ST 87501
  Leslie Nordby, prin.
Agua Fria ES, AGUA FRIA ST 87501
  Benjamin Baca, prin.
Alvord ES, HICKOX ST 87501
  Albert Ortega, prin.
Atalaya ES, CAMINO CABRA 87501
  Rose Ann Sena, prin.
Chaparral ES, YUCCA RD 87501
  Imelda Baca, prin.
El Dorado ES, #2 AVENIDA TORREON 87501
  Alfonso Garcia, prin.
Gilbert ES, 300 GRIFFIN ST 87501
  Maria Naranjo, prin.

Gonzales ES, 851 W ALAMEDA ST 87501
  George Bennett, prin.
Kaune ES, 1409 MONTEREY DR 87501
  Mariano Romero, prin.
Kearney ES
  901 AVENUE DE LAS CAMPANAS 87505
  Arthur Aragon, prin.
Larragoite ES, AGUA FRIA ST 87501
  Gilbert Archuleta, prin.
Martinez ES, SAN MATEO DR 87501
  James Starr, prin.
Nava ES, 2665 SIRINGO ROAD 87505
  Gloria Gomez, prin.
Pinon ES
  2921 CAMINO DE LOS CABALLO 87505
  Michael Mier, prin.
Salazar ES, 1300 OSAGE AVE 87501
  Richard Tolen, prin.
Sweeney ES, AIRPORT RD 87501
  Pedro Atencio, prin.
Wood Gormley ES, 141 E BOOTH ST 87501
  Rita Rubin, prin.
Other Schools – See Tesuque

Cristo Rey School, CAMINO DELORA 87501
Rio Grande School, 715 CAMINO CABRA 87501
St. Anne ES, 505 ALICIA ST 87501
St. Francis Cathedral School
  275 E ALAMEDA ST 87501

Santa Rosa, Guadalupe Co., Pop. Code 5
Santa Rosa AU
Sch. Sys. Enr. Code 3
Supt. – Charles Ward, 344 S 4TH ST 88435
MS, 244 S 4TH ST 88435 – Moises Herrera, prin.
ES, 658 S 5TH ST 88435 – Nora Garcia, prin.
Other Schools – See Anton Chico

Santo Domingo Pueblo, Sandoval Co., Pop. Code 4
Bernalillo AU
Supt. – See Bernalillo
Santo Domingo MS, P O BOX 100 87052
  Mary C. De Baca, prin.

Sapello, San Miguel Co.
Las Vegas City AU
Supt. – See Las Vegas
ES 87745 – Cipriano Aguilar, prin.

Seboyeta, Cibola Co.
Grants AU
Supt. – See Grants
ES 87055 – Loretta Miller, prin.

Shiprock, San Juan Co., Pop. Code 2
Central AU
Sch. Sys. Enr. Code 6
Supt. – William Horton, P O BOX 1179 87420
Tse' Bit'ai MS, P O BOX 1873 87420
  Elmer Hall, prin.
Mesa MS, P O BOX 936 87420
  Robert Pruett, prin.
Natanni Nez ES, P O BOX 280 87420
  Sylvia Ashley, prin.
Nizhoni ES, P O BOX 1147 87420
  Genevieve Jackson, prin.
Other Schools – See Fruitland, Kirtland, Newcomb, Tohatchi

Silver City, Grant Co., Pop. Code 6
Silver AU
Sch. Sys. Enr. Code 5
Supt. – Herb Torrez, P O BOX 1060 88062
Barrios ES, LITTLE WALNUT RD 88061
  Gerald Hunt, prin.
Schmitt ES, STATE HWY 90 S 88061
  Travis Columbus, prin.
Sixth Street ES, 405 W 6TH ST 88061
  Henry Munoz, prin.
Stout IS, 2600 N SWAN ST 88061
  Ernest Parra, prin.
Other Schools – See Cliff

Smith Lake, McKinley Co.
Gallup-McKinley AU
Supt. – See Gallup
ES, P O BOX A CPO 87323
  Claresia Montoya, prin.

Socorro, Socorro Co., Pop. Code 6
Socorro AU
Sch. Sys. Enr. Code 4
Supt. – Delbert Fraissinet, P O BOX 1157 87801
Sarracino MS, 1425 EL CAMINO REAL NW 87801
  Frank Jaramillo, prin.
Torres ES, 239 GARFIELD ST 87801
  Mary Wilburn, prin.
Zimmerly ES, 511 EL CAMINO REAL ST 87801
  Daniel Sanchez, prin.
Other Schools – See Polvadera, San Antonio

San Miguel School
  403 EL CAMINO REAL ST 87801

Springer, Colfax Co., Pop. Code 4
Springer AU
Sch. Sys. Enr. Code 2
Supt. – Robert Parnell, P O BOX 308 87747
Forrester ES, 311 MIRANDA 87747
  Lorence Gonzales, prin.
Wilferth MS, 311 MIRANDA 87747
  Lorence Gonzales, prin.

Sunland Park, Dona Ana Co., Pop. Code 4
Gadsden AU
Supt. – See Anthony

Desert View ES, P O BOX 280 88063
  Ana Banegas-Pena, prin.
Riverside MS, P O BOX 280 88063
  Lucille Housen, prin.
PS, P O BOX 2050 88063 – Felix Hernandez, prin.

Taos, Taos Co., Pop. Code 5
Taos AU
Sch. Sys. Enr. Code 5
Supt. – Edward Abeyta, P O BOX 677 87571
Arroyo Hondo ES, GENERAL DELIVERY 87501
  Mario Barela, prin.
Arroyo Seco ES, P O BOX 302 87501
  Mario Barela, prin.
Enos Garcia ES
  305 DON FERNANDO ROAD 87501
  Jerry Quintana, prin.
Rancho Do Taos MS, HWY 3 87501
  Jerry Quintana, prin.
Talpa ES, TALPA RD 87501 – Jerry Quintana, prin.
ES, 401 PLACITA RD 87501 – Mario Barela, prin.

Taos Christian Academy, P O BOX 1068 87571

Tatum, Lea Co., Pop. Code 3
Tatum AU
Sch. Sys. Enr. Code 2
Supt. – Dwayne Wood, P O BOX 685 88267
JHS 88267 – John Ingle, prin.
ES 88267 – David Willis, prin.

Tesuque, Santa Fe Co.
Santa Fe AU
Supt. – See Santa Fe
ES 87574 – Robert Lopez, prin.

Texico, Curry Co., Pop. Code 3
Texico AU
Sch. Sys. Enr. Code 2
Supt. – James Pierce, P O BOX 237 88135
JHS 88135 – Anna Southard, prin.
ES 88135 – David Lynn, prin.

Thoreau, McKinley Co., Pop. Code 3
Gallup-McKinley AU
Supt. – See Gallup
MS, P O BOX A 87365 – Larry Wilkinson, prin.
ES, P O BOX 8 87323 – Carpio Torres, prin.

Blessed Kateri Tekakwitha ES
  200 CENTRAL AVE 87323

Tierra Amarilla, Rio Arriba Co., Pop. Code 3
Chama Valley AU
Sch. Sys. Enr. Code 3
Supt. – J. Trujillo, P O BOX 10 87575
Chama MS, P O BOX 159 87575
  Ben Branch, prin.
MS, P O BOX 159 87575 – Manuel Valdez, prin.

ES, P O OBX 159 87575 – Carlos Casados, prin.
Other Schools – See Canjilon, Chama

Tijeras, Bernalillo Co., Pop. Code 2
Albuquerque AU
Supt. – See Albuquerque
Roosevelt MS, P O BOX 310 87059
  Rommie Compher, prin.
Montoya ES, P O OBX 310 87059
  Rommie Compher, prin.

Tohatchi, McKinley Co., Pop. Code 2
Central AU
Supt. – See Shiprock
Newcomb JHS, HCR 01 BOX 25 87325
  William Nidiffer, prin.
Naschitti ES 87325 – Rena Henry, prin.

Gallup-McKinley AU
Supt. – See Gallup
MS, P O BOX 322 87325 – Joe Cotner, prin.
ES, P O BOX 31 87325 – Jean Lawson, prin.

Trementina, San Miguel Co., Pop. Code 2
Las Vegas West AU
Supt. – See Las Vegas
ES, 179 BRIDGE ST 88439 – Rosalie Lopez, prin.

Tres Piedras, Taos Co.
Mesa Vista AU
Supt. – See El Rito
ES 87577 – Rubina Quinto, prin.

Truth or Consequences, Sierra Co., Pop. Code 6
Truth or Consequences AU
Sch. Sys. Enr. Code 4
Supt. – Janel Gilmer, P O BOX 952 87901
MS, NEW MIDDLE SCHOOL ROAD 87901
  Ken Lyon, prin.
ES 87901 – Stephanie Brownfield, prin.
Other Schools – See Arrey

Tucumcari, Quay Co., Pop. Code 6
Tucumcari AU
Sch. Sys. Enr. Code 4
Supt. – Guy Jacobus, P O BOX 1046 88401
JHS, 914 S 5TH ST 88401 – Pat Lujan, prin.
Buena Vista ES, 2400 S 8TH ST 88401
  Herman James, prin.
Granger MS, 913 S 3RD ST 88401
  Herman James, prin.
Mountain View ES
  1608 S ROCK ISLAND ST 88401
  Mike Kinsall, prin.
Zia ES, 702 E ALBER ST 88401
  Mike Kinsall, prin.

Tularosa, Otero Co., Pop. Code 5
Tularosa AU
Sch. Sys. Enr. Code 4
Supt. – Perry Andrews, 504 1ST ST 88352
JHS 88352 – Max Salcido, prin.
ES 88352 – Jerry Smith, prin.
Other Schools – See Mescalero

Vaughn, Guadalupe Co., Pop. Code 3
Vaughn AU
Sch. Sys. Enr. Code 2
Supt. – Kurt Knoernschild, P O BOX 158 88353
ES 88353 – Roman Garcia, prin.

Velarde, Rio Arriba Co., Pop. Code 2
Espanola AU
Supt. – See Espanola
ES 87582 – Benito Lucero, prin.

Wagon Mound, Mora Co., Pop. Code 2
Wagon Mound AU
Sch. Sys. Enr. Code 2
Supt. – Ray Gallegos, P O BOX 158 87752
ES 87752 – Paul Salas, prin.

Weed, Otero Co.
Alamogordo AU
Supt. – See Alamogordo
ES, P O BOX 548 88354 – Basil Curry, prin.

White Rock, Los Alamos Co.
Los Alamos AU
Supt. – See Los Alamos
Chamisa ES, 301 MEADOW LANE 87544
  Richard Grimes, prin.
Pinon ES, 90 GRAND CANYON DR 87544
  Richard Dunn, Jr., prin.

White Sands Missile Range, Dona Ana Co.
Las Cruces AU
Supt. – See Las Cruces
White Sands ES 88002 – Richard Schriver, prin.

Zuni, McKinley Co., Pop. Code 5
Zuni AU
Sch. Sys. Enr. Code 4
Supt. – Hayes Lewis, P O BOX A 87327
MS, P O BOX A 87327 – Jack Bradley, prin.
Dowa Yalanne ES, P O BOX D 87327
  Barbara Gordon, prin.

St. Anthony Zuni Indian School
  P O BOX 486 87327
Zuni Christian Reformed Mission School
  P O BOX 445 87327

NEW YORK

STATE EDUCATION DEPARTMENT
111 Education Building
Washington Ave., Albany 12234
(518) 474-5844

Commissioner of Education	Thomas Sobol
Executive Deputy Commissioner	Thomas Sheldon
Deputy Commissioner for Legal Affairs	Robert Diaz
Deputy Commissioner Elementary, Secondary Education	Lionel Mionelo
Deputy Commissioner School Improvement Planning	Arthur Walton
Deputy Commissioner Cultural Education	C. Huxley
Deputy Commissioner Vocational Rehabilitation	R. Switzer
Deputy Commissioner Higher & Professional Education	D. Nolan

BOARD OF REGENTS, UNIVERSITY OF THE STATE OF NEW YORK
Gordon M. Ambach, *Commissioner*   Albany 12224

BOARDS OF COOPERATIVE EDUCATIONAL SERVICES

Albany/Schoharie/Schenectady BOCES, Custer Quick, Supt.
  1015 WATERVLIET-SHAKER ROAD, Albany 12205
Broome/Delaware/Tioga BOCES, L. Distin, Supt.
  UPPER GLENWOOD ROAD, Binghamton 13905

Cattargus/Allegany/Erie/Wyoming BOCES, James Cross, Supt.
  P O BOX 424B, Olean 14760
Cayuga/Onondaga BOCES, Frank Ambrosie, Supt.
  234 S STREET ROAD, Auburn 13021

Clinton/Essex/Warren/Washington BOCES, William Fritz, Supt.
  P O BOX 455, Plattsburgh 12901
Delaware/Chenango/Madison/Otsego BOCES, F. Van Wickler, Supt.
  RURAL ROUTE 03, Norwich 13815

Dutchess BOCES, Duane Hutton, Supt.
SALT POINT TURNPIKE, Poughkeepsie 12603
Erie 1 BOCES, Robert Loretan, Supt.
2 PLEASANT AVE W, Lancaster 14086
Erie 2/Chautauqua/Cattaraugus BOCES, Gary Barr, Supt.
3340 BAKER ROAD, Orchard Park 14127
Franklin/Essex/Hamilton BOCES, David DeSantis, Supt.
P O BOX 28, Malone 12953
Genesee/Wyoming BOCES, Edwin Dunmire, Supt.
8250 STATE ST ROAD, Batavia 14020
Hamilton/Fulton/Montgomery BOCES, Kenneth Smith, Supt.
P O BOX 665, Johnstown 12095
Herkimer/Fulton/Hamilton/Otsego BOCES, William Busacker, Supt.
GROS BLVD, Herkimer 13350
Jeffrsn/Lewis/Hamltn/Herkmr/Oneida BOCES, Charles Bohlen, Supt.
OUTER ARSENAL ST ROAD, Watertown 13601
Livingston/Steuben/Wyoming BOCES, Charles Holowach, Supt.
LACKAWANNA AVE, Mount Morris 14510
Madison/Oneida BOCES, Edward Shafer, Supt.
SPRING ROAD, Verona 13478
Monroe 2/Orleans BOCES, Richard Haken, Supt.
3599 BIG RIDGE ROAD, Spencerport 14559
Monroe 1 BOCES, Joseph Farinola, Supt.
41 O'CONNOR ROAD, Fairport 14450

Nassau BOCES, Ira Singer, Supt.
VALENTINE RD & THE PLAIN RD, Westbury 11590
Oneida/Herkimer/Madison BOCES, Robert Sekowski, Supt.
P O BOX 70, New Hartford 13413
Onondaga/Cortland/Madison BOCES, Lee Peters, Supt.
P O BOX 4754, Syracuse 13211
Ontario/Seneca/Yates/Cayuga/Wayne BOCES, Harold Bowman, Supt.
RURAL ROUTE 02, Stanley 14561
Orange/Ulster BOCES, Emanuel Axelrod, Supt.
GIBSON ROAD, Goshen 10924
Orleans/Niagara BOCES, Richard Haken, Supt.
4232 SHELBY BASIN ROAD, Medina 14103
Oswego BOCES, Burton Ramer, Supt.
P O BOX 488, Mexico 13114
Otsego/Delaware/Schoharie/Greene BOCES, Austin Leahy,Jr., Supt.
REXMERE PARK, Stamford 12167
Putnam/Westchester BOCES, John Battles, Supt.
Yorktown Heights 10598
Rensselaer/Colmubia/Greene BOCES, John Sackett, Supt.
1550 SCHUURMAN ROAD, Castleton-on-Hudson 12033
Rockland BOCES, Anthony Campo, Supt.
61 PARROT ROAD, West Nyack 10994
Saratoga/Warren BOCES, B. Evans, Supt.
112 SPRING ST, Saratoga Springs 12866

Schuyler/Chemung/Tioga BOCES, Ronald Poletto, Supt.
431 PHILO ROAD, Elmira 14903
St. Lawrence/Lewis BOCES, William Hart, Supt.
P O BOX 231, Canton 13617
Steuben/Allegany BOCES, Rene Bouchard, Supt.
RURAL ROUTE 01, Bath 14810
Suffolk 1 BOCES, Raymond DeFeo, Supt.
215 OLD RIVERHEAD ROAD, Westhampton Beach 11978
Suffolk 2 BOCES, Edward Milliken, Supt.
201 E SUNRISE HWY, Patchogue 11772
Suffolk 3 BOCES, Edward Murphy, Supt.
507 DEER PARK ROAD, Dix Hills 11746
Sullivan BOCES, Gary Moore, Supt.
RURAL ROUTE 01 BOX 522, Liberty 12754
Tompkins/Seneca/Tioga BOCES, Roy Dexheimer, Supt.
555 WARREN ROAD, Ithaca 14850
Ulster BOCES, Laura Fleigner, Supt.
RURAL ROUTE 32 BOX 175, New Paltz 12561
Washington/Warren/Hamliton/Essex BOCES, Gerald Carozza, Supt.
WASHINGTON CO BLDG ANNEX, Hudson Falls 12839
Westchester BOCES, R. Lerer, Supt.
17 BERKLEY DR, Port Chester 10573

PUBLIC, PRIVATE, AND PAROCHIAL ELEMENTARY SCHOOLS

Accord, Ulster Co., Pop. Code 2
Rondout Valley Central SD
Sch. Sys. Enr. Code 4
Supt. – H. Ross O'Sullivan, P O BOX 9 12404
Rondout Valley JHS, P O BOX 9 12404
Peter Beckwith, prin.
Kerhonkson ES, P O BOX 9 12404
Thomas Sheldon, prin.
Marbletown ES, P O BOX 9 12404 – E. Fuhr, prin.
Rondout Valley MS, P O BOX 9 12404
Shelly Alexander, prin.
Rosendale ES, P O BOX 9 12404
Philip Buonfiglio, prin.

Adams, Jefferson Co., Pop. Code 4
South Jefferson Central SD
Sch. Sys. Enr. Code 4
Supt. – Kenneth Eysaman, 6 INSTITUTE ST 13605
Scholtz ES, 6 INSTITUTE ST 13605
M. Bovee, prin.
Other Schools – See Adams Center, Mannsville

Adams Center, Jefferson Co.
South Jefferson Central SD
Supt. – See Adams
Wilson ES, MAPLE AVENUE 13606
David Kane, prin.

Addison, Steuben Co., Pop. Code 4
Addison Central SD
Sch. Sys. Enr. Code 4
Supt. – A. Lyman Warner, 1 COLWELL ST 14801
Tuscarora ES, CLEVELAND DR 14801
Jon Thomas, prin.
Other Schools – See Cameron Mills

Afton, Chenango Co., Pop. Code 3
Afton Central SD
Sch. Sys. Enr. Code 3
Supt. – John Oates 13730
ES 13730 – Vernice Church, prin.

Akron, Erie Co., Pop. Code 5
Akron Central SD
Sch. Sys. Enr. Code 4
Supt. – David Fish, BLOOMINGDALE AVE 14001
ES, 47 BLOOMINGDALE AVE 14001
William Hite, prin.

Albany, Albany Co., Pop. Code 9
Albany CSD
Sch. Sys. Enr. Code 6
Supt. – David Brown, 1 ACADEMY PARK 12207
Hackett MS, 45 DELAWARE AVE 12202
Kevin Justice, prin.
Livingston MS, 315 NORTHERN BLVD 12210
Gerald Guzik, prin.
Arbor Hill ES, LARK DR 12210
Linda Chalmers, prin.
ES 16, 41 N ALLEN ST 12203 – Amelia Boel, prin.
ES 18, 43 BERTHA ST 12209
Agnes Edwards, prin.
ES 19, 1075 NEW SCOTLAND AVE 12208
Terrance White, prin.
ES 20, N PEARL & N SECOND 12204
Michael Carey, prin.
ES 23, 108 WHITEHALL RD 12209
Thomas Van Buren, prin.
ES 26, TREMONT STREET 12205
C. Gordon, prin.
ES 27, WESTERN AVE & RUSSELL ROAD 12203
John Canty, prin.
Giffen Memorial ES, 274 S PEARL ST 12202
M. Ford, prin.
O'Brien ES, LINCOLN PARK 12202
Walter Judd, prin.
Schuyler ES, 141 WESTERN AVE 12203
Jeremiah Spicer, prin.

Guilderland Central SD
Supt. – See Guilderland
Westmere ES, 6284 JOHNSTON RD 12203
Robert Oates, prin.

Menands UFD
Sch. Sys. Enr. Code 2
Supt. – Lyle Boyce, 17 WARDS LANE 12204
Menands ES, 17 WARDS LN 12204
Lyle Boyce, prin.

South Colonie Central SD
Sch. Sys. Enr. Code 6
Supt. – Thomas Mitchell
102 LORA LEE DR 12205
Lisha Kill MS, 100 WATERMAN AVE 12205
Joseph Sheperd, prin.
Sand Creek MS, 329 SAND CREEK ROAD 12205
Michael Norelli, prin.
Forest Park ES, 100 FOREST DR 12205
Gloria Francis, prin.
Shaker Road ES, 512 ALBANY SHAKER RD 12211
August Franze, prin.
Veeder ES, 25 VEEDER DR 12205
John Cocca, prin.

Albany Academy for Boys
135 ACADEMY ROAD 12208
Albany Academy for Girls
140 ACADEMY ROAD 12208
Doane Stuart School 12202
Pineview Christian Academy
WASHINGTON AVE EXT 12205
Blessed Sacrament ES, 605 CENTRAL AVE 12206
Cathedral Academy ES, 75 PARK AVE 12202
Christ the King ES, SUMTER AVE 12203
Hebrew Academy Capt District ES
SAND CRK & RUSSELL ROAD 12205
Holy Cross ES, 10 ROSEMONT ST 12203
Holy Names Lower MS
1065 NEW SCOTLAND AVE 12208
Our Saviour Lutheran ES
63 MOUNTAIN VIEW AVE 12205
St. Casimir ES, 315 SHERIDAN AVE 12206
St. Catherine of Siena ES, 35 HURST AVE 12208
St. James Institute ES, 50 SUMMIT AVE 12209
St. Teresa of Avila ES
8 HOLLYWOOD AVE 12208

Albertson, Nassau Co., Pop. Code 6
Herricks UFD
Supt. – See New Hyde Park
Herricks MS, HILLDALE DR 11507
John DeSilva, prin.
Searingtown ES, BEVERLY DRIVE 11507
Nancy Lindenauer, prin.

Mineola UFD
Supt. – See Mineola
Meadow Drive ES, MEADOW DRIVE 11507
Samuel Carpentier, prin.

Human Resources School
SEARINGTOWN ROAD 11507

Albion, Orleans Co., Pop. Code 5
Albion Central SD
Sch. Sys. Enr. Code 4
Supt. – Ronald Sodoma, 324 EAST AVE 14411
MS, 254 EAST AVE 14411 – Robert Huyck, prin.
MS, 254 EAST AVE 14411 – Betty Genter, prin.
PS, 324 EAST AVE 14411 – Donald Butts, prin.
Other Schools – See Waterport

Alden, Erie Co., Pop. Code 4
Alden Central SD
Sch. Sys. Enr. Code 4
Supt. – Thomas Boedicker, 13190 PARK ST 14004
MS, CRITTENDON ROAD 14004
G. McCormick, prin.
ES, CRITTENDEN ROAD 14004
Thomas Lyons, prin.
Townline ES, 11197 BROADWAY ST 14004
Margaret Ryan, prin.

St. John the Baptist ES
2028 SANDRIDGE RD 14004

Alexander, Genesee Co., Pop. Code 2
Alexander Central SD
Sch. Sys. Enr. Code 4
Supt. – Nelson Wellspeak
3314 BUFFALO ST 14005
ES, 3314 BUFFALO ST 14005 – Garry Stone, prin.

Alexandria Bay, Jefferson Co., Pop. Code 4
Alexandra Central SD
Sch. Sys. Enr. Code 3
Supt. – Ronald McLennan
34 BOLTON AVE 13607
Alexandria Center ES, 34 BOLTON AVE 13607
MyraJean Koster, prin.

Allegany, Cattaraugus Co., Pop. Code 4
Allegany Central SD
Sch. Sys. Enr. Code 4
Supt. – Thomas Nickler, N 4TH ST 14706
Allegany Central ES, 120 MAPLE AVE 14706
Diana Cianflocco, prin.

Almond, Allegany Co., Pop. Code 3
Alfred Almond Central SD
Sch. Sys. Enr. Code 3
Supt. – Gary Minns 14804
ES 14804 – Diana Luellen, prin.

Altamont, Albany Co., Pop. Code 4
Guilderland Central SD
Supt. – See Guilderland
ES, GRAND STREET 12009
Dominic Nuciforo, prin.

Altmar, Oswego Co., Pop. Code 2
Altmar Parish-Williamstown Central SD
Supt. – See Parish
ES, PULASKI STREET 13302
Gerry Hudson, prin.

Amagansett, Suffolk Co., Pop. Code 4
Amagansett UFD
Sch. Sys. Enr. Code 1
Supt. – Lloyd Peak, MAIN ST 11930
Amagansett ES, MAIN ST 11930
Lloyd Peak, prin.

Amenia, Dutchess Co., Pop. Code 6
Northeast Central SD
Sch. Sys. Enr. Code 2
Supt. – M. Rindsberg 12501
ES 12501 – John Ditondo, prin.
Webutuck MS, HAIGHT ROAD 12501
Janice Volpe, prin.
Other Schools – See Millerton

Kildonan School
RURAL ROUTE 01 BOX 294 12501

Amherst, Erie Co., Pop. Code 9
Amherst Central SD
Sch. Sys. Enr. Code 5
Supt. – William McPhee, 4301 MAIN ST 14226
MS, 55 KINGS HIGHWAY 14226
Anton Schwarzmueller, prin.
Smallwood Drive ES
300 SMALLWOOD DR 14226 – Bruce Burr, prin.
Windermere Boulevard ES
291 WINDERMERE BLVD 14226
David Maul, prin.

Sweet Home Central SD
Sch. Sys. Enr. Code 5
Supt. – James Finch
1901 SWEET HOME ROAD 14221
Sweet Home JHS, 4150 MAPLE ROAD 14226
Robert Kramer, prin.
Heritage Heights ES
2545 SWEET HOME RD 14120
Susan Mendel, prin.
Maplemere ES, 236 E MAPLEMERE RD 14221
Charles Taylor, prin.
Willow Ridge ES, 480 WILLOW RIDGE DR 14150
Charles Carle, prin.
Other Schools – See Tonawanda

Park School of Buffalo
4625 HARLEM ROAD   14226

Amityville, Suffolk Co., Pop. Code 6
Amityville UFD
Sch. Sys. Enr. Code 5
Supt. – Michael Walsh, 150 PARK AVE   11701
Northwest ES, COUNTY LINE ROAD   11701
Thomas DeBello, prin.
Park Avenue MS, 140 PARK AVE   11701
James Hackett, prin.

Bethesda ES, P O BOX 781   11701
St. Martin of Tours ES, 35 UNION AVE   11701

Amsterdam, Montgomery Co., Pop. Code 8
Amsterdam CSD
Sch. Sys. Enr. Code 5
Supt. – Alan Brown, 11 LIBERTY ST   12010
Lynch MS, COOLIDGE ROAD   12010
Claude Palczak, prin.
Bacon ES, HENRIETTA HEIGHTS   12010
Charles Loomis, prin.
Barkley ES, DE STEFANO STREET   12010
Jayne Steubing, prin.
Curie Eastside ES, BRICE STREET   12010
Lawrence Trzaskos, prin.
McNulty ES, COOLIDGE ROAD   12010
Edward Picinich, prin.
Tecler ES, NORTHERN BOULEVARD   12010
Nellie Bush, prin.

Broadalbin-Perth Central SD
Supt. – See Broadalbin
Perth ES, RURAL ROUTE 04   12010
Karen Sutton, prin.

Perth Bible Christian Academy
RURAL ROUTE 04   12010
St. Mary's Institute ES, 200 E MAIN ST   12010
St. Stanislaus ES, 42-44 CORNELL ST   12010

Andes, Delaware Co., Pop. Code 2
Andes Central SD
Sch. Sys. Enr. Code 2
Supt. – Charles Casler   13731
Andes Central S   13731 – Charles Casler, prin.

Andover, Allegany Co., Pop. Code 4
Andover Central SD
Sch. Sys. Enr. Code 2
Supt. – Jacquilyn Bellamy, 31-35 ELM ST   14806
S, 31-35 ELM ST   14806 – Charles Schroeder, prin.

Angelica, Allegany Co., Pop. Code 3
Angelica Central SD
Sch. Sys. Enr. Code 2
Supt. – Michael O'Brien, 21 E MAIN ST   14709
Angelica Central S, 21 E MAIN ST   14709
Dominic Digirolamo, prin.

Angola, Erie Co., Pop. Code 4
Evans-Brant Central SD
Sch. Sys. Enr. Code 5
Supt. – W. Houston, 8855 ERIE ROAD   14006
Hoag ES, 42 SUNSET BLVD   14006
Phillip Muck, prin.
Schmidt ES, 9455 LAKE SHORE RD   14006
Rosalyn Desantis, prin.
Waugh IS, 100 HIGH ST   14006
Michael Desantis, prin.
Other Schools – See Brant, Derby

Most Precious Blood ES, 24 PROSPECT ST   14006

Antwerp, Jefferson Co., Pop. Code 3
Indian River Central SD
Supt. – See Philadelphia
ES, ACADEMY STREET   13608
Dale Watkins, prin.

Apalachin, Tioga Co., Pop. Code 4
Owego-Apalachin Central SD
Supt. – See Owego
ES, PENNSYLVANIA AVENUE   13732
Robert Merrill, prin.

Aquebogue, Suffolk Co., Pop. Code 4
Riverhead Central SD
Supt. – See Riverhead
ES, MAIN RD   11931 – Gerard Corrado, prin.

Arcade, Wyoming Co., Pop. Code 4
Yorkshire-Pioneer Central SD
Supt. – See Yorkshire
ES, P O BOX 327   14009 – Mary Simons, prin.

Ardsley, Westchester Co., Pop. Code 5
Ardsley UFD
Sch. Sys. Enr. Code 4
Supt. – Stanley Toll, 500 FARM ROAD   10502
MS, 700 ASHFORD AVE   10502
Thomas Butera, prin.
Concord Road ES, CONCORD ROAD   10502
Rose Willner, prin.

Argyle, Washington Co., Pop. Code 2
Argyle Central SD
Sch. Sys. Enr. Code 3
Supt. – Lawrence Patzwald   12809
Argyle Central S, SALEM STREET   12809
Richard Broome, prin.

Arkport, Steuben Co., Pop. Code 3
Arkport Central SD
Sch. Sys. Enr. Code 3
Supt. – Richard Chubon, 35 EAST AVE   14807

Arkport ES, 35 EAST AVENUE   14807
William Locke, prin.

Armonk, Westchester Co., Pop. Code 6
Byram Hills Central SD
Sch. Sys. Enr. Code 4
Supt. – T. Maguire, 172 KING ST   10504
Crittenden MS, 10 MACDONALD AVE   10504
Jon Peterson, prin.
Coman Hill ES, 558 BEDFORD RD   10504
Kenneth Smith, prin.
Wampus ES, 41 WAMPUS AVE   10504
Clara Romano, prin.

Arverne, Queens Co.
Queens Borough SD 27
Supt. – See Ozone Park
Vernam ES, 4888 66TH STREET   11692
Eula Stephens, prin.

Astoria, Queens Co.

St. Demetrios School, 30-03 30TH DR   11102

Athens, Greene Co., Pop. Code 4
Coxsackie Athens Central SD
Supt. – See Coxsackie
ES, 51 THIRD ST   12015 – Edward Arthur, prin.

Athol Springs, Erie Co.

St. Francis of Assisi ES
SAINT FRANCIS DR   14010

Attica, Wyoming Co., Pop. Code 5
Attica Central SD
Sch. Sys. Enr. Code 4
Supt. – Ed Stores, 83 MAIN ST   14011
JHS, 3338 E MAIN ST ROAD   14011
Ernest Lusky, prin.
ES, 31 PROSPECT ST   14011 – Kent Bates, prin.
Other Schools – See Varysburg

Genesee-Wyoming Catholic Cent School
72 EAST AVE   14011

Auburn, Cayuga Co., Pop. Code 8
Auburn CSD
Sch. Sys. Enr. Code 6
Supt. – P. Kachris, 76 THORNTON AVE   13021
East MS, 157 FRANKLIN ST   13021
Paul Delpiano, prin.
West MS, 217 W GENESEE ST   13021
Michael Orofino, prin.
Casey Park ES, PULASKI STREET   13021
Gordon Lund, prin.
Genesee Street ES, 242 W GENESEE ST   13021
Robert Reardon, prin.
Herman Avenue ES, 2 N HERMAN AVE   13021
Paul Gagliano, prin.
Owasco ES, LETCHWORTH STREET   13021
Patricia Palmer, prin.
Seward ES, WHITEFRIAR DRIVE   13021
Anthony Gucciardi, prin.

Blessed Trinity ES, 101 E GENESEE ST   13021
SS. Peter & Paul ES, 130 WASHINGTON ST   13021
St. Hyacinth ES, 59 PULASKI ST   13021
St. Mary's ES, 17 CLYMER ST   13021

Aurora, Cayuga Co., Pop. Code 3
Southern Cayuga Central SD
Sch. Sys. Enr. Code 4
Supt. – A. Edward Dimiceli, DIST OFC   13026
Southern Cayuga S   13026 – Martin Nodzo, prin.

Au Sable Forks, Clinton Co., Pop. Code 5
Ausable Valley Central SD
Supt. – See Clintonville
ES   12912 – Joseph Kahn, prin.

Holy Name ES, PLEASANT ST   12912

Averill Park, Rensselaer Co., Pop. Code 4
Averill Park Central SD
Sch. Sys. Enr. Code 5
Supt. – Thomas Davis, P O BOX 248   12018
Algonquin MS, RURAL ROUTE 01   12018
Michael Purdy, prin.
Sand Lake ES, P O BOX 400   12018
George Raneri, prin.
Other Schools – See Troy, West Sand Lake

Avoca, Steuben Co., Pop. Code 4
Avoca Central SD
Sch. Sys. Enr. Code 3
Supt. – Carl Thompson, OLIVER ST   14809
Avoca Central S, OLIVER ST   14809
Sharon Muth, prin.

Avon, Livingston Co., Pop. Code 5
Avon Central SD
Sch. Sys. Enr. Code 4
Supt. – William McGee, 161 CLINTON ST   14414
Avon Central ES, CLINTON STREET   14414
Thomas Wallon, prin.

Babylon, Suffolk Co., Pop. Code 7
Babylon UFD
Sch. Sys. Enr. Code 4
Supt. – P. Nicolino, 171 RALPH AVE   11702
ES, 171 RALPH AVE   11702 – Esther Fusco, prin.
Babylon Memorial MS, 169 PARK AVE   11702
Marianne McCreery, prin.

Babylon Christian ES, 79 E MAIN ST   11702
St. Joseph ES, 41 CARL AVE   11702

Bainbridge, Chenango Co., Pop. Code 4
Bainbridge Guilford Central SD
Sch. Sys. Enr. Code 4
Supt. – R. Carroll, JULIAND ST   13733
Greenlawn MS, GREENLAWN AVENUE   13733
Rick Chase, prin.
Other Schools – See Guilford

Baldwin, Nassau Co., Pop. Code 8
Baldwin UFD
Sch. Sys. Enr. Code 6
Supt. – Rolland Jones
HIGH SCHOOL DRIVE   11510
JHS, SCHREIBER PLACE   11510
Raymond White, prin.
Brookside ES, 969 STANTON AVE E   11510
Robert Babb, prin.
Lenox ES, 555 LENOX RD   11510
William Gordon, prin.
Meadow ES, 850 JACKSON ST   11510
Thomas Hodge, prin.
Milburn ES, 2519 MILBURN AVE   11510
Deborah Martin, prin.
Plaza ES, W SEAMAN AVENUE   11510
Ann Edson, prin.
Shubert ES, CENTENNIAL AVE   11510
Frances O'Connor, prin.
Steele ES, CHURCH STREET   11510
John Ryan, prin.

St. Christopher ES, 15 PERSHING BLVD   11510

Baldwinsville, Onondaga Co., Pop. Code 6
Baldwinsville Central SD
Sch. Sys. Enr. Code 6
Supt. – Anthony Lease, E ONEIDA ST   13027
Elden ES, OSWEGO STREET   13027
Anne Jones, prin.
McNamara ES, OBRIEN ROAD   13027
Nancy Brown, prin.
Palmer ES, HICKS RD   13027
Nancy Maresca, prin.
Ray IS, VAN BUREN ROAD   13027
Gary Vandecarr, prin.
Reynolds ES, IDLEWOOD BOULEVARD   13027
William Demerio, prin.
Van Buren ES, 14 FORD ST   13027
Michael Denny, prin.

St. Mary's ES, 49 SYRACUSE ST   13027

Ballston Lake, Saratoga Co.
Burnt Hills Ballston Lake CSD
Supt. – See Scotia
Charlton Heights ES, OLD STAGE ROAD   12019
Stephen Honicki, prin.
Stevens ES   12019 – Arnold Redbord, prin.

Shenendehowa Central SD
Supt. – See Clifton Park
Chango ES, ROUND LAKE ROAD   12019
Thomas Koscielniak, prin.

Ballston Spa, Saratoga Co., Pop. Code 5
Ballston Spa Central SD
Sch. Sys. Enr. Code 5
Supt. – Paul Giacobbe, 70 MALTA AVE   12020
MS, RURAL ROUTE 67   12020
Stephen Toussaint, prin.
Malta Avenue ES, 70 MALTA AVE   12020
Philip Grayber, prin.
Milton Terrace ES, ROUTE 67   12020
Michael Glowacki, prin.
Wood Road ES, ROUTE 67   12020
Joseph Lopez, prin.

St. Mary's ES, 40 THOMPSON ST   12020

Bardonia, Rockland Co., Pop. Code 4
Clarkstown Central SD
Supt. – See West Nyack
ES, 360 BARDONIA RD   10954
Donald Kemp, prin.

Barker, Niagara Co., Pop. Code 3
Barker Central SD
Sch. Sys. Enr. Code 4
Supt. – Robert Melone, QUAKER ROAD   14012
ES, QUAKER ROAD   14012 – Norman Kahler, prin.

Batavia, Genesee Co., Pop. Code 7
Batavia CSD
Sch. Sys. Enr. Code 5
Supt. – David Van Scoy
39 WASHINGTON AVE   14020
MS, 96 ROSS ST   14020 – Nicholas Borrelli, prin.
Jackson ES, 411 S JACKSON ST   14020
Peter Arras, prin.
Kennedy ES, 166 VINE ST   14020
Angelo Branciforte, prin.
Morris ES, 80 UNION ST   14020
Andrew Steck, prin.

St. Anthony ES, 114 LIBERTY ST   14020
St. Joseph ES, 2 SUMMIT ST   14020
St. Mary ES, 40 WOODROW RD   14020

Bath, Steuben Co., Pop. Code 6
Bath Central SD
Sch. Sys. Enr. Code 4
Supt. – Charlotte Gregory, ELLAS AVE   14810
Lyon MS, 208 LIBERTY ST   14810
Allan Gay, prin.
Wightman ES, MAPLE HEIGHTS   14810
Theodore Bailey, prin.

Bayport, Suffolk Co., Pop. Code 6
Bayport-Blue Point UFD
Sch. Sys. Enr. Code 4
Supt. – George Reilly, 189 ACADEMY ST   11705
Young JHS, 602 SYLVAN AVE   11705
   John Whitney, prin.
Academy Street ES, 150 ACADEMY ST   11705
   Harriet Connor, prin.
Sylvan Avenue ES, 600 SYLVAN AVE   11705
   James Weik, prin.
Other Schools – See Blue Point

Bay Shore, Suffolk Co., Pop. Code 8
Bay Shore UFD
Sch. Sys. Enr. Code 5
Supt. – Crescent Bellamore
   75 W PERKAL ST   11706
MS, 393 BROOK AVE   11706
   Selven Powell, prin.
Brook Avenue ES, 45 BROOK AVE   11706
   Peter Bielitz, prin.
Clarkson ES, 1415 E 3RD AVE   11706
   Maggie Grant, prin.
Fifth Avenue ES, 217 5TH AVE   11706
   Frank Fallon, prin.
Gardiner Manor MS, 125 WOHSEEPEE DR   11706
   Lawrence Senecal, prin.
South Country MS, 885 HAMPSHIRE RD   11706
   Florence Wood, prin.

Brentwood UFD
Supt. – See Brentwood
Southwest ES, JOELSEN AVENUE   11706
   Austin Harney, prin.

Mark Country Day ES, P O BOX 188M   11706
St. Patrick ES, MONTAUK HWY   11706
St. Peter's Day ES, 500 S COUNTRY RD   11706

Bayside, Queens Co.
Queens Borough SD 25
Supt. – See Flushing
Public ES 130, 200-01 42ND AVE   11360
   Virginia Lee, prin.
Bay Terrace ES, 1825 212TH ST   11360
   Joel Seigerman, prin.

Queens Borough SD 26
Sch. Sys. Enr. Code 7
Supt. – Irwin Altman, 6115 OCEANIA ST   11364
Hawthorne IS, 6115 OCEANIA ST   11364
   Irving Kamil, prin.
Alley Pond ES
   218TH STREET & 67TH AVENUE   11364
   Stanley Weber, prin.
ES, 21145 46TH RD   11361
   Beverly Hirschorn, prin.
Crocheron ES, 21443 35TH AVE   11361
   Judith Ellner, prin.
Public ES 159, 20501 33RD AVE   11361
   Martin Greenbaum, prin.
Other Schools – See Bellerose, Douglaston, Floral
   Park, Flushing, Jamaica, Little Neck, Queens Village

Bayville, Nassau Co., Pop. Code 6
Locust Valley Central SD
Supt. – See Locust Valley
ES, MOUNTAIN AVENUE   11709
   Anne Young, prin.

Beacon, Dutchess Co., Pop. Code 7
Beacon CSD
Sch. Sys. Enr. Code 5
Supt. – Norman Palin, 88 SARGENT AVE   12508
Forrestal ES, 199 LIBERTY ST   12508
   Bruce Downer, prin.
Sargent ES, 445 WOLCOTT AVE   12508
   Vito Di Cesare,Jr., prin.
South Avenue ES, 60 SOUTH AVE   12508
   Joseph Vorbach, prin.
Other Schools – See Glenham

Beacon Christian Academy
   9 DELAVAN AVE   12508
St. Joachin ES, 60 LIBERTY ST   12508
St. John Evangelist ES, 31 WILLOW ST   12508

Beaver Falls, Lewis Co., Pop. Code 3
Beaver River Central SD
Sch. Sys. Enr. Code 4
Supt. – Hans Dellith   13305
Beaver River ES   13305 – Wayne Marcotte, prin.

Bedford, Westchester Co., Pop. Code 7
Bedford Central SD
Supt. – See Mount Kisco
Fox Lane MS, S BEDFORD ROAD   10506
   James Alloy, prin.

Rippowam Cisqua School, P O BOX 488   10506
St. Patrick ES, STATE ROAD   10506

Bedford Hills, Westchester Co., Pop. Code 5
Bedford Central SD
Supt. – See Mount Kisco
ES, BABBITT ROAD   10507
   Jacqueline Mandia, prin.
West Patent ES, 80 W PATENT RD   10507
   Kathryn Smith, prin.

Belfast, Allegany Co., Pop. Code 4
Belfast Central SD
Sch. Sys. Enr. Code 2
Supt. – Robert Bouldin   14711
S, KING STREET   14711 – Dennis Doell, prin.

Bellerose, Queens Co., Pop. Code 4
Queens Borough SD 26
Supt. – See Bayside
Public ES 133, 24805 86TH AVE   11426
   Felix Berman, prin.
Castlewood ES, 25212 72ND AVE   11426
   John Holst, prin.

Belleville, Jefferson Co., Pop. Code 2
Belleville Henderson Central SD
Sch. Sys. Enr. Code 3
Supt. – E. Ecker   13611
Union Academy S   13611 – Shawn Baker, prin.
Other Schools – See Henderson

Bellmore, Nassau Co., Pop. Code 7
Bellmore UFD
Sch. Sys. Enr. Code 3
Supt. – Abraham Neuwirth
   WINTHROP AVE   11710
Reinhard ES, 2750 S SAINT MARKS AVE   11710
   George Ringer, prin.
Shore Road ES, 2801 SHORE RD   11710
   Stewart Bruck, prin.
Winthrop Avenue ES, 580 WINTHROP AVE   11710
   Myra Neuwirth, prin.

Bellmore-Merrick Central SD
Supt. – See Merrick
Grand Avenue JHS, 2301 GRAND AVE   11710
   Frederick Gimpel, prin.

St. Barnabas ES, WASHINGTON AVE   11710

Bellport, Suffolk Co., Pop. Code 5
South Country Central SD
Supt. – See East Patchogue
MS, 35 KREAMER ST   11713
   Sheldon Stiefeld, prin.
Hampton Avenue MS
   599 BROOKHAVEN AVE   11713
   Curtis Fisher, prin.
Kreamer Street ES, 32 KREAMER ST   11713
   Brian McCarthy, prin.

Belmont, Allegany Co., Pop. Code 4
Belmont Central SD
Sch. Sys. Enr. Code 2
Supt. – Charles Smith, 24 SOUTH ST   14813
Belmont Central S, 24 SOUTH ST   14813
   James Arthur, prin.

Bemus Point, Chautauqua Co., Pop. Code 2
Bemus Point Central SD
Sch. Sys. Enr. Code 3
Supt. – Albert D'Attilio
   DUTCH HOLLOW ROAD   14712
Bemus MS, LIBERTY STREET   14712
   P. Sawyer, prin.
Other Schools – See Jamestown

Bergen, Genesee Co., Pop. Code 3
Byron Bergen Central SD
Sch. Sys. Enr. Code 4
Supt. – W. Hayes, TOWNLINE ROAD   14416
ES, WEST BERGEN ROAD   14416
   Thomas Biondolillo, prin.

Berlin, Rensselaer Co., Pop. Code 4
Berlin Central SD
Sch. Sys. Enr. Code 4
Supt. – Wayne Jones, P O BOX 259   12022
Cherry Plain ES, P O BOX 259   12022
   Jeanne Schultz, prin.
Grafton ES, P O BOX 259   12022
   David Sicko, prin.
Stephentown ES, P O BOX 259   12022
   David Sicko, prin.

Berne, Albany Co., Pop. Code 5
Berne Knox Westerlo Central SD
Sch. Sys. Enr. Code 4
Supt. – Robert Drake
   2021 HELDERBERG TRAIL   12023
Berne ES   12023 – Joseph Leombruno, prin.
Other Schools – See Westerlo

Bethpage, Nassau Co., Pop. Code 8
Bethpage UFD
Sch. Sys. Enr. Code 5
Supt. – John Somni, CHERRY AVE   11714
Kennedy JHS, BROADWAY   11714
   Clifford Jaeger, prin.
Campagne ES, 601 PLAINVIEW RD   11714
   Mary Quinn, prin.
Central Boulevard ES, 60 CENTRAL BLVD   11714
   Kenneth Blau, prin.
Other Schools – See Hicksville

Plainedge UFD
Supt. – See North Massapequa
West ES, STEWART & BOUNDARY   11714
   Sara Grillo, prin.

St. Martin of Tours ES, CENTRAL AVE   11714

Big Flats, Chemung Co., Pop. Code 6
Horseheads Central SD
Supt. – See Horseheads
ES, MAPLE STREET   14814
   Ronald Saccucci, prin.

Binghamton, Broome Co., Pop. Code 8
Binghamton CSD
Sch. Sys. Enr. Code 6
Supt. – Frank Cleary, 16 SAINT JOHN AVE   13905
East MS, 160 ROBINSON ST   13904
   Cornelius Lorden, prin.

West MS, W JUNIOR AVE   13905
   Muhammad Husami, prin.
Coolidge ES, 261 ROBINSON ST   13904
   David Constantine, prin.
Franklin ES, 262 CONKLIN AVE   13903
   David Stark, prin.
Jefferson ES, 151 HELEN ST   13905
   Dorothy DePue, prin.
Mac Arthur ES, 1123 VESTAL AVE   13903
   Thomas Peacock, prin.
Mann ES, 30 COLLEGE ST   13905
   Anthony Mesmer, prin.
Roosevelt ES, 9 OGDEN ST   13901
   Robert Kelly, prin.
Wilson ES, 287 PROSPECT ST   13905
   E. O'Hare, prin.

Chenango Forks Central SD
Sch. Sys. Enr. Code 4
Supt. – Norman Sweeney, P O BOX 204A   13903
Chenango Forks MS, P O BOX 204A   13903
   Ron Lilley, prin.
Harshaw PS, RURAL ROUTE 03   13901
   Robert Bundy, prin.
Other Schools – See Chenango Forks

Chenango Valley Central SD
Sch. Sys. Enr. Code 4
Supt. – Michael Grenis
   768 CHENANGO ST   13901
Chenango Bridge ES, 768 CHENANGO ST   13901
   Carmen Ciullo, prin.
Hillcrest MS, 768 CHENANGO ST   13901
   Thomas Personius, prin.
Port Dickinson ES, 768 CHENANGO ST   13901
   Joyce Westgate, prin.

Susquehanna Valley Central SD
Supt. – See Conklin
Brookside ES, RURAL ROUTE 01   13903
   Gary Worden, prin.

Central Baptist Christian Academy
   1606 UPPER FRONT ST   13901
St. Patrick's MS, 58 OAK ST   13905
St. John ES, 9 LIVINGSTON ST   13903
St. Stanislaus Kostka ES, 376 PROSPECT ST   13905
St. Thomas Aquinas ES, 3 AQUINAS ST   13905

Black River, Jefferson Co., Pop. Code 4
Carthage Central SD
Supt. – See Carthage
ES   13612 – Patricia Cameron, prin.

Blasdell, Erie Co., Pop. Code 5
Frontier Central SD
Supt. – See Hamburg
Blasdell ES Annex, 36 ARTHUR AVE   14219
   Susan Krickovich, prin.
ES, 3780 S PARK AVE   14219
   Stephen Maricich, prin.

Our Mother of Good Counsl ES
   15 OAKWOOD AVE   14219

Blauvelt, Rockland Co., Pop. Code 6
South Orangetown Central SD
Sch. Sys. Enr. Code 4
Supt. – Richard Olcott, VAN WYCK ROAD   10913
South Orangetown MS
   160 VAN WYCK ROAD   10913
   Lawrence Glickman, prin.
Cottage Lane MS, COTTAGE LN   10913
   Patricia Doyle, prin.
Other Schools – See Piermont, Tappan

St. Catherine ES, 174 WESTERN HWY S   10913

Blue Point, Suffolk Co., Pop. Code 5
Bayport-Blue Point UFD
Supt. – See Bayport
ES, 212 BLUE POINT AVE   11715
   Robert Luff, prin.

Bohemia, Suffolk Co., Pop. Code 6
Connetquot Central SD
Sch. Sys. Enr. Code 6
Supt. – John Maloney, 780 OCEAN AVE   11716
Bosti ES, BOURNE BOULEVARD   11716
   Robert Smith, prin.
Pearl ES, SMITHTOWN AVENUE   11716
   Gerald Devlin, prin.
Sycamore Avenue ES
   SYCAMORE AVENUE   11716 – Alvin Zivitz, prin.
Other Schools – See Oakdale, Ronkonkoma

St. John Nepomucene ES
   1150 LOCUST AVE   11716

Boiceville, Ulster Co.
Onteora Central SD
Sch. Sys. Enr. Code 4
Supt. – William Wilson   12412
Bennett ES   12412 – Brian Lane, prin.
Other Schools – See Phoenicia, West Hurley,
   Woodstock

Bolivar, Allegany Co., Pop. Code 4
Bolivar Central SD
Sch. Sys. Enr. Code 3
Supt. – Gary Hammond, 100 SCHOOL ST   14715
ES, 100 SCHOOL ST   14715
   Vincent Di Tanna, prin.

Bolton Landing, Warren Co., Pop. Code 3
Bolton Central SD
Sch. Sys. Enr. Code 2
Supt. – Dalton Marks, HORICON AVE 12814
Bolton Central S, HORICON AVE 12814
Dalton Marks, prin.

Boonville, Oneida Co., Pop. Code 4
Adirondack-Boonville Central SD
Sch. Sys. Enr. Code 4
Supt. – Raymond Borden, P O BOX 58 13309
ES, 110 FORD ST 13309 – Ralph Mirabelli, prin.
Other Schools – See Forestport, West Leyden

Bradford, Steuben Co., Pop. Code 3
Bradford Central SD
Sch. Sys. Enr. Code 2
Supt. – Nancy Zimar 14815
Bradford Central S, ROUTE 226 14815
Anne Shannon, prin.

Brant, Erie Co., Pop. Code 4
Evans-Brant Central SD
Supt. – See Angola
ES, BRANT AND N COLLINS RD 14027
Rosalyn Desantis, prin.

Brant Lake, Warren Co.
North Warren Central SD
Supt. – See Pottersville
Horicon ES 12815 – James Lagoy, prin.

Brasher Falls, St. Lawrence Co., Pop. Code 3
Brasher Falls Central SD
Sch. Sys. Enr. Code 4
Supt. – Richard Lane 13613
St. Lawrence ES 13613 – Richard Lane, prin.

Brentwood, Suffolk Co., Pop. Code 8
Brentwood UFD
Sch. Sys. Enr. Code 7
Supt. – Frank Mauro, 1 3RD AVE 11717
Hemlock ES, HEMLOCK PARK 11717
Joseph Graff, prin.
Laurel Park ES, SWAN PLACE 11717
Pat Hudson, prin.
Loretta Park ES, STAHLEY STREET 11717
Andrew Lovito, prin.
North ES, WHITE STREET 11717
Joseph Silva, prin.
Northeast ES, ARLINGTON ROAD 11717
Joseph Karzen, prin.
Oak Park ES, WISCONSIN AVENUE 11717
John Hoffmann, prin.
Pine Park ES, VOORHIS DRIVE 11717
Harvey Brickman, prin.
Southeast ES, MELODY LANE 11717
Christie Tedaldi, prin.
Twin Pines MS, VOORHIS DRIVE 11717
Peter Dimento, prin.
Other Schools – See Bay Shore

Academy of St. Joseph
BRENTWOOD ROAD 11717
St. Anne ES, 88 2ND AVE 11717

Brewerton, Onondaga Co., Pop. Code 4
Central Square Central SD
Supt. – See Central Square
ES, ROUTE 13029 – Michael Cunningham, prin.

Brewster, Putnam Co., Pop. Code 4
Brewster Central SD
Sch. Sys. Enr. Code 5
Supt. – Gregory Vogt
FARM TO MARKET ROAD 10509
Wells MS, ROUTE 312 10509
William Shannon, prin.
Garden Street ES, GARDEN STREET 10509
Maryann Noonan, prin.
Kennedy ES, FOGGINTOWN ROAD 10509
Caroline Temlock, prin.

Melrose ES, RURAL ROUTE 05 10509
St. Lawrence O'Toole ES
11-13 EASTVIEW AVE 10509

Briarcliff Manor, Westchester Co., Pop. Code 6
Briarcliff Manor UFD
Sch. Sys. Enr. Code 3
Supt. – Carol Harrington, INGHAM ROAD 10510
Todd ES, INGHAM RD 10510
Anita McCarthy, prin.

St. Theresa ES, 300 DALMENY RD 10510

Bridgehampton, Suffolk Co., Pop. Code 3
Bridgehampton UFD
Sch. Sys. Enr. Code 2
Supt. – Menzer Doud, MONTAUK HWY 11932
S, MONTAUK HIGHWAY 11932
Menzer Doud, prin.

Bridgeport, Madison Co.
Chittenango Central SD
Supt. – See Chittenango
ES, RURAL ROUTE 01 13030
Donna Crouse, prin.

Broadalbin, Fulton Co., Pop. Code 4
Broadalbin-Perth Central SD
Sch. Sys. Enr. Code 3
Supt. – Richard Sagar, SCHOOL ST 12025
Broadalbin-Perth MS, RURAL ROUTE 04 12010
Glenn Bellinger, prin.
ES, SCHOOL STREET 12025
Linda Nevulis, prin.

Other Schools – See Amsterdam

Broad Channel, Queens Co.
Queens Borough SD 27
Supt. – See Ozone Park
Broad Channel ES, 9 POWER RD 11693
Ann O'Keefe, prin.

Brockport, Monroe Co., Pop. Code 6
Brockport Central SD
Sch. Sys. Enr. Code 5
Supt. – D. Field, ALLEN ST 14420
MS, ALLEN ST 14420 – Wilson Buddle, prin.
Barclay ES, ALLEN STREET 14420
Joan Lennert, prin.
MS, ALLEN ST 14420 – Frank Balling, prin.
Ginther ES, ALLEN STREET 14420
Richard Knab, prin.

Nativity BVM ES, HOLLEY & UTICA STS 14420

Brocton, Chautauqua Co., Pop. Code 4
Brocton Central SD
Sch. Sys. Enr. Code 3
Supt. – Richard Gloss, 138 W MAIN ST 14716
ES, 138 W MAIN ST 14716 – Richard Gloss, prin.

Bronx, Bronx Co., Pop. Code 12
Bronx Borough SD 10
Sch. Sys. Enr. Code 8
Supt. – F. Goldberg, 3961 HILLMAN AVE 10463
Browning IS, 120 E 184TH ST 10468
Ira Goldberg, prin.
Patri IS, 2225 WEBSTER AVE 10457
Henry Shook, prin.
Belmont MS, 690 E 183RD ST 10458
Margaret Slattery, prin.
Bilingual ES
183RD ST & WASHINGTON AVE 10457
Felicita Serrano, prin.
Burnside Avenue ES, 1930 ANDREWS AVE 10453
Howard Safier, prin.
Creston ES, 125 E 181ST ST 10453
Phillip Werfel, prin.
Duyvil ES, 660 W 236TH ST 10463
David Rothstein, prin.
Dwight ES, 2424 JEROME AVE 10468
Helen McLoughlin, prin.
ES 206, 2280 AQUEDUCT AVE 10468
Carmen Jiminez, prin.
Kingsbridge MS, 3201 KINGSBRIDGE AVE 10463
Milton Fein, prin.
Marble Hill ES, 260 W KINGSBRIDGE RD 10463
Sheldon Lindenbaum, prin.
Norwood Heights ES
EAST 207TH ST & HULL AVE 10457
William Riley, prin.
Poe ES, 279 E 196TH ST 10458
Aramina Ferrer, prin.
Public ES 9, EAST 183RD & RYER AVENUE 10453
Charles Celauro, prin.
Public ES 59, 2185 BATHGATE AVE 10457
Seymour Perlin, prin.
Public ES 81, 5550 RIVERDALE AVE 10471
David Parker, prin.
Public ES 85, 2400 MARION AVE 10458
Winifred Washington, prin.
Public ES 86, 2756 RESERVOIR AVE 10468
Raymond Osinoff, prin.
Public ES 91, 2220 AQUEDUCT AVE 10453
Gloria Doyle, prin.
Public ES 94, 3530 KING COLLEGE PLACE 10467
Sheldon Salzberg, prin.
Public ES 205
23-2475 SOUTH BOULEVARD 10458
Gaeton Stella, prin.
Public ES 207, 3143 KINGSBRIDGE AVE 10463
C. McCrudden, prin.
Public ES 257, 2111 CROTONA AVE 10457
Carolyn Jones, prin.
Public ES 261, 2507 JEROME AVE 10468
Edward Flannery, prin.
Public ES 280, 149 E MOSHOLU PKWY 10467
Lowell Pollack, prin.
Public ES 291, 2246 JEROME AVE 10453
Gloria Burzi, prin.
Public MS 246, 2641 GRAND CONCOURSE 10468
Frank Gonzalez, prin.
Van Cortland ES, 3961 HILLMAN AVE 10463
Samuel Salant, prin.
Varian ES, 3010 BRIGGS AVE 10458
Della Jerome, prin.

Bronx Borough SD 11
Sch. Sys. Enr. Code 7
Supt. – Frank Arricale, 1250 ARNOW AVE 10469
Casals IS, 800 BAYCHESTER AVE 10475
Leonard Chesler, prin.
Castle Hill JHS, 1560 PURDY ST 10462
Marvin Rockley, prin.
Michelangelo IS, 2545 GUNTHER AVE 10469
Harlan Pruger, prin.
Northeast Education Park IS
700 BAYCHESTER AVE 10475
Patricia O'Rourke, prin.
Bronxwood ES, 1925 SCHIEFFELIN AVE 10466
Natalie Roberts, prin.
City Island ES, 200 CITY ISLAND AVE 10464
Ena Ellwanger, prin.
Disney ES, EINSTEIN LOOP 10452
MaryJane Whalen, prin.
Eggleston ES, 4318 KATONAH AVE 10470
Judith Weiss, prin.
Gun Hill Road ES, 3352 OLINVILLE AVE 10467
Dan Aguaro, prin.

Hutchinson ES, 1400 NEEDHAM AVE 10469
Inone Edwards, prin.
North Bronx ES, 650 BAYCHESTER AVE 10475
Beverly Taylor, prin.
Public ES 68, 4011 MONTICELLO AVE 10466
Gwendolyn Thomas, prin.
Public ES 76, 900 ADEE AVE 10469
Vincent Young, prin.
Public ES 83, 950 RHINELANDER AVE 10462
Ronald Imundi, prin.
Public ES 87, 1935 BUSSING AVE 10466
Maria Ciaiola, prin.
Public ES 89, 980 MACE AVE 10469
Jose Cordesco, prin.
Public ES 96, 650 WARING AVE 10467
Martin Unterberger, prin.
Public ES 97, 1375 MACE AVE 10469
Stephen Ucko, prin.
Public ES 103, 4125 CARPENTER AVE 10466
Marvin Fleishaker, prin.
Public ES 105, 725 BRADY AVE 10462
Rahla Gold, prin.
Public ES 106
2120 SAINT RAYMONDS AVE 10462
Anna Petsche, prin.
Public ES 108, 1166 NEILL AVE 10461
Victor Crecco, prin.
Seton Falls ES
3740 RAYCHESTER AVENUE 10466
William Wheeler, prin.
Sheridan ES, 715 E 225TH ST 10466
William Dana, prin.
Throop ES, 2750 THROOP AVE 10469
Meryl Natelli, prin.
Wakefield ES, 4550 CARPENTER AVE 10470
Joseph Kovaly, prin.
Waxman ES, 850 BAYCHESTER AVE 10475
Henry Bregman, prin.

Bronx Borough SD 12
Sch. Sys. Enr. Code 7
Supt. – P. Negroni, 1000 JENNINGS ST 10460
Gathings IS, 800 HOME ST 10456
Charles Dunn, prin.
Hansberry IS, 1970 W FARMS ROAD 10460
Leo Summergrad, prin.
Hernandez IS, 977 FOX ST 10459
Mario Vario, prin.
Barton ES, 1550 VYSE AVE 10460
Ida Reeves, prin.
Bristow ES, 1130 BRISTOW STREET 10459
Olga Labeet, prin.
Crescent ES, 2111 CROTONA AVE 10457
Alan Finkelstein, prin.
Farragut ES, 1825 PROSPECT AVE 10457
Susan Bailey, prin.
Fox ES, 920 E 167TH ST 10459
Beatrice Rubin, prin.
Loretan ES, 1827 ARCHER ST 10460
Vincent Locascio, prin.
Oller ES, 1550 CROTONA PARK E 10460
Beryl Banks, prin.
Public ES 66, 1001 JENNINGS ST 10460
Lorpis Cordero, prin.
Public ES 67, 2024 MOHEGAN AVE 10460
Jeffery Litt, prin.
Public ES 77, 1250 WARD AVE 10472
Leon Taylor, prin.
Public ES 92, 700 E 179TH ST 10457
Jerome Klein, prin.
Public ES 198, 1180 TINTON AVE 10456
Jaime Ortiz, prin.
Public ES 211, 560 E 179TH ST 10457
Irma Zardoya, prin.
Randolph ES, 1794 E 172ND ST 10472
Ralph Rogers, prin.
Twin Parks PS, 2050 PROSPECT AVE 10457
Carmen Ortiz, prin.
Twin Park MS, 2055 MAPES AVE 10460
Jacques Bonhomme, prin.
West Farms ES, 1000 E TREMONT AVE 10460
Ermine Holt, prin.
Young IS, 1919 PROSPECT AVE 10457
Eugene Jiminez, prin.

Bronx Borough SD 7
Sch. Sys. Enr. Code 7
Supt. – Carmen Rodriguez
501 COURTLANDT AVE 10451
Bilingual IS, 778 FOREST AVE 10456
Juan Fonseca, prin.
Burger IS, 345 BROOK AVE 10454
John Quinn, prin.
Gehrig IS, 250 E 156TH ST 10451
John Crawford, prin.
Robeson IS, 339 MORRIS AVE 10451
John Crawford, prin.
Rodriguez De Tio IS
600 SAINT ANN'S AVE 10455 – Joel Sklar, prin.
Banneker ES, 750 CONCOURSE VLG W 10451
Ralph Santalis, prin.
Bilingual ES, 811 E 149TH ST 10455
Luis Cartagena, prin.
Bronck ES, 165 BROWN PL 10454
Georgiana Kokason, prin.
Courtland ES, 335 E 152ND ST 10451
Madeline Golia, prin.
De Leon Elementary School
628 TINTON AVE 10455 – Arthur Raggio, prin.
Garrison ES, 425 GRAND CONCOURSE 10451
Carol Russo, prin.
Grove Hill ES, 757 CAULDWELL AVE 10456
Edward Levy, prin.

Hyatt ES, 333 E 135TH ST 10454
　Mary Rivera, prin.
Melrose ES, 758 COURTLANDT AVE 10451
　Arnold Santandreu, prin.
Port Morris ES, 564 JACKSON AVE 10455
　Jose Graciano, prin.
Public ES 65
　141ST STREET & CYPRESS AVE 10454
　Manuel Rodriguez, prin.
Saw Mill Brook ES, 468 E 140TH ST 10454
　Stanley Weinberg, prin.
St. Mary's Park ES, 519 SAINT ANNS AVE 10455
　Pedro Crespo, prin.
Willis Avenue ES, 383 E 139TH ST 10454
　Robert Wells, prin.
Wilton ES, 510 E 141ST ST 10454
　Aida Rosa, prin.
Zenger ES, 502 MORRIS AVE 10451
　James Wilson, prin.

Bronx Borough SD 9
Sch. Sys. Enr. Code 8
Supt. – Anne Wolinsky, 1377 JEROME AVE 10452
Clemente IS, 250 E 164TH ST 10456
　Nelson Abreu, prin.
Drew IS, 3630 3RD AVE 10456
　Hazel Cogar, prin.
IS 229, 275 HARLEM RIVER PARK 10453
　Felton Johnson, prin.
Macombs JHS, 1700 MACOMBS ROAD 10453
　Sanford Einhorn, prin.
Mott JHS, E 167TH ST & COLLEGE AVE 10456
　William Green, prin.
Sands IS, 1600 WEBSTER AVE 10457
　Calvin Hart, prin.
Tosacanini JHS, 1000 TELLER AVE 10456
　Bernard Krasnow, prin.
Claremont ES
　WASHINGTON & CLAREMONT PKY 10456
　Jo Marie Mounsey, prin.
Crotona ES, 1701 FULTON AVE 10457
　Stanley Kaminsky, prin.
Ehrenfeld ES, 1449 SHAKESPEARE AVE 10452
　Boston Chance, prin.
Hernandes ES, 1257 OGDEN AVE 10452
　Felix Gonzalez, prin.
Highbridge ES, 1257 OGDEN AVE 10452
　Robert Lerman, prin.
Hughes PS, 499 E 175TH ST 10457
　Clara Burgess, prin.
Lindlof ES, 175 W 166TH ST 10452
　Marjorie Dunbar, prin.
Morgan ES, 1245 WASHINGTON AVE 10456
　Marie Thomas, prin.
Morrisania ES, 1365 FULTON AVE 10456
　Lois Desvigne, prin.
Mt. Hope ES, 1861 ANTHONY AVE 10457
　Celedonio Felix, prin.
Public ES 53, 360 E 168TH ST 10456
　Matthew Barnwell, prin.
Public ES 55, 450 SAINT PAULS PL 10456
　William Plummer, prin.
Public ES 58
　EAST 176TH & WASHINGTON AVE 10457
　Rubi Lorans, prin.
Public ES 63, 1260 FRANKLIN AVE 10456
　Helen Foster, prin.
Public ES 73, 1020 ANDERSON AVE 10452
　Beryl Dorsett, prin.
Public ES 88, 1340 SHERIDAN AVE 10456
　Michael Mullee, prin.
Public ES 90, 1116 SHERIDAN AVE 10456
　Daniel Portelles, prin.
Public ES 229
　275 HARLEM RIVER PARK BR 10453
　Ellen Overton, prin.
Public MS 64, 1425 WALTON AVE 10452
　Howard Levine, prin.
Schoenfeld ES, 580 CROTONA PARK S 10456
　Leah Greenstein, prin.
Schoenfeld ES, 1691 WEEKS AVE 10457
　Roberto Batista, prin.
Schomberg ES, 2075 WEBSTER AVE 10457
　Arthur Aronstein, prin.
Sedgwick ES, 1771 POPHAM AVE 10453
　Angelo Sanchez, prin.
Sigel ES, 261 E 163RD ST 10451
　Hilda Gutierrez, prin.
Torres ES, 1155 CROMWELL AVE 10452
　David Cutie, prin.

Bronx Borough Sd 8
Sch. Sys. Enr. Code 7
Supt. – Max Messer
　650 WHITE PLAINS ROAD 10473
Einstein IS, 885 BOLTON AVE 10473
　Murray Scherer, prin.
Knowlton IS, 681 KELLY ST 10455
　Iraida Fuentes, prin.
Maleska IS, 456 WHITE PLAINS ROAD 10473
　Chester Cohen, prin.
Peninsula IS, 730 BRYANT AVE 10473
　Howard Thomas, prin.
Piagentini-Jones IS, 650 HOLLYWOOD AVE 10465
　Robert Barrett, prin.
Casanova ES, 660 FOX ST 10455
　Muriel Pagan, prin.
Clason ES, 800 TAYLOR AVE 10473
　Elizabeth Builder, prin.
Collins ES, 968 CAULDWELL AVE 10456
　Luther Ragin, prin.
Community MS, 1007 EVERGREEN AVE 10472
　Tobias Sumner, prin.

Dewey-Edison Avenue ES
　DEWEY & EDISON AVE 10465
　Helen Cardassi, prin.
Drake ES, 1290 SPOFFORD AVENE 10474
　Lora Lucks, prin.
Eagle ES, 916 EAGLE AVE 10456
　Larcelia Kebe, prin.
Hewitt ES, 750 PROSPECT AVE 10455
　Louis Carmona, prin.
Public ES 107, 1695 SEWARD AVE 10473
　Arthur Riegel, prin.
Public ES 60, 888 STEBBINS AVE 10459
　Jesus Barbosa, prin.
Public ES 69, 560 THIERIOT AVE 10473
　Augustin Lopez, prin.
Public ES 75, 984 FAILE ST 10459
　Eva Garcia, prin.
Public ES 93, 1535 STORY AVE 10473
　Jeanne Snyder, prin.
Public ES 119, 1075 PUGSLEY AVE 10472
　Pierre Lehmuller, prin.
Public ES 182, 601 NEWMAN AVE 10473
　Jeanne Locascio, prin.
Randall ES, 2060 LAFAYETTE AVE 10473
　Jeanne Rupp, prin.
Scala ES, 3040 ROBERTS AVE 10461
　Charles Lamontanaro, prin.
Throggs Neck ES, 3041 BRUCKNER BLVD 10461
　Barb Calvin, prin.
Unionport ES, 1070 CASTLE HILL AVE 10472
　Florence Kennedy, prin.

Glad Tidings Academy
　2 E VAN CORTLANDT AVE 10468
Mt. St. Michael JHS, 4300 MURDOCK AVE 10466
Our Savior Lutheran School
　1734 WILLIAMSBRIDGE ROAD 10461
Riverdale Country School
　5250 FIELDSTON ROAD 10471
Beth Jacob-Beth Miriam School
　2126 BARNES AVE 10458
Bible Church of Christ Christian ES
　1358 MORRIS AVE 10456
Blessed Sacrament ES, 1160 BEACH AVE 10472
Bronx-Manhattan SDA ES
　1440 PIMPTON AVE 10452
Christ the King ES
　1345 GRAND CONCOURSE 10452
Ethical Culture-the Fieldston ES
　4450 FIELDSTON RD 10471
Fielday ES, 5401 POST RD 10471
Grace Lutheran ES, 2930 VALENTINE AVE 10458
Greek American ES
　3573 BRUCKNER BLVD 10461
Holy Cross ES, 1846 RANDALL AVE 10473
Holy Family ES, 2169 BLACKROCK AVE 10472
Holy Rosary ES, 1500 ARNOW AVE 10469
Holy Spirit ES, 1960 UNIVERSITY AVE 10453
Horace Mann-Barnard ES
　4440 TIBBETT AVE 10471
Hudson ES, 1122 FOREST AVE 10456
Immaculate Conception ES, 378 E 151ST ST 10455
Immaculate Conception ES
　760 E GUN HILL RD 10467
Joytown ES, 2451 DEVOE TER 10468
Kinneret Day ES, 2600 NETHERLAND AVE 10463
Melrose Commnty ES, 838 BROOK AVE 10451
Nativity of the Blessed Lady ES
　3893 DYRE AVE 10466
Our Lady of Angels ES, 2865 CLALIN AVE 10468
Our Lady of Assumption ES
　1617 PARKVIEW AVE 10461
Our Lady of Grace ES
　3981 BRONXWOOD AVE 10466
Our Lady of Mercy ES, 2512 MARION AVE 10458
Our Lady of Mt. Carmel ES
　2465 BATHGATE AVE 10458
Our Lady Queen of Martyrs School
　71 ARDEN ST 10461
Our Lady of Refuge ES, 2708 BRIGGS AVE 10458
Our Lady of Solace ES
　1804 HOLLAND AVE 10462
Parkway ES, 986 E GUNHILL ROAD 10469
Regent ES, 719 E 216TH ST 10467
SS. Peter & Paul ES, 838 BROOK AVE 10451
SS. Philip & James ES, 1160 E 213TH ST 10469
Sacred Heart ES, 1651 ZEREGA AVE 10462
Sacred Heart MS, 1248 NELSON AVE 10452
Sacred Heart PS, 95 W 168TH ST 10452
Salanter Akiba Riverdale Academy
　655 W 254TH ST 10471
Santa Maria ES, 1510 ZEREGA AVE 10462
Scrolls ES, 3130 ROCHAMBEAU AVE 10467
St. Adalbert ES, 419 E 155TH ST 10455
St. Angela Merici ES, 266 E 163RD ST 10451
St. Ann ES, 3511 BAINBRIDGE AVE 10467
St. Anselm ES, 685 TINTON AVE 10455
St. Anthony ES, 4520 MATILDA AVE 10470
St. Anthony ES, 1776 MANSION ST 10460
St. Athanasius ES, 830 SOUTHERN BLVD 10459
St. Augustine ES, 1176 FRANKLIN AVE 10456
St. Barnabus ES, 413 E 241ST ST 10470
St. Benedict ES, 1016 EDISON AVE 10465
St. Brendan ES, 268 E 207TH ST 10467
St. Clare ES, 1911 HONE AVE 10461
St. Dominic ES, 1684 WHITE PLAINS RD 10462
St. Frances De Chantal ES
　2962 HARDING AVE 10465
St. Frances of Assisi ES
　4300 BAYCHESTER AVE 10466
St. Frances of Rome ES, 4321 BARNES AVE 10466
St. Francis Xavier ES, 1711 HAIGHT AVE 10461
St. Gabriel ES, 590 W 235TH ST 10463

St. Helena ES, 2050 BENEDICT AVE 10462
St. Jerome ES, 222 ALEXANDER AVE 10454
St. John Chrysostom ES, 1144 HOE AVE 10459
St. John ES, 3030 GODWIN TER 10463
St. John Vieny Cure of Ars ES
　2141 SEWARD AVE 10473
St. Joseph ES, 1946 BATHGATE AVE 10457
St. Lucy ES, 830 MACE AVE 10467
St. Luke ES, 608E E 139TH ST 10454
St. Margaret Mary ES, 121 E 177TH ST 10453
St. Margaret of Cortona ES
　452 W 260TH ST 10471
St. Martin of Tours ES, 695 E 182ND ST 10457
St. Mary ES, 3956 CARPENTER AVE 10466
St. Mary Star of Sea ES
　580 MINNIEFORD AVE 10464
St. Nicholas of Tolentine ES
　2335 UNIVERSITY AVE 10468
St. Philip Neri ES
　3031 GRAND CONCOURSE 10468
St. Pius V ES, 413 E 144TH ST 10454
St. Raymond ES, 2380 E TREMONT AVE 10462
St. Simon Stock ES, 2195 VALENTINE AVE 10457
St. Theresa ES, 2872 SAINT THERESA AVE 10461
St. Thomas Aquinas ES, 1909 DALY AVE 10460
Trinity Lutheran ES, 2125 WATSON AVE 10472
Villa Maria Academy
　3335 COUNTRY CLUB RD 10465
Visitation ES, 171 W 239TH ST 10463

Bronxville, Westchester Co., Pop. Code 6
Bronxville UFD
Sch. Sys. Enr. Code 4
Supt. – William Greenham
　81 PONDFIELD ROAD 10708
MS, PONDFIELD ROAD 10708 – John Kehoe, prin.
ES, 177 PONDFIELD RD 10708
　Daniel McCann, prin.

Chapel ES, 172 WHITE PLAINS RD 10708
St. Joseph ES, 30 MEADOW AVE 10708

Brookfield, Madison Co., Pop. Code 8
Brookfield Central SD
Sch. Sys. Enr. Code 2
Supt. – (—), FAIR ST 13314
Brookfield Central S, FAIR ST 13314
　James Tyler, prin.

Brookhaven, Suffolk Co., Pop. Code 10
South Country Central SD
Supt. – See East Patchogue
ES, 101 FIREPLACE NECK RD 11719
　Robert Esp, prin.
South Haven ES, MONTAUK HWY 11719
　Andrew Havens,Jr., prin.

Brooklyn, Kings Co., Pop. Code 12
Brooklyn Borough SD 13
Sch. Sys. Enr. Code 7
Supt. – J. Jerome Harris, 355 PARK PL 11238
Edmonds JHS, 300 ADELPHI ST 11205
　Beverly Hall, prin.
Key IS, 300 WILLOUGHBY AVE 11205
　John Graves, prin.
Macon IS, 141 MACON ST 11216
　Katherine Soloman, prin.
McKinney JHS, 101 PARK AVE 11205
　Mary Haynes, prin.
Ashford ES, 50 NAVY ST 11201
　Gwendolyn Wilson, prin.
Banneker ES, 114 KOSCIUSKO ST 11216
　Nannie Adams, prin.
Barnes ES, 195 SANFORD STREET 11205
　Melineze Lenhardt, prin.
Bedford Village ES, 50 JEFFERSON AVE 11216
　Yvette Poindexter, prin.
Behan ES, 419 WAVERLY AVE 11238
　Seymour Lerner, prin.
Bergen ES, 80 UNDERHILL AVE 11238
　Gerald Kornblum, prin.
Blum ES, 100 CLERMONT AVE 11205
　Barry Finkelman, prin.
Butler ES, 375 BUTLER ST 11217
　Gerome Shulman, prin.
Clinton Hill ES, 225 ADELPHI ST 11205
　Beatrice Thompson, prin.
Dekalb ES, 241 EMERSON PL 11205
　Barbara Goodard, prin.
Elliott ES, 51 ST EDWARDS ST 11205
　Evelyn Santiago, prin.
Jay ES, 37 HICKS ST 11201 – Roberta Bader, prin.
Latimer ES, 170 GATES AVE 11238
　Howard Sadowsky, prin.
Park Slope ES, 180 6TH AVE 11217
　Sharyn Goodman, prin.
Prescott ES, 31 NEW YORK AVE 11216
　Ruby Nottage, prin.
Putnam ES, 432 MONROE ST 11221
　Doreen Hall, prin.
Ray ES, 344 MONROE ST 11216
　Ruby Solomon, prin.
Williams ES, 209 YORK ST 11201
　Fannie Porter, prin.

Brooklyn Borough SD 14
Sch. Sys. Enr. Code 7
Supt. – William Rogers, 215 HEYWARD ST 11206
Campos ES, 215 HEYWARD ST 11206
　Ken Mittler, prin.
DeHostos IS, 101 WALTON ST 11206
　Alan Fierstein, prin.
Gaynor IS, 223 GRAHAM AVE 11206
　Henry Whitney, prin.

Hopkins IS, 70 TOMPKINS AVE 11206
  Linon Pretty, prin.
Bush ES, 101 MAUJER ST 11206
  Edward Averill, prin.
Clemente ES, 325 S 3RD ST 11211
  Harold Levine, prin.
Conselyea ES, 320 MANHATTAN AVE 11211
  Paul Corsello, prin.
Diego ES, 250 BERRY ST 11211
  Walter Gomoka, prin.
Dunkly ES, 157 WILSON ST 11211
  Steven Braustein, prin.
Dupont ES, 75 MESEROLE AVE 11222
  Eugene Levitt, prin.
Floyd ES, 211 THROOP AVE 11206
  Philip Nastasi, prin.
Franklin ES, 850 KENT AVE 11205
  Brunilda Graniela, prin.
Hylan ES, 60 COOK ST 11206 – Jose Garcia, prin.
Lindsey ES, 108 MONTROSE AVE 11206
  James Quail, prin.
Monitor ES, 124 MONITOR ST 11222
  John Musico, prin.
Perry ES, 131 NORMAN AVE 11222
  Joseph Caldone, prin.
Public ES 319, 360 KEAP ST 11211
  Charles Spirgel, prin.
Remsen ES, 325 BUSHWICK AVE 11206
  Patricia Clune, prin.
Stockton ES, 700 PARK AVE 11206
  Joseph Friscia, prin.
Tapia ES, 18 BEAVER ST 11206
  Maria Anderson, prin.
Ten Eyck ES, 207 BUSHWICK AVE 11206
  Albert Goldstein, prin.
Wayne ES, 370 MARCY AVE 11206
  John Lynch, prin.
Woodson ES, 545 WILLOUGHBY AVE 11206
  Donald Ashman, prin.
Woodworth ES, 208 N 5TH ST 11211
  Jeffrey Feingold, prin.

Brooklyn Borough SD 15
Sch. Sys. Enr. Code 7
Supt. – William Casey, 360 SMITH ST 11231
Alcott ES, 511 7TH AVE 11215
  Howard Sheikowitz, prin.
Bergen ES, 309 47TH ST 11220
  Blanca Ortiz, prin.
Bristow ES, 417 6TH AVE 11215
  Myron Yermak, prin.
Carroll ES, 330 SMITH ST 11231
  Phyllis Seehof, prin.
Cohen ES, 1 ALBEMARLE RD 11218
  Sylvia Oberferst, prin.
Dutcher ES, 515 4TH AVE 11215
  Gertrude Agoglia, prin.
Gowanus ES, 825 4TH AVE 11232
  Jack Spatola, prin.
Harrigan ES, 425 HENRY ST 11201
  Mary Zagami, prin.
Humphrey ES, NELSON & HICKS STREETS 11231
  Dorothy Joseph, prin.
Kimball ES, 1301 8TH AVE 11215
  Veola Harper, prin.
Livingston ES, 314 PACIFIC ST 11201
  Arthur Foresta, prin.
Longfellow ES, 5010 6TH AVE 11220
  Daniel Miller, prin.
Pacific ES, 450 PACIFIC ST 11217
  Millecent Goodman, prin.
Parkside ES, 70 OCEAN PKWY 11218
  Stephen Axelrod, prin.
Penn ES, 180 7TH AVE 11215
  Peter Heaney, prin.
Public ES 131
  4305 FORT HAMILTON PKY 11219
  Louis Staiano, prin.
Sprole ES, 317 HOYT ST 11231
  Beatrice Neu Melov, prin.
Sunset Park ES, 4305 7TH AVE 11232
  Yvette Aguirra, prin.
Windsor ES
  11 AVENUE & WINDSOR PLACE 11215
  Harvey Possner, prin.
Wolcott ES, 71 SULLIVAN ST 11231
  Patrick Daly, prin.

Brooklyn Borough SD 16
Sch. Sys. Enr. Code 7
Supt. – Minta Spain
  1010 LAFAYETTE AVE 11221
Attucks ES, 180 CHAUNCEY ST 11233
  Alice Uzoaga, prin.
Bruce ES, 820 HANCOCK ST 11233
  Thelma Simpkins, prin.
Cardwell ES, 616 QUINCY ST 11221
  Evelyn Castro, prin.
Carver ES, 265 RALPH AVE 11233
  Samuel Laitman, prin.
Lafayette ES, 787 LAFAYETTE AVE 11221
  Jean Kronenberg, prin.
McCooey ES, 500 MACON ST 11233
  Lester McDowell, prin.
Pulaski ES, 280 HART ST 11206
  Junious Watford, prin.
Quincy ES, 1014 LAFAYETTE AVE 11221
  Savannah Gillespie, prin.
Stevens ES, 990 DEKALB AVE 11221
  Barbara Thompson, prin.
Warren ES, 1001 HERKIMER ST 11233
  Thelma Peeples, prin.
Weeksville ES, 1580 DEAN ST 11213
  Joyce Washington, prin.

Wibecan ES, 794 MONROE ST 11221
  Robert Richardson, prin.
Woods ES, 130 ROCHESTER AVE 11213
  Noemi Wallace, prin.

Brooklyn Borough SD 17
Sch. Sys. Enr. Code 8
Supt. – Thelma Harper, 2 LINDEN BLVD 11226
Mahalia Jackson IS, 790 E NY AVE 11203
  Maishe Levitan, prin.
Marshall IS, 188 ROCHESTER AVE 11213
  Letha Terry, prin.
Albany Avenue ES
  E NEW YORK & ALBANY AVENUES 11203
  Eleanor Pittman, prin.
Brower ES, 900 ST MARKS AVE 11213
  Bernice Wiley, prin.
Caton Avenue ES, 18 MARLBOROUGH RD 11226
  Harold Wilson, prin.
Classon ES, 750 CLASSON AVE 11238
  Robert Jenkins, prin.
Crown ES, 330 CROWN ST 11225
  Erwin Kurs, prin.
Empire ES, 791 EMPIRE BLVD 11213
  Nellian Pilgrim, prin.
Foster-Laurie ES, 490 FENIMORE ST 11203
  Sheila Feinstein, prin.
Hegeman ES, 601 PARKSIDE AVE 11226
  Ron Evans, prin.
Johnston ES, 976 PRESIDENT ST 11225
  Marjorie Gill, prin.
Lincoln Terrace ES
  1100 E NEW YORK AVE 11212 – Jo Bruno, prin.
Malbin ES, 1023 NEW YORK AVE 11203
  Jean Yellon, prin.
Parkway ES, 1025 EASTERN PKY 11213
  Sharon Liddie, prin.
Public ES 138, 760 PROSPECT PL 11216
  Jean Louis, prin.
Public ES 398, 60 E 94TH ST 11212
  Heywood Feirstein, prin.
Public ES 399, 2707 ALBEMARLE RD 11226
  Mable Robertson, prin.
Robeson ES, 1600 PARK PL 11233
  Anita Johnson, prin.

Brooklyn Borough SD 18
Sch. Sys. Enr. Code 7
Supt. – H. Garner, 755 E 100TH ST 11236
Canarsie ES, AVENUE M & E 92ND STREET 11236
  Murray Soltano, prin.
Eastabrook ES, 10124 SEAVIEW AVE 11236
  Arthur Isman, prin.
Hyde Park ES, 4801 AVENUE D 11203
  Norman Desser, prin.
Kennedy-King ES, 1060 CLARKSON AVE 11212
  Judah Frank, prin.
Lazarus ES, 133 E 53RD ST 11203 – Ella Ivy, prin.
Lenox ES, LENOX ROAD & 39TH STREET 11203
  Mitchell Levine, prin.
Marshall ES, 1070 E 83RD ST 11236
  Julius Tutnauer, prin.
Public ES 233
  AVENUE B & E 93RD STREET 11236
  Harold Margulies, prin.
Rugby ES, 684 LINDEN BLVD 11203
  Myrna Wapner, prin.
Ryder ES, 1077 REMSEN AVE 11236
  Sheldon Cofsky, prin.
Schreiber ES, 1070 E 104TH ST 11236
  Norma Siegel, prin.
Ziefert ES
  TILDEN AVENUE & E 54 STREET 11203
  Robert Scaglioni, prin.

Brooklyn Borough SD 19
Sch. Sys. Enr. Code 7
Supt. – Levander Lily, 2057 LINDEN BLVD 11207
Cordero MS, 350 LINWOOD ST 11208
  Stephen Molinelli, prin.
East New York IS, 300 WYONA ST 11207
  Theodore Wexler, prin.
Gateway IS, 1426 FREEPORT LOOP 11239
  Richard Ferri, prin.
Gershwin JHS, 800 VAN SICLEN AVE 11207
  Milton Strong, prin.
Lincoln IS, 528 RIDGEWOOD AVE 11208
  Harold Zimmelman, prin.
Sinnott IS, 370 FOUNTAIN AVE 11208
  Jerry Krieger, prin.
Allen ES, 970 VERMONT ST 11207
  Arthella Addei, prin.
Arlington ES, 200 LINWOOD ST 11208
  Menotti Ciccone, prin.
Bolden ES, 111 BERRIMAN ST 11208
  Harvey Weintraub, prin.
Breuckelen ES, 875 WILLIAMS AVE 11207
  Audrey Delfyette, prin.
Brooklyn ES, 528 RIDGEWOOD AVE 11208
  Frances Ilivicky, prin.
Campos ES, 135 SCHENCK AVE 11207
  Roberta Cohen, prin.
Clemente ES, 557 PENNSYLVANIA AVE 11207
  Maria Power, prin.
Dumont ES, 574 RIDGEWOOD AVE 11208
  Jerry Rumsky, prin.
East New York ES, 700 SUTTER AVE 11207
  Leon Parker, prin.
Friedsam ES, 2944 PITKIN AVE 11208
  Brent Carrington, prin.
Goldman ES, 605 SHEPHERD AVE 11208
  Leonard Landsman, prin.
Jenkyns ES, 982 HEGEMAN AVE 11208
  Nancy Schuckman, prin.

Little Red ES, 158 RICHMOND ST 11208
  Roy Blash, prin.
New Lots ES, 580 HEGEMAN AVE 11207
  Lillian Oliveras, prin.
Old Mill ES, 755 WORTMAN AVE 11208
  Virginia Noville, prin.
Pitkin ES, 2781 PITKIN AVE 11208
  Victor Rodriguez, prin.
Public ES 190, 590 SHEFFIELD AVE 11207
  Jerry Cohen, prin.
Stark ES, 1400 PENNSYLVANIA AVE 11239
  Martin Rosansky, prin.
Warwick ES, 400 ASHFORD ST 11207
  Anita Harrison, prin.
Wheatley ES, 330 ALABAMA AVE 11207
  Stanley Lavnick, prin.
Wortman ES, 923 JEROME ST 11207
  Mildred Jones, prin.

Brooklyn Borough SD 20
Sch. Sys. Enr. Code 7
Supt. – Ralph Fabrizio, 1031 59TH ST 11219
Ditmas JHS, 700 CORTELYOU ROAD 11218
  Walter Verfenstein, prin.
Dyker Heights JHS, 8010 12TH AVE 11228
  Madeleine Brennan, prin.
McKinley JHS, 7305 FT HAMILTON PKWY 11228
  N. Donangelo, prin.
Shallow JHS, 6500 16TH AVE 11204
  Donald Delseni, prin.
Bath Beach ES, 1664 BENSON AVE 11214
  Patrick Marano, prin.
Bayview ES, 211 72ND ST 11209
  Richard Scarpaci, prin.
Benson ES, 1940 BENSON AVE 11214
  Robert Schwimmer, prin.
Blythebourne ES, 1031 59TH ST 11219
  Margaret Flanagan, prin.
Clarion ES, 6701 20TH AVE 11204
  Philip Tritt, prin.
Dyker ES, 1400 BENSON AVE 11228
  James Harrigan, prin.
Ft. Hamilton ES, 9115 FIFTH AVENUE 11209
  Denis Moore, prin.
Gladstone ES, 7601 19TH AVE 11214
  Dennis Gladstone, prin.
Homewood ES
  16TH AVENUE & 57TH STREET 11204
  Marvin Grosskopf, prin.
Kensington ES, 202 AVENUE C 11218
  Philip Lembo, prin.
Lefferts Park ES, 7115 15TH AVE 11228
  Carl Geraci, prin.
Lexington ES, 7109 6TH AVE 11209
  Dolores Grieco, prin.
Lombardi ES, 8101 15TH AVE 11228
  Salvatore Ferrera, prin.
Mapleton ES, 6015 18TH AVE 11204
  Joseph Maiello, prin.
Marin ES, 330 59TH ST 11220
  Francis McGuire, prin.
McKinley Park ES
  79TH STREET & SEVENTH AVE 11209
  Stanley Junemann, prin.
Ovington ES, 1225 69TH ST 11219
  Frederick Ergang, prin.
Public ES 185
  86TH STREET & RIDGE BLVD 11209
  Frank Landro, prin.
Public ES 192, 4715 18TH AVE 11204
  Bernice Jaffe, prin.
Public ES 247, 7000 21ST AVE 11204
  Robert Cohen, prin.
Rodney ES
  14TH AVENUE & 42ND STREET 11219
  Judith Stewart, prin.
Sampson ES, 5105 FORT HAMILTON PKY 11219
  Barry Mintzer, prin.

Brooklyn Borough SD 21
Sch. Sys. Enr. Code 7
Supt. – Donald Weber
  345 VAN SICKLEN ST 11223
Bensonhurst ES, 2075 84TH ST 11214
  Michael Miller, prin.
Berdy ES, 3314 NEPTUNE AVE 11224
  Augusto Martinez, prin.
Coney Island ES, 2951 W 3RD ST 11224
  Stuart Possner, prin.
Cosmopolitan ES
  1075 OCEANVIEW AVENUE 11235
  Joseph Alfieri, prin.
Elmwood ES, 1100 ELM AVE 11230
  Leonard Zeplin, prin.
Gravesend ES, 345 VAN SICKLEN ST 11223
  James Filatro, prin.
Hentz ES, 2950 W 25TH ST 11224
  Margaret Nichols, prin.
Highlawn ES
  STILLWELL AVENUE & AVENUE S 11223
  Louis Nezowitz, prin.
Homecrest ES, 1970 HOMECREST AVE 11229
  Lillian Dinofsky, prin.
Loftus ES, 2840 W 12TH ST 11224
  Edna Cohen, prin.
Marlboro ES
  AVENUE P & W FIRST STREET 11204
  Maurice Freeman, prin.
Mason ES, 6006 23RD AVE 11204
  Daniel Baris, prin.
Mead ES, AVENUE Z & SEVENTH STREET 11235
  Sheldon Thaler, prin.
Midwood ES, 1120 E 10TH ST 11230
  Louis Galinsky, prin.

Moody ES, 87 BAY 49TH ST   11214
  Miriam Corn, prin.
Public ES 253, 601 OCEANVIEW AVE   11230
  Margaret De Fazio, prin.
Rockefeller ES
  20TH AVENUE & 53RD STREET   11204
  James Anello, prin.
Sullivan ES, 1633 E 8TH ST   11223
  Lawrence Herstik, prin.
Surfside ES, 2929 W 30TH ST   11224
  Irwin Grossbard, prin.
Toscanini ES, 350 AVENUE X   11223
  Richard Breyer, prin.
Verrazano ES
  BENSON AVENUE & BAY 35TH   11214
  James Mullaney, prin.
Weiss ES, AVENUE S & E 2ND STREET   11223
  Gail Feuer, prin.

Brooklyn Borough SD 22
Sch. Sys. Enr. Code 7
Supt. – John Comer, 2525 HARING ST   11235
Cunningham JHS, 1875 E 17TH ST   11229
  Isidore Karbel, prin.
Hudde JHS, 2500 NOSTRAND AVE   11210
  Richard Arroyo, prin.
Man IS, 1420 E 68TH ST   11234 – Fred Zahn, prin.
Marine Park JHS, 1925 STUART ST   11229
  Albert Schwartz, prin.
Shell Bank IS, AVE X & BATCHELDER   11229
  Aaron Friedman, prin.
Bennett ES, AVENUE M & E 52ND STREET   11234
  Sidney Aronson, prin.
Bergen Beach ES, 7103 AVENUE T   11234
  Charles Langjahr, prin.
Gerritseh Beach ES, 2529 GERRITSEN AVE   11229
  Gerry Rosen, prin.
Glenwood Road ES, 2310 GLENWOOD RD   11210
  Lester Kostick, prin.
Hammarskjold ES, 1801 AVENUE Y   11235
  Daniel Gitter, prin.
Kelly ES, 1866 E 17TH ST   11229
  Saul Koren, prin.
Manhattan Beach ES, 131 IRWIN ST   11235
  Lillian Levy, prin.
Mill Basin ES, 6302 AVENUE U   11234
  Irving Rahinsky, prin.
Paedergat ES, 1801 AVENUE Y   11235
  Cynthia Kamen, prin.
Public ES 193, 2515 AVENUE L   11210
  Kathleen Cashin, prin.
Public ES 197, 1599 E 22ND ST   11210
  John Graziani, prin.
Public ES 198, 4105 FARRAGUT RD   11210
  Anthony Gaeta, prin.
Lamb ES, NECK ROAD & E 22ND STREET   11229
  Bernard Mendelson, prin.
Leary ES, 4011 FILLMORE AVE   11234
  Ralph Levy, prin.
Marcus ES
  NEWKIRK & CONEY ISLAND AVE   11230
  Janet Kramer, prin.
Nostrand ES, 1957 NOSTRAND AVE   11210
  Henry Rosenberg, prin.
Sheepshead Bay ES, 2675 E 29TH ST   11235
  George Greco, prin.
Snyder ES
  QUENTIN ROAD & 33RD STREET   11234
  Marita Regan, prin.
Amersfort ES, 3829 AVENUE K   11210
  Joan Lunney, prin.
Cortelyou ES, 330 RUGBY RD   11226
  Lawrence Levy, prin.
Wallengerg ES
  AVENUE W & KNAPP STREET   11229
  Myrna Neugesser, prin.

Brooklyn Borough SD 23
Sch. Sys. Enr. Code 7
Supt. – Michael Vega, 2240 DEAN ST   11233
Coleman JHS, 1137 HERKIMER ST   11233
  Gregory Coleman, prin.
Eiseman JHS, 985 ROCKAWAY AVE   11212
  Robert Adams, prin.
Marcus JHS, 210 CHESTER ST   11212
  Gilbert Grossman, prin.
Ocean Hill IS, 2021 BERGEN ST   11233
  Percy Jenkins, prin.
Bainbridge ES, 121 SARATOGA AVE   11233
  Frank Spradley, prin.
Christopher ES, 364 SACKMAN ST   11212
  Harold Golubichik, prin.
Dent ES, 111 BRISTOL ST   11212
  Rose English, prin.
Glenmore ES, 85 WATKINS ST   11212
  Humphrey Duncanson, prin.
Herkimer ES, 1355 HERKIMER ST   11233
  Albert Kisseloff, prin.
Houston ES, 51 CHRISTOPHER AVE   11212
  Richard Placente, prin.
James ES, 76 RIVERDALE AVE   11212
  Lester Young, prin.
Lott ES, 76 LOTT AVE   11212
  Hugh Griffith, prin.
McKelway ES, 2163 DEAN ST   11233
  Herbert Baldwin, prin.
Morrison ES, 241 MACDOUGAL ST   11233
  Pauline Riley, prin.
Public ES 184, 273 NEWPORT ST   11212
  Redell Osgood, prin.
Wallace ES, 220 WATKINS ST   11212
  Julia Washington, prin.
Waverly ES, 104 SUTTER AVE   11212
  Elizabeth Samuels, prin.

White ES, 411 THATFORD AVE   11212
  Herbert Ross, prin.

Brooklyn Borough SD 32
Sch. Sys. Enr. Code 7
Supt. – Marco Hernandez
  797 BUSHWICK AVE   11221
Fermi IS, 35 STARR ST   11221
  Dominick Lavelle, prin.
Hayes IS, 231 PALMETTO ST   11221
  Alberto Bryan, prin.
Schuyler IS, 1300 GREENE AVE   11237
  Loretta Boyce, prin.
Carter ES, 242 COOPER ST   11207
  Iran Pelcyger, prin.
Chauncey ES, 84 SCHAFFER ST   11207
  Vincent Gatto, prin.
De Gautier ES, 200 WOODBINE ST   11221
  Felix Vazquez, prin.
Evergreen Grove ES, 95 GROVE ST   11221
  Frank Lanza, prin.
Field ES, 88 WOODBINE ST   11221
  Gloria Saunders, prin.
Hale ES, 1314 PUTNAM AVE   11221
  Michael Dibisceglie, prin.
Irvington ES, 220 IRVING AVE   11237
  Anne Verrone, prin.
Jackson ES, 100 NOLL ST   11206
  Clara Baker, prin.
Johnson ES, 763 KNICKERBOCKER AVE   11207
  Irwin Weinstein, prin.
Kosciusko ES, 800 BUSHWICK AVE   11221
  Juan Martinez, prin.
Plymouth ES, 515 KNICKERBOCKER AVE   11237
  Theresa Higgins, prin.
Suydam ES, 100 IRVING AVE   11237
  Catherine Spatola, prin.

Adelphi Academy, 8515 RIDGE BLVD   11209
Bais Esther School, 1353 50TH ST   11219
Bais Rachel School ofBoro Park
  5301 14TH AVE   11219
Bais Yaakov Beth Jacob Academy
  1213 ELM AVE   11230
Berkeley Carroll Street School
  181 LINCOLN PLACE   11217
Beth Chana School for Girls
  620 BEDFORD AVE   11211
Beth Rivkah School for Girls
  2270 CHURCH AVE   11226
Bnos Yaakov Sch. for Girls HS
  62 HARRISON AVE   11211
Bnos Yerushalayim School
  12 FRANKLYN AVE   11211
Bobover Yeshiva Bnei Zion School
  1533 48TH ST   11219
Boro Hall Academy, 17 SMITH ST   11201
Brooklyn Friends School, 375 PEARL ST   11201
Epiphany Lutheran School
  721 LINCOLN PL   11216
Haitian Academy, 95 LEXINGTON AVE   11238
MSFTA Chsan Sofer & Rabbi Kluger
  1876 50TH ST   11204
Mesivta Haichel Hatorah School
  24-49 OCEAN AVE   11229
New Vistas Academy
  1886 NOSTRAND AVE   11226
Packer Collegiate Institute
  170 JORALEMON ST   11201
St. Ann's School, 129 PIERREPONT ST   11201
Talmud Torah Tolds Yosef
  105 HEYWARD ST   11206
Unid Tal Academy Tor V Yirah-Boro
  1356 53RD ST   11219
Unique Christian Academy
  22-22 CHURCH AVE   11226
Yeshira Machzekei Hadas, 1601 42ND ST   11204
Yeshiva & Msvta Karlin Stolin
  1818 54TH ST   11204
Yeshiva Farm Settlement School
  194 DIVISION AVE   11211
Yeshiva Riferes Elimelech, 5801 16TH AVE   11204
Yeshiva Torah Temimah
  555 OCEAN PKWY   11218
Yeshiva of Brooklyn for Girls
  1470 OCEAN PKWY   11230
Ahi Ezer Yeshiva ES, 2433 OLEAN PKWY   11235
Al-Karim ES, 876 PARK PL   11216
All Saints ES, 113 THROOP AVE   11206
Bais Brocho of Karlin ES, 1811 55TH ST   11204
Bais Issac Zui/Kesser Malka, 1019 46TH ST   11219
Bais Yaakov D'Chassidei Gur
  1681 42ND ST   11204
Bais Yaakov Dkhal Adas Yer
  563 BEDFORD AVE   11211
Bais Yaakov of Brooklyn ES, 1362 49TH ST   11219
Bais Yaakov of Eighteenth Avenue ES
  4419 18TH AVE   11204
Bais Yakov Adas Yereim ES
  5824 17TH AVE   11204
Bais Yitzchak ES, 1413 45TH ST   11219
Bay Ridge Christian Academy
  6324 7TH AVE   11220
Beer Hogolah Institute, 293 NEPTUNE AVE   11235
Beer Mordechai ES, 1670 OCEAN AVE   11230
Beikvei Hatzoin ES, 31 DIVISION AVE   11211
Bet Yaacov Ateret Torah School
  1750 E 4TH ST   11223
Beth Jacob School for Girls
  85 PARKVILLE AVE   11230
Beth Jacob of Boro Park ES, 1371 46TH ST   11219
Beth Jacob of Flatbush ES
  1981 HOMECREST AVE   11229
Beth Rachel Girls School, 227 MARCY AVE   11211

Beth Rivkah ES, 2270 CHURCH AVE   11226
Bethany Christian ES
  521 HOPKINSON AVE   11212
Bethel ES, 457 GRAND AVE   11238
Bethlehem Baptist Academy
  1962-84 LINDEN BLVD   11207
Bialik School-Flatbush Jewish Center
  500 CHURCH AVE   11218
Blessed Sacrament ES, 187 EUCLID AVE   11208
Bnei Shimon Yisroel of Sopron
  2Q5 HEWES ST   11211
Bnos Israel-East Flatbush ES
  1629 E 15TH ST   11229
Bnos Yakov ES, 1581 52ND ST   11219
Bnos Zion of Bobov School
  5000 14TH AVE   11219
Brooklyn Temple ES, 3 LEWIS AVE   11206
Concord Day ES, 833 MARCY AVE   11216
Crown Heights Yeshiva ES
  6363 AVENUE U   11234
Ebenezer Prep School, 5464 KINGS HWY   11203
Excelsior ES, 418 E 45TH ST   11203
Fantis Parochial ES, 195 STATE ST   11201
Flatbush ES, P O BOX 311   11226
Flatbush SDA ES, 5810 SNYDER AVE   11203
Good Shepherd ES, 1943 BROWN ST   11229
Grace Christian Education Center
  650 LIVONIA AVE   11207
Grayson Christian ES, 1237 EASTERN PKY   11213
Hanson Place ES, 38 LAFAYETTE AVE   11217
Holy Cross ES, 2520 CHURCH AVE   11226
Holy Cross Parochial ES, 8502 RIDGE BLVD   11209
Holy Family ES
  FLATLANDS & EAST 98TH ST   11236
Holy Ghost Ukranian Catholic ES
  161 N 5TH ST   11211
Holy Innocents ES, 249 E 17TH ST   11226
Holy Name of Jesus ES
  241 PROSPECT PARK W   11215
Holy Rosary ES, 180 BAINBRIDGE ST   11233
Holy Spirit ES, 560 STERLING PL   11238
Holy Spirit ES, 1668 46TH ST   11204
Hus Moravian ES, 153 OCEAN AVE   11225
Immaculate Heart of Mary ES
  3002 FT HAMILTON PKY   11218
Junior Academy, 856 QUINCY ST   11221
Leif Ericson Day ES, 1037 72ND ST   11228
Lubavitcher ES Chabad, 841 OCEAN PKY   11230
Lutheran ES-Bay Ridge
  440 OVINGTON AVE   11209
Magen David Yesh-Isaac Shlm
  50 AVENUE P   11204
Mary Queen of Heaven ES, 1326 E 57TH ST   11234
Mirrer Yeshiva ES, 1795 OCEAN PKY   11223
Most Holy Trinity ES
  140 MONTROSE AVE   11206
Most Precious Blood ES
  133-157 27TH AVE   11214
Mt. Moriah Chirstian Academy
  1149 EASTERN PKY   11213
Mt. Pisgah Christian Academy
  760 DEKALB AVE   11216
Mt. Roraima ES, 1915 FULTON ST   11233
Oholei Torah ES, 667 EASTERN PKY   11213
Our Lady Help-Christians ES
  1340 E 29TH ST   11210
Our Lady of Angels ES, 337-347 74TH ST   11209
Our Lady of Czestochowa ES, 169 25TH ST   11232
Our Lady of Grace ES, 385 AVENUE W   11223
Our Lady of Guadalupe ES, 1518 73RD ST   11228
Our Lady of Loretto ES, 2365 PACIFIC ST   11233
Our Lady of Lourdes ES
  2-12 ABERDEEN ST   11207
Our Lady of Miracles ES, 744 E 87TH ST   11236
Our Lady of Peach ES, 512 CARROLL ST   11215
Our Lady of Perpetual Help ES
  5902 6TH AVE   11220
Our Lady of Refuge ES, 1087 OCEAN AVE   11230
Our Lady of Solace ES, 2865 W 19TH ST   11224
Our Saviour ES, 250 HOOPER ST   11211
Parkway ES, 670 BROCKWAY PKWY   11236
Peter Pan ES, 1226 OCEAN PKY   11230
Pilgrim Baptist Christian Academy
  600 CENTRAL AVE   11207
Prospect Park Yeshiva ES, 1613 AVENUE R   11229
Queen of All Saints ES
  300 VANDERBILT AVE   11205
Rabbi Halpern Day ES, 1625 OCEAN AVE   11230
Regina Pacis ES, 1201 66TH ST   11219
Resurrection ES, 2335 GERRITSEN AVE   11229
Risen Christ Lutheran ES, 250 BLAKE AVE   11212
SDA Bilingual Union ES, 920 PARK PL   11213
SDA Ebenezer ES, 991 EASTERN PKY   11213
SS. Cyril & Methodius ES, 96 DUPONT ST   11222
SS. Peter & Paul ES, 288 BERRY ST   11211
SS. Simon & Jude ES, 294 AVENUE T   11223
Sacred Hearts and St. Stephens ES
  135 SUMMIT ST   11231
Shulamith ES for Girls, 1277 E 14TH ST   11230
Soterios Elenas Parochial ES, 224 18TH ST   11215
St. Agatha ES, 736 48TH ST   11220
St. Agnes Seminary, 2221 AVENUE R   11229
St. Angela Hall ES
  290 WASHINGTON AVE   11205
St. Anselm, 357 83RD ST   11209
St. Anthony of Alphonsus ES
  725 LEONARD ST   11222
St. Athanasius ES, 6120 BAY PKY   11204
St. Augustine-St. Frances Xavier ES
  763 PRESIDENT ST   11215
St. Bernadette ES, 1313 83RD ST   11228
St. Bernard ES, 2030 E 69TH ST   11234
St. Brendan ES, 1520 E 13TH ST   11230
St. Brigid ES, 438 GROVE ST   11237

St. Catharine-Alexandra ES, 1053 41ST ST 11219
St. Catherine of Genoa ES
  870 ALBANY AVE 11203
St. Cecilia ES, 1-15 MONITOR ST 11222
St. Charles Borromeo ES, 23 SIDNEY PL 11201
St. Edmund ES
  E 19TH ST AND AVENUE T 11229
St. Elizabeth Seton ES
  751 KNICKERBOCKER AVE 11221
St. Ephrem ES, 7415 FT HAMILTON PKWY 11228
St. Finbar ES, 1825 BATH AVE 11214
St. Fortunata ES, 2635 LINDEN BLVD 11208
St. Frances Cabrini ES, 21 BAY 11TH ST 11228
St. Frances Cabrini ES, 181 SUYDAM ST 11221
St. Frances of Chantal ES, 1273 57TH ST 11219
St. Francis of Assisi ES, 400 LINCOLN RD 11225
St. Francis of Paola ES
  201 CONSELYEA ST 11211
St. Jerome ES, 465 E 29TH ST 11226
St. John Cantius ES
  BLAKE AVE & VERMONT ST 11207
St. John Neumann ES, 237 JEROME ST 11207
St. John the Baptist ES, 80-82 LEWIS AVE 11206
St. John the Evangelist ES, 259 21ST ST 11215
St. John's ES, 19 WINTHROP ST 11225
St. Jude ES, 1696 CANARSIE RD 11236
St. Mark ES, 2602 E 19TH ST 11235
St. Mark's Day ES, 1346 PRESIDENT ST 11213
St. Mark's Lutheran ES
  626 BUSHWICK AVE 11206
St. Mary Mother of Jesus ES
  8401 23RD AVE 11214
St. Mary Star of the Sea ES, 477 COURT ST 11231
St. Michael's ES, 4222 4TH AVE 11232
St. Nicholas ES, 287 POWERS ST 11211
St. Patrick ES, 420 95TH ST 11209
St. Paul's Community Christian ES
  818 SCHENCK AVE 11207
St. Rita ES, 260 SHEPHERD AVE 11208
St. Rose of Lima ES, 259 PARKVILLE AVE 11230
St. Saviour ES, 701 8TH AVE 11215
St. Stanislaus Kostka ES, 10 NEWELL ST 11222
St. Stephen's Lutheran ES
  2806 NEWKIRK AVE 11226
St. Sylvester ES, 396 GRANT AVE 11208
St. Therese of Lisieux ES, 4410 AVENUE D 11203
St. Thomas Aquinas ES, 211 8TH ST 11215
St. Thomas Aquinas ES
  1501 HENDRICKSON ST 11234
St. Vincent De Paul ES, 180 N 7TH ST 11211
St. Vincent Ferrer ES
  1603 BROOKLYN AVE 11210
Tabernacle ES, 264 LEXINGTON AVE 11216
Talmud Taroh Imrei Chaim ES
  1480 43RD ST 11219
Talmud Tor Toldos Yakv Yosf
  1373 43RD ST 11219
Talmud Torah Toldos Hillel-Krasna
  631 BEDFORD AVE 11211
Three Hierarchs ES, 1724 AVENUE P 11229
Tifereth Mordechai Sholomo
  4405 14TH AVE 11219
Tomer Dvora ES, 4500 9TH AVE 11220
Tompkins Children ES, 730 PARK AVE 11206
United Talmudical Adamemy
  227 MARCY AVE 11211
Unity Catholic ES, 991 ST JOHNS PL 11213
Visitation Academy
  RIDGE BLVD AND 89TH ST 11209
Windmill Montessori School
  1317 AVENUE T 11229
Woodward Park ES
  49-50 PROSPECT PARK W 11215
Yechiva Chasdei Torah ES, 2025 67TH ST 11204
Yesh Beth Yitzchok Dsprinka
  575 BEDFORD AVE 11211
Yesh Mesivta Arugath Habrsm
  171-173 HOOPER ST 11211
Yeshiva Ahavas Israel ES, 6 LEE AVE 11211
Yeshiva Ateres Yisroel ES, 8101 AVENUE K 11236
Yeshiva Bais Ephraim ES, 2802 AVENUE J 11210
Yeshiva Beth Hillel of Krasna
  1364-66 42ND ST 11219
Yeshiva Imrei Yosef Spinka School
  5801 15TH AVE 11219
Yeshiva Kehilath Yakov School
  206 WILSON ST 11211
Yeshiva Kol Torah of Flatlands, 959 E 80 11236
Yeshiva Ohel Moshe ES, 7914 BAY PKY 11214
Yeshiva Rabbi Chaim Berlin
  1310 AVENUE I 11230
Yeshiva Rambam ES, 3300 KINGS HWY 11234
Yeshiva Rtzahd ES, 965 E 107TH ST 11236
Yeshiva Sharei Hayshr ES, 1449 50TH ST 11219
Yeshiva T'Tiferes Bunim ES
  52-02 13TH AVE 11219
Yeshiva Tifereth David ES, 1315 43RD ST 11219
Yeshiva Tifers Zvi ES, 4712 14TH AVE 11219
Yeshiva Toldos Yosef ES, 4706 10TH AVE 11219
Yeshiva Torah Vodaath ES, 452 E 9TH ST 11218
Yeshiva Toras Emes Kamenitz
  1650 56TH ST 11204
Yeshiva Yagdil Torah ES, 5110 18TH AVE 11204
Yeshiva Yesode Hatorah
  505 BEDFORD AVE 11211
Yeshiva Yesode Hatorah ES, 1350 50TH ST 11219
Yeshiva Yesodei Hytorah, 131 LEE AVE 11211
Yeshiva of Kings Bay ES, 2611 AVENUE Z 11235
Yeshiva of Manhattan Beach ES
  60 W END AVE 11235
Yeshivah of Flatbush ES, 919 E 10TH ST 11230
Yeshivat Ateret Torah ES
  901 QUENTIN RD 11223

Yeshivat Mizrachi L'Banim ES
  2810 NOSTRAND AVE 11229

Brownville, Jefferson Co., Pop. Code 4
Gen. Brown Central SD
Sch. Sys. Enr. Code 4
Supt. – D. Grant 13615
ES 13615 – William Archer, prin.
Other Schools – See Dexter

Brushton, Franklin Co., Pop. Code 3
Brushton Moira Central SD
Sch. Sys. Enr. Code 3
Supt. – David Moore, GALE ROAD 12916
Brushton ES, MAIN STREET 12916
  Robert Genaway, prin.

Buchanan, Westchester Co., Pop. Code 4
Hendrick Hudson Central SD
Supt. – See Montrose
Buchanan-Verplanck ES
  160 WESTCHESTER AVE 10511
  Francis Stein, prin.

Buffalo, Erie Co., Pop. Code 10
Buffalo CSD
Sch. Sys. Enr. Code 8
Supt. – Eugene Reville
  ROOM 712 CITY HALL 14202
Public MS 84, 462 GRIDER ST 14215
  Millicent Tonner, prin.
Badillo Community ES
  300 S ELMWOOD AVE 14201 – David Caban,
  prin.
Black Rock MS, 101 HERTEL AVE 14207
  John Bargnesi, prin.
Houghton MS, 1725 CLINTON ST 14206
  Jacqueline Morana, prin.
Indian Park MS, 76 BUFFUM ST 14210
  James Horrigan, prin.
Lincoln MS, 1369 BROADWAY ST 14212
  Frank Benbenek, prin.
Lorraine MS, 71 LORRAINE AVE 14220
  Lillian Kozminski, prin.
North Park MS, PARKSIDE & TACOMA 14216
  Robert Curtin, prin.
Public MS 56, 716 W DELAVAN AVE 14222
  Judith Ricca, prin.
Public MS 43, 161 BENZINGER ST 14206
  Ronald Romanowicz, prin.
Riverside MS, 238 ONTARIO ST 14207
  Donna Kogler, prin.
Roosevelt MS, 249 SKILLEN ST 14207
  Carol Needham, prin.
St. Lawrence MS
  756 SAINT LAWRENCE AVE 14216
  Robert Curtin, prin.
West Hertel MS, 489 HERTEL AVE 14207
  James Holland, prin.
Academic Challenge ES
  HICKORY AND S DIVISION 14204
  Edith James, prin.
Build Academy, 340 FOUGERON ST 14211
  Eunice Jackson, prin.
Campus East ES, 106 APPENHEIMER AVE 14214
  Priscilla Niedermeyer, prin.
Campus North ES, 120 MINNESOTA AVE 14214
  Anthony Catalfamo, prin.
Campus West ES, 1300 ELMWOOD AVE 14222
  Margaret Forrester, prin.
Futures ES, 295 CARLTON ST 14204
  Marva Daniel, prin.
Hillery Park MS, 73 PAWNEE PKY 14210
  Ruthetta Smikle, prin.
King Community ES, 487 HIGH ST 14211
  Anthony Palano, prin.
Montessori ES, 342 CLINTON ST 14204
  Rae Rosen, prin.
Olmsted ES West, 440 WEST AVE 14213
  Judith Ricca, prin.
Poplar Street Academy, 110 POPLAR AVE 14211
  Stephen Kraus, prin.
Public ES 12, 33 ASH ST 14204
  Philomena Daniels, prin.
Public ES 17, 1045 W DELAVAN AVE 14209
  Gillis Watson, prin.
Public ES 18, 118 HAMPSHIRE ST 14213
  Paul Williams, prin.
Public ES 19, 97 W DELAVAN AVE 14213
  Lloyd Elm, prin.
Public ES 3, 255 PORTER AVE 14201
  Victor Filadora, prin.
Public ES 31, 212 STANTON ST 14212
  Mildred Stallings, prin.
Public ES 33, 157 ELK ST 14210
  Charles Pezzino, prin.
Public ES 36, 10 DAYS PARK 14201
  Barbara Ribbeck, prin.
Public ES 38, 350 VERMONT ST 14213
  Leonard Testa, prin.
Public ES 4, 425 S PARK AVE 14204
  Jacqueline Woodbeck, prin.
Public ES 40, 245 ONEIDA ST 14206
  Frank Szumigala, prin.
Public ES 45, 141 HOYT ST 14213
  Francine Palmero, prin.
Public ES 53, 329 ROEHRER AVE 14208
  Donette Ruffin, prin.
Public ES 54, 2358 MAIN ST 14214
  Gilda Smith, prin.
Public ES 57, 231 SEARS ST 14212
  William Chambers, prin.
Public ES 59, 775 BEST ST 14211
  Carol Mitchell, prin.

Public ES 61, 453 LEROY AVE 14215
  Marion Canedo, prin.
Public ES 64
  AMHERST & LINCOLN PARKWAY 14216
  Judith Ricca, prin.
Public ES 68, 24 WESTMINSTER AVE 14215
  Guy Outlaw, prin.
Public ES 71, 156 NEWBURGH AVE 14211
  Marion Mayfield, prin.
Public ES 74, 126 DONALDSON RD 14208
  Joyce Harrington, prin.
Public ES 77, 370 NORMAL AVE 14213
  Peter Szlzap, prin.
Public ES 78, 345 OLYMPIC AVE 14215
  Michele Pozarny, prin.
Public ES 80, 600 HIGHGATE AVE 14215
  Michael Lucas, prin.
Public ES 81, 140 TACOMA AVE 14216
  Peter Delbello, prin.
Public ES 82, 230 EASTON AVE 14215
  Ophelia Nicholas, prin.
Public ES 90, 50 A ST 14211
  Goldie Williams, prin.
Follow-Thru ES, E UTICA & MASTEN 14208
  Donald Beck, prin.
Southside ES, 430 SOUTHSIDE PKY 14210
  Raymond Cooley, prin.
Triangle MS, 1515 S PARK AVE 14220
  Jill Bartkowski, prin.
Waterfront ES, 95 FOURTH ST 14202
  Patricia Sheffer, prin.

Cheektowaga Central SD
Supt. – See Cheektowaga
Pine Hill MS, 1635 E DELAVAN AVE 14215
  Frank Cantie, prin.

Cheektowago-Sloan UFD
Sch. Sys. Enr. Code 4
Supt. – James Mazgajewski
  166 HALSTEAD AVE 14212
Wilson MS, 166 HALSTEAD AVE 14212
  Dennis Piekarski, prin.
Other Schools – See Cheektowaga

Frontier Central SD
Supt. – See Hamburg
Woodlawn MS, 3656 MILESTRIP ROAD 14219
  Donald Griffin, prin.

Williamsville Central SD
Sch. Sys. Enr. Code 6
Supt. – Howard Welker, P O BOX 9070 14221
Other Schools – See East Amherst, Williamsville

Calasanctius School, 167 WINDSOR AVE 14209
Nardin Academy, 135 CLEVELAND AVE 14222
All Saints ES, 207 ESSER AVE 14207
Blessed Sacrament ES
  263 CLAREMONT AVE 14223
Cathedral ES, 1069 DELAWARE AVE 14209
Christ the King ES, 2 LAMARK DR 14226
College Learning Lab ES
  1300 ELMWOOD AVE 14222
Diocesan Education ES, 564 DODGE ST 14208
Elmwood Franklin ES
  104 NEW AMSTERDAM AVE 14216
Holy Angels ES, 348 PORTER AVE 14201
Holy Family ES, 920 TIFFT ST 14220
Holy Name of Jesus ES, 228 BRINKHAM ST 14211
Holy Spirit ES, 85 DAKOTA ST 14216
Kadimah School of Buffalo, 1 CAMBRIDGE AVE 14223
Luther Christian ES, 1085 EGGERT RD 14226
Mt. St. Joseph Academy ES, 2064 MAIN ST 14208
Nardin Academy ES, 135 CLEVELAND AVE 14222
Nazareth Lutheran School, 265 SKILLEN ST 14207
Our Lady of Black Rock ES
  16 GERMAIN ST 14207
Our Lady of Czestochowa School
  2769 S PARK AVE 14218
St. Agatha ES, 65 ABBOTT RD 14220
St. Agnes ES, 188 LUDINGTON ST 14206
St. Aloysius Gonzaga ES
  157 CLEVELAND DR 14215
St. Ambrose ES, 260 OKELL ST 14220
St. Andrew ES, CROCKER-FRANKLIN ST S 14212
St. Benedicts ES, 3980 MAIN ST 14226
St. Bernard ES, 1988 CLINTON ST 14206
St. Casimir ES, 1833 CLINTON ST 14206
St. Elizabeth ES, 89 MILITARY RD 14207
St. James ES, 21 DAVIDSON AVE 14215
St. John Gualbert ES, 111 GUALBERT AVE 14211
St. John Cantius ES, 82 BROWNELL ST 14212
St. John the Baptist ES
  BELMONT AND HIGHLAND 14223
St. Josaphat ES, 25 MANSION AVE 14206
St. Joseph ES, 3275 MAIN ST 14214
St. Lawrence ES, 26 WRIGHT AVE 14215
St. Leo's ES, 903 SWEET HOME RD 14226
St. Margaret ES
  HERTEL AND SARANAC STS 14216
St. Mark ES, 399 WOODWARD AVE 14214
St. Martin ES, 1125 ABBOTT RD 14220
St. Rose of Lima ES, 201 WINSTON RD 14216
St. Stanislaus ES, 128 WILSON ST 14212
St. Teresa ES, 16 HAYDEN ST 14210
St. Thomas Aquinas ES, 20 ATHOL ST 14220

Burnt Hills, Saratoga Co., Pop. Code 4
Burnt Hills Ballston Lake CSD
Supt. – See Scotia
MS, LAKE HILL ROAD 12027
  David Guilmette, prin.

Cadyville, Clinton Co.
Saranac Central SD
Supt. – See Saranac
ES 12918 – Gilbert Burnell, prin.

Cairo, Greene Co., Pop. Code 5
Cairo-Durham Central SD
Sch. Sys. Enr. Code 4
Supt. – Donald Gibson, P O BOX 780 12413
ES, MAIN STREET BOX 780 12413
Richard Booth, prin.
Other Schools – See Durham

Caledonia, Livingston Co., Pop. Code 4
Caledonia Mumford Central SD
Sch. Sys. Enr. Code 4
Supt. – Ray Chamberlin, 99 NORTH ST 14423
Caledonia Mumford ES, 99 NORTH ST 14423
Walter Pennington, prin.

Callicoon, Sullivan Co., Pop. Code 5
Delaware Valley Central SD
Sch. Sys. Enr. Code 3
Supt. – Charles Kozora, RURAL ROUTE 01 12723
Delaware Valley Central S
RURAL ROUTE 01 12723 – Edwin Chellis, prin.

Calverton, Suffolk Co., Pop. Code 3
Riverhead Central SD
Supt. – See Riverhead
Riley Avenue ES, RILEY AVENUE 11933
Gerald Martin, prin.

Cambria Heights, Queens Co.
Queens Borough SD 29
Supt. – See Queens Village
ES, 12045 235TH ST 11411 – Winston Joriso, prin.
Public ES 147, 21801 116TH AVE 11411
Dolores Nethersole, prin.

Cambridge, Washington Co., Pop. Code 4
Cambridge Central SD
Sch. Sys. Enr. Code 4
Supt. – Howard Bennett, 24 S PARK ST 12816
ES, 24 SOUTH PARK ST 12816
Gerald Benjamin, prin.

Camden, Oneida Co., Pop. Code 5
Camden Central SD
Sch. Sys. Enr. Code 5
Supt. – Richard McClements, 51 3RD ST 13316
MS, 32 UNION ST 13316 – Terry Schaal, prin.
ES, 1 OSWEGO ST 13316 – James Gordon, prin.
Other Schools – See Mc Connellsville, North Bay,
Taberg

Cameron Mills, Steuben Co.
Addison Central SD
Supt. – See Addison
Valley ES 14820 – Jon Thomas, prin.

Camillus, Onondaga Co., Pop. Code 4
West Genesee Central SD at Camillus
Sch. Sys. Enr. Code 5
Supt. – Rudolph Rubeis
5203 W GENESEE ST 13031
MS, IKE DIXON ROAD 13031
Richard Culkin, prin.
West Genesee MS, SANDERSON ROAD 13031
Joseph Pecori, prin.
East Hill ES, 333 BLACKMORE RD 13031
John Bome, prin.
Split Rock ES, RURAL ROUTE 01 13031
Robert Fugo, prin.
Stonehedge ES, 400 SANDERSON RD 13031
Donald Stebbins, prin.
Other Schools – See Syracuse

Campbell, Steuben Co., Pop. Code 5
Campbell Central SD
Sch. Sys. Enr. Code 3
Supt. – Stephen Morley, RURAL ROUTE 02 14821
ES, MAIN STREET 14821 – Gerald Brown, prin.

Canajoharie, Montgomery Co., Pop. Code 4
Canajoharie Central SD
Sch. Sys. Enr. Code 4
Supt. – T. Mickle, 10 ERIE BLVD 13317
JHS, 2 ERIE BLVD 13317 – O. Simonsen, prin.
East Hill MS 13317 – Oliver Simonsen, prin.
West Hill ES 13317 – Oliver Simonsen, prin.

Canandaigua, Ontario Co., Pop. Code 7
Canandaigua Central SD
Sch. Sys. Enr. Code 5
Supt. – John Eckhardt, 143 N PEARL ST 14424
Canandaigua Jr. Academy, 235 N MAIN ST 14424
Charles Carlson, prin.
MS, 470 S PEARL ST 14424 – David Diraddo, prin.
PS, WEST GIBSON STREET 14424
Eileen Gerace, prin.

St. Mary's ES, 16 GIBSON ST 14424

Canaseraga, Allegany Co., Pop. Code 3
Canaseraga Central SD
Sch. Sys. Enr. Code 2
Supt. – Michael Hall, E MAIN ST 14822
S, E MAIN ST 14822 – Michael Hall, prin.

Canastota, Madison Co., Pop. Code 5
Canastota Central SD
Sch. Sys. Enr. Code 4
Supt. – Vincent Albanese
220 N PETERBORO ST 13032
Peterboro Street ES, 220 N PETERBORO ST 13032
Edward Lee, prin.

Roberts Street MS, ROBERTS STREET 13032
Edward Lee, prin.
South Side ES, HIGH STREET 13032
Edward Lee, prin.

Candor, Tioga Co., Pop. Code 3
Candor Central SD
Sch. Sys. Enr. Code 3
Supt. – R. Barnes 13743
ES 13743 – George Wallace, prin.

Canisteo, Steuben Co., Pop. Code 5
Canisteo Central SD
Sch. Sys. Enr. Code 4
Supt. – Thomas McKeever
84 GREENWOOD ST 14823
ES, 120 GREENWOOD ST 14823
Nelson Mullen, prin.

Canton, St. Lawrence Co., Pop. Code 6
Canton Central SD
Sch. Sys. Enr. Code 4
Supt. – E. Stanley Howlett III, 99 STATE ST 13617
McKenney MS 13617 – D. Crosby III, prin.
Banford ES 13617 – Katherine Curro, prin.

St.Mary ES, 2 POWERS ST 13617

Cape Vincent, Jefferson Co., Pop. Code 3
Thousand Islands Central SD
Supt. – See Clayton
ES 13618 – William Montonna, prin.

Carle Place, Nassau Co., Pop. Code 6
Carle Place UFD
Sch. Sys. Enr. Code 4
Supt. – Albert Inserra, CHERRY LANE 11514
Cherry Lane ES, 168 CHERRY LN 11514
Gloria Weiner, prin.
Rushmore Avenue MS
251 RUSHMORE AVE 11514 – Patricia Kriss, prin.

Carmel, Putnam Co., Pop. Code 8
Carmel Central SD
Supt. – See Patterson
Fischer MS, 275 FAIR ST 10512
Thomas Higgins, prin.
Kent ES, ROUTE 52 10512
Robert Armitage, prin.
Kent PS, ROUTE 52 10512 – Karen Martin, prin.

St. James the Apostle ES
12 GLENEIDA AVE 10512

Caroga Lake, Fulton Co., Pop. Code 4
Wheelerville UFD
Sch. Sys. Enr. Code 2
Supt. – John Weiss 12032
Wheelerville ES 12032 – James Izzo, prin.

Carthage, Jefferson Co., Pop. Code 5
Carthage Central SD
Sch. Sys. Enr. Code 5
Supt. – Kenn Rishel
RURAL ROUTE 02 BOX 57B 13619
MS, RURAL ROUTE 02 BOX 57C 13619
James Newell, prin.
ES, BEAVER LN 13619 – William Tribol, prin.
West Carthage ES, 27 N JEFFERSON ST 13619
Oren Cook, prin.
Other Schools – See Black River, Great Bend

Augustinian ES Academy, 317 WEST ST 13619

Cassadaga, Chautauqua Co., Pop. Code 3
Cassadaga Valley Central SD
Supt. – See Sinclairville
ES, 175 MAPLE AVENUE 14718
Monique Valvo, prin.

Castleton-on-Hudson, Rensselaer Co., Pop. Code 4
East Greenbush Central SD
Supt. – See East Greenbush
Green Meadow ES, 1588 SCHUURMAN RD 12033
William Schwarz, prin.

Schodack Central SD
Sch. Sys. Enr. Code 3
Supt. – James Butterworth
1216 MAPLE HILL ROAD 12033
Maple Hill MS, 1216 MAPLE HILL ROAD 12033
Thomas Manko, prin.
Castleton ES
CAMPBELL & SCOTT AVENUES 12033
Gerald Friends, prin.

Cato, Cayuga Co., Pop. Code 2
Cato Meridian Central SD
Sch. Sys. Enr. Code 4
Supt. – Henry Safnauer 13033
Cato-Meridian ES 13033 – Deborah Bobo, prin.
Cato-Meridian MS 13033 – Thomas Manko, prin.

Catskill, Greene Co., Pop. Code 5
Catskill Central SD
Sch. Sys. Enr. Code 4
Supt. – John Shine, 347 W MAIN ST 12414
JHS, 347 W MAIN ST 12414
Buddy Lee Appel, prin.
Grandview MS, 10 GRANDVIEW AVE 12414
Melody Strudwick, prin.
Irving ES, ACADEMY STREET 12414
Larry Stewart, prin.

St. Patrick Catholic School
80 WOODLAND AVE 12414

Cattaraugus, Cattaraugus Co., Pop. Code 4
Cattaraugus Central SD
Sch. Sys. Enr. Code 3
Supt. – Frederick Thomsen, 1 CARTER ST 14719
Jefferson Street ES, JEFFERSON STREET 14719
Robert Hebert, prin.

Cayuga, Cayuga Co., Pop. Code 3
Union Springs Central SD
Supt. – See Union Springs
ES, CHAPPELL ROAD 13034 – David Jerva, prin.

Cazenovia, Madison Co., Pop. Code 5
Cazenovia Central SD
Sch. Sys. Enr. Code 4
Supt. – Donald Squires, 31 EMORY AVE 13035
Burton Street ES, BURTON STREET 13035
Richard Nichols, prin.
Green Street MS, GREEN STREET 13035
Paul Darnall, prin.

Cedarhurst, Nassau Co., Pop. Code 6
Lawrence UFD
Supt. – See Lawrence
ES 5, CEDARHURST & FIFTH 11516
Sabato Caponi, prin.

St. Joachim ES
CENTRAL AVENUE AND MCGLYNN 11516

Celoron, Chautauqua Co., Pop. Code 4
Southwestern Central SD
Supt. – See Jamestown
ES, DUNHAM AVE 14720 – Linda Swanson, prin.

Centereach, Suffolk Co., Pop. Code 8
Middle Country Central SD
Supt. – See Selden
Dawnwood MS, 43RD ST 11720 – John Reid, prin.
Holbrook Road ES, HOLBROOK ROAD 11720
Paul Tubin, prin.
Jericho ES, NORTH COLEMAN ROAD 11720
Paula Downs, prin.
North Coleman Road ES
NORTH COLEMAN ROAD 11720
Meryl Baumann, prin.
Oxhead Road ES, OXHEAD ROAD 11720
John Scirica, prin.

Center Moriches, Suffolk Co., Pop. Code 5
Center Moriches UFD
Sch. Sys. Enr. Code 4
Supt. – Clayton Huey, 511 MAIN ST 11934
Huey ES, 511 MAIN ST 11934
Martin Rubinstein, prin.

St. John the Evangelist ES, 2 ST JOHN'S PL 11934

Central Islip, Suffolk Co., Pop. Code 8
Central Islip UFD
Sch. Sys. Enr. Code 6
Supt. – James Gentilcore
50 WHEELER ROAD 11722
Reed MS, HALF MILE ROAD 11722
John Cassidy, prin.
Morrow ES, SYCAMORE LANE 11722
Donald Dapolito, prin.
Mulligan ES, BROADWAY 11722
John Heinz, prin.
Mulvey ES, BOULEVARD AVENUE 11722
Robert Di Martino, prin.
O'Neill ES, CLAYTON STREET 11722
Edward O'Donnell, prin.

St. John of God ES, 82 CARLETON AVE 11722

Central Square, Oswego Co., Pop. Code 4
Central Square Central SD
Sch. Sys. Enr. Code 5
Supt. – Paul Besser, MAIN ST 13036
Millard Hawk JHS 13036 – Keith Krause, prin.
ES 13036 – William McKee, prin.
Mallory ES 13036 – Robert Raymond, prin.
Other Schools – See Brewerton, Cleveland, Constantia

Central Valley, Orange Co., Pop. Code 3
Monroe-Woodbury Central SD
Sch. Sys. Enr. Code 5
Supt. – D. Alexander, EDUC CTR 10917
Monroe-Woodbury MS, RURAL ROUTE 32 10917
Richard Moomey, prin.
ES, SMITH CLOVE ROAD 10917
Charlene Bowler, prin.
Other Schools – See Monroe

Chadwicks, Oneida Co., Pop. Code 3
Sauquoit Valley Central SD
Supt. – See Sauquoit
Chadwicks JHS, 3354 ONEIDA ST 13319
Marianne Degraaf, prin.

Champlain, Clinton Co., Pop. Code 4
Northeastern Clinton Central SD
Sch. Sys. Enr. Code 4
Supt. – Christopher Degrandpre 12919
JHS 12919 – Raymond Lavoie, prin.
ES 12919 – Kristine Mulvihill, prin.
Other Schools – See Mooers, Rouses Point

St. Mary's ES, 47 MAIN ST 12919

Chappaqua, Westchester Co., Pop. Code 6
Chappaqua Central SD
Sch. Sys. Enr. Code 6
Supt. – John Connolly, P O BOX 21 10514
Bell MS, 50 SENTER ST 10514
Thomas Cardellichio, prin.

Grafflin ES, 650 KING ST 10514
  Dr. Michael Kirsch, prin.
Roaring Brook ES, 530 QUAKER RD 10514
  Mark Soss, prin.
Westorchard ES, GRANITE RD 10514
  Frederick Wilhelm, prin.

Chateaugay, Franklin Co., Pop. Code 3
  Chateaugay Central SD
  Sch. Sys. Enr. Code 3
  Supt. – Patrick Calnon, RIVER ST 12920
  ES, RIVER STREET 12920 – George Carlisto, prin.

Chatham, Columbia Co., Pop. Code 4
  Chatham Central SD
  Sch. Sys. Enr. Code 4
  Supt. – Lee Wilson, 48 WOODBRIDGE AVE 12037
  MS 12037 – Dolores Horan, prin.
  Dardess ES 12037 – John McGurgan, prin.

Chaumont, Jefferson Co., Pop. Code 3
  Lyme Central SD
  Sch. Sys. Enr. Code 2
  Supt. – Pasquale Caramanna, ACADEMY ST 13622
  Lyme Central S, P O BOX 219 13622
  Bill Moore, prin.

Chautauqua, Chautauqua Co., Pop. Code 5
  Chautauqua Central SD
  Sch. Sys. Enr. Code 2
  Supt. – R. Dimicco, P O BOX 1097 14722
  Turner ES 14722 – A. Jonus, prin.

Chazy, Clinton Co., Pop. Code 5
  Chazy UFD
  Sch. Sys. Enr. Code 3
  Supt. – Charles O'Connor 12921
  Chazy Central Rural ES
    CHAZY CENTRAL RURAL 12921
  Jerry Ducatte, prin.

Cheektowaga, Erie Co., Pop. Code 9
  Cheektowaga Central SD
  Sch. Sys. Enr. Code 4
  Supt. – Leslie Lewis, 3600 UNION ROAD 14225
  Union East ES, 3550 UNION RD 14225
    William Koepf, prin.
  Other Schools – See Buffalo

  Cheektowaga-Maryvale UFD
  Sch. Sys. Enr. Code 5
  Supt. – R. Binner, 1050 MARYVALE DR 14225
  Maryvale MS, 1050 MARYVALE DR 14225
    Burt Sellers, prin.
  Maryvale IS, 1050 MARYVALE DR 14225
    Charles Knight, prin.
  Maryvale PS, 1 NAGEL DR 14225
    James Mancuso, prin.

  Cheektowago-Sloan UFD
  Supt. – See Buffalo
  Roosevelt ES, 2495 WILLIAM ST 14206
    Victor Burgio, prin.

  Cleveland Hill UFD
  Sch. Sys. Enr. Code 4
  Supt. – Kenneth Dyl
    105 MAPLEVIEW ROAD 14225
  Cleveland Hill MS, MAPLEVIEW DR 14225
    Edward Knab, prin.
  Cleveland Hill ES, MAPLEVIEW DRIVE 14225
    Dale Hawkins, prin.

  Infant of Prague ES, 921 CLEVELAND DR 14225
  Most Holy Redeemer ES, 16 ALPINE PL 14225
  Mother of Divine Grace ES
    500 MARYVALE AVE 14225
  Our Lady Help Christian ES
    4115 UNION RD 14225
  Queen of Martyrs ES, 170 ROSEWOOD TER 14225

Chemung, Chemung Co., Pop. Code 4
  Waverly Central SD
  Supt. – See Waverly
  ES, NORTH STREET 14825
    Joseph McGuire, Jr., prin.

Chenango Forks, Broome Co., Pop. Code 7
  Chenango Forks Central SD
  Supt. – See Binghamton
  Kenyon MS, RURAL ROUTE 02 BOX 572 13746
    Carole Huff, prin.

Cherry Valley, Otsego Co., Pop. Code 3
  Cherry Valley-Springfield Central SD
  Sch. Sys. Enr. Code 2
  Supt. – C. Schrader, P O BOX E 13320
  Other Schools – See East Springfield, Springfield
    Center

Chester, Orange Co., Pop. Code 4
  Chester UFD
  Sch. Sys. Enr. Code 3
  Supt. – E. Stoddard, 1 MAPLE AVE 10918
  ES, 1 SURREY RD 10918
    William Castellane, prin.

  St. Columba School, 33 HIGH ST 10918

Chittenango, Madison Co., Pop. Code 5
  Chittenango Central SD
  Sch. Sys. Enr. Code 5
  Supt. – Mark Desanctis, RURAL ROUTE 02 13037
  Bolivar Road MS, RURAL ROUTE 03 13037
    Howard Beach, prin.
  Chittenango Station ES, RURAL ROUTE 02 13037
    Elizabeth Cornell, prin.

Lake Street MS, 100 LAKE ST 13037
  William Moth, prin.
Other Schools – See Bridgeport

Churchville, Monroe Co., Pop. Code 4
  Churchville Chili Central SD
  Sch. Sys. Enr. Code 5
  Supt. – David Ryan
    139 FAIRBANKS ROAD 14428
  Churchville-Chili MS
    139 FAIRBANKS ROAD 14428 – Joe Hoff, prin.
  ES, 36 W BUFFALO ST 14428
    George Wright, prin.
  Fairbanks Road ES, 175 FAIRBANKS RD 14428
    Ralph Maniscalco, prin.
  Other Schools – See Rochester

Cicero, Onondaga Co., Pop. Code 7
  North Syracuse Central SD
  Supt. – See North Syracuse
  ES, ROUTE 31 13039 – Robert Maloney, prin.

Cincinnatus, Cortland Co., Pop. Code 4
  Cincinnatus Central SD
  Sch. Sys. Enr. Code 3
  Supt. – Andrea Price 13040
  ES 13040 – Daryl Mattison, prin.

Circleville, Orange Co.
  Pine Bush Central SD
  Supt. – See Pine Bush
  MS, RURAL ROUTE 302 10919
    Barry Foster, prin.
  ES, ROUTE 302 10919 – Ralph Tavino, prin.
  Pakanasink ES, ROUTE 302 10919
    Steven Fisch, prin.

Clarence, Erie Co., Pop. Code 7
  Clarence Central SD
  Sch. Sys. Enr. Code 5
  Supt. – R. Moomaw, P O BOX T 14031
  JHS, P O BOX T 14031 – J. Ballard, prin.
  Ledgeview ES, 5150 OLD GOODRICH RD 14031
    Stephen Radi, prin.
  Other Schools – See Clarence Center, Williamsville

Clarence Center, Erie Co.
  Clarence Central SD
  Supt. – See Clarence
  ES, 9600 CLARENCE CENTER RD 14032
    Arnold Bartlett, prin.

Clarksville, Albany Co.
  Bethlehem Central SD
  Supt. – See Delmar
  Clarksville ES, OLIVE STREET 12041
    Cheryl MacCulloch, prin.

Claverack, Columbia Co., Pop. Code 6
  Hudson CSD
  Supt. – See Hudson
  ES 12513 – Carol Gans, prin.

Clay, Onondaga Co.
  North Syracuse Central SD
  Supt. – See North Syracuse
  Gillette Road MS, RURAL ROUTE 04 13041
    David Morton, prin.
  Lakeshore ES, 7180 LAKESHORE RD 13041
    Kathleen Gramet, prin.

Clayton, Jefferson Co., Pop. Code 4
  Thousand Islands Central SD
  Sch. Sys. Enr. Code 4
  Supt. – Gary Jadwin 13624
  ES 13624 – Sharon Coleman, prin.
  Other Schools – See Cape Vincent

Cleveland, Oswego Co., Pop. Code 3
  Central Square Central SD
  Supt. – See Central Square
  ES 13042 – David Redmore, prin.

Clifton Park, Saratoga Co., Pop. Code 7
  Shenendehowa Central SD
  Sch. Sys. Enr. Code 6
  Supt. – Edward McHale, P O BOX 57 12065
  Arongen ES, P O BOX 54 12065
    Richard Roberts, prin.
  Karigon ES, P O BOX 50 12065
    Douglas Johnson, prin.
  Okte ES, P O BOX 16 12065 – John Lewis, prin.
  Orenda ES, P O BOX 51 12065 – Ann Frantti, prin.
  Skano ES, P O BOX 52 12065 – Bruce Hull, prin.
  Tesago ES, P O BOX 53 12065
    Vincent Delucia, prin.
  Other Schools – See Ballston Lake

Clifton Springs, Ontario Co., Pop. Code 4
  Phelps-Clifton Springs Central SD
  Sch. Sys. Enr. Code 4
  Supt. – R. Heller 14432
  ES, TEFT AVENUE 14432 – John McGrath, prin.
  Other Schools – See Phelps

Clinton, Oneida Co., Pop. Code 4
  Clinton Central SD
  Sch. Sys. Enr. Code 4
  Supt. – James Torrance
    75 CHENANGO AVE 13323
  JHS, COLLEGE ST 13323 – Terrance Brewer, prin.
  ES, 75 CHENANGO AVE 13323
    Kevin Aubel, prin.

  St. Mary's ES, 5 PROSPECT ST 13323

Clinton Corners, Dutchess Co.

Upton Lake Christian School, P O BOX 63 12514

Clintonville, Clinton Co.
  Ausable Valley Central SD
  Sch. Sys. Enr. Code 4
  Supt. – James Lagoy 12924
  Other Schools – See Au Sable Forks, Keeseville

Clyde, Wayne Co., Pop. Code 4
  Clyde-Savannah Central SD
  Sch. Sys. Enr. Code 4
  Supt. – Fred Goodrich, 215 GLASGOW ST 14433
  ES, WAYNE AVENUE 14433
    James Sebring, prin.
  Other Schools – See Savannah

Clymer, Chautauqua Co., Pop. Code 4
  Clymer Central SD
  Sch. Sys. Enr. Code 3
  Supt. – R. Reagle 14724
  ES 14724 – Durwood Swanson, prin.
  Findley Lake ES 14724 – Durwood Swanson, prin.

Cobleskill, Schoharie Co., Pop. Code 6
  Cobleskill Central SD
  Sch. Sys. Enr. Code 4
  Supt. – Samuel Shevat, ELM ST 12043
  Aker MS, LARK ST 12043 – Samuel Warner, prin.
  Ryder ES, ELM STREET 12043
    William Miller, prin.

Coeymans, Albany Co., Pop. Code 6
  Ravena Coeymans Selkirk CSD
  Supt. – See Selkirk
  MS, CHURCH ST 12045 – George Montone, prin.

Cohocton, Steuben Co., Pop. Code 3
  Cohocton Central SD
  Sch. Sys. Enr. Code 2
  Supt. – Louis Rizzieri, 30 PARK AVE 14826
  Cohocton Central S, 30 PARK AVE 14826
    Timothy Bolton, prin.

Cohoes, Albany Co., Pop. Code 7
  Cohoes CSD
  Sch. Sys. Enr. Code 4
  Supt. – Michael Osnato, 2 JOHNSTON AVE 12047
  MS, 7 BEVAN ST 12047 – Frank Gorleski, prin.
  Harmony Hill ES, ELM ST 12047
    Gary Signor, prin.
  Lansing ES, 27 JAMES ST 12047
    Dominic Mucci, prin.
  Van Schaick Island ES
    150 CONTINENTAL AVE 12047
    Robert Archambault, prin.

  St. Agnes Catholic School
    45 JOHNSTON AVE 12047
  St. Marie School
    LEVERSEE & DUDLEY AVES 12047

Colden, Erie Co., Pop. Code 5
  Springville-Griff Institute SD
  Supt. – See Springville
  ES 14033 – Thomas Nemmer, prin.

Cold Spring, Putnam Co., Pop. Code 4
  Haldane Central SD of Philipstown
  Sch. Sys. Enr. Code 3
  Supt. – Dudley Hare, 10 CRAIGSIDE DR 10516
  Haldane ES 10516 – Joanne Marien, prin.

Cold Spring Harbor, Suffolk Co., Pop. Code 6
  Cold Spring Harbor Central SD
  Sch. Sys. Enr. Code 4
  Supt. – Francis Roberts, 334 MAIN ST 11724
  Other Schools – See Huntington, Syosset

College Point, Queens Co.
  Queens Borough SD 25
  Supt. – See Flushing
  Larkin ES, 12802 7TH AVE 11356
    Judith Engel, prin.
  Public ES 29, 12510 23RD AVE 11356
    Theresa Harris, prin.

Colton, St. Lawrence Co., Pop. Code 4
  Colton-Pierrepont Central SD
  Sch. Sys. Enr. Code 2
  Supt. – John Gratto 13625
  Colton Pierrepont ES 13625 – Joyce Monroe, prin.

Commack, Suffolk Co., Pop. Code 7
  Commack UFD
  Sch. Sys. Enr. Code 6
  Supt. – Joseph Del Russo, P O BOX 150 11725
  MS, VANDERBILT PKWY 11725
    Pamela Travis-Moore, prin.
  Burr IS, 235 BURR ROAD 11725
    Charles Heppeler, prin.
  Indian Hollow ES, 151 KINGS PARK RD 11725
    Fred Horowitz, prin.
  North Ridge ES, 300 TOWNLINE RD 11725
    Perry Bendicksen, prin.
  Rolling Hills ES, MCCULLOCH DRIVE 11725
    Gertrude Fishman, prin.
  Sawmill IS, 103 NEW HWY 11725
    Peter Flanagan, prin.
  Wood Park ES, 15 NEW HWY 11725
    George Baer, prin.

  Christ the King ES, 2 INDIAN HEAD RD 11725
  Schechter Day ES-Suffolk
    74 HAUPPAUGE RD 11725

Congers, Rockland Co., Pop. Code 6
  Clarkstown Central SD
  Supt. – See West Nyack

ES, 57 LAKE RD W   10920
  Elizabeth Carbone, prin.
Lake Wood ES, 77 LAKELAND AVE   10920
  Robert Looney, prin.

Rockland Country Day School, KINGS HWY   10920

Conklin, Broome Co., Pop. Code 6
Susquehanna Valley Central SD
Sch. Sys. Enr. Code 4
Supt. – V. Gerhard, 1040 CONKLIN ROAD   13748
Donnelly ES, P O BOX 250   13748
  Mary Charsky, prin.
Other Schools – See Binghamton, Kirkwood

Constableville, Lewis Co., Pop. Code 2
South Lewis Central SD
Supt. – See Turin
ES   13325 – John Hathway, prin.

Constantia, Oswego Co., Pop. Code 3
Central Square Central SD
Supt. – See Central Square
ES   13044 – Franklyn Dunham, prin.

Cooperstown, Otsego Co., Pop. Code 4
Cooperstown Central SD
Sch. Sys. Enr. Code 4
Supt. – Douglas Bradshaw, LINDEN AVE   13326
ES, 21 WALNUT ST   13326
  Douglas Geertgens, prin.

Copenhagen, Lewis Co., Pop. Code 3
Copenhagen Central SD
Sch. Sys. Enr. Code 3
Supt. – Michael Smith, MECHANIC ST   13626
ES, MECHANIC STREET   13626
  Michael Johndrow, prin.

Copiague, Suffolk Co., Pop. Code 7
Copiague UFD
Sch. Sys. Enr. Code 5
Supt. – George Apuzzi
  2650 GREAT NECK ROAD   11726
JHS, 2650 GREAT NECK ROAD   11726
  Albert Voorneveld, prin.
Deauville Gardens ES
  100 DEAUVILLE BLVD   11726
  Robert Donnellan, prin.
Great Neck Road ES
  1400 GREAT NECK RD   11726
  Catherine Quinn, prin.
Wiley ES, OFF SCUDDER AVENUE   11726
  Elizabeth Eide, prin.

Copiague Christian Academy
  2675 GREAT NECK RD   11726

Coram, Suffolk Co., Pop. Code 6
Longwood Central SD
Supt. – See Middle Island
ES, MOUNT SINAI ROAD   11727
  Edward Mavragis, prin.

Corfu, Genesee Co., Pop. Code 3
Pembroke Central SD
Sch. Sys. Enr. Code 4
Supt. – Richard Kelly
  RURAL ROUTE 05 & 77   14036
Pembroke IS, ALLEGHENY ROAD   14036
  Lawrence Sformo, prin.
Other Schools – See East Pembroke

Corinth, Saratoga Co., Pop. Code 5
Corinth Central SD
Sch. Sys. Enr. Code 4
Supt. – Thomas Gould, 105 OAK ST   12822
Main Sreet ES, 105 OAK ST   12822
  Marlene Kyea, prin.
Oak Street ES, 105 OAK ST   12822
  Marlene Kyea, prin.
Palmer Avenue ES, 105 OAK ST   12822
  Marlene Kyea, prin.

Corning, Steuben Co., Pop. Code 7
Corning CSD
Supt. – See Painted Post
Corning Free Academy MS, 11 W THIRD ST   14830
  Roger Grigsby, prin.
Northside Blodgett MS
  143 PRINCETON AVE   14830
  Sheldon Guss, prin.
Carder ES, STATE & WEST SIXTH STREET   14830
  Stephen Glantz, prin.
Gregg ES, FLINT AVENUE   14830
  Grant Sharman, prin.
Phillips ES, 120 CORNING BLVD   14830
  Grant Sharman, prin.
Severn ES, 51 MCMAHON AVE   14830
  Nicholas Rossi, prin.
Winfield Street ES, 194 WINFIELD ST   14830
  Ross Perry, prin.

All Saints Academy, 158 STATE ST   14830
Christian Learning Center, P O BOX 45   14830

Cornwall, Orange Co., Pop. Code 7
Cornwall Central SD
Supt. – See Cornwall on Hudson
ES, LEE RD   12518 – Robert Martens, prin.
Willow Avenue MS, 67 WILLOW AVE   12518
  John Shepard, prin.

Cornwall on Hudson, Orange Co., Pop. Code 5
Cornwall Central SD
Sch. Sys. Enr. Code 4
Supt. – Richard Brodow
  95 ACADEMY AVE   12520
ES, 234 HUDSON ST   12520 – Ronald Young, prin.
Other Schools – See Cornwall

St. Thomas of Canterbury ES
  336 HUDSON ST   12520

Corona, Queens Co.
Queens Borough SD 24
Supt. – See Middle Village
Da Vinci IS, 9850 50TH AVE   11368
  Louis Larocco, prin.
Fairview ES, 10701 OTIS AVE   11368
  Walter Liff, prin.
Lake ES, 99TH & ROOSEVELT AVENUE   11368
  Irene Nash, prin.
Meadow ES, 3474 113TH ST   11368
  Thomas Rooney, prin.

Queens Borough SD 30
Supt. – See Long Island City
Leverich ES, 9901 34TH AVE   11368
  Katheleen Murphy, prin.

Cortland, Cortland Co., Pop. Code 7
Cortland CSD
Sch. Sys. Enr. Code 5
Supt. – Harvey Kaufman
  VALLEY VIEW DR   13045
Barry ES, RAYMOND AVENUE   13045
  Fred Amante, prin.
Parker ES, 89 MADISON ST   13045
  Thomas Marzeski, prin.
Randall ES, RANDALL STREET   13045
  George Purcell, prin.
Smith ES, 33 WHEELER AVE   13045
  R. Carsello, prin.
Virgil ES, RURAL ROUTE 02   13045
  Lynn New, prin.

Cortland Christian Academy
  15 WEST ROAD   13045
St. Mary's ES, 61 N MAIN ST   13045

Coxsackie, Greene Co., Pop. Code 5
Coxsackie Athens Central SD
Sch. Sys. Enr. Code 4
Supt. – S. Delucia, 24 SUNSET BLVD   12051
ES, 24 SUNSET BLVD   12051
  Frank Gerrain, prin.
Other Schools – See Athens

Crompond, Westchester Co.
Lakeland CSD of Shrub Oak
Supt. – See Shrub Oak
Titus ES   10517 – John Millicker, prin.

Croton, Westchester Co., Pop. Code 6
Croton-Harmon UFD
Sch. Sys. Enr. Code 4
Supt. – D. Siegel, GERSTEIN ST   10520
Van Cortlandt MS, LARKIN PLACE   10520
  Joseph Zajac, prin.
Tompkins ES, ARMSTRONG DRIVE   10520
  Barbara Lofthouse, prin.

Croton Falls, Westchester Co., Pop. Code 4

St. Joseph ES, CROTON FLS RD   10519

Crown Point, Essex Co., Pop. Code 4
Crown Point Central SD
Sch. Sys. Enr. Code 2
Supt. – Alan McCartney, P O BOX 35   12928
Crown Point Central S, P O BOX 35   12928
  Alan McCartney, prin.

Cuba, Allegany Co., Pop. Code 4
Cuba Central SD
Sch. Sys. Enr. Code 3
Supt. – Richard Backer, 15 ELM ST   14727
ES, 16 ELM ST   14727 – Michael Kunz, prin.

Cuddebackville, Orange Co.
Port Jervis CSD
Supt. – See Port Jervis
Hamilton Bicentenia ES, ROUTE 209   12729
  Mary Haley, prin.

Cutchogue, Suffolk Co., Pop. Code 3

Sacred Heart ES, P O BOX 970   11935

Dalton, Livingston Co.
Dalton-Nunda Central SD
Supt. – See Nunda
Keshequa ES, CHURCH & MAPLE   14836
  Mary Jo McPhail, prin.

Dannemora, Clinton Co., Pop. Code 5
Saranac Central SD
Supt. – See Saranac
ES, BOUCK ST   12929 – Kenneth Cringle, prin.

Dansville, Livingston Co., Pop. Code 5
Dansville Central SD
Sch. Sys. Enr. Code 4
Supt. – Donald Bartalo, 285 MAIN ST   14437
PS, MAIN ST   14437 – Bonnie Trippi, prin.
Hyde MS, MAIN STREET   14437
  Nancy Hussey, prin.

St. Mary ES, 43 ELIZABETH ST   14437

Davenport, Delaware Co., Pop. Code 4
Charlotte Valley Central SD
Sch. Sys. Enr. Code 2
Supt. – David Whipple   13750
Charlotte Valley S, ROUTE 23   13750
  John Tucci, prin.

Deer Park, Suffolk Co., Pop. Code 8
Deer Park UFD
Sch. Sys. Enr. Code 5
Supt. – Ronald Paras, 81 LAKE AVE   11729
Adams ES, 172 OLD COUNTRY RD   11729
  Corynne Klein, prin.
Kennedy IS, 101 LAKE AVE   11729
  Leo O'Reilly, prin.
Moore ES, 239 CENTRAL AVE   11729
  Samuel Skidmore, prin.

SS. Cyril & Methods ES
  105 HALF HOLLOW RD   11729

De Kalb Junction, St. Lawrence Co., Pop. Code 4
Hermon-DeKalb Central SD
Sch. Sys. Enr. Code 3
Supt. – Richard Nelson
  RURAL ROUTE 01 BOX 13   13630
Hermon Dekalb ES   13630 – Russell Forbes, prin.

Delanson, Schenectady Co., Pop. Code 2
Duanesburg Central SD
Sch. Sys. Enr. Code 3
Supt. – C. Guyder   12053
Duanesburg ES   12053 – Diane McIver, prin.

Delevan, Cattaraugus Co., Pop. Code 4
Yorkshire-Pioneer Central SD
Supt. – See Yorkshire
ES, P O BOX 217   14042 – Michael Medden, prin.

Delhi, Delaware Co., Pop. Code 5
Delhi Central SD
Sch. Sys. Enr. Code 4
Supt. – R. Zajack   13753
Delaware Academy ES   13753
  Michelle Turner, prin.
Other Schools – See Treadwell

Delmar, Albany Co., Pop. Code 6
Bethlehem Central SD
Sch. Sys. Enr. Code 5
Supt. – Leslie Loomis, 90 ADAMS PL   12054
Bethlehem Central MS
  332 KENWOOD AVE   12054 – F. Burdick, prin.
Elsmere ES, 247 DELAWARE AVE   12054
  Dorothy Whitney, prin.
Hamagrael ES, 15 MCGUFFEY LN   12054
  Joseph Schaefer, prin.
Slingerland ES, 25 UNION AVE   12054
  David Murphy, prin.
Other Schools – See Clarksville, Glenmont

St. Thomas the Apostle ES, 42 ADAMS PL   12054

Depew, Erie Co., Pop. Code 7
Depew UFD
Sch. Sys. Enr. Code 5
Supt. – George Drescher, S TRANSIT ROAD   14043
MS, 5201 TRANSIT ROAD   14043
  Edward Mooradian, prin.
Cayuga Heights ES
  COMO PARK BOULEVARD   14043
  Eugene Hale, prin.

Lancaster Central SD
Supt. – See Lancaster
Sciole ES, 86 ALYS DR E   14043
  Arlene Boardway, prin.

Our Lady of Blessed Sacrament ES
  20 FRENCH RD   14043
SS. Peter & Paul ES, 52 BURLINGTON AVE   14043
St. Barnabas ES
  2099 GEORGE URBAN BLVD   14043
St. James ES, 500 TERRACE BLVD   14043

Deposit, Broome Co., Pop. Code 4
Deposit Central SD
Sch. Sys. Enr. Code 3
Supt. – Ernest Rebstock, 2ND ST   13754
ES, 121 SECOND ST   13754 – (—), prin.

Derby, Erie Co.
Evans-Brant Central SD
Supt. – See Angola
Highland ES, 6745 ERIR ROAD   14047
  James Lehnen, prin.
Jerusalem Corners ES
  999 STURGEON POINT RD   14047
  James Lehnen, prin.

De Ruyter, Madison Co., Pop. Code 3
De Ruyter Central SD
Sch. Sys. Enr. Code 3
Supt. – Dwayne Adsitt, 711 RAILROAD ST   13052
ES, 711 RAILROAD ST   13052
  Marilyn Phelan, prin.

De Witt, Onondaga Co., Pop. Code 7
Jamesville-DeWitt Central SD
Sch. Sys. Enr. Code 4
Supt. – Gene Spanneut, EDINGER DR   13214
ES, JAMESVILLE ROAD   13214
  Robert Dewey, prin.
Other Schools – See Jamesville

Manlius Pebble Hill School
  5300 JAMESVILLE ROAD   13214

Dexter, Jefferson Co., Pop. Code 4
Gen. Brown Central SD
Supt. – See Brownville
ES   13634 – George O'Brien, prin.

Dix Hills, Suffolk Co., Pop. Code 6
Half Hollow Hills Central SD
Supt. – See Melville
Forest Park ES, 30 DEFOREST RD   11746
Stanley Opas, prin.
Otsego ES, 55 OTSEGO AVE   11746
Joan Valle, prin.
Paumanok ES, 1 SEAMAN NECK RD   11746
Louis Guiliano, prin.
Signal Hill ES, 670 CALEDONIA RD   11746
Philip Carolan, prin.
Vanderbilt ES, 350 DEER PARK AVE   11746
Linda Bruno, prin.

Upper Room Christian School
722 DEER PARK ROAD   11746

Dobbs Ferry, Westchester Co., Pop. Code 7
Dobbs Ferry UFD
Sch. Sys. Enr. Code 3
Supt. – R. Gerson, BROADWAY   10522
MS, BROADWAY   10522 – John O'Mahoney, prin.
Springhurst ES, WALGROVE AVENUE   10522
Marjorie Castro, prin.

Sacred Heart ES, 535 BROADWAY   10522

Dolgeville, Herkimer Co., Pop. Code 5
Dolgeville Central SD
Sch. Sys. Enr. Code 4
Supt. – Robert Smith   13329
ES, MAIN STREET   13329 – Susan Benati, prin.

Douglaston, Queens Co.
Queens Borough SD 26
Supt. – See Bayside
Public ES 98, 4020 235TH ST   11363
Janet Bernsten, prin.

Dover Plains, Dutchess Co., Pop. Code 3
Dover UFD
Sch. Sys. Enr. Code 4
Supt. – J. Bruce McKenna, P O BOX 132   12522
Dover MS, SCHOOL STREET   12522
Margaret Dames, prin.
Other Schools – See Wingdale

Downsville, Delaware Co., Pop. Code 3
Downsville Central SD
Sch. Sys. Enr. Code 2
Supt. – Weston Hyde, P O BOX J   13755
Downsville Central S, P O BOX J   13755
Joseph Ivanenok, prin.

Dryden, Tompkins Co., Pop. Code 4
Dryden Central SD
Sch. Sys. Enr. Code 4
Supt. – John Wheeler, DRYDEN ROAD   13053
Cassavant ES, P O BOX 88   13053
George Burtis, prin.
IS, P O BOX 88   13053 – Ralph Undercoffler, prin.
PS, P O BOX 88   13053 – Leslie Cleland, prin.
Other Schools – See Freeville

Dundee, Yates Co., Pop. Code 4
Dundee Central SD
Sch. Sys. Enr. Code 3
Supt. – Donald Averill, 55 WATER ST   14837
ES, 55 WATER ST   14837 – Robert Delbono, prin.

Dunkirk, Chautauqua Co., Pop. Code 7
Dunkirk CSD
Sch. Sys. Enr. Code 4
Supt. – Terry Wolfenden
201 LAKE SHORE DRIVE E   14048
MS, 525 EAGLE ST   14048
Richard Peterson, prin.
Public ES 3, LAMPHERE STREET   14048
Louis Gugino, prin.
Public ES 4, CENTRAL AVENUE   14048
Robert Block, prin.
Public ES 5, BRIGHAM ROAD   14048
Richard Clifton, prin.
Public ES 6, BENTON STREET   14048
John Warren, prin.
Public ES 7, LAKE SHORE DRIVE EAST   14048
Leon Price, prin.

Holy Trinity ES, 1020 CENTRAL AVE   14048
St. Elizabeth Seton ES
336 WASHINGTON AVE   14048
St. Hyacinth ES, 12 N PANGOLIN ST   14048

Durham, Greene Co., Pop. Code 4
Cairo-Durham Central SD
Supt. – See Cairo
ES, ROUTE 145 BOX 53   12422
Janet Murray, prin.

Durhamville, Oneida Co.
Oneida CSD
Supt. – See Oneida
ES, MAIN STREET   13054
David Gillmeister, prin.

Earlville, Chenango Co., Pop. Code 3
Sherburne Earlville Central SD
Supt. – See Sherburne
MS, FAYETTE STREET   13332
Donald Dubois, prin.

East Amherst, Erie Co., Pop. Code 3
Williamsville Central SD
Supt. – See Buffalo
Dodge ES, 1900 DODGE RD   14051
Ronald Seaver, prin.

East Aurora, Erie Co., Pop. Code 6
East Aurora
Sch. Sys. Enr. Code 4
Supt. – Thomas Fowler-Finn, 430 MAIN ST   14052
MS, 430 MAIN ST   14052 – Dennis Leach, prin.
Main Street MS, 430 MAIN ST   14052
Dan Gard, prin.
Parkdale ES, 140 PARKDALE AVE   14052
Julia Weidemann, prin.

Iroquois Central SD
Supt. – See Elma
Wales ES, WOODCHUCK ROAD   14052
Denis Funseth, prin.

Immaculate Conception ES
510 OAKWOOD AVE   14052

East Bloomfield, Ontario Co., Pop. Code 3
East Bloomfield Central SD
Sch. Sys. Enr. Code 4
Supt. – R. Jack Siring   14443
Other Schools – See Holcomb

Eastchester, Westchester Co., Pop. Code 8
Eastchester UFD
Sch. Sys. Enr. Code 4
Supt. – Charles Murphy
580 WHITE PLAINS ROAD   10707
JHS, 550 WHITE PLAINS ROAD   10707
Donald Howard, prin.
Hutchinson ES, MILL ROAD   10709
Hugh Bartlett, prin.
Other Schools – See Scarsdale

Tuckahoe UFD
Sch. Sys. Enr. Code 3
Supt. – Anthony Mazzullo
69 CRAWFORD DRIVE   10707
Other Schools – See Yonkers

East Elmhurst, Queens Co.
Queens Borough SD 30
Supt. – See Long Island City
ES, 98TH STREET AND 25TH AVE   11369
Carmen Mathew, prin.
Public ES 148, 8902 32ND AVE   11369
Sal Romano, prin.

East Greenbush, Rensselaer Co., Pop. Code 7
East Greenbush Central SD
Sch. Sys. Enr. Code 5
Supt. – Robert Reidy, ADMIN CENTER   12061
Goff MS, GILLIGAN ROAD   12061
Robert Palozzi, prin.
Genet MS, TROY ROAD   12061
Stephen Lobban, prin.
Other Schools – See Castleton-on-Hudson, Nassau,
Rensselaer, Troy

Holy Spirit ES, HIGHLAND DR   12061

East Hampton, Suffolk Co., Pop. Code 4
East Hampton UFD
Sch. Sys. Enr. Code 4
Supt. – Cornelius O'Connell
76 NEWTOWN LANE   11937
MS, 76 NEWTOWN LANE   11937 – Jay Niles, prin.
Marshall ES, 30 CHURCH ST   11937
Dennis Donatuti, prin.

Springs UFD
Sch. Sys. Enr. Code 2
Supt. – William Lycke, 48 SCHOOL ST   11937
Springs ES, 48 SCHOOL ST   11937
Peter Lisi, prin.

Most Holy Trinity ES, 44 MEADOWAY   11937

East Islip, Suffolk Co., Pop. Code 7
East Islip UFD
Supt. – See Islip Terrace
Kennedy ES, 94 WOODLAND DR   11730
William Kohlmorgen, prin.
Timber Point ES, 180 TIMBERPOINT RD   11730
Vincent Sulpizio, prin.

Hewlett School of East Islip
52 SUFFOLK LANE   11730
St. Mary ES, 16 HARRISON AVE   11730

East Meadow, Nassau Co., Pop. Code 8
East Meadow UFD
Sch. Sys. Enr. Code 6
Supt. – Howard Koenig, CARMAN AVE   11554
Barnum Woods ES, ROSE & KALDA LANE   11554
Peter Valente, prin.
McVey ES, DEVON STREET & FRANKLIN   11554
William Coddington, prin.
Meadowbrook ES, N NEW BRIDGE ROAD   11554
Marilyn Wranek, prin.
Parkway ES, BELLMORE ROAD   11554
Selma Tannenbaum, prin.
Other Schools – See Westbury

New Covenant Christian School
757 BELLMORE AVE   11554
St. Raphael ES, 600 NEWBRIDGE RD   11554

East Moriches, Suffolk Co., Pop. Code 4
East Moriches UFD
Sch. Sys. Enr. Code 3
Supt. – Charles Tufano, 9 ADELAIDE AVE   11940
ES, 9 ADELAIDE AVE   11940
Suzanne Ericksen, prin.

East Northport, Suffolk Co., Pop. Code 7
Elwood UFD
Supt. – See Greenlawn
Elwood MS, 478 ELWOOD ROAD   11731
Arthur Strassle, prin.
Harley Avenue ES, HARLEY AVE   11731
Virginia Cancroft, prin.

Northport-East Northport UFD
Supt. – See Northport
MS, FIFTH AVE   11731 – William Muller, prin.
Bellerose ES, 253 BELLEROSE AVE   11731
Ira Goodman, prin.
Dickinson Avenue ES
DICKINSON AVENUE   11731 – John Scurti, prin.
Fifth Avenue ES, 1157 5TH AVE   11731
Clifford Bishop, prin.
Pulaski Road ES, 623 9TH AVE   11731
Irene Smithwick, prin.

St. Anthony of Padua ES, FIFTH AVE   11731
St. Paul's Lutheran Day ES
106 VERNON VALLEY RD   11731

East Norwich, Nassau Co., Pop. Code 5
Oyster Bay-East Norwich Central SD
Supt. – See Oyster Bay
Vernon MS, RURAL ROUTE 106   11732
Joseph Ferraro, prin.

East Patchogue, Suffolk Co., Pop. Code 6
South Country Central SD
Sch. Sys. Enr. Code 6
Supt. – James Gerardi, 189 DUNTON AVE   11772
Critz ES, 185 N DUNTON AVE   11772
Denis Desera, prin.
Other Schools – See Bellport, Brookhaven

East Pembroke, Genesee Co.
Pembroke Central SD
Supt. – See Corfu
Pembrook PS, MAIN RD   14056
Phillip Tabone, prin.

Eastport, Suffolk Co., Pop. Code 4
Eastport UFD
Sch. Sys. Enr. Code 3
Supt. – Richard Evans
MONTAUK HIGHWAY   11941
S, MONTAUK HIGHWAY   11941
J. Gagliano, prin.

East Quogue, Suffolk Co., Pop. Code 4
East Quogue UFD
Sch. Sys. Enr. Code 2
Supt. – Margaret Burns, CENTRAL AVE   11942
ES, 6 CENTRAL AVE   11942
Margaret Miller, prin.

East Rochester, Monroe Co., Pop. Code 6
East Rochester UFD
Sch. Sys. Enr. Code 4
Supt. – Joseph Ennis, 108 EAST AVE   14445
Morgan MS, 108 EAST AVE   14445
Joseph Bascom, prin.
Bird ES, 108 EAST AVE   14445
John Carlevatti, prin.

East Rockaway, Nassau Co., Pop. Code 7
East Rockaway UFD
Sch. Sys. Enr. Code 4
Supt. – Rob Parry   11518
Centre Avenue ES, 55 CENTRE AVE   11518
James Newman, prin.
Rhame Avenue ES, RHAME AVENUE   11518
Ralph Grandinetti, prin.

Lynbrook UFD
Supt. – See Lynbrook
Waverly Park ES
WAVERLY AND PEPPERIDGE   11518
Barbara Hayes, prin.

St. Raymond ES, 263 ATLANTIC AVE   11518

East Setauket, Suffolk Co., Pop. Code 3
Three Village Central SD
Supt. – See Setauket
Arrowhead ES, ARROWHEAD LANE   11733
Olga Carlin, prin.
Minnesauke ES, 75 BENNETS RD   11733
John Burns, prin.

First Steps Discovery Center, P O BOX U   11733

East Springfield, Otsego Co.
Cherry Valley-Springfield Central SD
Supt. – See Cherry Valley
Cherry Valley-Springfield JHS   13333
Charles Culbert, prin.

East Syracuse, Onondaga Co., Pop. Code 5
East Syracuse-Minoa Central SD
Sch. Sys. Enr. Code 5
Supt. – Fritz Hess, 407 FREMONT ROAD   13057
Fremont MS, RICHMOND ROAD WEST   13057
Linda Clarkson, prin.
Heman Street ES, 121 E HEMAN ST   13057
Mary Hilgenberg, prin.

Kinne Street MS, 230 KINNE ST   13057
  Carolyne Pfeifer, prin.
Woodland ES, 6320 FREMONT RD   13057
  Starr Canestraro, prin.
Other Schools – See Minoa

St. Matthew's ES, 214 KINNE ST   13057

East Williston, Nassau Co., Pop. Code 5
East Williston UFD
Sch. Sys. Enr. Code 4
Supt. – Darrell Lund
  100 E WILLISTON AVE   11596
North Side ES, 110 E WILLISTON AVE   11596
  Pat Corsentino, prin.
Other Schools – See Roslyn Heights

Eden, Erie Co., Pop. Code 6
Eden Central SD
Sch. Sys. Enr. Code 4
Supt. – Donald Fregelette, P O BOX 267   14057
ES, P O BOX 267   14057 – Kyle Eklum, prin.

Edmeston, Otsego Co., Pop. Code 4
Edmeston Central SD
Sch. Sys. Enr. Code 2
Supt. – John Holdorf, 7 NORTH ST   13335
Edmeston Central S, 11 NORTH STREET   13335
  Howard Heffron, prin.

Edwards, St. Lawrence Co., Pop. Code 3
Edwards-Knox Central SD
Supt. – See Russell
Edwards S, TROUT LAKE ST   13635
  James Antwine, prin.

Elba, Genesee Co., Pop. Code 3
Elba Central SD
Sch. Sys. Enr. Code 3
Supt. – S. Giansante, 57 S MAIN ST   14058
ES, 57 S MAIN ST   14058 – Robert Creme, prin.

Elbridge, Onondaga Co., Pop. Code 4
Jordan Elbridge Central SD
Supt. – See Jordan
ES, EAST MAIN STREET   13060
  Arlene Sardo, prin.

Eldred, Sullivan Co.
Eldred Central SD
Sch. Sys. Enr. Code 3
Supt. – J. Horan   12732
Eldred Central S, P O BOX 249   12732
  Albert Wojtaszek, prin.

Elizabethtown, Essex Co., Pop. Code 3
Elizabethtown-Lewis Central SD
Sch. Sys. Enr. Code 2
Supt. – James Chunco, COURT ST   12932
Elizabethtown-Lewis Central S, COURT ST   12932
  James Tromblee, prin.

Ellenburg Depot, Clinton Co., Pop. Code 4
Northern Adirondack Central SD
Sch. Sys. Enr. Code 4
Supt. – William Scott   12935
North Adirondack ES   12935 – Cynthia Forth, prin.

Ellenville, Ulster Co., Pop. Code 5
Ellenville Central SD
Sch. Sys. Enr. Code 4
Supt. – Arnold Elman, 28 MAPLE AVE   12428
ES, MAPLE AVENUE   12428
  Milton Lachterman, prin.

Ellicottville, Cattaraugus Co., Pop. Code 3
Ellicottville Central SD
Sch. Sys. Enr. Code 3
Supt. – D. Sirianni
  RURAL ROUTE 01 BOX 52   14731
ES   14731 – Mark Ward, prin.

Elma, Erie Co., Pop. Code 7
Iroquois Central SD
Sch. Sys. Enr. Code 5
Supt. – Joseph Riordan, P O BOX 32   14059
Iroquois MS, P O BOX 32   14059 – K. Bartoo, prin.
ES, P O BOX 32   14059 – Patricia Hansen, prin.
Other Schools – See East Aurora, Marilla

Annunciation BVM ES, 7580 CLINTON ST   14059

Elmhurst-A, Queens Co.
Queens Borough SD 24
Supt. – See Middle Village
ES, 8528 BRITTON AVE   11373
  Cleo Losecco, prin.
Moore ES, 5501 94TH ST   11373
  Jeremiah McCabe, prin.
Public ES 102, 5524 VAN HORN ST   11373
  Harvey Sherer, prin.

Elmira, Chemung Co., Pop. Code 8
Elmira CSD
Sch. Sys. Enr. Code 6
Supt. – James Carter, 951 HOFFMAN ST   14905
Broadway MS, 1000 BROADWAY   14904
  Earl Bush, prin.
Davis MS, E CLINTON AND LAKE ST   14901
  Daile Rose, prin.
Beecher ES, 310 SULLIVAN & EAST 2ND   14901
  George Welch, prin.
Booth ES, W SECOND & DAVIS STREETS   14901
  Eugene Augustine, prin.
Broadway ES, 1000 BROADWAY ST   14904
  Joseph Madero, prin.
Coburn ES, 216 MOUNT ZOAR ST   14904
  Donald Keddell, prin.

Diven ES, DIVISION & HALL STREETS   14901
  Pamela Mathes, prin.
Hendy Avenue ES, HENDY AVENUE   14905
  Charles Paternoster, prin.
Riverside ES, 409 RIVERSIDE AVE   14904
  John Goodwin, prin.
Washington ES
  422-448 W WASHINGTON AVE   14901
  Leroy Opelt, prin.
Other Schools – See Pine City

Elmira Christian Academy
  235 E MILLER ST   14904
Holy Family JHS, 1010 DAVDIS ST   14901
Holy Family Inter. School
  301 DEMAREST PKY   14905
Holy Family PS, 421 FULTON ST   14904

Elmira Heights, Chemung Co., Pop. Code 5
Elmira Heights Central SD
Sch. Sys. Enr. Code 4
Supt. – Charles Clemens
  ROBINWOOD AVE   14903
Cohen ES, ROBINWOOD AVE   14903
  Livia Trexler, prin.

Elmont, Nassau Co., Pop. Code 8
Elmont UFD
Sch. Sys. Enr. Code 5
Supt. – Richard Caliendo, ELMONT ROAD   11003
Carlson ES, BELMONT BOULEVARD   11003
  Peter Daraio, prin.
Covert Avenue ES, COVERT AVENUE   11003
  Margaret Pletta, prin.
Dutch Broadway ES, DUTCH BROADWAY   11003
  John Biot, prin.
Gotham Avenue ES, 300 GOTHAM AVE   11003
  Dennis Lawlor, prin.
Other Schools – See Roosevelt Field, Valley Stream

St. Boniface ES, 621 ELMONT RD   11003
St. Vincent De Paul ES, 1510 DEPAUL ST   11003

Elmsford, Westchester Co., Pop. Code 5
Elmsford UFD
Sch. Sys. Enr. Code 3
Supt. – Rob Pauline, S HILLSIDE AVE   10523
Grady ES, COBB LANE   10523
  Francel Walker, prin.

Our Lady of Mt. Carmel School
  59 E MAIN ST   10523

Endicott, Broome Co., Pop. Code 7
Union-Endicott Central SD
Sch. Sys. Enr. Code 6
Supt. – Dennis Sweeney, 1401 BROAD ST   13760
Snapp MS, 101 S LODER AVE   13760
  T. Kurkoski, prin.
Johnson ES, 715 PADEN ST   13760
  Chester Symancyk, prin.
Johnson ES, 201 HILL AVE   13760
  George Weigand, prin.
McGuinness IS
  1201 UNION CTR-MNE HW   13760
  David Zandy, prin.
Nichols ES, 401 HAYES AVE   13760
  James Fountaine, prin.
Watson ES, RIDGEFIELD ROAD   13760
  M. Visser, prin.
West PS, 1201 UNION CTR-MNE HW   13670
  Jean Donlon, prin.

Seton Catholic MS, 1112 BROAD ST   13760
St. Anthony of Padua ES, 906 JENKINS ST   13760
St. Joseph ES, 210 N JACKSON AVE   13760

Endwell, Broome Co., Pop. Code 7
Maine Endwell Central SD
Sch. Sys. Enr. Code 5
Supt. – Phillip Burkholder
  712 FARM TO MARKET ROAD   13760
Maine Endwell MS
  1119 FARM TO MARKET ROAD   13760
  Suzanne Prach, prin.
Brink ES, 3614 BRIAR LN   13760
  Donald Conning, prin.
Other Schools – See Maine

Evans Mills, Jefferson Co., Pop. Code 3
Indian River Central SD
Supt. – See Philadelphia
ES, MAIN STREET   13637
  Richard DeForest, prin.

Fabius, Onondaga Co., Pop. Code 2
Fabius-Pompey Central SD
Sch. Sys. Enr. Code 3
Supt. – Donald Trombley, MAIN ST   13063
ES, MAIN STREET   13063 – Bonnie Dunn, prin.

Fairport, Monroe Co., Pop. Code 6
Fairport Central SD
Sch. Sys. Enr. Code 6
Supt. – Myles Bigenwald
  38 CHURCH ST W   14450
Perrin MS, 85 POTTER PLACE   14450
  James Valentine, prin.
Brooks Hill ES, 181 HULBERT RD   14450
  Nancy Grouse, prin.
Dudley ES, 211 HAMILTON RD   14450
  Paul Earnst, prin.
Jefferson Avenue ES, 303 JEFFERSON AVE   14450
  Marilyn Gizzie, prin.
Northside MS, 181 HAMILTON RD   14450
  Gary Dunton, prin.

St. John of Rochester ES
  10 WICKFORD WAY   14450

Falconer, Chautauqua Co., Pop. Code 5
Falconer Central SD
Sch. Sys. Enr. Code 3
Supt. – Robert Niver, 2 EAST AVE N   14733
JHS, 2 EAST AVE N   14733 – Richard Wilson, prin.
Fenner MS   14733 – Kenneth Vossler, prin.
Other Schools – See Kennedy

Levant Christian School, P O BOX 236   14733

Fallsburg, Sullivan Co., Pop. Code 6
Fallsburg Central SD
Sch. Sys. Enr. Code 4
Supt. – John Galish   12733
Cosor ES, FALLSBURG   12733
  William Mintz, prin.

Farmingdale, Nassau Co., Pop. Code 6
Farmingdale UFD
Sch. Sys. Enr. Code 6
Supt. – Geoffrey Mattocks, VAN COTT AVE   11735
Howitt MS, VAN COTT AVE   11735
  Robert Schultz, prin.
East Memorial ES, MILL LANE   11735
  Stanley Saltzman, prin.
Northside ES, 1 POWELL PL   11735
  Rosalie Samuels, prin.
Woodward Parkway ES, WOODWARD PKY   11735
  Patricia Desch, prin.
Other Schools – See North Massapequa

St. Kilian ES, 50 CHERRY ST   11735

Farmingville, Suffolk Co., Pop. Code 6
Sachem Central SD
Supt. – See Holbrook
Lynwood Avenue ES, 50 LYNWOOD AVE   11738
  Rosemary Desimone, prin.
Tecumseh ES, 179 GRANNY RD   11738
  David Brewer, prin.

Faith Academy, 1070 PORTION ROAD   11738

Far Rockaway, Queens Co.
Queens Borough SD 27
Supt. – See Ozone Park
Piccolo IS, 1045 NAMEOKE ST   11691
  Vito Martino, prin.
Bay ES, 420 BEACH 51 ST   11691
  Homer Montague, prin.
Mott ES, 535 BRIAR PL   11691
  Herbert Tillem, prin.
Ocean ES, 825 HICKSVILLE RD   11691
  Eugene Kaserman, prin.
Public ES 104, 2601 MOTT AVE   11691
  Libby Grill, prin.
Public ES 106, 180 EAST 35TH STREET   11691
  Edward Levitan, prin.

Gordis Day ES, 445 BEACH 135TH ST   11694
St. Camillus ES, 185 BEACH 99TH ST   11694
St. Francis De Sales ES
  219 BEACH 129TH ST   11694
St. Mary Star of the Sea ES
  595 BEACH 19 ST   11691
St. Rose of Lima ES, 154 BEACH 84TH ST   11693
St. Virgilius ES, 16 NOEL RD   11693
Tapeinu ES, 710 HARTMAN LN   11691
Torah Academy for Girls, 444B SIXTH ST   11691
Yeshiva Darchei Torah ES
  257 BEACH 17 ST   11691

Fayetteville, Onondaga Co., Pop. Code 5
Fayetteville-Manlius Central SD
Sch. Sys. Enr. Code 5
Supt. – Philip Martin, 7173 MOTT ROAD   13066
Wellwood MS, 700 S MANLIUS ST   13066
  David Wheeler, prin.
ES, 710 S MANLIUS ST   13066
  Richard Parisi, prin.
Mott Road ES, 7173 MOTT ROAD   13066
  Carol Reed, prin.
Other Schools – See Manlius

Immaculate Conception ES
  400 SALT SPRINGS ST   13066

Fillmore, Allegany Co., Pop. Code 3
Fillmore Central SD
Sch. Sys. Enr. Code 3
Supt. – Eddie Husted, P O BOX 177   14735
Fillmore Central S, P O BOX 177   14735
  David Hanks, prin.

Fishers Island, Suffolk Co.
Fishers Island UFD
Sch. Sys. Enr. Code 1
Supt. – Thomas Roy, P O BOX A   06390
Fishers Island Central S, P O BOX A   06390
  Thomas Roy, prin.

Fishkill, Dutchess Co., Pop. Code 4
Wappingers Central SD
Supt. – See Wappingers Falls
Brinckerhoff ES, 10 WEDGEWOOD RD   12524
  Robert Morrison, prin.
ES, CHURCH STREET   12524 – L. Barton, prin.

St. Mary ES, JACKSON ST   12524

Floral Park, Nassau Co., Pop. Code 7
Floral Park-Bellrose UFD
Sch. Sys. Enr. Code 4
Supt. – William McDonald, 1 POPPY PL   11001
Childs ES, 12 ELIZABETH ST   11001
Frank Cozart, prin.
Floral Park Bellerose ES, 2 LARCH AVE   11001
Thomas Piro, prin.

Queens Borough SD 26
Supt. – See Bayside
Glen Oaks ES
8051 261 STREET & 81ST AVE   11004
John Gatto, prin.
Mayflower ES, 8515 258TH ST   11001
Jean Downey, prin.

Our Lady of Victory ES, 2 BELLMORE ST   11001
Our Lady of the Snows ES, 79-33 258TH ST   11004
St. Hedwig ES, 2 DEPAN AVE   11001

Florida, Orange Co., Pop. Code 4
Florida UFD
Sch. Sys. Enr. Code 3
Supt. – Michael Lesick
GOLDEN HILL BLDG   10921
Golden Hill ES, ROUND HILL ROAD   10921
Jean Parr, prin.

St. Joseph ES, 21 GLENMERE AVE   10921

Flushing, Queens Co.
Queens Borough SD 25
Sch. Sys. Enr. Code 8
Supt. – Jacklin Banone, 7030 164TH ST   11365
Bowne ES, 14230 BARCLAY AVE   11355
Sheldon Karnilow, prin.
Colden ES, 31 15 140TH STREET   11354
Lorenza Whitney, prin.
Dooley ES, 16702 45TH AVE   11358
David Leibowitz, prin.
Flushing Heights ES, 15901 59TH AVE   11365
Hellen Kurzban, prin.
Hart ES, 14736 26TH AVE   11354
Jeffrey Ratner, prin.
Jackson ES, 14111 HOLLY AVE   11355
Kurt Waldman, prin.
Jefferson ES, 153-01 SANFORD AVE   11355
Bruce Shames, prin.
Kissena ES, 6511 155 ST   11367
Norman Sherman, prin.
Klapper ES, 14439 GRAVETT RD   11367
Robert Roxenberg, prin.
Pomonk ES, 7010 164TH ST   11365
Elaine Lulka, prin.
Public ES 120, 5801 136TH ST   11355
Andrew Gruber, prin.
Public ES 154, 5 02 162ND STREET   11366
Margie Richardson, prin.
Queen Valley ES, 13801 77 AVE   11367
Joseph Cantara, prin.
State Street ES, 17111 35TH AVE   11358
Renee Sklar, prin.
Leigh ES, 7035 150 ST   11367 – Mary Fithian, prin.
Other Schools – See Bayside, College Point,
Whitestone

Queens Borough SD 26
Supt. – See Bayside
Bell ES, 7525 BELL BLVD   11364
Alvin Topol, prin.
Cloverdale ES, 23102 67TH AVE   11364
Malcolm Cooper, prin.
Fresh Meadow ES
67TH AVENUE & FRESH MEADOW   11365
Joel Schulman, prin.
King ES, 19502 69TH AVE   11365
John Gentile, prin.
Kingsbury ES, 21812 HARTLAND AVE   11364
Paul Arden, prin.
Oakland Gardens ES
5311 SPRINGFIELD BLVD   11364
Alvin Yurman, prin.
Golden ES, 20102 53RD AVE   11364
Stephen Berzok, prin.

Queens Borough SD 30
Supt. – See Long Island City
Public ES 2, 7510 21ST AVE   11370
Edward Goldstein, prin.

Garden School, 3316 79TH ST   11372
American Martyrs ES, 216-15 PECK AVE   11364
Ascension ES, 86-37 53RD AVE   11373
Blessed Sacrament ES, 34-20 94TH ST   11372
Bvm Help Christians ES, 70-20 47TH AVE   11377
Chapel Redeemer Lutheran ES
220-16 UNION TPKE   11364
Corpus Christi ES, 31-29 60TH ST   11377
Flushing Christian ES, 158-15 OAK AVE   11358
Forest Hills Montessori School
104-40 QUEENS BLVD   11375
Hebrew Academy of West Queens
34-25 82ND ST   11372
Highland ES, 193-10 PECK AVE   11365
Holy Cross ES, 56-01 61ST ST   11378
Holy Family ES, 74-15 175TH ST   11366
Holy Martyrs Armen Day ES
209-15 HORACE HARDING EXPY   11364
Holy Trinity ES, 14-45 143RD ST   11357
Immanuel Lutheran ES, 12-10 150TH ST   11357
Les Clochetts School, 35-45 223RD ST   11361
Lutheran ES of Flushing, 44-10 192ND ST   11358
Mary's Nativity ES, 146-28 JASMINE AVE   11355

Our Lady Queen of Martyrs ES
72-55 AUSTIN ST   11375
Our Lady of Fatima ES, 25-38 80TH ST   11370
Our Lady of Hope ES, 61-21 71ST ST   11379
Our Lady of Mercy ES, 70-25 KESSEL ST   11375
Our Lady of Sorrows ES, 35-34 105TH ST   11368
Our Lady of the Angelus ES, 9805 63RD DR   11374
Our Lady-Blessed Sacrament ES
34-45 202ND ST   11361
Our Saviour Lutheran ES
64-33 WOODHAVEN BLVD   11374
Queen of Peace ES, 141-25 77 RD   11367
Rabi Dov Revel Yesh, 71-02 113TH ST   11375
Redeemer Lutheran ES
69-26 COOPER AVE   11385
Redeemer Lutheran ES, 36-01 BELL BLVD   11361
Resurrectn Ascension ES, 85-25 61ST RD   11374
SDA ES of Jackson Heights
72-25 WOODSIDE AVE   11377
Sacred Heart ES, 84-05 78TH AVE   11385
Sacred Heart ES, 216-01 38TH AVE   11361
Schechter ES of Queens
76-16 PARSONS BLVD   11366
School of Transfiguration ES
98-07 38TH AVE   11368
Spyropoulos ES, 196-10 NORTHERN BLVD   11358
Sr. Clara Muhammed ES
105-01 NORTHERN BLVD   11368
St. Adalbert ES, 52-17 83RD ST   11373
St. Aloysius ES, 360 SENECA AVE   11385
St. Anastasia ES, 45-11 245TH ST   11362
St. Andrew Avellino ES, 35-50 158TH ST   11358
St. Ann ES, 142-45 58TH RD   11355
St. Bartholomew ES, 44-15 JUDGE ST   11373
St. Fidelis ES, 124-06 14TH AVE   11356
St. Gabriel ES, 26-26 97TH ST   11369
St. Joan of Arc ES, 35-27 82ND ST   11372
St. John Lutheran ES, 88-24 MYRTLE AVE   11385
St. John Lutheran ES, 123-07 22ND AVE   11356
St. Kevin ES, 45-50 195TH ST   11358
St. Leo ES, 104-19 49TH AVE   11368
St. Lukes ES, 16-01 150TH PL   11357
St. Margaret ES, 66-10 80TH ST   11379
St. Matthias ES, 5825 CATALPA AVE   11385
St. Mels ES, 154-24 26TH AVE   11354
St. Michael ES, 136-58 41ST AVE   11355
St. Pancras ES, 68-20 MYRTLE AVE   11385
St. Paul's Episcopal ES
13-21 COLLEGE POINT BLVD   11356
St. Robert Bellarmine ES, 56-10 214TH ST   11364
St. Sebastian ES, 39-76 58TH ST   11377
St. Stanislas Kostka ES, 61-17 GRAND AVE   11378
St. Teresa ES, 50-15 44TH ST   11377
Yeshiva Institute, 43-00 171ST ST   11358
Yeshiva Ohr Yisroel ES
66-20 THORNTON ST   11374
Yeshiva of Central Queens ES
147-37 70 RD   11367

Fonda, Montgomery Co., Pop. Code 4
Fonda-Fultonville Central SD
Sch. Sys. Enr. Code 4
Supt. – William Higgins   12068
Fonda Fultonville MS, CEMETERY ST   12068
John West, prin.
Fonda-Fultonville ES, CEMETERY STREET   12068
Donald Gregoire, prin.

Forest Hills, Queens Co.
Queens Borough SD 28
Sch. Sys. Enr. Code 7
Supt. – Cecelia Michaels, 7048 AUSTIN ST   11375
Grand Center Parkway ES, 7125 113TH ST   11375
Elinor Levy, prin.
Mandel ES, 6210 108TH ST   11375
Eita Carter, prin.
Remsen ES, 9302 69TH AVE   11375
Sydell Kane, prin.
School In The Garden, 2 RUSSELL PL   11375
Charles Bechtold, prin.
Other Schools – See Jamaica, Kew Gardens, Rego
Park, Richmond Hill, South Ozone Park

Queens Borough SD 33
Sch. Sys. Enr. Code 4
Supt. – Charles Schonhout
32-02 JUNCTION BLVD   11369
Armstrong IS, 32-02 JUNCTION BLVD   11369
David Brown, prin.

Kew Forest School
119-17 UNION TURNPIKE   11375

Forestport, Herkimer Co.
Adirondack-Boonville Central SD
Supt. – See Boonville
ES, ROUTE 28   13338 – Donald Porter, prin.

Forestville, Chautauqua Co., Pop. Code 3
Forestville Central SD
Sch. Sys. Enr. Code 3
Supt. – William Loftus   14062
ES, WATER STREET   14062
Richard Rodriguez, prin.

Fort Ann, Washington Co., Pop. Code 3
Ft. Ann Central SD
Sch. Sys. Enr. Code 4
Supt. – Richard Hogan, P O BOX 467   12827
S, P O BOX 467   12827 – John Whelan, prin.

Fort Covington, Franklin Co., Pop. Code 4
Salmon River Central SD
Sch. Sys. Enr. Code 4
Supt. – Robert Lewis
RURAL ROUTE 01 BOX 131   12937

Salmon River MS
RURAL ROUTE 01 BOX 131   12937
Emmett Favreau, prin.
Salmon River ES   12937 – Ronald Bombard, prin.
Other Schools – See Hogansburg

Fort Edward, Washington Co., Pop. Code 5
Ft. Edward UFD
Sch. Sys. Enr. Code 3
Supt. – Charles Mullen, 220 BROADWAY   12828
ES, 220 BROADWAY   12828 – Ella Collins, prin.

Hudson Falls Central SD
Supt. – See Hudson Falls
Burgoyne Avenue ES, 61 BURGOYNE AVE   12828
James Keenan, prin.

Fort Plain, Montgomery Co., Pop. Code 5
Ft. Plain Central SD
Sch. Sys. Enr. Code 4
Supt. – Stephen Uebbing, 1 WEST ST   13339
Hoag ES, HIGH STREET   13339
Walter Wheeler, prin.

Frankfort, Herkimer Co., Pop. Code 5
Frankfort Schuyler Central SD
Sch. Sys. Enr. Code 4
Supt. – Sam Colella, PALMER ST   13340
Reese Road ES, REESE ROAD   13340
Jon Loiacano, prin.
West Frankfort ES, RURAL ROUTE 02   13340
Francis Saraceno, prin.

Franklin, Delaware Co., Pop. Code 2
Franklin Central SD
Sch. Sys. Enr. Code 2
Supt. – Robert Bennett, P O BOX 888   13775
Franklin Central S, P O BOX 888   13775
Nan Gardiner, prin.

Franklin Square, Nassau Co., Pop. Code 8
Franklin Square UFD
Sch. Sys. Enr. Code 4
Supt. – Howard Rubin, WASHINGTON ST   11010
John Street ES, NASSAU BOULEVARD   11010
Walter Hawkins, prin.
Polk Street ES, POLK STREET   11010
Henry Montagni, prin.
Washington Street ES
762 WASHINGTON ST   11010
Marilyn Dreilinger, prin.

Valley Stream Hemp 13 UFD
Supt. – See Valley Stream
Willow Road ES, WILLOW ROAD   11010
John Hoffmann, prin.

St. Catherine of Siena ES
990 HOLZHEIMER ST   11010

Franklinville, Cattaraugus Co., Pop. Code 4
Franklinville Central SD
Sch. Sys. Enr. Code 3
Supt. – Richard Wachter, 32 N MAIN ST   14737
ES, 32 N MAIN ST   14737 – Robert O'Connor, prin.

Fredonia, Chautauqua Co., Pop. Code 7
Fredonia Central SD
Sch. Sys. Enr. Code 4
Supt. – James Merrins, 425 E MAIN ST   14063
MS, 425 E MAIN ST   14063 – Thomas Heary, prin.
MS, 425 E MAIN ST   14063 – Frank Grates, prin.
PS, E MAIN ST   14063 – Margaret Sauer, prin.

Fredonia Catholic ES, 32 MOORE AVE   14063

Freeport, Nassau Co., Pop. Code 8
Freeport UFD
Sch. Sys. Enr. Code 6
Supt. – John Bierwirth, P O BOX 50   11520
Dodd JHS, P O BOX 50   11520
Harding Morgan, prin.
Archer Street ES, BOX 50   11520
Thomas Haley, prin.
Atkinson MS, BOX 50   11520
George Coupe, prin.
Bayview Avenue ES, BOX 50   11520
Anthony Duhamel, prin.
Giblyn ES, BOX 50   11520 – James Glennon, prin.

Hi-Hello Day Care Center ES
212 S OCEAN AVE   11520
Our Holy Redeemer ES, 87 PINE ST   11520

Freeville, Tompkins Co., Pop. Code 2
Dryden Central SD
Supt. – See Dryden
Freeville ES   13053 – George Burtis, prin.

Frewsburg, Chautauqua Co., Pop. Code 4
Frewsburg Central SD
Sch. Sys. Enr. Code 3
Supt. – Paul Grekalski   14738
Jackson ES, IVORY STREET   14738
Sandra Willard, prin.

Friendship, Allegany Co., Pop. Code 4
Friendship Central SD
Sch. Sys. Enr. Code 2
Supt. – John Markell, MAIN ST   14739
Friendship Central S, RURAL ROUTE 01   14739
D. Mazur, prin.

Fulton, Oswego Co.
Fulton CSD
Sch. Sys. Enr. Code 5
Supt. – William Rasbeck
ROCHESTER & 4TH ST   13069

JHS, 167 S 4TH ST   13069 – James Simpson, prin.
Erie Street ES, ERIE STREET   13069
  Gordon Chesbro, prin.
Fairgrieve ES   13069 – Donald Kunzwiler, prin.
Lanigan ES, 59 BAKEMAN ST   13069
  Floyd Wallace, prin.
Oak Street ES, OAK STREET   13069
  Wayne Bleau, prin.
Phillips Street ES, PHILLIPS STREET   13069
  Gordon Chesbro, prin.
Volney ES, RURAL ROUTE 03   13069
  Harold Waugh, prin.

Fulton Catholic ES, 309 BUFFALO ST   13069

Gainesville, Wyoming Co., Pop. Code 2
Letchworth Gainesville Central SD
Sch. Sys. Enr. Code 4
Supt. – Michael Wesner, SCHOOL ROAD   14066
Lockwood ES, JORDAN ROAD   14066
  Clifford Bird, prin.

Galway, Saratoga Co., Pop. Code 2
Galway Central SD
Sch. Sys. Enr. Code 4
Supt. – Ronald Gillespie   12074
Henry ES, RURAL ROUTE 01   12074
  Joanne Sole, prin.

Garden City, Nassau Co., Pop. Code 7
Garden City UFD
Sch. Sys. Enr. Code 5
Supt. – Elliott Landon
  56 CATHEDRAL AVE   11530
MS, 98 CHERRY VALLEY AVE   11530
  Dominick Starace, prin.
Homestead ES
  HOMESTEAD-CLINCH AVENUE   11530
  George Marchal, prin.
Locust ES, BOYLSTON & LOCUST STREET   11530
  Marie Braccia, prin.
Stewart ES
  STEWART & CLINTON AVENUE   11530
  Marie Braccia, prin.
Stratford Avenue MS
  STRATFORD-WEYFORD TERRACE   11530
  George Marchal, prin.

Waldorf School, CAMBRIDGE AVE   11530
St. Anne's ES, 25 DARTMOUTH ST   11530
St. Joseph ES, 450 FRANKLIN AVE   11530

Garden City Park, Nassau Co., Pop. Code 3
New Hyde Park-Garden City UFD
Supt. – See New Hyde Park
Garden City Park ES
  CENTRAL AVENUE & THIRD   11040
  Joann Grim, prin.

Garnerville, Rockland Co.
Haverstraw-Stony Point Central SD
Supt. – See Stony Point
North Garnerville ES, CENTRAL HIGHWAY   10923
  Robert Steinberger, prin.

St. Gregory Barbargo ES, 29 CINDER RD   10923

Garrison, Putnam Co.
Garrison UFD
Sch. Sys. Enr. Code 2
Supt. – Carolyn Leary, RURAL ROUTE 09 D   10524
ES, ROUTE 9 D   10524 – William French, prin.

Gasport, Niagara Co., Pop. Code 3
Royalton Hartland Central SD
Supt. – See Middleport
ES, 4500 ORCHARD PL   14067
  Lawrence Shanley, prin.

Geneseo, Livingston Co., Pop. Code 6
Geneseo Central SD
Sch. Sys. Enr. Code 4
Supt. – Charles Little   14454
ES   14454 – E. Tay, prin.

Geneva, Ontario Co., Pop. Code 7
Border City UFD
Sch. Sys. Enr. Code 1
Supt. – C. Thomas Bailey
  467 BORDER CITY ROAD   14456
Border City Union Free S
  467 BORDER CITY RD   14456 – Bruce Viertel,
  prin.

Geneva CSD
Sch. Sys. Enr. Code 4
Supt. – Vincent Scalise, 400 W NORTH ST   14456
MS, 63 PULTENEY ST   14456
  Salvatore Scaglione, prin.
North ES, 400 WEST NORTH STREET   14456
  Mary Luckern, prin.
West Street ES, 30 WEST ST   14456
  Ethel Peters, prin.

St. Francis De Sales ES, 17 ELMWOOD AVE   14456

Georgetown, Madison Co.
Otselic Valley Central SD
Supt. – See South Otselic
ES, P O BOX 114   13072 – A. Schibeci, prin.

Germantown, Columbia Co., Pop. Code 4
Germantown Central SD
Sch. Sys. Enr. Code 3
Supt. – Peter Hughes
  RURAL ROUTE 01 BOX 35   12526
ES   12526 – Neal Burger, prin.

Ghent, Columbia Co., Pop. Code 5

Hawthorne Valley School
  ROAD 2 BOX 225   12075

Gilbertsville, Otsego Co., Pop. Code 2
Gilbertsville Central SD
Sch. Sys. Enr. Code 2
Supt. – Frederick Tarolli   13777
Gilbertsville Central S, ONE GROVE ST   13776
  Frederic Johnson, prin.

Gilboa, Schoharie Co., Pop. Code 4
Gilboa-Conesville Central SD
Sch. Sys. Enr. Code 2
Supt. – Thomas Markle   12076
Gilboa-Conesville Central S   12076
  David Sawyer, prin.

Glasco, Ulster Co., Pop. Code 4
Saugerties Central SD
Supt. – See Saugerties
Riccardi ES, P O BOX 127   12432
  Joseph Modica, prin.

Glen Cove, Nassau Co., Pop. Code 7
Glen Cove CSD
Sch. Sys. Enr. Code 5
Supt. – Florence Andresen
  150 DOSORIS LANE   11542
MS, 189 FOREST AVE   11542
  Carl LaPointe, prin.
Coles ES, CEDAR SWAMP ROAD   11542
  Robert Earthy, prin.
Connolly ES, 1 RIDGE DR   11542
  Lewis Baranello, prin.
Deasy ES, 2 DOSORIS LN   11542
  Francine Zausmer, prin.
Gribbin ES, SEAMAN ROAD   11542
  Teretta Charles, prin.
Landing ES, MCLOUGHLIN STREET   11542
  George Priest, prin.

St. Patrick's ES, 12 PEARSALL AVE   11542

Glendale, Queens Co.
Queens Borough SD 24
Supt. – See Middle Village
JHS, 78TH AVE & 74TH ST   11385
  Bernadette Boyle, prin.
Arkwright ES
  CENTRAL AVENUE & 69TH ST   11385
  David Levitman, prin.
Public ES 113, 8721 79TH AVE   11385
  Alan Gewirtz, prin.

Glenfield, Lewis Co.
South Lewis Central SD
Supt. – See Turin
ES   13343 – William Anderson, prin.

Glenham, Dutchess Co.
Beacon CSD
Supt. – See Beacon
ES, 5 CHASE DR   12527 – James Welling, prin.

Glen Head, Nassau Co.
North Shore Central SD
Supt. – See Sea Cliff
North Shore JHS, 505 GLENCOVE AVE   11545
  James Curran, prin.
ES, 7 SCHOOL ST   11545 – Joan Lewis, prin.

Green Vale ES, 250 VALENTINE LN   11545
St. Hyacinth ES, 319 CEDAR SWAMP RD   11545

Glenmont, Albany Co.
Bethlehem Central SD
Supt. – See Delmar
ES, ROUTE 9W   12077 – Donald Robillard, prin.

Glens Falls, Warren Co., Pop. Code 7
Glens Falls CSD
Sch. Sys. Enr. Code 5
Supt. – Dalen Showalter, 15 QUADE ST   12801
MS, 20 QUADE ST   12801 – Harriet Finch, prin.
Big Cross Street ES, 15 BIG CROSS ST   12801
  William Garrow, prin.
Jackson Heights ES, 24 JACKSON AVE   12801
  Paul Berkheimer, prin.
Kensington Road ES, 41 KENSINGTON RD   12801
  Richard Ost, prin.
Sanford Street ES, 10 SANFORD ST   12801
  Andrew Garuccio, prin.

Glens Falls Common SD
Sch. Sys. Enr. Code 2
Supt. – Donald Trombley
  120 LAWRENCE ST   12801
Wing ES, 120 LAWRENCE ST   12801
  Marilyn Pirkle, prin.

Queensbury UFD
Sch. Sys. Enr. Code 5
Supt. – J. Irion, 83 AVIATION ROAD   12801
Queensbury MS, 75 AVIATION ROAD   12801
  Michael Johnson, prin.
Queensbury ES, 83 AVIATION RD   12801
  Michael McCabe, prin.

St. Mary's Academy of N Country
  10 CHURCH ST   12801
St. Alphonsus ES, 37 BROAD ST   12801

Glenwood Landing, Nassau Co., Pop. Code 4
North Shore Central SD
Supt. – See Sea Cliff

ES, 60 CODY AVE   11547 – John Fallon, prin.

Gloversville, Fulton Co., Pop. Code 7
Gloversville CSD
Sch. Sys. Enr. Code 5
Supt. – George Krahl, 90 N MAIN ST   12078
Estee MS, 90 N MAIN ST   12078 – T. Morgan, prin.
Boulevard ES, EAST BOULEVARD   12078
  Ann Peluso, prin.
Kingsborough ES, 24 W ELEVENTH AVE   12078
  Donald Williams, prin.
McNab ES, W FULTON STREET   12078
  Jack Payne, prin.
Meco ES, RURAL ROUTE 03 BOX 40   12078
  Jack Payne, prin.
Park Terrace ES
  BLOOMINDALE AVENUE EXIT   12078
  Helen Maxwell, prin.

Our Lady of Mt. Carmel ES, 161 S MAIN ST   12078

Goldens Bridge, Westchester Co., Pop. Code 4
Katonah Lewisboro UFD
Supt. – See Katonah
Miller ES, ROUTE 138   10526 – Dale Truding, prin.

Gorham, Ontario Co.
Gorham-Middlesex Central SD
Supt. – See Rushville
ES   14461 – Eric Young, prin.

Goshen, Orange Co., Pop. Code 5
Goshen Central SD
Sch. Sys. Enr. Code 4
Supt. – Richard Nealon, MAIN ST BLDG   10924
Hooker MS, MCNALLY ST   10924
  K. Hubley, prin.
IS, MCNALLY STREET   10924 – Brenda Haas, prin.
Scotchtown Avenue ES
  SCOTCHTOWN AVENUE   10924
  Arthur Groves, prin.

Goshen Christian ES, RURAL ROUTE 02   10924
St. John's ES, 77 MURRAY AVE   10924

Gouverneur, St. Lawrence Co., Pop. Code 5
Gouverneur Central SD
Sch. Sys. Enr. Code 4
Supt. – Bonnie Bettinger
  133 E BARNEY ST   13642
East Side ES, SCHOOL STREET   13642
  Anthony Marchesano, prin.
Fowler ES, RURAL ROUTE 03   13642
  James Berry, prin.
West Side ES, WILSON STREET   13642
  Lauren Helena, prin.

St. James ES, SOUTH GORDON ST   13642

Gowanda, Cattaraugus Co., Pop. Code 5
Gowanda Central SD
Sch. Sys. Enr. Code 4
Supt. – J. Warren Adair, 24 PROSPECT ST   14070
Aldrich Street ES, ALDRICH STREET EXT   14070
  Estelle Crino, prin.
MS, SCHOOL STREET   14070
  Alona Forbes, prin.

St. Joseph ES, 71 E MAIN ST   14070

Grahamsville, Sullivan Co., Pop. Code 2
Tri Valley Central SD
Sch. Sys. Enr. Code 3
Supt. – J. Robert Kelz   12740
MS, P O BOX 420   12740 – Thomas Manell, prin.
Tri Valley ES   12740 – Daniel O'Rourke, prin.

Grand Island, Erie Co., Pop. Code 7
Grand Island Central SD
Sch. Sys. Enr. Code 5
Supt. – Lee Cravotta, 1100 RANSOM ROAD   14072
MS, 1100 RANSOM ROAD   14072
  Ronald Franke, prin.
Huth Road ES, 1773 HUTH RD   14072
  Marian Koppmann, prin.
Kaegebein ES, 1690 LOVE RD   14072
  George Wenner, prin.

St. Stephen ES, 2080 BASELINE RD   14072

Granville, Washington Co., Pop. Code 5
Granville Central SD
Sch. Sys. Enr. Code 4
Supt. – Robert Meldrum, 60 QUAKER ST   12832
JHS, 61 QUAKER ST   12832
  Douglas Burton, prin.
ES, 61 QUAKER ST   12832 – Robert Pedro, prin.
Other Schools – See Middle Granville

Great Bend, Jefferson Co.
Carthage Central SD
Supt. – See Carthage
ES, 7520 CHAMPION ST   13643 – Jan Delano, prin.

Great Neck, Nassau Co., Pop. Code 6
Great Neck UFD
Sch. Sys. Enr. Code 6
Supt. – William Shine
  345 LAKEVILLE ROAD   11020
Great Neck North MS, 77 POLO ROAD   11023
  Patrick Sullivan, prin.
Great Neck South MS
  349 LAKEVILLE ROAD   11020
  Salvatore Lipari, prin.
Baker ES, 69 BAKER HILL RD   11023
  Thaddeus Kuczinski, prin.

Kennedy ES, 1A GRASSFIELD RD   11024
  Catherine Moore, prin.
Lakeville ES, 4227 JAYSON AVENUE   11020
  Barbara Raber, prin.
Saddle Rock ES, 10 HAWTHORNE LN   11023
  Maureen Joy, prin.

North Shore Hebrew Academy
  26 OLD MILL RD   11023
St. Aloysius ES, 5 BREUER AVE   11023

Greece, Monroe Co., Pop. Code 8

St. Charles Borromeo ES, 64 MAIDEN LN   14616

Greene, Chenango Co., Pop. Code 4
Greene Central SD
Sch. Sys. Enr. Code 4
Supt. – Michael Picciano, 40 S CANAL ST   13778
MS, S CANAL ST   13778 – Frank Markowick, prin.
Green ES, E RIVER ROAD   13778
  Vincent Coletta, prin.

Greenfield Center, Saratoga Co.
Saratoga Springs CSD
Supt. – See Saratoga Springs
ES, RURAL ROUTE 01   12833
  Richard Lyman, prin.

Green Island, Albany Co., Pop. Code 5
Green Island UFD
Sch. Sys. Enr. Code 2
Supt. – Stephen Swinton
  171 HUDSON AVE   12183
Heatley S, 171 HUDSON AVE   12183
  Jerome Steele, prin.

St. Joseph ES, 117 GEORGE ST   12183

Greenlawn, Suffolk Co., Pop. Code 6
Elwood UFD
Sch. Sys. Enr. Code 4
Supt. – Joseph Laria, 100 KENNETH AVE   11740
Other Schools – See East Northport, Huntington

Harborfields Central SD
Sch. Sys. Enr. Code 5
Supt. – William Spendley
  2 OLDFIELD ROAD   11740
Oldfield MS, 2 OLDFIELD ROAD   11740
  Maurice Beaulieu, prin.
Lahey ES, 625 PULASKI RD   11740
  Stuart Bentsen, prin.

Greenport, Suffolk Co., Pop. Code 4
Greenport UFD
Sch. Sys. Enr. Code 3
Supt. – Carl Nelson, FRONT ST   11944
ES, 700 FRONT ST   11944 – Barbara Claps, prin.

Greenvale, Nassau Co.
Roslyn UFD
Supt. – See Roslyn
Harbor Hill ES, 3 GLEN COVE RD   11548
  Stephen Wachenfeld, prin.

Greenville, Greene Co., Pop. Code 2
Greenville Central SD
Sch. Sys. Enr. Code 4
Supt. – John Thero   12083
Ellis ES   12083 – Joann Morse, prin.

Greenwich, Washington Co., Pop. Code 4
Greenwich Central SD
Sch. Sys. Enr. Code 4
Supt. – J. Briglin, 10 GRAY AVE   12834
ES   12834 – Regina McManus, prin.

Greenwood, Steuben Co., Pop. Code 3
Greenwood Central SD
Sch. Sys. Enr. Code 2
Supt. – Grover Weeler   14839
Greenwood Central S, MAIN ST   14839
  Nancy Barkman, prin.

Greenwood Lake, Orange Co., Pop. Code 5
Greenwood Lake UFD
Sch. Sys. Enr. Code 3
Supt. – Ray Cole, WATERSTONE ROAD   10925
MS, P O BOX 8   10925 – William Perrego, prin.
ES, P O BOX 8   10925 – Wilma Volberg, prin.

Groton, Tompkins Co., Pop. Code 4
Groton Central SD
Sch. Sys. Enr. Code 4
Supt. – Gordon Klumpp
  GROTON CITY ROAD   13073
ES, 516 ELM ST   13073 – Joseph Amore, prin.

Guilderland, Albany Co., Pop. Code 3
Guilderland Central SD
Sch. Sys. Enr. Code 5
Supt. – Albert Pultz
  6011 STATE FARM ROAD   12084
Farnsworth MS, 6094 STATE FARM ROAD   12084
  Joseph Purcell, prin.
ES, 2211A WESTERN AVE   12084
  Martha Beck, prin.
Other Schools – See Albany, Altamont, Schenectady

Guilford, Chenango Co., Pop. Code 4
Bainbridge Guilford Central SD
Supt. – See Bainbridge
ES   13780 – Richard Howard, prin.

Hamburg, Erie Co., Pop. Code 7
Frontier Central SD
Sch. Sys. Enr. Code 7
Supt. – Richard Shands
  4432 BAY VIEW ROAD   14075
Cloverbank ES, 2761 CLOVERBANK RD   14075
  Carol Lovullo, prin.
Wanakah ES, 5120 ORCHARD AVE   14075
  Andrew Podlucky, prin.
Other Schools – See Blasdell, Buffalo, Lake View

Hamburg Central SD
Sch. Sys. Enr. Code 5
Supt. – L. Grell, 5305 ABBOTT ROAD   14075
Armor ES, 5301 ABBOTT RD   14075
  Martin Finnerty, prin.
Boston Valley ES, 7476 BACK CREEK RD   14075
  Gordon Blomquist, prin.
Charlotte Avenue ES
  301 CHARLOTTE AVE   14075
  Donald Wood, prin.
Union Pleasant Avenue ES
  150 PLEASANT AVE   14075 – John Connors, prin.

SS. Peter & Paul School, 68 E MAIN ST   14075
St. Bernadette ES, S 5890 ABBOTT RD   14075
St. Mary's of the Lake ES
  4737 LAKE SHORE RD   14075

Hamilton, Madison Co., Pop. Code 5
Hamilton Central SD
Sch. Sys. Enr. Code 3
Supt. – Thomas Coseo
  47 W KENDRICK AVE   13346
Hamilton Central S, 47 W KENDRICK AVE   13346
  Thomas Coseo, prin.

Hamlin, Monroe Co.

St. John's Christian ES, 1107 E LAKE RD   14464

Hammond, St. Lawrence Co., Pop. Code 2
Hammond Central SD
Sch. Sys. Enr. Code 2
Supt. – Robert Scofield   13646
Hammond Central S, MAIN ST   13646
  Robert Scofield, prin.

Hammondsport, Steuben Co., Pop. Code 4
Hammondsport Central SD
Sch. Sys. Enr. Code 3
Supt. – John Hogle, MAIN ST   14840
Curtiss Memorial ES
  BAUDER & LAKE STREET   14840
  Bruce Inglis, prin.

Hampton Bays, Suffolk Co., Pop. Code 5
Hampton Bays UFD
Sch. Sys. Enr. Code 4
Supt. – Patricia Horkan
  72 PONQUOGUE AVE   11946
ES, 72 PONQUOGUE AVE   11946
  Theodore Watt, prin.

Hancock, Delaware Co., Pop. Code 4
Hancock Central SD
Sch. Sys. Enr. Code 3
Supt. – Rob Urzillo, READ ST   13783
ES, WHEELER STREET EXTENSION   13783
  Linda Ivanenok, prin.

Hannibal, Oswego Co., Pop. Code 3
Hannibal Central SD
Sch. Sys. Enr. Code 4
Supt. – J. Hastings   13074
Cayuga Street MS   13074 – Dennis Kenney, prin.
Fairley ES   13074 – Joseph Occhino, prin.

Harpursville, Broome Co., Pop. Code 2
Harpursville Central SD
Sch. Sys. Enr. Code 4
Supt. – Albert Oatman   13787
Olmsted ES   13787 – Joseph Ranieri, prin.

Harrison, Westchester Co., Pop. Code 7
Harrison Central SD
Sch. Sys. Enr. Code 4
Supt. – Joseph Carbone
  UNION & NELSON AVES   10528
Klein MS, UNION & NELSON AVE   10528
  John Culhane, prin.
Harrison Avenue ES, 446 HARRISON AVE   10528
  John Russell, prin.
Parsons Memorial ES, 200 HALSTEAD AVE   10528
  Joseph Massi, prin.
Other Schools – See Purchase, White Plains

St. Gregory the Great School
  94 BROADWAY   10528

Harrisville, Lewis Co., Pop. Code 3
Harrisville Central SD
Sch. Sys. Enr. Code 3
Supt. – William Cartwright, P O BOX 189   13648
ES, P O BOX 189   13648
  William Cartwright, prin.

Hartford, Washington Co., Pop. Code 4
Hartford Central SD
Sch. Sys. Enr. Code 2
Supt. – Steve Dimuzio   12838
Hartford Central S   12838 – Clifford Moses, prin.

Hartsdale, Westchester Co., Pop. Code 7
Greenburgh Central SD
Sch. Sys. Enr. Code 4
Supt. – Robert Frelow
  475 W HARTSDALE AVE   10530
Highview ES, 200 N CENTRAL AVE   10530
  Rena Hersh, prin.
Other Schools – See White Plains

Sacred Heart School, 59 WILSON ST   10530

Hastings-on-Hudson, Westchester Co., Pop. Code 6
Greenburgh-Graham UFD
Sch. Sys. Enr. Code 2
Supt. – Vincent Ziccolella, 1 S BROADWAY   10706
Greenburgh-Graham ES, 1 S BROADWAY   10706
  Bessie Ford, prin.

Hastings On Hudson UFD
Sch. Sys. Enr. Code 4
Supt. – Mary Lou Dickinson
  FARRAGUT AVE   10706
Farragut MS, 282 FARRAGUT AVE   10706
  Renee Stalma, prin.
Hillside ES, EDGEWOOD AVENUE   10706
  R. Hildebrand, prin.

St. Matthew's School
  BWAY AND VILLARD AVE   10706

Hauppauge, Suffolk Co., Pop. Code 7
Hauppauge UFD
Sch. Sys. Enr. Code 5
Supt. – Jerome Malkan
  600 TOWNLINE ROAD   11788
MS, 600 TOWNLINE ROAD   11788
  Jerome Giaimo, prin.
Bretton Woods ES, CLUB LANE   11788
  Robert Morris, prin.
Other Schools – See Smithtown

Happy Acres ES, 358 HOFFMAN LN   11788

Haverstraw, Rockland Co., Pop. Code 6
Haverstraw-Stony Point Central SD
Supt. – See Stony Point
Haverstraw MS, 20 GRANT ST   10927
  Raymond Hagadorn, prin.
Neary ES, 20 GEORGE ST   10927
  Diana Greco, prin.

St. Peter's ES, 21 RIDGE ST   10927

Hawthorne, Westchester Co., Pop. Code 5
Mt. Pleasant Central SD
Supt. – See Thornwood
ES, 225 MEMORIAL DR   10532
  Barbara Cronin, prin.

Holy Rosary ES, 180 BRADHURST AVE   10532

Hempstead, Nassau Co., Pop. Code 8
Hempstead UFD
Sch. Sys. Enr. Code 6
Supt. – Clarence Pope
  185 PENINSULA BLVD   11550
Schultz MS, 70 GREENWICH ST   11550
  (—), prin.
Franklin ES, 335 S FRANKLIN ST   11550
  Sally Thompson, prin.
Fulton ES, 40 FULTON AVE   11550
  Vernon Gokey, prin.
Jackson Annex ES, 380 JACKSON ST   11550
  John Moore, prin.
Jackson MS, 451 JACKSON ST   11550
  Tyree Curry, prin.
Ludlum ES, 176 WILLIAM ST   11550
  Denise Cotton, prin.
Marshall ES, 15 E MARSHALL ST   11550
  Brezetta Bullock, prin.
Prospect ES, 265 PENINSULA BLVD   11550
  Archie Matthews, prin.
Rhodes ES, 270 WASHINGTON STREET   11550
  Bettye Howard, prin.

Rockville Centre UFD
Supt. – See Rockville Centre
Covert ES, LONG BEACH & WILLOW   11550
  Loretta Marshall, prin.

New Frontier Montessori School
  35 FULTON AVE   11550
Our Lady of Loretto ES
  120 GREENWICH ST   11550
Sacred Heart Seminary ES
  95 FULTON AVE   11550
St. Ladislaus ES, 436 FRONT ST   11550

Henderson, Jefferson Co.
Belleville Henderson Central SD
Supt. – See Belleville
ES, P O BOX 304   13650 – Doris Gorham, prin.

Henrietta, Monroe Co., Pop. Code 8
Rush Henrietta Central SD
Sch. Sys. Enr. Code 6
Supt. – R. Delaney
  2034 LEHIGH STATION ROAD   14467
Sherman ES, 50 AUTHORS AVE   14467
  Mark Turner, prin.
Winslow ES, 725 PINNACLE ROAD   14467
  Mary Welch, prin.
Other Schools – See Rochester, Rush, West Henrietta

Good Shepherd ES, 3288 E HENRIETTA RD   14467

Herkimer, Herkimer Co., Pop. Code 6
Herkimer Central SD
Sch. Sys. Enr. Code 4
Supt. – Robert Moorhead
  401 E GERMAN ST 13350
Bills ES, N WASHINTON STREET 13350
  Lawrence Orr, prin.
Foley JHS, 431 N BELLINGER ST 13350
  Harold Stoffolano, prin.

St. Francis De Sales ES, 220 HENRY ST 13350

Heuvelton, St. Lawrence Co., Pop. Code 3
Heuvelton Central SD
Sch. Sys. Enr. Code 3
Supt. – Lawrence Ames, WASHINGTON ST 13654
Heuvelton Central S 13654
  Lawrence Ames, prin.

Hewlett, Nassau Co., Pop. Code 5
Hewlett-Woodmere UFD
Sch. Sys. Enr. Code 5
Supt. – Bert Nelson, HENRIETTA PLACE 11557
Woodmere MS, 1170 PENINSULA BLVD 11557
  Barbara Kolb, prin.
ES, BROADWAY 11557 – Mildred David, prin.
Other Schools – See Valley Stream

Lawrence Country ES
  291 MEADOWVIEW AVE 11557
St. Joseph ES, 1355 NOEL AVE 11557
Yesh-Msvta Toras Chaim ES
  1170 WILLIAMS ST 11557

Hicksville, Nassau Co., Pop. Code 8
Bethpage UFD
Supt. – See Bethpage
Kramer ES, KRAMER LANE 11803
  Frank Cicione, prin.

Hicksville UFD
Sch. Sys. Enr. Code 5
Supt. – Cathy Fenton, DIVISION AVE 11801
MS, 215 JERUSALEM AVE 11801
  Gerald Klein, prin.
Burns Avenue ES, 40 BURNS AVE 11801
  Frank Burke, prin.
Dutch Lane ES, 50 STEWART AVE 11801
  Nancy DeSorbe, prin.
East Street ES, EAST STREET 11801
  William Granville, prin.
Fork Lane ES, FORK LANE 11801
  Carol Bentsen, prin.
Lee Avenue ES, SEVENTH STREET 11801
  John Mateer, prin.
Old Country Road ES, 49 RHODES LN 11801
  Geraldine Silver, prin.
Willet Avenue ES, 57 WILLET AVE 11801
  Michael Dunn, prin.
Woodland Avenue ES, 85 KETCHAM RD 11801
  Manus Clancy, prin.

Holy Family ES, 25 FORDHAM AVE 11801
Our Lady of Mercy ES
  520 S OYSTER BAY RD 11801
St. Ignatius Loyola ES, 30 E CHERRY ST 11801
Trinity Lutheran ES, 40 W NICHOLAI ST 11801

Highland, Ulster Co., Pop. Code 4
Highland Central SD
Sch. Sys. Enr. Code 4
Supt. – Ron Revelle
  PANCAKE HOLLOW ROAD 12528
MS, 71 MAIN ST 12528 – Carl Cioppa, prin.
ES, LOCKHART LANE 12528
  Michael Hinchey, prin.

St. Augustine ES, 35 PHILLIPS AVE 12528

Highland Falls, Orange Co., Pop. Code 5
Highland Falls Central SD
Sch. Sys. Enr. Code 4
Supt. – Herbert Donlan
  37 MOUNTAIN AVE 10928
MS, 40 MOUNTAIN AVE 10928
  Maureen Comer, prin.
ES, P O BOX 287 10928 – Maureen Comer, prin.

Sacred Heart ES, 7 COZZENS AVE 10928

Hillburn, Rockland Co., Pop. Code 3
Ramapo Central SD
Sch. Sys. Enr. Code 5
Supt. – Charles Grottenthaler
  MOUNTAIN AVE 10931
Other Schools – See Sloatsburg, Suffern

Hillsdale, Columbia Co., Pop. Code 4
Copake-Taconic Hills Central SD
Sch. Sys. Enr. Code 4
Supt. – Gerald Duffy 12529
Roeliff-Jansen MS 12529 – Gerald Sadoski, prin.
Roeliff-Jansen ES 12529 – Mary Modica, prin.
Other Schools – See Philmont

Hilton, Monroe Co., Pop. Code 5
Hilton Central SD
Sch. Sys. Enr. Code 5
Supt. – Arthur Herd, 100 SCHOOL LANE 14468
Williams MS, 200 SCHOOL LANE 14468
  Harold Garno, prin.
Northwood ES, 433 N GREECE ROAD 14468
  Norman Warren, prin.
Village ES, 90 SCHOOL LANE 14468
  Vernon Stevens, prin.

St. Paul Lutheran ES, 130 EAST AVE 14468

Hinsdale, Cattaraugus Co., Pop. Code 4
Hinsdale Central SD
Sch. Sys. Enr. Code 3
Supt. – Carl Saglimben, 3701 MAIN ST 14743
Hinsdale Central S, 3701 MAIN ST 14743
  Carl Saglimben, prin.

Hogansburg, Franklin Co.
Salmon River Central SD
Supt. – See Fort Covington
St. Regis Mohawk ES 13655
  William Mitchell, prin.

Holbrook, Suffolk Co., Pop. Code 7
Sachem Central SD
Sch. Sys. Enr. Code 7
Supt. – L. Adler, 245 UNION AVE 11741
Seneca JHS
  PATCHOGUE-HOLBROOK ROAD 11741
  Thomas McLaughlin, prin.
Grundy Avenue ES, 950 GRUNDY AVE 11741
  Donald Albrecht, prin.
Merriamc ES, 1090 BROADWAY AVE 11741
  Joan Adomsky, prin.
Nokomis ES, 151 HOLBROOK RD 11741
  Ralph Stile, prin.
Other Schools – See Farmingville, Holtsville, Lake
  Grove, Lake Ronkonkoma

Holcomb, Ontario Co., Pop. Code 3
East Bloomfield Central SD
Supt. – See East Bloomfield
Bloomfield ES, ROUTE 20C 14469
  Lansing Pfluke, prin.

Holland, Erie Co., Pop. Code 5
Holland Central SD
Sch. Sys. Enr. Code 4
Supt. – Peter Roswell, CANADA ST 14080
MS, PARTRIDGE ROAD 14080
  Karen Macgamwell, prin.
Brumsted ES, CANADA STREET 14080
  George Weissenberger, prin.

Holland Patent, Oneida Co., Pop. Code 3
Holland Patent Central SD
Sch. Sys. Enr. Code 4
Supt. – William Whitehall 13354
MS 13354 – Johnnie Jones, prin.
Floyd ES 13354 – Anthony Barretta, prin.
ES 13354 – Joseph Guarini, prin.

Holley, Orleans Co., Pop. Code 4
Holley Central SD
Sch. Sys. Enr. Code 4
Supt. – Robert Jaeger, N MAIN ST 14470
ES, NORTH MAIN STREET 14470
  John Heise, prin.
IS, NORTH MAIN ST 14470 – John Heise, prin.

Hollis, Queens Co.
Queens Borough SD 29
Supt. – See Queens Village
ES, 109TH AVENUE AND 203RD ST 11412
  Inez Allen, prin.
Woodhull ES, 19102 90TH AVE 11423
  Marvin Pinsky, prin.

St. Gerard Majella ES
  91ST AVE & 188TH ST 11423

Holtsville, Suffolk Co., Pop. Code 5
Sachem Central SD
Supt. – See Holbrook
Sagamore JHS, 57 DIVISION ST 11742
  Thomas Toscano, prin.
Chippewa ES, 31 MORRIS AVE 11742
  John Cassese, prin.
Tamarac ES, 50 SPENCE AVE 11742
  Guy Barber, prin.
Waverly Avenue ES, 1111 WAVERLY AVE 11742
  Walter Earley, prin.

Homer, Cortland Co., Pop. Code 5
Homer Central SD
Sch. Sys. Enr. Code 5
Supt. – John Grant, 80 S WEST ST 13077
IS, 58 CLINTON ST 13077 – Lawrence King, prin.
ES, CENTRAL PARK 13077
  Gary Harrington, prin.
Other Schools – See Truxton

Honeoye, Ontario Co., Pop. Code 2
Honeoye Central SD
Sch. Sys. Enr. Code 4
Supt. – Randolph Coon, P O BOX 170 14471
ES, P O BOX 170 14471 – James Wolinsky, prin.

Honeoye Falls, Monroe Co., Pop. Code 4
Honeoye Falls-Lima Central SD
Sch. Sys. Enr. Code 4
Supt. – James Frenck, 20 CHURCH ST 14472
Honeoye Falls-Lima MS, 20 CHURCH ST 14472
  Garcia Reed, prin.
Manor IS, 147 EAST ST 14472
  Daniel McCarthy, prin.
Other Schools – See Lima

Hoosick Falls, Rensselaer Co., Pop. Code 5
Hoosick Falls Central SD
Sch. Sys. Enr. Code 4
Supt. – Edward Szado, P O BOX 192 12090
ES, P O BOX 192 12090 – Stephen Johnson, prin.

St. Mary's Academy, 5 HIGH ST 12090

Hopewell Junction, Dutchess Co., Pop. Code 4
Wappingers Central SD
Supt. – See Wappingers Falls
Gayhead ES, ENTRY ROAD 12533
  John Campanella, prin.

St. Columba ES, ROUTE 82 BOX 368 12533

Hornell, Steuben Co., Pop. Code 7
Hornell CSD
Sch. Sys. Enr. Code 4
Supt. – H. Paul, 50 SENECA ST 14843
Bryant ES, TERRY STREET 14843
  William Loree, prin.
Columbian ES, 25 PEARL ST 14843
  William Loree, prin.
IS, 21 PARK ST 14843 – Robert Gaffney, prin.
North Hornell ES, AVONDALE AVENUE 14843
  Carol Topping, prin.

St. Ann ES, 27 ERIE AVE 14843

Horseheads, Chemung Co., Pop. Code 6
Horseheads Central SD
Sch. Sys. Enr. Code 5
Supt. – Donald Parker, BD OF EDUC BLDG 14845
MS, SING SING ROAD 14845
  Harry Hillman, prin.
Center Street ES, CENTER STREET 14845
  David Dallaportas, prin.
Gardner Road ES
  GARDNER ROAD SCHOOL 14845
  Denis Kingsley, prin.
Ridge Road ES, 200 RIDGE RD 14845
  Thomas Butterfield, prin.
Sing Sing Road ES, SING SING RD 14845
  Rose Tolbert, prin.
Other Schools – See Big Flats

St. Mary Our Mother ES
  811 WESTLAKE ST 14845

Howard Beach, Queens Co.
Queens Borough SD 27
Supt. – See Ozone Park
ES, 9801 159TH AVE 11414 – Julie Previds, prin.
Lindenwood ES, 15323 83RD ST 11414
  Sylvia Katkin, prin.
Rockwood Park ES, 15915 88TH ST 11414
  Guy Rossiello, prin.

Hudson, Columbia Co., Pop. Code 6
Hudson CSD
Sch. Sys. Enr. Code 4
Supt. – N. Howard, 401 STATE ST 12534
Edwards ES, 360 STATE ST 12534
  Hubert Hart, prin.
Greenport ES, 198 UNION TPKE 12534
  George Esposito, prin.
MS, 120 H HOWARD AVE 12534
  W. Keating, prin.
Other Schools – See Claverack

Hudson Falls, Washington Co., Pop. Code 6
Hudson Falls Central SD
Sch. Sys. Enr. Code 5
Supt. – John Zeis, 85 NOTRE DAME ST 12839
JHS, 83 NOTRE DAME ST 12839
  Nicholas Resetar, prin.
Dix Avenue ES, DIX AVENUE 12839
  Douglas Coughlin, prin.
Maple Street ES, 135 MAPLE ST 12839
  John Potter, prin.
Murphy ES, 2 CLARK ST 12839
  Leonard Goodrich, prin.
Other Schools – See Fort Edward

Hunter, Greene Co., Pop. Code 3
Hunter-Tannersville Central SD
Supt. – See Tannersville
ES 12442 – Richard Carter, prin.

Huntington, Suffolk Co., Pop. Code 9
Cold Spring Harbor Central SD
Supt. – See Cold Spring Harbor
Harbor ES, SCHOOL LANE 11743
  Ellen Bestlaimit, prin.

Elwood UFD
Supt. – See Greenlawn
Boyd ES, 286 CUBA HILL RD 11743
  Alan Vann, prin.

Huntington UFD
Sch. Sys. Enr. Code 5
Supt. – Richard Stock, P O BOX 1500 11743
Finley JHS, 20 GREENLAWN ROAD 11743
  Craig Springer, prin.
Flower Hill ES, GOLF LANE 11743
  Anthony Barresi, prin.
ES, LOWNDES AVE 11743 – Stephen Good, prin.
Jefferson ES, 253 OAKWOOD RD 11743
  Joan Skelly, prin.
Southdown ES, BROWNS ROAD 11743
  Philip Nardone, prin.
Other Schools – See Huntington Station

South Huntington UFD
Supt. – See Huntington Station
Oakwood ES, 264 W 22ND ST 11743
  Robert Harrington, prin.

St. Patrick ES, 360 W MAIN ST 11743

Huntington Station, Suffolk Co., Pop. Code 8
Half Hollow Hills Central SD
Supt. – See Melville
Chestnut Hill ES, 600 S SERVICE RD   11746
Edward Blair, prin.

Huntington UFD
Supt. – See Huntington
Washington ES, WHITSON ROAD   11746
(—), prin.

South Huntington UFD
Sch. Sys. Enr. Code 6
Supt. – Daniel Domenech, WESTON ST   11746
Stimson JHS, 401 OAKWOOD ROAD   11746
Marie Connelly, prin.
Birchwood ES, 121 WOLF HILL RD   11747
James Romanelli, prin.
Countrywood ES, OLD COUNTRY ROAD   11746
Emily Rodgers, prin.
Maplewood ES, SCHOOL LANE   11746
Howard Link, prin.
Silas Wood ES, 99 HARDING PL   11746
Sheila Montague, prin.
Other Schools – See Huntington

Long Island ES-Gifted
145 PIDGEON HILL RD   11746
St. Hugh of Lincoln ES
1450 NEW YORK AVE   11746

Hurley, Ulster Co., Pop. Code 5
Kingston CSD
Supt. – See Kingston
Myer ES   12433 – Frederick Wadnola, prin.

Hyde Park, Dutchess Co., Pop. Code 7
Hyde Park Central SD
Sch. Sys. Enr. Code 5
Supt. – Ernest Cannava, HAVILAND ROAD   12538
Haviland JHS, 20 HAVILAND ROAD   12538
R. Kuralt, prin.
ES, 65 S ALBANY POST RD   12538
Linda Relyea, prin.
Netherwood ES, NETHERWOOD ROAD   12538
John Kegan, prin.
North Park ES, ROUTE 9G   12538
Eileen Kerins, prin.
Smith ES, ROUTE 9G SMITH COURT   12538
Carol Meissner, prin.
Other Schools – See Poughkeepsie

Regina Coeli ES, 55 S ALBANY POST RD   12538

Ilion, Herkimer Co., Pop. Code 6
Ilion Central SD
Sch. Sys. Enr. Code 4
Supt. – J. Fusco, P O BOX 480   13357
Barringer Road ES, BARRINGER ROAD   13357
Salvatore Zito, prin.
Remington ES, 77 E NORTH ST   13357
Daniel Fleming, prin.

Annunciation ES, 60 WEST ST   13357

Indian Lake, Hamilton Co., Pop. Code 4
Indian Lake Central SD
Sch. Sys. Enr. Code 2
Supt. – Merton Burritt, HCR 01   12842
Indian Lake Central S, HCR 01   12842
Merton Burritt, prin.

Inlet, Hamilton Co.
Inlet Common SD
Sch. Sys. Enr. Code 1
Supt. – Peter Eckhardt, P O BOX 207   13360
ES, P O BOX 207   13360 – Jean Bird, prin.

Interlaken, Seneca Co., Pop. Code 3
South Seneca Central SD
Sch. Sys. Enr. Code 4
Supt. – John Plume, MAIN ST   14521
South Seneca ES, MAIN STREET   14847
Ray Vancuyck, prin.
South Seneca MS, MAIN ST   14847
Ray Vancuyck, prin.

Inwood, New York Co., Pop. Code 6
Lawrence UFD
Supt. – See Lawrence
ES 2, DONAHUE AVENUE   11696
Joseph Miller, prin.

Irvington, Westchester Co., Pop. Code 6
Abbott UFD
Sch. Sys. Enr. Code 2
Supt. – (—), 100 N BROADWAY   10533
Abbott S, 100 N BROADWAY   10533
Seabrew Ford, prin.

Irvington UFD
Sch. Sys. Enr. Code 4
Supt. – Stephen Fisher, N BROADWAY   10533
MS, 101 MAIN ST   10533 – Andrew Kerfut, prin.
Dows Lane ES, DOWS LANE   10533
Andrew Dowling, prin.

Immaculate Conception School
16 N BROADWAY   10533

Island Park, Nassau Co., Pop. Code 5
Island Park UFD
Sch. Sys. Enr. Code 3
Supt. – G. Marr, 150 TRAFALGAR BLVD   11558
Lincoln Orens MS, TRAFALGAR BLVD   11558
Sy Rosen, prin.

Hegarty ES, 98 RADCLIFFE RD   11558
Anthony Anechiarico, prin.

Islip, Suffolk Co., Pop. Code 10
Islip UFD
Sch. Sys. Enr. Code 5
Supt. – Michael Griffin, 215 MAIN ST   11751
MS, 211 MAIN ST   11751 – James Collins, prin.
Commack Road ES, COMMACK ROAD   11751
Everett Och, prin.
Sherwood ES, 305 SMITH AVE   11751
Marjorie Minicozzi, prin.

Islip Terrace, Suffolk Co., Pop. Code 6
East Islip UFD
Sch. Sys. Enr. Code 6
Supt. – Michael Griffin, 1 GARIEPY ST   11752
Islip Terrace JHS, 100 REDMAN ST   11752
Robert Stelling, prin.
Connetquot ES, 1 MERRICK ST   11752
Roseanne Amnunziato, prin.
Kinney ES, 1 SPUR DR S   11752
Christian Lavote, prin.
Other Schools – See East Islip

Ithaca, Tompkins Co., Pop. Code 8
Ithaca CSD
Sch. Sys. Enr. Code 6
Supt. – Gordon Bruno, P O BOX 549   14851
Boynton MS, 1601 N CAYUGA ST   14850
John Stewart, prin.
De Witt MS, 560 WARREN ROAD   14850
Gary Buchner, prin.
Belle Sherman ES, 501 MITCHELL ST   14850
Robert Navarro, prin.
Cayuga Heights ES, 110 E UPLAND RD   14850
Lynsey Plume, prin.
Central ES, 302 W BUFFALO ST   14850
Edward Wright, prin.
Enfield ES, RURAL ROUTE 05   14850
Nancy Brown, prin.
Fall Creek ES, 202 KING ST   14850
Iva Wong, prin.
Northeast ES, WINTHROP DRIVE   14850
Joseph Stone, prin.
South Hill ES, 520 HUDSON ST   14850
Michael Ouckama, prin.
Other Schools – See Slaterville Springs

Immaculate Conception ES
320 W BUFFALO ST   14850
Montessori School of Ithaca
120 E KING ROAD   14850

Jackson Heights, Queens Co.
Queens Borough SD 30
Supt. – See Long Island City
Pulitzer IS, 33-34 80TH ST   11372
Perry Sandler, prin.
ES, 7702 37TH AVE   11372 – Hadassa Legatt, prin.
McAuliffe ES, 9311 34TH AVE   11372
Thelma Prince, prin.

Jamaica, Queens Co.
Queens Borough SD 26
Supt. – See Bayside
Holliswood ES, 18910 RADNOR RD   11423
Carol Harris, prin.

Queens Borough SD 27
Supt. – See Ozone Park
Chester Park ES, 9725 108TH ST   11419
Jerry Spitz, prin.
Johnson ES, 12520 SUTPHIN BLVD   11434
M. Bradley, prin.

Queens Borough SD 28
Supt. – See Forest Hills
Briarwood ES
143RD STREET & 85TH ROAD   11435
Benjamin Dorogusker, prin.
Ellington ES
116TH AVENUE & 166TH STREET   11434
Ralph Satterthwaite, prin.
Higbie ES
137TH AVENUE & 173RD STREET   11434
Joan Burton, prin.
Huntington ES, 10920 UNION HALL ST   11433
Sheldon Roach, prin.
Maure ES, 13110 97TH AVE   11419
Norman Weisman, prin.
Public ES 160, 10950 INWOOD ST   11435
Rose Lee, prin.
Public ES 30, 12610 BEDELL ST   11434
Ursula Day, prin.
Public MS 86, 8741 PARSONS BLVD   11432
Harris Chandler, prin.
Smith PS, 90-30 & 90-50 150TH ST   11435
Anne Gargan, prin.
Talfourd Lawn ES, 14326 101ST AVE   11435
Joseph Locastro, prin.
Hammond MS, 8802 144TH ST   11435
Catherine Winter, prin.
Wordsworth ES, 15502 108TH AVE   11433
Ruth Harrod, prin.

Queens Borough SD 29
Supt. – See Queens Village
Anthony IS, 88-15 182ND ST   11423
Stanley Lisser, prin.
Adams ES
84TH AVENUE AND 172ND STRT   11432
Theresa Casey, prin.
Eastwood ES, 17901 90TH AVE   11432
Aura Zanzeni, prin.

Public ES 116, 10725 WREN PL   11433
Elaine Davis, prin.
Public ES 118, 19020 109TH RD   11412
Carl Solomon, prin.
Public ES 52
NEW YORK BLVD & 146TH TER   11434
Lloyd Backus, prin.
Springfield ES, 17937 137TH AVE   11434
Lawrence Saken, prin.
Wilkins ES, 21015 115TH AVE   11412
Erthel Mitchell, prin.

Christopher Robin School
222 16 MERRICK BLVD   11413
Allen Christian ES, 171-10 LINDEN BLVD   11434
Bais Yaakov Academy for Girls
124-50 METROPOLITAN AVE   11415
Cambria Center for Gifted Children
233-10 LINDEN BLVD   11411
Christ Lutheran ES
248-01 FRANCIS LEWIS BLVD   11422
Grace Lutheran Day ES
100-05 SPRINGFIELD BLVD   11429
Holy Trinity Community ES
90-20 191ST ST   11423
Ideal Montessori School, 87-41 165TH ST   11432
Immaculate Conception ES
179-14 DALNY RD   11432
Incarnation ES
8915 FRANCIS LEWIS BLVD   11427
Jamaica Day School-St. Demtrios
84-35 152ND ST   11432
Labre ES, 94-25 117TH ST   11419
Lakeview Educational Institute
194-15 LINDEN BLVD   11412
Linden ES, 137-01 228TH ST   11413
Our Lady of Cenacle ES, 87-25 136TH ST   11418
Our Lady of Grace ES, 158-20 101ST ST   11414
Our Lady of Lourdes ES, 92-80 220TH ST   11428
Our Lady of Perpetual Help ES
111-10 115TH ST   11420
Presentation of BVM ES
88-13 PARSONS BLVD   11432
SS. Joachim & Anne ES, 218-19 105TH AVE   11429
Sacred Heart ES, 115-50 221ST ST   11411
St. Anthony of Padua ES
125-18 ROCKAWAY BLVD   11420
St. Benedict Joseph Labre School
94-25 117TH ST   11419
St. Catherne of Sienna ES
118-34 RIVERTON ST   11412
St. Clare ES, 137-25 BROOKVILLE BLVD   11422
St. Clement Pope ES, 120-27 141ST ST   11436
St. Elizabeth ES, 94-01 85TH ST   11416
St. Gregory the Great ES, 244-44 87TH AVE   11426
St. Helen ES, 83-09 157TH AVE   11414
St. Joseph Parish Day ES, 99-10 217TH LN   11429
St. Mary Gate of Heaven ES
104-06 101ST AVE   11416
St. Nicholas of Tolentine ES
80-22 PARSONS BLVD   11432
St. Pascal Baylon ES, 112-35 199TH ST   11412
St. Peter Claver ES, 149-18 JAMAICA AVE   11435
St. Pius V ES, 105-12 LIVERPOOL ST   11435
St. Pius X ES, 147-65 249TH ST   11422
St. Stanislaus BM ES, 90-01 101ST AVE   11416
St. Teresa of Avila ES, 109-55 128TH ST   11420
St. Thomas Apostle ES, 8749 87TH ST   11421
Woodhull Day ES
196-10 WOODHULL AVE   11423
Yeshiva Tifereth Moshe
83-06 ABINGDON RD   11415
Yeshivat Ohr Haiim ES
82-52 ABINGTON RD   11415

Jamestown, Chautauqua Co., Pop. Code 8
Bemus Point Central SD
Supt. – See Bemus Point
Fluvanna ES, RURAL ROUTE 01   14701
P. Sawyer, prin.

Jamestown CSD
Sch. Sys. Enr. Code 6
Supt. – C. Tod Eagle, 200 E 4TH ST   14701
Jefferson MS, 195 MARTIN ROAD   14701
Primo Belluz, prin.
Bush ES, 150 PARDEE AVE   14701
Roger Gilbert, prin.
Fletcher ES, 301 COLE AVE   14701
Robert Herring, prin.
Lincoln ES, 301 FRONT ST   14701
Terrance Radecki, prin.
Love ES, 624 PINE ST   14701
Daniel Kathman, prin.
Persell MS, 375 BAKER ST   14701
Katherine Burch, prin.
Ring ES, 333 BUFFALO ST   14701
John Carlson, prin.
Rogers ES, 41 HEBNER ST   14701
Samuel Pellerito, prin.
Washington MS, 159 BUFFALO ST   14701
Ricardo Hammond, prin.

Southwestern Central SD
Sch. Sys. Enr. Code 4
Supt. – Donald Ogilivie, 600 HUNT ROAD   14701
Southwestern MS, 600 HUNT ROAD   14701
Gregory Paterniti, prin.
Other Schools – See Celoron, Lakewood

Bethel Baptist Christian Academy
200 HUNT ROAD   14701
SS. Peter & Paul ES, 1135 N MAIN ST   14701

Jamesville, Onondaga Co., Pop. Code 3
Jamesville-DeWitt Central SD
Supt. – See De Witt
Jamesville-DeWitt MS, RANDALL ROAD   13078
  Ronald Ramsden, prin.
ES   13078 – Robert Catney, prin.

Jasper, Steuben Co., Pop. Code 4
Jasper-Troupsburg Central SD
Sch. Sys. Enr. Code 2
Supt. – Frank Schmidt   14855
Jasper-Troupsburg JSHS, MAIN ST   14855
  Robert Cleeves, prin.
Other Schools – See Troupsburg

Jefferson, Schoharie Co., Pop. Code 4
Jefferson Central SD
Sch. Sys. Enr. Code 2
Supt. – Edward Roche   12093
Jefferson Central S, MAIN ST   12093
  John Righi, prin.

Jeffersonville, Sullivan Co., Pop. Code 3
Jeffersonville-Youngsville Central SD
Sch. Sys. Enr. Code 3
Supt. – D. Johnson, P O BOX 308   12748
S, P O BOX 308   12748 – Judith Highhouse, prin.
Other Schools – See Youngsville

Jericho, Nassau Co., Pop. Code 7
Jericho UFD
Sch. Sys. Enr. Code 4
Supt. – Rob Manheimer
  CEDAR SWAMP ROAD   11753
Cantiague ES, 698 CANTIAGUE ROCK RD   11753
  Marc Horowitz, prin.
Jackson ES, 58 MAYTIME DR   11753
  Gloria Tuchman, prin.

Solomon Schecter Day School-Nassau
  BARBARA LN   11753

Johnson City, Broome Co., Pop. Code 4
Johnson City Central SD
Sch. Sys. Enr. Code 5
Supt. – Albert Mamary
  666 REYNOLDS ROAD   13790
Johnson ES, 235 HARRY L DR   13790
  Arthur Chambers, prin.
Johnson MS, 100 ALBERT ST   13790
  R. Meehan, prin.
Lincoln ES, 30 CHERRY ST   13790
  Joseph Valentino, prin.

St. James ES, 147 MAIN ST   13790
Blessed Sacrament ES, 3 CENACLE PLZ   13790

Johnsonville, Rensselaer Co.
Brunswick Central SD
Supt. – See Troy
Parker ES, P O BOX 61   12094
  Darlene Egelston, prin.

Johnstown, Fulton Co., Pop. Code 6
Johnstown CSD
Sch. Sys. Enr. Code 4
Supt. – J. McNamara, 501 GLEBE ST   12095
Knox JHS, 400 PERRY ST   12095
  Anthony Eppolito, prin.
Glebe Street ES, GLEBE STREET   12095
  Donald Nickson, prin.
Jansen Avenue ES, JANSEN AVENUE   12095
  Richard Tucci, prin.
Pleasant Avenue ES, PLEASANT AVENUE   12095
  Roger Rooney, prin.
Warren Street ES, WARRENT STREET   12095
  Bertram Longbotham, prin.

Jordan, Onondaga Co., Pop. Code 4
Jordan Elbridge Central SD
Sch. Sys. Enr. Code 4
Supt. – William Phillips
  HAMILTON ROAD   13080
Ramsdell ES, CHAPEL STREET   13080
  Paul Hurst, prin.
Other Schools – See Elbridge

Katonah, Westchester Co., Pop. Code 5
Katonah Lewisboro UFD
Sch. Sys. Enr. Code 5
Supt. – Joseph Fletcher   10536
ES, 106 HUNTVILLE RD   10536
  Henry Brooks, prin.
Other Schools – See Goldens Bridge, South Salem

St. Mary-Assumption ES, 99 VALLEY RD   10536

Keene Valley, Essex Co.
Keene Central SD
Sch. Sys. Enr. Code 2
Supt. – John Stewart   12943
Keene Central S   12943 – John Stewart, prin.

Keeseville, Clinton Co., Pop. Code 4
Ausable Valley Central SD
Supt. – See Clintonville
ES, 52 MAIN ST   12944
  Richard McCormick, prin.

Kendall, Orleans Co., Pop. Code 4
Kendall Central SD
Sch. Sys. Enr. Code 4
Supt. – Harlow Fisher, KENDALL ROAD   14476
ES, KENDALL ROAD   14476 – J. Allen, prin.

Kenmore, Erie Co., Pop. Code 7
Kenmore UFD
Sch. Sys. Enr. Code 6
Supt. – John Helfrich, 1500 COLVIN BLVD   14223
Franklin MS, 540 PARKHURST BLVD   14223
  J. Martinke, prin.
Hoover MS, 249 THORNCLIFF ROAD   14223
  R. Coates, prin.
Kenmore MS, 155 DELAWARE ROAD   14217
  Florence Kern, prin.
Franklin ES, 500 PARKHURST BLVD   14223
  M. Cawley, prin.
Hoover ES, 199 THORNCLIFF RD   14223
  Michael Giallombardo, prin.
Jefferson ES, 250 ATHENS BLVD   14223
  Dorothy Vienne, prin.
Lindbergh ES, CROSBY AND IRVING TER   14223
  Lloyd Northey, prin.
Roosevelt ES, 283 WASHINGTON AVE   14217
  Stanley Penkacik, prin.
Other Schools – See Tonawanda

St. Andrew Country ES
  1545 SHERIDAN DR   14217
St. Paul ES, 47 VICTORIA BLVD   14217

Kennedy, Chautauqua Co.
Falconer Central SD
Supt. – See Falconer
Temple ES   14747 – Kenneth Vossler, prin.

Kew Gardens, Queens Co.
Queens Borough SD 28
Supt. – See Forest Hills
ES, 8237 KEW GARDENS RD   11415
  Benjamin Piltch, prin.

Kiamesha Lake, Sullivan Co.

Hebrew Day ES-Ulster, KIAMESHA LAKE   12751

Kinderhook, Columbia Co., Pop. Code 4
Kinderhook Central SD
Supt. – See Valatie
Vanburen ES, BROAD STREET   12106
  Jane Diamond, prin.

Kings Park, Suffolk Co., Pop. Code 6
Kings Park Central SD
Sch. Sys. Enr. Code 5
Supt. – Walter Arnold, 97 KOHR ROAD   11754
Rogers MS, 79 OLD DOCK ROAD   11754
  Mary Derose, prin.
Ft. Salonga ES, SUNKEN MEADOW ROAD   11754
  John McGovern, prin.
Parkview ES, 35 ROUNDTREE DR   11754
  Michael O'Brien, prin.

Kingston, Ulster Co., Pop. Code 7
Kingston CSD
Sch. Sys. Enr. Code 6
Supt. – L. Salzmann, 61 CROWN ST   12401
Bailey MS, MERILINA AVE   12401
  Patricia Majewski, prin.
Chambers ES
  945 ALBANY AVENUE EXTENSION   12401
  Ronald LeBlanc, prin.
Edson ES, MERILINA AVENUE   12401
  Robert Corcoran, prin.
Kennedy ES, 106 GROSS ST   12401
  Donald Shambo, prin.
Meagher ES, 21 WYNKOOP PL   12401
  Douglas Chisamore, prin.
Washington ES, 67 WALL ST   12401
  Vernon Outwater,Jr., prin.
Zena ES, ZENA & SAWKILL ROADS   12401
  Leon Hobbs, prin.
Other Schools – See Hurley, Lake Katrine, Port Ewen,
  Ulster Park

Good Shepherd ES, 83 E CHESTER ST   12401
Kingston Catholic ES, 159 BROADWAY   12401
St. Joseph ES, 235 WALL ST   12401

Kirkwood, Broome Co., Pop. Code 6
Susquehanna Valley Central SD
Supt. – See Conklin
Cedarhurst ES
  RURAL ROUTE 01 BOX 1825   13795
  Robert Callahan, prin.

Windsor Central SD
Supt. – See Windsor
Bell ES, RURAL ROUTE 02   13795
  Michael Farina, prin.

Knox, St. Lawrence Co.
Edwards-Knox Central SD
Supt. – See Russell
S, P O BOX 630   13684 – Joseph Zelinski, prin.

Lackawanna, Erie Co., Pop. Code 7
Lackawanna CSD
Sch. Sys. Enr. Code 5
Supt. – Thomas McDonnell
  30 JOHNSON STREET   14218
Franklin ES, 146 FRANKLIN ST   14218
  John Luba, prin.
Mckinley IS, 245 S SHORE BLVD   14218
  Robert Lisowski, prin.
Truman ES, 15 INNER DR   14218
  Nicholas Korach, prin.

Our Lady of Victory ES, 2760 S PARK AVE   14218

La Fargeville, Jefferson Co.
La Fargeville Central SD
Sch. Sys. Enr. Code 2
Supt. – Henry Henderson, P O BOX 138   13656
La Fargeville Central S   13656
  Henry Henderson, prin.

La Fayette, Onondaga Co.
La Fayette Central SD
Sch. Sys. Enr. Code 4
Supt. – J. Aiken, 7 RT 11 N   13084
Grimshaw ES, CHERRY VALLEY ROAD   13084
  James Barnello, prin.
Other Schools – See Nedrow

Lagrangeville, Dutchess Co.
Arlington Central SD
Supt. – See Poughkeepsie
La Grange ES, TODD HILL ROAD   12540
  David Craw, prin.

Lake George, Warren Co., Pop. Code 4
Lake George Central SD
Sch. Sys. Enr. Code 4
Supt. – Sherman Parker, 425 CANADA ST   12845
ES, ROUTE 9L   12845 – Robert Ross, prin.

Lake Grove, Suffolk Co., Pop. Code 6
Middle Country Central SD
Supt. – See Selden
Auer Memorial ES, WING STREET   11755
  Richard Hoff, prin.

Sachem Central SD
Supt. – See Holbrook
Wenonah ES, 251 HUDSON AVE   11755
  Thomas Myers, prin.

Lake Katrine, Ulster Co., Pop. Code 4
Kingston CSD
Supt. – See Kingston
Miller JHS, FORDING PL ROAD   12449
  Bythema Bagley, prin.
Crosby ES, NEIGHBORHOOD ROAD   12449
  Rita Wagner, prin.

Lake Luzerne, Warren Co., Pop. Code 5
Hadley-Luzerne Central SD
Sch. Sys. Enr. Code 3
Supt. – Harry Brooks, LAKE AVE   12846
Townsend MS, HYLAND DRIVE   12846
  Clinton Freeman, prin.
Hadley Luzerne ES, LAKE AVENUE   12846
  Clinton Freeman, prin.

Lakemont, Yates Co.

Freedom Academy, FREEDOM VILLAGE   14857

Lake Placid, Essex Co., Pop. Code 4
Lake Placid Central SD
Sch. Sys. Enr. Code 3
Supt. – Gerald Blair, 250 MAIN ST   12946
ES, OLD MILITARY ROAD   12946
  Donald Morrison, prin.

St. Agne's Parochial ES, 6 HILLCREST AVE   12946

Lake Ronkonkoma, Suffolk Co., Pop. Code 6
Sachem Central SD
Supt. – See Holbrook
Cayuga ES, 865 HAWKINS AVE   11779
  Dale Lemery, prin.
Gatelot Avenue ES, 65 GATELOT AVE   11779
  Henry Barton, prin.
Hiawatha ES, 97 PATCHOGUE RD   11779
  Maureen Bigham, prin.

St. Joseph ES, 25 CHURCH ST   11779

Lake View, Erie Co.
Frontier Central SD
Supt. – See Hamburg
Pinehurst ES, 6050 FAIRWAY CT   14085
  Andrew Podlucky, prin.

Southtowns Catholc ES, P O BOX 86   14085

Lakewood, Chautauqua Co., Pop. Code 5
Southwestern Central SD
Supt. – See Jamestown
MS, LAKEVIEW AVENUE   14750
  Brenda Malarkey, prin.

Lancaster, Erie Co., Pop. Code 7
Lancaster Central SD
Sch. Sys. Enr. Code 5
Supt. – Joseph Girardi, 177 CENTRAL AVE   14086
Aurora MS, 148 AURORA ST   14086
  Terrence Smerka, prin.
Como Park ES, 1985 COMO PARK BLVD   14086
  Rochford Harmon, prin.
Court Street ES, 91 COURT ST   14086
  Frank Rizzo, prin.
Hillview ES, TRANSIT PLEASANTVIEW   14086
  Kenneth Hamilton, prin.
Other Schools – See Depew

Our Lady of Pompeii ES
  129 LAVERACK AVE   14086
St. Mary's ES, SAINT MARYS HL   14086

Lansing, Tompkins Co., Pop. Code 5
Lansing Central SD
Sch. Sys. Enr. Code 4
Supt. – R. Buckley, 264 RIDGE ROAD   14882
MS, L6 LUDLOWVILLE ROAD   14882
  Thomas Jones, prin.

ES, 284 RIDGE RD   14882 – Creighton Lusk, prin.

Larchmont, Westchester Co., Pop. Code 3
Mamaroneck UFD
Supt. – See Mamaroneck
Hommocks MS, HOMMOCKS ROAD   10538
   Richard North, prin.
Central ES, 1100 PALMER AVE   10538
   Milton Meiskin, prin.
Chatsworth Avenue ES
   CHATSWORTH AVE   10538 – Joanne Stack, prin.
Murray Avenue ES, 200 MURRAY AVE   10538
   Elizabeth Dreier, prin.

French-American School
   111 LARCHMONT AVE   10538
SS. John & Paul School, 280 WEAVER ST   10538

Latham, Albany Co., Pop. Code 6
North Colonie Central SD
Supt. – See Newtonville
Shaker JHS
   445 WATERVLIET SHAKER ROAD   12110
   Russell Moore, prin.
Blue Creek ES, CLINTON ROAD   12110
   Maureen Flaherty, prin.
Boght Hills ES, P O BOX 300   12128
   James Girvin, prin.
Forts Ferry ES, 101 FORTS FERRY RD   12110
   Henry Boehning, prin.
Latham Ridge ES, MERCER AVENUE   12110
   Rose Jackson, prin.

Latham Christian Academy
   405 WTVLT-SHAKER ROAD   12110
St. Ambrose ES, 347 OLD LOUDON RD   12110

Laurel, Suffolk Co.
Laurel Common SD
Sch. Sys. Enr. Code 2
Supt. – Patricia Wall, MAIN ROAD   11948
ES, MAIN ROAD   11948 – Patricia Wall, prin.

Laurens, Otsego Co., Pop. Code 2
Laurens Central SD
Sch. Sys. Enr. Code 2
Supt. – Jeffrey Hahn   13796
Laurens Central S, MAIN ST   13796
   Pasquale Grasso, prin.

Lawrence, Nassau Co., Pop. Code 6
Lawrence UFD
Sch. Sys. Enr. Code 5
Supt. – Alvin Baron, 195 BROADWAY   11559
MS, 195 BROADWAY   11559
   Anthony Capobianco, prin.
ES 1, 260 CENTRAL AVE   11559
   George Cowie, prin.
Other Schools – See Cedarhurst, Inwood, Woodmere

Brandeis School, 25 FROST LN   11559
Hebrew Academy ES
   33 WASHINGTON AVE   11559

Le Roy, Genesee Co., Pop. Code 5
Le Roy Central SD
Sch. Sys. Enr. Code 4
Supt. – Gary Wilcox, 2-6 TRIGON PARK   14482
Wolcott Street ES   14482 – James Thompson, prin.

Holy Family ES, 44 LAKE ST   14482

Levittown, Nassau Co., Pop. Code 8
Island Trees UFD
Sch. Sys. Enr. Code 4
Supt. – Rich Segerdahl, ISLAND TREES 3   11756
Gallow ES, ISLAND TREES 5   11756
   Robert Feirsen, prin.
Sparke ES, ISLAND TREES 4   11756
   Mary Kivlighn, prin.
Stokes ES, ISLAND TREES 3   11756
   Madeline Montone, prin.

Levittown UFD
Sch. Sys. Enr. Code 6
Supt. – Herman Sirois, 1 CENTER LANE   11756
Salk MS, OLD JERUSALEM ROAD   11756
   P. Hall, prin.
Wisdom Lane MS, CENTER LANE   11756
   Robert Simko, prin.
Abbey Lane ES, ABBEY LANE   11756
   Rose Auteri, prin.
Gardiners Avenue ES
   610 GARDINERS AVE   11756 – John Furlong, prin.
Northside ES, 35 PELICAN RD   11756
   Lorraine Haviken, prin.
Summit Lane ES, 4 SUMMIT LN   11756
   Sally Evans, prin.
Other Schools – See Seaford, Wantagh

South Shore Christian ES
   40 FARMEDGE RD   11756
St. Bernard ES, 3100 HEMPSTEAD TPKE   11756

Lewiston, Niagara Co., Pop. Code 5
Niagara Wheatfield Central SD
Supt. – See Sanborn
Tuscarora ES, 2015 MOUNT HOPE RD   14092
   Charles Tortorete, prin.

St. Peter ES, 140 N 6TH ST   14092

Liberty, Sullivan Co., Pop. Code 5
Liberty Central SD
Sch. Sys. Enr. Code 4
Supt. – Richard Beruk, 167 N MAIN ST   12754

ES, 201 N MAIN ST   12754 – James Conway, prin.
Other Schools – See White Sulphur Springs

St. Peter ES, 2 LINCOLN PL   12754

Lima, Livingston Co., Pop. Code 4
Honeoye Falls-Lima Central SD
Supt. – See Honeoye Falls
ES, COLLEGE STREET   14485
   George Batterson, prin.

Lima Christian School
   1575 ROCHESTER ST   14485

Limestone, Cattaraugus Co., Pop. Code 1
Limestone UFD
Sch. Sys. Enr. Code 2
Supt. – John Pionzio, 100 MAIN ROAD   14753
Limestone Union Free S, 100 MAIN ROAD   14753
   John Pionzio, prin.

Lincolndale, Westchester Co.
Somers Central SD
Supt. – See Somers
Primrose ES, PRIMROSE ST   10540
   James Beaty, prin.

Lindenhurst, Suffolk Co., Pop. Code 8
Lindenhurst UFD
Sch. Sys. Enr. Code 6
Supt. – Anthony Pecorale, 350 DANIEL ST   11757
JHS, 350 S WELLWOOD AVE   11757
   Jack Diffily, prin.
Albany Avenue ES, 180 ALBANY AVENUE   11757
   Roy Mathison, prin.
Alleghany Avenue ES
   250 S ALLEGHANY AVE   11757
   Susan Stella, prin.
Bower ES, MONTAUK HIGHWAY   11757
   Bob Dennis, prin.
Daniel Street ES, 289 DANIEL ST   11757
   Renee Bennet, prin.
Harding Avenue ES, 2 HARDING AVE   11757
   Eric Freidman, prin.
Rall ES, NORTH WELLWOOD AVENUE   11757
   Robert Kersch, prin.
West Gates Avenue ES
   WEST GATES AVENUE   11757
   Jon Rothfeld, prin.

Our Lady of Perpetual Help ES
   240 S WELLWOOD AVE   11757

Lisbon, St. Lawrence Co., Pop. Code 5
Lisbon Central SD
Sch. Sys. Enr. Code 3
Supt. – Wayne Chesbrough   13658
Lisbon Central S   13658 – Philip Snyder, prin.

Little Falls, Herkimer Co., Pop. Code 6
Little Falls CSD
Sch. Sys. Enr. Code 4
Supt. – W. Bradt, 770 E MAIN ST   13365
Hall ES, 15 PETRIE ST   13365
   Salvatore Marchese, prin.
Monroe Street ES, 156 W MONROE ST   13365
   Leonard Hersh, prin.

Little Neck, Queens Co.
Queens Borough SD 26
Supt. – See Bayside
North Hills ES, 5740 MARATHON PKY   11362
   Berton Lax, prin.
Porter ES, 4177 LITTLE NECK PKY   11363
   Claire McIntee, prin.

Little Valley, Cattaraugus Co., Pop. Code 4
Little Valley Central SD
Sch. Sys. Enr. Code 2
Supt. – Timothy Wisniewski
   207 ROCK CITY ST   14755
Little Valley Central S, 207 ROCK CITY ST   14755
   Paul Stetz, prin.

Liverpool, Onondaga Co., Pop. Code 5
Liverpool Central SD
Sch. Sys. Enr. Code 7
Supt. – Jerome Melvin, 800 4TH ST   13088
Chestnut Hill MS
   204 SASLON PARK DRIVE   13088
   Carl Beck, prin.
MS, HICKORY & 7TH   13088 – R. Defazio, prin.
Soule Road MS, 8340 SOULE ROAD   13088
   L. Decoste, prin.
Chestnut Hill ES, 200 SASLON PARK DR   13088
   Margaret Masters, prin.
Crawford ES, 195 BLACKBERRY RD   13090
   Harry Desens, prin.
Donlin Drive ES, 299 DONLIN DR   13088
   Eugene Kinnison, prin.
Elmcrest ES, 350 WOODSPATH RD   13090
   Harry Faduski, prin.
ES, 910 2ND ST   13088 – Thomas Pendergast, prin.
Long Branch ES, 4035 LONG BRANCH RD   13090
   William Haber, prin.
Morgan Road ES, 4340 WETZEL RD   13090
   Phyllis Middleton, prin.
Perry ES, 7053 BUCKLEY RD   13088
   Roger Phillips, prin.
Soule Road ES, SOULE ROAD   13088
   Michael Roche, prin.
Wetzel Road ES, 4246 WETZEL RD   13090
   Robert Welcher, prin.

Livingston Manor, Sullivan Co., Pop. Code 4
Livingston Manor Central SD
Sch. Sys. Enr. Code 3
Supt. – Ken Gray   12758
ES   12758 – Carolyn Anklam, prin.

Livonia, Livingston Co., Pop. Code 4
Livonia Central SD
Sch. Sys. Enr. Code 4
Supt. – James Franklin, SPRING ST   14487
MS, SCHOOL ST   14487 – John Williams, prin.
PS, BIG TREE STREET   14487
   David De Loria, prin.

Lockport, Niagra Co., Pop. Code 7
Lockport CSD
Sch. Sys. Enr. Code 6
Supt. – Stephen McKinney
   130 BEATTIE AVE   14094
Clinton ES, 85 N ADAM ST   14094
   Donald Phillips, prin.
Cross ES, 319 WEST AVE   14094
   Christine Neal, prin.
Hunt ES, 50 RODGERS AVENUE   14094
   Edward Rybarczyk, prin.
Kelley ES, 610 12 EAST HIGH STREET   14094
   Freda Maiorana, prin.
Merritt ES, 389 GREEN ST   14094
   Thomas Mulvey, prin.
Pound ES, 51 HIGH ST   14094
   Terry Carbone, prin.
Southard ES, 6385 LOCUST STREET EXT   14094
   Thomas O'Shea, prin.
Upson ES, 28 HARDING AVE   14094
   Dennis Devine, prin.

Star Point Central SD
Sch. Sys. Enr. Code 4
Supt. – Lowell Brinnen
   4363 MAPLETON ROAD   14094
Starpoint ES, 4363 MAPLETON RD   14094
   Douglas Regan, prin.

Lockport Catholic ES, 160 CHESTNUT ST   14094
St. Peter Lutheran School
   4169 CHURCH RD   14094

Locust Valley, Nassau Co., Pop. Code 5
Locust Valley Central SD
Sch. Sys. Enr. Code 4
Supt. – D. Cande
   99 HORSE HOLLOW ROAD   11560
ES, RYEFIELD ROAD   11560
   Edward Tronolone, prin.
Other Schools – See Bayville

Friends Academy, 355 DUCK POND ROAD   11560
Portledge School, 355 DUCK POND ROAD   11560

Long Beach, Nassau Co., Pop. Code 8
Long Beach CSD
Sch. Sys. Enr. Code 5
Supt. – J. Oberman, LIDO BLVD   11561
JHS, LIDO BLVD   11561 – J. Jones, prin.
East ES, NEPTUNE BOULEVARD   11561
   William Silver, prin.
Lido ES, 237 LIDO BLVD   11561
   Donald Murphy, prin.
Lindell Boulevard ES
   LINDELL BOULEVARD   11561 – Lydia Parris, prin.
West ES, MARYLAND AVENUE   11561
   Robert Friedman, prin.

Hebrew Academy Long Beach
   530 W BROADWAY   11561
Long Beach Catholic ES
   735 W BROADWAY   11561

Long Island City, Queens Co.
Queens Borough SD 24
Supt. – See Middle Village
Fitzgerald ES, 3920 48TH AVE   11104
   Jack Birbiglia, prin.

Queens Borough SD 30
Sch. Sys. Enr. Code 7
Supt. – Angela Gimondo
   3625 CRESCENT ST   11106
Blackwell ES, 3715 13TH ST   11101
   Catherine Bala, prin.
Davy ES, 2370 31ST ST   11105
   Lucille Dibiase, prin.
Dutch Kills ES, 2505 37TH AVE   11101
   Daisy Martin, prin.
Hallett ES, 2245 41ST ST   11105
   Philip Zemmel, prin.
Public ES 122, 2121 DITMARS BLVD   11105
   Anthony Locurto, prin.
Public ES 150, 4001 43RD AVE   11104
   Irwin Berkowitz, prin.
Public ES 166, 3309 35TH AVE   11106
   Lorraine Cecere, prin.
Public ES 70, 3045 42ND ST   11103
   Thomas Cullen, prin.
Steinway ES, 2245 41ST ST   11105
   Joan Comyns, prin.
Thoreau ES, 2837 29TH ST   11102
   Helen Hanges, prin.
Van Alst ES, 1414 29TH AVE   11102
   Ann Bussel, prin.
Other Schools – See Corona, East Elmhurst, Flushing,
   Jackson Heights, Woodside

Evangel Christian ES, 32-71 41ST ST   11103
Immaculate Conception ES, 21-63 29TH ST   11105

Most Precious Blood ES, 32-52 37TH ST   11103
Our Lady of Mt. Carmel ES
   23-15 NEWTOWN AVE   11102
Queen of Angels ES, 41-12 44TH ST   11104
Queens Lutheran ES, 31-20 37TH ST   11103
St. Francis of Assisi ES, 21-18 46TH ST   11105
St. Joseph ES, 28-46 44TH ST   11103
St. Mary's ES, 10-24 49TH AVE   11101
St. Patrick ES, 39-37 28TH ST   11101
St. Raphael ES, 48-25 37TH ST   11101
St. Rita ES, 36-14 12TH ST   11106

Long Lake, Hamilton Co., Pop. Code 3
Long Lake Central SD
Sch. Sys. Enr. Code 2
Supt. – Harry Graham   12847
Long Lake Central S   12847 – Harry Graham, prin.

Loudonville, Albany Co., Pop. Code 6
North Colonie Central SD
Supt. – See Newtonville
ES, 341 OSBORNE RD   12211 – Harry Page, prin.
Southgate ES, 26 SOUTHGATE RD   12211
   Robert Farrell, prin.

Loudonville Christian ES, 374 LOUDON RD   12211
St. Pius X ES, 75 UPPER LOUDON RD   12211

Lowville, Lewis Co., Pop. Code 5
Lowville Central SD
Sch. Sys. Enr. Code 4
Supt. – William Wormuth
   7668 N STATE ST   13367
ES, 7668 N STATE ST   13367 – Gale Swiecki, prin.

St. Peter's ES, 5445 SHADY AVE   13367

Lynbrook, Nassau Co., Pop. Code 7
Lynbrook UFD
Sch. Sys. Enr. Code 5
Supt. – Bern Seiderman
   111 ATLANTIC AVE   11563
Lynbrook North MS, MERRICK ROAD   11563
   Donald Slover, prin.
Lynbrook South MS, 9 UNION AVE   11563
   Gary Rugg, prin.
Marion Street ES, MARION STREET   11563
   Alfred Solomon, prin.
West End ES, CLARK AVENUE   11563
   Nola Bacci, prin.
Other Schools – See East Rockaway

Malverne UFD
Supt. – See Rockville Centre
Davison Avenue ES
   DAVISON AVENUE P O   11563
   Phyllis Wright, prin.

Our Lady of Peace ES, 21 FOWLER AVE   11563

Lyndonville, Orleans Co., Pop. Code 3
Lyndonville Central SD
Sch. Sys. Enr. Code 3
Supt. – Richard Pucher, HOUSEL AVE   14098
ES, MAIN STREET   14098 – Russell Martino, prin.

Lyons, Wayne Co., Pop. Code 5
Lyons Central SD
Sch. Sys. Enr. Code 4
Supt. – Matthew Dirisio, 9 LAWRENCE ST   14489
ES, 98 WILLIAM ST   14489 – Judy Luce, prin.

Mc Connellsville, Oneida Co.
Camden Central SD
Supt. – See Camden
ES   13401 – Richard Keville, prin.

Macedon, Wayne Co., Pop. Code 2
Gananda Central SD
Sch. Sys. Enr. Code 3
Supt. – Larry Pedersen, P O BOX 609   14502
Mann ES, 1366 WATERFORD RD   14568
   Emma Klimek, prin.

Palmyra-Macedon Central SD
Supt. – See Palmyra
ES, 4 WEST STREET   14502
   Carmen Pagano, prin.

McGraw, Cortland Co., Pop. Code 4
McGraw Central SD
Sch. Sys. Enr. Code 3
Supt. – Donato Leopardi, P O BOX 556   13101
ES   13101 – William Swisher, prin.

Madison, Madison Co., Pop. Code 2
Madison Central SD
Sch. Sys. Enr. Code 3
Supt. – Arthur Wilson   13402
Madison Central S   13402 – Arthur Wilson, prin.

Madrid, St. Lawrence Co., Pop. Code 4
Madrid-Waddington Central SD
Sch. Sys. Enr. Code 3
Supt. – James Boyle   13660
ES   13660 – Carl Rose, prin.
Other Schools – See Waddington

Mahopac, Putnam Co., Pop. Code 6
Mahopac Central SD
Sch. Sys. Enr. Code 5
Supt. – Jerry Cicchelli   10541
JHS, BALDWIN PL ROAD   10541
   John Reilly, prin.
Austin Road ES, AUSTIN ROAD   10541
   Robert Meyer, prin.
Fulmar Road ES, FULMAR ROAD   10541
   Sandra Gould, prin.

Lakeview ES, LAKEVIEW ROAD   10541
   Stephen Ochser, prin.

St. John the Evangelist ES
   MSGR OBRIEN BLVD   10541

Maine, Broome Co., Pop. Code 6
Maine Endwell Central SD
Supt. – See Endwell
Maine Memorial ES, ROUTE 26   13802
   Michael Schafer, prin.

Malone, Franklin Co., Pop. Code 6
Malone Central SD
Sch. Sys. Enr. Code 5
Supt. – Donald Anderson   12953
JHS, WEBSTER ST   12953
   O. Kendall Bemis, prin.
Davis ES, WEBSTER STREET   12953
   Kathleen Schrader, prin.
Flanders ES, E MAIN STREET   12953
   Gary Goodin, prin.
St. Josephs ES, 111 ELM ST   12953
   Lynn Dufort, prin.

Bishop Smith Memorial ES
   17 WEBSTER ST   12953
Notre Dame ES, HOMESTEAD PK   12953

Malverne, Nassau Co., Pop. Code 6
Malverne UFD
Supt. – See Rockville Centre
Herber MS, OCEAN AVE   11565
   Raymond Rodecker, prin.
Downing ES, 55 LINDNER PL   11565
   Mary Freeley, prin.

Grace Lutheran ES, 400 HEMPSTEAD AVE   11565
Our Lady of Lourdes ES, 76 PARK BLVD   11565

Mamaroneck, Westchester Co., Pop. Code 7
Mamaroneck UFD
Sch. Sys. Enr. Code 5
Supt. – Norman Colb
   1000 W BOSTON POST ROAD   10543
Mamaroneck Avenue ES
   850 MAMARONECK AVE   10543
   Joseph Isidori, prin.
Other Schools – See Larchmont

Rye Neck UFD
Sch. Sys. Enr. Code 3
Supt. – C. Akin, 310 HORNIDGE ROAD   10543
Rye Neck MS, 300 HORNIDGE ROAD   10543
   Peter Mustich, prin.
Bellows ES, 200 CARROLL AVE   10543
   Alan Sturrock, prin.

Westchester Day School
   856 ORIENTA AVE   10543

Manchester, Ontario Co., Pop. Code 4
Manchester-Shortsville CSD
Supt. – See Shortsville
Red Jacket ES   14504 – Nancy Ruscio, prin.

Manhasset, Nassau Co., Pop. Code 6
Manhasset UFD
Sch. Sys. Enr. Code 4
Supt. – Don Harkness, MEMORIAL PLACE   11030
Munsey Park ES, HUNT LANE   11030
   Rhoda Pierre, prin.
Shelter Rock ES, 27 SHELTER ROCK RD   11030
   Richard Koebele, prin.

St. Mary's ES, 1340 NORTHERN BLVD   11030

Manlius, Onondaga Co., Pop. Code 6
Fayetteville-Manlius Central SD
Supt. – See Fayetteville
Eagle Hill MS, ENDERS ROAD   13104
   Donald Raw, prin.
Enders Road ES, ENDERS ROAD   13104
   Robert Storrier, prin.

Mannsville, Jefferson Co., Pop. Code 2
South Jefferson Central SD
Supt. – See Adams
Mannsville Manor ES   13661 – M. Bovee, prin.

Manorville, Suffolk Co.
South Manor UFD
Sch. Sys. Enr. Code 3
Supt. – Gary Schneider, DAYTON AVE   11949
South Street ES, SOUTH STREET   11949
   Benedict Merendino, prin.

Marathon, Cortland Co., Pop. Code 4
Marathon Central SD
Sch. Sys. Enr. Code 3
Supt. – M. Joseph, P O BOX 339   13803
Appleby ES, ALBRO ROAD   13803
   Joyce Duncan, prin.

Marcellus, Onondaga Co., Pop. Code 4
Marcellus Central SD
Sch. Sys. Enr. Code 4
Supt. – John Dowd, 2 REED PKWY   13108
Driver MS, REED PKWY   13108
   G. Morrissey, prin.
Heffernan ES, REED PARKWAY   13108
   Bren Price, prin.

Marcy, Oneida Co., Pop. Code 6
Whitesboro Central SD
Supt. – See Yorktown Heights

ES, MAYNARD DRIVE   13403
   Felix Guernier, prin.

Margaretville, Delaware Co., Pop. Code 3
Margaretville Central SD
Sch. Sys. Enr. Code 3
Supt. – Dennis McLean   12455
Margaretville Central S, MAIN ST   12455
   (—), prin.

Marilla, Erie Co., Pop. Code 5
Iroquois Central SD
Supt. – See Elma
ES, 11683 BULLIS RD   14102
   William Quick, prin.

Marion, Wayne Co., Pop. Code 5
Marion Central SD
Sch. Sys. Enr. Code 4
Supt. – B. Fleegel, 4034 WARNER ROAD   14505
ES, 3863 N MAIN ST   14505 – Carol Neff, prin.

Marlboro, Ulster Co., Pop. Code 6
Marlboro Central SD
Sch. Sys. Enr. Code 4
Supt. – J. Silvestri, PLATTEKILL ROAD   12542
MS, BIRDSALL AVE   12542 – Ed Sagarese, prin.
ES, ROUTE 9W   12542 – Debra Jackson, prin.
Other Schools – See Milton, Newburgh

Masonville, Delaware Co., Pop. Code 4
Sidney Central SD
Supt. – See Sidney
ES   13804 – Marlene Wilklow, prin.

Maspeth, Queens Co.
Queens Borough SD 24
Supt. – See Middle Village
Cowper JHS, 7002 54TH AVE   11378
   Patricia Ruddy, prin.
Maspeth ES, 6002 60TH ST   11378
   Catherine Anello, prin.

Massapequa, Nassau Co., Pop. Code 8
Massapequa UFD
Sch. Sys. Enr. Code 6
Supt. – Herbert Pluschau
   5478 MERRICK ROAD   11758
Fairfield ES, 330 MASSAPEQUA AVE   11758
   Bob Demblin, prin.
Lockhart ES, PITTSBURG AVENUE   11758
   Clara Goldberg, prin.
Unqua ES, 350 UNQUA RD   11758
   John Caruso, prin.
Other Schools – See Massapequa Park

Plainedge UFD
Supt. – See North Massapequa
Schwarting ES, JERUSALEM & FLOWER   11758
   Jeffrey Soloff, prin.

Grace Day ES, 23 CEDAR SHORE DR   11758
Montessori Childrens School
   CENTRAL & JERUSALEM AVE   11758
St. Rose of Lima ES, 4704 MERRICK RD   11758

Massapequa Park, Nassau Co., Pop. Code 7
Massapequa UFD
Supt. – See Massapequa
Birch Lane ES, 31 BIRCH LN   11762
   Alan Maher, prin.
East Lake ES, 154 E LAKE AVE   11762
   John Callow, prin.
Hawthorne ES, ROOSEVELT ROAD   11762
   William Romeika, prin.
McKenna MS, SPRUCE ST   11762
   Joseph Gaddone, prin.

Our Lady of Lourdes ES, 379 LINDEN ST   11762

Massena, St. Lawrence Co., Pop. Code 7
Massena Central SD
Sch. Sys. Enr. Code 5
Supt. – V. Sue Davis, 290 MAIN ST   13662
Leary JHS, RANSOM AVE & SCHOOL ST   13662
   Sandra Long, prin.
Jefferson ES, BAILEY ROAD   13662
   Harry Patterson, prin.
Louisville ES   13662 – Gary Wright, prin.
Madison ES, 290 MAIN ST   13662
   Carter Montross, prin.
Nightengale ES, NIGHTENGALE AVENUE   13662
   Michael Szeliga, prin.
Twin Rivers ES   13662 – Rod Crary, prin.

Trinity Catholic ES, 188 MAIN ST   13662

Mastic Beach, Suffolk Co., Pop. Code 6
William Floyd UFD
Sch. Sys. Enr. Code 6
Supt. – N. Poulos
   240 MASTIC BEACH ROAD   11951
Paca JHS, 240 MASTIC BEACH ROAD   11951
   Philip Marconi, prin.
Hobart ES, VAN BUREN STREET   11951
   Robert Wiggins, prin.
Smith ES, 240 MASTIC BEACH RD   11951
   Nicholas Cassone, prin.
Other Schools – See Moriches, Shirley

Mattituck, Suffolk Co., Pop. Code 4
Mattituck-Cutchogue UFD
Sch. Sys. Enr. Code 4
Supt. – R. Burns, P O BOX 1438   11952
Mattituck-Cutchogue ES, ROUTE 25   11952
   James Gilvarry, prin.

Mattydale, Onondaga Co., Pop. Code 6
North Syracuse Central SD
Supt. – See North Syracuse
Roxboro Road ES, ROXBORO ROAD   13211
Diane Fini, prin.
Roxboro Road MS, ROXBORO ROAD   13211
Nancy Brown, prin.

St. Margaret ES, 201 ROXBORO RD   13211

Maybrook, Orange Co., Pop. Code 4
Valley Central SD
Supt. – See Montgomery
ES, BROADWAY   12543
Anthony Cimorelli, prin.

Mayfield, Fulton Co., Pop. Code 3
Mayfield Central SD
Sch. Sys. Enr. Code 4
Supt. – William Gokey, SCHOOL ST   12117
ES, N MAIN STREET   12117
Ernest Clapper, prin.

Mayville, Chautauqua Co., Pop. Code 4
Mayville Central SD
Sch. Sys. Enr. Code 3
Supt. – Richard Casadonte, 2 ACADEMY ST   14757
ES, 2 ACADEMY ST   14757
Richard Casadonte, prin.

Mechanicville, Saratoga Co., Pop. Code 6
Mechanicville CSD
Sch. Sys. Enr. Code 4
Supt. – A. Cocozzo, 10 N MAIN ST   12118
ES, 10 N MAIN ST   12118 – Richard Moran, prin.

St. Paul Assumption Cent School
30 WILLIAM ST   12118

Medford, Suffolk Co., Pop. Code 5
Patchogue-Medford UFD
Supt. – See Patchogue
Eagle Drive ES, 1207 WAVE AVE   11763
John Waide, prin.
Tremont Avenue ES, 143 TREMONT AVE   11763
Raymond Cutter, prin.

Medina, Orleans Co., Pop. Code 6
Medina Central SD
Sch. Sys. Enr. Code 4
Supt. – David Gee, 1016 GWINN ST   14103
Oak Orchard ES, 335 W OAK ORCHARD ST   14103
Darryl Sanford, prin.
Towne ES, 181 BATES RD   14103
Joyce Derry, prin.

Melville, Suffolk Co., Pop. Code 6
Half Hollow Hills Central SD
Sch. Sys. Enr. Code 6
Supt. – Kevin McGuire, P O BOX 637   11747
Sunquam ES, 515 SWEET HOLLOW RD   11747
Ilsa Charette, prin.
Other Schools – See Dix Hills, Huntington Station

Crestwood Coutry Day ES
313 ROUND SWAMP RD   11747

Merrick, Nassau Co., Pop. Code 8
Bellmore-Merrick Central SD
Sch. Sys. Enr. Code 6
Supt. – Marc Bernstein
MEADOWBROOK & S STATE PKY   11566
Merrick Avenue JHS, MERRICK AVE   11566
Marvin Rosen, prin.
Other Schools – See Bellmore

Merrick UFD
Sch. Sys. Enr. Code 4
Supt. – Harriette Mortman
21 BABYLON ROAD   11566
Birch ES, 2400 CENTRAL PKY   11566
Andrew Perry, prin.
Chatterton ES, 108 MERRICK AVE N   11566
Richard Donges, prin.
Lakeside ES
MERRICK ROAD & BABYLON ROAD   11566
Judith Pastel, prin.

North Merrick UFD
Sch. Sys. Enr. Code 3
Supt. – June Irvin, 1775 OLD MILL ROAD   11566
Camp Avenue ES, 1712 MERRICK AVE N   11566
John Fried, prin.
Old Mill Road ES, 1775 OLD MILL RD   11566
Marianne Hurley, prin.
Other Schools – See North Merrick

Cure of Ars ES, 2303 MERRICK AVE S   11566

Mexico, Oswego Co., Pop. Code 4
Mexico Central SD
Sch. Sys. Enr. Code 5
Supt. – Robert McGruder
5390 ACADEMY ST   13114
MS   13114 – John Ruf, prin.
ES   13114 – Richard Carson, prin.
New Haven ES   13114 – Ann Pia, prin.
Palermo ES   13114 – Stephen Meisel, prin.

Middleburgh, Schoharie Co., Pop. Code 4
Middleburgh Central SD
Sch. Sys. Enr. Code 4
Supt. – W. Edward Ermlich, 181 MAIN ST   12122
ES, UPPER MAIN STREET   12122
Frances Reinl, prin.

Middle Granville, Washington Co.
Granville Central SD
Supt. – See Granville
Tanner ES   12849 – Daryl Hammond, prin.

Middle Island, Suffolk Co., Pop. Code 3
Longwood Central SD
Sch. Sys. Enr. Code 6
Supt. – Nick Muto
ROCKY PT-YAPHANK ROAD   11953
Longwood MS, YAPHANK RD   11953
Guy Mastrion, prin.
West Middle Island ES, SWEZEY LANE   11953
Robert Quinn, prin.
Other Schools – See Coram, Ridge, Yaphank

Middleport, Niagara Co., Pop. Code 4
Royalton Hartland Central SD
Sch. Sys. Enr. Code 4
Supt. – Gary Brader, 50 PARK AVE   14105
ES, STATE STREET   14105 – Geraldine Lupo, prin.
Other Schools – See Gasport

Middletown, Orange Co., Pop. Code 7
Middletown CSD
Sch. Sys. Enr. Code 6
Supt. – Carole Hankin, 223 WISNER AVE   10940
JHS, 112 GRAND AVE   10940
Domenic Leone, prin.
Academy Avenue ES, 47 ACADEMY AVE   10940
Colleen Sullivan, prin.
Chorley ES, 50 ROOSEVELT AVE   10940
Gary Wakeman, prin.
Liberty Street ES, LIBERTY STREET   10940
Antoinette Belfiglio, prin.
Mechanicstown ES, 425 E MAIN ST   10940
William Carter, prin.
Memorial ES
GARDNER AVENUE EXTENSION   10940
Robert Katulak, prin.
Truman Moon ES, 53 BEDFORD AVE   10940
Richard Delmoro, prin.

Harmony Christian School
ROUTE 211 EAST & BULL ROAD   10940
Our Lady of Mt. Carmel ES
205 WAWAYANDA AVE   10940
St. Joseph Parochial ES, 113 COTTAGE ST   10940

Middle Village, Queens Co.
Queens Borough SD 24
Sch. Sys. Enr. Code 8
Supt. – John Iorio, 6754 80TH ST   11379
Juniper Valley ES, 6926 65TH DR   11379
John Laville, prin.
Kole ES, 7915 PENELOPE AVE   11379
Dorthy Desanto, prin.
ES, 6754 80TH ST   11379 – Fred Izzo, prin.
Other Schools – See Corona, Elmhurst-A, Glendale,
Long Island City, Maspeth, Ridgewood, Woodside

Middleville, Herkimer Co., Pop. Code 3
West Canada Valley Central SD
Supt. – See Newport
MS   13406 – Mary Rommel, prin.

Milford, Otsego Co., Pop. Code 3
Milford Central SD
Sch. Sys. Enr. Code 2
Supt. – Bruce Burritt   13807
Milford Central S, W MAIN ST   13807
Michael Zollo, prin.

Millbrook, Dutchess Co., Pop. Code 4
Millbrook Central SD
Sch. Sys. Enr. Code 3
Supt. – Frank Schmidt
HIGH SCHOOL BLDG   12545
Alden Place MS, ALDEN PLACE   12545
John Yarochowicz, prin.
Elm Drive ES, ELM DRIVE   12545
John Yarochowicz, prin.

Dutchess Day ES
RURAL ROUTE 01 BOX 29A   12545
St. Joseph ES, NORTH AVE   12545

Miller Place, Suffolk Co., Pop. Code 5
Miller Place UFD
Sch. Sys. Enr. Code 5
Supt. – Robert Palguta
191 N COUNTRY ROAD   11764
North Country Road MS
191 N COUNTRY ROAD   11764
Harry Faulknor, prin.
Muller PS, 65 LOWER ROCKY POINT RD   11764
Grace Brindley, prin.
Sound Beach ES, 197 N COUNTRY RD   11764
Laddie Decker, prin.

Millerton, Columbia Co., Pop. Code 4
Northeast Central SD
Supt. – See Amenia
Millerton ES   12546 – John Ditondo, prin.

Milton, Ulster Co.
Marlboro Central SD
Supt. – See Marlboro
ES, MILTON TURNPIKE   12547
Thomas DeAngelo, prin.

Mineola, Nassau Co., Pop. Code 7
Mineola UFD
Sch. Sys. Enr. Code 5
Supt. – Robert Ricken, 200 EMORY ROAD   11501
MS, 200 EMORY ROAD   11501
Edward Shumsky, prin.

Hampton Street ES, 10 HAMPTON ST   11501
Noel Glick, prin.
Jackson Avenue ES, JACKSON AVENUE   11501
Ida Ayers, prin.
Other Schools – See Albertson

Corpus Christi ES, 120 SEARING AVE   11501
Nassau Lutheran ES
155 WASHINGTON AVE   11501

Minetto, Oswego Co., Pop. Code 3
Oswego CSD
Supt. – See Oswego
ES, GRANBY ROAD   13115 -- James Bartley, prin.

Minoa, Onondaga Co., Pop. Code 5
East Syracuse-Minoa Central SD
Supt. – See East Syracuse
ES, 421 MAIN ST N   13116
Russell Waldron, prin.

Fremont Christian Academy
112 EAST AVE   13116

Mohawk, Herkimer Co., Pop. Code 5
Mohawk Central SD
Sch. Sys. Enr. Code 4
Supt. – R. Heller, 28 GROVE ST   13407
Fisher ES, CHURCH STREET EXIT   13407
Ronald Behe, prin.

Mohegan Lake, Westchester Co., Pop. Code 4
Lakeland CSD of Shrub Oak
Supt. – See Shrub Oak
Van Cortlandtville ES, RURAL ROUTE 06   10547
Patrick Griffin, prin.
Washington ES, LEXINGTON AVENUE   10547
Joseph Kisslinger, prin.

Monroe, Orange Co., Pop. Code 6
Monroe-Woodbury Central SD
Supt. – See Central Valley
North Main Street ES, 212 N MAIN ST   10950
Douglas Goffman, prin.
Pine Tree ES, PINE TREE ROAD   10950
John Klahn, prin.

United Talmud Academy-Bais Rochel   10950
Sacred Heart ES, P O BOX 656   10950

Monsey, Rockland Co., Pop. Code 6
East Ramapo Central SD
Supt. – See Spring Valley
Elmwood MS, 43 ROBERT PITT DR   10952
Gerald Buckalter, prin.
Grandview ES, 46 GRANDVIEW AVE   10952
Henry Schult, prin.
Margetts ES, 25 MARGETTS RD   10952
Joel Elkind, prin.

Beth Rochel School for Girls
145 SADDLE RIVER RD   10952
United Talmudical Academy, P O BOX 188   10952
Yesh Ahavath Israel-Bnos Visnitz School
P O BOX 446   10952
Schreider Hebrew Academy
70 HIGHVIEW RD   10952
Talmud Torah Khal Adas Yereim
49 ROUTE 306   10952
Yeshiva Beth David ES, P O BOX 136   10952
Yeshiva Beth Mikroh ES, 23 W MAPLE AVE   10952
Yeshiva of Spring Valley ES
230 MAPLE AVE   10952

Montauk, Suffolk Co., Pop. Code 4
Montauk UFD
Sch. Sys. Enr. Code 2
Supt. – Frederic Philley, RURAL ROUTE 01   11954
ES, RURAL ROUTE 01 BOX 105   11954
William Loftus, prin.

Montgomery, Orange Co., Pop. Code 4
Valley Central SD
Sch. Sys. Enr. Code 4
Supt. – James Coonan
RURAL ROUTE 01 BOX 2   12549
Valley Central MS
RURAL ROUTE 01 BOX 2   12549 – W. Cocks, prin.
Berea ES, RURAL ROUTE 01 BOX 544   12549
Henry Morse, prin.
ES, 141 UNION ST   12549 – Margaret Lyons, prin.
Other Schools – See Maybrook, Newburgh, Walden

Monticello, Sullivan Co., Pop. Code 6
Monticello Central SD
Sch. Sys. Enr. Code 5
Supt. – R. Kaiser, 99 PORT JERVIS ROAD   12701
MS, 25 SAINT JOHN ST   12701 – L. Etkind, prin.
Cooke ES, ONEILL ROAD   12701
Harold Diamond, prin.
Rutherford MS, ATWELL LANE   12701
Michele Mitchell, prin.
Other Schools – See White Lake, Wurtsboro

Montour Falls, Schuyler Co., Pop. Code 4
Odessa-Montour Central SD
Supt. – See Odessa
Cate ES, CANAL STREET   14865
Sandra Young, prin.

Montrose, Westchester Co., Pop. Code 5
Hendrick Hudson Central SD
Sch. Sys. Enr. Code 4
Supt. – C. Eible, 61 TROLLEY ROAD   10548
Blue Mountain MS, P O BOX 14   10548
Oscar Scherer, prin.

Furnace Woods ES, P O BOX 24   10548
　　Joanne Falinski, prin.
Lindsey ES, 51 TROLLEY RD   10548
　　Thomas Blair, prin.
Other Schools – See Buchanan

Mooers, Clinton Co., Pop. Code 3
Northeastern Clinton Central SD
Supt. – See Champlain
ES   12958 – Thomas Graves, prin.

Moravia, Cayuga Co., Pop. Code 5
Moravia Central SD
Sch. Sys. Enr. Code 4
Supt. – A. Beaudry, 50 S MAIN ST   13118
Fillmore ES, 50 S MAIN STREET   13118
　　Judith Fenstermacher, prin.

Moriches, Suffolk Co.
William Floyd UFD
Supt. – See Mastic Beach
ES, LOUIS AVENUE   11953 – Paul Casciano, prin.

Morris, Otsego Co., Pop. Code 3
Morris Central SD
Sch. Sys. Enr. Code 2
Supt. – Elmo Barden   13808
Morris Central S   13808 – Wayne Hess, prin.

Morrisonville, Clinton Co.
Saranac Central SD
Supt. – See Saranac
ES, RURAL ROUTE 02 BOX 344   12962
　　Gilbert Burnell, prin.

St. Alexander's ES, ROUTE 22B   12962

Morristown, St. Lawrence Co., Pop. Code 2
Morristown Central SD
Sch. Sys. Enr. Code 3
Supt. – Beverly Ouderkirk   13664
Morristown Central S   13664
　　Raymond Kondrat, prin.

Morrisville, Madison Co., Pop. Code 5
Morrisville Eaton Central SD
Sch. Sys. Enr. Code 3
Supt. – Charles Molloy, P O BOX R   13408
Morrisville Eaton ES
　　57 EASTON STREET P O BOX R   13408
　　Baiba Peirce, prin.

Mount Kisco, Westchester Co., Pop. Code 6
Bedford Central SD
Sch. Sys. Enr. Code 5
Supt. – Paul Kelleher, P O BOX 180   10549
ES, HYATT AVENUE   10459 – John Finch, prin.
Other Schools – See Bedford, Bedford Hills, Pound
　　Ridge

Mount Marion, Ulster Co.
Saugarties Central SD
Supt. – See Saugarties
ES, P O BOX 438   12456 – Anthony Manley, prin.

Mount Morris, Livingston Co., Pop. Code 5
Mt. Morris Central SD
Sch. Sys. Enr. Code 3
Supt. – David Paciencia
　　BONNADONNA AVE   14510
ES, BONADONNA AVE   14510
　　David Saffer, prin.

Mount Sinai, Suffolk Co.
Mt. Sinai UFD
Sch. Sys. Enr. Code 4
Supt. – Peter Paciolla, N COUNTRY ROAD   11766
ES, NORTH COUNTRY ROAD   11766
　　Barbara Chu, prin.

Mount Upton, Chenango Co., Pop. Code 2
Mt. Upton Central SD
Sch. Sys. Enr. Code 2
Supt. – M. Klockowski, MAIN ST   13809
ES   13809 – Frederick Kirsch, prin.

Mount Vernon, Westchester Co., Pop. Code 8
Mt. Vernon CSD
Sch. Sys. Enr. Code 6
Supt. – W. Prattella
　　165 N COLUMBUS AVE   10553
Davis MS, 350 GRAMATAN AVE   10552
　　Peter Gentile, prin.
Nichols MS, 455 N HIGH ST   10552
　　Alfonzo Grimes, prin.
Columbus ES, 250 GRAMATAN AVE   10550
　　Peter Ragaglia, prin.
Fulton ES, 9 UNION LN   10553
　　Joan Morrison, prin.
Graham ES, 421 E 5TH ST   10553
　　Mario Sclafani, prin.
Grimes/Pennington ES
　　FAIRWAY & EAST DEVONIA   10552
　　Thomas Pesce, prin.
Hamilton ES, 20 OAK ST   10550
　　Diaquino DeFreitas, prin.
Holmes ES, 195 N COLUMBUS AVE   10553
　　Louis Cioffi, prin.
Lincoln ES, 170 E LINCOLN AVE   10552
　　George Albano, prin.
Longfellow ES, 625 S 4TH AVE   10550
　　Benjamin Soccodato, prin.
Parker ES, 461 S 6TH AVE   10550
　　Mary Spells, prin.
Traphagen ES, 95 OAKLAND AVE   10552
　　Neal Halperin, prin.

Washington ES
　　50 6TH AVENUE & SECOND ST   10550
　　Nellie Thornton, prin.

Milestone ES, 70 BROAD ST W   10552
Our Lady of Mt. Carmel ES, 19 S 10TH AVE   10550
Our Lady of Victory ES, 38 N 5TH AVE   10550
SS. Peter & Paul ES, 125 E BIRCH ST   10552
Sacred Heart ES, 71 SHARPE BLVD S   10550
St. Ursula ES, 183 RICH AVE   10550

Munnsville, Madison Co., Pop. Code 2
Stockbridge Valley Central SD
Sch. Sys. Enr. Code 3
Supt. – Ed Reid, MAIN ST   13409
Stockbrdg Valley Central S, MAIN ST   13409
　　Ed Reid, prin.

Nanuet, Rockland Co., Pop. Code 7
Nanuet UFD
Sch. Sys. Enr. Code 4
Supt. – Dr. David Rightmyer
　　101 CHURCH ST   10954
Barr MS, 143 CHURCH ST   10954
　　Peter Bydlik, prin.
Miller ES, 50 BLAUVELT RD   10954
　　Peter Smith, prin.

St. Anthony ES, 34 E ROUTE 59   10954

Naples, Ontario Co., Pop. Code 4
Naples Central SD
Sch. Sys. Enr. Code 3
Supt. – Walter Zerrahn, MAIN ST   14512
ES, ACADEMY STREET   14512
　　William Kelly, prin.

Narrowsburg, Sullivan Co.
Narrowsburg Central SD
Sch. Sys. Enr. Code 2
Supt. – Joseph Kilker   12764
Narrowsburg Central S, ERIE ST   12764
　　Joseph Kilker, prin.

Nassau, Rensselaer Co., Pop. Code 4
East Greenbush Central SD
Supt. – See East Greenbush
Sutherland ES, JOHN STREET   12123
　　Mark Sposato, prin.

Nedrow, Onondaga Co., Pop. Code 5
La Fayette Central SD
Supt. – See La Fayette
Onondaga Indian ES
　　RURAL ROUTE 01 BOX 270   13120
　　Kenneth McCaffery, prin.

Onondaga Central SD
Sch. Sys. Enr. Code 3
Supt. – P. Dolan, 201 HUDSON AVE   13120
Rockwell ES, 106 ROCKWELL RD   13120
　　William Silky, prin.
Wheeler ES, 4543 S ONONDAGA ROAD   13120
　　(—), prin.

Nesconset, Suffolk Co., Pop. Code 6
Smithtown Central SD
Supt. – See Smithtown
Great Hollow IS, 150 SOUTHERN BLVD   11767
　　Harry Ortgies, prin.
ES, GIBBS POND ROAD   11767
　　Mary Cahill, prin.
Tackan ES, 99 MIDWOOD AVE   11767
　　Patricia Friel, prin.

Newark, Wayne Co., Pop. Code 7
Newark Central SD
Sch. Sys. Enr. Code 5
Supt. – W. Rock, 701 PEIRSON AVE   14513
JHS, 316 W MILLER ST   14513 – Dennis Ford, prin.
Kelley MS, 710 PEIRSON AVE   14513
　　Peter Chamberlin, prin.
Lincoln ES, NORTH MAIN STREET   14513
　　Henry Hann, prin.
Perkins ES, WEST MAPLE AVENUE   14513
　　Robert Linehan, prin.

St. Michael ES, 320 S MAIN ST   14513

Newark Valley, Tioga Co., Pop. Code 4
Newark Valley Central SD
Sch. Sys. Enr. Code 4
Supt. – William Starkweather, WHIG ST   13811
Hall ES, WHIG STREET   13811 – Douglas Ido, prin.
MS, WHIG ST   13811 – Robert Gwinn, prin.

New Berlin, Chenango Co., Pop. Code 4
New Berlin Central SD
Sch. Sys. Enr. Code 3
Supt. – C. Thomas Bailey, BD EDUC BLDG   13411
ES, PRIMARY BUILDING   13411
　　Gerald Griffith, prin.

Newburgh, Orange Co., Pop. Code 7
Marlboro Central SD
Supt. – See Marlboro
Middle Hope ES, OVERLOOK DRIVE   12550
　　Janet Ceparano, prin.

Newburgh CSD
Sch. Sys. Enr. Code 6
Supt. – Phillip Leahy, 124 GRAND ST   12550
Balmville ES, 484 ROUTE 9W   12550
　　Robert Funck, prin.
Fostertown ES, RURAL ROUTE 01   12550
　　Peter Copeletti, prin.

Gardnertown Fundamental ES
　　RURAL ROUTE 03   12550 – Donald Dubois, prin.
Gidney Avenue Memorial ES
　　300 GIDNEY AVE   12550 – Thomas Donato, prin.
Horizon On Hudson ES
　　137 MONTGOMERY STREET   12550
　　Mary Joyce, prin.
Meadow Hill ES, 50 MEADOW HILL RD   12550
　　Ralph Pizzo, prin.
New Windsor ES, 175 QUASSAICK AVE   12550
　　Steven Runberg, prin.
Magnet PS, CHESTNUT STREET   12550
　　Mary Mahan, prin.
Temple Hill ES, 525 UNION AVE   12550
　　Lee Benton, prin.
Vails Gate ES, 320 OLD FORGE HILL RD   12550
　　Robert Moody, prin.
West Street ES, 39 WEST ST   12550
　　Joan Crosson, prin.

Valley Central SD
Supt. – See Montgomery
East Coldenham ES, 286-290 ROUTE 17K   12552
　　Harvey Gregory, prin.

Washingtonville Central SD
Supt. – See Washingtonville
Little Britain ES, BOX 97 ROUTE 207   12550
　　Marie Pillmeier, prin.

Bishop Dunn Memorial ES
　　50 GIDNEY AVE   12550
Leptondale Christian Acadmy
　　419 N PLANK RD   12550
Sacred Heart ES, 24 S ROBINSON AVE   12550
St. Francis of Assisi ES
　　245-247 RENWICK ST   12550

New City, Rockland Co., Pop. Code 8
Clarkstown Central SD
Supt. – See West Nyack
Laurel Plains ES, TEAKWOOD LANE   10956
　　John Delvecchio, prin.
Link ES, 55 RED HILL RD   10956 – Ruth Hess, prin.
Little Tor ES, 56 GREGORY ST   10956
　　Annemarie Romagnoli, prin.
ES, 60 CRESTWOOD DR   10956
　　Alan Lipman, prin.
Woodglen ES, 121 W PHILLIPS HILL RD   10956
　　Francis Stein, prin.

East Ramapo Central SD
Supt. – See Spring Valley
Summit Park ES, ROUTE 45   10956
　　Leo Chapdelaine, prin.

Rockland Learning Center
　　OLD MIDDLETOWN ROAD   10956
St. Augustine ES, 114 S MAIN ST   10956

Newcomb, Essex Co., Pop. Code 3
Newcomb Central SD
Sch. Sys. Enr. Code 2
Supt. – Edward Decker   12852
Newcomb Central S   12852 – Barbara Kearns, prin.

Newfane, Niagara Co., Pop. Code 6
Newfane Central SD
Sch. Sys. Enr. Code 4
Supt. – Wilbur Dunn
　　6273 CHARLOTTEVILLE ROAD   14108
MS, 2649 TRANSIT ROAD   14108
　　Dean Schaffer, prin.
MS, EAST AVE & TRANSIST ROAD   14108
　　Dean Schaffer, prin.
Newfane ES, 2909 TRANSIT RD   14108
　　Thomas Hicks, prin.

Newfield, Tompkins Co., Pop. Code 5
Newfield Central SD
Sch. Sys. Enr. Code 3
Supt. – Donald Hickman, 247 MAIN ST   14867
ES, 247 MAIN ST   14867 – Patricia Kendall, prin.

New Hartford, Oneida Co., Pop. Code 4
New Hartford Central SD
Sch. Sys. Enr. Code 5
Supt. – J. Meyer, 33 OXFORD ROAD   13413
Hughes ES, HIGBY ROAD   13413
　　Robert Loomis, prin.
Myles ES, CLINTON ROAD   13413
　　Michael Lafever, prin.
Oxford Road ES, OXFORD ROAD   13413
　　Ronald Evans, prin.

New Hyde Park, Nassau Co., Pop. Code 6
Herricks UFD
Sch. Sys. Enr. Code 5
Supt. – Leon Pierce, SHELTER ROCK ROAD   11040
Denton Avenue ES, 1050 DENTON AVE   11040
　　Eugene Goldwasser, prin.
Other Schools – See Albertson, Williston Park

New Hyde Park-Garden City UFD
Sch. Sys. Enr. Code 4
Supt. – Joseph Suriano
　　1950 HILLSIDE AVE   11040
Hillside ES, 150 MAPLE DR W   11040
　　Frank Calamusa, prin.
Manor Oaks/Bowie ES
　　1950 HILLSIDE AVE   11040
　　Kathleen Dyckes, prin.
New Hyde Park Road ES
　　300 NEW HYDE PARK RD   11040
　　George Schmidt, Jr., prin.
Other Schools – See Garden City Park

Holy Spirit ES, 13 S 6TH ST 11040
Notre Dame ES, 25 MAYFAIR RD 11040

New Paltz, Ulster Co., Pop. Code 5
New Paltz Central SD
Sch. Sys. Enr. Code 4
Supt. – Theodore Sturgis, 196 MAIN ST 12561
MS, S MANHEIM BLVD 12561 – Ira Glick, prin.
Duzine ES, SUNSET RDG 12561
Janice Krasilousky, prin.

Newport, Herkimer Co., Pop. Code 3
West Canada Valley Central SD
Sch. Sys. Enr. Code 3
Supt. – Richard Street 13416
ES 13416 – Mary Rommel, prin.
Other Schools – See Middleville

New Rochelle, Westchester Co., Pop. Code 8
New Rochelle CSD
Sch. Sys. Enr. Code 6
Supt. – James Gaddy, 515 NORTH AVE 10801
Leonard MS, 25 GERADA LANE 10804
Don Zaccagnino, prin.
Young MS, 270 CENTRE AVE 10805
Thelma Esteves, prin.
Columbus ES, 275 WASHINGTON AVE 10801
Lois Zabriskie, prin.
Davis ES, 80 ISELIN DR 10804
William Harrell, prin.
Jefferson ES, 131 WEYMAN AVE 10805
Donald Kuhn, prin.
Trinity ES, 180 PELHAM RD 10805
Gerald Kirshenbaum, prin.
Ward ES, 311 BROADFIELD RD 10804
Kenneth Regan, prin.
Webster ES, 95 GLENMORE DR 10801
Robert Stephens, prin.

Thornton-Donovan School
100 OVERLOOK CIRCLE 10804
Holy Family ES, 100 MOUNT JOY PL 10801
Holy Name of Jesus ES
70 PETERSVILLE RD 10801
Hudson Country Montessori School
340 QUARKER RIDGE ROAD 10804
Iona Grammar School, 173 STRATTON RD 10804
New Rochelle Catholic ES, 24 MAPLE AVE 10805
Our Lady of Perpetual Help ES
575 FOWLER AVE 10803
Westchester Area ES, 456 WEBSTER AVE 10801

New Suffolk, Suffolk Co., Pop. Code 3
New Suffolk Common SD
Sch. Sys. Enr. Code 1
Supt. – Harold Carr, 5TH AVE 11956
ES, 5TH ST 11956 – Ruth Nelson, prin.

Newtonville, Albany Co., Pop. Code 4
North Colonie Central SD
Sch. Sys. Enr. Code 5
Supt. – Charles Szuberla 12128
Other Schools – See Latham, Loudonville

New Windsor, Orange Co., Pop. Code 6

St. Joseph ES, 148 WINDSOR HWY 12550

New York, Pop. Code 12
Manhattan Borough SD 1
Sch. Sys. Enr. Code 7
Supt. – B. Mecklowitz
80 MONTGOMERY ST 10002
Bernstein ES, 327 CHERRY STREET 10002
Stanley Metzger, prin.
Burroughs ES
442 EAST HOUSTON STREET 10002
Alan Starsky, prin.
Castro ES, 100 ATTORNEY STREET 10002
Antonio Bilbao, prin.
Clemente ES, 333 EAST FOURTH STREET 10009
Leonard Greher, prin.
Levy ES, 185 FIRST AVENUE 10003
Martin Shapiro, prin.
Mangin ES, 525 EAST HOUSTON STREET 10002
Louise Burns, prin.
McKinley ES, 121 EAST THIRD STREET 10009
Lydia Dealvarez, prin.
Nightingale ES
285 DELANCEY STREET SOUTH 10002
Alexander Tare, prin.
Roosevelt ES
EAST 11TH STREET & AVENUE D 10009
Paul Flaumenhaft, prin.
Shaw ES, 610 EAST 12TH STREET 10009
Betty Machol, prin.
Silver ES, 166 ESSEX STREET 10002
Leonard Golubchick, prin.
Simon ES, 600 EAST SIXTH STREET 10009
Stanley Goldstein, prin.
Straus ES, 123 RIDGE STREET 10002
Estaban Barrientos, prin.
Szolds ES, 293 EAST BROADWAY 10002
Philip Thau, prin.

Manhattan Borough SD 2
Sch. Sys. Enr. Code 7
Supt. – Anthony Alvarado, 210 E 33RD ST 10016
Altman ES, 71 HESTER STREET 10002
Anthony Barry, prin.
Beekman Hill ES, 228 EAST 57TH STREET 10022
Irene Karras, prin.
Billard ES
FORT JAY GOVERNORS ISLAND 10004
Harry Apicos, prin.

Blake ES, 45 E 81ST ST 10028 – Elaine Fink, prin.
Charette ES, 490 HUDSON ST 10014
John Melser, prin.
Chelsea ES, 281 NINTH AVENUE 10001
John Natoli, prin.
De Soto ES, 143 BAXTER STREET 10013
Richard Kramer, prin.
Greenwich Village ES
116 WEST 11TH STREET 10011
Elliott Koreman, prin.
Harris ES, 320 WEST 21ST STREET 10011
Angelo Casillo, prin.
Howe ES, 520 WEST 45TH STREET 10036
John Economides, prin.
London ES, 122 HENRY STREET 10002
David Fong, prin.
Murray ES, 210 EAST 33RD STREET 10016
Milton Jones, prin.
O'Brien ES, 1763 FIRST AVENUE 10028
Genis Delaney, prin.
Ochs ES, 440 WEST 53RD STREET 10019
Robert Kinzelberg, prin.
Public ES 234, 292 GREENWICH ST 10007
Blossom Gelernter, prin.
Revere ES, 311 EAST 82RD STREET 10028
Harry Milner, prin.
Riis ES, 80 CATHERINE STREET 10038
Jacob Klein, prin.
Roosevelt Island ES, 585 MAIN ST 10044
Dorothy Bowser, prin.
Saint-Gaudens ES, 319 E 19TH ST 10003
Gena Cone, prin.
Smith ES, 8 HENRY STREET 10038
Jacob Wong, prin.
Stevenson ES, 419 EAST 66TH STREET 10021
Alan Cohen, prin.
Straus ES, 1700 THIRD AVENUE 10028
Edmund Fried, prin.
Taylor ES, 1458 YORK AVENUE 10021
Shelly Cohen, prin.
Wing ES, 40 DIVISION ST 10002
David Tom, prin.

Manhattan Borough SD 3
Sch. Sys. Enr. Code 7
Supt. – Anton Klein, 300 W 96TH ST 10025
Amsterdam ES, 210 WEST 61ST STREET 10023
Ina King, prin.
Anderson ES, 134 W 122ND ST 10027
Bernice Johnson, prin.
Bloom ES, 32 WEST 92ND STREET 10024
Sidney Morison, prin.
Dickinson ES, 735 W END AVE 10025
Luis Mercado, prin.
Jasper ES, 100 WEST 84TH STREET 10024
Bernadette O'Brien, prin.
Langston ES, 20 WEST 112TH STREET 10026
Pearl Jones, prin.
Locke MS, 21 W 111TH ST 10026
Corine Pettey, prin.
Newman ES, 370 WEST 120TH STREET 10027
Joy Cooke, prin.
Public ES 113, 240 W 113TH ST 10026
Elease Jackson, prin.
Public ES 145, 150 W 105TH ST 10025
Ann Budd, prin.
Public ES 166, 132 W 89TH ST 10024
Jack Regan, prin.
Rilleux MS, 41 W 117TH ST 10026
Linda Mininberg, prin.
ST. Nicholas ES, 220 WEST 121ST STREET 10027
Hobart Cope, prin.
Sherman ES, 160 W 78TH ST 10024
Naomi Hill, prin.
Simon ES, 234 WEST 109TH STREET 10025
Clara Ostrowski, prin.
Smith ES, 163 W 97TH ST 10025
Estelle Seittelman, prin.
Sojourner Truth ES, 34 W 118TH ST 10026
Linda Mininberg, prin.
Straus ES, 270 W 70TH ST 10023
Richard Boccadoro, prin.

Manhattan Borough SD 4
Sch. Sys. Enr. Code 7
Supt. – Carlos Medina, 319 E 117TH ST 10035
Cartier ES, 315 E 113TH ST 10029
Miguel Colondres, prin.
Galileo ES, 232 E 103RD ST 10029
Gustaro Torres, prin.
Henry ES, 19 E 103RD ST 10029
Lorraine Skeen, prin.
Johnson ES, 176 E 115TH ST 10029
Martino Black, prin.
Lanzetta ES, 216 E 120TH ST 10035
Nydia Sancho, prin.
Marcantonio ES, 433 EAST 100TH STREET 10029
Renee Lacorbiniere, prin.
Minuit ES, 1615 MADISON AVE 10029
Frederick Hellman, prin.
Paca ES, 319 E 117TH ST 10035
Lavinia Mancuso, prin.
Public ES 72, 131 E 104TH ST 10029
Marcelino Rodriguez, prin.
Public ES 101, 141 E 111TH ST 10029
Alex Castillo, prin.
Public ES 109, 215 E 99TH ST 10029
Marvin Galina, prin.
Public ES 112, 535 E 119TH ST 10035
Carlos Ramos, prin.
Public MS 206, 508 E 120TH ST 10035
Juana Dainis, prin.
Rivera ES, 219 E 109TH ST 10029
Norma Hurwitz, prin.

Short ES, 421 E 106TH ST 10029
Mamie Johnson, prin.
Stern ES, 160 E 120TH ST 10035
Robert Negron, prin.

Manhattan Borough SD 5
Sch. Sys. Enr. Code 7
Supt. – Bertrand Brown, 433 W 123RD ST 10027
Clemente IS, 625 W 133RD ST 10027
Samuel Williams, prin.
Douglas IS, 2581 7TH AVE 10039
David Bluford, prin.
Public JHS 275, 175 W 134TH STREET 10030
(—), prin.
Bethune ES, 222 W 134TH ST 10030
Steven Kaminsky, prin.
Bunche MS, 425 W 123RD ST 10027
Kay Richards, prin.
Cullen ES, 244 W 144TH ST 10030
Russell Cunningham, prin.
Douglas ES, 123 MORNINGSIDE DR 10027
Barbara Byrd, prin.
Finley ES, 425 W 130TH ST 10027
Vera Smith, prin.
La Guardia ES, 499 W 133RD ST 10027
Anthony Rodriguez, prin.
Moore ES, 2121 5TH AVE 10037
Edward Jackson, prin.
Mt. Morris ES
144-176 EAST 128TH STREET 10035
Jacqueline Bussey, prin.
Riverside ES, 2599 7TH AVE 10039
Joseph Sellers, prin.
Russworm ES, 2230 5TH AVE 10037
Cornelius Bass, prin.
Tappan ES, 2987 8TH AVE 10039
Edythe Ford, prin.
Tubman ES, 250 W 127TH ST 10027
Jeanette Hadley, prin.
Webb ES, 301 W 140TH ST 10030
Constance Wingate, prin.

Manhattan Borough SD 6
Sch. Sys. Enr. Code 7
Supt. – Anthony Amato, 665 W 182ND ST 10033
Inwood JHS, 650 ACADEMY ST 10034
Leonard Latronica, prin.
Public IS 223, 131ST ST & CONVENT AVE 10027
Miriam Sing, prin.
Roosevelt JHS, 511 W 182ND ST 10033
Howard Gross, prin.
Stitt IS, 401 W 164TH ST 10032
Donald Tippitt, prin.
Stowe IS, 6 EDGECOMBE AVE 10030
Margaret Maggs, prin.
Audubon ES, 560 W 169TH ST 10032
Blanca Batting, prin.
Cliffs ES, 349 CABRINI BLVD 10040
Richard Darwick, prin.
Dyckman Valley ES, 93 NAGLE AVE 10040
Stanley Kaplan, prin.
Ft. Washington ES, 185 WADSWORTH AVE 10033
Erick Irizarry, prin.
Humboldt ES, 586 W 177TH ST 10033
George Tomka, prin.
Powell ES, 1750 AMSTERDAM AVE 10031
Lloyd Campbell, prin.
Public ES 173
306 FORT WASHINGTON AVE 10033
Vivian Lieber, prin.
Public ES 189, 2580 AMSTERDAM AVE 10040
Elmer Sapadin, prin.
Schiff ES, 500 W 138TH ST 10031
Alejandro Rodriguez, prin.
Shorackappock ES, 512 W 212TH ST 10034
Mark Shapiro, prin.
Wright Brothers ES, 475 W 155TH ST 10032
Gilbert Musinger, prin.

Anglo-American School, 18 W 89TH ST 10028
Barnard School
554 FORT WASHINGTON AVE 10033
Birch Wathen School, 9 E 71ST ST 10021
Brearley School, 610 E 83RD ST 10028
Browning Boys School, 52 E 62ND ST 10021
Calhoun School, 433 END AVE 10024
Chapin School, 100 END AVE 10028
Collegiate School, 241 W 77TH ST 10024
Columbia Grammar & Prep School
5 W 93RD ST 10025
Convent of Sacred Heart, 1 E 91ST ST 10128
Dalton School, 108 E 89TH ST 10128
De La Salle Academy, 202 W 97TH ST 10025
Friends Seminary School, 222 E 16TH ST 10003
Hewitt School, 45 E 75TH ST 10021
Hunter College & Campus School
94TH ST AND PARK AVE 10128
King's Academy, 2341 3RD AVE 10035
Lenox School, 170 E 70TH ST 10021
Lycee Francais De New York
3-5 E 95TH ST 10028
Lyceum Francais Kennedy School
20 W 44TH ST 10036
Manhattan Christian School
401 W 205TH ST 10034
Marymount School, 1026-1028 5TH AVE 10028
McBurney School, 15 W 63RD ST 10023
Mesivta Tifereth Jerusalem School
141-147 E BROADWAY 10002
New Lincoln School, 210 E 77TH ST 10021
Nightingale Bamford School, 20 E 92ND ST 10128
Rabbi Samson Hirsch Yeshiva
85 BENNETT AVE 10033
Scuola D. Italia School, 10 LEROY ST 10014

Spence School, 22 E 91ST ST 10128
St. Hilda's & St. Hugh's School
  619 W 114TH ST 10025
St. Jean Baptist MS, 173 E 75TH ST 10021
Steiner School, 15 E 79TH ST 10021
Trinity Episcopal School, 139 W 91ST ST 10024
U.N. International School
  2450 E RIVER DR 10010
Walden School, 1 W 88TH ST 10024
All Saints ES, 1 E 130TH ST 10037
Annunciation ES, 461 W 131ST ST 10027
Ascension ES, 220 W 108TH ST 10025
Bank Street ES, 610 W 112TH ST 10025
Blessed Sacrament ES, 147 W 70TH ST 10023
Buckley ES, 113 E 73RD ST 10021
Caedmon ES, 416 E 80TH ST 10021
Cathedral ES, 1047 AMSTERDAM AVE 10025
City & Country ES, 147 W 13TH ST 10011
Corlears ES, 324 W 15TH ST 10011
Corpus Christi ES, 535 W 121ST ST 10027
Day ES, 1 E 92ND ST 10128
East Manhattan ES, 208 E 18TH ST 10003
Epiphany ES, 234 E 22ND ST 10010
Fleming ES, 35 E 62ND ST 10021
Good Shepherd ES, 620 ISHAM ST 10034
Grace Church ES, 86 4TH AVE 10003
Greenwich Village Neighborhood ES
  219 SULLIVAN ST 10012
Guardian Angel ES, 193 10TH AVE 10011
Holy Cross ES, 332 W 43RD ST 10036
Holy Name of Jesus ES, 202 W 97TH ST 10025
Immaculate Conception ES, 419 E 13TH ST 10009
Incarnation ES, 570 W 175TH ST 10033
Joshua Heschel ES, 270 W 89TH ST 10024
Little Red Schoolhouse ES
  196 BLEECKER ST 10012
Lower East Side International Comm. Scho
  137/141 DUANE ST 10013
Manhattan Country ES, 7 E 96TH ST 10128
Manhattan Day ES, 310 W 75TH ST 10023
Mary Help of Christians ES, 435 E 11TH ST 10009
Midtown Ethical Culture ES
  33 CENTRAL PARK W 10023
Modern ES, 539-43 W 152ND ST 10031
Mt. Carmel-Holy Rosary ES
  371 PLEASANT AVE 10035
Our Lady Queen of Angels ES
  232 E 113TH ST 10029
Our Lady Queen of Martyrs ES
  71 ARDEN ST 10040
Our Lady of Good Counsel ES
  323 E 91ST ST 10128
Our Lady of Lourdes ES, 468 W 143RD ST 10031
Our Lady of Pompeii ES, 240 BLEECKER ST 10014
Our Lady of Sorrows ES, 104 STANTON ST 10002
Park East Eshi Day School, 164 E 68TH ST 10021
Ramaz Lower ES, 125 E 85TH ST 10028
Resurrection ES, 282 W 151ST ST 10039
Rodeph Sholom Day ES, 10 W 84TH ST 10024
Sacred Heart of Jesus ES, 456 W 52ND ST 10019
St. Aloysius ES, 223 W 132ND ST 10027
St. Ann ES, 314 E 110TH ST 10029
St. Anthony ES, 60 MACDOUGAL ST 10012
St. Bernard ES, 327 W 13TH ST 10014
St. Bernard's ES, 4 E 98TH ST 10029
St. Brigid ES, 185 E 7TH ST 10009
St. Catherine of Genoa ES, 508 W 153RD ST 10031
St. Catherine of Siena ES, 420 E 69TH ST 10021
St. Cecilia ES, 220 E 106TH ST 10029
St. Charles Borromeo ES, 214 W 142ND ST 10030
St. Columba ES, 331 W 25TH ST 10001
St. David's ES, 12 E 89TH ST 10128
St. Elizabeth ES, 612 W 187TH ST 10033
St. Francis De Sales ES, 116 E 97TH ST 10029
St. Francis Xavier ES, 126 W 17TH ST 10011
St. George ES, 215 E 6TH ST 10003
St. Gregory the Great ES, 138 W 90TH ST 10024
St. Ignatius Loyola ES, 50 E 84TH ST 10028
St. James ES, 37 ST JAMES PL 10038
St. Joseph ES, 111 WASHINGTON PL 10014
St. Joseph ES, 420 E 87TH ST 10128
St. Joseph ES, 1-3 MONROE ST 10002
St. Joseph ES, 168 MORNINGSIDE AVE 10027
St. Jude ES, 433 W 204TH ST 10034
St. Lucy ES, 340 E 104TH ST 10029
St. Luke's ES, 487 HUDSON ST 10014
St. Mark the Evangelist ES, 55 W 138TH ST 10037
St. Matthew Lutheran ES
  200 SHERMAN AVE 10034
St. Michael's Montessori School
  225 W 99TH ST 10025
St. Patrick's ES, 233 MOTT ST 10012
St. Paul ES, 114 E 118TH ST 10035
St. Rose of Lima ES, 517 W 164TH ST 10032
St. Spyridon Parochial ES
  120 WADSWORTH AVE 10033
St. Stanislaus ES, 104 ST MARKS PL 10009
St. Stephen ES, 408 E 82ND ST 10028
St. Stephens School, 141 E 28TH ST 10016
St. Stephen of Hungary ES, 408 E 82ND ST 10028
St. Thomas Commnty ES
  259-61 W 123RD ST 10027
Stevenson ES, 132 E 78TH ST 10021
Town ES, 540 E 76TH ST 10021
Transfiguration ES, 29 MOTT ST 10013
Village Commnty ES, 272 W 10TH ST 10014
Yeshiva Chofetz Chaim of Radun School
  346 W 89TH ST 10024

New York Mills, Oneida Co., Pop. Code 5
New York Mills UFD
Sch. Sys. Enr. Code 3
Supt. – J. Semeniak, BURRSTONE ROAD 13417

S, BURRSTONE ROAD 13417
  Dewey Valentine, prin.

St. Mary's ES, SAINT STANISLAUS ST 13417

Niagara Falls, Niagara Co., Pop. Code 8
Niagara Falls CSD
Sch. Sys. Enr. Code 6
Supt. – William Sdao, 607 WALNUT AVE 14301
Gaskill JHS, 910 HYDE PARK BLVD 14301
  Jacqueline Kane, prin.
La Salle JHS, BUFFALO AVE & 76TH ST 14304
  Frank Orfano, prin.
Abate ES, 1625 LOCKPORT ST 14305
  Frank Delsignore, prin.
Hyde Park ES, 1620 HYDE PARK BLVD 14305
  Arthur McDonald, prin.
Kalfas ES, 1800 BEECH AVE 14305
  Thomas Orr, prin.
Mann ES, 1330 95TH ST 14304
  Ronald Walter, prin.
Maple Avenue ES
  MAPLE & MCKOON AVENUE 14303
  Sue Farley, prin.
Niagara Street ES
  NIAGARA & 25TH STREET 14305
  Gary Myers, prin.
Seventy Ninth Street ES, 551 79TH ST 14304
  Kate Maher, prin.
Sixtieth Street ES, LINDBERG AVENUE 14304
  Victoria Polka, prin.
Sixty Sixth Street ES
  66TH STREET & JOHN AVENUE 14304
  Thomas Franklin, prin.

Niagara Wheatfield Central SD
Supt. – See Sanborn
Colonial Village ES
  1456 SAUNDERS SETTLEMENT RD 14305
  Robert Filocamo, prin.
Military Road ES, 4185 MILITARY RD 14305
  Robert Arlington, prin.

Holy Ghost Lutheran ES, 6630 LUTHER ST 14304
Niagara Christian Academy, 601 28TH ST 14301
Our Lady of Mt. Carmel ES
  2499 INDEPENDENCE AVE 14301
Prince of Peace ES, 1055 N MILITARY RD 14304
Sacred Heart ES, 1112 SOUTH AVE 14305
St. John De La Salle ES
  8627 BUFFALO AVE 14304
St. Joseph ES, 625 TRONOLONE PL 14301
St. Teresa-Infant Jesus ES
  1018 COLLEGE AVE 14305

Nichols, Tioga Co., Pop. Code 3
Tioga Central SD
Supt. – See Tioga Center
ES 13812 – James Francis, prin.

Norfolk, St. Lawrence Co., Pop. Code 4
Norwood-Norfolk Central SD
Supt. – See Norwood
ES, HEPBURN STREET 13667
  Martin Manley, prin.

North Babylon, Suffolk Co., Pop. Code 8
North Babylon UFD
Sch. Sys. Enr. Code 5
Supt. – Frank Flood, 5 JARDINE PL 11703
Moses JHS, 250 PHELPS LANE 11703
  Alice Gordon, prin.
Deer Park Avenue ES
  DEER PARK AVENUE 11703
  Marion Vedder, prin.
Deluca ES, PHELPS LN 11703
  George Pincus, prin.
Parliament Place ES, PARLIAMENT PL 11703
  Ralph Pescuma, prin.
Woods Road ES, 110 WOODS RD 11703
  John Kohnken, prin.
Other Schools – See West Babylon

North Baldwin, Nassau Co.
Uniondale UFD
Supt. – See Uniondale
Grand Avenue ES, 711 SCHOOL DR 11510
  Robert Renner, prin.

North Bay, Oneida Co.
Camden Central SD
Supt. – See Camden
North Bay Area ES 13123 – Richard Keville, prin.

North Bellmore, Nassau Co., Pop. Code 7
North Bellmore UFD
Sch. Sys. Enr. Code 4
Supt. – Frank Marlow, MARTIN AVE 11710
Dinkelmeyer ES, WALTOFFER AVENUE 11710
  Isabel Stein, prin.
Gunther ES, REGENT PLACE 11710
  Laurance Anderson, prin.
Newbridge Road ES, 1601 NEWBRIDGE RD 11710
  Richard Benson, prin.
Saw Mill Road ES, SAW MILL ROAD 11710
  Toni Cincotta, prin.
Other Schools – See North Merrick

North Collins, Erie Co., Pop. Code 4
North Collins Central SD
Sch. Sys. Enr. Code 3
Supt. – John McDonough
  2045 SCHOOL ST 14111
ES, 10469 BANTLE RD 14111 – Jud Foy, prin.

North Creek, Warren Co., Pop. Code 3
Johnsburg Central SD
Sch. Sys. Enr. Code 2
Supt. – Clive Chambers 12853
Johnsburg Central S, P O BOX 380 12853
  Carl Flood, prin.

North Greece, Monroe Co.
Greece Central SD
Sch. Sys. Enr. Code 7
Supt. – John Yagielski, P O BOX 300 14515
Other Schools – See Rochester

North Massapequa, Nassau Co., Pop. Code 7
Farmingdale UFD
Supt. – See Farmingdale
Albany Avenue ES, 101 ALBANY AVE 11758
  William Johnston, prin.

Plainedge UFD
Sch. Sys. Enr. Code 5
Supt. – George Kane
  241 WYNGATE DRIVE 11758
Packard JHS, IDAHO AVE & CENTRAL 11758
  Anthony Pellegrino, prin.
Eastplain ES, MICHIGAN AVENUE 11758
  Dianne Catullo, prin.
Other Schools – See Bethpage, Massapequa

North Merrick, Nassau Co.
North Bellmore UFD
Supt. – See North Bellmore
Park Avenue ES
  PARK AVENUE & GROVE STREET 11566
  Michael Wolk, prin.

North Merrick UFD
Supt. – See Merrick
Fayette ES, 1057 MERRICK AVE N 11566
  Joseph Tucker, prin.

Sacred Heart ES, 730 MERRICK AVE N 11566

Northport, Suffolk Co., Pop. Code 6
Northport-East Northport UFD
Sch. Sys. Enr. Code 6
Supt. – William Brosnan
  110 ELWOOD ROAD 11768
Middleville MS, 69 MIDDLEVILLE ROAD 11768
  Peter Corradi, prin.
MS, 158 LAUREL AVE 11768
  Martin Nadler, prin.
Norwood Avenue ES, 25 NORWOOD RD 11768
  Peter Clark, prin.
Ocean Avenue ES, DOGWOOD ROAD 11768
  E. Welch, prin.
Other Schools – See East Northport

St. Philip Neri ES, 364 MAIN ST 11768

North Rose, Wayne Co.
North Rose-Wolcott Central SD
Supt. – See Wolcott
ES, SALTER ROAD 14516 – Linda Haensch, prin.

North Salem, Westchester Co., Pop. Code 5
North Salem Central SD
Sch. Sys. Enr. Code 3
Supt. – Anthony Sabella, RT 124 10560
Pequenakonck ES, ROUTE 124 10560
  Cheryl Cassano, prin.

North Syracuse, Onondaga Co., Pop. Code 6
North Syracuse Central SD
Sch. Sys. Enr. Code 6
Supt. – Thomas O'Rourke
  5355 W TAFT ROAD 13212
Allen Road ES, ALLEN ROAD 13212
  Joseph Dicarlo, prin.
Bear Road ES, 5590 BEAR RD 13212
  Karl Saile, prin.
Smith Road ES, 5959 SMITH RD 13212
  Harold Freeden, prin.
Other Schools – See Cicero, Clay, Mattydale

St. Rose of Lima ES, 411 S MAIN ST 13212

North Tarrytown, Westchester Co., Pop. Code 6
Pocantico Hills Central SD
Sch. Sys. Enr. Code 2
Supt. – Robert Morrison
  599 BEDFORD ROAD 10591
Pocantico Hills Central ES
  599 BEDFORD RD 10591 – Dolores Napello, prin.

Tarrytown UFD
Sch. Sys. Enr. Code 4
Supt. – H. Blueglass, 200 N BROADWAY 10591
Morse MS, POCANTICO STREET 10591
  Maria McCaskill, prin.
Other Schools – See Tarrytown

St. Teresa ES, 113 DEPEYSTER ST 10591

North Tonawanda, Niagara Co., Pop. Code 8
Niagara Wheatfield Central SD
Supt. – See Sanborn
Errick Road ES, 6839 ERRICK RD 14120
  Mary Maggiotto, prin.

North Tonawanda CSD
Sch. Sys. Enr. Code 6
Supt. – Michael Pavlovich
  175 HUMPHREY ST 14120
Payne JHS, 621 PAYNE AVE 14120
  Gloria Mierzwa, prin.

Reszel JHS, 1500 VANDERBILT AVE 14120
  Sandra Klimas, prin.
Drake ES, 380 DRAKE DR 14120
  Arlene Wallak, prin.
Gilmore ES, 789 GILMORE AVE 14120
  Ralph Irene, prin.
Grant ES, GRANT ST 14120 — Joel Rosokoff, prin.
Meadow ES, 455 MEADOW DR 14120
  Ronald Neal, prin.
Ohio ES, 625 OHIO ST 14120
  Charles Baker, prin.
Spruce ES, 195 SPRUCE ST 14120
  Roy Seiwell, prin.

First Baptist Christian School
  530 MEADOW DR 14120
Ascension-OLC ES, 75 KEIL ST 14120
St. John Lutheran ES, 6950 WARD RD 14120
St. Joseph ES, 1469 PAYNE AVE 14120
St. Mark Lutheran ES, 1135 OLIVER ST 14120
St. Matthew Lutheran ES, 875 EGGERT DR 14120
St. Paul Lutheran ES
  453 OLD FALLS BLVD 14120

Northville, Fulton Co., Pop. Code 4
Edinburg Common SD
Sch. Sys. Enr. Code 2
Supt. – Harry Brooks
  RURAL ROUTE 01 BOX 515 12134
Edinburg Common ES
  RURAL ROUTE 01 BOX 515 12134
  Roger McQuain, prin.

Northville Central SD
Sch. Sys. Enr. Code 3
Supt. – Gerald Fitzgerald, 3RD ST 12134
ES, THIRD STREET 12134
  Edward Meilinger, prin.

North White Plains, Westchester Co.
Valhalla UFD
Supt. – See Valhalla
Virginia Road ES, 72 VIRGINIA RD N 10603
  Harold Caplan, prin.

Norwich, Chenango Co., Pop. Code 6
Norwich CSD
Sch. Sys. Enr. Code 5
Supt. – Robert Cleveland, BD OF ED BLDG 13815
MS, MIDLAND DRIVE 13815
  Michael McCollough, prin.
Brown ES, BEEBE AVENUE 13815
  Paul Lupia, prin.
Gibson ES, RIDGELAND ROAD 13815
  Lelan Brookins, prin.

Valley Heights Christian Academy
  75 CALVARY DR 13815
St. Paul ES, 17 PROSPECT ST 13815

Norwood, St. Lawrence Co., Pop. Code 4
Norwood-Norfolk Central SD
Sch. Sys. Enr. Code 4
Supt. – T. Wodzinski 13668
ES, 26 PROSPECT ST 13668 – Charles Hager, prin.
Other Schools – See Norfolk

Nunda, Livingston Co., Pop. Code 4
Dalton-Nunda Central SD
Sch. Sys. Enr. Code 4
Supt. – Barry Schoenholz, MILL ST 14517
Other Schools – See Dalton

Nyack, Rockland Co., Pop. Code 6
Nyack UFD
Sch. Sys. Enr. Code 5
Supt. – Richard Greene, S HIGHLAND AVE 10960
JHS, S HIGHLAND AVE 10960
  J. Thomas Kane, prin.
Hilltop IS, DICKINSON AVE 10960
  Ernest Pelletier, prin.
Upper Nyack ES, 340 N BROADWAY 10960
  Barnet Ostrowsky, prin.
Other Schools – See Valley Cottage

St. Ann ES, 33 JEFFERSON ST 10960

Oakdale, Suffolk Co., Pop. Code 6
Connetquot Central SD
Supt. – See Bohemia
Idle Hour ES, 334 IDLE HOUR BLVD 11769
  Matthew Arnao, prin.

La Salle Military Academy
  MONTAUK HWY 11769

Oakfield, Genesee Co., Pop. Code 4
Oakfield Alabama Central SD
Sch. Sys. Enr. Code 4
Supt. – Norman Fagnan
  7011 LEWISTON ROAD 14125
Oakfield Alabama ES, 7011 LEWISTON RD 14125
  William Meyer, prin.

Ocean Beach, Suffolk Co., Pop. Code 2
Fire Island UFD
Sch. Sys. Enr. Code 1
Supt. – Alexander Van De Mark
  SURF ROAD 11770
Woodhull ES, SURF RD 11770
  Alexander Van De Mark, prin.

Oceanside, Nassau Co., Pop. Code 8
Oceanside UFD
Sch. Sys. Enr. Code 6
Supt. – Thomas Marcello, 145 MERLE AVE 11572

MS, ALICE & BEATRICE AVES 11572
  Enid D'Arrigo, prin.
Boardman ES, ALICE AND BEATRICE AVE 11572
  Bruce Misher, prin.
ES 2, 2731 TERRELL AVE 11572
  Donald Maresca, prin.
ES 3, 2852 FORTESQUE AVE 11572
  Jeffrey Schlissel, prin.
ES 5, N OCEANSIDE ROAD 11572
  Steven Kriss, prin.
ES 8, 3252 FULTON AVE 11572
  Ronald Schoen, prin.

St. Andrew's Episcopal School, P O BOX 98 11572
Crocker Country Day ES, P O BOX 36 11572

Odessa, Schuyler Co., Pop. Code 3
Odessa-Montour Central SD
Sch. Sys. Enr. Code 4
Supt. – Donald Gooley, P O BOX 48 14869
Hanlon MS, COLLEGE AVENUE 14869
  Harry Barrigar, prin.
Other Schools – See Montour Falls

Ogdensburg, St. Lawrence Co., Pop. Code 7
Ogdensburg CSD
Sch. Sys. Enr. Code 4
Supt. – Wesley Stitt, 1100 STATE ST 13669
Kennedy MS, PARK & DAVID STREET 13669
  Betty Mallott, prin.
Lincoln ES, 1515 KNOX ST 13669
  William Flynn, prin.
Madill ES, 800 JEFFERSON AVE 13669
  Richard Lockwood, prin.
Sherman ES, 619 FRANKLIN ST 13669
  William Flynn, prin.

Ogdensburg Catholic Cent School
  315 GATES ST 13669

Old Bethpage, Nassau Co.
Plainview-Old Bethpage Central SD
Supt. – See Plainview
ES, 1159 ROUND SWAMP RD 11804
  Gloria Bennardo, prin.

Old Forge, Herkimer Co., Pop. Code 3
Town of Webb UFD
Sch. Sys. Enr. Code 2
Supt. – Lawson Rutherford 13420
Town of Webb S, MAIN ST 13420
  Susan Webster, prin.

Old Westbury, Nassau Co., Pop. Code 5

School of the Holy Child
  25 STORE HILL ROAD 11568

Olean, Cattaraugus Co., Pop. Code 7
Olean CSD
Sch. Sys. Enr. Code 5
Supt. – John Edwards
  410 W SULLIVAN ST 14760
JHS, 420 N 7TH ST 14760 – Fred Nichols, prin.
Boardmanville ES, 622 MAIN ST 14760
  Doris Norton, prin.
East View ES, 690 EAST SPRING STREET 14760
  John Aceti, prin.
North Hill ES, 1001 N UNION ST 14760
  (—), prin.
Norton ES, 411 W HENLEY ST 14760
  Jon Baker, prin.
Washington West ES
  1626 WASHINGTON ST 14760
  Larry Miller, prin.

St. Mary of Angels ES, 205 W HENLEY ST 14760

Olmstedville, Essex Co.
Minerva Central SD
Sch. Sys. Enr. Code 2
Supt. – Raymond Ciccarelli 12857
Minerva Central S, P O BOX 67 12857
  Raymond Ciccarelli, prin.

Oneida, Madison Co., Pop. Code 7
Oneida CSD
Sch. Sys. Enr. Code 5
Supt. – Frederick Volp, EAST AVE 13421
North Broad Street ES, 230 N BROAD ST 13421
  Peter O'Brien, prin.
Oneida Castle ES, 1 FIRST ST 13421
  Lois Lang, prin.
Prior ES, EAST AVENUE 13421
  David Gillmeister, prin.
Seneca Street ES, 436 SENECA ST 13421
  David Clancy, prin.
Other Schools – See Durhamville, Wampsville

St. Patrick ES, 356 ELIZABETH ST 13421

Oneonta, Otsego Co., Pop. Code 7
Oneonta CSD
Sch. Sys. Enr. Code 4
Supt. – Lowell Foland, 290 CHESTNUT ST 13820
JHS, 130 EAST ST 13820 – Robert Grant, prin.
Center Street ES, 31 CENTER ST 13820
  John Cook, prin.
Greater Plains ES, W END AVE 13820
  R. Bellino, prin.
Riverside ES, HENRY STREET 13820
  Richard Picolla, prin.
Valleyview ES
  40 46 VALLEYVIEW STREET 13820
  John Higgins, prin.

St. Mary's ES, 38 WALNUT ST 13820

Ontario Center, Wayne Co., Pop. Code 6
Wayne Central SD
Sch. Sys. Enr. Code 4
Supt. – R. Spring, MACEDON ROAD 14520
Armstrong MS, MACEDON ROAD 14520
  Dan Talany, prin.
Freewill ES, 6076 ONTARIO CENTER RD 14520
  Dennis Fryer, prin.
Ontario MS, 6076 ONTARIO CENTER RD 14520
  Robert Pearles, Jr., prin.
Ontario PS, 6076 ONTARIO CENTER RD 14520
  Lucinda Van Hoover, prin.

Orchard Park, Erie Co., Pop. Code 5
Orchard Park Central SD
Sch. Sys. Enr. Code 5
Supt. – Charles Stoddart
  25 S LINCOLN AVE 14127
MS, 25 S LINCOLN AVE 14127
  Lurly Hunsberger, prin.
Eggert Road ES, 3580 EGGERT RD 14127
  Peter Walders, prin.
Ellicott Road ES, ELLICOTT RD 14127
  Robert Horvath, prin.
South Davis ES, S DAVIS ST 14127
  James Bodziak, prin.
Windom ES, SHELDON RD 14127
  Ronald Mellerski, prin.

Nativity of Our Lord ES
  4414 S BUFFALO ST 14127
Our Lady of the Sacred Heart ES
  S 3144 ABBOTT ROAD 14127
St. John Vianney ES
  2950 SW BOULEVARD 14127

Orient, Suffolk Co.
Oysterponds UFD
Sch. Sys. Enr. Code 2
Supt. – Charles Woznick, MAIN ROAD 11957
Oysterponds ES, MAIN RD 11957
  Charles Woznick, prin.

Oriskany, Oneida Co., Pop. Code 4
Oriskany Central UFD
Sch. Sys. Enr. Code 3
Supt. – Robert Bradley, UTICA ST 13424
Walbran ES 13424 – James Cufari, prin.

Ossining, Westchester Co., Pop. Code 7
Ossining UFD
Sch. Sys. Enr. Code 5
Supt. – John Humphrey, 83 CROTON AVE 10562
Dorner MS, CLAREMONT ROAD 10562
  Richard Maurer, prin.
Brookside ES, 2 PINESBRIDGE RD 10562
  Paul Fried, prin.
Claremont MS, 41 CLAREMONT RD 10562
  Bruce Bundy, prin.
Park ES, 22 EDWARD ST 10562
  H. Hallberg, prin.

St. Ann ES, 16 ELIZABETH ST 10562
St. Augustine ES, EAGLE PARK 10562

Oswego, Oswego Co., Pop. Code 7
Oswego CSD
Sch. Sys. Enr. Code 5
Supt. – Edward Garno, 233 W UTICA ST 13126
MS, 270 W 1ST ST 13126 – Edward Matott, prin.
Fitzhugh Park ES
  EAST BRIDGE & 10TH STREET 13126
  Gary Roy, prin.
Kingsford Park ES
  WEST FIFTH & NIAGARA STREET 13126
  Joseph Donovan, prin.
Leighton ES, 1 BUCCANEER ST 13126
  Jeffrey Davis, prin.
Riley ES, BUNNER STREET 13126
  Francis Witkowski, prin.
Other Schools – See Minetto

St. Mary's ES, 72 W 6TH ST 13126
St. Paul's Academy, 115 E 5TH ST 13126

Otego, Otsego Co., Pop. Code 4
Otego-Unadilla Central SD
Sch. Sys. Enr. Code 4
Supt. – Richard Molatch
  RURAL ROUTE 01 13825
ES, MAIN STREET 13825 – Peter Negri, prin.
Other Schools – See Unadilla

Owego, Tioga Co., Pop. Code 5
Owego-Apalachin Central SD
Sch. Sys. Enr. Code 5
Supt. – Francis Murphy, 38 TALCOTT ST 13827
Owego Apalachin MS, ELM ST 13827
  Nicholas Gatto, prin.
ES, GEORGE STREET 13827
  William Motsko, prin.
Other Schools – See Apalachin

St. Patrick ES, 309 FRONT ST 13827
Zion Lutheran ES
  RURAL ROUTE 02 BOX 237A 13827

Oxford, Chenango Co., Pop. Code 4
Oxford Academy & Central SD
Sch. Sys. Enr. Code 4
Supt. – D. Burroughs
  S WASHINGTON AVE 13830

Oxford Academy MS, FORT HILL 13830
 H. Grayson Stevens, prin.
Oxford Academy PS
 S WASHINGTON AVENUE 13830
 David Burroughs, prin.

Oyster Bay, Nassau Co., Pop. Code 10
Oyster Bay-East Norwich Central SD
Sch. Sys. Enr. Code 4
Supt. – Sidney Freund, MCCOUNTS LANE 11771
Roosevelt ES, W MAIN STREET 11771
 John Russo, prin.
Other Schools – See East Norwich

East Woods ES, 31 YELLOW COTE RD 11771
St. Dominic ES, 35 SCHOOL ST 11771

Ozone Park, Queens Co.
Queens Borough SD 27
Sch. Sys. Enr. Code 8
Supt. – Colman Genn, 90-15 SUTTER AVE 11417
Blackwell JHS, 93-11 101ST AVE 11416
 John Falco, prin.
Ampere ES, 8201 101ST AVE 11416
 Abby Kessler, prin.
Old South ES, 9015 SUTTER AVE 11417
 Alan Druckman, prin.
Other Schools – See Arverne, Broad Channel, Far
 Rockaway, Howard Beach, Jamaica, Richmond Hill,
 Rockaway Beach, Rockaway Park, South Ozone
 Park, Wood Haven

Nativity BVM ES
 92 ST & ROCKAWAY BLVD 11416

Painted Post, Steuben Co., Pop. Code 4
Corning CSD
Sch. Sys. Enr. Code 6
Supt. – George Hamaty, 165 CHARLES ST 14870
Erwin Valley ES, RURAL ROUTE 01 14870
 Richard Mayer, prin.
Pierce ES, RURAL ROUTE 01 14870
 John Castiglione, prin.
Presho ES, RURAL ROUTE 01 14870
 Richard Mayer, prin.
Smith ES, STANTON ST EXT 14870
 John Castiglione, prin.
Other Schools – See Corning

Palmyra, Wayne Co., Pop. Code 5
Palmyra-Macedon Central SD
Sch. Sys. Enr. Code 4
Supt. – James Tobin, 151 HYDE PKWY 14522
Palmyra Macedon MS, 151 HYDE PKWY 14522
 Earl Mehlenbacher, prin.
ES, 120 CANANDAIGUA ST 14522
 Vincent Caringi, prin.
Other Schools – See Macedon

Panama, Chautauqua Co., Pop. Code 3
Panama Central SD
Sch. Sys. Enr. Code 3
Supt. – Charles Pegan, RURAL ROUTE 01 14767
ES 14767 – Jack Engdahl, prin.

Parish, Oswego Co., Pop. Code 3
Altmar Parish-Williamstown Central SD
Sch. Sys. Enr. Code 4
Supt. – Oliver Blaise 13131
Altmar Parish-Williamstown MS
 CO ROUTE 22 13131 – Stanley Finkle, prin.
ES, UNION STREET 13131 – John Flower, prin.
Other Schools – See Altmar, Williamstown

Parishville, St. Lawrence Co., Pop. Code 4
Parishville-Hopkinton Central SD
Sch. Sys. Enr. Code 3
Supt. – Peter Lisi, SCHOOL ST 13672
ES, SCHOOL STREET 13672
 Annemarie Fitzrandolph, prin.

Patchogue, Suffolk Co., Pop. Code 7
Patchogue-Medford UFD
Sch. Sys. Enr. Code 6
Supt. – H. Read, 241 S OCEAN AVE 11772
Barton Avenue ES, 199 BARTON AVE 11772
 Frank Rossi, prin.
Bay Avenue ES, 114 BAY AVE 11772
 Angelo Truglio, prin.
Canaan ES, 59 FRY BLVD 11772
 Sandra Henik, prin.
Medford Avenue ES, 281 MEDFORD AVE 11772
 John Augustine, prin.
River Avenue ES, RIVER AVENUE 11772
 Antoinette Cutter, prin.
Other Schools – See Medford

Emanuel Lutheran ES, 179 E MAIN ST 11772
Patchogue Regional Catholic ES
 DIVISION ST 11772

Patterson, Putnam Co., Pop. Code 6
Carmel Central SD
Sch. Sys. Enr. Code 5
Supt. – G. Loewenberg, SOUTH ST 12563
ES, SOUTH STREET 12563
 Selly McCracken, prin.
Other Schools – See Carmel

Pattersonville, Schenectady Co.
Schalmont Central SD-Rotterdam
Supt. – See Schenectady
Mariaville ES, RURAL ROUTE 01 BOX 338 12137
 Gary Beadnell, prin.

Pavilion, Genesee Co., Pop. Code 3
Pavilion Central SD
Sch. Sys. Enr. Code 3
Supt. – R. Westacott, 7014 BIG TREE ROAD 14525
Bunce ES, 7071 YORK RD 14525
 Edward Orman, prin.

Pavilion Baptist School, 10983 LAKE ST 14525

Pawling, Dutchess Co., Pop. Code 4
Pawling Central SD
Sch. Sys. Enr. Code 4
Supt. – Vincent Vecchiarella, 7 HAIGHT ST 12564
ES, 7 HAIGHT ST 12564 – Barbara Gill, prin.

Pearl River, Rockland Co., Pop. Code 7
Pearl River UFD
Sch. Sys. Enr. Code 4
Supt. – A. Williamson, 37 FRANKLIN AVE 10965
Evans Park ES, 40 MARION PL 10965
 Diane Rodger, prin.
Franklin Avenue ES, 48 FRANKLIN AVE 10965
 Mary Evangelist, prin.
MS, 520 GILBERT AVE 10965
 Frank Auriema, prin.

St. Margaret ES, 33 N MAGNOLIA AVE 10965

Peekskill, Westchester Co., Pop. Code 7
Peekskill CSD
Sch. Sys. Enr. Code 4
Supt. – Donald Rickett, 1031 ELM ST 10566
MS, 212 RINGGOLD ST 10566
 Anthony Ciaglia, prin.
Hillcrest ES, 99 HORTON DR 10566
 Vincent Burruano, prin.
Oakside ES, JOHN STREET 10566
 James Taylor, prin.
Uriah Hill ES, PEMART AVENUE 10566
 James Pappas, prin.
Woodside ES, FRANKLIN STREET 10566
 John Gambino, prin.

Assumption ES, 920 1ST ST 10566
St. Columbanus School, 122 OREGON RD 10566

Pelham, Westchester Co., Pop. Code 6
Pelham UFD
Sch. Sys. Enr. Code 4
Supt. – Daniel Bryan, 17 FRANKLIN PL 10803
MS, COLONIAL AVE 10803 – J. Lohrfink, prin.
Colonial ES, 315 HIGHBROOK AVE 10803
 Joseph Longobardi, prin.
Hutchinson ES, LINCOLN AVENUE 10803
 Rocco Polera, prin.
Prospect Hill ES
 CLAY AND WASH AVENUES 10803
 Theodore Kusulas, prin.
Siwanoy ES, SIWANOY PLACE 10803
 Joan Campanella, prin.

Penfield, Monroe Co., Pop. Code 8
Penfield Central SD
Sch. Sys. Enr. Code 5
Supt. – Richard Mace
 2590 ATLANTIC AVE 14526
Bay Trail MS, 1760 SCRIBNER ROAD 14526
 Ron Bailey, prin.
Cobbles ES, GEBHARDT ROAD 14526
 William Gonyeo, prin.
Hill ES, 2126 PENFIELD RD 14526
 Mary Rapp, prin.
Scribner Road ES, 1750 SCRIBNER RD 14526
 Mark Miele, prin.
Other Schools – See Rochester

New Covenant Christian School
 P O BOX 468 14526
St. Joseph ES, 39 GEBHARDT RD 14526

Pennellville, Oswego Co.
Phoenix Central SD
Supt. – See Phoenix
ES, RURAL ROUTE 01 13132 – John Murray, prin.

Penn Yan, Yates Co., Pop. Code 6
Penn Yan Central SD
Sch. Sys. Enr. Code 4
Supt. – Dan Farsaci, 305 COURT ST 14527
MS, 655 LIBERTY ST 14527 – (—), prin.
ES, 101 MAPLE AVENUE 14527
 Richard Lent, prin.

St. Michael's School, 214 KEUKA ST 14527

Perry, Wyoming Co., Pop. Code 5
Perry Central SD
Sch. Sys. Enr. Code 4
Supt. – Per Omland, 59 LEICESTER ST 14530
ES, 59 LEICESTER ST 14530
 Eileen McAvoy, prin.

Peru, Clinton Co., Pop. Code 6
Peru Central SD
Sch. Sys. Enr. Code 5
Supt. – Norman Votraw
 HIGH SCHOOL BLDG 12972
IS, SCHOOL ST 12972 – Melvin Bruno, prin.
Primary Building ES 12972 – Rita Manly, prin.
Other Schools – See Plattsburgh A F B

St. Augustine, MAIN ST 12972

Phelps, Ontario Co., Pop. Code 4
Phelps-Clifton Springs Central SD
Supt. – See Clifton Springs

Midlakes JHS, W MAIN ST 14532
 Donald Dinolfo, prin.
ES, BANTA STREET 14532
 William Connolly, prin.

Philadelphia, Jefferson Co., Pop. Code 3
Indian River Central SD
Sch. Sys. Enr. Code 4
Supt. – H. Zygadlo, P O BOX 308 13673
ES, SAND STREET 13673 – David Rausch, prin.
Other Schools – See Antwerp, Evans Mills, Theresa

Philmont, Columbia Co., Pop. Code 4
Copake-Taconic Hills Central SD
Supt. – See Hillsdale
Ockawamick ES 12565
 Anthony Marchesano, prin.

Phoenicia, Ulster Co.
Onteora Central SD
Supt. – See Boiceville
ES 12464 – Randy Collins, prin.

Phoenix, Oswego Co., Pop. Code 4
Phoenix Central SD
Sch. Sys. Enr. Code 5
Supt. – J. Robert Johnson, 400 VOLNEY ST 13135
Dillon MS, 400 VOLNEY ST 13135
 Mark Montoney, prin.
Elm Street ES, 700 ELM ST 13135
 Richard McGuire, prin.
Other Schools – See Pennellville

Piermont, Rockland Co., Pop. Code 4
South Orangetown Central SD
Supt. – See Blauvelt
Tappan Zee ES, RURAL ROUTE 09 10968
 Carolyn Spence, prin.

Pine Bush, Orange Co., Pop. Code 4
Pine Bush Central SD
Sch. Sys. Enr. Code 5
Supt. – William Bassett, MAPLE AVE 12566
Russell ES, HOLLAND AVENUE 12566
 Jeanne Theis, prin.
Other Schools – See Circleville

Pine City, Chemung Co.
Elmira CSD
Supt. – See Elmira
ES 14871 – Margaret Drake, prin.

Pine Island, Orange Co., Pop. Code 3
Warwick Valley Central SD
Supt. – See Warwick
ES, SCHOOLHOUSE ROAD 10969
 R. Gibson, prin.

Pine Plains, Dutchess Co., Pop. Code 4
Pine Plains Central SD
Sch. Sys. Enr. Code 4
Supt. – Norris Gaynor, RURAL ROUTE 01 12567
Smith ES, ACADEMY STREET 12567
 Frank Perotti, prin.
Other Schools – See Stanfordville

Piseco, Hamilton Co.
Piseco Common SD
Sch. Sys. Enr. Code 1
Supt. – John Simons 12139
ES 12139 – John Simons, prin.

Pittsford, Monroe Co., Pop. Code 4
Pittsford Central SD
Sch. Sys. Enr. Code 6
Supt. – R. Hibschman, SUTHERLAND ST 14534
MS, BARKER ROAD 14534 – Sherman Craig, prin.
Jefferson Road ES, SCHOOL LANE 14534
 Carole Dedominicis, prin.
Park Road ES, PARK ROAD 14534
 Phillip Langton, prin.
Thornell Road ES, THORNELL ROAD 14534
 A. Parisi, prin.
Other Schools – See Rochester

St. Louis ES, 11 RAND PL 14534

Plainview, Nassau Co., Pop. Code 8
Plainview-Old Bethpage Central SD
Sch. Sys. Enr. Code 5
Supt. – Arthur Colver
 ADMIN BLDG JAMAICA AVE 11803
Mattlin MS, 40 WASHINGTON AVE 11803
 Lawrence Napolitano, prin.
Plainview-Old Bethpage MS
 33 BEDFORD ROAD 11803
 Howard Weinstock, prin.
Jamaica Avenue ES, 85 JAMAICA AVE 11803
 Norman Flaster, prin.
Parkway ES, 300 MANETTO HILL RD 11803
 Patricia Bergrin, prin.
Other Schools – See Old Bethpage

Good Shepherd Lutheran ES
 99 CENTRAL PARK RD 11803
Hebrew Academy/Mid Island School
 25 JOYCE ROAD 11803
Montessori School of Plainview
 992 OLD COUNTRY RD 11803
St. Pius X ES, 270 WASHINGTON AVE 11803

Plattekill, Ulster Co.
Wallkill Central SD
Supt. – See Wallkill
MS 12568 – Randolph Siegel, prin.

Plattsburgh, Clinton Co., Pop. Code 7
Beekmantown Central SD
Sch. Sys. Enr. Code 4
Supt. – David Walter, P O BOX 829 12901
Beekmantown ES, P O BOX 829 12901
James Sears, prin.
Cumberland Head ES, P O 829 12901
Ernest Craumer, prin.

Plattsburgh CSD
Sch. Sys. Enr. Code 4
Supt. – Arthur Momot, 106 OAK ST 12901
MS, 17 BROAD ST 12901
Richard McTigue, prin.
Bailey Avenue ES 12901 – Thomas Glasgow, prin.
Broad Street ES 12901 – Gilbert Duken, prin.
Monty Street ES 12901 – Thelma Dodson, prin.
Oak Street MS 12901 – Thomas Glasgow, prin.

St. John's Academy, 59 BROAD ST 12901
Notre Dame ES, 7 W ELIZABETH ST 12901
St. Peter's ES, 7 ST CHARLES ST 12901

Plattsburgh A F B, Clinton Co.
Peru Central SD
Supt. – See Peru
Northside ES 12903 – John Longware, prin.
Southside MS 12903 – James Howard, prin.

Pleasant Valley, Dutchess Co., Pop. Code 6
Arlington Central SD
Supt. – See Poughkeepsie
Traver Road ES, TRAVER ROAD 12569
Mary Landry, prin.
West Road IS, WEST ROAD 12569
Joseph Aquanni, prin.

Pleasantville, Westchester Co., Pop. Code 6
Pleasant UFD
Sch. Sys. Enr. Code 4
Supt. – Frank Gray, ROMER AVE 10570
ES, 350 BEDFORD RD 10570
Marilyn Glotzer, prin.

Poland, Herkimer Co., Pop. Code 3
Poland Central SD
Sch. Sys. Enr. Code 3
Supt. – Lorenzo Benati, P O BOX 8 13431
Poland Central S, P O BOX 8 13431
Jon Speich, prin.

Pomona, Rockland Co., Pop. Code 4

Bais Yaakov of Chofetz Chaim
CAMP HILL ROAD 10970

Port Byron, Cayuga Co., Pop. Code 4
Port Byron Central SD
Sch. Sys. Enr. Code 4
Supt. – Frank Ambrosie, 98 UTICA ST 13140
MS, MAPLE AVE 13140 – John Mormile, prin.
Gates ES, MAPLE AVENUE 13140
Rita Racette, prin.

Port Chester, Westchester Co., Pop. Code 7
Port Chester-Rye UFD
Sch. Sys. Enr. Code 5
Supt. – H. Mix, P O BOX 246 10573
MS, BOWMAN AVE 10573 – R. DeBuono, prin.
Edison ES, RECTORY STREET 10573
Frank Napolitano,Jr., prin.
Kennedy ES, 40 OLIVIA ST 10573
William Thompson,Jr., prin.
King Street ES, 697 KING ST 10573
Andrea Ragusa, prin.
Park Avenue ES, 75 PARK AVE 10573
Anthony Gioffre, prin.

Corpus Christi ES, 135 S REGENT ST 10573
Holy Rosary ES, 10 CENTRAL AVE 10573
Our Lady of Mercy School, 17 SPRING ST 10573

Port Ewen, Ulster Co., Pop. Code 5
Kingston CSD
Supt. – See Kingston
Graves ES, CLAY ROAD 12466
Raymond Monfette, prin.

Port Henry, Essex Co., Pop. Code 4
Moriah Central SD
Sch. Sys. Enr. Code 3
Supt. – Michael Singleton, HCR 01 BOX 7A 12974
Moriah ES, HCR 01 BOX 7A 12974
Allan Clark, prin.

Port Jefferson, Suffolk Co., Pop. Code 6
Brookhaven-Comsewogue UFD
Sch. Sys. Enr. Code 5
Supt. – Alan Austen, 290 NORWOOD AVE 11776
Kennedy JHS, 200 JAYNE BLVD 11776
Jack Zamek, prin.
Boyle Road ES, 424 BOYLE RD 11776
Constantino Basile, prin.
Clinton Avenue ES, 140 CLINTON AVE 11776
Shelley Saffer, prin.
Norwood Avenue ES, 290 NORWOOD AVE 11776
Andrew Cassidy, prin.

Port Jefferson UFD
Sch. Sys. Enr. Code 4
Supt. – Philip Magnerella
SCRAGGY HILL ROAD 11777
JHS, SPRING ST 11777 – Lawrence Lazar, prin.
ES, SCRAGGY HILL ROAD 11777
Sharon Miano, prin.

Infant Jesus ES, 110 MYRTLE AVE 11777

North Shore Christian ES, P O BOX 227 11776

Port Jervis, Orange Co., Pop. Code 6
Port Jervis CSD
Sch. Sys. Enr. Code 5
Supt. – Frank Moscati, P O BOX 1104 12771
MS, 118 E MAIN ST 12771 – T. Hoppey, prin.
Kuhl ES, 501 ROUTE 209 12771
William Montgomery, prin.
Sullivan Avenue ES, 1 SULLIVAN AVE 12771
Craig Onofry, prin.
Other Schools – See Cuddebackville

Trinity Catholic ES, P O BOX 1001 12771

Port Leyden, Lewis Co., Pop. Code 3
South Lewis Central SD
Supt. – See Turin
ES 13433 – Peter Stratton, prin.

Portville, Cattaraugus Co., Pop. Code 4
Portville Central SD
Sch. Sys. Enr. Code 4
Supt. – G. Christopher, ELM ST 14770
ES, ELM STREET 14770 – John Dubots, prin.

Port Washington, Nassau Co., Pop. Code 5
Port Washington UFD
Sch. Sys. Enr. Code 5
Supt. – William Heebink, 100 CAMPUS DR 11050
Weber JHS, PORT WASHINGTON BLVD 11050
Faith Cleary, prin.
Daly ES, 36 ROCKWOOD AVE 11050
Peter Faiella, prin.
Guggenheim ES, 38 POPLAR PL 11050
Thomas Lovett, prin.
Manorhaven ES, MOREWOOD OAKS 11050
Lee Aschenbrenner, prin.
Sousa ES, 101 SANDS POINT ROAD 11050
Richard Barry, prin.

St. Peter of Alcantara ES
1321 PORT WASHINGTON BLVD 11050

Potsdam, St. Lawrence Co., Pop. Code 7
Potsdam Central SD
Sch. Sys. Enr. Code 4
Supt. – Gary Snell, 29 LEROY ST 13676
Kingston MS, 29 LEROY ST 13676
Michael Loconti, prin.
Lawrence Avenue ES, 29 LEROY ST 13676
James Waterson, prin.

Campus Learning Center, MERRITT HALL 13676
St. Mary's ES, LAWRENCE AVE 13676

Pottersville, Warren Co.
North Warren Central SD
Sch. Sys. Enr. Code 3
Supt. – William Donlon 12860
MS 12860 – James Lagoy, prin.
Other Schools – See Brant Lake

Poughkeepsie, Dutchess Co., Pop. Code 8
Arlington Central SD
Supt. – T. Hasenpflug
232 DUTCHESS TURNPIKE 12603
Arlington MS, 5 DUTCHESS TPKE 12603
E. Fox, prin.
Titusville MS, GREEN MEADOW PK 12603
Anthony Celenza, prin.
Arlington ES, RAYMOND AVENUE 12603
Arthur May, prin.
Noxon Road ES, NOXON ROAD 12603
Grace Donahue, prin.
Overlook ES, OVERLOOK ROAD 12603
William Morrison, prin.
Other Schools – See Lagrangeville, Pleasant Valley,
Poughquag

Hyde Park Central SD
Supt. – See Hyde Park
Violet Avenue ES, 221 VIOLET AVE 12601
Charles Kortz, prin.

Poughkeepsie CSD
Sch. Sys. Enr. Code 5
Supt. – James Clarke
11 COLLEGE AVENUE 12603
MS, 55 COLLEGE AVE 12603
Frederick Hanlon, prin.
Clinton ES, 265 HOOKER AVE 12603
Frank Corliss, prin.
Columbus ES, 12 S PERRY ST 12601
Wayne Semelmacher, prin.
Krieger ES, 265 HOOKER AVE 12603
Susan Helman, prin.
Morse ES, 101 MANSION ST 12601
Antoinette Lyles, prin.
Smith MS, 400 CHURCH ST 12601
Robert Mountz, prin.
Warring ES, 283 MANSION ST 12601
Linda Mann, prin.

Spackenkill UFD
Sch. Sys. Enr. Code 4
Supt. – R. Woolley, 42 HAGAN DR 12603
Todd JHS, 11 CROFT ROAD 12603
Andrew Manca, prin.
Nassau Spackenkill ES, NASSAU ROAD 12601
Eileen Sicina, prin.
Spackenkill ES, 42 HAGAN DR 12603
John Pinna, prin.

Wappingers Central SD
Supt. – See Wappingers Falls

Kinry Road ES, KINRY ROAD 12603
John Cutler, prin.
Oak Grove ES, BROOKLAND DRIVE 12601
Henry Raiche,Jr., prin.
Vassar Road ES, 100 VASSAR RD 12603
Trudy Briggs, prin.

Poughkeepsie Day School
39 NEW HACKENSACK ROAD 12603
Tabernacle Christian Academy
153 ACADEMY ST 12601
Faith Christian Academy ES
254 SPACKENKILL RD 12603
Holy Trinity ES, 20 SPRINGSIDE AVE 12603
Our Lady of Mt. Carmel ES
15 MOUNT CARMEL PL 12601
St. Martin De Pores ES
38 CEDAR VALLEY RD 12603
St. Mary's ES, 26 S HAMILTON ST 12601
St. Peter ES, 416 VIOLET AVE 12601

Poughquag, Dutchess Co.
Arlington Central SD
Supt. – See Poughkeepsie
Beekman ES, LIME RIDGE ROAD 12570
Frederick Swartout, prin.

Pound Ridge, Westchester Co.
Bedford Central SD
Supt. – See Mount Kisco
ES, POUND RIDGE ROAD 10576
James Young, prin.

Prattsburg, Steuben Co., Pop. Code 4
Prattsburg Central SD
Sch. Sys. Enr. Code 3
Supt. – Harry Bartz 14873
Prattsburg Central S 14873
James McCormick, prin.

Pulaski, Oswego Co., Pop. Code 4
Pulaski Central SD
Sch. Sys. Enr. Code 4
Supt. – W. Leib, 7319 LAKE ST 13142
ES, 7319 LAKE ST 13142
Francis Bellardini, prin.

Purchase, Westchester Co.
Harrison Central SD
Supt. – See Harrison
ES, 90 PURCHASE ST 10577 – James Casale, prin.

Putnam Station, Washington Co.
Putnam Central SD
Sch. Sys. Enr. Code 1
Supt. – Lawrence Hendrix 12861
Putnam Central ES, LOWER ROAD 12861
Lawrence Hendrix, prin.

Putnam Valley, Putnam Co., Pop. Code 6
Putnam Valley Central SD
Sch. Sys. Enr. Code 3
Supt. – Maryann Doyle
OSCAWANA LAKE ROAD 10579
ES, OSCAWANA LAKE ROAD 10579
John Kleinegris, prin.

Queens Village, Queens Co.
Queens Borough SD 26
Supt. – See Bayside
Winchester ES, 8635 235TH CT 11427
Eileen Kramer, prin.

Queens Borough SD 29
Sch. Sys. Enr. Code 7
Supt. – Florence Fiiedlander
22110 JAMAICA AVE 11428
JHS, 21310 92ND AVE 11428 – Lewis Trazer, prin.
Belaire ES
89TH AVENUE & 207TH STREET 11427
James Gormly, prin.
Creedmoor ES, 9137 222ND ST 11428
Edward Funk, prin.
Harvard ES
104 12 SPRINGFIELD BOULEVARD 11428
Philip Ciani, prin.
Other Schools – See Cambria Heights, Hollis, Jamaica,
Rosedale, Saint Albans, Springfield Gardens

Quogue, Suffolk Co., Pop. Code 3
Quogue UFD
Sch. Sys. Enr. Code 1
Supt. – N. Paul Buscemi
EDGEWOOD ROAD 11959
ES, EDGEWOOD RD 11959 – Ralph Bell, prin.

Randolph, Cattaraugus Co., Pop. Code 4
Randolph Central SD
Sch. Sys. Enr. Code 4
Supt. – Edmund Harvey 14772
Chapman ES 14772 – Linda See, prin.

Ransomville, Niagara Co., Pop. Code 4
Wilson Central SD
Supt. – See Wilson
Stevenson ES, 3745 RANSOMVILLE RD 14131
Dennis Mallast, prin.

Raquette Lake, Hamilton Co.
Raquette Lake UFD
Sch. Sys. Enr. Code 1
Supt. – Peter Eckhardt 13436
ES 13436 – Deborah Fuge, prin.

Ravena, Albany Co., Pop. Code 5
Ravena Coeymans Selkirk CSD
Supt. – See Selkirk
JHS, ROUTE 92 12143 – Robert DeSarbo, prin.

ES, MOUNTAIN ROAD 12143
Dominic Nuciford, prin.

Red Creek, Wayne Co., Pop. Code 3
Red Creek Central SD
Sch. Sys. Enr. Code 4
Supt. – Edward Furletti 13143
Cuyler ES 13143 – Richard Drahms, prin.

Red Hook, Dutchess Co., Pop. Code 4
Red Hook Central SD
Sch. Sys. Enr. Code 4
Supt. – William Ledoux, MILL ROAD 12571
JHS, LINDEN AVE 12571
Thomas Turchetti, prin.
Mill Road ES, MILL ROAD 12571
Patricia Sherman, prin.

Rego Park, Queens Co.
Queens Borough SD 28
Supt. – See Forest Hills
Annadale Park ES, 6435 102ND ST 11374
Eli Nieman, prin.
Harding ES, 61 21 97TH PLACE 11374
Stanley Stern, prin.
Mount ES, 65 10 DIETERLE CRSNT 11374
William Bet, prin.
ES, 9306 63RD DR 11374
Robert Fredericks, prin.

Remsen, Oneida Co., Pop. Code 3
Remsen Central SD
Sch. Sys. Enr. Code 3
Supt. – Walter Doherty, DAVIS DR 13438
ES, DAVIS DRIVE 13438 – Anthony Nicotera, prin.

Remsenburg, Suffolk Co.
Remsenburg Speonk UFD
Sch. Sys. Enr. Code 1
Supt. – Joseph Loretan, OLD MILL ROAD 11960
Remsenburg-Speonk ES, OLD MILL RD 11960
Joseph Loretan, prin.

Rensselaer, Rensselaer Co., Pop. Code 6
East Greenbush Central SD
Supt. – See East Greenbush
Red Mill ES, MCCULLOCH PLACE 12144
John Craven, prin.

Rensselaer CSD
Sch. Sys. Enr. Code 4
Supt. – Stephen Urgenson, 905 3RD ST 12144
Van Rensselaer ES
199 WASHINGTON AVE 12144
Kathleen Mrozak, prin.

SS. Joseph's-John's Academy
1641 THIRD ST 12144
St. Mary ES, 149 COLUMBIA TPKE 12144

Retsof, Livingston Co.
York Central SD
Sch. Sys. Enr. Code 5
Supt. – Maurice Dalton, RT 63 14539
York Central ES, RURAL ROUTE 63 14539
Robert Hughes, prin.

Rexford, Saratoga Co.
Niskayuna Central SD
Supt. – See Schenectady
Glencliff ES, RIVERVIEW ROAD 12148
Martin Davis, prin.

Rhinebeck, Dutchess Co., Pop. Code 5
Rhinebeck Central SD
Sch. Sys. Enr. Code 4
Supt. – William Miles, P O BOX 351 12572
Bulkeley MS, P O BOX 351 12572
Patricia Jatul, prin.
Livingston ES, P O BOX 351 12572
Robert Kalman, prin.

North Dutchess Christ ES, ASTOR DR 12572

Richburg, Allegany Co., Pop. Code 2
Richburg Central SD
Sch. Sys. Enr. Code 2
Supt. – Robert Klucik, MAIN ST 14774
S, MAIN ST 14774 – Robert Klucik, prin.

Richfield Springs, Otsego Co., Pop. Code 4
Richfield Springs Central SD
Sch. Sys. Enr. Code 3
Supt. – Arthur Thompson, MAIN ST 13439
Richfield Springs Central S, P O BOX 631 13439
R. Erwin, prin.

Richmond Hill, Queens Co.
Queens Borough SD 27
Supt. – See Ozone Park
Eichler ES, 8610 114TH ST 11418
Philip Gold, prin.
Mann ES, 8650 109TH ST 11418
Kenneth Grover, prin.
Oxford ES, 8511 102ND ST 11418
Jay Rosler, prin.

Queens Borough SD 28
Supt. – See Forest Hills
Hillside Avenue ES, 8602 127TH ST 11418
Melvin Wenk, prin.

Holy Child Jesus ES
86TH AVE & 111TH ST 11418

Richmondville, Schoharie Co., Pop. Code 3
Richmondville Central SD
Sch. Sys. Enr. Code 2
Supt. – Anthony Marturano 12149
Richmondville Central S, 44 E MAIN ST 12149
John Traverse, prin.

Ridge, Suffolk Co., Pop. Code 4
Longwood Central SD
Supt. – See Middle Island
ES, RIDGE RD 11961 – Norman Howard, prin.

Ridgewood, Queens Co., Pop. Code 4
Queens Borough SD 24
Supt. – See Middle Village
IS 77, 976 SENECA AVE 11385
Joseph Quinn, prin.
JHS, 66-56 FOREST AVE 11385
Allen Formicella, prin.
Cambridge ES, 5909 ST FELIX AVE 11385
Max Hershberg, prin.
Richter ES, 559 CYPRESS AVENUE 11385
James Odowd, prin.
Seneca ES, 6085 CATALPA AVE 11385
Matthew Bromme, prin.
Williamsburg ES, 6285 FOREST AVE 11385
Edward Huckemeyer, prin.

Our Lady of Miracals Medal ES
61ST & BLEECKER STS 11385

Ripley, Chautauqua Co., Pop. Code 5
Ripley Central SD
Sch. Sys. Enr. Code 3
Supt. – Kenneth Wasmund, 12 N STATE ST 14775
Ripley Central S, 12 N STATE ST 14775
Ralph Scazafabo, prin.

Riverhead, Suffolk Co., Pop. Code 7
Riverhead Central SD
Sch. Sys. Enr. Code 5
Supt. – Richard Suprina
700 OSBORNE AVE 11901
MS, 600 HARRISON AVE 11901
Willie Patterson, prin.
Phillips Avenue ES, 141 PHILLIPS AVE 11901
Audrey Stupke, prin.
Pulaski Street MS, 300 PULASKI ST 11901
Edward Goldstein, prin.
Roanoke Avenue ES, 525 ROANOKE AVE 11901
George Mills, prin.
Other Schools – See Aquebogue, Calverton

Living Water Christian School
HUBBARD AVE & SH TR LANE 11901
St. Isidore ES, 515 MARCY AVE 11901
St. John the Evangelist ES
546 SAINT JOHNS PL 11901

Rochester, Monroe Co., Pop. Code 9
Brighton Central SD
Sch. Sys. Enr. Code 5
Supt. – John Shafter
220 IDLEWOOD ROAD 14618
Twelve Corners MS, 2643 ELMWOOD AVE 14618
Leroy Welkley, prin.
Council Rock PS, 600 GROSVENOR RD 14610
Mary Reed, prin.
French Road MS, 488 FRENCH ROAD 14618
James O'Connor, prin.

Churchville Chili Central SD
Supt. – See Churchville
Chestnut Ridge ES, 3560 CHILI AVE 14624
Jack Bates, prin.

East Irondequoit Central SD
Sch. Sys. Enr. Code 4
Supt. – Josephine Kehoe
600 PARDEE ROAD 14609
Eastridge JHS, 2350 RIDGE ROAD E 14622
Dale Berne, prin.
Durand-Eastman ES
95 POINT PLEASANT RD 14622
Ethel Furstenberg, prin.
Green ES, 800 BROWN RD 14622
Arthur Johnson, prin.
Laurelton/Pardee ES, 600 PARDEE RD 14609
Walter Kennedy, prin.

Gates-Chili Central SD
Sch. Sys. Enr. Code 5
Supt. – William Dadey
910 WEGMAN ROAD 14624
Gates Chili MS, 910 WEGMAN ROAD 14624
L. Benjamin, prin.
Armstrong ES, 3273 LYELL RD 14606
Dominick Abballe, prin.
Brasser ES, 1000 COLDWATER RD 14624
Richard Robillard, prin.
Paul Road ES, 571 PAUL RD 14624
Arthur Shilen, prin.
Walt Disney ES, 175 COLDWATER RD 14624
Kenneth Hutton, prin.

Greece Central SD
Supt. – See North Greece
Greece Athena MS, 800 LONG POND ROAD 14612
Ronald Nigro, prin.
Hoover Drive MS, 133 HOOVER DR 14615
Dan Doran, prin.
Arcadia MS, 120 ISLAND COTTAGE ROAD 14612
Douglas Skeet, prin.
Autumn Lane ES, 2089 MAIDEN LN 14626
Nelson Beetow, prin.

Barnard MS, 71 MAIDEN LN 14616
Robert Conrad, prin.
Brookside MS, 1144 LONG POND RD 14626
Lydia McCabe, prin.
Buckman Heights MS, 550 BUCKMAN RD 14615
Sue Whan, prin.
English Village ES, 800 TAIT AVE 14616
Frederick Dean, prin.
Hill ES, 320 W CRAIG HILL DR 14626
Dorothy Lindsay, prin.
Holmes Road ES, 300 HOLMES RD 14626
Deborah Johnson, prin.
Kirk Road MS, 299 KIRK RD 14612
George Anderson, prin.
Lakeshore MS, 1200 LATTA RD 14612
John Bartek, prin.
Longridge ES, 190 LONGRIDGE AVE 14616
Joan Thorton, prin.
Paddy Hill ES, 1801 LATTA RD 14612
Jean Biondolillo, prin.
Parkland ES, 1010 ENGLISH RD 14616
Wilford Clicquennoi, prin.

Penfield Central SD
Supt. – See Penfield
Indian Landing ES, 702 LANDING RD N 14625
Donald Shannon, prin.

Pittsford Central SD
Supt. – See Pittsford
Allen Creek ES, 3188 EAST AVE 14618
Elizabeth Dzwonoski, prin.

Rochester CSD
Sch. Sys. Enr. Code 8
Supt. – Pete McWalters, 131 W BROAD ST 14614
Charlotte MS, 4115 LAKE AVE 14612
Joseph Bivins, prin.
Douglass MS, 940 FERNWOOD PARK 14609
Bert Alexander, prin.
Jefferson MS, 1 EDGERTON PARK 14608
Wanda Belli, prin.
Lofton JHS, 54 OAKMAN ST 14605
Johnny Wilson, prin.
Rochester Community MS, 85 ADAMS ST 14608
Jack Heller, prin.
ES 1, 85 HILLSIDE AVE 14610
William Stroud, prin.
ES 12, 999 SOUTH AVE 14620
Barbara Wager, prin.
ES 14, 200 UNIVERSITY AVE 14605
George Leidecker, prin.
ES 16, 321 POST AVE 14619
Richard Rubin, prin.
ES 17, 158 ORCHARD ST 14611
Eleanor Johnson, prin.
ES 19, 465 SEWARD ST 14608
Nathaniel Waller, prin.
ES 2, 190 REYNOLDS ST 14608
Barbara McGriff, prin.
ES 22, 27 ZIMBRICH ST 14621
Richard Birch, prin.
ES 23, 170 BARRINGTON ST 14607
Samuel Montello, prin.
ES 25, 965 GOODMAN ST N 14609
Norma Bushorr, prin.
ES 28, 450 HUMBOLDT ST 14610
Robert Werner, prin.
ES 29, 88 KIRKLAND RD 14611
Sarah Moore, prin.
ES 30, 36 OTIS ST 14606 – Donald Stefano, prin.
ES 33, 500 WEBSTER AVE 14609
Norman Marten, prin.
ES 34, 530 LEXINGTON AVE 14613
Francis Scalise, prin.
ES 35, 194 FIELD ST 14620 – Peter Ciurca, prin.
ES 36, 85 SAINT JACOB ST 14621
Kristin Hondorf, prin.
ES 37, 353 CONGRESS AVE 14619
Richard Louck, prin.
ES 39, 145 MIDLAND AVE 14621
Michael Puleo, prin.
ES 4, 198 BRONSON AVE 14611
Thelma Hector, prin.
ES 41, 279 RIDGE RD W 14615
Carol Carson, prin.
ES 42, 3330 LAKE AVE 14612
Bevell Mason, prin.
ES 43, 1305 LYELL AVE 14606
Tim Wagner, prin.
ES 44, 820 CHILI AVE 14611 – Joan Miller, prin.
ES 46, 250 NEWCASTLE RD 14610
Bernard Strohmeyer, prin.
ES 5, 555 PLYMOUTH AVE N 14608
Michael Rohan, prin.
ES 50, 301 SENECA AVE 14621
Alexander Johnson, prin.
ES 52, 100 FARMINGTON RD 14609
Marianne Kenny, prin.
ES 6, 95 HERMAN ST 14605
Kenneth Hendel, prin.
ES 7, 31 BRYAN ST 14613 – Harvey Rubin, prin.
ES 8, 253 CONKEY AVE 14621
Rafaela O'Hara, prin.
ES 9, 485 CLINTON AVE N 14605
Anita Boggs, prin.
Rochester Commmunity ES, 85 ADAMS ST 14608
Jack Heller, prin.
Westside Early Childhood Center
15 COSTAR ST 14608 – Annette Moscato, prin.
World Of Inquiry ES
200 UNIVERSITY AVE 14605
William Pugh, prin.

Rush Henrietta Central SD
Supt. – See Henrietta
Crane ES, 85 SHELL EDGE DR 14623
  Dale Smith, prin.
Fyle ES, 133 VOLLMER PKY 14623
  Raymond Demeo, prin.

West Irondequoit Central SD
Sch. Sys. Enr. Code 5
Supt. – Joseph Sproule, 370 COOPER ROAD 14617
Dake MS, 350 COOPER ROAD 14617
  Paul Julien, prin.
Briarwood ES, 215 BRIARWOOD DR 14617
  Donald Yackel, prin.
Brookview ES, 300 BROOKVIEW DR 14617
  L. Wallace, prin.
Colebrook ES, 210 COLEBROOK DR 14617
  Edward Paulsen, prin.
Iroquois MS, 150 COLEBROOK DR 14617
  Edward Paulsen, prin.
Listwood ES 3, 25 LIST AVE 14617
  L. Wallace, prin.
Rogers MS, 219 NORTHFIELD RD 14617
  Holly Jones, prin.
Seneca ES, 4143 SAINT PAUL BLVD 14617
  Donald Yackel, prin.
Southlawn ES, 455 RAWLINSON RD 14617
  Holly Jones, prin.

Allendale Columbia School
  519 ALLENS CREEK ROAD 14618
Blessed Sacrament School, 546 OXFORD ST 14607
Faith Temple School
  1876 ELMWOOD AVE 14620
Harley School, 1981 CLOVER ST 14618
North Star Christian Academy
  332 SPENCERPORT ROAD 14606
Our Lady of Lourdes ES
  165 RHINECLIFF DR 14618
Rochester Christian Academy
  1612 BUFFALO ROAD 14624
Annunciation ES, 1787 NORTON ST 14609
Christ the King ES, 445 KINGS HWY S 14617
Corpus Christi ES, 880 MAIN ST E 14605
Greece Christian ES, 750 LONG POND RD 14612
Guardian Angels ES
  2061 E HENRIETTA RD 14623
Hillel ES, 191 FAIRFIELD DR 14620
Holy Cross ES, 4488 LAKE AVE 14612
Holy Family ES, 899 JAY ST 14611
Holy Ghost ES, 230 COLDWATER RD 14624
Holy Rosary ES, 420 LEXINGTON AVE 14613
Montessori School of Rochester
  170 SCHOLFIELD RD W 14617
Most Precious Blood ES, 179 STENSON ST 14606
Mother of Sorrows ES, 1777 LATTA RD 14612
Nazareth Hall ES, 180 RAINES PARK 14613
Our Lady of Good Counsl ES
  630 BROOKS AVE 14619
Our Lady of Perpetual Help ES
  1069 JOSEPH AVE 14621
Rochester Childrens ES, 941 SOUTH AVE 14620
Rochester Christian ES, 260 EMBURY RD 14625
Sacred Heart Cathedral ES
  311 FLOWER CITY PARK 14615
St. Ambrose ES, 31 EMPIRE BLVD 14609
St. Andrew ES, 901 PORTLAND AVE 14621
St. Anne ES, 151 E HENRIETTA RD 14620
St. Boniface ES, 15 WHALIN ST 14620
St. Cecilia ES, 2732 CULVER RD 14622
St. Helen ES, 150 LETTINGTON DR 14624
St. James ES, 119 BROCKLEY RD 14609
St. John Evangelist ES, 545 HUMBOLDT ST 14610
St. John the Evangelist ES
  2376 RIDGE RD W 14626
St. Lawrence ES, 1000 N GREECE RD 14626
St. Margaret Mary ES, 400 ROGERS PKY 14617
St. Monica ES, 841 GENESEE ST 14611
St. Philip Neri ES, 1772 CLIFFORD AVE 14609
St. Pius X ES, 3000 CHILI AVE 14624
St. Salome ES, 4280 CULVER RD 14622
St. Stanislaus ES, 1150 HUDSON AVE 14621
St. Theodore ES, 170 SPENCERPORT RD 14606
St. Thomas More ES, 2615 EAST AVE 14610
St. Thomas the Apostle ES
  41 COLEBROOK DR 14617

Rockaway Beach, Queens Co.
Queens Borough SD 27
Supt. – See Ozone Park
Beach Park ES, 245 B 79TH STREET 11693
  Vincent Ryan, prin.
Belle Harbor ES
  CRONSTON & B 135TH STREET 11694
  Arnold Wittenstein, prin.

Rockaway Park, Queens Co.
Queens Borough SD 27
Supt. – See Ozone Park
Seaside ES, 190 BEACH 110TH ST 11694
  Terrence Quinn, prin.

Rockville Centre, Nassau Co., Pop. Code 8
Malverne UFD
Sch. Sys. Enr. Code 4
Supt. – James Tolle, WOOFIELD ROAD 11570
Other Schools – See Lynbrook, Malverne

Rockville Centre UFD
Sch. Sys. Enr. Code 5
Supt. – William Johnson, SHEPARD ST 11570
South Side MS, 67 HILLSIDE AVE 11570
  Lawrence Vanderwater, prin.
Hewitt ES, HEMPSTEAD AVENUE 11570
  Joanne Spencer, prin.

Riverside ES, 110 RIVERSIDE DR 11570
  Patricia Bock, prin.
Watson ES, LAKEVIEW AVENUE 11570
  Ralph Campanella, prin.
Wilson ES, 25 BUCKINGHAM RD 11570
  Charles Gizzie, prin.
Other Schools – See Hempstead

St. Agnes Cathedral ES, 70 CLINTON AVE 11570

Rocky Point, Suffolk Co., Pop. Code 5
Rocky Point UFD
Sch. Sys. Enr. Code 5
Supt. – F. Carasiti
  ROCKY PT-YAPHANK ROAD 11778
Edgar MS, ROUTE 25A 11778
  Joseph Bartolotto, prin.
ES, ROCKY POINT ROAD 11778
  Minnie Dean, prin.

Rome, Oneida Co., Pop. Code 8
Rome CSD
Sch. Sys. Enr. Code 6
Supt. – Paul Doyle, 112 E THOMAS ST 13440
Bellamy ES, BRENNAN AVENUE 13440
  James Rizzo, prin.
Clinton ES, 427 ANN ST 13440
  Harry McKenna, prin.
Clough ES, BELL ROAD 13440
  Cheryl Gaffney, prin.
Columbus ES, 112 COLUMBUS AVE 13440
  Kathleen Lynch, prin.
Denti ES, 1001 RUBY ST 13440
  John Dellacontrada, prin.
Ft. Stanwix ES, 110 W LINDEN ST 13440
  Florence Barnett, prin.
Gansevoort ES, 758 W LIBERTY ST 13440
  Cheryl Johnson, prin.
Joy ES, TURIN ROAD M R 13440
  Robert Evangelist, prin.
Lake Delta ES, ELMER HILL RD 13440
  August Fiorenza, prin.
Ridge Mills ES
  7841 WESTERNVILLE ROAD 13440
  Vincent Grieco, prin.
Stokes ES, TURIN ROAD M R 13440
  Nazarene Fiore, prin.

St. Peters ES, 401 FLOYD AVE 13440
Transfiguration ES, 400 S JAMES ST 13440

Romulus, Seneca Co., Pop. Code 4
Romulus Central SD
Sch. Sys. Enr. Code 3
Supt. – James Piscitelli 14541
Romulus Central S 14541 – Barbara Quinn, prin.

Ronkonkoma, Suffolk Co., Pop. Code 7
Connetquot Central SD
Supt. – See Bohemia
Cherokee Street ES, CHEROKEE ST 11779
  Ronald Homa, prin.
Duffield ES, FIRST ST 11779
  Robert Liljequist, prin.
Slocum ES, JOHNSON AVENUE 11779
  William Ayres, prin.

Roosevelt, Nassau Co., Pop. Code 7
Roosevelt UFD
Sch. Sys. Enr. Code 5
Supt. – Rodgers Lewis
  240 DENTON PLACE 11575
Byas ES, UNDERHILL AVENUE 11575
  Earl Mosely, prin.
Centennial Avenue ES
  140 W CENTENNIAL AVE 11575
  Charles McIlwain, prin.
Daniels ES, OAKWOOD & ELMWOOD 11575
  Lois Baron, prin.
Rose ES, WASHINGTON AVENUE 11575
  Barbara Williams, prin.

Madassah Al-Aaraaf ES, 285 NASSAU RD 11575
Miss Shelley's Upward Prep School
  66 NASSAU ROAD 11575
Queen-Most Holy Rosary ES
  200 W CENTENNIAL AVE 11575

Roosevelt Field, Nassau Co.
Elmont UFD
Supt. – See Elmont
Stewart Manor ES, 501 STEWART AVE 11530
  Barbara Scherr, prin.

Roscoe, Sullivan Co.
Rosco Central SD
Sch. Sys. Enr. Code 2
Supt. – Theodore Sgouros 12776
Roscoe Central S 12776 – George Glantzis, prin.

Rosedale, Queens Co.
Queens Borough SD 29
Supt. – See Queens Village
Haberle ES, 25350 149TH AVE 11422
  Sheldon Silbermintz, prin.
ES, 13521 241ST ST 11422 – John Gleason, prin.
Sunrise ES, WELLER AVENUE & 253RD ST 11422
  Joseph Post, prin.

Rosendale, Ulster Co., Pop. Code 4

St. Peter's ES, JAMES ST 12472

Roslyn, Nassau Co., Pop. Code 4
Roslyn UFD
Sch. Sys. Enr. Code 5
Supt. – J. Segal, HARBOR HILL ROAD 11576
Other Schools – See Greenvale, Roslyn Heights

Buckley Contry Day ES, NORTH HILLS 11576

Roslyn Heights, Nassau Co., Pop. Code 6
East Williston UFD
Supt. – See East Williston
Willets Road MS, 455 WILLETS ROAD 11577
  Michael Gordon, prin.

Roslyn UFD
Supt. – See Roslyn
Roslyn MS, LOCUST LANE 11577
  Mira Martincich, prin.
East Hills ES, LOCUS LANE 11577
  Steven Kaplan, prin.

St. Mary's ES, 429 ROUNDHILL RD 11577

Rotterdam Junction, Schenectady Co., Pop. Code 3
Schalmont Central SD-Rotterdam
Supt. – See Schenectady
Woestina ES, MAIN STREET 12150
  M. Shipe, prin.

Rouses Point, Clinton Co., Pop. Code 4
Northeastern Clinton Central SD
Supt. – See Champlain
ES 12979 – John Huchro, prin.

Roxbury, Delaware Co., Pop. Code 4
Roxbury Central SD
Sch. Sys. Enr. Code 2
Supt. – Lee Quackenbush, MAIN ST 12474
Roxbury Central S, MAIN ST 12474
  Charles Strange, prin.

Rush, Monroe Co.
Rush Henrietta Central SD
Supt. – See Henrietta
Leary ES, 5509 E HENRIETTA RD 14543
  Lyria Hailstork, prin.

Rushford, Allegany Co., Pop. Code 4
Rushford Central SD
Sch. Sys. Enr. Code 2
Supt. – Robert Aronson, 9114 SCHOOL ST 14777
S, 9114 SCHOOL ST 14777 – James Shehein, prin.

Rushville, Ontario Co., Pop. Code 3
Gorham-Middlesex Central SD
Sch. Sys. Enr. Code 4
Supt. – Lynn Western 14544
Middlesex Valley ES 14544
  Ralph Casperson, prin.
Other Schools – See Gorham

Russell, St. Lawrence Co., Pop. Code 4
Edwards-Knox Central SD
Sch. Sys. Enr. Code 3
Supt. – Peter Hodge 13684
Other Schools – See Edwards, Knox

Rye, Westchester Co., Pop. Code 7
Rye CSD
Sch. Sys. Enr. Code 4
Supt. – Barry Farnham, 324 MIDLAND AVE 10580
MS, 1 PARSONS ST 10580 – Willis Bott, prin.
Midland ES, 324 MIDLAND AVE 10580
  Joseph Soury, prin.
Milton ES, 12 HEWLETT ST 10580
  Paul Berg, prin.
Osborn ES, 10 OSBORN RD 10580
  Su Klosek, prin.

Rye Country Day School, CEDAR ST 10580
Resurrection ES, 116 MILTON RD 10580

Rye Brook, Westchester Co.
Blind Brook-Rye SD
Sch. Sys. Enr. Code 3
Supt. – Ronald Valenti, NORTH RIDGE ST 10573
Ridge Street ES, NORTH RIDGE STREET 10573
  Bruno Ponterio, prin.

Sackets Harbor, Jefferson Co., Pop. Code 4
Sackets Harbor Central SD
Sch. Sys. Enr. Code 3
Supt. – Alson Dougherty, P O BOX 290 13685
Sackets Harbor Central S, P O BOX 290 13685
  Robert Wagoner, prin.

Sagaponack, Suffolk Co.
Sagaponack Common SD
Sch. Sys. Enr. Code 1
Supt. – Robert Fridah, MAIN ST 11901
ES, MAIN ST 11962 – Regina Guyer, prin.

Sag Harbor, Suffolk Co., Pop. Code 5
Sag Harbor UFD
Sch. Sys. Enr. Code 3
Supt. – Dominic Annacone, HAMPTON ST 11963
ES, HAMPTON STREET 11963
  Dominic Annacone, prin.

Tuller School at Maycroft, P O BOX 1991 11963
St. Andrew ES, DIVISION ST 11963

Saint Albans, Queens Co.
Queens Borough SD 29
Supt. – See Queens Village
ES, 18701 FOCH BLVD 11412
  Joseph Downey, prin.

Saint James, Suffolk Co., Pop. Code 7
Smithtown Central SD
Supt. – See Smithtown
Nesaquake IS, EDGEWOOD AVE 11780
  Fred Stellhorn, prin.
ES, 580 LAKE AVE 11780 – William Parker, prin.

Suffolk Lutheran School
  WOODLAWN & MORICHES RD 11780
Harbor Country Day ES
  17 THREE SISTERS RD 11780
SS. Philip & James ES, CLINTON AVE 11780

Saint Johnsville, Montgomery Co., Pop. Code 4
Oppenheim-Ephratah Central SD
Sch. Sys. Enr. Code 3
Supt. – Dale Schumacher
  RURAL ROUTE 02 13452
Oppenheim-Ephratah-Central S
  RURAL ROUTE 02 13472
  Terrence Wissick, prin.

St. Johnsville Central SD
Sch. Sys. Enr. Code 3
Supt. – David Lapone, 50 CENTER ST 13452
Robbins ES, MONROE STREET 13452
  John Burkhart, prin.

Saint Regis Falls, Franklin Co., Pop. Code 4
St. Regis Falls Central SD
Sch. Sys. Enr. Code 3
Supt. – Edwin Zacunski 12980
S 12980 – Carin Guarasci, prin.

Salamanca, Cattaraugus Co., Pop. Code 6
Salamanca CSD
Sch. Sys. Enr. Code 4
Supt. – Gerald Ackley
  50 IROQUOIS DRIVE 14779
Prospect ES, 215 PROSPECT AVE 14779
  Rosemarie Furlong, prin.
Seneca MS, 25 CENTER ST 14779
  Glen Goergen, prin.

Salem, Washington Co., Pop. Code 1
Salem Central SD
Sch. Sys. Enr. Code 3
Supt. – Wilfred Ross 12865
ES, E BROADWAY 12865 – Ann Baker, prin.

Sanborn, Niagara Co., Pop. Code 3
Niagara Wheatfield Central SD
Sch. Sys. Enr. Code 5
Supt. – Joel Radin
  2794 SAUNDERS SETTLEMENT RD 14132
Town MS
  2792 SAUNDERS SETTLEMENT RD 14132
  F. Pierce, prin.
Other Schools – See Lewiston, Niagara Falls, North
  Tonawanda

St. Peters Lutheran ES, 6168 WALMORE RD 14132

Sandy Creek, Oswego Co., Pop. Code 3
Sandy Creek Central SD
Sch. Sys. Enr. Code 4
Supt. – Jerald Quimby 13145
ES, P O BOX 248 13145 – Richard Gilbert, prin.

Saranac, Clinton Co., Pop. Code 3
Saranac Central SD
Sch. Sys. Enr. Code 4
Supt. – Donald Parks 12981
JHS 12981 – H. Alexander, prin.
ES 12981 – Harold Alexander, prin.
Other Schools – See Cadyville, Dannemora,
  Morrisonville

Saranac Lake, Franklin Co., Pop. Code 6
Saranac Lake Central SD
Sch. Sys. Enr. Code 4
Supt. – Thomas Christopher
  17 PETROVA AVE 12983
MS, 17 ROVA AVE 12983 – J. Videtti, prin.
ES, PETROVA AVE 12983 – Thomas Clark, prin.
ES, 17 PETROVA AVE 12983 – John Videtti, prin.

St. Bernard's ES, 32 RIVER ST 12983

Saratoga Springs, Saratoga Co., Pop. Code 7
Saratoga Springs CSD
Sch. Sys. Enr. Code 6
Supt. – Lawrence Zinn, 5 WELLS ST 12866
Caroline Street ES, 310 CAROLINE ST 12866
  Ronald Farra, prin.
Division Street ES, 220 DIVISION ST 12866
  Robert Treanor, prin.
Geyser Road ES, 49 GEYSER RD 12866
  Marcel Webb, prin.
Lake Avenue ES, 126 LAKE AVE 12866
  Marcia Henze, prin.
Nolan ES, RURAL ROUTE 01 12866
  Donald Hall, prin.
Other Schools – See Greenfield Center

St. Clement ES, 231 LAKE AVE 12866
St. Peter's ES, HAMILTON ST 12866

Saugerties, Ulster Co., Pop. Code 5
Saugarties Central SD
Sch. Sys. Enr. Code 5
Supt. – Daniel Lee
  WASHINGTON AVE EXT 12477
Cahill ES, P O BOX 389 12477
  Michael Piatek, prin.
Morse ES, P O BOX 3 12477
  Patrick Buonfiglio, prin.

Other Schools – See Glasco, Mount Marion

St. Mary of the Snow ES, 25 CEDAR ST 12477

Sauquoit, Oneida Co., Pop. Code 4
Sauquoit Valley Central SD
Sch. Sys. Enr. Code 4
Supt. – D. MacLane, 2601 ONEIDA ST 13456
Sauquoit Valley ES, 2601 ONEIDA STREET 13456
  Mary Brown, prin.
Other Schools – See Chadwicks

Savannah, Wayne Co.
Clyde-Savannah Central SD
Supt. – See Clyde
ES, GRAND AVE 13146 – Joseph Kolczynski, prin.

Savona, Steuben Co., Pop. Code 3
Savona Central SD
Sch. Sys. Enr. Code 3
Supt. – Robert Norton, 64 E LAMOKA AVE 14879
Savona Central S, 64 E LAMOKA AVE 14879
  Joan Barney, prin.

Sayville, Suffolk Co., Pop. Code 7
Sayville UFD
Sch. Sys. Enr. Code 5
Supt. – Joseph Verdone, ADMIN BLDG 11782
Lincoln Avenue ES, LINCOLN AVENUE 11782
  Mary Nolan, prin.
Sunrise Drive ES, SUNRISE DRIVE 11782
  Robert Rogers, prin.
Other Schools – See West Sayville

St. Lawrence ES, 200 MAIN ST 11782

Scarsdale, Westchester Co., Pop. Code 7
Eastchester UFD
Supt. – See Eastchester
Greenvale ES
  PARK DRIVE & MAPLE STREET 10583
  Jay Sherlach, prin.

Edgemont-Greenburgh UFD
Sch. Sys. Enr. Code 4
Supt. – Frank Calzi, GLENDALE ROAD 10583
Greenville ES, 1 GLENDALE RD 10583
  Jerry Schulman, prin.
Seely Place ES, 51 SEELY PL 10583
  Edward Kennedy, prin.

Scarsdale UFD
Sch. Sys. Enr. Code 5
Supt. – Samuel Cohen, 2 BREWSTER ROAD 10583
JHS, 134 MAMARONECK ROAD 10583
  Peter Telfer, prin.
Edgewood ES, ROOSEVELT PLACE 10583
  Vincent Dempsey, prin.
Fox Meadow ES, 4 BREWSTER RD 10583
  Joan McCann, prin.
Greenacres ES, HUNTINGTON AVENUE 10583
  Pauline Sternberg, prin.
Heathcote ES, 26 PALMER AVE 10583
  Lorraine Shepard, prin.
Quaker Ridge ES, 125 WEAVER ST 10583
  Ernest Machnits, prin.

Immaculate Heart of Mary School
  201 BOULEVARD 10583
Our Lady of Fatima School
  963 SCARSDALE RD 10583
St. Pius X School, 85 PALMER AVE 10583

Schaghticoke, Rensselaer Co., Pop. Code 3
Hoosic Valley Central SD
Sch. Sys. Enr. Code 4
Supt. – Joseph Colistra 12154
Hoosic Valley ES 12154 – Julia Hoover, prin.

Schenectady, Schenectady Co., Pop. Code 8
Guilderland Central SD
Supt. – See Guilderland
Lynnwood ES, REGINA DRIVE 12303
  Leonard Quint, prin.

Niskayuna Central SD
Sch. Sys. Enr. Code 5
Supt. – Theodore Foot
  VAN ANTWERP ROAD 12309
Iroquois MS, 2495 ROSENDALE ROAD 12309
  Naomi Woolsey, prin.
Craig ES, 2566 BALLTOWN RD 12309
  John O'Connor, prin.
Hillside ES, 1100 CORNELIUS AVE 12309
  Raymond Pressman, prin.
Rosendale ES, 2455 ROSENDALE RD 12309
  Thomas Buckley, prin.
Other Schools – See Rexford

Rotterdam-Mohanasen SD
Sch. Sys. Enr. Code 5
Supt. – Henry Grishman
  2072 CURRY ROAD 12303
Draper JHS, 2070 CURRY ROAD 12303
  Robert Killeen, prin.
Bradt ES, 2719 HAMBURG ST 12303
  Robert Parr, prin.
Pinewood ES, KINGS ROAD 12303
  George Carman, prin.

Schalmont Central SD-Rotterdam
Sch. Sys. Enr. Code 4
Supt. – Alan Longshore
  401 DUANESBURG ROAD 12306
Schalmont MS, 831 DUANESBURG ROAD 12306
  Ludwig Wallner, prin.

Jefferson MS, 100 PRINCETOWN RD 12306
  Ross Stagnitti, prin.
Pine Grove ES
  GIFFORD CHURCH ROAD 146 12306
  Laurence Weidler, prin.
Other Schools – See Pattersonville, Rotterdam Junction

Schenectady CSD
Sch. Sys. Enr. Code 6
Supt. – Richard Holzman
  108 N BRANDYWINE AVE 12307
Central Park MS, 425 ELM ST 12304
  David Wagner, prin.
Oneida MS, 1501 ONEIDA ST 12308
  Walter Leclair, prin.
Steinmetz MS, OAKWOOD AVE 12303
  Edmond Stevens, prin.
Elmer Avenue ES, 1 ELMER AVE 12308
  Robert Ceglerski, prin.
Fulton ES, ELEANOR STREET 12306
  Frank Austin, prin.
Hamilton ES
  7TH AVENUE & WEBSTER STREET 12303
  Robert Moolick, prin.
Howe/Open ES, BAKER AVENUE 12309
  Jack Hickey, prin.
King ES, STANLEY STREET 12307
  Julius Aycox, prin.
Lincoln ES, ROBINSON STREET 12304
  Anna Villa, prin.
Paige ES, ELLIOTT AVENUE 12304
  Paul Tyler, prin.
Pleasant Valley ES, FOREST ROAD 12303
  Roger Vanburen, prin.
Van Corlaer ES, 2300 GUILDERLAND AVE 12306
  Anthony Parisi, prin.
Woodlawn ES, 3301 WELLS AVE 12304
  Herbert Dieck, prin.
Yates ES, SALINA STREET 12308
  Charles Smith, prin.
Zoller ES, 1900 LANCASTER ST 12308
  Arnold Grosberg, prin.

New Life Academy, 150 CORLEAR AVE 12304
Brown ES, 1184 RUGBY RD 12308
Immaculate Conception ES, 520 BRADT ST 12306
Our Lady of Mt. Carmel ES
  1274 PLEASANT ST 12303
St. Anthony ES, 1840 VAN VRANKEN AVE 12308
St. Helen ES, 1801 UNION ST 12309
St. John the Evangelist ES, 806 UNION ST 12308
St. Luke's ES, 1252 ALBANY ST 12304
St. Madeleine Sophie ES
  3510 CARMEN RD 12303
St. Paul the Apostle ES, 16 VAN ZANDT ST 12304

Schenevus, Otsego Co., Pop. Code 3
Schenevus Central SD
Sch. Sys. Enr. Code 2
Supt. – Paul Fiacco, 100 MAIN ST 12155
Draper S, 100 MAIN ST 12155 – Mark Clark, prin.

Schoharie, Schoharie Co., Pop. Code 4
Schoharie Central SD
Sch. Sys. Enr. Code 4
Supt. – Peter Bassett, MAIN ST 12157
ES, MAIN STREET 12157 – Vernon Hobbs, prin.

Schroon Lake, Essex Co., Pop. Code 4
Schroon Lake Central SD
Sch. Sys. Enr. Code 2
Supt. – Daniel MacGregor 12870
Schroon Lake Central S, MAIN ST 12870
  Richard Kahn, prin.

Mountainside Christian Academy 12870

Schuylerville, Saratoga Co., Pop. Code 4
Schuylerville Central SD
Sch. Sys. Enr. Code 4
Supt. – Peter Brenner 12871
ES, 14-18 SPRING ST 12871
  Thomas Martin, prin.
IS, 14-18 SPRING ST 12871
  Richard Behrens, prin.

Scio, Allegany Co., Pop. Code 4
Scio Central SD
Sch. Sys. Enr. Code 2
Supt. – Louis Digiroland
  WASHINGTON ST 14880
Scio Central S, WASHINGTON ST 14880
  A. Thomas O'Grady, prin.

Scotia, Schenectady Co., Pop. Code 6
Burnt Hills Ballston Lake CSD
Sch. Sys. Enr. Code 5
Supt. – Richard O'Rourke
  50 CYPRESS DRIVE 12302
Pashley ES, 30 PASHLEY RD 12302
  James Denney, prin.
Other Schools – See Ballston Lake, Burnt Hills

Scotia-Glenville Central SD
Sch. Sys. Enr. Code 5
Supt. – Patrick Dicaprio, 1 WORDEN ROAD 12302
JHS, PRESTIGE PARKWAY 12302
  Anne Sterman, prin.
Glendaal ES, RURAL ROUTE 02 12302
  Frederick Gula, prin.
Lincoln ES, ALBION STREET 12302
  John Haher, prin.
Sacandaga ES, 1 SCHERMERHORN ST 12302
  Audrey Farnsworth, prin.

Schenectady Christian School
SACANDAGA ROAD 12302

Scottsville, Monroe Co., Pop. Code 4
Wheatland Chili Central SD
Sch. Sys. Enr. Code 3
Supt. – Henry Peris, 940 NORTH ROAD 14546
Connor ES, 13 BECKWITH AVE 14546
  Louise Sheinman, prin.

Sea Cliff, Nassau Co., Pop. Code 6
North Shore Central SD
Sch. Sys. Enr. Code 4
Supt. – Michael McGill
  112 FRANKLIN AVE 11579
ES, 280 CARPENTER AVE 11579
  Eileen Connelly, prin.
Other Schools – See Glen Head, Glenwood Landing

St. Boniface Martyr ES, 12 MAIN AVE 11579

Seaford, Nassau Co., Pop. Code 7
Levittown UFD
Supt. – See Levittown
Seaman Neck ES, 1100 CRESTLINE PL 11783
  Monroe Fremed, prin.

Seaford UFD
Sch. Sys. Enr. Code 5
Supt. – Dwayne Poll
  1600 WASHINGTON AVE 11783
MS, 3940 SUNSET AVE 11783
  Richard Humphrey, prin.
Seafood Harbor ES, 3501 BAYVIEW ST 11783
  Robert Aloise, prin.
Seaford Manor ES
  1590 WASHINGTON AVE 11783
  Virginia Portanova, prin.

Maria Regina ES, 40-45 JERUSALEM AVE 11783
St. James ES, 75 SEAMANS NECK RD 11783
St. William the Abbot ES
  2001 JACKSON AVE 11783

Selden, Suffolk Co., Pop. Code 7
Middle Country Central SD
Sch. Sys. Enr. Code 7
Supt. – Gerald Foley, 15 NEW LANE 11784
JHS, 22 JEFFERSON AVE 11784
  Elizabeth McCarville, prin.
Bicycle Path ES, BICYCLE PATH 11784
  Joseph Caliguri, prin.
Hawkins Path ES, HAWKINS PATH 11784
  Robert Berman, prin.
New Lane Memorial ES, NEW LANE 11784
  Paul Harren, prin.
Stagecoach ES, STAGECOACH ROAD 11784
  Robert Johnson, prin.
Other Schools – See Centereach, Lake Grove

Selkirk, Albany Co.
Ravena Coeymans Selkirk CSD
Sch. Sys. Enr. Code 4
Supt. – William Schwartz, THATCHER ST 12158
Becker ES, ROUTE 9W 12158
  Albert Keating, prin.
Other Schools – See Coeymans, Ravena

Seneca Falls, Seneca Co., Pop. Code 6
Seneca Falls Central SD
Sch. Sys. Enr. Code 4
Supt. – M. Douglas Zoller, 76 STATE ST 13148
MS, 95 TROY STREET 13148
  Gerald Macaluso, prin.
Knight ES, 98 CLINTON ST 13148
  Alan Foster, prin.
Stanton ES, 38 GARDEN ST 13148
  Ted Novak, prin.

St. Patrick ES, 81 W BAYARD ST 13148

Setauket, Suffolk Co., Pop. Code 6
Three Village Central SD
Sch. Sys. Enr. Code 6
Supt. – Joseph King, NICOLL ROAD 11733
Nassakeag ES, 500 POND PATH 11733
  Jack Schwartz, prin.
ES, MAIN STREET 11733 – Robert Bell, prin.
Other Schools – See East Setauket, Stony Brook

Sharon Springs, Schoharie Co., Pop. Code 3
Sharon Springs Central SD
Sch. Sys. Enr. Code 2
Supt. – Ronald Paquette 13459
Sharon Springs Central S 13459
  John Murray, prin.

Shelter Island, Suffolk Co., Pop. Code 3
Shelter Island UFD
Sch. Sys. Enr. Code 2
Supt. – Marlene Berman 11964
Shelter Island Central S, N FERRY ROAD 11964
  Marlene Berman, prin.

Sherburne, Chenango Co., Pop. Code 4
Sherburne Earlville Central SD
Sch. Sys. Enr. Code 4
Supt. – Joseph Martinelli, 15 UTICA ROAD 13460
Sherburne-Earlville JHS, ROUTE 12 13460
  Phyllis Dean, prin.
ES 13460 – Gayle Hellert, prin.
Other Schools – See Earlville

Sherman, Chautauqua Co., Pop. Code 3
Sherman Central SD
Sch. Sys. Enr. Code 3
Supt. – Raymond Cenni, PARK ST 14781
ES, PARK STREET 14781 – James Rorabach, prin.

Sherrill, Oneida Co., Pop. Code 5
Sherrill CSD
Supt. – See Verona
McAllister ES, KINSLEY STREET 13461
  Bonnie Tryon, prin.

Shirley, Suffolk Co., Pop. Code 6
William Floyd UFD
Supt. – See Mastic Beach
Floyd ES, LEXINGTON RD 11967
  Arlene Wild, prin.
Woodhull MS, FRANCIS LANDAU PL 11967
  John Deubel, prin.

Shoreham, Suffolk Co., Pop. Code 3
Shoreham-Wading River Central SD
Sch. Sys. Enr. Code 4
Supt. – Richard Doremus
  250 RURAL ROUTE 25A 11786
Shoreham-Wading River MS
  RANDALL ROAD 11786 – Cary Bell, prin.
Briarcliff ES, BRIARCLIFF ROAD 11786
  Mary Abata, prin.
Miller Avenue ES, MILLER AVENUE 11786
  Liala Strotman, prin.
Other Schools – See Wading River

Shortsville, Ontario Co., Pop. Code 4
Manchester-Shortsville CSD
Sch. Sys. Enr. Code 4
Supt. – Philip Grajko, RT 21 14548
Other Schools – See Manchester

Shrub Oak, Westchester Co., Pop. Code 2
Lakeland CSD of Shrub Oak
Sch. Sys. Enr. Code 6
Supt. – Leon Bock 10588
Lakeland-Copper Beech MS 10588
  James Rieger, prin.
Franklin ES 10588 – Frank Poli, prin.
Other Schools – See Crompond, Mohegan Lake,
  Yorktown Heights

St. Eliz Ann Seton School, 1375 MAIN ST 10588

Sidney, Delaware Co., Pop. Code 5
Sidney Central SD
Sch. Sys. Enr. Code 4
Supt. – Perry Berkowitz, 95 W MAIN ST 13838
MS, PEARL ST 13838 – B. Theobald, prin.
Other Schools – See Masonville, Sidney Center

Sidney Center, Delaware Co.
Sidney Central SD
Supt. – See Sidney
ES 13839 – Marlene Wilklow, prin.
Sidney ES 13839 – Stephen Paranya, prin.

Silver Creek, Chautauqua Co., Pop. Code 5
Silver Creek Central SD
Sch. Sys. Enr. Code 4
Supt. – Andrea Stein, DICKINSON ST 14136
ES, P O BOX 270 14136 – Michael Goth, prin.

Sinclairville, Chautauqua Co., Pop. Code 3
Cassadaga Valley Central SD
Sch. Sys. Enr. Code 3
Supt. – Kenneth Connolly
  SINCLAIR DRIVE 14782
ES, SINCLAIR DRIVE 14782
  Lawrence Griffin, prin.
Other Schools – See Cassadaga

Skaneateles, Onondaga Co., Pop. Code 5
Skaneateles Central SD
Sch. Sys. Enr. Code 4
Supt. – Walter Sullivan
  49E ELIZABETH ST 13152
MS, EAST ST 13152 – Tiffany Phillips, prin.
State IS, STATE STREET 13152
  William Britt, prin.
Waterman ES, EAST STREET 13152
  William Palombella, prin.

Slate Hill, Orange Co.
Minisink Valley Central SD
Sch. Sys. Enr. Code 5
Supt. – J. Iraci 10973
Minisink Valley MS 10973 – Frank Dimarco, prin.
Minisink Valley ES 10973 – Richard Warner, prin.

Slaterville Springs, Tompkins Co.
Ithaca CSD
Supt. – See Ithaca
Caroline ES, 2439 SLATERVILLE RD 14881
  Connie Tobias, prin.

Sloatsburg, Orange Co., Pop. Code 5
Ramapo Central SD
Supt. – See Hillburn
ES, 7 SECOND ST 10974
  Ronald Anagnostis, prin.

Smithtown, Suffolk Co., Pop. Code 9
Hauppauge UFD
Supt. – See Hauppauge
Forest Brook ES, LILAC LANE 11787
  Lydia McCaskey, prin.
Pines ES, HOLLY DRIVE 11787
  Richard Tynebor, prin.

Smithtown Central SD
Sch. Sys. Enr. Code 6
Supt. – John Keough, 26 NEW YORK AVE 11787
Accompsett IS, MEADOW ROAD 11787
  Robert Badeer, prin.
Accompsett ES, 1 LINCOLN ST 11787
  Gerald Klafter, prin.
Branch Brook ES, WEST RIDGELY ROAD 11787
  Richard Campisi, prin.
Dogwood ES, 50 DOGWOOD DR 11787
  Virginia Miller, prin.
Mt. Pleasant ES, 33 PLAISTED AVE 11787
  Kenneth Kavanagh, prin.
ES, 51 LAWRENCE AVE 11787 – Paul Graf, prin.
Other Schools – See Nesconset, Saint James

Hebrew Academy of Suffolk County
  525 VETERANS HWY 11787
Ivy League ES, 211 BROOKSITE DR 11787
Smithtown Christian ES, 2 HIGBIE DR 11787
St. Patrick's ES, 284 E MAIN ST 11787

Sodus, Wayne Co., Pop. Code 4
Sodus Central SD
Sch. Sys. Enr. Code 4
Supt. – Thomas Miller, MILL ST EXT 14551
IS, P O BOX 220 14551 – Roy Hyland, prin.
PS, P O BOX 220 14551 – Sharon Tari, prin.

Solvay, Onondaga Co., Pop. Code 6
Solvay UFD
Sch. Sys. Enr. Code 4
Supt. – L. Constantini
  HAZARD ST SCHOOL 13209
Hazard Street JHS, HAZARD ST 13209
  Timothy Barstow, prin.
Lakeland ES, WINCHELL ROAD 13209
  Michael Colabufo, prin.
ES, 701 WOODS RD 13209
  Phillip Mastroleo, prin.

Somers, Westchester Co., Pop. Code 7
Somers Central SD
Sch. Sys. Enr. Code 4
Supt. – James Monk, ROUTE 202 10589
JHS, ROUTE 202 10589 – Richard Holahan, prin.
IS, ROUTE 202 10589 – Carmen Macchia, prin.
Other Schools – See Lincolndale

Southampton, Suffolk Co., Pop. Code 5
Southampton UFD
Sch. Sys. Enr. Code 4
Supt. – Don Behnke, 70 LELAND LANE 11968
IS, 70 LELAND LANE 11968
  Richard Malone, prin.
ES, 30 PINE ST 11968 – Daniel Burns, prin.

Tuckahoe Community SD
Sch. Sys. Enr. Code 2
Supt. – Aurelio Colina, 468 MAGEE ST 11968
Tuckahoe ES, 468 MAGEE ST 11968
  Robert Moraghan, prin.

Our Lady of the Hamptons ES
  160 N MAIN ST 11968

South Dayton, Chautauqua Co., Pop. Code 3
Pine Valley-South Dayton Central SD
Sch. Sys. Enr. Code 2
Supt. – Franklin Russell 14138
Pine Valley ES 14138 – Franklin Russell, prin.

South Fallsburg, Sullivan Co.

Yeshivah Zichron Moshe
  LAUREL PARK ROAD 12779

South Glens Falls, Saratoga Co., Pop. Code 5
South Glens Falls Central SD
Sch. Sys. Enr. Code 5
Supt. – W. Wetherbee
  7914 BLUEBIRD ROAD 12801
Ballard ES, BALLARD ROAD 12803
  H. Butterfield, prin.
Harrison Avenue ES, 68 HARRISON AVE 12803
  James Baker, prin.
Moreau ES, 8112 BLUEBIRD ROAD 12803
  Steve Black, prin.
Tanglewood ES, TANGLEWOOD DRIVE 12803
  John Carayiannis, prin.

South Kortright, Delaware Co.
South Kortright Central SD
Sch. Sys. Enr. Code 2
Supt. – Martin Handler 13842
South Kortright Central S 13842
  Barbara Franz, prin.

South New Berlin, Chenango Co.
South New Berlin Central SD
Sch. Sys. Enr. Code 2
Supt. – Fred Hall 13843
South New Berlin Central S, N MAIN ST 13843
  Michael Sandore, prin.

Southold, Suffolk Co., Pop. Code 7
Southold UFD
Sch. Sys. Enr. Code 3
Supt. – Charles Nephew, OAKLAWN AVE 11971
MS, OAKLAWN AVE 11971 – R. Hilary, prin.
Peconic Lane PS, PECONIC LANE 11971
  Elizabeth Goldsmith, prin.

South Otselic, Chenango Co.
Otselic Valley Central SD
Sch. Sys. Enr. Code 3
Supt. – Thomas Helmer, MAPLE ST 13155

Other Schools – See Georgetown

South Ozone Park, Queens Co.
Queens Borough SD 27
Supt. – See Ozone Park
Church ES, 12915 150TH AVE 11420
　Leila Zuckerman, prin.
Morris ES, 11111 118TH ST 11420
　Robert Pavone, prin.
Public ES 96, 13001 ROCKAWAY BLVD 11420
　Beatrice Williams, prin.
Public ES 108, 10810 109TH AVE 11420
　Gloria Petitto, prin.
Public ES 123, 14501 119TH AVE 11436
　Yvonne Jackson, prin.
Public ES 155, 13002 115TH AVE 11420
　Robert Taylor, prin.
Witherspoon ES, 12628 150TH ST 11436
　Patrick McGettgan, prin.

Queens Borough SD 28
Supt. – See Forest Hills
Public ES 121, 12610 109TH AVE 11420
　Peter Derise, prin.

South Salem, Westchester Co., Pop. Code 3
Katonah Lewisboro UFD
Supt. – See Katonah
Lewisboro ES, BOUTON ROAD 10590
　Kenneth Waldemar, prin.
Meadow Pond ES
　RURAL ROUTE 02 BOX 97 10590
　John Boyle, prin.

Speculator, Hamilton Co., Pop. Code 2
Lake Pleasant Central SD
Sch. Sys. Enr. Code 2
Supt. – Edward Perkins 12164
Lake Pleasant ES 12164 – John Brewer,Jr., prin.

Spencer, Tioga Co., Pop. Code 3
Spencer-Van Etten Central SD
Supt. – See Van Etten
MS, CENTER STREET 14883
　Marcia Schwarz, prin.

Spencerport, Monroe Co., Pop. Code 5
Spencerport Central SD
Sch. Sys. Enr. Code 5
Supt. – J. Clement, 71 LYELL AVE 14559
Bernabi ES, 69 LYELL AVE 14559
　Sara Sprecher, prin.
Munn ES, 2233 MANITOU ROAD 14559
　Bonnie Seaburn, prin.
Town Line ES
　399 OGDEN PARMA TOWNLINE RD 14559
　Milton Ryan, prin.

St. John the Evangelist ES, 55 MARTHA ST 14559

Spring Brook, Erie Co.

St. Vincent De Paul ES
　RICE ROAD AND SENECA ST 14140

Springfield Center, Otsego Co.
Cherry Valley-Springfield Central SD
Supt. – See Cherry Valley
Cherry Valley-Springfield ES 13468
　Charles Culbert, prin.

Springfield Gardens, Queens Co.
Queens Borough SD 29
Supt. – See Queens Village
Springfield Gardens JHS
　132-55 RIDGEDALE ST 11413
　Celestine Miller, prin.
Brookfield ES, 14815 230TH ST 11413
　Louis Aranoff, prin.
Bunche ES
　218TH STREET & 132ND AVENUE 11413
　Daphne Driggriss, prin.
Laurelton ES, 22902 137TH AVE 11413
　Ellen Schlesinger, prin.
Public ES 251, 14451 ARTHUR ST 11413
　Millicent Gormandy, prin.
Robinson ES, 12115 LUCAS ST 11413
　Robert Anastasio, prin.

Spring Valley, Rockland Co., Pop. Code 7
East Ramapo Central SD
Sch. Sys. Enr. Code 6
Supt. – Jack Anderson, 50 S MAIN ST 10977
Colton MS, 40 GRANDVIEW AVE 10977
　Irwin Elkins, prin.
Eldorado MS, 5 ELDORADO DR 10977
　Frances Hunter, prin.
Fleetwood ES, 99 FLEETWOOD AVE 10977
　Neil Kaplicer, prin.
Hempstead ES
　UNION AND BRICK CHURCH 10977
　Linda Holmes, prin.
Hillcrest MS, 2 ADDISON BOYCE DR 10977
　Richard Poole, prin.
Other Schools – See Monsey, New City, Suffern

Green Meadow Waldor School
　HUNGRYHOLLOW ROAD & RT 45 10977
Gruss School for Girls
　15 ROOSEVELT NEW SQUARE 10977
Yeshiva of New Square School
　91 WASHINGTON AVE 10977
Gittelman Day ES, 4 WIDMAN CT 10977
St. Joseph ES, 245 N MAIN ST 10977

Springville, Erie Co., Pop. Code 5
Springville-Griff Institute SD
Sch. Sys. Enr. Code 4
Supt. – William Nennstiel
　307 NEWMAN ST 14141
Griffith Institute MS, 267 NEWMAN ST 14141
　Stephen Bell, prin.
ES, 283 NORTH ST 14141 – Robert Barnes, prin.
Other Schools – See Colden

St. Aloysius ES, 186 FRANKLIN ST 14141

Stamford, Delaware Co., Pop. Code 4
Stamford Central SD
Sch. Sys. Enr. Code 2
Supt. – William Lister, 1 RIVER ST 12167
Stamford Central S, 1 RIVER ST 12167
　Michael Prescott, prin.

Stanfordville, Dutchess Co.
Pine Plains Central SD
Supt. – See Pine Plains
Cold Springs ES 12581 – Elliott Golden, prin.

Star Lake, St. Lawrence Co., Pop. Code 3
Clifton Fine Central SD
Sch. Sys. Enr. Code 3
Supt. – Donald Belcer, P O BOX 75 13690
Clifton Fine ES, P O BOX 75 13690
　Donald Belcer, prin.

Staten Island, Richmond Co.
Richmond Borough SD 31
Sch. Sys. Enr. Code 8
Supt. – Louis DeSario
　211 DANIEL LOW TERRACE 10301
Barnes IS, 225 CLEVELAND AVE 10308
　Maureen O'Brien, prin.
Bernstein IS, 1270 HUGUENOT AVE 10312
　Joseph Corriero, prin.
Dreyfus IS, 101 WARREN ST 10304
　Bertram Levinson, prin.
Egbert IS, 333 MIDLAND AVE 10306
　David Kraus, prin.
Laurie IS, 32 FERNDALE AVE 10314
　Stanley Katzman, prin.
Markham IS, 20 HOUSTON ST 10302
　Ed Barbini, prin.
Morris IS, 445 CASTLETON AVE 10301
　Andrew Monahan, prin.
Paulo IS, HUGENOT & AMBOY AVES 10312
　Anthony Polomene, prin.
Prall IS, 11 CLOVE LAKE PLACE 10310
　Joseph Marone, prin.
Totten IS, ACADEMY & YETMAN AVES 10307
　Joseph Russo, prin.
Annadale ES, 200 JEFFERSON BLVD 10312
　Donald Juliano, prin.
Arrochar ES
　SAND LANE & MCFARLAND AVE 10305
　Arnold Magenheim, prin.
Austen ES, 44 MERRILL AVE 10314
　Angela Schleier, prin.
Bardwell ES, 1581 VICTORY BLVD 10314
　William Schorkopf, prin.
Bay Terrace ES, 330 DURANT AVE 10308
　Louis Anarumo, prin.
Boehm ES, 54 OSBORNE ST 10312
　Seymour Richman, prin.
Brown ES, 80 MAPLE PKY 10303
　Albert Quin, prin.
Carteret ES, 4108 VICTORY BLVD 10314
　Mitchell Checrallah, prin.
Clove Valley ES, 60 FOOTE AVE 10301
　Mafalda Coseglia, prin.
Cromwell ES, 421 LINCOLN AVE 10306
　Joan Rannie, prin.
Curtis ES, 780 POST AVE 10310
　John Campbell, prin.
Davis ES, 55 LAYTON AVE 10301
　Lewis Hayes, prin.
Dongan ES, 50 JEFFERSON ST 10304
　Henry Murphy, prin.
Driscoll ES, 80 MONROE AVE 10301
　Patricia Campbell, prin.
Elm Park ES, 168 HOOKER PL 10302
　Patricia Gilmartin, prin.
Eltingville ES, 380 GENESEE AVE 10312
　Doris Mims, prin.
Emerson ES, PALMA DRIVE 10304
　Lawrence Ambrosino, prin.
Gifford ES, 32 ELVERTON AVE 10308
　Anthony Caporaso, prin.
Graniteville ES, 1860 FOREST AVE 10303
　Melvin Selznick, prin.
Great Kills ES, LINDENWOOD ROAD 10308
　Mitchell Strear, prin.
Hankinson ES, ADELAIDE AVENUE 10306
　Richard Hutchinson, prin.
Huguenot ES, 103 12 KINGDOM AVENUE 10312
　Murray Brenner, prin.
Kreischer ES, NEDRA LANE 10309
　John Depalma, prin.
Leng ES, 1060 WILLOWBROOK RD 10314
　Robert Herman, prin.
Lindemeyer ES, 161 HYLAN BLVD 10305
　Emanuel Bierman, prin.
New Dorp ES
　CLAWSON STREET & LOCUST AVE 10306
　Jacob Siegler, prin.
Pleasant Plains ES, 80 S GOFF AVE 10309
　Alfred Abati, prin.
Port Richmond ES, 161 PARK AVE 10302
　Paul Gaor, prin.

Richmond Town ES, 30 NATICK ST 10306
　Louis Tagliani, prin.
South Beach ES, 41 REID AVE 10305
　Joseph Cugini, prin.
Thompson ES
　BUEL AND MASON AVENUES 10305
　Arron Stern, prin.
Tompkins ES, 144 KEATING PL 10314
　Frank Kelly, prin.
Tottenville ES, 58 SUMMIT ST 10307
　Carlo Ferrazzol, prin.
Tyler ES, 58 LAWRENCE AVE 10310
　Fred Chernow, prin.
Vanderbilt ES, 100 TOMPKINS AVE 10304
　Frank Carpenetta, prin.
Westerleigh ES
　FISKE & LEONARD AVENUES 10314
　Anthony Minardo, prin.
Whittier ES, 221 BROADWAY 10310
　Claire Simmons, prin.
Wilcox ES, 1075 TARGEE ST 10304
　Shelia Feinstein, prin.

Staten Island Academy
　715 TODT HILL ROAD 10304
Academy of St. Dorothy
　1305 HYLAN BLVD 10305
Assumption ES, 10 KINGSLEY PL 10301
Blessed Sacrament ES
　830 DELAFIELD AVE 10310
Building Blocks ES, 55 FOREST AVE 10301
Eltingville Lutheran ES, 300 GENESEE AVE 10312
Holy Rosary ES, 100 JEROME AVE 10305
Immaculate Conception ES
　104 GORDON ST 10304
Jewish Foundation School
　20 PARK HILL CIR 10304
Mt. Carmel St. Benedicta ES
　285 CLOVE RD 10310
New Dorp Christian Academy
　259 ROSE AVE 10306
Notre Dame Academy, 76 HOWARD AVE 10301
Our Lady Help-Christian ES
　23 SUMMIT ST 10307
Our Lady Queen of Peace ES
　22 STEELE AVE 10306
Our Lady Star of the Sea ES
　5411 AMBOY RD 10312
Our Lady of Good Counsel ES
　42 AUSTIN PL 10304
Rabbi Jacob Joseph-Girls, 984 POST AVE 10302
SS. Joseph & Thomas ES, 50 MAGUIRE AVE 10309
Sacred Heart ES, 301 N BURGHER AVE 10310
St. Adalbert ES, 355 MORNINGSTAR RD 10303
St. Ann ES, 125 CROMWELL AVE 10304
St. Charles ES, 200 PENN AVE 10306
St. Christopher ES, 15 LISBON PL 10306
St. Clare ES, 151 LINDENWOOD RD 10308
St. John Lutheran ES, 663 MANOR RD 10314
St. John Villa Academy, 57 CLEVELAND PL 10305
St. Joseph Hill Academy, 850 HYLAN BLVD 10305
St. Joseph Parochial ES
　139 ST MARYS AVE 10305
St. Margaret Mary ES, 556 LINCOLN AVE 10306
St. Mary ES, 1124 BAY ST 10305
St. Patrick ES, 3560 RICHMOND RD 10306
St. Paul ES, 129 CLINTON AVE 10301
St. Peter's ES, 300 RICHMOND TER 10301
St. Rita ES, 30 WELLBROOK AVE 10314
St. Roch ES, 465 VILLA AVE 10302
St. Sylvester ES, 884 TARGEE ST 10304
St. Teresa, 1632 VICTORY BLVD 10314
Staten Island Montessori
　500 BUTLER BLVD 10309
Trinity Lutheran ES, 309 ST PAULS AVE 10304
Yeshiva Rabbi Jacob Joseph-Boys
　3495 RICHMOND RD 10306

Stella Niagara, Niagara Co.

Stella Niagara Education Park
　4421 LOWER RIV RD 14144

Stillwater, Saratoga Co., Pop. Code 4
Stillwater Central SD
Sch. Sys. Enr. Code 4
Supt. – John Clark, N HUDSON AVE 12170
ES, PALMER AVENUE 12170
　Richard Toner, prin.

Stony Brook, Suffolk Co., Pop. Code 6
Three Village Central SD
Supt. – See Setauket
Mount ES, DEAN LANE 11790
　Deborah Blair, prin.

Stony Point, Rockland Co., Pop. Code 7
Haverstraw-Stony Point Central SD
Sch. Sys. Enr. Code 6
Supt. – A. Everhart, 117 W MAIN ST 10980
Farley MS, 271 CENTRAL DRIVE 10980
　Eugene White, prin.
ES, 10 GURNEE DR 10980 – Ted Lindenberg, prin.
Other Schools – See Garnerville, Haverstraw, Thiells,
　West Haverstraw

Immaculate Conception ES, EAST MAIN ST 10980

Suffern, Rockland Co., Pop. Code 7
East Ramapo Central SD
Supt. – See Spring Valley
Lime Kiln MS, 35 LIME KILN RD 10901
　Linda Cruz, prin.

Ramapo Central SD
Supt. – See Hillburn
JHS, HEMLON ROAD   10901
  Richard Kaufman, prin.
Cherry Lane ES, CHERRY LANE   10901
  Robert Drennen, prin.
Connor ES, CYPRESS ROAD   10901
  Paul Paparella, prin.
Montebello Road ES, 52 MONTEBELLO RD   10901
  Arlene Hoffman, prin.
Viola ES, 169 HAVERSTRAW RD   10901
  Paul Finch, prin.

Sacred Heart ES, 60 WASHINGTON AVE   10901
Yeshiva Chofetz Chaim ES
  24 HIGHVIEW RD   10901

Swormville, Erie Co.

St. Mary's ES, 6919 TRANSIT RD   14051

Syosset, Nassau Co., Pop. Code 7
Cold Spring Harbor Central SD
Supt. – See Cold Spring Harbor
West Side ES
  1597 LAUREL HOLLOW ROAD   11791
  T. Hilton, prin.

Syosset Central SD
Sch. Sys. Enr. Code 6
Supt. – Philip Tieman, 99 PELL LANE   11791
South Woods MS, 99 PELL LANE   11791
  James Dougherty, prin.
Thompson MS, ANN DRIVE   11791
  Mary Hausler, prin.
Baylis ES, WOODBURY ROAD   11791
  Bill Rhinehart, prin.
Berry Hill ES, 181 COLD SPRING RD   11791
  Dominick Cullire, prin.
Robbins Lane ES, 297 ROBBINS LN   11791
  Barbara Wood, prin.
South Grove ES, 50 COLONY LN   11791
  Eileen Gentilcore, prin.
Village ES, CONVENT ROAD   11791
  Corine Lipset, prin.
Willits ES, 99 NANA PL   11791
  Lynn Pombonyo, prin.
Other Schools – See Woodbury

St. Edward Confessor ES, 2 TEIBROOK AVE   11791

Syracuse, Onondaga Co., Pop. Code 9
Lyncourt UFD
Sch. Sys. Enr. Code 2
Supt. – Gloria Birmingham
  2709 COURT ST   13208
Lyncourt ES, 2709 COURT ST   13208
  Gloria Birmingham, prin.

Syracuse CSD
Sch. Sys. Enr. Code 7
Supt. – Lionel Meno, 725 HARRISON ST   13210
Clary MS, AMIDON DR   13205 – Albert Wolf, prin.
Grant MS, 2400 GRANT BLVD   13208
  Anthony Dibello, prin.
Levy MS, FELLOWS & HARVARD PLACE   13210
  Daniel Lowengard, prin.
Lincoln MS, 1613 JAMES ST   13203
  Letitia Collins, prin.
Shea MS, 1607 S GEDDES ST   13207
  Wayne O'Connor, prin.
Bellevue ES, 530 STOLP AVE   13207
  James Salviski, prin.
Delaware ES, 900 S GEDDES ST   13204
  Donnell Hicks,Jr., prin.
Elmwood ES, 1728 SOUTH AVE   13207
  Mary Gyder, prin.
Franklin ES, 428 S ALVORD ST   13208
  Dominick Sabatino, prin.
Frazer ES, 741 PARK AVE   13204
  Thomas Taylor, prin.
Hughes ES, 345 JAMESVILLE AVE   13210
  Karen Patton, prin.
Huntington ES, 400 SUNNYCREST RD   13206
  Yvonne Young, prin.
Hyde ES, 450 DURSTON AVE   13203
  Darlene Williams, prin.
King ES, 401 E CASTLE ST   13205
  Judith Brooks, prin.
Lemoyne ES, 1528 LEMOYNE AVE   13208
  Joanne Downes, prin.
Danforth Magnet ES
  309 W BRIGHTON AVE   13205
  Eugene Hannah, prin.
McKinley-Brighton ES, 141 W NEWELL ST   13205
  Mary Ellen Andrews, prin.
Meachem ES, 171 SPAULDING AVE   13205
  Donna Desiato, prin.
Porter ES, 512 EMERSON AVE   13204
  Octavia Wilcox, prin.
Roberts ES, 715 GLENWOOD AVE   13207
  John Barry, prin.
Seymour ES, 108 SHONNARD ST   13204
  Diane Rispoli, prin.
Smith ES, 1130 SALT SPRINGS RD   13224
  David Taddeo, prin.
Smith ES, 1226 LANCASTER AVE   13210
  Patricia Howard, prin.
Van Duyn ES, 401 LOOMIS AVE   13207
  Annie Rowland, prin.
Webster ES, 500 WADSWORTH ST   13208
  Margaret Nasemann, prin.
Weeks ES, 710 HAWLEY AVE   13203
  Sheila Elmer, prin.

West Genesee Central SD at Camillus
Supt. – See Camillus
Onondaga Road ES, 707 ONONDAGA RD S   13219
  Barry Guinn, prin.

Westhill Central SD
Sch. Sys. Enr. Code 4
Supt. – William Blydenburgh
  2709 COURT ST   13208
Onondaga Hill MS
  4860 ONONDAGA ROAD   13215
  J. Palumbo, prin.
Cherry Road MS, 201 CHERRY RD   13219
  Ronald Hill, prin.
Walberta Park PS, 400 WALBERTA ROAD   13219
  Suzanne Gilmour, prin.

Bishop Ludden JHS, 815 FAY RD   13219
Faith Heritage School, 3740 MIDLAND AVE   13205
Living Word Academy
  6101 COURT STREET ROAD   13206
Northside Catholic JHS, 923 N MCBRIDE ST   13208
Blessed Sacrament ES, 3129 JAMES ST   13206
Cathedral Academy
  420 MONTGOMERY ST   13202
Holy Cross ES, 4112 E GENESEE ST   13214
Holy Family ES, 130 CHAPEL DR   13219
Most Holy Rosary ES, 1031 BELLEVUE AVE   13207
Our Lady of Lourdes ES, 301 VALLEY DR   13207
Our Lady of Pompei ES
  915 N MCBRIDE ST   13208
Our Lady of Solace ES, 101 EAST ACE   13224
Sacred Heart ES, 1001 PARK AVE   13204
St. Ann ES, 4471 ONONDAGA BLVD   13219
St. Anthony of Padua ES
  417 W COLVIN ST   13205
St. Charles Borromeo ES, 200 W HIGH TER   13219
St. Daniel ES, 621 ROXFORD RD S   13208
St. James ES, 4837 S SALINA ST   13205
St. John the Baptist ES, 1406 PARK ST   13208
St. Lucy's ES, 422 GIFFORD ST   13204
St. Patrick's ES, 208 SCHUYLER ST   13204

Taberg, Oneida Co.
Camden Central SD
Supt. – See Camden
Annsville Area ES   13471 – John Covaleskie, prin.

Tannersville, Greene Co., Pop. Code 3
Hunter-Tannersville Central SD
Sch. Sys. Enr. Code 2
Supt. – Arthur Rood, MAIN ST   12485
Other Schools – See Hunter

Tappan, Rockland Co., Pop. Code 6
South Orangetown Central SD
Supt. – See Blauvelt
Schaefer ES, 40 LESTER DR   10983
  Joseph Zambito, prin.

Our Lady of the Sacred Heart ES
  100 KINGS HWY   10983

Tarrytown, Westchester Co., Pop. Code 7
Tarrytown UFD
Supt. – See North Tarrytown
Irving MS, BROADWAY & FRANKLIN   10591
  Rob Muller, prin.
Paulding ES, 154 N BROADWAY   10591
  Robert Capell, prin.

Hackley School, 293 BENEDICT AVE   10591
Transfiguration ES, 40 PROSPECT AVE   10591

Theresa, Jefferson Co., Pop. Code 3
Indian River Central SD
Supt. – See Philadelphia
ES, BRIDGE STREET   13691
  Frederic Bourcy, prin.

Thiells, Rockland Co.
Haverstraw-Stony Point Central SD
Supt. – See Stony Point
ES, ROSMAN ROAD   10984 – David Rounds, prin.

Thornwood, Westchester Co., Pop. Code 6
Mt. Pleasant Central SD
Sch. Sys. Enr. Code 4
Supt. – J. Whearty, COLUMBUS AVE   10594
Westlake MS, WESTLAKE ROAD   10594
  N. Castrataro, prin.
Columbus MS, 580 COLUMBUS AVE   10594
  Lorraine Iannuzzi, prin.
Other Schools – See Hawthorne

Ticonderoga, Essex Co., Pop. Code 5
Ticonderoga Central SD
Sch. Sys. Enr. Code 4
Supt. – Harry Frederick, AMHERST AVE   12883
MS, ALEXANDRIA AVE   12883
  Harold Bresett, prin.
ES, ALEXANDRIA AVENUE   12883
  William Bolton, prin.

St. Mary's ES, 301 AMHERST AVE   12883

Tioga Center, Tioga Co., Pop. Code 2
Tioga Central SD
Sch. Sys. Enr. Code 4
Supt. – Richard Pascuzzo   13845
Tioga MS   13845 – Pat Dougherty, prin.
Tioga ES   13845 – Joseph Swigonski, prin.
Other Schools – See Nichols

Tonawanda, Erie Co., Pop. Code 7
Kenmore UFD
Supt. – See Kenmore

Edison ES, 236 GRAYTON RD   14150
  Thomas Schwob, prin.
Hamilton ES, 44 WESTFALL DR   14150
  Leslie Racz, prin.
Holmes ES, 365 DUPONT AVE   14150
  Florence Gugino, prin.

Sweet Home Central SD
Supt. – See Amherst
Glendale ES, 101 GLENDALE DR   14150
  Richard McBride, prin.

Tonawanda CSD
Sch. Sys. Enr. Code 5
Supt. – Carl Mangee, 202 BROAD ST   14150
JHS, HINDS & FLETCHER ST   14150
  Richard Catlin, prin.
Fletcher ES, FLETCHER & GIBSON STREET   14150
  Michael Sheldon, prin.
Highland MS
  HIGHLAND AND MILTON ST   14150
  Jack Kearly, prin.
Mullen ES, MULLEN STREET   14150
  Joseph Spancic, prin.
Riverview MS, TAYLOR & HAMILTON   14150
  Thomas Robinson, prin.

St. Amelia ES, 2999 EGGERT RD   14150
St. Christopher's ES
  2660 NIAGARA FALLS BLVD   14150
St. Edmunds ES, 530 ELLICOTT CREEK RD   14150
St. Francis of Assisi ES, 70 ADAM ST   14150

Treadwell, Delaware Co.
Delhi Central SD
Supt. – See Delhi
Kellogg ES   13846 – Michelle Turner, prin.

Troupsburg, Steuben Co.
Jasper-Troupsburg Central SD
Supt. – See Jasper
Jasper-Troupsburg ES   14885 – John Cain, prin.

Troy, Rensselaer Co., Pop. Code 8
Averill Park Central SD
Supt. – See Averill Park
Poestenkill ES, 1 SCHOOL ROAD   12180
  Nancy Strong, prin.

Brunswick Central SD
Sch. Sys. Enr. Code 4
Supt. – Jerome Ochs
  RURAL ROUTE 03 BOX 200A   12180
Tamarac MS
  RURAL ROUTE 03 BOX 200A   12180
  Jerome Ochs, prin.
Tamarac ES, RURAL ROUTE 03 BOX 200A   12180
  Lauretta McGuirk, prin.
Other Schools – See Johnsonville

Brunswick Common SD
Sch. Sys. Enr. Code 2
Supt. – Joh McCarty, MENEMSHA LANE   12180
Washington ES, MENEMSHA LANE   12180
  John McCarty, prin.

East Greenbush Central SD
Supt. – See East Greenbush
Bell Top ES, 39 REYNOLDS RD   12180
  James Ferris, prin.

Lansingburgh CSD
Sch. Sys. Enr. Code 4
Supt. – Lee Bordick, 320 7TH AVE   12182
Rensselaer Park ES
  8TH AVENUE & 110TH STREET   12182
  Elizabeth Singer, prin.
Turnpike ES, NEW TURNPIKE ROAD   12182
  Gordon Brown, prin.

North Greenbush Common SD
Sch. Sys. Enr. Code 1
Supt. – Connie Hasselgren
  153 BLOOMINGROVE DR   12180
North Greenbush ES
  153 BLOOMINGROVE DR   12180
  Madeline Caruso, prin.

Troy CSD
Sch. Sys. Enr. Code 6
Supt. – Mario Scalzi, 400 GRAND ST   12180
Doyle MS, 1976 BURDETT AVE   12180
  James Gorman, prin.
Carroll Hill ES, 112 DELAWARE AVE   12180
  James Reid, prin.
Public ES 13, HARRISON & FIRST STREET   12180
  Norma Ebbs, prin.
Public ES 14, 1601 15TH ST   12180
  John Palladino, prin.
Public ES 16
  COLLINS & WALKER AVENUE   12180
  William Broderick, prin.
Public ES 18, 412 HOOSICK ST   12180
  Marvin Yowe, prin.
Public ES 2
  10TH STREET & MIDDLEBURG   12180
  Barbara Moak, prin.

Our Lady of Victory ES
  451 MARSHLAND CT   12180
Sacred Heart-St. Joseph's ES
  310 SPRING AVE   12180
St. Augustine's ES, 525 4TH AVE   12182
St. Patrick ES, 762 RIVER ST   12180

Trumansburg, Tompkins Co., Pop. Code 4
Trumansburg Central SD
Sch. Sys. Enr. Code 4
Supt. – John Delaney, BLDG 2 WHIG ST 14886
Doig MS, WHIG ST 14886 – Charles Wiltse, prin.
Building 2 ES, RURAL ROUTE 02 BOX 354 14886
  Joanne Brown, prin.

Truxton, Cortland Co., Pop. Code 3
Homer Central SD
Supt. – See Homer
ES, ACADEMY STREET 13158
  Carol Kurman, prin.

Tuckahoe, Westchester Co., Pop. Code 6

Immaculate Conception School
  WINTERHILL RD 10707

Tully, Onondaga Co., Pop. Code 4
Tully Central SD
Sch. Sys. Enr. Code 4
Supt. – Jack Shaw, 59 STATE ST 13159
ES, 59 STATE ST 13159 – James Bartley, prin.

Tupper Lake, Franklin Co., Pop. Code 5
Tupper Lake Central SD
Sch. Sys. Enr. Code 3
Supt. – T. McCarthy, HOSLEY AVE 12986
Quinn ES, HOSLEY AVENUE 12986
  Mary Sparks, prin.

Holy Ghost Academy ES, 98 MARION AVE 12986

Turin, Lewis Co., Pop. Code 2
South Lewis Central SD
Sch. Sys. Enr. Code 4
Supt. – Jack Mylan, JR-SR HS BLDG 13473
Other Schools – See Constableville, Glenfield, Port Leyden

Tuxedo Park, Orange Co., Pop. Code 3
Tuxedo UFD
Sch. Sys. Enr. Code 3
Supt. – Herbert Fliegner, RURAL ROUTE 17 10987
Tuxedo Union Free S, RURAL ROUTE 17 10987
  Carmine Antonelli, prin.

Tuxedo Park ES, P O BOX 756 10987

Ulster Park, Ulster Co.
Kingston CSD
Supt. – See Kingston
Devine ES, RURAL ROUTE 01 BOX 270 12487
  Raymond Yerkovich, prin.

Unadilla, Otsego Co., Pop. Code 4
Otego-Unadilla Central SD
Supt. – See Otego
ES, MAIN STREET 13849 – Ronald Hull, prin.

Uniondale, Nassau Co., Pop. Code 7
Uniondale UFD
Sch. Sys. Enr. Code 5
Supt. – Alan Hernandez
  933 GOODRICH ST 11553
California Avenue-Cornelius Court ES
  CALIFORNIA AVENUE 11553
  Robert Koster, prin.
Northern Parkway ES
  440 NORTHERN PKY 11553 – Sandra Grey, prin.
Smith Street ES, 780 SMITH ST 11553
  James Real, prin.
Walnut Street ES, 1270 WALNUT ST 11553
  Lois Small, prin.
Other Schools – See North Baldwin

St. Martha's ES, 530 HEMPSTEAD BLVD 11553

Union Springs, Cayuga Co., Pop. Code 4
Union Springs Central SD
Sch. Sys. Enr. Code 4
Supt. – Lawrence Kiley, 27 N CAYUGA ST 13160
Smith ES, 22 HOMER STREET 13160
  David Jerva, prin.
Other Schools – See Cayuga

Utica, Oneida Co., Pop. Code 8
Utica CSD
Sch. Sys. Enr. Code 6
Supt. – Francis Rodio, 13 ELIZABETH ST 13501
Albany ES, 1151 ALBANY ST 13501
  Anthony Zane, prin.
Columbus ES, 934 ARMORY DR 13501
  Michael Arcuri, prin.
Conkling ES, 1115 MOHAWK ST 13501
  Karen Kunkel, prin.
Herkimer ES, 420 KEYES RD 13502
  Margaret Buckley, prin.
Hughes ES, PROSPECT STREET 13501
  Fred Capozzella, prin.
Jefferson ES, BOOTH STREET 13502
  Margaret Beck, prin.
Jones ES, REMINGTON ROAD 13501
  Dominic Rasi, prin.
Kemble ES, 1604 KEMBLE ST 13501
  Patricia McNamara, prin.
Kernan ES, 929 YORK ST 13502
  Edward Keeler, prin.
King ES, 211 SQUARE ST 13501
  Anthony LePorte, prin.
Lincoln ES, 1010 MATHEWS AVE 13502
  Theresa Munski, prin.
Roosevelt ES, 1516 TAYLOR AVE 13501
  Philip Geraci, prin.
Seymour ES, 401 EUCLID RD 13502
  Arthur Perry, prin.

Sunset ES, 2521 SUNSET AVE 13502
  Dominic Rasi, prin.
Washington ES, 1216 OSWEGO ST 13502
  Theresa Munski, prin.
Wetmore ES, 405 WETMORE ST 13501
  Joseph Lubertine, prin.

Whitesboro Central SD
Supt. – See Yorktown Heights
Deerfield ES, 718 TRENTON RD 13502
  John Messina, prin.

Notre Dame JHS North, 309 GENESEE ST 13501
Notre Dame JHS-South, 10 BARTON AVE 13502
Blessed Sacrament ES
  1621 SAINT AGNES AVE 13501
Holy Trinity ES, 1208 LINCOLN AVE 13502
Our Lady of Lourdes ES, 10 BARTON AVE 13502
Sacred Heart ES, 1110 NEY AVE 13502
St. Agnes ES, 701 KOSSUTH AVE 13501
St. Francis De Sales School, 1119 ELM ST 13501
St. Peters ES, 19 HERKIMER RD 13502

Valatie, Columbia Co., Pop. Code 4
Kinderhook Central SD
Sch. Sys. Enr. Code 4
Supt. – Jerome Callahan
  CENT ADMIN OFFICE 12184
Crane MS, US ROUTE 09 12184 – (—), prin.
Crane ES, STATE FARM ROAD 12184
  David Peter, prin.
Glynn MS, CHURCH STREET 12184
  Jane Diamond, prin.
Other Schools – See Kinderhook

Valhalla, Westchester Co., Pop. Code 6
Mt. Pleasant-Blythedale UFD
Sch. Sys. Enr. Code 2
Supt. – Mariann Berlinger 10595
Blythedale S 10595 – Carol Squires, prin.

Valhalla UFD
Sch. Sys. Enr. Code 4
Supt. – George Port, 300 COLUMBUS AVE 10595
Columbus Avenue ES
  COLUMBUS AVENUE 10595
  Frank Ehrhart, prin.
Other Schools – See North White Plains

Holy Name of Jesus ES, 2 BROADWAY 10595

Valley Cottage, Rockland Co., Pop. Code 6
Nyack UFD
Supt. – See Nyack
Liberty ES, LAKE ROAD 10989
  Richard Adams, prin.
ES, LAKE ROAD 10989 – Edward Whalen, prin.

St. Paul ES, KINGS CT 10989

Valley Stream, Nassau Co., Pop. Code 8
Elmont UFD
Supt. – See Elmont
Alden Terrace ES, 1809 N CENTRAL AVE 11580
  Robert Aloise, prin.

Hewlett-Woodmere UFD
Supt. – See Hewlett
Ogden ES, LONGVIEW AVENUE 11581
  Carl Spinola, prin.

Valley Stream Hemp 13 UFD
Sch. Sys. Enr. Code 4
Supt. – Thomas Lee, CORONA AVE 11580
Dever ES, CORONA AVENUE 11582
  Stephanie Adams, prin.
Howell Road ES, 1475 HOWELL RD 11580
  Rosanne Keltos, prin.
Wheeler Avenue ES, WHEELER AVENUE 11582
  Jerry Keshian, prin.
Other Schools – See Franklin Square

Valley Stream Hemp 24 UFD
Sch. Sys. Enr. Code 3
Supt. – Richard Bonen, HORTON AVE 11581
Brooklyn Avenue ES, FIFTH STREET 11581
  David Tager, prin.
Buck ES, HORTON AVENUE 11581
  Diana Pirrone, prin.
Carbonaro ES, HUNGRY HARBOR & MILL 11581
  Matthew Melillo, prin.

Valley Stream Hemp 30 UFD
Sch. Sys. Enr. Code 3
Supt. – William Van Ness, SHAW AVE 11580
Clearstream Avenue ES
  60 CLEARSTREAM AVE 11580
  Richard Burbell, prin.
Forest Road ES, 16 FOREST RD 11581
  Raymond Brodeur,Jr., prin.
Shaw Avenue ES, 99 SHAW AVE 11580
  Patricia Callow, prin.

Blessed Sacrament ES, 50 ROSE AVE 11580
Holy Name of Mary ES, 90 S GROVE ST 11580

Van Etten, Tioga Co., Pop. Code 3
Spencer-Van Etten Central SD
Sch. Sys. Enr. Code 4
Supt. – Lawrence Pereira, DIST OFFICE 14889
ES 14889 – Cynthia Westbrook, prin.
Other Schools – See Spencer

Van Hornesville, Herkimer Co.
Hornesville-Young Central SD
Sch. Sys. Enr. Code 2
Supt. – Charles Messerich 13475

Young Central S 13475 – Theron Hotaling, prin.

Varysburg, Wyoming Co.
Attica Central SD
Supt. – See Attica
Sheldon ES, 2588 SCHOOL STREET 14167
  Margaret Borchert, prin.

Vernon, Oneida Co., Pop. Code 4
Sherrill CSD
Supt. – See Verona
Wettel ES, PETERBORO ROAD 13476
  Anthony Micaroni, prin.

Verona, Oneida Co., Pop. Code 6
Sherrill CSD
Sch. Sys. Enr. Code 5
Supt. – Albert Kouba, ROUTE 234 13478
Sherrill MS, ROUTE 31 13478 – Robert Biehl, prin.
George ES, MAIN STREET 13478
  Stephen Orcutt, prin.
Other Schools – See Sherrill, Vernon

Verona Beach, Oneida Co.
Sylvan Beach-Verona Comm. SD
Sch. Sys. Enr. Code 2
Supt. – Patricia Hughes 13162
Verona Beach Community ES
  VERONA BCH 13162 – Patricia Hughes, prin.

Vestal, Broome Co., Pop. Code 8
Vestal Central SD
Sch. Sys. Enr. Code 5
Supt. – Charles Moore, DIST OFFICE 13850
African Road JHS 13850 – Marlyn Geres, prin.
African Road ES 13850 – Joseph Colavito, prin.
Clayton Avenue ES 13850 – Tim McMullin, prin.
Glenwood ES 13850 – Philip Sciamanna, prin.
Tioga Hill ES 13850 – Bruce Theobald, prin.
Vestal Hills ES 13850 – Daniel Turner, prin.

Ross Corners Christian Academy
  2101 OWEGO RD 13850
Our Lady of Sorrows ES, 801 MAIN ST 13850

Victor, Ontario Co., Pop. Code 4
Victor Central SD
Sch. Sys. Enr. Code 5
Supt. – Richard Thomas 14564
JHS 14564 – Wayne Houseman, prin.
IS 14564 – Cheryl Dudley, prin.
PS 14564 – Paul Kelly, prin.

Voorheesville, Albany Co., Pop. Code 5
Voorheesville Central SD
Sch. Sys. Enr. Code 4
Supt. – Louise Gonan, ROUTE 85A 12186
ES, P O BOX 468 12186 – Donna Canavan, prin.

Waddington, Ontario Co., Pop. Code 3
Madrid-Waddington Central SD
Supt. – See Madrid
ES 13694 – Carl Rose, prin.

Wading River, Suffolk Co., Pop. Code 4
Shoreham-Wading River Central SD
Supt. – See Shoreham
ES, MANOR ROAD 11792
  Richard Anderson, prin.

Wainscott, Suffolk Co.
Wainscott Common SD
Sch. Sys. Enr. Code 1
Supt. – Robert Freidah, HOLLOW ROAD 11975
Wainscott Common ES, HOLLOW RD 11975
  Mary Laspia, prin.

Walden, Orange Co., Pop. Code 6
Valley Central SD
Supt. – See Montgomery
ES, 75 ORCHARD ST 12586 – John Schmoll, prin.

Most Precs Blood ES, 180 ULSTER AVE 12586

Wallkill, Ulster Co., Pop. Code 4
Wallkill Central SD
Sch. Sys. Enr. Code 5
Supt. – Don Andrews 12589
MS 12589 – James McGuire, prin.
Leptondale ES, RURAL ROUTE 02 BOX 435 12589
  Neil MacDonald, prin.
Ostrander ES 12589 – Leah Springer, prin.
Other Schools – See Plattekill

Walton, Delaware Co., Pop. Code 5
Walton Central SD
Sch. Sys. Enr. Code 4
Supt. – George Mack, STOCKTON AVE 13856
Townsend ES, NORTH STREET 13856
  Robert Holstead, prin.

Wampsville, Madison Co., Pop. Code 3
Oneida CSD
Supt. – See Oneida
Shortell MS, MARKELL DRIVE 13163
  Walter Thomas, prin.

Wantagh, Nassau Co., Pop. Code 7
Levittown UFD
Supt. – See Levittown
Lee Road ES, LEE ROAD 11793
  Renaldo Calabrese, prin.

Wantagh UFD
Sch. Sys. Enr. Code 5
Supt. – George Besculides, BELTAGH AVE 11793
MS, 3301 BELTAGH AVE 11793
  Carl Bonuso, prin.

Forest Lake ES, BELTAGH AVENUE   11793
   James Smith, prin.
Mandalay ES, 2601 BAYVIEW AVE   11793
   Lynne Dagostino, prin.
Wantagh ES
   BEECH STREET & DEMOTT PLACE   11793
   Donald Sternberg, prin.

Maplewood ES, 2166 WANTAGH AVE   11793
St. Frances De Chantal ES, IVY LN   11793

Wappingers Falls, Dutchess Co., Pop. Code 6
Wappingers Central SD
Sch. Sys. Enr. Code 7
Supt. – Dodge Watkins, 90 S REMSEN AVE   12590
Van Wyck JHS, HILLSIDE LAKE ROAD   12590
   John Biasotti, prin.
JHS, 90 S REMSEN AVE   12590
   Joseph Corrigan, prin.
Evans ES, ALBANY POST ROAD   12590
   Ronald Cole, prin.
Fishkill Plains ES, LAKE WALTON ROAD   12590
   Thomas Kenney, prin.
Myers Corners ES
   156 MYERS CORNERS RD   12590
   Justine Winters, prin.
Sheafe Road ES, 145 SHEAFE RD   12590
   Stephen Miller, prin.
Other Schools – See Fishkill, Hopewell Junction,
   Poughkeepsie

St. Mary ES, CONVENT AVE   12590

Warrensburg, Warren Co., Pop. Code 5
Warrensburg Central SD
Sch. Sys. Enr. Code 4
Supt. – Daniel Connor, 1 JAMES ST   12885
ES, 1 JAMES ST   12885 – Charles Devitto, prin.

Warsaw, Wyoming Co., Pop. Code 5
Warsaw Central SD
Sch. Sys. Enr. Code 4
Supt. – Edmund Kulakowski, W COURT ST   14569
ES, WEST COURT STREET   14569
   Don Felix, prin.

Warwick, Orange Co., Pop. Code 5
Warwick Valley Central SD
Sch. Sys. Enr. Code 5
Supt. – James Sailer, P O BOX E   10990
Warwick Valley MS, P O BOX E   10990
   John Russo, prin.
Kings ES, KINGS HIGHWAY   10990
   William Legrow, prin.
Park Avenue ES, PARK AVENUE   10990
   Gerald Decatur, prin.
Other Schools – See Pine Island

SS. Stephen & Edward ES, P O BOX 385   10990

Washingtonville, Orange Co., Pop. Code 4
Washingtonville Central SD
Sch. Sys. Enr. Code 5
Supt. – R. Miller, 52 W MAIN ST   10992
Round Hill ES, ROUTE 208   10992
   John Lantry, prin.
Taft ES, TOLEMAN ROAD   10992
   Judith McLaughlin, prin.
Other Schools – See Newburgh

Waterford, Saratoga Co., Pop. Code 4
Waterford-Halfmoon UFD
Sch. Sys. Enr. Code 3
Supt. – Ward Patton
   125 MIDDLETOWN ROAD   12188
ES, 125 MIDDLETOWN RD   12188
   Iona Johnston, prin.

Waterford Cent Catholic School, 12 6TH ST   12188

Waterloo, Seneca Co., Pop. Code 6
Waterloo Central SD
Sch. Sys. Enr. Code 4
Supt. – Michael Hunsinger
   202 W MAIN ST   13165
Main Street MS, MAIN ST   13165
   Richard Byndas, prin.
La Fayette MS, 71 INSLEE ST   13165
   Carol Emerson, prin.
Yase ES, WASHINGTON STREET   13165
   Nancy Milliman, prin.

St. Mary's ES, 35 CENTER ST   13165

Water Mill, Suffolk Co., Pop. Code 3

South Fork Christian ES
   RURAL ROUTE 01 BOX 561   11976

Waterport, Orleans Co.
Albion Central SD
Supt. – See Albion
ES, MAIN ST   14571 – Kim Houserman, prin.

Watertown, Jefferson Co., Pop. Code 8
Watertown CSD
Sch. Sys. Enr. Code 5
Supt. – Warren Fargo
   376 BUTTERFIELD AVE   13601
Case JHS, 1237 WASHINGTON ST   13601
   Philip Pratt, prin.
Knickerbocker ES
   729 KNICKERBOCKER DR   13601
   Irene Wilson, prin.
Meade ES, 531 MEADE ST   13601
   Roger Funnell, prin.

North ES, 171 HOARD ST   13601
   Marianne Malatino, prin.
Ohio Street ES, 1537 OHIO ST   13601
   Henry Hooker, prin.
Sherman ES, 836 SHERMAN ST   13601
   Donald Whitney, prin.
Starbuck ES, 430 E HOARD ST   13601
   Roger Funnell, prin.
Wiley MS, 1351 WASHINGTON ST   13601
   William Doull, prin.

Holy Family ES, 129 STERLING PL   13601
Sacred Heart ES, 320 W LYNDE ST   13601
St. Anthony ES, 870 ARSENAL ST   13601
St. Patrick's ES, 733 S MASSEY ST   13601

Waterville, Oneida Co., Pop. Code 4
Waterville Central SD
Sch. Sys. Enr. Code 4
Supt. – James McCarthy, MADISON ST   13480
Memorial Park ES, 145 E BACON ST   13480
   Paul Skinner, prin.

Watervliet, Albany Co., Pop. Code 7
Maplewood-Colonie Common SD
Sch. Sys. Enr. Code 2
Supt. – Barbara Nagler, 9 COHOES ROAD   12189
Maplewood ES, 9 COHOES RD   12189
   Barbara Nagler, prin.

Watervliet CSD
Sch. Sys. Enr. Code 4
Supt. – G. Perry, 10TH AVE & 25TH ST   12189
ES, 10TH AVENUE AND 25TH ST   12189
   Thomas Sands, prin.

St. Brigids ES, 700 5TH AVE   12189

Watkins Glen, Schuyler Co., Pop. Code 4
Watkins Glen Central SD
Sch. Sys. Enr. Code 4
Supt. – Wilfred Ross, 12TH ST   14891
MS, N DECATUR ST   14891
   Sandra Woolley, prin.
ES, GRANDVIEW AVENUE   14891
   Michael Yuhasz, prin.

Waverly, Tioga Co., Pop. Code 5
Waverly Central SD
Sch. Sys. Enr. Code 4
Supt. – Walter Cain, 15 FREDERICK ST   14892
Elm Street ES, 145 ELM STREET   14892
   William Baker, prin.
Lincoln Street ES, 45 LINCOLN ST   14892
   Floyd Williams, prin.
Other Schools – See Chemung

Wayland, Steuben Co., Pop. Code 4
Wayland Central SD
Sch. Sys. Enr. Code 4
Supt. – J. Burroughs, W NAPLES ST   14572
ES, WEST NAPLES STREET   14572
   Bradford Bowers, prin.

St. Joseph ES, 209 FREMONT ST   14572

Webster, Monroe Co., Pop. Code 6
Webster Central SD
Sch. Sys. Enr. Code 6
Supt. – K. Jack Syage, 119 SOUTH AVE   14580
Dewitt Road ES, 722 DEWITT RD   14580
   William Thompson, prin.
Klem Road North ES, 1015 KLEM RD   14580
   (—), prin.
Klem Road South ES, 1025 KLEM RD   14580
   Gerald Ryan, prin.
Plank Road North ES, 705 PLANK RD   14580
   Evajill Zulauf, prin.
Plank Road South ES, 715 PLANK ROAD   14580
   William Mackenzie, prin.
State Road ES, 1401 STATE RD   14580
   John Carpenter, prin.

Webster Christian School, 675 HOLT ROAD   14580
Holy Trinity ES, 1456 RIDGE RD   14580
St. Rita's ES, 1008 MAPLE DR   14580

Weedsport, Cayuga Co., Pop. Code 4
Weedsport Central SD
Sch. Sys. Enr. Code 3
Supt. – Gary Gilchrist, 2821 E BRUTUS ST   13166
ES, 8954 JACKSON STREET   13166
   Howard Lapidus, prin.

Wells, Hamilton Co., Pop. Code 3
Wells Central SD
Sch. Sys. Enr. Code 2
Supt. – Timothy Morell   12190
S, ROUTE 30   12190 – Timothy Morell, prin.

Wellsville, Allegany Co., Pop. Code 6
Wellsville Central SD
Sch. Sys. Enr. Code 4
Supt. – Thomas McGowan, 50 SCHOOL ST   14895
MS, 30 N BROOKLYN AVE   14895
   David Porter, prin.
ES, SCHOOL STREET   14895
   Robert Barnett, prin.

Immaculate Conception ES, 24 MAPLE AVE   14895

West Babylon, Suffolk Co., Pop. Code 8
North Babylon UFD
Supt. – See North Babylon
Belmont ES, BARNUM ST   11704
   Anita Cocheo, prin.

West Babylon UFD
Sch. Sys. Enr. Code 5
Supt. – John Roche
   10 FARMINGDALE ROAD   11704
JHS, 200 OLD FARMINGDALE ROAD   11704
   Melvin Noble, prin.
Forest Avenue ES, 200 FOREST AVE   11704
   Jerome Schiffman, prin.
Kennedy ES, 175 BROOKVALE AVE   11704
   Emanuel Campisi, prin.
Santapogue ES, 1130 HERZEL BLVD   11704
   Ethel Rigby, prin.
South Bay ES, 160 GREAT EAST NECK RD   11704
   Patricia Farrell, prin.
Tooker Avenue ES, 855 TOOKER AVE   11704
   Wayne Young, prin.

Westbury, Nassau Co., Pop. Code 7
East Meadow UFD
Supt. – See East Meadow
Bowling Green ES, 2368 STEWART AVE   11590
   Robert Merrifield, prin.

Westbury UFD
Sch. Sys. Enr. Code 5
Supt. – John Franco
   JERICHO TRPK & HITCHCOCK LN   11590
Drexel Avenue MS   11590 – Susan Nettler, prin.
Park ES   11590 – Delores Hunter, prin.
Powells Lane MS, POWELLS LANE   11590
   John Ogilvie, prin.

St. Brigid's ES, 101 MAPLE AVE   11590

Westerlo, Albany Co., Pop. Code 5
Berne Knox Westerlo Central SD
Supt. – See Berne
   Westerlo ES   12193 – Joseph Leombruno, prin.

Westfield, Chautauqua Co., Pop. Code 5
Westfield Central SD
Sch. Sys. Enr. Code 4
Supt. – Robert Olczak, 189 E MAIN ST   14787
ES, E MAIN STREET   14787
   Dennis Shively, prin.

Westhampton Beach, Suffolk Co., Pop. Code 4
Westhampton Beach UFD
Sch. Sys. Enr. Code 4
Supt. – Ed Broderick   11978
JHS, MILL ROAD   11978 – Phillip Debrita, prin.
ES, 340 MILL RD   11978 – Diana Lawlor, prin.

West Haverstraw, Rockland Co., Pop. Code 6
Haverstraw-Stony Point Central SD
Supt. – See Stony Point
ES, 67 BLAUVELT AVE   10993
   Thomas Manning, prin.

West Hempstead, Nassau Co., Pop. Code 7
West Hempstead UFD
Sch. Sys. Enr. Code 5
Supt. – Richard Varriale
   252 CHESTNUT ST   11552
Cornwell Avenue ES, 250 CORNWELL AVE   11552
   Charles Inghilterra, prin.
Washington ES, 347 WILLIAM ST   11552
   Helen Senesky, prin.

Hebrew Academy of Nassau
   609 HEMPSEAD AVE   11552
St. Thomas the Apostle ES
   12 WESTMINISTER RD   11552

West Henrietta, Monroe Co., Pop. Code 3
Rush Henrietta Central SD
Supt. – See Henrietta
Rush Henrietta JHS
   639 ERIE STATION ROAD   14586
   Roger Gorham, prin.

West Hurley, Ulster Co., Pop. Code 3
Onteora Central SD
Supt. – See Boiceville
ES   12491 – M. Carroll, prin.

West Islip, Suffolk Co., Pop. Code 7
West Islip UFD
Sch. Sys. Enr. Code 6
Supt. – William Bernhard, BEACH ST   11795
Bayview ES, SNEDECOR AVENUE   11795
   Andrew Pecoraro, prin.
Bellew ES, HIGBIE LANE   11795
   James Lanzarotta, prin.
Captree ES, SNEDECOR AVENUE   11795
   Douglas Simonton, prin.
Manetuck ES, VAN BUREN AVENUE   11795
   Robert Gaggin, prin.
Masera ES, UDALL ROAD   11795
   Michael Freyer, prin.
Oquenock ES, SPRUCE AVENUE   11795
   Carl Harris, prin.
Westbrook ES, HIGBIE LANE   11795
   Philip Harrigan, prin.

Our Lady of Lourdes ES, 44 TOOMEY RD   11795

West Lebanon, Columbia Co.
New Lebanon Central SD
Sch. Sys. Enr. Code 3
Supt. – Thaddeus Obloy   12195
Howard ES   12195 – Thaddeus Obloy, prin.

West Leyden, Lewis Co.
Adirondack-Boonville Central SD
Supt. – See Boonville
ES   13489 – Dean Bedgar, prin.

... ES, 375 WINECOFF SCHOOL RD   28025
.....rry Woods, prin.
.olf Meadow ES, 150 WOLFMEADOW DR   28025
  Allen Small, prin.
Other Schools – See Harrisburg, Kannapolis, Midland,
  Mount Pleasant

First Assembly Christian School
  154 HWY 601 BY PASS   28025

Connellys Springs, Burke Co.
Burke County SD
Supt. – See Morganton
Hildebrand ES, P O BOX 268-B   28612
  D. Sipe, prin.

Conover, Catawba Co., Pop. Code 5
Newton-Conover CSD
Supt. – See Newton
Shuford ES, RURAL ROUTE 05 BOX 636   28613
  David Poe, prin.

Concordia Lutheran ES, 115 5TH AVE SE   28613

Conway, Northampton Co., Pop. Code 3
Northampton County SD
Supt. – See Jackson
MS, P O BOX 307   27820 – Gary Newell, prin.

Cooleemee, Davie Co.
Davie County SD
Supt. – See Mocksville
ES, P O BOX 128   27014 – Vernon Thompson, prin.

Cordova, Richmond Co.
Richmond County SD
Supt. – See Hamlet
ES, P O BOX 149   28330 – Elijah Peterson, prin.

Cornelius, Mecklenburg Co., Pop. Code 4
Mecklenburg County SD
Supt. – See Charlotte
ES, 21126 CATAWBA AVE   28031
  Gayle Aughtry, prin.

Cove City, Craven Co., Pop. Code 2
Craven County SD
Supt. – See New Bern
Smith ES, BOX 150 KOONCETOWN RD   28523
  Allen Smith, prin.

Cramerton, Gaston Co., Pop. Code 4

Cramerton Christian Academy
  426 WOODLAWN ST   28032

Creedmoor, Granville Co., Pop. Code 4
Granville County SD
Supt. – See Oxford
Hawley MS, P O BOX 67   27522
  Abram Liles, prin.
ES, P O BOX 725   27522 – C. Weaver, prin.

Creston, Ashe Co.
Ashe County SD
Supt. – See Jefferson
Riverview ES, HCR BOX 133   28615
  Jerry Absher, prin.

Creswell, Washington Co., Pop. Code 2
Washington County SD
Supt. – See Plymouth
Creswell S, P O BOX 188   27928
  David Cahoon, prin.
MS, P O BOX 36   27928 – William Sermons, prin.

Crossnore, Avery Co.
Avery County SD
Supt. – See Newland
ES, P O BOX 10   28616 – Rodger Crenshaw, prin.

Crumpler, Ashe Co.
Ashe County SD
Supt. – See Jefferson
Healing Springs ES   28617 – Nancy Reeves, prin.
Nathans Creek ES
  RURAL ROUTE 01 BOX 150   28617
  James Blackburn, prin.

Cullowhee, Jackson Co., Pop. Code 5
Jackson County SD
Supt. – See Sylva
Camp Laboratory ES, P O BOX 2648   28723
  Arlin Middleton, prin.

Currituck, Currituck Co., Pop. Code 2
Currituck County SD
Sch. Sys. Enr. Code 4
Supt. – Jeanne Meiggs, P O BOX 40   27929
Knapp JHS   27929 – Maurice Green, prin.
Other Schools – See Knotts Island, Maple, Moyock,
  Poplar Branch

Dallas, Gaston Co., Pop. Code 5
Gaston County SD
Supt. – See Gastonia
Carr ES, 301 W CARPENTER ST   28034
  Peggy Ferguson, prin.
Costner ES, RURAL ROUTE 01 BOX 269   28034
  Glenn Dover, prin.
MS, 300 W CHURCH ST   28034
  Hiram Baucom, prin.

Dana, Henderson Co.
Henderson County SD
Supt. – See Hendersonville
ES, P O BOX 37   28724 – Carroll Mullins, prin.

Danbury, Stokes Co., Pop. Code 2
Stokes County SD
Sch. Sys. Enr. Code 6
Supt. – Dr. Kent Moseley, P O BOX 50   27016
Other Schools – See Germantown, King, Lawsonville,
  Pine Hall, Pinnacle, Sandy Ridge, Walnut Cove,
  Westfield

Davidson, Mecklenburg Co., Pop. Code 5
Mecklenburg County SD
Supt. – See Charlotte
ES, SOUTH ST BOX 398   28036
  Eugene Davis, prin.

Denton, Davidson Co., Pop. Code 3
Davidson County SD
Supt. – See Lexington
ES, P O BOX 967   27239 – Larry Talley, prin.

Denver, Lincoln Co., Pop. Code 2
Lincoln County SD
Supt. – See Lincolnton
Catawba Springs ES
  1701 LITTLE EGYPT ROAD   28037
  M. Chapman, prin.
Rock Springs ES, P O BOX 279   28037
  James Mundy, prin.

Dobson, Surry Co., Pop. Code 4
Surry County SD
Sch. Sys. Enr. Code 6
Supt. – Dr. David Martin, P O BOX 364   27017
Copeland ES, RURAL ROUTE 02   27017
  J. Smitherman, prin.
ES, P O BOX 248   27017 – Philip Cook, prin.
Other Schools – See Lowgap, Mount Airy, Pilot
  Mountain, Pinnacle, State Road, Westfield, White
  Plains

Drexel, Burke Co., Pop. Code 4
Burke County SD
Supt. – See Morganton
ES, P O BOX 488   28619 – Frances Huffman, prin.

Dublin, Bladen Co., Pop. Code 2
Bladen County SD
Supt. – See Elizabethtown
ES, P O BOX 307   28332 – James Hall, prin.

Dudley, Wayne Co., Pop. Code 2
Wayne County SD
Supt. – See Goldsboro
Brogden PS, RURAL ROUTE 02 BOX 17-B   28333
  Stuart Patten, prin.

Dunn, Harnett Co., Pop. Code 6
Harnett County SD
Supt. – See Lillington
MS   28334 – John Willoughby, prin.
Harnett PS   28334 – Jennie Brooks, prin.
Wayne Avenue MS   28334 – James Bennett, prin.

Sampson County SD
Supt. – See Clinton
Midway ES, RURAL ROUTE 05   28334
  Walton Keen, prin.
Plain View ES, RURAL ROUTE 05   28334
  Timothy Lee, prin.

Durham, Durham Co., Pop. Code 9
Durham CSD
Sch. Sys. Enr. Code 6
Supt. – Frank Weaver, P O BOX 2246   27702
Brogden MS, 1001 LEON ST   27704
  John Howard, prin.
Holton MS, 401 N DRIVER ST   27703
  Herbert Tatum, prin.
Rogers-Herr MS, CORNWALLIS ROAD   27707
  Donald Lowrance, prin.
Shepard MS, 2401 DAKOTA ST   27707
  John Hunter, prin.
Burton ES, LAKELAND ST   27701
  Lee Goode, prin.
Club Boulevard ES   27704 – Darryl Powell, prin.
East End ES, DOWD ST   27701 – (—), prin.
Fayettevlle Street ES, FAYETTEVILLE ST   27707
  Eula Henry, prin.
Harris ES, COOPER ST   27701
  Gertrude Williams, prin.
Holloway Street ES, HOLLOWAY ST   27701
  Thomas Taylor, Jr., prin.
Lakewood ES, 2520 VESSON AVE   27707
  William Woody, prin.
Morehead ES, ARNETTE AVE   27707
  Dennis Nichols, prin.
Pearson ES, UMSTEAD ST   27701
  Thelma Battle, prin.
Powe ES, NINTH ST   27705 – Ruth Murphy, prin.
Smith ES, 2410 E MAIN ST   27703
  Dr. Joseph Settle, prin.
Spaulding ES, 1531 S ROXBORO ST   27707
  Audrey Boykin, prin.
Watts ES, 700 WATTS ST   27701
  Dr. Michael Courtney, prin.

Durham County SD
Sch. Sys. Enr. Code 7
Supt. – Dr. Larry Coble, P O BOX 3823   27702
Githerns JHS, RURAL ROUTE 07   27707
  Dr. Elsa Woods, prin.
Lowes Grove JHS, 4418 S ALSTON AVE   27713
  J. Warren Elledge, prin.
Neal JHS, RURAL ROUTE 05   27704
  Dr. William Batchelor, prin.
Bethesda ES, 2009 S MIAMI BLVD   27703
  Clarence Hill, prin.

Bragtown MS, 320 BELVIN AVE   27704
  Edward Raeford, prin.
Eno Valley ES, 117 MILTON RD   27712
  Dr. Jane York, prin.
Glenn ES, 2415 E GEER ST   27704
  Arthur Grier, prin.
Hillandale ES, 2107 HILLANDALE RD   27705
  Dr. Isaac Thomas, prin.
Holt ES, 4019 HOLT SCHOOL RD   27704
  Gloria Elmore, prin.
Hope Valley ES, 3023 UNIVERSITY DR   27707
  Dr. Claud McCary, prin.
Lowes Grove ES, 4505 S ALSTON AVE   27713
  Charles Guess, prin.
Merrick-Moore ES, 2325 CHEEK RD   27704
  Phillip Rigdon, prin.
Oak Grove ES, 3810 WAKE FOREST RD   27703
  Mary Sharpe, prin.
Parkwood ES, 5207 REVERE RD   27713
  Sarah Spivey, prin.
Pearstown ES, 4915 BARBEE RD   27713
  Joanne Edelman, prin.
Other Schools – See Bahama

Carolina Friends School
  RURAL ROUTE 01 BOX 183   27705
Cresset Christian Academy
  3707 GARRETT ROAD   27707
Durham Academy, 3601 RIDGE ROAD   27705
Immaculate Catholic ES
  CHAPEL HILL STREET EXIT   27701

East Bend, Yadkin Co., Pop. Code 3
Yadkin County SD
Supt. – See Yadkinville
ES, P O BOX 129   27018 – Mike Crouse, prin.
Fall Creek ES, RURAL ROUTE 01 BOX 39   27018
  Mary Barriere, prin.

East Flat Rock, Henderson Co.
Henderson County SD
Supt. – See Hendersonville
MS, 101 E BLUE RIDGE RD   28726
  A. Collins, prin.
Hillandale ES, 900 W BLUE RIDGE RD   28726
  V. Thompson, prin.

East Spencer, Rowan Co.
Rowan County SD
Supt. – See Salisbury
North Rowan MS, P O BOX 428   28039
  Harold Thomas, prin.

Eden, Rockingham Co., Pop. Code 7
Eden CSD
Sch. Sys. Enr. Code 5
Supt. – Harold Matthews
  405 HIGHLAND DRIVE   27288
Burton Grove ES, 724 MCCONNELL AVE   27288
  Harold Kendrick, prin.
Central ES, 435 E STADIUM DR   27288
  John Thacker, prin.
Douglass ES, 1130 CENTER CHURCH RD   27288
  Lonnie Sechrist, prin.
Draper ES, 1719 E STADIUM DR   27288
  Bob Wilkes, prin.
Lakeside ES, 719 KENDALL ST   27288
  Fred Hampton, prin.
Leaksville-Spray MS, 609 COL ST   27288
  Fred Liner, prin.

Edenton, Chowan Co., Pop. Code 6
Chowan County SD
Sch. Sys. Enr. Code 3
Supt. – Dr. J. Dunn, P O BOX 207   27932
Walker ES, NORTH OAKUM ST   27932
  Ralph Cole, prin.
Other Schools – See Tyner

Efland, Orange Co.
Orange County SD
Supt. – See Hillsborough
Efland-Cheeks ES, STATE ROAD 1315   27243
  Rebecca Horne, prin.

Elizabeth City, Pasquotank Co., Pop. Code 7
Pasquotank County SD
Sch. Sys. Enr. Code 6
Supt. – Travis Twiford, Jr., P O BOX 2247   27909
MS, 306 N ROAD ST   27909
  Carlton Thornton, prin.
Central ES, RURAL ROUTE 06   27909
  Cecil Perry, prin.
Pasquotank MS, 1407 PEARTREE RD   27909
  James Britt, prin.
Sawyer ES, 1007 PARK ST   27909
  Rita Collie, prin.
Sheep Harney ES, 307 N ROAD ST   27909
  (—), prin.
Trigg MS, 1004 PARKVIEW DR   27909
  Walter Jolly, prin.
Weeksville ES, 606 ROANOKE AVE   27909
  Georgetta Jackson, prin.

Elizabethtown, Bladen Co., Pop. Code 5
Bladen County SD
Sch. Sys. Enr. Code 6
Supt. – W. Hair, P O BOX 37   28337
Bladen MS, P O BOX 638   28337
  Elbert Smith, prin.
Bladen Lakes ES, RURAL ROUTE 02   28337
  Daniel McLaurin, Jr., prin.
ES, P O BOX 966   28337 – Patricia Walker, prin.
Other Schools – See Bladenboro, Clarkton, D...
  Riegelwood, Tar Heel

Elkin, Surry Co., Pop. Code 5
Elkin CSD
Sch. Sys. Enr. Code 4
Supt. – Donald Lassiter, 241 CHURCH ST   28621
PS, 135 OLD VIRGINIA RD   28621
  Edward Lakey, prin.
North Elkin MS, 440 N ELKIN DRIVE   28621
  William Wagoner, prin.

Wilkes County SD
Supt. – See Wilkesboro
Eller ES, RURAL ROUTE 03 BOX 85   28621
  James Huffman, prin.

Elk Park, Avery Co., Pop. Code 3
Avery County SD
Supt. – See Newland
Beech Mountain ES
  RURAL ROUTE 01 BOX 406   28622
  Phillip Shomaker, prin.
ES, P O BOX 38   28622 – Buster Burleson, prin.

Ellenboro, Rutherford Co., Pop. Code 3
Rutherford County SD
Supt. – See Spindale
ES, P O BOX 68   28040 – Wayne York, prin.

Ellerbe, Richmond Co., Pop. Code 4
Richmond County SD
Supt. – See Hamlet
ES, P O BOX 30   28338 – Lewis Broadnax, prin.
Mineral Springs MS, P O BOX 160   28338
  Donald Pratt, prin.

Elm City, Wilson Co., Pop. Code 4
Nash County SD
Supt. – See Nashville
Coopers ES, RURAL ROUTE 02 BOX 209-A   27822
  B. Smith, prin.

Wilson County SD
Supt. – See Wilson
MS, P O BOX 729   27822 – S. Pofflemyer, prin.
ES, P O BOX 719   27822 – Luther Bryant, prin.
Gardners ES, RURAL ROUTE 03 BOX 167   27822
  Marvin Sessoms, prin.

Elon College, Alamance Co., Pop. Code 4
Alamance County SD
Supt. – See Graham
Western MS, RURAL ROUTE 01   27244
  Wilma Parrish, prin.
ES, 501 E HAGGARD AVE   27244
  Priscilla Starling, prin.
Ossipee ES, RURAL ROUTE 02 BOX 18   27244
  Wayne Beam, prin.

Enfield, Halifax Co., Pop. Code 5
Halifax County SD
Supt. – See Halifax
Eastman MS
  RURAL ROUTE 02 BOX 143A   27823
  Ralph Evans, prin.
MS, P O BOX 128   27823 – Claude Cooper, prin.
Inborden ES, P O BOX 457   27823
  Alfred Riddick, prin.
Pittman ES, RURAL ROUTE 03 BOX 286   27823
  Dock Brown, prin.
White Oak ES, RURAL ROUTE 02 BOX 160   27823
  Ruel Solomon, prin.

Engelhard, Hyde Co.
Hyde County SD
Supt. – See Swanquarter
Davis ES, RURAL ROUTE 01 BOX 44   27824
  James Lloyd, prin.

Ennice, Alleghany Co.
Alleghany County SD
Supt. – See Sparta
Glade Creek ES   28623 – James Sturgill, prin.

Erwin, Harnett Co., Pop. Code 5
Harnett County SD
Supt. – See Lillington
MS   28339 – Don Wilson, prin.
Gentry ES   28339 – Waylon Smith, prin.

Etowah, Henderson Co.
Henderson County SD
Supt. – See Hendersonville
ES, P O BOX 407   28729 – Malvern West, prin.

Eureka, Wayne Co., Pop. Code 2
Wayne County SD
Supt. – See Goldsboro
ES, P O BOX 208   27830 – Steve Taylor, prin.

Everetts, Martin Co., Pop. Code 2
Martin County SD
Supt. – See Williamston
North Everetts ES   27825 – Joseph Smith, prin.

Evergreen, Columbus Co.
Columbus County SD
Supt. – See Whiteville
ES, RURAL ROUTE 01 BOX 48   28438
  Donald Leggett, prin.

Fair Bluff, Columbus Co., Pop. Code 4
Columbus County SD
Supt. – See Whiteville
ES   28439 – Jimmy Turbeville, prin.

Fairmont, Robeson Co., Pop. Code 5
Robeson County SD
Supt. – See Lumberton
Fairgrove MS, RURAL ROUTE 01   28340
  Larece Hunt, prin.

Green Grove PS, RURAL ROUTE 01   28340
  Barry Harding, prin.

Fairview, Buncombe Co.
Buncombe County SD
Supt. – See Asheville
ES, P O BOX 160   28730 – Patricia Gowan, prin.

Faison, Duplin Co., Pop. Code 3
Sampson County SD
Supt. – See Clinton
Hargrove ES, RURAL ROUTE 02   28341
  John Allen, prin.

Faith, Rowan Co., Pop. Code 3
Rowan County SD
Supt. – See Salisbury
ES, P O BOX 161   28041 – Bobby Shive, prin.

Fallston, Cleveland Co., Pop. Code 3
Cleveland County SD
Supt. – See Shelby
ES, P O BOX 39   28042 – Mac Lancaster, prin.

Farmville, Pitt Co., Pop. Code 5
Pitt County SD
Supt. – See Greenville
MS, P O BOX 50   27828 – Richard Cutler, prin.
Bundy ES, P O BOX 1129   27828
  Edith Warren, prin.
Sugg ES, 807 S GEORGE ST   27828
  Tony Cates, prin.

Fayetteville, Cumberland Co., Pop. Code 8
Cumberland County SD
Sch. Sys. Enr. Code 8
Supt. – Dr. J. Britt, P O BOX 2357   28302
Ashley MS, 1301 ROBESON ST   28305
  Marie Parker, prin.
Auman ES, RURAL ROUTE 19 BOX 446   28304
  Daniel Goldner, prin.
Berrien ES, NORTH ST   28301
  Thurman Andrews, prin.
Brentwood ES, 1115 BINGHAM DR   28304
  Paris Jones, prin.
Cashwell ES, 2876 LEGION RD   28306
  M. Pierce, prin.
Cliffdale ES, 6450 CLIFFDALE RD   28314
  L Deaton Jr, prin.
College Lakes Elem School
  4963 ROSEHILL RD   28311 – O. Spivey,Jr., prin.
Coon ES, 913 HOPE MILLS RD   28304
  William Monroe, prin.
Cumberland Mills ES
  2576 HOPE MILLS RD   28306
  Sarah Washington, prin.
Cumberland Road ES
  2700 CUMBERLAND RD   28306
  Patrick Marks, prin.
Easom ES, 1610 WESTLAWN AVE   28305
  Miriam Smith, prin.
Eastover/Central ES
  RURAL ROUTE 01 BOX 346   28301 – J. Ray, prin.
Edgewood ES, 2517 RAMSEY ST   28301
  Dale Tompkins, prin.
Ferguson-Easley ES, SEABROOK ROAD   28301
  J. Purcell, prin.
Glendale Acres ES, 2915 SKYCREST DR   28304
  Betty Moses, prin.
Hall ES, 526 ANDREWS RD   28311
  Mack Virgil, prin.
Howard ES, 1608 CAMDEN RD   28306
  Vivian Woodall, prin.
Jones MS, B ST   28301 – Lisa Carter, prin.
Long Hill ES, 6456 RAMSEY ST   28311
  Lonnie McAllister, prin.
Martin ES, 240 N REILLY RD   28303
  Alice Smith, prin.
McArthur ES, 3809 VILLAGE DR   28304
  Joe Dunham, prin.
Montclair ES, 555 GLENSFORD DR   28314
  Paul Bass, prin.
Morganton Road ES, 102 BONANZA DR   28303
  Robert Riner, prin.
Owen ES, 4533 RAEFORD RD   28304
  Janet Mullen, prin.
Ponderosa ES, 311 BONANZA DR   28303
  K. Fipps, prin.
Seabrook ES, RURAL ROUTE 02 BOX 391   28301
  William Alphin, prin.
Seventy-First ES
  RURAL ROUTE 19 BOX 444   28304
  Robert Modlin, prin.
Sherwood Park ES, 2115 HOPE MILLS RD   28304
  Kenneth Edge, prin.
Souders ES, HILLVIEW AVE   28301
  Nelson Hendon, prin.
Sunnyside ES, RURAL ROUTE 02   28301
  Betty Smith, prin.
Vanstory Hills MS, 400 FOXHALL RD   28303
  Donald Dixon, prin.
Warrenwood ES, 4618 ROSEHILL RD   28311
  Donald Dawson, prin.
Westarea ES, 941 COUNTRY CLUB DR   28301
  Gwendolyn Edwards, prin.
Wilkins ES, 209 SKIBO RD   28303
  Billy Nobles, prin.
Willis ES, 1412 BELVEDERE AVE   28305
  Gary Hardin, prin.
Other Schools – See Hope Mills, Roseboro, Spring
  Lake, Stedman, Wade

———————————

Fayetteville Academy
  3200 CLIFFDALE ROAD   28303
St. Ann ES, 365 N COOL SPRING ST   28301

St. Patrick School
  1620 MARLBOROUGH RD   28304

Ferguson, Wilkes Co.
Wilkes County SD
Supt. – See Wilkesboro
Mt. Pleasant ES
  RURAL ROUTE 01 BOX 307   28624
  Robert Hartzog, prin.

Fleetwood, Ashe Co.
Ashe County SD
Supt. – See Jefferson
ES   28626 – Don Church, prin.

Fletcher, Henderson Co., Pop. Code 3
Henderson County SD
Supt. – See Hendersonville
ES, P O BOX 218   28732 – Michael Pressley, prin.

Forest City, Rutherford Co., Pop. Code 6
Rutherford County SD
Supt. – See Spindale
Cool Springs MS   28043 – Phillip Cook, prin.
Alexander ES, ALEXANDER STATION   28043
  Roger McCluney, prin.
Dunbar MS, 801 HARDIN RD   28043 – J. Neal, prin.
ES, OLD CAROLEEN ROAD   28043
  Robert Gammon, prin.
Harris ES, RURAL ROUTE 03 BOX 433   28043
  Bobby Tate, prin.
Mt. Vernon ES, RURAL ROUTE 02   28043
  Frank Wall, prin.
Shiloh ES, RURAL ROUTE 03   28043
  Phillip Miller, prin.

Fort Bragg, Cumberland Co.
Fort Bragg SD
Sch. Sys. Enr. Code 5
Supt. – Joseph Brust   28307
Albritton ES, P O BOX 70089   28307
  R. Ensley, prin.
Irwin MS, P O BOX 70089   28307
  Morris Hayes, prin.
Bowley ES, P O BOX 70089   28307
  Edgar Moneyhan, prin.
Butner ES, P O BOX 70089   28307 – (—), prin.
Holbrook ES, P O BOX 70089   28307
  Marian Carver, prin.
McNair ES, P O BOX 70089   28307
  Alexandra Haar, prin.
Murray ES, P O BOX 70089   28307
  Janey Idell, prin.
Pope ES, P O BOX 70089   28307
  Ronald Hicks, prin.

Four Oaks, Johnston Co., Pop. Code 4
Johnston County SD
Supt. – See Smithfield
ES, P O BOX 189   27524 – John Floyd, prin.

Franklin, Macon Co., Pop. Code 5
Macon County SD
Sch. Sys. Enr. Code 5
Supt. – Lonnie Crawford
  RURAL ROUTE 01   28734
Macon MS, RURAL ROUTE 09 BOX 1130   28734
  C. Sanders, prin.
Cartoogechaye ES, 420 HAYESVILLE HWY   28734
  Merritt Fouts, prin.
Cowee MS, 6 BRYSON BRANCH ROAD   28734
  William Dyar, prin.
Cullasaja ES, 17 RIVER RD   28734
  Claude Rogers,Jr., prin.
East Franklin ES, 37 WATAUGA ST   28734
  George Pattillo, prin.
Iotla ES, 136 IOTLA CHURCH RD   28734
  James Raby, prin.
Union ES, 66 CHEEK RD   28734 – Terry Bell, prin.
Other Schools – See Highlands, Otto, Topton

Franklinton, Franklin Co., Pop. Code 4
Franklinton CSD
Sch. Sys. Enr. Code 4
Supt. – Dr. Mel Sechrest, P O BOX 430   27525
ES, P O BOX 429   27525 – Denise Rhodes, prin.

Granville County SD
Supt. – See Oxford
Wilton ES, RURAL ROUTE 01 BOX 215   27525
  Jannie Preddy, prin.

Franklinville, Randolph Co., Pop. Code 3
Randolph County SD
Supt. – See Asheboro
ES, P O BOX 258   27248 – Emma Routh, prin.
Grays Chapel ES
  RURAL ROUTE 01 BOX 311   27248
  Gary Davis, prin.

Fremont, Wayne Co., Pop. Code 4
Wayne County SD
Supt. – See Goldsboro
ES, P O BOX 428   27830 – Shirley Bond, prin.

Fuquay-Varina, Wake Co., Pop. Code 5
Wake County SD
Supt. – See Raleigh
Fuquay MS, WOODROW ST   27526
  Carroll Reed, prin.
Fuquay ES, 6600 JOHNSON POND RD   27526
  D. Cotten, prin.
Lincoln Heights ES, 307 BRIDGE ST   27526
  Teresa Abron, prin.

Garland, Sampson Co., Pop. Code 3
Sampson County SD
Supt. – See Clinton

Clear Run MS, RURAL ROUTE 01 28441
   Tom Daughtry, prin.
ES 28441 – Gerald Johnson, prin.

Garner, Wake Co., Pop. Code 6
Wake County SD
Supt. – See Raleigh
Aversboro ES, 1605 AVERSBORO RD 27529
   Dr. B. Partin, prin.
East Garner MS, 100 W GARNER ROAD 27529
   R. Cobb, Jr., prin.
ES, 712 OLD GARNER ROAD 27529
   Joann O'Connell, prin.
Vandora Springs ES
   1300 VANDORA SPRINGS RD 27529
   Eddie Clinton, prin.

Garysburg, Northampton Co., Pop. Code 4
Northampton County SD
Supt. – See Jackson
ES, HWY 48 BOX 266 27831
   Lucy Edwards, prin.

Gaston, Northampton Co., Pop. Code 3
Northampton County SD
Supt. – See Jackson
JHS, P O BOX 258 27832 – John Pellam, prin.
Squire ES, HWY 48 BOX 217 27832
   Jasper Jones, prin.

Gastonia, Gaston Co., Pop. Code 8
Gaston County SD
Sch. Sys. Enr. Code 8
Supt. – George McSwain, P O BOX 1397 28053
Arlington ES, 1519 N WEBB ST 28052
   Dr. P. Sudderth, prin.
Bess ES, RURAL ROUTE 04 BOX 28-A 28054
   Frank Zinke, prin.
Chapel Grove ES, RURAL ROUTE 01 28052
   Jack Kimbro, prin.
Forest Heights ES, 2500 SEDGEFIELD DR 28052
   Robert Noblett, prin.
Gardner Park ES, 820 SHADY LN 28054
   Jacob Hord, Jr., prin.
Gastonia Central ES, EAST SECOND AVE 28052
   George Jaggers, prin.
Hancock ES, 905 N NEW HOPE RD 28054
   Bobby Guthrie, prin.
Lingerfeldt ES, CAROLINA AND MADISON 28052
   Dr. W. Little, prin.
New Hope ES, RURAL ROUTE 03 28054
   Kenneth White, prin.
Pleasant Ridge ES, 937 S MILLER ST 28052
   Ronald Withers, prin.
Rhyne ES, 1900 W DAVIDSON AVE 28052
   Eugene Hanna, prin.
Robinson ES, 3122 S UNION RD 28054
   Elmyra Jenkins, prin.
Sherwood ES, 1744 DIXIE ROAD 28054
   Leonard Earle, prin.
South Gastonia ES, 3005 S YORK RD 28052
   Jacob Schrum, prin.
Warlick ES, 1316 SPENCER MTN RD 28054
   John Senter, prin.
Woodhill ES, 1027 WOODHILL DR 28054
   T. Rowland, prin.
Other Schools – See Belmont, Bessemer City,
   Cherryville, Dallas, High Shoals, Lowell, Mc
   Adenville, Mount Holly, Stanley

Gaston Day School, 2001 AIRPORT ROAD 28054
St. Michael's ES, 704 ST MICHAELS LN 28052

Gates, Gates Co.
Gates County SD
Supt. – See Gatesville
Buckland ES, P O BOX 68 27937
   C. Don Gregory, prin.

Gatesville, Gates Co., Pop. Code 2
Gates County SD
Sch. Sys. Enr. Code 4
Supt. – John Perry, P O BOX 125 27938
MS, P O BOX 187 27938 – John Lane, Jr., prin.
Other Schools – See Gates, Sunbury

Germantown, Stokes Co.
Stokes County SD
Supt. – See Danbury
ES, RURAL ROUTE 01 BOX 1-A 27019
   A. Lovette, prin.

Gibson, Scotland Co., Pop. Code 3
Scotland County SD
Supt. – See Laurinburg
Gardner ES, P O BOX 337 28343
   Anthony Sassean, prin.

Gibsonville, Guilford Co., Pop. Code 4
Guilford County SD
Supt. – See Greensboro
ES, 500 CHURCH ST 27249 – Douglas Mabe, prin.

Glen Alpine, Burke Co., Pop. Code 3
Burke County SD
Supt. – See Morganton
ES, P O BOX 816 28628 – James Gordon, prin.

Glenville, Jackson Co., Pop. Code 2
Jackson County SD
Supt. – See Sylva
Blue Ridge S 28736 – Fred Harris, prin.

Glenwood, Mc Dowell Co.
McDowell County SD
Supt. – See Marion
ES 28737 – Larry Wilkerson, prin.

Gold Hill, Rowan Co.
Rowan County SD
Supt. – See Salisbury
Morgan ES, RURAL ROUTE 01 BOX 524 28071
   E. Taylor, prin.

Goldsboro, Wayne Co., Pop. Code 8
Goldsboro CSD
Sch. Sys. Enr. Code 5
Supt. – Kenneth Brinson, P O BOX 1757 27533
JHS, 801 LIONEL ST 27530 – Gerald Whitley, prin.
Carver Heights ES, 411 BUNCHE DR 27530
   William Charlton, prin.
Dillard MS, 1101 DEVEREAUX ST 27530
   M. Watson, prin.
North Drive ES, 1108 NORTH DR 27530
   James Gainey, prin.
School Street ES, 415 S VIRGINIA ST 27530
   Harvey Davis, Jr., prin.

Wayne County SD
Sch. Sys. Enr. Code 7
Supt. – Dr. Howard Sosne, 301 HERMAN N 27530
Belfast ES, RURAL ROUTE 07 BOX 308 27530
   Annie Edwards, prin.
Eastern Wayne ES
   RURAL ROUTE 10 BOX 108 27530
   David Rogers, prin.
Grantham ES, RURAL ROUTE 01 BOX 221 27530
   Melisia Gainey, prin.
Meadow Lane ES, 3500 E ASH ST 27530
   J. Turnage, prin.
Rosewood ES, RURAL ROUTE 05 27530
   William Turner, prin.
Other Schools – See Dudley, Eureka, Fremont, Mount
   Olive, Pikeville, Seven Springs

St. Mary's ES, 1110 EDGERTON ST 27530

Goldston, Chatham Co.
Chatham County SD
Supt. – See Pittsboro
Waters ES 27252 – Joe Jones, prin.

Graham, Alamance Co., Pop. Code 6
Alamance County SD
Sch. Sys. Enr. Code 7
Supt. – Robert Stockard, 609 RAY ST 27253
MS, 311 E PINE ST 27253 – Sam Fowler, prin.
Southern MS, RURAL ROUTE 04 BOX 660 27253
   G. Briggs, prin.
Jordan ES, RURAL ROUTE 02 BOX 439 27253
   Ted Bowen, prin.
North Graham ES, 1025 TROLLINGER RD 27253
   Dr. Buford Frye, prin.
South Graham ES, 320 IVEY ST 27253
   George Nall, prin.
Wilson ES, RURAL ROUTE 03 BOX 564 27253
   Carol Younger, prin.
Other Schools – See Burlington, Elon College, Haw
   River, Mebane, Snow Camp

Granite Falls, Caldwell Co., Pop. Code 5
Caldwell County SD
Supt. – See Lenoir
Baton ES, RURAL ROUTE 02 BOX 414 28630
   J. Watson, prin.
Dudley Shoals ES
   RURAL ROUTE 01 BOX 213 28630
   Renae Clark, prin.
ES, 60 N HIGHLAND AVE 28630
   Glenn Seabock, prin.
Saw Mills ES, RURAL ROUTE 04 BOX 301 28630
   Jim Caldwell, prin.

Granite Quarry, Rowan Co., Pop. Code 3
Rowan County SD
Supt. – See Salisbury
ES, P O BOX 279 28072 – Ralph Walton, prin.

Greenmountain, Yancey Co.
Mitchell County SD
Supt. – See Bakersville
Tipton Hill ES, RURAL ROUTE 01 28740
   Dean Myers, prin.

Yancy County SD
Supt. – See Burnsville
Clearmont ES, RURAL ROUTE 01 28740
   Blaine Whitson, prin.

Greensboro, Guilford Co., Pop. Code 9
Greensboro CSD
Sch. Sys. Enr. Code 7
Supt. – Dr. John Eberhart, P O BOX V 27402
Allen JHS, 1108 GLENDALE DRIVE 27406
   Harold Estep, prin.
Aycock ES, 811 CYPRESS ST 27405
   Ann Riffey, prin.
Jackson MS, 2200 ONTARIO ST 27403
   Jerry Hairston, prin.
Kiser MS, 718 BENJAMIN PARKWAY 27408
   Barry Williams, prin.
Lincoln MS, 1016 LINCOLN ST 27401
   G. Spencer Gwynn, prin.
Mendenhall MS, 205 WILLOUGHBY BLVD 27408
   Charles Wallace, prin.
Alderman ES, 4211 CHATEAU DR 27407
   Julia Banks, prin.
Archer ES, 2610 FOUR SEASONS BLVD 27407
   Samuel Cain, prin.
Bessemer ES, 918 HUFFINE MILL RD 27405
   Patricia Spicer, prin.
Bluford MS, 1901 TUSCALOOSA ST 27401
   Dr. Sandra Watkins, prin.

Claxton ES, 3720 PINETOP RD 27410
   Robert Strong, prin.
Cone ES, 2501 N CHURCH ST 27405
   Jane Andrews, prin.
Erwin Open MS, 3012 E BESSEMER AVE 27405
   Dan Jones, prin.
Foust ES, 2610 FLOYD ST 27406
   June Sofley, prin.
Frazier ES, 4215 GALWAY DR 27406
   David Johnson, Jr., prin.
Greene MS, 1501 BENJAMIN PKY 27408
   Charles Benton, prin.
Hampton ES, 2301 TRADE ST 27401
   Dr. Nancy Routh, prin.
Hunter MS, 1305 MERRITT DR 27407
   Lenwood Edwards, prin.
Irving Park ES, 1310 SUNSET DR 27408
   Alex Purcell, prin.
Jones ES, 502 SOUTH ST 27406
   Gertrude Morrow, prin.
Joyner ES, 3300 NORMANDY RD 27408
   Edward Allred, prin.
Lindley MS, 2700 CAMDEN RD 27403
   Shirley Morrison, prin.
Morehead MS, 4630 TOWER RD 27410
   Phillip Mobley, prin.
Murphey Traditional MS
   2306 ONTARIO ST 27403 – (—), prin.
Peck ES, 1601 W FLORIDA ST 27403
   Dan Cornelius, prin.
Peeler Open ES, 2200 RANDALL ST 27401
   Martha Hudson, prin.
Sternberger ES, 518 N HOLDEN RD 27410
   Peggy Branch, prin.
Vandalia ES, 407 W VANDALIA RD 27406
   Charles Monroe, prin.
Washington ES, 1110 E WASHINGTON ST 27401
   David Huneycutt, prin.
Wiley Traditional ES, 600 W TERRELL ST 27406
   Alma Stokes, prin.

Guilford County SD
Sch. Sys. Enr. Code 7
Supt. – Dr. Jerome Melton, P O BOX B-2 27402
Guilford MS, 401 COLLEGE RD 27410
   Oakley Mabe, prin.
Northwest Guilford MS
   5300 NW SCHOOL ROAD 27409
   Robert Boles, prin.
Southeast Guilford MS
   4825 WOODY MILL ROAD 27406
   Larry Dunn, prin.
Alamance ES, 3500 SE SCHOOL RD 27406
   Morris Blair, prin.
Brightwood ES, 2500 LEES CHAP ROAD 27405
   Roland Andrews, prin.
Guilford PS, 411 FRIENDWAY RD 27410
   Dr. D. Henderson, prin.
Rankin ES, 3301 SUMMIT AVE 27405
   Dorothy Richmond, prin.
Sedgefield ES, 2905 GROOMETOWN RD 27407
   Dr. Fred Wood, prin.
Southern ES, 5720 DRAKE RD 27406
   Mary Martin, prin.
Sumner ES, 1915 HARRIS DR 27406
   Luther Smith, prin.
Wharton ES, 116 PISGAH CHURCH RD 27405
   Dennis Kendrick, prin.
Other Schools – See Browns Summit, Colfax,
   Gibsonville, High Point, Jamestown, Liberty, Mc
   Leansville, Oak Ridge, Pleasant Garden, Sedalia,
   Stokesdale, Summerfield

Greensboro Day School, P O BOX 9361 27429
New Garden Friends School
   1128 NEW GARDEN ROAD 27410
Vandalia Christian School
   3919 PLEASANT GARDEN ROAD 27406
East Market Junior Academy
   1802 E MARKET ST 27401
Greensboro Montessori ES
   4915 GUILFORD SCHOOL RD 27410
Our Lady of Grace ES, 2205 W MARKET ST 27403
St. Pius X ES, 2200 N ELM ST 27408

Greenville, Pitt Co., Pop. Code 8
Pitt County SD
Sch. Sys. Enr. Code 7
Supt. – Edwin West, Jr., 1717 W 5TH ST 27834
Wellcome MS, RURAL ROUTE 06 BOX 76 27834
   C. Tadlock, prin.
Belvoir ES, RURAL ROUTE 04 BOX 43 27834
   Bruce Gray, prin.
Chicod ES, RURAL ROUTE 02 BOX 378 27858
   Charles Johnson, prin.
Eastern ES, CEDAR LANE 27834
   Glenn Strickland, prin.
Elmhurst ES, WEST BERKLEY ROAD 27834
   Stella Chambliss, prin.
Falkland ES, RURAL ROUTE 04 BOX 240 27834
   Shirley Carraway, prin.
Greenville MS, 600 W ARLINGTON BLVD 27834
   John Carstarphen, prin.
Pactolus ES, RURAL ROUTE 05 BOX 337 27834
   Selma Cherry, prin.
Saulter ES, FLEMING ST 27834
   Esther Warren, prin.
South Greenville ES, 800 HOWELL ST 27834
   Rebecca Oats, prin.
Third Street ES, WEST THIRD ST 27834
   Carolyn Ferebee, prin.
Wahl-Coates MS, EAST FIFTH ST 27834
   Judy Budacz, prin.

Wintergreen ES
 RURAL ROUTE 13 BOX 173 27858
 Clarence Gray, prin.
Other Schools – See Ayden, Bethel, Farmville,
 Grifton, Grimesland, Stokes, Winterville

Greenville Christian Academy
 2001 GREENVILLE BLVD SW 27834
St. Gabriel ES, 1100 WARD ST 27834
St. Peter ES, 2606 E 5TH ST 27858

Grifton, Lenoir Co., Pop. Code 4
Lenoir County SD
Supt. – See Kinston
Savannah MS, RURAL ROUTE 02 28530
 Levin Jones, prin.

Pitt County SD
Supt. – See Greenville
ES, P O BOX 158 28530 – Randy Collier, prin.

Grimesland, Pitt Co., Pop. Code 2
Pitt County SD
Supt. – See Greenville
Whitfield ES, P O BOX 129 27837
 Beth Ward, prin.

Grover, Cleveland Co., Pop. Code 3
King's Mountain CSD
Supt. – See Kings Mountain
ES, P O BOX 135 28073 – J. Scruggs, prin.

Halifax, Halifax Co., Pop. Code 2
Halifax County SD
Sch. Sys. Enr. Code 6
Supt. – Kenneth Brantley, P O BOX 468 27839
Other Schools – See Enfield, Hobgood, Hollister,
 Littleton, Roanoke Rapids, Scotland Neck

Weldon CSD
Supt. – See Weldon
Jackson ES, P O BOX 100 27839
 Robert Knight, prin.

Hallsboro, Columbus Co., Pop. Code 2
Columbus County SD
Supt. – See Whiteville
ES 28442 – Melvin Powell, prin.

Hamilton, Martin Co., Pop. Code 3
Martin County SD
Supt. – See Williamston
Andrews ES 27840 – Phillip Griffin, prin.

Hamlet, Richmond Co., Pop. Code 5
Richmond County SD
Sch. Sys. Enr. Code 6
Supt. – M. James, P O BOX 1259 28345
Fairview Heights ES, 104 HAMILTON ST 28345
 Earl Yates, prin.
Monroe Avenue MS, 400 MONROE AVE 28345
 Edward Ellis, prin.
Other Schools – See Cordova, Ellerbe, Hoffman,
 Rockingham

Hampstead, Pender Co., Pop. Code 2
Pender County SD
Supt. – See Burgaw
Topsail MS, P O BOX 279 28443
 E. Highsmith, prin.
Topsail PS, P O BOX 98 28443
 Mary Jordan, prin.

Hamptonville, Yadkin Co.
Yadkin County SD
Supt. – See Yadkinville
West Yadkin ES, RURAL ROUTE 03 BOX A 27020
 Jack Williams, prin.

Harkers Island, Carteret Co.
Carteret County SD
Supt. – See Beaufort
ES 28531 – William Blair, prin.

Harmony, Iredell Co., Pop. Code 2
Iredell County SD
Supt. – See Statesville
ES, RURAL ROUTE 02 28634 – D. Redmond, prin.

Harrells, Sampson Co.
Sampson County SD
Supt. – See Clinton
Bland ES 28444 – Ledell McIntyre, prin.

Harrells Christian Academy, P O BOX 88 28444

Harrisburg, Cabarrus Co., Pop. Code 4
Cabarrus County SD
Supt. – See Concord
ES, HWY 49 28075 – Richard Shaw, prin.

Havelock, Craven Co., Pop. Code 7
Craven County SD
Supt. – See New Bern
MS, 102 HIGH SCHOOL DRIVE 28532
 Alvin West, prin.
Barden ES, 200 CEDAR DR 28532
 Beatrice Smith, prin.
Bell ES, 500 HIGHWAY 101 28532
 E. Ricks, prin.
ES, 201 CUNNINGHAM BLVD 28532
 Pat Williams, prin.
West Havelock ES, P O BOX 189 28532
 Jerry Strickland, prin.

Annunciation ES, 246 E MAIN ST 28532

Haw River, Alamance Co., Pop. Code 4
Alamance County SD
Supt. – See Graham
ES, RURAL ROUTE 01 BOX 1 27258
 Dr. Lewis Franklin, prin.

Hayesville, Clay Co., Pop. Code 2
Clay County SD
Sch. Sys. Enr. Code 4
Supt. – Douglas Penland, P O BOX 178 28904
ES, P O BOX 487 28904 – Ernest Jones, prin.

Hays, Wilkes Co., Pop. Code 3
Wilkes County SD
Supt. – See Wilkesboro
Mountain View ES, RURAL ROUTE 01 28635
 Lewis Mitchell, prin.

Hazelwood, Haywood Co., Pop. Code 4
Haywood County SD
Supt. – See Waynesville
ES, 216 VIRGINIA AVE 28738
 Larry Leatherwood, prin.

Henderson, Vance Co., Pop. Code 7
Franklin County SD
Supt. – See Louisburg
Epsom ES, RURAL ROUTE 01 27536
 Monty Riggs, prin.

Vance County SD
Sch. Sys. Enr. Code 6
Supt. – Dr. Howard Maniloff
 128 CHURCH ST 27536
Eaton-Johnson MS, ROCK SPRING ST 27536
 Beverly Smith, prin.
Aycock ES, RURAL ROUTE 02 27536
 George Fowler, prin.
Carver ES, RURAL ROUTE 06 27536
 Michael Kita, prin.
Clarke Street ES, CLARK ST 27536
 Lynn Henderson, prin.
Dabney ES, RURAL ROUTE 08 27536
 Ronald Kinsley, prin.
New Hope ES, RURAL ROUTE 05 27536
 Carolyn Henry, prin.
Pinkston ES, ADAMS ST 27536
 Gladys Darensburg, prin.
Rollins ES, GARNETT ST EXT 27536
 Jerry Hoyle, prin.
Yancey ES, HAWKINS DR 27536
 Ronald Gregory, prin.
Other Schools – See Kittrell, Middleburg

Vance Academy
 RURAL ROUTE 04 BOX 213 27536

Hendersonville, Henderson Co., Pop. Code 6
Henderson County SD
Sch. Sys. Enr. Code 6
Supt. – Glen Marlow, 125 E ALLEN ST 28739
Atkinson ES, 2510 OLD KANUGA RD 28739
 T. Reed, prin.
Balfour ES, 2529 ASHEVILLE HWY 28739
 C. Smith,Jr., prin.
Edneyville ES, RURAL ROUTE 09 BOX 448 28739
 Swan Babb, prin.
Other Schools – See Dana, East Flat Rock, Etowah,
 Fletcher, Horse Shoe, Tuxedo

Hendersonville CSD
Sch. Sys. Enr. Code 4
Supt. – Charles Byrd, P O BOX 340 28793
JHS, 930 9TH AVE W 28739
 W. Keith Dalbec, prin.
Drysdale ES, NORTH MAIN ST 28739
 J. Ramsey, prin.
MS, 1039 RANDALL CIR 28739
 Thomas Williams, prin.

Immaculate ES, 711 BUNCOMBE ST 28739

Henrietta, Rutherford Co.
Rutherford County SD
Supt. – See Spindale
Tri-Community MS, P O BOX 649 28076
 James Beam, prin.
Proctor ES, P O BOX 337 28076
 Doris Francis, prin.

Hertford, Perquimans Co., Pop. Code 4
Perquimans County SD
Sch. Sys. Enr. Code 4
Supt. – Mary Jo Martin, P O BOX 337 27944
ES, P O BOX 397 27944 – William Tice, prin.
Other Schools – See Winfall

Hickory, Catawba Co., Pop. Code 7
Catawba County SD
Supt. – See Newton
Arndt MS, RURAL ROUTE 02 BOX 145 28601
 Kenneth Throneburg, prin.
Campbell ES, RURAL ROUTE 06 BOX 920 28601
 Elsie Combs, prin.
Mountain View ES
 RURAL ROUTE 12 BOX 467 28602
 Shirley Cunningham, prin.
Murray ES, RURAL ROUTE 11 BOX 91 28601
 Michael Barnett, prin.
St. Stephens ES, RURAL ROUTE 09 BOX 2 28601
 Frank Ridley, prin.
Sweetwater ES, 2110 MAIN AVE SE 28602
 Charles Lewis, prin.

Hickory CSD
Sch. Sys. Enr. Code 5
Supt. – Dr. Stuart Thompson
 432 4TH AVE SW 28601
College Park MS, 409 8TH AVE NE 28601
 Clinton Sigmon, prin.
Grandview MS, 737 12TH ST SW 28601
 Tanya Honeycutt, prin.
Jenkins ES, RURAL ROUTE 10 BOX 30 28601
 Beverly White, prin.
Longview ES, 2430 2ND AVE SW 28602
 Susan Arrowood, prin.
Oakwood ES, 366 4TH ST NW 28601
 Peggy Besse, prin.
Southwest ES, 1580 32ND ST SW 28602
 Dale Abernethy, prin.
Viewmont ES, 21 16TH AVE NW 28601
 James Killian, prin.

St. Stephen Lutheran ES, 2304 SPRINGS RD 28601

Hiddenite, Alexander Co., Pop. Code 3
Alexander County SD
Supt. – See Taylorsville
ES, RURAL ROUTE 01 BOX 350 28636
 (—), prin.

Highfalls, Moore Co.
Moore County SD
Supt. – See Carthage
ES, P O BOX 206 27259
 Raymond Vaughn,Jr., prin.

Highlands, Macon Co., Pop. Code 3
Macon County SD
Supt. – See Franklin
S, P O BOX 940 28741 – W. Brooks, prin.

High Point, Guilford Co., Pop. Code 8
Guilford County SD
Supt. – See Greensboro
Jay MS, 1201 FAIRFIELD ROAD 27263
 James Turner, prin.
Florence ES, 7605 FLORENCE SCHOOL DR 27260
 Thomas Stutts, prin.
Jay ES, 1311 SPRIGFIELD ROAD 27263
 Larry Wilson, prin.
Southwest ES, 4372 BARROW RD 27260
 James Battle, prin.
Union Hill ES, 3523 TRI LAKE ROAD 27260
 Pearl Hicks, prin.

High Point CSD
Sch. Sys. Enr. Code 6
Supt. – Dr. C. Owen Phillips, P O BOX 789 27261
Ferndale MS, 701 FERNDALE BLVD 27260
 William Shelton, prin.
Griffin MS, E WASHINGTON DRIVE 27260
 Ronald Krall, prin.
Northeast MS, 1710 MCGUINN ST 27260
 Gilda Scott, prin.
Fairview ES, 608 FAIRVIEW ST 27260
 John Schroeder, prin.
Johnson ES, 1601 JOHNSON ST 27262
 Jacqueline Garner, prin.
Kirkman Park ES, 715 E FARRISS AVE 27262
 Ina Hines, prin.
Montlieu Avenue ES
 1105 MONTLIEU AVE 27262 – Doris Davis, prin.
Northwood ES, 818 W LEXINGTON AVE 27260
 Michael Seamon, prin.
Oak Hill ES, 320 WRIGHTENBERRY ST 27260
 Jean Owen, prin.
Oak View ES, 614 OAK VIEW ROAD 27260
 Roland Hanes, prin.
Parkview Village ES, 506 HENRY PL 27260
 (—), prin.
Shadybrook ES, 503 SHADYBROOK DR 27260
 Betty Royal, prin.

Randolph County SD
Supt. – See Asheboro
Archdale ES, 207 TRINDALE RD 27263
 Celeste Smith, prin.
Trindale ES, 400 BALFOUR DR 27263
 John Waller, prin.

Wesleyan Academy
 1917 N CENTENNIAL ST 27260
Westchester Academy
 204 PINE TREE LANE 27260
Immaculate Heart of Mary ES
 605 BARBEE ST 27262

High Shoals, Gaston Co., Pop. Code 3
Gaston County SD
Supt. – See Gastonia
ES, P O BOX 9 28077 – Yates Maxwell, prin.

Hildebran, Burke Co., Pop. Code 3
Burke County SD
Supt. – See Morganton
ES, P O BOX 451 28637 – Ernest Stone, prin.

Hillsborough, Orange Co., Pop. Code 5
Orange County SD
Sch. Sys. Enr. Code 6
Supt. – Dan Lunsford, 200 E KING ST 27278
Stanford JHS, RURAL ROUTE 04 27278
 Alonzo McCullers, prin.
Brown ES, RURAL ROUTE 06 BOX 1005 27278
 William McCormick, prin.
Cameron Park ES, 240 E KING ST 27278
 Lindsay Tapp, prin.
Central ES, 154 HAYES ST 27278
 Wiley Shearin, prin.

Stanback MS, 402 N NASH ST   27278
Alton Creek, prin.
Other Schools – See Efland

Hobgood, Halifax Co., Pop. Code 2
Halifax County SD
Supt. – See Halifax
Shields ES, RURAL ROUTE 01 BOX 4   27843
John Hardy, prin.

Hobgood Academy, P O BOX 307   27843

Hoffman, Richmond Co., Pop. Code 2
Richmond County SD
Supt. – See Hamlet
ES   28347 – Derenda Garris, prin.

Hollister, Halifax Co.
Halifax County SD
Supt. – See Halifax
ES, RURAL ROUTE 01 BOX 59   27844
James Felton, prin.

Holly Ridge, Onslow Co., Pop. Code 2
Onslow County SD
Supt. – See Jacksonville
Dixon ES, RURAL ROUTE 01 BOX 321   28445
A. Everett, prin.

Hookerton, Greene Co., Pop. Code 2
Greene County SD
Supt. – See Snow Hill
East Greene MS, RURAL ROUTE 01   28538
Gail Edmondson, prin.

Hope Mills, Cumberland Co., Pop. Code 6
Cumberland County SD
Supt. – See Fayetteville
Collier ES, 3522 STURBRIDGE DR   28348
J. Twiddy, prin.
Grays Creek ES
RURAL ROUTE 01 BOX 272   28348
Elizabeth Lee, prin.
Legion Road ES, 3477 LEGION RD   28348
Ed Baldwin,Jr., prin.
Rockfish ES, P O BOX 426   28348
Jack McGinley, prin.

Horse Shoe, Henderson Co.
Henderson County SD
Supt. – See Hendersonville
Mills River ES, 96 SCHOOLHOUSE RD   28742
James Case, prin.

Hot Springs, Madison Co., Pop. Code 3
Madison County SD
Supt. – See Marshall
ES, P O BOX 247   28743 – John Wallin,Jr., prin.
Spring Creek ES, RURAL ROUTE 01   28743
Theresa Banks, prin.

Hudson, Caldwell Co., Pop. Code 5
Caldwell County SD
Supt. – See Lenoir
ES, 143 CEDAR VALLEY RD   28638
Joel Carroll, prin.

Huntersville, Mecklenburg Co., Pop. Code 4
Mecklenburg County SD
Supt. – See Charlotte
ES, P O BOX 458   28078 – Billy Presson, prin.
Long Creek ES
9213 BEATTIES FORD ROAD   28078
Bettye McCain, prin.

Hurdle Mills, Person Co.
Person County SD
Supt. – See Roxboro
Oak Lane ES, P O BOX 128   27541
Melinda Chambers, prin.

Icard, Burke Co., Pop. Code 7
Burke County SD
Supt. – See Morganton
ES, P O BOX 70   28666 – Robert Hennessee, prin.

Indian Trail, Union Co., Pop. Code 3
Union County SD
Supt. – See Monroe
Hemby Bridge ES, 751 FAIRVIEW RD   28079
(—), prin.
ES, P O BOX 70   28079 – George Miller, prin.

Iron Station, Lincoln Co., Pop. Code 2
Lincoln County SD
Supt. – See Lincolnton
ES, P O BOX 69   28080 – Jerry Payseur, prin.

Jackson, Northampton Co., Pop. Code 3
Northampton County SD
Sch. Sys. Enr. Code 5
Supt. – Dr. Willis McLeod, P O BOX 158   27845
Jackson-Eastside ES, HWY 305 BOX 453   27845
Dr. Carter Cherry, prin.
Other Schools – See Conway, Garysburg, Gaston,
Pendleton, Rich Square, Seaboard, Woodland

Jacksonville, Onslow Co., Pop. Code 7
Onslow County SD
Sch. Sys. Enr. Code 7
Supt. – E. Waters
200 GEORGETOWN ROAD   28540
MS, 401 NEW BRIDGE ST   28540
Edward Herring, prin.
Northwoods Park MS, 904 SIOUX DRIVE   28540
Alex Boyle, prin.
Bell Fork ES, 500 BELL FORK RD   28540
William Kelley, prin.

Blue Creek ES, 400 BURGAW HWY   28540
John Jones, prin.
Erwin ES, 323 NEW RIVER DR   28540
Sarde Howell, prin.
Morton ES, RURAL ROUTE 02   28546
William Batchelor, prin.
Northwoods ES, 617 HENDERSON DR   28540
Kay Glover, prin.
Parkwood ES, 2900 NORTHWOODS DR   28540
J. Holland, prin.
Summersill ES, RURAL ROUTE 05   28546
Doug Nicholson, prin.
Thompson ES, 1 HICKORY ST   28540
G. Williams, prin.
Other Schools – See Holly Ridge, Maysville,
Richlands, Swansboro

St. Francis of Assisi School, 7 EAST DR   28540

Jamestown, Guilford Co., Pop. Code 4
Guilford County SD
Supt. – See Greensboro
MS, RURAL ROUTE 02 BOX 19-B   27282
James Dunn, prin.
ES, 108 POTTER DR   27282 – Judy Stutts, prin.
Millis Road ES, 4310 MILLIS RD   27282
Wanda Szenasy, prin.

Jamesville, Martin Co., Pop. Code 3
Martin County SD
Supt. – See Williamston
S   27846 – Robert Jones, prin.

Jefferson, Ashe Co., Pop. Code 4
Ashe County SD
Sch. Sys. Enr. Code 5
Supt. – Dr. Roger Jackson, P O BOX 604   28640
ES, P O BOX 268   28640 – Gale Hurley, prin.
Other Schools – See Creston, Crumpler, Fleetwood,
Lansing, West Jefferson

Jonesville, Yadkin Co., Pop. Code 4
Yadkin County SD
Supt. – See Yadkinville
ES, 101 CEDARBROOK RD   28642
Joe Dezern, prin.

Kannapolis, Cabarrus Co., Pop. Code 8
Cabarrus County SD
Supt. – See Concord
Royal Oaks ES, 608 DAKOTA ST   28081
Richard Lapish, prin.

Kannapolis CSD
Sch. Sys. Enr. Code 5
Supt. – Dr. Grier Bradshaw, P O BOX 430   28082
MS, 525 E C ST   28081 – M. Taylor, prin.
Aycock ES, 611 S RIDGE AVE   28081
Tom Linn, prin.
Jackson Park ES, 700 RUTH AVE   28081
Doris Buchanan, prin.
Shady Brook ES, 903 ROGERS LAKE RD   28081
Bynum Phillips,Jr., prin.
Wilson ES, 1401 PINE ST EXIT   28081
Hydrick Stone, prin.
Wilson ES, 800 N WALNUT ST   28081
Otis Freeman, prin.

Kenansville, Duplin Co., Pop. Code 3
Duplin County SD
Sch. Sys. Enr. Code 6
Supt. – L. Guy,Jr., P O BOX 128   28349
Smith MS   28349 – Dan Wait, prin.
ES, P O BOX 98   28349 – Wilbur Carr, prin.
Other Schools – See Albertson, Beulaville, Calypso,
Chinquapin, Rose Hill, Wallace, Warsaw

Kenly, Johnston Co., Pop. Code 4
Johnston County SD
Supt. – See Smithfield
North Johnston MS
RURAL ROUTE 04 BOX 139   27542
Ann Parrish, prin.
Glendale-Kenly ES, P O BOX 279   27542
Melvin Woodard, prin.

Kernersville, Forsyth Co., Pop. Code 6
Forsyth County SD
Supt. – See Winston-Salem
Cash ES, 4700 OLD HOLLOW RD   27284
Thomas Webb, prin.
ES, MOUNTAIN ST   27284 – Kay McEntire, prin.
Sedge Garden ES, 475 SEDGE GARDEN RD   27284
J. Johnson, prin.
Union Cross ES, 4300 HIGH POINT RD   27284
P. Hairston, prin.

Kerwin Baptist Christian School
4520 OLD HOLLOW ROAD   27284

King, Stokes Co., Pop. Code 4
Stokes County SD
Supt. – See Danbury
IS, RURAL ROUTE 04   27021
Ronald Carroll, prin.
PS   27021 – Gareath Meadows, prin.

Kings Mountain, Cleveland Co., Pop. Code 6
King's Mountain CSD
Sch. Sys. Enr. Code 5
Supt. – Robert McRae, P O BOX 279   28086
Bethware ES, P O BOX 1487   28086
Hugh Holland, prin.
Central MS, 105 E RIDGE ST   28086
Glenda O'Shields, prin.
East ES, CLEVELAND AVE   28086
Cozell Vance, prin.

North ES, 900 RAMSEUR ST   28086
Joe Hopper, prin.
West ES, 500 W MOUNTAIN ST   28086
Shirley Bynum, prin.
Other Schools – See Grover

Kinston, Lenoir Co., Pop. Code 8
Kinston CSD
Sch. Sys. Enr. Code 6
Supt. – Dr. Duane Moore
307 ATLANTIC AVE   28501
Rochelle MS, 300 N ROCHELLE BLVD   28501
William Heath, prin.
Bynum MS, 100 BYNUM BLVD   28501
Elwood Meadows, prin.
Lewis MS, 501 N INDEPENDENT ST   28501
M. Wetherington, prin.
Northwest ES, OLD WELL ROAD   28501
Leroy Pittman, prin.
Sampson MS, 606 TOWER HILL RD   28501
Grady Bethel, prin.
Southeast MS, MCDANIEL ST   28501
Mildred Bryant, prin.
Teachers Memorial ES, 500 MARCELLA DR   28501
Stephen Scroggs, prin.

Lenoir County SD
Sch. Sys. Enr. Code 6
Supt. – Y. Allen, 201 E KING ST   28501
Woodington MS
RURAL ROUTE 05   BOX 274   28501
Vaughn Fowler, prin.
Banks ES, RURAL ROUTE 02   28501
Danny Price, prin.
Contentnea ES, RURAL ROUTE 01   28501
Deborah King, prin.
Moss Hill ES, RURAL ROUTE 04   28501
William Hill, prin.
Southwood ES, RURAL ROUTE 05   28501
Frank Abbott, prin.
Other Schools – See Grifton, La Grange, Pink Hill

Kipling, Harnett Co.
Harnett County SD
Supt. – See Lillington
Lafayette ES   27543 – Linda Turlington, prin.

Kittrell, Vance Co., Pop. Code 2
Vance County SD
Supt. – See Henderson
Vance ES, RURAL ROUTE 01   27544
John Streb, prin.

Kitty Hawk, Dare Co.
Dare County SD
Supt. – See Manteo
ES   27949 – Everette Walterhouse, prin.

Knightdale, Wake Co., Pop. Code 3
Wake County SD
Supt. – See Raleigh
ES, P O BOX 309   27545 – J. Mallette, prin.
Lockhart MS, P O BOX 189   27545
Mary Wiggs, prin.

Knotts Island, Currituck Co.
Currituck County SD
Supt. – See Currituck
ES   27950 – Frances Etheridge, prin.

La Grange, Lenoir Co., Pop. Code 5
Lenoir County SD
Supt. – See Kinston
Frink MS   28551 – B. Harrison, prin.
ES   28551 – Claude Willie III, prin.

Lake Toxaway, Transylvaina Co.
Transylvania County SD
Supt. – See Brevard
Henderson ES   28747 – Thomas Thomas, prin.

Landis, Rowan Co., Pop. Code 4
Rowan County SD
Supt. – See Salisbury
ES, 801 W RYDER AVE   28088
Christina Hall, prin.

Lansing, Ashe Co., Pop. Code 2
Ashe County SD
Supt. – See Jefferson
ES, P O BOX 98   28643 – Truett Eller, prin.

Lattimore, Cleveland Co., Pop. Code 2
Cleveland County SD
Supt. – See Shelby
ES, P O BOX 158   28089 – Linda Hendrick, prin.

Laurel Hill, Scotland Co.
Scotland County SD
Supt. – See Laurinburg
Carver ES, RURAL ROUTE 02 BOX 7   28351
James Tapp, prin.
PS, P O BOX 187   28351 – E. Blackwelder,Jr., prin.

Laurinburg, Scotland Co., Pop. Code 7
Scotland County SD
Sch. Sys. Enr. Code 6
Supt. – John Jones, 233 E CHURCH ST   28352
Johnson MS, MCGIRTS BRIDGE ROAD   28352
W. Newman, prin.
Shaw MS, RURAL ROUTE 02 BOX 293   28352
W. Thomas, prin.
Sycamore Lane MS
RURAL ROUTE 05   BOX 1   28352
Tommy Clarke, prin.
Central ES, 305 MCRAE ST   28352
Joyce McDow, prin.

Covington Street ES, 615 COVINGTON ST   28352
  L. Layiner, prin.
North Laurinburg ES
  RURAL ROUTE 04 BOX 10   28352
  P. Sullivan, prin.
South Scotland ES
  RURAL ROUTE 03 BOX 182   28352
  J. Massey, prin.
Washington Park ES
  1100 S CALEDONIA RD   28352 – J. Biggs, prin.
Other Schools – See Gibson, Laurel Hill, Wagram

Lawsonville, Stokes Co.
Stokes County SD
  Supt. – See Danbury
  ES, P O BOX 99   27022 – Bobby Martin, prin.

Leicester, Buncombe Co.
Buncombe County SD
  Supt. – See Asheville
  ES, RURAL ROUTE 02   28748
  Swann Payne, prin.

Leland, Brunswick Co., Pop. Code 2
Brunswick County SD
  Supt. – See Southport
  MS, P O BOX 40   28451 – Les Tubb, prin.
  Lincoln PS, P O BOX 10   28451
  Joseph Butler, prin.

Lenoir, Caldwell Co., Pop. Code 7
Caldwell County SD
  Sch. Sys. Enr. Code 7
  Supt. – Kenneth Roberts, P O BOX 1590   28645
  Gamewell MS, RURAL ROUTE 6 BOX 272   28645
  A. Tolbert, prin.
  MS, 332 GREENHAVEN DRIVE NW   28645
  E. Eppley, prin.
  Davenport MS, 901 COLLEGE AVE SW   28645
  Peggy Lowdermilk, prin.
  East Harper ES, 506 HARPER AVE NW   28645
  T. Crowe, prin.
  Gamewell ES, RURAL ROUTE 06 BOX 274   28645
  Joe Bost, prin.
  Kings Creek ES
  RURAL ROUTE 01 BOX 411-A   28645
  Charles Sherrill, prin.
  Lower Creek ES, 630 LOWER CREEK DR NE   28645
  John Frazier,Jr., prin.
  Oak Hill ES, RURAL ROUTE 02 BOX 252   28645
  Brent Helton, prin.
  Valmead ES, 116 ELIZABETH ST   28645
  Helen Hall, prin.
  West Lenoir ES, 125 MAPLE DR NW   28645
  Byron Talbert, prin.
  Whitnel ES, 116 HIBRITEN DR SW   28645
  John McCurry, prin.
Other Schools – See Collettsville, Granite Falls,
  Hudson, Patterson

Lewiston Woodville, Bertie Co., Pop. Code 2
Bertie County SD
  Supt. – See Windsor
  West Bertie ES, P O BOX 279   27849
  Euric Perry, prin.

Lewisville, Forsyth Co.
Forsyth County SD
  Supt. – See Winston-Salem
  ES, 6500 SCHOOL ST   27023 – Joe Hauser, prin.

Forsyth Country Day School   27023

Lexington, Davidson Co., Pop. Code 7
Davidson County SD
  Sch. Sys. Enr. Code 7
  Supt. – Dr. W. Max Walser, P O BOX 2057   27293
  Central MS, RURAL ROUTE 06 BOX 121   27292
  Stephen Teague, prin.
  Churchland ES
  RURAL ROUTE 05 BOX 1020   27292
  Lowell Roof, prin.
  Midway ES, RURAL ROUTE 12 BOX 2460   27292
  Phillip Kennedy, prin.
  Northwest ES
  RURAL ROUTE 08 BOX 3070   27292
  Patrick Harrison, prin.
  Reeds ES, RURAL ROUTE 22 BOX 160   27292
  Allan Thompson, prin.
  Silver Valley ES
  RURAL ROUTE 02 BOX 790   27292
  Gary Ball, prin.
  Southwood ES
  RURAL ROUTE 09 BOX 4371   27292
  Frank Austin, prin.
  Townsend ES, RURAL ROUTE 01 BOX 140   27292
  Ted Potts, prin.
Other Schools – See Denton, Linwood, Thomasville,
  Wallburg, Welcome

Lexington CSD
  Sch. Sys. Enr. Code 5
  Supt. – James Simeon, 1010 FAIR STREET   27292
  MS, HEMSTEAD ST   27292
  Johnnie Van Roekel, prin.
  Dunbar MS, 301 SMITH AVE   27292
  Becky Bloxam, prin.
  Pickett ES, BIESECKER ROAD   27292
  Arlene Morrow, prin.
  South Lexington ES
  900 COTTON GROVE RD   27292
  Ruth Parks, prin.
  Southwst Lexington ES, 434 CENTRAL AVE   27292
  Willard Moody, prin.

Sheets Memorial Christian School
  307 HOLT ST   27292

Liberty, Randolph Co., Pop. Code 4
Guilford County SD
  Supt. – See Greensboro
  Greene ES, 2217 NC 62 E   27298
  Paul Skiver, prin.

Randolph County SD
  Supt. – See Asheboro
  ES, P O BOX 1009   27298 – Stan Hedrick, prin.

Lilesville, Anson Co., Pop. Code 3
Anson County SD
  Supt. – See Wadesboro
  Bennett ES, P O BOX 218   28091
  Steve Dixon, prin.

Lillington, Harnett Co., Pop. Code 4
Harnett County SD
  Sch. Sys. Enr. Code 7
  Supt. – Ivo Wortman, 700 MAIN ST   27546
  MS   27546 – Ray Gilchrist, prin.
  Shawtown ES   27546 – Ned White, prin.
  Other Schools – See Angier, Buies Creek, Bunnlevel,
  Coats, Dunn, Erwin, Kipling, Mamers, Olivia,
  Sanford

Lincolnton, Lincoln Co., Pop. Code 5
Lincoln County SD
  Sch. Sys. Enr. Code 6
  Supt. – Dr. Martin Eaddy, P O BOX 400   28093
  Asbury ES, 310 SALEM RD   28092
  Rebecca Heavner, prin.
  Battleground MS, P O BOX 615   28093
  Gerald Schrum, prin.
  Love Memorial ES
  RURAL ROUTE 06 BOX 367   28092
  Cindy Poe, prin.
  Lowder MS, 350 KENNEDY DR   28092
  John Gilleland, prin.
  Massey MS, 1435 E MAIN ST   28092
  Judy Gilbert, prin.
  Oaklawn ES, 410 LINDEN ST   28092
  Dr. Clyde Smith, prin.
  Park ES, 311 MCBEE ST   28092
  Virginia Wright, prin.
  Other Schools – See Denver, Iron Station, Vale

Linwood, Davidson Co.
Davidson County SD
  Supt. – See Lexington
  Tyro MS, RURAL ROUTE 01   27299
  Randall Arnold, prin.

Littleton, Halifax Co., Pop. Code 3
Halifax County SD
  Supt. – See Halifax
  Aurelian Springs ES
  RURAL ROUTE 01 BOX 408   27850
  Eugene Richardson, prin.
  McIver ES, RURAL ROUTE 04 BOX 10   27850
  Lutricia Lynch, prin.

Locust, Stanly Co., Pop. Code 4
Stanly County SD
  Supt. – See Albemarle
  ES, 103 SCHOOL RD   28097 – G. White, prin.

Louisburg, Franklin Co., Pop. Code 5
Franklin County SD
  Sch. Sys. Enr. Code 5
  Supt. – Russell Allen, P O BOX 449   27549
  Gold Sand MS, RURAL ROUTE 06   27549
  Larry Rogers, prin.
  Best ES, RURAL ROUTE 04   27549
  R. Fleming, prin.
  Gold Sand ES, RURAL ROUTE 06   27549
  Henry Hedgepeth, prin.
  ES   27549 – Carl Harris, prin.
  Other Schools – See Bunn, Henderson, Youngsville

Lowell, Gaston Co., Pop. Code 5
Gaston County SD
  Supt. – See Gastonia
  ES, 1500 POWER DR   28098
  Samuel Carpenter, prin.

Lowgap, Surry Co.
Surry County SD
  Supt. – See Dobson
  Lowgap ES   27024 – John Haynes, prin.

Lucama, Wilson Co., Pop. Code 4
Wilson County SD
  Supt. – See Wilson
  Springfield MS, RURAL ROUTE 01   27851
  Randolph Sessoms, prin.
  ES, P O BOX 70   27851 – Hugh Flowers, prin.

Lumberton, Robeson Co., Pop. Code 7
Lumberton CSD
  Sch. Sys. Enr. Code 5
  Supt. – George Taylor, P O BOX 1187   28359
  Carroll MS, 300 BAILEY RD   28358
  A. Collins, prin.
  Hargrave ES, HARGRAVE ST   28358
  Mary Teets, prin.
  Knuckles ES, MARTIN L KING DR   28358
  Dr. Robert Jones, prin.
  Norment ES, GODWIN AVE   28358
  Robert Andrews, prin.
  Tanglewood ES, WEST 29TH ST   28358
  Laura Owens, prin.
  West Lumberton ES, SCHOOL STREET   28358
  Norman Sampson, prin.

Robeson County SD
  Sch. Sys. Enr. Code 7
  Supt. – P. Swett, P O BOX 1328   28359
  Magnolia S, RURAL ROUTE 08 BOX 350   28358
  Noah Woods, prin.
  Deep Branch ES
  RURAL ROUTE 04 BOX 483   28358
  Lindsey Quick, prin.
  East Robeson PS, RURAL ROUTE 07   28358
  Charles Kinlaw, prin.
  Long Branch ES, RURAL ROUTE 02   28358
  Stephen Stone, prin.
  Piney Grove ES, RURAL ROUTE 10   28358
  Grady Locklear, prin.
  Smiths/Allenton MS
  RURAL ROUTE 05 BOX 167   28358
  Anne Brinkley, prin.
  Other Schools – See Fairmont, Maxton, Parkton,
  Pembroke, Proctorville, Rowland, Shannon

St. Frances De Sales ES
  401 N SYCAMORE ST   28358

Mc Adenville, Gaston Co., Pop. Code 3
Gaston County SD
  Supt. – See Gastonia
  ES, P O BOX 128   28101 – Bobbie Holland, prin.

Mc Leansville, Guilford Co.
Guilford County SD
  Supt. – See Greensboro
  MS, P O BOX 48   27301 – Jeff German, prin.
  Northeast Guilford MS
  6720 MC LEANSVILLE ROAD   27301
  D. Kemp, prin.
  Madison ES, 3600 HINES CHAPEL RD   27301
  Don York, prin.

Madison, Rockingham Co., Pop. Code 5
Western Rockingham CSD
  Sch. Sys. Enr. Code 5
  Supt. – Dr. Charles Slemenda
  306 W DECATUR ST   27025
  Madison-Mayodan MS   27025 – J. Fowler, prin.
  Dillard ES, 810 CURE DR   27025
  Carol Summerlin, prin.
  Scott MS, 410 W DECATUR ST   27025
  Gail Collins, prin.
  Other Schools – See Mayodan, Stoneville

Maiden, Catawba Co., Pop. Code 5
Catawba County SD
  Supt. – See Newton
  Tuttle MS, RURAL ROUTE 01 BOX 38   28650
  William Crawford, prin.
  ES, 201 N MAIN AVE   28650 – L. McRee, prin.

Mamers, Harnett Co.
Harnett County SD
  Supt. – See Liflington
  Boone Trail ES   27552 – Donald Quinn, prin.

Manteo, Dare Co., Pop. Code 3
Dare County SD
  Sch. Sys. Enr. Code 4
  Supt. – James Harrell, P O BOX 640   27954
  MS   27954 – Gerald Roberson, prin.
  ES   27954 – G. Gaskill, prin.
  Other Schools – See Buxton, Kitty Hawk

Maple, Currituck Co.
Currituck County SD
  Supt. – See Currituck
  Central ES   27956 – Mark Stefanik, prin.

Maple Hill, Pender Co.
Pender County SD
  Supt. – See Burgaw
  ES, P O BOX 93   28454 – Samuel Bullock, prin.

Marble, Cherokee Co.
Cherokee County SD
  Supt. – See Murphy
  ES   28905 – Maynard Brown, prin.

Marion, McDowell Co., Pop. Code 5
McDowell County SD
  Sch. Sys. Enr. Code 6
  Supt. – Dr. David Ricketts, P O BOX 130   28752
  Eastfield ES, 711 E YANCEY ST   28752
  James Gorst, prin.
  ES, P O BOX 152   28752 – James Washburn, prin.
  North Cove ES, RURAL ROUTE 03   28752
  Earl Fender, prin.
  Pleasant Gardens ES, RURAL ROUTE 04   28752
  Jerry McNeely, prin.
  West Marion ES, 201 STEFFE ST   28752
  Pamela Gibbs, prin.
  Other Schools – See Glenwood, Nebo, Old Fort

Marshall, Madison Co., Pop. Code 5
Madison County SD
  Sch. Sys. Enr. Code 5
  Supt. – R. Edwards, P O BOX 308   28753
  MS, P O BOX 489   28753 – Fred Haynie, prin.
  Laurel ES, RURAL ROUTE 03   28753
  Vernon Ponder, prin.
  PS, P O BOX 758   28753 – Nancy Allen, prin.
  Walnut ES, WALNUT RURAL STATION   28753
  Troy Harrison, prin.
  Other Schools – See Hot Springs, Mars Hill

Mars Hill, Madison Co., Pop. Code 4
Madison County SD
  Supt. – See Marshall
  ES, P O BOX 340   28754
  Frederick Anderson, prin.

Marshville, Union Co., Pop. Code 4
Union County SD
　Supt. – See Monroe
　East Union MS, P O BOX 666　28103
　　J. McAfee, prin.
　ES, P O BOX 4607　28103 – William Walters, prin.
　New Salem ES, RURAL ROUTE 02　28103
　　Henry Morgan, prin.

Matthews, Mecklenburg Co., Pop. Code 4
Mecklenburg County SD
　Supt. – See Charlotte
　ES, 200 MCDOWELL ST　28105
　　Harold Hood, prin.
　McAlpine ES, 9100 CARSWELL LN　28105
　　Nancy Bell, prin.
　Olde Providence ES, 3800 REA ROAD　28105
　　Marianne Hickman, prin.

Union County SD
　Supt. – See Monroe
　Sun Valley MS
　　1409 WESLEY CHAPEL ROAD　28105
　　G. Faris, prin.

Maxton, Robeson Co., Pop. Code 5
Robeson County SD
　Supt. – See Lumberton
　Townsend MS, 331 N FLORENCE ST　28364
　　Vicki Jones, prin.
　Dean ES, 216 4TH ST　28364 – Howard Davis, prin.
　Oxendine ES, RURAL ROUTE 02　28364
　　Larry Brooks, prin.
　Prospect ES, RURAL ROUTE 03　28364
　　Kelly Sanderson, prin.

Mayodan, Rockingham Co., Pop. Code 5
Western Rockingham CSD
　Supt. – See Madison
　Duncan MS, 500 W MAIN ST　27027
　　Ralph Gilbert, prin.

Maysville, Jones Co., Pop. Code 3
Jones County SD
　Supt. – See Trenton
　ES, P O BOX 718　28555 – Fred Creech, prin.

Onslow County SD
　Supt. – See Jacksonville
　Tabernacle MS
　　RURAL ROUTE 01 BOX 581　28555
　　R. Whaley, prin.
　Silverdale ES, RURAL ROUTE 01 BOX 670　28555
　　Donald Parker, prin.

Mebane, Alamance Co., Pop. Code 5
Alamance County SD
　Supt. – See Graham
　Woodlawn MS, RURAL ROUTE 04　27302
　　Dr. John Phillips, prin.
　South Mebane ES, SOUTH THIRD ST　27302
　　Sondra Aheron, prin.
　Yoder ES, CHARLES ST　27302
　　Marshall Kidd, prin.

Caswell County SD
　Supt. – See Yanceyville
　Sweet Gum ES
　　RURAL ROUTE 03 BOX 388　27302
　　Melvin Paylor, prin.

Merry Hill, Bertie Co., Pop. Code 3
Bertie County SD
　Supt. – See Windsor
　Law ES, P O BOX 8　27957
　　Elizabeth Cayton, prin.

Lawrence Academy, P O BOX 36　27957

Micaville, Yancey Co.
Yancy County SD
　Supt. – See Burnsville
　ES　28755 – Gary Pate, prin.

Middleburg, Vance Co., Pop. Code 2
Vance County SD
　Supt. – See Henderson
　Young ES, P O BOX 160　27556
　　Ronald Williams, prin.

Middlesex, Nash Co., Pop. Code 3
Nash County SD
　Supt. – See Nashville
　ES, P O BOX 39　27557 – Carl Williams, prin.

Midland, Union Co.
Cabarrus County SD
　Supt. – See Concord
　Bethel ES, RURAL ROUTE 02 BOX 106　28107
　　D. Voigt, Jr., prin.

Millers Creek, Wilkes Co., Pop. Code 2
Wilkes County SD
　Supt. – See Wilkesboro
　IS, P O BOX 500　28651 – Ward Eller, prin.
　PS, P O BOX 499　28651 – Reggie Eller, prin.

Mill Spring, Polk Co., Pop. Code 2
Polk County SD
　Supt. – See Columbus
　ES　28756 – Rick Howell, prin.
　Sunny View ES, RURAL ROUTE 02　28756
　　Jerry Hensley, prin.

Milton, Caswell Co., Pop. Code 2
Caswell County SD
　Supt. – See Yanceyville
　Murphey ES, RURAL ROUTE 01 BOX 129　27305
　　Ray Reagan, prin.

Minneapolis, Avery Co.
Avery County SD
　Supt. – See Newland
　ES　28652 – Jerry Brown, prin.

Mocksville, Davie Co., Pop. Code 5
Davie County SD
　Sch. Sys. Enr. Code 5
　Supt. – William Steed, 220 CHERRY ST　27028
　Davie ES, RURAL ROUTE 05 BOX 540　27028
　　Linda Mercier, prin.
　ES, 295 CEMETERY ST　27028
　　Jefferson Albarty, prin.
　MS, RURAL ROUTE 08 BOX 7　27028
　　W. Campbell, prin.
　Pinebrook ES, RURAL ROUTE 02 BOX 390　27028
　　Larry Jones, prin.
　Other Schools – See Advance, Cooleemee

Moncure, Chatham Co.
Chatham County SD
　Supt. – See Pittsboro
　ES　27559 – Wade Lehman, prin.

Monroe, Union Co., Pop. Code 7
Monroe CSD
　Sch. Sys. Enr. Code 5
　Supt. – Dr. Thomas Batchelor
　　UNION CO CRTHSE #6　28110
　MS, 601 E SUNSET DRIVE　28110
　　Raymond Holman, prin.
　Benton Heights ES, 1200 CONCORD AVE　28110
　　Joseph Blanton, prin.
　Bickett MS, 501 LANCASTER AVE　28110
　　Frederick Ingold, prin.
　East ES, 515 ELIZABETH AVE　28110
　　Beatrice Colson, prin.

Union County SD
　Sch. Sys. Enr. Code 7
　Supt. – Nancy Davis, 500 N MAIN ST #700　28110
　Parkwood MS
　　3219 PARKWOOD SCHOOL ROAD　28110
　　Larry Stinson, prin.
　Piedmont MS, 2816 SIKESMILL ROAD　28110
　　Gwyn Griffin, prin.
　Fairview ES, 7516 CONCORD HWY　28110
　　Darrell Tomberlin, prin.
　Prospect ES, 3005 RUBEN RD　28110
　　Thomas Roberts, prin.
　Shiloh MS, 3828 OLD CHARLOTTE HWY　28110
　　(—), prin.
　Union ES
　　4311 OLD PAGELAND-MONROE RD　28110
　　C. Hargett, prin.
　Unionville ES, 4511 UNIONVILLE RD　28110
　　Bobby Shearon, prin.
　Wesley Chapel ES, 110 S POTTER RD　28110
　　Frances Davis, prin.
　Other Schools – See Indian Trail, Marshville,
　　Matthews, Waxhaw, Wingate

Mooresville, Iredell Co., Pop. Code 6
Iredell County SD
　Supt. – See Statesville
　Brawley MS, RURAL ROUTE 07　28115
　　Jerry Fox, prin.
　Shepherd ES, RURAL ROUTE 04　28115
　　W. Hall, prin.

Mooresville CSD
　Sch. Sys. Enr. Code 4
　Supt. – Dr. Samuel Houston, P O BOX 119　28115
　Park View ES, 217 W MCNEELY AVE　28115
　　Becky Wilson, prin.
　South ES, 839 S MAGNOLIA AVE　28115
　　Dr. Ruth Palmer, prin.
　Woods MS, 574 W MCLELLAND AVE　28115
　　C. Bankhead, Jr., prin.

Moravian Falls, Wilkes Co.
Wilkes County SD
　Supt. – See Wilkesboro
　ES, P O BOX 818　28654 – Nelta Church, prin.

Morehead City, Carteret Co., Pop. Code 5
Carteret County SD
　Supt. – See Beaufort
　MS　28516 – (—), prin.
　Camp Glen ES　28516 – Roy Styron, prin.
　Morehead MS　28557 – Treasure Edwards, prin.

St. Egbert ES, 1705 EVANS ST　28557

Morganton, Burke Co., Pop. Code 7
Burke County SD
　Sch. Sys. Enr. Code 7
　Supt. – Carlos Hicks, P O BOX 989　28655
　Chesterfield ES
　　RURAL ROUTE 03 BOX 945　28655
　　Don Sigmon, prin.
　Forest Hill ES, ANN ST　28655
　　Richard Peck, prin.
　Hillcrest ES, TENNESSEE ST　28655
　　Janice McMahon, prin.
　Mountain View ES, 100 ALPHABET LN　28655
　　Dr. Richard Peck, prin.
　Mull ES, RURAL ROUTE 04 BOX 140　28655
　　Donald Lovelace, prin.
　Oak Hill ES, RURAL ROUTE 05 BOX 11　28655
　　David McKinney, prin.
　Salem ES, 1311 SALEM RD　28655
　　Laton Horton, prin.
　Other Schools – See Connellys Springs, Drexel, Glen
　　Alpine, Hildebran, Icard, Rutherford College,
　　Valdese

Morven, Anson Co., Pop. Code 3
Anson County SD
　Supt. – See Wadesboro
　ES, P O BOX 33　28119 – Melton Ellerbe, prin.

Mount Airy, Surry Co., Pop. Code 6
Mt. Airy CSD
　Sch. Sys. Enr. Code 4
　Supt. – Robert Chilton, P O BOX 710　27030
　Jones ES, 215 JONES SCHOOL RD　27030
　　Donnie Johnson, prin.
　Tharrington ES, 315 CULBERT ST　27030
　　R. Williamson, prin.

Surry County SD
　Supt. – See Dobson
　Gentry MS, RURAL ROUTE 06　27030
　　B. Bledsoe, prin.
　Beulah ES, RURAL ROUTE 06　27030
　　Fred Goins, prin.
　Flat Rock ES, RURAL ROUTE 03　27030
　　Dr. Michelle Crews, prin.
　Franklin ES, 727 S FRANKLIN RD　27030
　　Harold Flippin, prin.

Mount Gilead, Montgomery Co., Pop. Code 4
Montgomery County SD
　Supt. – See Troy
　Highland MS, TROY ROAD　27306
　　Samuel Burris, prin.
　ES, P O BOX 308　27306 – Robert Gilman, prin.

Mount Holly, Gaston Co., Pop. Code 5
Gaston County SD
　Supt. – See Gastonia
　Pinewood ES, HWY 273 NORTH　28120
　　Charles Williamson, prin.
　Rankin ES, P O BOX 805　28120
　　Allan Craig, prin.

Mount Mourne, Iredell Co.
Iredell County SD
　Supt. – See Statesville
　ES　28123 – James Meadows, prin.

Mount Olive, Wayne Co., Pop. Code 5
Wayne County SD
　Supt. – See Goldsboro
　Carver ES, P O BOX 679　28365
　　Aaron Mozingo, prin.

Mount Pleasant, Cabarrus Co., Pop. Code 4
Cabarrus County SD
　Supt. – See Concord
　MS, P O BOX 877　28124 – Neil Shouse, prin.
　ES, P O BOX 368　28124 – T. Ford, prin.

Mount Ulla, Rowan Co., Pop. Code 4
Rowan County SD
　Supt. – See Salisbury
　ES, RURAL ROUTE 02 BOX 5　28125
　　Richard Seaboch, prin.

Moyock, Currituck Co.
Currituck County SD
　Supt. – See Currituck
　ES　27958 – Richard Wardle, prin.

Murfreesboro, Hertford Co., Pop. Code 5
Hertford County SD
　Supt. – See Winton
　Hertford County MS
　　RURAL ROUTE 01 BOX 422B　27855
　　Harvey Jones, prin.
　Riverview ES, RURAL ROUTE 01 BOX 337　27855
　　Landon Miales, prin.

Murphy, Cherokee Co., Pop. Code 4
Cherokee County SD
　Sch. Sys. Enr. Code 5
　Supt. – Donald Bentley, P O BOX 710　28906
　Hiwasee Dam S, RURAL ROUTE 04　28906
　　Michael Rogers, prin.
　Martins Creek ES, RURAL ROUTE 02　28906
　　Randall Barnett, prin.
　ES　28906 – William Hughes, prin.
　Peachtree ES, RURAL ROUTE 01　28906
　　Paul Vaught, Jr., prin.
　Ranger ES, RURAL ROUTE 06　28906
　　Charles Forrister, prin.
　Other Schools – See Andrews, Marble, Unaka

Nashville, Nash Co., Pop. Code 5
Nash County SD
　Sch. Sys. Enr. Code 7
　Supt. – C. Stroud, 930 EASTERN AVE　27856
　Cedar Grove ES
　　RURAL ROUTE 01 BOX 368　27856
　　Lina Bracey, prin.
　Greene JHS, 323 E 6TH ST　27856
　　Tim Perry, prin.
　ES, 209 E VIRGINIA AVE　27856
　　Leorita Hankerson, prin.
　Other Schools – See Bailey, Battleboro, Elm City,
　　Middlesex, Red Oak, Rocky Mount, Spring Hope,
　　Whitakers

Nebo, Mc Dowell Co., Pop. Code 3
McDowell County SD
　Supt. – See Marion
　ES　28761 – Jack Kirstein, prin.

New Bern, Craven Co., Pop. Code 7
Craven County SD
　Sch. Sys. Enr. Code 7
　Supt. – Dr. Ben Quinn, 222 BROAD ST　28560
　MacDonald MS, P O BOX 2445　28561
　　L. Eubanks, prin.

West Craven MS
    515 N WEST CRAVN MID SCH RD   28560
    Herbert Gray, prin.
Bangert ES, 3712 CANTERBURY RD   28562
    T. Ragland, prin.
Brinson Memorial ES
    319 NEUSE FOREST AVE   28560
    V. Barrow, prin.
Danyus MS, 622 WEST ST   28560
    Roland Pridgen, prin.
Oaks Road ES, 2811 OAKS RD   28560
    Susan Rivenbark, prin.
Trent Park ES, 2500 EDUCATIONAL DR   28562
    Richard Wilson, prin.
Other Schools – See Bridgeton, Cove City, Havelock,
    Vanceboro

St. Paul ES, 508 MIDDLE ST   28560

Newell, Mecklenburg Co., Pop. Code 3
Mecklenburg County SD
    Supt. – See Charlotte
ES, OLD CONCORD RD #163   28126
    Nancy Golson, prin.

Newland, Avery Co., Pop. Code 3
Avery County SD
    Sch. Sys. Enr. Code 5
    Supt. – Dr. Jerry Fee, P O BOX 397   28657
Avery County MS, P O BOX 697   28657
    Keith Tutterow, prin.
Newland ES, P O BOX 158   28657
    John Canupp, prin.
Riverside ES, RURAL ROUTE 03 BOX 362   28657
    Jack Buchanan, prin.
Other Schools – See Banner Elk, Crossnore, Elk Park,
    Minneapolis

New London, Stanly Co., Pop. Code 2
Stanly County SD
    Supt. – See Albemarle
ES, P O BOX 68   28127 – G. White, prin.

Newport, Carteret Co., Pop. Code 4
Carteret County SD
    Supt. – See Beaufort
ES   28570 – Robert Elkins, prin.

Newton, Catawba Co., Pop. Code 6
Catawba County SD
    Sch. Sys. Enr. Code 7
    Supt. – Dr. Emmett Floyd, P O BOX 1000   28658
Blackburn MS
    RURAL ROUTE 01 BOX 231   28658
    Bob Brooks, prin.
Balls Creek ES, RURAL ROUTE 02 BOX 566   28658
    Deborah Elliott, prin.
Startown ES, RURAL ROUTE 01   28658
    Nancy Jack, prin.
Other Schools – See Catawba, Claremont, Hickory,
    Maiden, Sherrills Ford, Vale

Newton-Conover CSD
    Sch. Sys. Enr. Code 5
    Supt. – Everette Simmons, P O BOX 149   28658
Newton-Conover MS, 211 W 26TH ST   28658
    Larry Harris, prin.
South Newton ES, 306 W 1ST ST   28658
    Mavis Hedrick, prin.
Thornton ES, 301 W 18TH ST   28658
    Stanley Everett, prin.
Other Schools – See Conover

Newton Grove, Sampson Co., Pop. Code 3
Sampson County SD
    Supt. – See Clinton
Hobbton ES   28366 – Jay Henderson, prin.

Norlina, Warren Co., Pop. Code 3
Warren County SD
    Supt. – See Warrenton
MS   27563 – C. Hege, prin.
Northside ES   27563 – Henry Greene, prin.

North Wilkesboro, Wilkes Co., Pop. Code 5
Wilkes County SD
    Supt. – See Wilkesboro
Fairplains ES, 14 SCHOOL ST   28659
    Jerry McGuire, prin.
Mulberry ES, RURAL ROUTE 01 BOX 227   28659
    Bill Cardwell, prin.
ES, RURAL ROUTE 05 BOX 199   28659
    John Burnette, prin.
Union ES, RURAL ROUTE 04 BOX 475   28659
    Dickie Welborn, prin.
Wright ES, 165 STATESVILLE RD   28659
    Coleen Bush, prin.

Norwood, Stanly Co., Pop. Code 4
Stanly County SD
    Supt. – See Albemarle
Aquadale ES, RURAL ROUTE 02   28128
    Bill West, prin.
ES, P O BOX 636   28128 – Pamela Morton, prin.

Oakboro, Stanly Co., Pop. Code 3
Stanly County SD
    Supt. – See Albemarle
ES, RURAL ROUTE 02 BOX 46   28129
    Joyce Steele, prin.

Oak City, Martin Co., Pop. Code 2
Martin County SD
    Supt. – See Williamston
West Martin ES   27857 – J. Horton, prin.

Oak Ridge, Guilford Co., Pop. Code 5
Guilford County SD
    Supt. – See Greensboro
ES, 2050 OAK RIDGE RD   27310
    Mamie Williams, prin.

Ocracoke, Hyde Co., Pop. Code 3
Hyde County SD
    Supt. – See Swanquarter
Ocracoke S, P O BOX 189   27960
    Bennett Utley, prin.

Old Fort, Mc Dowell Co., Pop. Code 3
McDowell County SD
    Supt. – See Marion
ES   28762 – Odell Parker, prin.

Olivia, Harnett Co.
Harnett County SD
    Supt. – See Lillington
Benhaven MS   28368 – Thomas Lasater, prin.

Otto, Macon Co.
Macon County SD
    Supt. – See Franklin
ES, P O BOX 186   28763 – Charles Cabe, prin.

Oxford, Granville Co., Pop. Code 6
Granville County SD
    Sch. Sys. Enr. Code 6
    Supt. – Dr. G. Thomas Houlihan
    P O BOX 927   27565
Potter MS, P O BOX 488   27565
    Michael Fedewa, prin.
Credle MS, 223 COLLEGE ST   27565
    Dr. Dorothy Pruitt, prin.
Toler-Oak Hill ES
    RURAL ROUTE 07 BOX 311   27565
    George Allen,Jr., prin.
West Oxford ES, RURAL ROUTE 06 BOX 26   27565
    Andrew Phillips,Jr., prin.
Other Schools – See Butner, Creedmoor, Franklinton,
    Stovall

Pantego, Beaufort Co., Pop. Code 2
Beaufort County SD
    Supt. – See Washington
MS, P O BOX 8   27860 – James Henderson, prin.
Beaufort County ES, P O BOX 98   27860
    Fred Wilson, prin.

Parkton, Robeson Co., Pop. Code 3
Robeson County SD
    Supt. – See Lumberton
S   28371 – Colon Lane, prin.

Patterson, Caldwell Co.
Caldwell County SD
    Supt. – See Lenoir
Happy Valley ES, P O BOX 130   28661
    J. Tucker, prin.

Peachland, Anson Co., Pop. Code 3
Anson County SD
    Supt. – See Wadesboro
MS, P O BOX 188   28133 – Jeraline Cole, prin.

Pelham, Caswell Co.
Caswell County SD
    Supt. – See Yanceyville
Duncan ES, RURAL ROUTE 01 BOX 476   27311
    Glen Parrott, prin.
ES, P O BOX 92   27311 – Diane Luquire, prin.

Pembroke, Robeson Co., Pop. Code 5
Robeson County SD
    Supt. – See Lumberton
ES   28372 – James Dial, prin.
MS   28372 – Rona Leach, prin.
Union Chapel ES, RURAL ROUTE 01   28372
    Wade Hunt, prin.

Pendleton, Northampton Co.
Northampton County SD
    Supt. – See Jackson
Hare ES, RURAL ROUTE 01 BOX 28   27862
    Rebecca Flynn, prin.

Penrose, Polk Co.
Transylvania County SD
    Supt. – See Brevard
ES   28766 – Peggy Singleton, prin.

Pfafftown, Forsyth Co.
Forsyth County SD
    Supt. – See Winston-Salem
Vienna ES, 1915 CHICKASHA RD   27040
    Patricia Compton, prin.

Pikeville, Wayne Co., Pop. Code 3
Wayne County SD
    Supt. – See Goldsboro
Nahunta ES, RURAL ROUTE 02 BOX 55   27863
    Joan Smiley, prin.
ES, P O BOX 189   27863 – Gareth Keene, prin.

Pilot Mountain, Surry Co., Pop. Code 4
Surry County SD
    Supt. – See Dobson
ES, P O BOX 97   27041 – Dr. W. Pipes, prin.

Pine Hall, Stokes Co.
Stokes County SD
    Supt. – See Danbury
ES   27042 – Jesse Lemons, prin.

Pinehurst, Moore Co., Pop. Code 4
Moore County SD
    Supt. – See Carthage

MS, P O BOX 951   28374 – Betty Martin, prin.
ES, P O BOX 1210   28374 – Janice Cagle, prin.

Pine Level, Johnston Co., Pop. Code 3
Johnston County SD
    Supt. – See Smithfield
Micro-Pine Level ES, P O BOX 68   27568
    Jack Temple, prin.

Pinetops, Edgecombe Co., Pop. Code 4
Edgecombe County SD
    Supt. – See Tarboro
South Edgecomb MS, P O BOX 88   27864
    James Lamm, prin.
Carver ES, P O BOX 48   27864
    Thomas Bogue, prin.

Pinetown, Beaufort Co.
Beaufort County SD
    Supt. – See Washington
ES, P O BOX 100   27865 – Gary Gaddy, prin.

Pineville, Mecklenburg Co., Pop. Code 4
Mecklenburg County SD
    Supt. – See Charlotte
Sterling MS, 9701 OLD PINEVILLE RD   28134
    Joyce Ambrose, prin.
ES, LOWRY ST   28134 – Robert Marshall, prin.

Piney Creek, Alleghany Co.
Alleghany County SD
    Supt. – See Sparta
ES   28663 – Duane Davis, prin.

Pink Hill, Lenoir Co., Pop. Code 3
Lenoir County SD
    Supt. – See Kinston
ES   28572 – Royce Swinson, prin.

Pinnacle, Stokes Co.
Stokes County SD
    Supt. – See Danbury
ES   27043 – Charles Bishop, prin.

Surry County SD
    Supt. – See Dobson
Shoals ES, RURAL ROUTE 02   27043
    O. Hauser, prin.

Pittsboro, Chatham Co., Pop. Code 4
Chatham County SD
    Sch. Sys. Enr. Code 6
    Supt. – Perry Harrison, P O BOX 128   27312
Horton MS, P O BOX 636   27312
    Ernest Alston, prin.
ES   27312 – Joe Burke, prin.
Other Schools – See Bennett, Bonlee, Goldston,
    Moncure, Siler City

Pleasant Garden, Guilford Co., Pop. Code 3
Guilford County SD
    Supt. – See Greensboro
ES, 4830 PLEASANT GARDEN RD   27313
    C. Willard, prin.

Plymouth, Washington Co., Pop. Code 5
Washington County SD
    Sch. Sys. Enr. Code 5
    Supt. – R. Alligood, P O BOX 747   27962
Pines ES   27962 – H. Estep, prin.
Other Schools – See Creswell, Roper

Polkton, Anson Co., Pop. Code 3
Anson County SD
    Supt. – See Wadesboro
ES, P O BOX 150   28135
    Elaine Scarborough, prin.

Polkville, Cleveland Co., Pop. Code 3
Cleveland County SD
    Supt. – See Shelby
ES, P O BOX 38   28136 – Joe Bowen, prin.

Pollocksville, Jones Co., Pop. Code 2
Jones County SD
    Supt. – See Trenton
ES, P O BOX 70   28573 – N. Boyd, prin.

Poplar Branch, Currituck Co.
Currituck County SD
    Supt. – See Currituck
Griggs ES   27965 – Fannie Newbern, prin.

Powellsville, Bertie Co., Pop. Code 2
Bertie County SD
    Supt. – See Windsor
White ES, P O BOX 9   27967
    Norman Cherry, prin.

Princeton, Johnston Co., Pop. Code 4
Johnston County SD
    Supt. – See Smithfield
S, P O BOX 38   27569 – Fred Bartholomew, prin.

Proctorville, Robeson Co., Pop. Code 2
Robeson County SD
    Supt. – See Lumberton
ES   28375 – Thomas Locklear, prin.

Raeford, Hoke Co., Pop. Code 5
Hoke County SD
    Sch. Sys. Enr. Code 6
    Supt. – Robert Nelson, 310 WOOLEY ST   28376
Upchurch MS, P O BOX 640   28376
    (—), prin.
McLauchlin ES, 326 N MAIN ST   28376
    Mitchell Tyler, prin.
Scurlock ES, RURAL ROUTE 02 BOX 505   28376
    George Wood, prin.

Turlington MS, 116 W PROSPECT AVE 28376
 Emma Mims, prin.
West Hoke ES, RURAL ROUTE 03 BOX 242 28376
 Milton Williams, prin.
Other Schools – See Red Springs

Raleigh, Wake Co., Pop. Code 9
Wake County SD
Sch. Sys. Enr. Code 8
Supt. – Robert Bridges
 3600 WAKE FOREST ROAD 27609
Carnage MS, 1425 CARNAGE DRIVE 27610
 Jeanette Beckwith, prin.
Carroll MS, 4520 SIX FORKS ROAD 27609
 Leon Herndon, prin.
Daniels MS, 2816 OBERLIN ROAD 27608
 Walt Sherlin, prin.
East Millbrook MS
 3801 SPRING FOREST ROAD 27604
 Patricia Gole, prin.
Ligon MS, 706 E LENOIR ST 27601
 Dan Bowers, prin.
Martin MS, 1701 RIDGE ROAD 27607
 David Coley, prin.
West Millbrook MS
 8115 STRICKLAND ROAD 27609
 N. Holshouser, prin.
Brentwood ES, 3426 INGRAM DR 27604
 Peg Bedini, prin.
Brooks ES, 700 NORTHBROOK DR 27609
 N. Adams, prin.
Bugg ES, 825 COOPER RD 27610
 Sally Bragg, prin.
Combs ES, 1600 LORIMER RD 27606
 Peggy Holliday, prin.
Conn ES, 1221 BROOKSIDE DR 27604
 Norma Haywood, prin.
Douglas ES, 600 ORTEGA RD 27609
 Pamela Hunsucker, prin.
Fuller ES, 806 CALLOWAY DR 27610
 Peggy Rodgers, prin.
Green ES, 5307 SIX FORKS RD 27609
 James McCall, prin.
Hunter ES, 1018 E DAVIE ST 27601
 Suzanne King, prin.
Jeffreys Grove ES, 6119 CREEDMOOR RD 27612
 George Cooper, prin.
Joyner ES, 2300 NOBLE RD 27608
 William Hooker, prin.
Lacy ES, 1820 RIDGE RD 27607
 Susan Jordan, prin.
Lynn Road ES, 1601 LYNN RD 27612
 Carolyn Earp, prin.
Millbrook ES, 1520 E MILLBROOK RD 27609
 Clifford Feather, prin.
North Ridge ES, 7120 HARPS MILL RD 27615
 Ann Hooker, prin.
Olds ES, 204 DIXIE TRL 27607
 Frank Koontz, prin.
Poe ES, 400 PEYTON ST 27610
 Thomas King, prin.
Powell ES, 1130 MARLBOROUGH RD 27610
 Patrick Kinlaw, prin.
Root ES, 3202 NORTHHAMPTON ST 27609
 Dr. Carolyn Earp, prin.
Smith ES, 1101 MAXWELL DR 27603
 Gailya Winters, prin.
Stough ES, 4210 EDWARDS MILL RD 27612
 Jack Nance, prin.
Swift Creek ES, 5601 HOLLY SPRINGS RD 27606
 Joann Cooper, prin.
Underwood ES, 1614 GLENWOOD AVE 27608
 Helen Collier, prin.
Vance ES, RURAL ROUTE 10 BOX 228 27603
 John Butler, prin.
Washington ES, 1000 FAYETTEVILLE ST 27601
 James Edwards, prin.
Wilburn ES, 3707 MARSH CREEK RD 27604
 Darryl Fisher, prin.
Wiley ES, 301 SAINT MARYS ST 27605
 Edward Gainor, prin.
York ES, 5201 BROOKHAVEN DR 27612
 Laverne Freitag, prin.
Other Schools – See Apex, Cary, Fuquay-Varina,
 Garner, Knightdale, Rolesville, Wake Forest,
 Wendell, Willow Spring, Zebulon

Ravenscroft School, P O BOX 19027 27619
Wake Christian Academy
 5500 ACADEMY DRIVE 27603
Cathedral ES, 204 HILLSBOROUGH ST 27603
Montessori School of Raleigh
 7005 LEADMINE RD 27615
Our Lady of Lourdes ES
 2710 OVERBROOK DR 27608

Ramseur, Randolph Co., Pop. Code 4
Randolph County SD
Supt. – See Asheboro
Coleridge ES, RURAL ROUTE 01 BOX 313 27316
 Mike York, prin.
ES, 146 JORDAN RD 27316 – Pat Foust, prin.

Randleman, Randolph Co., Pop. Code 4
Randolph County SD
Supt. – See Asheboro
MS, P O BOX 625 27317 – Debi Kime, prin.
ES, 100 SWAIM ST 27317 – Cindy Glascock, prin.

Red Oak, Nash Co., Pop. Code 2
Nash County SD
Supt. – See Nashville
ES, P O BOX 70 27868 – W. Thrower, prin.

Red Springs, Robeson Co., Pop. Code 5
Hoke County SD
Supt. – See Raeford
South Hoke ES
 RURAL ROUTE 01 BOX 645 28377
 Frank Richards, prin.

Red Springs CSD
Sch. Sys. Enr. Code 4
Supt. – John Ray, 130 MCNEIL DRIVE 28377
MS, 302 W 2ND AVE 28377
 Charles McNeill, prin.
Peterson ES, 503 W 4TH AVE 28377
 Anthony Parker, prin.

Reidsville, Rockingham Co., Pop. Code 7
Caswell County SD
Supt. – See Yanceyville
Stoney Creek ES
 RURAL ROUTE 01 BOX 320 27320
 Alma Spurlock, prin.

Reidsville CSD
Sch. Sys. Enr. Code 5
Supt. – Dr. John Kinlaw, 920 JOHNSON ST 27320
Franklin Street ES, 116 S FRANKLIN ST 27320
 James Spencer, prin.
Lawsonville Avenue ES
 212 LAWSONVILLE AVE 27320
 Bobby Moore, prin.
Moss Street ES, 419 MOSS ST 27320
 Ronald Somers, prin.
MS, 401 MOSS ST 27320
 Raymond Williams, prin.
South End ES, SOUTH PARK DR 27320
 Jeraldine Miller, prin.
Williamsburg ES
 RURAL ROUTE 10 BOX 296 27320
 Jerry Talley, prin.

Rockingham County SD
Supt. – See Wentworth
Bethany ES, RURAL ROUTE 04 BOX 151 27320
 Van Moore, prin.
Monroeton ES, RURAL ROUTE 06 BOX 828 27320
 Ronald Harris, prin.
Sadler ES, RURAL ROUTE 07 BOX 613 27320
 Linwood Faulcon, prin.

Richfield, Stanly Co., Pop. Code 2
Stanly County SD
Supt. – See Albemarle
ES, RURAL ROUTE 01 BOX 90 28137
 F. McIntyre, prin.

Richlands, Onslow Co., Pop. Code 3
Onslow County SD
Supt. – See Jacksonville
Trexler MS, P O BOX 188 28574
 Jerry Taylor, prin.
ES, P O BOX 67 28574 – Wayne Turner, prin.

Rich Square, Northampton Co., Pop. Code 4
Northampton County SD
Supt. – See Jackson
Rich Square-Creecy ES
 RURAL ROUTE 01 BOX 210 27869
 Dr. Mar Speller, prin.

Riegelwood, Columbus Co., Pop. Code 3
Bladen County SD
Supt. – See Elizabethtown
East Arcadia ES
 RURAL ROUTE 01 BOX 100 28456
 John Kirk, prin.

Columbus County SD
Supt. – See Whiteville
Acme-Delco ES 28456 – Norris Ebron, prin.

Roanoke Rapids, Halifax Co., Pop. Code 7
Halifax County SD
Supt. – See Halifax
Davie MS, RURAL ROUTE 01 BOX 191 27870
 Carolyn Johnson, prin.
Everetts ES, RURAL ROUTE 01 BOX 213 27870
 Donald Edwards, prin.

Roanoke Rapids CSD
Sch. Sys. Enr. Code 5
Supt. – Dr. Robert Clary
 536 HAMILTON ST 27870
Chaloner MS, P O BOX 970 27870
 Kathryn Landen, prin.
Hearne ES, 731 CEDAR ST 27870
 Deborah Bryan, prin.
Manning ES, 1102 BARRETT ST 27870
 Charles Snead, prin.
Medlin MS, 200 VANCE ST 27870
 Joseph Searcy, prin.

Halifax Academy
 RURAL ROUTE 02 BOX 355 27870

Roaring River, Wilkes Co.
Wilkes County SD
Supt. – See Wilkesboro
ES 28669 – Gaye Swaim, prin.

Robbins, Moore Co., Pop. Code 4
Moore County SD
Supt. – See Carthage
Elise MS, P O BOX 896 27325
 Charles Lambert, prin.
ES, P O BOX 188 27325 – Herb Cameron, prin.

Robbinsville, Graham Co., Pop. Code 4
Graham County SD
Sch. Sys. Enr. Code 4
Supt. – Lowell Crisp, P O BOX 605 28771
ES 28771 – Jack Lovin, prin.
Stecoah ES, RURAL ROUTE 02 BOX 114 28771
 Vickie Walsh, prin.

Robersonville, Martin Co., Pop. Code 4
Martin County SD
Supt. – See Williamston
JHS 27871 – Ernest Brooks, prin.
East End ES 27871 – Willie Peele, prin.

Rockingham, Richmond Co., Pop. Code 6
Richmond County SD
Supt. – See Hamlet
Ashley Chapel MS
 RURAL ROUTE 04 BOX 490 28379
 Marvin Spencer, prin.
Bell ES, FLOWERS & HAWTHORNE ST 28379
 Susan Eaves, prin.
Leak Street MS, P O BOX 1477 28379
 Thomas Clark, prin.
Rohanen PS, P O BOX 1311 28379
 Cathey Richardson, prin.
West Rockingham ES
 543 W WASHINGTON ST 28379
 John Hamer, prin.

Rockwell, Rowan Co., Pop. Code 4
Rowan County SD
Supt. – See Salisbury
ES, RURAL ROUTE 03 BOX 114 28138
 William Schnuit, prin.

Rocky Mount, Edgecombe Co., Pop. Code 7
Edgecombe County SD
Supt. – See Tarboro
West Edgecombe MS
 RURAL ROUTE 02 BOX 223 27801
 Thomas Worsley, prin.
Bulluck ES, RURAL ROUTE 04 BOX 374 27801
 Reuben Thompson, prin.

Nash County SD
Supt. – See Nashville
Benvenue ES, 1551 BENVENUE RD 27804
 James Wright, prin.
Benvenue MS, 1571 BENVENUE RD 27804
 Brenda Brown, prin.
Williford ES, 801 WILLIFORD ST 27803
 Calvin Whitaker, prin.

Rocky Mount CSD
Sch. Sys. Enr. Code 6
Supt. – J. Hare, P O BOX 1260 27802
Baskerville MS, STOKES ST 27801
 Ann Edge, prin.
Braswell ES, 220 S PEARL ST 27804
 Shirley Arrington, prin.
Englewood ES, ENGLEWOOD DR 27801
 Joan Hawley, prin.
Johnson ES, FAIRVIEW ROAD 27801
 Jim Armstrong, prin.
Parker MS, 1500 E VIRGINIA ST 27801
 Charles Davis, prin.
Pope MS, 336 COLEMAN AVE 27801
 Reba Bone, prin.

Falls Road Baptist School
 113 TREVATHAN ST 27801
Rocky Mount Academy
 1313 AVONDALE AVE 27801
Our Lady of Perpetual Help ES
 315 HAMMOND ST 27804

Rocky Point, Pender Co.
Pender County SD
Supt. – See Burgaw
Long Creek/Grady ES
 RURAL ROUE 01 BOX 360 28457
 Charlene Leister, prin.
ES, RURAL ROUTE 02 BOX 505 28457
 William Jordan, prin.

Rolesville, Wake Co., Pop. Code 2
Wake County SD
Supt. – See Raleigh
ES, P O BOX 40 27571 – Moira O'Connor, prin.

Ronda, Wilkes Co., Pop. Code 2
Wilkes County SD
Supt. – See Wilkesboro
Ronda-Clingman ES, RURAL ROUTE 02 28670
 Phillip Couch, prin.

Roper, Washington Co., Pop. Code 3
Washington County SD
Supt. – See Plymouth
Washington Union MS, P O BOX 188 27970
 Clifford Phifer, prin.

Roseboro, Sampson Co., Pop. Code 4
Cumberland County SD
Supt. – See Fayetteville
Beaver Dam ES, RURAL ROUTE 03 BOX 91 28382
 Ledmon Tyndall, prin.

Sampson County SD
Supt. – See Clinton
Roseboro-Salemburg MS 28382
 Richard Walters, prin.
Perry ES 28382 – Alphonza Williamson, prin.

Rose Hill, Duplin Co., Pop. Code 4
Duplin County SD
Supt. – See Kenansville

Charity MS, P O BOX 70   28458
  David Jordan, prin.
Rose Hill-Magnolia ES, P O BOX 340   28458
  Thomasine Kennedy, prin.

Rosman, Transylvania Co., Pop. Code 3
Transylvania County SD
Supt. – See Brevard
ES   28772 – Dawson Hogsed, prin.

Rowland, Robeson Co., Pop. Code 4
Robeson County SD
Supt. – See Lumberton
MS, 408 W CHAPEL ST   28383
  Donald Frye, prin.
Southside/Ashpole ES   28383 – Mabel Revels, prin.
Union ES, RURAL ROUTE 03   28383
  Rosemarie Lowry, prin.

Roxboro, Person Co., Pop. Code 6
Person County SD
Sch. Sys. Enr. Code 6
Supt. – Ronnie Bugnar, P O BOX 1078   27573
Bethel Hill ES, RURAL ROUTE 05 BOX 47   27573
  John Betterton,Jr., prin.
Bradsher ES, 404 S MORGAN ST   27573
  Stephen Knott, prin.
North ES, 815 HENDERSON RD   27573
  H. Carver, prin.
North End ES, RURAL ROUTE 02 BOX 122   27573
  Sandra Davis, prin.
South ES, P O BOX 418   27573
  Rickey Chambers, prin.
Woodland ES, P O BOX 448   27573
  Chuck Oakley, prin.
Other Schools – See Hurdle Mills, Timberlake

Ruffin, Rockingham Co., Pop. Code 6
Caswell County SD
Supt. – See Yanceyville
Cobb Memorial MS
  RURAL ROUTE 01 BOX 102   27326
  Kitty Blackwell, prin.

Rockingham County SD
Supt. – See Wentworth
Lincoln MS, RURAL ROUTE 02 BOX 265   27326
  Ralph Clayton, prin.
Happy Home ES
  RURAL ROUTE 02 BOX 223   27326
  Thomas Bolden, prin.

Rural Hall, Forsyth Co., Pop. Code 4
Forsyth County SD
Supt. – See Winston-Salem
ES   27045 – Reuben Slade, prin.

Rutherford College, Burke Co., Pop. Code 4
Burke County SD
Supt. – See Morganton
ES   28671 – D. Honeycutt, prin.

Rutherfordton, Rutherford Co., Pop. Code 5
Rutherford County SD
Supt. – See Spindale
New Hope MS, RIDGECREST AVE   28139
  Earnestine Kennedy, prin.
Gilkey ES, RURAL ROUTE 02 BOX 415   28139
  Fred Arrowood, prin.
Green Hill ES, RURAL ROUTE 05   28139
  John Calvert,Jr., prin.
Ruth ES, MOUNTAIN ST   28139
  William Mayberry, prin.
ES, MAPLE ST   28139 – Linda Edgerton, prin.

Saint Pauls, Robeson Co., Pop. Code 4
St. Pauls CSD
Sch. Sys. Enr. Code 4
Supt. – Thomas Paquin
  302 N OLD STAGE ROAD   28384
MS, 510 W SHAW ST   28384
  Dallas Freeman, prin.
ES, P O BOX 398   28384 – Willie Horsley, prin.

Salemburg, Sampson Co., Pop. Code 3
Sampson County SD
Supt. – See Clinton
ES, P O BOX 220   28385 – Anne Newman, prin.

Salisbury, Rowan Co., Pop. Code 7
Rowan County SD
Sch. Sys. Enr. Code 7
Supt. – C. Mobley, P O BOX 1348   28145
Hurley ES, RURAL ROUTE 06 BOX 602   28144
  Don Swanson, prin.
Knollwood ES
  RURAL ROUTE 02 BOX 679-A   28144
  Billy Shive, prin.
Other Schools – See China Grove, Cleveland, East
  Spencer, Faith, Gold Hill, Granite Quarry, Landis,
  Mount Ulla, Rockwell, Spencer, Woodleaf

Salisbury CSD
Sch. Sys. Enr. Code 5
Supt. – Dr. Marcus Smith, P O BOX 2349   28145
Knox MS, PARK ROAD W   28144
  William Robinson, prin.
Henderson MS, 1215 N MAIN ST   28144
  Frank Shaver, prin.
Isenberg PS, 2800 601 BYPASS   28144
  Paul Goble, prin.
Overton PS, PARK ROAD W   28144
  Ralph Brown, prin.

North Hills Christian School
  2740 W INNES ST   28144
Sacred Heart ES, 123 N ELLIS ST   28144

Saluda, Polk Co., Pop. Code 3
Polk County SD
Supt. – See Columbus
ES   28773 – Marvin Wagner, prin.

Sandy Ridge, Stokes Co.
Stokes County SD
Supt. – See Danbury
ES   27046 – James Grogan, prin.

Sanford, Lee Co., Pop. Code 7
Harnett County SD
Supt. – See Lillington
Johnsonville ES, RURAL ROUTE 06   27330
  Willie Brinkley, prin.

Lee County SD
Sch. Sys. Enr. Code 6
Supt. – William Johnson, P O BOX 1010   27331
Edwards ES, 3115 CEMETARY RD   27330
  Emily Lucas, prin.
Ingram ES, 3309 WICKER ST   27330
  N. Thompson, prin.
Iver ES, 7908 DEEP RIVER RD   27330
  Gary Moore, prin.
Jonesboro ES, P O BOX 1470   27331
  Linda Gales, prin.
St. Clair MS, 526 CROSS ST   27330
  Elaine Hotaling, prin.
Wicker MS, P O BOX 1129   27331
  Charles Alexander, prin.
Williams ES, P O BOX 1046   27331
  Neil MacDonald, prin.
Other Schools – See Broadway

Scotland Neck, Halifax Co., Pop. Code 5
Halifax County SD
Supt. – See Halifax
Brawley MS, P O BOX 449   27874
  Charles Swindell, prin.
Bakers ES, P O BOX 389   27874
  Thomas Sledge, prin.
Dawson ES, RURAL ROUTE 01 BOX 524-A   27874
  Ronald Hastye, prin.
PS, P O BOX 600   27874 – Robert Partin, prin.

Scotts, Iredell Co.
Iredell County SD
Supt. – See Statesville
ES   28699 – Edward Chenevey, prin.

Seaboard, Northampton Co., Pop. Code 3
Northampton County SD
Supt. – See Jackson
Seaboard-Coates ES, PARK ST BOX 308   27876
  Charles Tyner, prin.

Seagrove, Randolph Co., Pop. Code 2
Moore County SD
Supt. – See Carthage
Westmoore ES, RURAL ROUTE 02   27341
  Jack Burgess, prin.

Randolph County SD
Supt. – See Asheboro
ES, P O BOX 540   27341 – Pat Chappell, prin.

Sedalia, Guilford Co.
Guilford County SD
Supt. – See Greensboro
ES, 6120 BURLINGTON RD   27342
  Peggy Johnson, prin.

Selma, Johnson Co., Pop. Code 5
Johnston County SD
Supt. – See Smithfield
ES, P O BOX 147   27576 – Jerry Stevens, prin.

Seven Springs, Wayne Co., Pop. Code 2
Wayne County SD
Supt. – See Goldsboro
Spring Creek ES, P O BOX 297   28578
  M. Watson, prin.

Shallotte, Brunswick Co., Pop. Code 3
Brunswick County SD
Supt. – See Southport
MS, P O BOX 657   28459 – Mark Owens, prin.
Union PS, RURAL ROUTE 01 BOX 30   28459
  Clara Carter, prin.

Shannon, Robeson Co.
Robeson County SD
Supt. – See Lumberton
Rex-Rennert ES, RURAL ROUTE 01   28386
  Johnny Hunt, prin.

Shelby, Cleveland Co., Pop. Code 7
Cleveland County SD
Sch. Sys. Enr. Code 6
Supt. – Ellen Powell, 130 S POST ROAD   28150
Dover ES   28150 – Carole McDaniel, prin.
Elizabeth ES, 220 S POST RD   28150
  Courtney Madden, prin.
South Cleveland MS
  RURAL ROUTE 11 BOX 504   28150
  Jerry Simmons, prin.
Township Three ES, 1224 DAVIS RD   28150
  Tropzie McCluney, prin.
Washington ES
  RURAL ROUTE 01 BOX 225-C   28150
  Steve Borders, prin.
Other Schools – See Boiling Springs, Casar, Fallston,
  Lattimore, Polkville

Shelby SD
Sch. Sys. Enr. Code 5
Supt. – Dr. John Presson, 315 PATTON DR   28150

MS, 400 W MARION ST   28150
  Dina Braddy, prin.
Graham ES, 1100 BLANTON ST   28150
  Aileen Ford, prin.
Jefferson ES, 1166 WYKE RD   28150
  Donnie Tharrington, prin.
Love ES, 925 JAMES LOVE SCHOOL RD   28150
  Loyl Quinn, prin.
Marion ES, 410 FORREST HILL DR   28150
  Sarah Tallent, prin.

Sherrills Ford, Catawba Co.
Catawba County SD
Supt. – See Newton
ES   28673 – Harold Caldwell,Jr., prin.

Siler City, Chatham Co., Pop. Code 5
Chatham County SD
Supt. – See Pittsboro
Chatham MS, 439 E FIFTH ST   27344
  Brenda Griffin, prin.
ES, P O BOX 629   27344 – Linda McMasters, prin.
Silk Hope ES, RURAL ROUTE 03   27344
  James Watson, prin.

Skyland, Buncombe Co., Pop. Code 4
Buncombe County SD
Supt. – See Asheville
Estes ES, P O BOX 819   28776
  M. Stevenson, prin.

Smithfield, Johnston Co., Pop. Code 6
Johnston County SD
Sch. Sys. Enr. Code 7
Supt. – Dr. J. Ellerbe, HWY 70-E   27577
Smithfield-Selma MS, P O BOX 2270   27577
  Mike Walters, prin.
MS, 518 S THIRD ST   27577 – J. Creech, Jr., prin.
South Smithfield PS, 201 W SANDERS ST   27577
  J. Barbour, prin.
Other Schools – See Benson, Clayton, Four Oaks,
  Kenly, Pine Level, Princeton, Selma, Wilsons Mills,
  Zebulon

Smyrna, Carteret Co.
Carteret County SD
Supt. – See Beaufort
ES   28579 – Donald Willis, prin.

Snow Camp, Alamance Co.
Alamance County SD
Supt. – See Graham
Sylvan ES, RURAL ROUTE 02 BOX 11   27349
  Robert Woody,Jr., prin.

Snow Hill, Greene Co., Pop. Code 4
Greene County SD
Sch. Sys. Enr. Code 5
Supt. – Dr. W. Earl Watson
  301 KINGOLD BLVD   28580
Greene Central MS
  RURAL ROUTE 01 BOX 12   28580
  George Farrow, prin.
PS, 502 SE SECOND ST   28580
  Martha Carraway, prin.
West Greene MS, 303 KINGOLD BLVD   28580
  Raymond Smith, prin.
Other Schools – See Hookerton

Sophia, Randolph Co.
Randolph County SD
Supt. – See Asheboro
New Market ES, P O BOX 189   27350
  Fred Hemric, prin.

Southern Pines, Moore Co., Pop. Code 6
Moore County SD
Supt. – See Carthage
MS, 255 S MAY ST   28387
  Nathaniel Jackson, prin.
ES, P O BOX 146   28387 – Blanchie Carter, prin.

Wallace O'Neal Day School, P O BOX 290   28387

Southport, Brunswick Co., Pop. Code 5
Brunswick County SD
Sch. Sys. Enr. Code 6
Supt. – Dr. John Kaufhold, HWY 133   28461
South Brunswick MS   28461 – Robert Rhyne, prin.
ES, 9TH ST   28461 – Donald McNeill, prin.
Other Schools – See Ash, Bolivia, Leland, Shallotte

Sparta, Alleghany Co., Pop. Code 4
Alleghany County SD
Sch. Sys. Enr. Code 4
Supt. – Clarence Crouse, 1 PEACHTREE ST   28675
ES, P O BOX 789   28675 – Evelyn Hash, prin.
Other Schools – See Ennice, Piney Creek

Spencer, Rowan Co., Pop. Code 5
Rowan County SD
Supt. – See Salisbury
North Rowan PS, P O BOX 67   28159
  Dr. Elaine Stiller, prin.

Spindale, Rutherford Co., Pop. Code 5
Rutherford County SD
Sch. Sys. Enr. Code 7
Supt. – Roger Petty
  219 FAIRGROUND ROAD   28160
Carver MS, 900 CARVER ST   28160
  Don Hastings, prin.
ES, P O BOX 36   28160 – Carolyn Keever, prin.
Other Schools – See Bostic, Cliffside, Ellenboro,
  Forest City, Henrietta, Rutherfordton, Union Mills

Spring Hope, Nash Co., Pop. Code 4
Nash County SD
Supt. – See Nashville
Spaulding MS, P O BOX 99　27882
　Marvin Johnson, prin.
ES, P O BOX 10　27882 – Donna Carr, prin.

Spring Lake, Cumberland Co., Pop. Code 6
Cumberland County SD
Supt. – See Fayetteville
Black ES, 125 S THIRD ST　28390
　William Grady, prin.
Manchester ES, 611 SPRING AVE　28390
　Ander Dunham, Jr., prin.

Spruce Pine, Mitchell Co., Pop. Code 4
Mitchell County SD
Supt. – See Bakersville
Harris MS　28777 – William Buchanan, prin.
Deyton PS　28777 – Roger Burleson, prin.

Stanfield, Stanly Co., Pop. Code 2
Stanly County SD
Supt. – See Albemarle
Ridgecrest ES, RURAL ROUTE 01　28163
　W. Nash, prin.
ES, P O BOX 250　28163 – Bill Hinson, prin.

Stanley, Gaston Co., Pop. Code 4
Gaston County SD
Supt. – See Gastonia
Kiser MS, 311 E COLLEGE ST　28164
　Carroll Saunders, prin.
Springfield ES, 900 S MAIN ST　28164
　Richard Jordan, prin.

Stantonsburg, Wilson Co., Pop. Code 3
Wilson County SD
Supt. – See Wilson
ES, P O BOX 160　27883 – Terri Cobb, prin.

Star, Montgomery Co., Pop. Code 3
Montgomery County SD
Supt. – See Troy
Star-Biscoe ES, P O BOX 608　27356
　Robert Jackson, prin.

State Road, Surry Co.
Surry County SD
Supt. – See Dobson
Mountain Park ES, RURAL ROUTE 01　28676
　Ricky Dobbins, prin.

Statesville, Iredell Co., Pop. Code 7
Iredell County SD
Sch. Sys. Enr. Code 7
Supt. – Dr. Don Williams, P O BOX 709　28677
West Iredell MS, RURAL ROUTE 06　28677
　Glenn Weddington, prin.
Central ES, RURAL ROUTE 02　28677
　Bobby Patterson, prin.
East Iredell ES, 400 E IREDELL DR　28677
　Rose Dorton, prin.
Ebenezer ES, RURAL ROUTE 04　28677
　Dr. Peggy Gray, prin.
Henkel ES, RURAL ROUTE 03　28677
　Jonathan Byers, prin.
Monticello ES, RURAL ROUTE 13　28677
　Faye Rucker, prin.
Sharon ES, RURAL ROUTE 06　28677
　Frank Feeney, prin.
Wayside ES, RURAL ROUTE 07　28677
　Ronald Williams, prin.
Other Schools – See Cleveland, Harmony,
　Mooresville, Mount Mourne, Scotts, Troutman,
　Union Grove

Statesville CSD
Sch. Sys. Enr. Code 5
Supt. – Dr. B. Carson, P O BOX 911　28677
JHS, 321 CLEGG ST　28677 – Marlin Tate, prin.
Mills ES, 1410 PEARL ST　28677
　Pamela Aman, prin.
Mulberry Street ES, 501 S MULBERRY ST　28677
　Frank Harris, prin.
Northview ES, 625 N CAROLINA AVE　28677
　Bliss Payne, prin.
Pressly ES, 222 KNOX ST　28677
　James Millsaps, prin.
Rutherford ES, 410 GARFIELD ST　28677
　Roberta Ellis, prin.
Sherrill ES, 1400 4TH ST　28677
　Charles Hauser, prin.

Stedman, Cumberland Co., Pop. Code 3
Cumberland County SD
Supt. – See Fayetteville
ES, P O BOX 279　28391 – Jerry McCall, Jr., prin.

Stokes, Pitt Co.
Pitt County SD
Supt. – See Greenville
ES, RURAL ROUTE 01 BOX 198　27884
　Roscoe Locke, prin.

Stokesdale, Guilford Co.
Guilford County SD
Supt. – See Greensboro
ES, 8025 US 158　27357 – Michael Waggoner, prin.

Stoneville, Rockingham Co., Pop. Code 4
Western Rockingham CSD
Supt. – See Madison
S, P O BOX 21　27048 – Jeter Taylor, prin.
Stone MS, RURAL ROUTE 02 BOX 427　27048
　C. Howard Bigelow, prin.

Stony Point, Alexander Co., Pop. Code 4
Alexander County SD
Supt. – See Taylorsville
ES, P O BOX 78　28678 – Fredrick Ballard, prin.

Stovall, Granville Co., Pop. Code 2
Granville County SD
Supt. – See Oxford
Stovall-Shaw ES, P O BOX 38　27582
　Martha Zollicoffer, prin.

Sugar Grove, Watauga Co.
Watauga County SD
Supt. – See Boone
Bethel ES, RURAL ROUTE 01 BOX 161　28679
　Ron Henries, prin.
Cove Creek ES
　RURAL ROUTE 01 BOX 26A　28679
　Betty Nichols, prin.

Summerfield, Guilford Co., Pop. Code 3
Guilford County SD
Supt. – See Greensboro
Laughlin ES, 7911 SUMMERFIELD RD　27358
　Peggy Joyce, prin.
MS, 7515 TRAINER DR　27358 – Jesse Joyce, prin.

Sunbury, Gates Co.
Gates County SD
Supt. – See Gatesville
Cooper MS, P O BOX 58　27979
　Benjamin Saunders, prin.
ES, P O BOX 180　27979 – William Lawrence, prin.

Swannanoa, Buncombe Co., Pop. Code 7
Buncombe County SD
Supt. – See Asheville
MS, 161 BEE TREE ROAD　28778 – Olen Sisk, prin.
ES, 161 BEE TREE RD　28778 – W. Williams, prin.

Swanquarter, Hyde Co., Pop. Code 4
Hyde County SD
Sch. Sys. Enr. Code 3
Supt. – D. Coble, P O BOX 217　27885
Peay ES, P O BOX 249　27885
　Phillip Greene, Jr., prin.
Other Schools – See Engelhard, Ocracoke

Swansboro, Onslow Co., Pop. Code 3
Carteret County SD
Supt. – See Beaufort
White Oak ES, RURAL ROUTE 01　28584
　Raymond Whitby, prin.

Onslow County SD
Supt. – See Jacksonville
JHS, RURAL ROUTE 02　28584
　Paul Wiggins, prin.
ES, P O BOX 578　28584 – Eugene Taylor, prin.
MS, RURAL ROUTE 02　28584
　Gerald Pickett, prin.

Sylva, Jackson Co., Pop. Code 4
Jackson County SD
Sch. Sys. Enr. Code 5
Supt. – Dr. William Cowan, P O BOX 277　28779
Fairview ES, 507 E MAIN ST　28779
　Kenneth Nicholson, prin.
Scotts Creek ES, RURAL ROUTE 01　28779
　W. Bembry, prin.
Other Schools – See Cullowhee, Glenville, Whittier

Tabor City, Columbus Co., Pop. Code 5
Columbus County SD
Supt. – See Whiteville
S　28463 – Ronald Ward, prin.
Tabor City West MS　28463 – John Williams, prin.
Guideway ES, RURAL ROUTE 03　28463
　Sue Gore, prin.

Tarboro, Edgecombe Co., Pop. Code 6
Edgecombe County SD
Sch. Sys. Enr. Code 6
Supt. – Lee Hall, 412 PEARL ST　27886
Roberson ES, P O BOX 610　27886
　Evelyn Johnson, prin.
Other Schools – See Battleboro, Pinetops, Rocky
　Mount, Whitakers

Tarboro CSD
Sch. Sys. Enr. Code 5
Supt. – Dr. Philip Beaman, P O BOX 370　27886
Martin MS, 300 JOHNSTON ST E　27886
　Shelvia Whitehurst, prin.
Bridgers ES, PANOLA ST　27886
　Mary Felton, prin.
Pattillo MS, EAST AVE　27886
　Raymond Privott, prin.
Princeville ES, PRINCEVILLE　27886
　Ronnie Daughtr, prin.
Stocks ES, HOPE LODGE ST　27886
　Reginald Moss, prin.

Tar Heel, Bladen Co., Pop. Code 2
Bladen County SD
Supt. – See Elizabethtown
Plain View ES, RURAL ROUTE 01 BOX 144　28392
　Verdelle McMillan, prin.

Taylorsville, Alexander Co., Pop. Code 4
Alexander County SD
Sch. Sys. Enr. Code 6
Supt. – E. Wayne Trogdon
　HAPPY PLAINS DRIVE　28681
Bethlehem ES, RURAL ROUTE 01 BOX 130　28681
　Warren Hollar, prin.
Ellendale ES, RURAL ROUTE 02 BOX 116　28681
　Dewey Austin, prin.

Sugar Loaf ES, RURAL ROUTE 05 BOX 225　28681
　Joel Blackburn, prin.
ES, 121 7TH ST SW　28681 – Blake Jones, prin.
Wittenburg ES, RURAL ROUTE 06 BOX 486　28681
　R. Watts, prin.
Other Schools – See Hiddenite, Stony Point

Thomasville, Davidson Co., Pop. Code 7
Davidson County SD
Supt. – See Lexington
Brown MS　27360 – Doris Overcash, prin.
Ledford MS, RURAL ROUTE 04 BOX 786　27360
　Gilbert Buck, prin.
Fair Grove ES, 217 CEDAR LODGE RD　27360
　Carl Price, prin.
Hasty ES, RURAL ROUTE 06 BOX 140　27360
　Joyce Swicegood, prin.
Pilot ES, RURAL ROUTE 08 BOX 160　27360
　Jerry Koontz, prin.

Thomasville CSD
Sch. Sys. Enr. Code 5
Supt. – Ronald Singletary, P O BOX 548　27361
MS, 400 UNITY ST　27360 – Wayne Thrift, prin.
Colonial Drive ES, 211 W COLONIAL DR　27360
　Ottis Honeycutt, prin.
Kern Street ES, 200 KERN ST　27360
　James Graham, prin.
Liberty Drive ES, 401 LIBERTY DR　27360
　Thomas Beard, prin.

Timberlake, Person Co.
Person County SD
Supt. – See Roxboro
Helena ES, P O BOX 38　27583
　Josiah Thomas, prin.

Tobaccoville, Forsyth Co.
Forsyth County SD
Supt. – See Winston-Salem
Old Richmond ES
　6315 TOBACCOVILLE RD　27050
　T. Bigham, prin.

Topton, Macon Co., Pop. Code 2
Macon County SD
Supt. – See Franklin
Nantahala S　28781 – Richard Baldwin, prin.

Traphill, Wilkes Co.
Wilkes County SD
Supt. – See Wilkesboro
ES, P O BOX 6　28685 – Thomas Joines, prin.

Trenton, Jones Co., Pop. Code 2
Jones County SD
Sch. Sys. Enr. Code 4
Supt. – Curtis Rains, P O BOX 187　28585
Jones MS, P O BOX 310　28585 – Curtis Lee, prin.
Comfort ES, P O BOX 188　28585
　Linda Teal, prin.
ES, P O BOX 160　28585 – Lucille Taylor, prin.
Other Schools – See Maysville, Pollocksville

Trinity, Randolph Co., Pop. Code 7
Randolph County SD
Supt. – See Asheboro
Archdale Trinity MS, P O BOX 232　27370
　Robert Upchurch, prin.
Braxton Craven MS, P O BOX 250　27370
　John Maddocks, prin.
ES, P O BOX 161　27370 – K. Vestal, prin.

Troutman, Iredell Co., Pop. Code 4
Iredell County SD
Supt. – See Statesville
MS　28166 – Reginald Brown, prin.
ES　28166 – James Edmiston, prin.

Troy, Montgomery Co., Pop. Code 5
Montgomery County SD
Sch. Sys. Enr. Code 5
Supt. – Larry Ivey, P O BOX 427　27371
MS, 414 S MAIN ST　27371 – Frances Reaves, prin.
ES, 310 N RUSSELL ST　27371
　Larry Robinson, prin.
Other Schools – See Biscoe, Candor, Mount Gilead,
　Star

Tryon, Polk Co., Pop. Code 4
Polk County SD
Supt. – See Columbus
Green Creek ES, RURAL ROUTE 01　28782
　Willie Turner, prin.

Tryon CSD
Sch. Sys. Enr. Code 3
Supt. – V. Dusenbury, P O BOX 850　28782
ES, SCHOOL ST　28782 – Walker Williams, prin.

Tuxedo, Henderson Co., Pop. Code 3
Henderson County SD
Supt. – See Hendersonville
ES, P O BOX 7　28784 – Leslie Fisher, prin.

Tyner, Chowan Co., Pop. Code 2
Chowan County SD
Supt. – See Edenton
Chowan MS　27980 – Gilliam Underwood, prin.
White Oak ES, P O BOX 128　27980
　Clara Boswell, prin.

Unaka, Cherokee Co.
Cherokee County SD
Supt. – See Murphy
ES　28908 – Kathy Forrister, prin.

Union Grove, Wilkes Co.
Iredell County SD
Supt. – See Statesville
ES 28689 – Milton Bland,Jr., prin.

Union Mills, Rutherford Co.
Rutherford County SD
Supt. – See Spindale
MS 28167 – Regan Clark, prin.

Valdese, Burke Co., Pop. Code 5
Burke County SD
Supt. – See Morganton
ES, WEST MAIN ST 28690 – Glenn Yoder, prin.

Vale, Lincoln Co.
Catawba County SD
Supt. – See Newton
Banoak ES, RURAL ROUTE 03 BOX 16 28168
  J. Tallman, prin.

Lincoln County SD
Supt. – See Lincolnton
North Brook ES, RURAL ROUTE 04 BOX 56 28168
  Sara Miller, prin.
Union ES, RURAL ROUTE 02 BOX 37 28168
  Steve Miller, prin.

Valle Crucis, Watauga Co.
Watauga County SD
Supt. – See Boone
ES, RURAL ROUTE 01 BOX 396 28691
  Thomas McNeil, prin.

Vanceboro, Craven Co., Pop. Code 3
Craven County SD
Supt. – See New Bern
Vanceboro-Farm Life ES, P O BOX 98 28586
  Richard Bowers, prin.

Vass, Moore Co., Pop. Code 3
Moore County SD
Supt. – See Carthage
Vass-Lakeview ES, P O BOX 250 28394
  Dr. Jim Brock, prin.

Vaughan, Warren Co.
Warren County SD
Supt. – See Warrenton
ES 27586 – Shirley White, prin.

Wade, Cumberland Co., Pop. Code 2
Cumberland County SD
Supt. – See Fayetteville
District 7 ES, RURAL ROUTE 01 28395
  Sheryl Lewis, prin.

Wadesboro, Anson Co., Pop. Code 5
Anson County SD
Sch. Sys. Enr. Code 6
Supt. – Dr. James Sims, P O BOX 719 28170
Central ES, P O BOX 371 28170
  George Truman, prin.
MS, P O BOX 939 28170 – Rudd Jenson, prin.
Other Schools – See Ansonville, Lilesville, Morven,
  Peachland, Polkton

Wagram, Scotland Co., Pop. Code 3
Scotland County SD
Supt. – See Laurinburg
ES, RURAL ROUTE 01 BOX 20-A 28396
  Robert Young III, prin.

Wake Forest, Wake Co., Pop. Code 5
Wake County SD
Supt. – See Raleigh
Wake Forest-Rolesville MS, P O BOX 868 27587
  Marvin Pittman, prin.
ES, 136 W SYCAMORE AVE 27587
  C. Fisher, prin.

Walkertown, Forsyth Co., Pop. Code 4
Forsyth County SD
Supt. – See Winston-Salem
MS, 3175 RUXTON DRIVE 27051
  B. Henderson, prin.
ES, 2971 MAIN ST 27051 – Earl Parker, prin.

Gospel Light Christian School, P O BOX 38 27051

Wallace, Duplin Co., Pop. Code 5
Duplin County SD
Supt. – See Kenansville
ES, RURAL ROUTE 03 BOX 9 28466
  Cecil Beaman, prin.

Wallburg, Davidson Co.
Davidson County SD
Supt. – See Lexington
ES, P O BOX 65 27373 – Larry Garrison, prin.

Walnut Cove, Stokes Co., Pop. Code 4
Stokes County SD
Supt. – See Danbury
IS 27052 – Larry Durham, prin.
PS 27052 – Jane Williams, prin.

Warrenton, Warren Co., Pop. Code 3
Warren County SD
Sch. Sys. Enr. Code 5
Supt. – Michael Williams, P O BOX 110 27589
Graham MS 27589 – Willie Ramey III, prin.
Boyd ES 27589 – Walter Sweeney, prin.
Hawkins MS 27589 – Joseph Richardson, prin.
South Warren ES, RURAL ROUTE 02 27589
  Lucious Hawkins, prin.
Other Schools – See Norlina, Vaughan, Wise

Warsaw, Duplin Co., Pop. Code 5
Duplin County SD
Supt. – See Kenansville
JHS, 718 W COLLEGE ST 28398
  H. Bowden, prin.
ES, RURAL ROUTE 01 BOX 55 28398
  Paul Britt, prin.

Washington, Beaufort Co., Pop. Code 6
Beaufort County SD
Sch. Sys. Enr. Code 5
Supt. – Ethel Matthews, 321 SMAW ROAD 27889
Other Schools – See Aurora, Bath, Belhaven,
  Chocowinity, Pantego, Pinetown

Washington CSD
Sch. Sys. Enr. Code 5
Supt. – George Thigpen, 308 7TH ST 27889
Eastern ES, 947 HUDNELL ST 27889
  Robert Belcher, prin.
Small MS, 400 N HARVEY ST 27889
  Brenda Jones, prin.
Tayloe ES, 910 TARBORO ST 27889
  Michael Baker, prin.

Waxhaw, Union Co., Pop. Code 4
Union County SD
Supt. – See Monroe
ES, P O BOX 159 28173 – Paul Matheson, prin.
Western Union ES
  4111 WESTERN UNION SCH RD 28173
  Jerry Cross, prin.

Waynesville, Haywood Co., Pop. Code 6
Haywood County SD
Sch. Sys. Enr. Code 6
Supt. – Charles McConnell,Jr.
  1615 N MAIN ST 28786
Bethal ES, RURAL ROUTE 03 BOX 256 28786
  Charles Childers, prin.
Central ES, 506 S HAYWOOD ST 28786
  George McCorkle, prin.
Jonathan Valley ES, 165 HALL DR 28786
  Mary Fowler, prin.
Junaluska ES, 2301 ASHEVILLE RD 28786
  Dale Parris, prin.
Other Schools – See Canton, Clyde, Hazelwood

Weaverville, Buncombe Co., Pop. Code 4
Buncombe County SD
Supt. – See Asheville
MS, P O BOX 674 28787 – A. Taylor, prin.
Flat Creek ES, RURAL ROUTE 02 28787
  Ronnie Sams, prin.
Red Oak ES, 51 RED OAK SCHOOL RD 28787
  William Brigman, prin.
MS, P O BOX 674 28787 – Robert Nesbitt, prin.
Weaverville PS, P O BOX 654 28787
  Roy McGuinn, prin.

Welcome, Davidson Co., Pop. Code 4
Davidson County SD
Supt. – See Lexington
ES, P O BOX 849 27374 – Robert Rankin, prin.

Weldon, Halifax Co., Pop. Code 4
Weldon CSD
Sch. Sys. Enr. Code 4
Supt. – Dr. M. Fisher, P O BOX 31 27890
ES, P O BOX 112 27890 – Eva Howell, prin.
Other Schools – See Halifax

Wendell, Wake Co., Pop. Code 4
Wake County SD
Supt. – See Raleigh
Whitley MS, RURAL ROUTE 02 27591
  Michael Jordan, prin.
Carver ES, P O BOX 769 27591
  Alex Taylor, prin.
MS, WILSON AVE BOX 727 27591
  Elizabeth Rountree, prin.

Wentworth, Rockingham Co., Pop. Code 6
Rockingham County SD
Sch. Sys. Enr. Code 5
Supt. – Ira Trollinger, P O BOX 8 27375
ES, P O BOX 37 27375 – J. Meador, prin.
Other Schools – See Reidsville, Ruffin

West End, Moore Co., Pop. Code 3
Moore County SD
Supt. – See Carthage
ES, P O BOX 335 27376 – Joan Frye, prin.

Westfield, Stokes Co.
Stokes County SD
Supt. – See Danbury
Francisco ES, RURAL ROUTE 02 27053
  Jesse Martin, prin.
Reynolds ES, RURAL ROUTE 02 27053
  Barry Wall, prin.

Surry County SD
Supt. – See Dobson
ES, P O BOX 63 27053 – James Jessup, prin.

West Jefferson, Ashe Co., Pop. Code 3
Ashe County SD
Supt. – See Jefferson
ES, P O BOX 68 28694 – Bradley McNeill, prin.

Whitakers, Nash Co., Pop. Code 2
Edgecombe County SD
Supt. – See Tarboro
Willow Grove ES
  RURAL ROUTE 01 BOX 248 27891
  Gregory Todd, prin.

Nash County SD
Supt. – See Nashville
North Whitakers ES
  RURAL ROUTE 01 BOX 104-A 27891
  James Harfield, prin.
Swift Creek ES
  RURAL ROUTE 02 BOX 144 27891
  Carl Mills, prin.

Enfield Academy, P O BOX 700 27891

White Plains, Surry Co.
Surry County SD
Supt. – See Dobson
ES, P O BOX 77 27031 – Ben Bolick, prin.

Whiteville, Columbus Co., Pop. Code 6
Columbus County SD
Sch. Sys. Enr. Code 6
Supt. – R. Tyler, P O BOX 729 28472
Williams Twp. S, RURAL ROUTE 03 28472
  Denny McPherson, prin.
Old Dock ES, RURAL ROUTE 04 28472
  J. Formyduval,Jr., prin.
Other Schools – See Cerro Gordo, Chadbourn,
  Evergreen, Fair Bluff, Hallsboro, Riegelwood, Tabor
  City

Whiteville CSD
Sch. Sys. Enr. Code 5
Supt. – Dr. Jerry Paschal, P O BOX 609 28472
Central MS, 2085 MEMORY ST 28472
  Milton Frink, prin.
Edgewood MS, 305 E CALHOUN ST 28472
  Dr. Eugenia Blake, prin.
PS, HWY 74-76 28472 – Larry Hewett, prin.

Whittier, Jackson Co.
Jackson County SD
Supt. – See Sylva
Smokey Mountain ES, RURAL ROUTE 01 28789
  Lou Nicholson, prin.

Swain County SD
Supt. – See Bryson City
ES 28789 – Lambert Wilson, prin.

Wilkesboro, Wilkes Co., Pop. Code 4
Wilkes County SD
Sch. Sys. Enr. Code 7
Supt. – Marsh Lyall, 201 MAIN ST W 28697
ES, 1248 SCHOOL ST 28697 – Linda Little, prin.
Other Schools – See Boomer, Elkin, Ferguson, Hays,
  Millers Creek, Moravian Falls, North Wilkesboro,
  Roaring River, Ronda, Traphill

Willard, Pender Co.
Pender County SD
Supt. – See Burgaw
Penderlea ES
  RURAL ROUTE 01 BOX 335X 28478
  Vann Blake, prin.

Williamston, Martin Co., Pop. Code 6
Martin County SD
Sch. Sys. Enr. Code 6
Supt. – F. Boyd Bailey, 300 N WATTS ST 27892
JHS, P O BOX 427 27892
  William Matthews, prin.
Hayes MS 27892 – George James, prin.
Rodgers ES, RURAL ROUTE 04 27892
  Herman Daniels, prin.
PS 27892 – Mary Andrews, prin.
Other Schools – See Everetts, Hamilton, Jamesville,
  Oak City, Robersonville

Willow Spring, Wake Co.
Wake County SD
Supt. – See Raleigh
ES, P O BOX 38 27592 – Russell Manning, prin.

Wilmington, New Hanover Co., Pop. Code 8
New Hanover County SD
Sch. Sys. Enr. Code 7
Supt. – Dr. Richard Flynn, P O BOX 390 28402
Myrtle Grove MS, 901 PINER RD 28403
  George Lopatka, prin.
Noble JHS, 6520 MARKET ST 28405
  William Moore, prin.
Roland-Grise JHS, 4412 LAKE ST 28403
  Gary Widenhouse, prin.
Trask JHS, RURAL ROUTE 06 BOX 212 28405
  Hugh McManus, prin.
Virgo JHS, 813 NIXON ST 28401
  Russell Simmons, prin.
Williston JHS, 401 S 10TH ST 28401
  Arthalia Williams, prin.
Alderman ES, 2025 INDEPENDENCE BLVD 28403
  Justine Lerch, prin.
Bellamy ES, 70 SANDERS DR 28403
  Emma Jackson, prin.
Blair ES, 6510 MARKET ST 28405
  George Finch, prin.
Blount ES, 3702 PRINCESS PLACE DR 28405
  Inez Richardson, prin.
Bradley Creek ES
  6211 GREENVILLE LOOP RD 28403
  Henry Rivenbark, prin.
College Park ES, 5001 ORIOLE DR 28403
  Ralph Davis, prin.
Forest Hills ES, 602 COLONIAL DR 28403
  W. Maynard, prin.
Gregory ES, 319 S 10TH ST 28401
  Dorothy Deshields, prin.
Howe ES, 1020 MEARS ST 28401
  Gwendolyn Robinson, prin.

Johnson ES, 1100 MCRAE ST　28401
　Jacqueline O'Grady, prin.
Ogden ES, 421 MIDDLE SOUND RD　28405
　Michael Sabrinsky, prin.
Pine Valley ES, 440 JOHN S MOSBY DR　28403
　Fred Nelson, prin.
Roe ES, 2875 WORTH DR　28403
　Adelaide Kopotic, prin.
Snipes ES, 2150 CHESTNUT ST　28405
　Dennis Brandon, prin.
Sunset Park ES, 613 ALABAMA AVE　28401
　Julia Davis, prin.
Williams ES, 801 SILVER LAKE RD　28403
　Curtis Edwards, prin.
Winter Park ES, 204 S MACMILLAN AVE　28403
　Emma McCall, prin.
Wrightsboro ES, 640 CASTLE HAYNE RD　28401
　Steven Sneeden, prin.
Other Schools – See Carolina Beach, Wrightsville
　Beach

Cape Fear Academy
　4002 S COLLEGE ROAD　28403
Wilmington Christian Academy
　1401 N COLLEGE ROAD　28405
St. Mary's School, 217 S FOURTH ST　28401

Wilson, Wilson Co., Pop. Code 8
Wilson County SD
Sch. Sys. Enr. Code 7
Supt. – Thomas Dixon, P O BOX 2048　27894
Forest Hills MS, 1210 FOREST HILLS　27893
　Marshall Long, prin.
Speight MS, RURAL ROUTE 03　BOX 452　27893
　Lacy Taylor, prin.
Toisnot MS, 1301 CORBETT AVE　27893
　Henry Mercer, prin.
Adams ES, 639 E WALNUT ST　27893
　Dianne Pridgen, prin.
Barnes ES, RURAL ROUTE 05 BOX 57　27893
　Oneva Alston, prin.
Darden-Vick MS, 504 CARROLL ST E　27893
　Crawford Lane, prin.
Elvie Street MS, 723 ELVIE ST S　27893
　T. Lofton, prin.
Hearne ES, 300 W GOLD ST　27893
　W. Page, prin.
New Hope ES, 5212 NASH ST W　27893
　William Stott, prin.
Rock Ridge ES, RURAL ROUTE 02　27893
　Robert Caddell, prin.
Vinson-Bynum MS, 1601 TARBORO ST SW　27893
　Dalphine Perry, prin.
Wells ES, 1400 GROVE ST N　27893
　Christine Boyette, prin.
Winstead MS, 1713 DOWNING ST SW　27893
　Robert Pope, prin.
Other Schools – See Black Creek, Elm City, Lucama,
　Stantonsburg

Wilson Christian Academy, P O BOX 3818　27895

Wilsons Mills, Johnston Co.
Johnston County SD
Supt. – See Smithfield
ES, P O BOX 176　27593 – William Gilbert,Jr., prin.

Windsor, Bertie Co., Pop. Code 4
Bertie County SD
Sch. Sys. Enr. Code 5
Supt. – George Stancil, BERTIE IND PARK　27983
Askewville ES, P O BOX 38　27983
　Ray Kornegay, prin.
Southwestern ES, P O BOX 70　27983
　Glenwood Mitchell, prin.
Other Schools – See Aulander, Colerain, Lewiston
　Woodville, Merry Hill, Powellsville

Winfall, Perquimans Co.
Perquimans County SD
Supt. – See Hertford
Perquimans Union MS, P O BOX 117　27985
　Gary Stubbins, prin.

Perquimans Central ES, P O BOX 128　27985
　J. Kornegay, prin.

Wingate, Union Co., Pop. Code 5
Union County SD
Supt. – See Monroe
ES, P O BOX 127　28174 – Jerry Thomas, prin.

Winston-Salem, Forsyth Co., Pop. Code 9
Forsyth County SD
Sch. Sys. Enr. Code 8
Supt. – M. Jessup, P O BOX 2513　27102
Ashley MS, E 21ST ST　27105 – John Beaty, prin.
Atkins MS, 1215 N CAMERON AVE　27101
　Donald Golding, prin.
Cook MS, 920 W 11TH ST　27105
　Shirley Atkinson, prin.
Hanes MS, 28TH & IVY AVE　27105
　Nancy Gibson, prin.
Hill MS, 2300 TRYON ST　27107
　Ed Armstrong, prin.
Kennedy MS, 100 N HIGHLAND AVE　27101
　W. Holliday, prin.
Mineral Springs MS, 4559 OGBURN AVE　27105
　Kaye Shutt, prin.
Northwest MS, 5501 MURRAY ROAD　27106
　Michael Shrader, prin.
Paisley MS, 1400 GRANT AVE　27105
　Edward Hanes, prin.
Petree Optional MS
　3815 OLD GREENSBORO ROAD　27107
　Ron Caviness, prin.
Philo MS, 410 HAVERHILL ST　27107
　Dawn Wooten, prin.
Wiley MS, 1400 W NORTHWEST BLVD　27104
　Jay Wise, prin.
Bolton ES, 1250 BOLTON ST　27103
　James Kleu, prin.
Brunson ES, 155 N HAWTHORNE RD　27104
　Mary Isaacs, prin.
Easton ES, 734 E CLEMMONSVILLE RD　27107
　Norman King, prin.
Forest Park ES, 1900 MILFORD ST　27107
　Hoyt Wiseman, prin.
Griffith ES, 1385 W CLEMMONSVILLE RD　27127
　Bobbie McLeod, prin.
Hall-Woodard ES, 125 NICHOLSON RD　27107
　Peggy Tesh, prin.
Ibraham ES, 5036 OLD WALKERTOWN RD　27105
　A. Yarborough, prin.
Jefferson ES, 3500 SALLY KIRK RD　27106
　Fran Douthit, prin.
Kimberley Park ES, 1700 OLD CHERRY ST　27105
　W. Blackwell, prin.
Konnoak ES, 3200 RENON RD　27127
　Dr. Nelson Shearouse, prin.
Latham ES, 986 HUTTON ST　27101
　James McDaniel, prin.
Mineral Springs ES, 4527 OGBURN AVE　27105
　William Honeycutt, prin.
Moore ES, 451 KNOLLWOOD ST　27103
　Geneva Brown, prin.
Old Town ES, 3930 REYNOLDA RD　27106
　Chancel Brown, prin.
Sherwood Forest ES, 1055 YORKSHIRE RD　27106
　Hilda Barry, prin.
South Fork ES, 4332 COUNTRY CLUB RD　27104
　Rodger Eckard, prin.
Speas ES, WEST POLO ROAD　27106
　Thomas Gale, prin.
Whitaker ES
　BUENA VISTA-DARTMOUTH ROAD　27104
　Paul Stephens, prin.
Other Schools – See Clemmons, Kernersville,
　Lewisville, Pfafftown, Rural Hall, Tobaccoville,
　Walkertown

Our Lady of Mercy ES
　1900 SUNNYSIDE AVE　27127
St. John Lutheran ES
　2415 SILAS CREEK PKY　27103
St. Leo ES, 333 SPRINGDALE AVE　27104
The Summit ES, REYNOLDA ESTATES　27106

Winterville, Pitt Co., Pop. Code 4
Pitt County SD
Supt. – See Greenville
Cox MS, P O BOX 550　28590 – John Pinner, prin.
Robinson ES, P O BOX 509　28590
　Althea Weathington, prin.

Winton, Hertford Co., Pop. Code 3
Hertford County SD
Sch. Sys. Enr. Code 5
Supt. – George Norris, P O BOX 158　27986
Brown ES, P O BOX 38　27986
　Adron Jones,Jr., prin.
Other Schools – See Ahoskie, Murfreesboro

Wise, Warren Co.
Warren County SD
Supt. – See Warrenton
North Warren MS　27594 – Costel Evans, prin.

Woodland, Northampton Co., Pop. Code 3
Northampton County SD
Supt. – See Jackson
Woodland-Olney ES, MAIN ST　27897
　Helen Creech, prin.

Woodleaf, Rowan Co.
Rowan County SD
Supt. – See Salisbury
ES, P O BOX 10　27054 – Ray Shytle, prin.

Wrightsville Beach, New Hanover Co., Pop. Code 5
New Hanover County SD
Supt. – See Wilmington
ES, CORAL DR　28480 – H. Lennon, prin.

Yadkinville, Yadkin Co., Pop. Code 4
Yadkin County SD
Sch. Sys. Enr. Code 5
Supt. – Cleve Hollar, P O BOX 98　27055
Courtney ES, RURAL ROUTE 04 BOX 348　27055
　Thomas Wooten, prin.
Forbush ES, RURAL ROUTE 02 BOX 395　27018
　Herbert Baker, prin.
ES, P O BOX 518　27055 – Roger Nixon, prin.
Other Schools – See Boonville, East Bend,
　Hamptonville, Jonesville

Yanceyville, Caswell Co., Pop. Code 5
Caswell County SD
Sch. Sys. Enr. Code 5
Supt. – Dr. Lawrence Walker, P O BOX 160　27379
Dillard JHS　27379 – Larry Briggs, prin.
Oakwood ES, P O BOX 640　27379
　Gloria Wallace, prin.
Yancey MS, P O BOX 656　27379 – M. Battle, prin.
Other Schools – See Blanch, Burlington, Mebane,
　Milton, Pelham, Reidsville, Ruffin

Youngsville, Franklin Co., Pop. Code 2
Franklin County SD
Supt. – See Louisburg
ES　27596 – Clay Batchelor, prin.

Zebulon, Wake Co., Pop. Code 4
Johnston County SD
Supt. – See Smithfield
Corinth Holder ES, RURAL ROUTE 01　27597
　Haywood Watson, prin.

Wake County SD
Supt. – See Raleigh
ES, RURAL ROUTE 03 BOX 72　27597
　L. Liles, prin.

Zionville, Watauga Co.
Watauga County SD
Supt. – See Boone
Mabel ES, RURAL ROUTE 01 BOX 87　28698
　Mitchell Yates, prin.

NORTH DAKOTA

DEPARTMENT OF PUBLIC INSTRUCTION
600 Boulevard Ave., E., Bismarck 58505
(701) 224-2261

Superintendent of Public Instruction   Dr. Wayne Sanstead
Assistant Superintendent   Ronald Stastney

STATE BOARD OF PUBLIC SCHOOL EDUCATION
Dr. Vern Bennett, *Chairman*   Fargo 58103

STATE BOARD OF HIGHER EDUCATION
Jack Olin, *President*   12th Ave., W., Dickinson 58601

COUNTY SUPERINTENDENTS OF SCHOOLS

Adams County, Reva Frieze, Supt.
   P O BOX 150, Hettinger 58639
Barnes County, Pat Beil, Supt.
   Valley City 58072
Benson County, Jean Olson, Supt.
   P O BOX 347, Minnewaukan 58351
Billings County, Lana O'Brien, Supt.
   Medora 58645
Bottineau County, Dwane Getzlaff, Supt.
   Bottineau 58318
Bowman County, Lois Anderson, Supt.
   Bowman 58623
Burke County, Patricia Eckert, Supt.
   Bowbells 58721
Burleigh County, Eileen Mack, Supt.
   Bismarck 58504
Cass County, Joyce Holm, Supt.
   P O BOX 2806, Fargo 58108
Cavalier County, Shirley Peterson, Supt.
   901 3RD ST, Langdon 58249
Dickey County, Helen Sprouse, Supt.
   Ellendale 58436
Divide County, Wilma Anderson, Supt.
   Crosby 58730
Dunn County, Ella Mathisen, Supt.
   Manning 58642
Eddy County, Alice Allmaras, Supt.
   524 CENTRAL AVE, New Rockford 58356
Emmons County, Alvin M Tachosik, Supt.
   Linton 58552
Foster County, Sue Swanson, Supt.
   Carrington 58421
Golden Valley County, Kembel Dahl, Supt.
   P O BOX 35, Beach 58621
Grand Forks County, Kathryn Haltli, Supt.
   P O BOX 1435, Grand Forks 58206

Grant County, Deloris Roth, Supt.
   P O BOX 279, Carson 58529
Griggs County, Ardis Oettle, Supt.
   P O BOX 566, Cooperstown 58425
Hettinger County, (-), Supt.
   Mott 58646
Kidder County, Judy Fettig, Supt.
   Steele 58482
Lamoure County, Margaret Witt, Supt.
   P O BOX 235, La Moure 58458
Logan County, Gary Schumacker, Supt.
   Napoleon 58561
McHenry County, Corabelle Brown, Supt.
   Towner 58788
McIntosh County, Jerald Retzer, Supt.
   Ashley 58413
McKenzie County, Jessie Goddard, Supt.
   P O BOX 503, Watford City 58854
McLean County, James Fisher, Supt.
   P O BOX 10, Washburn 58577
Mercer County, Alice Husfloen, Supt.
   Stanton 58571
Morton County, William T Heisler, Supt.
   210 2ND AVE NW, Mandan 58554
Mountrail County, W. Ray Stewart, Supt.
   P O BOX 490, Stanley 58784
Nelson County, Grace Carlson, Supt.
   P O BOX 566, Lakota 58344
Oliver County, Alice Husfloen, Supt.
   Center 58530
Pembina County, Lois Olson, Supt.
   Cavalier 58220
Pierce County, Ioane Schmidt, Supt.
   Rugby 58368
Ramsey County, Caroline Horne, Supt.
   Devils Lake 58301

Ranson County, Sheryl Dagman, Supt.
   Lisbon 58054
Renville County, Shanette Haarsager, Supt.
   Mohall 58761
Richland County, Ted Schields, Supt.
   P O BOX 126, Wahpeton 58074
Rolette County, Dwane Getzlaff, Supt.
   Rolla 58367
Sargent County, Elaine Marquette, Supt.
   P O BOX 249, Forman 58032
Sheridan County, Anton Klein, Supt.
   P O BOX 667, McClusky 58463
Sioux County, Judy Fedder, Supt.
   P O BOX L, Fort Yates 58538
Slope County, Lois Anderson, Supt.
   P O BOX MM, Amidon 58620
Stark County, (-), Supt.
   P O BOX 130, Dickinson 58601
Steele County, Barbara Dekker, Supt.
   Finley 58230
Stutsman County, Joan Nayes, Supt.
   Jamestown 58401
Towner County, Patrick Delmore, Supt.
   Cando 58324
Traill County, Francis Colby, Supt.
   Hillsboro 58045
Walsh County, Lois Olson, Supt.
   Grafton 58237
Ward County, Everette Stromme, Supt.
   Minot 58701
Wells County, Sandra Olschlager, Supt.
   Fessenden 58438
Williams County, Grant Archer, Supt.
   Williston 58801

PUBLIC, PRIVATE, AND PAROCHIAL ELEMENTARY SCHOOLS

Abercrombie, Richland Co., Pop. Code 2
Richland SD 44
Supt. – See Colfax
Richland ES, P O BOX 139 58001
   Ron Julson, prin.

Adams, Walsh Co., Pop. Code 2
Adams SD 128
Sch. Sys. Enr. Code 2
Supt. – David Monson, P O BOX 76 58210
S, P O BOX 76 58210 – Dennis Hammer, prin.

Alamo, Williams Co., Pop. Code 2
Cottonwood Lake SD
Sch. Sys. Enr. Code 1
Supt. – Tony Grubb, P O BOX 57 58830
S, P O BOX 57 58830 – Tony Grubb, prin.

Alexander, McKenzie Co., Pop. Code 2
Alexander SD 2
Sch. Sys. Enr. Code 2
Supt. – Reid Straabe, P O BOX 66 58831
S, P O BOX 66 58831 – Darold Hitland, prin.

Almont, Morton Co., Pop. Code 2
Sims SD 8
Sch. Sys. Enr. Code 1
Supt. – Kasper N. Greff, P O BOX 128 58520
S, P O BOX 128 58520 – Ross Roemmich, prin.

Amenia, Cass Co., Pop. Code 1
Central Cass SD 17
Supt. – See Casselton
MS, P O BOX 57 58004 – Jack Fuller, prin.

Amidon, Slope Co., Pop. Code 1
Central Elementary SD 32
Sch. Sys. Enr. Code 1
Supt. – (—) 58620
ES 58620 – (—), prin.

Aneta, Nelson Co., Pop. Code 2
Aneta SD 20
Sch. Sys. Enr. Code 1
Supt. – Thomas Andler, P O BOX 257 58212
S, P O BOX 257 58212 – Larry Hoyt, prin.

Argusville, Cass Co., Pop. Code 2
Cass Valley North SD
Sch. Sys. Enr. Code 2
Supt. – Donald Muhs, P O BOX 38 58005
Cass Valley North ES, P O BOX 108 58005
   Jerry Srur, prin.

Ashley, McIntosh Co., Pop. Code 4
Ashley SD 9
Sch. Sys. Enr. Code 2
Supt. – B. McShane, P O BOX H 58413
S, P O BOX H 58413 – Floyd Schock, prin.

Baldwin, Burleigh Co.
Baldwin SD 29
Sch. Sys. Enr. Code 1
Supt. – (—), P O BOX 154 58521
ES, P O BOX 154 58521 – Genevieve Lyson, prin.

Balta, Pierce Co., Pop. Code 2
Balta SD 7
Sch. Sys. Enr. Code 1
Supt. – Donald Christianson, P O BOX 398 58313

S, P O BOX 398 58313
   Donald Christianson, prin.

Beach, Golden Valley Co., Pop. Code 4
Beach SD 3
Sch. Sys. Enr. Code 2
Supt. – John Adkins, P O BOX 368 58621
Lincoln ES, P O BOX 685 58621
   John Otterness, prin.

Belcourt, Rolette Co., Pop. Code 3
Belcourt SD 7
Sch. Sys. Enr. Code 4
Supt. – Daniel Jerome, P O BOX 440 58316
Turtle Mtn. Community MS, P O BOX 440 58316
   Louis Dauphinais, prin.
Turtle Mountain Community ES
   P O BOX 440 58316 – Teresa Delorme, prin.

Ojibwa Indian ES 58316

Belfield, Stark Co., Pop. Code 4
Billings County SD 1
Supt. – See Medora
Fryburg ES, RURAL ROUTE 03 BOX 19 58622
   Myron Johnson, prin.

Elm Grove SD 13
Sch. Sys. Enr. Code 2
Supt. – Walt V. Hoff, P O BOX 97 58622
S, P O BOX 97 58622 – Dennis Schmitz, prin.

Berthold, Ward Co., Pop. Code 2
Berthold SD 54
Sch. Sys. Enr. Code 2
Supt. – Kevin J. Keenaghan, P O BOX 185 58718
S, P O BOX 185 58718 – Clyde T. Huber, prin.

Beulah, Mercer Co., Pop. Code 5
Beulah SD 27
Sch. Sys. Enr. Code 4
Supt. – Dale T. Gilje, P O BOX 129 58523
MS, P O BOX 129 58523 – Dale Gilje, prin.
ES, P O BOX 129 58523 – Arthur Schilke, prin.

Binford, Griggs Co., Pop. Code 2
Binford SD 23
Sch. Sys. Enr. Code 2
Supt. – Lloyd K. Gjovik, P O BOX 38 58416
S, P O BOX 38 58416 – Larry Wold, prin.

Bismarck, Burleigh Co., Pop. Code 8
Apple Creek SD 39
Sch. Sys. Enr. Code 1
Supt. – (—), RURAL ROUTE 02 58501
Apple Creek ES, RURAL ROUTE 02 58504
Charlotte Knittel, prin.

Bismarck SD 1
Sch. Sys. Enr. Code 6
Supt. – Lowell Jensen, 400 AVE E 58501
Becep Center ES, 400 E AVENUE E 58501
Robert Stuckenbruck, prin.
Grimsrud ES, 716 W SAINT BENEDICT DR 58501
Rita Klemin, prin.
Highland Acres ES, 1200 PRAIRIE DR 58501
Ronald Becker, prin.
Lincoln ES, RURAL ROUTE 02 58504
(—), prin.
Miller ES 58501 – Maynard Dahl, prin.
Moore ES 58501 – John Wanser, prin.
Moses ES 58501 – Rolland Messmer, prin.
Murphy ES, 611 N 31ST ST 58501
Richard Buresh, prin.
Myhre ES 58501 – Harry Weisenberger, prin.
Northridge ES, 1727 N 3RD ST 58501
August Ritter, prin.
Pioneer ES, 14TH & BRAMAN 58501
Wayne Granfor, prin.
Richholt ES, 720 N 14TH ST 58501
Richard Buresh, prin.
Riverside ES, 406 S ANDERSON ST 58504
John Wanser, prin.
Roosevelt ES, 500 N ANDERSON ST 58501
Ronald Becker, prin.
Saxvik ES, 523 N 21ST ST 58501
Richard Buresh, prin.
Solheim ES 58501 – Don Prouty, prin.

Manning SD 45
Sch. Sys. Enr. Code 1
Supt. – (—), RURAL ROUTE 02 58501
Manning ES, RURAL ROUTE 02 BOX 161 58504
Vicki Bjornson, prin.

Naughton SD 25
Sch. Sys. Enr. Code 1
Supt. – (—), RURAL ROUTE 01 58501
Naughton ES, RURAL ROUTE 01 BOX 271 58501
Dianne Doerr, prin.

Telfer SD 46
Sch. Sys. Enr. Code 1
Supt. – (—), RURAL ROUTE 02 58501
Telfer ES, RURAL ROUTE 02 58504
Patricia Stein, prin.

Cathedral of the Holy Spirit ES
508 RAYMOND ST 58501
St. Annes ES, 13215 N 13TH ST 58501
St. Marys ES 58501

Bottineau, Bottineau Co., Pop. Code 5
Bottineau SD
Sch. Sys. Enr. Code 3
Supt. – James Holwell, 301 BRANDER ST 58318
ES 58318 – Terry Thirsk, prin.

Bowbells, Burke Co., Pop. Code 3
Bowbells SD 14
Sch. Sys. Enr. Code 2
Supt. – Rick Herbel, P O BOX 307 58721
S, P O BOX 307 58721 – Lyle C Olson, prin.

Bowdon, Wells Co., Pop. Code 2
Bowdon SD 23
Sch. Sys. Enr. Code 1
Supt. – Kent Hart, P O BOX 429 58418
S, P O BOX 429 58418 – Norbert J. Schlegel, prin.

Bowman, Bowman Co., Pop. Code 4
Bowman SD
Sch. Sys. Enr. Code 2
Supt. – Herbert Johnson, P O BOX H 58623
S, P O BOX H 58623 – Glenn Moser, prin.

Sheets SD 14
Sch. Sys. Enr. Code 1
Supt. – (—), RURAL ROUTE 01 BOX 21 58623
Cottage ES, RURAL ROUTE 01 BOX 21 58623
(—), prin.

Braddock, Emmons Co., Pop. Code 1
Braddock SD 7
Sch. Sys. Enr. Code 1
Supt. – Arthur Svalen, P O BOX 4 58524
S, P O BOX 4 58524 – Tim Dockter, prin.

Buchanan, Stutsman Co.
Buchanan SD 11
Sch. Sys. Enr. Code 2
Supt. – Denis Moen, P O BOX 97 58420
Pingree Buchanan ES, P O BOX 97 58420
Terrie Neys, prin.

Burlington, Ward Co., Pop. Code 3
United SD 7
Supt. – See Des Lacs
Burlington Des Lacs ES
301 WALLACE ST E 58722
James Goodman, prin.

Butte, McLean Co., Pop. Code 2
Butte SD 62
Sch. Sys. Enr. Code 1
Supt. – Richard Ringuette, P O BOX 287 58723
S, P O BOX 287 58723 – Arthur R. Kabanuk, prin.

Buxton, Traill Co., Pop. Code 2
Central Valley SD
Sch. Sys. Enr. Code 2
Supt. – Dale Duggan
HIGHWAY 81 BOX 152 58218
Central Valley S, HIGHWAY 81 BOX 152 58218
Robert Schneck, prin.

Calvin, Cavalier Co., Pop. Code 1
Border Central SD
Sch. Sys. Enr. Code 2
Supt. – John Roscoe 58323
Border Central 58323 – Mary Bollinger, prin.
Other Schools – See Sarles

Cando, Towner Co., Pop. Code 4
Southern SD 8
Sch. Sys. Enr. Code 2
Supt. – Albert Peterson, 418 2ND 58324
S, 418 2ND 58324 – Jon Kringen, prin.

Cannon Ball, Sioux Co., Pop. Code 2
Solen SD 3
Supt. – See Solen
ES 58528 – Lena George, prin.

Carpio, Ward Co., Pop. Code 2
Carpio SD 156
Sch. Sys. Enr. Code 2
Supt. – Marcia Mergenthal, P O BOX 168 58725
S, P O BOX 160 58725 – Patrick Dean, prin.

Carrington, Foster Co., Pop. Code 5
Carrington SD 10
Sch. Sys. Enr. Code 3
Supt. – Charles Brickner, 100 3RD AVE S 58421
ES, 232 9TH AVE N 58421 – Russell Miller, prin.

Carson, Grant Co., Pop. Code 2
Roosevelt SD 18
Sch. Sys. Enr. Code 2
Supt. – James Streifel, P O BOX 197 58529
Roosevelt S, P O BOX 197 58529
Jerome Sondag, prin.

Cartwright, McKenzie Co.
Horse Creek SD 32
Sch. Sys. Enr. Code 1
Supt. – (—), P O BOX 8 58838
Horse Creek ES, P O BOX 9 58838 – (—), prin.

Casselton, Cass Co., Pop. Code 4
Central Cass SD 17
Sch. Sys. Enr. Code 3
Supt. – Jerome Tjaden, P O BOX 250 58012
Central Cass S, P O BOX 250 58012
Steve Lorentzen, prin.
Other Schools – See Amenia

Cavalier, Pembina Co., Pop. Code 4
Cavalier SD
Sch. Sys. Enr. Code 3
Supt. – Melvin Olson, P O BOX N 58220
S, P O BOX N 58220 – Loren Scheer, prin.

Center, Oliver Co., Pop. Code 3
Center SD 18
Sch. Sys. Enr. Code 2
Supt. – Stanley Miller, P O BOX 248 58530
S, P O BOX 248 58530 – Leonard Shupe, prin.

Chaffee, Cass Co., Pop. Code 2
Chaffee SD 26
Sch. Sys. Enr. Code 1
Supt. – Brian Ramberg, P O BOX 110 58014
S, P O BOX 110 58014 – Brian Ramberg, prin.

Churchs Ferry, Ramsey Co., Pop. Code 2
Churchs Ferry SD 4
Sch. Sys. Enr. Code 1
Supt. – Winnifred Knutson 58325
S, P O BOX 157 58325 – Steven Stevenson, prin.

Colfax, Richland Co., Pop. Code 2
Richland SD 44
Sch. Sys. Enr. Code 2
Supt. – Ron Julson 58018
Other Schools – See Abercrombie

Columbus, Burke Co., Pop. Code 2
Columbus SD 34
Sch. Sys. Enr. Code 2
Supt. – Ronald Stammen, P O BOX 45 58727
ES, P O BOX 45 58727 – Beverly Baker, prin.

Cooperstown, Griggs Co., Pop. Code 4
Cooperstown SD 18
Sch. Sys. Enr. Code 2
Supt. – William Galloway, P O BOX 487 58425

Central ES, P O BOX 487 58425
Maynard Gunderson, prin.

Crary, Ramsey Co., Pop. Code 2
Crary SD 3
Sch. Sys. Enr. Code 1
Supt. – Samuel Tollefson
RURAL ROUTE 01 BOX 1A 58327
S, RURAL ROUTE 01 BOX 1A 58327
Dennis Nelson, prin.

Crosby, Divide Co., Pop. Code 4
Divide County SD 1
Sch. Sys. Enr. Code 2
Supt. – Ronald Stammen, P O BOX G 58730
Divide County ES, 300 2ND AVE N 58730
Donald Nielsen, prin.

Crystal, Pembina Co., Pop. Code 2
Valley SD 12
Supt. – See Hoople
Valley ES, P O BOX 128 58222
Gary Jackson, prin.

Davenport, Cass Co., Pop. Code 2
Kindred SD 2
Supt. – See Kindred
MS, HIGHWAY 16 58021 – James Kroshus, prin.

Deering, McHenry Co., Pop. Code 1
Thursby Butte SD 37
Sch. Sys. Enr. Code 1
Supt. – Michael Redman, P O BOX 197 58731
S, P O BOX 197 58731 – Michael Redman, prin.

Des Lacs, Ward Co., Pop. Code 2
United SD 7
Sch. Sys. Enr. Code 3
Supt. – Donald Strang, P O BOX 117 58733
Other Schools – See Burlington

Devils Lake, Ramsey Co., Pop. Code 6
Devils Lake SD 1
Sch. Sys. Enr. Code 4
Supt. – Richard Kunkel, COLLEGE DRIVE N 58301
Minnie ES, COLLEGE DRIVE S 58301
Julie Schuler, prin.
Prairie View ES, 12TH AVE 58301
Ronald Bommersbach, prin.
Sweetwater ES, 2ND AVE N 58301
John Geston, prin.

St. Joseph ES, 9TH ST & 10TH AVE 58301

Dickinson, Stark Co., Pop. Code 7
Dickinson SD 1
Sch. Sys. Enr. Code 5
Supt. – Ross Julson, P O BOX 1057 58602
Hagen JHS, W 4TH ST 58601 – Robert Burda, prin.
Berg ES 58602 – Louis Braun, prin.
Gladstone ES, P O BOX 1057 58602
L. Jessen, prin.
Heart River ES, P O BOX 1057 58602
Donald Stoxen, prin.
Jefferson ES, P O BOX 1057 58602
Clarence Corneil, prin.
Lincoln ES, P O BOX 1057 58602
Norman Jesperson, prin.
Roosevelt ES, P O BOX 1057 58602
Corenne Krieg, prin.

St. Joseph ES, 250 1ST SE 58601
St. Patricks ES, 145 3RD AVE W 58601
St. Wenceslaus ES, 515 E 3RD 58601

Dodge, Dunn Co., Pop. Code 2
Dodge SD 8
Sch. Sys. Enr. Code 1
Supt. – Curtis Herman, P O BOX 98 58625
ES, P O BOX 98 58625 – Darlene Reilly, prin.

Donnybrook, Ward Co., Pop. Code 2
Donnybrook SD 24
Sch. Sys. Enr. Code 1
Supt. – Arthur Grochow 58734
ES 58734 – Diane Zander, prin.

Drake, McHenry Co., Pop. Code 2
Drake SD 57
Sch. Sys. Enr. Code 2
Supt. – George Wieland, P O BOX 256 58736
S, P O BOX 256 58736 – Marvin Goplen, prin.

Drayton, Pembina Co., Pop. Code 4
Drayton SD 19
Sch. Sys. Enr. Code 2
Supt. – H. Richard Lavik, P O BOX 399 58225
S, P O BOX 399 58225 – Robert Klein, prin.

Driscoll, Burleigh Co., Pop. Code 2
Driscoll SD 36
Sch. Sys. Enr. Code 1
Supt. – Lester Fettig, P O BOX 46 58532
S, P O BOX 46 58532 – Gary Arlien, prin.

Dunseith, Rolette Co., Pop. Code 3
Dunseith SD
Sch. Sys. Enr. Code 2
Supt. – Myron Haugse, P O BOX 280 58329
ES, P O BOX 789 58329 – Dennis Martin, prin.

Edgeley, La Moure Co., Pop. Code 3
Edgeley SD 3
Sch. Sys. Enr. Code 2
Supt. – Arlyn Irion, P O BOX 37 58433
ES, P O BOX 37 58433
Myron Luttschwager, prin.

Willow Bank Colony ES, P O BOX 37　58433
　Myron Luttschwager, prin.

Edinburg, Walsh Co., Pop. Code 2
Edinburg SD 106
Sch. Sys. Enr. Code 2
Supt. – Robert Gibson　58227
S, P O BOX 6　58227 – John M. Evenson, prin.

Edmore, Ramsey Co., Pop. Code 2
Edmore SD 2
Sch. Sys. Enr. Code 2
Supt. – D. R. Schneider, P O BOX 188　58330
S, P O BOX 188　58330 – Mark Wisnewski, prin.

Egeland, Towner Co., Pop. Code 2
East Central SD 12
Sch. Sys. Enr. Code 1
Supt. – Wayne Lingen, P O BOX 128　58331
Bisbee-Egeland ES, P O BOX 128　58331
　Linda Flanagan, prin.

Eldridge, Stutsman Co.
Eldridge SD 12
Sch. Sys. Enr. Code 1
Supt. – (—)
　RURAL ROUTE 03　BOX 95　58401
ES, RURAL ROUTE 03　BOX 95　58401
　(—), prin.

Elgin, Grant Co., Pop. Code 3
Elgin SD 16
Sch. Sys. Enr. Code 2
Supt. – Richard Skarperud, P O BOX 70　58533
S, 110 N WEST　58533 – Wayne Dettmann, prin.

Ellendale, Dickey Co., Pop. Code 4
Ellendale SD 40
Sch. Sys. Enr. Code 2
Supt. – Kirk A Hansen, 321 N 1ST ST　58436
ES, P O BOX 400　58436 – Judy Bertsch, prin.
Maple River ES　58436 – Judy Bertsch, prin.

Emerado, Grand Forks Co., Pop. Code 3
Emerado SD 127
Sch. Sys. Enr. Code 2
Supt. – (—), P O BOX 67　58228
ES, P O BOX 67　58228 – Robert White, prin.

Enderlin, Ransom Co., Pop. Code 4
Enderlin SD 22
Sch. Sys. Enr. Code 2
Supt. – G. F. Muckenhirn, 410 BLUFF ST　58027
S, 410 BLUFF ST　58027 – Gary Harms, prin.

Esmond, Benson Co., Pop. Code 2
Esmond SD 25
Sch. Sys. Enr. Code 1
Supt. – Shirley Hageness, P O BOX 36　58332
S, P O BOX 36　58332 – Charles Miller, prin.

Fairfield, Billings Co.
Billings County SD 1
Supt. – See Medora
Glade ES　58627 – Myron Johnson, prin.
Snow ES　58627 – Myron Johnson, prin.
Thompson ES, P O BOX 37　58627
　Myron Johnson, prin.

Fairmount, Richland Co., Pop. Code 2
Fairmount SD 18
Sch. Sys. Enr. Code 2
Supt. – Kenneth Rusten, P O BOX 228　58030
S, P O BOX 228　58030 – William Raduenz, prin.

Fargo, Cass Co., Pop. Code 8
Fargo SD 1
Sch. Sys. Enr. Code 6
Supt. – Vern Bennett, 1104 2ND AVE S　58103
Agassiz JHS, 1305 9TH AVE S　58103
　Jerry L. Sheldon, prin.
Barton ES, 1417 S 6TH ST　58103
　Michele Vannote, prin.
Eielson ES, 1035 16TH ST S　58103
　Dennis Holmgren, prin.
Hawthorne ES, 555 8TH AVE S　58103
　Nancy Burkland, prin.
Jefferson ES, 315 16TH ST S　58103
　Martha Dicicco, prin.
Lewis & Clark ES, 1729 16TH ST S　58103
　Roger Olgard, prin.
Lincoln ES, 2120 9TH ST S　58103
　Charles Schulstad, prin.
Longfellow ES, 20 29TH AVE NE　58102
　George Booth, prin.
Madison ES, 1040 29TH ST NW　58102
　Elwood Stordahl, prin.
Mann ES, 1025 N 3RD ST　58103
　Ed Raymond, prin.
McKinley ES, 2930 8TH ST N　58102
　David Kahl, prin.
Roosevelt ES, 1026 10TH ST N　58102
　Kathryn Stigman, prin.
Washington ES, 1725 BROADWAY　58102
　Ronald Thorson, prin.

Grace Lutheran ES, 1025 14TH AVE S　58103
Holy Spirit ES, 1441 8TH ST N　58102
Nativity ES, 1825 11TH ST S　58103
St. Anthony Padua ES, 719 9TH ST S　58103

Fessenden, Wells Co., Pop. Code 3
Fessenden SD 40
Sch. Sys. Enr. Code 2
Supt. – Sherman Sylling, P O BOX 307　58438
S, P O BOX 307　58438 – Monty Benson, prin.

Fingal, Barnes Co., Pop. Code 2
Maple Valley SD
Supt. – See Tower City
ES, P O BOX 38　58031 – Loraine Olson, prin.

Finley, Steele Co., Pop. Code 3
Finley Sharon SD
Sch. Sys. Enr. Code 2
Supt. – Roger Rieger, P O BOX 447　58230
Finley Sharon S, P O BOX 447　58230
　Roger Rieger, prin.

Flasher, Morton Co., Pop. Code 2
Flasher SD 39
Sch. Sys. Enr. Code 2
Supt. – D. R. Emch, P O BOX 267　58535
S, P O BOX 267　58535 – R. C. Honrath, prin.

Oak Coulee SD 35
Sch. Sys. Enr. Code 1
Supt. – (—), RURAL ROUTE 01　58535
Oak Coulee ES, RURAL ROUTE 01　58535
　(—), prin.

Fordville, Walsh Co., Pop. Code 2
Fordville SD 79
Sch. Sys. Enr. Code 1
Supt. – Morgan J. Huset　58231
S, P O BOX 127　58231 – Dennis Dryburgh, prin.

Forman, Sargent Co., Pop. Code 3
Sargent Central SD
Sch. Sys. Enr. Code 2
Supt. – Leon Johnson, P O BOX 289　58032
Sargent Central S, P O BOX 289　58032
　B. Schumacher, prin.

Fort Ransom, Ransom Co., Pop. Code 1
Fort Ransom SD 6
Sch. Sys. Enr. Code 1
Supt. – (—)
　RURAL ROUTE 01　BOX 53A　58033
ES, RURAL ROUTE 01　BOX 53A　58033
　Vicki Dougherty, prin.

Fort Totten, Benson Co., Pop. Code 4
Fort Totten SD
Sch. Sys. Enr. Code 2
Supt. – Wayne Trottier,Jr., P O BOX 239　58335
Four Winds Community S, P O BOX 239　58335
　Charles Guthrie, prin.

Fort Yates, Sioux Co., Pop. Code 3
Fort Yates SD 4
Sch. Sys. Enr. Code 2
Supt. – John Ruegamer, P O BOX 428　58538
Fort Yates S, P O BOX 428　58538
　John Ruegamer, prin.

St. Bernards Mission School, P O BOX 394　58538

Fullerton, Dickey Co., Pop. Code 2
Fullerton SD 37
Sch. Sys. Enr. Code 1
Supt. – James Ham, P O BOX 39　58441
ES, P O BOX 39　58441 – James Ham, prin.

Gackle, Logan Co., Pop. Code 2
Gackle SD 14
Sch. Sys. Enr. Code 2
Supt. – Duane Zwinger, P O BOX 375　58442
S, P O BOX 375　58442 – Bernard Hummel, prin.

Galesburg, Traill Co., Pop. Code 2
Clifford-Galesburg SD 4
Sch. Sys. Enr. Code 2
Supt. – Marle Thorstad, P O BOX 499　58035
Clifford-Galesburg ES, P O BOX 69　58035
　Hilma Hovde, prin.

Garrison, McLean Co., Pop. Code 4
Garrison SD 51
Sch. Sys. Enr. Code 3
Supt. – Hy Schlieve, P O BOX 249　58540
Callies ES, P O BOX 249　58540
　Ladonna Whitmore, prin.

Glenburn, Renville Co., Pop. Code 2
Glenburn SD 26
Sch. Sys. Enr. Code 2
Supt. – Charles Dunlop, P O BOX 138　58740
S, P O BOX 138　58740 – Bruce Henderson, prin.

Glen Ullin, Morton Co., Pop. Code 4
Glen Ullin SD 48
Sch. Sys. Enr. Code 2
Supt. – Patrick Feist, HIGHWAY 10　58631
S, HIGHWAY 10　58631 – R. Johnson, prin.

Golden Valley, Mercer Co., Pop. Code 2
Golden Valley SD 20
Sch. Sys. Enr. Code 1
Supt. – Curtis Herman, P O BOX 158　58541
S, P O BOX 158　58541 – M. Beckwith, prin.

Golva, Golden Valley Co., Pop. Code 2
Lone Tree SD 6
Sch. Sys. Enr. Code 1
Supt. – Philip Nelson, P O BOX D　58632
S, P O BOX D　58632 – L. Wittmayer, prin.

Goodrich, Sheridan Co., Pop. Code 2
Goodrich SD 16
Sch. Sys. Enr. Code 1
Supt. – Rodney Scherbenske, P O BOX A　58444
S, P O BOX A　58444 – Kevin Rogers, prin.

Grace City, Foster Co., Pop. Code 1
Grace City SD 16
Sch. Sys. Enr. Code 1
Supt. – Gilbert Black, P O BOX 135　58445
S, P O BOX 135　58445 – Larry Tag, prin.

Grafton, Walsh Co., Pop. Code 6
Grafton SD 3
Sch. Sys. Enr. Code 4
Supt. – Julian Bjornson
　1548 SCHOOL ROAD　58237
Chase ES, 516 COOPER AVE　58237
　Wallace Feltman, prin.
Westview ES, 1301 MCHUGH AVE　58237
　Jerome Suda, prin.

Grand Forks, Grand Forks Co., Pop. Code 8
Grand Forks SD 1
Sch. Sys. Enr. Code 6
Supt. – Mark Sanford, P O BOX 6000　58206
Belmont ES, 407 CHESTNUT ST　58201
　Beth Randklev, prin.
Eielson ES　58201 – Don Heier, prin.
Franklin ES, 1016 S 20TH ST　58201
　Daniel Oshea, prin.
Lake Agassiz ES, 605 STANFORD ROAD　58201
　Wayne Peterson, prin.
Lewis & Clark ES, 11TH ST & 13TH AVE　58201
　Gary Mitchell, prin.
Lincoln ES, 400 PAKENHAM AVE　58201
　Sharon Gates, prin.
Nelson Kelly ES　58201 – Charles Zick, prin.
Twining ES, N LOUISIANA　58201
　John Klokstad, prin.
Viking ES, OAK & 22ND AVE S　58201
　Darrell Nottestad, prin.
West ES, 615 N 25TH ST　58201
　Carl Morken, prin.
Wilder ES　58201 – Michael Johnson, prin.
Winship ES, 1412 5TH AVE N　58201
　Glenn Gilbraith, prin.

Rye SD 25
Sch. Sys. Enr. Code 1
Supt. – (—), RURAL ROUTE 02　58201
Rye MS, RURAL ROUTE 02　58201
　Eilene Moxness, prin.

Holy Family ES, 1001 17TH AVE S　58201
St. Marys ES, 216 BELMONT ROAD　58201
St. Michaels ES, 504 5TH AVE N　58201

Granville, McHenry Co., Pop. Code 2
Granville SD 25
Sch. Sys. Enr. Code 2
Supt. – Gary Volk, P O BOX 158　58741
S, P O BOX 158　58741 – Hilman Ulland, prin.

Grassy Butte, McKenzie Co.
McKenzie County SD 1
Supt. – See Watford City
ES, P O BOX 205　58634
　Eugene Williamson, prin.

Grenora, Williams Co., Pop. Code 2
Grenora SD 99
Sch. Sys. Enr. Code 2
Supt. – M. A. Ulland, P O BOX 38　58845
S, P O BOX 138　58845 – Carlyle Norby, prin.

Gwinner, Sargent Co., Pop. Code 3
North Sargent SD 3
Sch. Sys. Enr. Code 2
Supt. – Delyle Willplecht, P O BOX 158　58040
North Sargent S, P O BOX 158　58040
　Walter Robinson, prin.

Hague, Emmons Co., Pop. Code 2
Bakker SD 10
Sch. Sys. Enr. Code 1
Supt. – (—)　58542
Bakker ES　58542 – Michele Meidinger, prin.

Hague SD 30
Sch. Sys. Enr. Code 2
Supt. – (—), P O BOX 185　58542
ES, P O BOX 185　58542 – Ervin Hirning, prin.

Odessa SD 9
Sch. Sys. Enr. Code 1
Supt. – (—), RURAL ROUTE 01　58542
Odessa ES, RURAL ROUTE 01　58542
　Arlouine Grad, prin.

Halliday, Dunn Co., Pop. Code 2
Halliday SD 19
Sch. Sys. Enr. Code 2
Supt. – L. A. Hendrickson, P O BOX 188　58636
S, P O BOX 188　58636 – Lloyd Hendrickson, prin.

Twin Buttes SD
Sch. Sys. Enr. Code 1
Supt. – Ronald Goetz　58636
Twin Buttes ES　58636 – Norman Bakke, prin.

Hankinson, Richland Co., Pop. Code 4
Hankinson SD 8
Sch. Sys. Enr. Code 2
Supt. – Clifford Rau, P O BOX 220　58041
S, 415 1ST AVE SE　58041 – Dennis Johnson, prin.
ES, P O BOX 220　57941 – Tom Tracy, prin.

Hannaford, Griggs Co., Pop. Code 2
Hannaford SD
Sch. Sys. Enr. Code 1
Supt. – Bruce Sedler, P O BOX 98　58448
S, P O BOX 98　58448 – Bruce Sedler, prin.

Hannover, Morton Co.
Springbrook SD 14
Sch. Sys. Enr. Code 1
Supt. – (—), HCR 03 BOX 89 58543
Springbrook ES, RURAL ROUTE BOX 84 58543
(—), prin.

Harvey, Wells Co., Pop. Code 5
Harvey SD 38
Sch. Sys. Enr. Code 3
Supt. – L. W. Nudell, 811 BURKE AVE 58341
ES 58341 – Robert Nelson, prin.

Harwood, Cass Co., Pop. Code 2
West Fargo SD
Supt. – See West Fargo
ES, 110 FREEDLAND 58042 – Jerry Barnum, prin.

Hatton, Traill Co., Pop. Code 3
Hatton SD 7
Sch. Sys. Enr. Code 2
Supt. – Roger Hulne, P O BOX 200 58240
S, P O BOX 200 58240 – Roger Hulne, prin.

Hazelton, Emmons Co., Pop. Code 2
Hazelton-Moffit SD
Sch. Sys. Enr. Code 2
Supt. – Edo Johnston, P O BOX 528 58544
ES, P O BOX 528 58544 – Dianne Kalberer, prin.

Hazen, Mercer Co., Pop. Code 4
Hazen SD 3
Sch. Sys. Enr. Code 3
Supt. – David H. Smette, P O BOX 487 58545
ES, P O BOX 487 58545 – Bea Weigum, prin.

Hebron, Morton Co., Pop. Code 4
Hebron SD 13
Sch. Sys. Enr. Code 2
Supt. – Donald Herbel, P O BOX Q 58638
S, 400 CHURCH AVE 58638 – George Ding, prin.

Hillsboro, Traill Co., Pop. Code 4
Hillsboro SD 9
Sch. Sys. Enr. Code 2
Supt. – Arthur Morlock, P O BOX 147 58045
ES, P O BOX 147 58045
William Schumacher, prin.

Hoople, Walsh Co.
Valley SD 12
Sch. Sys. Enr. Code 2
Supt. – James McGurran, P O BOX 143 58243
Other Schools – See Crystal

Hope, Steele Co., Pop. Code 2
Hope SD 10
Sch. Sys. Enr. Code 2
Supt. – Lyle Peterson, P O BOX 100 58046
S, P O BOX 100 58046 – Dennis Adair, prin.

Horace, Cass Co., Pop. Code 2
West Fargo SD
Supt. – See West Fargo
ES, 110 3RD AVE N 58047 – Jerry Barnum, prin.

Hunter, Cass Co., Pop. Code 2
Dakota SD 3
Sch. Sys. Enr. Code 2
Supt. – Helmuth Haberman, P O BOX 38 58048
Dakota ES, P O BOX 38 58048
Delores Carpenter, prin.

Hurdsfield, Wells Co., Pop. Code 2
Pleasant Valley SD
Sch. Sys. Enr. Code 1
Supt. – (—), P O BOX 165 58451
ES 58451 – Julie Hartman, prin.

Inkster, Grand Forks Co., Pop. Code 2
Midway SD 128
Sch. Sys. Enr. Code 2
Supt. – Kenneth Lanier
RURAL ROUTE 02 BOX 31 58244
Midway S, RURAL ROUTE 02 BOX 31 58244
Kenneth Henry, prin.
Forest River Colony ES
RURAL ROUTE 01 BOX 102 58244
Isabel Hovel, prin.

Jamestown, Stutsman Co., Pop. Code 7
Jamestown SD 1
Sch. Sys. Enr. Code 5
Supt. – Frank Fischer, P O BOX 269 58402
Franklin ES, 312 2ND ST SW 58401
Mary Walicski, prin.
Gussner ES 58402 – Mary Walicski, prin.
Lincoln ES, 319 5TH ST NE 58401
David Delaney, prin.
Roosevelt ES, 615 6TH AVE SE 58401
Jacob Wolf, Jr., prin.
Washington ES, 4TH AVE NW 58402
Dale Bayer, prin.

Anne Carlsen School, 7TH AVE NW 58401
St. Johns Academy, P O BOX 950 58402

Jud, La Moure Co., Pop. Code 2
Jud SD 5
Sch. Sys. Enr. Code 1
Supt. – James Vetter, P O BOX 487 58454
S, P O BOX 487 58454 – James Vetter, prin.

Karlsruhe, McHenry Co., Pop. Code 2
Karlsruhe SD 54
Sch. Sys. Enr. Code 1
Supt. – Donald Ost, P O BOX 365 58744
S, P O BOX 365 58744 – Donald Ost, prin.

Kathryn, Barnes Co., Pop. Code 1
Kathryn SD 93
Sch. Sys. Enr. Code 1
Supt. – Marc Almklov, P O BOX 197 58049
S, P O BOX 197 58049 – Dave Handt, prin.

Kenmare, Ward Co., Pop. Code 4
Kenmare SD 28
Sch. Sys. Enr. Code 2
Supt. – Arthur Grochow, P O BOX 667 58746
ES, P O BOX 667 58746 – Dale Norton, prin.

Kensal, Stutsman Co., Pop. Code 2
Kensal SD 19
Sch. Sys. Enr. Code 1
Supt. – LeRoy Bowman, P O BOX 8 58455
S, P O BOX 8 58455 – Allen Zerr, prin.

Killdeer, Dunn Co., Pop. Code 3
Killdeer SD 16
Sch. Sys. Enr. Code 2
Supt. – Ray E. Frank, 200 W HIGH ST 58640
S, 200 W HIGH ST 58640 – Roger Gunderson, prin.

Kindred, Cass Co., Pop. Code 3
Kindred SD 2
Sch. Sys. Enr. Code 2
Supt. – Adam Boschee, P O BOX 218 58051
S, P O BOX 218 58051 – Clair Bergene, prin.
Other Schools – See Davenport

Kramer, Bottineau Co., Pop. Code 1
Kramer SD 46
Sch. Sys. Enr. Code 1
Supt. – Elner Monson, P O BOX 8 58748
ES, P O BOX 8 58748 – Nina Moum, prin.

Kulm, La Moure Co., Pop. Code 3
Kulm SD 7
Sch. Sys. Enr. Code 2
Supt. – Gerald P. Harris, P O BOX G 58456
ES, P O BOX G 58456 – Marlys Taszarek, prin.

Lakota, Nelson Co., Pop. Code 3
Lakota SD 66
Sch. Sys. Enr. Code 2
Supt. – Elroy Hagen, P O BOX 388 58344
ES, P O BOX 388 58344 – Neil Dardis, prin.

La Moure, La Moure Co., Pop. Code 4
La Moure SD 8
Sch. Sys. Enr. Code 2
Supt. – Robert Kummeth, P O BOX 656 58458
S, P O BOX 656 58458 – Neil Taverna, prin.
ES, P O BOX 656 58458 – Susan Loe, prin.

Langdon, Cavalier Co., Pop. Code 4
Langdon SD 23
Sch. Sys. Enr. Code 3
Supt. – Delmar Lewis, 715 14TH AVE 58249
ES, 721 11TH AVE 58249
Dennis Throndset, prin.

St. Alphonsus ES 58249

Lankin, Walsh Co., Pop. Code 2
Lankin SD 39
Sch. Sys. Enr. Code 1
Supt. – Morgan Huset, P O BOX 126 58250
ES, P O BOX 126 58250 – Monica Hejlik, prin.

Lansford, Bottineau Co., Pop. Code 2
Lansford SD 35
Sch. Sys. Enr. Code 1
Supt. – Patrick Limke, P O BOX 8 58750
S, P O BOX 8 58750 – Patrick Limke, prin.

Larimore, Grand Forks Co., Pop. Code 4
Larimore SD 44
Sch. Sys. Enr. Code 3
Supt. – Clifford Moser, P O BOX 568 58251
ES, P O BOX 568 58251 – Bette Ritterman, prin.

Leeds, Benson Co., Pop. Code 3
Leeds SD 6
Sch. Sys. Enr. Code 2
Supt. – James Isaak, P O BOX K 58346
S, P O BOX K 58346 – Don Hoffman, prin.

Lefor, Stark Co.
Lefor SD 27
Sch. Sys. Enr. Code 1
Supt. – (—), P O BOX 188 58641
ES, P O BOX 188 58641 – Patricia Schatz, prin.

Lehr, Logan Co., Pop. Code 2
Lehr SD 10
Sch. Sys. Enr. Code 1
Supt. – Robert Scrivner, P O BOX 68 58460
S, P O BOX 68 58460 – Arnold Wetzel, prin.

Leonard, Cass Co., Pop. Code 2
Leonard SD 54
Sch. Sys. Enr. Code 2
Supt. – Steven Sedlmayr, P O BOX 368 58052
S, P O BOX 368 58052 – Richard Smith, prin.

Lidgerwood, Richland Co., Pop. Code 3
Lidgerwood SD 28
Sch. Sys. Enr. Code 2
Supt. – Dale Salberg, P O BOX 408 58053
S, P O BOX 408 58053 – Howard Grumbo, prin.

Lignite, Burke Co., Pop. Code 2
Burke Central SD
Sch. Sys. Enr. Code 2
Supt. – Harlind L. Ostrom, P O BOX 91 58752
Burke Central S, P O BOX 91 58752
Gerald Lokken, prin.

Linton, Emmons Co., Pop. Code 4
Linton SD 36
Sch. Sys. Enr. Code 3
Supt. – Dean Koppelman, P O BOX 884 58552
S, P O BOX 884 58552 – Steve Nelson, prin.

Lisbon, Ransom Co., Pop. Code 4
Lisbon SD 19
Sch. Sys. Enr. Code 3
Supt. – Elmer Lindstrom, P O BOX 593 58054
MS, P O BOX 593 58054 – Francis Bell, prin.
ES 58054 – Francis Bell, prin.

Litchville, Barnes Co., Pop. Code 2
Litchville SD 52
Sch. Sys. Enr. Code 1
Supt. – C. Kourajian, P O BOX 25 58461
S, P O BOX 25 58461 – R. Willson, prin.

Luverne, Steele Co., Pop. Code 1
Willow Lake SD 18
Sch. Sys. Enr. Code 1
Supt. – (—), P O BOX 177 58056
ES, P O BOX 177 58056 – (—), prin.

McClusky, Sheridan Co., Pop. Code 3
McClusky SD 19
Sch. Sys. Enr. Code 2
Supt. – W. A. Streightiff, P O BOX 426 58463
ES 58463 – Roger Olson, prin.

McHenry, Foster Co., Pop. Code 1
Glenfield-Sutton-McHenry SD
Sch. Sys. Enr. Code 2
Supt. – Kerwin Borgen, P O BOX P 58464
G S M ES 58464 – Jeanne Hoyt, prin.

McKenzie, Burleigh Co.
McKenzie SD 34
Sch. Sys. Enr. Code 1
Supt. – (—), P O BOX 150 58553
ES, P O BOX 150 58553 – Laverne Johnson, prin.

McVille, Nelson Co., Pop. Code 3
McVille SD 46
Sch. Sys. Enr. Code 2
Supt. – L. D. Peterson, P O BOX E 58254
S, P O BOX E 58254 – Maynard Loibl, prin.

Maddock, Benson Co., Pop. Code 3
Maddock SD 9
Sch. Sys. Enr. Code 2
Supt. – Les Kramer, P O BOX G 58348
S, P O BOX G 58348 – Gary Engberg, prin.

Makoti, Ward Co., Pop. Code 2
North Shore SD 158
Sch. Sys. Enr. Code 2
Supt. – Ken Scarbrough, P O BOX 127 58756
North Shore ES, P O BOX 127 58756
Michael Trudeau, prin.

Mandan, Morton Co., Pop. Code 7
Mandan SD 1
Sch. Sys. Enr. Code 5
Supt. – Pius Lacher, 905 8TH AVE NW 58554
JHS, 406 4TH ST NW 58554
Anton Engelhardt, prin.
Central ES, 406 NW 4TH ST 58554
Herman Schafer, prin.
Custer ES, 205 8TH AVE NE 58554
Herman Schafer, prin.
Lewis & Clark ES, 600 NW 14TH ST 58554
Ronald Biberdorf, prin.
Marmot ES 58554 – M. Conlon, prin.
Roosevelt ES, 305 10TH AVE NW 58554
Marley McDowall, prin.
Square Butte ES 58554 – M. Conlon, prin.
Stark ES, 405 8TH AVE SW 58554
M. Conlon, prin.

Sweet Briar SD
Sch. Sys. Enr. Code 1
Supt. – (—), RURAL ROUTE 04 58554
Sweet Briar ES, RURAL ROUTE 04 58554
(—), prin.

Shiloh Christian School
1000 COLLINS AVE 58554
Christ the King ES, 1100 3RD ST NW 58554
St. Joseph ES, 410 COLLINS AVE 58554

Mandaree, McKenzie Co.
Mandaree SD
Sch. Sys. Enr. Code 2
Supt. – Frank Taylor, P O BOX 488 58757
S, P O BOX 488 58757 – Tex Hall, prin.

Mantador, Richland Co., Pop. Code 1
Mantador SD 5
Sch. Sys. Enr. Code 1
Supt. – (—), P O BOX 2633 58058
ES, P O BOX 2633 58058 – Loretta Wieland, prin.

Manvel, Grand Forks Co.
Manvel SD 125
Sch. Sys. Enr. Code 2
Supt. – (—), P O BOX 98 58256
ES, P O BOX 98 58256 – Richard Ray, prin.

Mapleton, Cass Co., Pop. Code 2
Mapleton SD 7
Sch. Sys. Enr. Code 2
Supt. – (—), P O BOX 558 58059
ES, P O BOX 558 58059 – Clifford Puppe, prin.

Marion, La Moure Co., Pop. Code 2
Marion SD 9
Sch. Sys. Enr. Code 2
Supt. – Rudy Hanson, P O BOX 159 58466
S, P O BOX 159 58466 – Rudy Hanson, prin.

Marmarth, Slope Co., Pop. Code 2
Marmarth SD 12
Sch. Sys. Enr. Code 1
Supt. -- (—) 58643
ES 58643 – (—), prin.

Max, McLean Co., Pop. Code 2
Max SD 50
Sch. Sys. Enr. Code 2
Supt. – Norman Batterberry, P O BOX 297 58759
S, P O BOX 297 58759 – S. M. Hannegrefs, prin.

Maxbass, Bottineau Co., Pop. Code 2
Maxbass SD 28
Sch. Sys. Enr. Code 1
Supt. – Larry Brandvold, P O BOX 170 58760
ES, P O BOX 170 58760 – Arnold Kruse, prin.

Mayville, Traill Co., Pop. Code 4
Mayville-Portland SD
Sch. Sys. Enr. Code 3
Supt. – William Julson
    WESTWOOD ACRES 58257
Mayville-Portland ES 58257 – Peter Boe, prin.

Medina, Stutsman Co., Pop. Code 3
Medina SD 3
Sch. Sys. Enr. Code 2
Supt. – Jerry Fischer, P O BOX 547 58467
S, P O BOX 547 58467 – Alberta Moore, prin.

Medora, Billings Co., Pop. Code 1
Billings County SD 1
Sch. Sys. Enr. Code 1
Supt. – (—), P O BOX 307 58645
Connell ES, P O BOX 307 58645
    Myron Johnson, prin.
Demores ES, P O BOX 307 58645
    Myron Johnson, prin.
Little Missouri MS, P O BOX 127 58645
    Myron Johnson, prin.
West River ES, P O BOX 307 58645
    Myron Johnson, prin.
Other Schools – See Belfield, Fairfield

Menoken, Burleigh Co.
Menoken SD 33
Sch. Sys. Enr. Code 1
Supt. – (—), P O BOX D 58558
ES, P O BOX D 58558 – Glenda Walters, prin.

Michigan, Nelson Co., Pop. Code 3
Michigan SD 40
Sch. Sys. Enr. Code 2
Supt. – Duane Kratochvil, P O BOX 49 58259
S, P O BOX 49 58259 – Steven Lozeau, prin.

Milnor, Sargent Co., Pop. Code 3
Milnor SD 2
Sch. Sys. Enr. Code 2
Supt. – D. P. Fuhrman, 530 5TH ST 58060
S, P O BOX 86 58060 – Lenora Jensen, prin.
Sundale Colony ES, P O BOX 86 58060
    Lenora Jensen, prin.

Minnewaukan, Benson Co., Pop. Code 2
Minnewaukan SD 5
Sch. Sys. Enr. Code 2
Supt. – Myron Jury, P O BOX 348 58351
S, P O BOX 348 58351 – Ronald Carlson, prin.

Minot, Ward Co., Pop. Code 8
Bell SD 10
Sch. Sys. Enr. Code 2
Supt. – (—)
    RURAL ROUTE 04 BOX 157 58701
Bell ES, RURAL ROUTE 04 BOX 157 58701
    Larry Long, prin.

Eureka SD 19
Sch. Sys. Enr. Code 1
Supt. – (—), RURAL ROUTE 01 58701
Eureka ES, P O BOX 144 58702
    Betty Nelson, prin.

Minot SD 1
Sch. Sys. Enr. Code 6
Supt. – R. Edward Mundy, 215 2ND ST SE 58701
Hill JHS, 1000 6TH ST SW 58701
    Richard Westlake, prin.
Memorial JHS, 1 ROCKET ROAD 58704
    Larry Grindy, prin.
Belair ES, 501 25TH ST NW 58701
    John Andrus, prin.
Dakota ES, MAFB 58701 – Jim Collins, prin.
Edison ES, 701 17TH AVE SW 58701
    Ernest Medalen, prin.
Jefferson ES, 3800 11TH AVE SE 58701
    Douglas Hultberg, prin.
Lincoln ES, 1 SW 7TH 58701
    Grant Johnson, prin.
Longfellow ES, 600 16TH ST NW 58701
    Harlow Magnusson, prin.
McKinley ES, 5 5TH AVE NE 58701
    Curt Medalen, prin.
North Hill ES, 2215 NW 8 58701
    Francis Vetter, prin.
North Plains ES, MAFB 58701 – Gale Teske, prin.
Perkett ES, SW 18TH & 5TH AVE 58701
    Grant Johnson, prin.
Ramstad ES 58701 – Larry Wahlund, prin.

Roosevelt ES, 715 8TH ST NE 58701
    Curt Medalen, prin.
Sunnyside ES, 1000 5TH AVE SE 58701
    Michael Fogarty, prin.
Washington ES, 1001 2ND ST SE 58701
    Douglas Hultberg, prin.

Nedrose SD 4
Sch. Sys. Enr. Code 2
Supt. – (—), 6900 E BURDICK 58701
Nedrose ES, 6900 E BURDICK 58701
    John Melland, prin.

South Prairie SD 70
Sch. Sys. Enr. Code 2
Supt. – (—), RURAL ROUTE 03 58701
South Prairie ES
    RURAL ROUTE 03 BOX 251 58701
    Don Coe, prin.

Little Flower ES, 800 9TH AVE NW 58701
St. Leos ES, 208 1ST ST SE 58701

Minto, Walsh Co., Pop. Code 3
Minto SD 20
Sch. Sys. Enr. Code 2
Supt. – Harold A. Mach, P O BOX 377 58261
S, P O BOX 377 58261 – Frank M. Mitzell, prin.

Mohall, Renville Co., Pop. Code 4
Mohall SD 9
Sch. Sys. Enr. Code 2
Supt. – Milton Hoyt, P O BOX 187 58761
S, P O BOX 187 58761 – Todd Syverson, prin.

Montpelier, Stutsman Co., Pop. Code 1
Montpelier SD 14
Sch. Sys. Enr. Code 1
Supt. – Rick Maddock, P O BOX 10 58472
S, P O BOX 10 58472 – James Bakken, prin.

Mott, Hettinger Co., Pop. Code 4
Mott SD 6
Sch. Sys. Enr. Code 2
Supt. – Darrel Remington
    205 DAKOTA AVE 58646
S, 205 DAKOTA AVE 58646 – Norman Fries, prin.

Munich, Cavalier Co., Pop. Code 2
Munich SD 19
Sch. Sys. Enr. Code 2
Supt. – R. R. Fletschock, P O BOX 39 58352
S, P O BOX 39 58352 – Jack DeMaine, prin.

Napoleon, Logan Co., Pop. Code 4
Napoleon SD
Sch. Sys. Enr. Code 2
Supt. – Robert Tollefson, P O BOX 69 58561
S, 212 AVE D E 58561 – Wayne Lucht, prin.

Nash, Walsh Co.
Nash SD
Sch. Sys. Enr. Code 1
Supt. – (—) 58264
ES 58264 – James Wilebski, prin.

Neche, Pembina Co., Pop. Code 2
Neche SD 55
Sch. Sys. Enr. Code 2
Supt. – Larry Durand, P O BOX H 58265
S, P O BOX H 58265 – James Dinnigan, prin.

New England, Hettinger Co., Pop. Code 3
New England SD 9
Sch. Sys. Enr. Code 2
Supt. – Roger Pommerer, P O BOX 307 58647
S, P O BOX 307 58647 – Lawrence Lechler, prin.

New Leipzig, Grant Co., Pop. Code 2
New Leipzig SD 15
Sch. Sys. Enr. Code 2
Supt. – Ron Stahlecker, P O BOX 50 58562
S, P O BOX 50 58562 – Jack Maus, prin.

New Rockford, Eddy Co., Pop. Code 4
New Rockford SD 1
Sch. Sys. Enr. Code 2
Supt. – Dean Vorland, 430 1ST AVE N 58356
S, 430 1ST AVE N 58356 – Tim Guler, prin.

St. James ES, 127 2ND AVE N 58356

New Salem, Morton Co., Pop. Code 4
New Salem SD 7
Sch. Sys. Enr. Code 2
Supt. – Dale Hurt, P O BOX 378 58563
Prairie View ES, P O BOX 29 58563
    Rose Marie Gerhart, prin.

New Town, Mountrail Co., Pop. Code 4
New Town SD 1
Sch. Sys. Enr. Code 3
Supt. – Rollie Morud, P O BOX 700 58763
Loe ES, P O BOX 700 58763 – Bill Demaree, prin.

Northwood, Grand Forks Co., Pop. Code 4
Northwood SD 129
Sch. Sys. Enr. Code 2
Supt. – Mark Bernier, 204 S DOHENY ST 58267
S, P O BOX 250 58267 – John Holien, prin.

Nortonville, Stutsman Co.
Kennison SD 6
Sch. Sys. Enr. Code 1
Supt. – (—), P O BOX 156 58473
ES, P O BOX 156 58473 – Larae Hehr, prin.

Oakes, Dickey Co., Pop. Code 4
Oakes SD 41
Sch. Sys. Enr. Code 3
Supt. – Nicholas J. Roster, P O BOX 330 58474
ES 58474 – Jack Munsch, prin.

Oberon, Benson Co., Pop. Code 2
Oberon SD 16
Sch. Sys. Enr. Code 1
Supt. – (—), P O BOX 2 58357
ES, P O BOX 2 58357 – Kenneth Ploium, prin.

Oriska, Barnes Co., Pop. Code 2
Oriska SD 13
Sch. Sys. Enr. Code 1
Supt. – Richard Berg, P O BOX 427 58063
S, P O BOX 427 58063 – R. Mulvany, prin.

Osnabrock, Cavalier Co., Pop. Code 2
Osnabrock SD 1
Sch. Sys. Enr. Code 1
Supt. – Gerald Mikkelsen, P O BOX 57 58269
ES 58269 – Floyd McLeod, prin.

Page, Cass Co., Pop. Code 2
Page SD 80
Sch. Sys. Enr. Code 2
Supt. – Arthur Mitzel, P O BOX 26 58064
S, P O BOX 26 58064 – Richard Davidson, prin.

Palermo, Mountrail Co., Pop. Code 1
Palermo SD 83
Sch. Sys. Enr. Code 1
Supt. – (—), P O BOX 99 58769
ES, P O BOX 99 58769 – Karen Colbenson, prin.

Park River, Walsh Co., Pop. Code 4
Park River SD 78
Sch. Sys. Enr. Code 3
Supt. – Claude Sheldon, P O BOX 240 58270
ES, P O BOX 240 58270 – Richard Holand, prin.

Parshall, Mountrail Co., Pop. Code 4
Parshall SD 3
Sch. Sys. Enr. Code 2
Supt. – Henry Friedt, P O BOX 158 58770
ES, P O BOX 69 58770 – Kevin Erickson, prin.

Pembina, Pembina Co., Pop. Code 3
Pembina SD 1
Sch. Sys. Enr. Code 2
Supt. – Donald Brintnell, P O BOX 409 58271
S, P O BOX 409 58271 – Elroy Berg, prin.

Petersburg, Nelson Co., Pop. Code 2
Unity SD 80
Sch. Sys. Enr. Code 2
Supt. – Basil J. Duffey, P O BOX 37 58272
Unity S, P O BOX 37 58272 – James Stover, prin.

Pisek, Walsh Co., Pop. Code 2
Pisek SD 71
Sch. Sys. Enr. Code 1
Supt. – Wesley Sigette, P O BOX 25 58273
S, P O BOX 25 58273 – Kathy Myrvik, prin.

Plaza, Mountrail Co., Pop. Code 2
Plaza SD 137
Sch. Sys. Enr. Code 1
Supt. – Ken Scarbrough, P O BOX 38 58771
S, P O BOX 38 58771 – Janene Lee, prin.

Powers Lake, Burke Co., Pop. Code 2
Powers Lake SD 27
Sch. Sys. Enr. Code 2
Supt. – Clarence Weltz, P O BOX 346 58773
ES, P O BOX 346 58773 – Betty Ledene, prin.

Raleigh, Grant Co., Pop. Code 2
Leahy SD 34
Sch. Sys. Enr. Code 1
Supt. – (—)
    RURAL ROUTE 02 BOX 9A 58564
Leahy ES, RURAL ROUTE 02 BOX 9A 58564
    Judy Zins, prin.

Ray, Williams Co., Pop. Code 3
Nesson SD 2
Sch. Sys. Enr. Code 2
Supt. – G. Engebretson, P O BOX 564 58849
S, P O BOX 564 58849 – Arvin Larson, prin.

Reeder, Adams Co., Pop. Code 2
Reeder SD 3
Sch. Sys. Enr. Code 1
Supt. – Roland Stein, P O BOX 248 58649
S, P O BOX 248 58649 – Roland Stein, prin.

Regan, Burleigh Co., Pop. Code 1
Regan SD 2
Sch. Sys. Enr. Code 1
Supt. – (—), P O BOX 408 58477
ES, P O BOX 408 58477
    Linnett Schmidkunz, prin.

Regent, Hettinger Co., Pop. Code 2
Regent SD 14
Sch. Sys. Enr. Code 2
Supt. – Steven Rassier, P O BOX 219 58650
S, P O BOX 219 58650 – Duane Martin, prin.

Rhame, Bowman Co., Pop. Code 2
Mud Butte SD 30
Sch. Sys. Enr. Code 2
Supt. – Lawrence Sailer
    S ROUTE 02 BOX 26 58651
Mud Butte ES, RURAL ROUTE 02 BOX 26 58651
    (—), prin.

Rhame SD 17
Sch. Sys. Enr. Code 2
Supt. – Herbert Johnson, P O BOX 39 58651
S, P O BOX 39 58651 – Pam Nagel, prin.

Riverdale, McLean Co., Pop. Code 2
Riverdale SD 89
Sch. Sys. Enr. Code 2
Supt. – John Hurlimann, P O BOX 785 58565
S, P O BOX 785 58565 – Dave Bicknese, prin.

Robinson, Kidder Co., Pop. Code 2
Robinson SD 14
Sch. Sys. Enr. Code 1
Supt. – Kenneth Reed, P O BOX 38 58478
S, P O BOX 38 58478 – Marcia Steinwand, prin.

Rocklake, Towner Co., Pop. Code 2
North Central SD
Sch. Sys. Enr. Code 2
Supt. – D. Allen Halley, P O BOX 188 58365
North Central S, P O BOX 188 58365
   Arnold Jordan, prin.

Rogers, Barnes Co., Pop. Code 1
North Central SD 65
Sch. Sys. Enr. Code 2
Supt. – Alfred Borah, RURAL ROUTE 01 58479
North Central S, RURAL ROUTE 01 58479
   Clyde Eriksen, prin.

Rolette, Rolette Co., Pop. Code 3
Rolette SD 29
Sch. Sys. Enr. Code 2
Supt. – Merrill Krueger, P O BOX 97 58366
S, P O BOX 97 58366 – Wayne Johnson, prin.

Rolla, Rolette Co., Pop. Code 4
Mt. Pleasant SD 4
Sch. Sys. Enr. Code 2
Supt. – Norman Baumgarn, 114 NE 4TH 58367
Kyle ES, RURAL ROUTE 01 BOX 93 58367
   Helen Peterson, prin.

Rugby, Pierce Co., Pop. Code 5
Rugby SD 5
Sch. Sys. Enr. Code 3
Supt. – A. D. Bader, 1123 MAIN AVE S 58368
ES, 207 2ND ST SW 58368
   Ronald Reierson, prin.

Little Flower ES 58368

Saint Anthony, Morton Co.
Little Heart SD 4
Sch. Sys. Enr. Code 1
Supt. – (—) 58566
ES 58566 – Susan Mattson, prin.

Saint John, Rolette Co., Pop. Code 2
St. John SD 3
Sch. Sys. Enr. Code 2
Supt. – Donald Davis, P O BOX 358 58369
S, P O BOX 358 58369 – Carey Kakela, prin.

Saint Thomas, Pembina Co., Pop. Code 3
St. Thomas SD 43
Sch. Sys. Enr. Code 2
Supt. – Steven Dick, P O BOX 150 58276
S, P O BOX 150 58276 – David Hanson, prin.

Sarles, Cavalier Co., Pop. Code 2
Border Central SD
Supt. – See Calvin
Border Central ES, P O BOX 67 58372
   Mary Bollinger, prin.

Sawyer, Ward Co., Pop. Code 2
Sawyer SD 16
Sch. Sys. Enr. Code 2
Supt. – P. J. Blomberg, P O BOX 167 58781
S, P O BOX 167 58781 – G. Treft, prin.

Scranton, Bowman Co., Pop. Code 2
Scranton SD
Sch. Sys. Enr. Code 2
Supt. – Perry Nolan, P O BOX 126 58653
S, P O BOX 126 58653 – George Brackin, prin.

Selfridge, Sioux Co., Pop. Code 2
Selfridge SD 8
Sch. Sys. Enr. Code 1
Supt. – James Gross, P O BOX 45 58568
S, P O BOX 45 58568 – Russell Kronberg, prin.

Selz, Pierce Co.
Selz SD 31
Sch. Sys. Enr. Code 1
Supt. – (—), P O BOX 1 58373
ES, P O BOX 1 58373 – Magdalene Hoffart, prin.

Sheldon, Ransom Co., Pop. Code 2
Sheldon SD 2
Sch. Sys. Enr. Code 1
Supt. – Robert Molland
   RURAL ROUTE 01 BOX 1 58068
S, RURAL ROUTE 01 BOX 1 58068
   Robert Molland, prin.

Sherwood, Renville Co., Pop. Code 2
Sherwood SD 2
Sch. Sys. Enr. Code 1
Supt. – P. Pearson, P O BOX 9 58782
S, P O BOX 9 58782 – Terry L. Miller, prin.

Sheyenne, Eddy Co., Pop. Code 2
Sheyenne SD 12
Sch. Sys. Enr. Code 2
Supt. – Donald Busch, P O BOX 67 58374
S, P O BOX 67 58374 – Terry Otto, prin.

Solen, Sioux Co., Pop. Code 2
Solen SD 3
Sch. Sys. Enr. Code 2
Supt. – Bruce Meland, P O BOX 128 58570
Other Schools – See Cannon Ball

Souris, Bottineau Co., Pop. Code 2
Souris SD 29
Sch. Sys. Enr. Code 1
Supt. – Duane Paulsrud, P O BOX 106 58783
S, P O BOX 106 58783 – Duane Paulsrud, prin.

South Heart, Stark Co., Pop. Code 2
South Heart SD 9
Sch. Sys. Enr. Code 2
Supt. – Calvin Sailer, P O BOX 159 58655
S, P O BOX 159 58655 – D. Jablonsky, prin.

Spiritwood, Stutsman Co., Pop. Code 1
Spiritwood SD 26
Sch. Sys. Enr. Code 2
Supt. – (—), P O BOX X 58481
ES, P O BOX X 58481 – Marian Duff, prin.

Stanley, Mountrail Co., Pop. Code 4
Stanley SD 2
Sch. Sys. Enr. Code 3
Supt. – Douglas Degroote, P O BOX 10 58784
ES, P O BOX 10 58784 – Loren Mathson, prin.

Stanton, Mercer Co., Pop. Code 3
Stanton SD 22
Sch. Sys. Enr. Code 2
Supt. – Michael Ness, P O BOX 40 58571
S, P O BOX 40 58571 – Edwin Boger, prin.

Starkweather, Ramsey Co., Pop. Code 2
Starkweather SD 44
Sch. Sys. Enr. Code 2
Supt. – Thomas Birchem, P O BOX 45 58377
S, P O BOX 45 58377 – Dennis Dockter, prin.

Steele, Kidder Co., Pop. Code 3
Steele SD 26
Sch. Sys. Enr. Code 2
Supt. – V. Erdelt, P O BOX 380 58482
S, 501 4TH ST SE 58482 – Shabel Freije, prin.
Dawson ES, P O BOX 380 58482
   Donald Wick, prin.

Sterling, Burleigh Co.
Sterling SD 35
Sch. Sys. Enr. Code 1
Supt. – (—), P O BOX 68 58572
ES, P O BOX 68 58572 – Gwyn Tschosik, prin.

Strasburg, Emmons Co., Pop. Code 3
Strasburg SD 15
Sch. Sys. Enr. Code 2
Supt. – Clyde Hardesty, P O BOX 308 58573
S, P O BOX 308 58573 – James Eiseman, prin.

Streeter, Stutsman Co., Pop. Code 2
Streeter SD 42
Sch. Sys. Enr. Code 1
Supt. – Leland Ham, P O BOX 277 58483
S, P O BOX 277 58483 – Duane Baer, prin.

Surrey, Ward Co., Pop. Code 3
Surrey SD 41
Sch. Sys. Enr. Code 2
Supt. – Terry Mcleod, P O BOX 40 58785
S, P O BOX 40 58785 – Robert Briggs, prin.

Sykeston, Wells Co., Pop. Code 2
Sykes SD 39
Sch. Sys. Enr. Code 1
Supt. – Owen Wallace, ANSON & AVE B 58486
Sykes S, ANSON & AVE B 58486
   Robert Stringer, prin.

Tappen, Kidder Co., Pop. Code 2
Tappen SD 28
Sch. Sys. Enr. Code 2
Supt. – David Huwe, P O BOX 127 58487
S, P O BOX 127 58487 – Dale Kilmer, prin.

Taylor, Stark Co., Pop. Code 2
Taylor SD 3
Sch. Sys. Enr. Code 2
Supt. – Richard Cheatley, P O BOX 257 58656
ES, P O BOX 257 58656 – Richard Cheatley, prin.

Thompson, Grand Forks Co., Pop. Code 3
Thompson SD 61
Sch. Sys. Enr. Code 2
Supt. – Perry Bakke, P O BOX 02 58278
S, P O BOX 2 58278 – Allan Boedeker, prin.

Tioga, Williams Co., Pop. Code 4
Tioga SD 15
Sch. Sys. Enr. Code 3
Supt. – David S. Rust, P O BOX 279 58852
Central ES, P O BOX 69 58852
   Darrel Lambrecht, prin.
Hillcrest ES, P O BOX 69 58852
   Darrel Lambrecht, prin.

Tolna, Nelson Co., Pop. Code 2
Tolna SD 74
Sch. Sys. Enr. Code 2
Supt. – Eddie Poehls, P O BOX 198 58380
S, P O BOX 198 58380 – Janet Edlund, prin.

Tower City, Cass Co., Pop. Code 2
Maple Valley SD
Sch. Sys. Enr. Code 2
Supt. – Ronald Wendel 58071
West ES 58071 – Eldon Erickson, prin.
Other Schools – See Fingal

Towner, McHenry Co., Pop. Code 3
Newport SD
Sch. Sys. Enr. Code 2
Supt. – Larry Gregelman, P O BOX 338 58788
S, P O BOX 338 58788 – Richard Rogers, prin.

Trenton, Williams Co., Pop. Code 2
Eight Mile SD 6
Sch. Sys. Enr. Code 2
Supt. – Lincoln Napton, P O BOX 239 58853
Eight Mile S, P O BOX 239 58853
   Lincoln Napton, prin.

Turtle Lake, McLean Co., Pop. Code 3
Turtle Lake Mercer SD
Sch. Sys. Enr. Code 2
Supt. – Jerome Enget, P O BOX 160 58575
Turtle Lake Mercer S, P O BOX 160 58575
   Lui Ravnaas, prin.

Tuttle, Kidder Co., Pop. Code 2
Tuttle SD 20
Sch. Sys. Enr. Code 2
Supt. – Herb Kringen, P O BOX 214 58488
S, P O BOX 214 58488 – Leon Ableidinger, prin.

Underwood, McLean Co., Pop. Code 4
Underwood SD 8
Sch. Sys. Enr. Code 2
Supt. – Wade Faul, P O BOX 100 58576
S, 123 SUMMIT AVE 58576
   Edward Lockwood, prin.

Upham, McHenry Co., Pop. Code 2
Upham SD 29
Sch. Sys. Enr. Code 2
Supt. – Merlin Dahl, P O BOX 26 58789
S, P O BOX 26 58789 – Merlin Dahl, prin.

Valley City, Barnes Co., Pop. Code 6
Valley City SD 2
Sch. Sys. Enr. Code 4
Supt. – Robert Lentz, 460 CENTRAL AVE N 58072
JHS, 493 CENTRAL AVE N 58072
   Donald Bauer, prin.
Jefferson ES, 460 CENTRAL AVE N 58072
   Kenneth Bolstad, prin.
Washington ES, 460 CENTRAL AVE N 58072
   Leo Schmidt, prin.

St. Catherine School, 540 THIRD AVE NE 58072

Velva, McHenry Co., Pop. Code 4
Velva SD 1
Sch. Sys. Enr. Code 2
Supt. – Roger Slotsve, 101 W 4TH 58790
S, 101 W 4TH 58790 – Mike Norland, prin.

Verona, La Moure Co., Pop. Code 2
Verona SD 11
Sch. Sys. Enr. Code 1
Supt. – Robert Fenno, P O BOX 76 58490
S, P O BOX 76 58490 – R. Henrickson, prin.

Wahpeton, Richland Co., Pop. Code 6
Wahpeton SD 37
Sch. Sys. Enr. Code 4
Supt. – Daniel Tehle, 1021 11TH ST N 58075
Central MS, 212 3RD AVE N 58075
   Dennis Boumont, prin.
Central ES, 212 3RD AVE N 58075
   Wilfred Sauer, prin.
Dwight ES, 508 9TH ST N 58075
   Wilfred Sauer, prin.
Great Bend MS, 508 9TH ST N 58075
   Wilfred Sauer, prin.
Mooreton MS, 508 9TH ST N 58075
   Wilfred Sauer, prin.

St. Johns ES, 122 2ND ST N 58075

Walhalla, Pembina Co., Pop. Code 4
Walhalla SD 27
Sch. Sys. Enr. Code 2
Supt. – John Hvidsten, P O BOX 558 58282
S, P O BOX 558 58282 – Gary Nilsson, prin.

Warwick, Benson Co., Pop. Code 2
Warwick SD 29
Sch. Sys. Enr. Code 2
Supt. – Rocklyn Cofer, P O BOX 7 58381
S, P O BOX 7 58381 – Donald Tennancour, prin.

Washburn, McLean Co., Pop. Code 4
Washburn SD 4
Sch. Sys. Enr. Code 3
Supt. – Wesley Kessler, P O BOX 280 58577
S, P O BOX 280 58577 – Alfred Lowe, prin.

Watford City, McKenzie Co., Pop. Code 4
McKenzie County SD 1
Sch. Sys. Enr. Code 4
Supt. – R. L. Broeker, P O BOX 589 58854
Johnsons Corners ES
   RURAL ROUTE 03 BOX 19A 58854
   Eugene Williamson, prin.
ES, P O BOX 589 58854 – (—), prin.
Other Schools – See Grassy Butte

West Fargo, Cass Co., Pop. Code 7
West Fargo SD
Sch. Sys. Enr. Code 5
Supt. – M. Leidal, 207 MAIN AVE W 58078
Berger ES 58078 – Gerald Hagen, prin.
Eastwood ES, 500 10TH AVE E 58078
Edsel Kercher, prin.
South ES, 117 6TH AVE W 58078
Dean Hall, prin.
Westside ES, 945 7TH AVE W 58078
Louise Dardis, prin.
Other Schools – See Harwood, Horace

Wildrose, Williams Co., Pop. Code 2
Wildrose SD 91
Sch. Sys. Enr. Code 1
Supt. – Clifton Lee, P O BOX 697 58795
S, P O BOX 697 58795 – Clifton Lee, prin.

Williston, Williams Co., Pop. Code 7
New SD 8
Sch. Sys. Enr. Code 2
Supt. – (—), 1021 9TH AVE W 58801
Harney ES, 1021 9TH AVE W 58801
Ann Wills, prin.
Round Prairie ES, 1021 9TH AVE W 58801
Ann Wills, prin.
Stoney Creek ES, 1021 9TH AVE W 58801
Ann Wills, prin.
Twin Lake ES, 1021 9TH AVE W 58801
Ann Wills, prin.

Williston SD 1
Sch. Sys. Enr. Code 5
Supt. – Leon Olson, P O BOX 1407 58802
JHS, 612 1ST AVE W 58801 – Terry Bartness, prin.
Hagan ES, P O BOX 1407 58802
Garry Huber, prin.
Lewis & Clark ES, P O BOX 1407 58802
Warren Larson, prin.

McVay ES, P O BOX 1407 58802
Donald Roesler, prin.
Rickard ES, P O BOX 1407 58802
Larry Lynne, prin.
Webster ES, P O BOX 1407 58802
Donald Roesler, prin.
Wilkinson ES, P O BOX 1407 58802
David Hauser, prin.
_____

St. Josephs ES, 124 6TH ST W 58801

Willow City, Bottineau Co., Pop. Code 2
Willow City SD 13
Sch. Sys. Enr. Code 2
Supt. – James McQueen, P O BOX 37 58384
S, P O BOX 37 58384 – Morris Hovden, prin.

Wilton, McLean Co., Pop. Code 3
Grass Lake SD 3
Sch. Sys. Enr. Code 1
Supt. – (—) 58579
Grass Lake MS 58579 – Cynthia Lundgren, prin.

Montefiore SD 1
Sch. Sys. Enr. Code 2
Supt. – Gerald Christianson, P O BOX 157 58579
S, P O BOX 157 58579 – R. Norris, prin.

Wimbledon, Barnes Co., Pop. Code 2
Wimbledon Court SD
Sch. Sys. Enr. Code 2
Supt. – G. Gauderman, P O BOX 255 58492
Wimbledon Court S, P O BOX 255 58492
Dorothy Simenson, prin.

Wing, Burleigh Co., Pop. Code 2
Wing SD 28
Sch. Sys. Enr. Code 2
Supt. – Larry Nybladh, P O BOX M 58494
S, P O BOX M 58494 – Gary K. Simmons, prin.

Wishek, McIntosh Co., Pop. Code 4
Wishek SD 19
Sch. Sys. Enr. Code 2
Supt. – D. D. Zimmerman, P O BOX 247 58495
S, P O BOX 247 58495 – Cleo Boschee, prin.

Wolford, Pierce Co., Pop. Code 1
Wolford SD 1
Sch. Sys. Enr. Code 1
Supt. – Douglas Burlingame, P O BOX 478 58385
S, P O BOX 478 58385 – Douglas Burlingame, prin.

Woodworth, Stutsman Co., Pop. Code 2
Woodworth SD 30
Sch. Sys. Enr. Code 2
Supt. – Tom McGauley, P O BOX 66 58496
S, P O BOX 66 58496 – Kevin Synnott, prin.

Wyndmere, Richland Co., Pop. Code 3
Wyndmere SD 42
Sch. Sys. Enr. Code 2
Supt. – Dennis Nathan, P O BOX 248 58081
S, P O BOX 248 58081 – Val Welder, prin.

Zap, Mercer Co., Pop. Code 3
Zap SD 14
Sch. Sys. Enr. Code 2
Supt. – Arlyce Schulte, P O BOX 67 58580
S, P O BOX 67 58580 – Arlyce Schulte, prin.

Zeeland, McIntosh Co., Pop. Code 2
Zeeland SD 4
Sch. Sys. Enr. Code 2
Supt. – Clay Dunlap, P O BOX 2 58581
S, P O BOX 2 58581 – Clay Dunlap, prin.

OHIO

STATE DEPARTMENT OF EDUCATION
Ohio Departments Building
65 S. Front St., Columbus 43266
(614) 466-3304

Superintendent of Public Instruction	Franklin Walter
Director Computer Services & Statistical Reports	Eugene Miltko
Director Educational Services	E. Trent
Director Elementary & Secondary Education	Mary Poston
Director Equal Educational Opportunities	Hazel Flowers
Director Federal Assistance	Arlie Cox
Director Inservice Education	Nancy Eberhart
Director Personnel	Larry Cathell
Director Research & Communications	Margaret Trent
Director School Finance	James Van Keuren
Director School Food Service	Robert Koon
Director Special Education	Frank New
Director Teacher Education & Certification	Paul Hailey
Director Vocational & Career Education	Darrell Parks

STATE BOARD OF EDUCATION
Patricia Smith, *President*   415 Riley Ave., Worthington 43085

OHIO BOARD OF REGENTS
Alva Bonda, *Chairperson*   30 E. Broad St., Columbus 43266

COUNTY SUPERINTENDENTS OF SCHOOLS

Adams County, Walter Knauff, Supt.
3359 STATE RT 125, West Union 45693
Allen County, Richard Hart, Supt.
330 N ELIZABETH ST, Lima 45801
Ashland County, Gene Yeater, Supt.
CO OFC BLDG, Ashland 44805
Ashtabula County, Jerome Brockway, Supt.
CO OFC BLDG, Jefferson 44047

Athens County, Gerald Stotts, Supt.
26 W STIMSON AVE, Athens 45701
Auglaize County, Larry Goodes, Supt.
211 S BLACKHOOF ST, Wapakoneta 45895
Belmont County, Steven Grimm, Supt.
68323 BANNOCK COURT HOUSE, Saint Clairsville 43950

Brown County, Homer Castle, Supt.
ADMIN BLDG FAIRGROUNDS, Georgetown 45121
Butler County, George Hagen, Supt.
3RD & LUDLOW, Hamilton 45011
Carroll County, Bruce Schmidt, Supt.
401 W MAIN ST, Malvern 44644
Champaign County, Carroll Meadows, Supt.
P O BOX 269, Urbana 43078

Clark County, Roy Schmunk, Supt.
1115 N LIMESTONE ST, Springfield 45503
Clermont County, Robert Whitman, Supt.
809 EASTGATE DR #G, Cincinnati 45245
Clinton County, Carlton Binkley, Supt.
P O BOX 511, Wilmington 45177
Columbiana County, Paul Hood, Supt.
339 E LINCOLN WAY, Lisbon 44432
Coshocton County, Roger Ames, Supt.
23640 CR 202, Coshocton 43812
Crawford County, Ray Holland, Supt.
COURT HOUSE, Bucyrus 44820
Cuyahoga County, William Gesinsky, Supt.
5700 W CANAD ROAD, Valley View 44125
Darke County, Marlin Thompson, Supt.
504 S BROADWAY, Greenville 45331
Defiance County, Robert Breisinger, Supt.
506 COURT ST, Defiance 43512
Delaware County, Richard Coulter, Supt.
22 COURT ST, Delaware 43015
Erie County, Richard Acierto, Supt.
2902 COLUMBUS AVE, Sandusky 44870
Fairfield County, H. Klein, Supt.
125 W MAIN ST, Lancaster 43130
Fayette County, Stephen Yambor, Supt.
P O BOX 624, Washington Court House 43160
Franklin County, Don McIntyre, Supt.
1717 ALUM CREEK DRIVE, Columbus 43207
Fulton County, Eugene Winfield, Supt.
P O BOX 338, Wauseon 43567
Gallia County, Neil Johnson, Supt.
220 JACKSON PIKE, Gallipolis 45631
Geauga County, Mathew Galemmo, Supt.
211 MAIN ST, Chardon 44024
Greene County, Howard Post, Supt.
360 E ENON RD, Yellow Springs 45387
Guernsey County, Donald Jones, Supt.
CO BUILDING, Cambridge 43725
Hamilton County, Ralph Sinks, Supt.
11083 HAMILTON AVE, Cincinnati 45231
Hancock County, Bradley Cox, Supt.
604 LIMA AVE, Findlay 45840
Hardin County, Charles Renner, Supt.
COURT HOUSE ST, Kenton 43326
Harrison County, Ronald Pagano, Supt.
7205 CUMBERLAND ROAD SW, Bowerston 44695
Henry County, Robert Baker, Supt.
660 N PERRY ST, Napoleon 43545
Highland County, Pamela Nickell, Supt.
106 1/2 N HIGH ST, Hillsboro 45133
Holmes County, Richard Maxwell, Supt.
2 S CLAY ST, Millersburg 44654

Huron County, Don Schick, Supt.
180 MILAN AVE, Norwalk 44857
Jackson County, Howard Smith, Supt.
265 W CROSS ST, Oak Hill 45656
Jefferson County, Craig Closser, Supt.
2023 SUNSET BLVD, Steubenville 43952
Knox County, Bruce Hawkins, Supt.
106 E HIGH ST, Mount Vernon 43050
Lake County, James Porter, Supt.
P O BOX 490, Painesville 44077
Lawrence County, Oakley Collins, Supt.
COURT HOUSE, Ironton 45638
Licking County, Donald Boehm, Supt.
20 S 2ND ST, Newark 43055
Logan County, Max McGowan, Supt.
COURT & OPERA, Bellefontaine 43311
Lorain County, John Weber, Supt.
420 3RD ST, Elyria 44035
Lucas County, Thomas Baker, Supt.
1 GOVERNMENT CENTER, Toledo 43604
Madison County, Robert Parman, Supt.
59 N MAIN ST, London 43140
Mahoning County, Ronald Kendall, Supt.
2801 MARKET ST, Youngstown 44507
Marion County, James Traveline, Supt.
134 E CENTER ST, Marion 43302
Medina County, Homer Smith, Supt.
144 N BROADWAY ST, Medina 44256
Meigs County, John Reibel, Supt.
P O BOX 684, Pomeroy 45769
Mercer County, Ken Taylor, Supt.
311 S MAIN ST, Celina 45822
Miami County, Robert Weinfurtner, Supt.
P O BOX 130, Troy 45373
Monroe County, David Phillips, Supt.
304 MILL ST, Woodsfield 43793
Montgomery County, Raymond Hopper, Supt.
451 W THIRD ST, Dayton 45422
Morgan County, Budd Hegele, Supt.
P O BOX 509, Mc Connelsville 43756
Morrow County, Douglas Whitaker, Supt.
27 W HIGH ST, Mount Gilead 43338
Muskingum County, Larry Miller, Supt.
205 N 7TH ST, Zanesville 43701
Noble County, J. Strahler, Supt.
20977 STATE ROUTE 146, Sarahsville 43779
Ottawa County, James Getz, Supt.
314 W WATER ST, Oak Harbor 43449
Paulding County, Paul Clark, Supt.
102 S WILLIAMS ST, Paulding 45879
Perry County, Richard Fisher, Supt.
P O BOX 307, New Lexington 43764

Pickaway County, Donald Dowdy, Supt.
139 W FRANKLIN ST, Circleville 43113
Pike County, Larry Meredith, Supt.
P O BOX 578, Piketon 45661
Portage County, Donald Szostak, Supt.
224 W RIDDLE AVE, Ravenna 44266
Preble County, James Walker, Supt.
COURT HOUSE, Eaton 45320
Putnam County, Larry Bracken, Supt.
P O BOX 190, Ottawa 45875
Richland County, David Cardwell, Supt.
50 PARK AVE E, Mansfield 44902
Ross County, Rob Sigler, Supt.
P O BOX 326, Chillicothe 45601
Sandusky County, Gary Keller, Supt.
600 W STATE ST, Fremont 43420
Scioto County, William Platzer, Supt.
602 7TH ST #405, Portsmouth 45662
Seneca County, R. Lichtle, Supt.
244 S WASHINGTON ST, Tiffin 44883
Shelby County, Donald Flinn, Supt.
129 E COURT ST, Sidney 45365
Stark County, M. Herman Sims, Supt.
7800 COLUMBUS ROAD NE, Louisville 44641
Summit County, R. Louis Daugherty, Supt.
482 GRANT ST, Akron 44311
Trumbull County, Herbert Thomas, Supt.
347 N PARK AVE, Warren 44481
Tuscarawas County, Richard Ronald, Supt.
261 W HIGH AVE, New Philadelphia 44663
Union County, James Wright, Supt.
227 W 5TH ST, Marysville 43040
Van Wert County, David Rhoades, Supt.
116 N WALNUT ST, Van Wert 45891
Vinton County, Clyde Crewey, Supt.
MEMORIAL BLDG, Mc Arthur 45651
Warren County, Gerald Powell, Supt.
416 S EAST ST, Lebanon 45036
Washington County, P. Barton Cromer, Supt.
348 MUSKINGUM DR, Marietta 45750
Wayne County, Douglas Staggs, Supt.
2534 BURBANK ROAD, Wooster 44691
Williams County, Richard Harpster, Supt.
COURT HOUSE, Bryan 43506
Wood County, Dallas Gardner, Supt.
CO BLDG COURT HOUSE SQUARE, Bowling Green 43402
Wyandot County, Madelyn Jarvis, Supt.
295 STATE ROUTE 231, Sycamore 44882

PUBLIC, PRIVATE, AND PAROCHIAL ELEMENTARY SCHOOLS

Aberdeen, Brown Co., Pop. Code 4
Ohio Valley Local SD
Supt. – See West Union
ES, MAIN CROSS ST 45101
Charles Kimble, prin.

Ada, Hardin Co., Pop. Code 6
Ada EVD
Sch. Sys. Enr. Code 4
Supt. – Eugene Fries, 500 GRAND AVE 45810
ES, 500 GRAND AVE 45810
Dennis Anthony, prin.

Adamsville, Muskingum Co., Pop. Code 2
Tri-Valley Local SD
Supt. – See Dresden
ES, 7950 EAST ST 43802 – John Larson, prin.

Addyston, Hamilton Co., Pop. Code 4
Three Rivers Local SD
Supt. – See Cleves
Hitchens ES, 190 MAIN ST 45001
Donald Larrick, prin.

Adena, Harrison Co., Pop. Code 4
Buckeye Local SD
Supt. – See Rayland
ES, P O BOX 518 43901 – Ronald Ignac, prin.

Akron, Summit Co., Pop. Code 9
Akron CSD
Sch. Sys. Enr. Code 8
Supt. – Conrad Ott, 70 N BROADWAY ST 44308
Goodrich JHS, 700 LAFOLLETTE ST 44306
Alex Rachita, prin.
Goodyear MS, 49 N MARTHA AVE 44305
Anthony Marano, prin.
Hyre JHS, 2443 WEDGEWOOD DRIVE 44312
James Bell II, prin.
Innes MS, 1999 EAST AVE 44314
Greg Hinson, prin.
Jennings MS, 225 E TALLMADGE AVE 44310
Richard Roberts, prin.
Kent MS, 1445 HAMMEL ST 44306
Jerome Pecko, prin.
Litchfield MS, 1540 FARIFAX ROAD 44313
William Mannion, prin.
Perkins MS, 630 MULL AVE 44313
Donald Smith, prin.
Riedinger MS, 77 W THORTON ST 44311
Larry Johnson, prin.
Barber ES, 665 GARRY RD 44305
Thomas Royce, prin.
Barrett ES, 888 JONATHAN AVE 44306
Sam Orlando, prin.
Bettes ES, 1333 BETANA AVE 44310
Roy Copeland, prin.

Betty Jane ES, 444 DARROW RD 44305
James McCoy, prin.
Case ES, 1393 WESTVALE AVE 44313
John Dawson, prin.
Crosby ES, 235 SMITH ST 44303
Gloria Rittenhouse, prin.
Crouse ES, 1000 DIAGONAL RD 44320
Joseph Vassalotti, prin.
Erie Island ES, 1532 PEKHAM AVE 44320
Paul Dimascio, prin.
Essex ES, 1160 WINHURST DR 44313
Kenneth Mitchell, prin.
Fairlawn ES, 65 N MEADOWCROFT DR 44313
Bruce DeBarr, prin.
Findley ES, 65 W TALLMADGE AVE 44310
David Butz, prin.
Firestone Park ES, 1479 GIRARD ST 44301
Lynda Grieves, prin.
Forest Hill ES, 601 FOUSE ST 44310
James Anderson, prin.
Glover ES, 935 HAMMEL ST 44306
Carolyn Reed, prin.
Harris ES, 959 DAYTON ST 44310
Robert Mittiga, prin.
Hatton ES, 1933 BAKER AVE 44312
Paul Green, prin.
Heminger ES, 2228 11TH ST SW 44314
Joseph Cistone, prin.
Highland Park-Guinther ES
12222 W WATERLOO ROAD 44314
William Cline, prin.
Hill ES, 1065 AUSTIN AVE 44306
Barbara Whaley, prin.
Hotchkiss ES, 33 DORCAS AVE 44305
Dorothy Lower, prin.
Jackson ES, 1065 CLIFTON AVE 44310
Carl Mashek, prin.
King ES, 805 MEMORIAL PKY 44303
Moyra Culberston, prin.
Lawndale ES, 25TH ST SW 44314
Frances Kalapodis, prin.
Leggett ES, 619 SUMNER ST 44311
Connie Nolte, prin.
Lincoln ES, 175 W CROSIER ST 44311
Ronald Bishop, prin.
Park ES, 1413 MANCHESTER RD 44314
Dorothy Walsh, prin.
Mason ES, 366 BEAVER ST 44306
Patricia Durkin, prin.
McEbright ES, 349 COLE AVE 44301
Earl Nay, prin.
Pfeiffer ES, 2081 9TH ST SW 44314
Rochelle Riggins, prin.
Portage Path ES, 55 S PORTAGE PATH 44303
Henry Ereth, prin.

Rankin ES, 415 STORER AVE 44320
Barbara Tyler, prin.
Rimer ES, 2370 MANCHESTER RD 44314
Brenda Preer, prin.
Ritzman ES, 629 CANTON RD 44312
Karen Bennett, prin.
Robinson ES, 1156 4TH AVE 44306
Lawrence Marshall, prin.
Schumacher ES, 1031 GREENWOOD AVE 44320
Beverly Taylor, prin.
Seiberling ES, 400 BRITTAIN RD 44305
M. Scholl, prin.
Smith ES, 941 CHESTER AVE 44314
Warren Ferrell, prin.
Stewart PS, 1199 WOOSTER AVE 44307
Terry Cardine, prin.
Voris ES, 1875 GLENMOUNT AVE 44301
Joanne Shippy, prin.
Windemere ES, 2283 WINDEMERE AVE 44312
Alyce Simmons, prin.

Copley-Fairlawn CSD
Supt. – See Copley
Ft. Island PS, 496 TRUNKO RD 44313
Janet Monroe, prin.
Herberich IS, 2645 SMITH RD 44313
Eugene Nofsinger, prin.

Coventry Local SD
Sch. Sys. Enr. Code 4
Supt. – James Gides
3257 CORMANY ROAD 44319
Erwine MS, 1135 PORTAGE LAKES DRIVE 44319
Richard Kostko, prin.
Cottage Grove ES, 3185 DAISY AVE 44319
John Mazan, prin.
Lakeview ES, 2910 S MAIN ST 44319
Gerald Horak, prin.
Turkeyfoot ES
530 W TURKEYFOOT LAKE RD 44319
Donald Murray, prin.

Manchester Local SD
Sch. Sys. Enr. Code 4
Supt. – Marco Burnette
6075 MANCHESTER ROAD 44319
Manchester MS, 760 W NIMISILA ROAD 44319
Richard Brokow, prin.
Nolley ES, 6285 RENNINGER RD 44319
Jacqueline Carpas, prin.

Revere Local SD
Supt. – See Bath
Bath MS
1246 N CLEVELAND-MASSILLON 44313
James Nelson, prin.

Springfield Local SD
Sch. Sys. Enr. Code 5
Supt. – J. Gray, 2960 SANATORIUM ROAD 44312
Schrop JHS, 2215 PICKLE ROAD 44312
Paul Kovachick, prin.
Spring Hill MS, 660 LESSIG AVE 44312
Richard Currie, prin.
Milroy ES, 1639 KILLIAN RD 44312
Robert Jackson, prin.
Roosevelt ES, 3110 FARMDALE RD 44312
Dale Fraley, prin.
Young ES, 3258 NIDOVER DR 44312
R. Benczo, prin.
Other Schools – See Lakemore

Annunciation-St. John ES, 88 KENT ST 44305
Chapel Hill Christian South School
946 E TURKEYFOOT LAKE RD 44312
Christ the King ES, 1558 CREIGHTON AVE 44310
Immaculate Conception ES
2128 16TH ST SW 44314
Our Lady of Elms ES, 1230 W MARKET ST 44313
St. Anthony ES, 80 E YORK ST 44310
St. Francis De Sales ES
4009 MANCHESTER RD 44319
St. Hilary ES, 645 MOORFIELD RD 44313
St. Martha ES, 300 E TALLMADGE AVE 44310
St. Mary ES, 750 S MAIN ST 44311
St. Matthew ES, 2580 BENTON AVE 44312
St. Paul ES, 1580 BROWN ST 44301
St. Sebastian ES, 352 ELMDALE AVE 44320
St. Vincent De Paul ES, 17 S MAPLE ST 44303

Albany, Athens Co., Pop. Code 3
Alexander Local SD
Sch. Sys. Enr. Code 4
Supt. – Rick Rolston, P O BOX 337 45710
ES, P O BOX 188 45710 – Robert Bray, prin.
Other Schools – See New Marshfield, Shade

Alexandria, Licking Co., Pop. Code 2
Northridge Local SD
Supt. – See Johnstown
Northridge Alexandria ES, P O BOX 68 43001
Gregory Huffman, prin.

Alger, Hardin Co., Pop. Code 3
Upper Scioto Valley Local SD
Supt. – See Mc Guffey
MS 45812 – Ronald Pepple, prin.

Alliance, Stark Co., Pop. Code 7
Alliance CSD
Sch. Sys. Enr. Code 5
Supt. – Richard Tormasi
200 GLAMORGAN ST 44601
Stanton MS, 311 S UNION AVE 44601
David Root, prin.
State Street MS, 150 E STATE ST 44601
Michael Bosick, prin.
Liberty ES, 1800 S LIBERTY AVE 44601
Christophe Brown, prin.
Morgan ES, 935 GARWOOD ST 44601
Wanda Chidsey, prin.
North Lincoln ES, 530 N LINCOLN AVE 44601
Jerry Hodges, prin.
Parkway ES, 1490 PARKWAY BLVD 44601
Nancy Kile, prin.
Rockhill ES, 2400 ROCKHILL & 24TH ST 44601
Gail Singleton, prin.
South Lincoln ES, 284 W HIGH ST 44601
David Maxwell, prin.

Marlington Local SD
Sch. Sys. Enr. Code 5
Supt. – James Akenhead
10320 MOULIN AVE NE 44601
Marlington MS, 10325 MOULIN AVE NE 44601
J. Turner, prin.
Lexington ES, 12333 ATWATER AVE NE 44601
Raymond Asher, prin.
Washington ES, 5786 BEECHWOOD AVE 44601
Alan Andreani, prin.
Other Schools – See Louisville

West Branch Local SD
Supt. – See Beloit
Knox ES, 2900 KNOX SCHOOL RD 44601
Donald Denny, prin.
Maple Ridge ES, 13444 BANDY RD 44601
Frances French, prin.

Regina Coeli ES, 733 FERNWOOD BLVD 44601

Amanda, Fairfield Co., Pop. Code 3
Amanda-Clearcreek Local SD
Sch. Sys. Enr. Code 4
Supt. – Stephen Gahn, P O BOX 188 43102
ES, N SCHOOL ST #188 43102
Robert Christy, prin.
Other Schools – See Stoutsville

Amelia, Clermont Co., Pop. Code 4
West Clermont Local SD
Supt. – See Cincinnati
MS, CLOUGH PARK 45102 – Larry Lucas, prin.
ES, 5 E MAIN ST 45102 – Jenny Grisham, prin.
Holly Hill ES, 3520 STATE ROUTE 132 45102
David Jewell, prin.

St. Bernadette ES, 1453 LOCUST LAKE RD 45102

Amesville, Athens Co., Pop. Code 2
Federal Hocking Local SD
Supt. – See Stewart
ES, P O BOX 189 45711 – Cindy Hartman, prin.

Amherst, Lorain Co., Pop. Code 7
Amherst EVD
Sch. Sys. Enr. Code 5
Supt. – Howard Dulmage, 185 FOREST ST 44001
Nord JHS, 501 LINCOLN ST 44001
William Marley, prin.
Harris ES, 393 S LAKE ST 44001
Robert Wiersum, prin.
Powers ES, 401 WASHINGTON ST 44001
Robert Dinallo, prin.
Shupe MS, 600 SHUPE AVE 44001
Stephen Demko, prin.

St. Joseph ES, 175 SAINT JOSEPH DR 44001

Amsden, Seneca Co.
Lakota Local SD
Supt. – See Rising Sun
Lakota JHS
8351 W SENECA CITY ROAD 28 44803
Jeffery Szabo, prin.

Andover, Ashtabula Co., Pop. Code 4
Pymatuning Valley Local SD
Sch. Sys. Enr. Code 5
Supt. – Frank Little, RURAL ROUTE 06 44003
Pymatuning Valley MS, RURAL ROUTE 06 44003
Robert Dravesky, prin.
Pymatuning Valley PS, W MAIN ST 44003
James Miltner, prin.

Anna, Shelby Co., Pop. Code 4
Anna Local SD
Sch. Sys. Enr. Code 3
Supt. – Philip Cornett, 204 N 2ND 45302
ES, 204 N 2ND 45302 – Evonne Schnippel, prin.
McCarthyville ES, 9355 STATE ROUTE 119 45302
Louis Locker, prin.
Other Schools – See Kettlersville

Ansonia, Darke Co., Pop. Code 4
Ansonia Local SD
Sch. Sys. Enr. Code 4
Supt. – Norman Cutright, 600 E CANAL 45303
MS, 600 E CANAL ST 45303 – John Peters, prin.
ES, W CROSS 45303 – Judith Bergman, prin.

Antwerp, Paulding Co., Pop. Code 4
Antwerp Local SD
Sch. Sys. Enr. Code 4
Supt. – David Bagley, FRANKLIN ST 45813
ES, FRANKLIN ST 45813 – Jack Griner, prin.

Apple Creek, Wayne Co., Pop. Code 3
Southeast Local SD
Sch. Sys. Enr. Code 4
Supt. – Lynn Dildine, 9048 DOVER ROAD 44606
Lea MS, 9130 DOVER ROAD 44606
Willis Kaderly, prin.
ES, P O BOX 208 44606 – Gary Rogers, prin.
Other Schools – See Fredericksburg, Holmesville,
Mount Eaton

Arcadia, Hancock Co., Pop. Code 3
Arcadia Local SD
Sch. Sys. Enr. Code 3
Supt. – Ray Richardson
19033 STATE ROUTE 12 44804
ES, 19033 STATE ROUTE 12 44804
Richard Lehman, prin.

Arcanum, Darke Co., Pop. Code 4
Arcanum Butler Local SD
Sch. Sys. Enr. Code 4
Supt. – Howard Huston
2 WEINSENBARGER COURT 45304
Butler MS, 1481 STATE ROUTE 127 45304
Stephen Gruber, prin.
ES, 310 N MAIN ST 45304 – Ronald Mayo, prin.

Franklin-Monroe Local SD
Supt. – See Pitsburg
Franklin Monroe ES, 8982 HOGPATH RD 45304
Eugene Cullers, prin.

Archbold, Fulton Co., Pop. Code 5
Archbold-Area Local SD
Sch. Sys. Enr. Code 4
Supt. – David Lersch, 304 STRYKER ST 43502
MS, RURAL ROUTE 02 BOX 141A 43502
David Rex, prin.
ES, HOLLAND ST 43502 – Michael Sullivan, prin.

Gorham-Fayette Local SD
Supt. – See Fayette
Franklin MS, RURAL ROUTE 03 BOX 153 43502
John Winzeler, prin.

Arlington, Hancock Co., Pop. Code 4
Arlington Local SD
Sch. Sys. Enr. Code 3
Supt. – David Ingram, S MAIN 45814
ES, S MAIN 45814 – David Rossman, prin.

Lockland CSD
Supt. – See Lockland
Arlington ES, 607 CARTHAGE AVE 45215
Phillip Fox, prin.

Ashland, Ashland Co., Pop. Code 7
Ashland CSD
Sch. Sys. Enr. Code 5
Supt. – H. Doyle Davidson, P O BOX 156 44805
JHS, 345 COTTAGE ST 44805 – Rex Smith, prin.
Edison ES, 1202 MASTERS AVE 44805
James Minnich, prin.
Grant Street ES, 730 GRANT ST 44805
Ray Wiley, prin.

Lincoln ES, 30 W 11TH ST 44805
Steven Willeke, prin.
Montgomery ES, RURAL ROUTE 02 44805
Victor Knox, prin.
Osborn ES, 544 E MAIN ST 44805
Kyle Creasy, prin.
Pleasant Street ES, 317 PLEASANT ST 44805
George Scheff, prin.
Taft ES, BUDD AVE & SMITH ROAD 44805
Debra Krajcik, prin.

Crestview Local SD
Sch. Sys. Enr. Code 4
Supt. – Roger Barnes, RURAL ROUTE 01 44805
Other Schools – See Mansfield, Savannah

Mapleton Local SD
Sch. Sys. Enr. Code 4
Supt. – John Barahill, RURAL ROUTE 03 44805
Other Schools – See Nankin, Nova, Polk

Ashland Christian ES, 1144 W MAIN ST 44805
St. Edward ES, 433 COTTAGE ST 44805

Ashley, Delaware Co., Pop. Code 4
Buckeye Valley Local SD
Supt. – See Delaware
Buckeye Valley East ES, 522 HIGH ST 43003
John Klinge, prin.

Ashtabula, Ashtabula Co., Pop. Code 7
Ashtabula Area CSD
Sch. Sys. Enr. Code 6
Supt. – Elinor Scricca, P O BOX 290 44004
Columbus JHS, 1326 COLUMBUS AVE 44004
William Licate, prin.
West JHS, 1231 W 47TH ST 44004
John Rose, prin.
Chestnut ES, 5321 CHESTNUT AVE 44004
Charles Lotze, prin.
Jefferson ES, 2630 W 13TH ST 44004
Emily Fisher, prin.
McKinsey ES, 1113 BUNKER HILL RD 44004
John Meehl, prin.
Plymouth ES, PLYMOUTH ROAD 44003
Ronald Gaskell, prin.
Saybrook ES, 7911 DEPOT RD 44004
Dan Norman, prin.
State Road ES, 4200 STATE RD 44004
Rosemary Bernato, prin.
Station ES, 3703 STATION AVE 44004
Joel Peel, prin.
Washington ES, 917 LAKE AVE 44004
Theresa DiCesare, prin.

Buckeye Local SD
Sch. Sys. Enr. Code 4
Supt. – Roger Colucci
3436 EDGEWOOD DRIVE 44004
Braden JHS, 3436 EDGEWOOD DRIVE 44004
Joseph Donatone, prin.
Ridgeview ES, 3456 LIBERTY ST 44004
Jack Clements, prin.
Other Schools – See Kingsville, North Kingsville,
Pierpont

Christian Life Academy
2300 AUSTINBURG RD 44004
Mother of Sorrows ES, 1464 W 6TH ST 44004
Our Lady of Mt. Carmel ES
2150 COLUMBUS AVE 44004
St. Joseph ES, 3400 LAKE AVE 44004

Ashville, Pickaway Co., Pop. Code 4
Teays Valley Local SD
Sch. Sys. Enr. Code 5
Supt. – Benis Lutz, 28 MAIN ST E 43103
Teays Valley MS, 383 CIRCLEVILLE AVE 43103
Robert Jenkins, prin.
ES, 190 PLUM ST 43103 – Carol Hatem, prin.
Walnut ES, 16450 WINCHESTER RD S 43103
David Barnett, prin.
Other Schools – See Commercial Point

Athens, Athens Co., Pop. Code 7
Athens CSD
Sch. Sys. Enr. Code 5
Supt. – June Slobodian, P O BOX 788 45701
MS, 51-55 W STATE ST 45701
Paul Grippa, prin.
East ES, 3 WALLACE DR 45701
Denny Boger, prin.
Morrison ES, RURAL ROUTE 01 BOX 47 45701
John Gordon, prin.
West ES, 41 CENTRAL AVE 45701
Ted Reed, prin.
Other Schools – See Chauncey, The Plains

Athens Christian School, 10 S GREEN DR 45701

Attica, Seneca Co., Pop. Code 3
Seneca East Local SD
Sch. Sys. Enr. Code 4
Supt. – David Getter 44807
ES 44807 – Comer Carey, prin.
Other Schools – See Bellevue, Republic

Atwater, Portage Co., Pop. Code 3
Waterloo Local SD
Sch. Sys. Enr. Code 4
Supt. – Fred Crewse
1464 INDUSTRY ROAD 44201
Waterloo PS, 6660 WATERLOO RD 44201
Carolyn Vogenitz, prin.
Other Schools – See Randolph

Augusta, Carroll Co.
Carrollton EVD
Supt. – See Carrollton
ES, P O BOX 129 44607 – James Gow, prin.

Aurora, Portage Co., Pop. Code 6
Aurora CSD
Sch. Sys. Enr. Code 4
Supt. – James Costanza
102 E GARFIELD ROAD 44202
Harmon MS
130 AURORA HUDSON ROAD 44202
Jerry Brodsky, prin.
Craddock ES, HURD ROAD 44202
Doreene McDonald, prin.
Miller ES, 646 S CHILLICOTHE RD 44202
Doreene McDonald, prin.

Valley Christian Academy
646 S CHILLICOTHE RD 44202

Austinburg, Ashtabula Co., Pop. Code 3
Geneva Area CSD
Supt. – See Geneva
Austinburg ES, 3030 ROUTE 307 W 44010
Jerry Sykes, prin.

Austintown, Mahoning Co.

Immaculate Heart of Mary ES
4470 NORQUEST BLVD 44515
St. Joseph ES, 4565 NEW RD 44515

Avon, Lorain Co., Pop. Code 6
Avon Local SD
Sch. Sys. Enr. Code 4
Supt. – Richard Hronek
3075 STONEY RIDGE ROAD 44011
Avon East ES, 3100 NAGLE RD 44011
Joseph Paulchell, prin.

Holy Trinity ES, 2610 NAGLE RD 44011
St. Mary Immaculate ES
2680 STONEY RIDGE RD 44011

Avon Lake, Lorain Co., Pop. Code 7
Avon Lake CSD
Sch. Sys. Enr. Code 5
Supt. – Clayton Dusek
175 AVON BELDEN ROAD 44012
Learwood MS, 340 LEAR ROAD 44012
William Hamilton, prin.
Eastview ES, 230 LEAR RD 44012
Robert Godlewski, prin.
Erieview ES, 32630 ELECTRICE BLVD 44012
Ann Marley, prin.
Redwood ES, 32967 REDWOOD BLVD 44012
Daniel Trent, prin.
Westview ES, 155 MOORE RD 44012
Catherine Eggleston, prin.

St. Joseph ES, 32929 LAKE RD 44012

Bainbridge, Ross Co., Pop. Code 4
Paint Valley Local SD
Sch. Sys. Enr. Code 4
Supt. – T. Williamson, 7454 USR 50 45612
ES, 1/2 DEWEY AVE 45612 – Terry Childers, prin.
Other Schools – See Bourneville

Baltic, Tuscarawas Co., Pop. Code 3
Garaway Local SD
Supt. – See Sugarcreek
ES, P O BOX 266 43804 – Larry Miller, prin.

Baltimore, Fairfield Co., Pop. Code 5
Liberty Union-Thurston Local SD
Sch. Sys. Enr. Code 4
Supt. – John Ruff
621 W WASHINGTON ST 43105
Liberty Union MS
600 W WASHINGTON ST 43105
Max Beougher, prin.
Liberty Union ES, 1000 S MAIN ST 43105
Robert Drury, prin.

Barberton, Summit Co., Pop. Code 8
Barberton CSD
Sch. Sys. Enr. Code 5
Supt. – Ronald Clemmer
479 NORTON AVE 44203
Highland MS, 1152 BELLVIEW AVE 44203
Jay Whitman, prin.
Light MS, 292 ROBINSON AVE 44203
John Vargo, prin.
Johnson ES, 1340 AUBURN AVE 44203
Lynn Smith, prin.
Memorial ES, 291 W SUMMIT ST 44203
John Hoskinson, prin.
Oakdale ES, 165 3RD ST NE 44203
Gerald Anderson, prin.
Portage ES, 800 WOOSTER RD N 44203
Charles Rivers, prin.
Santrock ES, 88 19TH ST NW 44203
Robert Parsons, prin.
Woodford ES, 315 E STATE ST 44203
Jerry Mattingly, prin.

St. Augustine ES, 195 7TH ST NW 44203

Barnesville, Belmont Co., Pop. Code 5
Barnesville EVD
Sch. Sys. Enr. Code 4
Supt. – Kearney Lykins, 210 W CHURCH ST 43713

MS, 210 W CHURCH ST 43713
Arthur Monahan, prin.
ES, 210 W CHURCH ST 43713 – Frank Koci, prin.

Bartlett, Washington Co.
Warren Local SD
Supt. – See Vincent
MS, P O BOX 26 45713 – Jack Dunker, prin.

Bascom, Seneca Co.
Hopewell-Loudon Local SD
Sch. Sys. Enr. Code 3
Supt. – James Miccichi, P O BOX 400 44809
Hopewell-Loudon ES, P O BOX 400 44809
Douglas Picciuto, prin.

Batavia, Clermont Co., Pop. Code 4
Batavia Local SD
Sch. Sys. Enr. Code 4
Supt. – James Fite, 800 BAUER AVE 45103
ES, 215 BROADWAY ST 45103
Paul Sallada, prin.

Clermont-Northeastern Local SD
Sch. Sys. Enr. Code 4
Supt. – Thomas Rice
5347 HUTCHINSON ROAD 45103
Northeastern MS, 2792 STATE ROUTE 50 45103
Bennie Trail, prin.
Northeastern IS, 5347 HUTCHINSON RD 45103
Joann Beamer, prin.
Other Schools – See Owensville

West Clermont Local SD
Supt. – See Cincinnati
Willowville ES, 4529 SCHOOLHOUSE RD 45103
John Martin, prin.

Bath, Summit Co.
Revere Local SD
Sch. Sys. Enr. Code 5
Supt. – J. Klingensmith, P O BOX 176 44210
Revere MS, 3195 SPRING VALLEY ROAD 44210
Ed Wolski, prin.
Other Schools – See Akron, Richfield

Old Trail ES, 2315 IRA RD 44210

Bay Village, Cuyahoga Co., Pop. Code 7
Bay Village CSD
Sch. Sys. Enr. Code 5
Supt. – M. Bauer
377 DOVER CENTER ROAD 44140
Bay MS, 27725 WOLF ROAD 44140
David Wilson, prin.
Normandy ES, 26920 NORMANDY RD 44140
Harold Macri, prin.
Westerly ES, 30301 WOLF RD 44140
Lino Deanna, prin.

St. Raphael ES, 525 DOVER RD 44140

Beach City, Stark Co., Pop. Code 4
Fairless Local SD
Supt. – See Navarre
ES, 3RD AVE SW 44608 – Barry Askren, prin.

Beachwood, Cuyahoga Co., Pop. Code 6
Beachwood CSD
Sch. Sys. Enr. Code 4
Supt. – Lee McMurrin
24601 FAIRMOUNT BLVD 44122
MS, 2860 RICHMOND ROAD 44122
Margaret McCullough, prin.
Bryden ES, 25501 BRYDEN RD 44122
Deborah O'Brien, prin.
Hilltop MS, 24524 HILLTOP DR 44122
Daniel Johnston, prin.

Agnon ES, 26500 SHAKER BLVD 44122

Beallsville, Monroe Co., Pop. Code 3
Switzerland of Ohio Local SD
Supt. – See Woodsfield
ES, 52682 OHIO AVE 43716 – Starling Zink, prin.

Beaver, Pike Co., Pop. Code 2
Eastern Local SD
Sch. Sys. Enr. Code 4
Supt. – George Pendleton
1170 TILE MILL ROAD 45613
ES 45613 – (—), prin.
Other Schools – See Stockdale

Beavercreek, Greene Co., Pop. Code 8
Beavercreek Local SD
Supt. – See Xenia
Fairbrook ES, 2940 DAYTON XENIA RD 45385
Steven Huff, prin.
Main ES, 2940 DAYTON XENIA RD 45385
Mary Jo Scalzo, prin.
Parkwood ES, 2940 DAYTON XENIA RD 45385
Denton Brower, prin.
Shaw ES, 2940 DAYTON XENIA RD 45385
Steven Shank, prin.
Valley ES, 2940 DAYTON XENIA RD 45385
Dennis Montague, prin.

St. Luke ES, 1442 N FAIRFIELD RD 45432

Bedford, Cuyahoga Co., Pop. Code 7
Bedford CSD
Sch. Sys. Enr. Code 5
Supt. – Frank Ledonne
475 NORTHFIELD ROAD 44146
Heskett MS, 5771 PERKINS ROAD 44146
H. Brichacek, prin.

Aurora MS, 24200 AURORA RD 44146
Martha Motsco, prin.
Carylwood MS, 1387 CARYL DR 44146
Raymond Welling, prin.
Central MS, 799 WASHINGTON ST 44146
James Smith, prin.
Glendale ES, 400 W GLENDALE ST 44146
Daniel English, prin.

St. Mary ES, 232 UNION ST 44146
St. Pius X ES, 320 CENTER RD 44146

Bedford Heights, Cuyahoga Co., Pop. Code 7

New Covenant Christian ES
23600 COLUMBUS RD 44146

Bellaire, Belmont Co., Pop. Code 6
Bellaire CSD
Sch. Sys. Enr. Code 4
Supt. – Regis Woods, 3517 GUERNSEY ST 43906
First Ward MS, 1731 BELMONT ST 43906
Larry Dougherty, prin.
Gravel Hill MS, 46TH ST 43906
Robert Fialkowski, prin.
Indian Run ES, 4129 NOBLE ST 43906
Angeline Frantz, prin.
Key Ridge ES, KEY BELLAIRE ROAD 43906
Norman Brutchey, prin.
Rose Hill ES, 3400 FRANKLIN ST 43906
John Stinoski, prin.
West Bellaire ES, WASHINGTON ST 43906
Brett Merryman, prin.
Other Schools – See Neffs

St. John ES, 37TH & GUERNSEY ST 43906

Bellbrook, Greene Co., Pop. Code 6
Sugarcreek Local SD
Sch. Sys. Enr. Code 4
Supt. – A. Mikula, 60 E SOUTH ST 45305
MS, 3545 UPPER BELLBROOK ROAD 45305
Larry Will, prin.
Bell ES, 4122 N LINDA DR 45305
Paul Dunlap, prin.
Sugarcreek MS, 53 S EAST ST 45305
Alice Webb, prin.

Belle Center, Logan Co., Pop. Code 3
Benjamin Logan Local SD
Supt. – See Bellefontaine
Benjamin Logan ES, 107 SCHOOL ST 43310
Michael Moore, prin.

Bellefontaine, Logan Co., Pop. Code 7
Bellefontaine CSD
Sch. Sys. Enr. Code 5
Supt. – R. Carter, 820 LUDLOW ROAD 43311
MS, 509 PARK ROAD 43311 – Robert Bixler, prin.
Northeastern ES, 600 E BROWN AVE 43311
Eric Tom, prin.
Pine Avenue ES, 401 PINE AVE 43311
Deborah Ellis, prin.
Southeastern ES
COLTON AND HAMILTON STS 43311
Deborah Ellis, prin.
Western ES, 1130 W SANDUSKY AVE 43311
Jacqueline Kellogg, prin.

Benjamin Logan Local SD
Sch. Sys. Enr. Code 4
Supt. – Harold Keck
2091 STATE ROUTE 47 E 43311
Other Schools – See Belle Center, East Liberty,
Rushsylvania, West Mansfield

Belleville, Richland Co., Pop. Code 4
Clear Fork Valley Local SD
Sch. Sys. Enr. Code 4
Supt. – David Southward
RURAL ROUTE 03 44811
Other Schools – See Bellville, Butler

Bellevue, Huron Co., Pop. Code 6
Bellevue CSD
Sch. Sys. Enr. Code 4
Supt. – M. Yost, 125 NORTH ST 44811
JHS, NORTH ST 44811 – John Redd, prin.
Ellis ES, ELLIS AVE 44811 – Virginia Tesar, prin.
Lyme ES, RURAL ROUTE 01 44811
Jerrold Garman, prin.
Ridge ES, RIDGE DRIVE 44811
Michael Marshall, prin.
Shumaker ES, 1035 CASTALIA ST 44811
Charlotte Cole, prin.
Other Schools – See Clyde

Seneca East Local SD
Supt. – See Attica
Seneca-Huron ES, EAST CITY RT 24 44811
Comer Carey, prin.

Immaculate Conception ES
BROAD AND MAIN 44811

Bellville, Richland Co., Pop. Code 4
Clear Fork Valley Local SD
Supt. – See Belleville
ES, P O BOX 98 44813 – Ellen Wise, prin.

Belmont, Belmont Co., Pop. Code 3
Union Local SD
Sch. Sys. Enr. Code 4
Supt. – Robert Butts
66859 BELMONT MORRISTOWN RD 43718
ES, P O BOX 27 43718 – Samuel Lucas, prin.

Other Schools – See Bethesda, Flushing, Jacobsburg, Morristown

Beloit, Mahoning Co., Pop. Code 4
West Branch Local SD
Sch. Sys. Enr. Code 5
Supt. – Nancy Pinney, 14277 S MAIN ST 44609
ES, 17926 5TH ST 44609 – John Airhart, prin.
Other Schools – See Alliance, Damascus, Salem

Belpre, Washington Co., Pop. Code 6
Belpre CSD
Sch. Sys. Enr. Code 4
Supt. – Gary Stamm
2014 WASHINGTON BLVD 45714
MS, 2000 ROCKLAND AVE 45714
Steve Stahley, prin.
Stone ES, 2014 ROCKLAND AVE 45714
William Wotring, prin.

Bentonville, Adams Co.
Ohio Valley Local SD
Supt. – See West Union
ES, STATE ROUTE 41 45105
Clarence Wilkerson, prin.

Berea, Cuyahoga Co., Pop. Code 7
Berea CSD
Sch. Sys. Enr. Code 6
Supt. – David Cottrell, 390 FAIR ST 44017
Roehm MS, 7220 PLEASANT AVE 44017
John Marsick, prin.
Fairwood ES, 191 RACE ST 44017
Maria Ivanovich, prin.
Parknoll ES, 499 NOBOTTOM RD 44017
Dave Beveridge, prin.
Riveredge ES, 224 EMERSON AVE 44017
Rena Catron, prin.
Other Schools – See Brook Park, Middleburg Heights

St. Adalbert ES, 56 ADELBERT ST 44017
St. Mary ES, 265 BAKER ST 44017

Bergholz, Jefferson Co., Pop. Code 3
Edison Local SD
Supt. – See Hammondsville
Gregg ES, ROAD 1 43908 – Clarence Virtue, prin.

Berlin, Holmes Co., Pop. Code 2
East Holmes Local SD
Sch. Sys. Enr. Code 4
Supt. – Lewis Bevington, P O BOX 182 44610
Flat Ridge MS, P O BOX 310 44610
James Mast, prin.
ES, P O BOX 310 44610 – James Mast, prin.
Charm ES, P O BOX 310 44610 – James Mast, prin.
Wise ES, P O BOX 310 44610
Bruce Stambaugh, prin.
Other Schools – See Mount Hope, Walnut Creek, Winesburg

Berlin Center, Mahoning Co., Pop. Code 2
Western Reserve Local SD
Sch. Sys. Enr. Code 4
Supt. – C. Grist
13850 W AKRON-CANFIELD ROAD 44401
Western Reserve MS
15904 W AKRON-CANFIELD ROAD 44401
Rudolph Wyatt, prin.
Other Schools – See Ellsworth

Berlin Heights, Erie Co., Pop. Code 3
Berlin-Milan Local SD
Supt. – See Milan
Berlin-Milan MS, CENTER ST 44814
Robert Mitchell, prin.
Berlin ES, CENTER ST 44814
Deborah Miller, prin.

Bethel, Clermont Co., Pop. Code 4
Bethel-Tate Local SD
Sch. Sys. Enr. Code 4
Supt. – William Shula 45106
Hill East MS, FOSSYL DRIVE 45106
Steven Gill, prin.
Bick ES, STATE ROUTE 232 45106
David Weidner, prin.

Bethesda, Belmont Co., Pop. Code 4
Union Local SD
Supt. – See Belmont
ES, P O BOX 98 43719 – Samuel Lucas, prin.

Bettsville, Seneca Co., Pop. Code 3
Bettsville Local SD
Sch. Sys. Enr. Code 2
Supt. – J. Kelbley, P O BOX 6 44815
ES, P O BOX 6 44815 – James Kelbley, prin.

Beverly, Washington Co., Pop. Code 4
Fort Frye Local SD
Sch. Sys. Enr. Code 4
Supt. – Ronald Curry, 5TH ST 45715
ES, 5TH ST 45715 – Robert Forbes, prin.
Center ES, RURAL ROUTE 01 45715
Robert Forbes, prin.
Other Schools – See Lowell, Lower Salem

Bexley, Franklin Co., Pop. Code 7
Bexley CSD
Sch. Sys. Enr. Code 4
Supt. – Patricia Conran
348 S CASSINGHAM ROAD 43209
JHS, 250 S CASSINGHAM ROAD 43209
John Brandt, prin.
Cassingham ES, 250 S CASSINGHAM RD 43209
(—), prin.

Maryland Avenue ES
2754 MARYLAND AVE 43209
Linda Lucks, prin.
Montrose ES, 2754 MARYLAND AVE 43209
Terry Black, prin.

Bidwell, Gallia Co.
Gallia County Local SD
Supt. – See Gallipolis
Bidwell-Porter ES, P O BOX 18 45614
James Chestnut, prin.

Blacklick, Franklin Co.

Grace Brethren Christian East ES
7510 BROAD ST E 43004

Bladensburg, Knox Co.
East Knox Local SD
Supt. – See Howard
ES 43005 – Miles Burson, prin.

Blanchester, Clinton Co., Pop. Code 5
Blanchester Local SD
Sch. Sys. Enr. Code 4
Supt. – Rodney Lane, P O BOX 128 45107
MS, P O BOX 128 45107 – Phillip Horner, prin.
Main Street MS, E MAIN ST 45107
Ralph Pelfrey, prin.
Putnam ES, BALDWIN ST 45107
Roy Gross, prin.
Other Schools – See Midland

Little Miami Local SD
Supt. – See Morrow
Harlan-Butlerville ES
8276 STATE ROUTE 132 45107
Joyce Sanker, prin.

Bloomdale, Wood Co., Pop. Code 3
Elmwood Local SD
Sch. Sys. Enr. Code 4
Supt. – Russell Griggs
7650 JERRY CITY ROAD 44817
ES, 206 E VINE ST 44817 – Larry Coffelt, prin.
Other Schools – See Cygnet, Portage, Wayne

Bloomingburg, Fayette Co., Pop. Code 3
Miami Trace Local SD
Supt. – See Washington Court House
Miami Trace JHS, 103 MAIN STREET 43103
Roger Zimmerman, prin.

Bloomingdale, Jefferson Co., Pop. Code 2
Indian Creek Local SD
Supt. – See Mingo Junction
Wayne ES 43910 – Vincent Talarico, prin.

Bloomville, Seneca Co., Pop. Code 4
Tiffin CSD
Supt. – See Tiffin
Bloom Township ES, S MARION ST 44818
Larry Hedden, prin.

Wynford Local SD
Supt. – See Bucyrus
Wynford North ES
RURAL ROUTE 02 BOX 45 44818 – Joy Kear, prin.

Blue Creek, Adams Co.
Ohio Valley Local SD
Supt. – See West Union
Cedar Mills ES, 4910 STATE ROUTE 348 45616
David Worley, prin.
Jefferson ES, 8990 BLUE CREEK RD 45616
Jack Hazelbaker, prin.

Bluffton, Allen Co., Pop. Code 5
Bluffton EVD
Sch. Sys. Enr. Code 4
Supt. – Larry Brunswick
102 S JACKSON ST 45817
ES, 102 S JACKSON ST 45817 – Ib Thomsen, prin.

Boardman, Mahoning Co.

St. Charles ES, 7325 WESTVIEW DR 44512
St. Luke ES, 5225 SOUTH AVE 44512

Bolivar, Tuscarawas Co., Pop. Code 3
Tuscarawas Valley Local SD
Supt. – See Zoarville
ES, P O BOX 196 44612 – Fred Miller, prin.

Botkins, Shelby Co., Pop. Code 4
Botkins Local SD
Sch. Sys. Enr. Code 3
Supt. – James Degen, P O BOX 550 45306
ES, P O BOX 550 45306 – Connie Schneider, prin.

Bourneville, Ross Co.
Paint Valley Local SD
Supt. – See Bainbridge
Twin ES, 10699 UPPER TWIN RD 45617
Gary Newsome, prin.

Bowerston, Harrison Co., Pop. Code 2
Conotton Valley Union Local SD
Sch. Sys. Enr. Code 3
Supt. – Ronald Pagano
7205 CUMBERLAND ROAD SW 44695
ES, 600 MAIN ST 44695 – John Evanosky, prin.
Other Schools – See Sherrodsville

Bowersville, Greene Co., Pop. Code 2
Greeneview Local SD
Supt. – See Jamestown
Greeneview South ES, 5619 HUSSEY RD 45307
Keith Earley, prin.

Bowling Green, Wood Co., Pop. Code 8
Bowling Green CSD
Sch. Sys. Enr. Code 5
Supt. – Richard Cummings
140 S GROVE ST 43402
Conneaut ES, 542 HASKINS RD 43402
Judith Telb, prin.
Crim ES, CRIM & 1ST STS 43402
Mary Johnson, prin.
Kenwood ES, 710 KENWOOD AVE 43402
Tedde Eldridge, prin.
Ridge ES, 225 RIDGE ST 43402
Judith Paluck, prin.
South Main ES, 437 S MAIN ST 43402
Judith Paluck, prin.
Other Schools – See Custar

St. Aloysius ES, P O BOX 485 43402

Bradford, Miami Co., Pop. Code 4
Bradford EVD
Sch. Sys. Enr. Code 4
Supt. – Don Sheer, 712 N MIAMI AVE 45308
Bradford Central ES, SCHOOL ST 45308
Cherie Roeth, prin.

Bradner, Wood Co.
Lakota Local SD
Supt. – See Rising Sun
Lakota West ES, 218 E LIGHTNER ST 43406
Stephen Fogo, prin.

Brecksville, Cuyahoga Co., Pop. Code 7
Brecksville-Broadview Heights CSD
Sch. Sys. Enr. Code 5
Supt. – John Smith, 6638 MILL ROAD 44141
Brecksville-Broadview Heights MS
27 PUBLIC SQUARE 44141
Herbert Bradford, prin.
Chippewa ES, 8611 WIESE RD 44141
Carla Calevich, prin.
Highland Drive ES, 9457 HIGHLAND DR 44141
Cheryl Channel, prin.
Hilton ES, 6812 MILL RD 44141
Nicholas Carpas, prin.

Bremen, Fairfield Co., Pop. Code 4
Fairfield Union Local SD
Supt. – See West Rushville
ES, 210 STRAYER AVE 43107 – John Snider, prin.

Brewster, Stark Co., Pop. Code 4
Fairless Local SD
Supt. – See Navarre
ES, 245 FIFTH ST SE 44613 – Don Cooke, prin.

Bridgeport, Belmont Co., Pop. Code 5
Bridgeport EVD
Sch. Sys. Enr. Code 4
Supt. – Roger Stewart, 501 BENNETT ST 43912
Kirkwood MS, 503 BENNETT ST #L 43912
Robert Snyder, prin.
Westbrook IS, WATER ST 43912
David Obranovich, prin.
Other Schools – See Lansing

St. Joseph ES, 55505 NATIONAL RD 43912

Brilliant, Jefferson Co., Pop. Code 4
Buckeye Local SD
Supt. – See Rayland
ES, 1004 THIRD ST 43913 – Kent Stewart, prin.

Bristolville, Trumbull Co., Pop. Code 2
Bristol Local SD
Sch. Sys. Enr. Code 3
Supt. – James Levero, P O BOX 260 44402
Bristol ES, 1845 GREENVILLE RD NW 44402
Danice Bowser, prin.
Other Schools – See West Farmington

Broadview Heights, Cuyahoga Co., Pop. Code 7

Assumption ES, 9183 BROADVIEW RD 44147

Brookfield, Trumbull Co., Pop. Code 3
Brookfield Local SD
Sch. Sys. Enr. Code 4
Supt. – Jerry Raupach, P O BOX 209 44403
Other Schools – See Masury

Brooklyn, Cuyahoga Co., Pop. Code 7
Brooklyn CSD
Sch. Sys. Enr. Code 4
Supt. – Lewis Galante
9200 BIDDULPH AVE 44144
Brookridge ES, 4500 RIDGE RD 44144
David Petrus, prin.

St. Thomas More ES, 4180 N AMBER DR 44144

Brook Park, Cuyahoga Co., Pop. Code 8
Berea CSD
Supt. – See Berea
Ford MS, 17001 HOLLAND ROAD 44142
Barbara Webb, prin.
Memorial ES, 16900 HOLLAND RD 44142
Joseph DeNardi, prin.
Brookview ES, 14100 PARKMAN BLVD 44142
Ken Hartz, prin.

Brookville, Montgomery Co., Pop. Code 5
Brookville Local SD
Sch. Sys. Enr. Code 4
Supt. – James Davison, 325 SIMMONS AVE 45309
MS, 128 S HILL ST 45309 – Michael Gray, prin.

Westbrook ES, 100 JUNE PL 45309
James Boomershine, prin.

Brunswick, Medina Co., Pop. Code 8
Brunswick CSD
Sch. Sys. Enr. Code 6
Supt. – Terrance Furin
3643 CENTER ROAD 44212
Willetts Addition S, 1045 HADCOCK ROAD 44212
(—), prin.
Edwards MS, 1497 PEARL RD 44212
Sally Conaway, prin.
Willetts MS, 1045 HADCOCK RD 44212
Robert Sykora, prin.
Applewood ES, 3891 APPLEWOOD DR 44212
Benjamin Herrle, prin.
Memorial ES, 3845 MAGNOLIA DR 44212
Nance Hare, prin.
Crestview ES, 300 W 130TH ST 44212
Richard Vrable, prin.
Hickory Ridge ES
4628 HICKORY RIDGE AVE 44212
William Kubinski, prin.
Huntington ES, 1931 HUNTINGTON CIR 44212
James Schilling, prin.
Kidder ES, 3650 GRAFTON RD 44212
Michael Whitacre, prin.
Towslee ES, 3555 CENTER RD 44212
William Parschen, prin.

St. Ambrose ES, 923 PEARL RD 44212
St. Mark Lutheran School
1330 N CARPENTER ROAD 44212

Bryan, Williams Co., Pop. Code 6
Bryan CSD
Sch. Sys. Enr. Code 4
Supt. – Jack Raymond, 120 S BEECH ST 43506
MS, 1301 CENTER ST 43506 – T. Dominque, prin.
Lincoln ES, 301 E BUTLER ST 43506
Gene Linton, prin.
Pulaski-Jefferson ES, RURAL ROUTE 02 43506
John Miller, prin.
Washington ES, 510 AVENUE A ST 43506
Tom Breininger, prin.

St. Patrick ES, 610 S PORTLAND ST 43506

Buckland, Auglaize Co., Pop. Code 2
Wapakoneta CSD
Supt. – See Wapakoneta
Buckland ES, MAIN ST 45819
Donald Numbers, prin.

Bucyrus, Crawford Co., Pop. Code 7
Bucyrus CSD
Sch. Sys. Enr. Code 4
Supt. – William Hall, 1130 S WALNUT ST 44820
MS, 245 WOODLAWN AVE 44820
Thomas Armstrong, prin.
Carlisle ES, 501 EAST ST 44820
James Baublitz, prin.
Kilbourne ES, 1130 S WALNUT ST 44820
James Baublitz, prin.
Lincoln ES, 170 PLYMOUTH ST 44820
Joseph Short, prin.
Norton ES, 511 KALER AVE 44820
Charles Frobose, prin.

Colonel Crawford Local SD
Supt. – See North Robinson
Whetsone ES, 4063 MONNETT CHAPEL RD 44820
Kevin Ruth, prin.

Wynford Local SD
Sch. Sys. Enr. Code 4
Supt. – Robert Taylor
3288 HOLMES CENTER ROAD 44820
Wynford MS, 1141 MOUNT ZION ROAD 44820
Frank Levering, prin.
Wynford IS, 4401 STATE ROUTE 19 44820
Frank Levering, prin.
Other Schools – See Bloomville, Nevada

Holy Trinity ES, 740 TIFFIN ST 44820

Buford, Highland Co.
Lynchburg-Clay Local SD
Supt. – See Lynchburg
ES 45110 – Gregory Hawk, prin.

Burbank, Wayne Co., Pop. Code 2
North Central Local SD
Supt. – See Creston
ES, 125 SOUTH ST 44214 – Marlin Simms, prin.

Burgoon, Sandusky Co., Pop. Code 2
Lakota Local SD
Supt. – See Rising Sun
Lakota East ES, 1582 STATE ROUTE 590 S 43407
Edward Walden,Jr., prin.

Burkettsville, Mercer Co., Pop. Code 2
St. Henry Cons. Local SD
Supt. – See Saint Henry
MS, MAIN ST 45310 – Carl Hart, prin.

Burton, Geauga Co., Pop. Code 4
Berkshire Local SD
Sch. Sys. Enr. Code 4
Supt. – Arthur Langerman, 14531 MAIN ST 44021
ES, 13724 CARLTON ST 44021
David Scarberry, prin.
Troy ES, 17791 CLARIDON TROY RD 44021
Daniel Itschner, prin.
Other Schools – See East Claridon

Geuga Christian ES, RT 87 & WHITE ROAD 44021

Butler, Richland Co., Pop. Code 3
Clear Fork Valley Local SD
Supt. – See Belleville
ES, COLLEGE ST 44822 – Douglas Ramsey, prin.

Byesville, Guernsey Co., Pop. Code 5
Rolling Hills Local SD
Sch. Sys. Enr. Code 5
Supt. – Raymond Cook, RURAL ROUTE 01 43723
Meadowbrook MS
58607 MARIETTA ROAD 43723
Don Conaway, prin.
Brook ES, 58601 MARIETTA RD 43723
Sharon Miller, prin.
ES, 212 MAIN AVE 43723 – Irene Mailot, prin.
Other Schools – See Cambridge, Senecaville

Cadiz, Harrison Co., Pop. Code 5
Harrison Hills CSD
Supt. – See Hopedale
Central MS, 440 E MARKET ST 43907
John Alleman, prin.
Westgate ES, PEPPARD AVE 43907
Josephine Freeman, prin.

Caldwell, Nobel Co., Pop. Code 4
Caldwell EVD
Sch. Sys. Enr. Code 4
Supt. – Albert Shelton
516 FAIRGROUND ST 43724
ES, 44350 FAIRGROUND ROAD 43724
Samuel Sells, prin.

Caledonia, Marion Co., Pop. Code 3
River Valley Local SD
Supt. – See Marion
ES, NORTH MAIN ST 43314
Harvey Stoneman, prin.
ES, 3938 MARION-MT GILEAD RD 43314
John Boger, prin.

Cambridge, Guernsey Co., Pop. Code 7
Cambridge CSD
Sch. Sys. Enr. Code 5
Supt. – Robert Robinson
152 HIGHLAND AVE 43725
JHS, 701 STEUBENVILLE AVE 43725
Barbara Ballenger, prin.
Garfield ES, S 7TH ST 43725 – Tom Lodge, prin.
Liberty ES, ROUTE 21 N 43725
John Knapp, prin.
Lincoln ES, 710 N 4TH ST 43725
Art Clemenson, prin.
Oakland ES, 1300 CLAIRMONT AVE 43725
Paul Miller, prin.
Park ES, HIGHLAND AVE 43725
James Spisak, prin.
Washington ES, 916 FOSTER AVE 43725
John Knapp, prin.

East Muskingum Local SD
Supt. – See New Concord
Pike ES, 4533 PETERS CREEK RD 43725
Martha Moore, prin.

Rolling Hills Local SD
Supt. – See Byesville
Beech Grove ES, 8900 WHITAKER RD 43725
Irene Mailot, prin.

St. Benedict ES, 220 N 7TH ST 43725

Camden, Preble Co., Pop. Code 4
Preble-Shawnee Local SD
Sch. Sys. Enr. Code 4
Supt. – Lawrence Rentschler
124 BLOOMFIELD ST 45311
Shawnee MS
5495 SOMERS GRATIS ROAD 45311
Lucian Szlizewski, prin.
ES, 124 BLOOMFIELD ST 45311
Carl Trusty, prin.
Other Schools – See West Elkton

Campbell, Mahoning Co., Pop. Code 7
Campbell CSD
Sch. Sys. Enr. Code 4
Supt. – Matthew Bozic, 280 SIXTH ST 44405
Reed MS, 300 REED AVE 44405
James Cioffi, prin.
Gordon IS, 100 GORDON AVE 44405
Frank Richards, prin.
Penhale PS, 281 PENHALE AVE 44405
Robert Petruska, prin.

St. Joseph the Provider ES
633 PORTER AVE 44405

Canal Fulton, Stark Co., Pop. Code 5
Northwest Local SD
Sch. Sys. Enr. Code 5
Supt. – E. Frost, 8590 ERIE AVE N 44614
Northwest IS, 8540 ERIE AVE N 44614
Larry Minamyer, prin.
ES, 246 MARKET ST E 44614
Wendell Edwards, prin.
Stinson MS, 8510 ERIE AVE N 44614
Sherry Kapes, prin.
Other Schools – See Clinton

Sts. Philip & James ES, 532 HIGH ST NE 44614

Canal Winchester, Franklin Co., Pop. Code 5
Canal Winchester Local SD
Sch. Sys. Enr. Code 4
Supt. – Vernon Noggle, 131 FRANKLIN ST 43110
ES, 100 WASHINGTON ST 43110
Ray Mowery, prin.

Word of Life Christian Academy
10165 WRIGHT RD 43110

Canfield, Mahoning Co., Pop. Code 6
Canfield Local SD
Sch. Sys. Enr. Code 4
Supt. – James Watkins
100 WADSWORTH ST 44406
MS, 42 WADSWORTH ST 44406
Dante Zambrini, prin.
Campbell ES, 300 MORELAND DR 44406
Richard Taaffe, prin.
Hilltop ES, 400 HILLTOP BLVD 44406
Herbert Bartelmay, prin.

Canton, Stark Co., Pop. Code 8
Canton CSD
Sch. Sys. Enr. Code 7
Supt. – David Kaiser, 508 6TH ST SW 44707
Allen ES, 1114 GONDER AVE SE 44707
Stephanie Patrick, prin.
Baxter ES, 3408 13TH ST SW 44710
Jay Parrot, prin.
Belden ES, 2115 GEORGETOWN RD NE 44704
Fred Thompson, prin.
Belle Stone ES, 2100 ROWLAND AVE NE 44714
Victor Pitea, prin.
Cedar ES, 2823 9TH ST SW 44710
Michael DeComo, prin.
Clarendon ES, 412 CLARENDON AVE NW 44708
Howard Linz, prin.
Deuber ES, 815 DUEBER AVE SW 44706
Elaine Armbrust, prin.
Fairmount ES, 2701 COVENTRY BLVD NE 44705
Charles Wycuff, prin.
Gibbs ES, 1320 GIBBS AVE NE 44705
Audrey Sparks, prin.
Harter ES, 317 RAFF RD NW 44708
George Burwell, prin.
Lathrop ES, 401 14TH ST SE 44707
Minnie Hopkins, prin.
Mason ES, 316 30TH ST NW 44709
William Trbovich, prin.
McGregor ES, 2339 17TH ST SW 44706
Daniel Myers, prin.
Summit ES, 1033 TROY PL NW 44703
Robert Powell, prin.
Washington ES, 1220 9TH ST NE 44705
George Sams, prin.
Woodland ES
15034 WOODLAND AVE NW 44703
Ernest Leedy, prin.
Worley ES, 1340 23RD ST NW 44709
Thomas Calanni, prin.
Youtz ES, 1901 MIDWAY AVE NE 44705
Richard Barnes, prin.

Canton Local SD
Sch. Sys. Enr. Code 5
Supt. – Norman Poynter
4526 RIDGE AVE SW 44707
Faircrest Memorial MS
616 FAIRCREST ST SW 44706
Ronald Molnar, prin.
McDannel ES, 210 38TH ST SE 44707
Paul Davidson, prin.
Prairie College ES
3021 PRAIRIE COLLEGE ST SW 44706
Robert Graham, prin.
Walker ES, 3525 SANDY AVE SE 44707
Walter Linhart, prin.

Jackson Local SD
Supt. – See Massillon
Lake Cable ES
5335 VILLA PADOVA DR NW 44718
George Burwell, prin.

Perry Local SD
Supt. – See Massillon
Knapp ES, 5151 OAKCLIFF ST SW 44706
Paul Carver, prin.
Reedurban ES, 1221 PERRY DR SW 44710
James Hodinka, prin.
Whipple Heights ES, 4800 12TH ST NW 44708
Ben Miller, prin.

Plain Local SD
Sch. Sys. Enr. Code 6
Supt. – Larry Morgan, 901 44TH ST NW 44709
Pleasant View MS For Arts
3000 COLUMBUS RD NE 44705
Carmela Lioi, prin.
Taft MS, 3829 GUILFORD AVE NW 44718
Dennis Miller, prin.
Avondale ES, 3933 EATON RD NW 44708
Erick Hendrickson, prin.
Barr ES, 2000 47TH ST NE 44705
Wilbur Amacher, prin.
Day ES, 3101 38TH ST NW 44718
Gerald Mohn, prin.
Frazer ES, 3900 FRAZER AVE NW 44709
C. Digman, prin.
Other Schools – See North Canton

Heritage Christian Academy
2107 6TH ST SW 44706

Canton Country Day School
  3000 DEMINGTON AVE NW 44718
Our Lady of Peace ES, 1001 39TH ST NW 44709
St. Joan of Arc ES, 158 BORDNER AVE SW 44710
St. Joseph ES, 126 COLUMBUS AVE NW 44708
St. Michael ES
  3501 SAINT MICHAELS BLVD NW 44718
St. Peter ES, 702 CLEVELAND AVE NW 44702

Cardington, Morrow Co., Pop. Code 4
Cardington-Lincoln Local SD
Sch. Sys. Enr. Code 4
Supt. – Patrick Drouhard
  349 CHESTERVILLE AVE 43315
ES, NICHOLS ST 43315 – William Clauss, prin.

Carey, Wyandot Co., Pop. Code 5
Carey EVD
Sch. Sys. Enr. Code 4
Supt. – John Decker, 357 E SOUTH ST 43316
Crawford ES, 357 E SOUTH ST 43316
  Vernon Hull, prin.

Our Lady of Consolation ES, 401 CLAY ST 43316

Carlisle, Warren Co., Pop. Code 5
Carlisle Local SD
Sch. Sys. Enr. Code 5
Supt. – Daniel Shull, 724 FAIRVIEW DRIVE 45005
MS, 720 FAIRVIEW DRIVE 45005
  Mark Upton, prin.
ES, 100 JAMAICA RD 45005
  James Oldfield, prin.
PS, 310 JAMAICA RD 45005 – Robert Athy, prin.

Carroll, Fairfield Co., Pop. Code 3
Bloom Carroll Local SD
Sch. Sys. Enr. Code 4
Supt. – Richard Snelling, N BEAVER ST 43112
Bloom Carroll MS, N BEAVER STREET 43112
  Thomas Petty, prin.
ES, N BEAVER ST 43112 – Virginia Isele, prin.
Other Schools – See Lithopolis

Carrollton, Carroll Co., Pop. Code 5
Carrollton EVD
Sch. Sys. Enr. Code 5
Supt. – L. Pontuti, 80 3RD ST NE 44615
Bell-Herron MS, 80 3RD ST NE 44615
  Fred Boggs, prin.
Kilgore MS, 7211 GERMANO ROAD SE 44615
  Kevin Spears, prin.
ES, 80 3RD ST NE 44615 – Craig Winters, prin.
Harlem Springs ES
  3567 WASHINGTON ST SE 44615
  Norma Rutledge, prin.
Other Schools – See Augusta, Dellroy, Mechanicstown

Casstown, Miami Co., Pop. Code 2
Miami East Local SD
Sch. Sys. Enr. Code 4
Supt. – S. Warren
  4308 E STATE ROUTE 55 45312
ES, 4308 E STATE ROUTE 55 45312
  Roberta Wilson, prin.
Other Schools – See Conover, Fletcher, Troy

Castalia, Erie Co., Pop. Code 3
Margaretta Local SD
Sch. Sys. Enr. Code 4
Supt. – Don Ruck, 305 S WASHINGTON ST 44824
Bogart ES, BOGART ROAD 44824
  Fran Warner, prin.
Other Schools – See Vickery

Cedarville, Greene Co., Pop. Code 5
Cedar Cliff Local SD
Sch. Sys. Enr. Code 3
Supt. – James McGuire, P O BOX 45 45314
ES, P O BOX 45 45314 – Lois Stockwell, prin.

Celina, Mercer Co., Pop. Code 6
Celina CSD
Sch. Sys. Enr. Code 5
Supt. – Ralph Stelzer
  585 E LIVINGSTON ST 45822
MS, 615 HOLLY ST 45822 – Fred Wiswell, prin.
East ES, 615 E WAYNE ST 45822
  Mark Springer, prin.
Franklin ES, 6731 STATE ROUTE 219 45822
  (—), prin.
West ES, 1225 W LOGAN ST 45822
  Gary Whitaker, prin.

Immaculate Conception ES
  WAYNE AND WALNUT 45822

Centerburg, Knox Co., Pop. Code 4
Centerburg Local SD
Sch. Sys. Enr. Code 3
Supt. – Barbara Lambert, 175 UNION ST 43011
ES, PRESTON ST 43011 – Erma Morgan, prin.

Centerville, Montgomery Co., Pop. Code 7
Centerville CSD
Sch. Sys. Enr. Code 5
Supt. – Robert Kreiner, 111 VIRGINIA AVE 45459
Magsig MS, 192 W FRANKLIN ST 45459
  Jeff Kunst, prin.
Tower Heights MS, 195 N JOHANA DRIVE 45459
  Terry Riley, prin.
Cline ES, 99 VIRGINIA AVE 45459
  Patricia Buckingham, prin.
Stingley ES, 95 LINDEN DR 45459
  Gary Smiga, prin.
Weller ES, 9600 SHEEHAN RD 45458
  J. David Mays, prin.

Other Schools – See Dayton

Incarnation ES, 45 WILLIAMSBURG LN 45459

Chagrin Falls, Cuyahoga Co., Pop. Code 5
Chagrin Falls EVD
Sch. Sys. Enr. Code 4
Supt. – Arlene Rieger
  77 E WASHINGTON ST 44022
MS, 77 E WASHINGTON ST 44022
  Anthony Podijil, prin.
Gurney PS, 1155 BELL RD 44022
  Edward Wong, prin.
Sands MS, 400 E WASHINGTON ST 44022
  Patricia Gray, prin.

Kenston Local SD
Sch. Sys. Enr. Code 4
Supt. – L. Duane Tennant
  17419 SNYDER ROAD 44022
Kenston MS, 17419 SNYDER ROAD 44022
  Donald Menefee, prin.
Auburn ES, 11051 E WASHINGTON ST 44022
  Patricia Murphy, prin.
Gardiner ES, 9421 BAINBRIDGE RD 44022
  Patricia Murphy, prin.
Kenston IS, 17870 CHILLICOTHE RD 44022
  Richard Householder, prin.

St. Joan of Arc ES, 498 E WASHINGTON ST 44022

Chandlersville, Muskingum Co.
Franklin Local SD
Supt. – See Duncan Falls
ES 43727 – June Scott, prin.

Chardon, Geauga Co., Pop. Code 5
Chardon Local SD
Sch. Sys. Enr. Code 5
Supt. – Bruce Armstrong, 428 NORTH ST 44024
MS, 424 NORTH ST 44024
  Randolph Continenza, prin.
Hambden ES, 13871 GAR HWY 44024
  Dorothy Thompson, prin.
Maple ES, 308 MAPLE AVE 44024
  Millicent McClelland, prin.
Munson ES, 12687 BASS LAKE RD 44024
  Susan Miller, prin.
Park ES, 111 GOODRICH CT 44024
  Albert Hanson, prin.

Notre Dame ES, 13000 AUBURN RD 44024
St. Mary ES, 401 NORTH ST 44024

Chatfield, Crawford Co., Pop. Code 2
Buckeye Central Local SD
Supt. – See New Washington
Buckeye West ES, P O BOX 187 44825
  RuthAnn Noblet, prin.

Chauncey, Athens Co., Pop. Code 4
Athens CSD
Supt. – See Athens
ES, P O BOX 225 45719 – Clyde Jarvis, prin.

Cherry Fork, Adams Co., Pop. Code 2
Ohio Valley Local SD
Supt. – See West Union
Wayne MS, 14815 STATE ROUTE 136 #97 45618
  Sheila Roush, prin.

Chesapeake, Lawrence Co., Pop. Code 4
Chesapeake Union EVD
Sch. Sys. Enr. Code 4
Supt. – Dan Russell, P O BOX 458 45619
East MS, P O BOX 10 45619 – Fred Wood, prin.
West ES, P O BOX 358 45619 – Bob Harris, prin.

Cheshire, Gallia Co., Pop. Code 2
Gallia County Local SD
Supt. – See Gallipolis
Cheshire Kyger ES, RURAL ROUTE 01 45620
  James Page, prin.

Chester, Meigs Co., Pop. Code 4
Eastern Local SD
Supt. – See Reedsville
ES 45720 – Ron Hill, prin.

Chesterhill, Morgan Co., Pop. Code 2
Morgan Local SD
Supt. – See Mc Connelsville
Marion ES, P O BOX 115 43728
  Charles Cooper, prin.

Chesterland, Geauga Co., Pop. Code 4
West Geauga Local SD
Sch. Sys. Enr. Code 5
Supt. – Robert Gilson
  13445 CHILLICOTHE ROAD 44026
West Geauga JHS, 8611 CEDAR ROAD 44026
  Glenn Bitner, prin.
Lindsey ES, 11844 CAVES RD 44026
  Lloyd Schill, prin.
Other Schools – See Novelty

St. Anselm ES, 13013 CHILLICOTHE RD 44026

Chesterville, Morrow Co., Pop. Code 2
Highland Local SD
Supt. – See Sparta
Highland North ES, P O BOX 7 43317
  Steven Templin, prin.

Chillicothe, Ross Co., Pop. Code 7
Chillicothe CSD
Sch. Sys. Enr. Code 5
Supt. – Patricia Carr
  455 YOCTANGEE PARKWAY 45601
Mt. Logan MS, 841 E MAIN ST 45601
  Larry Ervin, prin.
Smith MS, 345 ARCH ST 45601
  Michael MacCarter, prin.
Allen ES, PLYLEYS LANE 45601
  Stanley Mitchell, prin.
Central ES, 40 W FIFTH ST 45601
  Betty Putman, prin.
Hopewell ES, 77 CUTRIGHT DR 45601
  Robert Imboden, prin.
McArthur ES, 1049 COLUMBUS ST 45601
  John Miller, prin.
Tiffin ES, S BRIDGE ST 45601
  Joseph Fisher, prin.
Worthington ES, 450 ALLEN AVE 45601
  William Vanvoorhis, prin.

Huntington Local SD
Sch. Sys. Enr. Code 4
Supt. – James McGuire
  188 HUNTSMAN ROAD 45601
Huntington ES, 188 HUNTSMAN RD 45601
  David Jones, prin.

Scioto Valley Local SD
Supt. – See Richmond Dale
Harrison ES, 6597 CHARLESTON PIKE 45601
  Rebecca Smallridge, prin.
Higby ES, 3477 HIGBY RD 45601
  Arrreta Hice, prin.

Union Scioto Local SD
Sch. Sys. Enr. Code 4
Supt. – Paul Folmer, 1432 EGYPT PIKE 45601
Union-Scioto IS, 1432 EGYPT PIKE 45601
  June Cormany, prin.
Union-Scioto PS, 1432 EGYPT PIKE 45601
  Bessie Angles, prin.

Zane Trace Local SD
Sch. Sys. Enr. Code 4
Supt. – James Dunkle
  946 STATE ROUTE 180 45601
Zane Trace MS, 946 STATE ROUTE 180 45601
  Leonard Johnson, prin.
Zane Trace ES, 946 STATE ROUTE 180 45601
  Donna Sever, prin.

Bishop Flaget ES, 570 PARSONS LN 45601

Cincinnati, Hamilton Co., Pop. Code 10
Cincinnati CSD
Sch. Sys. Enr. Code 8
Supt. – Lee Etta Powell, 230 E 9TH ST 45202
Bloom JHS, 1941 BAYMILLER ST 45214
  Dorothy Battle, prin.
Crest Hills MS, 1908 SEYMOUR AVE 45237
  Myron Kilgore, prin.
Gamble MS
  2601 WESTWOOD-NORTHERN BLVD 45211
  Charles Staley, prin.
Merry MS, 301 OAK ST 45219
  Elvin Turner, prin.
Peoples MS, 3030 ERIE AVE 45208
  William Thorman, prin.
Porter JHS, 1030 CUTTER ST 45203
  Edward Hawkins, prin.
Schwab ES, 4370 BEECH HILL AVE 45223
  Barbara Smitherman, prin.
Academy World Languages ES
  2030 FAIRFAX AVE 45207
  Gwendolyn Robinson, prin.
Anderson Place ES, 5051 ANDERSON PL 45227
  Alan James, prin.
Bond Hill ES, 1510 CALIFORNIA AVE 45237
  Marva Mitchell, prin.
Bramble ES, 4324 HOMER AVE 45227
  Jane Patterson, prin.
Burton ES, 876 GLENWOOD AVE 45229
  Dennis McNeal, prin.
Carson ES, 4323 GLENWAY AVE 45205
  Beverly Baughman, prin.
Carthage ES, 125 W NORTH BEND RD 45216
  Janet Weingartner, prin.
Central Fairmount ES, 2475 WHITE ST 45214
  Aurello Leon, prin.
Chase MS, 4151 TURRILL ST 45223
  Patricia Torrey, prin.
Cheviot ES, 4040 HARRISON AVE 45211
  Thomas Webb, prin.
Clifton ES, 3711 CLIFTON AVE 45220
  Mary Wagner, prin.
College Hill ES, 1625 CEDAR AVE 45224
  Jerry Boyle, prin.
Covedale ES, 5130 SIDNEY RD 45238
  Mary Kell, prin.
Douglass ES, 2825 ALMS PL 45206
  Thomas Haley, prin.
Eastern Hills ES, 6421 CORBLY RD 45230
  Annie Orr, prin.
Fairview ES, 2232 STRATFORD AVE 45219
  Frederick Veidt, prin.
Hartwell ES, 8320 VINE ST 45216
  James Gum, prin.
Hays ES, 1035 MOUND ST 45203
  Sheila Taylor, prin.
Heberle ES, 2015 FREEMAN AVE 45214
  Henri Bradshaw, prin.
Heinold ES, 2240 BALTIMORE AVE 45225
  Raymond Smith, prin.

Hoffman ES, 3060 DURRELL AVE 45207
  Theresa Henderson, prin.
Hyde Park ES, 3401 EDWARDS RD 45208
  Frank Mack, prin.
Kilgour ES, 1339 HERSCHEL AVE 45208
  Edwin Dawley, prin.
Kirby Road ES, 1710 BRUCE AVE 45223
  Roscoe Mickle, prin.
Linwood ES, 4900 EASTERN AVE 45226
  (—), prin.
Losantiville ES, 6701 ELBROOK AVE 45237
  Donald Embs, prin.
McKinley ES, 3905 EASTERN AVE 45226
  Joanne Perry, prin.
Midway ES, 3200 MIDWAY AVE 45238
  Maxine Watson, prin.
Millvale PS, 3277 BEEKMAN ST 45225
  John Listach, prin.
Mt. Airy ES, 5730 COLERAIN AVE 45239
  Meredythe Flynn, prin.
Mt. Washington ES, 1730 MEARS AVE 45230
  Gerald Porter, prin.
North Avondale ES
  615 CLINTON SPRINGS AVE 45229
  Phyllis Williams, prin.
North Fairmount ES
  2001 BALTIMORE AVE 45225
  Elizabeth Pearson, prin.
Oyler ES, 2121 HATMAKER ST 45204
  Russell Feth, prin.
Parham ES, 1835 FAIRFAX AVE 45207
  Betty Sommerville, prin.
Pleasant Hill ES, 1402 W NORTH BEND RD 45224
  Henri Frazier, prin.
Pleasant Ridge ES
  5945 MONTGOMERY RD 45213
  Roman Walton, prin.
Quebec Heights ES, 1655 ROSS AVERY RD 45205
  (—), prin.
Roberts Paideia ES, 1700 GRAND AVE 45214
  Patricia Surber, prin.
Rockdale ES, 305 ROCKDALE AVE 45229
  Frank Perry,Jr., prin.
Roll Hill ES, 2411 BALTIMORE AVE 45225
  Maude Thompson, prin.
Roosevelt ES, 1550 TREMONT ST 45214
  Benny Miles, prin.
Roselawn-Condon ES
  7735 GREENLAND PL 45237
  John Knoechel, prin.
Rothenberg ES, 241 E CLIFTON AVE 45210
  Louise Stallworth, prin.
Sands Montessori School, 940 POPLAR ST 45214
  Sandra Sommer, prin.
Sayler Park ES, 6700 HOME CITY AVE 45233
  Mary Rozier, prin.
Schiel Academic Arts Enrichment PS
  2821 VINE ST 45219 – Janet Parker, prin.
Silverton ES, 6829 STEWART RD 45236
  DeWolfe Turpeau, prin.
South Avondale ES, 636 PROSPECT PL 45229
  William Thomas, prin.
Swifton ES, 5771 RHODE ISLAND AVE 45237
  Clio Houp, prin.
Taft ES, 270 SOUTHERN AVE 45219
  Patrick McNeely, prin.
Vine ES, 2120 VINE ST 45210 – Greg Hook, prin.
Washburn ES, 1425 LINN ST 45214
  Jennifer Cottingham, prin.
Washington Park ES, 115 W 14TH ST 45210
  Helena Paul, prin.
Westwood ES, 2981 MONTANA AVE 45211
  Kenneth Barnes, prin.
Whittier ES, 945 HAWTHORNE AVE 45205
  Kenneth Sharp, prin.
Windsor ES, 937 WINDSOR ST 45206
  Wilbur Sanford, prin.
Winton Place ES, 4750 WINTON RD 45232
  Raymond Dornsife, prin.
Winton Terrace Phys Ed PS
  5300 WINNESTE AVE 45232
  Barbara Shells, prin.
Woodford PS, 6065 RED BANK RD 45213
  Gwendolyn Walton, prin.

Deer Park Comm. CSD
Sch. Sys. Enr. Code 4
Supt. – Robert Flury, 8688 DONNA LANE 45236
Amity MS, 4320 E GALBRAITH RD 45236
  Terry Murphy, prin.
Holmes ES, 8688 DONNA LN 45236
  Kathleen McKee, prin.
Howard ES, 4131 MATSON AVE 45236
  Jane Trout, prin.

Finneytown Local SD
Sch. Sys. Enr. Code 4
Supt. – Donald Schmidt
  8779 WINTON ROAD 45231
Cottonwood ES, 8513 COTTONWOOD DR 45231
  Julia Klinchok, prin.
Whitaker ES, 7400 WINTON RD 45224
  Everett Nissly, prin.

Forest Hills Local SD
Sch. Sys. Enr. Code 6
Supt. – Edward Hoffer
  7575 BEECHMONT AVE 45230
Ayer ES, 8471 FOREST RD 45255
  Paul Moser, prin.
Maddux ES, 943 ROSETREE LN 45230
  Diane Method, prin.
Mercer ES, 2600 BARTELS RD 45244
  Donald Stringfield, prin.

Sherwood ES, 7080 GRANTHAM WAY 45230
  Bruce McClure, prin.
Summit ES, 8400 NORTHPORT DR 45255
  Peggy Barns, prin.
Wilson ES, 2465 LITTLE DRY RUN RD 45244
  Rosemary Schroeder, prin.

Greenhills-Forest Park CSD
Sch. Sys. Enr. Code 6
Supt. – Charles Kron
  1215 W KEMPER ROAD 45240
Forest Park MS, 825 WAYCROSS ROAD 45240
  Howard Blevins, prin.
Greenhills MS, 8 ENFIELD ST 45218
  James Anthony, prin.
Beechwoods ES, 73 JUNEFIELD AVE 45218
  Ernest Spalding, prin.
Cameron Park ES, 626 WAYCROSS RD 45240
  Gladys Black, prin.
Forest View ES, 924 HALESWORTH DR 45240
  Harriet Rothert, prin.
Kemper Heights ES, 924 WAYCROSS RD 45240
  Linda Giuliano, prin.
Lakeside ES, 825 LAKERIDGE DR 45231
  Diane Arthur, prin.
Winton Forest ES, 1501 KINGSBURY DR 45240
  Richard Carboy, prin.

Indian Hill EVD
Sch. Sys. Enr. Code 4
Supt. – R. Boston, 6150 DRAKE ROAD 45243
Indian Hill MS, 6845 DRAKE ROAD 45243
  Robert Baas, prin.
Indian Hill ES, 6100 DRAKE RD 45243
  Gary Corn, prin.

Madeira CSD
Sch. Sys. Enr. Code 4
Supt. – John Rahe, 7465 LOANNES DRIVE 45243
Sellman MS, 6612 MIAMI AVE 45243
  Martin Strifler, prin.
Dumont ES, 7840 THOMAS DR 45243
  Theresa Deters, prin.

Mariemont CSD
Supt. – See Mariemont
Fairfax ES, 3847 SOUTHERN AVE 45227
  Jerry Sasson, prin.
Mariemont ES, 6750 WOOSTER PARK 45227
  Robert Denny, prin.

Milford EVD
Supt. – See Milford
Drake MS, 6205 DRAKE RD 45243
  Charles Cadle, prin.

Mt. Healthy CSD
Sch. Sys. Enr. Code 5
Supt. – David Distel, 1743 ADAMS ROAD 45231
North MS, 2170 STRUBLE ROAD 45231
  Randall Parsons, prin.
South MS, 1917 MILES ROAD 45231
  Carole Miller, prin.
Duvall ES, 1411 COMPTON RD 45231
  Hazel Ross, prin.
Frost ES, 2065 MISTYHILL DR 45240
  Edward Knabb, prin.
Greener ES, 2400 ADAMS RD 45231
  Ruth Forbeck, prin.
Hoop ES, 1738 COMPTON RD 45231
  Jerry Oberdorf, prin.
New Burlington ES
  10268 BURLINGTON RD 45231
  Clifford Strefelt, prin.
Ralph ES, 1310 ADAMS RD 45231
  Richard Pardini, prin.

New Richmond EVD
Supt. – See New Richmond
Pierce ES, 3437 BEHYMER RD 45245
  Elaine Rose, prin.

North College Hill CSD
Sch. Sys. Enr. Code 4
Supt. – Stanley Wernz
  1498 W GALBRAITH ROAD 45231
Becker ES, 6525 SIMPSON AVE 45239
  Brenda Hamrick, prin.
Clovernook ES, 1500 W GALBRAITH RD 45231
  Marian Schott, prin.

Northwest Local SD
Sch. Sys. Enr. Code 7
Supt. – Russell Sammons
  3240 BANNING ROAD 45239
Bevis ES, 10133 POTTINGER RD 45251
  George Bridges, prin.
Colerain ES, 4850 POOLE RD 45251
  Carrie Caldwell, prin.
Houston ES, 3310 COMPTON RD 45251
  Kay Walla, prin.
Monfort Heights ES, 3661 W FORK ROAD 45239
  William Duke, prin.
Pleasant Run ES, 11765 HAMILTON AVE 45231
  James Dunn, prin.
Struble ES, 2760 JONROSE AVE 45239
  Judith Reilly, prin.
Taylor ES, 3173 SPRINGDALE RD 45251
  Edward Myers, prin.
Weigel ES, 3242 BANNING RD 45239
  Alice Robbins, prin.
Welch ES, 12084 DEERHORN DR 45240
  Paul Bauer, prin.

Oak Hills Local SD
Sch. Sys. Enr. Code 6
Supt. – Louis Cardamone
  6479 BRIDGETOWN ROAD 45248
Delshire ES, 4402 GLENHAVEN RD 45238
  John McIntyre, prin.
Dulles ES, 6481 BRIDGETOWN RD 45248
  Hayes Wilcox, prin.
Harrison ES, 585 NEEB RD 45233
  Mark Koerner, prin.
Oakdale ES, 3850 VIRGINIA CT 45248
  Wayne Brown, prin.
Springmyer, 4179 EBENEZER RD 45248
  Allen Brodt, prin.

Princeton CSD
Sch. Sys. Enr. Code 6
Supt. – Richard Denoyer
  25 W SHARON AVE 45246
Princeton JHS, 11157 CHESTER ROAD 45246
  Lucius Ware, prin.
Evandale ES
  3940 GLENDALE-MILFORD RD 45241
  Bobby Cox, prin.
Glendale ES, 930 CONGRESS AVE 45246
  Aaron Mackey, prin.
Heritage Hill ES, 11961 CHESTERDALE RD 45246
  Wanda Mccollum, prin.
Lincoln Heights ES, 1200 LINDY AVE 45215
  Bettye Bennett, prin.
Lucas IS, 3900 COTTINGHAM DR 45241
  Noel Taylor, prin.
Sharonville ES, 11150 MAPLE ST 45241
  Robert Blaufuss, prin.
Springdale ES, 350 W KEMPER RD 45246
  Keith Perkins, prin.
Stewart ES, 11850 CONREY RD 45249
  Elmer Miller, prin.
Woodlawn ES, 31 RIDDLE RD 45215
  Kathryn Dickens, prin.

Sycamore CSD
Sch. Sys. Enr. Code 5
Supt. – Garth Errington
  4881 COOPER ROAD 45242
Sycamore JHS, 5757 COOPER ROAD 45242
  James Sears, prin.
Greene IS, 5200 ALDINE DR 45242
  C. Craig Harris, prin.
Blue Ash ES, 8522 KENWOOD RD 45236
  Kevin Boys, prin.
Maple Dale ES, 6100 HAGEWA DR 45242
  Philip Hackett, prin.
Montgomery ES, 9609 MONTGOMERY RD 45242
  Peggy Phillips, prin.

Three Rivers Local SD
Supt. – See Cleves
Miami Heights ES, 7670 BRIDGETOWN RD 45248
  Larry Bolin, prin.

West Clermont Local SD
Sch. Sys. Enr. Code 6
Supt. – John Abegglen
  550 CINCINNATI BATAVIA PK 45244
Glen Este MS, 4342 WITHAMSVILLE 45245
  Eldon Parker, prin.
Brantner Lane ES, 609 BRANTNER LN 45244
  Ben Ellis, prin.
Clough Pike ES, 808 CLOUGH RD 45245
  Jane Knudson, prin.
Merwin ES, 1040 GASKINS RD 45245
  Lewis Perry, prin.
Summerside ES, 4639 VERMONA DR 45245
  Patricia Stockman, prin.
Withamsville-Tobasco ES, 733 OHIO PIKE 45245
  Robert Farrell, prin.
Other Schools – See Amelia, Batavia

Wyoming CSD
Sch. Sys. Enr. Code 4
Supt. – Gary Payne, 700 REILY ROAD 45215
Wyoming MS, 17 WYOMING AVE 45215
  Robert Carovillano, prin.
Elm Avenue ES, 134 ELM AVE 45215
  Robert Carovillano, prin.
Hilltop ES, 425 OLIVER RD 45215
  Robert Carovillano, prin.
Vermont Avenue ES, 33 VERMONT AVE 45215
  Robert Carovillano, prin.

Cincinnati Country Day School
  6905 GIVEN ROAD 45243
Landmark Christian School
  500 OAK ROAD 45246
Our Lady of Victory ES, 808 NEEB RD 45233
Summit Country Day School
  2161 GRANDIN ROAD 45208
All Saints ES, 8939 MONTGOMERY RD 45236
Annunciation ES, 3545 CLIFTON AVE 45220
Bethany ES, 495 ALBION AVE 45246
Cardinal Pacelli ES, 927 ELLISON AVE 45226
Cincinnati Hebrew Day Chofetz
  7855 DAWN RD 45237
Concordia Lutheran School
  1133 CLIFTON HILLS AVE 45220
Corryville Catholic ES, 108 CALHOUN ST 45219
Cure of Ars ES, BERWICK & ROE 45227
Grace Lutheran ES, 3628 BOUDINOT AVE 45211
Guardian Angels ES
  6539 BEECHMONT AVE 45230
Immaculate Heart of Mary ES
  7820 BEECHMONT AVE 45255
Little Flower ES
  5555 LITTLE FLOWER AVE 45239

Nativity ES, 5936 RIDGE AVE 45213
Norwood Baptist Christian ES
20141 COURTLAND AVE 45212
Our Lady of Lords ES
5835 GLENWAY AVE 45238
Our Lady of Visitation ES, 3180 SOUTH RD 45248
Our Mother of Sorrows ES
7243 EASTLAWN DR 45237
Our Redeemer Lutheran School
6969 MONTGOMERY RD 45236
Price Hill Catholic ES, 3001 PRICE AVE 45205
Resurrection Academy, 11740 ILIFF AVE 45205
Springer Ed Foundation ES
2121 MADISON RD 45208
St. Agnes ES, 1600 CAROLINA AVE 45237
St. Aloysius Gonzaga ES
4390 BRIDGETOWN RD 45211
St. Aloysius on the Ohio ES
6218 PORTAGE ST 45233
St. Ann ES, 2940 W GALBRAITH RD 45239
St. Antoninus ES, 5425 JULMAR DR 45238
St. Bartholomew Consolidated ES
9375 WINTON RD 45231
St. Bernard ES, 7115 SPRINGDALE RD 45247
St. Boniface ES, PITTS AND PULLAN AVE 45223
St. Catherine of Sienna ES
3324 WUNDER AVE 45211
St. Cecilia ES, 4115 TAYLOR AVE 45209
St. Clare ES, 5800 SALVIA AVE 45224
St. Dominic ES, 371 PEDRETTI AVE 45238
St. Francis De Sales ES, 1602 MADISON RD 45206
St. Francis Seraph ES, 14 E LIBERTY ST 45210
St. Gertrude ES, 6551 MIAMI AVE 45243
St. Ignatius Loyola ES, 5222 N BEND RD 45247
St. James ES, 411 SPRINGFIELD RD 45215
St. James ES, 6111 CHEVIOT RD 45247
St. John the Baptist ES
5375 DRY RIDGE RD 45252
St. John the Evangelist ES
7131 PLAINFIELD RD 45236
St. Joseph ES, 745 EZZARD CHARLES DR 45203
St. Jude ES, 5940 BRIDGETOWN RD 45248
St. Lawrence ES, 1020 CARSON AVE 45205
St. Margaret Cortona ES, 4100 SIMPSON ST 45227
St. Margaret Mary ES
1820 W GALBRAITH RD 45239
St. Mark ES, 3500 MONTGOMERY RD 45207
St. Martin of Tours ES
3729 HARDING AVE 45211
St. Mary ES, 2845 ERIE AVE 45208
St. Pius ES, 3715 BORDEN ST 45223
St. Saviour ES, 4122 MYRTLE AVE 45236
St. Teresa of Avila ES, 1194 RULISON AVE 45238
St. Ursula Villa ES, 3660 VINEYARD PL 45226
St. Veronica ES, 4475 TOBASCO RD 45244
St. Vincent Ferrer ES
7754 MONTGOMERY RD 45236
St. Vivian ES, 885 DENIER PL 45224
St. William ES
4125 SAINT WILLIAMS AVE 45205
Yavneh Day ES, 8401 MONTGOMERY RD 45236

Circleville, Pickaway Co., Pop. Code 7
Circleville CSD
Sch. Sys. Enr. Code 5
Supt. – Roger Wolfe, 520 S COURT ST 43113
Everts MS, 520 S COURT ST 43113
Harold Cullum, prin.
Atwater ES, 870 ATWATER AVE 43113
Roger Born, prin.
Court Street ES, 1250 S COURT ST 43113
Gary Wasmer, prin.
Mound Street ES, 424 E MOUND ST 43113
Roger Born, prin.
Nicholas Drive ES, NICHOLAS DR 43113
Ty Ankrom, prin.

Logan Elm Local SD
Sch. Sys. Enr. Code 4
Supt. – Jack Maddox
9579 TARLTON ROAD 43113
McDowell Exchange JHS
9579 TARLTON ROAD 43113
Michael Jolley, prin.
Pickaway ES, 28158 KINGSTON PIKE 43113
Scott Wilson, prin.
Washington ES, 7990 STOUTSVILLE PIKE 43113
Charles Pritchard, prin.
Other Schools – See Kingston, Laurelville

Westfall Local SD
Supt. – See Williamsport
Jackson ES, 20010 FOX RD 43113
Jay Thomas, prin.

Clarington, Monroe Co., Pop. Code 3
Switzerland of Ohio Local SD
Supt. – See Woodsfield
ES, 205 CHURCH ST 43915 – Hattie Byers, prin.

Clarksburg, Ross Co., Pop. Code 2
Adena Local SD
Supt. – See Frankfort
ES, 10887 SIXTH ST 43115 – J. Miller, prin.

Clarksville, Clinton Co., Pop. Code 3
Clinton-Massie Local SD
Sch. Sys. Enr. Code 4
Supt. – Paul Schwamberger
2556 LEBANON ROAD 45113
Clinton-Massie ES, 2556 LEBANON RD 45113
Glenn Trout, prin.

Clay Center, Ottawa Co., Pop. Code 2
Genoa Area Local SD
Sch. Sys. Enr. Code 4
Supt. – Ivan Dangler, SUSAN ST 43408
Other Schools – See Curtice, Genoa

Clayton, Montgomery Co., Pop. Code 3
Northmont CSD
Supt. – See Englewood
Northmont JHS, 4810 NATIONAL ROAD 45315
James Krueckeberg, prin.

Cleveland, Cuyahoga Co., Pop. Code 11
Cleveland CSD
Sch. Sys. Enr. Code 8
Supt. – Alfred Tutela, 1380 E 6TH ST 44114
Audubon MS, 3055 EAST BLVD 44104
Arthur Lawson, prin.
Baker JHS, 3690 W 159TH ST 44111
Arthur Caliquire, prin.
Central MS, 2225 E 40TH ST 44103
Walker Russell, prin.
Davis MS, 10700 CHURCHILL AVE 44106
Delphya Gagliardi, prin.
Eliot MS, 15700 LOTUS DRIVE 44128
Mary Stokes, prin.
Empire MS, 9113 PARAMLEE AVE 44108
Willie Holmes, prin.
Gallagher MS, 6601 FRANKLIN BLVD 44102
Alvin Bradley, prin.
Hale MS, 3568 EAST BLVD 44105
Rose Davis, prin.
Hamilton MS, 3465 E 130TH ST 44120
Joseph Takacs, prin.
Hart JHS, 3901 E 74TH ST 44105
C. Dean Fleenor, prin.
Henry JHS, 11901 DURANT AVE 44108
Melvin Jones, prin.
Jamison MS, 13905 HARVARD AVE 44105
George Billingsley, prin.
Jefferson MS, 3145 W 46TH ST 44102
Darryl Smith, prin.
Lincoln MS, 1701 CASTLE AVE 44113
James Joyner, prin.
Mooney MS, 3213 MONTCLAIR AVE 44109
Sally Simon, prin.
Roosevelt MS, 800 LINN DRIVE 44108
Gilbert Freilano, prin.
Shuler JHS, 13501 TERMINAL AVE 44135
Marilyn Cargile, prin.
Spellacy JHS, 655 E 162ND ST 44110
Evelyn Pennington, prin.
Westropp MS, 19101 PURITAS AVE 44135
Leroy Lang, prin.
Willson MS, 1625 E 55TH ST 44103
Sandra Cohen, prin.
Wright MS, 11005 PARKHURST DRIVE 44111
Cynthia Metzger, prin.
Young MS, 17900 HARVARD AVE 44128
Betty English, prin.
Agassiz ES, 3595 BOSWORTH RD 44111
Margaret McNeeley, prin.
Almira ES, 3380 W 98TH ST 44102
Susan Molinari, prin.
Benesch ES, 5393 QUINCY AVE 44104
Allene Warren, prin.
Bethune MS, 11815 MOULTON AVE 44106
James Hobbs, prin.
Bolton ES, 9803 QUEBEC AVE 44106
Carolina Gwiazda, prin.
Brobst ES, 4840 W 192ND ST 44135
Juanita Flinner, prin.
Brooklawn ES
11801 WORTHINGTON AVE 44111
Grace Ellis, prin.
Bryant ES, 3121 OAK PARK AVE 44109
Edwin Stroh, prin.
Buckeye-Woodland ES, 9511 BUCKEYE RD 44104
Barbara Kozak, prin.
Buhrer MS, 1600 BUHRER AVE 44109
Janis Arnold, prin.
Carver MS, 2201 E 49TH ST 44103
Theodore Carter, prin.
Case ES, 4050 SUPERIOR AVE 44103
Sara Seals, prin.
Clark MS, 5550 CLARK AVE 44102
Thomas Mercer, prin.
Clement ES, 14311 WOODWORTH RD 44112
Robert McMahon, prin.
Cleaveland ES, 4092 E 146TH ST 44128
Dorothy Johnson, prin.
Corlett ES, 13013 CORLETT AVE 44105
David Keilin, prin.
Cranwood MS, 13604 CHRISTINE AVE 44105
Dorann Block, prin.
Denison ES, 3799 W 33RD ST 44109
Roye Thomas, prin.
DeSauze ES, 4747 E 176TH ST 44128
William Stuchal, prin.
Dickens ES, 3552 E 131ST ST 44120
William Talley, prin.
Dike ES, 2501 E 61ST ST 44104
Barbara Gunn, prin.
Dunbar ES, 2200 W 28TH ST 44113
Carol Glickhouse, prin.
East Clark ES, 885 E 146TH ST 44110
Peggie Brown, prin.
East Madison ES, 1130 ADDISON RD 44103
Doris Watts, prin.
Euclid Park ES, 17914 EUCLID AVE 44112
Barbara Rucker, prin.
Forest Hill Parkway ES, 450 E 112TH ST 44108
Lilloise Talley, prin.

Franklin MS, 1905 SPRING RD 44109
Robert Trask, prin.
Fullerton ES, 5920 FULLERTON AVE 44105
Robert Noble, prin.
Fulton ES, 3291 E 140TH ST 44120
Jane Cunningham, prin.
Fundamental ES, 5901 WHITTIER AVE 44103
Leonard Steiger, prin.
Garfield ES, 3800 W 140TH ST 44111
Barbara Clark, prin.
Giddings ES, 2250 E 71ST ST 44103
Elaine Banks, prin.
Gordon MS, 2121 W 67TH ST 44102
Bertha Dixson, prin.
Gracemount MS, 16200 GLENDALE AVE 44128
Judith Smith, prin.
Grdina ES, 3050 E 77TH ST 44104
George Beach, prin.
Halle MS, 7901 HALLE AVE 44102
Gladys Leftwich, prin.
Harper ES, 5515 IRA AVE 44144 – Floyd Lee, prin.
Hawthorne MS, 3575 W 130TH ST 44111
Walter Filipow, prin.
Hicks Montessori ES, 2409 BRIDGE AVE 44113
H. Booker, prin.
Howe MS, 1000 LAKEVIEW RD 44108
Joyce Haessler, prin.
Iowa-Maple ES, 12510 MAPLE AVE 44108
L. Shields, prin.
Ireland MS, 1800 E 63RD ST 44103
William Richardson, prin.
Jones ES, 4550 W 150TH ST 44135
Paul Crawley, prin.
Kentucky ES, 3805 TERRETT AVE 44113
Anita Isler, prin.
Lafayette Contemporary ES
12416 SIGNET AVE 44120 – John Nairus, prin.
Lake MS, 9201 HILLOCK AVE 44108
Opal Taylor, prin.
Landis ES, 10118 HAMPDEN AVE 44108
James Balotta, prin.
Longfellow ES, 650 E 140TH ST 44110
Claudia Cammon, prin.
MacArthur ES, 4401 VALLEYSIDE RD 44135
Antoinette Curtain, prin.
Marion-Sterling ES, 3033 CENTRAL AVE 44115
Neil Stone, prin.
Martin MS, 8200 BROOKLINE AVE 44103
Erma Spencer, prin.
McKinley MS, 3349 W 125TH ST 44111
Janice Olszowy, prin.
Memphis MS, 4103 MEMPHIS AVE 44109
Harold Ellis, prin.
Miles ES, 11918 MILES AVE 44105
Venerine Branham, prin.
Miles Park ES, 4090 E 93RD ST 44105
Mildred Foster, prin.
Standish ES, 1000 E 92ND ST 44108
James Eland, prin.
Morgan MS, 1440 E 92ND ST 44106
Mary Taylor, prin.
Mound ES, 5405 MOUND AVE 44105
Nancy Marks, prin.
Mt. Auburn ES
10110 MOUNT AUBURN AVE 44104
David Swann, prin.
MT. Pleasant MS, 11617 UNION AVE 44105
Robert Lloyd, prin.
Orchard ES, 4200 BAILEY AVE 44113
Teacola Offutt, prin.
Orr ES, 9711 LAMONT AVE 44106
James Holland, prin.
Pasteur ES, 815 LINN DR 44108
Norma Murray, prin.
Perry MS, 18400 SCHENELY AVE 44119
Jane Petshauer, prin.
Raper ES, 1601 E 85TH ST 44106
Rosa Schembri, prin.
Revere MS, 10706 SANDUSKY AVE 44105
Carol Cercek, prin.
Rice ES, 11529 BUCKEYE RD 44104
Gerald Hughes, prin.
Rickoff ES, 3500 E 147TH ST 44120
Jane Sembric, prin.
Riverside ES, 14601 MONTROSE AVE 44111
Nola Briskey, prin.
Roth ES, 12523 WOODSIDE AVE 44108
Barbara Eggleston, prin.
Scranton ES, 1991 BARBER AVE 44113
Lenore Floyd, prin.
Seltzer ES, 1468 W 98TH ST 44102
Bonnie Terrell, prin.
Stevenson ES, 3938 JO ANN DR 44122
Charles Russo, prin.
Tremont ES, 2409 W 10TH ST 44113
Richard Larrabee, prin.
Union MS, 6701 UNION AVE 44105
Sidney Henderson, prin.
Valley View ES, 17200 VALLEYVIEW AVE 44135
Inez Powell, prin.
Wade Park ES, 7600 WADE PARK AVE 44103
Harriett Young, prin.
Walton MS, 3409 WALTON AVE 44113
Saundra Wiggins, prin.
Ward MS, 4315 W 140TH ST 44135
Mildred Moylan, prin.
Warner MS, 8315 JEFFRIES AVE 44105
John Steffas, prin.
Watterson-Lake MS, 1422 W 74TH ST 44102
Barbara Spearman, prin.
Waverly ES, 1810 W 54TH ST 44102
Armitta Redmon, prin.
Wayne MS, 11711 WOODLAND AVE 44120
Donna Kolb, prin.

Willow ES, 5004 GLAZIER AVE 44127
 Adele Hampton, prin.
Woodland Hills ES, 9201 CRANE AVE 44105
 Katherine Dean, prin.

Cleveland Heights-University Heights CSD
Supt. – See University Heights
Roxboro MS, 2400 ROXBORO ROAD 44106
 James MaKee, prin.

Cuyahoga Heights Local SD
Sch. Sys. Enr. Code 3
Supt. – John Ramicone, 4820 E 71ST ST 44125
Cuyahoga Heights ES, 4880 E 71ST ST 44125
 Edward Mills, prin.

Mayfield CSD
Supt. – See Mayfield
Mayfield Center ES
 6625 WILSON MILLS RD 44143
 William Lauffer, prin.

South Euclid-Lyndhurst CSD
Supt. – See Lyndhurst
Southlyn ES, 1340 PROFESSOR RD 44124
 Vivian Noble, prin.

_____

Immaculate Heart Sacred ES
 6804 LANSING AVE 44105
Annunciation ES
 12913 BENNINGTON AVE 44135
Ascension ES, 4400 W 140TH ST 44135
Blessed Sacrament ES, 3389 FULTON RD 44109
Corpus Christi ES, 5007 ARCHMERE AVE 44144
Freedom Academy, 6000 MEMPHIS AVE 44144
Holy Name ES, 8328 BROADWAY AVE 44105
Holy Redeemer ES, 15720 KIPKING AVE 44110
Holy Rosary School, 12015 MAYRFIELD RD 44106
Immaculate Conception ES
 4129 SUPERIOR AVE 44103
Luther Memorial ES, 8607 SAUER AVE 44102
Mt. Pleasant Catholic ES, 3845 E 131ST ST 44120
Our Lady Lourdes ES, 3398 E 55TH ST 44127
Our Lady of Angels ES
 3644 ROCKY RIVER DR 44111
Our Lady of Good Counsel ES
 4419 PEARL RD 44109
Our Lady of Mt. Carmel West ES
 1355 W 70TH ST 44102
Our Lady of Peace ES
 12406 BUCKINGHAM AVE 44120
Our Lady of Perpetual Help ES
 18022 NEFF ROAD 44119
Ramah Junior Academy, 4770 LEE RD 44128
Sacred Heart of Jesus School
 6919 KRAKOW AVE 44105
St. Adalbert ES, 2345 E 83RD ST 44104
St. Agatha-St. Aolysius ES
 640 LAKEVIEW RD 44108
St. Benedict ES, 10615 LAMONTIER AVE 44104
St. Catherine ES, 3443 E 93RD ST 44104
St. Francis ES, 7206 MYRON AVE 44103
St. Henry ES, 18320 HARVARD AVE 44122
St. Hyacinth ES, 2971 E 61ST ST 44127
St. Ignatius ES, 10205 LORAIN AVE 44111
St. Jerome ES, 15100 LAKE SHORE BLVD 44110
St. John Cantius ES, 2265 W 10TH ST 44113
St. John Lutheran ES, 1027 E 176TH ST 44119
St. John Nepomucine ES
 3777 INDEPENDENCE RD 44105
St. Joseph Collinwood ES
 14405 SAINT CLAIR AVE 44110
St. Joseph Franciscan ES
 1027 SUPERIOR AVE 44113
St. Leo ES, 4900 BROADVIEW RD 44109
St. Mark ES, 15724 MONTROSE AVE 44111
St. Mark Lutheran ES, 4464 PEARL RD 44109
St. Mary Byzantine ES, 4600 STATE RD 44109
St. Mary ES, 716 E 156TH ST 44110
St. Mel ES, 14440 TRISKETT RD 44111
St. Patrick West Park ES
 17720 PURITAS AVE 44135
St. Rocco ES, 3205 FULTON RD 44109
St. Rose of Lima ES, 1441 W 116TH ST 44102
St. Stanislaus ES, 6615 FORMAN AVE 44105
St. Stephen ES, 1910 W 54TH ST 44102
St. Thomas Aquinas ES
 9101 SUPERIOR AVE 44106
St. Timothy ES, 13401 CRANWOOD DR 44105
St. Vincent De Paul ES
 13442 LORAIN AVE 44111
St. Vitus ES, 6111 GLASS AVE 44103
Sts. Philip & James ES
 3727 BOSWORTH RD 44111
Transfiguration ES, 7446 BROADWAY AVE 44105
Urban Community ES
 W 25TH AND WASHINGTON AVE 44113
West Park Lutheran ES
 13812 BELLAIRE RD 44135
Westside Baptist ES, 9407 MADISON AVE 44102

Cleveland Heights, Cuyahoga Co., Pop. Code 8
Cleveland Heights-University Heights CSD
Supt. – See University Heights
Monticello MS, 3665 MONTICELLO BLVD 44121
 Walter Maki, prin.
Oxford ES, 939 QUILLIAMS RD 44121
 Delores Vehar, prin.
Boulevard ES, 1749 LEE RD 44118
 Barbara Lindsay, prin.
Canterbury ES, 2530 CANTERBURY RD 44118
 Helen Moore, prin.
Coventry ES, 2843 WASHINGTON BLVD 44118
 Linda Gay, prin.

Fairfax ES, 3150 FAIRFAX RD 44118
 Awilda Hall, prin.
Noble ES, 1293 ARDOON ST 44121
 Roger Vince, prin.
Roxboro ES, 2405 ROXBORO RD 44106
 Rosemary Brickman, prin.

_____

Hebrew Academy, 1800 S TAYLOR ROAD 44118
Mosdos Ohr Hatorah ES
 3246 DESOTA AVE 44118
Raintree Academy, 14780 SUPERIOR RD 44118
Ruffing Montessori Ingalls ES
 3380 FAIRMOUNT BLVD 44118
St. Ann ES, 2160 STILLMAN RD 44118
St. Louis ES, 2463 N TAYLOR RD 44118

Cleves, Hamilton Co., Pop. Code 4
Three Rivers Local SD
Sch. Sys. Enr. Code 4
Supt. – Richard Scherer, P O BOX 128 45002
Three Rivers MS
 8575 BRIDGETOWN ROAD 45002
 Gary Smith, prin.
Young MS, 401 N MIAMI AVE 45002
 Robert Roszell, prin.
Other Schools – See Addyston, Cincinnati

Clinton, Summit Co., Pop. Code 4
Northwest Local SD
Supt. – See Canal Fulton
ES, 7927 FULTON ST 44216 – Gary Novak, prin.

Norton CSD
Supt. – See Norton
Grill ES, 6125 KUNGLE RD 44216
 Thomas Maroon, prin.

Clyde, Sandusky Co., Pop. Code 6
Bellevue CSD
Supt. – See Bellevue
York ES, 2314 E MCPHERSON 43410
 Beverly DeBlase, prin.

Clyde-Green Springs EVD
Sch. Sys. Enr. Code 5
Supt. – Stanley Mounts, 106 S MAIN ST 43410
JHS, 237 SPRING ST 43410 – Larry Schultz, prin.
South Main ES, 821 S MAIN ST 43410
 Stephen Puchta, prin.
Vine Street ES, 521 VINE ST 43410
 Rodney McMaster, prin.
Other Schools – See Green Springs

_____

St. Mary ES, 615 VINE ST 43410

Coal Grove, Lawrence Co., Pop. Code 5
Dawson-Bryant Local SD
Sch. Sys. Enr. Code 4
Supt. – Wayne White, 423 MARION PIKE 45638
Dawson-Bryant IS, 222 LANE ST 45638
 Steven Easterling, prin.
Monitor ES, RURAL ROUTE 04 BOX 52 45638
 Mary Deeds, prin.
Other Schools – See Ironton, Kitts Hill

Coalton, Jackson Co., Pop. Code 3
Wellston CSD
Supt. – See Wellston
ES 45621 – Gary Jenkins, prin.

Coldwater, Mercer Co., Pop. Code 5
Coldwater EVD
Sch. Sys. Enr. Code 4
Supt. – Wayne Miller, 217 N FIRST ST 45828
West ES, 220 N FIRST ST 45828
 Larry Benanzer, prin.

College Corner, Butler Co., Pop. Code 2
College Corner Local SD
Sch. Sys. Enr. Code 2
Supt. – Marilyn Crain, 230 RAMSEY ST 45003
College Corner Union S, 230 RAMSEY ST 45003
 Connie Smith, prin.

College Hill, Hamilton Co.

_____

Cincinnati Baptist ES
 7645 WINTON ROAD 45224

Collins, Huron Co.
Western Reserve Local SD
Supt. – See Wakeman
Western Reserve MS, RURAL ROUTE 01 44826
 Andrew Valachek, prin.
Hartland ES, ROAD 1 44826 – John Marshall, prin.

Columbiana, Columbiana Co., Pop. Code 5
Columbiana EVD
Sch. Sys. Enr. Code 4
Supt. – Roger Stiller
 720 NEW WATERFORD ROAD 44408
South Side MS
 720 NEW WATERFORD ROAD 44408
 Ronald Burger, prin.
Dixon PS, 333 N MIDDLE ST 44408
 John Scardino, prin.

Crestview Local SD
Sch. Sys. Enr. Code 4
Supt. – John Thomas
 3062 FAIRFIELD SCHOOL ROAD 44408
Crestview MS
 3062 FAIRFIELD SCHOOL ROAD 44408
 Kenneth Ekis, prin.
Other Schools – See New Waterford

Columbia Station, Lorain Co., Pop. Code 2
Columbia Local SD
Sch. Sys. Enr. Code 4
Supt. – Wilbur Watson
 25796 ROYALTON ROAD 44028
Columbia MS, 13646 W RIVER ROAD 44028
 Tod Conway, prin.
Copopa ES, 14168 W RIVER RD 44028
 Nicholas Anspach, prin.

Columbus, Franklin Co., Pop. Code 11
Columbus CSD
Sch. Sys. Enr. Code 8
Supt. – Ronald Etheridge, 270 E STATE ST 43215
Barrett MS, 345 E DESHLER AVE 43206
 William Lude, prin.
Beery MS, 2740 LOCKBOURNE ROAD 43207
 Charles Stack, prin.
Buckeye MS, 2950 PARSONS AVE 43207
 Thomas Simpson, prin.
Champion Alternative MS
 1270 HAWTHORNE AVE 43203
 Andrew Melton, prin.
Clinton MS, 3940 KARL ROAD 43224
 Larry Metz, prin.
Crestview MS, 251 E WEBER ROAD 43202
 Daniel Jerman, prin.
Dominion MS, 330 E DOMINION BLVD 43214
 Dolores Blankenship, prin.
Eastmoor MS, 3450 MEDWAY AVE 43213
 Phillip Hobbs, prin.
Everett MS, 100 W 4TH AVE 43201
 Ellsworth Foreman, prin.
Franklin Alternative MS
 1390 BRYDEN ROAD 43205 – Iris Fields, prin.
Hilltonia Alternative MS
 2345 W MOUND ST 43204 – Charles Pfeifer, prin.
Indianola MS, 420 E 19TH AVE 43201
 E. Borden, prin.
Johnson Park MS, 1130 S WAVERLY ST 43227
 Thomas Brown, prin.
Linmoor Alternative MS
 2001 HAMILTON AVE 43211 – George Rich, prin.
Medina MS, 1425 HUY ROAD 43224
 Charles Kellar, prin.
Mifflin Alternative MS, 3000 AGLER ROAD 43219
 Stephen Tankovich, prin.
Mohawk Alternative MS
 300 E LIVINGSTON AVE 43215
 John Brownley, prin.
Monroe Alternative MS
 474 N MONROE AVE 43203 – (—), prin.
Ridgeview MS, 4241 RUDY ROAD 43214
 Duane Pelkey, prin.
Sherwood Alternative MS
 1400 SHADY LANE ROAD 43227
 Steven Oldham, prin.
Southmoor MS, 1201 MOLER ROAD 43207
 McDaniel Marsh, prin.
Starling MS, 120 S CENTRAL AVE 43222
 Robert Cochrun, prin.
Wedgewood MS, 3771 EAKIN ROAD 43228
 Diane Warner, prin.
Westmoor MS, 3001 VALLEYVIEW DRIVE 43204
 Lynn Boetcher, prin.
Woodward Park MS, 5151 KARL ROAD 43229
 Jeffery Forster, prin.
Yorktown MS, 5600 E LIVINGSTON AVE 43232
 Jack Culp, prin.
Alpine ES, 1590 ALPINE DR 43229
 Lois Arend, prin.
Arlington Park ES, 2400 MOCK RD 43219
 John Westinghouse, prin.
Avalon ES, 5220 AVALON AVE 43229
 Reid Jamison, prin.
Avondale ES, 156 AVONDALE AVE 43222
 Essie Richardson, prin.
Beatty Park ES, 284 N 22ND ST 43203
 Fred Kouski, prin.
Beck Street ES, 387 E BECK ST 43206
 Barbara Blake, prin.
Berwick Alternative ES
 2595 SCOTTWOOD RD 43209
 Kenneth Havens, prin.
Binns ES, 1080 BINNS BLVD 43204
 Roger Veley, prin.
Brentnell Alternative ES
 1270 BRENTNELL AVE 43219 – H. Williams,
 prin.
Broadleigh ES, 3039 MARYLAND AVE 43209
 Keith Diehlmann, prin.
Burroughs ES, 2585 SULLIVANT AVE 43204
 Keith Rinehart, prin.
Cassady Alternative ES
 2500 N CASSADY AVE 43219
 Margaret Wilson, prin.
Cedarwood Alternative ES
 775 BARTFIELD DR 43207
 Mark Glassbrenner, prin.
Clarfield ES, 3220 GROVEPORT RD 43207
 Benny Banks, prin.
Clinton ES, 10 CLINTON HEIGHTS AVE 43202
 Meredith Snyder, prin.
Colerain ES, 429 E WEISHEIMER RD 43214
 Marjorie Clark, prin.
Como ES, 2989 REIS AVE 43224
 Nora Eramo, prin.
Cranbrook ES, 908 BRICKER BLVD 43221
 Robert Secrest, prin.
Dana Avenue ES, 300 DANA AVE 43223
 Carolyn Moxley, prin.
Deshler ES, 1234 E DESHLER AVE 43206
 Donald Tate, prin.

Devonshire Alternative ES
6286 AMBLESIDE DR 43229
Susan Fossmeyer, prin.
Douglas Alternative ES
43 S DOUGLASS ST 43205
Catherine Noble, prin.
Duxberry Park Alternative ES
1779 E MAYNARD AVE 43219
William Dwyer, prin.
Eakin ES, 3774 EAKIN RD 43228
George Zorich, prin.
East Columbus ES, 734 RARIG AVE 43219
Ernest Estice, prin.
East Linden ES, 2500 PERDUE AVE 43211
Erma Taylor, prin.
Eastgate ES, 1939 STRATFORD WAY 43219
Joseph Fuchala, prin.
Easthaven ES, 2360 GARNET PL 43232
Mitchell Truesdell, prin.
Fair Alternative ES, 1395 FAIR AVE 43205
Bernice Smith, prin.
Fairmoor ES, 3281 MAYFAIR PARK PL 43213
Lynne Wake, prin.
Fairwood Alternative ES
726 FAIRWOOD AVE 43205 – Marissa Craig, prin.
Fifth Alternative ES, 1300 FORSYTHE AVE 43201
Stanley Embry, prin.
Forest Park ES, 5535 SANDALWOOD BLVD 43229
Ruth Brown, prin.
Franklinton Alternative ES
617 W STATE ST 43215 – Evelyn Bell, prin.
Gables ES, 1680 BECKET AVE 43220
Jane Leach, prin.
Georgian Heights Alternative ES
784 GEORGIAN DR 43228
Elizabeth Mahaffey, prin.
Gladstone Alternative ES
1965 GLADSTONE AVE 43211
Ronald Leithe, prin.
Hamilton Alternative ES
2047 HAMILTON AVE 43211
Ronald Clark, prin.
Heyl Avenue ES, 760 REINHARD AVE 43206
(—), prin.
Highland ES, 40 S HIGHLAND AVE 43223
Gary Rader, prin.
Hubbard ES, 104 W HUBBARD AVE 43215
Diane Gosser, prin.
Hudson ES, 2323 LEXINGTON AVE 43211
Leroy Willis, prin.
Huy Road ES, 1545 HUY RD 43224
Edith Sidwell, prin.
Indiana Springs ES, 50 E HENDERSON RD 43214
Gwendolyn Lane, prin.
Indianola Alternative ES, 140 E 16TH AVE 43201
Thomas O'Mahoney, prin.
Innis ES, 3399 KOHR RD 43224
John Matchett, prin.
Kent ES, 1414 GAULT ST 43205
Lois Glover, prin.
Kenwood Alternative ES
3770 SHATTUCK AVE 43220
Roger Coffman, prin.
Koebel ES, 2521 FAIRWOOD AVE 43207
(—), prin.
Leawood ES, 1677 S HAMILTON RD 43227
Dale James, prin.
Lincoln Park ES, 1666 S 18TH ST 43207
Charles Mohr, prin.
Linden ES, 2626 CLEVELAND AVE 43211
John Stuck, prin.
Linden Park Alternative ES
1400 MYRTLE AVE 43211 – Lois Camealy, prin.
Livingston Avenue ES, 744 HEYL AVE 43206
Robert Pritts, prin.
Main Street ES, 1469 E MAIN ST 43205
Gregory Waddell, prin.
Maize Road ES, 4360 MAIZE RD 43224
Clarence Reavling, prin.
Maybury ES, 2633 MAYBURY RD 43232
(—), prin.
McGuffey ES, 2632 MCGUFFEY RD 43211
Floralou Carr, prin.
Medary ES, 2500 MEDARY AVE 43202
Marilyn Foreman, prin.
Moler ES, 1560 MOLER RD 43207
Steven Stone, prin.
North Linden ES, 1718 E COOKE RD 43224
Elmer Winner, prin.
Northtowne ES
4767 NORTHTOWNE BLVD 43229
John Rodeheffer, prin.
Oakland Park Alternative ES
3392 ATWOOD TER 43224 – (—), prin.
Oakmont ES, 5666 OAKMONT DR 43232
Robert Kimball, prin.
Ohio Avenue ES, 505 S OHIO AVE 43205
Will Thomas, prin.
Olde Orchard Alternative ES
800 MCNAUGHTON RD 43213 – Mary Six, prin.
Parkmoor ES, 1711 PENWORTH DR 43229
Larry Jones, prin.
Pilgrim ES, 440 TAYLOR AVE 43203
Lilliam Richardson, prin.
Reeb Avenue ES, 240 REEB AVE 43207
Nancy Zook, prin.
Salem ES, 1040 GARVEY RD 43229
Duane Stemen, prin.
Scioto Trail ES, 2951 S HIGH ST 43207
John Becker, prin.
Scottwood ES, 3392 SCOTTWOOD RD 43227
Patricia Brown, prin.
Second Avenue ES, 68 E 2ND AVE 43201
(—), prin.

Shady Lane ES, 1488 SHADY LANE RD 43227
Ronald Jackson, prin.
Siebert ES, 385 REINHARD AVE 43206
Dorene Miller, prin.
South Mifflin ES, 2355 MIDDLEHURST DR 43219
Mary Sykora, prin.
Southwood ES, 1500 S 4TH ST 43207
Fred Burt, prin.
Stewart Alternative ES, 40 STEWART AVE 43206
Clinton Hickman, prin.
Stockbridge ES, 3350 S CHAMPION AVE 43207
Catherine Crandall, prin.
Sullivant ES, 791 GRIGGS AVE 43223
Jerry Banks, prin.
Trevitt ES, 519 TREVITT ST 43203
(—), prin.
Weinland Park ES, 211 E 7TH AVE 43201
Earl Kelch, prin.
West Broad Street ES, 2744 W BROAD ST 43204
Charles Pfaltzgraf, prin.
West Mound ES, 2051 W MOUND ST 43223
Charles Knight, prin.
Westgate Alternative ES
3080 WICKLOW RD 43204
Krista Eisnaugle, prin.
Windsor Alternative ES, 1219 E 12TH AVE 43211
Joyce Biltz, prin.
Winterset ES, 4776 WINTERSET DR 43220
Constance Whitham, prin.

Groveport-Madison Local SD
Supt. – See Groveport
Groveport Madison MS North
5474 SEDALIA DRIVE 43232
Arthur Soroka, prin.
Asbury ES, 5127 HARBOR BLVD 43232
Sherry Kuehnle, prin.
Dunloe ES, 4200 GLENDENING DR 43232
Neil Lantz, prin.
Madison ES, 4600 MADISON SCHOOL DR 43232
Dennis Allen, prin.
Sedalia ES, 5400 SEDALIA DR 43232
John Heck, prin.

Hamilton Local SD
Sch. Sys. Enr. Code 4
Supt. – Elmo Kallner
4999 LOCKBOURNE ROAD 43207
Hamilton MS, 775 RATHMELL ROAD 43207
John Cornette, prin.
Hamilton Central ES, 1105 RATHMELL RD 43207
Ronald Miller, prin.
Other Schools – See Lockbourne

Hilliard CSD
Supt. – See Hilliard
Ridgewood ES, 4237 DUBLIN RD 43220
Arnold Miller, prin.

South-Western CSD
Supt. – See Grove City
Finland MS, 1825 FINLAND AVE 43223
Rodger Southward, prin.
Norton MS, 215 NORTON ROAD 43228
Billy Mullins, prin.
East Franklin ES, 1955 RICHMOND RD 43223
Margaret Idzkowski, prin.
Finland ES, 1835 FINLAND AVE 43223
Mary Winfield, prin.
Harmon ES, 2090 FRANK RD 43223
Lenn Turner, prin.
North Franklin ES, 1122 N HAGUE AVE 43204
Anne Hansen, prin.
Prairie-Lincoln ES, 4900 AMESBURY WAY 43228
Sandy Osterholtz, prin.
Prairie-Norton ES, 117 NORTON RD 43228
Donna Carter, prin.
Stiles ES, 4700 STILES AVE 43228
James Nelson, prin.
West Franklin ES, 3501 BRIGGS RD 43204
Keith Rife, prin.

Upper Arlington CSD
Supt. – See Upper Arlington
Windermere ES, 4101 WINDERMERE RD 43220
Alan Yarletts, prin.

Westerville CSD
Supt. – See Westerville
Hawthorne ES, 1 FARVIEW ROAD 43229
Vern Simpson, prin.

Columbus School for Girls
56 S COLUMBIA AVE 43209
Grace Brethren Christian School
5400 FOSTER AVE 43214
Liberty Christian Academy
5666 OAKMONT DRIVE 43227
Calumet Christian ES, 2774 CALUMET ST 43202
Christ the King ES
2855 E LIVINGSTON AVE 43209
Clintonville Academy
3916 INDIANOLA AVE 43214
Columbus Christian ES
1850 BOSTWICK RD 43227
Columbus Torah Academy
181 NOE-BIXBY RD 43213
Corpus Christi ES, 1256 LINWOOD AVE 43206
Grace Brethren Christian ES
50 WESTVIEW AVE 43214
Holy Name ES, 155 E PATTERSON AVE 43202
Holy Spirit ES, 4382 DUCHENE LN 43213
Immaculate Conception ES
366 E NORTH BROADWAY ST 43214
Learning Unlimited ES, 345 W 8TH AVE 43201

Learning Unlimited Ecole ES
5120 GODOWN RD 43220
Maranatha Christian ES, 4663 TRABUE RD 43228
Notre Dame ES, 2350 W MOUND ST 43204
Our Lady of Peace ES
40 E DOMINION BLVD 43214
Sonshine Christian Academy
508 BERKELEY RD 43205
St. Agatha ES, 2767 ANDOVER RD 43221
St. Andrew ES, 4081 REED RD 43220
St. Anthony ES, 1300 URBAN DR 43229
St. Augustine ES, 1567 LORETTA AVE 43211
St. Catharine ES, 2865 FAIR AVE 43209
St. Cecilia ES, 440 NORTON RD 43228
St. James the Less ES
1628 OAKLAND PARK AVE 43224
St. Joseph Montessori ES, 933 HAMLET ST 43201
St. Ladislas ES, 277 REEB AVE 43207
St. Leo ES, 221 HANFORD ST 43206
St. Mary ES, 700 S 3RD ST 43206
St. Mary Magdalene ES
2940 PARKSIDE RD 43204
St. Matthias ES, 1566 FERRIS RD 43224
St. Paul Lutheran ES, 322 STEWART AVE 43206
St. Philip the Apostle ES
1555 ELAINE ROAD 43227
St. Stephen ES, 4131 CLIME RD 43228
St. Thomas the Apostle ES
767 N CASSADY AVE 43219
St. Timothy ES, 1070 THOMAS LN 43220
Tree of Life Linden ES
1911 OAKLAND PARK AVE 43224
Trinity ES, 1381 IDA AVE 43212
Wellington ES, 3650 REED ROAD 43220

Columbus Grove, Putnam Co., Pop. Code 4
Columbus Grove Local SD
Sch. Sys. Enr. Code 3
Supt. – Gary Jones, 201 W CROSS ST 45830
MS, 201 W CROSS ST 45830
Douglas Ambroza, prin.
ES, 201 W CROSS ST 45830
Douglas Ambroza, prin.

St. Anthony Padua ES
518 W SYCAMORE ST 45830

Commercial Point, Pickaway Co., Pop. Code 2
Teays Valley Local SD
Supt. – See Ashville
Scioto ES, 20 W SCIOTO ST 43116
James Flanagan, prin.

Conesville, Coshocton Co., Pop. Code 2
River View Local SD
Supt. – See Warsaw
ES, 199 STATE ST 43811 – Andrew Duda, prin.

Conneaut, Ashtabula Co., Pop. Code 7
Conneaut Area CSD
Sch. Sys. Enr. Code 5
Supt. – Don Horwood, 263 LIBERTY ST 44030
Chestnut ES, 755 CHESTNUT ST 44030
Clyde Laughlin, prin.
Lake View ES, 670 LAKE VIEW AVE 44030
Joyce Shellhammer, prin.
Southeast ES, 400 MILL ST 44030
Jesse Howard, prin.
West Main ES, 836 MAIN ST 44030
Joyce Shellhammer, prin.
Other Schools – See Jacksontown

St. Frances Cabrini ES, 734 MILL ST 44030

Conover, Miami Co.
Miami East Local SD
Supt. – See Casstown
Miami East MS, 8025 E US ROUTE 36 45317
Mike Mullen, prin.

Continental, Putnam Co., Pop. Code 4
Continental Local SD
Sch. Sys. Enr. Code 3
Supt. – Cletus Biersack, P O BOX 479 45831
ES, P O BOX 479 45831 – Kyle Clark, prin.

Convoy, Van Wert Co., Pop. Code 4
Crestview Local SD
Sch. Sys. Enr. Code 4
Supt. – Steven Kellar 45832
Other Schools – See Van Wert, Wren

Coolville, Athens Co., Pop. Code 3
Federal Hocking Local SD
Supt. – See Stewart
ES, MAIN ST 45723 – Rick Martin, prin.

Copley, Summit Co., Pop. Code 6
Copley-Fairlawn CSD
Sch. Sys. Enr. Code 4
Supt. – Richard Cline
3797 RIDGEWOOD ROAD 44321
Copley-Fairlawn MS
1531 S CLEVELAND-MASSALLON 44321
George Verlaney, prin.
Arrowhead PS, 1600 RALEIGH BLVD 44321
Joanne Farkas, prin.
Other Schools – See Akron

Corning, Perry Co., Pop. Code 3
Southern Local SD
Supt. – See Hemlock
MS 43730 – Ned Gohring, prin.

Cortland, Trumbull Co., Pop. Code 6
Lakeview Local SD
Sch. Sys. Enr. Code 4
Supt. – Richard Raidel
  300 HILLMAN DRIVE 44410
ES, 264 PARK AVE 44410 – Joseph Guido,Jr., prin.
Lakeview MS, 640 WAKEFIELD DRIVE 44410
  Delores Uber, prin.
Other Schools – See Warren

Maplewood Local SD
Sch. Sys. Enr. Code 4
Supt. – D. McClain
  2414 GREENVILLE ROAD 44410
Maplewood East ES, 4174 GREENVILLE RD 44410
  Beverly Hoagland, prin.
Other Schools – See North Bloomfield

Mathews Local SD
Supt. – See Vienna
Currie ES, 3306 RIDGE RD 44410
  Dominic Mastropietro, prin.

Coshocton, Coshocton Co., Pop. Code 7
Coshocton CSD
Sch. Sys. Enr. Code 4
Supt. – John Berg
  1207 CAMBRIDGE ROAD 43812
MS, 132 S 7TH ST 43812 – William Pahl, prin.
Central ES, 724 WALNUT ST 43812
  Judith Maxwell, prin.
Lincoln ES, 801 CAMBRIDGE RD 43812
  Stanley Zurowski, prin.
South Lawn ES, 753 S LAWN AVE 43812
  Sharon Foster, prin.
Washington ES, 1517 CHESTNUT ST 43812
  Stanley Zurowski, prin.

River View Local SD
Supt. – See Warsaw
Pleasant Valley ES
  1160 CASSINGHAM HOLLOW DR 43812
  Wade Schuler, prin.

Sacred Heart ES, 39 BURT AVE 43812

Covington, Miami Co., Pop. Code 5
Covington EVD
Sch. Sys. Enr. Code 4
Supt. – David Jones, 25 N GRANT ST 45318
MS, 25 N GRANT ST 45318
  Steven Brandeberry, prin.
ES, 707 CHESTNUT ST 45318 – Joe Bledsoe, prin.

Crestline, Crawford Co., Pop. Code 6
Colonel Crawford Local SD
Supt. – See North Robinson
Leesville ES, 6910 LEESVILLE RD 44827
  Kevin Ruth, prin.

Crestline EVD
Sch. Sys. Enr. Code 4
Supt. – John Edgar, 511 S THOMAN ST 44827
MS, 215 N COLUMBUS ST 44827
  Daniel Vincent, prin.
Southeast ES, 300 E ARNOLD ST 44827
  John Leonard, prin.

Creston, Wayne Co., Pop. Code 4
North Central Local SD
Sch. Sys. Enr. Code 4
Supt. – Larry Acker, 350 S MAIN ST 44217
MS, 256 S MAIN ST 44217 – Rolland Seiple, prin.
Other Schools – See Burbank, Sterling

Cridersville, Allen Co., Pop. Code 4
Perry Local SD
Sch. Sys. Enr. Code 3
Supt. – Michael Lamb, RURAL ROUTE 06 45806
Perry ES, RURAL ROUTE 06 45806
  Linda Altstaetter, prin.

Wapakoneta CSD
Supt. – See Wapakoneta
Cridersville ES, 300 E MAIN ST 45806
  Daniel Graf, prin.

Crooksville, Perry Co., Pop. Code 5
Crooksville EVD
Sch. Sys. Enr. Code 4
Supt. – Larry Henry, 91 S BUCKEYE ST 43731
MS, 12400 TUNNEL HILL ROAD 43731
  Dennis Neff, prin.
ES, 12400 TUNNEL HILL RD 43731
  Dennis Neff, prin.

Morgan Local SD
Supt. – See Mc Connelsville
York ES, RURAL ROUTE 01 43731
  Richard Troup, prin.

Croton, Licking Co.
Northridge Local SD
Supt. – See Johnstown
Northridge Hartford ES
  10843 FOUNDATION RD 43013
  Wanda Green, prin.

Crown City, Gallia Co., Pop. Code 3
Gallia County Local SD
Supt. – See Gallipolis
Hannon Trace ES, RURAL ROUTE 01 45623
  Elton Savage, prin.

Curtice, Ottawa Co.
Genoa Area Local SD
Supt. – See Clay Center

Allen Central ES
  4865 N GENOA CLAY-CENTER RD 43412
  Gregory Towner, prin.

Oregon CSD
Supt. – See Oregon
Jerusalem ES, 535 S YONDATA RD 43412
  Charles Hyre, prin.

Custar, Wood Co., Pop. Code 2
Bowling Green CSD
Supt. – See Bowling Green
Milton ES, 22550 MERMILL RD 43511
  Elizabeth Rohrbacher, prin.

St. Louis ES, 22767 DEFIANCE PIKE 43511

Cutler, Washington Co.
Warren Local SD
Supt. – See Vincent
ES, P O BOX 68 45724 – Michael Swatzel, prin.

Cuyahoga Falls, Summit Co., Pop. Code 8
Cuyahoga Falls CSD
Sch. Sys. Enr. Code 6
Supt. – Ronald Overfield, 431 STOW AVE 44221
Bolich MS, 2630 13TH ST 44223
  William Sturm, prin.
Roberts MS, 3333 CHARLES ST 44221
  Thomas Ratcliff, prin.
Sill MS, 1910 SEARL ST 44221
  Charles McDermott, prin.
Dewitt ES, 425 FALLS AVE 44221
  Frank Barber, prin.
Lincoln ES, 3131 BAILEY RD 44221
  John Tomits, prin.
Newberry ES, 2800 13TH ST 44223
  James McCartney, prin.
Preston ES, 800 TALLMADGE RD 44221
  Carle Wyler, prin.
Price ES, 2610 DELMORE ST 44221
  David Lightel, prin.
Richardson ES, 2226 23RD ST 44223
  Robert Heath, prin.
Silver Lake ES, 2970 OVERLOOK RD 44224
  Joan Gulajski, prin.

Woodridge Local SD
Sch. Sys. Enr. Code 4
Supt. – Roger W. Edwards
  3313 NORTHAMPTON ROAD 44223
Woodridge ES, 3313 NORTHAMPTON RD 44223
  Stephen Snyder, prin.
Other Schools – See Peninsula

Chapel Hill Christian North School
  1090 HOWE AVE 44221
Immaculate Heart of Mary ES
  2859 LILLIS DR 44223
Redeemer Lutheran ES, 2141 5TH ST 44221
St. Joseph ES, 1909 3RD STSHORE BLVD 44221

Cygnet, Wood Co., Pop. Code 3
Elmwood Local SD
Supt. – See Bloomdale
Elmwood MS, WASHINGTON ST 43413
  Ronald Grimm, prin.

Dalton, Wayne Co., Pop. Code 4
Dalton Local SD
Sch. Sys. Enr. Code 4
Supt. – R. D. Pack, 177 MILL ST N 44618
MS, 151 W MAIN ST 44618 – John G. Leunk, prin.
ES, 151 W MAIN ST 44618 – Milton Troyer, prin.
Other Schools – See Kidron

Damascus, Columbiana Co.
West Branch Local SD
Supt. – See Beloit
West Branch ES 44619 – Cheryl Schoffman, prin.

Danville, Knox Co., Pop. Code 4
Danville Local SD
Sch. Sys. Enr. Code 3
Supt. – John Jurkowitz, P O BOX 30 43014
ES, P O BOX 30 43014 – Louise West, prin.

Darbydale, Franklin Co., Pop. Code 3
South-Western CSD
Supt. – See Grove City
ES, 7000 STATE ROUTE 665 43123
  Francis Shipley, prin.

Dayton, Montgomery Co., Pop. Code 9
Centerville CSD
Supt. – See Centerville
Watts MS, 7056 MCEWEN ROAD 45459
  Fred Lindley, prin.
Driscoll ES, 5767 MARSHALL RD 45429
  Gary Ogg, prin.
Hole ES, 180 W WHIPP RD 45459
  Tom Hannan, prin.
Normandy ES, 401 NORMANDY RIDGE RD 45459
  Margaret Barclay, prin.

Dayton CSD
Sch. Sys. Enr. Code 8
Supt. – Franklin Smith, 348 W FIRST ST 45402
Fairport MS, 1952 FAIRPORT AVE 45406
  Clarence Wade, prin.
Fairview MS, 2408 PHILADELPHIA DRIVE 45406
  Cheryl Johnson, prin.
Kiser MS, 1401 LEO ST 45404
  Barbara Minton, prin.
MacFarlane MS, 215 S SUMMIT ST 45407
  James Dorsey, prin.

Roth MS, 4535 HOOVER AVE 45417
  David Henderson, prin.
Stivers MS, 1313 E FIFTH ST 45422
  Timothy Nealon, prin.
Wright MS, 1361 HUFFMAN AVE 45403
  Louis Galiardi, prin.
Addams ES, 35 VICTORY DR 45427
  Williard Jenkins, prin.
Allen ES, 132 ALASKA ST 45404
  Laverne Daniels, prin.
Belle Haven ES, 4401 FREE PIKE 45416
  George Johnson, prin.
Brown PS, 48 E PARKWOOD DR 45405
  Herman Brown, prin.
Carlson ES, 807 S GETTYSBURG AVE 45408
  Thomas Greenwood, prin.
Cleveland ES, 1102 PURSELL AVE 45420
  Darlene Borgart, prin.
Cornell Heights MS, 2826 CAMPUS DR 45406
  David Medlar, prin.
Eastmont Park ES, 1480 EDENDALE RD 45432
  Elizabeth Davis, prin.
Edison ES, 228 N BROADWAY ST 45407
  Brenda Lee, prin.
Fairview ES, 1305 W FAIRVIEW AVE 45406
  Edward Baumer, prin.
Franklin ES, 2617 E FIFTH ST 45403
  Judith Oryan, prin.
Hickorydale ES, 2101 HICKORYDALE DR 45406
  Carrie Mallette, prin.
Jackson ES, 3201 MCCALL ST 45417
  Kenneth Dixon, prin.
Jefferson ES, 1231 N EUCLID AVE 45407
  Mildred McElroy, prin.
Jefferson PS, 1223 N EUCLID AVE 45407
  (—), prin.
Kemp MS, 816 SHEDBORNE AVE 45403
  James Lake, prin.
Lincoln Ige ES, 401 NASSAU ST 45410
  Grayce Toles, prin.
Loos MS, 45 WAMPLER AVE 45405
  Winifred Lee, prin.
Mann ES, 715 KREBS AVE 45419
  Alease Jones, prin.
McGuffey ES, 1032 WEBSTER ST 45404
  Sam Kurtz, prin.
McNary ES, 2400 HOOVER AVE 45407
  Lee Barnes, prin.
Meadowdale ES, 4448 THOMPSON DR 45416
  Barbara Goins, prin.
Miami Chapel MS
  1630 MIAMI CHAPEL RD 45408
  Raymond Swann, prin.
Patterson/Kennedy MS, 258 WYOMING ST 45409
  Paul Bryson, prin.
Residence Park MS, 833 ELMHURST RD 45417
  Eugene Richards, prin.
Ruskin MS, 275 MCCLURE ST 45410
  Sylvia Barrett, prin.
Troy ES, 1665 RICHLEY DR 45408
  Anastasia Bulcher, prin.
Valerie ES, 4020 BRADWOOD DR 45405
  Carolyn Wheeler, prin.
Van Cleve MS, 45 W HELENA ST 45405
  Lillian Walker, prin.
Webster MS, 1115 KEIFER ST 45404
  Dale VanTime, prin.
Whittier MS, 721 MIAMI CHAPEL RD 45408
  Donald Hubbard, prin.
Wogaman MS, 2716 GERMANTOWN ST 45408
  Malachi Williams, prin.
Wright MS, 200 S WRIGHT AVE 45403
  David Kreitzer, prin.

Jefferson Township Local SD
Sch. Sys. Enr. Code 4
Supt. – Herbert Franklin
  2989 S UNION ROAD 45418
Radcliff Heights MS, 120 KNOX AVE 45427
  William Schooler, prin.
Blairwood ES, 1241 BLAIRWOOD AVE 45418
  Katherine Arnold, prin.

Mad River Local SD
Sch. Sys. Enr. Code 5
Supt. – L. Draffen, 801 HARSHMAN ROAD 45431
Mad River MS, 1801 HARSHMAN ROAD 45424
  Donald Kuntz, prin.
Spinning Hills MS, 5001 EASTMAN AVE 45432
  Duane Bennett, prin.
Beverly Gardens ES, 5555 ENRIGHT AVE 45431
  J. Williams, prin.
Brantwood ES, 4350 SCHWINN DR 45404
  Norma Gaston, prin.
Saville ES, 5800 BURKHARDT RD 45431
  Joseph Moses, prin.
Stevenson ES, 805 HARSHMAN RD 45431
  Vicki Newsome, prin.

Miamisburg CSD
Supt. – See Miamisburg
Bauer ES, 6951 SPRINGBORO PIKE 45449
  Edmund Mershad, prin.

Northmont CSD
Supt. – See Englewood
Northwood ES, 6200 NORANDA DR 45415
  Robert Gentis, prin.

Northridge Local SD
Sch. Sys. Enr. Code 4
Supt. – C. W. Jarboe, 2011 TIMBER LANE 45414
Dennis MS, 5120 N DIXIE DRIVE 45414
  Stanley Kuck, prin.

Grafton Kennedy ES
2655 WAGONER FORD RD 45414
Mary Withrow, prin.
Morrison ES, 2235 ARTHUR AVE 45414
Tod Perez, prin.
Timberlane ES, 2131 TIMBER LN 45414
Donna Puckett, prin.

Oakwood CSD
Sch. Sys. Enr. Code 4
Supt. – D. Raisch, 20 RUBICON ROAD 45409
Harman ES, 735 HARMAN AVE 45419
James Eschbach, prin.
Smith ES, 1701 SHAFOR BLVD 45419
William Henry, prin.

Trotwood-Madison CSD
Supt. – See Trotwood
Trotwood-Madison JHS
3594 N SNYDER ROAD 45426
Willie Brown, prin.
Olivehill ES, 1250 OLIVE RD 45426
Roger Evans, prin.
Shilohview ES, 5600 ELGIN ROOF RD 45426
Genieve Caldwell, prin.
Townview ES, 5280 GARDENDALE AVE 45427
Donna Carpenter, prin.
Westbrook Village ES, 6500 WESTFORD RD 45426
Joseph Pizza, prin.

Vandalia-Butler CSD
Supt. – See Vandalia
Smith MS, 3625 LITTLE YORK ROAD 45414
James Dearmond, prin.
Murlin Heights ES, 8515 N DIXIE DR 45414
Gary Miller, prin.

West Carrollton CSD
Supt. – See West Carrollton
Holliday ES, 4100 S DIXIE DR 45439
Michael Dingledine, prin.
Nicholas ES, 3846 VANCE RD 45439
Gene Paul, prin.

Dayton Christian ES, 501 HICKORY ST 45410
Hillel Academy of Dayton
100 E WOODBURY DR 45415
Miami Valley School, 5151 DENISE DRIVE 45429
Corpus Christi ES, 200 HOMEWOOD AVE 45405
Dayton Catholic ES, 3805 KINGS HWY 45406
Dayton Christian North ES
325 HOMEWOOD AVE 45405
Dayton Christian South ES
2528 WILMINGTON PIKE 45419
Holy Angels ES, 223 L ST 45409
Holy Family ES, 121 S MONMOUTH ST 45403
Immaculate Conception S
2268 S SMITHVILLE RD 45420
Our Lady of Mercy ES, 545 ODLIN AVE 45405
Our Lady of Rosary ES
40 NOTRE DAME AVE 45404
Precious Blood ES, 4870 DENLINGER RD 45426
Queen of Martyrs ES
4128 CEDAR RIDGE RD 45414
Resurrection ES, 138 GRAMONT AVE 45417
St. Anthony ES, 825 CREIGHTON AVE 45410
St. Helen ES, 5086 BURKHARDT RD 45431
St. Peter ES, 6185 CHAMBERSBURG RD 45424
St. Rita ES, 251 ERDIEL DR 45415

Decatur, Brown Co.
Eastern Local SD
Supt. – See Sardinia
ES 45115 – Bonnie Kress, prin.

Defiance, Defiance Co., Pop. Code 7
Ayersville Local SD
Sch. Sys. Enr. Code 4
Supt. – Ken Jones, RURAL ROUTE 07 43512
Ayersville ES, RURAL ROUTE 07 43512
Ronald Zachrich, prin.

Defiance CSD
Sch. Sys. Enr. Code 5
Supt. – Gary Dowler, 629 ARABELLA ST 43512
JHS, 625 ARABELLA ST 43512 – Bill Mack, prin.
Brickell ES, 601 E 2ND ST 43512
Jerry Latta, prin.
MS, 801 S CLINTON ST 43512
Charles Beard, prin.
Slocum ES, 620 THURSTON ST 43512
Kevin Dangler, prin.
Spencer ES, 140 E BROADWAY ST 43512
Phil Furnas, prin.
Wayne ES, 1745 S CLINTON ST 43512
Robert Fetter, prin.

Northeastern Local SD
Sch. Sys. Enr. Code 4
Supt. – Joe Tumeo, RURAL ROUTE 03 43512
Tinora MS, RURAL ROUTE 03 43512
J. C. Roach, prin.
Noble ES, 10553 HALLER ST 43512
Eric Spiller, prin.
North Richland-Adams ES
RURAL ROUTE 04 43512 – Robert Brown, prin.
Tiffin ES, RURAL ROUTE 02 43512
Eric Spiller, prin.

St. John Evangelist ES, 800 5TH ST 43512
St. John Lutheran ES, 635 WAYNE AVE 43512
St. Mary ES, 702 WASHINGTON AVE 43512

De Graff, Logan Co., Pop. Code 4
Riverside Local SD
Sch. Sys. Enr. Code 3
Supt. – Phillip Trout, W MOORE ST 43318
Other Schools – See Quincy

Delaware, Delaware Co., Pop. Code 7
Buckeye Valley Local SD
Sch. Sys. Enr. Code 4
Supt. – Ronald Smith, 901 COOVER ROAD 43015
Other Schools – See Ashley, Ostrander, Radnor

Delaware CSD
Sch. Sys. Enr. Code 5
Supt. – Mark Stevens
248 N WASHINGTON ST 43015
Willis IS, 74 W WILLIAM ST 43015
Ralph Benziger, prin.
Carlisle ES, 746 US RT 37 WEST 43515
Kay Fisher, prin.
Conger ES, 10 CHANNING ST 43015
Patricia Bohmer, prin.
Smith ES, 355 N LIBERTY ST 43015
William Pasters, prin.
Woodward ES, 200 S WASHINGTON ST 43015
Walter Gibson, prin.

Olentangy Local SD
Sch. Sys. Enr. Code 4
Supt. – David Ritter
814 SHANAHAN ROAD 43015
Olentangy MS, 814 SHANAHAN ROAD 43015
Phillip Binkley, prin.
Olentangy ES, 814 SHANAHAN RD 43015
Larry Grover, prin.

Delaware Christian ES, 45 BELLE AVE 43015
St. Mary ES, 66 E WILLIAM ST 43015

Dellroy, Carroll Co., Pop. Code 2
Carrollton EVD
Supt. – See Carrollton
ES, P O BOX 93 44620 – Roy Ray, prin.

Delphos, Allen Co., Pop. Code 6
Delphos CSD
Sch. Sys. Enr. Code 4
Supt. – Bruce Sommers
234 N JEFFERSON ST 45833
Jefferson MS, 231 N JEFFERSON ST 45833
Mark Downey, prin.
Franklin ES, 300 E 4TH ST 45833
Mark Fuerst, prin.
Landeck ES, RURAL ROUTE 01 45833
Terry Moreo, prin.

St. John ES, 110 N PIERCE ST 45833

Delta, Fulton Co., Pop. Code 5
Pike-Delta-York Local SD
Sch. Sys. Enr. Code 4
Supt. – James Garber, 419 FERNWOOD ST 43515
MS, 419 FERNWOOD ST 43515
James McBride, prin.
ES, 419 FERNWOOD ST 43515
Thomas Lammers, prin.
Other Schools – See Wauseon

Dennison, Tuscarawas Co., Pop. Code 5
Claymont CSD
Sch. Sys. Enr. Code 5
Supt. – Franklin Gault, P O BOX 111 44621
Claymont MS, 220 N 3RD ST 44621
Donald Wright, prin.
Northside ES, 215 N 3RD ST 44621
John DeMuth, prin.
Park ES, JEWETT AVE 44621 – John DeMuth, prin.
Other Schools – See Uhrichsville

Immaculate Conception ES
100 SHERMAN ST 44621

Derby, Pickaway Co.
Westfall Local SD
Supt. – See Williamsport
ES, 12051 LONDON RD 43117 – Steve Best, prin.

Deshler, Henry Co., Pop. Code 4
Patrick Henry Local SD
Supt. – See Hamler
ES, 221 E MAPLE ST 43516 – Neil Flick, prin.

Dillonvale, Jefferson Co.
Buckeye Local SD
Supt. – See Rayland
Central ES, LIBERTY ST 43917
Stephen Dolfi, prin.

Martins Ferry CSD
Supt. – See Martins Ferry
Hilltop ES, RURAL ROUTE 02 43917
Anthony Collette, prin.

Dola, Hardin Co.
Hardin Northern Local SD
Sch. Sys. Enr. Code 3
Supt. – Terry Huffman
11589 STATE ROUTE 81 45835
Hardin Northern ES
11589 STATE ROUTE 81 45835
Sharon Bechtel, prin.

Donnelsville, Clark Co., Pop. Code 2
New Carlisle-Bethel Local SD
Supt. – See New Carlisle
ES, 150 E MAIN ST 45319 – Sharon Powers, prin.

Dover, Tuscarawas Co., Pop. Code 7
Dover CSD
Sch. Sys. Enr. Code 4
Supt. – F. William Zanders, 219 W 6TH ST 44622
MS, 220 W 6TH ST 44622
Donald Marshall, prin.
Dover Avenue ES, DOVER AVE & 13TH ST 44622
Renee Sattler, prin.
East ES, 325 BETSCHER AVE 44622
Glen Groh, prin.
Park MS, 2131 N WOOSTER AVE 44622
Edward Wallace, prin.
South ES, 280 SHAFER AVE 44622
Wayne Reese, prin.

St. Joseph ES, 600 N TUSCARAWAS AVE 44622

Doylestown, Wayne Co., Pop. Code 4
Chippewa Local SD
Sch. Sys. Enr. Code 4
Supt. – Rudy Yaksich, 257 HIGH ST 44230
Chippewa MS, 257 HIGH ST 44230
Marie Strayer, prin.
Hazel Harvey ES, 165 BROOKLYN AVE 44230
Bonnie Troyer, prin.

Sts. Peter & Paul ES, 169 W CLINTON ST 44230

Dresden, Muskingum Co., Pop. Code 4
Tri-Valley Local SD
Sch. Sys. Enr. Code 5
Supt. – Dean Sarbaugh
36 E MUSKINGUM AVE 43821
Jefferson ES, 1318 MAIN ST 43821
Roger Green, prin.
Other Schools – See Adamsville, Frazeysburg,
Nashport

Dublin, Franklin Co., Pop. Code 5
Dublin CSD
Sch. Sys. Enr. Code 5
Supt. – Phillip Price, 7030 COFFMAN RD 43017
Davis MS, 2400 SUTTER PKY 43017
Paul King, prin.
Deer Run ES, 8815 MANLEY ROAD 43017
Steve Anderson, prin.
Indian Run ES, 80 W BRIDGE ST 43017
Lynda Irvin, prin.
Olde Sawmill ES
2485 OLDE SAWMILL BLVD 43017
Susan Conner, prin.
Riverside ES, 3260 RIVERSIDE GREEN DR 43017
Nyra Terry, prin.
Scottish Corners ES, 5950 SELLS MILL DR 43017
John Laut, prin.
Thomas ES, 4671 TUTTLE RD 43017
Louis Staffilino, prin.
Wyandot ES, 5620 DUBLINSHIRE DR 43017
Jean Russell, prin.

Duncan Falls, Muskingum Co., Pop. Code 3
Franklin Local SD
Sch. Sys. Enr. Code 4
Supt. – Charles Bethel, P O BOX 428 43734
JHS, P O BOX 368 43734 – Terry Kopchak, prin.
ES, P O BOX 398 43734 – Thomas Patterson, prin.
Other Schools – See Chandlersville, Philo, Roseville

Dundee, Tuscarawas Co.
Garaway Local SD
Supt. – See Sugarcreek
ES 44624 – Larry Compton, prin.

East Canton, Stark Co., Pop. Code 4
Osnaburg Local SD
Sch. Sys. Enr. Code 4
Supt. – Ralph Waltman, BROWNING ST 44730
ES, 137 LIBERTY ST W 44730 – Neal Beans, prin.

East Claridon, Geauga Co.
Berkshire Local SD
Supt. – See Burton
Claridon ES, 14818 MAYFIELD RD 44033
Daniel Itschner, prin.

East Cleveland, Cuyahoga Co., Pop. Code 8
East Cleveland CSD
Sch. Sys. Enr. Code 6
Supt. – Rosie Doughty
15305 TERRACE ROAD 44112
Kirk MS, 14410 TERRACE ROAD 44112
(—), prin.
Caledonia ES, 914 CALEDONIA AVE 44112
Stella Loeb-Munson, prin.
Chambers ES, 14121 SHAW AVE 44112
John Whelan, prin.
Mayfair ES, 13916 MAYFAIR AVE 44112
Daisy Posey, prin.
Prospect ES, 1843 STANWOOD RD 44112
Elvin Jones, prin.
Rozelle ES, 12917 PHILLIPS AVE 44112
Louis Ernest, prin.
Superior ES, 1865 GARFIELD RD 44112
Brenda Wade, prin.

Christ The King Elem School
NOBLE AND TER RD 44112

Eastlake, Lake Co., Pop. Code 7
Willoughby-Eastlake CSD
Supt. – See Willoughby
MS, 36000 LAKE SHORE BLVD 44094
Don McCoy, prin.
Jefferson ES, 36010 LAKE SHORE BLVD 44094
Nancy Bradley, prin.

Longfellow ES, 35200 STEVENS BLVD   44094
  Robert Clampitt, prin.
Washington ES, 503 VEGAS DR   44094
  Jeffrey Hundt, prin.

St. Justin Martyr ES, 35741 STEVENS BLVD   44094

East Liberty, Logan Co.
Benjamin Logan Local SD
Supt. – See Bellefontaine
Benjamin Logan ES, P O BOX 7   43319
  Cheryl Chamberlain, prin.

East Liverpool, Columbiana Co., Pop. Code 7
Beaver Local SD
Supt. – See Lisbon
Calcutta ES, RUR RT 2-15482 ST RT 170   43920
  Gerald Barnes, prin.

East Liverpool CSD
Sch. Sys. Enr. Code 5
Supt. – Thomas Ash
  202 MAPLEWOOD AVE   43920
MS, W 8TH ST   43920 – Ken O'Hara, prin.
East ES, 1417 ETRURIA ST   43920
  Alma Kelly, prin.
La Croft ES, 2460 BORING LN   43920
  Richard Wolfe, prin.
North ES, 90 MAINE BLVD   43920
  Robert McVay, prin.
Westgate ES, 810 W 8TH ST   43920
  D. Edwards, prin.

East Liverpool Christian ES
  46682 FLORENCE ST   43920
St. Aloysius ES, 335 W FIFHT ST   43920

East Palestine, Columbiana Co., Pop. Code 6
East Palestine CSD
Sch. Sys. Enr. Code 4
Supt. – Milton Levy, 360 W GRANT ST   44413
MS, W NORTH AVE   44413 – Peter Chila, prin.
Taggart ES, 82 GARFIELD AVE   44413
  Charles Shreve, prin.
Unity ES, 49799 HCR 14   44413
  Charles Shreve, prin.

East Rochester, Columbiana Co.
Minerva Local SD
Supt. – See Minerva
West ES, 24604 U S ROUTE 30   44625
  Michael Gallina, prin.

East Sparta, Stark Co., Pop. Code 3
Sandy Valley Local SD
Supt. – See Magnolia
MS, 2195 POPLAR ST SE   44626
  Karen Williams, prin.

Eaton, Preble Co., Pop. Code 6
Eaton CSD
Sch. Sys. Enr. Code 4
Supt. – Charles Wiedenman
  307 N CHERRY ST   45320
Bruce MS, N CHERRY ST   45320
  Gregg Reink, prin.
Dixon-Isreal MS, RURAL ROUTE 04   45320
  George Henry, prin.
Hollingsworth East ES, 506 AUKERMAN ST   45320
  Lorrinda Saxby, prin.

Edgerton, Williams Co., Pop. Code 4
Edgerton Local SD
Sch. Sys. Enr. Code 3
Supt. – Dennis Lambes
  324 N MICHIGAN ST   43517
MS, EAST RIVER STREET   43517
  Charles Roberts, prin.
ES, 324 N MICHIGAN AVE   43517 – (—), prin.

Edison, Morrow Co., Pop. Code 3
Mt. Gilead EVD
Supt. – See Mount Gilead
ES, ST ROUTE 95 WEST   43320
  Stephanie Roarty, prin.

Edon, Williams Co., Pop. Code 3
Edon-Northwest Local SD
Sch. Sys. Enr. Code 3
Supt. – G. Kent Adams   43518
MS   43518 – William Wise, prin.
Northwest ES, RURAL ROUTE 02   43518
  William Wise, prin.

Elida, Allen Co., Pop. Code 4
Elida Local SD
Sch. Sys. Enr. Code 5
Supt. – Tom Jennell, 101 E NORTH ST   45807
MS, 4500 SUNNYDALE ST   45807
  Mike Estes, prin.
ES, 300 PIONEER RD   45807
  Stanley Strayer, prin.
Other Schools – See Gomer

Ellsworth, Mahoning Co.
Western Reserve Local SD
Supt. – See Berlin Center
ES, 6194 WARREN-SALEM RD   44416
  Joyce Galieti, prin.

Elmwood Place, Hamilton Co., Pop. Code 5
St. Bernard-Elmwood Place CSD
Supt. – See Saint Bernard
ES, 400 MAPLE ST   45216 – James Thomas, prin.

Elyria, Lorain Co., Pop. Code 8
Elyria CSD
Sch. Sys. Enr. Code 6
Supt. – William Halverson
  40710 GRISWOLD ROAD   44035
Eastern Heights JHS, 528 GARFORD AVE   44035
  John Joseph, prin.
Northwood MS, 700 GULF ROAD   44035
  Richard Ackerman, prin.
Westwood MS, 42350 ADELBERT ST   44035
  Roger McFrederick, prin.
Cascade ES, 233 BOND ST   44035
  Brenda Peaks, prin.
Crestwood ES, 42331 GRISWOLD RD   44035
  Linda Arter, prin.
Eastgate ES, 336 S LOGAN ST   44035
  Theodore Frierson, prin.
Ely ES, 312 GULF RD   44035 – Thomas Fox, prin.
Erie ES, 333 NAPLES DR   44035
  Bruce Kole, prin.
Franklin ES, 446 11TH ST   44035
  Connie Brown, prin.
Jefferson ES, 615 FOSTER AVE   44035
  Eileen Leuser, prin.
McKinley ES, 620 E RIVER ST   44035
  Richard Dargo, prin.
Oakwood ES, 925 SPRUCE ST   44035
  Gerald Gubeno, prin.
Prospect ES, 1410 PROSPECT AVE   44035
  Albert Eaton, prin.
Roosevelt ES, 121 W RIVER ST   44035
  Jack Penman, prin.
Spring Valley ES, 1005 ROSALEE AVE   44035
  Frank Humphrey, prin.
Windsor ES, 264 WINDSOR DR   44035
  Richard Sharrock, prin.

Midview Local SD
Supt. – See Grafton
East Carlisle ES, 1959 GRAFTON RD   44035
  William Reed, prin.

Kings Academy, 300 ABBE ROAD   44035
First Baptist Christian ES, P O BOX 929   44036
Open Door Christian ES, 8287 W RIDGE RD   44035
St. Jude ES, 594 POPLAR ST   44035
St. Mary ES, 237 FOURTH ST   44035
St. Vincent De Paul ES, 41315 N RIDGE RD   44035

Englewood, Montgomery Co., Pop. Code 7
Northmont CSD
Sch. Sys. Enr. Code 6
Supt. – Robert Mengerink
  4001 OLD SALEM ROAD   45322
Edgington ES, 515 N MAIN ST   45322
  David McMillen, prin.
ES, 702 ALBERT ST   45322 – Julie Wright, prin.
ES, 508 DURST DR   45322 – Kenneth Beiser, prin.
Northmoor ES, 4421 OLD SALEM RD   45322
  George Dietrich, prin.
Other Schools – See Clayton, Dayton, Phillipsburg, Union

Enon, Clark Co., Pop. Code 5
Mad River-Green Local SD
Supt. – See Springfield
Indian Valley MS, 510 ENON XENIA PIKE   45323
  Jeffrey Lewis, prin.
ES, 120 S XENIA DR   45323 – Mary Jung, prin.

Etna, Licking Co.
Southwest Licking Local SD
Supt. – See Kirkersville
ES, P O BOX 156   43018 – George Vickroy, prin.

Euclid, Cuyahoga Co., Pop. Code 8
Euclid CSD
Sch. Sys. Enr. Code 6
Supt. – Carl Hilling, 651 E 222ND ST   44123
Euclid Central MS, 20701 EUCLID AVE   44117
  William Dwyer, prin.
Forest Park MS, 27000 ELINORE AVE   44132
  Paul Kapostasy, prin.
Glenbrook ES, 23500 GLENBROOK BLVD   44117
  Richard Shisila, prin.
Jefferson ES, 1455 E 260TH ST   44132
  Henry Steinmetz, prin.
Lincoln ES, 280 E 206TH ST   44123
  Jeanne Ferrel, prin.
Roosevelt ES, 551 E 200TH ST   44119
  John McGowan, prin.
Upson ES, 490 E 260TH ST   44132
  Margie Pucsok, prin.

Holy Cross ES, 175 E 200TH ST   44119
St. Christine ES, 860 E 222ND ST   44123
St. Felicitas ES, 140 RICHMOND RD   44143
St. Paul ES, 1200 E 200TH ST   44117
St. Robert Bellarmine ES
  23802 LAKE SHORE BLVD   44123
St. Stephen Byzantine ES, 532 LLOYD RD   44132
St. William ES, 351 E 260TH ST   44132

Fairborn, Greene Co., Pop. Code 8
Fairborn CSD
Sch. Sys. Enr. Code 6
Supt. – Stephen Scovic
  306 E WHITTIER AVE   45324
Baker MS, 200 LINCOLN DRIVE   45324
  Thomas Swaim, prin.
Black Lane ES, 700 BLACK LN   45324
  Nancy Sayre, prin.
East ES, 100 LINCOLN DR   45324
  Michael Rarick, prin.

Five Points ES
  4 W DAYTON-YELLOW SPRINGS   45324
  Ronald McDermott, prin.
Palmer ES, 25 DELLWOOD DR   45324
  Joan Fine, prin.
South MS, 1020 S MAPLE AVE   45324
  Arthur Warthman, prin.
Wright ES, 480 W FUNDERBURG RD   45324
  Jacquelyn Woods, prin.

Mary Help of Christians ES
  934 N MAPLE AVE   45324

Fairfield, Butler Co., Pop. Code 8
Fairfield CSD
Sch. Sys. Enr. Code 6
Supt. – Larry Rodenberger
  5050 DIXIE HIGHWAY   45014
MS, 255 DONALD DRIVE   45014
  Erick Cook, prin.
Central ES, 5058 DIXIE HWY   45014
  Kathryn Accorinti, prin.
South ES, 5460 BIBURY DR   45014
  Catherine Milligan, prin.
West ES, 4700 E RIVER RD   45014
  Mabel Stitzel, prin.
Other Schools – See Hamilton

Sacred Heart ES, 400 NILLES RD   45014
Tri-County Christian School
  7350 DIXIE HIGHWAY   45014
La Valle ES, P O BOX 134   43944

Fairport Harbor, Lake Co., Pop. Code 5
Fairport Harbor EVD
Sch. Sys. Enr. Code 2
Supt. – David Sommers, 329 VINE ST   44077
McKinley ES, 602 PLUM ST   44077
  Alice Cunningham, prin.

Fairview Park, Cuyahoga Co., Pop. Code 7
Fairview Park CSD
Sch. Sys. Enr. Code 4
Supt. – John Babel, 20770 LORAIN ROAD   44126
Mayer JHS, 2100 CAMPUS AVE   44126
  Charles Kullik, prin.
Garnett ES, 4275 W 208TH ST   44126
  Mary Mohnacky, prin.
Parkview MS, 21620 MASTICK RD   44126
  Joseph Hruby, prin.

Messiah Lutheran ES, LORAIN & W 215TH   44126
St. Angela Merici ES, 20830 LORAIN RD   44126

Farmdale, Trumbull Co.
Joseph Badger Local SD
Supt. – See Kinsman
Gustavus ES, 4224 STATE ROUTE 87   44417
  Rocco Nero, prin.

Farmer, Defiance Co.
Central Local SD
Supt. – See Sherwood
ES, STATE ROUTE 249   43520
  Robert Lloyd, prin.

Farmersville, Montgomery Co., Pop. Code 3
Valley View Local SD
Supt. – See Germantown
ES, 202 JACKSON ST   45325 – Francis Pozzi, prin.

Fayette, Fulton Co., Pop. Code 4
Gorham-Fayette Local SD
Sch. Sys. Enr. Code 3
Supt. – Joseph Long, GAMBER ST   43521
Gorham Fayette ES, N EAGLE ST   43521
  John Winzeler, prin.
Other Schools – See Archbold

Fayetteville, Brown Co., Pop. Code 2
Fayetteville-Perry Local SD
Sch. Sys. Enr. Code 3
Supt. – J. Frazier, P O BOX 281   45118
MS, 60 EAST ST   45118 – Michael Wells, prin.
ES, 60 EAST ST   45118 – Julie Blaho, prin.

Felicity, Clermont Co., Pop. Code 3
Felicity-Franklin Local SD
Sch. Sys. Enr. Code 4
Supt. – Palmer Lowe, 415 WASHINGTON   45120
Felicity Franklin ES, WASHINGTON ST   45120
  Alice Hamilton, prin.

Findlay, Hancock Co., Pop. Code 8
Findlay CSD
Sch. Sys. Enr. Code 6
Supt. – Jan Patton, 227 S WEST ST   45840
Bigelow Hill ES, 300 HILLCREST AVE   45840
  Jerry Roth, prin.
Chamberlin Hill ES, 600 W YATES AVE   45840
  Marianne Anning, prin.
Franklin ES, 1100 BROAD AVE   45840
  J. Pelton, prin.
Jacobs ES, 600 JACOBS AVE   45840
  Christian Brooks, prin.
Jefferson ES, 204 FAIRLAWN PL   45840
  G. Philipp, prin.
Lincoln ES, 200 W LINCOLN ST   45840
  Joann Reeds, prin.
Northview ES, 133 LEXINGTON AVE   45840
  Thomas Elsea, prin.
Vance ES, 610 BRISTOL DR   45840
  John Richter, prin.
Washington ES, 701 N MAIN ST   45840
  David Rossman, prin.

Whittier ES, 733 WYANDOT ST 45840
Leslie Miller, prin.

Liberty-Benton Local SD
Sch. Sys. Enr. Code 3
Supt. – Wm. Butler
9050 W STATE ROUTE 12 45840
Liberty-Benton ES
9050 W STATE ROUTE 12 45840
Timothy Kruse, prin.

St. Michael ES, 701 ADAMS ST 45840

Fletcher, Miami Co., Pop. Code 2
Miami East Local SD
Supt. – See Casstown
ES, 4045 E US 36 45326 – Roberta Wilson, prin.

Flushing, Belmont Co., Pop. Code 4
Union Local SD
Supt. – See Belmont
ES, P O BOX 26 43977 – Robert Laipple, prin.

Forest, Hardin Co., Pop. Code 4
Riverdale Local SD
Supt. – See Mount Blanchard
ES, 311 W DIXON ST 45843
Steven Christopher, prin.

Fort Jennings, Putnam Co., Pop. Code 3
Jennings Local SD
Sch. Sys. Enr. Code 2
Supt. – F. Sukup, P O BOX 98 45844
ES, 130 W SECOND ST BOX 187 45844
David Miller, prin.

Fort Loramie, Shelby Co., Pop. Code 3
Fort Loramie Local SD
Sch. Sys. Enr. Code 3
Supt. – Norman Burkhardt
3640 STATE ROUTE 705 45845
ES, 35 ELM ST 45845 – Madeline Maurer, prin.

Fort Recovery, Mercer Co., Pop. Code 4
Southwest Local SD
Sch. Sys. Enr. Code 3
Supt. – Forest Yocum, P O BOX 612 45846
MS, W BUTLER ST 45846 – (—), prin.
Sharpsburg MS, 2454 SHARPSBURG RD 45846
Denny Howell, prin.
West ES, SOUTH WAYNE ST 45846
Denny Howell, prin.

Fostoria, Seneca Co., Pop. Code 7
Fostoria CSD
Sch. Sys. Enr. Code 5
Supt. – Jerry Argabrite, 114 W HIGH ST 44830
Emerson MS, 140 W HIGH ST 44830
Richard Van Mooy, prin.
Field ES, 6TH ST 44830 – Kenneth Watson, prin.
Holmes ES, 502 N GRANT ST 44830
Kathleen Herman, prin.
Longfellow ES, SANDUSKY AT TOWN ST 44830
Gregory Vay, prin.
Lowell ES, 129 ELM ST 44830 – Terry Piper, prin.
Riley ES, CORNER WALNUT & THOMAS 44830
Kenneth Goshe, prin.

St. Wendelin ES, 300 N WOOD ST 44830

Fowler, Trumbull Co., Pop. Code 5
Mathews Local SD
Supt. – See Vienna
Neal MS, P O BOX 37 44418 – John Sofikitis, prin.

Frankfort, Ross Co., Pop. Code 4
Adena Local SD
Sch. Sys. Enr. Code 4
Supt. – Ken Putnam, P O BOX 266-D 45628
ES, P O BOX 567 45628
Michael Kinnamon, prin.
Other Schools – See Clarksburg

Franklin, Warren Co., Pop. Code 7
Franklin CSD
Sch. Sys. Enr. Code 5
Supt. – Albert Porter, 150 E SIXTH ST 45005
JHS, 136 E SIXTH ST 45005
Thomas Wurzelbacher, prin.
Farrell ES, 513 PARK AVE 45005
James Vanderpool, prin.
Gerke ES, 312 SHERMAN DR 45005
Joann Feltner, prin.
Hunter ES, 4418 STATE ROUTE 122 45005
Michael McClusky, prin.
Pennyroyal ES, 4203 PENNYROYAL RD 45005
Margaret Engelhardt, prin.
Schenck ES, 350 ARLINGTON DR 45005
Anne Dowd, prin.
Wayne ES, 16 FARM AVE 45005
John Branson, prin.

Franklin Furnace, Scioto Co., Pop. Code 3
Green Local SD
Sch. Sys. Enr. Code 3
Supt. – Frank Barnett
RURAL ROUTE 02 BOX 13A 45629
Green ES, RURAL ROUTE 02 BOX 18AA 45629
Mark Cornwell, prin.

Frazeysburg, Muskingum Co., Pop. Code 4
Tri-Valley Local SD
Supt. – See Dresden
ES, N STATE ST 43822 – Donald Green, prin.

Fredericksburg, Wayne Co., Pop. Code 3
Southeast Local SD
Supt. – See Apple Creek
ES, P O BOX 249 44627 – Leslie Widder, prin.

Fredericktown, Knox Co., Pop. Code 4
Fredericktown Local SD
Sch. Sys. Enr. Code 4
Supt. – Rick Sulewski, W 2ND ST 43019
MS, 39 TAYLOR ST 43019 – Edward Erick, prin.
ES, TAYLOR ST 43019 – Morris James, prin.

Freeport, Harrison Co., Pop. Code 3
Harrison Hills CSD
Supt. – See Hopedale
ES, 113 N PHILADELPHIA 43973
Denver Kaiser, prin.

Fremont, Sandusky Co., Pop. Code 7
Fremont CSD
Sch. Sys. Enr. Code 6
Supt. – Kent Watkins, 211 S PARK AVE 43420
Atkinson ES, 1100 DELAWARE AVE 43420
Mary Kettner, prin.
Croghan ES, 1110 CHESTNUT ST 43420
William Rowley, prin.
Hayes ES, 916 HAYES AVE 43420
David McNelly, prin.
Lutz ES, 1929 BUCKLAND AVE 43420
William Krumnow, prin.
Otis ES, 718 N BRUSH ST 43420
John Brown, prin.
Stamm ES, 1038 MILLER ST 43420
Lyle Rowe, prin.
Other Schools – See Lindsey

Sacred Heart ES, 500 SMITH RD 43420
St. Ann ES, 1011 W STATE ST 43420
St. Joseph ES, 716 CROGHAN ST 43420

Fresno, Coshocton Co.
Ridgewood Local SD
Supt. – See West Lafayette
ES, 26366 HCR ROUTE 171 43824
Dennis Bahmer, prin.

Friendship, Scioto Co.
Washington Local SD
Supt. – See West Portsmouth
ES 45630 – George Essman, prin.

Gahanna, Franklin Co., Pop. Code 7
Gahanna-Jefferson CSD
Sch. Sys. Enr. Code 6
Supt. – Roger Viers, 160 HAMILTON ROAD 43230
Gahanna East MS, 730 CLOTTS ROAD 43230
Dennis Souder, prin.
Gahanna West MS, 350 N STYGLER ROAD 43230
John Allen, prin.
Chapelfield ES, 280 CHAPELFIELD RD 43230
Daniel Lister, prin.
Goshen Lane ES, 370 GOSHEN LN 43230
William Davis, prin.
High Point ES, 700 VENETIAN WAY 43230
Anthony Piehowicz, prin.
Jefferson ES, 136 CARPENTER RD 43230
Steven Montgomery, prin.
Lincoln ES, 515 HAVENS CORNERS RD 43230
Edgar Rarey, prin.
Royal Manor ES, 299 EMPIRE DR 43230
Daniel Rotella, prin.

Columbus Academy
4300 CHERRY BOTTOM ROAD 43230
Evangel Christian Academy
817 N HAMILTON RD 43230
St. Matthew ES
795 HAVENS CORNERS RD 43230

Galena, Delaware Co., Pop. Code 2
Big Walnut Local SD
Supt. – See Sunbury
Big Walnut Sixth MS, WALNUT ST 43021
Wesley Newland, prin.
Hylen Souders ES, 4121 MILLER PAUL RD 43021
Melissa Zarich, prin.

Galion, Crawford Co., Pop. Code 7
Galion CSD
Sch. Sys. Enr. Code 5
Supt. – Phillip Bunyard
200 W CHURCH ST 44833
MS, 200 W WALNUT ST 44833
Robert Casey, prin.
Crall ES, 702 S BOSTON ST 44833
Alfred Fairchild, prin.
Dawsett ES, 1051 DAWSETT AVE 44833
Thomas Bell, prin.
North ES, 200 WESTGATE DR 44833
Barbara Alesch, prin.
Renschville ES, 968 WINCHESTER RD 44833
David Chandler, prin.

Northmore Local SD
Sch. Sys. Enr. Code 4
Supt. – C. Stephen Oborn
5353 CO ROAD 29 44833
Other Schools – See Iberia, Shauck

St. Joseph ES, 141 N LIBERTY ST 44833

Gallipolis, Gallia Co., Pop. Code 6
Gallia County Local SD
Sch. Sys. Enr. Code 5
Supt. – Neil Johnson, 220 JACKSON PIKE 45631

Addaville ES, RURAL ROUTE 01 45631
Ronald Paxton, prin.
Other Schools – See Bidwell, Cheshire, Crown City,
Patriot, Vinton

Gallipolis CSD
Sch. Sys. Enr. Code 5
Supt. – Grant Sheppard, 61 STATE ST 45631
Clay ES, LOWER RIVER ROAD 45631
(—), prin.
Green ES, RURAL ROUTE 03 BOX 320 45631
Marvin McKelvey, prin.
Washington ES, 450 FOURTH AVE 45631
Jack Payton, prin.
Other Schools – See Rio Grande

Galloway, Fayette Co.
South-Western CSD
Supt. – See Grove City
Blton Hall ES, 1000 ALTON RD 43119
Carolyn Forrest, prin.

Gambier, Knox Co., Pop. Code 4
Mt. Vernon CSD
Supt. – See Mount Vernon
Wiggin Street ES, P O BOX 352 43022
Carol Owens, prin.

Garfield Heights, Cuyahoga Co., Pop. Code 8
Garfield Heights CSD
Sch. Sys. Enr. Code 5
Supt. – Charles Beshara
5640 BRIARCLIFF DRIVE 44125
MS, 4900 TURNEY ROAD 44125
Richard Golenski, prin.
Elmwood ES, 5275 TURNEY RD 44125
Donald Crosby, prin.
Foster ES, 12801 BANGOR AVE 44125
Frederick Baillis, prin.

St. John Lutheran ES, 11333 GRANGER RD 44125
St. Monica ES, 13633 ROCKSIDE RD 44125
St. Therese ES, 10608 PENFIELD AVE 44125
Sts. Peter & Paul ES, 4740 TURNEY RD 44125

Garrettsville, Portage Co., Pop. Code 4
James A. Garfield Local SD
Sch. Sys. Enr. Code 4
Supt. – William Frazier, 8233 PARK AVE 44231
Garfield MS, 8233 PARK AVE 44231
John Schwartzhof, prin.
Garfield ES, 10207 STATE ROUTE 88 44231
Michele Gaski, prin.

Gates Mills, Cuyahoga Co., Pop. Code 4
Mayfield CSD
Supt. – See Mayfield
ES, COLVIN ROAD 44040 – C Homansky, prin.

Gilmour Academy
CEDAR & SOM CENTER ROADS 44040
St. Francis Assisi ES, 6850 MAYFIELD RD 44040

Geneva, Ashtabula Co., Pop. Code 6
Geneva Area CSD
Sch. Sys. Enr. Code 5
Supt. – R. Taylor, 135 S EAGLE ST 44041
Geneva JHS, 819 SHERMAN ST 44041
Ronald Donatone, prin.
Cork ES, 314 STATE ROUTE 534 S 44041
William McNellie, prin.
Geneva ES, 119 S EAGLE ST 44041
Rita Zelei, prin.
Spencer ES, 4641 N RIDGE RD E 44041
Ralph Spaulding, prin.
Other Schools – See Austinburg

Assumption ES, 30 LOCKWOOD ST 44041

Genoa, Ottawa Co., Pop. Code 4
Genoa Area Local SD
Supt. – See Clay Center
JHS, 303 W 4TH ST 43430 – Charles Tank, prin.
Brunner MS, 1224 WEST ST 43430
John Tincher, prin.
Camper ES, 310 MAIN ST 43430
John Tincher, prin.

Georgetown, Brown Co., Pop. Code 5
Eastern Local SD
Supt. – See Sardinia
Ash Ridge ES, 9917 US ROUTE 62 45121
Susan Paeltz, prin.

Georgetown EVD
Sch. Sys. Enr. Code 4
Supt. – Robert Taylor
GREEN & CHERRY STS 45121
Reed ES, PLUM ST 45121 – Julie Weisner, prin.

Germantown, Montgomery Co., Pop. Code 6
Valley View Local SD
Sch. Sys. Enr. Code 4
Supt. – Leslie Harris, 64 COMSTOCK ST 45327
Valley View MS, 64 COMSTOCK ST 45327
John Wilson, prin.
ES, 110 COMSTOCK ST 45327
Frank Kozarec, prin.
Other Schools – See Farmersville

Gettysburg, Darke Co., Pop. Code 3
Greenville CSD
Supt. – See Greenville
ES, E MAIN ST 45328 – Neal Dalton, prin.

Gibsonburg, Sandusky Co., Pop. Code 4
Gibsonburg EVD
Sch. Sys. Enr. Code 4
Supt. – Bruce Smith, 300 S HARRISON ST 43431
Hilfiker ES, SUNSET AVE 43431
John Pertner, prin.

Gilboa, Putnam Co., Pop. Code 2
Pandora-Gilboa Local SD
Supt. – See Pandora
MS 45847 – Jeff Snook, prin.

Girard, Trumbull Co., Pop. Code 7
Girard CSD
Sch. Sys. Enr. Code 4
Supt. – S. Wright, 31 N WARD AVE 44420
Prospect JHS, 700 E PROSPECT ST 44420
Robert Foley, prin.
Summit ES, 2272 W LIBERTY ST EXT 44420
Stephen Koren, prin.
Washington Avenue
156 SMITHSONIAN ST 44420
Donald Rex, Jr., prin.
Woods MS, 443 TRUMBULL AVE 44420
Alison Harmon, prin.

St. Rose ES, 61 E MAIN ST 44420

Glandorf, Putnam Co., Pop. Code 3
Ottawa-Glandorf Local SD
Supt. – See Ottawa
ES 45848 – Thomas Weber, prin.

Glendale, Hamilton Co., Pop. Code 4

St. Gabriel ES, 18 W SHARON RD 45246

Glenford, Perry Co., Pop. Code 2
Northern Local SD
Supt. – See Thornville
ES, HIGH ST 43739 – Peggy Papritan, prin.

Glouster, Athens Co., Pop. Code 4
Morgan Local SD
Supt. – See Mc Connelsville
Homer Union ES, RURAL ROUTE 02 45732
Charles Cooper, prin.

Trimble Local SD
Sch. Sys. Enr. Code 4
Supt. – Judith Campbell
RURAL ROUTE 03 BOX 447 45732
Trimble MS, 18 CHERRY ST 45732
Darrell Dugan, prin.
Trimble ES, RURAL ROUTE 03 BOX 447 45732
Edwin Leatherwood, prin.

Gnadenhutten, Tuscarawas Co., Pop. Code 4
Indian Valley Local SD
Sch. Sys. Enr. Code 4
Supt. – William Wenger, P O BOX 171 44629
ES, P O BOX 130 44629 – Jack Campbell, prin.
Other Schools – See Midvale, Port Washington,
Tuscarawas

Gomer, Allen Co.
Elida Local SD
Supt. – See Elida
ES 45809 – Laree Little, prin.

Goshen, Clermont Co., Pop. Code 4
Goshen Local SD
Sch. Sys. Enr. Code 5
Supt. – Ralph Shell
GOSHEN ROAD AT STATE RT 28 45122
Spaulding MS, LINTON ROAD 45122
Bill Dennison, prin.
Cook ES, GOSHEN ROAD 45122
Phyllis Smith, prin.
IS, GOSHEN ROAD AT ST RTE 28-3 45122
Wanda Hill, prin.
Marr PS, GOSHEN ROAD 45122
Marie Chadwell, prin.

Grafton, Lorain Co., Pop. Code 4
Midview Local SD
Sch. Sys. Enr. Code 5
Supt. – Linda Huntley, 1097 ELM ST 44044
Midview MS, 2211 W CAPEL ROAD 44044
Richard Schibely, prin.
Belden ES, RURAL ROUTE 02 44044
Samuel Salvo, prin.
Brush ES, 555 N DURKEE RD 44044
Robert Maxwell, prin.
ES, 1111 ELM ST 44044 – Donna Lynch, prin.
Other Schools – See Elyria

Grand Rapids, Wood Co., Pop. Code 3
Otsego Local SD
Supt. – See Tontogany
MS, E 2ND ST 43522 – William Hale, prin.
ES, BRIDGE ST 43522 – Judith Lee, prin.

Grandview Heights, Franklin Co., Pop. Code 6
Grandview Heights CSD
Sch. Sys. Enr. Code 4
Supt. – Sherry Lahr, 1587 W 3RD AVE 43212
MS, 1240 OAKLAND AVE 43212
Jeannette Lauritsen, prin.
Edison ES, 1241 FAIRVIEW AVE 43212
Jeannette Lauritsen, prin.
Stevenson ES, 1065 OXLEY RD 43212
Todd Southern, prin.

Granville, Licking Co., Pop. Code 5
Granville EVD
Sch. Sys. Enr. Code 4
Supt. – James McCord, P O BOX 417 43023

MS, 130 N GRANGER ST 43023
Judith Lyons, prin.
ES, 310 N GRANGER ST 43023
James Knapp, prin.

Graysville, Monroe Co., Pop. Code 2
Switzerland of Ohio Local SD
Supt. – See Woodsfield
ES, 38861 STATE ROUTE 26 45734
Philip Ackerman, prin.

Graytown, Ottawa Co.
Benton Carroll Salem Local SD
Supt. – See Oak Harbor
ES, 1661 N GRAYTOWN RD 43432
Rosemary Schlievert, prin.

Green Camp, Marion Co., Pop. Code 2
Elgin Local SD
Supt. – See Marion
Elgin JHS, 447 HIGH ST 43322
Brian Napper, prin.

Greenfield, Highland Co., Pop. Code 6
Greenfield EVD
Sch. Sys. Enr. Code 4
Supt. – Joseph Carter, 200 N 5TH ST 45123
JHS, 200 N FIFTH ST 45123 – (—), prin.
ES, 200 N 5TH ST 45123 – Gail Thompson, prin.
McArthur PS, 200 N FIFTH ST 45123
(—), prin.
Other Schools – See Hillsboro, Rainsboro, South
Salem

Greenford, Mahoning Co.
South Range Local SD
Supt. – See North Lima
South Range West IS, P O BOX 86 44422
Donald Bobovnik, prin.

Greenhills, Hamilton Co., Pop. Code 5

Our Lady of Rosary ES, 19 FARRAGUT RD 45218

Greensburg, Summit Co.
Green Local SD
Sch. Sys. Enr. Code 5
Supt. – John Haschak
1900 GREENSBURG ROAD 44232
Green MS, 1711 STEESE ROAD 44232
Larry Brown, prin.
Greenwood ES, 2250 GRAYBILL RD 44232
James Kernen, prin.
Kleckner MS, 1900 GRE3ENSBURG RD 44232
Donn Force, prin.

Green Springs, Seneca Co., Pop. Code 4
Clyde-Green Springs EVD
Supt. – See Clyde
ES, 420 BROADWAY ST N 44836
Paul Nardini, prin.

Greenville, Darke Co., Pop. Code 7
Greenville CSD
Sch. Sys. Enr. Code 5
Supt. – Kenneth Peters, MEMORIAL HALL 45331
JHS, 100 CENTRAL AVE 45331
Michael Calland, prin.
East ES, E 5TH ST 45331 – Lee Elsass, prin.
North MS, SPRING ST 45331
Vivian Wagner, prin.
South ES, WAYNE AVE 45331 – John Dillon, prin.
Woodland Heights ES
7550 STATE ROUTE 118 45331
Douglas Cullers, prin.
Other Schools – See Gettysburg

St. Mary ES, 238 W THIRD ST 45331

Greenwich, Huron Co., Pop. Code 4
South Central Local SD
Sch. Sys. Enr. Code 3
Supt. – Lowell Etzler, RURAL ROUTE 01 44837
South Central ES, NEW ST 44837
Michael Schifer, prin.
Other Schools – See North Fairfield

Grove City, Franklin Co., Pop. Code 7
South-Western CSD
Sch. Sys. Enr. Code 4
Supt. – Bob Bowers, 2975 KINGSTON AVE 43123
Brook Park MS, 2803 SOUTHWEST BLVD 43123
Elaine Wank, prin.
Pleasant View MS, 3191 PARK ST 43123
Gregory Grinch, prin.
Pleasant View MS, 7255 KROPP ROAD 43123
Robert Skinner, prin.
Highland Park ES, 2600 CAMERON ST 43123
Philipp Bush, prin.
Monterey ES, 2584 DFENNIS LANE 43123
Connie Johnston, prin.
Richard Avenue ES, 3646 RICHARD AVE 43123
Barbara Orlos, prin.
Sommer ES, 3055 KINGSTON AVE 43123
Robert Merkle, prin.
Other Schools – See Columbus, Darbydale, Galloway,
Harrisburg

Our Lady of Perpetual Help ES
3752 BROADWAY ST 43123

Groveport, Franklin Co., Pop. Code 5
Groveport-Madison Local SD
Sch. Sys. Enr. Code 6
Supt. – Charles Barr
5055 HAMILTON ROAD 43125

Groveport-Madison MS South
4400 GLENDENNING DRIVE 43125
Tom Stahl, prin.
Glendening ES, 4200 GLENDENNING DR 43125
Janet Schultz, prin.
ES, 715 MAIN ST 43125
Thomas Stevenson, prin.
Other Schools – See Columbus

Grover Hill, Paulding Co., Pop. Code 2
Wayne Trace Local SD
Supt. – See Payne
ES, MONROE ST 45849 – James Shugars, prin.

Gypsum, Ottawa Co.
Port Clinton CSD
Supt. – See Port Clinton
Portage ES, LAKE ST AND STATE ROUT 43433
Kenneth Bogard, prin.

Hamden, Vinton Co., Pop. Code 4
Vinton County Local SD
Supt. – See Mc Arthur
ES 45634 – Carol Eberts, prin.

Hamersville, Brown Co., Pop. Code 3
Western Brown Local SD
Supt. – See Mount Orab
ES, P O BOX 205 45130 – Peggy McKinney, prin.

Hamilton, Butler Co., Pop. Code 8
Fairfield CSD
Supt. – See Fairfield
North ES, 6116 MORRIS RD 45011
Robert Fisher, prin.

Hamilton CSD
Sch. Sys. Enr. Code 7
Supt. – R. Quisenberry, 332 DAYTON ST 45011
Adams ES, S F ST & RIDGEWOOD AVE 45013
Irene Matthews, prin.
Buchanan ES
HANCOCK & HARMON AVES 45011
Raymond Flodin, prin.
Cleveland ES, 900 S BROOKWOOD AVE 45013
Judith Murray, prin.
Fillmore ES, 1125 MAIN ST 45013
Thomas Webster, prin.
Grant ES, CAMPBELL DR & GREENWOOD 45011
Raymond Flodin, prin.
Harrison ES, 150 KNIGHTSBRIDGE DR 45011
Howard Melvin, prin.
Hayes ES, 900 HOADLEY AVE 45015
Gloria Baker, prin.
Jefferson ES, 8TH AND CHESTNUT STS 45011
Harvey Cobbs, prin.
Lincoln ES, GRAY & N E STS 45013
William Brunner, prin.
Madison ES, 250 N NINTH ST 45011
James Barton, prin.
Monroe ES, CARRIAGE HILL LANE 45013
Herbert Johnson, prin.
Pierce ES, 2898 FREEMAN AVE 45015
Robert Brandner, prin.
Van Buren ES, LINCOLN & PARKAMO 45011
Susan Schnell, prin.

Lakota Local SD
Supt. – See West Chester
Liberty ES, 6040 PRINCETON RD 45011
Anne Jantzen, prin.

New Miami Local SD
Sch. Sys. Enr. Code 4
Supt. – Ebbie Gabb, 600 SEVEN MILE AVE 45011
New Miami MS, 606 SEVEN MILE AVE 45011
Dennis Byrd, prin.
New Miami ES, 600 N RIVERSIDE DR 45011
Orville Roach, prin.

Ross Local SD
Sch. Sys. Enr. Code 4
Supt. – James Bischoff
3371 HAMILTON-CLEVES ROAD 45013
Ross MS, 3371 HAMILTON-CLEVES ROAD 45013
Steve Miller, prin.
Elda ES, 3980 HAMILTON-CLEVES RD 45013
Cathy Jewett, prin.
Morgan ES, 3427 CHAPEL RD 45013
Michael Farmer, prin.

Immanuel Lutheran ES, 1285 MAIN ST 45013
Queen of Peace ES, 2550 MILLVILLE AVE 45013
St. Ann ES, 3064 PLEASANT AVE 45015
St. Joseph ES, 2ND AND HANOVER ST 45011
St. Julie Billiart School, P O BOX 1148 45011
St. Peter in Chains ES
451 RIDGELAWN AVE 45013
St. Stephen St. Veronica ES
1205 SHULER AVE 45011

Hamler, Henry Co., Pop. Code 3
Patrick Henry Local SD
Sch. Sys. Enr. Code 4
Supt. – John Wilhelm, RURAL ROUTE 01 43524
ES, MARION & COHN STS 43524
Dolores Spieles, prin.
Other Schools – See Deshler, Malinta

Hammondsville, Jefferson Co., Pop. Code 2
Edison Local SD
Sch. Sys. Enr. Code 5
Supt. – H. Swartzlander 43930
Other Schools – See Bergholz, Irondale, Richmond,
Toronto

Hanging Rock, Lawrence Co., Pop. Code 2
Rock Hill Local SD
Supt. – See Ironton
Rock Hill ES 4, RURAL ROUTE 04 BOX 52   45638
Bob Rucker, prin.

Hannibal, Monroe Co.
Switzerland of Ohio Local SD
Supt. – See Woodsfield
ES, 42634 MAIN ST   43931 – Hattie Byers, prin.

Hanoverton, Columbiana Co., Pop. Code 2
United Local SD
Sch. Sys. Enr. Code 4
Supt. – James Crawford, 8143 STATE RT 9   44423
United ES, 8143 STATE ROUTE 9   44423
Cynthia McMillin, prin.

Harpster, Wyandot Co., Pop. Code 2
Upper Sandusky EVD
Supt. – See Upper Sandusky
ES   43323 – Chloe Gatchell, prin.

Harrisburg, Franklin Co., Pop. Code 2
South-Western CSD
Supt. – See Grove City
ES, 1062 SCHOOL HOUSE LANE   43126
Carol Saunders, prin.

Harrison, Hamilton Co., Pop. Code 6
Southwest Local SD
Sch. Sys. Enr. Code 5
Supt. – E. Frank, 230 S ELM ST   45030
MS, 9860 WEST ROAD   45030
Don Jostworth, prin.
Crosby ES, 8382 NEW HAVEN RD   45030
Gregg Tracy, prin.
ES, 600 E BROADWAY ST   45030
Robert Stoll, prin.
Other Schools – See Hooven, Miamitown, North Bend

Christ Centered ES, P O BOX 115   45030
St. John the Baptist ES, 508 PARK AVE   45030

Harrod, Allen Co., Pop. Code 3
Allen East Local SD
Supt. – See Lafayette
Allen East MS, 9520 HARROD ROAD   45850
Joel Scott, prin.

Hartford, Licking Co., Pop. Code 2
Joseph Badger Local SD
Supt. – See Kinsman
ES, P O BOX 100   44424 – Rocco Nero, prin.

Hartville, Stark Co., Pop. Code 4
Lake Local SD
Sch. Sys. Enr. Code 5
Supt. – J. Lee, 227 LINCOLN ST SW   44632
ES, 245 BELLE ST SW   44632
Richard Warren, prin.
Lake MS, 225 LINCOLN ST SW   44632
Darlene Bucher, prin.
Other Schools – See Uniontown

Lake Center Christian ES
1360 WOODMONT ST NE   44632

Haskins, Wood Co., Pop. Code 3
Otsego Local SD
Supt. – See Tontogany
ES, FINDLAY RD   43525 – Ed Walden, prin.

Hayesville, Ashland Co., Pop. Code 3
Hillsdale Local SD
Supt. – See Jeromesville
ES   44838 – Raymond Bauer, prin.

Heath, Licking Co., Pop. Code 6
Heath CSD
Sch. Sys. Enr. Code 4
Supt. – Dan Dupps
107 LANCASTER DRIVE   43056
Fulton MS, 160 HEATH ROAD   43056
James Bowers, prin.
Garfield ES, 680 S 30TH ST   43056
Valerie Bailey, prin.

Hebron, Licking Co., Pop. Code 4
Lakewood Local SD
Sch. Sys. Enr. Code 4
Supt. – Douglas Grandstaff
4291 NATIONAL ROAD SE   43025
ES, 709 DEACON ST   43025 – James Riley, prin.
Lakewood MS, 9380 LANCER RD   43025
Arnold Johnson, prin.
Other Schools – See Jacksontown

Hemlock, Perry Co., Pop. Code 2
Southern Local SD
Sch. Sys. Enr. Code 4
Supt. – James Rosendahl
10397 STATE ROUTE 155 SE   43743
Other Schools – See Corning, Moxahala, New
Straitsville, Shawnee

Hicksville, Defiance Co., Pop. Code 5
Hicksville EVD
Sch. Sys. Enr. Code 4
Supt. – Carl Snyder, SMITH ST   43526
ES, ARTHUR ST   43526 – James Fetzer, prin.

Highland, Highland Co., Pop. Code 2
Fairfield Local SD
Supt. – See Leesburg
Fairfield-Highland ES, P O BOX 177   45132
Lawrence Fouch, prin.

Highland Heights, Cuyahoga Co., Pop. Code 6
Mayfield CSD
Supt. – See Mayfield
Millridge ES, 950 MILLRIDGE RD   44143
Robert Huntley, prin.

St. Paschal Baylon ES
5360 WILSON MILLS RD   44143

Hilliard, Franklin Co., Pop. Code 6
Hilliard CSD
Sch. Sys. Enr. Code 5
Supt. – Roger Nehls
5491 SCIOTO DARBY ROAD   43026
MS, 5380 SCIOTO DARBY ROAD   43026
Jeffrey Reinhard, prin.
Avery ES, 4388 AVERY RD   43026
Richard Sorg, prin.
Beacon ES, 3600 LACON RD   43026
Robert Searles, prin.
Brown ES, 2494 WALKER RD   43026
Robert Spicer, prin.
ES, 3859 MAIN ST   43026 – William Glenn, prin.
Reason ES, 4790 CEMETERY RD   43026
Mary Walker, prin.
Other Schools – See Columbus

St. Brendan School, 4475 DUBLIN RD   43026

Hillsboro, Highland Co., Pop. Code 6
Bright Local SD
Supt. – See Mowrystown
Belfast ES, 2024 STATE ROUTE 73   45133
Terressa Bobb, prin.
Concord ES, 2281 STATE ROUTE 136   45133
Mary Turner, prin.

Greenfield EVD
Supt. – See Greenfield
Petersburg ES, 9057 WATER ST   45133
John Miller, prin.

Hillsboro CSD
Sch. Sys. Enr. Code 4
Supt. – John Burton, 128 W WALNUT ST   45133
Marshall MS, 11090 STATE ROUTE 124   45133
Joe Temple, prin.
Washington MS, N E ST   45133
Byron Wisecup, prin.
Webster ES, 265 W WALNUT ST   45133
Terry Alexander, prin.

Hinckley, Medina Co.
Highland Local SD
Supt. – See Medina
ES, 1586 CENTER RD   44233 – John Giles, prin.

Hiram, Portage Co., Pop. Code 4
Crestwood Local SD
Supt. – See Mantua
ES, 8745 BANCROFT   44234 – Ted Poole, prin.

Holgate, Henry Co., Pop. Code 4
Holgate Local SD
Sch. Sys. Enr. Code 3
Supt. – John Mohler, 103 FRAZIER AVE   43527
ES, 103 FRAZIER ST   43527
Darlene Snyder, prin.

Holland, Lucas Co., Pop. Code 4
Springfield Local SD
Sch. Sys. Enr. Code 5
Supt. – George Tombaugh
7035 MADISON AVE   43528
Springfield JHS, KITTLE ROAD   43528
William Dais, prin.
Crissey ES, 2 GEISER RD   43528
Svea Cooke, prin.
ES, KITTLE RD   43528 – James Wightman, prin.
Other Schools – See Toledo

Hollansburg, Darke Co., Pop. Code 2
Tri-Village Local SD
Supt. – See New Madison
Tri-Village IS, P O BOX 10   45332
Shirley Verbanik, prin.

Holmesville, Holmes Co.
Southeast Local SD
Supt. – See Apple Creek
ES, P O BOX 8   44633 – Neely Summers, prin.

Homer, Licking Co.
Northridge Local SD
Supt. – See Johnstown
Northridge Homer ES
1227 HOMER RD NW   43027
John Loudermelt, prin.

Homerville, Medina Co.
Black River Local SD
Sch. Sys. Enr. Code 4
Supt. – Kurt Stanic, P O BOX 8   44235
Black River PS, P O BOX 8   44235
Linda Krieder, prin.
Other Schools – See Spencer, Sullivan

Hooven, Hamilton Co.
Southwest Local SD
Supt. – See Harrison
ES, CHIDLAW AVE   45033 – Fritz Monroe, prin.

Hopedale, Harrison Co., Pop. Code 3
Harrison Hills CSD
Sch. Sys. Enr. Code 5
Supt. – Lynn King, P O BOX 356   43976
ES, P O BOX 307   43976
Josephine Freeman, prin.

Other Schools – See Cadiz, Freeport, Jewett,
Tippecanoe

Hopewell, Muskingum Co.
West Muskingum Local SD
Supt. – See Zanesville
ES, 11100 WEST PIKE   43746
Robert Grayson, prin.

Houston, Shelby Co.
Hardin-Houston Local SD
Sch. Sys. Enr. Code 3
Supt. – Anthony Frierott
5300 HOUSTON ROAD   45333
Hardin-Houston MS, 5300 HOUSTON RD   45333
Sharon Dudek, prin.
Other Schools – See Sidney

Howard, Knox Co.
East Knox Local SD
Sch. Sys. Enr. Code 3
Supt. – Samuel Martin, P O BOX 222   43028
Other Schools – See Bladensburg

Hoytville, Hancock Co., Pop. Code 2
McComb Local SD
Supt. – See Mc Comb
Jackson MS   43529 – William Tatham, prin.

Hubbard, Trumbull Co., Pop. Code 6
Hubbard EVD
Sch. Sys. Enr. Code 5
Supt. – Clyde Metz, 150 HALL AVE   44425
Reed MS, 150 HALL AVE   44425
Geno Buonamici, prin.
Roosevelt ES, 110 ORCHARD AVE   44425
John Carlon, prin.

St. Patrick ES, 38 E WATER ST   44425

Huber Heights, Montgomery Co.
Huber Heights CSD
Sch. Sys. Enr. Code 6
Supt. – Richard Burke
5954 LONGFORD ROAD   45424
Menlo Park ES, 5701 ROSEBURY DR   45424
Larry Dale, prin.
Monticello ES, 6523 ALTER RD   45424
James Johnson, prin.
Rushmore ES, 7701 BERCHMAN DR   45424
John Dupre, prin.
Shenandoah ES, 5363 TILBURY RD   45424
Robert Lamendola, prin.
Titus ES, 7450 TAYLORSVILLE RD   45424
William Anderson, prin.
Valley Forge ES, 7191 TROY MANOR RD   45424
Bonita Benge, prin.
Weisenborn IS, 6061 OLD TROY PIKE   45424
Ron Sinclair, prin.

Hudson, Summit Co., Pop. Code 5
Hudson Local SD
Sch. Sys. Enr. Code 5
Supt. – Gerald Reeves, 77 N OVIATT ST   44236
MS, 120 N HAYDEN PARKWAY   44236
Joseph Siegferth, prin.
Evamere ES, 76 N HAYDEN PKY   44236
Marlene Heilman, prin.
ES, 34 N OVIATT ST   44236 – John Antonelli, prin.
McDowell MS, 280 N HAYDEN PKY   44236
Rosalie Dennis, prin.

Hudson Montessori ES, 7545 DARROW RD   44236

Huntsburg, Geauga Co.
Cardinal Local SD
Supt. – See Middlefield
ES, 12406 MADISON ROAD   44046
Lynne Muzik, prin.

Huntsville, Logan Co., Pop. Code 2
Indian Lake Local SD
Supt. – See Lewistown
Indian Lake ES, 222 NAPOLEON RD   43324
Larry Neal, prin.

Huron, Erie Co., Pop. Code 6
Huron CSD
Sch. Sys. Enr. Code 4
Supt. – Leslie Johnson, 329 OHIO ST   44839
McCormick MS, 325 OHIO ST   44839
Thomas Sprunk, prin.
Woodlands ES, 1810 MAPLE RD   44839
Joan Hogrefe, prin.

St. Peter ES, 429 HURON ST   44839

Iberia, Morrow Co.
Northmore Local SD
Supt. – See Galion
ES   43325 – E. Clark, prin.

Independence, Cuyahoga Co., Pop. Code 6
Independence Local SD
Sch. Sys. Enr. Code 3
Supt. – Guy Stella, 7733 STONE ROAD   44131
MS, 6565 BRECKSVILLE ROAD   44131
Daniel Potopsky, prin.
PS, 7600 HILLSIDE RD   44131
Judith Schulz, prin.

St. Michael ES, 6906 CHESTNUT RD   44131

Irondale, Jefferson Co., Pop. Code 3
Edison Local SD
Supt. – See Hammondsville
ES   43932 – Fred Burns, prin.

Ironton, Lawrence Co., Pop. Code 7
Dawson-Bryant Local SD
Supt. – See Coal Grove
Deering ES, RURAL ROUTE 01 45638
 Susan Vass, prin.

Ironton CSD
Sch. Sys. Enr. Code 4
Supt. – Charles Howard, 105 S FIFTH ST 45638
MS, 302 DELAWARE ST 45638
 Michael Whitehead, prin.
Campbell MS, 1111 S SIXTH ST 45638
 Steve Kingery, prin.
Kingsbury ES, 315 S SIXTH ST 45638
 Donald Miller, prin.
West Ironton MS, 3RD AND ELM STS 45638
 Charles Walters, prin.
Whitwell ES, 2213 S 4TH ST 45638
 Harold Patrick, prin.

Rock Hill Local SD
Sch. Sys. Enr. Code 4
Supt. – Lloyd Evans, RURAL ROUTE 03 45638
Rock Hill MS, RURAL ROUTE 03 45638
 James Wipert, prin.
Rock Hill ES 2, HCR RT 45638
 Samuel Hall, prin.
Rock Hill ES 3, RURAL ROUTE 03 45638
 Michael Hairston, prin.
Other Schools – See Hanging Rock, Pedro

St. Lawrence ES, 305 N SEVENTH ST 45638

Isle Saint George, Ottawa Co.
North Bass Local SD
Sch. Sys. Enr. Code 1
Supt. – James Getz, ISLE SAINT GEORGE 43436
North Bass ES, ISLE ST 43436
 Kamille Allen, prin.

Jackson, Jackson Co., Pop. Code 6
Jackson CSD
Sch. Sys. Enr. Code 5
Supt. – Michael Richardson
 379 E SOUTH ST 45640
Franklin ES, 4453 FRANKLIN VALLEY RD 45640
 Robert Bevins, prin.
ES, 236 SAVAGEVILLE SCHOOL RD 45640
 Robert Bevins, prin.
Kinnison ES, PORTSMOUTH ST 45640
 Carol Evans, prin.
Lick MS, 11507 US 35 WEST 45640
 George Wastier, prin.
Parkview ES, W SOUTH ST 45640
 Phillip Karl, prin.
Scioto ES, 4701 STATE ROUTE 776 45640
 Rodger Biggs, prin.
South Street ES, E SOUTH ST 45640
 Lieutriaci Willis, prin.

Oak Hill Union Local SD
Supt. – See Oak Hill
Bloomfield ES, 1325 DIXON RUN RD 45640
 Melvin Morgan, prin.

Jackson Center, Shelby Co., Pop. Code 4
Jackson Center Local SD
Sch. Sys. Enr. Code 3
Supt. – Donald Knight, 204 S LINDEN ST 45334
ES, 204 S LINDEN 45334 – Jerry Harmon, prin.

Jacksontown, Licking Co.
Conneaut Area CSD
Supt. – See Conneaut
Monroe ES, KELLOGGSVILLE RD 43030
 Jesse Howard, prin.

Lakewood Local SD
Supt. – See Hebron
ES, 9100 JACKSONTOWN RD SE 43030
 Joseph Ciricosta, prin.

Jacobsburg, Belmont Co.
Union Local SD
Supt. – See Belmont
Centerville ES, 46642 MAIN ST 43933
 John Koci, prin.

Jamestown, Greene Co., Pop. Code 4
Greeneview Local SD
Sch. Sys. Enr. Code 4
Supt. – John MacMillan
 53 N LIMESTONE ST 45335
Greeneview Central MS
 51 N LIMESTONE ST 45335 – Wayne Leis, prin.
Greeneview North ES
 1795 S CHARLESTON RD 45335
 Arthur Reiber, prin.
Other Schools – See Bowersville

Jasper, Pike Co.
Scioto Valley Local SD
Supt. – See Piketon
ES 45642 – Denny Chapman, prin.

Jefferson, Ashtabula Co., Pop. Code 5
Jefferson Area Local SD
Sch. Sys. Enr. Code 5
Supt. – Jerry Peterson
 108 E JEFFERSON ST 44047
ES, 108 E JEFFERSON ST 44047
 DeWayne Nicholes, prin.
Other Schools – See Rock Creek

Jeffersonville, Fayette Co., Pop. Code 4
Miami Trace Local SD
Supt. – See Washington Court House
ES, 23 W HIGH ST 43128 – Gordon McCarty, prin.

Jeromesville, Ashland Co., Pop. Code 3
Hillsdale Local SD
Sch. Sys. Enr. Code 4
Supt. – Arthur Eubanks
 405 TWP ROAD 1902 RT 1 44840
Other Schools – See Hayesville

Jewett, Harrison Co., Pop. Code 3
Harrison Hills CSD
Supt. – See Hopedale
Jewett-Scio ES, P O BOX 336 43986
 Robert Hugh, prin.

Johnstown, Licking Co., Pop. Code 5
Johnstown-Monroe Local SD
Sch. Sys. Enr. Code 4
Supt. – Sandra Vasu-Sarver
 13 E COSHOCTON ST 43031
Adams MS, 80 W MAPLE ST 43031
 James Romich, prin.
Oregon ES, 125 N OREGON ST 43031
 Linda Booth, prin.
Searfoss ES, 85 W DOUGLAS ST 43031
 Mary Thomas, prin.

Northridge Local SD
Sch. Sys. Enr. Code 4
Supt. – John Hollingsworth
 6097 JOHNSTOWN-UTICA ROAD 43031
Other Schools – See Alexandria, Croton, Homer

Junction City, Perry Co., Pop. Code 3
New Lexington CSD
Supt. – See New Lexington
ES 43748 – Michael Sherlock, prin.

Kalida, Putnam Co., Pop. Code 4
Kalida Local SD
Sch. Sys. Enr. Code 3
Supt. – Ronald Heitmeyer, P O BOX 269 45853
ES, P O BOX 358 45853 – Robert Williams, prin.

Keene, Coshocton Co.
River View Local SD
Supt. – See Warsaw
ES, HCR 01 BOX 27052 43828
 Wade Schuler, prin.

Kelleys Island, Erie Co., Pop. Code 2
Kelleys Island Local SD
Sch. Sys. Enr. Code 1
Supt. – Richard Acierto, P O BOX 349 43438
S, P O BOX 349 43438 – Patricia Seeholzer, prin.

Kent, Portage Co., Pop. Code 8
Field Local SD
Supt. – See Mogadore
Brimfield ES, 4182 STATE ROUTE 43 44240
 Richard Marks, prin.

Kent CSD
Sch. Sys. Enr. Code 5
Supt. – Donna Lightel, 321 DEPEYSTER ST 44240
Davey MS, PARK & PROSPECT STS 44240
 John Fender, prin.
Central ES
 N MANTUA ST AND PARK AVE 44240
 William Fankhauser, prin.
Franklin ES
 6662 CLEVELAND-CANTON ROAD 44240
 David Spencer, prin.
Holden ES, 132 W SCHOOL ST 44240
 Paul Bagocius, prin.
Longcoy ES, 1069 ELNO AVE 44240
 Mary Wiggins, prin.
Walls ES, 900 SORAMOR AVE 44240
 Thomas Shimmel, prin.

St. Patrick ES, 127 PORTAGE ST 44240

Kenton, Hardin Co., Pop. Code 6
Kenton CSD
Sch. Sys. Enr. Code 4
Supt. – Charles Taylor, 222 W CARROL ST 43326
MS, 300 ORIENTAL ST 43326
 Brent Wendling, prin.
Eastcrest ES, 409 MADISON ST 43326
 Richard Jones, prin.
Espy ES, 520 S DETROIT ST 43326
 Richard Jones, prin.
Hardin Central ES, 15128 STATE RT 67 E 43326
 David Jesse, prin.
Northwood ES, 530 GILMORE ST 43326
 Patricia Stiles, prin.
Westview ES, 401 SCOTT AVE 43326
 Dean Martino, prin.

Kettering, Montgomery Co., Pop. Code 8
Kettering CSD
Sch. Sys. Enr. Code 6
Supt. – John Goff, 3750 FAR HILLS AVE 45429
Beavertown ES, 2700 WILMINGTON PIKE 45419
 Robert Suter, prin.
Greenmont ES, 1 E WREN CIR 45420
 Yondal Combs, prin.
Indian Riffle ES, 3090 GLENGARRY DR 45420
 Joyce Hart, prin.
Kennedy ES, 5030 POLEN DR 45440
 Lorna Hinshaw, prin.
Oakview ES, 4001 ACKERMAN BLVD 45429
 Bertram Ruff, prin.
Orchard Park ES, 600 E DOROTHY LN 45419
 David Timpone, prin.
Prass ES, 2601 PARKLAWN DR 45440
 Richard Bowden, prin.
Southdale ES, 1200 W DOROTHY LN 45409
 Janice Thompson, prin.

Other Schools – See Moraine

Ascension ES, 2001 WOODMAN DR 45420
St. Albert the Great ES
 104 W DOROTHY LN 45429
St. Charles Borromeo ES
 4600 ACKERMAN BLVD 45429

Kettlersville, Shelby Co., Pop. Code 2
Anna Local SD
Supt. – See Anna
ES, 8833 NORTH 45336 – Carol Mescher, prin.

Kidron, Wayne Co., Pop. Code 3
Dalton Local SD
Supt. – See Dalton
ES, 4476 KIDRON RD 44636 – Phil Zuercher, prin.

Killbuck, Holmes Co., Pop. Code 3
West Holmes Local SD
Supt. – See Millersburg
ES, P O BOX 325 44637 – Roger Saurer, prin.

Kings Mills, Warren Co., Pop. Code 2
Kings Local SD
Sch. Sys. Enr. Code 4
Supt. – William Caudill
 5620 COLUMBIA ROAD 45034
Kings JHS, 5620 COLUMBIA ROAD 45034
 Charles Willis, prin.
MS, KINGS MILLS ROAD 45034
 Joseph Payne, prin.
Burns ES, 8471 COLUMBIA RD 45034
 Edward Groh, prin.
Other Schools – See South Lebanon

Kingston, Ross Co., Pop. Code 4
Logan Elm Local SD
Supt. – See Circleville
Saltcreek ES, 13190 STATE ROUTE 56 45644
 David Schiff, prin.

Kingsville, Ashtabula Co., Pop. Code 4
Buckeye Local SD
Supt. – See Ashtabula
ES, 5875 STATE ROUTE 193 44048
 James Hughes, prin.

Kinsman, Trumbull Co., Pop. Code 3
Joseph Badger Local SD
Sch. Sys. Enr. Code 4
Supt. – Lewis Strohm
 7000 CHAGRIN FALLS-GREENVLL 44428
Badger MS, 6144 YO CONNEUT ROAD 44428
 Allan Rummel, prin.
Other Schools – See Farmdale, Hartford

Kirkersville, Licking Co., Pop. Code 3
Southwest Licking Local SD
Sch. Sys. Enr. Code 5
Supt. – Terry Higgins, 195 N ST 43033
ES, P O BOX 401 43033 – Theresa Kucsma, prin.
Other Schools – See Etna, Pataskala

Kirtland, Lake Co., Pop. Code 6
Kirtland Local SD
Sch. Sys. Enr. Code 4
Supt. – Stephen Young
 9140 CHILLICOTHE ROAD 44094
MS, 9152 CHILLICOTHE ROAD 44094
 Glen Blabolil, prin.
ES, 9140 CHILLICOTHE RD 44094
 Jack Venen, prin.

Kitts Hill, Lawrence Co.
Dawson-Bryant Local SD
Supt. – See Coal Grove
Andis ES, RURAL ROUTE 01 45645
 Bill Stapleton, prin.

Kunkle, Williams Co.
North Central Local SD
Supt. – See Pioneer
North Central MS, P O BOX 92 43531
 Thomas Balser, prin.

Lafayette, Allen Co., Pop. Code 2
Allen East Local SD
Sch. Sys. Enr. Code 4
Supt. – Robert Mason
 105 N WASHINGTON ST 45854
Allen East PS
 105 N WASHINGTON STREET 45854
 Robert Wagner, prin.
Other Schools – See Harrod

LaGrange, Lorain Co., Pop. Code 4
Keystone Local SD
Sch. Sys. Enr. Code 4
Supt. – Ramon Rounds, 301 LIBERTY ST 44050
Keystone MS, 301 LIBERTY ST 44050
 Edward Bernetich, prin.
West Carlisle ES, 12079 STATE ROUTE 301 44050
 William Frey, prin.
Other Schools – See Wellington

Lake Milton, Mahoning Co., Pop. Code 3
Jackson-Milton Local SD
Supt. – See North Jackson
Lake Milton ES, 16670 MILTON AVE 44429
 Richard Christoff, prin.

Lakemore, Summit Co., Pop. Code 5
Springfield Local SD
Supt. – See Akron
ES, 1584 WILSON ST 44250 – Bruce Wilt, prin.

Lakeside, Ottawa Co., Pop. Code 3
  Danbury Local SD
    Sch. Sys. Enr. Code 3
    Supt. – Timothy Scherer
      9451 E HARBOR ROAD 43440
    Danbury ES, 9451 E HARBOR RD 43440
      Joyce Plummer, prin.

Lakeview, Logan Co., Pop. Code 4
  Indian Lake Local SD
    Supt. – See Lewistown
    Indian Lake ES, 850 W LAKE AVE 43331
      John Wells, prin.

Lakeville, Holmes Co.
  West Holmes Local SD
    Supt. – See Millersburg
    Lakeview MS, 14059 ST 226 PO BOX 68 44638
      Joseph Wengerd, prin.

Lakewood, Cuyahoga Co., Pop. Code 8
  Lakewood CSD
    Sch. Sys. Enr. Code 6
    Supt. – Daniel Kalish
      1470 WARREN ROAD 44107
    Emerson MS, 13439 CLIFTON BLVD 44107
      Charlane Bowden, prin.
    Harding MS, 16600 HILLIARD ROAD 44107
      Robert Hayden, prin.
    Mann MS, 1215 W CLIFTON BLVD 44107
      Edwin Isaly, prin.
    Franklin ES, 13465 FRANKLIN BLVD 44107
      Carolyn Kish, prin.
    Garfield ES, 13114 DETROIT AVE 44107
      Thomas Waddle, prin.
    Grant ES, 1470 VICTORIA AVE 44107
      Donald Paul, prin.
    Harrison ES, 2080 QUAIL ST 44107
      Thomas Zigman, prin.
    Hayes ES, 16401 DELAWARE AVE 44107
      John Dodd, prin.
    Lincoln ES, 15615 CLIFTON BLVD 44107
      Carl Lochard, prin.
    Madison ES, 16601 MADISON AVE 44107
      Thomas Lazor, prin.
    McKinley ES, 1351 W CLIFTON BLVD 44107
      Lois Welsch, prin.
    Roosevelt ES, 14237 ATHENS AVE 44107
      Elizabeth Mahoney, prin.
    Taft ES, 13701 LAKE AVE 44107
      Nancy Karabinus, prin.

  Lakewood Lutheran ES
    1419 LAKELAND AVE 44107
  St. Clement ES, 14505 MADISON AVE 44107
  St. Cyril & Methodius ES
    1639 ALAMEDA AVE 44107
  St. James ES, 17400 NORTHWOOD AVE 44107
  St. Luke ES, 13889 CLIFTON BLVD 44107

Lancaster, Fairfield Co., Pop. Code 8
  Fairfield Union Local SD
    Supt. – See West Rushville
    Fairfield-Union JHS
      6401 CIN-ZANESVILLE ROAD NE 43130
      Michael Destadio, prin.

  Lancaster CSD
    Sch. Sys. Enr. Code 6
    Supt. – John Baughman
      345 E MULBERRY ST 43130
    Ewing JHS, 825 E FAIR AVE 43130
      Carl Spencer, prin.
    Sherman JHS, 701 UNION ST 43130
      Gary Mauller, prin.
    Cedar Heights ES, 1515 CEDAR HILL RD 43130
      William Boyer, prin.
    East ES, 751 E WHEELING ST 43130
      Ronald Packard, prin.
    Medill ES, 1151 JAMES RD 43130
      Jerry White, prin.
    North ES, 710 N BROAD ST 43130
      David Todd, prin.
    Sanderson ES, 1450 MARIETTA RD NE 43130
      Paul Young, prin.
    South ES, 220 E WALNUT ST 43130
      Paul Given, prin.
    Tallmadge ES, 611 LEWIS AVE 43130
      Diana Eversole, prin.
    Tarhe ES, 425 N WHITTIER DR 43130
      Jerry Woodgeard, prin.
    West ES, 625 GARFIELD AVE 43130
      Shirley Wasem, prin.

  St. Mary ES, 309 E CHESTNUT ST 43130
  St. Bernadette ES, 1325 WHEELING RD NE 43130

Langsville, Meigs Co.
  Meigs Local SD
    Supt. – See Middleport
    Salem Center ES, 28764 STATE ROUTE 124 45741
      Charles Holliday, prin.

Lansing, Belmont Co.
  Bridgeport EVD
    Supt. – See Bridgeport
    PS, 68583 SCOTT AVE 43934
      Richard Everson, prin.

La Rue, Marion Co., Pop. Code 3
  Elgin Local SD
    Supt. – See Marion
    Elgin West ES, 350 N HIGH ST 43332
      Dennis Bame, prin.

Laurelville, Hocking Co., Pop. Code 3
  Logan Elm Local SD
    Supt. – See Circleville
    ES, 16138 PIKE ST 43135 – Charles Dean, prin.

Leavittsburg, Trumbull Co., Pop. Code 5
  Labrae Local SD
    Sch. Sys. Enr. Code 4
    Supt. – George Geordan
      1015 N LEAVITT ROAD 44430
    Labrae MS
      544 BRACEVLLE-ROBINSN RD SW 44444
      Albert Nye, prin.
    Bascom ES, 1015 N LEAVITT RD 44430
      Ruby Hawkins, prin.
    Leavitt MS, 4555 RISHER RD 44430
      Harry Benetis, prin.
    Other Schools – See Newton Falls

Lebanon, Warren Co., Pop. Code 6
  Lebanon CSD
    Sch. Sys. Enr. Code 5
    Supt. – H. Gardner, 25 OAKWOOD AVE 45036
    Berry JHS, 25 OAKWOOD AVE 45036
      David Winks, prin.
    Berry IS, 21 OAKWOOD AVE 45036
      Dale McVey, prin.
    Dunlavy ES, WATER ST 45036
      Charlotte Miller, prin.
    Holbrook ES, HOLBROOK AVE 45036
      E. Long, prin.
    Wright ES, S EAST ST 45036 – Charles Little, prin.

  St. Francis De Sales ES
    20 W DESALES AVE 45036

Leesburg, Highland Co., Pop. Code 4
  Fairfield Local SD
    Sch. Sys. Enr. Code 3
    Supt. – George Coffey,Jr., P O BOX 347 45135
    Other Schools – See Highland

Lees Creek, Clinton Co.
  East Clinton Local SD
    Sch. Sys. Enr. Code 4
    Supt. – J. Richard Gieringer
      LARRICK ROAD 45138
    Other Schools – See New Vienna, Sabina

Leetonia, Columbiana Co., Pop. Code 4
  Leetonia EVD
    Sch. Sys. Enr. Code 3
    Supt. – John Fieldhouse, 450 WALNUT ST 44431
    Orchard Hill MS, 450 WALNUT ST 44431
      Robert Eskay, prin.
    Other Schools – See Washingtonville

Leipsic, Putnam Co., Pop. Code 4
  Leipsic Local SD
    Sch. Sys. Enr. Code 3
    Supt. – Kenneth Boyer, 232 OAK ST 45856
    ES, 232 OAK ST 45856 – Richard Bryan, prin.

  St. Mary ES, 129 SAINT MARYS ST 45856

Lemoyne, Wood Co.
  Eastwood Local SD
    Supt. – See Pemberville
    ES, P O BOX 388 43441 – Marilyn Beckman, prin.

Lewisburg, Preble Co., Pop. Code 4
  Tri-County North Local SD
    Sch. Sys. Enr. Code 4
    Supt. – Phillip Dubbs
      108 N COMMERCE ST 45338
    Tri-County North MS, N COMMERCE ST 45338
      James Scherman, prin.
    Other Schools – See Verona

Lewistown, Logan Co.
  Indian Lake Local SD
    Sch. Sys. Enr. Code 4
    Supt. – Robert Van Osdol
      6210 STATE ROUTE 235 N 43333
    Indian Lake MS 43333 – James Jenkins, prin.
    Other Schools – See Huntsville, Lakeview

Lewisville, Monroe Co., Pop. Code 2
  Switzerland of Ohio Local SD
    Supt. – See Woodsfield
    ES, 33261 BACK ST 43754
      Philip Ackerman, prin.

Lexington, Richland Co., Pop. Code 5
  Lexington Local SD
    Sch. Sys. Enr. Code 5
    Supt. – Robert Earnest, 103 CLEVER LANE 44904
    JHS, 90 FREDERICK ST 44904
      William Ferguson, prin.
    Central ES, 90 FREDERICK ST 44904
      David Roberts, prin.
    Eastern MS, CASTOR ROAD 44904
      Louis Novak, prin.
    Western ES, WEST MAIN ST 44904
      Sarah Phillips, prin.

Liberty Center, Henry Co., Pop. Code 4
  Liberty Center Local SD
    Sch. Sys. Enr. Code 4
    Supt. – Myrna Ritterling, P O BOX 434 43532
    ES, P O BOX 434 43532
      Randal Chamberlain, prin.

Lima, Allen Co., Pop. Code 8
  Bath Local SD
    Sch. Sys. Enr. Code 4
    Supt. – Charles Montgomery
      2650 BIBLE ROAD 45801

  Bath MS, 2700 BIBLE ROAD 45801
    Paul Whittington, prin.
  Bath ES, 2501 SLABTOWN RD 45801
    Leroy Reed, prin.

  Lima CSD
    Sch. Sys. Enr. Code 6
    Supt. – Charles Buroker
      515 CALUMET AVE 45804
    Edison ES, 333 E VINE ST 45804
      Dave Shanks, prin.
    Emerson ES, EDWARDS AND BOYER 45801
      Patricia Woodley, prin.
    Faurot ES, 515 W ELM ST 45801
      Malcolm McCoy, prin.
    Irving ES, 1125 N METCALF ST 45801
      Virginia Cress, prin.
    Jefferson ES, 1300 S SUGAR ST 45804
      Leonard Crosley, prin.
    Lincoln ES, 516 S PIERCE ST 45804
      Larry Hutchinson, prin.
    Lowell ES, 1003 W SPRING ST 45805
      Kevin Fraley, prin.
    Mann ES, 1130 RICE AVE 45805
      James Kincaid, prin.
    Roosevelt ES, 1608 W SPRING ST 45805
      Linda Rolfe, prin.
    Washington-McKinley ES
      681 CALUMET AVE 45804 – Jean Synder, prin.
    Westwood ES, 501 N CABLE RD 45805
      Faith Rapp, prin.
    Whittier ES, 400 HOLMES AVE 45804
      Delbert Chalus, prin.

  Shawnee Local SD
    Sch. Sys. Enr. Code 5
    Supt. – (—), 3255 ZURMEHLY ROAD 45806
    Shawnee MS, 3235 ZURMEHLY ROAD 45806
      Corwin Croy, prin.
    Elmwood ES, 4295 SHAWNEE RD 45806
      James Thomason, prin.
    Maplewood ES, 1670 WONDERLICK RD 45805
      Ronald Clark, prin.

  St. Charles ES, 2175 W ELM ST 45805
  St. Gerard ES, 1311 N MAIN ST 45801
  St. Rose ES, 523 N WEST ST 45801

Lindsey, Sandusky Co., Pop. Code 3
  Fremont CSD
    Supt. – See Fremont
    Washington ES, 109 W LINCOLN ST 43442
      Kenneth Jenkins,Jr., prin.

Lisbon, Columbiana Co., Pop. Code 5
  Beaver Local SD
    Sch. Sys. Enr. Code 5
    Supt. – Nelson McCray
      13052 STATE ROUTE 7 44432
    Beaver MS, 13052 STATE ROUTE 7 44432
      Paul Metrovich, prin.
    Other Schools – See East Liverpool, Rogers, West Point

  Lisbon EVD
    Sch. Sys. Enr. Code 4
    Supt. – Clarence Means
      431 E CHESTNUT ST 44432
    Lincoln MS, 260 W PINE ST 44432
      Jeff Richardson, prin.
    McKinley ES, 441 E CHESTNUT ST 44432
      Howard Friend, prin.

Litchfield, Medina Co.
  Buckeye Local SD
    Supt. – See Medina
    ES, 9339 BROOKER RD 44253
      Carla Thomas, prin.

Lithopolis, Fairfield Co., Pop. Code 3
  Bloom Carroll Local SD
    Supt. – See Carroll
    Bloom ES, 200 MARKET ST 43136
      Marlo Mills, prin.

Little Hocking, Washington Co.
  Warren Local SD
    Supt. – See Vincent
    ES, RURAL ROUTE 01 BOX 45742
      Michael Swatzel, prin.

Lockbourne, Franklin Co., Pop. Code 2
  Hamilton Local SD
    Supt. – See Columbus
    Hamilton South ES
      ROUTE 317 AND SHOOK RD 43137
      Edgar Erlanger, prin.

Lockland, Hamilton Co., Pop. Code 5
  Lockland CSD
    Sch. Sys. Enr. Code 3
    Supt. – Nita Clayton, 210 N COOPER AVE 45215
    MS, 218 N COOPER AVE 45215
      Marlene Cole, prin.
    Lockland MS
      200 N COOPER AVE & LOCKLAND 45215
      Phillip Fox, prin.
    Other Schools – See Arlington

Lodi, Medina Co., Pop. Code 5
  Cloverleaf Local SD
    Sch. Sys. Enr. Code 5
    Supt. – Robert Szakovits
      8525 FRIENDSVILLE ROAD 44254
    ES, 301 MILL ST 44254
      Nicholas Moscalink, prin.

Other Schools — See Medina, Seville, Spencer, Westfield Center

Logan, Hocking Co., Pop. Code 6
Logan-Hocking CSD
Sch. Sys. Enr. Code 5
Supt. – Joseph Murtha, 57 S WALNUT ST 43138
Central ES, 80 NORTH ST 43138
    Ruth Spatar, prin.
East ES, 501 E MAIN ST 43138
    John Amann, prin.
Enterprise ES, 28841 CHIEFTAIN DR 43138
    Barbara Koehler, prin.
Green ES, 15663 STATE ROUTE 595 43138
    Paul DeBolt, prin.
West ES, 680 W HUNTER ST 43138
    Barbara Roach, prin.
West Logan ES, 1216 TRIMMER ST 43138
    Barbara Roach, prin.
Other Schools — See Rockbridge, South Bloomingville, Union Furnace

London, Madison Co., Pop. Code 6
Jonathan Alder Local SD
Supt. — See Plain City
Monroe ES, 5000 STATE ROUTE 38 43140
    Jon Fenton, prin.

London CSD
Sch. Sys. Enr. Code 4
Supt. – Jacob Froning, 60 S WALNUT ST 43140
MS, 60 S WALNUT ST 43140 – James Jones, prin.
Deercreek MS, 1730 CUMBERLAND RD 43140
    Douglas Roby, prin.
MS, 63 E FIRST ST 43140 – Douglas Roby, prin.
PS, 20 S WALNUT ST 43140 – Larry Powell, prin.
Somerford PS, 91 STATE RT 56 NW 43140
    Larry Powell, prin.

Madison-Plains Local SD
Sch. Sys. Enr. Code 4
Supt. – Frederic Reeder, 55 LINSON ROAD 43140
Madison-Plains MS
    9440 STATE ROUTE 38 SW 43140
    Tom Shoemaker, prin.
Fairfield ES, 5681 W JEFF-KIOUSVILLE SE 43140
    Bernie Hall, Jr., prin.
Madison Rural ES, 375 OLD XENIA RD SE 43140
    Walter Brown, prin.
Other Schools — See Mount Sterling, Sedalia

St. Patrick School, 226 ELM ST 43140

Londonberry, Ross Co.
Scioto Valley Local SD
Supt. — See Richmond Dale
ES, P O BOX 144 45647
    Charlotte Schumann, prin.

Lorain, Lorain Co., Pop. Code 8
Clearview Local SD
Sch. Sys. Enr. Code 4
Supt. – Wayne Ross, 4700 BROADWAY ST 44052
Durling MS, 100 N RIDGE RD W 44053
    William Jump, prin.
Vincent ES, 2303 N RIDGE RD E 44055
    Darrell Christian, prin.

Lorain CSD
Sch. Sys. Enr. Code 7
Supt. – John Pavic, 1020 W 7TH ST 44052
Whitter MS, E 32ND & SENECA AVE 44055
    David Karolak, prin.
Boone ES, 602 W 20TH ST 44052
    Herman Noland, prin.
Fairhome MS, ILLINOIS AVE & E STS 44052
    Stella Francis, prin.
Garfield MS, 205 W 30TH ST 44055
    Samuel Coleman, prin.
Homewood ES
    GOBLE & CHARLESTON AVES 44055
    John Matejcik, prin.
Irving MS, 4TH & HAMILTON AVE 44052
    Henry Harsar, prin.
Lakeview ES, 11TH ST & LAKEVIEW DR 44052
    Elba Armstrong, prin.
Larkmoor ES, 1100 LEROY ST 44052
    Charles Albright, prin.
Lincoln ES, 31ST & VINE ST 44055
    Ruben Lopez, prin.
Lowell ES, 3200 CLINTON AVE 44055
    E. Lange, prin.
Masson ES, EDGEWOOD DR & 40TH 44053
    Larry Melia, prin.
Meister Road ES, 3301 MEISTER RD 44053
    James Flanigan, prin.
Palm Avenue ES, 3330 PALM AVE 44055
    Sylvia Cooper, prin.
Washington ES, 2700 WASHINGTON AVE 44052
    William Tabak, prin.

Sheffield-Sheffield Lake CSD
Sch. Sys. Enr. Code 5
Supt. – Donald Chiavetta
    1824 HARRIS ROAD 44054
Sheffield MS, 1919 HARRIS ROAD 44054
    David Williams, prin.
Other Schools — See Sheffield Lake

St. Anthony Pudua ES, 1339 E ERIE AVE 44052
St. John the Baptist ES, 2140 E 36TH ST 44055
St. Mary ES, 307 W 7TH ST 44052
St. Nicholas Byzantine ES
    2707 W 40TH ST 44053
St. Peter ES, 3601 OBERLIN AVE 44053

Lore City, Guernsey Co., Pop. Code 2
East Guernsey Local SD
Supt. — See Old Washington
Madison ES, RURAL ROUTE 01 43755
    Thomas McVicker, prin.

Loudonville, Ashland Co., Pop. Code 5
Loudonville-Perrysville EVD
Sch. Sys. Enr. Code 4
Supt. – Tom Lavinder, 210 E MAIN ST 44842
Budd MS, 210 E MAIN ST 44842
    Nellie Wile, prin.
McMullen ES, 224 E BUSTLE ST 44842
    Sally Warbel, prin.
Other Schools — See Perrysville

Louisville, Stark Co., Pop. Code 6
Louisville CSD
Sch. Sys. Enr. Code 5
Supt. – David Mancini, 418 E MAIN ST 44641
Fairhope ES, 4001 ADDISON AVE NE 44641
    Wesley Hisey, prin.
ES, 1025 WASHINGTON AVE 44641
    Patricia Dilling, prin.
North Nimishillen ES
    7337 EASTON ST NE 44641 – David Snyder, prin.
Pleasant Grove ES
    9955 LOUISVILLE ST NE 44641
    Thomas McAlister, prin.

Marlington Local SD
Supt. — See Alliance
Marlboro ES, 8131 EDISON ST NE 44641
    Raymond Asher, prin.

Sacred Heart ES
    8267 NICKELPLATE AVE NE 44641
St. Louis ES, 214 N CHAPEL ST 44641

Loveland, Hamilton Co., Pop. Code 6
Loveland CSD
Sch. Sys. Enr. Code 4
Supt. – Ronald DeWitt
    757 S LEBANON ROAD 45140
MS, 600 LOVELAND-MADEIRA ROAD 45140
    Edward Lenney, prin.
Miami MS, 600 LOVELAND-MADEIRA RD 45140
    Warren McClellan, prin.
Mann ES
    6740 LOVELAND-MIAMIVILLE RD 45140
    Stephen Zinser, prin.

St. Columbian ES, 896 OAKLAND RD 45140

Lowell, Washington Co., Pop. Code 3
Fort Frye Local SD
Supt. — See Beverly
ES 45744 – Charlene Church, prin.

Lowellville, Mahoning Co., Pop. Code 4
Lowellville Local SD
Sch. Sys. Enr. Code 2
Supt. – Robert Kwiat, 2 E GRANT ST 44436
S, 2 E GRANT ST 44436 – Joseph Bertolini, prin.

Lower Salem, Washington Co., Pop. Code 2
Fort Frye Local SD
Supt. — See Beverly
Salem-Liberty ES, P O BOX 37 45745
    Charlene Church, prin.

Lucas, Richland Co., Pop. Code 3
Lucas Local SD
Sch. Sys. Enr. Code 3
Supt. – Robert Delane, P O BOX 307 44843
Heritage MS, P O BOX 307 44843
    William Seder, prin.
ES, P O BOX 307 44843 – Beverlee Powers, prin.

Lucasville, Scioto Co., Pop. Code 4
Northwest Local SD
Supt. — See Mc Dermott
Morgan ES, RURAL ROUTE 01 45648
    Betty Pietzer, prin.

Valley Local SD
Sch. Sys. Enr. Code 4
Supt. – Douglas Booth
    RURAL ROUTE 04 BOX 434A 45648
Valley MS, P O BOX 490 45648
    Paul Miller, prin.
Glendale ES, RURAL ROUTE 02 45648
    Gerald McGinnis, prin.
Valley ES, P O BOX 520 45648
    Robert Chestnut, prin.

Luckey, Wood Co., Pop. Code 3
Eastwood Local SD
Supt. — See Pemberville
ES, 524 KROTZER AVE 43443
    Marilyn Beckman, prin.

Lynchburg, Highland Co., Pop. Code 4
Lynchburg-Clay Local SD
Sch. Sys. Enr. Code 4
Supt. — See William Wills
    8250 STATE ROUTE 134 45142
Lynchburg-Clay ES, PEARL ST 45142
    Clo Davis, prin.
Other Schools — See Buford

Lyndhurst, Cuyahoga Co., Pop. Code 7
South Euclid-Lyndhurst CSD
Sch. Sys. Enr. Code 5
Supt. – Lawrence Marazza
    5044 MAYFIELD ROAD 44124
Memorial JHS, 1250 PROFESSOR ROAD 44124
    Larry Cirillo, prin.

Ridgebury ES, 1111 ALVEY RD 44124
    Michael Gigliotti, prin.
Sunview ES, 5520 MEADOW WOOD BLVD 44124
    Melvin Wasserman, prin.
Other Schools — See Cleveland, South Euclid

Billiart ES, 4982 CLUBSIDE RD 44124
Hawken ES, 5000 CLUBSIDE RD 44124
Ratner ES, 4900 ANDERSON RD 44124
St. Clare ES, 5655 MAYFIELD RD 44124

Lyons, Fulton Co., Pop. Code 3
Evergreen Local SD
Supt. — See Metamora
ES, 518 ADRIAN ST 43533 – Janet Pershing, prin.

Mc Arthur, Vinton Co., Pop. Code 4
Vinton County Local SD
Sch. Sys. Enr. Code 5
Supt. – Clyde Crewey, MEMORIAL BLDG 45651
Allensville ES
    STATE RT 01 P O BOX 1000 45651
    Troy Thacker, prin.
ES, 501 JEFFERSON AVE 45651
    Clyde Evans, prin.
Other Schools — See Hamden, Wilkesville, Zaleski

Mc Comb, Hancock Co., Pop. Code 4
McComb Local SD
Sch. Sys. Enr. Code 3
Supt. – Rahman Dyer, 328 S TODD ST 45858
ES, 328 S TODD ST 45858
    Bernice Salisbury, prin.
Other Schools — See Hoytville

Mc Connelsville, Morgan Co., Pop. Code 4
Morgan Local SD
Sch. Sys. Enr. Code 5
Supt. – Budd Hegele, P O BOX 509 43756
ES, 21 E JEFFERSON AVE 43756
    Robert Cosgray, prin.
Other Schools — See Chesterhill, Crooksville, Glouster, Malta, Pennsville, Stockport

Mc Cutchenville, Wyandot Co.
Mohawk Local SD
Supt. — See Sycamore
ES, 88505 STATE ROUTE 53 44844
    Linda Coleman, prin.

Mc Dermott, Scioto Co., Pop. Code 3
Northwest Local SD
Sch. Sys. Enr. Code 4
Supt. – A. McCoy, RURAL ROUTE 01 45652
ES 45652 – Howard Emnett, prin.
Union ES, RURAL ROUTE 01 45652
    Roby Bach, prin.
Other Schools — See Lucasville, Otway

Mc Donald, Trumbull Co., Pop. Code 5
McDonald Local SD
Sch. Sys. Enr. Code 4
Supt. – Richard Pachuk, 600 IOWA AVE 44437
Roosevelt ES, 400 ILLINOIS AVE 44437
    Anthony Russo, prin.

Macedonia, Summit Co., Pop. Code 6
Nordonia Hills CSD
Supt. — See Northfield
Ledgeview ES, 9130 SHEPARD RD 44056
    Keith Vandegrift, prin.

Mc Guffey, Hardin Co., Pop. Code 3
Upper Scioto Valley Local SD
Sch. Sys. Enr. Code 4
Supt. – Basilda Rockhold, S COURTRIGHT 45859
Other Schools — See Alger, Roundhead

Madison, Lake Co., Pop. Code 4
Madison Local SD
Sch. Sys. Enr. Code 5
Supt. – Jean Westfall, 6741 N RIDGE ROAD 44057
MS, 1941 RED BIRD ROAD 44057
    Robert Nobles, prin.
Kimball ES, 94 RIVER ST 44057
    John Kurila, prin.
North Madison ES, 6735 N RIDGE RD 44057
    Ansel Pierce, prin.
Red Bird ES, 1956 RED BIRD RD 44057
    Mary Snyder, prin.

Magnetic Spring, Union Co., Pop. Code 2
North Union Local SD
Supt. — See Richwood
Leesburg-Magnetic ES, P O BOX 96 43036
    Ruth Lowe, prin.

Magnolia, Stark Co., Pop. Code 3
Sandy Valley Local SD
Sch. Sys. Enr. Code 4
Supt. – W. Dieringer
    RURAL ROUTE 01 BOX 100 44643
ES, HARRISON ST BOX 397 44643
    David Spiker, prin.
Other Schools — See East Sparta, Waynesburg

Maineville, Warren Co., Pop. Code 2
Little Miami Local SD
Supt. — See Morrow
Hamilton-Maineville ES
    373 E FOSTER MAINEVILLE RD 45039
    Gregg Rolfsmeyer, prin.

Malinta, Henry Co., Pop. Code 2
Patrick Henry Local SD
Supt. — See Hamler
Malinta-Grelton ES, N HENRY ST BOX 87 43535
    Betsy Redd, prin.

Malta, Morgan Co., Pop. Code 3
Morgan Local SD
Supt. – See Mc Connelsville
ES, P O BOX 265 43758 – Richard Troup, prin.

Malvern, Carroll Co., Pop. Code 4
Brown Local SD
Sch. Sys. Enr. Code 4
Supt. – Bruce Schmidt, 401 W MAIN ST 44644
ES, 401 W MAIN ST 44644 – (—), prin.

Manchester, Adams Co., Pop. Code 4
Ohio Valley Local SD
Supt. – See West Union
Woolard ES, 315 E 9TH ST 45144
Rodney Wallace, prin.

Mansfield, Richland Co., Pop. Code 8
Crestview Local SD
Supt. – See Ashland
Union ES, RURAL ROUTE 02 44903
John Studebaker, prin.

Madison Local SD
Sch. Sys. Enr. Code 5
Supt. – Frederick Slater, 1379 GRACE ST 44905
Eastview ES, 1262 EASTVIEW DR 44905
Kathleen Romano, prin.
Lincoln Heights ES, 1035 GRACE ST 44905
Beverley Wenning, prin.
Madison South ES, 700 S ILLINOIS AVE 44907
Leroy Russell, prin.
Mifflin ES, RURAL ROUTE 11 44903
Martin Breitinger, prin.
Wooster Heights ES, 1419 GRACE ST 44905
Larry Young, prin.

Mansfield CSD
Sch. Sys. Enr. Code 6
Supt. – Mel Coleman, P O BOX 1448 44901
Appleseed MS, 314 CLINE AVE 44907
Larry Lewis, prin.
Sherman MS, 1138 SPRINGMILL ST 44906
Jennifer Morrison, prin.
Simpson MS, 218 4TH ST W 44903
D. Castle, prin.
Brinkerhoff ES, 240 EUCLID AVE 44903
Robert Coker, prin.
Carpenter ES, 71 CARPENTER RD 44903
Michael Ogden, prin.
Empire ES, 395 POMERENE RD 44905
Donna Malaniny, prin.
Hedges ES, 176 HEDGES ST 44902
Henry Griffith, prin.
Newman ES, 457 CENTRAL AVE 44905
Larry Kennedy, prin.
Prospect ES, 485 GILBERT AVE 44907
Charles Webster, prin.
Ranchwood ES, 1033 LARCHWOOD RD 44907
Albert Paetsch, prin.
Roseland ES, 1050 WYANDOTTE AVE 44906
Ivy Amos, prin.
Springmill ES, 1200 NESTOR DR 44906
Robert Adkins, prin.
Stadium ES, 215 TRIMBLE RD N 44906
James Harris, prin.
West Fifth Street ES, 150 W 5TH ST 44903
Sondra Asher, prin.
Woodland ES, 460 DAVIS RD 44907
James Tarantine, prin.

Ontario Local SD
Sch. Sys. Enr. Code 4
Supt. – Gregg Morris, 2200 BEDFORD BLVD 44906
Ontario MS, 3560 PARK AVE W 44906
Gene Hancock, prin.
Stingel ES, 416 SHELBY-ONTARIO RD 44906
Richard Wair, prin.

Mansfield Christian ES, 500 LOGAN RD 44907
St. Mary ES, 1630 ASHLAND RD 44905
St. Peter ES, 63 MULBERRY ST S 44902

Mantua, Portage Co., Pop. Code 4
Crestwood Local SD
Sch. Sys. Enr. Code 5
Supt. – Robert Thiede
4565 W PROSPECT ST 44255
Crestwood MS
10880 JOHN EDWARD DRIVE 44255
Robert Jurca, prin.
Mantua Center ES
11741 MANTUA CENTER RD 44255
Ted Poole, prin.
Mantua Village ES, 10803 MAIN ST 44255
Norman Brunelle, prin.
Other Schools – See Hiram, Ravenna

St. Joseph ES, 11045 SAINT JOSEPH BLVD 44255

Maple Heights, Cuyahoga Co., Pop. Code 8
Maple Heights CSD
Sch. Sys. Enr. Code 5
Supt. – Jack Neal, 5500 CLEMENT AVE 44137
MS, 5460 WEST BLVD 44137
Josephine Dodge, prin.
Dunham ES, 5965 DUNHAM RD 44137
Andrew Fetchik, prin.
Raymond ES, 18500 RAYMOND ST 44137
Claudette Burke, prin.
Rockside ES, 5740 LAWN AVE 44137
Henry Rish, prin.
Stafford ES, 19800 STAFFORD AVE 44137
George Hall, prin.

St. Martin of Tours ES, 14600 TURNEY RD 44137
St. Wenceslas ES, 5260 CATO ST 44137

Marengo, Morrow Co., Pop. Code 2
Highland Local SD
Supt. – See Sparta
Highland West ES, WALNUT ST 43334
Robert Rush, prin.

Maria Stein, Mercer Co.
Marion Local SD
Sch. Sys. Enr. Code 3
Supt. – R. Huelsman
1901 STATE ROUTE 716 45860
Marion ES, 7956 STATE ROUTE 119 45860
Hugh Aukerman, prin.

Mariemont, Hamilton Co., Pop. Code 5
Mariemont CSD
Sch. Sys. Enr. Code 4
Supt. – Donald Thompson
3900 PLAINVILLE ROAD 45227
Other Schools – See Cincinnati, Terrace Park

Marietta, Washington Co., Pop. Code 7
Frontier Local SD
Supt. – See New Matamoras
Lawrence ES, RURAL ROUTE 05 45750
Coletta Musick, prin.

Marietta Local SD
Sch. Sys. Enr. Code 5
Supt. – George Kingsmore, 701 N 3RD ST 45750
MS, 7TH & GLENDALE ST 45750
Robert Carmichael, prin.
Harmar ES, 100 FORT SQ 45750
Cheryl Carver, prin.
North Hills ES, COLEGATE ROAD 45750
Harry Fleming, prin.
Phillips ES, PIKE & ELMWOOD 45750
Joseph Toller, prin.
Putnam ES, 598 MASONIC PARK RD 45750
Harry Fleming, prin.
Washington ES, 401 WASHINGTON ST 45750
Marian Kurner, prin.
Other Schools – See Reno

Warren Local SD
Supt. – See Vincent
Warren ES, RURAL ROUTE 04 45750
Patrick Levine, prin.

St. John ES, RURAL ROUTE 02 45750
St. Mary ES, 320 MARION STREET 45750

Marion, Marion Co., Pop. Code 8
Elgin Local SD
Sch. Sys. Enr. Code 4
Supt. – Donald Bumgarner Supt
4616 LARUE PROSPECT RD W 43302
Other Schools – See Green Camp, La Rue, Prospect

Marion CSD
Sch. Sys. Enr. Code 6
Supt. – Stephen Stuart, 910 E CHURCH ST 43302
Baker MS, 400 PENSYLVANIA AVE 43302
Gerald Emery, prin.
Edison MS, 871 CHATFIELD ROAD 43302
Edwin Schoonmaker, prin.
Taft MS, 474 N STATE ST 43302
Ted Stolarczyk, prin.
Colonial Acres MS, 1565 AMHERST DR 43302
John Shank, prin.
Fair Park ES, 980 ROBINSON ST 43302
Robert Alexander, prin.
Glenwood ES, 317 LATOURETTE ST 43302
David White, prin.
Indian Mound ES, 625 BRIGHTWOOD DR 43302
Glen Gerber, prin.
Mark Street ES, 412 E MARK ST 43302
Rodney Banks, prin.
Oak Street ES, 565 OAK ST 43302
Michael Todd, prin.
Oakland ES, 765 UNCAPNER AVE 43302
Judy Aubry, prin.
Olney ES, 575 OLNEY AVE 43302
Terry Conley, prin.
Pearl Street ES, 436 PEARL ST 43302
Roger George, prin.
Silver Street ES, 750 SILVER ST 43302
Thomas Pannett, prin.
Washington ES, 300 PENNSYLVANIA AVE 43302
Jean Zoeller, prin.

Pleasant Local SD
Sch. Sys. Enr. Code 4
Supt. – C. Richard Arndt
3541 SMETZER ROAD 43302
Pleasant MS, 3507 SMELTZER ROAD 43302
Michael Terry, prin.
Pleasant ES, 1105 OWENS RD W 43302
Bruce Gast, prin.

Ridgedale Local SD
Supt. – See Morral
Grand Prairie ES
577 MARSEILLES-GALION RD 43302
Homer Comer, prin.

River Valley Local SD
Sch. Sys. Enr. Code 4
Supt. – David Kirkton
1239 COLS-SANDUSKY ROAD N 43302
River Valley MS
1190 COLS-SANDUSKY ROAD N 43302
Charles Osborne, prin.

Other Schools – See Caledonia, Waldo

Marion Christian ES
131 MARION-CARDINGTON RD E 43302
St. Mary ES, 274 N PROSPECT ST 43302

Mark Center, Defiance Co.
Central Local SD
Supt. – See Sherwood
Mark ES, P O BOX 30 43536
David Stallkamp, prin.

Marshallville, Wayne Co., Pop. Code 3
Green Local SD
Supt. – See Smithville
ES, CHESTNUT ST 44645
Edward Krahenbuhl, prin.

Martins Ferry, Belmont Co., Pop. Code 6
Martins Ferry CSD
Sch. Sys. Enr. Code 4
Supt. – William Parrett, 631 HANOVER ST 43935
South MS, BROADWAY & SCHOOL STS 43935
William Pratt, prin.
Elm ES, EUCLID ST 43935 – John Myers, prin.
North ES, ZANE & CENTER 43935
Nick Stankovich, prin.
Steeple Valley MS, 3105 COLERAIN PIKE 43935
Anthony Collette, prin.
Other Schools – See Dillonvale

St. Mary Central ES, 24 N 4TH ST 43935

Martinsville, Clinton Co., Pop. Code 3
Wilmington CSD
Supt. – See Wilmington
Holmes ES, STATE RT 730 45177
Willard Allen, prin.
Martinsville ES, CEMETERY RD 45146
Samuel Lewis, prin.

Marysville, Union Co., Pop. Code 6
Marysville EVD
Sch. Sys. Enr. Code 5
Supt. – Gary Meier, 1000 EDGEWOOD DR 43040
MS, 233 W 6TH ST 43040 – M. Sweeney, prin.
East ES, 6TH & CHESTNUT 43040
Karen Warner, prin.
Edgewood ES, 205 GROVE ST 43040
Greg Casto, prin.
Other Schools – See Raymond

St. John Lutheran ES
12741 STATE ROUTE 736 43040
Trinity Lutheran ES, 220 S WALNUT ST 43040

Mason, Warren Co., Pop. Code 6
Mason Local SD
Sch. Sys. Enr. Code 4
Supt. – David Lewis
200 NORTHCREST DRIVE 45040
MS, 211 N EAST ST 45040 – Dan Mooney, prin.
Mason Heights ES, 200 NORTHCREST DR 45040
Imogene Gilbert, prin.
Western Row MS, 755 WESTERN ROW RD 45040
Phyllis Bare, prin.

St. Susanna ES, 500 READING RD 45040

Massillon, Stark Co., Pop. Code 8
Jackson Local SD
Sch. Sys. Enr. Code 5
Supt. – Joe Larson
7984 FULTON DRIVE NW 44646
Jackson Memorial MS
7355 MUDBROOK ROAD NW 44646
Robert Glassburn, prin.
Amherst ES, 8750 JANE ST NW 44646
Joanne Mascaro, prin.
Sauder ES, 7503 MUDBROOK RD NW 44646
Forrest Westfall, prin.
Other Schools – See Canton

Massillon CSD
Sch. Sys. Enr. Code 5
Supt. – Alexander Paris
22 FEDERAL AVE NE 44646
Bowers ES, 1041-32ND NW 44646
Antonio Vincente, prin.
Emerson ES, 724 WALNUT RD SW 44646
Jack Peterson, prin.
Franklin ES, 1237 16TH ST SW 44646
Jeffery Thornberry, prin.
Gorrell ES, 2420 SCHULER AVE NW 44646
Russell Ramsey, prin.
Smith ES, 930 17TH ST NE 44646
Shirley Harper, prin.
Whittier ES, 1212 10TH ST NE 44646
Joseph Ehret, prin.
York ES, 2219 MASSACHUSETTS AVE SE 44646
Robert Otte, prin.

Perry Local SD
Sch. Sys. Enr. Code 6
Supt. – Gene Feucht, 4201 HARSH AVE SE 44646
Genoa ES, 519 GENOA ROAD 44646
Juanita Tietze, prin.
Pfeiffer MS, 4315 13TH ST SW 44646
Kenneth Hartwick, prin.
Watson ES, 515 MARION AVE NW 44646
Irene Splittorf, prin.
Other Schools – See Canton, Navarre

Tuslaw Local SD
Sch. Sys. Enr. Code 4
Supt. – Scott Romans
1723 MANCHESTER AVE NW 44646
Beech Grove ES
1548 MANMCHESTER AVE NW 44646
Jeffrey Thornberry, prin.
Moffitt Heights ES, 12035 MOFFITT ST SW 44646
Harry Chaplin, prin.
Newman ES, 11881 ORRVILLE ST NW 44646
Jeffrey Thornberry, prin.

Massillon Christian School
965 OVERLOOK AVE SW 44646
St. Barbara ES, 2825 LINCOLN WAY NW 44646
St. Mary ES, 726 1ST ST NE 44646

Masury, Trumbull Co., Pop. Code 6
Brookfield Local SD
Supt. – See Brookfield
Addison MS, 900 JUDSON RD 44438
John Young, prin.
Curtis ES, 832 N STATELINE RD 44438
Vincent Scoccia, prin.
Stevenson ES, 1144 BROADWAY ST 44438
Vincent Scoccia, prin.

Maumee, Lucas Co., Pop. Code 7
Maumee CSD
Sch. Sys. Enr. Code 5
Supt. – David Abbott, 2345 DETROIT AVE 43537
Fairfield ES, 1313 EASTFIELD DR 43537
Carol Mattews, prin.
Fort Miami ES, 716 ASKIN ST 43537
Randal Euckert, prin.
Union ES, CONANT & BROADWAY 43537
Kenneth Kwiatkowski, prin.
Wayne Trail ES, 1147 7TH ST 43537
David Amstutz, prin.

St. Joseph ES, 112 W BROADWAY ST 43537

Mayfield, Cuyahoga Co., Pop. Code 5
Mayfield CSD
Sch. Sys. Enr. Code 5
Supt. – Robert Stabile
784 SOM CENTER ROAD 44143
Other Schools – See Cleveland, Gates Mills, Highland
Heights, Mayfield Heights

Mayfield Heights, Cuyahoga Co., Pop. Code 7
Mayfield CSD
Supt. – See Mayfield
Lander ES, 1714 LANDER RD 44124
Donna Stovall, prin.

Mechanicsburg, Champaign Co., Pop. Code 4
Mechanicsburg EVD
Sch. Sys. Enr. Code 4
Supt. – Mark Gagyi, 60 HIGH ST 43044
Wilson ES, 60 HIGH ST 43044
Carol Daniels, prin.

Mechanicstown, Carroll Co.
Carrollton EVD
Supt. – See Carrollton
Willis ES, 8156 SALINEVILLE RD NE 44651
Debra Scott, prin.

Medina, Medina Co., Pop. Code 7
Buckeye Local SD
Sch. Sys. Enr. Code 4
Supt. – James Boyes
6695 NORWALK ROAD 44256
Buckeye MS, 3024 COLUMBIA ROAD 44256
Kim Meyer, prin.
York ES, 6695 NORWALK RD 44256
(—), prin.
Other Schools – See Litchfield, Valley City

Cloverleaf Local SD
Supt. – See Lodi
Lafayette ES, 6357 LAFAYETTE RD 44256
Timothy Burns, prin.

Highland Local SD
Sch. Sys. Enr. Code 4
Supt. – Robert Dunnerstick
3880 RIDGE ROAD 44256
Highland MS, 3940 RIDGE ROAD 44256
Nick Valentine, prin.
Other Schools – See Hinckley, Sharon Center

Medina CSD
Sch. Sys. Enr. Code 5
Supt. – Robert Fenn, P O BOX 408 44258
Medina Claggett JHS, 420 E UNION ST 44256
Thomas McKenna, prin.
Canavan ES, 825 LAWRENCE DR 44256
Curtis Kennedy,Jr., prin.
Fenn ES, 320 N SPRING GROVE ST 44256
Thomas Lehrer, prin.
Garfield ES, 234 S BROADWAY ST 44256
Joseph Hradek, prin.
Heritage ES, 833 GUILFORD BLVD 44256
Wesley Florian, prin.

First Baptist Christian ES
3646 MEDINA RD 44256
St. Francis Xavier ES
612 E WASHINGTON ST 44256

Medway, Clark Co., Pop. Code 4
New Carlisle-Bethel Local SD
Supt. – See New Carlisle
ES, 116 MIDDLE ST 45341 – Bill Back, prin.

Melmore, Seneca Co.
Mohawk Local SD
Supt. – See Sycamore
ES, P O BOX 69 44845 – Ronald Ruffing, prin.

Mendon, Mercer Co., Pop. Code 3
Mendon Union Local SD
Sch. Sys. Enr. Code 2
Supt. – Tucker Self, P O BOX 98 45862
Mendon-Union ES, P O BOX 98 45862
J. Schacht, prin.

Mentor, Lake Co., Pop. Code 8
Mentor EVD
Sch. Sys. Enr. Code 7
Supt. – Joseph Lesak, 6451 CENTER ST 44060
Bellflower ES, 6655 REYNOLDS RD 44060
Samuel Spinelli, prin.
Brentmoor ES
7671 JOHNNYCAKE RIDGE RD 44060
George Jaroscak, prin.
Center Street Village ES, 7482 CENTER ST 44060
Barbara Davis, prin.
Fairfax ES, 6465 CURTISS CT 44060
Gayle Cramer, prin.
Garfield ES, 7090 HOPKINS RD 44060
Kenneth Buckley, prin.
Headlands ES, 5028 FOREST RD 44060
Richard Kratche, prin.
Hopkins ES, 7565 HOPKINS RD 44060
Kathleen Bonnes, prin.
Morton ES, 9292 JORDAN DR 44060
Judyth Ulis, prin.
Orchard Hollow ES, 8700 HENDRICKS RD 44060
John Grund, prin.
Reynolds ES, 6176 REYNOLDS RD 44060
Thomas Doddridge, prin.
Rice ES, 7640 LAKE SHORE BLVD 44060
Carol Hoffman, prin.
Other Schools – See Mentor on the Lake

Lake Catholic ES, 6733 REYNOLDS RD 44060
St. Gabriel ES
9935 JOHNNYCAKE RIDGE RD 44060
St. Mary ES, 8540 MENTOR AVE 44060

Mentor on the Lake, Lake Co., Pop. Code 6
Mentor EVD
Supt. – See Mentor
Lake ES, 7625 PINEHURST DR 44060
Robert Archer, prin.

Mesopotamia, Trumbull Co.
Bloomfield-Mespo Local SD
Supt. – See North Bloomfield
ES, 4466 KINSMAN RD NW 44439
Charles Klamer, prin.

Metamora, Fulton Co., Pop. Code 3
Evergreen Local SD
Sch. Sys. Enr. Code 4
Supt. – Russell Griggs, P O BOX H 43540
Evergreen MS, 310 SWANTON ST 43540
Shirley Herlihy, prin.
Other Schools – See Lyons, Swanton

Miamisburg, Montgomery Co., Pop. Code 7
Miamisburg CSD
Sch. Sys. Enr. Code 5
Supt. – Gary Branson, 6TH & PARK AVE 45342
Wantz MS, 115 S 7TH ST 45342
David Wood, prin.
Bear ES, 545 SCHOOL ST 45342
Ruth Kimmet, prin.
Kinder ES, 536 E CENTRAL AVE 45342
Thomas Nicholas, prin.
Mound ES, 1108 RANGE AVE 45342
Jack Bartley, prin.
Twain ES, 822 N NINTH ST 45342
Jane Chance, prin.
Other Schools – See Dayton

Bishop Leibold School, 24 S THIRD WEST 45342

Miamitown, Hamilton Co., Pop. Code 3
Southwest Local SD
Supt. – See Harrison
ES, STATE AND MILL ST 45041
Carter Cordes, prin.

Middleburg Heights, Cuyahoga Co., Pop. Code 7
Berea CSD
Supt. – See Berea
Big Creek ES, 7247 BIG CREEK PKY 44130
Thomas Jones, prin.

St. Bartholomew ES, 14873 BAGLEY RD 44130

Middlefield, Geauga Co., Pop. Code 4
Cardinal Local SD
Sch. Sys. Enr. Code 4
Supt. – Norman Sommers, P O BOX 188 44062
Cardinal MS, S ELM ST 44062
Thomas Moss, prin.
Jordak ES, P O BOX 188 44062
Malcolm Garrett, prin.
Other Schools – See Huntsburg, Parkman

Middle Point, Van Wert Co., Pop. Code 3
Lincolnview Local SD
Supt. – See Van Wert
Lincolnview East ES 45863 – William Kelly, prin.

Middleport, Meigs Co., Pop. Code 5
Meigs Local SD
Sch. Sys. Enr. Code 5
Supt. – James Carpenter, 621 S 3RD AVE 45760

Meigs MS, 621 S 3RD AVE 45760
John Mora, prin.
Bradbury MS, 39105 BRADBURY RD 45760
Donald Hanning, prin.
ES, 659 PEARL ST 45760 – Donald Hanning, prin.
Other Schools – See Langsville, Pomeroy, Rutland

Middletown, Butler Co., Pop. Code 8
Lakota Local SD
Supt. – See West Chester
Liberty MS, 7055 DUTCHLAND PARKWAY 45044
Larry Glass, prin.

Madison Local SD
Sch. Sys. Enr. Code 4
Supt. – Charles Berny, 601 HILL ST 45042
Madison MS
1380 MIDDLETOWN EATON ROAD 45042
Ed Rudder, prin.
Poasttown ES
6600 TRENTON FRANKLIN RD 45042
Walker Williamson, prin.

Middletown CSD
Sch. Sys. Enr. Code 6
Supt. – Harry Eastridge, 1515 GIRARD AVE 45044
Vail MS, 1415 GIRARD AVE 45044
Thelma Hacker, prin.
Verity MS, 1900 JOHNS ROAD 45044
Larry Knapp, prin.
Amanda ES, 1215 OXFORD STATE RD 45044
Stephen Wolf, prin.
Creekview ES, 301 LORETTA ST 45044
John Shepard, prin.
Jefferson ES, 800 CHARLES ST 45042
Richard Gehm, prin.
Mayfield ES, 3325 BURBANK AVE 45044
Jesse Wilson, prin.
McKinley MS, 1210 S VERITY PKY 45044
Alan Spears, prin.
Oneida ES, 2901 YANKEE RD 45044
Carel Cosby,Jr., prin.
Roosevelt ES, 2701 CENTRAL AVE 45044
Donna Noggle, prin.
Rosedale ES, 4601 SOPHIE AVE 45042
John Petrocy, prin.
Taft ES, 1036 S VERITY PKY 45044
Sandra Locher, prin.
Wildwood ES, 3300 WILDWOOD RD 45042
Ronald Gadd, prin.
Wilson ES, 106 S HIGHVIEW RD 45044
Yvonne Hickman, prin.
Other Schools – See Monroe

Middletown Christian School
3023 N UNION ROAD 45042
John XXIII ES, 24 BALTIMORE ST 45044

Midland, Clinton Co., Pop. Code 2
Blanchester Local SD
Supt. – See Blanchester
Jefferson ES, STATE ROUTE 68 45148
Rick Burton, prin.

Midvale, Tuscarawas Co., Pop. Code 3
Indian Valley Local SD
Supt. – See Gnadenhutten
ES, P O BOX 246 44653 – Jack Campbell, prin.

Milan, Erie Co., Pop. Code 4
Berlin-Milan Local SD
Sch. Sys. Enr. Code 4
Supt. – Don Gfell, 140 MAIN ST S 44846
ES, 140 MAIN ST S 44846
Jeanine Williams, prin.
Other Schools – See Berlin Heights

Milford, Clermont Co., Pop. Code 6
Milford EVD
Sch. Sys. Enr. Code 6
Supt. – Bruce Jones, 525 LILA AVE 45150
Miami ES, 1039 GOSHEN PIKE 45150
Robin Zeuch, prin.
Milford Main MS, MAIN & LILA 45150
Harold Herron, prin.
Milford South ES, 777 GARFIELD AVE 45150
Joyce Richardson, prin.
Pleasant Hill ES, 5684 CROMLEY DR 45150
Charles Seipelt, prin.
Smith ES, 1052 JER-LES DR 45150
Alton Ison, prin.
Other Schools – See Cincinnati

St. Andrew ES, 555 MAIN ST 45150
St. Elizabeth Seton ES
5900 BUCKWHEAT RD 45150

Milford Center, Union Co., Pop. Code 3
Fairbanks Local SD
Sch. Sys. Enr. Code 3
Supt. – Stephen Weller
1158 STATE ROUTE 38 43045
Fairbanks MS, 1158 STATE ROUTE 38 43045
Jeff Squires, prin.
Fairbanks ES, MILFORD CENTER 43045
Mark Lotycz, prin.

Millbury, Wood Co., Pop. Code 3
Lake Local SD
Sch. Sys. Enr. Code 4
Supt. – Robert Walter, 28025 MAIN ST 43447
Lake JHS, 28100 LEMOYNE ROAD 43447
Carl Brubaker, prin.
Lake ES, 28150 LEMOYNE RD 43447
Thomas Mangold, prin.

ES, 28025 MAIN ST 43447 – Margaret West, prin.
Other Schools – See Walbridge

Miller City, Putnam Co., Pop. Code 2
Miller City-New Cleveland Local SD
Sch. Sys. Enr. Code 3
Supt. – William Kreinbrink, P O BOX 38 45864
ES, P O BOX 38 45864 – William Kreinbrink, prin.
Other Schools – See Ottawa

Millersburg, Holmes Co., Pop. Code 5
West Holmes Local SD
Sch. Sys. Enr. Code 5
Supt. – Dean Werstler, RURAL ROUTE 01 44654
West Holmes MS, 10 E JACKSON ST 44654
 Gary Gehm, prin.
Clark ES, 1390 ST RTE 83 RUR RT 03 44654
 Roger Saurer, prin.
ES, 219 E JACKSON ST 44654
 Robert Hoover, prin.
Other Schools – See Killbuck, Lakeville, Nashville

Millersport, Fairfield Co., Pop. Code 3
Walnut Township Local SD
Sch. Sys. Enr. Code 3
Supt. – Carl Berg, P O BOX 278 43046
ES, P O BOX 278 43046 – Barry Coleman, prin.

Mineral City, Tuscarawas Co., Pop. Code 3
Tuscarawas Valley Local SD
Supt. – See Zoarville
ES, P O BOX 428 44656 – Arline Mase, prin.
New Cumberland ES, RURAL ROUTE 01 44656
 Arline Mase, prin.

Mineral Ridge, Trumbull Co., Pop. Code 4
Weathersfield Local SD
Sch. Sys. Enr. Code 4
Supt. – Richard Murray, 3750 MAIN ST 44440
Seaborn ES, 3800 NILES CARVER RD 44440
 Cynthia Malgrew, prin.

Minerva, Stark Co., Pop. Code 2
Minerva Local SD
Sch. Sys. Enr. Code 5
Supt. – Robert Akenhead, 303 LATZER AVE 44657
Hazen MS, 401 N MARKET ST 44657
 Douglas Birks, prin.
Day ES, 130 BONNIEVIEW AVE 44657
 Donald Cassidy, prin.
Other Schools – See East Rochester, Robertsville

Minford, Scioto Co.
Minford Local SD
Sch. Sys. Enr. Code 4
Supt. – Dennis Meade, P O BOX 204 45653
MS, P O BOX 204 45653 – Jerry Ruark, prin.
ES, P O BOX 204 45653 – Timothy Allen, prin.

Mingo Junction, Jefferson Co., Pop. Code 5
Buckeye Local SD
Supt. – See Rayland
New Alexandria ES, ROAD 1 43938
 Alan Zerla, prin.

Indian Creek Local SD
Sch. Sys. Enr. Code 5
Supt. – Joseph Aguiar, 707 WILSON AVE 43938
Hills ES, 707 WILSON AVE 43938
 Sarah McCray, prin.
Other Schools – See Bloomingdale, Wintersville

St. Agnes ES, 212 MURDOCK ST 43938

Minster, Auglaize Co., Pop. Code 5
Minster Local SD
Sch. Sys. Enr. Code 3
Supt. – Halver Belcher
 RURAL ROUTE 01 BOX 175 45865
ES, 86 N HANOVER ST 45865
 Larry Prenger, prin.

Mogadore, Summit Co., Pop. Code 5
Field Local SD
Sch. Sys. Enr. Code 5
Supt. – Thomas Shoup, 1473 SAXE ROAD 44260
Suffield ES, 1128 WATERLOO RD 44260
 Paul Welch, prin.
Other Schools – See Kent

Mogadore Local SD
Sch. Sys. Enr. Code 3
Supt. – R. Larry Stucky
 144 S CLEVELAND AVE 44260
Somers ES, 3600 HERBERT ST 44260
 James Irvin, prin.

St. Joseph ES, 2617 WATERLOO RD 44260

Monclova, Lucas Co.
Anthony Wayne Local SD
Supt. – See Whitehouse
ES, MONCLOVA RD 43542
 Kenneth Machcinski, prin.

Monroe, Warren Co., Pop. Code 5
Middletown CSD
Supt. – See Middletown
ES, 225 MACREADY AVE 45050
 Charles Edwards, prin.

Monroeville, Huron Co., Pop. Code 4
Monroeville Local SD
Sch. Sys. Enr. Code 3
Supt. – Shirley Long, 101 WEST ST 44847
ES, 101 WEST ST 44847 – Sandra Zitner, prin.

Willard CSD
Supt. – See Willard

Greenfield ES, 2634 STATE ROUTE 162 44847
 Gerald Janosko, prin.

St. Joseph ES, 79 CHAPEL ST 44847

Montpelier, Williams Co., Pop. Code 5
Montpelier EVD
Sch. Sys. Enr. Code 4
Supt. – Charles Koch, 110 N EAST AVE 43543
Superior MS, RURAL ROUTE 03 43543
 Stephen Held, prin.
ES, N PLATT ST 43543 – Michael Pressler, prin.

Moraine, Montgomery Co., Pop. Code 6
Kettering CSD
Supt. – See Kettering
Meadows ES, 2600 HOLMAN ST 45439
 Richard Harter, prin.

Morral, Marion Co., Pop. Code 2
Ridgedale Local SD
Sch. Sys. Enr. Code 4
Supt. – Anthony Kazee
 3105 HILLMAN FORD ROAD 43337
Ridgedale MS
 3105 HILLMAN-FORD ROAD 43337
 Tom Crowe, prin.
MS, 175 NEFF ST 43337 – Charles Crisler, prin.
Other Schools – See Marion

Morristown, Belmont Co., Pop. Code 2
Union Local SD
Supt. – See Belmont
ES, P O BOX 1 43759 – Robert Laipple, prin.

Morrow, Warren Co., Pop. Code 4
Little Miami Local SD
Sch. Sys. Enr. Code 5
Supt. – Fred Williams
 5819 MORROW-ROSSBURG ROAD 45152
Little Miami JHS, 605 WELCH RD 45152
 Thomas Moffitt, prin.
ES, 10 MIRANDA ST 45152
 Kenneth Oliver, prin.
Other Schools – See Blanchester, Maineville

Mount Blanchard, Hardin Co., Pop. Code 2
Riverdale Local SD
Sch. Sys. Enr. Code 4
Supt. – John Roettger, 20613 STATE RT 37 45867
ES 45867 – Jeffrey Snook, prin.
Other Schools – See Forest, Wharton

Mount Eaton, Wayne Co., Pop. Code 2
Southeast Local SD
Supt. – See Apple Creek
ES, P O BOX 268 44659 – Bernard Comito, prin.

Mount Gilead, Morrow Co., Pop. Code 5
Mt. Gilead EVD
Sch. Sys. Enr. Code 4
Supt. – Paul Pendleton, P O BOX 239 43338
JHS, 145 N CHERRY ST 43338
 Steven Selvey, prin.
ES, 145 N CHERRY ST 43338 – Daniel Sipek, prin.
PS, 338 W PARK AVE 43338 – Daniel Sipek, prin.
Other Schools – See Edison

Mount Healthy, Hamilton Co., Pop. Code 6

Assumption ES, 1500 MCMAKIN AVE 45231

Mount Hope, Holmes Co.
East Holmes Local SD
Supt. – See Berlin
ES, P O BOX 74 44660 – Bruce Stambaugh, prin.

Mount Orab, Brown Co., Pop. Code 4
Western Brown Local SD
Sch. Sys. Enr. Code 4
Supt. – Robert Neu, P O BOX F 45154
ES, P O BOX E 45154 – Sherrill Callahan, prin.
Other Schools – See Hamersville

Mount Sterling, Madison Co., Pop. Code 4
Madison-Plains Local SD
Supt. – See London
ES, 94 W MAIN ST 43143 – Walter Brown, prin.

Miami Trace Local SD
Supt. – See Washington Court House
Madison Mills ES, 10346 HARRISON RD 43143
 Mary Spengler, prin.

Westfall Local SD
Supt. – See Williamsport
Monroe ES, 12364 ST RT 56 W 43143
 Lowell Anderson, prin.

Mount Vernon, Knox Co., Pop. Code 7
Mt. Vernon CSD
Sch. Sys. Enr. Code 5
Supt. – David Olsen, 105 E CHESTNUT ST 43050
MS, 301-5 N MULBERRY ST 43050
 Dinzle Brown, prin.
Columbia ES, 150 COLUMBUS RD 43050
 Robert Wells, prin.
East ES, 714 E VINE ST 43050
 Donald Garvic, prin.
Elmwood ES, 300 NEWARK RD 43050
 Kenneth Rhoades, prin.
Emmett ES, 108 MANSFIELD AVE 43050
 Sandra Chambers, prin.
Pleasant Street ES, 305 E PLEASANT ST 43050
 Jeffrey Kuntz, prin.
West ES, 900 W VINE ST 43050
 Pauline Riel, prin.
Other Schools – See Gambier

St. Vincent De Paul ES, 206 E CHESNUT ST 43050

Mount Victory, Hardin Co., Pop. Code 3
Ridgemont Local SD
Sch. Sys. Enr. Code 3
Supt. – Richard McGarvey, W TAYLOR ST 43340
Ridgemont ES, W TAYLOR 43340
 Ronald Hull, prin.

Mowrystown, Highland Co., Pop. Code 2
Bright Local SD
Sch. Sys. Enr. Code 3
Supt. – James Evilsizer, P O BOX 9 45155
Other Schools – See Hillsboro

Moxahala, Perry Co.
Southern Local SD
Supt. – See Hemlock
ES 43761 – Ned Gohring, prin.

Munroe Falls, Summit Co., Pop. Code 5
Stow CSD
Supt. – See Stow
Kimpton MS, 380 N RIVER ROAD 44262
 Edward Vandenbulke, prin.
Riverview ES, 240 N RIVER RD 44262
 Dan Nichols, prin.

Nankin, Ashland Co.
Mapleton Local SD
Supt. – See Ashland
ES 44848 – Daniel Ashbaugh, prin.

Napoleon, Henry Co., Pop. Code 6
Napoleon CSD
Sch. Sys. Enr. Code 4
Supt. – James Bernicke
 701 BRIARHEATH AVE 43545
Central MS, 303 W MAIN ST 43545
 Thomas Condit, prin.
Brillhart ES, ROHRS ST 43545
 Harold Jennings, prin.
Central ES, 315 W MAIN ST 43545
 Thomas Jenny, prin.
West ES, CLAIRMONT ST 43545
 Gary Ritchey, prin.

St. Augustine ES
 MONROE & E CLINTON STS 43545
St. John Lutheran School, 16-035 ROAD U 43545
St. Paul Lutheran ES
 1075 GLENWOOD AVE 43545

Nashport, Muskingum Co.
Licking Valley Local SD
Supt. – See Newark
Perry ES, 4661 LICKING VALLEY RD SE 43830
 Doug Anders, prin.

Tri-Valley Local SD
Supt. – See Dresden
ES, 6260 NEWARK RD 43830
 James McKee, prin.

Nashville, Holmes Co., Pop. Code 2
West Holmes Local SD
Supt. – See Millersburg
ES, ST 39 P O BOX 400 44661
 Joseph Wengerd, prin.

Navarre, Stark Co., Pop. Code 4
Fairless Local SD
Sch. Sys. Enr. Code 4
Supt. – Fred Blosser
 11885 NAVARRE ROAD SW 44662
Justus MS, 11836 NAVARRE ROAD SW 44662
 C. Fogle, prin.
ES, 148 MAIN ST N 44662 – Paul Warinner, prin.
Other Schools – See Beach City, Brewster

Perry Local SD
Supt. – See Massillon
Lohr ES, 5300 RICHVILLE DR SW 44662
 Chris McBurney, prin.
Richville ES, 6344 NAVARRE RD SW 44662
 Chris McBurney, prin.

St. Clement ES, 402 MARKET ST NE 44662

Neffs, Belmont Co.
Bellaire CSD
Supt. – See Bellaire
ES, 53299 PIKE ST 43940
 Lawrence Marinelli, prin.

Nelsonville, Athens Co., Pop. Code 5
Nelsonville-York CSD
Sch. Sys. Enr. Code 4
Supt. – Jacalyn Osborne, RURAL ROUTE 01 45764
Nelsonville-York MS, 189 FAYETTE ST 45764
 John Anderson, prin.
ES, PINEGROVE DR 45764
 Edward Swanson, prin.
Poston ES, RURAL ROUTE 01 45764
 Virginia Hedges, prin.
York ES, RURAL ROUTE 01 45764
 Virginia Hedges, prin.

Nevada, Wyandot Co., Pop. Code 3
Wynford Local SD
Supt. – See Bucyrus
Wynford South ES 44849 – Joy Kear, prin.

New Albany, Franklin Co., Pop. Code 2
Plain Local SD
Sch. Sys. Enr. Code 3
Supt. – Jack Porter
 6425 NEW ALBANY-CONDIT ROAD   43054
MS, 6425 NEW ALBANY-CONDIT ROAD   43054
 Vernon Fawcett, prin.
ES, 6425 NEW ALBANY-CONDIT RD   43054
 Shirley Latshaw, prin.

Newark, Licking Co., Pop. Code 8
Licking Valley Local SD
Sch. Sys. Enr. Code 4
Supt. – Donald Urban
 1379 LICKING VALLEY ROAD NE   43055
Licking Valley MS
 1379 LICKING VALLEY ROAD NE   43055
 Robert Tharp, prin.
Madison ES, 11037 MARNE RD NERD NE   43055
 Sue Smith, prin.
Mary Ann ES, 11152 WILKINS RUN RD NE   43055
 Ronald Walsh, prin.
Toboso ES, 2345 TOBOSO RD SE   43055
 William Weaver, prin.
Other Schools – See Nashport

Newark CSD
Sch. Sys. Enr. Code 6
Supt. – Robert Hite, E MAIN & 1ST ST   43055
Lincoln MS, 471 E MAIN ST   43055
 Raymond Kress, prin.
Roosevelt MS
 621 MOUNT VERNON ROAD   43055
 James O'Connor, prin.
Wilson MS, 805 W CHURCH ST   43055
 George Evans, prin.
Central IS, 116 W CHURCH ST   43055
 William Leedale, prin.
Central PS, 112 W MAIN ST   43055
 Gary Brown, prin.
Cherry Valley ES, 1040 W MAIN ST   43055
 Bill Booth, prin.
Clem ES, JEFFERSON ROAD   43055
 Barbara Heisel, prin.
Conrad ES, EVERETT AVE & ROSEHILL   43055
 Iris Wilson, prin.
Franklin ES, 533 BEACON RD   43055
 James Hoover, prin.
Hazelwood ES, 50 OBANNON AVE   43055
 Roger Abshire, prin.
Kettering ES, 599 ARLINGTON AVE   43055
 Sheila Hiles, prin.
Maholm ES, 96 MAHOLM ST   43055
 Sally Hannahs, prin.
McGuffey ES, N 24TH ST   43055 – Janet Barr, prin.
Miller ES, COUNTRY CLUB DR   43055
 Maria Duttera, prin.
North ES, DEO DRIVE   43055
 Stanley Kaiser, prin.

North Fork Local SD
Supt. – See Utica
Newton ES, 6645 MOUNT VERNON RD NE   43055
 Clarence Conley, prin.

Blessed Sacrament ES, 15 PENNY AVE   43055
St. Francis De Sales ES, 38 GRANVILLE ST   43055

New Boston, Scioto Co., Pop. Code 5
New Boston Local SD
Sch. Sys. Enr. Code 3
Supt. – Lowell Howard
 522 GLENWOOD AVE   45662
Oak IS, 824 HARRISONVILLE AVE   45662
 James Warren,Jr., prin.
Stanton PS, OHIO AVE   45662
 James Warren,Jr., prin.

New Bremen, Auglaize Co., Pop. Code 4
New Bremen Local SD
Sch. Sys. Enr. Code 3
Supt. – R. Stauffer, 202 S WALNUT ST   45869
ES, 202-210 S WALNUT ST   45869
 Trudy Kuenning, prin.

Newbury, Geauga Co.
Newbury Local SD
Sch. Sys. Enr. Code 3
Supt. – Robert Faehnle
 14775 AUBURN ROAD   44065
ES, 14775 AUBURN ROAD   44065
 Laurie Mental, prin.

St. Helen ES, 12060 KINSMAN RD   44065

New Carlisle, Clark Co., Pop. Code 6
New Carlisle-Bethel Local SD
Sch. Sys. Enr. Code 5
Supt. – Boyd Marcum
 9760 W NATIONAL ROAD   45344
MS, 1203 KENNISON AVE   45344
 Robert Coffield, prin.
Olive Branch MS
 9712 W NATIONAL ROAD   45344
 Peter Dedominici, prin.
Park Layne ES, 620 CLIFFSIDE DR   45344
 Walter Brown, prin.
Westlake ES, 621 WALSH DR   45344
 Matthew Curtis, prin.
Other Schools – See Donnelsville, Medway

Newcomerstown, Tuscarawas Co., Pop. Code 5
Newcomerstown EVD
Sch. Sys. Enr. Code 4
Supt. – Gary Sterrett, 702 S RIVER ST   43832
MS, RIVER ST   43832 – Daniel Murray, prin.

East ES, 137 S COLLEGE ST   43832
 James Overholt, prin.
West MS, 517 BEAVER ST   43832
 James Overholt, prin.

New Concord, Muskingum Co., Pop. Code 4
East Muskingum Local SD
Sch. Sys. Enr. Code 4
Supt. – James Mahoney
 13505 JOHN GLENN SCH ROAD   43762
East Muskingum MS
 13125 JOHN GLENN SCH ROAD   43762
 John Hazard, prin.
ES, 4 STORMONT ST   43762 – Don Burch, prin.
Other Schools – See Cambridge, Zanesville

New Haven, Huron Co.
Willard CSD
Supt. – See Willard
New Haven ES, PO BOX 176   44850
 Neil Lydy, prin.

New Holland, Pickaway Co., Pop. Code 3
Miami Trace Local SD
Supt. – See Washington Court House
ES, 110 S MAIN ST   43145
 Ronald Grottendick, prin.

New Knoxville, Auglaize Co., Pop. Code 3
New Knoxville Local SD
Sch. Sys. Enr. Code 2
Supt. – Martin Rehmert, 345 S MAIN ST   45871
ES, 345 S MAIN ST   45871 – Annett Kuck, prin.

New Lebanon, Montgomery Co., Pop. Code 5
New Lebanon Local SD
Sch. Sys. Enr. Code 4
Supt. – Milton Arter, 1105 W MAIN ST   45345
MS, 1100 W MAIN ST   45345
 Dale Thompson, prin.
ES, 1150 W MAIN ST   45345
 Dale Thompson, prin.

New Lexington, Perry Co., Pop. Code 6
New Lexington CSD
Sch. Sys. Enr. Code 4
Supt. – William King, 310 FIRST ST   43764
ES, 310 FIRST ST   43764 – Richard Eberts, prin.
Other Schools – See Junction City

St. Rose ES, WATER & HIGH ST   43764

New London, Huron Co., Pop. Code 4
New London Local SD
Sch. Sys. Enr. Code 4
Supt. – Stephen Schumm, 100 E MAIN ST   44851
Fitchville MS, 17 PARK AVE   44851
 Joseph Sexton, prin.
ES, 17 PARK AVE   44851 – Roger Knight, prin.

New Madison, Darke Co., Pop. Code 4
Tri-Village Local SD
Sch. Sys. Enr. Code 3
Supt. – Elmer Hinkle, S MAIN ST   45346
Other Schools – See Hollansburg, Palestine

New Marshfield, Athens Co.
Alexander Local SD
Supt. – See Albany
Waterloo ES   45766 – Robert Hoffman, prin.

New Matamoras, Washington Co., Pop. Code 3
Frontier Local SD
Sch. Sys. Enr. Code 4
Supt. – John Hoff, RURAL ROUTE 03   45767
Matamoras ES, P O BOX 338   45767
 Frank McCreery, prin.
Other Schools – See Marietta, Newport

New Middletown, Mahoning Co., Pop. Code 4
Springfield Local SD
Sch. Sys. Enr. Code 4
Supt. – L. David Ziegler
 11335 YOUNGSTWN-PITTSBRG RD   44442
Springfield IS
 11335 YOUNGSTWN-PITTSBRG RD   44442
 Leigh Klingensmith, prin.
New Middletown ES, 10580 MAIN ST   44442
 Gerald Kotchmar, prin.
Other Schools – See New Springfield

New Paris, Preble Co., Pop. Code 4
C. R. Coblentz Local SD
Sch. Sys. Enr. Code 4
Supt. – Dennis Curtin, 115 N SPRING ST   45347
Coblentz ES, 115 N SPRING ST   45347
 Michael Teufel, prin.
Other Schools – See West Manchester

New Philadelphia, Tuscarawas Co., Pop. Code 7
New Philadelphia CSD
Sch. Sys. Enr. Code 5
Supt. – Richard Gunmere
 248 FRONT AVE SW   44663
Welty MS, 315 4TH ST NW   44663
 Ted Gerber, prin.
Central ES, 145 RAY AVE NW   44663
 Karen Jenkins, prin.
East ES, 470 FAIR AVE NE   44663
 Richard Barker, prin.
South ES, 132 PROVIDENCE AVE SW   44663
 Lillian Devlin, prin.
Tuscarawas Avenue ES
 935 TUSCARAWAS AVE NW   44663
 Arline Smith, prin.
West ES, 232 TUSCARAWAS AVE NW   44663
 Hank Smith, prin.

York ES, RURAL ROUTE 02   44553
 David Branch, prin.

Sacred Heart ES, 320 FAIR AVE NE   44663

Newport, Washington Co.
Frontier Local SD
Supt. – See New Matamoras
ES, P O BOX 158   45768 – Michael Mason, prin.

New Richmond, Clermont Co., Pop. Code 5
New Richmond EVD
Sch. Sys. Enr. Code 5
Supt. – Jeffrey Sittason
 1139 BETHEL-NEW RICHMOND RD   45157
MS, 1135 BETHEL-NEW RICHMOND RD   45157
 Gregg Curless, prin.
Monroe ES, 2117 FRANKLIN-LAUREL RD   45157
 Carolyn McIntosh, prin.
ES, 1141 BETHEL-NEW RICHMOND RD   45157
 David Riel, prin.
Other Schools – See Cincinnati

New Riegel, Seneca Co., Pop. Code 2
New Riegel Local SD
Sch. Sys. Enr. Code 2
Supt. – Robert Brickner, P O BOX 126   44853
ES, P O BOX 126   44853 – Ronald Knopf, prin.

New Springfield, Mahoning Co.
Springfield Local SD
Supt. – See New Middletown
ES, 13900 GRANT ST   44443
 Gerald Kotchmar, prin.

New Straitsville, Perry Co., Pop. Code 3
Southern Local SD
Supt. – See Hemlock
ES, CLARK ST   43766 – Lucian Bennett,Jr., prin.

Newton Falls, Trumbull Co., Pop. Code 5
Labrae Local SD
Supt. – See Leavittsburg
Vaughn ES
 544 BRACEVILLE-ROBINSON NW   44444
 Patrick Gaia, prin.

Newton Falls EVD
Sch. Sys. Enr. Code 4
Supt. – Anthony D'Ambrosio
 909 1/2 MILTON BLVD   44444
JHS, 907 1/2 MILTON BLVD   44444
 Robert Force, prin.
Arlington ES, ARLINGTON ROAD   44444
 Sam Cappellino, prin.
Middle MS, RURAL ROUTE 01 BOX 909   44444
 Ronald Brown, prin.

Sts. Mary & Joseph ES, 709 MILTON BLVD   44444

New Vienna, Clinton Co., Pop. Code 4
East Clinton Local SD
Supt. – See Lees Creek
ES, 204 SECOND ST   45159
 Michael French, prin.

New Washington, Crawford Co., Pop. Code 4
Buckeye Central Local SD
Sch. Sys. Enr. Code 3
Supt. – John Hornsby, P O BOX 368   44854
Other Schools – See Chatfield, Tiro

St. Bernard ES, 320 E MANSFIELD ST   44854

New Waterford, Columbiana Co., Pop. Code 4
Crestview Local SD
Supt. – See Columbiana
Crestview ES, 46837 E STATE ST   44445
 Karen Barckert, prin.

Niles, Trumbull Co., Pop. Code 7
Niles CSD
Sch. Sys. Enr. Code 5
Supt. – John Bruno, 345 WARREN AVE   44446
Edison JHS, 36 W CHURCH ST   44446
 Barbara Weaver, prin.
Bonham ES, 120 E MARGARET AVE   44446
 Ignace Sebbio, prin.
Garfield ES, 101 W 3RD ST   44446
 John Vross, prin.
Jackson ES, 522 EMMA ST   44446
 Nick Bernard, prin.
Lincoln ES, 960 FREDERICK ST   44446
 Louie Tabor, prin.
Washington ES, 805 HARTZELL AVE   44446
 James Ford, prin.

Our Lady of Mt. Carmel ES
 309 N RHODES AVE   44446
St. Stephen ES, 45 S CHESTNUT AVE   44446

North Baltimore, Wood Co., Pop. Code 5
North Baltimore Local SD
Sch. Sys. Enr. Code 3
Supt. – Kenneth Cline, 110 S 2ND ST   45872
MS, 124 S 2ND ST   45872 – Gregory Hanson, prin.
Powell ES, 500 N MAIN ST   45872
 Donald King, prin.

North Bend, Hamilton Co., Pop. Code 3
Southwest Local SD
Supt. – See Harrison
Elizabethtown MS, RURAL ROUTE 01   45052
 Fritz Monroe, prin.

North Bloomfield, Trumbull Co.
Bloomfield-Mespo Local SD
Sch. Sys. Enr. Code 2
Supt. – Charles Klamer
   2077 PARK WEST ROAD   44450
Bloomfield MS, 2077 PARK WEST ROAD   44450
   Charles Klamer, prin.
Other Schools – See Mesopotamia

Maplewood Local SD
Supt. – See Cortland
Maplewood North ES
   1699 KINSMAN RD NE   44450
   Joseph Agresta, prin.

North Canton, Stark Co., Pop. Code 7
North Canton CSD
Sch. Sys. Enr. Code 5
Supt. – Robert Roden, 525 7TH ST NE   44720
MS, 200 CHARLOTTE ST NW   44720
   Mario Mattachione, prin.
Clearmount ES
   150 CLEARMOUNT AVE SE   44720
   Larry Marvin, prin.
Greentown ES, 3330 STATE ST NW   44720
   Paul Neiss, prin.
Northwood ES, 2525 HUME ST NW   44720
   Gloria Riefer, prin.
Orchard Hill ES, 1305 JONATHAN AVE SW   44720
   Mary Juersivich, prin.

Plain Local SD
Supt. – See Canton
Middlebranch MS
   7500 MIDDLEBRANCH AVE NE   44721
   Thomas Kauth, prin.
Plain Center ES, 1000 55TH ST NE   44721
   Philip Smith, prin.
Warstler ES, 2500 SCHNEIDER ST NE   44721
   Victor Drenta, prin.

St. Paul ES, 303 MAIN ST S   44720

North Fairfield, Huron Co., Pop. Code 3
South Central Local SD
Supt. – See Greenwich
South Central MS, ASHTABULA ST   44855
   Marie Strayer, prin.

Northfield, Summit Co., Pop. Code 5
Nordonia Hills CSD
Sch. Sys. Enr. Code 5
Supt. – Russel Haas
   9370 OLDE EIGHT ROAD   44067
Nordonia JHS, 73 LEONARD AVE   44067
   Wayne Greene, prin.
Eaton ES, 115 LEDGE RD   44067
   Carol Smagola, prin.
Rushwood ES, 8200 RUSHWOOD LN   44067
   William Lowery, prin.
Other Schools – See Macedonia

St. Barnabas ES, 9200 OLDE EIGHT RD   44067

North Jackson, Mahoning Co.
Jackson-Milton Local SD
Sch. Sys. Enr. Code 4
Supt. – Richard Rezek
   MAHONING AVE EXT   44451
Jackson-Milton MS
   14110 MAHONING AVE   44451
   James Infante, prin.
North Jackson ES, 10748 MAHONING AVE   44451
   Flora Direnzo, prin.
Other Schools – See Lake Milton

North Kingsville, Ashtabula Co., Pop. Code 5
Buckeye Local SD
Supt. – See Ashtabula
ES, 1343 E CENTER ST   44068 – Mary Taylor, prin.

North Lewisburg, Champaign Co., Pop. Code 4
Triad Local SD
Sch. Sys. Enr. Code 3
Supt. – John Merriman
   7920 BRUSH LAKE ROAD   43060
Triad ES, 7920 BRUSH LAKE RD   43060
   Richard Norviel, prin.

North Lima, Mahoning Co., Pop. Code 3
South Range Local SD
Sch. Sys. Enr. Code 4
Supt. – James Hall, 11836 SOUTH AVE   44452
South Range East ES, 11836 SOUTH AVE   44452
   Stephen Krivan, prin.
Other Schools – See Greenford

North Olmsted, Cuyahoga Co., Pop. Code 8
North Olmsted CSD
Sch. Sys. Enr. Code 5
Supt. – Dennis Allen
   27253 BUTTERNUT RIDGE ROAD   44070
MS, 27351 BUTTERNUT RIDGE ROAD   44070
   Michael Griffin, prin.
Butternut ES
   26669 BUTTERNUT RIDGE RD   44070
   Theodore Blank, prin.
Forest ES, 28963 TUDOR DR   44070
   William Burkhardt, prin.
Maple ES, 24101 MAPLE RIDGE ROAD   44070
   William Hotz, prin.
Pine ES, 4267 DOVER CENTER RD   44070
   Linda Ward, prin.
Spruce ES, 28590 WINDSOR DR   44070
   Sue Oswald, prin.

Kings Academy, P O BOX 302   44070
St. Brenden ES
   BRENDAN & KENNY LANES   44070
St. Richard ES, 26855 LORAIN RD   44070

North Ridgeville, Lorain Co., Pop. Code 7
North Ridgeville CSD
Sch. Sys. Enr. Code 5
Supt. – Paul Murphy
   35895 CENTER RIDGE ROAD   44039
Fields-Sweet MS, 8540 ROOT RD   44039
   Joseph Dudek, prin.
Lear North ES, 5580 LEAR NAGLE RD   44039
   Gayle Ritsko, prin.
Liberty ES, 5700 JAYCOX RD   44039
   Craig Phillips, prin.
Wilcox ES, 34580 BAINBRIDGE RD   44039
   Larry Bowersox, prin.

Lake Ridge Academy
   37501 CENTER RIDGE ROAD   44039
St. Peter ES, 35749 CENTER RIDGE RD   44039

North Robinson, Crawford Co., Pop. Code 2
Colonel Crawford Local SD
Sch. Sys. Enr. Code 4
Supt. – William Ferrell   44856
Crawford IS   44856 – John Roseberry, prin.
Other Schools – See Bucyrus, Crestline, Sulphur
   Springs

North Royalton, Cuyahoga Co., Pop. Code 7
North Royalton CSD
Sch. Sys. Enr. Code 5
Supt. – Albert Vasek
   6579 ROYALTON ROAD   44133
Albion MS, 9360 ALBION ROAD   44133
   A. Dolce, prin.
Royal View MS, 13220 RIDGE RD   44133
   Jefferey Lampert, prin.
Valley Vista ES, 4049 WALLINGS RD   44133
   Thomas List, prin.

St. Albert the Great ES
   6667 WALLINGS RD   44133

North Star, Darke Co., Pop. Code 2
Versailles EVD
Supt. – See Versailles
ES, P O BOX 159   45350 – Thomas Doseck, prin.

Northwood, Wood Co., Pop. Code 6
Northwood Local SD
Sch. Sys. Enr. Code 4
Supt. – Edison Barney
   600 LEMOYNE ROAD   43619
MS, 500 LEMOYNE ROAD   43619
   Kenneth Porter, prin.
Lark ES, 331 ANDRUS RD   43619
   Myrna Holland, prin.
Olney ES, 512 LEMOYNE RD   43619
   James Boyer, prin.

Norton, Summit Co., Pop. Code 7
Norton CSD
Sch. Sys. Enr. Code 4
Supt. – Clete Bulach
   4128 CLEVELAND-MASSILLON RD   44203
MS, 3300 CLEVELAND-MASSILLON RD   44203
   Bruce Kumer, prin.
ES, 4138 CLEVE-MASS RD   44203
   Sherry Marple, prin.
PS, 3163 GREENWICH RD   44203
   Joanne Anderson, prin.
Other Schools – See Clinton

Norwalk, Huron Co., Pop. Code 7
Norwalk CSD
Sch. Sys. Enr. Code 5
Supt. – Fred Walter, 134 BENEDICT AVE   44857
MS, 64 CHRISTIE AVE   44857
   Stephen Cillo, prin.
League ES, 16 E LEAGUE ST   44857
   Brent Sellers, prin.
Maplehurst ES, 195 SAINT MARYS ST   44857
   Michael Gordon, prin.
Pleasant ES, 16 S PLEASANT ST   44857
   Wayne Babcanec, prin.

St. Mary ES, 77 STATE ST   44857
St. Paul ES, 31 MILAN AVE   44857

Norwood, Hamilton Co., Pop. Code 8
Norwood CSD
Sch. Sys. Enr. Code 5
Supt. – David Query, 2132 WILLIAMS AVE   45212
MS, 2060 SHERMAN AVE   45212
   Donald Turner, prin.
Allison Street ES
   ALLISON AND COURTLAND AVE   45212
   Naomi Lykins, prin.
View ES, CARTHAGE & HANNAFORD   45212
   David Beamer, prin.
Sharpsburg ES, FOREST & SMITH   45212
   Donald Daly, prin.
Williams Avenue ES, 2132 WILLIAMS AVE   45212
   Larry Bird, prin.

Gressle ES, FLORAL & KENILWORTH   45212

Nova, Ashland Co.
Mapleton Local SD
Supt. – See Ashland
Ruggles-Troy MS   44859 – John Neighbor, prin.

Novelty, Geauga Co.
West Geauga Local SD
Supt. – See Chesterland
Westwood ES, 13738 CAVES RD   44072
   Henk Deree, prin.

Oak Harbor, Ottawa Co., Pop. Code 5
Benton Carroll Salem Local SD
Sch. Sys. Enr. Code 4
Supt. – Terry Clark
   11685 STATE ROUTE 163 W   43449
JHS, 315 N CHURCH ST   43449
   Daniel Kaylo, prin.
Carroll ES, 3536 STATE ROUTE 19 N   43449
   Terry Harsha, prin.
Waters ES, 220 E OTTAWA ST   43449
   Elwood Johns, prin.
Other Schools – See Graytown, Rocky Ridge

Oak Hill, Jackson Co., Pop. Code 4
Oak Hill Union Local SD
Sch. Sys. Enr. Code 4
Supt. – Howard Smith, 265 W CROSS ST   45656
Blackfork MS
   RURAL ROUTE 04 BOX 69-H   45656
   Dale Rawlins, prin.
Central MS, 202 MONROE ST   45656
   Homer Williams, prin.
Lewis ES, 1427 STATE ROUTE 140   45656
   Dale Rawlins, prin.
Oak View ES, 401 EVANS ST   45656
   Melvin Morgan, prin.
Other Schools – See Jackson

Oakwood, Paulding Co., Pop. Code 3
Paulding EVD
Supt. – See Paulding
ES, P O BOX 37   45873 – William Shugars, prin.

Oberlin, Lorain Co., Pop. Code 6
Firelands Local SD
Sch. Sys. Enr. Code 4
Supt. – Darrell Phillips
   11970 VERMILION ROAD   44074
Firelands ES, 10779 VERMILION ROAD   44074
   Pamela Goswick, prin.
Other Schools – See South Amherst

Oberlin CSD
Sch. Sys. Enr. Code 4
Supt. – Robert Murphy
   218 N PLEASANT ST   44074
Langston ES, 153 N MAIN ST   44074
   Larry Thomas, prin.
Eastwood ES, 198 E COLLEGE ST   44074
   Francine Toss, prin.
Prospect MS, 36 S PROSPECT ST   44074
   (—).

Ohio City, Van Wert Co., Pop. Code 3
Van Wert CSD
Supt. – See Van Wert
Ohio City ES, SHANES ST   45874
   Ronald Rase, prin.

Old Fort, Seneca Co.
Old Fort Local SD
Sch. Sys. Enr. Code 4
Supt. – C. Yaskowitz, P O BOX 64   44861
ES, P O BOX 64   44861 – Sandra Best, prin.

Old Washington, Guernsey Co., Pop. Code 2
East Guernsey Local SD
Sch. Sys. Enr. Code 4
Supt. – William Reese, P O BOX 128   43768
ES, P O BOX 128   43768 – Charles Byers, prin.
Other Schools – See Lore City, Quaker City

Olmsted Falls, Cuyahoga Co., Pop. Code 6
Olmsted Falls CSD
Sch. Sys. Enr. Code 4
Supt. – P. Joseph Madak
   7890 BROOKSIDE DRIVE   44138
MS, 26184 BAGLEY ROAD   44138
   Charles Murphy, prin.
Falls MS, 26350 BAGLEY RD   44138
   Gerald Neumann, prin.
Fitch ES, 7105 FITCH RD   44138
   Robert Rami, prin.
Lenox ES, 26470 BAGLEY RD   44138
   Margaret Gallagher, prin.

St. Mary of the Falls Elem Sch
   8262 COLUMBIA RD   44138

Oregon, Lucas Co., Pop. Code 7
Oregon CSD
Sch. Sys. Enr. Code 5
Supt. – Robert Pfefferle, 5721 SEAMAN ST   43616
Eisenhower MS, 331 N CURTICE ROAD   43616
   Ken Arndt, prin.
Fassett MS, 3025 STARR AVE   43616
   Lyle Nissen, prin.
Coy ES, 2630 PICKLE RD   43616
   Joseph Wasserman, prin.
Starr ES, 3230 STARR AVE   43616
   Martha Smock, prin.
Wynn ES, 5224 BAY SHORE ROAD   43616
   Donald Charlton, prin.
Other Schools – See Curtice

Orrville, Wayne Co., Pop. Code 6
Orrville CSD
Sch. Sys. Enr. Code 4
Supt. – Richard Thomas, 815 N ELLA ST   44667
JHS, 217 E CHURCH ST   44667
   James Curtis, prin.

Maple Street ES, 215 MAPLE ST   44667
 David Nawyn, prin.
North ES, MINERAL SPRING ST   44667
 Carolyn Johnson, prin.
Oak Street ES, OAK & VINE STS   44667
 Dennis Hartzler, prin.

Wayne County Christian ES
 2061 WADSWORTH RD   44667

Orwell, Ashtabula Co., Pop. Code 4
Grand Valley Local SD
 Sch. Sys. Enr. Code 4
 Supt. – Hiram Lynch, RT 45   44076
 Colebrook ES, RURAL ROUTE 01   44076
  Sara Perry, prin.
 Grand Valley ES, N MAPLE ST   44076
  Evelyn Henson, prin.
 Other Schools – See Rome, Windsor

Ostrander, Delaware Co., Pop. Code 2
Buckeye Valley Local SD
 Supt. – See Delaware
 Buckeye Valley West ES, 61 N THIRD ST   43061
  H. Bell, prin.

Ottawa, Putnam Co., Pop. Code 5
Miller City-New Cleveland Local SD
 Supt. – See Miller City
 New Cleveland MS, RURAL ROUTE 02   45875
  William Kreinbrink, prin.

Ottawa-Glandorf Local SD
 Sch. Sys. Enr. Code 4
 Supt. – Michael Ruhe, 630 GLENDALE AVE   45875
 ES, 751 E FOURTH ST   45875
  Mary Jo Williams, prin.
 Other Schools – See Glandorf

Sts. Peter & Paul ES, 320 N LOCUST ST   45875

Ottoville, Putnam Co., Pop. Code 3
Ottoville Local SD
 Sch. Sys. Enr. Code 3
 Supt. – Charles MacDonald, P O BOX 248   45876
 ES, P O BOX 248   45876 – Jose Flores, prin.

Otway, Scioto Co., Pop. Code 2
Northwest Local SD
 Supt. – See Mc Dermott
 ES, P O BOX 53   45657 – Howard McClay, prin.

Owensville, Clearmont Co., Pop. Code 3
Clermont-Northeastern Local SD
 Supt. – See Batavia
 Northeastern PS, S BROADWAY ST   45160
  Ruth Mitchell, prin.

St. Louis ES, P O BOX 85   45160

Oxford, Butler Co., Pop. Code 7
Talawanda CSD
 Sch. Sys. Enr. Code 5
 Supt. – Dennis Leone
  131 W CHESTNUT ST   45056
 McGuffey-Church MS, 14 N POPLAR   45056
  David McWilliams, prin.
 McGuffey-Millett MS, TALAWANDA ST   45056
  James Robinson, prin.
 McGuffey-Yeger MS
  5400 MORNING SUN RD   45056
  Phillip Caguin, prin.
 Marshall MS
  3260 OXFORD-MILLVILLE RD   45056
  Philip Cagwin, prin.
 Stewart MS, 315 S COLLEGE AVE   45056
  Marvin Wilhelm, prin.
 Kramer ES, LOCUST & SYCAMORE STS   45056
  William Bryan, prin.

Painesville, Lake Co., Pop. Code 7
Painesville CSD
 Sch. Sys. Enr. Code 5
 Supt. – Fritz Overs, 58 JEFFERSON ST   44077
 Hobart MS, 200 W WALNUT ST   44077
  Brent McGarvey, prin.
 Cedarbrook ES, 350 CEDARBROOK DR   44077
  Barbara Bertone, prin.
 Huntington ES, 979 N ST CLAIR ST   44077
  Norbert Smialek, prin.
 Lathrop ES, 61 ROOSEVELT DR   44077
  George Marko, prin.
 State Street ES, 348 S STATE ST   44077
  Med Johnson, prin.

Painesville Local SD
 Sch. Sys. Enr. Code 5
 Supt. – Earl Bardall, 585 RIVERSIDE DRIVE   44077
 Buckeye ES, 995 BUCKEYE RD   44077
  John Reed, prin.
 Hadden ES, 1800 MENTOR AVE   44077
  Toni Suydam, prin.
 Hale Road ES, 56 HALE RD   44077
  John Cassin, prin.
 Leroy ES, 13613 P'VILLE WARREN RD   44077
  John Bull, prin.
 Madison Avenue ES, 845 MADISON AVE   44077
  Charles Wacha, prin.
 Melridge ES, 6689 MELRIDGE DR   44077
  Ruth Stevenson, prin.

Our Shepherd Evangel Lutheran ES
 508 MENTOR AVE   44077
Phillips Lake Erie ES
 391 W WASHINGTON ST   44077
St. Mary ES, 268 N STATE ST   44077

Palestine, Darke Co., Pop. Code 2
Tri-Village Local SD
 Supt. – See New Madison
 Tri-Village PS, P O BOX B   45352
  Shirley Verbanik, prin.

Pandora, Putnam Co., Pop. Code 3
Pandora-Gilboa Local SD
 Sch. Sys. Enr. Code 3
 Supt. – Ray Graves, N JEFFERSON   45877
 ES, N JEFFERSON ST   45877
  Lloyd Harnishfeger, prin.
 Other Schools – See Gilboa

Parkman, Geauga Co.
Cardinal Local SD
 Supt. – See Middlefield
 ES, 18225 MADISON RD   44080
  Lynne Muzik, prin.

Parma, Cuyahoga Co., Pop. Code 8
Parma CSD
 Sch. Sys. Enr. Code 7
 Supt. – Walter Olszewski
  6726 RIDGE ROAD   44129
 Greenbriar JHS, 11810 HUFFMAN ROAD   44130
  Ronald Sterle, prin.
 Arlington ES, 7377 CHATEAU DR   44130
  Raymond Noss, prin.
 Dentzler ES, 3600 DENTZLER RD   44134
  Richard Delvichio, prin.
 Forrest ES, 11800 HUFFMAN RD   44130
  Marilynn Rankin, prin.
 Green Valley ES
  2401 W PLEASANT VALLEY R   44134
  Barbara Filipow, prin.
 Hammarskjold ES, 4040 TAMARACK DR   44134
  Patricia Matlin, prin.
 Muir ES, 5531 W 24TH ST   44134
  Howard Evans, prin.
 Parkview ES
  5210 STATE ROAD PKY BLVD   44134
  Elaine Kason, prin.
 Park ES, 6800 COMMONWEALTH BLVD   44130
  Christine Auginas, prin.
 Pleasantview ES, 7700 MALIBU DR   44130
  Richard Salisbury, prin.
 Renwood ES, 8020 DEERFIELD DR   44129
  Robert Myers, prin.
 Ridge-Brook ES, 7915 MANHATTAN AVE   44129
  Mary Orourke, prin.
 State Road ES, 6121 STATE RD   44134
  Wanda Ullman, prin.
 Thoreau Park ES, 5401 W 54TH ST   44129
  Helen Mize, prin.
 Other Schools – See Parma Heights, Seven Hills

Bethany Lutheran ES, 6041 RIDGE RD   44129
Bethel Christian Academy
 12901 W PLEASANT VALLEY RD   44130
Christian Centre ES, 5983 W 54TH ST   44129
Community ES, 6195 BROADVIEW RD   44134
Holy Family ES, 7367 YORK RD   44130
St. Anthony Pauda ES, 6800 STATE RD   44134
St. Bridget ES, 5620 HAUSERMAN RD   44130
St. Charles Borromeo ES
 7107 WILBER AVE   44129
St. Columbkille ES, 6740 BROADVIEW RD   44134
St. Francis De Sales ES, 3421 SNOW RD   44134
St. Josaphat ES, 5720 STATE RD   44134

Parma Heights, Cuyahoga Co., Pop. Code 7
Parma CSD
 Supt. – See Parma
 Pearl Road ES, 6125 PEARL RD   44130
  Beverly Cheselka, prin.

Incarnate Word Academy, 6618 PEARL RD   44130
Parma Heights Christian Academy
 8971 W RIDGEWOOD DR   44130
St. John Bosco ES, 6460 PEARL RD   44130

Pataskala, Licking Co., Pop. Code 4
Licking Heights Local SD
 Supt. – See Summit Station
 Jersey ES, 12201 MORSE RD SW   43062
  Barbara Heisel, prin.

Southwest Licking Local SD
 Supt. – See Kirkersville
 Watkins MS, 8808 WATKINS ROAD SW   43062
  Harry Gardner, prin.
 ES, 395 S HIGH ST   43062
  Mary Underwood, prin.

Patriot, Gallia Co.
Gallia County Local SD
 Supt. – See Gallipolis
 Southwestern ES, RURAL ROUTE 02   45658
  Lloyd Myers, prin.

Paulding, Paulding Co., Pop. Code 5
Paulding EVD
 Sch. Sys. Enr. Code 5
 Supt. – Stanley Searing, 405 N WATER ST   45879
 MS, 405 N WATER ST   45879 – (—), prin.
 ES, 405 N WATER ST   45879
  Stephen Young, prin.
 Other Schools – See Oakwood

Payne, Paulding Co., Pop. Code 4
Wayne Trace Local SD
 Sch. Sys. Enr. Code 4
 Supt. – John Ladd, W TOWNLINE ST   45880
 ES, W TOWNLINE   45880 – Edward Hook, prin.
 Other Schools – See Grover Hill

Pedro, Lawrence Co.
Rock Hill Local SD
 Supt. – See Ironton
 Rock Hill ES 1, RURAL ROUTE 01   45659
  Brenda Haas, prin.

Peebles, Adams Co., Pop. Code 4
Ohio Valley Local SD
 Supt. – See West Union
 Franklin ES, 8011 STATE ROUTE 73   45660
  Larry Shiveley, prin.
 ES, VINE ST BOX 307   45660 – James Castle, prin.

Pemberton, Shelby Co.
Fairlawn Local SD
 Supt. – See Sidney
 Fairlawn ES, P O BOX 24   45353 – Roy Jarvis, prin.

Pemberville, Wood Co., Pop. Code 4
Eastwood Local SD
 Sch. Sys. Enr. Code 4
 Supt. – William Smith
  4800 SUGAR RIDGE ROAD   43450
 ES, 120 COLLEGE AVE   43450
  Thomas Lingenfelder, prin.
 Webster ES, 17345 STATE ROUTE 199   43450
  Thomas Lingenfelder, prin.
 Other Schools – See Lemoyne, Luckey

Peninsula, Summit Co., Pop. Code 3
Woodridge Local SD
 Supt. – See Cuyahoga Falls
 Woodridge MS, 1930 BRONSON AVE   44264
  Thomas Yakubowski, prin.

Pennsville, Morgan Co.
Morgan Local SD
 Supt. – See Mc Connelsville
 ES, P O BOX 8   43770 – Robert Matthews, prin.

Pepper Pike, Cuyahoga Co., Pop. Code 6
Orange CSD
 Sch. Sys. Enr. Code 4
 Supt. – William Scoggan
  32000 CHAGRIN BLVD   44124
 Brady MS, 32000 CHAGRIN BLVD   44124
  Gail Allison, prin.
 Moreland Hills PS, 32000 CHAGRIN BLVD   44124
  Katie Shorter, prin.
 MS, 32000 CHAGRIN BLVD   44124
  Budd Dingwall, prin.

Perry, Lake Co., Pop. Code 3
Perry Local SD
 Sch. Sys. Enr. Code 4
 Supt. – Edgar Goodwin, 3961 MAIN ST   44081
 MS, 3843 MAIN ST   44081 – Douglas Jenkins, prin.
 Center Road MS, 3986 CENTER RD   44081
  Joseph Hambor, prin.
 Manchester ES, 4325 MANCHESTER AVE   44081
  Spencer Wiersma, prin.

Perrysburg, Wood Co., Pop. Code 7
Perrysburg EVD
 Sch. Sys. Enr. Code 5
 Supt. – John Bailey, 140 E INDIANA AVE   43551
 MS, 140 E INDIANA AVE   43551
  T. Waltzer, prin.
 Frank ES, 401 W SOUTH BOUNDARY ST   43551
  Terry Teopas, prin.
 Toth ES, 200 E 7TH ST   43551
  Carole Liebich, prin.
 Woodland MS, 27979 WHITE RD   43551
  Larry Studer, prin.

Rossford EVD
 Supt. – See Rossford
 Glenwood ES, 8950 AVENUE RD   43551
  Eugene Barrett, prin.

St. Rose ES, 217 E FRONT ST   43551

Perrysville, Ashland Co., Pop. Code 3
Loudonville-Perrysville EVD
 Supt. – See Loudonville
 JHS, 155 W 3RD ST   44864 – Steve Brown, prin.

Pettisville, Fulton Co.
Pettisville Local SD
 Sch. Sys. Enr. Code 2
 Supt. – Stephen Switzer, P O BOX 1   43553
 ES, P O BOX 1   43553 – Nancy Graber, prin.

Phillipsburg, Montgomery Co., Pop. Code 3
Northmont CSD
 Supt. – See Englewood
 ES, W MAIN ST   45354 – Philip Artz, prin.

Philo, Muskingum Co., Pop. Code 3
Franklin Local SD
 Supt. – See Duncan Falls
 IS, MARKET ST   43771 – Samuel Hutcheson, prin.

Pickerington, Fairfield Co., Pop. Code 5
Pickerington Local SD
 Sch. Sys. Enr. Code 5
 Supt. – Daniel Ross, 777 LONG ROAD   43147
 MS, 100 N EAST ST   43147 – James Barry, prin.
 Fairfield ES, 13000 COVENTRY AVE   43147
  H. Stemen, prin.
 ES, 775 LONG RD   43147
  Thomas Wilkinson, prin.
 Violet ES, 8855 EDUCATION DR   43147
  John Bryant, prin.

Pierpont, Ashtabula Co.
Buckeye Local SD
Supt. – See Ashtabula
ES, 1071 ROUTE 7 N 44082 – Ronald Coxon, prin.

Piketon, Pike Co., Pop. Code 4
Scioto Valley Local SD
Sch. Sys. Enr. Code 4
Supt. – Ernest Hamilton, P O BOX 600 45661
ES, 2379 SCHUSTER RD 45661
Gene Brushart, prin.
Other Schools – See Jasper

Western Local SD
Sch. Sys. Enr. Code 3
Supt. – Joseph Morrison
12599 STATE ROUTE 124 45661
Parker ES, 12599 STATE ROUTE 124 45661
Jack Stowers, prin.

Pioneer, Williams Co., Pop. Code 4
North Central Local SD
Sch. Sys. Enr. Code 3
Supt. – Gerald Smith, 201 WYANDOT ST 43554
North Central ES, 400 BAUBICE ST 43554
Thomas Balser, prin.
Other Schools – See Kunkle

Piqua, Miami Co., Pop. Code 7
Piqua CSD
Sch. Sys. Enr. Code 5
Supt. – Duane Bachman
316 N COLLEGE ST 45356
Bennett JHS, 625 S MAIN ST 45356
Robert Luby, prin.
Wilder MS, 1120 NICKLIN AVE 45356
Charles Rhyan, prin.
Favorite Hill ES, 950 SOUTH ST 45356
Robert Termuhlen, prin.
High Street ES, 1249 W HIGH ST 45356
Thomas Ringer, prin.
Nicklin Avenue ES, 818 NICKLIN AVE 45356
Louressa Yingst, prin.
South Street ES, 339 SOUTH ST 45356
Vonda Young, prin.
Springcreek ES, 145 E US 36 45356
James Wick, prin.
Washington ES, 800 N SUNSET DR 45356
Kenneth Amstutz, prin.

Piqua Catholic North Street ES
503 W NORTH ST 45356
Piqua Catholic Downing Street ES
218 S DOWNING 45356

Pitsburg, Darke Co., Pop. Code 2
Franklin-Monroe Local SD
Sch. Sys. Enr. Code 3
Supt. – Robert Lantz, P O BOX 78 45358
Other Schools – See Arcanum

Plain City, Madison Co., Pop. Code 4
Jonathan Alder Local SD
Sch. Sys. Enr. Code 4
Supt. – Douglas Carpenter
6440 KILBURY-HUBER ROAD 43064
Canaan MS, 7055 US ROUTE 42 S 43064
Lynne Gatsch, prin.
Other Schools – See London

Plainfield, Coshocton Co., Pop. Code 2
Ridgewood Local SD
Supt. – See West Lafayette
ES, P O BOX 448 43836 – Dennis Bahmer, prin.

Pleasant Hill, Miami Co., Pop. Code 4
Newton Local SD
Sch. Sys. Enr. Code 3
Supt. – L. Lehman, LONG ST 45359
Newton ES, P O BOX 68 45359
Janet Corbin, prin.

Pleasantville, Fairfield Co., Pop. Code 3
Fairfield Union Local SD
Supt. – See West Rushville
ES, 225 LINCOLN AVE 43148 – Gene Scott, prin.

Plymouth, Richland Co., Pop. Code 4
Plymouth Local SD
Sch. Sys. Enr. Code 4
Supt. – Jeffrey Slauson, 25 SANDUSKY ST 44865
ES, W BROADWAY 44865 – Mark Sheely, prin.
Other Schools – See Shiloh

Poland, Mahoning Co., Pop. Code 5
Poland Local SD
Sch. Sys. Enr. Code 4
Supt. – Robert Zorn, 53 COLLEGE ST 44514
MS, 47 COLLEGE ST 44514 – Thomas Shook, prin.
Dobbins ES, 3030 DOBBINS RD 44514
Mary Jones, prin.
McKinley ES, 47 ELM ST 44514
James Connolly, prin.
North ES, 361 JOHNSTON PL 44514
Carmella Smallhoover, prin.

Holy Family ES, 2731 CENTER RD 44514

Polk, Ashland Co., Pop. Code 2
Mapleton Local SD
Supt. – See Ashland
ES 44866 – Daniel Ashbaugh, prin.

Pomeroy, Meigs Co., Pop. Code 5
Meigs Local SD
Supt. – See Middleport
Harrisonville ES, 35359 STATE ROUTE 143 45769
Greg McCall, prin.

ES, 260 MULBERRY AVE 45769 – John Lisle, prin.
Salisbury ES, 41675 POMEROY PIKE 45769
Wendy Halar, prin.

Portage, Wood Co., Pop. Code 2
Elmwood Local SD
Supt. – See Bloomdale
ES, RURAL ROUTE 01 43451
Margaret McDowell, prin.

Port Clinton, Ottawa Co., Pop. Code 6
Port Clinton CSD
Sch. Sys. Enr. Code 5
Supt. – Dennis Rectenwald
431 PORTAGE DRIVE 43452
MS, E 4TH ST 43452 – Dale Van Lerberghe, prin.
Bataan Memorial ES, W 6TH ST 43452
Richard Linkous, prin.
Catawba ES, 3321 NW CATAWBA RD 43452
Kenneth Bogard, prin.
Jefferson ES, JEFFERSON & 5TH STS 43452
Michael Schifer, prin.
Other Schools – See Gypsum

Immaculate Conception ES, 109 W 4TH ST 43452

Portland, Meigs Co.
Southern Local SD
Supt. – See Racine
ES 45770 – Michaela Kucsma, prin.

Portsmouth, Scioto Co., Pop. Code 8
Clay Local SD
Sch. Sys. Enr. Code 3
Supt. – Ted Adams, RURAL ROUTE 06 45662
Rosemount ES, ROSE VALLEY ROAD 45662
Larry McNamer, prin.
Rubyville MS, RURAL ROUTE 06 45662
Larry McNamer, prin.

Portsmouth CSD
Sch. Sys. Enr. Code 5
Supt. – William Larson, 4TH & COURT ST 45662
Grant MS, 1225 4TH ST 45662
John Hendricks, prin.
McKinley MS, 1729 KINNEYS LANE 45662
Joseph Knapp, prin.
Portsmouth East MS
MARSHALL & FARNEY AVE 45662
Michael Flaig, prin.
Harding ES, 6135 HARDING AVE 45662
Wanda Kinker, prin.
Highland ES, 1511 HUTCHINS ST 45662
Hilda Drake, prin.
Lincoln ES, 1121 KINNEYS LN 45662
Jerry Skiver, prin.
Roosevelt ES, 1409 COLES BLVD 45662
Lana Perry, prin.
Wilson ES, 613 CAMPBELL AVE 45662
James Sinclair, prin.

Notre Dame ES, 1401 GALLIA ST 45662

Port Washington, Tuscarawas Co., Pop. Code 3
Indian Valley Local SD
Supt. – See Gnadenhutten
ES, P O BOX 8 43837 – (—), prin.

Powell, Delaware Co., Pop. Code 2
Worthington CSD
Supt. – See Worthington
Liberty ES, 1840 SUTTER PKY 43065
Jo Ann Triner, prin.
Sutter Park ES, 1850 SUTTER PKY 43065
James Baker, prin.

Powhatan Point, Belmont Co., Pop. Code 4
Switzerland of Ohio Local SD
Supt. – See Woodsfield
ES, 125 SECOND ST 43942 – Harold Blust, prin.

Proctorville, Lawrence Co., Pop. Code 3
Fairland Local SD
Sch. Sys. Enr. Code 4
Supt. – Jerry McConnell
RURAL ROUTE 04 BOX 201 45669
Fairland West MS
RURAL ROUTE 03 BOX 90 45669
John Lewis, prin.
Fairland East ES
RURAL ROUTE 01 BOX 593 45669
Henrietta Keyser, prin.

Prospect, Marion Co., Pop. Code 4
Elgin Local SD
Supt. – See Marion
Elgin South ES, 200 EAST ST N 43342
Timothy Hamilton, prin.

Put-in-Bay, Ottawa Co., Pop. Code 2
Put-in-Bay Local SD
Sch. Sys. Enr. Code 1
Supt. – Kelly Faris, P O BOX 38 43456
ES, P O BOX 659 43456 – Kelly Faris, prin.

Quaker City, Guernsey Co., Pop. Code 3
East Guernsey Local SD
Supt. – See Old Washington
ES, FAIR ST 43773 – Thomas McVicker, prin.

Quincy, Logan Co., Pop. Code 3
Riverside Local SD
Supt. – See De Graff
Riverside ES, P O BOX 189 43343
James McBrien, prin.

Racine, Meigs Co., Pop. Code 3
Southern Local SD
Sch. Sys. Enr. Code 3
Supt. – Bobby Ord, P O BOX 176 45771
Southern MS, P O BOX 326 45771
Jennings Beegle, prin.
Letart Falls ES, RURAL ROUTE 02 45771
Robert Beegle, prin.
ES, P O BOX 72 45771 – Donna Norris, prin.
Other Schools – See Portland, Syracuse

Radnor, Delaware Co., Pop. Code 4
Buckeye Valley Local SD
Supt. – See Delaware
Buckeye Valley MS
4230 STATE ROUTE 203 43066
Ruth Tarpy, prin.

Rainsboro, Highland Co.
Greenfield EVD
Supt. – See Greenfield
MS, 12916 BARRETTS MILLS ROAD 45165
John Miller, prin.

Randolph, Portage Co.
Waterloo Local SD
Supt. – See Atwater
Waterloo ES, 1776 STATE ROUTE 44 44265
Keith Ruhe, prin.

Ravenna, Portage Co., Pop. Code 7
Crestwood Local SD
Supt. – See Mantua
Shalersville ES, 4519 STATE ROUTE 303 44266
Linda Clapp, prin.

Ravenna CSD
Sch. Sys. Enr. Code 5
Supt. – Thomas King, 507 MAIN ST 44266
Brown MS, 228 SCRANTON ST 44266
Frank Seman, prin.
Carlin ES, 531 WASHINGTON AVE 44266
Vernon McElroy, prin.
Tappan ES, 310 BENNETT AVE 44266
Norman Stikes, prin.
West Main ES, 639 W MAIN ST 44266
James Boring, prin.
West Park ES, 1071 JONES ST 44266
George Groborchik, prin.
Willyard ES, 680 SUMMIT RD 44266
Harvey Warner, prin.

Southeast Local SD
Sch. Sys. Enr. Code 4
Supt. – D. Fedorchak
8423 TALLMADGE ROAD 44266
Southeast MS, 8301 TALLMADGE ROAD 44266
Brian Oglesbee, prin.
Southeast PS, 8301 TALLMADGE RD 44272
Richard Archer, prin.

Immaculate Conception ES
225 S SYCAMORE ST 44266

Rawson, Hancock Co., Pop. Code 2
Cory-Rawson Local SD
Sch. Sys. Enr. Code 3
Supt. – Walter Baney, 3930 C 26 45881
Cory Rawson MS, 3930 C 26 45881
John Spaeth, prin.
Cory-Rawson ES 45881 – Gerald Moyer, prin.

Rayland, Jefferson Co., Pop. Code 3
Buckeye Local SD
Sch. Sys. Enr. Code 5
Supt. – Anne Stephens, P O BOX 300 43943
Smithfield ES, RURAL ROUTE 01 43943
Gino Sgalla, prin.
Other Schools – See Adena, Brilliant, Dillonvale,
Mingo Junction, Tiltonsville

Raymond, Union Co.
Marysville EVD
Supt. – See Marysville
ES 43067 – Grant Kearns, prin.

Reading, Hamilton Co., Pop. Code 7
Reading Community CSD
Sch. Sys. Enr. Code 4
Supt. – Tom Varis
BONNELL & HALKER AVE 45215
Central Community ES
BONNELL & HALKER 45215
Kenneth Brand, prin.
Hilltop Community ES
BOLSER & SANBORN DR 45215
John Forsthoefel, prin.

Our Lady of Sacred Heart ES
162 SIEBENTHALER AVE 45215
Sts. Peter & Paul ES, 417 W VINVE ST 45215

Reedsville, Meigs Co.
Eastern Local SD
Sch. Sys. Enr. Code 4
Supt. – Daniel Apling, RURAL ROUTE 01 45772
Riverview ES, RURAL ROUTE 01 45772
Grace Weber, prin.
Other Schools – See Chester, Tuppers Plains

Reno, Washington Co.
Marietta CSD
Supt. – See Marietta
Reno ES, HCR 45773 – Gail Popp, prin.

Republic, Seneca Co., Pop. Code 3
Seneca East Local SD
Supt. – See Attica

Seneca East MS 44867 – Judy Watson, prin.
ES 44867 – David Getter, prin.

Reynoldsburg, Franklin Co., Pop. Code 7
Reynoldsburg CSD
Sch. Sys. Enr. Code 5
Supt. – Richard Ross
   6549 E LIVINGSTON AVE 43068
Ashton MS, 1482 JACKSON ST 43068
   Ralph Gillum, prin.
French Run ES, 1200 EPWORTH AVE 43068
   Charles Parsons, prin.
Graham Road ES, 1555 GRAHAM RD 43068
   Sharon Dawson, prin.
Mills ES, 6826 RETTON RD 43068
   Craig Seckel, prin.
Rose Hill ES, 760 ROSE HILL ROAD 43068
   Harold Scheiderer, prin.

St. Pius X ES, 1061 WAGGONER RD 43068

Richfield, Summit Co., Pop. Code 5
Revere Local SD
Supt. – See Bath
Hillcrest ES, 3080 REVERE RD 44286
   Katherine Yaussy, prin.
MS, 43115 W STREETSBORO ROAD 44286
   Darrell Hykes, prin.

Richmond, Jefferson Co., Pop. Code 3
Edison Local SD
Supt. – See Hammondsville
Pleasant Hill ES, P O BOX 386 43944
   William Swearingen, prin.
ES, P O BOX 386 43944 – Gerald DiLoreto, prin.

Richmond Dale, Ross Co., Pop. Code 3
Scioto Valley Local SD
Sch. Sys. Enr. Code 4
Supt. – Dennis Thompson
   757 JACKSON ST 45673
ES, P O BOX 108 45673 – Robert Hatfield, prin.
Other Schools – See Chillicothe, Londonberry

Richmond Heights, Cuyahoga Co., Pop. Code 7
Richmond Heights Local SD
Sch. Sys. Enr. Code 3
Supt. – G. Bowdouris
   447 RICHMOND ROAD 44143
MS, 447 RICHMOND ROAD 44143
   Patricia Raiff, prin.
ES, 447 RICHMOND RD 44143
   William Manley, prin.

Richwood, Union Co., Pop. Code 4
North Union Local SD
Sch. Sys. Enr. Code 4
Supt. – Tyrone Thomas
   401 N FRANKLIN ST 43344
North Union MS, 16 NORRIS ST 43344
   Neal Handler, prin.
Claibourne-Richwood ES, E OTTAWA 43344
   James Inskeep, prin.
Jackson ES, 12910 STATE ROUTE 739 43344
   David Wetterman, prin.
Other Schools – See Magnetic Spring

Rio Grande, Gallia Co., Pop. Code 3
Gallipolis CSD
Supt. – See Gallipolis
Rio Grande ES 45674 – Kenneth Farmer, prin.

Ripley, Brown Co., Pop. Code 4
Ripley-Union-Lewis Local SD
Sch. Sys. Enr. Code 4
Supt. – Charles Castle, 500 S 2ND ST 45167
ES, 25 N 2ND ST 45167 – Eugene Wright, prin.

St. Michael ES, 5TH 7 MARKET STS 45167

Rising Sun, Sandusky Co., Pop. Code 3
Lakota Local SD
Sch. Sys. Enr. Code 4
Supt. – Stan Heffner, P O BOX 5 43457
Lakota Central ES, P O BOX 5 43457
   Ann Mickey, prin.
Other Schools – See Amsden, Bradner, Burgoon

Rittman, Wayne Co., Pop. Code 6
Rittman EVD
Sch. Sys. Enr. Code 4
Supt. – Bill Spargur, 220 N FIRST ST 44270
MS, 75 N MAIN ST 44270
   Wayne G. Ambrose, prin.
North Street MS, 230 N FIRST ST 44270
   James Stafford, prin.
West Hill ES, 131 METZGER AVE 44270
   Charles Lyon, prin.

Robertsville, Stark Co.
Minerva Local SD
Supt. – See Minerva
ES, P O BOX 143 44670 – Timothy Hunston, prin.

Rockbridge, Hocking Co.
Logan-Hocking CSD
Supt. – See Logan
Rockbridge ES, 26730 MAIN ST 43149
   Dale Johnson, prin.

Rock Creek, Ashtabula Co., Pop. Code 3
Jefferson Area Local SD
Supt. – See Jefferson
ES, 2987 HIGH ST 44084 – Wayne Linek, prin.

Rockford, Mercer Co., Pop. Code 4
Parkway Local SD
Sch. Sys. Enr. Code 4
Supt. – Gary Graham 45882
Parkway ES, 401 S FRANKLIN ST 45882
   Robert Ransbottom, prin.
Other Schools – See Willshire

Rocky Ridge, Ottawa Co., Pop. Code 2
Benton Carroll Salem Local SD
Supt. – See Oak Harbor
ES, 1098 N WEST ST 43458 – Joseph Bibb, prin.

Rocky River, Cuyahoga Co., Pop. Code 7
Rocky River CSD
Sch. Sys. Enr. Code 5
Supt. – Victor Smole
   21600 CENTER RIDGE ROAD 44116
JHS, 1631 LAKEVIEW AVE 44116
   Kathleen Komnenovich, prin.
IS, 20140 LAKE RD 44116 – Charles Mealy, prin.
PS, 21600 CENTER RIDGE RD 44116
   Jean Rounds, prin.

Ruffing Montessori Rocky River ES
   1285 ORCHARD PARK DR 44116
St. Christopher ES, 1610 LAKEVIEW AVE 44116
St. Thomas Lutheran ES
   21165 DETROIT RD 44116

Rogers, Columbiana Co., Pop. Code 2
Beaver Local SD
Supt. – See Lisbon
ES, 8059 SPRUCEVALE RD 44455
   Elaine Humphrey, prin.

Rome, Adams Co., Pop. Code 2
Grand Valley Local SD
Supt. – See Orwell
Rome-Hartsgrove ES, ROUTE 6 & ROUTE 45 44085
   Patricia White, prin.

Rootstown, Portage Co.
Rootstown Local SD
Sch. Sys. Enr. Code 4
Supt. – Donald Crewse
   4190 STATE ROUTE 44 44272
MS, 4190 STATE ROUTE 44 44272
   Gary Savage, prin.
ES, 4190 STATE ROUTE 44 44272
   Fred Hyatt, prin.

Roseville, Muskingum Co.
Franklin Local SD
Supt. – See Duncan Falls
MS, 76 W ATHENS ROAD 43777
   James Sprague, prin.
ES, 35 ELM ST 43777 – Diane Jones, prin.

Rosewood, Champaign Co.
Graham Local SD
Supt. – See Saint Paris
Graham North ES, P O BOX 111 43070
   Glenn Lewis, prin.

Rossford, Wood Co., Pop. Code 6
Rossford EVD
Sch. Sys. Enr. Code 4
Supt. – Richard Bongiorno
   229 EAGLE POINT ROAD 43460
JHS, 701 SUPERIOR ST N 43460
   Fred Koester, prin.
Eagle Point ES, 203 EAGLE POINT RD 43460
   Joanne Johnson, prin.
Indian Hills ES, 401 GLENWOOD RD 43460
   Richard Knapp, prin.
Other Schools – See Perrysburg

Alter ES, 134 MAPLE ST 43460

Roundhead, Hardin Co.
Upper Scioto Valley Local SD
Supt. – See Mc Guffey
ES 43346 – Keith McGinnis, prin.

Rushsylvania, Logan Co., Pop. Code 3
Benjamin Logan Local SD
Supt. – See Bellefontaine
Benjamin Logan MS 43347
   Dwight Spencer, prin.

Rushville, Fairfield Co., Pop. Code 2
Fairfield Union Local SD
Supt. – See West Rushville
MS, 8155 RUSHVILLE RD 43150
   Frederick Burns, prin.

Russellville, Brown Co., Pop. Code 2
Eastern Local SD
Supt. – See Sardinia
MS 45168 – Gregory Stephenson, prin.

Russia, Shelby Co., Pop. Code 2
Russia Local SD
Sch. Sys. Enr. Code 2
Supt. – Steven Miller, P O BOX 8 45363
Russia Local ES, P O BOX 8 45363
   Vernon Rosenbeck, prin.

Rutland, Meigs Co., Pop. Code 3
Meigs Local SD
Supt. – See Middleport
ES, COLLEGE AVE 45775 – Greg McCall, prin.

Sabina, Clinton Co., Pop. Code 5
East Clinton Local SD
Supt. – See Lees Creek

ES, 246 W WASHINGTON ST 45169
   James Luck, prin.

Saint Bernard, Hamilton Co., Pop. Code 6
St. Bernard-Elmwood Place CSD
Sch. Sys. Enr. Code 4
Supt. – Roger Houck
   105 WASHINGTON AVE 45217
ES, 4515 TOWER AVE 45217
   Maurice Delk, prin.
Other Schools – See Elmwood Place

St. Clement ES, 4534 VINE ST 45217

Saint Clairsville, Belmont Co., Pop. Code 6
St. Clairsville-Richland CSD
Sch. Sys. Enr. Code 4
Supt. – Leslie Harris, 108 WOODROW AVE 43950
MS, 104 WOODROW AVE 43950
   Wayne Ogilbee, prin.
ES, 120 NORRIS ST 43950 – Jerry Albert, prin.

St. Mary ES, 226 W MAIN ST 43950

Saint Henry, Mercer Co., Pop. Code 4
St. Henry Cons. Local SD
Sch. Sys. Enr. Code 4
Supt. – James Dippold
   371 E COLUMBUS ST 45883
MS, 381 E COLUMBUS ST 45883
   Marvin Wourms, prin.
ES, 192 S WALNUT ST 45883 – Carl Hart, prin.
Other Schools – See Burkettsville

Saint Marys, Auglaize Co., Pop. Code 6
St. Marys CSD
Sch. Sys. Enr. Code 5
Supt. – Paul Blaine, W SOUTH ST 45885
McBroom MS, FRONT ST 45885
   Newton Triplett, prin.
East ES, ARMSTRONG ST 45885
   Charles Hole, prin.
Noble ES, RURAL ROUTE 01 BOX 181 45885
   Greg O'Connor, prin.
West ES, W HIGH ST 45885 – James Elking, prin.
Other Schools – See Wapakoneta

Holy Rosary ES, 128 S PINE ST 45885

Saint Paris, Champaign Co., Pop. Code 4
Graham Local SD
Sch. Sys. Enr. Code 4
Supt. – Frank Focht, P O BOX 910 43072
Graham MS, P O BOX 830 43072
   Steve Fine, prin.
Graham South ES
   2955 ST PARIS JACKSON RD 43072
   Daniel Eagle, prin.
Other Schools – See Rosewood, Urbana

Salem, Columbiana Co., Pop. Code 7
Salem CSD
Sch. Sys. Enr. Code 5
Supt. – Burton Schoffman
   1226 E STATE ST 44460
MS, 230 N LINCOLN AVE 44460
   Rob Delane, prin.
Buckeye ES, 1200 BUCKEYE AVE 44460
   Dennis Niederhiser, prin.
Prospect MS, 838 PROSPECT ST 44460
   Thomas Cupples, prin.
Reilly ES, 491 REILLY AVE 44460
   Marguerite Miller, prin.
Southeast MS, 2200 MERLE RD 44460
   Marjorie Kress, prin.

West Branch Local SD
Supt. – See Beloit
Goshen Center ES, 14003 S RANGE RD 44460
   John Airhart, prin.

St. Paul ES, 925 E STATE ST 44460

Salineville, Columbiana Co., Pop. Code 4
Southern Local SD
Sch. Sys. Enr. Code 4
Supt. – Anthony Krukowski
   38825 STATE ROUTE 39 43945
Southern Local MS, 54 W MAIN ST 43945
   Joann Felton, prin.
Highlandtown ES, 38825 STATE ROUTE 39 43945
   David Brookes, prin.
Other Schools – See Summitville, Wellsville

Sandusky, Erie Co., Pop. Code 8
Perkins Local SD
Sch. Sys. Enr. Code 4
Supt. – Ralph Roshong
   1210 E BOGART ROAD 44870
Perkins MS, 3700 SOUTH AVE 44870
   Larry Pitts, prin.
Furry ES, 310 DOUGLAS DR 44870
   Raymona Anderson, prin.
Meadowlawn MS, 1313 E STRUB RD 44870
   Alfred Weingart, prin.

Sandusky CSD
Sch. Sys. Enr. Code 5
Supt. – Gene Kleindienst
   407 DECATUR ST 44870
Jackson MS, 314 W MADISON ST 44870
   Dan McCarthy, prin.
Adams MS, 318 COLUMBUS AVE 44870
   James Thom, prin.
Campbell MS, 1215 CAMPBELL ST 44870
   Michael Delsignore, prin.

Hancock ES, 2314 HANCOCK ST 44870
  Terry Troutman, prin.
Madison ES, 910 W MADISON ST 44870
  William Biehl, prin.
Mills MS, 1918 MILLS ST 44870
  W. Schafer, prin.
Monroe ES, 328 E MONROE ST 44870
  Beverly Decker, prin.
Ontario MS, 924 ONTARIO ST 44870
  Ronald Maschari, prin.
Osborne ES, 920 W OSBORNE ST 44870
  Judith Monaghan, prin.
Venice Heights ES
  4501 VENICE HEIGHTS BLVD 44870
  James Chapple, prin.

Holy Angels ES, 1603 W JEFFERSON ST 44870
St. Mary ES, 514 DECATUR ST 44870
Sts. Peter & Paul ES, 514 JACKSON ST 44870

Sarahsville, Noble Co., Pop. Code 2
Noble Local SD
Sch. Sys. Enr. Code 4
Supt. – J. Strahler, 20977 STATE RT 146 43779
Shenandoah ES, 20977 STATE ROUTE 146 43779
  Charles Kozlesky, prin.

Sardinia, Brown Co., Pop. Code 3
Eastern Local SD
Sch. Sys. Enr. Code 4
Supt. – Thomas Miller, P O BOX 1 45171
ES, COLLEGE AVE 45171 – John Cushing, prin.
Other Schools – See Decatur, Georgetown, Russellville

Sardis, Monroe Co.
Switzerland of Ohio Local SD
Supt. – See Woodsfield
Midway ES, RURAL ROUTE 01 BOX 93 43946
  Alvin Thompson, prin.
ES, P O BOX 305 43946 – Alvin Thompson, prin.

Savannah, Ashland Co., Pop. Code 2
Crestview Local SD
Supt. – See Ashland
ES, P O BOX 14 44874 – David Petska, prin.

Scioto Furnace, Scioto Co.
Bloom-Vernon Local SD
Supt. – See South Webster
Scioto Furnace ES 45677 – Terry Cooper, prin.

Scottown, Lawrence Co.
Symmes Valley Local SD
Supt. – See Willow Wood
Symmes Valley ES 1 45678 – Hazel Wilson, prin.
Symmes Valley #3 ES 45678 – Eddie Hardy, prin.
Symmes Valley MS 4, HCR 45678
  Eddie Hardy, prin.

Seaman, Adams Co., Pop. Code 4
Ohio Valley Local SD
Supt. – See West Union
ES, BROADWAY AVE BOX J 45679
  Sheila Roush, prin.

Sebring, Mahoning Co., Pop. Code 6
Sebring Local SD
Sch. Sys. Enr. Code 3
Supt. – David Claypoole
  25 E INDIANA AVE 44672
Miller ES, 506 W VIRGINIA AVE 44672
  Robert Winn, prin.
Sebring ES, 306 W TEXAS AVE 44672
  Robert Winn, prin.

Sedalia, Madison Co.
Madison-Plains Local SD
Supt. – See London
Midway ES, 13880 MAIN SW 43151
  (—), prin.

Senecaville, Guernsey Co., Pop. Code 2
Rolling Hills Local SD
Supt. – See Byesville
Secrest ES, 58860 WINTERGREEN RD 43780
  Larry Touvell, prin.

Seven Hills, Cuyahoga Co., Pop. Code 7
Parma CSD
Supt. – See Parma
Hillside JHS, 1320 HILLSIDE RD 44131
  John Spinner, prin.
Glenn ES, 1300 E DARTMOOR AVE 44131
  William Clark, prin.

Seven Mile, Butler Co., Pop. Code 3
Edgewood CSD
Supt. – See Trenton
Edgewood JHS, 200 RITTER ST 45062
  Steve Moeckel, prin.

Seville, Medina Co., Pop. Code 4
Cloverleaf Local SD
Supt. – See Lodi
ES, 24 MAIN ST E 44273 – Carl Walley, prin.

Shade, Athens Co.
Alexander Local SD
Supt. – See Albany
ES 45776 – (—), prin.

Shadyside, Belmont Co., Pop. Code 5
Shadyside Local SD
Sch. Sys. Enr. Code 4
Supt. – Rob Henry, 3890 LINCOLN AVE 43947
Leona Avenue MS 43947 – David Sommers, prin.

Jefferson Avenue ES
  4900 JEFFERSON AVE 43947
  John Crunelle, prin.

Shaker Heights, Cuyahoga Co., Pop. Code 8
Shaker Heights CSD
Sch. Sys. Enr. Code 6
Supt. – Mark Freeman
  15600 PARKLAND DRIVE 44120
MS, 20600 SHAKER BLVD 44122
  Richard Peterjohn, prin.
Boulevard ES, 14900 DREXMORE RD 44120
  Rebecca Kimberly, prin.
Fernway ES, 17420 FERNWAY RD 44120
  Donald Coffee, prin.
Lomond ES, 17917 LOMOND BLVD 44122
  Lawrence Svec, prin.
Mercer ES, 23325 WIMBLEDON RD 44122
  Bernice Stokes, prin.
Onaway ES, 3115 WOODBURY RD 44120
  Margaret Lennard, prin.
Woodbury MS, 15400 S WOODLAND RD 44120
  Delores Groves, prin.

Hathaway Brown School
  19600 N PARK BLVD 44122
Laurel School, 1 LYMAN CIRCLE 44122
St. Dominic ES, 3455 NORWOOD RD 44122
University ES, 20701 BRANTLEY RD 44122

Sharon Center, Medina Co.
Highland Local SD
Supt. – See Medina
ES, P O BOX 179 44274 – Robert Hummel, prin.

Sharonville, Hamilton Co., Pop. Code 7

St. Michael ES, OAK ST & CREEK RD 45241

Shauck, Morrow Co.
Northmore Local SD
Supt. – See Galion
Johnsville ES 43349 – David Danhoff, prin.

Shawnee, Perry Co., Pop. Code 1
Southern Local SD
Supt. – See Hemlock
Miller JHS, P O BOX 26 43782
  Robert Towner, prin.

Sheffield Lake, Lorain Co., Pop. Code 7
Sheffield-Sheffield Lake CSD
Supt. – See Lorain
Barr MS, 2180 LAKE BREEZE RD 44054
  Jack Moskovitz, prin.
Forestlawn MS, 3975 FORESTLAWN AVE 44054
  Frederick Fastenau, prin.
Knollwood ES, 4975 OSTER RD 44054
  Lillian Baratko, prin.
Tennyson ES, 555 KENILWORTH AVE 44054
  David Karahuta, prin.

St. Thomas the Apostle ES, 715 HARRIS RD 44054

Shelby, Richland Co., Pop. Code 6
Shelby CSD
Sch. Sys. Enr. Code 5
Supt. – Terry Russell, P O BOX 31 44875
JHS, HIGH SCHOOL AVE 44875
  Mark Stock, prin.
Auburn ES, 109 AUBURN ST 44875
  Sharon Ickes, prin.
Central ES, 25 HIGH SCHOOL AVE 44875
  Dan Campbell, prin.
Dowds ES, 18 SENECA DR 44875
  Charles Fugate, prin.
Whitney ES, 111 E WHITNEY AVE 44875
  Steve Peebles, prin.

St. Mary ES, 26 WEST ST 44875

Sherrodsville, Carroll Co.
Conotton Valley Union Local SD
Supt. – See Bowerston
ES, MOUND ST 44675 – John Evanosky, prin.

Sherwood, Defiance Co., Pop. Code 3
Central Local SD
Sch. Sys. Enr. Code 4
Supt. – Douglas Johnson
  RURAL ROUTE 01 43556
Fairview JHS, RURAL ROUTE 01 43556
  Joseph Speiser, prin.
ES, P O BOX 4506 43556 – James Kline, prin.
Other Schools – See Farmer, Mark Center

Shiloh, Richland Co., Pop. Code 3
Plymouth Local SD
Supt. – See Plymouth
MS, MECHANIC ST 44878 – John Hart, prin.
Shiloh ES, MECHANIC ST 44878
  Mark Sheely, prin.

Shreve, Wayne Co., Pop. Code 4
Triway Local SD
Supt. – See Wooster
ES, 598 N MARKET ST 44676
  Robert Blanchard, prin.

Sidney, Shelby Co., Pop. Code 7
Fairlawn Local SD
Sch. Sys. Enr. Code 3
Supt. – Tom Coyne
  18800 JOHNSTON ROAD 45365
Other Schools – See Pemberton

Hardin-Houston Local SD
Supt. – See Houston
Hardin ES, 10207 STATE ROUTE 47 W 45365
  Sharon Dudek, prin.

Sidney CSD
Sch. Sys. Enr. Code 5
Supt. – Eugene Emter, 232 N MIAMI AVE 45365
Bridgeview MS, 320 E NORTH ST 45365
  Harold Schmiesing, prin.
Central ES, 102 N MIAMI AVE 45365
  Gerald Allen, prin.
Emerson ES, 901 CAMPBELL RD 45365
  John Scheu, prin.
Longfellow ES, 1250 PARK ST 45365
  Gary Reed, prin.
Lowell ES, 702 S MAIN AVE 45365
  (—), prin.
Northwood MS, 1152 SAINT MARYS RD 45365
  Sara Drake, prin.
Parkwood ES, 315 W RUSSELL RD 45365
  Ben Edmonds, prin.
Whittier ES, 425 BELMONT ST 45365
  Judith Bergman, prin.

Holy Angels ES, 120 E WATER ST 45365

Sinking Spring, Highland Co., Pop. Code 2
Ohio Valley Local SD
Supt. – See West Union
ES 45172 – Larry Shiveley, prin.

Smithville, Wayne Co., Pop. Code 4
Green Local SD
Sch. Sys. Enr. Code 4
Supt. – Roger Ramseyer, E MAIN ST 44677
Greene MS, 484 E MAIN ST 44677
  Richard Zimmerly, prin.
ES, 156 S MILTON ST 44677
  Terry Bauman, prin.
Other Schools – See Marshallville

Solon, Cuyahoga Co., Pop. Code 7
Solon CSD
Sch. Sys. Enr. Code 5
Supt. – Joseph Regano
  33675 SOLON ROAD 44139
Arthur Road MS, 33425 ARTHUR ROAD 44139
  Michael Doney, prin.
Lewis ES, 32345 CANNON RD 44139
  Janeen Oden, prin.
Orchard MS, 6800 SOM CENTER RD 44139
  R. Waugh, prin.
Roxbury ES, 6795 SOLON BLVD 44139
  Norman Wren, prin.

St. Rita ES, 32815 LINDEN DR 44139

Somerset, Perry Co., Pop. Code 4
Northern Local SD
Supt. – See Thornville
ES, HIGH ST 43783 – Jonn Simmons, prin.

Holy Trinity ES, 225 S COLUMBUS ST 43783

South Amherst, Lorain Co., Pop. Code 4
Firelands Local SD
Supt. – See Oberlin
South Amherst MS, 152 W MAIN ST 44001
  Robert Telloni, prin.
South Amherst ES, 152 W MAIN ST 44001
  Dennis Walters, prin.

South Bloomingville, Hocking Co.
Logan-Hocking CSD
Supt. – See Logan
ES, 21771 STATE ROUTE 664 43152
  Barbara Koehler, prin.

South Charleston, Clark Co., Pop. Code 4
Southeastern Local SD
Sch. Sys. Enr. Code 3
Supt. – Bruce Stewart
  195 E JAMESTOWN ST 45368
Miami View ES, 230 OLD CLIFTON ROAD 45368
  Rick Fry, prin.

South Euclid, Cuyahoga Co., Pop. Code 8
South Euclid-Lyndhurst CSD
Supt. – See Lyndhurst
Adrian ES, 1071 HOMESTEAD RD 44121
  Robert Evans, prin.
Lowden ES, 4106 LOWDEN RD 44121
  Sandra Weaver, prin.
Rowland ES, 4300 BAYARD RD 44121
  (—), prin.

Solomon Schecter Day ES
  1825 S GREEN RD 44121
St. Gregory the Great ES
  4478 RUSHTON RD 44121
St. John Lutheran ES, 4386 MAYFIELD RD 44121
St. Margaret Mary ES
  4205 BLUESTONE RD 44121

Southington, Trumbull Co.
Southington Local SD
Sch. Sys. Enr. Code 3
Supt. – Charles Jeffords
  4432 STATE ROUTE 305 44470
MS, 4432 STATE ROUTE 305 44470
  William Pfahler, prin.
Southington ES, 4432 STATE ROUTE 305 44470
  William Pfahler, prin.

South Lebanon, Warren Co., Pop. Code 5
Kings Local SD
Supt. – See Kings Mills
ES, 10 N HIGH ST   45065 – Kenneth Smith, prin.

South Point, Lawrence Co., Pop. Code 5
South Point Local SD
Sch. Sys. Enr. Code 5
Supt. – George York
RURAL ROUTE 03 BOX 25   45680
MS, RURAL ROUTE 03 BOX 122   45680
Ken Cook, prin.
Burlington ES, RURAL ROUTE 02 BOX 233   45680
Leslie York, prin.
South Point ES 2
501 WASHINGTON ST #2   45680
Gary Douglas, prin.

South Salem, Ross Co., Pop. Code 2
Greenfield EVD
Supt. – See Greenfield
Buckskin ES, P O BOX 69   45681
Mary Miller, prin.

South Vienna, Clark Co., Pop. Code 2
Northeastern Local SD
Supt. – See Springfield
ES, 140 W MAIN ST   45369 – Larry Shaffer, prin.

South Webster, Scioto Co., Pop. Code 3
Bloom-Vernon Local SD
Sch. Sys. Enr. Code 4
Supt. – Charles Lykins, P O BOX 237   45682
Bloom ES, P O BOX 237   45682
Terry Cooper, prin.
Other Schools – See Scioto Furnace, Wheelersburg

Sparta, Morrow Co., Pop. Code 2
Highland Local SD
Sch. Sys. Enr. Code 4
Supt. – Herschel Cornn, P O BOX 98   43350
Highland JHS, P O BOX 68   43350
John Jurkowitz, prin.
Highland East ES, P O BOX 69   43350
Michael Carder, prin.
Other Schools – See Chesterville, Marengo

Spencer, Medina Co., Pop. Code 3
Black River Local SD
Supt. – See Homerville
Black River MS, P O BOX 128   44275
Amanda Welch, prin.

Cloverleaf Local SD
Supt. – See Lodi
Chatham MS, 6306 AVON LAKE RD   44275
Timothy Burns, prin.

Spencerville, Allen Co., Pop. Code 4
Spencerville Local SD
Sch. Sys. Enr. Code 4
Supt. – Dale Kisler, 600 SCHOOL ST   45887
MS, 436 E 4TH ST   45887 – Charles Violet, prin.
Jennings MS, RURAL ROUTE 02   45887
Donald McClintock, prin.
ES, 436 E FOURTH ST   45887
Donald McClintock, prin.

Springboro, Warren Co., Pop. Code 5
Clearcreek Local SD
Sch. Sys. Enr. Code 4
Supt. – Don Dyck, 800 S MAIN ST   45066
JHS, 705 S MAIN ST   45066 – Gary Perkins, prin.
Clearcreek MS, 750 S MAIN ST   45066
Sandra Wray, prin.
Wright ES, 40 FLORENCE DR   45066
Victor Johantges, prin.

Ridgeville Christian School
946 E LOWER SPRINGBORO   45066

Springfield, Clark Co., Pop. Code 8
Mad River-Green Local SD
Sch. Sys. Enr. Code 5
Supt. – Darlene Duchene
1215 OLD MILL ROAD   45506
Hustead ES, 3600 HUSTEAD RD   45502
Rosa Strong, prin.
Other Schools – See Enon

Northeastern Local SD
Sch. Sys. Enr. Code 5
Supt. – Roger Compton
1414 BOWMAN ROAD   45502
Northridge ES, 4445 RIDGEWOOD ROAD E   45503
Frank Demma, prin.
Rolling Hills ES, 2613 MOOREFIELD RD   45502
Cynthia Fisher, prin.
Other Schools – See South Vienna

Northwestern Local SD
Sch. Sys. Enr. Code 4
Supt. – Charles Cornett, 5610 TROY ROAD   45502
Northwestern MS, 5610 TROY ROAD   45502
Milton Palmer, prin.
Northwestern ES, 5780 TROY RD   45502
(—), prin.

Springfield CSD
Sch. Sys. Enr. Code 7
Supt. – James Frantz, 49 E COLLEGE AVE   45504
Clark MS, 1315 W HIGH ST   45506
Richard Broderick, prin.
Franklin MS, 1525 KENWOOD AVE   45505
William Meyer, prin.
Hayward MS, 1700 CLIFTON AVE   45505
Craig Williams, prin.

Roosevelt MS, 1600 N LIMESTONE ST   45503
R. Bash, prin.
Schaefer MS, 130 S BURNETT ROAD   45505
J. Richard Wiggins, prin.
Emerson ES, 601 SELMA RD   45505
John Oda, prin.
Fulton ES, 631 S YELLOW SPRINGS ST   45506
Irene Davis, prin.
Grayhill ES, 251 MONTGOMERY AVE   45506
Dale Helmuth, prin.
Highlands ES, 1452 S WITTENBERG AVE   45506
Richard Yontz, prin.
Kenton ES, 1221 E HOME RD   45503
Marian Gochenour, prin.
Kenwood Heights ES, 1301 BEACON ST   45505
Jewell Hall, prin.
Lagonda ES, 2725 LAGONDA AVE   45503
David Calhoun, prin.
Lincoln ES, 1500 TIBBETTS AVE   45505
Edward Weisenbach, prin.
Mann ES, 521 MOUNT JOY ST   45505
Norman Knowlton, prin.
Perrin Woods ES, 431 W JOHN ST   45506
Andrew Heims, prin.
Snowhill ES, 531 W HARDING RD   45504
Pamela Young, prin.
Synder Park ES, 1600 MAIDEN LN   45504
Wanda Newport, prin.
Warder Park-Wayne ES
2251 HILLSIDE AVE   45503 – Donald Culler, prin.

Springfield Local SD
Sch. Sys. Enr. Code 4
Supt. – Larry Zerkle
1561 E POSSUM ROAD   45502
Possum ES, 2589 S YELLOW SPRINGS ST   45506
Thomas McGinnis, prin.
Reid ES, 3640 E HIGH ST   45505
Robert Willeman, prin.
Rockway ES, 3500 W NATIONAL RD   45504
Timothy Greenwood, prin.

Holy Trinity ES, 819 KENTON ST   45505
Ridgewood ES, 2420 SAINT PARIS PIKE   45504
Springfield Christian ES, 924 E HOME RD   45503
St. Bernard ES, 920 LAGONDA AVE   45503
St. Teresa ES, 137 FLORAL AVE   45504

Sterling, Wayne Co.
North Central Local SD
Supt. – See Creston
ES, 13323 KAUFFMAN AVE   44276
Wilbur Bowers, prin.

Steubenville, Jefferson Co., Pop. Code 8
Steubenville CSD
Sch. Sys. Enr. Code 5
Supt. – D. Keenan, P O BOX 189   43952
Harding MS, 1928 W MARKET ST   43952
Allen Hollowood, prin.
Buena Vista ES, SCHENLEY AVE   43952
Henry Gavarkavich, prin.
Garfield ES, 936 N 5TH ST   43952
Patricia Fletcher, prin.
Lincoln ES, 980 LINCOLN AVE   43952
Carmen Calfa, prin.
McKinley ES, W ADAMS ST   43952
Andrew Standardi, prin.
Roosevelt ES, 350 BELLEVIEW BLVD   43952
Joseph Pielech, prin.
Wells ES, 408 NORTH ST   43952
John Holub, prin.

All Saints MS, 243 S 7TH ST   43952
All Saints School, 415 N 4TH ST   43952
Aquinas Central ES
ROAD 3 LOVERS LANE   43952
Holy Rosary ES, 100 ETTA AVE   43952

Stewart, Athens Co.
Federal Hocking Local SD
Sch. Sys. Enr. Code 4
Supt. – Tim Lairson, P O BOX 117   45778
Federal Hocking MS, P O BOX 117   45778
James Watson, prin.
Other Schools – See Amesville, Coolville

Stockdale, Pike Co.
Eastern Local SD
Supt. – See Beaver
ES   45683 – Walter Bevins, prin.

Stockport, Morgan Co., Pop. Code 3
Morgan Local SD
Supt. – See Mc Connelsville
Windsor ES, P O BOX 288   43787
Robert Matthews, prin.

Stout, Adams Co.
Ohio Valley Local SD
Supt. – See West Union
Green ES, 2155 BLUE CREEK RD   45684
R. Lucas, prin.

Stoutsville, Fairfield Co., Pop. Code 3
Amanda-Clearcreek Local SD
Supt. – See Amanda
Clearcreek ES, 9096 WALNUT ST   43154
James Roe III, prin.

Stow, Summit Co., Pop. Code 8
Stow CSD
Sch. Sys. Enr. Code 6
Supt. – Dean Mizer, 3227 E GRAHAM RD   44224
Lakeview MS, 1819 GRAHAM RD   44224
Kim Lockhart, prin.

Echo Hills ES, 4405 STOW RD   44224
John Salter, prin.
Fishcreek ES, 5080 FISHCREEK RD   44224
Dennis Frisbee, prin.
Highland ES, 1843 GRAHAM RD   44224
Joan Sigafoos, prin.
Indian Trail ES, 3512 KENT RD   44224
Robert Woods, prin.
Woodland ES, 2908 GRAHAM RD   44224
Karen Schofield, prin.
Other Schools – See Munroe Falls

Holy Family ES, 3163 KENT RD   44224

Strasburg, Tuscarawas Co., Pop. Code 4
Strasburg-Franklin Local SD
Sch. Sys. Enr. Code 3
Supt. – Alan Osler, 140 N BODMER AVE   44680
Strasburg-Franklin ES
140 N BODMER AVE   44680 – Ed Bode, prin.

Streetsboro, Portage Co., Pop. Code 6
Streetsboro CSD
Sch. Sys. Enr. Code 4
Supt. – John Carney, 9000 KIRBY LANE   44241
MS, 1951 ANNALANE DRIVE   44241
George Wargo, prin.
Campus ES, 8955 KIRBY LN   44241
Dennis Ferguson, prin.
Wait ES, 899 FROST RD   44241
Virginia Patton, prin.

Strongsville, Cuyahoga Co., Pop. Code 8
Strongsville CSD
Sch. Sys. Enr. Code 6
Supt. – John Brown, 13200 PEARL ROAD   44136
Allen ES, 16400 PARK LANE DR   44136
James Gould, prin.
Chapman ES, 13883 DRAKE RD   44136
Walter Joyce, prin.
Drake ES, 20566 ALBION RD   44136
Jan Zmich, prin.
Muraski ES, 20270 ROYALTON RD   44136
Joseph Uher, prin.
Surrarrer ES, 9305 PRIEM RD   44136
Cathy Whelan, prin.
Whitney ES, 13548 WHITNEY RD   44136
Alexander Lutz, prin.
Zellers ES, 18199 COOK AVE   44136
Trent Lamb, prin.

St. Joseph & John Interparochi ES
12580 PEARL RD   44136

Struthers, Mahoning Co., Pop. Code 7
Struthers CSD
Sch. Sys. Enr. Code 4
Supt. – John Santillo, 172 SEXTON ST   44471
Sexton JHS, 128 SEXTON ST   44471
Robert Canter, prin.
Center ES, 75 CENTER ST   44471
Albert Toth, prin.
Fifth Street ES, 800 FIFTH ST   44471
(—), prin.
Lyon Plat ES, 520 NINTH ST   44471
James Fabilli, prin.
Manor Avenue ES, 230 E MANOR AVE   44471
Joanne Mcdanel, prin.

Holy Trinity ES, 250 N BRIDGE ST   44471
St. Nicholas ES, 762 FIFTH ST   44471

Stryker, Williams Co., Pop. Code 4
Stryker Local SD
Sch. Sys. Enr. Code 3
Supt. – David Nicholls, P O BOX 624   43557
ES, P O BOX 624   43557 – James Selgo, prin.

Sugarcreek, Tuscarawas Co., Pop. Code 4
Garaway Local SD
Sch. Sys. Enr. Code 4
Supt. – Douglas Spade, 146 DOVER ROAD   44681
Miller Avenue ES, 840 MILLER AVE   44681
Larry Compton, prin.
Ragersville ES, RURAL ROUTE 01   44681
Larry Miller, prin.
Other Schools – See Baltic, Dundee

Sugar Grove, Fairfield Co., Pop. Code 2
Berne Union Local SD
Sch. Sys. Enr. Code 4
Supt. – H. Seckinger, 506 N MAIN ST   43155
Berne Union ES, 506 N MAIN ST   43155
Joyce Sloan, prin.

Sullivan, Medina Co.
Black River Local SD
Supt. – See Homerville
Black River IS, P O BOX 7   44880
Linda Krieder, prin.

Sulphur Springs, Crawford Co.
Colonel Crawford Local SD
Supt. – See North Robinson
ES   44881 – Marjorie Brooks, prin.

Summit Station, Licking Co.
Licking Heights Local SD
Sch. Sys. Enr. Code 2
Supt. – Charles Crist
6539 SUMMIT ROAD SW   43073
Licking Heights MS
6539 SUMMIT ROAD SW   43073
Karl VanDeest, prin.

Summit ES, 6539 SUMMIT RD SW 43073
  Barbara Triplett, prin.
  Other Schools – See Pataskala

Summitville, Columbiana Co., Pop. Code 2
Southern Local SD
Supt. – See Salineville
Franklin ES, P O BOX 44 43962
  David Brookes, prin.

Sunbury, Delaware Co., Pop. Code 4
Big Walnut Local SD
Sch. Sys. Enr. Code 2
Supt. – Carl Martin, 105 BAUGHMAN ST 43074
Big Walnut IS, 70 HARRISON ST 43074
  Steven Butler, prin.
Big Walnut ES, 940 S OLD 3C RD 43074
  Richard Rosato, prin.
Other Schools – See Galena

Swanton, Fulton Co., Pop. Code 5
Evergreen Local SD
Supt. – See Metamora
Fulton ES, 10538 CO ROAD 4 43558
  Paul Cothrel, prin.

Swanton Local SD
Sch. Sys. Enr. Code 3
Supt. – Roy Vivian, 206 CHERRY ST 43558
JHS, 206 CHERRY ST 43558
  Ken Baumgartner, prin.
Crestwood ES, CRESTWOOD DR 43558
  William Brannan, prin.
Park ES, ELTON PARKWAY 43558
  Richard Ueberroth, prin.
Swanton Township ES
  12035 AIRPORT HWY 43558
  Richard Ueberroth, prin.

Holy Trinity-Swanton ES, 2-2639 US RT 20 43558
St. Richard ES, 333 BROOKSIDE DR 43558

Sycamore, Wyandot Co., Pop. Code 4
Mohawk Local SD
Sch. Sys. Enr. Code 2
Supt. – Madelyn Jarvis
  295 STATE ROUTE 231 44882
ES, W SAFFEL ST 44882 – James Lahoski, prin.
Other Schools – See Mc Cutchenville, Melmore

Sycamore Valley, Monroe Co.
Switzerland of Ohio Local SD
Supt. – See Woodsfield
Bethel ES, 36877 STATE ROUTE 260 43789
  Philip Ackerman, prin.

Sylvania, Lucas Co., Pop. Code 7
Sylvania CSD
Sch. Sys. Enr. Code 2
Supt. – Gordon Hoffman
  6850 MONROE ST 43560
Arbor Hills JHS, 5334 WHITEFORD ROAD 43560
  Thomas Hauman, prin.
McCord MS, 4304 MCCORD ROAD 43560
  Edwin Murbach, prin.
Highland ES, 7720 ERIE ST 43560
  Jack Smith, prin.
Hill View ES, 5425 WHITEFORD RD 43560
  Dale Wiltse, prin.
Maplewood ES, 6769 MAPLEWOOD AVE 43560
  William Baldridge, prin.
Sylvan ES, 4830 WICKFORD DR E 43560
  Margaret Yerman, prin.
Other Schools – See Toledo

St. Francis ES, 6832 CONVENT BLVD 43560
St. Joseph ES, 5411 MAIN ST 43560

Syracuse, Meigs Co., Pop. Code 3
Southern Local SD
Supt. – See Racine
ES, P O BOX 158326 45779
  James Lawrence, prin.

Tallmadge, Summit Co., Pop. Code 7
Tallmadge CSD
Sch. Sys. Enr. Code 3
Supt. – Daniel McCombs, 486 EAST AVE 44278
MS, 76 NORTH AVE 44278 – Richard Banig, prin.
Dunbar ES, 731 DUNBAR RD 44278
  Linda Jones, prin.
Munroe MS, 230 N MUNROE RD 44278
  Francis Martin, prin.

Akron Christian ES, 508 NEWTON ST 44278

Terrace Park, Hamilton Co., Pop. Code 4
Mariemont CSD
Supt. – See Mariemont
ES, 723 ELM AVE 45174 – Michele Hummel, prin.

The Plains, Athens Co., Pop. Code 4
Athens CSD
Supt. – See Athens
ES, P O BOX N 45780 – Shelley Conrath, prin.

Thompson, Geauga Co.
Ledgemont Local SD
Sch. Sys. Enr. Code 3
Supt. – Kathleen Ferrone
  16200 BURROWS ROAD 44086
Ledgemont ES, 16200 BURROWS RD 44086
  Donald Gentile, prin.

Thornville, Perry Co., Pop. Code 3
Northern Local SD
Sch. Sys. Enr. Code 4
Supt. – Steve Johnson
  3700 SHERIDAN DRIVE 43076
ES, P O BOX 246 43076 – Timothy Klingler, prin.
Other Schools – See Glenford, Somerset

Tiffin, Seneca Co., Pop. Code 7
Tiffin CSD
Sch. Sys. Enr. Code 5
Supt. – Larry Cook, 244 S MONROE ST 44883
Clinton ES, 2036 E TWP ROAD 122 44818
  Kay Assenheimer, prin.
Krout ES, GLENN ST 44883
  Winifred Place, prin.
Lincoln ES, 124 OHIO AVE 44883
  Kathy Wetta, prin.
Noble ES, MINERVA ST 44883
  Louis Dieguez, prin.
Washington ES, ELMER ST 44883
  George Dutt, prin.
Other Schools – See Bloomville

St. Joseph ES, 357 S WASHINGTON ST 44883
St. Mary ES, 75 S SANDUSKY ST 44883

Tiltonsville, Jefferson Co., Pop. Code 4
Buckeye Local SD
Supt. – See Rayland
ES, 109 GRANDVIEW AVE 43963
  Joseph Talarico, prin.

Tipp City, Miami Co., Pop. Code 6
Bethel Local SD
Sch. Sys. Enr. Code 3
Supt. – (—), 7490 S STATE ROUTE 201 45371
Bethel JHS, 7490 S STATE ROUTE 201 45371
  Stephen Liles, prin.
Bethel ES, 7490 S STATE ROUTE 201 45371
  David Henagen, prin.

Tipp City EVD
Sch. Sys. Enr. Code 4
Supt. – W. Dean Pond
  90 S TIPPECANOE DRIVE 45371
Ball MS, 575 N HYATT ST 45371
  Howard Parks, prin.
Tippecanoe Central MS
  223 W BROADWAY ST 45371 – John Ziegler,
  prin.
Broadway ES, 223 W BROADWAY ST 45371
  Ronald Martin, prin.
Coppock ES, 525 N HYATT ST 45371
  Adrienne Howell, prin.

Dayton Christian-Sugar Grove ES
  7875 KESSLER FREDERICK RD 45371

Tippecanoe, Harrison Co.
Harrison Hills CSD
Supt. – See Hopedale
MS, RURAL ROUTE 01 44699
  Denver Kaiser, prin.

Tiro, Crawford Co., Pop. Code 2
Buckeye Central Local SD
Supt. – See New Washington
Buckeye East ES, P O BOX 98 44887
  Ruthann Noblet, prin.

Toledo, Lucas Co., Pop. Code 10
Ottawa Hills Local SD
Sch. Sys. Enr. Code 3
Supt. – William Reimer
  2532 EVERGREEN ROAD 43606
Ottawa Hills ES, 3602 INDIAN RD 43606
  Anthony Judson, prin.

Springfield Local SD
Supt. – See Holland
Dorr Street ES, 1205 KING RD 43617
  Ralph Carroll, prin.

Sylvania CSD
Supt. – See Sylvania
Central Avenue ES, 7460 W CENTRAL AVE 43617
  Rene Greenberg, prin.
Stranahan ES
  3840 N HOLLAND-SYLVANIA RD 43615
  George Offenburg, prin.
Whiteford ES, 4708 WHITEFORD RD 43623
  John Hewitt, prin.

Toledo CSD
Sch. Sys. Enr. Code 8
Supt. – Ruth Scott, MANHATTAN AT ELM 43608
Byrnedale JHS, 3945 GLENDALE AVE 43614
  Alfred Mackie, prin.
DeVeaux JHS, 2626 SYLVANIA AVE W 43613
  John Hart, prin.
East Toledo JHS, 355 DEARBORN AVE 43605
  Gregg Libke, prin.
Jones JHS, 550 WALBRIDGE AVE 43609
  Alexander Davis, prin.
Leverett JHS, 1111 MANHATTAN BLVD E 43608
  Roger Moser, prin.
McTigue JHS, 5700 HILL AVE 43615
  Richard St. John, prin.
Old West End JHS, 3131 CAMBRIDGE ST 43610
  Pariss Coleman, prin.
Robinson JHS, 1007 GRAND AVE 43606
  Richard Jackson, prin.
Arlington ES, 700 TORONTO AVE 43609
  James Heer, prin.
Beverly ES, 4022 RUGBY DR 43614
  Sue Culver, prin.

Birmingham ES, 222 BAKEWELL ST 43605
  Robert Clark, prin.
Burroughs ES, 2404 SOUTH AVE 43609
  Paul Heintschel, prin.
Chase ES, 3315 MAYO ST 43611
  Katherine Zachel, prin.
Cherry ES, 3348 CHERRY ST 43608
  (—).
Crossgates ES, 3901 SHADYLAWN DR 43614
  Janice Reason, prin.
East Side Central ES, 815 NAVARRE AVE 43605
  Harriet Allen, prin.
Edgewater ES, 5549 EDGEWATER DR 43611
  Bonnie Sloan, prin.
Elmhurst ES, 4530 ELMHURST RD 43613
  David Schafer, prin.
Fall Meyer ES, 1800 KRIEGER DR 43615
  Millard Jackson, prin.
Franklin ES, 310 STEADMAN ST 43605
  Frank Nagy, prin.
Fulton ES, 333 MELROSE AVE 43610
  Roy Hodge, prin.
Garfield ES, 1103 N RAVINE PKY 43605
  Ronald McCullough, prin.
Glendale-Feilbach ES, 2317 CASS RD 43614
  Marcia Helman, prin.
Glenwood ES, 2860 GLENWOOD AVE 43610
  William Arner, prin.
Gunckel ES, 430 NEBRASKA AVE 43602
  James Sebree, prin.
Hale ES, 1800 UPTON AVE 43607 – (—), prin.
Harvard ES, 1949 GLENDALE AVE 43614
  Patricia Black, prin.
Hawkins ES, 5550 W BANCROFT ST 43615
  Donna Mather, prin.
Heather Downs ES
  1932 BIRCHWOOD AVE 43614
  Phyllis Tharp, prin.
Keyser ES, 3900 HILL AVE 43607
  Alvin Stephens, prin.
King ES, 1415 LAWRENCE AVE 43607
  Zoe Moore, prin.
LaGrange ES, 708 LAGRANGE ST 43604
  Gary Forquer, prin.
Larchmont ES, 1515 SLATER ST 43612
  Jeffrey Hanthorn, prin.
Lincoln ES, 1801 N DETROIT AVE 43606
  Helen Cohen, prin.
Longfellow ES, 4112 JACKMAN RD 43612
  Caroline Renz, prin.
Marshall ES, 415 COLBURN ST 43609
  Charles Hess, prin.
McKinley ES, 1901 W CENTRAL AVE 43606
  John Korenowsky, prin.
Mt. Vernon ES, 825 N BYRNE RD 43607
  Marie Bush, prin.
Navarre ES, 410 NAVARRE AVE 43605
  Dorothy Moreland, prin.
Newbury ES, 1040 NEWBURY ST 43609
  George Hathaway, prin.
Oakdale ES, 1620 E BROADWAY ST 43605
  Bruce Kuntz, prin.
Old Orchard ES, 2402 CHEITENHAM 43606
  Vincent Meyer, prin.
Ottawa River ES, 4801 290TH ST 43611
  Edrene Cole, prin.
Pickett ES, 1144 BLUM ST 43607
  Edna Robertson, prin.
Raymer ES, 1419 NEVADA ST 43605
  Ed Jacobs, prin.
Reynolds ES, 5000 NORWICH RD 43615
  Rose McDaniel, prin.
Riverside ES, 500 CHICAGO ST 43611
  Edward Kaser, prin.
Sherman ES, SHERMAN & WALNUT 43608
  (—), prin.
Spring ES, 730 SPRING ST 43608
  James Martin, prin.
Stewart ES, 707 AVONDALE AVE 43602
  Rita Mazurek, prin.
Walbridge ES, 1245 WALBRIDGE AVE 43609
  Thomas Creekmore, prin.
Washington ES, 514 PALMWOOD AVE 43602
  Gussie Hawkins, prin.
Westfield ES, 617 WESTERN AVE 43609
  John O'Toole, prin.
Whittier ES, 4215 WALKER AVE 43612
  Peter Whalen, prin.

Washington Local SD
Sch. Sys. Enr. Code 6
Supt. – Kenneth Bishop
  3505 LINCOLNSHIRE BLVD W 43606
Jefferson ES, 5530 WHITMER DRIVE 43613
  Cecil Martin, prin.
Washington JHS, 5700 WHITMER DRIVE 43613
  Gerald Ice, prin.
Greenwood ES, 760 NORTHLAWN DR 43612
  George Baker, prin.
Hiawatha ES, 3020 PHOTOS DR 43613
  Sandra Sheperd, prin.
Jackman ES, 2010 NORTHOVER RD 43613
  Arthur French, prin.
McGregor ES, 3535 MCGREGOR LN 43623
  Edward Stelnicki, prin.
Meadowvale ES, 2755 EDGEBROOK DR 43613
  Thomas French, prin.
Monac ES, 3845 CLAWSON AVE 43623
  Richard Luedtke, prin.
Shoreland ES, SUDER AVE & E HARBOR 43611
  Arthur Michaelis, prin.
Trilby ES, 5720 SECOR RD 43623
  Ernest Leroy, prin.

Wernert ES, 5050 DOUGLAS RD 43613
  George Bullock, prin.

Maumee Valley Country Day School
  1715 REYNOLDS ROAD S 43614
Toledo Christian Academy
  2303 BROOKFORD 43614
Blessed Sacrament ES
  2216 CASTLEWOOD DR 43613
Calvary Christian School
  5025 GLENDALE AVE 43614
Christ the King ES, 4100 HARVEST LN 43623
Gesu ES, 2045 PARKSIDE BLVD 43607
Good Shepherd ES, 541 UTAH ST 43605
Holy Rosary ES, 2565 YORK ST 43605
Ladyfield ES, 3837 SECOR RD 43623
Little Flower ES, 1620 OLIMPHIA RD 43615
Our Lady Lourdes ES, 6145 HILL AVE 43615
Our Lady of Perpetual Help ES
  2255 CENTRAL GROVE AVE 43614
Queen of Peace ES, 235 COURTLAND AVE 43609
Regina Coeli ES, 600 REGINA PKY 43612
Rosary Cathedral ES
  2535 COLLINGWOOD BLVD 43610
Sacred Heart ES, 824 6TH ST 43605
St. Adalbert ES
  3248 WARSAW AND OAKLAND 43608
St. Agnes ES, 3891 MARTHA AVE 43612
St. Angela Hall ES, 2436 PARKWOOD AVE 43620
St. Ann ES, 1120 HORACE ST 43606
St. Catherine ES, 1155 CORBIN RD 43612
St. Charles ES, 1850 AIRPORT HWY 43609
St. Clement ES, 3030 TREMAINSVILLE RD 43613
St. Hedwig ES, 225 DEXTER ST 43605
St. Hyacinth ES, 728 PARKSIDE BLVD 43607
St. James ES, 872 ORCHARD ST 43609
St. John ES, 2729 124TH ST 43611
St. John of Arc ES
  5950 HEATHERDOWNS BLVD 43614
St. Jude ES, 3648 VICTORY AVE 43607
St. Mary ES, 217 PAGE ST 43620
St. Michael ES, 2620 CHASE ST 43611
St. Patrick of Heatherdowns ES
  4201 HEATHERDOWNS BLVD 43614
St. Pius X ES, 2950 ILGER AVE 43606
St. Stephen ES, 2018 CONSAUL ST 43605
St. Teresa ES, 1462 WOODLAND AVE 43607
St. Thomas Aquinas ES, 1430 IDAHO ST 43605
St. Vincent De Paul ES, 1030 CLAY AVE 43608
Trinity Lutheran ES, 4560 GLENDALE AVE 43614
West Side Montessori ES
  2105 MCCORD RD 43615

Tontogany, Wood Co., Pop. Code 2
Otsego Local SD
  Sch. Sys. Enr. Code 4
  Supt. – Larry Busdeker, P O BOX 168 43565
  Other Schools – See Grand Rapids, Haskins, Weston

Toronto, Jefferson Co., Pop. Code 6
Edison Local SD
  Supt. – See Hammondsville
  Knoxville ES, RURAL ROUTE 02 43964
    Fred Burns, prin.

Toronto CSD
  Sch. Sys. Enr. Code 4
  Supt. – Franklin Vostatek, 840 FEDERAL ST 43964
  Karaffa MS, 1307 DENNIS WAY 43964
    Glen Dickinson, prin.
  Dennis MS, DENNIS WAY 43964
    Gary Wilson, prin.
  Lincoln ES, 300 BELMONT ST 43964
    Mary Risler, prin.

St. Francis ES
  FINDLEY AND LORETTA ST 43964

Trenton, Butler Co., Pop. Code 6
Edgewood CSD
  Sch. Sys. Enr. Code 5
  Supt. – Ron Kash, 5005 STATE ROUTE 73 45067
  Babeck ES, 100 MAPLE AVE 45067
    Dixie Davis, prin.
  Bloomfield ES, 300 N MIAMI ST 45067
    James Brandenburg, prin.
  Edgewood MS, 300 N MIAMI ST 45067
    William Kennel, prin.
  Other Schools – See Seven Mile

Trotwood, Montgomery Co., Pop. Code 6
Trotwood-Madison CSD
  Sch. Sys. Enr. Code 5
  Supt. – G. Mourouzis
    444 S BROADWAY ST 45426
  Broadmoor ES, 701 E MAIN ST 45426
    Margaret Henn, prin.
  Madison Park ES, 301 S BROADWAY ST 45426
    Donald Cook, prin.
  Other Schools – See Dayton

Troy, Miami Co., Pop. Code 7
Miami East Local SD
  Supt. – See Casstown
  Elizabeth ES, 5760 WALNUT GRV 45373
    Eric Hacker, prin.
  Staunton ES, 2801 N STRINGTOWN RD 45373
    Eric Hacker, prin.

Troy CSD
  Sch. Sys. Enr. Code 5
  Supt. – Michael Barnhart
    500 N MARKET ST 45373
  JHS, 556 N MARKET ST 45373
    Banna Smith, prin.

Concord ES, 3145 STATE ROUTE 718 45373
  Thomas Mercer, prin.
Cookson ES, MAPLECREST & MYSTIC 45373
  Michael Beamish, prin.
Heywood ES, 290 S RIDGE AVE 45373
  Cardiff Hall, prin.
Hook ES, 729 TRADE SQ W 45373
  Aldon Haines, prin.
Kyle ES, S PLUM ST 45373 – Marcia Rarick, prin.
Van Cleve ES, E MAIN ST 45373
  Alan Zunke, prin.

St. Patrick ES, 420 E WATER ST 45373
Troy Christian ES, 53 S NORWICH RD 45373

Tuppers Plains, Meigs Co.
Eastern Local SD
  Supt. – See Reedsville
  ES, ROUTE 681 45783 – Donald Shue, prin.

Tuscarawas, Tuscarawas Co., Pop. Code 3
Indian Valley Local SD
  Supt. – See Gnadenhutten
  MS, P O BOX 356 44682
    Robert McCutcheon, prin.

Twinsburg, Summit Co., Pop. Code 6
Twinsburg CSD
  Sch. Sys. Enr. Code 4
  Supt. – H. James Schulz
    10270 RAVENNA ROAD 44087
  Dodge MS, 10225 RAVENNA ROAD 44087
    Richard Dorr, prin.
  Bissell MS, 1811 GLENWOOD DR 44087
    Marybeth Bevan, prin.
  ES, 8897 DARROW RD 44087 – M. Corp, prin.
  Wilcox ES, 9198 DARROW RD 44087
    Don Crockett, prin.

Uhrichsville, Tuscarawas Co., Pop. Code 6
Claymont CSD
  Supt. – See Dennison
  Eastport Avenue ES, 1200 EASTPORT AVE 44683
    Pauline Shiltz, prin.
  Rush ES, RURAL ROUTE 02 44683
    Tony Scott, prin.
  Trenton Avenue ES, TRENTON AVE 44683
    Thomas Wolfe, prin.

Union, Montgomery Co., Pop. Code 6
Northmont CSD
  Supt. – See Englewood
  ES, 418 W MARTINDALE RD 45322
    Daniel Hall, prin.

Union City, Darke Co., Pop. Code 4
Mississinawa Valley Local SD
  Sch. Sys. Enr. Code 4
  Supt. – J. Roeth, RURAL ROUTE 05 45390
  Mississinawa Valley MS
    RURAL ROUTE 05 45390
    Michael Bannister, prin.
  Mississinawa Valley ES, 116 SYCAMORE 45390
    David Foltz, prin.

Union Furnace, Hocking Co.
Logan-Hocking CSD
  Supt. – See Logan
  ES 43158 – Tom Vogrin, prin.

Uniontown, Stark Co., Pop. Code 4
Lake Local SD
  Supt. – See Hartville
  ES, 13244 CLEVELAND AVE NW 44685
    John Sadler, prin.

University Heights, Cuyahoga Co., Pop. Code 7
Cleveland Heights-University Heights CSD
  Sch. Sys. Enr. Code 6
  Supt. – Irving Moskowitz
    2155 MIRAMAR BLVD 44118
  Wiley MS, 2181 MIRAMAR BLVD 44118
    James Cipolletti, prin.
  Belvoir ES, 2323 WRENFORD RD 44118
    Patricia Clary, prin.
  Other Schools – See Cleveland, Cleveland Heights

Gesu ES, 2450 MIRAMAR BLVD 44118

Upper Arlington, Franklin Co., Pop. Code 8
Upper Arlington CSD
  Sch. Sys. Enr. Code 6
  Supt. – Homer Mincy
    1950 N MALLWAY DRIVE 43221
  Hastings MS, 1850 HASTINGS LANE 43220
    Phoebe Wienke, prin.
  Jones MS, 2100 NW ARLINGTON AVE 43221
    Edward Orazen, prin.
  Barrington Road ES
    1780 BARRINGTON RD 43221
    Hugh Oakley, prin.
  Greensview ES, 4301 GREENSVIEW DR 43220
    Donald Guss, prin.
  Tremont ES, 2900 TREMONT RD 43221
    Barry Merrick, prin.
  Wickliffe ES, 2405 WICKLIFFE RD 43221
    Steven DeLapp, prin.
  Other Schools – See Columbus

Upper Sandusky, Wyandot Co., Pop. Code 6
Upper Sandusky EVD
  Sch. Sys. Enr. Code 4
  Supt. – Noah Garris, 390 W WALKER ST 43351
  Union JHS, 390 W WALKER ST 43351
    Thomas Patton, prin.
  Eden ES, RURAL ROUTE 01 43351
    Frank Shuleski, prin.

Marseilles ES, 20151 BROADWAY ST 43351
  Ralph Smith, prin.
Salem ES, RURAL ROUTE 02 43351
  Margaret Young, prin.
South Building ES, 444 S 8TH ST 43351
  Ellen Pool, prin.
Union Building ES, 390 W WALKER ST 43351
  Robert Elsmore, prin.
Other Schools – See Harpster

St. Peter ES, 310 N 8TH ST 43351

Urbana, Champaign Co., Pop. Code 7
Graham Local SD
  Supt. – See Saint Paris
  Graham East MS
    3263 N STATE ROUTE 560 43078
    Daniel Black, prin.

Urbana CSD
  Sch. Sys. Enr. Code 5
  Supt. – Stanley Imhulse, P O BOX 272 43078
  JHS, 500 WASHINGTON AVE 43078
    Mitchell Smith, prin.
  East ES, 630 WASHINGTON AVE 43078
    Kay Richards, prin.
  Local IS, 2468 RT 54 43078
    Mike Liskowiak, prin.
  North ES, 626 N RUSSELL ST 43078
    Brenda Riley, prin.
  South ES, 725 S MAIN ST 43078
    Joan Ware, prin.

West Liberty-Salem Local SD
  Supt. – See West Liberty
  Salem MS
    1425 KENNARD-KINGSCREEK RD 43078
    Laurence Amick, prin.

St. Mary ES, 229 WASHINGTON AVE 43078

Utica, Licking Co., Pop. Code 4
North Fork Local SD
  Sch. Sys. Enr. Code 4
  Supt. – Milton Meadows, 312 MAPLE AVE 43080
  MS, 260 JEFFERSON ST 43080
    Dennis Abend, prin.
  ES, P O BOX 956 43080 – Gerald Paisola, prin.
  Other Schools – See Newark

Valley City, Medina Co.
Buckeye Local SD
  Supt. – See Medina
  Liverpool ES, 6801 SCHOOL ST 44280
    Gerald Bammerlin, prin.

Van Buren, Hancock Co., Pop. Code 2
Van Buren Local SD
  Sch. Sys. Enr. Code 3
  Supt. – Jerrold Cramer, P O BOX 229 45889
  ES, P O BOX 229 45889 – Charlotte Vorwerk, prin.

Vandalia, Montgomery Co., Pop. Code 7
Vandalia-Butler CSD
  Sch. Sys. Enr. Code 5
  Supt. – Donald Keebaugh
    306 S DIXIE DRIVE 45377
  Morton ES, 231 W NATIONAL ROAD 45377
    Ralph Clay, prin.
  DeMitt ES, 1010 E OLD NATIONAL ROAD 45377
    Dennis Dyer, prin.
  Helke ES, 611 RANDLER AVE 45377
    Mary Wietzel, prin.
  Other Schools – See Dayton

St. Christopher ES, 405 E NATIONAL RD 45377

Vanlue, Hancock Co., Pop. Code 2
Vanlue Local SD
  Sch. Sys. Enr. Code 2
  Supt. – Mark Smith, 301 EAST ST 45890
  ES, 301 S EAST 45890 – Rodney Russell, prin.

Van Wert, Van Wert Co., Pop. Code 7
Crestview Local SD
  Supt. – See Convoy
  Crestview North ES, RURAL ROUTE 03 45891
    Kenneth Jerome, prin.

Lincolnview Local SD
  Sch. Sys. Enr. Code 3
  Supt. – Charles Cooper, P O BOX 270 45891
  Lincolnview Marsh MS, P O BOX 150 45891
    James Grant, prin.
  Lincolnview North MS
    RURAL ROUTE 02 BOX 103 45891
    Michael Inniger, prin.
  Other Schools – See Middle Point

Van Wert CSD
  Sch. Sys. Enr. Code 4
  Supt. – Steven Farnsworth
    CRAWFORD & JEFFERSON 45891
  Lincoln JHS, W CRAWFORD ST 45891
    William Swank, prin.
  Franklin ES
    FROTHINGHAM & WALNUT STS 45891
    Sue McGonnell, prin.
  Jefferson ES, BUCKEYE DR 45891
    Donald Miller, prin.
  Mann ES, E 3RD 45891 – David Roy, prin.
  Pleasant ES, RURAL ROUTE 04 45891
    Donald Miller, prin.
  Washington ES, 839 PROSPECT AVE 45891
    Michael Manken, prin.
  Wayne ES, 641 N JEFFERSON ST 45891
    David Roy, prin.

Other Schools – See Ohio City

St. Mary ES, 611 JENNINGS RD 45891

Vermilion, Erie Co., Pop. Code 7
Vermilion Local SD
Sch. Sys. Enr. Code 5
Supt. – Jack Hook, 5735 SOUTH ST 44089
Sailorway MS, 5355 SAILORWAY 44089
  Phillip Machcinski, prin.
Vermilion IS, 935 DECATUR ST 44089
  George Harizal, prin.
South Street ES, 5735 SOUTH ST 44089
  John Laslo, prin.

St. Mary ES, 5433 OHIO ST 44089

Verona, Preble Co., Pop. Code 3
Tri-County North Local SD
Supt. – See Lewisburg
Tri-County North PS, N MAIN ST 45378
  Suzanne Dorsey, prin.

Versailles, Darke Co., Pop. Code 4
Versailles EVD
Sch. Sys. Enr. Code 4
Supt. – Gregory Taylor, P O BOX 72 45380
ES, 130 W WARD ST #72 45380
  Thomas Doseck, prin.
MS, P O BOX 72 45380 – William Schuette, prin.
Other Schools – See North Star

Vickery, Sandusky Co.
Margaretta Local SD
Supt. – See Castalia
Townsend ES, 1783 N CO ROAD 294 43464
  Delores Meggitt, prin.

Vienna, Trumbull Co., Pop. Code 3
Mathews Local SD
Sch. Sys. Enr. Code 4
Supt. – Barry Morrison
  4429 WARREN SHARON ROAD NE 44473
Baker MS, SHERIDAN DR 44473
  Dominic Mastropietro, prin.
Other Schools – See Cortland, Fowler

Vincent, Washington Co., Pop. Code 2
Warren Local SD
Sch. Sys. Enr. Code 5
Supt. – Richard Helser, RURAL ROUTE 01 45784
Barlow-Vincent ES, RURAL ROUTE 01 45784
  Judith Coil, prin.
Other Schools – See Bartlett, Cutler, Little Hocking,
  Marietta

Vinton, Gallia Co., Pop. Code 2
Gallia County Local SD
Supt. – See Gallipolis
ES, RURAL ROUTE 02 BOX 160 45686
  Marilyn Reese, prin.

Wadsworth, Medina Co., Pop. Code 7
Wadsworth CSD
Sch. Sys. Enr. Code 5
Supt. – Charles Parsons, 360 COLLEGE ST 44281
Central MS, 151 MAIN ST 44281
  Stephen Dishauzi, prin.
Franklin ES, 148 CHESTNUT ST 44281
  Thomas Shumate, prin.
Isham Memorial ES, 348 COLLEGE ST 44281
  Daniel Williams, prin.
Lincoln ES, 268 N LYMAN ST 44281
  Richard Nettles, prin.
Overlook ES, 524 BROAD ST 44281
  Richard Nettles, prin.
Valley View ES, 160 W GOOD AVE 44281
  Roger Havens, prin.

Sacred Heart Jesus ES, 110 HUMBOLT AVE 44281

Wakeman, Huron Co., Pop. Code 3
Western Reserve Local SD
Sch. Sys. Enr. Code 4
Supt. – Billy Toney, RIVER ST 44889
ES, 28 RIVER ST 44889 – John Marshall, prin.
Other Schools – See Collins

Walbridge, Wood Co., Pop. Code 5
Lake Local SD
Supt. – See Millbury
ES, 200 E UNION ST 43465 – Margaret West, prin.

St. Jerome ES, 300 EARL ST 43465

Waldo, Marion Co., Pop. Code 2
River Valley Local SD
Supt. – See Marion
ES, 300 W MAIN ST 43356
  Sharon Bussard, prin.

Walnut Creek, Holmes Co.
East Holmes Local SD
Supt. – See Berlin
Chestnut Ridge ES, P O BOX 145 44687
  Gary Mast, prin.
ES, P O BOX 145 44687 – Gary Mast, prin.

Wapakoneta, Auglaize Co., Pop. Code 6
St. Marys CSD
Supt. – See Saint Marys
Moulton ES, RURAL ROUTE 02 BOX 118 45895
  Shirley McEvoy, prin.

Wapakoneta CSD
Sch. Sys. Enr. Code 5
Supt. – J. Bell, 3 N PINE ST 45895

Centennial ES, 700 S WATER ST 45895
  Joseph Carter, prin.
Northridge MS, 900 N BLACKHOOF ST 45895
  Charles Kuck, prin.
United Local ES, RURAL ROUTE 05 45895
  Donald Numbers, prin.
Other Schools – See Buckland, Cridersville

St. Joseph ES, RURAL ROUTE 04 45895

Warren, Trumbull Co., Pop. Code 8
Champion Local SD
Sch. Sys. Enr. Code 4
Supt. – John Leeper
  5759 MAHONING AVE NW 44483
Champion MS, 5435 KUSZMAUL AVE NW 44483
  John Christein, prin.
Champion Central ES
  5759 MAHONING AVE NW 44483
  Lee Seiple, prin.

Howland Local SD
Sch. Sys. Enr. Code 5
Supt. – Nick Macris, 8200 SOUTH ST SE 44484
Howland JHS, 8100 SOUTH ST SE 44484
  Robert Gribling, prin.
Howland Glen ES, 8000 BRIDLE LN NE 44484
  Randall Ribbon, prin.
Howland Springs ES
  9500 HOWLAND-SPRINGS RD SE 44484
  Larry Graber, prin.
Mines MS, 850 HOWLAND-WILSON RD NE 44484
  Barbara Wright, prin.
North Road MS, 863 NORTH RD SE 44484
  Charles Swindler, prin.

Lakeview Local SD
Supt. – See Cortland
Bazetta ES, 2755 BAZETTA RD NE 44481
  Joseph Toth, prin.

Lordstown Local SD
Sch. Sys. Enr. Code 4
Supt. – Ronald Schuster
  1824 SALT SPRINGS ROAD W 44481
Lordstown ES, 6540 TOD AVE SW 44481
  Philip Ginnetti, prin.

Warren CSD
Sch. Sys. Enr. Code 6
Supt. – John Peckyno
  261 MONROE ST NW 44483
East JHS, 1470 SOUTH ST SE 44483
  Edward Jenkins, prin.
Turner JHS, 1443 MAHONING AVE NW 44483
  Richard Crepage, prin.
West JHS, 1230 PALMYRA ROAD SW 44485
  Willard Mershon, prin.
Alden ES, 350 LOVELESS AVE SW 44485
  Frank Haniak, prin.
Devon ES
  833 CENTRAL PARKWAY AVE SE 44484
  Susan Ross, prin.
Dickey Avenue ES, 434 DICKEY AVE NW 44485
  David Leo, prin.
Elm Road ES, 361 ELM RD NE 44483
  Lee Pate, prin.
Emerson ES, 1619 DREXEL AVE NW 44485
  Daniel Cokrlic, prin.
Garfield ES, 2747 MONTCLAIR ST NE 44483
  Nancy Hahlen, prin.
Jefferson ES, 903 FIFTH ST SW 44485
  Alton Merrell, prin.
Laird Avenue ES, 565 LAIRD AVE SE 44484
  Martin Deak, prin.
Mann ES, 818 AUSTIN AVE SW 44485
  Sallie Kumik, prin.
McKinley ES, 1321 ELM RD NE 44483
  Virginia Kudrich, prin.
Roosevelt ES, 625 ROOSEVELT ST NW 44483
  Donald Spayd, prin.
Secrest ES, 1001 BENNETT AVE NW 44485
  S. Edgar, prin.

St. Mary ES, 261 ELM RD NE 44483
Blessed Sacrament ES, 3000 REEVES RD NE 44483
Howland Christian ES, 8957 MARKET ST E 44484
St. Cyril & Methodius ES
  175 LAIRD AVE NE 44483
St. James ES, 2106 ARBOR AVE SE 44484
St. Pius X ES, 1461 MONCREST DR NW 44485
Sts. Peter & Paul ES
  180 BELVEDERE AVE NE 44483
Warren Christian ES
  2640 PARKMAN RD NW 44485

Warrensville Heights, Cuyahoga Co., Pop. Code 7
Warrensville Heights CSD
Sch. Sys. Enr. Code 5
Supt. – Jack Hearnes
  4500 WARRENSVILLE CTR ROAD 44128
Dewey ES, 23401 EMERY RD 44128
  Mary Appleman, prin.
Eastwood ES, 4050 EASTWOOD LN 44122
  Franklin Jackson, prin.
Randallwood MS
  21865 CLARKWOOD PKY 44128
  Robert Lariccia, prin.
Westwood ES, 19000 GARDEN BLVD 44128
  Charles Pattillo, prin.

Warsaw, Coshocton Co., Pop. Code 3
River View Local SD
Sch. Sys. Enr. Code 5
Supt. – Don Rushing
  26496 STATE ROUTE 60 43844

River View MS, 26496 STATE ROUTE 60 43844
  Tom Gable, prin.
Union ES, 19781 STATE ROUTE 79 43844
  Dennis Blanford, prin.
ES, P O BOX 97 43844 – Welch Sprague, prin.
Other Schools – See Conesville, Coshocton, Keene

Washington Court House, Fayette Co., Pop. Code 7
Miami Trace Local SD
Sch. Sys. Enr. Code 5
Supt. – Stephen Yambor, P O BOX 624 43160
Chaffin ES, 2462 US ROUTE 35 NW 43160
  Norma Kirby, prin.
Eber MS
  22 BLOOMINGBRG N HOLLND NW 43160
  Ray Deeks, prin.
Staunton ES, 3091 LOCUST ST 43160
  Jerri Bomgardner, prin.
Wayne ES, 3978 NORTH ST SE 43160
  Paul Carpenter, prin.
Wilson ES, 1604 STATE ROUTE 41 SW 43160
  David Krupla, prin.
Other Schools – See Bloomingburg, Jeffersonville,
  Mount Sterling, New Holland

Washington Courthouse CSD
Sch. Sys. Enr. Code 4
Supt. – R. Thompson, 323 E PAINT ST 43160
Washington MS, 318 N NORTH ST 43160
  Thomas Gauldin, prin.
Belle Aire ES, 1120 HIGH ST 43160
  Peggy Zimmerman, prin.
Cherry Hill ES, 720 W OAKLAND AVE 43160
  Claudia Coe, prin.
Eastside ES, 506 S ELM ST 43160
  Rodger Mickle, prin.
Rose Avenue ES, 412 ROSE AVE 43160
  Claudia Coe, prin.

Washingtonville, Columbiana Co., Pop. Code 3
Leetonia EVD
Supt. – See Leetonia
Washingtonville ES, 105 SCHOOL ST 44490
  Robert Eskay, prin.

Waterford, Washington Co.
Wolf Creek Local SD
Sch. Sys. Enr. Code 3
Supt. – Ronald Thornton, P O BOX 67 45786
ES, P O BOX 41 45786 – Charles Boone, prin.
Other Schools – See Watertown

Waterloo, Lawrence Co.
Symmes Valley Local SD
Supt. – See Willow Wood
Symmes Valley ES 2 45688 – Neomia White, prin.

Watertown, Washington Co.
Wolf Creek Local SD
Supt. – See Waterford
ES, P O BOX 19 45787 – Paul Hickerson, prin.

Waterville, Lucas Co., Pop. Code 5
Anthony Wayne Local SD
Supt. – See Whitehouse
ES, 1 S RIVER RD 43566 – David Hilborn, prin.

Wauseon, Fulton Co., Pop. Code 6
Pike-Delta-York Local SD
Supt. – See Delta
York MS 43567 – Carolyn Scheid, prin.

Wauseon EVD
Sch. Sys. Enr. Code 4
Supt. – Neil Weber, 416 E ELM ST 43567
Burr Road MS, BURR ROAD 43567
  Richard Darcy, prin.
Elm Street ES, 440 E ELM ST 43567
  Carolyn Short, prin.

Waverly, Pike Co., Pop. Code 5
Waverly CSD
Sch. Sys. Enr. Code 4
Supt. – David Roberts, 500 E 2ND ST 45690
North MS, 610 E 3RD ST 45690
  Robert Bothel, prin.
East PS, 5TH ST 45690 – Robert Reagan, prin.
West MS, 410 CLOUGH ST 45690
  Roger Ramsey, prin.

Wayne, Wood Co., Pop. Code 3
Elmwood Local SD
Supt. – See Bloomdale
ES, SCHOLL HOUSE ST 43466
  Margaret McDowell, prin.

Waynesburg, Stark Co., Pop. Code 4
Sandy Valley Local SD
Supt. – See Magnolia
ES, W LISBON ST #430 44688
  Steven Gurewitz, prin.

St. James ES, 400 W LISBON ST 44688

Waynesfield, Auglaize Co., Pop. Code 3
Waynesfield-Goshen Local SD
Sch. Sys. Enr. Code 3
Supt. – Roy Cherry, P O BOX 98 43537
ES, P O BOX 98 45896 – Roy Cherry, prin.

Waynesville, Warren Co., Pop. Code 4
Wayne Local SD
Sch. Sys. Enr. Code 4
Supt. – Charles Williams, P O BOX 637 45068
ES, P O BOX 637 45068 – Byron Ames, prin.

Wellington, Lorain Co., Pop. Code 5
Keystone Local SD
Supt. – See LaGrange
Penfield ES, 40905 STATE ROUTE 18 44090
Timothy Jenkins, prin.

Wellington EVD
Sch. Sys. Enr. Code 4
Supt. – James McGlamery, 201 S MAIN ST 44090
McCormick MS, 201 S MAIN ST 44090
(—), prin.
Westwood ES, 305 UNION ST 44090
Nancy Urig, prin.

Wellston, Jackson Co., Pop. Code 6
Wellston CSD
Sch. Sys. Enr. Code 4
Supt. – Harry Gray
416 N PENNSYLVANIA AVE 45692
JHS, S NEW YORK AVE 45692
Carl Huntley, prin.
Bundy ES, 525 E 7TH ST 45692
Vance Ashley, prin.
Other Schools – See Coalton

Sts. Peter & Paul ES, 227 S NEW YORK AVE 45692

Wellsville, Columbiana Co., Pop. Code 6
Southern Local SD
Supt. – See Salineville
Number Sixteen ES, 20206 16 SCHOOL RD 43968
David Brookes, prin.

Wellsville CSD
Sch. Sys. Enr. Code 4
Supt. – L. Kent Yeager, 929 CENTER ST 43968
Daw MS, 929 CENTER ST 43968
James Brown, prin.
Fairview ES, 1151 OAKDALE AVE 43968
Allan Barlis, prin.
Garfield ES, 1600 LINCOLN AVE 43968
Paul Blevins, prin.
MacDonald ES, 9TH ST 43968 – Allan Barlis, prin.

West Alexandria, Preble Co., Pop. Code 4
Twin Valley Community Local SD
Sch. Sys. Enr. Code 4
Supt. – William Hughes, 1 S MAIN ST 45381
Lanier MS, 3225 STATE ROUTE 503 S 45381
Kathryn Rinehart, prin.
ES, 69 W THIRD ST 45381 – David Slater, prin.

West Carrollton, Montgomery Co., Pop. Code 7
West Carrollton CSD
Sch. Sys. Enr. Code 5
Supt. – Vance Ramage, 430 E PEASE AVE 45449
Russell ES, 123 ELEMENTARY DR 45449
Arvel Trent, prin.
Schnell ES, 5995 STUDENT ST 45449
Nancy Welch, prin.
Shade ES, 510 E PEASE AVE 45449
Barbara Gardecki, prin.
Other Schools – See Dayton

West Chester, Butler Co.
Lakota Local SD
Sch. Sys. Enr. Code 6
Supt. – Thomas Hayden
5030 TYLERSVILLE ROAD 45069
Hopewell MS, 8200 COX ROAD 45069
Robert Helsinger, prin.
Adena ES, 9316 MINUTEMAN WAY 45069
Cecilia Schmidt, prin.
Freedom ES, 6035 BECKETT RIDGE BLVD 45069
David Tobergte, prin.
Hopewell ES, 8300 COX RD 45069
Mary Westendorf, prin.
Union ES, 8735 CINCINNATI-DAYTON 45069
Ronald Brooks, prin.
Other Schools – See Hamilton, Middletown

West Elkton, Preble Co., Pop. Code 2
Preble-Shawnee Local SD
Supt. – See Camden
ES, P O BOX 97 45070 – Richard Speicher, prin.

Westerville, Franklin Co., Pop. Code 7
Westerville CSD
Sch. Sys. Enr. Code 7
Supt. – Ernest Husarik
336 S OTTERBEIN AVE 43081
Blendon MS, 223 S OTTERBEIN AVE 43081
Robert Schultz, prin.
Walnut Springs MS, 888 E WALNUT ST 43081
Ralph Collins, prin.
Annehurst ES, 925 W MAIN ST 43081
Steven DeRinger, prin.
Central College ES, 825 SUNBURY RD 43081
Don Snider, prin.
Cherrington ES, 522 CHERRINGTON RD 43081
Greg Sampson, prin.
Emerson MS, 44 N VINE ST 43081
Bette Marschall, prin.
Frost ES, 270 N SPRING RD 43081
Robert Abbott, prin.
Hanby MS, 56 S STATE ST 43081
Robert Abbott, prin.
Huber Ridge ES
5757 BUENOS AIRES BLVD 43081
Gary Kagarise, prin.
Longfellow ES, 120 HIAWATHA AVE 43081
Don Snider, prin.
Pointview ES, 720 POINTVIEW DR 43081
Richard Swartzmiller, prin.
Twain ES, 799 E WALNUT ST 43081
Jackie Nevels, prin.

Whittier ES, 130 E WALNUT ST 43081
Jack Geckeler, prin.
Other Schools – See Columbus

Worthington CSD
Supt. – See Worthington
Worthington Park ES, 500 PARK RD 43081
Jowanda Harkins, prin.

St. Paul ES, 61 MOSS RD 43081
Christ the King Christian ES
8600 WORTHINGTON ROAD 43081

West Farmington, Trumbull Co., Pop. Code 3
Bristol Local SD
Supt. – See Bristolville
Bristol-Farmington ES, 121 N SECOND ST 44491
James Betts, prin.

Westfield Center, Medina Co., Pop. Code 3
Cloverleaf Local SD
Supt. – See Lodi
Westfield ES, 9055 S LEROY RD 44251
Robert Hamad, prin.

West Jefferson, Madison Co., Pop. Code 5
Jefferson Local SD
Sch. Sys. Enr. Code 4
Supt. – Bill Stephan, P O BOX 47 43162
Jefferson Memorial MS, 177 S FREY AVE 43162
Don Schiff, prin.
Frey ES, 177 S FREY AVE 43162
Ron Minard, prin.
Norwood ES, 899 NORWOOD DR 43162
Thomas Phillips, prin.

West Lafayette, Coshocton Co., Pop. Code 4
Ridgewood Local SD
Sch. Sys. Enr. Code 4
Supt. – James Steinbrecher
225 W UNION AVE 43845
ES, 223 W UNION AVE 43845
Jerry Porteus, prin.
Other Schools – See Fresno, Plainfield

Westlake, Cuyahoga Co., Pop. Code 7
Westlake CSD
Sch. Sys. Enr. Code 5
Supt. – Keith Richards, 2282 DOVER ROAD 44145
Burneson MS, 2240 DOVER ROAD 44145
G. David Newman, prin.
Parkside MS, 24525 HILLIARD BLVD 44145
George Christ, prin.
Bassett ES, 2155 BASSETT RD 44145
Rick Hayman, prin.
Dover ES, 2300 DOVER ROAD 44145
Norman Siebenhar, prin.
Hilliard ES, 24365 HILLIARD BLVD 44145
Mary Flanagan, prin.
Holly Lane ES, 3057 HOLLY LN 44145
Rick Ruth, prin.

St. Bernadette ES, 2300 CLAGUE RD 44145
St. Paul Lutheran ES, 27981 DETROIT RD 44145

West Liberty, Logan Co., Pop. Code 4
West Liberty-Salem Local SD
Sch. Sys. Enr. Code 4
Supt. – Sherry Meadows
500 W COLUMBUS ST 43357
ES, 500 W COLUMBUS ST 43357
Sherry Meadows, prin.
Other Schools – See Urbana

West Manchester, Preble Co., Pop. Code 2
C. R. Coblentz Local SD
Supt. – See New Paris
Coblentz MS, RURAL ROUTE 01 45382
Mark Weedy, prin.

West Mansfield, Logan Co., Pop. Code 3
Benjamin Logan Local SD
Supt. – See Bellefontaine
Benjamin Logan ES, P O BOX 128 43358
Sheri Rice, prin.

West Milton, Miami Co., Pop. Code 5
Milton-Union EVD
Sch. Sys. Enr. Code 4
Supt. – Darlene Duchene, 112 S SPRING ST 45383
Milton-Union MS, 146 S SPRING ST 45383
Samuel Ison, prin.
Milton-Union ES, 43 WRIGHT RD 45383
Nicky Donaldson, prin.

Weston, Wood Co., Pop. Code 4
Otsego Local SD
Supt. – See Tontogany
ES, BROADWAY ST 43569 – James Robarge, prin.

West Point, Columbiana Co.
Beaver Local SD
Supt. – See Lisbon
ES, P O BOX 376 44492 – Elaine Humphrey, prin.

West Portsmouth, Scioto Co., Pop. Code 5
Washington Local SD
Sch. Sys. Enr. Code 4
Supt. – Jon Kiger, 13TH ST 45662
Nauvoo MS, 401 CALVERTS LN 45662
Robert Eichenlaub, prin.
Dry Run ES, 3171 GALENA PIKE 45662
William Haney, prin.
Jenkins ES, 10TH ST 45662 – Daniel Warner, prin.
Other Schools – See Friendship

West Rushville, Fairfield Co., Pop. Code 2
Fairfield Union Local SD
Sch. Sys. Enr. Code 4
Supt. – Clark Davis, P O BOX 67 43163
Other Schools – See Bremen, Lancaster, Pleasantville, Rushville

West Salem, Wayne Co., Pop. Code 4
Northwestern Local SD
Sch. Sys. Enr. Code 4
Supt. – John Morgan, RURAL ROUTE 01 44287
Congress MS, RURAL ROUTE 02 44287
Gary Guemelata, prin.
ES, 99 E BUCKEYE ST 44287 – David Knight, prin.
Other Schools – See Wooster

West Union, Adams Co., Pop. Code 5
Ohio Valley Local SD
Sch. Sys. Enr. Code 6
Supt. – Walter Knauff, 123 W MAIN ST 45693
Liberty MS, 3359 STATE ROUTE 125 45693
Linda Stepp, prin.
Tiffin MS, STATE ROUTE 125 45693
Linda Stepp, prin.
ES, 215 W SOUTH ST 45693
Nathaniel Grubb, prin.
Other Schools – See Aberdeen, Bentonville, Blue Creek, Cherry Fork, Manchester, Peebles, Seaman, Sinking Spring, Stout, Winchester

Adams County Christian School
212 SPARKS 45693

West Unity, Williams Co., Pop. Code 4
Millcreek-West Unity Local SD
Sch. Sys. Enr. Code 3
Supt. – J. Hutchinson, S DEFIANCE ST 43570
Hilltop ES, DEFIANCE ST 43570
Charles Johnston, prin.

Wharton, Wyandot Co., Pop. Code 2
Riverdale Local SD
Supt. – See Mount Blanchard
Wharton MS 43359 – J Hohn, prin.

Wheelersburg, Scioto Co., Pop. Code 5
Bloom-Vernon Local SD
Supt. – See South Webster
Vernon ES, RURAL ROUTE 02 BOX 256 45694
John Eaton, prin.

Wheelersburg Local SD
Sch. Sys. Enr. Code 3
Supt. – Frank Miller, P O BOX 340 45694
ES, RURAL ROUTE 01 45694
Gary Heimbach, prin.

White Cottage, Muskingum Co.
Maysville Local SD
Supt. – See Zanesville
Newton ES, P O BOX 157 43791
Jeff Childers, prin.

Whitehall, Franklin Co., Pop. Code 7
Whitehall CSD
Sch. Sys. Enr. Code 5
Supt. – Robert Zimpfer
625 S YEARLING ROAD 43213
Rosemore JHS, 4735 KAE AVE 43213
Ray Draghi, prin.
Beechwood ES, 455 BEECHWOOD RD 43213
Howard Martin, Jr., prin.
Etna Road ES, 4531 ETNA ST 43213
James Rodenmayer, prin.
Kae Avenue ES, 4738 KAE AVE 43213
Robert Ankney, prin.
Robinwood ES, 75 ROBINWOOD AVE 43213
James Carle, prin.

Whitehouse, Lucas Co., Pop. Code 4
Anthony Wayne Local SD
Sch. Sys. Enr. Code 5
Supt. – Randy Hardy, P O BOX 2487 43571
Fallen Timbers MS, 6119 FINZEL ROAD 43571
William Dick, prin.
ES, 6510 TEXAS ST 43571 – William Taylor, prin.
Other Schools – See Monclova, Waterville

Lial ES, 5900 DAVIS RD 43571

Wickliffe, Lake Co., Pop. Code 7
Wickliffe CSD
Sch. Sys. Enr. Code 4
Supt. – David Tanski, P O BOX 195 44092
MS, 29240 EUCLID AVE 44092
Gordon Gerber, prin.
ES, 1821 LINCOLN RD 44092
Dominic Mongiardo, prin.

All Sts./St. John Vianney ES
28702 EUCLID AVE 44092
Our Lady of Mt. Carmel ES
29840 EUCLID AVE 44092

Wilkesville, Vinton Co., Pop. Code 2
Vinton County Local SD
Supt. – See Mc Arthur
Wilton ES 45695 – Troy Thacker, prin.

Willard, Huron Co., Pop. Code 6
Willard CSD
Sch. Sys. Enr. Code 4
Supt. – Jerry Stackhouse, 955 S MAIN ST 44890
MS, 949 S MAIN ST 44890 – Stephen Eaton, prin.
Central ES, 206 W PEARL ST 44890
Alva Cummings, prin.

Richmond ES, 3565 SECTIONLINE ROAD 44890
David Hirschy, prin.
Other Schools – See Monroeville, New Haven

St. Francis Xavier School, 25 W PERRY ST 44890

Williamsburg, Clermont Co., Pop. Code 5
Williamsburg Local SD
Sch. Sys. Enr. Code 4
Supt. – Glenn Alexander, 549 W MAIN ST 45176
ES, 839 SPRING ST 45176
Robert Woodruff, prin.

Williamsport, Pickaway Co., Pop. Code 3
Westfall Local SD
Sch. Sys. Enr. Code 4
Supt. – Robert Debo
19463 PHERSON ROAD 43164
Westfall MS, 19545 PHERSON ROAD 43164
James Custis, prin.
Other Schools – See Circleville, Derby, Mount Sterling

Willoughby, Lake Co., Pop. Code 7
Willoughby-Eastlake CSD
Sch. Sys. Enr. Code 7
Supt. – Roger Lulow, 37047 RIDGE ROAD 44094
MS, 36901 RIDGE ROAD 44094 – Gary Barta, prin.
Edison ES, 5288 KAREN ISLE DR 44094
William Clark, prin.
Grant ES, 38281 HURRICANE DR 44094
Charles Roman, prin.
McKinley ES, LOST NATION ROAD 44094
Donald Schonauer, prin.
Other Schools – See Eastlake, Willowick

Immaculate Conception ES
37940 EUCLID AVE 44094
Willo Hill ES, 4200 STATE ROUTE 306 44094

Willowick, Lake Co., Pop. Code 7
Willoughby-Eastlake CSD
Supt. – See Willoughby
MS, 31500 ROYALVIEW DRIVE 44094
Thomas Mobily, prin.
Royalview ES, 31500 ROYALVIEW DR 44094
Joseph Bergant, prin.

St. Mary Magdalene ES, 32114 VINE ST 44094

Willow Wood, Lawrence Co.
Symmes Valley Local SD
Sch. Sys. Enr. Code 4
Supt. – James Payne, RURAL ROUTE 01 45696
Other Schools – See Scottown, Waterloo

Willshire, Van Wert Co., Pop. Code 3
Parkway Local SD
Supt. – See Rockford
Parkway MS, GREEN ST 45898
David Williamson, prin.

Wilmington, Clinton Co., Pop. Code 7
Wilmington CSD
Sch. Sys. Enr. Code 5
Supt. – Charles Dowler, 576 W MAIN ST 45177
Borror MS, 365 W LOCUST ST 45177
Fred Summers, prin.
Denver Place ES, 291 LORISH AVE 45177
Arlene Oehler, prin.
East End MS, 769 ROMBACH AVE 45177
Samuel Lewis, prin.
Other Schools – See Martinsville

Winchester, Adams Co., Pop. Code 4
Ohio Valley Local SD
Supt. – See West Union
ES, P O BOX 278 45697 – Stephen Darby, prin.

Windham, Portage Co., Pop. Code 5
Windham EVD
Sch. Sys. Enr. Code 4
Supt. – H. Robert Wert, 9530 BAUER AVE 44288
MS, 9530 BAUER AVE 44288
Cheryl Emrich, prin.
East MS, 9005 WILVERNE DR 44288
Donald Robinson, prin.
Thomas ES, 9600 COMMUNITY RD 44288
Margaret Miller, prin.

Windsor, Ashtabula Co.
Grand Valley Local SD
Supt. – See Orwell
ES, RURAL ROUTE 01 44099
Sharyn Vincent, prin.

Winesburg, Holmes Co.
East Holmes Local SD
Supt. – See Berlin
ES, P O BOX 133 44690 – Bruce Stambaugh, prin.

Wintersville, Jefferson Co., Pop. Code 5
Indian Creek Local SD
Supt. – See Mingo Junction
Bantam Ridge MS, BANTAM RIDGE ROAD 43952
Joseph Roshak, prin.
ES, 125 FERNWOOD RD 43952 – Evo Levi, prin.

Withamsville, Hamilton Co., Pop. Code 5

St. Thomas More ES, 800 OHIO PIKE 45245

Woodsfield, Monroe Co., Pop. Code 5
Switzerland of Ohio Local SD
Sch. Sys. Enr. Code 5
Supt. – David Phillips, 304 MILL ST 43793
ES, N PAUL ST 43793 – Glen Ayers, prin.

Other Schools – See Beallsville, Clarington,
Graysville, Hannibal, Lewisville, Powhatan Point,
Sardis, Sycamore Valley

St. Sylvester ES, 119 WAYNE ST 43793

Woodville, Sandusky Co., Pop. Code 4
Woodmore Local SD
Sch. Sys. Enr. Code 4
Supt. – Thomas Robey, MAIN & PINE ST 43469
Woodmore ES, MAIN AT PINE 43469
Jane Garling, prin.

Wooster, Wayne Co., Pop. Code 7
Northwestern Local SD
Supt. – See West Salem
Chester ES, 7509 W SMITHVILLE WESTER 44691
Richard Pantalone, prin.

Triway Local SD
Sch. Sys. Enr. Code 4
Supt. – Kevin DiDonato
3205 SHREVE ROAD 44691
Franklin ES, 2060 E MORELAND RD 44691
Bonnie Troyer, prin.
ES, 1071 DOVER RD 44691 – George Dean, prin.
Other Schools – See Shreve

Wooster CSD
Sch. Sys. Enr. Code 5
Supt. – Curtis Smith, 144 N MARKET ST 44691
Edgewood MS, 2695 GRAUSTARK PATH 44691
Jack Sleek, prin.
Beall Avenue ES, 716 BEALL AVE 44691
Peggy Archacki, prin.
Grant Street ES, 625 N GRANT ST 44691
Gerald Lanyi, prin.
Kean ES, 432 OLDMAN RD 44691
Gerald Lanyi, prin.
Layton ES, 1859 BURBANK RD 44691
Donald Drouhard, prin.
Lincoln Way ES, 905 PITTSBURG AVE 44691
Michael Mann, prin.
Melrose ES, 1641 SUNSET LN 44691
John Moritz, prin.
Parkview ES, 773 PARKVIEW DR 44691
Lewis Stern, prin.
Wayne ES, 1700 SMITHVILLE-WESTERN 44691
Jack Crafton, prin.

St. Mary Immaculate Conception School
535 E BOWMAN ST 44091

Worthington, Franklin Co., Pop. Code 7
Worthington CSD
Sch. Sys. Enr. Code 6
Supt. – John Hoeffler, 752 HIGH ST 43085
McCord MS, 1500 HARD RD 43085
Paul Kulik, prin.
Perry MS, 2341 SNOUFFER ROAD 43085
Bill Billinghurs, prin.
Worthingway MS, 6625 GUYER ST 43085
Paul Cynkar, prin.
Brookside ES, 6700 MCVEY BLVD 43085
Lynn Straker, prin.
Colonial Hills ES, 5800 GREENWICH ST 43085
Carol Price, prin.
Evening Street ES, 885 EVENING ST 43085
Donna Kelley, prin.
Granby ES, 1490 HARD RD 43085
Ronald Hopper, prin.
Wilson Hill ES, 6500 NORTHLAND RD 43085
Paul Zenisek, prin.
Worthington Estates ES, 6760 RIEBER ST 43085
Paul Jones, prin.
Worthington Hills ES
1221 CANDLEWOOD DR 43085
Kelley Stevens, prin.
Other Schools – See Powell, Westerville

St. Michael ES, 64 E SELBY BLVD 43085

Wren, Van Wert Co., Pop. Code 2
Crestview Local SD
Supt. – See Convoy
Crestview South ES 45899 – Kenneth Jerome, prin.

Xenia, Greene Co., Pop. Code 7
Beavercreek Local SD
Sch. Sys. Enr. Code 6
Supt. – Stanley Moreland
2940 DAYTON XENIA ROAD 45385
Other Schools – See Beavercreek

Xenia CSD
Sch. Sys. Enr. Code 6
Supt. – Robert Williams, 578 E MARKET ST 45385
Arrowood ES, 1694 PAWNEE DR 45385
Marcia Bayless, prin.
Cox ES, 506 DAYTON AVE 45385
Kenneth Rotroff, prin.
Kenton ES, 1087 W SECOND ST 45385
Pamela Mayo, prin.
McKinley ES, 819 COLORADO DR 45385
Wilgus Napier, prin.
Shawnee ES, 92 E ANKENEY MILL RD 45385
Linda Beaver, prin.
Spring Hill ES, 860 ORMSBY DR 45385
Robert Rose, prin.
Tecumseh ES
1058 OLD SPRINGFIELD PIKE 45385
Zosimo Garcia, prin.

St. Brigid ES, 312 FAIRFROUND RD 45385
Xenia Christian Day ES
1120 S DETROIT ST 45385

Xenia Nazarene Christian ES
1204 W SECOND ST 45385

Yellow Springs, Greene Co., Pop. Code 5
Yellow Springs EVD
Sch. Sys. Enr. Code 3
Supt. – Kenneth Yonkee
201 S WALNUT ST 45387
Mills Lawn ES, WALNUT ST 45387
Randall Newsome, prin.

Youngstown, Mahoning Co., Pop. Code 9
Austintown Local SD
Sch. Sys. Enr. Code 6
Supt. – Bernard Dunnan, 225 IDAHO ROAD 44515
Austintown MS, 5800 MAHONING AVE 44515
Daniel Bokesch, prin.
Ohl MS, 255 IDAHO ROAD 44515
Richard Denamen, prin.
Davis ES, 4302 MAPLE AVE 44515
Charles Eckberg, prin.
Lloyd ES, 5705 NORQUEST BLVD 44515
Thomas Moran, prin.
Lynn-Kirk ES, 4211 EVELYN RD 44511
Larry Kagle, prin.
Watson ES, 215 IDAHO RD 44515
Richard Evans, prin.
Woodside ES, 4105 ELMWOOD AVE 44515
Peter Morabito, prin.

Boardman Local SD
Sch. Sys. Enr. Code 6
Supt. – Richard Selby, 7410 MARKET ST 44512
Center MS, 7410 MARKET ST 44512
Edison Lugibihl, prin.
Glenwood MS, 7635 GLENWOOD AVE 44512
Anthony Alvino, prin.
Market Street ES, 5555 MARKET ST 44512
Donald Dailey, prin.
Robinwood Lane ES, 835 INDIANOLA RD 44512
Walter Yingling, prin.
Stadium Drive ES, 111 STADIUM DR 44512
Harold Cullar, prin.
West Boulevard ES, 6125 WEST BLVD 44512
Terry Samuels, prin.

Liberty Local SD
Sch. Sys. Enr. Code 4
Supt. – Grant Dieter, 4115 SHADY ROAD 44505
Guy MS, 4115 SHADY ROAD 44505
Mark Lucas, prin.
Blott ES, 4003 SHADY RD 44505
William Dunmire, prin.

Youngstown CSD
Sch. Sys. Enr. Code 7
Supt. – E. Catsoules, P O BOX 550 44501
Adams MS, 2537 COOPER ST 44502
Richard DeVincentis, prin.
Hayes MS, 1616 FORD AVE 44504
William Terlesky, prin.
North MS, 2724 MARINER AVE 44505
Fred Canning, prin.
Princeton MS, 2546 HILLMAN ST 44507
Larry Spires, prin.
Rogers MS, 2400 S SCHENLEY AVE 44511
Richard Saul, prin.
Bennett ES, 767 MABEL ST 44502
Lois Thornton, prin.
Bunn ES, 1825 SEQUOYA DR 44514
Mary Clark, prin.
Cleveland ES, 621 W PRINCETON AVE 44511
Joseph Reda, prin.
Haddow ES, 2800 OAK ST 44505
Walter Evanoski, prin.
Harding ES, 1903 CORDOVA AVE 44504
Samuel Leone, prin.
Harrison ES, 1387 COMMONWEALTH AVE 44505
Robert Mansfield, prin.
Hillman ES, 164 W MYRTLE AVE 44507
Victor Ugran, prin.
Jackson ES, 1813 WINDSOR AVE 44502
Geraldine Banks, prin.
Jefferson ES, 1514 VIRGINIA AVE 44510
Joseph Sculli, prin.
King ES, 706 COVINGTON ST 44510
Michael Orenic, prin.
Kirkmere ES, 2851 KIRK RD 44511
Marcella Crann, prin.
Lincoln ES, 1415 CHARLOTTE AVE 44506
Jack Dipinto, prin.
Madison ES, 84 MCGUFFEY RD 44505
Janet Sanders, prin.
Roosevelt ES, 1408 RIGBY ST 44506
Runita Adams, prin.
Sheridan ES, 3321 HUDSON AVE 44511
Carole Prestley, prin.
Taft ES, 3115 GIBSON ST 44502
Joseph Conley, prin.
West ES, 134 N HAZELWOOD AVE 44509
Anthony Deniro, prin.
White ES, 1061 LYDEN AVE 44505
Joseph Allegretto, prin.
Williamson ES, 58 WILLIAMSON AVE 44507
Edward Rakocy, prin.

Youngstown Christian School
125 WYCHWOOD LANE 44512
Byzantine Catholic Central ES
5512 YOUNGSTOWN-POLAND RD 44514
Calvary Christian Academy
1812 OAK HILL AVE 44507
Immaculate Conception ES, 810 OAK ST 44506
St. Ann Ukranian ES, 4310 KIRK RD 44511
St. Anthony ES, 1145 TURIN ST 44510

St. Brendan ES, 145 N GLENELLEN AVE   44509
St. Christine ES, 3125 S SCHENLEY AVE   44511
St. Dominic ES, 3404 SOUTHERN BLVD   44507
St. Edward ES, 211 REDONDO RD   44504
St. Matthias ES, 2800 SHADY RUN RD   44502
St. Patrick ES, 1400 OAK HILL AVE   44507
Watkins Christian Academy
   2122 E HIGH AVE   44505

Zaleski, Vinton Co., Pop. Code 2
Vinton County Local SD
Supt. – See Mc Arthur
ES   45698 – Troy Thacker, prin.

Zanesville, Muskingum Co., Pop. Code 8
East Muskingum Local SD
Supt. – See New Concord
Perry ES, 6975 E PIKE   43701
   Martha Moore, prin.

Maysville Local SD
Sch. Sys. Enr. Code 4
Supt. – Rodney Spohn, P O BOX 1818   43702
South Zanesville MS, 80 E MAIN ST   43701
   Bruce Keller, prin.
Springfield Bell ES, 1148 POTTS LN   43701
   Chris Ausmus, prin.
Other Schools – See White Cottage

West Muskingum Local SD
Sch. Sys. Enr. Code 4
Supt. – Charles Morehead, 4880 W PIKE   43701
West Muskingum MS, 100 KIMES ROAD   43701
   William Harbron, prin.
Dillon MS, 3005 DILLON SCHOOL DR   43701
   Jerrold May, prin.
Richey ES, 645 RICHEY RD   43701
   Jerrold May, prin.
Other Schools – See Hopewell

Zanesville CSD
Sch. Sys. Enr. Code 6
Supt. – James Robinson, 200 N 6TH ST   43701
Cleveland JHS, 714 PERSHING ROAD   43701
   Donald Plunkett, prin.
Roosevelt MS, 1275 ROOSEVELT AVE   43701
   H. Henderson, prin.
Garfield MS, 440 BRIGHTON BLVD   43701
   Jean Glenn, prin.
McIntire ES, 10-07 MCINTIRE AVE   43701
   Larry Morgan, prin.
McKinley ES, 1428 SHARON AVE   43701
   Richard Kanavel, prin.
Munson ES, 109 BRIGHTON BLVD   43701
   Jean Glenn, prin.
Pioneer MS, 20 9TH ST   43701
   Margaret Stainbrook, prin.

Pleasant Grove ES
   199 N PLEASANT GROVE RD   43701
   Richard Kanavel, prin.
Putnam Community ES
   920 MOXAHALA AVE   43701
   Douglas Butler, prin.
Sheridan ES, 1269 E MARKET ST   43701
   Margaret Stainbrook, prin.
Westview ES, 2256 DRESDEN RD   43701
   Anthony Reese, prin.
Wilson ES, 1065 SUPERIOR ST   43701
   Anthony Reese, prin.

St. Nicholas ES, 1030 E MAIN ST   43701
St. Thomas Aquinas ES, 139 N 5TH ST   43701

Zoarville, Carroll Co.
Tuscarawas Valley Local SD
Sch. Sys. Enr. Code 4
Supt. – Robert Bowden, P O BOX 92   44656
Other Schools – See Bolivar, Mineral City

OKLAHOMA

STATE DEPARTMENT OF EDUCATION
2500 N. Lincoln Blvd., Oklahoma City 73105
(405) 521-3301

Superintendent of Public Instruction	Gerald Hoeltzel
Associate Superintendent Financial & Administrative Services	Ed Huey
Associate Superintendent Federal/Special Services	Leroy Ireton
Associate Superintendent Instructional Services	Judy Leach

STATE BOARD OF EDUCATION
Gerald Hoeltzel, *President*   2500 N. Lincoln, Oklahoma City   73105

OKLAHOMA STATE REGENTS FOR HIGHER EDUCATION
Hans Brisch, *Chancellor*   500 Education Building, Oklahoma City   73105

COUNTY SUPERINTENDENTS OF SCHOOLS

Adair County, Harlene Green, Supt.
   Stilwell   74960
Alfalfa County, Kathryn Corr, Supt.
   300 S GRAND AVE, Cherokee   73728
Atoka County, Dale Wilson, Supt.
   200 E COURT ST, Atoka   74525
Beaver County, M. Rider, Supt.
   P O BOX 160, Beaver   73932
Beckham County, Peggy Dunlap, Supt.
   P O BOX 67, Sayre   73662
Blaine County, Marvin Daugherty, Supt.
   Watonga   73772
Bryan County, Jim Spivey, Supt.
   201 N 4TH AVE, Durant   74701
Caddo County, John Kusel, Supt.
   P O BOX 849, Anadarko   73005
Canadian County, Penny Haynes, Supt.
   P O BOX 849, El Reno   73036
Carter County, Henry Hicks, Supt.
   47 A ST SW, Ardmore   73401
Cherokee County, Don Crittenden, Supt.
   213 W DELAWARE ST, Tahlequah   74464
Choctaw County, Charlene Aubrey, Supt.
   304 E DUKE, Hugo   74743
Cimarron County, Loyd Fansher, Supt.
   P O BOX 817, Boise City   73933
Cleveland County, Merrill Roberson, Supt.
   201 S JONES AVE, Norman   73069
Coal County, Randall Erwin, Supt.
   2 N MAIN, Coalgate   74538
Comanche County, Don Duggins, Supt.
   P O BOX 9007, Lawton   73505
Cotton County, J. Darrel Riggins, Supt.
   301 N BROADWAY, Walters   73572
Craig County, Dixie Kirby, Supt.
   Vinita   74301

Creek County, Ed Wilkinson, Supt.
   1 S MISSION ST, Sapulpa   74066
Custer County, Duane Nicholas, Supt.
   P O BOX 300, Arapaho   73620
Delaware County, Jim Bradford, Supt.
   P O BOX 388, Jay   74346
Dewey County, Sherrill White, Supt.
   Taloga   73667
Ellis County, Sherrill White, Supt.
   Arnett   73832
Garfield County, Bob Meyer, Supt.
   114 W BROADWAY, Enid   73701
Garvin County, Kenneth Campbell, Supt.
   P O BOX 617, Pauls Valley   73075
Grady County, Hollis Myers, Supt.
   P O BOX 746, Chickasha   73018
Grant County, Carol Beggs, Supt.
   112 E GUTHRIE, Medford   73759
Greer County, Ola Sorrells, Supt.
   Mangum   73554
Harmon County, Lainial Gilbert, Supt.
   Hollis   73550
Harper County, M. Rider, Supt.
   Buffalo   73834
Haskell County, Dr. Larry Huff, Supt.
   P O BOX 409, Stigler   74462
Hughes County, Dr. Larry Huff, Supt.
   P O BOX 352, Holdenville   74848
Jackson County, Howard King, Supt.
   101 W BROADWAY, Altus   73521
Jefferson County, Alma Hooper, Supt.
   220 S MAIN ST, Waurika   73573
Johnston County, Jim Spivey, Supt.
   Tishomingo   73460
Kay County, Lavelle Wittmer, Supt.
   Newkirk   74647

Kingfisher County, Dr. Bill Siler, Supt.
   P O BOX 29, Kingfisher   73750
Kiowa County, Lainial Gilbert, Supt.
   P O BOX 73, Hobart   73651
Latimer County, Barbara Humphries, Supt.
   109 N CENTRAL, Wilburton   74578
LeFlore County, Suzanne Billingsley, Supt.
   P O BOX 130, Poteau   74953
Lincoln County, Bill Siler, Supt.
   LINCOLN ROAD, Chandler   74834
Logan County, Imogene Summers, Supt.
   P O BOX 310, Guthrie   73044
Love County, James Spivey, Supt.
   405 W MAIN, Marietta   73448
McClain County, Melvin Mackey, Supt.
   200 W WASHINGTON, Purcell   73080
McCurtain County, Charles Moyer, Supt.
   108 N CENTRAL, Idabel   74745
McIntosh County, Cleo Guthrie, Supt.
   P O BOX 431, Eufaula   74432
Major County, Sherrill White, Supt.
   500 E BROADWAY, Fairview   73737
Marshall County, Imogene Maxwell, Supt.
   100 PLAZA, Madill   73446
Mayes County, Bob Williams, Supt.
   P O BOX 947, Pryor   74361
Murray County, Bob Donaho, Supt.
   1000 W WYANDOTTE, Sulphur   73086
Muskogee County, S. Carroll, Supt.
   Muskogee   74401
Noble County, Bill Finley, Supt.
   Perry   73077
Nowata County, Barbara Dawson, Supt.
   700 W OSAGE, Nowata   74048
Okfuskee County, Patsy Wilson, Supt.
   Okemah   74859

Oklahoma County, Bob Clark, Supt.
320 NW ROBERT S KERR AVE, Oklahoma City 73102
Okmulgee County, J. Bennett, Supt.
P O BOX 249, Okmulgee 74447
Osage County, James Christie, Supt.
Pawhuska 74056
Ottawa County, Barbara Pollard, Supt.
Miami 74354
Pawnee County, Ralph Teague, Supt.
500 HARRISON, Pawnee 74058
Payne County, Robert Meyer, Supt.
Stillwater 74074
Pittsburg County, John Budzinsky, Supt.
201 E CARL ALBERT PKY, Mc Alester 74501
Pontotoc County, Pat Coffey, Supt.
P O BOX 1486, Ada 74821

Pottawatomie County, Jack Williams, Supt.
325 N BROADWAY, Shawnee 74801
Pushmataha County, Lewis Whitten, Supt.
P O BOX 70, Antlers 74523
Roger Mills County, Duane Nicholas, Supt.
Cheyenne 73628
Rogers County, Mary Lee Roden, Supt.
219 S MISSOURI AVE, Claremore 74017
Seminole County, Paul Lyon, Supt.
P O BOX 1102, Wewoka 74858
Sequoyah County, Norman Barton, Supt.
120 E CHICKASAW, Sallisaw 74955
Stephens County, Melvin Mackey, Supt.
12TH AND MAPLE STS, Duncan 73533
Texas County, M. Rider, Supt.
319 N MAIN ST, Guymon 73942

Tillman County, Bob Collins, Supt.
P O BOX 157, Frederick 73542
Tulsa County, Kara Wilson, Supt.
500 S DENVER AVE, Tulsa 74103
Wagoner County, Earl Garrison, Supt.
P O BOX 425, Wagoner 74467
Washington County, Donald Woford, Supt.
420 S JOHNSTONE #108, Bartlesville 74006
Washita County, Duane Nicholas, Supt.
P O BOX 290, Cordell 73632
Woods County, (-), Supt.
P O BOX 386, Alva 73717
Woodward County, M. Rider, Supt.
P O BOX 668, Woodward 73802

PUBLIC, PRIVATE, AND PAROCHIAL ELEMENTARY SCHOOLS

Achille, Bryan Co., Pop. Code 2
Achille ISD
Sch. Sys. Enr. Code 2
Supt. – Terry Evans, P O BOX 308 74720
ES, P O BOX 308 74720 – Nancy Hicks, prin.

Ada, Pontotoc Co., Pop. Code 7
Ada ISD
Sch. Sys. Enr. Code 4
Supt. – Zane Bowman, P O BOX 1359 74820
MS, 223 W 18TH ST 74820 – Albert Bare, prin.
Hayes ES, 500 S MISSISSIPPI AVE 74820
Jack Cooper, prin.
Washington ES, 600 S OAK AVE 74820
Rita Cloar, prin.
Williard ES, 817 3 9TH ST 74820
Phil Rhynes, prin.

Byng ISD
Sch. Sys. Enr. Code 4
Supt. – Marvin Stokes, RURAL ROUTE 03 74820
Byng MS, P O BOX 2509 74821
Betty Allred, prin.
Francis ES, P O BOX 2509 74821
Charles Kessinger, prin.
Homer ES, P O BOX 2509 74821
Sandra Looper, prin.

Latta ISD
Sch. Sys. Enr. Code 3
Supt. – Donald Hoover, RURAL ROUTE 01 74820
Latta ES, RURAL ROUTE 01 BOX 811 74820
Alton Wood, prin.

Pickett-Center SD
Sch. Sys. Enr. Code 2
Supt. – Patsy West, P O BOX 1363 74821
Pickett-Center ES, P O BOX 1363 74821
(—), prin.

Vanoss ISD
Sch. Sys. Enr. Code 2
Supt. – Kenneth Smith
RURAL ROUTE 05 BOX 119 74820
Vanoss ES, RURAL ROUTE 05 BOX 119 74820
Bill Ashley, prin.

Adair, Mayes Co., Pop. Code 3
Adair ISD
Sch. Sys. Enr. Code 3
Supt. – Jack Dryden, P O BOX 197 74330
MS, P O BOX 197 74330 – Jack Kinion, prin.
Hughes ES, P O BOX 197 74330
Kenneth Steidley, prin.

Adams, Texas Co.
Adams SD
Sch. Sys. Enr. Code 1
Supt. – Rita Adelman, P O BOX 628 73901
ES, P O BOX 628 73901 – (—), prin.

Afton, Ottawa Co., Pop. Code 4
Afton ISD
Sch. Sys. Enr. Code 2
Supt. – Milton Orr, P O BOX H 74331
ES, P O BOX 100 74331 – Randy Gardner, prin.

Cleora SD
Sch. Sys. Enr. Code 2
Supt. – Woodrow Goins, RURAL ROUTE 02 74331
Cleora ES, RURAL ROUTE 02 74331
(—), prin.

Agra, Lincoln Co., Pop. Code 2
Agra ISD
Sch. Sys. Enr. Code 2
Supt. – Wesley McFarland, P O BOX 279 74824
ES, P O BOX 279 74824 – John Spire, prin.

Albert, Caddo Co.
Oney ISD
Sch. Sys. Enr. Code 2
Supt. – Jerry Harris, P O BOX 128 73001
Oney ES, GENERAL DELIVERY 73001
Charlene Saunders, prin.

Albion, Pushmataha Co.
Albion SD
Sch. Sys. Enr. Code 1
Supt. – Kenneth Keeling, P O BOX 98 74521
ES, P O BOX 98 74521 – (—), prin.

Alex, Grady Co., Pop. Code 3
Alex ISD
Sch. Sys. Enr. Code 2
Supt. – Vernon Florence, P O BOX 188 73002
ES, P O BOX 188 73002 – Dale Smith, prin.

Aline, Alfalfa Co., Pop. Code 2
Aline-Cleo ISD
Sch. Sys. Enr. Code 2
Supt. – Harold Whipkey, P O BOX 49 73716
Aline-Cleo ES, P O BOX 49 73716
Greg Paris, prin.

Allen, Pontotoc Co., Pop. Code 3
Allen ISD
Sch. Sys. Enr. Code 2
Supt. – (—), P O BOX 430 74825
MS, P O BOX 430 74825 – Donald Johnson, prin.
ES, P O BOX 430 74825 – Loretta Borders, prin.

Altus, Jackson Co., Pop. Code 7
Altus ISD
Sch. Sys. Enr. Code 5
Supt. – Dr. Morris Foster, P O BOX 558 73522
Field ES, 902 E LIVEOAK ST 73521
Bob Kirk, prin.
Rivers ES, P O BOX 558 73522 – Tom Jones, prin.
Rogers ES, P O BOX 558 73522
David Grimes, prin.
Roosevelt ES, P O BOX 558 73522
Craig Cummins, prin.
Sunset ES, 1830 SUNSET DR 73521
Mark Whitlock, prin.
Washington ES, P O BOX 558 73522
Randy Ford, prin.

Navajo ISD
Sch. Sys. Enr. Code 2
Supt. – Gary Montgomery
RURAL ROUTE 02 73521
Navajo ES, RURAL ROUTE 02 73521
Lanita Southall, prin.

Alva, Woods Co., Pop. Code 6
Alva ISD
Sch. Sys. Enr. Code 4
Supt. – Lynn Hoskins, 14TH & BARNES 73717
JHS, 14TH & BARNES 73717 – Troy O'Hair, prin.
Lincoln MS, 1520 DAVIS ST 73717
Dr. Paul Resler, prin.
Longfellow ES, 101 BARNES AVE 73717
Beverly Owen, prin.
Washington ES, 701 BARNES AVE 73717
Harvey Reeg, prin.

Amber, Grady Co., Pop. Code 2
Amber-Pocasset ISD
Sch. Sys. Enr. Code 2
Supt. – W. Jackson, P O BOX 38 73004
Amber-Pocassett ES, P O BOX 38 73004
Hope Deaton, prin.

Ames, Major Co., Pop. Code 2
Ames ISD
Sch. Sys. Enr. Code 2
Supt. – Ted Roberts, P O BOX 508 73718
ES, P O BOX 508 73718 – Becky Markes, prin.

Anadarko, Caddo Co., Pop. Code 6
Anadarko ISD
Sch. Sys. Enr. Code 4
Supt. – Dr. W. Nixon, 1400 S MISSION ST 73005
IS, 1400 S MISSION ST 73005
Larry Wrede, prin.
East ES, 1400 S MISSION ST 73005
Eugene Akin, prin.
Sunset ES, 1400 S MISSION ST 73005
Jerry Ward, prin.

Antlers, Pushmataha Co., Pop. Code 5
Antlers ISD
Sch. Sys. Enr. Code 3
Supt. – Louis Maggia, 306 NE A 74523
Brantley ES, P O BOX 627 74523
Bob Cariker, prin.

Apache, Caddo Co., Pop. Code 4
Apache ISD
Sch. Sys. Enr. Code 3
Supt. – Jesse Wilburn, P O BOX 354 73006
MS, P O BOX 354 73006 – Linda Myers, prin.
ES, P O BOX 354 73006 – Rick Owens, prin.

Boone SD
Sch. Sys. Enr. Code 1
Supt. – Alan Van Deventer
RURAL ROUTE 02 BOX 177 73006
Boone ES, RURAL ROUTE 02 BOX 177 73006
(—), prin.

Broxton ISD
Sch. Sys. Enr. Code 2
Supt. – L'Roy Campbell
RURAL ROUTE 02 BOX 84 73006
Broxton ES, RURAL ROUTE 02 BOX 84 73006
Lloyd Dinse, prin.

Arapaho, Custer Co., Pop. Code 3
Arapaho ISD
Sch. Sys. Enr. Code 2
Supt. – Terry Selman, 214 N 12TH 73620
ES, P O BOX 160 73620 – Ginger Kauk, prin.

Ardmore, Carter Co., Pop. Code 7
Ardmore ISD
Sch. Sys. Enr. Code 5
Supt. – Dr. Howard Thomas, P O BOX 1709 73401
MS, P O BOX 1709 73402 – J. Thompson, prin.
Evans ES, P O BOX 1709 73402 – John Cobb, prin.
Franklin ES, P O BOX 1709 73402
Tom Choate, prin.
Jefferson ES, P O BOX 1709 73402
Darlene Kennedy, prin.
Lincoln ES, P O BOX 1709 73402
Donnell Cox, prin.
Northwest ES, P O BOX 1709 73402
Bobby Cole, prin.
Rogers ES, P O BOX 1709 73402
Linda Smith, prin.

Dickson ISD
Sch. Sys. Enr. Code 4
Supt. – James Harrod
RURAL ROUTE 04 BOX 122 73401
Dickson ES, RURAL ROUTE 04 BOX 122 73401
Phyllis Julian, prin.
Springdale ES, RURAL ROUTE 01 73401
Mike Harris, prin.

Plainview ISD
Sch. Sys. Enr. Code 4
Supt. – Larry Darbison
RURAL ROUTE 02 BOX 316 73401
Plainview MS, RURAL ROUTE 05 BOX 316 73401
Glenn Smith, prin.
Plainview ES, 1140 S PLAINVIEW 73401
Don Buck, prin.

Arkoma, Le Flore Co., Pop. Code 4
Arkoma ISD
Sch. Sys. Enr. Code 3
Supt. – Neil Brannon, P O BOX P 74901
Singleton ES, P O BOX P 74901
Nolen Branscum, prin.

Arnett, Ellis Co., Pop. Code 3
Arnett ISD
Sch. Sys. Enr. Code 2
Supt. – Jerry Pippin, P O BOX 317 73832
ES, P O BOX 317 73832 – Jerry Knowles, prin.

Asher, Pottawatomie Co., Pop. Code 3
Asher ISD
Sch. Sys. Enr. Code 2
Supt. – John Hamilton, P O BOX 168 74826
ES, P O BOX 168 74826 – Roy Watson, prin.

Atoka, Atoka Co., Pop. Code 5
Atoka ISD
Sch. Sys. Enr. Code 4
Supt. – Bill Crow, 202 W 1ST 74525
MS, P O BOX 488 74525 – Mark McPherson, prin.
Johnson MS, P O BOX 488 74525
Jim Wheeler, prin.
Thunderbird ES, P O BOX 488 74525
James Thomas, prin.

Bentley SD
Sch. Sys. Enr. Code 1
Supt. – Christopher Kellogg
RURAL ROUTE 05 74525
Bentley ES, RURAL ROUTE 05 BOX 136 74525
(—), prin.

Harmony SD
Sch. Sys. Enr. Code 2
Supt. – Tommy Lytle, RURAL ROUTE 02 74525

Harmony ES, RURAL ROUTE 02 74525
 (—), prin.

Tushka ISD
Sch. Sys. Enr. Code 2
Supt. – Ronald Meadows
 RURAL ROUTE 04 BOX T-26 74525
Other Schools – See Tushka

Avant, Osage Co., Pop. Code 2
Avant SD
Sch. Sys. Enr. Code 2
Supt. – (—), P O BOX 8 74001
ES, P O BOX 8 74001 – (—), prin.

Balko, Beaver Co.
Balko ISD
Sch. Sys. Enr. Code 2
Supt. – Richard Boothby
 RURAL ROUTE 01 BOX 37 73931
ES, RURAL ROUTE 01 BOX 37 73931
 Robert Kramer, prin.

Barnsdall, Osage Co., Pop. Code 4
Barnsdall ISD
Sch. Sys. Enr. Code 3
Supt. – Tommy Wilson, P O BOX 629 74002
ES, P O BOX 629 74002 – Bobby Baker, prin.

Bartlesville, Washington Co., Pop. Code 8
Bartlesville ISD
Sch. Sys. Enr. Code 6
Supt. – Dr. Gary Toothaker, P O BOX 1357 74003
Central MS, P O BOX 1357 74005
 Earl Sears, prin.
Madison MS, P O BOX 1357 74005
 John Ward, prin.
Hoover ES, P O BOX 1357 74005
 Mike Lamb, prin.
Kane ES, 801 SE 13TH 74003
 Jean Schwisow, prin.
Oak Park ES, P O BOX 1357 74005
 Fred Bailey, prin.
Phillips ES, P O BOX 1357 74005
 Jill Shackelford, prin.
Ranch Heights ES, P O BOX 1357 74005
 Dan Brock, prin.
Wayside ES, 3000 WAYSIDE DR 74006
 David Boone, prin.
Wilson ES, P O BOX 1357 74005
 Joye Butler, prin.

Osage Hills SD
Sch. Sys. Enr. Code 2
Supt. – Blan Cunningham
 RURAL ROUTE 05 BOX 416 74003
Osage Hills ES, RURAL ROUTE 05 BOX 416 74003
 (—), prin.

St. John School, 121 W 8TH ST 74003

Battiest, McCurtain Co.
Battiest ISD
Sch. Sys. Enr. Code 2
Supt. – Joe Wendt, P O BOX 199 74722
ES, P O BOX 199 74722 – Steve Lowrie, prin.

Bearden, Okfuskee Co.
Bearden SD
Sch. Sys. Enr. Code 1
Supt. – Leon McVeigh
 RURAL ROUTE 02 BOX 608 74859
Other Schools – See Okemah

Beaver, Beaver Co., Pop. Code 4
Beaver ISD
Sch. Sys. Enr. Code 3
Supt. – Jim Bouse, P O BOX 580 73932
ES, P O BOX 580 73932 – Ron Rist, prin.

Beggs, Okmulgee Co., Pop. Code 4
Beggs ISD
Sch. Sys. Enr. Code 3
Supt. – James Henson
 RURAL ROUTE 01 BOX 518 74421
MS, P O BOX 687 74421 – Paul McGee, prin.
ES, P O BOX 690 74421 – Marsha Norman, prin.

Bennington, Bryan Co., Pop. Code 2
Bennington ISD
Sch. Sys. Enr. Code 2
Supt. – Olan Isbell, P O BOX 10 74723
ES, P O BOX 10 74723 – Mary Knight, prin.

Bethany, Oklahoma Co., Pop. Code 7
Bethany ISD
Sch. Sys. Enr. Code 2
Supt. – G. Dickerson, 6721 NW 42 73008
MS, 6720 NW 42ND ST 73008
 Dr. Madalyn Long, prin.
Harris ES 73008 – Yvonne Cobb, prin.

Putnam City ISD
Supt. – See Oklahoma City
Apollo ES, 1901 N PENIEL AVE 73008
 Paul West, prin.
Lake Park ES, 8221 NW 30TH ST 73008
 Elbert Meeks, prin.
Overholser ES, 7900 NW 36TH ST 73008
 Dale Knowles, prin.
Western Oaks ES, 7200 NW 23RD ST 73008
 Dr. Linda Despain, prin.

Big Cabin, Craig Co., Pop. Code 2
Big Cabin ISD
Sch. Sys. Enr. Code 2
Supt. – Dr. Ted Hallum, P O BOX 178 74332
ES, P O BOX 178 74332 – Glenn Ward, prin.

Billings, Noble Co., Pop. Code 3
Billings ISD
Sch. Sys. Enr. Code 2
Supt. – Jerry McKeown, P O BOX 38 74630
ES, P O BOX 38 74630 – Mary Foltz, prin.

Binger, Caddo Co., Pop. Code 3
Binger ISD
Sch. Sys. Enr. Code 2
Supt. – Wayne Britton, P O BOX 280 73009
ES, P O BOX 280 73009 – (—), prin.

Bixby, Tulsa Co., Pop. Code 6
Bixby ISD
Sch. Sys. Enr. Code 4
Supt. – W. McKinney, P O BOX 160 74008
Brassfield ES, P O BOX 160 74008
 Don Kindle, prin.
Gray MS, P O BOX 160 74008 – Bob Paden, prin.

Blackwell, Kay Co., Pop. Code 6
Blackwell ISD
Sch. Sys. Enr. Code 4
Supt. – Dr. Richard Strahorn, 934 S 1ST 74631
MS, 934 S 1ST ST 74631 – Jim Jones, prin.
Huston Center MS, 934 S 1ST ST 74631
 Hessel Purdy, prin.
Parkside Center ES, 934 S 1ST ST 74631
 Dr. Dorothy Young, prin.
Washington ES, 934 S 1ST ST 74631
 Hessel Purdy, prin.

Union SD
Sch. Sys. Enr. Code 1
Supt. – Gayle Kuchera, RURAL ROUTE 02 74631
Union ES, RURAL ROUTE 02 74631
 (—), prin.

Blair, Jackson Co., Pop. Code 4
Blair ISD
Sch. Sys. Enr. Code 2
Supt. – Gary McLaughlin, P O BOX 428 73526
ES, P O BOX 428 73526 – Sue Von Tungeln, prin.

Blanchard, McClain Co., Pop. Code 4
Blanchard ISD
Sch. Sys. Enr. Code 4
Supt. – Neil Nuttall, P O BOX 38 73010
ES, P O BOX 38 73010 – Connie Korhonen, prin.

Bridge Creek ISD
Sch. Sys. Enr. Code 1
Supt. – Tom Anderson, RURAL ROUTE 01 73010
Bridge Creek ES, RURAL ROUTE 01 73010
 Jim Pothorst, prin.

Middleberg SD
Sch. Sys. Enr. Code 2
Supt. – Leon Burges, RURAL ROUTE 03 73010
Middleberg ES, RURAL ROUTE 03 73010
 (—), prin.

Bluejacket, Craig Co., Pop. Code 2
Bluejacket ISD
Sch. Sys. Enr. Code 2
Supt. – Richard Patterson, P O BOX 29 74333
ES, P O BOX 29 74333 – William Craig, prin.

Boise City, Cimarron Co., Pop. Code 4
Boise City ISD
Sch. Sys. Enr. Code 2
Supt. – Bill Terry, P O BOX 1116 73933
ES, P O BOX 1116 73933 – Terry Cayton, prin.

Bokchito, Bryan Co., Pop. Code 3
Bokchito ISD
Sch. Sys. Enr. Code 2
Supt. – David Dailey, P O BOX 161 74726
ES, P O BOX 161 74726 – Frank Birdsong, prin.

Bokoshe, Le Flore Co., Pop. Code 3
Bokoshe ISD
Sch. Sys. Enr. Code 2
Supt. – Eddie Ogdon, P O BOX 158 74930
ES, P O BOX 158 74930 – Ralph Pratt, prin.

Boley, Okfuskee Co., Pop. Code 2
Boley ISD
Sch. Sys. Enr. Code 2
Supt. – Ronald Walker, P O BOX 248 74829
ES, P O BOX 248 74829 – Glinda Mitchell, prin.

Boswell, Choctaw Co., Pop. Code 3
Boswell ISD
Sch. Sys. Enr. Code 2
Supt. – Jerry Combrink, P O BOX F 74727
ES, P O BOX F 74727
 Caroline Blankenship, prin.

Bowlegs, Seminole Co., Pop. Code 3
Bowlegs ISD
Sch. Sys. Enr. Code 2
Supt. – Doye Day, P O BOX 88 74830
ES, P O BOX 88 74830 – Glen Bryan, prin.

Bowring, Osage Co.
Bowring SD
Sch. Sys. Enr. Code 2
Supt. – Eddie Miles, P O BOX 668 74009
ES, P O BOX 668 74009 – (—), prin.

Boynton, Muskogee Co., Pop. Code 3
Boynton ISD
Sch. Sys. Enr. Code 2
Supt. – Donald Arney, P O BOX 127 74422
ES, P O BOX 127 74422 – John Schaublin, prin.

Bradley, Grady Co., Pop. Code 2
Bradley SD
Sch. Sys. Enr. Code 1
Supt. – John Wood, P O BOX 144 73011
ES, P O BOX 125 73011 – (—), prin.

Braggs, Muskogee Co., Pop. Code 2
Braggs ISD
Sch. Sys. Enr. Code 2
Supt. – Robert Davis, P O BOX 547 74423
ES, P O BOX 547 74423 – Larry Reynolds, prin.

Braman, Kay Co., Pop. Code 2
Braman ISD
Sch. Sys. Enr. Code 2
Supt. – Duncan Coons, P O BOX 130 74632
ES, P O BOX 130 74632 – Duncan Coons, prin.

Bray, Stephens Co., Pop. Code 3
Bray-Doyle ISD
Sch. Sys. Enr. Code 2
Supt. – Charles King, P O BOX 711 73055
ES, P O BOX 711 73055 – Bill Burton, prin.

Bristow, Creek Co., Pop. Code 5
Bristow ISD
Sch. Sys. Enr. Code 4
Supt. – Dr. W. Carmichael, 134 W 9TH 74010
Edison ES, 134 W 9TH AVE 74010
 Judy Vice, prin.
Washington ES, 134 W 9TH AVE 74010
 Gary Conway, prin.

Broken Arrow, Tulsa Co., Pop. Code 8
Broken Arrow ISD
Sch. Sys. Enr. Code 7
Supt. – Dr. C. Oliver, 601 S MAIN 74012
Central MS, 210 N MAIN ST 74012
 John Stockstill, prin.
Childers ES, 601 S MAIN ST 74012
 Dr. Barbara Evans, prin.
Haskell MS, 412 S 9TH ST 74012
 Tom Donathan, prin.
Sequoyah MS, 2701 S ELM PLACE 74012
 Steve Smith, prin.
Arrow Springs ES, 601 S MAIN ST 74012
 Mary Bias, prin.
Arrowhead ES, 1000 W NORMAN AVE 74012
 Gwen Collins, prin.
Indian Springs ES, 601 S MAIN ST 74012
 Dennis Griggs, prin.
Leisure Park ES, 4300 S JUNIPER PL 74011
 Patty Smith, prin.
Northeast ES, 320 E MIDWAY ST 74012
 Dan McDonald, prin.
Oak Crest ES, 405 E RICHMOND ST 74012
 John Burnett, prin.
Park Lane ES, 601 S MAIN ST 74012
 Bill Rampey, prin.
Southside ES, 509 W HOUSTON ST 74012
 John Weaver, prin.
Spring Creek ES, 601 S MAIN STREET 74012
 Linda Lantz, prin.
Vandever ES, 601 S MAIN ST 74012
 Ron Beckwith, prin.
Westwood ES, 601 S MAIN ST 74012
 Dr. Harriet Kuykendall, prin.
Wood ES, 601 S MAIN ST 74012
 Ron Salmon, prin.

Union ISD
Supt. – See Tulsa
Peters ES, 2900 W COLLEGE ST 74012
 Sue Barton, prin.

All Saints School, 299 S 9TH ST 74012

Broken Bow, McCurtain Co., Pop. Code 5
Broken Bow ISD
Sch. Sys. Enr. Code 4
Supt. – Gwyn Slaton, P O BOX 400 74728
MS, P O BOX 400 74728 – Howard Minor, prin.
Bennett MS, P O BOX 400 74728
 Charles Hubbard, prin.
Dierks ES, P O BOX 400 74728 – Tom Allen, prin.

Glover SD
Sch. Sys. Enr. Code 2
Supt. – Cheryl Van Buskirk
 RURAL ROUTE 03 BOX 385 74728
Glover ES, RURAL ROUTE 03 BOX 385 74728
 (—), prin.

Holly Creek SD
Sch. Sys. Enr. Code 2
Supt. – Charles Jones
 RURAL ROUTE 02 BOX 260 74728
Holly Creek ES
 RURAL ROUTE 02 BOX 260 74728
 (—), prin.

Lukfata SD
Sch. Sys. Enr. Code 2
Supt. – Michael Steele, P O BOX 940 74728
Lukfata ES, P O BOX 940 74728 – (—), prin.

Buffalo, Harper Co., Pop. Code 4
Buffalo ISD
Sch. Sys. Enr. Code 2
Supt. – Dr. Virgil Well, P O BOX 130 73834
ES, P O BOX 130 73834 – Joe Hart, prin.

Burbank, Osage Co., Pop. Code 2
Burbank SD
Sch. Sys. Enr. Code 1
Supt. – Nancy Sherrill, P O BOX 148 74633
ES, P O BOX 148 74633 – (—), prin.

Burlington, Alfalfa Co., Pop. Code 2
Burlington ISD
Sch. Sys. Enr. Code 2
Supt. – Gary Higgins, P O BOX 17 73722
ES, P O BOX 17 73722 – Joe Seely, prin.

Burneyville, Love Co.
Turner ISD
Sch. Sys. Enr. Code 2
Supt. – Frank Barrick, TURNER CIRCLE 73430
Turner ES, HCR 73 BOX 161 73430
   Jerry Garrett, prin.

Burns Flat, Washita Co., Pop. Code 4
Burns Flat ISD
Sch. Sys. Enr. Code 2
Supt. – Donald Lemke, P O BOX 129 73624
Rogers ES, P O BOX 129 73624
   George Auld, prin.

Butler, Custer Co., Pop. Code 2
Butler ISD
Sch. Sys. Enr. Code 2
Supt. – Larry Mills, P O BOX 127 73625
ES, P O BOX 127 73625 – Larry Haggard, prin.

Byars, McClain Co., Pop. Code 2
Byars SD
Sch. Sys. Enr. Code 1
Supt. – James Rhynes,Jr., P O BOX 8 74831
ES, P O BOX 8 74831 – (—), prin.

Cache, Comanche Co., Pop. Code 4
Cache ISD
Sch. Sys. Enr. Code 3
Supt. – Don Colwell, P O BOX 418 73527
ES, P O BOX 418 73527 – Margaret Fikes, prin.

Caddo, Bryan Co., Pop. Code 3
Caddo ISD
Sch. Sys. Enr. Code 2
Supt. – J. Edwards, P O BOX 128 74729
ES, P O BOX 128 74729 – Andrew Huggins, prin.

Calera, Bryan Co., Pop. Code 4
Calera ISD
Sch. Sys. Enr. Code 2
Supt. – H. Wingfield, P O BOX 386 74730
ES, P O BOX 386 74730 – Nancy Chappell, prin.

Calumet, Canadian Co., Pop. Code 2
Calumet ISD
Sch. Sys. Enr. Code 2
Supt. – Michael May, P O BOX 10 73014
ES, P O BOX 10 73014 – Jack Friesen, prin.

Maple SD
Sch. Sys. Enr. Code 2
Supt. – Joe Wells, RURAL ROUTE 01 73014
Maple ES, RURAL ROUTE 01 73014
   (—), prin.

Calvin, Hughes Co., Pop. Code 2
Calvin ISD
Sch. Sys. Enr. Code 2
Supt. – Charles Bundy, P O BOX 127 74531
ES, P O BOX 127 74531 – Beverly Chapman, prin.

Camargo, Dewey Co., Pop. Code 2
Camargo SD
Sch. Sys. Enr. Code 1
Supt. – Lewis Clem, P O BOX 67 73835
ES, P O BOX 67 73835 – (—), prin.

Cameron, Le Flore Co., Pop. Code 2
Cameron ISD
Sch. Sys. Enr. Code 2
Supt. – Charles Caughern, P O BOX 190 74932
ES, P O BOX 190 74932 – Levi Easton, prin.

Canadian, Pittsburg Co., Pop. Code 2
Canadian ISD
Sch. Sys. Enr. Code 2
Supt. – Bobby Yount, P O BOX 93 74425
ES, P O BOX 168 74425 – Hollis Weeks, prin.

Caney, Atoka Co., Pop. Code 2
Caney ISD
Sch. Sys. Enr. Code 2
Supt. – Ken Walker, P O BOX 368 74533
ES, P O BOX 368 74533 – Patricia Lahman, prin.

Canton, Blaine Co., Pop. Code 3
Canton ISD
Sch. Sys. Enr. Code 2
Supt. – Mike Fry, P O BOX 639 73724
ES, P O BOX 639 73724 – Donald Roberts, prin.

Canute, Washita Co., Pop. Code 3
Canute ISD
Sch. Sys. Enr. Code 2
Supt. – Ken Leddy, P O BOX 128 73626
ES, P O BOX 490 73626 – Jerald Calvert, prin.

Coweta ISD
Supt. – See Coweta
Northwest ES 73626 – Homerlene Burney, prin.

Carmen, Alfalfa Co., Pop. Code 3
Carmen-Dacoma ISD
Sch. Sys. Enr. Code 2
Supt. – Stephen Ward, P O BOX 129 73726
ES, P O BOX 129 73726 – Dale Ross, prin.

Carnegie, Caddo Co., Pop. Code 4
Alfalfa SD
Sch. Sys. Enr. Code 1
Supt. – Johnny Kitchens
   RURAL ROUTE 01 BOX 181 73015

Alfalfa ES, RURAL ROUTE 01 BOX 81 73015
   (—), prin.

Carnegie ISD
Sch. Sys. Enr. Code 3
Supt. – Harold Butler, P O BOX 159 73015
ES, P O BOX 159 73015 – Terry Kern, prin.

Carney, Lincoln Co., Pop. Code 3
Carney ISD
Sch. Sys. Enr. Code 2
Supt. – Charles O'Donnell, P O BOX 240 74832
ES, P O BOX 246 74832 – John Dickey, prin.

Carter, Beckham Co., Pop. Code 2
Carter ISD
Sch. Sys. Enr. Code 2
Supt. – Jerry Mason, P O BOX 520 73627
ES, P O BOX 520 73627 – Marilou Kistler, prin.

Cashion, Kingfisher Co., Pop. Code 3
Cashion ISD
Sch. Sys. Enr. Code 2
Supt. – Larry Mays, P O BOX 100 73016
ES, P O BOX 100 73016 – Wayne Hall, prin.

Catoosa, Rogers Co., Pop. Code 4
Catoosa ISD
Sch. Sys. Enr. Code 4
Supt. – Larry Lewis, P O BOX A 74015
Catoosa Lower ES, P O BOX A 74015
   Gary McKown, prin.
Catoosa Upper MS, P O BOX A 74015
   Perry Adams, prin.

Chelsea ISD
Supt. – See Chelsea
Longfellow IS, 306 W 6TH ST 74016
   Roger Thomas, prin.

Cement, Caddo Co., Pop. Code 3
Cement ISD
Sch. Sys. Enr. Code 2
Supt. – Danny Thornton, P O BOX 40 73017
ES, P O BOX 40 73017 – Iris Simmons, prin.

Centrahoma, Coal Co., Pop. Code 2
Centrahoma SD
Sch. Sys. Enr. Code 1
Supt. – Charles Canida, P O BOX 218 74534
ES, P O BOX 218 74534 – (—), prin.

Chandler, Lincoln Co., Pop. Code 5
Chandler ISD
Sch. Sys. Enr. Code 3
Supt. – Jerry Kashwer, 515 STEELE AVE 74834
Park Road MS, 515 STEELE AVE 74834
   Bill Delphon, prin.
East Side ES, 515 STEEELE AVE 74834
   Ronald Bowers, prin.
Memorial MS 74834 – Ronald Bowers, prin.

Chattanooga, Comanche Co., Pop. Code 2
Chattanooga ISD
Sch. Sys. Enr. Code 2
Supt. – Woody Gibbons, P O BOX 129 73528
ES, P O BOX 129 73528 – Woody Gibbons, prin.

Checotah, McIntosh Co., Pop. Code 5
Checotah ISD
Sch. Sys. Enr. Code 4
Supt. – Rick Moss, 320 W JEFFERSON 74426
MS, 320 W JEFFERSON ST 74426
   Lawrence Barnes, prin.
Marshall MS, 320 W JEFFERSON ST 74426
   Michael Rabon, prin.
Longfellow ES, 320 W JEFFERSON ST 74426
   Emma Waller, prin.

Chelsea, Rogers Co., Pop. Code 4
Alluwe ISD
Sch. Sys. Enr. Code 2
Supt. – (—)
   RURAL ROUTE 03 BOX 230 74016
Alluwe JHS 74016 – Bob Barnes, prin.
Alluwe ES, RURAL ROUTE 03 BOX 230 74016
   Clyde Branstetter, prin.

Chelsea ISD
Sch. Sys. Enr. Code 3
Supt. – Thomas Stiles, 300 W 6TH 74016
MS, 306 W 6TH ST 74016 – Art Goad, prin.
McIntosh ES, 306 W 6TH ST 74016
   Myrna Bengston, prin.
Other Schools – See Catoosa

Cherokee, Alfalfa Co., Pop. Code 4
Cherokee ISD
Sch. Sys. Enr. Code 3
Supt. – Merlin Overton, P O BOX 325 73728
ES, P O BOX 325 73728 – Jessie Reinhart, prin.

Cheyenne, Rogers Mills Co., Pop. Code 4
Cheyenne ISD
Sch. Sys. Enr. Code 2
Supt. – Galeard Roper, P O BOX 650 73628
ES, P O BOX 650 73628 – Larry Bradshaw, prin.

Chickasha, Grady Co., Pop. Code 7
Chickasha ISD
Sch. Sys. Enr. Code 5
Supt. – Dr. Weldon Perrin, P O BOX A 73023
MS, P O BOX A 73023
   Richard Weidenmaier, prin.
Brooks ES, P O BOX 669 73018
   Bob Holman, prin.
IS, P O BOX A 73023 – Bob Perry, prin.
Grand Avenue ES, P O BOX A 73023
   J. Freeny, prin.

Lincoln ES, P O BOX A 73023 – Pat Frost, prin.
Southwest ES, P O BOX A 73023
   Karen Williams, prin.
West ES, P O BOX A 73023
   Karen Williams, prin.

Friend SD
Sch. Sys. Enr. Code 2
Supt. – Kenneth Absher, RURAL ROUTE 03 73018
Friend ES, RURAL ROUTE 03 BOX 278 73018
   (—), prin.

Pioneer SD
Sch. Sys. Enr. Code 2
Supt. – Ron Gordon, RURAL ROUTE 02 73018
Pioneer ES, RURAL ROURTE 02 BOX 143 73018
   (—), prin.

Choctaw, Oklahoma Co., Pop. Code 6
Choctaw/Nicoma Park ISD
Sch. Sys. Enr. Code 8
Supt. – Dr. Dale Steans, 12880 NE 10 73020
ES, 14663 NE 10TH ST 73020 – David Ray, prin.
Griffith IS
   1861 INDIANA MERIDIAN ROAD 73020
   Gary Berglan, prin.
Indian Meridian ES, P O BOX 489 73020
   James Davis, prin.
Nicoma Park ES, P O BOX 947 73020
   Barbara Taylor, prin.
Nicoma Park IS, P O BOX 4070 73020
   Steven Allen, prin.
Westfall ES, 13239 NE 10TH ST 73020
   Joe Sturgeon, prin.

Chouteau, Mayes Co., Pop. Code 4
Chouteau-Mazie ISD
Sch. Sys. Enr. Code 3
Supt. – Marvin Rehl, P O BOX 969 74337
Chouteau-Mazie MS, P O BOX 969 74337
   Harvey Dooley, prin.
ES, P O BOX 969 74337 – Pamela Rehl, prin.
Mazie ES, P O BOX 969 74337
   Dennis Stutzman, prin.

Claremore, Rogers Co., Pop. Code 7
Claremore ISD
Sch. Sys. Enr. Code 5
Supt. – Dr. Bill Salwaechter, P O BOX 907 74017
Claremont ES, 318 E 8TH ST 74017
   Andy Hogan, prin.
Leeper MS, 101 W 11TH ST 74017
   Dr. Larry Howard, prin.
Roosa ES, 2001 N STOUX AVE 74017
   Marg Haltom, prin.
Westside ES, 200 N DAVIS AVE 74017
   Joe Newell, prin.

Justus SD
Sch. Sys. Enr. Code 2
Supt. – John Wood, P O BOX 864 74018
Justus ES, P O BOX 864 74018 – (—), prin.

Sequoyah ISD
Sch. Sys. Enr. Code 3
Supt. – Olan Graham
   RURAL ROUTE 03 BOX 200 74017
Sequoyah MS, RURAL ROUTE 03 BOX 200 74017
   John Rhine, prin.
Sequoyah ES, RURAL ROUTE 03 BOX 134 74017
   Burl Moore,Jr., prin.

Tiawah SD
Sch. Sys. Enr. Code 1
Supt. – Fred White
   RURAL ROUTE 07 BOX 256 74017
Tiawah ES, RURAL ROUTE 07 BOX 256 74017
   (—), prin.

Verdigris ISD
Sch. Sys. Enr. Code 2
Supt. – Terry Tillery
   RURAL ROUTE 08 BOX 128 74017
Verdigris ES, 6101 SW VERDIGRIS ROAD 74017
   Jim Anderson, prin.

Clayton, Pushmataha Co., Pop. Code 3
Clayton ISD
Sch. Sys. Enr. Code 2
Supt. – Preston Brown, P O BOX 190 74536
JHS, P O BOX 190 74536 – Fred Ferguson, prin.
Crain ES, P O BOX 190 74536
   Chester Knight, prin.

Cleveland, Pawnee Co., Pop. Code 5
Cleveland ISD
Sch. Sys. Enr. Code 4
Supt. – Charles Clayton, 211 E WICHITA 74020
MS, P O BOX 28 74020 – Max Caldwell, prin.
Terlton ES, P O BOX 28 74020 – Leon Day, prin.
West Side ES, 900 W DELAWARE ST 74020
   Robert Henderson, prin.

Clinton, Custer Co., Pop. Code 6
Clinton ISD
Sch. Sys. Enr. Code 4
Supt. – Joe Bingenheimer, P O BOX 729 73601
MS, P O BOX 729 73601 – Darryl Tincher, prin.
Nance ES, P O BOX 729 73601
   Joidell Salisbury, prin.
Southwest ES, P O BOX 729 73601
   Darrell Trissell, prin.
Washington MS, P O BOX 729 73601
   Roy Malson, prin.

Coalgate, Coal Co., Pop. Code 4
Coalgate ISD
Sch. Sys. Enr. Code 3
Supt. – Dr. John Linton, 100 W CEDAR 74538
MS, P O BOX 368 74538 – Allen Hicks, prin.
Emerson ES, P O BOX 368 74538
  Roy Campbell, prin.

Cottonwood SD
Sch. Sys. Enr. Code 1
Supt. – Robert Pickens, RURAL ROUTE 01 74538
Cottonwood ES
  RURAL ROUTE 01 BOX 28C 74538
  (—), prin.

Midway ISD
Supt. – See Council Hill
ES, P O BOX 98 74538 – Gemey Lackey, prin.

Olney ISD
Sch. Sys. Enr. Code 2
Supt. – Terry Ragan
  RURAL ROUTE 05 BOX 125 74538
Olney ES, RURAL ROUTE 05 BOX 125 74538
  Terry Ragan, prin.

Colbert, Bryan Co., Pop. Code 4
Colbert ISD
Sch. Sys. Enr. Code 2
Supt. – T. Owens, P O BOX 310 74733
East Ward MS, P O BOX 310 74733
  Kenneth Taylor, prin.
West Ward ES, P O BOX 310 74733
  Gerald Thompson, prin.

Colcord, Delaware Co., Pop. Code 3
Colcord ISD
Sch. Sys. Enr. Code 3
Supt. – Dan Edwards, P O BOX 188 74338
ES, P O BOX 188 74338 – Wilks Harper, prin.

Moseley SD
Sch. Sys. Enr. Code 2
Supt. – Bessie Duggan
  RURAL ROUTE 04 BOX 88 74338
Moseley ES, RURAL ROUTE 04 BOX 85 74338
  (—), prin.

Coleman, Johnston Co., Pop. Code 2
Coleman ISD
Sch. Sys. Enr. Code 2
Supt. – Perry Willis, P O BOX 218 73432
ES, P O BOX 218 73432 – Randy Brister, prin.

Collinsville, Tulsa Co., Pop. Code 5
Collinsville ISD
Sch. Sys. Enr. Code 4
Supt. – Pat Herald, 2400 W BROADWAY 74021
MS, 2400 W BROADWAY ST 74021
  Paul Davis, prin.
Washington MS, 2400 W BROADWAY ST 74021
  Tom Nichols, prin.
Wilson ES, 2400 W BROADWAY ST 74021
  Duane Cantrell, prin.

Comanche, Stephens Co., Pop. Code 4
Comanche ISD
Sch. Sys. Enr. Code 4
Supt. – Tommy Taylor, P O BOX 310 73529
JHS, P O BOX 310 73529 – Burl White, prin.
ES, P O BOX 310 73529 – James Chaffin, prin.
Liberty ES, P O BOX 310 73529
  Janice Montieth, prin.
Meridian ES, P O BOX 310 73529
  Jenene Bailey, prin.

Grandview SD
Sch. Sys. Enr. Code 1
Supt. – M. Lucille Baird
  GENERAL DELIVERY 73529
Grandview ES
  RURAL ROUTE 01 BOX 113 73529
  (—), prin.

Commerce, Ottawa Co., Pop. Code 5
Commerce ISD
Sch. Sys. Enr. Code 3
Supt. – Dick Currey, 420 D ST 74339
MS, 420 D ST 74339 – Jim Hutto, prin.
Alexander ES, 420 D STREET 74439
  Jack Redden, prin.

Connerville, Johnston Co.
Connerville SD
Sch. Sys. Enr. Code 1
Supt. – Colene Alexander, P O BOX 608 74859
ES, P O BOX 608 74836 – (—), prin.

Copan, Washington Co., Pop. Code 3
Copan ISD
Sch. Sys. Enr. Code 2
Supt. – Delbert Moreland, P O BOX 429 74022
ES, P O BOX 429 74022 – Betsy Graham, prin.

Cordell, Washita Co., Pop. Code 5
Cordell ISD
Sch. Sys. Enr. Code 3
Supt. – Jerry Burrows, P O BOX 290 73632
ES, P O BOX 290 73632 – Pat Bullard, prin.

Corn, Washita Co., Pop. Code 3
Washita Heights ISD
Sch. Sys. Enr. Code 2
Supt. – Mike Southall, P O BOX 8 73024
Washita Heights ES, P O BOX 8 73024
  F. McMullen, prin.

Council Hill, Muskogee Co., Pop. Code 2
Midway ISD
Sch. Sys. Enr. Code 2
Supt. – Roy King, P O BOX 127 74428
Other Schools – See Coalgate

Covington, Garfield, Pop. Code 3
Covington-Douglas ISD
Sch. Sys. Enr. Code 2
Supt. – Don Boynton, P O BOX 9 73730
Covington-Douglas ES, P O BOX 9 73730
  Mary Callas, prin.

Coweta, Wagoner Co., Pop. Code 5
Coweta ISD
Sch. Sys. Enr. Code 4
Supt. – Sam Farmer, P O BOX 550 74429
MS, P O BOX 550 74429 – Lloyd Keaton, prin.
Central ES, P O BOX 550 74429
  Mike Wallace, prin.
Other Schools – See Canute

Coyle, Logan Co., Pop. Code 2
Coyle ISD
Sch. Sys. Enr. Code 2
Supt. – Larry Northcutt, P O BOX 287 73027
ES, P O BOX 287 73027 – Gene Benson, prin.

Crawford, Roger Mills Co.
Crawford SD
Sch. Sys. Enr. Code 1
Supt. – Terrell Scroggins, P O BOX 17 73638
ES, P O BOX 17 73638 – (—), prin.

Crescent, Logan Co., Pop. Code 4
Crescent ISD
Sch. Sys. Enr. Code 3
Supt. – James Borin, P O BOX 719 73028
ES, P O BOX 719 73028 – Jim Childers, prin.

Cromwell, Seminole Co., Pop. Code 2
Butner ISD
Sch. Sys. Enr. Code 2
Supt. – Nolan Coker, P O BOX 157 74837
Butner ES, P O BOX 157 74837
  Jean Marquis, prin.

Crowder, Pittsburg Co., Pop. Code 2
Crowder ISD
Sch. Sys. Enr. Code 2
Supt. – David Jones, P O BOX B 74430
ES, P O BOX B 74430 – Concetta Gragg, prin.

Cushing, Payne Co., Pop. Code 6
Cushing ISD
Sch. Sys. Enr. Code 4
Supt. – Dr. Billy Childress, P O BOX 1609 74023
MS, 316 N STEELE ST 74023 – Ray Brumley, prin.
Deep Rock ES
  RURAL ROUTE 04 BOX 1965 74023
  Dr. John Carney, prin.
Harmony ES, RURAL ROUTE 01 74023
  Ed Williams, prin.
Harrison ES, 610 S NOBLE ST 74023
  Jay Evers, prin.
Sunnyside ES
  RURAL ROUTE 04 BOX 1050 74023
  Loren West, prin.
Wilson ES, 1411 E CHERRY ST 74023
  Kathryn Fisher, prin.

Oak Grove SD
Sch. Sys. Enr. Code 2
Supt. – Robert Brock
  RURAL ROUTE 02 BOX 355 74023
Oak Grove ES
  RURAL ROUTE 02 BOX 1500 74023
  (—), prin.

Custer City, Custer Co., Pop. Code 3
Custer ISD
Sch. Sys. Enr. Code 2
Supt. – Charles Thompson, P O BOX 200 73639
Custer ES, P O BOX 200 73639
  Karen Travis, prin.

Cyril, Caddo Co., Pop. Code 4
Cyril ISD
Sch. Sys. Enr. Code 2
Supt. – W. Whitman, P O BOX 449 73029
ES, P O BOX 449 73029 – Dwight Myers, prin.

Dale, Pottawatomie Co., Pop. Code 1
Dale ISD
Sch. Sys. Enr. Code 3
Supt. – Paul Lewis, P O BOX 748 74838
Jackson ES 74838 – John McClain, prin.

Davenport, Lincoln Co., Pop. Code 3
Davenport ISD
Sch. Sys. Enr. Code 2
Supt. – Glen Elliott, P O BOX 250 74026
ES, P O BOX 849 74026 – John Addison, prin.

Davidson, Tilman Co., Pop. Code 3
Davidson ISD
Sch. Sys. Enr. Code 2
Supt. – Phillip Ratcliff, P O BOX 338 73530
ES, P O BOX 338 73530 – Oleta Dunham, prin.

Davis, Murray Co., Pop. Code 5
Davis ISD
Sch. Sys. Enr. Code 3
Supt. – E. Wayne Byrd, 400 E ATLANTA 73030
MS, 400 E ATLANTA AVE 73030
  Allen Richardson, prin.
ES, 400 E ATLANTA AVE 73830
  Jim Clemons, prin.

Delaware, Nowata Co., Pop. Code 3
Delaware ISD
Sch. Sys. Enr. Code 2
Supt. – Don Sims, P O BOX 69 74027
ES, P O BOX 69 74027 – Dan Foster, prin.

Depew, Creek Co., Pop. Code 3
Depew ISD
Sch. Sys. Enr. Code 2
Supt. – Ivan Reeder, P O BOX 257 74028
ES, P O BOX 257 74028 – Arnold Dunn, prin.

Gypsy SD
Sch. Sys. Enr. Code 2
Supt. – John Britt
  RURAL ROUTE 01 BOX 400 74010
Gypsy ES, RURAL ROUTE 01 BOX 400 74028
  (—), prin.

Dewar, Okmulgee Co., Pop. Code 4
Dewar ISD
Sch. Sys. Enr. Code 2
Supt. – Harry Atkins, P O BOX A 74431
ES, P O BOX A 74431 – Roger Busse, prin.

Dewey, Washington Co., Pop. Code 5
Dewey ISD
Sch. Sys. Enr. Code 4
Supt. – Paul Smith, 1 BULLDOGGER ROAD 74029
JHS, 1 BULLDOGGER ROAD 74029
  Wendell Stacy, prin.
Lincoln ES, 1 BULLDOGGER ROAD 74029
  Gary Rhoton, prin.

Dibble, McClain Co., Pop. Code 2
Dibble ISD
Sch. Sys. Enr. Code 3
Supt. – Robert Perkins, P O BOX 9 73031
ES, P O BOX 9 73031 – Jerry Crawford, prin.

Dill City, Washita Co., Pop. Code 3
Dill City ISD
Sch. Sys. Enr. Code 2
Supt. – Jim Conger, P O BOX 188 73641
ES, P O BOX 188 73641 – Cindy Buckmaster, prin.

Dougherty, Murray Co., Pop. Code 2
Dougherty SD
Sch. Sys. Enr. Code 1
Supt. – (—), P O BOX 33 73032
ES, P O BOX 33 73032 – (—), prin.

Dover, Kingfisher Co., Pop. Code 3
Dover ISD
Sch. Sys. Enr. Code 2
Supt. – Steve Shiever, P O BOX 195 73734
ES, P O BOX 195 73734 – Teresa Loudermilk, prin.

Drummond, Garfield Co., Pop. Code 2
Drummond ISD
Sch. Sys. Enr. Code 2
Supt. – Robert Moore, P O BOX 220 73735
ES, P O BOX 220 73735 – Charlene Parker, prin.

Drumright, Creek Co., Pop. Code 5
Drumright ISD
Sch. Sys. Enr. Code 3
Supt. – Arthur Johnson
  801 S PENNSYLVANIA ST 74030
Edison MS, 301 S PENNSYLVANIA ST 74030
  Otis Stump, prin.
ES, 508 S SKINNER AVE 74030
  Benjamin Lacy, prin.

Olive ISD
Sch. Sys. Enr. Code 3
Supt. – Leroy Corbett
  RURAL ROUTE 01 BOX 337 74030
Olive ES, RURAL ROUTE 01 74030
  Beth Crabtree, prin.

Duke, Jackson Co., Pop. Code 2
Duke ISD
Sch. Sys. Enr. Code 2
Supt. – Bill Morgan, P O BOX 160 73532
ES, P O BOX 160 73932 – Arva Horschler, prin.

Duncan, Stephens Co., Pop. Code 7
Duncan ISD
Sch. Sys. Enr. Code 5
Supt. – Jack Atchley, P O BOX 1548 73533
JHS, P O BOX 1548 73534 – Don Dowhower, prin.
Emerson ES, P O BOX 1548 73534
  Joe Duncan, prin.
Irving ES, P O BOX 1548 73534
  John Millirons, prin.
Lee ES, P O BOX 1548 73534
  Nancy Leonard, prin.
Mann ES, P O BOX 1548 73534 – Irene Seay, prin.
Plato ES, P O BOX 1548 73534
  Don Dudley, prin.
Rogers ES, P O BOX 1548 73534
  Martha Burger, prin.
Twain ES, P O BOX 1548 73534
  Don Hendricks, prin.
Wilson ES, P O BOX 1548 73534
  Robert Ingle, prin.

Empire ISD
Sch. Sys. Enr. Code 3
Supt. – Billy Cox
  RURAL ROUTE 01 BOX 155 73533
Empire ES, RURAL ROUTE 01 BOX 155 73533
  Mary Herring, prin.

Durant, Bryan Co., Pop. Code 7
Blue ISD
Sch. Sys. Enr. Code 2
Supt. – James Marshall
RURAL ROUTE 01 BOX 181A 74701
Blue ES, RURAL ROUTE 01 BOX 181A 74701
John Carrell, prin.

Durant ISD
Sch. Sys. Enr. Code 5
Supt. – Dr. George Anderson
1801 UNIVERSITY 74701
MS, 405 N 5TH AVE 74701
Leonard Morgan, prin.
Irving ES, 405 N 5TH AVE 74701
Katy Stewart, prin.
Lee ES, 824 W LOUISIANA 74701
Mike Dills, prin.
Northwest Heights ES, 405 N 5TH AVE 74701
Dr. John Jackson, prin.
Washington ES, 405 N 5TH AVE 74701
Bill Fuller, prin.

Silo ISD
Sch. Sys. Enr. Code 3
Supt. – Larry Snider, HCR BOX 227 74701
Silo ES, HCR BOX 227 74701
Harold Trotter, prin.

Dustin, Hughes Co., Pop. Code 2
Dustin ISD
Sch. Sys. Enr. Code 2
Supt. – Wade Glover, P O BOX 390660 74839
ES, P O BOX 390660 74839
Richard Estorga, prin.

Eagletown, McCurtain Co., Pop. Code 2
Eagletown ISD
Sch. Sys. Enr. Code 2
Supt. – H. Coleman, P O BOX 38 74734
ES, P O BOX 38 74734 – Wayne Sloat, prin.

Eakly, Caddo Co., Pop. Code 2
Eakly ISD
Sch. Sys. Enr. Code 2
Supt. – Jimmy Buie, P O BOX 308 73033
ES, P O BOC 308 73033 – Jim Bluie, prin.

Earlsboro, Pottawatomie Co., Pop. Code 2
Earlsboro ISD
Sch. Sys. Enr. Code 2
Supt. – Billy Farnham, P O BOX 95 74840
ES, P O BOX 95 74840 – Sue Greenfield, prin.

Strother ISD
Supt. – See Seminole
Strother ES, RURAL ROUTE 01 74840
Frank Moore, prin.

Edmond, Oklahoma Co., Pop. Code 8
Deer Creek ISD
Sch. Sys. Enr. Code 3
Supt. – Dr. William White
RURAL ROUTE 01 BOX 137 73034
Deer Creek MS
RURAL ROUTE 01 BOX 137 73034
Jan Seely, prin.
Deer Creek ES
RURAL ROUTE 01 BOX 137 73034
Dr. Deborah Steller, prin.

Edmond ISD
Sch. Sys. Enr. Code 7
Supt. – Dr. Randall Raburn
1216 S RANKIN 73034
Cimarron MS, 3701 S BRYANT AVE 73034
Mona Warren, prin.
Sequoyah MS, 215 W DANFORTH ROAD 73034
Sandra Brothers, prin.
Chisholm ES, 2300 SE 33RD ST 73013
Barbara Mitchell, prin.
Clegern ES, 600 S JACKSON ST 73034
Mickey Hart, prin.
Dougherty ES, 19 N BLVD 73034
Ann Robinson, prin.
Freeman ES, 501 W HURD ST 73034
Dr. Nancy Wotring, prin.
Haskell ES, 1301 NW 150TH ST 73013
Bill Nowell, prin.
Northern Hills ES, 901 E WAYNE AVE 73034
Ann Sheldon, prin.
Risner ES, 2900 S RANKIN ST 73013
Glenn Norris, prin.
Rogers ES, 1215 E 9TH ST 73034
Dr. Rhonda Hamilton, prin.
Ross ES, 1901 THOMAS DR 73034
Mel Deering, prin.
Sunset ES, 401 W 9TH ST 73034
Barbara Siano, prin.

Oakdale SD
Sch. Sys. Enr. Code 2
Supt. – Kim Lanier
11901 N SOONER ROAD 73013
Oakdale ES 73013 – (—), prin.

Eldorado, Jackson Co., Pop. Code 3
Eldorado ISD
Sch. Sys. Enr. Code 2
Supt. – A. McDonald, P O BOX J 73537
ES, P O BOX J 73537 – Judith Hankins, prin.

Elgin, Comanche Co., Pop. Code 4
Elgin ISD
Sch. Sys. Enr. Code 3
Supt. – Lloyd Snow, P O BOX 369 73538

MS, P O BOX 369 73538 – Phil Harred, prin.
ES, P O BOX 369 73538 – Doug Garland, prin.

Stony Point SD
Sch. Sys. Enr. Code 1
Supt. – Patti Bray, RURAL ROUTE 01 73538
Stony Point ES
RURAL ROUTE 01 BOX 2200 73538
(—), prin.

Elk City, Beckham Co., Pop. Code 6
Elk City ISD
Sch. Sys. Enr. Code 4
Supt. – Don McDonald, 222 W BROADWAY 73644
Fairview ES, 222 W BROADWAY AVE 73644
Kenneth Hart, prin.
Grandview MS, 222 W BROADWAY AVE 73644
Terry Armstrong, prin.
Northeast ES, 222 W BROADWAY AVE 73644
Bob Kennemer, prin.
Pioneer ES, 222 W BROADWAY AVE 73644
Jim Coffey, prin.

Merritt Ind School Dist
Sch. Sys. Enr. Code 3
Supt. – Elmwood Simmons
RURAL ROUTE 04 73644
Merritt JHS, RURAL ROUTE 04 73644
Jim Richardson, prin.
Merritt ES, RURAL ROUTE 04 73644
Roger Woodson, prin.

Elmer, Jackson Co., Pop. Code 2
Southside ISD
Sch. Sys. Enr. Code 1
Supt. – Jessee Middick, RURAL ROUTE 01 73539
Southside ES, RURAL ROUTE 01 73539
Sandra Guy, prin.

Elmore City, Garvin Co., Pop. Code 3
Elmore City ISD
Sch. Sys. Enr. Code 2
Supt. – Dale Kirby, P O BOX 97 73035
ES, P O BOX 99 73035 – Laverne Kirby, prin.

Elmwood, Beaver Co.
Garrett SD
Sch. Sys. Enr. Code 1
Supt. – Eddie Thomas, ROUTE A BOX 31A 73935
Garrett ES, RURAL ROUTE 01 BOX 84 73932
(—), prin.

El Reno, Canadian Co., Pop. Code 7
Banner SD
Sch. Sys. Enr. Code 1
Supt. – (—)
RURAL ROUTE 02 BOX 121 73036
Banner ES, RURAL ROUTE 02 BOX 121 73036
(—), prin.

Darlington SD
Sch. Sys. Enr. Code 1
Supt. – Glen Meriwether, P O BOX 45-A 73036
Darlington ES
RURAL ROUTE 03 BOX 145-A 73036
(—), prin.

El Reno ISD
Sch. Sys. Enr. Code 4
Supt. – Leslie Roblyer, P O BOX 580 73036
Hillcrest ES, P O BOX 580 73036
Tom Cobble, prin.
Lincoln ES, P O BOX 580 73036
George Marshall, prin.
Webster ES, P O BOX 580 73036
Rick Horner, prin.
Witcher ES, P O BOX 580 73036
Jud Webster, prin.

Riverside SD
Sch. Sys. Enr. Code 2
Supt. – John Hoops, RURAL ROUTE 03 73036
Riverside ES, RURAL ROUTE 03 73036
(—), prin.

Enid, Garfield Co., Pop. Code 8
Chisholm ISD
Sch. Sys. Enr. Code 4
Supt. – Alan Livingston
RURAL ROUTE 06 BOX 102 73701
Chisholm ES 73701 – Lavonn McKnight, prin.

Enid ISD
Sch. Sys. Enr. Code 6
Supt. – Dr. Garland Keithly
500 S INDEPENDENCE 73701
Adams ES, 500 S INDEPENDENCE ST 73701
Galen Havner, prin.
Coolidge ES, 500 S INDEPENDENCE ST 73701
Mary Beach, prin.
Eisenhower ES, 500 S INDEPENDENCE ST 73701
Mary Butler, prin.
Garfield ES, 500 S INDEPENDENCE ST 73701
Walter Harrington, prin.
Glenwood ES, 500 S INDEPENDENCE ST 73701
Elizabeth Morris, prin.
Harrison ES, 500 S INDEPENDENCE ST 73701
Shirley Goertz, prin.
Hayes ES, 500 S INDEPENDENCE ST 73701
Barbara Erwin, prin.
Hoover ES, 500 S INDEPENDENCE ST 73701
Dr. Erma Austin, prin.
Lincoln ES, 500 S INDEPENDENCE ST 73701
Geneva Powell, prin.
McKinley ES, 500 S INDEPENDENCE ST 73701
Art Beelendorf, prin.

Monroe ES, 500 S INDEPENDENCE ST 73701
Loren Avery, prin.
Taft ES, 500 S INDEPENDENCE ST 73701
Ruth Erdner, prin.

St. Paul Lutheran School
1625 E BROADWAY AVE 73701

Erick, Beckham Co., Pop. Code 4
Erick ISD
Sch. Sys. Enr. Code 2
Supt. – Richard Deeds, P O BOX 9 73645
ES, P O BOX 9 73645 – Clifford Macklin, prin.

Eufaula, McIntosh Co., Pop. Code 5
Eufaula ISD
Sch. Sys. Enr. Code 4
Supt. – Dr. Larry Gill, P O BOX 609 74432
Cooper-McClain MS, P O BOX 609 74432
Deanna Broughton, prin.
Davis ES, P O BOX 609 74432
Beverly Brotton, prin.
Dixie ES, P O BOX 609 74432 – Peg Jordan, prin.

Fairfax, Osage Co., Pop. Code 4
Fairfax ISD
Sch. Sys. Enr. Code 2
Supt. – Felix Sikes, 100 N 6TH 74637
Crowder ES, P O BOX 487 74637
Burley Hathcoat, prin.

Fairland, Ottawa Co., Pop. Code 4
Fairland ISD
Sch. Sys. Enr. Code 4
Supt. – Earl Hudelson, P O BOX C 74343
ES, P O BOX 689 74343 – Ron Cash, prin.

Fairview, Major Co., Pop. Code 5
Fairview ISD
Sch. Sys. Enr. Code 3
Supt. – Bob Van Meter, 408 E BROADWAY 73737
Chamberlain MS, 1000 E ELM ST 73737
Garold Sullivan, prin.
Cornelsen ES, 1200 E ELM ST 73737
Donald Friesen, prin.

Progressive SD
Sch. Sys. Enr. Code 1
Supt. – Robert Eitzen
RURAL ROUTE 02 BOX 64A 73737
Progressive ES
RURAL ROUTE 02 BOX 64A 73737
(—), prin.

Fanshawe, Le Flore Co., Pop. Code 2
Fanshawe SD
Sch. Sys. Enr. Code 1
Supt. – Warner Hall, P O BOX 21 74935
ES, P O BOX 55 74935 – (—), prin.

Fargo, Ellis Co., Pop. Code 2
Fargo ISD
Sch. Sys. Enr. Code 2
Supt. – Larry Hixon, P O BOX 200 73840
ES, P O BOX 200 73840 – John Gilchrist, prin.

Farris, Atoka Co.
Farris SD
Sch. Sys. Enr. Code 2
Supt. – Bob Noak
RURAL ROUTE 01 BOX 31 74542
ES, RURAL ROUTE 01 BOX 31 74542
(—), prin.

Faxon, Comanche Co., Pop. Code 2
Faxon ISD
Sch. Sys. Enr. Code 1
Supt. – Lanetta Martin, P O BOX 95 73540
ES, P O BOX 95 73540 – (—), prin.

Felt, Cimarron Co.
Felt ISD
Sch. Sys. Enr. Code 1
Supt. – Mitchel Potter, P O BOX 47 73937
ES, P O BOX 47 73937 – Otha McDaniel, prin.

Fittstown, Pontotoc Co., Pop. Code 2
McLish ISD
Sch. Sys. Enr. Code 2
Supt. – J. Pryor, P O BOX 29 74842
McLish ES, P O BOX 29 74842
Robert Crow, prin.

Fletcher, Comanche Co., Pop. Code 4
Fletcher ISD
Supt. – See Marlow
ES, P O BOX 489 73541 – Lonnie Sanders, prin.

Forgan, Beaver Co., Pop. Code 3
Forgan ISD
Sch. Sys. Enr. Code 2
Supt. – Doug Rundle, P O BOX 458 73938
ES, P O BOX 406 73938 – Glen Kirkendall, prin.

Fort Cobb, Caddo Co., Pop. Code 3
Ft. Cobb ISD
Sch. Sys. Enr. Code 2
Supt. – Wayne Parrish, P O BOX 130 73038
ES, P O BOX 130 73038 – Tim Parker, prin.

Fort Gibson, Muskogee Co., Pop. Code 4
Ft. Gibson ISD
Sch. Sys. Enr. Code 4
Supt. – John Harrison, Jr., P O BOX 280 74434
MS, P O BOX 280 74434 – James Lasater, prin.
ES, P O BOX 280 74434 – Roger Shaw, prin.
Ft. Gibson ES South, P O BOX 280 74434
Ann Davis, prin.

Fort Sill, Comanche Co.
Lawton ISD
Supt. – See Lawton
Sheridan Road ES, 6500 SHERIDAN ROAD   73503
   Kenneth Schraner, prin.

Fort Supply, Woodward Co., Pop. Code 3
Ft. Supply ISD
Sch. Sys. Enr. Code 2
Supt. – Merle Hosler, P O BOX 160   73841
ES, P O BOX 160   73841 – Joyce Hunter, prin.

Fort Towson, Choctaw Co., Pop. Code 3
Ft. Towson ISD
Sch. Sys. Enr. Code 2
Supt. – James Gibbs, P O BOX 39   74735
ES, P O BOX 39   74735 – Jim Barker, prin.

Fox, Carter Co., Pop. Code 2
Fox ISD
Sch. Sys. Enr. Code 2
Supt. – Roy Snow, P O BOX 248   73435
ES, P O BOX 248   73435 – Don Osteen, prin.

Foyil, Rogers Co., Pop. Code 2
Foyil ISD
Sch. Sys. Enr. Code 2
Supt. – John Hollingsworth, P O BOX 49   74031
ES, P O BOX 49   74031 – David Archer, prin.

Frederick, Tillman Co., Pop. Code 6
Frederick ISD
Sch. Sys. Enr. Code 4
Supt. – Tony Risinger, P O BOX 370   73542
MS, P O BOX 490   73542 – Donald Mitchell, prin.
Central MS, P O BOX 669   73642
   Oscar Bennight, prin.
Brown ES   73542 – Paula Jacobs, prin.

Weaver SD
Sch. Sys. Enr. Code 1
Supt. – Clydia Heap
   RURAL ROUTE 02   BOX 24   73542
Weaver ES, RURAL ROUTE 02   BOX 24   73542
   (—), prin.

Freedom, Woods Co., Pop. Code 2
Freedom ISD
Sch. Sys. Enr. Code 1
Supt. – Don Rader, P O BOX 5   73842
ES, P O BOX 5   73842 – Jackie Bowers, prin.

Gage, Ellis Co., Pop. Code 3
Gage ISD
Sch. Sys. Enr. Code 2
Supt. – John Froage, P O BOX 7   73843
ES, P O BOX 7   73843 – Don Pittman, prin.

Gans, Sequoyah Co., Pop. Code 2
Gans ISD
Sch. Sys. Enr. Code 2
Supt. – Burley Middleton, P O BOX 52   74936
ES, P O BOX 52   74936 – Linda Peerson, prin.

Garber, Garfield Co., Pop. Code 4
Garber ISD
Sch. Sys. Enr. Code 2
Supt. – Bruce Mendenhall, P O BOX 539   73738
JHS, P O BOX 539   73738 – Ted Bentz, prin.
ES, P O BOX 548   73738 – Jan Marker, prin.

Garvin, McCurtin Co., Pop. Code 2
Forest Grove SD
Sch. Sys. Enr. Code 2
Supt. – Bob Dempsey, P O BOX 60   74736
Forest Grove ES, P O BOX 60   74736
   (—), prin.

Gate, Beaver Co., Pop. Code 2
Gate SD
Sch. Sys. Enr. Code 1
Supt. – Pat Howell, P O BOX 8   73844
ES, P O BOX 8   73844 – (—), prin.

Geary, Blaine Co., Pop. Code 4
Geary ISD
Sch. Sys. Enr. Code 3
Supt. – F. Brocato, P O BOX 188   73040
ES, P O BOX 188   73040 – Katheriene Hanes, prin.

Gene Autry, Carter Co., Pop. Code 2
Gene Autry SD
Sch. Sys. Enr. Code 1
Supt. – Snell Green, P O BOX 38   73436
ES, P O BOX 38   73436 – (—), prin.

Geronimo, Comanche Co., Pop. Code 3
Geronimo ISD
Sch. Sys. Enr. Code 2
Supt. – Denver Rowley, P O BOX 98   73543
ES, P O BOX 98   73543 – Madeline Kervin, prin.

Glencoe, Payne Co., Pop. Code 2
Glencoe ISD
Sch. Sys. Enr. Code 2
Supt. – Gene Slaton, P O BOX 218   74032
ES, P O BOX 218   74032 – Keith Childers, prin.

Glenpool, Tulsa Co., Pop. Code 5
Glenpool ISD
Sch. Sys. Enr. Code 4
Supt. – Dennis Chaffin, P O BOX 1149   74033
Glenpool MS, P O BOX 1149   74033
   Nancy Travers, prin.
ES, P O BOX 1149   74033 – Ron Metcalf, prin.

Goodwell, Texas Co., Pop. Code 4
Goodwell ISD
Sch. Sys. Enr. Code 2
Supt. – Junior Zollinger, P O BOX 580   73939
ES, P O BOX 580   73939 – Carol Nelson, prin.

Yarbrough ISD
Sch. Sys. Enr. Code 2
Supt. – Dr. Phillip Knight
   RURAL ROUTE 01   BOX 47   73939
Yarbrough ES, RURAL ROUTE 01   BOX 31   73939
   Betty Walters, prin.

Gore, Sequoyah Co., Pop. Code 2
Gore ISD
Sch. Sys. Enr. Code 2
Supt. – Robert Smith, P O BOX 580   74435
ES, P O BOX 580   74435 – Lou Evertson, prin.

Gum Springs SD
Sch. Sys. Enr. Code 1
Supt. – Beverly King
   RURAL ROUTE 01   BOX 129T   74435
Gum Springs ES
   RURAL ROUTE 01   BOX 129   74435
   (—), prin.

Gotebo, Kiowa Co., Pop. Code 2
Gotebo ISD
Sch. Sys. Enr. Code 1
Supt. – Steven Black, P O BOX 68   73041
ES   73041 – Karen Hestand, prin.

Gould, Harmon Co., Pop. Code 2
Gould ISD
Sch. Sys. Enr. Code 2
Supt. – Kenneth McClendon, P O BOX 69   73544
ES, P O BOX 69   73544
   Albert Motsenbocker, prin.

Gracemont, Caddo Co., Pop. Code 3
Gracemont ISD
Sch. Sys. Enr. Code 2
Supt. – James Edelen, P O BOX 5   73042
ES, P O BOX 5   73042 – Richard Allen, prin.

Graham, Carter Co.
Graham ISD
Sch. Sys. Enr. Code 2
Supt. – Bill Monroe, P O BOX 197   73437
ES, P O BOX 197   73437 – Roger Rounsaville, prin.

Grandfield, Tillman Co., Pop. Code 4
Grandfield ISD
Sch. Sys. Enr. Code 2
Supt. – Darrell Brite, P O BOX 639   73546
ES, P O BOX 639   73546 – Bill Querner, prin.

Granite, Greer Co., Pop. Code 4
Granite ISD
Sch. Sys. Enr. Code 2
Supt. – Dwight Hogg, P O BOX 98   73547
ES, P O BOX 98   73547 – Pam Griffis, prin.

Grant, Choctaw Co., Pop. Code 2
Grant ISD
Sch. Sys. Enr. Code 2
Supt. – Gerald Stegall, P O BOX 587   74738
ES, P O BOX 587   74738 – Perlita Brown, prin.

Greenfield, Blaine Co., Pop. Code 2
Greenfield ISD
Sch. Sys. Enr. Code 1
Supt. – George Smith, P O BOX 90   73043
ES, P O BOX 85   73043 – Connie George, prin.

Grove, Delaware Co., Pop. Code 5
Grove ISD
Sch. Sys. Enr. Code 4
Supt. – Joe Ethridge, P O BOX 789   74344
MS, P O BOX 550   74344 – Fred Clouse, prin.
ES, P O BOX 789   74344 – Zack Hamilton, prin.

Guthrie, Logan Co., Pop. Code 7
Guthrie ISD
Sch. Sys. Enr. Code 5
Supt. – Jack Herron, P O BOX 310   73044
JHS, 705 E OKLAHOMA ST   73044
   Earl Sykes, prin.
Central ES, P O BOX 310   73044 – (—), prin.
Cotteral ES, 2001 W NOBLE AVE   73044
   Gerald Collier, prin.
Faver MS, P O BOX 310   73044
   Claire Gatewood, prin.
Fogarty MS, 902 N WENTZ ST   73044
   John Haney, prin.

Guymon, Texas Co., Pop. Code 6
Guymon ISD
Sch. Sys. Enr. Code 4
Supt. – Clayton Goff, P O BOX 1307   73942
Academy ES, P O BOX 1307   73942
   Jess Nelson, prin.
Carrier ES, P O BOX 1307   73942
   Jess Nelson, prin.
Long ES, P O BOX 1307   73942 – Jess Nelson, prin.
Northeast ES, P O BOX 1307   73942
   Jess Nelson, prin.
Salyer ES, P O BOX 1307   73942
   Jess Nelson, prin.

Straight SD
Sch. Sys. Enr. Code 1
Supt. – Laura Hill
   RURAL ROUTE 01   BOX 89   73942
Straight ES, RURAL ROUTE 01   BOX 89   73942
   (—), prin.

Haileyville, Pittsburg Co., Pop. Code 3
Haileyville ISD
Sch. Sys. Enr. Code 2
Supt. – Gary Newberry, P O BOX 29   74546
ES, P O BOX 29   74536 – Stuart McPherson, prin.

Hammon, Rogers Mills Co., Pop. Code 3
Hammon ISD
Sch. Sys. Enr. Code 2
Supt. – Frank Kirchoffner
   GENERAL DELIVERY   73650
ES, P O BOX 279   73650 – Roy Malson, prin.

Hanna, McIntosh Co., Pop. Code 2
Hanna ISD
Sch. Sys. Enr. Code 2
Supt. – Bob Akin, P O BOX H   74845
ES, P O BOX H   74845 – Russell Byers, prin.

Hardesty, Texas Co., Pop. Code 2
Hardesty ISD
Sch. Sys. Enr. Code 1
Supt. – (—), P O BOX 129   73944
ES, P O BOX 129   73944 – (—), prin.

Harrah, Oklahoma Co., Pop. Code 5
Harrah ISD
Sch. Sys. Enr. Code 4
Supt. – Dr. Jim Morrel, 302 WALKER ST   73045
MS, 303 WALKER ST   73045 – Lloyd Walker, prin.
Babb MS, 20901 NE 10TH ST   73045
   Robert Odom, prin.
Reynolds ES, 701 HARRISON   73045
   Don Briix, prin.

Hartshorne, Pittsburg Co., Pop. Code 4
Hartshorne ISD
Sch. Sys. Enr. Code 3
Supt. – John Enloe, 520 S 5TH   74547
ES, 520 S 5TH ST   74547 – Larry Jennings, prin.

Haskell, Muskogee Co., Pop. Code 4
Haskell ISD
Sch. Sys. Enr. Code 3
Supt. – Thomas Dixon, 400 W MAIN   74436
White ES, P O BOX 278   74436
   Frank Holmes, prin.

Haworth, McCurtain Co., Pop. Code 2
Haworth ISD
Sch. Sys. Enr. Code 3
Supt. – Herman Horn, P O BOX 98   74740
ES, P O BOX 99   74740 – Donald Ray, prin.

Haywood, Pittsburg Co.
Haywood SD
Sch. Sys. Enr. Code 2
Supt. – Terry Beck, GENERAL DELIVERY   74548
ES, GENERAL DELIVERY   74548 – (—), prin.

Healdton, Carter Co., Pop. Code 5
Healdton ISD
Sch. Sys. Enr. Code 3
Supt. – Dr. Kathy Roberts, P O BOX 490   73438
MS, P O BOX 490   73438 – Dennis Idleman, prin.
Sunset ES, P O BOX 490   73438
   Larry Munholland, prin.

Heavener, Le Flore Co., Pop. Code 5
Heavener ISD
Sch. Sys. Enr. Code 3
Supt. – Dan Foreman, P O BOX 698   74937
ES, P O BOX 698   74937 – Joann Riggs, prin.

Helena, Alfalfa Co., Pop. Code 3
Helena-Goltry ISD
Sch. Sys. Enr. Code 2
Supt. – Ed Winn, P O BOX 287   73741
Helena-Goltry JHS, P O BOX 287   73741
   Buddy Taylor, prin.
Helena-Goltry ES, P O BOX 287   73741
   Ron Frech, prin.

Hendrix, Bryan Co., Pop. Code 2
Yuba ISD
Sch. Sys. Enr. Code 2
Supt. – Hall Alexander, RURAL ROUTE 01   74741
Yuba ES, RURAL ROUTE 01   74741
   Sharron Dunham, prin.

Hennessey, Kingfisher Co., Pop. Code 4
Hennessey ISD
Sch. Sys. Enr. Code 3
Supt. – Kenneth New, 707 E OKLA   73742
Binkley MS, 604 E OKLAHOMA ST   73742
   Don Harris, prin.
ES, 130 S MITCHELL ROAD   73742
   Don Harris, prin.

Henryetta, Okmulgee Co., Pop. Code 6
Henryetta ISD
Sch. Sys. Enr. Code 4
Supt. – Jim Wills, 618 W MAIN   74437
JHS, P O BOX 130   74437 – Chelsea Cook, prin.
ES, 618 W MAIN ST   74437 – Max Duncan, prin.

Ryal SD
Sch. Sys. Enr. Code 1
Supt. – Louis Hicks, RURAL ROUTE 02   74437
Ryal ES, RURAL ROUTE 02   74437 – (—), prin.

Wilson ISD
Sch. Sys. Enr. Code 2
Supt. – Fred Adams
   RURAL ROUTE 01   BOX 260   74437
Wilson ES, RURAL ROUTE 01   BOX 274   74437
   George Christy, prin.

Hinton, Caddo Co., Pop. Code 4
Hinton ISD
Sch. Sys. Enr. Code 3
Supt. – Jimmy Holmes, P O BOX 1036 73047
MS, P O BOX 1036 73047 – Max Townsend, prin.
ES, P O BOX 1036 73047 – Steve Freeman, prin.

Hitchcock, Blaine Co., Pop. Code 2
Hitchcock SD
Sch. Sys. Enr. Code 1
Supt. – Steven Ray, P O BOX 138 73744
ES, HIGHWAY 08 BOX 139 73744
(—), prin.

Hobart, Kiowa Co., Pop. Code 5
Hobart ISD
Sch. Sys. Enr. Code 3
Supt. – June Knight, P O BOX 899 73651
MS, P O BOX 899 73651 – Kenneth O'Neal, prin.
Field MS, P O BOX 899 73651
  Stephen Boyd, prin.
Willard ES, P O BOX 899 73651
  Randy Allison, prin.

Hodgen, Le Flore Co.
Hodgen SD
Sch. Sys. Enr. Code 2
Supt. – Charles Caughern,Jr., P O BOX 6 74939
ES, P O BOX 69 74939 – (—), prin.

Holdenville, Hughes Co., Pop. Code 6
Holdenville ISD
Sch. Sys. Enr. Code 4
Supt. – W. Andrew Young, 112 E 9TH 74848
Parkview ES, P O BOX 977 74848
  Dale McLoud, prin.
Thomas MS, P O BOX 977 74848
  Larry Miller, prin.

Moss ISD
Sch. Sys. Enr. Code 2
Supt. – Bennie Taylor
  RURAL ROUTE 02 BOX 57 74848
Moss ES, RURAL ROUTE 02 BOX 57 74848
  Bennie Taylor, prin.

Hollis, Harmon Co., Pop. Code 5
Arnett ISD
Sch. Sys. Enr. Code 1
Supt. – R. Sherrill, RURAL ROUTE 02 73550
Arnett ES, RURAL ROUTE 02 73550
  Larry Powers, prin.

Hollis ISD
Sch. Sys. Enr. Code 3
Supt. – Ed Robinson, 415 N MAIN 73550
ES 73550 – Tim Love, prin.

Hominy, Osage Co., Pop. Code 5
Hominy ISD
Sch. Sys. Enr. Code 3
Supt. – Gerald Christy, P O BOX 400 74035
MS, P O BOX 400 74035 – Ronald Watkins, prin.
Mann ES, P O BOX 400 74035 – Max Sullins, prin.

Hooker, Texas Co., Pop. Code 4
Hooker ISD
Sch. Sys. Enr. Code 2
Supt. – Bill Goodwin, P O BOX 247 73945
ES, P O BOX 247 73945 – James Taylor, prin.

Howe, Le Flore Co., Pop. Code 3
Howe ISD
Sch. Sys. Enr. Code 2
Supt. – Ray Pebsworth, P O BOX 259 74940
ES, P O BOX 259 74940 – Gary Morgan, prin.

Hugo, Choctaw Co., Pop. Code 6
Goodland SD
Sch. Sys. Enr. Code 1
Supt. – Bob Bone, GOODLAND ROUTE 74743
Goodland ES, GOODLAND ROUTE 74743
  (—), prin.

Hugo ISD
Sch. Sys. Enr. Code 4
Supt. – Phil Kaniatobe, 208 N 2ND 74743
JHS, 208 N 2ND ST 74743 – Mike Armes, prin.
Field ES, 208 N 2ND ST 74743
  Shelby Koonce, prin.
Franklin ES, 208 N 2ND ST 74743
  Mike Armes, prin.
Lee ES, 208 N 2ND ST 74743
  Shelby Koonce, prin.
Mann ES, 208 N 2ND ST 74743
  Gary Smith, prin.
Washington ES, 208 N 2ND ST 74743
  Gary Smith, prin.

Hulbert, Cherokee Co., Pop. Code 3
Hulbert ISD
Sch. Sys. Enr. Code 2
Supt. – J. McGowan, P O BOX 125 74441
ES, P O BOX 125 74441 – Darrell Wilson, prin.

Lost City SD
Sch. Sys. Enr. Code 2
Supt. – Barney Mitchell,Jr.
  RURAL ROUTE 03 74441
Lost City ES, RURAL ROUTE 03 74441
  (—), prin.

Norwood SD
Sch. Sys. Enr. Code 2
Supt. – James Moss
  RURAL ROUTE 01 BOX 537 74441
Norwood ES, RURAL ROUTE 01 BOX 537 74441
  (—), prin.

Shady Grove SD
Sch. Sys. Enr. Code 2
Supt. – Raymond Webb, RURAL ROUTE 02 74441
Shady Grove ES, RURAL ROUTE 02 74441
  (—), prin.

Hydro, Caddo Co., Pop. Code 3
Hydro ISD
Sch. Sys. Enr. Code 2
Supt. – Delbert Handke, P O BOX 5 73048
ES, P O BOX 5 73048 – Ed Royalty, prin.

Idabel, McCurtain Co., Pop. Code 6
Denison SD
Sch. Sys. Enr. Code 2
Supt. – Ailean Harris
  RURAL ROUTE 01 BOX 29A 74745
Denison ES, RURAL ROUTE 04 BOX 230 74745
  (—), prin.

Idabel ISD
Sch. Sys. Enr. Code 4
Supt. – Jerry Shinn, P O BOX 29 74745
MS, P O BOX 29 74745 – Doyle Burns, prin.
Central MS, P O BOX 29 74745
  Meredith Cockrell, prin.
George ES, P O BOX 29 74745
  Mally Randolph, prin.
Southeast ES, P O BOX 29 74745
  Meredith Cockrell, prin.

Indiahoma, Comanche Co., Pop. Code 2
Indiahoma ISD
Sch. Sys. Enr. Code 2
Supt. – R. McKinley, P O BOX 8 73552
ES, P O BOX 8 73552 – Rick Carothers, prin.

Indianola, Pittsburg Co., Pop. Code 2
Indianola ISD
Sch. Sys. Enr. Code 2
Supt. – Joe Kitchens, P O BOX G 74442
ES, P O BOX G 74442 – Gary Walden, prin.

Inola, Rogers Co., Pop. Code 4
Inola ISD
Sch. Sys. Enr. Code 3
Supt. – Jim Peters, P O BOX 789 74036
MS, P O BOX 789 74036 – Tom Sullivan, prin.
ES, P O BOX 8199 74036 – Billy Hill, prin.

Jay, Delaware Co., Pop. Code 4
Jay ISD
Sch. Sys. Enr. Code 2
Supt. – Dr. Roy Drake, P O BOX C-1 74346
MS, P O BOX C-1 74346 – Glen Hamby, prin.
ES, P O BOX C-1 74346 – Kenny Holland, prin.

Jenks, Tulsa Co., Pop. Code 6
Jenks ISD
Sch. Sys. Enr. Code 6
Supt. – Dr. Gene Buinger, 1ST & B 74037
Central MS, 1ST & B STREET 74037
  Keith Churchill, prin.
East MS, 1ST & B STREET 74037
  Bill Jordan, prin.
Central ES, 1ST & B ST 74037 – Susan Oare, prin.
East ES, 1ST & B ST 74037 – Gene Harris, prin.
West ES, 1ST & B ST 74037 – Don Worley, prin.

Jennings, Pawnee Co., Pop. Code 2
Jennings SD
Sch. Sys. Enr. Code 2
Supt. – James Hubbard, P O BOX 128 74038
ES, P O BOX 439 74038 – (—), prin.

Jet, Alfalfa Co., Pop. Code 2
Jet-Nash ISD
Sch. Sys. Enr. Code 2
Supt. – Lynn Kinnamon, P O BOX 188 73749
Jet-Nash ES, P O BOX 188 73749
  Ocus Murphy, prin.

Jones, Oklahoma Co., Pop. Code 4
Jones ISD
Sch. Sys. Enr. Code 3
Supt. – Dr. Earl Myers, 3RD & HAWAII 73049
Jones-State Center MS, P O BOX C 73049
  William Stevens, prin.
PS, P O BOX 670 73049 – Carrol McEwen, prin.
IS, P O BOX 670 73049
  Charles Montalbano, prin.

Kansas, Delaware Co., Pop. Code 2
Kansas ISD
Sch. Sys. Enr. Code 3
Supt. – Jim Burgess, P O BOX 196 74347
ES, P O BOX 196 74347 – Phillip Odle, prin.

Kaw City, Kay Co., Pop. Code 2
Kaw CSD
Sch. Sys. Enr. Code 1
Supt. – Ben Sanders, P O BOX 150 74641
ES, P O BOX 150 74641 – (—), prin.

Kellyville, Creek Co., Pop. Code 3
Kellyville ISD
Sch. Sys. Enr. Code 3
Supt. – Dwight Davidson, P O BOX 655 74039
ES, P O BOX 99 74039 – Rick Watson, prin.

Keota, Haskell Co., Pop. Code 3
Keota ISD
Sch. Sys. Enr. Code 2
Supt. – Dwight Henry, P O BOX 160 74941
ES, P O BOX 160 74941 – Tommy Roberson, prin.

Ketchum, Craig Co., Pop. Code 2
Ketchum ISD
Sch. Sys. Enr. Code 2
Supt. – Bill London, P O BOX 720 74349
JHS, P O BOX 145 74349 – Larry Callison, prin.
ES, P O BOX 720 74349 – Tom Hood, prin.

Keyes, Cimarron Co., Pop. Code 3
Keyes ISD
Sch. Sys. Enr. Code 2
Supt. – Richard Dally, P O BOX 47 73947
ES, P O BOX 47 73947 – Dick Clifford, prin.

Kiefer, Creek Co., Pop. Code 3
Kiefer ISD
Sch. Sys. Enr. Code 2
Supt. – John Coker, P O BOX 850 74041
Oliver ES, P O BOX 850 74041
  Aneta Wilkinson, prin.

Kildare, Kay Co., Pop. Code 2
Kildare SD
Sch. Sys. Enr. Code 2
Supt. – Paula Barber
  RURAL ROUTE 05 BOX 1215 74601
ES, RURAL ROUTE 05 BOX 1215 74601
  (—), prin.

Kingfisher, Kingfisher Co., Pop. Code 5
Kingfisher ISD
Sch. Sys. Enr. Code 4
Supt. – C. Jack Harrell, P O BOX 29 73750
Gilmour PS, P O BOX 29 73750 – Sam Wood, prin.
MS, 1400 OAK STREET 73750
  Bert Rickner, prin.

Kingston, Marshall Co., Pop. Code 4
Kingston ISD
Sch. Sys. Enr. Code 2
Supt. – James Caldwell, P O BOX 370 73439
MS, P O BOX 458 73439 – Randall Monroe, prin.
ES, P O BOX 370 73439 – Gary Canada, prin.

Kinta, Haskell Co., Pop. Code 2
Kinta ISD
Sch. Sys. Enr. Code 2
Supt. – Bill Smith, P O BOX 219 74552
ES, P O BOX 219 74552 – Jack Reasnor, prin.

Kiowa, Pittsburg Co., Pop. Code 3
Kiowa ISD
Sch. Sys. Enr. Code 2
Supt. – Dennis Trammell, P O BOX 6 74553
ES, P O BOX 6 74553 – Royce Casey, prin.

Konawa, Seminole Co.
Konawa ISD
Sch. Sys. Enr. Code 3
Supt. – Charles McFarland, P O BOX 127 74849
ES, RURAL ROUTE 01 BOX 3 74849
  Ted Oliphant, prin.

Vamoosa SD
Sch. Sys. Enr. Code 1
Supt. – Laquita Hucklebery
  RURAL ROUTE 3 74849
Vamoosa ES, RURAL ROUTE 02 74849
  (—), prin.

Krebs, Pittsburg Co., Pop. Code 4
Krebs SD
Sch. Sys. Enr. Code 2
Supt. – Danny Jabara, P O BOX 67 74554
ES, P O BOX 67 74554 – (—), prin.

Kremlin, Garfield Co., Pop. Code 2
Kremlin-Hillsdale ISD
Sch. Sys. Enr. Code 2
Supt. – Robert Grider, P O BOX 198 73753
Kremlin-Hillsdale ES, P O BOX 198 73753
  Mary Light, prin.

Lahoma, Garfield Co., Pop. Code 3
Lahoma ISD
Sch. Sys. Enr. Code 2
Supt. – W. Hassler, P O BOX 8 73754
ES, P O BOX 8 73754 – A. Ledwig, prin.

Lamont, Grant Co., Pop. Code 3
Deer Creek-Lamont ISD
Sch. Sys. Enr. Code 2
Supt. – Kenneth Rose, P O BOX 10 74643
Deer Creek-Lamont ES, P O BOX 10 74643
  Ray Higginbotham, prin.

Lane, Atoka Co.
Lane SD
Sch. Sys. Enr. Code 2
Supt. – Jack Humphrey, P O BOX 31 74555
ES, P O BOX 39 74555 – (—), prin.

Langston, Logan Co., Pop. Code 2
Langston SD
Sch. Sys. Enr. Code 1
Supt. – Clara Richard, P O BOX 300 73050
ES, P O BOX 300 73050 – (—), prin.

Laverne, Harper Co., Pop. Code 4
Laverne ISD
Sch. Sys. Enr. Code 2
Supt. – Jerry Lee Merritt, P O BOX 40 73848
MS, P O BOX 40 73848 – Mac Branscum, prin.
ES, P O BOX 40 73848 – Bill Heaton, prin.

Lawton, Comanche Co., Pop. Code 8
Bishop SD
Sch. Sys. Enr. Code 2
Supt. – Carl Fred Bishop
  RURAL ROUTE 03 73501

Bishop ES, RURAL ROUTE 03 BOX 14 73501
(—), prin.

Flower Mound SD
Sch. Sys. Enr. Code 2
Supt. – Kay Johnson
RURAL ROUTE 02 BOX 80 73501
Flower Mound ES
RURAL ROUTE 02 BOX 80 73501 – (—), prin.

Lawton ISD
Sch. Sys. Enr. Code 7
Supt. – Dick Neptune, P O BOX 1009 73501
Adams ES, 3501 NW FERRIS AVE 73505
Cathie Blodgett, prin.
Almor West ES, 6902 SW DELTA AVE 73505
Carolyn Mayes, prin.
Bish ES, 5611 NW ALLAN A DALE LANE 73505
Rebecca McKeown, prin.
Brockland ES, 6205 NW FERRIS AVE 73505
Bill Miracle, prin.
Carriage Hills ES, 215 SE WARWICK WAY 73501
Les Hastings, prin.
Cleveland ES, 1202 SW 27TH ST 73505
Ardeth Hearn, prin.
Country Club Heights ES, 714 SW 45TH ST 73505
Kendall Lamb, prin.
Crosby Park ES, 1602 NW HORTON BLVD 73505
Lynn Fitz, prin.
Douglass ES, 102 E GROVE 73501
Jody Sherry, prin.
Edison ES, 5801 NW COLUMBIA 73505
Bill Davis, prin.
Eisenhower ES, 315 SW 52ND ST 73505
Mikel Morris, prin.
Garfield ES, 2701 NW BELL AVE 73505
Terry Martin, prin.
Geronimo Road ES
5727 GERONIMO ROAD 73503 – Sam Smith,
prin.
Hoover ES, 1614 NW 47TH ST 73505
Elmer Butler, prin.
Howell ES, 2402 SW E AVE 73505
Howard Smith, prin.
Jackson ES, 2201 N LINDY AVE 73505
Elbert Bentley, prin.
Jefferson ES, 1401 NW BESSIE AVE 73507
Marcille Covey, prin.
Kuntz ES, 4814 NW FLOYD AVE 73505
Don Wright, prin.
Lee ES, 501 NW WOODRIDGE DR 73507
Jerry Ryder, prin.
Lincoln ES, 602 SW PARK AVE 73501
Barbara Morgan, prin.
Park Lane ES, P O BOX 1009 73502
Ken Baden, prin.
Pecan Grove ES, 32 NW 40TH ST 73505
Rodney Mastin, prin.
Pioneer Park ES, 3005 NE ANGUS PLACE 73507
Bill Ingram, prin.
Rogers ES, 1608 SW 9TH ST 73501
Vic Stoll, prin.
Roosevelt ES, 1502 SW I AVE 73501
Junior Nation, prin.
Sullivan Village ES
3802 SE ELMHURST LANE 73501
Lorene Sullivan, prin.
Swinney ES, 1431 NW 23RD ST 73505
Clayton Alexander, prin.
Taft ES, 1701 NW TAFT AVE 73507
James Hickerson, prin.
Washington ES, P O BOX 1009 73502
Tom Munson, prin.
Western Hills ES, 5402 NW KINYON AVE 73505
Jenny Reno, prin.
Westwood ES, 1908 NW 38TH ST 73505
Helen Trotter, prin.
Whittier ES, 1115 NW LAIRD AVE 73507
Marlene Jones, prin.
Wilson ES, 102 NW 17TH ST 73507
Rundell Edison, prin.
Woodland Hills ES
405 NW WOODLAWN DR 73515
Jack Bozarth, prin.
Other Schools – See Fort Sill

St. Mary School, 611 A AVE 73502

Leedey, Dewey Co., Pop. Code 2
Leedey ISD
Sch. Sys. Enr. Code 2
Supt. – Gene Velharticky, P O BOX 67 73654
ES, P O BOX 67 73654 – Sherman Lauder, prin.

Le Flore, Le Flore Co., Pop. Code 2
Le Flore ISD
Sch. Sys. Enr. Code 2
Supt. – Dorsey Adams, P O BOX 67 74942
ES, P O BOX 67 74942 – Peggy McAlister, prin.

Lenapah, Nowata Co., Pop. Code 2
Lenapah ISD
Sch. Sys. Enr. Code 2
Supt. – Lewis Mann, P O BOX 157 74042
ES, P O BOX 159 74042 – Stan Mavity, prin.

Leon, Love Co., Pop. Code 2
Leon SD
Sch. Sys. Enr. Code 1
Supt. – Tommy Hestily, P O BOX 506 73441
ES, P O BOX 506 73441 – (—), prin.

Leonard, Tulsa Co.
Leonard SD
Sch. Sys. Enr. Code 2
Supt. – Glyn Ritter, P O BOX 37 74043
ES, P O BOX 37 74043 – Glyn Ritter, prin.

Lexington, Cleveland Co., Pop. Code 4
Lexington ISD
Sch. Sys. Enr. Code 3
Supt. – Wayne Maxwell, P O BOX C 73051
MS, P O BOX C 73051 – Ed Fisher, prin.
ES, P O BOX C 73051 – Don McQuerrey, prin.

Lindsay, Garvin Co., Pop. Code 5
Lindsay ISD
Sch. Sys. Enr. Code 4
Supt. – Robert Howard, 302 SW 8TH ST 73052
Lindsay MS, 302 SW 8TH ST 73052
Bob Ashley, prin.
ES, 302 SW 8TH ST 73052
Claude Cameron, prin.

Locust Grove, Mayes Co., Pop. Code 4
Locust Grove ISD
Sch. Sys. Enr. Code 3
Supt. – Joe Ballard, P O BOX 399 74352
MS, P O BOX 399 74352 – Clarence Austin, prin.
ES, P O BOX 399 74362 – Roy Flanary, prin.

Lone Grove, Carter Co., Pop. Code 5
Lone Grove ISD
Sch. Sys. Enr. Code 4
Supt. – Ron Schnee, P O BOX 1330 73443
MS, P O BOX E 73443 – Gary Scott, prin.
ES, P O BOX 1330 73443 – Dan Hull, prin.

Lone Wolf, Kiowa Co., Pop. Code 3
Lone Wolf ISD
Sch. Sys. Enr. Code 2
Supt. – Harold Hayes,Jr., P O BOX 158 73655
ES, P O BOX 158 73655 – Jim Tepe, prin.

Longdale, Blaine Co., Pop. Code 2
Longdale SD
Sch. Sys. Enr. Code 2
Supt. – Jerry Lee, P O BOX B 73755
ES, P O BOX 267 73755 – (—), prin.

Lookeba, Caddo Co., Pop. Code 2
Lookeba-Sickles ISD
Sch. Sys. Enr. Code 2
Supt. – Dennis Byrd
RURAL ROUTE 01 BOX 34 73053
Lookeba-Sickles ES
RURAL ROUTE 01 BOX 34 73053
Larry Pendleton, prin.

Luther, Oklahoma Co., Pop. Code 4
Luther ISD
Sch. Sys. Enr. Code 3
Supt. – Jess Thomason, P O BOX 430 73054
MS, P O BOX 430 73054 – Dennis Delano, prin.
ES, P O BOX 430 73054 – Bill Florer, prin.

Mc Alester, Pittsburg Co., Pop. Code 7
Frink-Chambers SD
Sch. Sys. Enr. Code 2
Supt. – Doy Adams, RURAL ROUTE 03 74501
Frink-Chambers ES
RURAL ROUTE 03 BOX 65 74501 – (—), prin.

Mc Alester ISD
Sch. Sys. Enr. Code 5
Supt. – Dr. Lucy Smith, P O BOX 1027 74501
Puterbaugh MS, P O BOX 1027 74502
Leslie Smith, prin.
Doyle ES, P O BOX 1027 74502 – Jay White, prin.
Emerson ES, P O BOX 1027 74502
Fred Goodson, prin.
Field ES, P O BOX 1027 74502
Jim Davidson, prin.
Gay ES, P O BOX 1027 74502
Charlotte Wilson, prin.
Jefferson ES, P O BOX 1027 74502
Charles Wood, prin.
Rogers ES, P O BOX 1027 74502
Jim Northcutt, prin.

Tannehill SD
Sch. Sys. Enr. Code 2
Supt. – Rocky Stone, P O BOX 1848 74502
Tannehill ES, P O BOX 1848 74502
(—), prin.

Mc Curtain, Haskell Co., Pop. Code 3
McCurtain SD
Sch. Sys. Enr. Code 2
Supt. – Bob Byrum, P O BOX 189 74944
ES, P O BOX 189 74944 – Perry Arnwine, prin.

Mc Loud, Pottawatomie Co., Pop. Code 5
McLoud ISD
Sch. Sys. Enr. Code 4
Supt. – Dr. John Kessinger
MC LOUD ROAD 74851
MS 74851 – Doug VanScoyoc, prin.
ES, P O BOX 40 74851 – Deborah Lobdell, prin.

White Rock SD
Sch. Sys. Enr. Code 2
Supt. – Warren Boles
RURAL ROUTE 02 BOX 325 74851
White Rock ES
RURAL ROUTE 02 BOX 325 74851
(—), prin.

Macomb, Pottawatomie Co., Pop. Code 1
Macomb ISD
Sch. Sys. Enr. Code 2
Supt. – H. Dale Smart, P O BOX 688 74852
ES, P O BOX 688 74852 – Sandra Starks, prin.

Madill, Marshall Co., Pop. Code 5
Madill ISD
Sch. Sys. Enr. Code 4
Supt. – Jim Archer, 609 S 5TH AVE 73446
MS, 609 S 5TH AVE 73446 – Larry Davison, prin.
ES, 701 W TISHOMINGO ST 73446
Neil Duncan, prin.

Mangum, Greer Co., Pop. Code 5
Mangum ISD
Sch. Sys. Enr. Code 3
Supt. – Gary Tyler, 400 N PENN 73554
Edison ES, 400 N PENNSYLVANIA ST 73554
Dave Roberts, prin.

Manitou, Tillman Co., Pop. Code 2
Manitou SD
Sch. Sys. Enr. Code 1
Supt. – Jerry Cupp, P O BOX 38 73555
ES, P O BOX 38 73555 – (—), prin.

Mannford, Creek Co., Pop. Code 4
Mannford ISD
Sch. Sys. Enr. Code 4
Supt. – Robert Hightower, P O BOX 100 74044
MS, P O BOX 100 74044 – R. Owsley, prin.
ES, P O BOX 100 74044 – Nancy Martin, prin.

Mannsville, Johnson Co., Pop. Code 3
Mannsville ISD
Sch. Sys. Enr. Code 2
Supt. – Charles Mason, P O BOX 68 73447
ES, P O BOX 68 73447 – (—), prin.

Marble City, Sequoyah Co., Pop. Code 2
Marble CSD
Sch. Sys. Enr. Code 2
Supt. – Larry Couch, P O BOX 1 74945
ES, P O BOX 10 74945 – (—), prin.

Marietta, Love Co., Pop. Code 4
Greenville SD
Sch. Sys. Enr. Code 1
Supt. – Larry Buck, RURAL ROUTE 01 73448
Greenville ES, RURAL ROUTE 01 73448
(—), prin.
Marietta ISD
Sch. Sys. Enr. Code 3
Supt. – Jim Langston Supt, P O BOX 289 73448
MS, P O BOX 289 73448 – Troy Owens, prin.
ES, P O BOX 289 73448 – Marjorie Hobbs, prin.

Marland, Noble Co., Pop. Code 2
Marland ISD
Sch. Sys. Enr. Code 2
Supt. – Ralph Jones, P O BOX 637 74644
ES, P O BOX 637 74644 – Debra Stolhand, prin.

Marlow, Stephens Co., Pop. Code 6
Central High ISD
Sch. Sys. Enr. Code 2
Supt. – Leonard Garrison
RURAL ROUTE 03 BOX 249 73055
Central ES, RURAL ROURTE 03 BOX 249 73055
Larry Malcom, prin.

Fletcher ISD
Sch. Sys. Enr. Code 2
Supt. – Gary Ledford, 409 N ASH ST 73055
Other Schools – See Fletcher

Marlow ISD
Sch. Sys. Enr. Code 4
Supt. – Ray McCarter, 510 W MAIN 73055
MS, P O BOX 73 73055 – John DeYong, prin.
ES, P O BOX 73 73055 – Jim Thomas, prin.

Martha, Jackson Co., Pop. Code 2
Martha SD
Sch. Sys. Enr. Code 1
Supt. – Nick Schnorrenberg, P O BOX 277 73556
ES, P O BOX 277 73556 – (—), prin.

Mason, Okfuskee Co.
Mason ISD
Sch. Sys. Enr. Code 2
Supt. – (—)
RURAL ROUTE 01 BOX 143B 74852
ES, RURAL ROUTE 01 BOX 143-B 74859
James Wade, prin.

Maud, Pottawatomie Co., Pop. Code 4
Maud ISD
Sch. Sys. Enr. Code 2
Supt. – Connie Ramsey, P O BOX 130 74854
MS 74854 – Tom Rigney, prin.
ES, P O BOX 130 74854 – Karen Pearcy, prin.

Maysville, Garvin Co., Pop. Code 4
Maysville ISD
Sch. Sys. Enr. Code 3
Supt. – Larry Garner, P O BOX 780 73057
ES, P O BOX 780 73057 – Gary Reynolds, prin.

Medford, Grant Co., Pop. Code 4
Medford ISD
Sch. Sys. Enr. Code 2
Supt. – Roy Dean Innis, 301 N MAIN 73759
ES, 303 N MAIN STREET 73759
Steve Struble, prin.

Medicine Park, Comanche Co., Pop. Code 2
Medicine Park SD
Sch. Sys. Enr. Code 1
Supt. – Bob Dismuke, PARK BOX 174 73557
ES, P O BOX 174 73557 – (—), prin.

Meeker, Lincoln Co., Pop. Code 4
Meeker SD
Sch. Sys. Enr. Code 3
Supt. – Hulen Howe, P O BOX 68 74855
MS, P O BOX 68 74855 – Darrell Roe, prin.
ES, P O BOX 338 74855 – Herschel Stearman, prin.

Miami, Ottawa Co., Pop. Code 7
Miami ISD
Sch. Sys. Enr. Code 4
Supt. – Dr. Charles Head, 4TH & G SE 74354
Nichols ES, 504 14TH AVE NW 74354
  Larry Williams, prin.
Rockdale ES, 2116 ROCKDALE ROAD 74354
  Marilyn Kemp, prin.
Roosevelt ES, 129 G ST NE 74354
  Doug Spillman, prin.
Washington ES, 20TH & B ST NE 74354
  Joe Lannan, prin.
Wilson ES, 308 G ST NW 74354
  Mabel Dowler, prin.

Midwest City, Oklahoma Co., Pop. Code 8
Midwest City-Del City ISD
Sch. Sys. Enr. Code 7
Supt. – Dr. John Folks, P O BOX 10630 73110
Bailey ES, 3301 W SUNVALLEY DR 73110
  Morri Rose, prin.
Barnes ES, 10551 SE 59TH ST 73150
  James Watson, prin.
Country Estates ES, 1609 FELIX PLACE 73110
  Chris Caram, prin.
Del City ES, 2400 EPPERLY DR 73115
  Celeste Scott, prin.
Eastside ES, 600 N KEY BLVD 73110
  Robert O'Hern, prin.
Epperly Heights ES, 3805 DEL ROAD 73115
  James Johnson, prin.
Highland Park ES, 5301 S DIMPLE AVE 73135
  David Bibens, prin.
Parkview ES, 5701 MACKELMAN DR 73135
  David Rhoades, prin.
Ridgecrest ES, 137 W RIDGEWOOD DR 73110
  Lonnie McGuire, prin.
Soldier Creek ES, 9021 SE 15TH ST 73130
  Royce Gambill, prin.
Sooner-Rose ES, 5601 SE 15TH ST 73110
  Don Watson, prin.
Steed ES, 2118 FLANNERY DR 73110
  Darrel Eike, prin.
Tinker ES, 4402 MCNARNEY AVE 73145
  Marvella Sharpe, prin.
Townsend ES, 4100 EPPERLY DR 73115
  Seay Sanders, prin.
Traub ES, 6500 SE 15TH ST 73110
  Edith Adams, prin.
Other Schools – See Oklahoma City

St. Philip Neri School, 1121 FELIX PLACE 73110

Milburn, Johnston Co., Pop. Code 2
Fillmore SD
Sch. Sys. Enr. Code 1
Supt. – Charles Driggers
  RURAL ROUTE 01 BOX 65A 73450
Fillmore ES, P O BOX 86 73450 – (—), prin.

Milburn ISD
Sch. Sys. Enr. Code 2
Supt. – Jimmie Heard, P O BOX 276 73450
ES, P O BOX 276 73450 – Maxine Enloe, prin.

Milfay, Creek Co.
Milfay SD
Sch. Sys. Enr. Code 1
Supt. – Paul Allee, P O BOX 218 74046
ES, P O BOX 219 74046 – (—), prin.

Mill Creek, Johnston Co., Pop. Code 2
Mill Creek ISD
Sch. Sys. Enr. Code 2
Supt. – Ray Dodd, P O BOX 105 74856
ES, P O BOX 105 74856
  Lawanna Sue Harden, prin.

Minco, Grady Co., Pop. Code 4
Minco ISD
Sch. Sys. Enr. Code 2
Supt. – Dennis Klugh, P O BOX 428 73059
ES, P O BOX 428 73059 – Ann Wegener, prin.

Moffett, Sequoyah Co., Pop. Code 2
Moffett SD
Sch. Sys. Enr. Code 1
Supt. – Bill Horton, P O BOX 98 74946
ES, P O BOX 180 74946 – (—), prin.

Monroe, Le Flore Co.
Monroe SD
Sch. Sys. Enr. Code 2
Supt. – Floyis Clay, RURAL ROUTE 02 74947
ES, P O BOX 818 74947 – (—), prin.

Moore, Cleveland Co., Pop. Code 8
Moore ISD
Sch. Sys. Enr. Code 7
Supt. – Jerry Rippetoe
  400 N BROADWAY ST 73160
Apple Creek ES, 1101 SE 14TH STREET 73160
  Belinda Rogers, prin.

Central ES, 123 NW 2ND ST 73160
  Jim Hines, prin.
Fairview ES, 2431 SW 89TH ST 73159
  Mike Messerli, prin.
Houchin ES, 3200 WEBSTER ST 73160
  Paul Roberts, prin.
Kelly ES, 1900 N JANEWAY AVE 73160
  Jamie Chuculate, prin.
Lower Central ES, 123 NW 2ND STREET 73160
  Brenda Bain, prin.
Northmoor ES, 400 N BROADWAY ST 73160
  Debbie Arato, prin.
Plaza Towers ES, 852 SW 11TH ST 73160
  Pat Faurot, prin.
Santa Fe ES, 501 N SANTA FE ST 73160
  Scott Blythe, prin.
Sky Ranch ES, 9501 S WESTERN AVE 73139
  Bonnie Lightfoot, prin.
Southgate ES, 500 N NORMAN AVE 73160
  John Bailey, prin.
Upper Central MS
  400 N BROADWAY STREET 73160
  Jim Hines, prin.
Winding Creek ES, 1409 NE 12TH ST 73160
  Chris Bolen, prin.
Other Schools – See Oklahoma City

Mooreland, Woodward Co., Pop. Code 4
Mooreland ISD
Sch. Sys. Enr. Code 2
Supt. – David Self, P O BOX 75 73852
ES, P O BOX 75 73852 – M. Kendall, prin.

Morris, Okmulgee Co., Pop. Code 4
Liberty SD
Sch. Sys. Enr. Code 1
Supt. – James McReynolds
  RURAL ROUTE 01 BOX 68 74445
Liberty ES, RURAL ROUTE 01 BOX 68 74445
  (—), prin.

Morris ISD
Sch. Sys. Enr. Code 3
Supt. – Don Shoemake, P O BOX 1 74445
MS, P O BOX 1 74445 – Derril Etchison, prin.
ES, P O BOX 1 74445 – Robert Greenlee, prin.

Morrison, Noble Co., Pop. Code 3
Morrison ISD
Sch. Sys. Enr. Code 2
Supt. – Jim Frazier, P O BOX 176 73061
ES, P O BOX 176 73061
  Charlotte Chatburn, prin.

Mounds, Creek Co., Pop. Code 4
Liberty ISD
Sch. Sys. Enr. Code 2
Supt. – David Martin
  RURAL ROUTE 01 BOX 308 74047
Liberty MS, RURAL ROUTE 01 BOX 354 74047
  Steve Reynolds, prin.
Liberty ES, RURAL ROUTE 01 BOX 354 74047
  Tom Padalino, prin.

Mounds ISD
Sch. Sys. Enr. Code 3
Supt. – Boyd Linduff, P O BOX 189 74047
JHS, P O BOX 128 74047 – Frank Paullus, prin.
ES, P O BOX 188 74047 – Frank Adams, prin.

Mountain View, Kiowa Co., Pop. Code 4
Mountain View ISD
Sch. Sys. Enr. Code 2
Supt. – Darrell Thompson, P O BOX B 73062
ES, P O BOX B 73062 – Phyllis Gaskill, prin.

Moyers, Pushmataha Co.
Moyers SD
Sch. Sys. Enr. Code 1
Supt. – Jim Washburn, P O BOX 488 74557
ES, P O BOX 488 74557 – (—), prin.

Muldrow, Sequoyah Co., Pop. Code 5
Belfonte SD
Sch. Sys. Enr. Code 2
Supt. – Kenneth Harvell
  RURAL ROUTE 03 BOX 282 74948
Belfonte ES, RURAL ROUTE 03 BOX 282 74948
  (—), prin.

Liberty SD
Sch. Sys. Enr. Code 2
Supt. – Leroy Taylor
  RURAL ROUTE 02 BOX 128 74948
Liberty ES, RURAL ROUTE 02 BOX 128 74948
  (—), prin.

Muldrow ISD
Sch. Sys. Enr. Code 4
Supt. – Roger Sharp, P O BOX 1080 74948
MS, P O BOX 1080 74948 – Monty Wight, prin.
ES, P O BOX 1080 74948 – Dean Pratt, prin.

Muskogee, Muskogee Co., Pop. Code 8
DuBois SD
Sch. Sys. Enr. Code 2
Supt. – William Abernathy
  RURAL ROUTE 04 BOX 429 74401
DuBois ES, RURAL ROUTE 04 BOX 429 74401
  (—), prin.

Hilldale ISD
Sch. Sys. Enr. Code 4
Supt. – Dean Hughes
  RURAL ROUTE 08 BOX 141 74401
Hilldale MS, RURAL ROUTE 08 BOX 141 74401
  Clarence Holland, prin.

Hilldale ES, RURAL ROUTE 08 BOX 141 74401
  Larrie Reynolds, prin.

Muskogee ISD
Sch. Sys. Enr. Code 6
Supt. – Dr. James Christian, 570 N 6TH ST 74401
Cherokee ES, 570 N 6TH ST 74401
  Shirley Garde, prin.
Creek ES, 570 N 6TH STREET 74401
  Jim Rogers, prin.
Franklin ES, 570 N 6TH ST 74401
  Gary Stevenson, prin.
Goetz ES, 2412 HASKELL BLVD 74403
  Spencer Wilkinson, prin.
Grant-Foreman ES, 570 N 6TH ST 74401
  Don Peavler, prin.
Harris-Jobe ES, 570 N 6TH ST 74401
  James McPherson, prin.
Irving ES, 1100 N J ST 74403
  Marguerite Waldroop, prin.
Pershing ES, 570 N 6TH ST 74401
  Barbara Freedman, prin.
Sadler ES, 570 N 6TH ST 74401
  Mike Garde, prin.
Whittier ES, 570 N 6TH ST 74401
  Ellen McCue, prin.

St. Joseph School, 323 N VIRGINIA ST 74403

Mustang, Canadian Co., Pop. Code 6
Mustang ISD
Sch. Sys. Enr. Code 6
Supt. – B. Rowley, 906 S HEIGHTS DR 73064
MS, P O BOX 107 73064 – Don Snider, prin.
North MS, P O BOX 107 73064
  David Steiner, prin.
Lakehoma ES, 906 S HEIGHTS DR 73064
  Larry Bruce, prin.
ES, 906 S HEIGHTS DR 73064
  Ann Morgan, prin.
Mustang Valley ES, 906 S HEIGHTS DR 73064
  Jack Perry, prin.

Mutual, Woodward Co., Pop. Code 2
Sharon-Mutual ISD
Sch. Sys. Enr. Code 2
Supt. – Dr. Irvin Garrison, P O BOX 1 73853
Sharon-Mutual ES, P O BOX 1 73853
  Guy Winters, prin.

Nashoba, Pushmataha Co.
Nashoba SD
Sch. Sys. Enr. Code 1
Supt. – Mike Kirkes, P O BOX 107 74558
ES, P O BOX 17 74558 – (—), prin.

Newcastle, McClain Co., Pop. Code 5
Newcastle ISD
Sch. Sys. Enr. Code 4
Supt. – Terry Brown, P O BOX B 73065
MS, P O BOX 557 73065 – Roy Giles, prin.
ES, P O BOX B 73065 – Paula Pace, prin.

Newkirk, Kay Co., Pop. Code 4
Newkirk ISD
Sch. Sys. Enr. Code 3
Supt. – Ray Sinor, P O BOX 91 74647
MS, P O BOX 91 74647 – Jim Wiersig, prin.
ES, P O BOX 91 74647 – Gary Reed, prin.

Peckham SD
Sch. Sys. Enr. Code 1
Supt. – Gary Young
  RURAL ROUTE 01 247 74647
Peckham ES, RURAL ROUTE 01 BOX 247 74647
  (—), prin.

Ninnekah, Grady Co., Pop. Code 2
Ninnekah ISD
Sch. Sys. Enr. Code 3
Supt. – Ray Craig, P O BOX 275 73067
ES, P O BOX 275 73067 – John Nations, prin.

Noble, Cleveland Co., Pop. Code 5
Noble ISD
Sch. Sys. Enr. Code 5
Supt. – William Martin, P O BOX 499 73068
Crosstimbers ES, P O BOX 559 73068
  Katherine Daily, prin.
Hubbard ES, P O BOX 499 73068
  Coy Tugman, prin.
Pioneer IS, P O BOX 559 73068
  Karen Smith, prin.

Norman, Cleveland Co., Pop. Code 8
Little Axe ISD
Sch. Sys. Enr. Code 4
Supt. – Dr. Joe Work
  RURAL ROUTE 02 BOX 266 73071
Little Axe ES, RURAL ROUTE 02 BOX 266 73071
  Dr. Beverly Renner, prin.
Little Axe IS, RURAL ROUTE 02 BOX 266 73071
  James Clifford, prin.

Norman ISD
Sch. Sys. Enr. Code 6
Supt. – Dr. James Gray, 1133 W MAIN 73070
Irving MS, 1920 E ALAMEDA ST 73071
  Ken Muncy, prin.
Longfellow MS, 1809 STUBBEMAN AVE 73069
  Teena Nations, prin.
Whitter MS, 2000 W BROOKS ST 73069
  Jim Smith, prin.
Adams ES, 817 DENISON DR 73069
  Don Lynn, prin.
Cleveland ES, 500 N SHERRY AVE 73069
  Carla Kimberling, prin.

Eisenhower ES, 1415 FAIRLAWN DR 73071
Dr. Judi Ford, prin.
Lakeview ES, RURAL ROUTE 04 BOX 195 73071
Lynne Miller, prin.
Jackson ES, 520 WYLIE ROAD 73069
Dottie Caldwell, prin.
Jefferson ES, 726 E HUGHBERT ST 73071
Pat Wiggins, prin.
Kennedy ES, 621 SUNRISE ST 73071
Betty Shoeman, prin.
Lincoln ES, 915 CLASSEN BLVD 73071
Dr. Rupel Jones, prin.
Madison ES, 500 JAMES DR 73072
Katy DeFord, prin.
McKinley ES, 728 S FLOOD AVE 73069
David Goin, prin.
Monroe ES, 1601 MCGEE DR 73072
Mickey Herron, prin.
Wilson ES, 808 N PETERS AVE 73069
Dr. Christie Seely, prin.

Robin Hill SD
Sch. Sys. Enr. Code 2
Supt. – Mary Sulivant
RURAL ROUTE 03 BOX 236 73071
Robin Hill ES, 4801 E FRANKLIN ROAD 73071
(—), prin.

Mt. Childrens House of Norman
606 S SANTE FE AVE 73069

Nowata, Nowata Co., Pop. Code 5
Nowata ISD
Sch. Sys. Enr. Code 4
Supt. – Troy Compston 74048
MS, 700 W OSAGE AVE 74048
B. McDaniel, prin.
ES, 707 W OSAGE AVE 74048
Donna Kelly, prin.

Oaks, Delaware Co., Pop. Code 3
Oaks-Mission ISD
Sch. Sys. Enr. Code 2
Supt. – Alfred Forrest, P O BOX 70 74359
Oaks-Mission ES, P O BOX 70 74359
Donald Mayes, prin.

Ochelata, Washington Co., Pop. Code 2
Caney Valley ISD
Supt. – See Ramona
ES, RURAL ROUTE 01 BOX 932 74051
Don Brake, prin.

Oilton, Creek Co., Pop. Code 4
Oilton ISD
Sch. Sys. Enr. Code 2
Supt. – Greg Kasbaum, P O BOX E 74052
Kennedy ES, P O BOX E 74052
Juanita Parker, prin.

Okarche, Kingfisher Co., Pop. Code 4
Okarche ISD
Sch. Sys. Enr. Code 2
Supt. – Richard Buswell, 215 N 4TH 73762
ES, P O BOX 276 73762 – Mickey Wilson, prin.

Okay, Wagoner Co., Pop. Code 3
Okay ISD
Sch. Sys. Enr. Code 2
Supt. – Thelbert Echols, P O BOX 188 74446
ES, P O BOX 188 74446 – Betty Smallwood, prin.

Okeene, Blaine Co., Pop. Code 4
Okeene ISD
Sch. Sys. Enr. Code 2
Supt. – Robert Hooladay, P O BOX 409 73763
ES, P O BOX 409 73763 – Ron Pittman, prin.

Okemah, Okfuskee Co., Pop. Code 5
Bearden SD
Supt. – See Bearden
Bearden ES, RURAL ROUTE 02 BOX 608 74859
(—), prin.

Okemah ISD
Sch. Sys. Enr. Code 3
Supt. – H. Holloway, 2ND & DATE 74859
MS, 2ND & DATE ST 74859
Dr. Larry McKinney, prin.
Oakes ES, 2ND AND OATE ST 74859
Leslie Steele, prin.

Oklahoma City, Oklahoma Co., Pop. Code 10
Crooked Oak ISD
Sch. Sys. Enr. Code 3
Supt. – Roger Holloway, 1901 SE 15TH ST 73129
Crooked Oak MS, 1901 SE 15TH ST 73129
Alford Nichols, prin.
Central Oak MS, 1901 SE 15TH ST 73129
Dennis McClanahan, prin.
West Oak Park ES, 1901 SE 15TH ST 73129
(—), prin.

Crutcho SD
Sch. Sys. Enr. Code 2
Supt. – Elvie Ellis
RURAL ROUTE 04 BOX 193 73111
Crutcho ES 73141 – (—), prin.

Midwest City-Del City ISD
Supt. – See Midwest City
Pleasant Hill ES, 4324 NE 36TH ST 73121
Dwayne Cleveland, prin.

Millwood ISD
Sch. Sys. Enr. Code 4
Supt. – Dr. Leon Edd, 6724 EASTERN AVE 73111
Millwood IS 73111 – Charlene Factory, prin.

Millwood ES, 6724 MARTIN L KING AVE 73111
Vivian Miller, prin.

Moore ISD
Supt. – See Moore
Briarwood ES, 14901 S HUDSON AVE 73170
Mike Ossenkop, prin.
Kingsgate ES, 1400 W KINGSGATE ROAD 73159
Rod Godfredson, prin.
Red Oak ES
11224 S PENNSYLVANIA AVE 73170
Dr. Dick Heatly, prin.

Oklahoma City ISD
Sch. Sys. Enr. Code 8
Supt. – Dr. Arthur Steller
900 N KLEIN AVE 73106
Eisenhower MS, 1301 NE 101ST ST 73114
Dr. Phillip Odom, prin.
Harding MS, 3333 N SHARTEL AVE 73118
Charles Rundell, prin.
Jackson MS, 2601 S VILLA AVE 73108
Rafael White, prin.
Jefferson MS, 6800 S BLACKWELDER AVE 73159
Joe Hodges, prin.
Moon MS, 1901 NE 13TH ST 73117
Dwight Jones, prin.
Rogers MS, 4000 SPENCER ROAD 73084
Ron Maxfield, prin.
Roosevelt MS, 3233 SW 44TH ST 73119
Jan Graham, prin.
Taft MS, 2901 NW 23RD ST 73107
James Senter, prin.
Webster MS, 6708 S SANTA FE AVE 73139
Robert Higgins, prin.
Adams ES, 3416 SW 37TH ST 73119
Joe Hornbeak, prin.
Arcadia ES, P O BOX A 73007
Shirley Konechney, prin.
Arthur ES, 5100 S INDEPENDANCE AVE 73119
Sue Clark, prin.
Bodine ES, 5301 S BRYANT AVE 73129
Henry Walding, prin.
Britton ES, 1215 NW 95TH ST 73114
Dessie Edwards, prin.
Buchanan ES, 4126 NW 18TH ST 73107
Roxie McBride, prin.
Capitol Hill 5th Grade Center
2717 S ROBINSON AVE 73109
Norma Cole, prin.
Classen 5th Grade Center
1901 N ELLISON AVE 73106
Jesse Thompson, prin.
Columbus ES
2402 S PENNSYLVANIA AVE 73108
Judy Jones, prin.
Coolidge ES, 5212 S VILLA AVE 73119
Doy Burchell, prin.
Creston Hills PS, 2240 NE 19TH ST 73111
Doris Henry, prin.
Dewey PS, 3500 S LINDSAY AVE 73129
Lexye Tomlinson, prin.
Dunbar ES, 900 N KLEIN AVE 73106
Odette Scobey, prin.
Edgemere ES, 3220 N WALKER AVE 73118
Bill Parker, prin.
Edwards PS, 1123 NE GRAND BLVD 73117
Ruby Rolfe, prin.
Field ES, 1515 N KLEIN AVE 73106
Virginia Thompson, prin.
Fillmore ES, 5200 S BLACKWELDER AVE 73119
Dale Reeder, prin.
Garden Oaks PS, 3401 NE 16TH ST 73117
(—), prin.
Gatewood ES, 1821 NW 21ST ST 73106
Billie McElroy, prin.
Hawthorne ES, 2300 NW 15TH ST 73107
Jean Hendrickson, prin.
Hayes ES, 6900 S BYERS AVE 73149
Wendell Edwards, prin.
Heronville ES, 1240 SW 29TH ST 73109
Orgel Ware, prin.
Hillcrest ES, 6421 S MILLER BLVD 73159
Jerry Black, prin.
Hoover 5th/6th Grade Center
2401 NW 115TH ST 73120 – Wanda Hume, prin.
Johnson ES, 1810 SHEFFIELD ROAD 73120
Dr. Donna Hicks, prin.
Kaiser ES, 3101 N LYON BLVD 73112
Carol Berry, prin.
King ES, 1537 NE 24TH ST 73111
Robert Brown, prin.
Lafayette ES, 500 SW 44TH ST 73109
Julie Bailey, prin.
Lee ES, 424 SW 29TH ST 73109
Dorris Burleigh, prin.
Linwood ES, 3416 NW 17TH ST 73107
Marilyn Davis, prin.
Longfellow ES, 1201 NE 48TH ST 73111
Beverly Story, prin.
Madison ES, 3117 N INDEPENDENCE AVE 73112
Audrey Baker, prin.
Mann ES, 1195 45TG ST 73117
Oneida Christian, prin.
Monroe ES, 4810 N LINN AVE 73112
Jeanee Adams, prin.
Nichols Hills ES, 8400 GREYSTONE AVE 73120
Thelma Sughru, prin.
North Highland ES
8400 N ROBINSON AVE 73114
Donna Wallace, prin.
Oakridge ES, 4100 LEONHARDT DR 73115
Ilene Marshall, prin.

Page-Woodson 5th Year Center
600 N HIGH AVE 73117 – Townes Watson, prin.
Parker ES, 12700 NE 42ND ST 73084
Oneta James, prin.
Parmelee ES, 6700 S HUDSON AVE 73139
Christina Kiser, prin.
Pierce ES, 4101 SW 27TH ST 73108
George Dinse, prin.
Polk ES, 3806 N PROSPECT AVE 73111
Jerry Bowerman, prin.
Prairie Queen ES
6609 S BLACKWELDER AVE 73159
Bill Shehorne, prin.
Putnam Heights ES, 1601 NW 36TH ST 73118
Martha Galbreath, prin.
Quail Creek ES
11700 THORN RIDGE ROAD 73120
Ancil Warren, prin.
Rancho Village ES, 1401 JOHNSTON DR 73119
Gay Littlepage, prin.
Ridgeview ES, 10010 RIDGEVIEW DR 73120
Jessie Davis-Wesley, prin.
Rockwood ES, 3101 SW 24TH ST 73108
Myrna Moore, prin.
Sequoyah ES, 2400 NW 36TH ST 73112
LaRita Aragon, prin.
Shidler ES, 1415 S BYERS AVE 73129
Eugene King, prin.
Shields Heights ES, 301 SE 38TH ST 73129
Raymond Mitchell, prin.
Southern Hills ES, 7800 S KENTUCKY AVE 73159
Jerry Wallace, prin.
Stand Watie ES, 3517 S LINN AVE 73119
James Brewer, prin.
Stonegate ES, 2525 NW 112TH ST 73120
Richard Danner, prin.
Telstar ES, 9521 NE 16TH ST 73130
Neil Ginsterblum, prin.
Twain ES, 2451 W MAIN ST 73107
Fred Pahlke,Jr., prin.
Western Village ES, 1508 NW 106TH ST 73114
Waylan Ables, prin.
Wheeler ES, 501 SE 25TH ST 73129
Charles Lewis, prin.
Willow Brook ES, 8105 NE 10TH ST 73110
Bob Dixson, prin.
Wilson ES, 2215 N WALKER AVE 73103
Linda Foure, prin.
Other Schools – See Spencer

Putnam City ISD
Sch. Sys. Enr. Code 7
Supt. – R. Downs, 5401 NW 40TH ST 73122
Central IS, 5430 NW 40TH ST 73122
Joan Wernersbach, prin.
Central ES, 5728 NW 40TH ST 73122
Lesley Schmidt, prin.
Coronado Heights ES
5911 N SAPULPA AVE 73112
Robert Shelton, prin.
Dennis ES, 6501 WESTBROOK DR 73162
Robert Woodson, prin.
Harvest Hills ES, 8201 NW 104TH ST 73162
Bill Spaeth, prin.
Hilldale ES, 4801 NW 16TH ST 73127
Sonya Allison, prin.
Kirkland ES, 6020 N INDEPENDENCE AVE 73112
Bill Tomlinson, prin.
Northridge ES, 8501 NW 82ND ST 73132
Doyle Ivester, prin.
Rogers ES, 8201 NW 122ND ST 73142
Fred Rhodes, prin.
Rollingwood ES, 6301 N ANN ARBOR AVE 73122
Kathy Nauman, prin.
Tulakes ES, 6600 GALAXIE DR 73132
Joe Siano, prin.
Wiley Post ES, 6920 W BRITTON ROAD 73132
Ann Mullerborg, prin.
Windsor Hills ES
2909 N ANN ARBOR AVE 73127
Janee Scott, prin.
Other Schools – See Bethany

Schwartz SD
Sch. Sys. Enr. Code 2
Supt. – Dennis Watson, 12001 SE 104 73165
Schwartz ES, 12001 SE 104TH ST 73165
(—), prin.

Western Hts. ISD
Sch. Sys. Enr. Code 4
Supt. – Bruce Miller
340 N COUNCIL ROAD 73127
Council Grove ES, 7721 MELROSE LANE 73127
Delores Perdue, prin.
Glenn ES, 6500 S LAND AVE 73159
Dowell Cluck, prin.
Greenvale ES, 901 GREENVALE ROAD 73127
John Hames, prin.
Winds West ES, 8300 SW 37TH ST 73179
Charles Hahn, prin.

Casady School
9500 N PENNSYLVANIA AVE 73120
Heritage Hall School, 1400 NW 115TH ST 73114
Westminister Upper Day School
540 NW 44TH ST 73118
Christ the King School
1900 GUILFORD LANE 73120
Corpus Christi School, 1025 NE 15TH ST 73117
John Carroll School, 1121 NW 31ST ST 73118
Rosary School, 1910 NW 19TH ST 73106
Sacred Heart School
2700 S SHARTEL AVE 73109

St. Charles Borromeo School
    5000 N GROVE AVE 73122
St. Eugene School, 2400 W HEFNER ROAD 73120
St. James School, 1224 SW 41ST ST 73109
St. John's Parish Day School
    5201 N BROOKLINE AVE 73112
Trinity Episcopal School, 1120 E HEFNER 73131
Villa Teresa School, 1216 CLASSEN DRIVE 73103
Westminster Day School
    4400 N SHARTEL AVE 73118

Okmulgee, Okmulgee Co., Pop. Code 7
Nuyaka SD
Sch. Sys. Enr. Code 1
Supt. – Carl King
    RURAL ROUTE 04 BOX 140 74447
Nuyaka ES, RURAL ROUTE 04 BOX 140 74447
    (—), prin.

Okmulgee ISD
Sch. Sys. Enr. Code 5
Supt. – George Hayes, P O BOX 1346 74447
MS, P O BOX 1346 74447
    Howard Williams, prin.
Eastside ES, P O BOX 1346 74447
    Ted Butler, prin.
Westside ES, P O BOX 1346 74447
    Dwight Wilson, prin.

Twin Hills SD
Sch. Sys. Enr. Code 2
Supt. -- Robert Pinkston, RURAL ROUTE 02 74447
Twin Hills ES, RURAL ROUTE 02 BOX 266 74447
    (—), prin.

Oktaha, Muskogee Co., Pop. Code 2
Oktaha ISD
Sch. Sys. Enr. Code 2
Supt. – Jerry Needham, P O BOX 746 74450
ES, P O BOX 9 74450 – Neoma Buckley, prin.

Olustee, Jackson Co., Pop. Code 3
Olustee ISD
Sch. Sys. Enr. Code 2
Supt. – Roger Allen, P O BOX 7 73560
ES, P O BOX 70 73560 – H. Mitchell, prin.

Omega, Kingfisher Co.
Lomega ISD
Sch. Sys. Enr. Code 2
Supt. – Gayle Hajny, RURAL ROUTE 01 73764
Lomega ES, RURAL ROUTE 01 BOX 1 73764
    Steve Mendell, prin.

Oologah, Rogers Co., Pop. Code 3
Oologah-Talala ISD
Sch. Sys. Enr. Code 4
Supt. – Keith Ballard, P O BOX 189 74053
MS, P O BOX 189 74053 – Dan Willott, prin.
ES, P O BOX 189 74053 – Joe Mosely, prin.

Optima, Texas Co., Pop. Code 2
Optima SD
Sch. Sys. Enr. Code 1
Supt. – Fern Boring, P O BOX 68 73948
ES, P O BOX 68 73948 – (—), prin.

Orlando, Logan Co., Pop. Code 2
Mulhall-Orlando ISD
Sch. Sys. Enr. Code 2
Supt. – Horace Sprouse, P O BOX 8 73073
Mulhall-Orlando ES, P O BOX 8 73073
    Peggy Yost, prin.

Owasso, Tulsa Co., Pop. Code 6
Owasso ISD
Sch. Sys. Enr. Code 5
Supt. – Dale Johnson, 1500 N ASH 74055
MS, 86TH ST N & MAIN 74055 – Dale Pride, prin.
Ator Heights ES, 1500 N ASH ST 74055
    Tim Taylor, prin.
Barnes ES, 1500 N ASH ST 74055
    Dan Siemens, prin.
Mills ES, 1500 N ASH ST 74055
    Martin Stovall, prin.
Smith ES, 12223 E 91ST 74055
    Ron Hughes, prin.

Paden, Okfuskee Co., Pop. Code 2
Paden ISD
Sch. Sys. Enr. Code 2
Supt. – Gary Pollard, P O BOX 218 74860
ES, P O BOX 277 74860 – Floyd Hamilton, prin.

Panama, Le Flore Co., Pop. Code 4
Panama ISD
Sch. Sys. Enr. Code 3
Supt. – L. Johnson, P O BOX 550 74951
MS, P O BOX 550 74951 – Lundy Kiger, prin.
ES, P O BOX 550 74951 – Gary Gunter, prin.

Panola, Latimer Co.
Panola ISD
Sch. Sys. Enr. Code 2
Supt. – Kenneth Kitchens, P O BOX 6 74559
ES, P O BOX 6 74559 – Jahue Dodd, prin.

Paoli, Garvin Co., Pop. Code 3
Paoli ISD
Sch. Sys. Enr. Code 2
Supt. – John Wilson, P O BOX 278 73074
ES, P O BOX 278 73074 – William Lawson, prin.

Park Hill, Cherokee Co.
Keys SD
Sch. Sys. Enr. Code 2
Supt. – Jackie Grass, RURAL ROUTE 02 74451
Keys ES, HCR 69 BOX 151 74451 – (—), prin.

Pauls Valley, Garvin Co., Pop. Code 6
Pauls Valley ISD
Sch. Sys. Enr. Code 4
Supt. – Joe Ogle, P O BOX 679 73075
MS, P O BOX 679 73075 – Gail Holder, prin.
Jackson ES, P O BOX 679 73075
    Jerry McCreary, prin.
Jefferson MS, P O BOX 679 73075
    Charles Fryar, prin.

Whitebead SD
Sch. Sys. Enr. Code 2
Supt. – Linda Pesterfield
    RURAL ROUTE 03 BOX 214 73075
Whitebead ES, RURAL ROUTE 03 BOX 214 73075
    (—), prin.

Pawhuska, Osage Co., Pop. Code 5
Pawhuska ISD
Sch. Sys. Enr. Code 4
Supt. – Jim Wilson, 1505 N LYNN 74056
JHS, 1505 LYNN AVE 74056 – Marvin Potter, prin.
Indian Camp MS, 1500 LYNN AVE 74056
    Terry Young, prin.
ES, 1500 LYNN AVE 74056
    Patsy Simmons, prin.

Pawnee, Pawnee Co., Pop. Code 4
Pawnee ISD
Sch. Sys. Enr. Code 3
Supt. – Ned Williams 74058
JHS, P O BOX 410 74058 – David Tanner, prin.
ES, P O BOX 410 74058 – Kenneth Drake, prin.

Peggs, Cherokee Co.
Peggs SD
Sch. Sys. Enr. Code 2
Supt. – Janell Meigs, P O BOX 486 74452
ES, P O BOX 486 74452 – (—), prin.

Perkins, Payne Co., Pop. Code 4
Perkins-Tryon ISD
Sch. Sys. Enr. Code 4
Supt. – Don Dale, P O BOX 549 74059
Perkins-Tryon MS, P O BOX 549 74059
    C. Owings, prin.
ES, P O BOX 549 74059 – Joe Hrencher, prin.
Tryon ES, P O BOX 187 74059
    Jarrell Browning, prin.

Pernell, Garvin Co.
Pernell ISD
Sch. Sys. Enr. Code 2
Supt. – Rick Webb, P O BOX 87 73076
ES, P O BOX 87 73076 – Ginger Mulkey, prin.

Perry, Noble Co., Pop. Code 6
Perry ISD
Sch. Sys. Enr. Code 4
Supt. – Larry Fry, 900 FIR AVE 73077
ES, 900 FIR ST 73077 – Carol Williams, prin.

Sumner ISD
Sch. Sys. Enr. Code 1
Supt. – Rauni Sherrell, RURAL ROUTE 03 73077
Sumner ES, RURAL ROUTE 03 73077
    (—), prin.

Christ Lutheran School, 1314 N 7TH ST 73077

Picher, Ottawa Co., Pop. Code 4
Picher-Cardin ISD
Sch. Sys. Enr. Code 3
Supt. – Joe Layton, P O BOX 280 74360
Picher-Cardin ES, P O BOX 280 74360
    Larry Heatherly, prin.

Piedmont, Canadian Co., Pop. Code 4
Piedmont ISD
Sch. Sys. Enr. Code 3
Supt. – Dr. Leonard Hall
    RURAL ROUTE 01 73078
ES, 917 PIEDMONT ROAD N 73078
    Sally Howard, prin.

Pittsburg, Pittsburg Co., Pop. Code 2
Pittsburg ISD
Sch. Sys. Enr. Code 2
Supt. – George Ellis, P O BOX 118 74560
ES, P O BOX 118 74560 – John McPhetridge, prin.

Pocola, Le Flore Co., Pop. Code 5
Pocola ISD
Sch. Sys. Enr. Code 3
Supt. – Larry Sockey, P O BOX 308 74902
ES, P O BOX 308 74902
    Thomas Humphreville, prin.

Ponca City, Kay Co., Pop. Code 8
McCord SD
Sch. Sys. Enr. Code 2
Supt. – Boyd Braden, 99 SHERIDAN AVE 74601
McCord ES, 99 SHERWIN AVE 74604
    (—), prin.

Ponca City ISD
Sch. Sys. Enr. Code 6
Supt. – Dr. Larry Robinson, P O BOX 271 74601
Garfield ES, 601 S 7TH ST 74601
    H. Ritcheson, prin.
Liberty ES, 505 W LIBERTY ST 74602
    Larry Leatherman, prin.
Lincoln ES, 700 W BROADWAY AVE 74601
    Elizabeth Watson, prin.
Roosevelt ES, 815 E HIGHLAND ST 74602
    David Shelton, prin.
Trout ES, 2109 E PROSPECT ST 74602
    Perry Pederson, prin.

Union ES, 2617 N UNION 74602
    Ralph Purget, prin.
Washington ES, 1615 N 7TH ST 74601
    Tom Sipe, prin.
Woodlands ES
    2005 E WOODLANDS ROAD 74604
    Ron McCleary, prin.

First Lutheran School
    N FOURTH & LIBERTY STS 74601
St. Mary's School, 415 S 7TH ST 74601

Pond Creek, Grant Co., Pop. Code 3
Pond Creek-Hunter ISD
Sch. Sys. Enr. Code 2
Supt. – James White, P O BOX 25 73766
Pond Creek-Hunter MS 73766
    Steve Hendrix, prin.
Pond Creek-Hunter ES, P O BOX 25 73766
    Max Moore, prin.

Porter, Wagoner Co., Pop. Code 3
Porter ISD
Sch. Sys. Enr. Code 2
Supt. – Lee Cobb, P O BOX 120 74454
ES, P O BOX 120 74454 – Carolyn Jones, prin.

Porum, Muskogee Co., Pop. Code 3
Porum ISD
Sch. Sys. Enr. Code 2
Supt. – Jerry Clark, P O BOX 189 74455
ES, P O BOX 189 74455 – Horace Tatum, prin.

Poteau, Le Flore Co., Pop. Code 6
Poteau ISD
Sch. Sys. Enr. Code 4
Supt. – Dr. Bert Corr, 300 N WALTER 74953
Kidd JHS, 300 N WALKER 74953
    Alice Smith, prin.
Central ES, 307 MOCKINGBIRD LN 74953
    Cloyis Clay, prin.

Prague, Lincoln Co., Pop. Code 4
Prague ISD
Sch. Sys. Enr. Code 3
Supt. – David Cox, NBU 3504 74864
MS, NBU 3504 74864 – Jackie Hargrove, prin.
ES 74864 – Judy Hightower, prin.

Preston, Okmulgee Co., Pop. Code 2
Preston ISD
Sch. Sys. Enr. Code 2
Supt. – Jim Waller, P O BOX 418 74456
ES, P O BOX 418 74456 – Ron Cunningham, prin.

Prue, Osage Co., Pop. Code 3
Prue ISD
Sch. Sys. Enr. Code 2
Supt. – Dr. David Owens, P O BOX 130 74060
ES, P O BOX 130 74060 – Delbert Daniels, prin.

Pryor, Mayes Co., Pop. Code 6
Osage SD
Sch. Sys. Enr. Code 2
Supt. – Randy Wassam
    RURAL ROUTE 01 BOX 163 74361
Osage ES, RURAL ROUTE 01 BOX 163 74361
    (—), prin.

Pryor ISD
Sch. Sys. Enr. Code 4
Supt. – Dr. Larry Burdick, 521 SE 1ST 74361
Jefferson ES, 521 SE 1ST ST 74361
    Wesley Kelley, prin.
Lincoln ES, 521 SE 1ST ST 74361
    Lavonne Ward, prin.
Roosevelt ES, 521 SE 1ST ST 74361
    Ailsa Vojvoda, prin.
Washington ES, 521 SE 1ST ST 74361
    Bill Hixson, prin.

Purcell, McClain Co., Pop. Code 5
Purcell ISD
Sch. Sys. Enr. Code 3
Supt. – George Hatfield, 919 N 9TH 73080
MS, 919 N 9TH AVE 73080 – Danny Jacobs, prin.
ES, 809 N 9TH AVE 73080
    Pat Frankenberg, prin.

Quapaw, Ottawa Co., Pop. Code 4
Quapaw ISD
Sch. Sys. Enr. Code 3
Supt. – David Hardage, 300 W 1ST 74363
ES, P O BOX 767 74363 – Max Hoskins, prin.

Quinton, Pittsburg Co., Pop. Code 4
Quinton ISD
Sch. Sys. Enr. Code 3
Supt. – Arthur Schofield, P O BOX 670 74561
ES, P O BOX 670 74561 – Keith Votravis, prin.

Ralston, Pawnee Co., Pop. Code 2
Ralston ISD
Sch. Sys. Enr. Code 2
Supt. – Phyllis Rottman, P O BOX 229 74650
ES, P O BOX 229 74650 – Bill Brown, prin.

Ramona, Washington Co., Pop. Code 3
Caney Valley ISD
Sch. Sys. Enr. Code 2
Supt. – Virginia Webb, P O BOX B 74061
Other Schools – See Ochelata

Randlett, Cotton Co., Pop. Code 2
Big Pasture ISD
Sch. Sys. Enr. Code 2
Supt. – Joe Ferguson, P O BOX 426 73562

Big Pasture ES, P O BOX 167 73562
 Ben Bernard, prin.

Rattan, Pushmataha Co., Pop. Code 2
 Rattan ISD
 Sch. Sys. Enr. Code 2
 Supt. – Loyd Deaton, P O BOX 44 74562
 ES, P O BOX 44 74562 – Charles Walls, Jr., prin.

Ravia, Johnson Co., Pop. Code 2
 Ravia SD
 Sch. Sys. Enr. Code 2
 Supt. – David Duncan, P O BOX 299 73455
 ES, P O BOX 299 73455 – (—), prin.

Red Oak, Latimer Co., Pop. Code 3
 Red Oak ISD
 Sch. Sys. Enr. Code 2
 Supt. – Rod McDonald, P O BOX 310 74563
 JHS, P O BOX 310 74563 – Larry Culwell, prin.
 ES, P O BOX 310 74563 – Greg McGowen, prin.

Red Rock, Noble Co., Pop. Code 2
 Red Rock ISD
 Sch. Sys. Enr. Code 2
 Supt. – Dr. Bob Piguet, P O BOX 130 74651
 ES, P O BOX 96 74651 – Philip Stidham, prin.

Reydon, Rogers Mills Co., Pop. Code 2
 Reydon ISD
 Sch. Sys. Enr. Code 2
 Supt. – Stanley Lamb, P O BOX 37 73660
 ES, P O BOX 37 73660 – Charles Callum, prin.

Ringling, Jefferson Co., Pop. Code 4
 Ringling ISD
 Sch. Sys. Enr. Code 2
 Supt. – E. Bural, P O BOX 1010 73456
 JHS, P O BOX 1010 73456 – Rick Gandy, prin.
 ES, P O BOX 1010 73456 – Bill Renfro, prin.

Ringwood, Major Co., Pop. Code 2
 Ringwood ISD
 Sch. Sys. Enr. Code 2
 Supt. – Jim Knox, P O BOX 115 73768
 ES, P O BOX 235 73768 – Susan Fike, prin.

Ripley, Payne Co., Pop. Code 2
 Ripley ISD
 Sch. Sys. Enr. Code 2
 Supt. – A. Matlock, P O BOX 65 74062
 ES, P O BOX 65 74062 – Geraldine Johnson, prin.

Roff, Pontotoc Co., Pop. Code 3
 Roff ISD
 Sch. Sys. Enr. Code 2
 Supt. – Alvin Minor, P O BOX 157 74865
 ES, P O BOX 157 74865 – Joe Moon, prin.

Roland, Sequoyah Co., Pop. Code 4
 Roland ISD
 Sch. Sys. Enr. Code 4
 Supt. – Carl Matlock
  RURAL ROUTE 01 BOX 1 74954
 ES, RURAL ROUTE 01 BOX 1 74954
  Bryce Dalke, prin.

Roosevelt, Kiowa Co., Pop. Code 2
 Roosevelt ISD
 Sch. Sys. Enr. Code 2
 Supt. – Gary Swart, P O BOX 303 73564
 ES, P O BOX 303 73564 – Gary Swart, prin.

Rush Springs, Grady Co., Pop. Code 4
 Rush Springs ISD
 Sch. Sys. Enr. Code 3
 Supt. – Mike McElroy, P O BOX 308 73082
 MS, P O BOX 308 73082 – Morris McKay, prin.
 ES, P O BOX 308 73082 – Max Laing, prin.

Ryan, Jefferson Co., Pop. Code 4
 Ryan ISD
 Sch. Sys. Enr. Code 2
 Supt. – Terry Kellner, P O BOX C 73565
 ES, P O BOX C 73565 – Steve Freeman, prin.

Saint Louis, Pottawatomie Co., Pop. Code 2
 St. Louis SD
 Sch. Sys. Enr. Code 1
 Supt. – Dale Smith, P O BOX 128 74866
 ES, P O BOX 128 74866 – (—), prin.

Salina, Mayes Co., Pop. Code 4
 Kenwood SD
 Sch. Sys. Enr. Code 2
 Supt. – Garland Lane, RURAL ROUTE 01 74365
 Kenwood ES, RURAL ROUTE 01 BOX 179 74365
  Jacqueline Schrader, prin.

 Salina ISD
 Sch. Sys. Enr. Code 3
 Supt. – Don Woodson, P O BOX 98 74365
 MS, P O BOX 98 74365 – Sally Cox, prin.
 ES, P O BOX 98 74365 – Albert Sellers, prin.

 Wickliffe SD
 Sch. Sys. Enr. Code 2
 Supt. – Michael Whalen
  RURAL ROUTE 01 BOX 130 74365
 Wickliffe ES, RURAL ROUTE 01 BOX 130 74365
  Michael Whalen, prin.

Sallisaw, Sequoyah Co., Pop. Code 6
 Brushy SD
 Sch. Sys. Enr. Code 2
 Supt. – Darlus Edwards, P O BOX 507 74955
 Brushy ES, P O BOX 507 74955 – (—), prin.

Central ISD
 Sch. Sys. Enr. Code 2
 Supt. – Bobby Barbee
  RURAL ROUTE 01 BOX 36 74955
 Central ES, RURAL ROUTE 01 BOX 36 74955
  Alfred Fullbright, prin.

Sallisaw ISD
 Sch. Sys. Enr. Code 5
 Supt. – Bill Patton, 312 S WALNUT 74955
 MS, 1206 E CREEK ST 74955
  Dwight Phillips, prin.
 Eastside MS, 136 S DOGWOOD ST 74955
  Ron Wyrick, prin.
 Liberty ES, 200 W CREEK ST 74955
  Bob Workman, prin.

Sand Springs, Tulsa Co., Pop. Code 7
 Anderson SD
 Sch. Sys. Enr. Code 2
 Supt. – Mickey Back
  RURAL ROUTE 05 BOX 161 74063
 Anderson ES, W ANDERSON ROAD 74063
  (—), prin.

 Keystone SD
 Sch. Sys. Enr. Code 2
 Supt. – Albert Randolph
  RURAL ROUTE 03 BOX 900 74063
 Keystone ES, RURAL ROUTE 03 BOX 900 74063
  (—), prin.

 Sand Springs ISD
 Sch. Sys. Enr. Code 6
 Supt. – Dr. Wendell Sharpton, P O BOX 970 74063
 Angus Valley ES, P O BOX 970 74063
  Dale Flynn, prin.
 Central ES, P O BOX 970 74063
  Mary Carter, prin.
 Garfield MS, P O BOX 970 74063
  Denis Clark, prin.
 Limestone ES, P O BOX 970 74063
  Robert Purser, prin.
 Pratt ES, P O BOX 970 74063
  Richard Berumen, prin.
 Twin Cities ES, P O BOX 970 74063
  Paul Gage, prin.

Sapulpa, Creek Co., Pop. Code 7
 Lone Star SD
 Sch. Sys. Enr. Code 3
 Supt. – David Pritz, P O BOX 1170 74067
 Lone Star ES, P O BOX 1170 74067
  (—), prin.

 Pretty Water SD
 Sch. Sys. Enr. Code 2
 Supt. – Eddie Peters
  RURAL ROUTE 04 BOX 411 74066
 Pretty Water ES
  RURAL ROUTE 04 BOX 411 74066
  (—), prin.

 Sapulpa ISD
 Sch. Sys. Enr. Code 5
 Supt. – Dr. Randall Raburn, 1 S MISSION 74066
 Garfield ES 74066 – Bob Alfred, prin.
 Jefferson MS, 1 S MISSION ST 74066
  Bob Alfred, prin.
 Liberty ES, 1 S MISSION ST 74066
  James Long, prin.
 MS, 1 S MISSION 74066 – Tim Cameron, prin.
 South Heights ES, 1 S MISSION ST 74066
  Jim DeLoache, prin.
 Washington ES, 1 S MISSION ST 74066
  Dr. Ben Hazlett, prin.
 Woodlawn ES, 1 S MISSION ST 74066
  Edwin Swift, prin.
 Other Schools – See Tulsa

Sasakwa, Seminole Co., Pop. Code 2
 Sasakwa ISD
 Sch. Sys. Enr. Code 2
 Supt. – Eldon Moffitt, P O BOX 323 74867
 ES, P O BOX 323 74867 – Leon Thompson, prin.

Savanna, Pittsburg Co., Pop. Code 3
 Savanna ISD
 Sch. Sys. Enr. Code 2
 Supt. – Bob Cooley, P O BOX 266 74565
 ES, P O BOX 266 74565 – Gary Canada, prin.

Sayre, Beckham Co., Pop. Code 5
 Sayre ISD
 Sch. Sys. Enr. Code 3
 Supt. – Paul Conner, 716 NE 66TH ST 73662
 ES, 716 NE 66TH ST 73662 – Andrea Reed, prin.

Schulter, Okmulgee Co., Pop. Code 2
 Schulter ISD
 Sch. Sys. Enr. Code 2
 Supt. – Kenneth Speer 74460
 ES, P O BOX 203 74460 – Carroll Brooksher, prin.

Seiling, Dewey Co., Pop. Code 4
 Seiling ISD
 Sch. Sys. Enr. Code 3
 Supt. – Gerald Daugherty, P O BOX 425 73663
 ES, P O BOX 780 73663 – Bobby Russell, prin.

Seminole, Seminole Co., Pop. Code 6
 Pleasant Grove ISD
 Sch. Sys. Enr. Code 2
 Supt. – J. Badgett
  RURAL ROUTE 01 BOX 247 74868
 Pleasant Grove ES
  RURAL ROUTE 01 BOX 247 74868
  Sue Taylor, prin.

Seminole ISD
 Sch. Sys. Enr. Code 4
 Supt. – Dr. Audie Woodard, P O BOX 1031 74868
 Northwood MS, P O BOX 1031 74818
  Ernest Carter, prin.
 Wilson ES, P O BOX 1031 74818
  Betty Smith, prin.

Strother ISD
 Sch. Sys. Enr. Code 2
 Supt. – James Begin, RURAL ROUTE 03 74868
 Other Schools – See Earlsboro

Varnum ISD
 Sch. Sys. Enr. Code 2
 Supt. – Jeff Gray
  RURAL ROUTE 04 BOX 148 74868
 Varnum ES, RURAL ROUTE 04 BOX 148 74868
  Dwight Grady, prin.

Sentinel, Washita Co., Pop. Code 4
 Sentinel ISD
 Sch. Sys. Enr. Code 2
 Supt. – Danny Rennels, P O BOX 9 73664
 ES, P O BOX 9 73664 – Gomer Skelley, prin.

Shady Point, Le Flore Co., Pop. Code 2
 Shady Point SD
 Sch. Sys. Enr. Code 2
 Supt. – Ray Bell, P O BOX C 74956
 ES, P O BOX 6 74956 – (—), prin.

Shattuck, Ellis Co., Pop. Code 4
 Shattuck ISD
 Sch. Sys. Enr. Code 2
 Supt. – Steven Crawford, P O BOX 159 73858
 ES, P O BOX 159 73858 – James Beers, prin.

Shawnee, Pottawatomie Co., Pop. Code 8
 Bethel ISD
 Sch. Sys. Enr. Code 4
 Supt. – Belvin Cantrell
  RURAL ROUTE 04 BOX 402 74801
 Bethel ES, RURAL ROUTE 04 BOX 402 74801
  Gary Bourbonnais, prin.

 Grove SD
 Sch. Sys. Enr. Code 2
 Supt. – Bob Green, RURAL ROUTE 03 74801
 Grove ES, 200 N BRYAN ST 74801 – (—), prin.

 North Rock Creek SD
 Sch. Sys. Enr. Code 2
 Supt. – Michael Lackey, RURAL ROUTE 03 74801
 North Rock Creek ES
  RURAL ROUTE 03 BOX 67 74801 – (—), prin.

 Pleasant Grove SD
 Sch. Sys. Enr. Code 2
 Supt. – Gene Hill, 300 S BRYAN ST 74801
 Pleasant Grove ES, 1927 E WALNUT ST 74801
  Arlene Ritter, prin.

 Shawnee ISD
 Sch. Sys. Enr. Code 5
 Supt. – Terry LaValley, 326 N UNION ST 74801
 Franklin ES, 326 N UNION ST 74801
  Marilyn Bradford, prin.
 Jefferson ES, 800 N LOUISA ST 74801
  Paul Pounds, prin.
 Mann ES, DRAPER & WHITTAKER 74801
  Jesse Field, prin.
 Rogers ES, 326 N UNION ST 74801
  Janice Rosenbaum, prin.
 Sequoyah ES, 326 N UNION ST 74801
  James Taffee, prin.
 Washington MS, 326 N UNION ST 74801
  Rocky Arrington, prin.
 Wilson MS, 1830 N BEARD ST 74801
  Roger Pritchard, prin.

 South Rock Creek SD
 Sch. Sys. Enr. Code 2
 Supt. – Bob Smith
  RURAL ROUTE 05 BOX 377 74801
 South Rock Creek ES
  RURAL ROUTE 05 BOX 377 74801
  (—), prin.

Shidler, Osage Co., Pop. Code 3
 Shidler ISD
 Sch. Sys. Enr. Code 2
 Supt. – Vernon Young, P O BOX 85 74652
 ES, P O BOX 85 74652 – Richard Conrad, prin.

Skiatook, Osage Co., Pop. Code 5
 Skiatook ISD
 Sch. Sys. Enr. Code 4
 Supt. – Jim Newman, P O BOX 217 74070
 MS, P O BOX 217 74070 – Tom Jones, prin.
 Central MS, P O BOX 217 74070
  Tom Maddox, prin.
 Marrs ES, P O BOX 217 74070 – Joyce Jech, prin.

Smithville, McCurtain Co., Pop. Code 2
 Smithville ISD
 Sch. Sys. Enr. Code 2
 Supt. – Claude Eberle, P O BOX 8 74957
 Octavia ES, P O BOX 8 74957
  Ellen Hensley, prin.
 MS, P O BOX 8 74957 – Kenneth Smith, prin.

Snyder, Kiowa Co., Pop. Code 4
 Snyder ISD
 Sch. Sys. Enr. Code 3
 Supt. – John McKee, P O BOX 368 73566
 ES, P O BOX 368 73566 – Don Woody, prin.

Soper, Choctaw Co., Pop. Code 2
Soper ISD
 Sch. Sys. Enr. Code 2
 Supt. – Olen Jestis, P O BOX 218 74759
 ES, P O BOX 218 74759 – Bob Edge, prin.

South Coffeyville, Nowata Co., Pop. Code 3
South Coffeyville ISD
 Sch. Sys. Enr. Code 2
 Supt. – Robert Donald, 600 E 5TH 74072
 ES, P O BOX 190 74072 – (—), prin.

Sparks, Lincoln Co., Pop. Code 3
Sparks SD
 Sch. Sys. Enr. Code 1
 Supt. – Jim Oakley, P O BOX 128 74869
 ES, P O BOX 129 74869 – (—), prin.

Spavinaw, Mayes Co., Pop. Code 3
Spavinaw SD
 Sch. Sys. Enr. Code 2
 Supt. – Jerry Lane, P O BOX 46 74366
 ES, P O BOX 46 74366 – Jerry Lane, prin.

Spencer, Oklahoma Co., Pop. Code 5
Oklahoma City ISD
 Supt. – See Oklahoma City
 Green Pastures 5th Grade Center
  4300 POST ROAD 73084 – Audrey Baker, prin.
 ES, 8700 NE 50TH ST 73084
  Dr. Delores Parker, prin.
 Star ES, 8917 NE 23RD ST 73084
  Sharon Creager, prin.

Sperry, Tulsa Co., Pop. Code 4
Sperry ISD
 Sch. Sys. Enr. Code 3
 Supt. – Harry Red Eagle, P O BOX 610 74073
 MS, P O BOX 908 74073 – David Jobe, prin.
 ES, P O BOX 610 74073 – John Harchar, prin.

Spiro, Le Flore Co., Pop. Code 4
Spiro ISD
 Sch. Sys. Enr. Code 4
 Supt. – J. L. Williams, P O BOX 188 74959
 MS, P O BOX 188 74959 – Ronnie Parent, prin.
 ES, 600 W BROADWAY ST 74959
  Jim Glenn, prin.

Springer, Carter Co., Pop. Code 3
Springer ISD
 Sch. Sys. Enr. Code 2
 Supt. – Rip Tidwell, P O BOX 249 73458
 ES, P O BOX 249 73458 – Jerry Clark, prin.

Sterling, Comanche Co., Pop. Code 3
Sterling ISD
 Sch. Sys. Enr. Code 2
 Supt. – Calvin Monroe, P O BOX 158 73567
 ES, P O BOX 158 73567 – Robert Danilavez, prin.

Stidham, McIntosh Co., Pop. Code 1
Stidham SD
 Sch. Sys. Enr. Code 1
 Supt. – Danny Williams
  GENERAL DELIVERY 74461
 ES, GENERAL DELIVERY 74461 – (—), prin.

Stigler, Haskell Co., Pop. Code 5
Stigler ISD
 Sch. Sys. Enr. Code 4
 Supt. – Bill Wilson, 302 NW E ST 74462
 MS, 302 NW E ST 74462 – Rick Prentice, prin.
 ES, 302 NW E ST 74462 – Ed Bell, prin.

Stillwater, Payne Co., Pop. Code 8
Stillwater ISD
 Sch. Sys. Enr. Code 5
 Supt. – Dr. William Hodges, P O BOX 879 74074
 Highland Park ES, P O BOX 879 74076
  Randy Stevens, prin.
 Rogers ES, P O BOX 879 74076
  Furman Clark, prin.
 Sangre Ridge ES, P O BOX 879 74076
  Karen White, prin.
 Skyline ES, P O BOX 879 74076
  Dr. O. Wikoff, prin.
 MS, P O BOX 879 74076 – John Mills, prin.
 Westwood ES, P O BOX 879 74076
  Terry Hopper, prin.

Stilwell, Adair Co., Pop. Code 4
Bell SD
 Sch. Sys. Enr. Code 2
 Supt. – Benjamin Poindexter, P O BOX 346 74960
 Bell ES, P O BOX 346 74960 – (—), prin.

Cave Springs ISD
 Sch. Sys. Enr. Code 2
 Supt. – Wayne Green
  RURAL ROUTE 01 BOX 300 74960
 Cave Springs ES
  RURAL ROUTE 01 BOX 300 74960
  Terry Mays, prin.

Dahlonegah SD
 Sch. Sys. Enr. Code 2
 Supt. – Kenneth Limore, RURAL ROUTE 01 74960
 Dahlonegah ES, RURAL ROUTE 01 74960
  (—), prin.

Greasy SD
 Sch. Sys. Enr. Code 2
 Supt. – Nellie Mays, RURAL ROUTE 01 74960
 Greasy ES, RURAL ROUTE 01 74960
  (—), prin.

Maryetta SD
 Sch. Sys. Enr. Code 2
 Supt. – Carthel Means, RURAL ROUTE 04 74960
 Maryetta ES, RURAL ROUTE 04 74960
  (—), prin.

Peavine SD
 Sch. Sys. Enr. Code 2
 Supt. – Willie Means, P O BOX 389 74960
 Peavine ES, P O BOX 389 74960 – (—), prin.

Rocky Mountain SD
 Sch. Sys. Enr. Code 1
 Supt. – D. Merrill
  RURAL ROUTE 01 BOX 112 74960
 Rocky Mountain ES
  RURAL ROUTE 01 BOX 112 74960
  (—), prin.

Stilwell ISD
 Sch. Sys. Enr. Code 4
 Supt. – Pat Martin, HWY 100 W 74960
 MS, 4 N 6TH ST 74960 – John Perry, prin.
 ES, HIGHWAY 100 W 74960 – Jerry Knight, prin.

Zion SD
 Sch. Sys. Enr. Code 2
 Supt. – Charles Benham, P O BOX 347 74960
 Zion ES, P O BOX 347 74960 – (—), prin.

Stonewall, Pontotoc Co., Pop. Code 3
Stonewall ISD
 Sch. Sys. Enr. Code 2
 Supt. – Floyd Gibson
  RURAL ROUTE 02 BOX 1A 74871
 ES, P O BOX 365 74871 – Gerald Stewart, prin.

Stratford, Garvin Co., Pop. Code 4
Stratford ISD
 Sch. Sys. Enr. Code 3
 Supt. – William Stokes, P O BOX 589 74872
 ES, P O BOX 589 74872 – Tawana Jones, prin.

Stringtown, Atoka Co., Pop. Code 4
Stringtown ISD
 Sch. Sys. Enr. Code 2
 Supt. – Bill Potts, P O BOX 130 74569
 ES, P O BOX 130 74569 – John Harris, prin.

Stroud, Lincoln Co., Pop. Code 5
Stroud ISD
 Sch. Sys. Enr. Code 3
 Supt. – Dean Morrison, 212 W 7TH 74079
 MS, P O BOX 236 74079 – Bill Terry, prin.
 ES, 212 W 7TH ST 74079 – Dennis Bookout, prin.

Stuart, Hughes Co., Pop. Code 2
Stuart ISD
 Sch. Sys. Enr. Code 2
 Supt. – Harold Lasiter, P O BOX 145 74570
 ES, RURAL ROUTE 01 BOX 7 74570
  Sherry Cates, prin.

Sulphur, Murray Co., Pop. Code 6
Sulphur ISD
 Sch. Sys. Enr. Code 4
 Supt. – Lloyd Snow, 1021 W 9TH 73086
 MS, 800 W WYNN 73086 – Keith Foreman, prin.
 ES, 1021 W 9TH STREET 73086
  Linda Besett, prin.

Sweetwater, Roger Mills Co.
Sweetwater ISD
 Sch. Sys. Enr. Code 2
 Supt. – Dr. Phillip Williams
  RURAL ROUTE 01 BOX 6 73666
 ES, RURAL ROUTE 01 BOX 6 73666
  Glen Harmon, prin.

Swink, Choctaw Co.
Swink SD
 Sch. Sys. Enr. Code 2
 Supt. – Robert Covert, P O BOX 73 74761
 ES, P O BOX 73 74761 – (—), prin.

Taft, Muskogee Co., Pop. Code 2
Moton ISD
 Sch. Sys. Enr. Code 2
 Supt. – Alexander Springs, P O BOX AB 74463
 Moton ES, P O BOX AB 74463 – Lois Lowe, prin.

Tahlequah, Cherokee Co., Pop. Code 6
Briggs SD
 Sch. Sys. Enr. Code 2
 Supt. – Speedie Chaffin
  RURAL ROUTE 03 BOX 100 74464
 Briggs ES, RURAL ROUTE 03 BOX 656 74464
  (—), prin.

Grand View SD
 Sch. Sys. Enr. Code 2
 Supt. – Jimmie Bilby, P O BOX 1188 74465
 Grand View ES
  RURAL ROUTE 04 BOX 195 74464
  (—), prin.

Lowrey SD
 Sch. Sys. Enr. Code 2
 Supt. – Denver Spears, P O BOX 70 74465
 Lowrey ES, HC-11 BOX 190-1 74464
  (—), prin.

Tahlequah ISD
 Sch. Sys. Enr. Code 5
 Supt. – Dr. Otis LoVette, P O BOX 517 74464
 Cherokee ES, 800 GOINGSNAKE ST 74464
  Jerry Casady, prin.
 Greenwood ES, 400 E ROSS ST 74464
  Jim White, prin.

Sequoyah ES, 425 S COLLEGE AVE 74464
  Janice Dick, prin.

Woodall SD
 Sch. Sys. Enr. Code 2
 Supt. – Randall Davis
  RURAL ROUTE 05 BOX 226 74464
 Woodall ES, RURAL ROUTE 05 BOX 226 74464
  (—), prin.

Talihina, Le Flore Co., Pop. Code 4
Buffalo Valley ISD
 Sch. Sys. Enr. Code 2
 Supt. – Orin Harrington
  RURAL ROUTE 02 BOX 3505 74571
 Buffalo Valley ES
  RURAL ROUTE 02 BOX 3505 74571
  Glenda Turner, prin.

Talihina ISD
 Sch. Sys. Enr. Code 3
 Supt. – Ray Henson, P O BOX 38 74571
 ES, P O BOX 38 74571 – Joe Bush, prin.

Taloga, Dewey Co., Pop. Code 2
Taloga ISD
 Sch. Sys. Enr. Code 2
 Supt. – Reith Claflin, P O BOX 158 73667
 ES, P O BOX 158 73667 – Georgia Horne, prin.

Tecumseh, Pottawatomie Co., Pop. Code 6
Tecumseh ISD
 Sch. Sys. Enr. Code 4
 Supt. – Jim Myers, 302 S 9TH 74873
 MS, 302 S 9TH ST 74873 – Don Anderson, prin.
 Barnard ES, 315 E LOCUST ST 74873
  Marjorie Bingham, prin.
 Cross Timbers MS, 302 S 9TH ST 74873
  Yvonne Raney, prin.
 Krouch ES, 302 S 9TH ST 74873
  Louise Mclin, prin.

Temple, Cotton Co., Pop. Code 4
Temple ISD
 Sch. Sys. Enr. Code 2
 Supt. – Bob Martin, P O BOX 400 73568
 ES, P O BOX 400 73568 – Terry Stricker, prin.

Terral, Jefferson Co., Pop. Code 3
Terral ISD
 Sch. Sys. Enr. Code 1
 Supt. – Don Garrison, P O BOX 340 73569
 ES, P O BOX 340 73569 – Kay Martin, prin.

Texhoma, Texas Co., Pop. Code 3
Plainview SD
 Sch. Sys. Enr. Code 1
 Supt. – Jim Bob Brown
  RURAL ROUTE 01 BOX 71 74740
 Plainview ES, RURAL ROUTE 01 BOX 71 73949
  (—), prin.

Texhoma ISD
 Sch. Sys. Enr. Code 2
 Supt. – Mel Yates
  RURAL ROUTE 01 BOX 71 73949
 MS, P O BOX 648 73949 – Odes Brown, prin.
 ES, P O BOX 648 73949 – Ben Ingham, prin.

Thackerville, Love Co., Pop. Code 2
Thackerville ISD
 Sch. Sys. Enr. Code 2
 Supt. – Clifford Boatright, P O BOX 170 73459
 ES, P O BOX 170 73459 – Ken Chancy, prin.

Thomas, Custer Co., Pop. Code 4
Thomas ISD
 Sch. Sys. Enr. Code 2
 Supt. – Dwaine Schneider, P O BOX 190 73669
 ES, P O BOX 190 73669 – Ed Beck, prin.

Tipton, Tillman Co., Pop. Code 4
Tipton ISD
 Sch. Sys. Enr. Code 2
 Supt. – Larry Osborne, P O BOX 340 73570
 ES, P O BOX 340 73570 – Doyle Chambers, prin.

Tishomingo, Johnston Co., Pop. Code 5
Tishomingo ISD
 Sch. Sys. Enr. Code 3
 Supt. – S. Littlepage
  RURAL ROUTE 01 BOX 47 73460
 MS, P O BOX 548 73460 – Rex Lokey, prin.
 Memorial ES, RURAL ROUTE 01 BOX 47 73460
  Donald Rowland, prin.

Tom, McCurtain Co.
Tom SD
 Sch. Sys. Enr. Code 2
 Supt. – Milton Glass
  RURAL ROUTE 01 BOX 183 74740
 ES, HCR 60 BOX 1130 74740 – (—), prin.

Tonkawa, Kay Co., Pop. Code 5
Tonkawa ISD
 Sch. Sys. Enr. Code 3
 Supt. – Ron Hodges, P O BOX 10 74653
 ES, P O BOX 10 74653 – Nancy Jackson, prin.

Tullahassee, Wagoner Co., Pop. Code 2
Carter G. Woodson ISD
 Sch. Sys. Enr. Code 2
 Supt. – John Gamble, P O BOX 1257 74466
 Woodson ES, P O BOX 1257 74466
  James Newton, prin.

Tulsa, Tulsa Co., Pop. Code 10
Academy Central SD
Sch. Sys. Enr. Code 2
Supt. – Dr. Norman Zielinski
1789 W SEMINOLE ST 74127
Academy Central ES 74127 – (—), prin.

Allen-Bowden SD
Sch. Sys. Enr. Code 2
Supt. – Nita Rusher
RURAL ROUTE 13 BOX 371A 74107
Allen-Bowden ES
RURAL ROUTE 13 BOX 371 A 74107
(—), prin.

Berryhill ISD
Sch. Sys. Enr. Code 3
Supt. – Leonard Wood
3128 S 63RD WEST AVE 74107
Berryhill ES, 3128 S 63RD WEST AVE 74107
Berlene Mace, prin.

Mingo SD
Sch. Sys. Enr. Code 2
Supt. – Louis Galluzzi
RURAL ROUTE 03 BOX 94 74115
Mingo ES, 4588 N MINGO ROAD 74116
(—), prin.

Sapulpa ISD
Supt. – See Sapulpa
Oakridge ES, 6500 S 43RD WEST AVE 74132
John Shouse, prin.

Tulsa ISD
Sch. Sys. Enr. Code 8
Supt. – Dr. Larry Zenke, P O BOX 45208 74145
Byrd MS, 7502 E 57TH ST 74145
Carol Croskery, prin.
Carver MS, 624 N OKLAHOMA 74106
Bobbie Johnson, prin.
Cleveland MS, 724 N BIRMINGHAM AVE 74110
Wayne Kendall, prin.
Clinton MS, 2224 W 41ST ST 74107
Garry Jones, prin.
Foster MS, 12121 E 21ST ST 74129
Manuel Domingos, prin.
Gilcrease MS, 5550 N CINCINNATI AVE 74126
June Hughes, prin.
Hamilton MS, 2316 N NORWOOD PLACE 74115
Irvin Brown, prin.
Lewis and Clark MS, 737 S 113 E AVE 74128
Kenneth Yates, prin.
Madison MS, 4132 W CAMERON ST 74127
Michael Hacker, prin.
Monroe MS, 2010 E 48TH NORTH ST 74130
Jewell Maynard, prin.
Nimitz MS, 3111 E 56TH ST 74105
Marolyn Hunnicutt, prin.
Skelly MS, 3027 S NEW HAVEN 74147
Gerald Hicks, prin.
Whitney MS, 2177 S 67TH EAST AVE 74129
Charles Claunts, prin.
Wilson MS, 1127 S COLUMBIA AVE 74104
Robert Maxie, prin.
Addams ES, P O BOX 470208 74147
Martha McCain, prin.
Alcott ES, 525 E 46TH ST 74126
Joan Gilford, prin.
Anderson ES, 1921 E 29TH STREET 74147
Leroy Alfred, prin.
Barnard ES, 2324 E 17TH ST 74104
Pat Randall, prin.
Bell ES, 6304 E ADMIRAL BLVD 74115
Phil Mauser, prin.
Bryant ES, 6201 E VIRGIN ST 74115
Joe Bernardi, prin.
Burroughs ES
1824 B KCUBCUBBATU AVE 74106
Jane Looney, prin.
Carnegie ES, 4309 E 56TH ST 74135
Carol Caldwell, prin.
Cherokee ES, 6001 N PEORIA AVE 74126
Brady Cypert, prin.
Chouteau ES, 575 N 39TH WEST AVE 74127
Michael Burk, prin.
Clinton ES, 1740 N HARVARD AVE 74115
Gary Coots, prin.
Columbus ES, 10620 E 27TH ST 74129
Elwyn Pruitt, prin.
Cooper ES, 1808 S 123RD EAST AVE 74128
Sue Allen, prin.
Disney ES, 11702 E 25TH ST 74129
Charles Carlile, prin.
Eliot ES, 1432 E 36TH ST 74105
Roger Tomlinson, prin.
Emerson ES, 909 N BOSTON AVE 74106
Catherine Frederick, prin.
Field ES, 1116 W 22ND ST 74107 – Joe Craig, prin.
Greeley ES, 105 E 63RD NORTH ST 74126
Percy Perry, prin.
Grimes ES, 3213 E 56TH ST 74105
Norman Ahrend, prin.
Grissom ES, 6646 S 73RD EAST AVE 74133
Elizabeth Miller, prin.
Hawthorne ES, 1105 E 33RD NORTH ST 74106
Wanda Reed, prin.
Henry ES, 3820 E 41ST ST 74135
Jolly Meadows, prin.
Hoover ES, 2327 S DARLINGTON AVE 74114
Kathleen Wilhite, prin.
Houston ES, 5402 N CINCINNATI AVE 74126
Willie Mackey, prin.
Jackson ES, 2137 N PITTSBURG AVE 74115
Duane Wilson, prin.

Kendall ES, 715 S COLUMBIA AVE 74104
Shirley Stanley, prin.
Kerr ES, 202 S 117TH EAST AVE 74128
Alice Spears, prin.
Key ES, 5702 S IRVINGTON AVE 74135
Gordon McDaniel, prin.
Lanier ES, 1727 S HARVARD AVE 74112
Debbie Howard, prin.
Lee ES, 1920 S CINCINNATI AVE 74119
Sharon Atcheson, prin.
Lincoln ES, 1515 S PEORIA AVE 74120
Linda Mayes, prin.
Lindbergh ES, 931 S 89TH EAST AVE 74112
John Knox, prin.
Lindsey ES, 2740 E 41ST ST 74110
Matthew Atkinson, prin.
MacArthur ES, 2182 S 73RD EAST AVE 74129
Robert Geneva, prin.
Marshall ES, 1142 E 56TH ST 74105
Margaret Erling, prin.
McClure ES, 1770 E 61ST ST 74136
John Simmons, prin.
McKinley ES, 6703 E KING ST 74115
Robin Gooldy, prin.
Mitchell ES, 733 N 73RD EAST AVE 74115
Diane Montgomery, prin.
Park ES, 3205 W 39TH ST 74107
Jean Swanson, prin.
Peary ES, 10818 E 17TH ST 74128
Larry Constien, prin.
Penn ES, 2138 E 48TH ST N 74130
Mozelle Lewis, prin.
Phillips ES, 3613 S HUDSON AVE 74135
Caroldean Tomlinson, prin.
Remington ES, 2524 W 53RD ST 74107
Grace Dean, prin.
Robertson ES, 2720 W 48TH ST 74107
Ed Creekppaum, prin.
Roosevelt ES, 1202 W EASTON ST 74127
Manyles Gaines, prin.
Salk ES, 7625 E 58TH ST 74145 – Jerry Carr, prin.
Sandburg ES, 18580 E 3RD ST 74108
Athena Rogers, prin.
Sequoyah ES, 3441 E ARCHER ST 74115
Roger Geary, prin.
Skelly ES, 2940 S 90 E AVE 74129
Ron Bradshaw, prin.
Springdale ES, 2510 E PINE ST 74110
Corene Tennant, prin.
Twain ES, 541 S 43RD WEST AVE 74127
Betty McIlvain, prin.
Whitman ES, 39F24 N LANSING AVE 74106
Q. Williams, prin.
Whittier ES, 68 N LEWIS AVE 74110
Don Walker, prin.
Wright ES, 1202 E 45TH PL 74105
Woodrow Norwood, prin.

Union ISD
Sch. Sys. Enr. Code 4
Supt. – Dr. Wesley Jarman
5656 S 129TH EAST AVE 74134
Anderson ES, 5656 S 129TH EAST AVE 74134
Darrell Wood, prin.
Boevers ES, 3433 S 133RD EAST AVE 74134
Faye Pride, prin.
Briarglen ES, 5656 S 129TH EAST AVE 74134
Marvis Jarvis, prin.
Clark ES, 3656 S 103RD EAST AVE 74146
Mildred Phillips, prin.
Darnaby ES, 7625 E 87TH ST 74133
Patti Pitcock, prin.
Grove ES, 10202 E 62ND ST 74133
Joe Bates, prin.
Seventh Grade Center
5656 S 129TH EAST AVE 74134
Larry Elliott, prin.
Other Schools – See Broken Arrow

_____

Holland Hall School, 5666 E 81ST ST 74137
Holy Family School, 820 S BOULDER AVE 74119
Immaculate Conception School
926 N OSAGE DRIVE 74106
Marquette School, 1519 S QUINCY AVE 74120
Monte Cassino ES, 2206 S LEWIS AVE 74114
St. Catherine School, 2515 W 46TH ST 74107
St. Mary School, 1365 E 49TH PLACE 74105
St. Pius X School, 1717 S 75TH EAST AVE 74112
SS. Peter and Paul School
1420 N 67TH EAST AVE 74115
Undercroft Montessori School
3745 S HUDSON AVE 74135

Tupelo, Coal Co., Pop. Code 3
Tupelo ISD
Sch. Sys. Enr. Code 2
Supt. – Palmer Mosely, P O BOX 310 74572
ES, P O BOX 310 74572 – Nancy Sanders, prin.

Turpin, Beaver Co.
Turpin ISD
Sch. Sys. Enr. Code 2
Supt. – Gerald Danley, P O BOX 187 73950
ES, P O BOX 187 73950 – Bill Jackson, prin.

Tushka, Atoka Co., Pop. Code 2
Tushka ISD
Supt. – See Atoka
ES, RURAL ROUTE 04 BOX T-26 74525
Jerry Cartwright, prin.

Tuskahoma, Pushmataha Co.
Tuskahoma SD
Sch. Sys. Enr. Code 1
Supt. – Leigh Keeling, P O BOX 97 74574
ES, P O BOX 97 74574 – (—), prin.

Tuttle, Grady Co., Pop. Code 5
Tuttle ISD
Sch. Sys. Enr. Code 4
Supt. – Hershel Busby, P O BOX H 73089
JHS, P O BOX H 73089 – James Stewart, prin.
MS, P O BOX H 73089 – James Cobble, prin.
ES, P O BOX H 73089 – James Cobble, prin.

Twin Oaks, Delaware Co.
Leach SD
Sch. Sys. Enr. Code 2
Supt. – Virgil Smith, P O BOX 211 74368
Leach ES, P O BOX 211 74368 – (—), prin.

Tyrone, Texas Co., Pop. Code 3
Tyrone ISD
Sch. Sys. Enr. Code 2
Supt. – John Montgomery, P O BOX 168 73951
ES, P O BOX 168 73951 – James Hogg, prin.

Union City, Canadian Co., Pop. Code 3
Union City ISD
Sch. Sys. Enr. Code 2
Supt. – Ben Grove, RURAL ROUTE 01 73090
ES, P O BOX 279 73090 – Rebecca Wright, prin.

Valliant, McCurtain Co., Pop. Code 3
Valliant ISD
Sch. Sys. Enr. Code 4
Supt. – Larry Landreth, P O BOX 777 74764
MS, P O BOX 777 74764 – Maurice Jackson, prin.
ES, P O BOX 777 74764 – Melvin Fenley, prin.

Velma, Stephens Co., Pop. Code 3
Velma-Alma ISD
Sch. Sys. Enr. Code 3
Supt. – Glenn Haswell, P O BOX 8 73091
Velma-Alma ES, P O BOX 8 73091
Barbara Wood, prin.

Verden, Grady Co., Pop. Code 3
Verden ISD
Sch. Sys. Enr. Code 2
Supt. – S. Cook, P O BOX 99 73092
ES, P O BOX 99 73092 – Carlos McBride, prin.

Vian, Sequoyah Co., Pop. Code 4
Vian ISD
Sch. Sys. Enr. Code 3
Supt. – Bob Hill, P O BOX 434 74962
MS, P O BOX 434 74962 – Bill Reynolds, prin.
ES, P O BOX 434 74962 – William Willis, prin.

Vici, Dewey Co., Pop. Code 3
Vici ISD
Sch. Sys. Enr. Code 2
Supt. – Michael Parkhurst, P O BOX 60 73859
ES, P O BOX 60 73859 – G. Taylor, prin.

Vinita, Craig Co., Pop. Code 6
Vinita ISD
Sch. Sys. Enr. Code 3
Supt. – Jerry Greenwood, P O BOX 408 74301
Halsell JHS, P O BOX 408 74301
Jeff Williams, prin.
Halsell ES, P O BOX 408 74301
Jim Dishman, prin.
Rogers MS, P O BOX 408 74301
Jerry Lingo, prin.
Southeast ES, P O BOX 408 74301
C. McCord, prin.

White Oak ISD
Sch. Sys. Enr. Code 2
Supt. – George Wickliffe
RURAL ROUTE 04 BOX 274 74301
White Oak ES, RURAL ROUTE 04 BOX 274 74301
Shirley Youngblood, prin.

Wagoner, Wagoner Co., Pop. Code 6
Wagoner ISD
Sch. Sys. Enr. Code 4
Supt. – Cecil Ford, P O BOX 707 74477
Central MS, 402 NE 2ND ST 74467
Cloyd O'Dell, prin.
Ellington ES, 601 SE 6TH ST 74467
Don Yates, prin.
Maple Park ES, 700 N STORY AVE 74467
Bill Teague, prin.

Wainwright, Muskogee Co., Pop. Code 2
Wainwright SD
Sch. Sys. Enr. Code 1
Supt. – Jim Ogden, P O BOX 188 74468
ES, P O BOX 188 74468 – (—), prin.

Wakita, Grant Co., Pop. Code 3
Wakita ISD
Sch. Sys. Enr. Code 2
Supt. – Donny Darrow, P O BOX 45 73771
ES, P O BOX 45 73771 – Gerald Miller, prin.

Walters, Cotton Co., Pop. Code 5
Walters ISD
Sch. Sys. Enr. Code 3
Supt. – Terry Simpson, 418 S BROADWAY 73572
MS, 418 S BROADWAY ST 73572
M. G. Philpott, prin.
ES, 418 S BROADWAY ST 73572
Tom Rowley, prin.

Wanette, Pottawatomie Co., Pop. Code 2
Wanette ISD
Sch. Sys. Enr. Code 2
Supt. – Jerry Layman, P O BOX 161 74878
ES, P O BOX 16I1 74878 – Jerry Thompson, prin.

Wann, Nowata Co., Pop. Code 2
Wann ISD
Sch. Sys. Enr. Code 2
Supt. – Bob Biggs, P O BOX 100 74083
ES, P O BOX 100 74083 – Tim Kilpatrick, prin.

Wapanucka, Johnston Co., Pop. Code 2
Wapanucka ISD
Sch. Sys. Enr. Code 2
Supt. – Randel Johnson, P O BOX 88 73461
ES, P O BOX 88 73461 – Ronald Germany, prin.

Warner, Muskogee Co., Pop. Code 4
Warner ISD
Sch. Sys. Enr. Code 3
Supt. – Don Perryman
   RURAL ROUTE 01 BOX A5 74469
ES, RURAL ROUTE 01 BOX A 74469
   Lanny Riggs, prin.

Washington, McClain Co., Pop. Code 2
Washington ISD
Sch. Sys. Enr. Code 3
Supt. – L. McAlister, P O BOX 98 73093
ES, P O BOX 98 73093 – Mike King, prin.

Watonga, Blaine Co., Pop. Code 5
Watonga ISD
Sch. Sys. Enr. Code 3
Supt. – (—), P O BOX 310 73772
MS, P O BOX 310 73772 – Geraldine Weber, prin.
ES, P O BOX 640 73772 – Grant Boyd, prin.

Watson, McCurtain Co.
Watson SD
Sch. Sys. Enr. Code 1
Supt. – Frank Makinson, P O BOX 8 74963
ES, P O BOX 8 74963 – (—), prin.

Watts, Adair Co., Pop. Code 2
Skelly SD
Sch. Sys. Enr. Code 1
Supt. – Larry Duncan, RURAL ROUTE 01 74964
Skelly ES, RURAL ROUTE 01 BOX 167A 74964
   (—), prin.

Watts ISD
Sch. Sys. Enr. Code 2
Supt. – Jack Ritchie, P O BOX 10 74964
ES, P O BOX 10 74964 – Nancy Boswood, prin.

Waukomis, Garfield Co., Pop. Code 4
Pioneer-Pleasant Vale ISD
Sch. Sys. Enr. Code 3
Supt. – Bob Bush, RURAL ROUTE 01 73773
Pioneer-Pleasant Vale ES
   RURAL ROUTE 01 BOX 219 73773
   James Shields, prin.

Waukomis ISD
Sch. Sys. Enr. Code 3
Supt. – (—), P O BOX 729 73773
MS, P O BOX 70 73773 – Robert Walsh, prin.
ES, P O BOX 729 73773 – (—), prin.

Waurika, Jefferson Co., Pop. Code 4
Waurika ISD
Sch. Sys. Enr. Code 2
Supt. – Gary Ferguson, 600 E FLORIDA 73573
ES, 600 EDUCATION AVE 73573 – Jon Jones, prin.

Wayne, McClain Co., Pop. Code 3
Wayne ISD
Sch. Sys. Enr. Code 3
Supt. – Jo Ann Bates, P O BOX 40 73095
MS, P O BOX 40 73095 – David Powell, prin.
ES, P O BOX 40 73095 – Oscar Cannon, prin.

Waynoka, Woods Co., Pop. Code 4
Waynoka ISD
Sch. Sys. Enr. Code 2
Supt. – Glen Love, 313 WAYNOKA 73860
ES, RURAL ROUTE 01 73860 – Bill Evans, prin.

Weatherford, Custer Co., Pop. Code 6
Weatherford ISD
Sch. Sys. Enr. Code 4
Supt. – Richard O'Hara
   WEATHERFORD EAST STATION 73096
Thompson JHS, 516 N BROADWAY ST 73096
   James Westfahl, prin.
Burcham ES, 516 N BROADWAY ST 73096
   Tom Gage, prin.
East ES, 516 N BROADWAY ST 73096
   Mary Page, prin.
West MS, 516 N BROADWAY ST 73096
   Carol Gaunt, prin.

Webbers Falls, Muskogee Co., Pop. Code 2
Webbers Falls ISD
Sch. Sys. Enr. Code 2
Supt. – David Harriman, P O BOX 188 74470
ES, P O BOX 188 74470 – Louise Carter, prin.

Welch, Craig Co., Pop. Code 3
Welch ISD
Sch. Sys. Enr. Code 2
Supt. – Jim Woody, P O BOX 189 74369
ES, P O BOX 297 74369 – Jack Eden, prin.

Weleetka, Okfuskee Co., Pop. Code 4
Graham SD
Sch. Sys. Enr. Code 2
Supt. – D. Chancey, RURAL ROUTE 01 74880
Graham ES, RURAL ROUTE 01 74880
   Stanley White, prin.

Weleetka ISD
Sch. Sys. Enr. Code 2
Supt. – Tom Cameron, P O BOX 278 74880
Spence Memorial MS, P O BOX 278 74880
   Ruth Pennington, prin.
PS, P O BOX 278 74880 – Linda Fisher, prin.

Welling, Cherokee Co.
Tenkiller SD
Sch. Sys. Enr. Code 2
Supt. – Ron Cambiano, P O BOX 191 74471
Tenkiller ES, RURAL ROUTE 01 BOX 750 74471
   (—), prin.

Wellston, Lincoln Co., Pop. Code 3
Wellston ISD
Sch. Sys. Enr. Code 2
Supt. – Thomas Crawley, P O BOX 60 74881
MS, P O BOX 38 74881 – Janice Johnson, prin.
ES, P O BOX 60 74881 – Janice Johnson, prin.

Westville, Adair Co., Pop. Code 4
Christie SD
Sch. Sys. Enr. Code 1
Supt. – Norma Marshall, RURAL ROUTE 02 74965
Christie ES, RURAL ROUTE 02 74965
   (—), prin.

Westville ISD
Sch. Sys. Enr. Code 3
Supt. – Travis Slaton, P O BOX 410 74965
ES, P O BOX 410 74965 – Richard Olinger, prin.

Wetumka, Hughes Co., Pop. Code 4
Wetumka ISD
Sch. Sys. Enr. Code 3
Supt. – Ron Renfrow, P O BOX 8 74883
ES, P O BOX 307 74883 – Jess Durham, prin.

Wewoka, Seminole Co., Pop. Code 6
Justice SD
Sch. Sys. Enr. Code 1
Supt. – William Harrison,Jr.
   RURAL ROUTE 01 BOX 246 74884
Justice ES, RURAL ROUTE 01 BOX 246 74884
   (—), prin.

New Lima ISD
Sch. Sys. Enr. Code 2
Supt. – Bryce Hill, P O BOX 67 74884
New Lima ES, RURAL ROUTE 01 BOX 96 74884
   Cozetta Gordon, prin.

Nobletown SD
Sch. Sys. Enr. Code 1
Supt. – Bob Alexander, RURAL ROUTE 02 74884
Nobletown ES, RURAL ROUTE 02 BOX 403 74884
   (—), prin.

Wewoka ISD
Sch. Sys. Enr. Code 4
Supt. – Richard Sloan, P O BOX 870 74884
Cowart MS, P O BOX 870 74884
   Wilma Cooper, prin.
ES, P O BOX 870 74884 – Joe Moon, prin.

Whitefield, Haskell Co., Pop. Code 2
Whitefield SD
Sch. Sys. Enr. Code 1
Supt. – Ted Green, P O BOX 188 74472
ES, P O BOX 188 74472 – (—), prin.

Whitesboro, Le Flore Co.
Whitesboro ISD
Sch. Sys. Enr. Code 2
Supt. – Jim Olive, P O BOX 206 74577
ES, P O BOX 206 74577 – Frieda McClellan, prin.

Wilburton, Latimer Co., Pop. Code 5
Wilburton ISD
Sch. Sys. Enr. Code 4
Supt. – John Shero, 301 W CADDO 74578
ES, 1201 W BLAIR AVE 74578
   Albert Shelton, prin.

Wilson, Carter Co., Pop. Code 4
Wilson ISD
Sch. Sys. Enr. Code 3
Supt. – Gary Labeth, P O BOX 730 73463
MS, P O BOX 730 73463 – Harland Smith, prin.
ES, P O BOX 730 73463 – Kenneth Longest, prin.

Zaneis SD
Sch. Sys. Enr. Code 1
Supt. – Calvin Wade
   RURAL ROUTE 02 BOX 37 73463
Zaneis ES, RURAL ROUTE 02 BOX 37 73463
   (—), prin.

Wister, Le Flore Co., Pop. Code 2
Wister ISD
Sch. Sys. Enr. Code 2
Supt. – Charles Bullard, P O BOX 246 74966
ES, P O BOX 489 74966 – Evelyn Campbell, prin.

Woodward, Woodward Co., Pop. Code 7
Woodward ISD
Sch. Sys. Enr. Code 7
Supt. – Burl Bartlett, P O BOX 668 73801
Cedar Heights ES, P O BOX 668 73802
   Ron Littau, prin.
Highland Park ES, P O BOX 668 73802
   Phillip Kenny, prin.
Madison Park ES, P O BOX 668 73802
   Sharon Yeager, prin.
Mann ES, P O BOX 668 73802
   Sharon Yeager, prin.
Oak Park ES, P O BOX 668 73802
   Ron Littau, prin.
Westwood ES, P O BOX 668 73802
   Phillip Kenny, prin.
Woodward 5th & 6th Grade Center
   P O BOX 668 73802 – Jasper Overton, prin.

Wright City, McCurtain Co., Pop. Code 4
Wright City ISD
Sch. Sys. Enr. Code 3
Supt. – Terry Davidson, P O BOX 329 74766
ES, P O BOX 329 74766 – David Hawkins, prin.

Wyandotte, Ottawa Co., Pop. Code 2
Turkey Ford SD
Sch. Sys. Enr. Code 1
Supt. – Philip Bowles, RURAL ROUTE 01 74370
Turkey Ford ES
   RURAL ROUTE 01 BOX 142 74370
   (—), prin.

Wyandotte ISD
Sch. Sys. Enr. Code 3
Supt. – Bobby Martin, P O BOX 360 74370
ES, P O BOX 360 74370 – Jim Nichols, prin.

Wynnewood, Garvin Co., Pop. Code 5
Joy SD
Sch. Sys. Enr. Code 1
Supt. – Ron Boles, P O BOX 57 73098
Joy ES, RURAL ROUTE 01 BOX 57 73098
   (—), prin.

Walker SD
Sch. Sys. Enr. Code 1
Supt. – Judy Staggs, RURAL ROUTE 01 73098
Walker ES, RURAL ROUTE 01 BOX 168 73098
   (—), prin.

Wynnewood ISD
Sch. Sys. Enr. Code 2
Supt. – James Potts, P O BOX 9 73098
MS, 702 ROBERT KERR BLVD 73098
   Tom McKay, prin.
Central ES, P O BOX 9 73098 – Jim Stark, prin.

Wynona, Osage Co., Pop. Code 3
Wynona ISD
Sch. Sys. Enr. Code 2
Supt. – Gregory Holleyman, P O BOX 700 74084
ES, P O BOX 700 74084 – Donald John, prin.

Yale, Payne Co., Pop. Code 4
Yale ISD
Sch. Sys. Enr. Code 3
Supt. – Robert DeLay, 322 N C ST 74085
ES, 322 N C STREET 74085 – Glen Williams, prin.

Yukon, Canadian Co., Pop. Code 7
Yukon ISD
Sch. Sys. Enr. Code 6
Supt. – Dr. Darrell Hill, 950 POPLAR AVE 73099
Independence MS, 500 E VANDERMENT 73099
   Rita Billbe, prin.
Central ES, 600 MAPLE AVE 73099
   Donna Randolph, prin.
Myers ES, 1200 S 1ST ST 73099
   Wayne Beam, prin.
Parkland ES, 2201 S CORNWELL DR 73099
   Janice McComas, prin.
Ranchwood ES, 607 ANNAWOOD ST 73099
   Dwayne Bunch, prin.
Shedeck ES, 2100 HOLLY AVE 73099
   Jane Kennedy, prin.
Skyview ES, 2800 N MUSTANG ROAD 73099
   Joe Hanska, prin.
Surrey Hills ES, 10700 HASTINGS AVE 73099
   Janet Lee, prin.

St. John Nepomuk School
   600 SOUTH 11TH 73099

OREGON

STATE DEPARTMENT OF EDUCATION
700 Pringle Parkway, S.E., Salem 97310
(503) 378-3573

Superintendent of Public Instruction	Verne Duncan
Deputy Superintendent	Ronald Burge
Associate Superintendent Curriculum & School Improvement	Bob Burns
Associate Superintendent Special Student Services	Jerry Fuller
Associate Superintendent School District Services	Milt Baum
Associate Superintendent Vocational Technical Education	Monty Multanen

STATE BOARD OF EDUCATION
Donald Kruse, *Chairperson*   700 Pringle Pkwy., Salem   97310

EDUCATION SERVICE DISTRICTS

Baker ESD, Ruth Whitnah, Supt.
  2100 MAIN ST, Baker 97814
Clackamas ESD, R. Klein, Supt.
  P O BOX 216, Marylhurst 97036
Clatsop ESD, Richard Laughlin, Supt.
  3194 MARINE DRIVE, Astoria 97103
Columbia ESD, Roland Lippold, Supt.
  P O BOX 900, Saint Helens 97051
Coos ESD, Robert Work, Supt.
  1350 TEAKWOOD AVE, Coos Bay 97420
Curry ESD, Sam Wilson, Supt.
  P O BOX 786, Gold Beach 97444
Deschutes ESD, Dennis Douglass, Supt.
  221 NW KANSAS AVE, Bend 97701
Douglas ESD, Vernon Bittner, Supt.
  1871 NE STEPHENS ST, Roseburg 97470
Gilliam ESD, H. James Burton, Supt.
  P O BOX 637, Condon 97823
Grant ESD, Robert Batty, Supt.
  P O BOX 99, Canyon City 97820

Harney ESD, Ed Schumacher, Supt.
  P O BOX 72, Burns 97720
Jackson ESD, Shelby Price, Supt.
  101 N GRAPE ST, Medford 97501
Jefferson ESD, Darrell Wright, Supt.
  1355 BUFF ST, Madras 97741
Lake ESD, Donald Knowles, Supt.
  118 SOUTH E ST, Lakeview 97630
Lane ESD, James Maxwell, Supt.
  1200 HIGHWAY 99 N, Eugene 97402
Linn-Benton ESD, Gerald Bennett, Supt.
  905 4TH AVE SE, Albany 97321
Malheur ESD, Leroy Paulsen, Supt.
  P O BOX 610, Vale 97918
Marion ESD, Ron Wilkerson, Supt.
  3400 PORTLAND ROAD NE, Salem 97303
Multnomah ESD, Allan Thede, Supt.
  P O BOX 16657, Portland 97216
Polk ESD, Peyton Lieuallen, Supt.
  322 MAIN ST, Dallas 97338

Sherman ESD, Dale Coles, Supt.
  HCR 01 BOX 95, Moro 97039
Tillamook ESD, William Molendyke, Supt.
  2410 5TH ST, Tillamook 97141
Umatilla ESD, Boyd Swent, Supt.
  P O BOX 38, Pendleton 97801
Union ESD, Ken Kramer, Supt.
  RURAL ROUTE 04 BOX 4778, La Grande 97850
Wallowa ESD, Dave Smyth, Supt.
  301 WEST NORTH ST, Enterprise 97828
Wasco ESD, F. Krauss, Supt.
  422 E 3RD ST, The Dalles 97058
Washington ESD, Lee Christiansen, Supt.
  17705 NW SPRINGVILLE ROAD, Portland 97229
Wheeler ESD, Daniel Barker, Supt.
  P O BOX 206, Fossil 97830
Yamhill ESD, James Redmond, Supt.
  800 E 2ND ST, Mc Minnville 97128

PUBLIC, PRIVATE, AND PAROCHIAL ELEMENTARY SCHOOLS

Adel, Lake Co.
  Adel SD 21
  Sch. Sys. Enr. Code 1
  Supt. – (—) 97620
  ES 97620 – David Greiner, prin.

Adrian, Malheur Co., Pop. Code 2
  Adrian SD 61
  Sch. Sys. Enr. Code 2
  Supt. – Irvin Easom, P O BOX 108 97901
  ES, P O BOX 108 97901 – Irvin Easom, prin.

Agness, Curry Co.
  Agness SD 4
  Sch. Sys. Enr. Code 1
  Supt. – (—) 97406
  ES 97406 – Patricia Cox, prin.

Albany, Linn Co., Pop. Code 8
  Greater Albany SD 8J
  Sch. Sys. Enr. Code 6
  Supt. – Dr. Robert Williams
    718 7TH AVE SW 97321
  Calapooia MS, 830 24TH AVE SE 97321
    Paul Nys, prin.
  Memorial MS, 1050 QUEEN AVE SW 97321
    Merl Helms, prin.
  North Albany MS
    1205 NW ALBANY ROAD 97321
    Bob Bayman, prin.
  Central ES, 336 9TH AVE SW 97321
    Ralph Younce, prin.
  Clover Ridge ES
    2953 CLOVER RIDGE ROAD NE 97321
    Martin Meyer, prin.
  Fir Grove ES, 5355 NW SCENIC DRIVE 97321
    Cynthia Coady, prin.
  Lafayette ES, 3122 MADISON ST SE 97321
    Wilmer Leichty, prin.
  Liberty ES, 2345 LIBERTY ST SW 97321
    Shary Wortman, prin.
  North Albany ES
    815 NW THORNTON LAKE DRIVE 97321
    Hazel Brentlinger, prin.
  Oak ES, 3610 OAK ST SE 97321
    Lavae Robertson, prin.

Oak Grove ES
  1500 NW OAK GROVE DRIVE 97321
  Cynthia Coady, prin.
Periwinkle ES, 2196 21ST AVE SE 97321
  Marilee Fitzpatrick, prin.
South Shore ES, 910 BAIN ST SE 97321
  Joan Boylan, prin.
Sunrise ES, 730 19TH AVE SE 97321
  Moe Chester, prin.
Takena ES, 1210 TAKENA ST SW 97321
  Ralph Younce, prin.
Waverly ES, 425 COLUMBUS ST SE 97321
  Tom Anderson, prin.
Other Schools – See Crabtree, Tangent

Albany Private ES, 420 3RD AVE SE 97321
St. Mary's ES, 815 S BROADALBIN ST SW 97321

Aloha, Washington Co.
  Beaverton SD 48J
  Supt. – See Beaverton
  Aloha Park ES, 17770 SW BLANTON ST 97007
    Douglas Smith, prin.
  Beaver Acres ES, 2125 SW 170TH AVE 97006
    Lee Wick, prin.

  Reedville SD 29
  Supt. – See Hillsboro
  Butternut Creek ES
    20394 SW FLORENCE ST 97007
    Nadine Zimmerlund, prin.
  Indian Hills ES, 21260 SW ROCK ROAD 97006
    Doug Mattson, prin.
  Reedville ES, 2695 SW 209TH AVE 97006
    Marilyn Eide, prin.

  Faith Bible Christian School, P O BOX 5335 97006
  Pacific Christian Montessori, P O BOX 6297 97007

Alsea, Benton Co., Pop. Code 2
  Alsea SD 7J
  Sch. Sys. Enr. Code 2
  Supt. – Gus Forester, P O BOX B 97324
  ES, P O BOX B 97324 – Gary Sunderland, prin.

Amity, Yamhill Co., Pop. Code 4
  Amity SD 4J
  Sch. Sys. Enr. Code 3
  Supt. – George Lanning, P O BOX 138 97101
  MS, 115 CHURCH ST 97101
    George Lanning, prin.
  ES, P O BOX 138 97101 – Herb Romey, prin.

  Perrydale SD 21
  Sch. Sys. Enr. Code 2
  Supt. – Joseph Curelo
    7445 PERRYDALE ROAD 97101
  Perrydale ES, 7445 PERRYDALE ROAD 97101
    Joseph Curelo, prin.

Applegate, Jackson Co., Pop. Code 3
  Applegate SD 40
  Sch. Sys. Enr. Code 2
  Supt. – Bruce Matheny
    14188 HIGHWAY 238 97530
  ES 97530 – Bruce Matheny, prin.

Arch Cape, Clatsop Co.

  Fire Mountain ES, P O BOX 96 97102

Arlington, Gilliam Co., Pop. Code 3
  Arlington SD 3
  Sch. Sys. Enr. Code 2
  Supt. – Laurence Jones, P O BOX 10 97812
  ES, P O BOX 460 97812 – Terry Mahler, prin.

  Olex SD 11
  Sch. Sys. Enr. Code 1
  Supt. – (—), HCR 97812
  Olex ES, HCR 97812 – Lynnette Holdahl, prin.

Arock, Malheur Co.
  Arock SD 81
  Sch. Sys. Enr. Code 1
  Supt. – (—) 97902
  Jones ES 97902 – Linda Pelroy, prin.

Ashland, Jackson Co., Pop. Code 7
  Ashland SD 5
  Sch. Sys. Enr. Code 5
  Supt. – John Daggett, 885 SISKIYOU BLVD 97520
  Bellview ES, 1070 TOLMAN CREEK ROAD 97520
    Erik Jorgensen, prin.

Briscoe ES, 265 N MAIN ST 97520
　Karl Hesse, prin.
Helman ES, 705 HELMAN ST 97520
　Neil Richardson, prin.
Lincoln ES, 320 BEACH ST 97520
　Rose Davis, prin.
Walker ES, 364 WALKER AVE 97520
　Marvin Dunn, prin.

Pinehurst SD 94
Sch. Sys. Enr. Code 1
Supt. – (—), 15337 HIGHWAY 66 97520
Pinehurst ES, 15337 HIGHWAY 66 97520
　Laurie Grupe, prin.
_____

Chautauqua Ranch ES, 1497 E MAIN ST 97520
_____

Ashwood, Jefferson Co.
Ashwood SD 8
Sch. Sys. Enr. Code 1
Supt. – (—) 97711
ES, P O BOX 2 97711 – Sharon Cyrus, prin.

Astoria, Clatsop Co., Pop. Code 6
Astoria SD 1
Sch. Sys. Enr. Code 4
Supt. – Stuart Kammerman
　3196 MARINE DRIVE 97103
MS, 1100 KLASKANINE AVE 97103
　John Jenson, prin.
Astor ES, 3550 FRANKLIN AVE 97103
　Judy Bigby, prin.
Gray ES, 785 ALAMEDA ST 97103
　Ross Bailey, prin.

Columbia SD 5J
Supt. – See Westport
Lahti ES, RURAL ROUTE 06 BOX 226 97103
　Robert Theis, prin.

Lewis & Clark SD 5
Sch. Sys. Enr. Code 2
Supt. – John Stuckey
　RURAL ROUTE 03 BOX 145 97103
Lewis & Clark ES
　RURAL ROUTE 03 BOX 145 97103
　(—), prin.

Olney SD 11
Sch. Sys. Enr. Code 1
Supt. – Robert Guenther
　RURAL ROUTE 01 BOX 806 97103
Olney ES, RURAL ROUTE 01 BOX 806 97103
　Robert Guenther, prin.
_____

Star of the Sea ES, 1411 GRAND AVE 97103
_____

Athena, Umatilla Co., Pop. Code 3
Athena-Weston SD 29J
Sch. Sys. Enr. Code 3
Supt. – Verle Bechtel, P O BOX 240 97813
ES, P O BOX 510 97813 – Gaylord Salter, prin.
Other Schools – See Weston

Aumsville, Marion Co., Pop. Code 4
Aumsville SD 11
Sch. Sys. Enr. Code 2
Supt. – Ernest Teal, 572 N 11TH ST 97325
ES, 572 N 11TH ST 97325 – Ernest Teal, prin.

North Santiam SD 126
Sch. Sys. Enr. Code 1
Supt. – Patricia Stewart
　8902 SANTIAM LOOP SE 97325
North Santiam ES
　8902 SANTIAM LOOP SE 97325
　Patricia Stewart, prin.

West Stayton SD 61
Sch. Sys. Enr. Code 1
Supt. – Douglas Smith
　11463 W STAYTON ROAD SE 97325
West Stayton ES
　11463 W STAYTON ROAD SE 97325
　(—), prin.

Aurora, Marion Co., Pop. Code 3
North Marion SD 15
Sch. Sys. Enr. Code 4
Supt. – Wilbur Brown
　20256 GRIM ROAD NE 97002
North Marion MS, 20246 GRIM ROAD NE 97002
　Richard Overfield, prin.
North Marion ES, 20237 GRIM ROAD NE 97002
　Margaret Dutton, prin.

Baker, Baker Co., Pop. Code 6
Baker SD 5J
Sch. Sys. Enr. Code 4
Supt. – Charles Wiltse,Jr., 2090 4TH ST 97814
MS, 2025 4TH ST 97814 – Frank Bishop, prin.
Brooklyn ES, 1350 WASHINGTON AVE 97814
　Jerry Peacock, prin.
North Baker ES, 2725 7TH ST 97814
　Pat Braswell, prin.
South Baker ES, 1285 3RD ST 97814
　Dennis Axness, prin.

Bandon, Coos Co., Pop. Code 4
Bandon SD 54
Sch. Sys. Enr. Code 3
Supt. – Dave Hamilton, 455 SW 9TH ST 97411
Harbor Lights MS, 390 SW 9TH ST 97411
　Peter Petros, prin.
Ocean Crest ES, 1040 ALLEGHENY AVE 97411
　James Cowan, prin.

Banks, Washington Co. Pop. Code 2
Banks SD 13
Sch. Sys. Enr. Code 3
Supt. – Will Duke, P O BOX 38 97106
JHS, P O BOX 386 97106 – Gene Harp, prin.
ES, P O BOX 367 97106 – Art Anderson, prin.
Buxton ES, P O BOX 367 97106
　Art Anderson, prin.
_____

St. Francis of Assisi School
　RURAL ROUTE 02 BOX 62 97106
_____

Beaver, Tillamook Co.
Beaver SD 8
Sch. Sys. Enr. Code 2
Supt. – John Starr 97108
ES 97108 – John Starr, prin.

Beavercreek, Clackamas Co.
Oregon City SD 62
Supt. – See Oregon City
ES, 21944 S YEOMAN ROAD 97004
　Mary Ann Deffenbaugh, prin.

Schuebel SD 80
Sch. Sys. Enr. Code 2
Supt. – Fred Proett
　23931 S SCHUEBEL SCH ROAD 97004
Schuebel ES
　23931 S SCHUEBEL SCH ROAD 97004
　Fred Proett, prin.

Beaverton, Washington Co., Pop. Code 8
Beaverton SD 48J
Sch. Sys. Enr. Code 7
Supt. – Boyd Applegarth, P O BOX 200 97075
Barnes ES, 13730 SW WALKER ROAD 97005
　Tony Fernandez, prin.
Bethany ES, 3305 NW 174TH AVE 97006
　Betty Flad, prin.
Chehalem ES, 15555 SW DAVIS ROAD 97007
　Glenn Rutherford, prin.
Cooper Mountain ES, 7670 SW 170TH AVE 97007
　Linda Borquist, prin.
Elmonica ES, 450 SW 173RD AVE 97006
　Jeanne Sabbe, prin.
Fir Grove ES, 6300 SW WILSON AVE 97005
　Alan Deckard, prin.
Greenway ES, 9150 SW DOWNING DRIVE 97005
　Candace Stevens, prin.
Hassell ES, 18100 SW BANY ROAD 97007
　Michael Smith, prin.
Hazeldale ES
　20080 SW FARMINGTON ROAD 97007
　Toni Painter, prin.
Hiteon ES, 13800 SW BROCKMAN ROAD 97005
　Bob Blanchard, prin.
Kinnaman ES, 4205 SW 193RD ST 97005
　Patricia Sharp, prin.
McKay ES
　7485 SW SCHOLLS FERRY ROAD 97005
　Marv Holstein, prin.
McKinley ES, 1500 NW 185TH AVE 97006
　Judith Taccogna, prin.
Oak Hills ES, 2625 NW 153RD AVE 97006
　Mark Carlton, prin.
Raleigh Hills ES, P O BOX 200 97005
　Shelly King, prin.
Rock Creek ES, P O BOX 200 97075
　Dorothy Danner, prin.
Terra Linda ES, P O BOX 200 97075
　Arlene Norman, prin.
Vose ES, 11350 SW DENNY ROAD 97005
　Jack Kirby, prin.
Walker ES, 11940 SW LYNNFIELD LANE 97005
　Molly Stewart, prin.
West Tualatin View ES, P O BOX 200 97075
　Mei-Ling Shiroishi, prin.
Other Schools – See Aloha, Portland
_____

Holy Trinity ES, 13755 SW WALKER ROAD 97005
Pilgrim Lutheran ES, 5650 SW HALL BLVD 97005
St. Cecilia ES, 12250 SW 5TH ST 97005
St. Mary of the Valley School
　4440 SW 148TH AVE 97007
Tualatin Valley Junior Academy
　21975 W BASELINE ROAD 97006
_____

Bend, Deschutes Co., Pop. Code 7
Bend Administrative SD 1
Sch. Sys. Enr. Code 6
Supt. – Murl Anderson, 520 NW WALL ST 97701
Cascade JHS, 19740 SW CENTURY DRIVE 97702
　Lowell Pearce, prin.
Pilot Butte JHS, 1501 NE PENN AVE 97701
　Brian Lauchlan, prin.
Bear Creek ES, 51 SE 13TH ST 97702
　Betty Lewis, prin.
Buckingham ES, 62560 HAMBY ROAD 97701
　Marion Morehouse, prin.
Jewell ES, 20501 RAE ROAD 97702
　Marvin Anderson, prin.
Juniper ES, 1300 NE NORTON AVE 97701
　Paul Danford, prin.
Kenwood ES, 701 NW NEWPORT AVE 97701
　Herbert Ekstrom, prin.
Kingston ES, 1101 NW 12TH ST 97701
　Herbert Ekstrom, prin.
Thompson ES, 437 NW WALL ST 97701
　Herbert Ekstrom, prin.
Other Schools – See La Pine

Redmond SD 2J
Supt. – See Redmond

Tumalo ES, 19835 2ND ST 97701
　Carl Williquette, prin.
_____

Central Oregon Academy in Bend
　22580 MARTEE LANE 97701
Sylvan Learning Center
　1560 NW NEWPORT AVE 97701
Tamarak Learning Center, 1468 NW 3RD 97701
St. Francis of Assisi School
　720 NW BOND ST 97701

Blachly, Lane Co., Pop. Code 2
Blachly SD 90
Sch. Sys. Enr. Code 2
Supt. – John Rollofson
　20264 BLACHLY GRANGE ROAD 97412
Triangle Lake ES
　20264 BLACHLY GRANGE ROAD 97412
　John Rollofson, prin.

Blodgett, Benton Co.
Philomath SD 17J
Supt. – See Philomath
ES, COAST HWY 97326 – Wendell Seat, prin.

Bly, Klamath Co., Pop. Code 3
Klamath County SD
Supt. – See Klamath Falls
Gearhart ES, P O BOX 47 97622
　Douglas Smith, prin.

Boardman, Morrow Co., Pop. Code 4
Morrow SD 1
Supt. – See Lexington
ES, P O BOX 529 97818 – Susan Tolar, prin.

Bonanza, Klamath Co., Pop. Code 2
Klamath County SD
Supt. – See Klamath Falls
ES, P O BOX 128 97623 – Jack Musser, prin.

Bonneville, Hood River Co.
Bonneville SD 46
Supt. – See Cascade Locks
ES 97014 – Warren Linville, prin.

Boring, Clackamas Co.
Boring SD 44
Sch. Sys. Enr. Code 2
Supt. – Michael McDonough
　12240 SE SCHOOL AVE 97009
MS, 27801 SE DEE ST 97009
　Marilyn Heaton, prin.
ES, 12240 SE SCHOOL AVE 97009
　Michael McDonough, prin.

Cottrell SD 107
Sch. Sys. Enr. Code 2
Supt. – Joanne Yatvin
　36225 SE PROCTOR ROAD 97009
Cottrell ES, 36225 SE PROCTOR ROAD 97009
　Joanne Yatvin, prin.

Damascus Un. SD 26
Sch. Sys. Enr. Code 3
Supt. – Joseph Bucher,Jr.
　14151 SE 242ND AVE 97009
Damascus MS, 14151 SE 242ND AVE 97009
　Dennis Paldi, prin.
Damascus Deep Creek ES
　15600 SE 232ND DRIVE 97009
　Al Fitzpatrick, prin.

Sandy ESD 46
Supt. – See Sandy
Kelso ES, 34651 SE KELSO ROAD 97009
　Mary Smith, prin.
_____

Hood View Junior Academy, P O BOX 128 97009

Brogan, Malheur Co.
Brogan SD 1
Sch. Sys. Enr. Code 1
Supt. – (—) 97903
ES 97903 – Pamela Hug, prin.

Brookings, Curry Co., Pop. Code 5
Brookings-Harbor SD 17
Sch. Sys. Enr. Code 4
Supt. – Jim Stuckey, P O BOX 640 97415
Azalea MS, 564 FERN ST 97415
　Jim Mercer, prin.
Kalmiopsis ES, P O BOX 640 97415
　Jim Phelps, prin.

Upper Chetco SD 23
Sch. Sys. Enr. Code 1
Supt. – (—)
　99603 N BANK CHETCO RVR RD 97415
Upper Chetco ES
　99603 N BANK CHETCO RVR RD 97415
　Peggyann Barrier, prin.
_____

Brookings SDA ES, 18881 CORNETT ROAD 97415

Brooks, Marion Co.
Brooks SD 31
Sch. Sys. Enr. Code 2
Supt. – Lavonne Bush
　9075 PUEBLO AVE NE 97305
ES, P O BOX 9216 97305 – Lavonne Bush, prin.

Parkersville SD 82
Sch. Sys. Enr. Code 1
Supt. – (—), 9496 WABASH DRIVE NE 97305
Parkersville ES, 9496 WABASH DR NE 97305
　Victor Barnick, prin.

Pioneer SD 13
Sch. Sys. Enr. Code 1
Supt. – (—), 10653 71ST AVE NE 97305
Pioneer ES, 10653 71ST AVE NE 97305
Nancy Baier, prin.

Brothers, Deschutes Co.
Brothers SD 15
Sch. Sys. Enr. Code 1
Supt. – (—) 97712
ES 97712 – (—), prin.

Brownsville, Linn Co., Pop. Code 4
Central Linn SD 552
Supt. – See Halsey
ES, RURAL ROUTE 01 BOX 107 97327
Wade Doerfler, prin.

Burns, Harney Co., Pop. Code 5
Andrews SD 29
Sch. Sys. Enr. Code 1
Supt. – (—), ANDREWS HCR BOX 5 97720
Andrews ES, ANDREWS STAR ROUTE 97720
(—), prin.

Double O SD 28
Supt. – See Princeton
Double O ES, P O BOX 953 97720
Eileen Gill, prin.

Harney County SD 1
Sch. Sys. Enr. Code 3
Supt. – Richard Adair
800 N FAIRVIEW AVE 97720
Lincoln JHS, 550 N COURT AVE 97720
Roy Reed, prin.
Filmore ES, 779 W FILMORE ST 97720
Ramona Revak, prin.
Slater ES, 800 N FAIRVIEW AVE 97720
Helen Patton, prin.

Butte Falls, Jackson Co., Pop. Code 2
Butte Falls SD 91
Sch. Sys. Enr. Code 2
Supt. – Harvey Boyle, P O BOX 167 97522
ES, P O BOX 197 97522 – Harvey Boyle, prin.

Camas Valley, Douglas Co., Pop. Code 2
Camas Valley SD 21J
Sch. Sys. Enr. Code 2
Supt. – Grayson Gerard, P O BOX 57 97416
ES, P O BOX 57 97416 – Grayson Gerard, prin.

Camp Sherman, Jefferson Co.
Black Butte SD 41
Sch. Sys. Enr. Code 1
Supt. – (—) 97730
Black Butte ES, P O BOX 150 97730
Toni Foster, prin.

Canby, Clackamas Co., Pop. Code 6
Canby SD 86
Sch. Sys. Enr. Code 4
Supt. – Milton Dennison, 117 NE 3RD AVE 97013
Ackerman JHS, 350 SE 13TH AVE 97013
Michael Zagyna, prin.
Eccles ES, 562 NW 5TH ST 97013
Norman Trotter, prin.
Knight MS, 501 N GRANT ST 97013
Dennis Cone, prin.
Philander Lee ES, 1110 S IVY ST 97013
Douglas Gingerich, prin.

Molalla SDA ES, 8950 S SCHNEIDER ROAD 97013

Cannon Beach, Clatsop Co., Pop. Code 4
Seaside SD 10
Supt. – See Seaside
ES, P O BOX 277 97110 – Nancy O'Donnell, prin.

Canyon City, Grant Co., Pop. Code 3
John Day SD 3
Supt. – See John Day
Izee ES, OZEE ROUTE 97820
Peggy Bedortha, prin.

Canyonville, Douglas Co., Pop. Code 4
South Umpqua SD 19
Supt. – See Myrtle Creek
ES, P O BOX 745 97417 – Frank Braudt, prin.

Carlton, Yamhill, Pop. Code 4
Carlton SD 11
Sch. Sys. Enr. Code 2
Supt. – Mark Hyder, P O BOX 338 97111
ES, P O BOX 338 97111 – Mark Hyder, prin.

Cascade Locks, Hood River Co., Pop. Code 3
Bonneville SD 46
Sch. Sys. Enr. Code 1
Supt. – Warren Linville, P O BOX 729 97014
Other Schools – See Bonneville

Hood River County SD
Supt. – See Hood River
ES, P O BOX 279 97014 – David Sears, prin.

Cave Junction, Josephine Co., Pop. Code 4
Josephine County Unit SD
Supt. – See Grants Pass
Byrne MS, 101 S JUNCTION AVE 97523
Kenneth Hoback, prin.
Evergreen ES, P O BOX 313 97523
John Simpson, prin.

Cave Junction SDA ES
4300 HOLLAND LOOP ROAD 97523
The Dome ES, 9367 TAKIMA ROAD 97523

Central Point, Jackson Co., Pop. Code 6
Central Point SD 6
Sch. Sys. Enr. Code 5
Supt. – Clarence Baker, 451 N 2ND ST 97502
ES, 450 S 4TH ST 97502 – Harrell Oxner, prin.
Jewett ES, 1001 MANZANITA ST 97502
Robert Dais, prin.
Richardson ES, 200 N PINE ST 97502
Kathy Tompkins, prin.
Sams Valley ES
14235 TABLE ROCK ROAD 97502
Lawrence Shearer, prin.
Other Schools – See Gold Hill

Central Assembly Christian School
310 N 10TH ST 97502

Charleston, Coos Co., Pop. Code 3
Coos Bay SD 9
Supt. – See Coos Bay
ES, SEVEN DEVILS ROAD 97420
Victoria Jenkins, prin.

Chiloquin, Klamath Co., Pop. Code 3
Klamath County SD
Supt. – See Klamath Falls
ES, P O BOX 375 97624 – Marjorie Wolf, prin.

Clackamas, Clackamas Co., Pop. Code 3
North Clackamas SD 12
Supt. – See Milwaukie
ES, 15301 SE 92ND AVE 97015
Roger Capps, prin.
Concord ES, 15301 SE 92ND AVE 97015
Jan O'Berg, prin.
Sunnyside ES, 13401 SE 132ND AVE 97015
Charles Hopman, prin.

Clatskanie, Columbia Co., Pop. Code 4
Columbia SD 5J
Supt. – See Westport
MS, P O BOX 188 97016 – W. Reinhart, prin.
ES, P O BOX 327 97016 – Dewey James, prin.
Quincy-Mayger ES
RURAL ROUTE 01 BOX 1148 97016
(—), prin.

Vernonia SD 47J
Supt. – See Vernonia
Mist ES, P O BOX 29 97016 – Sandi Wilson, prin.

Cloverdale, Tillamook Co., Pop. Code 2
Cloverdale SD 22
Sch. Sys. Enr. Code 2
Supt. – Gary Anderson 97112
Cloverdale MS, 36925 HWY 101 S 97112
Gary Anderson, prin.
ES, 36925 HIGHWAY 101 S 97112
Gary Anderson, prin.

Colton, Clackamas Co., Pop. Code 5
Colton SD 53
Sch. Sys. Enr. Code 3
Supt. – Chuck Vater, 31158 S WALL ST 97017
MS, 30205 S WALL ST 97017 – Barbara Ritt, prin.
ES, 30437 S GRAYS HILL ROAD 97017
Kenneth Manns, prin.

Columbia City, Columbia Co., Pop. Code 3
St. Helens SD 502
Supt. – See Saint Helens
ES, P O BOX 339 97018 – Richard Carlson, prin.

Condon, Gilliam Co., Pop. Code 3
Condon SD 25J
Sch. Sys. Enr. Code 2
Supt. – H. Burton, P O BOX 615 97823
ES, P O BOX 615 97823 – H. Burton, prin.

Coos Bay, Coos Co., Pop. Code 7
Coos Bay SD 9
Sch. Sys. Enr. Code 5
Supt. – Giles Parker, P O BOX 509 97420
Sunset MS, 1191 MICHIGAN AVE 97420
Thomas Jacobson, prin.
Blossom Gulch ES, 10TH & ANDERSON 97420
Suzanne Marchant, prin.
Bunker Hill ES, HIGHWAY 101 S 97420
Gary Smith, prin.
Madison ES, MADISON ST 97420
Chuck Howard, prin.
Milner Crest ES, 13TH & HEMLOCK 97420
Jeff Fagan, prin.
Other Schools – See Charleston, Eastside

Coquille, Coos Co., Pop. Code 5
Coquille SD 8
Sch. Sys. Enr. Code 4
Supt. – Jim Harris, 140 E 10TH ST 97423
Coquille Valley MS, 1115 N BAXTER ST 97423
Carl Wilson, prin.
Fairview ES, P O BOX 3010 97423
Archie Flood, prin.
Jefferson ES, 17TH & HEMLOCK STS 97423
Ronald Ramsey, prin.
Lincoln ES, 1366 N GOULD ST 97423
George Johnson, prin.

Corbett, Multnomah Co., Pop. Code 5
Corbett SD 39
Sch. Sys. Enr. Code 3
Supt. – Dale Nees
36004 E CROWN POINT HIGHWAY 97019
MS, 35800 E CROWN POINT HIGHWAY 97019
Larry McClellan, prin.
MS, 36115 E CROWN POINT HWY 97019
Fred Martin, prin.

Springdale ES
32405 E CROWN POINT HWY 97019
Fred Martin, prin.

Cornelius, Washington Co., Pop. Code 5
Forest Grove SD 15
Supt. – See Forest Grove
ES, P O BOX 546 97113 – Ray Haag, prin.
Echo Shaw ES, 914 S LINDEN ST 97113
Jack Beu, prin.

Cherry Grove Academy
RURAL ROUTE 04 BOX 138-A 97113
Emmaus Christian School, 860 N ADAIR ST 97113

Corvallis, Benton Co., Pop. Code 8
Corvallis SD 509J
Sch. Sys. Enr. Code 6
Supt. – Thomas D. Wogaman
1555 SW 35TH ST 97333
Cheldelin IS, 987 NE CONIFER BLVD 97330
(—), prin.
Highland View IS
1920 NW HIGHLAND DRIVE 97330
Holly Endersby, prin.
Western View IS, 1435 SW 35TH ST 97333
Margo Garton, prin.
Adams ES, 1615 SW 35TH ST 97333
Marie Melin, prin.
Fairplay ES, 3855 NE HIGHWAY 20 97330
Lois Rawers, prin.
Garfield ES, 1205 NW GARFIELD AVE 97330
Gloria Gibbs, prin.
Harding ES, 510 NW 31ST ST 97330
Irene Golden, prin.
Hoover ES, 3838 NW WALNUT BLVD 97330
Terry Vaughn, prin.
Inaval ES
GREENBERRY&BELLFOUNTAIN RDS 97330
Lynn Lahey, prin.
Jefferson ES, 1825 NW 27TH ST 97330
Montie Markham, prin.
Lincoln ES, 110 SE ALEXANDER AVE 97333
Dan Hays, prin.
Mt. View ES, 340 NE GRANGER AVE 97330
John Schaer, prin.
Wilson ES, 2701 NW SATINWOOD ST 97330
Bob Mittleider, prin.

Montessori Learning Center
625 NW 25TH ST 97330
Sundance ES, 2870 SW MORRIS 97333
Zion Lutheran School
2800 NW TYLER AVE 97330

Cottage Grove, Lane Co., Pop. Code 6
South Lane SD 45J3
Sch. Sys. Enr. Code 5
Supt. – Lane DuBose, P O BOX 218 97424
Bohemia ES, 721 STATE ROUTE ST 97424
Bruce Kelsh, prin.
Culp Creek-Dorena ES
37895 ROW RIVER ROAD 97424
Gerard Settelmeyer, prin.
Delight Valley ES
79980 DELIGHT VALLEY SCH RD 97424
(—), prin.
Harrison ES, 10TH AND HARRISON AVE 97424
Sue Wickizer, prin.
Latham ES, 32112 LATHAM ROAD 97424
Dave Browne, prin.
London ES, 72388 LONDON ROAD 97424
Dave Browne, prin.

Oak Park Christian School, 152 S M ST 97424

Cove, Union Co., Pop. Code 2
Cove SD 15
Sch. Sys. Enr. Code 2
Supt. – Gene Mills, P O BOX 68 97824
ES, P O BOX 68 97824 – Gene Mills, prin.

Crabtree, Linn Co.
Greater Albany SD 8J
Supt. – See Albany
ES, P O BOX 80 97335 – Martin Meyer, prin.

Crane, Harney Co.
Harney County SD 4
Sch. Sys. Enr. Code 1
Supt. – Henry Thew, P O BOX 828 97732
ES 97732 – Henry Thew, prin.

Crawfordsville, Linn Co.
Sweet Home SD 55
Supt. – See Sweet Home
ES 97336 – Rob Younger, prin.

Creswell, Lane Co., Pop. Code 4
Creswell SD 40
Sch. Sys. Enr. Code 4
Supt. – Dave Cellers, 182 S 2ND ST 97426
MS, 655 W OREGON AVE 97426
Dennis Biggerstaff, prin.
Creslane ES, 996 A ST #W 97426
Chalmers Blatch, prin.

Creswell Christian ES, P O BOX 217 97426

Culver, Jefferson Co., Pop. Code 3
Culver SD 4
Sch. Sys. Enr. Code 2
Supt. – John Cunnion, P O BOX 228 97734
ES, P O BOX 228 97734 – John Cunnion, prin.

Dallas, Polk Co., Pop. Code 6
Dallas SD 2
Sch. Sys. Enr. Code 4
Supt. – Gary Burton, 111 SW ASH ST 97338
LaCreole JHS, 701 SE LACREOLE DRIVE 97338
  John LaFountaine, prin.
Bridgeport ES, 17475 BRIDGEPORT ROAD 97338
  Richard Purkerson, prin.
Lyle ES, 185 SW LEVENS ST 97338
  Darrell Jones, prin.
Oakdale Heights ES, 1375 SW MAPLE ST 97338
  Dave Voves, prin.
Whitworth ES, 1151 SE MILLER AVE 97338
  Melvin McCutcheon, prin.
Other Schools – See Monmouth, Rickreall

Days Creek, Douglas Co., Pop. Code 2
Days Creek SD 15
Sch. Sys. Enr. Code 2
Supt. – Gerald Rust, P O BOX 10 97429
ES, P O BOX 10 97429 – Gerald Rust, prin.
Other Schools – See Tiller

Dayton, Yamhill Co., Pop. Code 4
Dayton SD 8
Sch. Sys. Enr. Code 3
Supt. – Steve Johnson, 526 FERRY ST 97114
ES, 526 FERRY ST 97114 – Robert Dittmer, prin.

Dayville, Grant Co., Pop. Code 2
Dayville SD 16J
Sch. Sys. Enr. Code 1
Supt. – Nancy Canon, P O BOX C 97825
ES, P O BOX C 97825 – Nancy Canon, prin.

Detroit, Marion Co., Pop. Code 2
Detroit SD 123J
Sch. Sys. Enr. Code 2
Supt. – Dennis Mills, P O BOX 500 97342
ES 97342 – Dennis Mills, prin.

Diamond, Harney Co.
Diamond SD 7
Sch. Sys. Enr. Code 1
Supt. – (—) 97722
ES 97722 – A. Rushton, prin.

Dillard, Douglas Co., Pop. Code 3
Winston-Dillard SD 116
Sch. Sys. Enr. Code 4
Supt. – John Rogers, P O BOX 288 97432
Lookingglass ES, P O BOX 288 97432
  Gary Frazier, prin.
McGovern ES, P O BOX 288 97432
  Emerson Hall, prin.
Tenmile ES, P O BOX 288 97432
  Guy Hankins, prin.
Other Schools – See Winston

Drain, Douglas Co., Pop. Code 4
North Douglas SD 22
Sch. Sys. Enr. Code 3
Supt. – Charles Jackson, P O BOX 428 97435
North Douglas ES, P O BOX 338 97435
  Dorothy Keechi, prin.

Drewsey, Harney Co.
Drewsey SD 13
Sch. Sys. Enr. Code 1
Supt. – (—), P O BOX 105 97904
ES 97904 – (—), prin.

Pine Creek SD 5
Sch. Sys. Enr. Code 1
Supt. – (—) 97904
Pine Creek ES 97904 – Kim Robinson, prin.

Dufur, Wasco Co., Pop. Code 3
Dufur SD 29
Sch. Sys. Enr. Code 2
Supt. – Lawrence Wolfgram, P O BOX 98 97021
ES, P O BOX 98 97021 – Gary Delvin, prin.

Dundee, Yamhill Co., Pop. Code 4
Newberg SD 29J
Supt. – See Newberg
ES 97115 – Larry Derry, prin.

Eagle Point, Jackson Co., Pop. Code 5
Eagle Point SD 9
Sch. Sys. Enr. Code 5
Supt. – Stephen Miller, P O BOX 548 97524
JHS, P O BOX 218 97524 – Jan Donnelly, prin.
Hale ES, P O BOX 197 97524
  Sam Chimento, prin.
Little Butte IS, P O BOX 549 97524
  Eleanor Mitchell, prin.
Other Schools – See Shady Cove, Trail, White City

Eastside, Coos Co., Pop. Code 4
Coos Bay SD 9
Supt. – See Coos Bay
Millicoma MS, 2ND AVE E 97420
  Wayne Young, prin.
ES, 936 D ST 97420 – Ann Ulum, prin.

Echo, Umatilla Co., Pop. Code 3
Echo SD 5
Sch. Sys. Enr. Code 2
Supt. – Jim Carlson, P O BOX 359 97826
ES, P O BOX 359 97826 – (—), prin.

Eddyville, Lincoln Co., Pop. Code 4
Lincoln County SD
Supt. – See Newport
ES 97343 – Ron LaBreche, prin.

Elgin, Union Co., Pop. Code 4
Elgin SD 23
Sch. Sys. Enr. Code 3
Supt. – Joy Delgado, P O BOX 68 97827
Mayfield ES, P O BOX 638 97827
  Marc Williamson, prin.

Elkton, Douglas Co., Pop. Code 2
Elkton SD 34
Sch. Sys. Enr. Code 2
Supt. – Bill Karwacki, P O BOX 390 97436
ES, P O BOX 440 97436 – Bill Karwacki, prin.

Elmira, Lane Co., Pop. Code 2
Fern Ridge SD 28J
Sch. Sys. Enr. Code 4
Supt. – Les Wolfe
  88834 TERRITORIAL ROAD 97437
Fern Ridge MS
  88831 TERRITORIAL ROAD 97437
  Donna Hein, prin.
ES, 88960 TERRITORIAL ROAD 97437
  Bonnie Swan, prin.
Other Schools – See Eugene, Noti, Veneta

Enterprise, Wallowa Co., Pop. Code 4
Enterprise SD 21
Sch. Sys. Enr. Code 3
Supt. – Larry Christman, P O BOX 520 97828
ES, P O BOX 520 97828 – Robert Eddy, prin.

Troy SD 54
Sch. Sys. Enr. Code 1
Supt. – (—), HCR 62 BOX 76 97828
Troy ES, HCR 62 BOX 76 97828
  Theodore Zeller, prin.

Estacada, Clackamas Co., Pop. Code 4
Estacada SD 108
Sch. Sys. Enr. Code 4
Supt. – Gail Perkins, P O BOX 519 97023
JHS, P O BOX 519 97023 – Steve Mauritz, prin.
Eagle Creek ES, P O BOX 519 97023
  (—), prin.
ES, 250 NE MAIN ST 97023 – Paula Stewart, prin.
River Mill ES, 850 N BROADWAY ST 97023
  (—), prin.

Eugene, Lane Co., Pop. Code 9
Bethel SD 52
Sch. Sys. Enr. Code 5
Supt. – Kent Hunsaker
  4640 BARGER DRIVE 97402
Cascade MS, 1525 ECHO HOLLOW ROAD 97402
  Steve Waddell, prin.
Shasta MS, 4656 BARGER DRIVE 97402
  Randy Harvey, prin.
Clear Lake ES, 4646 BARGER DRIVE 97402
  Mary Louise Noble, prin.
Danebo ES, 1265 CANDELIGHT DRIVE 97402
  Pamela Ellis, prin.
Fairfield ES, 3455 ROYAL AVE 97402
  Jim Winger, prin.
Irving ES, 3200 HYACINTH ST 97404
  Fred Merten, prin.
Malabon ES, 1380 TANEY ST 97402
  Lee Holden, prin.

Crow-Applegate-Lorane SD 66
Sch. Sys. Enr. Code 2
Supt. – R. Beebe
  85955 TERRITORIAL ROAD 97402
Crolane MS, 85955 TERRITORIAL ROAD 97402
  T. Thrower, prin.
Applegate ES, 85955 TERRITORIAL ROAD 97402
  Thal Thrower, prin.
Other Schools – See Lorane

Eugene SD 4J
Sch. Sys. Enr. Code 7
Supt. – Margaret Nichols
  200 N MONROE ST 97402
Jefferson MS, 1650 W 22ND AVE 97405
  Jeannine Bertrand, prin.
Kelly MS, 850 HOWARD AVE 97404
  Ted Calhoun, prin.
Kennedy MS, 2200 BAILEY HILL ROAD 97405
  Dick Hicks, prin.
Madison MS, 875 WILKES DRIVE 97404
  Cecil Kribs, prin.
Monroe MS, 2800 BAILEY LANE 97401
  Lynne George, prin.
Roosevelt MS, 680 E 24TH AVE 97405
  Jim Slemp, prin.
Spencer Butte MS, 500 E 43RD AVE 97405
  Jerry Henderson, prin.
Young MS, 2555 GILHAM ROAD 97401
  Evelyn Matthews, prin.
Adams ES, 950 W 22ND AVE 97405
  Nick Maskel, prin.
Awbrey Park ES, 158 SPRING CREEK DR 97404
  Tom Henry, prin.
Bailey Hill ES
  2295 FOUR OAKS GRANGE ROAD 97405
  Wally Bryant, prin.
Coburg ES, 91274 N COBURG ROAD 97401
  Cindy Stults, prin.
Crest Drive ES, 1155 CREST DRIVE 97405
  Sallie Walker, prin.
Edgewood ES, 577 E 46TH AVE 97405
  Kenar Charkoudian, prin.
Edison ES, 1328 E 22ND AVE 97403
  Karrin Emmert, prin.
Gilham ES, 3147 GILHAM ROAD 97401
  Tom Hochstatter, prin.

Harris ES, 1150 E 29TH AVE 97403
  Cliff Lind, prin.
Howard ES, 700 HOWARD AVE 97404
  Nancy Hunsdon, prin.
McCornack ES, 1968 BRITTANY ST 97405
  Margaret Johnson, prin.
Meadowlark ES, 1500 QUEENS WAY 97401
  Ernest Carbajal, prin.
Parker ES, 3875 KINCAID ST 97405
  Earl Harris, prin.
Patterson ES, 1510 W 15TH AVE 97402
  Virgil Erickson, prin.
River Road ES, 120 HILLIARD LANE 97404
  Roger Diddock, prin.
Santa Clara ES, 2685 RIER ROAD 97404
  Thomas Tomlinson, prin.
Spring Creek ES, 560 IRVINGTON DRIVE 97404
  Carolyn Hult, prin.
Twin Oaks ES, 85916 BAILEY HILL ROAD 97405
  Janice Jurisich, prin.
Washington ES, 3515 HARLOW ROAD 97401
  Dennis Arendt, prin.
Westmoreland ES, 1717 CITY VIEW ST 97402
  Gerald Keener, prin.
Whiteaker ES, 21 N GRAND ST 97402
  Paul Randall, prin.
Willagillespie ES
  1125 WILLAGILLESPIE ROAD 97401
  Amanda Seabloom, prin.
Willakenzie ES, 3057 WILLAKENZIE ROAD 97401
  Virginia Schwartzrock, prin.
Willard ES, 2855 LINCOLN ST 97405
  Arline DeFrank, prin.

Fern Ridge SD 28J
Supt. – See Elmira
Central ES, 87230 CENTRAL ROAD 97402
  Steve Tritten, prin.

Springfield SD 19
Supt. – See Springfield
Goshen ES, 34020 B ST 97405
  Dallas Lommen, prin.

Eugene Christian ES
  4500 W AMAZON DRIVE 97405
Eugene Montessori School
  2255 OAKMONT WAY 97401
Eugene Waldorf ES, 1350 MCLEAN 97405
O'Hara Catholic ES, 715 W 18TH AVE 97402
Paideia ES, 45 RUSTIC 97401
St. Paul Catholic School, 1201 SATRE ST 97401
Williamette Christian School
  P O BOX 22108 97402

Fairview, Multnomah Co., Pop. Code 4
Reynolds SD 7
Supt. – See Troutdale
ES, SECOND & MAIN STS 97024
  David Reynolds, prin.

Falls City, Polk Co., Pop. Code 3
Falls City SD 57
Sch. Sys. Enr. Code 2
Supt. – Eugene Marcy
  81 E NORTH MAIN ST 97344
ES, 177 PROSPECT AVE 97344
  Patricia Sowby, prin.

Fields, Harney Co.
Fields Trout Creek SD 33
Sch. Sys. Enr. Code 1
Supt. – (—) 97710
ES 97710 – Tim Buchman, prin.

Finn Rock, Lane Co., Pop. Code 1
McKenzie SD 68
Sch. Sys. Enr. Code 2
Supt. – Edward Curtis
  51187 BLUE RIVER DRIVE 97488
McKenzie River ES
  51187 BLUE RIVER DRIVE 97488
  Anne Raftree, prin.

Florence, Lane Co., Pop. Code 5
Siuslaw SD 97J
Sch. Sys. Enr. Code 4
Supt. – Glenn Butler
  RURAL ROUTE 02 BOX 4 97439
Siuslaw MS 97439 – J. Browne, prin.
Rhododendron MS 97439 – Duane Wright, prin.
Siuslaw ES 97439 – Emmett Devereux, prin.

Forest Grove, Washington Co., Pop. Code 7
Forest Grove SD 15
Sch. Sys. Enr. Code 5
Supt. – Gary Lucas, 1343 PACIFIC AVE 97116
Armstrong MS, 1777 MOUNT VIEW LANE 97116
  Mike Totman, prin.
McCall MS, 1341 PACIFIC AVE 97116
  Georgia Deetz, prin.
Central ES, 1728 MAIN ST 97116
  Robert Gales, prin.
Clark ES, 2516 B ST 97116
  Thelma Rueppell, prin.
Dilley ES, RURAL ROUTE 01 BOX 39 97116
  Jack Cadd, prin.
Gale ES, 3130 18TH AVE 97116
  Roger Moore, prin.
Other Schools – See Cornelius, Gales Creek

Country School
  RURAL ROUTE 03 BOX 95 97116
Visitation ES, RURAL ROUTE 02 BOX 221 97116

Fort Rock, Lake Co.
North Lake SD 14
Supt. – See Silver Lake
PS, CABIN LAKE ROAD 97735
Mike Costello, prin.

Fossil, Wheeler Co., Pop. Code 3
Fossil SD 21
Sch. Sys. Enr. Code 2
Supt. – Daniel Barker, P O BOX 206 97830
ES, P O BOX 287 97830 – Daniel Barker, prin.

Foster, Linn Co.
Sweet Home SD 55
Supt. – See Sweet Home
ES, P O BOX 747 97345 – James Riggs, prin.

Frenchglen, Harney Co.
Frenchglen SD 16
Sch. Sys. Enr. Code 1
Supt. – Deby Hammond 97736
ES 97736 – L. Hurley, prin.

Gales Creek, Washington Co.
Forest Grove SD 15
Supt. – See Forest Grove
ES 97117 – Mike Smith, prin.

Gardiner, Douglas Co., Pop. Code 2
Reedsport SD 105
Supt. – See Reedsport
Jewett MS, P O BOX 10 97441
Rodney Mebius, prin.

Garibaldi, Tillamook Co., Pop. Code 3
Neah-Kah-Nie SD 56
Supt. – See Rockaway
ES, P O BOX 317 97118 – Maynard Frank, prin.

Gaston, Washington Co., Pop. Code 2
Gaston SD 511J
Sch. Sys. Enr. Code 3
Supt. – Fred Loomis, P O BOX 68 97119
JHS 97119 – Fred Loomis, prin.
ES 97119 – David Wells, prin.

Laurelwood ES, RURAL ROUTE 02 97119

Gates, Marion Co., Pop. Code 2
Mill City-Gates SD 129J
Supt. – See Mill City
ES, P O BOX 457 97346 – (–), prin.

Gearhart, Clatsop Co., Pop. Code 3
Seaside SD 10
Supt. – See Seaside
ES, 180 S LINCOLN ST 97138 – Jim White, prin.

Gervais, Marion Co., Pop. Code 4
Gervais SD 76
Sch. Sys. Enr. Code 2
Supt. – David Nuss, P O BOX 176 97026
ES, P O BOX 176 97026 – David James, prin.

Sacred Heart ES, 515 N 7TH AVE 97383

Gilchrist, Klamath Co., Pop. Code 2
Klamath County SD
Supt. – See Klamath Falls
ES, P O BOX 668 97737 – Duane Barstad, prin.

Gladstone, Clackamas Co., Pop. Code 6
Gladstone SD 115
Sch. Sys. Enr. Code 4
Supt. – Joe Ghaffari, P O BOX 165 97027
Kraxberger MS, 1777 WEBSTER ROAD 97027
Richard Thompson, prin.
ES, 645 CHICAGO AVE 97027 – John Wetten, prin.

Serendipity Academy, P O BOX 156 97027
Rivergate SDA ES, 1505 OHLSON ROAD 97027

Glendale, Douglas Co., Pop. Code 3
Glendale SD 77
Sch. Sys. Enr. Code 3
Supt. – Donald Currey, P O BOX E 97442
ES, P O BOX E 97442 – Donald Currey, prin.

Glide, Douglas Co., Pop. Code 1
Glide SD 12
Sch. Sys. Enr. Code 3
Supt. – Scott Mutchie, 301 GLIDE LOOP DR 97443
JHS 97443 – Gordon Duvaul, prin.
ES 97443 – Stan Johns, prin.
Other Schools – See Idleyld Park, Roseburg

Gold Beach, Curry Co., Pop. Code 4
Gold Beach SD 3
Sch. Sys. Enr. Code 2
Supt. – Joe Taber, 520 LEITH ROAD 97444
Riley Creek MS, 520 LEITH ROAD 97444
Lawrence Doyle, prin.
PS, 120 S ELLENSBURG AVE 97444
Joe Taber, prin.

Gold Hill, Jackson Co., Pop. Code 3
Central Point SD 6
Supt. – See Central Point
Hanby JHS, 806 6TH AVE 97525
Mary Barker, prin.
Patrick ES, 1500 2ND AVE 97525
Bob Bowers, prin.

Grand Ronde, Polk Co.
Willamina SD 30J
Supt. – See Willamina
ES, P O BOX 7 97347 – Don Keller, prin.

Grants Pass, Josephine Co., Pop. Code 7
Grants Pass SD 7
Sch. Sys. Enr. Code 5
Supt. – Dale Smith, 223 S E M ST 97526
North MS, 1725 N W HIGHLAND AVE 97526
Jack Woodhead, prin.
South MS, 350 W HARBECK ROAD 97527
Larry Moynihan, prin.
Allen Dale ES, 2320 WILLIAMS HIGHWAY 97527
Neil Murphy, prin.
Highland ES, 1845 NW HIGHLAND AVE 97526
Peggy Rosendahl, prin.
Lincoln ES, 1132 NE 10TH ST 97526
Larry Thornton, prin.
Redwood ES, 1385 DOWELL ROAD 97527
Forrest Bell, prin.
Riverside ES, 1200 SE HARVEY DRIVE 97526
Armand Olson, prin.

Josephine County Unit SD
Sch. Sys. Enr. Code 6
Supt. – John Mayfield, 706 NW A ST 97526
Fleming MS, 6001 MONUMENT DRIVE 97526
Jerry Dawson, prin.
Lincoln Savage MS
8551 NEW HOPE ROAD 97527
Craig Binkley, prin.
Ft. Vannoy ES, 5250 UPPER RIVER ROAD 97526
Midge Renton, prin.
Fruitdale ES, 1560 HAMILTON LANE 97527
Gail Jones, prin.
Jerome Prairie ES, 2555 WALNUT AVE 97527
Vince Matt, prin.
Madrona ES, 520 DETRICK DRIVE 97527
Jim Elliott, prin.
Manzanita ES, 310 SAN FRANCISCO AVE 97526
Janice Olson, prin.
Other Schools – See Cave Junction, Selma, Williams, Wolf Creek

Grants Pass SDA Junior Academy
1121 NE 7TH ST 97526
Lifeskills Academy, 516 STEWART ROAD 97526

Grass Valley, Sherman Co., Pop. Code 2
South Sherman SD 17J
Sch. Sys. Enr. Code 2
Supt. – Latrelle Smoot, P O BOX 68 97029
South Sherman ES, P O BOX 68 97029
Latrelle Smoot, prin.

Gresham, Multnomah Co., Pop. Code 8
Gresham SD 4
Sch. Sys. Enr. Code 5
Supt. – James Jenkins, P O BOX 655 97030
McCarty MS, 1400 SE 5TH ST 97030
Tom Markley, prin.
Russell MS
3625 E POWELL VALLEY ROAD 97080
wally Scherler, prin.
East Gresham ES, 900 SE 5TH ST 97080
Jay Greenwood, prin.
Hall ES, 2505 NE 23RD ST 97030
Glory Yankauskas, prin.
Highland ES, 295 NE 24TH ST 97030
Jack Barger, prin.
Hollydale ES, 505 SW BIRDSDALE AVE 97030
Jan Baxter, prin.
North Gresham ES, 1001 SE 217TH AVE 97030
Ronald Clawson, prin.
Powell Valley ES
4825 E POWELL VALLEY ROAD 97080
Annie Painter, prin.
West Gresham ES, 330 W POWELL BLVD 97030
John Stanley, prin.

Orient SD 6J
Sch. Sys. Enr. Code 3
Supt. – James Buck
29805 SE ORIENT DRIVE 97030
East Orient MS, 7431 SE 302ND AVE 97030
Tom Greene, prin.
West Orient ES, 29805 SE ORIENT DRIVE 97080
Chuck Tomac, prin.

New Country School
2229 E BURNSIDE ST #70 97080
Mt. Hood Christian School
3445 SE HILLYARD ROAD 97080
Portland Adventist ES, 3990 NW 1ST ST 97030

Halfway, Baker Co., Pop. Code 2
Pine Eagle SD 61
Sch. Sys. Enr. Code 2
Supt. – Michael Keown, P O BOX 677 97834
ES, P O BOX 677 97834 – Andrew Koopmen, prin.
Other Schools – See Richland

Halsey, Linn Co., Pop. Code 3
Central Linn SD 552
Sch. Sys. Enr. Code 3
Supt. – Francis Dummer
32433 HIGHWAY 228 97348
Central Linn MS, P O BOX 258 97348
Tom Endersby, prin.
Other Schools – See Brownsville, Shedd

Harper, Malheur Co.
Harper SD 66
Sch. Sys. Enr. Code 1
Supt. – Jim Payne, P O BOX 800 97906
ES 97906 – Jim Payne, prin.

Harrisburg, Linn Co., Pop. Code 4
Harris SD 46
Sch. Sys. Enr. Code 1
Supt. – (—), 31414 HARRIS DRIVE 97446
Harris ES, 31414 HARRIS DRIVE 97446
Mary Strutz, prin.

Harrisburg SD 42J
Sch. Sys. Enr. Code 2
Supt. – Doss Bradford, P O BOX 247 97446
ES, P O BOX 247 97446 – Doss Bradford, prin.

Wyatt SD 63J
Sch. Sys. Enr. Code 1
Supt. – (—), 21211 COBURG ROAD 97446
Wyatt ES, 21211 COBURG ROAD 97446
Randall Crowson, prin.

Hebo, Tillamook Co.
Hebo SD 13J
Sch. Sys. Enr. Code 1
Supt. – Michael Walsh, P O BOX 259 97122
ES, P O BOX 259 97122 – Michael Walsh, prin.

Helix, Umatilla Co., Pop. Code 2
Helix SD 1
Sch. Sys. Enr. Code 2
Supt. – Jim Nerdin, P O BOX 398 97835
ES, P O BOX 398 97835 – Jim Nerdin, prin.

Heppner, Morrow Co., Pop. Code 4
Morrow SD 1
Supt. – See Lexington
ES, P O BOX 367 97836 – Donald Cole, prin.

Hermiston, Umatilla Co., Pop. Code 6
Hermiston SD 8
Sch. Sys. Enr. Code 5
Supt. – Al Meunier, 341 NE 3RD ST 97838
Larive JHS, 199 E RIDGEWAY AVE 97838
Shannon Gorham, prin.
Highland Hills ES, 450 SE 10TH ST 97838
Martin Neyman, prin.
Rocky Heights ES, 650 W STANDARD AVE 97838
James Bates, prin.
Sunset ES, 300 E CATHERINE AVE 97838
Philip Starkey, prin.
West Park ES, 555 SW 7TH ST 97838
Evelyn Huston, prin.

Hillsboro, Washington Co., Pop. Code 8
Farmington View SD 58J
Sch. Sys. Enr. Code 2
Supt. – Marilyn McGlasson
RURAL ROUTE 02 BOX 100 97123
Farmington View ES
RURAL ROUTE 02 BOX 100 97123
Marilyn McGlasson, prin.

Groner SD 39
Sch. Sys. Enr. Code 2
Supt. – Therman Striplin
RURAL ROUTE 06 BOX 300 97123
Groner ES, RURAL ROUTE 06 BOX 300 97123
Therman Striplin, prin.

Hillsboro SD 7
Sch. Sys. Enr. Code 5
Supt. – Roy Ottley, 215 SE 6TH AVE 97123
Boscow ES, 452 NE 3RD AVE 97124
Ed Bettencourt, prin.
Brookwood ES, 3960 SE CEDAR ST 97123
Carole Viebrock, prin.
Eastwood ES, 2100 NE LINCOLN ST 97124
Roger Close, prin.
Henry ES, 1060 SE 24TH AVE 97123
Analyne Flanagan, prin.
Hill ES, 440 E OAK ST 97123
Walt Thomas, prin.
McKinney ES, 535 NW DARNIELLE DRIVE 97124
Kenneth Rupp, prin.
Minter Bridge ES
1750 SE JACQUELIN DRIVE 97123
Crystal Dipaola, prin.
Mooberry ES, 1230 NE 10TH AVE 97124
Jean Bomber, prin.

Reedville SD 29
Sch. Sys. Enr. Code 4
Supt. – David Gillespie
2425 SW 219TH AVE 97123
Ladd Acres ES, 2425 SW 219TH AVE 97123
Allen Huggett, prin.
Witch Hazel ES
4995 SE WITCH HAZEL ROAD 97123
Jim Biller, prin.
Other Schools – See Aloha

West Union SD 1
Sch. Sys. Enr. Code 3
Supt. – Cliff Tetreault
RURAL ROUTE 05 BOX 230 97124
West Union ES
RURAL ROUTE 05 BOX 230 97124
Roy Nickerson, prin.
Other Schools – See Portland

St. Matthew ES, 221 SE WALNUT ST 97123
Sylvan Learning Center, 230 NE 2ND AVE 97124

Hines, Harney Co., Pop. Code 4
Hines SD 30
Sch. Sys. Enr. Code 2
Supt. – Ken Blackburn, P O BOX 38 97738
ES, P O BOX 38 97738 – Ken Blackburn, prin.

Hood River, Hood River Co., Pop. Code 5
Hood River County SD
Sch. Sys. Enr. Code 5
Supt. – James Carnes, P O BOX 920 97031
MS, 1601 MAY AVE 97031 – Jack Bimrose, prin.
Wy'East MS, 3000 WY'EAST ROAD 97031
  Betty Shalhope, prin.
May Street ES, 911 MAY AVE 97031
  James Sims, prin.
Pine Grove ES, 2405 EASTSIDE ROAD 97031
  Douglas Mahurin, prin.
Westside ES, 36895 BELMONT DRIVE 97031
  Pat Evenson-Brady, prin.
Other Schools – See Cascade Locks, Odell, Parkdale

Hubbard, Marion Co., Pop. Code 4
Ninety-One SD 91
Sch. Sys. Enr. Code 2
Supt. – Floyd Lapp
  5811 WHISKEY HILL ROAD NE 97032
Ninety-one ES
  5811 WHISKEY HILL ROAD NE 97032
  Ronald Camp, prin.

Huntington, Baker Co., Pop. Code 3
Huntington SD 16J
Sch. Sys. Enr. Code 2
Supt. – Mel Munn 97907
ES 97907 – (—), prin.

Idleyld Park, Douglas Co.
Glide SD 12
Supt. – See Glide
Toketee Falls ES 97447 – Martin Hilgers, prin.

Imbler, Union Co., Pop. Code 2
Imbler SD 11
Sch. Sys. Enr. Code 2
Supt. – Nick Eddy, P O BOX 164 97841
ES, P O BOX 164 97841 – Nick Eddy, prin.

Imnaha, Wallowa Co.
Joseph SD 6
Supt. – See Joseph
ES, P O BOX W 97842 – Char Williams, prin.

Independence, Polk Co., Pop. Code 5
Central SD 13J
Sch. Sys. Enr. Code 4
Supt. – John Dracon, 1610 MONMOUTH ST 97351
Talmadge MS, 510 16TH ST 97351
  Richard Hornaday, prin.
Hill ES, 750 5TH ST 97351
  Glenn Brostrom, prin.
ES, 150 4TH ST 97351 – Laticia Antonson, prin.
Other Schools – See Monmouth, Rickreall

Ione, Morrow Co., Pop. Code 2
Morrow SD 1
Supt. – See Lexington
ES, P O BOX 167 97843 – Dick Allen, prin.

Irrigon, Morrow Co., Pop. Code 3
Morrow SD 1
Supt. – See Lexington
Columbia JHS, P O BOX K 97844
  Vic Marchek, prin.
Houghton ES, P O BOX B 97844
  Michael Tolar, prin.

Jacksonville, Jackson Co., Pop. Code 4
Medford SD 549
Supt. – See Medford
ES, P O BOX 9 97530 – Charles Lockridge, prin.
Ruch ES, 156 UPPER APPLEGATE ROAD 97530
  Joani Bristol, prin.

Jefferson, Marion Co., Pop. Code 4
Jefferson SD 14J
Sch. Sys. Enr. Code 3
Supt. – Glenn Dorn, 596 N 3RD ST 97352
MS, 1334 N 2ND ST 97352 – Jim Moskal, prin.
ES, 615 N 2ND ST 97352 – J. Garza, prin.

John Day, Grant Co., Pop. Code 4
John Day SD 3
Sch. Sys. Enr. Code 3
Supt. – Dean Nodine, P O BOX 537 97845
JHS, 116 NW BRIDGE ST 97845
  Patrick Echanis, prin.
Humbolt ES, P O BOX 545 97845
  Lester Still, prin.
Other Schools – See Canyon City, Seneca

Jordan Valley, Malheur Co., Pop. Code 2
Jordan Valley SD 3
Sch. Sys. Enr. Code 2
Supt. – (—) 97910
ES 97910 – Alberta Shook, prin.

Joseph, Wallowa Co., Pop. Code 3
Joseph SD 6
Sch. Sys. Enr. Code 2
Supt. – Mike McCulloch, P O BOX W 97846
JHS, P O BOX W 97846
  William McCadden, prin.
ES, P O BOX W 97846 – Mike McCulloch, prin.
Other Schools – See Imnaha

Junction City, Lane Co., Pop. Code 5
Junction City SD 69
Sch. Sys. Enr. Code 4
Supt. – Ivan Launstein, P O BOX 408 97448
Oaklea MS, 1515 ROSE ST 97448
  Sara Jane Bates, prin.
Laurel ES, 1401 LAUREL ST 97448
  John Davies, prin.

Territorial ES, 1401 LAUREL ST 97448
  Mary Jo Simone, prin.

Christ's Center, 530 W 7TH AVE 97448

Juntura, Malheur Co.
Juntura SD 12
Sch. Sys. Enr. Code 1
Supt. – (—) 97911
ES 97911 – Tom White, prin.

Keno, Klamath Co.
Klamath County SD
Supt. – See Klamath Falls
ES, P O BOX 187 97627 – Pete Whitehead, prin.

Klamath Falls, Klamath Co., Pop. Code 7
Klamath County SD
Sch. Sys. Enr. Code 6
Supt. – Marvin Evans
  2450 SUMMERS LANE 97603
Brixner JHS, 4272 HOMEDALE ROAD 97603
  Wayne Johannes, prin.
Henley JHS, 7925 HIGHWAY 39 97603
  Leonard Harrington, prin.
Fairhaven ES, RURAL ROUTE 03 BOX 223 97601
  Wayne Snoozy, prin.
Ferguson ES, 2901 HOMEDALE ROAD 97603
  Douglas Woods, prin.
Henley ES, 8205 HIGHWAY 39 97603
  Harold Shimek, prin.
Peterson ES, 4856 CLINTON AVE 97603
  Gary Wells, prin.
Shasta ES, 1951 MADISON ST 97603
  Arthur Lapsley, prin.
Stearns ES, 3641 CREST ST 97603
  George Hanson, prin.
Other Schools – See Bly, Bonanza, Chiloquin,
  Gilchrist, Keno, Malin, Merrill

Klamath Falls SD 1
Sch. Sys. Enr. Code 4
Supt. – E. Ferguson, 475 S ALAMEDA AVE 97603
Ponderosa JHS, 2554 MAIN ST 97601
  Kenneth Womer, prin.
Conger ES, CALIFORNIA AVE & DELTA ST 97601
  Barbara Lund, prin.
Fairview ES, 1017 DONALD ST 97601
  Galen Mann, prin.
Mills ES, 520 E MAIN 97601 – Leo Olsen, prin.
Pelican ES, 501 MCLEAN ST 97601
  Wayne Johannes, prin.
Riverside ES, 707 CYPRESS AVE 97601
  Brant Baldini, prin.
Roosevelt ES, 1125 N ELDORADO AVE 97601
  Miriam Lindgren, prin.

Klamath Christian Academy
  235 S LAGUNA ST 97601
Sacred Heart HS, 429 N 8TH ST 97601

Lafayette, Yamhill Co., Pop. Code 4
Mc Minnville SD 40
Supt. – See Mc Minnville
Wascher ES, P O BOX 788 97127
  Mary Ringer, prin.

La Grande, Union Co., Pop. Code 7
La Grande SD 1
Sch. Sys. Enr. Code 5
Supt. – Richard Prather, 1208 4TH ST 97850
MS, 1108 4TH ST 97850 – James Thompson, prin.
Ackerman ES, 8TH ST & "J" AVE 97850
  Ed Morgan, prin.
Central ES, 402 K AVE 97850
  Ramon Westenskow, prin.
Greenwood ES, 2300 N SPRUCE ST 97850
  Judy Peterson, prin.
Island City ES
  RURAL ROUTE 04 BOX 4194 97850
  Pasco Arritola, prin.
Riveria ES, 2607 2ND ST 97850
  Larry Glaze, prin.
Willow ES, 1305 WILLOW ST 97850
  Larry Glaze, prin.

Lake Oswego, Clackamas Co., Pop. Code 7
Lake Oswego SD 7J
Sch. Sys. Enr. Code 6
Supt. – William Kurach, P O BOX 70 97034
JHS, 2500 COUNTRY CLUB ROAD 97034
  Rudolph Mundy, prin.
Waluga JHS, 4700 JEAN ROAD 97034
  Charles Actor, prin.
Bryant ES, 4750 JEAN ROAD 97035
  Jan Burgess, prin.
Forest Hills ES, 1133 ANDREWS ROAD 97034
  William Johnson, prin.
Hallinan ES, 16800 HAWTHORNE CT 97034
  William Morris, prin.
Lake Grove ES
  15777 BOONES FERRY ROAD 97035
  Weldon Starkey, prin.
River Grove ES, 5850 MCEWAN ROAD 97035
  Russell Pearce, prin.
Uplands ES, 2055 WEMBLEY PARK ROAD 97034
  Kathleen McCarney, prin.
Westridge ES, 3400 ROYCE WAY 97034
  Jean Fairbairn, prin.

Bethlehem Christian School
  1500 GREENTREE AVE 97034
Our Lady of the Lake School, 7165 A AVE 97034

Lakeview, Lake Co., Pop. Code 5
Lake County SD 5
Sch. Sys. Enr. Code 1
Supt. – (—), HCR 60 BOX 2650 97630
Union ES, HCR 60, BOX 2650 97630
  Ralph Paull, prin.

Lake County SD 7
Sch. Sys. Enr. Code 3
Supt. – Howard Ottman, P O BOX 1069 97630
Daly MS, 220 S H ST 97630
  Gerald Prickett, prin.
Fremont/Hay ES, S I ST 97630
  Jerry Owen, prin.

La Pine, Deschutes Co.
Bend Administrative SD 1
Supt. – See Bend
ES, P O BOX 305 97739 – Ellen Youngbluth, prin.

Lebanon, Linn Co., Pop. Code 7
Crowfoot SD 89
Sch. Sys. Enr. Code 3
Supt. – Bob Nelson, P O BOX 127 97355
Seven Oak MS, P O BOX 127 97355
  Robert Nelson, prin.
Crowfoot MS, 410 CROWFOOT ROAD 97355
  Wallace Clausen, prin.
Waterloo ES, 8 STAR(WATERLOO) 97355
  Judie Rhoads, prin.

Gore SD 81
Sch. Sys. Enr. Code 1
Supt. – Walt Blomberg, 37180 GORE DRIVE 97355
Gore ES, 37180 GORE DRIVE 97355
  Walt Blomberg, prin.

Hamilton Creek SD 33
Sch. Sys. Enr. Code 2
Supt. – David Odegard
  32135 BERLIN ROAD 97355
Hamilton Creek ES, 32135 BERLIN ROAD 97355
  David Odegard, prin.

Lacomb SD 73
Sch. Sys. Enr. Code 2
Supt. – Eldon Wortman
  34110 EAST LACOMB ROAD 97355
Lacomb ES, 34110 EAST LACOMB ROAD E 97355
  Eldon Wortman, prin.

Lebanon SD 16
Sch. Sys. Enr. Code 4
Supt. – William Lane, P O BOX 518 97355
MS, 60 MAIN ST 97355 – Tom Leonard, prin.
Cascades ES, 7TH ST & AIRPORT ROAD 97355
  Phil Atkinson, prin.
Green Acres ES, 10TH & SHERMAN STS 97355
  Judy Isaacson, prin.
Queen Anne ES, 142 E ELMORE ST 97355
  Ron Nelson, prin.

Sand Ridge SD 30
Sch. Sys. Enr. Code 1
Supt. – (—), 35935 SAND RIDGE ROAD 97355
Sand Ridge ES, 35935 ROCK HILL DRIVE 97355
  Phil Jackson, prin.

Sodaville SD 13
Sch. Sys. Enr. Code 1
Supt. – Patrick Cariati
  30581 SODAVILLE MT HOME RD 97355
Sodaville ES
  30581 SODAVILLE-MTN HOME RD 97355
  Patrick Cariati, prin.

Tennessee SD 102
Sch. Sys. Enr. Code 1
Supt. – Dan Hundley
  37575 TENNESSEE SCHOOL DR 97355
Tennessee ES
  37575 TENNESSEE SCHOOL DR 97355
  Dan Hundley, prin.

Lexington, Morrow Co., Pop. Code 2
Morrow SD 1
Sch. Sys. Enr. Code 4
Supt. – Doyle McCaslin, P O BOX 368 97839
Other Schools – See Boardman, Heppner, Ione, Irrigon

Lincoln City, Lincoln Co., Pop. Code 6
Lincoln County SD
Supt. – See Newport
Delake ES, 540 N HWY 101 97367
  Warren Kenton, prin.
Oceanlake MS, 2420 N 22ND ST 97367
  Robert Andersen, prin.
Taft ES, 1545 SE 50TH 97367 – Tom Correia, prin.

Long Creek, Grant Co., Pop. Code 2
Long Creek SD 17
Sch. Sys. Enr. Code 2
Supt. – Carroll Aebi, P O BOX 546 97856
ES, P O BOX 546 97856 – Carroll Aebi, prin.

Lorane, Lane Co.
Crow-Applegate-Lorane SD 66
Supt. – See Eugene
ES, 80304 OLD LORANE ROAD 97451
  Richard Beebe, prin.

Lowell, Lane Co., Pop. Code 3
Lowell SD 71
Sch. Sys. Enr. Code 2
Supt. – Ronald Johnson, 65 S PIONEER ST 97452
Lundy ES, 45 S MOSS ST 97452
  Ron Johnson, prin.

Lyons, Linn Co., Pop. Code 3
Mari-Linn SD 29J
Sch. Sys. Enr. Code 2
Supt. – Jan Miller
  RURAL ROUTE 01 BOX 278 97358
Mari-Linn ES, RURAL ROUTE 01 BOX 278 97358
  Jan Miller, prin.

Mc Minnville, Yamhill Co., Pop. Code 7
Mc Minnville SD 40
Sch. Sys. Enr. Code 5
Supt. – Michael Brott, 1500 N BAKER ST 97128
MS, 1715 E 19TH ST 97128 – Leon Mayer, prin.
Adams ES, 13TH & COWLS STS 97128
  Gary Williams, prin.
Columbus ES, 600 S BAKER ST 97128
  Bruce Waltz, prin.
Cook ES, LAFAYETTE AVE 97128
  Marie Bettiol, prin.
Memorial ES, 501 W 14TH ST 97128
  Colin Cameron, prin.
Newby ES, 1125 W 2ND ST 97128
  Laurel Adams, prin.
Other Schools – See Lafayette

St. James ES, 206 N KIRBY ST 97128

Madras, Jefferson Co., Pop. Code 4
Jefferson SD 509J
Sch. Sys. Enr. Code 4
Supt. – Darrell Wright, 1355 BUFF ST 97741
JHS, 655 4TH ST 97741 – Stanley Pine, prin.
Buff MS, 1301 BUFF ST 97741
  Suzanne Harrison, prin.
ES, 408 10TH ST 97741 – Glenn Miller, prin.
Metolius ES, 420 BUTTE AVE 97741
  Keith Johnson, prin.
Other Schools – See Warm Springs

Malin, Klamath Co., Pop. Code 3
Klamath County SD
Supt. – See Klamath Falls
ES, P O BOX 25 97632 – David Davis, prin.

Manzanita, Tillamook Co., Pop. Code 2

Whitmore School, P O BOX 353 97130

Mapleton, Lane Co., Pop. Code 3
Mapleton SD 32
Sch. Sys. Enr. Code 2
Supt. – John Campbell, P O BOX 388 97453
ES, P O BOX 97 97453 – (—), prin.

Marcola, Lane Co., Pop. Code 2
Marcola Sd 79J
Sch. Sys. Enr. Code 2
Supt. – Don Hopkins 97454
ES 97454 – Rick Swan, prin.

Marion, Marion Co.
Marion SD 20
Sch. Sys. Enr. Code 1
Supt. – James Briles, P O BOX 268 97359
ES, P O BOX 268 97359 – James Briles, prin.

Maupin, Wasco Co., Pop. Code 2
Maupin SD 84
Sch. Sys. Enr. Code 2
Supt. – Russell Snodgrass, P O BOX 346 97037
ES, P O BOX 346 97037 – Russell Snodgrass, prin.

Medford, Jackson Co., Pop. Code 8
Medford SD 549
Sch. Sys. Enr. Code 6
Supt. – Steve Wisely, 500 MONROE ST 97501
Hedrick JHS, 1501 E JACKSON ST 97504
  Carolyn Hayes, prin.
McLoughlin JHS, 320 W 2ND ST 97501
  Cliff Gibson, prin.
Griffin Creek ES
  2430 GRIFFIN CREEK ROAD 97501
  David Jenkins, prin.
Hoover ES, 2323 SISKIYOU BLVD 97504
  Ed Nicholson, prin.
Howard ES, 286 MACE ROAD 97501
  Richard Stebbins, prin.
Jackson ES, 630 W JACKSON ST 97501
  Phillip Meager, prin.
Jefferson ES, 333 HOLMES AVE 97501
  Randy Gravon, prin.
Kennedy ES, 2860 N KEENE WAY DRIVE 97504
  Robert Hartwig, prin.
Lone Pine, 3158 LONE PINE ROAD 97504
  Robert Goerke, prin.
Oak Grove ES
  2838 JACKSONVILLE HIGHWAY 97501
  Jae Johnson, prin.
Roosevelt ES, 112 LINDLEY ST 97504
  William Klenke, prin.
Washington ES, 610 S PEACH ST 97501
  Stephanie Johnson, prin.
Wilson ES, 1400 JOHNSON ST 97504
  Lois Rosmarin, prin.
Other Schools – See Jacksonville

Phoenix-Talent SD 4
Supt. – See Phoenix
Orchard Hill ES, 1011 LA LOMA DRIVE 97504
  Tim Mobley, prin.

Grace Christian ES
  649 CRATER LAKE AVE 97504
Rogue River Junior Academy
  3675 S STAGE ROAD 97501
Sacred Heart ES, 431 S IVY ST 97501

Mehama, Linn Co.
Stayton SD 77J
Supt. – See Stayton
ES 97384 – Carole Twede, prin.

Merrill, Klamath Co., Pop. Code 3
Klamath County SD
Supt. – See Klamath Falls
ES, P O BOX 468 97633 – David Davis, prin.

Mill City, Linn Co., Pop. Code 4
Mill City-Gates SD 129J
Sch. Sys. Enr. Code 3
Supt. – David Willard, P O BOX 1447 97360
MS, P O BOX 198 97360 – Robert Williams, prin.
Other Schools – See Gates

Milton-Freewater, Umatilla Co., Pop. Code 6
Ferndale SD 10
Sch. Sys. Enr. Code 2
Supt. – William Keyser
  RURAL ROUTE 03 BOX 179 97862
Pleasant View MS
  RURAL ROUTE 02 BOX 314 97862
  Gary Sunderland, prin.
Ferndale MS, RURAL ROUTE 03 BOX 179 97862
  William Keyser, prin.
Fruitvale ES, RURAL ROUTE 02 BOX 259 97862
  Gary Sunderland, prin.
Tum-A-Lum ES, RURAL ROUTE 03 97862
  William Keyser, prin.

Milton-Freewater SD 31
Sch. Sys. Enr. Code 3
Supt. – Cliff Walters, 105 NW 8TH AVE 97862
Central MS, 306 SW 2ND AVE 97862
  Cliff Walters, prin.
Freewater MS, 17 NW 8TH AVE 97862
  Judy Chesnut, prin.
Grove ES, 129 SE 15TH AVE 97862
  Steve Haugen, prin.

Milton-Stateline SDA School
  RURAL ROUTE 03 BOX 233 97862

Milwaukie, Clackamas Co., Pop. Code 7
North Clackamas SD 12
Sch. Sys. Enr. Code 7
Supt. – B. Schellenberg
  4444 SE LAKE ROAD 97222
Ickes JHS, 7726 SE HARMONY ROAD 97222
  Elaine Drakulich, prin.
McLoughlin JHS
  14450 SE JOHNSON ROAD 97222
  Kelly Hood, prin.
JHS, 2300 SE HARRISON ST 97222
  Brian Kleiner, prin.
Rowe JHS, 3606 SE LAKE ROAD 97222
  Robert Adrian, prin.
Bilquist ES, 15708 SE WEBSTER ROAD 97267
  Charles Hinds III, prin.
Campbell ES, 11326 SE 47TH AVE 97222
  Larry Weber, prin.
Leweling ES, 5325 SE LOGUS ROAD 97222
  Ron Orme, prin.
Linwood ES, 11909 SE LINWOOD AVE 97222
  Gary Salyers, prin.
ES, 11250 SE 27TH AVE 97222
  Edward Steele, prin.
North Oak Grove ES
  2150 SE TORBANK ROAD 97222
  Lynne Smith, prin.
Oak Grove ES, 1901 SE OAK GROVE BLVD 97267
  Richard Phillips, prin.
Riverside ES, 16303 SE RIVER ROAD 97267
  Robert Orr, Jr., prin.
View Acres ES
  4828 SE VIEW ACRES ROAD 97267
  James Stell, prin.
Whitcomb ES, 7400 SE THOMPSON ROAD 97222
  Vicki Chambers, prin.
Wichita ES, 6031 SE KING ROAD 97222
  William Engle, prin.
Other Schools – See Clackamas, Portland

Oregon City SD 62
Supt. – See Oregon City
Candy Lane ES, 5901 SE HULL AVE 97267
  Jack Drumm, prin.
Jennings Lodge ES, 18521 SE RIVER ROAD 97267
  Jack Drumm, prin.

Christ the King ES
  7414 SE MICHAEL DRIVE 97222
St. John the Baptist School
  10956 SE 25TH AVE 97222

Mitchell, Wheeler Co., Pop. Code 2
Mitchell SD 55
Sch. Sys. Enr. Code 1
Supt. – Michael Carroll, P O BOX 247 97750
ES, P O BOX 247 97750 – Michael Carroll, prin.

Molalla, Clackamas Co., Pop. Code 5
Dickey Prairie SD 25
Sch. Sys. Enr. Code 1
Supt. – Lyman Bruce
  16897 S CALLAHAN ROAD 97038
Dickey Prairie ES
  16897 S CALLAHAN ROAD 97038
  Lyman Bruce, prin.

Maple Grove SD 87
Sch. Sys. Enr. Code 1
Supt. – Lyman Bruce
  39214 S SAWTELL ROAD 97038

Maple Grove ES, 39214 S SAWTELL ROAD 97038
  Lyman Bruce, prin.

Molalla SD 35
Sch. Sys. Enr. Code 4
Supt. – William Jordan
  910 TOLIVER ROAD 97038
MS, P O BOX 225 97038 – Robert Backstrom, prin.
PS, P O BOX 206 97038 – Barbara Sandgren, prin.

Rural Dell SD 92
Sch. Sys. Enr. Code 2
Supt. – Thomas Cowan
  10500 S HIGHWAY 211 97038
Rural Dell ES, 10500 S HIGHWAY 211 97038
  Thomas Cowan, prin.

Monmouth, Polk Co., Pop. Code 6
Central SD 13J
Supt. – See Independence
ES, 958 CHURCH ST E 97361
  Richard Beight, prin.

Dallas SD 2
Supt. – See Dallas
Pedee ES, RURAL ROUTE 02 BOX 124 97361
  Dave Davis, prin.

Luckiamute ES, 265 CLAY ST W 97361

Monroe, Benton Co., Pop. Code 2
Alpine SD 26
Sch. Sys. Enr. Code 1
Supt. – Dave Manley, 25114 ALPINE RD 97456
Alpine ES, RURAL ROUTE 02 BOX 200 97456
  Dave Manley, prin.

Bellfountain SD 23
Sch. Sys. Enr. Code 1
Supt. – (—), 25398 DAWSON ROAD 97456
Bellfountain ES, 25398 DAWSON ROAD 97456
  Nelson O'Mealey, prin.

Irish Bend SD 24
Sch. Sys. Enr. Code 1
Supt. – (—), 26698 ALPINE RD 97456
Irish Bend ES, 26192 OLD RIVER ROAD 97456
  Nancy Canon, prin.

Monroe ESD 25J
Sch. Sys. Enr. Code 2
Supt. – William Stogsdill, P O BOX 288 97456
ES, P O BOX 288 97456 – William Stogsdill, prin.

Monument, Grant Co., Pop. Code 2
Monument SD 8
Sch. Sys. Enr. Code 2
Supt. – Maynord Simenson, P O BOX 127 97864
ES 97864 – Maynord Simenson, prin.

Mosier, Wasco Co., Pop. Code 2
Chenowith SD 9
Supt. – See The Dalles
ES, P O BOX 306 97040 – Ken Tessen, prin.

Mount Angel, Marion Co., Pop. Code 5
Butte Creek SD 67J
Sch. Sys. Enr. Code 2
Supt. – John Peters, 37569 S HIGHWAY 213 97362
Butte Creek ES, 37569 S HIGHWAY 213 97362
  John Peters, prin.

Monitor SD 142J
Sch. Sys. Enr. Code 2
Supt. – Thom Guthrie
  12465 MERIDIAN ROAD NE 97362
Monitor ES, 12465 MERIDIAN ROAD NE 97362
  Thom Guthrie, prin.

Mt. Angel SD 91
Sch. Sys. Enr. Code 3
Supt. – Frank Ellis, 890 E MARQUAM ST 97362
MS, 460 E MARQUAM ST 97362
  Mel Hurley, prin.
St. Mary's ES, 590 E COLLEGE ST 97362
  Mike Amon, prin.

Mount Vernon, Grant Co., Pop. Code 3
Mt. Vernon SD 6
Sch. Sys. Enr. Code 2
Supt. – H. Burton, P O BOX 648 97865
ES, P O BOX 648 97865 – Joan Bennett, prin.

Mulino, Clackamas Co.
Clarkes SD 32
Sch. Sys. Enr. Code 2
Supt. – Allan Barker
  19100 S WINDY CITY ROAD 97042
Clarkes ES, 19100 S WINDY CITY ROAD 97042
  Alan Barker, prin.

Mulino SD 84
Sch. Sys. Enr. Code 2
Supt. – Earl Miller, P O BOX 838 97042
ES, P O BOX 838 97042 – Earl Miller, prin.

Myrtle Creek, Douglas Co., Pop. Code 5
South Umpqua SD 19
Sch. Sys. Enr. Code 4
Supt. – Richard Risener
  558 SW CHADWICK LANE 97457
Coffenberry JHS, 591 RICE ST 97457
  Bill Burnett, prin.
ES, 651 NE DIVISION ST 97457 – (—), prin.
Tri City ES, 546 SW CHADWICK LANE 97457
  Donald Dick, prin.
Other Schools – See Canyonville

Myrtle Point, Coos Co., Pop. Code 5
Myrtle Point SD 41
Sch. Sys. Enr. Code 4
Supt. – Tom Roe, 212 SPRUCE ST　97458
Bridge ES, P O BOX 115m　97458
　Ivan Watts, prin.
Maple ES, 413 C ST　97458 – Bob Miles, prin.
Myrtle Crest ES
　903 MYRTLE CREST LANE　97458
　Tom Howard, prin.

Nehalem, Tillamook Co., Pop. Code 2
Neah-Kah-Nie SD 56
Supt. – See Rockaway
ES, P O BOX 190　97131 – Laurel Woodworth, prin.

Newberg, Yamhill Co., Pop. Code 7
Newberg SD 29J
Sch. Sys. Enr. Code 5
Supt. – H. Smith, 1421 DEBORAH ROAD　97132
Renne MS, 620 E 6TH ST　97132
　Paul Jellum, prin.
Springbrook MS, 2015 EMERY DR　97132
　Judy Wayland, prin.
Central ES, 415 E SHERIDAN ST　97132
　Marcia Garrick, prin.
Edwards ES, 6TH & EDWARDS STS　97132
　Gary Fendall, prin.
Rush ES, 1400 DEBORAH ROAD　97132
　Eric Johnson, prin.
Young ES, RURAL ROUTE 03　BOX 287　97132
　Kate Copenhaver, prin.
Other Schools – See Dundee

CS Lewis Community School, P O BOX 938　97132
Chehalem Valley Christian School
　RURAL ROUTE 03　BOX 487　97132

Newport, Lincoln Co., Pop. Code 6
Lincoln County SD
Sch. Sys. Enr. Code 6
Supt. – John Erickson, P O BOX 1110　97365
MS, 311 NE EADS ST　97365
　Clayton Ockert, prin.
Case ES, 459 NE 12TH ST　97365
　Carl Jorgensen, prin.
Yaquina View ES, 351 SE HARNEY ST　97365
　Ron Hutchison, prin.
Other Schools – See Eddyville, Lincoln City, Siletz,
　Toledo, Waldport

Yaquina Christian School, P O BOX 1068　97365

North Bend, Coos Co., Pop. Code 6
North Bend SD 13
Sch. Sys. Enr. Code 5
Supt. – James Ulum, 1313 AIRPORT LANE　97459
JHS, 16TH & PACIFIC ST　97459
　Ronald Handke, prin.
Bangor ES, 11TH & MADRONA STS　97459
　Avadna Boshears, prin.
Glasgow ES, 550 DOVE LANE　97459
　Sally Prouty, prin.
Hillcrest ES, 1100 MAINE ST　97459
　James Adams, prin.
North Bay ES, VIKING WAY　97459
　Richard Lillebo, prin.
Roosevelt ES, 2389 SHERMAN AVE　97459
　Russell Hasegawa, prin.
Sunny Hill ES, 3161 N BAY DRIVE　97459
　Ruth Kennedy, prin.

Kingsview Christian School
　1850 CLARK ST　97459

North Plains, Washington Co., Pop. Code 3
North Plains SD 70
Sch. Sys. Enr. Code 2
Supt. – Robert Duffy, P O BOX 688　97133
ES, P O BOX 190　97133 – Robert Duffy, prin.

North Powder, Union Co., Pop. Code 2
North Powder SD 8J
Sch. Sys. Enr. Code 2
Supt. – Arnold Coe, 3RD & G STS　97867
ES, P O BOX 10　97867 – Arnold Coe, prin.

Noti, Lane Co.
Fern Ridge SD 28J
Supt. – See Elmira
ES, 22713 HWY 126　97461 – Ken Johnson, prin.

Nyssa, Malheur Co., Pop. Code 5
Nyssa SD 26
Sch. Sys. Enr. Code 4
Supt. – Dennis Savage, 810 ADRIAN BLVD　97913
JHS, 804 ADRIAN BLVD　97913 – D. Martin, prin.
ES, 1 N 7TH ST　97913 – Denzel Weeks, prin.

Oakland, Douglas Co., Pop. Code 3
Oakland SD 1
Sch. Sys. Enr. Code 3
Supt. – Joseph Reed, P O BOX 818　97462
Lincoln MS, P O BOX 818　97462
　Roger Stewart, prin.
ES, P O BOX 818　97462 – James Dale, prin.

Oakridge, Lane Co., Pop. Code 5
Oakridge SD 76
Sch. Sys. Enr. Code 3
Supt. – Kenneth Carver, 76499 ROSE ST　97463
ES, 48119 W 1ST ST　97463 – James Swan, prin.
Other Schools – See Westfir

Odell, Hood River Co.
Hood River County SD
Supt. – See Hood River

Mid Valley ES, P O BOX 188　97044
　Kenneth Sparks, prin.

Ontario, Malheur Co., Pop. Code 6
Annex SD 29
Sch. Sys. Enr. Code 1
Supt. – Jack Lortz, 402 ANNEX RD　97914
Annex ES, ANNEX ROAD　97914
　Jack Lortz, prin.

Ontario SD 8
Sch. Sys. Enr. Code 5
Supt. – Dave Cloud, 497 SW 3RD AVE　97914
Aiken ES, 1297 W IDAHO AVE　97914
　(—), prin.
Alameda ES, 1252 ALAMEDA DRIVE　97914
　Myron Carpenter, prin.
Cairo ES, 531 HWY 20-25　97914
　Wayne Strong, prin.
Lindbergh ES, 482 SE 3RD ST　97914
　John McDonough, prin.
Pioneer ES, 4744 PIONEER ROAD　97914
　Irene Bates, prin.
Roberts ES, 590 NW 8TH ST　97914
　(—), prin.

St. Peter ES, 98 SW 9TH ST　97914

Ophir, Curry Co.
Ophir SD 12
Sch. Sys. Enr. Code 1
Supt. – (—), P O BOX 158　97464
ES　97464 – James Shockley, prin.

Oregon City, Clackamas Co., Pop. Code 7
Carus SD 29
Sch. Sys. Enr. Code 2
Supt. – John Young, 14412 S CARUS ROAD　97045
Carus ES, 14412 S CARUS ROAD　97045
　Jim Mabbott, prin.

Oregon City SD 62
Sch. Sys. Enr. Code 6
Supt. – Charles Clemans, P O BOX 591　97045
Eastham ES, 1404 7TH ST　97045
　Gordon Layden, prin.
Gaffney Lane ES, 13521 S GAFFNEY LANE　97045
　Bob Light, prin.
Holcomb ES, 14625 S HOLCOMB BLVD　97045
　Alan Heitschmidt, prin.
King ES, 995 S S END ROAD　97045
　Lance Margeson, prin.
McLoughlin ES, 19230 S S END ROAD　97045
　Al Gallagher, prin.
Mt. Pleasant ES, 1232 LINN AVE　97045
　Warren Burley, prin.
Park Place ES, 16075 S FRONT AVE　97045
　Dick Miller, prin.
Other Schools – See Beavercreek, Milwaukie

Redland SD 116
Sch. Sys. Enr. Code 3
Supt. – Clark Bray
　18131 S REDLAND ROAD　97045
Redland ES, 18131 S REDLAND ROAD　97045
　Gail Wilkinson, prin.

Associated Education Services HS
　20499 S MOLALLA AVE　97045
St. John's Catholic School, 516 5TH ST　97045

Paisley, Lake Co., Pop. Code 2
Paisley SD 11
Sch. Sys. Enr. Code 2
Supt. – Maurice Thorne, P O BOX 97　97636
ES　97636 – Maurice Thorne, prin.

Parkdale, Hood River Co., Pop. Code 4
Hood River County SD
Supt. – See Hood River
ES, P O BOX 69　97041 – Anthony Turner, prin.

Paulina, Crook Co.
Crook County Unit SD
Supt. – See Prineville
ES　97754 – Phil Fischer, prin.

Pendleton, Umatilla Co., Pop. Code 7
Pendleton SD 16
Sch. Sys. Enr. Code 5
Supt. – Marshall Keating
　1207 SW FRAZER AVE　97801
Hawthorne ES, 1308 SW EMIGRANT AVE　97801
　Richard Pratt, prin.
Lincoln ES, 107 NW 10TH ST　97801
　Duane Whitten, prin.
McKay Creek ES, 1500 SW 44TH ST　97801
　Creagh Hawes, prin.
Sherwood Heights ES
　3111 SW MARSHALL AVE　97801
　Jerry Archer, prin.
Washington ES, 1205 SE BYERS AVE　97801
　William Anderson, prin.
West Hills ES, 1700 NW 15TH DRIVE　97801
　Duane Whitten, prin.

Harris Junior Academy
　3121 SW HAILEY AVE　97801

Philomath, Benton Co., Pop. Code 5
Philomath SD 17J
Sch. Sys. Enr. Code 4
Supt. – Leroy Edwards, P O BOX 591　97370
MS, P O BOX 271　97370 – Ruth Daniels, prin.
Kings Valley ES, 239 S 16TH ST　97370
　Wendell Seat, prin.

ES, P O BOX 71　97370 – Wendell Seat, prin.
Other Schools – See Blodgett

Phoenix, Jackson Co., Pop. Code 4
Phoenix-Talent SD 4
Sch. Sys. Enr. Code 4
Supt. – Joseph Diamond, P O BOX 698　97535
ES, P O BOX 727　97535 – James Buck, prin.
Other Schools – See Medford, Talent

Pilot Rock, Umatilla Co., Pop. Code 4
Pilot Rock SD 2
Sch. Sys. Enr. Code 2
Supt. – Darce Driskel, P O BOX BB　97868
ES, P O BOX A　97868 – Darce Driskel, prin.

Pistol River, Curry Co.
Pistol River SD 16
Sch. Sys. Enr. Code 1
Supt. – (—)　97444
ES　97444 – Judith Biesen, prin.

Pleasant Hill, Lane Co., Pop. Code 6
Pleasant Hill SD 1
Sch. Sys. Enr. Code 4
Supt. – J. Howard, 36386 HIGHWAY 58　97455
JHS, 36386 HIGHWAY 58　97455
　R. Darling, prin.
MS, 36386 HWY 58　97455 – Stan Paine, prin.
Trent PS, 36386 HIGHWAY 58　97455
　Polly Tripp, prin.

Emerald Junior Academy
　35582 ZEPHYR WAY　97455

Plush, Lake Co.
Plush SD 18
Sch. Sys. Enr. Code 1
Supt. – (—)　97637
ES　97637 – Wayne Wollenweber, prin.

Portland, Multnomah Co., Pop. Code 10
Beaverton SD 48J
Supt. – See Beaverton
Cedar Mill ES, 10265 NW CORNELL ROAD　97229
　Tom Morris, prin.
Montclair ES, 7250 SW VERMONT CT　97223
　Don Hunt, prin.
Raleigh Park ES, 3670 SW 78TH AVE　97225
　Ed Robinson, prin.
Ridgewood ES, 10100 SW INGLEWOOD ST　97225
　Barbara Marrion, prin.

Centennial SD 28J
Sch. Sys. Enr. Code 5
Supt. – G. Benson
　18135 SE BROOKLYN ST　97236
Centennial MS, 17650 SE BROOKLYN ST　97236
　Clark Brody, prin.
Lynch Meadows ES
　18009 SE BROOKLYN ST　97236
　Jacine Vieira, prin.
Lynch View ES, 1546 SE 169TH PLACE　97233
　Billy Van Horn, prin.
Lynch Wood ES, 3615 SE 174TH AVE　97236
　Al Doan, prin.
Oliver MS, 15840 SE TAYLOR ST　97233
　Ronald Hoppes, prin.
PS, 15811 SE MAIN ST　97233
　Ellen Seawell, prin.
Pleasant Valley ES
　17625 SE FOSTER ROAD　97236
　Jim Donovan, prin.

David Douglas SD 40
Sch. Sys. Enr. Code 6
Supt. – Anthony Palermini
　1500 SE 130TH AVE　97233
Light ES, 10800 SE WASHINGTON ST　97216
　Daryl Girod, prin.
Ott MS, 12500 SE RAMONA ST　97236
　A. Jean Bruck, prin.
Cherry Park ES, 1930 SE 104TH AVE　97216
　Rodger Dalgleish, prin.
Gilbert Heights ES
　12839 SE HOLGATE BLVD　97236
　Rea Janes, prin.
Gilbert Park ES, 13132 SE RAMONA ST　97236
　Richard St. Claire, prin.
Lincoln Park ES, 13200 SE LINCOLN ST　97233
　Douglas Sharp, prin.
Menlo Park ES, 12900 NE GLISAN ST　97230
　George Martin, prin.
Mill Park ES, 1900 SE 117TH AVE　97216
　Ruth Wehling, prin.
Ventura Park ES, 145 SE 117TH AVE　97216
　Doris Minard, prin.
West Powellhurst ES, 2921 SE 116TH AVE　97266
　Harriet Jackson, prin.

North Clackamas SD 12
Supt. – See Milwaukie
Ardenwald ES, 8950 SE 36TH AVE　97222
　Dave Larson, prin.
Happy Valley ES, 13865 SE KING ROAD　97236
　Terry Spahr, prin.

Parkrose SD 3
Sch. Sys. Enr. Code 5
Supt. – Ronald Zook
　10636 NE PRESCOTT ST　97220
Parkrose MS, 11800 NE SHAVER ST　97220
　Marvin Chapman, prin.
Prescott ES, 10410 NE PRESCOTT ST　97220
　Kay Struckman, prin.
Russell ES, 2700 NE 127TH AVE　97230
　Preston Butcher, prin.

Sacramento ES
11400 NE SACRAMENTO ST 97220
Lillian Hosman, prin.
Shaver ES, 3701 NE 131ST PLACE 97230
Michael Furrer, prin.
Sumner ES, 8678 NE SUMNER ST 97220
Gary Dietderich, prin.

Portland SD 1J
Sch. Sys. Enr. Code 8
Supt. – Matthew Prophet, P O BOX 3107 97208
Metro Learning Center School
2033 NW GLISAN ST 97209 – Mike Harris, prin.
Beaumont MS, 4043 NE FREMONT ST 97212
Thomas Marineau, prin.
Binnsmead MS, 2225 SE 87TH AVE 97216
Donna Manning, prin.
Fernwood MS, 3255 NE HANCOCK ST 97212
John Ubik, prin.
George MS, 10000 N BURR 97203
Linda Simington, prin.
Gray MS, 5505 SW 23RD AVE 97201
Wes Bartholomaus, prin.
Green MS, 1315 N AINSWORTH ST 97217
Pat Burke, prin.
Gregory Heights MS
7334 NE SISKIYOU ST 97213 – Tom Lydon, prin.
Hosford MS, 2303 SE 28TH PLACE 97214
Dan Klee, prin.
Kellogg MS, 6909 SE POWELL BLVD 97206
Sue Parker, prin.
Lane MS, 7200 SE 60TH 97206 – Ron Reilly, prin.
Markham MS, 10625 SW 35TH AVE 97219
Delores Crawford, prin.
Mt. Tabor MS, 5800 SE ASH ST 97215
Ken Wait, prin.
Portsmouth MS, 5103 N WILLIS BLVD 97203
Tom Pickett, prin.
Sellwood MS, 8300 SE 15TH AVE 97202
Bill Beck, prin.
Tubman MS, 2231 N FLINT AVE 97227
Paul Coakley, prin.
West Sylvan MS
8111 SW WEST SLOPE DRIVE 97225
Leigh Wilcox, prin.
Whitaker MS, 5700 NE 39TH AVE 97211
Don Starr, prin.
Abernethy ES, 2421 SE ORANGE AVE 97214
Frank Scotto, prin.
Ainsworth ES, 2425 SW VISTA AVE 97201
Ruth Ann Angell, prin.
Alameda ES, 2732 NE FREMONT ST 97212
Charles Nakvasil, prin.
Applegate ES, 7650 N COMMERCIAL AVE 97217
Joy Pruitt, prin.
Arleta ES, 5109 SE 66TH AVE 97206
Jeanne Pace, prin.
Astor ES, 5601 N YALE ST 97203
Robert Whitmore, prin.
Atkinson ES, 5800 SE DIVISION ST 97206
John Withers, prin.
Ball ES, 4221 N WILLIS BLVD 97203
Bruce Craft, prin.
Beach ES, 1710 N HUMBOLDT ST 97217
Mike Verbout, prin.
Boise/Eliot ES, 620 N FREMONT ST 97227
Betty Campbell, prin.
Bridger ES, 7910 SE MARKET ST 97215
Judy Koford, prin.
Bridlemile ES, 4300 SW 47TH DRIVE 97221
Peter Hamilton, prin.
Brooklyn ES, 3830 SE 14TH AVE 97202
Rosemary Daniels, prin.
Buckman ES, 320 SE 16TH AVE 97214
Addie O'Brien, prin.
Capitol Hill ES, 8401 SW 17TH AVE 97219
Ralph Hodges, prin.
Chapman ES, 1445 NW 26TH AVE 97210
Joan Liapes, prin.
Chief Joseph ES, 2409 N SARATOGA ST 97217
Mary MacDougall, prin.
Clarendon ES, 9325 N VAN HOUTEN AVE 97203
Lynne Smith, prin.
Clark ES, 1231 SE 92ND AVE 97216
Dan McCall, prin.
Creston ES, 4701 SE BUSH ST 97206
Greg Wolleck, prin.
Duniway ES, 7700 SE REED COLLEGE PL 97202
Allan Luethe, prin.
Edwards ES, 1715 SE 32ND PLACE 97214
Candace Beck, prin.
Faubion ES, 3039 NE PORTLAND BLVD 97211
Kathleen Yarnell, prin.
Glencoe ES, 825 SE 51ST AVE 97215
James Williams, prin.
Gregory Heights 6th Grade Center
8020 NE TILLAMOOK ST 97213
Tom Lydon, prin.
Grout ES, 3119 SE HOLGATE BLVD 97202
Ron Hanlon, prin.
Hayhurst ES, 5037 SW IOWA ST 97221
Hal Folmar, prin.
Hollyrood PS, 3560 NE HOLLYROOD CT 97212
Olliemae Phillips, prin.
Humboldt ES, 4915 N GANTENBEIN AVE 97217
Lela Roberts, prin.
Irvington ES, 1320 NE BRAZEE ST 97212
Pam Shelly, prin.
John ES, 7439 N CHARLESTON AVE 97203
Willie Poinsette, prin.
Kelly ES, 9030 SE COOPER ST 97266
John Spathas, prin.
Kenton ES, 7528 N FENWICK AVE 97217
Jeff Sachtler, prin.

King ES, 4906 NE 6TH AVE 97211
Harriet Adair, prin.
Laurelhurst ES, 840 NE 41ST AVE 97232
Olliemae Phillips, prin.
Lee ES, 2222 NE 92ND AVE 97220
Miguel Salinas, prin.
Lent ES, 5105 SE 97TH AVE 97266
Bob Ralston, prin.
Lewis ES, 4401 SE EVERGREEN ST 97206
Janet Whitaker, prin.
Llewellyn ES, 6301 SE 14TH AVE 97202
Mary Van Cleave, prin.
Maplewood ES, 7452 SW 52ND AVE 97219
Lester Baker, prin.
Marysville ES, 7733 SE RAYMOND ST 97206
Gwen Gerald, prin.
Meek ES, 4039 NE ALBERTA CT 97211
Joe Williams, prin.
Peninsula ES, 8125 N EMERALD AVE 97217
David Lindstrom, prin.
Richmond ES, 2276 SE 41ST AVE 97214
Renee Staub, prin.
Rigler ES, 5401 NE PRESCOTT ST 97218
Larry Fleckenstein, prin.
Rose City Park ES, 2334 NE 57TH AVE 97213
Ed Bettencourt, prin.
Sabin ES, 4013 NE 18TH AVE 97212
Michael Jordan, prin.
Scott ES, 6700 NE PRESCOTT ST 97218
Louis Tesch, prin.
Sitton ES, 9930 N SMITH ST 97203
John Alkire, prin.
Skyline ES, 11536 NW SKYLINE BLVD 97231
Robert McAllister, prin.
Smith ES, 8935 SW 52ND AVE 97219
Peggy Miller, prin.
Stephenson ES, 2627 SW STEPHENSON ST 97219
David Masunaga, prin.
Sunnyside ES, 3421 SE SALMON ST 97214
Doug Marshall, prin.
Vernon ES, 2044 NE KILLINGSWORTH ST 97211
Betsy Geddes, prin.
Vestal ES, 161 NE 82ND AVE 97220
Bertha Little, prin.
Whitman ES, 7326 SE FLAVEL ST 97206
Greg Jones, prin.
Wilcox ES, 833 NE 74TH AVE 97213
Thelma Brown, prin.
Woodlawn ES, 7200 NE 11TH AVE 97211
Linda Harris, prin.
Woodmere ES, 6540 SE 78TH AVE 97206
Diana Leitner, prin.
Woodstock ES, 5601 SE 50TH AVE 97206
Syd Steinbock, prin.
Youngson ES, 2704 SE 71ST AVE 97206
Lee Delance, prin.

Reynolds SD 7
Supt. – See Troutdale
Lee MS, 1121 NE 172ND AVE 97230
George Swart, prin.
Rockwood MS, 740 SE 182ND AVE 97233
LaDyle Simpson, prin.
Alder ES, 17200 SE ALDER ST 97233
Anita Harder, prin.
Davis ES, 19501 NE DAVIS ST 97230
Donnise Brown, prin.
Glenfair ES, 15300 NE GLISAN ST 97230
Marvin Daniels, prin.
Hartley ES, 701 NE 185TH PLACE 97230
Mervin Peters, prin.
Scott ES, 14700 NE SACRAMENTO ST 97230
Leroy Scott, prin.
Wilkes ES, 17020 NE WILKES ROAD 97230
Wayne Travillion, prin.

Riverdale SD 51J
Sch. Sys. Enr. Code 2
Supt. – Claude Offenbacher
11733 SW BREYMAN AVE 97219
Riverdale ES, 11733 SW BREYMAN AVE 97219
Claude Offenbacher, prin.

Sauvie Island SD 19
Sch. Sys. Enr. Code 1
Supt. – El Duane Whatley
1445 NW CHARLTON ROAD 97231
Sauvie Island ES
14445 NW CHARLTON ROAD 97231
El Duane Whatley, prin.

West Union SD 1
Supt. – See Hillsboro
Lenox ES, 21200 NW ROCK CREEK BLVD 97229
Betsy Jeronen, prin.

Catlin-Gabel School
8625 SW BARNES ROAD 97225
Columbia Christian HS
9101 E BURNSIDE ST 97216
Oregon Episcopal School
6300 SW NICOL ROAD 97223
Portland Christian Schools
12456 NE BRAZEE ST 97230
All Saints ES, 601 NE 39TH AVE 97232
Belmont,Inc. ES, 3841 SE BELMONT ST 97214
Cathedral ES, 110 NW 17TH AVE 97209
Franciscan Montessori Earth School
14030 NE SACRAMENTO ST 97230
French American School
1849 SW 58TH AVE 97221
Holy Cross ES, 5202 N BOWDOIN ST 97203
Holy Family ES, 7425 SE 39TH AVE 97202
Holy Redeemer ES
127 N PORTLAND BLVD 97217

Our Lady of Sorrows School
5239 SE WOODSTOCK BLVD 97206
Pope John XXIII ES
7654 N DELAWARE AVE 97217
Portland ES, 16301 SE DIVISION 97236
Sacred Heart ES, 3822 SE 11TH AVE 97202
St. Agatha ES, 1516 SE MILLER ST 97202
St. Charles ES, 5420 NE 42ND AVE 97206
St. Clare ES, 1807 SW FREEMAN ST 97219
St. Ignatius ES, 3330 SE 43RD AVE 97206
St. John Fisher ES, 7101 SW 46TH AVE 97219
St. Pius X ES, 1260 NW SALTZMAN ROAD 97229
St. Stephen's ES, 4235 SE SALMON ST 97215
St. Therese ES, 1260 NE 132ND AVE 97230
St. Thomas More ES
3521 SW PATTON ROAD 97221
The Madeleine ES, 3240 NE 23RD AVE 97212
Trinity Lutheran School
5520 N KILLINGSWORTH ST 97218
Tucker-Maxon Oral School
2860 SE HOLGATE BLVD 97202
Wesley Christian Academy
11456 NE KNOTT ST 97220
West Hills Christian School
7945 SW CAPITOL HILL ROAD 97219

Port Orford, Curry Co., Pop. Code 4
Port Orford-Langlois SD 2J
Sch. Sys. Enr. Code 2
Supt. – P. Romney, P O BOX 8 97465
Blanco JHS, P O BOX 8 97465 – John Black, prin.
ES, P O BOX 28 97465 – Donald Tate, prin.

Powell Butte, Crook Co.
Crook County Unit SD
Supt. – See Prineville
ES 97753 – (—), prin.

Powers, Coos Co., Pop. Code 3
Powers SD 31
Sch. Sys. Enr. Code 2
Supt. – Al Samples, P O BOX 479 97466
ES, P O BOX 479 97466 – Al Samples, prin.

Prairie City, Grant Co., Pop. Code 4
Prairie City SD 4
Sch. Sys. Enr. Code 2
Supt. – Otis Falls, P O BOX 345 97869
ES, P O BOX 345 97869 – Otis Falls, prin.

Princeton, Harney Co.
Double O SD 28
Sch. Sys. Enr. Code 1
Supt. – (—), HCR 72 BOX 270-E 97721
Other Schools – See Burns

Sodhouse SD 32
Sch. Sys. Enr. Code 1
Supt. – (—), HCR 72 BOX 270-E 97721
Sodhouse ES, HRC 32 BOX 230E 97721
Glenda Jones, prin.

Prineville, Crook Co., Pop. Code 6
Crook County Unit SD
Sch. Sys. Enr. Code 4
Supt. – Robert Wininger, 1390 SE 2ND ST 97754
Crook County MS, 1400 SE 2ND ST 97754
Ron Wilkinson, prin.
Crooked River ES, 631 E 3RD ST 97754
Frederick Hasse, prin.
Ochoco ES, 900 MADRAS HIGHWAY 97754
Royce Chadwick, prin.
Other Schools – See Paulina, Powell Butte

Prospect, Jackson Co., Pop. Code 2
Prospect SD 59
Sch. Sys. Enr. Code 2
Supt. – Lee Anderson, P O BOX 40 97536
ES 97536 – Don Alexander, prin.

Rainier, Columbia Co., Pop. Code 4
Columbia County SD 13
Sch. Sys. Enr. Code 4
Supt. – Gene Carlson, P O BOX 318 97048
MS, P O BOX 500 97048 – Harry Price, prin.
Goble ES, 70024 GOBLE ROAD 97048
Lawrence Wallace, prin.
Hudson Park ES
28170 OLD RAINIER ROAD 97048
Robert Ward, prin.
ES, P O BOX 319 97048 – J. Brown, prin.

Redmond, Deschutes Co., Pop. Code 6
Redmond SD 2J
Sch. Sys. Enr. Code 5
Supt. – Richard Slaven
716 SW EVERGREEN AVE 97756
Obsidian JHS, 1335 SW OBSIDIAN AVE 97756
Lois Northrup, prin.
Brown ES, 850 W ANTLER AVE 97756
Richard LeFrancis, prin.
EVERGREEN ES, 437 S 9TH ST 97756
Carl Williquette, prin.
Hill ES, 830 SW CASCADE AVE 97756
Richard LeFrancis, prin.
Lynch ES, 1314 SW KALAMA AVE 97756
Richard Rice, prin.
Tuck MS, 209 NW 10TH ST 97756
Gary Williams, prin.
Other Schools – See Bend, Terrebonne

Reedsport, Douglas Co., Pop. Code 5
Ash Valley SD 125
Sch. Sys. Enr. Code 1
Supt. – (—), HCR 4 BOX 75 97467
Ash Valley ES, HCR 4 BOX 75 97467
Shirley Baxter, prin.

Reedsport SD 105
Sch. Sys. Enr. Code 4
Supt. – Clark Lund, 100 RANCH ROAD 97467
Highland ES, HIGHLAND DRIVE 97467
Robert Townsend, prin.
Other Schools – See Gardiner

Richland, Baker Co., Pop. Code 2
Pine Eagle SD 61
Supt. – See Halfway
ES 97870 – David Bird, prin.

Rickreall, Polk Co.
Central SD 13J
Supt. – See Independence
Oak Grove ES, 2700 OAK GROVE ROAD 97371
Glenn Brostrom, prin.

Dallas SD 2
Supt. – See Dallas
ES 97371 – Wayne Osborn, prin.

Riddle, Douglas Co., Pop. Code 4
Riddle SD 70
Sch. Sys. Enr. Code 3
Supt. – Duane Lyons, P O BOX 45 97469
ES, P O BOX 45 97469 – Gerald Archer, prin.

Riley, Harney Co.
Suntex SD 10
Sch. Sys. Enr. Code 1
Supt. – (—) 97758
Suntex ES 97758 – (—), prin.

Rockaway, Tillamook Co., Pop. Code 3
Neah-Kah-Nie SD 56
Sch. Sys. Enr. Code 3
Supt. – Garey Mark, P O BOX 28 97136
Other Schools – See Garibaldi, Nehalem

Rogue River, Jackson Co., Pop. Code 4
Rogue River SD 35
Sch. Sys. Enr. Code 4
Supt. – Carl Shaff, P O BOX A 97537
MS, P O BOX A 97537 – David Montesano, prin.
Evans Valley ES, P O BOX 1045 97537
George Blue, prin.
ES, P O BOX 1045 97537 – Richard Springer, prin.

Christian Life of Rogue River School
270 W EVANS CREEK ROAD 97537

Roseburg, Douglas Co., Pop. Code 7
Douglas County SD 4
Sch. Sys. Enr. Code 6
Supt. – Richard Eisenhauer
1419 NW VALLEY VIEW DRIVE 97470
Sunnyslope IS, 2230 SW CANNON AVE 97470
Robert Siebum, prin.
Eastwood ES, 2550 SE WALDON AVE 97470
Jim Knapp, prin.
Fir Grove ES, 1360 W HARVARD BLVD 97470
Thad Sprague, prin.
Fullerton IV ES
2560 W BRADFORD DRIVE 97470
Michael Sheppard, prin.
Green PS, 4498 SW CARNES ROAD 97470
Richard Fulwyler, prin.
Hucrest ES, 1810 NW KLINE ST 97470
Ronald Singler, prin.
Melrose ES, 2960 MELROSE ROAD 97470
Gary Gries, prin.
Rose ES, 948 SE ROBERTS AVE 97470
Lee Patersen, prin.
Other Schools – See Winchester

Glide SD 12
Supt. – See Glide
Deer Creek ES, 18515 DIXONVILLE ROAD 97470
Armin Freeman, prin.

Umpqua Valley Christian School
3013 STEWART PARKWAY DR 97470
Douglas County Christian School
2079 NW WITHERSPOON AVE 97470
Roseburg Junior Academy
1633 NW TROOST ST 97470
St. Joseph ES, 630 W STANTON ST 97470

Rufus, Sherman Co., Pop. Code 2
Rufus SD 3
Sch. Sys. Enr. Code 1
Supt. – Jerome Anderson 97050
ES 97050 – Jerome Anderson, prin.

Saint Helens, Columbia Co., Pop. Code 6
St. Helens SD 502
Sch. Sys. Enr. Code 4
Supt. – Gus Spiropulos, 474 N 16TH ST 97051
JHS, 354 N 15TH ST 97051 – Donald Hogan, prin.
Condon ES, 1051 COLUMBIA BLVD 97051
Robert Kunders, prin.
Gumm ES, 251 SAINT HELENS ST 97051
Richard Carlson, prin.
McBride ES, 295 S VERNONIA ROAD 97051
Raymond Justice, prin.
Yankton ES, 33035 PITTSBURG ROAD 97051
Raymond Justice, prin.
Other Schools – See Columbia City

Saint Paul, Marion Co., Pop. Code 2
St. Paul SD 45
Sch. Sys. Enr. Code 2
Supt. – Charles Geis, 601 MAIN ST NE 97137
ES, P O BOX 44 97137 – Vince Drago, prin.

St. Paul School, P O BOX 188 97137

Salem, Marion Co., Pop. Code 8
Buena Crest SD 134
Sch. Sys. Enr. Code 1
Supt. – (—), 8485 RIVER ROAD NE 97303
Buena Crest ES, 8485 RIVER ROAD NE 97303
J. Scott, prin.

Eldriedge SD 60
Sch. Sys. Enr. Code 1
Supt. – Fred Niemiec
10327 RIVER ROAD NE 97303
Eldriedge ES, 10327 RIVER ROAD NE 97303
Fred Niemiec, prin.

Pratum SD 50
Sch. Sys. Enr. Code 1
Supt. – (—)
8995 SUNNYVIEW ROAD NE 97305
Pratum ES, 8995 SUNNYVIEW ROAD NE 97305
Rosemary McNeely, prin.

Salem/Keizer SD 24J
Sch. Sys. Enr. Code 8
Supt. – Homer Kearns, P O BOX 12024 97309
Judson MS, 4512 JONES ROAD SE 97302
(—), prin.
Leslie MS, 710 HOWARD ST SE 97302
Gaye Stewart, prin.
Parrish MS, 802 CAPITOL ST NE 97301
Richard Krepel, prin.
Waldo MS, 2805 LANSING AVE NE 97303
Mike Kolb, prin.
Walker MS, 1075 8TH ST NW 97304
Patricia Mack, prin.
Whiteaker MS
1605 LOCKHAVEN DRIVE NE 97303
David Cook, prin.
Auburn ES, 4612 AUBURN ROAD NE 97301
John Trujillo, prin.
Baker ES, 1515 SAGINAW ST S 97302
Rose Marie Marsh, prin.
Bethel ES, 6580 STATE ST 97301
Dave Cronk, prin.
Brush College ES
2623 COAKES FERRY ROAD NW 97304
Dave King, prin.
Bush ES, 755 UNIVERSITY ST SE 97301
Jenifer Billman, prin.
Candalaria ES, 935 HANSEN AVE S 97302
Tom Snider, prin.
Chapman Hill ES
1482 DOAKS FERRY ROAD NW 97304
Dick Kemper, prin.
Clear Lake ES
7990 WHEATLAND ROAD N 97303
Beverlyn Sevall, prin.
Cummings ES, 613 CUMMINGS LANE N 97303
Leon Bousha, prin.
Englewood ES, 1132 19TH ST NE 97301
Kathleen Bebe, prin.
Eyre ES, 4868 BUFFALO DRIVE SE 97301
Marilyn Campbell, prin.
Four Corners ES, 500 ELMA AVE SE 97301
Dave Cronk, prin.
Fruitland ES, 6425 FRUITLAND ROAD NE 97301
John Trujillo, prin.
Grant ES, 725 MARKET ST NE 97301
Charles Goforth, prin.
Gubser ES, 6610 14TH AVE NE 97303
Melvin Hurley, prin.
Hayesville ES, 4545 WARD DR NE 97305
Catherine Mink, prin.
Hazel Green ES
5774 HAZEL GREEN ROAD NE 97305
Beverlyn Sevall, prin.
Highland ES, 530 HIGHLAND AVE NE 97303
Michele Evans, prin.
Hoover ES, 1104 SAVAGE ROAD NE 97301
Ron Lee, prin.
Keizer ES, 5600 MCCLURE ST N 97303
David Guile, prin.
Kennedy ES, 4912 NOREN AVE NE 97303
Glenda Melton, prin.
Lake Labish ES
7495 PORTLAND ROAD NE 97305
Susan Lee, prin.
Liberty ES, 4871 LIBERTY ROAD S 97306
Starla Thomas, prin.
McKinley ES, MCGILCHRIST ST SE 97302
Rose Marie Marsh, prin.
Middle Grove ES
4950 SILVERTON ROAD NE 97305
Susan Lee, prin.
Morningside ES, 3513 12TH ST SE 97302
Tom Tyler, prin.
Myers ES, 2160 JEWEL ST NW 97304
Curt Gettis, prin.
Pringle ES, 4985 BATTLE CREEK ROAD SE 97302
Nanci Schneider, prin.
Richmond ES, 466 RICHMOND AVE SE 97301
Grant Foster, prin.
Rosedale ES, 6974 BATES ROAD S 97306
Mollie Brown, prin.
Salem Heights ES, 3495 LIBERTY ROAD S 97302
Warren Webster, prin.
Schirle ES, 4875 JUSTICE WAY S 97302
Tom Paterson, prin.
Scott ES, 4700 ARIZONA AVE NE 97305
Torry Johnson, prin.
Sumpter ES, 525 ROCKWOOD ST SE 97306
Rex Neiger, prin.
Swegle ES, 4485 MARKET ST NE 97301
James Weil, prin.
Washington ES, 3165 LANSING AVE NE 97303
Steve Arndt, prin.

Wright ES, 4060 LONE OAK ROAD SE 97302
John Taylor, prin.

Vinyard Academy, 355 BELMONT ST NE 97301
Livingstone Junior Academy
5771 FRUITLAND ROAD NE 97301
Mid-Valley Christian School
4453 COUNTRY LANE NE 97303
Montessori Children's House
7625 SUNNYSIDE ROAD SE 97306
Queen of Peace Catholic School
4227 LONE OAK ROAD SE 97302
Salem Academy MS
250 COLLEGE DRIVE NW 97304
St. Joseph ES, 373 WINTER ST NE 97301
St. Vincent DePaul School
1015 COLUMBIA ST NE 97303
The Heritage ES, 685 COURT ST NE 97301

Sandy, Clackamas Co., Pop. Code 5
Bull Run SD 45
Sch. Sys. Enr. Code 2
Supt. – Jerry McGuire
41515 THOMAS ROAD 97055
Bull Run ES, 41515 SE THOMAS ROAD 97055
Jerry McGuire, prin.

Sandy ESD 46
Sch. Sys. Enr. Code 4
Supt. – Leland Chapman, P O BOX 547 97055
Cedar Ridge MS, P O BOX 547 97055
Darrell Shepherd, prin.
Firwood ES, 42900 SE TRUBEL ROAD 97055
John Wuitschick, prin.
ES, P O BOX 547 97055 – Verne Buhler, prin.
Other Schools – See Boring

Scappoose, Columbia Co., Pop. Code 5
Scappoose SD 1J
Sch. Sys. Enr. Code 4
Supt. – Jack Blair, P O BOX V 97056
MS, P O BOX N 97056 – Delburt Powell, prin.
Petersen MS, 52181 SW E M WATTS ROAD 97056
Peter McHugh, prin.
Watts ES, 5200 SE THIRD PLACE 97056
Michael Judah, prin.
Other Schools – See Warren

Scio, Linn Co., Pop. Code 3
Lourdes SD 124
Sch. Sys. Enr. Code 1
Supt. – (—), 39059 JORDAN ROAD 97374
Lourdes ES, 39059 JORDAN ROAD 97374
Diane Duda, prin.

Scio SD 95
Sch. Sys. Enr. Code 3
Supt. – Ellis Mason, 38875 NW 1ST AVE 97374
MS, 38875 NW 1ST AVE 97374
Larry Armbrust, prin.
Centennial ES, 38875 NW 1ST AVE 97374
Larry Armbrust, prin.

Scotts Mills, Marion Co., Pop. Code 2
Scotts Mills SD 73J
Sch. Sys. Enr. Code 2
Supt. – David Mikkelsen, P O BOX 40 97375
ES, P O BOX 40 97375 – David Mikkelsen, prin.

Seaside, Clatsop Co., Pop. Code 6
Jewell SD 8
Sch. Sys. Enr. Code 2
Supt. – Bernard Adamson
ELSIE RT BOX 1280 97138
Jewell ES, ELSIE ROUTE, BOX 1280 97138
Bernard Adamson, prin.

Seaside SD 10
Sch. Sys. Enr. Code 4
Supt. – Harold Riggan
1801 S FRANKLIN ST 97138
Broadway MS, 1120 BROADWAY ST 97138
Donald Wickersham, prin.
Seaside Heights ES, 1720 SPRUCE DRIVE 97138
Douglas Ayles, prin.
Other Schools – See Cannon Beach, Gearhart

Selma, Josephine Co.
Josephine County Unit SD
Supt. – See Grants Pass
ES, 18255 REDWOOD HIGHWAY 97538
Donald McCoy, prin.

Seneca, Grant Co., Pop. Code 2
John Day SD 3
Supt. – See John Day
ES 97873 – Robert Nelson, prin.

Shady Cove, Jackson Co., Pop. Code 4
Eagle Point SD 9
Supt. – See Eagle Point
MS, P O BOX 138 97539 – Charlotte Smith, prin.

Shedd, Linn Co.
Central Linn SD 552
Supt. – See Halsey
ES, 31700 FAYETTEVILLE DRIVE 97377
Wade Doerfler, prin.

Sheridan, Yamhill Co., Pop. Code 4
Sheridan SD 48J
Sch. Sys. Enr. Code 3
Supt. – Ian Grabenhorst
339 NW SHERMAN ST 97378
Chapman MS, 332 SW CORNWALL ST 97378
Harry Shipman, prin.
Faulconer ES, 339 NW SHERMAN ST 97378
Ian Grabenhorst, prin.

Delphian School
20950 SW ROCK CREEK ROAD 97378
West Valley Academy, P O BOX 192 97378
Bridge Christian ES, 917 S BRIDGE ST 97378

Sherwood, Washington Co., Pop. Code 4
Sherwood SD 88J
Sch. Sys. Enr. Code 4
Supt. – Bill Hill, 400 N SHERWOOD BLVD 97140
IS, 400 N SHERWOOD BLVD 97140
   Betty Saltzman, prin.
Hopkins ES, 800 SHERWOOD BLVD 97140
   Pete Miller, prin.

Siletz, Lincoln Co., Pop. Code 4
Lincoln County SD
Supt. – See Newport
ES 97380 – Mike Darcy, prin.

Silver Lake, Lake Co.
North Lake SD 14
Sch. Sys. Enr. Code 2
Supt. – Mike Costello, P O BOX 40 97638
MS, P O BOX 40 97638 – Mike Costello, prin.
Other Schools – See Fort Rock

Silverton, Marion Co., Pop. Code 6
Bethany SD 63
Sch. Sys. Enr. Code 1
Supt. – Richard Sunderland
   11824 HAZELGREEN ROAD NE 97381
Bethany ES
   11824 HAZELGREEN ROAD NE 97381
   Richard Sunderland, prin.

Central Howell SD 540
Sch. Sys. Enr. Code 2
Supt. – Jeffrey Gunter
   8832 SILVERTON ROAD NE 97381
Central Howell ES
   8832 SILVERTON ROAD NE 97381
   Jeffrey Gunter, prin.

Evergreen SD 10
Sch. Sys. Enr. Code 1
Supt. – (—)
   3727 CASCADE HIGHWAY NE 97381
Evergreen ES, 3727 CASCADE HWY NE 97381
   Finley Couch, prin.

North Howell SD 51
Sch. Sys. Enr. Code 1
Supt. – (—), 9410 RAMBLER DRIVE NE 97381
North Howell ES
   9410 RAMBLER DRIVE NE 97381
   Stephen Caputo, prin.

Silver Crest SD 93
Sch. Sys. Enr. Code 2
Supt. – (—), 365 LOAR ROAD SE 97381
Silver Crest ES, 365 LOAR ROAD SE 97381
   Shirley Bates, prin.

Silverton SD 4
Sch. Sys. Enr. Code 4
Supt. – Craig Roessler, 201 WESTFIELD ST 97381
Twain JHS, 925 CHURCH ST 97381
   Carol Beatty, prin.
Field ES, 410 N WATER ST 97381
   Evelyn Irwin, prin.
Frost MS, 201 WESTFIELD ST 97381
   Judith Keeney, prin.

Victor Point SD 42
Sch. Sys. Enr. Code 2
Supt. – (—)
   RURAL ROUTE 03 BOX 65A 97381
Point ES, 1175 VICTOR POINT ROAD SE 97381
   Lloyd Barnes, prin.

Christian Learning Center, P O BOX 164 97381

Sisters, Deschutes Co., Pop. Code 3
Sisters SD 6
Sch. Sys. Enr. Code 2
Supt. – Judith May, P O BOX 99 97759
ES, P O BOX 99 97759 – Earl Armbruster, prin.

Spray, Wheeler Co., Pop. Code 2
Spray SD 1
Sch. Sys. Enr. Code 1
Supt. – Don Coffey, P O BOX 230 97874
ES, P O BOX 230 97874 – Don Coffey, prin.

Springfield, Lane Co., Pop. Code 8
Springfield SD 19
Sch. Sys. Enr. Code 6
Supt. – Paul Plath, 525 MILL ST 97477
Briggs MS, 2355 YOLANDA AVE 97477
   Gary Connor, prin.
Hamlin MS, 326 CENTENNIAL BLVD 97477
   (—), prin.
MS, 1084 G ST 97477 – Don Buckley, prin.
Thurston MS, 6300 THURSTON ROAD 97478
   Lee Wacker, prin.
Brattain ES, 425 N 10TH ST 97477
   Dallas Lommen, prin.
Camp Creek ES
   37770 UPPER CAMP CREEK ROAD 97478
   Len Arney, prin.
Centennial ES, 1315 ASPEN ST 97477
   John Halgren, prin.
Douglas Gardens ES, 3680 JASPER ROAD 97478
   Bruce Smolnisky, prin.
Lee ES, 755 HARLOW ROAD 97477
   Linda Forbes, prin.

Maple ES, 2109 J ST 97477
   Phyllis Vanderzanden, prin.
Moffitt ES, 1544 N 5TH ST 97477
   Wendell Walmsley, prin.
Mohawk ES, 91166 SUNDERMAN ROAD 97478
   Suzanne Painter, prin.
Mt. Vernon ES, 725 S 42ND ST 97478
   Mel Kaiser, prin.
Page ES, 1300 HAYDEN BRIDGE ROAD 97477
   Kathleen Mathson, prin.
Ridgeview ES, 526 N 66TH ST 97478
   Jay Rickford, prin.
Thurston ES, 7345 THURSTON ROAD 97478
   Roy Van Horn, prin.
Walterville ES, 40589 MCKENZIE HWY 97478
   Len Arney, prin.
Yolanda ES, 2350 YOLANDA AVE 97477
   Richard Barr, prin.
Other Schools – See Eugene

Stanfield, Umatilla Co., Pop. Code 4
Stanfield SD 61
Sch. Sys. Enr. Code 3
Supt. – James Carlson, P O BOX 158 97875
Stanfield MS, P O BOX 189 97875
   Alan Neerenberg, prin.
West ES, P O BOX 219 97875
   Robert MacPherson, prin.

Stayton, Marion Co., Pop. Code 5
Stayton SD 77J
Sch. Sys. Enr. Code 3
Supt. – Gretta Merwin, 1021 SHAFF ROAD 97383
MS, 1021 SHAFF ROAD 97383
   Michael Loretz, prin.
ES, 922 N 1ST AVE 97383 – David Gentry, prin.
Other Schools – See Mehama

St. Mary's Catholic School
   1066 N 6TH AVE 97383
Staton Private School, P O BOX 493 97383

Sublimity, Marion Co., Pop. Code 4
Sublimity SD 7
Sch. Sys. Enr. Code 2
Supt. – Barry Gourley, P O BOX 96 97385
ES 97385 – Barry Gourley, prin.

Sunriver, Deschutes Co.

Sunriver Preporatory School, P O BOX 3132 97707

Sutherlin, Douglas Co., Pop. Code 5
Sutherlin SD 130
Sch. Sys. Enr. Code 4
Supt. – Richard Smith, P O BOX 500 97479
JHS, P O BOX 1164 97479 – Gerry Galbraith, prin.
East Sutherlin PS, P O BOX E 97479
   Gary King, prin.
West IS, 531 N COMSTOCK ST 97479
   Greg Knee, prin.

Southerlin SDA ES, P O BOX 633 97479

Sweet Home, Linn Co., Pop. Code 6
Sweet Home SD 55
Sch. Sys. Enr. Code 4
Supt. – William Hampton, 1920 LONG ST 97386
JHS, 880 22ND AVE 97386
   William Starnes, prin.
Hawthorne ES, 3205 LONG ST 97386
   Harold Schollian, prin.
Holley ES, RURAL ROUTE 02 BOX 259 97386
   Harold Schollian, prin.
Oak Heights ES, 605 ELM ST 97386
   Larry Graves, prin.
Other Schools – See Crawfordsville, Foster

Talent, Jackson Co., Pop. Code 5
Phoenix-Talent SD 4
Supt. – See Phoenix
JHS, P O BOX 255 97540 – Stephen Trout, prin.
ES, P O BOX 296 97540 – Bill Mayer, prin.

Oak Meadow ES
   10798 YANK GULCH ROAD 97540

Tangent, Linn Co., Pop. Code 2
Greater Albany SD 8J
Supt. – See Albany
ES, 32100 OLD OAK DRIVE 97389
   Shary Wortman, prin.

Terrebonne, Deschutes Co.
Redmond SD 2J
Supt. – See Redmond
ES, P O BOX 66 97760 – Della Brandt, prin.

The Dalles, Wasco Co., Pop. Code 7
Chenowith SD 9
Sch. Sys. Enr. Code 3
Supt. – Peter Christensen, 3632 W 10TH ST 97058
Chenowith MS, 3718 W 13TH ST 97058
   Dick Kessler, prin.
Chenowith PS, 922 CHENOWITH LOOP W 97058
   Denny Peterson, prin.
Other Schools – See Mosier

Petersburg SD 14
Sch. Sys. Enr. Code 1
Supt. – Howard Fetz
   3855 FIFTEEN MILE ROAD 97058
Petersburg ES 97058 – Howard Fetz, prin.

The Dalles SD 12
Sch. Sys. Enr. Code 4
Supt. – Leslie Bradbury, 220 E 10TH ST 97058

JHS, 1401 I ST 97058 – Dave Beasley, prin.
Colonel Wright ES, 610 W 14TH ST 97058
   K. Baumgartner, prin.
Dry Hollow ES, 1314 E 19TH ST 97058
   Daryl Corey, prin.
Wilson ES, 1413 E 12TH ST 97058
   Jerry Christensen, prin.

St. Mary's Academy
   1112 CHERRY HEIGHTS ROAD 97058

Tigard, Washington Co., Pop. Code 7
Tigard SD 23J
Sch. Sys. Enr. Code 6
Supt. – Russell Joki
   13137 SW PACIFIC HIGHWAY 97223
Durham ES, 8040 SW DURHAM ROAD 97224
   Scott Baker, prin.
Lewis ES, 12615 SW 72ND AVE 97223
   Art Rutkin, prin.
Metzger ES, 10255 SW 90TH AVE 97223
   Maryalice Russell, prin.
Templeton ES, 9500 SW MURDOCK ST 97224
   Debbie Beeson-Merkel, prin.
ES, 12985 SW GRANT AVE 97223
   Gayle Collum, prin.
Woodward ES, 12325 SW KATHERINE ST 97223
   Art Hass, prin.
Other Schools – See Tualatin

Gaarde Christian School
   11265 SW GAARDE ST 97224
St. Anthony ES
   12645 SW PACIFIC HIGHWAY 97223

Tillamook, Tillamook Co., Pop. Code 5
Tillamook SD 9
Sch. Sys. Enr. Code 4
Supt. – Bruce Anderson
   6825 OFFICERS ROW 97141
JHS, 3906 ALDER LANE 97141
   Norman Lehman, prin.
East ES, 3905 ALDER LANE 97141
   William Leininger, prin.
Liberty ES, 1700 9TH ST 97141
   Harold Grassley, prin.
South Prairie ES, 6855 S PRAIRIE ROAD 97141
   Janis Swan, prin.
Wilson ES, 2513 3RD ST 97141
   Harold Grassley, prin.

Tiller, Douglas Co.
Days Creek SD 15
Supt. – See Days Creek
ES, P O BOX C 97484 – Gerald Rust, prin.

Toledo, Lincoln Co., Pop. Code 5
Lincoln County SD
Supt. – See Newport
MS, 600 NE STURDEVANT 97391
   Gail Tipton, prin.
Arcadia MS, 1811 ARCADIA ROAD 97391
   Robert Folkers, prin.
Harrison ES, 321 SE 3RD ST 97391
   Kathy Larrabee, prin.

Trail, Jackson Co.
Eagle Point SD 9
Supt. – See Eagle Point
Elk Trail ES, 591 ELK CREEK ROAD 97541
   Charleen Brown, prin.

Troutdale, Multnomah Co., Pop. Code 6
Reynolds SD 7
Sch. Sys. Enr. Code 6
Supt. – Hudson Lasher
   1424 NE 201ST AVE 97060
Sweetbriar ES, 501 SE SWEETBRIAR LANE 97060
   Bettianne Goetz, prin.
ES, 648 SE HARLOW AVE 97060
   Julie Moyer, prin.
Other Schools – See Fairview, Portland

Tualatin, Washington Co., Pop. Code 6
Tigard SD 23J
Supt. – See Tigard
Bridgeport ES, 5505 SW BORLAND ROAD 97062
   Marilyn Adair, prin.
Byrom ES, 21800 SW 91ST AVE 97062
   Fred Puhl, prin.
ES, 19945 SW BOONES FERRY ROAD 97062
   Nancy Longaker, prin.

Community Chrisitan School
   P O BOX 1183 97062

Turner, Marion Co., Pop. Code 4
Cloverdale SD 144
Sch. Sys. Enr. Code 1
Supt. – (—)
   9666 PARRISH GAP ROAD SE 97392
Cloverdale ES
   9666 PARRISH GAP ROAD SE 97392
   Bill Dollar, prin.

Turner SD 79
Sch. Sys. Enr. Code 2
Supt. – Stephen Rusk, P O BOX 129 97392
ES, P O BOX 129 97392 – Stephen Rusk, prin.

Tygh Valley, Wasco Co.
Tygh Valley Grade SD 40
Sch. Sys. Enr. Code 1
Supt. – Ronald Worrell, P O BOX 38 97063
ES 97063 – Ronald Worrell, prin.

Ukiah, Umatilla Co., Pop. Code 2
Ukiah SD 80
Sch. Sys. Enr. Code 1
Supt. – Richard Erdrich, P O BOX 218 97880
ES, P O BOX 218 97880 – Richard Erdrich, prin.

Umatilla, Umatilla Co., Pop. Code 5
Umatilla SD 6
Sch. Sys. Enr. Code 3
Supt. – George Fenton,Jr., P O BOX 131 97882
Brownell MS, P O BOX 131 97882
    John Thomas, prin.
McNary Heights ES, P O BOX 131 97882
    William Delong, prin.

Umpqua, Douglas Co.
Umpqua SD 45
Sch. Sys. Enr. Code 1
Supt. – Frank Cardiff
    806 HUBBARD CREEK ROAD 97486
ES, 806 HUBBARD CREEK ROAD 97486
    Frank Cardiff, prin.

Union, Union Co., Pop. Code 4
Union SD 5
Sch. Sys. Enr. Code 2
Supt. – Carl Holmes, P O BOX K 97883
ES, P O BOX 868 97883 – Carl Holmes, prin.

Unity, Baker Co., Pop. Code 2
Burnt River SD 30J
Sch. Sys. Enr. Code 1
Supt. – June Williams, P O BOX 8 97884
Burnt River ES, P O BOX 8 97884
    June Williams, prin.

Vale, Malheur Co., Pop. Code 4
Vale SD 15
Sch. Sys. Enr. Code 3
Supt. – Robert Crawford, 403 E SAINT W 97918
ES, 403 E SAINT W 97918 – David Enright, prin.

Willowcreek SD 42
Sch. Sys. Enr. Code 1
Supt. – (—)
    RURAL ROUTE 02 BOX 2695 97918
Willowcreek ES
    RURAL ROUTE 02 BOX 2695 97918
    Lana Andrews, prin.

Veneta, Lane Co., Pop. Code 4
Fern Ridge SD 28J
Supt. – See Elmira
ES, P O BOX 370 97487 – Phil Bertrand, prin.

Vernonia, Columbia Co., Pop. Code 4
Vernonia SD 47J
Sch. Sys. Enr. Code 3
Supt. – Ed Danielson, 475 BRIDGE ST 97064
Lincoln ES, 1462 BRIDGE ST 97064
    Sunny Hunteman, prin.
Washington MS, 199 BRIDGE ST 97064
    Gary Wilson, prin.
Other Schools – See Clatskanie

Waldport, Lincoln Co., Pop. Code 4
Lincoln County SD
Supt. – See Newport
MS, P O BOX C 97394 – Ron Corbell, prin.
ES, P O BOX 830 97394 – Kathy Godinet, prin.

Wallowa, Wallowa Co., Pop. Code 3
Wallowa SD 12
Sch. Sys. Enr. Code 2
Supt. – Dave Smyth, P O BOX 425 97885
ES, P O BOX 425 97885 – Dale Johnson, prin.

Wamic, Wasco Co.
Wamic SD 42
Sch. Sys. Enr. Code 1
Supt. – Kenneth Reinke, P O BOX 707 97063
ES 97063 – Rosemary Sjoli, prin.

Warm Springs, Jefferson Co.
Jefferson SD 509J
Supt. – See Madras
ES, P O BOX 5 97761 – Jane Nimocks, prin.

Warren, Columbia Co., Pop. Code 2
Scappoose SD 1J
Supt. – See Scappoose
ES, 34555 BERG ROAD 97053
    Rolland Rethmeier, prin.

Warrenton, Clatsop Co., Pop. Code 4
Warrenton-Hammond SD 30
Sch. Sys. Enr. Code 3
Supt. – William Hilton
    820 SW CEDAR AVE 97146
ES, 820 SW CEDAR ST 97146
    Bernard LaCasse, prin.

Wasco, Sherman Co., Pop. Code 2
Wasco Grade SD 7
Sch. Sys. Enr. Code 1
Supt. – Rick Eggers 97065
ES 97065 – Rick Eggers, prin.

Welches, Clackamas Co.
Welches SD 13
Sch. Sys. Enr. Code 2
Supt. – Judith Warren
    E SALMON RIVER ROAD 97067
ES, SALMON RIVER PARK ROAD 97067
    Terry Prochaska, prin.

Westfir, Lane Co.
Oakridge SD 76
Supt. – See Oakridge
Westridge JHS, 46433 WESTFIR ROAD 97492
    Deborah Cameron, prin.

West Linn, Clackamas Co., Pop. Code 7
West Linn SD 3J
Sch. Sys. Enr. Code 5
Supt. – Dealous Cox, P O BOX 100 97068
Bolton MS, 5933 HOLMES ST 97068
    Marilyn Seger, prin.
Willamette MS, 1403 12TH ST 97068
    Kenton Hill, prin.
Cedar Oak Park ES
    4515 CEDAR OAK DRIVE 97068
    Kenneth Welch, prin.
Stafford ES, 19875 SW STAFFORD ROAD 97068
    Susan Miller, prin.
Sunset ES, 2351 OXFORD ST 97068
    Nancy Hays, prin.
Other Schools – See Wilsonville

Weston, Umatilla Co., Pop. Code 3
Athena-Weston SD 29J
Supt. – See Athena
Athena-Weston JHS, P O BOX 158 97886
    C. Janson, prin.
ES, P O BOX 188 97886 – Clifford Janson, prin.

Westport, Columbia Co., Pop. Code 3
Columbia SD 5J
Sch. Sys. Enr. Code 4
Supt. – Duane Scott
    WESTPORT SCHOOL ROAD 97016
Other Schools – See Astoria, Clatskanie

White City, Jackson Co., Pop. Code 2
Eagle Point SD 9
Supt. – See Eagle Point

ES, 2830 MAPLE CT 97503 – William Jones, prin.
IS, 7837 HALE WAY 97503
    Gerald Aebischer, prin.

Willamina, Yamhill Co., Pop. Code 4
Willamina SD 30J
Sch. Sys. Enr. Code 3
Supt. – Michael Wsiaki, P O BOX 127 97396
MS, P O BOX 499 97396 – Kathleen Shelley, prin.
ES, P O BOX 499 97396 – Joan Rivenbark, prin.
Other Schools – See Grand Ronde

Tri-City Christian School, P O BOX 957 97396

Williams, Josephine Co.
Josephine County Unit SD
Supt. – See Grants Pass
ES, P O BOX 88 97544 – Juanita Drummond, prin.

Horizon ES, 1960 E FORK ROAD 97544

Wilsonville, Clackamas Co., Pop. Code 5
West Linn SD 3J
Supt. – See West Linn
Wood MS, 11055 SW WILSONVILLE ROAD 97070
    Penny McDonald, prin.
ES, 30275 SW BOONES FERRY ROAD 97070
    Glenn Moran, prin.

Winchester, Douglas Co., Pop. Code 3
Douglas County SD 4
Supt. – See Roseburg
ES, P O BOX 778 97495
    Kathleen Crenshaw, prin.

Winston, Douglas Co., Pop. Code 5
Winston-Dillard SD 116
Supt. – See Dillard
JHS, P O BOX 1689 97496 – (—), prin.

Abba Christian ES
    8186 UPPER OLALLA ROAD 97496

Wolf Creek, Josephine Co.
Josephine County Unit SD
Supt. – See Grants Pass
ES, P O BOX 325 97497 – David Wells, prin.

Woodburn, Marion Co., Pop. Code 7
Woodburn SD 103
Sch. Sys. Enr. Code 4
Supt. – Keith Robinson
    965 N BOONES FERRY ROAD 97071
JHS, BOONES FERRY ROAD & HWY 214 97071
    Paul Shaffer, prin.
Muir ES, 1800 W HAYES ST 97071
    Kathy Larson, prin.
Washington ES, 777 E LINCOLN ST 97071
    Jacqueline Blalock, prin.
MS, 1041 N BOONES FERRY ROAD 97071
    Milt Parker, prin.

St. Lukes ES, 529 HARRISON ST 97071

Yamhill, Yamhill Co., Pop. Code 3
Yamhill SD 16
Sch. Sys. Enr. Code 3
Supt. – Bill Bentley, P O BOX 188 97148
ES, P O BOX 188 97148 – T Bessonette, prin.

Yoncalla, Douglas Co., Pop. Code 3
Yoncalla SD 32
Sch. Sys. Enr. Code 2
Supt. – George Robbins, P O BOX 568 97499
ES, P O BOX 568 97499 – Mike Lambert, prin.

PENNSYLVANIA

STATE DEPARTMENT OF EDUCATION
333 Market St., Harrisburg 17126
(717) 783-6788

Secretary of Education	Thomas Gilhool
Office of Press & Communications	Timothy Potts
Office of Policy & Government Relations	Vacant
Office of Basic Education	Donna Wall
Office of Higher Education	Charles Fuget
Office of Research Planning & Program Evaluation	Vacant

STATE BOARD OF EDUCATION
Sister M. Lawreace Antoun, *Chairperson*   P.O. Box 911, Harrisburg   17126

PENNSYLVANIA COUNCIL OF HIGHER EDUCATION
William Smith, *Chairperson*   333 Market St., Harrisburg   17126

INTERMEDIATE UNITS

Intermediate Unit 1, Harry Brownfield, Supt.
1148 S WOOD ST, California 15419
Pittsburgh/Mt. Oliver IU 2, Richard Wallace,Jr., Supt.
341 S BELLEFIELD AVE, Pittsburgh 15213
Allegheny IU 3, Edgar Holtz, Supt.
200 COMMERCE COURT, Pittsburgh 15219
Midwestern IU 4, Gary Miller, Supt.
453 MAPLE ST, Grove City 16127
Northwest Tri-County IU 5, John Leuenberger, Supt.
252 WATERFORD ST #5, Edinboro 16412
Riverview IU 6, Arnold Hillman, Supt.
RT 322 E, Shippenville 16254
Westmoreland IU 7, R. Gene Malarbi, Supt.
222 E PITTSBURGH ST, Greensburg 15601
Appalachia IU 8, Joseph Tarris, Supt.
119 PARK ST, Ebensburg 15931
Seneca Highlands IU 9, Dr. Frank Rackish, Supt.
119 S MECHANIC ST, Smethport 16749
Central IU 10, Dr. Nancy Robbins, Supt.
RURAL ROUTE 01 BOX 374, West Decatur 16878
Tuscarora IU 11, Dale Heller, Supt.
RURAL ROUTE 01 BOX 70A, Mc Veytown 17051

Lincoln IU 12, I. Karam, Supt.
P O BOX 70, New Oxford 17350
Lancaster/Lebanon IU 13, Harry Zechman, Supt.
1110 ENTERPRISE RD, East Petersburg 17520
Berks County IU 14, Roger Hertz, Supt.
P O BOX 4097, Reading 19606
Capital Area IU 15, Dr. John Nagle, Supt.
26 N 9TH ST, Lemoyne 17043
Central Susquehanna IU 16, Patrick Toole, Supt.
P O BOX 213, Lewisburg 17837
Blast IU 17, Clair Goodman,Jr., Supt.
469 HEPBURN ST, Williamsport 17701
Luzerne IU 18, Dr. Thomas O'Donnell, Supt.
P O BOX 1649, Kingston 18704
Northeastern Educational IU 19, Paul Bebla, Supt.
OLD PLANK RD, Mayfield 18433
Colonial Northampton IU 20, Dr. John Abbruzzese,Jr., Supt.
P O BOX 179, Nazareth 18064
Carbon/Lehigh IU 21, Jerry Stout, Supt.
2370 MAIN ST, Schnecksville 18078

Bucks County IU 22, A. William Vantine, Supt.
CROSS KEYS BLDG, Doylestown 18901
Montgomery County IU 23, Dennis Harken, Supt.
300 MONTGOMERY AVE #23, Erdenheim 19118
Chester County IU 24, John Baillie, Supt.
150 JAMES HANCE COU, Exton 19341
Delaware County IU 25, James Shields, Supt.
6TH & OLIVE STS, Media 19063
Philadelphia IU 26, Constance Clayton, Supt.
PARKWAY AT 21ST ST, Philadelphia 19103
Beaver Valley IU 27, Francis Matika, Supt.
225 CENTER GRANGE ROAD, Aliquippa 15001
Arin IU 28, Dr. Thomas Carey, Supt.
RT 422 BOX 175, Shelocta 15774
Schuylkill IU 29, R. Alspach, Supt.
P O BOX 130, Mar Lin 17951

PUBLIC, PRIVATE, AND PAROCHIAL ELEMENTARY SCHOOLS

Abington, Montgomery Co., Pop. Code 6
Abington SD IU 23
Sch. Sys. Enr. Code 6
Supt. – Dr. Louis Hebert
1841 SUSQUEHANNA ST 19001
Highland ES, 1301 EDGE HILL ROAD 19001
Lennox McKinley, prin.
Overlook ES, 2001 OLD WELSH RD 19001
Robert Wolfe, prin.
Other Schools – See Elkins Park, Glenside, Huntingdon Valley, Roslyn, Willow Grove

Our Lady of Help Christian ES
CRATER AND MARIAN RDS 19001

Adamstown, Lancaster Co., Pop. Code 4
Cocalico SD IU 13
Supt. – See Denver
ES, P O BOX 39 19501 – R. Buck, prin.

Akron, Lancaster Co., Pop. Code 5
Ephrata Area SD IU 13
Supt. – See Ephrata
ES, 125 S ELEVENTH ST 17501
Thomas Legath, prin.

Albion, Erie Co., Pop. Code 4
Northwestern SD IU 5
Sch. Sys. Enr. Code 4
Supt. – Dr. Lynn Corder, 1 HARTHAN WAY 16401
Northwestern ES
JOHN WILLIAMS AVENUE 16401
David Olson, prin.
Other Schools – See East Springfield

Alburtis, Lehigh Co., Pop. Code 4
East Penn SD IU 21
Supt. – See Emmaus
ES, N 3RD STREET 18011 – Richard Gorton, prin.

Aldan, Delaware Co., Pop. Code 5
William Penn SD IU 25
Supt. – See Yeadon

ES, PROVIDENCE ROAD AND WOODLAW 19018
Michael Shaika, prin.

Aleppo, Greene Co., Pop. Code 3
West Greene SD IU 1
Supt. – See Waynesburg
MS, 550 EAST MAIN STREET 15310
Samuel Steinmiller, prin.

Alexandria, Huntington Co., Pop. Code 2
Juniata Valley SD IU 11
Sch. Sys. Enr. Code 4
Supt. – Ellis Griffith, RURAL ROUTE 01 16611
Juniata Valley ES, RURAL ROUTE 01 16611
H. Silvey, prin.

Aliquippa, Beaver Co., Pop. Code 7
Aliquippa SD IU 27
Sch. Sys. Enr. Code 4
Supt. – Anthony Cerilli
LAUGHLIN BLDG MAIN ST 15001
ES, SHEFFIELD ROAD 21ST STREET 15001
Irene Hoover, prin.

Center Area SD IU 27
Supt. – See Monaca
Center Grange ES
225 CENTER GRANGE RD 15001
Edward Elder, prin.

Hopewell Area SD
Sch. Sys. Enr. Code 5
Supt. – Steve Mulik, 1215 LONGVUE AVE 15001
Hopewell JHS, 2121 BRODHEAD ROAD 15001
Stanley Yukica, prin.
Hopewell ES, 3000 KANE RD 15001
Ralph Gaudio, prin.
Independence ES, RURAL ROUTE 01 15001
Ralph Gaudio, prin.
Raccoon ES, 3949 PATTERSON RD 15001
Ralph Gaudio, prin.

Our Lady of Fatima ES, 3005 FATIMA DR 15001

Rhema Christian ES, JACK ST 15001
St. Titus ES, 107 SYCAMORE ST 15001

Allentown, Lehigh Co., Pop. Code 9
Allentown CSD IU 21
Sch. Sys. Enr. Code 7
Supt. – Dr. Richard Cahn, P O BOX 328 18105
Harrison-Morton MS, 2ND & TURNER ST 18102
Kenneth Moyer, prin.
Raub MS, 100 S SAINT CLOUD ST 18104
Robert Doran, prin.
South Mountain MS
EMAUS AVE & S CHURCH ST 18103
Bruce Hutchinson, prin.
Trexler MS, 15TH & GREENLEAF STS 18103
Raymond O'Connell, prin.
Central ES
TURNER AND LUMBER STREETS 18102
David Borbe, prin.
Cleveland ES, 424 N 9TH ST 18102
Bernard O'Brien, prin.
Dodd ES, MOHAWK S CHURCH STREETS 18103
Robert Bennett, prin.
Jackson ES, 517 N 15TH ST 18102
Bernard O'Brien, prin.
Jefferson ES
8TH AND SAINT JOHN STREET 18103
Gene Capers, prin.
Lehigh Park ES
1708 20 CORONADO STREET 18103
Robert Foster, prin.
McKinley ES, 1124 W TURNER ST 18102
Robert Foster, prin.
Mosser ES, DAUPHIN E UNION STREETS 18103
Joseph Burke, prin.
Muhlenberg ES
21ST WASHINGTON STREETS 18104
Thomas Check, prin.
Ritter ES, PLYMOUTH E WASHINGTON 18103
Dennis Blankowitsch, prin.

550

Roosevelt ES
   W SUSQUHANNA AND SOUTH 2ND   18103
   Lenore Kohl, prin.
Sheridan ES, 2ND & LIBERTY ST   18102
   Wayne Trumbauer, prin.
Union Terrace ES
   UNION STEET WEST OF 19TH   18104
   Robert Laudenslager, prin.
Washington ES, 9TH & WASHINGTON ST   18102
   Ralph Todd, prin.

Parkland SD IU 21
Supt. – See Orefield
Cetronia ES, 3635 W HAMILTON ST   18104
   Charles Klein, prin.
Fogelsville ES, RURAL ROUTE 06 BOX 487   18106
   Joseph Altieri, prin.
Kratzer ES, 2200 MAIN BLVD   18104
   William Urland, prin.
Parkway Manor ES, N PARKWAY ROAD   18104
   Julius Horvath, prin.

Salisbury SD IU 21
Sch. Sys. Enr. Code 6
Supt. – F. Laird Evans
   1140 SALISBURY ROAD   18103
Truman ES, 1400 GASKILL ST   18103
   George Carver, prin.
Western Salisbury ES
   3201 DEVONSHIRE RD   18103
   Thomas Brunner, prin.

Cathedral St. Catherine ES, 210 N 18TH ST   18104
Holy Spirit ES, 508 RIDGE AVE   18102
Lehigh Christian Academy
   689 S HILLVIEW RD   18103
Our Lady of Help Christian ES
   934 HANOVER AVE   18103
Sacred Heart of Jesus ES, 325 N 4TH ST   18102
St. Frances of Assisi ES
   1035 W WASHINGTON ST   18102
St. Paul ES, 3RD & SUSQUEHANNA ST   18103
St. Thomas More ES, 1040 FLEXER AVE   18103
Swain ES, 1100 S 24TH ST   18103

Allenwood, Union Co.
Montgomery Area SD IU 17
Supt. – See Montgomery
Elimsport ES, RURAL ROUTE 01   17810
   Terry Kirschler, prin.

Allison Park, Allegheny Co., Pop. Code 6
Hampton Twp. SD IU 3
Sch. Sys. Enr. Code 6
Supt. – Kenneth Scholtz
   4482 MT ROYAL BLVD   15101
Hampton MS, 4589 SCHOOL ROAD   15101
   Harold Sarver, prin.
Central ES, 4480 MOUNT ROYAL BLVD   15101
   M. Neal, prin.
Wyland ES, 2284 WYLAND AVE   15101
   Richard Baker, prin.
Other Schools – See Gibsonia

North Allegheny SD IU 3
Supt. – See Pittsburgh
Hosack ES, 9275 PEEBLES RD   15101
   Walter Schwartz, prin.

Shaler Area SD IU 3
Supt. – See Glenshaw
Burchfield ES, 1500 BURCHFIELD RD   15101
   Diane Kirk, prin.

Eden Chrsitian Academy
   2326 DUNCAN AVE   15101
Proivdence Heights Alpha ES
   9000 BABCOCK BLVD   15101
St. Ursula ES, 3937 KIRK AVE   15101

Altoona, Blair Co., Pop. Code 8
Altoona Area SD IU 8
Sch. Sys. Enr. Code 6
Supt. – Dr. Dennis Murray
   5TH AVE & 15TH ST   16602
Baker ES, WARD AVENUE   16602
   Robert Duffett, prin.
Curtin ES
   WEST CHESTNUT AVENUE & 30   16601
   James Sturniolo, prin.
Irving ES
   CHERRY AVENUE & 1ST STREET   16601
   Mary Jo Jubelirer, prin.
Juniata ES, 420 8TH AVE JUNIATA   16601
   Daniel Daniels, prin.
Juniata Gap ES, JUNIATA GAP ROAD   16601
   Mary Jo Jubelirer, prin.
Logan ES, 301 SYCAMORE ST   16602
   Mary Ray, prin.
Penn-Lincoln ES, 411 12TS STREET   16602
   Dennis Keller, prin.
Pleasant Valley ES
   3401 PLEASANT VALLEY BLVD   16602
   Robert Duffett, prin.
Washington-Jefferson ES
   FIRST AVENUE & 5TH STREET   16602
   Carl Dunn, prin.
Wright ES, 1800 11TH ST   16601
   Jeanne Hair, prin.

McNeils Catholic ES, 1304 13TH AVE   16601
Our Lady Mt. Carmel ES, 1012 8TH AVE   16602
Our Lady of Lourdes ES
   2719 W CHESTNUT AVE   16601
Sacred Heart ES, 2006 6TH AVE   16602

St. John Evangelist ES, 311 LOTZ AVE   16602
St. Mary ES, 1400 4TH AVE   16602
St. Rose of Lims ES, 5519 6TH AVE   16602
St. Therese ES, 424 WOPSONONCIK AVE   16601

Alverton, Westmoreland Co., Pop. Code 2
Southmoreland SD IU 7
Supt. – See Scottdale
Southmoreland JHS, P O BOX B   15612
   A. Scott Logan, prin.
ES   15612 – William Nelson, prin.

Ambler, Montgomery Co., Pop. Code 6
Hatsboro-Horsham SD IU 23
Supt. – See Horsham
Simmons ES, 1125 LIMEKILN PIKE   19002
   Rita Klein, prin.

Wissahickon SD IU 23
Sch. Sys. Enr. Code 5
Supt. – Bruce Kowalski
   601 KNIGHT ROAD   19002
Wissahickon MS, 500 HOUSTON ROAD   19002
   Austin Snyder, prin.
Mattison Avenue ES, MATTISON AVENUE   19002
   Claudia Harley, prin.
Shady Grove MS
   LEWIS LANE SKIPPACK PK   19002
   David Adler, prin.
Other Schools – See Blue Bell, Norristown

Ambler Catholic ES, 251 FOREST AVE   19002
Ambler Catholic ES, 251 FOREST AVE   19002

Ambridge, Beaver Co., Pop. Code 6
Ambridge Area SD IU 27
Sch. Sys. Enr. Code 5
Supt. – Dr. Joseph Dimperio
   740 PARK ROAD   15003
Highland ES, 1051 HIGHLAND AVE   15003
   W. Grime, prin.
Ridge Road ES, 1893 ZEHNDER RD   15003
   Jesse McGee, prin.
Wayne ES, 21ST AND LENZ AVENUE   15003
   James Bergandy, prin.
Other Schools – See Baden, Freedom

Ambridge Area Catholic ES
   GLENWOOD & EIGHT AVE   15003

Amity, Washington Co.
Trinity Area SD IU 1
Supt. – See Washington
ES, RURAL ROUTE 01   15311
   Ray McCullough, prin.

Anita, Jefferson Co.
Punxsutawney Area SD IU 6
Supt. – See Punxsutawney
Parkview ES, MAIN STREET   15711
   Rosalie Astorino, prin.

Annville, Lebanon Co., Pop. Code 5
Annville-Cleona SD IU 13
Sch. Sys. Enr. Code 4
Supt. – Dr. Carole Spahr, S WHITE OAK ST   17003
ES, S WHITE OAK MARSHAL   17003
   Marion Miller, prin.
North Annville ES, RURAL ROUTE 01   17003
   Marion Miller, prin.
Other Schools – See Cleona

Northern Lebanon SD IU 13
Supt. – See Fredericksburg
East Hanover ES, RURAL ROUTE 02   17003
   Gary Messinger, prin.

Apollo, Armstrong Co., Pop. Code 4
Apollo-Ridge SD IU 28
Supt. – See Spring Church
ES, 616 1ST ST   15613 – Dr. June Merryman, prin.

Kiski Area SD IU 7
Supt. – See Vandergrift
North Washington ES, 600 RTE 66   15613
   William Kerr, prin.
Washington ES, 180 RTE 66   15613
   William Kerr, prin.

St. James ES, 109 OWENS VIEW AVE   15613

Archbald, Lackawanna Co., Pop. Code 6
Valley View SD IU 19
Sch. Sys. Enr. Code 4
Supt. – Daniel Corazzi, COLUMBUS DR   18403
Other Schools – See Eynon, Peckville

St. Thomas Aquinas ES, 400 CHURCH ST   18403

Ardmore, Montgomery Co., Pop. Code 6
Lower Merion SD IU 23
Sch. Sys. Enr. Code 6
Supt. – James Pugh
   301 E MONTGOMERY AVE   19003
Other Schools – See Bala-Cynwyd, Gladwyne, Merion
   Station, Narberth, Penn Wynne

Torah Academy
   ARGYLE & WYNNEWD ROADS   19003

Arendtsville, Adams Co., Pop. Code 3
Upper Adams SD IU 12
Supt. – See Biglerville
ES, FOHL AVE   17303 – Gayle Griffie, prin.

Armagh, Indiana Co., Pop. Code 2
United SD IU 28
Sch. Sys. Enr. Code 4
Supt. – Dr. James Hartman, P O BOX 168   15920
United ES, P O BOX 168   15920
   Charles Mack, prin.

Arnold, Westmoreland Co., Pop. Code 6
New Kensington-Arnold SD IU 7
Supt. – See New Kensington
Valley MS, 1701 ALCOA DRIVE   15068
   Richard Romito, prin.
Berkey ES, 1739 VICTORIA AVE   15068
   Thomas Rocchi, prin.

Ashland, Schuylkill Co., Pop. Code 5
North Schuylkill SD IU 29
Supt. – See Frackville
ES, RURAL ROUTE 01   17921 – Paula Peron, prin.

Tri-Valley SD IU 29
Supt. – See Valley View
Barry ES, RURAL ROUTE 01   17921
   Thomas Kuczawa, prin.

Aston, Delaware Co., Pop. Code 6
Chichester SD IU 25
Supt. – See Boothwyn
Hilltop ES, 401 CHERRY TREE RD   19014
   Marilyn Brien, prin.

Penn-Delco SD IU 25
Sch. Sys. Enr. Code 5
Supt. – Harry Hill, 95 CONCORD ROAD   19014
Northley MS, CONCORD ROAD   19014
   William Snyder, prin.
Green Ridge ES, CONCORD ROAD   19014
   Paul Hagy, prin.
Pennell ES, PENNELL ROAD AT WEI   19014
   John Monaghan, prin.
Other Schools – See Brookhaven

American Christian ES
   2140 BRIDGEWATER RD   19014
St. Joseph ES, 251 CONCORD RD   19014

Atglen, Chester Co., Pop. Code 3
Octorara Area SD IU 24
Sch. Sys. Enr. Code 4
Supt. – R. McAdams
   RURAL ROUTE 01 BOX 65   19310
Octorara Area Inter S, P O BOX 65   19310
   Richard Gilpin, prin.
Octorara ES, RURAL ROUTE 01 BOX 65   19310
   Karen Brofee, prin.

Fallowfield Church ES, P O BOX 279   19310

Athens, Bradford Co., Pop. Code 5
Athens Area SD IU 17
Sch. Sys. Enr. Code 5
Supt. – W. Hutz, 204 WILLOW ST   18810
Rowe MS, PENNSYLVANIA AVE   18810
   Eugene Cerutti, prin.
Lynch ES, PENNSYLVANIA AVENUE   18810
   James Priester, prin.
Main ES, 220 S RIVER ST   18810
   Paul Hewitt, prin.
Other Schools – See East Smithfield, Gillett, Ulster

Atlasburg, Washington Co., Pop. Code 3
Burgettstown Area SD IU 1
Supt. – See Burgettstown
ES   15004 – (—), prin.

Austin, Potter Co., Pop. Code 3
Austin Area SD IU 9
Sch. Sys. Enr. Code 3
Supt. – Charylene Philp, P O BOX 7   16720
ES, COSTELLO AVENUE   16720
   Charylene Philp, prin.

Avella, Washington Co., Pop. Code 4
Avella Area SD IU 1
Sch. Sys. Enr. Code 3
Supt. – William Grega
   RURAL ROUTE 02 BOX 192   15312
ES, RURAL ROUTE 02   15312
   Charles Gersna, prin.

Avoca, Luzerne Co., Pop. Code 5

St. Mary's ES, 746 SPRING ST   18641

Baden, Beaver Co., Pop. Code 6
Ambridge Area SD IU 27
Supt. – See Ambridge
Economy ES
   3151 CONWAY WALLROSE RD   15005
   Jesse McGee, prin.
State Street ES, HARMONY ROAD   15005
   James Bergandy, prin.

Mt. Gallitzin Academy
   ROUTE 65 AND STATE ST   15005

Bainbridge, Lancaster Co.
Elizabethtown Area SD IU 13
Supt. – See Elizabethtown
ES, SECOND STREET   17502
   Norma Zwally, prin.

Bala-Cynwyd, Montgomery Co., Pop. Code 6
Lower Merion SD IU 23
Supt. – See Ardmore
MS, 510 BRYN MAWR AVE   19004
   Robert Cummings, prin.

Cynwyd ES, 101 W LEVERING MILL RD   19004
  John Hartmire, prin.

St. Matthias ES, 122 BRYN MAWR AVE   19004

Bally, Berks Co., Pop. Code 4

Most Blessed Sacrament ES
  SEVENTH AND PINE ST   19503

Bangor, Northampton Co., Pop. Code 6
Bangor Area SD IU 20
  Sch. Sys. Enr. Code 5
  Supt. – Wilford Ottey, 44 S 3RD ST   18013
  ES, 36 S 4TH ST   18013 – Dorothy Ruggiero, prin.
  Five Points ES, RURAL ROUTE 02   18013
    John Reinhart, prin.
  Washington ES, 381 WASHINGTON BLVD   18013
    Dorothy Ruggiero, prin.

Barnesboro, Cambria Co., Pop. Code 5
Northern Cambria SD IU 8
  Sch. Sys. Enr. Code 4
  Supt. – Milton Morozowich
    600 JOSEPH ST   15714
  Northern Cambria MS, 600 JOSEPH ST   15714
    Robert Williams, prin.
  Northern Cambria ES, 600 JOSEPH ST   15714
    Robert Williams, prin.

North Cambria Catholic ES
  805 CHESTNUT AVE   15714

Barto, Berks Co.
Boyertown Area SD IU 14
  Supt. – See Boyertown
  Washington ES
    RURAL ROUTE 02 BOX 792   19504
    Thomas Smythe, prin.

Herman, Butler Co.

St. Mary Assumption ES, P O BOX 21   16039

Bath, Northampton Co.
Northampton Area SD IU 20
  Supt. – See Northampton
  Moore Township ES
    2835 MOUNTAIN VIEW DR   18014
    Darrell Crook, prin.
  Wolf ES, ALLEN STREET   18014
    Leslie Muthard, prin.

Sacred Heart ES, 115 WASHINGTON ST   18014

Beaver, Beaver Co., Pop. Code 6
Beaver Area SD IU 27
  Sch. Sys. Enr. Code 4
  Supt. – John Haddad, 855 F 2ND ST   15009
  Brighton Township ES
    4900 TUSCARAWAS RD   15009
    William Lohr, prin.
  College Square ES, 375 COLLEGE AVE   15009
    Albert Camp, prin.

Sts. Peter & Paul ES, 370 E END AVE   15009

Beaver Falls, Beaver Co., Pop. Code 7
Big Beaver Falls Area SD IU 27
  Sch. Sys. Enr. Code 4
  Supt. – Dr. Jean Higgins, 820 16TH ST   15010
  MS, 1601 8TH AVE   15010 – George Potter, prin.
  Central ES
    15TH STREET AND 9TH AVENUE   15010
    Timothy Pigza, prin.
  South ES
    4TH AVENUE AND PINE STREET   15010
    Timothy Pigza, prin.
  Other Schools – See Koppel

Blackhawk SD IU 27
  Sch. Sys. Enr. Code 4
  Supt. – Dr. Martha Johnston, 1601 8TH AVE   15010
  Highland MS, 402 SHENANGO ROAD   15010
    Edward Smith, prin.
  Patterson ES, 701 DARLINGTON ROAD   15010
    Robert Delgreco, prin.
  Other Schools – See Darlington

Riverside Beaver County SD IU 27
  Supt. – See Ellwood City
  Riverside PS, RURAL ROUTE 02   15010
    Joan Mansell, prin.

St. Mary ES, 609 10TH ST   15010
St. Philomena School, 4001 6TH AVE   15010

Beavertown, Snyder Co., Pop. Code 3
Midd-West SD IU 16
  Supt. – See Middleburg
  Beaver-Adams ES, RURAL ROUTE 01   17813
    David Angstadt, prin.

Bedford, Bedford Co., Pop. Code 5
Bedford Area SD IU 8
  Sch. Sys. Enr. Code 5
  Supt. – Jerry Dunkle, 330 E JOHN ST   15522
  MS, E WATSON ST   15522
    Robert Gervinski, prin.
  IS, RURAL ROUTE 05 BOX 364   15522
    Deryl Clark, prin.
  PS, SOURTH JULIANA STREET   15522
    Patricia Dorner, prin.
  Colerain ES, RURAL ROUTE 04   15522
    Cathy Cessna, prin.

Cumberland Valley ES
  RURAL ROUTE 03 BOX 138   15522
  James Norman, prin.
Other Schools – See Everett, Hyndman

St. Thomas Apostle ES, P O BOX 666   15522

Bedminster, Bucks Co., Pop. Code 5
Pennridge SD IU 22
  Supt. – See Perkasie
  ES, E HOLLAND RD   18910 – David Wagner, prin.

Beech Creek, Clinton Co., Pop. Code 3
Keystone Central SD IU 10
  Supt. – See Lock Haven
  ES, VESPER STREET   16822 – Thomas Croce, prin.

Bellefonte, Centre Co., Pop. Code 6
Bellefonte Area SD IU 10
  Sch. Sys. Enr. Code 5
  Supt. – Dr. Frederick Sample
    301 N ALLEGHENY ST   16823
  MS, 100 N SCHOOL ST   16823 – Elton Abel, prin.
  ES, 100 W LINN ST   16823 – Timothy Miller, prin.
  Benner ES, RURAL ROUTE 04 BOX 170B   16823
    Eileen Dillon, prin.
  Marion-Walker ES
    RURAL ROUTE 02 BOX 330X   16823
    H. Mencer, prin.
  Other Schools – See Pleasant Gap

Centre County Christian Academy
  P O BOX 47   16823
St. John the Evangelist ES
  116 E BISHOP ST   16823

Belle Vernon, Fayette Co., Pop. Code 4
Belle Vernon Area SD IU 7
  Sch. Sys. Enr. Code 5
  Supt. – G. Caruso, RURAL ROUTE 02   15012
  Marion ES, 500 PERRY AVE   15012
    Miles Kelley, prin.
  Rostraver ES, RURAL ROUTE 02   15012
    Raymond Ciferno, prin.

Chapel Christian School, 318 RIDGE ROAD   15012
St. Sebastian ES, 815 BROAD AVE   15012

Belleville, Mifflin Co.
Mifflin County SD IU 11
  Supt. – See Lewistown
  Union Township ES, RURAL ROUTE 02   17004
    George Bailor, prin.

Belleville Mennonite School, P O BOX 847   17004

Bellevue, Allegheny Co., Pop. Code 7

Assumption ES, 35 N JACKSON AVE   15202

Bellwood, Blair Co., Pop. Code 4
Bellwood-Antis SD IU 8
  Sch. Sys. Enr. Code 4
  Supt. – Michael Sakash, 400 MARTIN ST   16617
  Bellwood-Antis MS, MARTIN STREET   16617
    Robert Fisher, prin.
  Myers ES, MARTIN STREET   16617
    James Bilka, prin.
  North Side MS, NORTH THIRD STREET   16617
    Robert Fisher, prin.
  South Side MS, BOYLE STREET   16617
    James Bilka, prin.

Bendersville, Adams Co., Pop. Code 3
Upper Adams SD IU 12
  Supt. – See Biglerville
  ES, RAMPIKE HILL   17306 – Gayle Griffie, prin.

Bensalem, Bucks Co., Pop. Code 8
Bensalem Twp. SD IU 22
  Sch. Sys. Enr. Code 6
  Supt. – Dr. Robert Dampman
    3000 DONALLEN DRIVE   19020
  Armstrong MS, 2201 STREET ROAD   19020
    William Nichols, prin.
  Shafer MS, 3333 HULMEVILLE ROAD   19020
    Gary Rowe, prin.
  Snyder MS, 3333 HULMEVILLE ROAD   19020
    C. Pearson, prin.
  Belmont Hills ES, 5000 NESHAMINY BLVD   19020
    Robert Wurst, prin.
  Cornwells ES, 2400 BRISTOL PIKE   19020
    James Marchesani, prin.
  Faust ES, 2901 BELLVIEW DR   19020
    James Watson, Jr., prin.
  Rush ES, 3400 HULMEVILLE RD   19020
    Melvin Montanye, prin.
  Struble ES, 4300 BENSALEM BLVD   19020
    Frederick Straffe, prin.
  Valley ES, 3100 DONALLEN DR   19020
    Alan Bernabei, prin.

Our Lady of Fatima ES
  SAINT AND MECANICSVILLE RD   19020
St. Charles Borromeo ES
  1704 BRISTOL PIKE   19020
St. Ephrem ES, 5340 HULMEVILLE RD   19020

Bentleyville, Washington Co., Pop. Code 5
Bentworth SD IU 1
  Sch. Sys. Enr. Code 4
  Supt. – Reid Smith, 620 WASHINGTON ST   15314
  MS, 620 WASHINGTON ST   15314
    Anthony Conn, prin.
  Other Schools – See Eighty Four, Ellsworth

Benton, Columbia Co., Pop. Code 3
Benton Area SD IU 16
  Sch. Sys. Enr. Code 3
  Supt. – Dr. Linda Shea, RURAL ROUTE 02   17814
  Appleman ES, RURAL ROUTE 02   17814
    Jeffrey Walters, prin.

Berlin, Somerset Co., Pop. Code 4
Berlin-Brothersvalley SD IU 8
  Sch. Sys. Enr. Code 4
  Supt. – John Smrek, 1025 MAIN ST   15530
  Berlin Brothersvalley ES, 1025 MAIN ST   15530
    John Cornish, prin.

Bernville, Berks Co., Pop. Code 3
Tulpehocken Area SD IU 14
  Sch. Sys. Enr. Code 4
  Supt. – Charles Snyder, RURAL ROUTE 02   19506
  Penn Bernville ES, RURAL ROUTE 02   19506
    William Hunter, prin.
  Other Schools – See Bethel, Rehrersburg

Berrysburg, Dauphin Co., Pop. Code 2
Upper Dauphin Area SD IU 15
  Supt. – See Lykens
  ES, 801 WOOD ST   17005 – Rose Radzievich, prin.

Berwick, Columbia Co., Pop. Code 7
Berwick Area SD IU 16
  Sch. Sys. Enr. Code 5
  Supt. – David Force, 500 N MARKET ST   18603
  Fourteenth Street ES, 1401 N MARKET ST   18603
    Ronald Garrison, prin.
  Orange Street ES, 845 ORANGE ST   18603
    Charles Hestor, prin.
  Salem ES, 810 E 10TH ST   18603
    Alfred Melito, prin.
  Other Schools – See Nescopeck

Holy Family Consolidate ES
  728 WASHINGTON ST   18603

Berwyn, Chester Co., Pop. Code 4
Tredyffrin-Easttown SD IU 24
  Sch. Sys. Enr. Code 5
  Supt. – George Garwood
    1ST & BRIDGE AVES   19312
  Beaumont ES
    BEAUMONT AND NEWTOWN ROAD   19312
    Janet Bernhardt, prin.
  Hillside ES, 507 HOWELLVILLE RD   19312
    Anthony Paladino, prin.
  Other Schools – See Devon, Wayne

St. Monica ES
  FIRST AND WOODSIDE AVES   19312

Bessemer, Lawrence Co., Pop. Code 4
Mohawk Area SD IU 4
  Sch. Sys. Enr. Code 4
  Supt. – Edmund Retort   16112
  Mohawk ES, MOHAWK SCHOOL ROAD   16112
    James Verlotte, prin.

Bethel, Berks Co.
Tulpehocken Area SD IU 14
  Supt. – See Bernville
  MS, RURAL ROUTE 02   19507
    L. Messersmith, prin.

Bethel Park, Allegheny Co., Pop. Code 8
Bethel Park SD IU 3
  Sch. Sys. Enr. Code 5
  Supt. – Dr. Robert MacNaughton
    301 CHURCH ROAD   15102
  Independence MS
    2807 BETHEL CHURCH ROAD   15102
    Robert David, prin.
  Bethel Memorial ES
    3301 SOUTH PARK RD   15102
    Frederick Bowman, prin.
  Logan ES, 5851 KEYSTONE DR   15102
    William Raymer, prin.
  McMillan ES, 199 CAMBRIDGE RD   15102
    Albert Guiliano, prin.
  Penn ES, 110 WOODLET LN   15102
    James Wolf, prin.
  Washington ES, 431 MCMURRAY RD   15102
    Vance Sanford, prin.
  Other Schools – See Pittsburgh

Faith Community Christian School
  35 HIGHLAND ROAD   15102
St. Germaine School, 7001 BAPTIST RD   15102
St. Valentine ES, 2709 MESTA ST   15102

Bethlehem, Northampton Co., Pop. Code 8
Bethlehem Area SD IU 20
  Sch. Sys. Enr. Code 7
  Supt. – Thomas Doluisio
    1516 SYCAMORE ST   18017
  Broughal MS, 125 W PACKER AVE   18015
    Joe Petraglia, prin.
  East Hills MS, 2005 CHESTER AVE   18017
    Monty Perfetti, prin.
  Nitschmann MS, 909 W UNION BLVD   18018
    A. Thomas Kartsotis, prin.
  Northeast MS, 1110 FERNWOOD ST   18018
    David Shelly, prin.
  Buchanan ES, 1621 CATASAUQUA RD   18017
    James Ackerman, prin.
  Calypso ES, 1021 CALYPSO AVE   18018
    Shirley Bilheimer, prin.
  Clearview ES, 2121 ABINGTON RD   18018
    John Roman, prin.

Donegan ES, 1210 E 4TH ST 18015
  Marie Proctor, prin.
Fountain Hill ES, 1330 CHURCH ST 18015
  James Dundon, prin.
Governor Wolf ES, 1920 BUTZTOWN RD 18017
  Foster Leonhardt, prin.
Hanover ES, 3890 JACKSONVILLE RD 18017
  John Burke, prin.
Jefferson ES, 404 EAST NORTH STREET 18018
  Michael Loupos, prin.
Lincoln ES, 1810 RENWICK ST 18017
  Rebecca Bartholomew, prin.
Marvine ES, 1400 LEBANON ST 18017
  Gilbert Lopez, prin.
Miller Heights ES, 3605 ALLEN ST 18017
  George Neupauer, prin.
Packer ES, 1650 KENWOOD DR 18017
  Patricia Derrico, prin.
Penn ES, 1002 MAIN ST 18018
  Dominic Russo, prin.
Spring Garden ES, 901 NORTH BLVD 18017
  Richard Pappas, prin.
Other Schools — See Easton, Freemansburg

Bethlehem Christ Day ES
  3100 HECKTOWN RD 18017
Holy Child ES, SIOUX STA & GREENE CT 18015
Holy Infancy ES
  FOURTH AND WEBSTER ST 18015
Moravian Academy Lower MS
  422 HECKEWELDER PL 18018
Notre Dame of Beth ES
  1835 CATASAUQUA RD 18018
Our Lady of Perpetual Help ES
  3229 SANTEE RD 18017
Sacred Heart ES, 1814 2ND ST 18017
St. Anne's ES, HICKORY ST AND EASTON 18017
St. Michael Archangel ES
  RURAL ROUTE 03 18015
Sts. Cyril & Methodius ES
  520 BUCHANAN ST 18015
Sts. Simon & Jude ES, 714 W BROAD ST 18018

Bigler, Clearfield Co.
Clearfield Area SD IU 10
Supt. — See Clearfield
Bradford Township ES 16825
  Raymond Luke, prin.

Biglerville, Adams Co., Pop. Code 3
Upper Adams SD IU 12
Sch. Sys. Enr. Code 4
Supt. — Robert G. Witten, N MAIN ST 17307
ES, N MAIN ST 17307 — Ronald Ebbert, prin.
Other Schools — See Arendtsville, Bendersville

Big Run, Jefferson Co., Pop. Code 3
Punxsutawney Area SD IU 6
Supt. — See Punxsutawney
ES, MAIN STREET 15715 — Terrence Veitz, prin.

Bird In Hand, Lancaster Co.
Conestoga Valley SD IU 13
Supt. — See Lancaster
Johns ES, RURAL ROUTE 01 17505
  Beverly Breniser, prin.

Weavertown Menn ES, 73 ORCHARD RD 17505

Birdsboro, Berks Co., Pop. Code 5
Daniel Boone Area SD IU 14
Sch. Sys. Enr. Code 4
Supt. — Dr. Rita Jones, P O BOX 307 19508
Roosevelt MS
  3RD AND JEFFERSON STREETS 19508
  Roger Weinhold, prin.
Other Schools — See Douglassville

Twin Valley SD IU 14
Supt. — See Elverson
Robeson ES, RURAL ROUTE 03 BOX 2042 19508
  Terrence Siedel, prin.

Berks Christian School
  926 PHILADELPHIA TERRACE 19508

Black Lick, Indiana Co., Pop. Code 4
Blairsville-Saltsburg SD IU 28
Supt. — See Blairsville
Burrell ES 15716 — John Boylan, prin.

Blain, Perry Co., Pop. Code 2
West Perry SD IU 15
Supt. — See Elliottsburg
ES 17006 — Wayne Reisinger, prin.

Blairsville, Indiana Co., Pop. Code 5
Blairsville-Saltsburg SD IU 28
Sch. Sys. Enr. Code 4
Supt. — Gerald J. Clawson
  195 N WALNUT ST 15717
JHS, 195 N WALNUT ST 15717
  Louis Oliver, prin.
Third Ward ES, 145 S WALNUT ST 15717
  John Boylan, prin.
Other Schools — See Black Lick, Saltsburg

Sts. Simon & Jude ES, 329 E CAMPBELL ST 15717

Blanchard, Centre Co., Pop. Code 3
Keystone Central SD IU 10
Supt. — See Lock Haven
Liberty Curtin ES
  RURAL ROUTE 01 BOX 90 16826
  Wesley Burrows, prin.

Blandon, Berks Co., Pop. Code 4
Fleetwood Area SD IU 14
Supt. — See Fleetwood
Maier ES, MAIER BOULEVARD 19510
  Nancy Allmon, prin.

Bloomsburg, Columbia Co., Pop. Code 7
Bloomsburg Area SD IU 16
Sch. Sys. Enr. Code 4
Supt. — Alex J. Dubil
  12TH & RAILROAD STS 17815
MS, 1ST & CENTER STS 17815
  Robert Rupp, prin.
Beaver-Main ES, RURAL ROUTE 03 17815
  James Harris, prin.
Evans Memorial ES, 59 PERRY AVE 17815
  James Harris, prin.
Memorial ES, 5TH AND MARKET STREET 17815
  Karen Hess, prin.

Central Columbia SD IU 16
Sch. Sys. Enr. Code 4
Supt. — Horace Reynolds
  4777 OLD BERWICK ROAD 17815
Central Columbia MS
  4777 OLD BERWICK ROAD 17815
  Joe Kelly, prin.
Scott ES, 250 WORMAN ST 17815
  John Yastishock, prin.
Other Schools — See Mifflinville

Bloomsburg Christian School
  728 E 5TH ST 17815
St. Columbia ES, 40 E 3RD ST 17815

Blossburg, Tioga Co., Pop. Code 4
Southern Tioga SD IU 17
Supt. — See Mansfield
ES, 133 HANNIBAL ST 16912
  Ronald Miller, prin.

Blue Ball, Lancaster Co., Pop. Code 3
Eastern Lancaster County SD IU 13
Supt. — See New Holland
ES, P O BOX 427 17506 — Walter Wunderly, prin.

Blue Bell, Montgomery Co., Pop. Code 3
Wissahickon SD IU 23
Supt. — See Ambler
ES, SYMPHONY LANE 19422 — John Knebl, prin.

St. Helena ES, P O BOX 85 19422
Oak Lane Day ES, 137 STENTON AVE 19422

Bobtown, Greene Co., Pop. Code 4
Southeastern Green SD IU 1
Supt. — See Greensboro
ES, P O BOX 58 15315 — Robert Long, prin.

Boiling Springs, Cumberland Co., Pop. Code 4
Cumberland Valley SD IU 15
Supt. — See Mechanicsburg
Monroe ES, 1240 BOILING SPRINGS RD 17007
  Randall Pletcher, prin.

South Middleton SD IU 15
Sch. Sys. Enr. Code 4
Supt. — Dr. Robert Miller, 4 FORGE ROAD 17007
South Middleton Upper MS, 4 FORGE RD 17007
  Lee Devenney, prin.
Other Schools — See Mount Holly Springs

Bolivar, Westmoreland Co., Pop. Code 3
Ligonier Valley SD IU 7
Supt. — See Ligonier
Fairfield ES, RURAL ROUTE 01 15923
  Daniel McDonald, prin.

Boothwyn, Delaware Co., Pop. Code 5
Chichester SD IU 25
Sch. Sys. Enr. Code 5
Supt. — John A. Kaczenski, P O BOX 2100 19061
ES, 1414 MEETINGHOUSE RD 19061
  Barbara Kenney, prin.
Other Schools — See Aston, Linwood, Marcus Hook

Boswell, Somerset Co., Pop. Code 4
North Star SD IU 8
Sch. Sys. Enr. Code 4
Supt. — James Smith, 1200 MORRIS AVE 15531
North Star Central ES, 1200 MORRIS AVE 15531
  Francis Fregly, prin.
Other Schools — See Jennerstown, Kantner

Bowmansville, Lancaster Co.
Eastern Lancaster County SD IU 13
Supt. — See New Holland
Brecknock ES, P O BOX 158 17507
  Jonathan Green, prin.

Boyers, Butler Co.
Moniteau SD IU 4
Supt. — See West Sunbury
Marion ES, RURAL ROUTE 01 16020
  James Wetzel, prin.

Boyertown, Berks Co., Pop. Code 5
Boyertown Area SD IU 14
Sch. Sys. Enr. Code 6
Supt. — James Replogle
  911 MONTGOMERY AVE 19512
ES, 100 S MADISON ST 19512 — Lee Moyer, prin.
Earl ES, RURAL ROUTE 03 BOX 570 19512
  Kermit Bartholomew, prin.
Other Schools — See Barto, Gilbertsville, New
  Berlinville, Pine Forge

Brackenridge, Allegheny Co., Pop. Code 5
Highlands SD IU 3
Supt. — See Natrona Heights
Fairmount ES, PENN & ROUP STREETS 15014
  Albert Porter, prin.

Braddock, Allegheny Co., Pop. Code 6

Good Shepherd ES, 1025 BRADDOCK AVE 15104

Bradenville, Westmoreland Co., Pop. Code 4
Derry Area SD IU 7
Supt. — See Derry
ES, RURAL ROUTE BOX 157 15620
  Thomas Pavlik, prin.

Bradford, McKean Co., Pop. Code 7
Bradford Area SD IU 9
Sch. Sys. Enr. Code 5
Supt. — Dr. Elmer Myers, P O BOX 375 16701
Blaisdell ES, 265 CONSTITUTION AVE 16701
  Gary Lucas, prin.
Blaisdell Foundation ES
  150 KENNEDY STREET 16701
  Maureen O'Mara, prin.
West Branch ES, 645 W WASHINGTON ST 16701
  Samuel Johnson, prin.
Other Schools — See Custer City, Derrick City, Lewis
  Run

St. Bernard ES, 95 E CORYDON ST 16701

Bradfordwoods, Allegheny Co., Pop. Code 4
North Allegheny SD IU 3
Supt. — See Pittsburgh
ES, FOREST ROAD 15015 — Robert Vilscek, prin.

Breezewood, Bedford Co.
Everett Area SD IU 8
Supt. — See Everett
ES 15533 — James Droz, prin.

Brentwood, Allegheny Co., Pop. Code 7
Brentwood Borough SD IU 3
Supt. — See Pittsburgh
Elroy Avenue ES
  ELROY E. FRANCIS STREET 15227
  Jacquelyn Rauz, prin.
Moore ES, ELTON DALEWOOD STREET 15227
  Jacquelyn Rauz, prin.

Bridgeport, Montgomery Co., Pop. Code 5
Upper Merion Area SD IU 23
Supt. — See King of Prussia
ES, FORD STREET 19405
  Salvatore Rotondo, prin.

Sacred Heart of Jesus ES, 635 E FOUTH ST 19405
St. Augustine Our Lord Mt. ES
  BUSH AND RAMBO STS 19405

Bridgeville, Allegheny Co., Pop. Code 6
Chartiers Valley SD IU 3
Supt. — See Pittsburgh
Roberts ES, VANADIUM ROAD 15017
  Williams Rodgers, prin.
Washington ES, 528 DEWEY AVE 15017
  Edward Ewaskey, prin.

Center Christian Academy
  3831 WASHINGTON PIKE 15017
St. Agatha ES, 220 STATION ST 15017

Bristol, Bucks Co., Pop. Code 7
Bristol Borough SD IU 22
Sch. Sys. Enr. Code 4
Supt. — Michael McCool, 420 BUCKLEY ST 19007
Snyder ES, 420 BUCKLEY ST 19007
  John Girotti, prin.

Bristol Twp. SD IU 22
Sch. Sys. Enr. Code 6
Supt. — Joseph Kaufman, 800 COATES AVE 19007
Lafayette ES, 4201 FAYETTE DR 19007
  Kenneth McKinney, prin.
Other Schools — See Croydon, Levittown

St. Ann ES, 430 JEFFERSON AVE 19007
St. Mark ES, 1024 RADCLIFFE ST 19007

Brockway, Jefferson Co., Pop. Code 4
Brockway Area SD IU 6
Sch. Sys. Enr. Code 4
Supt. — Stephen Zarlinski, 96 NORTH ST 15824
North Street ES, 95 NORTH ST 15824
  Patrick Wright, prin.

Brodbecks, York Co.
South Western SD IU 12
Supt. — See Hanover
Manheim ES, RURAL ROUTE 02 BOX 188 17329
  Donald Stock, prin.

Brodheadsville, Monroe Co., Pop. Code 2
Pleasant Valley SD IU 20
Sch. Sys. Enr. Code 5
Supt. — Dr. John B. Nye 18322
Mills MS 18322 — Don Rinker, prin.
Chestnuthill ES, 120 PENN STREET 18322
  Harrie Blood, prin.
Other Schools — See Kresgeville, Kunkletown

Brogue, York Co.
Red Lion Area SD IU 12
Supt. — See Windsor
Chanceford ES. BOX 1400 17309
  Judith James, prin.

Clearview ES, P O BOX 340 17309
  Judith James, prin.

Brookhaven, Delaware Co., Pop. Code 6
  Chester Upland SD IU 25
  Supt. – See Chester
  Toby Farms ES
    TRIMBLE AND BRIDGEWATER 19015
    William Jones, prin.

  Penn-Delco SD IU 25
  Supt. – See Aston
  Coebourn ES, 1 COEBURN BLVD 19015
    Fred Passante, prin.
  Parkside ES, EDGMONT AVENUE 19015
    John Jennings, prin.

  Our Lady of Charity ES, 245 UPLAND RD 19015

Brooklyn, Susquehanna Co.
  Mountain View SD IU 19
  Supt. – See Kingsley
  ES 18813 – Margaret Coombs, prin.

Brookville, Jefferson Co., Pop. Code 5
  Brookville Area SD IU 6
  Sch. Sys. Enr. Code 4
  Supt. – J. Grottenthale, 265 BARNETT ST 15825
  Hickory Grove ES, JENKS STREET 15825
    John Stuchell, prin.
  Northside ES, P O BOX 479 15825
    John Stuchell, prin.
  Pinecreek ES, RURAL ROUTE 01 15825
    John Stuchell, prin.

Broomall, Delaware Co., Pop. Code 7
  Marple-Newtown SD IU 25
  Supt. – See Newtown Square
  Paxon Hollow JHS 19008 – James Best, prin.
  Loomis ES, S CENTRAL BOULEVARD 19008
    Eugene Pertchack, prin.
  Russell ES, SPROUL NEW ARDMORE 19008
    David Paxson, prin.
  Worrall ES, JPENNVIEW HEARTH ROAD 19008
    Dr. Richard Herbster, prin.

  St. Pius X ES, 204 LAWRENCE RD 19008

Brownstown, Cambria Co., Pop. Code 3
  Conestoga Valley SD IU 13
  Supt. – See Lancaster
  ES, SCHOOL LANE 17508
    Larry Donmoyer, prin.

Brownsville, Fayette Co., Pop. Code 5
  Brownsville Area SD IU 1
  Supt. – See Republic
  Cox-Donahey ES
    RURAL ROUTE 01 RT 166 15417
    Joseph Nepa, prin.
  Hiller ES, LEWIS ST 15417 – Debra Suba, prin.

  Brownsville Catholic ES
    300 SHAFFNER AVE 15417

Bruin, Butler Co., Pop. Code 3
  Karns City Area SD IU 4
  Supt. – See Karns City
  ES, HARPER AND HILLCREST 16022
    Harry O'Donnell, prin.

Bryn Athyn, Montgomery Co., Pop. Code 3

  Bryn Athyn Church ES, P O BOX 277 19009

Bryn Mawr, Montgomery Co., Pop. Code 7
  Haverford Twp. SD IU 25
  Supt. – See Havertown
  Coopertown ES
    HIGHLAND LANE AND COOP 19010
    Carol Plater, prin.

  Radnor Twp. SD IU 25
  Supt. – See Wayne
  Ithan ES, CLYDE AND SPROUL RD 19010
    Muriel Hopp, prin.

  Baldwin School
    MORRIS AND MONTGOMERY AVE 19010
  Country Day School of the Sacred Heart
    480 S BRYN MAWR AVE 19010
  Shipley School, 814 YARROW ST 19010
  St. Aloysius Academy
    401 S BRYN MAWR AVE 19010
  St. Thomas of Good Council ES
    PENNSWOOD AND LANCASTER 19010

Buckingham, Bucks Co., Pop. Code 2
  Central Bucks SD IU 22
  Supt. – See Doylestown
  ES, P O BOX 158 18912 – Carolyn Ambler, prin.

Burgettstown, Washington Co., Pop. Code 4
  Burgettstown Area SD IU 1
  Sch. Sys. Enr. Code 4
  Supt. – Eugene Sangiuliano, 99 MAIN ST 15021
  Hanover ES, RURAL ROUTE 01 15021
    Robert Peach, prin.
  Raccoon ES, RURAL ROUTE 03 15021
    (—), prin.
  Other Schools – See Atlasburg, Eldersville, Langeloth

  Our Lady of Lourdes ES, 620 S MAIN ST 15021

Burnham, Mifflin Co., Pop. Code 4
  Mifflin County SD IU 11
  Supt. – See Lewistown

ES, 101 N BEECH ST 17009
  Kenneth Barrett, prin.

Butler, Butler Co., Pop. Code 7
  Butler Area SD IU 4
  Sch. Sys. Enr. Code 6
  Supt. – Dr. Robert Paserba
    167 NEW CASTLE ROAD 16001
  Butler Area JHS, E NORTH ST 16001
    Vincent Burke, prin.
  Brittain ES
    PENN & WASHINGTON STREET 16001
    Sara Jones, prin.
  Broad Street ES
    BROAD & NORTH CASTLE STREET 16001
    Dominic Virgallito, prin.
  Center Avenue ES, CENTER AT LINCOLN 16001
    David Hillhouse, prin.
  Center Township ES, 950 MERCER RD 16001
    David Hillhouse, prin.
  McQuistion ES, MCQUISTION ROAD 16001
    Charles Kreinbucher, prin.
  Meridian ES, SPARKS AVENUE 16001
    Thomas Hughes, prin.
  Northwest ES, STALEY AVENUE 16001
    Vera Jones, prin.
  Oakland Township ES, 545 CHICORA RD 16001
    John Zgibor, prin.
  Summit ES, 351 BRINKER RD 16001
    Charles Kreinbucher, prin.
  Other Schools – See Connoquenessing, Fenelton

  Slippery Rock Area SD IU 4
  Supt. – See Slippery Rock
  Franklin Township MS, 139 RIEGER RD 16001
    Donald Downing, prin.

  South Butler County SD IU 4
  Supt. – See Saxonburg
  Jefferson ES, RURAL ROUTE 04 16001
    Thomas Tibbott, prin.
  Penn ES, 199 AIRPORT ROAD 16001
    Thomas Tibbott, prin.

  Butler Catholic ES, 515 E LOCUST ST 16001
  Holy Speulcher ES, RURAL ROUTE 06 16001

Cabot, Butler Co.
  South Butler County SD IU 4
  Supt. – See Saxonburg
  Winfield ES, 707 WINFIELD RD 16023
    Garry Molloy, prin.

  St. Lukes Lutheran ES, P O BOX 314 16023

Cairnbrook, Somerset Co., Pop. Code 4
  Shade-Central CSD IU 8
  Sch. Sys. Enr. Code 3
  Supt. – Hubert Donahue, MCGREGOR AVE 15924
  ES, 6TH & MCGREGOR AVENUE 15924
    Madeline Keri, prin.

Cambridge Springs, Crawford Co., Pop. Code 4
  Penncrest SD IU 5
  Supt. – See Saegertown
  ES, 130 STEELE ST 16403 – William Hayes, prin.

  Schooling Pro Rege, P O BOX 205 16403

Camp Hill, Cumberland Co., Pop. Code 6
  Camp Hill SD IU 15
  Sch. Sys. Enr. Code 3
  Supt. – William R. Freed
    2627 CHESTNUT ST 17011
  Hoover MS
    24TH STREET DICKINSON AVENU 17011
    Richard Lundvall, prin.
  Schaeffer ES
    29TH AND CHESTNUT STREETS 17011
    Robert Coffman, prin.

  East Pennsboro Area SD IU 15
  Supt. – See Enola
  West Creek Hills ES, 400 ERFORD RD 17011
    William Fry, prin.

  West Shore SD IU 15
  Supt. – See Lemoyne
  Allen MS, 4225 GETTYSBURG ROAD 17011
    Joseph Marcin, prin.
  Highland ES, 1325 CARLISLE RD 17011
    James Starr, prin.
  Lower Allen ES
    4100 OLD GETTYSBURG RD 17011
    Deloris McElroy, prin.

  Good Shepherd ES
    34TH AND MARKET STS 17011

Canonsburg, Washington Co., Pop. Code 7
  Canon-McMillan SD IU 1
  Sch. Sys. Enr. Code 5
  Supt. – Donald W. Strang
    1 N JEFFERSON AVE 15317
  Borland Manor ES, 30 GIFFIN DR 15317
    Richard Kern, prin.
  First Street ES, FIRST STREET 15317
    Rita Polansky, prin.
  Hills-Hendersonville ES
    320 MAYVIEW ROAD 15317
    Frank Brettschneid, prin.
  South Central Avenue ES
    230 S CENTRAL AVE 15317
    Susan Stonebraker, prin.
  Other Schools – See Cecil, Eighty Four, Muse

St. Patrick ES
    HUTCHINSON MURDOCK ST 15317

Canton, Bradford Co., Pop. Code 4
  Canton Area SD IU 17
  Sch. Sys. Enr. Code 4
  Supt. – Richard Neff, 139 E MAIN ST 17724
  ES, 141 EAST UN ST 17724 – James Arnold, prin.

Carbondale, Lackawanna Co., Pop. Code 7
  Carbondale Area SD IU 19
  Sch. Sys. Enr. Code 4
  Supt. – Dr. Joseph Como
    BROOKLYN ST ROUTE 6 18407
  Roosevelt ES
    SALEM AVENUE AND PARK ST 18407
    Dominick Famularo, prin.
  Other Schools – See Simpson

  Our Lady of Mt. Carmel ES
    2733 FAIRVIEW ST 18407
  St. Rose ES, 7 AVE CHURCH ST 18407

Cardale, Fayette Co.
  Brownsville Area SD IU 1
  Supt. – See Republic
  ES, 201 S HANOVER ST 15420
    Alfred Grant, prin.

Carlisle, Cumberland Co., Pop. Code 7
  Big Spring SD IU 15
  Supt. – See Newville
  Plainfield ES
    RURAL ROUTE 04 BOX 222A 17013
    Jay Shuman, prin.

  Carlisle Area SD IU 15
  Sch. Sys. Enr. Code 6
  Supt. – Dr. Robert Stowell, 623 W PENN ST 17013
  Lamberton ES, 777 S HANOVER ST 17013
    Kermit Leitner, prin.
  Wilson MS, 900 WAGGONER'S GAP ROAD 17013
    John Friend, prin.
  Bellaire ES, WAGGONERS GAP ROAD 17013
    Mary Durham, prin.
  Crestview ES, RURAL ROUTE 02 17013
    Robert Alspaugh, prin.
  Hamilton ES, CLAY STREET 17013
    Richard Greger, prin.
  Letort ES, E SOUTH AND S BEDFORD 17013
    Robert Tabachini, prin.
  Mooreland ES, WILSON STREET 17013
    Richard Ocker, prin.
  North Dickinson ES
    151 N DICKINSON SCHOOL RD 17013
    Pamela Ehly, prin.
  Other Schools – See Mount Holly Springs

  Cumberland Valley SD IU 15
  Supt. – See Mechanicsburg
  Middlesex ES, 250 N MIDDLESEX RD 17013
    Ralph Johnson, prin.

  Grace Baptist Christian School
    777 W NORTH ST 17013
  St. Patrick ES, 87 MARCH DR 17013

Carmichaels, Greene Co., Pop. Code 3
  Carmichaels Area SD IU 1
  Sch. Sys. Enr. Code 4
  Supt. – Dr. Dolores A. Zoldos
    300 W GREENE ST 15320
  Central ES, 215 S MARKET ST 15320
    Terry Ganocy, prin.
  Other Schools – See Crucible, Nemacolin

Carnegie, Allegheny Co., Pop. Code 7
  Carlynton SD IU 3
  Sch. Sys. Enr. Code 4
  Supt. – Dr. Frank Ameruoso
    435 KINGS HWY 15106
  ES, FRANKLIN AVENUE 15106
    Robert Fuller, prin.
  Other Schools – See Crafton

  Chartiers Valley SD IU 3
  Supt. – See Pittsburgh
  Heidelberg ES, 1819 ELLSWORTH AVE 15106
    Philip Cartier, prin.
  Nixon ES, 1000 LINDSAY RD 15106
    Philip Cartier, prin.
  Shepard ES, 175 MCMICHAEL RD 15106
    Edward Ewaskey, prin.

  St. Ignatius ES, 127 FINLEY AVE 15106
  St. Luke ES, 316 3RD AVE 15106

Carrolltown, Cambria Co., Pop. Code 4
  Cambria Heights SD IU 8
  Supt. – See Patton
  MS 15722 – Michael Johnson, prin.

  St. Benedict ES, CHURCH ST 15722

Cashtown, Adams Co.
  Gettysburg SD IU 12
  Supt. – See Gettysburg
  Franklin Township ES 17310 – L. Ruggles, prin.

Cassville, Huntingdon Co., Pop. Code 2
  Southern Huntingdon County SD IU 11
  Supt. – See Orbisonia
  Trough Creek Valley ES, RURAL ROUTE 01 16623
    Kenneth Beck, prin.

Castanea, Clinton Co., Pop. Code 4
Keystone Central SD IU 10
Supt. – See Lock Haven
ES, LOGAN AVENUE 17726 – Thomas Ryan, prin.

Castle Shannon, Allegheny Co., Pop. Code 7

St. Anne ES, 4040 WILLOW AVE 15234

Catasauqua, Lehigh Co., Pop. Code 6
Catasauqua Area SD IU 21
Sch. Sys. Enr. Code 4
Supt. – F. J. Farrell, 201 N 14TH ST 18032
Lincoln MS, 330 HOWERTOWN ROAD 18032
Frank Snyder, prin.
Sheckler ES, 201 N 14TH ST 18032
Edward Bruchak, prin.

Catawissa, Columbia Co., Pop. Code 4
Southern Columbia Area SD IU 16
Sch. Sys. Enr. Code 4
Supt. – Margaret Jessick
RURAL ROUTE 02 BOX 372B 17820
Hartman ES, RURAL ROUTE 02 BOX 372C 17820
Roy Clippinger, prin.

Cecil, Washington Co., Pop. Code 3
Canon-McMillan SD IU 1
Supt. – See Canonsburg
ES, RURAL ROUTE 04 15321
Frank Brettschneid, prin.

Center Valley, Lehigh Co.
Southern Lehigh SD IU 21
Sch. Sys. Enr. Code 4
Supt. – Michael F. Greene
RURAL ROUTE 01 BOX 13 18034
Southern Lehigh MS
RURAL ROUTE 01 BOX 13 18034
John Yeager, prin.
Hopewell ES, RURAL ROUTE 02 BOX 219 18034
Robert Csizma, prin.
Other Schools – See Coopersburg

Centre Hall, Centre Co., Pop. Code 4
Penns Valley Area SD IU 10
Supt. – See Spring Mills
Centre Hall Potter ES
143 NORTH HOFFER STREET 16828
Ruth Rishel, prin.

Chadds Ford, Delaware Co.
Unionville-Chadds Ford SD IU 24
Supt. – See Unionville
ES 19317 – Frederick Darling, prin.

Chalfont, Bucks Co., Pop. Code 5
Central Bucks SD IU 22
Supt. – See Doylestown
Butler ES, 200 BRITTANY DR 18914
Eugene Gourley, prin.

St. Jude ES, 323 W BUTLER AVE 18914

Chambersburg, Franklin Co., Pop. Code 7
Chambersburg Area SD IU 12
Sch. Sys. Enr. Code 6
Supt. – Edwin Sponseller, 511 S SIXTH ST 17201
Chambersburg Area MS
1151 E MCKINLEY ST 17201
James Papoutsis, prin.
Buchanan ES, 730 E WASHINGTON ST 17201
Charles Manning, prin.
Coldbrook ES, 756 S COLDBROOK AVE 17201
Jack Goodhart, prin.
Duffield ES, 2168 MONT ALTO RD 17201
Joann Young, prin.
Falling Spring ES
1006 FALLING SPRING RD 17201
Paul Sick, prin.
Gordy ES, 401 MILLER ST 17201
Margaret Reasey, prin.
Grandview ES, 5538 CUMBERLAND HWY 17201
James Taylor, prin.
Guilford Hills ES, 2105 LINCOLN WAY E 17201
Mary Frey, prin.
Hamilton Heights ES, 1589 JOHNSON RD 17201
Susan Perry, prin.
King Street ES, EAST KING STREET 17201
Bonita Cockley, prin.
New Franklin ES, 3584 WAYNE RD 17201
Brian MacKey, prin.
Portico MS, 5222 FORT MCCORD RD 17201
Patricia Stumbaugh, prin.
Sharpe ES, 850 BROAD ST 17201
Cynthia Campbell, prin.
South Hamilton ES
1019 WARM SPRING RD 17201
Jeanine Hocker, prin.
Stevens ES, 800 HOLLYWELL AVE 17201
William Cockley, prin.
Other Schools – See Fayetteville, Lurgan, Marion,
Scotland, Upperstrasburg

Cumberland Valley Christian School
600 MILLER ST 17201
Shalom Christian Academy
126 SOCIAL ISLAND ROAD 17201
Corpus Christi ES, N 2 AND GRANT STS 17201

Charleroi, Washington Co., Pop. Code 6
Charleroi Area SD IU 1
Sch. Sys. Enr. Code 4
Supt. – Donald A. Celaschi, FECSEN DRIVE 15022

Crest Avenue ES
SIXTH STREET AND CREST AVE 15022
Francis Vescio, prin.
Fallowfield ES, RURAL ROUTE 01 15022
Francis Vescio, prin.
Meadow Avenue MS
4TH ST MEADOW AVENUE 15022
Francis Vescio, prin.

St. Jerome ES
6TH AND WASHINGTON AVE 15022

Cheltenham, Montgomery Co., Pop. Code 6
Cheltenham Twp. SD IU 23
Supt. – See Elkins Park
ES, ASHBOURNE RD AND FRON 19012
Helen Fox, prin.

Presentation BVM ES
107 OLD SOLDIERS RD 19012
St. Joseph ES
BONCOURER AND WATERS RD 19012

Chester, Delaware Co., Pop. Code 8
Chester Upland SD IU 25
Sch. Sys. Enr. Code 6
Supt. – Harold Smith
18TH & MELROSE AVE 19013
Pulaski MS, 7TH & HARWICK STS 19013
Joseph Madzelan, prin.
Showalter MS, 10TH AND LLOYD ST 19013
Toney Lucas, prin.
Smedley MS, 17TH AND UPLAND ST 19013
J. Harold Hughes, prin.
Columbus ES, 10TH & FULTON ST 19013
Wendell Sharpe,Jr., prin.
Penn ES, HIGHLAND AVENUE TWP LINE 19013
Sylvester Pompilii, prin.
Stetser ES, 17TH AND MELROSE AVENUE 19061
Thomas Kelley, prin.
Washington ES
7TH AND CENTRAL AVENUE 19013
Daniel Petino, prin.
Wetherill ES, 24TH POTTER STREETS 19013
Pamela DeJarnette, prin.
Other Schools – See Brookhaven, Upland

Holy Ghost ES, 3010 W 3RD ST 19013
Immaculate Heart of Mary ES
229 NORRIS ST 19013
Resurrection of Our Lord ES
10TH & HIGHLAND AVE 19013
St. Francis De Sales School, 39 NEW ROAD 19014
St. Hedwig ES, 2609 W 4TH ST 19013
St. Robert ES, 1902 PROVIDENCE AVE 19013

Chester Springs, Chester Co.

Montgomery ES, 1 ROUTE 113 19425

Cheswick, Allegheny Co., Pop. Code 4
Allegheny Valley SD IU 3
Sch. Sys. Enr. Code 4
Supt. – Don G. McGhee, PEARL AVE 15024
Acmetonia ES, PEARL STREET 15024
Ralph Varrato, prin.
Other Schools – See Springdale

Deer Lakes SD IU 3
Sch. Sys. Enr. Code 4
Supt. – John Disanti, RURAL ROUTE 05 15024
Deer Lakes MS, RURAL ROUTE 05 15024
James Yaconis, prin.
East Union Road ES, RURAL ROUTE 05 15024
James Yaconis, prin.
Other Schools – See Creighton

Cheswick Christian Academy
1407 PITTSBURGH ST 15024

Chicora, Butler Co., Pop. Code 4
Karns City Area SD IU 4
Supt. – See Karns City
ES, ALLISON HALLAM AVENUES 16025
Harry O'Donnell, prin.

Chinchilla, Lackawanna Co., Pop. Code 4
Abington Heights SD IU 19
Supt. – See Clarks Summit
South Abington ES, NORTHERN BLVD #16 18410
Allan Rose, prin.

Christiana, Lancaster Co., Pop. Code 4
Solanco SD IU 13
Supt. – See Quarryville
Bart-Colerain ES, 1336 NOBLE RD 17509
Kathleen Legenstein, prin.

Clairton, Allegheny Co., Pop. Code 7
Clairton CSD IU 3
Sch. Sys. Enr. Code 4
Supt. – Carmen Sarnicola, 535 5TH ST 15025
MS, 734 MILLER AVE 15025
John Invernizzi, prin.
PS, 501 WADDELL AVE 15025 – (—), prin.

West Jefferson Hills SD IU 3
Supt. – See Pittsburgh
Gill Hall ES, 829 GILL HALL RD 15025
John Ward,Jr., prin.
Roosevelt ES, 105 OAK RD 15025
W. Coulson, prin.

Clairton Central Catholic ES
336 WILSON AVE 15025

Clarence, Centre Co.
Bald Eagle Area SD IU 10
Supt. – See Wingate
MS, RURAL ROUTE 16829 – Sandra Rockey, prin.

Clarendon, Warren Co., Pop. Code 3
Warren County SD IU 5
Supt. – See Warren
Allegheny Valley ES, MAIN STREET 16313
John Johnson, prin.

Claridge, Westmoreland Co.
Penn-Trafford SD IU 7
Supt. – See Harrison City
Penn MS 15623 – T. Perich, prin.
McCullough ES, OOL 15623
John Meneghini, prin.

Clarion, Clarion Co., Pop. Code 6
Clarion Area SD IU 6
Sch. Sys. Enr. Code 4
Supt. – Joseph Fotos, 800 BOUNDARY ST 16214
Clarion Area ES, 800 BOUNDARY ST 16214
Thomas Shirey, prin.

Immaculate Conception ES, 729 MAIN ST 16214

Clarks Summit, Lackawanna Co., Pop. Code 6
Abington Heights SD IU 19
Sch. Sys. Enr. Code 6
Supt. – Elvin LaCoe, 218 E GROVE ST 18411
Abington Heights MS, RURAL ROUTE 04 18411
F. Oravec, prin.
Grove Street ES, 218 EAST GROVE STREET 18411
William Carlin, prin.
Newton-Ransom ES, RURAL ROUTE 02 18411
Allan Rose, prin.
Other Schools – See Chinchilla, Waverly

Our Lady of Peace ES
410 N ABINGTON RD 18411
Summit Baptist Academy, 625 MOBLE RD 18411

Claysburg, Blair Co., Pop. Code 4
Claysburg-Kimmel SD IU 8
Sch. Sys. Enr. Code 4
Supt. – James O'Harrow 16625
Roosevelt MS, BEDFORD STREET 16625
Thomas Moore, prin.
Other Schools – See Queen

Claysville, Washington Co., Pop. Code 4
McGuffey SD IU 1
Sch. Sys. Enr. Code 5
Supt. – Elizabeth A. Logan, P O BOX 431 15323
McGuffey MS, RURAL ROUTE 01 15323
Charles Mahoney, prin.
Blaine-Buffalo ES, RURAL ROUTE 01 15323
Raymond Pizzi, prin.
ES, MAIN STREET 15323 – Linda Barnhart, prin.
East-West Finley ES, RURAL ROUTE 01 15323
John McCullough, prin.
Other Schools – See Washington, West Alexander

Clearfield, Clearfield Co., Pop. Code 6
Clearfield Area SD IU 10
Sch. Sys. Enr. Code 5
Supt. – Stanley Rakowsky, P O BOX 710 16830
Centre ES, RURAL ROUTE 04 16830
Gordon Tomb, prin.
Clearfield Area MS, P O BOX 710 16830
R. Rishel, prin.
Goshen ES, RURAL ROUTE 02 16830
Raymond Luke, prin.
Leonard ES, 5TH & MARKET STREETS 16830
Gordon Tomb, prin.
Plymptonville ES, SHAW STREET 16830
Gordon Tomb, prin.
Third Ward ES, MILL ROAD 16830
Raymond Luke, prin.
Other Schools – See Bigler, Glen Richey, Lecontes
Mills

Clearfield Alli Christian School
RURAL ROUTE 02 BOX 257 16830
St. Francis ES, 230 S SECOND ST 16830

Clearville, Bedford Co.
Everett Area SD IU 8
Supt. – See Everett
Mann-Monroe ES, RURAL ROUTE 02 15535
Richard Border, prin.

Cleona, Lebanon Co., Pop. Code 4
Annville-Cleona SD IU 13
Supt. – See Annville
ES, LINCOLN WALNUT STREETS 17042
Marion Miller, prin.

Clifford, Susquehanna Co.
Mountain View SD IU 19
Supt. – See Kingsley
ES 18413 – Margaret Coombs, prin.

Clifton Heights, Delaware Co., Pop. Code 6
Upper Darby SD IU 25
Supt. – See Drexel Hill
Westbrook Park ES
SPRINGFIELD & BISHOP AVE 19018
David Priebe, prin.

Our Lady of Fatima ES, 10 FATIMA DR 19018

Clymer, Indiana Co., Pop. Code 4
Penns Manor Area SD IU 28
Sch. Sys. Enr. Code 5
Supt. – M. Monaghan, RURAL ROUTE 02 15728

Penns Manor ES, RURAL ROUTE 02 15728
Edward Meshanko, prin.

Coal Center, Washington Co., Pop. Code 2
California Area SD IU 1
Sch. Sys. Enr. Code 4
Supt. – James Johnston, RURAL ROUTE 01 15423
California Area ES, RURAL ROUTE 01 15423
Ronald Keppich, prin.

Coatesville, Chester Co., Pop. Code 7
Coatesville Area SD IU 24
Sch. Sys. Enr. Code 6
Supt. – Louis Laurento
1515 E LINCOLN HWY 19320
Gordon MS, 351 KERSEY ST 19320
William Brunson, prin.
North Brandywine MS
200 REECEVILLE ROAD 19320 – Al Bullock, prin.
South Brandywine MS
RURAL ROUTE 03 BOX 121 19320
Judith MacCloskey, prin.
Benner ES, 545 E LINCOLN HWY 19320
Elaine Clayton, prin.
East Fallowfield ES, RURAL ROUTE 01 19320
Michael Leonard, prin.
Friendship ES, 300 REECEVILLE RD 19320
Michael Givler, prin.
Kings Highway ES
RURAL ROUTE 06 BOX 263 19320
David Hemingway, prin.
Rainbow ES, 50 COUNTRY CLUB RD 19320
Eva Andrew, prin.
Other Schools – See Thorndale

Coatesville Catholic ES
605 E LINCOLN HWY 19320
Lan-Chester Christian School
1400 OLIVE ST 19320

Cochranton, Crawford Co., Pop. Code 4
Crawford Central SD IU 5
Supt. – See Meadville
Cochranton Area ES, RURAL ROUTE 04 16314
Lynn Dickson, prin.

Codorus, York Co.
Spring Grove Area SD IU 12
Supt. – See Spring Grove
Jefferson ES, P O BOX 217 17311
Carol Kling, prin.

Cogan Station, Lycoming Co.
Williamsport Area SD IU 17
Supt. – See Williamsport
Hepburn-Lycoming ES, RURAL ROUTE 02 17728
R. Marks, prin.

Collegeville, Montgomery Co., Pop. Code 5
Methacton SD IU 23
Supt. – See Fairview Village
Arrowhead ES, RURAL ROUTE 02 19426
James Brown, prin.

Perkiomen Valley SD IU 23
Supt. – See Schwenksville
Perkiomen Valley MS
3RD AVENUE TRAPPE 19426
Richard Devaney, prin.
Perkiomen Valley South ES
3RD AVENUE TRAPPE 19426
Joanne Waddell, prin.

Spring-Ford Area SD IU 23
Sch. Sys. Enr. Code 5
Supt. – William Welliver
199 BECHTEL ROAD 19426
Other Schools – See Oaks, Royersford, Spring City

St. Eleanor ES, 406 MAIN ST 19426

Collingdale, Delaware Co., Pop. Code 6
Southeast Delco SD IU 25
Supt. – See Folcroft
Harris ES, SHARON AND BLACKSTONE 19023
Catherine Crossett, prin.

St. Joseph ES, 1012 BARTRAM AVE 19023

Columbia, Lancaster Co., Pop. Code 7
Columbia Borough SD IU 13
Sch. Sys. Enr. Code 4
Supt. – D. K. Detwiler
901 IRONVILLE PIKE 17512
Park ES, 50 S 6TH ST 17512
Robert McConaghy, prin.
Taylor Street ES, 45 N 9TH ST 17512
Robert McConaghy, prin.

Holy Trinity ES
FOURTH AND CHERRY STS 17512
St. Peter School, 125 S SECOND ST 17512

Columbia Cross Roads, Bradford Co.
Troy Area SD IU 17
Supt. – See Troy
Springfield Township ES
RURAL ROUTE 02 16914
Dr. Roger Goodman, prin.

Columbus, Warren Co., Pop. Code 2
Corry Area SD IU 5
Supt. – See Corry
ES, MAIN STREET EXTENDED 16405
Richard Patterson, prin.

Colwyn, Delaware Co., Pop. Code 5
William Penn SD IU 25
Supt. – See Yeadon
ES, 2ND AND PINE STREETS 19023
M. Dzedzej, prin.

Commodore, Indiana Co.
Purchase Line SD IU 28
Sch. Sys. Enr. Code 4
Supt. – Dwight E. Brocious
RURAL ROUTE 01 BOX 241-A 15729
Purchase Line South ES
RURAL ROUTE 01 BOX 374 15729
Earl Winsheimer, prin.
Other Schools – See Mahaffey

Concordville, Delaware Co.
Garnet Valley SD IU 25
Sch. Sys. Enr. Code 4
Supt. – Dr. Vernon Wyland, P O BOX 233 19331
Concord MS, P O BOX 233 19331
John McCoy, prin.
Green ES, P O BOX 233 19331 – David Fry, prin.

Conestoga, Lancaster Co.
Penn Manor SD IU 13
Supt. – See Millersville
ES, RURAL ROUTE 01 17516
Diane Denison, prin.

Confluence, Somerset Co., Pop. Code 3
Turkeyfoot Valley Area SD IU 8
Sch. Sys. Enr. Code 3
Supt. – Pete Forno, RURAL ROUTE 01 15424
Turkeyfoot Valley ES
RURAL ROUTE 01 BOX 78 15424
Albert Packan, prin.

Conneaut Lake, Crawford Co., Pop. Code 3
Conneaut SD IU 5
Supt. – See Linesville
Conneaut Lake-Sadsbry ES
630 LINE STREET 16316 – Henry Eberhart, prin.
Greenwood ES
RURAL ROUTE 03 BOX 469 16316
Henry Eberhart, prin.

Conneautville, Crawford Co., Pop. Code 3
Conneaut SD IU 5
Supt. – See Linesville
Conneaut Valley ES
RURAL ROUTE 03 BOX 197 16406
Robert Cryder, prin.

Connellsville, Fayette Co., Pop. Code 7
Connellsville Area SD IU 1
Sch. Sys. Enr. Code 6
Supt. – Dr. John Phillips, 125 N 7TH ST 15425
Bullskin ES, 125 PLEASANT VALLEY RD 15425
Wanda Reynolds, prin.
Connell ES, 700 PARK ST 15425
Vincent Dipaolo, prin.
Connellsville Township ES
730 ROCKRIDGE RD 15425
Wanda Reynolds, prin.
Dunbar Township ES, 711 RIDGE BLVD 15425
William Baer, prin.
South Side ES, 1135 RACE ST 15425
(—), prin.
Other Schools – See Dunbar, Melcroft, Normalville

Conn Area Catholic ES
110 N PROSPECT ST 15425

Connoquenessing, Butler Co., Pop. Code 3
Butler Area SD IU 4
Supt. – See Butler
ES, CONNOQUENESSING SCHOOL ROAD 16027
Dominic Virgallito, prin.

Conshohocken, Montgomery Co., Pop. Code 6
Colonial SD IU 23
Supt. – See Plymouth Meeting
ES, 3RD AVENUE AND HARRY ST 19428
Patricia Iannelli, prin.
Ridge Park ES
KARRS LA AND LITTLE AVE 19428
John Canterbury, prin.

St. Cosmas & Damian ES
FIFTH AVE AND MAPLE ST 19428
St. Mary School, 1ST AVE AND MAPLE ST 19428
St. Matthew ES, 205 FAYETTE ST 19428

Conway, Beaver Co., Pop. Code 5
Freedom Area SD IU 27
Supt. – See Freedom
ES, 2ND AVENUE 15027 – Eugene Cercone, prin.

Conyngham, Luzerne Co., Pop. Code 4
Hazleton Area SD IU 18
Supt. – See Hazleton
ES, MAIN ST 18219 – Harold Getz, prin.

Coopersburg, Lehigh Co., Pop. Code 5
Southern Lehigh SD IU 21
Supt. – See Center Valley
ES, 317 E STATE ST 18036 – Julia Moore, prin.
Liberty Bell ES, 960 W OXFORD ST 18036
Julia Moore, prin.
Lower Milford ES
RURAL ROUTE 02 BOX 567 18036
Robert Csizma, prin.

Cooperstown, Venango Co., Pop. Code 3
Oil City Area SD IU 6
Supt. – See Oil City

Oakland ES, RURAL ROUTE 01 16317
Kenneth Nelson, prin.

Valley Grove SD IU 6
Supt. – See Franklin
ES, 2 CHURCH STREET 16317
Eugene Sheffer, prin.

Coplay, Lehigh, Pop. Code 5
Parkland SD IU 21
Supt. – See Orefield
Ironton ES, RURAL ROUTE 01 18037
Richard Houck, prin.

Christ the King ES, 22 S 5TH ST 18037

Coraopolis, Allegheny Co., Pop. Code 6
Cornell SD IU 3
Sch. Sys. Enr. Code 3
Supt. – Joseph R. Karlik
1099 MAPLE ST EXT 15108
Cornell ES, 1099 MAPLE ST EXT 15108
Orlando Falcione, prin.

Montour Sd IU 3
Sch. Sys. Enr. Code 5
Supt. – Dr. Richard Davis, GRANT ST 15108
Williams JHS, PORTERS HOLLOW ROAD 15108
Steve Wargo, prin.
Forest Grove ES, 1 FOREST GROVE RD 15108
Ross Mastrean, prin.
Other Schools – See Mc Kees Rocks, Pittsburgh

Moon Area SD IU 3
Sch. Sys. Enr. Code 5
Supt. – Donald Deep
1407 BEERS SCHOOL ROAD 15108
Allard ES, 170 SHAFER RD 15108
Charles Franklin, prin.
Bon Meade ES, 1595 BROADHEAD RD 15108
Alexander Meta, prin.
Hyde ES, 110 WALL RIDGE DRIVE 15108
John Sheffler, prin.
Pleasant View ES
1301 CORAOPOLIS HTS RD 15108
Richard Davis, prin.

St. Joseph ES, 1313 5TH AVE 15108
St. Malacy ES, 343 FOREST GROVE RD 15108

Cornwall, Lebanon Co., Pop. Code 5
Cornwall-Lebanon SD IU 13
Supt. – See Lebanon
ES, 1825 S FIFTH AVENUE 17016
Ira Light, prin.

Corry, Erie Co., Pop. Code 6
Corry Area SD IU 5
Sch. Sys. Enr. Code 5
Supt. – John McCracken, 800 E SOUTH ST 16407
Concord ES, 230 EAST ST 16407
James Anundson, prin.
Conelway ES, RURAL ROUTE 03 16407
Richard Patterson, prin.
Wright ES, 426 WRIGHT ST 16407
John Linden, prin.
Other Schools – See Columbus, Spartansburg

St. Thomas ES, 229 W WASHINGTON ST 16407

Coudersport, Potter Co., Pop. Code 5
Coudersport Area SD IU 9
Sch. Sys. Enr. Code 3
Supt. – Dr. Joseph DeRenzis, SCHOOL ST 16915
ES, 14 S MAIN ST 16915 – Thomas Todd, prin.

Cowansville, Armstrong Co.
Armstrong SD IU 28
Supt. – See Ford City
Sugarcreek ES, RURAL ROUTE 01 16218
Richard Grabiec, prin.

Crafton, Allegheny Co., Pop. Code 6
Carlynton SD IU 3
Supt. – See Carnegie
ES, 1874 CRAFTON BLVD 15205
Joseph Covelli, prin.

Creighton, Allegheny Co., Pop. Code 4
Deer Lakes SD IU 3
Supt. – See Cheswick
Kennedy Memorial ES
120 CRAWFORD RUN RD 15030
James Yaconis, prin.

Cresco, Monroe Co.
Pocono Mountain SD IU 20
Supt. – See Swiftwater
Barrett ES 18326 – Thomas Kopetskie, prin.

Monsignor McHugh ES, RURAL ROUTE 01 18326

Cresson, Cambria Co., Pop. Code 4
Penn Cambria SD IU 8
Sch. Sys. Enr. Code 4
Supt. – Russell Strange, 214 POWELL AVE 16630
ES, 205 6TH STREET 16630
Richard Sweeney, prin.
Other Schools – See Gallitzin, Lilly

St. Aloysius ES, 850 WILLIAM PENN HWY 16630
St. Francis Xavier ES, 220 POWELL AVE 16630

Cressona, Schuylkill Co., Pop. Code 4
Blue Mountain SD IU 29
Supt. – See Orwigsburg
MS, 45 WILDER ST 17929 – Robert Long, prin.

Croydon, Bucks Co., Pop. Code 6
Bristol Twp. SD IU 22
Supt. – See Bristol
Devine ES, KEYSTONE STREET 19020
Jennaro Rose, prin.
Maple Shade ES, PROSPECT AVENUE 19020
Joseph Trachy, prin.

St. Thomas Aquinas ES
BRISTOL PK AND WALNUT 19020

Crucible, Greene Co., Pop. Code 3
Carmichaels Area SD IU 1
Supt. – See Carmichaels
ES, 215 S MARKET STREET 15325
Terry Ganocy, prin.

Curwensville, Clearfield Co., Pop. Code 5
Curwensville Area SD IU 10
Sch. Sys. Enr. Code 4
Supt. – Robert Dreibelbis, 650 BEECH ST 16833
ES, 650 BEECH ST 16833
Richard McKnight, prin.
Other Schools – See Grampian

Custer City, McKean Co.
Bradford Area SD IU 9
Supt. – See Bradford
ES, DEFOE ST 16725 – J. Hare, prin.

Dallas, Luzerne Co., Pop. Code 5
Dallas SD IU 18
Sch. Sys. Enr. Code 5
Supt. – Gerald Wycallis, P O BOX 2000 18612
ES, HILDEBRANDT ROAD 18612
Ruth Tetschner, prin.
Other Schools – See Trucksville

Gate of Heaven ES, 10 MACHELL AVE 18612

Dallastown, York Co., Pop. Code 5
Dallastown Area SD IU 12
Sch. Sys. Enr. Code 5
Supt. – A. Neil Harvey, RURAL ROUTE 01 17313
Dallastown Area MS, RURAL ROUTE 01 17313
Donald E. Myers, prin.
ES, S CHARLES STREET 17313
Barry Rohrbaugh, prin.
Other Schools – See York

St. Joseph ES, 271 E MAIN ST 17313

Dalmatia, Northumberland Co.
Line Mountain SD IU 16
Supt. – See Herndon
ES, RURAL ROUTE 01 BOX 293 17017
Gary Gonsar, prin.

Dalton, Lackawanna Co., Pop. Code 4
Lackawanna Trail SD IU 19
Supt. – See Factoryville
ES, 16 MILL STREET 18414 – James Evans, prin.

Tunkhannock Area SD IU 18
Supt. – See Tunkhannock
Mill City ES, RURAL ROUTE 02 18414
Ernestine Swetland, prin.

Damascus, Wayne Co.
Wayne Highlands SD IU 19
Supt. – See Honesdale
Damascus Area ES 18415 – Thomas Jenkins, prin.

Danboro, Bucks Co., Pop. Code 3
Central Bucks SD IU 22
Supt. – See Doylestown
Gayman ES, POINT PLEASANT PIKE 18916
George Kallenbach, prin.

Danville, Montour Co., Pop. Code 6
Danville Area SD IU 16
Sch. Sys. Enr. Code 5
Supt. – William Opdenhoff
PINE & E MAHONING STS 17821
ES, ROUTE 11 17821 – Shelley Crawford, prin.
Liberty Valley ES, RURAL ROUTE 01 17821
Charles Hughes, prin.
Mahoning Cooper ES, 1605 BLOOM RD 17821
Charles Hughes, prin.
Riverside ES, RURAL ROUTE 06 17868
Shelley Crawford, prin.
Other Schools – See Washingtonville

St. Jospeh ES, 9 BLOOM ST 17821

Darby, Delaware Co., Pop. Code 7
William Penn SD IU 25
Supt. – See Yeadon
Park Lane ES, PARK LANE 19023
Robert Wetzel, prin.
Walnut Street ES
6TH AND WALNUT STREETS 19023
M. Gaskill, prin.

Blessed Virgin Mary ES
51 MACDADE BLVD 19023

Darlington, Beaver Co., Pop. Code 2
Blackhawk SD IU 27
Supt. – See Beaver Falls
Northwest ES, RURAL ROUTE 02 BOX 1 16115
W. Byrne, prin.

Dauphin, Dauphin Co., Pop. Code 3
Central Dauphin SD IU 15
Supt. – See Harrisburg

Middle Paxton ES
931 PETERS MOUNTAIN RD 17018
John Osuch,Jr., prin.

Davidsville, Somerset Co.
Conemaugh Twp. Area SD IU 8
Sch. Sys. Enr. Code 4
Supt. – Dr. Albert Reynolds, P O BOX 407 15928
Other Schools – See Jerome, Johnstown

Dawson, Fayette Co., Pop. Code 3
Frazier SD IU 1
Supt. – See Perryopolis
Brownfield ES, RURAL ROUTE 01 15428
John Strickler, prin.

Dayton, Armstrong Co., Pop. Code 3
Armstrong SD IU 28
Supt. – See Ford City
ES, GRANT AVENUE 16222
Herbert Crawford, prin.

Defiance, Bedford Co.
Tussey Mountain SD IU 8
Supt. – See Saxton
ES, RURAL ROUTE 03 BOX 138 16633
Stanley Gresko, prin.

Delta, York Co., Pop. Code 3
South Eastern SD IU 12
Supt. – See Fawn Grove
Delta-Peach Bottom ES
RURAL ROUTE 01 BOX 40 17314
M. Parlett, prin.

Denver, Lancaster Co., Pop. Code 4
Cocalico SD IU 13
Sch. Sys. Enr. Code 4
Supt. – Dr. William Worley, 800 S 4TH ST 17517
Cocalico MS, S 6TH ST 17517
Joseph Geesey, prin.
ES, S 4TH STREET 17517 – David Burns, prin.
Other Schools – See Adamstown, Reamstown,
Schoeneck

Gehmans Menn ES
RURAL ROUTE 03 BOX 336 17517

Derrick City, McKean Co.
Bradford Area SD IU 9
Supt. – See Bradford
ES 16701 – Maureen O'Mara, prin.

Derry, Westmoreland Co., Pop. Code 5
Derry Area SD IU 7
Sch. Sys. Enr. Code 4
Supt. – Robert Critchfield
RURAL ROUTE 01 BOX 169 15627
Grandview MS, 81 DERRY RD 15627
Michael Metil, prin.
Other Schools – See Bradenville, Latrobe, New Derry

St. Joseph ES, E SECOND AVE 15627

Devault, Chester Co., Pop. Code 2
Great Valley SD IU 24
Sch. Sys. Enr. Code 5
Supt. – William Fitzpatrick
CHARLESTOWN ROAD 19432
Charlestown ES, CHARLESTOWN RD 19432
Sandra Griffin, prin.
Other Schools – See Malvern

Devon, Chester Co.
Tredyffrin-Easttown SD IU 24
Supt. – See Berwyn
ES, FAIRFIELD AND SUGARTO 19333
Marta Stevens, prin.

Episcopal Academy, 905 S WATERLOO RD 19333

Dickson City, Lackawanna Co., Pop. Code 6
Mid Valley SD IU 19
Supt. – See Throop
Mid Valley PS, CARMALT STREET 18519
Gerald Luchansky, prin.

St. Mary Visitation ES, P O BOX 9038 18519

Dillsburg, York Co., Pop. Code 4
Northern York County SD IU 15
Sch. Sys. Enr. Code 5
Supt. – John F. Allison
149 S BALTIMORE ST 17019
Northern MS, RURAL ROUTE 02 17019
Richard Nilsen, prin.
ES, 202 S CHESTNUT ST 17019
Larry Rhone, prin.
Northern ES, RURAL ROUTE 02 17019
Mark Hagenbuch, prin.
Other Schools – See Wellsville

Dimock, Susquehanna Co., Pop. Code 3
Elk Lake SD IU 19
Sch. Sys. Enr. Code 4
Supt. – Richard Serfass, P O BOX 133 18816
Elk Lake ES, P O BOX 133 18816
Dale Grosvenor, prin.

Dingmans Ferry, Pike Co.
Delaware Valley SD IU 20
Supt. – See Milford
Dingman-Delaware ES
RURAL ROUTE 01 BOX 94-F 18328
Richard Maggs, prin.

Donora, Washington Co., Pop. Code 6
Ringgold SD IU 1
Supt. – See Monongahela
ES, FOURTH AND WADDELL 15033
Margaret Protz, prin.

Donora Catholic School
2ND ST EXTENSION 15033

Douglassville, Berks Co., Pop. Code 3
Daniel Boone Area SD IU 14
Supt. – See Birdsboro
Amity ES, RURAL ROUTE 02 BOX 84 19518
Barry Clippinger, prin.
Monocacy ES, RURAL ROUTE 01 19518
Roger Weinhold, prin.

Dover, York Co., Pop. Code 4
Dover Area SD IU 12
Sch. Sys. Enr. Code 5
Supt. – J. Daniel Collins, E CANAL ST 17315
Dover Area MS, 4500 INTERMEDIATE AVE 17315
Kenneth Walter, prin.
ES, 109 E CANAL ST 17315 – Suzanne Krug, prin.
Leib ES, 2925 OAKLAND RD 17315
William O'Donnell, prin.
Weigelstown ES, 3205 CARLISLE RD 17315
Harry Platts, prin.
Other Schools – See East Berlin

Downingtown, Chester Co., Pop. Code 6
Downingtown Area SD IU 24
Sch. Sys. Enr. Code 6
Supt. – Dr. Ronald Gray
122 WALLACE AVE 19335
Beaver Creek ES, 601 W PENNA AVE 19335
Ernest Faulkner, prin.
Brandywine-Wallace ES
435 DILWORTH RD 19335 – Carl Deutsch, prin.
East Ward ES, 435 WASHINGTON AVE 19335
Richard Orth, prin.
Lionville ES, 518 LIONVILLE RD 19335
O. Davison, prin.
Uwchlan Hills ES, 50 PECK RD 19335
Donald Phillips, prin.
West Bradford ES
1475 BROAD RUN ROAD 19335
Robert Clegg, prin.
Other Schools – See Uwchland

St. Joseph ES, 240 MANOR AVE 19335

Doylestown, Bucks Co., Pop. Code 6
Central Bucks SD IU 22
Sch. Sys. Enr. Code 6
Supt. – Robert Winters, 315 W STATE ST 18901
Doyle ES, 260 NORTH ST 18901
Merton Keller, prin.
Kutz ES, 1950 TURK RD 18901
Corinne Cody, prin.
Linden ES, 480 LINDEN AVE 18901
Louis Tenaglia, prin.
Other Schools – See Buckingham, Chalfont, Danboro,
New Britain, Warrington

Our Lady of Mt. Carmel ES
E ASHLAND ST 18901

Dresher, Montgomery Co., Pop. Code 3
Upper Dublin SD IU 23
Sch. Sys. Enr. Code 5
Supt. – Dr. Clair Brown,Jr.
530 TWINING ROAD 19025
Sandy Run MS, 520 TWINING ROAD 19025
Valerie Mahla, prin.
Jarrettown ES, 1520 LIMEKILN PIKE 19025
Henry Ferguson, prin.
Other Schools – See Fort Washington, Willow Grove

Phil Mont Christ Academy
1701 JARRETTOWN RD 19025

Drexel Hill, Delaware Co., Pop. Code 8
Upper Darby SD IU 25
Sch. Sys. Enr. Code 6
Supt. – Joseph Batory
BOND AVE & BURMONT ROAD 19026
MS, STATE ROAD & PENN AVE 19026
Charles Granger, prin.
Aronimink ES
BOND AVENUE BURMONT ROAD 19026
Merle Horowitz, prin.
Garrettford ES, 3820 GARRETT RD 19026
Wayne McAllister, prin.
Hillcrest ES
BOND AVENUE AND AGNEW DR 19026
Mary Sweet, prin.
Other Schools – See Clifton Heights, Upper Darby

School of the Holy Child ES
450 PENN AVE 19026
St. Andrew's ES, 535 MASON AVE 19026
St. Bernadette ES
BOND AND TURNER AVES 19026
St. Charles Borromeo ES
3407 DENNISON AVE 19026
St. Dorothy ES, 1201 BURMONT RD 19026

Drumore, Lancaster Co.
Solanco SD IU 13
Supt. – See Quarryville
ES, 1158 OSCEOLA DR 17518
Kathleen Legenstein, prin.

Drums, Luzerne Co.
Hazleton Area SD IU 18
Supt. – See Hazleton
ES 18222 – Elizebeth Brndjar, prin.

Du Bois, Clearfield Co., Pop. Code 6
Du Bois Area SD IU 6
Sch. Sys. Enr. Code 5
Supt. – Michael Ferko, 500 LIBERTY BLVD 15801
Du Bois Area JHS, 404 LIBERTY BLVD 15801
A. Sebring, prin.
Highland Street ES
RURAL ROUTE 02 BOX 525 15801
Fred Kovalyak, prin.
Juniata ES, JUNIATA STREET 15801
Rita Wray, prin.
Oklahoma ES, RURAL ROUTE 03 15801
Donald Smith, prin.
Wasson Avenue ES, 300 WASSON AVE 15801
Fred Kovalyak, prin.
Other Schools – See Luthersburg, Penfield,
Reynoldsville, Sykesville

First Baptist Church Academy
MAPLE AVE EXT 15801
St. Catherine ES, 514 W WEBER AVE 15801

Duke Center, McKean Co., Pop. Code 4
Otto-Eldred SD IU 9
Sch. Sys. Enr. Code 4
Supt. – William Stavisky 16729
Other Schools – See Eldred, Rixford

Dunbar, Fayette Co., Pop. Code 4
Connellsville Area SD IU 1
Supt. – See Connellsville
Dunbar Boro ES, RURAL ROUTE 01 15431
William Baer, prin.

Duncannon, Perry Co., Pop. Code 4
Susquenita SD IU 15
Sch. Sys. Enr. Code 4
Supt. – Dr. Steven Messner
RURAL ROUTE 03 BOX 685 17020
Susquenita ES, RURAL ROUTE 03 BOX 685 17020
Robert Miller, prin.

Duncansville, Blair Co., Pop. Code 4
Hollidaysburg Area SD IU 8
Supt. – See Hollidaysburg
Allegheny ES, RURAL ROUTE 02 BOX 45 16635
Ann Mitchell, prin.
Allegheny ES, RURAL ROUTE 04 BOX 213 16635
Ann Mitchell, prin.

Blair County Christian School, P O BOX 840 16635

Dunmore, Lackawanna Co., Pop. Code 7
Dunmore SD IU 19
Sch. Sys. Enr. Code 4
Supt. – Joseph Haggerty
QUINCY AVE & WARREN ST 18509
ES, QUINCY AND WARREN ST 18512
Robert Sheehan, prin.

St. Anthony ES, 208 SMITH ST 18512
St. Mary of Mt. Carmel ES
325 CHESTNUT ST 18512

Duquesne, Allegheny Co., Pop. Code 7
Duquesne CSD IU 3
Sch. Sys. Enr. Code 4
Supt. – Dr. John Buchovecky, S 3RD ST 15110
ES, SOUTH SIXTH STREET 15110
Christine Bannon, prin.

Duquesne Catholic ES, 12 NORMAN ST 15110

Duryea, Luzerne Co., Pop. Code 6

Holy Rosary ES, 110 STEPHENSON ST 18642

Dushore, Sullivan Co., Pop. Code 3
Sullivan County SD IU 17
Sch. Sys. Enr. Code 4
Supt. – Jack Shaw, P O BOX 346 18614
Other Schools – See Laporte, Mildred

Eagleville, Montgomery Co., Pop. Code 4
Methacton SD IU 23
Supt. – See Fairview Village
ES, 125 SUMMIT AVE 19403 – David Davis, prin.

East Berlin, Adams Co., Pop. Code 4
Bermudian Springs SD IU 12
Supt. – See York Springs
ES, FOURTH STREET 17316
Ronald Snyder, prin.

Dover Area SD IU 12
Supt. – See Dover
Kralltown ES, RURAL ROUTE 01 17316
Harry Platts, prin.

East Brady, Clarion Co., Pop. Code 4
Armstrong SD IU 28
Supt. – See Ford City
ES, P O BOX 308 16028 – Richard Grabiec, prin.

East Freedom, Blair Co.
Spring Cove SD IU 8
Supt. – See Roaring Spring
Freedom ES, P O BOX 210 16637
Howard Benner, prin.

East Greenville, Montgomery Co., Pop. Code 4
Upper Perkiomen SD IU 23
Sch. Sys. Enr. Code 5
Supt. – Thomas Persing, 201 W 5TH ST 18041
Upper Perkiomen MS, JEFFERSON ST 18041
Celine Matz, prin.
Other Schools – See Green Lane, Hereford, Red Hill

St. Philip Neri ES, 26 E SIXTH ST 18041

East Lansdowne, Delaware Co., Pop. Code 5
William Penn SD IU 25
Supt. – See Yeadon
ES, EMERSON & MELROSE AVE 19050
Joseph Bruni, prin.

St. Cyril Alex ES, EMERSON & LEWIS AVE 19050

East Mckeesport, Allegheny Co., Pop. Code 5

St. Bellarmine ES, 1301 FIFHT AVE 15035

East Millsboro, Fayette Co.
Brownsville Area SD IU 1
Supt. – See Republic
Central ES, RURAL ROUTE 01 15433
William Snyder, prin.

Easton, Northampton Co., Pop. Code 8
Bethlehem Area SD IU 20
Supt. – See Bethlehem
Farmersville ES, 7036 WM PENN HWY 18042
David Ongiri, prin.

Easton Area SD IU 20
Sch. Sys. Enr. Code 6
Supt. – Dr. William Moloney
811 NORTHAMPTON ST 18042
Easton Area MS, 12TH & NORTHAMPTON 18042
Robert Kearn, prin.
Cheston ES, GRANT AND COAL STREET 18042
Thomas Murphy, prin.
Forks ES, 1709 RICHMOND RD 18042
David Freytag, prin.
March ES, MONROE REEDER STREETS 18042
Karl Hettle, prin.
Palmer ES, 3050 GREEN POND RD 18042
William Kahres, prin.
Paxinosa ES, 1315 ECHO TRL 18042
Roger Wrazien, prin.
Tracy ES, 1243 TATAMY RD 18042
Thomas Blackton, prin.

Wilson Area SD IU 20
Sch. Sys. Enr. Code 5
Supt. – Albert Zarbatany
21ST & WASHINGTON BLVD 18042
Lauer MS, FIRMSTONE & BALATA STS 18042
Dennis Harper, prin.
Avona ES, 24TH FRONT STREETS 18042
Guy Fulmer, prin.
Williams ES, 2660 MORGAN HILL RD 18042
Guy Fulmer, prin.
Wilson Borough ES
21 AND WASHINGTON BLVD 18042
Guy Fulmer, prin.

Easton Catholic ES, NINTH & LEHIGH STS 18042
St. Jane Francis ES
1900 WASHINGTON BLVD 18042

East Petersburg, Lancaster Co., Pop. Code 5
Hempfield SD IU 13
Supt. – See Landisville
East Petersburg ES, 5700 LEMON ST 17520
John Ernst, prin.

East Prospect, York Co., Pop. Code 3
Eastern York SD IU 12
Supt. – See Wrightsville
Canadochly ES, OAK LN 17317
Donald Eckert,Jr., prin.

East Smithfield, Bradford Co.
Athens Area SD IU 17
Supt. – See Athens
Child ES, 1000 HEWIT STREET 18817
Raymond Hughes, prin.

East Springfield, Erie Co.
Northwestern SD IU 5
Supt. – See Albion
Springfield ES, BOND STREET 16411
Robert Fontana, prin.

East Stroudsburg, Monroe Co., Pop. Code 6
East Stroudsburg Area SD IU 20
Sch. Sys. Enr. Code 5
Supt. – John Lambert, P O BOX 298 18301
Bunnell JHS, P O BOX 298 18301
Allen Fields, prin.
Hill ES, 151 E BROAD ST 18301
Arthur Gray, prin.
Middle Smithfield ES
RURAL ROUTE 06 BOX 573 18301
Gregory Naudascher, prin.
North Courtland MS, P O BOX 298 18301
William Pinkowski, prin.
Smithfield ES
RURAL ROUTE 05 BOX 214B 18301
William Pinkowski, prin.

Notre Dame ES, 78 RIDGEWAY ST 18301

East Vandergrift, Westmoreland Co., Pop. Code 3
Kiski Area SD IU 7
Supt. – See Vandergrift

East Vandergrift ES, 434 MCKINLEY AVE 15629
William Kerr, prin.

Ebensburg, Cambria Co., Pop. Code 5
Central Cambria SD IU 8
Sch. Sys. Enr. Code 4
Supt. – Philip Evans
RURAL ROUTE 02 BOX 422 15931
Central Cambria MS
205 W HIGHLAND AVE 15931
Ronald Ponchione, prin.
Cambria ES, RURAL ROUTE 04 BOX 800 15931
Kenneth Letso, prin.
Other Schools – See Johnstown

Holy Name ES, 215 W HORNER ST 15931

Eddystone, Delaware Co., Pop. Code 5
Ridley SD IU 25
Supt. – See Folsom
ES, 9TH & SIMPSON ST 19013
Joseph Wallen, prin.

Edinboro, Erie Co., Pop. Code 6
General McLane SD IU 5
Sch. Sys. Enr. Code 5
Supt. – Therese Walter
11771 EDINBORO ROAD 16412
Parker MS, 11781 EDINBORO ROAD 16412
Patricia Crist, prin.
ES, 5390 RTE 6N 16412 – Donnan Stoicovy, prin.
Other Schools – See Mc Kean

Eighty Four, Washington Co.
Bentworth SD IU 1
Supt. – See Bentleyville
Somerset ES, RURAL ROUTE 02 BOX 489 15330
Anthony Conn, prin.

Canon-McMillan SD IU 1
Supt. – See Canonsburg
Wylandville ES, RURAL ROUTE 01 15330
Richard Kern, prin.

Eldersville, Washington Co.
Burgettstown Area SD IU 1
Supt. – See Burgettstown
ES 15036 – (—), prin.

Elderton, Armstrong Co., Pop. Code 2
Armstrong SD IU 28
Supt. – See Ford City
ES 15736 – Dr. Jon Drew, prin.

Eldred, McKean Co., Pop. Code 4
Otto-Eldred SD IU 9
Supt. – See Duke Center
Eldred Boro ES, BENNETT STREET 16731
Robert Falk, prin.
Eldred Township ES
INDIAN CREEK ROAD RFD 16731
Robert Falk, prin.

Elizabeth, Allegheny Co., Pop. Code 8
Elizabeth-Forward SD IU 3
Sch. Sys. Enr. Code 5
Supt. – Donna Shultz
1950 SCENERY DRIVE 15037
Central ES, 401 ROCK RUN RD 15037
Wesley Luckey, prin.
ES, 207 S 3RD AVE 15037 – Thomas Rowles, prin.
Other Schools – See Mc Keesport, Monongahela

St. Michael School, SIXTH & BAYARD STS 15037

Elizabethtown, Lancaster Co., Pop. Code 6
Elizabethtown Area SD IU 13
Sch. Sys. Enr. Code 5
Supt. – Robert Kratz, 600 E HIGH ST 17022
Elizabethtown Area MS, 600 E HIGH ST 17022
Gerald Lorson, prin.
East High Street ES, 800 E HIGH ST 17022
Deborah Weaver, prin.
Fairview ES, 1852 ELIZABETHTOWN RD 17022
Norma Zwally, prin.
Mill Road ES, 35 ELM AVE 17022
Ruth Rastatter, prin.
Other Schools – See Bainbridge, Rheems

Lower Dauphin SD IU 15
Supt. – See Hummelstown
Conewago ES, 2809 HERSHEY RD 17022
H. Kline, prin.

Mt. Calvary Christian School
HOLLY & HILLSIDE AVE 17022
St. Peters Catholic ES, P O BOX 386 17022

Elizabethville, Dauphin Co., Pop. Code 4
Upper Dauphin Area SD IU 15
Supt. – See Lykens
ES, 801 WOOD STREET 17023
Rose Radzievich, prin.

Elkins Park, Montgomery Co., Pop. Code 7
Abington SD IU 23
Supt. – See Abington
McKinley ES, 370 CEDAR RD 19117
Janet Vassian, prin.

Cheltenham Twp. SD IU 23
Sch. Sys. Enr. Code 5
Supt. – Dr. Charles Stefanski
ASHBOURNE ROAD & WASHINGTON 19117
MS, 2ND ST AND TOOKANY DRIVE 19117
Joseph Kircher,Jr., prin.

Myers ES
MONTGOMERY AND UNION AVENUE   19117
Alice Jefferson, prin.
Other Schools – See Cheltenham, Glenside, Wyncote

St. James ES, 8310 BROOKSIDE RD   19117

Elkland, Tioga Co., Pop. Code 4
Northern Tioga SD IU 17
Sch. Sys. Enr. Code 4
Supt. – Kenneth Schoonover
117 COATES AVE   16920
Wood ES, 101 COATES AVE   16920
James Gardner, prin.
Other Schools – See Tioga, Westfield

Elliottsburg, Perry Co.
West Perry SD IU 15
Sch. Sys. Enr. Code 5
Supt. – Winston Cleland
RURAL ROUTE 01   17024
Green Park ES, RURAL ROUTE 01   17024
Tim Scott, prin.
Other Schools – See Blain, New Bloomfield,
Shermans Dale

Ellsworth, Washington Co., Pop. Code 4
Bentworth SD IU 1
Supt. – See Bentleyville
Bentworth MS, PINE ST   15331
Edward Palla, prin.

Ave Maria ES, P O BOX 590   15331

Ellwood City, Lawrence Co., Pop. Code 6
Ellwood City Area SD IU 4
Sch. Sys. Enr. Code 4
Supt. – John DeCaro, 501 CRESCENT AVE   16117
Ewing Park ES, WOOD STREET   16117
Francis Keller,Jr.,prin.
Hartman ES, CRESCENT AVENUE & 4TH   16117
George Garda, prin.
North Side ES, ORCHARD NORTH STREET   16117
David Ialongo, prin.
Perry Township ES, PORTERSVILLE ROAD   16117
Dominick Magnifico, prin.
Walnut Ridge ES
AETNA DRIVE & SUNSET ROAD   16117
Paul Frederick, prin.

Riverside Beaver County SD IU 27
Sch. Sys. Enr. Code 4
Supt. – James Hoy
RURAL ROUTE 02 BOX 4010   16117
Riverside MS
RURAL ROUTE 02 BOX 4010   16117
J. Meehan, prin.
Other Schools – See Beaver Falls

Purification BVM ES
3RD AND LAWRENCE AVE   16117

Elmora, Cambria Co.
Cambria Heights SD IU 8
Supt. – See Patton
Bakerton ES   15737 – Harold Gabrielson, prin.

Elverson, Chester Co., Pop. Code 3
Owen J. Roberts SD IU 24
Supt. – See Pottstown
Warwick MS, ROUTE 23 RD 1   19520
Joseph Clark, prin.

Twin Valley SD IU 14
Sch. Sys. Enr. Code 5
Supt. – Creeden Coulson
RURAL ROUTE 02   19520
Twin Valley ES, RURAL ROUTE 02 BOX 54   19520
Linda Leisey, prin.
Other Schools – See Birdsboro, Honey Brook,
Morgantown

Emlenton, Venango Co., Pop. Code 3
Allegheny-Clarion Valley SD IU 6
Supt. – See Foxburg
ES   16373 – Betty Ditz, prin.

Emmaus, Lehigh Co., Pop. Code 7
East Penn SD IU 21
Sch. Sys. Enr. Code 6
Supt. – William Leary
640 MACUNGIE AVE   18049
Jefferson ES, 525 NORTH ST   18049
Neil Moyer, prin.
Lincoln ES, 235 SEEM ST   18049
Joseph Pavone, prin.
Vera Cruz ES, RURAL ROUTE 01   18049
Neil Moyer, prin.
Other Schools – See Alburtis, Macungie, Old
Zionsville, Wescosville

Emmaus Baptist Academy
30 COLEBROOK AVE   18049
St. Ann ES, SIXTH & FAIRVIEW ST   18049

Emporium, Cameron Co., Pop. Code 5
Cameron County SD IU 9
Sch. Sys. Enr. Code 4
Supt. – Dr. Douglas Bleggi
601 WOODLAND AVE   15834
East Fourth Street MS
EAST FOURTH STREET   15834
Charles Eckenroth, prin.
Woodland ES, WOODLAND AVENUE   15834
Charles Eckenroth, prin.

Enola, Cumberland Co., Pop. Code 5
Cumberland Valley SD IU 15
Supt. – See Mechanicsburg
Shaull ES, 1920 GOOD HOPE RD   17025
William Wishard, prin.

East Pennsboro Area SD IU 15
Sch. Sys. Enr. Code 4
Supt. – Dr. Glenn Zehner, 890 VALLEY ST   17025
East Pennsboro MS, 529 N ENOLA DRIVE   17025
Keith Voelker, prin.
East Pennsboro ES, 529R N ENOLA DR   17025
Carole Capriotti, prin.
Other Schools – See Camp Hill

Ephrata, Lancaster Co., Pop. Code 7
Ephrata Area SD IU 13
Sch. Sys. Enr. Code 5
Supt. – Theodore Soistmann
803 OAK BLVD   17522
JHS, HAMMON AVE   17522 – Luther Snook, prin.
Bergstrasse ES, RURAL ROUTE 03   17522
Edward Gordon, prin.
Clay ES, 250 CLAY SCHOOL RD   17522
Joseph Smith,Jr., prin.
Highland ES, 99 HIGHLAND AVE   17522
Daniel Felix, prin.
Lincoln ES, APPLE STREET   17522
Joseph Smith,Jr., prin.
Washington ES, 26 MARSHALL ST   17522
Ralph Homsher, prin.
Other Schools – See Akron

Ephrata Mennonite School
598 STEVENS ROAD   17522
Farmersville Mennonite School
RURAL ROUTE 04   17522
Hinkletown Menn ES, RURAL ROUTE 03   17522
Our Mother of Perpetual Help ES
330 N CHURCH AVE   17522

Erie, Erie Co., Pop. Code 9
Erie CSD IU 5
Sch. Sys. Enr. Code 7
Supt. – Joe Rodriguez, 1511 PEACH ST   16501
Gridley MS, 816 N PARK AVE   16502
Robert Scypinski, prin.
Roosevelt MS, 2300 CRANBERRY ST   16502
Paul Perowicz, prin.
Wayne MS, 650 EAST AVE   16503
Donna Carney, prin.
Wilson MS, 718 E 28TH ST   16504
Helen Jackson, prin.
Burton ES, 1661 BUFFALO RD   16510
Gregory Myers, prin.
Cleveland ES, 1540 W 38TH ST   16508
Mario Pecoraro, prin.
Connell ES, 1820 E 38TH ST   16510
Pat Conley, prin.
Diehl ES, 2327 FAIRMOUNT PKY   16510
Phillip Rewers, prin.
Edison ES, 1921 EAST LAKE ROAD   16511
Milton Simon, prin.
Emerson ES, 1006 W 10TH ST   16502
Ronald Fronzaglia, prin.
Glenwood ES, 3503 PEACH ST   16508
Joseph Rose, prin.
Harding ES, 820 LINCOLN AVE   16505
Donald Kenton, prin.
Irving ES, 2310 PLUM ST   16502
Joseph Sulkowski, prin.
Jefferson ES, 239 E 38TH ST   16504
Michael Burenko, prin.
Lincoln ES, 831 E 31ST ST   16504
Gerald Mifsud, prin.
McKinley ES, 2212 EAST AVE   16503
Brenda Meredith, prin.
Perry ES, 955 W 29TH ST   16508
Phyllis Shioleno, prin.
Pfeiffer-Burleigh ES, 235 E 11TH ST   16503
Phyllis Hensley, prin.

Harbor Creek SD IU 5
Supt. – See Harborcreek
Clark ES, 3650 DEPOT RD   16510
Michele Campbell, prin.
Klein ES, 5325 EAST LAKE ROAD   16511
James Tracy, prin.
Rolling Ridge ES, 3700 RIDGE PKY   16510
R. Miller, prin.

Iroquois Area SD IU 5
Sch. Sys. Enr. Code 4
Supt. – Lawrence Devine
4231 MORSE AVE   16511
Lawrence Park MS, 4231 MORSE ST   16511
Frank Bova, prin.
Other Schools – See Wesleyville

Millcreek Twp. SD IU 5
Sch. Sys. Enr. Code 6
Supt. – Robert Agnew, 3740 W 26TH ST   16506
Westlake MS, 4330 W LAKE ROAD   16505
Joseph Cuzzola, prin.
Wilson MS, 900 W 54TH ST   16509
Kenneth Borland, prin.
Asbury ES, 3814 ASBURY RD   16506
Robert Case, prin.
Belle Valley ES, 1762 NORCROSS RD   16510
Mary Mahon, prin.
Chestnut Hill ES, 1001 W 54TH ST   16509
Mary Mahon, prin.
Grandview ES, 4301 LANCASTER RD   16506
Larry Stevens, prin.

Ridgefield ES, 3227 HIGHLAND RD   16506
Dennis Libra, prin.
Tracy ES, 2920 W 12TH ST   16505
Robert Scarpitti, prin.
Vernondale ES, 1432 WILKINS RD   16505
Robert Pollifrone, prin.

Wattsburg Area SD IU 5
Supt. – See Wattsburg
Greene Township MS, RURAL ROUTE 05   16509
Kimberly Grove, prin.

Bethel Christian School of Erie
1781 W 38TH ST   16508
Blessed Sacrament ES
2510 GREENGARDEN RD   16502
Cathedral Center ES, 160 W 11TH ST   16501
Holy Family ES, 1153 E 9TH ST   16503
Holy Rosary ES, 1012 E 28TH ST   16504
Holy Trinity ES, 641 E 22ND ST   16503
Mt. Calvary ES, 426 EAGLE POINT BLVD   16511
Our Lady of Mt. Carmel ES
1531 E GRANDVIEW BLVD   16510
Our Lady of Peace ES, 2401 W 38TH ST   16506
Our Lady's Cristian ES, 606 LOWELL AVE   16505
Sacred Heart ES, 2501 PLUM ST   16502
St. Andrew ES, 606 RASPBERRY ST   16502
St. Boniface ES, 7621 WATTSBURG RD   16509
St. George ES, 1612 BRYANT ST   16509
St. James ES, 2602 BUFFALO RD   16510
St. John the Baptist ES, 504 E 27TH ST   16504
St. Jospeh ES, 139 W 24TH ST   16502
St. Luke ES, 425 E 38TH ST   16504
St. Mary ES, 310 E 10TH ST   16503
St. Patrick ES, 217 E 4TH ST   16507
St. Stanislaus ES, 1203 WALLACE ST   16503
The Erie Day ES, 1372 W 6TH ST   16505
Villa Maria ES, 819 W 8TH ST   16502

Essington, Delaware Co., Pop. Code 4
Interboro SD IU 25
Supt. – See Prospect Park
Tinicum ES, 1ST & SENECA ST   19029
B. Davis, prin.

Etters, York Co.
West Shore SD IU 15
Supt. – See Lemoyne
Newberry ES, 2055 OLD TRAIL RD   17319
Joseph Gargiulo, prin.

Evans City, Butler Co., Pop. Code 4
Seneca Valley SD IU 4
Supt. – See Harmony
ES, 345 W MAIN ST   16033 – Dean Yobp, prin.

Everett, Bedford Co., Pop. Code 4
Bedford Area SD IU 8
Supt. – See Bedford
Snake Spring ES
RURAL ROUTE 01 BOX 304   15537
Betty Calhoun, prin.

Everett Area SD IU 8
Sch. Sys. Enr. Code 4
Supt. – Edward Vollbrecht
E SOUTH ST EXT   15537
Chaneysville Cove ES, HCR 04   15537
Charles Perrin, prin.
Everett Area ES, E FIRST AVE   15537
Kenneth Albaugh, prin.
Other Schools – See Breezewood, Clearville

Exeter, Luzerne Co., Pop. Code 6
Wyoming Area SD IU 18
Sch. Sys. Enr. Code 5
Supt. – Robert Fumanti, MEMORIAL ST   18643
Kennedy ES, 58 PENN AVE   18643
Richard Ascani, prin.
Other Schools – See Pittston, West Pittston, Wyoming

Export, Westmoreland Co., Pop. Code 4
Franklin Regional SD IU 7
Supt. – See Murrysville
Duff ES, 5870 KENNEDY AVE   15632
David Reese, prin.

Kiski Area SD IU 7
Supt. – See Vandergrift
Mamont ES, RURAL ROUTE 02   15632
William Kerr, prin.

Exton, Chester Co.
West Chester Area SD IU 24
Supt. – See West Chester
ES, 301 HENDRICKS AVE   19341
John Bullock, prin.

Sts. Philip & James ES
ROUTE 30 AND SHIP RD   19341

Eynon, Lackawanna Co.
Valley View SD IU 19
Supt. – See Archbald
Roosevelt ES, BETTY STREET   18403
John Scagliotti, prin.

Factoryville, Wyoming Co., Pop. Code 3
Lackawanna Trail SD IU 19
Sch. Sys. Enr. Code 4
Supt. – Dr. John Micco, RURAL ROUTE 01   18419
ES, COLLEGE AVENUE   18419
James Evans, prin.
Other Schools – See Dalton, Fleetville, Nicholson

Fairchance, Fayette Co., Pop. Code 4
Albert Galltn Area SD IU 1
Supt. – See Uniontown

ES, 25 S MAIN ST 15436
  Stephen Kezmarsky, prin.

Fairfield, Adams Co., Pop. Code 3
  Fairfield Area SD IU 12
  Sch. Sys. Enr. Code 3
  Supt. – Carol Saylor, P O BOX 245 17320
  ES, P O BOX 245 17320 – Jack Inskip, prin.

Fairless Hills, Bucks Co.
  Pennsbury SD IU 22
  Supt. – See Fallsington
  Penn MS, 600 S OLDS BLVD 19030
    Ross Bartleson, prin.
  Oxford Valley ES, 430 TRENTON RD 19030
    Carol Sandford, prin.
  Village Park ES, UNITY DR 19030
    Dennis Lowe, prin.

  Faith Baptist Christian Academy
    1515 WISTAR ROAD 19030
  Pen Ryn ES, 235 S OLDS BLVD 19030
  St. Francis Cabrini ES, GOBLE CT 19030

Fairview, Erie Co., Pop. Code 4
  Fairview SD IU 5
  Sch. Sys. Enr. Code 4
  Supt. – R. Alan Zito, 7460 MCCRAY ROAD 16415
  Garwood MS, 4967 GARWOOD ST 16415
    Greg Baran, prin.
  Chestnut ES, 7554 CHESTNUT ST 16415
    Wayne Bubnis, prin.

Fairview Village, Montgomery Co., Pop. Code 2
  Methacton SD IU 23
  Sch. Sys. Enr. Code 5
  Supt. – Laird Warner
    KRIEBEL MILL ROAD 19403
  Other Schools – See Collegeville, Eagleville,
    Norristown, Trooper

Fallsington, Bucks Co.
  Pennsbury SD IU 22
  Sch. Sys. Enr. Code 6
  Supt. – Dr. Joseph Farese
    134 YARDLEY AVE 19054
  Other Schools – See Fairless Hills, Levittown,
    Morrisville, Yardley

Farmington, Fayette Co.
  Uniontown Area SD IU 1
  Supt. – See Uniontown
  Wharton ES, RURAL ROUTE 01 15437
    J. Thomas, prin.

Farrell, Mercer Co., Pop. Code 6
  Farrell Area SD IU 4
  Sch. Sys. Enr. Code 4
  Supt. – John Sava, 1600 ROEMER BLVD 16121
  Farrell Area ES, 1600 ROEMER BLVD 16121
    Louis Mastrian, prin.

  Monsignor Geno Monti ES, 1225 UNION ST 16121

Fawn Grove, York Co., Pop. Code 3
  South Eastern SD IU 12
  Sch. Sys. Enr. Code 4
  Supt. – Dr. Luther Natter, P O BOX 157 17321
  South Eastern MS
    RURAL ROUTE 01 BOX 27A 17321
    Bernard Loman, prin.
  Fawn ES, RURAL ROUTE 01 BOX 28 17321
    M. Parlett, prin.
  Other Schools – See Delta, Stewartstown

Fayette City, Fayette Co., Pop. Code 3
  Frazier SD IU 1
  Supt. – See Perryopolis
  Central ES, RURAL ROUTE 01 15438
    Linda Nelson, prin.

Fayetteville, Franklin Co., Pop. Code 4
  Chambersburg Area SD IU 12
  Supt. – See Chambersburg
  ES, 8 E MAIN ST 17222 – P. Peters, prin.

Feasterville, Bucks Co., Pop. Code 6
  Neshaminy SD IU 22
  Supt. – See Langhorne
  Lower Southampton ES, 7 SCHOOL LN 19047
    Nicholas Iampietro, prin.
  Poquessing ES, 300 HEIGHTS LN 19047
    Richard McPhillips, prin.

Fenelton, Butler Co.
  Butler Area SD IU 4
  Supt. – See Butler
  Clearfield ES, RURAL ROUTE 01 16034
    John Zgibor, prin.

Finleyville, Washington Co., Pop. Code 2
  Ringgold SD IU 1
  Supt. – See Monongahela
  Finley MS, RURAL ROUTE 88 15332
    Richard Borchilo, prin.

  South Hills Christian School, ROUTE 88 15332

Fishertown, Bedford Co.
  Chestnut Ridge SD IU 8
  Sch. Sys. Enr. Code 4
  Supt. – Larry Giovacchini 15539
  Chestnut Ridge MS 15539 – James Dull, prin.
  Other Schools – See New Paris

Fleetville, Lakawanna Co.
  Lackawanna Trail SD IU 19
  Supt. – See Factoryville

Benton ES, COLLEGE AVE 18420
  James Evans, prin.

Fleetwood, Berks Co., Pop. Code 5
  Brandywine Heights Area SD IU 14
  Supt. – See Topton
  Rockland Center ES, RURAL ROUTE 01 19522
    Ruth Bloom, prin.

  Fleetwood Area SD IU 14
  Sch. Sys. Enr. Code 4
  Supt. – Dr. Gary McCartney
    409 N RICHMOND ST 19522
  MS, 110 W ARCH ST 19522
    Charles Hostetler, prin.
  Fleetwood ES, 101 W VINE ST 19522
    Mary Klinedinst, prin.
  Richmond ES
    RURAL ROUTE 04 BOX 4032 19522
    Mary Klinedinst, prin.
  Other Schools – See Blandon

Flinton, Cambria Co.
  Glendale SD IU 10
  Sch. Sys. Enr. Code 4
  Supt. – Edward Turchick, RURAL ROUTE 16640
  Glendale ES, RURAL ROUTE 16640
    Harry Cree, prin.

Flourtown, Montgomery Co., Pop. Code 6

  St. Genevieves ES, 1237 BETHLEHEM PIKE 19031

Folcroft, Delaware Co., Pop. Code 6
  Southeast Delco SD IU 25
  Sch. Sys. Enr. Code 5
  Supt. – William Donato, P O BOX 328 19032
  Delcroft ES
    SCHOOL LN AND DELMAR DR 19032
    Bernadette George, prin.
  Other Schools – See Collingdale, Glenolden, Sharon
    Hill

Folsom, Delaware Co., Pop. Code 6
  Ridley SD IU 25
  Sch. Sys. Enr. Code 5
  Supt. – John Cochran, 1001 MORTON AVE 19033
  Edgewood ES, 8TH & EDGEWOOD AVE 19033
    A. Ersek, prin.
  Other Schools – See Eddystone, Morton, Ridley Park,
    Swarthmore, Woodlyn

Ford City, Armstrong Co., Pop. Code 5
  Armstrong SD IU 28
  Sch. Sys. Enr. Code 6
  Supt. – Dr. William Williams, 410 MAIN ST 16226
  Lenape ES, 2300 CENTER AVE 16226
    Robert Randolph, prin.
  Other Schools – See Cowansville, Dayton, East Brady,
    Elderton, Kittanning, Rural Valley, Templeton

  Ford City Catholic ES, 726 4TH AVE 16226

Forest City, Susquehanna Co., Pop. Code 4
  Forest City Reg. SD IU 19
  Sch. Sys. Enr. Code 3
  Supt. – Michael De Stefano
    100 SUSQUEHANNA ST 18421
  Forest City Regional ES
    100 SUSQUEHANNA ST 18421
    Ann Cyzeski, prin.

Fort Washington, Montgomery Co., Pop. Code 5
  Upper Dublin SD IU 23
  Supt. – See Dresher
  ES, 1264 FORT WASHINGTON AVE 19034
    Harry Franklin, prin.

  Germantown Academy, 340 MORRIS ROAD 19034
  Open Door Christian Academy
    FT WASHINGTON AVE 19034

Forty Fort, Luzerne Co., Pop. Code 6
  Wyoming Valley West SD IU 18
  Supt. – See Kingston
  Dana Street ES, 50 DANA ST 18704
    Nelson Kile, prin.

Foxburg, Clarion Co., Pop. Code 2
  Allegheny-Clarion Valley SD IU 6
  Sch. Sys. Enr. Code 4
  Supt. – Gerald Peairs, P O BOX 345 16036
  Other Schools – See Emlenton, Parker, Saint
    Petersburg

Frackville, Schuylkill Co., Pop. Code 6
  North Schuylkill SD IU 29
  Sch. Sys. Enr. Code 5
  Supt. – Charles Greco
    S CENTER AND OAK ST 17931
  ES, S CENTER & OAK ST 17931
    Carl Pyzowski, prin.
  Other Schools – See Ashland, Girardville, Ringtown

  Holy Family ES
    29 S BROAD MOUNTAIN AVE 17931

Franklin, Venango Co., Pop. Code 6
  Franklin Area SD IU 6
  Sch. Sys. Enr. Code 5
  Supt. – Bob Morris, P O BOX 350 16323
  MS, RURAL ROUTE 01 16323 – R. Muse, prin.
  Central ES, 1276 OTTER ST 16323
    Terry Peterson, prin.
  Sandycreek ES, RURAL ROUTE 01 16323
    Gerald Wendt, prin.

Seventh Street ES, 310 7TH ST 16323
    Gerald Wendt, prin.
  Other Schools – See Harrisville, Polk, Utica

  Valley Grove SD IU 6
  Sch. Sys. Enr. Code 4
  Supt. – J. Kockler, 429 WILEY AVE 16323
  Rocky Grove ES, 317 WILEY AVE 16323
    Eugene Sheffer, prin.
  Sugarcreek ES, RURAL ROUTE 03 16323
    Eugene Sheffer, prin.
  Other Schools – See Cooperstown

  St. Patrick ES, 952 BUFFALO ST 16323

Fredericksburg, Lebanon Co., Pop. Code 4
  Northern Lebanon SD IU 13
  Sch. Sys. Enr. Code 5
  Supt. – Richard Wendler 17026
  ES, N PINE GROVE STREET 17026
    Michael Miller, prin.
  Other Schools – See Annville, Jonestown

Fredericktown, Washington Co., Pop. Code 4
  Bethlehem-Center SD IU 1
  Sch. Sys. Enr. Code 4
  Supt. – Max Williams
    RURAL ROUTE 01 BOX 28-C 15333
  Bethlehem-Center ES
    RURAL ROUTE 01 BOX 28C 15333
    Beverly Krill, prin.

Fredonia, Mercer Co., Pop. Code 3
  Reynolds SD IU 4
  Supt. – See Greenville
  Fredonia-Delaware ES, RURAL ROUTE 2 16124
    Fred Ray, prin.

Freeburg, Snyder Co., Pop. Code 3
  Selinsgrove Area SD IU 16
  Supt. – See Selinsgrove
  Freeburg-Washington ES 17827
    Randall Young, prin.

Freedom, Beaver Co., Pop. Code 4
  Ambridge Area SD IU 27
  Supt. – See Ambridge
  Ambridge Area JHS, RURAL ROUTE 01 15042
    Paul Dinello, prin.

  Freedom Area SD IU 27
  Sch. Sys. Enr. Code 4
  Supt. – Robert Cercone, 1701 8TH AVE 15042
  Freedom Area MS, 1701 8TH AVE 15042
    Anthony Mullen, prin.
  Big Knob ES, RURAL ROUTE 01 15042
    Casper Depaolis, prin.
  Other Schools – See Conway

Freeland, Luzerne Co., Pop. Code 5
  Hazleton Area SD IU 18
  Supt. – See Hazleton
  ES, 400 ALVIN ST 18224 – George Leitner, prin.

Freemansburg, Northampton Co., Pop. Code 4
  Bethlehem Area SD IU 20
  Supt. – See Bethlehem
  ES, 501 MONROE ST 18017 – Richard Laury, prin.

Freeport, Armstrong Co., Pop. Code 4
  Freeport Area SD IU 28
  Sch. Sys. Enr. Code 4
  Supt. – E. Garlitz, P O BOX C 16229
  Freeport Area JHS, 325 4TH ST 16229
    E. Prusick, prin.
  ES, 408 HIGH ST 16229 – William Blose, prin.
  South Buffalo Township ES
    562 FREEPORT RD 16229 – William Blose, prin.
  Other Schools – See Sarver

Friedens, Somerset Co., Pop. Code 3
  Somerset Area SD IU 8
  Supt. – See Somerset
  ES, RURAL ROUTE 01 15541 – Carl Kahl, prin.

Friedensburg, Schuylkill Co.
  Blue Mountain SD IU 29
  Supt. – See Orwigsburg
  Wayne ES, RURAL ROUTE 17933
    Robert Long, prin.

Friendsville, Susquehanna Co., Pop. Code 1
  Montrose Area SD IU 19
  Supt. – See Montrose
  Choconut Valley ES
    RURAL ROUTE 01 BOX 111B 18818
    Stephen Placko, prin.

Galeton, Potter Co., Pop. Code 4
  Galeton Area SD IU 9
  Sch. Sys. Enr. Code 3
  Supt. – Frank Flamish, 3 BRIDGE ST 16922
  ES, 3 BRIDGE ST 16922 – (—), prin.

Gallitzin, Cambria Co., Pop. Code 4
  Penn Cambria SD IU 8
  Supt. – See Cresson
  ES, MAXWELL & DIVISION 16641
    Richard Sweeney, prin.

  St. Patrick ES, 811 CHURCH ST 16641

Gap, Lancaster Co., Pop. Code 4
  Pequea Valley SD IU 13
  Supt. – See Kinzers
  Salisbury ES, RURAL ROUTE 01 BOX 73 17527
    James Streaker, prin.

Fairhaven Christian ES
RURAL ROUTE 02 BOX 2378A   17527

Gastonville, Washington Co.
Ringgold SD IU 1
Supt. – See Monongahela
ES, RURAL ROUTE 01   15336 – Harry Miale, prin.

Geigertown, Berks Co.

High Point Baptist Academy   19523

Gettysburg, Adams Co., Pop. Code 6
Gettysburg SD IU 12
Sch. Sys. Enr. Code 5
Supt. – Dr. Dorothy Bollinger
900 BIGLERVILLE ROAD   17325
Eisenhower ES
EAST BROADWAY EXTENDED   17325
William Foreman, prin.
Gettys ES, BIGLERVILLE ROAD   17325
L. Gilbert, prin.
Keefauver ES
EAST CONFEDERATE AVENUE   17325
Ronald Miller, prin.
Meade ES, SPRINGS AVENUE   17325
Deborah Sponseller, prin.
Other Schools – See Cashtown

St. Francis Xavier ES, 45 W HIGH ST   17325

Gibsonia, Allegheny Co., Pop. Code 4
Hampton Twp. SD IU 3
Supt. – See Allison Park
Poff ES, 2990 HABERLEIN RD   15044
Gerald Goga, prin.

Pine-Richland SD IU 3
Sch. Sys. Enr. Code 4
Supt. – Stephen Storkel
4046 EWALT ROAD   15044
Pine MS, RURAL ROUTE 01   15044
Dr. Sherry Burtnett, prin.
Hance ES, 5518 MOLNAR DR   15044
Elio Allasia, prin.
Washington ES, 5847 MERIDIAN RD   15044
Elio Allasia, prin.
Other Schools – See Wexford

Gilbertsville, Montgomery Co.
Boyertown Area SD IU 14
Supt. – See Boyertown
ES, CONGO ROAD   19525 – Thomas Smythe, prin.

Gillett, Bradford Co.
Athens Area SD IU 17
Supt. – See Athens
Burnham ES, RURAL ROUTE 03 BOX 114   16925
Raymond Hughes, prin.

Girard, Erie Co., Pop. Code 5
Girard SD IU 5
Sch. Sys. Enr. Code 4
Supt. – Lydia Axelrod, 1135 LAKE ST   16417
Rice Avenue MS, 1100 RICE AVE   16417
Dr. Rudy Lascek, prin.
Other Schools – See Lake City

Girard Alliance Christian Academy
229 RICE AVE   16417
St. John the Evangelist ES, 101 OLIN AVE   16417

Girardville, Schuylkill Co., Pop. Code 4
North Schuylkill SD IU 29
Supt. – See Frackville
ES, 200 A ST   17935 – Carl Pyzowski, prin.

Immaculate Heart ES
MAIN AND RICHARDS STS   17935

Gladwyne, Mongomery Co., Pop. Code 5
Lower Merion SD IU 23
Supt. – See Ardmore
ES, 230 RIGHTERS MILL RD   19035
Connie Demedio, prin.

Childrens House ES
920 YOUNGSFORD RD   19035

Glassport, Allegheny Co., Pop. Code 6
South Allegheny SD IU 3
Supt. – See Mc Keesport
Glassport Central ES
THIRD & OHIO AVENUE   15045 – H. Pierce, prin.

Glen Campbell, Indiana Co., Pop. Code 2
Punxsutawney Area SD IU 6
Supt. – See Punxsutawney
Banks Township ES, RURAL ROUTE 01   15742
D. Smith, prin.

Glen Mills, Delaware Co.

St. Thomas Apostle ES
430 VALLEYBROOK RD   19342

Glenolden, Delaware Co., Pop. Code 6
Interboro SD IU 25
Supt. – See Prospect Park
ES, MACDADE & KNOWLES   19036
John Whitig, prin.

Southeast Delco SD IU 25
Supt. – See Folcroft
Ashland MS
ASHLAND AND BARTRAM AVE   19036
Ellen Sosangelis, prin.

Darby Township ES
SCHOOL LANE AND RIVEL   19036
Lee Janiczek, prin.

St. George ES, 11 LAMONT AVE   19036

Glen Richey, Clearfield Co.
Clearfield Area SD IU 10
Supt. – See Clearfield
ES, MAIN STREET   16837 – Gordon Tomb, prin.

Glen Rock, York Co., Pop. Code 4
Southern York County SD IU 12
Sch. Sys. Enr. Code 5
Supt. – Richard Hupper, P O BOX 128   17327
Southern MS, P O BOX 128   17327
John Wright, prin.
Friendship ES, RURAL ROUTE 03   17327
David Sherrer, prin.
Southern ES, P O BOX 128   17327
Ray Lingenfelter, prin.

Glenshaw, Allegheny Co., Pop. Code 8
Shaler Area SD IU 3
Sch. Sys. Enr. Code 5
Supt. – Dr. Robert Perry
2800 MOUNT ROYAL BLVD   15116
Jeffery ES, 201 WETZEL RD   15116
William Baker, prin.
Rogers ES, 705 SCOTT AVE   15116
Paul Surloff, prin.
Other Schools – See Allison Park, Pittsburgh

St. Bonaventure ES
2001 MOUNT ROYAL BLVD   15116
St. Mary's ES, 2510 MIDDLE RD   15116

Glenside, Montgomery Co., Pop. Code 7
Abington SD IU 23
Supt. – See Abington
Glenside-Weldon ES, 409 N EASTON RD   19038
Lorraine Hirsh, prin.

Cheltenham Twp. SD IU 23
Supt. – See Elkins Park
ES, LIMEKILN PK HARRISON   19038
Paul Kilrain, prin.

Queen of Peace ES, 835 N HILLS AVE   19038
St. Luke Evangelist ES
2330 FAIRHILL AVE   19038

Grampian, Clearfield Co., Pop. Code 2
Curwensville Area SD IU 10
Supt. – See Curwensville
Penn-Grampian ES
RURAL ROUTE 01 BOX 194   16838
Richard McKnight, prin.

Grantville, Dauphin Co.
Lower Dauphin SD IU 15
Supt. – See Hummelstown
East Hanover ES
RURAL ROUTE 02 BOX 3210   17028
Irvin Engle, prin.

Granville, Mifflin Co.
Mifflin County SD IU 11
Supt. – See Lewistown
ES, GARDEN VIEW   17029
Kenneth Goodling, prin.

Gratz, Dauphin Co., Pop. Code 3
Upper Dauphin Area SD IU 15
Supt. – See Lykens
ES, 801 WOOD STREET   17030
Rose Radzievich, prin.

Graysville, Greene Co.
West Greene SD IU 1
Supt. – See Waynesburg
ES, RURAL ROUTE 01   15337
Samuel Steinmiller, prin.

Greencastle, Franklin Co., Pop. Code 5
Greencastle-Antrim SD IU 12
Sch. Sys. Enr. Code 4
Supt. – Kendrick McCall
500 LEITERSBURG ST   17225
Greencastle-Antrim MS, 370 RIDGE AVE   17225
Dale Gearhart, prin.
Greencastle-Antrim ES
500 LEITERSBURG ST   17225 – Frank Lewis, prin.
Shady Grove ES
1442 BUCHN TRAIL EAST   17225
Frank Lewis, prin.
South Antrim ES, 842 S WASHINGTON ST   17225
Frank Lewis, prin.

Green Lane, Montgomery Co., Pop. Code 3
Upper Perkiomen SD IU 23
Supt. – See East Greenville
ES, GREEN LANE   18054 – Charles Wayes, prin.

Greensboro, Greene Co., Pop. Code 2
Southeastern Green SD IU 1
Sch. Sys. Enr. Code 4
Supt. – Alton Fell, Jr., RURAL ROUTE 01   15338
Penn Pitt ES, RURAL ROUTE 01   15338
Robert Long, prin.
Other Schools – See Bobtown

Greensburg, Westmoreland Co., Pop. Code 7
Greater Latrobe SD IU 7
Supt. – See Latrobe
Mountain View ES
311 MOUNT VIEW DRIVE   15601
Frank Farrell, prin.

Greensburg-Salem SD IU 7
Sch. Sys. Enr. Code 5
Supt. – Robert Nevin, 11 PARK ST   15601
Nicely ES, 55 MCLAUGHLIN DR   15601
Ronald Silvis, prin.
Welty Street ES, 810 WELTY ST   15601
Harold Christopher, prin.
West Pittsburgh Street ES
571 W PITTSBURGH ST   15601 – John Vitale, prin.
Other Schools – See New Alexandria

Hempfield Area SD IU 7
Sch. Sys. Enr. Code 6
Supt. – Dr. Margaret Smith
RURAL ROUTE 06 BOX 76   15601
Bovard ES, RURAL ROUTE 12 BOX 525   15601
John Bindas, prin.
East Hempfield ES, 555 RIAL LN   15601
Merle Johnson, prin.
Ft. Allen ES, RURAL ROUTE 01 BOX 168   15601
Merle Johnson, prin.
Maxwell ES, 1101 OLD SALEM RD   15601
John Bindas, prin.
St. Clair ES, 1900 GAY AVE   15601
Edward Bunting, prin.
West Point ES, SAINT ANDREWS DR   15601
Edward Bunting, prin.
Other Schools – See Irwin, Manor, New Stanton

Greensburg Catholic ES, 820 CARBON RD   15601
Cathedral ES, 330 N MAIN ST   15601
St. Bruno ES, 1709 POPLAR ST   15601
St. Paul ES, 820 CARBON RD   15601

Greenville, Mercer Co., Pop. Code 6
Greenville Area SD IU 4
Sch. Sys. Enr. Code 4
Supt. – Dr. Patricia Homer
9 DONATION ROAD   16125
East MS, COLUMBIA AVENUE   16125
John Ziegler, prin.
Hempfield ES, 60 FREDONIA RD   16125
Janet Hoffman, prin.

Reynolds SD IU 4
Sch. Sys. Enr. Code 4
Supt. – Maddox Stokes
531 REYNOLDS ROAD   16125
Reynolds MS, 1609 BRENTWOOD DR   16125
Fred Ray, prin.
West Salem ES, 425 S GOOD HOPE RD   16125
Fred Ray, prin.
Other Schools – See Fredonia, Transfer

St. Michael ES, 80 N HIGH ST   16125

Grindstone, Fayette Co.
Brownsville Area SD IU 1
Supt. – See Republic
Colonial ES, RURAL ROUTE 01   15442
Walter Shimborske, prin.

Grove City, Mercer Co., Pop. Code 6
Grove City Area SD IU 4
Sch. Sys. Enr. Code 4
Supt. – Dr. Robert Post
611 HIGHLAND AVE   16127
Grove City Area JHS, 130 E MAIN ST   16127
Francis Staph, prin.
Highland ES, 611 HIGHLAND AVE   16127
Richard Bonnar, prin.
Hillview MS, 482 E MAIN ST   16127
Richard Bonnar, prin.
Park ES, 511 HIGHLAND AVE   16127
Richard Bonnar, prin.

Guys Mills, Crawford Co., Pop. Code 4
Penncrest SD IU 5
Supt. – See Saegertown
Maplewood ES, RURAL ROUTE 01   16327
Frank Santoro, prin.

Hadley, Mercer Co.
Commodore Perry SD IU 4
Sch. Sys. Enr. Code 2
Supt. – Oliver Rodax, RURAL ROUTE 01   16130
Commodore Perry S, RURAL ROUTE 01   16130
Bruce Dunham, prin.

Halifax, Dauphin Co., Pop. Code 3
Halifax Area SD IU 15
Sch. Sys. Enr. Code 2
Supt. – Mark Drumheller
RURAL ROUTE 03 BOX 7   17032
Halifax Area MS, RURAL ROUTE 03 BOX 7   17032
James Scott, prin.
Enders-Fisherville ES, RURAL ROUTE 01   17032
John Fronk, prin.
MS, RURAL ROUTE 01   17032 – John Fronk, prin.

Hamburg, Berks Co., Pop. Code 5
Hamburg Area SD IU 14
Sch. Sys. Enr. Code 4
Supt. – J. Gilmartin, WINDSOR ST   19526
MS, 680 E STATE ST   19526 – Philip Kistler, prin.
Tilden ES, 524 W STATE ST   19526
Robert Shoener, prin.
Other Schools – See Shartlesville, Shoemakersville,
Strausstown

Hamlin, Wayne Co.
Western Wayne SD IU 19
Supt. – See South Canaan
ES   18427 – D. Peet, prin.

Hanover, York Co., Pop. Code 7
Conewago Valley SD IU 12
Supt. – See New Oxford
Conewago Township ES, 1189 W ELM AVE 17331
Bernard Anthony,Jr., prin.

Hanover Public SD IU 12
Sch. Sys. Enr. Code 4
Supt. – Solomon Lausch
190 E WALNUT ST 17331
MS, 195 STOCK ST 17331 – James Little, prin.
Clearview ES, 100 CLEARVIEW RD 17331
Donald Bair, prin.
Hanover Street ES, 101 E HANOVER ST 17331
Ann Mellott, prin.
Washington ES, 301 MOUL AVE 17331
Donald Bair, prin.

South Western SD IU 12
Sch. Sys. Enr. Code 5
Supt. – D. Schaeberle
225 BOWMAN ROAD 17331
Markle IS, 225 BOWMAN ROAD 17331
Fred Marsh, prin.
Baresville ES, 135 SANFORD AVE 17331
Donald Stock, prin.
Park Hills ES, 137 W GRANGER ST 17331
Gene Bowser, prin.
West Manheim ES, 2412 BALTIMORE PIKE 17331
Richard Houseknecht, prin.
Other Schools – See Brodbecks

Sacred Heart ES, 55 BASILICA DR 17331
St. Joseph ES, 236 BALTIMORE ST 17331
St. Vincent DePaul ES, 224 THIRD ST 17331

Harborcreek, Erie Co., Pop. Code 3
Harbor Creek SD IU 5
Sch. Sys. Enr. Code 5
Supt. – Robert Mulvin
6375 BUFFALO ROAD 16421
Other Schools – See Erie

Harford, Susquehanna Co.
Mountain View SD IU 19
Supt. – See Kingsley
ES, COLLEGE STREET 18823
Margaret Coombs, prin.

Harleysville, Montgomery Co., Pop. Code 4
North Penn SD IU 23
Supt. – See Lansdale
Nash ES, BSTRD ROAD AND LIBERTY BE 19438
Dr. Helen Larson, prin.

Souderton Area SD IU 23
Supt. – See Souderton
Lower Salford ES, 250 MAPLE AVE 19438
Lowell Tinner, prin.
Salford Hills ES, 2720 BARNDT RD 19438
Hugh Jones, prin.

Harmony, Butler Co., Pop. Code 4
Seneca Valley SD IU 4
Sch. Sys. Enr. Code 5
Supt. – Donald Lee, RURAL ROUTE 01 16037
Other Schools – See Evans City, Mars, Zelienople

Harrisburg, Dauphin Co., Pop. Code 8
Central Dauphin SD IU 15
Sch. Sys. Enr. Code 6
Supt. – Carolyn Dumaresq
600 RUTHERFORD ROAD 17109
Chamber Hill ES
6450 CHAMBERS HILL RD 17111
Dr. James Dostich, prin.
Fishing Creek Valley ES
1524 PINE TREE AVE 17112
Howard Kauffman, prin.
Linglestown ES, 1044 N MOUNTAIN RD 17112
William Beaver, prin.
North Side ES, 4520 DEVONSHIRE RD 17109
Kenneth Beard, prin.
Paxtang ES
SWAN AND RUTHERFORD STREETS 17111
Linda Dolan, prin.
Paxtonia ES, 6135 JONESTOWN RD 17112
Robert Cook, prin.
Phillips ES, 100 OAKMONT RD 17109
Harold Kauffman, prin.
Rutherford ES, 65TH AND CLEARFIELD ST 17111
Dr. James Dostich, prin.
South Side ES, 4525 UNION DEPOSIT RD 17111
Edward Shadle, prin.
West Hanover ES, 7740 MANOR DR 17112
Gary Wendt, prin.
Other Schools – See Dauphin, Steelton

Harrisburg CSD IU 15
Sch. Sys. Enr. Code 6
Supt. – Donald Carroll, P O BOX 2645 17105
Rowland IS, 1901 WAYNE AVE 17109
James Musmanno, prin.
Scott IS, 1901 WAYNE AVE 17109
James Parker, prin.
Camp Curtin Early Childhood ES
2900 N 6TH ST 17110 – Janet McVey, prin.
Downey Early Childhood
1313 MONROE ST 17103 – Lloyd Seaman, prin.
Foose Early Childhood
1301 SYCAMORE ST 17104
Janet Esworthy, prin.
Franklin ES, 1205 N 6TH ST 17102
JoAnn Griffin, prin.
Hamilton ES, 1701 N 6TH ST 17102
Richard Baker, prin.

Lincoln Early Childhood, 1601 STATE ST 17103
Dr. Marshall Layton, prin.
Marshall MS, 301 HALE AVE 17104
Janie Dodd, prin.
Melrose MS, 2041 BERRYHILL ST 17104
Ronald Dixon, prin.
Shimmell Early Childhood, 548 S 17TH ST 17104
Patricia Prim, prin.
Steele MS, 2537 N 5TH ST 17110
Carolyn Carter, prin.
Woodward MS, 1001 N 18TH ST 17103
Samuel Lester, prin.

Susquehanna Twp. SD IU 15
Sch. Sys. Enr. Code 4
Supt. – Thomas Holtzman
3550 ELMERTON AVE 17109
Susquehanna Twp. MS, 801 WOOD ST 17109
James Shadle, prin.
Hoover MS, 1910 LINGLESTOWN RD 17110
Dennis Brehm, prin.
Lindemuth ES, 1201 N PROGRESS AVE 17109
Linda Geesaman, prin.

Christian School Association
P O BOX 6010 17112
Cathedral ES, LIBERY AND CHURCH ST 17101
Holy Family ES, 555 S 25TH ST 17104
Holy Name of Jesus ES
6190 ALLENTOWN BLVD 17112
St. Catherine LaBour ES, 4020 DERRY ST 17111
St. Margaret Mary ES, 2826 HERR ST 17103
St. Stephen's Episcopal ES
215 N FRONT ST 17101
Town & Country Day School
2910 BRISBAN ST 17111
Yeshiva Academy of Harrisburg
100 VAUGHEN ST 17110

Harrison City, Westmoreland Co.
Penn-Trafford SD IU 7
Sch. Sys. Enr. Code 4
Supt. – Joseph Marasti, ADMIN BLDG 15636
Other Schools – See Claridge, Irwin, Jeannette,
Trafford

Christian Fellowship ES, P O BOX 446 15636

Harrisonville, Fulton Co.
Forbes Road SD IU 11
Sch. Sys. Enr. Code 4
Supt. – Charles Dunn, HCR 74 BOX 222 17228
Forbes Road ES, HCR 74 BOX 220 17228
David Hoover II, prin.

Harrisville, Venango Co., Pop. Code 4
Franklin Area SD IU 6
Supt. – See Franklin
Victory ES, RURAL ROUTE 01 16038
Robert Scheer, prin.

Slippery Rock Area SD IU 4
Supt. – See Slippery Rock
Har-Mer ES, PRAIRIE STREET 16038
Bruce Golmic, prin.

Harveys Lake, Luzerne Co., Pop. Code 4
Lake-Lehman SD IU 18
Supt. – See Lehman
Lake-Noxen ES 18618 – Robert Kunkle, prin.

Hastings, Cambria Co., Pop. Code 4
Cambria Heights SD IU 8
Supt. – See Patton
Cambria Hts. MS, P O BOX 480 16646
Michael Johnson, prin.

St. Bernard ES, SPANGLER ST 16646

Hatboro, Montgomery Co., Pop. Code 6
Hatsboro-Horsham SD IU 23
Supt. – See Horsham
Blair Mill ES, BENDER ROAD 19040
Eleano Seif, prin.
Crooked Billet ES
MEADOWBROOK & PENN ST 19040
Nancy Bobkoskie, prin.

Upper Moreland Twp. SD IU 23
Supt. – See Willow Grove
Upper Moreland MS
4000 ORANGEMENS ROAD 19040
William Lessa, prin.
Round Meadow ES, BYBERRY ROAD 19040
Charles Ross, prin.

St. John Bosco ES, 215 E COUNTY LINE RD 19040

Hatfield, Montgomery Co., Pop. Code 5
North Penn SD IU 23
Supt. – See Lansdale
ES, FAIRGROUND ROAD 19440
Barbara Steven, prin.
Kulp ES, HATFIELD VALLEY ROAD 19440
Janell Holtz, prin.
Pennfield MS, 4TH FOOT ROAD 19440
Joan Stough, prin.

St. Marie Goretti ES, HARFIELD VLY RD 19440

Haverford, Montgomery Co., Pop. Code 8

Haverford School, 450 LANCASTER AVE 19041
Friends ES, 851 BUCK LN 19041

Havertown, Delaware Co., Pop. Code 5
Haverford Twp. SD IU 25
Sch. Sys. Enr. Code 5
Supt. – Ewald Kalmbach
1801 DARBY ROAD 19083
Haverford MS, 1701 DARBY ROAD 19083
Michael Bianco, prin.
Chatham Park ES
ALLSTON AND GLEN ARBO 19083
Richard Shaeffer, prin.
Lynnewood ES, 1400 LAWRENCE RD 19083
Edward Pratt, prin.
Manoa ES, MANOA ROAD AND FURLON 19083
Michael Walker, prin.
Oakmont ES, EAGLE ROAD HATHAWAY L 19083
Audrone Meskauskas, prin.
Other Schools – See Bryn Mawr

Annunciation BVM ES
421 BROOKLINE BLVD 19083
Sacred Heart ES
N MANOA RD AND WILSON AVE 19083
St. Denis ES, 300 E EAGLE RD 19083
SS Colman John Neumann School
HIGHLAND LN & RADNOR RD 19083

Hawley, Wayne Co., Pop. Code 4
Wallenpaupack Area SD IU 19
Sch. Sys. Enr. Code 4
Supt. – Thomas Peifer, HCR 02 18428
Wallenpaupack Area MS, HCR 02 18428
Michael Silsby, prin.
ES, ACADEMY STREET 18428
Thomas Kennedy, prin.
Wallenpaupak North ES
BLOOMING GROVE 18428
Thomas Kennedy, prin.
Other Schools – See Newfoundland

Hawthorn, Clarion Co., Pop. Code 3
Redbank Valley SD IU 6
Supt. – See New Bethlehem
Redbank-Hawthorn ES, TRUITTSBURG RD 16230
Charles Evans, prin.

Hazleton, Luzerne Co., Pop. Code 8
Hazleton Area SD IU 18
Sch. Sys. Enr. Code 6
Supt. – Eugene Gatty
CHURCH & WALNUT STS 18201
Arthur Street ES, ARTHUR 9TH STREETS 18201
Anthony Valente, prin.
Hazle ES, 23RD AND MCKINLEY STREET 18201
John Roman, prin.
Heights Terrace ES, 275 MILL ST 18201
Eugene Gallagher, prin.
Locust Street ES, LOCUST 11TH STREETS 18201
Frank Antonelli, prin.
Thomas ES, GRANT 4TH STREETS 18201
Frank Antonelli, prin.
Other Schools – See Conyngham, Drums, Freeland,
Mc Adoo, Nuremberg, Sugarloaf, West Hazleton

Holy Trinity ES, 35 N CHURCH ST 18201
Monsignour Molino ES, 225 E 4TH ST 18201
St. Gabriel ES, 154 S WYOMING ST 18201
St. John Byzantine ES, 201 N WYOMING ST 18201
St. Joseph Memorial ES, 600 N LAUREL ST 18201

Hellam, York Co.
Eastern York SD IU 12
Supt. – See Wrightsville
Kreutz Creek ES, N LEE STREET 17406
Eugene Gruver, prin.

Hellertown, Northampton Co., Pop. Code 6
Saucon Valley SD IU 20
Sch. Sys. Enr. Code 4
Supt. – Dr. M. David Preston
1050 MAIN ST 18055
Lower Saucon MS, 1200 WASSERGASS RD 18055
Douglas Koch, prin.
Reinhard ES, 315 NORTHAMPTON ST 18055
William Yerger, prin.

St. Teresa ES, 300 LEONARD ST 18055

Hereford, Berks Co.
Upper Perkiomen SD IU 23
Supt. – See East Greenville
ES 18056 – Anita Bieler, prin.

Herminie, Westmoreland Co.
Yough SD IU 7
Sch. Sys. Enr. Code 5
Supt. – Earl Lutz, 99 LOWBER ROAD 15637
Good ES 15637 – Lawrence Nemec, prin.
Other Schools – See Lowber, Ruffs Dale, Smithton,
West Newton

St. Edward ES, ST EDWARD SQUARE 15637

Hermitage, Mercer Co., Pop. Code 7
Hermitage SD IU 4
Sch. Sys. Enr. Code 4
Supt. – Thomas Hawkins, P O BOX 1227 16148
MS, 123 N HERMITAGE ROAD 16148
John Young, prin.
Bartman ES, P O BOX 1227 16148
William Swanson, prin.
Delahunty MS, P O BOX 1227 16148
Allan Rummel, prin.
ES, P O BOX 1227 16148 – Hugh Phythyon, prin.

Notre Dame ES, 2335 HIGHLAND RD 16148

Herndon, Northumberland Co., Pop. Code 2
Line Mountain SD IU 16
Sch. Sys. Enr. Code 4
Supt. – David Landis
 RURAL ROUTE 01 BOX 43A 17830
Other Schools – See Dalmatia, Leck Kill, Shamokin,
 Trevorton

Hershey, Dauphin Co., Pop. Code 6
Derry Twp SD IU 15
Sch. Sys. Enr. Code 4
Supt. – Barbara Hasson
 HOMESTEAD ROAD 17033
MS, E GRANADA AVE 17033 – Joseph Galli, prin.
ES, HOMESTEAD RD 17033
 Dr. Jane Karper, prin.

Lower Dauphin SD IU 15
Supt. – See Hummelstown
South Hanover ES, W 3RD STREET 17033
 Robert Santarelli, prin.

Milton Hershey School, P O BOX 830 17033
St. Joan of Arc ES, 329 W AREBA AVE 17033

Hickory, Washington Co., Pop. Code 3
Fort Cherry SD IU 1
Supt. – See Mc Donald
ES, WABASH AVENUE BOX 37 15340
 Milton Diaz, prin.

Hilltown, Bucks Co.

St. Agnes-Sacred Heart ES, BROAD ST 18927

Holland, Bucks Co.
Council Rock SD IU 22
Supt. – See Richboro
ES, CRESCENT AND BEVERLY 18966
 Christopher Cresswell, prin.
Rolling Hills ES
 340 MIDDLE HOLLAND RD 18966
 Harry Fritz, prin.

St. Bede Venerable ES
 1053 E HOLLAND RD 18966

Hollidaysburg, Blair Co., Pop. Code 6
Hollidaysburg Area SD IU 8
Sch. Sys. Enr. Code 5
Supt. – Dr. Leo Gensante
 201-15 JACKSON ST 16648
Blair ES, RURAL ROUTE 01 BOX 379 16648
 Dean Benton, prin.
Frankstown ES
 RURAL ROUTE 03 BOX 592 16648
 Dean Benton, prin.
MS, 1000 HEWITT ST 16648
 Barry Michelone, prin.
Longer ES, 1320 UNION ST 16648
 Edward Kohlmeyer, prin.
Other Schools – See Duncansville

Hollidaysburg ES, 314 CLARK ST 16648

Hollsopple, Somerset Co., Pop. Code 3

Johnstown Christian School
 RURAL ROUTE 02 15935

Holtwood, Lancaster Co.
Penn Manor SD IU 13
Supt. – See Millersville
Martic ES, RURAL ROUTE 02 17532
 Louise Hardinger, prin.

Homer City, Indiana Co., Pop. Code 4
Homer-Center SD IU 28
Sch. Sys. Enr. Code 4
Supt. – Joseph Marcoline 15748
Homer Center ES 15748
 Dr. Kathleen Kelley, prin.

Homestead, Allegheny Co., Pop. Code 6
Steel Valley SD IU 3
Supt. – See Munhall
Barrett ES, 221 E 12TH AVE 15120
 Doris Hyde, prin.

St. Mary Magdaline ES, 127 E 10TH AVE 15120

Honesdale, Wayne Co., Pop. Code 6
Wayne Highlands SD IU 19
Sch. Sys. Enr. Code 5
Supt. – J. Sutton, 474 GROVE ST 18431
Wayne Highlands MS, 482 GROVE ST 18431
 J. Clift, prin.
Lincoln ES, WILLOW AVENUE 18431
 Leroy Spoor, prin.
Stourbridge ES, PARK ST 18431
 Leroy Spoor, prin.
Other Schools – See Damascus, South Canaan

Honedale Catholic ES, 329 CLIFF ST 18431

Honey Brook, Chester Co., Pop. Code 4
Twin Valley SD IU 14
Supt. – See Elverson
ES, RURAL ROUTE 03 BOX 5 19344
 David Woods, prin.

Honey Grove, Juniata Co.
Juniata County SD IU 11
Supt. – See Mifflintown
Lack-Tuscarora ES, RURAL ROUTE 01 17035
 Stephen Bahorik, prin.

Hookstown, Beaver Co., Pop. Code 2
South Side Area SD IU 27
Sch. Sys. Enr. Code 4
Supt. – George Szymanski
 RURAL ROUTE 01 BOX 410 15050
South Side MS
 RURAL ROUTE 01 BOX 410 15050
 D. Chewning, prin.
South Side ES, RURAL ROUTE 01 BOX 410 15050
 William Schiffhauer, prin.

Horsham, Montgomery Co.
Hatsboro-Horsham SD IU 23
Sch. Sys. Enr. Code 5
Supt. – Dr. Gerald Strock
 229 MEETINGHOUSE ROAD 19044
Keith Valley MS, 411 BABYLON ROAD 19044
 Harrison Woodruff, prin.
Hallowell ES, 200 MAPLE AVE 19044
 George Plosa, prin.
Other Schools – See Ambler, Hatboro

St. Catherine of Siena ES, 317 WITMER RD 19044

Houston, Washington Co., Pop. Code 4
Chartiers-Houston SD IU 1
Sch. Sys. Enr. Code 4
Supt. – Dorothy Dillomuth
 2080 W PIKE ST 15342
Chartiers-Houston MS, 2050 W PIKE ST 15342
 Paul Lapcevic, prin.
Allison Park ES, 803 MCGOVERN RD 15342
 William Hill, prin.

Central Christian Academy
 145 MCGOVERN RD 15342

Houtzdale, Clearfield Co., Pop. Code 4
Moshannon Valley SD IU 10
Sch. Sys. Enr. Code 4
Supt. – Don Evans
 RURAL ROUTE 01 BOX 111 16651
Moshannon Valley ES
 RURAL ROUTE 01 BOX 314 16651
 Tom Snyder, prin.

Howard, Centre Co., Pop. Code 3
Bald Eagle Area SD IU 10
Supt. – See Wingate
ES, CHURCH STREET 16841
 Faye Marshall, prin.

Hughesville, Lycoming Co., Pop. Code 4
East Lycoming SD IU 17
Sch. Sys. Enr. Code 4
Supt. – Thomas Paternostro
 CEMETARY ST 17737
Ashkar ES, 334 S BROAD ST 17737
 Steven Moyer, prin.
Other Schools – See Lairdsville, Picture Rocks

Hummelstown, Dauphin Co., Pop. Code 5
Lower Dauphin SD IU 15
Sch. Sys. Enr. Code 5
Supt. – Dr. George Sauers, 291 E MAIN ST 17036
Lower Dauphin MS, 201 S HANOVER ST 17036
 Paul Shirk, prin.
Nye MS, SHORT AND JOHN STREETS 17036
 Wendell Poppy, prin.
Price ES, HIGH AND WATER STREETS 17036
 Wendell Poppy, prin.
Other Schools – See Elizabethtown, Grantville,
 Hershey, Middletown

Mountain View Christian School
 34 SIPE AVE 17036

Hunlock Creek, Luzerne Co.
Northwest Area SD IU 18
Supt. – See Shickshinny
ES, RURAL ROUTE 01 18621
 Richard Belles, prin.

Huntingdon, Huntingdon Co., Pop. Code 6
Huntingdon Area SD IU 11
Sch. Sys. Enr. Code 5
Supt. – Norman Smith
 723 PORTLAND AVE 16652
Huntingdon Area MS, 2500 CASSADY AVE 16652
 Thomas Giles, prin.
Alfarata ES, 14TH & MOORE STREET 16652
 Donald McCloy, prin.
Jackson-Miller ES
 RURAL ROUTE 02 BOX 173 16652
 Donald McCloy, prin.
Smith ES, 5TH & ONEIDA STREETS 16652
 Donald McCloy, prin.
Smithfield-Juniata ES
 710 MOUNT VERNON AVE 16652
 Donald McCloy, prin.
Woodcock Valley ES
 RURAL ROUTE 01 BOX 107 16652
 Donald McCloy, prin.
Other Schools – See Mill Creek

Huntingdon Valley, Montgomery Co., Pop. Code 6
Abington SD IU 23
Supt. – See Abington
Rydal ES, 1160 HUNTINGDON PIKE 19006
 Cornelius McCarthy, prin.

Lower Moreland Twp. SD IU 23
Sch. Sys. Enr. Code 4
Supt. – Dr. Robert Pellicone
 555 RED LION ROAD 19006

Lower Moreland MS, 2551 MURRAY AVE 19006
 Debra Bruner, prin.
Pine Road ES, 3737 PINE RD 19006
 Gail Garber, prin.

Greater Philadelphia SDA Jr. Academy
 1845 BYBERRY ROAD 19006
St. Albert the Great ES, 214 WELSH RD 19006
Valley Christian ES
 2364 HUNTINGDON PIKE 19006

Huntington Mills, Luzerne Co.
Northwest Area SD IU 18
Supt. – See Shickshinny
ES 18622 – Dorothy Deitterick, prin.

Hyndman, Bedford Co., Pop. Code 4
Bedford Area SD IU 8
Supt. – See Bedford
ES, CHURCH STREET 15545
 Sylva Willison, prin.
Londonderry IS, RURAL ROUTE 01 15545
 Robert Hine, prin.

Immaculata, Chester Co.

Villa Maria Ac. Lower ES, KING RD 19345

Imperial, Allegheny Co., Pop. Code 4
West Allegheny SD IU 3
Sch. Sys. Enr. Code 4
Supt. – Dr. Reggie Bonfield, P O BOX 55 15126
West Allegheny MS, RURAL ROUTE 01 15126
 Charles Hughey, prin.
Wilson ES, RURAL ROUTE 01 15126
 Frank Bruno, prin.
Other Schools – See Oakdale

Indiana, Indiana Co., Pop. Code 7
Indiana Area SD IU 28
Sch. Sys. Enr. Code 5
Supt. – David Laird, 501 E PIKE 15701
East Pike ES, 501 EAST PIKE 15701
 Kenneth Belgie, prin.
Eisenhower ES, 1460 SCHOOL ST 15701
 Harry McFarland, prin.
Franklin ES, 95 BEN FRANKLIN RD S 15701
 Dr. Walter Kealey, Jr., prin.
Mann ES, 204 S 5TH ST 15701
 Paul Gallagher, prin.

St. Bernard ES, 351 N 5TH ST 15701

Industry, Beaver Co., Pop. Code 4
Western Beaver County SD IU 27
Supt. – See Midland
Snyder MS, RURAL ROUTE 02 15052
 Roland Delaney, prin.

Ingomar, Allegheny Co.
North Allegheny SD IU 3
Supt. – See Pittsburgh
ES, INGOMAR RD 15127 – Abe Comunale, prin.

Intercourse, Lancaster Co., Pop. Code 3
Pequea Valley SD IU 13
Supt. – See Kinzers
Leacock ES, P O BOX 120 17534
 Rachelle Bonfield, prin.

Irwin, Westmoreland Co., Pop. Code 5
Hempfield Area SD IU 7
Supt. – See Greensburg
West Hempfield ES, RURAL ROUTE 03 15642
 Cheryl Troglio, prin.

Norwin SD IU 7
Sch. Sys. Enr. Code 6
Supt. – Charles Lauffer
 281 MCMAHON DRIVE 15642
Pennsylvania Avenue ES
 1015 PENNSYLVANIA AVE 15642
 Ruth Tully, prin.
Other Schools – See North Huntingdon

Penn-Trafford SD IU 7
Supt. – See Harrison City
Sunrise ES, RURAL ROUTE 02 15642
 Paul Bergamasco, prin.

Immaculate Conception ES, 308 2ND ST 15642

Jamestown, Mercer Co., Pop. Code 3
Jamestown Area SD IU 4
Sch. Sys. Enr. Code 3
Supt. – David Shaffer, P O BOX 217 16134
Jamestown Area ES, P O BOX 217 16134
 Mary Reames, prin.

Jeannette, Westmoreland Co., Pop. Code 7
Jeannette CSD IU 7
Sch. Sys. Enr. Code 4
Supt. – Vincent Aiello, P O BOX 418 15644
MS, P O BOX 418 15644 – Paul Noonan, prin.
FT. Pitt ES, HARRISON AVENUE 15644
 Geraldine McCartney, prin.
Gaskill ES, GASKILL AVENUE 15644
 Geralding McCartney, prin.
Other Schools – See Rochester

Penn-Trafford SD IU 7
Supt. – See Harrison City
Harrison Park ES, HARRISON PARK 15644
 John Meneghini, prin.

Sacred Heart ES, N SEVENTH ST 15644

Jefferson, Greene Co., Pop. Code 2
Jefferson-Morgan SD IU 1
Sch. Sys. Enr. Code 3
Supt. – K. Macek, P O BOX 158 15344
Jefferson-Morgan ES
   GREENE STREET BOX 158 15344
   V. Monas, prin.

Jenkintown, Montgomery Co., Pop. Code 5
Jenkintown SD IU 23
Sch. Sys. Enr. Code 3
Supt. – David Barrett III
   325 HIGHLAND AVE 19046
ES, W AND HIGHLAND AVE 19046
   Ernest Simon, prin.

Abington Friends School
   575 WASHINGTON LANE 19046
Immaculate Conception ES, 606 WEST AVE 19046

Jennerstown, Somerset Co., Pop. Code 3
North Star SD IU 8
Supt. – See Boswell
North Star West ES 15547 – Francis Fregly, prin.

Jermyn, Lackawanna Co., Pop. Code 4
Lakeland SD IU 19
Sch. Sys. Enr. Code 4
Supt. – Robert Ghigiarelli
   RURAL ROUTE 01 18433
Scott ES, RURAL ROUTE 01 18433
   Carl Klach, prin.
Other Schools – See Mayfield

Jerome, Somerset Co., Pop. Code 4
Conemaugh Twp. Area SD IU 8
Supt. – See Davidsville
ES, P O BOX 396 15937 – William Ackman, prin.

Jersey Shore, Lycoming Co., Pop. Code 5
Jersey Shore Area SD IU 17
Sch. Sys. Enr. Code 5
Supt. – Gary Mowery, 201 S BROAD ST 17740
Avis ES, RURAL ROUTE 01 BOX 246 17740
   Raymond Hill, prin.
Jersey Shore ES, 601 LOCUST ST 17740
   John Eisenhauer, prin.
Salladasburg ES
   RURAL ROUTE 03 BOX 98 17740
   Eugene Kurzejewski, prin.
Other Schools – See Williamsport

Jessup, Lackawanna Co., Pop. Code 5

St. Michael ES, 316 FIRST AVE 18434

Jim Thorpe, Carbon Co., Pop. Code 6
Jim Thorpe Area SD IU 21
Sch. Sys. Enr. Code 3
Supt. – Thomas Sangiuliano
   1105 CENTER ST 18229
Jim Thorpe Area JHS, 410 CENTER AVE 18229
   Jeffery James, prin.
Morris ES, 150 W 10TH ST 18229
   Virginia Smith, prin.

St. Joseph ES, 27 W 6TH ST 18229

Johnsonburg, Elk Co., Pop. Code 5
Johnsonburg Area SD IU 9
Sch. Sys. Enr. Code 4
Supt. – Frank Carnovale, ELK AVE 15845
ES, ROUTE 219 15845 – Barbara Lias, prin.

Holy Rosary ES, 605 MARKET ST 15845

Johnstown, Cambria Co., Pop. Code 8
Central Cambria SD IU 8
Supt. – See Ebensburg
Jackson ES, RURAL ROUTE 06 BOX 177 15909
   Ronald Rufrano, prin.

Conemaugh Twp. Area SD IU 8
Supt. – See Davidsville
Central ES, RURAL ROUTE 04 BOX 49 15905
   Joseph DiBartola, prin.

Conemaugh Valley SD IU 8
Sch. Sys. Enr. Code 5
Supt. – Joseph Ondrejik
   1451 FRANKSTOWN ROAD 15902
Conemaugh Valley ES
   1451 FRANKSTOWN RD 15902
   Frances Gaborek, prin.
East Taylor ES, RURAL ROUTE 01 BOX 130 15906
   Frances Gaborek, prin.

Ferndale Area SD IU 8
Sch. Sys. Enr. Code 3
Supt. – Richard Rodgers
   100 DARTMOUTH AVE 15905
Ferndale ES, 100 DARTMOUTH AVE 15905
   Barry Haddle, prin.

Greater Johnstown SD IU 8
Sch. Sys. Enr. Code 5
Supt. – Dr. Levi Hollis
   220 MESSENGER ST 15902
Greater Johnstown JHS, 280 DECKER AVE 15906
   Donald Hartnett, prin.
Chandler ES, 280 GARFIELD ST 15906
   Robert Beatty, prin.
Cypress ES, 325 CYPRESS AVE 15902
   John Sholtis, prin.
Meadowvale ES, 220 MESSENGER ST 15902
   Edward Minium, prin.

Roxbury ES, 11 19 SELL STREET 15905
   Barbara Casavant, prin.
Westwood ES, 196 WESTGATE DRVIE 15905
   Donna Spangler, prin.

Richland SD IU 8
Sch. Sys. Enr. Code 4
Supt. – Elizabeth Matgouranis
   340 THEATRE DR 15904
Richland MS, 1740 HIGHFIELD ST 15904
   Nick Campitelli, prin.
Rachel Hill MS, 338 THEATRE DR 15904
   John Korch, prin.
University Park ES
   321 SCHOOLHOUSE RD 15904
   John Korch, prin.

Westmont Hilltop SD IU 8
Sch. Sys. Enr. Code 4
Supt. – Gary Estadt, 827 DIAMOND BLVD 15905
Westmont Hilltop MS
   827 DIAMOND BLVD 15905
   Austin Greenland, prin.
Westmont Hilltop ES
   600 GOUGHER STREET 15905
   Paul Ponchione, prin.

Central Catholic ES, 751 RAILROAD ST 15901
Our Mother of Sorrow ES, 430 TIOGA ST 15905
St. Andrew ES, 1629 FERNDALE AVE 15905
St. Benedict ES, 2306 BEDFORD ST 15905
St. Clement ES, 110 LINDBERG AVE 15905
St. Patrick ES, 625 PARK AVE 15902
West End Catholic ES, 917 CHESTNUT ST 15906

Jones Mills, Westmoreland Co.
Mt. Pleasant Area SD IU 7
Supt. – See Mount Pleasant
Donegal ES, RURAL ROUTE 01 15646
   Dan Landy, prin.

Jonestown, Lebanon Co., Pop. Code 3
Northern Lebanon SD IU 13
Supt. – See Fredericksburg
ES, N LANCASTER ST 17038
   Gary Messinger, prin.
Lickdale ES, RURAL ROUTE 01 17038
   Michael Miller, prin.

Kane, McKean Co., Pop. Code 5
Kane Area SD IU 9
Sch. Sys. Enr. Code 4
Supt. – Dr. Charles Amuso
   W HEMLOCK AVE 16735
Kane Area MS, 400 W HEMLOCK AVE 16735
   Richard Buckley, prin.
Chestnut Street ES, 226 CHESTNUT ST 16735
   Danette Sarvey, prin.
Other Schools – See Mount Jewett

Kantner, Somerset Co.
North Star SD IU 8
Supt. – See Boswell
North Star East MS, 15548 – Jack Dickey, prin.
North Start East ES, L 15548 – Francis Fregly, prin.

Karns City, Butler Co., Pop. Code 2
Karns City Area SD IU 4
Sch. Sys. Enr. Code 3
Supt. – Dr. David Pisani, HS BLDG 16041
Other Schools – See Bruin, Chicora

Kemblesville, Chester Co.
Avon-Grove SD IU 24
Supt. – See West Grove
ES, RURAL ROUTE 01 19347 – John Neill, prin.

Kempton, Berks Co.
Kutztown Area SD IU 14
Supt. – See Kutztown
Albany ES 19529 – Dennis Lesher, prin.

Kennerdell, Venango Co.
Cranberry Area SD IU 6
Supt. – See Seneca
Rockland ES, RURAL ROUTE 01 16374
   Edward Schick, prin.

Kennett Square, Chester Co., Pop. Code 5
Kennett Cons. SD IU 24
Sch. Sys. Enr. Code 4
Supt. – Dr. Larry Bosley
   130 W MULBERRY ST 19348
Kennett MS, S UNION ST 19348
   Jerome Cammarata, prin.
Greenwood ES, GREENWOOD ROAD 19348
   Susan Kampf, prin.
Lang ES
   CENTER AND MULBERRY STREET 19348
   Andrew Augustine, prin.
Other Schools – See Toughkenamon

St. Patrick ES, 210 MEREDITH ST 19348
Upland Country Day School
   420 WEST STREET ROAD 19348

Kersey, Elk Co.
St. Mary's Area SD IU 9
Supt. – See Saint Marys
Fox Township ES, MAIN STREET 15846
   Marion Johnson, prin.

Kimberton, Chester Co., Pop. Code 3

Kimberton Waldorf School
   W 7 STARS ROAD 19442
St. Basil the Great ES, P O BOX 463 19442

King of Prussia, Montgomery Co., Pop. Code 7
Upper Merion Area SD IU 23
Sch. Sys. Enr. Code 5
Supt. – Charles Scott
   435 CROSSFIELD ROAD 19406
Upper Merion MS, CROSSFIELD ROAD 19406
   Jacqueline Hollrah, prin.
Caley Road ES, CALEY ROAD 19406
   Dennis Barcaro, prin.
Candlebrook ES, PRICE FREDERICK ROAD 19406
   Marilyn Fitzgerald, prin.
Other Schools – See Bridgeport, Wayne

Mother Divine Providence ES
   405 ALLENDALE RD 19406

Kingsley, Susquehanna Co.
Mountain View SD IU 19
Sch. Sys. Enr. Code 4
Supt. – Dr. Andrew Chichura
   RURAL ROUTE 01 18826
Other Schools – See Brooklyn, Clifford, Harford

Kingston, Luzerne Co., Pop. Code 7
Wyoming Valley West SD IU 18
Sch. Sys. Enr. Code 6
Supt. – Ellwood Jacoby, 450 N MAPLE AVE 18704
Wyoming Valley West MS, CHESTER ST 18704
   D. Leapline, prin.
Chester Street ES, CHESTER STREET 18704
   William Bosso, prin.
Pringle Street ES, 230 PRINGLE ST 18704
   John Lagoski, prin.
Schuyler Avenue ES, SCHUYLER AVENUE 18704
   Nelson Kile, prin.
Third Avenue ES, THIRD AVENUE 18704
   William Bosso, prin.
Other Schools – See Forty Fort, Larksville, Plymouth

Wyoming Seminary, 201 N SPRAGUE AVE 18704
St. Hedwig ES, 16 PULASKI ST 18704

Kintnersville, Bucks Co.
Palisades SD IU 22
Sch. Sys. Enr. Code 4
Supt. – Tom Free
   RURAL ROUTE 02 BOX 15 18930
Durham-Nockamixon ES
   RURAL ROUTE 02 BOX 14 18930
   Frank Kuebler, prin.
Other Schools – See Pipersville, Quakertown, Upper
   Black Eddy

Kinzers, Lancaster Co., Pop. Code 2
Pequea Valley SD IU 13
Sch. Sys. Enr. Code 4
Supt. – Dr. Ann Keim
   RURAL ROUTE 01 BOX 81 17535
Pequea Valley IS
   RURAL ROUTE 01 BOX 81 17535
   Eric Dreibelbis, prin.
Other Schools – See Gap, Intercourse, Paradise

Kittanning, Armstrong Co., Pop. Code 6
Armstrong SD IU 28
Supt. – See Ford City
JHS, 210 N MCKEAN ST 16201
   Dr. William Jones, prin.
Central ES, NORTH MCKEAN STREET 16201
   Dr. William Jones, prin.
Kittanning Township ES
   RURAL ROUTE 01 16201 – Dr. Jon Drew, prin.
North Buffalo ES, RURAL ROUTE 04 16201
   Gary Thomas, prin.
Spaces ES, RURAL ROUTE 02 16201
   Dr. William Jones, prin.
West Hills ES, 838 BUTLER RD 16201
   Gary Thomas, prin.

St. Mary ES, 351 N JEFFERSON ST 16201

Klingerstown, Schuylkill Co.
Tri-Valley SD IU 29
Supt. – See Valley View
Mahantongo ES, RURAL ROUTE 01 17941
   Thomas Kuczawa, prin.

Knox, Clarion Co., Pop. Code 4
Keystone SD IU 6
Sch. Sys. Enr. Code 4
Supt. – W. Regester, P O BOX 370 16232
Keystone ES, P O BOX 370 16232
   Peter Miller, prin.

Koppel, Beaver Co., Pop. Code 4
Big Beaver Falls Area SD IU 27
Supt. – See Beaver Falls
Big Beaver ES, FRIENDSHIP DR 16136
   Timothy Pigza, prin.
Koppel ES, 2ND AVE 16136 – Timothy Pigza, prin.

Kresgeville, Carbon Co.
Pleasant Valley SD IU 20
Supt. – See Brodheadsville
Polk ES 18333 – Harrie Blood, prin.

Kulpmont, Northumberland Co., Pop. Code 5
Mt. Carmel Area SD IU 16
Supt. – See Mount Carmel
ES, 11TH & SPRUCE ST 17834 – Rita Bolesta, prin.

Assumption BVM ES
   9TH & CHESTNUT ST 17834

Kunkletown, Monroe Co.
Pleasant Valley SD IU 20
Supt. – See Brodheadsville

Eldred ES, RURAL ROUTE 02 BOX 11   18058
  Sandra Feilin, prin.

Kutztown, Berks Co., Pop. Code 5
Kutztown Area SD IU 14
Sch. Sys. Enr. Code 4
Supt. – Dr. Richard Karr
  CONSTITUTION BLVD & TREXLER   19530
JHS, RURAL ROUTE 10 BOX 125A   19530
  Terry Lindenmath, prin.
ES, NORMAL AND CONSTITUTO   19530
  Robert Loose, prin.
Maxatawny ES
  RURAL ROUTE 01 BOX 444   19530
  Dennis Lesher, prin.
Other Schools – See Kempton, Lenhartsville

Northwestern Lehigh SD IU 21
Supt. – See New Tripoli
Weisenberg ES
  RURAL ROUTE 02 BOX 253   19530
  Gail Farnham, prin.

Laceyville, Wyoming Co., Pop. Code 2
Wyalusing Area SD IU 17
Supt. – See Wyalusing
ES, RURAL ROUTE 02   18623
  Paulette Conrad, prin.

Lafayette Hill, Montgomery Co., Pop. Code 6
Colonial SD IU 23
Supt. – See Plymouth Meeting
Whitemarsh ES, 4120 JOSHUA RD   19444
  Albert Erb, prin.

St. Philip Neri ES, 3015 CHESTNUT ST   19444

Lahaska, Bucks Co.

Buckingham Friends ES, P O BOX 158   18931

Lairdsville, Lycoming Co.
East Lycoming SD IU 17
Supt. – See Hughesville
Renn ES, LAUREL STREET   17742
  Steven Moyer, prin.

Lake Ariel, Wayne Co., Pop. Code 2
North Pocono SD IU 19
Supt. – See Moscow
Jefferson ES, RURAL ROUTE 03   18436
  Matthew Farrell, prin.

Western Wayne SD IU 19
Supt. – See South Canaan
MS, RURAL ROUTE 03   18436
  Andrew Falonk, prin.

Canaan Christian Academy
  RURAL ROUTE 02 BOX 378   18436

Lake City, Erie Co., Pop. Code 4
Girard SD IU 5
Supt. – See Girard
Elk Valley ES, 2556 MAPLE AVE   16423
  John Lovett, prin.

Lamar, Clinton Co., Pop. Code 4
Keystone Central SD IU 10
Supt. – See Lock Haven
Porter Township ES, P O BOX 276   16848
  Lynn Grieb, prin.

Lampeter, Lancaster Co., Pop. Code 2
Lampeter-Strasburg SD IU 13
Sch. Sys. Enr. Code 4
Supt. – Melvin Rosier, P O BOX 216   17537
Meylin MS, 1007 VILLAGE ROAD   17537
  G. Myers, prin.
Hans Herr MS, 1007 VILLAGE RD   17537
  Robert Frick, prin.
Walnut Run ES, 1007 VILLAGE RD   17537
  Robert Frick, prin.
Other Schools – See Strasburg, Willow Street

Lancaster, Lancaster Co., Pop. Code 8
Conestoga Valley SD IU 13
Sch. Sys. Enr. Code 5
Supt. – D. Witmer
  2110 HORSESHOE ROAD   17601
Fritz ES, 845 HORNIG RD   17601 – A. Stoner, prin.
Smoketown ES, 2426 OLD PHILA PIKE   17602
  Jerre Pietsch, prin.
Other Schools – See Bird In Hand, Brownstown, Leola

Hempfield SD IU 13
Supt. – See Landisville
Centerville JHS, 865 CENTERVILLE ROAD   17601
  Richard Mearig, prin.
Centerville ES, 901 CENTERVILLE RD   17601
  Ray Mentzer, prin.

Lancaster SD IU 13
Sch. Sys. Enr. Code 6
Supt. – Dr. Roger Place, P O BOX 150   17603
Buchanan ES, 340 S WEST END AVE   17603
  Marianne Herzog, prin.
Burrowes ES, 1001 E ORANGE ST   17602
  David Rentschler, prin.
Fulton ES, 225-239 W ORANGE STREET   17603
  John Bender, prin.
Hamilton ES, WABANK AND CHARLES RD   17603
  Jere Kenderdine, prin.
King ES, S DUKE AND NINTH STREETS   17602
  Raymond Smith, prin.
Lafayette ES, SAINT JOESPH STREET   17603
  Henry Papiernik, prin.

Martin ES, 1990 WABANK RD   17603
  David Rentschler, prin.
Price ES, 615 FAIRVIEW AVE   17603
  Robert Lehr, prin.
Ross ES, 650 N QUEEN ST   17603
  Joseph Rader, prin.
Washington ES, 620 S ANNE AND CHESAP   17602
  Terry Mancini, prin.
Wharton ES, MARY AND NEW STREETS   17603
  Jere Kenderdine, prin.
Wickersham ES
  RESERVOIR AND LEHIGH AVENUE   17602
  Fred Shultz, prin.

Manheim Twp. SD IU 13
Sch. Sys. Enr. Code 5
Supt. – A. Lawrence Gagnon, P O BOX 5134   17601
Manheim Twp. MS, P O BOX 5134   17601
  Lawrence Large, prin.
Brecht ES, 1250 LITITZ PIKE   17601
  John Reigel, prin.
Bucher ES, 450 CANDLEWYCK RD   17601
  Rose Stetler, prin.
Neff ES, P O BOX 5134   17601
  Warren Keith, prin.
Nitrauer ES, 811 ASHBOURNE AVE   17601
  Richard Kephart, prin.
Schaeffer ES, 875 PLEASURE RD   17601
  Robert Feltman, prin.

Penn Manor SD IU 13
Supt. – See Millersville
Hambright ES, 25 MILLERSVILLE RD   17603
  Donald Stewart, prin.

Calvary Baptist Christian School
  530 MILTON ROAD   17602
Lancaster Christian School
  651 LAMPETER ROAD   17602
Lancaster Country Day School
  725 HAMILTON ROAD   17603
The Living Word Academy
  2384 NEW HOLLAND PARK   17601
Assumption BVM ES, 32 W VINE ST   17603
New Danville Menn ES, RURAL ROUTE 06   17603
Sacred Heart of Jesus ES, 235 NEVIN ST   17603
St. Anne ES, LIBERTY AND DUKE STS   17602
St. Anthony Padua ES, 521 E ORANGE ST   17602
St. Joseph ES, S MULBERRY AND VINE ST   17603
St. Leo the Great ES, 2427 MARIETTA AVE   17601

Landisville, Lancaster Co., Pop. Code 4
Hempfield SD IU 13
Sch. Sys. Enr. Code 5
Supt. – Dr. Earl Horton, STANLEY AVE   17538
ES, 300 CHURCH ST   17538 – Lynda Schmid, prin.
Other Schools – See East Petersburg, Lancaster,
  Mount Joy, Mountville, Rohrerstown

Langeloth, Washington Co.
Burgettstown Area SD IU 1
Supt. – See Burgettstown
ES, MAIN ST   15054 – (—), prin.

Langhorne, Bucks Co., Pop. Code 4
Neshaminy SD IU 22
Sch. Sys. Enr. Code 6
Supt. – Bernard Hoffman
  2001 OLD LINCOLN HIGHWAY   19047
Heckman ES, E MAPLE AVE & CHERRY ST   19047
  Irwin Shanken, prin.
Hoover ES, 501 TRENTON RD   19047
  Richard Marotto, prin.
Tawanka ES, 2055 BROWNSVILLE RD   19047
  Robert Gormley, prin.
Other Schools – See Feasterville, Levittown

Assumption ES
  BRISTOL AND MEADOW RD   19047

Lansdale, Montgomery Co., Pop. Code 7
North Penn SD IU 23
Sch. Sys. Enr. Code 6
Supt. – Dr. Frances Rhodes, 400 PENN ST   19446
Inglewood ES, ALLENTOWN ROAD   19446
  John Schickling, prin.
Knapp ES, KNAPP ROAD   19446
  Leta Thompson, prin.
Oak Park ES, 500 SQUIRREL LN   19446
  Allen Koehler, prin.
York Avenue ES, 700 YORK AVE   19446
  Norman Miller, prin.
Other Schools – See Harleysville, Hatfield, North
  Wales

Calvary Baptist Christian School
  1450 S VALLEY FORGE ROAD   19446
Corpus Christi ES
  920 SUMNEYTOWN PIKE   19446
St. Stanislaus ES, 493 E MAIN ST   19446

Lansdowne, Delaware Co., Pop. Code 7
William Penn SD IU 25
Supt. – See Yeadon
Ardmore Avenue ES
  ARDMORE AND ESSEX AVE   19050
  Robert Cella, prin.

St. Philomena ES, 13 N HIGHLAND AVE   19050

Lansford, Carbon Co., Pop. Code 5
Panther Valley SD IU 21
Sch. Sys. Enr. Code 4
Supt. – Dr. Richard Miller, P O BOX 40   18232
Panther Valley MS, P O BOX 7   18232
  Robert Thear, prin.

Other Schools – See Nesquehoning

Our Lady of the Valley ES, 30 E BERSCH ST   18232
St. Michael ES
  WATER AND WALNUT STS   18232

Laporte, Sullivan Co., Pop. Code 2
Sullivan County SD IU 17
Supt. – See Dushore
Sullivan County ES
  RURAL ROUTE 01 BOX 78   18626
  Richard Robinson, prin.

Larksville, Luzerne Co., Pop. Code 5
Wyoming Valley West SD IU 18
Supt. – See Kingston
State Street ES, STATE STREET   18704
  John Lagoski, prin.

Latrobe, Westmoreland Co., Pop. Code 7
Derry Area SD IU 7
Supt. – See Derry
Loyalhanna ES, 1256 SAINT CLAIR ST   15650
  Thomas Pavlik, prin.

Greater Latrobe SD IU 7
Sch. Sys. Enr. Code 5
Supt. – Dr. C. Richard Nichols
  410 MAIN ST   15650
Baggaley ES, RURAL ROUTE 06 BOX 495   15650
  Dr. Gene Leonard, prin.
ES, 1501 LIGONIER ST   15650
  Mark Schaeffer, prin.
Other Schools – See Greensburg

Holy Family ES, 323 CHESTNUT ST   15650
St. John the Evangelist ES
  310 SAINT JOHNS DR   15650
St. Vincent ES, 605 LLOYD AVE   15650

Laureldale, Berks Co., Pop. Code 5
Muhlenberg SD IU 14
Sch. Sys. Enr. Code 4
Supt. – James Morrell
  801 E BELLEVUE AVE   19605
Muhlenberg MS, 801 E BELLEVUE AVE   19605
  Roger Bauer, prin.
Cole MS, KUTZTOWN ROAD   19605
  A. Daecher, prin.
Muhlenberg ES
  SHARP AVENUE AND KUTZTOWN   19605
  Linda Lutz, prin.

Laurelton, Union Co.
Mifflinburg Area SD IU 16
Supt. – See Mifflinburg
ES, RURAL ROUTE 01   17835 – Paul Reeder, prin.

Lebanon, Lebanon Co., Pop. Code 8
Cornwall-Lebanon SD IU 13
Sch. Sys. Enr. Code 5
Supt. – Edward Phillips
  15 EVERGREEN ROAD   17042
Cedar Crest MS, 101 EVERGREEN ROAD   17042
  Joseph Sakalosky, prin.
Ebenezer ES, 452 EBENEZER RD   17042
  Thomas Quinn, prin.
South Lebanon ES, 1825 S 5TH AVE   17042
  Karen Light, prin.
Other Schools – See Cornwall

Lebanon SD IU 13
Sch. Sys. Enr. Code 5
Supt. – William Starr, 1000 S 8TH ST   17042
JHS, 8TH & CHURCH   17042 – E. Grier, prin.
Harding ES
  SIXTH AND CHESTNUT STREET   17042
  Robert Buchan, prin.
Houck ES, 3RD AVENUE AND E LEHMAN   17042
  Joseph Elder, Jr., prin.
Northwest ES
  NINTH AND MAPLE STREETS   17042
  Robert Okonak, prin.
Southeast ES, 5TH AND E PERSHING AVE   17042
  Joseph Elder, Jr., prin.
Southwest ES, 14TH & WOODLAND ST   17042
  Elizabeth Wile, prin.

Lebanon Christian Academy
  875 ACADEMY DR   17042
St. Mary's ES, 740 WILLOW ST   17042

Leck Kill, Northumberland Co.
Line Mountain SD IU 16
Supt. – See Herndon
ES, STAR ROUTE BOX 18   17836
  Gary Gonsar, prin.

Lecontes Mills, Clearfield Co.
Clearfield Area SD IU 10
Supt. – See Clearfield
Girard ES   16850 – Raymond Luke, prin.

Leechburg, Armstrong Co., Pop. Code 5
Kiski Area SD IU 7
Supt. – See Vandergrift
Allegheny-Hyde Park IS, RURAL ROUTE 05   15656
  Samuel Paolo, prin.
Weinels ES, RURAL ROUTE 03   15656
  Barbara Altmire, prin.

Leechburg Area SD IU 28
Sch. Sys. Enr. Code 4
Supt. – R. Nigro, 200 SIBERIAN AVE   15656
Gilpin ES, RURAL ROUTE 01   15656
  Larry Blumer, prin.

MS, 200 SIBERIAN AVE 15656
  Larry Blumer, prin.

Leesport, Berks Co., Pop. Code 4
Schuylkill Valley SD IU 14
Sch. Sys. Enr. Code 5
Supt. – John O'Connell 19533
Schuylkill Valley IS
  RURAL ROUTE 01 BOX 1486 19533
  Rob Springer, prin.
Schuylkill Valley ES
  RURAL ROUTE 01 BOX 1486 19533
  Bernard Wallace, prin.

Lehighton, Carbon Co., Pop. Code 6
Lehighton Area SD IU 21
Sch. Sys. Enr. Code 5
Supt. – Robert Nagle
  200 BEAVER RUN ROAD 18235
JHS, 110 N 3RD ST 18235 – James Smith, prin.
East Penn ES, RURAL ROUTE 07 BOX 189 18235
  Jill Delong, prin.
First Ward ES, 325 ALUM ST 18235
  Norman Frey, prin.
Franklin ES, RURAL ROUTE 04 BOX 85 18235
  Gene Camoni, prin.
Mahoning ES, RURAL ROUTE 01 BOX 108 18235
  Lee Getz, prin.
Shull-David ES, 200 BEAVER RUN RD 18235
  Dennis Serfass, prin.
Third Ward ES, 335 N 4TH ST 18235
  Michele Yasson, prin.

Palmerton Area SD IU 21
Supt. – See Palmerton
Towamensing ES, RURAL RAOUTE 03 18235
  Sara Stroup, prin.

Sts. Peter & Paul ES, 242 N 3RD ST 18235

Lehman, Luzerne Co., Pop. Code 4
Lake-Lehman SD IU 18
Sch. Sys. Enr. Code 4
Supt. – Dr. Charles Borchetta
  ADMIN BUILDING 18627
Lehman-Jackson ES 18627 – Charles James, prin.
Other Schools – See Harveys Lake, Sweet Valley

Lemont, Centre Co., Pop. Code 5
State College Area SD IU 10
Supt. – See State College
MS, P O BOX 96 16851 – Carl Morris, prin.

Lemoyne, Cumberland Co., Pop. Code 5
West Shore SD IU 15
Sch. Sys. Enr. Code 6
Supt. – Larry Sayre, 1000 HUMMEL AVE 17043
MS, 7TH & MARKET STS 17043
  Jean Dyszel, prin.
Herman Avenue ES
  6TH AND HERMAN AVE 17043
  Ronald Shuey, prin.
Washington Heights MS
  7TH & WALNUT ST 17043 – Ronald Shuey, prin.
Other Schools – See Camp Hill, Etters, Lewisberry,
  Mechanicsburg, New Cumberland

Lenhartsville, Berks Co., Pop. Code 2
Kutztown Area SD IU 14
Supt. – See Kutztown
Greenwich Lenhartsville ES
  RURAL ROUTE 01 19534 – Dennis Lesher, prin.

Leola, Lancaster Co., Pop. Code 4
Conestoga Valley SD IU 13
Supt. – See Lancaster
Conestoga Valley JHS, 11 SCHOOL DRIVE 17540
  John Cunningham, prin.
ES, 36 HILLCREST AVE 17540
  Beverly Breniser, prin.

Levittown, Bucks Co., Pop. Code 8
Bristol Twp. SD IU 22
Supt. – See Bristol
Barton ES, BLUE RIDGE DRIVE 19057
  Leonard Schwartz, prin.
Buchanan ES, HAINES ROAD 19055
  Willa Kaal, prin.
Emerson ES, MILL CREEK ROAD 19057
  Susan Shock, prin.
Fitch ES, GREENBROOK DRIVE 19055
  Mary Delia, prin.
Lincoln ES, 10 PLUMSTREE PLACE 19056
  Louis Saltzgueber, prin.
Washington ES, 275 CRABTREE DR 19055
  Regina Cesario, prin.

Neshaminy SD IU 22
Supt. – See Langhorne
Everitt ES, FORSYTHIA DRIVE SOUTH 19056
  Rodney Bauer, prin.
Miller ES, 10 COBALT RIDGE DR STREET 19057
  Joseph Botzer, prin.
Pearl Buck ES, 143 TOP ROAD 19056
  Neal Young, prin.
Schweitzer ES, 10 HARMONY RD 19056
  Charles Weber, prin.

Pennsbury SD IU 22
Supt. – See Fallsington
Disney ES, LAKESIDE DRIVE 19054
  Edward O'Byrne, prin.
Manor ES, PENN VALLEY ROAD 19054
  Raymond Naylor, prin.
Penn Valley ES, NORTH TURN LANE 19054
  John Hutchings, prin.

Lower Bucks Christian Academy
  6401 MILLCREEK 19058
Hope Lutheran ES
  MIL CRK PKWY & HAINES RD 19055
Immaculate Conception ES
  3810 OXFORD VALLY RD 19057
Queen of Universe ES, 2443 TRENTON RD 19056
St. Joseph the Worker ES
  9168 NEW FALLS RD 19054
St. Michael Archangel ES
  130 LEVITTOWN PKY 19054

Lewisberry, York Co., Pop. Code 2
West Shore SD IU 15
Supt. – See Lemoyne
Fishing Creek ES, 510 FISHING CREEK RD 17339
  Richard Shepps, prin.
Mt. Zion ES, 850 LEWISBERRY RD 17339
  Phyliss Meckley, prin.

Lewisburg, Union Co., Pop. Code 6
Lewisburg Area SD IU 16
Sch. Sys. Enr. Code 4
Supt. – Dr. Donald Eichhorn, P O BOX 351 17837
MS, 2051 WASHINGTON AVE 17837
  Joseph Galanti, prin.
Kelly ES, RURAL ROUTE 03 BOX 305 17837
  T. Morris, prin.
Linntown ES, 1901 WASHINGTON AVE 17837
  David Heberlig, prin.
South Ward ES, 208 S 4TH ST 17837
  T. Morris, prin.

Mifflinburg Area SD IU 16
Supt. – See Mifflinburg
Buffalo Cross Road ES
  249 JOHNSON MILL RD 17837 – Paul Los, prin.

Lewis Run, McKean Co., Pop. Code 3
Bradford Area SD IU 9
Supt. – See Bradford
Ryan ES, HCR 01 BOX 136 16738 – J. Hare, prin.

Lewistown, Mifflin Co., Pop. Code 6
Mifflin County SD IU 11
Sch. Sys. Enr. Code 6
Supt. – Dr. Robert Bohn, 514 W 4TH ST 17044
MS, HIGHLAND PARK 17044
  William Hartman, prin.
Buchanan ES, FRANKLIN AVENUE 17044
  Kenneth Goodling, prin.
East Derry ES, RURAL ROUTE 03 17044
  Kenneth Barrett, prin.
Seventh Ward ES
  SUSQUEHANNA AVENUE 17044
  Daniel McClenahen, prin.
Other Schools – See Belleville, Burnham, Granville,
  Mc Clure, Mc Veytown, Milroy, Reedsville,
  Yeagertown

Sacred Heart of Jesus ES
  110 N DORCAS ST 17044

Liberty, Tioga Co., Pop. Code 2
Southern Tioga SD IU 17
Supt. – See Mansfield
ES, RURAL ROUTE 01 BOX 2C 16930
  Robert Wirth, prin.

Library, Allegheny Co., Pop. Code 5
South Park SD IU 3
Sch. Sys. Enr. Code 4
Supt. – William Torlidas
  2178 RIDGE ROAD 15129
South Park MS, 2500 STEWART ROAD 15129
  Douglas Broglie, prin.
ES, 6450 PLEASANT ST 15129
  Lawrene Muir, prin.
Stewart ES, BROWNSVILLE RD 15129
  Lawrence Muir, prin.
Other Schools – See Pittsburgh

St. Joan of Arc ES, 6470 LIBRARY RD 15129

Ligonier, Westmoreland Co., Pop. Code 4
Ligonier Valley SD IU 7
Sch. Sys. Enr. Code 5
Supt. – M. Carnahan, 120 E MAIN ST 15658
Mellon ES, RURAL ROUTE 03 15658
  Stanton Harvey, prin.
Other Schools – See Bolivar, New Florence,
  Stahlstown

Holy Trinity ES, 327 W VINCENT ST 15658
Valley School of Ligonier ES, P O BOX 616 15658

Lilly, Cambria Co., Pop. Code 4
Penn Cambria SD IU 8
Supt. – See Cresson
ES, MAIN STREET 15938
  Richard Sweeney, prin.

Limerick, Montgomery Co.

Chapel Christian Academy
  378 W RIDGE PIKE 19468

Linden, Lycoming Co.
Williamsport Area SD IU 17
Supt. – See Williamsport
Woodward Township ES
  RURAL ROUTE 01 17744 – Donna Flaig, prin.

Linesville, Crawford Co., Pop. Code 4
Conneaut SD IU 5
Sch. Sys. Enr. Code 5
Supt. – Andrew Pollus, 302 E ERIE ST 16424
Schafer ES, RURAL ROUTE 03 BOX 135E 16424
  Douglas Melby, prin.
Other Schools – See Conneaut Lake, Conneautville

Linwood, Delaware Co., Pop. Code 5
Chichester SD IU 25
Supt. – See Boothwyn
ES, 1400 HUDDELL AVE 19061
  Anthony Seman, Jr., prin.

Holy Savior St. J Fishe ES, 122 E RIDGE RD 19061

Lititz, Lancaster Co., Pop. Code 6
Warwick SD IU 13
Sch. Sys. Enr. Code 5
Supt. – John Bonfield, 301 W ORANGE ST 17543
Warwick ES, 401 MAPLE ST 17543
  James Diehm, prin.
Beck ES, 418 E LEXINGTON RD 17543
  Joseph Narkiewicz, prin.
Kissel Hill ES, 215 LANDIS VALLEY RD 17543
  Robert Heron, prin.
ES, 20 S CEDAR ST 17543
  Dr. Gail Ekstrand, prin.

Lititz Area Menn ES, 1050 E NEWPORT RD 17543
Lititz Christian ES, 501 W LINCOLN AVE 17543

Littlestown, Adams Co., Pop. Code 5
Littlestown Area SD IU 12
Sch. Sys. Enr. Code 4
Supt. – John Smarsh, MAPLE AVE 17340
Maple Avenue MS, MAPLE AVE 17340
  John Bream, prin.
Rolling Acres ES, 150 E MYRTLE ST 17340
  William Shoemaker, prin.

Liverpool, Perry Co., Pop. Code 3
Juniata County SD IU 11
Supt. – See Mifflintown
Susquehanna Township ES
  RURAL ROUTE 01 17045 – Gerald Hibbs, prin.

Lock Haven, Clinton Co., Pop. Code 6
Keystone Central SD IU 10
Sch. Sys. Enr. Code 6
Supt. – Earle Hummel, 95 W FOURTH ST 17745
Dickey ES, 102 S FAIRVIEW ST 17745
  Jane Oakley, prin.
McGhee ES, 101 W FOURTH ST 17745
  Don Sweeley, prin.
Robb MS, HENDERSON STREET 17745
  Dennis Bryon, prin.
Woodward ES, RURAL ROUTE 01 17745
  Christian Dwyer, prin.
Other Schools – See Beech Creek, Blanchard,
  Castanea, Lamar, Loganton, Mill Hall, Renovo,
  Woolrich

Lock Haven Catholic ES, 311 W WATER ST 17745

Loganton, Clinton Co., Pop. Code 2
Keystone Central SD IU 10
Supt. – See Lock Haven
Sugar Valley Area S 17726
  Kenneth Sohmer, prin.

Loretto, Cambria Co., Pop. Code 4

St. Michael ES, P O BOX 67 15940

Lowber, Westmoreland Co.
Yough SD IU 7
Supt. – See Herminie
ES 15660 – Robert Cunningham, prin.

Lower Burrell, Westmoreland Co., Pop. Code 7
Burrell SD IU 7
Sch. Sys. Enr. Code 4
Supt. – Gerald Malecki
  PUCKETY CHURCH ROAD 15068
Huston MS, 500 PERRY AVE 15068
  Dr. Anna Palermo, prin.
Bon Air ES 15068 – Lawrence Murphy, Jr., prin.
Stewart ES 15068 – Paul Serlucco, prin.

St. Maragret Mary ES
  3055 LEECHBURG RD 15068

Loysburg, Bedford Co.
Northern Bedford County SD IU 8
Sch. Sys. Enr. Code 4
Supt. – Dr. Lanny Ross 16659
Northern Bedford County ES
  HCR 01 BOX 200 16659 – J. Dean, prin.

Lucinda, Clarion Co.

St. Josephs ES, ROUTE 66 16235

Lurgan, Franklin Co.
Chambersburg Area SD IU 12
Supt. – See Chambersburg
ES, 8888 ROXBURY RD 17232 – Jean Pinci, prin.

Luthersburg, Clearfield Co.
Du Bois Area SD IU 6
Supt. – See Du Bois
ES, ROBINSON STREET 15848
  Donald Smith, prin.

Luzerne, Luzerne Co., Pop. Code 5

Sacred Heart ES, 545 CHARLES ST   18709

Lykens, Dauphin Co., Pop. Code 4
Upper Dauphin Area SD IU 15
Sch. Sys. Enr. Code 4
Supt. – Dr. Andrew Hills, RURAL ROUTE   17048
Upper Dauphin Area MS, RURAL ROUTE   17048
Robert Franklin, prin.
ES, 801 WOOD STREET   17048
Rose Radzievich, prin.
Other Schools – See Berrysburg, Elizabethville, Gratz

Mc Adoo, Schuylkill Co., Pop. Code 5
Hazleton Area SD IU 18
Supt. – See Hazleton
Mc Adoo-Kelayres ES, KELAYRES ROAD   18237
William Weed, prin.

Mcadoo Catholic ES, 35 N CLEVELAND ST   18237

Mc Alisterville, Juniata Co., Pop. Code 3
Juniata County SD IU 11
Supt. – See Mifflintown
Fayette Township ES   17049 – Gerald Hibbs, prin.

Mc Clellandtown, Fayette Co., Pop. Code 3
Albert Galltn Area SD IU 1
Supt. – See Uniontown
German Central ES
RURAL ROUTE 01 BOX 389E   15458
William Morganosky, prin.

Mc Clure, Snyder Co., Pop. Code 4
Midd-West SD IU 16
Supt. – See Middleburg
West Beaver ES, P O BOX 220   17841
Donald Goodwin, prin.

Mifflin County SD IU 11
Supt. – See Lewistown
Decatur ES, RURAL ROUTE 01   17841
Kenneth Barrett, prin.

Mc Connellsburg, Fulton Co., Pop. Code 4
Central Fulton SD IU 11
Sch. Sys. Enr. Code 4
Supt. – R. Swadley, E CHERRY ST   17233
ES, E CHERRY ST   17233 – Louise Hine, prin.

Mc Donald, Washington Co., Pop. Code 5
Fort Cherry SD IU 1
Sch. Sys. Enr. Code 4
Supt. – John Manion
RURAL ROUTE 04 BOX 145   15057
ES, 105 COAL ST   15057 – Milton Diaz, prin.
Robinson ES, RURAL ROUTE 01 BOX 265A   15057
Milton Diaz, prin.
Other Schools – See Hickory

South Fayette Twp. SD IU 3
Sch. Sys. Enr. Code 4
Supt. – Joel Carr
RURAL ROUTE 02 BOX 207A   15057
South Fayette Township ES
RURAL ROUTE 02 BOX 207A   15057
David McDougal, prin.

Mc Kean, Erie Co., Pop. Code 2
General McLane SD IU 5
Supt. – See Edinboro
ES, 5120 WEST RIDGE RD   16426
Jerome Englert, prin.

Mc Keesport, Allegheny Co., Pop. Code 8
Elizabeth-Forward SD IU 3
Supt. – See Elizabeth
Greenock ES, 1101 GREENOCK-B   15135
Thomas Rowles, prin.
Mt. Vernon ES, 2400 GREENOCK-B   15135
Thomas Rowles, prin.

McKeesport Area SD IU 3
Sch. Sys. Enr. Code 6
Supt. – Myles Stepanovich, 2225 5TH AVE   15132
Cornell MS, 1600 CORNELL ST   15132
Frank McLaughlin, prin.
McClure MS, 500 LONGVUE DRIVE   15131
Adolph Vay, prin.
Centennial ES, 1601 BEAVER ST   15132
Joseph Fiori, prin.
Eleventh Ward ES, 438 28TH ST   15132
Morrell Dodds, prin.
Grandview ES, 2130 GRANDVIEW AVE   15132
Morrell Dodds, prin.
Washington ES, 1818 SUMAC ST   15132
Dennis DeVirgilio, prin.
White Oak ES, 1415 CALIFORNIA AVE   15131
Shirley Golofski, prin.

South Allegheny SD IU 3
Sch. Sys. Enr. Code 4
Supt. – Charles Lalley
2743 WASHINGTON BLVD   15133
Manor ES, GLENDALE ST   15133
Robert Piatt, prin.
Port Vue ES, ROMINE AVENUE   15133
Bernard Kalocay, prin.
Other Schools – See Glassport

Wilson Christian Academy
2910 LIBERTY WAY   15133
McKeesport Central Catholic School
2412 VERSAILLES AVE   15132
St. Joseph Regional Catholic ES
1125 ROMINE AVE   15133

Mc Kees Rocks, Allegheny Co., Pop. Code 6
Montour Sd IU 3
Supt. – See Coraopolis
Burkett ES, 5501 STEUBENVILLE PIKE   15136
Vince Valicenti, prin.

Sto-Rox SD IU 3
Sch. Sys. Enr. Code 4
Supt. – Patrick Mancini
600 RUSSELLWOOD AVE   15136
Bryan MS, 1123 WAYNE AVE   15136
Elaine Palahunik, prin.
Fenton ES, ELIZABETH & MAIN STREET   15136
Robert Raymond, prin.
Foster ES, 800 RUSSELLWOOD AVE   15136
Robert Raymond, prin.
Hamilton ES, 19 MAY AVE   15136
Raymond Pusker, prin.

McKees Rocks Catholic ES
115 MARGARET ST   15136

Mc Murray, Washington Co., Pop. Code 4
Peters Twp. SD IU 1
Sch. Sys. Enr. Code 5
Supt. – Dr. Dennis Urso
616 E MCMURRAY ROAD   15317
Peters Twp. MS, 625 E MCMURRAY ROAD   15317
James Johnson, prin.
Elm Grove ES, 225 THOMPSONVILLE RD   15317
Harry Casciotti,Jr., prin.
Pleasant Valley ES, 250 E MCMURRAY RD   15317
Dennis McWreath, prin.
Other Schools – See Venetia

Mc Sherrystown, Adams Co., Pop. Code 5

Annunciation BVM School, 316 NORTH ST   17344

Macungie, Lehigh Co., Pop. Code 4
East Penn SD IU 21
Supt. – See Emmaus
Lower Macungie ES
RURAL ROUTE 02 BOX 185   18062
Dr. Margaret Geosits, prin.
ES, E MAIN STREET   18062
Richard Gorton, prin.
Shoemaker MS, E FAIRVIEW STREET   18062
Robert Leidich, prin.

Salem Christian School, RURAL ROUTE 01   18062

Mc Veytown, Mifflin Co., Pop. Code 2
Mifflin County SD IU 11
Supt. – See Lewistown
Strodes Mills MS, RURAL ROUTE 02   17051
William Barger, prin.
Strodes Mills ES, RURAL ROUTE 02   17051
William Barger, prin.

Mahaffey, Clearfield Co., Pop. Code 3
Purchase Line SD IU 28
Supt. – See Commodore
Purchase Line North ES
RURAL ROUTE 01 BOX 135   15757
JoAnn Jacobs, prin.

Mahanoy City, Schuylkill Co., Pop. Code 6
Mahonoy Area SD IU 29
Sch. Sys. Enr. Code 4
Supt. – Elbur Techentin, P O BOX 58   17948
Mahanoy Area IS, 400 E SOUTH ST   17948
John Murtin, prin.

Mahanoy City Catholic ES
S CATAWISSA ST   17948

Malvern, Chester Co., Pop. Code 5
Great Valley SD IU 24
Supt. – See Devault
Wayne MS, DEVON & GRUBB ROADS   19355
Stephen Swymer, prin.
Markley ES, CHURCH ROAD   19355
Sally Winterton, prin.
Sugartown ES, SUGARTOWN ROAD   19355
Donald Fraatz, prin.

St. Patrick ES, 126 CHANNING AVE   19355

Manchester, York Co., Pop. Code 4
Northeastern York SD IU 12
Sch. Sys. Enr. Code 4
Supt. – Dr. David Krauser, 41 HARDING ST   17345
Northeastern JHS, HARTMAN ST   17345
W. Schaeffer, prin.
Orendorf ES, 101 S HARTMAN ST   17345
David Ginder, prin.
Other Schools – See Mount Wolf, York, York Haven

Manheim, Lancaster Co., Pop. Code 6
Manheim Central SD IU 13
Sch. Sys. Enr. Code 4
Supt. – Lewis Jury, 71 N HAZEL ST   17545
Manheim Central JHS, E GRAMBY ST   17545
L. Stitzel, prin.
Burgard ES, 237 W FERDINAND ST   17545
Drew Scheffey, prin.
Fairland ES, RURAL ROUTE 01   17545
Mary Adams, prin.
Mastersonville ES, RURAL ROUTE 04   17545
Priscilla Feir, prin.
Sporting Hill ES, 65 COLEBROOK RD   17545
Priscilla Feir, prin.
Stiegel ES, HIGH AND HAZEL STREETS   17545
Mary Adams, prin.

White Oak ES, RURAL ROUTE 05   17545
Priscilla Feir, prin.
Other Schools – See Mount Joy

Manheim Church Day ES
RURAL ROUTE 06 BOX 482   17545

Manor, Westmoreland Co., Pop. Code 4
Hempfield Area SD IU 7
Supt. – See Greensburg
ES, BROADWAY & BLAINE   15665
Cheryl Troglio, prin.

Mansfield, Tioga Co., Pop. Code 5
Southern Tioga SD IU 17
Sch. Sys. Enr. Code 4
Supt. – Ronald Boyanowski
DORSETT DRIVE   16933
Miller ES, DORSETT DR   16933
John Novak, prin.
Other Schools – See Blossburg, Liberty, Trout Run

Maple Glen, Montgomery Co.

St. Alphonsus ES, 29 CONWELL DR   19002

Mapleton Depot, Huntingdon Co.
Mt. Union Area SD IU 11
Supt. – See Mount Union
Mapleton-Union ES, RURAL ROUTE 01   17052
John Miller, prin.

Marcus Hook, Delaware Co., Pop. Code 5
Chichester SD IU 25
Supt. – See Boothwyn
Hook ES, 8TH & MARCUS   19061
Paul Blanford, prin.

Marienville, Forest Co., Pop. Code 3
Forest Area SD IU 6
Supt. – See Tionesta
East Forest ES, BIRCH STREET   16239
Arthur Van Nort, prin.

Marietta, Lancaster Co., Pop. Code 5
Donegal SD IU 13
Supt. – See Mount Joy
Riverview ES, RT 441   17547
James Lawrence, prin.

Marion, Franklin Co., Pop. Code 3
Chambersburg Area SD IU 12
Supt. – See Chambersburg
ES, P O BOX 248   17235 – Frederick Nickey, prin.

Marion Center, Indiana Co., Pop. Code 2
Marion Center Area SD IU 28
Sch. Sys. Enr. Code 4
Supt. – J. Mallino   15759
ES   15759 – George Hood, prin.

Markleton, Somerset Co.
Rockwood Area SD IU 8
Supt. – See Rockwood
Middlecreek ES, RURAL ROUTE 01   15551
Malcolm Buchanan, prin.

Markleysburg, Fayette Co., Pop. Code 2
Uniontown Area SD IU 1
Supt. – See Uniontown
McMullen MS, P O BOX 110-B   15459
J. Thomas, prin.
Marclay ES, RURAL ROUTE 01   15459
J. Thomas, prin.

Mars, Butler Co., Pop. Code 4
Mars Area SD IU 4
Sch. Sys. Enr. Code 3
Supt. – Dr. William Pettigrew, P O BOX 897   16046
Mars Area MS
RURAL ROUTE 02 BOX 138   16046
Mark Feris, prin.
Adams IS, RURAL ROUTE 02   16046
Sara Werlinich, prin.
PS, P O BOX 897   16046 – Sara Werlinich, prin.
Other Schools – See Valencia

Seneca Valley SD IU 4
Supt. – See Harmony
Haine ES, HAINES SCHOOL ROAD   16046
Robert Shoemaker, prin.
Rowan ES, RURAL ROUTE 01   16046
Beverly Krill, prin.

Martinsburg, Blair Co., Pop. Code 4
Spring Cove SD IU 8
Supt. – See Roaring Spring
Benson ES
SOUTH MULBERRY & WOODLA   16662
Rodney Green, prin.
Martin MS, EAST SPRING STREET   16662
Rodney Green, prin.

Masontown, Fayette Co., Pop. Code 5
Albert Galltn Area SD IU 1
Supt. – See Uniontown
Masontown Central ES
W CHURCH AND WASHINGTON   15461
Judith Psenicska, prin.

All Saints ES, 100 S WASHINGTON ST   15461

Mayfield, Lackawanna Co., Pop. Code 4
Lakeland SD IU 19
Supt. – See Jermyn
Mayfield ES, LINDEN & LACKAWANNA   18433
Carl Klach, prin.

Maytown, Lancaster Co., Pop. Code 3
Donegal SD IU 13
Supt. – See Mount Joy
ES, RIVER STREET   17550 – James Lawrence, prin.

Meadowbrook, Montgomery Co., Pop. Code 4

The Meadowbrook ES, 1641 HAMPTON RD   19046

Meadville, Crawford Co., Pop. Code 7
Crawford Central SD IU 5
Sch. Sys. Enr. Code 6
Supt. – Dr. Robert Bender, 719 N MAIN ST   16335
East End ES, 640 WALNUT ST   16335
Joanne Darling, prin.
First District ES, 725 N MAIN ST   16335
Anthony Bevacqua, prin.
Kerrtown ES, MERCER PIKE   16335
Vincent Pisani, prin.
Neason Hill ES, RURAL ROUTE 06   16335
Fred Bloom, prin.
Second District ES, 1216 S MAIN ST   16335
Anthony Stellato, prin.
Other Schools – See Cochranton

Calvary Baptist Christian Academy
543 RANDOLPH ST   16335
Seton ES, 385 PINE ST   16335

Mechanicsburg, Cumberland Co., Pop. Code 6
Cumberland Valley SD IU 15
Sch. Sys. Enr. Code 6
Supt. – Dr. Orr Brenneman
6746 CARLISLE PIKE   17055
Good Hope MS, 451 SKYPORT ROAD   17055
Robert Crobak, prin.
Middle School West, 6746 CARLISLE PIKE   17055
Eugene Baldwin, prin.
Green Ridge ES, 1 GREEN RIDGE RD   17055
Richard Smith, prin.
Hampden ES, 441 SKYPORT RD   17055
Donald Zeigler, prin.
Silver Spring ES, 6746 CARLISLE PIKE   17055
Harold Pamraning, prin.
Sporting Hill ES, 210 S SPORTING HILL RD   17055
Richard Roth, prin.
Other Schools – See Boiling Springs, Carlisle, Enola

Mechanicsburg Area SD IU 15
Sch. Sys. Enr. Code 5
Supt. – Dr. Robert Curtis, 500 S BROAD ST   17055
IS, 100 S ELMWOOD AVE   17055
Leonard Ference, prin.
Broad Street ES, 200 S BROAD ST   17055
Frank Coffey, prin.
Filbert Street ES, 505 S FILBERT ST   17055
Jack Wagoner, prin.
Northside ES, 411 N WALNUT ST   17055
Marlin Lippert, prin.
Shepherdstown ES, 1849 S YORK ST   17055
Paul Healey, prin.
Upper Allen MS, 1790 S MARKET ST   17055
Norma Mateer, prin.
Other Schools – See Shiremanstown

West Shore SD IU 15
Supt. – See Lemoyne
Rossmoyne MS, 1225 ROSSMOYNE RD   17055
Deloris McElroy, prin.

Emmanuel Baptist Christian Academy
4681 E TRINDLE ROAD   17055
Faith Tabernacle School
1410 GOOD HOPE ROAD   17055
St. Joseph ES, 400 E SIMPSON ST   17055

Media, Delaware Co., Pop. Code 6
Rose Tree Media SD IU 25
Sch. Sys. Enr. Code 5
Supt. – Henry Nacrelli
901 N PROVIDENCE ROAD   19063
Springton Lake MS
1900 N PROVIDENCE ROAD   19063
David Leibig, prin.
Glenwood ES, 122 S PENNELL RD   19063
Richard Dunlap, prin.
ES, STATE AND MONROE STREETS   19063
John Laird, prin.
Rose Tree ES, 1101 FIRST AVE   19063
Harry Dissinger, prin.

The Christian Academy
704 S OLD MIDDLETOWN ROAD   19063
Benchmark ES, 2107 N PROVIDENCE RD   19063
Media Provid Friends School
125 W THIRD ST   19063
Nativity BVM ES, 30 E FRANKLIN ST   19063
St. Mary Magdalene ES
2430 N PROVIDENCE RD   19063

Mehoopany, Wyoming Co.
Tunkhannock Area SD IU 18
Supt. – See Tunkhannock
ES, RURAL ROUTE 02   18629
Susann Barziloski, prin.

Melcroft, Fayette Co.
Connellsville Area SD IU 1
Supt. – See Connellsville
Saltlick ES, STAR ROUTE   15462
Billy Pritts, prin.

Mercer, Mercer Co., Pop. Code 5
Mercer Area SD IU 4
Sch. Sys. Enr. Code 4
Supt. – J. Stephens, P O BOX 32   16137

Mercer Area ES, 301 LAMOR RD   16137
Eugene Blakley, prin.

Mercersburg, Franklin Co., Pop. Code 4
Tuscarora SD IU 12
Sch. Sys. Enr. Code 5
Supt. – Ted Rabold, 118 E SEMINARY ST   17236
Buchanan MS, 5191 FT LOWDON ROAD   17236
Patrick Crawford, prin.
ES, 30 SOUTH PARK AVENUE   17236
Philip Shuman, prin.
Montgomery ES, 9138 FORT LOUDON RD   17236
Philip Shuman, prin.
Mountain View ES, 2311 LEMAR RD   17236
Harold Yeager, prin.
Other Schools – See Saint Thomas

Merion Station, Montgomery Co., Pop. Code 6
Lower Merion SD IU 23
Supt. – See Ardmore
Merion ES, 549 BOWMAN AVE   19066
Marvin Gold, prin.

Episcopal Academy
376 N LATCHES LANE   19066
Waldron Mercy Academy
513 MONTGOMERY AVE   19066

Mertztown, Berks Co.
Brandywine Heights Area SD IU 14
Supt. – See Topton
Longswamp ES, RURAL ROUTE 01   19539
Robert Hassler, prin.

Meyersdale, Somerset Co., Pop. Code 5
Meyersdale Area SD IU 8
Sch. Sys. Enr. Code 4
Supt. – D. Duppstadt, RURAL ROUTE 03   15552
Meyersdale Area ES, RURAL ROUTE 03   15552
Thomas Houser, prin.

Middleburg, Snyder Co., Pop. Code 4
Midd-West SD IU 16
Sch. Sys. Enr. Code 4
Supt. – Dr. Barry Smith, 568 E MAIN ST   17842
ES, 600 WAGENSELLER ST   17842
Harold Kratzer, prin.
Other Schools – See Beavertown, Mc Clure, Mount
Pleasant, Penns Creek

Middletown, Dauphin Co., Pop. Code 7
Lower Dauphin SD IU 15
Supt. – See Hummelstown
Londonderry ES, 260 SCHOOLHOUSE RD   17057
Kenneth Allwine, prin.

Middletown Area SD IU 15
Sch. Sys. Enr. Code 5
Supt. – Leon Calabrese, 55 W WATER ST   17057
Feaser MS, 214 N RACE ST   17057
Russ Eppinger, prin.
Demey ES, CATHERINE ROOSEVELT   17057
Joseph Rasimas, prin.
Fink ES, 150 RACE ST   17057
Audrey Utley, prin.
Kunkel ES, FULLING MILL ROAD   17057
Margaret Viehdorfer, prin.
Mansberger ES
WOOD AND ANN STREETS   17057
Ray Thompson, prin.

Seven Sorrows BVM ES
RACE AND CONEWAGO ST   17057

Midland, Beaver Co., Pop. Code 5
Midland Borough SD IU 27
Sch. Sys. Enr. Code 2
Supt. – William Donley
9TH & MIDLAND AVE   15059
Neel ES, 7TH AND OHIO AVENUE   15059
William Donley, prin.

Western Beaver County SD IU 27
Sch. Sys. Enr. Code 4
Supt. – Albert Troiano
RURAL ROUTE 01 BOX 22   15059
Fairview ES, RURAL ROUTE 01   15059
Roland Delaney, prin.
Other Schools – See Industry

Mifflin, Juniata Co., Pop. Code 3
Juniata County SD IU 11
Supt. – See Mifflintown
Mountain View ES   17058 – Thomas Wert, prin.

Mifflinburg, Union Co., Pop. Code 5
Mifflinburg Area SD IU 16
Sch. Sys. Enr. Code 4
Supt. – Dr. David Witmer, P O BOX 285   17844
Mifflinburg Area MS, EAST MARKET ST   17844
Thomas Muchler, prin.
ES, 115 SHIPTON ST   17844
Josephine McCauley, prin.
Other Schools – See Laurelton, Lewisburg, New Berlin

Mifflintown, Juniata Co., Pop. Code 3
Juniata County SD IU 11
Sch. Sys. Enr. Code 4
Supt. – Kenneth Stuck, 7TH ST   17059
Fermanagh-Mifflintown ES
SEVENTH STREET   17059 – Thomas Wert, prin.
Walker Township ES, RURAL ROUTE 02   17059
Stephen Bahorik, prin.
Other Schools – See Honey Grove, Liverpool, Mc
Alisterville, Mifflin, Port Royal, Richfield,
Thompsontown

Mifflinville, Columbia Co., Pop. Code 4
Central Columbia SD IU 16
Supt. – See Bloomsburg
ES, RACE ST   18631 – John Yastishock, prin.

Mildred, Sullivan Co.
Sullivan County SD IU 17
Supt. – See Dushore
Turnpike Area ES, CHERRY STREET   18632
Richard Robinson, prin.

Milford, Pike Co., Pop. Code 4
Delaware Valley SD IU 20
Sch. Sys. Enr. Code 4
Supt. – James Melody, HCR 01 BOX 379A   18337
Delaware Valley MS
RURAL ROUTE 06-209   18337 – William Day,
prin.
Delaware Valley MS, HCR 1 BOX 379D   18337
Sonya Cole, prin.
Other Schools – See Dingmans Ferry, Shohola

Mill Creek, Huntingdon Co., Pop. Code 2
Huntingdon Area SD IU 11
Supt. – See Huntingdon
Brady-Henderson Mll ES, P O BOX B   17060
Donald McCloy, prin.

Millersburg, Dauphin Co., Pop. Code 5
Millersburg Area SD IU 15
Sch. Sys. Enr. Code 4
Supt. – W. Knisely, 799 CENTER ST   17061
Millersburg Area MS, 799 CENTER ST   17061
M. Stephen Boston, prin.
Lenkerville ES, SOUTH MARKET STREET   17061
Alton Zerby, prin.

Millerstown, Perry Co., Pop. Code 3
Greenwood SD IU 15
Sch. Sys. Enr. Code 3
Supt. – Norman Shea, 405 E SUNBURY ST   17062
Greenwood ES   17062 – Norman Shea, prin.

Millersville, Lancaster Co., Pop. Code 6
Penn Manor SD IU 13
Sch. Sys. Enr. Code 4
Supt. – Noel Taylor   17551
Eshleman ES, LEAMAN AVENUE   17551
William Wood, prin.
Other Schools – See Conestoga, Holtwood, Lancaster,
Pequea, Washington Boro, Willow Street

Millerton, Tioga Co.
Troy Area SD IU 17
Supt. – See Troy
Wells Township ES, RURAL ROUTE 02   16936
Dr. Roger Goodman, prin.

Mill Hall, Clinton Co., Pop. Code 4
Keystone Central SD IU 10
Supt. – See Lock Haven
Lamar Township ES
RURAL ROUTE 01 BOX 90   17751
Carol Livingston, prin.
ES, B E N AVENUE   17751
Charles Randecker, prin.

Mill Village, Erie Co., Pop. Code 2
Ft. LeBoeuf SD IU 5
Supt. – See Waterford
ES, RURAL ROUTE 06   16427
Raymond Whitmer, prin.

Millvale, Allegheny Co., Pop. Code 5

St. Nicholas ES, 24 MARYLAND AVE   15209

Millville, Columbia Co., Pop. Code 3
Millville Area SD IU 16
Sch. Sys. Enr. Code 4
Supt. – P. Phillip Bollenbacher
P O BOX 260   17846
MS, P O BOX 300   17846 – Lorraine Young, prin.
Pine ES, P O BOX 300   17846 – Mary Lewis, prin.

Milmont Park, Delaware Co., Pop. Code 4

Our Lady of Peace ES
REESE AND MILMONT STS   19033

Milroy, Mifflin Co., Pop. Code 4
Mifflin County SD IU 11
Supt. – See Lewistown
Armagh Township ES
BROAD STREET EXTENDED   17063
George Bailor, prin.

Milton, Northumberland Co., Pop. Code 6
Milton Area SD IU 16
Sch. Sys. Enr. Code 5
Supt. – James Baugher, P O BOX 397   17847
ES, LIMESTONE ROAD   17847
Joseph Kowalski, prin.
Other Schools – See Montandon, New Columbia

Meadowbrook Christian School
RURAL ROUTE 02 BOX 338   17847

Minersville, Schuylkill Co., Pop. Code 6

Holy Redeemer ES, LINE ST AND OAK ST   17954
St. Elizabeth Ann Seton ES
534 SUNBURY ST   17954

Miquon, Montgomery Co.

Miquon ES, HARTS LN   19452

Monaca, Beaver Co., Pop. Code 6
Center Area SD IU 27
Sch. Sys. Enr. Code 4
Supt. – Dr. Victor Morrone
  BAKER ROAD EXT   15061
Center JHS, BAKER ROAD EXT   15061
  Samuel Gagliardi, prin.
Todd Lane MS, TODD LN   15061
  John Zigerelli, prin.
Other Schools – See Aliquippa

Monaca SD IU 27
Sch. Sys. Enr. Code 3
Supt. – Michael Siget, 1500 ALLEN AVE   15061
Fourth Ward MS, WALNUT STREET   15061
  Dr. Edward Wozniak, prin.
Mangin ES, INDIANA AND 10TH ST   15061
  Dr. Edward Wozniak, prin.

St. John the Baptist ES
  15TH AND VIRGINA AVE   15061

Monessen, Westmoreland Co., Pop. Code 7
Monessen CSD IU 7
Sch. Sys. Enr. Code 4
Supt. – T. Wilkinson, ROSTRAVER ST   15062
ES, ROSTRAVER ST   15062
  Joseph Garofolo, prin.

Monongahela, Washington Co., Pop. Code 6
Elizabeth-Forward SD IU 3
Supt. – See Elizabeth
Penn ES, RURAL ROUTE 03 BOX 400   15063
  Wesley Lucky, prin.

Ringgold SD IU 1
Sch. Sys. Enr. Code 5
Supt. – James Lopresti, 1200 CHESS ST   15063
Carroll MS, 120 ALEXANDER AVE   15063
  Edward Repka, prin.
ES, 1200 CHESS ST   15063 – William Garlitz, prin.
Other Schools – See Donora, Finleyville, Gastonville

Transfiguration ES, 731 CHESS ST   15063

Monroeton, Bradford Co.
Towanda Area SD IU 17
Supt. – See Towanda
Monroe-Franklin ES, RURAL ROUTE 01   18832
  Joyce Vandusen, prin.

Monroeville, Allegheny Co., Pop. Code 8
Gateway SD IU 3
Sch. Sys. Enr. Code 5
Supt. – Dr. Wayne Doyle
  2609 MOSSIDE BLVD   15146
Gateway JHS
  OLD WM PENN AND HAYMAK   15146
  George Kocerka, prin.
Evergreen ES, 3831 EVERGREEN DR   15146
  Roger Guella, prin.
Gateway Upper MS
  MOSS SIDE BOULEVARD   15416
  James Held, prin.
Ramsey ES, 2200 RAMSEY RD   15146
  W. Kuch, prin.
University Park ES, NOEL DR   15146
  Marjorie Hawkins, prin.
Other Schools – See Pitcairn

Greater Works Academy
  301 COLLEGE PARK DRIVE   15146
North American Marytrs ES
  2526 HAYMAKER RD   15146
St. Bernadette ES, 245 AZALEA DR   15146

Montandon, Northumberland Co.
Milton Area SD IU 16
Supt. – See Milton
ES   17850 – Joseph Kowalski, prin.

Montgomery, Lycoming Co., Pop. Code 4
Montgomery Area SD IU 17
Sch. Sys. Enr. Code 4
Supt. – David Robbins, 120 PENN ST   17752
ES, 120 PENN ST   17752 – Terry Kirschler, prin.
Other Schools – See Allenwood

Montoursville, Lycoming Co., Pop. Code 6
Loyalsock Twp. SD IU 17
Supt. – See Williamsport
Four Mile ES, 2800 FOUR MILE DR   17754
  Brooks Nancarrow, prin.

Montoursville Area SD IU 17
Sch. Sys. Enr. Code 4
Supt. – John Zimmerman
  1304 WEAVER ST   17754
McCall MS, 600 WILLOW ST   17754
  J. Kustanbauter, prin.
Loyalsock Valley ES, RURAL ROUTE 02   17754
  Thomas O'Mealy, prin.
Lyter ES, 900 SPRUCE ST   17754
  Henry Wenzel,Jr., prin.

Montrose, Susquehanna Co., Pop. Code 4
Montrose Area SD IU 19
Sch. Sys. Enr. Code 4
Supt. – J. Rodger Lewis, RURAL ROUTE 03   18801
Lathrop Street ES, 14 LATHROP ST   18801
  Harry Klein, prin.
Other Schools – See Friendsville

Moosic, Lacawanna Co., Pop. Code 6
Riverside SD IU 19
Supt. – See Taylor

ES, KRIEG AVENUE AND SCHOOL ST   18518
  William Kasulis, prin.

Morgantown, Berks Co., Pop. Code 3
Twin Valley SD IU 14
Supt. – See Elverson
ES, NORTH & MULBERRY STREET   19543
  Elaine Wright, prin.

Conestoga Christian School
  RURAL ROUTE 02   BOX 124   19543

Morrisdale, Clearfield Co., Pop. Code 3
West Branch Area SD IU 10
Sch. Sys. Enr. Code 4
Supt. – John McDannel, P O BOX 248   16858
West Branch ES
  RURAL ROUTE 02 BOX 194   16858
  Ronald Guth, prin.

Morrisville, Bucks Co., Pop. Code 6
Morrisville Boro SD IU 22
Sch. Sys. Enr. Code 4
Supt. – Dr. James McDowelle
  550 W PALMER ST   19067
Grandview ES, 80 GRANDVIEW AVE   19067
  Barry White, prin.
Manor Park ES, PENN AVE   19067
  Barry White, prin.
Reiter ES, HARPER AND HILLCREST   19067
  Jo Ann Agoglia, prin.

Pennsbury SD IU 22
Supt. – See Fallsington
Roosevelt ES, 185 WALTON DR   19067
  Norman Gross, prin.

Holy Trinity ES
  227 N PENNSYLVANIA AVE   19067
St. John Evangelist ES, 728 BIG OAK RD   19067

Morton, Delaware Co., Pop. Code 4
Ridley SD IU 25
Supt. – See Folsom
Amosland ES, AMOSLAND ROAD   19070
  Thomas Pugh, prin.

Lady of Perpetual Help ES
  948 AMOSLAND RD   19070

Moscow, Lackawanna Co., Pop. Code 4
North Pocono SD IU 19
Sch. Sys. Enr. Code 5
Supt. – John Buscarini, CHURCH ST   18444
North Pocono MS, CHURCH ST   18444
  William Wright, prin.
Covington ES, RURAL ROUTE 03   18444
  Clifton Walls, prin.
Elmhurst ES, RURAL ROUTE 02   18444
  Matthew Farrell, prin.
Madisonville ES, RURAL ROUTE 01   18444
  Clifton Walls, prin.
ES, ACADEMY STREET   18444
  Clifton Walls, prin.
Other Schools – See Lake Ariel

Mountain Top, Luzerna Co., Pop. Code 4
Crestwood Sd IU 18
Sch. Sys. Enr. Code 4
Supt. – Dr. Richard Deane
  281 S MOUNTAIN BLVD   18707
Fairview ES, 117 SPRUCE ST   18707
  Bernard Okuniewski, prin.
Rice ES, RURAL ROUTE 08   18707
  Stephen Beres, prin.

St. Jude ES, MOUNTAIN BLVD-ROUTE 309   18707

Mount Carmel, Northumberland Co., Pop. Code 6
Mt. Carmel Area SD IU 16
Sch. Sys. Enr. Code 4
Supt. – Joseph Warner, 600 W 5TH ST   17851
ES, 4TH AND VINE STREETS   17851
  Mary Krakowski, prin.
Other Schools – See Kulpmont

Holy Spirit ES, 250 WEST AVE   17851

Mount Holly Springs, Cumberland Co., Pop. Code 4
Carlisle Area SD IU 15
Supt. – See Carlisle
Mt. Holly Springs ES, CHESTNUT STREET   17065
  E. Shank,Jr., prin.

South Middleton SD IU 15
Supt. – See Boiling Springs
Rice ES, 805 HOLLY PIKE   17065
  Dean Clepper, prin.

Mount Jewett, McKean Co., Pop. Code 4
Kane Area SD IU 9
Supt. – See Kane
ES, MAIN STREET   16740 – Julie Thompson, prin.

Mount Joy, Lancaster Co., Pop. Code 6
Donegal SD IU 13
Sch. Sys. Enr. Code 4
Supt. – Woodrow Sites, P O BOX 297   17552
Donegal MS, S POPLAR ST   17552
  William Fenstermaker, prin.
Grandview ES, ORCHARD ROAD   17552
  Jacques Gibble, prin.
Seiler ES, S BARBARA STREET   17552
  Mary Dougherty, prin.
Other Schools – See Marietta, Maytown

Hempfield SD IU 13
Supt. – See Landisville
Farmdale ES, RURAL ROUTE 03   17552
  Michael Nicklaus, prin.

Manheim Central SD IU 13
Supt. – See Manheim
Elm Tree ES, RURAL ROUTE 03 BOX 264   17552
  Drew Scheffey, prin.

Kraybill Menn ES
  RURAL ROUTE 01 BOX 234   17552

Mount Morris, Greene Co., Pop. Code 3
Central Green SD IU 1
Supt. – See Waynesburg
Perry ES, 176 NORTH PORTER STREET   15349
  Charlotte Minehart, prin.

Mount Penn, Berks Co., Pop. Code 5
Antietam SD IU 14
Supt. – See Reading
ES, 24 AND CUMBERLAND STREETS   19606
  John Bruchak,Jr., prin.

Mount Pleasant, Westmoreland Co., Pop. Code 6
Midd-West SD IU 16
Supt. – See Middleburg
Perry-West Perry ES
  RURAL ROUTE 02 BOX 272   17853
  William Houser, prin.

Mt. Pleasant Area SD IU 7
Sch. Sys. Enr. Code 5
Supt. – John Grecco, RURAL ROUTE 04   15666
Norvelt ES, RURAL ROUTE 01 BOX 169A   15666
  Robert Patterson, prin.
Ramsay ES, 300 EAGLE ST   15666
  Dan Landy, prin.
Rumbaugh ES
  RURAL ROUTE 04 BOX 1200   15666
  Robert Patterson, prin.
Other Schools – See Jones Mills

Mt. Carmel Christian School
  RURAL ROUTE 02   15666
Holy Trinity Catholic School
  222 SUMMIT ST   15666
Verna Montessori ES
  RURAL ROUTE 02 BOX 348   15666

Mount Union, Huntingdon Co., Pop. Code 5
Mt. Union Area SD IU 11
Sch. Sys. Enr. Code 4
Supt. – Harold Estep, 28 W MARKET ST   17066
Kistler ES, RURAL ROUTE 01   17066
  John Miller, prin.
ES, WEST MARKET STREET   17066
  Jean Vadella, prin.
Shirley Township ES, RURAL ROUTE 01   17066
  John Miller, prin.
Other Schools – See Mapleton Depot

Mountville, Lancaster Co.
Hempfield SD IU 13
Supt. – See Landisville
ES, 120 COLLEGE AVE   17554
  Gerald Doerr, prin.

Mount Wolf, York Co., Pop. Code 4
Northeastern York SD IU 12
Supt. – See Manchester
ES, SIXTH AND MAPLE STREETS   17347
  William Kleinfelter, prin.

Muncy, Lycoming Co., Pop. Code 5
Muncy SD IU 17
Sch. Sys. Enr. Code 4
Supt. – Thomas Scholvin, W PENN ST   17756
Myers ES, NEW STREET   17756
  James Weaver, prin.

Munhall, Allegheny Co., Pop. Code 7
Steel Valley SD IU 3
Sch. Sys. Enr. Code 4
Supt. – Dr. Gerard Longo
  220 E OLIVER ROAD   15120
Woodlawn ES, 300 WOODLAWN AVE   15120
  R. Wright, prin.
Park ES, MAIN & CAMBRIA STREETS   15120
  Deane Lopus, prin.
Other Schools – See Homestead

St. John the Baptist ES, 427 E 10TH AVE   15120
St. Therese ES, 3 ST THERESE CT   15120

Murrysville, Westmoreland Co., Pop. Code 7
Franklin Regional SD IU 7
Sch. Sys. Enr. Code 5
Supt. – Dr. Paul Johnson
  3210 SCHOOL ROAD   15668
Franklin Regional MS
  4660 OLD WM PENN HWY   15668
  Louis Cowan, prin.
Newlonsburg ES, 3170 SCHOOL RD   15668
  David Reese, prin.
Sloan ES, 4121 SARDIS RD   15668
  Samuel Shaneyfelt, prin.
Other Schools – See Export

Mother of Sorrows ES
  3264 EVERGREEN DR   15668

Muse, Washington Co., Pop. Code 4
Canon-McMillan SD IU 1
Supt. – See Canonsburg
ES, MAIN ST   15350 – Rita Polansky, prin.

Myerstown, Lebanon Co., Pop. Code 5
Eastern Lebanon County SD IU 13
Sch. Sys. Enr. Code 4
Supt. – Karl Martin, P O BOX 268   17067
Eastern Lebanon County MS, P O BOX 268   17067
Frank Bergman, prin.
Jackson ES, 558 W MAIN AVE   17067
Ronald Hetrick, prin.
ES, S RAILROAD STREET   17067
Brenda Haverstick, prin.
Other Schools – See Richland, Schaefferstown

Grace Christian School
430 E LINCOLN AVE   17067
Myerstown Mennonite School
739 E LINCOLN AVE   17067

Nanticoke, Luzerne Co., Pop. Code 7
Greater Nanticoke Area SD IU 18
Sch. Sys. Enr. Code 4
Supt. – D. Charles Davis, P O BOX 126   18634
MS, 555 E MAIN ST   18634
Dennis Matzoni, prin.
Kennedy ES, KOSCIUSZKO ST   18634
Dr. Mariellen Scott, prin.
Lincoln MS, 613 KOSCIUSZKO ST   18634
Dr. Mariellen Scott, prin.
Smith ES, ROBERT STREET   18634
Ralph Ferraro, prin.

Pope John Paul II ES, 529 S HANOVER ST   18634

Nanty Glo, Cambria Co., Pop. Code 5
Blacklick Valley SD IU 8
Sch. Sys. Enr. Code 4
Supt. – Donald Thomas, 555 BIRCH ST   15943
Blacklick Valley ES, 1000 RAILROAD ST   15943
Kenneth Martinazzi, prin.

St. Mary's ES, 1051 ROBERTS ST   15943

Narberth, Montgomery Co., Pop. Code 5
Lower Merion SD IU 23
Supt. – See Ardmore
Welsh Valley MS
1320 HAGY'S FORD ROAD   19072
William Brubaker, prin.
Penn Valley ES, 301 RIGHTERS MILL RD   19072
Judy Vietri, prin.

St. Margret ES, 227 N NARBERTH AVE   19072

Narvon, Lancaster Co.
Eastern Lancaster County SD IU 13
Supt. – See New Holland
Caernarvon ES
RURAL ROUTE 03 BOX 151   17555
Alice Hummer, prin.

Natrona Heights, Allegheny Co., Pop. Code 7
Highlands SD IU 3
Sch. Sys. Enr. Code 5
Supt. – Dr. Louis Baldassare
CALIFORNIA AT 11TH AVE   15065
Birdville ES, ADAMS STREET   15065
Joseph Kocon, prin.
Fawn ES, RURAL ROUTE 01 BOX 460   15065
Joseph Kocon, prin.
ES, 1415 FREEPORT RD   15065
Albert Porter, prin.
Other Schools – See Brackenridge, Tarentum

Blessed Sacrament ES
800 MONTANA AVE   15065

Nazareth, Northampton Co., Pop. Code 6
Nazareth Area SD IU 20
Sch. Sys. Enr. Code 5
Supt. – John Jenkins, 8 CENTER SQUARE   18064
Bushkill ES, 960 BUSHKILL CENTER RD   18064
Kenneth Butz, prin.
Lower Nazareth ES, 4422 NEWBURG RD   18064
Joseph Polinski, prin.
Shafer ES, LIBERTH STREET   18064
John Caprari, prin.

Pen Argyl Area SD IU 20
Supt. – See Pen Argyl
Plainfield ES, 539 SCHOOL RD   18064
John Dentith, prin.

Holy Family ES, 500 W CENTER ST   18064

Needmore, Fulton Co.
Southern Fulton SD IU 11
Supt. – See Warfordsburg
ES, RURAL ROUTE 02   17238 – Larry Truax, prin.

Nemacolin, Greene Co., Pop. Code 4
Carmichaels Area SD IU 1
Supt. – See Carmichaels
ES, 215 S MARKET STREET   15351
Stan Ferek, prin.

Nescopeck, Luzerne Co., Pop. Code 4
Berwick Area SD IU 16
Supt. – See Berwick
ES, 315 DEWEY ST   18635 – Ronald Garrison, prin.

Nesquehoning, Carbon Co., Pop. Code 5
Panther Valley SD IU 21
Supt. – See Lansford
ES, DOUGLAS STREET   18240
Kathleen Polastre, prin.

New Albany, Bradford Co., Pop. Code 2
Wyalusing Area SD IU 17
Supt. – See Wyalusing
ES, RURAL ROUTE 01   18833
Eloise Corson, prin.

New Alexandria, Westmoreland Co., Pop. Code 3
Greensburg-Salem SD IU 7
Supt. – See Greensburg
Metzgar ES, C C HALL DRIVE   15670
William Hurrianko, prin.

New Berlin, Union Co., Pop. Code 3
Mifflinburg Area SD IU 16
Supt. – See Mifflinburg
ES, PLUM AND HIGH STREETS   17855
Terry Gessner, prin.

New Berlinville, Berks Co., Pop. Code 4
Boyertown Area SD IU 14
Supt. – See Boyertown
Colebrookdale ES, S MADISON ST   19545
Ruth Webster, prin.

New Bethlehem, Clarion Co., Pop. Code 4
Redbank Valley SD IU 6
Sch. Sys. Enr. Code 4
Supt. – Dr. R. David Farley
RURAL ROUTE 03 BOX 224   16242
Mahoning ES, RURAL ROUTE 01   16242
Charles Evans, prin.
New Bethlehem-South Bethlehem ES
VINE STREET   16242 – Charles Evans, prin.
Other Schools – See Hawthorn

New Bloomfield, Perry Co., Pop. Code 3
West Perry SD IU 15
Supt. – See Elliottsburg
West Perry JHS, RURAL ROUTE 02   17068
Donald Albright, prin.

New Brighton, Beaver Co., Pop. Code 6
New Brighton Area SD IU 27
Sch. Sys. Enr. Code 4
Supt. – J. Ross, 3225 43RD ST   15066
MS, ALLEGHENY & PENN AVE   15066
Jon Best, prin.
ES, 3200 43RD ST   15066 – David Pietro, prin.

Beaver County Christian School
601 PENN AVE   15066

New Britain, Bucks Co., Pop. Code 5
Central Bucks SD IU 22
Supt. – See Doylestown
Pine Run ES, 383 W BUTLER AVE   18901
Donald McClintock, prin.

New Castle, Lawrence Co., Pop. Code 8
Laurel SD IU 4
Sch. Sys. Enr. Code 4
Supt. – A. Bulazo
RURAL ROUTE 04 BOX 30   16101
Laurel ES, RURAL ROUTE 04 BOX 52   16101
Keith Kennedy, prin.

Neshannock Twp. SD IU 4
Sch. Sys. Enr. Code 4
Supt. – J. Scungio, 301 MITCHELL ROAD   16105
Neshannock Memorial ES
299 MITCHELL RD   16105
Dr. Herbert Hunt, prin.

New Castle Area SD IU 4
Sch. Sys. Enr. Code 5
Supt. – J. Martin, 708 W WASHINGTON ST   16101
Franklin JHS, 921 CUNNINGHAM AVE   16101
Amen Hassen, prin.
Kennedy ES, 326 LAUREL BLVD   16101
Mabel Paige, prin.
Lincoln-Garfield ES
708 W WASHINGTON ST   16101 – (-)_, prin.
Lockley ES, 900 E MAIN ST   16101
Pat George, prin.
Mahoning ES, 210 N CEDAR ST   16102
Pat George, prin.
McGill ES, 420 FERN ST   16101
Chris Kiriakou, prin.
Stevens ES, 831 HARRISON ST   16101
Pat George, prin.
Washington IS, EUCLID AVE   16105
George Gabriel, prin.
West Side ES, 708 W WASHINGTON ST   16101
Mabel Paige, prin.

Shenango Area SD IU 4
Sch. Sys. Enr. Code 4
Supt. – William Foster
2501 OLD PITTSBURGH ROAD   16101
Shenango Area ES, 2501 OLD PGH RD   16101
Marilyn Sanfilippo, prin.

Union Area SD IU 4
Sch. Sys. Enr. Code 3
Supt. – Domenic Ionta, 2106 CAMDEN AVE   16101
Union Area MS, 2106 CAMDEN AVE   16101
John Leitera, prin.
Union Memorial ES, 500 S SCOTLAND LN   16101
Joseph Yasher, prin.

St. Vitus ES, 915 S JEFFERSON ST   16101

New Columbia, Union Co.
Milton Area SD IU 16
Supt. – See Milton
White Deer ES   17856 – Joseph Kowalski, prin.

New Cumberland, Cumberland Co., Pop. Code 6
West Shore SD IU 15
Supt. – See Lemoyne
MS, 9TH & BRANDT AVE   17070
Michael Murphy, prin.
Fairview ES, 480 LEWISBERRY RD   17070
Edwin Resser, prin.
Hillside ES, 7TH AND SHARON STREETS   17070
J. Henry, prin.

St. Theresa ES, 1200 BRIDGE ST   17070

New Derry, Westmoreland Co., Pop. Code 3
Derry Area SD IU 7
Supt. – See Derry
ES, RURAL ROUTE 97   15671
Thomas Pavlik, prin.

New Florence, Westmoreland Co., Pop. Code 3
Ligonier Valley SD IU 7
Supt. – See Ligonier
Laurel Valley MS, RURAL ROUTE 01   15944
Daniel McDonald, prin.

Newfoundland, Wayne Co.
Wallenpaupack Area SD IU 19
Supt. – See Hawley
Wallenpaupack South ES, P O BOX 155   18445
Joyce Nicksick, prin.

New Freedom, York Co., Pop. Code 4

New Freedom Christian School
P O BOX 519   17349

New Freeport, Greene Co.
West Greene SD IU 1
Supt. – See Waynesburg
Springhill-Freeport ES, RURAL ROUTE 01   15352
Samuel Steinmiller, prin.

New Holland, Lancaster Co., Pop. Code 5
Eastern Lancaster County SD IU 13
Sch. Sys. Enr. Code 5
Supt. – L. Lloyd Ruoss, 101 E MAIN ST   17557
ES, 101 E MAIN ST   17557
Joseph Longenecker, prin.
Summit Valley MS, RURAL ROUTE 02   17557
Donna Searle, prin.
Other Schools – See Blue Ball, Bowmansville, Narvon

New Hope, Bucks Co., Pop. Code 4
New Hope-Solebury SD IU 22
Sch. Sys. Enr. Code 3
Supt. – Irene Bender, 180 W BRIDGE ST   18938
Other Schools – See Solebury

New Kensington, Westmoreland Co., Pop. Code 7
New Kensington-Arnold SD IU 7
Sch. Sys. Enr. Code 5
Supt. – Richard Rosenberger
ROUTE 56 AT 7TH ST   15068
Edgewood ES, KNOLLWOOD ROAD   15068
James Girardi, prin.
Ft. Crawford ES, 400 3RD ST   15068
James Girardi, prin.
Greenwald Memorial ES, ELMTREE RD   15068
Thomas Rocchi, prin.
Martin ES, 7TH STREET ROAD   15068
James Girardi, prin.
Other Schools – See Arnold

Mt. St. Peter ES, 100 FREEPORT RD   15068
St. Joseph ES, 1129 LEISHMAN AVE   15068
St. Mary School, 837 KENNEKTH AVE   15068

New Milford, Susquehanna Co., Pop. Code 4
Blue Ridge SD IU 19
Sch. Sys. Enr. Code 4
Supt. – Edward Harris, RURAL ROUTE 02   18834
Blue Ridge ES, RURAL ROUTE 02   18834
Mario Salati, prin.

New Oxford, Adams Co., Pop. Code 4
Conewago Valley SD IU 12
Sch. Sys. Enr. Code 5
Supt. – Dr. William Landauer
130 BERLIN ROAD   17350
ES, 116 N BERLIN AVE   17350 – D. Shupp, prin.
Other Schools – See Hanover

Immaculate Conception BVM School
101 N PETER ST   17350

New Paris, Bedford Co., Pop. Code 2
Chestnut Ridge SD IU 8
Supt. – See Fishertown
Chestnut Ridge Central ES
RURAL ROUTE 01   15554
Richard McDermott, prin.
New Paris Central ES, RURAL ROUTE 02   15554
Richard McDermott, prin.

New Philadelphia, Schuylkill Co., Pop. Code 4

Holy Cross ES, 47 WIGGAN ST   17959

Newport, Perry Co., Pop. Code 4
Newport SD IU 15
Sch. Sys. Enr. Code 4
Supt. – John Amsler, RURAL ROUTE 03   17074
ES, RURAL ROUTE 03   17074
Daniel Rathfon, prin.

New Providence, Lancaster Co.
Solanco SD IU 13
Supt. – See Quarryville

Providence ES, 137 TRUCE RD   17560
Kenneth Zieber, prin.

Newry, Blair Co., Pop. Code 2

St. Patricks Parish, P O BOX 398   16665

New Ringgold, Schuylkill Co., Pop. Code 2
Tamaqua Area SD IU 29
Supt. – See Tamaqua
West Penn Township ES
RURAL ROUTE 02   17960 – Thomas Ponting, prin.

New Stanton, Westmoreland Co., Pop. Code 5
Hempfield Area SD IU 7
Supt. – See Greensburg
Stanwood ES, RURAL ROUTE 01 BOX 255   15672
John Rankin, prin.

Newtown, Bucks Co., Pop. Code 5
Council Rock SD IU 22
Supt. – See Richboro
Chancellor Street ES
30 N CHANCELLOR ST   18940
Michael Beatrice, prin.
Feinstone ES
EAGLE AND PINEVILLE ROADS   18940
Richard Wentz, prin.
Goodnoe MS, 298 FROST LN   18940
Michael Beatrice, prin.

Newtown Friends ES, P O BOX 69   18940
St. Andrew ES, 138 S SYCAMORE ST   18940

Newtown Square, Delaware Co., Pop. Code 6
Marple-Newtown SD IU 25
Sch. Sys. Enr. Code 5
Supt. – Stephen Frederick
120 MEDIA LINE ROAD   19073
Culbertson ES, 3530 GOSHEN RD   19073
John Hughes, prin.
Other Schools – See Broomall

Delaware County Christian School
464 MALIN ROAD   19073
St. Anastasia ES, 3305 W CHESTER P   19073

New Tripoli, Lehigh Co.
Northwestern Lehigh SD IU 21
Sch. Sys. Enr. Code 4
Supt. – Dr. David Fallinger
RURAL ROUTE 02   BOX 67   18066
Northwestern ES
RURAL ROUTE 02 BOX 67   18066
Brad Cressman, prin.
Other Schools – See Kutztown

Newville, Cumberland Co., Pop. Code 4
Big Spring SD IU 15
Sch. Sys. Enr. Code 5
Supt. – Warren Howard, P O BOX 98   17241
Big Spring MS, P O BOX 98   17241
Glenn Gow, prin.
Centerville ES, RURAL ROUTE 01 BOX 107   17241
Arthur McCarter, prin.
Frankford ES, RURAL ROUTE 03 BOX 102   17241
John Bonitz, prin.
Mifflin ES, RURAL ROUTE 02 BOX 160   17241
John Bonitz, prin.
ES, RURAL ROUTE 02 BOX 6   17241
Lee Clouse, prin.
Other Schools – See Carlisle, Walnut Bottom

New Wilmington, Lawrence Co., Pop. Code 5
Wilmington Area SD IU 4
Sch. Sys. Enr. Code 4
Supt. – Dr. Leon Ahlum, 400 WOOD ST   16142
New Wilmington ES, 450 WOOD ST   16142
Edward Pandoiti, prin.
Other Schools – See Pulaski, Volant

Nicholson, Wyoming Co., Pop. Code 3
Lackawanna Trail SD IU 19
Supt. – See Factoryville
ES, HARDING STREET   18446 – James Evans, prin.

Normalville, Fayette Co.
Connellsville Area SD IU 1
Supt. – See Connellsville
Springfield ES, 1135 RACE STREET   15469
Billy Pritts, prin.

Norristown, Montgomery Co., Pop. Code 8
Colonial SD IU 23
Supt. – See Plymouth Meeting
Colonial MS, 716 BELVOIR ROAD   19401
Theodore Thomas, prin.

Methacton SD IU 23
Supt. – See Fairview Village
Arcola MS, EAGLEVILLE ROAD   19401
Andrew Case, prin.

Norristown Area SD IU 23
Sch. Sys. Enr. Code 6
Supt. – James Holton
401 N WHITEHALL ROAD   19403
East Norriton MS, 330 ROLAND DRIVE   19401
Patricia Hopkins, prin.
Eisenhower MS, 1601 MARKLEY ST   19401
John Haines, prin.
Stewart MS, MARSHALL & SELMA STS   19401
Joseph Howell, prin.
Burnside ES, MAIN STREET BURNSIDE   19403
John Sweeney, prin.
Cole Manor ES, 2350 SPRINGVIEW RD   19401
Doris Harris, prin.

Fly ES, 2920 POTSHOP ROAD   19403
Theresa Carfagno, prin.
Gotwals ES, 1 E OAK ST   19401
Gary Engler, prin.
Hancock ES, ARCH AND SUMMIT STREET   19401
Carl Glover, prin.
Marshall Street ES, 1525 W MARSHALL ST   19403
Clifford Rogers, prin.

Wissahickon SD IU 23
Supt. – See Ambler
Stony Creek ES, 1721 YOST RD   19401
Gary Bundy, prin.

Epiphany of Our Lord ES
3040 WALTON RD   19401
Holy Saviour ES, WALNUT & AIRY STS   19401
Penn Christian Academy
50 W GERMANTOWN PIKE   19401
St. Francis of Assisi ES
601 BUTTONWOOD ST   19401
St. Patrick ES, GREEN AND CHESTNUT ST   19401
St. Paul ES, 351 E JOHNSON HWY   19401
St. Teresa of Avila ES
2550 S PARKVIEW DR   19403
St. Titus ES, 3000 KEENWOOD RD   19403
Visitation BVM ES, RURAL ROUTE 01   19403

Northampton, Northampton Co., Pop. Code 6
Northampton Area SD IU 20
Sch. Sys. Enr. Code 6
Supt. – Edwin Coyle, 1617 LAUBACH AVE   18067
Franklin ES, 9TH AND LINCOLN AVENUE   18067
Edward Reichard, prin.
Washington ES, 24TH AND MAIN STREET   18067
Edward Reichard, prin.
Wolf ES, 17TH AND LINCOLN AVENUE   18067
Edward Reichard, prin.
Other Schools – See Bath, Walnutport

Our Lady of Hungary ES
1314 NEWPORT AVE   18067
St. John the Baptist School 3
1357 NEWPORT AVE   18067

North Apollo, Armstrong Co., Pop. Code 4
Apollo-Ridge SD IU 28
Supt. – See Spring Church
ES, WILSON AVE   15673
Dr. June Merryman, prin.

North Braddock, Allegheny Co., Pop. Code 6
Woodland Hills SD IU 3
Supt. – See Pittsburgh
Fairless IS, 531 JONES AVE   15104
Frank Marino, prin.

North East, Erie Co., Pop. Code 5
North East SD IU 5
Sch. Sys. Enr. Code 5
Supt. – Robert Towsey, 50 E DIVISION ST   16428
Davis ES, 50 E DIVISION ST   16428
Thomas Savidge, prin.
Heard Memorial MS, 40 NORTH LAKE ST   16428
Robert Rhodes, prin.

Wattsburg Area SD IU 5
Supt. – See Wattsburg
Greenfield Township ES
10941 STATION RD   16428 – Judy Hunt, prin.

St. Gregory ES, 140 W MAIN ST   16428

North Huntingdon, Westmoreland Co.
Norwin SD IU 7
Supt. – See Irwin
Hartford Heights ES, 15020 ARDARA RD   15642
Paul Davis, prin.
Hillcrest ES, 11091 MOCKINGBIRD DR   15642
Marlynn Sidehamer, prin.
Scull ES, 780 BRUSH HILL RD   15642
David Cunningham, prin.
Shaw ES, 1219 MORRIS AVENUE SHWT   15642
Kerry Weber, prin.
Stewartsville ES, 101 CARPENTER LN   15642
Neil Hamilton, prin.

St. Agnes Roman Catholic ES
11400 SAINT AGNES LN   15642

Northumberland, Northumberland Co., Pop. Code 5
Shikellamy SD IU 16
Supt. – See Sunbury
Priestley ES, RURAL ROUTE 01   17857
David Doran, prin.
Rice ES, 4TH AND HANOVER STREETS   17857
John Gotaskie, prin.
Second Street ES
2ND AND ORANGE STREETS   17857
Dave Doran, prin.

Northumberland Christian School
2ND & QUEEN STS   17857

North Versailles, Allegheny Co., Pop. Code 7
East Allegheny SD IU 3
Sch. Sys. Enr. Code 4
Supt. – Dr. Richard Napolitan
1150 JACKS RUN ROAD   15137
Green Valley PS, CRESTVIEW DIRVE   15137
Lillian Naccarati, prin.
Other Schools – See Wilmerding

Praise Christian Academy, 245 FOSTER RD   15137

North Wales, Montgomery Co., Pop. Code 5
North Penn SD IU 23
Supt. – See Lansdale
Gwyn-Nor ES, 151 HANCOCK RD   19454
Marianne Kaemmer, prin.
Montgomery ES, 1221 STUMP ROAD   19454
Judith Clark, prin.
ES, SECOND AND SUMMIT STREETS   19454
Thomas Shugar, prin.
Pennbrook MS, 1201 E WALNUT ST   19454
Richard Dormuth, prin.

St. Rose of Lima ES, PENNSYLVANIA AVE   19454

North Warren, Warren Co., Pop. Code 4
Warren County SD IU 5
Supt. – See Warren
ES, STATE STREET   16365 – James Graziano, prin.

Norwood, Delaware Co., Pop. Code 6
Interboro SD IU 25
Supt. – See Prospect Park
ES, 558 SENECA AVE   19074
Ralph Bagnato, prin.

St. Gabriel's ES, 233 MOHAWK AVE   19074

Nuremberg, Luzerne Co.
Hazleton Area SD IU 18
Supt. – See Hazleton
ES   18241 – Ray Schneider, prin.

Oakdale, Allegheny Co., Pop. Code 4
West Allegheny SD IU 3
Supt. – See Imperial
McKee ES, ROUTE 978   15071
Charles Fazekas, prin.

Oakmont, Allegheny Co., Pop. Code 6
Riverview SD IU 3
Sch. Sys. Enr. Code 4
Supt. – R. Knapp, 701 10TH ST   15139
Tenth Street ES
PENNA AVENUE & 10TH STREET   15139
Stanley Sofish, prin.
Other Schools – See Verona

St. Irenaeus ES, 637 4TH ST   15139

Oaks, Montgomery Co.
Spring-Ford Area SD IU 23
Supt. – See Collegeville
ES, GREEN TREE RD   19456
James Leiderman, prin.

Oil City, Venango Co., Pop. Code 7
Cranberry Area SD IU 6
Supt. – See Seneca
Pinoak ES, 3 SOUTH WEST BOULEVARD   16301
Nicholas Bodnar, prin.

Oil City Area SD IU 6
Sch. Sys. Enr. Code 5
Supt. – Stephen Pikna, 202 CRAWFORD ST   16301
JHS, 69 SPRING ST   16301 – John Downing, prin.
Hasson Heights ES, 833 GRANVIEW RD   16301
Thomas Huston, prin.
Lincoln ES, HARRIOTT & WASHINGTON   16301
Darrell Smith, prin.
Riverview MS, 69 SPRING ST   16301
John Downing, prin.
Seventh Street ES
WEST SEVENTH & ORANGE   16301
Kenneth Nelson, prin.
Smedley Street ES, 310 SMEDLEY ST   16301
Thomas Huston, prin.
Other Schools – See Cooperstown

St. Stephen ES, 214 REED ST   16301

Old Forge, Lackawanna Co., Pop. Code 6
Old Forge SD IU 19
Sch. Sys. Enr. Code 3
Supt. – Daniel Donovan, MOOSIC ROAD   18518
ES, WEST GRACE STREET   18518
Bart Giacometti, prin.

St. Mary's ES, 216 W GRACE ST   18518

Old Zionsville, Lehigh Co.
East Penn SD IU 21
Supt. – See Emmaus
Kings Highway ES, ROUTE 29   18068
Richard Gorton, prin.

Oley, Berks Co., Pop. Code 4
Oley Valley SD IU 14
Sch. Sys. Enr. Code 4
Supt. – Robert Lesko   19547
Oley Valley MS   19547 – R. Klucharich, prin.
ES   19547 – Alan Bartlett, prin.
Other Schools – See Reading

Olyphant, Lackawanna Co., Pop. Code 6
Mid Valley SD IU 19
Supt. – See Throop
Mid Valley MS
LINCOLN & SUSQUEHANNA AVE   18447
Gerald Luchansky, prin.

Sts. Cyril Methodius ES, 133 RIVER ST   18447

Orbisonia, Huntingdon Co., Pop. Code 3
Southern Huntingdon County SD IU 11
Sch. Sys. Enr. Code 4
Supt. – Harry King, P O BOX 68   17243

Other Schools – See Cassville, Rockhill Furnace,
Shade Gap, Three Springs

Orefield, Lehigh Co.
Parkland SD IU 21
Sch. Sys. Enr. Code 6
Supt. – Carmen Riola 18069
Kernsville ES, KERNSVILLE ROAD 18069
Edward Roth, prin.
Other Schools – See Allentown, Coplay, Schnecksville

Oreland, Montgomery Co., Pop. Code 6
Springfield Twp. SD IU 23
Sch. Sys. Enr. Code 4
Supt. – Thomas Davis
1901 E PAPER MILL ROAD 19075
Enfield MS, 1901 E PAPER MILL ROAD 19075
Theresa Felix, prin.
Enfield ES, CHURCH AND PAPER MILL 19075
Ronald Mutchnik, prin.
Other Schools – See Philadelphia

Holy Martyrs ES
ULMER AND ALLISON AVE 19075

Orwigsburg, Schuylkill Co., Pop. Code 5
Blue Mountain SD IU 29
Sch. Sys. Enr. Code 5
Supt. – Raymond Froling, REDDALE ROAD 17961
Blue Mountain ES, 675 REDDALE RD 17961
Edward Cope, prin.
Blue Mountain MS 17961 – William Toomey, prin.
Other Schools – See Cressona, Friedensburg

Osceola Mills, Clearfield Co., Pop. Code 4
Philipsburg-Osceola Area SD IU 10
Supt. – See Philipsburg
ES, COAL & BLANCHARD STREET 16666
Bettyann Benjamin, prin.
Rush Consolidated ES, RURAL ROUTE 01 16666
Bettyann Benjamin, prin.

Ottsville, Bucks co.

St. John the Baptist School
RURAL ROUTE 01 BOX 246 A 18942

Oxford, Chester Co., Pop. Code 5
Oxford Area SD IU 24
Sch. Sys. Enr. Code 4
Supt. – Dr. Sharron Nelson, 119 S 5TH ST 19363
Oxford Area IS, 602 GARFIELD ST 19363
Ronald Reidinger, prin.
Hopewell S C ES, 536 HODGSON ST 19363
Carol Gilmore, prin.
Nottingham MS, 736 GARFIELD ST 19363
James Householder, prin.

Palmerton, Carbon Co., Pop. Code 6
Palmerton Area SD IU 21
Sch. Sys. Enr. Code 5
Supt. – Ronald Mihalko
171 DELAWARE AVE 18071
Palmerton Area JHS
3RD AND LAFAYETTE AVE 18071
Thaddeus Kosciolek, prin.
Palmer MS, THIRD AND LAFAYETTE 18071
(–), prin.
Other Schools – See Lehighton

St. John Neuman ES
3RD & LAFAYETTE AVE 18071

Palmyra, Lebanon Co., Pop. Code 6
Palmyra Area SD IU 13
Sch. Sys. Enr. Code 5
Supt. – James Dell, PARK DRIVE 17078
Forge Road ES, SOUTH FORGE ROAD 17078
Jon Whittle, prin.
Northside ES
SPRUCE AND GRANT STREETS 17078
Jon Whittle, prin.
Pine Street ES
W PINE AND COLLEGE STREET 17078
Jon Whittle, prin.

Paoli, Chester Co., Pop. Code 6

St. Norbert ES, 6 GREENLAWN RD 19301

Paradise, Lancaster Co.
Pequea Valley SD IU 13
Supt. – See Kinzers
ES, 3293 LINCOLN HWY E 17562
Rachelle Bonfield, prin.

Linville ES, 295 S DINZER RD 17562

Parker, Armstrong Co., Pop. Code 3
Allegheny-Clarion Valley SD IU 6
Supt. – See Foxburg
ES, RURAL ROUTE 03 16049
Barry Wineland, prin.

Moniteau SD IU 4
Supt. – See West Sunbury
Washington ES, RURAL ROUTE 03 16049
James Wetzel, prin.

Patton, Cambria Co., Pop. Code 4
Cambria Heights SD IU 8
Sch. Sys. Enr. Code 4
Supt. – Russell DeFrahn, 510 BEECH AVE 16668
Cambria Heights ES, 510 BEECH AVE 16668
Harold Gabrielson, prin.
Other Schools – See Carrolltown, Elmora, Hastings

Peach Bottom, Lancaster Co.
Solanco SD IU 13
Supt. – See Quarryville
Fulton ES, RURAL ROUTE 01 BOX 3A 17563
Thomas Brackbill, prin.

Peckville, Lackawanna Co.
Valley View SD IU 19
Supt. – See Archbald
Elementary Center School, MAIN STREET 18452
Fred Rosetti, prin.
Lincoln ES, BROOK STREET 18452
John Scagliotti, prin.

Pen Argyl, Northampton Co., Pop. Code 5
Pen Argyl Area SD IU 20
Sch. Sys. Enr. Code 4
Supt. – Russell Roper, P O BOX 92 18072
Pen Argyl Area JHS, 501 W LAUREL AVE 18072
Edward Fishler, prin.
Wind Gap MS, 1620 TEELS RD 18072
Thomas Ciccarelli, prin.
Other Schools – See Nazareth

Immaculate Conception ES
BABBITT & HELLER AVE 18072

Penfield, Clearfield Co.
Du Bois Area SD IU 6
Supt. – See Du Bois
ES, RURAL ROUTE 03 15849 – Rita Wray, prin.

Penndel, Bucks Co., Pop. Code 5

Our Lady of Grace ES
338 HULMEVILLE AVE 19047

Penns Creek, Snyder Co.
Midd-West SD IU 16
Supt. – See Middleburg
ES, P O BOX 38 17862 – Gregg Wetzel, prin.

Penn Wynne, Montgomery Co., Pop. Code 5
Lower Merion SD IU 23
Supt. – See Ardmore
ES, 250 HAVERFORD RD 19151
James Werkiser, prin.

Pequea, Lancaster Co., Pop. Code 5
Penn Manor SD IU 13
Supt. – See Millersville
Marticville MS, RURAL ROUTE 01 17565
G. Campbell, prin.

Perkasie, Bucks Co., Pop. Code 6
Pennridge SD IU 22
Sch. Sys. Enr. Code 6
Supt. – John Slattery, 1506 N 5TH ST 18944
Pennridge Central JHS, 1500 N 5TH ST 18944
K. Patrick Svanson, prin.
Pennridge South JHS
S 5TH AND CEDAR ST 18944
Blaine Strunk, prin.
Deibler ES, 1122 SCHWENKMILL RD 18944
William Woehr, prin.
ES, 601 N 7TH ST 18944 – Alfred Bolinsky, prin.
Seylar ES, 612 H W CALOWHILL ROAD 18944
Jack Newell, prin.
Other Schools – See Bedminster, Sellersville

Perryopolis, Fayette Co., Pop. Code 4
Frazier SD IU 1
Sch. Sys. Enr. Code 4
Supt. – H. Dale Winger, P O BOX 302 15473
Perry ES, 407 CONSTITUTION ST 15473
Barbara Mehalov, prin.
Other Schools – See Dawson, Fayette City

Philadelphia, Philadelphia Co., Pop. Code 12
Philadelphia CSD IU 26
Sch. Sys. Enr. Code 8
Supt. – Constance Clayton
PARKWAY AT 21 ST 19103
Lamberton S, 75TH & WOODBINE 19151
Marilyn Kraft, prin.
Poe S, 18TH & SNYDER AVE 19145
Dr. Emilio Matticoli, prin.
Baldi MS, VERREE & ALBURGER 19115
Max Ehrlich, prin.
Clemente MS, 5TH AND LUZERNE ST 19140
Walter Scruggs, prin.
Conwell MS
JASPER AND CLEARFIELD ST 19134
Joseph Sweeney, prin.
Fitler MS, SEYMOUR & KNOX STS 19144
William Crumley, prin.
Hill MS, TULPEHOCKEN & CRITT 19138
Ed McHugh, prin.
Labrum MS
HAWLEY & BROOKVIEW ROADS 19154
Myron Mostovoy, prin.
Leeds MS, E MOUNT PLEASANT AVE 19150
Albert Session, prin.
Lewis MS, TULPEHOCKEN & ARDLEIGH 19138
Dorothy Rush, prin.
Meehan MS, 3001 RYAN AVE 19152
Gabriel Pascuzzi, prin.
Pepper MS, 84TH & LYONS 19153
Albert Newman, prin.
Pickett MS, WAYNE & CHELTEN AVES 19144
Samuel Gottlieb, prin.
Rhodes MS, 29TH & CLEARFIELD 19132
John Miceli, prin.
Rush MS
KNIGHTS AND FAIRDALE ROAD 19154
Edward Itzenson, prin.

Thomas MS, 9TH AND JOHNSTON ST 19148
Robert McCarthy, prin.
Tilden MS, 66TH & ELMWOOD AVE 19142
O. Raymond Harper, prin.
Turner MS, 59TH & BALTIMORE AVE 19143
Robert Chapman, prin.
Vare MS, 24TH & SNYDER 19145
Yvonne Jones, prin.
Vare MS, MORRIS AND MOYAMENSIN 19148
Ambrose Actiolivia, prin.
Adaire ES, PALMER AND THOMPSON 19123
Patricia Reilly, prin.
Alcorn ES 19146 – Regina Jones, prin.
Allen ES, ROBBINS AND BATTERSBY 19149
Bruce Bell, prin.
Allen ES, 31ST AND LEHIGH AVENUE 19132
Catherine Draper, prin.
Anderson ES
61ST AND COBBS CRK PARK 19143
Dr. Norman Washington, prin.
Arthur ES
20TH AND CATHARINE STREETS 19146
Eugene Koller, prin.
Bache-Martin ES 19130 – Cedric Carter, prin.
Barry ES, 59TH AND RACE STREET 19139
James Barksdale, prin.
Barton ES, B & WYOMING AVE 19120
Dr. William Wingel, prin.
Belmont ES, 41ST & BROWN ST 19104
Sophie Hayward, prin.
Bethune ES, OLD YORK RD & ONTARIO ST 19140
Dahlia Johnson, prin.
Birney ES, 9TH AND LINDLEY AVENUE 19141
Dr. Arnold Oblon, prin.
Blaine Academics Plus
30TH AND BERKS STREETS 19121
Madeline Cartwright, prin.
Blankenburg ES
46TH AND GIRARD AVENUE 19131
Dr. Agnes Barksdale, prin.
Bregy ES 19145 – Michael Iannelli, prin.
Bridesburg ES, RICHMOND & NORRIS ST 19125
Dr. Henry Barsky, prin.
Brown Academics Plus
SERGEANT & JASPER ST 19125
John Dinnien, prin.
Brown Academics Plus
FRANKFORD & STANWOOD 19136
Alyson Fronton, prin.
Bryant Academics Plus
60TH & CATHERINE ST 19143
Dr. Ida Peterson, prin.
Carnell ES, FRONTENAC ST 19111
Quintin Robinson, prin.
Cassidy ES, LANSDOWNE EAST OF 6 19151
Jerome Drossner, prin.
Catharine ES
66TH AND CHESTER AVENUE 19142
Dr. John Dolan, prin.
Childs ES 19146 – Frances Williams, prin.
Cleveland ES, 19TH STREET N OF ERIE 19140
Nancy Kane, prin.
Clymer ES, 12TH AND RUSH STREETS 19133
Dr. William Tate, prin.
Comegys ES, 51ST AND GREENWAY 19143
Sybil Waldman, prin.
Comly ES, BYBERRY AND KELVIN ROAD 19116
Richard Shohen, prin.
Cook-Wissahickon ES
RIGHTER & E SALAIGNAC ST 19128
Rita Spelkoman, prin.
Cramp ES
HOWARD AND ONTARIO STREET 19140
Gaeton Zorzi, prin.
Creighton ES, TABOR RD AND FOULKRO 19120
Raymond Levy, prin.
Crossan Academics Plus
BINGHAM & BLEIGH AVE 19111
Carrie Rice, prin.
Daroff ES, 57TH AND VINE STREET 19139
Barbara Foxworth, prin.
Decatur ES, ACADEMY & WILLITS RD 19114
Elaine Chernicoff, prin.
Dick ES, 25TH AND DIAMOND STREET 19121
Nilsa Gonzalez, prin.
Disston ES, KNORR AND COTTAGE 19135
James Adams, prin.
Dobson ES, UMBRIA AND HERMITAGE 19127
William McClain, prin.
Douglass ES, 22ND & NORRIS ST 19121
James Kane, prin.
Drew ES, WARREN AND DEKALB STS 19145
Olin Johnson, prin.
Duckrey ES
15TH AND DIAMOND STREET 19121
Michael Clayton, prin.
Dunbar Adademics Plus
12TH NORTH OF COLUM 19122
Marilyn Kraft, prin.
Durham ES, 16TH & LOMBARD 19146
Shively Willingham, prin.
Edmonds ES, SEDGWICK AND THOURON 19150
Brenda Fishman, prin.
Edmunds ES, LARGE & DYRE ST 19124
Dr. Frederick Zorn, prin.
Elkin ES, D AND CLEARFIELD STREETS 19134
Leonard Kaltz, prin.
Elwood ES, 13TH & OAKLANE 19126
Harris Lewin, prin.
Emien ES, CHEW AND UPSAL 19119
Dolores Seiberlich, prin.
Fairhill ES, MARSHALL & PORTER ST 19148
Dr. Marylouise De Nicola, prin.

Farrell ES
  CASTOR AND FOX CHASE ROAD 19152
  Aaron Levin, prin.
Fell ES, 9TH AND OREGON AVENUE 19148
  Michelle Chaplin, prin.
Feltonville Academics Plus
  RISING SUN AND ROCK 19120 – Joyce Kail, prin.
Ferguson Academics Plus
  7TH & PORTER ST 19148
  Barbara Montoya, prin.
Finletter Academics
  N FRONT & GODFREY AVE 19120
  Leonard Sussman, prin.
Fitzpatrick ES
  KNIGHTS ROAD AND CHALFO 19154
  Frederick Rabinowitz, prin.
Forrest ES, COTTAGE & BLEIGH ST 19136
  Robert Scarcelle, prin.
Fox Chase Academics Plus
  RHAWN AND RIDGEWAY 19111
  William Lee, prin.
Frank ES, BOWLER AND HOFF 19103
  Barbara Shohen, prin.
Franklin Academics Plus
  RISING SUN AND CHEL 19120
  Richard Becker, prin.
Fulton ES, HAINES EAST OF GERM 19144
  Marvin Kaplan, prin.
Gideon ES, 29TH & GLENWOOD AVE 19121
  Addie Johnson, prin.
Gompers ES, 57TH & WYNNEFIELD AVE 19131
  Claudia Solomon, prin.
Greenberg ES
  ALICIA STREET AND SHARON L 19115
  Arthur Romanelli, prin.
Greenfield ES, 23RD AND CHESTNUT STS 19103
  Angelo Milicia, prin.
Hackett ES, YORK AND SEPVIVA STREETS 19125
  Eugene Strolle, prin.
Hamilton ES 19119 – Dr. Sylvia Jones, prin.
Hancock ES
  MORRELL STREET AND CROWN L 19114
  Rochelle Agris, prin.
Hanna ES, 58TH AND MEDIA 19131
  Dr. James Clements, prin.
Harrington ES
  53RD AND BALTIMORE AVE 19116
  Dr. Lawrence Colvin, prin.
Harrison ES
  11TH AND THOMPSON STREET 19122
  Rosamond Lindsey, prin.
Harrity ES 19143 – Nancy Donahue, prin.
Hartranft ES, 7TH OF YORK ST N 19133
  Dr. Maurice Weeks, prin.
Henry ES, 601 CARPENTER LN 19119
  Ronald Brown, prin.
Heston Academics Plus
  54TH & LANSDOWNE AVE 19131
  Richard Phipps,Jr., prin.
Hill ES, 32ND & RIDGE AVE 19132
  Helen Webb, prin.
Holme ES, ACADEMY & WILLITS RD 19114
  Henry Carroll, prin.
Hopkinson ES, L & LUZERNE ST 19124
  Dr. William Garbernia, prin.
Houston ES, ALLEN AND RURAL LN 19191
  Patricia Magee, prin.
Howe Academics Plus
  13TH AND GRANGE STREET 19141
  Janis Butler, prin.
Huey ES, 52ND & PINE ST 19139
  Richard Lawrence, prin.
Hunter ES, MASCHER & ASHDALE ST 19120
  Kathleen Quinn, prin.
Jackson ES, 12TH & FEDERAL 19147
  Renee Yampolsky, prin.
Jenks Academics PS
  13TH AND PORTER STREET 19148
  Adele Cassidy, prin.
Jenks ES, GERMANTOWN & HIGH ST 19144
  Patrick Gillan, prin.
Kearny ES 19123 – Leonard Rovner, prin.
Kelley ES, 28TH & OXFORD ST 19121
  Anthony Bellos, prin.
Kelly ES, PULASKI AVENUE AND HANSB 19144
  William Seiberlich, prin.
Kenderton ES, 15TH & ONTARIO ST 19140
  Dr. Edna McCrae, prin.
Key ES, 8TH AND WOLF ST 19148
  Helenmarie McLaughlin, prin.
Kinsey ES, 65TH & LIMEKILN PIKE 19138
  Ellen Denofa, prin.
Kirkbride ES, 7TH & DICKINSON ST 19147
  Jacqueline Wolf, prin.
Lawton ES, BENNER & DITMAN ST 19135
  Joan Miller, prin.
Lea ES, 47TH & LOCUST ST 19139
  Dr. John Grelis, prin.
Leidy ES, BELMONT AVE & EDGELY RD 19131
  William Snyder, prin.
Levering ES, RIDGE AVE AND GERHARD 19128
  Raymond Ostrowski, prin.
Lingelbach ES
  WAYNE AVENUE AND JOHNSON 19144
  Joanruth Hirschman, prin.
Locke ES
  46TH AND HAVERFORD AVENUE 19143
  Sandra Cunningham, prin.
Loesche ES
  TOMLINSON & BUSTLETON AVE 19116
  John Gallagher, prin.
Logan ES, 17TH AND LINDLEY AVENUE 19141
  Delores Gross, prin.

Longstreth ES, 57TH AND WILLOWS AVE 19143
  Dr. Domenic Matteo, prin.
Lowell ES, 5TH & NEDRO AVE 19120
  Shirley Sherman, prin.
Ludlow ES, 6TH & MASTER ST 19122
  Soledad Gillespie, prin.
Mann Academics Plus, 54TH & BERKS ST 19131
  Mamie Bryan, prin.
Marshall ES, SELLERS AND GRISCOM 19124
  Gerald Weisman, prin.
Mayfair ES, PRINCETON AND HAWTHOR 19149
  Alice Acosta, prin.
McCall ES, 7TH & DELANCEY ST 19106
  Leonard Rovner, prin.
McCloskey ES
  GOWEN AVENUE AND PICKE 19150
  Gerald Klein, prin.
McClure ES, 6TH & HUNTING PARK AVE 19140
  Julio Feldman, prin.
McDaniel ES 19145 – James Jones, prin.
McKinley ES
  ORKNEY AND DIAMOND STREET 19122
  Carmen Derivera, prin.
McMichael ES
  35TH AND FAIRMOUNT AVE 19104
  Russell Sgro, prin.
Meade ES 19121 – Mark Levin, prin.
Meredith ES 19147 – Angelo Branca, prin.
Mifflin ES, MIDVALE AVE AND CON 19129
  Richard Slusarski, prin.
Mitchell ES
  56TH AND KINGSESSING AVE 19143
  Vernon Jones, prin.
Moffet ES
  HOWARD AND OXFORD STREETS 19122
  Bruce Rachild, prin.
Moore Academics Plus
  SUMMERDALE & LONGSHORE AVE 19111
  Donald Leporea, prin.
Morris ES, 26TH & THOMPSON ST 19121
  Verneta Harvey, prin.
Morrison ES, 3RD & DUNCANNON AVE 19120
  Alan Katz, prin.
Morton ES
  63RD AND ELMWOOD AVENUE 19139
  Robert Mack, prin.
Nebinger ES, 6TH & CARPENTER ST 19147
  Arthur Rubin, prin.
Olney ES, TABOR RD AND WATER ST 19120
  Eugene Gruber, prin.
Palumbo ES 19147 – Sandra Cunningham, prin.
Pastorius ES, CHELTEN AVENUE AND SPR 19138
  Elvedine Wilkerson, prin.
Patterson ES, 70TH AND BUIST AVE 19143
  Dr. James Knopf, prin.
Peirce ES, 23RD AND CAMBRIA STREET 19132
  Carol Mullin, prin.
Peirce ES, 24TH AND CHRISTIAN STREET 19146
  Martin Glassman, prin.
Pennell Academics Plus
  OGONTZ AND NEDRO AVENUE 19141
  Donald Wittenberg, prin.
Pennypacker ES
  WASHINGTON LANE AND T 19138
  Adrienne Carpenter, prin.
Penrose ES, S 78TH & ESTE AVE 19153
  Francis Salandria, prin.
Pollock ES
  WELSH ROAD N OF HOLME CIR 19152
  Estelle Freeman, prin.
Potter-Thomas ES
  6TH AND CLEARFIELD ST 19133
  Felecita Melendez, prin.
Powell ES, 36TH & POWELTON AVE 19104
  James Otto, prin.
Pratt-Arnold ES
  22ND AND SUSQUEHANNA AVE 19132
  Mary Flynn, prin.
Prince Hall ES
  GODFREY AVENUE AND LIMEL 19141
  Gwendolyn Scott, prin.
Reynolds ES, 24TH & JEFFERSON ST 19121
  Marlene Panek, prin.
Rhawnhurst ES, CASTOR ADN BORBECK 19152
  Zeldan Weisbein, prin.
Rhoads ES 19139 – C. Akers, prin.
Richmond Academics Plus
  ANN & BELGRADE ST 19134 – Eileen Dwell, prin.
Rowen ES, 19TH AND HAINES STREET 19126
  Steven Dash, prin.
Sharswood ES, 2ND & WOLF ST 19148
  Arlene Robin, prin.
Shawmont ES
  SHAWMONT AVENUE & EVA ST 19128
  Frederick Donatucci, prin.
Sheppard ES
  HOWARD AND CAMBRIA STREET 19133
  Joan Poolos, prin.
Sheridan ES, G & ONTARIO ST 19134
  Marshall Gorodetzer, prin.
Smedley ES, BRIDGE & CHARLES ST 19124
  Edward Szymant, prin.
Smith Academics Plus
  19TH AND WHARTON STREETS 19146
  Murray Ginsburg, prin.
Solis-Cohen Academics Plus
  TYSON AND HORROCKS 19149
  Albert Schaaf, prin.
Southwark ES, 9TH & MIFFLIN ST 19148
  Doris Peltzman, prin.
Spring Garden ES
  12TH AND MELON STREET 19123
  (—), prin.

Spruance ES
  LEVICK AND HORROCKS STREET 19149
  Carl Walz, prin.
Stanton ES, 16TH & CUMBERLAND ST 19132
  Mary Lou Diarenzo, prin.
Stanton ES, 17TH AND CHRISTIAN ST 19146
  Jeanne Iezzi, prin.
Stearne ES, HEDGE & UNITY ST 19124
  Gemma Geigert, prin.
Steel ES, WAYNE AVENUE AND BRISTOL 19140
  Dr. Oscar Henkinson, prin.
Sullivan ES, HARBISON AVENUE AND SA 19124
  Herman Bell, prin.
Taggart ES, 4TH & PORTER ST 19148
  Judy Know, prin.
Taylor ES, RANDOLPH & ERIE AVE 19140
  Dr. Martin Eilberg, prin.
Walton ES, 28TH & HUNTINGDON ST 19132
  Jeanette Floyd, prin.
Waring ES, 18TH AND GREEN STREETS 19130
  Paul Somerville, prin.
Washington Academics, 44TH & ASPEN ST 19104
  Harold Trawick, prin.
Washington ES, 5TH & FEDERAL ST 19147
  (—), prin.
Webster ES, 3400 FRANKFORD AVE 19134
  Dr. Barbara Porges, prin.
Welsh ES, 4TH & YORK ST 19133
  Steven Alper, prin.
Whittier ES, 27TH & CLEARFIELD ST 19132
  Linda Gotlieb, prin.
Willard ES, EMERALD & ORLEANS ST 19134
  Dante Lombardi, prin.
Wilson ES
  46TH AND WOODLAND AVENUE 19143
  John Matthews, prin.
Wister ES, WAKEFIELD & BRINGHURS ST 19144
  Barbara Daly, prin.
Wright ES, 28TH AND DAUPHIN STREETS 19132
  Alvin Kressman, prin.
Ziegler ES, SAUL AND COMLY 19149
  Dr. Oswald Giulii, prin.

Springfield Twp. SD IU 23
Supt. – See Oreland
Erdenheim ES, 500 HAWS LN 19118
  Marjorie Summerville, prin.

———

Cedar Grove Christian Academy
  TABOR ROAD & RISING SUN 19120
Chestnut Hill Academy
  50 W WILLOW GROVE AVE 19118
Christ Independant Baptist Academy
  1618 20 WOMRATH ST 19124
Evelyn Graves Christian Academy
  5447 CHESTER AVE 19143
Faith Tabernacle School
  3611-15 N RANDOLPH 19140
Friends Central School
  N 68TH AND CITY AVE 19151
Friends Select School
  17TH & BEN FRANKLIN PKY 19103
Germantown Friends School
  31 W COULTER ST 19144
Girard College School
  GIRARD & CORINTHIAN 19121
Springside School, 8000 CHEROKEE ST 19118
Sr. Clara Muhammad School
  4700 WYALUSING AVE 19131
William Penn Charter School
  3000 W SCHOOL HOUSE LANE 19144
All Saints ES, 4629 E THOMPSON ST 19137
Annunciation ES
  12TH AND WHARTON STS 19147
Ascension of Our Lord ES
  735 E WESTMORELAND ST 19134
Calvary Temple Christian Academy
  3301 S 20TH ST 19145
Cecilian Academy ES
  100 W CAPENTER LN 19119
Christ the King ES
  3205 CHESTERFIELD RD 19114
Epiphany of Our Lord ES
  13TH & JACKSON ST 19148
Frankford Friends ES
  PENN AND ORTHODOX STS 19124
Gesu ES, 1700 W THOMPSON ST 19121
Good Shepherd ES
  66TH ST CHESTER AVE 19142
Greene Street Friends ES, 5511 GREENE ST 19144
Hebrew Academy of N.E. Philadelphia
  9225 OLD BUSTLETON AVE 19115
Holmesburg Baptist Church ES
  7927 FRANKFORD AVE 19136
Holy Child ES, 5218 N BROAD ST 19141
Holy Cross ES, 148 E MOUNT AIRY AVE 19119
Holy Family ES, 240 HERMITAGE ST 19127
Holy Innocents ES, 1312 E BRISTOL ST 19124
Holy Name of Jesus ES
  E BERKS & GAULS ST 19125
Holy Redeemer ES, 915 VINE ST 19107
Holy Spirit ES
  19TH AND SIGR HARTRANFT ST 19145
Immaculate Conception ES, 811 N 8TH ST 19123
Immaculate Heart of Mary ES
  815 CATHEDRAL RD 19128
Immanuel Lutheran School
  COTTMAN AVE & PLMTO 19111
Incarnation Our Lord ES
  425 LINDLEY AVE 19120
King of Peace ES, S 26TH & REED ST 19146
Lehigh Christian Academy
  934 ALBURGER AVE 19115
Lotus Academy, 62 W HARVEY ST 19144

Mater Dolorosa ES, PAUL AND RUAN STS 19124
Maternity BVM ES, 9322 BUSTLETON AVE 19115
Most Blessed Sacerment ES
    56TH AND CHESTER AVE 19143
Most Precious Blood ES
    28TH AND SEDGLEY STS 19121
Mother Divine Grace ES
    2918 E THOMPSON ST 19134
Mt. Airy Christ Day School
    7800 OGONTZ AVE 19150
Nativity BVM ES, BELGRADE & MADISON 19134
Nazareth Academy ES, 4701 GRANT AVE 19114
Norwood Fontbonne Academy
    8891 GERMANTOWN AVE 19118
Our Lady Consolation ES
    PRINCETON AVE & EDMUN 19135
Our Lady Rosary ES, 344 N FELTON ST 19139
Our Lady of Calvary ES, 11023 KIPLING LN 19154
Our Lady of Help Christian ES
    E ALGHY AVE AND CHATHAM 19134
Our Lady of Holy Souls ES
    19TH AND ATLANTIC 19140
Our Lady of Loreto ES, 2412 S 62ND ST 19142
Our Lady of Lourdes ES
    63RD AND LANCASTER AVE 19151
Our Lady of Mt. Carmel ES, 2329 S 3RD ST 19148
Our Lady of Ransom ES
    6740 ROOSEVELT BLVD 19149
Our Lady of Victory ES
    54TH AND SUMMER STS 19139
Our Mother Consolation ES
    17 E CHESTNUT HILL AVE 19118
Our Mother of Sorrow ES, 1020 N 48TH ST 19131
Presentation BVM ES, 230 HAVERFORD AVE 19151
Redeemer Lutheran ES, 3212 RYAN AVE 19136
Resurrection ES, 2020 SHELMIRE SCHOOL 19152
Sacred Heart ES, THIRD & REED STS 19147
Sanctuary Christian Academy
    5923-41 WALNUT ST 19139
Spruce Hill Christian ES
    4115 BALTIMORE AVE 19104
St. Adalbert ES, 3236 EDGEMONT ST 19134
St. Aloysius, 1624 S 26TH ST 19145
St. Ambrose, 405 E ROOSEVELT BLVD 19120
St. Anne ES, 2343 TUCKER AVE 19125
St. Anselm ES, 12670 DUNKS FERRY RD 19154
St. Athanslius Immaculate Conception ES
    7105 LIMEKLIN PIKE 19138
St. Barbara ES, 5339 LEBANON AVE 19131
St. Barnabas ES, 6332 BUIST AVE 19142
St. Bartholomew ES
    JACKSON & SANGER ST 19124
St. Benedict ES
    MEDARY AVENUE AND OPAL ST 19141
St. Bernard ES, 7340 JACKSON ST 19136
St. Bonaventure ES
    2834 N HUTCHINSON ST 19133
St. Boniface ES, 142 W DIAMOND ST 19122
St. Bridgets ES, 3636 STANTON ST 19129
St. Callistus ES
    68TH ADN LANSDOWNE AVE 19151
St. Carthage ES, 6225 CEDAR AVE 19143
St. Casimir ES, 338 WHARTON ST 19147
St. Cecilia ES, 525 RHAWN ST 19111
St. Charles Borromeo ES
    2019 MONTROSE ST 19146
St. Christopher ES, 13301 PROCTOR RD 19116
St. Clement-Ireneus ES
    72ND AND PASCHALL AVE 19142
St. Columbia ES, 2320 W LEHIGH AVE 19132
St. Dominic ES, 8510 FRANKFORD AVE 19136
St. Donato ES, 405 N 65TH ST 19151
St. Edmond ES, 23RD AND MIFFLIN STS 19145
St. Edward's ES, 709 W YORK ST 19133
St. Elizabeth ES
    23RD AND MONTGOMERY S 19121
St. Frances DeSales ES, 912 S 47TH ST 19143
St. Frances Xavier ES
    24TH AND WALLACE 19130
St. Gabriel ES, 2916 DICKINSON ST 19146
St. George ES, 2700 E VENANGO ST 19134
St. Helena ES, 6101 N 5TH ST 19120
St. Henry ES, 5TH & CAYUGA ST 19140
St. Hugh ES, 3533 N MASCHER ST 19140
St. Ignatius Loyola ES, 640 N 43RD ST 19104
St. Jerome ES
    HOLME AND STAMFORD ST 19136
St. Joan of Arc ES, 3550 FRANKFORD AVE 19134
St. John Cantius ES, 4435 ALMOND ST 19137
St. John the Baptist ES, 119 RECTOR ST 19127
St. Josaphat ES, 6932 DITMAN ST 19135
St. Josaphat ES, 137 GRAPE ST 19127
St. Joschim ES, PENN AND CHURCH STS 19124
St. Katherine Siena ES
    9720 FRANKFORD AVE 19114
St. Laurentius ES, 1612 E BERKS ST 19125
St. Leo's ES, KEYSTONE & BENNER ST 19135
St. Lucy's ES, 146 GREEN LN 19127
St. Malachy ES, 1415 N 11TH ST 19122
St. Martha ES, 11321 ACADEMY RD 19154
St. Martin De Porres ES, 49 W LOGAN ST 19144
St. Martin of Tours ES
    5450 ROOSEVELT BLVD 19124
St. Mary Assumption ES
    171 CONARROE ST 19127
St. Mary Czestochowa ES
    5900 ELMWOOD AVE 19143
St. Mary Interparoch ES
    5TH & LOCUST ST 19106
St. Matthew ES, 3040 COTTMAN AVE 19149
St. Micheal ES, 1429 N 2ND ST 19122
St. Monica ES, 1720 W RITNER ST 19145
St. Nicholas ES, 9TH AND PEIRCE STS 19130
St. Paul ES, 916 CHRISTIAN ST 19147

St. Peter the Apostle ES, 1009 N 5TH ST 19123
St. Peter's ES, 319 LOMBARD ST 19147
St. Raymond ES, 7940 WILLIAMS AVE 19150
St. Richard ES, 1827 POLLOCK ST 19145
St. Rita's ES, CARLISLE AND ELLSWORT 19146
St. Rose of Lima ES
    1516 N WANAMAKER ST 19131
St. Stephen ES, BROAD AND BUTLER STS 19140
St. Theresa of Child Jesus ES
    UPSAL & CHEW AVE 19119
St. Thomas Aquinas ES
    18TH & MORRIS STS 19145
St. Timothy ES, 3033 LEVICK ST 19149
St. Veronica ES, 3521 N 6TH ST 19140
St. William ES, 6238 RISING SUN AVE 19111
Stella Maris ES, 814 BIGLER ST 19148
The Philadelphia ES, 2501 LOMBARD ST 19146
The YMCA Academy
    4601 HAVERFORD AVE 19139
Timothy Academy, 2637 N 4TH ST 19133
Transfiguration ES, 5501 CEDAR AVE 19143
Visitation ES, B ST AND LEHIGH AVE 19125
West Oak Lane Christian Academy
    7401 LIMEKILN PIKE 19138

Philipsburg, Centre Co., Pop. Code 5
Philipsburg-Osceola Area SD IU 10
Sch. Sys. Enr. Code 5
Supt. – Dr. Joseph Mainello, 200 SHORT ST 16866
North Lincoln Hill ES, SHORT STREET 16866
    Lawrence Salvetto, prin.
ES, NINTH STREET 16866
    Chester Peterson, prin.
Other Schools – See Osceola Mills, Wallaceton

Phoenixville, Chester Co., Pop. Code 7
Phoenixville Area SD IU 24
Sch. Sys. Enr. Code 5
Supt. – Dr. Robert Murray, 1120 GAY ST 19460
Barkley ES, 320 2ND AVE 19460
    Joseph Dougherty, prin.
East Pikeland ES, RURAL ROUTE 02 19460
    Demetra Haines, prin.
Schuylkill, 330 S WHITEHORSE RD 19460
    Frank Orlando, prin.
Second Avenue ES, 69 2ND AVE 19460
    Joseph Dougherty, prin.
_____

Our Lady Fatima School Secane
    10 FATIMA DR 19460
Phoenixville Catholic ES
    3RD AND BUTTONWOOD ST 19460

Picture Rocks, Lycoming Co., Pop. Code 3
East Lycoming SD IU 17
Supt. – See Hughesville
Ferrell ES, LAUREL ST 17762
    Steven Moyer, prin.

Pine Forge, Berks Co.
Boyertown Area SD IU 14
Supt. – See Boyertown
New Hanover ES
    RURAL ROUTE 03 BOX 570 19548
    Carl Yescavage, prin.
ES, P O BOX 570 19548
    Kermit Bartholomew, prin.

Pine Grove, Schuylkill Co., Pop. Code 4
Pine Grove Area SD IU 29
Sch. Sys. Enr. Code 4
Supt. – Edward Brewer, 2ND & SCHOOL ST 17963
Pine Grove Area MS, SCHOOL ST 17963
    Edward Kimmel, prin.
ES, SCHOOL ST 17963 – Joyce Romberger, prin.
Other Schools – See Tremont

Pine Grove Mills, Centre Co.
State College Area SD IU 10
Supt. – See State College
Ferguson Township ES, 215 W MAIN ST 16868
    William Keenan, prin.

Pipersville, Bucks Co.
Palisades SD IU 22
Supt. – See Kintnersville
Tinicum ES, RURAL ROUTE 01 18947
    Eileen Wessel, prin.

Pitcairn, Allegheny Co., Pop. Code 5
Gateway SD IU 3
Supt. – See Monroeville
Pitcairn Building 3 ES, 435 AGATHA ST 15140
    Alex Balla, prin.

Pittsburgh, Allegheny Co., Pop. Code 10
Avonworth SD IU 3
Sch. Sys. Enr. Code 4
Supt. – Dr. Bruno Raso, 234 DICKSON AVE 15202
Avon MS, 200 DICKSON AVE 15202
    Ronald McClymonds, prin.
Ohio Township ES, 1320 ROOSEVELT RD 15237
    Ronald McClymonds, prin.

Baldwin-Whitehall SD IU 3
Sch. Sys. Enr. Code 5
Supt. – Dr. Charles Faust
    4900 CURRY ROAD 15236
Harrison JHS, 129 WINDVALE DRIVE 15236
    James Bruni, prin.
McAnnulty ES, 5151 MCANULTY RD 15236
    Ronald Lenzi, prin.
Paynter ES, 3454 PLEASANTVUE DR 15227
    Wayne Paulos, prin.
Whitehall ES, 4900 CURRY RD 15236
    Albert Pollak, prin.

Bethel Park SD IU 3
Supt. – See Bethel Park
Lincoln ES, 1524 HAMILTON RD 15234
    James Willison, prin.

Brentwood Borough SD IU 3
Sch. Sys. Enr. Code 4
Supt. – Dr. Eugene Bolt
    3601 BROWNSVILLE ROAD 15227
Other Schools – See Brentwood

Chartiers Valley SD IU 3
Sch. Sys. Enr. Code 5
Supt. – P. Boggio
    2030 SWALLOW HILL ROAD 15220
Chartiers Valley MS
    2030 SWALLOW HILL ROAD 15220
    Edward Dlugos, prin.
Foxcroft ES, 808 HOPE STREET EXIT 15220
    William Rodgers, prin.
Other Schools – See Bridgeville, Carnegie

Fox Chapel Area SD IU 3
Sch. Sys. Enr. Code 5
Supt. – Dr. Daniel Freeman
    611 FIELD CLUB ROAD 15238
Dorseyville JHS, 550 SAXONBURG ROAD 15238
    Charles Lodge, prin.
Fairview ES, 710 DORSEYVILLE RD 15238
    Robert Condron, prin.
Hartwood ES, 548 SAXONBURG RD 15238
    Wanda Dickson, prin.
Kerr ES, 341 KITTANNING PIKE 15215
    Jon Gorsin, prin.
O'Hara ES, 115 CABIN LN 15238
    Harry Vidmar, prin.

Keystone Oaks SD IU 3
Sch. Sys. Enr. Code 5
Supt. – Dr. Chester Kent
    1000 KELTON AVE 15216
Neff MS, 3200 ANNAPOLIS AVE 15216
    Barbara Doak, prin.
Aiken ES, 881 GREENTREE RD 15220
    F. Beyer, prin.
Hillsdale ES, 1444 HILLSDALE AVE 15216
    James Daley, prin.
Kelton ES, 1098 KELTON AVE 15216
    Robert Pletcher, prin.
Myrtle MS, 3724 MYRTLE AVE 15234
    James Taylor, prin.
Vernridge ES, 850 BALDWIN AVE 15234
    James Taylor, prin.

Montour Sd IU 3
Supt. – See Coraopolis
Ingram ES, 40 VANCOUVER ST 15205
    John Mosimann, prin.

Mt. Lebanon SD IU 3
Sch. Sys. Enr. Code 6
Supt. – Allan Blacka, 7 HORSMAN DR 15228
Mt. Lebanon JHS
    11 CASTLE SHANNON BLVD 15228
    John Wagner, prin.
Foster ES, 700 VERMONT AVE 15234
    Barbara Float, prin.
Hoover ES, 37 ROBB HOLLOW RD 15243
    Shirley Davidson, prin.
Howe ES, 400 BROADMOOR AVE 15228
    Richard Flick, prin.
Jefferson ES, 11 MOFFETT ST 15243
    Larry Snyder, prin.
Lincoln ES, 2 RALSTON PL 15216
    Donald Dunbar, prin.
Markham ES, 165 CRESCENT DR 15228
    Pamela Boyd, prin.
Washington ES, 735 WASHINGTON RD 15228
    Leo Crawford, prin.

North Allegheny SD IU 3
Sch. Sys. Enr. Code 6
Supt. – Lawrence Bozzomo
    200 HILLVUE LANE 15237
Carson MS, 200 HILLVUE LANE 15237
    Willard Brown, prin.
Ingomar ES, INGOMAR HEIGHTS ROAD 15237
    Steve Duchi, prin.
Espe ES, 8711 OLD PERRY HWY 15237
    Linda Barnhart, prin.
McKnight ES, 500 CUMBERLAND RD 15237
    Stanley Zimmerman, prin.
Peebles ES, 8625 PEEBLES RD 15237
    Steve Morris, prin.
Other Schools – See Allison Park, Bradfordwoods,
    Ingomar, Sewickley

North Hills SD IU 3
Sch. Sys. Enr. Code 5
Supt. – James Higgins
    200 MCINTYRE ROAD 15237
Highcliff ES, 156 PEONY AVE 15229
    John Norris, prin.
Northway ES, 495 BROWNS LN 15237
    Milton Moratis, prin.
Perrysville ES, 950 PERRY HWY 15237
    Milton Moratis, prin.
Ross ES, 90 HOUSTON RD 15237
    Charles Hannan, prin.
Seville ES, 100 ENGER AVE 15214
    John Norris, prin.
West View ES, 498 PERRY HWY 15229
    Robert Irvin, prin.

Northgate SD IU 3
Sch. Sys. Enr. Code 4
Supt. – James Manley, 90 GRANT AVE 15202
Avalon ES, 721 CALIFORNIA AVE 15202
  Dr. Paul Kirsch, prin.
Lincoln ES, 435 LINCOLN AVE 15202
  Paul Kirsch, prin.

Penn Hills SD IU 3
Sch. Sys. Enr. Code 6
Supt. – Dr. Joseph Saeli
  12200 GARLAND DRIVE 15235
Dible ES, 1079 JEFFERSON RD 15235
  John Slagle, prin.
Hebron ES, 102 DUFF RD 15235
  Dr. Edward Bitler, prin.
Washington ES, 2501 MAIN ST 15235
  Dr. Jesse Jones, prin.
Other Schools – See Verona

Pittsburgh CSD IU 2
Sch. Sys. Enr. Code 8
Supt. – R. Wallace, 341 S BELLEFIELD AVE 15213
Allegheny MS, 810 ARCH ST 15212
  Robert Pipkin, prin.
Arsenal MS, 40TH AND BUTLER ST 15201
  Ruthane Reginella, prin.
Columbus Traditional Academy
  1805 BUENA VISTA ST 15212 – Ted Soens, prin.
Frick MS, 107 THACKERAY ST 15213
  Ernestine Reed, prin.
Gladstone MS, 327 HAZELWOOD AVE 15207
  Theodore Vasser, prin.
Greenway MS, 1400 CRUCIBLE ST 15205
  Lloyd Briscoe, prin.
Knoxville MS, 324 CHARLES ST 15210
  William Nicholson, prin.
Milliones MS, 3117 CENTRE AVE 15219
  Delphina Briscoe, prin.
Prospect MS, 3 COWAN ST 15211
  Carl Jurkiewicz, prin.
Reizenstein MS, 129 DENNISTON AVE 15206
  Roberta Feldman, prin.
Rogers Center for Performing Arts
  5525 COLUMBO ST 15206 – Neal Huguley, prin.
Shiller Classical Academy
  1018 PERALTA ST 15212 – Gussie Johnson, prin.
Sterrett Classical Academy
  7110 REYNOLDS ST 15208 – Carl Berdnik, prin.
Washington Polytech Academy
  169 40TH ST 15201 – James Dickson, prin.
Arlington ES, 2500 JONQUIL WAY 15210
  Jacob Minsinger, prin.
Beechwood ES, 810 ROCKLAND AVENUE 15216
  Patricia Kupec, prin.
Belmar ES, 7109 HERMITAGE ST 15208
  Samuel Howard, prin.
Beltzhoover ES, 320 CEDARHURST ST 15210
  Joseph Puzio, prin.
Bon Air ES, 252 FORDYCE ST 15210
  Jerry Minsinger, prin.
Brookline ES, 500 WOODBOURNE AVE 15226
  Bette Mucha, prin.
Burgwin ES, 5401 GLENWOOD AVE 15207
  Robert Scherer, prin.
Carmalt ES, 1583 BREINING ST 15226
  Geroge Witkovich, prin.
Chartiers ES, 3799 CHARTIERS AVE 15204
  Willie Ellard, prin.
Chatham ES, 227 BONVUE ST 15214
  Lester Young, prin.
Clayton ES, 1901 CLAYTON ST 15214
  Johnny Jiggetts, prin.
Colfax ES, 2332 BEECHWOOD BLVD 15217
  Patsy Nysewander, prin.
Concord ES
  BROWNVILLE ROAD & BISCAYNE 15210
  Frank Casne, prin.
Crescent ES, 8080 BENNETT ST 15221
  Gayle Griffin, prin.
Dilworth International Studys
  6200 STANTON AVE 15206 – Edward Kress, prin.
East Hills ES, 2150 EAST HILLS DR 15221
  Richard Nicklos, prin.
Fort Pitt ES, 5101 HILLCREST ST 15224
  Joseph Hightower, prin.
Friendship ES, 201 GRAHAM 15206
  James Boyd, prin.
Fulton ES, 5799 HAMPTON ST 15206
  Paula Howard, prin.
Grandview ES, 845 MCLAIN ST 15210
  Richard Sternberg, prin.
Greenfield ES, 1 ALGER STREET 15207
  William Brim, prin.
Homewood Montessori Magnet
  7100 HAMILTON AVE 15208
  Donald Pederson, prin.
King ES, 50 MONTGOMERY PL 15212
  Patricia Fisher, prin.
Lemington ES, 7061 LEMINGTON AVE 15206
  Rachel Jones, prin.
Liberty ES, 601 FILBERT ST 15232
  Patricia Reidbord, prin.
Lincoln ES, 328 LINCOLN AVE 15206
  Erma Williams, prin.
Linden ES, 725 S LINDEN AVE 15208
  James Hrabovsky, prin.
Madison ES, 3401 MILWAUKEE ST 15219
  Vivian Williams, prin.
Manchester ES, 1612 MANHATTAN ST 15233
  Kenneth Barbour, prin.
Mann ES, 2819 SHADELAND AVE 15212
  Lonnie Folino, prin.

McKelvy ES, 2055 BEDFORD AVE 15219
  Roberta Cartus, prin.
Mifflin ES, 1290 MIFFLIN RD 15207
  Thomas Mattox, prin.
Miller ES, 61 REED ST 15219
  Henry Stephens, prin.
Minadeo ES, 6502 LILAC ST 15217
  Frank Smizik, prin.
Morrow ES, 1611 DAVIS AVE 15212
  James Chapas, prin.
Murray ES, 800 RECTENWALD STREET 15210
  James Robinson, prin.
Northview Heights ES
  310 MOUNT PLEASANT RD 15214
  Lawrence Nee, prin.
Overbrook ES, 2140 SAW MILL RUN 15210
  Dr. Joseph Michaels, prin.
Phillips ES, 1901 SARAH ST 15203
  Elmer Parks, prin.
Regent Square ES
  HENRIETTA MILTON STREET 15218
  Janet Thompson, prin.
Roosevelt ES, 200 THE BOULEVARD 15210
  Jerry Minsinger, prin.
Schaeffer Traditional A
  1235 CLAIRHAVEN ST 15205 – Isa Leita, prin.
Sheraden ES, 3128 ALLENDALE ST 15204
  Maxine Klimasara, prin.
Spring Garden ES
  1501 SPRING GARDEN AVE 15212
  John Watson, prin.
Stevens ES, 822 CRUCIBLE ST 15220
  Donald O'Rourke, prin.
Sunnyside ES, 4799 STANTON AVE 15201
  Paul Pollock, prin.
Vann ES, 631 WATT ST 15219
  Doris Brevard, prin.
Weil ES, 2250 CENTRE AVE 15219
  Donus Crawford, prin.
Westwood ES, 508 SHADYHILL RD 15205
  Janet Bell, prin.
Whittier ES, 150 MERIDAN ST 15211
  Natalie Kunkel, prin.

Plum Borough SD IU 3
Sch. Sys. Enr. Code 5
Supt. – John Cummings
  200 SCHOOL ROAD 15239
Center ES, 201 CENTER-NEW TEXAS RD 15239
  Nick Borrelli, prin.
Holiday Park ES, 4795 HAVANA DR 15239
  Theodore Peshkopia, prin.
Regency Park ES, 606 MILLERS LN 15239
  Louis Lazzaro, prin.
Renton ES, 1480 RENTON RD 15239
  Lawrence Popovich, prin.
Stevenson ES, 313 HOLIDAY PARK DR 15239
  Dr. Charlotte Fontana, prin.

Shaler Area SD IU 3
Supt. – See Glenshaw
Marzolf Road ES
  101 MARZOLF ROAD EXIT 15209
  Walter Engle, prin.
Reserve ES, 2107 LONSDALE ST 15212
  Michael Nealon, prin.

South Park SD IU 3
Supt. – See Library
Broughton ES, 935 SCHANG RD 15236
  Lawrence Muir, prin.

Upper St. Clair SD IU 3
Supt. – See Upper Saint Clair
Baker ES, 2300 MORTON RD 15241
  John Gido, prin.
Boyce MS, 1500 BOYCE RD 15241
  Robert Furman, prin.
Eisenhower ES, 100 WARWICK DR 15241
  Robert Broggi, prin.
Streams ES, 1560 ASHLAWN DR 15241
  Patricia Dunkis, prin.

West Jefferson Hills SD IU 3
Sch. Sys. Enr. Code 5
Supt. – Dr. Richard St. Clair
  P O BOX 18019 15236
Pleasant Hills MS
  NTNL DR & OLD CLAIRTON ROAD 15236
  Joseph Bayto, prin.
McClellan ES, MCCLELLAN DRIVE 15236
  Alan Cook, prin.
Pleasant Hills ES, 5 AUDREY DR 15236
  John Ward,Jr., prin.
Other Schools – See Clairton

Woodland Hills SD IU 3
Sch. Sys. Enr. Code 6
Supt. – John Dunlap
  4240 GREENSBURG PIKE 15221
Dickson IS, SCHOYER AVENUE 15218
  James Hay, prin.
Edgewood PS, 241 MAPLE AVE 15218
  Thomas Guerrieri, prin.
Shaffer PS, 37 GARDEN TERRACE 15221
  Patricia Quinn, prin.
Wilkins PS, 362 CHURCHILL ROAD 15235
  Richard Carretta, prin.
Other Schools – See North Braddock, Rankin

───────────────

Ellis School, 6425 5TH AVE 15206
Hillel Academy of Pittsburg
  5685 BEACON ST 15217
North Hills Christian School
  P O BOX 11161 15237

Shady Side Academy
  423 FOX CHAPEL ROAD 15238
Trinity Christian School
  9100 FRANKSTOWN ROAD 15235
Winchester Thurston School
  555 MOREWOOD AVE 15213
Yeshiva Achei Tmimim School
  2100 WIGHTMAN ST 15217
All Saints ES, 19 DEWEY ST 15223
Carlow College Campus School
  3333 5TH AVE 15213
Fox Chapel Country Day School
  620 SQUAW RUN RD E 15238
Holy Innocents ES, 3021 LANDIS ST 15204
Holy Rosary ES, 7120 KELLY ST 15208
Holy Trinity ES, P O BOX 15567 15244
Immaculate Conception ES
  321 EDMOND ST 15224
Immaculate Heart of Mary ES
  3029 PAULOWNA ST 15219
Lawrenceville Catholic School
  223 37TH ST 15201
Most Holy Name ES, 1515 TINSBURY ST 15212
Nativity ES, 5811 CURRY RD 15236
Nativity of Our Lord ES
  4072 FRANKLIN RD 15214
Our Lady of Loreto ES, 1901 PIONEER AVE 15226
Our Lady of Grace ES
  1734 BOWER HILL RD 15243
Resurrection ES, 1100 CREEDMORE AVE 15226
Sacred Heart ES, 325 EMERSON ST 15206
Sacred Heart ES, 125 NORTH AVE 15202
South Side Catholic School
  155 S 15TH STREET 15203
St. Agnes ES, 120 ROBINSON ST 15213
St. Albert the Great ES
  3151 CHURCHVIEW AVE 15227
St. Aloyius ES, 3614 MOUNT TROY RD 15212
St. Ann ES, 413 EVERGREEN AVE 15209
St. Anselm ES, 7436 MCCLURE AVE 15218
St. Anthony's ES, 100 HOWARD ST 15209
St. Athanasuis ES, 2 WENTWORTH AVE 15229
St. Bartholomew ES, 111 ERGARDT DR 15235
St. Basil ES, 1803 CONCORDIA ST 15210
St. Bede ES, 6920 EDGERTON AVE 15208
St. Benedict of Moor ES
  2900 BEDFORD AVE 15219
St. Bernard ES, 401 WASHINGTON RD 15216
St. Canice ES, 201 ROCHELLE ST 15210
St. Catherine Siena ES
  1915 BROADWAY AVE 15216
St. Cyril of Alexandria ES
  3854 BRIGHTON RD 15212
St. Edmunds Academy
  5705 DARLINGTON RD 15217
St. Elizabeth ES, GROVE PL 15236
St. Francis Xavier School
  3250 CALIFORNIA AVE 15212
St. Gabriel School, 5200 GREENRIDGE DR 15236
St. George ES, 843 CLIMAX ST 15210
St. Henry ES, 2429 CHARCOT ST 15210
St. James ES, S MAIN AND SANCTUS ST 15220
St. James ES, 721 REBECCA AVE 15221
St. John the Baptist ES
  418 UNITY CENTER RD 15239
St. Joseph ES, 323 PEARL ST 15224
St. Joseph ES, 434 ORMSBY AVE 15210
St. Kieran ES, 5326 CARNEGIE ST 15201
St. Leo ES, 1215 SCHIMMER ST 15212
St. Louise De Marillac ES
  310 MCMURRAY RD 15241
St. Margaret ES, 915 ALICE ST 15220
St. Martin ES, 1000 LOGUE ST 15220
St. Mary ES, 211 GARNIER ST 15215
St. Mary of the Mount ES, 115 BIGHAM ST 15211
St. Matthew Lutheran School
  600 E NORTH AVE 15212
St. Maurice ES, 2001 ARDMORE BLVD 15221
St. Norbert ES 15234
St. Paul Cathedral ES, 136 N CRAIG ST 15213
St. Peter ES, 711 W COMMONS 15212
St. Philip ES, 52 W CRAFTON AVE 15205
St. Philomena ES, 6424 FORWARD AVE 15217
St. Pius X ES, 2690 WADDINGTON AVE 15226
St. Raphael ES, 1154 CHISLETT ST 15206
St. Rosalia ES, 411 GREENFIELD AVE 15207
St. Scholastica ES, 205 BRILLIANT AVE 15215
St. Sebastian ES, 307 SIEBERT RD 15237
St. Stephen ES, 134 E ELIZABETH ST 15207
St. Sylvester ES, 30 W WILLOCK RD 15227
St. Teresa ES, 800 AVILA CT 15237
St. Thomas More ES, 134 FORT COUCH RD 15241
St. Wendelin ES, 2720 CUST AVE 15227
St. Winifred ES, 550 SLEEPY HOLLOW RD 15228
Sts. Simon Jude ES, 1625 GREENTREE RD 15220
The Falk School, UNIV OF PITT 15261

Pittsfield, Warren Co.
Warren County SD IU 5
Supt. – See Warren
  ES, P O BOX 200 16340 – Gordon Sutton, prin.

Pittston, Luzerne Co., Pop. Code 6
Pittston Area SD IU 18
Sch. Sys. Enr. Code 5
Supt. – Gerald Musto, 5 STOUT ST 18640
Pittston Area MS, NEW ST 18640
  Constantino Turco, prin.
Lincoln ES, DEFOE STREET 18640
  John DeGennari, prin.
Pittston City ES, NEW ST 18640
  James Giordina, prin.

Wyoming Area SD IU 18
Supt. – See Exeter

Harding ES, RURAL ROUTE 01 18643
 Sarah Dymond, prin.

Sacred Heart of Jesus ES
 219 LACKAWANNA AVE 18641
St. John the Baptist ES, 12 WILLIAM ST 18640
St. Mary's Assumption ES, 41 CARROLL ST 18640
Wyoming Area Catholic ES
 1690 WYOMING AVE 18643

Plains, Luzerne Co., Pop. Code 6
Wilkes-Barre Area SD IU 18
Supt. — See Wilkes-Barre
Maffett Street ES, 125 MAFFETT ST 18705
 MaryAnne Toole, prin.

Pleasant Gap, Venango Co., Pop. Code 4
Bellefonte Area SD IU 10
Supt. — See Bellefonte
ES, 230 S MAIN ST 16823 — H. Mencer, prin.

Pleasantville, Venango Co., Pop. Code 4
Titusville Area SD IU 6
Supt. — See Titusville
ES, 374 N MAIN ST 16341 — Dennis Ledebur, prin.

Plumsteadville, Bucks Co.

Plumstead Christian School, P O BOX 216 18949

Plymouth, Luzerne Co., Pop. Code 6
Wyoming Valley West SD IU 18
Supt. — See Kingston
Main Street ES, MAIN STREET 18651
 William Bosso, prin.

Ebenezer Faith Christian School
 P O BOX 99 18651
Holy Child ES, 103 WILLOW ST 18651

Plymouth Meeting, Montgomery Co., Pop. Code 5
Colonial SD IU 23
Sch. Sys. Enr. Code 4
Supt. — Richard Creasey
 230 FLOURTOWN ROAD 19462
Colonial ES, 230 FLOURTOWN RD 19462
 William Wilson, prin.
Plymouth ES, 542 PLYMOUTH RD 19462
 Sheryl Solow, prin.
Other Schools — See Conshohocken, Lafayette Hill,
 Norristown

Plymouth Meeting Fr. ES
 GERMANTOWN AND BUTLER 19462

Pocono Pines, Monroe Co.
Pocono Mountain SD IU 20
Supt. — See Swiftwater
Tobyhanna ES 18350 — Edward Vogue, prin.

Point Marion, Fayette Co., Pop. Code 4
Albert Galltn Area SD IU 1
Supt. — See Uniontown
Friendship Hill ES, RURAL ROUTE 01 15474
 Judith Psenicska, prin.
ES, UNION STREET 15474 — Paul Boord, prin.

Polk, Venango Co., Pop. Code 4
Franklin Area SD IU 6
Supt. — See Franklin
ES, CHURCH STREET EXTENTION 16342
 Robert Scheer, prin.

Portage, Cambria Co., Pop. Code 5
Portage Area SD IU 8
Sch. Sys. Enr. Code 5
Supt. — James Hepner, 750 MEADE ST 15946
Portage Area ES, 700 MEADE STREET 15946
 Andrew Kittell, prin.
Portage Area MS, 700 MEADE ST 15946
 Andrew Kittel, prin.

St. Joseph ES, 612 PROSPECT ST 15946

Port Allegany, McKean Co., Pop. Code 5
Port Allegany SD IU 9
Sch. Sys. Enr. Code 5
Supt. — Ronald Ungerer, 200 OAK ST 16743
ES, CLYDE LYNCH DR 16743
 Dr. James Holt, prin.

Port Carbon, Schuylkill Co., Pop. Code 5

St. Stephen's ES, 214 VALLEY ST 17965

Portersville, Butler Co., Pop. Code 2
Slippery Rock Area SD IU 4
Supt. — See Slippery Rock
Muddy Creek-Portersville ES, ROUTE 488 16051
 Donald Downing, prin.

Portersville Church ES 16051

Port Matilda, Centre Co., Pop. Code 3
Bald Eagle Area SD IU 10
Supt. — See Wingate
ES 16870 — Marsha Fisk, prin.

State College Area SD IU 10
Supt. — See State College
Matternville ES
 RURAL ROUTE 01 BOX 354 16870
 Paul Solley, prin.

Port Royal, Juniata Co., Pop. Code 3
Juniata County SD IU 11
Supt. — See Mifflintown

Tuscarora Valley ES, 401 8TH ST 17082
 Stephen Bahorik, prin.

Port Trevorton, Snyder Co.
Selinsgrove Area SD IU 16
Supt. — See Selinsgrove
Champman-Union ES
 RURAL ROUTE 01 BOX 615 17864
 Maureen Wagner, prin.

Pottstown, Montgomery Co., Pop. Code 7
Owen J. Roberts SD IU 24
Sch. Sys. Enr. Code 5
Supt. — Roy Claypool, RURAL ROUTE 01 19464
Roberts MS, RURAL ROUTE 01 19464
 Frank Scalise, prin.
East Coventry MS, SANATOGA ROAD RD 1 19464
 Kenneth Swart, prin.
French Creek Valley ES, ROUTE 23 RD 2 19464
 Joseph Clark, prin.
North Coventry ES, 873 S HANOVER ST 19464
 Raymond Gualtieri, prin.
Other Schools — See Elverson, Spring City

Pottsgrove SD IU 23
Sch. Sys. Enr. Code 5
Supt. — Dr. Alvin Coleman
 1301 KAUFFMAN ROAD 19464
Pottsgrove IS, 1329 BUCHERT ROAD 19464
 J. Benton McCue, prin.
Ringing Rocks ES, 1401 KAUFFMAN RD 19464
 Stanley Terzopolos, prin.
Other Schools — See Sanatoga, Stowe

Pottstown SD IU 23
Sch. Sys. Enr. Code 5
Supt. — Dr. Ray Feick, BEACH & PENN STS 19464
JHS, FRANKLIN & EAST STS 19464
 William Smith, prin.
Barth ES, WALNUT AND RYAN STREETS 19464
 Thomas Henry, prin.
Edgewood ES
 MORRIS AND MINTZER STREET 19464
 William Bartman, prin.
Franklin ES, 970 N FRANKLIN ST 19464
 Fred Brown, prin.
Lincoln ES, EIGHTH AND YORK STREETS 19464
 Gaylord Conquest, prin.
Rupert ES
 SOUTH AND MT. VERNON STREET 19464
 Lemmon Stevenson, prin.

St. Aloysius ES, 3RD AND HANOVER STS 19464
St. Peter's ES, 1126 SOUTH ST 19464
Wyndcroft ES, 401 ROSEDALE DR 19464

Pottsville, Schuylkill Co., Pop. Code 7
Minersville Area SD IU 29
Sch. Sys. Enr. Code 5
Supt. — M. Brady, RURAL ROUTE 01 17901
Liewellyn ES, RURAL ROUTE 01 BOX 1259 17901
 Lawrence Palko, prin.
Minersville Area ES
 RURAL ROUTE 01 BOX 1259 17901
 Lawrence Palko, prin.

Pottsville Area SD IU 29
Sch. Sys. Enr. Code 5
Supt. — William Davidson
 1501 LAUREL BLVD 17901
Lengel MS, 1541 W LAUREL BLVD 17901
 John Keating, prin.
Clarke ES, 16TH MT HOPE AVENUE 17901
 Patricia Pacenta, prin.

All Saints Catholic ES
 7TH ST AND HOWARD AVE 17901

Primos-Secane, Delaware Co., Pop. Code 4

St. Eugene ES, 100 OAK LANE 19018

Prospect, Butler Co., Pop. Code 4
Slippery Rock Area SD IU 4
Supt. — See Slippery Rock
Prospect Boro ES 16052 — Donald Downing, prin.

Prospect Park, Delaware Co., Pop. Code 6
Interboro SD IU 25
Sch. Sys. Enr. Code 5
Supt. — Edmond Sacchetti
 9TH & WASHINGTON AVE 19076
ES, 10TH AND PENNA AVE 19076
 Jamie Nachman, prin.
Other Schools — See Essington, Glenolden, Norwood

Pulaski, Lawrence Co., Pop. Code 4
Wilmington Area SD IU 4
Supt. — See New Wilmington
New Bedford ES, RURAL ROUTE 01 16143
 Edward Pandoiti, prin.
MS, RURAL ROUTE 01 16143
 Edward Pandoiti, prin.

Punxsutawney, Jefferson Co., Pop. Code 6
Punxsutawney Area SD IU 6
Sch. Sys. Enr. Code 5
Supt. — S. Willar, P O BOX 478 15767
Punxsutawney Area JHS
 200 N JEFFERSON ST 15767
 Anthony Parise, prin.
Bell Township ES, RURAL ROUTE 02 15767
 Elizabeth Depp, prin.
Jenks Hill ES, 200 JENKS AVE 15767
 Ernest Huey, prin.
Longview ES, RURAL ROUTE 01 15767
 Richard Craffiusii, prin.

Mapleview ES, RURAL ROUTE 04 15767
 Michael McIntyre, prin.
West End ES, 221 CENTER ST 15767
 J. Frantz, prin.
Wilson ES, EAST MAHONING STREET 15767
 Robert Barone, prin.
Other Schools — See Anita, Big Run, Glen Campbell

Sts. Cosmas & Damian ES
 615 CHESTNUT ST 15767

Quakertown, Bucks Co., Pop. Code 6
Palisades SD IU 22
Supt. — See Kintnersville
Springfield ES
 PLEASANT VALLEY STAR ROAD 18951
 Frank Kuebler, prin.

Quakertown Comm. SD IU 22
Sch. Sys. Enr. Code 5
Supt. — George Taylor, 600 PARK AVE 18951
Haycock ES, RURAL ROUTE 04 18951
 Barbara Scott, prin.
Neidig ES, 201 N PENROSE ST 18951
 Barbara Scott, prin.
Pfaff ES, RURAL ROUTE 02 18951
 Dr. Leslie Fetterman, prin.
ES, 123 S 7TH ST 18951
 James Moczydlowski, prin.
Richland ES, 500 FAIRVIEW AVE 18951
 Ronald Freed, prin.
Tohickon Valley ES
 2082 OLD BETHLEHEM PK 18951
 Harry Morgan, prin.

Quakertown Church Day School
 143 ROCKY RIDGE RD 18951
St. Isidore ES, 603 W BROAD ST 18951

Quarryville, Lancaster Co., Pop. Code 4
Solanco SD IU 13
Sch. Sys. Enr. Code 5
Supt. — Dr. Elizabeth Logna, 121 S HESS ST 17566
Swift MS, RURAL ROUTE 03 17566
 Leon Trager, prin.
Swift MS, 1866 ROBERT FULTON HWY 17566
 J. Drue Miles, prin.
Little Britain MS, 416 NOTTINGHAM RD 17566
 Thomas Brackbill, prin.
ES, 211 S HESS ST 17566 — Austin Kreeger, prin.
Other Schools — See Christiana, Drumore, New
 Providence, Peach Bottom

Queen, Bedford Co.
Claysburg-Kimmel SD IU 8
Supt. — See Claysburg
ES 16670 — Thomas Moore, prin.

Quincy, Franklin Co.
Waynesboro Area SD IU 12
Supt. — See Waynesboro
Mont Alto ES, P O BOX 188 17247
 Timothy Lafferty, prin.
Mowrey ES 1, PARK ST 17247
 Timothy Lafferty, prin.
Mowrey MS 2, P O BOX 188 17247
 Timothy Lafferty, prin.

Rankin, Allegheny Co., Pop. Code 5
Woodland Hills SD IU 3
Supt. — See Pittsburgh
IS, 4TH & MOUND ST 15104
 David Shestack, prin.

Reading, Berks Co., Pop. Code 8
Antietam SD IU 14
Sch. Sys. Enr. Code 3
Supt. — John DiNunzio, 100 ANTIETAM RD 19606
Other Schools — See Mount Penn

Exeter Twp. SD IU 14
Sch. Sys. Enr. Code 5
Supt. — Dr. Ronald Dick
 3650 PERKIOMEN AVE 19606
Jacksonwald ES, 49 CHURCH LANE RD 19606
 Robert Hoch, prin.
Lausch ES, 200 ELM ST 19606
 Philip Rabena, prin.
Lorane ES, RITTENHOUSE DRIVE 19606
 Kathy Entrekin, prin.

Oley Valley SD IU 14
Supt. — See Oley
Alsace ES, RURAL ROUTE 04 19606
 Alan Bartlett, prin.

Reading SD IU 14
Sch. Sys. Enr. Code 7
Supt. — Dr. James Henderson
 8TH & WASHINGTON STS 19601
Ford ES, OLD WYOMISSING ROAD 19611
 Judith Malick, prin.
Glenside ES
 SCHUYLKILL AVENUE LACKA 19601
 Stella Leonati, prin.
Lauers Park ES
 SECOND AND ELM STREETS 19601
 Gordon Hoodak, prin.
Northwest ES
 CLINTON AND W DOUGLAS 19601
 John Crossan, prin.
Riverside ES, 1400 CENTRE AVE 19601
 Mary Zerkowski, prin.
Sixteenth and Haak ES
 HAAK AND 16TH STREETS 19602
 Walter Levan, prin.

Stout ES, 10TH AND SPRUCE STREETS 19602
  Grace Jones, prin.
Tenth and Green ES, N 10TH & GREEN ST 19604
  William Manderbach, prin.
Thirteenth and Green ES
  GREEN ST AT 13TH 19604
  Garrett Hyneman, prin.
Thirteenth and Union ES
  13TH AND UNION STREETS 19604
  C. Moyer, prin.
Twelfth and Marian ES
  N 12TH & MARION ST 19604
  Richard Holder, prin.
Tyson-Schoener ES
  5TH AND SPRUCE STREETS 19602
  Sara Shipe, prin.

Wilson SD IU 14
Supt. – See West Lawn
Lincoln Park ES, 400 DORCHESTER AVE 19609
  Joseph Toy, prin.

Reading SDA Jr. Academy
  309 KENHORST BLVD 19607
Cabrini Academy, 240 FRANKLIN ST 19602
Holy Garden Angels ES
  3125 KUTZTOWN RD 19605
Sacred Heart ES, 701 FRANKLIN ST 19611
St. Catharine Siena ES
  2330 PERKIOMEN AVE 19606
St. Ignatius Loyola ES
  2710 SAINT ALBANS DR 19609
St. Joseph ES, 1040 N 8TH ST 19604
St. Margaret ES, THIRD AND SPRING STS 19601
St. Peter ES, 225 S 5TH ST 19602

Reamstown, Lancaster Co., Pop. Code 4
Cocalico SD IU 13
Supt. – See Denver
ES 17567 – R. Buck, prin.

Reamstown Menn ES 17567

Rebersburg, Centre Co.
Penns Valley Area SD IU 10
Supt. – See Spring Mills
Miles Township ES, RURAL ROUTE 01 16872
  Wayne Dorman, prin.

Red Hill, Montgomery Co., Pop. Code 4
Upper Perkiomen SD IU 23
Supt. – See East Greenville
ES, 5TH ST 18076 – Charles Wayes, prin.

Red Lion, York Co., Pop. Code 6
Red Lion Area SD IU 12
Supt. – See Windsor
Red Lion Area JHS
  CHARLES & HENRIETTA STS 17356
  Paul DiPangrazio, prin.
Gable ES, EAST GAY STREET 17356
  Kathy Geiger, prin.
Moore ES, COUNTRY CLUB ROAD 17356
  Kathy Geiger, prin.
North Hopewell-Winterstown ES
  P O BOX 241 17356 – Martin Weiss, prin.
Pleasant View ES, P O BOX 44 17356
  Bradley Stell, prin.

Red Lion Christian School
  RURAL ROUTE 03 17356

Reedsville, Mifflin Co., Pop. Code 3
Mifflin County SD IU 11
Supt. – See Lewistown
Brown Township ES, GARDEN VIEW 17084
  George Bailor, prin.

Rehrersburg, Berks Co.
Tulpehocken Area SD IU 14
Supt. – See Bernville
Tulpehocken ES
  RURAL ROUTE 04 BOX 4032 19550
  L. Messersmith, prin.

Renovo, Clinton Co., Pop. Code 4
Keystone Central SD IU 10
Supt. – See Lock Haven
ES, 7TH & ONTARIO AVENUE 17764
  Charles Barnum, prin.

Republic, Fayette Co., Pop. Code 4
Brownsville Area SD IU 1
Sch. Sys. Enr. Code 5
Supt. – Dexston Reed, P O BOX 752 15475
Redstone MS, P O BOX 752 15475
  John Mazzocco, prin.
Other Schools – See Brownsville, Cardale, East
  Millsboro, Grindstone

Holy Rosary ES, P O BOX 797 15475

Reynoldsville, Jefferson Co., Pop. Code 5
Du Bois Area SD IU 6
Supt. – See Du Bois
Johnson ES, JACKSON STREET 15851
  Thomas Vizza, prin.

Rheems, Lancaster Co.
Elizabethtown Area SD IU 13
Supt. – See Elizabethtown
ES, P O BOX 389 17570 – Ruth Rastatter, prin.

Richboro, Bucks Co., Pop. Code 4
Council Rock SD IU 22
Sch. Sys. Enr. Code 6
Supt. – John Byrne
  151 TWINING FORD ROAD 18954
ES, 1060 2ND STREET PIKE 18954
  J. Ogelby, prin.
Other Schools – See Holland, Newtown,
  Southampton, Wrightstown

Richfield, Juniata Co.
Juniata County SD IU 11
Supt. – See Mifflintown
Monroe Township ES 17086 – Gerald Hibbs, prin.

Richland, Lebanon Co., Pop. Code 4
Eastern Lebanon County SD IU 13
Supt. – See Myerstown
Ft. Zeller ES, RURAL ROUTE 01 17087
  Ronald Hetrick, prin.

Ridgway, Elk Co., Pop. Code 6
Ridgway Area SD IU 9
Sch. Sys. Enr. Code 4
Supt. – H. Sharp, 213 FILLMORE AVE 15853
Ridgway Area MS, BOOT JACK ROAD 15853
  Francis Grandinetti, prin.
Centennial MS, 300 CENTER ST 15853
  Dr. Hugo Marnatti, prin.
Central ES
  SOUTH BROAD & SOUTH STREET 15853
  Dr. Hugo Marnatti, prin.

St. Leo ES, 117 DEPOT ST 15853

Ridley Park, Delaware Co., Pop. Code 6
Ridley SD IU 25
Supt. – See Folsom
Lakeview ES, 333 CONSTITUTION AVE 19078
  Audrey Lesky, prin.
Leedom ES, E CHESTER PIKE 19078
  Dr. Richard Picard, prin.

St. Madeline-St. Rose ES
  TOME & RODGERS ST 19078

Rimersburg, Clarion Co., Pop. Code 4
Union SD IU 6
Sch. Sys. Enr. Code 4
Supt. – Robert Harris, RURAL ROUTE 02 16248
ES, RURAL ROUTE 01 BOX 23 16248
  Darrell Shick, prin.
Other Schools – See Sligo

Ringtown, Schuylkill Co., Pop. Code 3
North Schuylkill SD IU 29
Supt. – See Frackville
ES, HANCOCK STREET 17967
  Carl Pyzowski, prin.

Rixford, McKean Co.
Otto-Eldred SD IU 9
Supt. – See Duke Center
ES 16745 – Robert Falk, prin.

Roaring Spring, Blair Co., Pop. Code 5
Spring Cove SD IU 8
Sch. Sys. Enr. Code 4
Supt. – Ivan Shibley, 230 POPLAR ST 16673
ES, CEMETERY AND POPLAR ST 16673
  Howard Benner, prin.
Taylor MS, RURAL ROUTE 01 16673
  Rick Miller, prin.
Other Schools – See East Freedom, Martinsburg

Robertsdale, Huntingdon Co., Pop. Code 3
Tussey Mountain SD IU 8
Supt. – See Saxton
ES 16674 – William Ross, prin.

Robesonia, Berks Co., Pop. Code 4
Conrad Weiser Area SD IU 14
Sch. Sys. Enr. Code 4
Supt. – Terry Reber, P O BOX 7 19551
Other Schools – See Wernersville, Womelsdorf

Rochester, Beaver Co., Pop. Code 5
Jeannette CSD IU 7
Supt. – See Jeannette
Seneca Heights ES, 200 PARK ST 15644
  Geraldine McCartney, prin.

Rochester Area SD IU 27
Sch. Sys. Enr. Code 4
Supt. – Dr. Samuel DePaul, 540 RENO ST 15074
Rochester Area S, 540 RENO ST 15074
  Ronald Mento, prin.

Beaver Valley Christian Academy
  350 ADAMS ST 15074

Rockhill Furnace, Huntingdon Co., Pop. Code 2
Southern Huntingdon County SD IU 11
Supt. – See Orbisonia
Rockhill ES, P O BOX 184 17249
  Kenneth Beck, prin.

Rockwood, Somerset Co., Pop. Code 4
Rockwood Area SD IU 8
Sch. Sys. Enr. Code 4
Supt. – Jack Romesberg, P O BOX G 15557
ES, BOX G 15557 – Malcolm Buchanan, prin.
Other Schools – See Markleton

Rohrerstown, Lancaster Co., Pop. Code 4
Hempfield SD IU 13
Supt. – See Landisville

ES, ROHRERSTOWN ROAD 17571
  Harry Goodman, prin.

Rome, Bradford Co., Pop. Code 2
Northeast Bradford SD IU 17
Sch. Sys. Enr. Code 4
Supt. – Fredrick Dinse, RURAL ROUTE 01 18837
Northeast Bradford ES, RURAL ROUTE 01 18837
  Thomas Neilson, prin.

Rosemont, Montgomery Co., Pop. Code 5

Agnes Irwin School, S ITHAN AVE 19010
Rosemont Holy Child ES
  1344 MOTGOMERY AVE 19010

Roseto, Northampton Co.

Faith Christian School, 122 DANTE ST 18013
Our Lady of Mt. Carmel ES, 80 RIDGE ST 18013

Roslyn, Montgomery Co., Pop. Code 7
Abington SD IU 23
Supt. – See Abington
ES, 2565 SUSQUEHANNA ST 19001
  Janice Kline, prin.

Faith Chrisitian ES, 2450 HAMILTON AVE 19001
St. John of the Cross ES
  2801 WOODLAND RD 19001

Royersford, Montgomery Co., Pop. Code 5
Spring-Ford Area SD IU 23
Supt. – See Collegeville
Spring-Ford MS
  S 7TH & WASHINGTON ST 19468
  William Marion, prin.
Limerick ES, 81 LIMERICK CENTER RD 19468
  (—), prin.
ES, 4TH AVENUE WASH ST 19468
  David Willauer, prin.
MS, 200 S 5TH AVE 19468 – David Willauer, prin.

Area Catholic Sacred ES
  LEWIS RD & WALNUT ST 19468

Ruffs Dale, Westmoreland Co.
Southmoreland SD IU 7
Supt. – See Scottdale
ES 15679 – William Nelson, prin.

Yough SD IU 7
Supt. – See Herminie
Mendon ES, RURAL ROUTE 01 15679
  John Johnson, prin.

Rural Valley, Armstrong Co., Pop. Code 4
Armstrong SD IU 28
Supt. – See Ford City
Shannock Valley ES 16249 – Gerald Fouse, prin.

Russell, Warren Co.
Warren County SD IU 5
Supt. – See Warren
Lander ES, RURAL ROUTE 03 BOX 3264 16345
  Susan Chase, prin.
ES, RURAL ROUTE 01 BOX 1032 16345
  Kenneth Fitzsimmons, prin.
Scandia ES, RURAL ROUTE 01 BOX 1484 16345
  Kenneth Fitzsimmons, prin.

Rydal, Montgomery Co.

St. Hilary of Poiters ES
  920 SUSQUEHANNA RD 19046

Saegertown, Crawford Co., Pop. Code 3
Penncrest SD IU 5
Sch. Sys. Enr. Code 5
Supt. – Dennis Livi 16433
MS, 420 NORTH ST 16433 – Richard Baker, prin.
Brookhouser MS, RURAL ROUTE 01 16433
  Thomas Miller, prin.
Cussewago ES, RURAL ROUTE 03 16433
  William Hayes, prin.
Euclid ES, EUCLID AVENUE 16433
  Thomas Miller, prin.
Other Schools – See Cambridge Springs, Guys Mills,
  Townville

Saint Clair, Schuylkill Co., Pop. Code 5
St. Clair Area SD IU 29
Sch. Sys. Enr. Code 3
Supt. – Dr. Ralph Lutz, 227 S MILL ST 17970
ES, 227 S MILL ST 17970 – Bernadette Meck, prin.

St. Clair Catholic ES
  NICHOLS AND HANCOCK 17970

Saint Marys, Elk Co., Pop. Code 6
St. Mary's Area SD IU 9
Sch. Sys. Enr. Code 5
Supt. – Richard Luke
  977 S SAINT MARYS ROAD 15857
MS, 977 S SAINT MARYS ROAD 15857
  John Caribardi, prin.
South St. Marys Street ES
  370 S SAINT MARYS ST 15857
  John Esenwine, prin.
Other Schools – See Kersey, Weedville

Queen of the World ES, 134 QUEENS RD 15857
Sacred Heart ES, 337 CENTER ST 15857
St. Mary's ES, 325 CHURCH ST 15857

Saint Petersburg, Clarion Co., Pop. Code 2
Allegheny-Clarion Valley SD IU 6
Supt. – See Foxburg
ES, RURAL ROUTE 02 16054 – Stuart Estes, prin.

Saint Thomas, Franklin Co., Pop. Code 3
Tuscarora SD IU 12
Supt. – See Mercersburg
ES, 70 SCHOOL HOUSE RD #24 17252
Harold Yeager, prin.

Salina, Westmoreland Co.
Kiski Area SD IU 7
Supt. – See Vandergrift
Bell Township ES, P O BOX B 15680
William Kerr, prin.

Salisbury, Somerset Co., Pop. Code 3
Salisbury-Elk Lick SD IU 8
Sch. Sys. Enr. Code 3
Supt. – Russell Wilson, SMITH AVE 15558
Salisbury-Elk Lick ES, SMITH AVENUE 15558
David Knepper, prin.

Saltsburg, Indiana Co., Pop. Code 3
Apollo-Ridge SD IU 28
Supt. – See Spring Church
Elders Ridge ES
RURAL ROUTE 01 BOX 128 15681
Myrtle Creigh, prin.

Blairsville-Saltsburg SD IU 28
Supt. – See Blairsville
ES, 250 3RD ST 15681 – Joseph Emrick, prin.

Sanatoga, Chester Co.
Pottsgrove SD IU 23
Supt. – See Pottstown
Lower Pottsgrove ES
815 N PLEASANTVIEW RD 19464
James Boyce, prin.

Sarver, Armstrong Co.
Freeport Area SD IU 28
Supt. – See Freeport
Buffalo Township ES, 500 SARVER RD 16055
James Quinn, prin.

Saxonburg, Butler Co., Pop. Code 4
South Butler County SD IU 4
Sch. Sys. Enr. Code 5
Supt. – Dr. Merrill Arnold, KNOCK ROAD 16056
Clinton ES, RURAL ROUTE 01 BOX 301 16056
Garry Molloy, prin.
ES, KNOCH ROAD BOX 627 16056
Garry Molloy, prin.
Other Schools – See Butler, Cabot

Saxton, Bedford Co., Pop. Code 3
Tussey Mountain SD IU 8
Sch. Sys. Enr. Code 4
Supt. – Dr. Walter Curfman 16678
Saxton-Liberty ES, MIFFLIN STREET 16678
Dennis Rourke, prin.
Other Schools – See Defiance, Robertsdale

Sayre, Bradford Co., Pop. Code 6
Sayre Area SD IU 17
Sch. Sys. Enr. Code 4
Supt. – Paul Kelley, 333 W LOCKHART ST 18840
Litchfield Township ES, RURAL ROUTE 01 18840
Ralph Yanuzzi, prin.
Snyder ES, 130 WARREN ST 18840
Ralph Yanuzzi, prin.

Epiphany ES, 627 STEVENSON ST 18840

Schaefferstown, Lebanon Co., Pop. Code 3
Eastern Lebanon County SD IU 13
Supt. – See Myerstown
ES, LANCASTER CARPENTER 17088
Brenda Haverstick, prin.

Schnecksville, Lehigh Co.
Parkland SD IU 21
Supt. – See Orefield
ES, RURAL ROUTE 01 18078
Stephen Szilagyi, prin.

Schoeneck, Lancaster Co.
Cocalico SD IU 13
Supt. – See Denver
ES, S 4TH STREET 17574 – David Burns, prin.

Schuylkill Haven, Schuylkill Co., Pop. Code 6
Schuylkill Haven Area SD IU 29
Sch. Sys. Enr. Code 4
Supt. – E. Surmacz, 120 HAVEN ST 17972
Schuylkill Haven MS, HAVEN ST 17972
Kim LeVan, prin.
East Ward ES, UNION STREET 17972
Richard Rada, prin.
South Ward ES, PARKWAY 17972
Richard Rada, prin.

St. Ambrose ES, 302 RANDEL ST 17972

Schwenksville, Montgomery Co., Pop. Code 4
Perkiomen Valley SD IU 23
Sch. Sys. Enr. Code 4
Supt. – William Westcott, P O BOX 338 19473
Perkiomen Valley North ES
PERKIOMEN AVENUE 19473
Michael Friedberg, prin.
Other Schools – See Collegeville

St. Mary School, SPRING MOUNT RD 19473

Sciota, Monroe Co.
Stroudsburg Area SD IU 20
Supt. – See Stroudsburg
Hamilton Township ES
1100 N 9TH STREET 18354
Scott Houseknecht, prin.

Scotland, Franklin Co.
Chambersburg Area SD IU 12
Supt. – See Chambersburg
ES, 3832 MAIN ST 17254 – George Wagner, prin.

Scottdale, Westmoreland Co., Pop. Code 6
Southmoreland SD IU 7
Sch. Sys. Enr. Code 5
Supt. – Dr. John Kenney
PARKER AVE & N HIGH 15683
ES, NORTH CHESTNUT STREET 15683
Margaret Brooks, prin.
Other Schools – See Alverton, Ruffs Dale

St. John the Baptist ES
504 S BROADWAY ST 15683

Scranton, Lackawanna Co., Pop. Code 8
Scranton CSD IU 19
Sch. Sys. Enr. Code 6
Supt. – Thomas O'Donnell
425 N WASHINGTON AVE 18503
East Scranton IS, 528 QUINCY AVE 18510
Joseph Caputo, prin.
South Scranton IS
SLOCUM AVE & MAPLE 18505
Vincent Rizzo, prin.
West Scranton IS
PARROTT AVE & FELLOWS ST 18504
Michael Langan, prin.
Adams ES, 927 CAPOUSE AVE 18509
Emile Mazzei, prin.
Armstrong ES, CLEARVIEW AT LINCOLN 18508
Joseph Doyle, prin.
Audubon ES
COLFAX AND MULBERRY STREET 18510
Vincent Gross, prin.
Bancroft ES
LAWALL STREET AND ALBRIGHT 18508
Joseph Kennedy, prin.
Kennedy ES
PROSPECT AVE & SAGINA ST 18505
Louis Nardella, prin.
Lincoln-Jackson ES
ACADEMY AND S HYDE PR 18505
Ann McDonough, prin.
Marshall ES
N LINCOLN AVENUE AND ORA 18504
John McAuliffe, prin.
McNichols ES, 1111 S IRVING AVE 18505
Martin Kuhn, prin.
Morris ES
BOULEVARD AVENE AND COL ST 18509
Thomas Jordan, prin.
Prescott ES, PRESCOTT AVE AND MYRTL 18510
George Roskos, prin.
Sumner ES, SUMNER AND SWETLAND 18504
Paul Dougherty, prin.
Whitter ES, 700 ORCHARD ST 18505
Louise Alimenti, prin.
Willard ES, 1100 EYNON ST 18504
George Noone, prin.

St. Paul's ES, 1527 PENN AVE 18509
Holy Rosary ES, 312 WILLIAM ST 18508
Nativity of Our Lord ES, 638 HEMLOCK ST 18505
St. Ann's Monaster ES
1228 SAINT ANNS ST 18504
St. Clare ES, 2215 N WASHINGTON AVE 18509
St. Mary Assmption ES, 430 RIVER ST 18505
St. Patrick ES, 115 S LINCOLN AVE 18504

Selinsgrove, Snyder Co., Pop. Code 6
Selinsgrove Area SD IU 16
Sch. Sys. Enr. Code 5
Supt. – Dr. Karl Rohrbach, 400 18TH ST 17870
Selinsgrove Area MS, 400 18TH ST 17870
Elwood Stetler, prin.
Jackson-Penn ES, RURAL ROUTE 01 17870
Lynn Fiedler, prin.
Monroe Township ES
RURAL ROUTE 04 BOX 127 17870
Leonard Lawrence, prin.
ES, 600 BROAD ST 17870 – Francis Newton, prin.
Other Schools – See Freeburg, Port Trevorton

Sellersville, Bucks Co., Pop. Code 5
Pennridge SD IU 22
Supt. – See Perkasie
Grasse ES, 600 RICKERT RD 18960
Gregory Nolan, prin.
ES, BROADWAY AND RIDGE AVE 18960
Peter Lamana, prin.

Faith Christian Academy, P O BOX 360 18960
Upper Bucks Christian School
754 E ROCKWILL ROAD 18960
St. Agnes School of the Sacred Heart
427 MAIN ST 18960

Seneca, Venango Co., Pop. Code 3
Cranberry Area SD IU 6
Sch. Sys. Enr. Code 4
Supt. – Mary Ann Nobers, P O BOX 553 16346
Cranberry ES, RURAL ROUTE 01 BOX 553 16346
Edward Schick, prin.

Steffee ES, RURAL ROUTE 02 BOX 297 16346
Nicholas Bodnar, prin.
Other Schools – See Kennerdell, Oil City, Venus

Seven Valleys, York Co., Pop. Code 2
Spring Grove Area SD IU 12
Supt. – See Spring Grove
ES, P O BOX 7 17360 – Carol Kling, prin.

Sewickley, Allegheny Co., Pop. Code 5
North Allegheny SD IU 3
Supt. – See Pittsburgh
Franklin ES, RURAL ROUTE 01 15143
Campbell Witherspoon, prin.

Quaker Valley SD IU 3
Sch. Sys. Enr. Code 4
Supt. – Leroy Kite, 400 CHESTNUT ROAD 15143
Edgeworth ES, 200 MEADOW LN 15143
Mike Schnirel, prin.
Osborne ES, 1414 BEAVER ST 15143
Nancy Auer, prin.

Sewickley Academy, 315 ACADEMY AVE 15143
St. James ES, BANK AND BROAD STS 15143

Shade Gap, Huntingdon Co., Pop. Code 2
Southern Huntingdon County SD IU 11
Supt. – See Orbisonia
ES, HCR 62 BOX 408 17255 – Kenneth Beck, prin.

Shamokin, Northumberland Co., Pop. Code 7
Line Mountain SD IU 16
Supt. – See Herndon
West Cameron ES
RURAL ROUTE 02 BOX 538 17872
Gary Gonsar, prin.

Shamokin Area SD IU 16
Sch. Sys. Enr. Code 5
Supt. – Joseph Swatski, 2000 W STATE ST 17872
Shamokin Area MS, 8TH & ARCH ST 17872
Edward Binkoski, prin.
ES, 3000 W STATE STREET 17872
Sylvestor Schicatano, prin.

Queen of Peace ES, 201 N SHAMOKIN ST 17872

Shanksville, Somerset Co., Pop. Code 2
Shanksville-Stonycreek SD IU 8
Sch. Sys. Enr. Code 3
Supt. – Gary Singel, P O BOX 128 15560
Shanksville-Stoneycreek S
1025 E MAIN ST 15560 – Curtis Kerns, prin.

Sharon, Mercer Co., Pop. Code 7
Sharon CSD IU 4
Sch. Sys. Enr. Code 5
Supt. – Donald Thomas, 215 FORKER BLVD 16146
Case Avenue ES, 36 CASE AVE 16146
Richard Rubano, prin.
Musser ES, LESLIE & CEDAR STREET 16146
Fred Hoffman, prin.
West Hill ES, ELLSWORTH NORTH IRVINE 16146
William Dunsmore, prin.

St. Joseph ES, 760 E STATE ST 16146

Sharon Hill, Delaware Co., Pop. Code 6
Southeast Delco SD IU 25
Supt. – See Folcroft
ES, 701 COATES ST 19079
Eugene Abraham, prin.

Holy Spirit ES, 1028 SCHOOL ST 19079

Sharpsville, Mercer Co., Pop. Code 6
Sharpsville Area SD IU 4
Sch. Sys. Enr. Code 4
Supt. – S. Schubel, 100 W RIDGE AVE 16150
Snyder MS, 100 W RIDGE AVE 16150
Samuel Liburdi, prin.
Seventh Street ES, 701 SEVENTH STREET 16150
Christ Hodges, prin.
South Pymatuning ES
3637 TAMARACK DR 16150
Christ Hodges, prin.

Shartlesville, Berks Co.
Hamburg Area SD IU 14
Supt. – See Hamburg
Upper Bern ES, P O BOX 31 19554
Dennis Bowers, prin.

Sheffield, Warren Co., Pop. Code 4
Warren County SD IU 5
Supt. – See Warren
ES, PICKERING STREET 16347
John Johnson, prin.

Shenandoah, Schuylkill Co., Pop. Code 6
Shenandoah Valley SD IU 29
Sch. Sys. Enr. Code 3
Supt. – John Kubeika, W CENTER ST 17976
Shenandoah Valley ES, 39 N WHITE ST 17976
Thomas Shaffer, prin.

Annunciation St. George ES
CHESTNUT AND CHERRY ST 17976
Sts. Casimir St. Stanslaus ES
233 N JARDIN ST 17976

Shermans Dale, Perry Co.
West Perry SD IU 15
Supt. – See Elliottsburg
Carroll ES, RURAL ROUTE 01 17090
Ronald Hummel, prin.

Shickshinny, Luzerne Co., Pop. Code 4
Northwest Area SD IU 18
Sch. Sys. Enr. Code 4
Supt. – Gerald Bau, RURAL ROUTE 02 18655
Garrison Memorial ES, W VINE STREET 18655
Jane Ackerman, prin.
Other Schools – See Hunlock Creek, Huntington Mills

Shillington, Berks Co., Pop. Code 6
Governor Mifflin SD IU 14
Sch. Sys. Enr. Code 5
Supt. – Dr. Jack Harf, 10 S WAVERLY ST 19607
Brecknock ES, BOX C750 10 S WAVERL 19607
Christ Bucculo, prin.
Cumru ES, PHILADELPHIA AVENUE 19607
James Watts, prin.
Intermediate MS, 600 GOVERNORS DR 19607
Stephen Gancar,Jr., prin.

St. John Baptist Delasal ES
105 N WYOMISSING AVE 19607

Shinglehouse, Potter Co., Pop. Code 4
Oswayo Valley SD IU 9
Sch. Sys. Enr. Code 3
Supt. – Dr. Larry Henry, P O BOX 368 16748
Oswayo Valley S 16748 – John Hertlein, prin.

Shippensburg, Cumberland Co., Pop. Code 6
Shippensburg Area SD IU 15
Sch. Sys. Enr. Code 5
Supt. – Dale Baker, 317 N MORRIS ST 17257
Burd ES
RICHWALTER AND BRAD STREET 17257
Dale Hess, prin.
Grayson ES, LURGAN AVENUE 17257
Lawrence Basler, prin.
Rowland School For Young Children
SHIPPENSBURG UNIV 17257 – Mary Taylor, prin.

Shiremanstown, Cumberland Co., Pop. Code 4
Mechanicsburg Area SD IU 15
Supt. – See Mechanicsburg
ES, 41 S LOCUST ST 17011 – Judith Ingram, prin.

Bible Baptist School, 201 W MAIN ST 17011
Christ Adademy Camp Hill, P O BOX 3189 17011

Shoemakersville, Berks Co., Pop. Code 4
Hamburg Area SD IU 14
Supt. – See Hamburg
Perry ES, 201 4TH ST 19555
Janet Schadler, prin.

Shohola, Pike Co.
Delaware Valley SD IU 20
Supt. – See Milford
Smith Nelson Shohola ES
TWIN LAKES ROAD 18458 – Robert Smith, prin.

Sidman, Cambria Co.
Forest Hills SD IU 8
Sch. Sys. Enr. Code 5
Supt. – Alex Afton, P O BOX 158 15955
Forest Hills ES, P O BOX 158 15955
William Wantiez, prin.

Simpson, Lackawanna Co., Pop. Code 4
Carbondale Area SD IU 19
Supt. – See Carbondale
Fell ES, JOHN STREET 18407 – John Petak, prin.

Sinking Spring, Berks Co., Pop. Code 5
Wilson SD IU 14
Supt. – See West Lawn
Lower Heidelberg ES, RURAL ROUTE 05 19608
Marjorie Miller, prin.
ES, 630 VESTER PL 19608 – Marjorie Miller, prin.

Sipesville, Somerset Co.
Somerset Area SD IU 8
Supt. – See Somerset
ES, 209 W PATRIOT ST 15561 – Carl Kahl, prin.

Slatington, Lehigh Co., Pop. Code 5
Northern Lehigh SD IU 21
Sch. Sys. Enr. Code 4
Supt. – Dr. Michael Clark
1201 SHADOW OAKS LANE 18080
Peters ES, RURAL ROUTE 01 18080
Donald Muenker, prin.
ES, 1201 SHADOW OAKS LN 18080
Gerald Zinner, prin.
Other Schools – See Walnutport

Sligo, Clarion Co., Pop. Code 3
Union SD IU 6
Supt. – See Rimersburg
ES, RURAL ROUTE 01 BOX 209B 16255
Darrell Shick, prin.

Slippery Rock, Butler Co., Pop. Code 5
Slippery Rock Area SD IU 4
Sch. Sys. Enr. Code 5
Supt. – Dr. Gerald Heller, KEISTER ROAD 16057
Slippery Rock Area MS, KEISTER ROAD 16057
Ken Mills, prin.
Slippery Rock Area ES, RURAL ROUTE 03 16057
Bruce Golmic, prin.
Other Schools – See Butler, Harrisville, Portersville, Prospect

Smethport, McKean Co., Pop. Code 4
Smethport Area SD IU 9
Sch. Sys. Enr. Code 4
Supt. – Paul Hite, W KING ST 16749
ES, 414 S MECHANIC ST 16749
Richard Shildt, prin.

Smithfield, Fayette Co., Pop. Code 4
Albert Galltn Area SD IU 1
Supt. – See Uniontown
ES, RURAL ROUTE 01 BOX 35A 15478
Paul Boord, prin.

Smithton, Westmoreland Co., Pop. Code 3
Yough SD IU 7
Supt. – See Herminie
Barren Run ES, RURAL ROUTE 01 15479
Daniel Pergola, prin.

Smoketown, Lancaster Co.

Locust Grove Menn ES
2257 OLD PHILA PIKE 17576

Snow Shoe, Centre Co., Pop. Code 3
Bald Eagle Area SD IU 10
Supt. – See Wingate
ES 16874 – Kathleen Rounds, prin.

Solebury, Bucks Co.
New Hope-Solebury SD IU 22
Supt. – See New Hope
New Hope-Solebury ES, SUGAN RD 18963
Melvin Sonier, prin.

Somerset, Somerset Co., Pop. Code 6
Somerset Area SD IU 8
Sch. Sys. Enr. Code 5
Supt. – Dr. Dennis Afton
S COLUMBIA AVE 15501
Maple Ridge ES, RURAL ROUTE 04 15501
Carl Kahl, prin.
Patriot Street ES, 209 W PATRIOT ST 15501
Carl Kahl, prin.
Other Schools – See Friedens, Sipesville

St. Peter ES, 433 W CHURCH ST 15501
St. Peter ES, 433 W CHURCH ST 15501

Souderton, Montgomery Co., Pop. Code 6
Souderton Area SD IU 23
Sch. Sys. Enr. Code 5
Supt. – Alexander Grande
139 HARLEYSVILLE PIKE 18964
Crouthamel ES, 143 S SCHOOL LN 18964
George Balzer, prin.
Franconia ES, 366 HARLEYSVILLE PIKE 18964
Mark Garis, prin.
West Broad Street ES, 342 W BROAD ST 18964
David Kratz, prin.
Other Schools – See Harleysville

Penn View Christ ES, 420 COWPATH RD 18964

Southampton, Bucks Co.
Centennial SD IU 22
Supt. – See Warminster
Davis ES, 475 MAPLE AVE 18966
Lawrence Belli, prin.
Stackpole ES, 1350 STRATHMANN DR 18966
Charles Loughery, prin.

Council Rock SD IU 22
Supt. – See Richboro
Churchville ES, 100 NEW RD 18966
David Hunter, prin.

Our Lady of Good Counsel ES
2ND ST PK AND KNOWLES 18966

South Canaan, Wayne Co., Pop. Code 4
Wayne Highlands SD IU 19
Supt. – See Honesdale
Preston ES 18459 – Robert Ford, prin.

Western Wayne SD IU 19
Sch. Sys. Enr. Code 4
Supt. – Patricia Leamy 18459
Other Schools – See Hamlin, Lake Ariel, Waymart

South Erie, Erie Co.
Ft. LeBoeuf SD IU 5
Supt. – See Waterford
Robison ES, 1651 W ROBISON RD 16509
Debra Spaulding, prin.
Summit Central ES, 1264 TOWNHALL RD 16509
Debra Spaulding, prin.

South Williamsport, Lycoming Co., Pop. Code 6
South Williamsport Area SD IU 17
Sch. Sys. Enr. Code 4
Supt. – James Revello, 700 PERCY ST 17701
Central ES, 555 W MOUNTAIN AVE 17701
Bruce Mosser, prin.
Other Schools – See Williamsport

Spartansburg, Crawford Co., Pop. Code 2
Corry Area SD IU 5
Supt. – See Corry
Sparta ES, WATER STREET 16434
James Anundson, prin.

Spraggs, Greene Co.
Central Green SD IU 1
Supt. – See Waynesburg
Wayne ES, RURAL ROUTE 01 15362
Charlotte Minehart, prin.

Spring Church, Armstrong Co.
Apollo-Ridge SD IU 28
Sch. Sys. Enr. Code 5
Supt. – R. Cogar, P O BOX 219 15686
Apollo-Ridge MS, HCR BOX 46B 15686
Guy De Toma, prin.

Sunnyside ES, P O BOX 147 15686
Myrtle Creigh, prin.
Other Schools – See Apollo, North Apollo, Saltsburg

Spring City, Chester Co., Pop. Code 5
Owen J. Roberts SD IU 24
Supt. – See Pottstown
Vincent ES, ROUTE 23 RD 1 19475
Kenneth Swart, prin.

Spring-Ford Area SD IU 23
Supt. – See Collegeville
ES, 190 WALL STREET 19475
Margaret Stengel, prin.

Springdale, Allegheny Co., Pop. Code 5
Allegheny Valley SD IU 3
Supt. – See Cheswick
Colfax ES, 430 COLFAX ST 15144
Ralph Varrato, prin.

St. Alphonsus ES, 744 PITTSBURGH ST 15144

Springfield, Delaware Co., Pop. Code 8
Springfield SD IU 25
Sch. Sys. Enr. Code 5
Supt. – C. McLaughlin, 111 W LEAMY AVE 19064
Richardson MS, 20 W WOODLAND AVE 19064
Donald Eckert, prin.
Sabold ES, E THOMSON AVENUE 19064
James Johnson, prin.
Scenic Hills ES
HILLVIEW AND CLAREMON 19064
John Deangelis, prin.

Holy Cross ES, 240 N BISHOP AVE 19064
St. Francis Assisi ES, 112 SAXER AVE 19064
St. Kevin ES, SPROUL RD & THOMPSON 19064

Spring Grove, York Co., Pop. Code 4
Spring Grove Area SD IU 12
Sch. Sys. Enr. Code 5
Supt. – Dr. Alan Lindquist
220 W JACKSON ST 17362
MS, 50 N EAST ST 17362 – James Myers, prin.
Heidelberg ES, RURAL ROUTE 03 17362
Philip Hempfing, prin.
ES, COLLEGE AVENUE 17362
Philip Hempfing, prin.
Other Schools – See Codorus, Seven Valleys, Thomasville, York

Spring House, Bucks Co., Pop. Code 3

Gwynedd Mercy Academy
NORRISTOWN RD 19477

Spring Mills, Centre Co., Pop. Code 2
Penns Valley Area SD IU 10
Sch. Sys. Enr. Code 4
Supt. – F. Bogert, RURAL ROUTE 02 16875
Gregg Township ES
143 NORTH HOFFER STREET 16875
P. Michaels, prin.
Penns Valley ES, RURAL ROUTE 02 16875
Karen Keller, prin.
Other Schools – See Centre Hall, Rebersburg

Stahlstown, Westmoreland Co.
Ligonier Valley SD IU 7
Supt. – See Ligonier
Cook Township ES 15687 – Stanton Harvey, prin.

State College, Centre Co., Pop. Code 8
State College Area SD IU 10
Sch. Sys. Enr. Code 6
Supt. – Dr. Seldon Whitaker
131 W NITTANY AVE 16801
State College Area JHS
2180 SCHOOL DRIVE 16803 – J. Casey, prin.
Boalsburg Panorama ES
240 VILLA CREST DR 16801 – Paul Solley, prin.
Corl Street ES, 235 CORL ST 16801
Cameron Bausch, prin.
Easterly Parkway ES, 234 EASTERLY PKY 16801
Cameron Bausch, prin.
Fairmount Avenue ES, 411 S FRASER ST 16801
William Keenan, prin.
Houserville ES, 217 SCHOLL ST 16801
Carl Morris, prin.
Park Forest ES, 2181 SCHOOL DR 16803
John Cox, prin.
Radio Park ES, 800 CIRCLEVILLE RD 16803
Peter Carpenter, prin.
Other Schools – See Lemont, Pine Grove Mills, Port Matilda

Our Lady Victory ES, 800 WESTERLY PKY 16801

Steelton, Dauphin Co., Pop. Code 6
Central Dauphin SD IU 15
Supt. – See Harrisburg
Tri Community ES
MONROE & CYPRESS ST 17113
Robert Griffith, prin.

Steelton-Highspire SD IU 15
Sch. Sys. Enr. Code 4
Supt. – David Meckley
4TH & WALNUT STS 17113
Steelton-Highspire ES
4TH AND WALNUT STREETS 17113
Stephanie Acri, prin.

St. John Neuman ES, 825 S 2ND ST 17113

Stewartstown, York Co., Pop. Code 4
South Eastern SD IU 12
Supt. – See Fawn Grove
ES, RURAL ROUTE 02 BOX 2001   17363
M. Parlett, prin.

Stoneboro, Mercer Co., Pop. Code 4
Lakeview SD IU 4
Sch. Sys. Enr. Code 5
Supt. – Samuel Wilson, RURAL ROUTE 01   16153
Lakeview MS, RURAL ROUTE 01   16153
Fred McConnell, prin.
Oakview ES, RURAL ROUTE 01   16153
Kent Smith, prin.

Stowe, Chester Co., Pop. Code 5
Pottsgrove SD IU 23
Supt. – See Pottstown
West Pottsgrove ES, GROSSTOWN ROAD   19464
Jeffrey Hohman, prin.

Strasburg, Lancaster Co., Pop. Code 4
Lampeter-Strasburg SD IU 13
Supt. – See Lampeter
ES, FULTON AND FRANKLIN STREET   17579
Nancy Hoop, prin.

Strattanville, Clarion Co., Pop. Code 3
Clarion-Limestone Area SD IU 6
Sch. Sys. Enr. Code 4
Supt. – Dr. Jerry Long, RURAL ROUTE 01   16258
Clarion-Limestone ES
RURAL ROUTE 01 BOX 205   16258
Ralph Seigworth, prin.
ES, WASHINGTON STREET   16258
Ralph Seigworth, prin.

Strausstown, Berks Co., Pop. Code 2
Hamburg Area SD IU 14
Supt. – See Hamburg
ES, P O BOX 156   19559 – Gary Wilhelm, prin.

Stroudsburg, Monroe Co., Pop. Code 6
Stroudsburg Area SD IU 20
Sch. Sys. Enr. Code 5
Supt. – Salvatore Illuzzi, 1100 W MAIN ST   18360
MS, CHIPPERFIELD DRIVE   18360
Elizabeth Burak, prin.
Clearview ES, N 5TH STREET   18360
Judith Landry, prin.
Morey ES, 1040 W MAIN ST   18360
Patricia Trancredi, prin.
Ramsey ES, THOMAS STREET   18360
Judith Landry, prin.
Other Schools – See Sciota

Sugargrove, Warren Co., Pop. Code 3
Warren County SD IU 5
Supt. – See Warren
ES, SCHOOL STREET   16350 – Susan Chase, prin.

Sugarloaf, Luzerne Co.
Hazleton Area SD IU 18
Supt. – See Hazleton
MS   18249 – Harold Getz, prin.

Sunbury, Northumberland Co., Pop. Code 7
Shikellamy SD IU 16
Sch. Sys. Enr. Code 5
Supt. – Dr. Clyde Colwell
350 ISLAND BLVD   17801
Rice MS, 4TH & HANOVER STS   17801
John Gotaskie, prin.
MS, 115 FAIRMOUNT AVE   17801
Trevor Lewis, prin.
Beck ES, 600 ARCH ST   17801
Theodore Andrewlevich, prin.
Edison ES
4TH AND GREENOUGH STREET   17801
Dave Doran, prin.
Ft. Augusta ES, SUSQUEHANA AND PACK   17801
Barrie Wirth, prin.
Maclay ES
SOUTH AND SECOND STREETS   17801
Barrie Wirth, prin.
Oaklyn ES, RURAL ROUTE 02   17801
Gerald Sanders, prin.
Other Schools – See Northumberland

St. Michael Archangel ES, 20 N FRONT ST   17801

Susquehanna, Susquehanna Co., Pop. Code 4
Susquehanna Comm. SD IU 19
Sch. Sys. Enr. Code 4
Supt. – William Stracka, P O BOX 5A   18847
Susquehanna Community ES
RURAL ROUTE 03 BOX 5A   18847
Robert Keyes, prin.

Swarthmore, Delaware Co., Pop. Code 6
Ridley SD IU 25
Supt. – See Folsom
Grace Park ES, SEVENTH AVE   19081
Joseph Fleischut, prin.

Wallingford-Swarthmore SD IU 25
Supt. – See Wallingford
Swarthmore-Rtldg ES, 100 COLLEGE AVE   19081
Sandra Sparrow, prin.

Notre Dame DeLourdes School
1000 FAIRVIEW RD   19081

Sweet Valley, Luzerne Co.
Lake-Lehman SD IU 18
Supt. – See Lehman
Ross ES, 1ST AND CENTER STREET   18656
Robert Kunkle, prin.

Swiftwater, Monroe Co., Pop. Code 2
Pocono Mountain SD IU 20
Sch. Sys. Enr. Code 5
Supt. – Dr. Linford Werkheiser
P O BOX 200   18370
Other Schools – See Cresco, Pocono Pines,
Tannersville, Tobyhanna

Sykesville, Jefferson Co., Pop. Code 4
Du Bois Area SD IU 6
Supt. – See Du Bois
ES, P O BOX J   15865 – Thomas Vizza, prin.

Tamaqua, Schuylkill Co., Pop. Code 6
Tamaqua Area SD IU 29
Sch. Sys. Enr. Code 4
Supt. – H. Bruce Geiger, P O BOX 112   18252
Tamaqua Area JHS   18252
Frederick Bausch, prin.
Rush ES, RURAL ROUTE 02   18252
Thomas Ponting, prin.
ES, W ELM AND NESCOPEC STREET   18252
Thomas Ponting, prin.
Other Schools – See New Ringgold

St. Jerome ES, 250 W BROAD ST   18252

Tannersville, Monroe Co., Pop. Code 3
Pocono Mountain SD IU 20
Supt. – See Swiftwater
Pocono ES   18372 – John Savidge, prin.

Tarentum, Allegheny Co., Pop. Code 6
Highlands SD IU 3
Supt. – See Natrona Heights
Grandview ES
9TH AVENUE AND ROSS ST   15084
William Heasley, prin.

Taylor, Lackawanna Co., Pop. Code 6
Riverside SD IU 19
Sch. Sys. Enr. Code 4
Supt. – John Rooney, 610 S MAIN ST   18517
ES, 607 S MAIN ST   18517 – Louis Nykaza, prin.
Other Schools – See Moosic

Templeton, Armstrong Co., Pop. Code 3
Armstrong SD IU 28
Supt. – See Ford City
ES, 212 CLAY STREET   16259
Herbert Crawford, prin.

Thomasville, York Co.
Spring Grove Area SD IU 12
Supt. – See Spring Grove
Paradise ES, RURAL ROUTE 01   17364
Nancy Baird, prin.
ES, RURAL ROUTE 02 BOX 4621   17364
Nancy Baird, prin.

Thompsontown, Juaniata Co., Pop. Code 3
Juniata County SD IU 11
Supt. – See Mifflintown
Thompsontown-Deleware ES   17094
Thomas Wert, prin.

Thorndale, Chester Co., Pop. Code 4
Coatesville Area SD IU 24
Supt. – See Coatesville
Cain ES, 3609 LINCOLN HWY   19372
Camie Arvay, prin.

Three Springs, Huntingdon Co., Pop. Code 3
Southern Huntingdon County SD IU 11
Supt. – See Orbisonia
Spring Farms ES
RURAL ROUTE 01 BOX 1876   17264
Kenneth Beck, prin.

Throop, Lackawanna Co., Pop. Code 5
Mid Valley SD IU 19
Sch. Sys. Enr. Code 4
Supt. – Joseph Crotti, UNDERWOOD ROAD   18512
Other Schools – See Dickson City, Olyphant

Tidioute, Warren Co., Pop. Code 3
Warren County SD IU 5
Supt. – See Warren
ES, 241 MAIN ST   16351
Patrick Cronmiller, prin.

Tioga, Tioga Co., Pop. Code 3
Northern Tioga SD IU 17
Supt. – See Elkland
J. L. T. ES, RURAL ROUTE   16946
Keith Graver, prin.

Tionesta, Forest Co., Pop. Code 3
Forest Area SD IU 6
Sch. Sys. Enr. Code 3
Supt. – Dr. Gordon Snow, P O BOX 388   16353
West Forest ES, VINE STREET   16353
Gordon Snow, prin.
Other Schools – See Marienville

North Clarion County SD IU 6
Sch. Sys. Enr. Code 3
Supt. – Richard Priester, P O BOX 194   16353
North Clarion County ES
RURAL ROUTE 01 BOX 194   16353
David Stake, prin.

Titusville, Crawford Co., Pop. Code 6
Titusville Area SD IU 6
Sch. Sys. Enr. Code 5
Supt. – Richard Carr
221 N WASHINGTON ST   16354
Cherrytree ES, RURAL ROUTE 03   16354
Robert Omer, prin.

Hydetown ES, RURAL ROUTE 04   16354
Robert Omer, prin.
Main Street ES, 117 W MAIN ST   16354
Robert Morris, prin.
Other Schools – See Pleasantville

St. Titus ES, 528 W MAIN ST   16354

Tobyhanna, Monroe Co., Pop. Code 3
Pocono Mountain SD IU 20
Supt. – See Swiftwater
Coolbaugh ES   18466 – Thomas Kopetskie, prin.

Topton, Berks Co., Pop. Code 4
Brandywine Heights Area SD IU 14
Sch. Sys. Enr. Code 4
Supt. – Dr. Glen Smartschan   19562
Brandywine Heights MS
BRANDYWINE HEIGHTS   19562
W. Cooperman, prin.
District Topton ES
BARKLEY AND WEISS STREETS   19562
Ruth Bloom, prin.
Other Schools – See Fleetwood, Mertztown

Toughkenamon, Chester Co., Pop. Code 3
Kennett Cons. SD IU 24
Supt. – See Kennett Square
New Garden ES, NEW GARDEN ROAD   19374
John Carr, Jr., prin.

Towanda, Bradford Co., Pop. Code 5
Towanda Area SD IU 17
Sch. Sys. Enr. Code 4
Supt. – Thomas Holland
101 N FOURTH ST   18848
MS, STATE ST   18848 – Donald Butler, prin.
Morrow ES, 101 N FOURTH ST   18848
Joyce Vandusen, prin.
Other Schools – See Monroeton, Wysox

St. Agnes ES, 102 THIRD ST   18848

Tower City, Schuylkill Co., Pop. Code 4
Williams Valley SD IU 29
Sch. Sys. Enr. Code 4
Supt. – Edwin Schlegel, RURAL ROUTE 01   17980
Williams Valley Elementary Plus 1
E GRAND AVENUE   17980 – David Michael, prin.
Other Schools – See Williamstown

Townville, Crawford Co., Pop. Code 2
Penncrest SD IU 5
Supt. – See Saegertown
Maplewood MS, RURAL ROUTE 01   16360
W. Houck, prin.

Trafford, Westmoreland Co., Pop. Code 5
Penn-Trafford SD IU 7
Supt. – See Harrison City
MS, 100 BRINTON AVE   15085
Ronald Darragh, prin.
Level Green ES, RURAL ROUTE 01   15085
Paul Bergamasco, prin.
ES, 100 BRINTON AVE   15085
Ronald Darragh, prin.

St. Regis ES, HOMEWOOD AVE   15085

Transfer, Mercer Co.
Reynolds SD IU 4
Supt. – See Greenville
ES, RURAL ROUTE 01   16154 – Fred Ray, prin.

Tremont, Schuylkill Co., Pop. Code 4
Pine Grove Area SD IU 29
Supt. – See Pine Grove
ES, CLAY STREET   17981 – Joyce Romberger, prin.

Trevorton, Northumberland Co., Pop. Code 4
Line Mountain SD IU 16
Supt. – See Herndon
Line Mountain MS, 500 W SHAMOKIN ST   17881
Bryan Balavage, prin.
ES, 500 SHAMOKIN STREET   17881
Gary Gonsar, prin.

Trooper, Montgomery Co., Pop. Code 5
Methacton SD IU 23
Supt. – See Fairview Village
Woodland ES, 2700 WOODLAND AVE   19403
Morgan Rinker III, prin.

Trout Run, Lycoming Co.
Southern Tioga SD IU 17
Supt. – See Mansfield
Cogan House ES, RD   17771 – Robert Wirth, prin.

Williamsport Area SD IU 17
Supt. – See Williamsport
Lewis Township ES   17771 – R. Marks, prin.

Troy, Bradford Co., Pop. Code 4
Troy Area SD IU 17
Sch. Sys. Enr. Code 4
Supt. – B. Schoonover, P O BOX 67   16947
MS, HIGH & KING ST   16947 – Clyde Moate, prin.
Croman ES, 250 CANTON ST   16947
Dr. Roger Goodman, prin.
ES, RURAL ROUTE 02 BOX 142A   16947
Dr. Roger Goodman, prin.
Other Schools – See Columbia Cross Roads, Millerton

Trucksville, Luzerne Co., Pop. Code 4
Dallas SD IU 18
Supt. – See Dallas
Westmoreland ES, 106 S LEHIGH ST   18708
Samuel Barbose, prin.

Tunkhannock, Wyoming Co., Pop. Code 4
Tunkhannock Area SD IU 18
Sch. Sys. Enr. Code 5
Supt. – Kent Kresge, 200 FRANKLIN AVE 18657
MS, 41 PHILADELPHIA AVE 18657
  Russell Hons, prin.
Evans Falls ES, RURAL ROUTE 05 18657
  Ernestine Swetland, prin.
Roslund ES, DIGGER DRIVE 18657
  Susann Barziloski, prin.
Other Schools – See Dalton, Mehoopany

Turbotville, Northumberland Co., Pop. Code 3
Warrior Run SD IU 16
Sch. Sys. Enr. Code 4
Supt. – Samuel Cooper, P O BOX 151A 17772
Warrior Run MS, P O BOX 151A 17772
  John Zeigler, prin.
ES, RURAL ROUTE 02 BOX 151 17772
  Gordon Thomas, prin.
Watsontown ES
  RURAL ROUTE 02 BOX 151 17772
  Gordon Thomas, prin.

Turtle Creek, Allegheny Co., Pop. Code 6

Faith Christian School, 801 THOMPSON ST 15145
St. Colman ES, 547 HUNTER ST 15145

Tyrone, Blair Co., Pop. Code 6
Tyrone Area SD IU 8
Sch. Sys. Enr. Code 4
Supt. – William Miller
  1317 LINCOLN AVE 16686
Adams ES, 1747 ADAMS AVE 16686
  Bradley Aults, prin.
Lincoln ES, 1317 LINCOLN AVE 16686
  John Vendetti, prin.
Logan ES, 1400 LOGAN AVE 16686
  John Vendetti, prin.
Other Schools – See Warriors Mark

St. Matthew ES, 1105 CAMRON AVE 16686

Ulster, Bradford Co.
Athens Area SD IU 17
Supt. – See Athens
Sheshequin-Ulster ES, SECOND STREET 18850
  Paul Hewitt, prin.

Ulysses, Potter Co., Pop. Code 3
Northern Potter SD IU 9
Sch. Sys. Enr. Code 3
Supt. – Robert Smith, RURAL ROUTE 01 16948
Northern Potter ES, RURAL ROUTE 01 16948
  Wesley Kuratomi, prin.

Union City, Erie Co., Pop. Code 5
Union City Area SD IU 5
Sch. Sys. Enr. Code 4
Supt. – Dr. William Young, 91 MILES ST 16438
ES, 91 MILES ST 16438 – Joseph Vergona, prin.

Uniontown, Fayette Co., Pop. Code 7
Albert Galltn Area SD IU 1
Sch. Sys. Enr. Code 5
Supt. – M. Tippet
  RURAL ROUTE 05 BOX 175 15401
Swaney ES, RURAL ROUTE 05 BOX 171 15401
  Stephen Kezmarsky, prin.
Other Schools – See Fairchance, Mc Clellandtown,
  Masontown, Point Marion, Smithfield

Laurel Highlands SD IU 01
Sch. Sys. Enr. Code 5
Supt. – Ronald Sheba, 304 BAILEY AVE 15401
Laurel Highlands MS, 18 HOOKTON AVE 15401
  Melvin Sepic, prin.
Clark ES, 200 WATER ST 15401
  William Martin, prin.
Hatfield ES, 370 DERRICK AVE 15401
  William Ainsley, prin.
Hutchinson ES
  RURAL ROUTE 02 BOX 492-X 15401
  Frank Yezioro, prin.
Kennedy ES, CHAFFEE STREET EXIT 15401
  Shirley Juriga, prin.
Marshall ES, RURAL ROUTE 01 15401
  William Raho, prin.

Uniontown Area SD IU 1
Sch. Sys. Enr. Code 5
Supt. – James Burns, 23 E CHURCH ST 15401
Franklin ES, 351 MORGANTOWN ST 15401
  Harry Coffman, prin.
Lafayette ES, 303 CONNELLSVILLE ST 15401
  Roland Baer, prin.
Menallen ES, RURAL ROUTE 06 BOX 272 15401
  Nick Galie, prin.
Other Schools – See Farmington, Markleysburg,
  Vanderbilt

St. John Evangelist ES, 88 PENNA AVE 15401
St. John the Baptist ES, 201 E MAIN ST 15401
St. Mary ES, 17 GILMORE ST 15401

Unionville, Chester Co., Pop. Code 2
Unionville-Chadds Ford SD IU 24
Sch. Sys. Enr. Code 5
Supt. – Dr. Charles Garris, ROUTE 82 19375
MS 19375 – C. Patton, prin.
ES 19375 – Thomas Wood, prin.
Other Schools – See Chadds Ford

United, Westmoreland Co.

St. Florians ES, P O BOX 188 15689

Upland, Delaware Co., Pop. Code 5
Chester Upland SD IU 25
Supt. – See Chester
Main Street ES, 704 MAIN ST 19015
  Jesse Richardson, prin.

Upper Black Eddy, Bucks Co.
Palisades SD IU 22
Supt. – See Kintnersville
Bridgeton ES, SWAMP ROAD 18972
  Eileen Wessel, prin.

Upper Darby, Delaware Co., Pop. Code 8
Upper Darby SD IU 25
Supt. – See Drexel Hill
Beverly Hills MS
  GARRETT RD & SHERBROOK BLVD 19082
  Melvyn Brodsky, prin.
Bywood ES, AVON & MADEIRA RD 19082
  Stuart Yowell, prin.
Highland Park ES, W CHESTER PK LYNN B 19082
  David Sanderson, prin.
Stonehurst Hills ES
  RUSKIN LANE TIMBERLAK 19082
  Gail Apfel, prin.

St. Alice ES, 131 COPLEY RD 19082
St. Laurence ES, 8245 W CHESTER PIKE 19082

Upper Saint Clair, Allegheny Co., Pop. Code 4
Upper St. Clair SD IU 3
Sch. Sys. Enr. Code 4
Supt. – Dr. Robert Christiana
  1820 MCLAUGHLIN RUN ROAD 15241
Ft. Couch MS, 515 FORT COUCH ROAD 15241
  Thomas Harshman, prin.
Other Schools – See Pittsburgh

Upperstrasburg, Franklin Co.
Chambersburg Area SD IU 12
Supt. – See Chambersburg
Letterkenny ES 17265 – Donna Shives, prin.

Utica, Venango Co., Pop. Code 2
Franklin Area SD IU 6
Supt. – See Franklin
ES 16362 – Terry Peterson, prin.

Uwchland, Chester Co.
Downingtown Area SD IU 24
Supt. – See Downingtown
Pickering Valley ES, P O BOX 250 19480
  Donald Hopson, prin.

Valencia, Butler Co., Pop. Code 2
Mars Area SD IU 4
Supt. – See Mars
Middlesex IS, RURAL ROUTE 03 BOX 77 16059
  Sara Werlinich, prin.

Valley View, Schuylkill Co., Pop. Code 4
Tri-Valley SD IU 29
Sch. Sys. Enr. Code 4
Supt. – Richard Spotts, 1801 W MAIN ST 17983
Hegins Hubley ES, 1801 W MAIN ST 17983
  Thomas Kuczawa, prin.
Other Schools – See Ashland, Klingerstown

Vanderbilt, Fayette Co., Pop. Code 3
Uniontown Area SD IU 1
Supt. – See Uniontown
Franklin ES, RURAL ROUTE 01 15486
  Nick Galie, prin.

Vandergrift, Westmoreland Co., Pop. Code 6
Kiski Area SD IU 7
Sch. Sys. Enr. Code 5
Supt. – Stephen Vak, 200 POPLAR ST 15690
IS, 420 FRANKLIN AVE 15690
  George Capretto, prin.
Adams ES, 200 LINCOLN AVE 15690
  Barbara Altmire, prin.
Laurel Point MS, RURAL ROUTE 01 15690
  Barbara Altmire, prin.
North Vandergrift ES, 151 LINCOLN AVE 15690
  Barbara Altmire, prin.
Wilson ES, 224 LONGFELLOW ST 15690
  Barbara Altmire, prin.
Other Schools – See Apollo, East Vandergrift, Export,
  Leechburg, Salina

St. Gertrude ES, 315 FRANKLIN AVE 15690

Venetia, Washington Co.
Peters Twp. SD IU 1
Supt. – See Mc Murray
ES, 300 VENETIA RD 15367 – Janet Ocel, prin.

Venus, Venango Co.
Cranberry Area SD IU 6
Supt. – See Seneca
Pinegrove ES, RURAL ROUTE 01 16364
  Nicholas Bodnar, prin.

Verona, Allegheny Co., Pop. Code 5
Penn Hills SD IU 3
Supt. – See Pittsburgh
Forbes ES, 5785 SALTSBURG RD 15147
  Robert Swanson, prin.
Penn ES
  WILLIAM PENN SCHOOL STREET 15147
  Craig Cunningham, prin.
Shenandoah ES, 700 IDAHO AVE 15147
  Emory Casey, prin.

Riverview SD IU 3
Supt. – See Oakmont

Verner ES, 700 1ST ST 15147
  Felicia Renard, prin.

St. Joseph ES, 825 2ND ST 15147

Volant, Lawrence Co., Pop. Code 2
Wilmington Area SD IU 4
Supt. – See New Wilmington
East Lawrence ES, RURAL ROUTE 02 16156
  Edward Pandoiti, prin.

Wallaceton, Clearfield Co., Pop. Code 2
Philipsburg-Osceola Area SD IU 10
Supt. – See Philipsburg
Wallaceton-Boggs ES
  PITTSVILLE MONROESVILL HWY 16876
  Chester Peterson, prin.

Wallingford, Delaware Co., Pop. Code 5
Wallingford-Swarthmore SD IU 25
Sch. Sys. Enr. Code 5
Supt. – George Slick
  200 S PROVIDENCE ROAD 19086
Nether Providence MS
  200 S PROVIDENCE ROAD 19086
  Gene Herninko, prin.
Nether Providence ES, 410 MOORE RD 19086
  Louis Tancredi, prin.
ES, 20 S PROVIDENCE RD 19086
  Robert Rice, prin.
Other Schools – See Swarthmore

St. John Chrysostom ES
  605 S PROVIDENCE RD 19086

Walnut Bottom, Cumberland Co.
Big Spring SD IU 15
Supt. – See Newville
Jacksonville ES 17266 – Arthur McCarter, prin.

Walnutport, Northampton Co., Pop. Code 4
Northampton Area SD IU 20
Supt. – See Northampton
Lehigh Township ES
  800 BLUE MOUNTAIN DR 18088
  Craig Moyer, prin.

Northern Lehigh SD IU 21
Supt. – See Slatington
ES, LINCOLN AVENUE 18088
  Donald Muenker, prin.

Warfordsburg, Fulton Co.
Southern Fulton SD IU 11
Sch. Sys. Enr. Code 3
Supt. – William Printz 17267
ES, RURAL ROUTE 02 17267 – Clyde Booth, prin.
Other Schools – See Needmore

Warminster, Bucks Co., Pop. Code 8
Centennial SD IU 22
Sch. Sys. Enr. Code 6
Supt. – Harry Harhigh
  CENTENNIAL ROAD 18974
Leary ES, 157 HENRY AVE 18974
  John Dietz, prin.
Longstreth ES, 999 ROBERTS RD 18974
  Sherry Weinberg, prin.
McDonald ES, 666 REEVES LN 18974
  Arnold Lindley, prin.
Willow Dale ES, 720 NORRISTOWN RD 18974
  Michael Webb, prin.
Other Schools – See Southampton

Nativity of Our Lord ES, 585 W STREET RD 18974

Warren, Warren Co., Pop. Code 7
Warren County SD IU 5
Sch. Sys. Enr. Code 6
Supt. – Ronald Snyder
  EAST ST & 3RD AVE 16365
Beaty-Warren MS, 2 E 3RD AVE 16365
  Elizabeth Bauer, prin.
Home Street ES, 200 HOME ST 16365
  Joseph Tassone,Jr., prin.
Irvinedale ES, 18 HOHMAN RD 16365
  Anthony Marino, prin.
Jefferson ES, JEFFERSON CONEWANGO 16365
  James Graziano, prin.
Lacy ES, 1607 PENNA AVE E 16365
  Anthony Marino, prin.
Market Street ES, MARKET STREET 16365
  Joseph Tassone,Jr., prin.
McClintock ES, 1209 PENNA AVE W 16365
  Joseph Tassone,Jr., prin.
Pleasant Township ES, 84 MCKINLEY AVE 16365
  Anthony Marino, prin.
South Street ES
  SOUTH STREET & PENNA AVE E 16365
  Kenneth Fitzsimmons, prin.
Other Schools – See Clarendon, North Warren,
  Pittsfield, Russell, Sheffield, Sugargrove, Tidioute,
  Youngsville

St. Joseph's ES, 608 PENNA AVE W 16365

Warrington, Bucks Co., Pop. Code 5
Central Bucks SD IU 22
Supt. – See Doylestown
Barclay ES, 2015 PALOMINO DR 18976
  James Brown, prin.
Titus ES, 2333 LOWER BARNESS RD 18976
  Lee Benner, prin.

St. Joseph St. Robert ES
  VALLEY RD AND COLUMBI 18976

Warriors Mark, Huntingdon Co.
Tyrone Area SD IU 8
Supt. – See Tyrone
ES 16877 – Bradley Aults, prin.

Washington, Washington Co., Pop. Code 7
McGuffey SD IU 1
Supt. – See Claysville
Walker ES, RURAL ROUTE 06 15301
John McCullough, prin.

Trinity Area SD IU 1
Sch. Sys. Enr. Code 5
Supt. – James Husk, PARK AVE 15301
Trinity MS, 50 SCENIC DRIVE 15301
Angel Rodriguez, prin.
Laboratory ES, 99 MANSE ST 15301
Yvonne Beverina, prin.
Log Pile ES, RURAL ROUTE 03 15301
Yvonne Beverina, prin.
Lone Pine ES, RURAL ROUTE 08 BOX 43 15301
Ray McCullough, prin.
North Franklin ES, 1041 GABBY AVE 15301
John Marano, prin.
Patten ES, SCHOOL STREET 15301
Ray McCullough, prin.
Windsor ES, 252 CAMERON RD 15301
Ray McCullough, prin.
Wolfdale ES, 2170 JEFFERSON AVE 15301
Yvonne Beverina, prin.
Other Schools – See Amity

Washington SD IU 1
Sch. Sys. Enr. Code 4
Supt. – Donald Hartswick
ALLISON & HALLAM AVE 15301
Washington-Park MS, 801 E WHEELING ST 15301
James Hanna, prin.
Washington Park ES, 801 E WHEELING ST 15301
James Hanna, prin.

Kennedy ES, 111 W SPRUCE ST 15301
St. Hillary ES, 340 HENDERSON AVE 15301

Washington Boro, Lancaster Co.
Penn Manor SD IU 13
Supt. – See Millersville
Central Manor ES
RURAL ROUTE 01 BOX 476 17582
Gerald Sheckart, prin.
Letort ES, RURAL ROUTE 01 17582
Diane Denison, prin.

Washingtonville, Montour Co., Pop. Code 2
Danville Area SD IU 16
Supt. – See Danville
Delong Memorial ES 17884
Charles Hughes, prin.

Waterford, Erie Co., Pop. Code 4
Ft. LeBoeuf SD IU 5
Sch. Sys. Enr. Code 4
Supt. – J. Wolf, 122 E 2ND ST 16441
Ft. LeBoeuf MS, 865 CHERRY ST 16441
Gary Rilling, prin.
ES, 323 CHERRY STREET 16441
Raymond Whitmer, prin.
Other Schools – See Mill Village, South Erie

Watsontown, Northumberland Co., Pop. Code 4

Watsontown Christian Academy
RURAL ROUTE 03 BOX 453 17777

Wattsburg, Erie Co., Pop. Code 3
Wattsburg Area SD IU 5
Sch. Sys. Enr. Code 5
Supt. – L. Hurlburt, P O BOX 219 16442
MS, P O BOX 119 16442 – Gerald Rosati, prin.
Wattsburg Central ES, LOWVILLE STREET 16442
Judy Hunt, prin.
Other Schools – See Erie, North East

Waverly, Lackawanna Co., Pop. Code 3
Abington Heights SD IU 19
Supt. – See Clarks Summit
ES, SCHOOL ST 18471 – Doris Lindsley, prin.

Waymart, Wayne Co., Pop. Code 4
Western Wayne SD IU 19
Supt. – See South Canaan
Wilson ES, RURAL ROUTE 02 18472
Levern Meritt, prin.

Wayne, Delaware Co., Pop. Code 6
Radnor Twp. SD IU 25
Sch. Sys. Enr. Code 5
Supt. – John DeFlaminis
135 S WAYNE AVE 19087
Radnor MS, 131 S WAYNE AVE 19087
E. Dodd, prin.
ES, 651 W WAYNE AVE 19087
Charles Shupe,Jr., prin.
Other Schools – See Bryn Mawr

Tredyffrin-Easttown SD IU 24
Supt. – See Berwyn
New Eagle ES, PUGH ROAD STRAFFORD 19087
Thomas Tobin, prin.
Valley Forge ES, 99 WALKER RD 19087
Stoughton Watts, prin.

Upper Merion Area SD IU 23
Supt. – See King of Prussia
Roberts ES, CROTON ROAD 19087
Harry Marshall, prin.

Woodlynde School
W VALLEY & UPPER GULPH 19087
Armenian Sister Academy
440 UPPER GULPH RD 19087
St. Katherine ES
MIDLAND & ABERDEEN AVE 19087

Waynesboro, Franklin Co., Pop. Code 6
Waynesboro Area SD IU 12
Sch. Sys. Enr. Code 5
Supt. – Dr. Michael Moskalski, P O BOX 72 17268
Fairview Avenue ES, 200 FAIRVIEW AVE 17268
Gerald Stouffer, prin.
Hooverville ES, 10829 BUCHANAN TRL E 17268
Bernard Zaborowski, prin.
Summitview ES, 840 E 2ND ST 17268
Ronald Snowberger, prin.
Other Schools – See Quincy

St. Andrew's ES, 213 E MAIN ST 17268

Waynesburg, Greene Co., Pop. Code 5
Central Green SD IU 1
Sch. Sys. Enr. Code 5
Supt. – Nancy Davis, P O BOX 472 15370
Miller MS, 126 E LINCOLN ST 15370
Allen Nixdorf, prin.
East Franklin ES, 300 NORTH STREET 15370
Craig Younken, prin.
East Ward ES, 176 N PORTER ST 15370
Charlotte Minehart, prin.
Whiteley ES, RURAL ROUTE 03 15370
Craig Younken, prin.
Other Schools – See Mount Morris, Spraggs

West Greene SD IU 1
Sch. Sys. Enr. Code 5
Supt. – Frank Blout
RURAL ROUTE 05 BOX 36-B 15370
Other Schools – See Aleppo, Graysville, New Freeport

Weatherly, Carbon Co., Pop. Code 5
Weatherly Area SD IU 21
Sch. Sys. Enr. Code 3
Supt. – Clyde Blair, SPRING & E MAIN STS 18255
Weatherly Area MS, EVERGREEN AVE 18255
John Kudlick, prin.
Weatherly ES, SIXTH STREET 18255
John Kudlick, prin.

Weedville, Elk Co.
St. Mary's Area SD IU 9
Supt. – See Saint Marys
Bennetts Valley ES 15868 – Marion Johnson, prin.

Wellsboro, Tioga Co., Pop. Code 5
Wellsboro Area SD IU 17
Sch. Sys. Enr. Code 4
Supt. – Dr. David Spearly, 2 CHARLES ST 16901
MS, 9 NICHOLS ST 16901 – Terry Erway, prin.
Gill ES, 10 SHERMAN ST 16901
William Wenner, prin.
Lappla ES, 32 MEADE ST 16901
William Wenner, prin.

Canyon Christian Academy
RURAL ROUTE 02 16901

Wellsville, York Co., Pop. Code 2
Northern York County SD IU 15
Supt. – See Dillsburg
ES, RURAL ROUTE 03 17365 – W. Martz, prin.

Wernersville, Berks Co., Pop. Code 4
Conrad Weiser Area SD IU 14
Supt. – See Robesonia
South Heidelberg ES, RURAL ROUTE 03 19565
Dennis Roule, prin.
ES, 63 PINE ST 19565 – Dennis Roule, prin.

Wescosville, Lehigh Co.
East Penn SD IU 21
Supt. – See Emmaus
ES, LIBERTY LANE 18106
Margaret Geosits, prin.

Wesleyville, Erie Co., Pop. Code 5
Iroquois Area SD IU 5
Supt. – See Erie
ES, 2138 WILLOW ST 16510
James Robbins, prin.

West Alexander, Washington Co., Pop. Code 2
McGuffey SD IU 1
Supt. – See Claysville
ES, LIBERTY STREET 15376
Raymond Pizzi, prin.

West Chester, Chester Co., Pop. Code 7
West Chester Area SD IU 24
Sch. Sys. Enr. Code 6
Supt. – Thomas Kent, 629 PAOLI PIKE 19380
Fugett MS, 500 ELLIS LANE 19380
Dr. Robert Shapley, prin.
Pierce MS, 1314 BURKE ROAD 19380
R. Clark, prin.
Stetson MS, 1060 WILMINGTON PARK 19382
R. London, prin.
East Bradford ES, RURAL ROUTE 01 19380
Franklin Tibbs, prin.
East Goshen ES, 800 N CHESTER RD 19382
Dr. Grace Bulls, prin.
Fern Hill ES, 915 LINCOLN AVE 19380
Joyce Bernhardt, prin.
Glen Acres ES, 1150 DELANCEY PL 19382
Ida Norrell, prin.

Hillsdale ES, 725 W MARKET ST 19382
Lee McFadden, prin.
Howse ES, 641 BOOT ROAD 19380
Donald Pitt, prin.
Westtown-Thornbury ES
150 WESTBOURNE ROAD 19380
Ronald Grimm, prin.
Wood ES, 1470 JOHNNYS WAY 19382
Peter Longmire, prin.
Other Schools – See Exton

West Chester Christian School
1237 PAOLI PIKE 19380
St. Agnes ES, 211 W GAY ST 19380
Sts. Simon & Jude ES, 6 S CHESTER RD 19382
West Chester Friends ES, 415 N HIGH ST 19380

Westfield, Tioga Co., Pop. Code 4
Northern Tioga SD IU 17
Supt. – See Elkland
Cowanesque Valley ES, MAPLE STREET 16950
Thomas Huzey, prin.

West Grove, Chester Co., Pop. Code 4
Avon-Grove SD IU 24
Sch. Sys. Enr. Code 4
Supt. – Ronald Ferrari, 20 PROSPECT AVE 19390
Engle MS, SCHOOL HOUSE ROAD 19390
Robert Pittman, prin.
Avon Grove ES, RURAL ROUTE 01 19390
Philip Pyle, prin.
Other Schools – See Kemblesville

Assumption BVM ES, STATE RD 19390

West Hazleton, Luzerne Co., Pop. Code 5
Hazleton Area SD IU 18
Supt. – See Hazleton
Encke ES, MONROE AVENUE 18201
Robert Katrishen, prin.

Tranfiguration ES, 214 W GREEN ST 18201

West Lawn, Berks Co., Pop. Code 4
Wilson SD IU 14
Sch. Sys. Enr. Code 5
Supt. – S. Dubelle, GRANDVIEW BLVD 19609
Cornwall Terrace ES, IROQUIS AVENUE 19609
Niles Stoudt, prin.
West Wyomissing ES, 2173 GARFIELD AVE 19609
Joseph Toy, prin.
Whitfield ES
VAN REED ROAD AND DWIGH 19609
Darlene Gorka, prin.
Other Schools – See Reading, Sinking Spring,
Wyomissing

West Middlesex, Mercer Co., Pop. Code 4
West Middlesex Area SD IU 4
Sch. Sys. Enr. Code 4
Supt. – Albert Jones, W LOW BLDG 16159
Low ES, SCHOOL ST 16159 – Daniel Paga, prin.
Oakview MS
SCHOOL ST & S NEWCASTLE 16159
Daniel Paga, prin.

West Mifflin, Allegheny Co., Pop. Code 8
West Mifflin Area SD IU 3
Sch. Sys. Enr. Code 5
Supt. – John Kresovich
515 CAMP HOLLOW ROAD 15122
MS, 371 CAMP HOLLOW ROAD 15122
Bert Ogden, prin.
Barton ES, 764 BEVERLY DR 15122
William Scharritter, prin.
Emerson ES, 1850 PENNSYLVANIA AVE 15122
Joseph Coccaro, prin.
Homeville ES, 4315 ELIZA ST 15122
James Gdovic, prin.
New England ES, STATE ROUTE 885 15122
William Scharritter, prin.

Lavelle Memorial ES, 1 MAJKA DR 15122
St. Agnes ES, 653 SAINT AGNES LN 15122

West Newton, Westmoreland Co., Pop. Code 5
Yough SD IU 7
Supt. – See Herminie
ES, 1208 VINE ST 15089 – Stanley Vlosich, prin.

Westover, Clearfield Co., Pop. Code 3
Harmony SD IU 10
Sch. Sys. Enr. Code 3
Supt. – Derry Stufft, RURAL ROUTE 01 16692
Harmony Area S, RURAL ROUTE 01 16692
James Sybert, prin.

West Pittston, Luzerne Co., Pop. Code 6
Wyoming Area SD IU 18
Supt. – See Exeter
Wyoming Area MS, MONTGOMERY AVE 18643
Lawrence Brogna, prin.
Luzerne Avenue ES, 313 LUZERNE AVE 18643
Richard Ascani, prin.

West Reading, Berks Co., Pop. Code 5
Wyomissing Area SD IU 14
Supt. – See Wyomissing
MS, 4TH AVENUE AND CHESTNUT 19611
James Derr, prin.

West Sunbury, Butler Co., Pop. Code 2
Moniteau SD IU 4
Sch. Sys. Enr. Code 4
Supt. – Robert Hartnett, RURAL ROUTE 01 16061

McKinney ES, RURAL ROUTE 01   16061
  James Wetzel, prin.
Other Schools – See Boyers, Parker

Westtown, Chester Co., Pop. Code 6

Westtown School   19395

Wexford, Allegheny Co., Pop. Code 3
Pine-Richland SD IU 3
Supt. – See Gibsonia
ES, BROWN ROAD   15090 – Elio Allasia, prin.

St. Alexis ES, 10090 OLD PERRY HWY   15090
St. Alphonsus ES, 201 CHURCH RD   15090

Whitehall, Lehigh Co., Pop. Code 7
Whitehall-Coplay SD IU 21
Sch. Sys. Enr. Code 5
Supt. – Daniel Yakubecek
  2940 MACARTHUR ROAD   18052
Whitehall-Coplay MS
  2930 MACARTHUR ROAD   18052
  Robert Rothenberger, prin.
Gockley ES, 2932 MACARTHUR RD   18052
  Mary Fekula, prin.
Steckel ES, 2928 MACARTHUR RD   18052
  Richard Brownell, prin.

St. Elizabeth ES, 431 PERSHING BLVD   18052

White Oak, Allegheny Co., Pop. Code 6

St. Anglea Merici ES
  1640 FAWCETT AVEE   15131

Wilkes-Barre, Luzerne Co., Pop. Code 8
Hanover Area SD IU 18
Sch. Sys. Enr. Code 4
Supt. – Dr. Dominick Graziano
  1600 SANS SOUCI PARKWAY   18702
Hanover Green ES, MAIN ROAD   18702
  Alberta Griffiths, prin.
Hanover Memorial ES, 98 ST MARYS RD   18702
  Mary Budinas, prin.
Lynwood ES, COLLEY FIRST STREETS   18702
  Dennis Puhalla, prin.

Wilkes-Barre Area SD IU 18
Sch. Sys. Enr. Code 6
Supt. – Leo Solomon, 730 S MAIN ST   18711
Bear Creek Township ES
  RURAL ROUTE 01   18702 – Michael Novosel, prin.
Calvin-Parsons ES, 991 SCOTT ST   18705
  William Sokola, prin.
Cotton Avenue ES, 42 COTTON AVE   18705
  Michael Novossel, prin.
Dodson ES, 80 JONES ST   18702
  John Brislin, prin.
Flood ES, 565 N WASHINGTON ST   18705
  Donald Sabatino, prin.
Heights ES, 1 S SHERMAN ST   18702
  Michael Ferrence, prin.
Kistler ES, 301 OLD RIVER RD   18702
  Philip Walsh, prin.
Mackin ES, 13 27 HILLARD STREET   18702
  William Sokola, prin.
Other Schools – See Plains

St. Ignatius MS, 316 N MAPLE AVE   18704
Holy Name of Jesus ES
  1133 WYOMING AVE   18704
Holy Saviour ES, 35 WORRALL ST   18702
Holy Trinity ES, 119 HUGHES ST   18704
North End Catholic ES, 522 MADISON ST   18705
Sacred Heart of Jesus ES, 421 MADISON ST   18705
St. Aloysius ES, 321 BARNERY ST   18702
St. Boniface ES, 221 BLACKMAN ST   18702
Sts. Nicholas & Mary ES
  242 S WASHINGTON ST   18701
Sts. Peter & Paul ES, 12 HUDSON RD   18705

Wilkinsburg, Allegheny Co., Pop. Code 7
Wilkinsburg SD IU 3
Sch. Sys. Enr. Code 4
Supt. – Walter Watson, 718 WALLACE AVE   15221
Johnston ES, 1256 FRANKLIN AVE   15221
  Alecia Gibbs, prin.
Kelly ES, 400 KELLY AVE   15221
  Donald Sobel, prin.
Turner ES, 1833 LAKETON RD   15221
  Roslynne Wilson, prin.

Williamsburg, Blair Co., Pop. Code 4
Williamsburg Comm. SD IU 8
Sch. Sys. Enr. Code 3
Supt. – Lee Swinsburg, 515 W 3RD ST   16693
Williamsburg Community ES
  SAGE HILL DRIVE   16693 – Jan Srock, prin.

Williamsport, Lycoming Co., Pop. Code 8
Jersey Shore Area SD IU 17
Supt. – See Jersey Shore
Nippenose Valley ES
  RURAL ROUTE 03 BOX 267   17701
  Eugene Kurzejewski, prin.

Loyalsock Twp. SD IU 17
Sch. Sys. Enr. Code 4
Supt. – Donald Byerly
  1225 CLAYTON AVE   17701
Loyalsock Twp. JHS
  2101 LOYALSOCK DRIVE   17701 – R. Straub,
  prin.

Becht ES, CLAYTON AND SHERIDAN   17701
  Raymond Thompson, prin.
Other Schools – See Montoursville

South Williamsport Area SD IU 17
Supt. – See South Williamsport
Duboistown ES, 126 SUMMER ST   17701
  Richard Zuber, prin.

Williamsport Area SD IU 17
Sch. Sys. Enr. Code 6
Supt. – Oscar Knade, 201 W 3RD ST   17701
Curtin MS, 100 PACKER ST   17701
  Jay Fetterman, prin.
Lycoming Valley MS, 1825 HAYS LANE   17701
  William Swisher, prin.
Roosevelt MS, 2800 W 4TH ST   17701
  Jay Livziey, prin.
Cochran ES, 1500 CHERRY ST   17701
  Charmaine Cunningham, prin.
Jackson ES
  WAYNE AND HILLSIDE AVENUE   17701
  Richard Bittner, prin.
Lose ES, 1121 MEMORIAL AVE   17701
  Byron Campbell, prin.
Round Hills ES, 136 GRIMESVILLE RD   17701
  Donna Flaig, prin.
Sheridan ES, 915 SHERIDAN ST   17701
  Herbert Seltzer,Jr., prin.
Stevens ES, 1150 LOUISA ST   17701
  Ragnar Franzen, prin.
Other Schools – See Cogan Station, Linden, Trout Run

Immaculate Conception ES
  RURAL ROUTE 03 BOX 169   17701
St. Ann's ES, 1225 NORTHWAY RD   17701
St. Boniface ES, 710 FRANKLIN ST   17701
St. Joseph's ES, 711 W EDWIN ST   17701

Williamstown, Dauphin Co., Pop. Code 4
Williams Valley SD IU 29
Supt. – See Tower City
Williams Valley Elementary Plus 2
  JULIAN STREET   17098 – David Michael, prin.
Williams Valley Elementary Plus 3
  JULIAN STREET   17098 – David Michael, prin.

Willow Grove, Montgomery Co., Pop. Code 7
Abington SD IU 23
Supt. – See Abington
Willow Hill ES, 1700 COOLIDGE AVE   19090
  Joanne Weaver, prin.

Upper Dublin SD IU 23
Supt. – See Dresher
Fitzwater ES, SCHOOL LANE   19090
  Ellen Milgrim, prin.

Upper Moreland Twp. SD IU 23
Sch. Sys. Enr. Code 5
Supt. – Paul Beck, TERWOOD ROAD   19090
Cold Spring ES, REED STREET   19090
  James Stephenson, prin.
Other Schools – See Hatboro

St. David ES, EASTON RD AT SMT   19090

Willow Hill, Franklin Co.
Fannett-Metal SD IU 12
Sch. Sys. Enr. Code 3
Supt. – Ben Van Horn   17271
Fannett-Metal ES   17271 – Sandara Miley, prin.

Willow Street, Lancaster Co., Pop. Code 4
Lampeter-Strasburg SD IU 13
Supt. – See Lampeter
ES, 9 MAIN ST   17584 – Nancy Hoop, prin.

Penn Manor SD IU 13
Supt. – See Millersville
Pequea ES, RURAL ROUTE 03 BOX 128A   17584
  William Wood, prin.

Wilmerding, Allegheny Co., Pop. Code 4
East Allegheny SD IU 3
Supt. – See North Versailles
Westinghouse MS, MARGUERITE AVENUE   15148
  Carmen Violi, prin.

Windber, Somerset Co., Pop. Code 6
Windber Area SD IU 8
Sch. Sys. Enr. Code 4
Supt. – Salvatore Marro
  2301 GRAHAM AVE   15963
Windber Area MS, 2301 GRAHAM AVE   15963
  Glenn Gaye, prin.
East End ES, GRAHAM AVENUE   15963
  Mathew Pavlovich, prin.
Hoffman Avenue ES, HOFFMAN AVENUE   15963
  Mathew Pavlovich, prin.
Maple Drive ES, RUMM MAPLE DR   15963
  Mathew Pavlovich, prin.
West End ES, 12TH AND SOMERSET   15963
  Glenn Gaye, prin.

Windsor, York Co., Pop. Code 4
Red Lion Area SD IU 12
Sch. Sys. Enr. Code 5
Supt. – Dale Reinecker
  28 WINDSOR ROAD #34   17366
Other Schools – See Brogue, Red Lion, York

Wingate, Centre Co.
Bald Eagle Area SD IU 10
Sch. Sys. Enr. Code 5
Supt. – Dr. Richard Grove, P O BOX 4   16880
ES, THEATER DRIVE   16880
  Dr. Elizabeth Llewellyn, prin.

Other Schools – See Clarence, Howard, Port Matilda,
  Snow Shoe

Womelsdorf, Berks Co., Pop. Code 4
Conrad Weiser Area SD IU 14
Supt. – See Robesonia
New Womelsdorf ES, S THIRD ST   19567
  George Wentling, prin.

Woodlyn, Delaware Co., Pop. Code 6
Ridley SD IU 25
Supt. – See Folsom
ES, SCHOOL LANE AND COLSO   19094
  Dr. Warren Bowden, prin.

Woolrich, Clinton Co., Pop. Code 3
Keystone Central SD IU 10
Supt. – See Lock Haven
ES, RURAL ROUTE 01   17779
  Calvin Young, prin.

Wormleysburg, Cumberland Co., Pop. Code 5

Harrisburg Academy, 10 ERFORD ROAD   17043

Wrightstown, Bucks Co.
Council Rock SD IU 22
Supt. – See Richboro
ES, PENNS PARK ROAD   18940
  Thomas Walsh, prin.

Wrightsville, York Co., Pop. Code 4
Eastern York SD IU 12
Sch. Sys. Enr. Code 4
Supt. – Robert McGraw
  RURAL ROUTE 02 BOX 150   17368
ES, 300-350 CHESTNUT STREET   17368
  Saundra Hoover, prin.
Other Schools – See East Prospect, Hellam

Wyalusing, Bradford Co., Pop. Code 3
Wyalusing Area SD IU 17
Sch. Sys. Enr. Code 4
Supt. – Warner Stark, P O BOX 157   18853
Camptown ES, RURAL ROUTE 01   18853
  Albert Minetola, prin.
ES, RURAL ROUTE 02 BOX 264   18853
  Robert Dibble, prin.
Other Schools – See Laceyville, New Albany

Wyncote, Montgomery Co., Pop. Code 6
Cheltenham Twp. SD IU 23
Supt. – See Elkins Park
Cedarbrook MS, 300 LONGFELLOW ROAD   19095
  John Townsend, prin.
ES, RICES MILL & BARKER RD   19095
  Dontina Jackson, prin.

Ancillae Assumption Academy
  2025 CHURCH RD   19095

Wyoming, Luzerne Co., Pop. Code 5
Wyoming Area SD IU 18
Supt. – See Exeter
Tenth Street ES, TENTH STREET   18644
  Thomas Jones, prin.

Wyomissing, Berks Co., Pop. Code 6
Wilson SD IU 14
Supt. – See West Lawn
Berkshire Height ES
  N 7TH AND WYOMISSING   19610
  Joseph Toy, prin.

Wyomissing Area SD IU 14
Sch. Sys. Enr. Code 4
Supt. – David Magill
  GIRARD & EVANS AVE   19610
Wyomissing Hills ES, WOODLAND ROAD   19610
  James Derr, prin.
Other Schools – See West Reading

Wysox, Bradford Co.
Towanda Area SD IU 17
Supt. – See Towanda
ES, RURAL ROUTE 01   18854
  Joyce Vandusen, prin.

Yardley, Bucks Co., Pop. Code 5
Pennsbury SD IU 22
Supt. – See Fallsington
Pennwood MS, RURAL ROUTE 01   19067
  Roger Hedeman, prin.
Edgewood ES
  EDGEWOOD & OXFORD VAL RD   19067
  Ralph Nuzzolo, prin.
Makefield ES, 95 MAKEFIELD RD   19067
  Robert Chast, prin.
Quarry Hill ES, 1625 QUARRY RD   19067
  Bruce Johnson, prin.

Abrams Hebrew Academy
  31 W COLLEGE AVE   19067
Grey Nun Academy, 1750 QUARRY RD   19067
St. Ignatius ES, READING AVE   19067

Yeadon, Delaware Co., Pop. Code 7
William Penn SD IU 25
Sch. Sys. Enr. Code 5
Supt. – John Dirnbauer
  BELL AVE & MACDADE BLVD   19050
Evans ES
  BAILY ROAD AND CHURCH LANE   19050
  James Banks, prin.
Other Schools – See Aldan, Colwyn, Darby, East
  Lansdowne, Lansdowne

St. Louis ES, 801 W COBBS CREEK PKY   19050

Yeagertown, Mifflin Co., Pop. Code 4
Mifflin County SD IU 11
Supt. – See Lewistown
Derry ES, GREENWOOD AVE 17099
  Kenneth Barrett, prin.

York, York Co., Pop. Code 8
Central York SD IU 12
Sch. Sys. Enr. Code 5
Supt. – W. Snyder, 275 E 7TH AVE 17404
Central York MS, 1950 N HILLS ROAD 17402
  Linda Estep, prin.
Hayshire ES, 2801 HAYSHIRE DR 17402
  Barbara Snare, prin.
North Hills ES, 1330 NORTH HLS RD 17402
  Jeffrey Fox, prin.
Roundtown ES, 570 CHURCH RD 17404
  Jeffrey Fox, prin.
Stony Brook ES, 250 SILVER SPUR DR 17402
  Richard Burd, prin.

Dallastown Area SD IU 12
Supt. – See Dallastown
Leaders Heights ES, RURAL ROUTE 08 17403
  Dr. Richard Mauro, prin.
Loganville-Springfield ES
  RURAL ROUTE 08 17403 – Robert Grove, prin.
Ore Valley ES, RURAL ROUTE 03 17402
  Barry Rohrbaugh, prin.
York Township ES, 2500 S QUEEN ST 17402
  Richard Ault, prin.

Northeastern York SD IU 12
Supt. – See Manchester
Conewago ES, 570 COPENHAFFER RD 17404
  Joseph Snoke, prin.

Red Lion Area SD IU 12
Supt. – See Windsor
Locust Grove ES
  RURAL ROUTE 27 BOX 136 17402
  Bradley Stell, prin.

Spring Grove Area SD IU 12
Supt. – See Spring Grove
New Salem ES
  RURAL ROUTE 28 BOX 140N 17404
  Carol Kling, prin.

West York Area SD IU 12
Sch. Sys. Enr. Code 4
Supt. – Albert Glennon
  2605 W MARKET ST 17404
West York Area JHS, 1800 BANNISTER ST 17404
  Barbara Rupp, prin.
Lincolnway ES, 2625 W PHILA STREET 17404
  Norman Shimmel, prin.
Loucks ES, 1381 W POPLAR ST 17404
  Laura George, prin.
Martin ES, 1731 W PHILA ST 17404
  Norman Shimmel, prin.
Trimmer MS, 1900 BRENDA RD 17404
  Kenneth Klawitter, prin.
Wallace ES, 2065 HIGH ST 17404
  Kenneth Klawitter, prin.

York CSD IU 12
Sch. Sys. Enr. Code 6
Supt. – Jack Van Newkirk, P O BOX 1927 17405
Penn MS, 415 E BOUNDARY AVE 17403
  Ronald Trimmer, prin.
Smith MS, 701 TEXAS AVE 17404
  Dr. Julia Harris, prin.
Davis ES, 300 S OGONTZ ST 17403
  David Kochik, prin.
Devers ES, 801 CHANCEFORD AVE 17404
  Joseph Bender, prin.
Ferguson ES, 525 N NEWBERRY ST 17404
  George Glatfelter, prin.
Goode ES, 251 N BROAD ST 17403
  Richard Hall, prin.
Jackson ES, 177 E JACKSON ST 17403
  Richard Barley, prin.
Lincoln ES, 599 W KING ST 17404
  Michael Fogle, prin.
McKinley ES, 600 MANOR ST 17403
  Dennis Fry, prin.

York Suburban SD IU 12
Sch. Sys. Enr. Code 4
Supt. – Robert Dovey
  HOLLYWOOD DR & SOUTHERN RD 17403
York Suburban MS, SUNDALE DRIVE 17402
  Jere Eckenroth, prin.
East York ES, ERIEN DR 17402
  Sharon Whittle, prin.
Indian Rock ES, 1500 INDIAN ROCK DA 17403
  Bonni Kunerroth, prin.

Christian School of York
  907 GREENBRIER ROAD 17404
Immaculate Conception BVM ES
  323 S GEORGE ST 17403
St. John Lutheran ES
  2580 MOUNT ROSE AVE 17402
St. Joseph ES, 2945 KINGSTON RD 17402
St. Patrick ES, 231 S BEAVER ST 17403
St. Rose of Lima ES, 459 W KING ST 17404

York Haven, York Co., Pop. Code 3
Northeastern York SD IU 12
Supt. – See Manchester
ES, S HARTMAN STREET 17370
  William Kleinfelter, prin.

York Springs, Adams Co., Pop. Code 3
Bermudian Springs SD IU 12
Sch. Sys. Enr. Code 4
Supt. – W. Reese Lichtel
  BERMUDIAN SPRINGS CRK ROAD 17372
Bermudian Springs MS, RURAL ROUTE 02 17372
  Gerald Soltis, prin.
ES, P O BOX 501 17372 – Ronald Snyder, prin.
Other Schools – See East Berlin

Youngstown, Westmoreland Co., Pop. Code 2

Sacred Heart ES, P O BOX 328 15696

Youngsville, Warren Co., Pop. Code 4
Warren County SD IU 5
Supt. – See Warren
ES, 232 SECOND ST 16371
  Robert McCullough, prin.

Warren County Christian School
  ROUTE 6W 16371

Zelienople, Butler Co., Pop. Code 5
Seneca Valley SD IU 4
Supt. – See Harmony
Connoquenessing Valley ES
  BEAVER & PGH STREETS 16063
  Donald Tylinski, prin.

St. Gregory ES, 115 PINE ST 16063

RHODE ISLAND

STATE DEPARTMENT OF EDUCATION
22 Hayes St., Providence 02908
(401) 277-2031

Commissioner of Education	Dr. J. Troy Earhart
Assistant Commissioner	Dr. Kenneth Mellor
Director Administration & Finance	Robert Whitaker
Director School Support Services	Edward Costa
Director Vocational & Adult Education	Dr. Frank Santoro
Director Management Information & Evaluation	Dr. Janice Baker
Director School/Teacher Accreditation	Edward Dambruch
Director Special Populations	Dr. Phil Zarlengo
Director Civil Rights & Personnel	Frank Walker
Director Literacy & Dropout Prevention	Marie DiBiasio

BOARD OF REGENTS FOR ELEMENTARY & SECONDARY EDUCATION
Augustine Capotosto, Jr., *Chairperson*   22 Hayes St., Providence   02908

RHODE ISLAND OFFICE OF HIGHER EDUCATION
Dr. Eleanor McMahon, *Commissioner*   199 Promenade St., Providence   02908

PUBLIC, PRIVATE, AND PAROCHIAL ELEMENTARY SCHOOLS

Ashaway, Washington Co., Pop. Code 4
Chariho SD
Supt. – See Wood River Junction
ES, P O BOX 857   02804 – Bonnie Ursillo, prin.

Barrington, Bristol Co., Pop. Code 7
Barrington SD
Sch. Sys. Enr. Code 4
Supt. – Dr. Philip Streifer
   283 COUNTRY ROAD   02806
MS, MIDDLE HWY   02806 – Robert Miller, prin.
Barrington Middle Highway MS
   MIDDLE HWY   02806 – David Steele, prin.
Hampden Meadows ES
   NEW MEADOW ROAD   02806 – Jean Leary, prin.
Nayatt ES, 400 NAYATT RD   02806
   Robert Hassan, prin.
Primrose Hill ES, MIDDLE HWY   02806
   Paul Osmon, prin.

Barrington Christian Academy
   OLD COUNTRY ROAD   02806
St. Luke ES, WALDRON AVE   02806

Block Island, Newport Co., Pop. Code 2
New Shoreham SD
Sch. Sys. Enr. Code 2
Supt. – Dr. Esther Campbell, HIGH ST   02807
Block Island Consolidated S, P O BOX 249   02807
   Dr. Esther Campbell, prin.

Bradford, Washington Co., Pop. Code 4
Westerly SD
Supt. – See Westerly
ES, CHURCH ST   02808
   Carolyn Longolucco, prin.

Bristol, Bristol Co., Pop. Code 7
Bristol SD
Sch. Sys. Enr. Code 4
Supt. – Gerald Bourgeois, 151 STATE ST   02809
Byfield ES, 220 HIGH ST   02809
   Naomi Carpenter, prin.
Colt-Andrews MS, 570 HOPE ST   02809
   James Alves, prin.
Guiteras MS, 35 WASHINGTON ST   02809
   F. Fanger, prin.
Reynolds ES, 235 HIGH ST   02809
   Naomi Carpenter, prin.
Rockwell ES, 1225 HOPE ST   02809
   Naomi Carpenter, prin.

Our Lady of Mt. Carmel ES, 127 STATE ST   02809
St. Elizabeth ES, 10 MONROE AVE   02809

Carolina, Washington Co., Pop. Code 2
Chariho SD
Supt. – See Wood River Junction
Charlestown ES
   363 CAROLINA BACK ROAD   02813
   Allen Nichols, prin.

Central Falls, Providence Co., Pop. Code 7
Central Falls SD
Sch. Sys. Enr. Code 5
Supt. – Roland Deneault, 21 HEDLEY AVE   02863
Broad Street ES, 405 BROAD ST   02863
   Irene Gouveia, prin.
Calcutt MS, 112 WASHINGTON ST   02863
   Allen Shunney, prin.
Hunt ES, 14 KENDALL ST   02863
   Ann Prosser, prin.
Risk ES, 949 DEXTER ST   02863
   Carol Shore, prin.
Robertson ES, 135 HUNT ST   02863
   Veronica Magnan, prin.
Other Schools – See Lincoln

Holy Trinity ES, 325 COWDEN ST   02863
St. Matthew/Notre Dame ES
   909 LONSDALE AVE   02863

Chepachet, Providence Co., Pop. Code 3
Glocester SD
Supt. – See North Scituate
ES, MAIN ST   02814 – Mary Ferns, prin.

Clayville, Providence Co.
Scituate SD
Supt. – See North Scituate
ES, FIELD HILL ROAD   02815
   Harold Wright, prin.

Coventry, Kent Co., Pop. Code 8
Coventry SD
Sch. Sys. Enr. Code 6
Supt. – Raymond Spear, 60 WOOD ST   02816
JHS, 19 FOSTER DRIVE   02816
   James Palumbo, prin.
Blackrock ES, LAFORGE DR   02816
   David Moss, prin.
Hopkins Hill ES, JOHNSON BLVD   02816
   Arthur Bradstreet, prin.
Oak Haven ES, PETTINE ST   02816
   Joanne Olson, prin.
Tiogue ES, E SHORE DR   02816
   John Ruzanski, prin.
Washington Oak ES, FLAT RIVER ROAD   02816
   Dr. James Brown, prin.
Other Schools – See Greene

Father John Doyle ES, 341 S MAIN ST   02816
Our Lady of Czenstochowa ES
   222 MACARTHUR BLVD   02816

St. Vincent De Paul School
   SAINT VINCENT DE PAUL ST   02816

Cranston, Providence Co., Pop. Code 8
Cranston SD
Sch. Sys. Enr. Code 6
Supt. – Dr. Joseph J. Picano Jr.
   P O BOX 9969   02910
Arlington ES, 155 PRINCESS AVE   02920
   Marie Benjamin, prin.
Dutemple ES, 32 GARDEN ST   02910
   Rose Vestri, prin.
Eden Park ES, 180 OAKLAND AVE   02910
   Barbara Simone, prin.
Garden City ES, 70 PLANTATIONS DR   02920
   Dennis Laven, prin.
Gladstone Street ES, 50 GLADSTONE ST   02920
   George Gagnon, prin.
Glen Hills ES, GLEN HILLS DR   02920
   John Vestri, prin.
Horton ES, 1196 PARK AVE   02910
   Linda Casey, prin.
Oak Lawn ES, 36 STONEHAM ST   02920
   Edward Mitchell, prin.
Peters ES, 15 MAYBERRY ST   02920
   Donald Noack, prin.
Stadium ES, 100 CRESCENT AVE   02910
   William Brannon, prin.
Stone Hill ES, 21 VILLAGE AVE   02920
   James Cofone, prin.
Waterman ES, 722 PONTIAC AVE   02910
   William Condon, prin.
Woodridge ES, 401 BUDLONG RD   02920
   Philip Abbatomarco, prin.
Other Schools – See Providence

Cranston-Johnston ES, 43 POPLAR DR   02920
St. Mary ES, 85 CHESTER AVE   02920
St. Matthew ES, 1301 ELMWOOD AVE   02910

Cumberland, Providence Co., Pop. Code 8
Cumberland SD
Sch. Sys. Enr. Code 5
Supt. – Dr. Rodney McFarlin
   2600 MENDON ROAD   02864
MS, 280 HIGHLAND AVE   02864
   Robert Wallace, prin.
North Cumberland MS
   30 NATE WHIPPLE HWY   02864
   Joseph Nasif,Jr., prin.
Ashton ES, SCOTT RD   02864
   Raymond Vallee, prin.
Central ES, CLARK ST   02864 – David Moore, prin.
Community ES, WHIPPLE ROAD   02864
   John Smith, prin.
Cumberland Hill ES
   175 MANVILLE HILL RD   02864
   Edward Lesiak, prin.
Cumberland Hill Annex ES
   3357 MENDON RD   02864 – Edward Lesiak, prin.
Garvin Memorial ES
   DIAMOND HILL ROAD   02864
   Thomas Stepka, prin.
St. Patrick MS, 269 BROAD ST   02864
   David Moore, prin.

Mercymount Country Day School
   75 WRENTHAM RD   02864

East Greenwich, Kent Co., Pop. Code 7
East Greenwich SD
Sch. Sys. Enr. Code 4
Supt. – David Connolly, 5 DIVISION ST   02818
Cole JHS, 100 CEDAR AVE   02818
   Joseph Militello, prin.
Eldredge ES, 101 FIRST AVE   02818
   Francis Gallo, prin.
Frenchtown ES, FRENCHTOWN ROAD   02818
   Joan Sousa, prin.
Hanaford ES, LABARON DR   02818
   Dr. Donald Holder, prin.
Meadowbrook Farms ES, 2 CHESTNUT DR   02818
   Marie Kojian, prin.

Warwick SD
Supt. – See Warwick
Potowomut ES, 225 POTOWOMUT RD   02818
   Margaret Adams, prin.

Rocky Hill School, IVES ROAD   02818
Our Lady of Mercy Regional ES, 4TH AVE   02818

East Providence, Providence Co., Pop. Code 8
East Providence SD
Sch. Sys. Enr. Code 6
Supt. – John Degoes, 80 BURNSIDE AVE   02915
Grove Avenue ES, 100 GROVE AVE   02914
   Diane Santos, prin.
Hennessey ES, 175 FORT ST   02914
   Stanley Traverse, prin.
Kent Heights ES, 2674 PAWTUCKET AVE   02914
   Thomas Labonte, prin.
Orlo Avenue ES, 25 ORLO AVE   02914
   Patricia Piver, prin.
Tristam Burges ES, 1169 S BROADWAY   02914
   Stanley Traverse, prin.
Whiteknact ES, 261 GROSVENOR AVE   02914
   Edward Bochner, prin.
Other Schools – See Riverside, Rumford

Sacred Heart ES, 56 PURCHASE ST   02914
The Gordon ES, 45 MAXFIELD AVE   02914

Esmond, Providence Co., Pop. Code 5
Smithfield SD
Sch. Sys. Enr. Code 4
Supt. – David Reilly, 47 FARNUM PIKE   02917
Gallagher JHS, INDIAN RUN TRAIL   02917
   Charles Bresnahan, prin.
Laperche ES, LIMEOCK ROAD   02917
   Barry Dana, prin.
McCabe ES, PLEASANT VIEW AVE   02917
   Dr. James Paras, prin.
Old County Road ES, 208 OLD COUNTY RD   02917
   Andrew Tournas, prin.
Other Schools – See Greenville

Exeter, Washington Co., Pop. Code 5
Exeter-West Greenwich SD
Sch. Sys. Enr. Code 4
Supt. – John Eldridge
   NOOSENECK HILL ROAD   02822
Metcalf ES, NOOSENECK HILL ROAD   02822
   George Finch, prin.
Wawaloam ES, RURAL ROUTE 102   02822
   Christine Davidson, prin.
Other Schools – See West Greenwich

Foster, Providence Co., Pop. Code 5
Foster SD
Supt. – See North Scituate
Paine ES, FOSTER CENTER ROAD   02825
   Gerard Tetreault, prin.

Greene, Kent Co.
Coventry SD
Supt. – See Coventry
Western Coventry ES
   RURAL ROUTE 117 BOX 157   02827
   Barry Ricci, prin.

Greenville, Providence Co., Pop. Code 6
Smithfield SD
Supt. – See Esmond
Winsor ES, PUTNAM AVE   02828
   Leslie Improta, prin.

St. Philip ES, 618 PUTNAM PIKE   02828

Harrisville, Providence Co., Pop. Code 4
Burrillville SD
Sch. Sys. Enr. Code 5
Supt. – Dennis Flynn, OLD VICTORY HWY   02830
Callahan ES, SCHOOL ST   02830
   Edward Mara, prin.
Levy ES, MAIN ST   02830 – Allan Drury, prin.
Other Schools – See Pascoag

Hope, Providence Co.
Scituate SD
Supt. – See North Scituate
ES, RURAL ROUTE 116   02831
   Carl Johnson, prin.

Hope Valley, Washington Co., Pop. Code 4
Chariho SD
Supt. – See Wood River Junction
ES, MAIN ST   02832 – (—), prin.

Jamestown, Newport Co., Pop. Code 5
Jamestown SD
Sch. Sys. Enr. Code 3
Supt. – Phyllis Schmidt, P O BOX 318   02835
ES, P O BOX 318   02835 – Phyllis Schmidt, prin.

Johnston, Providence Co., Pop. Code 7
Johnston SD
Sch. Sys. Enr. Code 5
Supt. – Dr. Ralph Jasparro
   345 CHERRY HILL ROAD   02919
Ferri MS, 10 MEMORIAL AVE   02919
   Frederick Pasquariello, prin.
Barnes ES, BARNES AVE   02919
   Richard Allaire, prin.
Brown Avenue ES, 14 BROWN AVE   02919
   John Guiliano, prin.
Calef ES, WAVELAND ST   02919
   Frank Giuliano, prin.
Graniteville ES, 6 COLLINS AVE   02919
   Barbara Lysik, prin.
Thornton ES, 4 SCHOOL ST   02919
   Arlene Iannazzi, prin.
Winsor Hill ES, 100 THERESA ST   02919
   Joseph Hopkins, prin.

St. Rocco ES, 931 ATWOOD AVE   02919

Lincoln, Providence Co., Pop. Code 7
Central Falls SD
Supt. – See Central Falls
Fairlawn/Lincoln ES, PARKER ST   02865
   Irene Gouveia, prin.

Lincoln SD
Sch. Sys. Enr. Code 5
Supt. – Franklin Peters
   1624 LONSDALE AVE   02865
Lincoln Central ES, 1215 GREAT RD   02865
   Stephen Hofgren, prin.
Lonsdale ES, 230 RIVER RD   02865
   Ronald Tibbetts, prin.
Saylesville ES, WOODLAND ST   02865
   Sam Williams, prin.
Other Schools – See Manville

Little Compton, Newport Co., Pop. Code 5
Little Compton SD
Sch. Sys. Enr. Code 2
Supt. – Donald Gavin, THE COMMONS 02837
Wilbur ES, THE COMMONS 02837
Carl Mock, prin.

Manville, Providence Co.
Lincoln SD
Supt. – See Lincoln
Northern Lincoln ES, NEW RIVER RD 02838
Franklin Peters, prin.

Middletown, Newport Co., Pop. Code 7
Middletown SD
Sch. Sys. Enr. Code 5
Supt. – D. William Wheetley
350 E MAIN ROAD 02840
Gaudet MS, 1017 AQUIDNECK AVE 02840
Vincent Guillano, prin.
Aquidneck ES, 100 RESERVOIR RD 02840
Joseph Ruggiero, prin.
Kennedy ES, WEST MAIN ROAD 02840
John Chapman, prin.
Oliphant ES, WEST MAIN ROAD 02840
Rosemarie Kraeger, prin.

Newport County Catholic ES
909 W MAIN RD 02840
The New ES, FOREST AVE 02840

Narragansett, Washington Co., Pop. Code 7
Narragansett SD
Sch. Sys. Enr. Code 4
Supt. – Dr. F. William Davis, 25 5TH AVE 02882
ES, 55 MUMFORD RD 02882 – David Hayes, prin.

Newport, Newport Co., Pop. Code 8
Newport SD
Sch. Sys. Enr. Code 5
Supt. – Dr. Donald Beaudette, MARY ST 02840
Thompson JHS, 39 BROADWAY ST 02840
Arthur Dring,Jr., prin.
Carey ES, NARRAGANSETT AVE 02840
Michael Towey, prin.
Coggeshall ES, 130 VAN ZANDT AVE 02840
Timothy Ryan, prin.
Cranston-Calvert ES, 10 CRANSTON AVE 02840
Daniel Bolhouse, prin.
Sheffield ES, 519 BROADWAY 02840
Robert Coulombe, prin.
Sullivan ES, 9 DEXTER ST 02840
Michael Segerson, prin.
Underwood ES, HARRISON AVE 02840
Edward Walsh, prin.

St. Joseph Cluny ES, BRENTON ROAD 02840
St. Michaels Country ES
180 RHODE ISLAND AVE 02840

North Kingstown, Washington Co., Pop. Code 7
North Kingstown SD
Sch. Sys. Enr. Code 5
Supt. – Dr. Josephine Kelleher
100 FAIRWAY DR 02852
Davisville MS, 200 SCHOOL ST 02852
E. Jane Kondon, prin.
Wickford MS, 250 TOWER HILL ROAD 02852
Martin Hellewell, prin.
Davisville ES, 50 E COURT 02852
Robert Stearns, prin.
Forest Park ES, 50 WOODLAWN DR 02852
Carol Shipman, prin.
Hamilton ES, 25 SALISBURY AVE 02852
Manuel Perry, prin.
Quidnessett ES, 166 MARK DR 02852
William Wilson, prin.
Stony Lane ES, 825 STONEY LN 02852
Roy Seitsinger, prin.
Wickford ES, 99 PHILLIPS ST 02852
Kenneth O'Grady, prin.

North Providence, Providence Co., Pop. Code 8
North Providence SD
Sch. Sys. Enr. Code 5
Supt. – Richard Shadoian, 9 GEORGE ST 02911
Birchwood MS, BIRCHWOOD DR 02904
Joseph Pasonelli, prin.
Ricci ES, INTERVALE AVE 02911
Charles Graves, prin.
Other Schools – See Providence

North Scituate, Providence Co., Pop. Code 2
Foster SD
Sch. Sys. Enr. Code 4
Supt. – Gerard Tetreault
RURAL ROUTE 02 BOX 498B 02857
Other Schools – See Foster

Foster-Glocester SD
Sch. Sys. Enr. Code 4
Supt. – Clifton Boyle
RURAL ROUTE 02 BOX 498 B 02857
Ponaganset MS
RURAL ROUTE 02 BOX 498 02857
Patrick Hannigan, prin.

Glocester SD
Sch. Sys. Enr. Code 3
Supt. – Clifton Boyle
RURAL ROUTE 02 BOX 498B 02857
Fogarty Memorial ES, RURAL ROUTE 02 02857
(—), prin.
Other Schools – See Chepachet

Scituate SD
Sch. Sys. Enr. Code 4
Supt. – A. Manning, MAIN ST 02857
ES, INSTITUTE LN 02857 – Gerry Leonard, prin.
Other Schools – See Clayville, Hope

Pascoag, Providence Co., Pop. Code 5
Burrillville SD
Supt. – See Harrisville
ES, 101 SAYLES AVE 02859
Patricia Daloisio, prin.

Northwest Catholic ES, 4 FR HOLLAND PL 02859

Pawtucket, Providence Co., Pop. Code 8
Pawtucket SD
Sch. Sys. Enr. Code 6
Supt. – Dr. Richard Charlton, PARK PLACE 02860
Goff JHS, 947 NEWPORT AVE 02861
Clifford Wallace, prin.
Jenks JHS, 350 DIVISION ST 02860
Joseph Cunha, prin.
Slater JHS, 281 MINERAL SPRING AVE 02860
Walter Guest III, prin.
Baldwin ES, 50 WHITMAN ST 02860
Robert Moran, prin.
Cunningham ES, 40 BALDWIN ST 02860
Richar Cooney, prin.
Curtis Memorial ES, 582 BENEFIT ST 02861
John Kanakry, prin.
Curvin-McCabe ES, 466 COTTAGE ST 02861
Jacqueline Walsh, prin.
Fallon Memorial ES, 62 LINCOLN AVE 02861
Edward Molloy,Jr., prin.
Greene ES, 285 SMITHFIELD AVE 02860
George LaPorte, prin.
Little ES, 60 S BEND ST 02860
Barbara Romani, prin.
Potter-Burns ES, 973 NEWPORT AVE 02861
Audrey Calistra, prin.
Varieur ES, 486 PLEASANT ST 02860
George Treanor, prin.
Winters ES, 481 BROADWAY 02860
Eleanor Byrnes, prin.

Our Lady of Consolation ES
45 WEBSTER ST 02860
St. Cecilia ES, 755 CENTRAL AVE 02861
St. Leo the Great ES, 723 CENTRAL AVE 02861
St. Mary ES, 167 GEORGE ST 02860
St. Teresa ES, 140 WOOD HAVEN ROAD 02861
Woodlawn Catholic Regional ES
61 HOPE ST 02860

Peace Dale, Wakefield Co., Pop. Code 5
South Kingstown SD
Supt. – See Wakefield
South Kingstown JHS
CURTIS CORNER ROAD 02883
Robert Smith, prin.

Portsmouth, Newport Co., Pop. Code 7
Portsmouth SD
Sch. Sys. Enr. Code 5
Supt. – Henry Diodati, 29 MIDDLE ROAD 02871
MS, 125 JEPSON LANE 02871
Donald Vacchi, prin.
Elmhurst ES, GLEN ROAD 02871
Albert Honneman, prin.
Hathaway ES, TALLMAN AVE 02871
Lawrence Jones, prin.
Melville ES, 1351 W MAIN RD 02871
Russell Carter, prin.

St. Philomena ES, CORYS LN 02871

Providence, Providence Co., Pop. Code 9
Cranston SD
Supt. – See Cranston
Barrows ES, 9 BEACHMONT AVE 02905
Craig Jamieson, prin.
Edgewood Highland MS
160 PAWTUXET AVE 02905
Charles Morris, Jr., prin.
Norwood Avenue ES, 205 NORWOOD AVE 02905
Vincent Rozen, prin.
Rhodes ES, 160 SHAW AVE 02905
Dr. Margaret Day, prin.

North Providence SD
Supt. – See North Providence
Centredale ES, 41 ANGELL AVE 02911
Charles Shadoian, prin.
Greystone ES, 100 MORGAN AVE 02911
Robert Wiese, prin.
Marieville ES
1135 MINERAL SPRING AVE 02904
Deborah Capuano, prin.
McGuire ES, 55 CENTRAL AVE 02911
Marie Klement, prin.
Olney ES, 1378 DOUGLAS AVE 02904
Joseph Simeone, prin.
Whelan ES, 1440 MINERAL SPRING AVE 02904
Paul Morry, prin.

Providence SD
Sch. Sys. Enr. Code 7
Supt. – Joseph Almagno, 480 CHARLES ST 02904
Bishop MS, 101 SESSIONS ST 02906
Robert Lee, prin.
Bridgham MS, 1655 WESTMINSTER ST 02909
Thomas Mezzanotte, prin.
Greene MS, 721 CHALKSTONE AVE 02908
James Dolan, prin.

Perry MS, 370 HARTFORD AVE 02909
John Hernandez, prin.
Williams MS, 278 THURBERS AVE 02905
Paul Vorro, prin.
Windmill IS, 110 PAUL ST 02904
Anthony Rao, prin.
Broad Street ES, 1450 BROAD ST 02905
Maureen Taylor, prin.
Camden Avenue ES, 60 CAMDEN AVE 02908
Dr. Judith Barry, prin.
D'Abate ES, 60 KOSSUTH ST 02909
Bernice Graser, prin.
Flynn ES, 220 BLACKSTONE ST 02905
Samuel Greenstein, prin.
Fogarty ES, 199 OXFORD ST 02905
Lummer Jennings, prin.
Fox Point ES, 455 WICKENDEN ST 02903
Veretta Jungwirth, prin.
Kennedy ES, 195 NELSON ST 02908
Eillen McCormick, prin.
King ES, 35 CAMP ST 02906
Stephen Kane, prin.
Laurel Hill Avenue ES
85 LAUREL HILL AVE 02909 – Isabella Lee, prin.
Lauro Memorial ES, 99 KENYON ST 02903
Frank Spaziano, prin.
Messer Annex ES, 245 ALTHEA ST 02909
Frank Pallotta, prin.
Messer ES, 158 MESSER ST 02909
Frank Pallotta, prin.
Reservoir Avenue ES, 156 RESERVOIR AVE 02907
Joseph Renzulli, prin.
Sackett Street ES, 159 SACKETT ST 02907
Joseph Renzulli, prin.
Stuart ES, 188 PRINCETON AVE 02907
Meredith Costa, prin.
Webster Avenue ES, 191 WEBSTER AVE 02909
Joseph Degnan, prin.
West Broadway ES, 7 BAINBRIDGE AVE 02909
Dr. Anthony Tutalo, prin.
West ES, 145 BEAUFORT ST 02908
Louis Filippelli, prin.
Windmill Street 2 ES, 977 BRANCH AVE #2 02904
Anthony Rao, prin.
Windmill Street 1 ES, 425 BRANCH AVE #1 02904
Anthony Rao, prin.
Windmill Street MS, 110 PAUL ST 02904
Anthony Rao, prin.

Bishop McVinney ES, 155 HARRISON ST 02907
Lincoln School, 301 BUTLER AVE 02906
Moses Brown School, 250 LLOYD AVE 02906
Providence Hebrew Day School
450 ELMGROVE AVE 02906
Wheeler School, 216 HOPE ST 02906
Bishop McVinney ES, 155 GORDON AVE 02905
Blessed Sacrament ES, 240 REGENT AVE 02908
Holy Ghost ES, 35 SWISS ST 02909
Holy Name ES
LOCUST ST AND MT HOPE AVE 02906
Monsignor Bove School, 525 BRANCH AVE 02904
Solomon Schechter ES, 99 TAFT AVE 02906
St. Augustine ES
635 MOUNT PLEASANT AVE 02908
St. Bartholemew ES
315 LAUREL HILL AVE 02909
St. Mary ES, 30 BARTON ST 02909
St. Patrick Word of God ES, 244 SMITH ST 02908
St. Paul ES, 1789 BROAD ST 02905
St. Paul Lutheran School, 12 CARTER ST 02907
St. Pius V ES, 49 ELMHURST AVE 02908
St. Raymond ES, 260 HIGHLAND AVE 02906
St. Teresa ES, 17 POPE ST 02909
St. Thomas Regional ES
15 EDENDALE AVE 02911

Riverside, Providence Co.
East Providence SD
Supt. – See East Providence
Meadowcrest ES, 60 BART DR 02915
John Savage, prin.
Oldham ES, 640 BULLOCKS POINT AVE 02915
Judith Richardson, prin.
Silver Spring ES, 120 SILVER SPRING AVE 02915
Michael Martinous, prin.
Waddington ES, 101 LEGION WAY 02915
Ann Higginbotham, prin.
Watters ES, 33 HOPPIN AVE 02915
John Savage, prin.

St. Brendan ES, 55 TURNER AVE 02915
St. Mary Academy Bay View ES
3070 PAWTUCKET AVE 02915

Rumford, Providence Co.
East Providence SD
Supt. – See East Providence
Thompson ES, 215 FERRIS AVE 02916
David Kelleher, prin.
Union ES, 1320 PAWTUCKET AVE 02916
David Kelleher, prin.
Wilson ES, 54 BOURNE AVE 02916
Anthony Ferris, prin.

St. Margaret ES, 42 BISHOP AVE 02916

Slatersville, Providence Co., Pop. Code 4
North Smithfield SD
Supt. – See Woonsocket
Halliwell Memorial MS, GREAT ROAD 02876
Eugene Peloquin, prin.
Kendall-Dean ES, GREEN ST 02876
Juliette Elias, prin.

Tiverton, Newport Co., Pop. Code 7
Tiverton SD
Sch. Sys. Enr. Code 4
Supt. – John Edwards
    100 N BRAYTON ROAD 02878
MS, 10 QUINTAL DRIVE 02878
    Louis Bitar, prin.
Ft. Barton ES, 99 LAWTON AVE 02878
    Joseph Pavao, prin.
Pocasset ES, 242 MAIN RD 02878
    John Pacheco, prin.
Ranger ES, 1185 STAFFORD RD 02878
    Samuel Williamson, prin.

Wakefield, Washington Co., Pop. Code 5
South Kingstown SD
Sch. Sys. Enr. Code 5
Supt. – Arthur Campbell, 71 COLUMBIA ST 02883
Hazard MS, 67 COLUMBIA ST 02879
    Paul Johnson, prin.
Matunuck ES, 380 MATUNUCK BEACH RD 02879
    Richard Corcoran, prin.
Peace Dale ES, 59 KERSEY RD 02883
    Marc Ladin, prin.
South Road ES, 1157 SOUTH RD 02879
    Patricia Gallivan, prin.
ES, 37 HIGH ST 02879 – John Fratiello,Jr., prin.
Other Schools – See Peace Dale, West Kingston

Monsignor Matthew F. Clarke ES
    TOWER HILL ROAD 02880

Warren, Bristol Co., Pop. Code 7
Warren SD
Sch. Sys. Enr. Code 4
Supt. – James Hoebbel
    SCHOOLHOUSE ROAD 02885
Quirk JHS, 790 MAIN ST 02885
    George Manyan, prin.
Child Street ES, CHILD ST 02885
    Louis Perella, prin.
Cole MS, ASYLUM ROAD 02885
    Romeo Blooin, prin.
Main Street ES, 689 MAIN ST 02885
    Louis Perella, prin.

Warwick, Kent Co., Pop. Code 8
Warwick SD
Sch. Sys. Enr. Code 7
Supt. – Dr. Elliott LeFaiver
    34 WARWICK LAKE AVE 02889
Aldrich JHS, 789 POST ROAD 02888
    Anthony Carcieri, prin.
Gorton JHS, 69 DRAPER AVE 02889
    Robert Nicholson, prin.
Cedar Hill ES, 35 RED CHIMNEY DR 02886
    Mitchell Asadorian, prin.
Drum Rock ES, 575 CENTERVILLE RD 02886
    Patricia Tomasso, prin.
Francis ES, 325 MIANTONOMO DR 02888
    Arlene Militello, prin.
Greene ES, 51 DRAPER AVE 02889
    Murry Winkleman, prin.
Greenwood ES, SHARON ST 02886
    David Desjardins, prin.
Holden ES, 61 HOXSIE AVE 02889
    Albert Berger, prin.
Holliman ES, 70 DEBORAH RD 02888
    Bert Finan, prin.
Hoxsie ES, 55 GLENWOOD DR 02889
    Walter Freeman, prin.
Lippitt ES, 30 ALMY ST 02886
    Robert Bushell, prin.

Norwood ES, 266 NORWOOD AVE 02888
    Vincent Monti, prin.
Oakland Beach ES
    383 OAKLAND BEACH AVE 02886
    Richard Sousa, prin.
Park ES, 40 ASYLUM RD 02886
    Richard Maresca, prin.
Rhodes ES, 110 SHERWOOD AVE 02888
    Frank Romasso, prin.
Robertson ES, 70 NAUSAUCKET ROAD 02886
    Nancy Dorch, prin.
Scott ES, 833 CENTERVILLE RD 02886
    Sheila Stanley, prin.
Sherman ES, 120 KILLEY AVE 02889
    Brian Pendergast, prin.
Warwick Neck ES, 155 ROCKY POINT AVE 02889
    Kathryn Webb, prin.
Wickes ES, 50 CHILD LN 02886
    Raymond Hodges, prin.
Wyman ES, 1 COLUMBIA AVE 02888
    Anthony Destefanis, prin.
Other Schools – See East Greenwich

St. Francis ES, 610 JEFFERSON BLVD 02886
St. Kevin ES, 39 CATHEDRAL RD 02889
St. Peter ES, 120 MAYFAIR RD 02888
St. Rose of Lima ES
    200 BRENTWOOD AVE 02886
St. Timothy ES, 101 LAKE SHORE DR 02889

Westerly, Washington Co., Pop. Code 7
Westerly SD
Sch. Sys. Enr. Code 5
Supt. – Salvatore Augeri, 28 CHESTNUT ST 02891
Babcock MS, HIGHLAND AVE 02891
    William Barrs, prin.
Dunns Corners ES, 10 PLATEAU RD 02891
    Joseph Celico, prin.
State Street ES, STATE ST 02891
    Dr. Joyce Duerr, prin.
Tower Street ES, TOWER ST 02891
    Carolyn Longolucco, prin.
Other Schools – See Bradford

St. Pius X ES, 32 ELM ST 02891

West Greenwich, Kent Co., Pop. Code 5
Exeter-West Greenwich SD
Supt. – See Exeter
Lineham ES, WOOSENECK HILL ROAD 02816
    Christine Davidson, prin.

West Kingston, Washington Co., Pop. Code 3
South Kingstown SD
Supt. – See Wakefield
ES, MINISTERIAL ROAD 02892
    Richard Hines, prin.

West Warwick, Kent Co., Pop. Code 8
West Warwick SD
Sch. Sys. Enr. Code 5
Supt. – Thomas Sweeney,Jr.
    300 PROVIDENCE ST 02893
Duffy ES, 10 HARRIS AVE 02893
    W. Lovett, prin.
Horgan ES, 124 PROVIDENCE ST 02893
    W. Lovett, prin.
Providence Street MS
    819 PROVIDENCE ST 02893
    Robert McKenna, prin.
Providence Street Annex ES
    820 PROVIDENCE ST 02893
    Robert McKenna, prin.
Quinn ES, 1 BROWN ST 02893
    Pasco Dipadua, prin.

Monsignor Vincent ES, 17 SAINT JOHN ST 02893
Notre Dame Regional ES, 107 SUMMIT AVE 02893
St. James ES, 19 SAINT MARY ST 02893
St. Joseph ES
    WAKEFIELD ST & INTERVALE RD 02893

Wood River Junction, Washington Co., Pop. Code 2
Chariho SD
Sch. Sys. Enr. Code 4
Supt. – Robert Andreotti
    445 SWITCH ROAD 02894
Other Schools – See Ashaway, Carolina, Hope Valley,
    Wyoming

Woonsocket, Providence Co., Pop. Code 8
North Smithfield SD
Sch. Sys. Enr. Code 4
Supt. – Charles Shunney
    RURAL ROUTE 02 02895
St. Paul Street ES, ST PAUL ST 02895
    Juliette Elias, prin.
Other Schools – See Slatersville

Woonsocket SD
Sch. Sys. Enr. Code 6
Supt. – Timothy Conners, 108 HIGH ST 02895
Bernon Heights ES, 657 LOGEE ST 02895
    Dennis Gentili, prin.
Citizens Memorial ES, WINTHROP ST 02895
    Louis Lamoureux, prin.
Coleman MS, 96 SECOND AVE 02895
    Robert Jones, prin.
East Woonsocket ES, 990 MENDON RD 02895
    Daniel Andrews, prin.
Fifth Avenue ES, 65 FIFTH AVE 02895
    Ellen Dagnenica, prin.
George Street MS, 25 GEORGE ST 02895
    Raymond Rabidoux, prin.
Globe Park ES, 192 AVENUE A 02895
    Maurice Aubin, prin.
Grove Street ES, 320 GROVE ST 02895
    Raymond Sutherland, prin.
Harris ES, 60 HIGH SCHOOL ST 02895
    Richard Crepeau, prin.
Kendrick Avenue ES, 72 KENDRICK AVE 02895
    Ann Stratton, prin.
Pothier ES, 1044 SOCIAL ST 02895
    Raymond Rabidoux, prin.
Second Avenue ES, 196 SECOND AVE 02895
    (—), prin.
Social Street ES, 706 SOCIAL ST 02895
    Ann Stratton, prin.
Summer Street ES, 219 SUMMER ST 02895
    Richard Crepeau, prin.
Vose Street ES, 388 VOSE ST 02895
    Raymond Sutherland, prin.

Mercymount Country Day School
    WRENTHAM RD 02895
Monsignor Gadoury ES, 1371 PARK AVE 02895
Our Lady of Victories Regional ES
    148 SPRING ST 02895
St. Joseph Regional ES, 1210 MENDON RD 02895

Wyoming, Washington Co., Pop. Code 3
Chariho SD
Supt. – See Wood River Junction
Richmond ES, RURAL ROUTE 138 BOX 01 02898
    Pasquale Nappi, prin.

SOUTH CAROLINA

STATE DEPARTMENT OF EDUCATION
Rutledge Building
1429 Senate St., Columbia 29201
(803) 734-8500

Superintendent of Education	Dr. Charles Williams
Deputy Superintendent Administration & Planning	Robert Hill
Deputy Superintendent Instruction	Sidney Cooper
Deputy Superintendent Finance & Operations	Carl Garris
Deputy Superintendent Public Accountability	Robert Paskel

STATE BOARD OF EDUCATION
Dr. Charles Williams, *Administrative Officer*　　1006 Rutledge Building, Columbia　29201

SOUTH CAROLINA COMMISSION ON HIGHER EDUCATION
Fred Sheheen, *Commissioner*　　1333 Main St. #650, Columbia　29201

PUBLIC, PRIVATE, AND PAROCHIAL ELEMENTARY SCHOOLS

Abbeville, Abbeville Co., Pop. Code 6
Abbeville County SD
Sch. Sys. Enr. Code 5
Supt. – W. Richard Garrett, P O BOX 520　29620
Wright MS, P O BOX 848　29620
　Ed Crawford, prin.
Antreville ES, RURAL ROUTE 04　29620
　Dale Martin, prin.
Greenville Street ES, P O BOX 578　29620
　David Havird, prin.
Westwood ES, P O BOX 188　29620 – (—), prin.
Other Schools – See Calhoun Falls, Donalds, Due West

Aiken, Aiken Co., Pop. Code 7
Aiken County SD
Sch. Sys. Enr. Code 7
Supt. – Joseph Brooks, P O BOX 1137　29802
Kennedy MS, 659 PINE LOG ROAD　29801
　George Rogers, prin.
Schofield MS, 220 SUMTER ST NE　29801
　William Price, prin.
ES, 2050 PINE LOG RD　29801
　Lynette Rinehart, prin.
East Aiken ES, RURAL ROUTE 06 BOX 760　29801
　David Davis, prin.
Lever ES, RURAL ROUTE 04 BOX 495　29801
　William Summer, prin.
Millbrook ES, 650 PINE LOG RD　29801
　Christine Sanders, prin.
North Aiken ES, 123 RUTLAND DR　29801
　Geneva Thompson, prin.
Oakwood-Windsor ES
　RURAL ROUTE 06 BOX 1170　29801
　Jerry Swing, prin.
Redcliffe ES, 2880 ATOMIC RD　29801
　Jane Slay, prin.
Other Schools – See Bath, Belvedere, Clearwater,
　Gloverville, Graniteville, Jackson, Langley, New
　Ellenton, North Augusta, Ridge Spring, Wagener,
　Warrenville

Mead Hall ES, P O BOX 1057　29802
St. Mary Help of Christians School
　118 YORK ST SW　29801
South Aiken Baptist Christian School
　980 DOUGHERTY RD　29801

Alcolu, Clarendon Co., Pop. Code 3
Clarendon SD 2
Supt. – See Manning
MS, P O BOX 169　29001 – Jerry Coker, prin.

Allendale, Allendale Co., Pop. Code 5
Allendale County SD
Sch. Sys. Enr. Code 4
Supt. – Dr. Dill Gamble, P O BOX 458　29810
MS, HWY 278 E　29810 – Wilda Robinson, prin.
PS, P O BOX 738　29810 – Mattie Drayton, prin.
Other Schools – See Fairfax

Allendale Academy, 623 N MAIN ST　29810

Anderson, Anderson Co., Pop. Code 8
Anderson SD 5
Sch. Sys. Enr. Code 7
Supt. – Karen Callison, P O BOX 439　29622
Lakeside MS, 115 PEARMAN DAIRY ROAD　29621
　Joseph Keaton, prin.

McCants MS, 105 S FANT ST　29624
　Melvin Poore, prin.
Southwood MS, 1110 SOUTHWOOD ST　29624
　Jacky Stamps, prin.
Calhoun Street ES, 1520 E CALHOUN ST　29621
　Dan Shaw, prin.
Centerville ES, 1529 WHITEHALL RD　29625
　Michael Ruthsatz, prin.
Concord ES, 2701 CALROSSIE RD　29621
　Kay McKee, prin.
Homeland Park ES, 3519 WILMONT ST　29624
　(—), prin.
Nevitt Forest ES, 1401 BOLT DR　29621
　Larry Knighton, prin.
New Prospect ES
　NEW PROSPECT CHURCH ROAD　29621
　William Jones, prin.
South Fant Street ES, 1700 S FANT ST　29624
　Jason Rucker, prin.
Varennes ES, RURAL ROUTE 13 BOX 18　29624
　Dr. Mary Paul, prin.
West Franklin Street ES
　1100 W FRANKLIN ST　29624
　Jonathan Jennings, prin.
West Market Street ES
　1909 W MARKET ST　29624
　Charles Wooten, prin.
Whitehall ES, 702 WHITEHALL RD　29625
　Elizabeth Terry, prin.

Oakwood Christian School
　304 PEARMAN DAIRY ROAD　29621
St. Joseph's School-Anderson
　1200 CORNELIA RD　29621

Andrews, Georgetown Co., Pop. Code 5
Georgetown County SD
Supt. – See Georgetown
Rosemary MS, P O BOX 4　29510
　Doreatha Pierce, prin.
PS, P O BOX 217　29510 – R. King, prin.

Williamsburg County SD
Supt. – See Kingstree
Blakeley-Wiliamsburg ES
　RURAL ROUTE 04 BOX 91　29510
　James Evans, prin.

Andrews Academy, P O BOX 468　29510

Arcadia, Spartanburg Co., Pop. Code 4
Spartanburg SD 6
Supt. – See Spartanburg
ES, P O BOX 45　29320 – Charles Butler, prin.

Aynor, Horry Co., Pop. Code 3
Horry County SD
Supt. – See Conway
ES, RURAL ROUTE 01 BOX 3　29511
　James Gerrald, prin.
Horry ES, RURAL ROUTE 01 BOX 286　29511
　Robert Bell, prin.

Ballentine, Richland Co., Pop. Code 2
Lexington SD 5
Sch. Sys. Enr. Code 7
Supt. – Dr. H. Corley, P O BOX 938　29002
Other Schools – See Chapin, Columbia, Irmo

Bamberg, Bamberg Co., Pop. Code 5
Bamberg SD 1
Sch. Sys. Enr. Code 4
Supt. – Jack Steadman, P O BOX 526　29003
ES, P O BOX 546　29003 – W. Ginn, prin.
Carroll MS, P O BOX 949　29003
　R. McCollum, prin.
Other Schools – See Ehrhardt

Barnwell, Barnwell Co., Pop. Code 6
Barnwell SD 45
Sch. Sys. Enr. Code 5
Supt. – James Benson, 2208 HAGOOD AVE　29812
Guinyard-Butler MS, 2211 ALLEN ST　29812
　Jeff Still, prin.
ES, 1610 MARLBORO AVE　29812
　Carolyne Sailors, prin.

Batesburg, Lexington Co., Pop. Code 5
Lexington SD 3
Sch. Sys. Enr. Code 4
Supt. – Thomas Smith
　707 E COLUMBIA AVE　29006
Batesburg-Leesville MS
　721 E COLUMBIA AVE　29006
　Robert Williams, prin.
Batesburg-Leesville MS
　338 W COLUMBIA AVE　29006 – John Stone, prin.
Batesburg-Leesville PS
　800 SUMMERLAND AVE　29006
　Jerry Koon, prin.

King Academy
　RURAL ROUTE 01 BOX 287　29006

Bath, Aiken Co., Pop. Code 4
Aiken County SD
Supt. – See Aiken
Jefferson ES, P O BOX 340　29816
　Lawana McKenzie, prin.

Beaufort, Beaufort Co., Pop. Code 6
Beaufort County SD
Sch. Sys. Enr. Code 7
Supt. – Dr. Terry Terrill, P O BOX 309　29901
ES, 1800 PRINCE ST　29902 – Mary Walters, prin.
Ladys Island ES, HCR 05 BOX 800　29902
　Eugene Matthews, prin.
Mossy Oaks ES, 2600 MOSSY OAKS RD　29902
　John Marvin, prin.
Shell Point ES, SAVANNAH HWY　29902
　Mary Towery, prin.
Other Schools – See Bluffton, Burton, Dale, Daufuskie
　Island, Frogmore, Hilton Head Island, Port Royal

Beaufort Academy, HCR 05　29902

Belton, Anderson Co., Pop. Code 6
Anderson SD 1
Supt. – See Williamston
Cedar Grove ES, RURAL ROUTE 04　29627
　Brenda Ellison, prin.

Anderson SD 2
Supt. – See Honea Path
MS, 102 CHEROKEE ROAD　29627
　Dan Hawkins, prin.
MS, 202 WATKINS ST　29627 – Michael Hall, prin.
PS, 218 BANNISTER ST　29627
　Ronald Walfield, prin.

Wright ES, RURAL ROUTE 01 29627
 (—), prin.

Belvedere, Aiken Co.
 Aiken County SD
 Supt. – See Aiken
 ES, RHOMBOLD PLACE 29841
  Hubert Turner, prin.

Bennettsville, Marlboro Co., Pop. Code 6
 Marlboro County SD
 Sch. Sys. Enr. Code 6
 Supt.– Dr. Floyd Wright, 122 BROAD ST 29512
 MS, 801 COUNTRY CLUB DRIVE 29512
  Herbert Ash, prin.
 MS, FAYETTEVILLE AVE 29512 – John Lee, prin.
 IS, RURAL ROUTE 03 BOX 3 29512
  Clyde Murphy, prin.
 PS, 301 JEFFERSON ST 29512 – W. Collins, prin.
 Other Schools – See Blenheim, Clio, Mc Coll, Wallace

 Marlboro Academy
  RURAL ROUTE 03 BOX 52 29512

Bethune, Kershaw Co., Pop. Code 2
 Kershaw County SD
 Supt. – See Camden
 MS, P O BOX 217 29009 – R. Small, prin.
 ES, P O BOX 477 29009 – Fred Stephens, prin.

Bishopville, Lee Co., Pop. Code 5
 Lee County SD
 Sch. Sys. Enr. Code 5
 Supt. – John Wall, P O BOX 507 29010
 MS, 600 N MAIN ST 29010 – John Tindall, prin.
 PS, 603 N DENNIS AVE 29010
  Ina Livingston, prin.
 Other Schools – See Lynchburg, Mayesville, Rembert

 Lee Academy, P O BOX 488 29010

Blacksburg, Cherokee Co., Pop. Code 4
 Cherokee SD
 Supt. – See Gaffney
 MS, P O BOX 398 29702 – Charles Byars, prin.
 PS, P O BOX 607 29702 – Hal Howington, prin.

Blackville, Barnwell Co., Pop. Code 5
 Barnwell SD 19
 Sch. Sys. Enr. Code 4
 Supt. – R. Huggins, P O BOX 185 29817
 MS, P O BOX 186 29817 – William Scott, prin.
 Macedonia ES, P O BOX 307 29817
  William Sandiffer, prin.

 Davis Academy, P O BOX 338 29817

Blair, Fairfield Co.
 Fairfield County SD
 Supt. – See Winnsboro
 McCrorey-Liston ES
  RURAL ROUTE 01 BOX 154 29015
  Evelyn Henry, prin.

Blenheim, Marlboro Co.
 Marlboro County SD
 Supt. – See Bennettsville
 ES, P O BOX 350 29516 – Fred Thomas, prin.

Bluffton, Beaufort Co., Pop. Code 3
 Beaufort County SD
 Supt. – See Beaufort
 McCracken MS, P O BOX 228 29910
  Dorothy Gnann, prin.
 Riley ES, P O BOX 198 29910
  Elizabeth Hyman, prin.

Blythewood, Richland Co., Pop. Code 1
 Richland SD 2
 Supt. – See Columbia
 Hanberry MS, P O BOX 40 29016
  Jo Hecker, prin.
 Bethel MS, P O BOX 40 29016 – Jo Hecker, prin.
 ES, P O BOX 20 29016 – (—), prin.

Bowman, Orangeburg Co., Pop. Code 4
 Orangeburg SD 2
 Sch. Sys. Enr. Code 3
 Supt. – Dr. Joseph Rice, P O BOX 36 29018
 ES, P O BOX 158 29018 – Dr. Thomas Smith, prin.

 Bowman Academy, P O BOX 98 29018

Branchville, Orangeburg Co., Pop. Code 4
 Orangeburg SD 8
 Sch. Sys. Enr. Code 3
 Supt. – Nelson Perry 29432
 ES, P O BOX 188 29432 – Robert Dufford, prin.

Brunson, Hampton Co., Pop. Code 3
 North SD 1
 Supt. – See Hampton
 ES, P O BOX 130 29911 – Roger Terry, prin.

Buffalo, Union Co., Pop. Code 4
 Union County SD
 Supt. – See Union
 ES, HWY 215 E 29321 – Eugene Palmer, prin.

Burton, Beaufort Co., Pop. Code 2
 Beaufort County SD
 Supt. – See Beaufort
 Broad River MS
  RURAL ROUTE 01 BOX 357 29902
  Irvin White, prin.

Cades, Beaufort Co.
 Williamsburg County SD
 Supt. – See Kingstree
 Cades Hebron ES
  RURAL ROUTE 01 BOX 58 29518
  Debra Ellis, prin.

Calhoun Falls, Abbeville Co., Pop. Code 4
 Abbeville County SD
 Supt. – See Abbeville
 Calhoun ES, P O BOX 216 29628 – (—), prin.

Camden, Kershaw Co., Pop. Code 6
 Kershaw County SD
 Sch. Sys. Enr. Code 6
 Supt. – Robert Falls, DUBOSE CT 29020
 MS, CHESTNUT FERRY ROAD 29020
  Clyde Jones, prin.
 Antioch ES, RURAL ROUTE 01 BOX 78 29020
  (—), prin.
 Baron DeKalb ES
  RURAL ROUTE 03 BOX 210 29020
  Henry Baggett III, prin.
 MS, CAMPBELL ST 29020 – Andrew James, prin.
 PS, 1301 LYTTLETON ST 29020
  Brent Penrod, prin.
 Pine Tree Hill ES, 1213 LAKESHORE DR 29020
  Myra Canipe, prin.
 Other Schools – See Bethune, Cassatt, Elgin, Kershaw,
  Lugoff

Cameron, Calhoun Co., Pop. Code 3
 Calhoun SD
 Supt. – See Saint Matthews
 St. John ES, P O BOX 398 29030
  Joyce Jones, prin.

Campobello, Spartanburg Co., Pop. Code 2
 Spartanburg SD 1
 Sch. Sys. Enr. Code 5
 Supt. – Dr. James Littlefield, P O BOX 218 29322
 Campobello-Gramling ES
  RURAL ROUTE 02 BOX 158 29322
  William Sapp, prin.
 Holly Springs-Motlow ES
  RURAL ROUTE 02 BOX 251 29322
  David Craft, prin.
 Other Schools – See Inman, Landrum

Cassatt, Kershaw Co.
 Kershaw County SD
 Supt. – See Camden
 Midway ES, RURAL ROUTE 01 29032
  Bob Jones, prin.

Cayce, Lexington Co., Pop. Code 7
 Lexington SD 2
 Supt. – See West Columbia
 S, 800 LEXINGTON AVE 29033
  Dr. Dorinda Donohoe, prin.
 Busbee MS, 1407 DUNBAR ROAD 29033
  Joseph English, prin.
 Davis ES, 2305 FRINK ST 29033
  John Litton, prin.
 Taylor ES, 103 ANN LN 29033
  Phillip Fretwell, prin.

Central, Pickens Co., Pop. Code 4
 Pickens SD
 Supt. – See Easley
 ES, RURAL ROUTE 01 BOX 311 29630
  Anne Rauton, prin.

Chapin, Lexington Co., Pop. Code 2
 Lexington SD 5
 Supt. – See Ballentine
 ES, RURAL ROUTE 04 BOX 219 29036
  Dr. Joan Warlick, prin.

Charleston, Charleston Co., Pop. Code 8
 Berkeley County SD
 Supt. – See Moncks Corner
 Marrington MS, GEARING AVE 29408
  John Harper, prin.
 Fishburne ES, 6215 N MURRAY AVE 29406
  J. Prosser, prin.
 Marrington ES, O GEARING ST 29408
  Helen Condor, prin.
 Menriv Park ES, O PULASKI ST 29408
  Robert Wickersham, prin.

 City of Charleston Constituent
 Sch. Sys. Enr. Code 6
 Supt. – D. Mack, 103 CALHOUN ST 29403
 Courtney MS, 382 MEETING ST 29403
  Charles Holmes, prin.
 Rivers MS, 1002 KING ST 29403
  Walter Burke, prin.
 Buist ES, 103 CALHOUN ST 29403
  Jean Murray, prin.
 Fraser ES, 63 COLUMBUS ST 29403
  Carlretta Wright, prin.
 Memminger ES, 20 BEAUFAIN ST 29401
  James Goldsmith, prin.
 Mitchell ES, 220 NASSAU ST 29403
  Jacqulyn Brown, prin.
 Sanders ES, 805 MORRISON DR 29403
  James Edwards, prin.
 Simons ES, 741 KING ST 29403
  Nat Washington, prin.

 Cooper River Constituent
 Supt. – See North Charleston
 Birney MS, 7750 PINEHURST ST 29418
  Michael Casey, prin.
 Brentwood MS, 2685 LEEDS AVE 29405
  Annette Goodwin, prin.

 Toole MS, CARNER AVE 29405
  Edward McClain, prin.
 Burns ES, 3750 DORCHESTER RD 29405
  Roy Davis, prin.
 Chicora ES, 1912 SUCCESS ST 29405
  Wheeler Hughes, prin.
 Corcoran ES, 8617 VISTA VIA ROAD 29405
  Paul Ricciardi, prin.
 Ford ES, 3180 AZALEA DR 29405
  Eugene Willis, prin.
 Goodwin ES, 5501 DORCHESTER RD 29418
  Mache Larkin, prin.
 Hunley Park ES, 1000 MICHIGAN AVE 29404
  James Walker, prin.
 Lambs ES, RURAL ROUTE 02 BOX 29 29418
  Kenneth Skipper, prin.
 Midland Park ES
  2415 MIDLAND PARK RD 29418
  William Mayer, prin.
 Pepperhill ES, 3300 CREOLA RD 29420
  Judy Waldo, prin.

 James Island Constituent
 Sch. Sys. Enr. Code 5
 Supt. – Gary Awkerman
  1825 CAMP ROAD #B 29412
 Ft. Johnson MS, 1825 CAMP ROAD 29412
  John Rhodes, prin.
 James Island MS, 1484 CAMP ROAD 29412
  Franklin McCrea, prin.
 Harbor View ES, 1576 HARBOR VIEW RD 29412
  Kathleen Harris, prin.
 Murray-Lasaine ES, 691 RIVERLAND DR 29412
  Blondell Kidd, prin.
 Stiles Point ES, 883 MIKELL DR 29412
  R. Hanna, prin.

 St. Andrews Constituent
 Sch. Sys. Enr. Code 6
 Supt. – William Jefferson
  725 WAPPOO ROAD 29407
 Hall MS, 3183 ASHLEY RIVER ROAD 29407
  Charles Marshall, prin.
 Williams MS, RURAL ROUTE 13 29407
  James Mobley, prin.
 Ashley River ES
  40 WALLACE SCHOOL ROAD 29406
  Rose Myers, prin.
 Oakland ES, 2728 ARLINGTON DR 29407
  Robert Walton, prin.
 Orange Grove ES
  1225 ORANGE BRANCH RD 29407
  (—), prin.
 Springfield ES, 2741 CLOVER ST 29414
  John Halfacre, prin.
 St. Andrew's ES, 30 CHADWICK DR 29407
  Floyd Funderberg, prin.
 Stono Park ES, 1699 GARDEN ST 29407
  William Meeks, prin.

 St. Johns Constituent SD
 Sch. Sys. Enr. Code 4
 Supt. – Gary Awkerman
  1825 CAMP ROAD #B 29412
 Other Schools – See Johns Island, Wadmalaw Island

 Ashley Hall School, P O BOX 248 29402
 First Baptist Church School
  48 MEETING ST 29401
 Low Country Academy, 2120 WOOD AVE 29414
 Northside Christian School
  7800 NORTHSIDE DRIVE 29418
 Porter-Gaud School, ALBERMARIE POINT 29407
 Blessed Sacrament ES, 7 ST TERESA DR 29407
 Cathedral ES, 120 BROAD ST 29401
 Charleston Day School, 51 ARCHDALE ST 29401
 Divine Redeemer School, 1104 FORT DR 29406
 Evangel Christian School
  2957 SAVANNAH HWY 29414
 Mason Prep School, 56 HALSEY BLVD 29401
 Nativity ES, 1061 FOLLY RD 29412
 Northwood Christian School
  8717 RIVERS AVE 29418
 Sacred Heart School, 888 KING ST 29403
 Towne Montessori School
  56 LEINBACH DR 29407

Cheraw, Chesterfield Co., Pop. Code 6
 Chesterfield SD
 Supt. – See Chesterfield
 Long JHS, P O BOX 993 29520
  Edward Shuford, prin.
 MS, 220 GREENE ST 29520 – M. Hicks, prin.
 PS, 334 CHRISTIAN ST 29520
  Peggy Nolan, prin.
 Smalls ES, FRONT ST 29520
  Wilkin Williams, prin.

Chesnee, Spartanburg Co., Pop. Code 4
 Spartanburg SD 2
 Supt. – See Spartanburg
 ES, 3231 OLD FURNACE RD 29323
  Dan Broome, prin.
 ES, 212 N ALABAMA AVE 29323
  Bennie Bishop, prin.
 Cooley Springs-Fingerville ES
  140 COOLEY SPRINGS SCH RD 29323
  Robert Ledfor, prin.

Chester, Chester Co., Pop. Code 6
 Chester SD
 Sch. Sys. Enr. Code 6
 Supt. – Samuel Wooten
  121 COLUMBIA ST 29706

JHS, 112 CALDWELL ST   29706
  Dr. Ellen Cauthen, prin.
College Street ES, 109 HINTON ST   29706
  Harry Robbins, prin.
Jones/Gayle MS, 157 COLUMBIA ST   29706
  Larry Heath, prin.
Southside ES, 72 BYPASS   29706
  Sam Rollins, prin.
Other Schools — See Edgemoor, Fort Lawn, Great
  Falls, Richburg

Chesterfield, Chesterfield Co., Pop. Code 4
Chesterfield SD
  Sch. Sys. Enr. Code 6
  Supt. — Joe Bradham, 141 MAIN ST W   29709
MS, 344 EAST BLVD   29709 — Jerry Burns, prin.
Edwards ES, P O BOX 30   29709
  Sue Bourne, prin.
Other Schools — See Cheraw, Jefferson, Mc Bee,
  Pageland, Patrick, Ruby

Clearwater, Aiken Co.
Aiken County SD
  Supt. — See Aiken
ES, P O BOX 397   29822
  William McKinney, prin.

Clemson, Pickens Co., Pop. Code 6
Pickens SD
  Supt. — See Easley
Morrison ES, 230 FRONTAGE RD   29631
  Jean Perry, prin.

Clinton, Laurens Co., Pop. Code 6
Laurens SD 56
  Sch. Sys. Enr. Code 5
  Supt. — Dr. Charles Cummins, P O BOX 484   29325
Bell Street MS, RURAL ROUTE 03   29325
  J. Claude Underwood, prin.
Dendy MS, P O BOX 295   29325
  Henry Simmons, prin.
Bailey ES, P O BOX 517   29325
  Thelma Thompson, prin.
ES, P O BOX 747   29325 — Randall Wright, prin.
Eastside ES, P O BOX 745   29325
  Betty Strock, prin.
Other Schools — See Joanna

Thornwell School, P O BOX 1157   29325

Clio, Marlboro Co., Pop. Code 4
Marlboro County SD
  Supt. — See Bennettsville
ES, P O BOX 577   29525 — James Myers, prin.

Clover, York Co., Pop. Code 5
York SD 2
  Sch. Sys. Enr. Code 5
  Supt. — Bill Floyd   29710
JHS, RURAL ROUTE 05   29710
  James Johnson, prin.
Bethany ES, 337 MAYNARD GRAYSON RD   29710
  Texie Fowler, prin.
Bethel ES, 6000 HWY 55 E   29710
  Robert Parker,Jr., prin.
MS, 103 WILSON ST   29710 — Randolph Lee, prin.
Kinard ES, 201 PRESSLEY ST   29710
  Amarintha Whitener, prin.

Columbia, Richland Co., Pop. Code 8
Lexington SD 5
  Supt. — See Ballentine
Harbison West ES, 257 CROSSBOW DR   29212
  Flora Kennedy, prin.
Leaphart ES, 120 PINEY GROVE RD   29210
  Kenneth Frick, prin.
Nursery Road ES, 6706 NURSERY RD   29212
  Dr. Mary Kennerly, prin.
Seven Oaks ES, 2800 ASHLAND RD   29210
  Larry Houk, prin.

Richland SD 1
  Sch. Sys. Enr. Code 8
  Supt. — Dr. John Stevenson
    1616 RICHLAND ST   29201
Alcorn MS, 5100 FAIRFIELD ROAD   29203
  Gladys Cureton, prin.
Crayton MS, 5000 CLEMSON AVE   29206
  Ellen Cooper, prin.
Gibbes-Heyward MS
    500 SUMMERLEA DRIVE   29203
  Kenneth Richardson, prin.
Hand MS, 2600 WHEAT ST   29205
  Charles Cothran, prin.
Perry MS, 2600 BARHAMVILLE ROAD   29204
  Kenneth Law, prin.
St. Andrews MS, 1231 BLUEFIELD DRIVE   29210
  Carlos Smith, prin.
Sanders MS, 6000 ALIDA ST   29203
  Faye Diggs, prin.
Arden ES, 1300 ASHLEY ST   29203
  Dr. Verna Green, prin.
Bradley ES, 3032 PINE BELT RD   29204
  Thomas Edwards, prin.
Brennen ES, 4438 DEVEREAUX RD   29205
  Richard Moore, prin.
Burnside ES, 7300 PATTERSON DR   29209
  Willie Ross, prin.
Burton ES, 5026 FARROW RD   29203
  Roger Wiley, prin.
Carver ES, 2100 WAVERLY ST   29204
  Marc Brown, prin.
Caughman Road ES, 7725 CAUGHMAN RD   29209
  George Goley, prin.

Crane Creek ES
    RURAL ROUTE 05 BOX 244   29203
  Thelma Brooks, prin.
Greenview ES, 726 EASTER ST   29203
  Helen Jones, prin.
Hyatt Park ES, 4200 MAIN ST   29203
  Lilly White, prin.
Lyon Street ES, 1310 LYON ST   29204
  Barbara Harvey, prin.
McCants ES, 3501 LYLES ST   29201
  George Harkness, prin.
Meadowlake ES, 525 GALWAY LN   29209
  Lynn Robertson, prin.
Mill Creek ES, 925 UNIVERSAL DR   29209
  Sue Goodwin, prin.
Moore ES, 333 ETIWAN AVE   29205
  Joanne Wilkes, prin.
Nance ES, 2611 GRANT ST   29203
  Dr. Eugene George, prin.
Pack ES, 3602 THURMOND ST   29204
  James Hardy, prin.
Rhame ES, 1300 ARROWWOOD RD   29210
  Dr. Ted Wachter, prin.
Roosevelt Village ES, MACRAE ST   29203
  (—), prin.
Rosewood ES, 3300 ROSEWOOD DR   29205
  Carol Stewart, prin.
South Kilbourne ES, 400 S KILBOURNE RD   29205
  Cleo Herbert, prin.
Sandel ES, 2700 SEMINOLE RD   29210
  Betty Prudence, prin.
Satchel Ford Road ES
    5901 SATCHELFORD RD   29206
  Bernadette Scott, prin.
Terrace ES, 6429 BISHOP AVE   29203
  Matthew Cannon, prin.
Thomas ES, 6001 WESTON AVE   29203
  Jacquelin Duckett, prin.
Watkins ES, 2612 COVENANT RD   29204
  Evelyn Cohens, prin.
Other Schools — See Eastover, Gadsden, Hopkins

Richland SD 2
  Sch. Sys. Enr. Code 7
  Supt. — Dr. John Hudgens
    6831 BROOKFIELD ROAD   29206
Dent MS, 2719 DECKER BLVD   29206
  J. Earl Rankin, prin.
Wright MS, 2740 ALPINE ROAD   29223
  Ann O'Quinn, prin.
Conder ES, 8161 BROOKFIELD RD   29223
  Nancy Martin, prin.
Forest Lake ES, 6801 BROOKFIELD RD   29206
  Beverly Foster, prin.
Keels ES, 7801 SPRINGVIEW ST   29223
  Richard Inabinet, prin.
Nelson ES, 225 N BRICKYARD RD   29223
  Sarah Wallace, prin.
Windsor ES, 2839 HOBKIRK RD   29223
  Evelyn Horne, prin.
Other Schools — See Blythewood, Elgin

Hammond Academy, 845 GALWAY LANE   29209
Heathwood Hall Episcopal School
    3000 S BELTLINE ROAD   29201
Sloans School, 171 STARLIGHT AVE   29210
Covenant Presbyterian Day School
    2801 STEPP DR   29204
St. Andrews Christian Academy
    P O BOX 21688   29221
St. John Neumann School, 721 POLO RD   29223
St. Joseph's ES, 3700 DEVINE ST   29205
St. Martin De Porres School, 1500 OAK ST   29340
St. Peters ES, P O BOX 1896   29202
Timmerman School
    2219 ATASCADERO DR   29206

Conway, Horry Co., Pop. Code 7
Horry County SD
  Sch. Sys. Enr. Code 7
  Supt. — John Dawsey, P O BOX 1739   29526
MS, 1104 ELM ST   29526
  Dr. Gilbert Stefanides, prin.
West Conway MS, P O BOX 920   29526
  Cynthia Brockington, prin.
MS, 304 12TH AVE   29526
  Michael Eddings, prin.
PS, 1620 SHERWOOD DR   29526
  Doris Garrison, prin.
Homewood ES, 2701 N MAIN ST   29526
  Paul Hickman, prin.
Kingston ES, RURAL ROUTE 05 BOX 398   29526
  Scott Alexander, prin.
Pee Dee ES, RURAL ROUTE 08 BOX 522   29526
  Amanda Sessions, prin.
South Conway ES, 3001 4TH AVE   29526
  Dr. Samuel Dusenbury, prin.
Waccamaw ES
    RURAL ROUTE 06 BOX 20E   29526
  Dr. Michael Borovicka, prin.
Other Schools — See Aynor, Galivants Ferry, Green
  Sea, Loris, Myrtle Beach, North Myrtle Beach

Waccamaw Academy, P O BOX 870   29526

Cordova, Orangeburg Co., Pop. Code 2
Orangeburg SD 4
  Sch. Sys. Enr. Code 4
  Supt. — J. Herring, P O BOX A   29039
Carver-Edisto MS, P O BOX 65   29039
  Raymond Schultz, prin.
Edisto PS, P O BOX A   29039
  Thomas Smith, prin.

Cottageville, Colleton Co., Pop. Code 2
Colleton County SD
  Supt. — See Walterboro
ES, P O BOX 194   29435 — Daniel Green, prin.

Coward, Florence Co., Pop. Code 2
Florence SD 3
  Supt. — See Lake City
Lynch ES, P O BOX 140   29530
  Jane Matthews, prin.

Cowpens, Spartanburg Co., Pop. Code 4
Spartanburg SD 3
  Supt. — See Glendale
ES, P O BOX 828   29330 — Thomas Abbott, prin.

Cross, Berkeley Co., Pop. Code 6
Berkeley County SD
  Supt. — See Moncks Corner
ES, RURAL ROUTE 01 BOX 2   29436
  Carolyn Gillens, prin.
Sandridge ES, RURAL ROUTE 01 BOX 75   29436
  Lynette Smith, prin.

Dale, Georgetown Co.
Beaufort County SD
  Supt. — See Beaufort
Davis ES   29914 — Sam Murray, prin.

Dalzell, Sumter Co., Pop. Code 2

Sumter Academy   29040

Darlington, Darlington Co., Pop. Code 6
Darlington SD
  Sch. Sys. Enr. Code 7
  Supt. — Dr. Terry Grier
    RM 304 COURTHOUSE   29532
Dargan JHS, P O BOX 520   29532
  Jack Dearhart, prin.
Gary MS, P O BOX 73   29532 — Otto Wingate, prin.
Brockington ES, P O BOX 135   29532
  Fred Ellison, prin.
Cain ES, P O BOX 784   29532
  Henrietta Pauley, prin.
Pate ES, P O BOX 496   29532
  Harvey Drawdy, prin.
Spring ES, P O BOX 498   29532 — Jane Brandt, prin.
St. John's ES, P O BOX 69   29532
  Wilbur Baughan, prin.
Other Schools — See Hartsville, Lamar, Society Hill

Daufuskie Island, Beaufort Co.
Beaufort County SD
  Supt. — See Beaufort
Fields ES, GENERAL DELIVERY   29915
  Catherine Campbell, prin.

Denmark, Bamberg Co., Pop. Code 5
Bamberg SD 2
  Sch. Sys. Enr. Code 4
  Supt. — Roy Holloway, P O BOX 345   29042
Denmark-Olar MS, P O BOX 343   29042
  R. Cooper, prin.
Denmark-Olar ES, P O BOX 246   29042
  Watson Cleckley, prin.

Dillon, Dillon Co., Pop. Code 6
Dillon SD 2
  Sch. Sys. Enr. Code 5
  Supt. — Dr. R. James Roquemore
    401 W WASHINGTON ST   29536
East ES, 1103 E HARRISON ST   29536
  Susanne Black, prin.
Gordon MS, MULLINS HWY   29536
  Dolphus Carter, prin.
Martin JHS, Maple Campus, 901 S 9TH AVE   29536
  (—), prin.
South Dillon ES, 900 S 16TH AVE   29536
  Peggy Stafford, prin.
Stewart Heights PS, P O BOX 1266   29536
  Jayne Lee, prin.

Avalon Academy, P O BOX 1246   29536

Donalds, Abbeville Co., Pop. Code 2
Abbeville County SD
  Supt. — See Abbeville
ES, P O BOX 146   29638 — Bobby Smith, prin.

Due West, Abbeville Co., Pop. Code 4
Abbeville County SD
  Supt. — See Abbeville
ES, P O BOX 488   29639 — Joseph Reynolds, prin.

Duncan, Spartanburg Co., Pop. Code 4
Spartanburg SD 5
  Sch. Sys. Enr. Code 5
  Supt. — Dr. Marvin Woodson, P O BOX 307   29334
Hill MS, P O BOX 277   29334
  David Henderson, prin.
ES, 100 S DANTZLER RD   29334
  Paul Black, prin.
Other Schools — See Lyman, Reidville, Startex,
  Wellford

Easley, Pickens Co., Pop. Code 7
Anderson SD 1
  Supt. — See Williamston
Concrete ES, RURAL ROUTE 07 BOX 274   29640
  (—), prin.

Pickens SD
  Sch. Sys. Enr. Code 7
  Supt. — Dr. David Sawyer
    RURAL ROUTE 08 BOX 375   29640
Crosswell ES, 800 KAY DR   29640
  Henry Hunt, prin.

Dacusville ES, RURAL ROUTE 05 BOX 147   29640
  David Cox, prin.
East End ES, 505 E 2ND AVE   29640
  Donald Batson, prin.
Forest Acres ES, MCALISTER RD   29640
  Sandra Bandy, prin.
McKissick ES, 112 MARY ANN ST   29640
  Glenn Turner, prin.
West End ES, 314 PELZER HWY   29640
  Doug Limbaugh, prin.
Other Schools – See Central, Clemson, Liberty, Pickens, Six Mile

Easley Christian School, P O BOX 546   29641

Eastover, Richland Co., Pop. Code 3
Richland SD 1
Supt. – See Columbia
Webber ES, 140 WEBBER SCHOOL RD   29044
  Jerry Hollis, prin.

Edgefield, Edgefield Co., Pop. Code 5
Edgefield County SD
Sch. Sys. Enr. Code 5
Supt. – Clarence Dickert, P O BOX 608   29824
Parker ES, 325 CREST RD   29824
  Ray Wilson, prin.
Other Schools – See Johnston, North Augusta, Trenton

Edgemoor, Chester Co.
Chester SD
Supt. – See Chester
Lewisville ES, RURAL ROUTE 01 BOX 120   29712
  Patricia Hensley, prin.

Edisto Beach, Colleton Co., Pop. Code 2
Colleton County SD
Supt. – See Walterboro
PS   29438 – Roslyn Tracy, prin.

Edisto Island, Colleton Co.
St. Paul Constituent
Supt. – See Yonges Island
Edwards ES, 1960 JANE EDWARDS RD   29438
  Alveria Bowens, prin.

Effingham, Florence Co.
Florence SD 1
Supt. – See Florence
Carter ES, RURAL ROUTE 01 BOX 591   29541
  Howard Worrell, prin.
Savannah Grove ES
  RURAL ROUTE 03 BOX 455   29541
  Lionel Brown, prin.

Ehrhardt, Bamberg Co., Pop. Code 2
Bamberg SD 1
Supt. – See Bamberg
ES, GENERAL DELIVERY BOX 949   29081
  Jack Sease, prin.

Jackson Academy, P O BOX 98   29081

Elgin, Kershaw Co., Pop. Code 3
Kershaw County SD
Supt. – See Camden
Blaney ES, P O BOX 186   29045
  Carl Robinson, prin.

Richland SD 2
Supt. – See Columbia
North Springs ES, 4200 CLEMSON RD   29045
  James Price, prin.

Elloree, Orangeburg Co., Pop. Code 3
Orangeburg SD 7
Sch. Sys. Enr. Code 3
Supt. – Dr. Owen Bush   29047
ES, P O BOX K   29047 – Robert McCants, prin.

Estill, Hampton Co., Pop. Code 4
Hampton SD 2
Sch. Sys. Enr. Code 4
Supt. – Albert Eads, P O BOX 1028   29918
MS, P O BOX 817   29918 – James Bullard, prin.
ES, P O BOX 1027   29918 – Evelyn Smith, prin.

Henry Academy, P O BOX 847   29918

Eutawville, Orangeburg Co., Pop. Code 3
Orangeburg SD 3
Supt. – See Holly Hill
St. James MS, P O BOX 325   29048
  James McDaniel, prin.
Gaillard PS, RURAL ROUTE 01 BOX 485   29048
  Ida Bailey, prin.

Fairfax, Allendale Co., Pop. Code 4
Allendale County SD
Supt. – See Allendale
Allendale-Fairfax MS
  RURAL ROUTE 02 BOX 221-A   29827
  Joe Singleton, prin.
ES, P O BOX 910   29827 – Lewis Bryan, prin.

Fairforest, Spartanburg Co., Pop. Code 3
Spartanburg SD 6
Supt. – See Spartanburg
MS, P O BOX A   29336 – Bob Jackson, prin.
ES, P O BOX B   29336 – Larry Irvin, prin.

Fair Play, Oconee Co.
Oconee County SD
Supt. – See Walhalla
ES, P O BOX 8   29643 – John Smith, prin.

Florence, Florence Co., Pop. Code 8
Florence SD 1
Sch. Sys. Enr. Code 7
Supt. – Thomas Truitt, 319 S DARGAN ST   29501
Moore MS, 1101 CHERAW DRIVE   29501
  Patricia Hanna, prin.
Southside MS, 200 HOWE SPRINGS ROAD   29501
  Patsy Slice, prin.
Williams MS, 1119 N IRBY ST   29501
  Lionel Johnson, prin.
Briggs ES, 1012 CONGAREE DR   29501
  Martin Smith, prin.
Carver ES, 1001 W SUMTER ST   29501
  Dorothy Ellerbe, prin.
Delmae Heights ES, 1211 S CASHUA DR   29501
  Cynthia Young, prin.
Greenwood ES, 2300 HOWE SPRINGS RD   29501
  Randall Barnes, prin.
Lester ES, 3500 E PALMETTO ST   29501
  Evelyn Heyward, prin.
McLaurin ES, 1400 MCMILLAN LN   29501
  Rebecca Smith, prin.
North Vista ES, 1200 N IRBY ST   29501
  Clarence Alston, prin.
Royall ES, 1400 WOODS RD   29501
  Julie Smith, prin.
Timrod ES, RURAL ROUTE 06 BOX 72   29501
  Linda Huggins, prin.
Wallace ES, RURAL ROUTE 04   29500
  Larry Leasure, prin.
Other Schools – See Effingham

Byrnes Academy, RURAL ROUTE 06   29501
Florence Christian School, 2308 S IRBY ST   29501
Marantha Christian School
  2624 W PALMETTO ST   29501
All Saints Episcopal Day School
  1425 CHEROKEE RD   29501
Christian Assembly School
  1501 SIESTA DR   29501
St. Anthony's Parish School, P O BOX 5327   29502
Wesleyan School & Day Care School
  2299 MECHANICSVILLE RD   29501

Fort Lawn, Chester Co., Pop. Code 2
Chester SD
Supt. – See Chester
ES, P O BOX 36   29714 – Sol Foster, prin.

Fort Mill, York Co., Pop. Code 5
Lancaster SD
Supt. – See Lancaster
Indian Land ES, RURAL ROUTE 02   29715
  Paul Cook, prin.

York SD 4
Sch. Sys. Enr. Code 5
Supt. – C. Joseph Bonds, P O BOX 369   29715
MS, BANKS ST   29715 – Linda Allen, prin.
MS, P O BOX 370   29715 – James Epps, prin.
PS, P O BOX 399   29715 – Molly Coggins, prin.

Frogmore, Beaufort Co.
Beaufort County SD
Supt. – See Beaufort
St. Helena ES, RURAL ROUTE 03 BOX 895   29920
  Mildred Wilson, prin.

Fountain Inn, Greenville Co., Pop. Code 5
Greenville County SD
Supt. – See Greenville
Bryson MS, P O BOX 338   29644
  Susan Hoover, prin.
ES, 311 N MAIN ST   29644 – Donald Skelton, prin.

Gadsden, Richland Co.
Richland SD 1
Supt. – See Columbia
ES, P O BOX 40   29052
  Dr. Alphonso Counts, prin.

Gaffney, Cherokee Co., Pop. Code 7
Cherokee SD
Sch. Sys. Enr. Code 6
Supt. – John Ewing, P O BOX 460   29342
Alma ES, 2901 FLORENCE AVE   29340
  Salley Peeler, prin.
Beam ES, RURAL ROUTE 03 BOX 82   29340
  Zara Barnhill, prin.
Bramlett ES, 301 SPRUCE ST   29340
  Francis Sarratt, prin.
Central ES, 301 S JOHNSON ST   29340
  Alfred McGaha, prin.
Corinth ES, RURAL ROUTE 04 BOX 330   29340
  Terry Price, prin.
Draytonville ES
  RURAL ROUTE 06 BOX 123   29340
  Billy Elmore, prin.
Goucher ES, RURAL ROUTE 04 BOX 402   29340
  Barbara Rhodes, prin.
Lee ES, 401 OVERBROOK DR   29340
  Bertha Harris, prin.
Limestone ES, 130 LEADMINE ST   29340
  Jane Queen, prin.
Macedonia ES, RURAL ROUTE 07 BOX 575   29340
  Lucious Jones, prin.
Morgan ES, RURAL ROUTE 03 BOX 83   29340
  Archie Fowler, prin.
Vaughan ES, RURAL ROUTE 01   29340
  Sarah Bonner, prin.
Other Schools – See Blacksburg

Heritage Christian School
  RURAL ROUTE 08 BOX 740   29342

Galivants Ferry, Horry Co.
Horry County SD
Supt. – See Conway
Midland ES, RURAL ROUTE 03   29544
  Kenneth Frye, prin.

Gaston, Lexington Co., Pop. Code 3
Lexington SD 4
Supt. – See Swansea
Mack ES, 161 GASTON ST   29053
  Gregg Riley III, prin.

Georgetown, Georgetown Co., Pop. Code 7
Georgetown County SD
Sch. Sys. Enr. Code 7
Supt. – C. Dodson, P O BOX 720   29442
Beck MS, P O BOX 1747   29442
  Celestine Pringle, prin.
Choppee MS
  RURAL ROUTE 03 BOX 422-A   29440
  Hughie Peterson,Jr., prin.
Browns Ferry ES
  RURAL ROUTE 04 BOX 700   29440
  Joseph Bryant, prin.
Kensington ES, 86 KENSINGTON BLVD   29440
  Capers Johnston, prin.
Maryville ES, P O BOX 8129   29440
  Charles Huff III, prin.
McDonald ES, 12 MCDONALD RD   29440
  Bonnie Lee, prin.
Plantersville ES, HCR 01 BOX 532   29440
  Levi Keith, prin.
Sampit ES, RURAL ROUTE 01 BOX 242   29440
  Thomas Robinson, prin.
Other Schools – See Andrews, Hemingway, Pawleys Island

First Baptist Church School, P O BOX K   29442

Gilbert, Lexington Co., Pop. Code 2
Lexington SD 1
Supt. – See Lexington
ES, P O BOX AF   29054 – Nancy Harman, prin.

Glendale, Spartanburg Co., Pop. Code 4
Spartanburg SD 3
Sch. Sys. Enr. Code 5
Supt. – Dr. James Buie, P O BOX 267   29346
Other Schools – See Cowpens, Pacolet, Spartanburg

Gloverville, Aiken Co., Pop. Code 4
Aiken County SD
Supt. – See Aiken
ES, P O BOX 358   29828 – Gloria Rush, prin.

Goose Creek, Berkeley Co., Pop. Code 7
Berkeley County SD
Supt. – See Moncks Corner
Sedgefield MS, CHARLES GIBSON BLVD   29445
  Willis Sanders, prin.
Westview MS, 101 WESTVIEW DRIVE   29445
  Lewis Quick, prin.
Boulder Bluff ES, RURAL ROUTE 10   29445
  Brooks Moore, prin.
Howe Hall ES, P O BOX 37   29445
  C. Bianchi, prin.
Westview ES, 100 WESTVIEW DR   29445
  Michael Heitzler, prin.

Graniteville, Aiken Co., Pop. Code 4
Aiken County SD
Supt. – See Aiken
Leavelle-McCampbell MS, CANAL ST   29829
  Alfonso Lamback, prin.
Byrd ES, 1 WILLIS CIR   29829
  Claude Prather, prin.

Gray Court, Laurens Co., Pop. Code 3
Laurens SD 55
Supt. – See Laurens
Gray Court-Owings MS, P O BOX 187   29645
  Eugene Marlar, prin.
Hickory Tavern ES, RURAL ROUTE 01   29645
  John Topping, prin.
Pleasant View ES, P O BOX 128   29645
  Carolyn Shortt, prin.

Great Falls, Chester Co., Pop. Code 5
Chester SD
Supt. – See Chester
MS, P O BOX 448   29055 – Debra Carpenter, prin.
ES, 301 DEARBORN ST   29055
  Dr. James Linder, prin.

Greeleyville, Williamsburg Co., Pop. Code 3
Williamsburg County SD
Supt. – See Kingstree
ES, P O BOX 128   29056 – Ralph Fennell,Jr., prin.

Green Pond, Colleton Co.
Colleton County SD
Supt. – See Walterboro
Brown ES, P O BOX 305   29446
  Marvin Jones, prin.

Green Sea, Horry Co.
Horry County SD
Supt. – See Conway
Green Sea-Floyds MS, P O BOX 128   29545
  Zebedee Pack, prin.
Green Sea-Floyds ES, P O BOX 148   29545
  Shirley Huggins, prin.

Greenville, Greenville Co., Pop. Code 8
Greenville County SD
Sch. Sys. Enr. Code 8
Supt. – Dr. Thomas Kerns, P O BOX 2848   29602

Beara MS, RURAL ROUTE 03 29611
  David Russell, prin.
Beck MS, 302 MCALISTER ROAD 29607
  Dennis Varner, prin.
MS, 16 HUDSON GROVE 29615
  Scarlette Owens, prin.
Hughes MS, 122 DEOYLEY AVE 29605
  Karen Moore, prin.
Lakeview MS
  3801 OLD BUNCOMBE ROAD 29609
  Paul Goble, prin.
League MS, 125 TWINE LAKE ROAD 29609
  Dennis Pelletier, prin.
Parker MS, 900 WOODSIDE AVE 29611
  Jessie Bowens, prin.
Sevier MS, 101 SUNNYDALE DRIVE 29609
  Peggy Martin, prin.
Tanglewood MS
  2801 OLD EASLEY BRIDGE ROAD 29611
  James Gardner, prin.
Alexander ES, 1601 BRAMLETT RD 29611
  Robert Jones, prin.
Armstrong ES, RURAL ROUTE 03 29611
  Nancy Anderson, prin.
Arrington ES, 925 N FRANKLIN RD 29609
  Anthony Hester, prin.
Augusta Circle ES, 100 WINYAH ST 29605
  Sandra Welch, prin.
Bakers Chapel ES
  200 OLD PIEDMONT HWY 29611
  Nancy Farnsworth, prin.
Berea ES, 104 FARRS BRIDGE RD 29611
  Robert Crouch, prin.
Blythe ES, 100 BLYTHE DR 29605
  Katherine Howard, prin.
Duncan Chapel ES
  200 DUNCAN CHAPEL RD 29609
  Joanne Thomas, prin.
Collins ES, 1200 PARKINGS MILL ROAD 29607
  Betty Spencer, prin.
Cone ES, 500 GRIDLEY ST 29609
  Thomas Huber, prin.
East Gantt ES, RURAL ROUTE 04 BOX 1A 29605
  Robert Cashion, prin.
East North Street ES, 1720 E NORTH ST 29607
  Charles Franchina, prin.
ES, RURAL ROUTE 14 29607
  Harvey Ferguson, prin.
ES, 625 PIEDMONT HWY 29605
  Zach Nabers III, prin.
Hollis ES, 14 8TH ST 29611 – James Nance, prin.
Lake Forest ES, 31 SHANNON DR 29615
  Sara Utsey, prin.
Laurel Creek ES, 421 DALLAS DR 29607
  William Stevenson, prin.
Mitchell Road ES, 4124 E NORTH ST 29615
  Barbara Campbell, prin.
Monaview ES, 1006 W PARKER RD 29611
  James Patterson, prin.
Paris ES, 1004 PIEDMONT PARK RD 29609
  Jackson House, prin.
Pelham Road ES, 1 ALL STAR WAY 29615
  Pat Borenstein, prin.
Sans Souci ES, 302 PERRY RD 29609
  Willie Sullivan, prin.
Sirrine ES, 301 E DORCHESTER BLVD 29605
  Gerald Haynes, prin.
Stone ES, 412 WILTON ST 29609
  Francis Allgood, prin.
Summit Drive ES, 424 SUMMIT DR 29609
  Allan Goodlett, prin.
Welcome ES, 36 E WELCOME RD 29611
  Frank Sutherland, prin.
Westcliffe ES, 105 EASTBOURNE RD 29611
  John Hamilton, prin.
Other Schools – See Fountain Inn, Greer, Marietta,
  Mauldin, Pelzer, Piedmont, Simpsonville, Taylors,
  Travelers Rest
_____

Christ Church Episcopal School
  P O BOX 10128 29603
Emmanuel Academy, 106 DUPONT DR 29607
Hampton Park Christian School
  RURAL ROUTE 12 29609
Shannon Forest Christian School
  829 GARLINGTON ROAD 29615
Tabernacle Christian School
  3931 WHITE HORSE ROAD 29611
Haynsworth School, 228 E PARK AVE 29601
Jones ES, WADE HAMPTON BLVD 29614
Mitchell Road Christian Academy
  207 MITCHELL RD 29615
Our Lady of the Rosary School, 2 JAMES DR 29605
St. Mary's ES, 101 HAMPTON AVE 29601

Greenwood, Greenwood Co., Pop. Code 7
Greenwood SD 50
  Sch. Sys. Enr. Code 6
  Supt. – Dr. Robert Watson, P O BOX 248 29648
  Brewer IS, 927 E CAMBRIDGE AVE 29646
    Sidney Hopkins, prin.
  East End IS, E CAMBRIDGE AVE 29646
    Shirley Crosby, prin.
  Lakeview PS, CENTE ST 29646
    Gay McHugh, prin.
  Mathews PS, P O BOX 2087 29646
    Joann Burroughs, prin.
  Merrywood PS, 100 MERRYWOOD DR 29646
    Jean Ledvina, prin.
  Oakland ES, 1802 E DURST AVE 29646
    Eleanor Rice, prin.
  Pinecrest ES, 220 E NORTHSIDE DR 29646
    Janell Alston, prin.

Woodfields PS, 304 WOODFIELDS ST 29646
  Patricia Vahjen, prin.
Other Schools – See Hodges
_____

Cambridge Academy, 103 EASTMAN ST 29646
Community Christian School
  P O BOX 2026 29646
East Side Christian School, P O BOX 907 29648

Greer, Greenville Co., Pop. Code 7
Greenville County SD
  Supt. – See Greenville
  Blue Ridge MS
    2423 TYGER BRIDGE ROAD 29651
    Charles Bright, prin.
  MS, 301 CHANDLER ROAD 29651
    Marion Waters, prin.
  Buena Vista ES, 310 S BATESVILLE RD 29650
    Judith Green, prin.
  Crestview ES, RURAL ROUTE 09 29651
    Margaret Thomason, prin.
  East Greer ES, 200 MORGAN ST 29651
    Carol Sherron, prin.
  Skyland ES, RURAL ROUTE 02 29651
    Robert Tyson, prin.
  Tryon Street ES, 108 TRYON ST 29650
    Sue Link, prin.
  Woodland ES, 209 WEST RD 29650
    Betty Payne, prin.

Gresham, Marion Co., Pop. Code 2
Marion SD 4
  Sch. Sys. Enr. Code 3
  Supt. – W. Saffold
    RURAL ROUTE 01 BOX 499 29546
  Brittons Neck ES
    RURAL ROUTE 01 BOX 499 29546
    David Anderson, prin.

Hampton, Hampton Co., Pop. Code 5
North SD 1
  Sch. Sys. Enr. Code 5
  Supt. – C. Phillips, P O BOX 177 29924
  ES, P O BOX 687 29924 – E. Boland, prin.
  Other Schools – See Brunson, Varnville, Yemassee

Hanahan, Berkeley Co., Pop. Code 7
Berkeley County SD
  Supt. – See Moncks Corner
  MS, 5815 N MURRAY AVE 29406
    H. Dukes, prin.

Hardeeville, Jasper Co., Pop. Code 4
Jasper County SD
  Supt. – See Ridgeland
  West Hardeeville ES, P O BOX 525 29927
    Larry Duncan, prin.
_____

Abundant Life Academy, P O BOX 310 29927

Harleyville, Dorchester Co., Pop. Code 3
Dorchester SD 4
  Supt. – See Saint George
  Jenkins Hill ES
    RURAL ROUTE 01 BOX 196 29448
    Mildred Brown, prin.
_____

Mims Academy, P O BOX 248 29448

Hartsville, Darlington Co., Pop. Code 6
Darlington SD
  Supt. – See Darlington
  Carolina ES, 719 W CAROLINA AVE 29550
    Dr. Allen McCutchen, prin.
  North Hartsville MS, 110 SCHOOL DR 29550
    (—), prin.
  West Hartsville ES
    RURAL ROUTE 02 BOX 91 29550
    Dr. Frank Bouknight, prin.
  Sonovista ES, 401 SOCIETY AVE 29550
    Sharon Griggs, prin.
  Southside ES, 1615 BLANDING DR 29550
    (—), prin.
  Thornwell ES, 604 E HOME AVE 29550
    Claude Wint, prin.
  Washington Street ES
    325 W WASHINGTON ST 29550
    Annie Peterson, prin.
_____

Emmanuel Baptist School
  RURAL ROUTE 01 BOX 82 29550

Heath Springs, Lancaster Co., Pop. Code 3
Lancaster SD
  Supt. – See Lancaster
  ES, RURAL ROUTE 03 BOX 128 29058
    Terry Clyburn, prin.

Hemingway, Williamsburg Co., Pop. Code 3
Georgetown County SD
  Supt. – See Georgetown
  Pleasant Hill MS
    RURAL ROUTE 03 BOX 178 29554
    Denise Appewhite, prin.
  Deep Creek ES, RURAL ROUTE 03 BOX 463 29554
    Don Swett, prin.

Williamsburg County SD
  Supt. – See Kingstree
  MS, P O BOX 977 29554 – James Gray, prin.
  PS, RURAL ROUTE 01 BOX 350 29554
    Marion Lee, prin.

Hickory Grove, York Co., Pop. Code 2
York SD 1
  Supt. – See York

Hickory Grove-Sharon ES, P O BOX 97 29717
  H. Stephenson, prin.

Hilton Head Island, Beaufort Co.
Beaufort County SD
  Supt. – See Beaufort
  Hilton Head ES, 25 SCHOOL RD 29926
    Henry Noble, prin.
_____

Hilton Head Christian Academy
  12 ARROW ROAD 29928
Hilton Head Prep School
  8 FOXGRAPE ROAD 29928

Hodges, Greenwood Co., Pop. Code 2
Greenwood SD 50
  Supt. – See Greenwood
  MS, P O BOX 499 29653
    Mary Lou Goodman, prin.

Holly Hill, Orangeburg Co., Pop. Code 4
Orangeburg SD 3
  Sch. Sys. Enr. Code 5
  Supt. – David Longshore, P O BOX 98 29059
  Dantzler MS, RURAL ROUTE 01 BOX 157 29059
    Booker Whetstone, prin.
  MS, P O BOX 878 29059 – James Myers, prin.
  PS, P O BOX 278 29059 – Gerald Wright, prin.
  Providence PS, RURAL ROUTE 01 BOX 190 29059
    Lucia Shuler, prin.
  Other Schools – See Eutawville, Vance
_____

Holly Hill Academy, P O BOX 757 29059

Honea Path, Anderson Co., Pop. Code 5
Anderson SD 2
  Sch. Sys. Enr. Code 5
  Supt. – Roger Burnett, RURAL ROUTE 02 29654
  MS, 107 BOCK AVE 29654 – Tillie Parker, prin.
  Honea Path ES-Watkins, S MAIN ST 29654
    Lee Rawl, prin.
  Honea Path ES-Gantt, E GREER ST 29654
    Lee Rawl, prin.
  Other Schools – See Belton

Hopkins, Richland Co., Pop. Code 6
Richland SD 1
  Supt. – See Columbia
  MS, RURAL ROUTE 01 29061
    Ellen Mosley, prin.
  ES, RURAL ROUTE 03 BOX 64 29061
    Thedrick Pigford, prin.
  Horrell Hill ES, 455 HORRELL HILL BLVD 29061
    Parthenia Satterwhite, prin.

Huger, Berkeley Co., Pop. Code 1
Berkeley County SD
  Supt. – See Moncks Corner
  Cainhoy ES, RURAL ROUTE 01 HWY 98 29450
    Clara Cooper, prin.

Inman, Spartanburg Co., Pop. Code 4
Spartanburg SD 1
  Supt. – See Campobello
  Mabry JHS, 10 W MILLER ST 29349
    Louis Jarrell, prin.
  ES, 25 OAKLAND AVE 29349 – Sam Fuller, prin.
  New Prospect ES
    RURAL ROUTE 09 BOX 337 29349
    Geary Jolley, prin.

Spartanburg SD 2
  Supt. – See Spartanburg
  Boiling Springs ES
    700 DOUBLE BRIDGE RD 29349
    Sheilia Davis, prin.
  Boiling Springs MS
    1850 OLD FURNACE RD 29349
    Allen Bogan, prin.
  Hendrix ES, RURAL ROUTE 05 BOX 116 29349
    Jack Littlefield, prin.

Irmo, Richland Co., Pop. Code 5
Lexington SD 5
  Supt. – See Ballentine
  Dutch Fork ES, P O BOX 869 29063
    Dr. Anne Scott, prin.
  ES, P O BOX 707 29063 – Marcia Loadholt, prin.

Iva, Anderson Co., Pop. Code 4
Anderson SD 3
  Sch. Sys. Enr. Code 4
  Supt. – Roy Herron, P O BOX 118 29655
  ES, P O BOX 268 29655 – Charles Hayes, prin.
  Other Schools – See Starr

Jackson, Aiken Co., Pop. Code 4
Aiken County SD
  Supt. – See Aiken
  MS, DUAL LANE HIGHWAY 29831
    David Caver, prin.

Jefferson, Chesterfield Co., Pop. Code 3
Chesterfield SD
  Supt. – See Chesterfield
  ES, P O BOX 156 29718 – Allen Teal, prin.

Joanna, Laurens Co., Pop. Code 4
Laurens SD 56
  Supt. – See Clinton
  Joanna-Woodson ES, 510 S ELLIS ST 29351
    James Longshore, prin.

Johns Island, Charleston Co., Pop. Code 6
St. Johns Constituent SD
  Supt. – See Charleston
  Haut Gap MS, 1861 BOHICKET ROAD 29455
    James Coaxum, prin.

Angel Oak ES, 6134 CHISOLM RD   29455
Ruby Martin, prin.
Mount Zion ES, 3464 RIVER RD   29455
Cheryl Boan, prin.

Sea Island Academy, 2024 ACADEMY DR   29455

Johnsonville, Florence Co., Pop. Code 4
Florence SD 5
Sch. Sys. Enr. Code 4
Supt. – Paul Shaw, P O BOX 98   29555
MS, P O BOX 67   29555 – D. Ray McAlister, prin.
ES, P O BOX 1078   29555 – James Weaver, prin.

Johnston, Edgefield Co., Pop. Code 5
Edgefield County SD
Supt. – See Edgefield
MS, P O BOX 116   29832 – Robert Heflin, prin.
PS, P O BOX J   29832 – Diane Murrell, prin.

Wardlaw Academy
RURAL ROUTE 01 BOX 92   29832

Jonesville, Union Co., Pop. Code 4
Union County SD
Supt. – See Union
ES, P O BOX 218   29353 – Jean Carlisle, prin.

Kershaw, Kershaw Co., Pop. Code 4
Kershaw County SD
Supt. – See Camden
Mt. Pisgah ES, RURAL ROUTE 04   29067
James Morton, prin.

Lancaster SD
Supt. – See Lancaster
Jackson MS, RURAL ROUTE 02   29067
(—), prin.
MS, RURAL ROUTE 03 BOX 209   29067
Charles Clyburn, prin.
Flat Creek ES, RURAL ROUTE 03   29067
Tony Brasington, prin.
PS, 108 ROLLINS AVE   29067
Imogene Blackmon, prin.

Kingstree, Williamsburg Co., Pop. Code 5
Williamsburg County SD
Sch. Sys. Enr. Code 6
Supt. – Floride Martin, P O BOX 1067   29556
JHS, 710 3RD AVE   29556
Dr. Sandra Steiner, prin.
Anderson PS, 500 LEXINGTON AVE   29556
(—), prin.
MS, 500 N ACADEMY ST   29556
Gary Chandler, prin.
Other Schools – See Andrews, Cades, Greeleyville, Hemingway, Nesmith

Williamsburg Academy, P O BOX 770   29556

Ladson, Berkeley Co.
Berkeley County SD
Supt. – See Moncks Corner
College Park MS, UNIVERSITY DRIVE   29456
Richard Van Brunt, prin.
College Park ES, DAVIDSON DR   29456
James Hinson, prin.

Cooper River Constituent
Supt. – See North Charleston
ES, LADSON ROAD   29456
James Humphries, prin.

Dorchester SD 2
Supt. – See Summerville
Oakbrook MS, 4704 OLD FORT ROAD   29456
Garland Crump, prin.
Oakbrook ES, 4700 OLD FORT ROAD   29456
Patsy Pye, prin.

La France, Anderson Co., Pop. Code 3
Anderson SD 4
Supt. – See Pendleton
ES, P O BOX 487   29656 – Walter Johnson, prin.

Lake City, Florence Co., Pop. Code 6
Florence SD 3
Sch. Sys. Enr. Code 5
Supt. – James Hyman, P O BOX 128   29560
McNair JHS, P O BOX 1019   29560
Jerome Ballard, prin.
Lake City 2 MS, P O BOX 1267   29560
W. Murdaugh, prin.
Lake City I ES, P O BOX 1207   29560
(—), prin.
PS, P O BOX 1726   29560 – Cheryl Floyd, prin.
Other Schools – See Coward, Olanta, Scranton

Carolina Academy
351 S COUNTRY CLUB ROAD   29560

Lake View, Dillon Co., Pop. Code 3
Dillon SD 1
Sch. Sys. Enr. Code 4
Supt. – D. Rogers, P O BOX 644   29563
ES, P O BOX 685   29563 – Dian Scott, prin.
MS, P O BOX 744   29563 – Gerlan Nance, prin.

Lamar, Darlington Co., Pop. Code 4
Darlington SD
Supt. – See Darlington
Spaulding JHS, P O BOX 128   29069
Eddie Pauley, prin.
ES, P O BOX 769   29069 – (—), prin.
Spaulding ES, P O BOX 849   29069
John Bloom, prin.

Lancaster, Lancaster Co., Pop. Code 6
Lancaster SD
Sch. Sys. Enr. Code 6
Supt. – Ernest Mathis, P O BOX 130   29720
Brooklyn Springs ES, 502 BILLINGS DR   29720
Bernadine King, prin.
Buford ES, RURAL ROUTE 09   29720
Gene Starnes, prin.
Central ES, 302 W DUNLAP ST   29720
Elizabeth Hutchinson, prin.
Clinton ES, 408 CLINTON AVE   29720
Ed Jackson, prin.
Dobson ES, P O BOX 128   29720 – (—), prin.
Erwin ES, 201 N LOCUSTWOOD AVE   29720
(—), prin.
McDonald Green ES, RURAL ROUTE 08   29720
Martha Noblitt, prin.
North ES, RODDY DR   29720 – Bill Smith, prin.
South Side ES, 500 HAMPTON ROAD   29720
Audrey Prus, prin.
Other Schools – See Fort Mill, Heath Springs, Kershaw

Landrum, Spartanburg Co., Pop. Code 4
Spartanburg SD 1
Supt. – See Campobello
Earle ES, 100 REDLAND RD   29356
Janie Summers, prin.

Langley, Aiken Co.
Aiken County SD
Supt. – See Aiken
Langley-Bath-Clearwater MS, P O BOX 327   29834
James Gallman, prin.

Latta, Dillon Co., Pop. Code 4
Dillon SD 3
Sch. Sys. Enr. Code 4
Supt. – Robert McBryde,Jr., P O BOX 458   29565
Latimer MS, 502 WILLIS ST   29565
Isaiah Armstrong, prin.
PS, 602 N RICHARDSON ST   29565
James Kimmell, prin.

Laurens, Laurens Co., Pop. Code 7
Laurens SD 55
Sch. Sys. Enr. Code 6
Supt. – Raleigh Buchanan, P O BOX 388   29360
JHS, P O BOX 288   29360 – W. Ramey, prin.
Ford ES, P O BOX 266   29360 – James Pitts, prin.
PS, P O BOX 385   29360 – Thomas Childress, prin.
Morse ES, P O BOX 329   29360
Gwendolyn Adams, prin.
Sanders MS, P O BOX 366   29360
James Jennings, prin.
Other Schools – See Gray Court

Lexington, Lexington Co., Pop. Code 4
Lexington SD 1
Sch. Sys. Enr. Code 7
Supt. – Dr. J. Floyd, P O BOX 219   29072
MS, 702 N LAKE DRIVE   29072
Charles Gatch, prin.
ES, AZALEA DR   29072 – John Mitchum, prin.
IS, 420 HENDRIX ST   29072 – Janice Duncan, prin.
Oak Grove ES, 479 OAK DR   29072
William Long, prin.
Red Bank ES, 246 COMMUNITY DR   29072
Glenda Loftis, prin.
Other Schools – See Gilbert, Pelion

Liberty, Pickens Co., Pop. Code 5
Pickens SD
Supt. – See Easley
MS, 310 W MAIN ST   29657
Dennis Somerville, prin.
ES, 151 N HILLCREST ST   29657
Mike Mahaffey, prin.

Little Mountain, Newberry Co., Pop. Code 2
Newberry County SD
Supt. – See Newberry
ES, RURAL ROUTE 01 BOX A-1   29075
Lannie Griffeth, prin.

Lockhart, Union Co., Pop. Code 1
Union County SD
Supt. – See Union
ES, P O BOX 220   29364 – (—), prin.

Loris, Horry Co., Pop. Code 4
Horry County SD
Supt. – See Conway
Daisy ES, RURAL ROUTE 04 BOX 62   29569
Carolyn Chestnut, prin.
ES, 4350 SPRING ST   29569 – Charles Camp, prin.
MS, 3410 CHURCH ST   29569
James McCall, prin.

Lugoff, Kershaw Co., Pop. Code 4
Kershaw County SD
Supt. – See Camden
Lugoff-Elgin MS, P O BOX 68   29078
Larry Patrick, prin.
ES, P O BOX 38   29078 – Amy McLester, prin.

Lyman, Spartanburg Co., Pop. Code 4
Spartanburg SD 5
Supt. – See Duncan
ES, 84 GROCE RD   29365 – Frank Cook, prin.

Lynchburg, Lee Co., Pop. Code 3
Lee County SD
Supt. – See Bishopville
Fleming MS, P O BOX 218   29080
Leroy Gary, prin.

Sumter SD 2
Supt. – See Sumter
St. John ES, RURAL ROUTE 01 BOX 97   29080
George Gibson, prin.

Hudgens Academy, RURAL ROUTE 02   29080

Manning, Clarendon Co., Pop. Code 5
Clarendon SD 2
Sch. Sys. Enr. Code 5
Supt. – Dr. Sylvia Weinberg, P O BOX 1252   29102
MS, 311 W BOYCE ST   29102
Kenneth Mance, prin.
PS, 125 N BOUNDARY ST   29102
Cynthia Boland, prin.
Other Schools – See Alcolu

Marietta, Greenville Co., Pop. Code 3
Greenville County SD
Supt. – See Greenville
Slater-Marietta ES, RURAL ROUTE 02   29661
Janet Welch, prin.

Marion, Marion Co., Pop. Code 6
Marion SD 1
Sch. Sys. Enr. Code 5
Supt. – Charles Bethea
616 E NORTHSIDE AVE   29571
Johnakin MS, GURLEY ST   29571
Andrew Eaddy, prin.
Easterling ES, 600 NORTHSIDE AVE   29571
Dennis Triplett, prin.
MS, 719 N MAIN ST   29571 – Jackie Jackson, prin.
Southside ES, EUTAW ST   29571 – (—), prin.

Mauldin, Greenville Co., Pop. Code 6
Greenville County SD
Supt. – See Greenville
ES, P O BOX 96   29662 – Michelle Meekins, prin.

Mayesville, Sumter Co., Pop. Code 3
Lee County SD
Supt. – See Bishopville
Lower Lee ES, RURAL ROUTE 01 BOX 293   29104
John Haynesworth, prin.

Sumter SD 2
Supt. – See Sumter
Mayesville Instructional ES, P O BOX 128   29104
Martha Gary, prin.

Mayo, Spartanburg Co.
Spartanburg SD 2
Supt. – See Spartanburg
ES, P O BOX 128   29368 – William Browning, prin.

Mc Bee, Chesterfield Co., Pop. Code 3
Chesterfield SD
Supt. – See Chesterfield
ES, P O BOX 368   29101
Ernest Witherspoon, prin.

Mc Clellanville, Charleston Co., Pop. Code 2
St. James Santee Constituent
Supt. – See Mount Pleasant
St. James Santee ES, 8900 HWY 17 N   29458
Juanita Middleton, prin.

Mc Coll, Marlboro Co., Pop. Code 5
Marlboro County SD
Supt. – See Bennettsville
Adamsville MS
RURAL ROUTE 01 BOX 395   29570
Cherry Charpia, prin.
PS, N MARLBORO ST   29570 – Hazel King, prin.

Mc Cormick, Mc Cormick Co., Pop. Code 4
McCormick SD
Sch. Sys. Enr. Code 4
Supt. – Charles Parnell,Jr., P O BOX 548   29835
MS, P O BOX 458   29835 – F. Pierce, prin.
ES, 615 CLAYTON   29835 – J. R. Curtis, prin.

Long Cane Academy, P O BOX 666   29835

Moncks Corner, Berkeley Co., Pop. Code 5
Berkeley County SD
Sch. Sys. Enr. Code 8
Supt. – Charles Gibson, P O BOX 608   29461
Berkeley MS, HIGHWAY 17A   29461
L. Snider, prin.
Macedonia MS, RURAL ROUTE 03   29461
Nicke Gaspers, prin.
Berkeley ES, 107 E MAIN ST   29461
Ruth Lusk, prin.
Bonner ES, RURAL ROUTE 03 BOX 329   29461
Linda Harrelson, prin.
Ready IS, 100 READY ST   29461
Joseph Myers, prin.
Whitesville ES
RURAL ROUTE 06 BOX 249   29461
Charles Rogers, prin.
Other Schools – See Charleston, Cross, Goose Creek, Hanahan, Huger, Ladson, Saint Stephen, Summerville

Lord Berkeley Academy, 204 W MAIN ST   29461

Moore, Spartanburg Co.
Spartanburg SD 6
Supt. – See Spartanburg
Blackstock ES, RURAL ROUTE 02 BOX 80   29369
Don King, prin.

Mount Pleasant, Charleston Co., Pop. Code 7
Moultrie Constituent
Sch. Sys. Enr. Code 6
Supt. – Lynda Davis, 665 COLEMAN BLVD   29464

Laing MS, RURAL ROUTE 01 BOX 170H 29464
  Walter Pusey, prin.
Moultrie MS, 645 COLEMAN BLVD 29464
  Thomas Ferguson, prin.
Edwards ES, 855 VON KOLNITZ RD 29464
  Thomas Lee, prin.
Moore ES, RURAL ROUTE 01 BOX 390 29464
  John Collins, prin.
ES, 605 CENTER ST 29464
  Marian Mentavlos, prin.
Whitesides ES, RURAL ROUTE 01 29464
  David Schlachter, prin.
Other Schools – See Sullivans Island

St. James Santee Constituent
Sch. Sys. Enr. Code 3
Supt. – Lynda Davis, 665 COLEMAN BLVD 29464
Other Schools – See Mc Clellanville

East Cooper School, P O BOX 442 29464
Trident Academy, P O BOX 804 29464
Christ our King ES, 1183 RUSSELL DR 29464

Mullins, Marion Co., Pop. Code 6
Marion SD 2
Sch. Sys. Enr. Code 5
Supt. – Dr. W. Foil, P O BOX 689 29574
Palmetto MS, 305 O'NEAL ST 29574
  Herman Wallace, prin.
McCormick ES, 1123 SANDY BLUFF RD 29574
  John Lane, prin.
North Mullins PS, 105 CHARLES ST 29574
  Cynthia Lane, prin.
Palmetto MS, 200 BROAD ST 29574
  Vicki Kirby, prin.
Other Schools – See Nichols

Marion SD 3
Supt. – See Rains
Pleasant Grove ES
  RURAL ROUTE 01 BOX 403 29574
  Willie Sue Best, prin.

Pee Dee Academy, P O BOX 449 29574

Myrtle Beach, Horry Co., Pop. Code 7
Horry County SD
Supt. – See Conway
MS, 3301 OAK ST 29577 – Betty Reid, prin.
St. James MS, 121 ST JAMES RD 29577
  Wendell Shealy, prin.
Socastee MS, P O BOX 91 29578
  Roger Bryan, prin.
Forestbrook ES, ROUTE 11 BOX 2000 29577
  Robert Vaughn, prin.
Lakewood ES, RURAL ROUTE 02 29575
  W. David James, prin.
MS, 3101 OAK ST 29577 – Dr. John Sprawls, prin.
PS, 612 29TH AVE N 29577
  Rosemary Quickel, prin.
Socastee ES, ST JAMES ROAD 29577
  Samuel Floyd, prin.

Calvary Christian School
  23 DICK POND ROAD 29577
Coastal Academy, 904 65TH AVE N 29577
Risen Christ Lutheran School
  10595 N HWY 17 NORTH 29577
St. Andrews ES, 36TH AVENUE N 29577

Neeses, Orangeburg Co., Pop. Code 3
Orangeburg SD 1
Supt. – See Springfield
ES, P O BO X126 29113 – Billy Colvin, prin.

Nesmith, Williamsburg Co.
Williamsburg County SD
Supt. – See Kingstree
Battery Park ES
  RURAL ROUTE 01 BOX 172 29580
  Janie Cooper, prin.

Newberry, Newberry Co., Pop. Code 6
Newberry County SD
Sch. Sys. Enr. Code 6
Supt. – Dr. Vance Johnson, P O BOX 718 29108
JHS, 1829 NANCE ST 29108
  William Floyd, prin.
Boundary ES, 1406 BOUNDARY ST 29108
  Henry Reeders, prin.
Gallman MS, 540 BRANTLEY ST 29108
  Charles Layton, prin.
Rueben ES, RURAL ROUTE 04 BOX 273 29108
  Mildred Kramer, prin.
Speers Street PS, P O BOX 8 29108
  Harvey Kirkland, prin.
Other Schools – See Little Mountain, Pomaria,
  Prosperity, Whitmire

Newberry Academy, P O BOX 669 29108

New Ellenton, Aiken Co., Pop. Code 5
Aiken County SD
Supt. – See Aiken
MS, 814 MAIN ST S 29809 – William Ward, prin.
Greendale ES, 505 S BOUNDARY AVE 29809
  Teresa Pope, prin.

New Zion, Clarendon Co.
Clarendon SD 3
Supt. – See Turbeville
East Clarendon ES, P O BOX 7 29111
  Richard Knowlton, prin.

Nichols, Marion Co., Pop. Code 3
Marion SD 2
Supt. – See Mullins
ES, P O BOX 209 29581 – Judith Pace, prin.

Ninety Six, Greenwood Co., Pop. Code 4
Greenwood SD 52
Sch. Sys. Enr. Code 4
Supt. – Gerald Robinson
  119 S CAMBRIDGE ST 29666
MS, KINARD AVE 29666 – Ray Frick, prin.
ES, 121 S CAMBRIDGE ST 29666
  Nancy Milner, prin.

North, Orangeburg Co., Pop. Code 4
Orangeburg SD 6
Sch. Sys. Enr. Code 3
Supt. – Joseph Lefft, P O BOX 640 29112
ES, P O BOX 218 29112 – Marshall Lynn, prin.

North Augusta, Aiken Co., Pop. Code 7
Aiken County SD
Supt. – See Aiken
Knox MS, 1804 WELLS ROAD 29841
  Joseph Padget, prin.
MS, 725 OLD EDGEFIELD ROAD 29841
  F. Hyers, prin.
Hammond Hill ES
  901 W WOODLAWN AVE 29841
  Frances Bell, prin.
ES, 400 E SPRING GROVE AVE 29841
  E. Watkins, prin.

Edgefield County SD
Supt. – See Edgefield
Merriwether ES, 430 MURRAH RD 29841
  David Mathis, prin.

Victory Christian School
  620 MARTINTOWN ROAD 29841
Our Lady of Peace School
  856 OLD EDGEFIELD RD 29841
Walden Hall Montessori School
  1896 KNOBCONE AVE 29841

North Charleston, Charleston Co., Pop. Code 8
Cooper River Constituent
Sch. Sys. Enr. Code 7
Supt. – Matilda Dunston
  4720 JENKINS AVE 29406
Morningside MS, ASTER ST 29406
  Archie Franchini, prin.
Berry ES, 250 IROQUOIS T 29406
  Molly Kuntz, prin.
McNair ES, SPRUILL AVE 29405
  Gideon Pearson, prin.
ES, DURANT AND MARQUIS AVES 29406
  William Hayes, prin.
Park Circle ES, 4444 SIMS ST 29406
  Frank Thrift, prin.
Remount Road ES, 1825 REMOUNT RD 29406
  (–), prin.
Other Schools – See Charleston, Ladson

Ferndale Baptist School
  400 PIEDMONT AVE 29406

North Myrtle Beach, Horry Co., Pop. Code 5
Horry County SD
Supt. – See Conway
North Myrtle Beach MS
  RURAL ROUTE 02 BOX 48 29582
  Michael Blanton, prin.
North Myrtle Beach MS, RIUTE 02 BOX 98 29582
  W. Terry Blackwell, prin.
PS, 800 YE OLDE KINGS HWY 29582
  David Dickson, prin.

Norway, Orangeburg Co., Pop. Code 3

Heritage Hall Academy, P O BOX 456 29113

Olanta, Florence Co., Pop. Code 3
Florence SD 3
Supt. – See Lake City
ES, P O BOX 628 29114 – Sharon Askins, prin.

Orangeburg, Orangeburg Co., Pop. Code 7
Orangeburg SD 5
Sch. Sys. Enr. Code 6
Supt. – Dr. J. Wilsford, 578 ELLIS AVE NE 29115
Belleville MS, 1255 BELLEVILLE ROAD NE 29115
  James Howard, prin.
Bennett MS, 919 BENNETT ST NE 29115
  Rebecca Williams, prin.
Brookdale MS, 394 BROOKDALE DRIVE NE 29115
  Charlie Spell, prin.
Marshall ES, 1441 MARSHALL ST NE 29115
  Gerald Runager, prin.
Mellichamp ES, 350 MURRAY RD SW 29115
  Elizabeth Whetsell, prin.
Nix ES, 770 STILTON ST NE 29115
  (–), prin.
Rivelon ES, 350 RIVELON RD SW 29115
  Thomas Eklund, prin.
Sheridan ES, 139 HILLSBORO ST NE 29115
  Jean Oswald, prin.
Whittaker ES, 790 WHITTAKER PKY SE 29115
  Harry Nesmith, prin.

Garden City Christian Sch
  630 BROUGHTON ST SW 29115
Orangeburg Christian School
  P O BOX 1325 29116

Orangeburg Prep School
  2651 NORTH ROAD NW 29115
Holy Trinity School, 2202 RIVESIDE DR 29115

Pacolet, Spartanburg Co., Pop. Code 4
Spartanburg SD 3
Supt. – See Glendale
ES, P O BOX 99 29372 – Richard Wheeler, prin.

Pageland, Chesterfield Co., Pop. Code 5
Chesterfield SD
Supt. – See Chesterfield
MS, P O BOX 187 29728 – Jerry Hough, prin.
Petersburg ES, P O BOX 428 29728
  Charles Williams, prin.

Pamplico, Florence Co., Pop. Code 4
Florence SD 2
Sch. Sys. Enr. Code 4
Supt. – Dr. T. Paul Vivian
  RURAL ROUTE 01 BOX 36-B 29583
Hannah-Pamplico ES, P O BOX 67 29583
  Dr. D. Wayne Brazell, prin.
Hannah-Pamplico MS, P O BOX 158 29583
  Beverly Emanuel, prin.

New Prospect Christian School
  RURAL ROUTE 02 BOX 84-D 29583

Patrick, Chesterfield Co., Pop. Code 2
Chesterfield SD
Supt. – See Chesterfield
Plainview ES, RURAL ROUTE 01 BOX 87 29584
  Dr. John Williams, prin.

Pauline, Spartanburg Co.
Spartanburg SD 6
Supt. – See Spartanburg
Pauline-Glenn Springs ES, P O BOX 195 29374
  James Sloan, prin.

Pawleys Island, Georgetown Co., Pop. Code 3
Georgetown County SD
Supt. – See Georgetown
Waccamaw ES, P O BOX 778 29585
  Carl Hughes, prin.

Pelion, Lexington Co., Pop. Code 2
Lexington SD 1
Supt. – See Lexington
ES, P O BOX 158 29123 – Darrell Barringer, prin.

Pelzer, Anderson Co., Pop. Code 2
Anderson SD 1
Supt. – See Williamston
PS, P O BOX 255 29669 – Brenda Ellison, prin.
West Pelzer PS, 10 W STEWART ST 29669
  Elizabeth Griffith, prin.

Greenville County SD
Supt. – See Greenville
Fork Shoals ES, RURAL ROUTE 03 29669
  Harold Mims, prin.
Woodside ES, RURAL ROUTE 03 BOX 159 29669
  Charles Heyward, prin.

Pendleton, Anderson Co., Pop. Code 5
Anderson SD 4
Sch. Sys. Enr. Code 4
Supt. – Dr. W. Chaiken, P O BOX 545 29670
JHS, P O BOX 707 29670
  Irvin Cunningham, prin.
ES, P O BOX 237 29670 – Grady Gambrell, prin.
Riverside ES, P O BOX 248 29670
  James Woodson, prin.
Other Schools – See La France, Townville

Pickens, Pickens Co., Pop. Code 5
Pickens SD
Supt. – See Easley
Ambler ES, RURAL ROUTE 01 29671
  Gordon Turner, prin.
Hagood ES, SPARKS LANE 29671
  Katherine Porter, prin.
Holly Springs ES, RURAL ROUTE 03 29671
  Gary Looper, prin.
Lewis ES, RURAL ROUTE 02 BOX 371 29671
  Sue Rickman, prin.
ES, HAMPTON AVE EXT 29671 – Edgar Cox, prin.

Piedmont, Greenville Co., Pop. Code 6
Anderson SD 1
Supt. – See Williamston
Wren MS, RURAL ROUTE 01 29673
  Gregory Cantrell, prin.
Spearman PS, RURAL ROUTE 07 BOX 314 29673
  Wayne Fowler, prin.
Wren PS, RURAL ROUTE 07 BOX 499 29673
  Fletcher Martin, prin.

Greenville County SD
Supt. – See Greenville
Woodmont MS
  RURAL ROUTE 02 BOX 289 29673
  David Ledbetter, prin.
Cleveland ES, CHURCH ST 29673
  Robert Brown, prin.
Grove ES, RURAL ROUTE 05 BOX 506 29673
  Eugene Hinton, prin.

Pinewood, Sumter Co., Pop. Code 3
Sumter SD 2
Supt. – See Sumter
Manchester ES, RURAL ROUTE 01 29125
  Joan Sagona, prin.

Pomaria, Newberry Co., Pop. Code 2
Newberry County SD
Supt. – See Newberry
Garmany MS, RURAL ROUTE 01 BOX 170   29126
  David Jenkins, prin.
ES, RURAL ROUTE 01 BOX 75   29126
  David Jenkins, prin.

Port Royal, Beaufort Co., Pop. Code 5
Beaufort County SD
Supt. – See Beaufort
ES, P O BOX 68   29935 – Bob Smith, prin.

Prosperity, Newberry Co., Pop. Code 3
Newberry County SD
Supt. – See Newberry
Mid.-Carolina JHS, RURAL ROUTE 01   29127
  Clarence Chick, prin.
ES, P O BOX 279   29127
  Theodore Kennedy, prin.
Rikard MS, RURAL ROUTE 03 BOX 17-A   29127
  Boyden Brown, prin.

Rains, Marion Co.
Marion SD 3
Sch. Sys. Enr. Code 3
Supt. – Robtert Johnson   29589
Rains-Centenary MS, P O BOX 439   29589
  Nathaniel Gilchrist, prin.
Other Schools – See Mullins

Ravenel, Charleston Co., Pop. Code 4
St. Paul Constituent
Supt. – See Yonges Island
Ellington ES
  5600 ELLINGTON SCHOOL RD   29470
  Theodore Coker, prin.

Reidville, Spartanburg Co.
Spartanburg SD 5
Supt. – See Duncan
ES, P O BOX 185   29375 – Toni McCullough, prin.

Rembert, Sumter Co.
Lee County SD
Supt. – See Bishopville
West Lee PS, RURAL ROUTE 01 BOX 360   29128
  Gordon Correll, prin.

Sumter SD 2
Supt. – See Sumter
Rafting Creek ES
  RURAL ROUTE 02 BOX 189   29128
  Ida Barboza, prin.

Richburg, Chester Co., Pop. Code 2
Chester SD
Supt. – See Chester
Lewisville MS, P O BOX 56   29729
  Eugene Neely, prin.

Ridgeland, Jasper Co., Pop. Code 4
Jasper County SD
Sch. Sys. Enr. Code 5
Supt. – (—), P O BOX 848   29936
ES, P O BOX 850   29936 – Robert Barron, prin.
Other Schools – See Hardeeville

Heyward Academy
  RURAL ROUTE 02 BOX 333   29936

Ridge Spring, Saluda Co., Pop. Code 3
Aiken County SD
Supt. – See Aiken
Ridge Spring-Monetta ES, P O BOX 386   29129
  Dan Bates, prin.

Ridgeville, Dorchester Co., Pop. Code 3
Dorchester SD 2
Supt. – See Summerville
Givhans MS, RURAL ROUTE 03 BOX 1235   29472
  Cheryl Powell, prin.

Dorchester SD 4
Supt. – See Saint George
Clay Hill ES, P O BOX 218   29472
  Jerry Montjoy, prin.

Ridgeway, Fairfield Co., Pop. Code 2
Fairfield County SD
Supt. – See Winnsboro
Geiger ES, RURAL ROUTE 02 BOX 7   29130
  T. Cook, prin.

Rock Hill, York Co., Pop. Code 8
Rock Hill SD 3
Sch. Sys. Enr. Code 7
Supt. – Dr. Joseph Gentry, P O BOX 10072   29731
Belleview ES, 501 BELLEVIEW RD   29730
  Dan Mitchell, prin.
Ebenezer Avenue ES, 242 EBENEZER AVE   29730
  Allen Bogan, prin.
Ebinport ES, 2142 INDIA HOOK RD   29730
  Mildred Huey, prin.
Finley Road ES, 1089 FINLEY RD   29730
  Brenda Bolt, prin.
Independence ES, 132 S SPRINGDALE RD   29730
  Samuel Cason, prin.
Lesslie ES, RURAL ROUTE 06 BOX 73   29730
  Dorothy Hutchison, prin.
Mt. Gallant ES
  4664 MOUNT GALLANT RD   29730
  Betty Conner, prin.
Northside ES, 840 ANNAFREL ST   29730
  Edmonia McFadden, prin.
Oakdale ES, RURAL ROUTE 02 BOX 413   29730
  Larry Doggett, prin.

Richmond Drive ES, 1162 RICHMOND DR   29730
  Barbara Beam, prin.
Rosewood ES, ROSEWOOD DR   29730
  Allen Leonard, prin.
Sunset Park MS, 1036 OGDEN RD   29730
  Tony Reid, prin.
Sylvia Circle ES, 929 SYLVIA CIR   29730
  Mary Snipes, prin.
York Road ES, 2254 W MAIN ST   29730
  James Graham, prin.

Catawba School, 2650 INDIA HOOK ROAD   29730
Trinity Christian School
  505 UNIVERSITY DRIVE   29730
St. Anne's ES, 648 S JONES AVE   29730
Westminster Christian School
  1300 INDIA HOOK RD   29730

Roebuck, Spartanburg Co.
Spartanburg SD 6
Supt. – See Spartanburg
Gable MS, P O BOX 246   29376 – Joseph Cox, prin.
IS, P O BOX 247   29376 – Wayne Harris, prin.
PS, P O BOX 248   29376 – James Stephens, prin.

Ruby, Chesterfield Co., Pop. Code 2
Chesterfield SD
Supt. – See Chesterfield
ES, P O BOX 7   29741 – Gary Douglas, prin.

Ruffin, Colleton Co., Pop. Code 2
Colleton County SD
Supt. – See Walterboro
Bells ES, RURAL ROUTE 01 BOX 109   29475
  William Smith, prin.

Saint George, Dorchester Co., Pop. Code 4
Dorchester SD 4
Sch. Sys. Enr. Code 5
Supt. – Ed Laughinghouse, 500 RIDGE ST   29477
Williams Memorial MS, P O BOX 907   29477
  Kenneth Jenkins, prin.
ES, 201 JOHNSON ST   29477
  William Carter, prin.
Other Schools – See Harleyville, Ridgeville

Dorchester Academy, P O BOX 901   29477

Saint Matthews, Calhoun Co., Pop. Code 4
Calhoun SD
Sch. Sys. Enr. Code 4
Supt. – Donna Elmore, P O BOX 215   29135
Ford MS, AGNES ST   29135 – Jim Franklin, prin.
Guinyard ES Campus B
  RURAL ROUTE 01 BOX 618   29135
  Griffin Miller, prin.
Guinyard ES Campus A
  RURAL ROUTE 02 BOX 557   29135
  Griffin Miller, prin.
Other Schools – See Cameron

Calhoun Academy, P O BOX 526   29135

Saint Stephen, Berkeley Co., Pop. Code 4
Berkeley County SD
Supt. – See Moncks Corner
MS, P O BOX 308   29479 – Kenneth Coffey, prin.
Gourdine ES, HCR 01 BOX 202   29479
  Dorie Gaillard, prin.
ES, P O BOX 338   29479 – David Brisbon, prin.

Saluda, Saluda Co., Pop. Code 5
Saluda SD
Sch. Sys. Enr. Code 4
Supt. – Nelle Taylor, 404 N WISE ROAD   29138
Riverside MS
  404 N BAUKNIGHT FERRY ROAD   29138
  N. Burton, prin.
Hollywood ES, RURAL ROUTE 01 BOX 335   29138
  Philip Flynn, prin.
ES, 200 MATTHEWS DR   29138 – Alice Pyatt, prin.

Scranton, Florence Co., Pop. Code 3
Florence SD 3
Supt. – See Lake City
ES, P O BOX 129   29591 – Gloria Gardner, prin.

Seneca, Oconee Co., Pop. Code 6
Oconee County SD
Supt. – See Walhalla
JHS, P O BOX 607   29679 – Alphonzo Gaines, prin.
Gignilliat Park MS, 615 N TOWNVILLE ST   29678
  Andrew Inabinet, prin.
Kellett ES, 500 ADAMS ST   29678
  Paul Dover, prin.
Keowee ES, RURAL ROUTE 01 BOX 214   29678
  Norman Cason, prin.
Northside ES, 710 N TOWNVILLE ST   29678
  Clarence Breazeale, prin.
Ravenel ES, 1700 DAVIS CREEK RD   29678
  (—), prin.
Utica MS, 50 GODDARD AVE   29678
  Charles Thompson, prin.

Shaw A F B, Sumter Co., Pop. Code 6
Sumter SD 2
Supt. – See Sumter
High Hills MS, FRIERSON ROAD   29152
  Harold Nettles, prin.

Simpsonville, Greenville Co., Pop. Code 6
Greenville County SD
Supt. – See Greenville
Hillcrest MS
  RURAL ROUTE 04 GARRISON RD   29681
  Herbert Dozier, prin.

Bethel ES, 111 BETHEL SCHOOL RD   29681
  Richard Barker, prin.
Bryson ES, RURAL ROUTE 02 BOX 253   29681
  Betty McConaghy, prin.
Morton ES, 310 BENSON ST   29681
  (—), prin.
Plain ES, 106 NEELY FERRY RD   29681
  Judy James, prin.
ES, 315 E COLLEGE ST   29681
  Shirley Chapman, prin.

Southside Christian School
  111 WOODRUFF ROAD   29681

Six Mile, Pickens Co., Pop. Code 2
Pickens SD
Supt. – See Easley
ES, RURAL ROUTE 01   29682
  Joe Tankersley, prin.

Smoaks, Colleton Co., Pop. Code 2
Colleton County SD
Supt. – See Walterboro
MS, RURAL ROUTE 01 BOX 216-A   29481
  William Dowdy, prin.

Society Hill, Darlington Co., Pop. Code 3
Darlington SD
Supt. – See Darlington
Rosenwald ES, P O BOX 127   29593
  Alvin Heatley, prin.
St. David's ES, P O BOX 50   29593
  Donald Myers, prin.

Spartanburg, Spartanburg Co., Pop. Code 8
Spartanburg SD 2
Sch. Sys. Enr. Code 6
Supt. – John Liston, RURAL ROUTE 06   29303
Other Schools – See Chesnee, Inman, Mayo

Spartanburg SD 3
Supt. – See Glendale
Cannon ES, RURAL ROUTE 01 BOX 246   29302
  Donna Lipscomb, prin.
Clifdale ES, RURAL ROUTE 12 BOX 115   29302
  Robert Glenn, prin.

Spartanburg SD 6
Sch. Sys. Enr. Code 6
Supt. – Dr. David Eubanks
  1493 W O EZELL BLVD   29301
Dawkins MS
  150 LINCOLN SCHOOL ROAD   29301
  Susan Hendrix, prin.
Bobo ES, 495 POWELL MILL RD   29301
  Leon Hayes, prin.
Lone Oak ES, 7314 LONE OAK RD   29303
  Gwendolyn Smith, prin.
West View ES, 400 OAK GROVE RD   29301
  Kathleen Campbell, prin.
Woodland Heights ES, 1216 REIDVILLE RD   29301
  Robert Pettis, prin.
Other Schools – See Arcadia, Fairforest, Moore,
  Pauline, Roebuck

Spartanburg SD 7
Sch. Sys. Enr. Code 7
Supt. – (—), P O BOX 970   29304
Boyd ES, 1505 FERNWOOD RD   29302
  Thomas Huber, prin.
Chapman ES, RURAL ROUTE 06   29303
  David Steven, prin.
Cleveland ES, 698 HOWARD ST   29303
  Arthur Brewton, prin.
Houston ES, 1475 SKYLYN DR   29302
  Lellaree Greene, prin.
Madden ES, 498 W CENTENNIAL ST   29303
  Fred Woods, prin.
Park Hills ES, 301 CRESCENT AVE   29301
  Doris Tidwell, prin.
Pine Street ES, PINE & BOYD STS   29302
  Thomas Stokes, prin.
Todd ES, 170 CEDAR SPRINGS RD   29302
  Robert Page, prin.
Wright ES, 310 CAULDER AVE   29301
  Dr. Judy Bazemore, prin.

Spartanburg Day School
  1701 SKYLYN DRIVE   29302
St. Paul the Apostle School
  152 ALABAMA ST   29302
Westgate Christian School
  1990 REIDVILLE ROAD   29301

Springfield, Orangeburg Co., Pop. Code 3
Orangeburg SD 1
Sch. Sys. Enr. Code 4
Supt. – Claude Terry, P O BOX 337   29146
MS, P O BOX 338   29146 – William Brannen, prin.
Other Schools – See Neeses

Starr, Anderson Co., Pop. Code 2
Anderson SD 3
Supt. – See Iva
Starr-Iva MS, P O BOX 68   29684
  Bill Daniel, prin.
ES, P O BOX 96   29684 – J. Bevill, prin.

Startex, Spartanburg Co.
Spartanburg SD 5
Supt. – See Duncan
ES, P O BOX 39   29377 – Homer Fowler, prin.

Sullivans Island, Charleston Co., Pop. Code 4
Moultrie Constituent
Supt. – See Mount Pleasant
ES, P O BOX Q   29482 – Fleming Harris, prin.

Summerton, Clarendon Co., Pop. Code 4
Clarendon SD 1
Sch. Sys. Enr. Code 4
Supt. – Dr. Milton Marley, P O BOX 38 29148
Spring Hill MS
 RURAL ROUTE 01 BOX 539 29148
 (—), prin.
St. Paul PS, RURAL ROUTE 01 BOX 162 29148
 Robert Godfrey, prin.

Clarendon Hall School, P O BOX 608 29148

Summerville, Dorchester Co., Pop. Code 6
Berkeley County SD
Supt. – See Moncks Corner
Sangaree ES, RURAL ROUTE 11 29483
 William Schupp, prin.
Sangaree IS, RURAL ROUTE 11 29483
 Ronald Graham, prin.

Dorchester SD 2
Sch. Sys. Enr. Code 7
Supt. – William Reeves
 102 GREENWAVE BLVD 29483
Alston Mid., 500 BRYAN ST 29483
 Robert Polk, prin.
DuBose MS, 1000 DUBOSE DR 29483
 Anthony Lemon, prin.
Flowertown ES, 20 KING CHARLES CIR 29485
 Joseph Pye, prin.
Knightsville ES
 535 W OLD ORANGEBURG RD 29483
 Charles Stoudenmire, prin.
Newington MS, 10 KING CHARLES CIR 29485
 Mike Burrell, prin.
Rollings MS, 815 S MAIN ST 29483
 Eugene Limehouse, prin.
Spann ES, 901 S MAGNOLIA ST 29483
 Joseph Cummings, prin.
ES, 835 S MAIN ST 29483 – E. Sires, prin.
Other Schools – See Ladson, Ridgeville

Pinewood-Summerville School
 808 W OLD ORANGEBURG RD 29483
Summerville Catholic School
 226 BLACK OAK BLVD 29483

Sumter, Sumter Co., Pop. Code 7
Sumter SD 17
Sch. Sys. Enr. Code 6
Supt. – Dr. Lawrence Derthick
 P O BOX 1180 29151
Alice Drive MS, 40 MILLER ROAD 29150
 Ellison Lawson, prin.
Bates MS, 700 BAILEY ST 29150
 Erthlay Witherspoon, prin.
Alice Drive ES, 251 ALICE DR 29150
 Zona Jefferson, prin.
Crosswell Drive ES, 11 CROSSWELL DR 29150
 Edward Myers, prin.
Lemira ES, 952 FULTON ST 29150
 Wesley Fudger, prin.
Millwood ES, PINEWOOD ROAD 29150
 Joe Kirven, prin.
Wilder ES, 900 FLORAL AVE 29150
 Geraldine Ingersoll, prin.
Willow Drive ES, 26 WILLOW DR 29150
 Eli Baker, prin.

Sumter SD 2
Sch. Sys. Enr. Code 6
Supt. – Elijah McCants, P O BOX 2425 29150
Cherryvale ES, 1420 FURMAN DR 29154
 Henrietta Green, prin.
Davis ES, RURAL ROUTE 05 29150
 Rachel Schwartz, prin.
Oakland ES, OAKLAND PLANTATION 29150
 Dr. Roosevelt Miott, prin.
Shaw Heights ES
 FRIERSON ROAD SHAW AFB 29152
 Virginia Ray, prin.
Other Schools – See Lynchburg, Mayesville,
 Pinewood, Rembert, Shaw A F B, Wedgefield

Sumter Christian Schools, P O BOX 1855 29151
Wilson Hall School, P O BOX 246 29150
St. Anne's ES, 11 S MAGNOLIA ST 29150
St. Jude PS, P O BOX 1589 29150
Temple Baptist Christian School
 120 PINEWOOD ROAD 29150

Swansea, Lexington Co., Pop. Code 3
Lexington SD 4
Sch. Sys. Enr. Code 4
Supt. – Robert English, P O BOX 128 29160
MS, RURAL ROUTE 01 BOX 22C 29160
 Robert Maddox, prin.
ES, 1195 W HUTTO ROAD 29160
 Cecil McClary, prin.
IS, 295 N LAWRENCE AVE 29160
 Robert Taylor, prin.
Other Schools – See Gaston

Tamassee, Oconee Co.
Oconee County SD
Supt. – See Walhalla
ES, P O BOX 68 29686 – Larry Brown, prin.

Taylors, Greenville Co., Pop. Code 7
Greenville County SD
Supt. – See Greenville
Northwood MS, 710 IKES ROAD 29687
 Harold McClain, prin.
Brook Glenn ES, 2003 E LEE RD 29687
 Tom Sizemore, prin.

Brushy Creek ES, 700 BRUSHY CREEK RD 29687
 Geraldine Martin, prin.
Hampton ES, 200 WADDELL RD 29687
 Joe Dickey, prin.
ES, 809 REID SCHOOL ROAD 29687
 Mary Woods, prin.

Academy of Arts School
 525 TAYLORS ROAD 29687

Timmonsville, Florence Co., Pop. Code 4
Florence SD 4
Sch. Sys. Enr. Code 4
Supt. – Dr. Ernest Nicholson, 612 S HILL ST 29161
Johnson MS, P O BOX 250 29161
 Willie Sneed, prin.
Brockinton ES, 401 N BROCKINGTON ST 29161
 Isaiah Echols, prin.

Townville, Anderson Co.
Anderson SD 4
Supt. – See Pendleton
ES, P O BOX 10 29689 – J. Carroll, prin.

Travelers Rest, Greenville Co., Pop. Code 5
Greenville County SD
Supt. – See Greenville
Northwest MS, RURAL ROUTE 02 BOX 173 29690
 Phil Edge, prin.
Ebenezer ES, RURAL ROUTE 04 BOX 256 29690
 Janet Campbell, prin.
Gateway ES, RURAL ROUTE 05 29690
 Glenn Wright, prin.
ES, 21 CENTER ST 29690 – Rosalie Burnett, prin.

Trenton, Edgefield Co., Pop. Code 2
Edgefield County SD
Supt. – See Edgefield
Douglas ES, P O BOX 69 29847 – Alva Lewis, prin.

Turbeville, Clarendon Co., Pop. Code 3
Clarendon SD 3
Sch. Sys. Enr. Code 4
Supt. – J. Lee McCormick, P O BOX 270 29162
East Clarendon MS, P O BOX 67 29162
 (—), prin.
Other Schools – See New Zion

Union, Union Co., Pop. Code 7
Union County SD
Sch. Sys. Enr. Code 6
Supt. – Dr. Karen Callison, P O BOX 907 29379
Sims JHS, P O BOX F 29379 – D. Howard, prin.
Excelsior ES, 300 CULP ST 29379
 Algemena Ray, prin.
Foster Park ES, 103 KENNEDY CIR 29379
 Glenn Hibbard, prin.
Monarch ES, RURAL ROUTE 06 BOX 137 29379
 (—), prin.
MS, P O BOX 907 29379 – Mike Cassells, prin.
Other Schools – See Buffalo, Jonesville, Lockhart

Vance, Orangeburg Co., Pop. Code 1
Orangeburg SD 3
Supt. – See Holly Hill
PS, RURAL ROUTE 01 BOX 1 29163
 Reginald McNeely, prin.

Varnville, Hampton Co., Pop. Code 4
North SD 1
Supt. – See Hampton
North District MS, P O BOX 368 29944
 Willie Coker, prin.
ES, P O BOX 367 29944 – Peggy Parker, prin.

Wadmalaw Island, Charleston Co.
St. Johns Constituent SD
Supt. – See Charleston
Frierson ES, 6133 MAYBANK HWY 29487
 Edward Simmons, prin.

Wagener, Aiken Co., Pop. Code 3
Aiken County SD
Supt. – See Aiken
Corbett MS, P O BOX 188 29164
 Frank Roberson, prin.
Busbee ES, RURAL ROUTE 01 BOX C 29164
 Marguerite Derrick, prin.

Walhalla, Oconee Co., Pop. Code 5
Oconee County SD
Sch. Sys. Enr. Code 7
Supt. – James Brown, P O BOX 220 29691
MS, 201 RAZORBACK LANE 29691
 Troy Hawkins, prin.
Pine Street ES, 415 S PINE ST 29691
 Phillip Chewining, prin.
ES, P O BOX 370 29691 – Bob Long, prin.
Other Schools – See Fair Play, Seneca, Tamassee,
 Westminster

Wallace, Marlboro Co., Pop. Code 5
Marlboro County SD
Supt. – See Bennettsville
Kollock PS, P O BOX 247 29596
 James Porterfield, prin.
ES, P O BOX 127 29596 – (—), prin.

Walterboro, Colleton Co., Pop. Code 6
Colleton County SD
Sch. Sys. Enr. Code 6
Supt. – A. Smoak, P O BOX 290 29488
Colleton MS, N LEMACKS ST 29488
 F. Smalls, prin.
Black Street PS, 120 SMITH ST 29488
 Nancy Carter, prin.
Colleton MS, 500 FOREST CIRCLE 29488
 Eleanor Adams, prin.

Forest Hill ES, 611 GREENRIDGE ROAD 29488
 Margarine Hamilton, prin.
Hampton Street MS, 494 HAMPTON ST 29488
 Roger Hudson, prin.
Other Schools – See Cottageville, Edisto Beach, Green
 Pond, Ruffin, Smoaks, Yemassee

Calhoun Academy, P O BOX 1426 29488

Ware Shoals, Greenwood Co., Pop. Code 4
Greenwood SD 51
Sch. Sys. Enr. Code 4
Supt. – J. McAbee, 42 SPARKS AVE 29692
JHS, P O BOX 269 29692 – J. Graves, prin.
MS, P O BOX 279 29692 – Larry Shirley, prin.
PS, P O BOX 269 29692 – John Snead, prin.

Warrenville, Aiken Co.
Aiken County SD
Supt. – See Aiken
ES, P O BOX 398 29851 – Glenn Sanders, prin.

Wedgefield, Sumter Co.
Sumter SD 2
Supt. – See Sumter
Delaine ES, RURAL ROUTE 01 BOX 372 29168
 Marilyn Adams, prin.

Wellford, Spartanburg Co., Pop. Code 4
Spartanburg SD 5
Supt. – See Duncan
ES, P O BOX D 29385 – Judy Watson, prin.

West Columbia, Lexington Co., Pop. Code 7
Lexington SD 2
Sch. Sys. Enr. Code 6
Supt. – Michael Woodall, 715 9TH ST 29169
Fulmer MS, 1614 WALTERBORO ST 29169
 Christopher Clancy, prin.
Northside MS, 1218 BATCHELOR ST 29169
 Marion Thompkins, prin.
Pine Ridge MS, 735 PINE RIDGE DRIVE 29169
 Marilyn Ward, prin.
B. C. North 1 ES, 114 HOOK AVE 29169
 Kay Gossett, prin.
Congaree ES, 1221 RAMBLIN RD 29169
 Steve Patterson, prin.
Pair ES, 2325 PLATT SPRINGS RD 29169
 Lauren Allen, prin.
Pineview ES, 3035 LEAPHART RD 29169
 Don Ackerman, prin.
Saluda River ES, 1520 DUKE ST 29169
 Jean Westbrook, prin.
Springdale ES, 361 WATTLING RD 29169
 Dr. Thomas Smith, prin.
Wood ES, 737 PINE RIDGE DR 29169
 Dianne Gregory, prin.
Other Schools – See Cayce

Grace Christian School, 416 DENHAM ST 29169

Westminster, Oconee Co., Pop. Code 5
Oconee County SD
Supt. – See Walhalla
Oakway MS, RURAL ROUTE 02 29693
 William Highsmith, prin.
MS, P O BOX 614 29693 – Bryan Jenkins, prin.
Oakway ES, RURAL ROUTE 02 29693
 Donald Moore, prin.
ES, 206 HAMILTON DR 29693
 Michael Bobo, prin.

Whitmire, Newberry Co., Pop. Code 4
Newberry County SD
Supt. – See Newberry
Carver MS, 51 SATTERWHITE ST 29178
 (—), prin.
Park Street ES, P O BOX 295 29178
 (—), prin.

Williamston, Anderson Co., Pop. Code 5
Anderson SD 1
Sch. Sys. Enr. Code 6
Supt. – Reginald Christopher, P O BOX 98 29697
Palmetto MS, P O BOX 545 29697
 Roger Wolfe, prin.
Palmetto PS, 1 ROBERTS BLVD 29697
 Marshall Whitley, prin.
Other Schools – See Belton, Easley, Pelzer, Piedmont

Williston, Barnwell Co., Pop. Code 5
Williston SD 29
Sch. Sys. Enr. Code 4
Supt. – William Kight, P O BOX 508 29853
Williston-Elko MS, P O BOX 508 29853
 Lee Davis, prin.
Edwards ES, P O BOX 508 29853
 Benjamin Hayes, prin.

Winnsboro, Fairfield Co., Pop. Code 5
Fairfield County SD
Sch. Sys. Enr. Code 5
Supt. – Harris Heath, P O BOX 622 29180
Fairfield MS, RURAL ROUTE 05 BOX 50 29180
 Bill King, prin.
Fairfield PS, RURAL ROUTE 02 BOX 9E 29180
 Elizabeth Spearman, prin.
Miller ES, RURAL ROUTE 01 BOX 101C 29180
 Harvey Chapman, prin.
Mt. Zion IS, P O BOX 207 29180
 Carl Jackson, prin.
Other Schools – See Blair, Ridgeway

Winn Academy
 RURAL ROUTE 2 OLD CHSTR RD 29180

Woodruff, Spartanburg Co., Pop. Code 6
Spartanburg SD 4
Sch. Sys. Enr. Code 4
Supt. – William Howell, P O BOX 669   29388
MS, P O BOX 639   29388 – John Cannon, prin.
PS, P O BOX 339   29388 – James Call, prin.

Yemassee, Hampton Co., Pop. Code 4
Colleton County SD
Supt. – See Walterboro
Jonesville ES, RURAL ROUTE 02 BOX 50   29945
Dan Dobison, prin.

North SD 1
Supt. – See Hampton
Fennell ES, P O BOX 427   29945
Daniel Harley, prin.

Yonges Island, Charleston Co., Pop. Code 1
St. Paul Constituent
Sch. Sys. Enr. Code 4
Supt. – John Brockington
RURAL ROUTE 01 BOX 272-A   29494
Schroder MS, RURAL ROUTE 01   29494
Robert Ephraim, prin.
Blaney ES, 7184 HWY 162   29494
Josiah Washington, prin.
Hughes ES, 8548 WILLTOWN ROAD   29494
Ellamae Washington, prin.
Other Schools – See Edisto Island, Ravenel

York, York Co., Pop. Code 6
York SD 1
Sch. Sys. Enr. Code 5
Supt. – Dr. Ellison Smith, P O BOX 770   29745
JHS, 1280 JOHNSON ROAD   29745
Wilbert Holmes, prin.
Jefferson PS, 37 PINCKNEY ST   29745
William Lowry, prin.
Johnson MS, 400 E JEFFERSON ST   29745
William Plaxco, prin.
Other Schools – See Hickory Grove

Blessed Hope Baptist School, P O BOX 627   29745

SOUTH DAKOTA

STATE DEPARTMENT OF EDUCATION
Kneip Building
700 N. Illinois St., Pierre 57501
(605) 733-3243

State Superintendent of Education	Henry Kosters
Manager School Standards/Other Programs	Clint Berndt
Director Instructional Services	Karon Schaack
Director Adult, Vocational Technical Education	Larry Zikmund

STATE BOARD OF EDUCATION
Noel Hamiel, *President*   Yankton

PUBLIC, PRIVATE, AND PAROCHIAL ELEMENTARY SCHOOLS

Aberdeen, Brown Co., Pop. Code 8
Aberdeen SD 6-1
Sch. Sys. Enr. Code 5
Supt. – Dan Hoke, 203 3RD AVE SE   57401
Hedger ES   57401 – Mary Schwab, prin.
Lee ES   57401 – Duane Alm, prin.
Lincoln ES   57401 – Luther Schumacher, prin.
Neil ES   57401 – Mark Degroot, prin.
Overby ES   57401 – Tom Berg, prin.
Simmons ES   57401 – Abby Erani, prin.
Tiffany ES   57401 – Earl Martell, prin.

Roncalli MS, 505 3RD AVE SE   57401
Roncalli ES, 424 2ND AVE NE   57401

Agar, Sully Co., Pop. Code 2
Agar SD 58-1
Sch. Sys. Enr. Code 1
Supt. – George Levin, P O BOX 398   57520
MS   57520 – George Levin, prin.
ES   57520 – George Levin, prin.
Prairie View ES   57520 – George Levin, prin.

Alcester, Union Co., Pop. Code 3
Alcester SD 61-1
Sch. Sys. Enr. Code 2
Supt. – Don Zinger, P O BOX 248   57001
JHS   57001 – Jerry Joachim, prin.
ES   57001 – Dan Solberg, prin.
Hudson ES   57001 – Dan Solberg, prin.

Alexandria, Hanson Co., Pop. Code 3
Hanson SD 30-1
Sch. Sys. Enr. Code 2
Supt. – Darwin Peterson, P O BOX 490   57311
Hanson JHS   57311 – Jim Goodall, prin.
ES, P O BOX 490   57311 – Coraine Goodall, prin.
Farmer ES, P O BOX 490   57311
Coraine Goodall, prin.
Millbrook Colony ES, P O BOX 490   57311
Coraine Goodall, prin.
Oaklane Colony ES, P O BOX 490   57311
Coraine Goodall, prin.

Alpena, Jerauld Co., Pop. Code 2
Alpena SD 36-1
Sch. Sys. Enr. Code 2
Supt. – Wallace Weatherford, P O BOX 38   57312
ES   57312 – Dr. Delores Kleinsasser, prin.

Arlington, Kingsbury Co., Pop. Code 3
Arlington SD 38-1
Sch. Sys. Enr. Code 4
Supt. – Donald Meyer, P O BOX 359   57212
JHS   57212 – Lowell Gilbertson, prin.
ES   57212 – Leo Tschetter, prin.

Armour, Douglas Co., Pop. Code 3
Armour SD 21-1
Sch. Sys. Enr. Code 2
Supt. – Richard Fuller, P O BOX 427   57313
MS   57313 – Linda Spease, prin.
ES   57313 – Linda Spease, prin.

Artesian, Sanborn Co., Pop. Code 2
Artesian SD 55-1
Sch. Sys. Enr. Code 2
Supt. – Richard Christensen, P O BOX 7   57314
MS   57314 – Colleen Moody, prin.
ES   57314 – Colleen Moody, prin.

Astoria, Deuel Co., Pop. Code 2
Astoria SD 19-1
Sch. Sys. Enr. Code 1
Supt. – Norris Oerter, P O BOX 38   57213
ES   57213 – Norris Oerter, prin.

Avon, Bon Homme Co., Pop. Code 3
Avon SD 4-1
Sch. Sys. Enr. Code 2
Supt. – John Fathke, P O BOX 407   57315
JHS   57315 – Georgeann Dykstra, prin.
ES, P O BOX 407   57315 – John Fathke, prin.

Baltic, Minnehaha Co., Pop. Code 3
Baltic SD 49-1
Sch. Sys. Enr. Code 2
Supt. – Dean Johnson, P O BOX 309   57003
JHS   57003 – Frederick Clark, prin.
ES   57003 – Dean Poppinga, prin.

Barnard, Brown Co.
Elm Valley SD 6-2
Sch. Sys. Enr. Code 2
Supt. – Leighton Getty, P O BOX 6   57426
ES   57426 – Leighton Getty, prin.
Other Schools – See Frederick

Batesland, Shannon Co.
Shannon County SD 65-1
Sch. Sys. Enr. Code 3
Supt. – Donald Standing Elk, P O BOX 578   57716
MS   57716 – Jean Reeves, prin.
Red Shirt Table ES   57716
A. Whirlwind Horse, prin.
Rockyford ES   57716 – A. Whirlwind Horse, prin.
Wolf Creek ES   57716 – Robert Truijillo, prin.

Belle Fourche, Butte Co., Pop. Code 5
Belle Fourche SD 9-1
Sch. Sys. Enr. Code 2
Supt. – Louis Graslie, 706 JACKSON ST   57717
Roosevelt MS   57717 – Jean Dahlinger, prin.

Gay Park ES   57717 – William O'Dea, prin.
South Park MS   57717 – William O'Dea, prin.

Beresford, Union Co., Pop. Code 4
Beresford SD 61-2
Sch. Sys. Enr. Code 3
Supt. – C. Carnes, 301 W MAPLE ST   57004
MS, 301 W MAPLE ST   57004
Charles VonEschen, prin.
ES   57004 – Charles Voneschen, prin.

Big Stone City, Grant Co., Pop. Code 3
Big Stone CSD 25-1
Sch. Sys. Enr. Code 2
Supt. – Burton Nypen, P O BOX 108   57216
ES   57216 – Violet Griepp, prin.

Bison, Perkins Co., Pop. Code 2
Bison SD 52-1
Sch. Sys. Enr. Code 2
Supt. – Gerry Heck, P O BOX 9   57620
JHS   57620 – Lester Krause, prin.
ES   57620 – Dale Kari, prin.
Strool ES   57620 – Dale Kari, prin.
Union ES   57620 – Dale Kari, prin.

Bonesteel, Gregory Co., Pop. Code 2
Bonesteel-Fairfax SD 26-5
Sch. Sys. Enr. Code 2
Supt. – Richard Parry, P O BOX 97   57317
Bonesteel-Fairfax JHS   57317
Dennis Leonard, prin.
Bonesteel-Fairfax ES   57317 – Trudie Myers, prin.

Bowdle, Edmunds Co., Pop. Code 3
Bowdle SD 22-1
Sch. Sys. Enr. Code 2
Supt. – Richard Ulrich, P O BOX 563   57428
JHS   57428 – Craig Kono, prin.
ES   57428 – Richard Ulrich, prin.

Brandon, Minnehaha Co., Pop. Code 5
Brandon Valley SD 49-2
Sch. Sys. Enr. Code 4
Supt. – Carleton Holt
301 S SPLITROCK BLVD   57005
Brandon Valley JHS   57005 – G. Gulson, prin.
IS   57005 – Marvin Sharkey, prin.
PS   57005 – Elaine Gordon, prin.
Valley Springs ES   57005 – Kathryn Hoxeng, prin.

Bridgewater, McCook Co., Pop. Code 3
Bridgewater SD 43-6
Sch. Sys. Enr. Code 2
Supt. – Steve McCormick, P O BOX 350   57319
JHS   57319 – Brenda Kwasniewski, prin.
ES   57319 – Kathleen Lloyd, prin.

Bristol, Day Co., Pop. Code 2
Bristol SD 18-1
Sch. Sys. Enr. Code 2
Supt. – Darrell Hildebrandt, P O BOX 107 57219
JHS 57219 – Darrell Hildebrant, prin.
ES 57219 – Patricia Holzhauser, prin.

Britton, Marshall Co., Pop. Code 4
Britton SD 45-1
Sch. Sys. Enr. Code 2
Supt. – Thomas Butler, P O BOX 190 57430
JHS 57430 – Donald Kirkegaard, prin.
ES 57430 – Noreem Jochim, prin.

Brookings, Brookings Co., Pop. Code 7
Brookings SD 5-1
Sch. Sys. Enr. Code 5
Supt. – Robert Jostad, 601 4TH ST 57006
MS, 601 4TH ST 57006 – Dan Nelles, prin.
Central ES 57006 – Wayne Thompson, prin.
Hillcrest ES, 304 15TH AVE 57006
   Richard Brubakken, prin.
Medary ES 57006 – Hugh Ackman, prin.

Buffalo, Harding Co., Pop. Code 2
Harding County SD 31-1
Sch. Sys. Enr. Code 2
Supt. – Charles Maxon, P O BOX 367 57720
JHS, P O BOX 367 57720 – Charles Maxon, prin.
ES 57720 – Dr. Robert Migneault, prin.
Camp Crook ES 57720
   Dr. Robert Migneault, prin.
Cox ES 57720 – Dr. Robert Migneault, prin.
Govert ES 57720 – Dr. Robert Migneault, prin.
Lincoln ES 57720 – Dr. Robert Migneault, prin.
Norbeck ES 57720 – Dr. Robert Migneault, prin.
Painter ES 57720 – Dr. Robert Migneault, prin.
Reva ES 57720 – Dr. Robert Migneault, prin.

Burke, Gregory Co., Pop. Code 3
Burke SD 26-2
Sch. Sys. Enr. Code 2
Supt. – Jack Broome, P O BOX 382 57523
ES 57523 – Audrey Brevik, prin.
Lucas ES 57523 – Audrey Brevik, prin.

Canistota, McCook Co., Pop. Code 3
Canistota SD 43-1
Sch. Sys. Enr. Code 2
Supt. – Robert Wilson, P O BOX 8 57012
ES 57012 – Donald Kom, prin.

Canova, Miner Co., Pop. Code 2
Howard SD 48-3
Supt. – See Howard
ES 57321 – Alyce Lundberg, prin.

Canton, Lincoln Co., Pop. Code 5
Canton SD 41-1
Sch. Sys. Enr. Code 3
Supt. – Dr. Joe Gertsema, 112 ELDER AVE E 57013
JHS 57013 – David Beckman, prin.
Jacobson ES 57013 – John Eckert, prin.
Lawrence ES, 724 N SANBORN 57013
   John Eckert, prin.

Carthage, Miner Co., Pop. Code 2
Carthage SD 48-2
Sch. Sys. Enr. Code 1
Supt. – Fred Grimme, P O BOX 146 57323
ES 57323 – Fred Grimme, prin.

Castlewood, Hamlin Co., Pop. Code 3
Castlewood SD 28-1
Sch. Sys. Enr. Code 2
Supt. – Jeff Taylor, P O BOX 98 57223
JHS 57223 – Jeff Taylor, prin.
ES 57223 – Mary Jane Tereick, prin.

Centerville, Turner Co., Pop. Code 3
Centerville SD 60-1
Sch. Sys. Enr. Code 2
Supt. – John Erickson, P O BOX 100 57014
ES 57014 – Norma Thomson, prin.

Chamberlain, Brule Co., Pop. Code 4
Chamberlain SD 7-1
Sch. Sys. Enr. Code 4
Supt. – Duane Roehrick, P O BOX 119 57325
MS 57325 – Harry Haaen, prin.
American ES 57325 – Mahylen Niles, prin.
ES 57325 – Mahylen Niles, prin.
Cooper ES 57325 – Mahylen Niles, prin.
Oacoma ES 57325 – Mahylen Niles, prin.
Ola ES 57325 – Mahylen Niles, prin.
Prairie Center ES 57325 – Mahylen Niles, prin.
Pukwana ES 57325 – Mahylen Niles, prin.

St. Joseph's Indian School, P O BOX 89 57326

Chester, Lake Co., Pop. Code 2
Chester Area SD 39-1
Sch. Sys. Enr. Code 2
Supt. – John Pederson, P O BOX 159 57016
JHS 57016 – Donald Loomis, prin.
Franklin ES 57016 – Joan Hilmoe, prin.

Clark, Clark Co., Pop. Code 4
Clark SD 12-2
Sch. Sys. Enr. Code 3
Supt. – Roland Smit, P O BOX 220 57225
JHS 57225 – Michael White, prin.
ES 57225 – Terry Vander Vorst, prin.

Clear Lake, Deuel Co., Pop. Code 4
Clear Lake SD 19-2
Sch. Sys. Enr. Code 3
Supt. – Donald Jorgenson, P O BOX 667 57226

JHS 57226 – Roger Hansen, prin.
ES 57226 – Donald Fuehrer, prin.
Goodwin ES 57226 – Donald Fuehrer, prin.

Colman, Moody Co., Pop. Code 3
Colman SD 50-1
Sch. Sys. Enr. Code 2
Supt. – Roger Fritz, P O BOX I 57017
JHS 57017 – Terrance Stulken, prin.
ES 57017 – Shirley Haar, prin.

Colome, Tripp Co., Pop. Code 2
Colome SD 59-1
Sch. Sys. Enr. Code 2
Supt. – Francis Blaine, P O BOX 367 57528
JHS 57528 – Jerold Grayot, prin.
ES 57528 – Francis Blaine, prin.

Conde, Spink Co., Pop. Code 2
Conde SD 56-1
Sch. Sys. Enr. Code 1
Supt. – Gerald Schlueter, P O BOX 328 57434
ES 57434 – Darlene Dirksen, prin.

Corsica, Douglas Co., Pop. Code 3
Corsica SD 21-2
Sch. Sys. Enr. Code 2
Supt. – Vern DeGeest, P O BOX 299 57328
MS 57328 – Gwen Rothenberger, prin.
ES, P O BOX 299 57328
   Gwen Rothenberger, prin.

Cresbard, Faulk Co., Pop. Code 2
Cresbard SD 24-1
Sch. Sys. Enr. Code 2
Supt. – Roland Stekl, P O BOX 128 57435
JHS 57435 – Frank Larson, prin.
ES 57435 – Roland Stekl, prin.

Custer, Custer Co., Pop. Code 4
Custer SD 16-1
Sch. Sys. Enr. Code 4
Supt. – William Gaskins
   527 MONTGOMERY ST 57730
JHS 57730 – Dean Keith, prin.
ES 57730 – Bruce McKee, prin.
Fairburn ES 57730 – Bruce McKee, prin.
Hermosa ES 57730 – Bruce McKee, prin.
Pringle ES 57730 – Bruce McKee, prin.
Spring Creek ES 57730 – Bruce McKee, prin.

Dell Rapids, Minnehaha Co., Pop. Code 4
Dell Rapids SD 49-3
Sch. Sys. Enr. Code 3
Supt. – Dr. Stephen Doerr
   1216 GARFIELD AVE 57022
JHS 57022 – Douglas Druse, prin.
ES 57022 – Dr. John Jewett, prin.

St. Mary's Grade School, 602 E 8TH ST 57022

Delmont, Douglas Co., Pop. Code 2
Delmont SD 21-3
Sch. Sys. Enr. Code 2
Supt. – John Spiegel, P O BOX 96 57330
JHS 57330 – Russell Weller, prin.
ES 57330 – John Spiegel, prin.
Greenwood Colony ES 57330 – John Spigel, prin.

De Smet, Kingsbury Co., Pop. Code 4
DeSmet SD 38-2
Sch. Sys. Enr. Code 2
Supt. – Donovan Twite, P O BOX K 57231
MS 57231 – Leslie Grabowska, prin.
Wilder ES 57231 – (—), prin.

Doland, Spink Co., Pop. Code 2
Doland SD 56-2
Sch. Sys. Enr. Code 2
Supt. – Joel Druley, P O BOX 385 57436
JHS 57436 – Gene Turner, prin.
ES 57436 – Susan Gose, prin.

Dupree, Ziebach Co., Pop. Code 3
Dupree SD 64-2
Sch. Sys. Enr. Code 2
Supt. – Rodney Jones, P O BOX 96 57623
JHS 57623 – Curtis Johnson, prin.
ES 57623 – Leora Burgee, prin.

Eagle Butte, Dewey Co., Pop. Code 2
Eagle Butte SD 20-1
Sch. Sys. Enr. Code 4
Supt. – Gerald Stapert, P O BOX 260 57625
JHS 57625 – Cynthia McCrea, prin.
PS 57625 – Duane Ross, prin.
IS 57625 – Jeanne Bowman, prin.
Ridgeview ES 57625 – Jeanne Bowman, prin.

Edgemont, Fall River Co., Pop. Code 4
Edgemont SD 23-1
Sch. Sys. Enr. Code 2
Supt. – Donald Sondergard, P O BOX 29 57735
MS 57735 – Allan Beyer, prin.
ES 57735 – Donald Sondergard, prin.

Elk Mountain SD 16-2
Sch. Sys. Enr. Code 1
Supt. – Jack Pope, HCR 59 BOX 46 57735
Elk Mountain ES 57735 – Jack Pope, prin.

Egan, Moody Co., Pop. Code 2
Eagan SD 50-2
Sch. Sys. Enr. Code 2
Supt. – Henry Hauck, P O BOX 8 57024
JHS 57024 – Mike Cullen, prin.
ES 57024 – Elaine Brown, prin.

Elk Point, Union Co., Pop. Code 4
Elk Point SD 61-3
Sch. Sys. Enr. Code 2
Supt. – Dennis Jensen, P O BOX 578 57025
MS 57025 – Don Long, prin.
ES 57025 – Don Long, prin.

Elkton, Brookings Co., Pop. Code 3
Elkton SD 5-3
Sch. Sys. Enr. Code 2
Supt. – Gordon Fuhr, P O BOX 190 57026
JHS 57026 – Donald Magnus, prin.
ES 57026 – Kathie Tuntland, prin.

Ellsworth A F B, Pennington Co., Pop. Code 5
Douglas SD 51-1
Sch. Sys. Enr. Code 5
Supt. – John Sweet, PATRIOT DRIVE 57706
Vandenburg MS 57706 – Robert Froehlich, prin.
Badger Clark ES 57706 – Janet Hensley, prin.
Carrousel ES 57706 – Joan Lankowitz, prin.
Case MS 57706 – Elizabeth Bowers, prin.

Emery, Hanson Co., Pop. Code 2
Emery SD 30-2
Sch. Sys. Enr. Code 2
Supt. – John Stanton, P O BOX 265 57332
JHS 57332 – Dean Christensen, prin.
ES 57332 – John Stanton, prin.

Estelline, Hamlin Co., Pop. Code 3
Estelline SD 28-2
Sch. Sys. Enr. Code 2
Supt. – Errol Johnson, P O BOX F 57234
ES 57234 – Sharon Delzer, prin.

Ethan, Davison Co., Pop. Code 2
Ethan SD 17-1
Sch. Sys. Enr. Code 2
Supt. – Bob Ruth, P O BOX 169 57334
MS 57334 – Bob Ruth, prin.
ES 57334 – William Fritzemeier, prin.

Eureka, McPherson Co., Pop. Code 4
Eureka SD 44-1
Sch. Sys. Enr. Code 2
Supt. – Sherlock Hirning, P O BOX 10 57437
JHS 57437 – Harvey Diedtrich, prin.
ES 57437 – Sherlock Hirning, prin.

Faith, Meade Co., Pop. Code 3
Faith SD 46-2
Sch. Sys. Enr. Code 2
Supt. – Dennis Fernau, P O BOX 619 57626
JHS 57626 – Carol Johnson, prin.
Cottonwood ES 57626 – Carol Johnson, prin.
ES 57626 – Carol Johnson, prin.
Maurine ES 57626 – Carol Johnson, prin.
Plainview ES 57626 – Carol Johnson, prin.

Faulkton, Faulk Co., Pop. Code 3
Faulkton SD 24-2
Sch. Sys. Enr. Code 2
Supt. – John Cruzeiro, P O BOX 308 57438
JHS 57438 – Newell Ordal, prin.
ES 57438 – John Cruzeiro, prin.

Flandreau, Moody Co., Pop. Code 4
Flandreau SD 50-3
Sch. Sys. Enr. Code 3
Supt. – Mark Froke, 600 W 1ST AVE 57028
MS, 606 W 2ND AVE 57028
   Richard Thomas, prin.
Spafford ES 57028 – Roxann Voorhees, prin.

Florence, Codington Co., Pop. Code 2
Florence SD 14-1
Sch. Sys. Enr. Code 2
Supt. – Larry Johnke, P O BOX 66 57235
ES 57235 – Eldon Clarke, prin.

Fort Pierre, Stanley Co., Pop. Code 4
Stanley County SD 57-1
Sch. Sys. Enr. Code 3
Supt. – Sherman Monroe, P O BOX 37 57532
Stanley County JHS 57532 – Rodney Link, prin.
Cheyenne ES 57532 – Sharyl Gottschalk, prin.
ES 57532 – Sharyl Gottschalk, prin.
Hayes ES 57532 – Sharyl Gottschalk, prin.
New Liberty ES 57532 – Sharyl Gottschalk, prin.
Orton ES 57532 – Sharyl Gottschalk, prin.

Frederick, Brown Co., Pop. Code 2
Elm Valley SD 6-2
Supt. – See Barnard
Elm Walley JHS 57441 – Doyne Jensen, prin.

Freeman, Hutchinson Co., Pop. Code 4
Freeman SD 33-1
Sch. Sys. Enr. Code 2
Supt. – Alvin Mudder, P O BOX 220 57029
JHS 57029 – Bruce Wendling, prin.
ES 57029 – Laverne Diede, prin.
Tschetter Colony ES 57029 – Laverne Diede, prin.
Wolf Creek Colony ES 57029
   Laverne Diede, prin.

Garretson, Minnehaha Co., Pop. Code 3
Garretson SD 49-4
Sch. Sys. Enr. Code 2
Supt. – Robert Arend, P O BOX C 57030
JHS 57030 – Mark Greguson, prin.
ES, P O BOX C 57030 – Jon Starkey, prin.

Gary, Deuel Co., Pop. Code 2
Gary SD 19-3
Sch. Sys. Enr. Code 1
Supt. – William Bird, P O BOX 100 57237
ES 57237 – Racheal Westgard, prin.

Gayville, Yankton Co., Pop. Code 2
Gayville-Volin SD 63-1
Sch. Sys. Enr. Code 2
Supt. – Ward Thelen, P O BOX 158 57031
Gayville-Volin JHS 57031 – Ward Thelen, prin.
Volin ES 57031 – Nancy Farg, prin.

Geddes, Charles Mix Co., Pop. Code 2
Geddes Comm. SD 11-2
Sch. Sys. Enr. Code 2
Supt. – Richard Rockafellow, P O BOX 125 57342
JHS 57342 – R. Rockafellow, prin.
ES 57342 – Aldeene Mulder, prin.

Gettysburg, Potter Co., Pop. Code 4
Gettysburg SD 53-1
Sch. Sys. Enr. Code 2
Supt. – Donald Quimby, 100 E KING AVE 57442
JHS 57442 – Thomas Fairbanks, prin.
ES 57442 – Jerold Bender, prin.

Glenham, Walworth Co., Pop. Code 2
Glenham SD 62-1
Sch. Sys. Enr. Code 1
Supt. – W. Warren, P O BOX 38 57631
ES 57631 – W. Warren, prin.

Gregory, Gregory Co., Pop. Code 4
Gregory SD 26-4
Sch. Sys. Enr. Code 3
Supt. – David Gellerman, P O BOX 438 57533
MS 57533 – Michael Dacy, prin.
ES 57533 – Mark Krogstrand, prin.
Iona ES 57533 – Mark Krogstrand, prin.

Groton, Brown Co., Pop. Code 4
Groton SD 6-3
Sch. Sys. Enr. Code 3
Supt. – Robert Olson, P O BOX 146 57445
JHS 57445 – Larry Ball, prin.
ES 57445 – William Ganje, prin.

Harrisburg, Lincoln Co., Pop. Code 3
Harrisburg SD 41-2
Sch. Sys. Enr. Code 3
Supt. – Leon Swier, P O BOX 187 57032
JHS 57032 – James Hargens, prin.
ES 57032 – Janice Eversole, prin.

Harrold, Hughes Co., Pop. Code 2
Harrold SD 32-1
Sch. Sys. Enr. Code 2
Supt. – Steven Selchert, P O BOX 160 57536
ES 57536 – George Wang, prin.
West Bend ES 57536 – George Wang, prin.

Hartford, Minnehaha Co., Pop. Code 4
West Central SD 49-7
Sch. Sys. Enr. Code 3
Supt. – W. Willer, P O BOX 259 57033
West Central JHS 57033 – Aaron Herman, prin.
ES 57033 – Aaron Herman, prin.
Humboldt ES 57033 – Regina Lebeda, prin.

Hayti, Hamlin Co., Pop. Code 2
Hamlin SD 28-3
Sch. Sys. Enr. Code 3
Supt. – Gene Carr, P O BOX 298 57241
Hazel ES 57241 – Mary Pietila, prin.
Lake Norden ES 57241 – Mary Pietila, prin.

Hecla, Brown Co., Pop. Code 2
Hecla-Houghton SD 6-4
Sch. Sys. Enr. Code 2
Supt. – Greg East, P O BOX 185 57446
MS 57446 – Robert Grebel, prin.
ES 57446 – Robert Grebel, prin.

Henry, Codington Co., Pop. Code 2
Henry SD 14-2
Sch. Sys. Enr. Code 2
Supt. – Michael Steinhoff, P O BOX 8 57243
ES 57243 – Q. Miles, prin.

Herreid, Campbell Co., Pop. Code 3
Herreid SD 10-1
Sch. Sys. Enr. Code 2
Supt. – Alvin Winckler, P O BOX 276 57632
JHS 57632 – Ray Wikenheiser, prin.
ES 57632 – Alvin Winckler, prin.

Highmore, Hyde Co., Pop. Code 4
Hyde SD 34-1
Sch. Sys. Enr. Code 2
Supt. – John Biegler, P O BOX 416 57345
ES 57345 – Phyllis Scott, prin.
Illinois ES 57345 – Phyllis Scott, prin.
Stephan ES 57345 – Phyllis Scott, prin.

Hill City, Pennington Co., Pop. Code 3
Hill City SD 51-2
Sch. Sys. Enr. Code 3
Supt. – Orville Creighton, P O BOX 659 57745
JHS 57745 – Detlev Prautzsch, prin.
ES 57745 – John Halter, prin.
Keystone ES 57745 – John Halter, prin.

Hitchcock, Beadle Co., Pop. Code 2
Hitchcock SD 2-1
Sch. Sys. Enr. Code 2
Supt. – Dale Schneider, P O BOX 8 57348
ES 57348 – Wanda Gebhardt, prin.

Hosmer, Edmunds Co., Pop. Code 2
Hosmer SD 22-2
Sch. Sys. Enr. Code 2
Supt. – William Sorensen, P O BOX 26 57448
ES 57448 – Patricia Hollan, prin.

Hot Springs, Fall River Co., Pop. Code 5
Hot Springs SD 23-2
Sch. Sys. Enr. Code 4
Supt. – Emanuel Moran
  1609 UNIVERSITY AVE 57747
MS, 1609 UNIVERSITY 57747
  Vern Hagedorn, prin.
Buffalo Gap ES 57747 – Dean Cook, prin.
ES, 1609 UNIVERSITY 57747 – Dean Cook, prin.
Oral ES 57747 – Dean Cook, prin.

Hoven, Potter Co., Pop. Code 3
Hoven SD 53-2
Sch. Sys. Enr. Code 2
Supt. – Mike Elsberry, P O BOX 128 57450
JHS 57450 – Larry Birchem, prin.
Copp ES 57450 – Mike Elsberry, prin.
Fayette ES 57450 – Mike Elsberry, prin.
Lebanon ES 57450 – Mike Elsberry, prin.
Lincoln-Lucas ES 57450 – Mike Elsberry, prin.
Tolstoy ES 57450 – Mike Elsberry, prin.

———————————

St. Anthony's School, P O BOX 188 57450

Howard, Miner Co., Pop. Code 4
Howard SD 48-3
Sch. Sys. Enr. Code 2
Supt. – Loren Scott, P O BOX E 57349
JHS 57349 – Earl Nebelsick, prin.
Cloverleaf Colony ES 57349
  John Bjorkman, prin.
ES 57349 – John Bjorkman, prin.
Other Schools – See Canova

Hurley, Turner Co., Pop. Code 2
Hurley SD 60-2
Sch. Sys. Enr. Code 2
Supt. – Robert Graham, P O BOX 278 57036
JHS 57036 – Ron Wiblemo, prin.
ES 57036 – Robert Graham, prin.

Huron, Beadle Co., Pop. Code 7
Huron SD 2-2
Sch. Sys. Enr. Code 4
Supt. – Robert Taylor
  535 ILLINOIS AVE SW 57350
MS 57350 – Eugene Johnson, prin.
Buchanan ES 57350 – Joseph Thomas, prin.
Huron Colony ES 57350 – John Van Wyhe, prin.
Jefferson ES 57350 – John Van Wyhe, prin.
Madison ES 57350 – Loren Struble, prin.
McKinley ES 57350 – Joseph Thomas, prin.
Riverside Colony ES 57350
  John Van Wyhe, prin.
Washington ES 57350 – John Liedle, prin.

———————————

St. Martin's Catholic School
  522 OREGON AVE SE 57350

Ipswich, Edmunds Co., Pop. Code 4
Ipswich SD 22-3
Sch. Sys. Enr. Code 2
Supt. – Russ Monroe, P O BOX 306 57451
JHS 57451 – Edwin Miller, prin.
ES 57451 – Camille Geditz, prin.
Rosette Colony ES 57451 – Camille Geditz, prin.

Irene, Turner Co., Pop. Code 3
Irene SD 63-2
Sch. Sys. Enr. Code 2
Supt. – Allan Alexander, P O BOX 5 57037
JHS 57037 – Alvin Wiebenga, prin.
ES 57037 – Allan Alexander, prin.

Iroquois, Beadle Co., Pop. Code 2
Iroquois SD 2-3
Sch. Sys. Enr. Code 2
Supt. – Robert Callahan, P O BOX 166 57353
JHS 57353 – Donald Olson, prin.
Cavour ES 57353 – Paul Kingery, prin.
Pearl Creek Colony ES 57353 – Paul Kingery, prin.

Isabel, Dewey Co., Pop. Code 2
Isabel SD 20-2
Sch. Sys. Enr. Code 2
Supt. – Charles Begeman, P O BOX 134 57633
ES 57633 – Delfred Brinkman, prin.

Java, Walworth Co., Pop. Code 2
Java SD 62-2
Sch. Sys. Enr. Code 1
Supt. – B. Wasko, P O BOX 187 57452
ES 57452 – B. Wasko, prin.

Jefferson, Union Co., Pop. Code 3
Jefferson SD 61-6
Sch. Sys. Enr. Code 3
Supt. – Merle Pickner, P O BOX 309 57038
MS, P O BOX 309 57038 – David Nitzschke, prin.
McCook ES, P O BOX 309 57038
  David Nitzschke, prin.

Kadoka, Jackson Co., Pop. Code 3
Kadoka SD 35-1
Sch. Sys. Enr. Code 2
Supt. – Joe Blando, P O BOX 99 57543
Interior ES 57543 – Randall Rueter, prin.
ES 57543 – Randall Reuter, prin.
Longvalley ES 57543 – Randall Reuter, prin.
Wanblee ES 57543 – Randall Reuter, prin.

Kimball, Brule Co., Pop. Code 3
Kimball SD 7-2
Sch. Sys. Enr. Code 2
Supt. – Glenn Turner, P O BOX 479 57355
Grass Range Colony ES 57355
  Glenn Turner, prin.
ES 57355 – Glenn Turner, prin.
Lyons ES 57355 – Glenn Turner, prin.
Richland ES 57355 – Glenn Turner, prin.

Lake Andes, Charles Mix Co., Pop. Code 4
Andes Central SD 11-1
Sch. Sys. Enr. Code 2
Supt. – William Carda, P O BOX 39 57356
Andes Central MS 57356 – Bruce Hart, prin.
Andes Central ES 57356 – Joanne Hinckley, prin.

Lake Preston, Kingsbury Co., Pop. Code 3
Lake Preston SD 38-3
Sch. Sys. Enr. Code 2
Supt. – Calvin Higgins, P O BOX 38 57249
JHS 57249 – Paul Nelson, prin.
ES 57249 – Monte Scheel, prin.

Langford, Marshall Co., Pop. Code 2
Langford SD 45-2
Sch. Sys. Enr. Code 2
Supt. – L. Wattier, P O BOX 127 57454
JHS, P O BOX 127 57454 – Trevor Osborne, prin.
ES, P O BOX 127 57454 – Janet Neff, prin.

Lead, Lawrence Co., Pop. Code 5
Lead-Deadwood SD 40-1
Sch. Sys. Enr. Code 4
Supt. – Robert Stuerman, 320 MAIN ST S 57754
MS 57754 – Peggy Pieper, prin.
Central ES 57754 – Elden Titus, prin.
Deadwood ES 57754 – Peggy Pieper, prin.
West Lead ES 57754 – Elden Titus, prin.

Lemmon, Perkins Co., Pop. Code 4
Lemmon SD 52-2
Sch. Sys. Enr. Code 3
Supt. – Victor Erlacher, 209 3RD ST W 57638
JHS 57638 – Duane Knabel, prin.
Center ES 57638 – Wendell McNeely, prin.
ES 57638 – Wendell McNeely, prin.
Progress ES 57638 – Wendell McNeely, prin.

Lennox, Lincoln Co., Pop. Code 4
Lennox SD 41-4
Sch. Sys. Enr. Code 4
Supt. – James Stoeckman, 208 W 5TH AVE 57039
Chancellor MS 57039 – Verlyn Schmidt, prin.
MS 57039 – Verlyn Schmidt, prin.
Tea MS 57039 – Roger DeGroot, prin.
Worthing MS 57039 – Roger Degroot, prin.
Chancellor ES 57039 – Verlyn Schmidt, prin.
ES 57039 – Verlyn Schmidt, prin.
Tea ES 57039 – Roger Degroot, prin.
Worthing ES 57039 – Roger Degroot, prin.

Leola, McPherson Co., Pop. Code 3
Leola SD 44-2
Sch. Sys. Enr. Code 2
Supt. – William Freitag, P O BOX 350 57456
JHS 57456 – Marvin Maule, prin.
ES 57456 – William Freitag, prin.
Longlake Colony ES 57456 – William Freitag, prin.
Spring Creek Colony ES 57456
  William Freitag, prin.

Letcher, Sanborn Co., Pop. Code 2
Letcher SD 55-3
Sch. Sys. Enr. Code 1
Supt. – Roger Kahle, P O BOX 68 57359
ES 57359 – William McDowall, prin.
Upland Colony ES 57359
  William McDowall, prin.

Lodgepole, Pekins Co., Pop. Code 1
Northwest SD 52-3
Sch. Sys. Enr. Code 1
Supt. – Duane Nelson, P O BOX 248 57640
Fredlund ES 57640 – Duane Nelson, prin.
ES 57640 – Duane Nelson, prin.
Sidney ES 57640 – Duane Nelson, prin.
Swanson ES 57640 – Duane Nelson, prin.

Lyons, Minnehaha Co., Pop. Code 3
Tri-Valley SD 49-6
Sch. Sys. Enr. Code 3
Supt. – Dr. Ralph Herring, P O BOX 8 57041
Tri-Valley MS 57041 – Dr. Ralph Herring, prin.
Colton ES 57041 – Dan Yost, prin.

Mc Intosh, Corson Co., Pop. Code 2
McIntosh SD 15-1
Sch. Sys. Enr. Code 2
Supt. – Frank Seiler, P O BOX 417 57641
JHS 57641 – Robert Braun, prin.
ES 57641 – Olaus Njos, prin.

Mc Laughlin, Corson Co., Pop. Code 3
Mc Laughlin SD 15-2
Sch. Sys. Enr. Code 2
Supt. – Jerry Kleinsasser, P O BOX 468 57642
MS, P O BOX 790 57642 – Keith Wilson, prin.
ES 57642 – Keith Wilson, prin.

Madison, Lake Co., Pop. Code 6
Lake Central SD 39-2
Sch. Sys. Enr. Code 4
Supt. – William Jiricek, 800 NE 9TH ST 57042
Lake Central JHS 57042 – Dale Waba, prin.
Colony ES 57042 – James Maroon, prin.
Garfield ES 57042 – Daniel Walsh, prin.
Lincoln ES 57042 – Elizabeth Bortnem, prin.

Washington ES 57042 – James Maroon, prin.

St. Thomas School, 401 N VAN EPS AVE 57042

Marion, Turner Co., Pop. Code 3
Marion SD 60-3
Sch. Sys. Enr. Code 2
Supt. – Dale Waysman, P O BOX 207 57043
ES 57043 – Richard Ellefson, prin.

Martin, Bennett Co., Pop. Code 4
Bennett County SD 3-1
Sch. Sys. Enr. Code 3
Supt. – Denzil Rush, P O BOX 580 57551
Central ES 57551 – Frank Finney, prin.
ES 57551 – Frank Finney, prin.
Tuthill ES 57551 – Frank Finney, prin.
Vetal ES 57551 – Frank Finney, prin.

Mellette, Spink Co., Pop. Code 2
Northwestern SD 56-3
Sch. Sys. Enr. Code 2
Supt. – Donald Swain, P O BOX 45 57461
Northwestern MS 57461
  Merle Bomesberger, prin.
ES, P O BOX 45 57461 – Merle Bomesberger, prin.

Menno, Hutchinson Co., Pop. Code 3
Menno SD 33-2
Sch. Sys. Enr. Code 2
Supt. – T. Archie Ireland, P O BOX 346 57045
JHS 57045 – Ervin Ptak, prin.
Jamesville Colony ES 57045 – T. Ireland, prin.
Maxwell Colony ES 57045 – T. Ireland, prin.
ES 57045 – T. Ireland, prin.

Midland, Haakon Co., Pop. Code 2
Midland SD 27-2
Sch. Sys. Enr. Code 2
Supt. – Eldor Larson, P O BOX 226 57552
JHS 57552 – Steve Selchert, prin.
ES 57552 – Eldor Larson, prin.

Milbank, Grant Co., Pop. Code 5
Milbank SD 25-4
Sch. Sys. Enr. Code 4
Supt. – George Smith, P O BOX 1190 57252
JHS, 305 N 5TH ST 57252 – Marlin Smart, prin.
ES 57252 – Pete Carvell, prin.

St. Lawrence School, 113 S 6TH ST 57252

Miller, Hand Co., Pop. Code 4
Miller SD 29-1
Sch. Sys. Enr. Code 3
Supt. – Tom Marso, P O BOX 257 57362
Como ES 57362 – Ardessa Moser, prin.
ES 57362 – Paul Scissons, prin.
Millerdale Colony ES 57362
  Ardessa Moser, prin.
Mondamin ES 57362 – Ardessa Moser, prin.
Ree Heights ES 57362 – Ardessa Moser, prin.

Mission, Todd Co., Pop. Code 3
Todd County SD 66-1
Sch. Sys. Enr. Code 4
Supt. – T. Larry Thacker, P O BOX 87 57555
Todd County JHS 57555 – Leila Hall, prin.
Happy Valley ES 57555 – Marvin Pickner, prin.
He Dog ES 57555 – Ruth Kornely, prin.
Klein ES 57555 – Marvin Pickner, prin.
Lakeview ES 57555 – Marvin Pickner, prin.
Littleburg ES 57555 – Marvin Pickner, prin.
North Mission ES 57555 – Beverly McKenzie, prin.
Okreek ES 57555 – Nancy Piper, prin.
Rosebud ES 57555 – Douglas Daughters, prin.
South Mission MS 57555 – Mildred Moran, prin.
Spring Creek ES 57555 – Marvin Pickner, prin.

Mitchell, Davison Co., Pop. Code 7
Mitchell SD 17-2
Sch. Sys. Enr. Code 5
Supt. – Dr. John Christinsen
  117 E 4TH AVE 57301
MS 57301 – Deborah Dusseau, prin.
Field ES 57301 – Mary Wilson, prin.
Litchfield ES 57301 – Edwin Olson,Jr., prin.
Longfellow ES 57301 – Merry Bleeker, prin.
Rockport Colony ES 57301 – Dennis Champ, prin.
Rosedale Colony ES 57301 – Dennis Champ, prin.
Whittier ES 57301 – Dennis Champ, prin.

Holy Family School, 200 N KIMBALL ST 57301
Holy Spirit School, 1400 W CEDAR AVE 57301

Mobridge, Walworth Co., Pop. Code 5
Mobridge SD 62-3
Sch. Sys. Enr. Code 3
Supt. – Dr. Iro C. Mogen, 114 10TH ST E 57601
Beadle ES 57601 – Bert Cameron, prin.
Davis ES 57601 – Bert Cameron, prin.

Montrose, McCook Co., Pop. Code 2
Montrose SD 43-2
Sch. Sys. Enr. Code 2
Supt. – Carl Nielsen, P O BOX 8 57048
JHS 57048 – Todd Payer, prin.
ES 57048 – Carl Nielsen, prin.

Mount Vernon, Davison Co., Pop. Code 2
Mt. Vernon SD 17-3
Sch. Sys. Enr. Code 2
Supt. – Francis Determan, P O BOX 46 57363
MS 57363 – Warren Thomas, prin.
ES 57363 – Warren Thomas, prin.

Murdo, Jones Co., Pop. Code 3
Jones County SD 37-3
Sch. Sys. Enr. Code 2
Supt. – Jack Cranston, P O BOX 109 57559
Jones County MS 57559 – Jerald Applebee, prin.
Draper ES 57559 – Jack Cranston, prin.
ES 57559 – Jack Cranston, prin.

New Effington, Roberts Co., Pop. Code 2
New Effington SD 54-3
Sch. Sys. Enr. Code 2
Supt. – Harvey DeJong, P O BOX 8 57255
ES 57255 – Robert Hansen, prin.

Newell, Butte Co., Pop. Code 3
Newell SD 9-2
Sch. Sys. Enr. Code 2
Supt. – Richard Auch, P O BOX 99 57760
JHS 57760 – Edward Wegner, prin.
Moreau ES 57760 – Trula Fields, prin.
ES 57760 – Trula Fields, prin.
Nisland ES 57760 – Trula Fields, prin.

New Underwood, Pennington Co., Pop. Code 3
New Underwood SD 51-3
Sch. Sys. Enr. Code 2
Supt. – B. Stepina, P O BOX 128 57761
Farmingdale ES 57761 – Scott Pickner, prin.
Harmony ES 57761 – Scott Pickner, prin.
ES 57761 – Scott Pickner, prin.

Oelrichs, Fall River Co., Pop. Code 2
Oelrichs SD 23-3
Sch. Sys. Enr. Code 1
Supt. – Jerry Hills, P O BOX 65 57763
ES 57763 – Francis Mitchell, prin.
Smithwick ES 57763 – Francis Mitchell, prin.

Oldham, Kingsbury Co., Pop. Code 2
Oldham SD 38-4
Sch. Sys. Enr. Code 1
Supt. – Dal Williams, P O BOX N 57051
ES 57051 – Edward Buys, prin.

Onida, Sully Co., Pop. Code 3
Sully Buttes SD 58-2
Sch. Sys. Enr. Code 2
Supt. – Donald Rykhus, P O BOX FHS-1 57564
MS 57564 – Tom Ludens, prin.
Blunt ES 57564 – Don Rykhus, prin.
ES 57564 – Don Rykhus, prin.

Orient, Faulk Co., Pop. Code 1
Polo SD 29-2
Sch. Sys. Enr. Code 1
Supt. – Lew Gomer
  RURAL ROUTE 01 BOX 83 57467
Polo MS 57467 – Douglas Benton, prin.
Polo ES 57467 – Sharon Wieseler, prin.

Parker, Turner Co., Pop. Code 3
Parker SD 60-4
Sch. Sys. Enr. Code 2
Supt. – Darrell Salter, P O BOX 517 57053
JHS 57053 – Wallace Hortness, prin.
ES 57053 – Darrell Salter, prin.

Parkston, Hutchinson Co., Pop. Code 4
Parkston SD 33-3
Sch. Sys. Enr. Code 3
Supt. – J. Moen, 401 N 1ST ST 57366
JHS 57366 – Douglas Chapman, prin.
Dimock MS 57366 – Wesley Nelson, prin.
New Elm Spring Colony ES 57366
  Wesley Nelson, prin.
ES 57366 – Wesley Nelson, prin.

Philip, Haakon Co., Pop. Code 4
Haakon SD 27-1
Sch. Sys. Enr. Code 2
Supt. – Ted Kunz, P O BOX 730 57567
MS 57567 – Gale Patterson, prin.
Alfalfa Valley ES, P O BOX 730 57567
  Bruce Tusberg, prin.
Cheyenne ES, P O BOX 730 57567
  Bruce Tusberg, prin.
Deep Creek ES, P O BOX 730 57567
  Bruce Tusberg, prin.
Elbon ES, P O BOX 730 57567
  Bruce Tusberg, prin.
Hart ES, P O BOX 730 57567
  Bruce Tusberg, prin.
King ES, P O BOX 730 57567
  Bruce Tusberg, prin.
Milesville ES 57567 – Bruce Tusberg, prin.
Old Trail ES 57567 – Bruce Tusberg, prin.
Ottumwa ES, P O BOX 730 57567
  Bruce Tusberg, prin.
ES, P O BOX 730 57567 – Bruce Tusberg, prin.
Plum Creek ES, P O BOX 730 57567
  Bruce Tusberg, prin.

Pierre, Hughes Co., Pop. Code 7
Pierre SD 32-2
Sch. Sys. Enr. Code 5
Supt. – D. Tessier, 302 E DAKOTA AVE 57501
Buchanan ES 57501 – Dave Kaul, prin.
Jefferson ES 57501 – Dave Patten, prin.
McKinley ES 57501 – Dan Cronin, prin.
Raber ES 57501 – Dan Cronin, prin.
Washington ES 57501 – Margaret Logan, prin.

St. Joseph School, 210 E BROADWAY AVE 57501

Pine Ridge, Shannon Co.

Red Cloud HS, MISSION DR 57770

Plankinton, Aurora Co., Pop. Code 3
Plankinton SD 1-1
Sch. Sys. Enr. Code 2
Supt. – James Paulsen, P O BOX 190 57368
JHS 57368 – Joe Schlimgen, prin.
ES, P O BOX 190 57368 – James Paulsen, prin.

Platte, Charles Mix Co., Pop. Code 4
Platte Comm. SD 11-3
Sch. Sys. Enr. Code 3
Supt. – James Walker, P O BOX 157 57369
MS 57369 – Vernal Andersen, prin.
Castalia ES 57369 – Darrell Mueller, prin.
Cedar Grove Colony ES 57369
  Darrell Mueller, prin.
LaRoche ES 57369 – Darrell Mueller, prin.
Platte Colony ES 57369 – Darrell Mueller, prin.
ES 57369 – Darrell Mueller, prin.
Torrey Lake ES 57369 – Darrell Mueller, prin.

Pollock, Campbell Co., Pop. Code 2
Pollock SD 10-2
Sch. Sys. Enr. Code 2
Supt. – John Lafave, P O BOX 207 57648
ES 57648 – Sylvia LaFave, prin.

Porcupine, Shannon Co.

Our Lady of Lourdes School, P O BOX 7 57772

Presho, Lyman Co., Pop. Code 3
Lyman SD 42-1
Sch. Sys. Enr. Code 2
Supt. – Chris Anderson, P O BOX 160 57568
Lyman MS 57568 – Richard Willard, prin.
Kennebec ES 57568 – Richard Willard, prin.
ES 57568 – Richard Willard, prin.
Reliance ES 57568 – Richard Willard, prin.

Ramona, Lake Co., Pop. Code 2
Ramona SD 39-3
Sch. Sys. Enr. Code 1
Supt. – Douglas Degen, P O BOX 8 57054
JHS 57054 – John Putnam, prin.
ES 57054 – Diane Spilde, prin.

Rapid City, Pennington Co., Pop. Code 8
Rapid City Area SD 51-4
Sch. Sys. Enr. Code 7
Supt. – Dr. William Dean, 809 SOUTH ST 57701
Beadle ES 57701 – Linda Petersen, prin.
Bergquist ES 57701 – Lois Cersosimo, prin.
Black Hawk ES, 300 6TH ST 57701
  Harold Brenden, prin.
Canyon Lake ES 57701 – Chuck McLain, prin.
Cleghorn Canyon ES 57701 – Nancy Hall, prin.
Garfield ES 57701 – Steven Hengen, prin.
Grandview ES 57701 – James Gandy, prin.
Knollwood Heights ES 57701
  James Waltman, prin.
Lincoln ES 57701 – Bill Hines, prin.
Mann ES 57701 – Robert Rose, prin.
Meadowbrook ES 57701 – Jim Meszaros, prin.
Pinedale ES 57701 – Sam Zimiga, prin.
Rapid Valley East ES 57701 – Janet Luce, prin.
Robbinsdale ES 57701 – Jim Schuh, prin.
South Canyon ES, 218 NORDBY 57701
  Nancy Whitcher, prin.
Tallent ES 57701 – Dr. Phyllis Dixon, prin.
Valley View ES 57701 – Robert Herz, prin.
Wilson ES 57701 – Mary Heilman, prin.

St. Elizabeth Seton Central School
  431 OAKLAND ST 57701
Zion Lutheran School, 501 QUINCY ST 57701

Redfield, Spink Co., Pop. Code 5
Redfield SD 56-4
Sch. Sys. Enr. Code 3
Supt. – Donald Danielson, P O BOX 560 57469
JHS 57469 – Robert Luce, prin.
ES 57469 – Betty Schlueter, prin.

Revillo, Grant Co., Pop. Code 2
Grant-Deuel SD 25-3
Sch. Sys. Enr. Code 2
Supt. – Lawrence Furney
  RURAL ROUTE 01 BOX 9 57259
JHS 57259 – Barry Pickner, prin.
Grant-Deuel ES 57259 – Lawrence Furney, prin.

Roscoe, Edmunds Co., Pop. Code 2
Roscoe SD 22-4
Sch. Sys. Enr. Code 2
Supt. – Gerald Beutler, P O BOX 8 57471
JHS 57471 – Gerold Beck, prin.
ES 57471 – Gerald Beutler, prin.

Rosholt, Roberts Co., Pop. Code 2
Rosholt SD 54-4
Sch. Sys. Enr. Code 2
Supt. – Gene Harstad, P O BOX 106 57260
ES 57260 – Iva Wenzel, prin.
White Rock Colony ES 57260 – Iva Wenzel, prin.

Roslyn, Day Co., Pop. Code 2
Roslyn SD 18-2
Sch. Sys. Enr. Code 2
Supt. – R. Glad, P O BOX 196 57261
JHS 57261 – Marc Frankenstein, prin.
ES 57261 – Richard Glad, prin.

Rutland, Lake Co., Pop. Code 1
Rutland SD 39-4
Sch. Sys. Enr. Code 2
Supt. – Dal Williams, P O BOX 89 57057

JHS   57057 – Dorman Hansen, prin.
ES   57057 – Arvilla Dilly, prin.

Salem, McCook Co., Pop. Code 4
Salem SD 43-3
Sch. Sys. Enr. Code 2
Supt. – Dale Weber, P O BOX 310   57058
Jr. H.S.   57058 – Arlon McNeely, prin.
ES   57058 – Arlon McNeely, prin.

St. Mary's School, 205 W ESSEX AVE   57058

Scotland, Bon Homme Co., Pop. Code 4
Scotland SD 4-3
Sch. Sys. Enr. Code 2
Supt. – Eugene Schneider, P O BOX 327   57059
JHS   57059 – William Snoozy, prin.
Kaylor ES   57059 – Terry Kluthe, prin.
Lesterville ES   57059 – Terry Kluthe, prin.
ES   57059 – Terry Kluthe, prin.

Selby, Walworth Co., Pop. Code 3
Selby SD 62-4
Sch. Sys. Enr. Code 2
Supt. – Donald Akre, P O BOX 324   57472
JHS   57472 – Don Vogt, prin.
ES   57472 – Selma Groth, prin.

Sioux Falls, Minnehaha Co., Pop. Code 8
Sioux Falls SD 49-5
Sch. Sys. Enr. Code 7
Supt. – Dr. John Harris, 201 E 38TH ST   57105
Addams ES   57117 – Mike Hansen, prin.
Anderson ES   57117 – Jan Dangel, prin.
Bancroft ES   57117 – Ken Cross, prin.
Cleveland ES   57103 – Carol Brown, prin.
Dunn ES   57117 – Doug Erickson, prin.
Field ES   57117 – Sid Stallinga. prin.
Franklin ES   57103 – Rodney Unruh, prin.
Frost ES   57117 – Dick Hubble, prin.
Garfield ES   57117 – Pam Sessler, prin.
Hawthorne ES   57117 – Colleen Bee, prin.
Hayward ES   57117 – David Mendel, prin.
Howe ES   57117 – Lois Lampkin, prin.
Irving ES   57117 – Kathy Coulter, prin.
Jefferson ES   57117 – Doug Kuhlman, prin.
Kennedy ES   57117 – Doris Johnson, prin.
Lincoln ES   57117 – Lyle Farrand, prin.
Longfellow ES   57117 – Ken Iseminger, prin.
Lowell ES   57117 – Pat Croston, prin.
Mann ES   57117 – Dr. Robert Hemre, prin.
Renberg ES   57117 – Larry Anderson, prin.
Twain ES   57117 – John Gauer, prin.
Wilder ES   57117 – Fred Aderhold, prin.

Calvin Christian School, 700 S SNEVE AVE   57103
Christ the King School, 1801 S LAKE AVE   57105
Little Flower ES, 217 N SHERMAN AVE   57103
Sioux Falls Lutheran School
    308 W 37TH ST   57105
St. Joseph Cathedral School, 601 W 4TH ST   57104
St. Lambert School, 16TH & BAHNSON   57103
St. Mary's School, 2001 S 5TH AVE   57105

Sisseton, Roberts Co., Pop. Code 5
Sisseton SD 54-5
Sch. Sys. Enr. Code 4
Supt. – M. Rebenberg, 302 MAPLE ST E   57262
Thollehauge MS   57262 – Verlin Hosmer, prin.
Peever ES   57262 – Mylo Hoffman, prin.
Westside ES   57262 – Mylo Hoffman, prin.

South Shore, Codington Co., Pop. Code 2
South Shore SD 14-3
Sch. Sys. Enr. Code 2
Supt. – Max Nawroth, P O BOX 638   57263
JHS   57263 – Charles Stormo, prin.
ES   57263 – Glenn Elmore, prin.

Spearfish, Lawrence Co., Pop. Code 6
Spearfish SD 40-2
Sch. Sys. Enr. Code 4
Supt. – Dr. James Anderson
    400 HUDSON ST E   57783
JHS   57783 – Tom Riedel, prin.
Central ES   57783 – Kay Burke, prin.
East MS   57783 – Kay Burke, prin.
West ES   57783 – Perry Hansen, prin.

Spencer, McCook Co., Pop. Code 2
Spencer SD 43-4
Sch. Sys. Enr. Code 1
Supt. – John Stanton, P O BOX 66   57374
JHS   57374 – Pat McCormick, prin.
ES   57374 – John Stanton, prin.

Stickney, Aurora Co., Pop. Code 2
Stickney SD 1-2
Sch. Sys. Enr. Code 2
Supt. – Frank Odens, P O BOX 67   57375
ES   57375 – Genevieve Hargreaves, prin.

Sturgis, Meade Co., Pop. Code 6
Meade SD 46-1
Sch. Sys. Enr. Code 5
Supt. – Dr. Barry Furze, 1230 DOUGLAS ST   57785
Williams MS, 1425 CEDAR   57785
    Lonny Harter, prin.
Alkali ES, 1230 DOUGLAS   57785
    William Burke, prin.
Atall ES, 1230 DOUGLAS   57785
    William Burke, prin.
Badger Clark ES, 1119 3RD ST   57785
    Wilbur Stader, prin.
Bear Butte ES   57785 – Wilbur Stader, prin.
Case ES, 1119 3RD ST   57785
    Wilbur Stader, prin.

Elm Springs ES, 1230 DOUGLAS   57785
    William Burke, prin.
Enning ES, 1230 DOUGLAS   57785
    William Burke, prin.
Erskine ES, 1119 3RD ST   57785
    Wilbur Stader, prin.
Hereford ES, 1230 DOUGLAS   57785
    William Burke, prin.
Hope ES, 1230 DOUGLAS   57785
    William Burke, prin.
Lakeside ES, 1230 DOUGLAS   57785
    William Burke, prin.
Opal ES, 1230 DOUGLAS   57785
    William Burke, prin.
Piedmont ES, 1230 DOUGLAS   57785
    Wayne Musilek, prin.
Primary Building ES, 1119 3RD ST   57785
    Wilbur Stader, prin.
Red Top ES, 1230 DOUGLAS   57785
    William Burke, prin.
Stagebarn ES, 1230 DOUGLAS   57785
    Wayne Musilek, prin.
Stoneville ES, 1230 DOUGLAS   57785
    William Burke, prin.
Sulphur Creek ES   57785 – William Burke, prin.
Union Center ES, 1230 DOUGLAS   57785
    William Burke, prin.
United ES, 1230 DOUGLAS   57785
    William Burke, prin.
Wetz ES, 1230 DOUGLAS   57785
    William Burke, prin.
Whitewood ES, 1230 DOUGLAS   57785
    William Burke, prin.

Summit, Roberts Co., Pop. Code 2
Summit SD 54-6
Sch. Sys. Enr. Code 2
Supt. – Edward Wickre, P O BOX 791   57266
JHS   57266 – Edward Wickre, prin.
ES   57266 – Darlene Tonsager, prin.

Timber Lake, Dewey Co., Pop. Code 3
Timber Lake SD 20-3
Sch. Sys. Enr. Code 2
Supt. – Carl Remmers, P O BOX 100   57656
JHS   57656 – Loris Lindskov, prin.
ES   57656 – Bonita Ehly, prin.

Tripp, Hutchinson Co., Pop. Code 3
Tripp SD 33-4
Sch. Sys. Enr. Code 2
Supt. – G. Schnieder, P O BOX 430   57376
MS   57376 – Marilyn Kepplinger, prin.
ES   57376 – Marilyn Kepplinger, prin.

Tulare, Spink Co., Pop. Code 2
Tulare SD 56-5
Sch. Sys. Enr. Code 2
Supt. – Barry Erickson, P O BOX 108   57476
Glendale Colony ES   57476 – Martha Koester, prin.
Spink Colony ES   57476 – Martha Koester, prin.
ES   57476 – Martha Koester, prin.

Tyndall, Bon Homme Co., Pop. Code 4
Bon Homme SD 4-2
Sch. Sys. Enr. Code 3
Supt. – Larry Lickfelt, P O BOX 28   57066
JHS   57066 – Delight Paulson, prin.
Hutterische Colony ES   57066
    Delight Paulson, prin.
Springfield ES   57066 – Delight Paulson, prin.
Tabor ES   57066 – Delight Paulson, prin.
ES   57066 – Delight Paulson, prin.

Veblen, Marshall Co., Pop. Code 2
Veblen SD 45-3
Sch. Sys. Enr. Code 2
Supt. – Herbert Samson, P O BOX E   57270
JHS   57270 – Donald Warren, prin.
ES   57270 – Herbert Samson, prin.

Vermillion, Clay Co., Pop. Code 6
Vermillion SD 13-1
Sch. Sys. Enr. Code 4
Supt. – John Bonaiuto, 127 LINDEN AVE   57069
MS   57069 – John Grinde, prin.
Austin ES   57069 – Robert Bowker, prin.
Jolly ES   57069 – Robert Bowker, prin.

St. Agnes School, 909 E LEWIS ST   57069

Viborg, Turner Co., Pop. Code 3
Viborg SD 60-5
Sch. Sys. Enr. Code 2
Supt. – Dan Moran, P O BOX 397   57070
JHS   57070 – James Holbeck, prin.
ES, P O BOX 397   57070 – Nancy Allen, prin.

Volga, Brookings Co., Pop. Code 4
Sioux Valley SD 5-5
Sch. Sys. Enr. Code 3
Supt. – Ronald Bennett, P O BOX 268   57071
Sioux Valley JHS   57071 – C. Grebner, prin.
Sioux Valley ES   57071 – Virgil Newman, prin.

Wagner, Charles Mix Co., Pop. Code 4
Wagner Community SD 11-4
Sch. Sys. Enr. Code 3
Supt. – Dale Hall, P O BOX 310   57380
JHS   57380 – Roger Wiltz, prin.
ES   57380 – Roberta Rehwaldt, prin.

Wakonda, Clay Co., Pop. Code 2
Wakonda SD 13-2
Sch. Sys. Enr. Code 2
Supt. – Larry Wynia, P O BOX 268   57073

JHS   57073 – Ronald Flynn, prin.
ES   57073 – L. Anderson, prin.

Wakpala, Corson Co., Pop. Code 2
Smee SD 15-3
Sch. Sys. Enr. Code 2
Supt. – Patrick Mullen, P O BOX B   57658
ES   57658 – Eldon Sting, prin.

Wall, Pennington Co., Pop. Code 3
Wall SD 51-5
Sch. Sys. Enr. Code 2
Supt. – K. Poppe, P O BOX 414   57790
Big White ES   57790 – Patrick Deering, prin.
Pleasant Ridge ES   57790 – Patrick Deering, prin.
Scenic ES   57790 – Patrick Deering, prin.
ES   57790 – Patrick Deering, prin.
Wasta ES   57790 – Patrick Deering, prin.

Warner, Brown Co., Pop. Code 2
Warner SD 6-5
Sch. Sys. Enr. Code 2
Supt. – L. Tobin, P O BOX 68   57479
MS   57479 – Lewis Borge, prin.
ES   57479 – Donneley Kay, prin.

Watertown, Codington Co., Pop. Code 7
Watertown SD 14-4
Sch. Sys. Enr. Code 5
Supt. – Ernest Edwards, P O BOX 730   57201
Garfield ES   57201 – Derril Chapman, prin.
Grant ES   57201 – Curt Ehresmann, prin.
Lincoln ES   57201 – Lee Konvalin, prin.
McKinley ES   57201 – Dennis Arnold, prin.
Mellette ES   57201 – Marly Wilson, prin.
Roosevelt ES   57201 – Harry Johnson, prin.

St. Martin's Lutheran School
    1200 SECOND ST NE   57201

Waubay, Day Co., Pop. Code 3
Waubay SD 18-3
Sch. Sys. Enr. Code 2
Supt. – Dennis Nelson, P O BOX E   57273
JHS   57273 – Gene Furness, prin.
ES   57273 – Lloyal Saugstad, prin.

Waverly, Codington Co., Pop. Code 1
Waverly SD 14-5
Sch. Sys. Enr. Code 1
Supt. – Bernard Pugh, P O BOX 80   57202
JHS   57202 – Rodger Gross, prin.
ES   57202 – Bernard Pugh, prin.

Webster, Day Co., Pop. Code 4
Webster SD 18-4
Sch. Sys. Enr. Code 3
Supt. – Arnold Anderson, 1 E 8TH AVE   57274
JHS   57274 – Bruce Olson, prin.
ES   57274 – Charles Overby, prin.

Wessington, Beadle Co., Pop. Code 2
Wessington SD 2-4
Sch. Sys. Enr. Code 2
Supt. – Douglas Voss, P O BOX 167   57381
JHS   57381 – Randy Barendeau, prin.
ES   57381 – Douglas Voss, prin.

Wessington Springs, Jerauld Co., Pop. Code 4
Wessington Springs SD 36-2
Sch. Sys. Enr. Code 2
Supt. – James Heinert, P O BOX 449   57382
Spring Valley Colony ES   57382
    Patrick Dowd, prin.
ES   57382 – Patrick Dowd, prin.

White, Brookings Co., Pop. Code 2
Deubrook SD 5-2
Sch. Sys. Enr. Code 2
Supt. – Douglas Nelson, P O BOX 346   57276
Deubrook JHS   57276 – Don Ray, prin.
Toronto ES   57276 – Mary Cypher, prin.

White Lake, Aurora Co., Pop. Code 2
White Lake SD 1-3
Sch. Sys. Enr. Code 2
Supt. – Elwood Baird, P O BOX 246   57383
JHS   57383 – Daniel Guericke, prin.
ES   57383 – Elwood Baird, prin.

White River, Mellette Co., Pop. Code 3
White River SD 47-1
Sch. Sys. Enr. Code 2
Supt. – Dr. Don Barnhart, P O BOX 273   57579
MS   57579 – Don Barnhart, prin.
Big White ES   57579 – Marc Christianson, prin.
Norris ES   57579 – Marc Christianson, prin.
Prairie View ES   57579 – Marc Christianson, prin.
Ring Thunder ES   57579 – Marc Christianson, prin.
Running Bird ES   57579 – Marc Christianson, prin.
ES   57579 – Marc Christianson, prin.

Willow Lake, Clark Co., Pop. Code 2
Willow Lake SD 12-3
Sch. Sys. Enr. Code 2
Supt. – Leland Poppen, P O BOX 237   57278
JHS   57278 – Gary Skoglund, prin.
ES   57278 – Leland Poppen, prin.

Wilmot, Roberts Co., Pop. Code 3
Wilmot SD 54-7
Sch. Sys. Enr. Code 2
Supt. – Wayne Johnson, P O BOX 100   57279
JHS   57279 – Robert Tennis, prin.
ES   57279 – Oscar Kapfenstein, prin.

Winner, Tripp Co., Pop. Code 5
  Winner SD 59-2
  Sch. Sys. Enr. Code 4
  Supt. – Arnold Wold, P O BOX 231   57580
  MS   57580 – Terry Eckstaine, prin.
  Beaver Creek ES   57580 – David Wrotenbury, prin.
  Central ES   57580 – John Wranek, prin.
  East Side ES   57580 – John Wranek, prin.
  Eden ES   57580 – David Wrotenbury, prin.
  Hamill ES   57580 – David Wrotenbury, prin.
  Ideal ES   57580 – David Wrotenbury, prin.
  King ES   57580 – David Wrotenbury, prin.
  Milboro ES   57580 – David Wrotenbury, prin.
  Plainview ES   57580 – David Wrotenbury, prin.
  Star Prairie ES   57580 – David Wrotenbury, prin.
  Star Valley ES   57580 – David Wrotenbury, prin.
  Weaver ES   57580 – David Wrotenbury, prin.
  West Side ES   57580 – John Wranek, prin.

Wolsey, Beadle Co., Pop. Code 2
  Wolsey SD 2-5
  Sch. Sys. Enr. Code 2
  Supt. – Thomas Halvorson, P O BOX 187   57384
  ES   57384 – Thomas Halvorson, prin.

Wood, Mellette Co., Pop. Code 2
  Wood SD 47-2
  Sch. Sys. Enr. Code 1
  Supt. – Chris Anderson, P O BOX 458   57585
  Witten ES   57585 – Gayla Frederickson, prin.
  ES   57585 – Gayla Frederickson, prin.

Woonsocket, Sanborn Co., Pop. Code 3
  Woonsocket SD 55-4
  Sch. Sys. Enr. Code 2
  Supt. – Dr. Larry Davis, P O BOX 428   57385
  JHS   57385 – Jens Andree, prin.
  ES   57385 – Dr. Larry Davis, prin.

Yankton, Yankton Co., Pop. Code 7
  Yankton SD 63-3
  Sch. Sys. Enr. Code 5
  Supt. – Maurice Haugland, 1900 FERDIG ST   57078
  MS   57078 – Lee Kanago, prin.
  Beadle ES   57078 – Carolyn Pesicka, prin.
  Lincoln ES   57078 – Robert Walser, prin.
  Mission Hill ES   57078 – Lee Kanago, prin.
  Stewart ES   57078 – Sophie Merrigan, prin.
  Utica ES   57078 – Lee Kanago, prin.
  Webster ES   57078 – Bruce Blumer, prin.

  Sacred Heart School, 504 CAPITAL ST   57078

TENNESSEE

STATE DEPARTMENT OF EDUCATION
100 Cordell Hull Building, Nashville 37219
(615) 741-2731

Commissioner of Education	Charles Smith
Deputy Commissioner	Nebraska Mays
Assistant Commissioner Finance & Administration	Mike Gower
Assistant Commissioner Vocational Education	Marvin Flatt
Assistant Commissioner Career Ladder/Certification	Frances Prince
Assistant Commissioner General Education Curriculum	Estel Mills
Assistant Commissioner School Approval	Tom Cannon

STATE BOARD OF EDUCATION
Dr. Brent Poulton, *Executive Director*   122 Cordell Hull Building, Nashville   37219

HIGHER EDUCATION COMMISSION
Dr. Wayne Brown, *Executive Director*   501 Union Building #300, Nashville   37219

PUBLIC, PRIVATE, AND PAROCHIAL ELEMENTARY SCHOOLS

Adamsville, McNairy Co., Pop. Code 4
  Hardin County SD
  Supt. – See Savannah
  West Hardin ES, RURAL ROUTE 01   38310
    Bryan Black, prin.

  McNairy County SD
  Supt. – See Selmer
  ES, P O BOX 335   38310 – Luzell Hughes, prin.

Afton, Greene Co.
  Greene County SD
  Supt. – See Greeneville
  Newmansville ES, RURAL ROUTE 02   37616
    William Seneker, prin.

Alamo, Crockett Co., Pop. Code 5
  Alamo SD
  Sch. Sys. Enr. Code 2
  Supt. – Virginia Mohunoro, 326 E PARK ST   38001
  ES, 326 E PARK ST   38001
    Virginia Mohunoro, prin.

  Crockett County SD
  Sch. Sys. Enr. Code 4
  Supt. – Bill Emerson, RURAL ROUTE 02   38001
  Crockett County JHS
    RURAL ROUTE 01 BOX 102   38001
    Pauline Elliot, prin.
  Other Schools – See Friendship, Gadsden, Maury City

Alcoa, Blount Co., Pop. Code 6
  Alcoa CSD
  Sch. Sys. Enr. Code 4
  Supt. – William Bailey, 500 FARADAY ST   37701
  MS, HOWE ST   37701 – Vaughn D. Belcher, prin.
  ES, SPRINGBROOK ROAD   37701
    Dr. Robert Delozier, prin.

Algood, Putnam Co., Pop. Code 4
  Putnam County SD
  Supt. – See Cookeville

  ES, 288N E MAIN ST   38501
    Richard Norton, prin.

Allardt, Fentress Co., Pop. Code 3
  Fentress County SD
  Supt. – See Jamestown
  ES   38504 – Clyde Maddox,Jr., prin.

Allons, Overton Co.
  Clay County SD
  Supt. – See Celina
  Maple Grove ES, RURAL ROUTE 01   38541
    Jerry Collins, prin.

  Overton County SD
  Supt. – See Livingston
  ES   38541 – Dolphus Dial, prin.

Altamont, Grundy Co., Pop. Code 3
  Grundy County SD
  Sch. Sys. Enr. Code 5
  Supt. – Keith Brewer, P O BOX 97   37301
  North ES   37301 – Janette Sartain, prin.
  Other Schools – See Coalmont, Laager, Palmer, Pelham, Tracy City

Andersonville, Anderson Co.
  Anderson County SD
  Supt. – See Clinton
  ES   37705 – Greg Hamilton, prin.

Antioch, Davidson Co.
  Davidson County SD
  Supt. – See Nashville
  Cole ES, 5060 COLEMONT DR   37013
    Edward Counter, prin.

Apison, Hamilton Co.
  Hamilton County SD
  Supt. – See Chattanooga
  ES, 11206 OLD E BRAINERD   37302
    Esther Taj, prin.

Arlington, Shelby Co., Pop. Code 4
  Shelby County SD
  Supt. – See Memphis
  Shadowlawn MS
    4734 SHADOWLAWN ROAD   38002
    Rob Hatton, prin.
  ES, 11825 DOUGLAS ST   38002
    Carol Matthews, prin.
  Barrets ES, 10280 GODWIN RD   38002
    Bonita Grumme, prin.

Ashland City, Cheatham Co., Pop. Code 4
  Cheatham County SD
  Sch. Sys. Enr. Code 5
  Supt. – Jere Jordan, 102 ELIZABETH ST   37015
  ES, 108 ELIZABETH ST   37015
    Millie Miles, prin.
  East Cheatham ES, RURAL ROUTE 02   37015
    David Chester, prin.
  Other Schools – See Chapmansboro, Kingston Springs, Pegram, Pleasant View

Athens, McMinn Co., Pop. Code 7
  Athens CSD
  Sch. Sys. Enr. Code 4
  Supt. – Dr. Robin L. Pierce
    943 CRESTWAY DRIVE   37303
  City Park ES   37303 – Joseph Buchanan, prin.
  Ingelside ES, 200 GUILLE ST   37303
    Ben Wilson, prin.
  North City ES, PALOS ST   37303
    Luke Sewell, prin.
  Westside ES, 700 WILSON ST   37303
    Ann Dodson, prin.

  McMinn County SD
  Sch. Sys. Enr. Code 6
  Supt. – James Hoyal, COURTHOUSE   37303
  Baker ES, RURAL ROUTE 03   37303
    Jack Garner, prin.

Idlewild ES, RURAL ROUTE 01 37303
    James Patterson, prin.
    Other Schools – See Calhoun, Englewood, Etowah,
    Niota, Riceville

Auburntown, Cannon Co., Pop. Code 2
    Cannon County SD
    Supt. – See Woodbury
    Auburn ES 37016 – Roger Turney, prin.

Bartlett, Shelby Co., Pop. Code 7
    Shelby County SD
    Supt. – See Memphis
    Alturia ES, 6641 DEERMONT DR 38134
        Augustus Johnson, prin.
    ES, 5650 WOODLAWN ST 38134
        Rose Powell, prin.
    Ellendale ES, 6950 DAWN HILL RD 38134
        James Jonakin, prin.
    Elmore Park ES, 6330 ALTHORNE RD 38134
        Page Watson, prin.
    Oak ES, 3573 OAK RD 38134
        Dr. Julianne Robertson, prin.

Baxter, Putnam Co., Pop. Code 4
    Putnam County SD
    Supt. – See Cookeville
    ES 38544 – Donna Shanks, prin.

Bean Station, Grainger Co.
    Grainger County SD
    Supt. – See Rutledge
    ES, RURAL ROUTE 03 BOX 428 37708
        Gary Jackson, prin.

Beech Bluff, Madison Co.
    Madison County SD
    Supt. – See Jackson
    ES 38313 – Bill Wheatley, prin.

Bells, Crockett Co., Pop. Code 4
    Bells SD
    Sch. Sys. Enr. Code 2
    Supt. – Bill Emerson, P O BOX A 38006
    ES, P O BOX A 38006 – Linda Bridges, prin.

Benton, Polk Co., Pop. Code 4
    Polk County SD.
    Sch. Sys. Enr. Code 5
    Supt. – Danny Rogers, P O BOX A 37307
    ES 37307 – William Moats, prin.
    Other Schools – See Ducktown, Oldfort, Turtletown

Bethel Springs, McNairy Co., Pop. Code 3
    McNairy County SD
    Supt. – See Selmer
    ES, P O BOX 38 38315 – Alvin Wilson, prin.

Bethpage, Sumner Co.
    Sumner County SD
    Supt. – See Gallatin
    ES, P O BOX 68 37022 – (—), prin.
    North Sumner ES, RURAL ROUTE 02 37022
        John Holer, prin.

Big Rock, Stewart Co.
    Stewart County SD
    Supt. – See Dover
    North Stewart ES, RURAL ROUTE 01 37023
        Terry Burkhart, prin.

Big Sandy, Benton Co., Pop. Code 3
    Benton County SD
    Supt. – See Camden
    S, MAIN ST 38221 – Steve Baker, prin.

Birchwood, Hamilton Co.
    Hamilton County SD
    Supt. – See Chattanooga
    ES, HWY 60 37308 – James Hale, prin.

Blountville, Sullivan Co., Pop. Code 3
    Sullivan County SD
    Sch. Sys. Enr. Code 7
    Supt. – Jim Fleming, P O BOX 306 37617
    MS, RURAL ROUTE 05 BOX 282 37617
        Lawrence Garland, prin.
    Holston MS, RURAL ROUTE 07 BOX 198 37617
        David Burrell, prin.
    ES, RURAL ROUTE 05 BOX 376 37617
        Jerry Ford, prin.
    Central Heights ES
        RURAL ROUTE 01 BOX 86 37617
        Jerry Mays, prin.
    Holston ES, RURAL ROUTE 07 BOX 198 37617
        Patrinka Quillen, prin.
    Other Schools – See Bluff City, Bristol, Kingsport,
    Piney Flats

Bluff City, Sullivan Co., Pop. Code 2
    Sullivan County SD
    Supt. – See Blountville
    MS 37618 – Ed Scarbrogh, prin.
    ES, P O BOX 280 37618 – Albert Buchanan, prin.

Bogota, Dyer Co.
    Dyer County SD
    Supt. – See Dyersburg
    ES 38007 – David Lovell, prin.

Bolivar, Hardeman Co., Pop. Code 6
    Hardeman County SD
    Sch. Sys. Enr. Code 6
    Supt. – Billy Joe Sanders, P O BOX 112 38008
    ES 38008 – Ben Carr, prin.
    Other Schools – See Grand Junction, Hornsby,
    Middleton, Toone, Whiteville

Bradford, Gibson Co., Pop. Code 4
    Bradford CSD
    Sch. Sys. Enr. Code 3
    Supt. – Bobby McCartney, P O BOX 220 38316
    S, P O BOX 70 38316 – Joe Denning, prin.

Bradyville, Cannon Co.
    Cannon County SD
    Supt. – See Woodbury
    Woodland ES, RURAL ROUTE 01 37026
        John Todd, prin.

Brentwood, Williamson Co., Pop. Code 6
    Davidson County SD
    Supt. – See Nashville
    Granbery ES, 495 HILL ROAD 37027
        Robert Sadler, prin.

    Williamson County SD
    Supt. – See Franklin
    Northside MS, 624 GRANNY WHITE PIKE 37027
        Bob Hardison, prin.
    Lipscomb ES, 8011 CONCORD RD 37027
        Jesse Frank, prin.
    Scales ES, MURRAY LN 37027
        Viva Bosland, prin.

Briceville, Anderson Co.
    Anderson County SD
    Supt. – See Clinton
    ES 37710 – Wayne Patton, prin.

Brighton, Tipton Co.
    Tipton County SD
    Supt. – See Covington
    ES, P O BOX C 38011 – Timothy Fite, prin.

Bristol, Sullivan Co., Pop. Code 7
    Bristol CSD
    Sch. Sys. Enr. Code 5
    Supt. – Dr. Wm. J. Morrell
        615 EDGEMONT AVE 37620
    Vance JHS, 815 EDGEMONT AVE 37620
        Ralph Erwin, prin.
    Anderson ES 37620 – Rebecca Walters, prin.
    Avoca ES, 2440 VOLUNTEER PKWY 37620
        Donna Raines, prin.
    Central ES, EDGEMONT AVE 37620
        L. Johnson, prin.
    Fairmount ES, CYPRESS ST 37620
        John Clark, Jr., prin.
    Haynesfield ES, 201 BLUFF CITY HWY 37620
        Steve Dixon, prin.
    Holston View ES, KING COLLEGE ROAD 37620
        C. Wise, prin.

    Sullivan County SD
    Supt. – See Blountville
    Holston Valley MS, RURAL ROUTE 04 37620
        James Flannagan, prin.
    Akard Memorial ES
        RURAL ROUTE 14 BOX 266 37620
        Sam Morton, prin.
    East Cherokee ES, RURAL ROUTE 04 37620
        Wilbert Roberts, prin.
    Emmett ES, RURAL ROUTE 04 37620
        Bill Hamilton, prin.
    Valley Pike ES, 2305 CAROLINA AVE 37620
        Kenneth Haga, prin.
    Weavers ES, RURAL ROUTE 01 BOX 274 37620
        Jonathon Morrell, prin.

Brownsville, Haywood Co., Pop. Code 6
    Haywood County SD
    Sch. Sys. Enr. Code 5
    Supt. – W. W. Cox, 900 E MAIN ST 38012
    Anderson MS, 520 W MAIN ST 38012
        Ben Morrison, prin.
    Sunny Hill MS
        RURAL ROUTE 03 BOX 9548 38012
        William Kendrick, prin.
    East Side ES, RURAL ROUTE 06 38012
        Elvin Wells, prin.
    Haywood ES, 313 N GRAND AVE 38012
        Jerry Smith, prin.

Bruceton, Carroll Co., Pop. Code 4
    Hollow Rock-Bruceton SD
    Sch. Sys. Enr. Code 3
    Supt. – Bob McMackins, P O BOX 135 38317
    Central ES, P O BOX 135 38317
        Steve Wilkerson, prin.

Buchanan, Henry Co.
    Henry County SD
    Supt. – See Paris
    ES 38222 – Gordon Taylor, prin.

Bulls Gap, Hawkins Co., Pop. Code 3
    Hawkins County SD
    Supt. – See Rogersville
    ES, P O BOX 67 37711 – Carl Starnes, prin.
    St. Clair ES, RURAL ROUTE 01 37711
        Annette Beach, prin.

Burns, Dickson Co., Pop. Code 3
    Dickson County SD
    Supt. – See Charlotte
    ES, GENERAL DELIVERY 37029
        Kenneth Fussell, prin.

Butler, Johnson Co.
    Carter County SD
    Supt. – See Elizabethton
    Little Milligan ES, RURAL ROUTE 02 37640
        Jerry Calhoun, prin.

    Johnson County SD
    Supt. – See Mountain City
    Dry Run ES, RURAL ROUTE 01 37640
        Gary Manuel, prin.

Byrdstown, Pickett Co., Pop. Code 3
    Pickett County SD
    Sch. Sys. Enr. Code 3
    Supt. – Charles Mitchell
        WOODLANN DRIVE 38549
    Pickett County ES, P O BOX 68 38549
        Harlan Copeland, prin.

Calhoun, McMinn Co., Pop. Code 3
    McMinn County SD
    Supt. – See Athens
    ES 37309 – David Pierce, prin.

Camden, Benton Co., Pop. Code 5
    Benton County SD
    Sch. Sys. Enr. Code 5
    Supt. – Allen Dean Presson, P O BOX 148 38320
    Briarwood MS, BRIARWOOD ST 38320
        Randall Robertson, prin.
    ES, 208 WASHINGTON ST 38320
        Clyde Duncan, prin.
    Other Schools – See Big Sandy, Holladay

Carthage, Smith Co., Pop. Code 5
    Smith County SD
    Sch. Sys. Enr. Code 5
    Supt. – Wayne Lankford, 100 MAIN ST 37030
    ES, 150 SKYLINE DR 37030
        Robby Richardson, prin.
    Defeated ES, RURAL ROUTE 01 37030
        David Nixon, prin.
    Union Heights ES, RURAL ROUTE 02 37030
        B. Owen, prin.
    Other Schools – See Elmwood, Gordonsville, Pleasant
    Shade

Caryville, Campbell Co., Pop. Code 4
    Campbell County SD
    Supt. – See Jacksboro
    Stony Fork S, RURAL ROUTE 02 BOX 328 37714
        Hugh Perry, prin.
    ES 37714 – Robert Massengill, prin.
    Ridgewood ES, RURAL ROUTE 01 37714
        Clifford Kohlmeyer, prin.

Cedar Grove, Carroll Co.
    West Carroll SD
    Supt. – See Mc Lemoresville
    West Carroll PS, RURAL ROUTE 02 38321
        Linda Inman, prin.

Cedar Hill, Robertson Co., Pop. Code 2
    Robertson County SD
    Supt. – See Springfield
    Byrns S, RURAL ROUTE 01 37032
        John Mantooth, prin.

Celina, Clay Co., Pop. Code 4
    Clay County SD
    Sch. Sys. Enr. Code 4
    Supt. – L. Mayfield Brown, P O BOX 188 38551
    ES 38551 – Peggy Davis, prin.
    Other Schools – See Allons, Red Boiling Springs

Centerville, Hickman Co., Pop. Code 5
    Hickman County SD
    Sch. Sys. Enr. Code 5
    Supt. – Wayne Qualls, 108 COLLEGE AVE 37033
    Hickman County MS
        109 E HACKBERRY ST 37033
        Douglas True, prin.
    ES, OLD DICKSON RD 37033 – Gary Spicer, prin.
    Other Schools – See Lyles

Chapel Hill, Marshall Co., Pop. Code 3
    Marshall County SD
    Supt. – See Lewisburg
    Forrest S, P O BOX 97 37034 – Dean Delk, prin.

Chapmansboro, Cheatham Co.
    Cheatham County SD
    Supt. – See Ashland City
    West Cheatham ES, RURAL ROUTE 01 37035
        Elizabeth Ferrell, prin.

Charleston, Bradley Co., Pop. Code 3
    Bradley County SD
    Supt. – See Cleveland
    S, P O BOX 258 37310 – Norman Dillon, prin.

Charlotte, Dickson Co., Pop. Code 3
    Dickson County SD
    Sch. Sys. Enr. Code 6
    Supt. – Noah Daniel, P O BOX 218 37036
    ES, P O BOX 70 37036 – George Freeman, Jr., prin.
    Other Schools – See Burns, Dickson, Vanleer, White
    Bluff

Chattanooga, Hamilton Co., Pop. Code 9
    Chattanooga CSD
    Sch. Sys. Enr. Code 7
    Supt. – Clifford Hendrix, 1161 40TH ST E 37407
    Chattanooga Arts & Sciences S
        865 E 3RD ST 37403 – Mary Ann Holt, prin.
    Alton Park MS, 200 37TH ST E 37410
        Ervin Mitchell, prin.
    Brainerd MS, 4201 CHERRYTON DRIVE 37411
        Andrew Frierson, prin.
    Dalewood MS
        1300 SHALLOWFORD ROAD 37411
        Morris Chapman, prin.
    East Lake MS, 3600 13TH AVE 37407
        Reeves Fairey, prin.

North Chattanooga MS
  1301 DALLAS ROAD 37405
  Arlandres Horton, prin.
Orchard Knob MS
  500 N HIGHLAND PARK AVE 37404
  Amelia Allen, prin.
Tyner MS, 6837 TYNER ROAD 37421
  Randall Wall, prin.
Barger ES, 4808 BRAINERD RD 37411
  Christine Hicks, prin.
Clifton Hills ES, 1815 E 32ND ST 37407
  Sarah Jones, prin.
Donaldson ES, 926 W 37TH ST 37410
  Herman Grier, prin.
Dupont ES, 4134 HIXSON PIKE 37415
  Darwin Lane, prin.
East Brainerd ES, 7453 E BRAINERD RD 37421
  Dr. Kathleen Conner, prin.
East Lake ES, 3700 13TH AVE 37407
  Joe Shadwick, prin.
East Side ES, 2200 MAIN ST E 37404
  Mary Shannon, prin.
Garber ES, 2225 ROANOKE AVE 37406
  Dr. Oscar Allen, prin.
Hardy ES, 2115 DODSON AVE 37406
  Sullivan Ruff, prin.
Hillcrest ES, 4302 BONNY OAKS DR 37416
  Robert Hope, prin.
Howard ES, 100 E 25TH STREET 37408
  Mary Gee, prin.
Lakeside ES, 4930 HIGHWAY 58 37416
  Eleanor Matthews, prin.
Normal Park ES, 1009 MISS AVE 37405
  Dr. Betty Martin, prin.
North Chattanooga ES
  1219 MISSISSIPPI AVE W 37405 – Tee Carr, prin.
Orchard Knob ES
  400 N ORCHARD KNOB AVE 37404
  Sara Cotton, prin.
Rivermont ES, 3330 HIXSON PIKE 37415
  William Hodges, prin.
Shepherd ES, 7126 TYNER RD 37421
  Louis Perfetti, prin.
Valley View ES, 701 BROWNS FERRY RD 37419
  Fred Carr, prin.
Woodmore ES, 800 WOODMORE LN 37411
  Raymond Swoffard, prin.
Other Schools – See Hixson

Hamilton County SD
Sch. Sys. Enr. Code 7
Supt. – Don Loftis, 1161 40TH ST E 37407
East Ridge JHS, 4400 BENNETT ROAD 37412
  Ben Johnson, prin.
Red Bank JHS, 3715 DAYTON BLVD 37415
  William Smith, prin.
Alpine Crest ES, STAGG ROAD 37415
  Charlotte Stiles, prin.
East Ridge ES, 1014 JOHN ROSS RD 37412
  Delbert Hale, prin.
McBrien ES, 1501 TOMBRAS AVE 37412
  Donald Beard, prin.
Red Bank ES, 3901 DAYTON BLVD 37415
  Bill Hampton, prin.
Spring Creek ES, 1100 SPRING CREEK RD 37412
  Jim Booth, prin.
Westview ES, 9629 E BRAINERD RD 37421
  James Kelley, prin.
White Oak ES, 901 ALTAMONT RD 37415
  Willena Byrd, prin.
Other Schools – See Apison, Birchwood, Harrison,
  Hixson, Lookout Mountain, Ooltewah, Sale Creek,
  Signal Mountain, Soddy-Daisy

Chattanooga Christian School
  3354 BROAD ST 37409
Avondale SDA School, 1824 WILSON ST 37406
Our Lady of Perpetual Help School
  501 S MOORE RD 37412
St. Jude School, 930 ASHLAND TER 37415
The Bright School, HIXSON PIKE 37405
The Lutheran School, 800 BELVOIR AVE 37412

Christiana, Rutherford Co.
Rutherford County SD
Supt. – See Murfreesboro
ES, RURAL ROUTE 01 37037 – Jane Harrell, prin.

Chuckey, Greene Co.
Greene County SD
Supt. – See Greeneville
ES, RURAL ROUTE 01 BOX 445 37641
  Tony Kerns, prin.

Washington County SD
Supt. – See Jonesborough
South Central ES, RURAL ROUTE 04 37641
  Dr. Roy Gillis, prin.

Church Hill, Hawkins Co., Pop. Code 5
Hawkins County SD
Supt. – See Rogersville
MS, P O BOX 38 37642 – James Saller, prin.
Carters Valley ES, RURAL ROUTE 04 37642
  James Childress, prin.
ES, P O BOX 365 37642 – Archie McMillan, prin.
McPheeters Bend ES, RURAL ROUTE 02 37642
  Charles Ladd, prin.
Mt. Carmel ES, 121 CHERRY ST 37642
  Quentin Dykes, prin.

Clairfield, Claiborne Co.
Clairborne County SD
Supt. – See Tazewell
ES 37715 – David Peterson, prin.

Clarkrange, Fentress Co., Pop. Code 5
Fentress County SD
Supt. – See Jamestown
ES 38553 – Clinton Linder, prin.

Clarksburg, Carroll Co., Pop. Code 2
South Carroll SD
Sch. Sys. Enr. Code 2
Supt. – Charles Meals, P O BOX 15 38324
S, P O BOX 15 38324 – Charles Meals, prin.

Clarksville, Montgomery Co., Pop. Code 8
Montgomery County SD
Sch. Sys. Enr. Code 7
Supt. – Johnny Miller, 501 FRANKLIN ST 37040
Greenwood MS, 430 GREENWOOD AVE 37040
  Joe Roberts, prin.
New Providence MS
  146 CUNNINGHAM LANE 37042
  James Darke, prin.
Richview MS, 2350 MEMORIAL DRIVE 37043
  Ewing Burchett, prin.
Barksdale ES, 1920 MADISON ST 37043
  Vernon Cooper, prin.
Burt MS, 110 BAILEY ST 37040
  Irene Gudgeon, prin.
Cumberland Heights ES, RURAL ROUTE 12 37040
  Wayne Mittler, prin.
Darden ES, 609 EAST ST 37042
  Flora Richbourg, prin.
East Montgomery ES
  RURAL ROUTE 08 BOX 255 37043
  Samuel Winters, prin.
Moore ES, 1350 MADISON ST 37040
  Lettie Kendall, prin.
Ringgold ES, RURAL ROUTE 09 BOX 437 37042
  Kenneth Hudson, prin.
Smith ES, 740 GREENWOOD AVE 37040
  Richard Billmyer, prin.
St. Bethlehem ES
  RURAL ROUTE 15 BOX 153 37040
  Evelyn Bell, prin.
Other Schools – See Cunningham, Woodlawn

Clarksville Academy, 710 N 2ND ST 37040

Cleveland, Bradley Co., Pop. Code 8
Bradley County SD
Sch. Sys. Enr. Code 6
Supt. – Dr. George Nerren, P O BOX 399 37364
Black Fox ES, RURAL ROUTE 06 37311
  Herbert Lackey, prin.
Blue Springs ES, RURAL ROUTE 01 37311
  Lebron Montgomery, prin.
East Cleveland ES
  1450 STRAWBERRY LN NE 37311
  Gerald Lillard, prin.
Hopewell ES, 5350 FREEWILL RD NW 37312
  Charles Flowers, prin.
Michigan Avenue ES
  RURAL ROUTE 09 BOX 144 37312
  David Holloway, prin.
North Lee ES, 205 SEQUOIA RD NW 37312
  Robert Ingram, prin.
Oak Grove ES, DURKEE ROAD 37311
  Roger Rowe, prin.
Prospect ES
  2450 PROSPECT SCHOOL RD NW 37312
  Terry Caywood, prin.
Taylors ES, BATGES PIKE 37311
  John Driver, prin.
Trewhitt ES, RURAL ROUTE 04 BOX 17 37311
  Sam Ledford, prin.
Valley View ES
  RURAL ROUTE 08 BOX 795 37311
  David Robinson, prin.
Waterville ES, RURAL ROUTE 01 37311
  Marvin Kirkpatrick, prin.
Other Schools – See Charleston, Mc Donald

Cleveland CSD
Sch. Sys. Enr. Code 5
Supt. – Dr. Donald Yates
  4300 MOUSE CREEK ROAD NW 37311
JHS, 852 RAIDER DRIVE NW 37311
  Ashley Smith, prin.
Arnold ES, 473 8TH ST NW 37311
  Leslie Cox, prin.
Blythe Avenue ES, 1075 BLYTHE AVE SE 37311
  Robert Dryman, prin.
Bower ES, 604 20TH ST SE 37311
  Robert Henley, Jr., prin.
Mayfield ES, 1201 MAGNOLIA AVE NE 37311
  Duane Shriver, prin.
Ross ES, 4340 MOUSE CREEK RD NW 37312
  Ann Culbreth, prin.
Stuart ES, 802 20TH ST NW 37311
  Edna Howard, prin.

Clinton, Anderson Co., Pop. Code 6
Anderson County SD
Sch. Sys. Enr. Code 6
Supt. – Charles Webber, COURTHOUSE 37716
Dutch Valley ES, RURAL ROUTE 02 37716
  Arnold Swain, prin.
Marlow ES, RURAL ROUTE 05 BOX 188 37716
  Roy Johnson, prin.
Shinliver ES, RURAL ROUTE 07 BOX 70 37716
  Linda Yarbrough, prin.
Other Schools – See Andersonville, Briceville,
  Devonia, Heiskell, Lake City, Norris, Oliver Springs,
  Powell

Clinton SD
Sch. Sys. Enr. Code 4
Supt. – H. Morrow, 209 HICKS ST N 37716
ES, 209 HICKS ST N 37716 – Gary Lukat, prin.
North Clinton ES, 305 BEETS ST 37716
  Tommy Giles, prin.
South Clinton ES
  RURAL ROUTE 06 BOX 118-1 37716
  Tim Stewart, prin.

Coalfield, Morgan Co., Pop. Code 5
Morgan County SD
Supt. – See Wartburg
S 37719 – Estel Underwood, prin.

Coalmont, Grundy Co., Pop. Code 3
Grundy County SD
Supt. – See Altamont
ES 37313 – Kenneth Driver, prin.

Collegedale, Hamilton Co., Pop. Code 5

Spalding ES, COLLEGE DR 37315

College Grove, Williamson Co.
Williamson County SD
Supt. – See Franklin
ES, RURAL ROUTE 01 37046 – Harold Ford, prin.

Collierville, Shelby Co., Pop. Code 6
Shelby County SD
Supt. – See Memphis
MS, 1101 N BYHALIA ROAD 38017
  Sherry Jamison, prin.
ES, 3414 PETERSON LAKE RD 38017
  Hazel Richmond, prin.

Collinwood, Wayne Co., Pop. Code 4
Wayne County SD
Supt. – See Waynesboro
MS, RURAL ROUTE 01 BOX 300 38450
  Bob Montgomery, prin.
ES, RURAL ROUTE 01 BOX 300 38450
  David Walker, prin.

Columbia, Maury Co., Pop. Code 8
Maury County SD
Sch. Sys. Enr. Code 6
Supt. – Bill Hobbs, 401 W 9TH ST 38401
Baker ES, HAMPSHIRE PARK 38401
  Eloise Dabney, prin.
Brown ES, CORD DR 38401 – Cecil Cathey, prin.
College Hill ES, P O BOX 770 38401
  Dr. Janet Edgin, prin.
Highland Park ES, 1612 HIGHLAND AVE 38401
  W. Whitlatch, prin.
McDowell ES, 714 W 7TH ST 38401
  Larry DuVall, prin.
Riverside ES, 205 CARTER ST 38401
  Vernon Brooks, prin.
Other Schools – See Culleoka, Hampshire, Mount
  Pleasant, Santa Fe, Spring Hill

Cookeville, Putnam Co., Pop. Code 7
Jackson County SD
Supt. – See Gainesboro
Dodsons Branch ES, RURAL ROUTE 03 38501
  Virginia Henshaw, prin.

Putnam County SD
Sch. Sys. Enr. Code 6
Supt. – Robert Hargis, 442 E SPRING ST 38501
Capshaw ES, 577 E HUDGENS ST 38501
  Leslie Roberts, prin.
Northeast ES, 575 OLD KENTUCKY RD 38501
  Arthur Thompson, prin.
Park View ES, 545 SCOTT AVE 38501
  Hollis Loftis, prin.
Sycamore ES, CRESCENT DR 38501
  Jerry Maynard, prin.
Whitson ES, 199 JERE WHITSON RD 38501
  Rhea Wilson, prin.
Other Schools – See Algood, Baxter, Monterey

Cordova, Shelby Co.
Shelby County SD
Supt. – See Memphis
Mt. Pisgah ES, 1444 PISGAH RD 38018
  Elizabeth Lane, prin.

St. Benedict HS
  2100 GERMANTOWN ROAD 38018

Cornersville, Marshall Co., Pop. Code 3
Marshall County SD
Supt. – See Lewisburg
S, RURAL ROUTE 01 37047 – Joe McKinney, prin.

Corryton, Knox Co., Pop. Code 4
Knox County SD
Supt. – See Knoxville
ES, 7200 CORRYTON RD 37721
  George Martin, prin.
Gibbs ES, RURAL ROUTE 04 37721
  Janet Cruze, prin.

Cosby, Cocke Co.
Cocke County SD
Supt. – See Newport
S, RURAL ROUTE 01 37722 – Fred James, prin.
Smoky Mountain ES, RURAL ROUTE 03 37722
  Paul Cogburn, prin.

Sevier County SD
Supt. – See Sevierville
Jones Cove ES, RURAL ROUTE 02 37722
  Mike Bookhart, prin.

Cottage Grove, Henry Co., Pop. Code 2
Henry County SD
Supt. – See Paris
ES 38224 – Don Cate, prin.

Cottontown, Sumner Co.
Sumner County SD
Supt. – See Gallatin
Oakmont ES, RURAL ROUTE 02 37048
Carl Newby, prin.

Counce, Hardin Co., Pop. Code 2
Hardin County SD
Supt. – See Savannah
South Side ES 38326 – Michael Alexander, prin.

Covington, Tipton Co., Pop. Code 6
Covington SD
Sch. Sys. Enr. Code 4
Supt. – Ray Newbill
764 BERT JOHNSTON AVE 38019
ES, 760 BERT JOHNSTON AVE 38019
Gordon Stone, prin.

Tipton County SD
Sch. Sys. Enr. Code 6
Supt. – Hyatt Williams, P O BOX 486 38019
Covington Crestview ES
RURAL ROUTE 02 BOX 800 38019
John Wells, prin.
Other Schools – See Brighton, Drummonds, Munford

Cowan, Franklin Co., Pop. Code 4
Franklin County SD
Supt. – See Winchester
ES, CUMBERLAND ST 37318
Raymond Council, prin.

Crab Orchard, Cumberland Co., Pop. Code 4
Cumberland County SD
Supt. – See Crossville
ES, GENERAL DELIVERY 37723
Roger Woody, prin.

Crawford, Overton Co.
Overton County SD
Supt. – See Livingston
Wilson ES, RURAL ROUTE 01 38554
Joe Core, prin.

Cross Plains, Robertson Co., Pop. Code 3
Robertson County SD
Supt. – See Springfield
East Robertson S, RURAL ROUTE 01 37049
Mark Stubblefield, prin.

Crossville, Cumberland Co., Pop. Code 6
Cumberland County SD
Sch. Sys. Enr. Code 6
Supt. – Arlon Way, P O BOX 567 38555
ES, 4TH ST 38555 – Maureen Hodges, prin.
Homestead ES, RURAL ROUTE 12 BOX 97 38555
Dana Winningham, prin.
North Cumberland ES
RURAL ROUTE 01 BOX 630 38555
Bruce Simmons, prin.
South Cumberland ES
RURAL ROUTE 11 BOX 316D 38555
Gordon Davis, prin.
Other Schools – See Crab Orchard, Pleasant Hill,
Rockwood

Culleoka, Maury Co.
Maury County SD
Supt. – See Columbia
S, RURAL ROUTE 01 BOX 128 38451
Harry Underwood, prin.

Cunningham, Montgomery Co.
Montgomery County SD
Supt. – See Clarksville
Central ES, RURAL ROUTE 01 BOX 4 37052
Nancy Grant, prin.

Dandridge, Jefferson Co., Pop. Code 4
Jefferson County SD
Sch. Sys. Enr. Code 6
Supt. – William Taylor, P O BOX 190 37725
Maury MS, P O BOX 336 37725 – Tom Bettis, prin.
ES, P O BOX 0 37725 – Eldridge Bryant, prin.
Piedmont ES, RURAL ROUTE 05 BOX 321 37725
Bertie French, prin.
Other Schools – See Jefferson City, New Market,
Strawberry Plains, Talbott, White Pine

Dayton, Rhea Co., Pop. Code 6
Dayton SD
Sch. Sys. Enr. Code 3
Supt. – Richard Fisher, 502 S CHERRY ST 37321
Dayton City ES, 502 S CHERRY ST 37321
Richard Fisher, prin.

Rhea County SD
Sch. Sys. Enr. Code 5
Supt. – Dr. Patricia Christi, MONTAGUE ST 37321
Frazier ES, RURAL ROUTE 01 BOX 606 37321
Dallas Smith, prin.
Rhea Central ES, 208 E 4TH AVE 37321
Patrick Conner, prin.
Waldens Ridge ES
RURAL ROUTE 03 BOX 86 37321
Dicke Kucharski, prin.
Other Schools – See Evensville, Graysville, Spring
City

Decatur, Meigs Co., Pop. Code 4
Meigs County SD
Sch. Sys. Enr. Code 4
Supt. – Robert Greene, P O BOX 68 37322
Meigs Consolidated S, P O BOX 128 37322
Dorie Harmon, prin.
Cedar Valley ES
RURAL ROUTE 03 BOX 100 37322
Roy Lillard, prin.
Fairview ES, RURAL ROUT3 01 BOX 573 37322
Phyllis Bryant, prin.
Other Schools – See Georgetown, Ten Mile

Decaturville, Decatur Co., Pop. Code 4
Decatur County SD
Sch. Sys. Enr. Code 4
Supt. – J. Wayne Stanfill, P O BOX 160 38329
ES 38329 – Danny Adkisson, prin.
Other Schools – See Parsons, Scotts Hill

Decherd, Franklin Co., Pop. Code 4
Franklin County SD
Supt. – See Winchester
ES, BRATTON ST 37324 – Carl Burnette, prin.
Oak Grove ES, RURAL ROUTE 03 37324
Wayne Photon, prin.

Del Rio, Cocke Co.
Cocke County SD
Supt. – See Newport
ES, RURAL ROUTE 01 37727 – Connie Ball, prin.

Denmark, Madison Co., Pop. Code 1
Madison County SD
Supt. – See Jackson
ES, 980 DENMARK ROAD 38391
Ernest Golden, prin.

Devonia, Anderson Co.
Anderson County SD
Supt. – See Clinton
Rosedale ES, RURAL ROUTE 01 BOX 425 37728
Douglas MacAllister, prin.

Dickson, Dickson Co., Pop. Code 6
Dickson County SD
Supt. – See Charlotte
ES, 120 W BROAD ST 37055 – Gary Brunett, prin.
Oakmont ES, 220 MCLEMORE ST 37055
Linda Fox, prin.
Sullivan J. E. MS, HENSLEE DR 37055
Warner Martin, prin.

Dover, Stewart Co., Pop. Code 4
Stewart County SD
Sch. Sys. Enr. Code 4
Supt. – Van Riggins, P O BOX 40 37058
ES, P O BOX 130 37058 – Phillip Wallace, prin.
Other Schools – See Big Rock

Doyle, White Co., Pop. Code 2
White County SD
Supt. – See Sparta
ES 38559 – Michael Ryan, prin.

Dresden, Weakley Co., Pop. Code 4
Weakley County SD
Sch. Sys. Enr. Code 6
Supt. – Ernestine McWherter, P O BOX 71 38225
JHS, N WILSON ST 38225 – Richard Barber, prin.
ES, N WILSON ST 38225 – Winnie Moore, prin.
Other Schools – See Gleason, Greenfield, Martin,
Palmersville, Sharon

Drummonds, Tipton Co.
Tipton County SD
Supt. – See Covington
ES, P O BOX 178 38023 – Morris Jones, prin.

Ducktown, Polk Co.
Polk County SD
Supt. – See Benton
ES 37326 – David Cook, prin.

Duff, Campbell Co.
Campbell County SD
Supt. – See Jacksboro
Wynn-Habersham S
RURAL ROUTE 01 BOX 286 37729
E. Morton, prin.
White Oak ES, RURAL ROUTE 01 37729
Raymond Kahre, prin.

Dunlap, Sequatchie Co., Pop. Code 5
Sequatchie County SD
Sch. Sys. Enr. Code 4
Supt. – Myrna Barker, P O BOX 488 37327
Sequatchie County JHS, P O BOX 728 37327
Ed Hobbs, prin.
Griffith ES, P O BOX 818 37327
Idell Payne, prin.
Sequatchie County MS, P O BOX 788 37327
Jimmy Worley, prin.

Dyer, Gibson Co., Pop. Code 4
Gibson CSD
Sch. Sys. Enr. Code 4
Supt. – Bill Carey, P O BOX D 38330
ES, 322 E COLLEGE ST 38330
Lynn Tucker, prin.
Other Schools – See Medina, Rutherford, Trenton,
Yorkville

Dyersburg, Dyer Co., Pop. Code 7
Dyer County SD
Sch. Sys. Enr. Code 5
Supt. – Dr. Dwight L. Hedge
159 EVERETT ST 38024

Dyer County Central ES, HORNBROOK ST 38024
Bobby Bowen, prin.
Fifth Consolidated ES, P O BOX 1270 38025
Anne Kirk, prin.
Other Schools – See Bogota, Finley, Fowlkes,
Newbern, Trimble

Dyersburg CSD
Sch. Sys. Enr. Code 5
Supt. – Dr. Wade Roby, 1025 PHILLIPS ST 38024
MS, 305 COLLEGE ST 38024 – Edward Eller, prin.
IS, TIBBS ST 38024 – Oscar Bruce, prin.
PS, LEWIS AVE 38024 – Maurice Jones, prin.

Eagleville, Rutherford Co., Pop. Code 2
Rutherford County SD
Supt. – See Murfreesboro
S 37060 – James Russ, prin.

Eidson, Hawkins Co., Pop. Code 4
Hawkins County SD
Supt. – See Rogersville
Clinch S, RURAL ROUTE 01 37731
Melville Bailey, prin.

Elizabethton, Carter Co., Pop. Code 7
Carter County SD
Sch. Sys. Enr. Code 6
Supt. – John Hall, ACADEMY ST 37643
Happy Valley MS
RURAL ROUTE 11 BOX 3400 37643
Jerry Hinkle, prin.
Siam MS, RURAL ROUTE 01 BOX 2965 37643
W. Wilkins, prin.
Hunter ES, RURAL ROUTE 07 BOX 2785 37643
Harley Carden, prin.
Keenburg ES, RURAL ROUTE 09 BOX 256 37643
James Ellis, prin.
Southside ES, RURAL ROUTE 09 37643
(—), prin.
Unaka ES, RURAL ROUTE 10 BOX 1150 37643
Ronald Taylor, prin.
Valley Forge ES
RURAL ROUTE 08 BOX 330 37643
John Hopson, prin.
Other Schools – See Butler, Hampton, Johnson City,
Roan Mountain, Watauga

Elizabethton CSD
Sch. Sys. Enr. Code 5
Supt. – David Wetzel
RURAL ROUTE 09 BOX 8 37643
Dugger JHS, 306 E ST W 37643
Larry White, prin.
East Side ES, SIAM ROAD 37643
Frank Baker, prin.
McCormick ES, CEDAR AVE 37643
W. Armstrong, prin.
West Side ES, BURGIE ST 37643
Thomas Little, prin.

Elkton, Giles Co., Pop. Code 3
Giles County SD
Supt. – See Pulaski
ES 38455 – Larry Gillespie, prin.

Elmwood, Smith Co.
Smith County SD
Supt. – See Carthage
Forks River ES, RURAL ROUTE 01 38560
Ronnie Scudder, prin.

Englewood, McMinn Co., Pop. Code 4
McMinn County SD
Supt. – See Athens
ES 37329 – David Decker, prin.

Erin, Houston Co., Pop. Code 4
Houston County SD
Sch. Sys. Enr. Code 4
Supt. – O. S. Uffelman, P O BOX 209 37061
ES, HWY 13 37061 – Jack Norwood, prin.
Other Schools – See Tennessee Ridge

Erwin, Unicoi Co., Pop. Code 5
Unicoi County SD
Sch. Sys. Enr. Code 5
Supt. – Ronald Wilcox, 600 ELM AVE N 37650
Evans ES, 600 MOHAWK DR S 37650
D. Rogers, prin.
Love Chapel ES, RURAL ROUTE 03 37650
Tommy Clouse, prin.
Martin Chapel ES, 900 HOBACK AVE 37650
James Hatcher, prin.
Rock Creek ES, E ERWIN RD 37650
Hazel Higgins, prin.
Temple Hill ES, RURAL ROUTE 02 37650
Steve White, prin.
Other Schools – See Flag Pond, Unicoi

Estill Springs, Franklin Co., Pop. Code 4
Franklin County SD
Supt. – See Winchester
Rock Creek ES, RURAL ROUTE 01 37330
Danny Brown, prin.

Ethridge, Lawrence Co., Pop. Code 3
Lawrence County SD
Supt. – See Lawrenceburg
ES, 601 RED HILL RD 38456
Melvin Allison, prin.

Etowah, McMinn Co., Pop. Code 5
Etowah SD
Sch. Sys. Enr. Code 2
Supt. – Michael Reeves,Sr., 858 8TH ST 37331
ES, 858 8TH ST 37331
Dr. Nancy Boardman, prin.

McMinn County SD
Supt. – See Athens
Mountain View ES, RURAL ROUTE 02   37331
  (—), prin.

Evensville, Rhea Co., Pop. Code 2
Rhea County SD
Supt. – See Dayton
ES, RURAL ROUTE 02 BOX 140   37332
  Phyllis Smith, prin.

Fairview, Williamson Co., Pop. Code 5
Williamson County SD
Supt. – See Franklin
MS, 1928 FAIRVIEW BLVD W   37062
  Terry Blackman, prin.
ES, 1708 FAIRVIEW BLVD W   37062
  Robert Cantrell, prin.

Fall Branch, Washington Co.
Washington County SD
Supt. – See Jonesborough
ES   37656 – Susan Kiernan, prin.

Fayetteville, Lincoln Co., Pop. Code 6
Fayetteville CSD
Sch. Sys. Enr. Code 3
Supt. – Dr. R. Earl Thomas
  219 COLLEGE ST E   37334
Askins ES, 901 SHADY LN   37334
  Barbara Vannatta, prin.

Lincoln County SD
Sch. Sys. Enr. Code 5
Supt. – Robert Gray, 208 DAVIDSON ST E   37334
Eighth District ES, 1107 HEDGEMONT AVE   37334
  Greg Holder, prin.
Highland Rim ES, RURAL ROUTE 08   37334
  Leonard McGrath, prin.
Other Schools – See Flintville, Petersburg, Taft

Finley, Dyer Co.
Dyer County SD
Supt. – See Dyersburg
ES, P O BOX K   38030 – Danny Walden, prin.

Flag Pond, Unicoi Co.
Unicoi County SD
Supt. – See Erwin
ES, RURAL ROUTE 01   37657
  Michael Scott, prin.

Flintville, Lincoln Co., Pop. Code 5
Lincoln County SD
Supt. – See Fayetteville
ES, RURAL ROUTE 01 BOX 274   37335
  Louis Bledsoe, prin.

Fowlkes, Dyer Co.
Dyer County SD
Supt. – See Dyersburg
Powell ES, P O BOX 98   38033 – Fay Bowen, prin.

Franklin, Williamson Co., Pop. Code 7
Franklin CSD
Sch. Sys. Enr. Code 5
Supt. – Joseph D. Brown
  303 FAIRGROUND ST   37064
ES, 1408 CANNON ST   37064 – Kay Awalt, prin.
MS, 303 FAIRGROUND ST   37064
  Mary Mills, prin.
Johnson ES, MT HOPE ST   37064
  Laura Bracy, prin.
Liberty ES, 600 LIBERTY PIKE   37064
  Bill Marley, prin.

Williamson County SD
Sch. Sys. Enr. Code 7
Supt. – Kenneth Fleming
  1320 W MAIN #202   37064
Grassland MS, RURAL ROUTE 05   37064
  Ann Vaughan, prin.
Page MS, RURAL ROUTE 01   37064
  Mayes Waters, prin.
Grassland ES, RURAL ROUTE 07   37064
  William Hurt, prin.
Hillsboro ES, RURAL ROUTE 06   37064
  Gary York, prin.
Trinity ES, RURAL ROUTE 05   37064
  Brenda Cratty, prin.
Other Schools – See Brentwood, College Grove,
  Fairview, Nolensville, Primm Springs, Thompsons
  Station

Harpeth Academy, 150 FRANKLIN RD   37064

Friendship, Crockett Co., Pop. Code 3
Crockett County SD
Supt. – See Alamo
ES, P O BOX 67   38034 – Nancy Colvett, prin.

Friendsville, Blount Co., Pop. Code 3
Blount County SD
Supt. – See Maryville
ES, P O BOX 119   37737 – Leroy Painter, prin.

Gadsden, Crockett Co., Pop. Code 3
Crockett County SD
Supt. – See Alamo
ES, RURAL ROUTE 01   38337 – Hal Fisher, prin.

Gainesboro, Jackson Co., Pop. Code 4
Jackson County SD
Sch. Sys. Enr. Code 4
Supt. – Ed Smith, P O BOX 95   38562
Fox MS, 707 SCHOOL DRIVE   38562
  Angelia Smith, prin.

ES, 611 S MAIN ST   38562
  Jimmy Anderson, prin.
Other Schools – See Cookeville

Gallatin, Sumner Co., Pop. Code 7
Sumner County SD
Sch. Sys. Enr. Code 7
Supt. – Benny Bills
  117 E WINCHESTER ST   37066
MS, 695 SCOTTSVILLE PIKE   37066
  Jim Gilmore, prin.
Guild ES, HWY 109 S   37066 – Joe Brown, prin.
Howard ES, LONG HOLLOW PARK   37066
  Tom Hughes, prin.
Stewart MS, SMALL ST   37066
  Andrew Turner, prin.
Union MS, 516 CARSON ST   37066
  Pat Webb, prin.
Other Schools – See Bethpage, Cottontown,
  Goodlettsville, Hendersonville, Portland,
  Westmoreland, White House

Gatlinburg, Sevier Co., Pop. Code 5
Sevier County SD
Supt. – See Sevierville
Pi Beta Phi ES   37738 – Al Cardiel, prin.

Georgetown, Meigs Co.
Meigs County SD
Supt. – See Decatur
Eastview ES, RURAL ROUTE 01 BOX 257   37336
  Chris Ziegler, prin.

Germantown, Shelby Co., Pop. Code 7
Shelby County SD
Supt. – See Memphis
MS, 2734 CROSS COUNTRY DRIVE   38138
  Theodore Wells, prin.
Dogwood ES, 8945 DOGWOOD RD   38138
  Patsy Smith, prin.
Farmington ES, 2085 CORDES RD   38138
  Hazel Goodale, prin.
ES, 2730 CROSS COUNTRY DR   38138
  Marjorie Bradford, prin.
Riverdale ES, 7391 NESHOBA RD   38138
  (—), prin.

Gladeville, Wilson Co.
Wilson County SD
Supt. – See Lebanon
ES   37071 – Jane Atwood, prin.

Gleason, Weakley Co., Pop. Code 4
Weakley County SD
Supt. – See Dresden
S, FRONT ST   38229 – Jerry Simmons, prin.

Goodlettsville, Davidson Co., Pop. Code 6
Davidson County SD
Supt. – See Nashville
MS, 300 S MAIN ST   37072 – Hugh Price, prin.
ES, 514 DONALD ST   37072 – Mary Granstaff, prin.
Old Center ES, 1245 S MAIN ST   37072
  Helen Stratton, prin.
Union Hill ES, 1538 UNION HILL RD   37072
  Everett Hamner, prin.

Sumner County SD
Supt. – See Gallatin
Millersville ES, 1225 LOUISVILLE HWY   37072
  Phoebe Kitts, prin.

Gordonsville, Smith Co., Pop. Code 3
Smith County SD
Supt. – See Carthage
S, MAIN ST   38563 – Carol Sykes, prin.
New Middleton ES, RURAL ROUTE 01   38563
  Becky Hackett, prin.

Grand Junction, Hardeman Co., Pop. Code 2
Hardeman County SD
Supt. – See Bolivar
ES   38039 – Allie Greene, prin.

Gray, Washington Co.
Washington County SD
Supt. – See Jonesborough
Boones Creek ES
  RURAL ROUTE 15 BOX 289   37615
  Reece Jamerson, prin.
ES, RURAL ROUTE 11 BOX 2   37615
  Jane Wright, prin.

Graysville, Rhea Co., Pop. Code 4
Rhea County SD
Supt. – See Dayton
ES   37338 – Barbara Mauldin, prin.

Greenback, Loudon Co., Pop. Code 3
Loudon County SD
Supt. – See Loudon
S, CHILHOWEE AVE   37742 – Helen Cole, prin.

Greenbrier, Robertson Co., Pop. Code 5
Robertson County SD
Supt. – See Springfield
MS, HIGHWAY 41   37073 – Faye Taylor, prin.
ES, HWY 41   37073 – Clyde Witherspoon, prin.

Greeneville, Greene Co., Pop. Code 7
Greene County SD
Sch. Sys. Enr. Code 6
Supt. – James Parham, 111 UNION ST   37743
Baileyton ES, BAILEYTON STATION   37743
  Kenneth Bailey, prin.
Camp Creek ES, RURAL ROUTE 10   37743
  Lena Ensor, prin.

DeBusk ES, RURAL ROUTE 04   37743
  Bill Jones, prin.
Doak ES, TUSCULUM STATION   37743
  John Howe, prin.
Glenwood ES, RURAL ROUTE 01   37743
  Larry Neas, prin.
Greystone ES, RURAL ROUTE 09   37743
  Paul Fox,Jr., prin.
Nolachuckey ES, RURAL ROUTE 04   37743
  Buford Neas, prin.
Ottway ES, RURAL ROUTE 06   37743
  Owen Hensley,Jr., prin.
Sunnyside ES, RURAL ROUTE 10   37743
  Jerry Scott, prin.
West Pines ES, RURAL ROUTE 12   37743
  William Huffman, prin.
Other Schools – See Afton, Chuckey, Mohawk,
  Mosheim

Greeneville CSD
Sch. Sys. Enr. Code 5
Supt. – Dr. Ben Hankins, P O BOX 1420   37744
MS, 909 VANN ROAD   37743 – Joyce Bales, prin.
Eastview ES, BERNARD AVE   37743
  Robert Keasling, prin.
Henard ES, 920 VANN RD   37743 – R. Jordan, prin.
Highland ES, 208 N HIGHLAND AVE   37743
  J. Sams, prin.
Tusculum View ES, 1617 LAFAYETTE ST   37743
  Kenneth Grubb, prin.

Greenfield, Weakley Co., Pop. Code 4
Weakley County SD
Supt. – See Dresden
ES, 319 W MAIN ST   38230 – Richard Ward, prin.

Grimsley, Fentress Co.
Fentress County SD
Supt. – See Jamestown
ES   38565 – Cecil Franklin, prin.

Halls, Lauderdale Co., Pop. Code 4
Lauderdale County SD
Supt. – See Ripley
ES, WEST TIGRETT   38040 – David Carmack, prin.

Hampshire, Maury Co.
Maury County SD
Supt. – See Columbia
S, RURAL ROUTE 01   BOX 22   38461
  Rex Hines, prin.

Hampton, Carter Co., Pop. Code 3
Carter County SD
Supt. – See Elizabethton
ES, RURAL ROUTE 02 BOX 58   37658
  Gary Smith, prin.

Harriman, Roane Co., Pop. Code 6
Harriman CSD
Sch. Sys. Enr. Code 4
Supt. – Lucille Buttram, 1001 ROANE ST   37748
Cumberland MS, CUMBERLAND ST   37748
  James Reeves, prin.
South Harriman MS
  RURAL ROUTE 06 BOX 25   37748
  Ray Andrews, prin.
Bowers ES, RURAL ROUTE 06 BOX 122   37748
  Marion Crabtree, prin.
Central ES, 500 GEORGIA ST   37748
  William Powers, prin.
Walnut Hill ES, RURAL ROUTE 05 BOX 56   37748
  Larry Sills, prin.

Roane County SD
Supt. – See Kingston
Dyllis ES, RURAL ROUTE 02   37748
  Donald McKinney, prin.
Midtown ES, RURAL ROUTE 08 BOX 188   37748
  Jim Whittenbarger, prin.

Harrison, Hamilton Co., Pop. Code 2
Hamilton County SD
Supt. – See Chattanooga
Brown MS, 5716 HWY 58   37341
  Curtis Drake, prin.
ES, 5637 HWY 58   37341 – C. Fraley, prin.

Harrogate, Claiborne Co.
Clairborne County SD
Supt. – See Tazewell
Forge Ridge S, RURAL ROUTE 02   BOX 164   37752
  (—), prin.
Livesay MS, P O BOX 460   37752
  Don Wilder, prin.
Myers ES   37752 – Troy Poore, prin.

Hartford, Cocke Co.
Cocke County SD
Supt. – See Newport
Grassy Fork ES, RURAL ROUTE 01   37753
  Martha Lowe, prin.
ES, GENERAL DELIVERY   37753
  Alfred Hogan, prin.

Hartsville, Trousdale Co., Pop. Code 5
Trousdale County SD
Sch. Sys. Enr. Code 4
Supt. – Jim B. Satterfield, 214 BROADWAY   37074
Trousdale County ES   37074 – Floyd Jackson, prin.

Heiskell, Knox Co.
Anderson County SD
Supt. – See Clinton
Fairview ES, RURAL ROUTE 01   37754
  Pattie Ragsdale, prin.

Henderson, Chester Co., Pop. Code 5
Chester County SD
Sch. Sys. Enr. Code 4
Supt. – Kathy Coatney, P O BOX 327   38340
Chester County JHS, HIGHWAY 100 E   38340
Joann Jones, prin.
East Chester County ES, HWY 100 E   38340
Linda Patterson, prin.
North Chester County MS, 524 LURAY AVE   38340
Harold James, prin.
West Chester County ES, HWY 100 W   38340
Guy Weaver, prin.
Other Schools – See Jacks Creek

Hendersonville, Sumner Co., Pop. Code 8
Sumner County SD
Supt. – See Gallatin
Hunter MS, RURAL ROUTE 01   37075
Tom Bruce, prin.
Beech ES, RURAL ROUTE 01   37075
Sam Massey, prin.
Berry ES, 138 INDIAN LAKE RD   37075
Vaun Smith, prin.
ES, 115 GAIL DR   37075 – Bobby Timmons, prin.
Indian Lake ES, 505 INDIAN LAKE RD   37075
Jane Reynolds, prin.
Lakeside Park ES, 204 DOLPHUS DR   37075
Opal Poe, prin.
Walton Ferry ES, 732 WALTON FERRY RD   37075
B. Russell, prin.
Wessington Place ES, 140 SCOTCH ST   37075
George Whitten, prin.

Henry, Henry Co., Pop. Code 2
Henry County SD
Supt. – See Paris
ES   38231 – Jerry Muzzall, prin.

Hermitage, Davidson Co.
Davidson County SD
Supt. – See Nashville
Dupont MS, 431 TYLER DRIVE   37076
Nelda Watts, prin.
Dodson ES, 4401 CHANDLER RD   37076
Carl Ross, prin.
ES, 6000 PLANTATION DR   37076
Willie Nixon, prin.

Hilham, Overton Co.
Overton County SD
Supt. – See Livingston
ES   38568 – James Bilbrey, prin.

Hillsboro, Coffee Co.
Coffee County SD
Supt. – See Manchester
ES, RURAL ROUTE 02 BOX 140   37342
James Simons, prin.

Hixson, Hamilton Co.
Chattanooga CSD
Supt. – See Chattanooga
Big Ridge ES
5210 CASSANDRA SMITH RD   37343
Mary Uchytil, prin.
ES, WINDING LANE   37343
Kenneth Wilson, prin.

Hamilton County SD
Supt. – See Chattanooga
Falling Water ES, 715 ROBERTS MILL RD   37343
Charles Peavyhouse, prin.
Ganns Mid Valley ES
1609 THRASHER PIKE   37343
Warren Roberts, prin.
McConnell ES, 8629 COLUMBUS RD   37343
Sandra Black, prin.

Hohenwald, Lewis Co., Pop. Code 5
Lewis County SD
Sch. Sys. Enr. Code 4
Supt. – Kenny Graves, 206 S COURT ST   38462
Lewis County MS, PARK AVE   38462
William Lynch, prin.
Lewis County ES, S OAK ST   38462
Barbara Hinson, prin.

Holladay, Benton Co.
Benton County SD
Supt. – See Camden
ES   38341 – Robert Bowling, prin.

Hornbeak, Obion Co., Pop. Code 2
Obion County SD
Supt. – See Union City
Black Oak ES, SHAWTOWN ROAD   38232
Ronnie Yoes, prin.

Hornsby, Hardeman Co., Pop. Code 2
Hardeman County SD
Supt. – See Bolivar
ES   38044 – Hugholene Barnes, prin.

Humboldt, Gibson Co., Pop. Code 7
Humboldt CSD
Sch. Sys. Enr. Code 5
Supt. – J. Ralph Mays, 1421 OSBORNE   38343
East End ES, 1560 N 30TH AVE   38343
Ann Williams, prin.
Main Street ES, 1751 E MAIN ST   38343
Catherine Forsyth, prin.
Stigall MS, 200 N 1ST AVE   38343
Neal Jones, prin.

Huntingdon, Carroll Co., Pop. Code 5
Huntingdon CSD
Sch. Sys. Enr. Code 4
Supt. – Billy Crum, P O BOX 648   38344

MS   38344 – Lynn Twyman, prin.
PS   38344 – Clarnece Barham,Jr., prin.

Huntland, Franklin Co., Pop. Code 3
Franklin County SD
Supt. – See Winchester
S, GORE ST   37345 – Randall Brewer, prin.

Huntsville, Scott Co., Pop. Code 3
Scott County SD
Sch. Sys. Enr. Code 5
Supt. – Edgar Culver, P O BOX 37   37756
MS   37756 – Frank Blakeley, prin.
Fairview ES   37756 – T. Lay, prin.
ES   37756 – George Sexton, prin.
Other Schools – See Oneida, Robbins, Winfield

Huron, Henderson Co.
Henderson County SD
Supt. – See Lexington
West Over ES   38345 – Nancy Wilson, prin.

Jacksboro, Campbell Co., Pop. Code 4
Campbell County SD
Sch. Sys. Enr. Code 6
Supt. – Kenneth Miller, P O BOX 445   37757
MS   37757 – Linda Agee, prin.
ES   37757 – Eugene Lawson, prin.
Other Schools – See Caryville, Duff, Jellico, La
Follette, Newcomb, Pioneer

Jacks Creek, Chester Co.
Chester County SD
Supt. – See Henderson
ES, GENERAL DELIVERY   38347
Jimmy Dyer, prin.

Jackson, Madison Co., Pop. Code 8
Jackson CSD
Sch. Sys. Enr. Code 6
Supt. – Thomas Allen, 100 E MAIN ST   38301
Alexander ES, 900 N HIGHLAND AVE   38301
Buford Matlock, prin.
Douglass ES, ISELIN ST   38301
Louvella McClellan, prin.
Highland Park ES, 617 W FOREST AVE   38301
David Bratcher, prin.
ES, 211 OLD HICKORY BLVD   38301
C. Powers, prin.
Lincoln ES, BERRY ST   38301
Mavis Johnson, prin.
Parkview ES, CHESTER ST   38301
Cleo Boyd, prin.
West Jackson ES, 227 MCCOWAT ST   38301
Macine Stewart, prin.
Whitehall ES, 532 WHITEHALL ST   38301
Phinehas Hegmon, prin.

Madison County SD
Sch. Sys. Enr. Code 6
Supt. – Buddy McMillin
701 S HIGHLAND AVE   38301
East MS, RURAL ROUTE 08   38305
Stanley Smith, prin.
Malesus ES, BOLIVAR HWY   38301
Jimmy Arnold, prin.
Nova ES, RURAL ROUTE 04   38305
Lora Murchison, prin.
Pope ES, RURAL ROUTE 01   38305
Leeoard Pearson, prin.
Young ES, 236 D ST   38301 – Jimmy Morris, prin.
Other Schools – See Beech Bluff, Denmark, Pinson

Episcopal Day School
1981 HOLLYWOOD DR   38305
St. Mary's School, 1665 HIGHWAY 45 BYP   38305

Jamestown, Fentress Co., Pop. Code 4
Fentress County SD
Sch. Sys. Enr. Code 5
Supt. – Casper Wright, P O BOX L   38556
Pine Haven ES, RC ROUTE   38556
Georgia Tate, prin.
Roslin ES, RURAL ROUTE 01   38556
Shirley York, prin.
West Fentress ES, RURAL ROUTE 03   38556
Ernest Campbell, prin.
York ES, P O BOX 310   38556
David Conatser, prin.
Other Schools – See Allardt, Clarkrange, Grimsley,
Pall Mall

Jasper, Marion Co., Pop. Code 5
Marion County SD
Sch. Sys. Enr. Code 5
Supt. – John Shelley
326 BETSY PACK DRIVE   37347
MS   37347 – Earline Ross, prin.
ES   37347 – Richard Sisemore, prin.
Other Schools – See Monteagle, South Pittsburg,
Whitwell

Jefferson City, Jefferson Co., Pop. Code 6
Jefferson County SD
Supt. – See Dandridge
Jefferson MS, HIGHWAY 11 E   37760
Phil Kindred, prin.
Jefferson ES, HWY 11 EAST   37760
Bill Nolen, prin.

Jellico, Campbell Co., Pop. Code 5
Campbell County SD
Supt. – See Jacksboro
ES   37762 – Gene Prewitt, prin.

Joelton, Davidson Co.
Davidson County SD
Supt. – See Nashville
MS, 3500 OLD CLARKSVILLE PIKE   37080
Sharon Anthony, prin.
ES, 5880 WHITES CREEK PIKE   37080
Robert Dorris, prin.
Morny ES, 5880 EATONS CREEK RD   37080
Dollene Myles, prin.

Johnson City, Washington Co., Pop. Code 8
Carter County SD
Supt. – See Elizabethton
Central ES, RURAL ROUTE 05 BOX 440   37601
Clyde Curde, prin.
Happy Valley ES, RURAL ROUTE 05   37601
Larry Bunton, prin.

Johnson City CSD
Sch. Sys. Enr. Code 6
Supt. – Dr. Mike Simmons
P O BOX 1517   37605
Cherokee ES, RURAL ROUTE 10   37604
Wendell Messimer, prin.
Fairmont ES, 1405 LESTER HARRIS RD   37601
John Phillips, prin.
Johnson ES, 820 MARKET ST W   37604
Jerry Cole, prin.
Keystone ES, 603 BERT ST   37601
Barbara Beckett, prin.
King Springs ES, KINGS SPRINGS ROAD   37601
Sarah Odom, prin.
North Side ES, CHILHOWIE & N ROAN STS   37601
Lorenzo Wyatt, prin.
South Side ES, SOUTHWEST & BOYD STS   37601
John Boyd, prin.
Stratton ES, 500 OAKLAND AVE E   37601
Gerald Malcolm, prin.
Towne Acres ES, 2310 LARKSPUR DR   37604
Annette Bowman, prin.

Washington County SD
Supt. – See Jonesborough
University S, EAST TN STATE UNIV   37614
Sam Humphreys, prin.
Boones Creek MS
RURAL ROUTE 14   BOX 495   37615
Max Williams, prin.
Asbury ES, 2002 INDIAN RIDGE RD   37604
Hobart Powell, prin.

St. Mary School, 227 1/2 MARKET ST E   37604

Jonesborough, Washington Co., Pop. Code 5
Washington County SD
Sch. Sys. Enr. Code 6
Supt. – John McKinney
405 W COLLEGE ST   37659
MS, 308 FOREST DRIVE   37659
Terry Crowe, prin.
ES, 306 FOREST DR   37659 – Gary Fair, prin.
Lamar ES, RURAL ROUTE 08   37659
Jerry Boswell, prin.
Sulphur Springs ES, RURAL ROUTE 05   37659
Helen Zeller, prin.
Other Schools – See Chuckey, Fall Branch, Gray,
Johnson City, Limestone

Kenton, Obion Co., Pop. Code 4
Obion County SD
Supt. – See Union City
ES, 300 N COLLEGE ST   38233 – Sandy Pitts, prin.

Kingsport, Sullivan Co., Pop. Code 8
Kingsport CSD
Sch. Sys. Enr. Code 6
Supt. – Charles Tollett, 1701 E CENTER ST   37664
Palmer Center S, 1609 FORT HENRY DRIVE   37664
Lowell Biller, prin.
Robinson MS, JESSIE ST   37664
William Clark, prin.
Sevier MS, 1200 WATEREE ST   37660
Jana Lewis, prin.
Jackson ES, 600 JACKSON ST   37660
Dr. Gary Martin, prin.
Jefferson ES, 2216 WESTMORELAND AVE   37664
Dalton Bloomer, prin.
Johnson ES, ORMOND DR   37664
Thomas Milam, prin.
Lincoln ES, 1000 SUMMER ST   37664
Edmund Abbott, prin.
Washington ES, 205 E SEVIER AVE   37660
Richard Everroad, prin.

Sullivan County SD
Supt. – See Blountville
Colonial Heights MS, 415 LEBANON ROAD   37663
Norman Tunnell, prin.
Ketron MS, 3301 BLOOMINGDALE PIKE   37660
Clyde Groseclose, prin.
Lynn View MS, 256 WALKER ST   37665
David Ward, prin.
Sullivan MS, 4154 S WILCOX DRIVE   37660
Prezzel Quillen, prin.
Brookside ES, 301 BROOKSIDE DR   37660
Sherman Harrison, prin.
Cedar Grove ES, 100 COLEY ST   37660
Orville Cantrell, prin.
Gravely ES, 647 GRAVELLY RD   37660
Ray Willis, prin.
Indian Springs ES, RURAL ROUTE 13   37664
F. Brown, prin.
Kingsley ES, 100 EMORY LN   37660
Sharon Crutchfield, prin.
Lynn Garden ES, 1500 WOODLAND AVE   37665
James Dixon, prin.

Perry ES, RURAL ROUTE 12   37663
  Leatrice Prescott, prin.
Rock Springs ES
  RURAL ROUTE 17 BOX 75   37664
  Allen Hendrickson, prin.
Sullivan ES, 209 ROSEMONT ST   37660
  Waymond Begley, prin.
West View ES, 1051 LAKE ST   37660
  Steve Odom, prin.

Kingston, Roane Co., Pop. Code 5
Roane County SD
Sch. Sys. Enr. Code 6
Supt. – Jess Plemons, 100 BLUFF ROAD   37763
Cherokee MS
  200 PAINT ROCK FERRY ROAD   37763
  Jody McLoud, prin.
ES, 520 CUMBERLAND ST W   37763
  Robert Morton, prin.
Midway ES, RURAL ROUTE 01 BOX 188   37763
  Glenn Wheaton, prin.
Other Schools – See Harriman, Oliver Springs,
  Rockwood

Kingston Springs, Cheatham Co., Pop. Code 4
Cheatham County SD
Supt. – See Ashland City
ES, MT PLEASANT ROAD   37082
  Betty Davidson, prin.

Knoxville, Knox Co., Pop. Code 9
Knox County SD
Sch. Sys. Enr. Code 8
Supt. – Earl Hoffmeister, P O BOX 2188   37901
Bearden MS, 1000 FRANCIS ROAD NW   37919
  Mary Kanipe, prin.
Beardsley MS, 1201 COLLEGE ST NW   37921
  Emily Walker, prin.
Cedar Bluff MS
  707 CEDAR BLUFF ROAD NW   37923
  George Perry, prin.
Christenberry MS
  925 OGLEWOOD AVE NE   37917
  John Harris, prin.
Doyle MS, 2021 TIPTON STATION RD SW   37920
  Alvin Scott, prin.
Farragut MS, 200 W END AVE NW   37922
  Don Rhodes, prin.
Gresham MS, 500 GRESHAM ROAD NE   37918
  Leo Cooper, prin.
Halls MS, 4317 EMORY ROAD NE   37938
  James Ivey, prin.
Karns MS
  2925 GREY HENDRIX ROAD NW   37931
  James Monroe, prin.
Northwest MS
  5301 PLEASANT RIDGE ROAD NW   37912
  Howard Rash, prin.
South MS, 801 TIPTON AVE SE   37920
  Gary Mahoney, prin.
Spring Hill MS, MILDRED DRIVE   37914
  Herman Baker, prin.
Vine MS, 1401 VINE AVE SE   37915
  Elnora Williams, prin.
Whittle Springs MS
  2700 WHITE OAK LANE NE   37917
  Charles Branam, prin.
Anderson ES, 4808 PROSPECT RD SE   37920
  Dr. Sherry Morgan, prin.
Ball Camp ES
  9801 MIDDLEBROOK PIKE NW   37931
  Dr. Ray Ross, prin.
Beardem ES, 5717 KINGSTON PIKE W   37919
  William McNabb, prin.
Beaumont ES, 1211 BEAUMONT AVE NW   37921
  Ronald Hopper, prin.
Bell ES, 4415 WASHINGTON PIKE NE   37917
  Margie LeCoultre, prin.
Blue Grass ES, 8901 BLUEGRASS RD SW   37922
  Joe Stewart, prin.
Bonny Kate ES, RURAL ROUTE 10   37920
  Lewis Robinette, prin.
Brickey ES, RURAL ROUTE 02   37938
  John McCloud, prin.
Brownlow ES, 1305 LUTTRELL ST NE   37917
  Lester Myers, prin.
Burnett ES, 4521 BROWNS GAP RD NE   37918
  James Prince, prin.
Cedar Bluff IS, 709 CEDAR BLUFF RD NW   37923
  Fred Nidiffer, prin.
Cedar Bluff PS, 705 CEDAR BLUFF RD NW   37923
  Joyce Core, prin.
Chilhowee ES, 5005 ASHEVILLE HWY E   37914
  Vicki Andrews, prin.
East Port ES, 2036 BETHEL AVE SE   37915
  Dr. Mildred Phillips, prin.
Fair Garden ES, 400 FERN ST SE   37914
  Myles Hicks, prin.
Farragut IS, 208 W END AVE NW   37922
  Robert Frazier, prin.
Farragut PS
  509 CAMPBELL STATION RD NW   37922
  Muriel Chreist, prin.
Flenniken ES, 115 FLENNIKEN ST SW   37920
  Jill Carroll, prin.
Fountain City ES
  2910 MONTBELLE DR NE   37918
  C. Privette, prin.
Gap Creek ES, RURAL ROUTE 19   37920
  Winston Davis, prin.
Giffin ES, BEECH ST   37920 – Karen Milani, prin.
Green ES, 800 PAYNE AVE   37915
  Dr. Lula Powell, prin.
Greene ES, 3001 BROOKS RD SE   37914
  Blenza Davis, prin.

Halls ES, 7502 ANDERSONVILLE PIKE NE   37938
  Scott Hayes, prin.
Inskip ES, 4701 HIGH SCHOOL RD NE   37912
  Barbara McGarity, prin.
Karns IS, 8109 BEAVER RIDGE RD NW   37931
  Fred Russell, prin.
Karns PS, 8108 BEAVER RIDGE RD NW   37931
  Ben Burnette, Jr., prin.
Lincoln Park ES
  535 CHICAMAUGA AVE NE   37917
  Anne Loy, prin.
Lonsdale ES, 1317 LOUISIANA AVE NW   37921
  Dr. Anita Padial, prin.
Maynard ES, 737 COLLEGE ST NW   37921
  Della Oliver, prin.
Mooreland Heights ES
  5315 MAGAZINE RD SW   37920
  Betty Sparks, prin.
Morris ES, 2308 WASHINGTON PIKE NE   37917
  Joyce Greene, prin.
Mt. Olive ES, 2507 MARYVILLE PIKE SW   37920
  Robert Huff, prin.
New Hopewell ES
  757 KIMBERLIN HEIGHTS RD SE   37920
  Mayford Galyon, prin.
Norwood ES, 1909 MERCHANTS DR NW   37912
  J. Beeler, prin.
Oakwood ES, 232 CHURCHWELL AVE NE   37917
  Sheryl Kerley, prin.
Pleasant Ridge ES
  3013 WALNOAKS RD NW   37921
  Donna Parrott, prin.
Pond Gap ES, 1400 HOLLYWOOD DR NW   37909
  Richard Casado, prin.
Ridgedale ES, 2900 RIDGEDALE RD NW   37921
  William Crosland, prin.
Ritta ES, RURAL ROUTE 12   37918 – J. Jones, prin.
Rocky Hill ES, 1200 MORRELL RD SW   37919
  Joseph Dent, prin.
Sequoyah ES, 942 SOUTHGATE RD SW   37919
  Mary Wishart, prin.
Shannondale ES
  5316 SHANNONDALE RD NE   37918
  Christine Williams, prin.
South Knox ES, 801 SEVIER AVE SE   37920
  Linda Bell, prin.
Sterchi ES, 900 OAKLETT RD NE   37912
  Nancy Maland, prin.
Sunnyview ES, 412 BAGWELL RD NE   37924
  William Thomas, prin.
West Haven ES, 3620 SISK RD NW   37921
  Arleen DeLozier, prin.
West Hills ES, 409 VANOSDALE RD NW   37909
  Wayne Smith, prin.
West View ES, 1714 MINGLE AVE NW   37921
  Andrew Shockley, prin.
Other Schools – See Corryton, Mascot, Powell,
  Strawberry Plains

First Lutheran School
  1207 BROADWAY NE   37917
Sacred Heart School
  711 NORTHSHORE DR SW   37919
St. Joseph School, 1810 HOWARD RD NE   37918

Kodak, Sevier Co.
Sevier County SD
Supt. – See Sevierville
Northview ES, RURAL ROUTE 01   37764
  Lloyd McDaniels, prin.

Kyles Ford, Hancock Co.
Hancock County SD
Supt. – See Sneedville
Ford ES   37765 – Morris Reed, prin.

Laager, Grundy Co.
Grundy County SD
Supt. – See Altamont
Swiss Memorial ES   37349 – Paul Cooke, prin.

Lafayette, Macon Co., Pop. Code 5
Macon County SD
Sch. Sys. Enr. Code 5
Supt. – Terry Marsh, 501 COLLEGE ST   37083
Central MS, 905 SYCAMORE ST   37083
  J. Watson, prin.
Fairlane ES, 305 FAIRLANE DR   37083
  Melabaline Wilson, prin.
Other Schools – See Red Boiling Springs,
  Westmoreland

La Follette, Campbell Co., Pop. Code 6
Campbell County SD
Supt. – See Jacksboro
MS, 1116 MIDDLESBORO HWY   37766
  Rob Malicote, prin.
College Hill ES, RURAL ROUTE 03   37766
  William Pyle, prin.
East La Follette ES   37766 – James Davis, prin.
Stinking Creek ES, RURAL ROUTE 03   37766
  Roger Walden, prin.
Valley View ES
  RURAL ROUTE 01 BOX 450   37766
  Don Poston, prin.
West La Follette ES   37766 – Robert Greene, prin.

Lake City, Anderson Co., Pop. Code 4
Anderson County SD
Supt. – See Clinton
MS, RURAL ROUTE 01 BOX 208   37769
  Jim Stewart, prin.
ES, LINDSAY ST   37769 – L. Madron, prin.
Medford ES, RURAL ROUTE 01   37769
  E. Jan Moore, prin.

Lascassas, Rutherford Co.
Rutherford County SD
Supt. – See Murfreesboro
ES   37085 – Larry Stewart, prin.

Laurel Bloomery, Johnson Co.
Johnson County SD
Supt. – See Mountain City
Laurel ES   37680 – Eric Taylor, prin.

La Vergne, Rutherford Co., Pop. Code 6
Rutherford County SD
Supt. – See Murfreesboro
ES   37086 – Sharon Summar, prin.

Lawrenceburg, Lawrence Co., Pop. Code 7
Lawrence County SD
Sch. Sys. Enr. Code 6
Supt. – Garner Exell, WEST GAINES ST   38464
Coffman MS, 111 LAFAYETTE ST   38464
  David James, prin.
Crockett ES, 510 W POINT RD   38464
  Gari Lynn, prin.
ES, 600 PROSSER RD   38464 – Larry Morrow, prin.
New Prospect ES, 4520 PULASKI HWY   38464
  Billy Walters, prin.
Sowell ES, 510 SEVENTH ST   38464
  Bruce Edwards, prin.
West Highland ES, 140 BRINK ST   38464
  Mary Conn, prin.
Other Schools – See Ethridge, Leoma, Loretto,
  Summertown

Sacred Heart School, 222 BERGER ST   38464

Lebanon, Wilson Co., Pop. Code 7
Lebanon CSD
Sch. Sys. Enr. Code 4
Supt. – Cordell Winfree
  507 COLES FERRY PIKE   37087
Baird MS, 509 COLES FERRY PIKE   37087
  Andy Brummett, prin.
Byars Dowdy ES
  DAWSON LN AT HICKORY RDG RD   37087
  Kenneth Watts, prin.
Houston ES, OAKDALE DR   37087
  Robert Johnson, prin.

Wilson County SD
Sch. Sys. Enr. Code 6
Supt. – Felix Smallwood, 218 E HIGH ST   37087
Carroll Oakland ES
  RURAL ROUTE 11 BOX 378   37087
  William Repsher, prin.
Southside ES, RURAL ROUTE 06   37087
  Karl Puryear, prin.
Tuckers Cross Roads ES, RURAL ROUTE 01   37087
  Jimmy Allen, prin.
Other Schools – See Gladeville, Mount Juliet,
  Watertown

Lenoir City, Loudon Co., Pop. Code 6
Lenoir City CSD
Sch. Sys. Enr. Code 4
Supt. – Harold B. Duff, 104 A ST   37771
MS, 100 FOURTH AVE   37771
  Jerry Burnett, prin.
ES, 200 KELLY LN   37771 – Gerald Augustus, prin.

Loudon County SD
Supt. – See Loudon
North MS, RURAL ROUTE 01   37771
  Joe Malloy, prin.
Eatons ES, RURAL ROUTE 01 BOX 9-B   37771
  Larry Duff, prin.
Highland Park ES, EAST LEE HWY   37771
  David Meers, prin.

Leoma, Lawrence Co.
Lawrence County SD
Supt. – See Lawrenceburg
ES, RURAL ROUTE 02   38468
  Robert McIlwain, prin.

Lewisburg, Marshall Co., Pop. Code 6
Marshall County SD
Sch. Sys. Enr. Code 5
Supt. – Jack Keny, 700 JONES CIRCLE   37091
Connelly MS, 300 FIFTH AVE N   37091
  Hugh Adams, prin.
Marshall ES, HIGH SCHOOL DR   37091
  Barbara Lee, prin.
Westhills MS, ELLINGTON PKWY   37091
  John Pierce, prin.
Other Schools – See Chapel Hill, Cornersville

Lexington, Henderson Co., Pop. Code 6
Henderson County SD
Sch. Sys. Enr. Code 5
Supt. – John Graves, P O BOX 190   38351
Bargerton ES, RURAL ROUTE 04   38351
  Howard Coffman, prin.
Pin Oak ES, RURAL ROUTE 03   38351
  Mike Todd, prin.
South Haven ES
  RURAL ROUTE 05 BOX 6000   38351
  Joe Tate, prin.
Other Schools – See Huron, Reagan, Wildersville

Lexington SD
Sch. Sys. Enr. Code 3
Supt. – Walter Medearis, 162 MONROE ST   38351
Caywood ES, 162 MONROE ST   38351
  Walter Medearis, prin.

Liberty, De Kalb Co., Pop. Code 2
DeKalb County SD
Supt. – See Smithville
West ES 37095 – W. Hobson, prin.

Limestone, Washington Co.
Washington County SD
Supt. – See Jonesborough
West View ES, RURAL ROUTE 03 37681
Earl Henley, prin.

Linden, Perry Co., Pop. Code 4
Perry County SD
Sch. Sys. Enr. Code 4
Supt. – Lannie Dedrick, P O BOX 909 37096
ES, RURAL ROUTE 01 BOX 10A 37096
Glyn Mercer, prin.
Other Schools – See Lobelville

Livingston, Overton Co., Pop. Code 5
Overton County SD
Sch. Sys. Enr. Code 5
Supt. – Edwin Garrett, 112 BUSSELL ST 38570
MS 38570 – Michael Garrett, prin.
Roberts ES 38570 – Willie Beaty, prin.
Other Schools – See Allons, Crawford, Hilham,
Rickman

Lobelville, Perry Co., Pop. Code 3
Perry County SD
Supt. – See Linden
ES, SCHOOL ST 37097 – Linda Fesmire, prin.

Lookout Mountain, Hamilton Co., Pop. Code 4
Hamilton County SD
Supt. – See Chattanooga
ES, 321 N BRAGG AVE 37350
Marvin Lane, prin.

Loretto, Lawrence Co., Pop. Code 4
Lawrence County SD
Supt. – See Lawrenceburg
South Lawrence ES, P O BOX 310 38469
Paul Blair, prin.

Loudon, Loudon Co., Pop. Code 5
Loudon County SD
Sch. Sys. Enr. Code 5
Supt. – A. Edward Headlee, P O BOX D 37774
Ft. Loudon MS, RURAL ROUTE 04 BOX 51 37774
R. Akins, prin.
ES, RURAL ROUTE 04 37774 – Bob Yates, prin.
Steekee ES, RURAL ROUTE 02 37774
Jerldine Boone, prin.
Other Schools – See Greenback, Lenoir City,
Philadelphia

Louisville, Blount Co.
Blount County SD
Supt. – See Maryville
Mid Settlements ES
RURAL ROUTE 01 BOX 91 37777
Wendell Huffstetler, prin.

Luttrell, Union Co., Pop. Code 3
Union County SD
Supt. – See Maynardville
ES, TAZEWELL PARK 37779
Randy Arnwine, prin.

Lyles, Hickman Co.
Hickman County SD
Supt. – See Centerville
East ES, RURAL ROUTE 01 37098
Jerry Burlison, prin.

Lynchburg, Moore Co., Pop. Code 3
Moore County SD
Sch. Sys. Enr. Code 3
Supt. – Wayne Stewart, P O BOX 219 37352
ES 37352 – A. Roenfeldt, prin.

Lynnville, Giles Co., Pop. Code 2
Giles County SD
Supt. – See Pulaski
Richland ES, RURAL ROUTE 01 BOX 215 38472
Rayburn Hickman, prin.

Macon, Fayette Co.
Fayette County SD
Supt. – See Somerville
Southwest ES, P O BOX 2871 38048
Allen Yancey,Jr., prin.

Madison, Davidson Co., Pop. Code 7
Davidson County SD
Supt. – See Nashville
Neelys Bend MS
1251 NEELYS BEND ROAD 37115
Jesse Cabler, prin.
Amqui ES, 319 ANDERSON LN 37115
Arthur Irvin, prin.
Chadwell ES, 321 PORT DR 37115
Donna Hudson, prin.
Gateway ES, 1524 MONTICELLO AVE 37115
Homer Wright, prin.
Neelys Bend ES, 1300 NEELYS BEND RD 37115
Levelle Boyd, prin.
Stratton ES, 610 GALLATIN RD S 37115
Charles Spurlock, prin.

Madison Campus ES
1515 SUTHERLAND DR 37115
St. Joseph School, 1225 GALLATIN RD S 37115

Madisonville, Monroe Co., Pop. Code 5
Monroe County SD
Sch. Sys. Enr. Code 6
Supt. – Theodore Belcher, COURTHOUSE 37354
JHS 37354 – (—), prin.
ES 37354 – Mary Jordon, prin.
Other Schools – See Tellico Plains, Vonore

Manchester, Coffee Co., Pop. Code 6
Coffee County SD
Sch. Sys. Enr. Code 5
Supt. – Dr. Joe Brandon
210 E MCCLEAN ST 37355
East Coffee ES
RURAL ROUTE 04 BOX 4822 37355
Richard Crosslin, prin.
New Union ES
RURAL ROUTE 06 BOX 6202 37355
Ray Winton, prin.
North Coffee ES
RURAL ROUTE 02 BOX 2258 37355
Wayne Clouse, prin.
Other Schools – See Hillsboro, Normandy, Tullahoma

Manchester CSD
Sch. Sys. Enr. Code 4
Supt. – Bill Pack, 209 E MCLEAN ST 37355
College Street ES, 405 COLLEGE ST 37355
Charles Sain, prin.
Westwood ES, 912 OAKDALE ST 37355
Roy Bush, prin.

Martin, Weakley Co., Pop. Code 6
Weakley County SD
Supt. – See Dresden
JHS, 670 N MCCOMB ST 38237
William Jones, prin.
MS, 300 S COLLEGE ST 38237
James Dunn, prin.
PS, 215 S COLLEGE ST 38237
Joan Pritchett, prin.

Maryville, Blount Co., Pop. Code 1
Blount County SD
Sch. Sys. Enr. Code 7
Supt. – Mae Owenby
301 COURTHOUSE ST 37801
Eagleton MS, 325 BENJAMIN AVE 37801
Rob Maxey, prin.
Binfield ES, RURAL ROUTE 11 BOX 307 37801
Jerry Bailey, prin.
Bungalow ES
1010 MIDDLESETTLEMENTS RD 37801
Charles Finley, prin.
Eagleton ES, 110 MAIN RD 37801
Neubert Harless, prin.
Fairview ES, RURAL ROUTE 10 BOX 51 37801
Cynthia Nichols, prin.
Hubbard ES, RURAL ROUTE 12 BOX 147 37801
Richard Cooper, prin.
Lanier ES, RURAL ROUTE 04 BOX 369 37801
Frank Kidd, prin.
Montvale ES, RURAL ROUTE 14 BOX 56A 37801
Gle Keown, prin.
Porter ES, RURAL ROUTE 03 BOX 66A 37801
Ronald Campbell, prin.
Other Schools – See Friendsville, Louisville,
Rockford, Townsend, Walland

Maryville CSD
Sch. Sys. Enr. Code 5
Supt. – J. Harrell Harrison
400 W BROADWAY AVE 37801
Fort Craig ES, 520 S WASHINGTON AVE 37801
David Berry, prin.
Houston ES, 330 MELROSE ST 37801
Jan Click, prin.
Sevier ES, SEQUOYAH AVE 37801
Larry Holt, prin.

Mascot, Knox Co.
Knox County SD
Supt. – See Knoxville
East Knox County ES
9315 RUTLEDGE PARK 37806 – Judy Cupp, prin.

Mason, Tipton Co., Pop. Code 2
Fayette County SD
Supt. – See Somerville
Northwest ES, RURAL ROUTE 01 38049
Robert Chapman, prin.

Maury City, Crockett Co., Pop. Code 3
Crockett County SD
Supt. – See Alamo
ES, MAURY CITY ELEMENTARY 38050
Harold Garrett, prin.
ES 38050 – Hilda Mount, prin.

Maynardville, Union Co., Pop. Code 3
Union County SD
Sch. Sys. Enr. Code 4
Supt. – David Coppock 37807
Big Ridge ES, HICKORY VALLEY RAOD 37807
Donald Goforth, prin.
ES, OLD HWY 33 BOX H 37807
Dr. Eddie Shoffner, prin.
Other Schools – See Luttrell, Sharps Chapel

Mc Donald, Bradley Co.
Bradley County SD
Supt. – See Cleveland
ES, RURAL ROUTE 01 37353 – Darline Bell, prin.

Mc Ewen, Humphreys Co., Pop. Code 4
Humphreys County SD
Supt. – See Waverly
S 37101 – Glen Shivvers, prin.

Mc Kenzie, Carroll Co., Pop. Code 6
Mc Kenzie CSD
Sch. Sys. Enr. Code 4
Supt. – Joe F. Williams, 203 W BELL AVE 38201
JHS, 106 W WOODROW AVE 38201
James Jackson, prin.
ES, 213 W BROOKS AVE 38201
Billy Rogers, prin.

Mc Lemoresville, Carroll Co., Pop. Code 2
West Carroll SD
Sch. Sys. Enr. Code 4
Supt. – Fred Martin, P O BOX 279 38235
West Carroll PS, P O BOX 219 38235
Charles Dameron, prin.
Other Schools – See Cedar Grove, Trezevant

Mc Minnville, Warren Co., Pop. Code 7
Warren County SD
Sch. Sys. Enr. Code 6
Supt. – Ron Martin, 109 LYON ST 37110
Biles ES, 201 LOCUST ST 37110
Jimmy Blankenship, prin.
Centertown ES, RURAL ROUTE 01 37110
Janie Moore, prin.
Dibrell ES, RURAL ROUTE 04 37110
Bob Bonner, prin.
Irving College ES, RURAL ROUTE 02 37110
Samuel Boyd, prin.
North MS, RURAL ROUTE 08 BOX 41 37110
Byron Chambers, prin.
West ES, 400 CLARK BLVD 37110
Bryan Knight, prin.
Other Schools – See Morrison, Rock Island, Viola

Medina, Gibson Co., Pop. Code 3
Gibson CSD
Supt. – See Dyer
ES, 117 COLLEGE 38355 – Calvin Bailey, prin.

Memphis, Shelby Co., Pop. Code 11
Memphis CSD
Sch. Sys. Enr. Code 8
Supt. – Dr. W. W. Herenton
2597 AVERY AVE 38112
Avon S, 310 AVON RD 38117
Josephine Allsop, prin.
Raligh Egypt JHS, 4315 ALICE ANN DRIVE 38128
Leslie Fortner, prin.
Vance JHS, 673 VANCE AVE 38126
Fred Brown, prin.
White Station JHS, 5456 MASON ROAD 38119
Barb Branch, prin.
Alcy ES, 1750 E ALCY RD 38114
Christine Johnson, prin.
Alton ES, 2020 ALTON AVE 38106
Bernice Garrett, prin.
Berclair ES, 810 N PERKINS RD 38122
Jack Simpson, prin.
Bethel Grove ES, 2459 ARLINGTON AVE 38114
Dave Bond, prin.
Brookmeade ES, 3777 EDENBURG DR 38127
Barbara Olds, prin.
Brownsville ES, 5292 BANBURY AVE 38134
James Fleming, prin.
Bruce ES, 1206 CARR AVE 38104
Marvin Harris,Jr., prin.
Caldwell ES, 230 HENRY AVE 38107
Halloe Robinson, prin.
Campus ES, MEMPHIS STATE UNIV CAM 38152
Debbie Riley, prin.
Carnes ES, 943 LANE AVE 38105
Cleophus Hudson,Jr., prin.
Charjean ES, 2140 CHARJEAN RD 38114
Helen Bates, prin.
Cherokee ES, 3061 KIMBALL AVE 38114
William Reese, prin.
Coleman ES, 3210 RALEIGH MILL ROAD 38128
Roy Laughlin, prin.
Corning ES, 1662 DABBS AVE 38127
Jim Hester, prin.
Coro Lake ES, 1560 DREW RD 38109
Catherine Mitchell, prin.
Cromwell ES, 4989 CROMWELL AVE 38118
Eugene Callaway, prin.
Cummings ES, 1037 CUMMINGS ST 38106
Robert Terrell, prin.
Delano ES, 1716 DELANO AVE 38127
David Moore, prin.
DeMonst ES, 320 CARPENTER ST 38112
Patricia Garrett, prin.
Denver ES, 1940 FRAYSER BLVD 38127
Betty Frost, prin.
Double Tree ES, 4560 DOUBLE TREE RD 38109
Hattie Jackson, prin.
Douglass ES, 1650 ASH ST 38108
Herman Holeyfield, prin.
Dunbar ES, 2606 SELECT AVE 38114
Dora Purdy, prin.
Dunn Avenue ES, 1500 DUNN AVE 38106
Dr. Sarah Chandler, prin.
Egypt ES, 4160 KAREN CV 38128
Lee Presley, prin.
Evans ES, 4949 COTTONWOOD RD 38118
Margaret Woods, prin.
Fairley ES, 4950 FAIRLEY RD 38109
Edward Only, prin.

Florida ES, 1560 FLORIDA ST 38109
  Lawrence Garrett, prin.
Ford Road ES, 3336 FORD RD 38109
  Curtis Mitchell, prin.
Fox Meadows ES, 2960 EMERALD DR 38115
  Barbara Bolton, prin.
Frayser ES, 1602 DELLWOOD AVE 38127
  Rosemary Bennett, prin.
Gardenview ES, 4075 HARTZ DR 38116
  Dr. Bobbie Smothers, prin.
Georgia Avenue ES, 690 MISSISSIPPI BLVD 38126
  Fay Lee, prin.
Georgian Hills ES, 3930 LEWEIR ST 38127
  Gene Holland, prin.
Goodlett ES, 3001 S GOODLETT ST 38118
  William Clark, prin.
Gordon ES, 780 DECATUR ST 38107
  Shirley Kendrick,Jr., prin.
Grahamwood ES, 3950 SUMMER AVE 38122
  Margaret Taylor, prin.
Grandview Heights ES, 2342 CLIFTON AVE 38127
  William Williams, prin.
Grant ES, 190 CHELSEA AVE 38107
  Joseph Wilkerson, prin.
Graves ES, 3398 GRAVES RD 38116
  Comodore Primous, prin.
Guthrie ES, 951 CHELSEA AVE 38107
  Roy Logan, prin.
Hamilton ES, 1378 ETHLYN AVE 38106
  Phillip Dean, prin.
Hanley ES, 680 HANLEY ST 38114
  Ruby Payne, prin.
Hawkins Mill ES
  4295 MOUNTAIN TERRACE ST 38127
  Arnold Harris, prin.
Hill ES, 1372 LATHAM ST 38106
  Arthur Hull, prin.
Hollywood ES, 1346 BRYAN ST 38108
  Makeda Baruti, prin.
Idlewild ES, 1950 LINDEN AVE 38104
  Dr. Joyce Jones, prin.
Jackson ES, 3925 WALES AVE 38108
  Billy Scott, prin.
Kansas ES, 1353 KANSAS ST 38106
  William Cox, prin.
Kingsbury ES, 4055 BAYLISS AVE 38108
  Raymond Abernathy, prin.
Klondike ES, 1250 VOLLINTINE AVE 38107
  Annie Saunders, prin.
Knight Road ES, 3237 KNIGHT RD 38118
  Robert Baker, prin.
Lakeview ES, 5132 JONETTA ST 38109
  Thomas Yarbrough, prin.
LaRose ES, 851 WELLINGTON ST 38126
  Eleanor Tinnon, prin.
Lauderdale ES, 955 S LAUDERDALE ST 38126
  Lora Sandridge, prin.
Levi ES, 3939 U S HIGHWAY 61 S 38109
  Theodore Johnson, prin.
Lincoln ES, 1566 S ORLEANS ST 38106
  Dr. Leon Davis, prin.
Locke ES, 688 SAINT PAUL AVE 38126
  Joseph Carr, prin.
Macon ES, 968N N MENDENHALL RD 38122
  Graham Griffith, prin.
Magnolia ES, 2061 LIVEWELL CIR 38114
  Jacqueline Sales, prin.
Manor Lake ES, 4900 HORN LAKE RD 38109
  Betty Hendon, prin.
Newberry ES, 5540 NEWBERRY AVE 38115
  Judith Byrd, prin.
Norris ES, 1490 NORRIS AVE 38106
  Otto Lashley, prin.
Oakhaven ES, 3795 BISHOPS BRIDGE RD 38118
  Edwin Dilworth,Jr., prin.
Oakshire ES, 1765 E HOLMES RD 38116
  Morris Busby, prin.
Orleans ES, 1400 MCMILLAN ST 38106
  Charles Jones, prin.
Peabody ES, 2086 YOUNG AVE 38104
  Jimmy Gillespie, prin.
Raineshaven ES, 430 IVAN RD 38109
  Carolyn McGhee, prin.
Ralgh Bart Meadows ES
  5195 TWIN WOODS AVE 38134
  William Walk, prin.
Richland ES, 5440 RICH RD 38119
  Dr. Joyce Jensen, prin.
Ridgeway ES, 1775 RIDGEWAY RD 38119
  Paul Taylor, prin.
Riverview ES, 260 JOUBERT AVE 38109
  Samuel Polk, prin.
Rozelle ES, 993 ROLAND ST 38114
  Charlene Turner, prin.
Scenic Hills ES, 3450 SCENIC HWY 38128
  W. Bingham, prin.
Shady Grove ES, 5360 SHADY GROVE RD 38119
  Patricia Driscoll, prin.
Shannon ES, 2248 SHANNON AVE 38108
  Ethel Gardner, prin.
Sharpe ES, 3431 SHARPE AVE 38111
  Donald Miller, prin.
Sheffield ES, 4290 CHUCK AVE 38118
  Billy Mitchell, prin.
Sherwood ES, 3717 VANUYS RD 38111
  Diane Canepa, prin.
Snowden ES, 1870 N PARKWAY 38112
  Carolyn Pittman, prin.
South Park ES, 1736 GETWELL RD 38111
  Juna Pickering, prin.
Spring Hill ES
  3796 RALEIGH FRAYSER RD 38128
  Walton Bailey,Jr., prin.

Springdale ES, 880 N HOLLYWOOD ST 38108
  Rita Porter, prin.
Stafford ES, 1237 COLLEGE ST 38106
  Utillus Phillips, prin.
Treadwell ES, 3538 GIVEN AVE 38122
  John Renick, prin.
Vollentine ES, 1682 VOLLINTINE AVE 38107
  Bertharine Young, prin.
Walker ES, 322 KING RD 38109
  Arthur Bowles, prin.
Wells Station ES
  1610 WELLS STATION RD 38108
  Roy Hopkins, prin.
Westhaven ES, 4585 HODGE RD 38109
  George Watkins, prin.
Westside ES, 3347 DAWN DR 38127
  Michael Rowland, prin.
Westwood ES, 778 PARKROSE RD 38109
  Opal Bowen, prin.
White Station ES, 518 S PERKINS RD 38117
  R. Duncan, prin.
Whitehaven ES
  4783 ELVIS PRESLEY BLVD 38116
  Wilma Proctor, prin.
Whites Chapel ES, 3966 SEWANEE RD 38109
  Edward Gaskin, prin.
Whitney ES, 1219 WHITNEY AVE 38127
  James Howell, prin.
Willow Oaks ES, 4417 WILLOW RD 38117
  Harold Draper, prin.
Winchester ES, 3587 BOEINGSHIRE DR 38116
  Gerald Beibers, prin.

Shelby County SD
Sch. Sys. Enr. Code 8
Supt. – James Anderson
  160 S HOLLYWOOD ST 38112
Kirby MS, 6670 E RAINES ROAD 38115
  John Sadowski, prin.
Capleville ES, 4326 E SHELBY DR 38118
  Velma Rice, prin.
Crump ES, 4405 CRUMP RD 38115
  Elizabeth Donnelly, prin.
Northaven ES, 5157 N CIRCLE RD 38127
  Raymond Dunavant, prin.
Ross ES, 4890 ROSS RD 38115
  David Carlisle, prin.
Other Schools – See Arlington, Bartlett, Collierville,
  Cordova, Germantown, Millington

Hutchison School, 1740 RIDGEWAY RAOD 38119
Lausanne School, 1381 W MASSEY ROAD 38119
St. Mary's Episcopal School
  60 PERKINS EXTENDED 38117
Alcy SDA Junior Academy
  1325 E ALCY RD 38106
Blessed Sacrament School, 2568 HALE AVE 38112
Christ the King Lutheran School
  5296 PARK AVENUE 38119
Holy Cross Lutheran School
  4327 ELVIS PRESLEY BLVD 38116
Holy Rosary School, 4841 PARK AVE 38117
Immaculate Conception ES
  1669 CENTRAL AVE 38104
Immanuel Lutheran School
  6319 RALEIGH LANGRANGE RD 38134
Lamplighter Montessori School
  1021 MOSBY RD 38116
Memphis Hebrew Academy
  390 S WHITE STATION RD 38117
Our Lady of Sorrows School
  3690 THOMAS ST 38127
St. Agnes ES
  4830 WALNUT GROVE ROAD 38117
St. Ann School, 6529 STAGE RD 38134
St. Anne School, 670 S HIGHLAND ST 38111
St. Augustine ES, 1169 KERR AVE 38106
St. Dominic School for Boys, 30 AVON RD 38117
St. George's Day School, 8259 U S HWY 72 38138
St. John School, 2718 LAMAR AVE 38114
St. Louis School, 5192 SHADY GROVE RD 38117
St. Luke's Episcopal School
  246 S BELVEDERE BLVD 38104
St. Michael School, 3880 FORREST AVE 38122
St. Paul School, 1425 E SHELBY DR 38116

Michie, McNairy Co., Pop. Code 3
McNairy County SD
Supt. – See Selmer
ES, RURAL ROUTE 01 BOX 225 38357
  Allen Phillips, prin.

Middleton, Hardeman Co., Pop. Code 3
Hardeman County SD
Supt. – See Bolivar
ES 38052 – Harold Ross, prin.

Milan, Gibson Co., Pop. Code 6
Milan CSD
Sch. Sys. Enr. Code 4
Supt. – Wylie Wheeler, P O BOX 528 38358
Park Avenue MS, 450 SMITH ST 38358
  Jerry Johnson, prin.
Clark ES, HARRIS ST 38358
  Wallace Burnett, prin.
McKellar MS, 535 N MAIN ST 38358
  Harold Brady, prin.

Millington, Shelby Co., Pop. Code 7
Shelby County SD
Supt. – See Memphis
MS, 4964 CUBA-MILLINGTON ROAD 38053
  Roger Deans, prin.
Harrold ES, 4943 W UNION RD 38053
  Robert Steele, prin.

Jeter ES, 7662 BENJESTOWN RD 38053
  Mary McNeil, prin.
Lucy ES, 6269 AMHERST RD 38053
  Dr. Evelyn Jewell, prin.
Millington East ES, 6467 NAVY RD 38053
  Bettye Goddard, prin.
ES, 4954 EASLEY AVE 38053
  Penelope Eilert, prin.
Millington South ES
  4885 BILL KNIGHT RD 38053
  Mike Simpson, prin.
Woodstock ES
  5909 WOODSTOCK-CUBA RD 38053
  John Strong, prin.

Minor Hill, Giles Co., Pop. Code 3
Giles County SD
Supt. – See Pulaski
ES, P O BOX 99 38473 – Willard Davis, prin.

Mohawk, Greene Co., Pop. Code 3
Greene County SD
Supt. – See Greeneville
McDonald ES 37810 – Steve Wallin, prin.

Monteagle, Grundy Co., Pop. Code 4
Marion County SD
Supt. – See Jasper
ES 37356 – Billy Layne, prin.

Monterey, Putnam Co., Pop. Code 5
Putnam County SD
Supt. – See Cookeville
Uffelman ES, 112 N ELM ST 38574
  Eddie Nipper, prin.

Mooresburg, Hawkins Co.
Hawkins County SD
Supt. – See Rogersville
ES, RURAL ROTUE 01 37811
  Shirley Begley, prin.

Morrison, Warren Co., Pop. Code 3
Warren County SD
Supt. – See Mc Minnville
ES, GENERAL DELIVERY 37357
  Donald Prater, prin.

Morristown, Hamblen Co., Pop. Code 7
Hamblen County SD
Sch. Sys. Enr. Code 6
Supt. – Herbert H. Harville
  210 E MORRIS BLVD 37814
Lincoln Heights MS, 219 LINCOLN AVE 37814
  Ed Goan, prin.
Meadowview MS
  1623 MEADOWVIEW LANE 37814
  William Welch, prin.
West View MS, 555 W ECONOMY ROAD 37814
  Sanford Harville, prin.
Alpha MS
  5959 W ANDREW JOHNSON HWY 37814
  George Johnson, prin.
Alpha PS, 5626 OLD HIGHWAY 11E 37814
  (—), prin.
Fairview ES
  2125 FAIRVIEW RD 37814 – Bill Carroll, prin.
Hay ES, 501 BRITTON CT 37814
  Eddie Amos, prin.
Hillcrest ES, 407 S LIBERTY HILL RD 37813
  Madge Susong, prin.
Lincoln Heights ES, 215 LINCOLN AVE 37813
  Melvine Blevine, prin.
Manley ES
  3685 W ANDREW JOHNSON HWY 37814
  Ralph Livesay,Jr., prin.
Union Heights ES, 3366 ENKA HWY 37813
  Lynn Sullivan, prin.
West ES, 235 CONVERSE ELM ST 37814
  William Harrison, prin.
Witt ES, 4650 S DAVY CROCKETT PKY 37813
  Kenneth Helton, prin.
Other Schools – See Russellville, Whitesburg

Moscow, Fayette Co., Pop. Code 2
Fayette County SD
Supt. – See Somerville
Moscow Springhill ES, RURAL ROUTE 03 38057
  Willie Waddell, prin.

Mosheim, Greene Co., Pop. Code 4
Greene County SD
Supt. – See Greeneville
ES 37818 – Alford Taylor, prin.

Mountain City, Johnson Co., Pop. Code 4
Johnson County SD
Sch. Sys. Enr. Code 5
Supt. – John Payne, 211 N CHURCH ST 37683
Johnson County MS
  500A FAIRGROUND LANE 37683
  C. Courtner, prin.
Doe ES, RURAL ROUTE 03 37683
  Thomas Barry, prin.
ES, 301 DONNELLY ST 37683
  Gerald Buckles, prin.
Neva ES, RURAL ROUTE 01 37683
  Virginia Moorhouse, prin.
Shouns ES, RURAL ROUTE 04 37683
  Morris Woodring, prin.
Other Schools – See Butler, Laurel Bloomery, Shady
  Valley, Trade

Mount Juliet, Wilson Co., Pop. Code 5
Wilson County SD
Supt. – See Lebanon

Lakeview ES, RURAL ROUTE 04   37122
  James Robinson, prin.
ES   37122 – Steve Brown, prin.
Stoner Creek ES   37122 – Linda Johnson, prin.
West End ES, RURAL ROUTE 02   37122
  Robert Stokes, prin.

Mount Pleasant, Maury Co., Pop. Code 5
  Maury County SD
  Supt. – See Columbia
  Woody ES, 600 LOCUST ST   38474
    John Gibson, prin.

Munford, Tipton Co., Pop. Code 4
  Tipton County SD
  Supt. – See Covington
  ES, P O BOX P   38058 – William Smith, prin.

Murfreesboro, Rutherford Co., Pop. Code 8
  Murfreesboro SD
  Sch. Sys. Enr. Code 5
  Supt. – John Jones, 400 N MAPLE ST   37130
  Bellwood ES, 435 SANBYRN DR   37130
    Tom Hartley, prin.
  Bradley Model ES, 511 MERCURY BLVD   37130
    Zane Cantrell, prin.
  Hobgood ES, 307 S BAIRD LN   37130
    Dr. William Strang, prin.
  Neilson MS, CLARK BLVD   37130
    Robert Crowder, prin.
  Neilson PS, JONES BLVD   37130
    Louise Cooper, prin.
  Northfield ES, 550 W NORTHFIELD BLVD   37129
    Mark Edwards, prin.
  Rogers ES, 1807 GREENLAND DR   37130
    Barbara Tuckson, prin.

  Rutherford County SD
  Sch. Sys. Enr. Code 7
  Supt. – Jerry Gaither
    502 MEMORIAL BLVD   37130
  Central MS, 701 E MAIN ST   37130
    Tom Tenpenney, prin.
  Buchanan ES, RURAL ROUTE 06   37130
    Harris Hooper, prin.
  Hill ES, RURAL ROUTE 03   37129
    George Campbell, prin.
  McFadden ES, 221 BRIDGE AVE   37129
    Donald Johnson, prin.
  Pittard ES, MIDDLE TN STATE U BOX 4   37132
    Dr. Ronald Kersey, prin.
  Other Schools – See Christiana, Eagleville, Lascassas,
    La Vergne, Readyville, Rockvale, Smyrna

Nashville, Davidson Co., Pop. Code 10
  Davidson County SD
  Sch. Sys. Enr. Code 8
  Supt. – Charles O. Frazier
    2601 BRANSFORD AVE   37204
  Bass MS, 5200 DELAWARE AVE   37209
    James Turbeyville, prin.
  Bellevue MS, 656 COLICE JEANNE ROAD   37221
    Buford Moran, prin.
  Cameron MS, 1034 1ST AVE S   37210
    Gerald Martin, prin.
  East MS, 110 GALLATIN ROAD   37206
    Elbert Ross, prin.
  Ewing Park MS, 3411 KNIGHT ROAD   37207
    Helen Adams, prin.
  Highland Heights MS, 123 DOUGLAS AVE   37207
    James Armsrong, prin.
  Litton MS, 4600 GALLATIN ROAD   37216
    Phil Boeing, prin.
  McMurray MS, 520 MCMURRAY DRIVE   37211
    Ron Webb, prin.
  Meigs Magnet MS, 712 RAMSEY ST   37206
    Anne Whitefield, prin.
  Moore MS, 4425 GRANNY WHITE PIKE   37204
    L. Batson, prin.
  Two Rivers MS, 2991 MCGAVOCK PIKE   37214
    Rob Eskew, prin.
  West End MS, 3529 WEST END AVE   37205
    Paul Mays, prin.
  Wright MS, 180 MCCALL ST   37211
    James Thompson, prin.
  Allen ES, 500 SPENCE LN   37210
    Dr. Riley Elliot, prin.
  Baxter MS, 3515 GALLATIN RD   37216
    George Northern, prin.
  Bellshire ES, 1128 BELL GRIMES LN   37207
    Dr. B. Crawford, prin.
  Berry ES, 2200 WINFORD AVE   37211
    Dr. H. McCallister, prin.
  Binkley ES, 4700 W LONGDALE DR   37211
    Dr. Karen Barron, prin.
  Bordeaux ES, 1910 S HAMILTON RD   37218
    Gwendolyn Smith, prin.
  Brick Church MS
    3230 BRICK CHURCH PIKE   37207
    Thomas Ward, prin.
  Brookmeade ES, 1015 DAVIDSON RD   37205
    Charles Tarkington, prin.
  Buena Vista MS, 1531 9TH AVE N   37208
    Martha Butler, prin.
  Charlotte Park ES, 480 ANNEX AVE   37209
    Ray Scott, prin.
  Cockrill ES, 610 49TH AVE N   37209
    Geraldine Butts, prin.
  Cotton ES, 1033 GREENWOOD AVE   37206
    William Boyd, prin.
  Cumberland ES, 3500 HYDES FERRY RD   37218
    Dr. Carolyn Tucker, prin.
  Dalewood ES, 1460 MCGAVOCK PIKE   37216
    Paul Webb, prin.

Eakin ES, 2400 FAIRFAX AVE   37212
  Don Hudson, prin.
Early MS, 2013 25TH AVE N   37208
  Betty Triplett, prin.
Fall-Hamilton ES, 165 RAINS AVE   37203
  James Meriwether, prin.
Glencliff ES, 158 OLD ANTIOCH PARK   37211
  Ronald Pounders, prin.
Glendale MS, 800 THOMPSON AVE   37204
  Carol Hutson, prin.
Glengarry ES, 200 FINLEY DR   37217
  Lora Hall, prin.
Glenview ES, 1115 THOMPSON PL   37217
  Dr. Flora Gutterman, prin.
Gower ES, 650 OLD HICKORY BLVD   37209
  Patricia Kircher, prin.
Gra-Mar ES, 575 JOYCE LN   37216
  John Young, prin.
Green ES, 3500 HOBBS RD   37215
  Mary Wiggins, prin.
Hall ES, 498 HOGAN RD   37220
  Dr. Gloria McMahan, prin.
Harpeth Valley ES, 7840 OLD HARDING RD   37221
  Russell Mays, prin.
Haynes MS, 510 W TRINITY LN   37207
  Dr. William Waters, prin.
Haywood ES, 3790 TURLEY DR   37211
  Evelyn Bennett, prin.
Head MS, 500 20TH AVE N   37203
  Josephine Jacobs, prin.
Hickman ES, 3125 IRONWOOD DR   37214
  George Brinkman, prin.
Hill ES, 150 DAVIDSON RD   37205
  Dr. Louise MacKay, prin.
Howe ES, 1928 GREENWOOD AVE   37206
  Mary Lewis, prin.
Inglewood ES, 1700 RIVERSIDE DR   37216
  Rogert Mingle, prin.
Johnson MS, 1200 2ND AVE S   37210
  Mary Lane, prin.
Joy ES, 1900 LISCHEY AVE   37207
  Minnie Sowell, prin.
Kings Lane MS, 3200 KINGS LN   37218
  Keknneth McKay, prin.
Kirkpatrick ES, 1000 SEVIER ST   37206
  John Lifsey, prin.
Lakeview ES, 110 STEWARTS FERRY PIKE   37214
  Gilmon Jenkins, prin.
Lawrence MS, 1110 12TH AVE S   37203
  Dr. George Kersey, prin.
Lockeland MS, 105 S 17TH ST   37206
  Dr. Maurice McDonald, prin.
McCann ES, 1300 56TH AVE N   37209
  Howard Allen, prin.
McGavock ES, 275 MCGAVOCK PIKE   37214
  (—), prin.
McKissack MS, 915 38TH AVE N   37209
  (—), prin.
Mills ES, 4106 KENNEDY AVE   37216
  Nancy Edwards, prin.
Napier ES, 60 FAIRFIELD AVE   37210
  J. Taylor, prin.
Paragon Mills ES
  260 PARAGON MILLS RD   37211
  James Bass, prin.
Park Avenue ES, 3703 PARK AVE   37209
  Steve Barron, prin.
Pennington ES, 2940 DONNA HILL DR   37214
  Dr. Robert Halpin, prin.
Priest ES, 1700 OTTER CREEK RD   37215
  Dorothy Butler, prin.
Rose Park MS, 1025 9TH AVE S   37203
  Oliver Smith, prin.
Rosebank ES, 1012 PRESTON DR   37206
  William Hooper, prin.
Ross ES, 1300 ORDWAY PL   37206
  Emma Buford, prin.
Shwab ES, 1500 DICKERSON RD   37207
  Bargara Harris, prin.
Stokes MS, 3701 BELMONT BLVD   37215
  Dr. H. Miller, prin.
Sylvan Park ES, 4801 UTAH AVE   37209
  Carole Candiles, prin.
Tusculum ES, 4917 NOLENSVILLE RD   37211
  Larry Huggins, prin.
Una ES, 2018 MURFREESBORO ROAD   37217
  (—), prin.
Wade ES, 5022 OLD HYDES FERRY RD   37218
  Dr. Thurman Pate,Jr., prin.
Warner ES, 626 RUSSELL ST   37206
  Carlene Bowers, prin.
Westmeade ES, 6641 CLEARBROOK DR   37205
  Helen Richardson, prin.
Wharton MS, 1625 18TH AVE N   37208
  Dr. Pauline Maupin, prin.
Whitsitt ES, 110 WHITSETT RD   37210
  Robert Wright, prin.
Other Schools – See Antioch, Brentwood,
  Goodlettsville, Hermitage, Joelton, Madison, Old
  Hickory, Whites Creek

University School of Nashville
  2000 EDGEHILL AVE   37212
Christ the King School
  3105 BELMONT BLVD   37212
Ensworth School, 211 ENSWORTH AVE   37205
Greater Nashvle SDA Jr. Academy
  3307 BRICK CHURCH PIKE   37207
Harding Academy
  HARDING PL AND WINDSOR DR   37205
Holy Rosary Academy, 190 GRAYLYNN DR   37214
Oak Hill School, 4815 FRANKLIN RD   37220
Overbrook School, 4210 HARDING RD   37205

St. Ann School, 5105 CHARLOTTE AVE   37209
St. Bernard Nongraded Academy
  2021 21ST AVE S   37212
St. Edward School, 190 THOMPSON LN   37211
St. Henry School, 6401 HARDING RD   37205
St. Pius X School, 2750 TUCKER RD   37218
St. Vincent De Paul School
  1708 HEIMAN ST   37208

Newbern, Dyer Co., Pop. Code 5
  Dyer County SD
  Supt. – See Dyersburg
  ES, 320 WASHINGTON ST   38059
    Carlton Cherry, prin.

Newcomb, Campbell Co.
  Campbell County SD
  Supt. – See Jacksboro
  ES   37819 – Kenneth Johnson, prin.

New Johnsonville, Humphreys Co., Pop. Code 4
  Humphreys County SD
  Supt. – See Waverly
  Lakeview ES   37134 – Jessie McNeil, prin.

New Market, Jefferson Co., Pop. Code 4
  Jefferson County SD
  Supt. – See Dandridge
  ES, P O BOX 197   37820 – Gary Strange, prin.

Newport, Cocke Co., Pop. Code 6
  Cocke County SD
  Sch. Sys. Enr. Code 5
  Supt. – Charles Seehorn, COLLEGE ST   37821
  Bridgeport ES, RURAL ROUTE 04   37821
    Steve Davidson, prin.
  Centerview ES, RURAL ROUTE 03   37821
    David Bible, prin.
  Edgemont ES, RURAL ROUTE 01   37821
    Dale Campbell, prin.
  Northwest ES
    RURAL ROUTE 06   BOX 1330   37821
    H. Gregory, prin.
  Other Schools – See Cosby, Del Rio, Hartford,
    Parrottsville

  Newport SD
  Sch. Sys. Enr. Code 3
  Supt. – Dr. James Gaddis, 202 COLLEGE ST   37821
  ES, 202 COLLEGE ST   37821 – James Gaddis, prin.

New Tazewell, Claiborne Co., Pop. Code 4
  Clairborne County SD
  Supt. – See Tazewell
  Midway ES   37825 – Leonard Bundren, prin.
  Tazewell New T. ES   37825 – Steve Minton, prin.

Niota, McMinn Co., Pop. Code 3
  McMinn County SD
  Supt. – See Athens
  ES   37826 – Robert Mahoney, prin.

Nolensville, Williamson Co.
  Williamson County SD
  Supt. – See Franklin
  ES, RURAL ROUTE 01 BOX 3   37135
    Ann Gordon, prin.

Normandy, Bedford Co., Pop. Code 2
  Coffee County SD
  Supt. – See Manchester
  Jones ES, RURAL ROUTE 01 BOX 107   37360
    Linda Walden, prin.

Norris, Anderson Co., Pop. Code 4
  Anderson County SD
  Supt. – See Clinton
  Norris MS   37828 – David Vaccaro, prin.
  ES   37828 – Ellayn Crossno, prin.

Oakdale, Morgan Co., Pop. Code 2
  Morgan County SD
  Supt. – See Wartburg
  Oakdale S   37829 – Paul Scarbrough, prin.

Oakland, Fayette Co., Pop. Code 2
  Fayette County SD
  Supt. – See Somerville
  ES, P O BOX 388   38060 – Odalia Jones, prin.

Oak Ridge, Anderson Co., Pop. Code 8
  Oak Ridge CSD
  Sch. Sys. Enr. Code 5
  Supt. – Dr. Robert Smallridge
    NEW YORK AVE   37830
  Glenwood ES, 125 AUDUBON RD   37830
    Howe Irwin, prin.
  Linden ES, 700 ROBERTSVILLE RD   37830
    Lana Yarbrough, prin.
  Willow Brook ES, 298 ROBERTSVILLE RD   37830
    George Walker, prin.
  Woodland ES, MARIETTA CIRCLE   37830
    Karleen Richter, prin.

St. Mary School, 323 VERMONT AVE   37830

Oldfort, Polk Co.
  Polk County SD.
  Supt. – See Benton
  South Polk ES   37362 – Andrew Harbison, prin.

Old Hickory, Davidson Co., Pop. Code 6
  Davidson County SD
  Supt. – See Nashville
  Dupont MS, 2001 HADLEY AVE   37138
    Paul Burgess, prin.
  Dupont ES, 1311 9TH ST   37138
    Faye Goodman, prin.

Jackson ES, 110 SHUTE LN 37138
Betty Cannon, prin.

Oliver Springs, Anderson Co., Pop. Code 5
Anderson County SD
Supt. – See Clinton
Norwood ES, 669 TRI CO BLVD 37840
Ernest Payne, prin.

Morgan County SD
Supt. – See Wartburg
Joyner ES, RURAL ROUTE 01 BOX 110-A 37840
Ronald Wilson, prin.

Roane County SD
Supt. – See Kingston
ES, P O BOX A 37840 – Richard Davis,Jr., prin.

Oneida, Scott Co., Pop. Code 5
Oneida CSD
Sch. Sys. Enr. Code 4
Supt. – Larry Miller, 110 BANK ST 37841
ES, P O BOX 1015 37841 – Lynn Williamson, prin.

Scott County SD
Supt. – See Huntsville
Burchfield ES, RURAL ROUTE 03 37841
Dwaine Limburg, prin.

Ooltewah, Hamilton Co., Pop. Code 3
Hamilton County SD
Supt. – See Chattanooga
MS, P O BOX 470 37363 – Betty Robinson, prin.
Mountain Oaks ES, 5610 CHERRY ST 37363
Russell Ayers, prin.
ES, 9232 LEE HWY 37363 – William Elsea, prin.
Snow Hill ES, 9042 CAREER LN 37363
Rodney Thompson, prin.

Pall Mall, Fentress Co.
Fentress County SD
Supt. – See Jamestown
ES 38577 – Daryl Rains, prin.

Palmer, Grundy Co., Pop. Code 4
Grundy County SD
Supt. – See Altamont
ES 37365 – Eugene Watson, prin.

Palmersville, Weakley Co., Pop. Code 4
Weakley County SD
Supt. – See Dresden
S, ZION ROAD 38241 – Rob Montgomery, prin.

Paris, Henry Co., Pop. Code 7
Henry County SD
Sch. Sys. Enr. Code 5
Supt. – Frank R. Gallimore, P O BOX 47 38242
Grove JHS, 900 GROVE ST 38242
Lucas Welch, prin.
Other Schools – See Buchanan, Cottage Grove, Henry,
Puryear, Springville

Paris SD
Sch. Sys. Enr. Code 4
Supt. – Larry Vick, 402 LEE ST 38242
Inman ES, 400 HARRISON ST 38242
Joy Call, prin.
Porter ES, 500 WALNUT ST 38242
Keith Chilcutt, prin.
Rhea ES, LONE OAK ROAD 38242
J. Underwood, prin.

Parrottsville, Cocke Co., Pop. Code 2
Cocke County SD
Supt. – See Newport
ES, RURAL ROUTE 02 37843 – Larry Blazer, prin.

Parsons, Decatur Co., Pop. Code 4
Decatur County SD
Supt. – See Decaturville
JHS 38363 – Grafton Dodd, prin.
ES 38363 – Patricia Wentworth, prin.

Pegram, Cheatham Co., Pop. Code 4
Cheatham County SD
Supt. – See Ashland City
ES, DOGWOOD LN 37143 – Martha Frazer, prin.

Pelham, Grundy Co.
Grundy County SD
Supt. – See Altamont
ES 37366 – Lloyd Carden, prin.

Petersburg, Lincoln Co., Pop. Code 3
Lincoln County SD
Supt. – See Fayetteville
Boonshill ES, RURAL ROUTE 02 37144
Delton Ashby, prin.
ES, RURAL ROUTE 02 BOX 20 37144
Janine Wilson, prin.

Philadelphia, Loudon Co., Pop. Code 3
Loudon County SD
Supt. – See Loudon
ES, SPRING ST 37846 – Edward Waller III, prin.

Pigeon Forge, Sevier Co., Pop. Code 4
Sevier County SD
Supt. – See Sevierville
MS, 215 PINE MOUNTAIN ROAD 37863
Jerry Wear, prin.
PS, 300 WEARS VALLEY RD 37863
Max Watson, prin.

Pikeville, Bledsoe Co., Pop. Code 4
Bledsoe County SD
Sch. Sys. Enr. Code 4
Supt. – Thad Colvard, P O BOX 369 37367

Dill ES, RURAL ROUTE 02 37367
Bennett Roynton, prin.
ES 37367 – Venia McJunkin, prin.
Rigsby ES, RURAL ROUTE 05 37367
Leon Hitchcox, prin.
Wheeler ES, RURAL ROUTE 04 37367
Michael Snyder, prin.

Piney Flats, Sullivan Co.
Sullivan County SD
Supt. – See Blountville
Hughes ES, RURAL ROUTE 02 BOX 153 37686
Dwight Mason, prin.

Pinson, Madison Co.
Madison County SD
Supt. – See Jackson
ES, P O BOX 30 38366 – Robert Morrison, prin.

Pioneer, Campbell Co.
Campbell County SD
Supt. – See Jacksboro
Elk Valley ES, RURAL ROUTE 02 37847
Gilbert Lay, prin.

Pleasant Hill, Cumberland Co., Pop. Code 2
Cumberland County SD
Supt. – See Crossville
ES, P O BOX 8 38578 – Dane Sorrell, prin.

Pleasant Shade, Smith Co.
Smith County SD
Supt. – See Carthage
ES, RURAL ROUTE 01 37145
Sherry Shoulders, prin.

Pleasant View, Cheatham Co., Pop. Code 6
Cheatham County SD
Supt. – See Ashland City
Sycamore MS, RURAL ROUTE 01 37146
William Sapp, prin.
ES, CHURCH ST 37146 – Tom Pardue, prin.

Portland, Sumner Co., Pop. Code 5
Sumner County SD
Supt. – See Gallatin
MS, HIGHWAY 109 S 37148 – Bob Little, prin.
Hardison ES, 300 GIBSON ST 37148
Glenn Gregory, prin.
Riggs MS, RURAL ROUTE 03 37148
Hilman Key, prin.

Highland SDA School, 400 HIGHLAND CIR 37148

Powell, Knox Co., Pop. Code 6
Anderson County SD
Supt. – See Clinton
Claxton ES, RT 8 BOX 166 CLINTON HWY 37849
V. Stonecipher, prin.

Knox County SD
Supt. – See Knoxville
MS, 5329 EMORY ROAD NW 37849
Benton Stewart, prin.
Cooper Ridge ES, RURAL ROUTE 06 37849
Charles Cameron, prin.
ES, 1711 SPRING ST 37849 – Freda Eidson, prin.

Primm Springs, Hickman Co.
Williamson County SD
Supt. – See Franklin
Pinewood Heights ES
RURAL ROUTE 01 BOX 138 38476
Wayne Fox, prin.

Pulaski, Giles Co., Pop. Code 6
Giles County SD
Sch. Sys. Enr. Code 5
Supt. – James Abernathy
720 W FLOWER ST 38478
Bridgeforth MS, BRIDGEFORTH CIRCLE 38478
Charles Brener, prin.
ES, 606 S CEDAR LN 38478 – Warren Burns, prin.
Other Schools – See Elkton, Lynnville, Minor Hill

Puryear, Henry Co., Pop. Code 3
Henry County SD
Supt. – See Paris
ES 38251 – Gary Smith, prin.

Ramer, McNairy Co., Pop. Code 2
McNairy County SD
Supt. – See Selmer
ES, P O BOX 8 38367 – Freddie Moore, prin.

Readyville, Cannon Co.
Cannon County SD
Supt. – See Woodbury
West Side ES, RURAL ROUTE 02 37149
Ronald Basham, prin.

Rutherford County SD
Supt. – See Murfreesboro
Kittrell ES, RURAL ROUTE 01 37149
Billy Summers, prin.

Reagan, Henderson Co.
Henderson County SD
Supt. – See Lexington
South Side ES 38368 – Neal Wright, prin.

Red Boiling Springs, Macon Co., Pop. Code 4
Clay County SD
Supt. – See Celina
Hermitage Springs S 37150 – Ron Roberts, prin.

Macon County SD
Supt. – See Lafayette
S 37150 – Charles Biles, prin.

Riceville, McMinn Co.
McMinn County SD
Supt. – See Athens
ES 37370 – William Bridges, prin.

Rickman, Overton Co., Pop. Code 2
Overton County SD
Supt. – See Livingston
ES 38580 – Kenneth Dodson, prin.

Ridgely, Lake Co., Pop. Code 4
Lake County SD
Supt. – See Tiptonville
Kendall ES, 200 W COLLEGE ST 38080
Howard Todd, prin.

Ridgetop, Robertson Co., Pop. Code 4
Robertson County SD
Supt. – See Springfield
Watauga ES, P O BOX 195 37152
Roy McConnell, prin.

Ripley, Lauderdale Co., Pop. Code 6
Lauderdale County SD
Sch. Sys. Enr. Code 5
Supt. – Phillip Jackson
402 S WASHINGTON 38063
Lauderdale MS, 230 GRIGGS AVE 38063
Walter Harris, prin.
ES, 225 VOLZ AVE 38063 – Jack Phillips, prin.
Other Schools – See Halls

Rives, Obion Co., Pop. Code 2
Obion County SD
Supt. – See Union City
ES 38253 – Donnie Braswell, prin.

Roan Mountain, Carter Co., Pop. Code 5
Carter County SD
Supt. – See Elizabethton
Cloudland ES, RURAL ROUTE 01 37687
Carter Blevins, prin.

Robbins, Scott Co.
Scott County SD
Supt. – See Huntsville
ES 37852 – Donald Branim, prin.

Rockford, Blount Co., Pop. Code 3
Blount County SD
Supt. – See Maryville
ES, RURAL ROUTE 02 BOX 51 37853
William Crisp, prin.

Rock Island, Warren Co.
Warren County SD
Supt. – See Mc Minnville
East ES, RURAL ROUTE 03 BOX 110 38581
Charles Collier, prin.

Rockvale, Rutherford Co.
Rutherford County SD
Supt. – See Murfreesboro
ES 37153 – Richard Wise, prin.

Rockwood, Roane Co., Pop. Code 6
Cumberland County SD
Supt. – See Crossville
Pine View ES, RURAL ROUTE 01 BOX 419 37854
Lawrence Buck, prin.

Roane County SD
Supt. – See Kingston
Ridge View ES, 625 PUMPHOUSE RD 37854
M. Honeycutt, prin.

Rogersville, Hawkins Co., Pop. Code 5
Hawkins County SD
Sch. Sys. Enr. Code 6
Supt. – Robert Cooper, 200 N DEPOT ST 37857
MS, 950 MCKINNEY AVE E 37857
Joe Davis, prin.
Hawkins ES, 1121 E MAIN ST 37857
Douglas Seal, prin.
Keplar ES, RURAL ROUTE 06 37857
Tommy Dykes, prin.
Other Schools – See Bulls Gap, Church Hill, Eidson,
Mooresburg, Surgoinsville

Rogersville SD
Sch. Sys. Enr. Code 3
Supt. – Dr.Gary Peevely
116 W BROADWAY ST 37857
ES, 116 W BROADWAY ST 37857
Dr. Gary Peevely, prin.

Russellville, Hamblen Co., Pop. Code 3
Hamblen County SD
Supt. – See Morristown
East Ridge MS, P O BOX 192A 37860
Glen Kanipe, prin.
ES, 5655 OLD RUSSELLVILLE PIKE 37860
Sam Taylor, prin.

Rutherford, Gibson Co., Pop. Code 4
Gibson CSD
Supt. – See Dyer
ES, 108 W KNOX 38369 – James Orr, prin.

Rutledge, Grainger Co., Pop. Code 4
Grainger County SD
Sch. Sys. Enr. Code 5
Supt. – Vernon Coffey, P O BOX 38 37861
MS, P O BOX 67 37861 – Keith Rich, prin.
Joppa ES, RURAL ROUTE 01 BOX 235A 37861
Steve McLane, prin.
ES, P O BOX 67 37861 – Keith Rich, prin.
Other Schools – See Bean Station, Washburn

Sale Creek, Hamilton Co., Pop. Code 5
Hamilton County SD
Supt. – See Chattanooga
S, 211 PATTERSON ROAD 37373
Dave Testerman, prin.

Saltillo, Hardin Co., Pop. Code 2
Hardin County SD
Supt. – See Savannah
ES 38370 – Kenny Harris, prin.

Santa Fe, Maury Co., Pop. Code 5
Maury County SD
Supt. – See Columbia
S, P O BOX F 38482 – Ken Jackson, prin.

Savannah, Hardin Co., Pop. Code 6
Hardin County SD
Sch. Sys. Enr. Code 5
Supt. – Dr. Elizabeth Ralston
616 HARLEM ST 38372
Cerro Gordo ES, RURAL ROUTE 06 38372
Jean Holbert, prin.
Nixon ES, RURAL ROUTE 04 38372
Lonnie Barnett, prin.
North Savannah ES, TENNESSEE ST 38372
Billy Garrard, prin.
South ES, RURAL ROUTE 07 BOX 175 38372
Kenneth Smith, prin.
Walker ES, RURAL ROUTE 04 38372
Patricia White, prin.
Walnut Grove ES, RURAL ROUTE 01 38372
Linda Gean, prin.
Whites ES, RURAL ROUTE 05 38372
Margaret Jerrolds, prin.
Other Schools – See Adamsville, Counce, Saltillo

Scotts Hill, Henderson Co., Pop. Code 3
Decatur County SD
Supt. – See Decaturville
S 38374 – Charles Woody, prin.

Selmer, McNairy Co., Pop. Code 5
McNairy County SD
Sch. Sys. Enr. Code 5
Supt. – Estel Mills 38375
MS, 635 POPLAR AVE 38375
Frank Congiardo, prin.
ES, 533 POPLAR AVE 38375
Carolyn Giesler, prin.
Other Schools – See Adamsville, Bethel Springs, Michie, Ramer

Sevierville, Sevier Co., Pop. Code 5
Sevier County SD
Sch. Sys. Enr. Code 6
Supt. – T. Mack Sharpe, 226 CEDAR ST 37862
MS, 550 HIGH ST 37862 – Mary Teaque, prin.
Catons Chapel ES, RURAL ROUTE 09 37862
Bill Hatcher, prin.
New Center ES, RURAL ROUTE 08 37862
Nina Manning, prin.
Pittman Center ES, RURAL ROUTE 09 37862
Jerry Wear, prin.
PS, 224 CEDAR ST 37862 – Andrea Roe, prin.
Wearwood ES, RURAL ROUTE 07 37862
John Enloe, prin.
Other Schools – See Cosby, Gatlinburg, Kodak, Pigeon Forge, Seymour

Sewanee, Franklin Co., Pop. Code 5
Franklin County SD
Supt. – See Winchester
ES, UNIVERSITY DR 37375 – Ruth Ramseur, prin.

Seymour, Sevier Co., Pop. Code 1
Sevier County SD
Supt. – See Sevierville
MS, 732 BOYDS CREEK HWY 37865
John Wade, prin.
ES, 717 BOYDS CREEK HWY 37865
Bill Smith, prin.

Shady Valley, Johnson Co.
Johnson County SD
Supt. – See Mountain City
ES 37688 – Richard Blevins, prin.

Sharon, Weakley Co., Pop. Code 4
Weakley County SD
Supt. – See Dresden
S, N WOODLAWN DRIVE 38255
Don Capps, prin.

Sharps Chapel, Union Co.
Union County SD
Supt. – See Maynardville
ES 37866 – Fredrick West, prin.

Shelbyville, Bedford Co., Pop. Code 7
Bedford County SD
Sch. Sys. Enr. Code 6
Supt. – Earl Harris, 500 MADISON ST 37160
Harris MS, 400 ELM ST 37160
Terry Saylor, prin.
Eakin ES, 1100 GLENOAKS RD 37160
Don Shelton, prin.
East Side ES, 421 ELLIOTT ST 37160
Jimmy Woodson, prin.
Liberty ES, RURAL ROUTE 04 37160
Bernard Bydalek, prin.
South Side ES, 903 S CANNON BLVD 37160
Ralph McBride, prin.
Thomas ES, 515 TATE AVE 37160
Pat Gore, prin.
Other Schools – See Unionville, Wartrace

Sherwood, Franklin Co.
Franklin County SD
Supt. – See Winchester
ES, HWY 124 37376 – Mark Clifton, prin.

Signal Mountain, Hamilton Co., Pop. Code 6
Hamilton County SD
Supt. – See Chattanooga
JHS, 315 AULT ROAD 37377 – Helen White, prin.
Bachman ES, 2815 ANDERSON PIKE 37377
Elizabeth Fassnacht, prin.
ES, 809 KY AVE 37377 – Norbert Kier, prin.
Thrasher MS, 1301 JAMES BLVD 37377
S. Wheeler, prin.

Smithville, De Kalb Co., Pop. Code 5
DeKalb County SD
Sch. Sys. Enr. Code 5
Supt. – Aubrey Turner,Jr., 104 S 3RD ST 37166
DeKalb County MS 37166 – Tucker Hendrix, prin.
ES 37166 – Glen Page, prin.
Other Schools – See Liberty

Smyrna, Rutherford Co., Pop. Code 6
Rutherford County SD
Supt. – See Murfreesboro
Francis JHS, P O BOX 249 37167
Don Jernigan, prin.
Colemon ES, LONGSTREET DR 37167
Leonard Zachery, prin.
MS, P O BOX 815 37167 – Elam Carlton, prin.
Smyrna MS West, P O BOX 835 37167
Nelda Harrison, prin.
PS, P O BOX 305 37167 – Terry Davenport, prin.
Youree ES, P O BOX 67 37167 – Don Odom, prin.

Sneedville, Hancock Co., Pop. Code 4
Hancock County SD
Sch. Sys. Enr. Code 4
Supt. – Mike Antrican, P O BOX 187 37869
Hancock Central ES 37869 – Dennis Greene, prin.
Mathis ES 37869 – Debra Reed, prin.
Mulberry Gap ES 37869 – Fred Jones, prin.
Other Schools – See Kyles Ford, Treadway

Soddy-Daisy, Hamilton Co., Pop. Code 6
Hamilton County SD
Supt. – See Chattanooga
JHS, 200 TURNER ROAD 37379
Jane Barker, prin.
Allen ES, 9811 DALLAS HOLLOW RD 37379
Nesha Upton, prin.
Daisy ES, 620 SEQUOYAH RD 37379
Kenneth Barker, prin.
Mowbray ES, 1709 MOWBRAY PIKE 37379
DeVota Barnes, prin.
Soddy ES, 260 SCHOOL ST 37379
Freddie Schmid, prin.

Somerville, Fayette Co., Pop. Code 4
Fayette County SD
Sch. Sys. Enr. Code 6
Supt. – Dr. Warner Dickerson, P O BOX 10 38068
Central ES, RURAL ROUTE 04 38068
William Weddle, prin.
Jefferson ES, RURAL ROUTE 05 38068
Andrew Perry, prin.
ES, 412 S MAIN ST 38068 – Lillie Fletcher, prin.
Other Schools – See Macon, Mason, Moscow, Oakland

South Fulton, Obion Co., Pop. Code 5
Obion County SD
Supt. – See Union City
ES, 202 SMITH ST 38257 – Clifford Wright, prin.

South Pittsburg, Marion Co., Pop. Code 5
Marion County SD
Supt. – See Jasper
ES 37380 – Richard Lawson, prin.

Richard CSD
Sch. Sys. Enr. Code 2
Supt. – Laura Raulston
1620 HAMILTON AVE 37380
Hardy Memorial ES, 1620 HAMILTON AVE 37380
Laura Raulston, prin.

Sparta, White Co., Pop. Code 5
White County SD
Sch. Sys. Enr. Code 5
Supt. – James Rascoe, 136 BAKER ST 38583
White County MS, 216 HIGH SCHOOL ST 38583
Roy Heady, prin.
Bon De Croft ES, P O BOX 265 38583
Barry Roberts, prin.
Cassville ES, RURAL ROUTE 04 BOX 347 38583
Dennis Wood, prin.
Findlay ES, RURAL ROUTE 02 BOX 111 38583
David Whiteaker, prin.
Woodland Park ES, RURAL ROUTE 03 38583
David McCulley, prin.
Other Schools – See Doyle, Walling

Speedwell, Claiborne Co.
Clairborne County SD
Supt. – See Tazewell
Powell Valley ES 37870 – Kenneth West, prin.

Spencer, Van Buren Co., Pop. Code 4
Van Buren County SD
Sch. Sys. Enr. Code 3
Supt. – Albert Jones,Jr., P O BOX 98 38585
Mountain View ES, RURAL ROUTE 01 38585
Herbert VanWinkle, prin.
ES 38585 – Larry Yates, prin.

Spring City, Rhea Co., Pop. Code 4
Rhea County SD
Supt. – See Dayton
ES, P O BOX 367 37381 – James Pemberton, prin.

Springfield, Robertson Co., Pop. Code 7
Robertson County SD
Sch. Sys. Enr. Code 6
Supt. – Jerome Ellis
22ND AND WOODLAND ST 37172
MS, 5TH AVE W 37172 – Dick Stewart, prin.
Bransford ES, BRANSFORD DR 37172
Robert Farmer, prin.
Cheatham Park ES, 4TH AVE W 37172
Steve Moss, prin.
Coopertown ES, RURAL ROUTE 01 37172
Charles Dudas, prin.
Krisle ES, RURAL ROUTE 05 37172
Marlin Sholar, prin.
Westside MS, RURAL ROUTE 02 37172
Ronnie Meador, prin.
Other Schools – See Cedar Hill, Cross Plains, Greenbrier, Ridgetop, White House

Spring Hill, Maury Co., Pop. Code 3
Maury County SD
Supt. – See Columbia
ES, HWY 31 37174 – Noel Evans, prin.

Springville, Henry Co.
Henry County SD
Supt. – See Paris
ES 38256 – Charles Cate, prin.

Strawberry Plains, Knox Co.
Jefferson County SD
Supt. – See Dandridge
Strong ES, P O BOX 280 37871 – Martin Dail, prin.

Knox County SD
Supt. – See Knoxville
Carter MS, RURAL ROUTE 02 37871
Sandra Hamilton, prin.
Carter ES, RURAL ROUTE 02 37871
Bill Huffaker, prin.

Summertown, Lawrence Co., Pop. Code 4
Lawrence County SD
Supt. – See Lawrenceburg
ES, P O BOX 48 38483 – Dan Putman, prin.

Sunbright, Morgan Co., Pop. Code 5
Morgan County SD
Supt. – See Wartburg
S 37872 – James Jones, prin.

Surgoinsville, Hawkins Co., Pop. Code 4
Hawkins County SD
Supt. – See Rogersville
MS, RURAL ROUTE 01 BOX 44 37873
Ken McNabb, prin.
ES, P O BOX 239 37873 – Carroll Raines, prin.

Sweetwater, Monroe Co., Pop. Code 5
Sweetwater CSD
Sch. Sys. Enr. Code 4
Supt. – Joe Sherlin, MONROE ST 37874
JHS 37874 – Sam Parker, prin.
Brown MS 37874 – August Hadorn, prin.
ES 37874 – Stephen Hickey, prin.

Taft, Lincoln Co.
Lincoln County SD
Supt. – See Fayetteville
Blanche ES, RURAL ROUTE 02 BOX 64 38488
Buford Beadle, prin.

Talbott, Hamlden Co.
Jefferson County SD
Supt. – See Dandridge
ES, RURAL ROUTE 01 37877 – Keith Craig, prin.

Tazewell, Claiborne Co., Pop. Code 4
Clairborne County SD
Sch. Sys. Enr. Code 6
Supt. – Dennis Peters, P O BOX 179 37879
Soldiers Memorial MS
RURAL ROUTE 01 BOX 55 37879
Lynn Barnard, prin.
Springdale ES 37879 – Janet Barnard, prin.
Other Schools – See Clairfield, Harrogate, New Tazewell, Speedwell

Tellico Plains, Monroe Co., Pop. Code 3
Monroe County SD
Supt. – See Madisonville
JHS 37385 – Bruce Beaty, prin.
Ball Play ES, RURAL ROUTE 03 37385
Dale Toomey, prin.
Coker Creek ES, RURAL ROUTE 02 37385
Rex Yates, prin.
Rural Vale ES, RURAL ROUTE 01 37385
Carol Best, prin.
ES 37385 – Mitchell Millsaps, prin.

Ten Mile, Meigs Co.
Meigs County SD
Supt. – See Decatur
ES, RURAL ROUTE 01 BOX 5 37880
Mary Woody, prin.

Tennessee Ridge, Houston Co., Pop. Code 4
Houston County SD
Supt. – See Erin
ES 37178 – Arvel Atkins, prin.

Thompsons Station, Williamson Co.
Williamson County SD
Supt. – See Franklin

Bethesda ES, RURAL ROUTE 02 37179
Michael Harris, prin.

Tiptonville, Lake Co., Pop. Code 4
Lake County SD
Sch. Sys. Enr. Code 4
Supt. – James W. Wilson, P O BOX 397 38079
Newton ES, 819 CHURCH ST 38079
Tommy Lovell, prin.
Other Schools – See Ridgely

Toone, Hardeman Co., Pop. Code 2
Hardeman County SD
Supt. – See Bolivar
ES 38381 – Henry Parramore,Jr., prin.

Townsend, Blount Co., Pop. Code 2
Blount County SD
Supt. – See Maryville
ES 37882 – Margie Carico, prin.

Tracy City, Grundy Co., Pop. Code 4
Grundy County SD
Supt. – See Altamont
Tracy ES 37387 – Ronnie Fults, prin.

Trade, Johnson Co.
Johnson County SD
Supt. – See Mountain City
ES 37691 – Vickie Livesay, prin.

Treadway, Hancock Co.
Hancock County SD
Supt. – See Sneedville
Flat Gap ES 37883 – Sydney Seal, prin.

Trenton, Gibson Co., Pop. Code 5
Gibson CSD
Supt. – See Dyer
Spring Hill ES, RURAL ROUTE 03 BOX 144 38382
Thomas Walters, prin.

Trenton CSD
Sch. Sys. Enr. Code 4
Supt. – Larry J. Ridings, 201 W 10TH ST 38382
Trenton MS East, 201 W TENTH ST 38382
Willie Bond, prin.
ES, 805 S COLLEGE ST 38382 – Andy Leach, prin.

Trezevant, Carroll Co., Pop. Code 3
West Carroll SD
Supt. – See Mc Lemoresville
West Carroll MS, HARBER ST 38258
Thomas Dees, prin.

Trimble, Dyer Co., Pop. Code 3
Dyer County SD
Supt. – See Dyersburg
ES 38259 – Kenneth Galloway, prin.

Troy, Obion Co., Pop. Code 4
Obion County SD
Supt. – See Union City
Hillcrest ES, RURAL ROUTE 02 38260
Charles Morris, prin.

Tullahoma, Coffee Co., Pop. Code 7
Coffee County SD
Supt. – See Manchester
Hickerson ES, RURAL ROUTE 02 BOX 103 37388
Reggie Johnson, prin.

Tullahoma CSD
Sch. Sys. Enr. Code 5
Supt. – Donald E. Embry
1001 S JACKSON ST N 37388
East MS, 900 COUNTRY CLUB DRIVE 37388
Rob Osteen, prin.
West MS, 301 DECHERD ST W 37388
John Wilson, prin.
Bel Aire ES, 500 STONE BLVD 37388
James Waters, prin.
East Lincoln ES, E LINCOLN ST 37388
Mike Robinson, prin.
Farrar ES, 215 WESTSIDE DR 37388
Sylvia Jones, prin.
Lee ES, LAYNE ST 37388 – Marilyn Morris, prin.

St. Paul the Apostle School
306 W GRIZZARD ST 37388

Turtletown, Polk Co.
Polk County SD.
Supt. – See Benton
ES 37391 – Rosella Carruth, prin.

Unicoi, Unicoi Co.
Unicoi County SD
Supt. – See Erwin
ES, RURAL ROUTE 01 37692
William Nuss, prin.

Union City, Obion Co., Pop. Code 7
Obion County SD
Sch. Sys. Enr. Code 5
Supt. – Vinson Thompson, P O BOX 747 38261
Lake Road ES, HWY 22 38261
Gary Houston, prin.
Other Schools – See Hornbeak, Kenton, Rives, South
Fulton, Troy

Union City CSD
Sch. Sys. Enr. Code 4
Supt. – Baxter Wheatley, P O BOX 749 38261
MS, 1111 HIGH SCHOOL DRIVE 38261
Bill Dowell, prin.
Central ES, 512 E COLLEGE ST 38261
Mary Welch, prin.
East Side MS, MILES AVE 38261
Donnie Cox, prin.

Unionville, Bedford Co., Pop. Code 5
Bedford County SD
Supt. – See Shelbyville
Community S, RURAL ROUTE 02 37180
Ed Gray, prin.

Vanleer, Dickson Co., Pop. Code 2
Dickson County SD
Supt. – See Charlotte
ES, RURAL ROUTE 01 BOX 238 37181
Janey Thomas, prin.

Viola, Warren Co., Pop. Code 1
Warren County SD
Supt. – See Mc Minnville
ES, P O BOX 38 37394 – Clyde Hale, prin.

Vonore, Monroe Co., Pop. Code 3
Monroe County SD
Supt. – See Madisonville
ES 37885 – Jean Black, prin.

Walland, Blount Co., Pop. Code 2
Blount County SD
Supt. – See Maryville
MS, RURAL ROUTE 01 37886 – (—), prin.
Rocky Branch ES, RURAL ROUTE 01 37886
John Sloan, prin.

Walling, White Co.
White County SD
Supt. – See Sparta
Central View ES, RURAL ROUTE 01 38587
Sue Carmichael, prin.

Wartburg, Morgan Co., Pop. Code 3
Morgan County SD
Sch. Sys. Enr. Code 5
Supt. – Allan Nance, P O BOX 348 37887
Central ES 37887 – Ken Vespie, prin.
Other Schools – See Coalfield, Oakdale, Oliver
Springs, Sunbright

Wartrace, Bedford Co., Pop. Code 3
Bedford County SD
Supt. – See Shelbyville
Cascade S, RURAL ROUTE 02 37183
Hal Skelton, prin.

Washburn, Grainger Co.
Grainger County SD
Supt. – See Rutledge
Washburn S, P O BOX 8 37888 – R. Coffey, prin.

Watauga, Carter Co., Pop. Code 2
Carter County SD
Supt. – See Elizabethton
Range ES, RURAL ROUTE 01 37694
Dallas Williams, prin.

Watertown, Wilson Co., Pop. Code 4
Wilson County SD
Supt. – See Lebanon
ES 37184 – Joe Mills, prin.

Waverly, Humphreys Co., Pop. Code 5
Humphreys County SD
Sch. Sys. Enr. Code 5
Supt. – James Long, 103 S CHURCH ST 37185
JHS 37185 – (—), prin.
ES 37185 – Enid Barber, prin.
Other Schools – See Mc Ewen, New Johnsonville

Waynesboro, Wayne Co., Pop. Code 4
Wayne County SD
Sch. Sys. Enr. Code 5
Supt. – Rick Brewer, P O BOX 658 38485
MS, P O BOX 657 38485 – Gailand Grinder, prin.
ES, P O BOX 216 38485 – Robert Cole, prin.
Other Schools – See Collinwood

Westmoreland, Sumner Co., Pop. Code 4
Macon County SD
Supt. – See Lafayette
Westside ES, RURAL ROUTE 02 37186
David Woods, prin.

Sumner County SD
Supt. – See Gallatin
ES, AUSTIN PEAY HWY 37186
Jimmy Brown, prin.

White Bluff, Dickson Co., Pop. Code 4
Dickson County SD
Supt. – See Charlotte
ES, P O BOX A 37187 – Kenneth Kerne, prin.

White House, Sumner Co., Pop. Code 4
Robertson County SD
Supt. – See Springfield
ES, 200 ELEMENTARY DR 37188
Robert Woodall, prin.

Sumner County SD
Supt. – See Gallatin
MS, P O BOX M 37188 – Carl Fussell, prin.

White Pine, Jefferson Co.
Jefferson County SD
Supt. – See Dandridge
ES, P O BOX A 37890 – David Jones, prin.

Whitesburg, Hamblen Co.
Hamblen County SD
Supt. – See Morristown
ES, 7859 E ANDREW JOHNSON HWY 37891
William Southern, prin.

Whites Creek, Davidson Co.
Davidson County SD
Supt. – See Nashville
Green ES, 4020 WHITES CREEK PIKE 37189
Ricky Binkley, prin.

Whiteville, Hardeman Co., Pop. Code 4
Hardeman County SD
Supt. – See Bolivar
ES, P O BOX 659 38075 – Yvonne Allen, prin.

Whitwell, Marion Co., Pop. Code 4
Marion County SD
Supt. – See Jasper
Crossroads ES, RURAL ROUTE 04 37397
Linda Hooper, prin.
Griffith Creek ES, RURAL ROUTE 03 37397
Landon Pickett, prin.
ES 37397 – Willie Hooper, prin.

Wildersville, Henderson Co.
Henderson County SD
Supt. – See Lexington
Beaver ES, RURAL ROUTE 01 38388
Kenneth Reed, prin.

Winchester, Franklin Co., Pop. Code 6
Franklin County SD
Sch. Sys. Enr. Code 6
Supt. – Dr. Jessie Warren, P O BOX 129 37398
Broadview ES, RURAL ROUTE 04 37398
Peggy Soderbom, prin.
Clark Memorial MS, 500 N JEFFERSON ST 37398
Danny Smith, prin.
Sharp ES, S COLLEGE ST 37398
Suzanne McDowell, prin.
Other Schools – See Cowan, Decherd, Estill Springs,
Huntland, Sewanee, Sherwood

Good Shepherd School
RURAL ROUTE 02 BOX 30 37398

Winfield, Scott Co.
Scott County SD
Supt. – See Huntsville
ES 37892 – James Hughett, prin.

Woodbury, Cannon Co., Pop. Code 4
Cannon County SD
Sch. Sys. Enr. Code 4
Supt. – Joe Davenport, 212 E WATER ST 37190
East Side ES, RURAL ROUTE 02 37190
Ann Bartholomew, prin.
Short Mountain ES, RURAL ROUTE 02 37190
Donald Hampton, prin.
ES, 500 W COLONIAL ST 37190
Joseph Haltom, prin.
Other Schools – See Auburntown, Bradyville,
Readyville

Woodlawn, Montgomery Co.
Montgomery County SD
Supt. – See Clarksville
ES, RURAL ROUTE 01 37191 – Lee Wallace, prin.

Yorkville, Gibson Co., Pop. Code 2
Gibson CSD
Supt. – See Dyer
ES, P O BOX 37 38389 – Richard Binkley, prin.

TEXAS

TEXAS EDUCATION AGENCY
1701 N. Congress Ave., Austin 78701
(512) 463-9734

Commissioner of Education	W. Kirby
Deputy Commissioner Education Quality	Carl Candoli
Deputy Commissioner Curriculum & Program Development	Victoria Bergin
Deputy Commissioner Finance & Compliance	Thomas Anderson
Deputy Commissioner Internal Management	James Hill
Deputy Commissioner Research & Information	Lynn Moak

STATE BOARD OF EDUCATION
Jon Brumley, *Chairperson*   Fort   Worth

COORDINATING BOARD, TEXAS COLLEGE AND UNIVERSITY SYSTEM
Dr. Kenneth Ashworth, *Commissioner of Higher Education*   P.O. Box 12788, Austin   78711

PUBLIC, PRIVATE, AND PAROCHIAL ELEMENTARY SCHOOLS

Abbott, Hill Co., Pop. Code 2
Abbott ISD
Sch. Sys. Enr. Code 2
Supt. – Harley Johnson, P O BOX 226   76621
S   76621 – Rob Johnston, prin.

Abernathy, Hale Co., Pop. Code 5
Abernathy ISD
Sch. Sys. Enr. Code 3
Supt. – Charles Floyd, 505 7TH ST   79311
MS   79311 – Steve Guerrant, prin.
ES, 505 7TH ST   79311 – Larry Aldridge, prin.

Abilene, Taylor Co., Pop. Code 8
Abilene ISD
Sch. Sys. Enr. Code 7
Supt. – Wayne Blevins, P O BOX 981   79604
Franklin MS, 1200 MERCHANT ST   79603
   Royce Curtis, prin.
Jefferson MS, 1741 S 14TH ST   79602
   Joe Humphrey, prin.
Lincoln MS, 1699 S 1ST ST   79602
   Robert Starr, prin.
Madison MS, 3145 BARROW ST   79605
   Mac Hurley, prin.
Mann MS, 2545 MIMOSA DRIVE   79603
   Glenn Petty, prin.
Alta Vista ES, 1929 S 11TH ST   79602
   Edgar Willard, prin.
Austin ES, 2341 GREENBRIAR DR   79605
   Sam Thomas, prin.
Bonham ES, 4250 POTOMAC AVE   79605
   Martha Murphy, prin.
Bowie ES   79604 – Bill Walker, prin.
College Heights ES, 1450 N 17TH ST   79601
   Hubert Pickett, prin.
Crockett ES, 3282 S 13TH ST   79605
   James Stovall, prin.
Dyess ES, DYESS AIR FORCE BASE   79607
   David Jones, prin.
Fannin ES, 2726 N 18TH ST   79603
   Kay McMahon, prin.
Jackson ES, 2650 S 32ND ST   79605
   Don Rogers, prin.
Johnston ES, 3602 N 12TH ST   79603
   Preston Parker, prin.
Jones ES, 2002 JAMESON ST   79603
   Ann Jones, prin.
Lee ES, 1026 N PIONEER DR   79603
   Robert Warner, prin.
Locust ES, 625 S 8TH ST   79602
   Tommie Allen, prin.
Long ES, 3600 SHERRY LANE   79603
   Pat Dudley, prin.
Reagan ES, 5340 HARTFORD ST   79605
   Pat Pool, prin.
Taylor ES, 916 N 13TH ST   79601
   Cam Hurst, prin.
Valley View ES, 1840 N 8TH ST   79603
   Kelly Moore, prin.

Wylie ISD
Sch. Sys. Enr. Code 4
Supt. – Marion Shelton
   7049 BUFFALO GAP ROAD   79606
Wylie MS, 3158 BELTWAY SOUTH   79606
   Dub Preston, prin.
Butterfield ES   79605 – Sue Humphrey, prin.
Wylie ES   79605 – Gary Hosch, prin.

Abilene Christian School
   2550 N JUDGE ELY   79601
St. John's Episcopal School
   1500 SHERMAN DRIVE   79605

Ackerly, Dawson Co., Pop. Code 2
Sands ISD
Sch. Sys. Enr. Code 2
Supt. – James Blake, P O BOX 218   79713
Sands JHS   79713 – Rick Mantooth, prin.
Sands ES   79713 – Lon McDonald, prin.

Addison, Dallas Co., Pop. Code 6

Trinity Christian School
   17001 ADDISON ROAD   75248

Adrian, Oldham Co., Pop. Code 2
Adrian ISD
Sch. Sys. Enr. Code 2
Supt. – Pat Blankenship, P O BOX 189   79001
S   79001 – Ted Hale, prin.

Afton, Dickens Co.
Patton Springs ISD
Sch. Sys. Enr. Code 2
Supt. – J. Barlow, P O BOX 2   79220
Patton Spring ES   79220 – Edward Shepler, prin.

Agua Dulce, Nueces Co., Pop. Code 3
Agua Dulce ISD
Sch. Sys. Enr. Code 2
Supt. – Tim Black, P O BOX 250   78330
ES   78330 – Jon Borhauer, prin.

Alanreed, Gray Co.
Alanreed ISD
Sch. Sys. Enr. Code 1
Supt. – Bill Adams, P O BOX B   79002
ES   79002 – Bill Adams, prin.

Alba, Wood Co., Pop. Code 3
Alba-Golden ISD
Sch. Sys. Enr. Code 3
Supt. – Elton Caldwell
   RURAL ROUTE 02 BOX 212H   75410
Alba-Golden ES   75410 – Ferrell Wright, prin.

Albany, Shackelford Co., Pop. Code 4
Albany ISD
Sch. Sys. Enr. Code 3
Supt. – Terry Harlow, P O BOX 188   76430
Smith ES   76430 – Gene Williams, prin.

Aledo, Parker Co., Pop. Code 4
Aledo ISD
Sch. Sys. Enr. Code 4
Supt. – Gerald Adams, P O BOX D   76008
MS   76008 – Randal Cahoon, prin.
MS   76008 – Willard Stuard, prin.
ES   76008 – Judy Ratlief, prin.

Alice, Jim Wells Co., Pop. Code 7
Alice ISD
Sch. Sys. Enr. Code 6
Supt. – Henry Herrera, 1801 E MAIN ST   78332
DuBose MS   78332 – Flynn Dennis, prin.
Garcia ES, OLD KINGSVILLE ROAD   78332
   Claudina Hernandez, prin.

Hillcrest ES, 1400 MORNINGSIDE DR   78332
   Amy Koenning, prin.
Memorial MS   78332 – Noel Estrada, prin.
Nayer ES, 501 CACTUS AVE   78332
   Ramon Garcia, prin.
Noonan ES, 701 W 3RD ST   78332
   Steve Lile, prin.
Saenz ES, 800 S JOHNSON ST   78332
   Candelario Ruiz, prin.
Salazar ES, 1028 PIERCE ST   78332
   Armengol Farias, prin.
Schallert ES, 1301 N TEXAS BLVD   78332
   Roberto Carrasco, prin.

St. Elizabeth ES, 615 E 5TH ST   78332
St. Joseph ES, 311 DEWEY AVE   78332

Alief, Harris Co., Pop. Code 8
Alief ISD
Sch. Sys. Enr. Code 7
Supt. – Wayne Blevins, P O BOX 68   77411
Albright MS   77411 – Dennis Paul, prin.
MS, P O BOX 68   77411 – Cathy Yasilli, prin.
Killough MS, P O BOX 68   77411
   Betty Murdock, prin.
Alexander ES, P O BOX 68   77411
   Jane Franklin, prin.
Boone ES, P O BOX 68   77411
   Carol Hankins, prin.
Chambers ES, P O BOX 68   77411
   Rick Greenwood, prin.
Chancellor ES, P O BOX 68   77411
   Bertha Jamison, prin.
Cummings ES, P O BOX 68   77411
   Patty Stevens, prin.
Flem Rees ES, P O BOX 68   77411
   James Keel, prin.
Hearne ES   77411 – Judy Miller, prin.
Heflin ES, P O BOX 68   77411
   Linda Shubert, prin.
Kennedy ES, P O BOX 68   77411
   Lillie Wilson, prin.
Liestman ES, P O BOX 68   77411
   Paula Smith, prin.
Mahanay ES, P O BOX 68   77411
   Fran Reasoner, prin.
Martin ES, P O BOX 68   77411
   Nancy Bowser, prin.
Petrosky ES, P O BOX 68   77411
   Betty Schroeder, prin.
Smith ES, P O BOX 68   77411 – Lucy Leta, prin.
Youens ES, P O BOX 68   77411
   Tami Ciarella, prin.
Other Schools – See Houston

Allen, Collin Co., Pop. Code 6
Allen ISD
Sch. Sys. Enr. Code 5
Supt. – Gene Davenport, P O BOX 13   75002
Ford MS, 630 PARK PLACE DR   75002
   Joe Champion, prin.
Boyd ES, 900 JUPITER ROAD   75002
   Rickie Clements, prin.
Reed ES, 1200 RIVERCREST BLVD   75002
   Norma Lewis, prin.
Rountree ES, 800 E MAIN ST   75002
   James Marion, prin.

Story ES, 1550 EDELWEISS DR 75002
  Russ Bratcher, prin.
Vaughan ES 75002 – (—), prin.

Peeblebrook Montessori School
  612 PEBBLEBROOK DR 75002

Allison, Wheeler Co.
  Allison ISD
  Sch. Sys. Enr. Code 1
  Supt. – David Mims, P O BOX 50 79003
  ES 79003 – (—), prin.

Alpine, Brewster Co., Pop. Code 6
  Alpine ISD
  Sch. Sys. Enr. Code 4
  Supt. – Charles Lamb, P O BOX 419 79831
  JHS, 705 W AVENUE D 79830
    Eldefonso Garcia, prin.
  ES, 200 W AVENUE A 79830
    Albert Hallford, prin.

Altair, Colorado Co.
  Rice Cons. ISD
  Sch. Sys. Enr. Code 4
  Supt. – Harold King, P O BOX 338 77412
  Eagle Lake MS 77412 – Charles Abel, prin.
  Eagle Lake PS 77412 – H. Benge, prin.
  Garwood ES 77412 – John Mader, prin.
  Sheridan ES 77412 – W. Gohlke, prin.

Alto, Cherokee Co., Pop. Code 4
  Alto ISD
  Sch. Sys. Enr. Code 3
  Supt. – John Cook, P O BOX 130 75925
  ES 75925 – Faye Rogers, prin.

Alvarado, Johnson Co., Pop. Code 5
  Alvarado ISD
  Sch. Sys. Enr. Code 4
  Supt. – S. Pruitt, P O BOX 387 76008
  MS, 103 CAMPUS DRIVE 76009
    Donna Magee, prin.
  Alvarado ES-North 76009 – Kathy Amburn, prin.
  MS 76009 – Jerald McCanlies, prin.
  Lillian ES 76009 – Karen Sero, prin.

Alvin, Brazoria Co., Pop. Code 7
  Alvin ISD
  Sch. Sys. Enr. Code 6
  Supt. – William Hasse, 605 W HOUSE ST 77511
  JHS, 2300 W SOUTH ST 77511
    Linda Robinson, prin.
  Harby JHS, 1500 HEIGHTS 77511
    Cliff Whitlock, prin.
  MS, 1910 ROSHARON ROAD 77511
    Patricia Sigler, prin.
  ES, 2401 W PARK DR 77511
    Beverly Walker, prin.
  Disney MS, 500 MUSTANG ROAD 77511
    Carolyn Wheeler, prin.
  Longfellow MS, 1200 E HOUSE ST 77511
    Jennifer Schaeffer, prin.
  Manvel ES, 7029 MASTERS 77511
    James Orr, prin.
  Stevenson ES, 4715 MUSTANG ROAD 77511
    Bob Verdine, prin.
  Twain PS, 610 E CLEMENS 77511 – J. Wood, prin.
  Other Schools – See Manvel

Alvord, Wise Co., Pop. Code 3
  Alvord ISD
  Sch. Sys. Enr. Code 2
  Supt. – Larry Wilson, P O BOX 85 76225
  JHS 76225 – Martha Hancock, prin.
  ES 76225 – Martha Lawson, prin.

Amarillo, Potter Co., Pop. Code 9
  Amarillo ISD
  Sch. Sys. Enr. Code 8
  Supt. – Lamar Lively, 910 W 8TH AVE 79101
  Austin MS, 1808 WIMBERLY ROAD 79109
    M. Miller, prin.
  Bonham MS, 5600 W 49TH AVE 79109
    Linda Gleghorn, prin.
  Bowie MS, 3001 E 12TH AVE 79104
    J. Krodel, prin.
  Crockett MS, 4720 FLOYD AVE 79106
    Jan Bowser, prin.
  Fannin MS, 4623 S RUSK ST 79110
    S. Barela, prin.
  Houston MS, 815 S INDEPENDENCE ST 79106
    David Smith, prin.
  Mann MS, 610 N BUCHANAN ST 79107
    Michael Mugits, prin.
  Travis MS, 2815 MARTIN ROAD 79107
    Charles Ritchie, prin.
  Avondale ES, 1500 S AVONDALE ST 79106
    Earlene Petropoulos, prin.
  Belmar ES, 6342 ADIRONDACK TRL 79106
    Charles Higley, prin.
  Bivins ES, 1500 S FANNIN ST 79102
    Doyce Wilhelm, prin.
  Carver Academy ES 79102 – Margaret Lynch, prin.
  Coronado ES, 3210 WIMBERLY ROAD 79109
    Mary Settle, prin.
  Eastridge ES, 1314 EVERGREEN ST 79107
    Carolyn Rice, prin.
  Emerson ES, 700 N LINCOLN ST 79107
    Jack Lewis, prin.
  Forest Hill ES, 3601 E AMARILLO BLVD 79107
    Loretta Johns, prin.
  Glenwood ES, 2407 S HOUSTON ST 79103
    Betty Solis, prin.
  Hamlet ES, 705 SYCAMORE ST 79107
    Frank Bowers, prin.

Humphrey's-Highland ES
  1301 S DALLAS ST 79104 – Gerald Watson, prin.
Lamar ES, 3800 S LIPSCOMB ST 79110
  Gaylia Cochran, prin.
Landergin ES, 3209 S TAYLOR ST 79110
  Jerry Pybus, prin.
Lawndale ES, 2215 S BIVINS ST 79103
  Shirley Thomas, prin.
Lee ES, 119 NE 15TH AVE 79107
  Lola Whitaker, prin.
Mesa Verde ES, 4011 BEAVER DR 79107
  Richard Ross, prin.
Oak Dale ES, 2711 S HILL ST 79103
  David Walvoord, prin.
Olsen Park ES, 2409 ANNA ST 79106
  William Mote, prin.
Paramount Terrace ES, 3906 W 40TH AVE 79109
  M. Powell, prin.
Pleasant Valley ES, 4413 RIVER ROAD 79108
  Pat Phillips, prin.
Puckett ES, 6700 OAKHURST DR 79109
  Bill Hill, prin.
Ridgecrest ES, 5306 W 37TH AVE 79109
  Margaret Frost, prin.
Rogers ES, 920 N MIRROR ST 79107
  Sible Roethke, prin.
San Jacinto ES, 3400 W 4TH AVE 79106
  Mary Reeve, prin.
Sanborn ES, 700 S ROBERTS ST 79102
  Salvador Martinez, prin.
Sleepy Hollow ES, 3501 REEDER DR 79121
  Denzil Bencini, prin.
South Georgia ES, 5018 SUSAN DR 79110
  Ronald Price, prin.
South Lawn ES, 4719 BOWIE ST 79110
  Don McMahon, prin.
Sunrise ES, 5123 E 14TH AVE 79104
  Allen Herron, prin.
Western Plateau ES 79109 – Harvest Riedt, prin.
Whittier ES, 2004 N MARRS ST 79107
  Patricia Williams, prin.
Willis ES, 3500 W 11TH AVE 79106
  Beverly Williams, prin.
Windsor ES 79101 – Julia Green, prin.
Wolflin ES, 2026 S HUGHES ST 79109
  Jerry Imel, prin.

Canyon ISD
  Supt. – See Canyon
Sundown Lane ES, 4616 SUNDOWN LANE 79118
  Cynthia Anderson, prin.

Highland Park ISD
  Sch. Sys. Enr. Code 2
  Supt. – Michael Salvato, P O BOX 30430 79120
  Highland Park ES, P O BOX 30430 79120
    Danny Cochran, prin.

River Road ISD
  Sch. Sys. Enr. Code 4
  Supt. – Gene Andrews
    RURAL ROUTE 09 BOX 1 79108
  Rolling Hills ES, W CHERRY AVE 79108
    William Dupree, prin.
  Willow Vista MS, 7600 PAVILLARD DR 79108
    George Malkuch, prin.

Amarillo Christian ES, P O BOX 7308 79114
Our Lady of Guadalupe School
  1108 S HOUSTON ST 79102
St. Andrews Day School
  1601 S GEORGIA ST 79102
St. Joseph ES, 4118 S BONHAM ST 79110
St. Lawrence ES, 2300 N SPRING ST 79107
St. Mary's ES, 1200 S ASHINGTON ST 79102
Trinity Lutheran School
  5005 INTERSTATE 40 W 79106

Amherst, Lamb Co., Pop. Code 3
  Amherst ISD
  Sch. Sys. Enr. Code 2
  Supt. – Kermit Sorrells, P O BOX 248 79312
  S, 100 N MAIN 79312 – Joel Parsons, prin.

Anahuac, Chambers Co., Pop. Code 4
  Anahuac ISD
  Sch. Sys. Enr. Code 4
  Supt. – Gene Best, P O BOX 369 77514
  JHS, P O BOX 849 77514 – Sue Kruger, prin.
  ES, P O BOX 399 77514 – Cecil Fuller, prin.

Anderson, Grimes Co., Pop. Code 2
  Anderson-Shiro Cons. ISD
  Sch. Sys. Enr. Code 2
  Supt. – Thomas Poe, P O BOX 289 77830
  ES, P O BOX 289 77830
    Chesley Ketchersio, prin.

Andrews, Andrews Co., Pop. Code 7
  Andrews ISD
  Sch. Sys. Enr. Code 5
  Supt. – J. Pennington, 405 NW 3RD ST 79714
  MS 79714 – Gary Petross, prin.
  Clearfork ES 79714 – Fred Nelson, prin.
  Devonian ES 79714 – Moody Conner, prin.
  Glorieta ES 79714 – Ann McCabe, prin.
  San Andres ES 79714 – James Ketcham, prin.
  Underwood ES 79714 – Jerry McWilliams, prin.

Angleton, Brazoria Co., Pop. Code 7
  Angleton ISD
  Sch. Sys. Enr. Code 6
  Supt. – E. Wall, 1900 N DOWNING ROAD 77515
  MS, 1800 N DOWNING ROAD 77515
    Darlene O'Brien, prin.
  Northside ES 77515 – Don Hood, prin.

Rancho Isabella ES, 100 CORRAL LANE 77515
  Stan Lindner, prin.
Southside ES, 1200 PARKLANE ST 77515
  Don West, prin.
Westside ES, 300 S WALKER ST 77515
  Dennis Chaloupka, prin.

Anna, Collin Co., Pop. Code 3
  Anna ISD
  Sch. Sys. Enr. Code 2
  Supt. – A. Mosby, P O BOX 157 75003
  Anna MS 75003 – Christy Benedict, prin.
  ES 75003 – Beverly Hogan, prin.

Anson, Jones Co., Pop. Code 5
  Anson ISD
  Sch. Sys. Enr. Code 3
  Supt. – Roger Huber
    1509 COMMERCIAL AVE 79501
  MS, 922 AVENUE M 79501 – Marvin Ansley, prin.
  ES 79501 – Mona Conger, prin.

Anthony, El Paso Co., Pop. Code 5
  Anthony ISD
  Sch. Sys. Enr. Code 3
  Supt. – Harrell Holder, P O BOX B 79951
  S, 900 S 6TH ST 79821 – Gert Peck, prin.

Anton, Hockley Co., Pop. Code 4
  Anton ISD
  Sch. Sys. Enr. Code 2
  Supt. – Max Washington, P O BOX 309 79313
  ES 79313 – Ershel Bird, prin.

Apple Springs, Trinity Co.
  Apple Springs ISD
  Sch. Sys. Enr. Code 2
  Supt. – A. Tidwell, P O BOX 125 75926
  ES 75926 – Lyndon Langford, prin.

Aquilla, Hill Co., Pop. Code 2
  Aquilla ISD
  Sch. Sys. Enr. Code 2
  Supt. – Elroy Otte, P O BOX 209 76622
  S 76622 – Clarence McDaniel, prin.

Aransas Pass, San Patricio Co., Pop. Code 6
  Aransas Pass ISD
  Sch. Sys. Enr. Code 4
  Supt. – Glenn Acker, P O BOX AA 78336
  Blunt ES, 600 W HARRISON BLVD 78336
    Hector Acevedo, prin.
  Faulk ES, 430 S 8TH ST 78336
    William Ratliff, prin.
  Kieberger ES, 748 W GOODNIGHT AVE 78336
    Lester Ferguson,Jr., prin.
  Noble MS 78336 – Lester Ferguson, prin.

Archer City, Archer Co., Pop. Code 4
  Archer City ISD
  Sch. Sys. Enr. Code 3
  Supt. – Donald Shearmire, P O BOX 926 76351
  ES, P O BOX 926 76351 – Bill Taliaferro, prin.

Argyle, Denton Co., Pop. Code 4
  Argyle ISD
  Sch. Sys. Enr. Code 2
  Supt. – T. Marlin, P O BOX 989 76226
  ES 76226 – D. Angore, prin.

Arlington, Tarrant Co., Pop. Code 9
  Arlington ISD
  Sch. Sys. Enr. Code 8
  Supt. – Donald Wright
    1203 W PIONEER PARKWAY 76013
  Amos ES, 3100 DANIEL DR 76014
    Judy Cox, prin.
  Atherton ES, 2101 OVERBROOK DR 76014
    Shirley Cole, prin.
  Bebensee ES 76013 – Malcolm Turner, prin.
  Berry ES, 1800 JOYCE ST 76010
    Gwen Wilkins, prin.
  Blanton ES, 1800 S COLLINS ST 76010
    Linda English, prin.
  Butler ES, 2121 MARGARET DR 76012
    Joyce Meesey, prin.
  Corey ES, 5201 KELLY ELLIOTT ROAD 76017
    Randall Gribbon, prin.
  Crow ES, 1201 COKE DR 76010
    Anita Gribbin, prin.
  Ditto ES, 3001 QUAIL LANE 76016
    Janna Graham, prin.
  Duff ES, 3100 LYNNWOOD DR 76013
    Linda Clark, prin.
  Dunn ES, 2201 WOODSIDE DR 76013
    Joy Read, prin.
  Fitzgerald ES, 5201 CREEK VALLEY DR 76018
    Tom Wheeler, prin.
  Foster ES, 1025 HIGH POINT ROAD 76015
    Barbara Syptak, prin.
  Goodman ES, 1400 REBECCA LANE 76014
    Ann Weatherford, prin.
  Hill ES, 2020 W TUCKER BLVD 76013
    S. West, prin.
  Johns ES, 1900 SHERRY ST 76010
    Patricia Evans, prin.
  Key ES, 3621 ROOSEVELT DR 76016
    E. Mayhugh, prin.
  Little ES, 4215 LITTLE ROAD 76016
    Alvin Miller, prin.
  Miller ES
    6401 W PLEASANT RIDGE ROAD 76016
    Floyd Sanders, prin.
  Morton ES, 2900 BARRINGTON PL 76014
    Harold Smith, prin.
  Pope ES, 901 CHESTNUT DR 76012
    J. Bradham, prin.

Rankin ES, 1900 OLEANDER ST 76010
Kenneth Rigdon, prin.
Roark ES, 2401 ROVERTS CIRCLE 76010
James Rose, prin.
Roquemore ES, 2001 VAN BUREN DR 76011
Jeanne Paull, prin.
Sherrod ES, 2626 LINCOLN DR 76006
Kenneth Blackford, prin.
Short ES, 2000 CALIFORNIA LANE 76015
Flo Jones, prin.
South Davis ES, 2001 S DAVIS DR 76013
Connie Petrie, prin.
Speer ES, 811 FULLER ST 76012
Rebecca Henley, prin.
Starrett ES 76013 – Robert Windham, prin.
Swift ES, 1101 S FIELDER ROAD 76013
W. Bryant, prin.
Thornton ES, 2301 E PARK ROW DR 76010
Reg Day, prin.
Wimbish ES, 1601 WRIGHT ST 76012
C. Andrews, prin.
Wood ES, 3300 PIMLICO DR 76017
Charlene Brinkley, prin.

Oakridge School
5900 W PIONEER PARKWAY 76013
Arlington Country Day ES, P O BOX 5862 76005
Grace Lutheran School, 210 W PARK ROW 76010
St. Albans Episcopal School, P O BOX 308 76004
St. Maria Goretti ES, 1200 S DAVIS DR 76013

Arp, Smith Co., Pop. Code 3
Arp ISD
Sch. Sys. Enr. Code 3
Supt. – Rudy Eddington, P O BOX 70 75750
JHS 75750 – Lindsay Marshall, prin.
ES 75750 – Keith Robbins, prin.

Asherton, Dimmit Co., Pop. Code 4
Asherton ISD
Sch. Sys. Enr. Code 2
Supt. – Lucille Gardner, P O BOX 398 78827
ES 78827 – Jose Talamantez, prin.

Aspermont, Stonewall Co., Pop. Code 4
Aspermont ISD
Sch. Sys. Enr. Code 2
Supt. – L. Dunn, P O BOX 549 79502
JHS 79502 – Alex Long, prin.
ES 79502 – Cecil Robinson, prin.

Athens, Henderson Co., Pop. Code 7
Athens ISD
Sch. Sys. Enr. Code 5
Supt. – Wayne Martin, P O BOX 112 75751
MS, 610 E COLLEGE 75751 – Ted Hull, prin.
IS, 307 MADOLE ST 75751 – James Freeman, prin.
Bel Air ES, 1201 BEL AIR DR 75751
Louis De Rosa, prin.
South Athens ES, ROBBINS ROAD 75751
Kenneth Lewis, prin.

Atlanta, Cass Co., Pop. Code 6
Atlanta ISD
Sch. Sys. Enr. Code 4
Supt. – J. Cox, 315 N BUCKNER ST 75551
JHS, HIGH SCHOOL LANE 75551
Lewis Lincoln, prin.
ES, WADE ST 75551 – Waymon Burleson, prin.
PS, CASS HWY 75551 – Gus Schuhmann, prin.

Aubrey, Denton Co., Pop. Code 3
Aubrey ISD
Sch. Sys. Enr. Code 3
Supt. – James Monaco
RURAL ROUTE 02 BOX 63 76227
ES, RURAL ROUTE 02 BOX 6 76227
H. Brockett, prin.

Austin, Travis Co., Pop. Code 10
Austin ISD
Sch. Sys. Enr. Code 8
Supt. – John Ellis, 6100 N GUADALUPE ST 78752
Bedichek MS, 6800 BILL HUGHES ROAD 78745
Ed Elliott, prin.
Burnet MS, 8401 HATHAWAY DRIVE 78758
James Wilson, prin.
Covington MS 78752 – William Armentrout, prin.
Dobie MS, 1200 E RUNDBERG LANE 78753
Yolanda Rocha, prin.
Fulmore MS, 2010 BRACKENRIDGE ST 78704
Vicky Baldwin, prin.
Kealing JHS 78752 – Selena Cash, prin.
Lamar MS, 6201 WYNONA AVE 78757
Floyd Odom, prin.
Martin JHS, 1601 HASKELL ST 78702
Martin Bera, prin.
Murchison MS, 3700 NORTH HILLS DRIVE 78731
Isabel Cortez, prin.
Mendez MS 78752 – Fortunato Vera, prin.
O'Henry MS, 2610 W 10TH ST 78703
John Brown, prin.
Pearce JHS, 6401 N HAMPTON DRIVE 78723
Barbara Williams, prin.
Porter MS, 2206 PRATHER LANE 78704
Frances Bush, prin.
Allan ES, 4900 GONZALES ST 78702
Anita Coy, prin.
Allison ES, 515 VARGAS ROAD 78741
Alfred Estrello, prin.
Andrews ES, 6801 NORTHEAST DR 78723
Ray Evans, prin.
Barrington ES, 400 COOPER DR 78753
Amelia Mendez, prin.
Barton Hills ES, 2108 BARTON HILLS DR 78704
Sue Searles, prin.

Becker ES, 906 W MILTON ST 78704
Judy Taylor, prin.
Blackshear ES, 1712 E 11TH ST 78702
Ida Hunt, prin.
Blanton ES, 5408 WESTMISTER DR 78723
Greg Swimelar, prin.
Boone ES 78752 – Stella Cook, prin.
Brentwood ES, 6700 ARROYO SECA 78757
Katherine Williams, prin.
Brooke ES, 3100 E 45TH ST 78702
Graciela Morales, prin.
Brown ES, 505 W ANDERSON LANE 78752
Leticia Hinojosa, prin.
Bryker Woods ES, 3309 KERBEY LANE 78703
Mary Kinkel, prin.
Campbell ES, 1600 CHICON ST 78702
Rita Hunt, prin.
Casis ES, 2710 EXPOSITION BLVD 78703
Amy Kinkade, prin.
Cook ES, 1511 CRIPPLE CREEK DR 78758
John Combs, prin.
Cunningham ES, 2200 BERKELEY AVE 78745
B. Henry, prin.
Dawson ES, 3001 S 1ST ST 78704
Dan Akery, prin.
Doss ES, 7005 NORTHLEDGE DR 78731
Wayne King, prin.
Govalle ES, 3601 GOVALLE AVE 78702
Elida Bera, prin.
Graham ES, 1005 E BRAKER LANE 78753
Andrew Guerrero, prin.
Gullett ES, 6310 TREADWELL BLVD 78731
Diane Crowe, prin.
Harris ES, 1711 WHELESS LANE 78723
Ruth Bailey, prin.
Highland Park ES, 4900 FAIRVIEW DR 78731
Claudia Tousek, prin.
Hill ES, 8601 TALLWOOD DR 78759
Glenda Adkinson, prin.
Houston ES, 5409 PONCIANA DR 78744
Iona Jaimes, prin.
Joslin ES, 4500 MANCHACA ROAD 78745
Eugenio Hinojosa, prin.
Kocurek ES 78752 – Rudy Munguia, prin.
Langford ES, 2206 BLUE MEADOW DR 78744
Arturo Arce, prin.
Lee ES, 3308 HAMPTON ROAD 78705
Mary Clayton, prin.
Linder ES, 2800 METCALFE ROAD 78741
Armando Saenz, prin.
Maplewood ES, 3808 MAPLEWOOD AVE 78722
Carol Brandon, prin.
Mathews ES, 906 W LYNN ST 78703
Elma Berrones, prin.
Menchaca ES, 12120 MANCHACA ROAD 78748
Bill Brandon, prin.
Metz ES, 2101 WILLOW ST 78702
Jorge Rodriguez, prin.
Norman ES, 4101 TANNEHILL LANE 78721
Jane Runnels, prin.
Oak Hill ES, 6101 PATTON ROAD 78735
Scott Bass, prin.
Oak Springs ES
3601 WEBBERVILLE ROAD 78702
Patrick Johnson, prin.
Odom ES, 1010 TURTLE CREEK BLVD 78745
Carol Moring, prin.
Ortega ES, 1135 GARLAND AVE 78721
Priscilla Malone, prin.
Palm ES 78752 – Valerie Walker, prin.
Patton ES, 6001 WESTCREEK DR 78749
Sheila Anderson, prin.
Pease ES, 1106 RIO GRANDE ST 78701
Douglas Hall, prin.
Pecan Springs ES, 3100 ROGGE LAND 78723
Lorraine Phillips, prin.
Pillow ES, 3025 CROSSCREEK DR 78758
Belia Nichols, prin.
Pleasant Hill ES, 6405 CIRCLE S ROAD 78745
Mildred Beyer, prin.
Reilly ES, 405 DENSON DR 78752
Elaine Farrington, prin.
Ridgetop ES, 5005 CASWELL AVE 78751
Alma Perry, prin.
Saint Elmo ES, 600 W SAINT ELMO ROAD 78745
Hulberto Saenz, prin.
Sanchez ES, 73 SAN MARCOS ST 78702
Ed Leo, prin.
Sims ES, 1203 SPRINGDALE ROAD 78721
Louis Hubbard, prin.
Summitt ES, 12207 BRIGADOON LANE 78727
Verginia Stevens, prin.
Sunset Valley ES, 3001 JONES ROAD 78745
Betty Sanders, prin.
Travis Heights ES, 2010 ALAMEDA DR 78704
Janet Kennedy, prin.
Walnut Creek ES, 401 W BRAKER LANE 78753
Martha Neeley, prin.
Webb MS, 610 E SAINT JOHNS AVE 78752
Bernard Riesold, prin.
Widen ES 78752 – Lucia Duncan, prin.
Williams ES, 500 MAIRO ST 78748
Mary Stinson, prin.
Winn ES, 3500 SUSQUEHANNA LANE 78723
Cecil Wright, prin.
Wooldridge ES
1412 NORSEMAN TERRACE 78758
Joe Lowe, prin.
Wooten ES, 1406 DALE DR 78758
Hector Dominguez, prin.
Zavala ES, 310 CANADIAN ST 78702
Roberto Perez, prin.
Zilker ES, 1900 BLUEBONNET LANE 78704
Gilbert Cantu, prin.

Eanes ISD
Sch. Sys. Enr. Code 5
Supt. – D. Rogers, 601 CAMP CRAFT ROAD 78746
Hill Country MS
1300 WALSH TARLTON LANE 78746
Mary Bull, prin.
West Ridge MS 78746 – Barry Aidman, prin.
Cedar Creek MS, 3301 PINNACLE ROAD 78746
Bob Judge, prin.
Eanes ES, 4101 BEE CAVES ROAD 78746
Carmyn Douglas, prin.
Forest Trail MS, 1203 S LOOP 360 78746
James Veitenheimer, prin.
Valley View ES, 1201 S LOOP 360 78746
Betty Courtney, prin.

Lake Travis ISD
Sch. Sys. Enr. Code 4
Supt. – Walter Howard
670 N RANCH ROAD 620 78734
Lake Travis MS, 3322 S RANCH ROAD 620 78734
Dennis Brent, prin.
Lake Travis ES, 607 N RANCH ROAD 620 78734
Sandy Leibick, prin.

Round Rock ISD
Supt. – See Round Rock
Grisham MS
10805 SCHOOL HOUSE LANE 78750
Linda Herrington, prin.
Forest North ES, 13414 BROADMEADE ST 78729
Carolyn Hood, prin.
Laurel Mountain ES
13401 POND SPRINGS RD 78729
Eleece Moffatt, prin.
North Oaks ES, 1104 OAK VIEW DR 78759
Kathy Caraway, prin.
Purple Sage ES
11606 EL SALIDO PARKWAY 78750
Terri Hunt, prin.
Spicewood ES, 116Y01 OLSON DR 78750
Jerry Landers, prin.

Allandale Baptist School
10500 JOLLYVILLE 78759
Hyde Park Baptist School
3901 SPEEDWAY ST 78751
Kirby Hall School, 306 W 29TH ST 78705
Bannockburn ES, 3901 SPEEDWAY 78751
Brentwood Christian School
11908 N LAMAR BLVD 78753
Nazarene Christian School
6711 MANCHACA ROAD 78745
Our Savior Lutheran School
800 PARMER LANE 78727
Reedemer Lutheran School
1500 W ANDERSON LANE 78757
Resurrection Episcopal School
2008 JUSTIN LANE 78757
Sacred Heart ES, 5911 REICHER DR 78723
St. Andrew's ES, 1112 W 31ST ST 78705
St. Austin's ES, 1911 SAN ANTONIO ST 76705
St. Ignatius Martyr School
120 W OLTORF ST 78704
St. Ignatius Martyr School
120 W OLTORF ST 78704
St. Louis ES, 2114 SAINT JOSEPH BLVD 78757
St. Martins Lutheran School
606 W 15TH ST 78701
St. Mary's Cathredal School
910 SAN JACINTO BLVD 78701
St. Paul Lutheran ES, 3407 RED RIVER ST 78705

Avalon, Ellis Co.
Avalon ISD
Sch. Sys. Enr. Code 2
Supt. – Pepper Wells, P O BOX 455 76623
S 76623 – Phyllis Mikulak, prin.

Avery, Red River Co., Pop. Code 3
Avery ISD
Sch. Sys. Enr. Code 2
Supt. – Jack Allen, P O BOX 97 75554
ES 75554 – Pat Davis, prin.

Avinger, Cass Co., Pop. Code 3
Avinger ISD
Sch. Sys. Enr. Code 2
Supt. – Henry Willis
RURAL ROUTE 02 BOX 22 75630
ES 75630 – Charles Traylor, prin.

Axtell, McLennan Co.
Axtell ISD
Sch. Sys. Enr. Code 3
Supt. – William Crockett, P O BOX 429 76624
ES 76624 – Stan Harris, prin.

Azle, Tarrant Co., Pop. Code 6
Azle ISD
Sch. Sys. Enr. Code 5
Supt. – William Ortego, 300 ROE ST 76020
JHS 76020 – D. Hufstedler, prin.
MS, 301 CHURCH ST 76020
Deborah Mangieri, prin.
Eagle Heights ES, P O BOX 1347 76020
Robert Gathright, prin.
Liberty ES 76020 – Bob Price, prin.
Silver Creek ES 76020 – Fred Weir, prin.
Walnut Creek MS, 1010 BOYD ROAD 76020
Thomas Hicks, prin.

Baird, Callahan Co., Pop. Code 4
Baird ISD
Sch. Sys. Enr. Code 2
Supt. – Bill Gunn, P O BOX 1147 79504
ES 79504 – Jackie Pruet, prin.

Ballinger, Runnels Co., Pop. Code 5
Ballinger ISD
Sch. Sys. Enr. Code 4
Supt. – Rodney Gordon, P O BOX 231 76821
JHS 76821 – Jim Stubblefield, prin.
ES, BROAD AVE 76821 – Wadena McAlister, prin.

Balmorhea, Reeves Co., Pop. Code 3
Balmorhea ISD
Sch. Sys. Enr. Code 2
Supt. – R. Clanton, P O BOX 368 79718
S 79718 – Jack Hoffman, prin.

Bandera, Bandera Co., Pop. Code 3
Bandera ISD
Sch. Sys. Enr. Code 4
Supt. – Ted Dockery, P O BOX 727 78003
JHS 78003 – Newell Donahoo, prin.
Alkek ES 78003 – Al Kindla, prin.

Bangs, Brown Co., Pop. Code 4
Bangs ISD
Sch. Sys. Enr. Code 3
Supt. – Deral Edwards, P O BOX 969 76823
JHS, P O BOX 969 76823 – B. Rankin, prin.
Stephens ES, P O BOX 969 76823
Elvin Hutchins, prin.

Banquete, Nueces Co., Pop. Code 3
Banquete ISD
Sch. Sys. Enr. Code 3
Supt. – Otis Burroughs, P O BOX 369 78339
JHS 78339 – Edwin Stuart, prin.
ES 78339 – Julia Strubhart, prin.

Barksdale, Edwards Co.
Nueces Canyon Consolidated ISD
Sch. Sys. Enr. Code 2
Supt. – James Deatherage, P O BOX 118 78828
Nuces Canyon ES 78828 – Warren Colwell, prin.

Bartlett, Bell Co., Pop. Code 4
Bartlett ISD
Sch. Sys. Enr. Code 2
Supt. – Johnnie Hauerland, P O BOX 170 76511
MS 76511 – F. Pierce, prin.
ES, 300 W BELL 76511 – F. Pierce, prin.

Bastrop, Bastrop Co., Pop. Code 5
Bastrop ISD
Sch. Sys. Enr. Code 5
Supt. – Patrick Deviney, 1602 HILL ST 78602
MS 78602 – Wiley Alexander, prin.
ES, AUSTIN & MARION 78602
Rebecca Smith, prin.
IS 78602 – Betty Evans, prin.
PS, 1203 HILL ST 78602 – Sheila Mills, prin.

Bay City, Matagorda Co., Pop. Code 7
Bay City ISD
Sch. Sys. Enr. Code 5
Supt. – David Damerall, P O BOX 631 77414
JHS, 2417 16TH ST 77414
William Murphree, prin.
McAllister JHS 77414 – John Keys, prin.
Cherry ES, 2509 8TH ST 77414
Rudolph Martin, prin.
Holmes MS, P O BOX 631 77414
Charles Coney, prin.
Pierce ES, 2400 4TH ST 77414
Rebecca Walker, prin.
Roberts MS, P O BOX 631 77414
Peggy O'Neal, prin.

Holy Cross ES, 2001 KATY AVE 77414

Baytown, Harris Co., Pop. Code 8
Goose Creek ISD
Sch. Sys. Enr. Code 7
Supt. – Bill Kennedy, P O BOX 30 77522
JHS 77520 – Charles Polk, prin.
Cedar Bayou JHS 77520 – Herman Boatman, prin.
Gentry JHS 77522 – Phyllis Dean, prin.
Mann JHS 77520 – Al Dennis, prin.
Alamo ES, 1801 AUSTIN ST 77520
Billie Hinton, prin.
Austin ES
3022 MASSEY TOMPKINS ROAD 77521
Sandra Northcutt, prin.
Bowie ES, 2200 CLAYTON DR 77520
Brenda Pickens, prin.
Carver ES, 800 CARVER ST 77520
Joy Wristers, prin.
Crockett ES, 3400 BARKALOO ROAD 77521
Wynona Montgomery, prin.
Harlem ES, 2623 BROAD ST 77521
Kay Hurzeler, prin.
Lamar ES, 816 W PRUETT ST 77520
Barb Wilson, prin.
Pumphrey ES, 4901 FAIRWAY DR 77521
Joy Rutledge, prin.
San Jacinto ES, 2615 VIRGINIA ST 77520
Diana Maldonado, prin.
Smith ES 77522 – Suzanne Howard, prin.
Travis ES, 100 ROBIN ROAD 77520
W. Busch, prin.
Other Schools – See Highlands

St. Joseph ES, 1811 CAROLINA ST 77520

Beaumont, Jefferson Co., Pop. Code 9
Beaumont ISD
Sch. Sys. Enr. Code 7
Supt. – O. Mike Taylor, P O BOX 672 77704
Austin MS, 3410 AUSTIN ST 77706
Bill Lackey, prin.
Bowie MS, 3525 CLEVELAND ST 77703
Edward Senigaur, prin.
Crockett MS, 1400 ROYAL ST 77701
Alma Harris, prin.
Marshall MS, 6455 GLADYS ST 77706
Loyd Davis, prin.
South Park MS, 350 E WOODROW ST 77705
J. Allardyce, prin.
Odom MS, 2550 W VIRGINIA ST 77705
Marvin Durden, prin.
Vincent MS, 350 ELDRIDGE DRIVE 77707
James Breaux, prin.
Amelia ES, 565 S MAJOR DR 77707
Sidney Calame, prin.
Bingman ES, 5265 KENNETH AVE 77705
Ed Williams, prin.
Blanchette ES, 2400 LELA ST 77705
Clarence Francois, prin.
Caldwood ES, 102 BERKSHIRE LANE 77707
Harold Steward, prin.
Curtis ES, 6225 N CIRCUIT DR 77706
Elijah Moye, prin.
Dowling ES, 1300 NORTH ST 77701
Sally Blewett, prin.
Dunbar ES, 825 JACKSON ST 77701
Edna Joseph, prin.
Fehl ES, 3350 BLANCHETTE ST 77701
Cathy Chavis, prin.
Field ES, 4315 CONCORD ROAD 77703
Charles Etheridge, prin.
Fletcher ES, 1050 AVENUE E 77701
Iris Williams, prin.
French ES, 1900 POPE ST 77703
Elmo Chaison, prin.
Guess ES, 8055 VOTH ROAD 77708
Hoyt Simmons, prin.
Howell MS 77705 – Sandra Henderson, prin.
Lucas ES, 1750 E LUCAS DR 77703
Betty Cooper, prin.
Martin ES 77703 – Michael Ryals, prin.
Ogden ES, 2300 VICTORIA ST 77701
Howard Mills, prin.
Pietzsch ES, 4301 HIGHLAND AVE 77705
J. Judith, prin.
Price MS, 3350 WAVERLY ST 77705
Floyd Broussard, prin.

Hamshire-Fannett ISD
Supt. – See Hamshire
Hamshire-Fannett MS 77705
Marcus Rector, prin.

Catholic in the Pines MS
2350 EASTEX FREEWAY 77703
Wilson HS, 8001 OLD VOTH ROAD 77708
All Saints Episcopal ES
4108 DELAWARE ST 77706
Assumption ES, 4440 CHAISON ST 77705
Our Mother of Mercy ES, 3380 SARAH ST 77705
Ridgewood ES, 8001 OLD VOTH ROAD 77708
St. Anne ES, 375 N 11TH ST 77702
St. Anthony's Cathedral ES, P O BOX 3309 77704

Beckville, Panola Co., Pop. Code 3
Beckville ISD
Sch. Sys. Enr. Code 3
Supt. – Andrew Nutt, P O BOX 37 75631
MS 75631 – Jerry Stout, prin.
ES 75631 – C. Thomas, prin.

Bedford, Tarrant Co., Pop. Code 7
Hurst-Euless-Bedford ISD
Sch. Sys. Enr. Code 7
Supt. – F. Watson, 1849 CENTRAL DRIVE 76022
Bedford Heights ES
1000 CUMMINGS DRIVE 76021 – Eva Orr, prin.
Bell Manor ES, 1300 WINCHESTER WAY 76022
Carolyn Hill, prin.
Shadybrook ES
2601 SHADY BROOK DRIVE 76021
Steven Green, prin.
Spring Garden ES, 2400 CUMMINGS ROAD 76021
Bill Barnes, prin.
Stonegate ES, 900 BEDFORD ROAD 76022
Joyce Early, prin.
Other Schools – See Euless, Hurst

Beeville, Bee Co., Pop. Code 7
Beeville ISD
Sch. Sys. Enr. Code 5
Supt. – H. Reynolds, 1900 N ADAMS ST 78102
Jefferson JHS, 701 E HAYES ST 78102
Bob Wingenter, prin.
Fadden-McKeown ES
2001 S SAINT MARYS ST 78102 – T. J. Pfeil, prin.
Hall ES, 1100 W HUNTINGTON ST 78102
Max Luna, prin.
Madderra-Flournoy MS, 501 E LOTT ST 78102
Rudolfo Garcia, prin.
Tyler ES, 815 N TYLER ST 78102
Clint Cowart, prin.

Our Lady of Victory School
707 N AVENUE E 78102
St. Joseph ES, 410 N TYLER ST 78102
St. Philips Episcopal School
105 N ADAMS ST 78102

Bellevue, Clay Co., Pop. Code 2
Bellevue ISD
Sch. Sys. Enr. Code 2
Supt. – Arbuary Ritter, P O BOX 38 76228
S 76228 – Dan Webb, prin.

Bells, Grayson Co., Pop. Code 3
Bells ISD
Sch. Sys. Enr. Code 3
Supt. – Ron Rowell, P O BOX 7 75414
MS 75414 – James Bankston, prin.
ES 75414 – Gerald Beckham, prin.

Bellville, Austin Co., Pop. Code 5
Bellville ISD
Sch. Sys. Enr. Code 4
Supt. – Bill Shaver, 404 E MAIN ST 77418
JHS, 404 E MAIN ST 77418 – Sam Atwood, prin.
O'Bryant-Spicer ES, 414 S TESCH ST 77418
George Schulz, prin.
West End ES 77418 – Marsha Manley, prin.

Belton, Bell Co., Pop. Code 7
Belton ISD
Sch. Sys. Enr. Code 5
Supt. – J. Pirtle, P O BOX 269 76513
JHS 76513 – Joe Brooks, prin.
Central ES, 400 E 4TH AVE 76513
Bob McFarland, prin.
Lakewood ES, FM 2305 76513
Jeannette Kelley, prin.
Leon Heights ES, 1501 N MAIN ST 76513
Wayne Carpenter, prin.
Miller Heights ES, FAIRWAY ST 76513
Ralph Masters, prin.
Southwest ES, CONNELL ST 76513
Ed Wilks, prin.

Benavides, Duval Co., Pop. Code 4
Benavides ISD
Sch. Sys. Enr. Code 3
Supt. – Reynaldo Chapa, P O BOX P 78341
JHS 78341 – Ramon Tanguma, prin.
PS 78341 – J. Garcia, prin.
Realitos ES 78341 – Victoriana Leal, prin.

Ben Bolt, Jim Wells Co.
Ben Bolt-Palito Blanco ISD
Sch. Sys. Enr. Code 2
Supt. – Julio Dominguez, P O BOX 547 78342
MS 78342 – Ruben Gaza, prin.
Palito Blanco ES 78342 – Adam Martinez, prin.

Benjamin, Knox Co., Pop. Code 2
Benjamin ISD
Sch. Sys. Enr. Code 1
Supt. – Ben Grill, P O BOX 166 79505
S 79505 – (—), prin.

Ben Wheeler, Van Zandt Co., Pop. Code 5
Martins Mill ISD
Sch. Sys. Enr. Code 2
Supt. – William McEachern
RURAL ROUTE 02 BOX 280 75754
Martins Mills S 75754 – Robert Wyman, prin.

Big Bend National Park, Brewster Co.
San Vicente ISD
Sch. Sys. Enr. Code 1
Supt. – Rudy Lopez, P O BOX 36 79834
San Vicente ES 79834 – (—), prin.

Big Lake, Reagan Co., Pop. Code 5
Reagan ISD
Sch. Sys. Enr. Code 4
Supt. – Joe White, 1111 E TWELFTH ST 76932
Reagan MS, 500 N PENNSYLVANIA AVE 76932
Daniel Schaefer, prin.
Reagan ES, 501 N TEXAS AVE 76932
Jerry Burleson, prin.

Big Sandy, Upshur Co., Pop. Code 4
Big Sandy ISD
Sch. Sys. Enr. Code 3
Supt. – Charles Penney, P O BOX 598 75755
ES 75765 – Donna Varnado, prin.

Big Spring, Howard Co., Pop. Code 7
Big Spring ISD
Sch. Sys. Enr. Code 5
Supt. – William McQueary, P O BOX 590 79721
Runnels JHS 79720 – Tom Henry, prin.
Bauer ES, 108 NW 9TH ST 79720
Jean Broughton, prin.
College Heights ES, 1801 GOLIAD ST 79720
Janice Rosson, prin.
Goliad MS 79721 – Jim Holmes, prin.
Kentwood ES, MERRILY & ANN 79720
Andre Clark, prin.
Marcy ES, OLD SAN ANGELO HWY 79721
Royce Cox, prin.
Moss ES, FORDHAM AVE 79720
Ronald Moss, prin.
Washington ES
BIRDWELL & MONTICELLO 79720
Wendell Ware, prin.

St. Mary's Episcopal School
118 CEDAR ROAD 79720

Big Wells, Dimmit Co., Pop. Code 3
Carrizo Springs Consolidated ISD
Supt. – See Carrizo Springs
ES 78830 – Gustavo Marinez, prin.

Bishop, Nueces Co., Pop. Code 5
Bishop Consolidated ISD
Sch. Sys. Enr. Code 4
Supt. – Nathan Lee, P O BOX 788 78343
JHS 78343 – Glynn Hill, prin.
East Side ES 78343 – Carmen Gonzalez, prin.
Petronila ES 78343 – Charles Jones, prin.

Blackwell, Nolan Co., Pop. Code 2
Blackwell ISD
Sch. Sys. Enr. Code 2
Supt. – James Connel, P O BOX 505 79506
ES 79506 – Gary Snith, prin.

Blanco, Blanco Co., Pop. Code 4
Blanco ISD
Sch. Sys. Enr. Code 3
Supt. – Larry Moehnke, P O BOX 340 78606
ES 78606 – Joe Summy, prin.

Blanket, Brown Co., Pop. Code 2
Blanket ISD
Sch. Sys. Enr. Code 2
Supt. – Winifred Dodds
RURAL ROUTE 01 BOX 12A 76432
ES 76432 – Don Weaver, prin.

Bledsoe, Cochran Co.
Bledsoe ISD
Sch. Sys. Enr. Code 1
Supt. – Hiram Sharp, P O BOX 78 79314
ES 79314 – Mary Stanton, prin.

Bloomburg, Cass Co., Pop. Code 2
Bloomburg ISD
Sch. Sys. Enr. Code 2
Supt. – Ron Surrott, P O BOX 156 75556
ES 75556 – Billy Frost, prin.

Blooming Grove, Navarro Co., Pop. Code 3
Blooming Grove ISD
Sch. Sys. Enr. Code 3
Supt. – Marshall McMillan, P O BOX 258 76626
ES 76626 – Wanda Barton, prin.

Bloomington, Victoria Co., Pop. Code 4
Bloomington ISD
Sch. Sys. Enr. Code 3
Supt. – Bob Harraid, P O BOX 158 77951
Bloomington Int. S 77951 – K. Marshall, prin.
ES 77951 – Gary Zeplin, prin.
Placedo ES 77951 – Ernestina Garcia, prin.

Blue Ridge, Collin Co., Pop. Code 2
Blue Ridge ISD
Sch. Sys. Enr. Code 2
Supt. – James Cole, P O BOX 8 75004
ES 75004 – Garold Spurrier, prin.

Bluff Dale, Erath Co.
Bluff Dale ISD
Sch. Sys. Enr. Code 1
Supt. – Kay Todd, P O BOX 101 76433
ES 76433 – Kay Todd, prin.

Blum, Hill Co., Pop. Code 2
Blum ISD
Sch. Sys. Enr. Code 2
Supt. – Jim Todd, P O BOX 548 76627
ES 76627 – David Hodges, prin.

Boerne, Kendall Co., Pop. Code 5
Boerne ISD
Sch. Sys. Enr. Code 5
Supt. – Joseph Doenges, 123 W JOHNS RD 78006
MS, 240 JOHNS ROAD 78006
Sandra Radtke, prin.
MS, 601 E ADLER 78006 – Dianne Kyle, prin.
Fabra ES 78006 – John Biggs, prin.

Bogata, Red River Co., Pop. Code 4
Talco-Bogata Cons. ISD
Sch. Sys. Enr. Code 3
Supt. – Harold Cowley, P O BOX 125 75417
ES 75417 – Earl Stubblefield, prin.
Talco ES 75417 – Bill Vickers, prin.

Boling, Wharton Co., Pop. Code 3
Boling ISD
Sch. Sys. Enr. Code 3
Supt. – Thomas Luce, P O BOX 278 77420
Iago JHS 77420 – Bobby Knox, prin.
Newgulf ES 77420 – Clifford Curry, prin.

Bonham, Fannin Co., Pop. Code 6
Bonham ISD
Sch. Sys. Enr. Code 4
Supt. – Charles Hopp, P O BOX 490 75418
Rather JHS 75418 – John Snead, prin.
Bailey-Inglish ES 75418 – Bill Manhart, prin.
Evans MS, 1300 N MAIN ST 75418
Bill Houston, prin.

Booker, Lipscomb Co., Pop. Code 4
Booker ISD
Sch. Sys. Enr. Code 2
Supt. – C. Craighead, P O BOX 288 79005
JHS 79005 – Steve Burleson, prin.
ES 79005 – Bob Kirksey, prin.

Borger, Hutchinson Co., Pop. Code 7
Borger ISD
Sch. Sys. Enr. Code 5
Supt. – Larry Coffman, 9TH & WEATHERLY 79007
MS 79007 – James Jones, prin.
Central ES, 800 N MCGEE ST 79007
Allen Jenkins, prin.
Crockett ES, KAYE ST 79007
Manuel Kesner, prin.

Gateway ES, STERLING & WEST DR 79007
Shirley Jameson, prin.

St. John's ES, 201 SAINT JOHNS ROAD 79007

Bovina, Parmer Co., Pop. Code 4
Bovina ISD
Sch. Sys. Enr. Code 3
Supt. – Robert Owen, P O BOX 70 79009
ES 79009 – Sue Nuttall, prin.

Bowie, Montague Co., Pop. Code 6
Bowie ISD
Sch. Sys. Enr. Code 4
Supt. – Bobby Bain, P O BOX 1168 76230
JHS, P O BOX 1168 76230
Thomas McMurray, prin.
MS 76230 – Lelia Hix, prin.
PS 76230 – Charles Gifford, prin.

Gold Burg ISD
Sch. Sys. Enr. Code 2
Supt. – R. Preston, RURAL ROUTE 01 76230
Ringgold ES 76255 – Tommie Stilwell, prin.

Montague ISD
Supt. – See Montague
Montague ES 76255 – R. Hamric, prin.

Boyd, Wise Co., Pop. Code 3
Boyd ISD
Sch. Sys. Enr. Code 3
Supt. – Larry Enis, P O BOX 608 76023
MS, P O BOX 608 76023 – Bruce Frost, prin.
ES 76023 – Linda Ware, prin.
MS 76023 – Lynn Todd, prin.

Boys Ranch, Oldham Co.
Boys Ranch ISD
Sch. Sys. Enr. Code 2
Supt. – Garland Rattan, P O BOX 219 79105
ES 79010 – Buddy Sparks, prin.

Brackettville, Kinney Co., Pop. Code 4
Brackett ISD
Sch. Sys. Enr. Code 3
Supt. – Bobby McCall, P O BOX 586 78832
Jones ES 78832 – Steve Mills, prin.

Brady, McCulloch Co., Pop. Code 6
Brady ISD
Sch. Sys. Enr. Code 4
Supt. – Al Chance, 1000 S WALL ST 76825
JHS, 200 W 4TH ST 76825 – Larry Blair, prin.
China IS, 205 W CHINA ST 76825
Albert Thompson, prin.
North Ward ES, 500 W VICTORIA ST 76825
Janice Brown, prin.
South Ward ES, 500 W 11TH ST 76825
Caroline Parks, prin.

Breckenridge, Stephens Co., Pop. Code 6
Breckenridge ISD
Sch. Sys. Enr. Code 4
Supt. – Wayne Bingham, 208 N MILLER ST 76024
JHS, 500 W LINDSEY ST 76024
Joe Jackson, prin.
East ES, 1310 N ELM ST 76024 – P. Grimes, prin.
North ES 76024 – William Calvert, prin.
South MS 76024 – William Ash, prin.

Bremond, Robertson Co., Pop. Code 4
Bremond ISD
Sch. Sys. Enr. Code 2
Supt. – Joe Phariss, P O BOX 190 76629
ES 76629 – Ronnie Groholski, prin.

St. Mary ES, 6 N MAIN ST 76604

Brenham, Washington Co., Pop. Code 7
Brenham ISD
Sch. Sys. Enr. Code 5
Supt. – Gerald Anderson, P O BOX 1147 77833
MS 77833 – Ben Seeker, prin.
Alton ES, 304 KERR ST 77833 – E. Faykus, prin.
ES, 201 E 6TH ST 77833 – Marilyn Mortimer, prin.
IS, 2201 E STONE 77833 – Gerald Krause, prin.

Grace Lutheran School
1212 W JEFFERSON ST 77833

Bridge City, Orange Co., Pop. Code 6
Bridge City ISD
Sch. Sys. Enr. Code 5
Supt. – Glenn Pearson, P O BOX 847 77611
JHS, 2690 TEXAS AVE 77611
Ralph Wallace, prin.
Hatton ES, 1-35 W ROUND BONCH ROAD 77611
Larry Buchman, prin.
Sims ES, 425 ROVERTS AVE 77611
Ella Staggs, prin.

Bridgeport, Wise Co., Pop. Code 5
Bridgeport ISD
Sch. Sys. Enr. Code 4
Supt. – John Brooks, 1407 CARPENTER ST 76026
MS, 1400 HIGHWAY 1400 76026
Walton Vincent, prin.
ES, 1608 CATES ST 76026 – Joseph Duncan, prin.

Briscoe, Wheeler Co.
Briscoe ISD
Sch. Sys. Enr. Code 1
Supt. – L. Salmon, P O BOX 399 79011
S, P O BOX 138 79011 – Bob Downs, prin.

Broaddus, San Augustine Co., Pop. Code 2
Broaddus ISD
Sch. Sys. Enr. Code 2
Supt. – T. Marion Neill, P O BOX 58 75929
S, P O BOX 58 75929 – (—), prin.

Bronte, Coke Co., Pop. Code 3
Bronte ISD
Sch. Sys. Enr. Code 2
Supt. – Michael Hartman, P O BOX 670 76933
ES, P O BOX 670 76933 – Shirley Coleman, prin.

Brookeland, Jasper Co., Pop. Code 2
Brookeland ISD
Sch. Sys. Enr. Code 2
Supt. – Robert Roy, P O BOX 8 75931
ES 75931 – John Lynch, prin.

Brookesmith, Brown Co.
Brookesmith ISD
Sch. Sys. Enr. Code 2
Supt. – Don Davis, P O BOX 706 76827
ES 76827 – Marvin McClure, prin.

Brookshire, Waller Co., Pop. Code 4
Royal ISD
Sch. Sys. Enr. Code 4
Supt. – Frank Jackson, P O BOX 247 77423
Royal IS, 4010 4TH 77423 – Hervey Vaclavik, prin.
Royal PS, 4101 7TH 77423 – Robert Dunk, prin.
Other Schools – See Pattison

Brownfield, Terry Co., Pop. Code 7
Brownfield ISD
Sch. Sys. Enr. Code 5
Supt. – Don Hendley, 601 TAHOKA ROAD 79316
MS, 1001 E BROADWAY ST 79316
C. Arnold, prin.
IS, 302 E MAIN ST 79316 – Jesse Geron, prin.
Colonial Heights ES, 1100 W REPPTO ST 79316
Fred Cawthon, prin.
Oak Grove ES, 1000 E CACTUS LANE 79316
Charley Hargrave, prin.

Union ISD
Sch. Sys. Enr. Code 1
Supt. – Charles Clark
RURAL ROUTE 05 BOX 53 79316
Union S 79316 – Glen Cunningham, prin.

Brownsboro, Henderson Co., Pop. Code 3
Brownsboro ISD
Sch. Sys. Enr. Code 4
Supt. – John Saunders, P O BOX 465 75756
JHS 75756 – Tony Volentine, prin.
ES 75756 – Aaron Stripling, prin.
PS 75756 – Anthony Bruner, prin.
Chandler ES 75756 – Jerry Houston, prin.

Brownsville, Cameron Co., Pop. Code 8
Brownsville ISD
Sch. Sys. Enr. Code 8
Supt. – R. Besteiro, 1900 PRICE RD 78521
Central IS, 610 PALM BLVD 78520
Alfredo Garcia, prin.
Cummings IS 78520 – Estela Aguirre, prin.
Faulk IS, 2000 ROOSEVELT ST 78521
Nelson Permenter, prin.
Oliveira IS 78521 – Carlos Garza, prin.
Perkins Inter. HS, 4750 AUSTIN ROAD 78521
Hector Hernandez, prin.
Stell IS 78520 – Guadalupe Rocha, prin.
Burns ES, W TEJON ROAD 78520
Leonel Escobedo, prin.
Canales ES, 1811 E 18TH ST 78520
Joe Yanez, prin.
Castaneda ES, 3110 E 30TH ST 78521
(—), prin.
Clearwater ES, 610 PALM BLVD 78520
Robert Rodriguez, prin.
Cromack ES, 1102 E MADISON ST 78520
Minerva Saldivar, prin.
Del Castillo ES, 105 MORNINGSIDE ROAD 78521
Manfred Del Castillo, prin.
Egly ES, 445 LAND O LAKES DR 78521
Hesiquio Perez, prin.
El Jardin ES, 6911 BOCA CHICA BLVD 78521
Humberto Garza, prin.
Garden Park ES, 855 MILITARY ROAD 78520
Ophelia Haywood, prin.
Garza ES, 200 ESPERANZA ROAD 78521
Carlos Alvarado, prin.
Gonzales ES, 4450 COFFEEPORT ROAD 78520
Neida Soto, prin.
Longoria ES, 2400 E VAN BUREN ST 78520
Sharon Moore, prin.
Martin ES, 1701 STANFORD AVE 78520
Adan Salinas, prin.
Morningside ES
1025 MORNINGSIDE ROAD 78521
Oscar Cantu, prin.
Palm Grove ES, 7942 SOUTHMOST ROAD 78521
Irma Salinas, prin.
Perez ES, 2364 SHIDLER DR 78521
Henry Kenneson, prin.
Putegnat ES, 730 E 8TH ST 78520
Severino Saenz, prin.
Resaca ES, 901 E FILMORE ST 78520
Raguel Ybarra, prin.
Russell ES, 800 LAKESIDE BLVD 78520
Rachael Ayala, prin.
Sharp ES, 1439 PALM BLVD 78520
Jerry Osborn, prin.
Skinner ES, 411 W ST CHARLES ST 78520
David Espurvoa, prin.
Southmost ES 78520 – Nancy Mejia, prin.

Vermillion Road ES, 6895 FM 802 78520
  Angel Martinez, prin.
Victoria Heights ES, 2801 E 13TH ST 78521
  Victorio Avila, prin.
Villanueva ES, 7 MILITARY ROAD 78520
  Raul Vasquez, prin.
Webb ES, 1315 POLK ST 78520
  Francisco Saldivar, prin.

First Baptist School
  1600 BOCA CHICA BLVD 78520
Immaculate Conception ES
  1235 E JEFFERSON ST 78520
Incarnate Word Academy
  224 RESACA BLVD 78520
St. Mary's ES, 1300 LOS EBANOS BLVD 78520

Brownwood, Brown Co., Pop. Code 7
Brownwood ISD
Sch. Sys. Enr. Code 5
Supt. – James Lancaster, P O BOX 730 76804
JHS 76801 – Roland Graves, prin.
Central Six MS, 901 B AVENUE 76801
  Leon Williams, prin.
Coggin ES, 1005 B AVENUE 76801
  Walter Hamilton, prin.
East ES 76804 – Sue Ragsdale, prin.
Northwest ES, 311 BLUFFVIEW DR 76801
  James Brasher, prin.
South ES, 1600 K AVENUE 76801
  Norman Stegemoller, prin.
Woodland Heights ES, 3900 4TH ST 76801
  Gary Chamberlain, prin.

Bruni, Webb Co., Pop. Code 2
Webb Cons. ISD
Sch. Sys. Enr. Code 2
Supt. – Charles Little, P O BOX 206 78344
MS 78344 – Ezequiel Lopez, prin.
Oilton ES 78344 – Carlos Herrera, prin.

Bryan, Brazos Co., Pop. Code 8
Bryan ISD
Sch. Sys. Enr. Code 7
Supt. – Guy Gorden, 101 N TEXAS 77803
Bonham ES, 2801 WILKES ROAD 77802
  Virginia Wentrcek, prin.
Bowie ES, 401 W 26TH ST 77803
  David Ogden, prin.
Carver MS 77803 – Joe Herndon, prin.
Crockett ES, 401 ELM AVE 77801
  Ernest Johnson, prin.
Fannin ES, 1200 BAKER AVE 77803
  Carolyn Taylor, prin.
Henderson ES, 801 MATOUS DR 77802
  Jimmy Anding, prin.
Houston ES, 4501 CANTERBURY DR 77802
  Dana Marable, prin.
Johnson ES, 3800 OAK HILL DR 77802
  Carolyn Davis, prin.
Jones MS, 1400 PECAN ST 77803
  Harry Crenshaw, prin.
Kemp MS 77802 – Paul Kunz, prin.
Lamar MS, 1901 W VILLA MARIA ROAD 77801
  Judy Hughson, prin.
Milam ES, 1201 RIDGEDALE ST 77803
  Linda Asberry, prin.
Navarro ES 77803 – Doris Ruffino, prin.
Ross ES, 3300 PARKWAY TERR 77802
  Linda Sasse, prin.
Travis ES, 901 E 25TH ST 77803
  Randy Caperton, prin.

St. Michael's Academy
  2505 S COLLEGE AVE 77801
St. Joseph ES, 109 N PRESTON AVE 77803

Bryson, Jack Co., Pop. Code 3
Bryson ISD
Sch. Sys. Enr. Code 2
Supt. – J. Stanfield, P O BOX 309 76027
ES 76027 – Delmar Day, prin.

Buckholts, Milam Co., Pop. Code 2
Buckholts ISD
Sch. Sys. Enr. Code 2
Supt. – J. Hauk, P O BOX 248 76518
S 76518 – Martha Henry, prin.

Buda, Hays Co., Pop. Code 3
Hays Cons. ISD
Sch. Sys. Enr. Code 5
Supt. – Clyde Greer
  RURAL ROUTE 02 BOX 22 78610
Dahlstrom MS 78610 – James Miller, prin.
Kyle MS 78810 – Armando Chapa, prin.
IS 78610 – Nolan Kunkel, prin.
PS 78610 – Lavon May, prin.
Green ES 78610 – Silas Wade, prin.
Kyle ES 78610 – Magdalena Arredondo, prin.

Buffalo, Leon Co., Pop. Code 4
Buffalo ISD
Sch. Sys. Enr. Code 3
Supt. – Ray Elam, P O BOX C 75831
ES 75831 – Thomas Middlebrook, prin.

Bullard, Smith Co., Pop. Code 3
Bullard ISD
Sch. Sys. Enr. Code 3
Supt. – P. Wood, P O BOX 105 75757
MS 75757 – Richard Tedder, prin.
ES 75757 – Lynette Hughes, prin.

Buna, Jasper Co., Pop. Code 4
Buna ISD
Sch. Sys. Enr. Code 4
Supt. – Jerry Smith, P O BOX 1087 77612
JHS 77612 – Thomas Saunders, prin.
ES 77612 – Anthony Michalsky, prin.

Burkburnett, Wichita Co., Pop. Code 7
Burkburnett ISD
Sch. Sys. Enr. Code 5
Supt. – Danny Taylor, 408 GLENDALE ST 76354
JHS, 108 S AVE D 76354 – J. Phillips, prin.
Evans ES, 1015 S BERRY ST 76354
  Overton Ray, prin.
Hardin ES, 100 N AVENUE D 76354
  Gerald Combs, prin.
Tower ES 76354 – Stanley Owen, prin.

Burkeville, Newton Co.
Burkeville ISD
Sch. Sys. Enr. Code 2
Supt. – Joe Gassiott, P O BOX 218 75932
ES 75932 – Jack Miller, prin.

Burleson, Johnson Co., Pop. Code 7
Burleson ISD
Sch. Sys. Enr. Code 6
Supt. – Gordon Cockerham
  1160 SW WILSHIRE BLVD 76028
Frazier ES, 900 SW HILLSIDE DR 76028
  Naomi Coontz, prin.
Mound ES, 205 SW THOMAS ST 76028
  Robert Griswold, prin.
Nola Dunn ES, 201 S DOBSON ST 76028
  Harold Moore, prin.
Norwood ES, 619 EVELYN LANE 76028
  Bill King, prin.
Taylor ES 76028 – Judy Hajek, prin.

Burnet, Burnet Co., Pop. Code 5
Burnet Cons. ISD
Sch. Sys. Enr. Code 4
Supt. – T. Scott, 308 E BRIER LANE 78611
JHS 78611 – Marvin Stewart, prin.
Bertram ES 78611 – Jerry Sanders, prin.
ES, 608 N VANDERVEER ST 78611
  Mary Harris, prin.
MS, 308 E BRIER LANE 78611
  Charles Williams, prin.

Burton, Washington Co., Pop. Code 2
Burton ISD
Sch. Sys. Enr. Code 2
Supt. – Gary Herbert, P O BOX 37 77835
ES 77835 – Marcus Broesche, prin.

Bushland, Potter Co.
Bushland ISD
Sch. Sys. Enr. Code 2
Supt. – David Jones, P O BOX 60 79012
Bushland ES 79012 -- Fred Lunsford, prin.

Byers, Clay Co., Pop. Code 3
Byers ISD
Sch. Sys. Enr. Code 2
Supt. – J. Priddy, P O BOX 217 76357
ES 76357 – Joseph Turner, prin.

Bynum, Hill Co., Pop. Code 2
Bynum ISD
Sch. Sys. Enr. Code 2
Supt. – David Deaver, P O BOX 68 76631
S 76631 – David Deaver, prin.

Caddo Mills, Hunt Co., Pop. Code 4
Caddo Mills ISD
Sch. Sys. Enr. Code 3
Supt. – R. Smith, P O BOX 160 75005
MS 75005 – David Turner, prin.
ES 75005 – Mark Shambeck, prin.

Caldwell, Burleson Co., Pop. Code 5
Caldwell ISD
Sch. Sys. Enr. Code 4
Supt. – Anthony Kneupper
  203 N GRAY ST 77836
MS 77836 – Ed Presley, prin.
ES 77836 – John Meckel, prin.
IS 77836 – Jo Lock, prin.

Calvert, Robertson Co., Pop. Code 4
Calvert ISD
Sch. Sys. Enr. Code 2
Supt. – W. Ivy, P O BOX 07 77837
Spigner ES 77837 – Nemo Comfort, prin.

Cameron, Milam Co., Pop. Code 6
Cameron ISD
Sch. Sys. Enr. Code 4
Supt. – B. Dulin, 504 E 10TH ST 76520
Thomas JHS 76520 – John Matlock, prin.
Henderson MS, 208 E 10TH ST 76520
  Terry Wyatt, prin.
Milam ES, 504 E 10TH ST 76520
  Terry Wyatt, prin.

Campbell, Hunt Co., Pop. Code 3
Campbell ISD
Sch. Sys. Enr. Code 2
Supt. – James Calvert, P O BOX 157 75422
ES 75422 – Price Thrall, prin.

Canadian, Hemphill Co., Pop. Code 5
Canadian ISD
Sch. Sys. Enr. Code 3
Supt. – Jim Pollard, 800 HILLSIDE ST 79014
MS 79014 – L. Scroggins, prin.

Baker MS, 723 CHEYENNE AVE 79014
  David Taylor, prin.
ES, 500 DOGWOOD ST 79014
  Karen Minyen, prin.

Canton, Van Zandt Co., Pop. Code 5
Canton ISD
Sch. Sys. Enr. Code 4
Supt. – T. Harvey, 225 W ELM ST 75103
MS 75103 – Max Callahan, prin.
ES, 225 W ELM ST 75103 – Larry Davis, prin.

Canutillo, El Paso Co., Pop. Code 4
Canutillo ISD
Sch. Sys. Enr. Code 5
Supt. – Wilson Knapp, P O BOX 100 79835
MS 79835 – Robert Mendoza, prin.
PS 79835 – Charles Wendler, prin.

Canyon, Randall Co., Pop. Code 7
Canyon ISD
Sch. Sys. Enr. Code 6
Supt. – Mike King, P O BOX 899 79015
JHS, 606 8TH ST 79015 – Duane Chapman, prin.
Valleyview JHS 79015 – Bob Sloan, prin.
Arden Road ES 79015 – Vondean Mcgregor, prin.
Hinger IS, 1005 21ST ST 79015
  Jerry Bigham, prin.
Howe ES, 5108 PICO AMARILLO 79015
  Donna Clopton, prin.
Lakeview ES 79015 – Earleen Huff, prin.
Reeves PS, 1005 21ST ST 79015
  Karen Rich, prin.
Other Schools – See Amarillo

Carbon, Eastland Co., Pop. Code 2
Carbon ISD
Sch. Sys. Enr. Code 2
Supt. – Ed Stumm, P O BOX 608 76435
S 76435 – John Rodgers, prin.

Carmine, Fayette Co., Pop. Code 2
Round Top-Carmine ISD
Sch. Sys. Enr. Code 2
Supt. – Jack Flinn, P O BOX 385 78932
Round Top ES 78932 – Ronald Goehring, prin.

Carrizo Springs, Dimmit Co., Pop. Code 6
Carrizo Springs Consolidated ISD
Sch. Sys. Enr. Code 5
Supt. – Enrique Uribe, 102 N 5TH ST 78834
JHS, HCR 01 78834 – Marcelino Costilla, prin.
Central ES, 402 N 7TH ST 78834
  Rosa Castaneda, prin.
Middle MS, HWY 85 N 78834 – C. Baker, prin.
North ES, 612 N 7TH ST 78834
  Patsy Vivion, prin.
Other Schools – See Big Wells

Carrollton, Dallas Co., Pop. Code 8
Carrollton-Farmers Branch ISD
Sch. Sys. Enr. Code 7
Supt. – B. Davis, P O BOX 186 75006
Blalack JHS, 1706 PETERS COLONY ROAD 75007
  Lora Folsom, prin.
Perry JHS, 1709 E BELT LINE ROAD 75006
  Lee Alviod, prin.
Blanton ES, 2525 SCOTT MILL ROAD 75006
  Linda Hawkins, prin.
ES, 1805 PEARL ST 75006 – Cloyd Hastings, prin.
Central ES, 1800 COX DR 75006
  Linda Stromberg, prin.
Country Place ES, 2115 RAINTREE DR 75006
  Barry Dodson, prin.
Davis ES, 3205 DORCHESTER DR 75007
  Carolyn Rogers, prin.
Farmers Branch ES 75011 – Joan Burk, prin.
Furneaux ES, 3210 FURNEAUX LANE 75007
  Robert McCrummen, prin.
Good ES, 2025 DENTON DR 75006
  Sharon McFerren, prin.
Kent ES 75011 – (—), prin.
Las Colinas ES 75011 – Beverly Rodgers, prin.
McCoy ES, 2425 MCCOY ROAD 75006
  Eddie Taylor, prin.
McLaughlin ES
  1500 WEBB CHAPEL ROAD 75006
  Joan Shelley, prin.
Montgomery ES 75011 – Ree McKensie, prin.
Rosemeade ES, 3550 KIMBERLY DR 75007
  Marie Huie, prin.
Sheffield ES, 1810 KELLY BLVD 75006
  George Wells, prin.
Stark ES 75011 – Larry Conner, prin.
Woodlake ES, 2915 SCOTT MILL ROAD 75007
  Dorothy Wells, prin.
Other Schools – See Dallas, Farmers Branch

Prince of Peace Lutheran School
  2115 FRANKFORD 75007

Carthage, Panola Co., Pop. Code 6
Carthage ISD
Sch. Sys. Enr. Code 5
Supt. – Mac Wheat, P O BOX D 75633
JHS 75633 – Russell Porter, prin.
Baker-Koonce MS, N DANIELS ST 75633
  Jeretta Thompson, prin.
Libby ES, DAVIS ST 75633
  Eberline Nugent, prin.

Castroville, Medina Co., Pop. Code 4
Medina Valley ISD
Sch. Sys. Enr. Code 4
Supt. – Wendell McAndrew, P O BOX P 78009

Medina Valley JHS, P O BOX P 78009
  F. Keller, prin.
Medina Valley ES 78009 – Leslie Tschirhart, prin.
Medina Valley IS, P O BOX P 78009
  Willie Allen, prin.

Cayuga, Anderson Co.
Cayuga ISD
Sch. Sys. Enr. Code 3
Supt. – Joe Woodland, P O BOX 427 75832
Cayuga ES 75832 – E. Scarborough,Jr., prin.

Cedar Hill, Dallas Co., Pop. Code 6
Cedar Hill ISD
Sch. Sys. Enr. Code 5
Supt. – Albert Thomas, P O BOX 248 75104
Mid S, P O BOX 248 75104 – John Rich, prin.
Bray ES, 218 BROAD ST 75104
  Gary Sneed, prin.
IS, 649 E BELT LINE ROAD 75104
  Victor Leos, prin.
Hi Pointe ES, 1351 HIGH POINTE LANE 75104
  Charlesetta Williams, prin.
Highland ES, 830 WHITNEY ST 75104
  Jay Miller, prin.
Plummer ES, 1203 S CLARK ROAD 75104
  Doris Wortham, prin.

Cedar Park, Williamson Co., Pop. Code 5
Leander ISD
Supt. – See Leander
Faubion ES, 1209 CYPRESS CREEK RD 78613
  Carolyn Mabarak, prin.

Good Shepherd Lutheran ES, P O BOX 64 78613

Celeste, Hunt Co., Pop. Code 3
Celeste ISD
Sch. Sys. Enr. Code 2
Supt. – C. Larry LaFauers, P O BOX 67 75423
ES, P O BOX 67 75423 – Marcia Cruse, prin.
IS 75423 – Don Williams, prin.

Celina, Collin Co., Pop. Code 4
Celina ISD
Sch. Sys. Enr. Code 3
Supt. – Truett Mobley, P O BOX 188 75009
MS, 601 S COLORADO DR 75009
  Jerry Moore, prin.
ES, FM 455 75009 – Joe Stubblefield, prin.

Center, Shelby Co., Pop. Code 6
Center ISD
Sch. Sys. Enr. Code 4
Supt. – H. Halvorson, 404 MOSBY ST 75935
JHS, 624 MALONE DRIVE 75935
  Lyndon Jobe, prin.
ES, 314 NACOGDOCHES ST 75935
  Margaret Hathorn, prin.
Intermediate MS 75935 – James Allen, prin.
Moffett PS 75935 – (—), prin.

Excelsior ISD
Sch. Sys. Enr. Code 1
Supt. – Melvin Holland
  RURAL ROUTE 02 BOX 816 75935
Excelsior ES 75935 – (—), prin.

Center Point, Kerr Co., Pop. Code 3
Center Point ISD
Sch. Sys. Enr. Code 2
Supt. – Burt Slater, P O BOX 377 78010
ES 78010 – Vester Joiner, prin.

Centerville, Leon Co., Pop. Code 3
Centerville ISD
Sch. Sys. Enr. Code 3
Supt. – Pierce Beard, P O BOX 218 75833
ES 75833 – Jeff Hyndman, prin.
MS 75833 – James Boozer, prin.

Channelview, Harris Co., Pop. Code 7
Channelview ISD
Sch. Sys. Enr. Code 5
Supt. – B. Hamblen, 1403 SHELDON ROAD 77530
Johnson JHS 77530 – W. Bigott, prin.
Cobb MS, 914 DELL DALE ST 77530
  Roger Martin, prin.
Crenshaw PS, 16204 WOOD DR 77530
  Patricia Schuler, prin.
De Zavala MS, 16150 SECOND STREET 77530
  Dossie Bruce, prin.
McMullan PS, 1290 DELL DALE ST 77530
  Glenn Barrett, prin.
Schochler PS, 910 DERRPASS ST 77530
  Ben Cooner, prin.

Channing, Hartley Co., Pop. Code 2
Channing ISD
Sch. Sys. Enr. Code 2
Supt. – Ky Sherrod, P O BOX A 79018
ES 79018 – Don Johnson, prin.

Chapman Ranch, Nueces Co.
Santa Cruz ISD
Sch. Sys. Enr. Code 1
Supt. – W. David, P O BOX 147 78347
ES 78347 – (—), prin.

Charlotte, Atascosa Co., Pop. Code 4
Charlotte ISD
Sch. Sys. Enr. Code 3
Supt. – R. Sinks, P O BOX 489 78011
JHS 78011 – Randy Gates, prin.
ES 78011 – Clyde Thompson, prin.

Cherokee, San Saba Co.
Cherokee ISD
Sch. Sys. Enr. Code 2
Supt. – Oliver Altizer, P O BOX S 76832
ES 76832 – Charles Perry, prin.

Chester, Tyler Co., Pop. Code 2
Chester ISD
Sch. Sys. Enr. Code 2
Supt. – Gary Gazaway, P O BOX 28 75936
ES 75936 – Jim Morris, prin.

Chico, Wise Co., Pop. Code 3
Chico ISD
Sch. Sys. Enr. Code 3
Supt. – Kenneth Manning, P O BOX 95 76030
MS 76030 – Doyle Reynolds, prin.
ES 76030 – Doyle Reynolds, prin.

Childress, Childress Co., Pop. Code 6
Childress ISD
Sch. Sys. Enr. Code 4
Supt. – Gary Grogan, P O BOX 179 79201
JHS, 700 COMMERCE ST 79201
  Anita Pitchford, prin.
ES 79201 – John Parker, prin.

Chillicothe, Hardeman Co., Pop. Code 4
Chillicothe ISD
Sch. Sys. Enr. Code 2
Supt. – Monte Pannell, P O BOX 518 79225
ES, AVE L & S 4 79225 – Larry Palmer, prin.

Chilton, Falls Co., Pop. Code 2
Chilton ISD
Sch. Sys. Enr. Code 2
Supt. – Richard Gott, P O BOX 488 76632
S 76632 – Burnell Hall, prin.

China, Jefferson Co., Pop. Code 4
Hardin-Jefferson ISD
Supt. – See Sour Lake
Henderson JHS, P O BOX 278 77613
  C. Styles, prin.

China Spring, McLennan Co.
China Spring ISD
Sch. Sys. Enr. Code 3
Supt. – Jim Carpenter 76633
MS 76633 – Charles Pierce, prin.
ES 76633 – Bob Baker, prin.

Chireno, Nacogdoches Co., Pop. Code 2
Chireno ISD
Sch. Sys. Enr. Code 2
Supt. – Bill Metteauer, P O BOX 85 75937
ES 75937 – Harold Hagle, prin.

Christoval, Tom Green Co., Pop. Code 3
Christoval ISD
Sch. Sys. Enr. Code 2
Supt. – John Reeves, P O BOX 162 76935
ES 76935 – Buddy Luce, prin.

Cibolo, Guadalupe Co., Pop. Code 3
Schertz-Cibolo-U. City ISD
Supt. – See Schertz
IS, RURAL ROUTE 03 BOX 705 78108
  Steve Ogle, prin.
Wiederstein ES, P O BOX 560 78108
  Linda Guy, prin.

Cisco, Eastland Co., Pop. Code 5
Cisco ISD
Sch. Sys. Enr. Code 3
Supt. – C. Saunders, P O BOX 1645 76437
JHS 76437 – Jim Puryear, prin.
ES 76437 – Robert Lindsey, prin.

Clarendon, Donley Co., Pop. Code 4
Clarendon ISD
Sch. Sys. Enr. Code 3
Supt. – J. Walker, P O BOX 610 79226
ES 79226 – Floyd Guinn, prin.

Clarksville, Red River Co., Pop. Code 5
Clarksville ISD
Sch. Sys. Enr. Code 4
Supt. – Mack Humphrey, P O BOX 1016 75426
JHS 75426 – William Mabry, prin.
ES, 107 S SPRUCE ST 75426
  James Brantley, prin.
IS, 107 S SPRUCE ST 75426
  Suzanne Lowe, prin.

Claude, Armstrong Co., Pop. Code 4
Claude ISD
Sch. Sys. Enr. Code 2
Supt. – J. Hawthorne, P O BOX 209 79019
S 79019 – W. Burcham, prin.

Cleburne, Johnson Co., Pop. Code 7
Cleburne ISD
Sch. Sys. Enr. Code 6
Supt. – Kermit Heimann
  103 S WALNUT ST 76031
JHS, 204 S BUFFALO ST 76031
  Frank Hyde, prin.
Adams ES, 1005 S ANGLIN ST 76031
  Lonnie Borden, prin.
Coleman ES, 920 W WESTHILL DR 76031
  Harry King, prin.
Cooke ES, 902 PHILLIPS ST 76031
  Charles Head, prin.
Fulton MS, 311 FEATHERSTON ST 76031
  Douglas Johnson, prin.
Gerard ES 76031 – Carolyn Cody, prin.

Irving ES, 1108 N ANGLIN ST 76031
  Riley Dunn, prin.
Liberty Chapel ES 76031 – Lynda Ballard, prin.
Long ES, 425 GRANBURY ST 76031
  Juanita White, prin.

Cleveland, Liberty Co., Pop. Code 6
Cleveland ISD
Sch. Sys. Enr. Code 5
Supt. – Linden Parrish, 103 LEGION ST 77327
JHS 77327 – Curtis Brinkley, prin.
Northside IS, 1522 N BLAIR AVE 77327
  Charles McLin, prin.
Southside ES, 216 E DALLAS ST 77327
  Gwendolyn Brinkley, prin.

Tarkington ISD
Sch. Sys. Enr. Code 4
Supt. – Ken Miller
  RURAL ROUTE 06 BOX 130 77327
Tarkington JHS 77327 – Perry Cowan, prin.
Tarkington ES, TARKINGTON PRARIE 77327
  Bob Saunders, prin.

Clifton, Bosque Co., Pop. Code 5
Clifton ISD
Sch. Sys. Enr. Code 3
Supt. – R. Liardon, 1102 N AVE N 76634
ES, 706 W 11TH ST 76634 – M. Brown, prin.

Clint, El Paso Co., Pop. Code 4
Clint ISD
Sch. Sys. Enr. Code 4
Supt. – Charles Downer, P O BOX 779 79836
JHS 79836 – Carlos Lopez, prin.
Desert Hills ES 79836 – Manuel Jimenez, prin.
Montana Vista ES, P O BOX 779 79836
  Ricardo Estrada, prin.
Surratt ES, P O BOX 779 79836
  Max Glover, prin.

Clute, Brazoria Co., Pop. Code 6
Brazosport ISD
Supt. – See Freeport
Clute Int. S, 421 E MAIN ST 77531
  Larry Meche, prin.

Our Lady Queen of Peace School
  1600 HIGHWAY 2064 77531

Clyde, Callahan Co., Pop. Code 5
Clyde ISD
Sch. Sys. Enr. Code 4
Supt. – Bobby Spence, P O BOX 479 79510
JHS 79510 – Brian Barrows, prin.
ES 79510 – Ed Brady, prin.
Hamby ES 79510 – Vicki Thomas, prin.

Eula ISD
Sch. Sys. Enr. Code 1
Supt. – William Harlan
  RURAL ROUTE 01 BOX 229A 79510
Eula S 79510 – J. Wilson, prin.

Coahoma, Howard Co., Pop. Code 4
Coahoma ISD
Sch. Sys. Enr. Code 3
Supt. – Gary Rotan, P O BOX 110 79511
JHS 79511 – Al Phillips, prin.
ES 79511 – Mike Turner, prin.

Coldspring, San Jacinto Co., Pop. Code 2
Coldspring-Oakhurst ISD
Sch. Sys. Enr. Code 2
Supt. – Cole Pugh, P O BOX 39 77331
Lincoln JHS 77331 – J. Le Flore, prin.
Coldspring-Oakhurst MS 77331
  Harold Stone, prin.
Street ES 77331 – I. Thomson, prin.

Coleman, Coleman Co., Pop. Code 6
Coleman ISD
Sch. Sys. Enr. Code 4
Supt. – Arthur Casey, Jr., P O BOX 900 76834
JHS 76834 – Tim Parrott, prin.
ES, W 5TH 76834 – Edward Pryor, prin.

Panther Creek Cons. SD
Sch. Sys. Enr. Code 2
Supt. – Charles Bryant, GOULDBUSK RT 76834
Panther Creek MS 76888 – Ted Bedwell, prin.
Panther Creek ES 76834 – Jack Cosby, prin.

College Station, Brazos Co., Pop. Code 8
College Station ISD
Sch. Sys. Enr. Code 6
Supt. – Raymond Chancellor
  100 ANDERSON ST 77840
A & M JHS 77840 – Alan Stolt, prin.
College Hills ES, 101 WILLIAMS ST 77840
  Robert Garner, prin.
Oakwood MS, 106 HOLIK DR 77840
  Gerald Wynn, prin.
South Knoll ES, 1220 BOSWELL ST 77840
  B. Holland, prin.
Southwood Valley ES 77840 – Dan Stribling, prin.

Colleyville, Tarrant Co., Pop. Code 6
Grapevine-Colleyville ISD
Supt. – See Grapevine
MS, 1100 BOGART ST 76034 – T. Taylor, prin.

Collinsville, Grayson Co., Pop. Code 3
Collinsville ISD
Sch. Sys. Enr. Code 2
Supt. – Archie Scott, P O BOX 268 76233
ES 76233 – S. Quattlebaum, prin.

Colmesneil, Tyler Co., Pop. Code 3
Colmesneil ISD
Sch. Sys. Enr. Code 2
Supt. – J. Handley, P O BOX 37 75938
ES 75938 – Diane Duhon, prin.

Colorado City, Mitchell Co., Pop. Code 6
Colorado ISD
Sch. Sys. Enr. Code 4
Supt. – Jim Ramsey, P O BOX 1268 79512
Colorado MS, 300 E 12TH ST 79512
James McLean, prin.
Hutchinson MS, 440 CEDAR ST 79512
William Jeffries, prin.
Kelley ES, 1435 ELM ST 79512
Bob Lemons, prin.

Columbus, Colorado Co., Pop. Code 5
Columbus ISD
Sch. Sys. Enr. Code 4
Supt. – John Saul, P O BOX 578 78934
JHS 78934 – Tommy Blair, prin.
ES, 1324 BOWIE ST 78934
Thomas Rowland, prin.

St. Anthony ES, 635 BONHAM ST 78934

Comanche, Comanche Co., Pop. Code 5
Comanche ISD
Sch. Sys. Enr. Code 4
Supt. – H. Jefferies, 405 N LANE ST 76442
Jeffries JHS 76442 – Bill Pope, prin.
IS, 205 E HIGHLAND 76442 – Susan Carruth, prin.
PS, 700 N PEARL ST 76442 – James Wilson, prin.

Comfort, Kendall Co., Pop. Code 3
Comfort ISD
Sch. Sys. Enr. Code 3
Supt. – T. Gene Williams, P O BOX 398 78013
ES 78013 – Kenneth Petermann, prin.

Commerce, Hunt Co., Pop. Code 6
Commerce ISD
Sch. Sys. Enr. Code 4
Supt. – Patricia Pope, P O BOX 1251 75428
MS 75428 – Sherry Rector, prin.
Day ES 75428 – Anna Blohm, prin.
Williams MS, WASHINGTON ST 75428
Bud Jones, prin.

Como, Hopkins Co., Pop. Code 3
Como-Pickton ISD
Sch. Sys. Enr. Code 3
Supt. – Joe Minter, P O BOX 416 75431
Como-Pickton S 75431 – Gary McCain, prin.

Comstock, Val Verde Co.
Comstock ISD
Sch. Sys. Enr. Code 2
Supt. – Jack Skiles, P O BOX 905 78837
S 78837 – (—), prin.

Conroe, Montgomery Co., Pop. Code 7
Conroe ISD
Sch. Sys. Enr. Code 7
Supt. – Richard Griffin
702 N THOMPSON ST 77301
Travis JHS, 1100 N THOMPSON 77301
Chris Kattner, prin.
Washington JHS, 507 AVENUE K 77301
Andrew Shell, prin.
York JHS 77301 – Hartwell Brown, prin.
Anderson ES, N 3RD ST 77301
Herbert Lamp, prin.
Armstrong ES, 110 GLADSTELL ST 77301
Dorothy Neathery, prin.
Austin ES, 702 N THOMPSON ST 77301
Michael Phythian, prin.
Creighton ES, 702 N THOMPSON ST 77301
Anne Coker, prin.
Crockett IS, 701 N 3RD ST 77301
Charlie Loyd, prin.
Houser IS
27370 OAK RIDGE SCHOOL ROAD 77385
George Branch, prin.
Houston ES, 601 W LEWIS ST 77301
Walter Jett, prin.
Oak Ridge ES, 9401 INTERSTATE 45 S 77385
Pat Nichol, prin.
Reaves IS, 1717 LOOP 336 W 77304
Dru Ann Davis, prin.
Rice ES, 804 GLADSTELL ROAD 77304
Valarie Thompson, prin.
Ride ES, 702 N THOMPSON ST 77301
Kay Richardson, prin.
Runyan ES, 1101 FOSTER DR 77301
Judith Robert, prin.
San Jacinto ES, 702 N THOMPSON ST 77301
Dixie Jackson, prin.
Other Schools – See Grangerland, Spring, The Woodlands

Sacred Heart ES, 105 N FRAZIER ST 77301

Converse, Bexar Co., Pop. Code 5
Judson ISD
Sch. Sys. Enr. Code 7
Supt. – G. Elolf, P O BOX 249 78109
ES, 102 SCHOOL ST 78109 – Arnold Griffin, prin.
Miller Point ES 78109 – Frances Anderson, prin.
Spring Meadows ES 78109 – William Dalton, prin.
Other Schools – See San Antonio, Universal City

St. Monica ES, 502 NORTH ST 78109

Coolidge, Limestone Co., Pop. Code 3
Coolidge ISD
Sch. Sys. Enr. Code 2
Supt. – Clarence Hollingsworth
P O BOX 1026 76635
S 76635 – David Lee, prin.

Cooper, Delta Co., Pop. Code 4
Cooper ISD
Sch. Sys. Enr. Code 3
Supt. – F. Wilkerson, 440 SW 3RD ST 75432
JHS 75432 – Glen Harris, prin.
ES 75432 – Glen Harris, prin.

Coppell, Dallas Co., Pop. Code 5
Coppell ISD
Sch. Sys. Enr. Code 4
Supt. – David Stanfield
1201 WRANGLER DRIVE 75019
MS, 400 MOCKINGBIRD 75019 – Vern Edin, prin.
Austin ES, 161 S MOORE ROAD 75019
Debra Nelson, prin.
Lee ES 75019 – Bruce MacDonald, prin.
Pinkerton ES 75019 – Mary King, prin.

Copperas Cove, Coryell Co., Pop. Code 7
Copperas Cove ISD
Sch. Sys. Enr. Code 6
Supt. – Richard Kirkpatrick, P O BOX 580 76522
JHS 76522 – Gail Milligan, prin.
Avenue E MS, E AVENUE E 76522
Robert Weiss, prin.
Fairview ES, 900 MAIN AVE 76522
Mike Wilburn, prin.
Halstead ES, N MAIN ST 76522
Joe Donaldson, prin.
Jewell ES, ROSE & 5TH 76522 – Mary Glass, prin.
Stevens ES, CUMMINGS & SYCAMORE 76522
Wayne Turner, prin.
Walker ES 76522 – James Sneed, prin.

Corpus Christi, Nueces Co., Pop. Code 9
Calallen ISD
Sch. Sys. Enr. Code 5
Supt. – Fred Zachary
4602 CORNETT DRIVE 78410
Calallen MS, 4602 CORNETT DRIVE 78410
Larry Smith, prin.
Annaville ES, 3901 HILLTOP ROAD 78410
Clifford Crenshaw, prin.
Calallen/Wood Rivr ES 78410
Tamlyn Jones, prin.
East ES 78410 – Carlos Cruz, prin.
Magee ES 78410 – David Andrews, prin.

Corpus Christi ISD
Sch. Sys. Enr. Code 8
Supt. – Charles Benson, P O BOX 110 78403
Baker MS, 3445 PECAN ST 78411
Richard Harbin, prin.
Cunningham MS, 4321 PRESCOTT ST 78416
Arnold Saavedra, prin.
Driscoll MS, 261 DRISCOLL DRIVE 78408
Curtis Clerkley, prin.
Martin MS, 3502 GREENWOOD DRIVE 78416
Roy Torres, prin.
Seale MS, 1707 AYERS ST 78404
Raymond Davis, prin.
Shannon MS, 5922 BROCKHAMPTON 78414
(—), prin.
Allen ES, 2002 ELIZABETH ST 78404
Sylvia Villarreal, prin.
Calk ES, 4621 MARIE ST 78411 – Rolor Ray, prin.
Carroll Lane ES, 4120 CARROLL LANE 78411
Deborak McAden, prin.
Casa Linda ES, 1540 CASA GRANDE DR 78411
Sylvia Rosales, prin.
Central Park ES, 3602 MCARDLE ROAD 78415
Dottie Pittman, prin.
Chula Vista Fine Arts ES
1761 HUDSON ST 78416 – Anson Nash, prin.
Club Estates ES, 5222 MERGANSER DR 78413
Jose Salinas, prin.
Coles ES, 924 WINNEBAGO ST 78401
Delia Villarreal, prin.
Crockett ES, 2625 BELTON ST 78416
Mary Gonzales, prin.
Crossley ES, 2512 KOEPKE ST 78407
Raul Prezas, prin.
Evans ES, 1315 COMANCHE ST 78401
Millard Reynolds, prin.
Fannin ES, 2730 GOLLIHAR ROAD 78415
H. Pearson, prin.
Fisher ES, 601 TEXAN TRAIL 78411
Joe Guerra, prin.
Garcia ES, 4401 GREENWOOD DR 78416
Roger Frank, prin.
Gibson ES, 5723 HAMPSHIRE ROAD 78408
Albert Villarreal, prin.
Houston ES, 363 NORTON ST 78415
Gilbert Silva, prin.
Kostorys ES, 3602 PANAMA DR 78415
Quince Mitchell, prin.
Lamar ES, 2212 MORRIS ST 78405
Faye Webb, prin.
Lexington ES, 2901 MCARDLE ROAD 78415
Jerald Brooks, prin.
Los Encinos ES, 1826 FRIO ST 78417
Yolanda Gonzalez, prin.
Lozano ES, 650 ORSAGE ST 78405
Maggie Ramirez, prin.
Meadowbrook ES
901 MEADOWBROOK DR 78412
Susan Marshall, prin.

Menger ES, 2209 S ALAMEDA ST 78404
Karen Grant, prin.
Montclair ES, 5241 KENTNER ST 78412
Delia Marichalar, prin.
Moore ES, 6121 DURANT 78414
Chris Garza, prin.
Oak Park ES, 3701 MUELLER ST 78408
Judy Maroney, prin.
Prescott ES, 1945 GOLLIHAR ROAD 78416
Claude Melton, prin.
Sanders ES, 4102 REPUBLIC DR 78413
Charles Blasingame, prin.
Schanen ES, 5717 KILLARMET DR 78413
Hector Garciz, prin.
Shaw ES, 844 VIRGINIA AVE 78405
Terri Alaniz, prin.
Smith ES, 6902 WILLIAMS DR 78412
Hector Hinojosa, prin.
Travis ES, 1645 TARLTON ST 78415
Guadalupe Guerrero, prin.
Windsor Park Gifted/Talent ES
4525 S ALAMEDA ST 78412
Virginia Harris, prin.
Woodlawn ES, 1110 WOODLAWN DR 78412
John Boeye, prin.
Yeager ES, 5414 TRIPOLI DR 78411
(—), prin.
Zavala ES, 3201 HIGHLAND AVE 78405
Eduardo Torres, prin.

Flour Bluff ISD
Sch. Sys. Enr. Code 5
Supt. – W. Claborn, 2505 WALDRON ROAD 78418
Flour Bluff JHS, 2505 WALDRON ROAD 78418
Walter Dennis, prin.
Flour Bluff ES 78418 – Charles Thompson, prin.
Flour Bluff IS 78418 – Kay Mecom, prin.
Flour Bluff PS 78418 – Ralph Gowens, prin.

London ISD
Sch. Sys. Enr. Code 2
Supt. – Anne Baker
RURAL ROUTE 03 BOX 350 78415
London ES 78415 – Anne Baker, prin.

Tuloso-Midway ISD
Sch. Sys. Enr. Code 5
Supt. – Suzanne Nelson, 9760 LEBRANCH 78410
Tuloso-Midway JHS, 1925 TULOSO ROAD 78409
Ana Marie Elizondo, prin.
Tuloso-Midway Central S
1925 TULOSO ROAD 78409
Melodie McClarren, prin.
Tuloso-Midway IS, 1925 TULOSO ROAD 78409
Phyllis McBride, prin.

West Oso ISD
Sch. Sys. Enr. Code 4
Supt. – Doris Henderson
5050 ROCKFORD DRIVE 78416
Allen MS 78416 – (—), prin.
West Oso JHS, 1115 BLOOMINGTON ST 78416
Roger Trevino, prin.
Kennedy ES, 5040 ROCKFORD DR 78416
Indalecio Vela, prin.
Skinner MS, 1001 BLOOMINGTON ST 78416
Lillie Satterwhite, prin.

Incarnate Word JHS, 2917 AUSTIN ST 78404
Central Catholic School
1218 COMANCHE STREET 78401
Christ the King ES, 1625 ARLINGTON DR 78415
Holy Family ES, 2513 NOGALES ST 78416
Incarnate Word ES, 450 CHAMBERLAIN ST 78404
Most Precious Blood School
3502 SARATOGA BLVD 78415
Our Lady of Perpetual Help School
5814 WILLIAMS DR 78412
SS Cyril and Methodius School
5002 KOSTORYZ ROAD 78415
Sacred Heart School, 1218 COMANCHE ST 78401
St. James Episcopal ES
602 S CARANCAHUA ST 78401
St. Patrick ES, 3350 S ALAMEDA ST 78411
St. Pius X ES, 747 ST PIUS DR 78412
St. Theresa ES, 1253 LANTANA ST 78407
Trinity Lutheran ES
808 LOUISIANA PARKWAY AVE 78404

Corrigan, Polk Co., Pop. Code 4
Corrigan-Camden ISD
Sch. Sys. Enr. Code 4
Supt. – Jacob Sherman, S HOME ST #01060 75939
Corrigan-Camden JHS 75939 – John Thomas, prin.
Corrigan-Camden IS 75939 – Harlan Parrish, prin.
Corrigan-Camden PS 75939 – Robert Barrett, prin.

Corsicana, Navarro Co., Pop. Code 7
Corsicana ISD
Sch. Sys. Enr. Code 5
Supt. – M. Culwell, 312 W 1ST AVE 75110
MS, 1520 DOBBIN ROAD 75110
Gilbert Hall, prin.
Bowie ES, 1440 W LEXINGTON DR 75110
Bill Humbert, prin.
Drane ES 75110 – Earl Scarborough, prin.
Fannin ES, 3201 N BEATON ST 75110
Cleo Lee, prin.
Houston ES, 1213 W 4TH AVE 75110
J. Thompson, prin.
Lee ES, 2200 W 4TH AVE 75110
James Gleason, prin.
Lincoln ES, 1101 E 13TH AVE 75110
William Alexander, prin.

Travis ES, 1009 W 13TH AVE   75110
  Sharon Eddins, prin.

Mildred ISD
  Sch. Sys. Enr. Code 2
  Supt. – Douglas Lane
    RURAL ROUTE 06 BOX 113   75110
  Mildred ES   75110 – Paula McNeel, prin.

James Collins Catholic ES
  3000 W HIGHWAY 22   75110

Cotton Center, Hale Co.
  Cotton Center ISD
  Sch. Sys. Enr. Code 2
  Supt. – Monte Lee, P O BOX 51   79021
  S   79021 – Kenneth Landers, prin.

Cotulla, La Salle Co., Pop. Code 5
  Cotulla ISD
  Sch. Sys. Enr. Code 4
  Supt. – Henry Sollers, P O BOX 699   78014
  Burks ES, 601 CENTER ST   78014
    Louisa Franklin, prin.
  Encinal ES   78014 – James Holmes, prin.
  Newman MS, 506 CARRIZO ST   78014
    Louisa Franklin, prin.
  Ramirez ES   78014 – Louisa Franklin, prin.

Coupland, Williamson Co.
  Coupland ISD
  Sch. Sys. Enr. Code 1
  Supt. – Coleman Bailey, P O BOX 217   78615
  ES   78615 – (—), prin.

Covington, Hill Co., Pop. Code 2
  Covington ISD
  Sch. Sys. Enr. Code 2
  Supt. – Charles Moore, P O BOX 67   76636
  S   76636 – Hank Strauch, prin.

Crandall, Kaufman Co., Pop. Code 3
  Crandall ISD
  Sch. Sys. Enr. Code 4
  Supt. – D. Harrison, P O BOX 128   75114
  JHS   75114 – Seth Adams, prin.
  IS   75114 – Sewell Glenn, prin.
  Raynes ES   75114 – Stephen Fleener, prin.

Crane, Crane Co., Pop. Code 5
  Crane ISD
  Sch. Sys. Enr. Code 4
  Supt. – Joe Allen, 511 W 8TH ST   79731
  JHS, 511 W 8TH   79731 – Jesse McWhorter, prin.
  ES, 300 W 7TH ST   79731 – Dan Dillard, prin.

Cranfills Gap, Bosque Co., Pop. Code 2
  Cranfills Gap ISD
  Sch. Sys. Enr. Code 2
  Supt. – John Bryant, P O BOX 67   76637
  S   76637 – Charles McGehee, prin.

Crawford, McLennan Co., Pop. Code 3
  Crawford ISD
  Sch. Sys. Enr. Code 2
  Supt. – Kenneth Judy, P O BOX 120   76638
  ES   76638 – Lee Yearwood, prin.

Crockett, Houston Co., Pop. Code 6
  Crockett ISD
  Sch. Sys. Enr. Code 4
  Supt. – P. Irby, P O BOX 481   75835
  JHS, P O BOX 481   75835 – Jim Powell, prin.
  ES, P O BOX 481   75835 – Sheila Crone, prin.
  IS, P O BOX 481   75835 – Walter Moffitt, prin.

Crockett Episcopal ES, P O BOX 671   75835

Crosby, Harris Co., Pop. Code 4
  Crosby ISD
  Sch. Sys. Enr. Code 5
  Supt. – Don Hendrix, P O BOX C   77532
  MS   77532 – Ernest Sylva, prin.
  ES   77532 – Roy Gilbert, prin.
  PS   77532 – Jane Eaton, prin.
  Drew IS, 223 RED OAK AVE   77532
    George Dean, prin.

Sacred Heart ES, 907 RUNNEBERG ROAD   77532

Crosbyton, Crosby Co., Pop. Code 4
  Crosbyton ISD
  Sch. Sys. Enr. Code 3
  Supt. – Jerry Scott, 204 S HARRISON ST   79322
  JHS, 204 S HARRISON ST   79322
    Wynn Robinson, prin.
  ES, 204 S HARRISON ST   79322 – Chet Dye, prin.

Cross Plains, Callahan Co., Pop. Code 4
  Cross Plains ISD
  Sch. Sys. Enr. Code 2
  Supt. – Lee Thompson, P O BOX 669   76443
  ES   76443 – Ray Womack, prin.

Crowell, Foard Co., Pop. Code 4
  Crowell ISD
  Sch. Sys. Enr. Code 2
  Supt. – L. Wall, P O BOX 239   79227
  ES   79227 – Mark Stretcher, prin.

Crowley, Tarrant Co., Pop. Code 6
  Crowley ISD
  Sch. Sys. Enr. Code 5
  Supt. – S. Poynter, P O BOX 688   76036
  Stevens MS, 1016 HWY 1187   76036
    Richard Allie, prin.
  Bess Race ES, 512 PEACH ST   76036
    Tom Tomlin, prin.

Deer Creek ES, 1301 S CROWLEY ROAD   76036
  Jim Johnson, prin.
Meadow Creek ES   76036 – Mary Harris, prin.
Sycamore ES
  1601 COUNTRY MANOR ROAD   76036
  David Walker, prin.

Crystal City, Zavala Co., Pop. Code 6
  Crystal City ISD
  Sch. Sys. Enr. Code 4
  Supt. – David Serna, 805 E CROCKETT ST   78839
  Fly JHS, 711 E CROCKETT ST   78839
    Juan Orona, prin.
  Juarez MS   78839 – Mercedes Casarez, prin.
  Zavala ES   78839 – Ray Espinosa, prin.

Cuero, DeWitt Co., Pop. Code 6
  Cuero ISD
  Sch. Sys. Enr. Code 4
  Supt. – Derrith Welch
    405 PARK HEIGHTS DRIVE   77954
  JHS   77954 – John Hancock, prin.
  French ES, 505 HENRY ST   77954
    Denzil McMurrey, prin.
  Hunt MS, 805 N HUNT ST   77954
    James Rabe, prin.

St. Michael ES, 208 N MCLEOD ST   77954

Cumby, Hopkins Co., Pop. Code 3
  Cumby ISD
  Sch. Sys. Enr. Code 2
  Supt. – James Allcorn, P O BOX 848   75433
  ES   75433 – Pat Crawford, prin.

Miller Grove ISD
  Sch. Sys. Enr. Code 2
  Supt. – Tommy Turner
    RURAL ROUTE 02 BOX 101   75433
  Miller Grove S, RURAL ROUTE 02   75433
    Richard Benson, prin.

Cushing, Nacogdoches Co., Pop. Code 3
  Cushing ISD
  Sch. Sys. Enr. Code 2
  Supt. – Jerry Whitaker, P O BOX 337   75760
  S   75760 – Lynn Moore, prin.

Daingerfield, Morris Co., Pop. Code 5
  Daingerfield-Lone Star ISD
  Sch. Sys. Enr. Code 4
  Supt. – Sheilia Hurtte, P O BOX V   75638
  JHS   75638 – J. Davis, prin.
  Lone Star ES   75638 – Vestal Harrell, prin.
  South MS, 701 LINDA DRIVE   75638
    Decker May, prin.

Daisetta, Liberty Co., Pop. Code 4
  Hull-Daisetta ISD
  Sch. Sys. Enr. Code 3
  Supt. – Kenneth Voytek, P O BOX 477   77533
  Hull-Daisetta JHS   77533 – Troy Dagle, prin.
  Hull-Daisetta ES   77533 – John Freeman, prin.

Dalhart, Dallam Co., Pop. Code 6
  Dalhart ISD
  Sch. Sys. Enr. Code 4
  Supt. – Ned Burns, P O BOX 590   79022
  JHS   79022 – Geneva Priddy, prin.
  ES, 1401 TENNESSEE BLVD   79022
    Roy Woods, prin.
  Finch MS   79022 – Thomas Sherrill, prin.

St. Anthony ES, 1302 OAK AVE   79022

Dallas, Dallas Co., Pop. Code 11
  Carrollton-Farmers Branch ISD
  Supt. – See Carrollton
  North Carrollton JHS
    12532 NUESTRA DRIVE   75230
    Kathy McWhorter, prin.

Dallas ISD
  Sch. Sys. Enr. Code 7
  Supt. – Marvin Edwards, 3700 ROSS AVE   75204
  Anderson MS   75204 – Wilber Williams, prin.
  Atwell MS, 1303 REYNOLDSTON LANE   75232
    Robert Yowell, prin.
  Browne MS, 3333 SPRAGUE DRIVE   75233
    Lincoln Butler, prin.
  Cary MS, 3978 KILLION DRIVE   75229
    Joy Barnhart, prin.
  Comstock MS, 7044 HODDE ST   75217
    Richard Allen, prin.
  Edison MS, 2940 SINGLETON BLVD   75212
    Joe Granado, prin.
  Florence MS, 1625 N MASTERS DRIVE   75217
    Robert Quast, prin.
  Franklin MS, 6920 MEADOW ROAD   75230
    Glenda Lassiter, prin.
  Gaston MS, 9565 MERCER DRIVE   75228
    Linda Isaacks, prin.
  Greiner MS, 625 S EDGEFIELD AVE   75208
    Oscar Rodriguez, prin.
  Hill MS, 505 EASTON ROAD   75218
    Bill Poteet, prin.
  Holmes MS, 2001 E KIEST BLVD   75216
    Carl Williams, prin.
  Hood MS, 7625 HUME DRIVE   75227
    Arthur Gillum, prin.
  Hulcy MS, 9339 S POLK ST   75232
    Leon King, prin.
  Long MS, 6116 REIGER AVE   75214
    Larry Smith, prin.
  Longfellow MS   75204 – Ora Lee Watson, prin.
  Marsh MS, 3838 CROWN SHORE DRIVE   75244
    Torance Vandygriff, prin.

Metropolitan MS, 912 S ERVAY ST   75201
  Sam Pugh, prin.
Rusk MS, 2929 INWOOD ROAD   75235
  Cele Rodriquez, prin.
Seagoville MS   75259 – Louis Moore, prin.
Spence MS, 4001 CAPITOL AVE   75204
  Joe Espinosa, prin.
Stockard MS, 2300 S RAVINIA DRIVE   75211
  Frank Romero, prin.
Stone MS, 4747 VETERANS DRIVE   75216
  Warren Baker, prin.
Storey MS, 3000 MARYLAND AVE   75216
  Joseph Brew, prin.
Adams ES, 3700 ROSS AVE   75204 – (—), prin.
Adams ES, 8239 LAKE JUNE ROAD   75217
  (—), prin.
Alexander ES, 1830 GOLDWOOD DR   75232
  Bob Simmons, prin.
Allen MS, 5220 NOMAS ST   75212
  Joseph Lopez, prin.
Anderson ES
  620 N SAINT AUGUSTINE DR   75217
  Manual Corrasco, prin.
Arcadia Park ES, 911 N MOROCCO AVE   75211
  John Chapel, prin.
Arlington Park ES, 5606 WAYSIDE DR   75235
  Mary Davis, prin.
Bayles ES, 2444 TELEGRAPH AVE   75228
  Jack Sisco, prin.
Blair ES, 7720 GAYGLEN DR   75217
  James Money, prin.
Blaton ES, 8915 GREENMOUND AVE   75227
  Richard Cox, prin.
Bonham ES, 2617 N HENDERSON AVE   75206
  Christobal Carrizales, prin.
Bowie ES, 301 N LANCASTER AVE   75203
  Yvonne Thompson, prin.
Brown ES, 2801 PARK ROW AVE   75215
  Selena Dorsey, prin.
Bryan ES, 2001 DEER PATH DR   75216
  Ruby Abel, prin.
Buckner ES, 400 ELLA AVE   75217
  Sally Dysart, prin.
Budd ES, 2121 S MARSALIS AVE   75216
  Charmaine Price, prin.
Burleson MS, 6300 ELAM ROAD   75217
  Katie Smith, prin.
Burnet ES, 3200 KINKAID DR   75220
  W. Toney Poulos, prin.
Bushman ES, 4200 BONNIE VIEW ROAD   75216
  Claudis Allen, prin.
Cabell ES, 12701 TEMPLETON TRL   75234
  Jacqulyn Irvan, prin.
Caillet ES, 3033 MERRELL ROAD   75229
  Ouida Ploeger, prin.
Carpenter ES, 2121 TOSCA LANE   75224
  George Woodrow, prin.
Carr ES, 1952 BAYSIDE ST   75212
  Jessie McNeil, prin.
Carver ES, 3719 GREENLEAF ST   75212
  Beatrice Vickers, prin.
Casa View ES, 2100 N FAROLA DR   75228
  Wayne Phillips, prin.
Central ES, 600 N KAUFMAN   75204
  Bill Frazier, prin.
City Park ES   75204 – Maria Gonzales, prin.
Cochran ES, 6000 KEENELAND PKWY   75211
  Marcus Gifford, prin.
Colonial ES, 1824 PENNSYLVANIA AVE   75215
  Marilyn Calhoun, prin.
Conner ES, 3037 GREEN MEADOW DR   75228
  Danny Salinas, prin.
Cowart ES, 1515 S RAVINIA DR   75211
  Walter Nelson, prin.
Crockett ES, 401 N CARROLL AVE   75246
  Al Miranda, prin.
Darrell ES, 4730 S LANCASTER ROAD   75216
  Fred Jackson, prin.
Davis ES, 1111 W KIEST BLVD   75224
  Chauncey Hightower, prin.
De Zavala ES, 3501 MARK   75204
  Fernando Lozano, prin.
Donald ES, 1218 PHINNEY AVE   75211
  W. Durrett, prin.
Dorsey ES, 133 N SAINT AUGUSTINE DR   75217
  Mary Cherbonnier, prin.
Dunbar ES, 4200 METROPOLITAN AVE   75210
  Annette Mitchell, prin.
Earhart ES
  3531 N WESTMORELAND ROAD   75212
  Rita Newman, prin.
Ervin ES, 3722 BLACK OAK DR   75241
  Robert Craft, prin.
Fannin ES, 4800 ROSS AVE   75204
  Edward Torres, prin.
Field ES, 2151 ROYAL LANE   75229
  Jack Gilliam, prin.
Foster ES, 3700 CLOVER LANE   75220
  Olivia Henderson, prin.
Frazier PS, 4600 SPRING AVE   75210
  Rubye Snow, prin.
Gill ES, 10910 FERGUSON ROAD   75228
  Will Sanders, prin.
Gooch ES, 4030 CALCULUS ROAD   75244
  Carolyn Schroeder, prin.
Hall ES, 2120 KEATS DR   75211
  Jack London, prin.
Harllee ES, 1216 E 8TH ST   75203
  Mabel Thomas, prin.
Harris ES, 4212 E GRAND AVE   75223
  Roscoe Smith, prin.
Hawthorne ES, 7800 UMPHRESS ROAD   75217
  Larry Norrell, prin.

Henderson ES, 2200 S EDGEFIELD AVE 75224
  Will Crowder, prin.
Hexter ES, 9720 WATERVIEW ROAD 75218
  Martha Lochner, prin.
Hogg ES, 1144 N MADISON AVE 75208
  Yolanda Cruz, prin.
Hooe ES, 2419 GLADSTONE DR 75211
  James Ross, prin.
Hotchkiss Montessori Acad
  6929 TOWN NORTH DR 75231
  Andrew Martin, prin.
Houston ES, 2827 THROCKMORTON ST 75219
  Graciela Escobedo, prin.
Ireland ES, 1515 N JIM MILLER ROAD 75217
  Opal Smith, prin.
Jackson MS, 2929 STAG ROAD 75241
  Sherwin Allen, prin.
Jackson ES, 5828 E MOCKINGBIRD LANE 75206
  Juanita Anderson, prin.
Johnston ES, 2020 MOUSER LANE 75203
  Cornell Thomas, prin.
Jones ES, 3901 MEREDITH ST 75211
  Arturo Salazar, prin.
Kiest ES 75204 – Richard McCook, prin.
Kleberg ES, 1450 EDD ROAD 75253
  Monty Boren, prin.
Knight ES, 2615 ANSON ROAD 75235
  William Scales, prin.
Lagow ES, 637 EDGEWORTH DR 75217
  Joe Waddill,Jr., prin.
Lakewood ES, 3000 HILLBROOK ST 75214
  Larry Wilburn, prin.
Lanier ES, 1400 WALMSLEY AVE 75208
  Rina Davis, prin.
Lee ES, 2911 DELMAR AVE 75206
  Linda Kimm, prin.
Lee ES, 7808 RACINE DR 75232
  Henry Smith, prin.
Lipscomb ES, 5801 WORTH ST 75214
  Michael Stiles, prin.
Lisbon ES 75204 – Cheryl Malone, prin.
Macon ES, 650 HOLCOMB ROAD 75217
  Charles Knox, prin.
Maple Lawn ES, 3120 INWOOD ROAD 75235
  Armando Murillo, prin.
Marcus ES, 2911 NORTHAVEN ROAD 75229
  Eva Vera, prin.
Marsalis ES, 5640 S MARSALIE AVE 75241
  Betty Davis, prin.
Marshall ES, 915 BROOKMERE DR 75216
  Eddye Oneal, prin.
Martinez ES, 3700 ROSS AVE 75204
  (—), prin.
Mcmillan PS, 3700 ROSS AVE 75204
  Jeanae Lewis, prin.
McNair ES, 3700 ROSS AVE 75204
  Carolyn Bailey, prin.
Milam ES, 4200 MCKINNEY AVE 75205
  Thomas Hood, prin.
Miller ES, 3111 BONNIE VIEW ROAD 75216
  Hazel Partee, prin.
Mills ES, 1515 LYNN HAVEN AVE 75216
  Pauline Davis, prin.
Moseley ES, 10400 RYLIE ROAD 75217
  Thurston Bridges, prin.
Mt. Auburn ES, 6012 E GRAND AVE 75223
  Arturo Cantu, prin.
Navarro ES, 3530 KINGBRIDGE ST 75212
  Thalia Matherson, prin.
Oliver MS, 4010 IDAHO AVE 75216
  Darrell Harris,Jr., prin.
Patton IS 75204 – Howard Kirven, prin.
Peabody ES, 3010 RAYDELL PL 75211
  Domingo Regalado, prin.
Pease ES, 2914 CUMMINGS ST 75216
  Theodore Lee, prin.
Peeler ES, 810 S LLEWELLYN AVE 75208
  Alberto Orozco, prin.
Pershing ES, 5715 MEADERS LANE 75229
  Mary Poulos, prin.
Polk ES, 6911 VICTORIA AVE 75209
  Charles Shaffner, prin.
Preston Hollow ES
  6423 WALNUT HILL LANE 75230
  Susie Oliphint, prin.
Ray ES, 2211 CADDO ST 75204
  Marilyn Mask, prin.
Reagan ES, 201 N ADAMS AVE 75208
  Cecilia Anzaldua, prin.
Reilly ES, 11230 LIPPITT AVE 75218
  Sandra Chertkov, prin.
Reinhardt ES, 10122 LOSA DR 75218
  Don Smith, prin.
Rhoads ES, 4401 S 2ND AVE 75210
  Barbara Patrick, prin.
Rice ES, 2425 PINE ST 75215
  Louise Smith, prin.
Roberts ES, 4919 E GRAND AVE 75223
  Martin Riojas, prin.
Rogers ES, 5314 ABRAMS ROAD 75214
  Rex Cole, prin.
Rosemont ES, 719 N MONTCLAIR AVE 75208
  W. Ferrell, prin.
Rowe ES, 4918 HOVENKAMP DR 75227
  Robert Ward, prin.
Runyan ES, 10750 CRADLEROCK DR 75217
  Robert Arwine, prin.
Russell MS, 3031 S BECKLEY AVE 75224
  George Willis, prin.
San Jacinto ES, 7900 HUME DR 75227
  Wayne Neu, prin.
Sanger ES, 8410 SAN LEANDRO DR 75218
  Mary Bolden, prin.
Seagoville ES 75204 – Stacy Mosley, prin.

Seguin ES, 111 W CORNING AVE 75224
  Cubie Evans, prin.
Sequoyah MS, 3635 GREENLEAF ST 75212
  Alvin Brossette,Jr., prin.
Silberstein ES, 5940 HOLLIS AVE 75227
  Joe McCalister, prin.
Starks ES, 3033 TIPS BLVD 75216
  Roosevelt Vaughn,Jr., prin.
Stemmons ES, 2727 KNOXVILLE ST 75211
  R. Upchurch, prin.
Stevens Park ES
  2615 W COLORADO BLVD 75211
  Don Clark, prin.
Terry ES, 6661 GREENSPAN AVE 75232
  John Brashear, prin.
Thompson ES, 5700 BEXAR ST 75215
  Don Williams, prin.
Thornton ES, 6011 OLD OX ROAD 75241
  Farris Sharp, prin.
Titche ES, 9560 HIGHFIELD DR 75227
  James Fox, prin.
Travis ES, 3001 MCKINNEY AVE 75204
  Maria Villalon, prin.
Truett ES, 1811 GROSS ROAD 75228
  Linda Solis, prin.
Turner ES, 5505 S POLK ST 75232
  Waylan Wallace, prin.
Twain ES, 724 GREEN COVE LANE 75232
  Frank Puntenney, prin.
Tyler ES, 2333 CALYPSO ST 75212
  Oneida Bradford, prin.
Urban Park ES, 6901 MILITRY PKWY 75227
  Jim Tate, prin.
Walnut Hill ES, 10115 MIDWAY ROAD 75229
  Kenneth Brashear, prin.
Webster ES, 3815 S FRANKLIN ST 75233
  James Reed, prin.
Weiss ES, 8601 WILLOUGHBY BLVD 75232
  Dean Watson, prin.
Wheatley ES, 2908 METROPOLITAN AVE 75215
  Patricia Pickles, prin.
Williams ES, 4518 POMONA ROAD 75209
  Marvin Grantham, prin.
Winnetka ES, 1151 S EDGEFIELD AVE 75208
  Joe Davis, prin.
Young MS, 4601 VETERANS DR 75216
  Harnell Williams, prin.

Highland Park ISD
Sch. Sys. Enr. Code 5
Supt. – W. Power
  7015 WESTCHESTER DRIVE 75205
McCulloch MS, 3520 NORMANDY AVE 75205
  Cecil Floyd, prin.
Armstrong ES 75205 – Kenneth Thomas, prin.
Bradfield ES, 4300 SOUTHERN AVE 75205
  Elaine Prude, prin.
Hyer ES, 3920 CARUTH BLVD 75225
  Louis Powers, prin.
University Park ES, 3505 AMHERST AVE 75225
  Charles Cole, prin.

Richardson ISD
Supt. – See Richardson
Bowie ES, 7643 LA MANGA DR 75248
  Dennis Johnson, prin.
Brentfield ES, 6767 BRENTFIELD DR 75248
  Harold Havard, prin.
Dobie ES, 14040 ROLLING HILLS LANE 75240
  Tom Savay, prin.
Forrestridge ES, 10330 BUNCHBERRY DR 75243
  Ray Hartman,Jr., prin.
Hamilton Park ES, 8301 TOWNS ST 75243
  Sue Francis, prin.
Northwood Hills ES
  14532 MEANDERING WAY 75240
  Everett Williams, prin.
Prestonwood ES, 6525 LA COSA DR 75248
  Mike Murphy, prin.
Spring Creek ES, 7667 ROUNDROCK ROAD 75248
  Jim Smith, prin.
Spring Valley ES
  13535 SPRING GROVE AVE 75240
  Judy Neslage, prin.

Wilmer-Hutchins ISD
Sch. Sys. Enr. Code 5
Supt. – Charles Matthews
  3820 E ILLINOIS AVE 75216
Kennedy-Curry JHS, 6605 SEBRING DRIVE 75241
  Richard Shaw, prin.
Alta Mesa ES, 2901 MORGAN DR 75241
  Ann Lee, prin.
White ES, 3820 E ILLINOIS AVE 79216
  Tommie Lydia, prin.
Other Schools – See Hutchins, Wilmer

Dallas Christian School, P O BOX 28295 75228
Fairhill School, 6039 CHURCHILL WAY 75230
First Baptist School, P O Box 868 75221
Greenhill School, 14255 MIDWAY ROAD 75244
Hockaday School, 11600 WELCH ROAD 75229
Lakehill Prep School
  2720 HILLSIDE DRIVE 75214
Lobias Murray School
  330 E ANN ARBOR AVE 75216
St. Marks School, 10600 PRESTON ROAD 75230
Tyler Street Christian Academy
  927 W 10TH ST 75208
Winston School, 5707 ROYAL LANE 75229
Akiba ES, 6210 CHURCHILL WAY 75230
Christ the King ES, 8017 PRESTON ROAD 75225
Dallas City Temple School 75203
Dallas-Oak Cliff SDA School 75224

First Baptist of East Dallas ES, P O BOX 868 75221
Good Shepherd Episcopal ES
  11122 MIDWAY ROAD 75229
Grace Lutheran School
  1523 S BECKLEY AVE 75224
Highland Park Presbyterian School
  3821 UNIVERSITY BLVD 75205
Holy Cross Lutheran School
  11425 MARSH LANE 75229
Holy Trinity ES, 3815 OAK LAWN AVE 75219
Houston Montessori Class
  2827 THROCKMORTON ST 75219
John XXIII ES, 2801 HARLANDALE AVE 75216
Lamplighter School, 11611 INWOOD ROAD 75229
Mary Immaculate ES, 14032 DENNIS LANE 75234
Montessori School of Park Cities
  4011 INWOOD ROAD 75209
Our Lady of Perpetual Help ES
  7625 CORTLAND AVE 75235
Our Redeemer ES, 7611 PARK LANE 75225
Parish ES, 14115 HILLCREST ROAD 75240
Scofield Christian ES
  7730 ABRAMS ROAD 75231
Solomon Schechter Academy
  7111 STARBUCK DR 75252
St. Anthony ES, 3732 MYRTLE ST 75215
St. Augustine ES
  1064 N ST AUGUSTINE DR 75217
St. Bernard ES, 1420 OLD GATE LANE 75218
St. Cecilia ES, 635 MARYCLIFF ROAD 75208
St. Elizabeth ES, 4019 S HAMPTON ROAD 75224
St. John's Episcopal ES
  848 HARTER ROAD 75218
St. Mary of Carmel ES
  1716 SINGLETON BLVD 75212
St. Michael ES
  8011 DOUGLAS AT COLGATE 75225
St. Monica ES, 4140 WALNUT HILL LANE 75229
St. Patrick ES, 9635 FERNDALE ROAD 75238
St. Philip ES, 8151 MILITARY PARKWAY 75227
St. Phillip's Episcopal ES
  1500 PENNSYLVANIA AVE 75215
St. Pius X ES
  3030 GUS THOMASSON ROAD 75228
St. Rita ES, 12525 INWOOD ROAD 75244
St. Thomas Aquinas ES
  3741 ABRAMS ROAD 75214
Winston School, 5707 ROYAL LANE 75229
Zion Lutheran ES, 6121 E LOVERS LANE 75214

Damon, Brazoria Co.
Damon ISD
Sch. Sys. Enr. Code 2
Supt. – Leonard Duckworth, P O BOX 8 77430
ES 77430 – (—), prin.

Danbury, Brazoria Co., Pop. Code 4
Danbury ISD
Sch. Sys. Enr. Code 3
Supt. – Robert Reeves, P O BOX 378 77534
MS 77534 – Patrick Callahan, prin.
ES 77534 – Michael Cortright, prin.

Darrouzett, Lipscomb Co., Pop. Code 2
Darrouzett ISD
Sch. Sys. Enr. Code 1
Supt. – Melvin Williams, P O BOX 98 79024
S 79024 – Dean Foshee, prin.

Dawson, Navarro Co., Pop. Code 3
Dawson ISD
Sch. Sys. Enr. Code 2
Supt. – William Brown, P O BOX 2788 76639
ES 76639 – Kenneth Murray, prin.

Dayton, Liberty Co., Pop. Code 5
Dayton ISD
Sch. Sys. Enr. Code 5
Supt. – Will Moore, P O BOX 248 77535
Wilson JHS 77535 – Larry Wadzeck, prin.
Austin ES, 702 S CLEVELAND ST 77535
  Charles Childs, prin.
Colbert MS, COLBERT ST 77535
  Gytha Mcnair, prin.
Richter MS, 2400 N WINFREE ST 77535
  Mike Day, prin.

Decatur, Wise Co., Pop. Code 5
Decatur ISD
Sch. Sys. Enr. Code 4
Supt. – Kenneth McKay, P O BOX 390 76234
MS 76234 – J. Carson, prin.
ES 76234 – Carmelina Holloway, prin.
IS 76234 – David Mosley, prin.

Deer Park, Harris Co., Pop. Code 7
Deer Park ISD
Sch. Sys. Enr. Code 6
Supt. – Lynn Hale, 203 IVY AVE 77536
Bonnette JHS, 5010 PASADENA BLVD 77536
  Dan Lamb, prin.
JHS, 410 E 9TH ST 77536 – Ed Mays, prin.
Carpenter ES, 5002 PASADENA BLVD 77536
  Robert Garcia, prin.
Dabbs ES, 302 E LAMBUTH LANE 77536
  James Wuthrich, prin.
Deepwater MS 77536 – Harry Fuller, prin.
ES, 2920 LUELLA AVE 77536
  John Simmons, prin.
Lynchburg ES, 203 IVY AVE 77536
  Kinney Moore, prin.
Parkwood ES, 203 IVY AVE 77536
  Ed Mills, prin.
San Jacinto ES, 601 E 8TH ST 77536
  Louis Guisti, prin.
Other Schools – See Pasadena

De Kalb, Bowie Co., Pop. Code 4
De Kalb ISD
Sch. Sys. Enr. Code 4
Supt. – Allen Cooper, 152 SW MAPLE ST 75559
JHS, 845 SW FRONT ST 75559
  Wayne Mahone, prin.
ES 75559 – James Tidwell, prin.

Hubbard ISD
Sch. Sys. Enr. Code 1
Supt. – Ron McMillion
  RURAL ROUTE 01 BOX 274 75559
Hubbard ES 75559 – (—), prin.

De Leon, Commanche Co., Pop. Code 4
DeLeon ISD
Sch. Sys. Enr. Code 3
Supt. – James Perkins, P O BOX 256 76444
ES, 201 E PECAN ST 76444 – Bill Johnson, prin.

Dell City, Hudspeth Co., Pop. Code 2
Dell City ISD
Sch. Sys. Enr. Code 2
Supt. – Kay Karr, P O BOX 37 79837
S 79837 – Bob Richardson, prin.

Del Rio, Val Verde Co., Pop. Code 8
Juno Cons. SD
Sch. Sys. Enr. Code 1
Supt. – Sergio Gonzalez, P O BOX 1266 78841
Juno ES 78840 – Lorrie Hickman, prin.

San Felipe-Del Rio Cons. ISD
Sch. Sys. Enr. Code 6
Supt. – Richard Evins, P O BOX 1229 78841
Del Rio MS 78840 – Roberto Chavira, prin.
Buena Vista ES, P O BOX 420128 78841
  Patricia Younts, prin.
Chavira ES, HWY 277 S 78840
  Juan Olivares,Jr., prin.
East Side ES, 1009 AVENUE J 78840
  Linda Spivey, prin.
Garfield ES, 300 LAS BEGAS ROAD 78840
  Ricardo Jimenez, prin.
Lamar ES, 301 WATERS AVE 78840
  Leticia Cuellar, prin.
Memorial MS 78842 – Rogelio Musquiz, prin.
North Heights ES, 1100 AVENUE C 78840
  Edna Blanks, prin.
San Felipe MS 78842 – Roberto Zaragoza, prin.

Sacred Heart ES, 209 E GREENWOOD ST 78840
St. James Episcopal School
  206 W GREENWOOD ST 78840

Del Valle, Travis Co., Pop. Code 3
Del Valle ISD
Sch. Sys. Enr. Code 6
Supt. – Edward Neal 78617
JHS 78617 – Susan Oglesbee, prin.
Baty ES 78617 – John Schwartz, prin.
Hillcrest MS 78617 – Jackie Thornton, prin.
Hornsby-Dunlap ES 78617
  Marianne Casarez, prin.
Popham ES 78617 – Joan DeLucca, prin.
Smith ES 78617 – Bernard Blanchard, prin.

Denison, Grayson Co., Pop. Code 7
Denison ISD
Sch. Sys. Enr. Code 5
Supt. – Bill Jacobs, 800 S MIRICK AVE 75020
McDaniel MS, 701 W MAIN ST 75020
  Gary Birdsong, prin.
Golden Rule ES, 800 W FLORENCE ST 75020
  Paul Jennings, prin.
Houston ES, 1100 W MORGAN ST 75020
  Katherine Dean, prin.
Hyde Park ES, 1700 S HYDE PARK AVE 75020
  D. McKnight, prin.
Lamar ES, 508 E MUNSON ST 75020
  Carole Linsteadt, prin.
Layne ES, 1000 LAYNE DR 75020
  Gordon Rutledge, prin.
Mayes ES, 201 JENNIE LANE 75020
  Harriet Steward, prin.
Terrell ES, WASHINGTON & RUSK AVE 75020
  Gregory Roman, prin.

Selwyn School, 3333 UNIVERSITY DRIVE 76201

Denver City, Yoakum Co., Pop. Code 5
Denver City ISD
Sch. Sys. Enr. Code 4
Supt. – Howard Pollard, P O BOX A 79323

JHS, 603 MUSTANG DRIVE 79323
  William Gravitt, prin.
IS, 1001 N F AVE 79323 – Wendell Solis, prin.
PS, 500 S AVENUE C 79323
  Brenda Massey, prin.
Kelley ES, 500 N SOLAND AVE 79323
  Eddie Allen, prin.

De Soto, Dallas Co., Pop. Code 7
DeSoto ISD
Sch. Sys. Enr. Code 5
Supt. – F. Moates, 200 E BELT LINE ROAD 75115
JHS, 601 BELT LINE ROAD E 75115
  William Richardson, prin.
West JHS, 800 N WESTMORELAND 75115
  David Robbins, prin.
Amber Terrace IS, 224 AMBER LANE 75115
  Carlene Stricklin, prin.
Belt Line ES, 200 E BELT LINE ROAD 75115
  Peggy Trammell, prin.
Cockrell Hill ES
  425 COCKRELL HILL ROAD 75115
  Price Minter, prin.
Meadows IS, 1016 MEADOWS PKWY 75115
  Richard Clark, prin.
Moates ES 75115 – Eddie Mae Geren, prin.
Northside ES, 525 RAY AVE 75115
  Ron Cagle, prin.
Young ES, 707 N YOUNG BLVD 75115
  Dorothy McMeans, prin.

Detroit, Red River Co., Pop. Code 3
Detroit ISD
Sch. Sys. Enr. Code 2
Supt. – John Lands
  RURAL ROUTE 02 BOX 44B 75436
ES, RURAL ROUTE 02 BOX 44B 75436
  Charles Sharp, prin.

Devers, Liberty Co., Pop. Code 3
Devers ISD
Sch. Sys. Enr. Code 1
Supt. – James Hardy, P O BOX 488 77538
ES 77538 – James Hardy, prin.

Devine, Medina Co., Pop. Code 5
Devine ISD
Sch. Sys. Enr. Code 4
Supt. – Dale Hatley, P O BOX 1 78016
MS, 900 ATKINS AVE 78016 – Jim Davis, prin.
Ciavarra ES 78016 – Linda Stanton, prin.

Deweyville, Newton Co., Pop. Code 3
Deweyville ISD
Sch. Sys. Enr. Code 3
Supt. – Earl Luce, P O BOX 408 77614
MS 77614 – Jim Sheppard, prin.
ES 77614 – Joy Scarborough, prin.

D'Hanis, Medina Co., Pop. Code 3
D'Hanis ISD
Sch. Sys. Enr. Code 2
Supt. – Maurice Zerr, P O BOX 307 78850
S 78850 – Amos Finger, prin.

Diana, Upshur Co., Pop. Code 2
New Diana ISD
Sch. Sys. Enr. Code 3
Supt. – Norton Lovell, P O BOX 26 75640
New Diana JHS, P O BOX 26 75640
  J. Mcghee, prin.
New Diana ES 75640 – Robert Hunt, prin.

Diboll, Angelina Co., Pop. Code 6
Diboll ISD
Sch. Sys. Enr. Code 4
Supt. – James Dunlop, P O BOX 550 75941
Temple JHS 75941 – Dale Anderson, prin.
ES 75941 – Helen Cheshire, prin.

Dickinson, Galveston Co., Pop. Code 6
Dickinson ISD
Sch. Sys. Enr. Code 6
Supt. – N. Ohlendorf, P O BOX Z 77539
McAdams JHS, 4007 VIDEO ST 77539
  Alton Morgan, prin.
PS 77359 – David Dunham, prin.
Dunbar MS, 2901 23RD ST 77539
  Linda Hanson, prin.
Hughes Road MS, 11901 HUGHES ROAD 77539
  Norma Deats, prin.
Little ES 77359 – Mickey Barlow, prin.
Silbernagel ES 77359 – William Crocker, prin.

True Cross ES, 400 PINE DR 77539

Dilley, Frio Co., Pop. Code 5
Dilley ISD
Sch. Sys. Enr. Code 3
Supt. – Tommy Sanders, P O BOX 18040 78017
Harper MS 78017 – Albert Burton, prin.
ES 78017 – Marilyn Smyth, prin.

Dime Box, Lee Co., Pop. Code 2
Dime Box ISD
Sch. Sys. Enr. Code 2
Supt. – Larry Pennington, P O BOX 157 77853
S 77853 – Byron Welch, prin.

Dimmitt, Castro Co., Pop. Code 6
Dimmitt ISD
Sch. Sys. Enr. Code 4
Supt. – R. Ryan, 608 W HALSELL ST 79027
MS, 805 W JONES 79027 – Neil Bryan, prin.
Richardson ES 79027 – Charles Miller, prin.

Dodd City, Fannin Co., Pop. Code 2
Dodd City ISD
Sch. Sys. Enr. Code 2
Supt. – B. Matthews
  RURAL ROUTE 01 BOX 02 75438
S 75438 – Ryan Lehtinen, prin.

Donna, Hidalgo Co., Pop. Code 6
Donna ISD
Sch. Sys. Enr. Code 6
Supt. – Roel Smith, 116 N 10TH ST 78537
Todd JHS 78537 – Evaristo Guerrero, prin.
Austin ES 78537 – Juan Garcia, prin.
ES 78537 – Maria Ochoa, prin.
Guzman ES 78537 – Florence Hollembeak, prin.
Lenoir MS 78537 – Francisco Olvera, prin.
Moye MS 78537 – Andres Martinez, prin.
Runn ES 78537 – Maria Munoz, prin.

Douglass, Nacogdoches Co.
Douglass ISD
Sch. Sys. Enr. Code 2
Supt. – Steve Cooper, P O BOX 38 75943
ES 75943 – Robert Baker, prin.

Dripping Springs, Hays Co.
Dripping Springs ISD
Sch. Sys. Enr. Code 4
Supt. – G. Julian Shaddix, P O BOX 479 78620
MS 78620 – Keith Burnett, prin.
ES 78620 – Richard Stark, prin.

Driscoll, Nueces Co., Pop. Code 3
Driscoll ISD
Sch. Sys. Enr. Code 2
Supt. – Milton Jirasek, P O BOX 238 78351
ES 78351 – Franklin White, prin.

Dublin, Erath Co., Pop. Code 5
Dublin ISD
Sch. Sys. Enr. Code 3
Supt. – Roy Neff, P O BOX D 76446
JHS 76446 – Baker Conger, prin.
ES 76446 – Ermanell Hurst, prin.

Dumas, Moore Co., Pop. Code 7
Dumas ISD
Sch. Sys. Enr. Code 5
Supt. – R. Pennington, P O BOX 615 79029
Cactus ES, P O BOX 615 79029
  Charles Napp, prin.
Green Acres ES, 300 OAK AVE 79029
  Bill Greene, prin.
Hillcrest ES, 524 PEAR DR 79029
  Lawrence Bussard, prin.
Morningside ES, 623 POWELL AVE 79029
  Eldridge Ledbetter, prin.
Sunset ES, 300 W 14TH ST 79029
  Don Phillips, prin.

Duncanville, Dallas Co., Pop. Code 8
Duncanville ISD
Sch. Sys. Enr. Code 6
Supt. – Ed Stevens, 802 S MAIN ST 75137
Byrd JHS, 1040 W WHEATLAND ROAD 75116
  Joe Howell, prin.
Reed JHS, 530 E FREEMAN ST 75116
  Mel Morris, prin.
Acton ES, 9240 COUNTY VIEW 75137
  Lynda Opitz, prin.
Alexander ES, 510 SOFTWOOD DR 75137
  Jo Ann Slauson, prin.
Central ES, 302 E FREEMAN ST 75116
  Cynthia Hartgraves, prin.
Daniel IS, 802 MAIN ST S 75137
  Shirley King, prin.
Fairmeadows ES
  100 E FAIRMEADOWS DR 75116
  Becky Minnis, prin.
Hardin IS, 802 MAIN ST S 75137
  Ron Golden, prin.
Hastings ES, 602 W CENTER ST 75116
  Vicky Dearing, prin.
Merrifield ES, FOUTS AVE 75137
  Eva Cannon, prin.
Smith ES, 1010 BIG STONE GAP ROAD 75137
  Logan Casada, prin.

Eagle Pass, Maverick Co., Pop. Code 7
Eagle Pass ISD
Sch. Sys. Enr. Code 6
Supt. – Walter Williams, P O BOX 1409 78853
Austin ES, MADISON & LEONA 78853
  Leopoldo Moncado, prin.
Benavides ES, MESA DR 78852
  Cecilio Ibarra, prin.
Darr ES 78853 – Graciela Gonzalez, prin.
Glass ES, 1501 BOEHMER AVE 78852
  Salvador Gonzalez, prin.
Graves ES, 720 KELSO DR 78852
  Jose De La Garza, prin.
Kirchner ES 78853 – Ray Hallard, prin.
Lee ES, 300 S MONROE ST 78852
  Jesus Sanchez, prin.
San Luis ES, 2090 WILLIAMS ST 78852
  Julian Lerma, prin.
Seco Mines ES, 2900 DIAZ ST 78852
  Jesus Rubio, prin.

Our Lady of Refuge ES, 977 WASHINGTON 78852

Early, Brown Co., Pop. Code 4
Early ISD
Sch. Sys. Enr. Code 4
Supt. – Bob Beard, P O BOX 3315 76803
MS 76801 – Gary Kaseberg, prin.
ES 76803 – Betty Morris, prin.

Earth, Lamb Co., Pop. Code 4
Springlake-Earth ISD
Sch. Sys. Enr. Code 3
Supt. – Robert Conkin, P O BOX 436 79031
Springlake JHS 79031 – C. Slover, prin.
Springlake ES 79031 – William Verden, prin.

East Bernard, Wharton Co., Pop. Code 4
East Bernard ISD
Sch. Sys. Enr. Code 3
Supt. – Dwight Winkler, 727 FITZGERALD 77435
JHS 77435 – Roy Tucker, prin.
ES 77435 – J. Osborne, prin.

Eastland, Eastland Co., Pop. Code 5
Eastland ISD
Sch. Sys. Enr. Code 4
Supt. – Keith Watkins, P O BOX 31 76448
JHS 76448 – Donald Hughes, prin.
Siebert ES 76448 – Loys Allmand, prin.

Ector, Fannin Co., Pop. Code 3
Ector ISD
Sch. Sys. Enr. Code 2
Supt. – B. Finnell, P O BOX 128 75439
S 75439 – Nema Morris, prin.

Edcouch, Hidalgo Co., Pop. Code 5
Edcouch-Elsa ISD
Sch. Sys. Enr. Code 5
Supt. – Daniel Hernandez, P O BOX 127 78538
Edcouch-Elsa JHS, P O BOX 127 78538
Jose Martinez, prin.
Central MS, P O BOX 127 78538
Guadalupe Castillo, prin.
ES, P O BOX 127 78538 – Mary Reyes, prin.
Kennedy ES, P O BOX 127 78538
Sandra Cisneros, prin.

Monte Alto ISD
Sch. Sys. Enr. Code 2
Supt. – Jose Borrego
RURAL ROUTE 01 BOX 116 78538
Monte Alto ES
RURAL ROUTE 01 BOX 116 78538
Gaudencio Alaniz, prin.

Eddy, McLennan Co., Pop. Code 2
Bruceville-Eddy ISD
Sch. Sys. Enr. Code 3
Supt. – J. Payne, P O BOX 99 76524
Bruceville-Eddy ES 76524 – Clay Davis, prin.

Eden, Concho Co., Pop. Code 4
Eden Consolidated ISD
Sch. Sys. Enr. Code 2
Supt. – Larry Taylor, P O BOX X 76837
S 76837 – R. Marsh, prin.

Edgewood, Van Zandt Co., Pop. Code 4
Edgewood ISD
Sch. Sys. Enr. Code 3
Supt. – Ellis Carroll, P O BOX 6 75117
Edgewood MS 75117 – James Laprade, prin.
ES 75117 – Arthur Jones, prin.

Edinburg, Hidalgo Co., Pop. Code 7
Edinburg ISD
Sch. Sys. Enr. Code 7
Supt. – J. Chapman, P O BOX 990 78540
JHS 78540 – Ramiro Corona, prin.
Edinburg North JHS 78539 – J. Salinas, prin.
Edinburg South JHS 78539 – Gene Gutierrez, prin.
Austin ES, 1023 E KUHN ST 78539
Eduardo Gonzalez, prin.
Brewster ES, 18 MI N HWY 281 78539
Cipriano Pena, prin.
De La Vina ES, 1001 S JACKSON ROAD 78539
Gilberto Garza,Jr., prin.
Gonzalez ES, 2401 S SUGAR ROAD 78539
Cristina Darnall, prin.
Hargill ES 78539 – Edna Olivarez, prin.
Houston ES, 315 W MCINTYRE ST 78539
Francisco Lumbreras, prin.
Jefferson ES, 904 S 12 AVE 78539
Ruby Benedict, prin.
Lamar ES, 1200 W SCHUNIOR ST 78539
Mercedes Ramirez, prin.
LBJ ES, 1801 E SPRAGUE ST 78539
Octavio Perez,Jr., prin.
Lee ES, 1215 SPRAGUE ST 78539
Donald Profitt, prin.
Lincoln ES, 1319 E LOVETT ST 78539
Jose Manzano, prin.
Lull ES 78540 – Shirley Hensley, prin.
McCook ES 78539 – Judy Keller, prin.
San Carlos ES 78540 – Dolores Edwards, prin.
Travis ES, 1200 E TABASCO 78539
Soledad Guzman, prin.

St. Joseph's ES, 119 W FAY ST 78539

Edna, Jackson Co., Pop. Code 6
Edna ISD
Sch. Sys. Enr. Code 4
Supt. – John Sutton, P O BOX D 77957
JHS, 505 W GAYLE ST 77957
Mike Rainbolt, prin.
Austin MS, 112 W ASH ST 77957
Kenneth Airheart, prin.

Carver ES, 1128 2ND ST 77957
William Bryan,Jr., prin.

El Campo, Wharton Co., Pop. Code 7
El Campo ISD
Sch. Sys. Enr. Code 5
Supt. – Joe Thedford, 6700 W NORRIS ST 77437
MS, 1409 MCCLURE ST 77437
George Nohavitza, prin.
Hutchins ES, AVE I 77437 – Suzanne Yates, prin.
Myatt ES 77437 – Gilbert Vela, prin.
Northside MS, 200 W CHURCH ST 77437
Roy Johnson, prin.

St. Philip ES, 302 W CHURCH ST 77437

Eldorado, Schleicher Co., Pop. Code 4
Schleicher ISD
Sch. Sys. Enr. Code 3
Supt. – J. Weldon Moore, P O BOX W 76936
MS 76936 – Scott Barton, prin.
ES 76936 – Glen Nix, prin.

Electra, Wichita Co., Pop. Code 5
Electra ISD
Sch. Sys. Enr. Code 3
Supt. – D. Windham, 400 E ROOSEVELT ST 76360
JHS, 621 S BAILEY AVE 76360
Olan Bourland, prin.
Dinsmore ES, 700 S MAIN ST 76360
Pat Watkins, prin.

Elgin, Bastrop Co., Pop. Code 5
Elgin ISD
Sch. Sys. Enr. Code 4
Supt. – Paul Willis, P O BOX 351 78621
JHS, 920 W 2ND ST 78621 – David Solomon, prin.
MS, 1002 N AVENUE C 78621
Nancy Graham, prin.
PS, 1001 W 2ND ST 78621 – Jo Frazier, prin.

Elkhart, Anderson Co., Pop. Code 4
Elkhart ISD
Sch. Sys. Enr. Code 3
Supt. – Wesley Taylor, P O BOX C 75839
ES 75839 – Johnnie Keeling, prin.

Elmaton, Matagorda Co.
Tidehaven ISD
Sch. Sys. Enr. Code 3
Supt. – Allen Dusek, P O BOX B 77440
Tidehaven IS 77440 – Robert Tomlinson, prin.
Blessing ES 77440 – William Glasscock, prin.
Markham ES 77440 – Tyrus Mills,Jr., prin.

El Paso, El Paso Co., Pop. Code 10
El Paso ISD
Sch. Sys. Enr. Code 8
Supt. – Ronald McLeod, P O BOX 20100 79998
Bassett MS, 4400 ELM ST 79930
Efren Yturralde, prin.
Guillen IS, 900 S COTTON ST 79901
Ramon Peregrino, prin.
Henderson MS, 5505 COMANCHE AVE 79905
Nicasio Cobos, prin.
Ross MS 79925 – Mary Lou Martinez, prin.
Wiggs MS, 1300 CIRCLE DR 79902
Patricia Multhauf, prin.
Alamo ES, 508 S HILLS ST 79901
Elifas Zamora, prin.
Alta Vista ES, 3500 LA LUZ AVE 79903
Kay Tidwell, prin.
Aoy ES, 901 S CAMPBELL ST 79901
Ben Gomersall, prin.
Beall ES, 320 S PIEDRAS ST 79905
David Elias, prin.
Bliss ES, 401 SHERIDAN ROAD 79906
Rosemary Lyons, prin.
Bonham ES, 7024 CIELO VISTA DR 79925
Hilario Hernandez, prin.
Bradley ES, 5330 SWEETWATER DR 79924
Cecilia Stephens, prin.
Burleson ES, 4400 BLANCO AVE 79905
Felie Truitt, prin.
Burnet ES, 3700 THOMASON AVE 79904
Carmen LaFarelle, prin.
Cielo Vista ES, 900 BASIL CT 79925
Jenny Pohan, prin.
Clardy ES, 5508 DELTA DR 79905
Tino Valenzuela, prin.
Clendenin ES, 4201 ELM ST 79930
Fernando Carrasco, prin.
Coldwell ES, 4101 ALTURA AVE 79903
James Richardson, prin.
Collins ES, 4860 TROPICANA AVE 79924
Ginny Hunt, prin.
Cooley ES, 107 N COLLINGSWORTH ST 79905
Irene Trejo, prin.
Crockett ES, 3200 WHEELING AVE 79930
Rose Pereira, prin.
Crosby ES, 5411 WREN AVE 79924
Alfredo Quintela, prin.
Douglass ES, 101 S EUCALYPTUS ST 79905
Gloria Boyer, prin.
Dowell ES, 5249 BASTILLE AVE 79924
Maria Bedoya, prin.
Fannin ES, 5425 SALEM DR 79924
Robert Leavitt, prin.
Hart ES, 1110 PARK DR 79902
Arturo Lightbourn, prin.
Hawkins ES, 5816 STEPHENSON AVE 79905
Guadalupe Varela, prin.
Hillside ES, 4500 CLIFTON AVE 79903
Eduardo Herrera, prin.
Houston ES, 2851 GRANT AVE 79930
Martin Sandidge, prin.

Hughey ES, 6400 WIELAND WAY 79925
Margaret Frederick, prin.
Johnson ES, 499 CABARET DR 79912
Rachel Hamilton, prin.
Lamar ES, 1440 E CLIFF DR 79902
Ted Taylor, prin.
Lee ES, 7710 PANDORA ST 79904
Jackie Morgan, prin.
Lindberg ES, 250 LINDBERGH AVE 79932
Roger Mansfield, prin.
Logan ES 79907 – Maria Castillo, prin.
MacArthur ES 79998 – Shelby Martin, prin.
Mesita ES, 500 ALETHEA PARK DR 79902
Miriam Lait, prin.
Milam ES, 5000 LUKE ST 79908
Carolyn Grantham, prin.
Newman ES, 10275 ALCAN ST 79924
John Black, prin.
Park ES, 3601 EDGAR PARK AVE 79904
Alice Price, prin.
Polk ES, 940 BELVIDERE ST 79912
Frank Davis, prin.
Putnam ES, 6508 FIESTA DR 79912
Ralph Yturralde, prin.
Rivera ES, 6445 ESCONDIDO DR 79912
Georgina Alva, prin.
Roberts ES, 341 THORN AVE 79932
Robert Gonzalez, prin.
Roosevelt ES, 616 E FIFTH AVE 79901
Salvador Pena, prin.
Rusk ES, 3601 N COPIA ST 79930
Roberto Gonzalez, prin.
Schuster ES, 5515 WILL RUTH AVE 79924
Nancy Archer, prin.
Stanton ES, 5414 HONDO PASS DR 79924
Cecilia Doran, prin.
Travis ES, 5000 N STEVENS ST 79930
Ira Barbe, prin.
Vilas ES, 220 LAWTON DR 79902
Fred Vasquez, prin.
Wainwright ES, 4500 LAWRENCE AVE 79904
Evangelina Sanchez, prin.
Western Hills ES 79912 – Susan Yturralde, prin.
Whitaker ES, 4700 RUTHERFORD 79924
Dorothy McCarthy, prin.
White ES, 4256 ROXBURY DR 79922
Charolotte Craigo, prin.
Zavala ES, 51 N HAMMETT ST 79905
Irene Trejo, prin.

Fabens ISD
Supt. – See Fabens
O'Donnell MS 79838 – Lionel Rubio, prin.

Socorro ISD
Sch. Sys. Enr. Code 7
Supt. – R. Jerry Barber
12300 EASTLAKE DR 79927
Campestre ES 79927 – Arturo Olivas, prin.
Cooper ES, 1515 REBECCA ANN DR 79927
Michael Quatrini, prin.
Escontrias ES, 313 N RIO VISTA ROAD 79927
Alfonso Cardenas, prin.
Hilley ES 79927 – Dona DeScamps, prin.
Horizon Heights ES 79927 – Lorenzo Nieto, prin.
Hueco ES 79927 – Robert Martinez, prin.
Rojas ES, 500 BAUMAN ROAD 79927
Armando Bustamante, prin.
Vista Del Sol ES, 12300 E LAKE DR 79927
David Solis, prin.

Ysleta ISD
Sch. Sys. Enr. Code 8
Supt. – Mauro Reyna, 9660 SIMS 79925
Camino Real MS 79925 – (—), prin.
Desert View MS, 1641 BILLIE MARIE 79936
Maynard Pike, prin.
Eastwood MS, 2612 CHASWOOD DRIVE 79935
Laura Brown, prin.
Indian Ridge MS 79925 – (—), prin.
Parkland MS, 8253 MCELROY AVE 79907
Bob Beauford, prin.
Ranchland Hills MS, 7615 YUMA DR 79915
Leo Pleasants, prin.
Riverside MS, 515 VOCATIONAL DRIVE 79915
Felipe Candelaria, prin.
Valley View MS, 8674 N LOOP DR 79907
Luis Teijeiro, prin.
Yselta MS, 8691 INDEPENDENCE DRIVE 79907
Rudy Murillo, prin.
Ascarate ES, 7090 ALAMEDA AVE 79915
Nellie Morales, prin.
Cadwallader ES, 7998 ALAMEDA AVE 79915
Pete Castro, prin.
Capistrano ES, 240 MECCA DR 79907
Jose Salgado, prin.
Cedar Grove ES, 218 BARKER ROAD 79915
William Whitman, prin.
Del Norte Heights ES
1800 WINSLOW ROAD 79915
Gloria Polanco, prin.
Desertaire ES 79925 – (—), prin.
Mission Valley ES 79925 – (—), prin.
Dolphin ES, 9790 PICKEREL DR 79924
Gerald Whitman, prin.
East Point ES, 2400 ZANZIBAR ROAD 79925
Kirk Irwin, prin.
Eastwood Heights ES, 10530 JANWAY DR 79925
Genevieve Scott, prin.
Eastwood Knolls ES
10000 BUCKWOOD AVE 79925
Carmen Zamora, prin.
Edgemere ES, 10300 EDGEMERE BLVD 79925
Robert Attridge, prin.

Glen Cove ES, 10955 SAM SNEAD DR   79936
    Richard Gore, prin.
Hacienda Heights ES
    7530 ACAPULCO AVE   79915
    Avelardo Trujillo, prin.
Lancaster ES, 9230 ELGIN DR   79907
    Richard Armendariz, prin.
Le Barron Park ES, 920 BURGUNDY DR   79907
    Joe Urias, prin.
Loma Terrace ES, 8200 TYLAND CT   79907
    James Thompson, prin.
Marian Manor ES
    8300 FORREST HAVEN CT   79907
    Tom Carson, prin.
Mesa Vista ES, 8032 ALAMO AVE   79907
    Thelma Aguirre, prin.
North Loop ES, 412 EMERSON ST   79915
    Alice Davis, prin.
Parkland ES, 5920 QUAIL AVE   79924
    Mason Boone, prin.
Pasodale ES, 8253 MCELROY AVE   79907
    Helen Henry, prin.
Pebble Hills ES, 11145 EDGEMERE BLVD   79936
    Walter Cross, prin.
Presa ES, 128 PRESA PL   79907
    Marcelino Franco, prin.
Ramona ES, 351 NICHOLS ROAD   79915
    Sharon Duncan, prin.
Sageland ES, 7901 SANTA MONICA CT   79915
    Mary Peatschman, prin.
Scotsdale ES, 2901 MCRAE BLVD   79925
    Billie Benton, prin.
South Loop ES, 520 SOUTHSIDE ROAD   79907
    Jose Banales, prin.
Thomas Manor ES, 7900 JERSEY ST   79915
    Fred Alvarado, prin.
Tierra Del Sol ES
    1832 TOMMY AARON DR   79936
    Aubrey Tucker, prin.
Vista Hills ES, 10801 LA SUBIDA DR   79935
    Rebecca O'Neill, prin.
Ysleta ES, 9009 ALAMEDA VE   79907
    Victor Valdivia, prin.

Loretto Academy MS, 1300 HARDAWAY   79903
Radford School, 2001 RADFORD ST   79903
Blessed Sacrament ES, 9001 DIANA DR   79904
Father Yermo ES, 237 TOBIN PLACE   79905
Holy Trinity ES, 10000 PHEASANT ROAD   79924
Loretto ES, 4625 CLIFTON AVE   79903
Our Lady of Assumption ES
    4805 BYRON ST   79930
Our Lady of Mt. Carmel ES   79930
Our Lady of the Valley ES
    8600 WINCHESTER ROAD   79907
St. Clement's Episcopal ES
    804 N FLORENCE ST   79902
St. Joseph ES, 1300 LAMAR ST   79903
St. Patrick ES, 1111 N STANTON ST   79902
St. Pius X ES, 1007 GERONIMO DR   79905
St. Raphael's ES, 2301 ZANZIBAR ROAD   79925

Elysian Fields, Harrison Co., Pop. Code 2
Elysian Fields ISD
Sch. Sys. Enr. Code 3
Supt. – J. Brian Nichols, P O BOX 120   75642
JHS, P O BOX 120   75642 – Bill Short, prin.
ES, P O BOX 119   75642 – Charles Crawford, prin.

Emory, Rains Co., Pop. Code 3
Rains ISD
Sch. Sys. Enr. Code 4
Supt. – Jerry Gideon, P O BOX 247   75440
Rains JHS, P O BOX 247   75440
    Bob Clopton, prin.
Rains ES   75440 – Emery Cathey, prin.

Ennis, Ellis Co., Pop. Code 7
Ennis ISD
Sch. Sys. Enr. Code 5
Supt. – David Cochran, 116 W ENNIS AVE   75119
JHS, 501 N GAINES ST   75119 – John Huff, prin.
Austin ES, 1500 AUSTIN DR   75119
    Troy Selzer, prin.
Bowie ES, 600 E ML KING DR   75119
    Lynda Maxey, prin.
Houston ES, W HWY 34   75119
    Beauford Thomason, prin.
Travis ES, 200 N SHAWNEE ST   75119
    Doris Gerron, prin.

St. John ES, 701 S PARIS ST   75119

Era, Cooke Co., Pop. Code 2
Era ISD
Sch. Sys. Enr. Code 2
Supt. – Dale Smiley, P O BOX 98   76238
S   76238 – Sharon Durham, prin.

Etoile, Nacogdoches Co.
Etoile ISD
Sch. Sys. Enr. Code 1
Supt. – Jim Carr, P O BOX 98   75944
ES   75944 – (—), prin.

Euless, Tarrant Co., Pop. Code 7
Hurst-Euless-Bedford ISD
Supt. – See Bedford
Lakewood ES, 1600 DONLEY DRIVE   76039
    Russell Chapman, prin.
Midway Park ES, 409 N ECTOR DRIVE   76039
    Joy Busey, prin.
North Euless ES, 1101 DENTON DRIVE   76039
    Betty Vines, prin.

Oakwood Terrace ES, 700 RANGER ST   76040
    Mike Wagner, prin.
South Euless ES, 605 S MAIN ST   76040
    Jack Thayer, prin.
Wilshire ES, 420 WILSHIRE DRIVE   76040
    Tommie Boaz, prin.

Mid-Cities Learning Center
    RURAL ROUTE 01   BOX 257   76040
St. Vincent Episcopal ES
    3201 W PIPELINE ROAD   76040

Eustace, Henderson Co., Pop. Code 3
Eustace ISD
Sch. Sys. Enr. Code 3
Supt. – Tony Jones, P O BOX 188   75124
IS   75124 – George Peacock, prin.
PS   75124 – Gilbert Thompson, prin.

Evadale, Jasper Co., Pop. Code 3
Evadale ISD
Sch. Sys. Enr. Code 2
Supt. – R. Fling, P O BOX 497   77615
ES   77615 – Thomas Westbrook, prin.

Evant, Coryell Co., Pop. Code 2
Evant ISD
Sch. Sys. Enr. Code 2
Supt. – J. Williams, P O BOX 339   76525
JHS, P O BOX 339   76525 – Bill Brister, prin.
ES, P O BOX 339   76525 – Linda Yarbrough, prin.

Everman, Tarrant Co., Pop. Code 6
Everman ISD
Sch. Sys. Enr. Code 5
Supt. – Joe Bean, 608 TOWNLEY DRIVE   76140
JHS, 8901 OAK GROVE ROAD   76140
    A. O'Connor, prin.
Bishop ES, 501 VAUGHN AVE   76140
    Don Heizer, prin.
Hommel ES, 308 W ENON AVE   76140
    Kathy Tomlin, prin.
Ray ES, 7309 SHERIDAN ROAD   76134
    Bill Gilbert, prin.
Souder ES, 201 N FOREST HILL DR   76140
    Mildred Bayless, prin.

Fabens, El Paso Co., Pop. Code 5
Fabens ISD
Sch. Sys. Enr. Code 4
Supt. – Eli Casey, P O BOX 697   79838
JHS   79838 – Stephen Beyer, prin.
Risinger ES, 810 NORTHEAST CAMP   79838
    Don Holes, prin.
Other Schools – See El Paso

Fairfield, Freestone Co., Pop. Code 5
Fairfield ISD
Sch. Sys. Enr. Code 4
Supt. – A. Whitaker
    125 N BATEMAN ROAD   75840
JHS   75840 – David Price, prin.
ES   75840 – Maurice Burleson, prin.
IS   75840 – James Clark, prin.

Falfurrias, Brooks Co., Pop. Code 6
Brooks ISD
Sch. Sys. Enr. Code 4
Supt. – A. Byington, P O BOX 589   78355
MS   78355 – G. Almendarez, prin.
Encino ES   78355 – Jose Garza, prin.
MS, 100 E ALLEN ST   78355
    Patrick Romero, prin.
Lasater ES, S CALDWELL ST   78355
    Norma Villarreal, prin.

La Gloria ISD
Sch. Sys. Enr. Code 1
Supt. – Raul Flores
    RURAL ROUTE 01   BOX 87C   78355
La Gloria ES   78355 – Raul Flores, prin.

Falls City, Karnes Co., Pop. Code 3
Falls City ISD
Sch. Sys. Enr. Code 2
Supt. – Luther Thomas, P O BOX 399   78113
ES   78113 – Roy Pargmann, prin.

Farmers Branch, Dallas Co., Pop. Code 7
Carrollton-Farmers Branch ISD
Supt. – See Carrollton
Field JHS, 13551 DENNIS LANE   75234
    Conan Reinken, prin.

Farmersville, Collin Co., Pop. Code 4
Farmersville ISD
Sch. Sys. Enr. Code 3
Supt. – James Dickson, P O BOX 472   75031
MS   75031 – Marvin Schkade, prin.
Tatum ES, N WASHINGTON   75031
    Robert Sellman, prin.

Farwell, Parmer Co., Pop. Code 4
Farwell ISD
Sch. Sys. Enr. Code 2
Supt. – John Grigsby, P O BOX F   79325
JHS, P O BOX F   79325 – Jerry Owen, prin.
ES   79325 – James Craig, prin.

Fayetteville, Fayette Co., Pop. Code 2
Fayetteville ISD
Sch. Sys. Enr. Code 2
Supt. – Ray Bethke, P O BOX 129   78940
ES   78940 – Clem Gully, prin.

Ferris, Ellis Co., Pop. Code 4
Ferris ISD
Sch. Sys. Enr. Code 4
Supt. – James Harrison, P O BOX 59   75125
JHS   75125 – Gary Patterson, prin.
ES   75125 – Michael Grantz, prin.

Flatonia, Fayette Co., Pop. Code 4
Flatonia ISD
Sch. Sys. Enr. Code 2
Supt. – James Schroeder, P O BOX 189   78941
ES   78941 – Ben Carson, prin.

Florence, Williamson Co., Pop. Code 3
Florence ISD
Sch. Sys. Enr. Code 3
Supt. – Clinton Ogilvie II, P O BOX 489   76527
JHS   76527 – Lawrence Hanke, prin.
ES   76527 – Marilyn Stone, prin.

Floresville, Wilson Co., Pop. Code 5
Floresville ISD
Sch. Sys. Enr. Code 4
Supt. – Joe Robinson, 1103 FOURTH ST   78114
JHS, 1813 TRAIL ST   78114 – Hurvey Elliot, prin.
ES   78114 – Thomas Mowles, prin.
IS   78114 – Carolyn Pullin, prin.
PS   78114 – Allan Drozd, prin.

Sacred Heart ES, 1007 TRAIL ST   78114

Floydada, Floyd Co., Pop. Code 5
Floydada ISD
Sch. Sys. Enr. Code 4
Supt. – Jerry Cannon
    226 WEST CALIFORNIA ST   79235
JHS, 910 N 5TH ST   79235 – Joe Christian, prin.
Andrews MS, 215 N WHITE ST   79235
    Charles Tyer, prin.
Duncan ES, 1011 S 8TH ST   79235
    Bobbie Weir, prin.

Follett, Lipscomb Co., Pop. Code 3
Follett ISD
Sch. Sys. Enr. Code 2
Supt. – J. Kyle Collier, P O BOX 28   79034
S, P O BOX 28   79034 – Randel Beaver, prin.

Forestburg, Montague Co.
Forestburg ISD
Sch. Sys. Enr. Code 2
Supt. – Hollis Adams, P O BOX 415   76239
ES   76239 – R. Halford, prin.

Forney, Kaufman Co., Pop. Code 4
Forney ISD
Sch. Sys. Enr. Code 4
Supt. – Roy Hartman, 811 S BOIS DARC ST   75126
MS   75126 – Robert Peters, prin.
IS   75126 – Georgia Power, prin.
PS   75126 – Marsha Taylor, prin.

Forsan, Howard Co., Pop. Code 2
Forsan ISD
Sch. Sys. Enr. Code 3
Supt. – J. Poynor, P O BOX A   79733
Elbow ES   79733 – W. Cregar, prin.

Fort Davis, Jeff Davis Co., Pop. Code 3
Ft. Davis ISD
Sch. Sys. Enr. Code 2
Supt. – Ray Labeff, P O BOX 1339   79734
Anderson ES   79734 – Barbara Dirks, prin.

Fort Hancock, Hudspeth Co., Pop. Code 3
Ft. Hancock ISD
Sch. Sys. Enr. Code 2
Supt. – Bill Franklin, P O BOX 98   79839
S   79839 – Jim Liner, prin.

Fort Hood, Bell Co., Pop. Code 8
Killeen ISD
Supt. – See Killeen
Smith MS, 51000 COPPERAS COVE ROAD   76544
    Jerry Lewis, prin.

Fort Stockton, Pecos Co., Pop. Code 6
Fort Stockton ISD
Sch. Sys. Enr. Code 5
Supt. – J. Ryan, P O BOX 1628   79735
MS, 205 N OKLAHOMA ST   79735
    Manuel Espino, prin.
Alamo ES, MARATHON HWY   79735
    Ira Henslee, prin.
Apache ES, 208 W EIGHTEENTH ST   79735
    Charles Roberts, prin.
Comanche ES, 803 N ROAD   79735
    Robert Alfaro, prin.
IS, 1100 W SECOND ST   79735
    Billy Espino, prin.

Fort Worth, Tarrant Co., Pop. Code 10
Birdville ISD
Sch. Sys. Enr. Code 7
Supt. – Joe Fox, 6125 E BELKNAP ST   76117
New MS   76117 – Allen Morrow, prin.
Birdville ES, 3126 BEWLEY ST   76117
    Marvin Fuller, prin.
Foster Village ES
    6800 SPRINGDALE LANE   76180
    Howard Nix, prin.
Francisco ES, 3701 LAYTON ST   76117
    Claudine Thomas, prin.
Glenview ES, 3900 NORTON DR   76118
    Juan Menchaca, prin.
Hardeman ES, 6100 WHISPERING LANE   76148
    Joe Hallford, prin.

Holiday Heights ES
5221 SUSAN LEE LANE 76180 – Joe Wilson, prin.
Mullendore ES, 6125 E BELKNAP ST 76117
Richard Richeson, prin.
North Ridge ES 76117 – Don Williams, prin.
Porter ES, 6125 E BELKNAP ST 76117
Gay Ingram, prin.
Richland ES, 3250 SCRUGGS PARK DR 76118
Lynn Farmer, prin.
Smith ES 76117 – David Bach, prin.
Smithfield ES, 6724 SMITHFIELD ROAD 76180
Wanda Strong, prin.
Snow Heights ES, 4801 VANCE ROAD 76180
Janelle Bourgeois, prin.
South Birdville ES, 2600 SOLONA ST 76117
Ray Willis, prin.
Stowe ES, 4200 DOELINE ST 76117
Franklin Earney, prin.
Thomas ES, 8200 O BRIEN WAY 76180
Cecil Hill, prin.
Watauga ES, 5937 WHITLEY ROAD VE 76148
Georgene Mais, prin.
West Birdville ES, 3001 LAYTON ST 76117
Marta White, prin.

Castleberry ISD
Sch. Sys. Enr. Code 5
Supt. – C. Winn, 315 CHURCHILL ROAD 76114
Marsh MS, 415 HAGG DRIVE 76114
J. Pollard, prin.
Castleberry ES, 1101 MERRITT ST 76114
Carroll Gilbreath, prin.
Cato MS 76114 – Larry Meeks, prin.
North Castleberry ES, 5300 BUCHANAN ST 76114
Joy James, prin.

Eagle Mt.-Saginaw ISD
Sch. Sys. Enr. Code 5
Supt. – William Anderson, P O BOX 79160 76179
Wayside MS, 1300 OLD DECATUR ROAD 76179
Weldon Hafley, prin.
Bryson ES, 1201 OLD DECATUR ROAD 76179
Bill Williams, prin.
Eagle Mountain ES, BOAT CLUB ROAD 76179
Jim Schulz, prin.
Elkins ES 76179 – Ed Wade, prin.
La Gililland ES 76179 – Angela Averhoff, prin.
Saginaw ES, 300 W MCLEROY BLVD 76179
Danny Jordan, prin.

Fort Worth ISD
Sch. Sys. Enr. Code 8
Supt. – Don Roberts
3210 W LANCASTER AVE 76107
Elliott ES 76107 – Thylis Chambless, prin.
Jara ES 76107 – Bertha Guzman, prin.
Park West ES 76107 – Everett Hackworth, prin.
Daggett MS, 1108 CARLOCK ST 76110
Richard Galindo, prin.
Dunbar MS, 100 WILLE ST 76119
Pat Turner, prin.
Elder MS, 709 NW 21ST ST 76106
Mary Jara Wright, prin.
Forest Oak MS, 3221 PECOS ST 76119
Raymond Wright, prin.
Handley MS, 2801 PATINO ROAD 76112
Dewey York, prin.
James MS 76105 – George Thompson, prin.
Kirkpatrick MS 76112 – Mildred Sims, prin.
Leonard MS, 8900 CHAPIN ROAD 76116
A Erwin, prin.
McLean MS, 3816 STADIUM DRIVE 76109
Clifford Helbert, prin.
Meacham MS, 3600 WEBER ST 76106
Grace Daum, prin.
Meadowbrook MS
2001 ELDERVILLE ROAD 76103
Herman Baldwin, prin.
Monnig MS, 3136 BIGHAM BLVD 76116
Tom Maxwell, prin.
Morningsdide MS 76104 – Odessa Ravin, prin.
Riverside MS, 1600 BOLTON ST 76111
George Morgan, prin.
Rosemont MS, 1501 W SEMINARY DRIVE 76115
Joe Martinez, prin.
Stripling MS, 3210 W LANCASTER 76107
Anita Whiteside, prin.
Wedgewood MS, 3909 WILKIE WAY 76133
Billie Younger, prin.
Benbrook ES, 800 MERCEDES ST 76126
Jonna Murray, prin.
Burton Hill ES, 519 BURTON HILL ROAD 76114
Ewell Crawford, prin.
Carter Park ES, 1204 E BROADUS AVE 76115
James Jones, prin.
Clarke ES, 3300 S HENDERSON ST 76110
Tom Janes, prin.
Clayton ES, 2000 PARK PLACE AVE 76110
Susan Smith, prin.
Como ES, 4000 HORNE ST 76107
Laverne Williams, prin.
Daggett ES, 958 PAGE AVE 76110
Jo McCormack, prin.
De Zavala ES, 1419 COLLEGE AVE 76104
Jim Arteaga, prin.
Denver Avenue ES, 1412 DENVER AVE 76106
Micaela Camacho, prin.
Diamond Hill ES, 3000 OSCAR AVE 76106
Luis Flores, prin.
Dillow ES, 4000 AVENUE N 76105
Frankie Batts, prin.
Dunbar MS 76107 – Helen Curtis, prin.
East Handley ES, 2617 MIMS ST 76112
Richard Anderson, prin.

Eastern Hills ES, 5917 SHELTON ST 76112
Joy Craig, prin.
Eastland ES 76119 – Mildred Butler, prin.
Forest Hill ES, 5615 FOREST HILL DR 76119
Harlean Beal, prin.
Glencrest MS 76119 – Wyvonia Ruffin, prin.
Glen Park ES, 3601 PECOS ST 76119
Ray Roberts, prin.
Green ES
4612 DAVID STRICKLAND ROAD 76119
Norman Myers, prin.
Greenbriar ES, 1605 GRADY LEE ST 76134
Ben Hamilton, prin.
Helbing ES, 3524 N CRUMP ST 76106
Juanita Silva, prin.
Hubbard ES, 1333 W SPURGEON ST 76115
Cora Torres, prin.
Kirkpatrick ES, 3229 LINCOLN AVE 76106
Donald Fulbright, prin.
Logan ES, 2300 DILLARD ST 76105
Simuel Williams, prin.
McDonald ES, 1850 BARRON LANE 76112
Julia Stokes, prin.
McRae ES, 3316 AVENUE N 76105
Shirlene Potts, prin.
Meadowbrook ES
4330 MEADOWBROOK DR 76103
Ron McManus, prin.
Merrett ES, 7325 KERMIT AVE 76116
Robert Rodriguez, prin.
Mitchell Blvd ES, 3601 MITCHELL BLVD 76105
Beverly Oakes, prin.
Moore ES, 1809 NE 36TH ST 76106
Bettie Reyes, prin.
Morningside ES, 2601 EVANS AVE 76104
Marguerite Johnson, prin.
Nash ES, 401 SAMUELS AVE 76102
Eunice Lopez, prin.
Howell ES, 1324 KINGS HWY 76117
Barbara Hryekewicz, prin.
North Hi Mount ES, 3801 W 7TH ST 76107
Shirley Capps, prin.
Oakhurst ES, 2700 YUCCA AVE 76111
Clint McClendon, prin.
Oaklawn ES, 3220 HARDEMAN ST 76119
Constance Person, prin.
Pate ES, 3800 ANGLIN DR 76119
Robert Barbour, prin.
Peak ES, 1212 ELMWOOD AVE 76104
Elbert Parker, prin.
Phillips ES, 3020 BINGHAM BLVD 76116
Carlene Dennis, prin.
Ridglea Hills ES
6817 CUMBERLAND ROAD 76116
Phenelope Omami, prin.
Rosen ES, 2613 ROOSEVELT AVE 76106
Fred Castillo, prin.
Sagamore Hill ES, 701 S HUGHES AVE 76103
Mary Williams, prin.
Sellars ES, 4200 DORSEY ST 76119
Jim White, prin.
Shulkey ES, 5533 WHITMAN AVE 76133
Ava Chambers, prin.
South Fort Worth ES, 900 W FOGG ST 76110
Richard Wilson, prin.
South Hi Mount ES, 4101 BIRCHMAN AVE 76107
Robert Plummer, prin.
South Hills ES, 3009 BILGLADE ROAD 76133
Barb Hryekewicz, prin.
Springdale ES, 3207 HOLLIS ST 76111
Margaret Carr, prin.
Stevens ES, 6161 WRIGLEY WAY 76133
Robert Forrester, prin.
Sunrise ES, 3409 STALCUP ROAD 76119
Beatrice Douglas, prin.
Tanglewood ES, 3060 OVERTON PARK W 76109
Millicent Jones, prin.
Turner ES, 3001 AZLE AVE 76106
Cynthia Davis, prin.
Van Zandt-Guinn ES, 501 MISSOURI AVE 76104
Alma Parish, prin.
Walton ES, 5816 RICKENBACKER PL 76112
Constance Davis, prin.
Washington Heights ES
3215 N HOUSTON ST 76106 – Carlos Ayala, prin.
Waverly Park ES, 3604 CIMMARON TRL 76116
James Smith, prin.
Westcliff ES, 4300 CLAY AVE 76117
Alicia Hyman, prin.
Westcreek ES, 3401 WALTON AVE 76133
Earl Nance, prin.
Western Hills ES, 2805 LAREDO DR 76116
Evelene Jones, prin.
Williams ES, 901 BAURLINE ST 76111
Betty Sandley, prin.
Worth Heights ES, 519 E BUTLER ST 76110
Elda Gonzalez, prin.

Lake Worth ISD
Sch. Sys. Enr. Code 4
Supt. – Arthur Gegory
6800 TELEPHONE ROAD 76135
Hodgkins S 76135 – Gail Johnson, prin.
Howry MS, 6800 TELEPHONE ROAD 76135
Dewayne Kennemore, prin.
Morris ES, 6800 TELEPHONE ROAD 76135
Marilyn Miller, prin.

Masonic Home ISD
Sch. Sys. Enr. Code 2
Supt. – J. Stewart, P O BOX 15040 76119
Masonic Home S, P O BOX 15040 76119
Bill Holt, prin.

White Settlement ISD
Supt. – See White Settlement
Brewer MS, 1000 S CHERRY LANE 76108
Homer Dear, prin.

All Saints Parish Day School
8200 TUMBLEWEED TRAIL 76108
Ft. Worth Academy MS 76102
Ft. Worth Christian School
7517 BOGART DRIVE 76180
Ft. Worth Country Day School
4200 COUNTRY DAY LANE 76109
Trinity Valley School, 6101 MCCART AVE 76133
All Saints ES, 2006 N HOUSTON ST 76106
All Saints Parish Day School
8200 TUMBLEWEED TRAIL 76108
Ft. Worth Academy ES 76102
Holy Family ES, 6146 PERSHING AVE 76107
Our Lady of Victory ES
3320 HEMPHILL ST 76110
Our Mother of Mercy ES
1003 E TERRELL AVE 76104
Redeemer Lutheran School
4513 WILLIAMS ROAD 76116
Southwest Christian School
4600-B ALTAMESA BLVD 76133
St. Andrew's Inter Parochial ES
3304 DRYDEN ROAD 76109
St. George ES, 824 HUDGINS AVE 76111
St. John the Apostle School
7421 GLENVIEW DR 76180
St. Mary's School, 1320 S JENNINGS AVE 76104
St. Paul Lutheran School
1800 W FREEWAY 76102
St. Peter ES, 1201 S CHERRY LANE 76108
St. Rita ES, 712 WELLER BLVD 76112
White Lake ES, 501 OAKLAND BLVD 76103
Worth Heights Montessori School
519 E BUTLER ST 76110
Zion Lutheran School, 1112 EAGLE DR 76111

Franklin, Robertson Co., Pop. Code 4
Franklin ISD
Sch. Sys. Enr. Code 3
Supt. – Thomas Phillips, P O BOX 369 77856
Reynolds ES 77856 – Tom Cole, prin.

Frankston, Anderson Co., Pop. Code 4
Frankston ISD
Sch. Sys. Enr. Code 3
Supt. – Bill Alexander, P O BOX 428 75763
S 75763 – G. Ousley, prin.

Fredericksburg, Gillespie Co., Pop. Code 6
Doss Cons. SD
Sch. Sys. Enr. Code 1
Supt. – Jay Weinheimer, P O BOX 351 78624
Doss ES 78624 – Carrie Bierschwale, prin.

Fredericksburg ISD
Sch. Sys. Enr. Code 4
Supt. – Robert Caster, 202 W TRAVIS ST 78624
MS 78624 – Lawrence Pesek, prin.
IS, 202 W TRAVIS ST 78624 – Mike Wuest, prin.
PS, S ADAMS ST 78624 – Barbara Grona, prin.
Other Schools – See Stonewall

St. Mary ES, 202 S ORANGE ST 78624

Freeport, Brazoria Co., Pop. Code 7
Brazosport ISD
Sch. Sys. Enr. Code 7
Supt. – Patricia Shell, P O BOX Z 77541
Velasco ES, 500 N B AVE 77541
Anna Brodie, prin.
MS 77541 – Douglas Reed, prin.
Austin ES, AUSTIN ST 77541
Gayla Sterzinger, prin.
Fleming ES, 431 W 4TH ST 77541
Jackie Reed, prin.
Long ES, 1200 W 11TH ST 77541
Helen Brewer, prin.
Ogg ES, 400 W MARION 77541
James Moore, prin.
Polk ES, GLEN FOREST DR 77541
Horace Driskill, prin.
Roberts ES, 110 S CEDAR LAKE 77541
Ludina Bush, prin.
Other Schools – See Clute, Lake Jackson

Freer, Duval Co., Pop. Code 5
Freer ISD
Sch. Sys. Enr. Code 4
Supt. – J. Doughty, P O BOX 240 78357
JHS, 615 NORTON AVE 78357
John Goodin, prin.
Thomas ES 78357 – Saul Hinojosa, prin.

Friendswood, Galveston Co., Pop. Code 7
Friendswood ISD
Sch. Sys. Enr. Code 5
Supt. – T. Thomas, 302 LAUREL DRIVE 77546
Intermed. S, 402 LAUREL DRIVE 77546
Wiley Murrell, prin.
Cline PS, 505 BRIARMEADOW AVE 77546
Gary Morris, prin.
Westwood MS, 506 W EDGEWOOD DR 77546
Mary Ward, prin.

Friona, Parmer Co., Pop. Code 5
Friona ISD
Sch. Sys. Enr. Code 4
Supt. – Hal Ratcliff, P O BOX 607 79035
JHS 79035 – Thomas Johnson, prin.
ES 79035 – Jerry Shelton, prin.

Frisco, Collin Co., Pop. Code 5
Frisco ISD
Sch. Sys. Enr. Code 4
Supt. – J. Wakeland, P O BOX 910 75034
JHS 75034 – Charles Mooneyham, prin.
Acker ES, P O BOX 649 75034
Charlotte Mooneyham, prin.
Rogers MS, 10500 ROGERS 75034
Patricia Kramer, prin.

McKinney ISD
Supt. – See Mc Kinney
Finch ES 75034 – Bob Rountree, prin.

Fritch, Hutchinson Co., Pop. Code 4
Sanford ISD
Sch. Sys. Enr. Code 4
Supt. – C. Cunningham, P O BOX 1287 79036
Sanford-Fritch JHS, P O BOX 1287 79036
Ken Hayes, prin.
Sanford-Fritch ES 79036 – Dale Howard, prin.
Sanford-Fritch MS 79036 – Joe Thornton, prin.

Frost, Navarro Co., Pop. Code 3
Frost ISD
Sch. Sys. Enr. Code 2
Supt. – Billy Burton, P O BOX K 76641
ES 76641 – Thomas Campbell, prin.

Fruitvale, Van Zandt Co., Pop. Code 2
Fruitvale ISD
Sch. Sys. Enr. Code 2
Supt. – Don Travis, P O BOX 77 75127
ES, P O BOX 77 75127 – Movita Maciel, prin.

Gail, Gordon Co.
Borden County ISD
Sch. Sys. Enr. Code 2
Supt. – James McLeroy, P O BOX 95 79738
Borden S 79738 – M. McMeans, prin.

Gainesville, Cooke Co., Pop. Code 7
Callisburg ISD
Sch. Sys. Enr. Code 3
Supt. – L. Hawkins, RURAL ROUTE 02 76240
Callisburg JHS 76240 – Grace Rains, prin.
Rad Ware ES 76240 – Gerald Langston, prin.

Gainesville ISD
Sch. Sys. Enr. Code 5
Supt. – Charlie Uselton, P O BOX 801 76240
MS, 421 N DENTON ST 76240
Edward Green, prin.
Edison ES, 1 EDISON DR 76240
Sherian Keeling, prin.
Franklin ES, 400 HARVEY ST 76240
Patrick Hermes, prin.
Lee ES, 900 N GRAND AVE 76240
Bill Roberg, prin.
Lindsay ES, 801 S LINDSAY ST 76240
Mary Moore, prin.
McMurray ES, 801 S GRAND AVE 76240
Velton Williams, prin.
Washington ES, 1201 LINDSAY ST 76240
Nancy Fisher, prin.

Sivells Bend ISD
Sch. Sys. Enr. Code 1
Supt. – Orville Anderle, HCR 76240
Sivells Bend ES 76240 – Orville Anderle, prin.

Walnut Bend ISD
Sch. Sys. Enr. Code 1
Supt. – W. Hunt
RURAL ROUTE 06 BOX 394 76240
Walnut Bend ES 76240 – W. Hunt, prin.

St. Mary ES, 931 N WEAVER ST 76240

Galena Park, Harris Co., Pop. Code 6
Galena Park ISD
Sch. Sys. Enr. Code 7
Supt. – Don Hooper, P O BOX 565 77547
MS, 1600 3RD ST 77547 – John Manison, prin.
Cimmarron ES, P O BOX 565 77547
Mike Barkley, prin.
Cloverleaf ES, P O BOX 565 77547
Kenneth Bush, prin.
ES, 401 N MAIN ST 77547
Robert McCollum, prin.
Green Valley ES, P O BOX 565 77547
Margaret Goolsbee, prin.
Jacinto City ES, P O BOX 565 77547
Leonard Jones, prin.
MacArthur ES, 1801 N MAIN ST 77547
Fran Keal, prin.
North Shore ES, P O BOX 565 77547
Joyce Weir, prin.
Pyburn ES, P O BOX 565 77547
B. Stanfield, prin.
Tice ES, P O BOX 565 77547 – Earl Cobb, prin.
Woodland Acres ES, P O BOX 565 77547
Huey Cook, prin.
Other Schools – See Houston

Our Lady of Fatima ES, 1702 9TH ST 77547

Galveston, Galveston Co., Pop. Code 8
Galveston ISD
Sch. Sys. Enr. Code 6
Supt. – James Pickett, P O BOX 660 77553
Central MS, 3014 AVENUE I 77550
Tom Lasater, prin.
Alamo ES, 5200 AVE M #1/2 77551
Elbert Clay, prin.
Austin IS 77553 – Gregory Smith, prin.
Bolivar ES 77553 – Phyllis Kingsbury, prin.

Burnet ES, 5501 AVENUE S 77550
Josh Hernandez, prin.
Morgan ES, 1410 37TH ST 77550
Barbara McIlveen, prin.
Oppe ES 77553 – Carole Streiff, prin.
Parker ES, 6820 JONES DR 77551
Mary Cook, prin.
Rosenberg ES, 721 10TH ST 77550
Patricia Williams, prin.
San Jacinto ES, 1110 MOODY AVE 77550
Irene Dillon, prin.
Weis IS 77553 – Tommie Boudreaux, prin.

Galveston Catholic School
2601 URSULINE ST 77550
Trinity Episcopal ES, 720 TREMONT ST 77550

Ganado, Jackson Co., Pop. Code 4
Ganado ISD
Sch. Sys. Enr. Code 3
Supt. – R. Dale Cosby, P O BOX D 77962
ES, 310 S 5TH 77962 – William Stroman, prin.

Garden City, Glasscock Co.
Glasscock ISD
Sch. Sys. Enr. Code 2
Supt. – Donn Stringer, P O BOX 9 79739
Glasscock County ES 79739 – Robert Kelso, prin.

Garland, Dallas Co., Pop. Code 9
Garland ISD
Sch. Sys. Enr. Code 8
Supt. – Eli Douglas, 720 STADIUM DRIVE 75040
Austin Academy for Excellence MS
1125 BEVERLY DRIVE 75040 – Ann Plyler, prin.
Brandenburg MS, 626 NICKENS ROAD 75043
Jerry Halpin, prin.
Bussey MS, 1204 TRAVIS ST 75040
L. Nichols, prin.
Houston MS, 2232 SUSSEX DRIVE 75041
B. Willis, prin.
Jackson MS, 1310 BOBBIE LANE 75042
Henry Brackett, prin.
Lyles MS, 4655 COUNTRY CLUB ROAD 75041
Debbie Wester, prin.
Memorial MS, 2825 S 1ST ST 75041
B. Williamson, prin.
O'Banion MS, 700 BIRCHWOOD DRIVE 75043
J. Brown, prin.
Sellers MS, 1009 MARS DRIVE 75040
Larry Holmes, prin.
Webb MS, 1610 SPRING CREEK DRIVE 75040
Robert Thompson, prin.
Back ES, 720 STADIUM DR 75040
Mel Barto, prin.
Beaver ES, 3232 MARCH LANE 75042
John Tucker, prin.
Bradfield ES, 3817 BUCKNELL DR 75042
Ken Gossett, prin.
Bullock ES, 3909 EDGEWOOD DR 75042
Weldon Bowden, prin.
Caldwell ES, 3400 SATURN ROAD 75041
Charles Cooper, prin.
Centerville ES, 600 E KINGSLEY ROAD 75041
Jeanette O'Neal, prin.
Club Hill ES, 1330 COLONEL DR 75043
Keith Harrison, prin.
Cooper ES, 1220 KINGSBRIDGE DR 75040
Mary Dollar, prin.
Daugherty ES, 501 W MILLER ROAD 75041
Pamela Howeth, prin.
Davis ES, 1621 MCCALLUM DR 75042
Kay Kuner, prin.
Ethridge ES, 2301 SAM HOUSTON DR 75042
Penny Campbell, prin.
Freeman ES, 1221 W WALNUT ST 75040
Mitt Price, prin.
Golden Meadows ES, 1726 TRAVIS ST 75042
Winston Ferrell, prin.
Handley ES, 3725 BROADWAY BLVD 75043
John Driver, prin.
Heather Glen ES, 5119 HEATHER GLEN DR 75043
Cleburne Raney, prin.
Herfeurth ES 75040 – Larry Rhodes, prin.
Hickman ES, 3114 PINEWOOD DR 75042
Bill Johnson, prin.
Hillside Academy ES, 2014 DAIRY ROAD 75041
Fred Dillard, prin.
Kimberlin Academy
1520 CUMBERLAND DR 75040
Martha Craft, prin.
Luna ES 75040 – Mike Richey, prin.
Montclair ES, 5200 BROADMOOR DR 75043
Phyllis Parker, prin.
Northlake ES, 1626 BOSQUE DR 75040
Bill Stevens, prin.
Park Crest ES, 2232 PARKCREST DR 75041
Bob McDonald, prin.
Roach ES, 1811 MAYFIELD AVE 75041
Mary Echols, prin.
Shorehaven ES, 600 SHOREHAVEN DR 75040
Jewell Reed, prin.
Shugart ES, 4726 ROSE HILL ROAD 75043
Lura Townsend, prin.
Southgate ES, 1115 MAYFIELD AVE 75041
Nelda Gentsch, prin.
Spring Creek ES, 1510 SPRING CREEK DR 75040
Ron Taylor, prin.
Toler ES, 3520 GUTHRIE ROAD 75043
Les Green, prin.
Vial ES, 126 CREEKVIEW DR 75043
Sandra Click, prin.
Walnut Glen ES, 3101 EDGEWOOD DR 75042
Larry Allen, prin.

Watson ES, 2601 DAIRY ROAD 75041
Frank Reid, prin.
Weaver ES
805 PLEASANT VALLEY ROAD 75040
Dean Nelson, prin.
Williams ES, 1821 OLD GATE LANE 75042
Mary Day, prin.
Other Schools – See Rowlett

Mesquite ISD
Supt. – See Mesquite
Price ES, 630 STOUD 75043 – Juaniza Cross, prin.

Good Shepherd ES, 214 S GARLAND AVE 75040

Garrison, Nacogdoches Co., Pop. Code 4
Garrison ISD
Sch. Sys. Enr. Code 3
Supt. – Vernis Rogers, P O BOX 510 75946
ES 75946 – Ray Smith, prin.

Gary, Panola Co., Pop. Code 2
Gary ISD
Sch. Sys. Enr. Code 2
Supt. – Russell Porter, P O BOX 189 75643
S 75643 – S. Yarbrough, prin.

Gatesville, Coryell Co., Pop. Code 6
Gatesville ISD
Sch. Sys. Enr. Code 4
Supt. – Tracy Barnes, 2537 E MAIN ST 76528
JHS 76528 – Roland Lambert, prin.
MS, 2537 E MAIN ST 76528 – Dennis Taylor, prin.
PS, S 26TH ST 76528 – Donald Edwards, prin.

Gause, Milam Co., Pop. Code 2
Gause ISD
Sch. Sys. Enr. Code 1
Supt. – James Askew, P O BOX 38 77857
ES 77857 – (—), prin.

Georgetown, Williamson Co., Pop. Code 6
Georgetown ISD
Sch. Sys. Enr. Code 5
Supt. – Jim Gunn, 603 LAKEWAY 78628
JHS 78626 – Richard McCormick, prin.
Williams MS, 603 LAKEWAY DR 78628
Jo Ann Ford, prin.
PS, 1600 LAUREL ST 78626 – Mard Herrick, prin.
Frost ES 78628 – Vernon Killen, prin.
Northside MS, 1313 WILLIAMS DR 78628
Mike Coulter, prin.
Westside PS, W 17TH 78626 – Pete Zenner, prin.

Zion Lutheran School, RURAL ROUTE 02 78626

George West, Live Oak Co., Pop. Code 5
George West ISD
Sch. Sys. Enr. Code 4
Supt. – Charles Williams, P O BOX G 78022
JHS, P O BOX 430 78022 – A. Viertel, prin.
MS 78022 – Steve Lackey, prin.
PS 78022 – Frank Sales, prin.

Geronimo, Guadalupe Co.
Navarro ISD
Sch. Sys. Enr. Code 3
Supt. – Larry McGough, P O BOX 10 78115
Navarro ES 78115 – Jeffery Menking, prin.

Giddings, Lee Co., Pop. Code 5
Giddings ISD
Sch. Sys. Enr. Code 4
Supt. – C. Buck, P O BOX 389 78942
MS 78942 – Thomas Campbell, prin.
ES, INDUSTRY ST 78942 – Robert French, prin.

Immanual Lutheran School
382 N GRIMES ST 78942

Gilmer, Upshur Co., Pop. Code 6
Gilmer ISD
Sch. Sys. Enr. Code 4
Supt. – Joe Smith, P O BOX 40 75644
JHS 75644 – B. Traylor, prin.
ES, W SCOTT ST 75644 – Harmon Camp, prin.
IS 75644 – Sandra Young, prin.

Harmony ISD
Sch. Sys. Enr. Code 3
Supt. – Ray Thompson, RURAL ROUTE 04 75644
MS, RURAL ROUTE 04 75644
Sherwin Yocum, prin.
James Poole ES 75644 – William Taylor, prin.

Union Hill ISD
Sch. Sys. Enr. Code 2
Supt. – Weldon Snodgrass, P O BOX 370 75644
Union Hill ES, 200 BROADWAY ST 75644
Sharon Long, prin.

Gladewater, Gregg Co., Pop. Code 6
Gladewater ISD
Sch. Sys. Enr. Code 4
Supt. – O. Johnston, 700 MELBA ST #A 75647
MS 75647 – Wiley Wilkerson, prin.
Broadway ES 75647 – Harold Keller, prin.
Gay Avenue PS 75647 – David Tankersley, prin.
Weldon IS 75564 – Don Williams, prin.

Sabine ISD
Sch. Sys. Enr. Code 4
Supt. – Gloria Berry
RURAL ROUTE 01 BOX 189 75647
Sabine JHS 75647 – Jerry Welty, prin.
Sabine ES, RURAL ROUTE 01 BOX 189 75647
Marilynn Lantrip, prin.

Sabine IS, RURAL ROUTE 01 BOX 189 75647
Bobby Fortson, prin.

Union Grove ISD
Sch. Sys. Enr. Code 3
Supt. – Dan Rose, P O BOX 1447 75647
Union Grove ES, P O BOX 1447 75647
Joe Johnson, prin.

Glen Rose, Somervell Co., Pop. Code 4
Glen Rose ISD
Sch. Sys. Enr. Code 4
Supt. – John Jones, P O BOX 996 76043
JHS 76043 – Thomas Prisoc, prin.
ES 76043 – Gary Buckingham, prin.

Godley, Johnson Co., Pop. Code 3
Godley ISD
Sch. Sys. Enr. Code 3
Supt. – Kenneth Bateman, P O BOX 128 76044
MS 76044 – Gene Loflin, prin.
ES 76044 – Maureen Green, prin.

Goldthwaite, Mills Co., Pop. Code 4
Goldthwaite ISD
Sch. Sys. Enr. Code 3
Supt. – H. Grayson Wetzel, P O BOX 608 76844
ES 76844 – Marilyn Johanson, prin.

Goliad, Goliad Co., Pop. Code 4
Goliad ISD
Sch. Sys. Enr. Code 4
Supt. – James Young, P O BOX 830 77963
MS 77963 – James Jenkins, prin.
PS, 101 W HIGH 77963 – Letitia Robinson, prin.

Gonzales, Gonzales Co., Pop. Code 6
Gonzales ISD
Sch. Sys. Enr. Code 5
Supt. – Erwin Ckodre, P O BOX 157 78629
JHS 78629 – Bob Johnson, prin.
East Avenue ES, P O BOX 905 78629
Herbert Karnau, prin.
North Avenue MS, 1032 SAINT JOSEPH ST 78629
Don Rainey, prin.

Goodrich, Polk Co., Pop. Code 2
Goodrich ISD
Sch. Sys. Enr. Code 2
Supt. – Don Reynolds, P O BOX 193 77335
ES 77335 – Janet Gaston, prin.

Gordon, Palo Pinto Co., Pop. Code 3
Gordon ISD
Sch. Sys. Enr. Code 2
Supt. – Randy Savage, 112-116 RUSK ST 76453
ES 76453 – Nelson Campbell, prin.

Goree, Knox Co., Pop. Code 3
Goree ISD
Sch. Sys. Enr. Code 2
Supt. – E. Hosea, P O BOX 156 76363
S 76363 – George Cotton, prin.

Gorman, Eastland Co., Pop. Code 4
Gorman ISD
Sch. Sys. Enr. Code 2
Supt. – G. Maxfield, P O BOX 8 76454
ES 76454 – Allan Gibbs, prin.

Graford, Palo Pinto Co., Pop. Code 2
Graford ISD
Sch. Sys. Enr. Code 2
Supt. – William Stidham, P O BOX 09 76045
S 76045 – Dorothy Stidham, prin.

Graham, Young Co., Pop. Code 6
Graham ISD
Sch. Sys. Enr. Code 5
Supt. – Bobby Parker, Jr.
100 KENTUCKY ST 76046
JHS 76046 – Keith Hardin, prin.
Crestview ES
1317 OLD JACKSBORO ROAD 76046
Charles Richardson, prin.
Shawnee ES, 912 CHERRY ST 76046
Ken Ford, prin.
Woodland ES, 1219 CLIFF DR 76046
Joe Garvey, prin.

Granbury, Hood Co., Pop. Code 5
Granbury ISD
Sch. Sys. Enr. Code 5
Supt. – Jerry Christian, P O BOX 520 76048
MS 76048 – L. Williams, prin.
Acton ES 76048 – Ronald Babers, prin.
Baccus ES 76048 – S. Hollingsworth, prin.
ES, 200 N JONES ST 76048
Sylvia Campbell, prin.
IS, 600 W BRIDGE ST 76048
Marsha Grissom, prin.
Roberson ES, PALUXY 76048 – Tom Taylor, prin.

Grandfalls, Ward Co., Pop. Code 3
Grandfalls-Royalty ISD
Sch. Sys. Enr. Code 2
Supt. – Kenneth Norris, P O BOX 10 79742
Grandfalls Royalty JHS 79742 – J. Stocks, prin.
Grandfalls-Royalty ES, 109 AVENUE C 79742
Robert Norris, prin.

Grand Prairie, Dallas Co., Pop. Code 8
Grand Prairie ISD
Sch. Sys. Enr. Code 7
Supt. – Marvin Crawford, P O BOX 1170 75051
Adams MS, 833 TARRANT ROAD 75050
Bebe Bingham, prin.

Jackson MS, 305 W WARRIOR TRAIL 75051
Phillip Farris, prin.
Jefferson MS, 1309 PINE ST 75050
Greg Farr, prin.
Kennedy MS, 2205 SE 4TH ST 75051
Joe Jackson, prin.
Lee MS, 401 E GRAND PRAIRIE ROAD 75051
Gary Gilbreath, prin.
Truman MS 75052 – Michael Brinkley, prin.
Austin ES, 815 NW 7TH ST 75050
Delmas Morton, prin.
Bonham ES, 1301 E CORAL WAY 75051
Rudy Lopez, prin.
Bowie ES, 425 ALICE DR 75051 – Judy Hall, prin.
Crockett ES, 501 E GRAND PRAIRIE ROAD 75051
Beverly Flanary, prin.
Dalworth ES, 1933 SPIKES ST 75051
Marva Dixon, prin.
Dickinson ES, 1902 PALMER TRL 75052
Susan Sharp, prin.
Eisenhower ES, 2102 N CARRIER PKWY 75050
Frances Bostic, prin.
Fannin ES, 301 NE 28TH ST 75050
Pat Laster, prin.
Garner ES, 145 POLO ROAD 75052
George Angle, prin.
Hill ES, 4213 S BELT LINE ROAD 75052
Kenneth Johnston, prin.
Houston ES, 1502 COLLEGE ST 75050
Doylene White, prin.
Johnson ES, 605 STONEWALL DR 75051
Dennis Hale, prin.
Lamar ES, 2099 WALNUT ST 75050
Keith Jerden, prin.
Milam ES, 2030 PROCTOR ST 75051
Dale Brown, prin.
Rayburn ES, 2800 REFORMA ST 75051
H. Jackson, prin.
Travis ES, 525 NE 15TH ST 75050
Wayne Van Bevers, prin.
Zavala ES, 3501 MARK DR 75051
Gene Berryhill, prin.

Immaculate Conception ES
400 NE 17TH ST 75050
St. Andrew's Episcopal School
727 HILL ST 75050

Grand Saline, Van Zandt Co., Pop. Code 5
Grand Saline ISD
Sch. Sys. Enr. Code 3
Supt. – Gerald Gilbert
400 STADIUM DRIVE 75140
MS 75140 – J. Witt, prin.
ES 75140 – Wayne Gore, prin.

Grandview, Johnson Co., Pop. Code 4
Grandview ISD
Sch. Sys. Enr. Code 3
Supt. – Harold Pinkerton, P O BOX 310 76050
JHS 76050 – Alan Neff, prin.
ES 76050 – Randy Rice, prin.

Granger, Williamson Co., Pop. Code 4
Granger ISD
Sch. Sys. Enr. Code 2
Supt. – Raymond Etheridge, P O BOX 578 76530
ES 76350 – Leslie Michalik, prin.

Grangerland, Montgomery Co.
Conroe ISD
Supt. – See Conroe
Milam ES, HIGHWAY 3083 77302
Kathy Sharples, prin.

Grapeland, Houston Co., Pop. Code 4
Grapeland ISD
Sch. Sys. Enr. Code 3
Supt. – James Caveness, P O BOX 248 75844
JHS 75844 – Larry Hughes, prin.
ES 75844 – Jerry Boyd, prin.

Grapevine, Tarrant Co., Pop. Code 7
Grapevine-Colleyville ISD
Sch. Sys. Enr. Code 5
Supt. – E. Sigler, 3051 W HIGHWAY 26 76051
MS, 730 E WORTH ST 76051 – Linda Koch, prin.
Bear Creek ES 76051 – Kathryn Land, prin.
Cannon ES, 1300 W COLLEGE ST 76051
Denise Weber, prin.
Colleyville ES 76051 – Martha Walker, prin.
Dove ES, 1932 DOVE ROAD 76051
Linda Holifield, prin.
Taylor ES 76051 – Neal Odle, prin.
Timberline ES, 3220 TIMERLINE DR 76051
Julia Lyda, prin.
Other Schools – See Colleyville

Greenville, Hunt Co., Pop. Code 7
Greenville ISD
Sch. Sys. Enr. Code 6
Supt. – John Wilson, P O BOX 1022 75401
MS, 3201 STANFORD ST 75401
William Smith, prin.
Bowie ES, 6000 STONEWALL ST 75401
Patricia Gilbert, prin.
Carver ES, 2504 CARVER ST 75401
Sarah Wright, prin.
Crockett ES, HWY 34 N 75401
Joe Skillerns, prin.
Houston ES, 3923 HENRY ST 75401
Gwendolyn Willems, prin.
Lamar ES, 4004 MOULTON ST 75401
Jearl Dunavin, prin.

Travis ES, 3005 DIVISION ST 75401
James Evans, prin.
Travis IS 75401 – Charles Sivley, prin.

Gregory, San Patricio Co., Pop. Code 5
Gregory-Portland ISD
Sch. Sys. Enr. Code 5
Supt. – James Hall, P O BOX 338 78359
Austin ES 78359 – Katherine Conoly, prin.
Other Schools – See Portland

Groesbeck, Limestone Co., Pop. Code 5
Groesbeck ISD
Sch. Sys. Enr. Code 4
Supt. – E. Ellis, P O BOX 559 76642
JHS, P O BOX 559 76642 – Don Driscoll, prin.
ES, 800 W TRINITY ST 76642
Gerald Gibson, prin.
Whitehurst MS, 801 N ELLIS ST 76642
Glynis Rosas, prin.

Groom, Carson Co., Pop. Code 3
Grandview-Hopkins ISD
Sch. Sys. Enr. Code 1
Supt. – Jess Baker
RURAL ROUTE 01 BOX 27 79039
Grandview-Hopkins ES 79039 – Jess Baker, prin.

Groom ISD
Sch. Sys. Enr. Code 2
Supt. – Rex Peeples, P O BOX 550 79039
S 79039 – Kenneth Sweat, prin.

Groves, Jefferson Co., Pop. Code 7
Port Neches ISD
Supt. – See Port Neches
MS, 3901 CLEVELAND AVE 77619
David Garrett, prin.
Taft ES, 2500 TAFT AVE 77619
Donald Mott, prin.
Van Buren ES, 64090 VAN BUREN ST 77619
Rebecca Walker, prin.

Groveton, Trinity Co., Pop. Code 4
Centerville ISD
Sch. Sys. Enr. Code 2
Supt. – James Davis
RURAL ROUTE 01 BOX 146 75845
Centerville ES 75845 – Colleen Moore, prin.

Groveton ISD
Sch. Sys. Enr. Code 3
Supt. – John Reynolds, P O BOX 728 75845
ES, P O BOX 580 75845 – Joe Driskell, prin.

Grulla, Starr Co., Pop. Code 4
Rio Grande City ISD
Supt. – See Rio Grande City
Grulla JHS 78548 – Merardo Bando, prin.

Gruver, Hansford Co., Pop. Code 4
Gruver ISD
Sch. Sys. Enr. Code 3
Supt. – Tommy Cathey, P O BOX 650 79040
JHS, P O BOX 709 79040 – Bill Duncan, prin.
ES, 405 GARRETT 79040 – Bob Burgoon, prin.

Gunter, Grayson Co., Pop. Code 3
Gunter ISD
Sch. Sys. Enr. Code 2
Supt. – R. Cohagan, P O BOX 98 75058
ES 75058 – Cheyrl Cohagan, prin.

Gustine, Comanche Co., Pop. Code 2
Gustine ISD
Sch. Sys. Enr. Code 2
Supt. – Steve Davidson, P O BOX 169 76455
S 76455 – Roy Newsom, prin.

Guthrie, King Co., Pop. Code 2
Guthrie Common SD
Sch. Sys. Enr. Code 2
Supt. – N. Edward Kendall, P O BOX 1 79236
S 79236 – Clayton Hubbart, prin.

Hale Center, Hale Co., Pop. Code 4
Hale Center ISD
Sch. Sys. Enr. Code 3
Supt. – Marlin Dodds, P O BOX M 79041
MS 79041 – D. Harkins, prin.
Aikin ES, N AVE K 79041 – T. Clark, prin.

Hallettsville, Lavaca Co., Pop. Code 5
Ezzell ISD
Sch. Sys. Enr. Code 2
Supt. – Donald Madden
RURAL ROUTE 03 BOX 162-C 77964
Ezzell ES 77964 – (—), prin.

Hallettsville ISD
Sch. Sys. Enr. Code 3
Supt. – Robert Haas, P O BOX 368 77964
JHS, 410 S RUSSELL ST 77964
David Kalich, prin.
ES 77964 – Joe Clark, prin.

Vysehrad ISD
Sch. Sys. Enr. Code 1
Supt. – Edward Pustka
RURAL ROUTE 04 BOX 289-A 77964
Vysehrad ES 77964 – Edward Pustka, prin.

Sacred Heart ES, 313 S TEXANA ST 77964

Hallsville, Harrison Co., Pop. Code 4
Hallsville ISD
Sch. Sys. Enr. Code 5
Supt. – Bob Browning, P O BOX 810 75650
JHS 75650 – Charles McGough, prin.

ES, P O BOX 810   75650 – Billie Martin, prin.
IS, P O BOX 810   75650 – Gwen Allbright, prin.
MS, P O BOX 810   75650 – Jimmie Ross, prin.

Hamilton, Hamilton Co., Pop. Code 5
Hamilton ISD
Sch. Sys. Enr. Code 3
Supt. – Clyde Raibourn, P O BOX 392   76531
ES   76531 – Elizabeth Abernathy, prin.

Hamlin, Jones Co., Pop. Code 5
Hamlin ISD
Sch. Sys. Enr. Code 3
Supt. – Wayne King, P O BOX 338   79520
MS   79520 – S. Ferguson, prin.
ES   79520 – Joe Dean, prin.

Hamshire, Jefferson Co., Pop. Code 2
Hamshire-Fannett ISD
Sch. Sys. Enr. Code 4
Supt. – Robert Nicks, P O BOX 223   77622
Hamshire-Fannett ES   77622
Connie McCray, prin.
Other Schools – See Beaumont

Happy, Swisher Co., Pop. Code 3
Happy ISD
Sch. Sys. Enr. Code 2
Supt. – Bill Mayfield, P O BOX 458   79042
ES, P O BOX 458   79042 – Deborah Keefer, prin.

Hardin, Liberty Co., Pop. Code 3
Hardin ISD
Sch. Sys. Enr. Code 4
Supt. – Billy Bob Parker, P O BOX 330   77561
JHS   77561 – Monty Upton, prin.
ES   77561 – Allen Sheffield, prin.

Harker Heights, Bell Co., Pop. Code 6
Killeen ISD
Supt. – See Killeen
Harker Heights ES, HARLEY DR   76543
Gladys Swindle, prin.

Harleton, Harrison Co.
Harleton ISD
Sch. Sys. Enr. Code 3
Supt. – Curtis Williams, P O BOX 7   75651
JHS   75651 – Morris Jones, prin.
ES, P O BOX 307   75651 – Jane McGill, prin.

Harlingen, Cameron Co., Pop. Code 8
Harlingen ISD
Sch. Sys. Enr. Code 7
Supt. – T. Carl McMillan
1409 E HARRISON ST   78550
Coakley JHS   78550 – William Pietro, prin.
Vernon JHS   78550 – Noe Salinas, prin.
Austin ES, 700 E AUSTIN ST   78550
Juana Lawson, prin.
Bonham ES, 2400 E JEFFERSON ST   78550
Christina Garcia, prin.
Bowie ES, 309 W LINCOLN AVE   78550
Jean Pearce, prin.
Crockett ES, 1406 W JEFFERSON ST   78550
Jane Terry, prin.
Dishman ES, 1409 E HARRISON ST   78550
Geraldine Dusek, prin.
Houston ES, 301 E TAFT ST   78550
Sue Bennett, prin.
Jefferson ES, 601 J ST   78550
Librado Hernandez, prin.
Lamar ES, 1100 MCLARRY ROAD   78550
Cesar Morales, prin.
Long ES, 2601 N 7TH ST   78550 – Lee Means, prin.
Memorial MS   78550 – Guillermo Rodriguez, prin.
Milam ES, 1215 RANGERVILLE ROAD   78552
Amador Galvan, prin.
Stuart ES, W STATE HWY   78550
Cheryl Gray, prin.
Travis ES, 600 E POLK ST   78550
Placido Cortez, prin.
Treasure Hills ES, 2525 HAINE DR   78550
Frances Payne, prin.
Wilson ES   78550 – Tony Rodriguez, prin.
Zavala ES, 1111 N B ST   78550 – (—), prin.

Calvary Christian ES, 1815 N 7TH ST   78550
Harlingen SDA Church School
P O BOX 3539   78551
St. Anthony ES, 1015 E HARRISON ST   78550
St. Paul Lutheran ES, 602 MORGAN BLVD   78550

Harper, Gillespie Co., Pop. Code 2
Harper ISD
Sch. Sys. Enr. Code 2
Supt. – James Ward, P O BOX 68   78631
S   78631 – Judy Reimer, prin.

Harrold, Wilbarger Co.
Harrold ISD
Sch. Sys. Enr. Code 1
Supt. – Chester Juroska, P O BOX 418   76364
S   76364 – Ronald Brandon, prin.

Hart, Castro Co., Pop. Code 4
Hart ISD
Sch. Sys. Enr. Code 3
Supt. – Phil Barefield, P O BOX 487   79043
ES   79043 – Jack Burkhalter, prin.

Hartley, Hartley Co.
Hartley ISD
Sch. Sys. Enr. Code 2
Supt. – Preston Cleveland, P O BOX 56   79044
S   79044 – Lee Montgomery, prin.

Haskell, Haskell Co., Pop. Code 5
Haskell ISD
Sch. Sys. Enr. Code 3
Supt. – James Kemp, P O BOX 937   79521
ES, 306 S AVENUE G   79521 – James Lisle, prin.

Paint Creek ISD
Sch. Sys. Enr. Code 1
Supt. – Jerry Morgan
RURAL ROUTE 02   BOX 46   79521
Paint Creek S, RURAL ROUTE 02   BOX 190   79521
Max Calk, prin.

Hawkins, Wood Co., Pop. Code 4
Hawkins ISD
Sch. Sys. Enr. Code 3
Supt. – Wendell McGuire, P O BOX L   75765
MS   75765 – Robert Pool, prin.
ES, P O BOX L   75765 – Dwayne Hickey, prin.

Hawley, Jones Co., Pop. Code 3
Hawley ISD
Sch. Sys. Enr. Code 3
Supt. – Cecil Davis, P O BOX D   79525
ES   79525 – Edmund Womack, prin.

Hearne, Robertson Co., Pop. Code 6
Hearne ISD
Sch. Sys. Enr. Code 4
Supt. – H. Bonorden, 401 WHEELOCK ST   77859
JHS   77859 – M. Grenwelge, prin.
Blackshear MS, 1401 W 3RD ST   77859
Norris McDaniel, prin.
East Side ES, 1102 RILEY ST   77859
Jack Bradley, prin.

Hebbronville, Jim Hogg Co., Pop. Code 5
Jim Hogg County ISD
Sch. Sys. Enr. Code 4
Supt. – Roberto Alvarez, P O BOX 880   78361
JHS, P O BOX 880   78361
Humberto Gonzalez, prin.
ES, 112 W LUCILLE ST   78361
Jose Castellano, prin.

Hedley, Donley Co., Pop. Code 2
Hedley ISD
Sch. Sys. Enr. Code 1
Supt. – Glyndol Holland, P O BOX 38   79237
S   79237 – Bryan Hill, prin.

Hemphill, Sabine Co., Pop. Code 4
Hemphill ISD
Sch. Sys. Enr. Code 3
Supt. – Douglas Butler, P O BOX 550   75948
ES   75948 – Harvel Walker, prin.

Hempstead, Waller Co., Pop. Code 5
Hempstead ISD
Sch. Sys. Enr. Code 4
Supt. – B. Caesar, P O BOX 1007   77445
JHS, P O BOX 1007   77445 – Walter Baker, prin.
ES, P O BOX 1007   77445
William Broderick, prin.
MS   77445 – Mary Ragston, prin.

Henderson, Rusk Co., Pop. Code 7
Henderson ISD
Sch. Sys. Enr. Code 5
Supt. – Jerry Christian, P O BOX 728   75653
MS   75652 – Jerry Melton, prin.
Central ES   75653 – Gena Gardiner, prin.
Chamberlain ES   75653 – Bill Blanton, prin.
Montgomery ES   75653 – Albert Smith, prin.
Northside MS   75653 – G. Deason, prin.

Henrietta, Clay Co., Pop. Code 5
Henrietta ISD
Sch. Sys. Enr. Code 3
Supt. – Thomas Davenport
16700 E CRAFTON   76365
ES, 1600 E CRAFTON ST   76365
Billye Nobles, prin.

Midway ISD
Sch. Sys. Enr. Code 2
Supt. – Toby Howard, RURAL ROUTE 02   76365
Midway S, RURAL ROUTE 02   76365
John Guice, prin.

Hereford, Deaf Smith Co., Pop. Code 7
Hereford ISD
Sch. Sys. Enr. Code 5
Supt. – Charles Greenawalt, 136 AVE F   79406
JHS   79045 – Raymond Schroeder, prin.
Aikman ES, 900 K AVE   79045
John Poindexter, prin.
Bluebonnet MS, 221 16TH ST   79045
Howard Birdwell, prin.
Northwest ES, 400 MOREMAN ST   79045
Gary Billingsley, prin.
Shirley MS, 239 H AVE   79045
John Dominguez, prin.
Tierra Blanca ES, 300 COLUMBIA DR   79045
Phillip Shook, prin.
West Central MS, 120 CAMPBELL ST   79045
George Ochs, prin.

Walcott ISD
Sch. Sys. Enr. Code 1
Supt. – Bill McLaughlin, RURAL ROUTE 04   79045
Walcott ES   79045 – Bill McLaughlin, prin.

St. Anthony's ES, 114 SUNSET DR   79045

Hermleigh, Scurry Co., Pop. Code 2
Hermleigh ISD
Sch. Sys. Enr. Code 2
Supt. – Jerry Church, P O BOX 195   79526
S   79526 – T. Riley, prin.

Hewitt, McLennan Co., Pop. Code 6
Midway ISD
Supt. – See Waco
ES, 900 PANTHER DR   76643 – Bill Killian, prin.

Hico, Hamilton Co., Pop. Code 4
Hico ISD
Sch. Sys. Enr. Code 2
Supt. – Leon Murdoch, P O BOX 218   76457
S   76457 – Everitt Ables, prin.

Hidalgo, Hidalgo Co., Pop. Code 4
Hidalgo ISD
Sch. Sys. Enr. Code 4
Supt. – Alejo Salinas, P O BOX D   78557
Diaz JHS   78557 – Leo Pena, prin.
ES, 604 FLORA   78557 – Manuel Elizondo, prin.
Kelly ES   78557 – Trine Barron, prin.

Higgins, Lipscomb Co., Pop. Code 3
Higgins ISD
Sch. Sys. Enr. Code 2
Supt. – L. Blocker, P O BOX 238   79046
S   79046 – L. Blocker, prin.

High Island, Galveston Co., Pop. Code 2
High Island ISD
Sch. Sys. Enr. Code 2
Supt. – David Anthony, P O BOX 246   77623
ES   77623 – Crocket DuBose, prin.

Highlands, Harris Co., Pop. Code 5
Goose Creek ISD
Supt. – See Baytown
JHS, 1212 N WALLISVILLE ROAD   77562
Carol Fontenot, prin.
MS, 200 N WALLISVILLE ROAD   77562
Larry Topfer, prin.
Hopper PS, 405 E HOUSTON ST   77562
Sheila Liles, prin.

Hillsboro, Hill Co., Pop. Code 6
Hillsboro ISD
Sch. Sys. Enr. Code 4
Supt. – Maurice English, P O BOX 459   76645
JHS, P O BOX 977   76645 – Will Lowrance, prin.
Franklin ES, P O BOX 418   76645
Anna Alivenshine, prin.
IS   76645 – Larry Brown, prin.

Hitchcock, Galveston Co., Pop. Code 6
Hitchcock ISD
Sch. Sys. Enr. Code 4
Supt. – William Banks, 8117 HIGHWAY 6   77563
Crosby JHS   77563 – Ken Kendall, prin.
Northside ES   77563 – Rose Archie, prin.
Stewart MS, 8100 BARRY AVE   77563
James Knapp, prin.

Our Lady of Lourdes ES, P O BOX 557   77563

Hockley, Harris Co., Pop. Code 7
Waller ISD
Supt. – See Waller
Roberts Road ES   77447 – Mary Brooker, prin.

Holland, Bell Co., Pop. Code 3
Holland ISD
Sch. Sys. Enr. Code 2
Supt. – J. Bowman, P O BOX 217   76534
ES   76534 – Barbara Hill, prin.

Holliday, Archer Co., Pop. Code 4
Holliday ISD
Sch. Sys. Enr. Code 3
Supt. – Dan Owen, P O BOX H   76366
MS   76366 – Jake Cottrell, prin.
ES, 751 COLLEGE   76366 – Carol Magee, prin.

Hondo, Medina Co., Pop. Code 6
Hondo ISD
Sch. Sys. Enr. Code 4
Supt. – Newell Woolls, P O BOX 307   78861
McDowell JHS   78861 – Tim Coyle, prin.
Meyer ES   78861 – R. Nations, prin.

Honey Grove, Fannin Co., Pop. Code 4
Honey Grove Consolidated ISD
Sch. Sys. Enr. Code 3
Supt. – Harvey Milton, 107 BOIS DARC ST   75446
ES   75446 – Beverly Felts, prin.

Hooks, Bowie Co., Pop. Code 2
Hooks ISD
Sch. Sys. Enr. Code 4
Supt. – Ken Hall, P O BOX 39   75561
JHS   75561 – David Hanes, prin.
ES, E 28TH   75561 – Grover Godfrey, prin.

Leary ISD
Sch. Sys. Enr. Code 2
Supt. – Franklin Wray, P O BOX 519   75561
Leary ES, P O BOX 519   75561 – (—), prin.

Houston, Harris Co., Pop. Code 12
Aldine ISD
Sch. Sys. Enr. Code 8
Supt. – M. Donaldson
14910 ALDINE WESTFIELD ROAD   77032
Aldine JHS
14910 ALDINE WESTFIELD ROAD   77032
Wilbert Johnson, prin.
Drew MS   77091 – Pat Nash, prin.

Grantham MS, 13300 CHRISMAN 77039
  John Amshoff, prin.
Hambrick JHS, 4600 ALDINE MAIL ROAD 77039
  Ralph Ramirez, prin.
Hoffman MS, 6101 W LITTLE YORK 77091
  Mary Raby, prin.
Shotwell MS, 6515 TRAIL VALLEY WAY 77086
  James Murrell, prin.
Stovall JHS, 11201 AIRLINE DRIVE 77037
  Jody Tyson, prin.
Anderson Fifth Grade ES
  7401 WHEATLEY ST 77088
  Nancy Bennett, prin.
Bethune Fourth & Fifth Grade ES
  2500 S VICTORY DR 77088 – Linda Smith, prin.
Black ES 77022 – (—), prin.
Carmichael ES, 6902 SILVER STAR DR 77086
  Charlotte Utley, prin.
Carroll ES, 222 RAYMAC ST 77037
  Kenneth Ryan, prin.
Colonial Hills ES, 14701 HENRY ROAD 77060
  Weaver Odom, prin.
Conley ES, 3345 W GREENS ROAD 77066
  Linda Clarke, prin.
Dunn ES 77022 – Patricia Lawrence, prin.
Ermel ES, 7103 WOODSMAN TRAIL 77040
  Priscilla Newman, prin.
Francis ES, 14815 LEE ROAD 77032
  Bette Koudelka, prin.
Gray ES 77022 – (—), prin.
Hidden Valley ES, 9325 DEER TRAIL DR 77088
  James Godwin, prin.
Inwood ES, 5815 W LITTLE YORK ROAD 77091
  Cleba Leschper, prin.
Johnson ES, 5801 HAMILL ROAD 77039
  Dorothea Jenkins, prin.
Magrill ES
  14910 ALDINE WESTFIELD ROAD 77032
  Cecil Jones, prin.
Mendel ES, 3735 TOPPING ST 77093
  Jack Ludwick, prin.
Oakwilde ES, 3007 HARTWICK ROAD 77093
  William Worsham, prin.
Oleson ES, 12345 VICKERY ST 77039
  Dora Murray, prin.
Orange Grove ES
  4515 MOUNT HOUSTON ROAD 77093
  Jeanette Verwold, prin.
Raymond ES, 1605 CONNORVALE ROAD 77039
  David Brenek, prin.
Sammons ES, 2301 FRICK ROAD 77038
  Jane Conner, prin.
Stephens ES
  14910 ALDINE WESTFIELD ROAD 77032
  Melanie Pritchett, prin.
Thompson ES, 220 CASA GRANDE DR 77060
  Patricia Sanders, prin.
Other Schools – See Humble

Alief ISD
Supt. – See Alief
Holub MS, 9515 S DAIRY ASHFORD ST 77099
  Colin Stanton, prin.
Olle MS, 9200 BOONE ROAD 77099
  Linda Sheeman, prin.

Clear Creek ISD
Supt. – See League City
Clear Lake IS, 15545 EL CAMINO REAL 77062
  Alan Schultz, prin.

Cypress-Fairbanks ISD
Sch. Sys. Enr. Code 8
Supt. – Donald Thornton, P O BOX 692003 77269
Arnold JHS, 22602 HEMPSTEAD ROAD 77040
  Charles Goodson, prin.
Bleyl JHS, 10800 MILLS ROAD 77070
  Bill Martin, prin.
Campbell JHS 77064 – Leonard Brautigam, prin.
Cook JHS 77269 – Jan Aragon, prin.
Labay JHS 77269 – Bob Warner, prin.
Watkins JHS 77269 – Titika Liollio, prin.
Adam ES, P O BOX 692003 77269
  Sandra Lawrence, prin.
Bane ES, 5805 KAISER ST 77040
  Debbie Emery, prin.
Dean JHS 77040 – Charles Wilson, prin.
Emmott ES, 11750 STEEPLE WAY BLVD 77065
  Norma Ault, prin.
Francone ES, 11250 PERRY ROAD 77064
  Arlene Robison, prin.
Frazier ES, 8300 LITTLE RIVER ROAD 77064
  Gwen Keith, prin.
Hancock ES, 13801 SCHROEDER ROAD 77070
  Beth Coleman, prin.
Holbrook ES, 6402 LANGFIELD ROAD 77092
  Susan Cichon, prin.
Holmsley ES, 7315 HUDSON OAKS DR 77095
  Barbara Goldstein, prin.
Horne ES, 14950 W LITTLE YORK ROAD 77084
  Nancy Sampson, prin.
Jowell ES 77269 – Barb Birkes, prin.
Lamkin ES, 11521 TELGE ROAD 77040
  Mary Stevens, prin.
Lieder ES, 17003 KIETH HARROW BLVD 77084
  Robbie Sheridan, prin.
Lowery ES, 15950 RIDGE PARK DR 77095
  Jane Andre, prin.
Matzke ES, 13102 JONES ROAD 77070
  Jane Tipps, prin.
Millsap ES, 12424 HUFFMEISTER ROAD 77065
  Jane Little, prin.
Moore ES, 13734 LAKEWOOD FOREST DR 77070
  Betty Rennell, prin.

Owens ES, 7939 JACKRABBIT ROAD 77095
  Melissa Ehrhardt, prin.
Post ES, 7600 EQUADOAR ST 77040
  Tom Danish, prin.
Wilson ES, 18015 KIETH HARROW BLVD 77084
  Barbara Fine, prin.
Yeager ES, 13615 CHAMPION FOREST DR 77069
  Margaret Gleason, prin.

Galena Park ISD
Supt. – See Galena Park
Cunningham MS 77015 – Corliss Rogers, prin.
North Shore MS
  13801 HOLLY PARK DRIVE 77015
  Raymond Kilgo, prin.
Woodland Acres MS
  12947 MYRTLE LANE 77015
  David Hopkins, prin.

Houston ISD
Sch. Sys. Enr. Code 9
Supt. – Joan Raymond
  3830 RICHMOND AVE 77027
Attucks MS, 4330 BELLFORT ST 77051
  Rudolph Wilson, prin.
Black MS, 1575 CHANTILLY LANE 77018
  Ana Guzman, prin.
Burbank MS, 315 BERRY ROAD 77022
  Erna Dempsey, prin.
Clifton MS, 3830 RICHMOND 77027
  Mira Baptiste, prin.
Contemporary Learning Center MS
  1906 CLEBURNE ST 77004
  Naurita Daniels, prin.
Cullen MS, 6900 SCOTT ST 77021
  Margaret Stroud, prin.
Deady MS, 2500 BROADWAY ST 77012
  Lydia Long, prin.
Dowling MS, 14000 STANCLIFF ST 77045
  La France Harris, prin.
Edison MS, 6901 AVE I 77011
  Carlos Pomares, prin.
Fleming MS, 4910 OCTAVIA ST 77026
  Ellis Douglas, prin.
Fondren MS, 6333 S BRAESWOOD BLVD 77096
  Caroline Lavois, prin.
Fonville MS, 725 E LITTLE YORK ROAD 77076
  Doyle Lakin, prin.
Gregory-Lincoln MS, 1101 TAFT ST 77019
  Margaret Kilgo, prin.
Hamilton MS, 139 E 20TH ST 77008
  Diana Mulet, prin.
Hartman MS, 7111 WESTOVER ST 77087
  Arnold Ramirez, prin.
Henry MS, 10702 E HARDY ST 77093
  Mary Thornton, prin.
Hogg MS, 1100 MERRILL ST 77009
  Nancy Hill, prin.
Holland MS 77029 – Edmund Broussard, prin.
Jackson MS, 5100 POLK ST 77023
  Cecilia Saenz, prin.
Johnston MS, 10410 MANHATTAN DRIVE 77096
  F. Turner, prin.
Key MS, 4000 KELLEY ST 77026
  Charles Henderson, prin.
Lanier MS, 2600 WOODHEAD ST 77098
  Letitia Codner, prin.
Long MS, 6501 BELLAIRE BLVD 77074
  Robert Parquharson, prin.
Marshall MS, 1115 NOBLE ST 77009
  L. Brown, prin.
McReynolds MS, 5910 MARKET ST 77020
  Richard Zamora, prin.
Pershing MS, 7000 BRAES BLVD 77025
  Claude Cunningham, prin.
Revere MS, 10502 BRIAR FOREST DRIVE 77042
  Dorothea Smith, prin.
Ryan MS, 2610 ELGIN ST 77004
  Roger Rideau, prin.
Sharpstown MS, 8330 TRIOLA LANE 77036
  J. Douglas Hooten, prin.
Smith MS, 3415 LYONS AVE 77020
  Fred Lewis, prin.
Terrell MS, 4610 CROSSTIMBERS ST 77016
  Carolyn Lindsey, prin.
Thomas MS, 5655 SELINSKY ROAD 77048
  Teresa Le Noir, prin.
Welch MS, 11544 S GESSNER DRIVE 77071
  Deborah Parker, prin.
Williams MS, 6100 KNOX ST 77091
  Ron Johnson, prin.
Woodson MS, 10720 SOUTHVIEW ST 77047
  Richard Gardner, prin.
Alcott ES, 5859 BELLFORT ST 77033
  Annie Haynes, prin.
Allen ES, 400 VICTORIA DR 77022
  Warren Ervin, prin.
Almeda ES, 14249 BRIDGEPORT ROAD 77047
  Nancy Nichols, prin.
Anderson ES, 5727 LUDINGTON DR 77035
  Georgia Hanna, prin.
Ashford ES, 1815 SHANNON VALLEY DR 77077
  Glenda Alvarey, prin.
Askew ES, 11200 WOODLODGE DR 77027
  (—), prin.
Atherton ES, 2011 SOLO ST 77020
  Nobelton Jones, prin.
Barrick ES, 12001 WINFREY LANE 77076
  Sara Gallo, prin.
Bastian ES, 7350 CALHOUN ROAD 77033
  Artice Hedgeman, prin.
Bell ES, 12323 SHAFTSBURY DRIVE 77031
  Elizabeth Howell, prin.

Benbrook ES, 4026 BOLIN ROAD 77092
  Mary Polhemus, prin.
Berry ES, 2310 BERRY ROAD 77093
  Marion Norris, prin.
Blackshear ES, 2900 HOLMAN ST 77004
  George Mundine, prin.
Bonham ES, 8302 BRAES RIVER DR 77074
  Susan Givens, prin.
Bonner ES, 8100 ELROD ST 77017
  Febe Urbina, prin.
Bowie ES, 7501 CURRY ROAD 77093
  Betty Pouncey, prin.
Braeburn ES, 7707 RAMPART ST 77081
  Bonnie Hughes, prin.
Briargrove ES, 6145 SAN FELIPE ST 77057
  Mary Cook, prin.
Briscoe ES, 321 FOREST HILL BLVD 77011
  Felipa Young, prin.
Brock ES, 1417 HOUSTON AVE 77007
  Clyde Hough, prin.
Brookline ES, 6301 SOUTH LOOP EAST 77012
  Norman Luther, prin.
Browning ES, 607 NORTHWOOD ST 77009
  Maria Barrientes, prin.
Bruce ES, 713 BRINGHURST ST 77020
  Charles Bryant, prin.
Burbank ES, 216 TIDWELL ROAD 77022
  Walter Day, prin.
Burnet ES, 5403 CANAL ST 77011
  Gonzalo Campos, prin.
Burrus ES, 701 E 33RD ST 77022
  Flossie Sylvester, prin.
Cage ES 77027 – Alan Vaughan, prin.
Carnegie ES, 10401 SCOTT ST 77051
  Freddie Kinnard, prin.
Chatham ES, 8110 BERTWOOD ST 77016
  Beverly Cashaw, prin.
Clinton Park ES, 158 MISSISSIPPI ST 77029
  Willie Coffin, prin.
Codwell ES, 5225 TAVENOR LANE 77048
  Loraine Bridgewater, prin.
Concord ES, 5426 CAVALCADE ST 77026
  Joan Graham, prin.
Condit ES, 3830 RICHMOND AVE 77027
  Doris Pasquali, prin.
Coop ES
  10130 ALDINE WESTFIELD ROAD 77093
  Mary Cherbonnier, prin.
Cornelius ES, 7475 WESTOVER ST 77087
  Martha Wong, prin.
Crawford ES, 1510 JENSEN DR 77020
  Charles Taylor, prin.
Crockett ES, 2212 CROCKETT ST 77007
  Elida Troutman, prin.
Cunningham ES, 5100 GULFTON ST 77081
  Rosemary Garza, prin.
DeChaumes ES, 155 COOPER ROAD 77076
  John Woods, prin.
Dezavala ES, 7521 AVENUE J 77012
  Sylvia Valverde, prin.
Dodson ES, 1808 SAMPSON ST 77003
  O. Curtis, prin.
Dogan ES, 4202 LIBERTY ROAD 77026
  Virginia Collins, prin.
Douglass ES, 3000 TRULLEY ST 77004
  LaSalle Donnell, prin.
Dow ES, 1900 KANE ST 77007
  Margaret Amaya, prin.
Durham ES, 4803 BRINKMAN ST 77018
  Sandra Satterwhite, prin.
Durkee ES, 7301 NORDLING ROAD 77076
  Alvin Frankel, prin.
Easter ES, 4435 WEAVER ROAD 77016
  Elna Kennedy, prin.
Eighth Avenue ES, 727 WAVERLY ST 77007
  Arthur Adams, prin.
Eliot ES, 6411 LAREDO ST 77020
  Margaret Acosta, prin.
Elrod ES, 6230 DUMFRIES DR 77096
  Joan Cullinane, prin.
Emerson ES, 9533 SKYLINE DRIVE 77063
  Herman Caldwell, prin.
Fairchild ES, 8701 DELILAH ST 77033
  Dolores Sandling, prin.
Field ES, 701 E 17TH ST 77008
  Mary Nikirk, prin.
Foerster ES, 14200 FONMEADOW DR 77035
  Yolande Eugere, prin.
Fondren ES, 12405 CARLSBAD ST 77085
  James Brock, prin.
Foster ES, 3913 WARD ST 77021
  Donald Hunter, prin.
Franklin ES, 7100 CANAL ST 77011
  Jesse Pryor, prin.
Frost ES, 5650 SELINSKY ROAD 77048
  Alice Griffin, prin.
Garden Oaks ES, 901 SUE BARNETT DR 77018
  Jean Dodd, prin.
Garden Villas ES, 7185 SANTA FE DR 77061
  Herbert Karpicke, prin.
Golfcrest ES, 7414 FAIRWAY DR 77087
  Laura Jeanes, prin.
Gordon ES 77027 – Bob Taylor, prin.
Gregg ES, 6701 ROXBURY ROAD 77087
  Harold Routt, prin.
Gregor-Lincoln ES, 1101 TAFT ST 77019
  Margaret Kilgo, prin.
Grimes ES, 9220 JUTLAND ROAD 77033
  Judy Allen, prin.
Grissom ES, 4901 SIMSBROOK DR 77045
  Pat Finch, prin.
Harris ES, 801 BORADWAY ST 77012
  George Smith, prin.
Harris ES 77027 – Gloria Howard, prin.

Hartsfield ES, 5001 PERRY ST   77021
  Lori Collins, prin.
Harvard ES, 810 HARVARD ST   77007
  Richard Resin, prin.
Helms ES, 503 W 21ST ST   77008
  Teodoro Villarreal, prin.
Henderson ES, 1800 DISMUKE ST   77023
  Herlinda Garcia, prin.
Henderson ES, 701 SOLO ST   77020
  Lois Pettis, prin.
Herod ES, 5628 JASON ST   77096
  Nancy Nichols, prin.
Highland Heights ES, 865 PAUL QUINN ST   77091
  Helen Ward, prin.
Hobby ES, 4021 WOODMONT DR   77045
  Ray Williams, prin.
Hohl ES, 5320 YALE ST   77091
  Lawrence Brown, prin.
Holden ES, 810 W 28TH ST   77008
  Linda Miller, prin.
Horn ES, 4535 PINE ST   77081
  Mary Ashmore, prin.
Houston Gardens ES   77028 – Glyn Johnson, prin.
Isaacs ES, 3830 PICKFAIR ST   77026
  Leon Pettis, Jr., prin.
Jannowski ES, 7500 BAUMAN ROAD   77022
  Rita Poimbeauf, prin.
Jefferson ES, 5000 SHARMAN ST   77009
  Armandina Farias, prin.
Jones ES, 2311 CANAL ST   77003
  Charles Ross, prin.
Jones ES, 1800 STUART ST   77004
  Bessie Hickman, prin.
Kashmere Gardens ES
  4901 LOCKWOOD DR   77026
  Alberta Smith, prin.
Kelso ES, 5800 SOUTHMUND ST   77033
  Debra Hayes, prin.
Kennedy ES, 306 CROSSTIMBERS ST   77022
  Will Evans, prin.
Kolter ES, 9710 RUNNYMEADE DR   77096
  Elaine Allen, prin.
Lamar ES, 2209 GENTRY ST   77009
  Rebecca Cazares, prin.
Langston ES, 2814 QUITMAN ST   77026
  James Brewer, prin.
Lantrip ES   77023 – Gloria Silva, prin.
Law ES, 12401 S COAST DR   77047
  Jean Alexander, prin.
Lee ES, 2101 SOUTH ST   77009 – (—), prin.
Lewis ES, 7649 ROCKHILL ST   77061
  Sue Payne, prin.
Lockhart ES, 3501 SOUTHMORE BLVD   77004
  Mary Wilson, prin.
Longfellow ES, 3614 MURWORTH DR   77025
  Linda Bair, prin.
Looscan ES, 3800 ROBERTSON ST   77009
  Sandra Cantu, prin.
Love ES, 1120 W 13TH ST   77008
  Patsy Cavazos, prin.
Lovett ES, 8814 S RICE AVE   77096
  Annie Smith, prin.
MacArthur ES, 5909 ENGLAND ST   77021
  Bobbye Harris, prin.
MacGregor ES, 4801 LA BRANCH ST   77004
  Karin Shipman, prin.
Mading ES, 8511 CRESTMONT ST   77033
  Johnnie Johnson, prin.
Twain ES   77025 – Sally Clyburn, prin.
McDade ES, 5815 HIRSCH ROAD   77026
  Ethel Lewis, prin.
McNamara ES, 8714 MCAVOY DR   77074
  Carolyn Spears, prin.
Memorial ES, 6401 ARNOT ST   77007
  Thelma Garza, prin.
Milam ES, 5000 CENTER ST   77007
  John Bell, prin.
Mitchell ES, 10900 GULFDALE DR   77075
  Rosa Graham, prin.
Montgomery ES, 4000 SIMSBROOK DR   77045
  Alice Rains, prin.
Neff ES, 8100 CARVEL LANE   77036
  Esther Chess, prin.
Northline ES, 821 E WITCHER LANE   77076
  Sarah Cordray, prin.
Oak Forest ES, 1401 W 43RD ST   77018
  Sharon Koonce, prin.
Oates ES, 10044 WALLISVILLE ROAD   77013
  Maria Diaz, prin.
Osborne ES   77027 – Gloria Jones, prin.
Park Place ES, 3701 HASTINGS ST   77017
  Laura Covington, prin.
Parker ES, 10626 ATWELL DR   77096
  Jean Crouchet, prin.
Patterson ES, 5302 ALLENDALE ROAD   77017
  Barbara Turner, prin.
Peck ES, 5116 ARVILLA LANE   77021
  Anita Ellis, prin.
Petersen ES, 14404 WATERLOO DR   77045
  Anne Scardino, prin.
Pilgrim ES, 3315 BARRINGTON ROAD   77056
  Kermit Harper, prin.
Piney Point ES, 8921 PAGEWOOD LANE   77063
  Betty Van Maszewski, prin.
Pleasants ES, 1305 BENSON ST   77020
  Herbert Elmore, prin.
Pleasantville ES, 1431 GELLHORN DR   77029
  Elmyra Turner, prin.
Poe ES, 5100 HAZARD ST   77098
  Martha Schumacher, prin.
Port Houston ES, 1800 MCCARTY ST   77029
  (—), prin.
Pugh ES, 1147 KRESS ST   77020
  Judith Premazon, prin.

Red ES, 4520 TONAWANDA DR   77035
  Virginia Westmoreland, prin.
Reynolds ES, 9601 ROSEHAVEN DR   77051
  Marine Hanchett, prin.
Rhoads ES, 4103 BRISBANE ST   77047
  Althea Cooper, prin.
River Oaks ES, 2008 KIRBY DR   77019
  Michele Pola, prin.
Roberts ES   77030 – Charlotte Haynes, prin.
Rogers ES   77027 – (—), prin.
Roosevelt ES, 6700 FULTON ST   77022
  Earleane Bell, prin.
Ross ES, 2819 BAY ST   77026
  Dalton Hughes, prin.
Rucker ES, 5201 VINETT ST   77017
  Mike Billette, prin.
Rusk ES, 2805 GARROW ST   77003
  Patricia Gonzale, prin.
Ryan ES, 4000 HARDY ST   77009
  Luella Sims, prin.
Sanchez ES, 2700 BERKLEY ST   77012
  Augustine Marcellus, prin.
Sanderson ES, 7115 LOCKWOOD DR   77016
  Iris Ashley, prin.
Scarborough ES, 3021 LITTLE YORK ROAD   77093
  Victoria Mauldin, prin.
Scott ES, 3300 RUSSELL ST   77026
  Ed Perry, prin.
Scroggins ES, 400 BOYLES ST   77020
  San Juana Elizondo, prin.
Shearn ES, 9802 STELLA LINK ROAD   77025
  Doris Bilton, prin.
Sherman ES, 1505 LORRAINE ST   77009
  Hilda Stickney, prin.
Sinclair ES, 6410 GROVEWOOD LANE   77008
  Elizabeth Deuble, prin.
Smith ES, 4802 CHRYSTELL LANE   77092
  Doris Roy, prin.
Southmayd ES, 1800 CORAL ST   77012
  Gloria Villarrial, prin.
Stevens ES, 1910 LA MONTE LANE   77018
  Jessie Grant, prin.
Stevenson ES, 2116 RADCLIFFE ST   77007
  Alberto Ramirez, prin.
Sunnyside ES, 3555 BELLFORT ST   77051
  Charles Tilmon, prin.
Sutton ES, 7402 ALBACAORE DR   77074
  R. Davis, prin.
Thompson ES, 3535 DIXIE DR   77021
  Billie Johnson, prin.
Tijerina ES, 6501 SHERMAN ST   77011
  Jacel Morgan, prin.
Travis ES, 3311 BEAUCHAMP ST   77009
  Celia Ramirez, prin.
Turner ES, 3200 ROSEDALE ST   77004
  Andre Hornsby, prin.
Wainwright ES, 5330 MILWEE ST   77092
  Jerome Vinklarek, prin.
Walnut Bend ES, 10620 BRIAR FOREST DR   77042
  Bonnie Hughes, prin.
Wesley ES, 800 DILLARD ST   77091 – T. Lott, prin.
West University ES
  3756 UNIVERSITY BLVD   77005
  Anne Patterson, prin.
Wharton ES, 900 W GRAY ST   77019
  Siro Guitierrez, prin.
Whidby ES, 7625 SPRINGHILL ST   77021
  Vivian Harrison, prin.
White ES, 9001 TRIOLA LANE   77036
  Margaret Beltran, prin.
Whittier ES, 10511 LA CROSSE ST   77029
  Jeanine Poth, prin.
Rogers ES, 3830 RICHMOND   77027
  Anna Bruner, prin.
Wilson ES, 2100 YUPON ST   77006
  Ferne Pernoud, prin.
Windsor Village ES, 14440 POLO ST   77085
  Alma Allen, prin.

Katy ISD
Supt. – See Katy
Mayde Creek JHS   77084 – Kenneth Egger, prin.
Bear Creek ES, 4815 HICKORY DOWNS DR   77084
  Sandra Shenkir, prin.
Mayde Creek ES
  2698 GREENHOUSE ROAD   77084
  Elsie Huang, prin.
Nottingham Country ES
  20500 KINGSLAND BLVD   77094
  Malcolm Smith, prin.
Sundown ES, 20100 SAUMS   77084
  Ursula Stephens, prin.

Klein ISD
Supt. – See Spring
Wunderlich IS   77066 – Kay Dawdy, prin.
Epps Island ES
  7403 SMILING WOOD LANE   77086
  Merri Lebo, prin.
Greenwood Forest ES
  12100 MISTY VALLEY DR   77066
  Darrel Luedeker, prin.
Kaiser ES, 13430 BEAMER ROAD   77089
  Dennis Redford, prin.
Nitsch ES
  4702 W MOUNT HOUSTON ROAD   77088
  James Cain, prin.

North Forest ISD
Sch. Sys. Enr. Code 7
Supt. – Robert Jones, P O BOX 23278   77228
Elmore MS, 8200 TATE ST   77028
  Willie Edwards, prin.

Kirby MS
  9709 E HOUSTON-DYERSDALE RD   77078
  Adley Richard, prin.
Northwood MS
  10750 HOMESTEAD ROAD   77016
  J. Lundy, prin.
Oak Village MS, 6602 WINFIELD ROAD   77050
  Lillian Parker, prin.
East Houston ES, 8115 E HOUSTON ROAD   77028
  Tom Dover, prin.
Fonwood ES   77228 – Ben Petteway, prin.
Hilliard ES   77228 – Rufus Allen, prin.
Keahey ES   77228 – Essie Thomas, prin.
Lakewood ES   77228 – (—), prin.
Mount Houston ES   77228 – Roy Ford, prin.
Rogers ES   77228 – Maxine Craig, prin.
Shadydale ES, 5905 TIDWELL ROAD   77016
  Mary Holman, prin.
Tidwell ES, 8000 TIDWELL ROAD   77028
  Theodore Merrell, prin.

Pasadena ISD
Supt. – See Pasadena
Beverly Hills IS, 10415 FUQUA ST   77089
  Thomas Baccaro, prin.
Thompson IS, 11309 SAGEDOWNE LANE   77089
  E. Ritchey, prin.
Atkinson ES, 9602 KINGSPOINT ROAD   77075
  Hollis Powell, prin.
Burnett ES, 11825 TEANECK DR   77089
  Sally Sherrod, prin.
Frazier ES, 10503 HUGHES ROAD   77089
  Sharon Oakes, prin.
Freeman ES, 2323 THETA ST   77034
  Judy Bowers, prin.
Garfield ES, 10301 HARTSOOK ST   77034
  Gilberto De Leon, prin.
Genoa ES, 12900 ALMEDA ROAD   77045
  Erwin Peterson, prin.
Jessup ES, P O BOX 1799   77501
  Doris Rusciano, prin.
Meador ES, 10701 SEAFORD DR   77089
  Stephen Laymon, prin.
Stuchbery ES, 11210 HUGHES ROAD   77089
  Nancy Teichelman, prin.

Sheldon ISD
Sch. Sys. Enr. Code 5
Supt. – Max Nichter
  8540 C E KING PARKWAY   77044
King JHS, 8540 C E KING PARKWAY   77044
  Mike Null, prin.
Monahan ES, 8901 DEEP VALLEY DR   77044
  James Blanscet, prin.
Parkway ES, 8540 C E KING PARKWAY   77044
  R. Thompson, prin.
Royalwood ES, 7715 ROYALWOOD DR   77049
  Stephanie Cravens, prin.
Sheldon ES   77044 – J. White, prin.
Sheldon IS   77044 – (—), prin.

Spring Branch ISD
Sch. Sys. Enr. Code 8
Supt. – Harold Guthrie
  955 CAMPBELL ROAD   77024
Landrum JHS   77055 – Linda Watkins, prin.
Memorial JHS, 12550 VINDON DRIVE   77024
  M. Eldridge, prin.
Spring Branch JHS
  1000 PINEY POINT ROAD   77024
  Tom Byrd, prin.
Spring Forrest JHS
  14240 MEMORIAL DRIVE   77079
  B. Allison, prin.
Spring Oaks JHS
  2150 SHADOWDALE DRIVE   77043
  Ken Young, prin.
Spring Woods JHS   77080 – Gracie Clouse, prin.
Bunker Hill ES   77024 – Connie Myers, prin.
Edgewood ES, 8655 EMNORA LANE   77080
  Dorothy Greer, prin.
Frostwood ES   77024 – Jean Quigg, prin.
Hollibrook ES, 3602 HOLLISTER ST   77080
  Suzanne Still, prin.
Housman ES, 6820 HOMESTEAD ROAD   77028
  Pam Stout, prin.
Hunters Creek ES   77024 – Ruth Stafford, prin.
Meadow Wood ES, 14230 MEMORIAL DR   77079
  Barb Moore, prin.
Memorial Drive ES   77024 – Gloria Fishman, prin.
Nottingham ES   77079 – Jim Felle, prin.
Pine Shadows ES, 9900 NEENS RIAD   77080
  Jackie Day, prin.
Ridgecrest ES, 2015 RIDGECREST DR   77055
  S. Calendar, prin.
Rummel Creek ES   77079 – Shirley Lincoln, prin.
Shadow Oaks ES   77043 – Yvonne Gill, prin.
Sherwood ES
  1700 SHERWOOD FOREST ST   77043
  Marcia McCall, prin.
Spring Branch ES, 1700 CAMPBELL ROAD   77080
  Suzanne Fennell, prin.
Spring Shadow ES   77080 – Linda Reed, prin.
Terrace ES, 955 CAMPBELL ROAD   77024
  Evelyn Clark, prin.
Thornwood ES, 955 CAMPBELL ROAD   77024
  Mable Henderson, prin.
Valley Oaks ES, 8390 WESTVIEW DR   77055
  Vicki Hardway, prin.
Westwood ES, 2100 SHADOWDALE DR   77043
  Elise Tapp, prin.
Wilchester ES, 13618 SAINT MARYS LANE   77079
  Martha Bair, prin.
Woodview ES, 9749 CEDARDALE DR   77055
  Joyce Ryan, prin.

Spring ISD
Sch. Sys. Enr. Code 7
Supt. – Gordon Anderson
16717 ELLA BLVD 77090
Bammel MS 77090 – J. Riddle, prin.
Wells MS, 4033 GLADERIDGE DRIVE 77068
Gene LaForge, prin.
Anderson ES, 16717 ELLA BLVD 77090
Jean Polarolo, prin.
Bammel ES, 17309 RED OAK DR 77090
Karen Archer, prin.
Beneke ES 77090 – Judy Frost, prin.
Jenkins ES, 16717 ELLA BLVD 77090
Chris Kuhlmann, prin.
Link ES, 2815 RIDGE HOLLOW DR 77067
David Scarpino, prin.
Meyer ES, 16330 FOREST WAY DR 77090
Milton Cooper, prin.
Oak Creek ES, 3975 GLADERIDGE DR 77068
Pat Reynolds, prin.
Ponderosa ES, 17202 BUTTE CREEK ROAD 77090
Peggy Black, prin.
Salyers ES, 16717 ELLA BLVD 77090
Rosalind Keck, prin.
Smith ES 77090 – Marjorie Cain, prin.
Other Schools – See Spring

Awty International School, P O BOX 55489 77255
Briarwood School
12207 WHITTINGTON DRIVE 77077
Broadway Baptist School, 1020 CORAL ST 77012
Duchesne Academy of the Sacred Heart
10202 MEMORIAL DRIVE 77024
Hebrew Academy
5435 S BRAESWOOD BLVD 77096
Kinkaid School
201 KINKAID SCHOOL DRIVE 77024
Memorial Hall School, 3721 DACOMA ST 77092
Northland Christian School
2700 F M 1960 ROAD W 77068
Northwest Academy
4211 WATONGA BLVD 77092
Second Baptist School
6400 WOODWAY DR 77057
Seton Catholic JHS, 801 ROSELANE ST 77037
St. John's School, 2401 CLAREMONT ST 77019
Westbury Christian School
10420 HILLCROFT ST 77096
All Saints ES, 215 E 10TH ST 77008
Annunciation Orthodox ES
3511 YOAKUM BLVD 77006
Ascension Episcopal School
2525 SEAGLER ROAD 77042
Baptist Temple ES, 230 W 20TH ST 77008
Beth Yeshurun ES, 4525 BEECHNUT ST 77096
Bethany Lutheran ES, 522 LINDALE ST 77022
Blessed Sacrament ES, 4015 SHERMAN ST 77003
Carethers SDA School, 5878 BELLFORT ST 77058
Corpus Christi ES, 4005 CHEENA DR 77025
Holy Ghost School
6920 CHIMNEY ROCK ROAD 77081
Holy Name ES, 1912 MARION ST 77009
Holy Spirit Episcopal ES
12535 PERTHSHIRE ROAD 77024
Immaculate Heart of Mary ES
7535 AVENUE L 77012
Immanuel-Bethlehem ES, 306 E 15TH ST 77008
Lutheran North ES, 215 RITTENHOUSE ST 77076
Memorial Lutheran ES
5800 WESTHEIMER ROAD 77057
Our Lady of Guadalupe ES, 2410 ANN ST 77003
Our Lady of Mt. Carmel ES
6703 WHITEFRIARS DR 77087
Our Mother of Mercy ES, 2000 BENSON ST 77020
Our Savior Lutheran ES
4425 N SHEPHERD DR 77018
Pilgrim Lutheran School
8601 CHIMNEY ROCK 77096
Queen of Peace ES, 2320 OAKCLIFF ST 77023
Redd ES, 4820 STRACK ROAD 77069
Redd Reading Center ES
5310 PALMETTO ST 77081
Resurrection ES, 916 MAJESTIC ST 77020
Resurrection School, 916 MAJESTIC ST 77020
River Oaks Baptist ES
2300 WILLOWICK ROAD 77027
School of the Woods ES, 1321 WIRT ROAD 77055
Sharpstown Christian School
8405 BONHOMME ROAD 77074
St. Agnes Baptist ES, 3730 S ACRES DRIVE 77047
St. Ambrose ES, 4213 MANGUM ROAD 77092
St. Anne's ES, 2120 W HEIMER ROAD 77098
St. Augustine ES
5500 LAUREL CREEK WAY 77017
St. Barnabas Episcopal School
107 E EDGEBROOK DR 77034
St. Catherine Montessori School
2510 WESTRIDGE ST 77054
St. Cecelia ES, 11740 JOAN OF ARC DR 77024
St. Charles Borromeo ES
501 TIDWELL ROAD 77022
St. Christopher ES
8134 PARK PLACE BLVD 77017
St. Francis De Sales ES, 8100 ROOS ROAD 77036
St. Francis Episcopal Day School
345 PINEY POINT ROAD 77024
St. Francis of Assisi ES, 5100 DABNEY ST 77026
St. Jerome Catholic ES
8825 KEMPWOOD DR 77080
St. John Lutheran School, 404 66TH ST 77011
St. Mark Lutheran School
1515 HILLENDAHL BLVD 77055

St. Mark's Episcopal ES
3816 BELLAIRE BLVD 77025
St. Mary ES, 3006 ROSEDALE ST 77004
St. Matthew Lutheran School
5315 MAIN ST 77004
St. Michael Catholic ES, 1833 SAGERD 77056
St. Peter the Apostle ES
6220 LA SALETTE ST 77021
St. Phillip Neri ES, 10950 S PARK BLVD 77048
St. Rose of Lima ES, 3604 BRINKMAN ST 77018
St. Theresa ES, 6622 HASKELL ST 77007
St. Thomas Apostle Day School
P O BOX 58824 77258
St. Thomas More ES, 5927 WIGTON DR 77096
St. Vincent De Paul ES
6802 BUFFALO SPEEDWAY 77025
The Hebrew Academy ES
5435 S BRAESWOOD BLVD 77096
Torah Day ES, 10900 FONDREN ROAD 77096
Trinity Messiah Lutheran School
800 HOUSTON AVE 77007
Varnett ES, P O BOX 1457 77251
Village ES, 13077 WEST ELLA 77077

Howe, Grayson Co., Pop. Code 4
Howe ISD
Sch. Sys. Enr. Code 3
Supt. – Pete Simmons, P O BOX 1878 75059
MS 75059 – Tom Skipworth, prin.
ES, ROBERTS 75059 – Darlene Pyland, prin.

Hubbard, Hill Co., Pop. Code 4
Hubbard ISD
Sch. Sys. Enr. Code 2
Supt. – Bill Eitel, P O BOX 218 76648
ES 76648 – Wayne Kilgo, prin.
MS 76648 – Kathleen Connor, prin.

Huffman, Harris Co., Pop. Code 3
Huffman ISD
Sch. Sys. Enr. Code 4
Supt. – Douglass Shands, P O BOX 69 77336
MS 77336 – Glenn Lemke, prin.
Bowen ES, 24403 LAKE HOUSTON PKWY 77336
Lewine Foster, prin.
Huffman IS 77336 – Laura Traywick, prin.

Hughes Springs, Cass Co., Pop. Code 4
Hughes Springs ISD
Sch. Sys. Enr. Code 3
Supt. – Leland Cockrill, P O BOX 398 75656
JHS 75656 – Bob Stewart, prin.
ES, 700 N RUSSELL 75656 – Carolyn Smires, prin.

Humble, Harris Co., Pop. Code 6
Aldine ISD
Supt. – See Houston
Teague MS, 21700 RAYFORD ROAD 77338
Sue Wooten, prin.

Humble ISD
Sch. Sys. Enr. Code 7
Supt. – Michael Say, P O BOX 2000 77347
Atascocita MS 77392 – Ron Westerfeld, prin.
Creekwood MS, P O BOX 2000 77347
Paul Roser, prin.
MS, 1131 WILSON ROAD 77338
Walter Denny, prin.
Kingwood MS
3000 WOODLAND HILLS DR 77339
Margaret Puckett, prin.
Bear Branch ES 77347 – Margaret Long, prin.
Deerwood ES 77347 – Pat Dinhoble, prin.
Elm Grove ES 77347 – Coleen Killingsworth, prin.
Foster ES 77347 – Carol Suell, prin.
Greentree ES 77347 – Nancy Pinkerton, prin.
ES 77338 – Robert Cunningham, prin.
Lakeland ES 77347 – Betty Brewster, prin.
North Belt ES 77347 – William Mackey, prin.
Oaks ES 77347 – Jane Nelson, prin.
Pineforest ES 77347 – Nancy Morrison, prin.
Timbers ES 77347 – Charlotte Coffelt, prin.
Willow Creek ES 77347 – John Widmier, prin.
Woodland Hills ES 77347 – Diane Lazarine, prin.

Hunt, Kerr Co.
Hunt ISD
Sch. Sys. Enr. Code 2
Supt. – James Hesson, P O BOX 259 78024
ES 78024 – James Hesson, prin.

Huntington, Angelina Co., Pop. Code 4
Huntington ISD
Sch. Sys. Enr. Code 4
Supt. – H. Chafin, P O BOX 328 75949
JHS 75949 – William Castleberry, prin.
ES 75949 – Jennifer Jones, prin.

Huntsville, Walker Co., Pop. Code 7
Huntsville ISD
Sch. Sys. Enr. Code 6
Supt. – (—), P O BOX 959 77340
JHS 77340 – Earnest Grover, prin.
Mance Park JHS 77340 – Clayton Waits, prin.
Gibbs ES 77340 – Joyce Merchant, prin.
Houston ES, 341 OLD MADISONVILLE RD 77340
Morris Johnson, prin.
Johnson ES 77340 – Elmo Feazell, prin.
Stewart ES 77340 – Regina Ginsel, prin.

Hurst, Tarrant Co., Pop. Code 8
Hurst-Euless-Bedford ISD
Supt. – See Bedford
Bellaire ES, 501 BELLAIRE DRIVE 76053
Jo Singleton, prin.
Donna Park ES, 1125 SCOTT DR 76053
Price Lee, prin.

Harrison Lane ES, 1000 HARRISON LANE 76053
Carol Small, prin.
Hurst Hills ES, 525 BILLIE RUTH LANE 76053
Bill Goode, prin.
Shady Oaks ES, 1400 CAVENDER DRIVE 76053
Bob Yarbrough, prin.
West Hurst ES
501 N PRECINCT LINE ROAD 76053
Darlene Chapman, prin.

Hutchins, Dallas Co., Pop. Code 5
Wilmer-Hutchins ISD
Supt. – See Dallas
ES, 700 N DENTON ST 75141
John Ryan, Jr., prin.
Winn IS, 1701 S MILLERS FERRY ROAD 75141
Dorsey Lewis, prin.

Hutto, Williamson Co., Pop. Code 3
Hutto ISD
Sch. Sys. Enr. Code 3
Supt. – Ernest Laurence, P O BOX 128 78634
ES 78634 – Thomas Gola, prin.

Idalou, Lubbock Co., Pop. Code 4
Idalou ISD
Sch. Sys. Enr. Code 3
Supt. – Robert Moore, P O BOX 1338 79329
JHS 79329 – Richard Belt, prin.
ES, P O BOX 1399 79329 – Emory Grayson, prin.

Imperial, Pecos Co., Pop. Code 3
Buena Vista ISD
Sch. Sys. Enr. Code 2
Supt. – Max Fly, P O BOX 310 79743
Buena Vista ES, P O BOX 310 79743
Elwen Wilson, prin.

Ingleside, San Patricio Co., Pop. Code 6
Ingleside ISD
Sch. Sys. Enr. Code 4
Supt. – G. Mircovich, P O BOX HH 78362
Taylor JHS 78362 – Gene Schreiber, prin.
Blaschke-Sheldon MS 78362
Luis Rodriguez, prin.
Cook ES 78362 – Brenda Richardson, prin.

Ingram, Kerr Co., Pop. Code 3
Ingram ISD
Sch. Sys. Enr. Code 3
Supt. – Carol Moffett, 700 HWY 39 78025
ES 78025 – Donald Williams, prin.

Iola, Grimes Co.
Iola ISD
Sch. Sys. Enr. Code 2
Supt. – Larry Curry, P O BOX 159 77861
ES, P O BOX 159 77861 – Kim Holland, prin.

Iowa Park, Wichita Co., Pop. Code 6
Iowa Park Cons. ISD
Sch. Sys. Enr. Code 4
Supt. – Glen Mitchell, P O BOX 898 76367
JHS, 412 E CASH ST 76367 – James Alsup, prin.
Bradford MS, 800 S TEXOWA ST 76367
Charles Davis, prin.
Kidwell ES, 1200 N 3RD ST 76367
Ronald Woods, prin.

Ira, Scurry Co.
Ira ISD
Sch. Sys. Enr. Code 2
Supt. – Jay Martin, P O BOX 248 79527
S 79527 – Larry Long, prin.

Iraan, Pecos Co., Pop. Code 4
Iraan-Sheffield ISD
Sch. Sys. Enr. Code 3
Supt. – Roy Dodds, P O BOX 486 79744
JHS 79744 – Don Malone, prin.
ES 79744 – Gerald Ritchie, prin.
Sheffield ES 79744 – William McClure, prin.

Iredell, Bosque Co., Pop. Code 2
Iredell ISD
Sch. Sys. Enr. Code 2
Supt. – Charles Yarbrough, P O BOX 39 76649
S 76449 – Kary Owens, prin.

Irving, Dallas Co., Pop. Code 9
Irving ISD
Sch. Sys. Enr. Code 7
Supt. – William McKinney, P O BOX 2637 75061
Austin JHS, 825 E UNION BOWER ROAD 75061
Kenneth Tillman, prin.
Bowie JHS, 600 E 6TH ST 75060
James Puryear, prin.
Crockett JHS, 2431 HANCOCK ST 75061
Lane Ladewig, prin.
Houston JHS
4625 N COUNTRY CLUB ROAD 75038
William Althoff, prin.
Lamar JHS, 219 CRANDALL ROAD 75060
William McAlister, prin.
Travis JHS, 1600 FINLEY ROAD 75062
Max Whitley, prin.
Barton ES, 2931 CONFLANS ROAD 75061
Judy Melton, prin.
Brandenburg ES, 2800 HILLCREST DR 75062
Evelyn Clifton, prin.
Britain ES, 631 EDMONDSON DR 75060
Larry Wilkinson, prin.
Brown ES, 2501 W 10TH ST 75060
Kenneth Wages, prin.
Elliott ES, 1900 S STORY ROAD 75060
Barbara Kemp, prin.

Farine ES, 615 METKER ST 75062
 Wallace Wimbish, prin.
Good ES, 1200 E UNION BOWER ROAD 75061
 Earl Cook, prin.
Haley J. ES, 224 S MACARTHUR BLVD 75060
 Artice Tate, prin.
Haley T. ES, 3900 W NORTHGATE DR 75062
 Myrna Lancaster, prin.
Hanes ES, 2730 CHEYENNE ST 75062
 John Pickens, prin.
Johnston ES, 2801 RUTGERS DR 75062
 Barbara Jasper, prin.
Keyes ES, 115 W GRAUWYLER ROAD 75061
 Robert Voelkle, prin.
Lee ES, 1600 CARLISLE ST 75062
 Cecil Carson, prin.
Lively ES, 1800 E PLYMOUTH DR 75061
 A. Brazil, prin.
Schulze ES, 16000 E SHADY GROVE ROAD 75060
 Douglas Baum, prin.
Townley ES, 1030 W VILBIG ST 75060
 Margaret Young, prin.

Holy Family of Nazareth ES
 2323 CHEYENNE ST 75062
Redeemer Montessori School
 120 E ROCHELLE ROAD 75062
St. Luke ES, 1023 SCHULZE DR 75060

Italy, Ellis Co., Pop. Code 4
Italy ISD
Sch. Sys. Enr. Code 3
Supt. – George Scott, P O BOX 909 76651
Stafford ES, 515 HARRIS ST 76651
 David Roland, prin.

Itasca, Hill Co., Pop. Code 4
Itasca ISD
Sch. Sys. Enr. Code 3
Supt. – Harvey Wilson, P O BOX 567 76055
ES 76055 – Larry Baer, prin.

Ivanhoe, Fannin Co.
Sam Rayburn ISD
Sch. Sys. Enr. Code 2
Supt. – Jim Smith
 RURAL ROUTE 01 BOX 127 75447
Rayburn ES, RURAL ROUTE 01 BOX 127 75447
 Judy Kissinger, prin.

Jacksboro, Jack Co., Pop. Code 5
Jacksboro ISD
Sch. Sys. Enr. Code 3
Supt. – Ray Crass, 812 W BELKNAP ST 76056
Lowrance MS, 117 N 4TH ST 76056
 Larry Johnson, prin.
ES, 119 N 4TH ST 76056 – Truetta Walker, prin.

Jacksonville, Cherokee Co., Pop. Code 7
Jacksonville ISD
Sch. Sys. Enr. Code 5
Supt. – Harry Beavers, P O BOX 631 75766
MS, P O BOX 631 75766 – Bill Stewart, prin.
East Side ES, 111 FORT WORTH ST 75766
 Jean Mixon, prin.
IS, TROUP HIGHWAY 75766 – James Spivey, prin.
Wright ES, 215 KICKAPOO ST 75766
 Rose Cunningham, prin.

Jarrell, Williamson Co.
Jarrell ISD
Sch. Sys. Enr. Code 2
Supt. – Larry Hausenfluke, P O BOX 429 76537
ES 76537 – Vince Trevino, prin.

Jasper, Jasper Co., Pop. Code 6
Jasper ISD
Sch. Sys. Enr. Code 5
Supt. – Arthur Kees, 128 PARK LANE 75951
MS 75951 – Billy Burt, prin.
Parnell ES, 151 PARK LANE 75951
 Elwin Watson, prin.
Rowe MS, HIGHWAY 190 E 75951
 Preston Moore, prin.

Trinity Episcopal ES, 105 COLLIER ST 75951

Jayton, Kent Co., Pop. Code 3
Jayton-Girard ISD
Sch. Sys. Enr. Code 2
Supt. – Gary Harrell, P O BOX 167 79528
ES 79528 – Eugene Harris, prin.

Jefferson, Marion Co., Pop. Code 5
Jefferson ISD
Sch. Sys. Enr. Code 4
Supt. – James Richardson, 510 S LINE ST 75657
MS 75657 – Arthur Wesley, prin.
ES 75657 – Carol Harrell, prin.

Stanton ISD
Supt. – See Stanton
Stanton ES 75657 – Jim White, prin.

Jewett, Leon Co., Pop. Code 3
Leon ISD
Sch. Sys. Enr. Code 3
Supt. – E. McAdams, P O BOX 157 75846
Leon JHS 75846 – Starley Cogdell, prin.
Leon ES 75846 – Jay Winn, prin.

Joaquin, Shelby Co., Pop. Code 3
Joaquin ISD
Sch. Sys. Enr. Code 3
Supt. – Charles Thompson, P O BOX 338 75954
Fellowship ES 75935 – Elmer Mathews, prin.

Johnson City, Blanco Co., Pop. Code 3
Johnson City ISD
Sch. Sys. Enr. Code 3
Supt. – Quentin Burnett, P O BOX 98 78636
ES 78636 – Orville Westbrook, prin.
IS 78636 – Orville Westbrook, prin.

Jonesboro, Coryell Co.
Jonesboro ISD
Sch. Sys. Enr. Code 2
Supt. – James Tollett, P O BOX 125 76538
S 76538 – J. Lightsey, prin.

Joshua, Johnson Co., Pop. Code 4
Joshua ISD
Sch. Sys. Enr. Code 4
Supt. – Bob Hawes, P O BOX 40 76058
MS 76058 – R. Loflin, prin.
ES 76058 – Randolph Garner, prin.
IS 76058 – Marion Mccarroll, prin.

Jourdanton, Atascosa Co., Pop. Code 5
Jourdanton ISD
Sch. Sys. Enr. Code 4
Supt. – James Hill, 200 ZANDERSON AVE 78026
JHS 78026 – Robert Rutkowski, prin.
ES 78026 – Don McAskill, prin.

Junction, Kimble Co., Pop. Code 5
Junction ISD
Sch. Sys. Enr. Code 3
Supt. – George Wright, 1700 COLLEGE ST 76849
MS 76849 – Dale Ethridge, prin.
ES 76849 – Jerry Massingill, prin.

Justin, Denton Co., Pop. Code 3
Northwest ISD
Sch. Sys. Enr. Code 5
Supt. – J. Ammons
 RURAL ROUTE 01 BOX 39A 76247
Northwest MS 76247 – Robert Hines, prin.
Haslet ES 76247 – Beverly Watson, prin.
ES 76247 – Celene Claude, prin.
Lakeview ES 76247 – Sharon Caplan, prin.
Roanoke MS 76247 – Beverly Watson, prin.
Seven Hills ES 76247 – Mary Wall, prin.

Karnack, Harrison Co., Pop. Code 3
Karnack ISD
Sch. Sys. Enr. Code 3
Supt. – Ralph Ussery, P O BOX 259 75661
ES, FM ROAD #134 77661
 Cozzette Warren, prin.

Karnes City, Karnes Co., Pop. Code 5
Karnes City ISD
Sch. Sys. Enr. Code 3
Supt. – William Gary, P O BOX 38 78118
JHS, 311 N ESPLANADE 78118
 Richard Moody, prin.
ES 78118 – Roger Sides, prin.
Other Schools – See Panna Maria

Katy, Harris Co., Pop. Code 6
Katy ISD
Sch. Sys. Enr. Code 7
Supt. – Linda Woodward, P O BOX 159 77492
JHS, 6501 HIGHWAY BLVD 77450
 Roosevelt Alexander, prin.
Memorial Park JHS 77492 – Mike Cargill, prin.
West Memorial JHS
 22311 PROVINCIAL BLVD 77450
 James Tays, prin.
Cimarron ES, 1100 PEEK ROAD 77450
 Ellen Massey, prin.
Hutsell ES, 5360 FRANZ ROAD 77449
 Melvin Nash, prin.
ES, 5726 6TH ST 77449 – Nancy Justice, prin.
Memorial Parkway ES
 21603 PARK TREE LANE 77450
 Sara Eggleston, prin.
West Memorial ES
 22605 PROVINCIAL BLVD 77450
 Freddye Coussons, prin.
Williamsburg Settlemt ES
 22555 PRINCE GEORGE LANE 77449
 Diane Winborn, prin.
Wolfe ES 77449 – Tom Wilson, prin.
Other Schools – See Houston

Kaufman, Kaufman Co., Pop. Code 5
Kaufman ISD
Sch. Sys. Enr. Code 4
Supt. – Kenneth English
 1000 S HOUSTON ST 75142
JHS 75142 – Ed Crouch, prin.
PS 75142 – Kathy Covington, prin.
Nash MS, 4001 S HOUSTON ST 75142
 Bruce Curran, prin.
Phillips ES 75142 – Mary Edwards, prin.

Keene, Johnson Co., Pop. Code 5
Keene ISD
Sch. Sys. Enr. Code 2
Supt. – Wanda Smith, P O BOX 656 76059
ES, 302 PECAN ST 76059 – Billie Hopps, prin.

Keene Adventist School, 302 PECAN ST 76059

Keller, Tarrant Co., Pop. Code 5
Keller ISD
Sch. Sys. Enr. Code 5
Supt. – Thomas Myers, P O BOX B 76248
Fossil Hill MS 76248 – Norman Baxter, prin.
MS 76248 – Randy Baker, prin.
Bear Creek IS 76248 – Daniel Davis, prin.
Florence ES 76248 – Suzanne Pettit, prin.
Heritage ES 76248 – John Walkinshaw, prin.
ES 76248 – Sue Boothe, prin.
Parkview ES 76248 – Vicki Frost, prin.
Whitley Road ES 76248 – Sharon Isbell, prin.

Kemp, Kaufman Co., Pop. Code 4
Kemp ISD
Sch. Sys. Enr. Code 4
Supt. – L. Williamson, P O BOX 389 75143
MS 75143 – Phil Rogers, prin.
IS 75143 – Dennis Parkins, prin.
PS, 1301 S MAIN 75143 – Richard Dale, prin.

Kendleton, Fort Bend Co., Pop. Code 3
Kendleton ISD
Sch. Sys. Enr. Code 2
Supt. – James Davis, P O BOX 705 77451
Powell Point ES 77451 – Flora Smith, prin.

Kenedy, Karnes Co., Pop. Code 5
Kenedy ISD
Sch. Sys. Enr. Code 4
Supt. – William Chapman, P O BOX 149 78119
JHS, 501 HIGHWAY 719 78119
 George Dumont, prin.
ES, FM 719 78119 – Kenneth Anderson, prin.

Kennard, Houston Co., Pop. Code 2
Kennard ISD
Sch. Sys. Enr. Code 2
Supt. – Kenton Miller, P O BOX 38 75847
ES 75847 – Emmit Roach, prin.

Kennedale, Tarrant Co., Pop. Code 5
Kennedale ISD
Sch. Sys. Enr. Code 4
Supt. – G. Cockerham, P O BOX 467 76060
JHS, 120 W MANSFIELD HIGHWAY 76060
 Ronald Burns, prin.
Arthur MS 76060 – Lynda Ives, prin.
PS 76060 – James Delaney, prin.

Kerens, Navarro Co., Pop. Code 4
Kerens ISD
Sch. Sys. Enr. Code 3
Supt. – Lloyd Smith, P O BOX 310 75144
S 75144 – George Edwards, prin.

Kermit, Winkler Co., Pop. Code 6
Kermit ISD
Sch. Sys. Enr. Code 4
Supt. – Charlie Helmer, P O BOX S 79745
JHS 79745 – Herman Barrs, prin.
East PS, SCHOOL ST 79745
 Ted Westmoreland, prin.
Purple Sage MS, N EAST AVE 79745
 Kenneth Mays, prin.

Kerrville, Kerr Co., Pop. Code 7
Divide ISD
Sch. Sys. Enr. Code 1
Supt. – Larry Corder, P O BOX 275 78028
Divide ES 78028 – Larry Corder, prin.

Kerrville ISD
Sch. Sys. Enr. Code 5
Supt. – Mike Barry, 1009 BARNETT ST 78028
Peterson JHS, 605 TIVY ST 78028
 G. Miears, prin.
Daniels ES, 2002 SINGING WIND DR 78028
 Lucy Ament, prin.
Nimitz ES, 100 VALLEY VIEW 78028
 Ted Schwarz, prin.
Starkey ES, 1009 BARNETT ST 78028
 Debra Wells, prin.

Notre Dame ES, 923 MAIN ST 78028

Kilgore, Gregg Co., Pop. Code 7
Kilgore ISD
Sch. Sys. Enr. Code 5
Supt. – Edward Little
 711 N LONGVIEW ST 75662
Laird MS, 711 N LONGVIEW ST 75662
 Jim Griffin, prin.
Chandler ES, CHANDLER ST 75662
 Nancy Grisham, prin.
Eastview MS, LUDER ST 75662
 Jerome Towns, prin.
Elder ES, TYLER HIGHWAY 75662
 Bill Salmon, prin.

Killeen, Bell Co., Pop. Code 8
Killeen ISD
Sch. Sys. Enr. Code 7
Supt. – Charles Patterson, P O BOX 967 76540
Eastern Hills MS
 300 INDIAN TRAIL ROAD 76543
 Dale Lusk, prin.
Fairway MS 76541 – Joe Maines, prin.
Manor MS, 1700 S WS YOUNG DRIVE 76541
 James Seifert, prin.
Nolan MS 76541 – Kathleen Moore, prin.
Rancier MS, 902 N 10 ST 76541 – A. Powell, prin.
Bellaire ES, 108 W JASPER DR 76542
 Johnny Watson, prin.
Clarke ES, 51600 COMANCHE AVE 76544
 Martha Crow, prin.
Clifton Park ES, TRIMMIER ROAD 76541
 Melvin Smith, prin.
Duncan ES, 52400 HOPI ROAD 76544
 Peggy Cutler, prin.
East Ward ES, E RANCIER AVE 76541
 Patricia Carney, prin.
Fowler ES, 1020 TRIMMIER ROAD 76541
 W. Thomas, prin.

Hay Branch ES, 6101 WESTCLIFF ROAD 76543
    Alice Douse, prin.
Haynes ES, ZEPHYR ROAD 76541
    Ron Gawryszewski, prin.
Marlboro ES, PARKHILL DR 76543
    Marge Haedge, prin.
Meadows ES, 422 27TH ST 76544
    Jeanette Cavitt, prin.
Peebles ES, NWS YOUNG & POAGE AVE 76543
    Anna Connell, prin.
Pershing Park ES
    1702 WILLOW SPRINGS ROAD 76542
    Davina Spencer, prin.
Sugar Loaf ES
    JANIS DR & BARBARA LANE 76542
    Steve Caruso, prin.
West Ward ES, DEAN & HILLCREST AVE 76541
    Bernice Moland, prin.
Willow Springs ES
    OLD COPPERAS CV ROAD 76542
    Gladys Driver, prin.
Other Schools – See Fort Hood, Harker Heights,
    Nolanville

St. Joseph ES, 2901 E RANCIER AVE 76543

Kingsville, Kleberg Co., Pop. Code 8
Kingsville ISD
Sch. Sys. Enr. Code 6
Supt. – Kent Pogue, P O BOX 871 78364
Gillett MS 78363 – Ronald Williams, prin.
Memorial MS 78363 – Adela Williams, prin.
Colston MS, 900 N 17TH ST 78363
    Sherwood Thompson, prin.
Harrel ES, 925 E JOHNSTON AVE 78363
    Judith Coleman, prin.
Harvey ES, 1301 E KENEDY AVE 78363
    Linda Cantu, prin.
Kleberg MS, 900 S 6TH ST 78363
    Tony Morales, prin.
Lamar ES, 631 E FORDYCE AVE 78363
    Elida Ramirez, prin.
McRoberts MS, 400 W CORRAL AVE 78363
    Rodolfo Calderon, prin.
Perez ES, 1111 E AILSIE AVE 78363
    Kenneth Wilkinson, prin.

Laureles ISD
Sch. Sys. Enr. Code 1
Supt. – Donald Trant, P O BOX 592 78364
Laureles ES 78363 – Mary Wright, prin.

Ricardo ISD
Sch. Sys. Enr. Code 2
Supt. – Rollin Smith
    RURAL ROUTE 01 BOX 366 78363
Ricardo ES 78363 – Eugenia Bissett, prin.

Santa Gertrudis ISD
Sch. Sys. Enr. Code 1
Supt. – Donald Trant, P O BOX 592 78364
Santa Gertrudis ES 78363 – Carolyn Regan, prin.

Epiphany Episcopal School, P O BOX 1258 78363
St. Gertrude ES, 400 E CAESER AVE 78363
St. Martin ES, 400 E NETTIE AVE 78363

Kingwood, Harris Co.

Pines Montessori ES
    3535 CEDAR KNOLLS DRIVE 77339
West Oaks–Ft. Bend ES
    6500 HORNWOOD DR 77074

Kirbyville, Jasper Co., Pop. Code 4
Kirbyville ISD
Sch. Sys. Enr. Code 4
Supt. – Joe Folk, 206 E MAIN ST 75956
JHS, 109 E PINE ST 75956 – Robert Corley, prin.
Consolidated ES, BEAUMONT HIGHWAY 75956
    Preston Shoubrouek, prin.

Knippa, Uvalde Co.
Knippa ISD
Sch. Sys. Enr. Code 2
Supt. – David Malone, P O BOX 98 78870
S 78870 – Dan Bielfeldt, prin.

Knox City, Knox Co., Pop. Code 4
Knox City-O'Brien ISD
Sch. Sys. Enr. Code 2
Supt. – Clead Cheek, P O BOX 697 79529
O'Brien MS 79529 – Charles Reed, prin.
ES, 300 N 4TH 79529 – Johnny Rinehart, prin.

Kopperl, Bosque Co.
Kopperl ISD
Sch. Sys. Enr. Code 2
Supt. – Jim Malone, P O BOX 67 76652
S 76652 – Donald Reed, prin.

Kountze, Hardin Co., Pop. Code 5
Kountze ISD
Sch. Sys. Enr. Code 4
Supt. – Harold Ramm, P O BOX 460 77625
JHS, P O BOX 460 77625 – Patricia Pickett, prin.
ES 77625 – Jesse Hawthorne, prin.

Kress, Swisher Co., Pop. Code 3
Kress ISD
Sch. Sys. Enr. Code 2
Supt. – James Lanier, P O BOX 38 79052
ES, P O BOX 970 79052 – Jack McCraw, prin.

Krum, Denton Co., Pop. Code 3
Krum ISD
Sch. Sys. Enr. Code 3
Supt. – Bennie Enis, P O BOX 158 76249
MS, P O BOX 158 76249 – Ray Lea, prin.
Dyer ES, P O BOX 158 76249 – Troy Hamm, prin.

Ladonia, Fannin Co., Pop. Code 3
Fannindel ISD
Sch. Sys. Enr. Code 2
Supt. – Alfred Conley, 601 W MAIN ST 75449
Fannindel ES, 601 W MAIN ST 75449
    Glen Fields, prin.

Lago Vista, Travis Co.
Lago Vista ISD
Sch. Sys. Enr. Code 2
Supt. – Marion Czaja, P O BOX 929 78641
MS 78645 – Keith Mahler, prin.
ES 78641 – Larry Gibson, prin.

La Feria, Cameron Co., Pop. Code 5
La Feria ISD
Sch. Sys. Enr. Code 4
Supt. – W. Green, P O BOX 1157 78559
Vail MS 78559 – Carlos Verduzco, prin.
Houston PS 78559 – Ruth Johnson, prin.
Roosevelt MS 78559 – Reyes Rodriguez,Jr., prin.

Weslaco ISD
Supt. – See Weslaco
Houston ES 78559 – Karen Heilman, prin.
Roosevelt ES, W JESSAMINE 78559
    Anna Smith, prin.

La Grange, Fayette Co., Pop. Code 5
La Grange ISD
Sch. Sys. Enr. Code 4
Supt. – Fred Weaver, P O BOX 100 78945
MS 78945 – L. Calley, prin.
Hermes ES 78945 – David Ehler, prin.

Sacred Heart ES, 545 E PEARL ST 78945

La Joya, Hidalgo Co., Pop. Code 4
La Joya ISD
Sch. Sys. Enr. Code 6
Supt. – Roberto Zamora, P O BOX J 78560
Schunior JHS, P O BOX J 78560
    Juan Salinas, prin.
De La Garza ES 78560 – Irene Garcia, prin.
Flores MS 78560 – Jose Pena, prin.
Kennedy ES 78560 – Roberto Vela, prin.
Leo ES 78560 – Jose Arredondo,Jr., prin.
Memorial ES 78560 – Benito Saenz,Jr., prin.
Other Schools – See Sullivan City

Lake Dallas, Denton Co., Pop. Code 5
Lake Dallas ISD
Sch. Sys. Enr. Code 4
Supt. – B. Jameson, P O BOX 548 75065
MS 75065 – Mike Pierson, prin.
MS, 190 TEXAS 75065 – Melonae Peters, prin.
PS, SHADY SHORES DR 75065
    Deon Quisenberry, prin.

Lake Jackson, Brazoria Co., Pop. Code 7
Brazosport ISD
Supt. – See Freeport
IS 77566 – Melvin Blair, prin.
Beutel ES, 300 LIGUSTRUM ST 77566
    Nancy Swenson, prin.
Brannen ES, 802 THAT WAY ST 77566
    Johnnie McWilliams, prin.
Ney ES, 308 WINDING WAY ST 77566
    George Lea, prin.

Lakeview, Hall Co., Pop. Code 2
Lakeview ISD
Sch. Sys. Enr. Code 2
Supt. – Wilford Arthur, P O BOX 48 79239
S 79239 – Rick Guy, prin.

La Marque, Galveston Co., Pop. Code 7
La Marque ISD
Sch. Sys. Enr. Code 6
Supt. – Mike Moses, P O BOX 7 77568
JHS, 1711 MAGNOLIA DRIVE 77568
    John Washington, prin.
Bayou Road MS, 1431 BAYOU ROAD 77568
    Curtis McGowan, prin.
Highlands ES, 2401 MAGNOLIA DR 77568
    Crawford Helms, prin.
Inter City ES, 600 WISTERIA ST 77568
    Kyle Wargo, prin.
Lake Road ES 77568 – Don Shumate, prin.
Lamar ES, 1101 DELMAR DR 77568
    Doug Johnson, prin.
Simms ES, 400 FULTON ST N 77568
    Barbara Trahan, prin.
Westlawn ES, 1217 VAUTHIER ST 77568
    Thomasine Allen, prin.

Queen of Peace ES, 1228 CEDAR DR 77568

Lamesa, Dawson Co., Pop. Code 7
Klondike ISD
Sch. Sys. Enr. Code 2
Supt. – Carl Foster
    RURAL ROUTE 01 BOX 276A 79331
Klondike ES 79331 – Van Kountz, prin.

Lamesa ISD
Sch. Sys. Enr. Code 5
Supt. – Neal Chastain, P O BOX 261 79331
MS 79331 – Paul Wade, prin.
Central MS 79331 – Paul Wade, prin.

North ES, N 14TH ST 79331
    George Schreiber, prin.
Rogers ES, NE 3RD ST 79331
    Randy Simmans, prin.
South ES, 2000 S 8TH ST 79331
    Gene Borkowsky, prin.

Lampasas, Lampasas Co., Pop. Code 6
Lampasas ISD
Sch. Sys. Enr. Code 4
Supt. – Jerry Doyle, 207 W EIGHTH ST 76550
MS 76550 – George Morley, prin.
PS, 904 S BROAD ST 76550
    William Hammett, prin.
Whitis MS, 500 S WILLIS ST 76550
    Timothy Petty, prin.

Lancaster, Dallas Co., Pop. Code 7
Lancaster ISD
Sch. Sys. Enr. Code 5
Supt. – Larry Groppel, P O BOX 400 75146
JHS 75146 – Don Berry, prin.
Houston ES 75134 – Tresa Long, prin.
IS, 1355 W BELT LINE ROAD 75146
    Joe Mcmeans, prin.
Millbrook ES, 630 MILLBROOK DR 75146
    Steve Waddell, prin.
Pleasant Run ES
    4267 W PLEASANT RUN ROAD 75146
    Jerry DeLong, prin.
West Main ES, 531 W MAIN ST 75146
    Dan Eubank, prin.

St. Francis of Assisi ES, 1537 ROGERS AVE 75134

Laneville, Rusk Co.
Laneville ISD
Sch. Sys. Enr. Code 2
Supt. – Steven Ervin, P O BOX 127 75667
S 75667 – Ann Lock, prin.

La Porte, Harris Co., Pop. Code 6
La Porte ISD
Sch. Sys. Enr. Code 6
Supt. – Robert Williams
    301 E FAIRMONT PARKWAY 77571
Baker JHS, 3201 UNDERWOOD ROAD 77571
    B. Phillips, prin.
JHS 77571 – Larry Cox, prin.
Lomax JHS 77571 – James Sitton, prin.
Bayshore MS 77571 – Martha Love, prin.
College Park ES 77571 – Mervin Risner, prin.
ES 77571 – Valton Hazelton, prin.
Lomax ES 77571 – John Still, prin.
Reid ES 77571 – Charles Wilder, prin.
Rizzuto ES 77571 – Gary Millard, prin.

La Pryor, Zavala Co., Pop. Code 3
La Pryor ISD
Sch. Sys. Enr. Code 3
Supt. – Leland Edge IV, P O BOX 519 78872
ES 78872 – Elmer Lechler, prin.

Laredo, Webb Co., Pop. Code 8
Laredo ISD
Sch. Sys. Enr. Code 7
Supt. – V. Trevino, 1702 HOUSTON ST 78040
Cigarroa MS 78040 – Cecilia Moreno, prin.
Christen JHS, 2001 SANTA MARIA AVE 78040
    Roberto Castro, prin.
JHS, 2502 GALVESTON ST 78043
    Alonzo Ramirez, prin.
Memorial MS 78040 – Pedro Lara, prin.
Bruni ES 78040 – Luis Garcia, prin.
Buenos Aires ES, 508 CLARK BLVD 78040
    Arturo Gutierrez, prin.
Daiches ES, 1401 GREEN ST 78040
    Alfonso Ornelas, prin.
Dovalina ES, 1700 ANNA AVE 78040
    Leonor Daves, prin.
Farias ES, 1510 CHICAGO ST 78041
    George Andrews, prin.
Hachar ES, 1208 MARKET ST 78040
    Ignacio Vallone, prin.
Heights ES 78040 – Carlos Cruz, prin.
Kawas ES, 2100 S MILMO AVE 78043
    Esther Boubel, prin.
Leyendecker ES, 1311 GARDEN ST 78040
    Francisco Inocencio, prin.
MacDonell ES, 1606 BENAVIDES ST 78040
    Violeta Moreno, prin.
Martin Jr. ES, 16000 MONTERREY AVE 78040
    Pedro Trevino,Jr., prin.
Milton ES, 2502 E ELM ST 78043
    Carlos Garza, prin.
Ochoa ES, 3000 GUADALUPE ST 78043
    Cynthia Conchas, prin.
Pierce ES, 800 E EISTETTER ST 78041
    Rodolfo Lopez, prin.
Ryan ES, 2401 CLARK BLVD 78043
    Adalberto Jaime, prin.
Sanchez ES, 211 E ASH ST 78040
    Olga Salinas, prin.
Santa Maria ES, 3817 SANTA MARIA AVE 78041
    Carlos Carranco, prin.
Santo Nino ES, 2702 BISMARK ST 78043
    Cesar Salinas, prin.
Tarver ES, 3200 TILDLEN AVE 78040
    Amparo Benavidez, prin.
Zachry ES, 3200 CHACOTA ST 78043
    Corina Mojica, prin.

United ISD
Sch. Sys. Enr. Code 6
Supt. – James Wood
    201 LINDENWOOD DRIVE 78041

United IS, 900 E DEL MAR BLVD 78041
  Eduardo Perales, prin.
Clark ES 78041 – Richard Perales, prin.
Clark MS, 500 W HILLSIDE ROAD 78041
  Neida Estringel, prin.
Finley ES 78041 – Humberto Adame, prin.
Newman ES, 1300 VISTA HERMOSA ST 78041
  Juanita Lira, prin.
Nye ES, 101 E DEL MAR BLVD 78041
  Olga Herrera, prin.
Perez ES 78041 – Rogelio Perez, prin.
Salinas ES, 1000 W CENTURY DR 78043
  Juanita Guajardo, prin.
Trautmann ES, 810 LINDENWOOD DR 78041
  Reynaldo Rodriguez, prin.
United IS 78041 – Bertha Dominguez, prin.

Blessed Sacrament ES, 1501 BARTLETT ST 78043
Mary Help of Christians ES
  100 W DEL MAR BLVD 78041
Our Lady of Guadalupe ES
  1718 SAN JORGE AVE 78040
St. Peter's Memorial ES
  1519 HOUSTON ST 78040
United Day ES, 1601 CLARK BLVD 78043
Ursuline Academy ES
  1300 GALVESTON ST 78040

Larue, Henderson Co.
  La Poynor ISD
  Sch. Sys. Enr. Code 2
  Supt. – Douglas Steger, RURAL ROUTE 02 75770
  La Poyner ES 75770 – Don Gordon, prin.

Lasara, Willacy Co.
  Lasara ISD
  Sch. Sys. Enr. Code 2
  Supt. – Abel Cavazos, P O BOX 57 78561
  ES 78561 – Hector Gonzales, prin.

Latexo, Houston Co., Pop. Code 2
  Latexo ISD
  Sch. Sys. Enr. Code 2
  Supt. – Clifford Price, P O BOX 975 75849
  ES 75849 – Jack Patton, prin.

La Vernia, Wilson Co., Pop. Code 3
  La Vernia ISD
  Sch. Sys. Enr. Code 3
  Supt. – Preston Stephens, P O BOX 309 78121
  IS 78121 – Paul Kalkwarf, prin.
  ES 78121 – Marie Gerlich, prin.

La Villa, Hidalgo Co., Pop. Code 4
  La Villa ISD
  Sch. Sys. Enr. Code 3
  Supt. – Alejos Salazar, P O BOX 9 78562
  La Villa ES 78562 – Palmira Lozano, prin.

Lazbuddie, Parmer Co.
  Lazbuddie ISD
  Sch. Sys. Enr. Code 2
  Supt. – Joe Hall, P O BOX A 79053
  S 79053 – Roy Willingham, prin.

League City, Galveston Co., Pop. Code 7
  Clear Creek ISD
  Sch. Sys. Enr. Code 7
  Supt. – Charles Thacker, 2301 E MAIN ST 77573
  Bay ES, P O BOX 799 77573
    Peter Quattrini, prin.
  Bayou ES, P O BOX 799 77573
    Martha Daniel, prin.
  Clear Lake ES, P O BOX 799 77573
    Kenneth Royal, prin.
  Greene ES, P O BOX 799 77573
    Claire Stout, prin.
  Hall ES 77573 – Barry Beck, prin.
  Landolt ES, P O BOX 799 77573
    Mary Howard, prin.
  ES 77573 – David Davis, prin.
  McWhirter MS, P O BOX 799 77573
    Glenna Shields, prin.
  Ross ES 77573 – John Myer, prin.
  Stewart ES, P O BOX 799 77573
    Michael Clayton, prin.
  Weber ES, P O BOX 799 77573
    Charles Winsor, prin.
  Webster PS 77573 – Dona Ammons, prin.
  Whitcomb ES, P O BOX 799 77573
    Mary Richardson, prin.
  White ES, P O BOX 799 77573
    Leslie Talley, prin.
  Other Schools – See Houston, Seabrook, Webster

St. Mary ES, 1612 E WALKER ST 77573

Leakey, Real Co., Pop. Code 2
  Leakey ISD
  Sch. Sys. Enr. Code 2
  Supt. – Gerald Singleton, P O BOX 808 78873
  S 78873 – David Harp, prin.

Leander, Williamson Co., Pop. Code 4
  Leander ISD
  Sch. Sys. Enr. Code 5
  Supt. – Tom Glenn, P O BOX 218 78641
  JHS 78641 – Ronald Lafevers, prin.
  Block House Creek ES 78641
    Bonnie Shaffer, prin.
  Cypress ES 78641 – Donna MacDonnell, prin.
  Giddens ES, 300 S WEST DR 78641
    Elizabeth Parker, prin.
  Other Schools – See Cedar Park

Lefors, Gray Co., Pop. Code 3
  Lefors ISD
  Sch. Sys. Enr. Code 2
  Supt. – W. Earl Ross, 209 E 5TH 79054
  ES 79054 – Bill Crockett, prin.

Leggett, Polk Co.
  Leggett ISD
  Sch. Sys. Enr. Code 2
  Supt. – Edwin Walker, P O BOX 68 77350
  ES 77350 – Wayne Geeslin, prin.

Lenorah, Martin Co.
  Grady ISD
  Sch. Sys. Enr. Code 2
  Supt. – Gary Harrell, P O BOX 4 79749
  Grady S 79749 – Richard Gibson, prin.

Leonard, Fannin Co., Pop. Code 4
  Leonard ISD
  Sch. Sys. Enr. Code 3
  Supt. – L. Tucker, P O BOX G 75452
  MS, P O BOX G 75452 – John Neuman, prin.
  ES 75452 – Elizabeth Treadway, prin.

Levelland, Hockley Co., Pop. Code 7
  Levelland ISD
  Sch. Sys. Enr. Code 5
  Supt. – Max Newman, 1103 HOUSTON ST 79336
  Cactus Drive ES, 500 CACTUS DR 79336
    Delano Phillips, prin.
  Capitol ES, ELLIS ST 79336
    Kenneth Foster, prin.
  MS 79336 – Lester Driver, prin.
  South ES, 1500 C AVE 79336
    Mark Holcomb, prin.
  West ES, 500 WEST AVE 79336
    Dale Albright, prin.

Lewisville, Denton Co., Pop. Code 7
  Lewisville ISD
  Sch. Sys. Enr. Code 7
  Supt. – Clayton Downing, P O BOX 217 75067
  Delay MS, 136 W PURNELL ROAD 75067
    Clint Mosely, prin.
  Griffin MS 75067 – Ben Swearingen, prin.
  Hedrick MS, 1526 BELLAIRE LANE 75067
    Dean Tackett, prin.
  Lamar MS, P O BOX 217 75067 – Brent Buck, prin.
  Milliken MS, 2103 SAVAGE LANE 75067
    Barbara Stagner, prin.
  Camey ES, 4949 ARBOR GLEN ROAD 75056
    Diane Thornton, prin.
  Central ES 75067 – Carol Fisher, prin.
  College Street ES, 350 W COLLEGE ST 75067
    Dan Van Horne, prin.
  Degan ES 75067 – Michael DeBolt, prin.
  Flower Mound ES 75067 – Connie Gall, prin.
  Hedrick ES, 1532 BELLAIRE LANE 75067
    Gary Goldsmith, prin.
  Highland Village ES 75067 – Dan Holder, prin.
  Indian Creek ES 75067 – Lucille Smith, prin.
  Lakeland ES 75067 – Stephen Polzer, prin.
  McAuliffe ES, P O BOX 217 75067
    Mary Ritchie, prin.
  Owen ES, P O BOX 217 75067
    Marilyn Spence, prin.
  Peters Colony ES, 5101 NASH DR 75056
    David Spence, prin.
  Stewarts Creek ES 75067 – Jill Spanheimer, prin.
  Timbercreek ES
    1900 TIMBERCREEK ROAD 75028
    Don Harvey, prin.

Lexington, Lee Co., Pop. Code 4
  Lexington ISD
  Sch. Sys. Enr. Code 3
  Supt. – C. Peterson, P O BOX 248 78947
  MS 78947 – Geary McManus, prin.
  ES 78947 – Larry Nichols, prin.

Liberty, Liberty Co., Pop. Code 6
  Liberty ISD
  Sch. Sys. Enr. Code 4
  Supt. – Allen Brown, 1600 GRAND AVE 77575
  MS 77575 – Ken Whiteker, prin.
  MS, 1202 BOWIE ST 77575 – Nell Almond, prin.
  San Jacinto ES, 2525 GRAND AVE 77575
    Nylds Hinch, prin.

Liberty Hill, Williamson Co., Pop. Code 2
  Liberty Hill ISD
  Sch. Sys. Enr. Code 4
  Supt. – Louine Noble, P O BOX 68 78642
  MS 78642 – Richard Hastings, prin.
  ES 78642 – Peggy McCullough, prin.

Lindale, Smith Co., Pop. Code 4
  Lindale ISD
  Sch. Sys. Enr. Code 4
  Supt. – Richard Capps, P O BOX 370 75771
  JHS, P O BOX 370 75771 – Jane Holbrook, prin.
  IS 75771 – Jim Woodson, prin.
  PS 75771 – Jasper Huff, prin.

Linden, Cass Co., Pop. Code 4
  Linden-Kildare ISD
  Sch. Sys. Enr. Code 4
  Supt. – W. Parker, P O BOX 840 75563
  Linden-Kildare JHS 75563 – Mark Smith, prin.
  ES, KAUFMAN 75563 – Jack York, prin.

Lindsay, Cooke Co., Pop. Code 3
  Lindsay ISD
  Sch. Sys. Enr. Code 2
  Supt. – Henry Schroeder, P O BOX 145 76250
  ES 76250 – Gilbert Hermes, prin.

Lingleville, Erath Co.
  Lingleville ISD
  Sch. Sys. Enr. Code 2
  Supt. – G. Rice, P O BOX 134 76461
  S 76461 – Jerry Brock, prin.

Lipan, Hood Co., Pop. Code 2
  Lipan ISD
  Sch. Sys. Enr. Code 2
  Supt. – Wallace Price, P O BOX 188 76462
  S 76462 – Terry Antonie, prin.

Little Elm, Denton Co., Pop. Code 3
  Little Elm ISD
  Sch. Sys. Enr. Code 3
  Supt. – Elmer Russell, P O BOX 9 75068
  MS, 500 COTTONWOOD PARK DR 75068
    Linda Blase, prin.
  ES 75068 – Carol Baker, prin.

Littlefield, Lamb Co., Pop. Code 6
  Littlefield ISD
  Sch. Sys. Enr. Code 4
  Supt. – Jerry Blakely, P O BOX 606 79339
  JHS, 105 N LAKE AVE 79339 – C. Rogers, prin.
  Littlefield MS 1, 120 N WESTSIDE AVE 79339
    Sam Burnett, prin.
  PS, 214 N WESTSIDE AVE 79339
    Anna Ketchum, prin.

Livingston, Polk Co., Pop. Code 5
  Big Sandy ISD
  Sch. Sys. Enr. Code 2
  Supt. – Thomas Foster
    RURAL ROUTE 03 BOX 422 77351
  Big Sandy S 77351 – Thomas Foster, prin.

  Livingston ISD
  Sch. Sys. Enr. Code 5
  Supt. – David Montgomery, P O BOX 1297 77351
  JHS 77351 – Randy Burchfield, prin.
  ES, 701 N WILLIS AVE 77351 – Dan Tinney, prin.
  MS, 223 N WILLIS AVE 77351
    Sandra Sherman, prin.

Llano, Llano Co., Pop. Code 5
  Llano ISD
  Sch. Sys. Enr. Code 4
  Supt. – Dorman Moore, 1402 OATMAN ST 78643
  JHS, 1400 OATMAN ST 78643
    Richard Gilbert, prin.
  ES, 1600 OATMAN ST 78643
    Joe Studebaker, prin.

Lockhart, Caldwell Co., Pop. Code 6
  Lockhart ISD
  Sch. Sys. Enr. Code 5
  Supt. – Roy Dollar, P O BOX 120 78644
  JHS 78644 – Herbert Schulze, prin.
  Clear Fork ES 78644 – Donna Moore, prin.
  IS, 1011 SCHEH ST 78644 – Charles Red, prin.
  Plum Creek ES, 710 FLORES ST 78644
    La Vell Walker, prin.

Lockney, Floyd Co., Pop. Code 4
  Lockney ISD
  Sch. Sys. Enr. Code 3
  Supt. – W. Hallmark, P O BOX 428 79241
  JHS, P O BOX 550 79241 – Terry Ellison, prin.
  ES, P O BOX 127 79241 – Joyce Evans, prin.

Lohn, McCulloch Co.
  Lohn ISD
  Sch. Sys. Enr. Code 2
  Supt. – Marlene Shelton, P O BOX 277 76852
  S 76852 – Leon Freeman, prin.

Lolita, Jackson Co., Pop. Code 3
  Industrial ISD
  Supt. – See Vanderbilt
  Industrial JHS 77971 – Donald Egg, prin.

Lometa, Lampasas Co., Pop. Code 3
  Lometa ISD
  Sch. Sys. Enr. Code 2
  Supt. – Richard Stockman, P O BOX 250 76853
  S 76853 – Charles Fields, prin.

Lone Oak, Hunt Co., Pop. Code 2
  Lone Oak ISD
  Sch. Sys. Enr. Code 2
  Supt. – Bob Fannin, P O BOX 38 75453
  JHS 75453 – John Stahmer, prin.
  ES 75453 – Jack McClendon, prin.

Longview, Gregg Co., Pop. Code 8
  Longview ISD
  Sch. Sys. Enr. Code 6
  Supt. – R. McMichael, P O BOX 3268 75606
  Forest Park MS, 1515 LAKE DRIVE 75601
    Mary Schmitz, prin.
  Foster MS, 410 S GREEN ST 75601
    Beth Bassett, prin.
  Judson MS, JUDSON ROAD 75606
    Brent Taylor, prin.
  Bramlette ES, 111 TUPELO DR 75601
    Eddie Cannon, prin.
  Foster ES, 16TH ST 75602 – Boyce Jones, prin.
  Hudson ES, 1609 LILLY ST 75602
    Murlene Waits, prin.
  Johnston ES, JUDSON ROAD 75601
    Benette Cippele, prin.
  McClure MS, 500 MELBA ST 75602
    Gary Whitwell, prin.
  McQueen PS 75606 – Nancy Ballard, prin.
  Pinewood Park ES, 209 W GLENN ST 75602
    Charles Newhouse, prin.

South Ward ES, S MOBBERLY AVE 75602
  Lorna Bonner, prin.
Valley View ES, 1601 ALPINE ST 75601
  Jack Tillery, prin.
Ware ES, W GARFIELD ST 75602
  Carol Gray, prin.

Pine Tree ISD
Sch. Sys. Enr. Code 5
Supt. – Leland Frase, P O BOX 5878 75608
Pine Tree 6th Grade ES 75608
  Gary Sanders, prin.
Pine Tree 7th Grade ES 75608
  Derrell Murphy, prin.
Pine Tree ES, BIRCH ST 75604
  Lanell Dowell, prin.
Pine Tree IS, PINE TREE ROAD 75604
  J. Bardwell, prin.
Pine Tree PS, 2180 W LOOP 281 75604
  Myrle Cariker, prin.

Spring Hill ISD
Sch. Sys. Enr. Code 4
Supt. – D. Michael Crossland
  RURAL ROUTE 08 BOX 33 75605
Spring Hill JHS
  RURAL ROUTE 08 BOX 33 75605
  Bob Moore, prin.
Spring Hill ES 75605 – Martha Mauldin, prin.
Spring Hill MS 75605 – Tom Barnett, prin.

St. Mary ES, 405 HOLLYBROOK DR 75601

Loop, Gaines Co.
Loop ISD
Sch. Sys. Enr. Code 2
Supt. – Jay Watson, P O BOX 917 79342
S 79342 – Richard Roberts, prin.

Loraine, Mitchell Co., Pop. Code 3
Loraine ISD
Sch. Sys. Enr. Code 2
Supt. – Glenn Sanders, P O BOX 457 79532
S 79532 – Doug Foshee, prin.

Lorena, McLennan Co., Pop. Code 3
Lorena ISD
Sch. Sys. Enr. Code 3
Supt. – K. Riley, P O BOX 97 76655
MS 76655 – Herman Roessler, prin.
ES 76655 – Margaret Cummings, prin.

Lorenzo, Crosby Co., Pop. Code 4
Lorenzo ISD
Sch. Sys. Enr. Code 2
Supt. – Jim Norris, P O BOX 520 79343
ES 79343 – (—), prin.

Los Fresnos, Cameron Co., Pop. Code 4
Los Fresnos Consolidated ISD
Sch. Sys. Enr. Code 5
Supt. – A. Vallado, P O BOX 309 78566
JHS, P O BOX 309 78566 – Fernando Rosillo, prin.
Las Yescas ES 78566 – Manuel Salinas, prin.
Lopez-Riggins ES 78566 – Susan Fox, prin.
MS 78566 – Dora Ruiz, prin.
Villareal ES 78566 – Joe Ceballos, prin.

Los Indios, Cameron Co.
San Benito Cons. ISD
Supt. – See San Benito
ES, P O BOX 68 78567 – Jesus Rocha, prin.

Lott, Falls Co., Pop. Code 3
Westphalia ISD
Sch. Sys. Enr. Code 1
Supt. – David Kelm
  RURAL ROUTE 02 BOX 58D 76656
Westphalia ES 76656 – (—), prin.

Louise, Wharton Co., Pop. Code 3
Louise ISD
Sch. Sys. Enr. Code 2
Supt. – Chester St. Clair III, P O BOX 97 77455
S 77455 – Jesse Smelley, prin.

Lovelady, Houston Co., Pop. Code 3
Lovelady ISD
Sch. Sys. Enr. Code 2
Supt. – Howard Tucker, P O BOX 250 75851
ES 75851 – Fred Gamble, prin.

Lubbock, Lubbock Co., Pop. Code 9
Lubbock ISD
Sch. Sys. Enr. Code 8
Supt. – E. Leslie, 1628 19TH ST 79401
Alderson JHS, 219 WALNUT AVE 79403
  Curtis Gipson, prin.
Arnett ES, 701 E QUEENS ST 79403
  Luis Cardenas, prin.
Bayless ES, 2115 58TH ST 79412
  Elvin Kelly, prin.
Bean ES, 3001 AVENUE N 79405
  Barbara Mezack, prin.
Bowie ES, 2902 CHICAGO AVE 79407
  Joe Williams, prin.
Bozeman ES, 3101 E 2ND ST 79403
  Carolyn Solomon, prin.
Brown ES, 2315 36TH ST 79412
  Kelly Eubank, prin.
Dupre ES, 2008 AVENUE T 79411
  Harold Young, prin.
Guadulupe ES, 101 N AVENUE P 79401
  Gale Lambert, prin.
Hardwick ES, 1420 CHICAGO AVE 79416
  Rachel Harmon, prin.

Harwell ES, 4101 AVENUE D 79404
  Lucy Gutierrez, prin.
Haynes ES, 3802 60TH ST 79413
  Nettie Edwards, prin.
Hodges ES, 5001 AVENUE P 79412
  Dennis Hargrove, prin.
Honey ES, 3615 86TH ST 79423
  Larry Mullicam, prin.
Hunt ES, 415 N IVORY AVE 79403
  Vernita Holmes, prin.
Iles ES, 2401 DATE AVE 79404
  Linda Andersen, prin.
Jackson ES, 201 VERNON AVE 79415
  Richard Ybarra, prin.
Maedgen ES, 4401 NASHVILLE AVE 79413
  Frank Mullican, prin.
Mahon ES, 2010 CORNELL ST 79415
  Kay Tavenor, prin.
Martin ES, 3315 E BROADWAY ST 79403
  Betty Dixon, prin.
Matthews MS 79401 – Jesse Garza, prin.
McWhorter ES, 2711 1ST ST 79415
  Bill Gonzales, prin.
Murfee ES, 6901 NASHVILLE DR 79413
  Sue Bounds, prin.
Overton ES, 2902 LOUISVILLE AVE 79410
  Drew Jackson, prin.
Parkway ES, 406 N ZENITH AVE 79403
  Raymond Peppers, prin.
Parsons ES, 2811 58TH ST 79413
  Ed Mullins, prin.
Posey ES, 1301 REDBUD AVE 79403
  Charles Taylor, prin.
Ramirez ES 79401 – Carl Knight, prin.
Rush ES, 4702 15TH ST 79416
  Toni Hancock, prin.
Smith ES 79401 – Dan McPherson, prin.
Stewart ES, 4815 46TH ST 79414
  Jerry Hale, prin.
Stubbs ES, 3516 TOLEDO AVE 79414
  Charles Mayfield, prin.
Tubbs ES, 3311 BATES ST 79415
  Sim Larkins, prin.
Waters ES, 3006 78TH ST 79423
  Bettye Wright, prin.
Wester ES, 4602 CHICAGO AVE 79414
  James Baker, prin.
Wheatley ES, 1802 E 28TH ST 79404
  Hattie Gipson, prin.
Wheelock ES, 3008 42ND ST 79413
  Louise Stuart, prin.
Whiteside ES, 7508 ALBANY AVE 79424
  Denzil Minyard, prin.
Williams ES, 4812 58TH ST 79414
  Carroll Lockett, prin.
Wilson ES, 2807 25TH ST 79410
  Drew Foster, prin.
Wolffarth ES, 3202 ERSKINE ST 79415
  Armando Garcia, prin.
Wright ES, 1302 ADRIAN ST 79403
  Roy Carnes, prin.

Lubbock-Cooper ISD
Sch. Sys. Enr. Code 4
Supt. – Mary Vinson
  RURAL ROUTE 06 BOX 400 79412
Cooper JHS, RURAL ROUTE 06 BOX 400 79412
  Oliver Thompson, prin.
Cooper ES 79412 – James Gordon, prin.

Roosevelt ISD
Sch. Sys. Enr. Code 4
Supt. – D. Taylor
  RURAL ROUTE 01 BOX 402 79401
Roosevelt ES 79041 – Stan Wheeler, prin.

Lubbock Christian School, 5601 19TH ST 79407
All Saint's Episcopal School
  P O BOX 64545 79464
Christ the King ES, 4011 54TH ST 79413
St. John Neumann ES, 5838 22ND ST 79407

Lueders, Jones Co., Pop. Code 2
Lueders-Avoca ISD
Sch. Sys. Enr. Code 2
Supt. – George Blanch, P O BOX 168 79533
Lueders-Avoca ES 79533 – (—), prin.

Lufkin, Angelina Co., Pop. Code 8
Hudson ISD
Sch. Sys. Enr. Code 4
Supt. – Joe Smith
  RURAL ROUTE 05 BOX 3420 75901
Hudson JHS 75901 – Michael Patrick, prin.
Hudson ES 75901 – John McGilvra, prin.

Lufkin ISD
Sch. Sys. Enr. Code 6
Supt. – Jack Darnell, P O BOX 1407 75902
Anderson ES, 381 CHAMPIONS DR 75901
  Helen Strohschein, prin.
Brandon ES 75901 – Sandra McEntire, prin.
Brookhollow ES, 1009 LIVE OAK DR 75901
  Herbert Cross, prin.
Coston ES, 707 TRENTON ST 75901
  Virginia Casper, prin.
Garrett ES, KURTH DR 75901
  Robert Kuykendall, prin.
Herty ES, 2804 PAUL AVE 75901
  Clarence Luedke, prin.
Kurth ES, 521 YORK DR 75901
  Kenneth Saint Ama, prin.
Lufkin Dunbar IS 75901 – Joe Deason, prin.
Redland ES 75901 – Roger Kelly, prin.

Slack ES, 1305 FULLER SPRINGS DR 75901
  James Martinec, prin.
Trout ES 75901 – R. Miller,Jr., prin.

St. Cyprian's ES
  1115 S JOHN REDDITT DRIVE 75901
St. Patrick's ES, 2116 LOWRY ST 75901

Luling, Caldwell Co., Pop. Code 6
Luling ISD
Sch. Sys. Enr. Code 4
Supt. – George Bujnoch, 216 E BOWIE ST 78648
JHS, 214 E TRAVIS ST 78648
  Gilbert Gerdes, prin.
MS, 122 E HOUSTON ST 78648
  Leonard Shanklin, prin.
PS, 118 W BOWIE ST 78648
  Nolan Alexander, prin.

Lumberton, Hardin Co., Pop. Code 4
Lumberton ISD
Supt. – See Silsbee
IS 77711 – (—), prin.
PS 77711 – Lani Randall, prin.

Lyford, Willacy Co., Pop. Code 4
Lyford ISD
Sch. Sys. Enr. Code 4
Supt. – Jose Flores, P O BOX 220 78569
JHS 78569 – A. Correa, prin.
ES 78569 – Darlene Perez, prin.
Travis MS 78569 – Albino Infante, prin.

Lytle, Atascosa Co., Pop. Code 4
Lytle ISD
Sch. Sys. Enr. Code 3
Supt. – Paul Fleming, P O BOX 745 78052
JHS 78052 – Walter Stein, prin.
ES 78052 – Siewchan Lackan, prin.

Mabank, Kaufman Co., Pop. Code 4
Mabank ISD
Sch. Sys. Enr. Code 4
Supt. – James Engelmann, P O BOX C 75147
JHS 75147 – W. Lundy, prin.
IS 75147 – Robert Ray, prin.
PS 75147 – Bonny Cain, prin.

Mc Allen, Hidalgoro, Pop. Code 8
McAllen ISD
Sch. Sys. Enr. Code 7
Supt. – Pablo Perez, 2000 N 23RD ST 78501
Brown JHS 78501 – Steve Ellis, prin.
Lamar JHS 78501 – Maria Vitello, prin.
Lincoln JHS 78501 – Eutiquio Rivas, prin.
Morris JHS 78501 – William Parry, prin.
Travis JHS 78501 – Nicholas Gonzalez, prin.
Alvarez ES, 2606 GUMWOOD AVE 78501
  Pablo Munoz, prin.
Austin ES, 2100 FIR AVE 78501
  Anne Mangham, prin.
Bonham ES, 2400 JORDAN ROAD 78503
  Rose Flores, prin.
Crockett ES, 2112 N MAIN ST 78501
  Mariaelena Champion, prin.
Escandon MS, 2901 COLBATH ROAD 78503
  Eunice Santa Ana, prin.
Fields ES, 500 DALLAS AVE 78501
  David McKeand, prin.
Garza ES, 6300 N 29TH ST 78504
  Roseella Ortega, prin.
Houston ES, 1101 S 16TH ST 78501
  Arnoldo Rodriguez, prin.
Jackson ES, 500 HIGHLAND AVE 78501
  Reynaldo Torres,Jr., prin.
McAuliffe ES 78501 – Joanetta Ellis, prin.
Milam ES, 3800 N MAIN ST 78501
  Roger Larson, prin.
Navarro MS, 2100 W HACKBERRY AVE 78501
  Hector Guerra, prin.
Rayburn ES, 7000 N MAIN 78504
  Delia Longoria, prin.
Roosevelt ES, 4801 S 26TH ST 78503
  Jose Perez, prin.
Seguin ES, 2200 S 29TH ST 78503
  Blanca Sanchez, prin.
Thigpen ES, 520 S 23RD ST 78501
  Eileen Davis, prin.
Wilson ES, 1200 W HACKBERRY AVE 78501
  Priscila Martinez, prin.
Zavala MS, 2500 GALVESTON AVE 78501
  Doris Palmquist, prin.

Our Lady of Sorrows ES, 702 N 12TH ST 78501
St. Paul Lutheran School, 300 PECAN BLVD 78501

Mc Camey, Upton Co., Pop. Code 4
McCamey ISD
Sch. Sys. Enr. Code 3
Supt. – Bill Little, P O BOX 1069 79752
MS 79752 – Joe Neill, prin.
ES, E 11TH 79752 – Al Stone, prin.

Mc Caulley, Fisher Co.
McCaulley ISD
Sch. Sys. Enr. Code 1
Supt. – Henry Hunter, P O BOX 187 79534
ES 78534 – Henry Hunter, prin.

Mc Dade, Bastrop Co.
McDade ISD
Sch. Sys. Enr. Code 1
Supt. – Thomas Baca, P O BOX 4858 78650
ES 78650 – (—), prin.

Mc Gregor, McLennan Co., Pop. Code 5
McGregor ISD
Sch. Sys. Enr. Code 4
Supt. – L. Westbrook, P O BOX 356   76657
Isbill JHS, 323 S VAN BUREN ST   76657
  W. Zacharias, prin.
Jenkins ES   76657 – Jack Keltner, prin.

Mc Kinney, Collin Co., Pop. Code 7
Lovejoy ISD
Sch. Sys. Enr. Code 2
Supt. – Robert Puster, F M ROAD #1378   75069
Lovejoy ES   75069 – James Hill, prin.

McKinney ISD
Sch. Sys. Enr. Code 5
Supt. – Jack Cockrill
  800 N MCDONALD ST   75069
Faubion JHS   75069 – Rick Smotherman, prin.
Burks ES, 1801 HILL ST   75069
  Ron Gauthier, prin.
Caldwell IS, 601 W LOUISIANA   75069
  Judy Bratcher, prin.
Greer ES, 510 HEARD ST   75069
  Joyce Owen, prin.
Slaughter IS, 2706 WOLFORD   75069
  Barney Edwards, prin.
Webb ES, 2706 WOLFORD ST   75069
  Dave Adams, prin.
Other Schools – See Frisco

Mc Lean, Gray Co., Pop. Code 4
McLean ISD
Sch. Sys. Enr. Code 2
Supt. – J. Rutheford, P O BOX K   79057
S   79057 – Griffin/Cook, prin.

Mc Leod, Cass Co.
McLeod ISD
Sch. Sys. Enr. Code 2
Supt. – Gary Watson, P O BOX 538   75565
ES, 600 MAIN ST   75565 – Marilyn Felkins, prin.

Madisonville, Madison Co., Pop. Code 5
Madisonville Consolidated ISD
Sch. Sys. Enr. Code 4
Supt. – Norman Plemons, P O BOX 879   77864
JHS   77864 – Sidney Baker, prin.
ES, 300 W SCHOOL ST   77864
  Glenda Blair, prin.
IS   77864 – Sarah Warren, prin.

Magnolia, Motgomery Co., Pop. Code 3
Magnolia ISD
Sch. Sys. Enr. Code 5
Supt. – Steve Jones, P O BOX 88   77355
JHS, P O BOX 476   77355
  Patricia Yarbrough, prin.
Bear Branch ES, 8040 KEN LAKE   77355
  Barbara Sultemeier, prin.
ES   77355 – Beverly Robison, prin.
IS, P O BOX 907   77355 – (—), prin.

Malakoff, Henderson Co., Pop. Code 4
Cross Roads ISD
Sch. Sys. Enr. Code 3
Supt. – D. McKinnerney, RURAL ROUTE 01   75148
Cross Roads JHS   75148 – Glenda Wisenbaker, prin.
Cross Roads ES   75148 – V. Darden, prin.

Malakoff ISD
Sch. Sys. Enr. Code 4
Supt. – Walter Bingham, P O BOX 489   75148
JHS   75148 – David McKee, prin.
ES   75148 – Dave Smith, prin.
IS   75148 – Bill Preston, prin.

Malone, Hill Co., Pop. Code 2
Malone ISD
Sch. Sys. Enr. Code 1
Supt. – David Wood, P O BOX 38   76660
ES   76660 – David Wood, prin.

Manor, Travis Co., Pop. Code 4
Manor ISD
Sch. Sys. Enr. Code 4
Supt. – Noel Jett, P O BOX L   78653
JHS   78653 – J. Fugua, prin.
ES   78653 – John Grasshoff, prin.

Mansfield, Tarrant Co., Pop. Code 6
Mansfield ISD
Sch. Sys. Enr. Code 5
Supt. – Joe Starnes, 605 E BROAD ST   76063
Worley MS, 500 PLEASANT RIDGE DRIVE   76063
  Jerry Gray, prin.
Anderson ES   76063 – Ronnie Lee, prin.
Boren ES, 1400 COUNTRY CLUB DR   76063
  Sarah Jandrucko, prin.
Harmon ES   76063 – Myrna Cline, prin.
IS, 1015 E BROAD ST   76063 – James White, prin.
Nash ES, 800 E BROAD ST   76063
  Judy Miller, prin.
Ponder ES, 102 PLEASANT RIDGE DR   76063
  Pat Jones, prin.
Rendon ES, 605 E BROAD ST   76063
  Martha Reid, prin.

Manvel, Brazoria Co., Pop. Code 5
Alvin ISD
Supt. – See Alvin
Manvel JHS   77578 – Bill Knapick, prin.

Maple, Bailey Co.
Three Way ISD
Sch. Sys. Enr. Code 2
Supt. – Don Parker, P O BOX 87   79344
Three Way S   79344 – Lloyd Mowery, prin.

Marathon, Brewster Co., Pop. Code 3
Marathon ISD
Sch. Sys. Enr. Code 2
Supt. – Marshall Bise, P O BOX 416   79842
ES   79842 – Larry Letbetter, prin.

Marble Falls, Burnet Co., Pop. Code 5
Marble Falls ISD
Sch. Sys. Enr. Code 4
Supt. – Harold Horne,Jr.
  2001 BROADWAY ST   78654
JHS, 2007 BROADWAY ST   78654
  Kenneth McIlvain, prin.
MS, 1909 BROADWAY ST   78654
  Tom Rhea, prin.
PS, 1800 PONY CIR   78654 – Bill Rives, prin.

Marfa, Presidio Co., Pop. Code 4
Marfa ISD
Sch. Sys. Enr. Code 3
Supt. – C. Robinson, P O BOX T   79843
ES   79843 – William Plumbley, prin.
Redford ES   79843 – Tiburcio Acosta, prin.

St. Mary's Cathedral School
206 SOUTH AUSTIN   79843

Marietta, Cass Co., Pop. Code 2
Marietta ISD
Sch. Sys. Enr. Code 1
Supt. – Joel Sain, P O BOX 187   75566
ES   75566 – (—), prin.

Marion, Guadalupe Co., Pop. Code 3
Marion ISD
Sch. Sys. Enr. Code 3
Supt. – Thomas Stockstill, P O BOX 127   78124
MS   78124 – Dennis Dreyer, prin.
Krueger ES   78124 – Harold Dekunde, prin.

Marlin, Falls Co., Pop. Code 6
Marlin ISD
Sch. Sys. Enr. Code 4
Supt. – Joe Campbell, 213 GREEN ST   76661
MS   76661 – Murray Wise, prin.
ES   76661 – Rockney Terry, prin.
IS   76661 – Gayle Pelzel, prin.

Marshall, Harrison Co., Pop. Code 7
Marshall ISD
Sch. Sys. Enr. Code 6
Supt. – Patsy Smith, P O BOX 879   75671
JHS, 201 S COLLEGE ST   75670
  Ora Johnson, prin.
Carver ES, 2302 HOLLAND ST   75670
  Ben Bennett, prin.
Crockett ES, 700 JASPER DR   75670
  Reba Schumacher, prin.
Houston MS, 2905 E TRAVIS ST   75670
  Charles Peden, prin.
Lee ES, 1315 CALLAWAY ST   75670
  Gene Stinson, prin.
Moore ES, 2303 NORWOOD ST   75670
  Orlette Ross, prin.
South Marshall ES, 1600 MEADOW ST   75670
  Jake Matthews, prin.
Travis ES, 300 W CAROLANNE BLVD   75670
  Charles Bertrand, prin.
Young MS, 1501 SANFORD ST   75670
  Vernon May, prin.

St. Joseph ES, 2307 S GARRETT ST   75670
Trinity Episcopal ES, 103 N GROVE ST   75670

Mart, McLennan Co., Pop. Code 4
Mart ISD
Sch. Sys. Enr. Code 3
Supt. – T. Smith, P O BOX 120   76664
IS, WACO HIGHWAY   76664 – E. Ridling, prin.
ES   76664 – W. Hoskins, prin.

Martinsville, Nacogdoches Co.
Martinsville ISD
Sch. Sys. Enr. Code 2
Supt. – C. Scarborough, P O BOX 49   75958
S, P O BOX 49   75958 – Donna Collom, prin.

Mason, Mason Co., Pop. Code 4
Mason ISD
Sch. Sys. Enr. Code 3
Supt. – Ted Kerr, P O BOX 410   76856
ES, 801 COLLEGE   76856 – Henry Hohn, prin.

Matador, Motley Co., Pop. Code 4
Motley County ISD
Sch. Sys. Enr. Code 2
Supt. – Ronald Cummings, P O BOX 310   79244
Motley County ES   79244 – Oran Hamilton, prin.

Matagorda, Matagorda Co.
Matagorda ISD
Sch. Sys. Enr. Code 2
Supt. – Sam Burnes, P O BOX 208   77457
ES   77457 – (—), prin.

Mathis, San Patricio Co., Pop. Code 6
Mathis ISD
Sch. Sys. Enr. Code 4
Supt. – Olan McCraw, P O BOX 1177   78368
JHS   78368 – Dan Murphy, prin.
Hardin ES, 500 E SAINT MARYS ST   78368
  Rochelle Lueckemeye, prin.
IS, 510 E SAINT MARYS ST   78368
  William Williams, prin.
Weber ES, 313 S DUVAL ST   78368
  John Box, prin.

Maud, Bowie Co., Pop. Code 4
Maud ISD
Sch. Sys. Enr. Code 2
Supt. – Robert Stinnett, P O BOX 308   75567
S   75587 – William Humphrey, prin.

May, Brown Co.
May ISD
Sch. Sys. Enr. Code 2
Supt. – Donald Rhodes, P O BOX 38   76857
May ES   76857 – Don Lee, prin.

Maydelle, Cherokee Co.
Maydelle ISD
Sch. Sys. Enr. Code 2
Supt. – J. McGregor, P O BOX 13   75772
S   75772 – William Edwards,Jr., prin.

Maypearl, Ellis Co., Pop. Code 3
Maypearl ISD
Sch. Sys. Enr. Code 2
Supt. – Joe Penn, P O BOX 40   76064
ES   76064 – Ronnie Derryberry, prin.

Meadow, Terry Co., Pop. Code 3
Meadow ISD
Sch. Sys. Enr. Code 2
Supt. – Jim Thomas, P O BOX 217   79345
S   79345 – Lance Morton, prin.

Medina, Bandera Co.
Medina ISD
Sch. Sys. Enr. Code 2
Supt. – Jerry Huie, P O BOX 1415   78055
S   78055 – Dale Naumann, prin.

Megargel, Archer Co., Pop. Code 2
Megargel ISD
Sch. Sys. Enr. Code 2
Supt. – J. Phil Barefield, P O BOX 39   76370
ES, P O BOX 39   76370 – Jim Lee, prin.

Melissa, Collin Co., Pop. Code 3
Melissa ISD
Sch. Sys. Enr. Code 2
Supt. – James Masters, P O BOX 127   75071
MS, P O BOX 127   75071 – Shirley Temples, prin.
Melissa Ridge ES   75071 – Shirley Temples, prin.

Memphis, Hall Co., Pop. Code 5
Memphis ISD
Sch. Sys. Enr. Code 3
Supt. – L. Neal Hindman, P O BOX 460   79245
JHS, P O BOX 460   79245 – Lewis Riley, prin.
Austin MS, 515 S 9TH ST   79245
  Frankye Goldston, prin.
Travis ES, 710 N 12TH ST   79245
  Jo Ann Bailey, prin.

Menard, Menard Co., Pop. Code 4
Menard ISD
Sch. Sys. Enr. Code 2
Supt. – Bob Miller, P O BOX 729   76859
ES   76859 – Harold Miller, prin.

Mercedes, Hidalgo Co., Pop. Code 7
Mercedes ISD
Sch. Sys. Enr. Code 5
Supt. – Monte Churchill, P O BOX 419   78570
JHS, 839 S OHIO ST   78570
  Eliezar Marroquin, prin.
Graham MS, 838 S OHIO ST   78570
  Alejandro Estrada, prin.
Kennedy ES, 801 HIDALGO ST   78570
  Elvira Gracia, prin.
Taylor MS, 900 N MISSOURI ST   78570
  Alvin Smith, prin.
Travis ES   78570 – J. Pinkerton, prin.

Meridian, Bosque Co., Pop. Code 4
Meridian ISD
Sch. Sys. Enr. Code 2
Supt. – Harold McCreary, P O BOX 306   76665
S   76665 – James Hardin, prin.

Merit, Hunt Co.
Bland ISD
Sch. Sys. Enr. Code 2
Supt. – Larry Johnson, P O BOX 216   75072
Bland ES   75072 – Alfred Shipp, prin.

Merkel, Taylor Co., Pop. Code 4
Merkel ISD
Sch. Sys. Enr. Code 4
Supt. – James Logan, P O BOX 430   79536
MS   79536 – Gaylon Brnovak, prin.
ES, 1512 5TH ST   79536 – Ed Ammons, prin.
Other Schools – See Tye

Mertzon, Irion Co., Pop. Code 3
Irion County ISD
Sch. Sys. Enr. Code 2
Supt. – Paul Gothard, P O BOX 469   76941
Iron ES   76941 – John Schuch, prin.

Mesquite, Dallas Co., Pop. Code 8
Mesquite ISD
Sch. Sys. Enr. Code 7
Supt. – John Horn, 405 E DAVIS ST   75149
Agnew MS, 701 WILKINSON DRIVE   75149
  Bill Porter, prin.
McDonald MS, 2930 N TOWN EAST BLVD   75150
  Ron Pardun, prin.
New MS, 3700 S BELT LINE ROAD   75181
  James Maines, prin.
Vanston MS   75150 – Michael Coffey, prin.
Wilkinson MS   75149 – David Allred, prin.

Beasley ES, 919 GREEN CANYON DR 75150
  Gayle Owen, prin.
Black ES, 328 NEWSOME ROAD 75149
  Weldon Hogan, prin.
Cannaday ES 75149 – Denise Kutch, prin.
Florence ES, 4621 GLENEAGLE ST 75150
  Nancy Frehner, prin.
Floyd ES, 3025 HICKORY TREE ROAD 75180
  Aubrey Perry, prin.
Galloway ES, 2329 CANDLEBERRY DR 75149
  Clyde May, prin.
Hanby ES, 912 CASCADE ST 75149
  Cathy Rideout, prin.
Hodges ES, SPRING OAKS DR 75149
  Robert Wilson, prin.
Kimball ES, 4010 CORYELL WAY 75150
  R. Luce, prin.
Lawrence ES, 3811 RICHMAN DR 75150
  William Sefzik, prin.
McKenzie ES, 3535 STEPHENS GREEN 75150
  Howard Payne, prin.
McWhorter ES
  1700 HICKORY TREE ROAD 75149
  Richard Haverkamp, prin.
Motley ES, 7319 MOTLEY DR 75150
  James Mitchell, prin.
Pirrung ES, 405 E DAVIS 75149
  Alane Malone, prin.
Porter ES, 517 VIA AVENIDA 75150
  Arlen McLain, prin.
Range ES, 2600 BAMBOO ST 75150
  Timothy Strobel, prin.
Rugel ES, 2701 SYBIL DR 75149
  Wilburn Nichols, prin.
Rutherford ES, 1601 SIERRA DR 75149
  Jean Stuart, prin.
Seabourn ES, 2300 SANDY LANE 75149
  Orville Pinson, prin.
Shands ES, 4836 SHANDS DR 75150
  Mary McCoy, prin.
Shaw ES, 707 PURPLE SAGE TRAIL 75149
  Larry Benningfield, prin.
Tisinger ES, 1331 NORTHRIDGE DR 75149
  Frank Brooks, prin.
Tosch ES, 2424 LARCHMONT DR 75150
  Cathy Tanton, prin.
Other Schools – See Garland

Mexia, Limestone Co., Pop. Code 6
Mexia ISD
Sch. Sys. Enr. Code 4
Supt. – B. Funderburk
  616 N RED RIVER ST 76667
JHS 76667 – T. Wilkins, prin.
McBay ES 76667 – Bill Brown, prin.
Sims IS 76667 – Warner Hancock, prin.

Meyersville, De Witt Co.
Meyersville ISD
Sch. Sys. Enr. Code 2
Supt. – Laura Whitson, 1000 SCHOOL RD 77974
ES 77974 – (—), prin.

Miami, Roberts Co., Pop. Code 3
Miami ISD
Sch. Sys. Enr. Code 2
Supt. – Allan Dinsmore, P O BOX 368 79059
S 79059 – (—), prin.

Midland, Midland Co., Pop. Code 8
Greenwood ISD
Sch. Sys. Enr. Code 4
Supt. – Tim Outlaw
  RURAL ROUTE 01 BOX 143D 79701
Greenwood S 79701 – Bob Pheil, prin.

Midland ISD
Sch. Sys. Enr. Code 7
Supt. – Joseph Baressi, P O BOX 2298 79702
Alamo JHS, 3800 STOREY AVE 79703
  David Adams, prin.
Goddard JHS, 2500 HAYNES DRIVE 79705
  James Cox, prin.
San Jacinto JHS 79701 – Jack Ratcliff, prin.
Bonham ES, 909 BONHAM ST 79703
  Carl Pirkle, prin.
Bowie ES, 805 ELK AVE 79701
  Bob Watkins, prin.
Burnet ES, 900 RAYMOND DR 79703
  Toby Ward, prin.
Crockett ES, 401 E PARKER AVE 79701
  Roberto Banda, prin.
De Zavala ES, 705 N LEE ST 79701
  Robert Stewart, prin.
Emerson ES, 2800 MOSS AVE 79705
  Clyde Hobbs, prin.
Fannin ES, 2400 FANNIN AVE 79705
  Stanton Burrill, prin.
Henderson ES, 4800 GRACELAND DR 79703
  Jack Hightower, prin.
Houston ES, 2000 W LOUISIANA AVE 79701
  Dorsey Rushing, prin.
Jones ES, 4919 SHADY LANE DR 79703
  Marillyn Odum, prin.
Lamar ES, 3200 KESSLER AVE 79701
  Beverly Ihinger, prin.
Long ES, 4200 CEDAR SPRING DR 79703
  Melinda Phillips, prin.
Milam ES, 301 E DORMARD AVE 79705
  Clinton Adams, prin.
Parker ES, 3800 NORWOOD ST 79707
  Joe Cummins, prin.
Pease ES, 1700 E MAGNOLIA AVE 79705
  John McAfee, prin.

Rusk ES, 2601 WEDGEWOOD ST 79707
  William Sherman, prin.
Santa Rita ES, 5306 WHITMAN DR 79705
  William Maurer, prin.
Scharbauer ES, 2115 HEREFORD BLVD 79701
  Mamie Williams, prin.
South ES, 201 W DAKOTA AVE 79701
  Rob Van Stavern, prin.
Travis ES, 900 E GIST AVE 79701
  Romeo Canales, prin.
Washinton ES, 1800 E WALL ST 79701
  Michael Worley, prin.

Midland Christian School
  2001 CULVER ST 79705
St. Ann's ES, 2000 W TEXAS AVE 79701
Trinity School of Midland
  3500 W WADLEY AVE 79707

Midlothian, Ellis Co., Pop. Code 5
Midlothian ISD
Sch. Sys. Enr. Code 4
Supt. – Jim Norris, 925 S 9TH ST 76065
MS 76065 – Frank Seale, prin.
Baxter ES 76065 – Melanie Wallace, prin.
Irvin MS, 800 W AVENUE H 76065
  Randall Hill, prin.
Mills ES, LAKE ROAD 76065 – Pam Norman, prin.

Milano, Milam Co., Pop. Code 2
Milano ISD
Sch. Sys. Enr. Code 2
Supt. – James Hubert, P O BOX 145 76556
Milano East ES 76556 – Don Hafley, prin.

Miles, Runnels Co., Pop. Code 3
Miles ISD
Sch. Sys. Enr. Code 2
Supt. – James Whitehead, P O BOX 308 76861
S 76861 – Robert McCarson, prin.

Milford, Ellis Co., Pop. Code 3
Milford ISD
Sch. Sys. Enr. Code 2
Supt. – Miles Broughton, P O BOX 545 76670
S 76670 – Dean Burbank, prin.

Millsap, Parker Co., Pop. Code 2
Millsap ISD
Sch. Sys. Enr. Code 3
Supt. – James Scott, P O BOX 100 76066
ES 76066 – Charles White, prin.

Mineola, Wood Co., Pop. Code 5
Mineola ISD
Sch. Sys. Enr. Code 4
Supt. – Bill Knight, 308 UNIVERSITY 75773
MS 75773 – Jerry Cloud, prin.
MS, W PATTON 75773 – Donald Phillips, prin.
PS 75773 – Mavis De La Rosa, prin.

Mineral Wells, Palo Pinto Co., Pop. Code 7
Mineral Wells ISD
Sch. Sys. Enr. Code 5
Supt. – Bill Perrin, 102 NW 6TH AVE 76067
JHS 76067 – Dan Patton, prin.
Grimes ES, 1806 NE 1ST AVE 76067
  Russell McClure, prin.
Houston ES, 1200 SW 4TH AVE 76067
  Pat Caudill, prin.
Lamar ES, 2012 SE 12TH ST 76067
  Don McEwen, prin.
Lee IS, 1200 SE 14TH AVE 76067
  Clarence Holliman, prin.
Travis ES, 701 SE 9TH AVE 76067
  Bill Patterson, prin.

Mirando City, Webb Co., Pop. Code 2
Mirando City ISD
Sch. Sys. Enr. Code 2
Supt. – Benford Frizzell, P O BOX 471 78369
Mirando ES 78369 – Nora Black, prin.

Mission, Hidalgo Co., Pop. Code 7
Mission Consolidated ISD
Sch. Sys. Enr. Code 6
Supt. – Rafael Cantu, 1116 N CONWAY ST 78572
JHS, 1201 BRYCE DRIVE 78572
  John Abbenante, prin.
White JHS 78572 – Linda Alaniz, prin.
Alton ES 78572 – J. Villarreal, prin.
Bryan ES 78572 – Alicia Vela, prin.
Cantu ES 78572 – Daniel King, prin.
Castro ES 78572 – Santos Ramirez, prin.
Leal ES 78572 – Ramon Benavides, prin.
Marcell ES 78572 – Aurora Delgado, prin.
Mims ES 78572 – Hurla Midkiff, prin.
O'Grady ES 78572 – J. Sanchez, prin.
Pearson ES 78572 – Mona Parras, prin.
Roosevelt ES 78572 – Alicia Vela, prin.

Sharyland ISD
Sch. Sys. Enr. Code 4
Supt. – James McDaniel, P O BOX 753 78572
Sharyland/Gray JHS 78572 – Bill Atchison, prin.
Sharyland I ES 78572 – Elizabeth Garrett, prin.
Sharyland II MS 78572 – Rick Powell, prin.

Our Lady of Guadalupe ES
  615 N DUNLAP AVE 78572

Missouri City, Fort Bend Co., Pop. Code 7
Fort Bend ISD
Supt. – See Sugar Land
JHS, 200 LOUISIANA ST 77489
  Ronald Hartman, prin.
Quail Valley JHS 77459 – Michael Leach, prin.

Mobeetie, Wheeler Co., Pop. Code 2
Mobeetie ISD
Sch. Sys. Enr. Code 1
Supt. – David Summers, P O BOX 197 79061
S, P O BOX 197 79061 – Vicki Lewis, prin.

Monahans, Ward Co., Pop. Code 6
Monahans-Wickett-Poyte ISD
Sch. Sys. Enr. Code 5
Supt. – Richard Bain, 606 S BETTY ST 79756
Walker JHS, 611 S BETTY ST 79756
  Elmo Freeman, prin.
Edwards ES, 804 S DWIGHT ST 79756
  Edward Middlebrooks, prin.
Sudderth MS, CAROL & E 79756
  Jim Jordan, prin.
Tatom ES, 1600 S CALVIN ST 79756
  John Ratcliff, prin.
Other Schools – See Wickett

Montague, Montague Co.
Montague ISD
Sch. Sys. Enr. Code 1
Supt. – R Hamric, P O BOX 78 76251
Other Schools – See Bowie

Mont Belvieu, Chambers Co., Pop. Code 4
Barbers Hill ISD
Sch. Sys. Enr. Code 4
Supt. – Louis Bates, P O BOX 1108 77580
MS, P O BOX 1108 77580 – Dan Grimes, prin.
Barbers Hill IS, P O BOX 1108 77580
  Ladell Sanders, prin.
Barbers Hill PS, P O BOX 1108 77580
  Sandra Tilton, prin.

Montgomery, Montgomery Co., Pop. Code 2
Montgomery ISD
Sch. Sys. Enr. Code 4
Supt. – G. Underwood, P O BOX 1475 77356
JHS 77356 – Gaylon Prince, prin.
ES 77356 – Margaret Looper, prin.
IS 77356 – Rebecca Atkinson, prin.

Moody, McLennan Co., Pop. Code 4
Moody ISD
Sch. Sys. Enr. Code 3
Supt. – Marcus Anderson, P O BOX 448 76557
ES 76557 – Swede Erlund, prin.

Moran, Shackelford Co., Pop. Code 2
Moran ISD
Sch. Sys. Enr. Code 1
Supt. – Stephen Beyer, P O BOX 98 76464
ES 75454 – Willis Godwin III, prin.

Morgan, Bosque Co., Pop. Code 2
Morgan ISD
Sch. Sys. Enr. Code 2
Supt. – Leon Hickox, P O BOX 128 76471
S 76671 – Robert Holt, prin.

Morgan Mill, Erath Co.
Morgan Mill ISD
Sch. Sys. Enr. Code 1
Supt. – Dewey Edwards, P O BOX 8 76465
ES 76465 – Dean Edwards, prin.

Morse, Hansford Co.
Pringle-Morse ISD
Sch. Sys. Enr. Code 1
Supt. – Roy Harris, P O BOX 109 79062
Pringle-Morse ES 79062 – Roy Harris, prin.

Morton, Cochran Co., Pop. Code 5
Morton ISD
Sch. Sys. Enr. Code 3
Supt. – Charles Skeen
  500 W BUCHANAN AVE 79346
JHS 79346 – Richard Houston, prin.
ES 79346 – Margaret Masten, prin.

Moulton, Lavaca Co., Pop. Code 4
Moulton ISD
Sch. Sys. Enr. Code 2
Supt. – T. Hoyer, P O BOX C 77975
ES 77975 – Kenneth Fishbeck, prin.

Mount Calm, Hill Co., Pop. Code 2
Mt. Calm ISD
Sch. Sys. Enr. Code 1
Supt. – Hershel Strickland, P O BOX 105 76673
ES 76673 – (—), prin.

Mount Enterprise, Rusk Co., Pop. Code 2
Mt. Enterprise ISD
Sch. Sys. Enr. Code 2
Supt. – J. Webb, P O BOX 130 75681
ES 75681 – Paul Moore, prin.

Mount Pleasant, Titus Co., Pop. Code 7
Chapel Hill ISD
Sch. Sys. Enr. Code 2
Supt. – Jim Sumners, RURAL ROUTE 01 75455
Chapel Hill ES 75493 – Kay Lathem, prin.

Harts Bluff ISD
Sch. Sys. Enr. Code 2
Supt. – M. Barron
  RURAL ROUTE 06 BOX 302 75455
Harts Bluff ES, RURAL ROUTE 06 BOX 302 75455
  Rickey Logan, prin.

Mt. Pleasant ISD
Sch. Sys. Enr. Code 5
Supt. – Jack Murray, P O BOX 1117 75455
Wallace JHS 75455 – Willie Williams, prin.
Brice ES, P O BOX 1117 75455 – Jerry Tierce, prin.

Corprew IS, SCHOOL ST 75455
　Robert Cochran, prin.
Fowler ES, 1006 W 6TH ST 75455
　A. Taylor, prin.
Sims ES, 1801 1ST ST 75455
　Bruce Theobald, prin.

Mount Vernon, Franklin Co., Pop. Code 4
Mt. Vernon ISD
Sch. Sys. Enr. Code 4
Supt. – W. Sears, P O BOX 98 75457
JHS 75457 – R. Robinson, prin.
ES 75457 – Larry Hahn, prin.
IS 75457 – Robert Attaway, prin.

Muenster, Cooke Co., Pop. Code 4
Muenster ISD
Sch. Sys. Enr. Code 2
Supt. – Charles Coffey, P O BOX 608 76252
ES 76252 – Gwen Trubenbach, prin.

Sacred Heart School, 141 E 6TH ST 76252

Muleshoe, Bailey Co., Pop. Code 5
Muleshoe ISD
Sch. Sys. Enr. Code 4
Supt. – Tom Jinks, 514 W AVE G 79347
Watson JHS 79347 – Bob Graves, prin.
DeShazo MS 79347 – (—), prin.
Dillman ES 79347 – Barbara Finney, prin.

Mullin, Mills Co., Pop. Code 2
Mullin ISD
Sch. Sys. Enr. Code 2
Supt. – Harley Ethridge, P O BOX 128 76864
S, P O BOX 128 76864 – Rick Wiedebusch, prin.

Mumford, Robertson Co.
Mumford ISD
Sch. Sys. Enr. Code 1
Supt. – Pete Bienski, P O BOX 268 77867
ES 77867 – (—), prin.

Munday, Knox Co., Pop. Code 4
Munday ISD
Sch. Sys. Enr. Code 2
Supt. – Doyle Lowrance, P O BOX 300 76371
ES, 1111 W MAIN 76371 – Douglas Donoho, prin.

Murchison, Henderson Co., Pop. Code 3
Murchison ISD
Sch. Sys. Enr. Code 2
Supt. – James McPherson, P O BOX 38 75778
ES 75778 – (—), prin.

Nacogdoches, Nacogdoches Co., Pop. Code 8
Central Heights ISD
Sch. Sys. Enr. Code 2
Supt. – James Bogue
　RURAL ROUTE 06 BOX 382 75961
Central Heights S 75961 – Bob Lee, prin.

Nacogdoches ISD
Sch. Sys. Enr. Code 6
Supt. – M. Rector, P O BOX 1521 75963
Rusk MS 75961 – Steve Green, prin.
Brooks-Quinn-Jones PS 75963
　Frances Nations, prin.
Carpenter ES, 1005 LEROY ST 75961
　Evelyn Jackson, prin.
Fredonia ES, 1326 S FREDONIA ST 75961
　Donald Wyatt, prin.
Marshall ES, 422 W COX ST 75961
　Sally Allen, prin.
Raguet ES, 2708 RAGUET ST 75961
　G. Neal, prin.

Christ Episcopal School, 502 E STARR AVE 75961

Nash, Bowie Co., Pop. Code 4
Texarkana ISD
Supt. – See Texarkana
ES, 324 N KINGS HIGHWAY 75569
　Dale Vickers, prin.

Natalia, Medina Co., Pop. Code 4
Natalia ISD
Sch. Sys. Enr. Code 3
Supt. – J. Barta, P O BOX 300 78059
JHS 78059 – Amy Schacht, prin.
ES 78059 – Ira Wells, prin.

Navasota, Grimes Co., Pop. Code 6
Navasota ISD
Sch. Sys. Enr. Code 5
Supt. – Ben Hansen, P O BOX 511 77868
JHS 77868 – W. Hood, prin.
ES, NEAL ST 77868 – Sharon Lyons, prin.
Webb ES, 1604 STACEY ST 77868
　Allen Clark, prin.

Nazareth, Castro Co., Pop. Code 2
Nazareth ISD
Sch. Sys. Enr. Code 2
Supt. – John Mason, P O BOX 189 79063
S 79063 – J. Peggram, prin.

Neches, Anderson Co.
Neches ISD
Sch. Sys. Enr. Code 2
Supt. – Arthur Sloan, P O BOX 310 75779
ES 75779 – Gary Holcomb, prin.

Nederland, Jefferson Co., Pop. Code 7
Nederland ISD
Sch. Sys. Enr. Code 5
Supt. – Charles Thomas, 220 N 17TH ST 77627
Central MS 77627 – Beverly Krohn, prin.

Wilson MS, P O BOX 1088 77627
　J. Winkle, prin.
Helena Park ES, 2800 HELENA AVE 77627
　Carrol Dial, prin.
Highland Park ES, 200 S 6TH ST 77627
　David Coco, prin.
Hillcrest ES, 2611 AVE H 77627
　John Verret, prin.
Langham ES, 800 12TH ST 77627
　Wilfred Noel, prin.

Needville, Fort Bend Co., Pop. Code 4
Needville ISD
Sch. Sys. Enr. Code 4
Supt. – Leroy Miksch, P O BOX 412 77461
MS, P O BOX 412 77461 – Charles Roehling, prin.
ES 77461 – Roxie Crawford, prin.

Nevada, Collin Co.
Community ISD
Sch. Sys. Enr. Code 3
Supt. – Ed Burleson, P O BOX 938 75073
Community MS 75073 – Joe Cashon, prin.
Community ES 75073 – Ruth Cashon, prin.

New Boston, Bowie Co., Pop. Code 5
Malta ISD
Sch. Sys. Enr. Code 1
Supt. – Clarence Davis
　RURAL ROUTE 02 BOX 240 75570
Malta ES, RURAL ROUTE 03 BOX 169 75570
　(—), prin.

New Boston ISD
Sch. Sys. Enr. Code 4
Supt. – Roy Cagle, 600 N MCCOY BLVD 75570
JHS, RURAL ROUTE 02 BOX 362 75570
　J. May, prin.
Crestview ES, 604 HOSPITAL DR 75570
　James Coffman, prin.

New Braunfels, Comal Co., Pop. Code 7
Comal ISD
Sch. Sys. Enr. Code 6
Supt. – Bill Brown
　1421 E US HIGHWAY 81 78130
Canyon MS 78130 – Rusty Brockman, prin.
Bulverde PS 78130 – Marlene Moore, prin.
Bulverde MS 78130 – (—), prin.
Comal ES, RURAL ROUTE 06 BOX 595 78132
　Barbara Miller, prin.
Frazier ES, 1441 E U S HIGHWAY 81 78130
　Sidney Ridgway, prin.
Goodwin PS, 1297 CHURCHHILL ST 78130
　James Dry, prin.
Mountain Valley ES 78130 – Carroll Welch, prin.
Other Schools – See Wetmore

New Braunfels ISD
Sch. Sys. Enr. Code 5
Supt. – Charles Bradberry, P O BOX 311688 78131
MS, 659 S GUENTHER ST 78130
　William Karnau, prin.
Lone Star ES, 144 S HIDALGO ST 78130
　Marilyn Buckner, prin.
Memorial ES, 1200 W COUNTY LNE ROAD 78130
　Karen Simpson, prin.
Schurz MS, 633 W COLL ST 78130
　Jane MacDonald, prin.
Seele MS, 540 HOWARD ST 78130
　Elaine Reagan, prin.

SS Peter and Paul ES, 198 W BRIDGE ST 78130

New Caney, Montgomery Co., Pop. Code 2
New Caney ISD
Sch. Sys. Enr. Code 6
Supt. – Wilburn Echols, P O BOX 53 77357
MS 77357 – Joe Hines, prin.
Aikin ES 77357 – Jeanette Loving, prin.
ES 77357 – Betty Wyatt, prin.
IS 77357 – Sue Smith, prin.
Porter ES 77357 – Gloria Hammack, prin.

Newcastle, Young Co., Pop. Code 3
Newcastle ISD
Sch. Sys. Enr. Code 2
Supt. – Ben Daws, P O BOX 128 76372
ES 76372 – Clarence Spieker, prin.

New Deal, Lubbock Co., Pop. Code 3
New Deal ISD
Sch. Sys. Enr. Code 3
Supt. – Allan Gamblin, P O BOX 280 79350
MS 79350 – Hugh Norwood, prin.
ES, P O BOX 240 79350 – Nancy Cooper, prin.

New Home, Lynn Co., Pop. Code 2
New Home ISD
Sch. Sys. Enr. Code 2
Supt. – Tom Templeton, P O BOX 248 79383
ES 79383 – Glenn Kreger, prin.

New London, Rusk Co., Pop. Code 3
West Rusk ISD
Sch. Sys. Enr. Code 3
Supt. – Douglas Moore, P O BOX 168 75682
West Rusk JHS, P O BOX 168 75682
　Johnny Thompson, prin.
Gaston ES 75682 – Evelyn Anthony, prin.
London ES 75682 – E. Mullins, prin.

New Summerfield, Cherokee Co., Pop. Code 2
New Summerfield ISD
Sch. Sys. Enr. Code 2
Supt. – David Clegg, P O BOX 107 75780
S 75780 – Stanley Wade, prin.

Newton, Newton Co., Pop. Code 4
Newton ISD
Sch. Sys. Enr. Code 4
Supt. – M. Davis, P O BOX 448 75966
JHS 75966 – Hershel Hall, prin.
Bleakwood ES 75966 – Wilma Jones, prin.
ES 75966 – Jeanine McEwin, prin.

New Waverly, Walker Co., Pop. Code 3
New Waverly ISD
Sch. Sys. Enr. Code 3
Supt. – Alvin Davis, P O BOX 38 77358
MS 77358 – James Youngblood, prin.
Rudd ES 77358 – Vergie Klawinski, prin.

Nixon, Gonzales Co., Pop. Code 4
Nixon-Smiley ISD
Sch. Sys. Enr. Code 3
Supt. – M. Gene Ellis, P O BOX 400 78140
Nixon-Smiley MS 78140 – Wayne Stewart, prin.
ES, 802 N RANCHO ROAD 78140
　Lynda McDonald, prin.
Smiley ES 78140 – Wayne Stewart, prin.

Nocona, Montague Co., Pop. Code 5
Nocona ISD
Sch. Sys. Enr. Code 2
Supt. – Richard Brown, P O BOX 210 76255
MS 76255 – Terry Dooley, prin.
ES 76255 – Acce Atkinson, prin.

Prairie Valley ISD
Sch. Sys. Enr. Code 2
Supt. – James Braiser
　RURAL ROUTE 03 BOX 550 76255
Prairie Valley ES 76255 – Ann Fitts, prin.

Nolanville, Bell Co., Pop. Code 4
Killeen ISD
Supt. – See Killeen
ES, 901 NOLANVILLE ROAD 76559
　Johne Little, prin.

Nordheim, De Witt Co., Pop. Code 2
Nordheim ISD
Sch. Sys. Enr. Code 2
Supt. – Vance Frosch, P O BOX 08 78141
S 78141 – John Fortner, prin.

Normangee, Leon Co., Pop. Code 3
Normangee ISD
Sch. Sys. Enr. Code 2
Supt. – Roddy McIver, P O BOX 219 77871
ES, P O BOX 219 77871 – James Vinson, prin.

North Zulch, Madison Co., Pop. Code 2
North Zulch ISD
Sch. Sys. Enr. Code 2
Supt. – M. Gayle Cosby, P O BOX 158 77872
ES 77864 – Glenn Connor, prin.

Novice, Coleman Co., Pop. Code 2
Novice ISD
Sch. Sys. Enr. Code 2
Supt. – E. Farmer, P O BOX 205 79538
S 79538 – Robert Sharp, prin.

Oakwood, Leon Co., Pop. Code 3
Oakwood ISD
Sch. Sys. Enr. Code 2
Supt. – Ronnie Durham, P O BOX 198 75855
ES 75855 – Jim Nedbalek, prin.

Odem, San Patricio Co., Pop. Code 4
Odem-Edroy ISD
Sch. Sys. Enr. Code 4
Supt. – Arturo Almendarez, P O BOX AC 78370
JHS 78370 – Alfredo Acevedo, prin.
ES 78370 – Daniel Baen,Jr., prin.

Odessa, Ector Co., Pop. Code 8
Ector County ISD
Sch. Sys. Enr. Code 8
Supt. – Hugh Hayes, P O BOX 3912 79760
Alamo ES, 801 E 23RD ST 79761
　Joe Ramirez, prin.
Austin ES, 200 E 9TH ST 79761
　Don Chesser, prin.
Blanton ES, P O BOX 3912 79760
　Dan Waters, prin.
Burleson ES, 3800 N GOLDER AVE 79764
　Luis Salcido, prin.
Burnet ES, PERMIAN DR 79762 – Jay Davis, prin.
Cameron ES, 2400 W 8TH ST 79763
　Doris Weaver, prin.
Dowling ES, 17TH & MAPLE 79760
　Phyllis Calzada, prin.
El Magnet/Reagan ES 79760 – Merita Hart, prin.
El Magnet/Travis ES 79760 – Kay Watson, prin.
El Magnet At Hays ES 79760 – Joan Sanders, prin.
El Magnet At Milam ES 79760 – Jo Meeks, prin.
El Magnet At Noel ES 79760 – Irma Chavez, prin.
El Magnet/Blackshear ES 79760
　Bruce Almond, prin.
El Magnet/Ireland ES 79760 – Jimmy Jones, prin.
Fly ES, 9500 WESTVIEW 79760
　Bill Patterson, prin.
Goldsmith ES, 800 MIDLAND ST 79760
　Harold McKelvain, prin.
Goliad ES, P O BOX 3912 79760
　Danny Keener, prin.
Gonzales ES, DISNEY ST 79760
　Nelson Allison, prin.
Houston ES, 37TH & MCKNIGHT 79760
　Edmon Lang, prin.
Lamar ES, 610 JEFFERSON AVE 79761
　Hector Mendez, prin.

Pease ES, W 22ND & SAN FERNANDO 79760
    Bert Mann, prin.
Ross ES, 4600 N EVERLADE AVE 79762
    Will Guster, prin.
San Jacinto ES, P O BOX 3912 79763
    Horton Kidd, prin.
Zavala ES, PINE & CLIFFORD 79760
    Don Norwood, prin.

St. Johns Episcopal Day School
    401 WEST COUNTY ROAD 79760
St. Mary's ES, 1703 ADAMS AVE 79761

O'Donnell, Lynn Co., Pop. Code 4
    O'Donnell ISD
    Sch. Sys. Enr. Code 2
    Supt. – Dale Read, P O BOX 487 79351
    JHS 79351 – I. Hopkins, prin.
    ES 79351 – Bill Clopton, prin.

Oglesby, Coryell Co., Pop. Code 2
    Oglesby ISD
    Sch. Sys. Enr. Code 2
    Supt. – A. Standridge, P O BOX 158 76561
    S 76561 – James Brown, prin.

Olney, Young Co., Pop. Code 5
    Olney ISD
    Sch. Sys. Enr. Code 3
    Supt. – Larry Jones, P O BOX 67 76374
    JHS 76374 – Ben Setliff, prin.
    ES, 801 W HAMILTON ST 76374
        Gerald Butler, prin.

Olton, Lamb Co., Pop. Code 4
    Olton ISD
    Sch. Sys. Enr. Code 3
    Supt. – Ray Kinnison, P O BOX 388 79064
    JHS 79064 – Vernon Paul, prin.
    Webb ES 79054 – Ken Hoskins, prin.

Omaha, Morris Co., Pop. Code 3
    Pewitt ISD
    Sch. Sys. Enr. Code 3
    Supt. – Howard Carver, P O BOX 1106 75571
    Pewitt JHS 75571 – Richard Kitchens, prin.
    Pewitt ES 75571 – Randy Dungan, prin.

Onalaska, Polk Co., Pop. Code 2
    Onalaska ISD
    Sch. Sys. Enr. Code 2
    Supt. – Travis Gibson, P O BOX 1000 77360
    ES 77360 – Ronald Eilers, prin.
    MS 77360 – Ronald Eilers, prin.

Orange, Orange Co., Pop. Code 7
    Little Cypress-Mauriceville ISD
    Sch. Sys. Enr. Code 5
    Supt. – George Skipper
        RURAL ROUTE 08 BOX 220 77630
    Little Cypress JHS, RURAL ROUTE 08 77630
        Eunive Trahan, prin.
    Mauriceville MS 77630 – John Rayburn, prin.
    Little Cypress ES 77630 – Robert Miller,Jr., prin.
    Little Cypress IS 77630 – Ellis Boyd, prin.
    Mauriceville ES 77630 – Pauline Hargrove, prin.

    West Orange-Cove Cons. ISD
    Sch. Sys. Enr. Code 5
    Supt. – Jerome Bourgeois, P O BOX 1107 77631
    West Orange MS 77630 – Lenora George, prin.
    Anderson ES, 902 W PARK AVE 77630
        Kathaleen Rodgers, prin.
    Bancroft ES, 2300 41ST ST 77630
        Wayne McCamey, prin.
    Jones ES, 1704 14TH ST 77630
        Ken Wernig, prin.
    North IS 77630 – Phyllis Logan, prin.
    Oates ES, P O BOX 1107 77631
        Thelma Dowies, prin.

    St. Mary ES, 2600 BOB HALL ROAD 77630

Orangefield, Orange Co., Pop. Code 3
    Orangefield ISD
    Sch. Sys. Enr. Code 4
    Supt. – Michael Moehler, P O BOX 228 77639
    JHS 77639 – Raylin Johnston, prin.
    McLewis ES 77639 – J. Quarles, prin.
    ES 77639 – Mike Martin, prin.

Orange Grove, Jim Wells Co., Pop. Code 4
    Orange Grove ISD
    Sch. Sys. Enr. Code 4
    Supt. – Guy Martin, P O BOX 534 78372
    Slater MS, P O BOX 534 78372 – James Sims, prin.
    ES, P O BOX 534 78372 – Frederick Brand, prin.
    IS 78372 – Margaret Victor, prin.

Orchard, Fort Bend Co., Pop. Code 2
    Wallis-Orchard ISD
    Supt. – See Wallis
    Brazos JHS 77464 – Jackie Ellis, prin.

Ore City, Upshur Co., Pop. Code 4
    Ore City ISD
    Sch. Sys. Enr. Code 3
    Supt. – T. Ferguson, P O BOX 100 75683
    JHS 75683 – Carolyn Coleman, prin.
    ES 75683 – Jim Davis, prin.

Overton, Rusk Co., Pop. Code 4
    Leveretts Chapel ISD
    Sch. Sys. Enr. Code 2
    Supt. – Bill Ward, RURAL ROUTE 02 75684
    Leveretts Chapel S 75684 – Dan Chadwick, prin.

Overton ISD
    Sch. Sys. Enr. Code 2
    Supt. – Bill Davis, P O BOX 130 75684
    ES 75684 – Mary Plemmons, prin.

Ozona, Crockett Co., Pop. Code 5
    Crockett Co. Consolidated Common SD
    Sch. Sys. Enr. Code 3
    Supt. – Garland Davis, P O BOX 400 76943
    JHS 76943 – H. Hooper, prin.
    IS 76943 – Sherry Scott, prin.
    PS 76943 – Walter Spiller, prin.

Paducah, Cottle Co., Pop. Code 4
    Paducah ISD
    Sch. Sys. Enr. Code 2
    Supt. – John Brinson, P O BOX P 79248
    Goodwin ES 79248 – Jimmie Sandlin, prin.

Paint Rock, Concho Co., Pop. Code 2
    Paint Rock ISD
    Sch. Sys. Enr. Code 2
    Supt. – Rich Wood, P O BOX 277 76866
    S 76866 – Daniel Ferrell, prin.

Palacios, Matagorda Co., Pop. Code 5
    Palacios ISD
    Sch. Sys. Enr. Code 4
    Supt. – William Reaves, 1209 12TH ST 77465
    JHS 77465 – Michael Witte, prin.
    Central ES, 1001 5TH ST 77465
        Richard Joyce, prin.
    East Side MS, 901 2ND ST 77465
        Linda Reaves, prin.

Palestine, Anderson Co., Pop. Code 7
    Palestine ISD
    Sch. Sys. Enr. Code 5
    Supt. – L. Thornton, P O BOX 440 75802
    MS 75801 – Jerry Mayo, prin.
    Houston PS, 1000 E LAMAR ST 75801
        Patricia Hamil, prin.
    Northside ES, HWY 155 75802
        Carlton Tucker, prin.
    Rusk PS, 420 W PALESTINE AVE 75801
        Freta Parkes, prin.
    Southside ES, GILLESPIE ROAD 75801
        Billie Pipes, prin.
    Story MS, P O BOX 440 75801
        Diane Thompson, prin.
    Washington ES, W HAMLETT ST 75801
        Richard Smith, prin.

    Westwood ISD
    Sch. Sys. Enr. Code 4
    Supt. – Marvin Thompson, P O BOX 260 75802
    Westwood JHS, P O BOX 260 75802
        Elaine Wilmore, prin.
    Westwood MS, 2305 SALT WORKS RD 75801
        Mary Gibson, prin.
    Westwood PS, 1701 W POINT TAP 75801
        Clyce Marshall, prin.

Palmer, Ellis Co., Pop. Code 4
    Palmer ISD
    Sch. Sys. Enr. Code 3
    Supt. – B. Earl Richardson, P O BOX 278 75152
    MS 75152 – Ronald Levingston, prin.
    ES, P O BOX 790 75152 – Jack Bardwell, prin.

Palo Pinto, Palo Pinto Co., Pop. Code 3
    Palo Pinto ISD
    Sch. Sys. Enr. Code 1
    Supt. – J. Pat Narcomey, P O BOX 280 76072
    ES, P O BOX 280 76072 – Pat Narcomey, prin.

Pampa, Gray Co., Pop. Code 7
    Pampa ISD
    Sch. Sys. Enr. Code 5
    Supt. – Harry Griffith, 321 W ALBERT ST 79065
    MS, 2401 CHARLES ST 79065
        Oneal Westbrook, prin.
    Austin ES 79065 – Bill Jones, prin.
    Baker ES, 300 E TUKE ST 79065
        John Welborn, prin.
    Lamar ES, 1234 S NELSON ST 79065
        Tim Powers, prin.
    Mann ES, 400 N FAULKNER ST 79065
        Tom Lindsey, prin.
    Travis ES, 2300 PRIMROSE LANE 79065
        Jack Bailey, prin.
    Wilson ES, 801 E BROWNING AVE 79065
        Raymond Thornton, prin.

    St. Matthew's Episcopal Day School
        727 W BROWNING AVE 79065
    St. Vincent De Paul School
        2300 N HOBART ST 79065

Panhandle, Carson Co., Pop. Code 4
    Panhandle ISD
    Sch. Sys. Enr. Code 3
    Supt. – Ronnie Teichelman, P O BOX 1030 79068
    JHS, P O BOX 1030 79068 – C. Gill, prin.
    ES, 106 W 9TH 79068 – Gary Laramore, prin.

Panna Maria, Karnes Co.
    Karnes City ISD
    Supt. – See Karnes City
    ES 78144 – Richard Moody, prin.

Paradise, Wise Co., Pop. Code 4
    Paradise ISD
    Sch. Sys. Enr. Code 3
    Supt. – Robert Lacy, P O BOX 6758 76073
    ES 76073 – Wally Shackleford, prin.

Paris, Lamar Co., Pop. Code 8
    Chisum ISD
    Sch. Sys. Enr. Code 3
    Supt. – J. Brooks, RURAL ROUTE 04 75460
    Chisum ES 75460 – Robert Ballard, prin.

    Paris ISD
    Sch. Sys. Enr. Code 5
    Supt. – Elaine Ballard, P O BOX 1159 75460
    Crockett MS, 655 28TH ST NW 75460
        Philip Nance, prin.
    Travis MS, 3270 GRAHAM ST 75460
        Ralph Rodgers, prin.
    Aiken ES, 3100 PINE MILL ROAD 75460
        Jim Preston, prin.
    Justiss ES, 401 18TH ST NW 75460
        Loren Stephens, prin.

Pasadena, Harris Co., Pop. Code 9
    Deer Park ISD
    Supt. – See Deer Park
    Deepwater JHS, 501 GLENMORE DRIVE 77503
        Don McGhee, prin.

    Pasadena ISD
    Sch. Sys. Enr. Code 8
    Supt. – E. Luty, P O BOX 1799 77501
    Jackson IS, 100 JACKSON AVE 77506
        Ben Lenamon, prin.
    Miller IS, 1002 FAIRMONT PARKWAY 77504
        James Smith, prin.
    Park View IS, 3003 DABNEY DRIVE 77502
        James satterwhite, prin.
    Queens IS 77502 – Robert Tyler, prin.
    San Jacinto IS, 3102 SAN AUGUSTINE AVE 77503
        David Post, prin.
    Southmore IS, 1300 HOUSTON AVE 77502
        Robert Fawcett, prin.
    Bailey ES, 2707 LAFFERTY ROAD 77502
        Jeanette Bradley, prin.
    Fisher ES, 2220 GRUNEWALD DR 77502
        Jean Palmer, prin.
    Gardens ES, 1105 HARRIS AVE 77506
        Celia Payne, prin.
    Golden Acres ES, 5233 HOLLY AVE 77503
        Bob Kelley, prin.
    Jensen ES, 3514 TULIP ST 77504
        John Lowe, prin.
    Kruse ES, 201 BROADWAY AVE 77506
        Sylvia Valverde, prin.
    McMasters ES, 1011 BENNETT DR 77503
        Diana Alvarez, prin.
    Moore ES 77501 – Gerald Davis, prin.
    Parks ES, 3302 SAN AUGUSTINE AVE 77503
        Dorethea Norville, prin.
    Pearl Hall ES, AVE N & 13 77501
        Doyle Little, prin.
    Pomeroy ES, 920 BURKE ROAD 77506
        Pam Ainsworth, prin.
    Red Bluff ES, 416 BEARLE ST 77506
        Carole Lusby, prin.
    Richey ES, 700 RICHEY ST 77506
        Nina Hobdy, prin.
    Smith ES, 206 PEREZ 77501 – Jonah Boyd,Jr., prin.
    Smythe ES, 2202 PASADENA BLVD 77502
        Emily Timmons, prin.
    South Shaver ES, 2020 SHAVER ST 77502
        Joyce Eversole, prin.
    Sparks ES, 2503 SOUTHMORE AVE 77502
        Gayle Holder, prin.
    Teague ES, 4200 CRENSHAW ROAD 77504
        Gene Henson, prin.
    Williams ES, 1522 SCARBOROUGH LANE 77502
        Tim Cone, prin.
    Young ES, 4221 FOX MEADOW LANE 77504
        Shirlyn Ross, prin.
    Other Schools – See Houston, South Houston

    St. Pius V ES, 812 MAIN ST 77506
    Zion Lutheran ES, 1117 MAIN ST 77506

Pattison, Waller Co., Pop. Code 2
    Royal ISD
    Supt. – See Brookshire
    Royal MS 77466 – H. Nail, prin.

Pattonville, Lamar Co.
    Prairiland ISD
    Sch. Sys. Enr. Code 4
    Supt. – Leslie Taylor
        RURAL ROUTE 01 BOX 39 75468
    Blossom ES 75468 – L. Stout, prin.
    DePort ES 75468 – Larry Salter, prin.

Pawnee, Bee Co.
    Pawnee ISD
    Sch. Sys. Enr. Code 2
    Supt. – Douglas Arnold, P O BOX 568 78145
    ES 78145 – Lacy Pogue, prin.

Pearland, Brazoria Co., Pop. Code 7
    Pearland ISD
    Sch. Sys. Enr. Code 6
    Supt. – G. Bullard, P O BOX 7 77588
    IS 77581 – J. Anderson, prin.
    Carleton ES 77588 – Christine Knight, prin.
    Harris ES 77588 – (—), prin.
    Jamison MS 77588 – Robert Richter, prin.
    Lawhon ES 77588 – Alice Martinez, prin.
    Shadycrest ES 77588 – Jack Harvey, prin.

Pearsall, Frio Co., Pop. Code 6
    Pearsall ISD
    Sch. Sys. Enr. Code 4
    Supt. – Tom Morris, 522 E FLORIDA ST 78061
    JHS 78061 – Ben Wilson, prin.

IS, 523 E FLORIDA ST 78061 – Mike Salinas, prin.
Westside ES, 1005 N WILLOW ST 78061
  Rolando Trevino, prin.

Peaster, Parker Co.
Peaster ISD
Sch. Sys. Enr. Code 2
Supt. – Philip Bledsoe, P O BOX 278 76074
S 76074 – Weldon Turner, prin.

Pecos, Reeves Co., Pop. Code 7
Pecos-Barstow-Toyah ISD
Sch. Sys. Enr. Code 5
Supt. – Harvey Ramsey, P O BOX 869 79772
Pecos JHS-8th 79772 – Bud Gossett, prin.
Pecos JHS-7th 79772 – F. Talamantez, prin.
Austin ES, 1501 W VETERANS BLVD 79772
  Beatrice Jenkins, prin.
Barstow ES 79772 – Sandra Bailey, prin.
Haynes ES, 800 E 11TH ST 79772
  Gomesinda Olibas, prin.
Lamar ES, OAK & F ST 79772
  Robert Hernandez, prin.
ES, 901 S WILLOW ST 79772
  Joyce Mussey, prin.

Pecos SDA School 79772

Penelope, Hill Co., Pop. Code 2
Penelope ISD
Sch. Sys. Enr. Code 2
Supt. – Bill Sparks, P O BOX 68 76676
S 76676 – Bill Sparks, prin.

Perrin, Jack Co., Pop. Code 4
Perrin-Whitt CISD
Sch. Sys. Enr. Code 2
Supt. – Bob Cannon, P O BOX 39 76075
JHS 76075 – Russell Cotton, prin.
ES 76075 – W. Whaley, prin.

Perryton, Ochiltree Co., Pop. Code 6
Perryton ISD
Sch. Sys. Enr. Code 4
Supt. – Zearl Fiskin, P O BOX 1048 79070
JHS, 510 S ETON ST 79070 – Dale Parvin, prin.
Central ES, 410 S ETON ST 79070
  Kenneth Splawn, prin.
Wright ES, 1702 S GRINNELL ST 79070
  S. Pierce, prin.

Petersburg, Hale Co., Pop. Code 4
Petersburg ISD
Sch. Sys. Enr. Code 2
Supt. – Bert Grimes, P O BOX 160 79250
ES, P O BOX 160 79250 – Charles Thompson, prin.

Petrolia, Clay Co., Pop. Code 3
Petrolia ISD
Sch. Sys. Enr. Code 2
Supt. – Troy Bratcher, P O BOX 176 76377
S, P O BOX 176 76377 – G. Linton, prin.

Pettus, Bee Co., Pop. Code 3
Pettus ISD
Sch. Sys. Enr. Code 2
Supt. – H. Jefferson, P O BOX D 78146
ES, P O BOX D 78146 – Elizabeth Crabb, prin.

Pflugerville, Travis Co., Pop. Code 3
Pflugerville ISD
Sch. Sys. Enr. Code 6
Supt. – Robert Spoonemore, P O BOX 778 78660
MS 78660 – Fred Fasel, prin.
Westview MS 78660 – Boni Duran, prin.
Dessau ES 78660 – Pat Rueter, prin.
Northwest ES 78660 – Robert Toth, prin.
Parmer Lane ES 78660 – Linda Rowold, prin.
ES, 15801 DESSAU ROAD 78660
  Randall Reese, prin.
Timmerman ES, 800 W PECAN ST 78660
  Erbie Rodgers, prin.

Pharr, Hidalgo Co., Pop. Code 7
Pharr-San Juan-Alamo ISD
Supt. – See San Juan
Johnson JHS 78577 – Jose Garza, prin.
Bowie ES, P O BOX Y 78577
  Lydia Savedra, prin.
Buckner MS, 1001 N FIR ST 78577
  Jose Sanchez, prin.
Buell ES, 218 E JUAREZ ST 78577
  Eva Martinez, prin.
Carnahan ES, 317 W GORE ST 78577
  Marla Guerra, prin.
Clover ES, N SAN JUAN ROAD 78577
  Ruben Solis, prin.
Doedyns MS, N SAN JUAN ROAD 78577
  Alma Prado, prin.
Farias MS, N ALAMO ROAD 78577
  Ramiro Vargas, prin.
Ford ES, E POLK ST 78577
  Maria Del Pilar Garza, prin.
Franklin ES, 314 BIRCH 78577
  Alfonso Licon, prin.
Garza-Pena ES, E GASLINE ROAD 78577
  Porfirio Rodriguez, prin.
Garza-Pena PS, E GASLINE ROAD 78577
  Marcia Garza, prin.
Longoria ES, P O BOX 654 78577
  Berta Palacios, prin.
Napper ES, 903 N FLAG ST 78577
  Anna Perez, prin.
Palmer ES, 703 E SAM HOUSTON ST 78577
  Salvador Flores, prin.
Ramirez MS, P O BOX F 78577
  Esteban Garcia, prin.

Whitney MS, 1600 W KELLY ST 78577
  Baldomero Cantu, prin.

Valley View ISD
Sch. Sys. Enr. Code 4
Supt. – Leonel Galaviz
  RURAL ROUTE 01 BOX 122 78577
Valley View IS 78577 – Norma Anzaldua, prin.
Valley View PS 78577 – Santos Perez, prin.

Trinity Episcopal Day School
  202 S ASTER ST 78577

Pilot Point, Denton Co., Pop. Code 4
Pilot Point ISD
Sch. Sys. Enr. Code 3
Supt. – Earl Tate, P O BOX 455 76258
Gee JHS 76258 – C. Purcell, prin.
ES 76258 – Linda Medearis, prin.

Pineland, Sabine Co., Pop. Code 4
West Sabine ISD
Sch. Sys. Enr. Code 3
Supt. – Jackie Hilton, P O BOX 8 75968
West Sabine ES 75968 – Janet Carriger, prin.

Pittsburg, Camp Co., Pop. Code 5
Pittsburg ISD
Sch. Sys. Enr. Code 4
Supt. – L. Curtis Culwell, 302 TEXAS ST 75686
MS, 303 BROACH ST 75686 – Donald Fry, prin.
IS, LAFAYETTE ST 75686
  Roxanne Crouch, prin.
PS, E FULTON ST 75686 – Jerry Bass, prin.

Plains, Yoakum Co., Pop. Code 4
Plains ISD
Sch. Sys. Enr. Code 4
Supt. – Dean Andrews, P O BOX 479 79355
JHS 79355 – Jim Conner, prin.
ES 79355 – John Nance, prin.

Plainview, Hale Co.
Plainview ISD
Sch. Sys. Enr. Code 6
Supt. – Dennis Townsend, P O BOX 1540 79073
Estacado JHS, 2500 W 20TH ST 79072
  Wendell Dunlap, prin.
Ash MS, 908 ASH ST 79072 – Dell Brown, prin.
College Hill ES, 707 CANYON ST 79072
  Ronald Miller, prin.
Coronado JHS, 1201 GALVESTON ST 79072
  Derrell Kunkel, prin.
Edgemere ES, 2600 W 20TH ST 79072
  Don Williams, prin.
Highland ES, 1707 W 11TH ST 79072
  Joanne Cagle, prin.
Hillcrest ES, 315 NW ALPINE DR 79072
  Larry Mc Nutt, prin.
Lakeside MS, 1800 JOLIET ST 79072
  Romey Fennell,Jr., prin.
Thunderbird ES, 1200 W 32ND ST 79072
  L. Williams, prin.

Plano, Collin Co., Pop. Code 8
Plano ISD
Sch. Sys. Enr. Code 8
Supt. – H. Hendrick, 1517 AVE H 75074
Armstrong MS, 3805 TIMBERLINE DRIVE 75074
  D. Beavert, prin.
Bowman MS, 2501 JUNIPER ROAD 75074
  Joe Chesney, prin.
Carpenter MS, 1501 CROSSBEND 75075
  David Dooley, prin.
Haggard MS, 2401 WESTSIDE DRIVE 75075
  Tom Salmon, prin.
Schimelpfenig MS, 75023 – Tom Leyden, prin.
Wilson MS, 1001 CUSTER ROAD 75075
  Beverly Sellers, prin.
Aldridge ES, 75074 – James Bloomer, prin.
Barron ES, 3300 P AVE 75074
  Sharon Gunn, prin.
Brinker ES 75074 – Joan Heiting, prin.
Carlisle ES, 6525 OLD ORCHARD DR 75023
  Charles McCasland, prin.
Christie ES, 3801 RAINER ROAD 75023
  Jane Fletcher, prin.
Davis ES, 2701 PARKHAVEN DR 75075
  Don Dunlap, prin.
Dooley ES, 2425 SAN GABRIEL DR 75074
  Sandra Wysong, prin.
Forman ES, 3600 TIMBERLINE DR 75074
  Mary Fossier, prin.
Harrington ES, 2528 COUNTRY PLACE DR 75075
  Susan Dantzler, prin.
Hendrick ES, 1517 AVE H 75074
  Jacqueline Russell, prin.
Huffman ES, 5510 CHANNEL ISLE DR 75075
  Carol Gardner, prin.
Hughston ES, 2601 CROSS BEND ROAD 75023
  Luanne Collins, prin.
Jackson ES, 1101 JACKSON DR 75075
  Carolyn Warterfield, prin.
Mathews ES, 1517 AVE H 75074
  Deborah Sanders, prin.
Meadows ES, 1600 RIGSBEE DR 75074
  Chuck Clotfelter, prin.
Memorial ES, 2600 R AVE 75074
  Charles Greer, prin.
Mendenhall ES, 1313 18TH ST 75074
  Martha Hunt, prin.
Saigling ES, 3600 MATTERHORN DR 75075
  Janie Milner, prin.
Shepard ES, 1000 WILSON DR 75075
  Robert Sewell, prin.

Sigler ES, 1400 JANWOOD DR 75075
  Margaret Reynolds, prin.
Thomas ES, 6537 BLUE RIDGE TRL 75023
  Elizabeth Kirby, prin.
Weatherford ES, 2941 MOLLIMAR DR 75075
  Janice Havard, prin.
Wells ES, 3427 MISSION RIDGE ROAD 75023
  Nell Pearce, prin.

Faith Lutheran School, 1701 E PARK BLVD 75074
St. Mark Catholic ES, 1201 ALMA DR 75075

Pleasanton, Atascosa Co., Pop. Code 6
Pleasanton ISD
Sch. Sys. Enr. Code 5
Supt. – Darrell Pool, 831 STADIUM DRIVE 78064
JHS, 831 STADIUM DRIVE 78064
  Norman Porter, prin.
Campbellton ES 78064 – Michael Dworaczyk, prin.
Leming ES 78064 – Aaron Guajardo, prin.
ES, 616 MAIN ST 78064 – Arth Whitley, prin.
PS 78064 – Margaret Coleman, prin.

Point Comfort, Calhoun Co., Pop. Code 4
Calhoun County ISD
Supt. – See Port Lavaca
ES, JESTER 77978 – John Woods, prin.

Pollok, Angelina Co.
Central ISD
Sch. Sys. Enr. Code 4
Supt. – Joe Crane
  RURAL ROUTE 01 BOX 39 75969
Central JHS 75969 – Dudley Dickens, prin.
Central ES 75969 – K. Nerren, prin.

Ponder, Denton Co., Pop. Code 2
Ponder ISD
Sch. Sys. Enr. Code 2
Supt. – Emmett Baker, P O BOX 278 76259
ES 76259 – Linda Monaco, prin.

Poolville, Parker Co., Pop. Code 2
Poolville ISD
Sch. Sys. Enr. Code 2
Supt. – Bill Allen, P O BOX 96 76076
S 76076 – Robert Clark, prin.

Port Aransas, Nueces Co., Pop. Code 4
Port Aransas ISD
Sch. Sys. Enr. Code 2
Supt. – Dale Pitts, P O BOX 1297 78373
Brundrett MS, P O BOX 1297 78373
  Ernest Page, prin.
Olsen ES, 100 S STATION 78373
  Jim Littlefield, prin.

Port Arthur, Jefferson Co., Pop. Code 8
Port Arthur ISD
Sch. Sys. Enr. Code 7
Supt. – Joe Pitts, P O BOX 1388 77641
Edison MS, 3501 12TH ST 77642
  Joe Herod, prin.
Wilson MS, 1500 LAKESHORE DRIVE 77640
  Sylvester Page, prin.
DeQueen ES, 7 ST & DEQUEEN 77641
  Bob Durham, prin.
Dowling ES, 62 ST & PAT 77641
  Kathy Attaway, prin.
Franklin ES, 10 ST & MOBILE 77641
  Charlie Vanatta, prin.
Houston ES, 36 ST & 5 AVE 77641
  Doris Gill, prin.
Lee ES, 3939 DELAWARE DR 77642
  Glenn Park, prin.
Pease ES, 5924 JADE AVE 77640
  Elizabeth Braggs, prin.
Travis-Opportunity ES
  LAKEVIEW AVE & LEWIS DR 77641
  Morris Lee, prin.
Tyrrell ES, 4401 FERNDALE DR 77642
  Charlotte Edmons, prin.
Washington ES, 401 W 12TH ST 77640
  Norman Traylor, prin.

Central Catholic ES 77640
St. Catherine ES, 3840 WOODROW DR 77642

Port Isabel, Cameron Co., Pop. Code 5
Port Isabel ISD
Sch. Sys. Enr. Code 4
Supt. – Martin Pena, P O BOX AH 78578
JHS, 202 PORT ROAD 78578
  Raul Villarreal, prin.
Derry MS, 2ND & MICHIGAN 78578
  Bertha Zamora, prin.
Garriga ES 78578 – Cecilia Castillo, prin.

Portland, San Patricio Co., Pop. Code 6
Gregory-Portland ISD
Supt. – See Gregory
Gregory-Portland JHS
  4200 WILDCAT DRIVE 78374
  Donald Sheldon, prin.
Andrews ES, 1100 LANG ROAD 78374
  Lloyd Goldsmith, prin.
Clark ES, 1100 AUSTIN ST 78374
  Pat McDonald, prin.
East Cliff ES, 200 FULTON PLACE 78374
  Louise Moser, prin.

Port Lavaca, Calhoun Co., Pop. Code 7
Calhoun County ISD
Sch. Sys. Enr. Code 5
Supt. – Elvis Arterbury, P O BOX DD 77979
Travis MS, 705 N NUECES ST 77979
  Juan Rodriguez, prin.

Crockett MS, 1512 JACKSON ST 77979
  Janette Barlow, prin.
Harrison ES, 110 E ASH ST 77979
  Wilbert Treybig, prin.
Jackson MS, 1418 JACKSON ST 77979
  Janette Barlow, prin.
Jefferson ES, N COMMERCE ST 77979
  Bob Meloy, prin.
Madison MS, N COMMERCE ST 77979
  Leroy Wiese, prin.
Port O'Connor ES 77979 – Marilyn Herren, prin.
Roosevelt ES, 300 ALCOA DR 77979
  Apolonio Carrion, prin.
Other Schools – See Point Comfort, Seadrift

Port Neches, Jefferson Co., Pop. Code 7
Port Neches ISD
Sch. Sys. Enr. Code 5
Supt. – Zach Byrd, P O BOX 877 77651
Groves MS, P O BOX 877 77651
  Wayne Beasley, prin.
MS, 2131 LLANO ST 77651 – Howard Frey, prin.
MS, 2101 LLANO ST 77651 – Charles Riley, prin.
Ridgewood ES 77651 – Charlie Reynolds, prin.
Woodcrest ES, 1522 HEISLER ST 77651
  Wynell Hollomon, prin.
Other Schools – See Groves

Post, Garza Co., Pop. Code 5
Post ISD
Sch. Sys. Enr. Code 4
Supt. – W. Shiver, P O BOX 70 79356
MS, 405 W 8TH ST 79356 – L. Davis, prin.
ES, 309 W 8TH ST 79356 – Dan Rankin, prin.

Poteet, Atascosa Co., Pop. Code 5
Poteet ISD
Sch. Sys. Enr. Code 4
Supt. – Dale Summit, P O BOX 138 78065
JHS 78065 – James Henry, prin.
ES, SCHOOL DR 78065 – Gerald Nowotny, prin.

Poth, Wilson Co., Pop. Code 4
Poth ISD
Sch. Sys. Enr. Code 3
Supt. – Larry Stavinoha, P O BOX 248 78147
JHS 78147 – Leroy Schneider, prin.
ES 78147 – Tim Braniff, prin.

Pottsboro, Grayson Co., Pop. Code 3
Pottsboro ISD
Sch. Sys. Enr. Code 3
Supt. – C. Chambless, P O BOX 555 75076
MS 75076 – Ronny Ray, prin.
ES 75076 – Larry Cassell, prin.

Pottsville, Hamilton Co.
Pottsville ISD
Sch. Sys. Enr. Code 1
Supt. – David Lewein, P O BOX 174 76565
S 76565 – (—), prin.

Powderly, Lamar Co.
North Lamar ISD
Sch. Sys. Enr. Code 5
Supt. – R. Chadwick, P O BOX 68 75473
Bailey MS 75473 – B. Brown, prin.
Everett ES 75473 – Sherry Workman, prin.
Parker ES 75473 – Raymond Allen, prin.

Prairie Lea, Caldwell Co.
Prairie Lea ISD
Sch. Sys. Enr. Code 2
Supt. – Maebeth Bagley, P O BOX 12 78661
ES 78661 – Bill Nicholas, prin.

Elgin SDA School 78661

Premont, Jim Wells Co., Pop. Code 5
Premont ISD
Sch. Sys. Enr. Code 3
Supt. – Jose Johnson, P O BOX 530 78375
JHS 78375 – Luis Guerra, prin.
Premont Central MS, 400 CORA 78375
  Luis Guerra, prin.
PS, 100 NW 1ST 78375 – Luz Alanis, prin.

Presidio, Presidio Co., Pop. Code 3
Presidio ISD
Sch. Sys. Enr. Code 3
Supt. – Rene Franco, P O BOX S 79845
JHS 79845 – Armando Carrasco, prin.
Candelaria ES 79845 – (—), prin.
ES 79845 – (—), prin.

Price, Rusk Co., Pop. Code 3
Carlisle ISD
Sch. Sys. Enr. Code 2
Supt. – J. Henderson, P O BOX 187 75687
Carlisle S 75687 – T. Robertson, prin.

Priddy, Mills Co.
Priddy ISD
Sch. Sys. Enr. Code 1
Supt. – Rick Davidson, P O BOX 40 76870
S 76870 – Melvin Eilers, prin.

Princeton, Collin Co., Pop. Code 5
Princeton ISD
Sch. Sys. Enr. Code 4
Supt. – Bob Aldridge, P O BOX B 75077
Clark MS, P O BOX B 75077 – Larry Latham, prin.
Princeton ES 75077 – Susan Williamson, prin.

Progreso, Hidalgo Co., Pop. Code 3
Progreso ISD
Sch. Sys. Enr. Code 4
Supt. – Alfonso Obregon, Jr., P O BOX 613 78579

JHS 78579 – Homero Garcia, prin.
ES 78579 – Pete Ramirez, prin.

Prosper, Collin Co., Pop. Code 3
Prosper ISD
Sch. Sys. Enr. Code 2
Supt. – William Rushing, P O BOX 107 75078
ES 75078 – Tom Cooper, prin.

Quanah, Hardeman Co., Pop. Code 5
Quanah ISD
Sch. Sys. Enr. Code 3
Supt. – Stanley Jaggers, P O BOX 150 79252
Travis MS 79252 – Terry Allen, prin.
Reagan ES, 205 E 8TH ST 79252
  Gayle McKinley, prin.

Queen City, Cass Co., Pop. Code 4
Queen City ISD
Sch. Sys. Enr. Code 4
Supt. – Sidney Lane, P O BOX 128 75572
MS 75572 – Douglas Devine, prin.
Hileman ES 75572 – Eugene Sloan, prin.

Quinlan, Hunt Co., Pop. Code 4
Boles Home ISD
Sch. Sys. Enr. Code 2
Supt. – Graham Sweeney
  RURAL ROUTE 03 BOX 48 75474
Boles Home ES 75474 – Jack Thomason, prin.

Quinlan ISD
Sch. Sys. Enr. Code 4
Supt. – Charlie Thompson, P O BOX 466 75474
MS, RURAL ROUTE 03 BOX 18 75474
  Thomas Idom, prin.
Butler MS 75474 – Patricia Higgins, prin.
Cannon ES 75474 – Charles Wilson, prin.

Quitaque, Briscoe Co., Pop. Code 3
Turkey-Quitaque ISD
Supt. – See Turkey
Valley S 79255 – J. Maupin, prin.

Quitman, Wood Co., Pop. Code 4
Quitman ISD
Sch. Sys. Enr. Code 4
Supt. – Noel Jackson, P O BOX 488 75783
JHS, P O BOX 488 75783 – Delbert Ballard, prin.
ES, 902 E GOODE ST 75783
  Ronald Beeson, prin.

Ralls, Crosby Co., Pop. Code 4
Ralls ISD
Sch. Sys. Enr. Code 3
Supt. – J. Apple, P O BOX AD 79357
MS 79357 – Tom Morris, prin.
ES, 1401 16TH 79357 – Steve Myers, prin.

Ranger, Eastland Co., Pop. Code 5
Ranger ISD
Sch. Sys. Enr. Code 3
Supt. – Jerry Jackson
  RURAL ROUTE 03 BOX 12D 76470
ES 76470 – Glynn Wilson, prin.

Rankin, Upton Co., Pop. Code 4
Rankin ISD
Sch. Sys. Enr. Code 2
Supt. – Bobby Dodds, P O BOX 66 79778
MS 79778 – Melvin Wimberley, prin.
ES 79778 – Gary Kuhlmann, prin.

Raymondville, Willacy Co., Pop. Code 6
Raymondville ISD
Sch. Sys. Enr. Code 5
Supt. – Byron Secrest, 1 BEARKAT BLVD 78580
Green JHS 78580 – Joe Herod, prin.
Pittman IS 78580 – Barbara Nicholson, prin.
Pittman PS 78580 – Sylvia Hembree, prin.
Smith ES 78580 – Frank Solis, prin.

Red Oak, Ellis Co., Pop. Code 4
Red Oak ISD
Sch. Sys. Enr. Code 5
Supt. – R. Edd Burleson, P O BOX 262 75154
JHS 75154 – Gary Autrey, prin.
ES, 306 METHODIST ST 75154
  Ray Hernandez, prin.
IS 75154 – Steve Nash, prin.
Shields ES 75154 – Karen Miller, prin.
Wooden ES, FM 2377 75154 – Joy Shaw, prin.

Redwater, Bowie Co., Pop. Code 2
Redwater ISD
Sch. Sys. Enr. Code 3
Supt. – Joe Lee, P O BOX 347 75573
JHS 75573 – Wayland Lacy, prin.
ES 75573 – Robert Eitel, prin.

Refugio, Refugio Co., Pop. Code 5
Refugio ISD
Sch. Sys. Enr. Code 3
Supt. – Ben Colwell, P O BOX 190 78377
MS 78377 – Glen Pfeil, prin.
Stricklin PS, 101 CROCKETT ST 78377
  Michael Kellner, prin.

Rice, Ellis Co.
Rice ISD
Sch. Sys. Enr. Code 2
Supt. – Jerry Eddins, P O BOX 68 75155
ES 75156 – Tom Herrin, prin.

Richards, Grimes Co., Pop. Code 2
Richards ISD
Sch. Sys. Enr. Code 2
Supt. – Ron Reed, P O BOX 308 77873
ES 77873 – Ronnie Reed, prin.

Richardson, Dallas Co., Pop. Code 8
Richardson ISD
Sch. Sys. Enr. Code 8
Supt. – Arzell Ball
  400 S GREENVILLE AVE 75081
Aikin ES
  12300 PLEASANT VALLEY LANE 75080
  Jody Westbrook, prin.
Arapaho ES, 1300 CYPRESS DR 75080
  Brenda Bottles, prin.
Big Springs ES 75081 – Frances Smith, prin.
Canyon Creek ES, 2100 COPPER RIDGE DR 75080
  Greta Scobie, prin.
Dartmouth ES, 417 DARMOUTH LANE 75081
  Melanie Cook, prin.
Dover ES, 700 DOVER DR 75080
  Weldon Morgan, prin.
Greenwood Hills ES
  1313 WEST SHORE DR 75080
  Carolyn Bedinghaus, prin.
Harben ES, 600 S GLENVILLE DR 75081
  Rudy Rogers, prin.
Lake Highlands ES 75081 – Libby Vernon, prin.
Merriman Park ES
  400 S GREENVILLE AVE 75081
  Bill Passmore, prin.
Mohawk ES, 1500 MIMOSA DR 75080
  Darryl Cross, prin.
Moss Haven ES 75081 – Mary Mamantov, prin.
Northlake ES 75081 – Nancy Bingamon, prin.
Northrich ES, 1301 CUSTER ROAD 75080
  Ken Stephens, prin.
O'Henry ES 75081 – Larry Bedinghaus, prin.
Prairie Creek ES
  2120 E PRAIRIE CREEK DR 75080
  David Sanders, prin.
Richardson Heights ES
  100 N FLOYD ROAD 75080 – Otis Ratliff, prin.
Richardson Terrace ES
  300 N DOROTHY DR 75081 – Ann Hampton, prin.
Richland ES, 550 BUCKINGHAM ROAD 75081
  Jane Olson, prin.
Skyview ES 75081 – Pam Smith, prin.
Springridge ES
  1801 E SPRING VALLEY ROAD 75081
  Ann Adams, prin.
Stults Road ES 75081 – Mike Thomas, prin.
Twain ES, 1200 LARKSPUR DR 75081
  Billie Cox, prin.
Wallace ES 75081 – Gene Peer, prin.
White Rock ES 75081 – Bob Parks, prin.
Yale ES, 1900 E COLLINS BLVD 75081
  John Phillips, prin.
Other Schools – See Dallas

Glenwood School, 851 S GREENVILLE AVE 75081
St. Paul the Apostle ES
  720 S FLOYD ROAD 75080

Richland Springs, San Saba Co., Pop. Code 2
Richland Springs ISD
Sch. Sys. Enr. Code 2
Supt. – Bill Crabbs, P O BOX E 76871
S 76871 – Roy Smith, prin.

Richmond, Fort Bend Co., Pop. Code 6

Calvary Episcopal ES, 1201 AUSTIN ST 77469

Riesel, McLennan Co., Pop. Code 3
Riesel ISD
Sch. Sys. Enr. Code 2
Supt. – Ronald Urbantke, P O BOX 40 76682
S 76682 – William Wren, prin.

Rio Grande City, Starr Co., Pop. Code 6
Rio Grande City ISD
Sch. Sys. Enr. Code 6
Supt. – A. Garcia, 1 S FORT RINGGOLD ST 78582
Ringgold JHS 78582 – Walter Watson, prin.
Grulla ES, 1 S FORT RINGGOLD ST 78582
  Constancio Salinas, prin.
Guerra ES 78582 – Minerva Alanis, prin.
La Union ES 78582 – Felicia Garza, prin.
North PS 78582 – Noe Lopez, prin.
Ringgold ES 78582 – Alfredo Garcia, prin.
Ringgold IS 78582 – Julio Saenz, prin.
Other Schools – See Grulla

Immaculate Conception ES
  305 N BRITTON AVE 78582

Rio Hondo, Cameron Co., Pop. Code 4
Rio Hondo ISD
Sch. Sys. Enr. Code 4
Supt. – Marvin Huckle, P O BOX 220 78583
JHS 78583 – Faustino Rivas, prin.
ES, 400 MADERO 78583 – Alfredo Garcia, prin.

Rio Vista, Johnson Co., Pop. Code 3
Rio Vista ISD
Sch. Sys. Enr. Code 3
Supt. – Douglas Mullins, P O BOX 369 76093
ES 76093 – Sharron Miles, prin.

Rising Star, Eastland Co., Pop. Code 4
Rising Star ISD
Sch. Sys. Enr. Code 2
Supt. – Donald Bryan, P O BOX 37 76471
Ward ES 76471 – Weldon Hill, prin.

Riviera, Kleberg Co., Pop. Code 2
Riviera ISD
Sch. Sys. Enr. Code 2
Supt. – Orville Ballard, P O BOX 98 78379
Nanny ES 78379 – Ramiro De La Paz, prin.

Robert Lee, Coke Co., Pop. Code 4
Robert Lee ISD
Sch. Sys. Enr. Code 2
Supt. – Jerry Gibbs, SANCO ROUTE 76945
S 76945 – J. Tennison, prin.

Robstown, Nueces Co., Pop. Code 7
Robstown ISD
Sch. Sys. Enr. Code 5
Supt. – Amancio Cantu, 801 N 1ST ST 78380
Seale JHS, 401 E AVE G 78380
Dalia Rodriguez, prin.
Lotspeich ES, 1000 RUBEN CHAVEZ ROAD 78380
Erenesto Carrillo, prin.
Martin MS, 701 N 1ST ST 78380
Lydia Ramon, prin.
MS 78380 – Frank Perez, prin.
Salazar ES, BUENA VISTA 78380
Alma Guiterrez, prin.
San Pedro ES, 800 W AVE D 78380
Adan Botello, prin.

St. Anthony ES, 203 DUNNE AVE 78380
St. John Parochial School, 109 W AVE F 78380

Roby, Fisher Co., Pop. Code 3
Roby ISD
Sch. Sys. Enr. Code 2
Supt. – J. Laurie, P O BOX 487 79543
ES 79543 – Mick Early, prin.

Rochelle, McCulloch Co.
Rochelle ISD
Sch. Sys. Enr. Code 2
Supt. – K. Mitchell, P O BOX 167 76872
S 76872 – Joe Skalak, prin.

Rochester, Haskell Co., Pop. Code 2
Rochester ISD
Sch. Sys. Enr. Code 2
Supt. – Thomas Walker, P O BOX 97 79544
ES 79544 – Dick Sloan, prin.

Rockdale, Milam Co., Pop. Code 6
Rockdale ISD
Sch. Sys. Enr. Code 4
Supt. – Walter Pond, P O BOX 632 76567
JHS, P O BOX 632 76567 – Travis Grindle, prin.
ES, 625 W BELTON AVE 76567
Kathleen Simmons, prin.

Rockport, Aransas Co., Pop. Code 5
Aransas County ISD
Sch. Sys. Enr. Code 5
Supt. – Karen Hall, P O BOX 907 78382
Rockport-Fulton JHS 78382 – Paul Tressa, prin.
Fulton ES 78382 – Steve Herring, prin.
Live Oak ES, FM ROAD 881 78382
Joy Pleasant, prin.
ES 78382 – William Spears III, prin.

Sacred Heart ES, 111 N CHURCH ST 78382

Rocksprings, Edwards Co., Pop. Code 4
Rocksprings ISD
Sch. Sys. Enr. Code 2
Supt. – Joe Connell, P O BOX 157 78880
ES 78880 – R. Meadows, prin.

Rockwall, Rockwall Co., Pop. Code 6
Rockwall ISD
Sch. Sys. Enr. Code 5
Supt. – J. Williams
801 E WASHINGTON ST 75087
MS 75087 – Chuck King, prin.
Cullins Lake Point ES 75087
Charlotte Evans, prin.
Dobbs ES, E INTERURBAN ST 75087
Jerry Hollon, prin.
Reinhardt ES, 615 HIGHLAND ST 75087
Jo Glass, prin.
ES, I 30 75087 – Paul Hamm, prin.
IS, 901 E INTERURBAN ST 75087
Nathan Crawford, prin.

Rogers, Bell Co., Pop. Code 4
Rogers ISD
Sch. Sys. Enr. Code 3
Supt. – Jack Whitis, P O BOX A 76569
ES 76569 – Gary Lange, prin.

Roma, Starr Co., Pop. Code 5
Roma ISD
Sch. Sys. Enr. Code 5
Supt. – Eleuterio Garza, P O BOX 187 78584
JHS 78584 – Raul Munoz, prin.
Esocobares ES 78584 – Ludivina Ybarra, prin.
IS 78584 – Roberto Guerra, prin.
Scott ES 78584 – Ludivina Ybarra, prin.

Ropesville, Hockley Co., Pop. Code 2
Ropes ISD
Sch. Sys. Enr. Code 2
Supt. – Fred Satterwhite, P O BOX 7 79358
JHS 79358 – Anniece Willis, prin.
Ropes ES 79358 – Lena Locke, prin.

Roscoe, Nolan Co., Pop. Code 4
Highland ISD
Sch. Sys. Enr. Code 2
Supt. – Tom Harkey, RURAL ROUTE 01 79545
Highland S 79545 – Robert Sanford, prin.

Roscoe ISD
Sch. Sys. Enr. Code 2
Supt. – B. Spurgin, P O BOX 188 79545
ES 79545 – Rudy Raughton, prin.

Rosebud, Falls Co., Pop. Code 4
Rosebud-Lott ISD
Sch. Sys. Enr. Code 3
Supt. – Wayne Pierce, P O BOX 638 76570
Rosebud-Lott JHS 76570 – George Ganze, prin.
Lott ES, TRAVIS 76570 – Bob Collier, prin.
IS, 202 S COLLEGE 76570 – P. Hoelscher, prin.
PS, HWY 77 S 76570 – Nelda Jones, prin.

Rosenberg, Fort Bend Co., Pop. Code 7
Lamar Cons. ISD
Sch. Sys. Enr. Code 7
Supt. – Ron Caloss, 930 E STADIUM DRIVE 77471
George JHS 77471 – W. Balderach, prin.
Lamar JHS, 4201 AIRPORT AVE 77471
Gene Tomas, prin.
Beasley ES 77471 – Sidney Pastor, prin.
Bowie ES 77471 – Kenneth Lince, prin.
Crockett MS 77471 – Winfred Rhodes, prin.
Huggins ES 77471 – Billie Egger, prin.
Jackson MS, 301 3RD ST 77471
Mike Vernon, prin.
Lee ES 77471 – Lelia Brummett, prin.
Long ES 77471 – Doris Whileyman, prin.
Meyer IS 77471 – David Santos, prin.
Navarro ES, 930 E STADIUM DR 77471
Judi Vernon, prin.
Smith ES 77471 – Bob Massey, prin.
Taylor MS 77471 – Cass Keen, prin.
Travis ES, 2700 AVE K 77471
Richard Stadnicki, prin.
Williams ES 77471 – Robert Haley, prin.

Holy Rosary ES, 1408 JAMES ST 77471

Rotan, Fisher Co., Pop. Code 4
Hobbs ISD
Sch. Sys. Enr. Code 1
Supt. – Dale Gibson
RURAL ROUTE 01 BOX 1086 79546
Hobbs ES 79546 – (—), prin.

Rotan ISD
Sch. Sys. Enr. Code 3
Supt. – Alton Fields
102 MCKINLEY AVE N 79546
JHS 79546 – Marshall Hill, prin.
ES, 100 N TYLER AVE 79546
David Hargrove, prin.

Round Rock, Williamson Co., Pop. Code 7
Round Rock ISD
Sch. Sys. Enr. Code 7
Supt. – Brent Rock
1311 ROUND ROCK AVE 78681
Canyon Vista MS 78681 – Don Dalton, prin.
Chisholm Trail MS 78664 – Alan Veach, prin.
Deerpark MS 78681 – Jeff Rhodes, prin.
Fulkes MS 78664 – Gene Stokes, prin.
Anderson Mill ES 78681 – Jannelle Sanders, prin.
Berkman ES, 400 W ANDERSON AVE 78664
Leonard Kiely, prin.
Bluebonnet ES 78681 – Barbara Perry, prin.
Brushy Creek ES, 3800 STONEBRIDGE DR 78681
Connie Parker, prin.
Deepwood ES, 705 DEEPWOOD DR 78681
Sara Fogg, prin.
Double File Trail ES 78681 – David Moore, prin.
Live Oak ES 78681 – Marla McGhee, prin.
Old Town ES 78681 – Sandy Apperly, prin.
Pond Springs ES 78681 – Royce Swaim, prin.
Robertson ES 78681 – Robert Carlton, prin.
Voigt ES, 1201 CUSHING DR 78664
Rosemary Cone, prin.
Wells Branch ES, 1311 ROUND ROCK AVE 78681
Tom Hansen, prin.
Other Schools – See Austin

Rowena, Runnels Co.
Olfen ISD
Sch. Sys. Enr. Code 1
Supt. – Thomas McNew
RURAL ROUTE 01 BOX 115 76875
Olfen ES, RURAL ROUTE 01 BOX 115 76875
T. McNew, prin.

Rowlett, Dallas Co., Pop. Code 6
Garland ISD
Supt. – See Garland
Coyle MS, SKYLINE DRIVE 75088
Larry Butler, prin.
ES, 3315 CARLA DR 75088 – Bill Kirk, prin.

Roxton, Lamar Co., Pop. Code 3
Roxton ISD
Sch. Sys. Enr. Code 2
Supt. – Anthony Daugherty, P O BOX 307 75477
ES 75477 – Golda Humphries, prin.

Royse City, Rockwall Co., Pop. Code 4
Royse City ISD
Sch. Sys. Enr. Code 4
Supt. – William Fort, P O BOX 479 75089
MS 75089 – Ernest Smith, prin.
ES 75089 – Gary Evers, prin.

Rule, Haskell Co., Pop. Code 4
Rule ISD
Sch. Sys. Enr. Code 2
Supt. – Lavon Beakley, P O BOX 307 79547
S 79547 – A. Kutch, prin.

Runge, Karnes Co., Pop. Code 4
Runge ISD
Sch. Sys. Enr. Code 2
Supt. – Thomas Galbreath, P O BOX 158 78151
ES 78151 – James Franklin, prin.

Rusk, Cherokee Co., Pop. Code 5
Rusk ISD
Sch. Sys. Enr. Code 4
Supt. – T. Murray, 204 E 3RD ST 75785
JHS 75785 – William Curtis, prin.
ES 75785 – Charles Horton, prin.
PS 75785 – Beth Long, prin.

Sabinal, Uvalde Co., Pop. Code 4
Sabinal ISD
Sch. Sys. Enr. Code 3
Supt. – Jim Ryan, P O BOX 338 78881
S 78881 – Sollers/Shudde, prin.

Sabine Pass, Jefferson Co., Pop. Code 3
Sabine Pass ISD
Sch. Sys. Enr. Code 2
Supt. – John Villot, P O BOX 1148 77655
S, P O BOX 1148 77655 – Bob Chumley, prin.

Sadler, Grayson Co., Pop. Code 2
S & S Cons. ISD
Sch. Sys. Enr. Code 3
Supt. – Michael Stevens, P O BOX 641 76264
S And S MS 76264 – Mack Pate, prin.
S And Cons ES 76264 – Martha Inbert, prin.

Saint Jo, Montague Co., Pop. Code 4
St. Jo ISD
Sch. Sys. Enr. Code 2
Supt. – J. Freeman, P O BOX L 76265
ES 76265 – Rebecca Harris, prin.

Salado, Bell Co.
Salado ISD
Sch. Sys. Enr. Code 2
Supt. – N. Kinsey, P O BOX 98 76571
Arnold ES 76571 – Laurice McClellan, prin.

Saltillo, Hopkins Co.
Saltillo ISD
Sch. Sys. Enr. Code 2
Supt. – Kerry Garmon, P O BOX 138 75478
S 75478 – Carol Henderson, prin.

Samnorwood, Collingsworth Co.
Samnorwood ISD
Sch. Sys. Enr. Code 1
Supt. – W. Martindale, P O BOX 765 79077
ES 79077 – Jim Brown, prin.

San Angelo, Tom Green Co., Pop. Code 8
Grape Creek-Pulliam ISD
Sch. Sys. Enr. Code 3
Supt. – Dan Grounds
RURAL ROUTE 01 BOX 140 76901
Grape Creek ES 76901 – Jackie Dyer, prin.

San Angelo ISD
Sch. Sys. Enr. Code 7
Supt. – Bill Graves, 1621 UNIVERSITY AVE 76904
Lincoln JHS, 4100 BOWIE ST 76903
Steve Van Hoozer, prin.
Alta Loma ES, 1700 N GARFIELD ST 76901
Larry White, prin.
Austin ES, 700 N VAN BUREN ST 76901
Janet Hudgins, prin.
Belaire ES, 700 STEPHEN ST 76905
Herman Rubio, prin.
Blackshear ES, 2223 BROWN ST 76903
Thomas Hurt, prin.
Bonham ES 76904 – John Krupala, prin.
Bowie ES, 3700 FOREST TRAIL 76904
Sydna Easley, prin.
Bradford ES, 1202 E 22ND ST 76903
Morris Hartgraves, prin.
Crockett ES, 2104 JOHNSON AVE 76904
Betty Evans, prin.
Day ES, 3026 N OAKES ST 76903
Gloria Weatherman, prin.
Fannin ES, 1702 WILSON ST 76901
Donald Mauldin, prin.
Fort Concho ES, 205 E AVENUE C 76903
John Chapa, prin.
Glenmore ES, 323 PENROSE ST 76903
Gary Ledford, prin.
Goliad ES, 3902 GOLIAD ST 76903
(—), prin.
Holiman ES, 1201 MONTAGUE ST 76905
Eddie Heath, prin.
McGill ES, 201 MILLSPAUGH ST 76901
Eloise Amos, prin.
Reagan ES, 1600 VOLNEY ST 76903
Phil Burroughs, prin.
Rio Vista ES, 2800 BEN FICKLIN ROAD 76903
Santos Elizondo, prin.
Sam Houston ES, 310 W AVENUE M 76903
Alma Contreras, prin.
San Jacinto ES, 800 SPAULDING ST 76903
Brenda Rios, prin.
Santa Rita ES, 615 S MADISON ST 76901
Susan Van Hoozer, prin.
Travis ES, 2909 A & M AVE 76904
Linda Sylva, prin.

Angelo Catholic School, 19 S OAKES ST 76903
San Angelo SDA School 76903
Trinity Lutheran ES
1326 KENWOOD DRIVE 76903

San Antonio, Bexar Co., Pop. Code 11
Alamo Heights ISD
Sch. Sys. Enr. Code 5
Supt. – Charles Slater
7101 BROADWAY ST 78209

Alamo Heights JHS
7607 N NEW BRAUNFELS AVE 78209
Linda Foster, prin.
Cambridge ES, 1001 TOWNSEND AVE 78209
Paul Rode, prin.
Howard ES, 7800 BROADWAY ST 78209
Elvira Ortiz, prin.
Woodridge ES, 100 WOODRIDGE DR 78209
Penny Simone, prin.

East Central ISD
Sch. Sys. Enr. Code 6
Supt. – Anthony Constanzo
7382 S F M 1628 78263
Oak Crest MS
9789 NW SULPHUR SPRING ROAD 78263
Peggy Caravantes, prin.
Salado MS, 3602 S W W WHITE ROAD 78222
Peggy Caravantes, prin.
Glenn ES, 7284 S F M 1628 78263
Roland Gusman, prin.
Harmony ES, 12271 DONOP 78263
Kenneth Hanson, prin.
Pecan Valley ES
3966 E SOUTHCROSS BLVD 78222
Eugene Sekula, prin.
Sinclair ES, 6126 SINCLAIR ROAD 78222
Curtis Jungman, prin.

Edgewood ISD
Sch. Sys. Enr. Code 7
Supt. – J. Vasquez, 5338 W COMMERCE ST 78237
Brentwood MS, 1626 THOMPSON PLACE 78226
Abel Reyna, prin.
Garcia JHS, 3366 RUIZ ST 78228
Antonio Rodriguez, prin.
Truman MS, 1018 NW 34TH ST 78228
Rosendo Valdez, prin.
Wrenn JHS, 627 S ACME ROAD 78237
Richard Bocanegra, prin.
Burleson ES, 4415 MONTEREY ST 78237
Maria Leandro, prin.
Cenizo Park ES, 2800 ARBOR PLACE 78228
Estela Flores, prin.
Coronado/Escobar ES 78237
David Gonzales, prin.
Frey ES, 900 S SAN EDUARDO AVE 78237
(—), prin.
Gardendale ES, 1730 ATHEL AVE 78237
Luciana Cristadoro, prin.
Gonzalez ES, 2803 CASTROVILLE ROAD 78237
Lucy Hall, prin.
Guerra ES, 2002 HERBERT LANE 78227
Naomi Brown, prin.
Hoelscher ES, 1602 THOMPSON PL 78226
Margaret Harvey, prin.
Johnson ES, 6516 W COMMERCE ST 78227
Tom Hill, prin.
Las Palmas ES, 115 LAS PALMAS DR 78237
Dorothy Collins, prin.
Loma Park ES, 400 AURORA DR 78228
Raquel Escobar, prin.
Perales ES, 1507 CERALVO ST 78237
Carolynn Copley, prin.
Roosevelt ES, 3823 FORTUNA CT 78237
Anetta Ryan, prin.
Stafford ES, 611 SW 36TH ST 78237
Margaret Luna, prin.
Williams ES 78237 – Ralph Longoria, prin.
Winston ES
2500 S GENERAL MCMULLEN DR 78226
James Ryan, prin.

Ft. Sam Houston ISD
Sch. Sys. Enr. Code 4
Supt. – Thomas Mosely
1900 WINANS ROAD 78234
Ft. Sam Houston ES 78234 – Anne Stephens, prin.

Harlandale ISD
Sch. Sys. Enr. Code 7
Supt. – Yvonne Katz
102 GENEVIEVE DRIVE 78285
Harlandale MS, 300 W HUFF AVE 78214
Santiago Zamora, prin.
Kingsborough MS, 422 E ASHLEY ROAD 78221
Bill Ivy, prin.
Leal MS, 743 SOUTHCROSS 78221
Angelo Russo, prin.
Terrell Wells MS, 422 HUTCHINS PLACE 78221
Virginia Aguiar, prin.
Adams ES, 135 E SOUTHCROSS BLVD 78214
Dixie Yarbrough, prin.
Bell ES, 2717 PLEASANTON ROAD 78221
Bonnie Marlow, prin.
Bellaire ES, 142 E AMBER ST 78285
Bill Harris, prin.
Collier ES, 834 W SOUTHCROSS BLVD 78211
Rodolfo Torres, prin.
Columbia Heights ES, 1610 FITCH ST 78211
Guillermo Zavala, prin.
Flanders ES, 934 FLANDERS AVE 78211
Yolanda Escobedo, prin.
Gilbert ES, 931 E SOUTHCROSS BLVD 78214
Roland Cadena, prin.
Gillette ES, 625 GILLETTE BLVD 78221
Robert Hittson, prin.
Morrill ES, 5200 S FLORES ST 78214
Monica Flores, prin.
Rayburn ES, 635 RAYBURN DR 78221
Febe Herrera, prin.
Scheh ES, 906 MARCH ROAD 78214
Frances Rodriguez, prin.
Schulze ES, 9131 YETT BLVD 78221
Jim Armstrong, prin.

Stonewall ES, 804 STONEWALL ST 78211
Mary Vasys, prin.
Vestal ES, 1111 W VESTAL PL 78221
Bartholomew Mora, prin.
Wright ES, 115 E HUFF AVE 78214
Emmett Krachala, prin.

Judson ISD
Supt. – See Converse
Kirby JHS, 5441 SEGUIN ROAD 78219
Charles Neumeyer, prin.
Crestview ES, 7710 NARROW PASS ST 78233
Beverley Hans, prin.
Kirby ES, 2440 ACKERMAN ROAD 78219
Joe Hopkins, prin.
Live Oak ES, 12301 WELCOME DRIVE 78233
John Stahl, prin.
Park Village ES, 5855 E MIDCROWN DRIVE 78218
George Ammermann, prin.
Woodlake ES, 5501 E LAKE BEND ST 78244
Calvin Hutzler, prin.

Lackland ISD
Sch. Sys. Enr. Code 3
Supt. – Michael Nelms, 228 PUCKET ST 78236
Lackland ES 78236 – Catherine Meskil, prin.

North East ISD
Sch. Sys. Enr. Code 8
Supt. – Arnold Oates
10333 BROADWAY ST 78217
Bradley MS, 14819 HEIMER ROAD 78232
Audrey Villarreal, prin.
Eisenhower MS, 8231 BLANCO ROAD 78216
Anthony Petri, prin.
Garner MS
4302 HARRY WURZBACH HIGHWAY 78209
Wesley Davis, prin.
Jackson MS, 4538 VANCE JACKSON ROAD 78230
Shirley Kearns, prin.
Krueger MS, 438 LANARK DRIVE 78218
Walter Howard, prin.
Nimitz MS, 5426 BLANCO ROAD 78216
Bob Niehoff, prin.
White MS, 5623 CASTLE KNIGHT 78218
Gary Short, prin.
Wood MS, 6145 WENZEL 78233
Tom Defosset, prin.
Camelot ES, 7410 RAY BON DR 78218
Reba Locke, prin.
Castle Hills ES, 101 HONEYSUCKLE DR 78213
Pope Crook, prin.
Clear Spring ES, 4311 CLEAR SPRING DR 78217
Richard Kirk, prin.
Coker ES, 302 HEIMER ROAD 78232
Cathryn Johnson, prin.
Colonial Hills ES, 2627 KERRYBROOK CT 78230
Charles Carr, prin.
Dellview ES, 7235 DEWHURST ROAD 78213
John Michel, prin.
East Terrell Hills ES, 4415 BLOOMDALE 78218
Louise Riley, prin.
El Dorado ES, 12634 EL SENDERO ST 78233
Billie Rigby, prin.
Harmony Hills ES, 10727 MEMORY LANE 78216
Newell Whitney, prin.
Hidden Forest ES, 802 SILVER SPURCE ST 78232
Mary Watkins, prin.
Larkspur ES, 11330 BELAIR DR 78213
Rosalyn Bornmann, prin.
Montgomery ES, 7047 MONTGOMERY 78239
Linzel Kennedy, prin.
Northern Hills ES, 13901 HIGGINS ROAD 78217
Don Wilkinson, prin.
Northwood ES, 519 PIKE ROAD 78209
Susan Wood, prin.
Oak Grove ES
3250 NACOGDOCHES ROAD 78217
William Kays, prin.
Olmos ES, 1103 ALLENA DR 78213
Cindy Fairall, prin.
Regency Place ES, 2635 E BITTERS ROAD 78217
Rita Houston, prin.
Ridgeview ES, 8223 MCCULLOUGH AVE 78216
Mary Gerza, prin.
Stahl ES, 5222 STAHL ROAD 78247
Raymond Bordelon, prin.
Thousand Oaks ES
16080 HENDERSON PASS 78232
Rand Dyer, prin.
Walzem ES, 4618 WALZEM ROAD 78218
Virgil Wadsack, prin.
West Avenue ES, 3915 W AVE 78213
Pablo Tijerina, prin.
Wilshire ES, 6523 CASCADE PL 78218
David Manning, prin.
Windcrest ES, 465 FAIRCREST DR 78239
Sondra Burris, prin.
Woodstone ES, 5602 FOUNTAINWOOD ST 78233
John Naranjo, prin.

Northside ISD
Sch. Sys. Enr. Code 8
Supt. – Jack Jordan, 5900 EVERS ROAD 78238
Hobby MS, 11843 VANCE JACKSON ROAD 78230
Jay Dubose, prin.
Jones MS, 1256 PINN ROAD 78227
Debbie Zuberbueler, prin.
Neff MS, 5227 EVERS ROAD 78238
Steve Skipper, prin.
Pease MS, 201 HUNT LANE 78245
Richard Krueger, prin.
Rayburn MS, 1400 CEDARHURST DRIVE 78227
David Doyle, prin.
Rudder MS 78238 – Lewis Patton, prin.

Stevenson MS 78250 – Linda Garcia, prin.
Sul Ross MS, 3630 CALLAGHAN ROAD 78228
Ruben Perez, prin.
Zachry MS 78238 – Dean Krueger, prin.
Adams Hill ES, 9627 ADAMS HL 78245
Tom Prince, prin.
Boone ES, 6614 SPRING TIME ST 78249
Charles Harms, prin.
Braun Station ES, 8600 TEZEL ROAD 78250
James Carson, prin.
Cable ES, 1706 PINN ROAD 78227
Lupe Gonzales, prin.
Cody ES, 10403 DUGAS DR 78245
Fred Dyas, prin.
Colonies North ES
9915 NORTHAMPTON DR 78230
Pat Blattman, prin.
Coon ES, 435 S SAN DARIO AVE 78237
Robert Coyle, prin.
Esparza ES, 5700 HEMPHILL DR 78228
Yolanda Molina, prin.
Forest Hills ES, 2902 WHITE TAIL DR 78228
Benito Resendiz, prin.
Galm ES 78238 – Gil Marshall, prin.
Glass ES 78238 – William Bechtol, prin.
Glenn ES, 400 JAMAICA ST 78227
Roberto Zarate, prin.
Glenoaks ES, 5103 NEWCOME ST 78229
Dorothy Sweet, prin.
Helotes ES 78023 – Mary Mitchell, prin.
Hull ES, 7320 REMUDA DR 78227
Linda Christy, prin.
Knowlton ES, 9500 TIMBER PATH 78250
Tom Zuberbueler, prin.
Lackland City ES, 101 DUMONT DR 78227
Jerry Allen, prin.
Leon Valley ES, 7111 HUEBNER ROAD 78240
James Resendez, prin.
Linton ES, 2103 OAKHILL ROAD 78238
Mary Turk, prin.
Locke Hill ES, 5050 DE ZAVALA ROAD 78249
Shirley Howsman, prin.
Meadow Village ES
1406 MEADOW WAY DR 78227
James Adair, prin.
Northwest Crossing ES 78238 – Mary Allen, prin.
Oak Hills Terrace ES
5710 CARY GRANT DR 78240
Fran Rhodes, prin.
Passmore ES, 2215 PINN ROAD 78227
Neal Howell, prin.
Scobee ES 78238 – Eleanor Elder, prin.
Shenandoah ES
11431 VANCE JACKSON BLVD 78230
Linda Zarakas, prin.
Sunset Hills ES, 519 CLEARVIEW DR 78228
William Bechtol, prin.
Thunderbird Hills ES, 6003 THUNDER DR 78238
Lawrence Powell, prin.
Timberwilde ES, 8838 TIMBERWILDE ST 78250
Bobbye Behlau, prin.
Valley Hi ES, 8503 RAY ELLISON BLVD 78227
Fred Pizzini, prin.
Westwood Terrace ES
7615 BRONCO LANE 78227 – Jane Lunn, prin.

San Antonio ISD
Sch. Sys. Enr. Code 8
Supt. – Victor Rodriguez, 141 LAVACA ST 78210
Connell JHS, 400 HOT WELLS BLVD 78223
Marvin Foster, prin.
Cooper JHS, 1700 TAMPICO ST 78207
Andrew Guerrero, prin.
Davis JHS, 463 HOLMGREEN ROAD 78220
Royal Hammond, prin.
Harris JHS, 325 PRUITT AVE 78204
Anna Lopez, prin.
Irving JHS, 1300 DELGADO ST 78207
Ray Bibb, prin.
King JHS, 141 LAVACA ST 78210
Dee Whorton, prin.
Longfellow JHS, 1130 E SUNSHINE DRIVE 78228
(—), prin.
Lowell JHS, 919 THOMPSON PLACE 78226
Sandra Scheideman, prin.
Mann JHS, 2123 W HUISACHE AVE 78201
Ernest Longoria, prin.
Page JHS, 401 BERKSHIRE AVE 78210
Eugene Hall, prin.
Poe JHS, 814 ARANSAS AVE 78210
John Almaguer, prin.
Rhodes JHS, 3000 TAMPICO ST 78207
Bohn Hilliard, prin.
Rogers JHS, 314 GALWAY ST 78223
Caroyl Green, prin.
Tafolla JHS, 1303 W DURANGO BLVD 78207
Sherrill Nicholson, prin.
Twain JHS, 2411 SAN PEDRO AVE 78212
Steve Johnson, prin.
Whittier JHS, 2101 EDISON DRIVE 78201
Alfred Gutierrez, prin.
Wheatley MS, 419 GABRIEL 78202
Juretta Marshall, prin.
Cotton ES, 1616 BLANCO ROAD 78212
Acelie Villareal, prin.
Arnold ES 78210 – James Pryor, prin.
Austin ES, 621 W EUCLID AVE 78212
Edward Millsap, prin.
Ball ES, 343 KOEHLER COURT 78223
Sylvia Marcus, prin.
Barkley ES, 1112 S ZARZAMORA ST 78207
Margaret Cantu, prin.
Baskin ES, 630 CRESTVIEW DR 78201
Nancy Runnels, prin.

Beacon Hill ES, 1411 W ASHBY PL 78201
  Gloria Rodriguez, prin.
Bonham ES, 925 S SAINT MARYS ST 78205
  Anita Ayala, prin.
Bowden ES, 515 WILLOW 78202
  Joan Pytel, prin.
Brackenridge ES, 1214 GUADALUPE ST 78207
  Richard Tobin, prin.
Brewer ES, 906 MERIDA ST 78207
  Sylvia Reyna, prin.
Briscoe ES, 2015 S FLORES ST 78204
  Sylvia Sutton, prin.
Burnet ES, 406 BARRERA ST 78210
  Katie Jones, prin.
Cameron ES, 3635 BELGIUM LANE 78219
  Ellina Perry, prin.
Carvajal ES, 225 ARIZONA AVE 78207
  Lina Flores, prin.
Collins Garden ES, 167 HARRIMAN PL 78204
  Jacinto Guzman, prin.
Crockett ES, 2215 MORALES ST 78207
  Rogelio Selvera, prin.
De Zavala ES, 2311 SAN LUIS ST 78207
  Mary Rodriguez, prin.
Douglass MS, 318 MARTIN L KING DR 78203
  Mardrette Clack, prin.
Fenwick ES, 1930 WAVERLY AVE 78228
  Stephen Catalani, prin.
Forbes ES, 6718 PECAN VALLEY DR 78223
  George Steele, prin.
Foster ES, 6718 PECAN VALLEY DR 78223
  James Boriack, prin.
Franklin ES, 1915 W OLMOS DR 78201
  Florence Carvajal, prin.
Gates ES, 510 MORINGVIEW DR 78220
  Donald McC'ure, prin.
Graebner ES, 530 HOOVER AVE 78225
  James Utley, prin.
Green ES, 122 W WHITTIER ST 78210
  Patricia Anderson, prin.
Hawthorne ES, 115 W JOSEPHINE ST 78212
  Paul Henson, prin.
Herff ES, 996 S HACKBERRY 78210
  Maria Buescher, prin.
Highland Hills ES, 734 GLAMIS AVE 78223
  Raquel Sosa, prin.
Highland Park ES, 635 RIGSBY AVE 78210
  Judy Lusted, prin.
Hillcrest ES, 211 W MALONE AVE 78214
  Teresa Cantu, prin.
Hirsch ES, 4826 SEABREEZE DR 78220
  Bill Terrell, prin.
Huppertz ES, 247 BANGOR DR 78228
  Lanelle Anderson, prin.
Bowie ES, 439 ARBOR PLACE 78207
  Priscilla Armstead, prin.
Kelly ES, 1026 THOMPSON PL 78226
  Alicia Wilson, prin.
King ES, 1001 CERALVO ST 78207
  Ruben Sierra, prin.
Knox ES, 302 TIPTON AVE 78204
  Gloria Martinez, prin.
Lamar ES, 201 PARLAND PL 78209
  Gail Fordyce, prin.
Madison ES, 2900 W WOODLAWN AVE 78228
  Ed Tobia, prin.
Margil ES, 601 N LAS MORAS ST 78207
  Genevieve Guerrero, prin.
Maverick ES, 107 RALEIGH PL 78201
  Peggy Stark, prin.
Miller ES, 207 LINCOLNSHIRE DR 78220
  Earl Bullock, prin.
Neal ES, 3407 CAPITOL AVE 78201
  Linda Tankersley, prin.
Nelson ES, 1014 WAVERLY AVE 78201
  Eloise Sowell, prin.
Ogden ES, 2215 LEAL ST 78207
  Maria Marquez, prin.
Pershing ES, 600 SANDMEYER ST 78208
  Gloria Barrera, prin.
Pfeiffer ES, 4551 DIETRICH ROAD 78219
  Douglas Dever, prin.
Riverside Park ES, 202 SCHOOL ST 78210
  Marvene Elliott, prin.
Rodriguez ES, 3626 W DURGANGO BLVD 78207
  Alicia Wilson, prin.
Rogers ES, 600 MCILUANINE ST 78212
  Yolanda Borrego, prin.
Ruiz ES, 1912 VERA CRUZ 78207
  George Sanchez, prin.
Schenck ES, 101 KATE SCHENCK AVE 78223
  John MacKechney, prin.
Smith ES, 823 S GEVERS ST 78203
  Ida Mackenzie, prin.
Steel ES, 722 HAGGIN ST 78210
  Phil Mendez, prin.
Stewart ES, 1950 RIGSBY AVE 78210
  Margaret Robinson, prin.
Storm ES, 435 BRADY BLVD 78207
  Lionel Gonzales, prin.
Tynan ES, 925 GULF 78202 – Jo Sherrill, prin.
Washington ES, 1823 NOLAN 78202
  Jacquelyn Banks, prin.
Wilson ES, 1421 CLOWER 78201
  Lucila Solis, prin.
Travis ES, 1915 N MAIN AVE 78212
  Will Taylor, prin.
Woodlawn ES, 1717 W MAGNOLIA AVE 78201
  Maureen Fitzgerald, prin.
Woodlawn Hills ES, 110 W QUILL DR 78228
  Graydon Love, prin.
White ES 78210 – Janice Jehl, prin.

South San Antonio ISD
Sch. Sys. Enr. Code 7
Supt. – Herbert Harper, 2515 SIOUX ST 78224
Abraham Kazen MS, 1520 GILLETTE BLVD 78224
  Manuel Bejarano, prin.
Dwight MS, 2454 W SOUTHCROSS BLVD 78211
  Lauro Montalvo, prin.
Shepard MS, 5558 RAY ELLISON BLVD 78242
  Harry Baker, prin.
Armstrong ES, 7111 APPLE VALLEY DR 78242
  Vicki Lozano, prin.
Athens ES, 2707 W GERALD AVE 78211
  Ruben Flores, prin.
Five Palms ES, 7138 FIVE PALMS DR 78242
  Donald Crook, prin.
Hutchins ES, 1919 HUTCHINS PL 78224
  Robert Flores, prin.
Kindred ES, 7811 KINDRED ST 78224
  Albert Casillas, prin.
Olivares ES, 1450 GILLETTE BLVD 78224
  Rupert Nunez, prin.
Palo Alto ES 78211 – John Burks, prin.
Price ES, 245 PRICE AVE 78211
  Frank Gonzales, prin.
Royalgate ES, 6100 ROYALGATE DR 78242
  Luis Rodriguez, prin.

Southside ISD
Sch. Sys. Enr. Code 5
Supt. – Ron Geyer
  1610 MARTINEZ-LOSOYA ROAD 78221
Southside MS
  1610 MARTINEZ-LOSOYA ROAD 78221
  Ray Conner, prin.
Losoya IS
  1610 MARTINEZ-LOSOYA ROAD 78221
  Tony Luna, prin.
Pearce PS
  1610 MARTINEZ-LOSOYA ROAD 78221
  Margaret McCaughtry, prin.

Southwest ISD
Sch. Sys. Enr. Code 6
Supt. – Richard Clifford
  RURAL ROUTE 09 BOX 205 78227
Southwest JHS, FARM ROAD 2536 78227
  William Holmes, prin.
Big Country ES 78227 – Clifford Cleborne, prin.
Hidden Cove ES 78227 – Sylvia Glass, prin.
Sky Harbour ES 78227 – Alfred Trevino, prin.
Southwest Bob Hope ES
  3014 REFORMA DR 78211 – Lou Jackson, prin.
Southwest ES 78227 – Floyd Worley, prin.
Southwest MS, FM 2536 78227
  Faith Ballard, prin.
Sun Valley ES, 6803 SW LOOP 410 78227
  Margaret Simpson, prin.
Southwest Indian Creek ES
  RURAL ROUTE 09 BOX 205AF 78227
  Wil Bachman, prin.

Keystone School, 119 E CRAIG PLACE 78212
St. Mary's Hall, P O BOX 33430 78265
Blessed Sacrament ES, 600 OBLATE DR 78216
Christ the King ES, 2626 PEREZ ST 78207
Christian Heritage School
  703 TRAFALGAR ROAD 78216
Concordia Lutheran School
  1826 BASSE ROAD 78213
Holy Name ES, 3814 NASH BLVD 78223
Holy Rosary ES
  155 CAMINO SANTA MARIA ST 78228
Holy Spirt ES, 770 W RAMSEY ROAD 78216
Kriterion Montessori School
  611 W ASHBY PLACE 78212
Little Flower ES, 905 KENTUCKY AVE 78201
Mt. Olive Lutheran School
  8138 WESTSHIRE DR 78227
Mt. Sacred Heart Boys ES
  619 MOUNT SACRED HEART ROAD 78216
Mt. Sacred Heart Girls ES
  5810 BIANCO ROAD 78216
Our Lady of Guadalupe School
  1401 EL PASO ST 78207
Our Lady of Perp Help ES
  RURAL ROUTE 20 BOX 196 78218
Redeemer Lutheran School
  2507 FREDERICKSBURG ROAD 78201
Resurrection Episcopal School
  5909 WALZEM ROAD 78218
San Antonio Academy
  117 E FRENCH PLACE 78212
San Antonio Junior Academy
  117 E FRENCH PLACE 78212
Shepherd of the Hills School
  6914 WURZBACH ROAD 78240
St. Ann ES, 210 SAINT ANN 78201
St. Anthony ES, 205 W HUISACHE AVE 78212
St. Benedict ES, 4535 LORD ROAD 78220
St. Cecilia ES, 118 LOWELL ST 78210
St. Gerard ES, 1619 IOWA ST 78203
St. Gregory ES, 700 DEWHURST ROAD 78213
St. James ES, 907 W THEO AVE 78225
St. John Berchmans ES
  1147 CUPPLES ROAD 78226
St. John Bosco ES, 5630 W COMMERCE ST 78237
St. John ES, 502 S AUDUBON DR 78212
St. Joseph ES, 2372 W SOUTHCROSS BLVD 78211
St. Leo ES, 119 OCTAVIA PL 78214
St. Luke ES, 4603 MANITOU 78228
St. Luke's Episcopal School
  11 SAINT LUKES LANE 78209
St. Margaret Mary ES, 1202 FAIR AVE 78223
St. Mark's Day Care School, 315 PECAN ST 78205

St. Martin Hall ES, 411 SW 24TH ST 78225
St. Mary ES, 207 N SAINT MARYS ST 78205
St. Mary Magdalen ES, 1700 CLOWER 78201
St. Paul ES, 307 JOHN ADAMS DR 78228
St. Peter Prince of Apostles ES
  112 MARCIA PL 78209
St. Philip of Jesus ES, 134 E LAMBERT ST 78204
St. Pius X ES, 7734 RUBIN REST DR 78209
St. Thomas More ES, 4427 MOANA DR 78218
Westside Catholic ES 78207

San Augustine, San Augustine Co., Pop. Code 5
San Augustine ISD
Sch. Sys. Enr. Code 4
Supt. – Doug Stewart
  HIGH SCHOOL DRIVE 75972
IS, 1002 BARRETT ST 75972
  Warren Norvell, prin.
ES, 101 S MILAM ST 75972 – Linda Muse, prin.

San Benito, Cameron Co., Pop. Code 7
San Benito Cons. ISD
Sch. Sys. Enr. Code 6
Supt. – Manuel Gomez, 195 W ADELE ST 78586
Cabaza JHS, 500 N DOWLING ST 78586
  Gumecinda Robles, prin.
Booth South ES, 705 ZARAGOSA ST 78586
  Gloria Rocha, prin.
Booth North ES, 705 ZARAGOZA 78586
  Beatriz Rodriguez, prin.
Cash ES, 400 PONCIANA ST 78586
  Luke Oliver, prin.
Downs ES, 1302 N DOWLING ST 78586
  Rogelio Cano, prin.
Jordan IS, 700 N MCCOLLOUGH 78586
  Helen Lara, prin.
La Encantada ES 78586 – Will Montemayor, prin.
La Paloma ES 78586 – Sylvia Lara, prin.
Landrum ES, 450 S DOWLING ST 78586
  J. Munoz, prin.
Rangerville ES 78586 – Jesus Rocha, prin.
Roberts ES, 650 BIDDLE ST 78586
  Manuel Becerra, prin.
Sullivan ES, 900 ELIZABETH ST 78586
  Sara Galarza, prin.
Other Schools – See Los Indios

Sanderson, Terrell Co., Pop. Code 4
Terrell County ISD
Sch. Sys. Enr. Code 2
Supt. – Bill Daugherty, P O BOX 747 79848
JHS 79848 – Manley Holmes, prin.
ES 79848 – Manley Holmes, prin.

San Diego, Duval Co., Pop. Code 6
San Diego ISD
Sch. Sys. Enr. Code 4
Supt. – Eloy Guerra, 609 W LABBE ST 78384
Jaime JHS, 609 W LABBE ST 78384
  Elijio Uresti, prin.
Collins PS, 609 W LABBE ST 78384
  Jesus Maldonado, prin.
Parr MS 78384 – Elijio Uresti,Jr., prin.

San Elizario, El Paso Co., Pop. Code 3
San Elizario ISD
Sch. Sys. Enr. Code 3
Supt. – Allen Boyd, P O BOX 920 79849
MS, 122700 SOCORRO DR 79849
  Robert Longoria, prin.
ES 79849 – (—), prin.

Sanger, Denton Co., Pop. Code 5
Sanger ISD
Sch. Sys. Enr. Code 4
Supt. – Jim Coulston, P O BOX 188 76266
MS 76266 – Jack Biggerstaff, prin.
Chisholm Trail ES, P O BOX 188 76266
  Travis Underwood, prin.
IS 76266 – Alice Madden, prin.

San Isidro, Starr Co., Pop. Code 2
San Isidro ISD
Sch. Sys. Enr. Code 2
Supt. – Carlos Lopez, P O BOX 1 78588
ES 78588 – Miguel Gonzales,Jr., prin.

San Juan, Hidalgo Co., Pop. Code 6
Pharr-San Juan-Alamo ISD
Sch. Sys. Enr. Code 7
Supt. – Augusto Guerra, P O BOX 938 78589
Alamo JHS 78589 – Scott Owings, prin.
Austin JHS 78589 – Eleazar Romero, prin.
Pharr MS 78589 – Raul Garza, prin.
MS 78589 – Heron Ramirez, prin.
Sorensen ES, 715 S STANDARD AVE 78589
  Irma Garza, prin.
Other Schools – See Pharr

San Marcos, Hays Co., Pop. Code 7
San Marcos ISD
Sch. Sys. Enr. Code 6
Supt. – H. Fuller, P O BOX 1087 78667
Goodnight JHS, 607 PETER GARZA DRIVE 78666
  Bea Flores, prin.
Bowie MS, 1205 HIGHWAY 123 78666
  Rufus Doyle, prin.
Crockett ES 78666 – Pat Curtin, prin.
Dezavala ES 78667 – Yolanda Almenadez, prin.
Lamar IS, 500 W HUTCHISON ST 78666
  Carl Jake, prin.
Travis MS 78666 – Bernard Callender, prin.

San Perlita, Willacy Co., Pop. Code 2
San Perlita ISD
Sch. Sys. Enr. Code 2
Supt. – Jim Crow, P O BOX 37 78590
S 78590 – Raul Chapa, prin.

San Saba, San Saba Co., Pop. Code 4
San Saba ISD
Sch. Sys. Enr. Code 3
Supt. – W. Grusendorf, 607 W STOREY ST 76877
JHS 76877 – Richard Barker, prin.
ES 76877 – Louise Oswald, prin.
IS 76877 – Richard Barker, prin.

Santa Anna, Coleman Co., Pop. Code 4
Santa Anna ISD
Sch. Sys. Enr. Code 2
Supt. – Gerald Brister, P O BOX 99 76878
ES 76878 – J. Burns, prin.

Santa Fe, Galveston Co.
Santa Fe ISD
Sch. Sys. Enr. Code 5
Supt. – Roy Wollam, P O BOX 370 77510
JHS 77510 – Earl Routh, prin.
ES 77510 – Gerald Cleveland, prin.
IS 77510 – Marianne Butler, prin.
Wollam ES 77510 – Debra King, prin.

Santa Maria, Cameron Co.
Santa Maria ISD
Sch. Sys. Enr. Code 2
Supt. – Silverio Pena, P O BOX 448 78592
ES 78592 – Jesse Munoz, prin.

Santa Rosa, Cameron Co., Pop. Code 4
Santa Rosa ISD
Sch. Sys. Enr. Code 4
Supt. – Luis Sanchez, P O.BOX 368 78593
MS, HWY 107 78593 – Andres Contreras, prin.
ES 78593 – Hilario Ramirez, prin.

Santo, Palo Pinto Co., Pop. Code 2
Santo ISD
Sch. Sys. Enr. Code 2
Supt. – Robert Stathem, P O BOX 67 76472
ES 76472 – Jack Davis, prin.

Saratoga, Hardin Co., Pop. Code 3
West Hardin ISD
Sch. Sys. Enr. Code 3
Supt. – Merlin Tilley, P O BOX 128 77585
West Hardin JHS 77585 – Oscar Whitmire, prin.
West Hardin ES 77585 – Danny Bell, prin.

Sarita, Kenedy Co.
Kenedy County Wide Common SD
Sch. Sys. Enr. Code 1
Supt. – Gilbert Wheeler, P O BOX 155 78385
Noias ES 78385 – Gilbert Wheeler, prin.
ES 78385 – Gilbert Wheeler, prin.

Savoy, Fannin Co., Pop. Code 3
Savoy ISD
Sch. Sys. Enr. Code 2
Supt. – John Kay, P O BOX 446 75479
S 75497 – Jerry Newell, prin.

Schertz, Guadalupe Co., Pop. Code 6
Schertz-Cibolo-U. City ISD
Sch. Sys. Enr. Code 5
Supt. – Byron Steele, 1060 AERO AVE 78154
Corbett JHS, 301 MAIN 78154
  Richard Walpole, prin.
ES, 701 CURTISS ST 78154
  Marion Dolford, prin.
Other Schools – See Cibolo, Universal City

Schulenburg, Fayette Co., Pop. Code 4
Schulenburg ISD
Sch. Sys. Enr. Code 3
Supt. – Greg Gant, 517 NORTH ST 78956
ES 78956 – George Schultz, prin.

St. Rose of Lima ES, 400 BLACK ST 78956

Scurry, Kaufman Co., Pop. Code 2
Scurry-Rosser ISD
Sch. Sys. Enr. Code 3
Supt. – Bill Blythe
  RURAL ROUTE 01 BOX 14 75158
Scurry-Rosser MS 75158 – James Whitworth, prin.
Scurry-Rosser ES 75158 – Tom Hooper, prin.

Seabrook, Harris Co., Pop. Code 5
Clear Creek ISD
Supt. – See League City
Seabrook Inter., 2401 MEYER ROAD 77586
  Jimmy Stephens, prin.

Seadrift, Calhoun Co., Pop. Code 4
Calhoun County ISD
Supt. – See Port Lavaca
Fannin MS 77983 – Susan Brooks, prin.
ES 77983 – Susan Brooks, prin.

Seagraves, Gaines Co., Pop. Code 5
Seagraves ISD
Sch. Sys. Enr. Code 3
Supt. – Don Blankenship, P O BOX 577 79359
JHS 79359 – Douglas Karr, prin.
ES 79359 – Michael Harris, prin.

Sealy, Austin Co., Pop. Code 5
Sealy ISD
Sch. Sys. Enr. Code 4
Supt. – Thomas Golson, 939 WEST ST 77474
JHS 77474 – A. Stuessel, prin.
Selman ES 77474 – Donald Fairweather, prin.

Seguin, Guadalupe Co., Pop. Code 7
Seguin ISD
Sch. Sys. Enr. Code 6
Supt. – James Lehmann, P O BOX 31 78156
Briesemeister MS 78155 – Herminia Uresti, prin.
Saegert MS, 118 BOWIE ST 78155
  Milton Witt, prin.
Ball ES, 620 W KREZDORN ST 78155
  Clarence Little,Jr., prin.
Erskine MS, 216 E COLLEGE ST 78155
  Pat Watkins, prin.
Jefferson Avenue ES, 215 SHORT AVE 78155
  Jennie Hines, prin.
Koennecke ES 78156 – David Gettig, prin.
McQueeney ES 78156 – Carolyn Carr, prin.
Patlan ES 78156 – Gretchen Ricker, prin.
Weinert MS, 1111 BRUNS ST 78155
  Stan Wieding, prin.

St. James ES, 510 S AUSTIN ST 78155

Seminole, Gaines Co., Pop. Code 6
Seminole ISD
Sch. Sys. Enr. Code 4
Supt. – Charles Bright, P O BOX 900 79360
JHS, P O BOX 900 79360 – Tom Rogers, prin.
MS, P O BOX 900 79360 – Doug Harriman, prin.
PS 79342 – Roy Winters, prin.
Young ES 79360 – Ronnie Gandy, prin.

Seymour, Baylor Co., Pop. Code 5
Seymour ISD
Sch. Sys. Enr. Code 3
Supt. – Charles Barron, 409 W IDAHO ST 76380
ES, 300 E IDAHO ST 76380 – Don Gilstrap, prin.

Shallowater, Lubbock Co., Pop. Code 4
Shallowater ISD
Sch. Sys. Enr. Code 4
Supt. – C. Hohertz, P O BOX 220 79363
MS 79363 – Bill Garland, prin.
ES 79363 – Gary Sherman, prin.

Shamrock, Wheeler Co., Pop. Code 5
Lela ISD
Sch. Sys. Enr. Code 1
Supt. – (—)
  RURAL ROUTE 02 BOX 26 79079
Lela ES 79079 – Wayne Johnson, prin.

Shamrock ISD
Sch. Sys. Enr. Code 3
Supt. – Ron Gregory, 100 S ILLINOIS ST 79079
JHS 79079 – Tommy Waldrop, prin.
ES 79079 – Tommy Waldrop, prin.

Shelbyville, Shelby Co.
Shelbyville ISD
Sch. Sys. Enr. Code 3
Supt. – Bob Collins, P O BOX 325 75973
S 75973 – Burley Lamb, prin.

Shepherd, San Jacinto Co., Pop. Code 4
Shepherd ISD
Sch. Sys. Enr. Code 4
Supt. – R. Corn, P O BOX 429 77371
JHS 77371 – Roger Williams, prin.
ES 77331 – Helen Currie, prin.

Sherman, Grayson Co., Pop. Code 8
Sherman ISD
Sch. Sys. Enr. Code 6
Supt. – J. McDougal, P O BOX 1156 75090
Piner MS, 402 W PECAN ST 75090
  Charles Byler, prin.
Crutchfield ES, 521 S DEWEY AVE 75090
  Clarence Phipps, prin.
Dillingham IS 75090 – Lou Jones, prin.
Fairview ES, 501 W TAYLOR ST 75090
  D. Johnson, prin.
Jefferson ES, 608 N LEE ST 75090
  Charles Templeton, prin.
Perrin ES 75090 – David Parker, prin.
Wakefield ES, 400 SUNSET BLVD 75090
  Bonnie Avard, prin.
Washington ES, 8155 TRAVIS ST 75090
  Ruby Williams, prin.

Glad Tidings School, P O BOX 2102 75090
St. Mary ES, 713 S TRAVIS ST 75090

Shiner, Lavaca Co., Pop. Code 4
Shiner ISD
Sch. Sys. Enr. Code 3
Supt. – James Stewart, P O BOX 804 77984
ES 77984 – John Lewis, prin.

St. Ludmilas Academy
  424 SAINT LUDMILA ST 77984

Sidney, Comanche Co.
Sidney ISD
Sch. Sys. Enr. Code 2
Supt. – D. Andrews, P O BOX 290 76474
S 76474 – Jim Ball, prin.

Sierra Blanca, Hudspeth Co., Pop. Code 3
Allamoore Common SD
Sch. Sys. Enr. Code 1
Supt. – Samuel Bray, P O BOX 68 79851
Allamoore ES 79851 – Trava Sparks, prin.

Sierra Blanca ISD
Sch. Sys. Enr. Code 2
Supt. – Tom Tasma, P O BOX 308 79851
S 79851 – David Kyser, prin.

Silsbee, Hardin Co., Pop. Code 6
Lumberton ISD
Sch. Sys. Enr. Code 4
Supt. – Richard Ownby, P O BOX 8123 77711
MS 77711 – D. Sue Horne, prin.
Other Schools – See Lumberton

Silsbee ISD
Sch. Sys. Enr. Code 5
Supt. – Herbert Muckleroy, 415 W AVE N 77656
MS 77656 – Ronald Nash, prin.
Kirby ES 77656 – Leonard Barnett, prin.
Read-Turrentine ES, S 7TH ST 77656
  Bill Conway, prin.
Reeves MS 77656 – Fred Miller, prin.

Silverton, Briscoe Co., Pop. Code 3
Silverton ISD
Sch. Sys. Enr. Code 2
Supt. – David Cavitt, P O BOX 597 79257
S 79257 – Stan Fogerson, prin.

Simms, Bowie Co.
Simms ISD
Sch. Sys. Enr. Code 2
Supt. – Michael Jansen, P O BOX 8 75574
Bowie ES 75574 – Mel Hamilton, prin.

Sinton, San Patricio Co., Pop. Code 6
Sinton ISD
Sch. Sys. Enr. Code 4
Supt. – Sam May, P O BOX 1337 78387
Smith JHS, 900 S SAN PATRICIO ST 78387
  Reynaldo Torres, prin.
Lamar ES 78387 – Henry Gonzales, prin.
Odem MS 78370 – Leo Canion, prin.
Welder ES 78387 – Randel Lee, prin.

Skellytown, Carson Co., Pop. Code 3
Spring Creek ISD
Sch. Sys. Enr. Code 1
Supt. – Susan Perez
  RURAL ROUTE 01 BOX 48 79080
Spring Creek ES 79080 – Susan Perez, prin.

Skidmore, Bee Co., Pop. Code 3
Skidmore-Tynan ISD
Sch. Sys. Enr. Code 3
Supt. – D. Ross, P O BOX 408 78389
Skidmore/Tynan JHS 78389 – Ruben Corkill, prin.
Skidmore-Tynan ES 78389 – Ruben Corkill, prin.

Slaton, Lubbock Co., Pop. Code 6
Slaton ISD
Sch. Sys. Enr. Code 4
Supt. – Jerry Hogue, 300 S 9TH ST 79364
JHS, 1000 S 10TH ST 79364 – Pete Villalba, prin.
Austin MS 79364 – Ernest Davis, prin.
West Ward ES 79364 – Maybelle Kern, prin.

St. Joseph ES, 20TH & W DIVISION STS 79364

Slidell, Wise Co.
Slidell ISD
Sch. Sys. Enr. Code 2
Supt. – Daniel Jones, P O BOX 68 76267
S 76267 – Eugene Franklin, prin.

Slocum, Anderson Co.
Slocum ISD
Sch. Sys. Enr. Code 2
Supt. – Raymond Trotter,Jr.
  RURAL ROUTE 02 75839
S 75839 – Gary Bottoms, prin.

Smithville, Bastrop Co., Pop. Code 5
Smithville ISD
Sch. Sys. Enr. Code 4
Supt. – D. Hestand, P O BOX 479 78957
JHS 78957 – Gene Sampson, prin.
Brown ES, 4TH & HARRIS ST 78957
  Dawton Hughes, prin.
MS 78957 – Leslie Hurta, prin.

Smyer, Hockley Co., Pop. Code 2
Smyer ISD
Sch. Sys. Enr. Code 2
Supt. – David Foote, P O BOX 192 79367
JHS 79367 – Sarah Morrison, prin.
ES 79367 – Harlan White, prin.

Snook, Burleson Co., Pop. Code 2
Snook ISD
Sch. Sys. Enr. Code 3
Supt. – Larry Horn, P O BOX 87 77878
S 77878 – M. Schoeneman, prin.

Snyder, Scurry Co., Pop. Code 7
Snyder ISD
Sch. Sys. Enr. Code 5
Supt. – Dalton Moseley, 2901 37TH ST 79549
JHS 79549 – Charles Anderson, prin.
Central ES, 27TH & AVE K 79549
  L. Monroe, prin.
East ES, 3600 A AVE 79549 – Jim Erwin, prin.
North ES, LUBBOCK HWY 79549
  Tom Alvis, prin.
Northeast ES, 13TH & AVE 1 79549
  Wayne Kennedy, prin.
Stanfield ES, 4300 V AVE 79549
  Bob Travis, prin.
West ES, 3601 EL PASO AVE 79549
  Geraldine Parker, prin.

Somerset, Bexar Co., Pop. Code 4
Somerset ISD
Sch. Sys. Enr. Code 4
Supt. – Joe Martinez, P O BOX 278 78069

JHS 78069 – Shirley Johnson, prin.
ES 78069 – Abelardo Villareal, prin.

Somerville, Burleson Co., Pop. Code 4
Somerville ISD
Sch. Sys. Enr. Code 3
Supt. – George Williford, P O BOX 458 77879
JHS 77879 – Jim Edge, prin.
ES 77879 – Don Krumrey, prin.

Sonora, Sutton Co., Pop. Code 5
Sonora ISD
Sch. Sys. Enr. Code 4
Supt. – James Bible, 807 S CONCHO AVE 76950
JHS 76950 – Smith Neal, prin.
PS 76950 – Clay Cade, prin.
IS 76950 – Miguel Ramos, prin.

Sour Lake, Hardin Co., Pop. Code 4
Hardin-Jefferson ISD
Sch. Sys. Enr. Code 4
Supt. – J. Miller, P O BOX 490 77659
China ES, P O BOX 490 77659
   Sandra Sherman, prin.
ES, P O BOC 340 77659 – James Burke, prin.
Other Schools – See China

South Houston, Harris Co., Pop. Code 7
Pasadena ISD
Supt. – See Pasadena
IS, 900 COLLEGE AVE 77587 – Lucas Vegas, prin.
ES, 900 MAIN ST 77587 – Joseph Karlen, prin.

Southlake, Tarrant Co., Pop. Code 5
Carroll ISD
Sch. Sys. Enr. Code 4
Supt. – John Lowrey, P O BOX 838 76051
Carroll MS 76092 – Jackie Mayfield, prin.
Carroll ES 76092 – Nancy Henderson, prin.
Johnson ES 76092 – Jane Cousins, prin.

Southland, Garza Co., Pop. Code 2
Southland ISD
Sch. Sys. Enr. Code 2
Supt. – K. Fritz Leifeste II, P O BOX 117 79368
ES 79368 – Peggy Wheeler, prin.

Spade, Lamb Co.
Spade ISD
Sch. Sys. Enr. Code 2
Supt. – Van Carr, P O BOX 396 79369
S 79369 – Rollie McNutt, prin.

Spearman, Hansford Co., Pop. Code 5
Spearman ISD
Sch. Sys. Enr. Code 3
Supt. – Larry Butler, 403 E 11TH AVE 79081
JHS 79081 – Richard Olsen, prin.
ES, 511 TOWNSEND ST 79081 – Eddie Gage, prin.

Splendora, Montgomery Co., Pop. Code 3
Splendora ISD
Sch. Sys. Enr. Code 4
Supt. – William Shaw, P O BOX 168 77372
Dukes JHS 77372 – Leon Cubillas, prin.
ES 77372 – Donette Weatherly, prin.
IS 77372 – Jim Burns, prin.

Spring, Harris Co., Pop. Code 3
Conroe ISD
Supt. – See Conroe
Ford ES, 25460 RICHARD ROAD 77386
   Rebecca Holland, prin.
Hailey ES, 12051 SAWMILL ROAD 77380
   Pat Pribilski, prin.
Lamar ES, 1200 WOODLANDS PARKWAY 77380
   Jane Durbin, prin.
Wilkerson IS, 12312 SAWMILL ROAD 77380
   James Crabb, prin.

Klein ISD
Sch. Sys. Enr. Code 7
Supt. – D. Collins
   7200 SPRING CYPRESS ROAD 77379
Doerre IS 77379 – Larry Whitehead, prin.
Hildebrandt IS
   22800 HILDEBRANDT ROAD 77389
   Laurence Liles, prin.
Kleb IS, 16503 STUEBNER AIRLINE RD 77379
   Larry Fricke, prin.
Klein IS 77379 – Don Rather, prin.
Strack IS, 18027S KUYKENDAHL ROAD 77379
   Gary Jones, prin.
Benfer ES, 18027B KUYKENDAHL ROAD 77379
   Maryanna Richardson, prin.
Brill ES, 9102 HERST 77379 – Don Simme, prin.
Ehrhardt ES, 6603 ROSEBROOK LANE 77379
   Teresa Johnson, prin.
Kuehnle Elementary School 77379 – (—), prin.
Haude ES, 3111 LOUETTA ROAD 77388
   Jan Simonton, prin.
Krahn ES, 9502 EDAY DR 77379
   Carolyn Sims, prin.
Lemm ES, 19034 JOANLEIGH DR 77388
   Gay Cook, prin.
Northampton ES, 6404 ROOT ROAD 77389
   Linda Farmer, prin.
Roth ES, 21623 CASTLEMONT LANE 77388
   Betty Dodd, prin.
Theiss ES, 17440 THEISS MAIL ROUTE RD 77379
   Pat Wallace, prin.
Other Schools – See Houston

Spring ISD
Supt. – See Houston
Wunsche S, 800 SPRING CYPRESS ROAD 77373
   Denise Drexler, prin.

Dueitt MS, 5119 TREASCHWIG ROAD 77373
   Nancy Matlock, prin.
Twin Creeks MS
   27100 CYPRESS WOOD DR 77373
   Mike Mier, prin.
Hirsch ES, 2633 TRAILING VINE 77373
   Marlene Lindsay, prin.
Winship ES, 2175 SPRING CREEK DR 77373
   Marshall Priest, prin.

Oaks Academy ES
   17810 SPRING CREEK FOREST 77379
St. Edward ES
   2601 SPRING STUEBNER ROAD 77389
Trinity Lutheran ES
   18926 KLEIN CHURCH ROAD 77379

Springtown, Parker Co., Pop. Code 4
Springtown ISD
Sch. Sys. Enr. Code 4
Supt. – Conny Martin, P O BOX 249 76082
MS 76082 – Michael Gilley, prin.
Springtown Hinkle MS 76082 – Carl Moore, prin.
Springtown Upper ES 76082 – Carl Moore, prin.
Springtown Watson ES 76082
   Lynn Browning, prin.

Spur, Dickens Co., Pop. Code 4
Spur ISD
Sch. Sys. Enr. Code 2
Supt. – Curt Parsons, P O BOX 550 79370
ES, 412 E HILL ST 79370 – Fred Walker, prin.

Spurger, Tyler Co., Pop. Code 2
Spurger ISD
Sch. Sys. Enr. Code 2
Supt. – Gerald Lancaster, P O BOX 38 77660
ES 77660 – Jim McWilliams, prin.

Stafford, Fort Bend Co., Pop. Code 5
Fort Bend ISD
Supt. – See Sugar Land
Dulles ES, 500 DULLES AVE 77477
   Cletha Perrin, prin.
Meadows ES, 12037 PENDER LANE 77477
   Terry Harris, prin.

Stafford Metro SD
Sch. Sys. Enr. Code 4
Supt. – James Woodfin
   1625 STAFFORDSHIRE 77477
MS 77477 – Charles Wood, prin.
ES 77477 – Ron Roberson, prin.

Advent Episcopal School
   605 DULLES AVE 77477

Stamford, Jones Co., Pop. Code 5
Stamford ISD
Sch. Sys. Enr. Code 3
Supt. – Allen Norman, P O BOX 1238 79553
Oliver ES 79553 – Zenita Gardner, prin.
Reynolds MS 79553 – Harley McCasland, prin.

Stanton, Martin Co., Pop. Code 4
Stanton ISD
Sch. Sys. Enr. Code 3
Supt. – Lloyd Mitchell, P O BOX 730 79782
JHS 79782 – John McGregor, prin.
Other Schools – See Jefferson

Star, Mills Co.
Star ISD
Sch. Sys. Enr. Code 1
Supt. – Pat Hicks, P O BOX 838 76880
S 76880 – Pat Hicks, prin.

Stephenville, Erath Co., Pop. Code 7
Huckabay ISD
Sch. Sys. Enr. Code 2
Supt. – James Stone, P O BOX 182 76401
S, P O BOX 182 76401 – William Brock, prin.

Stephenville ISD
Sch. Sys. Enr. Code 5
Supt. – Ben Gilbert, 726 N CLINTON ST 76401
MS 76401 – E. Henderson, prin.
Central ES, 780 W WASHINGTON ST 76401
   Wayne Ford, prin.
Chamberlin ES, 1601 W FREY ST 76401
   Roger McQueary, prin.
IS 76401 – Louise Woolley, prin.

Three Way ISD
Sch. Sys. Enr. Code 1
Supt. – Arley Echols, P O BOX 161 76401
Three Way ES 76410 – (—), prin.

Sterling City, Sterling Co., Pop. Code 3
Sterling City ISD
Sch. Sys. Enr. Code 2
Supt. – James Thompson, P O BOX 765 76951
S 76951 – Ron Krejci, prin.

Stockdale, Wilson Co., Pop. Code 4
Stockdale ISD
Sch. Sys. Enr. Code 3
Supt. – Bennie Wolff, P O BOX 7 78160
JHS 78160 – Glenn Thompson, prin.
ES 78160 – Jo Ann Salmon, prin.
IS 78160 – Glenn Thompson, prin.

Stonewall, Gillespie Co., Pop. Code 4
Fredericksburg ISD
Supt. – See Fredericksburg
ES 78671 – Harvey Eckert, prin.

Stratford, Sherman Co., Pop. Code 4
Stratford ISD
Sch. Sys. Enr. Code 3
Supt. – Elwyn Bass, P O BOX 108 79084
JHS 79084 – James Taliaferro, prin.
Mary Allen ES 79084 – Steve Haynes, prin.

Strawn, Palo Pinto Co., Pop. Code 3
Strawn ISD
Sch. Sys. Enr. Code 2
Supt. – J. Gibson, P O BOX 428 76475
S 76475 – Louie Bailey, prin.

Sudan, Lamb Co., Pop. Code 4
Sudan ISD
Sch. Sys. Enr. Code 4
Supt. – W. McAlpin, P O BOX 249 79371
ES 79371 – Tom Lacewell, prin.

Sugar Land, Fort Bend Co., Pop. Code 6
Fort Bend ISD
Sch. Sys. Enr. Code 8
Supt. – Rodney LeBoeuf, P O BOX 1004 77487
Dulles JHS 77487 – Fred Ikler, prin.
First Colony JHS 77487 – David Goodman, prin.
Hodges Bend JHS, P O BOX 1004 77487
   Mary Ann Reynolds, prin.
McAuliffe JHS, 16650 S POST OAK 77487
   John Merriweather, prin.
JHS 77487 – Vernon Madden, prin.
Austin Parkway ES 77487 – (—), prin.
Blue Ridge ES 77487 – Clement Boulte, prin.
Briargate ES 77487 – Bessie Ford, prin.
Colony Bend ES, 2720 PLANTERS ST 77479
   Blair Hysmith, prin.
Highlands ES, 2022 COLONIST PARK DR 77487
   Barb Kulpinsky, prin.
Hunters Glen ES 77487 – Patricia Rainbow, prin.
Jones ES 77487 – Vicki Delgado, prin.
Lakeview ES, 300 LAKEVIEW DR 77478
   Tony Christian, prin.
Lantern Lane ES 77487 – Bruce Drennan, prin.
Mission Bend ES 77487 – La Ray Ledger, prin.
Mission Glen ES, 16103 MISSION GLEN 77487
   Carol Allin, prin.
Palmer ES 77487 – Patricia Conway, prin.
Pecan Grove ES 77487 – Sandra Campos, prin.
Quail Valley ES 77487 – Toni Mamula, prin.
Ridgegate ES 77487 – Cecil Tielke, prin.
Ridgemont ES 77487 – Raymond Robertson, prin.
Settlers Way ES 77487 – (—), prin.
Sugar Mill ES 77487 – William Harris, prin.
Townewest ES
   13927 OLD RICHMONT ROAD 77478
   Michael McDonald, prin.
Other Schools – See Missouri City, Stafford

Faith Lutheran School
   800 BROOKS STREET 77478

Sullivan City, Hidalgo Co., Pop. Code 2
La Joya ISD
Supt. – See La Joya
Benavides ES, POST OFFICE ROAD 78595
   Wilfrido Garcia, prin.

Sulphur Bluff, Hopkins Co.
Sulphur Bluff ISD
Sch. Sys. Enr. Code 2
Supt. – Bruce Fielden, P O BOX 7 75481
S 75481 – J. Morton, prin.

Sulphur Springs, Hopkins Co., Pop. Code 7
North Hopkins ISD
Sch. Sys. Enr. Code 2
Supt. – Tom Long
   RURAL ROUTE 03 BOX 486 75482
North Hopkins S
   RURAL ROUTE 03 BOX 486 75482
   Jim Day, prin.

Sulphur Springs ISD
Sch. Sys. Enr. Code 5
Supt. – Dan Durham, 631 CONNALLY ST 75482
MS, 800 BELL ST 75482 – Foy Williams, prin.
Austin ES, 808 DAVIS ST S 75482
   Tona Hudson, prin.
Bowie ES, 1400 MOCKINGBIRD LANE 75482
   Jackie Brice, prin.
Douglas IS, 600 CALVERT ST 75482
   Lewis Watts, prin.
Houston ES, 411 COLLEGE ST 75482
   Lewis Teer, prin.
Lamar ES, 825 CHURCH ST 75482
   Vaden Richey, prin.
Travis ES, 130 GARRISON ST 75482
   Bill Lindley, prin.

Sundown, Hockley Co., Pop. Code 4
Sundown ISD
Sch. Sys. Enr. Code 3
Supt. – G. Lasater, P O BOX 1110 79372
JHS 79372 – Truitt Mitchell, prin.
ES 79372 – Mike Motheral, prin.

Sunnyvale, Dallas Co., Pop. Code 4
Sunnyvale ISD
Sch. Sys. Enr. Code 2
Supt. – Gwinn Blankenship
   RURAL ROUTE 02 BOX 955 75182
ES 75182 – (—), prin.

Sunray, Moore Co., Pop. Code 4
Sunray ISD
Sch. Sys. Enr. Code 3
Supt. – Ken Oller, P O BOX L 79086
ES 79086 – Richard Bucy, prin.

Sweeny, Brazoria Co., Pop. Code 5
Sweeny ISD
Sch. Sys. Enr. Code 4
Supt. – Pat Patterson, P O BOX 307 77480
JHS 77480 – Booker Holbert, prin.
ES, SYCAMORE ST 77480 – Nancy Hanson, prin.

Sweet Home, Lavaca Co.
Sweet Home ISD
Sch. Sys. Enr. Code 1
Supt. – Marian Fikac, P O BOX 326 77987
ES 77987 – (—), prin.

Sweetwater, Nolan Co., Pop. Code 7
Sweetwater ISD
Sch. Sys. Enr. Code 5
Supt. – Drennon Daves
  207 MUSGROVE ST 79556
MS 79556 – Joe Marlett, prin. '
Cowen ES, 701 W FIFTH ST 79554
  Barron Bird, prin.
East Ridge ES, 1101 HOYT ST 79556
  Ben High, prin.
Nolan MS, 805 E THIRD ST 79556
  Scarlett Whitteker, prin.
Southeast ES 79556 – Webster Williams, prin.

Taft, San Patricio Co., Pop. Code 5
Taft ISD
Sch. Sys. Enr. Code 4
Supt. – A. McMillin, 731 MCINTYRE ST 78390
JHS 78390 – Emiliano Alaniz, prin.
East MS 78390 – Claudio Salinas, prin.
Petty ES 78390 – Mary Robertson, prin.

Tahoka, Lynn Co., Pop. Code 5
Tahoka ISD
Sch. Sys. Enr. Code 3
Supt. – Duane Carter, P O BOX 1230 79373
ES, 2121 N 3RD 79373 – Gaylon Gassiot, prin.

Tatum, Rusk Co., Pop. Code 4
Tatum ISD
Sch. Sys. Enr. Code 4
Supt. – Jack Clemmons, P O BOX 808 75691
MS 75691 – David Stanley, prin.
MS 75691 – John DeBrock, prin.
PS 75691 – Debbie McGriff, prin.

Taylor, Williamson Co.
Taylor ISD
Sch. Sys. Enr. Code 5
Supt. – Michael Caplinger
  602 W TWELFTH ST 76574
MS, 410 W 7TH ST 76574 – Larry Sutton, prin.
Johnson MS 76574 – Ivan Leschber, prin.
Northside ES, 2500 NORTH DR 76574
  Doug Ruthven, prin.

Thrall ISD
Supt. – See Thrall
Thrall ES 76578 – Elsa Lieberum, prin.

St. Mary's ES, 520 WASHBURN ST 76574

Teague, Freestone Co., Pop. Code 5
Dew ISD
Sch. Sys. Enr. Code 1
Supt. – W. Fleetwood, RURAL ROUTE 02 75860
Dew ES 75860 – W. Fleetwood, prin.

Teague ISD
Sch. Sys. Enr. Code 4
Supt. – Jesse Harwell, P O BOX 830 75860
Mounger ES, 300 S TENTH AVE 75860
  Carl Shields, prin.
IS 75860 – Gary Barker, prin.

Temple, Bell Co., Pop. Code 8
Academy ISD
Sch. Sys. Enr. Code 3
Supt. – J. Holland, RURAL ROUTE 02 76502
Academy JHS, HWY 195 76502
  Joann Hopper, prin.
Academy ES 76502 – Garmen Compton, prin.

Temple ISD
Sch. Sys. Enr. Code 6
Supt. – Marilyn Hoster, P O BOX 788 76503
Bonham MS, 4600 MIDWAY DRIVE 76502
  Marcia Pope, prin.
Lamar MS, 2120 N 1ST ST 76501
  Ron Henson, prin.
Travis MS, 1500 S 19TH ST 76501
  Melody Johnson, prin.
Bethune/Mega Comet ES, 10TH & AVE J 76503
  Helen Pope, prin.
Cater ES, 4201 LARK TRL 76502
  Lanny Cawthon, prin.
Dickson ES, 1100 S 33RD ST 76504
  Tina Wright, prin.
Emerson ES, 14 E AVENUE B 76501
  Odilia Leal, prin.
Freeman Heights ES, 300 S 27TH ST 76504
  Martin Brubaker, prin.
Jefferson ES, 400 W WALKER AVE 76501
  Jean Sykes, prin.
Lanier ES, 201 N 8TH ST 76501
  Leontene English, prin.
Merideth-Dunbar/Comet MS, 1900 E AVE J 76501
  Bonnie Martin, prin.
Reagan/Comet ES, 1000 S 5TH ST 76504
  Vanny Bolsins, prin.
Scott ES, 2301 W AVENUE P 76504
  Pamela Johnson, prin.
Thornton ES, 2900 PIN OAK DR 76502
  Peg Dooley, prin.

Western Hills ES, 600 ARAPAHO ST 76504
  Dorothy Powell, prin.

Immanual Lutheran School
  2901 W AVENUE S 76504
McGowen Stephens Episcopal School
  317 N 1ST ST 76501
St. Mary's ES, 1004 S 7TH ST 76504

Tenaha, Shelby Co., Pop. Code 4
Tenaha ISD
Sch. Sys. Enr. Code 2
Supt. – Russell Marshall, P O BOX 308 75974
ES 75974 – Carolyn Hooker, prin.

Terlingua, Brewster Co.
Terlingua Cons. SD
Sch. Sys. Enr. Code 1
Supt. – Jim Stovall, P O BOX 256 79852
ES 79852 – (—), prin.

Terrell, Kaufman Co., Pop. Code 7
Terrell ISD
Sch. Sys. Enr. Code 5
Supt. – James Wood, 212 W HIGH ST 75160
MS, 701 TOWN NORTH DRIVE 75160
  William Reynolds, prin.
Burnett ES, 921 S ROCKWALL AVE 75160
  Sandra Williams, prin.
Kennedy ES, S ROCKWELL ST 75160
  Jean Price, prin.
Langwith MS 75160 – Joe Arnold, prin.

Texarkana, Bowie Co., Pop. Code 8
Liberty-Eylau ISD
Sch. Sys. Enr. Code 5
Supt. – Max Harris, 2901 F C I ROAD 75501
Liberty-Eylau JHS
  2300 BUCHANAN ROAD 75501
  Luther Groce, prin.
Liberty-Eylau IS 75501 – J. Holcombe, prin.
Liberty-Eylau PS 75501 – Nolan Bryant, prin.

Pleasant Grove ISD
Sch. Sys. Enr. Code 4
Supt. – Leon Blake, 5605 COOKS LANE 75503
Pleasant Grove MS, 5605 COOKS LANE 75503
  James Richardson, prin.
Pleasant Grove ES, 6421 RICHMOND ROAD 75503
  Roxanne Schoen, prin.

Red Lick ISD
Sch. Sys. Enr. Code 2
Supt. – Richard Hervey
  RURAL ROUTE 05 BOX 395 75501
Red Lick ES 75501 – (—), prin.

Texarkana ISD
Sch. Sys. Enr. Code 6
Supt. – Gary Collins
  4241 SUMMERHILL ROAD 75503
Pine Street MS 75501 – George Kirtley, prin.
Westlawn MS, 410 WESTLAWN DRIVE 75501
  Dwight Duncan, prin.
Dunbar ES, 2315 W 10TH ST 75501
  Ethel Jones, prin.
Fifteenth Street ES, 2600 W 15TH ST 75501
  George Moore, prin.
Highland Park ES, 2401 WALNUT ST 75503
  Blaine Sapaugh, prin.
Kennedy ES, 2100 COLLEGE DR 75503
  Marcus Heldt, prin.
Wake Village ES 75503 – James Goff, prin.
Other Schools – See Nash

St. James ES, 5501 N STATE LINE 75503

Texas City, Galveston Co., Pop. Code 8
Texas City ISD
Sch. Sys. Enr. Code 6
Supt. – Leonard Merrell, P O BOX 1150 77592
Blocker MS 77590 – R. Carter, prin.
Fry IS, 1400 5TH AVE N 77590
  James Jiminez, prin.
Heights ES, 300 N LOGAN ST 77590
  Thomas Sterling, prin.
Kohfeldt ES, 701 14TH ST N 77590
  Alice Rhame, prin.
Northside ES, 2300 21ST ST N 77590
  W. Marshall, prin.
Roosevelt-Wilson ES, 300 14TH AVE N 77590
  Rik Hawkins, prin.

Our Lady of Fatima ES, 1600 9TH AVE N 77590

Texhoma, Sherman Co., Pop. Code 2
Texhoma ISD
Sch. Sys. Enr. Code 2
Supt. – Odes Brown, P O BOX 709 73949
MS, P O BOX 709 73949 – (—), prin.

Texline, Dallam Co., Pop. Code 2
Texline ISD
Sch. Sys. Enr. Code 2
Supt. – Ellis Ivey II, P O BOX 68 79087
S 79087 – James Noyles, prin.

The Woodlands, Montgomery Co.
Conroe ISD
Supt. – See Conroe
Neal Knox JHS, 12104 SAWMILL ROAD 77381
  Thomas Randle, prin.
Loch ES, 27505 GLEN LOCH DR 77380
  Bonnie Wilkinson, prin.

Thorndale, Milam Co., Pop. Code 4
Thorndale ISD
Sch. Sys. Enr. Code 2
Supt. – Jerry Doherty, P O BOX 336 76577
ES 76577 – Suzanne Lenz, prin.

St. Paul Lutheran School, P O BOX 277 76577

Thrall, Williamson Co., Pop. Code 3
Thrall ISD
Sch. Sys. Enr. Code 2
Supt. – Thomas Bowman, P O BOX 398 76578
Other Schools – See Taylor

Three Rivers, Live Oak Co., Pop. Code 4
Three Rivers ISD
Sch. Sys. Enr. Code 3
Supt. – James Keese, P O BOX 640 78071
JHS 78071 – Curry Newport, prin.
ES 78071 – Charles Arnott, prin.

Throckmorton, Throckmorton Co., Pop. Code 4
Throckmorton ISD
Sch. Sys. Enr. Code 2
Supt. – Ward Cooksey, COLLEGE ST 76083
ES 76083 – Johnnie Dormier, prin.

Tilden, McMullen Co., Pop. Code 2
McMullen County ISD
Sch. Sys. Enr. Code 2
Supt. – Frank Franklin, P O BOX 255 78072
McMullen County S 78072 – Jim Bauman, prin.

Timpson, Shelby Co., Pop. Code 4
Timpson ISD
Sch. Sys. Enr. Code 3
Supt. – R. Higginbotham, P O BOX 370 75975
ES 75975 – Lloyd Goolsby, prin.

Tioga, Grayson Co., Pop. Code 3
Tioga ISD
Sch. Sys. Enr. Code 1
Supt. – David Wolf, P O BOX 158 76271
ES 76271 – (—), prin.

Tivoli, Refugio Co., Pop. Code 2
Austwell-Tivoli ISD
Sch. Sys. Enr. Code 2
Supt. – B. Welkener, P O BOX B 77990
Austwell ES 77990 – Disidoro Martinez, prin.
MS 77990 – Anthony Aguirre, prin.

Tolar, Hood Co., Pop. Code 2
Tolar ISD
Sch. Sys. Enr. Code 2
Supt. – Cecil Todd, P O BOX 74 76476
ES 76476 – Charles Carroll, prin.

Tomball, Harris Co.
Tomball ISD
Sch. Sys. Enr. Code 5
Supt. – H. Harrington, 221 W MAIN ST 77375
Beckendorf JHS, 1110 BAKER DRIVE 77375
  James Boyle, prin.
Decker Prairie ES, 221 W MAIN ST 77375
  Michael McWhirter, prin.
Lakewood ES 77375 – Robert Fontenot, prin.
ES 77375 – Michael Williams, prin.

St. Anne Catholic ES, 1111 S CHERRY ST 77375
Tomball Lutheran ES, 911 HICKS ST 77375

Tom Bean, Grayson Co., Pop. Code 3
Tom Bean ISD
Sch. Sys. Enr. Code 3
Supt. – J. Hollensed, P O BOX 128 75489
MS 75489 – Suzanne Jennings, prin.
ES 75489 – Patricia Madison, prin.

Tornillo, El Paso Co., Pop. Code 2
Tornillo ISD
Sch. Sys. Enr. Code 2
Supt. – David Marcum, P O BOX 170 79853
ES 79853 – Harry Eskew, prin.

Trent, Taylor Co., Pop. Code 2
Trent ISD
Sch. Sys. Enr. Code 2
Supt. – R. Don Gibson, P O BOX 105 79561
S 79561 – Edward Donahue, prin.

Trenton, Fannin Co., Pop. Code 3
Trenton ISD
Sch. Sys. Enr. Code 2
Supt. – Ed Derr, P O BOX 5 75490
ES 75490 – Doris Reagan, prin.

Trinidad, Henderson Co., Pop. Code 4
Trinidad ISD
Sch. Sys. Enr. Code 2
Supt. – William Hamm, P O BOX 349 75163
S 75163 – Bennie King, prin.

Trinity, Trinity Co., Pop. Code 4
Trinity ISD
Sch. Sys. Enr. Code 4
Supt. – Robert Henderson, P O BOX 752 75862
JHS 75862 – Alfred Wiedeman, prin.
Lansberry ES 75862 – Phillip Langlais, prin.

Troup, Smith Co., Pop. Code 4
Troup ISD
Sch. Sys. Enr. Code 3
Supt. – Gene Whitsell, P O BOX 578 75789
MS, P O BOX 578 75789 – Michael Payne, prin.
ES, P O BOX 578 75789 – James Branham, prin.

Troy, Bell Co., Pop. Code 4
Troy ISD
Sch. Sys. Enr. Code 3
Supt. – John Gibler, P O BOX 288 76579
MS 76579 – Ronnie Gilliland, prin.
ES, LOWER TROY ROAD 76579
  Peter Thauwald, prin.

Tulia, Swisher Co., Pop. Code 6
Tulia ISD
Sch. Sys. Enr. Code 4
Supt. – Mike Vinyard, 702 NW 8TH ST 79088
JHS, 401 NE 3RD ST 79088 – Don Stout, prin.
Tulia East Ward MS, 800 NW 9TH ST 79088
  Julie Parkinson, prin.
Tulia Highland ES 79088 – Bill Hicks, prin.

Turkey, Hall Co., Pop. Code 3
Turkey-Quitaque ISD
Sch. Sys. Enr. Code 2
Supt. – Wilburn Leeper, P O BOX 397 79261
Other Schools – See Quitaque

Tuscola, Taylor Co., Pop. Code 3
Jim Ned ISD
Sch. Sys. Enr. Code 3
Supt. – R. Kenneth Crouch, P O BOX 9 79562
Buffalo Gap ES 79562 – Oran Egger, prin.
Lawn ES 79562 – Rodney Stockstill, prin.

Tye, Taylor Co., Pop. Code 4
Merkel ISD
Supt. – See Merkel
ES 79536 – Harry Taylor, prin.

Tyler, Smith Co., Pop. Code 8
Chapel Hill ISD
Sch. Sys. Enr. Code 5
Supt. – John Johnston
  RURAL ROUTE 07 BOX 878A 75707
Chapel Hill MS 75708 – Leroy Johnson, prin.
Jackson ES 75707 – Julia Ballenger, prin.
Wise ES 75707 – Robert Fleet, prin.

Tyler ISD
Sch. Sys. Enr. Code 7
Supt. – Jack Davidson, P O BOX 2035 75710
Boulter MS, 2926 GARDEN VALLEY ROAD 75702
  Dale Barnes, prin.
Dogan MS, 2621 N BORDER AVE 75702
  George McDowell, prin.
Hogg MS, 920 S BROADWAY AVE 75701
  Rex White, prin.
Hubbard MS, 1300 HUBBARD DRIVE 75703
  S. Bell, prin.
Moore MS, 1200 S TIPTON ST 75701
  Al Harris, prin.
Stewart MS, 2800 W SHAW ST 75701
  Gerald Barnes, prin.
Austin ES 75710 – Gladys Johnson, prin.
Bell ES, 1409 E HANKERSON ST 75701
  Dewey Williams, prin.
Birdwell ES, 1919 S KENNEDY AVE 75701
  Shirley Franklin, prin.
Bonner ES, 235 S SAUNDERS AVE 75702
  Orenthia Mason, prin.
Clarkston ES, 2819 SHENANDOAH DR 75701
  Charles Douthey, prin.
Dixie ES 75710 – Arless Wilson, prin.
Douglas ES, 1508 N HAYNIE AVE 75702
  John Love, prin.
Gary ES, 730 S CHILTON AVE 75701
  Tom Rhodes, prin.
Griffin ES, 3000 N BORDER AVE 75702
  James Ray, prin.
Jones ES, 2521 W FRONT ST 75702
  Michael Berrier, prin.
Orr ES, 3001 ORR DR 75702 – Don Dudley, prin.
Owens ES 75710 – Betty Cox, prin.
Peete ES 75710 – Therelee Washington, prin.
Ramey ES 75710 – Virginia Dodd, prin.
Rice ES, OLD BULLARD ROAD 75710
  Ed McMillan, prin.
Woods ES, 809 CLYDE DR 75701
  Grace Good, prin.

Thomas Gorman MS, 1405 SE LOOP 323 75701
All Saints Episcopal ES
  3811 BRIARWOOD ROAD 75709
East Texas Christian Academy
  P O BOX 8201 75711
St. Gregory ES, 500 S COLLEGE 75702

Universal City, Bexar Co., Pop. Code 7
Judson ISD
Supt. – See Converse
Kitty Hawk JHS
  840 OLD CIMARRON TRAIL 78148
  Steve Blackmon, prin.
Coronado Village ES, 213 AMISTAD BLVD 78148
  Patricia Russell, prin.
Olympia ES, 8439 ATHENIAN 78148
  Harold Uecker, prin.

Randolph Field ISD
Sch. Sys. Enr. Code 4
Supt. – John Armstrong, P O BOX 2217 78148
Randolph ES 78148 – Barbara Baker, prin.

Schertz-Cibolo-U. City ISD
Supt. – See Schertz
Rose Garden ES, 506 NORTH BLVD 78148
  David Pevoto, prin.

Utopia, Uvalde Co., Pop. Code 2
Utopia ISD
Sch. Sys. Enr. Code 2
Supt. – J. McFadin, P O BOX 218 78884
S 78884 – (—), prin.

Uvalde, Uvalde Co., Pop. Code 7
Uvalde Cons. ISD
Sch. Sys. Enr. Code 5
Supt. – Paul Curtis, P O BOX 1909 78802
Anthon ES, BENSON ROAD 78801
  Judith Tindol, prin.
Batesville ES 78801 – Rex Jackson, prin.
Benson MS 78802 – Bruno Mata, prin.
Dalton ES, 600 N FOURTH ST 78801
  Elizabeth Knippa, prin.
Robb MS, GERALDINE ST 78801
  Willis Springfield, prin.
MS 78802 – Valeriano Ibarra, prin.

Sacred Heart ES, 401 W LEONA ST 78801

Valentine, Jeff Davis Co., Pop. Code 2
Valentine ISD
Sch. Sys. Enr. Code 1
Supt. – J. Lusk, P O BOX 188 79854
ES 79854 – (—), prin.

Valley Mills, Bosque Co., Pop. Code 4
Valley Mills ISD
Sch. Sys. Enr. Code 2
Supt. – Les Farmer, P O BOX 518 76689
ES 76689 – Charles Symank, prin.

Valley View, Cooke Co., Pop. Code 3
Valley View ISD
Sch. Sys. Enr. Code 3
Supt. – Bert Glascock, P O BOX 125 76272
S 76272 – B. West, prin.

Van, Van Zandt Co., Pop. Code 4
Van ISD
Sch. Sys. Enr. Code 4
Supt. – John Dosher, P O BOX 697 75790
JHS 75790 – Jeffrey Turner, prin.
Rhodes ES 75790 – Edward Darragh, prin.

Wills Point ISD
Supt. – See Wills Point
Wills Point S 75790 – Grace Lamar, prin.

Van Alstyne, Grayson Co., Pop. Code 4
Van Alstyne ISD
Sch. Sys. Enr. Code 3
Supt. – Charles Williams, P O BOX 518 75095
JHS, P O BOX 699 75095 – Jerry Page, prin.
ES, P O BOX 699 75095 – Carl Vawter, prin.

Vanderbilt, Jackson Co., Pop. Code 3
Industrial ISD
Sch. Sys. Enr. Code 3
Supt. – Jerald Jimerson, P O BOX 2067 77991
Inez ES 77991 – Marion Carter, prin.
Laward ES 77991 – Gary Thedford, prin.
ES 77991 – Bruce Sanders, prin.
Other Schools – See Lolita

Van Horn, Culberson Co., Pop. Code 5
Culberson County ISD
Sch. Sys. Enr. Code 3
Supt. – Mario Sotelo, P O BOX 898 79855
JHS 79855 – Sheila Joyner, prin.
Eagle ES 79856 – Donna Hill, prin.
Guadalupe ES 79856 – Donna Hill, prin.

Van Vleck, Matagorda Co., Pop. Code 4
Van Vleck ISD
Sch. Sys. Enr. Code 4
Supt. – Kenneth Loveless, P O BOX 0 77482
JHS 77482 – Ramona Pate, prin.
ES 77482 – Terry Sullivan, prin.
IS 77482 – Harold Williams, prin.

Vega, Oldham Co., Pop. Code 3
Vega ISD
Sch. Sys. Enr. Code 2
Supt. – Leonard Kent, P O BOX 219 79092
ES 79092 – James Thompson, prin.

Venus, Johnson Co., Pop. Code 3
Venus ISD
Sch. Sys. Enr. Code 3
Supt. – Preston Holland, P O BOX 364 76084
ES 76084 – Jerry Brand, prin.

Veribest, Tom Green Co.
Veribest ISD
Sch. Sys. Enr. Code 2
Supt. – Willie Siler, P O BOX 475 76886
ES 76886 – (—), prin.

Vernon, Wilbarger Co., Pop. Code 7
Northside ISD
Sch. Sys. Enr. Code 2
Supt. – J. Reed, RURAL ROUTE 01 76384
Northside S, RURAL ROUTE 04 76384
  Galen Smart, prin.

Vernon Cons. ISD
Sch. Sys. Enr. Code 5
Supt. – E. Davis, P O BOX 2160 76384
IS, 2201 YAMPARIKA ST 76384
  Don Coats, prin.
Central ES, 1300 PARADISE ST 76384
  Kay Gibbons, prin.
McCord ES 76384 – Louis Boynton, prin.
Shive MS, 3130 BACON ST 76384
  Max Tatum, prin.

Victoria, Victoria Co., Pop. Code 8
McFaddin ISD
Sch. Sys. Enr. Code 1
Supt. – Jack Goins, 1905 LEARY LANE 77901
McFaddin ES 77901 – (—), prin.

Nursery ISD
Sch. Sys. Enr. Code 1
Supt. – Linda Lockhart, 1905 LEARY LANE 77901
Nursery ES 77901 – (—), prin.

Victoria ISD
Sch. Sys. Enr. Code 7
Supt. – Larry Vaughn, P O BOX 1759 77902
Crain IS 77901 – Leonard Svrcek, prin.
Howell IS 77901 – Kenneth Ballard, prin.
Welder IS 77901 – Harold Cade, prin.
Aloe ES 77902 – Maxine Ross, prin.
Dudley Magnet ES, 3307 CALLIS ST 77901
  Annette Scott, prin.
Gross ES, 1208 S NAVARRO ST 77901
  Israel Salinas, prin.
Guadalupe ES 77902 – Felix Salinas, prin.
Hopkins ES, HOPKINS ROAD 77901
  Rudolfo Torres, prin.
Juan Linn ES, 1500 N DEPOT ST 77902
  Martha Jones, prin.
Martin De Leon ES 77902 – Lionel Cardosa, prin.
Mission Valley ES, 306 E COMMERCIAL ST 77901
  James Anderson, prin.
Mitchell ES 77902 – Wendy Crater, prin.
O'Connor ES, 3402 BOBOLINK ST 77901
  Efren De Leon, prin.
Rowland ES, 2706 LEARY LANE 77901
  Sue Gibbs, prin.
Shields ES, 3400 BLUEBONNET ST 77902
  Luis Rodriguez, prin.
Smith ES, 2901 ERWIN ST 77901
  Susana Mathis, prin.
Stanly ES, 102 SALEM ROAD 77904
  Frank Hogan, prin.
Vickers ES, 708 CLASCOW 77904
  Lorene Azbill, prin.
Wood ES 77902 – Felix Salinas, prin.

Devereux School, P O BOX 2666 77902
Nazareth Academy ES
  206 W CONVENT ST 77901
Our Lady of Victory ES
  1309 E MESQUITE LANE 77901
The Parish School, 1501 N GLASS ST 77901

Vidor, Orange Co., Pop. Code 7
Vidor ISD
Sch. Sys. Enr. Code 6
Supt. – Robert Brezina, 120 E BOLIVAR ST 77662
JHS, NORTH FREEWAY 77662
  Edith Peacock, prin.
Oak Forest ES, 2400 HIGHWAY 12 77662
  Richard Sessions, prin.
Pine Forest ES, 4150 N MAIN ST 77662
  Will Hayes, prin.
ES, 400 E RAILROAD ST 77662
  Marlene Locke, prin.
MS 77662 – Ray Brock, prin.

Waco, McLennan Co., Pop. Code 9
Bosqueville ISD
Sch. Sys. Enr. Code 2
Supt. – Roy Trussell
  RURAL ROUTE 03 BOX 470 76708
Bosqueville S 76708 – C. Hammond, prin.

Connally ISD
Sch. Sys. Enr. Code 4
Supt. – G. Peoples, 715 N RITA ST 76705
Connally JHS, 715 N RITA ST 76705
  Frances Baldwin, prin.
Connally ES 76705 – Cecil Friend, prin.

Gholson ISD
Sch. Sys. Enr. Code 2
Supt. – Bill West
  RURAL ROUTE 05 BOX 498 76705
Gholson ES 76705 – (—), prin.

Hallsburg ISD
Sch. Sys. Enr. Code 2
Supt. – Garland Byrd, RURAL ROUTE 07 76705
Hallsburg ES 76705 – (—), prin.

La Vega ISD
Sch. Sys. Enr. Code 4
Supt. – J. James, 3100 BELLMEAD DRIVE 76705
Miles MS 76705 – Woodrow Logan, prin.
East La Vega MS, 3100 BELLMEAD DR 76705
  Donald Richardson, prin.
La Vega ES, 3100 WHEELER ST 76705
  Shirley Wills, prin.
La Vega PS 76705 – Harold Dodson, prin.

Midway ISD
Sch. Sys. Enr. Code 5
Supt. – M. Dameron
  9101 WOODWAY DRIVE 76710
Midway JHS, MCGREGOR HIGHWAY 76710
  Randy Albers, prin.
Speegleville ES 76710 – Walter Drake, prin.
Spring Valley ES 76712 – C. Lewis, prin.
Woodway ES, 9101 WOODWAY DR 76712
  Charlotte Walker, prin.
Other Schools – See Hewitt

Robinson ISD
Sch. Sys. Enr. Code 4
Supt. – J. Morris, 500 W LYNDALE ST 76706

Robinson JHS, 500 W LYNDALE ST 76706
  James Curlee, prin.
Robinson ES 76706 – Gary Hawkins, prin.
Rosenthal MS 76706 – Curtis Collier, prin.

Waco ISD
Sch. Sys. Enr. Code 7
Supt. – Jim Hensley, P O BOX 27 76703
Lake Air MS, 4601 COBBS DRIVE 76710
  Jay McCullough, prin.
Tennyson MS, 6100 TENNYSON DRIVE 76710
  Jean Lessman, prin.
University MS, 1800 IRVING LEE ST 76711
  Rudy Lopez, prin.
Wiley MS, 1030 E LIVE OAK ST 76704
  Willie Williams, prin.
Alta Vista ES, 3637 ALTA VISTA DR 76706
  Martha Anderson, prin.
Cedar Ridge ES, 2115 MERIDIAN AVE 76708
  Peg Bills, prin.
Crestview ES, 1120 N NEW ROAD 76710
  Hazel Rowe, prin.
Dean-Highland ES, 1800 N 33RD ST 76707
  Pat Marlin, prin.
Hines ES, 1102 PAUL QUINN ST 76704
  Helen Bailey, prin.
Kendrick ES, 1801 KENDRICK LANE 76711
  Nilean Folmar, prin.
Lake Waco ES, 3005 EDNA AVE 76708
  R. Barksdale,Jr., prin.
Meadowbrook ES 76703 – (—), prin.
Mountainview ES, 5901 BISHOP ST 76710
  Raymond Weldon, prin.
North Waco ES, 2015 ALEXANDER ST 76708
  Fhae Lee, prin.
Parkdale ES, 6400 EDMOND AVE 76710
  Alice Lang, prin.
Provident Heights ES
  2415 CUMBERLAND ST 76703
  Patricia Fuller, prin.
South Waco ES, 1410 JAMES AVE 76706
  Beulah Johnson, prin.
Sul Ross ES 76703 – Yolanda Lopez, prin.
Viking Hills ES, 7200 VIKING DR 76710
  Mary Edwards, prin.

Waco Christian School, 816 N NEW ROAD 76710
St. Louis ES, 2208 N 23RD ST 76708
St. Mary of the Assumption ES
  1301 WASHINGTON AVE 76701
Trinity Lutheran ES, 6125 BOSQUE BLVD 76710

Waelder, Gonzales Co., Pop. Code 3
Waelder ISD
Sch. Sys. Enr. Code 2
Supt. – Robert Carruthers,Jr., P O BOX 516 78959
ES, 105 N AVE C 78959 – Norman Woolsey, prin.

Waka, Ochiltree Co.
Waka ISD
Sch. Sys. Enr. Code 1
Supt. – Edward Gilliland, P O BOX 32 79093
ES 79093 – Ed Gilliland, prin.

Wall, Tom Green Co.
Wall ISD
Sch. Sys. Enr. Code 3
Supt. – Charles Spieker, P O BOX 259 76957
Fairview MS 76957 – Ted Hallford, prin.
ES 76957 – Wilbert Jost, prin.

Waller, Waller Co., Pop. Code 4
Waller ISD
Sch. Sys. Enr. Code 5
Supt. – Hugh Mixon, P O BOX 377 77484
JHS, P O BOX 757 77484 – Howard Hawkins, prin.
Holleman ES 77484 – Margaret Martin, prin.
MS 77484 – Almeta Washington, prin.
Other Schools – See Hockley

Wallis, Austin Co., Pop. Code 4
Wallis-Orchard ISD
Sch. Sys. Enr. Code 3
Supt. – Delton Weise, P O BOX E 77485
Orchard ES 77485 – Ralph McCord, prin.
ES 77485 – Nelson Kieke, prin.
Other Schools – See Orchard

Walnut Springs, Bosque Co., Pop. Code 3
Walnut Springs ISD
Sch. Sys. Enr. Code 2
Supt. – D. Edwards, P O BOX 63 76690
S 76690 – Walter Langston, prin.

Warren, Tyler Co., Pop. Code 2
Warren ISD
Sch. Sys. Enr. Code 3
Supt. – Joe Woodland, P O BOX 69 77664
JHS 77664 – Nancey Atkinson, prin.
Fred ES 77664 – Allen Mitchell, prin.
ES 77664 – H. Pitts, prin.

Waskom, Harrison Co., Pop. Code 4
Waskom ISD
Sch. Sys. Enr. Code 3
Supt. – William Edmundson, P O BOX 748 75692
Waskom MS 75692 – Jack Thomas, prin.
ES 75692 – Terry Slone, prin.

Water Valley, Tom Green Co.
Water Valley ISD
Sch. Sys. Enr. Code 2
Supt. – Dan Harris, P O BOX 722 76958
ES, 101 S COMMERCE 76958
  Burel Jameson, prin.

Waxahachie, Ellis Co., Pop. Code 7
Waxahachie ISD
Sch. Sys. Enr. Code 5
Supt. – David Montgomery, P O BOX 977 75165
JHS 75165 – Carolyn McCreight, prin.
Dunaway ES, P O BOX 977 75165
  Billinelle Currie, prin.
Northside ES, 801 BROWN ST 75165
  Jim Ray, prin.
Shackelford ES, P O BOX 977 75165
  Dolores Moore, prin.
Turner MS, 614 N GETZENDANER ST 75165
  David Wyer, prin.
Wilemon ES, 102 W 2ND ST 75165
  John Hauser, prin.

Weatherford, Parker Co., Pop. Code 7
Brock ISD
Sch. Sys. Enr. Code 2
Supt. – David Rice
  RURAL ROUTE 06 BOX 95 76086
S, RURAL ROUTE 06 BOX 95 76086
  Bill Conrad, prin.

Garner ISD
Sch. Sys. Enr. Code 2
Supt. – Robert Duvall
  RURAL ROUTE 05 BOX 120 76086
Garner ES 76086 – (—), prin.

Weatherford ISD
Sch. Sys. Enr. Code 5
Supt. – Joe Tison, P O BOX N 76086
MS, 902 CHARLES ST 76086 – Bill Atchley, prin.
Austin ES 76086 – Jack Hartsfield, prin.
Bowie ES, 902 N ELM ST 76086
  James Tabor, prin.
Crockett ES, 1015 JAMISON ST 76086
  Bill Zinke, prin.
Curtis IS 76086 – Jerry Wilhelm, prin.
Houston ES, 1309 CHARLES ST 76086
  Bill Wright, prin.
Travis ES, 602 W WATER ST 76086
  Leland Harper, prin.

Webster, Harris Co., Pop. Code 4
Clear Creek ISD
Supt. – See League City
Webster Inter. 77598 – John Seidensticker, prin.

Weimar, Colorado Co., Pop. Code 4
Weimar ISD
Sch. Sys. Enr. Code 3
Supt. – Wayne Wise, 101 N WEST ST 78962
JHS, 409 N EAGLE ST 78962 – J. Hudec, prin.
ES 78962 – Robert Long, prin.

St. Michael ES, 103 E NORTH ST 78962

Weinert, Haskell Co., Pop. Code 2
Weinert ISD
Sch. Sys. Enr. Code 1
Supt. – H. Guess, P O BOX 8 76388
S 76388 – Chesley Forehand, prin.

Welch, Dawson Co., Pop. Code 2
Dawson ISD
Sch. Sys. Enr. Code 2
Supt. – Jim Airhart, P O BOX 180 79377
Dawson ES 79377 – Bill Pierce, prin.

Wellington, Collingsworth Co., Pop. Code 5
Wellington ISD
Sch. Sys. Enr. Code 3
Supt. – Lawrence Ward, 606 15TH ST 79095
S, 812 15TH ST 79095 – (—), prin.

Wellman, Terry Co., Pop. Code 2
Wellman ISD
Sch. Sys. Enr. Code 2
Supt. – Raymond Lusk, P O BOX 68 79378
S 79378 – Donald Paris, prin.

Wells, Cherokee Co., Pop. Code 3
Wells ISD
Sch. Sys. Enr. Code 2
Supt. – Victoria Williams, P O BOX 160 75976
ES 75976 – Richard Hawthorne, prin.

Weslaco, Hidalgo Co., Pop. Code 7
Weslaco ISD
Sch. Sys. Enr. Code 7
Supt. – A. Rico, P O BOX 266 78596
Hoge JHS, 603 E 6TH ST 78596
  Aurelio Barbosa, prin.
Airport ES 78596 – Martha Pullen, prin.
Border ES 78596 – Rodolfo Silva, prin.
Cuellar MS 78596 – Mario Hernandez, prin.
Margo ES 78596 – J. Murphy, prin.
Mid Valley ES 78596 – Marlee Payne, prin.
Other Schools – See La Feria

Valle Grande ES, P O BOX 1126 78596

West, McLennan Co., Pop. Code 4
West ISD
Sch. Sys. Enr. Code 4
Supt. – T. Sandifer, P O BOX 156 76691
MS 76691 – Harvey Siems, prin.
ES, 209 N HARRISON ST 76691
  Phillip Gerik, prin.

St. Mary's ES, 507 W SPRUCE ST 76691

Westbrook, Mitchell Co., Pop. Code 2
Westbrook ISD
Sch. Sys. Enr. Code 2
Supt. – David Casey, P O BOX 98 79565
S, P O BOX 98 79565 – R. Hollis, prin.

West Columbia, Brazoria Co., Pop. Code 5
Columbia-Brazoria ISD
Sch. Sys. Enr. Code 5
Supt. – Howard Pickle, P O BOX 158 77486
JHS, P O BOX 158 77486 – Gary Chandler, prin.
Brazoria ES 77486 – L. McCaskill, prin.
Brazoria IS 77486 – Hazel Austin, prin.
Brown IS 77486 – Frank Reid, prin.
ES 77486 – Patsy Martin, prin.
Wild Peach ES 77486 – Brenda Heffernan, prin.

Westhoff, De Witt Co., Pop. Code 2
Westhoff ISD
Sch. Sys. Enr. Code 1
Supt. – Irene Hahn, P O BOX 38 77994
ES 77994 – Irene Hahn, prin.

Westminster, Collin Co., Pop. Code 2
Westminster ISD
Sch. Sys. Enr. Code 2
Supt. – V. Tate, P O BOX 610 75096
ES 75096 – Thomas Holman, prin.

Wetmore, Comal Co.
Comal ISD
Supt. – See New Braunfels
Smithson Valley MS
  RURAL ROUTE 03 BOX 3006 78218
  Patrick Hollis, prin.

Wharton, Wharton Co., Pop. Code 6
Wharton ISD
Sch. Sys. Enr. Code 5
Supt. – Henry Morse, P O BOX 1240 77488
JHS 77488 – James Durley, prin.
Alabama Road ES
  1607 N ALABAMA ROAD 77488
  Margaret Carmichael, prin.
Canton Street MS, 1619 CANTON ST 77488
  Kenneth Hewett, prin.

Wheeler, Wheeler Co., Pop. Code 4
Kelton ISD
Sch. Sys. Enr. Code 1
Supt. – N. Johnson
  RURAL ROUTE 01 BOX 157 79096
Kelton S, RURAL ROUTE 01 BOX 157 79096
  Ross Coffey, prin.

Wheeler ISD
Sch. Sys. Enr. Code 2
Supt. – Doyle Wilson, P O BOX 1010 79096
S, P O BOX 1010 79096 – Clayton Neal, prin.

White Deer, Carson Co., Pop. Code 4
White Deer ISD
Sch. Sys. Enr. Code 3
Supt. – Tom Harkey, P O BOX 517 79097
Skellytown ES 79097 – Kenneth Cox, prin.
ES 79097 – Robert Laurie, prin.

Whiteface, Cochran Co., Pop. Code 2
Whiteface Consolidated ISD
Sch. Sys. Enr. Code 2
Supt. – R. Smotherman, P O BOX 7 79379
ES 79379 – Homer Edwards, prin.

Whitehouse, Smith Co., Pop. Code 4
Whitehouse ISD
Sch. Sys. Enr. Code 5
Supt. – T. Marshall Neill, P O BOX 458 75791
Holloway MS 75791 – Greg Whitman, prin.
Brown ES 75791 – Thomas Luce, prin.
Cain ES, TROUP HWY 75791 – Nora Tucker, prin.
Higgins S, 104 HIGHWAY 110 N 75791
  Larry Sullivan, prin.

White Oak, Gregg Co., Pop. Code 5
White Oak ISD
Sch. Sys. Enr. Code 4
Supt. – R. Proctor
  200 S WHITE OAK ROAD 75693
MS 75693 – J. Johns, prin.
IS 75693 – Jack Hale, prin.
PS 75693 – Bettye Carr, prin.

Whitesboro, Grayson Co., Pop. Code 5
Whitesboro ISD
Sch. Sys. Enr. Code 4
Supt. – Jerry Dickson, P O BOX 130 76273
JHS 76273 – Harold Tamplen, prin.
ES, 211 COLLEGE ST 76273
  Charles Brown, prin.

White Settlement, Tarrant Co., Pop. Code 7
White Settlement ISD
Sch. Sys. Enr. Code 5
Supt. – Clabe Welch, P O BOX 5187 76108
Blue Haze ES 76108 – Gaila Arthur, prin.
Liberty ES 76108 – K. Martin, prin.
North ES 76108 – George Ford, prin.
West ES 76108 – Eldon Krivanek, prin.
Other Schools – See Fort Worth

Whitewright, Grayson Co., Pop. Code 4
Whitewright ISD
Sch. Sys. Enr. Code 3
Supt. – Larry Threadgill, P O BOX 518 75491
MS 75491 – Howard Hodge, prin.
ES 75491 – Howard Roach, prin.

Whitharral, Hockley Co.
Whitharral ISD
Sch. Sys. Enr. Code 2
Supt. – Louis McCormack, P O BOX H   79380
S   79380 – Philip Warren, prin.

Whitney, Hill Co., Pop. Code 4
Whitney ISD
Sch. Sys. Enr. Code 4
Supt. – Hollis Jean, P O BOX 68   76692
JHS, P O BOX 518   76692 – Gwen Eubank, prin.
ES   76692 – Kay Thiele, prin.

Wichita Falls, Wichita Co., Pop. Code 8
City View ISD
Sch. Sys. Enr. Code 3
Supt. – Delbert Mahan
   1023 CITY VIEW DRIVE   76305
City View ES   76305 – Michael Smith, prin.

Wichita Falls ISD
Sch. Sys. Enr. Code 7
Supt. – Leslie Carnine, P O BOX 2570   76307
Barwise JHS, 3807 GRANT   76308
   Nina McNeil, prin.
Kirby JHS, 1715 LOOP 11   76305
   Dan Huddleston, prin.
McNiel JHS, 4712 BARNETT   76310 – J. Ozee, prin.
Zundelowitz JHS, 1706 POLK ST   76309
   Robert Hill, prin.
Alamo ES, 1912 11TH ST   76301
   Patricia Haywood, prin.
Austin ES, 1309 13TH ST   76301
   Dalton Clark, prin.
Bonham ES, 3101 ARMORY ROAD   76302
   Eddie Waldrip, prin.
Burgess ES, 3106 MAURINE ST   76305
   William Shelton, prin.
Crockett ES, 3015 AVENUE I   76309
   Gary Cardwell, prin.
Cunningham ES   76307 – Robert Mobley, prin.
Fain ES, 1562 NORMAN ST   76302
   Judith Pipes, prin.
Fannin ES, 710 BURKBURNETT ROAD   76304
   Robert Sparks, prin.
Fowler ES, 5100 RIDGECREST DR   76310
   Gerald Phelps, prin.
Franklin ES, 2112 SPEEDWAY AVE   76308
   Linda Bonham, prin.
Haynes ES, 1705 KATHERINE DR   76306
   William Lukert, prin.
Houston ES, 2500 GRANT ST   76309
   Lanny Gilley, prin.
Huey ES, 1513 N 6TH ST   76304
   Delfina Martinez, prin.
Jefferson ES, 4628 MISTLETOE DR   76310
   Dorothy Ozee, prin.
Lamar ES, 2206 LUCAS AVE   76303
   William Phillips, prin.
McGaha ES, 1615 MIDWESTERN PKWY   76302
   Davis Lowe, prin.
Milam ES, 2960 STEARNS AVE   76308
   Norma Hill, prin.
Sheppard A F B ES, 301 ANDERSON DR   76311
   Claude Rogers, prin.
Washington MS, 1300 HARDING ST   76303
   Deborah Taylor, prin.

Notre Dame Schools, 2821 LANSING BLVD   76309
Notre Dame ES, 4060 YORK ST   76309
St. Paul Lutheran School
   2222 BROOK AVE   76301
The Episcopal School
   3801 W CAMPUS DRIVE   76308

Wickett, Ward Co., Pop. Code 3
Monahans-Wickett-Pyote ISD
Supt. – See Monahans
Gensler ES   79788 – Bill Shoemake, prin.

Wildorado, Oldham Co.
Wildorado ISD
Sch. Sys. Enr. Code 1
Supt. – Bill Wood, P O BOX 146   79098
ES   79098 – Bill Wood, prin.

Willis, Montgomery Co., Pop. Code 4
Willis ISD
Sch. Sys. Enr. Code 5
Supt. – J. Reeves, P O BOX 377   77378
Hardy JHS   77378 – Fred Rush, prin.
Roark ES   77378 – Linda Reeves, prin.
Turner IS   77378 – Jay Martin, prin.
ES   77378 – Tim Drake, prin.

Wills Point, Van Zandt Co., Pop. Code 5
Wills Point ISD
Sch. Sys. Enr. Code 4
Supt. – Gerald Rosebure, P O BOX 30   75169
MS   75169 – Jon Whittemore, prin.
IS   75169 – Larry Turner, prin.
Other Schools – See Van

Wilmer, Dallas Co., Pop. Code 4
Wilmer-Hutchins ISD
Supt. – See Dallas
ES, 211 WALNUT ST   75172
   Geraldine Hobson, prin.

Wilson, Lynn Co., Pop. Code 3
Wilson ISD
Sch. Sys. Enr. Code 2
Supt. – David Williams, P O BOX 9   79381
ES   79381 – Ted Dockery, prin.

Wimberly, Hays Co.
Wimberly ISD
Sch. Sys. Enr. Code 3
Supt. – Lloyd Treadwell, P O BOX 1809   78676
Bowen MS   78676 – Larry Lorenz, prin.
Scudder PS   78676 – Larry Lorenz, prin.

Windthorst, Archer Co., Pop. Code 2
Windthorst ISD
Sch. Sys. Enr. Code 2
Supt. – H. Neeb, P O BOX 65   76389
ES   76389 – Leonard Schenk, prin.

Winfield, Titus Co., Pop. Code 2
Winfield ISD
Sch. Sys. Enr. Code 1
Supt. – Gerald Hampton, P O BOX 298   75493
ES, P O BOX 298   75493 – (—), prin.

Wingate, Taylor Co.
Wingate ISD
Sch. Sys. Enr. Code 1
Supt. – Edd Farmer, P O BOX 107   79566
Other Schools – See Winters

Wink, Winkler Co., Pop. Code 4
Wink-Loving ISD
Sch. Sys. Enr. Code 2
Supt. – John Sollis, P O BOX 637   79789
ES   79789 – Maxie Watts, prin.

Winnie, Chambers Co., Pop. Code 4
East Chambers ISD
Sch. Sys. Enr. Code 3
Supt. – Keith Davis, P O BOX 417   77665
East Chambers JHS, P O BOX 417   77665
   George Morris, prin.
East Chambers ES   77665 – Sidney Bertrand, prin.

Winnsboro, Wood Co., Pop. Code 5
Winnsboro ISD
Sch. Sys. Enr. Code 4
Supt. – Jerry Hardy, 207 PINE ST E   75494
Memorial MS, 605 S CHESTNUT   75494
   Jim Whittle, prin.
ES, 310 COKE ROAD W   75494
   Bettye Herlocker, prin.

Winona, Smith Co., Pop. Code 2
Winona ISD
Sch. Sys. Enr. Code 3
Supt. – Jack Fry, P O BOX 218   75792
JHS   75792 – Ron Foster, prin.
ES   75792 – Luther Lawless, prin.

Winters, Runnels Co., Pop. Code 5
Wingate ISD
Supt. – See Wingate
Wingate ES   79567 – (—), prin.

Winters ISD
Sch. Sys. Enr. Code 3
Supt. – T. Lancaster, P O BOX 125   79567
ES   79567 – L. Hounsel, prin.

Woden, Nacogdoches Co.
Woden ISD
Sch. Sys. Enr. Code 3
Supt. – W. King, P O BOX 24   75978
JHS   75978 – Keith Lowery, prin.
ES   75978 – Carolyn Gartman, prin.

Wolfe City, Hunt Co., Pop. Code 4
Wolfe City ISD
Sch. Sys. Enr. Code 2
Supt. – John Sneed, P O BOX L   75496
JHS   75496 – Jim Felty, prin.
ES   75496 – Carole Williams, prin.

Wolfforth, Lubbock Co., Pop. Code 4
Frenship ISD
Sch. Sys. Enr. Code 5
Supt. – Paul Whitton, P O BOX 100   79382
Frenship JHS   79382 – Smythie Lawrence, prin.
Casey ES   79382 – Larry Donaldson, prin.
Crestview ES   79382 – Rod Davis, prin.
Friendship IS   79382 – Terry Kohnhorst, prin.
North Ridge ES   79382 – Rod Davis, prin.
Reese ES   79382 – Dan Newberry, prin.

Woodsboro, Refugio Co., Pop. Code 4
Woodsboro ISD
Sch. Sys. Enr. Code 3
Supt. – Milton Denham, P O BOX Y   78393
JHS   78393 – Bill Cooper, prin.
ES, 704 LOCKE   78393 – Finley Barth, prin.

Woodson, Throckmorton Co., Pop. Code 2
Woodson ISD
Sch. Sys. Enr. Code 2
Supt. – G. Freeman, P O BOX 287   76091
S   76091 – Dan Bellah, prin.

Woodville, Tyler Co., Pop. Code 5
Woodville ISD
Sch. Sys. Enr. Code 4
Supt. – Dorman Jackson, P O BOX 429   75979
MS   75979 – Robert Borel, prin.
ES, 306 KIRBY DR   75979
   Lawilda Chapman, prin.
IS   75979 – Mary Rainey, prin.

Wortham, Freestone Co., Pop. Code 4
Wortham ISD
Sch. Sys. Enr. Code 2
Supt. – Sandra Lowery, P O BOX 247   76693
ES   76693 – Johnny Singleton, prin.

Wylie, Collin Co., Pop. Code 5
Wylie ISD
Sch. Sys. Enr. Code 4
Supt. – D. Whitt, P O BOX 490   75098
MS, P O BOX 490   75098 – Bob McAdams, prin.
Akin ES   75098 – Ron Ferguson, prin.
Birmingham ES, 700 W BROWN ST   75098
   Joy Russell, prin.
Hartman ES, 510 S BIRMINGHAM ST   75098
   Cherilou Cox, prin.

Yantis, Wood Co., Pop. Code 2
Yantis ISD
Sch. Sys. Enr. Code 2
Supt. – P. Ponder, P O BOX 149   75497
S   75497 – Joe Taylor, prin.

Yoakum, Dewitt Co., Pop. Code 6
Yoakum ISD
Sch. Sys. Enr. Code 4
Supt. – Harvey Schneider, P O BOX 737   77995
JHS, 115 MCKINNON ST   77995 – C. Dullye, prin.
IS   77995 – Nancy West, prin.
PS, 701 W GRAND AVE   77995 – J. Allee, prin.

St. Joseph ES, ORANGE & ORTH STS   77995

Yorktown, Dewitt Co., Pop. Code 4
Yorktown ISD
Sch. Sys. Enr. Code 3
Supt. – W. Stephenson, P O BOX 487   78164
JHS   78164 – Ed Seidel, prin.
ES, 416 W 4TH   78164 – Elsie Hamilton, prin.

Zapata, Zapata Co., Pop. Code 4
Zapata ISD
Sch. Sys. Enr. Code 4
Supt. – Antonio Molina, P O BOX 158   78076
JHS   78076 – Eliseo Perez, prin.
Benavides ES   78076 – Arturo Martinez, prin.
MS   78076 – Grace Gutierrez, prin.
Zapata North ES   78076
   Anselmo Trevino, Jr., prin.
Zapata South ES   78076
   Humberto Gonzalez, Jr., prin.

Zavalla, Angelina Co., Pop. Code 3
Zavalla ISD
Sch. Sys. Enr. Code 2
Supt. – J. Edmons, P O BOX 45   75980
ES   75980 – Milton Hudspeth, prin.

Zephyr, Brown Co.
Zephyr ISD
Sch. Sys. Enr. Code 2
Supt. – T. Howard, P O BOX 708   76890
ES   76890 – Gary Bufe, prin.

UTAH

STATE OFFICE OF EDUCATION
250 E. 5th, S., Salt Lake City 84111
(801) 533-7500

Superintendent of Public Instruction	James Moss
Associate Superintendent Administration	Scott Bean
Associate Superintendent Research & Development	Kolene Granger
Associate Superintendent Operations	Bruce Griffin

STATE BOARD OF EDUCATION
James Moss, *Executive Director*   250 E. 5th, S., Salt Lake City   84111

UTAH STATE BOARD OF REGENTS
William Rolfe Kerr, *Commissioner of Higher Education*   3 Triad Center, Salt Lake City

PUBLIC, PRIVATE, AND PAROCHIAL ELEMENTARY SCHOOLS

Alpine, Utah Co., Pop. Code 5
Alpine SD
Supt. – See American Fork
ES, 400 E 300 N 84003 – (—), prin.

Altamont, Duchesne Co., Pop. Code 2
Duchesne SD
Supt. – See Duchesne
ES, P O BOX 40 84001 – Lawrence Henry, prin.

American Fork, Utah Co., Pop. Code 7
Alpine SD
Sch. Sys. Enr. Code 8
Supt. – Steven Baugh, 50 N CENTER ST 84003
Barratt ES, 168 N 900 E 84003
  Cristi Dehler, prin.
Forbes ES, 281 N 200 E 84003
  John Bushman, prin.
Greenwood ES, 50 E 200 S 84003
  Bruce Wathen, prin.
Highland ES, 10865 N 6000 W 84003
  Daniel Adams, prin.
Shelley ES, 550 N 2ND W 84003
  Melinda Sherrell, prin.
Other Schools – See Alpine, Cedar Fort, Lehi, Lindon, Manila, Orem, Pleasant Grove

Antimony, Garfield Co., Pop. Code 1
Garfield SD
Supt. – See Panguitch
ES 84712 – Marjorie Robinson, prin.

Bear River City, Box Elder Co., Pop. Code 3
Box Elder SD
Supt. – See Brigham City
ES, P O BOX 159 84301 – Patricia Crandall, prin.

Beaver, Beaver Co., Pop. Code 4
Beaver SD
Sch. Sys. Enr. Code 4
Supt. – Lynn Haslem, 290 N MAIN 84713
Belnap ES 84713 – Val Smith, prin.
Other Schools – See Milford, Minersville

Beryl, Iron Co.
Iron SD
Supt. – See Cedar City
Escalante Valley ES, HCR BOX 38 84714
  Wayne Mifflin, prin.

Bicknell, Wayne Co., Pop. Code 2
Wayne SD
Sch. Sys. Enr. Code 3
Supt. – Robert Painter, 95 W 1ST N 84715
Wayne MS, 265 N 400 W 84715
  Dale Tiffany, prin.
Other Schools – See Hanksville, Loa

Bingham Canyon, Salt Lake Co., Pop. Code 5
Jordan SD
Supt. – See Sandy
Bingham MS, BINGHAM CANYON 84006
  N. Tullos, prin.

Blanding, San Juan Co., Pop. Code 5
San Juan SD
Supt. – See Monticello
ES, P O BOX 405 84511 – Donald Jack, prin.
Halls Crossing ES
  HALLS CROSSING MARINA 84511
  Barbara Bennett, prin.
Lyman MS 84511 – Chris Johnson, prin.

Bluff, San Juan Co.
San Juan SD
Supt. – See Monticello
ES 84512 – Albert Kuipers, prin.

Boulder, Garfield Co., Pop. Code 2
Garfield SD
Supt. – See Panguitch
ES 84716 – Sue Bassett, prin.

Bountiful, Davis Co., Pop. Code 8
Davis SD
Supt. – See Farmington
South Davis JHS, 298 W 2600 S 84010
  Dale Rees, prin.
Adelaide ES, 731 W 3600 S 84010
  Terry Verlan, prin.
Boulton ES, 2611 S ORCHARD DR 84010
  Stephen Burningham, prin.
ES, 1620 S 50 W 84010 – Velda Morrow, prin.
Holbrook ES, 1018 E 250 N 84010
  Marilyn Oberg, prin.
Meadowbrook ES, 695 N 2ND W 84010
  Elizabeth Beck, prin.
Muir ES, 2275 S DAVIS BLVD 84010
  Jesse Taylor, prin.
Oak Hills ES, 1235 E 600 S 84010
  Talmadge Robinson, prin.
Orchard ES, 928 W 4400 S 84010
  Wayne Stanger, prin.
Tolman ES, 300 E 1200 N 84010
  Bowen Lewis, prin.
Valley View ES, 1395 S 600 E 84010
  Linda Davis, prin.
Washington ES, 340 W 650 S 84010
  Deon Stevens, prin.

St. Olaf School, 1793 S ORCHARD DR 84010

Brigham City, Box Elder Co., Pop. Code 7
Box Elder SD
Sch. Sys. Enr. Code 7
Supt. – Darrell White, 230 W 2ND S 84302
Box Elder JHS, 18 S 5TH E 84302
  LaMar Bourne, prin.
Bunderson ES, 641 E 2ND N 84302
  Marilyn Anderson, prin.
Central ES, 210 S MAIN ST 84302
  Richard Williams, prin.
Foothill ES, 890 N 1ST E 84302
  Richard Dunn, prin.
Lake View ES, 851 S 2ND W 84302
  Jerry Wilde, prin.
Lincoln ES, 271 N 1ST W 84302
  Steven Johnson, prin.
Mountain View ES, 650 E 7TH S 84302
  Val Bennett, prin.
Perry ES, RURAL ROUTE 02 84302
  Fred Green, prin.
Other Schools – See Bear River City, Corinne, Fielding, Garland, Grouse Creek, Honeyville, Howell, Park Valley, Snowville, Tremonton, Willard

Castle Dale, Emery Co., Pop. Code 4
Emery SD
Supt. – See Huntington
ES 84513 – Sid Lancaster, prin.

Cedar City, Iron Co., Pop. Code 7
Iron SD
Sch. Sys. Enr. Code 6
Supt. – Dee Stapley, P O BOX 879 84720
MS, 450 W CENTER ST 84720 – Randy Ence, prin.

Cedar East ES, 225 E COLLEGE AVE 84720
  Paul Radmall, prin.
Cedar North ES, 550 W 200 N 84720
  Dee Smith, prin.
Cedar South ES, 499 W 400 S 84720
  Alan Garfield, prin.
Fiddlers Canyon ES, 475 E 1935 N 84720
  Stephen Baker, prin.
Other Schools – See Beryl, Enoch, Parowan

Cedar Fort, Utah Co., Pop. Code 2
Alpine SD
Supt. – See American Fork
Cedar Valley ES, 40 E CENTER 84013
  Jim Melville, prin.

Centerville, Davis Co., Pop. Code 6
Davis SD
Supt. – See Farmington
ES, 350 N 100 E 84014 – Ofelia Wade, prin.
Reading ES, 360 W 2025 N 84014
  Maynard Whitesides, prin.
Stewart ES, 1155 N MAIN ST 84014
  Jay Tolman, prin.
Taylor ES, 293 E PAGES LN 84014
  Jean Madsen, prin.

Circleville, Piute Co., Pop. Code 2
Piute SD
Supt. – See Junction
ES 84723 – Dan Westwood, prin.

Clearfield, Davis Co., Pop. Code 7
Davis SD
Supt. – See Farmington
Antelope ES, 200 S MAIN 84015
  Keith Webb, prin.
Hill Field ES, 389 S 1000 E 84015
  Duane Stoker, prin.
Holt ES, 448 N 1000 W 84015 – Julie Goble, prin.
South Clearfield ES, 990 E 700 S 84015
  Marilyn Dahl, prin.
Wasatch ES, 270 CENTER ST 84015
  Kent Beckman, prin.

Cleveland, Emery Co., Pop. Code 3
Emery SD
Supt. – See Huntington
ES 84518 – Dan Wells, prin.

Clinton, Davis Co., Pop. Code 6
Davis SD
Supt. – See Farmington
ES, 1101 N 1800 N 84015 – Craig Poll, prin.
West Clinton ES, 1800 N 2800 W 84015
  George Cook, prin.

Coalville, Summit Co., Pop. Code 4
North Summit SD
Sch. Sys. Enr. Code 3
Supt. – Derwin Francom, P O BOX 497 84017
North Summit MS, P O BOX 497 84017
  Blaine Dearden, prin.
North Summit ES, P O BOX 497 84017
  Kay Richins, prin.

Corinne, Box Elder Co., Pop. Code 3
Box Elder SD
Supt. – See Brigham City
ES, 2275 N 3900 W 84307 – Brent Larsen, prin.

Delta, Millard Co., Pop. Code 4
Millard SD
Sch. Sys. Enr. Code 5
Supt. – Kenneth Topham, P O BOX 666 84624

MS, 351 E 300 N 84624 – Eleanor Dalton, prin.
Delta North ES, 55 N 100 E 84624
  Scott Bassett, prin.
Delta South ES, 450 S CENTER ST 84624
  Barbara Nielson, prin.
Other Schools – See Fillmore, Garrison

Draper, Salt Lake Co., Pop. Code 6
Jordan SD
Supt. – See Sandy
ES, 1080 E 12660 S 84020 – Spencer Young, prin.

Duchesne, Duchesne Co., Pop. Code 4
Duchesne SD
Sch. Sys. Enr. Code 5
Supt. – Dennis Mower, P O BOX 446 84021
ES, P O BOX 370 84021 – Lowell Caldwell, prin.
Other Schools – See Altamont, Myton, Neola,
  Roosevelt, Tabiona

Dugway, Tooele Co., Pop. Code 5
Tooele SD
Supt. – See Tooele
ES, BLDG 5000 VALDEZ CIR 84022
  David Watson, prin.

Dutch John, Daggett Co.
Daggett SD
Supt. – See Manila
Flaming Gorge ES, P O BOX 187 84023
  Gerold Erickson, prin.

East Layton, Davis Co., Pop. Code 5
Davis SD
Supt. – See Farmington
ES, 2470 E CHERRY LANE 84040
  Neal Smith, prin.

Enoch, Iron Co., Pop. Code 3
Iron SD
Supt. – See Cedar City
ES, 4701 N WAGON WHEEL DR 84720
  Gary Roper, prin.

Enterprise, Washington Co., Pop. Code 3
Washington SD
Supt. – See Saint George
ES, P O BOX 459 84725 – Theron Randall, prin.

Ephraim, Sanpete Co., Pop. Code 5
South Sanpete SD
Supt. – See Manti
MS, 550 E 100 N 84627 – T. Rees, prin.
ES, 151 S MAIN ST 84627 – James Petersen, prin.

Escalante, Garfield Co., Pop. Code 3
Garfield SD
Supt. – See Panguitch
ES 84726 – Marianne Saras, prin.

Eureka, Juab Co., Pop. Code 3
Tintic SD
Sch. Sys. Enr. Code 2
Supt. – F. Openshaw 84628
ES, P O BOX 210 84628 – Gordon Grimstead, prin.
Other Schools – See Trout Creek, Wendover

Fairview, Sanpete Co., Pop. Code 3
North Sanpete SD
Supt. – See Mount Pleasant
ES, 651 E 150 N 84629 – Larry Seely, prin.

Farmington, Davis Co., Pop. Code 5
Davis SD
Sch. Sys. Enr. Code 8
Supt. – Richard Kendell, 45 E STATE ST 84025
ES, 50 W 200 S 84025 – Kenneth Bullock, prin.
Knowlton ES, 801 SHEPARD LANE 84025
  Glen Tonge, prin.
Other Schools – See Bountiful, Centerville, Clearfield,
  Clinton, East Layton, Kaysville, Layton, Ogden,
  Sunset, Syracuse, West Bountiful, West Point,
  Woods Cross

Ferron, Emery Co., Pop. Code 4
Emery SD
Supt. – See Huntington
ES 84523 – Morris Mower, prin.

Fielding, Box Elder Co., Pop. Code 2
Box Elder SD
Supt. – See Brigham City
ES, P O BOX 98 84311 – Karl Starr, prin.

Fillmore, Millard Co., Pop. Code 4
Millard SD
Supt. – See Delta
ES, 430 S 500 W 84631 – Charles Ferguson, prin.
MS, 435 S 500 W 84631 – LaVoy Starley, prin.

Fountain Green, Sanpete Co., Pop. Code 3
North Sanpete SD
Supt. – See Mount Pleasant
ES 84632 – Clark Walker, prin.

Garland, Box Elder Co., Pop. Code 4
Box Elder SD
Supt. – See Brigham City
ES, 250 S MAIN ST 84312 – Donald Potter, prin.

Garrison, Millard Co.
Millard SD
Supt. – See Delta
ES 84728 – Judy Dalton, prin.

Goshen, Utah Co., Pop. Code 3
Nebo SD
Supt. – See Spanish Fork
ES, 10 N CENTER 84633 – Garth Bird, prin.

Grantsville, Tooele Co., Pop. Code 5
Tooele SD
Supt. – See Tooele
MS, 318 S HALE ST 84029
  Donald Lindsay, prin.
ES, 175 W MAIN ST 84029 – Cleo Riggs, prin.

Green River, Emery Co., Pop. Code 4
Emery SD
Supt. – See Huntington
Book Cliff ES 84525 – Blaine Evans, prin.

Grouse Creek, Box Elder Co.
Box Elder SD
Supt. – See Brigham City
ES 84313 – Carol Warburton, prin.

Gunnison, Sanpete Co., Pop. Code 4
South Sanpete SD
Supt. – See Manti
Gunnison Valley ES 84634
  Rodney Anderson, prin.

Hanksville, Wayne Co.
Garfield SD
Supt. – See Panguitch
Ticaboo ES, P O BOX 1 84734 – Roy Strom, prin.

Wayne SD
Supt. – See Bicknell
ES 84734 – Judy Sip, prin.

Heber City, Wasatch Co., Pop. Code 5
Wasatch SD
Sch. Sys. Enr. Code 5
Supt. – Henry Jolley, 173 E 2ND N 84032
Wasatch MS, 200 E 800 S 84032
  David Giles, prin.
Central ES, 301 S MAIN ST 84032
  Marlin Larsen, prin.
North ES, 101 E 100 N 84032
  Marilyn Baird, prin.
Smith ES, 235 E 500 N 84032 – Earl Dayton, prin.
Other Schools – See Midway

Helper, Carbon Co., Pop. Code 5
Carbon SD
Supt. – See Price
Mauro ES, 20 2ND AVE 84526
  Joseph Bonacci, prin.

Hildale, Washington Co., Pop. Code 4
Washington SD
Supt. – See Saint George
Phelps ES 84601 – Frederick Neilson, prin.

Honeyville, Box Elder Co., Pop. Code 3
Box Elder SD
Supt. – See Brigham City
ES, P O BOX 39 84314 – Joan Stokes, prin.

Hooper, Weber Co.
Weber SD
Supt. – See Ogden
Country View ES, 4650 W 4800 S 84315
  Larry Charlton, prin.
ES, 5500 S 5900 W 84315 – Jerry Lerohl, prin.
Kanesville ES, 3112 S 3500 W 84315
  Don Clarke, prin.

Howell, Box Elder Co., Pop. Code 2
Box Elder SD
Supt. – See Brigham City
ES, 16020 N 17400 W 84316 – Janet Coombs, prin.

Huntington, Emery Co., Pop. Code 4
Emery SD
Sch. Sys. Enr. Code 5
Supt. – Ernest Weeks, 130 N MAIN 84528
ES, 90 E 100 N 84528 – Leon Bawden, prin.
Other Schools – See Castle Dale, Cleveland, Ferron,
  Green River, Orangeville

Huntsville, Weber Co., Pop. Code 3
Weber SD
Supt. – See Ogden
Valley ES, 7436 E 200 S 84317 – Val Parrish, prin.

Hurricane, Washington Co., Pop. Code 4
Washington SD
Supt. – See Saint George
MS, 34 S 100 W 84737 – Dan Spendlove, prin.
ES, 63 S 100 W 84737 – Dennis Beatty, prin.

Hyde Park, Cache Co., Pop. Code 4
Cache SD
Supt. – See Logan
Cedar Ridge MS, 65 N 200 W 84318
  Brian Chambers, prin.

Hyrum, Cache Co., Pop. Code 5
Cache SD
Supt. – See Logan
South Cache MS, 29 N 4TH W 84319
  Tom Bailey, prin.
Lincoln ES, 62 W 1ST S 84319
  William Bertolio, prin.

Ibapah, Tooele Co.
Tooele SD
Supt. – See Tooele
ES 84034 – Robert Arthur, prin.

Junction, Piute Co., Pop. Code 2
Piute SD
Sch. Sys. Enr. Code 2
Supt. – Neal Hollingshead, COURTHOUSE 84740
Other Schools – See Circleville, Marysvale

Kamas, Summit Co., Pop. Code 4
South Summit SD
Sch. Sys. Enr. Code 3
Supt. – V. Edrington, 350 E 3RD S 84036
South Summit MS 84036 – Douglas Beer, prin.
South Summit ES 84036 – Myrl Louder, prin.

Kanab, Kane Co., Pop. Code 4
Kane SD
Sch. Sys. Enr. Code 4
Supt. – Nils Bayles, 190 E CENTER ST 84741
Big Water S 84741 – Clint Nielsen, prin.
MS 84741 – Evan Henderson, prin.
ES 84741 – Robert Johnson, prin.
Other Schools – See Orderville

Kaysville, Davis Co., Pop. Code 6
Davis SD
Supt. – See Farmington
Burton ES, 827 E 200 S 84037 – Kent Larsen, prin.
Columbia ES, 378 S 50 W 84037
  Dale Barnett, prin.
ES, 50 N 100 E 84037 – Charles Dyer, prin.
Morgan ES, 1065 THORNFIELD ROAD 84037
  Henry Emery, prin.

Kearns, Salt Lake Co., Pop. Code 7
Granite SD
Supt. – See Salt Lake City
Bacchus ES, 5925 S 5975 W 84118
  Richard Hyland, prin.
Beehive ES, 5655 S 5220 W 84118
  Marcie McDonald, prin.
Gourley ES, 4905 S 4300 W 84118
  Claudia Wasden, prin.
Oquirrh Hills ES, 5241 S 4280 W 84118
  Dale Hartvigsen, prin.
Silver Hills ES, 5770 W 5100 S 84118
  William Mansell, prin.
Smith ES, 2150 W 6200 S 84118
  Delbert Lambert, prin.
South Kearns ES, 4430 W 5570 S 84118
  Catherine Perryman, prin.
West Kearns ES, 4900 S 4620 W 84118
  William Anderson, prin.
Western Hills ES, 5190 HEATH AVE 84118
  Paul Hansen, prin.

Koosharem, Sevier Co., Pop. Code 2
Sevier SD
Supt. – See Richfield
ES 84744 – Tarval Torgersen, prin.

Laketown, Rich Co., Pop. Code 2
Rich SD
Supt. – See Randolph
Rich JHS 84038 – Blaine Robertson, prin.
North Rich ES 84038 – Blaine Robertson, prin.

Lapoint, Uintah Co.
Uintah SD
Supt. – See Vernal
ES 84039 – Errol Merkley, prin.

La Sal, San Juan Co.
San Juan SD
Supt. – See Monticello
ES 84530 – Barbara Redd, prin.

La Verkin, Washington Co., Pop. Code 4
Washington SD
Supt. – See Saint George
ES, P O BOX 288 84745 – Charlene Mendoza, prin.

Layton, Davis Co., Pop. Code 7
Davis SD
Supt. – See Farmington
Adams ES, 2500 N 2200 E 84041
  Forest Barker, prin.
Crestview ES, 185 W GOLDEN AVE 84041
  Melvin Kleinman, prin.
King ES, 601 E 1000 N 84041
  Steve Whitesides, prin.
ES, 319 W GENTILE ST 84041
  Dolores Hansen, prin.
Lincoln ES, 591 W 2000 N 84041
  Ralph Davis, prin.
Syracuse ES, 1503 S 2000 W 84075
  Richard Baird, prin.
Vae View ES, 1750 W 1600 N 84041
  Randall Jensen, prin.
Whitesides ES, 233 COLONIAL ST 84041
  Emer Winward, prin.

Lehi, Utah Co., Pop. Code 6
Alpine SD
Supt. – See American Fork
JHS, 152 N CENTER ST 84043
  Arthur Dowdle, prin.
ES, 765 N CENTER ST 84043
  Paul Rasband, prin.
Meadow ES, 176 S 500 W 84043 – Jack Reid, prin.
Sego Lily ES, 550 E 900 N 84043
  Richard Rowley, prin.

Lewiston, Cache Co., Pop. Code 4
Cache SD
Supt. – See Logan
ES, 107 E 2ND S 84320 – LeRoy Goodey, prin.

Lindon, Utah Co., Pop. Code 5
Alpine SD
Supt. – See American Fork
ES, 30 N MAIN ST 84062 – Ted Maag, prin.

Loa, Wayne Co., Pop. Code 2
Wayne SD
Supt. – See Bicknell
ES, 50 S 100 E 84747 – Burke Torgerson, prin.

Logan, Cache Co., Pop. Code 8
Cache SD
Sch. Sys. Enr. Code 7
Supt. – Clark Puffer, 2063 N 12TH E 84321
Bowen ES, 348 W 3RD N 84321 – Prent Klag, prin.
North Park ES, 2800 N 8TH E 84321
   Richard Roberts, prin.
River Heights ES, 420 S 5TH E 84321
   Merlin Leonhardt, prin.
Other Schools – See Hyde Park, Hyrum, Lewiston,
   Millville, Providence, Richmond, Smithfield,
   Wellsville

Logan SD
Sch. Sys. Enr. Code 6
Supt. – Gary Carlston, 101 W CENTER ST 84321
Mt. Logan MS, 875 N 2ND E 84321
   Donald Jeppesen, prin.
Adams ES, 530 N 4TH E 84321
   Larry Jacobsen, prin.
Bowen ES, USU-UMC 67 84322 – Prent Klag, prin.
Ellis ES, 348 W 3RD N 84321
   Melvin Mecham, prin.
Hillcrest ES, 960 N 14TH E 84321
   David Welch, prin.
Riverside ES, 420 S 5TH E 84321
   Clark Ballard, prin.
Wilson ES, 89 S 5TH E 84321
   Clark Ballard, prin.
Woodruff ES, 650 S 10TH E 84321
   Wendell Shepherd, prin.

Magna, Salt Lake Co., Pop. Code 6
Granite SD
Supt. – See Salt Lake City
Copper Hills ES, 7635 W 3715 S 84044
   Julene Oliver, prin.
Lake Ridge ES, 7400 W 3400 S 84044
   Jerry Pulsipher, prin.
ES, 8500 W 3100 S 84044 – Larry Peterson, prin.
Pleasant Green ES, 8201 W 2700 S 84044
   Portia Peterson, prin.
Webster ES, 9228 W 2700 S 84044
   Cyndy Cannell, prin.

Manila, Daggett Co., Pop. Code 2
Alpine SD
Supt. – See American Fork
ES, 1726 N 600 W 84062 – John Burton, prin.

Dagett SD
Sch. Sys. Enr. Code 2
Supt. – Vermon Barney, P O BOX 248 84046
ES, P O BOX 248 84046 – Vermon Barney, prin.
Other Schools – See Dutch John

Manti, Sanpete Co., Pop. Code 4
South Sanpete SD
Sch. Sys. Enr. Code 4
Supt. – Lewis Mullins, 39 S MAIN ST 84642
ES, 90 W 1ST S 84642 – Kirk Anderson, prin.
Other Schools – See Ephraim, Gunnison

Mapleton, Utah Co., Pop. Code 5
Nebo SD
Supt. – See Spanish Fork
ES, 120 W MAPLE ST 84664
   Ralph Poulsen, prin.

Marysvale, Piute Co., Pop. Code 2
Piute SD
Supt. – See Junction
Oscarson ES 84750 – William Winn, prin.

Mexican Hat, San Juan Co.
San Juan SD
Supt. – See Monticello
ES, P O BOX 157 84531 – Herb Frazier, prin.

Midvale, Salt Lake Co., Pop. Code 7
Jordan SD
Supt. – See Sandy
Copperview ES, 8449 S 150 W 84047
   Charles Weber, prin.
East Midvale ES, 6990 S 300 E 84047
   David Wilson, prin.
ES, 385 E CENTER ST 84047 – Dale Ahlberg, prin.
Midvalley ES, 217 E 7800 S 84047
   Lamar Beckstead, prin.

Midway, Wasatch Co., Pop. Code 4
Wasatch SD
Supt. – See Heber City
ES, 225 S 100 E 84049 – Harvey Horner, prin.

Milford, Beaver Co., Pop. Code 4
Beaver SD
Supt. – See Beaver
ES 84751 – Robert Puffer, prin.

Millville, Cache Co., Pop. Code 3
Cache SD
Supt. – See Logan
ES, 67 S MAIN 84326 – Mary Cadez, prin.

Minersville, Beaver Co., Pop. Code 3
Beaver SD
Supt. – See Beaver
ES, P O BOX 189 84752 – Douglas Albrecht, prin.

Moab, Grand Co., Pop. Code 6
Grand SD
Sch. Sys. Enr. Code 4
Supt. – Glen Taylor, 264 S 4TH E 84532
Grand County MS, 217 E CENTER ST 84532
   Diana Kopka, prin.
Red Rock ES, 685 MILL CREEK DR 84532
   Margaret Hopkin, prin.

Mona, Juab Co., Pop. Code 3
Juab SD
Supt. – See Nephi
ES, 260 E 200 S 84645 – Norman Wall, prin.

Monroe, Sevier Co., Pop. Code 4
Sevier SD
Supt. – See Richfield
South Sevier MS, 430 S 100 W 84754
   Randy Johnson, prin.
ES, 40 W CENTER 84754 – Ray Hunt, prin.

Montezuma Creek, San Juan Co.
San Juan SD
Supt. – See Monticello
ES, P O BOX 538 84534 – Clayton Long, prin.

Monticello, San Juan Co., Pop. Code 4
San Juan SD
Sch. Sys. Enr. Code 5
Supt. – Hal Jensen, P O BOX 219 84535
ES, P O BOX 189 84535 – Timothy Taylor, prin.
Other Schools – See Blanding, Bluff, La Sal, Mexican
   Hat, Montezuma Creek

Morgan, Morgan Co., Pop. Code 4
Morgan SD
Sch. Sys. Enr. Code 4
Supt. – Joseph Ball, P O BOX 530 84050
MS, 75 N 100 E 84050 – Robert Richins, prin.
ES, 344 E YOUNG ST 84050 – Paul Mecham, prin.

Moroni, Sanpete Co., Pop. Code 4
North Sanpete SD
Supt. – See Mount Pleasant
North Sanpete MS 84646 – Courtney Syme, prin.
ES 84646 – Perry Christensen, prin.

Mount Pleasant, Sanpete Co., Pop. Code 4
North Sanpete SD
Sch. Sys. Enr. Code 4
Supt. – Brent Thorne, 41 W MAIN ST 84647
ES 84647 – Reed Miller, prin.
Other Schools – See Fairview, Fountain Green,
   Moroni, Spring City

Murray, Salt Lake Co., Pop. Code 8
Murray SD
Sch. Sys. Enr. Code 6
Supt. – Ron Stephens, 147 E 5065 S 84107
Grant ES, 661 W 6181 S 84123
   Steven Hirase, prin.
Horizon ES, 5180 GLENDON ST 84123
   David Smith, prin.
Liberty ES, 140 W 6100 S 84107
   Brent Bateman, prin.
Longview ES, 6240 LONGVIEW DR 84107
   Martha Kupferschmidt, prin.
McMillan ES, 315 E 5900 S 84107
   Beck Sheffield, prin.
Parkside ES, 5175 S 495 E 84107
   Steven Smith, prin.
Viewmont ES, 745 W 5720 S 84123
   Robert Freeman, prin.

Myton, Duchesne Co., Pop. Code 2
Duchesne SD
Supt. – See Duchesne
ES, P O BOX 186 84052 – Evan Cramer, prin.

Neola, Duchesne Co., Pop. Code 3
Duchesne SD
Supt. – See Duchesne
ES, P O BOX 204 84053 – Gerald Mitchell, prin.

Nephi, Juab Co., Pop. Code 5
Juab SD
Sch. Sys. Enr. Code 4
Supt. – Kirk Wright, 305 E 1ST N 84648
Juab MS, 475 E 800 N 84648 – Norman Wall, prin.
ES, 380 E 200 N 84648 – Betty Mikkelsen, prin.
Other Schools – See Mona

Ogden, Weber Co., Pop. Code 8
Davis SD
Supt. – See Farmington
South Weber ES, 1285 LESTER DR 84405
   Jeannine Crabtree, prin.

Ogden SD
Sch. Sys. Enr. Code 7
Supt. – James West, 2444 ADAMS AVE 84401
Central MS, 781 25TH ST 84401
   Robert Francis, prin.
Highland MS, 325 GRAMERCY AVE 84404
   Dwayne Hansen, prin.
Mound Fort MS, 1396 LIBERTY AVE 84404
   Vern Call, prin.
Mt. Ogden MS, 3260 HARRISON BLVD 84403
   Catherine Ortega, prin.
Bonneville ES, 490 GRAMERCY AVE 84404
   Larry Carrillo, prin.
Dee ES, 550 22ND ST 84401 – Stephen Felt, prin.
Edison ES, 935 E 1050 N 84404
   Henry Dickamore, prin.
Gramercy ES, 1270 GRAMERCY AVE 84404
   Beverly Wilcox, prin.
Grandview ES, 960 39TH ST 84403
   Shauna Eccles, prin.
Hillcrest ES, 130 N ECCLES AVE 84404
   Jeanette Graham, prin.
Lewis ES, 455 28TH ST 84401
   John Crossley, prin.
Lincoln ES, 1235 CANFIELD DR 84404
   Grant Hawkes, prin.
Lynn ES, 605 GRANT AVE 84404
   Rich Moore, prin.
Mann ES, 1300 9TH ST 84404 – Ladd Chase, prin.
Mountain View ES, 170 15TH ST 84404
   David Hunter, prin.
Polk ES, 2615 POLK AVE 84401
   Dale Thompson, prin.
Smith ES, 3301 GRAMERCY AVE 84403
   Bruce Marchant, prin.
Taylor ES, 2120 TAYLOR AVE 84401
   Reed Spencer, prin.
Wasatch ES, 3370 POLK AVE 84403
   Shirley Bergeson, prin.

Weber SD
Sch. Sys. Enr. Code 7
Supt. – Jay Taggart, 5320 S ADAMS AVE 84405
Bates ES, 850 E 3100 N 84414 – Maloy Hales, prin.
Child ES, 655 E 5500 S 84405 – Paul Bryner, prin.
Club Heights ES, 100 E 4150 S 84405
   Evelene Rice, prin.
Farr West ES, 2190 W 2700 N 84404
   Karen Ballif, prin.
Green Acres ES, 640 E 1900 N 84414
   James Shupe, prin.
Lomond View ES, 3644 N 900 W 84414
   Lynne Greenwood, prin.
Mar-Lon Hills ES, 4400 MADISON AVE 84403
   Roberta Grow, prin.
North Ogden ES, 474 E 2650 N 84414
   Penny Dodart, prin.
Parkview ES, 586 40TH ST 84403
   Sheila Stephens, prin.
Pioneer ES, 250 N 1600 W 84404
   Norm Devries, prin.
Plain City ES, 4394 W 2425 N 84404
   Scott Ballif, prin.
Riverdale MS, 1160 W 4400 S 84405
   Rodney Vaterlaus, prin.
Roosevelt ES, 190 W 5100 S 84405
   Scott Spencer, prin.
Uintah ES, 6115 S 2250 E 84403
   William Warner, prin.
Washington Terrace ES, 125 E 4475 S 84405
   Cheryl Nash, prin.
West Weber ES, 4178 W 900 S 84404
   Allan Clarke, prin.
Other Schools – See Hooper, Huntsville, Roy

St. Joseph ES, 2980 QUINCY AVE 84403
St. Paul Lutheran School
   3329 HARRISON BLVD 84403

Orangeville, Emery Co., Pop. Code 4
Emery SD
Supt. – See Huntington
Cottonwood ES 84537 – Kirk Sitterud, prin.

Orderville, Kane Co., Pop. Code 1
Kane SD
Supt. – See Kanab
Valley ES 84758 – Shirl Spencer, prin.

Orem, Utah Co., Pop. Code 8
Alpine SD
Supt. – See American Fork
Aspen ES, 945 W 2000 N 84057 – Jim Gray, prin.
Bonneville ES, 800 W 1245 N 84057
   Brent Milne, prin.
Cascade ES, 160 N 800 E 84057
   Kathryn Spencer, prin.
Cherry Hill ES, 250 E 1650 S 84058
   Darrell Jensen, prin.
Geneva ES, 400 W 665 N 84057
   Wayne Crabb, prin.
Hillcrest ES, 651 E 1400 N 84058
   Gary Seastrand, prin.
Northridge ES, 1660 N 50 E 84057
   Bruce Farrer, prin.
Orchard ES, 1035 N 800 E 84057
   Byron Nicholls, prin.
ES, 450 W 400 N 84058
   Marilyn Laughridge, prin.
Scera Park ES, 450 S 400 E 84057
   John Crandall, prin.
Sharon ES, 525 N 400 E 84057
   Kathy Witbeck, prin.
Suncrest ES, 200 N 700 W 84057
   Michael Pratt, prin.
Vineyard ES, 950 W 800 S 84058
   Dennis Knuckles, prin.
Westmore ES, 1150 S MAIN ST 84058
   Stanley Butler, prin.
Windsor ES, 1315 N MAIN ST 84057
   Stephen Cherrington, prin.

Panguitch, Garfield Co., Pop. Code 4
Garfield SD
Sch. Sys. Enr. Code 4
Supt. – Jerold Judd, 90 S 400 E 84759
MS 84759 – Bennett Josie, prin.
ES 84759 – Nick Reynolds, prin.
Other Schools – See Antimony, Boulder, Escalante,
   Hanksville, Tropic

Park City, Summit Co., Pop. Code 5
Park City SD
Sch. Sys. Enr. Code 4
Supt. – Ronald McIntire, P O BOX 680310 84068

Treasure Mountain MS, P O BOX 1920   84060
  Brian Schiller, prin.
Parleys Park ES, P O BOX 1718   84060
  Linda Singer, prin.

Park Valley, Box Elder Co.
Box Elder SD
Supt. – See Brigham City
ES   84329 – Carol Spackman, prin.

Parowan, Iron Co., Pop. Code 4
Iron SD
Supt. – See Cedar City
ES, 100 N 128 W   84761 – Kevin Porter, prin.

Payson, Utah Co., Pop. Code 6
Nebo SD
Supt. – See Spanish Fork
Barnett ES, 333 E 400 N   84651 – Joe Spencer, prin.
Parkview ES, 360 S 1ST E   84661
  Ryan Creer, prin.
MS, 250 S MAIN   84651 – Tom Hudson, prin.
Taylor ES, 40 S 5TH W   84651 – Lynn Jones, prin.
Wilson ES, 590 W 5TH S   84651
  Roger Bushman, prin.

Pleasant Grove, Utah Co., Pop. Code 7
Alpine SD
Supt. – See American Fork
JHS, 810 N 100 E   84062 – Kent Rowley, prin.
Central ES, 95 N 400 E   84062
  Stan Harward, prin.
Grovecrest ES, 200 E 1100 N   84062
  Scot Westover, prin.
Valley View ES, 941 ORCHARD DR   84062
  Norman Barton, prin.

Price, Carbon Co., Pop. Code 6
Carbon SD
Sch. Sys. Enr. Code 6
Supt. – Ell Sorenson, P O BOX B   84501
Castle Heights ES, 750 HOMESTEAD BLVD   84501
  John Angotti, prin.
Creekview ES, 590 W 500 S   84501
  Paul Crookston, prin.
Durrant ES, 651 N 6TH E   84501
  Gary Arnold, prin.
Westridge MS, 251 W 400 N   84501
  Gary Wilson, prin.
Other Schools – See Helper, Sunnyside, Wellington

Notre Dame School, 210 N 6TH E   84501

Providence, Cache Co., Pop. Code 5
Cache SD
Supt. – See Logan
Spring Creek MS, 350 E 100 N   84332
  Holly Peterson, prin.
ES, 91 E CENTER ST   84332 – Bill Lindauer, prin.

Provo, Utah Co., Pop. Code 8
Provo SD
Sch. Sys. Enr. Code 7
Supt. – James Bergera, 280 W 940 N   84604
Dixon JHS, 750 W 2ND N   84601
  Robert Gentry, prin.
Farrer JHS, 100 N 6TH E   84601
  Thomas Carter, prin.
Canyon Crest ES, 4664 CANYON ROAD   84604
  Karla Thompson, prin.
Edgemont ES, 550 E 3600 N   84604
  Gerald Langton, prin.
Franklin ES, 355 S 700 W   84601
  Elaine Burgener, prin.
Grandview ES, 1591 JORDAN AVE   84604
  Grady Edenfield, prin.
Joaquin ES, 550 N 6TH E   84601
  Marlin Palmer, prin.
Maeser ES, 150 S 5TH E   84601
  Douglas Gardner, prin.
Provost ES, 629 S 10TH E   84601
  David Moyle, prin.
Rock Canyon ES, 2405 N 650 E   84604
  Raymond Harrison, prin.
Sunset View ES, 525 S 16TH W   84601
  Patti Harrington, prin.
Timpanogos ES, 449 N 5TH W   84601
  Rosemarie Smith, prin.
Wasatch ES, 1080 N 10TH E   84604
  A. Samuel Roberts, prin.
Westridge ES, 1720 W 1460 N   84604
  John Bone, prin.

Randolph, Rich Co., Pop. Code 3
Rich SD
Sch. Sys. Enr. Code 3
Supt. – Martell Menlove, P O BOX 67   84064
South Rich ES   84064 – Martell Menlove, prin.
Other Schools – See Laketown

Richfield, Sevier Co., Pop. Code 6
Sevier SD
Sch. Sys. Enr. Code 5
Supt. – Brent Rock, 195 E 5TH N   84701
Red Hills MS, 400 S 600 W   84701
  Russell Peterson, prin.
Ashman ES, 70 N 2ND W   84701
  Ronald Utley, prin.
Pahvant ES, 240 W 500 N   84701
  Elwood Willis, prin.
Other Schools – See Koosharem, Monroe, Salina

Richmond, Cache Co., Pop. Code 4
Cache SD
Supt. – See Logan

North Cache MS, 571 S 2ND W   84333
  Sherm Lindhardt, prin.
Park ES, 90 S 100 W   84333 – Dean Phillips, prin.

Riverton, Salt Lake Co., Pop. Code 6
Jordan SD
Supt. – See Sandy
Oquirrh Hills MS, 12949 S 2700 W   84065
  Earl Behrmann, prin.
Monte Vista ES, 11121 S 2799 W   84065
  Lyle Thacker, prin.
ES, 12830 S 1700 W   84065 – Tom Hicks, prin.
Rosamond ES, 12195 S 2010 W   84065
  Beverly Thompson, prin.
South Jordan ES, 1350 W 1400 S   84065
  Barry Newbold, prin.
Southland ES, 12675 S 2700 W   84065
  Bernett Baldwin, prin.
Welby ES, 4130 W 9580 S   84065
  Kirk Denison, prin.

Roosevelt, Duchesne Co., Pop. Code 5
Duchesne SD
Supt. – See Duchesne
East ES, 700 E 4 N   84066 – Paul Chambers, prin.
MS, 437 N 300 W #425   84066
  Ken McKenzie, prin.

Uintah SD
Supt. – See Vernal
Todd ES, RURAL ROUTE 01 BOX 152   84066
  Dale Harrison, prin.

Roy, Weber Co., Pop. Code 7
Weber SD
Supt. – See Ogden
Lakeview ES, 2025 W 5000 S   84067
  William Lythgoe, prin.
Midland ES, 3100 W 4800 S   84067
  Robert Wood, prin.
Municipal ES, 5775 S 2200 W   84067
  Sheron Christensen, prin.
North Park ES, 4230 S 2175 W   84067
  Larry Neves, prin.
ES, 2888 W 5600 S   84067 – Mike Skeen, prin.
Valley View ES, 2465 W 4500 S   84067
  Don Jensen, prin.

Saint George, Washington Co., Pop. Code 7
Washington SD
Sch. Sys. Enr. Code 7
Supt. – Steven Peterson
  189 W TABERNACLE ST   84770
Dixie MS, 825 S 100 E   84770
  Frances Christensen, prin.
Pine View MS, 2145 E 130 N   84770
  Dale Barlow, prin.
Bloomington ES, 425 MAN OF WAR RD   84770
  Wynn Turek, prin.
Panorama ES, 301 N 2200 E   84770
  Kent Christensen, prin.
St. George East ES, 453 S 600 E   84770
  W. Whatcott, prin.
St. George West ES, 12 N 300 W   84770
  Leon Jones, prin.
Sunset ES, 495 N WESTRIDGE DR   84770
  Dean Losee, prin.
Woodward MS, 15 S 100 W   84770
  Don Powell, prin.
Other Schools – See Enterprise, Hildale, Hurricane,
  La Verkin, Santa Clara, Springdale, Washington

Salem, Utah Co., Pop. Code 4
Nebo SD
Supt. – See Spanish Fork
ES, 140 W 100 S   84653 – Brent Hawkins, prin.

Salina, Sevier Co., Pop. Code 4
Sevier SD
Supt. – See Richfield
North Sevier MS, 135 N 100 W   84654
  Boyd Gurney, prin.
ES, 210 W 3RD N   84654 – William Jolley, prin.

Salt Lake City, Salt Lake Co., Pop. Code 9
Granite SD
Sch. Sys. Enr. Code 8
Supt. – Loren Burton, 340 E 3545 S   84115
Arcadia ES, 3461 W 4850 S   84118
  Joyce Gray, prin.
Bennion ES, 5775 SIERRA GRANDE DR   84118
  Kenneth Higgins, prin.
Canyon Rim ES, 3005 S 29TH E   84109
  Rose Coshow, prin.
Cottonwood ES, 5205 HOLLADAY BLVD   84117
  Jim McCasland, prin.
Crestview ES, 2100 LINCOLN LANE   84124
  Joann Steffensen, prin.
Driggs ES, 4340 S 2700 E   84124
  Morris Goates, prin.
Eastwood ES, 3305 WASATCH BLVD   84109
  Carol Beasley, prin.
Edward ES, 1655 E 33RD S #3   84106
  Marianna Sullivan, prin.
Fox Hills ES, 3775 W 6020 S   84118
  Varon Howell, prin.
Fremont ES, 4249 S 1425 W   84123
  John Erlacher, prin.
Hill View ES, 4405 S 1025 E   84124
  Paul McCarty, prin.
Holladay ES, 4580 S 2300 E   84117
  John Allen, prin.
Lincoln ES, 501 E 3900 S   84107
  Leon Tobler, prin.
Meadow Moor ES, 5315 S 1700 E   84117
  Kevin Hague, prin.

Mill Creek ES, 3761 S 1100 E   84106
  Sherman Johansen, prin.
Morningside ES, 4170 S 3000 E   84124
  Susan Denton, prin.
Moss ES, 4399 S 500 E   84107 – Jane Lindsay, prin.
Oakwood ES, 5815 HIGHLAND DR   84121
  Jeffrey Day, prin.
Penn ES, 1670 SIGGARD DR   84106
  Marilyn Copeland, prin.
Plymouth ES, 5220 S 1470 W   84123
  Mary Rudelich, prin.
Roosevelt ES, 3225 S 800 E   84106
  Glen Drew, prin.
Rosecrest ES, 2420 FISHER LN   84109
  Edna Erlinger, prin.
Taylorsville ES, 2010 W 4230 S   84119
  Varon Howell, prin.
Twin Peaks ES, 5325 S 1045 E   84117
  Wynne Weight, prin.
Upland Terrace ES, 3700 S 2860 E   84109
  Sundee Listello, prin.
Vista ES, 4925 S 2200 W   84118
  Donald Christensen, prin.
Westbrook ES, 3451 W 6200 S   84118
  Cliff Degraw, prin.
Whittier ES, 5975 W 3500 S   84120
  Ted Williams, prin.
Wilson ES, 2825 S 200 E   84115
  Paul LeFevor, prin.
Woodstock ES, 6015 S 13TH E   84121
  Paul Trane, prin.
Other Schools – See Kearns, Magna, West Jordan,
  West Valley

Jordan SD
Supt. – See Sandy
Bella Vista ES, 2131 E 7000 S   84121
  Edwin Deboard, prin.
Butler ES, 2700 E 7000 S   84121
  Daniel Anderson, prin.
Canyon View ES, 3050 E 7800 S   84121
  Robert Wood, prin.
Cottonwood Heights ES, 2415 E 7600 S   84121
  Frank Shaw, prin.
Mountview ES, 1651 E 7000 S   84121
  Terry Klenk, prin.
Ridgecrest ES, 1800 E 7200 S   84121
  Bruce Barnson, prin.

Salt Lake City SD
Sch. Sys. Enr. Code 7
Supt. – John Bennion
Bryant IS, 40 S 800 E   84102 – Larry Jensen, prin.
Clayton IS, 1471 S 1800 E   84108
  Larry Odem, prin.
Glendale IS, 1430 ANDREW AVE   84104
  Rick McCandless, prin.
Hillside IS, 2375 GARFIELD AVE   84108
  Scott Bowles, prin.
Northwest IS, 1400 GOODWIN AVE   84116
  James McCoy, prin.
Salt Lake IS, 233 W 200 N   84103
  James Andersen, prin.
Backman ES, 1450 W 6TH N   84116
  James DeNeff, prin.
Beacon Heights ES, 1850 S 2500 E   84108
  Maria Peterson, prin.
Bennion ES, 429 S 8TH E   84102
  Phyllis White, prin.
Bonneville ES, 1145 S 1900 E   84108
  Shauna Carl, prin.
Dilworth ES, 1953 S 2100 E   84108
  E. Dilworth Newman, prin.
Edison ES, 466 CHEYENNE ST   84104
  Lexie Somerville, prin.
Emerson ES, 1017 HARRISON AVE   84105
  Dorothy Cosgrove, prin.
Ensign ES, 775 12TH AVE   84103
  Ann Cook, prin.
Franklin ES, 1100 W 400 S   84104
  Lawrence Gonzales, prin.
Guadalupe ES, 120 N 600 W   84116
  Suzanne Weiss, prin.
Hawthorne ES, 644 MILTON AVE   84105
  Cosette Joesten, prin.
Highland Park ES, 1738 E 2700 S   84106
  Sally Trost, prin.
Indian Hills ES, 2496 ST MARYS DR   84108
  Steve Borovatz, prin.
Jackson ES, 750 W 200 N   84116
  Peter Gallegos, prin.
Lincoln ES, 1090 ROBERTA ST   84111
  Keith Langford, prin.
Lowell ES, 134 D ST   84103
  Marti Frankovich, prin.
Meadowlark ES, 497 MORTON DR   84116
  William Romine, prin.
Mountain View ES
  1415 CALIFORNIA AVE   84104
  Nancy Larsen, prin.
Newman ES, 1269 COLORADO ST   84116
  Mary Hancey, prin.
Nibley Park ES, 2785 S 8OO E   84106
  Marilyn Phillips, prin.
Parkview ES, 1250 MEAD AVE   84104
  Jan Wilde, prin.
Riley ES, 1431 S 900 W   84104
  Patricia Rowse, prin.
Rose Park ES, 1130 STERLING DR   84116
  Rosanne Jackson, prin.
Rosslyn Heights ES, 2291 S 2000 E   84106
  Gail Mladejovsky, prin.
Uintah ES, 1227 S 1500 E   84105
  Dale Harding, prin.

Wasatch ES, 30 R ST 84103
  Kenneth Harris, prin.
Washington ES, 420 N 200 W 84103
  Dolores Riley, prin.
Whittier ES, 1568 S 300 E 84115
  Lewis Gardiner, prin.

Christ Lutheran ES, 240 E 5600 S 84107
Cosgriff Memeorial School
  2335 REDONDO AVE 84108
Our Lady of Lourdes School, 1065 E 7TH S 84102
Redeemer Lutheran School
  1955 STRATFORD AVE 84106
Rowland Hall St. Marks School
  205 E 3370 S 84103
St. Ann ES, 430 E 21ST S 84115
St. Vincent School, 1385 SPRING LANE 84117

Sandy, Salt Lake Co., Pop. Code 8
  Jordan SD
  Sch. Sys. Enr. Code 8
  Supt. – Raymond Whittenburg
    9361 S 300 E 84070
  Crescent View MS, 1150 S 300 E 84070
    L. Bruce Garrison, prin.
  Eastmont MS, 10100 S 1300 E 84094
    Glayde Hill, prin.
  Indian Hills MS, 1180 SANDERS ROAD 84070
    J. Paul Kochevar, prin.
  Mt. Jordan MS, 9360 S 300 E 84070
    Roger Miner, prin.
  Alta View ES, 865 E 10380 S 84070
    Jennie Stage, prin.
  Altara ES, 800 E 11000 S 84070
    Nancy Moore, prin.
  Bell View ES, 800 E 9800 S 84070
    Max Welcker, prin.
  Brookwood ES, 8640 SNOWBIRD DR 84092
    Brent Palmer, prin.
  Crescent ES, 11100 S 230 E 84070
    Bill Drossos, prin.
  East Sandy ES, 8295 S 870 E 84070
    Diane Dickman, prin.
  Edgemont ES, 1085 E 9800 S 84070
    Moya Kessig, prin.
  Granite ES, 9760 S 3100 E 84092
    Charles Jeppson, prin.
  Lone Peak ES, 11515 HIGH MESA DR 84092
    Keith Wilson, prin.
  Oakdale ES, 1900 CREEK ROAD 84092
    Jerry Chapman, prin.
  Park Lane ES, 9955 S 2300 E 84092
    Denney Berrett, prin.
  Peruvian ES, 1545 E 8425 S 84092
    Ronald Jarrett, prin.
  Quail Hollow ES, 2625 NEWCASTLE DR 84092
    Cheryl Lebo, prin.
  ES, 8725 S 280 E 84070 – Dan Barney, prin.
  Silver Mesa ES, 8920 S 1700 E 84092
    Bonnie Dahl, prin.
  Sprucewood ES, 12025 S 1000 E 84070
    Susan Turner, prin.
  Sunrise ES, 1520 E 11265 S 84092
    Sharon Griener, prin.
  Willow Canyon ES, 9650 S 1700 E 84092
    Gilbert Stevenson, prin.
  Other Schools – See Bingham Canyon, Draper,
    Midvale, Riverton, Salt Lake City, South Jordan,
    West Jordan

Santa Clara, Washington Co., Pop. Code 4
  Washington SD
  Supt. – See Saint George
  ES, 2950 W CRESTVIEW DR 84765
    Donald Fawson, prin.

Santaquin, Utah Co., Pop. Code 4
  Nebo SD
  Supt. – See Spanish Fork
  ES, 25 S 400 W 84655 – Chris Sorensen, prin.

Smithfield, Cache Co., Pop. Code 5
  Cache SD
  Supt. – See Logan
  Summit ES, 80 W CENTER ST 84335
    Loyal Green, prin.

Snowville, Box Elder Co., Pop. Code 2
  Box Elder SD
  Supt. – See Brigham City
  ES 84336 – Peggy Smith, prin.

South Jordan, Salt Lake Co., Pop. Code 6
  Jordan SD
  Supt. – See Sandy
  Jordan Ridge ES, 2636 W 9800 S 84065
    Kreig Kelley, prin.

Spanish Fork, Utah Co., Pop. Code 6
  Nebo SD
  Sch. Sys. Enr. Code 7
  Supt. – J. Wayne Nelson, 350 S MAIN ST 84660
  Brockbank ES, 340 W 540 N 84660
    Ronald Bills, prin.
  Larsen ES, 1175 E FLONETTE AVE 84660
    Sterling Argyle, prin.
  Park ES, 90 N 600 E 84660 – Howard Creer, prin.
  Rees ES, 185 E 400 N 84660 – Ray Mecham, prin.
  IS, 600 S 820 E 84660 – Lee Hill, prin.
  Other Schools – See Goshen, Mapleton, Payson,
    Salem, Santaquin, Springville

Spring City, Sanpete Co., Pop. Code 3
  North Sanpete SD
  Supt. – See Mount Pleasant
  ES 84662 – Arlea Howell, prin.

Springdale, Washington Co., Pop. Code 2
  Washington SD
  Supt. – See Saint George
  ES 84767 – Leon Lewis, prin.

Springville, Utah Co., Pop. Code 6
  Nebo SD
  Supt. – See Spanish Fork
  Art City ES, 121 N 900 E 84663
    Richard Dotson, prin.
  Brookside ES, 750 E 400 S 84663
    Dennis Tuckett, prin.
  Grant ES, 105 S 400 E 84663 – Clara Clark, prin.
  Sage Creek ES, 1050 S 7TH E 84663
    Bradford Walker, prin.
  MS, 485 S 100 E 84663 – George Rasband, prin.
  Westside ES, 500 S MAIN ST 84663
    Peter Fawson, prin.

Sunnyside, Carbon Co., Pop. Code 3
  Carbon SD
  Supt. – See Price
  Peterson ES 84539 – Fern Wilkerson, prin.

Sunset, Davis Co., Pop. Code 6
  Davis SD
  Supt. – See Farmington
  Doxey ES, 944 N 250 W 84015 – Pat McKay, prin.
  Fremont ES, 2525 N 160 W 84015
    Arvel Beckstead, prin.
  ES, 2014 N 250 W 84015 – John Olearain, prin.

Syracuse, Davis Co., Pop. Code 5
  Davis SD
  Supt. – See Farmington
  Cook ES, 1175 W 1350 S 84075
    Ruth Kunkel, prin.

Tabiona, Duchesne Co., Pop. Code 2
  Duchesne SD
  Supt. – See Duchesne
  ES, P O BOX 446 84072 – Robert Park, prin.

Tooele, Tooele Co., Pop. Code 7
  Tooele SD
  Sch. Sys. Enr. Code 6
  Supt. – Michael Jacobsen, 66 W VINE ST 84074
  JHS, 412 W VINE ST 84074 – Louis Killpack, prin.
  East ES, 150 S 7TH ST 84074 – Robert Kroff, prin.
  Harris ES, 251 N 1ST ST 84074
    Claude Segura, prin.
  Stansbury ES, 485 COUNTRY CLUB 84074
    Cheryl Miller, prin.
  Tooele Central ES, 55 N 1ST W 84074
    Albert Arellano, prin.
  West ES, 400 W 400 S 84074 – John Barrus, prin.
  Other Schools – See Dugway, Grantsville, Ibapah,
    Vernon

Tremonton, Box Elder Co., Pop. Code 5
  Box Elder SD
  Supt. – See Brigham City
  Bear River MS, 400 E 4TH N 84337
    Jim Baty, prin.
  McKinley ES, 121 W 5TH S 84337
    Ray Timothy, prin.
  North Park ES, 50 E 7TH N 84437
    Lavar Douglas, prin.

Tropic, Garfield Co., Pop. Code 2
  Garfield SD
  Supt. – See Panguitch
  Bryce Valley ES 84776 – Lowell Mecham, prin.

Trout Creek, Juab Co.
  Tintic SD
  Supt. – See Eureka
  West Desert ES 84083 – Fred Openshaw, prin.

Vernal, Uintah Co., Pop. Code 6
  Uintah SD
  Sch. Sys. Enr. Code 6
  Supt. – Grant Drollinger, 635 W 200 S 84078
  Ashley ES, 350 N 1150 W 84078
    Frank Andreasen, prin.
  Central ES, 250 S VERNAL AVE 84078
    Ken Morgan, prin.
  Davis ES, 4101 S 2500 E 84078 – Dixie Allen, prin.
  Discovery ES, 650 W 1200 S 84078
    Carol Latham, prin.
  Maeser ES, 2670 W 1000 N 84078
    Lyle Southam, prin.
  Naples ES, 1971 S 1500 E 84078
    Larry Klein, prin.
  MS, 161 N 1000 W 84078
    Leonard Sullivan, prin.
  Other Schools – See Lapoint, Roosevelt

Vernon, Tooele Co., Pop. Code 2
  Tooele SD
  Supt. – See Tooele
  ES 84080 – David Watson, prin.

Washington, Washington Co., Pop. Code 5
  Washington SD
  Supt. – See Saint George
  ES, 300 N 300 E 84780 – Robert Everett, prin.

Wellington, Carbon Co., Pop. Code 4
  Carbon SD
  Supt. – See Price
  ES, P O BOX 407 84542 – Ralph Dyett, prin.

Wellsville, Cache Co., Pop. Code 4
  Cache SD
  Supt. – See Logan
  ES, 90 E 1ST S 84339 – Clair Larkin, prin.

Wendover, Tooele Co., Pop. Code 4
  Tintic SD
  Supt. – See Eureka
  Callao ES, CALLAO RT 84083
    Fred Openshaw, prin.

West Bountiful, Davis Co., Pop. Code 5
  Davis SD
  Supt. – See Farmington
  ES, 750 W 400 N 84087 – Noel Williams, prin.

West Jordan, Salt Lake Co., Pop. Code 8
  Granite SD
  Supt. – See Salt Lake City
  Bridger ES, 5368 CYCLAMEN WAY 84084
    Verna Tripp, prin.

  Jordan SD
  Supt. – See Sandy
  Jensen MS, 8105 S 3200 W 84084
    Marvin Reid, prin.
  MS, 7550 S 1700 W 84084
    Sidney Beveridge, prin.
  Columbia ES, 3505 W 7800 S 84088
    Brenda Hales, prin.
  Heartland ES, 1451 W 7000 S 84084
    J. Dale Christensen, prin.
  Majestic ES, 7430 S 1700 W 84084
    James Madsen, prin.
  Mountain Shadows ES, 5255 W 7000 S 84084
    Calvin Newbold, prin.
  Oquirrh ES, 7165 PADDINGTON ROAD 84084
    Denis Lyons, prin.
  Riverside ES, 8737 S 1220 W 84088
    Stephen Burnside, prin.
  Terra Linda ES, 8400 S 3400 W 84088
    Ray Whitlock, prin.
  ES, 7220 S 2370 W 84084 – Richard Allred, prin.
  Westland ES, 2925 W 7180 S 84084
    Larry Fryer, prin.
  Westvale ES, 8660 S 2300 W 84084
    Susan Westergard, prin.

West Point, Davis Co., Pop. Code 4
  Davis SD
  Supt. – See Farmington
  ES, 3788 W 300 N 84015 – Les Broadhead, prin.

West Valley, Salt Lake Co.
  Granite SD
  Supt. – See Salt Lake City
  Academy Park ES, 4580 WESTPOINT DR 84120
    Gloria Rupp, prin.
  Farnsworth ES, 4225 W 3751 S 84120
    Karen Sterling, prin.
  Frost ES, 3444 W 4400 S 84119
    Janice Wright, prin.
  Granger ES, 2450 W 3800 S 84119
    Donald Norton, prin.
  Hillsdale ES, 3275 W 3100 S 84119
    Bonnie Newman, prin.
  Hillside ES, 4283 S 6000 W 84120
    Reed Wahlquist, prin.
  Hunter ES, 4351 S 5400 W 84120
    Sharon Prescott, prin.
  Jackling ES, 3760 S 4610 W 84120
    Lynn Burton, prin.
  Monroe ES, 4450 W 3100 S 84120
    Claudia Seeley, prin.
  Oakridge ES, 4325 JUPITER DR 84120
    Richard Davis, prin.
  Orchard ES, 6744 W 3800 S 84120
    Archie McCarrie, prin.
  Pioneer ES, 3860 S 3380 W 84119
    Dorene Squires, prin.
  Redwood ES, 2650 S REDWOOD RD 84119
    Rex Becker, prin.
  Rolling Meadows ES
    2950 WHITEHALL DR 84119
    Susan McGhie, prin.
  Sandberg ES, 3900 S 5325 W 84120
    Louis Jensen, prin.
  Stansbury ES, 3050 S 2700 W 84119
    Kent Johnson, prin.
  Truman ES, 4639 S 3200 W 84119
    Frank Hall, prin.
  Valley Crest ES, 5240 W 3100 S 84120
    Ann Gerson, prin.

Willard, Box Elder Co., Pop. Code 4
  Box Elder SD
  Supt. – See Brigham City
  ES, 30 S MAIN 84340 – Wade Hyde, prin.

Woods Cross, Davis Co., Pop. Code 5
  Davis SD
  Supt. – See Farmington
  ES, 1100 S 745 W 84087 – Garvin Carlile, prin.

VERMONT

STATE DEPARTMENT OF EDUCATION
State Office Building
120 State St., Montpelier 05602
(802) 828-3135

Commissioner of Education	Richard Mills
Deputy Commissioner	Bruce Richardson
Director Administrative Services	Peter Ryan
Director Basic Education	Douglas Walker
Director Adult & Vocational-Technical Education	Gerard Asselin
Director Special & Compensatory Education	Marc Hull

STATE BOARD OF EDUCATION
Martha O'Connor, *Chairperson*   Brattleboro   05301

VERMONT HIGHER EDUCATION PLANNING COMMISSION
Suzanne Villanti, *Executive Director*   109 State St., Montpelier   05620

PUBLIC, PRIVATE, AND PAROCHIAL ELEMENTARY SCHOOLS

Albany, Orleans Co., Pop. Code 2
Orleans Central Supervisory Union
Supt. – See Orleans
Albany Village MS   05820 – Sandy Kepler, prin.

Alburg, Grand Isle Co., Pop. Code 2
Grand Isle Supervisory Union
Supt. – See North Hero
Alburg Community ES, P O BOX 80   05440
    (—), prin.

Arlington, Bennington Co., Pop. Code 4
Bennington-Rutland Supervisory Union
Supt. – See Manchester Center
Sunderland ES, P O BOX 1500   05250
    Edward Houlihan, prin.

Southwest Vermont Supervisory Union
Supt. – See Bennington
Fisher ES   05250 – Roberta Barone, prin.

Ascutney, Windsor Co.
Windsor Southeast Supervisory Union
Supt. – See Windsor
Weathersfield MS, P O BOX 28   05030
    Gordon Schnare, prin.

Bakersfield, Franklin Co., Pop. Code 2
Franklin Northeast Supervisory Union
Supt. – See Richford
MS, ACADEMY DR BOX 17   05441
    Michael Deweese, prin.

Barnard, Windsor Co.
Windsor Central Supervisory Union
Supt. – See Woodstock
Barnard Central ES   05031
    Georgena Holden, prin.

Barnet, Caledonia Co., Pop. Code 4
Caledonia Central Supervisory Union
Supt. – See Danville
MS   05821 – Joanne Hickey, prin.

Barre, Washington Co., Pop. Code 6
Barre City Supervisory SD
Sch. Sys. Enr. Code 4
Supt. – Charles Johnson, WASHINGTON ST   05641
Spaulding MS, 60 WASHINGTON ST   05641
    Charles Decker, prin.
Barre Lincoln ES, 114 HILL ST   05641
    Laura Johnson, prin.
Brook Street ES   05641 – Gordon Willard, prin.
Mathewson ES, 71 ELM ST   05641
    Earline Marsh, prin.
North Barre ES, BECKLEY STREET   05641
    James Taffel, prin.
Ward Five ES, HUMBERT STREET   05641
    Donald LaPointe, prin.

Barre Town Supervisory District
Sch. Sys. Enr. Code 2
Supt. – Brian O'Regan, RURAL ROUTE 02   05641
Barretown ES
    RURAL ROUTE 02   BOX 4323   05641
    David James, prin.

St. Monica's ES, 73 SUMMER ST   05641

Barton, Orleans Co., Pop. Code 4
Orleans Central Supervisory Union
Supt. – See Orleans
ES   05822 – Jeffrey Taylor, prin.

St. Paul's ES, EASTERN AVE   05822

Bellows Falls, Windham Co., Pop. Code 5
Windham Northeast Supervisory Union
Sch. Sys. Enr. Code 4
Supt. – Hugh Haggerty
    8 1/2 ATKINSON ST   05101
MS, SCHOOL ST   05101 – Herbert Werden, prin.
Rockingham Central ES, SCHOOL ST EXT   05101
    Robert Campbell, prin.
Other Schools – See Chester, Grafton, Putney, Saxtons
    River, Westminster

Bellvidere Center, Lamoille Co., Pop. Code 2
Lamoille North Supervisory Union
Supt. – See Hyde Park
Belvedere Central ES, RURAL ROUTE   05442
    Richard Spaulding, prin.

Bennington, Bennington Co., Pop. Code 7
Southwest Vermont Supervisory Union
Sch. Sys. Enr. Code 5
Supt. – (—), 604 MAIN ST   05201
Mt. Anthony JHS, 640 MAIN ST   05201
    Martha Rudd, prin.
ES, 128 PARK ST   05201 – Ernest LaFontaine, prin.
Catamount ES, 230 SCHOOL ST   05201
    Nicholas Charest, prin.
Monument ES, 2 MAIN ST   05201
    Robert Marcoux, prin.
Stark ES, 9 WILLOW RD   05201
    Thomas Driscoll, prin.
Whitney ES, GAGE STREET   05201
    Joyce Horst, prin.
Woodford Hollow ES, HCR   05201
    Nancy Arseneau, prin.
Other Schools – See Arlington, North Bennington,
    Pownal, Shaftsbury

Sacred Heart ES, 307 SCHOOL ST   05201

Benson, Rutland Co., Pop. Code 3
Addison-Rutland Supervisory Union
Supt. – See Fair Haven
ES   05731 – Richard Beriau, prin.

Bethel, Windsor Co., Pop. Code 4
Windsor Northwest Supervisory Union
Sch. Sys. Enr. Code 3
Supt. – Terrance McCannell   05032
ES   05032 – John Bacon, prin.
Stockbridge ES, RURAL ROUTE 02   05032
    Edwin Fava, prin.
Other Schools – See Granville, Hancock, Rochester

Bomoseen, Rutland Co.
Addison-Rutland Supervisory Union
Supt. – See Fair Haven
Castleton ES, P O BOX 337   05732
    Andrew Olanoff, prin.

Bondville, Bennington Co.
Windham Central Supervisory Union
Supt. – See Newfane
Winhall ES, RURAL ROUTE   05340
    Kim Kiniry, prin.

Bradford, Orange Co., Pop. Code 3
Orange East Supervisory Union
Sch. Sys. Enr. Code 4
Supt. – Robert Marquis, P O BOX 396   05033
ES, FAIRGROUND ROAD   05033
    Russell Collins, prin.
Other Schools – See East Corinth, Fairlee, Newbury,
    Thetford, Vershire, West Fairlee

Brandon, Rutland Co., Pop. Code 5
Rutland Northeast Supervisory Union
Sch. Sys. Enr. Code 4
Supt. – William Mathis, 2 UNION ST   05733
Leicester Central ES, RURAL ROUTE 02   05733
    Eleanor Holsman, prin.
Neshobe ES, RURAL ROUTE 03   05733
    Bertram Coolidge, prin.
Sudbury Country ES, RURAL ROUTE 01   05733
    Mark Pelletier, prin.
Other Schools – See Chittenden, Pittsford, Whiting

Brattleboro, Windham Co., Pop. Code 7
Windham Southeast Supervisory Union
Sch. Sys. Enr. Code 5
Supt. – James Cusick, 230 MAIN ST   05301
JHS   05301 – Eric Hammerlund, prin.
Acadmey ES, 204 WESTERN AVE   05301
    Lawrence Alper, prin.
Canal Street ES   05301 – Mark Taft, prin.
Green Street ES   05301 – Robert Neubauer, prin.
Guilford Central ES, RURAL ROUTE 03   05301
    Charlotte Levens, prin.
Oak Grove MS, 2 MORELAND AVE   05301
    Mark Taft, prin.
Walnut Street MS   05301 – Robert Neubauer, prin.
Other Schools – See Putney, Vernon

St. Michael's ES, 23 WALNUT ST   05301

Bridgewater, Windsor Co., Pop. Code 2
Windsor Central Supervisory Union
Supt. – See Woodstock
Bridgewater Village ES   05034
    William Cossabooon, prin.

Brideport, Addison Co., Pop. Code 3
Addison Central Supervisory Union
Supt. – See Middlebury
Bridport Central ES
    RURAL ROUTE 22A BOX 35   05734
    Keith Shearer, prin.

Bristol, Addison Co., Pop. Code 4
Addison Northeast Supervisory Union
Sch. Sys. Enr. Code 4
Supt. – James Lombardo, 9 AIRPORT DR   05443
MS, PARK ST   05443 – Terrance Evarts, prin.
Lincoln Community ES
    RURAL ROUTE 01 BOX 123   05443
    Rick Ebel, prin.
Mountain Street ES   05443 – Terrance Evarts, prin.
Other Schools – See Monkton, New Haven, Starksboro

Brookfield, Orange Co., Pop. Code 3
Orange Southwest Supervisory Union
Supt. – See Randolph
ES, RURAL ROUTE 01 BOX 39   05036
Clayton Gage, prin.

Brownsville, Windsor Co.
Windsor Southeast Supervisory Union
Supt. – See Windsor
Bridge ES   05037 – Eleanor Robinson, prin.

Burlington, Chittenden Co., Pop. Code 8
Burlington Supervisory SD
Sch. Sys. Enr. Code 6
Supt. – Paul Danyow
150 COLCHESTER AVE   05401
Edmunds MS, 265 MAIN ST   05401
Robert Levis, prin.
Hunt MS, 1364 NORTH AVE   05401
Nelson Wentworth, prin.
Barnes ES, NORTH STREET   05401
Steve Hamilton, prin.
Champlin ES, PINE STREET   05401
Roland Limoge, prin.
Edmunds ES, 265 MAIN ST   05401
Diane Chattman, prin.
Flynn ES, NORTH AVE   05401
Edward White, prin.
Smith ES, 322 ETHAN ALLEN PKY   05401
Eleanore McNamara, prin.
Thayer ES, 1364 NORTH AVE   05401
Mary Ellen Beard, prin.
Wheeler ES, ARCHIBALD & SPRING   05401
Howard Goodrich, prin.

Christ the King ES, 136 LOCUST ST   05401
Mater Christi ES, 50 MANSFIELD AVE   05401
St. Joseph's ES, 20 ALLEN ST   05401

Cabot, Washington Co., Pop. Code 2
Washington Northeast Supervisory Union
Supt. – See Plainfield
S   05647 – (—), prin.

Cambridge, Lamoille Co., Pop. Code 2
Lamoille North Supervisory Union
Supt. – See Hyde Park
Fletcher ES, RURAL ROUTE   05444
Howard Wooden, prin.

Canaan, Essex Co., Pop. Code 4
Essex North Supervisory Union
Sch. Sys. Enr. Code 2
Supt. – Donald Sipe   05903
ES   05903 – Wayne Murray, prin.
Other Schools – See Norton

Castleton, Rutland Co., Pop. Code 5
Addison-Rutland Supervisory Union
Supt. – See Fair Haven
Castleton Village MS, P O BOX 68   05735
Andrew Olanoff, prin.

Charlotte, Chittenden Co., Pop. Code 5
Chittendon South Supervisory Union
Supt. – See Shelburne
Charlotte Central ES   05445 – Rick Detwiler, prin.

Chelsea, Orange Co., Pop. Code 4
Orange-Windsor Supervisory Union
Supt. – See South Royalton
S   05038 – David Savidge, prin.

Chester, Windsor Co., Pop. Code 5
Windham Northeast Supervisory Union
Supt. – See Bellows Falls
Athens ES, RURAL ROUTE 03   05143
Virginia Marshall, prin.

Windsor Southwest Supervisory Union
Sch. Sys. Enr. Code 4
Supt. – Paul Ippolito   05143
Chester Andover ES, MAIN STREET   05143
John Perry, prin.
Other Schools – See Londonderry, Proctorsville

Chittenden, Rutland Co., Pop. Code 3
Rutland Northeast Supervisory Union
Supt. – See Brandon
Barstow ES   05737 – David Wolk, prin.

Colchester, Chittenden Co., Pop. Code 7
Colchester Supervisory SD
Sch. Sys. Enr. Code 6
Supt. – R. Grimley, P O BOX 27   05446
JHS, P O BOX 30   05446 – B. Fitzgerald, prin.
Mallets Bay MS, P O BOX 28   05446
Roger Moyer, prin.
Porters Point ES, P O BOX 32   05446
Martin Waldron, prin.
Union Memorial ES, MAIN STREET   05446
George Costello, prin.

Concord, Essex Co., Pop. Code 4
Essex-Caledonia Supervisory SD
Sch. Sys. Enr. Code 3
Supt. – Gordon Flight   05824
Other Schools – See Gilman, Granby, Guildhall,
Lower Waterford, Lunenburg

Coventry, Orleans Co., Pop. Code 3
Orleans-Essex North Supervisory Union
Supt. – See Derby
Coventry Village ES   05825 – Richard Lussier, prin.

Craftsbury, Orleans Co., Pop. Code 3
Orleans Southwest Supervisory Union
Supt. – See Hardwick
ES   05826 – Robert Libby, prin.

Cuttingsville, Rutland Co., Pop. Code 3
Rutland South Supervisory Union
Supt. – See North Clarendon
Shrewsbury Mountain MS   05738
Wallace Lorimer, prin.
Shrewsbury Northam ES   05738
Wallace Lorimer, prin.

Danby, Rutland Co., Pop. Code 2
Bennington-Rutland Supervisory Union
Supt. – See Manchester Center
Currier Memorial ES   05739 – Robert Bushey, prin.

Danville, Caledonia Co., Pop. Code 4
Caledonia Central Supervisory Union
Sch. Sys. Enr. Code 3
Supt. – Richard Fagnant, P O BOX 216   05828
Other Schools – See Barnet, East Hardwick,
Hardwick, Mc Indoe Falls, Passumpsic, Peacham,
Saint Johnsbury, West Danville

Derby, Orleans Co., Pop. Code 3
Orleans-Essex North Supervisory Union
Sch. Sys. Enr. Code 5
Supt. – A. John LaRock   05829
North Country JHS   05829 – Susan Ginnett, prin.
Other Schools – See Coventry, Derby Line, Island
Pond, Jay, Lowell, Morgan, Newport, Newport
Center, North Troy, West Charleston, Westfield

Derby Line, Orleans Co., Pop. Code 3
Orleans-Essex North Supervisory Union
Supt. – See Derby
Derby ES, ELM STREET   05830
David Elwood, prin.
Holland ES, RURAL ROUTE   05830
Mark Johnson, prin.

Dorset, Bennington Co., Pop. Code 3
Bennington-Rutland Supervisory Union
Supt. – See Manchester Center
ES, MORSE HILL RD   05251 – John Meagher, prin.

East Barre, Washington Co., Pop. Code 3
Orange North Supervisory Union
Supt. – See South Barre
Orange Center ES, HCR 20 BOX 6   05649
(—), prin.

East Corinth, Orange Co., Pop. Code 3
Orange East Supervisory Union
Supt. – See Bradford
Union 36 ES   05040 – Bernard Bisson, prin.

East Dover, Windham Co., Pop. Code 3
Windham Central Supervisory Union
Supt. – See Newfane
Dover ES, BOX HC300   05341 – Frank Vara, prin.

East Fairfield, Franklin Co., Pop. Code 2
Franklin Central Supervisory Union
Supt. – See Saint Albans
ES   05448 – Kenneth Wade, prin.

East Hardwick, Caledonia Co., Pop. Code 5
Caledonia Central Supervisory Union
Supt. – See Danville
Walden Star MS, RURAL ROUTE BOX 116   05836
Patricia Ainsworth, prin.

East Haven, Essex Co., Pop. Code 2
Caledonia North Supervisory Union
Supt. – See Lyndonville
East Haven River ES   05850
Marlin Devenger, prin.

East Montpelier, Washington Co., Pop. Code 4
Washington Central Supervisory Union
Supt. – See Montpelier
ES, P O BOX 188   05651 – Thomas Sparrow, prin.

East Randolph, Orange Co., Pop. Code 5
Orange Southwest Supervisory Union
Supt. – See Randolph
Randolph East ES   05041 – Regina Miller, prin.

Eden, Lamoille Co., Pop. Code 3
Lamoille North Supervisory Union
Supt. – See Hyde Park
Eden Central ES   05652 – Barbara Smigiel, prin.

Enosburg Falls, Franklin Co., Pop. Code 4
Franklin Northeast Supervisory Union
Supt. – See Richford
ES, DICKINSON AVE   05450 – Larry Messier, prin.

Essex Junction, Chittenden Co., Pop. Code 6
Chittenden Central Supervisory Union
Sch. Sys. Enr. Code 5
Supt. – Robert Harrison
7 MEADOW TERRACE   05452
Lawton MS, 104 MAPLE ST   05452
John Bossange, prin.
Fleming MS, PROSPECT STREET   05452
Barry Meigs, prin.
Hiawatha ES, 25 HIAWATHA AVE   05452
Peter Hunt, prin.
Summit Street ES   05452 – Barry Meigs, prin.
Other Schools – See Westford

Essex Supervisory SD
Sch. Sys. Enr. Code 3
Supt. – Raymond Proulx   05452

Essex MS, 40 FOSTER ROAD   05452
Howard Magnant, prin.
Essex ES, 16 BROWNS RIVER RD   05452
George Clapp, prin.
Founders Memorial MS
168 SAND HILL RD   05452 – Edmond Jones, prin.

Fairfax, Franklin Co., Pop. Code 4
Franklin West Supervisory Union
Sch. Sys. Enr. Code 4
Supt. – Donald Collins, P O BOX 152   05454
Bellows Free Academy   05454
Richard Brown, prin.
Other Schools – See Saint Albans

Fairfield, Franklin Co.
Franklin Central Supervisory Union
Supt. – See Saint Albans
Fairfield Center MS   05455 – Kenneth Wade, prin.
Fairfield Common ES   05455
Kenneth Wade, prin.

Fair Haven, Rutland Co., Pop. Code 5
Addison-Rutland Supervisory Union
Sch. Sys. Enr. Code 3
Supt. – Raymond Pentkowski
3 N PARK PLACE   05743
ES, MAIN ST   05743 – Wayne Cooke, prin.
West Haven ES, RURAL ROUTE 22A   05743
James Webber, prin.
Other Schools – See Benson, Bomoseen, Castleton,
Orwell

Fairlee, Orange Co., Pop. Code 3
Orange East Supervisory Union
Supt. – See Bradford
ES, SARGENT ROAD   05045
Elizabeth Silvester, prin.

Ferrisburg, Addison Co., Pop. Code 4
Addison Northwest Supervisory Union
Supt. – See Vergennes
ES   05456 – Marjorie Von Ohlsen, prin.

Franklin, Franklin Co., Pop. Code 4
Franklin Northwest Supervisory Union
Supt. – See Swanton
ES, P O BOX 146   05457 – Robert Hamilton, prin.

Gilman, Essex Co., Pop. Code 3
Essex-Caledonia Supervisory SD
Supt. – See Concord
MS   05904 – Charles Witters, prin.

Glover, Orleans Co., Pop. Code 3
Orleans Central Supervisory Union
Supt. – See Orleans
ES   05839 – Stephen Laurie, prin.

Grafton, Windham Co., Pop. Code 3
Windham Northeast Supervisory Union
Supt. – See Bellows Falls
Grafton Central ES   05146 – William Murphy, prin.

Granby, Essex Co., Pop. Code 1
Essex-Caledonia Supervisory SD
Supt. – See Concord
ES   05840 – Sandra Morehouse, prin.

Grand Isle, Grand Isle Co., Pop. Code 4
Grand Isle Supervisory Union
Supt. – See North Hero
ES, P O BOX 307   05458 – (—), prin.

Granville, Addison Co., Pop. Code 2
Windsor Northwest Supervisory Union
Supt. – See Bethel
Granville Village ES   05747
Martin Tewksbury, prin.

Greensboro, Orleans Co., Pop. Code 3
Orleans Southwest Supervisory Union
Supt. – See Hardwick
ES   05841 – Jan Travers, prin.

Guildhall, Essex Co., Pop. Code 2
Essex-Caledonia Supervisory SD
Supt. – See Concord
ES   05905 – Ellen Fraser, prin.

Hancock, Addison Co., Pop. Code 2
Windsor Northwest Supervisory Union
Supt. – See Bethel
Hancock Branch ES   05748
Martin Tewksbury, prin.
Hancock Village MS   05748
Martin Tewksbury, prin.

Hardwick, Caledonia Co., Pop. Code 5
Caledonia Central Supervisory Union
Supt. – See Danville
Walden South ES   05843 – Lloyd Berry, prin.

Orleans Southwest Supervisory Union
Sch. Sys. Enr. Code 4
Supt. – Bruce Richardson   05843
ES   05843 – Robert Pequignot, prin.
Other Schools – See Craftsbury, Greensboro, Wolcott,
Woodbury

Hartford, Windsor Co., Pop. Code 6
Hartford Supervisory SD
Supt. – See White River Junction
ES   05047 – Michael Livingston, prin.

Hartland, Windsor Co., Pop. Code 4
Windsor Southeast Supervisory Union
Supt. – See Windsor
ES   05048 – Peter Richards, prin.

Highgate Center, Franklin Co., Pop. Code 4
Franklin Northwest Supervisory Union
Supt. – See Swanton
Highgate MS, SCHOOL STREET   05459
  Merritt Clark, prin.
Highgate ES, SCHOOL STREET   05459
  (—), prin.

Hinesburg, Chittenden Co., Pop. Code 5
Chittendon South Supervisory Union
Supt. – See Shelburne
ES, P O BOX 130   05461 – Harold Morse, prin.

Huntington, Chittenden Co., Pop. Code 4
Chittendon East Supervisory Union
Supt. – See Richmond
Brewster Peirce ES
  RURAL ROUTE 01 BOX 158   05462
  James Osborne, prin.

Hyde Park, Lamoille Co., Pop. Code 2
Lamoille North Supervisory Union
Sch. Sys. Enr. Code 4
Supt. – Gayle Utley, P O BOX 4133   05655
ES   05655 – David Potter, prin.
Other Schools – See Bellvidere Center, Cambridge,
  Eden, Jeffersonville, Johnson, Waterville

Irasburg, Orleans Co., Pop. Code 3
Orleans Central Supervisory Union
Supt. – See Orleans
Albany Hilltop ES, RURAL ROUTE   05845
  Jane Davis, prin.
ES   05845 – James Riccio, prin.

Island Pond, Essex Co., Pop. Code 4
Orleans-Essex North Supervisory Union
Supt. – See Derby
Brighton ES, P O BOX 411   05846
  Marie Commoss, prin.

Isle La Motte, Grand Isle Co., Pop. Code 2
Grand Isle Supervisory Union
Supt. – See North Hero
ES   05463 – Beth Savage, prin.

Jacksonville, Windham Co., Pop. Code 2
Windham Southwest Supervisory Union
Sch. Sys. Enr. Code 3
Supt. – Joseph Loretan   05342
Whitingham S, P O BOX 199   05342
  John Doty, prin.
Other Schools – See Readsboro, Stamford, West
  Halifax, Wilmington

Jamaica, Windham Co., Pop. Code 3
Windham Central Supervisory Union
Supt. – See Newfane
Jamaica Villlage ES   05343 – John Procopio, prin.

Jay, Orleans Co., Pop. Code 2
Orleans-Essex North Supervisory Union
Supt. – See Derby
Jay Village ES, RURAL ROUTE   05859
  Judy LeBlanc, prin.

Jeffersonville, Lamoille Co., Pop. Code 2
Lamoille North Supervisory Union
Supt. – See Hyde Park
Cambridge ES   05464 – Donald Lange, prin.

Jericho, Chittenden Co., Pop. Code 4
Chittendon East Supervisory Union
Supt. – See Richmond
ES   05465 – Christine Barnes, prin.

Johnson, Lamoille Co., Pop. Code 4
Lamoille North Supervisory Union
Supt. – See Hyde Park
ES, SCHOOL STREET   05656
  Stanley Harvey, prin.

Killington, Rutland Co.
Windsor Central Supervisory Union
Supt. – See Woodstock
Sherbourne ES, P O BOX 287   05751
  Gary Netsch, prin.

Lake Elmore, Lamoille Co.
Lamoille South Supervisory Union
Supt. – See Morrisville
ES   05657 – Eunice Green, prin.

Londonderry, Windham Co., Pop. Code 4
Windsor Southwest Supervisory Union
Supt. – See Chester
Flood Brook ES, P O BO X68   05148
  Matthew Carroll, prin.

Lowell, Orleans Co., Pop. Code 3
Orleans-Essex North Supervisory Union
Supt. – See Derby
Lowell Village ES   05847 – James Starr, prin.

Lower Waterford, Caledonia Co., Pop. Code 3
Essex-Caledonia Supervisory SD
Supt. – See Concord
Waterford ES   05848 – Roger Couture, prin.

Ludlow, Windsor Co., Pop. Code 4
Rutland-Windsor Supervisory Union
Sch. Sys. Enr. Code 3
Supt. – Lanning Nicoloff, 92-A MAIN ST   05149
ES, 45 MAIN ST   05149 – Thomas Lavalley, prin.
Other Schools – See Mount Holly, Plymouth

Lunenburg, Essex Co., Pop. Code 4
Essex-Caledonia Supervisory SD
Supt. – See Concord

East Concord ES, RURAL ROUTE   05906
  Roger Boyington, prin.
Lunenburg Village ES   05906
  Charles Witters, prin.

Lyndon, Caledonia Co., Pop. Code 5
Caledonia North Supervisory Union
Supt. – See Lyndonville
Lyndon Corner MS   05849
  Rebecca Reynolds, prin.

Lyndon Center, Caledonia Co., Pop. Code 2
Caledonia North Supervisory Union
Supt. – See Lyndonville
Baker ES   05850 – Rebecca Reynolds, prin.
Lyndon Center Campus ES   05850
  Rebecca Reynolds, prin.

Lyndonville, Caledonia Co., Pop. Code 4
Caledonia North Supervisory Union
Sch. Sys. Enr. Code 4
Supt. – Norman Messier, P O BOX 107   05851
MS   05851 – Carl Anderson, prin.
Red Village ES, RURAL ROUTE   05851
  Rebecca Reynolds, prin.
Squabble Hollow ES, RURAL ROUTE   05851
  Rebecca Reynolds, prin.
Other Schools – See East Haven, Lyndon, Lyndon
  Center, Sheffield, Sutton, West Burke

Mc Indoe Falls, Caledonia Co.
Caledonia Central Supervisory Union
Supt. – See Danville
McIndoes ES   05050 – Joanne Hickey, prin.

Manchester Center, Bennington Co., Pop. Code 4
Bennington-Rutland Supervisory Union
Sch. Sys. Enr. Code 3
Supt. – Wade Sherer   05255
Manchester ES, MEMORIAL AVE   05255
  Richard Leadem, prin.
Other Schools – See Arlington, Danby, Dorset, Pawlet,
  Rupert, West Pawlet, West Rupert

Marlboro, Windham Co., Pop. Code 3
Windham Central Supervisory Union
Supt. – See Newfane
ES   05344 – Constance Barton, prin.

Marshfield, Washington Co., Pop. Code 4
Washington Northeast Supervisory Union
Supt. – See Plainfield
Twinfield ES   05658 – John Wells, prin.

Middlebury, Addison Co., Pop. Code 6
Addison Central Supervisory Union
Sch. Sys. Enr. Code 4
Supt. – Dale Lamphear, 3 CHARLES AVE   05753
Cornwall Memorial ES
  RURAL ROUTE 02 BOX 705   05753
  Ronald Rubin, prin.
ES 4, 51 COURT ST #4   05753
  Henry Scipione, prin.
Weybridge ES, RURAL ROUTE 01   05753
  Joanne Hickey, prin.
Other Schools – See Brideport, Ripton, Salisbury,
  Shoreham

Middletown Springs, Rutland Co., Pop. Code 3
Rutland Southwest Supervisory Union
Supt. – See Poultney
Middletown Springs Village ES   05757
  Ronald Ryan, prin.

Milton, Chittenden Co., Pop. Code 4
Milton Supervisory SD
Sch. Sys. Enr. Code 4
Supt. – A. Keith Ober, P O BOX 21   05468
ES, 42 HERRICK AVE   05468
  Wesley McClellan, prin.
IS, SCHOOL STREET   05468
  Wesley McClellan, prin.

Monkton, Addison Co., Pop. Code 4
Addison Northeast Supervisory Union
Supt. – See Bristol
Monkton Central ES   05469
  Raymond Pellegrini, prin.

Montgomery Center, Franklin Co., Pop. Code 3
Franklin Northeast Supervisory Union
Supt. – See Richford
ES   05471 – Gyneth Lumbra, prin.

Montpelier, Washington Co., Pop. Code 6
Montpelier Supervisory SD
Sch. Sys. Enr. Code 3
Supt. – Edwin Jacobs, 58 BARRE ST   05602
Main Street MS, 170 MAIN ST   05602
  Janet Jamieson, prin.
Union ES, PARK AVE   05602 – Mary Ober, prin.

Washington Central Supervisory Union
Sch. Sys. Enr. Code 3
Supt. – Lyman Amsden   05602
Berlin ES, RURAL ROUTE 04   05602
  Burns Page, prin.
Middlesex Rumney ES
  RURAL ROUTE 03 BOX 2100   05602
  Allen Freund, prin.
Other Schools – See East Montpelier, Plainfield,
  Worcester

St. Michael's ES, 46 BARRE ST   05602

Moretown, Washington Co., Pop. Code 4
Washington West Supervisory Union
Sch. Sys. Enr. Code 4
Supt. – Richard Moser, P O BOX 1065   05660
ES   05660 – Jean Eisele, prin.
Other Schools – See Waitsfield, Warren, Waterbury

Morgan, Orleans Co., Pop. Code 2
Orleans-Essex North Supervisory Union
Supt. – See Derby
Hatton ES, P O BOX 57   05853
  Mark Johnson, prin.

Morrisville, Lamoille Co., Pop. Code 4
Lamoille South Supervisory Union
Sch. Sys. Enr. Code 4
Supt. – Alice Angney, P O BOX 338   05661
MS, ROUTE 15A   05661 – Otho Thompson, prin.
ES, COPLEY AVE   05661 – Otho Thompson, prin.
Other Schools – See Lake Elmore, Stowe

Mount Holly, Rutland Co., Pop. Code 3
Rutland-Windsor Supervisory Union
Supt. – See Ludlow
Mt. Holly Central ES, P O BOX 45   05758
  John Notte, prin.

Newbury, Orange Co., Pop. Code 4
Orange East Supervisory Union
Supt. – See Bradford
ES, RURAL ROUTE 05 BOX 165   05051
  John Sanborn, prin.

Newfane, Windham Co., Pop. Code 2
Windham Central Supervisory Union
Sch. Sys. Enr. Code 3
Supt. – Thomas Lewis, P O BOX 186   05345
Brookline ES, RURAL ROUTE BOX 1510   05345
  Joyce Pamelen, prin.
ES, RURAL ROUTE 01 BOX 1936   05345
  Art Benedict, prin.
Other Schools – See Bondville, East Dover, Jamaica,
  Marlboro, Townshend, Wardsboro, West
  Townshend

New Haven, Addison Co., Pop. Code 4
Addison Northeast Supervisory Union
Supt. – See Bristol
Beeman ES, RURAL ROUTE BOX 3   05472
  Robbe Brook, prin.

Newport, Orleans Co., Pop. Code 5
Orleans-Essex North Supervisory Union
Supt. – See Derby
Hillside ES, 150 SIAS AVE   05855
  Raymond Ladue, prin.
Lakeview ES, SCHOOL STREET   05855
  Raymond Ladue, prin.

Sacred Heart ES, PROSPECT ST   05855

Newport Center, Orleans Co.
Orleans-Essex North Supervisory Union
Supt. – See Derby
Newport Town ES   05857 – Baxter McNeal, prin.

North Bennington, Bennington Co., Pop. Code 4
Southwest Vermont Supervisory Union
Supt. – See Bennington
ES   05257 – Phillip Viereck, prin.

North Clarendon, Rutland Co., Pop. Code 2
Rutland South Supervisory Union
Sch. Sys. Enr. Code 4
Supt. – Henry Burnham, P O BOX 87   05759
Clarendon ES, P O BOX 7   05759
  Robert Snarski, prin.
Other Schools – See Cuttingsville, Wallingford

Northfield, Washington Co., Pop. Code 4
Washington South Supervisory Union
Sch. Sys. Enr. Code 2
Supt. – Charles Memoe, 19 MAPLE AVE   05663
Comiskey MS, 1 GARVEY HL   05663
  Dean Baker, prin.
ES, 66 S MAIN ST   05663 – Dean Baker, prin.
Northfield Falls ES, SCHOOL STREET   05663
  Dean Baker, prin.
Other Schools – See Roxbury

North Hero, Grand Isle Co., Pop. Code 2
Grand Isle Supervisory Union
Sch. Sys. Enr. Code 3
Supt. – Armand Premo   05474
ES, P O BOX 144A   05474 – George Bedrin, prin.
Other Schools – See Alburg, Grand Isle, Isle La Motte,
  South Hero

North Pomfret, Windsor Co., Pop. Code 3
Windsor Central Supervisory Union
Supt. – See Woodstock
ES   05053 – Lynn Fersuson, prin.
Pomfret Hewittvlle ES   05053
  Patricia Meyer, prin.

North Troy, Orleans Co., Pop. Code 3
Orleans-Essex North Supervisory Union
Supt. – See Derby
Troy ES, MAIN STREET   05859
  Robert Henderson, prin.

Norton, Essex Co.
Essex North Supervisory Union
Supt. – See Canaan
Norton Village ES   05907 – Karen Farrar, prin.

Orleans, Orleans Co., Pop. Code 3
Orleans Central Supervisory Union
Sch. Sys. Enr. Code 4
Supt. – Paul Henry   05860
Brownington Central ES, RURAL ROUTE   05860
  Ellwood Guyette, prin.
ES   05860 – Charles Ginnett, prin.
Other Schools – See Albany, Barton, Glover, Irasburg

Orwell, Addison Co., Pop. Code 3
Addison-Rutland Supervisory Union
Supt. – See Fair Haven
ES, MAIN STREET   05760 – William Nelson, prin.

Passumpsic, Caledonia Co.
Caledonia Central Supervisory Union
Supt. – See Danville
ES   05861 – Joanne Hickey, prin.

Pawlet, Rutland Co., Pop. Code 4
Bennington-Rutland Supervisory Union
Supt. – See Manchester Center
ES, RURAL ROUTE 01 BOX 1530   05761
  (—), prin.

Peacham, Caledonia Co., Pop. Code 3
Caledonia Central Supervisory Union
Supt. – See Danville
ES   05862 – Evelyn Howard, prin.

Perkinsville, Windsor Co., Pop. Code 2
Windsor Southeast Supervisory Union
Supt. – See Windsor
Weathersfield ES   05151 – Gordon Schnare, prin.

Pittsford, Rutland Co., Pop. Code 5
Rutland Northeast Supervisory Union
Supt. – See Brandon
Lothrop ES, RURAL ROUTE 07   05763
  John Duval, prin.

Plainfield, Washington Co., Pop. Code 3
Washington Central Supervisory Union
Supt. – See Montpelier
Calais ES, RURAL ROUTE 02   05667
  Wanda Wilbur, prin.

Washington Northeast Supervisory Union
Sch. Sys. Enr. Code 2
Supt. – Glenn Yankee   05667
Other Schools – See Cabot, Marshfield

Plymouth, Windsor Co., Pop. Code 2
Rutland-Windsor Supervisory Union
Supt. – See Ludlow
ES, HCR   05056 – Joanne Williamson, prin.

Poultney, Rutland Co., Pop. Code 4
Rutland Southwest Supervisory Union
Sch. Sys. Enr. Code 3
Supt. – H. Alan Brown, 3 MAIN ST   05764
ES, 15 ALLEN AVE   05764 – John Poljacik, prin.
Other Schools – See Middletown Springs,
  Wallingford, Wells, West Rutland

Pownal, Bennington Co., Pop. Code 5
Southwest Vermont Supervisory Union
Supt. – See Bennington
ES, RURAL ROUTE 01 BOX 97   05261
  Ray Lambert, prin.

Proctor, Rutland Co., Pop. Code 4
Rutland Central Supervisory Union
Supt. – See Rutland
ES, 14 SCHOOL ST   05765 – John Kaldy, prin.

Proctorsville, Windsor Co., Pop. Code 2
Windsor Southwest Supervisory Union
Supt. – See Chester
Cavendish Town ES, P O BOX 236   05153
  Michael Lannon, prin.

Putney, Windham Co., Pop. Code 4
Windham Northeast Supervisory Union
Supt. – See Bellows Falls
Westminster West ES, RURAL ROUTE 03   05346
  Claire Oglesby, prin.

Windham Southeast Supervisory Union
Supt. – See Brattleboro
Dummerston East MS
  RURAL ROUTE 02 BOX 680   05346
  Timothy Parsons, prin.
Dummerston West ES
  RURAL ROUTE 02 BOX 680   05346
  Timothy Parsons, prin.
Putney Central ES
  RURAL ROUTE 03 BOX 30   05346
  Michael Friel, prin.

Quechee, Windsor Co.
Hartford Supervisory SD
Supt. – See White River Junction
ES   05059 – Bruce Franzen, prin.

Randolph, Orange Co., Pop. Code 4
Orange Southwest Supervisory Union
Sch. Sys. Enr. Code 4
Supt. – Roger Bourassa, P O BOX 250   05060
Braintree Lower MS, RURAL ROUTE   05060
  Floyd Cone, prin.
Braintree Upper ES, RURAL ROUTE   05060
  Floyd Cone, prin.
Randolph Village ES, 28 N MAIN ST   05060
  Steve Metcalf, prin.
Other Schools – See Brookfield, East Randolph,
  Randolph Center

Randolph Center, Orange Co.
Orange Southwest Supervisory Union
Supt. – See Randolph
Randolph ES   05061 – Jane Currier, prin.

Reading, Windsor Co., Pop. Code 3
Windsor Central Supervisory Union
Supt. – See Woodstock
ES   05062 – Armando Vilaseca, prin.

Readsboro, Bennington Co., Pop. Code 3
Windham Southwest Supervisory Union
Supt. – See Jacksonville
ES, RURAL ROUTE BOX 56   05350
  David Switz, prin.

Richford, Franklin Co., Pop. Code 4
Franklin Northeast Supervisory Union
Sch. Sys. Enr. Code 4
Supt. – Raymond McNulty, P O BOX 130   05476
Berkshire ES, RURAL ROUTE   05476
  Edward Wilkens, prin.
ES, P O BOX 725   05476 – Donald Martin, prin.
Other Schools – See Bakersfield, Enosburg Falls,
  Montgomery Center

Richmond, Chittenden Co., Pop. Code 3
Chittendon East Supervisory Union
Sch. Sys. Enr. Code 4
Supt. – Harold Boyden   05477
Camels Hump MS, BROWNS TRACE RD   05477
  Robert Goudreau, prin.
ES, BRIDGE STREET   05477
  James Massingham, prin.
Other Schools – See Huntington, Jericho, Underhill,
  Underhill Center, Waterbury

Ripton, Addison Co., Pop. Code 2
Addison Central Supervisory Union
Supt. – See Middlebury
Ripton Hollow ES   05766 – Robert Risch, prin.

Rochester, Windsor Co., Pop. Code 4
Windsor Northwest Supervisory Union
Supt. – See Bethel
S, RURAL ROUTE 01 BOX 100   05767
  Jerry West, prin.

Roxbury, Addison Co.
Washington South Supervisory Union
Supt. – See Northfield
Roxbury Village ES   05669 – Shirley Nelson, prin.

Rupert, Bennington Co., Pop. Code 3
Bennington-Rutland Supervisory Union
Supt. – See Manchester Center
Rupert Village ES   05768 – Madeline Leach, prin.

Rutland, Rutland Co., Pop. Code 7
Rutland Central Supervisory Union
Sch. Sys. Enr. Code 4
Supt. – Richard Zani, P O BOX G   05701
Dana ES, E CENTER STREET   05701
  Dorothy Kraft, prin.
Rutland Town ES, POST RD   05701
  Robert Bell, prin.
Rutland Lincoln ES, LINCOLN AVE   05701
  John Stempek, prin.
Rutland Northeast ES
  OFF TEMPLE STREET   05701 – Cheryl Evans, prin.
Rutland Northwest ES, PIERPONT AVE   05701
  Paul Kerns, prin.
Rutland Southeast ES, ALLEN STREET   05701
  Virginia Anderson, prin.
Other Schools – See Proctor, West Rutland

Rutland Central Supervisory Union
Sch. Sys. Enr. Code 4
Supt. – Richard Zani, P O BOX G   05701
Dana ES, E CENTER STREET   05701
  Dorothy Kraft, prin.
Rutland Town ES, POST RD   05701
  Robert Bell, prin.
Rutland Lincoln ES, LINCOLN AVE   05701
  John Stempek, prin.
Rutland Northeast ES
  OFF TEMPLE STREET   05701 – Cheryl Evans, prin.
Rutland Northwest ES, PIERPONT AVE   05701
  Paul Kerns, prin.
Rutland Southeast ES, ALLEN STREET   05701
  Virginia Anderson, prin.

Christ the King ES, 60 S MAIN ST   05701

Saint Albans, Franklin Co., Pop. Code 6
Franklin Central Supervisory Union
Sch. Sys. Enr. Code 4
Supt. – James Aitchison, 40 KINGMAN ST   05478
St. Albans Town MS, 165 S MAIN ST   05478
  Edwin Brehaut, prin.
St. Albans City ES, BELLOWS ST   05478
  Frederick O'Brien, prin.
Other Schools – See East Fairfield, Fairfield, Saint
  Albans Bay

Franklin West Supervisory Union
Supt. – See Fairfax
Georgia ES, RURAL ROUTE 02   05478
  Marvin Alderman, prin.

Saint Albans Bay, Franklin Co.
Franklin Central Supervisory Union
Supt. – See Saint Albans
Callaghan Memorial ES   05481
  David MacCallum, prin.

Saint Johnsbury, Caledonia Co., Pop. Code 6
Caledonia Central Supervisory Union
Supt. – See Danville
Danville ES, RURAL ROUTE 02   05819
  Eleanore Belding, prin.

St. Johnsbury Supervisory SD
Sch. Sys. Enr. Code 4
Supt. – Joseph Kasprzak   05819
MS, 24 WESTERN AVE   05819
  David Cameron, prin.
Arlington ES, 13 SCHOOL ST   05819
  Kerry Keenan, prin.
Lincoln Street ES, 11 LINCOLN ST   05819
  Marion Sharik, prin.
Portland MS, 99 PORTLAND ST   05819
  Richard Watson, prin.
St. Johnsbury Adams ES, 65 SUMMER ST   05819
  Mary Bentley, prin.
St. Johnsbury Center ES
  SCHOOLS STREET   05863 – Mary Bentley, prin.
Summer Street MS, 58 SUMMER ST   05819
  Duane Gorham, prin.

Salisbury, Addison Co., Pop. Code 3
Addison Central Supervisory Union
Supt. – See Middlebury
Salisbury Village MS   05769 – Anne Johnston, prin.
West Salisbury ES   05769 – Anne Johnston, prin.

Saxtons River, Windham Co., Pop. Code 3
Windham Northeast Supervisory Union
Supt. – See Bellows Falls
ES, SCHOOL STREET   05154
  Thomas Crossett, prin.

Shaftsbury, Bennington Co., Pop. Code 5
Southwest Vermont Supervisory Union
Supt. – See Bennington
ES, EAST STREET   05262 – Samuel Carrara, prin.

Sharon, Windsor Co., Pop. Code 3
Orange-Windsor Supervisory Union
Supt. – See South Royalton
ES, P O BOX 2   05065 – Reginald Blair, prin.

Sheffield, Caledonia Co., Pop. Code 2
Caledonia North Supervisory Union
Supt. – See Lyndonville
Millers Run ES   05866 – Kaye Greene, prin.

Shelburne, Chittenden Co., Pop. Code 5
Chittendon South Supervisory Union
Sch. Sys. Enr. Code 5
Supt. – William Crocoll, P O BOX 127   05482
MS   05482 – John Winton, prin.
ES, RURAL ROUTE 04 BOX 69   05482
  Alfred Mercaldo, prin.
Other Schools – See Charlotte, Hinesburg, Williston

Sheldon, Franklin Co., Pop. Code 4
Franklin Northwest Supervisory Union
Supt. – See Swanton
ES   05483 – Sara Denny, prin.

Shoreham, Addison Co., Pop. Code 3
Addison Central Supervisory Union
Supt. – See Middlebury
ES   05770 – (—), prin.

South Barre, Washington Co., Pop. Code 3
Orange North Supervisory Union
Sch. Sys. Enr. Code 3
Supt. – David Bisson, P O BOX 367   05670
Other Schools – See East Barre, Washington,
  Williamstown

South Burlington, Chittenden Co., Pop. Code 7
South Burlington Supervisory SD
Sch. Sys. Enr. Code 4
Supt. – Fred Tuttle, 550 DORSET ST   05401
MS, 530 S DORSET ST   05401
  Mark Kennedy, prin.
Chamberlin ES, 262 WHITE ST   05403
  Marilyn Dunn, prin.
Orchard ES, BALDWIN AVE   05401
  Anne Browne, prin.
ES, WILLSITON ROAD   05401
  Roderick Marcotte, prin.

South Hero, Grand Isle Co., Pop. Code 4
Grand Isle Supervisory Union
Supt. – See North Hero
Folsom ES, SOUTH STREET   05486
  Judi Maynard, prin.

South Pomfret, Windsor Co., Pop. Code 3
Windsor Central Supervisory Union
Supt. – See Woodstock
MS   05067 – Dale West, prin.

South Royalton, Windsor Co., Pop. Code 2
Orange-Windsor Supervisory Union
Sch. Sys. Enr. Code 4
Supt. – Richard Sawyer, P O BOX 240   05068
S, RURAL ROUTE 02 BOX 11   05068
  Shaun Pickett, prin.
Other Schools – See Chelsea, Sharon, South Strafford,
  Tunbridge

South Strafford, Orange Co., Pop. Code 3
Orange-Windsor Supervisory Union
Supt. – See South Royalton
Newton ES   05070 – Robert Murray, prin.

Springfield, Windsor Co., Pop. Code 7
Springfield Supervisory SD
Sch. Sys. Enr. Code 4
Supt. – David MacDonald, 60 PARK ST   05156

Riverside MS, 13 FAIRGROUND ROAD 05156
    Rodney Tulonen, prin.
Springfield Park Street MS, 60 PARK ST 05156
    Richard DeYoung, prin.
Springfield Union ES, 43 UNION ST 05156
    Charles Meyers, prin.
Springfield Elm Hill ES, 10 HOOVER ST 05156
    Kathy Davignon, prin.

Stamford, Bennington Co., Pop. Code 3
Windham Southwest Supervisory Union
Supt. – See Jacksonville
ES, P O BOX 718 05352 – Leo Ethier, prin.

Starksboro, Addison Co., Pop. Code 4
Addison Northeast Supervisory Union
Supt. – See Bristol
Robinson ES, P O BOX 10 05487
    Molly McClaskey, prin.

Stowe, Lamoille Co., Pop. Code 3
Lamoille South Supervisory Union
Supt. – See Morrisville
ES, P O BOX 160 05672 – Rebecca Tarrant, prin.

Sutton, Caledonia Co., Pop. Code 3
Caledonia North Supervisory Union
Supt. – See Lyndonville
Sutton Village ES 05687 – Lucien Belanger, prin.

Swanton, Franklin Co., Pop. Code 5
Franklin Northwest Supervisory Union
Sch. Sys. Enr. Code 4
Supt. – John Robb, P O BOX 123 05488
ES, GRAND AVE 05488 – Mary Lynn Riggs, prin.
MS, 21 CHURCH ST 05488
    Mary Lynn Riggs, prin.
Other Schools – See Franklin, Highgate Center,
    Sheldon

Thetford, Orange Co., Pop. Code 4
Orange East Supervisory Union
Supt. – See Bradford
ES 05074 – Robert Johnston, prin.

Townshend, Windham Co., Pop. Code 3
Windham Central Supervisory Union
Supt. – See Newfane
Townshend Village ES 05353
    Esther Lamoria, prin.

Tunbridge, Orange Co., Pop. Code 3
Orange-Windsor Supervisory Union
Supt. – See South Royalton
Tunbridge Central ES 05077
    Bruce Bellemeur, prin.

Underhill, Chittenden Co., Pop. Code 2
Chittendon East Supervisory Union
Supt. – See Richmond
Browns River MS
    RURAL ROUTE 01 BOX 183 05489
    Paul Corologos, prin.
ES, STEAM MILL RD 05489 – Joseph Obrien, prin.

Underhill Center, Chittenden Co., Pop. Code 4
Chittendon East Supervisory Union
Supt. – See Richmond
ES 05490 – Alan Pasell, prin.

Vergennes, Addison Co., Pop. Code 4
Addison Northwest Supervisory Union
Sch. Sys. Enr. Code 4
Supt. – Arnold Lanni, 185 MAIN ST 05491
Addison ES, RURAL ROUTE 01 BOX 134 05491
    Veronica Berreen, prin.
ES, 43 EAST ST 05491 – Robert Aldrich, prin.
Other Schools – See Ferrisburg

Vernon, Windham Co., Pop. Code 4
Windham Southeast Supervisory Union
Supt. – See Brattleboro
ES 05354 – Carol Virkler, prin.

Vershire, Orange Co., Pop. Code 2
Orange East Supervisory Union
Supt. – See Bradford
Vershire Village ES 05079
    Stefanie Johnston, prin.

Waitsfield, Washington Co., Pop. Code 4
Washington West Supervisory Union
Supt. – See Moretown
Fayston ES 05673 – Robert Stanton, prin.
ES 05673 – Carol Hosford, prin.

Wallingford, Rutland Co., Pop. Code 4
Rutland South Supervisory Union
Supt. – See North Clarendon
Wallingford Village ES 05773 – Walter Goetz, prin.

Rutland Southwest Supervisory Union
Supt. – See Poultney

Tinmouth Center ES
    RURAL ROUTE 01 BOX 211 05773
    Nelson Jaquay, prin.

Wardsboro, Windham Co., Pop. Code 3
Windham Central Supervisory Union
Supt. – See Newfane
ES, RURAL ROUTE 100 BOX 185 05355
    Mark Cembalisty, prin.

Warren, Washington Co., Pop. Code 3
Washington West Supervisory Union
Supt. – See Moretown
ES 05674 – Katie Woodruff, prin.

Washington, Orange Co., Pop. Code 3
Orange North Supervisory Union
Supt. – See South Barre
Washington Village ES 05675
    Kathleen Lengel, prin.

Waterbury, Washington Co., Pop. Code 4
Chittendon East Supervisory Union
Supt. – See Richmond
Smilie ES, RURAL ROUTE 02 05676
    Henrietta Barup, prin.

Washington West Supervisory Union
Supt. – See Moretown
Duxbury ES, RURAL ROUTE 02 05676
    Andrea Erchak, prin.
ES, 47 STOWE ST 05676 – William Riegel, prin.

Waterville, Lamoille Co., Pop. Code 2
Lamoille North Supervisory Union
Supt. – See Hyde Park
Waterville Central ES 05492 – Maylo Baker, prin.

Wells, Rutland Co., Pop. Code 3
Rutland Southwest Supervisory Union
Supt. – See Poultney
Wells Village ES 05774 – Jean Oakman, prin.

Wells River, Orange Co., Pop. Code 2
Blue Mountain Union 21
Sch. Sys. Enr. Code 2
Supt. – Theodore Whalen 05081
Blue Mountain Union S 21
    RURAL ROUTE 1 BOX 50A 05081
    David Baker, prin.

West Burke, Caledonia Co.
Caledonia North Supervisory Union
Supt. – See Lyndonville
Burke Hollow MS 05871 – Robert Vincze, prin.
Newark ES 05871 – Beverly Lawson, prin.
West Burke Village ES 05871
    Robert Vincze, prin.

West Charleston, Orleans Co.
Orleans-Essex North Supervisory Union
Supt. – See Derby
Charleston ES 05872 – Linda Studer, prin.

West Danville, Caledonia Co.
Caledonia Central Supervisory Union
Supt. – See Danville
Walden Heights MS 05873 – Lloyd Berry, prin.
Noyesville ES, RFD 05873 – Chip Hedler, prin.

West Fairlee, Orange Co., Pop. Code 2
Orange East Supervisory Union
Supt. – See Bradford
West Fairlee Village ES 05083
    Carol Cottrell, prin.

Westfield, Orleans Co., Pop. Code 2
Orleans-Essex North Supervisory Union
Supt. – See Derby
ES, RURAL ROUTE 01 05874
    Scott Boskind, prin.

Westford, Chittenden Co., Pop. Code 4
Chittenden Central Supervisory Union
Supt. – See Essex Junction
ES 05494 – Armando Velaseca, prin.

West Halifax, Windham Co., Pop. Code 2
Windham Southwest Supervisory Union
Supt. – See Jacksonville
Halifax West ES 05358 – James Law, prin.

Westminster, Windham Co., Pop. Code 2
Windham Northeast Supervisory Union
Supt. – See Bellows Falls
Westminster Center ES 05158
    Claire Oglesby, prin.

West Pawlet, Rutland Co., Pop. Code 2
Bennington-Rutland Supervisory Union
Supt. – See Manchester Center
MS, ROUTE 153 05775 – Susan Caiazza, prin.

West Rupert, Bennington Co., Pop. Code 2
Bennington-Rutland Supervisory Union
Supt. – See Manchester Center
MS 05776 – Madeline Leach, prin.

West Rutland, Rutland Co., Pop. Code 4
Rutland Central Supervisory Union
Supt. – See Rutland
S 05777 – Richard Trogisch, prin.

Rutland Southwest Supervisory Union
Supt. – See Poultney
Ira ES, RURAL ROUTE 05777
    Kathryn Bernhardt, prin.

West Townshend, Windham Co.
Windham Central Supervisory Union
Supt. – See Newfane
Windham ES, P O BOX 108 05359
    Brian Sackett, prin.

White River Junction, Windsor Co., Pop. Code 4
Hartford Supervisory SD
Sch. Sys. Enr. Code 4
Supt. – John Frank, 2 TAFT AVE 05001
Hartford Memorial MS, 30 HIGHLAND AVE 05001
    Francis Duncan, prin.
White River ES 05001 – Christopher Ashley, prin.
Other Schools – See Hartford, Quechee, Wilder

Whiting, Addison Co., Pop. Code 2
Rutland Northeast Supervisory Union
Supt. – See Brandon
Whiting Village ES, P O BOX 27 05778
    Susan Kellogg. prin.

Wilder, Windsor Co., Pop. Code 4
Hartford Supervisory SD
Supt. – See White River Junction
ES 05088 – Phyllis Bettis, prin.

Williamstown, Orange Co., Pop. Code 4
Orange North Supervisory Union
Supt. – See South Barre
ES 05679 – Cleland Selby, prin.

Williston, Chittenden Co., Pop. Code 5
Chittendon South Supervisory Union
Supt. – See Shelburne
Williston Central ES, 705 WILLISTON RD 05495
    Marion Stroud, prin.

Wilmington, Windham Co., Pop. Code 4
Windham Southwest Supervisory Union
Supt. – See Jacksonville
Deerfield Valley ES, ROUTE 100 N 05363
    Donald Finck, prin.

Windsor, Windsor Co., Pop. Code 5
Windsor Southeast Supervisory Union
Sch. Sys. Enr. Code 4
Supt. – Donald Saltmarsh, 147 MAIN ST 05089
ES 05089 – Paul Whalen, prin.
Other Schools – See Ascutney, Brownsville, Hartland,
    Perkinsville

Winooski, Chittenden Co., Pop. Code 6
Winooski Supervisory SD
Sch. Sys. Enr. Code 3
Supt. – Joseph Anger, 3 NORMAN ST 05404
Kennedy ES, 70 NORMAND ST 05404
    Roderick Ross, prin.

St. Francis Xavier ES, 7 SAINT PETER ST 05404

Wolcott, Lamoille Co., Pop. Code 3
Orleans Southwest Supervisory Union
Supt. – See Hardwick
ES 05680 – Merri Greenia, prin.

Woodbury, Washington Co., Pop. Code 3
Orleans Southwest Supervisory Union
Supt. – See Hardwick
Woodbury Village ES 05681 – Helen Dix, prin.

Woodstock, Windsor Co., Pop. Code 4
Windsor Central Supervisory Union
Sch. Sys. Enr. Code 4
Supt. – Howard Goodrow, MOUNT TOM 05091
ES, 15 SOUTH ST 05091 – Norman Frates, prin.
Other Schools – See Barnard, Bridgewater, Killington,
    North Pomfret, Reading, South Pomfret

Worcester, Washington Co., Pop. Code 3
Washington Central Supervisory Union
Supt. – See Montpelier
ES, CALAIS ROAD 05682
    Christina Johnston, prin.

VIRGINIA

STATE DEPARTMENT OF EDUCATION
P.O. Box 6-Q, Richmond 23216
(804) 225-2023

Superintendent of Public Instruction	Dr. S. John Davis
Deputy Superintendent Compliance, Field Services	Vincent Cibbarelli
Deputy Superintendent Curriculum, Instruction, Personnel Services	Dr. E. Howerton, Jr.
Assistant Superintendent for General & Vocational Education	Dr. Callie Shingleton
Associate Superintendent Financial & Support Services	Myron Cale
Assistant Superintendent Special Ed. & Pupil Personnel	Randle Edwards
Assistant Superintendent Educational Technology	Ida Hill

STATE BOARD OF EDUCATION
Robert DeFord, *President*   2712 Southern Blvd. #100, Virginia Beach   23352

STATE COUNCIL OF HIGHER EDUCATION
Gordon Davies, *Director*   101 N. 14th St., Richmond   23219

PUBLIC, PRIVATE, AND PAROCHIAL ELEMENTARY SCHOOLS

Abingdon, Washington Co., Pop. Code 5
Washington County SD
Sch. Sys. Enr. Code 6
Supt. – Raynard Hale, 780 THOMPSON DR   24210
ES, RURAL ROUTE 03   24210
    Jone Sutherland, prin.
Greendale ES, RURAL ROUTE 03 BOX 241   24210
    Ronald Walls, prin.
Hayters Gap ES
    RURAL ROUTE 08 BOX 404   24210
    Thomas Hall, prin.
Stanley ES, 297 STANLEY ST   24210
    Bob Hammond, prin.
Watauga ES, RURAL ROUTE 01 BOX 260   24210
    Donald Thayer, prin.
Other Schools – See Bristol, Damascus, Glade Spring,
    Meadowview, Mendota

Accomac, Accomack Co., Pop. Code 3
Accomack County SD
Sch. Sys. Enr. Code 6
Supt. – Charles Kline   23301
Smith MS   23301 – Edward Smith, prin.
Accomac ES   23301 – Margaret Miles, prin.
Other Schools – See Bloxom, Chincoteague,
    Mappsville, Melfa, Painter, Parksley, Tangier

Afton, Nelson Co.
Nelson County SD
Supt. – See Lovingston
Rockfish Valley ES   22920 – Clarke Magruder, prin.

Alberta, Brunswick Co., Pop. Code 2
Brunswick County SD
Supt. – See Lawrenceville
Red Oak ES, P O BOX 398   23821
    Thomas Smith, prin.

Aldie, Loudoun Co.
Loudoun County SD
Supt. – See Leesburg
ES, MEETING HOUSE LN   22001
    William Raye, prin.

Alexandria, (Indep. City), Pop. Code 9
Alexandria CSD
Sch. Sys. Enr. Code 6
Supt. – Dr. Paul Masem
    3801 W BRADDOCK ROAD   22302
Adams ES, 5651 RAYBURN AVE   22311
    Rita Hunt, prin.
Barrett ES, 1115 MARTHA CUSTIS DR   22302
    Catherine Malone, prin.
Henry ES, 4643 TANEY AVE   22304
    Ardelia Hunter, prin.
Jefferson-Houston ES, 1501 CAMERON ST   22314
    Dr. Cecelia Krill, prin.
Kelly Magnet ES
    3600 COMMONWEALTH AVE   22305
    Betty Hobbs, prin.
Lyles-Crouch MS, 530 S SAINT ASAPH ST   22314
    Elwood Lewis, prin.
MacArthur ES, 1101 JANNEYS LN   22302
    Jalna Jones, prin.
Mason ES, 2601 CAMERON MILLS RD   22302
    Marvin Maygarden, prin.

Maury ES, 600 RUSSELL RD   22301
    Mildred Lockridge, prin.
Mt. Vernon ES
    2601 COMMONWEALTH AVE   22305
    Phyllis Past, prin.
Polk ES, 5000 POLK AVE   22304
    Sylvia Garrett, prin.
Ramsay ES, 5700 SANGER AVE   22311
    Sidney Houston, prin.

Fairfax County SD
Supt. – See Fairfax
Glasgow MS, 4101 FAIRFAX PKWY   22312
    Dr. William Johnson, prin.
Holmes MS, 6525 MONTROSE ST   22312
    Vera Blake, prin.
Sandburg MS, 8428 FORT HUNT ROAD   22308
    Linda Whitfield, prin.
Twain MS, 4700 FRANCONIA ROAD   22310
    Foster Morse, prin.
Whitman MS, 2500 PARKERS LANE   22306
    Eugene Jordan, prin.
Belle View ES, 6701 FORT HUNT RD   22307
    E. Thompson, prin.
Bren Mar ES, 6344 BERYL RD   22312
    Ellen Schoetzau, prin.
Bucknell ES, 6925 UNIVERSITY DR   22307
    Nancy Manning, prin.
Bush Hill ES, 5927 WESTCHESTER ST   22310
    C. Davis, prin.
Cameron ES, 3434 CAMPBELL DR   22303
    George Towery, prin.
Clermont ES, 5720 CLERMONT DR   22310
    E. Whitley, prin.
Fort Hunt ES, 8832 LINTON LN   22308
    Janet Trout, prin.
Franconia ES, 6043 FRANCONIA RD   22310
    Garry McClincey, prin.
Groveton ES, 6900 HARRISON LN   22306
    Cynthia Buck, prin.
Hayfield ES, 7633 TELEGRAPH RD   22310
    Edwin Grady III, prin.
Hollin Meadows ES, 2310 NORDOK PL   22306
    Bernice Johnson, prin.
Hybla Valley ES, 3415 LOCKHEED BLVD   22306
    Blanche Delaine, prin.
Mt. Eagle ES, 6116 N KINGS HWY   22303
    David Lunter, prin.
Mt. Vernon Woods ES, 4015 FIELDING ST   22309
    Reginald Romaine, prin.
Parklawn ES, 4116 BRADDOCK RD   22312
    Susan Akroyd, prin.
Riverside ES
    8410 OLD MOUNT VERNON RD   22309
    John Spataro, prin.
Rose Hill ES, 6301 ROSE HILL DR   22310
    Sandra Culmer, prin.
Stratford Landing ES, 8484 RIVERSIDE RD   22308
    Beverly Peterson, prin.
Washington Mill ES
    9100 CHERRYTREE DR   22309
    Norman Lubus, prin.
Waynewood ES
    1205 WAYNEWOOD BLVD   22308
    Kathleen Parzych, prin.

Weyanoke ES, 6520 BRADDOCK RD   22312
    R. Padgett, prin.
Woodlawn ES, 8505 HIGHLAND LN   22309
    William Dudgeon,Jr., prin.
Woodley Hills ES
    8718 OLD MT VERNON ROAD   22309
    Dr. Joan Freck, prin.

St. Agnes School, JEFFERSON PARK   22302
Blessed Sacrament PS
    1417 W BRADDOCK RD   22302
Immanuel Lutheran School
    109 BELLAIRE RD   22301
Queen of Apostles School, 4409 SANO ST   22312
St. Louis School, 2901 POPKINS LN   22306
St. Mary Parochial School, 400 GREEN ST   22314
St. Rita School, 3801 RUSSELL RD   22305

Altavista, Campbell Co., Pop. Code 5
Campbell County SD
Supt. – See Rustburg
MS   24517 – David Gorsline,Jr., prin.
Moseley Heights ES, FRANKLIN AVE   24517
    Joan Woodson, prin.

Amelia Court House, Amelia Co., Pop. Code 3
Amelia County SD
Sch. Sys. Enr. Code 4
Supt. – William Sailer, P O BOX 167   23002
Amelia ES, P O BOX 187   23002
    Ruby Dillard, prin.
Amelia MS, P O BOX 219   23002
    Susan Barnard, prin.

Amherst, Amherst Co., Pop. Code 4
Amherst County SD
Sch. Sys. Enr. Code 5
Supt. – Dr. Russell Watson, P O BOX 459   24521
ES, P O BOX 310   24521 – Edward Hopkins, prin.
Central ES, P O BOX 560   24521
    Grady Davis, prin.
Temperance ES, RURAL ROUTE 04   24521
    Howard Anderson, prin.
Other Schools – See Madison Heights, Monroe

Annandale, Fairfax Co., Pop. Code 8
Fairfax County SD
Supt. – See Fairfax
Poe MS, 7000 CINDY LANE   22003
    Barbara Nissen, prin.
Annandale Terrace ES, 7604 HERALD ST   22003
    Beverly Woody, prin.
Braddock ES, 7825 HERITAGE DR   22003
    Harold Price, prin.
Camelot ES, 8100 GUINEVERE DR   22003
    Joseph Rucker, prin.
Canterbury Woods ES, 4910 WILLET DR   22003
    Mary Dietze, prin.
Columbia ES, 6720 ALPINE DR   22003
    Mark Summers, prin.

Holy Spirit School, 8800 BRADDOCK RD   22003
St. Michael School
    7401 SAINT MICHAELS LN   22003

Appalachia, Wise Co., Pop. Code 4
Wise County SD
Supt. – See Wise
ES, RURAL ROUTE 01 BOX 259-F 24216
James Clark, prin.

Appomattox, Appomattox Co., Pop. Code 4
Appomattox County SD
Sch. Sys. Enr. Code 4
Supt. – L. Walton 24522
MS, 300 N CHURCH ST 24522
Hezteine Foster, prin.
MS, 600 W CONFEDERATE BLVD 24522
Janice Marston, prin.
PS, 500 FERGUSON AVE 24522
Carolyn Coleman, prin.

Ararat, Patrick Co.
Patrick County SD
Supt. – See Stuart
Blue Ridge ES, P O BOX 30 24053
Fred Brim, prin.

Arcola, Loudoun Co.
Loudoun County SD
Supt. – See Leesburg
ES, P O BOX 24A 22010 – Louis Tiano, prin.

Arlington, Arlington Co., Pop. Code 9
Arlington County SD
Sch. Sys. Enr. Code 7
Supt. – Arthur Gosling, 1426 N QUINCY ST 22207
Jefferson MS, 125 S OLD GLEBE ROAD 22204
Sharon Steindam. prin.
Kenmore MS
200 S CARLIN SPRINGS ROAD 22204
Walter Taylor, prin.
Swanson MS, 5800 WASHINGTON BLVD 22205
Lawrence Grove, prin.
Williamsburg MS, 3600 N HARRISON ST 22207
William Michael, prin.
Abingdon ES, 3035 S ABINGDON ST 22206
Margaret Dirner, prin.
Ashlawn ES, 5950 8TH RD N 22205
Camay Murphy, prin.
Barcroft ES, 625 S WAKEFIELD ST 22204
Ellen Kahan, prin.
Barrett ES, 4401 N HENDERSON RD 22203
Dr. Herbert Ware, prin.
Drew ES, 3500 24TH ST S 22206
William Young, prin.
Glebe ES, 1770 N GLEBE RD 22207
William Vollin, prin.
Glencarlyn ES, 737 S CARLIN SPRINGS RD 22204
Dr. Walter Penders, prin.
Henry ES, 701 S HIGHLAND ST 22204
Douglas Bullock, prin.
Jamestown ES, 3700 N DELAWARE ST 22207
Dr. Lionel Seitzer, prin.
Key ES, 2300 KEY BLVD 22201
Dr. Paul Wireman, prin.
Long Branch ES, 33 N FILLMORE ST 22201
Margery Tracy, prin.
McKinley ES, 1030 N MCKINLEY RD 22205
Silvia Koch, prin.
Nottingham ES, 5900 LITTLE FALLS RD 22207
Edward Reynolds, prin.
Oakridge ES, 1414 24TH ST S 22202
Nancy King, prin.
Page, 1501 N LINCOLN ST 22201
Dr. G Miller, prin.
Randolph ES, 1306 S QUINCY ST 22204
Gloria Hoffman, prin.
Taylor ES, 2600 N STUART ST 22207
Dr. Ralph Stone, prin.
Tuckahoe ES, 6550 26TH ST N 22213
Marjorie Tuccillo, prin.

Cathedral St. Thomas More School
105 N THOMAS ST 22203
Our Savior Lutheran School
825 S TAYLOR ST 22204
St. Agnes School, 2024 N RANDOLPH ST 22207
St. Ann School, 980 N FREDERICK ST 22205
St. Charles School, 3299 FAIRFAX DR 22201

Arrington, Nelson Co., Pop. Code 1
Nelson County SD
Supt. – See Lovingston
Nelson MS 22922 – T. Mabry, prin.

Arvonia, Buckingham Co., Pop. Code 3
Buckingham County SD
Supt. – See Buckingham
ES, P O BOX 157 23004 – Gloria Wood, prin.

Ashburn, Loudoun Co., Pop. Code 2
Loudoun County SD
Supt. – See Leesburg
ES, P O BOX 16 22011 – Laurie McDonald, prin.

Ashland, Hanover Co., Pop. Code 5
Hanover County SD
Sch. Sys. Enr. Code 7
Supt. – Dr. S. Baker, 200 BERKLEY ST 23005
Liberty MS, RURAL ROUTE 03 BOX 631 23005
William Sadler, prin.
Clay ES, 310 S JAMES ST 23005
Melvin Hall,Jr., prin.
Elmont ES, RURAL ROUTE 01 BOX 1100 23005
Robert Crummette, prin.
Gandy MS, 705 HENRY ST 23005
Dr. Sue Burgess, prin.
Other Schools – See Beaverdam, Mechanicsville, Montpelier

Atkins, Smyth Co., Pop. Code 2
Smyth County SD
Supt. – See Marion
ES, RURAL ROUTE 01 BOX 155 24311
Edgar Waddell, prin.

Austinville, Wythe Co., Pop. Code 3
Carroll County SD
Supt. – See Hillsville
Laurel ES, RURAL ROUTE 01 24312
Robert Utz, prin.

Wythe County SD
Supt. – See Wytheville
ES, RURAL ROUTE 02 BOX 12 24312
Foy Crowder, prin.

Axton, Henry Co.
Henry County SD
Supt. – See Collinsville
Irisburg ES, RURAL ROUTE 03 BOX 120 24054
William Bullins, prin.

Bandy, Tazewell Co.
Tazewell County SD
Supt. – See Tazewell
ES 24602 – James Hammond, prin.

Bassett, Henry Co., Pop. Code 5
Henry County SD
Supt. – See Collinsville
MS, RURAL ROUTE 05 BOX 299 24055
Stephen Burton, prin.
Campbell Court ES
RURAL ROUTE 07 BOX 10 24055
Robert Pettit,Jr., prin.
Sanville ES, RURAL ROUTE 01 BOX 321 24055
Lewis Morgan, prin.

Bastian, Bland Co., Pop. Code 2
Bland County SD
Supt. – See Bland
ES, P O BOX 10 24314 – Ruth Groseclose, prin.

Bealeton, Fauquier Co.
Fauquier County SD
Supt. – See Warrenton
Walter ES, RURAL ROUTE 02 BOX 148-A 22712
Lois Atkins, prin.

Beaverdam, Hanover Co.
Hanover County SD
Supt. – See Ashland
ES, RURAL ROUTE 01 BOX 190 23015
Bradford Ashley, prin.

Bedford, (Indep. City), Pop. Code 6
Bedford County SD
Sch. Sys. Enr. Code 6
Supt. – Dr. John Kent, 310 S BRIDGE ST 24523
MS, LONGWOOD AVE & PEAKS ST 24523
William Whitaker, prin.
PS, COLLEGE ST 24523 – Roy Monk, prin.
Body Camp ES, RURAL ROUTE 03 24523
Conley Wallace, prin.
Other Schools – See Big Island, Forest, Goode, Goodview, Huddleston, Lynchburg, Moneta, Montvale, Thaxton

Bent Mountain, Roanoke Co.
Roanoke County SD
Supt. – See Salem
Bent Mountain ES, 10148 TINSLEY LN 24059
Lois Board, prin.

Bergton, Rockingham Co.
Rockingham County SD
Supt. – See Harrisonburg
ES, P O BOX 48 22811 – Edward Powell, prin.

Berryville, Clarke Co., Pop. Code 4
Clarke County SD
Sch. Sys. Enr. Code 4
Supt. – W. Johnson, P O BOX 351 22611
Williams MS, 301 JOSEPHINE ST 22611
William Weimer, prin.
ES, 317 W MAIN ST 22611 – Paul Jones, prin.
Cooley MS, RURAL ROUTE 03 BOX 5640 22611
Dr. G. Brown, prin.
Other Schools – See Boyce

Big Island, Bedford Co., Pop. Code 2
Bedford County SD
Supt. – See Bedford
ES 24526 – Johnny Lawson, prin.

Big Rock, Buchanan Co., Pop. Code 2
Buchanan County SD
Supt. – See Grundy
ES, P O BOX 195 24603 – Marcum Keene, prin.

Big Stone Gap, Wise Co., Pop. Code 5
Wise County SD
Supt. – See Wise
Powell Valley MS, P O BOX 280 24219
George Collins, prin.
Powell Valley ES, P O BOX 857 24219
Frank Cloud,Jr., prin.

Birchleaf, Dickenson Co.
Dickenson County SD
Supt. – See Clintwood
Sandlick ES 24220 – Dr. Tommy Street, prin.

Blacksburg, Montgomery Co., Pop. Code 8
Montgomery County SD
Supt. – See Christiansburg
MS, S MAIN ST 24060 – Donald Kelsey, prin.

Beeks ES, 709 AIRPORT RD 24060
Mary Kivlighan, prin.
Harding Avenue ES, 429 HARDING AVE 24060
Gary McCoy, prin.
Linkous ES, 813 TOMS CREEK RD 24060
Ray Vandyke, prin.
Prices Fork ES, RURAL ROUTE 02 24060
Dr. James Sellers, prin.

Blackstone, Nottoway Co., Pop. Code 5
Nottoway County SD
Supt. – See Nottoway
MS 23824 – Milton Johnson, prin.
PS, EAST ST 23824 – Edward Gates,Jr., prin.

Blairs, Pittsylvania Co., Pop. Code 6
Pittsylvania SD
Supt. – See Chatham
JHS, RURAL ROUTE 01 BOX 31 24527
James Bryant III, prin.
Southside ES, RURAL ROUTE 01 BOX 32-A 24527
Jesse Bennett,Jr., prin.

Bland, Bland Co., Pop. Code 2
Bland County SD
Sch. Sys. Enr. Code 4
Supt. – Milton Maxton, P O BOX 128 24315
S, RURAL ROUTE 01 BOX 218 24315
Roger Thompson, prin.
Hollybrook ES
RURAL ROUATE 01 BOX 287 24315
Donna Wolcott, prin.
Other Schools – See Bastian, Ceres, Rocky Gap

Bloxom, Accomack Co., Pop. Code 2
Accomack County SD
Supt. – See Accomac
ES 23308 – Thelma Miller, prin.

Bluefield, Tazewell Co., Pop. Code 6
Tazewell County SD
Supt. – See Tazewell
Graham MS 24605 – Bryan Bush, prin.
Dudley ES 24605 – Brenda Lawson, prin.
Graham MS 24605 – Dr. Robert Brown, prin.

Blue Ridge, Botetourt Co., Pop. Code 4
Botetourt County SD
Supt. – See Fincastle
Colonial ES, RURAL ROUTE 01 BOX 330 24064
Dr. Diana Bishop, prin.

Boissevain, Tazewell Co., Pop. Code 3
Tazewell County SD
Supt. – See Tazewell
Abbs Valley-Boissevain ES 24606
Nyoka Money, prin.

Bon Air, Richmond Co., Pop. Code 7
Chesterfield County SD
Supt. – See Chesterfield
ES, 8701 POLK ST 23235
Dr. Irving Driscoll,Jr., prin.

St. Michael's Episcopal School
8706 QUAKER LN 23235

Boones Mill, Franklin Co., Pop. Code 2
Franklin County SD
Supt. – See Rocky Mount
ES, RURAL ROUTE 03 BOX 151 24065
Anne Tyler, prin.

Bowling Green, Caroline Co., Pop. Code 3
Caroline County SD
Sch. Sys. Enr. Code 5
Supt. – Dr. William Asbury, P O BOX 529 22427
Caroline MS, P O BOX 99 22427
Stanley Jones, prin.
MS, P O BOX E 22427 – Carolyn Davis, prin.
PS, DRAWER H 22427
Blanche Washington, prin.
Other Schools – See Ruther Glen

Boyce, Clarke Co., Pop. Code 2
Clarke County SD
Supt. – See Berryville
ES, P O BOX 65 22620 – John McCuan, prin.

Powhatan School
RURAL ROUTE 2A BOX 177A 22620

Boydton, Mecklenburg Co., Pop. Code 2
Mecklenburg County SD
Sch. Sys. Enr. Code 6
Supt. – Dr. J. Austin, P O BOX 190 23917
ES, RURAL ROUTE 02 BOX 218-A 23917
Doris Hester, prin.
Other Schools – See Chase City, Clarksville, La
Crosse, Skipwith, South Hill, Union Level

Boykins, Southampton Co., Pop. Code 3
Southhampton County SD
Supt. – See Courtland
ES, P O BOX 367 23827 – Riddick Parker, prin.

Bridgewater, Rockingham Co., Pop. Code 5
Rockingham County SD
Supt. – See Harrisonburg
Wayland MS 22812 – James Gresham, prin.
ES, P O BOX 5 22812 – Edmund Price, prin.

Bristol, (Indep. City), Pop. Code 7
Bristol CSD
Sch. Sys. Enr. Code 5
Supt. – David Lenker, 222 OAK ST 24201
Virginia MS, 501 PIEDMONT ST 24201
William Shanks, prin.

Douglass ES, OAKVIEW & RANDALL STS 24201
  Harold Rife, prin.
Highland View ES, 1405 EADS AVE 24201
  Don Mumpower, prin.
Jackson ES, 2045 EUCLID AVE 24201
  Robert Jones, prin.
Van Pelt ES, 200 SPRING HILL TER 24201
  Larry Lusk, prin.
Washington-Lee ES
  900 WASHINGTON & LEE DR 24201
  Tom Parker, prin.

Washington County SD
Supt. – See Abingdon
High Point ES
  ROUTE 01, SINKING CRK ROAD 24201
  Guessner Musick, prin.
Valley Institute ES, 3644 GATE CITY HWY 24201
  W. Church, prin.
Wallace ES, 1376 WALLACE RD 24201
  Sloan Southerlin,Jr., prin.

St. Anne Catholic School, 350 EUCLID AVE 24201

Bristow, Prince William Co.

Linton Hall School
  9535 LINTON HALL RD 22013

Broadway, Rockingham Co., Pop. Code 4
Rockingham County SD
Supt. – See Harrisonburg
Myers MS, P O BOX 517 22815
  Ronald Smith, prin.

Brookneal, Charlotte Co., Pop. Code 4
Campbell County SD
Supt. – See Rustburg
ES 24528 – Sandra Owen, prin.

Brownsburg, Rockbridge Co., Pop. Code 2
Rockbridge County SD
Supt. – See Lexington
MS 24415 – Russell Fleshman, prin.

Buchanan, Botetourt Co., Pop. Code 4
Botetourt County SD
Supt. – See Fincastle
ES, P O BOX 639 24066 – William Watson, prin.

Buckingham, Buckingham Co., Pop. Code 2
Buckingham County SD
Sch. Sys. Enr. Code 4
Supt. – M. Kay 23921
ES, HC-02 BOX 375 23921 – H. Adams, prin.
Other Schools – See Arvonia, Dillwyn, New Canton

Buena Vista, (Indep. City), Pop. Code 6
Buena Vista CSD
Sch. Sys. Enr. Code 4
Supt. – Dr. James Bradford, P O BOX 110 24416
McCluer MS, 2329 CHESTNUT AVE 24416
  Robert Williams, prin.
Enderly Heights ES, 101 WOODLAND AVE 24416
  William Hammack, prin.
Kling ES, 3400 LOMBARDY AVE 24416
  Barbara Cash, prin.

Rockbridge County SD
Supt. – See Lexington
Mountain View ES, RURAL ROUTE 01 24416
  B. Claytor, prin.

Burke, Fairfax Co.
Fairfax County SD
Supt. – See Fairfax
Cherry Run ES, 9732 IRONMASTER DR 22015
  Elaine Smith, prin.
Terra-Centre ES
  6000 BURKE CENTRE PKY 22015
  Stephen Gossin, prin.
White Oaks ES, 6130 SHIPLETT BLVD 22015
  Dr. Carolyn Buckenmaier, prin.

Burkeville, Nottoway Co., Pop. Code 3
Nottoway County SD
Supt. – See Nottoway
MS 23922 – James Dyson, prin.

Callao, Northumberland Co., Pop. Code 2
Northumberland County SD
Supt. – See Heathsville
ES 22435 – Malcolm Davis, prin.

Callaway, Franklin Co.
Franklin County SD
Supt. – See Rocky Mount
ES 24067 – Dr. Claude Nolen,Jr., prin.

Cana, Carroll Co., Pop. Code 1
Carroll County SD
Supt. – See Hillsville
Mt. Bethel ES, RURAL ROUTE 01 BOX 437 24317
  Olen Webb, prin.
St. Paul ES, RURAL ROUTE 02 24317
  John Midkiff, prin.

Cape Charles, Northampton Co., Pop. Code 4
Northampton County SD
Supt. – See Eastville
ES, 23 PARK ROW 23310 – Betty Spooner, prin.

Capron, Southampton Co., Pop. Code 2
Southhampton County SD
Supt. – See Courtland
ES, P O BOX 164 23829 – Barbara Edwards, prin.

Carrsville, Isle of Wight Co.
Isle of Wight County SD
Supt. – See Isle of Wight
ES 23315 – Richard Crawford, prin.

Carson, Dinwiddie Co.
Prince George County SD
Supt. – See Prince George
ES, 19806 HALIFAX RD 23830 – Jan Peyrot, prin.

Castlewood, Russell Co., Pop. Code 6
Russell County SD
Supt. – See Lebanon
ES, RURAL ROUTE 03 24224
  Aaron Osborne, prin.
Clinch River ES, RURAL ROUTE 01 24224
  Charlie Collins, prin.
Copper Creek ES
  RURAL ROUTE 02 BOX 33 24224
  Charles Duty, prin.

Catlett, Fauquier Co.
Fauquier County SD
Supt. – See Warrenton
Pearson ES, RURAL ROUTE 02 BOX 10 22019
  A. Thorp, prin.

Cedar Bluff, Tazewell Co., Pop. Code 4
Tazewell County SD
Supt. – See Tazewell
ES, P O BOX C 24609 – Bruce Russell, prin.
Rivermont ES
  RURAL ROUTE 01 BOX 264 A 24609
  James Hammond, prin.

Centreville, Fairfax Co.
Fairfax County SD
Supt. – See Fairfax
ES, 13800 BRADDOCK RD 22020
  Gregory Lock,Jr., prin.
Cub Run ES, 5301 SULLY STATION RD 22020
  Janet LeBel, prin.
London Towne ES, 6100 STONE RD 22020
  Al Migliara,Jr., prin.

Ceres, Bland Co.
Bland County SD
Supt. – See Bland
ES, RURAL ROUTE 01 BOX 74-A 24318
  Anne Cassell, prin.

Chantilly, Fairfax Co., Pop. Code 2
Fairfax County SD
Supt. – See Fairfax
Franklin MS, 3300 LEES CORNER ROAD 22021
  Douglas Rice, prin.
Rocky Run MS
  4400 STRINGFELLOW ROAD 22021
  Dr. Richard Lavine, prin.
Brookfield ES, 4200 LEES CORNER RD 22021
  Joanne Ibbotson, prin.

St. Timothy School
  13809 POPLAR TREE RD 22021

Charles City, Charles City Co.
Charles City County SD
Sch. Sys. Enr. Code 4
Supt. – Willie Townes
  RURAL ROUTE 02 BOX 2 23030
Charles City County MS
  RURAL ROUTE 03 BOX 290 23030
  Bessie Cooper, prin.
Charles City County MS
  RURAL ROUTE 02 BOX 50 23030
  Clarence Hawkes, prin.
Other Schools – See Providence Forge

Charlotte Court House, Charlotte Co., Pop. Code 3
Charlotte County SD
Sch. Sys. Enr. Code 4
Supt. – Paul Stapleton, P O BOX 387 23923
Central MS, P O BOX 367 23923
  Thomas Elder, prin.
Jeffress MS, P O BOX 55 23923
  Mary Dupee, prin.
Other Schools – See Keysville, Phenix, Saxe

Charlottesville, (Indep. City), Pop. Code 8
Albermarle County SD
Sch. Sys. Enr. Code 6
Supt. – N. Andrew Overstreet
  401 MCINTIRE ROAD 22901
Burley MS, 901 ROSE HILL DRIVE 22901
  Thomas Zimorski, prin.
Jouett MS, 2065 LAMBS ROAD 22901
  James Helvin, prin.
Walton MS, RURAL ROUTE 01 BOX 200 22901
  William Banks, prin.
Greer ES, 2055 LAMBS RD 22901
  Fulton Marshall,Jr., prin.
Hollymead ES, 2775 POWELL CREEK DR 22901
  John Cruickshank, prin.
Lewis ES, 1610 OWENSVILLE RD 22901
  Sylvia Henderson, prin.
Murray ES, RURAL ROUTE 12 BOX 229 22901
  Sylvia Henderson, prin.
Robinson ES, RURAL ROUTE 09 BOX 413 22901
  Charles Simmons, prin.
Rose Hill ES, 1200 FORREST ST 22901
  Gerald Terrell, prin.
Woodbrook ES, 202 WOODBROOK DR 22901
  Keith Hammon, prin.
Other Schools – See Crozet, Earlysville, Esmont,
  Keswick, North Garden, Scottsville

Charlottesville CSD
Sch. Sys. Enr. Code 5
Supt. – Dr. Vincent Cibbarelli
  1562 DAIRY ROAD 22903
Buford MS, 617 9TH ST SW 22903
  Dr. Helen Stiff, prin.
Burnley-Moran ES, 1300 LONG ST 22901
  Bonnie Wescott, prin.
Clark ES, FOURTH ST NW 22901
  S. Hamrick, prin.
Greenbrier ES, 2228 GREENBRIER DR 22901
  Dr. Robert Knighton, prin.
Jackson-Via ES, 508 HARRIS RD 22903
  Mozell Booker, prin.
Johnson ES, 1645 CHERRY AVE 22903
  David Garrett, prin.
Venable ES, 406 14TH ST NW 22903
  Dr. Charles Dempsey, prin.
Walker MS, 1564 DAIRY ROAD 22903
  Ralph Law, prin.

St. Ann's Belfield School, 2132 IVY ROAD 22903

Chase City, Mecklenburg Co., Pop. Code 5
Mecklenburg County SD
Supt. – See Boydton
ES, RURAL ROUTE 02 BOX 60 23924
  Helen Hill, prin.

Chatham, Pittsylvania Co., Pop. Code 4
Pittsylvania SD
Sch. Sys. Enr. Code 6
Supt. – John Neely, P O BOX 232 24531
Central MS, P O BOX B 24531
  Emma Austin, prin.
ES, P O BOX 531 24531 – Diane Mangus, prin.
Climax ES, RURAL ROUTE 03 BOX 86A 24531
  Reuben Doss, prin.
Spring Garden ES
  RURAL ROUTE 01 BOX 97 24531
  Charles Miller,Jr., prin.
Union Hall ES, RURAL ROUTE 06 BOX 234 24531
  Isaac Jackson, prin.
Other Schools – See Blairs, Danville, Dry Fork,
  Gretna, Hurt, Ringgold

Check, Floyd Co.
Floyd County SD
Supt. – See Floyd
ES, RURAL ROUTE 01 24072 – Robert Peak, prin.

Cheriton, Northampton Co., Pop. Code 3
Northampton County SD
Supt. – See Eastville
ES 23316 – Ann Bonniwell, prin.

Chesapeake, (Indep. City), Pop. Code 9
Chesapeake CSD
Sch. Sys. Enr. Code 8
Supt. – Dr. C. Fred Bateman
  P O BOX 15204 23320
Truitt MS, 1100 HOLLY AVE 23324
  Samuel Leary, prin.
Western Branch MS
  4201 HAWKSLEY DRIVE 23321
  Craig Jones, prin.
Butts Road ES
  1000 MOUNT PLEASANT RD 23320
  Janet Garner, prin.
Camelot ES, 2901 GUENEVERE DR 23323
  Rebecca Adams, prin.
Carver MS, BROAD ST 23324
  Charles Jubilee, prin.
Chittum ES, 2008 DOCK LANDING RD 23321
  Meredith Garrett, prin.
Crestwood MS, 1240 GREAT BRIDGE BLVD 23320
  Edna Faulk, prin.
Deep Creek ES, 2809 FOREHAND DR 23323
  Harmor Booker, prin.
Deep Creek IS
  140 GEORGE WASHINGTON HWY N 23323
  Charles Brabble, prin.
Georgetown ES, 436 PROVIDENCE RD 23325
  Glenn Brown, prin.
Great Bridge ES, 408 CEDAR RD 23320
  Eugene Welton, prin.
Great Bridge IS, 369 BATTLEFIELD BLVD S 23320
  Rick West, prin.
Greenbrier ES, 1551 EDEN WAY S 23320
  Linda Smith, prin.
Hickory ES, 2710 BATTLEFIELD BLVD S 23322
  Dr. Elsie Craig, prin.
Norfolk Highlands ES, 1120 LILAC AVE 23325
  Ruth Boone, prin.
Park ES, 2700 BORDER RD 23324
  Steve Lassiter, prin.
Portlock ES, 1857 VARSITY DR 23324
  Robert Martin, prin.
Southeastern ES
  1853 BATTLEFIELD BLVD S 23322
  Marc Rittman, prin.
Southwestern ES, 4410 AIRLINE BLVD 23321
  Curtis Myers, prin.
Sparrow Road MS, 1605 SPARROW RD 23325
  Kerry Bierma, prin.
Treakle ES, 2500 GILMERTON RD 23323
  Dr. Diane Martin, prin.
Western Branch MS, 4013 TERRY DR 23321
  Ted Carpenter, prin.
Western Branch PS, 4122 TERRY DR 23321
  G. Short, prin.
Williams ES, 1100 BATTLEFIELD BLVD N 23320
  Daisy Kessler, prin.
Wright ES, 600 PARK AVE 23324
  Dr. Dean Jones, prin.

Chester, Chesterfield, Pop. Code 6
Chesterfield County SD
Supt. – See Chesterfield
Carver MS
12400 BRANDERS BRIDGE ROAD 23831
T. Tilley, prin.
MS, 3900 HUNDRED ROAD W 23831
Michael Rose, prin.
Curtis ES, 3600 HUNDRED RD W 23831
Bruce Tetlow, prin.
Enon ES, 2001 HUNDRED RD E 23831
Basil Furr, prin.
Harrowgate ES, 15501 HARROWGATE RD 23831
Leonard Rogers, prin.
Wells ES, 13101 CHESTER RD S 23831
Dr. Sheila Leckie, prin.

Chesterfield, Chesterfield Co., Pop. Code 1
Chesterfield County SD
Sch. Sys. Enr. Code 8
Supt. – Dr. Eugene Davis, P O BOX 10 23832
Chalkley ES, 3301 TURNER RD 23832
Glen Dewire, prin.
Gates ES, 10001 COURTHOUSE ROAD EXT 23832
W. Smith III, prin.
Jacobs Road ES, 8800 JACOBS RD 23832
Linda Cosby, prin.
Other Schools – See Bon Air, Chester, Ettrick,
Matoaca, Midlothian, Moseley, Richmond

Chilhowie, Smyth Co., Pop. Code 4
Smyth County SD
Supt. – See Marion
ES, P O BOX 348 24319 – Greever Crouse,Jr., prin.

Chincoteague, Accomack Co., Pop. Code 4
Accomack County SD
Supt. – See Accomac
ES 23336 – Horst Seibert, prin.

Christiansburg, Montgomery Co., Pop. Code 7
Montgomery County SD
Sch. Sys. Enr. Code 6
Supt. – Harold Dodge, P O BOX 29 24073
MS, 208 COLLEGE ST 24073
Richard Ballengee, prin.
Bethel ES, RURAL ROUTE 01 24073
L. Johnson, prin.
MS, WADES LANE 24073 – Douglas Morgan, prin.
PS, 105 DEPOT ST W 24073 – John Callahan, prin.
Other Schools – See Blacksburg, Elliston, Radford,
Riner, Shawsville

Church Road, Dinwiddie Co.
Dinwiddie County SD
Supt. – See Dinwiddie
Midway ES, RURAL ROUTE 01 BOX 255 23833
George Rapp, prin.

Churchville, Augusta Co.
Augusta County SD
Supt. – See Fishersville
ES 24421 – Richard Landis, prin.

Clarksville, Mecklenburg Co., Pop. Code 4
Mecklenburg County SD
Supt. – See Boydton
ES, RURAL ROUTE 01 BOX 1 23927
Joe Davidson, prin.

Clear Brook, Frederick Co., Pop. Code 2
Frederick County SD
Supt. – See Winchester
Stonewall ES
RURAL ROUTE 01 BOX 312-A 22624
Dewayne Raines, prin.

Cleveland, Russell Co.
Russell County SD
Supt. – See Lebanon
MS, P O BOX 66 24225 – Myrl Allen, prin.
ES, P O BOX 248 24225 – Lewis Barton, prin.

Clifton, Fairfax Co., Pop. Code 2
Fairfax County SD
Supt. – See Fairfax
ES, 7010 CLIFTON RD 22024
Dr. Patricia Heiselberg, prin.
Union Mill ES, 13611 SPRINGSTONE DR 22024
Dr. Brenda Spratt, prin.

Clifton Forge, (Indep. City), Pop. Code 6
Alleghany Highlands SD
Supt. – See Covington
Clifton MS, COMMERCIAL ST 24422
Roy Putnam, prin.
ES, CHURCH & A STS 24422
Joseph Simpson, prin.
Sharon ES, RURAL ROUTE 01 24422
Charles Burger, prin.

Clinchco, Dickenson Co., Pop. Code 3
Dickenson County SD
Supt. – See Clintwood
ES 24226 – Robert Musick, prin.

Clinchport, Scott Co., Pop. Code 1
Scott County SD
Supt. – See Gate City
Fairview ES, RURAL ROUTE 03 24244
Danny Calhoun, prin.
Rye Cove ES, RURAL ROUTE 04 BOX 59 24244
John Vicars, prin.

Clintwood, Dickenson Co., Pop. Code 4
Dickenson County SD
Sch. Sys. Enr. Code 5
Supt. – John Dotson, P O BOX 1127 24228

ES, P O BOX 585 24228 – Bob Baker, prin.
Longs Fork ES, P O BOX 600 24228
Clyde Wright, prin.
Other Schools – See Birchleaf, Clinchco, Nora

Clover, Halifax Co., Pop. Code 2
Halifax County SD
Supt. – See Halifax
ES, P O BOX 98 24534 – Mary Wilkerson, prin.

Cloverdale, Botetourt Co., Pop. Code 3
Botetourt County SD
Supt. – See Fincastle
ES, RURAL ROUTE 605 24077 – Paul Garber, prin.

Cluster Springs, Halifax Co.
Halifax County SD
Supt. – See Halifax
MS, P O BOX 171 24535 – Roderick Hunt, prin.

Coeburn, Wise Co., Pop. Code 5
Wise County SD
Supt. – See Wise
MS, P O BOX 670 24230 – C. Hubbard, prin.
PS, P O BOX 130 24230 – Nolan Kilgore, prin.

Collinsville, Henry Co., Pop. Code 6
Henry County SD
Sch. Sys. Enr. Code 6
Supt. – Virgil Poore, P O BOX 958 24078
ES, 306 OAKLAND DR 24078
Charles Clifton, prin.
Smith MS, 100 SCHOOL DR 24078
Rudolph Johnson, prin.
Other Schools – See Axton, Bassett, Fieldale,
Martinsville, Ridgeway, Spencer, Stanleytown

Colonial Beach, Westmoreland Co., Pop. Code 4
Colonial Beach CSD
Sch. Sys. Enr. Code 3
Supt. – Dr. Donald Warner
300 GARFIELD AVE 22443
Colonial Beach S, 315 N DOUGLAS ST 22443
John Sessoms, prin.

Westmoreland County SD
Supt. – See Montross
Washington District ES 22443
Frances Jenkins, prin.

Colonial Heights, (Indep. City), Pop. Code 7
Colonial Heights CSD
Sch. Sys. Enr. Code 5
Supt. – Herman Bartlett, 512 BOULEVARD 23834
MS, 500 CONDUIT ROAD 23834
Frank Morgan, prin.
Lakeview ES, TASWELL AVE 23834
Donald Schmidt, prin.
North ES, 3201 DALE AVE 23834
Marvin Clipp, prin.
Tussing ES, 5501 CONDUIT RD 23834
Leslie Fryar, prin.

Concord, Appomattox Co.
Campbell County SD
Supt. – See Rustburg
ES 24538 – Leonard Frady, prin.

Courtland, Southampton Co., Pop. Code 3
Southhampton County SD
Sch. Sys. Enr. Code 4
Supt. – Dr. Howard Wainwright
P O BOX 26 23837
Southampton MS, RURAL ROUTE 01 23837
James Ricks, prin.
ES, P O BOX 27 23837 – Howard Benton, prin.
Other Schools – See Boykins, Capron, Franklin, Ivor

Southampton Academy Upper HS
320 OLD PLANK ROAD 23837

Covington, (Indep. City), Pop. Code 6
Alleghany Highlands SD
Sch. Sys. Enr. Code 5
Supt. – Dr. E. Mark Pace
110 ROSEDALE AVE 24426
Boiling Spring ES, RURAL ROUTE 04 24426
James Hodges,Jr., prin.
Callaghan ES, RURAL ROUTE 01 24426
Paul Linkenhoker, prin.
Other Schools – See Clifton Forge, Hot Springs,
Lowmoor

Covington CSD
Sch. Sys. Enr. Code 4
Supt. – Dr. William Sibley
340 E WALNUT ST 24426
Jeter-Watson MS, PINE & MERCER STS 24426
Willis Shawver, prin.
Edgemont ES, 451 W PARK ST 24426
Tom Robertson, prin.

Craigsville, Augusta Co., Pop. Code 3
Augusta County SD
Supt. – See Fishersville
ES, P O BOX 130 24430 – Gerald Zaccaria, prin.

Crewe, Notoway Co., Pop. Code 4
Nottoway County SD
Supt. – See Nottoway
ES, P O BOX 107 23930 – Jack Stamper, prin.

Critz, Patrick Co.
Patrick County SD
Supt. – See Stuart
Hardin-Reynolds MS 24052 – Larry Belcher, prin.

Crozet, Albemarle Co., Pop. Code 4
Albermarle County SD
Supt. – See Charlottesville
Henley MS, RURAL ROUTE 01 BOX 519 22932
Sharon Harris, prin.
Brownsville ES
RURAL ROUTE 01 BOX 518 22932
Anne Norford, prin.
ES, RURAL ROUTE 03 BOX 188 22932
Charles Witt,Jr., prin.

Crozier, Goochland Co.
Goochland County SD
Supt. – See Goochland
Randolph ES
1552 SHEPPARDTOWN ROAD 23039
Carol Brallier, prin.

Culpeper, Culpeper Co., Pop. Code 6
Culpepper County SD
Sch. Sys. Enr. Code 5
Supt. – Tony Stewart, P O BOX 631 22701
Binns MS, NORTH MAIN ST EXT 22701
Robert Heffern, prin.
Farmington ES, 500 SUNSET LN 22701
Gail Brewer, prin.
Richardson MS
1401 OLD FREDERICKSBURG RD 22701
Charles Oliver, prin.
Sample ES, 2520 ORANGE RD 22701
William Simms, prin.
Sycamore Park ES, 145 RADIO LN 22701
Dr. Robert Borges, prin.

Cumberland, Cumberland Co., Pop. Code 2
Cumberland County SD
Sch. Sys. Enr. Code 4
Supt. – James Irons, RURAL ROUTE 01 23040
ES, RURAL ROUTE 01 BOX 230 23040
C. Magruder, prin.

Dahlgren, King George Co., Pop. Code 3
King George County SD
Supt. – See King George
Potomac ES, P O BOX 314 22448
Philip Worrell, prin.

Damascus, Washington Co., Pop. Code 4
Washington County SD
Supt. – See Abingdon
ES, RURAL ROUTE 01 BOX 7-A 24236
David McFarlane, prin.

Dante, Dickenson Co., Pop. Code 4
Russell County SD
Supt. – See Lebanon
ES, P O BOX 727 24237 – James Elkins, prin.

Danville, (Indep. City), Pop. Code 8
Danville CSD
Sch. Sys. Enr. Code 6
Supt. – Larry Leonard
313 MUNICIPAL BLDG 24541
Coates ES, 1727 WESTOVER DR 24541
Carolyn Harris, prin.
Forest Hills ES
155 MOUNTAIN VIEW AVE 24541
Daphine Hall, prin.
Gibson MS, 1215 INDUSTRIAL AVE 24541
Ruby Hodges, prin.
Glenwood ES, HALIFAX RD 24540
Barbara Bennett, prin.
Grove Park ES, 1070 S MAIN ST 24541
Robert Chandler, prin.
Johnson ES, 680 ARNETT BLVD 24540
Mildred Watlington, prin.
Park Avenue ES, 611 PARK AVE 24541
Sue Davis, prin.
Schoolfield ES, BALTIMORE AVE 24541
Suzanne Jones, prin.
Taylor MS, 825 PINEY FOREST RD 24540
Dorothy Harris, prin.
WEST Townes Lea ES
439 CEDARBROOK DR 24541
Virginia Robertson, prin.
Westmoreland MS, 540 GAY ST 24541
Samuel Massie, prin.
Wilson MS, 1005 N MAIN ST 24540
William Wolford, prin.
Woodberry Hills ES, 614 AUDUBON DR 24540
Elmore Lyons, prin.

Pittsylvania SD
Supt. – See Chatham
Brosville MS, RURAL ROUTE 01 BOX 1280 24541
William Reece, prin.
Mt. Hermon ES, 1809 FRANKLIN TPKE 24540
Jennie Wagner, prin.
Stony Mill ES
RURAL ROUTE 06 BOX 1834 24541
George Grekos, prin.

William T. Sutherlin Academy
RURAL ROUTE 05 BOX 1398 24540
Sacred Heart School, 540 CENTRAL BLVD 24540

Davenport, Buchanon Co.
Buchanan County SD
Supt. – See Grundy
Council ES, P O BOX 70 24239
Larry Ashby, prin.

Dayton, Rockingham Co., Pop. Code 4
Rockingham County SD
Supt. – See Harrisonburg
ES, P O BOX 278 22821 – Edward Byrd, prin.

Ottobine ES, RURAL ROUTE 01 BOX 328   22821
  Charles Wright, prin.

Deerfield, Augusta Co.
Augusta County SD
Supt. — See Fishersville
ES   24432 — Garold Senger,Jr., prin.

Dendron, Surry Co., Pop. Code 2
Surry County SD
Supt. — See Surry
Surry ES, RURAL ROUTE 01 BOX 15A   23839
  Flossie Gilchrist, prin.

Dillwyn, Buckingham Co., Pop. Code 3
Buckingham County SD
Supt. — See Buckingham
MS, P O BOX 608   23936 — James Blevins, prin.
PS, RURAL ROUTE 01 BOX 8   23936
  Ossie Harris,Jr., prin.

Dinwiddie, Dinwiddie Co., Pop. Code 2
Dinwiddie County SD
Sch. Sys. Enr. Code 5
Supt. — Dr. Richard Vaughn, P O BOX 7   23841
MS, RURAL ROUTE 01 BOX 122   23841
  Charlie Taylor, prin.
Southside ES, RURAL ROUTE 01 BOX 1294   23841
  Cornelia Roberts, prin.
Other Schools — See Church Road, Mc Kenney,
  Petersburg

Disputanta, Prince George Co., Pop. Code 2
Prince George County SD
Supt. — See Prince George
Burrowsville ES, 18701 JAMES RIVER DR   23842
  Jan Peyrot, prin.
Harrison ES, 12900 EAST QUAKER RD   23842
  Raymond Sutton, prin.
South ES, 13400 PRINCE GEORGE DR   23842
  Hugh Mumford, prin.

Draper, Wythe Co.
Pulaski County SD
Supt. — See Pulaski
ES   24324 — James Neblett,Jr., prin.

Dryden, Lee Co., Pop. Code 2
Lee County SD
Supt. — See Jonesville
S, P O BOX 89   24243 — Jake Doss, prin.

Dry Fork, Pittsylvania Co.
Pittsylvania SD
Supt. — See Chatham
Whitmell ES, RURAL ROUTE 01 BOX 322   24549
  C. Huffman, prin.

Dublin, Pulaski Co., Pop. Code 4
Pulaski County SD
Supt. — See Pulaski
MS, P O BOX 1067   24084 — Paul Phillips, prin.
ES, P O BOX 1106   24084 — C. Bruce, prin.
Newbern ES, RURAL ROUTE 01 BOX 154   24084
  James Neblett,Jr., prin.

Duffield, Scott Co., Pop. Code 2
Lee County SD
Supt. — See Jonesville
Stickleyville ES
  RURAL ROUTE 01 BOX 141-S   24244
  Lisa Poe, prin.

Scott County SD
Supt. — See Gate City
Duffield-Pattnsvle ES, P O BOX 363   24244
  Dan Meade, prin.

Dugspur, Carroll Co.
Carroll County SD
Supt. — See Hillsville
ES, RURAL ROUTE 02   24325
  Dr. Bernard Talley, prin.

Dumfries, Prince William Co., Pop. Code 5
Prince William County SD
Supt. — See Manassas
ES, 300 CAMERON ST   22026
  Nicolette Rinaldo, prin.
Henderson ES, 3799 WATERWAY DR   22026
  Ruby Strickland, prin.
Pattie ES, 16125 DUMFRIES RD   22026
  Ralph Sebastian, prin.

Dungannon, Scott Co., Pop. Code 2
Scott County SD
Supt. — See Gate City
ES, P O BOX 280   24245 — Tom Green, prin.

Eagle Rock, Botetourt Co., Pop. Code 2
Botetourt County SD
Supt. — See Fincastle
ES, P O BOX 15-A   24085 — Bobby Kiker, prin.

Earlysville, Albermarle Co.
Albermarle County SD
Supt. — See Charlottesville
Wood ES, STAR ROUTE 01 BOX 22   22936
  Dr. Charlene Gill, prin.

Eastville, Northampton Co., Pop. Code 2
Northampton County SD
Sch. Sys. Enr. Code 5
Supt. — G. Young   23347
Other Schools — See Cape Charles, Cheriton, Exmore,
  Machipongo

Edinburg, Shenandoah Co., Pop. Code 3
Shenandoah County SD
Supt. — See Woodstock
MS, P O BOX 97   22824 — Bill Smitherman, prin.

Elk Creek, Grayson Co.
Grayson County SD
Supt. — See Independence
ES, P O BOX 104   24326
  Carolyn Richardson, prin.

Elkton, Rockingham Co., Pop. Code 4
Rockingham County SD
Supt. — See Harrisonburg
MS, 401 E SPOTSWOOD TRAIL   22827
  Joseph Dudash, prin.
ES, 302 W B ST   22827 — Carlos Diehl,Jr., prin.

Elliston, Montgomery Co., Pop. Code 3
Montgomery County SD
Supt. — See Christiansburg
Elliston-Lafayette ES, RURAL ROUTE 11 E   24087
  Lois Hinkle, prin.

Emporia, (Indep. City), Pop. Code 5
Greensville SD
Sch. Sys. Enr. Code 5
Supt. — Dr. Arnold Saari, P O BOX 1156   23847
Belfield MS, RURAL ROUTE 03 BOX 352   23847
  Ulysses Russell, prin.
ES, 114 S MAIN ST   23847 — Virginia Young, prin.
Hicksford ES, WASHINGTON PARK   23847
  Larance Adams, prin.
Zion MS, RURAL ROUTE 01   23847
  Larance Adams, prin.

Esmont, Albermarle Co.
Albermarle County SD
Supt. — See Charlottesville
Yancey ES, RURAL ROUTE 01 BOX 285   22937
  Carolyn Page, prin.

Ettrick, Chesterfield Co., Pop. Code 5
Chesterfield County SD
Supt. — See Chesterfield
ES, 20910 CHESTERFIELD AVE   23803
  Jeffrey Beatman, prin.

Ewing, Lee Co., Pop. Code 2
Lee County SD
Supt. — See Jonesville
Elydale ES, RURAL ROUTE 02 BOX 457   24248
  Ernie Chadwell, prin.
ES, P O BOX 279   24248 — Jerry Hounshell, prin.

Exmore, Northampton Co., Pop. Code 4
Northampton County SD
Supt. — See Eastville
Exmore-Willis Wharf ES, P O BOX 685   23350
  Perry Whitley,Jr., prin.
Hare Valley ES, RURAL ROUTE 01   23350
  Rex Ingram, prin.

Broadwater Academy, P O BOX 546   23350

Fairfax, (Indep. City), Pop. Code 7
Fairfax County SD
Sch. Sys. Enr. Code 9
Supt. — Dr. Robert Spillane
  10700 PAGE AVE   22030
Bonnie Brae ES, 5404 SIDEBURN RD   22032
  Kay Eckler, prin.
Sangster ES, 7500 RESERVATION DR   22153
  C. Bright, prin.
Frost MS, 4101 PICKETT ROAD   22032
  Dr. Gary Miller, prin.
Lanier MS, 3710 BEVAN DRIVE   22030
  Ronald Savage, prin.
Fairfax Villa ES, 10900 SANTA CLARA DR   22030
  Maryanne Roesch, prin.
Fairhill ES, 3001 CHICHESTER LN   22031
  David Chubb, prin.
Green Acres ES, 4401 SIDEBURN RD   22030
  Susan Oblon, prin.
Greenbriar East ES
  13006 POINT PLEASANT DR   22033
  Karen Johnston, prin.
Greenbriar West ES
  13300 POPLAR TREE RD   22033
  Mary Roots, prin.
Jermantown ES, 3616 JERMANTOWN RD   22030
  Lynne Pope, prin.
Laurel Ridge ES
  10110 COMMONWEALTH BLVD   22032
  E. Gill, prin.
Layton Hall ES, 3705 OLD LEE HWY   22030
  Mary Garman, prin.
Lees Corner ES, 13500 HOLLINGER AVE   22033
  Nancy Roberson, prin.
Little Run ES, 4511 OLLEY LN   22032
  Janice Poates, prin.
Mantua ES, 9107 HORNER CT   22031
  Joseph Ross, prin.
Mosby Woods ES, 9819 FIVE OAKS RD   22031
  Emily Williams, prin.
Navy ES, 3500 W OX RD   22033
  Dr. Barbara Fry, prin.
Oak View ES, 5004 SIDEBURN RD   22032
  Virginia Mealing, prin.
Olde Creek ES, 9524 OLD CREEK DR   22032
  Dr. Patricia Sisson, prin.
Wakefield Forest ES, 4011 IVA LN   22032
  Regenia Dalton, prin.
Westmore ES, 11000 BERRY ST   22030
  Ken Buterbaugh, prin.

Other Schools — See Alexandria, Annandale, Burke,
  Centreville, Chantilly, Clifton, Fairfax Station, Falls
  Church, Fort Belvoir, Great Falls, Herndon, Lorton,
  Mc Lean, Oakton, Reston, Springfield, Vienna

St. Leo School, 3704 OLD LEE HWY   22030

Fairfax Station, Fairfax Co.
Fairfax County SD
Supt. — See Fairfax
Silverbrook ES, 9350 CROSSPOINTE DR   22039
  S. McCall, prin.
Fairview ES, 5815 OX RD   22039
  James Walters, prin.

Fairfield, Rockbridge Co.
Rockbridge County SD
Supt. — See Lexington
ES, P O BOX 162   24435 — Harry Stone, prin.

Falls Church, (Indep. City), Pop. Code 6
Fairfax County SD
Supt. — See Fairfax
Jackson MS, 3020 GALLOWS ROAD   22042
  Leslie Kent, prin.
Longfellow MS
  2000 WESTMORELAND ST   22043
  Maurice Burnsworth, prin.
Baileys ES, 6111 KNOLLWOOD DR   22041
  Dr. Gloria McDonell, prin.
Beech Tree ES, 3401 BEECHTREE LN   22042
  Carol Bradley, prin.
Belvedere ES, 6540 COLUMBIA PIKE   22041
  Sheila Bender, prin.
Glen Forest ES, 5829 GLEN FOREST DR   22041
  Judy Estep, prin.
Graham Road ES, 3036 GRAHAM RD   22042
  Alan Manor, prin.
Haycock ES, 6616 HAYCOCK RD   22043
  Courtney Pelley, prin.
Lemon Road ES, 7230 IDYLWOOD RD   22043
  E. Burchett, prin.
Pine Spring ES, 7607 WILLOW LN   22042
  Suzanne Walters, prin.
Shrevewood ES, 7525 SHREVE RD   22043
  Veronica Minor, prin.
Sleepy Hollow ES
  3333 SLEEPY HOLLOW RD   22044
  Ercell Binns, prin.
Timber Lane ES, 2737 WEST ST   22046
  Dr. Cosimo Renzi, prin.
Westgate ES, 7500 MAGARITY RD   22043
  John Russ, prin.
Westlawn ES, 3200 WESTLEY RD   22042
  Lynn Stanleigh, prin.
Woodburn ES, 3401 HEMLOCK DR   22042
  Margaret Keel, prin.

Falls Church CSD
Sch. Sys. Enr. Code 4
Supt. — Dr. Warren Pace
  210 E BROAD ST #100   22046
Jefferson ES, 601 S OAK ST   22046
  William Thomas, prin.

St. Anthony School
  3301 GLEN CARLYN RD   22041
St. James School, W BROAD & SPRING STS   22046
St. Philip School, 7506 SAINT PHILIPS CT   22042

Falls Mills, Tazewell Co.
Tazewell County SD
Supt. — See Tazewell
ES   24613 — Deaton Jones, prin.

Falmouth, Stafford Co.
Stafford County SD
Supt. — See Stafford
Drew MS, 725 CAMBRIDGE ST   22405
  Donald Dixon, prin.
Gayle MS, 610 GAYLE ST   22405
  David Ward, prin.
ES, 1000 FORBES ST   22405 — W. Burke, prin.

Fancy Gap, Carroll Co.
Carroll County SD
Supt. — See Hillsville
ES, RURAL ROUTE 01   24328 — Robert Utz, prin.

Farmville, Prince Edward Co., Pop. Code 6
Prince Edward County SD
Sch. Sys. Enr. Code 4
Supt. — Dr. J. Anderson
  RURAL ROUTE 04 BOX 370   23901
Prince Edward PS
  RURAL ROUTE 05 BOX 680   23901
  Nancy Iverson, prin.
Prince Edward MS
  RURAL ROUTE 05 BOX 680   23901
  Maurice Finney, prin.

Prince Edward Academy, P O BOX 328   23901

Ferrum, Franklin Co., Pop. Code 2
Franklin County SD
Supt. — See Rocky Mount
ES, RURAL ROUTE 03 BOX 317   24088
  Larry Meadors, prin.

Fieldale, Henry Co., Pop. Code 4
Henry County SD
Supt. — See Collinsville
Carver MS, P O BOX 837   24089 — Linda Dorr, prin.
ES, P O BOX 68   24089 — Aubrey Price, prin.

Fincastle, Botetourt Co., Pop. Code 2
Botetourt County SD
Sch. Sys. Enr. Code 5
Supt. – Dr. Clarence McClure, P O BOX 309 24090
Botetourt MS, RURAL ROUTE 02 BOX 41 24090
John Jenkins, prin.
Breckinridge ES, P O BOX 175 24090
Weldon Martin, prin.
Other Schools – See Blue Ridge, Buchanan,
Cloverdale, Eagle Rock, Troutville

Fishersville, Augusta Co., Pop. Code 3
Augusta County SD
Sch. Sys. Enr. Code 6
Supt. – Edward Clymore
RURAL ROUTE 01 BOX 252 22939
Wilson ES, RURAL ROUTE 01 BOX 251 22939
Albert Costa, prin.
Other Schools – See Churchville, Craigsville,
Deerfield, Fort Defiance, Mount Solon, New Hope,
Staunton, Stuarts Draft, Verona, Waynesboro,
Weyers Cave

Floyd, Floyd Co., Pop. Code 2
Floyd County SD
Sch. Sys. Enr. Code 4
Supt. – Omar Ross
RURAL ROUTE 01 BOX 4-A 24091
ES, RURAL ROUTE 01 24091
Randy Gallimore, prin.
Other Schools – See Check, Radford, Willis

Forest, Bedford Co., Pop. Code 2
Bedford County SD
Supt. – See Bedford
ES, RURAL ROUTE 02 24551 – Emily Helms, prin.
New London Academy ES
RURAL ROUTE 01 24551 – Jack West, prin.

Fork Union, Fluvanna Co., Pop. Code 5
Fluvanna County SD
Supt. – See Palmyra
ES, RURAL ROUTE 01 BOX 64-A 23055
D. Watson, prin.

Fort Belvoir, Fairfax Co.
Fairfax County SD
Supt. – See Fairfax
Barden ES, 1017 BELVOIR RD 22060
Virlinda Snyder, prin.
Cheney ES, 1741 MEERES RD 22060
Charles Gray, prin.
Markham ES, 950 BARLOW RD 22060
Dr. Robert Sisson,Jr., prin.

Fort Blackmore, Stokes Co.
Scott County SD
Supt. – See Gate City
ES, RURAL ROUTE 01 24250
Mescal Baker, prin.

Fort Defiance, Augusta Co., Pop. Code 1
Augusta County SD
Supt. – See Fishersville
Stewart MS, P O BOX 37 24437
Glen Patterson, prin.

Franklin, (Indep. City), Pop. Code 6
Franklin CSD
Sch. Sys. Enr. Code 4
Supt. – Dr. Alfred Butler IV
800 W 2ND AVE 23851
King ES, 507 1/2 3RD AVE W 23851
Donald Spengeman, prin.
Morton MS, MORTON ST 23851
Pauline Gotham, prin.

Southampton County SD
Supt. – See Courtland
Hunterdale ES, 825 HUNTERDALE RD 23851
William Pruett, prin.

Fredericksburg, (Indep. City), Pop. Code 7
Fredericksburg CSD
Sch. Sys. Enr. Code 4
Supt. – J. Garnett, 817 PRINCESS ANNE ST 22401
Walker-Grant MS, GUNNERY ROAD 22401
Richard Griffin, prin.
Mercer ES, 2100 COWAN BLVD 22401
Susan Regan, prin.

Spotsylvania County SD
Supt. – See Spotsylvania
Battlefield MS, 4078 LEAVELLS ROAD 22401
Dwight Frazier,Jr., prin.
Battlefield ES, 11108 LEAVELLS RD 22401
B. Marcus, prin.
Chancellor ES, 5995 PLANK RD 22401
Thelma Forbes, prin.
Lee Hill ES, RURAL ROUTE 03 BOX 581 22401
Michael Cotter, prin.
Salem ES, 4501 JACKSON RD 22401
Fred Wells,Jr., prin.
Spotswood ES, 400 LORRAINE AVE 22401
Constance Braxton, prin.

Stafford County SD
Supt. – See Stafford
Ferry Farm ES, 20 PENDLETON RD 22405
William Kennedy, prin.
Grafton Village ES
RURAL ROUTE 07 BOX 990 22405
Randall Washburn, prin.

Montfort Academy School
700 SUNKEN RD 22401

Fries, Grayson Co., Pop. Code 3
Carroll County SD
Supt. – See Hillsville
Vaughn ES, P O BOX 328 24330
H. Robert Leonard, prin.

Grayson County SD
Supt. – See Independence
Providence ES, RURAL ROUTE 02 BOX 85 24330
Reginald Gardner, prin.

Front Royal, Warren Co., Pop. Code 7
Warren County SD
Sch. Sys. Enr. Code 5
Supt. – Dr. James Cook
111 E CRISER ROAD 22630
Warren MS, W 15TH ST 22630
Dr. John Blanton, prin.
Jeffries ES, CRISER ROAD 22630
D. Mishler, prin.
Keyser ES, 1015 E STONEWALL DR 22630
Michael Kitts, prin.
Morrison ES, 40 CRESCENT ST 22630
Anne Sager, prin.
Rhodes ES, 224 W STRASBURG ROAD 22630
Margaret Holmes, prin.

Fulks Run, Rockingham Co.
Rockingham County SD
Supt. – See Harrisonburg
ES, P O BOX 609 22830 – Edward Powell, prin.

Gainesville, Prince William Co., Pop. Code 3
Prince William County SD
Supt. – See Manassas
Tyler ES, 14500 JOHN MARSHALL HWY 22065
Robert Rowell, prin.

Galax, (Indep. City), Pop. Code 6
Carroll County SD
Supt. – See Hillsville
Gladeville ES, RURAL ROUTE 04 24333
James Jessee, prin.
Oakland ES, RURAL ROUTE 03 24333
Edward May, prin.

Galax CSD
Sch. Sys. Enr. Code 4
Supt. – Dr. Jeanne Kent, 223 LONG ST 24333
ES, 300 JEFFERSON ST S 24333
Mary Coulson, prin.

Grayson County SD
Supt. – See Independence
Baywood ES, RURAL ROUTE 01 24333
J. C. Roudebush III, prin.
Fairview ES, RURAL ROUTE 02 BOX 129 24333
John Nichols, prin.

Gate City, Scott Co., Pop. Code 4
Scott County SD
Sch. Sys. Enr. Code 5
Supt. – Fred Fugate, 261 E JACKSON ST 24251
Shoemaker ES, 125 SHOEMAKER DR 24251
E. Rhoton, prin.
Yuma ES, RURAL ROUTE 03 24251
Darryl Johnson, prin.
Other Schools – See Clinchport, Duffield,
Dungannon, Fort Blackmore, Hiltons, Nickelsville,
Weber City

Gladehill, Franklin Co.
Franklin County SD
Supt. – See Rocky Mount
ES, P O BOX 96 24092 – Gary Hunt, prin.

Glade Spring, Washington Co., Pop. Code 4
Washington County SD
Supt. – See Abingdon
ES, P O BOX 1023 24340
Richard Buchanan, prin.

Gladys, Campbell Co.
Campbell County SD
Supt. – See Rustburg
ES 24554 – P. Hamilton, prin.

Glen Allen, Henrico Co.
Henrico County SD
Supt. – See Highland Springs
ES, 11101 MILL RD 23060
Dr. Robert Siegel, prin.
Longdale ES, 1351 COLE BLVD 23060
Judith Johnston, prin.

Gloucester, Gloucester Co., Pop. Code 5
Gloucester County SD
Sch. Sys. Enr. Code 6
Supt. – Robert Mitchell, P O BOX 770 23061
MS, RURAL ROUTE 04 23061 – Daniel Fary, prin.
Botetourt ES, RURAL ROUTE 05 BOX 242 23061
Bernard Robins, prin.
Petsworth ES, RURAL ROUTE 02 BOX 525 23061
John Briggs, prin.
Walker ES, RURAL ROUTE 04 BOX 540 23061
James Diggs, prin.
Other Schools – See Hayes, Wicomico

Goochland, Goochland Co., Pop. Code 2
Goochland County SD
Sch. Sys. Enr. Code 4
Supt. – Charles Nunley, P O BOX 169 23063
MS, RURAL ROUTE 02 BOX 275 23063
William Fenn, prin.
Byrd ES, 2704 HADENSVILLE FIFE RD 23063
Betty Wolfrey, prin.

ES, 3150 RIVER RD W 23063
Barbara Brown, prin.
Other Schools – See Crozier

Goode, Bedford Co.
Bedford County SD
Supt. – See Bedford
Otter River ES, RURAL ROUTE 01 24556
Bruce Shafferman, prin.

Goodview, Bedford Co.
Bedford County SD
Supt. – See Bedford
Stewartsville ES 24095 – Faye Craghead, prin.

Gordonsville, Orange Co., Pop. Code 4
Orange County SD
Supt. – See Orange
Barbour ES 22942 – Charles Higgins, prin.

Grafton, York Co.
York County SD
Sch. Sys. Enr. Code 6
Supt. – Dr. Judith Ball, 302 DARE ROAD 23692
Dare ES, 230 DARE RD 23692
Dell Stinnette, prin.
Grafton Bethel ES, 410 LAKESIDE DR 23692
Fay Clark, prin.
Other Schools – See Hampton, Langley A F B,
Seaford, Tabb, Williamsburg, Yorktown

Great Falls, Fairfax Co.
Fairfax County SD
Supt. – See Fairfax
Forrestville ES
1085 UTTERBACK STORE RD 22066
Carole Taylor, prin.
ES, 701 WALKER RD 22066 – Jina Ross, prin.

Gretna, Pittsylvania Co., Pop. Code 4
Pittsylvania County SD
Supt. – See Chatham
MS, P O BOX 308 24557 – Paul Martin, prin.
ES, P O BOX 595 24557 – Robert Hedrick, prin.
Mt. Airy ES, RURAL ROUTE 02 BOX 248 24557
Raymond Ramsey, prin.

Grottoes, Augusta Co., Pop. Code 4
Rockingham County SD
Supt. – See Harrisonburg
ES 24441 – Gary Shell, prin.

Grundy, Buchanan Co., Pop. Code 4
Buchanan County SD
Sch. Sys. Enr. Code 6
Supt. – Paul Hatfield, P O BOX 833 24614
Bevins ES, STAR ROUTE BOX 8-B 24614
Robert Branham, prin.
Dennis ES, RURAL ROUTE 04 BOX 358-H 24614
William Parish III, prin.
Harman ES, RURAL ROUTE 02 BOX 351 24614
Gerald Arrington, prin.
Vansant ES, RURAL ROUTE 04 BOX 218 24614
Leroy Jones, prin.
Other Schools – See Big Rock, Davenport, Hurley,
Oakwood, Vansant, Whitewood

Hague, Westmoreland Co.
Westmoreland County SD
Supt. – See Montross
Cople ES 22469 – Ellen McKenney, prin.

Halifax, Halifax Co., Pop. Code 3
Halifax County SD
Sch. Sys. Enr. Code 6
Supt. – Dr. Paul Jones, P O BOX 805 24558
ES, RURAL ROUTE 01 BOX 838 24558
Harold McAdams, prin.
Sinai ES, RURAL ROUTE 01 BOX 674-A 24558
Michael Wilborne, prin.
Other Schools – See Clover, Cluster Springs, Nathalie,
Scottsburg, South Boston, Turbeville, Vernon Hill,
Virgilina

South Boston SD
Sch. Sys. Enr. Code 3
Supt. – Dr. Paul Jones, P O BOX 805 24558
Other Schools – See South Boston

Hamilton, Loudoun Co., Pop. Code 3
Loudoun County SD
Supt. – See Leesburg
ES, 54 S KERR ST 22068 – Nancy McManus, prin.

Hampton, (Indep. City), Pop. Code 9
Hampton CSD
Sch. Sys. Enr. Code 7
Supt. – Dr. Don Musselman
1819 NICKERSON BLVD 23663
Davis MS, 1435 TODDS LANE 23666
William Pearson, prin.
Eaton MS, 2108 CUNNINGHAM DRIVE 23666
Bertram Sexton, prin.
Lindsay MS, 2636 BRIARFIELD ROAD 23661
Ashby Williams, prin.
Spratley MS, 339 WOODLAND ROAD 23669
Cornelius Sherman, prin.
Syms MS, 170 FOX HILL ROAD 23669
Arnetta Washington, prin.
Aberdeen ES, 1424 ABERDEEN RD 23666
Joseph Ramsey, prin.
Armstrong ES, 3401 MATOAKA RD 23661
Dr. Betty Peters, prin.
Asbury ES, 140 BEACH RD 23664
Joseph Tatum, prin.
Barron ES, 45 FOX HILL RD 23669
Michael Anastasio, prin.

Bassette ES, 671 BELL ST 23661
Deborah Jackson, prin.
Booker ES, 160 APOLLO DR 23669
Douglas Brown, prin.
Bryan ES, 1021 N MALLORY ST 23663
Eunice Frazier, prin.
Burbank ES, 40 TIDEMILL LN 23666
Mary Yarborough, prin.
Cary ES, 2009 ANDREWS BLVD 23663
Elva Riddick, prin.
Cooper ES, 200 MARCELLA RD 23666
Patricia Johnson, prin.
Forrest ES, 1406 TODDS LN 23666
Richard Byrd, prin.
Kraft ES, 600 CONCORD DR 23666
John Lockett, Jr., prin.
Langley ES, 16 ROCKWELL RD 23669
Girard Chambers III, prin.
Lee ES, 1646 BRIARFIELD RD 23669
Paul Fleming, prin.
Machen ES, 20 SACRAMENTO DR 23666
James Graham, prin.
Mallory ES, 331 BIG BETHEL RD 23666
James Newman, prin.
Merrimack ES, 2113 WOODMANSEE DR 23663
Arnold Baker, prin.
Moton MS, 339 OLD BUCKROE RD 23663
Clark Eversole, prin.
Phillips ES, 703 LEMASTER AVE 23669
Brenda Hitt, prin.
Smith ES, 379 WOODLAND RD 23669
Effie Lawson, prin.
Tarrant ES, 1589 WINGFIELD DR 23666
Ira Luck, prin.
Tucker-Capps ES, 113 WELLINGTON DR 23666
Jacqueline Spangler, prin.
Tyler ES, 57 SALINA ST 23669
Donald Williams, prin.
Wythe ES, 200 CLAREMONT AVE 23661
Leonard Singleton, prin.

York County SD
Supt. – See Grafton
Tabb ES, 3710 BIG BETHEL RD 23666
B. Helms, prin.

St. Mary Star of the Sea School
14 N WILLARD AVE 23663

Harrisonburg, (Indep. City), Pop. Code 7
Harrisonburg CSD
Sch. Sys. Enr. Code 5
Supt. – C. Alan Hiner, 317 S MAIN ST 22801
Harrison MS, 395 S HIGH ST 22801
Dr. Barry Raebeck, prin.
Keister ES, 100 MARYLAND AVE 22801
Bruce Hamilton, prin.
Spotswood ES, 400 MOUNTAIN VIEW DR 22801
Sheryl Wyse, prin.
Waterman ES, 451 CHICAGO AVE 22801
James Snyder, prin.

Rockingham County SD
Sch. Sys. Enr. Code 6
Supt. – Dr. David Andes
304 CO OFC BLDG 22801
Mt. Clinton ES, RURAL ROUTE 04 BOX 94 22801
B. Emswiler, prin.
Pleasant Valley ES
215 PLEASANT VALLEY RD 22801
Gar Miley, prin.
Other Schools – See Bergton, Bridgewater, Broadway,
Dayton, Elkton, Fulks Run, Grottoes, Keezletown,
Linville, Mc Gaheysville, Penn Laird, Port
Republic, Timberville

Hartwood, Stafford Co.
Stafford County SD
Supt. – See Stafford
ES, RURAL ROUTE 02 BOX 475 22471
Catherine Walker, prin.

Hayes, Gloucester Co.
Gloucester County SD
Supt. – See Gloucester
Achilles ES, RURAL ROUTE 02 BOX 95 23072
Steven Frey, prin.

Haymarket, Prince William Co., Pop. Code 2
Prince William County SD
Supt. – See Manassas
Gainesville MS
14550 JOHN MARSHALL HWY 22069
Barry Rosenberg, prin.

Heathsville, Northumberland Co., Pop. Code 4
Northumberland County SD
Sch. Sys. Enr. Code 4
Supt. – J. Larry Hoover, P O BOX 258 22473
Northumberland MS, P O BOX 108 22473
D. Clint Stables, prin.
Other Schools – See Callao, Reedville

Henry, Franklin Co.
Franklin County SD
Supt. – See Rocky Mount
ES, RURAL ROUTE 01 24102
James Pearson, prin.

Herndon, Fairfax Co., Pop. Code 7
Fairfax County SD
Supt. – See Fairfax
Crossfield ES, 2791 FOX MILL RD 22071
Nathan Emery, prin.

Dranesville ES
1515 POWELL TAVERN PLACE 22070
Gioia Forman, prin.
MS, 901 LOCUST ST 22070 – Dale Sander, prin.
Clearview ES, 12635 BUILDERS RD 22070
Dr. Bernard Gross, prin.
Floris ES, 2708 CENTREVILLE RD 22071
Marcia Sweedler, prin.
Fox Mill ES, 2601 VIKING DR 22071
Bette Schwarzman, prin.
ES, 630 DRANESVILLE RD 22070
Wayne Chester, prin.
Hutchison ES, 13209 PARCHER AVE 22070
Frank Mehm, prin.
Oak Hill ES, 3210 KINROSS CIR 22071
Carolyn Boxley, prin.

St. Joseph School, 750 PEACHTREE ST 22070

Highland Springs, Henrico Co., Pop. Code 6
Henrico County SD
Sch. Sys. Enr. Code 8
Supt. – Dr. William Bosher, P O BOX 40 23075
Fair Oaks ES, 201 HENNINGS ROAD 23075
Rebecca Grant, prin.
ES, 600 PLEASANT ST 23075
Betty Wiedemann, prin.
Other Schools – See Glen Allen, Richmond, Sandston

Hillsboro, Loudoun Co., Pop. Code 1
Loudoun County SD
Supt. – See Leesburg
ES, P O BOX 86 22132 – Kenny Vance, prin.

Hillsville, Carroll Co., Pop. Code 4
Carroll County SD
Sch. Sys. Enr. Code 5
Supt. – Dr. R. Phillips, P O BOX 1328 24343
Gladesboro ES, RURAL ROUTE 02 24343
Charles Childress, prin.
ES, P O BOX 38 24343 – Joe Bunn, prin.
Sylvatus ES, RURAL ROUTE 04 24343
Ralph Martin, Jr., prin.
Other Schools – See Austinville, Cana, Dugspur,
Fancy Gap, Fries, Galax, Lambsburg, Laurel Fork,
Woodlawn

Hiltons, Scott Co.
Scott County SD
Supt. – See Gate City
Hilton ES, P O BOX 56 24258 – Marie Miller, prin.

Hiwassee, Pulaski Co.
Pulaski County SD
Supt. – See Pulaski
Snowville ES, RURAL ROUTE 01 BOX 186 24347
Judith Barr, prin.

Honaker, Russell Co., Pop. Code 4
Russell County SD
Supt. – See Lebanon
ES, P O BOX 744 24260 – B. Sample, prin.

Hopewell, (Indep. City), Pop. Code 7
Hopewell CSD
Sch. Sys. Enr. Code 5
Supt. – Dr. Steven Ballowe, P O BOX 270 23860
Woodson MS
1000 WINSTON CHURCHILL DR 23860
J. P. Tiller, prin.
Copeland ES, 205 APPOMATTOX ST 23860
Janet Covington, prin.
Dupont ES, 300 S 18TH AVE 23860
Susan Jones, prin.
James ES, 2700 COURT HOUSE RD 23860
Yvonne Jones, prin.
Woodlawn ES, 1100 DINWIDDIE AVE 23860
Larry Landes, prin.

St. James School, 105 N 6TH AVE 23860

Hot Springs, Bath Co., Pop. Code 3
Alleghany Highlands SD
Supt. – See Covington
Falling Spring ES, RURAL ROUTE 02 24445
Charles Patton, prin.

Bath County SD
Supt. – See Warm Springs
Valley ES, RURAL ROUTE 02 BOX 84 24445
James Stephenson, prin.

Huddleston, Bedford Co.
Bedford County SD
Supt. – See Bedford
ES, RURAL ROUTE 01 24104 – Aaron Dixon, prin.

Hurley, Buchanan Co.
Buchanan County SD
Supt. – See Grundy
MS, RURAL ROUTE 01 BOX 111 24620
Marvin Lewis, prin.
Justus ES, RURAL ROUTE 01 BOX 15 24620
Roger Dotson, prin.

Hurt, Pittsylvania Co., Pop. Code 4
Pittsylvania SD
Supt. – See Chatham
ES, 315 PROSPECT RD 24563 – G. Jefferson, prin.

Independence, Grayson Co., Pop. Code 4
Grayson County SD
Sch. Sys. Enr. Code 4
Supt. – Dr. Sidney Harvey, P O BOX 219 24348
Bridle Creek ES, RURAL ROUTE 03 24348
Ira Gentry, Jr., prin.
ES, P O BOX A 24348 – Robert Statzer, prin.

Other Schools – See Elk Creek, Fries, Galax, Trout
Dale, Whitetop

Isle of Wight, Isle of Wight Co.
Isle of Wight County SD
Sch. Sys. Enr. Code 5
Supt. – Dr. Vito Morlino, P O BOX 78 23397
Other Schools – See Carrsville, Smithfield, Windsor

Isle of Wight Academy, P O BOX 105 23397

Ivor, Southampton Co., Pop. Code 2
Southhampton County SD
Supt. – See Courtland
ES, P O BOX 169 23866 – Louis Clayton, prin.

Jarratt, Sussex Co., Pop. Code 3
Sussex County SD
Supt. – See Sussex
Jefferson ES 23867 – J. Kimberlin, prin.

Jewell Ridge, Buchanon Co., Pop. Code 3
Tazewell County SD
Supt. – See Tazewell
ES 24622 – William Rhodes, prin.

Jonesville, Lee Co., Pop. Code 3
Lee County SD
Sch. Sys. Enr. Code 5
Supt. – Jerry Bishop, P O BOX 710 24263
Flatwoods S, RURAL ROUTE 02 24263
James Rosenbaum, prin.
ES, P O BOX 734 24263 – Earl Sumpter, prin.
Other Schools – See Dryden, Duffield, Ewing, Keokee,
Pennington Gap, Rose Hill, Saint Charles

Keezletown, Rockingham Co.
Rockingham County SD
Supt. – See Harrisonburg
ES 22832 – Garry Rupert, prin.

Kenbridge, Lunenburg Co., Pop. Code 4
Lunenburg County SD
Supt. – See Victoria
MS 23944 – W. Seamster, prin.
PS 23944 – Rhoecus Cousins, prin.

Keokee, Lee Co., Pop. Code 2
Lee County SD
Supt. – See Jonesville
S, P O BOX 93 24265 – Omer Elkins, prin.

Keswick, Albermarle Co.
Albermarle County SD
Supt. – See Charlottesville
Stony Point ES
RURAL ROUTE 01 BOX 282-A 22947
Marion Henshaw, prin.

Keysville, Charlotte Co., Pop. Code 3
Charlotte County SD
Supt. – See Charlotte Court House
Eureka ES, RURAL ROUTE 01 BOX 289 23947
Steven Baker, prin.

Kilmarnock, Lancaster Co., Pop. Code 3
Lancaster County SD
Sch. Sys. Enr. Code 4
Supt. – Dr. William Chapman
P O BOX 2000 22482
Lancaster MS, SCHOOL & BRENT STS 22482
Randolph Latimore, prin.
Other Schools – See Lancaster

King & Queen Court House, King & Queen Co.
King & Queen County SD
Sch. Sys. Enr. Code 3
Supt. – Robert Deronda, P O BOX 97 23085
Other Schools – See Saint Stephen Church, Shanghai

King George, King George Co., Pop. Code 2
King George County SD
Sch. Sys. Enr. Code 4
Supt. – J. Dennis
RURAL ROUTE 01 BOX 513 22485
MS, 71 W DAHLGREN ROAD 22485
Patricia Barrett, prin.
ES, RURAL ROUTE 03 BOX 79 22485
George McCrum, prin.
Other Schools – See Dahlgren

King William, King William Co., Pop. Code 2
King William County SD
Sch. Sys. Enr. Code 4
Supt. – Dr. Nicholas Maschal, P O BOX 185 23086
Hamilton-Holmes ES 23086 – Evelyn Woods, prin.

West Point CSD
Sch. Sys. Enr. Code 2
Supt. – Dr. George Stainback, P O BOX 185 23086
Other Schools – See West Point

La Crosse, Mecklenburg Co., Pop. Code 3
Mecklenburg County SD
Supt. – See Boydton
ES, RURAL ROUTE 01 BOX 224 23950
Sherman Graham, prin.

Lambsburg, Carroll Co.
Carroll County SD
Supt. – See Hillsville
ES, RURAL ROUTE 01 24351 – Olen Webb, prin.

Lancaster, Lancaster Co.
Lancaster County SD
Supt. – See Kilmarnock
Lancaster PS, P O BOX 10 22503
Peter Olenick III, prin.

Langley A F B, Hampton Co.
York County SD
Supt. – See Grafton
Bethel Manor ES
FIRST AVENUE CAPEHART   23665
Sandros Ayscue,Jr., prin.

Laurel Fork, Carroll Co.
Carroll County SD
Supt. – See Hillsville
ES   24352 – Charles Childress, prin.

Lawrenceville, Brunswick Co., Pop. Code 4
Brunswick County SD
Sch. Sys. Enr. Code 5
Supt. – J. Grady Martin, P O BOX 309   23868
Powellton ES, RURAL ROUTE 02   23868
Carlton Clarke, prin.
Sturgeon ES, RURAL ROUTE 01 BOX 146-A   23868
John Hicks,Jr., prin.
Totaro ES, RURAL ROUTE 01 BOX 239A   23868
Esther Maclin, prin.
Other Schools – See Alberta

Brunswick Academy, HWY 606 N   23868

Lebanon, Russell Co., Pop. Code 5
Russell County SD
Sch. Sys. Enr. Code 6
Supt. – Larry Massie, P O BOX 8   24266
ES, P O BOX 668   24266 – Roger Taylor, prin.
MS, P O BOX 217   24266 – James Warner, prin.
Oak Grove ES, RURAL ROUTE 03 BOX 340   24266
Charles Puckett, prin.
Other Schools – See Castlewood, Cleveland, Dante,
Honaker, Rosedale, Swords Creek

Leesburg, Loudoun Co., Pop. Code 6
Loudoun County SD
Sch. Sys. Enr. Code 7
Supt. – David Thomas, 20 UNION ST NW   22075
Simpson MS, RURAL ROUTE 01 BOX 372   22075
Francis Fera, prin.
Catoctin ES, 311 CATOCTIN CIR SW   22075
Fred Drummond,Jr., prin.
ES, 323 PLAZA ST NE   22075
William Whitmore,Jr., prin.
Lucketts ES, RURAL ROUTE 04 BOX 584   22075
William Prokopchak, prin.
Other Schools – See Aldie, Arcola, Ashburn,
Hamilton, Hillsboro, Lincoln, Lovettsville,
Middleburg, Purcellville, Round Hill, Sterling,
Waterford

Loudoun Country Day School
237 FAIRVIEW ST NW   22075

Lexington, (Indep. City), Pop. Code 6
Lexington CSD
Sch. Sys. Enr. Code 2
Supt. – Dr. Elizabeth Morie
300A WHITE ST   24450
Lylburn-Downing MS, 300 DIAMOND ST   24450
Clyde Keen, prin.
Harrington-Waddell ES, PENDLETON PL   24450
Michael Rettig, prin.

Rockbridge County SD
Sch. Sys. Enr. Code 5
Supt. – Glen Stark
417 MORNINGSIDE DRIVE   24450
Highland Belle MS
RURAL ROUTE 01 BOX 229   24450
Roy Gray, prin.
Central ES, CENTRAL RD   24450
Alice Waddell, prin.
Effinger ES, RURAL ROUTE 02 BOX 352   24450
Sam Johnson, prin.
Other Schools – See Brownsburg, Buena Vista,
Fairfield, Natural Bridge Station

Lincoln, Loudoun Co.
Loudoun County SD
Supt. – See Leesburg
ES   22078 – Mary Brecht, prin.

Linville, Rockingham Co.
Rockingham County SD
Supt. – See Harrisonburg
Linville-Edom ES
RURAL ROUTE 01 BOX 37   22834
Dale Warner, prin.

Lorton, Fairfax Co.
Fairfax County SD
Supt. – See Fairfax
Gunston ES, 10100 GUNSTON RD   22079
Dr. Elizabeth Henderson, prin.

Louisa, Louisa Co., Pop. Code 3
Louisa County SD
Supt. – See Mineral
Jefferson ES, RURAL ROUTE 01 BOX 165   23093
Mary Clarke, prin.
Trevilians ES, RURAL ROUTE 03 BOX 2090   23093
Patricia Mahone, prin.

Lovettsville, Loudoun Co., Pop. Code 3
Loudoun County SD
Supt. – See Leesburg
ES, P O BOX 370   22080 – Ronald Dyer, prin.

Lovingston, Nelson Co., Pop. Code 5
Nelson County SD
Sch. Sys. Enr. Code 4
Supt. – R. Adams   22949
MS   22949 – Donald Farmer, prin.

Other Schools – See Afton, Arrington, Roseland,
Schuyler, Shipman

Lowmoor, Alleghany Co.
Alleghany Highlands SD
Supt. – See Covington
Central ES   24457 – Lorenza Carter III, prin.

Luray, Page Co., Pop. Code 5
Page County SD
Sch. Sys. Enr. Code 5
Supt. – James Campbell, 735 W MAIN ST   22835
ES, 555 FIRST ST   22835 – J. Cubbage,Jr., prin.
Other Schools – See Rileyville, Shenandoah, Stanley

Lynchburg, (Indep. City), Pop. Code 8
Bedford County SD
Supt. – See Bedford
Boonsboro ES, RURAL ROUTE 04   24503
Marlene Clark, prin.

Campbell County SD
Supt. – See Rustburg
Brookville MS, 1113 LAXTON ROAD   24502
Terry Hoggatt, prin.
Leesville Road ES, 861 LEESVILLE RD   24502
J. Lewis, prin.
Tomahawk ES, 8501 TIMBERLAKE RD   24502
Charles Booker, prin.

Lynchburg CSD
Sch. Sys. Enr. Code 6
Supt. – Dr. J. Spagnolo, P O BOX 1599   24505
Dunbar MS, POLK & 12TH STS   24504
Roger Roberts, prin.
Linkhorne MS, 2525 LINKHORNE DRIVE   24503
Donald Martin, prin.
Sandusky MS, 805 CHINOOK PLACE   24502
Gilliam Cobbs, prin.
Bass-Hutcherson ES, SEABURY AVE   24501
Nina Bibb, prin.
Bedford Hills ES, 1900 INDIAN HILL RD   24503
Reuben Womack, prin.
Heritage ES, 501 LEESVILLE RD   24502
Nancy Farley, prin.
Kizer-Dearington ES
401 MONTICELLO AVE   24501
Lois Booker, prin.
Linkhorne ES, 2501 LINKHORNE DR   24503
Merle Herndon, prin.
Munro ES, 4641 LOCKSVIEW RD   24503
Charles McClung, prin.
Payne ES, 12TH & FLOYD STS   24504
Jack St. Clair, prin.
Perrymont ES, 409 PERRYMONT AVE   24502
Consuella Woods, prin.
Sandusky ES, 5800 APACHE LN   24502
Fred Fauber, prin.
Sheffield ES, 1350 FENWICK DR   24502
Eveline Wood, prin.

Holy Cross School
2125 LANGHORNE ROAD   24501

Mc Gaheysville, Rockingham Co.
Rockingham County SD
Supt. – See Harrisonburg
ES, RURAL ROUTE 01 BOX 208   22840
W. Price, prin.

Machipongo, Northampton Co.
Northampton County SD
Supt. – See Eastville
Northampton MS   23405 – Calvin Brickhouse, prin.
MS   23405 – Jeanette Garner, prin.

Mc Kenney, Dinwiddie Co., Pop. Code 2
Dinwiddie County SD
Supt. – See Dinwiddie
Sunnyside McKenney ES, P O BOX 250   23872
Melvin Alsbrook, prin.

Mc Lean, Fairfax Co., Pop. Code 7
Fairfax County SD
Supt. – See Fairfax
Cooper MS, 977 BALLS HILL ROAD   22101
Susan Decorpo, prin.
Chesterbrook ES, 1753 KIRBY RD   22101
Helen Knoke, prin.
Churchill Road ES, 7100 CHURCHILL RD   22101
Susan Warner, prin.
Kent Gardens ES, 1717 MELBOURNE DR   22101
Dr. Robinetta Hooker, prin.
Sherman ES, 6630 BRAWNER ST   22101
Marilyn Fawley, prin.
Spring Hill ES, 8201 LEWINSVILLE RD   22102
Elizabeth Keahey, prin.

Langley School, 1411 BALLS HILL RD   22101
Potomac School
1301 POTOMAC SCHOOL RD   22101
St. John School, 6422 LINWAY TER   22101
St. Luke School, 7005 GEORGETOWN PIKE   22101

Madison, Madison Co., Pop. Code 2
Madison County SD
Sch. Sys. Enr. Code 4
Supt. – C. Jack Harner, P O BOX 647   22727
Criglersville ES
RURAL ROUTE 02 BOX 300   22727
Zed French, prin.
MS   22727 – John Dwyer, prin.
PS   22727 – William Mitchell, prin.
Yowell MS   22727 – John Anderson, prin.

Madison Heights, Amherst Co., Pop. Code 5
Amherst County SD
Supt. – See Amherst
Amelon ES, 200 AMER CT   24572
Ralph Steele, prin.
Elon ES, RURAL ROUTE 01 BOX 282   24572
Bettie Douglas, prin.
James River ES, 529 COLONY RD   24572
Louise Faulconer, prin.
Seminole ES, 110 PHELPS RD   24572
Jane Andes, prin.

Manassas, (Indep. City), Pop. Code 7
Manassas CSD
Sch. Sys. Enr. Code 5
Supt. – Russell Thomas
9000 TUDOR LANE   22110
Dean MS, 9601 PRINCE WILLIAM ST   22110
Ann Yeck, prin.
Baldwin ES, 9705 MAIN ST   22110
Dr. Alice Howard, prin.
Carr Round ES, 10100 HASTINGS DR   22110
Hilda Boyd, prin.
Haydon ES, 9075 PARK AVE   22110
Robert Thomas, prin.
Weems ES, 8750 WEEMS RD   22110
Gloria Jackson, prin.

Manassas Park CSD
Supt. – See Manassas Park
Manassas Park ES, 101 TREMONT ST   22111
Joyia Raftelis, prin.

Prince William County SD
Sch. Sys. Enr. Code 8
Supt. – Dr. Edward Kelly, P O BOX 389   22110
Marsteller ES, 8730 SUDLEY ROAD   22110
James Addington, prin.
Parkside MS, 8602 MATHIS AVE   22111
Frederick Melnichek, prin.
Saunders MS, 13557 SPRIGGS RD   22111
Rick Fitzgerald, prin.
Stonewall MS, 10100 LOMOND DRIVE   22110
Allan Nixon, prin.
Bennett ES, 9305 STONEWALL RD   22110
Graham Spencer, prin.
Coles ES, 7405 HOADLY RD   22111
Robert Blevins, prin.
Loch Lomond ES, 7900 AUGUSTA RD   22111
Matthew Brooks, prin.
Parkside ES, 8600 MATHIS AVE   22110
Ronald Despirito, prin.
Sinclair ES, 7801 GARNER DR   22110
Dr. Paul Banks, prin.
Sudley ES, 9744 COPELAND DR   22110
Dan Bennett, prin.
West Gate ES, 8031 URBANNA RD   22110
Dr. Richard Keeler, prin.
Yorkshire ES, 7610 OLD CENTREVILLE RD   22111
Otelia Frazier, prin.
Other Schools – See Dumfries, Gainesville,
Haymarket, Nokesville, Triangle, Woodbridge

All Saints Parochial School
9294 STONEWALL RD   22110

Manassas Park, (Indep. City), Pop. Code 6
Manassas Park CSD
Sch. Sys. Enr. Code 4
Supt. – Jim Stuart, 140-A KENT DRIVE   22111
JHS, 8200 EUCLID AVE   22111
William Minehart, prin.
Conner MS, 8230 CONNER DR   22111
Olrin Boone, prin.
Other Schools – See Manassas

Mappsville, Accomack Co.
Accomack County SD
Supt. – See Accomac
North Accomack ES   23407 – Mark Flynn, prin.

Marion, Smyth Co., Pop. Code 6
Smyth County SD
Sch. Sys. Enr. Code 6
Supt. – Marvin Winters, P O BOX 987   24354
MS, P O BOX 850   24354 – N. Lewis Clay, prin.
MS, 820 STAGE ST   24354
William Graybeal, prin.
PS, 1042 STAGE ST   24354 – David Helms, prin.
Other Schools – See Atkins, Chilhowie, Saltville,
Sugar Grove

Marshall, Fauquier Co., Pop. Code 3
Fauquier County SD
Supt. – See Warrenton
Coleman MS, P O BOX 68   22115
Emerson Smith,Jr., prin.
Northwestern ES
RURAL ROUTE 02 BOX 116   22115
Claude Thompson, prin.

Martinsville, (Indep. City), Pop. Code 7
Franklin County SD
Supt. – See Rocky Mount
Snow Creek ES, RURAL ROUTE 05   24112
Thomas Sawyers, prin.

Henry County SD
Supt. – See Collinsville
Leatherwood MS
RURAL ROUTE 01 BOX 409   24112
Charles Craddock, prin.
Figsboro ES, RURAL ROUTE 02 BOX 245   24112
Gary Joyce, prin.
Hairston ES, RURAL ROUTE 03 BOX 366   24112
James Napper, prin.

Mt. Olivet ES, RURAL ROUTE 01 BOX 601 24112
  Jean Philpotts, prin.
Rich Acres ES, RURAL ROUTE 06 BOX 181 24112
  Curtis Shelton, prin.

Martinsville CSD
Sch. Sys. Enr. Code 5
Supt. – Dr. James Calkins, P O BOX 5548 24115
MS, 30 CLEVELAND AVE 24112
  Gayle Keith, prin.
Clearview ES, 800 AINSLEY ST 24112
  Nancy Brammer, prin.
Druid Hills ES, 746 INDIAN TRL 24112
  Joan Montgomery, prin.
Harris MS, 710 SMITH RD 24112
  Willis Via, prin.
Henry ES, 1810 E CHURCH ST EXT 24112
  John Vartenisian, prin.

Carlisle School, P O BOX 5388 24115

Mathews, Mathews Co., Pop. Code 2
Mathews County SD
Sch. Sys. Enr. Code 4
Supt. – Harry Ward, P O BOX 368 23109
MS, P O BOX 339 23109 – Melvin Fry, prin.
Lee-Jackson ES, P O BOX 219 23109
  W. Wilburn, prin.

Matoaca, Chesterfield Co., Pop. Code 7
Chesterfield County SD
Supt. – See Chesterfield
MS, 20300 HALLOWAY AVE 23803
  Dr. John Baskerville, prin.
ES, 6627 E RIVER RD 23803
  Stephen Degaetani, prin.

Max Meadows, Wythe Co., Pop. Code 2
Wythe County SD
Supt. – See Wytheville
ES, P O BOX 216 24360 – Curtis Campbell, prin.

Meadows of Dan, Patrick Co.
Patrick County SD
Supt. – See Stuart
ES 24120 – Wendell Smith, prin.

Meadowview, Washington Co., Pop. Code 3
Washington County SD
Supt. – See Abingdon
ES, P O BOX 340 24361 – Thomas Merrihue, prin.
Rhae Valley ES, RURAL ROUTE 01 24361
  Charles Rector, prin.

Mechanicsville, Hanover Co., Pop. Code 6
Hanover County SD
Supt. – See Ashland
Battlefield Park ES
  RURAL ROUTE 12 BOX 242 23111
  Theresa Stimpson, prin.
Cold Harbor ES
  RURAL ROUTE 08 BOX 220 23111
  Joan Willis, prin.
Henry ES, 6138 MANN DR 23111
  Stephen Goldsmith, prin.
ES, 1403 ATLEE RD 23111 – Hugh Reese, prin.
Pearsons Corner ES, 2456 ASHCAKE RD 23111
  John Saunders,Jr., prin.
Rural Point ES
  RURAL ROUTE 07 BOX 23A 23111
  William Young IV, prin.

Melfa, Accomack Co., Pop. Code 2
Accomack County SD
Supt. – See Accomac
South Accomack ES
  RURAL ROUTE BOX 409 23410
  B. Krawchuk, prin.

Mendota, Washington Co.
Washington County SD
Supt. – See Abingdon
Hamilton ES, P O BOX 67 24270
  Richard Gardner, prin.

Middleburg, Loudoun Co., Pop. Code 3
Loudoun County SD
Supt. – See Leesburg
Banneker ES, RURAL ROUTE 01 BOX 225 22117
  Lillie Spriggs, prin.
ES, P O BOX 25 22117 – Mary Phelps, prin.

Hill School, P O BOX 65 22117

Midland, Fauquier Co.
Fauquier County SD
Supt. – See Warrenton
Southeastern ES
  RURAL ROUTE 01 BOX 153 22728 – J. Wine,
  prin.

Midlothian, Chesterfield Co., Pop. Code 8
Chesterfield County SD
Supt. – See Chesterfield
MS, 13501 MIDLOTHIAN TPKE 23113
  Larry Buchanan, prin.
Robious MS, 11632 ROBIOUS ROAD 23113
  William Gillespie, prin.
Swift Creek MS
  3700 OLD HUNDRED ROAD 23113
  Lois Graham, prin.
Clover Hill ES
  5700 WOODLAKE VILLAGE PKWY 23113
  Dolores Cale, prin.
Crenshaw ES
  11901 BAILEY BRIDGE ROAD 23113
  James Raines, prin.

Evergreen ES
  1701 EVERGREEN EAST PKY 23113
  Jean Ridgeway, prin.
Robious ES, 11630 ROBIOUS RD 23113
  Bernard Monroe, prin.
Swift Creek ES, 13800 GENITO RD 23112
  John Temple,Jr., prin.
Watkins ES, 501 COALFIELD RD 23113
  Shirley White, prin.

Millboro, Bath Co.
Bath County SD
Supt. – See Warm Springs
ES, P O BOX F 24460 – John Jenkins, prin.

Mineral, Louisa Co., Pop. Code 2
Louisa County SD
Sch. Sys. Enr. Code 5
Supt. – Dr. William Thomas, P O BOX 7 23117
Louisa MS, P O BOX 448 23117
  Lewis Stephens, prin.
Jouett ES, RURAL ROUTE 02 BOX 303 23117
  Judith Lewis, prin.
Other Schools – See Louisa

Moneta, Bedford Co.
Bedford County SD
Supt. – See Bedford
Staunton River Annex MS
  RURAL ROUTE 02 24121 – Paul Sherman, prin.
ES 24121 – Alton Vincent, prin.

Monroe, Amherst Co., Pop. Code 2
Amherst County SD
Supt. – See Amherst
Pleasant View ES, RURAL ROUTE 02 24574
  Howard Anderson, prin.

Monterey, Highland Co., Pop. Code 2
Highland County SD
Sch. Sys. Enr. Code 2
Supt. – Dr. Jack Gold, P O BOX 250 24465
Highland ES, P O BOX 310 24465
  Randolph Hooke, prin.

Montpelier, Hanover Co.
Hanover County SD
Supt. – See Ashland
South Anna ES
  RURAL ROUTE 02 BOX 186 23192
  Elwood Kelley, prin.

Montross, Westmoreland Co., Pop. Code 2
Westmoreland County SD
Sch. Sys. Enr. Code 4
Supt. – C. Pierce, P O BOX 406 22520
MS 22520 – John Brown, prin.
Other Schools – See Colonial Beach, Hague

Montvale, Bedford Co.
Bedford County SD
Supt. – See Bedford
ES 24122 – Ann Boothe, prin.

Moseley, Pohatan Co.
Chesterfield County SD
Supt. – See Chesterfield
Grange Hall ES, 19301 HULL ST RD 23120
  David McCrum, prin.

Mount Jackson, Shenandoah Co., Pop. Code 4
Shenandoah County SD
Supt. – See Woodstock
Ashby Lee ES, P O BOX 68 22842
  Jane Gaidos, prin.
Triplett MS, P O BOX 423 22842
  Esten Lambert, prin.

Mount Solon, Augusta Co.
Augusta County SD
Supt. – See Fishersville
North River ES
  RURAL ROUTE 01 BOX 180 22843
  Gerald Livick, prin.

Narrows, Giles Co., Pop. Code 5
Giles County SD
Supt. – See Pearisburg
ES, 501 WOLF ST W 24124 – Ronald Skeens, prin.

Naruna, Campbell Co., Pop. Code 2
Campbell County SD
Supt. – See Rustburg
Campbell MS 24576 – Linda Gray, prin.

Nathalie, Halifax Co.
Halifax County SD
Supt. – See Halifax
Jennings ES, RURAL ROUTE 01 BOX 591 24577
  James Wood, prin.
Meadville ES, RURAL ROUTE 01 BOX 262 24577
  Joseph Griles, prin.
Volens MS, RURAL ROUTE 03 BOX 57 24577
  Jackie Yesalavich, prin.

Natural Bridge Station, Rockbridge Co., Pop. Code 5
Rockbridge County SD
Supt. – See Lexington
Natural Bridge ES, P O BOX A 24579
  Eileen Head, prin.

New Canton, Buckingham Co.
Buckingham County SD
Supt. – See Buckingham
Gold Hill MS, RURAL ROUTE 01 23123
  Claiborne Johnson, prin.

New Castle, Craig Co., Pop. Code 2
Craig County SD
Sch. Sys. Enr. Code 3
Supt. – M. Helems, P O BOX 245 24127
McCleary ES, P O BOX 247 24127
  K. Smith, prin.

New Hope, Augusta Co.
Augusta County SD
Supt. – See Fishersville
ES, P O BOX 18 24469 – William Fauber, prin.

New Kent, New Kent Co.
New Kent County SD
Sch. Sys. Enr. Code 4
Supt. – B. Alexander, P O BOX 110 23124
New Kent County PS 23124
  Frederick Balmer,Jr., prin.
Other Schools – See Quinton

New Market, Shenandoah Co., Pop. Code 4
Shenandoah County SD
Supt. – See Woodstock
MS, 277 JOHN SEVIER ROAD 22844
  Gary Rutz, prin.

Newport News, (Indep. City), Pop. Code 9
Newport News CSD
Sch. Sys. Enr. Code 8
Supt. – Donald Bruno, P O BOX 6130 23606
Carver MS, 6160 JEFFERSON AVE 23605
  Jean Beckerdite, prin.
Dozier MS, 432 INDUSTRIAL PARK DRIVE 23602
  Dr. Guy Quesenberry, prin.
Hines MS, 6150 JEFFERSON AVE 23605
  Bob James, prin.
Huntington MS, 3401 ORCUTT AVE 23607
  Frederick Cheeks, prin.
Reservoir MS, 15638 WARWICK BLVD 23602
  William Birchette III, prin.
Briarfield ES, 5720 MARSHALL AVE 23605
  June Webb, prin.
Charles ES, 101 YOUNGS RD 23602
  Lucy Hancock, prin.
Dunbar-Erwin ES, 726 16TH ST 23607
  Henry Godfrey, prin.
Dutrow ES, 60 CURTIS TIGNOR RD 23602
  Henry Schwarting, prin.
Epes ES, 855 LUCAS CREEK RD 23602
  Leslie Stanley, prin.
Greenwood ES, 13460 WOODSIDE LN 23602
  Peter Bender, prin.
Hidenwood ES, 501 BLOUNT POINT RD 23606
  Ann Mouser, prin.
Hilton ES, 225 RIVER RD 23601
  Carolyn Felling, prin.
Jenkins ES, 80 MENCHVILLE RD 23602
  Mary Spells, prin.
Lee Hall ES, 17346 WARWICK BLVD 23603
  Louann McIntosh, prin.
Magruder ES, 1712 CHESTNUT AVE 23607
  Frances Graham, prin.
Marshall ES, 743 23RD ST 23607
  Marian Travis, prin.
McIntosh ES, 185 RICHNECK RD 23602
  Frederick Holcomb, prin.
Nelson ES, 826 MOYER RD 23602
  Lawrence Vaught,Jr., prin.
Newsome Park ES, 4200 MARSHALL AVE 23607
  Jean Beckerdite, prin.
Palmer ES, 675 OYSTER POINT RD 23602
  Michael Hickman, prin.
Richneck ES, 205 TYNER DR 23602
  Rebecca Luckett, prin.
Riverside ES, 1100 COUNTRY CLUB RD 23606
  Maedean Northam, prin.
Sanford ES, 480 COLONY RD 23602
  Margaret Huneycutt, prin.
Saunders ES, 853 HAPERSVILLE ROAD 23601
  Louise Wylie, prin.
Sedgefield ES, 804 MAIN ST 23605
  Patricia Yoder, prin.
South Morrison ES, 746 ADAMS DR 23601
  Dianne Suber, prin.
Washington ES, 3700 CHESTNUT AVE 23607
  Carol Lambiotte, prin.
Watkins ES, 21 BURNS DR 23601
  Tommy Willis, prin.
Yates ES, 73 MAXWELL LN 23606
  Donna Pultz, prin.

Our Lady of Mt. Carmel School
  52 HARPERSVILLE RD 23601

Nickelsville, Scott Co., Pop. Code 2
Scott County SD
Supt. – See Gate City
ES, P O BOX 136 24271 – Thomas Hillman, prin.

Nokesville, Prince William Co., Pop. Code 2
Prince William County SD
Supt. – See Manassas
ES, 12625 FITZWATER DR 22123
  Dr. Kenneth Pettit, prin.

Nora, Dickenson Co., Pop. Code 2
Dickenson County SD
Supt. – See Clintwood
Ervinton ES 24272 – Ruby Rasnick, prin.

Norfolk, (Indep. City), Pop. Code 10
Norfolk CSD
Sch. Sys. Enr. Code 8
Supt. – Dr. Gene Carter, P O BOX 1357 23501

Azalea MS
7721 AZALEA GARDENS ROAD 23518
Greta Gustavson, prin.
Blair MS, 730 SPOTSWOOD AVE 23517
Michael Caprio, prin.
Campostella MS
1106 CAMPOSTELLA ROAD 23523
Charles Corprew, prin.
Lake Taylor MS, 1380 KEMPSVILLE ROAD 23502
Joel Wagner, prin.
Northside MS, 8720 GRANBY ST 23503
Frank Steadman, prin.
Norview MS, 6325 SEWELLS PT ROAD 23513
Jack Leslie, prin.
Rosemont MS, 1401 AUBURN AVE 23513
James Jordan, prin.
Ruffner MS, 489 TIDEWATER DRIVE 23504
Robert Clark, prin.
Bay View ES, 1434 BAY VIEW BLVD 23503
Jean Farrow, prin.
Bowling Park ES
2861 E PRINCESS ANNE RD 23504
Herman Clark,Jr., prin.
Calcott ES, 137 WESTMONT AVE 23503
Watkins Davenport, prin.
Camp Allen ES, 501 C ST 23505
Delores Fitzgerald, prin.
Chesterfield Heights ES
2915 WESTMINSTER AVE 23504
Carolyn Umphlett, prin.
Coleman Place ES, 2450 RUSH ST 23513
John Harvey, prin.
Crossroads ES, 7920 TIDEWATER DR 23505
Barbara Leathers, prin.
Diggs Park ES, 1530 CYPRESS ST 23523
Delores Wilson, prin.
Fairlawn ES, 1132 WADE ST 23502
Mary Raiss, prin.
Ghent ES, 200 SHIRLEY AVE 23517
Dr. Julia Kidwell, prin.
Granby ES, 7101 NEWPORT AVE 23505
Joseph Thain, prin.
Ingleside ES, 976 INGLESIDE RD 23502
Dr. Bonita Bill, prin.
Jacox ES, 1300 MARSHALL AVE 23504
Mervin McCoy, prin.
Larchmont ES, 5210 HAMPTON BLVD 23508
Ed Hall, prin.
Larrymore ES, 7600 HALPRIN DR 23518
Peggie Robertson, prin.
Lindenwood ES, 2700 LUDLOW ST 23504
Mamie Ratliff, prin.
Little Creek MS, 7900 TARPON PL 23518
Robert Hahne, prin.
Little Creek PS, 7901 NANCY DR 23518
Helen Shropshire, prin.
Meadowbrook ES, 7620 SHIRLAND AVE 23505
Bernard Chapel, prin.
Monroe ES, 446 VIRGINIA AVE 23508
Dr. James Robinson, prin.
Norview ES, 6401 CHESAPEAKE BLVD 23513
Leon Bonds, prin.
Oakwood ES, 900 ASBURY AVE 23513
Janice Root, prin.
Ocean View ES, 9501 MASON CREEK RD 23503
Leverett Trump, prin.
Oceanair ES, 600 DUDLEY AVE 23503
John Saunders, prin.
Poplar Halls ES, 5523 PEBBLE LN 23502
Jean Alexander, prin.
Roberts Park ES
2600 E PRINCESS ANNE RD 23504
Belva Keeling, prin.
Sewells Point ES, 7928 HAMPTON BLVD 23505
Charles Stevenson, prin.
Sherwood Forest ES
3035 SHERWOOD FOREST LN 23513
N. Boothby,Jr., prin.
St. Helena ES, 903 S MAIN ST 23523
Carolyn Sands, prin.
Suburban Park ES, 310 THOLE ST 23505
Audrey Mills, prin.
Tarrallton ES, 2080 TARRALLTON DR 23518
Charles Clay, prin.
Taylor ES, 1129 W PRINCESS ANNE RD 23507
Martha Cannon, prin.
Tidewater Park ES
1045 E BRAMBLETON AVE 23504
Cheryl Bunch, prin.
Tucker ES, 2300 BERKLEY AVENUE EXT 23523
Clifford Copeland, prin.
Willard ES, 3425 TIDEWATER DR 23509
Lillian Brinkley, prin.
Willoughby ES, 9500 4TH VIEW ST 23503
William Jennings, prin.
Young Park ES, 543 E OLNEY RD 23510
Jennifer Blonts, prin.

Norfolk Academy, 1585 WESLEYAN DRIVE 23502
Norfolk Christian School, 255 THOLE ST 23505
Norfolk Collegiate School
7336 GRANBY ST 23505
Christ the King School
3401 TIDEWATER DR 23509
Ghent Montessori School
610 MOWBRAY ARCH 23507
Holy Trinity School
154 W GOVERNMENT AVE 23503
St. Mary Academy, 921 HOLT ST 23504
St. Pius X School, 7813 HALPRIN DR 23518
Trinity Lutheran School, 6001 GRANBY ST 23505

North Garden, Albermarle Co.
Albermarle County SD
Supt. – See Charlottesville
Red Hill ES, RURAL ROUTE 01 BOX 87 22959
Richard Spitler, prin.

North Tazewell, Tazewell Co.
Tazewell County SD
Supt. – See Tazewell
ES 24630 – Fred Dean, prin.
Springville ES, RURAL ROUTE 02 24630
Deaton Jones, prin.

Norton, (Indep. City), Pop. Code 5
Norton CSD
Sch. Sys. Enr. Code 3
Supt. – Albert Armentrout, P O BOX 498 24273
ES, 205 PARK AVE NE 24273
Albert Johnson, prin.

Nottoway, Nottoway Co., Pop. Code 2
Nottoway County SD
Sch. Sys. Enr. Code 4
Supt. – Howard Mustian,Jr. 23955
MS 23955 – Sherman Vaughn, prin.
Other Schools – See Blackstone, Burkeville, Crewe

Oakton, Fairfax Co.
Fairfax County SD
Supt. – See Fairfax
ES, 3000 CHAIN BRIDGE RD 22124
Fay Morrisson, prin.

Oakwood, Buchanan Co., Pop. Code 2
Buchanan County SD
Supt. – See Grundy
Garden ES 24631 – Richard Dailey, prin.
Garden MS 24631 – Clarence Brown, prin.

Orange, Orange Co., Pop. Code 5
Orange County SD
Sch. Sys. Enr. Code 5
Supt. – Dr. Renfro Manning, P O BOX 349 22960
Prospect Heights MS, 200 CAROLINE ST 22960
John Burks, prin.
ES, 230 MONTEVISTA AVE 22960
Thomas Short,Jr., prin.
Other Schools – See Gordonsville, Unionville

Grymes Memorial School, P O BOX 1160 22960

Painter, Accomack Co., Pop. Code 2
Accomack County SD
Supt. – See Accomac
Central MS 23420 – Lummie Smith, prin.

Palmyra, Fluvanna Co., Pop. Code 5
Fluvanna County SD
Sch. Sys. Enr. Code 4
Supt. – Wayne White, P O BOX 419 22963
Fluvanna MS
RURAL ROUTE 01 BOX 29-A 22963
Willa Powell, prin.
Central MS, RURAL ROUTE 01 BOX 29 22963
Emogene Johnson, prin.
Columbia ES, RURAL ROUTE 02 BOX 219 22963
D. Watson, prin.
Cunningham ES
RURAL ROUTE 02 BOX 137 22963
Dr. Hilda Pendergrass, prin.
ES, RURAL ROUTE 01 BOX 430 22963
Wayne Guenther, prin.
Other Schools – See Fork Union

Parksley, Accomack Co., Pop. Code 3
Accomack County SD
Supt. – See Accomac
MS 23421 – William Parker, prin.

Patrick Springs, Patrick Co.
Patrick County SD
Supt. – See Stuart
ES, RURAL ROUTE 01 BOX 10 24133
Ilene Pons, prin.

Pearisburg, Giles Co., Pop. Code 4
Giles County SD
Sch. Sys. Enr. Code 5
Supt. – Harold Absher
RURAL ROUTE 01 BOX 52 24134
Johnston MS, 1410 WENONAH AVE 24134
Armistead Booker, prin.
McClaugherty ES, 1001 HENSON AVE 24134
Curtis Coulson, prin.
Other Schools – See Narrows, Pembroke, Rich Creek

Pembroke, Giles Co., Pop. Code 4
Giles County SD
Supt. – See Pearisburg
Eastern ES, P O BOX 569 24136
James Wheeler,Jr., prin.

Pennington Gap, Lee Co., Pop. Code 4
Lee County SD
Supt. – See Jonesville
Elk Knob ES, RURAL ROUTE 02 BOX 193 24277
Glen Perkins, prin.
Pennington ES, 600 W MORGAN AVE 24277
Mark Carter, prin.

Penn Laird, Rockingham Co.
Rockingham County SD
Supt. – See Harrisonburg
Montevideo MS 22846 – Charles Rodeffer, prin.

Petersburg, (Indep. City), Pop. Code 8
Dinwiddie County SD
Supt. – See Dinwiddie

Rohoic ES, RURAL ROUTE 04 BOX 335 23803
Thomas Green, prin.

Petersburg CSD
Sch. Sys. Enr. Code 6
Supt. – Edwin Betts,Jr., 141 WYTHE ST E 23803
Peabody MS, 725 WESLEY ST 23803
Waide Robinson, prin.
Hill ES, TALLEY AVE 23803
Arlene Anderson, prin.
Lee ES, 51 GIBBONS AVE 23803
Gwendolyn Carter, prin.
Stuart ES, PLEASANTS LN 23803
Joan Walker, prin.
Virginia Avenue ES, 1000 DIAMOND ST 23803
Janet Mason, prin.
Walnut Hill ES, 300 S BOULEVARD 23805
Floyd Henderson, prin.
Westview ES, PATTERSON & CARVER STS 23803
Shirley Webb, prin.

St. Joseph ES, 123 FRANKLIN ST 23803

Phenix, Charlotte Co., Pop. Code 2
Charlotte County SD
Supt. – See Charlotte Court House
ES 23959 – Barbara Clark, prin.

Poquoson, (Indep. City), Pop. Code 6
Posquoson CSD
Sch. Sys. Enr. Code 4
Supt. – Dr. Raymond Vernall
P O BOX 2068 23662
JHS, 985 POQUOSON AVE 23662
Roger Tomlinson, prin.
ES, 1033 POQUOSON AVE 23662
Mary Weston, prin.

Port Republic, Rockingham Co.
Rockingham County SD
Supt. – See Harrisonburg
ES, P O BOX 50 24471 – Charles McDonald, prin.

Portsmouth, (Indep. City), Pop. Code 9
Portsmouth CSD
Sch. Sys. Enr. Code 7
Supt. – Dr. T. Cherry, P O BOX 988 23707
Churchland MS, 4051 RIVER SHORE ROAD 23703
Robert Little, prin.
Waters MS, 6700 ROOSEVELT BLVD 23701
Gerard Gavin, prin.
Brighton MS, 1101 JEFFERSON ST 23704
Charles Bowens III, prin.
Churchland Academy ES
4061 RIVERSHORE ROAD 23703
Bernard Mamlin, prin.
Churchland MS, 5601 MICHAEL LN 23703
Betty Bartlett, prin.
Churchland PS, 5700 HEDGEROW LN 23703
Patricia Holmes, prin.
Douglass Park ES
GRAND AND SHELBY STS 23701
Viola Morgan, prin.
Highland-Biltmore ES
10 INDEPENDENCE ST 23701
James Weaver, prin.
Hodges Manor MS, 1201 CHEROKEE RD 23701
Dr. Sheila Hill, prin.
Hunt MS, 1800 HIGH ST 23704
Kenneth Hopkins, prin.
Hurst ES, 18 DAHLGREN AVE 23702
William Wiseman, prin.
Lakeview ES, 1300 HORNE AVE 23701
Marlene Randall, prin.
Mapp MS, 21 ALDEN AVE 23702
Lindell Wallace, prin.
Olive Branch MS, 415 MIMOSA RD 23701
Margarette Bartlett, prin.
Park View ES, 1401 CRAWFORD PKY 23704
Vikki Maida, prin.
Port Norfolk ES, 3101 DETROIT ST 23707
Isaac Askew, prin.
Shea Terrace ES, 253 CONSTITUTION AVE 23704
William Slate, prin.
Simonsdale ES, 132 BYERS AVE 23701
Eunice Southall, prin.
Tyler ES, 3649 HARTFORD ST 23707
Gloria Gowings, prin.
Westhaven ES, 3700 CLIFFORD ST 23707
Dora Harris, prin.

Portsmouth Catholic School
2301 OREGON AVE 23701

Pound, Wise Co., Pop. Code 4
Wise County SD
Supt. – See Wise
Adams ES, P O BOX 767 24279 – Bob Varner, prin.

Powhatan, Powhatan Co., Pop. Code 2
Powhatan County SD
Sch. Sys. Enr. Code 4
Supt. – Maynard Bean
2320 SKAGGS ROAD 23139
Pocahontas MS
4290 ANDERSON HIGHWAY 23139
Richard Stewart, prin.
ES, 4111 OLD BUCKINGHAM RD 23139
Linda Poorbaugh, prin.

Prince George, Prince George Co.
Prince George County SD
Sch. Sys. Enr. Code 5
Supt. – Dr. James Rooks, P O BOX 8 23875
Beazley MS, 6700 COURTHOUSE RD 23875
Charles Saunders, prin.

North ES, 11100 OLD STAGE RD 23875
  Ralph Collins, prin.
Walton MS, 4101 COURTHOUSE RD 23875
  Thelma Face, prin.
Other Schools — See Carson, Disputanta

Providence Forge, New Kent Co.
Charles City County SD
Supt. — See Charles City
Charles City County PS
  RURAL ROUTE 01 BOX 209 23140
  Brenda Gore, prin.

Pulaski, Pulaski Co., Pop. Code 7
Pulaski County SD
Sch. Sys. Enr. Code 6
Supt. — K. Dobson, P O BOX 909 24301
MS, 500 PICO TERRACE 24301
  Harold Lambert, prin.
Claremont ES, BROWN RD 24301
  Joan Pearman, prin.
Critzer MS, RURAL ROUTE 02 BOX 37A 24301
  Dr. John Johnston, prin.
Jefferson ES, 85 1ST ST SW 24301
  Betty Plott, prin.
Northwood ES, 100 NORTHWOOD DR 24301
  Jeanne Whitman, prin.
Other Schools — See Draper, Dublin, Hiwassee,
  Radford

Purcellville, Loudoun Co., Pop. Code 4
Loudoun County SD
Supt. — See Leesburg
Blue Ridge MS, 551 E A ST 22132
  Joseph Mauck, prin.
Emerick ES, 440 S NURSERY AVE 22132
  Carol Thomson, prin.

Quinton, New Kent Co.
New Kent County SD
Supt. — See New Kent
New Kent County MS 23141
  Howard Ormond, prin.

Radford, (Indep. City), Pop. Code 7
Floyd County SD
Supt. — See Floyd
Indian Valley ES, STAR ROUTE 24141
  Bonnie Smith, prin.

Montgomery County SD
Supt. — See Christiansburg
Belview ES, RURAL ROUTE 04 BOX 229 24141
  Thomas Martin, prin.

Pulaski County SD
Supt. — See Pulaski
Riverlawn ES, RURAL ROUTE 04 BOX 381 24141
  E. Martin, prin.

Radford CSD
Sch. Sys. Enr. Code 4
Supt. — Dr. Michael Wright, P O BOX 3698 24143
Dalton MS, 109 DEHAVEN DRIVE 24141
  Robert Young, prin.
Belle Heth MS, 810 2ND AVE 24141
  R. Glass, prin.
McHarg ES, 1220 WADSWORTH ST 24141
  Dr. Betty Henry, prin.

Raven, Buchanan Co., Pop. Code 4
Tazewell County SD
Supt. — See Tazewell
ES 24639 — Jean Nicholson, prin.

Reedville, Northumberland Co., Pop. Code 2
Northumberland County SD
Supt. — See Heathsville
Fairfields ES, RURAL ROUTE 01 BOX 80 22539
  Faye Pittman, prin.

Remington, Culpeper Co.
Fauquier County SD
Supt. — See Warrenton
Pierce ES 22734 — Margaret Pierce, prin.

Reston, Fairfax Co., Pop. Code 6
Fairfax County SD
Supt. — See Fairfax
Hughes MS, 11401 RIDGE HTS ROAD 22091
  R. Edgar Thacker, prin.
Armstrong ES, 11900 LAKE NEWPORT RD 22094
  Dr. O. Chaplain, prin.
Dogwood ES, 12300 GLADE DR 22091
  Prentice Christian,Jr., prin.
Forest Edge ES, 1501 BECONTREE LN 22090
  William Stewart, prin.
Hunters Woods ES, 2401 COLTS NECK RD 22091
  Linda Goldberg, prin.
Lake Anne ES, 11510 N SHORE DR 22090
  Dr. Amanda Griggs, prin.
Sunrise Valley ES
  10824 CROSS SCHOOL RD 22091
  Dr. Maryann Chung, prin.
Terraset ES, 11411 RIDGE HEIGHTS RD 22091
  John Prohaska, prin.

Rich Creek, Giles Co., Pop. Code 3
Giles County SD
Supt. -- See Pearisburg
ES, P O BOX J 24147 — Armistead Booker, prin.

Richlands, Tazewell Co., Pop. Code 6
Tazewell County SD
Supt. — See Tazewell
MS, RT 460 24641 — Woodrow Mullins, prin.
ES 24641 — Claude Reedy,Jr., prin.

Richmond, (Indep. City), Pop. Code 9
Chesterfield County SD
Supt. — See Chesterfield
Falling Creek MS, 4724 HOPKINS ROAD 23234
  John Stith, prin.
Providence MS, 900 STARLIGHT LANE 23235
  William Morris, prin.
Salem Church MS
  9700 SALEM CHURCH ROAD 23237
  Edward Witthoefft, prin.
Bellwood ES, 9536 DAWNSHIRE RD 23237
  Kenneth Wynne, prin.
Bensley ES, 6600 STRATHMORE RD 23237
  Dr. Edith Seibel, prin.
Beulah ES, 4216 BEULAH RD 23237
  James Taylor, prin.
Crestwood ES, 7600 WHITTINGTON DR 23225
  Mary Slater, prin.
Davis ES, 415 S PROVIDENCE RD 23236
  Wayne Baker, prin.
Falling Creek ES, 4800 HOPKINS RD 23234
  Donald Bechtel, prin.
Gordon ES, 11701 GORDON SCHOOL RD 23236
  Charles Gurkin, prin.
Greenfield ES, 10751 SAVOY RD 23235
  C. Slonaker, prin.
Hening ES, 5230 CHICORA DR 23234
  Toy Dowdy, prin.
Hopkins Road ES, 6000 HOPKINS RD 23234
  Mildred Bell, prin.
Providence ES
  11001 W PROVIDENCE ROAD 23236
  Wes Hicks, prin.
Reams Road ES, 10141 REAMS RD 23236
  Dr. Irvin Williams, prin.
Salem Church ES
  9600 SALEM CHURCH RD 23237
  Eloise Huff, prin.

Henrico County SD
Supt. — See Highland Springs
Brookland MS, 9200 LYDELL DRIVE 23228
  Annette Monroe, prin.
Byrd MS, 9400 QUIOCCASIN ROAD 23233
  Dr. William Ware, prin.
Fairfield MS, 5121 STOP NINE MILE ROAD 23223
  Thomas Walls, prin.
Moody MS, 7800 WOODMAN ROAD 23228
  Geneva Webb, prin.
Rolfe MS, 7800 MESSER ROAD 23231
  Bernard Perkins III, prin.
Tuckahoe MS, 9000 THREE CHOPT ROAD 23229
  Dr. T. Anderson, prin.
Adams ES, 600 S LABURNUM AVE 23223
  Diane Halley, prin.
Baker ES, 6651 WILLSON RD 23231
  Diana Winston, prin.
Carver ES, 1801 LAUDERDALE DR 23233
  Susan Brown, prin.
Chamberlayne ES
  8200 SAINT CHARLES RD 23227
  William Lyon, prin.
Crestview ES, 1901 CHARLES ST 23226
  Eugene Keeton,Jr., prin.
Davis ES, 8801 NESSLEWOOD RD 23229
  Gary Blair, prin.
Dumbarton ES, 9000 HUNGARY RD 23228
  Barbara Childress, prin.
Gayton ES, 12481 CHURCH RD 23233
  Meredith Henry, prin.
Glen Lea ES, 3909 AUSTIN AVE 23222
  J. Traylor, prin.
Holladay ES, 7300 GALAXIE RD 23228
  Robin Priddy, prin.
Johnson ES, 5600 BETHLEHEM RD 23230
  Nancy Harris, prin.
Laburnum ES, 500 MERRIWEATHER AVE 23222
  Charlotte Melton, prin.
Lakeside ES, 6700 CEDAR CROFT ST 23228
  Faye Thompson, prin.
Longan ES, 9200 MAPLEVIEW AVE 23229
  D. Bradley, prin.
Maybeury ES, 901 MAYBEURY DR 23229
  Ronald Odom, prin.
Montrose ES, 4901 BRITTLES LN 23231
  Paxton Black, prin.
Pemberton ES, 1400 PEMBERTON RD 23233
  A. Hall,Jr., prin.
Pinchbeck ES, 1225 GASKINS RD N 23233
  Marie Hendricks, prin.
Ratcliffe ES, 2901 THALEN ST 23223
  Herbert Monroe, prin.
Ridge ES, 8910 THREE CHOPT RD 23229
  Robert Norris, prin.
Short Pump ES
  11401 OLD THREE CHOPT RD 23233
  Rachel Alley, prin.
Skipwith ES, 2401 SKIPWITH RD 23229
  Dr. David Moore, prin.
Three Chopt ES, 1600 SKIPWITH RD 23229
  Lucy Guy, prin.
Trevvett ES, 2300 TREVVETT DR 23228
  Harold Singleton,Jr., prin.
Tuckahoe ES, 701 FOREST AVE 23229
  Hobby Neale, prin.
Varina ES, 2551 NEW MARKET RD 23231
  Teresa Forrest, prin.

Richmond CSD
Sch. Sys. Enr. Code 8
Supt. — James Tyler, 301 N 9TH ST 23219
Binford MS, 1701 FLOYD AVE 23220
  Jacqueline Cameron, prin.

Boushall MS, 3400 HOPKINS ROAD 23234
  Willie Carr, prin.
East End MS, 701 N 37TH ST 23223
  William Joyner, prin.
Henderson MS, 4319 OLD BROOK ROAD 23227
  Dr. Beverly Braxton, prin.
Hill MS, 3400 PATTERSON AVE 23221
  Edward Pruden, prin.
Mosby MS, 1000 MOSBY ST 23223
  Dr. Roy West, prin.
Thompson MS, 7824 FOREST HILL AVE 23225
  Kenneth Geiger, prin.
Bellevue ES, 2301 E GRACE ST 23223
  Sylvia Richardson, prin.
Blackwell ES, 1600 EVERETT ST 23224
  William Johnson,Jr., prin.
Broad Rock ES, 4615 FERGUSON LN 23234
  John Dillard, prin.
Carver ES, 1110 W LEIGH ST 23220
  Deloris Pitt, prin.
Cary ES, 3021 MAPLEWOOD AVE 23221
  Dr. Russell Cooley, prin.
Chimborazo ES, 3000 E MARSHALL ST 23223
  Calvin Gay, prin.
Clark Springs ES, 1101 DANCE ST 23220
  Barbara Walker, prin.
Elkhardt MS, 6300 HULL ST ROAD 23224
  John Lane, prin.
Fairfield Court ES, 2510 PHAUP ST 23223
  Elizabeth York, prin.
Fisher ES, 3701 GARDEN RD 23235
  Dr. Mary Murphy, prin.
Fox ES, 2300 HANOVER AVE 23220
  Barbara Grey, prin.
Francis ES, 5146 SNEAD RD 23224
  Hellmut Herdey, prin.
Ginter Park ES
  3817 CHAMBERLAYNE AVE 23227
  A. Ooghe,Jr., prin.
Greene ES, 1745 CATALINA DR 23224
  Robert Johnson, prin.
Henry ES, 3411 SEMMES AVE 23225
  Connie Edwards, prin.
Lee ES, 3101 KENSINGTON AVE 23221
  Gregory Musik, prin.
Mason ES, 813 N 28TH ST 23223
  William Bjork, prin.
Maymont ES, 1211 S ALLEN AVE 23220
  Dr. Alexander Dill,Jr., prin.
Munford ES, 211 WESTMORELAND ST 23226
  Dale Kalkofen, prin.
Norrell ES, 2120 FENDALL AVE 23222
  Russell Harris,Jr., prin.
Oak Grove/Bellmede ES
  2200 INGRAM AVE 23224
  Dr. Raymond Tarkington, prin.
Overby-Sheppard ES, 2300 1ST AVE 23222
  Herbert Crockett, prin.
Redd ES, 5601 JAHNKE RD 23225
  James Jervis, prin.
Reid ES, 1301 WHITEHEAD RD 23225
  Ronald Herman, prin.
Southampton ES, 3333 CHEVERLY RD 23225
  Sylvia Robinson, prin.
Stuart ES, 3101 FENDALL AVE 23222
  Mildred Bruce, prin.
Summer Hill ES, 2717 ALEXANDER AVE 23234
  Dr. Fred Stokes, prin.
Swansboro ES, 3160 MIDLOTHIAN TPKE 23224
  Dr. Ronald Carey, prin.
Westover Hills ES, 1211 JAHNKE RD 23225
  Lillian Greene, prin.
Whitcomb Court ES, 2100 SUSSEX ST 23223
  Alga Evans, prin.
Woodville ES, 2000 N 28TH ST 23223
  Dr. Leon Harding, prin.

Collegiate School
  201 N MOORELAND ROAD 23229
St. Catherines School, 6001 GROVE AVE 23226
St. Christophers School
  711 ST CHRISTOPHER'S ROAD 23226
St. Edward Epiphany School
  10701 W HUGUENOT ROAD 23235
All Saints Catholic School
  3418 NOBLE AVE 23222
Luther Memorial School
  1301 ROBIN HOOD RD 23227
Our Lady of Lourdes School
  8200 WOODMAN RD 23228
Richmond Montessori School
  499 N PARHAM RD 23229
St. Benedict School, 3102 GROVE AVE 23221
St. Bridget School, 6011 YORK RD 23226
St. Mary School, 9501 GAYTON RD 23229
St. Patrick School, 2600 E GRACE ST 23223

Ridgeway, Henry Co., Pop. Code 3
Henry County SD
Supt. — See Collinsville
Mason MS, RURAL ROUTE 03 24148
  James Grandinetti, prin.
ES, CHURCH ST 24148 — Harriett Copeland, prin.

Rileyville, Page Co.
Page County SD
Supt. — See Luray
Springfield ES, RURAL ROUTE 01 22650
  John Shuda, prin.

Riner, Montgomery Co., Pop. Code 7
Montgomery County SD
Supt. — See Christiansburg

ES, RURAL ROUTE 08 24149
Jennifer Stuart, prin.

Ringgold, Pittsylvania Co., Pop. Code 1
Pittsylvania SD
Supt. – See Chatham
Dan River MS, RURAL ROUTE 03 BOX 949 24586
Dr. Nancy McMurray, prin.
Kentuck ES, RURAL ROUTE 02 BOX 1136 24586
Robert Fowlkes, prin.

Roanoke, (Indep. City), Pop. Code 9
Roanoke CSD
Sch. Sys. Enr. Code 7
Supt. – Dr. Frank Tota, P O BOX 13145 24031
Crystal Spring ES
2720 CAROLINA AVE SW 24014
William Lalik, prin.
Fairview ES, 648 WESTWOOD BLVD NW 24017
Philip Jepson, prin.
Fallon Park ES, 502 19TH ST SE 24013
Judith Gorham, prin.
Fishburn Park ES
3057 COLONIAL AVE SW 24015
Thomas Dunleavy, prin.
Forest Park ES, 2730 MELROSE AVE NW 24017
Carolyn Haley, prin.
Garden City ES
3718 GARDEN CITY BLVD SE 24014
Linda Wright, prin.
Grandin Court ES
2815 SPESSARD AVE SW 24015
Dr. Marsha Christy, prin.
Huff Lane MS, 4412 HUFF LN NW 24012
Helen Harris, prin.
Hurt Park ES, 1525 SALEM AVE SW 24016
Dorothy Lash, prin.
Lincoln Terrace ES, 1802 LIBERTY RD NW 24012
William Sinkler, prin.
Monterey ES, 4501 OLIVER RD NE 24012
Warren Crawford, prin.
Morningside ES, 1716 WILSON ST SE 24013
James McCorkindale, prin.
Northwest ES, 1122 19TH ST NW 24017
Margaret Thompson, prin.
Oakland ES, 3229 WILLIAMSON RD NW 24012
Irene Elliott, prin.
Preston Park ES, 3142 PRESTON AVE NW 24012
Irene Elliott, prin.
Raleigh Court ES, 2202 GRANDIN RD SW 24015
Clark Vandergrift, prin.
Round Hill ES, 2020 OAKLAND BLVD NE 24012
Virginia Stuart, prin.
Virginia Heights ES
1210 AMHERST ST SW 24015
Gary Galbreath, prin.
Wasena ES, 1125 SHERWOOD AVE SW 24015
Thomas Dunleavy, prin.
Westside ES, 1441 WESTSIDE BLVD NW 24017
Elizabeth Alls, prin.

Roanoke County SD
Supt. – See Salem
Back Creek ES, 7130 BENT MOUNTAIN RD 24018
Lucille Wolfrey, prin.
Burlington ES
6533 PETERS CREEK RD NW 24019
George Gearhart, prin.
Cave Spring ES
5404 SPRINGLAWN AVE SW 24018
L. James,Jr., prin.
Clearbrook ES, 5205 FRANKLIN RD SW 24014
David Trumbower, prin.
Glen Cove ES, 5901 COVE RD NW 24019
Mary Divers, prin.
Green Valley ES, 3838 OVERDALE DR SW 24018
Douglas Kingery, prin.
Mountain View ES, 6001 PLANTATION RD 24019
Thompson Hall, prin.
Mt. Pleasant ES
3216 MOUNT PLEASANT BLVD SE 24014
Ellen Walton, prin.
Oak Grove ES, 5005 GRANDIN RD SW 24018
Margaret Moles, prin.
Penn Forest ES, 6328 MERRIMAN RD SW 24018
Patricia Sales, prin.

North Cross School
4254 COLONIAL AVE SW 24018
Roanoke Catholic ES, 620 N JEFFERSON ST 24022

Rocky Gap, Bland Co., Pop. Code 4
Bland County SD
Supt. – See Bland
S, P O BOX 9 24366 – Charlie Puckett, prin.

Rocky Mount, Franklin Co., Pop. Code 5
Franklin County SD
Sch. Sys. Enr. Code 6
Supt. – Leonard Gereau
RURAL ROUTE 06 BOX 320A 24151
Franklin MS, RURAL ROUTE 01 BOX 574 24151
Dr. Samuel Campbell, prin.
MS, RURAL ROUTE 06 BOX 329 24151
John Busher, prin.
Sontag ES, RURAL ROUTE 02 24151
William Robey, prin.
Waid ES, 332 COURT ST E 24151
Laverne Tiggle, prin.
Other Schools – See Boones Mill, Callaway, Ferrum,
Gladehill, Henry, Martinsville, Wirtz

Rosedale, Russell Co.
Russell County SD
Supt. – See Lebanon

Belfast Elk Garden ES, P O BOX G 24280
Edward Hibbitts,Jr., prin.

Rose Hill, Lee Co., Pop. Code 3
Lee County SD
Supt. – See Jonesville
ES, P O BOX 9 24281 – Wade Wilson, prin.

Roseland, Nelson Co.
Nelson County SD
Supt. – See Lovingston
Fleetwood ES 22967 – Malcom Drumheller, prin.

Round Hill, Loudoun Co., Pop. Code 3
Loudoun County SD
Supt. – See Leesburg
ES, 20 HIGH ST 22141 – Evalyn Collier, prin.

Rural Retreat, Wythe Co., Pop. Code 4
Wythe County SD
Supt. – See Wytheville
ES, P O BOX 10 24368 – James Phipps, prin.

Rustburg, Campbell Co., Pop. Code 2
Campbell County SD
Sch. Sys. Enr. Code 6
Supt. – Dr. G. Nolley, P O BOX 99 24588
MS 24588 – Charles Arthur III, prin.
Fray ES 24588 – Thomas Webb, prin.
Yellow Branch ES, RURAL ROUTE 01 24588
Mary Watts, prin.
Other Schools – See Altavista, Brookneal, Concord,
Gladys, Lynchburg, Naruna

Ruther Glen, Caroline Co.
Caroline County SD
Supt. – See Bowling Green
Ladysmith MS
RURAL ROUTE 04 BOX 83C-1 22546
Walter Young, prin.
Ladysmith PS, RURAL ROUTE 01 BOX 73 22546
Leslie Roberson, prin.

Saint Charles, Lee Co., Pop. Code 2
Lee County SD
Supt. – See Jonesville
ES, P O BOX O 24282 – Charles Ledger, prin.

Saint Paul, Wise Co., Pop. Code 3
Wise County SD
Supt. – See Wise
ES, P O BOX X 24283 – Clyde Neff, prin.

Saint Stephen Church, King & Queen Co.
King & Queen County SD
Supt. – See King & Queen Court House
Lawson-Marrott ES 23148 – Henry Albert,Jr., prin.

Salem, (Indep. City), Pop. Code 7
Roanoke County SD
Sch. Sys. Enr. Code 7
Supt. – Bayes Wilson, 526 S COLLEGE AVE 24153
Ft. Lewis ES, 3115 W MAIN ST 24153
W. Urquhart, prin.
Glenvar ES, 4750 TOBEY RD 24153
Frederic Dixon, prin.
Masons Cove ES, 3370 BRADSHAW RD 24153
Dr. Mitchell Bowman, prin.
Other Schools – See Bent Mountain, Roanoke, Vinton

Salem CSD
Sch. Sys. Enr. Code 5
Supt. – Dr. Walter Hunt
19 N COLLEGE AVE 24153
Lewis MS, 616 S COLLEGE AVE 24153
Lewis Campbell, prin.
Carver ES, 6 E 4TH ST 24153
Dr. Joseph Coleman, prin.
East Salem ES, 1765 BOULEVARD 24153
James Kelley,Jr., prin.
South Salem ES, 1600 CAROLYN RD 24153
Martha Smith, prin.
West Salem ES, 520 N BRUFFEY ST 24153
John Millard, prin.

Saltville, Smyth Co., Pop. Code 4
Smyth County SD
Supt. – See Marion
Northwood MS, RURAL ROUTE 03 24370
Gordon Jones, prin.
Rich Valley ES, RURAL ROUTE 03 24370
John Morgan, prin.
ES, P O BOX C 24370 – W. Rhea, prin.

Saluda, Middlesex Co., Pop. Code 5
Middlesex County SD
Sch. Sys. Enr. Code 4
Supt. – James Goforth 23149
Middlesex ES 23149 – Philip Iovino, prin.

Sandston, Henrico Co., Pop. Code 5
Henrico County SD
Supt. – See Highland Springs
Donahoe ES, 1801 GRAVES RD 23150
Dr. Ernest Sanders, prin.
ES, 7 NAGLEE AVE 23150 – I. Mitchell, prin.
Seven Pines ES, 301 BEULAH RD 23150
Thomas Fernald, prin.

Saxe, Charlotte Co.
Charlotte County SD
Supt. – See Charlotte Court House
Bacon ES 23967 – Otis Lovelace,Jr., prin.

Schuyler, Albemarle Co., Pop. Code 2
Nelson County SD
Supt. – See Lovingston
ES 22969 – Goldie Jones, prin.

Scottsburg, Halifax Co., Pop. Code 2
Halifax County SD
Supt. – See Halifax
Clays Mill ES, RURAL ROUTE 01 BOX 377 24589
Elizabeth Francisco, prin.
MS, RURAL ROUTE 01 BOX 67 24589
E. Ingram, prin.

Scottsville, Fluvanna Co., Pop. Code 2
Albemarle County SD
Supt. – See Charlottesville
ES, RURAL ROUTE 04 BOX 177 24590
William Steigman,Jr., prin.

Seaford, York Co., Pop. Code 4
York County SD
Supt. – See Grafton
ES, 1105 SEAFORD RD 23696
Macon Moye, prin.

Seven Fountains, Shenandoah Co.
Shenandoah County SD
Supt. – See Woodstock
Ft. Valley ES, P O BOX 105 22653
Peter Clements, prin.

Shanghai, King & Queen Co.
King & Queen County SD
Supt. – See King & Queen Court House
King & Queen ES, P O BOX 270 23110
Charles Shipp, prin.

Shawsville, Montgomery Co., Pop. Code 7
Montgomery County SD
Supt. – See Christiansburg
ES, RURAL ROUTE 11 E 24162
Dale Margheim, prin.

Shenandoah, Page Co., Pop. Code 4
Page County SD
Supt. – See Luray
Grove Hill ES, RURAL ROUTE 01 22849
James Odell, prin.
ES, 529 FOURTH ST 22849 – Gary Pence, prin.

Shipman, Nelson Co., Pop. Code 2
Nelson County SD
Supt. – See Lovingston
Ryan ES 22971 – Louis Thurman, prin.

Skipwith, Mecklenburg Co.
Mecklenburg County SD
Supt. – See Boydton
MS, RURAL ROUTE 01 BOX 55A 23968
Jerome Watson, prin.

Smithfield, Isle of Wight Co., Pop. Code 5
Isle of Wight County SD
Supt. – See Isle of Wight
Hardy ES, P O BOX 409 23430
Frederick Stanton,Jr., prin.
MS, 800 MAIN ST 23430 – Lloyd Martin, prin.

South Boston, (Indep. City), Pop. Code 6
Halifax County SD
Supt. – See Halifax
South of Dan ES
RURAL ROUTE 04 BOX 389 24592
Carter Hicks, prin.

South Boston SD
Supt. – See Halifax
Friend MS, 601 MARSHALL AVE 24592
Doyle Bryson, prin.
Washington-Coleman ES
1927 JEFFRESS BLVD 24592
Nathaniel Brooks, prin.

South Hill, Mecklenburg Co., Pop. Code 5
Mecklenburg County SD
Supt. – See Boydton
Park View MS, RURAL ROUTE 01 BOX 192 23970
Marlyn Walker, prin.
MS, 313 FRANKLIN ST 23970
Vinson Harris, prin.
PS, 1050 PLANK RD 23970 – John Best, prin.

Speedwell, Wythe Co.
Wythe County SD
Supt. – See Wytheville
ES, P O BOX B 24374 – Sidney Crockett, prin.

Spencer, Henry Co.
Henry County SD
Supt. – See Collinsville
Spencer Penn ES
RURAL ROUTE 01 BOX 156 24165
C. Joyce, prin.

Sperryville, Rappahannock Co., Pop. Code 2
Rappahannock County SD
Sch. Sys. Enr. Code 3
Supt. – Dr. David Gangel, P O BOX 273 22740
Rappahannock ES, P O BOX 274 22740
Bernard Chesshir, prin.

Spotsylvania, Spotsylvania Co., Pop. Code 1
Spotsylvania County SD
Sch. Sys. Enr. Code 7
Supt. – L. Robert McDaniel, P O BOX 338 22553
MS, RURAL ROUTE 06 BOX 9 22553
Charles Harris III, prin.
Wright MS, RURAL ROUTE 06 BOX 225 22553
Mary Barton, prin.
Berkley ES, RURAL ROUTE 08 BOX 610 22553
Corliss Talley,Jr., prin.
Courtland ES, 6601 SMITH STATION RD 22553
Thomas Burleson, prin.

Lee ES, RURAL ROUTE 05 BOX 55 22553
  Helen Gilmore, prin.
Livingston ES, RURAL ROUTE 03 BOX 660 22553
  Clyde Coleman, prin.
Other Schools – See Fredericksburg

Springfield, Fairfax Co., Pop. Code 7
  Fairfax County SD
  Supt. – See Fairfax
  Irving MS, 8100 OLD KEENE MILL ROAD 22152
    Edward Barker, prin.
  Key MS, 6402 FRANCONIA ROAD 22150
    Donna Carr, prin.
  Kings Glen MS
    5401 DANBURY FOREST DR 22151
    Franklin Freeman, prin.
  Cardinal Forest ES
    8600 FORRESTER BLVD 22152
    Marilyn Arwood, prin.
  Crestwood ES, 6010 HANOVER AVE 22150
    Dr. M. Mayo, prin.
  Forestdale ES, 6530 ELDER AVE 22150
    Susan Byrne, prin.
  Garfield ES, 7101 OLD KEENE MILL RD 22150
    Otha Davis, prin.
  Hunt Valley ES, 7107 SYDENSTRICKER RD 22152
    Saundra Wolstenholme, prin.
  Keene Mill ES, 6310 BARDU AVE 22152
    Gwynneth Mudd, prin.
  Kings Park/King Glen ES
    5400 HARROW WAY 22151
    Lenore Plissner, prin.
  Lynbrook ES, 5801 BACKLICK RD 22150
    Shirley Eaton, prin.
  Newington Forest ES
    8001 NEWINGTON FOREST AVE 22153
    Robert Holderbaum, prin.
  North Springfield ES, 7602 HEMING CT 22151
    James Ross, prin.
  Orange Hunt ES
    6820 SYDENSTRICKER RD 22152
    Margaret Readyhough, prin.
  Ravensworth ES, 5411 NUTTING DR 22151
    Dr. Marilyn Helvie, prin.
  Rolling Valley ES, 6703 BARNACK DR 22152
    Mary Dill, prin.
  Springfield Estates ES
    6200 CHARLES C GOFF DR 22150
    Agnes Brown, prin.
  West Springfield ES, 6802 DELAND DR 22152
    Jane Crim, prin.

St. Bernadette School
  7602 OLD KEENE MILL RD 22152

Stafford, Stafford Co.
  Stafford County SD
  Sch. Sys. Enr. Code 7
  Supt. – Sidney Faucett
    1729 JEFFERSON DAVIS HWY 22554
  MS, 2160 JEFFERSON DAVIS HWY 22554
    F. Coleman Starnes, prin.
  Wright MS, 100 WOOD DRIVE 22554
    Napolean Harper, prin.
  Garrisonville ES, 100 WOOD DR 22554
    Andre Nougaret, prin.
  Moncure ES, 244 GARRISONVILLE RD 22554
    Rita Berkey, prin.
  ES, 1349 COURTHOUSE RD 22554
    Stephen Butters, prin.
  Widewater ES, 101 DEN RICH RD 22554
    Anne Knicely, prin.
  Other Schools – See Falmouth, Fredericksburg,
    Hartwood

Stanardsville, Greene Co., Pop. Code 2
  Greene County SD
  Sch. Sys. Enr. Code 4
  Supt. – K. Comer, P O BOX 98 22973
  Green ES, 1 MONROE DR 22973
    William Wade,Jr., prin.
  Monroe MS, 3 MONROE DRIVE 22973
    Clinton Estes, prin.

Stanley, Page Co., Pop. Code 4
  Page County SD
  Supt. – See Luray
  ES, P O BOX 26 22851 – John Smith, prin.

Stanleytown, Henry Co., Pop. Code 3
  Henry County SD
  Supt. – See Collinsville
  ES, RURAL ROUTE 04 BOX 516 24168
    Walter Turner, prin.

Staunton, (Indep. City), Pop. Code 7
  Augusta County SD
  Supt. – See Fishersville
  Beverley Manor ES
    RURAL ROUTE 01 BOX 5 24401
    George Earhart, prin.
  Riverheads ES, RURAL ROUTE 02 BOX 353 24401
    Robin Crowder, prin.

  Staunton CSD
  Sch. Sys. Enr. Code 5
  Supt. – Kenneth Frank, P O BOX 2626 24401
  Shelburne MS, 300 GRUBERT AVE 24401
    John Maurer, prin.
  Dixon ES, 1751 SHUTTLEMILL ROAD 24401
    Joseph Wine,Jr., prin.
  McSwain ES, 1100 N COALTER ST 24401
    Linda Lunsford, prin.
  Ware ES, 330 GRUBERT AVE 24401
    Ronnie Cartwright, prin.

Weller ES, 600 GREENVILLE AVE 24401
  James Kivlighan, prin.

Stephens City, Frederick Co., Pop. Code 4
  Frederick County SD
  Supt. – See Winchester
  Aylor MS, P O BOX 357 22655
    Colin Steele, prin.
  Bass-Hoover ES
    RURAL ROUTE 02 BOX 24C 22655
    Larry Shobe, prin.

Sterling, Loudoun Co., Pop. Code 6
  Loudoun County SD
  Supt. – See Leesburg
  Seneca Ridge MS, 98 SENECA RIDGE DR 22170
    Charles Haydt, prin.
  MS, 201 W HOLLY AVE 22170
    Terrence Hill, prin.
  Guilford ES, 600 W POPLAR RD 22170
    Carol Shackleford, prin.
  Meadowland ES
    729 S SUGARLAND RUN DR 22170
    Dennis Young, prin.
  Rolling Ridge ES, 500 E FREDERICK DR 22170
    Wayne Mills, prin.
  ES, 200 W CHURCH RD 22170 – Susan Mills, prin.
  Sugarland ES, 65 SUGARLAND RUN DR 22170
    Bernice Nicewicz, prin.
  Sully ES, 300 CIRCLE DR 22170
    Margery Hathorn, prin.

Strasburg, Shenandoah Co., Pop. Code 4
  Shenandoah County SD
  Supt. – See Woodstock
  Sandy Hook ES
    RURAL ROUTE 03 BOX 795 22657
    David Brill, prin.
  MS, 207 HIGH ST 22657 – Paul Sorrell,Jr., prin.

Stuart, Patrick Co., Pop. Code 4
  Patrick County SD
  Sch. Sys. Enr. Code 5
  Supt. – Dennis Witt, P O BOX 346 24171
  ES, STAPLES AVE 24171 – Edward West, prin.
  Other Schools – See Ararat, Critz, Meadows of Dan,
    Patrick Springs, Woolwine

Stuarts Draft, Augusta Co., Pop. Code 3
  Augusta County SD
  Supt. – See Fishersville
  MS, RURAL ROUTE 01 BOX 113 24477
    George Kidd, prin.
  ES, 356 N MAIN ST 24477 – Troy Rexrode II, prin.

Suffolk, (Indep. City), Pop. Code 8
  Suffolk CSD
  Sch. Sys. Enr. Code 6
  Supt. – C. Suggs, P O BOX 1549 23434
  Driver MS, 4270 DRIVER LANE 23435
    W. Barnes, prin.
  Southwestern MS
    9301 SOUTHWESTERN BLVD 23437
    Edward Darden, prin.
  Washington MS, 415 WALNUT ST 23434
    Johnnie Edwards, prin.
  Bowser ES, 4540 NANSEMOND PKY 23435
    Karen Brickey, prin.
  Elephants Fork ES
    2316 WILLIAM REID DR 23434
    Walter Biggs, prin.
  Holland ES, 6620 HOLLAND ROAD 23437
    Janice Cawthorn, prin.
  Jefferson ES, CLAY & FREEMASON STS 23434
    Frederick McCain, prin.
  Kilby ES, 111 KILBY SHORES DR 23434
    W. White, prin.
  Mt. Zion ES, 3624 PRUDEN BLVD 23434
    Christina Gray, prin.
  Nansemond Parkway ES
    3012 NANSEMOND PKY 23434
    Jean Summerville, prin.
  Oakland ES, 5505 GODWIN BLVD 23434
    John Sammons,Jr., prin.
  Robertson ES, 132 ROBERTSON ST 23438
    William Krupp, prin.

Nansemond-Suffolk Academy
  P O BOX 1249 23434

Sugar Grove, Smyth Co., Pop. Code 2
  Smyth County SD
  Supt. – See Marion
  ES, P O BOX 8 24375 – Samuel Hambrick, prin.

Surry, Surry Co.
  Surry County SD
  Sch. Sys. Enr. Code 4
  Supt. – Clarence Penn, P O BOX 317 23883
  Other Schools – See Dendron

Sussex, Sussex Co.
  Sussex County SD
  Sch. Sys. Enr. Code 4
  Supt. – J. Semones 23884
  Other Schools – See Jarratt, Wakefield, Waverly

Swords Creek, Russell Co.
  Russell County SD
  Supt. – See Lebanon
  Givens ES, RURAL ROUTE 01 BOX 219 24649
    James Hughes, prin.
  ES, P O BOX 129 24649 – Dan Brown, prin.

Tabb, York Co.
  York County SD
  Supt. – See Grafton

MS, 300 YORKTOWN ROAD 23602
  James Carmines, prin.
Mt. Vernon ES, 310 MOUNT VERNON DR 23602
  Julia Williams, prin.

Tangier, Accomack Co., Pop. Code 3
  Accomack County SD
  Supt. – See Accomac
  S 23440 – Dennis Crockett, prin.

Tappahannock, Essex Co., Pop. Code 4
  Essex County SD
  Sch. Sys. Enr. Code 4
  Supt. – W. Harrow 22560
  Essex MS 22560 – Russel Jarrett, prin.
  ES 22560 – Mary Maschal, prin.

Tazewell, Tazewell Co., Pop. Code 5
  Tazewell County SD
  Sch. Sys. Enr. Code 6
  Supt. – Frank Cosby, P O BOX 469 24651
  MS, 100 BULL DOG AVE 24651
    John Peters, prin.
  Cove ES, RURAL ROUTE 01 24651
    Virginia Russell, prin.
  ES 24651 – Dr. Charles Grindstaff, prin.
  Thompson Valley MS, RURAL ROUTE 01 24651
    Anna Neel, prin.
  Other Schools – See Bandy, Bluefield, Boissevain,
    Cedar Bluff, Falls Mills, Jewell Ridge, North
    Tazewell, Raven, Richlands

Thaxton, Bedford Co.
  Bedford County SD
  Supt. – See Bedford
  ES 24174 – Michael Johnson, prin.

Timberville, Rockingham Co., Pop. Code 4
  Rockingham County SD
  Supt. – See Harrisonburg
  Plains ES, 225 AMERICAN LEGION DR 22853
    Larry Huffman, prin.

Toms Brook, Shenandoah Co., Pop. Code 2
  Shenandoah County SD
  Supt. – See Woodstock
  ES, RURAL ROUTE 01 22660
    Stephen Stickler, prin.

Triangle, Prince William Co., Pop. Code 5
  Prince William County SD
  Supt. – See Manassas
  Graham Park MS
    3513 GRAHAM PARK ROAD 22172
    Joyce Harte, prin.
  ES, 3615 LIONSFIELD RD 22172
    Carleton Moyer, prin.

St. Francis of Assisi School
  18825 FULLER HEIGHTS RD 22172

Trout Dale, Grayson Co., Pop. Code 2
  Grayson County SD
  Supt. – See Independence
  Flatridge ES, RURAL ROUTE 02 BOX 223 24378
    Chester Cole, prin.

Troutville, Botetourt Co., Pop. Code 2
  Botetourt County SD
  Supt. – See Fincastle
  ES, RURAL ROUTE 04 BOX 64 24175
    Sandra Tunnell, prin.

Turbeville, Halifax Co.
  Halifax County SD
  Supt. – See Halifax
  ES, P O BOX 658 24596 – Christine Powell, prin.

Union Level, Mecklenburg Co.
  Mecklenburg County SD
  Supt. – See Boydton
  Buckhorn ES, RURAL ROUTE 01 BOX 275 23973
    Dan Cameron, prin.

Unionville, Orange Co.
  Orange County SD
  Supt. – See Orange
  Lightfoot MS 22567 – Mary Sutherland, prin.
  ES 22567 – Leonard Nicholson, prin.

Vansant, Buchanan Co., Pop. Code 3
  Buchanan County SD
  Supt. – See Grundy
  Prater ES, RURAL ROUTE 01 BOX 493 24656
    Gene Counts, prin.

Vernon Hill, Halifax Co.
  Halifax County SD
  Supt. – See Halifax
  Wilson ES, RURAL ROUTE 01 BOX 10-A 24597
    Henry Richardson, prin.

Verona, Augusta Co., Pop. Code 4
  Augusta County SD
  Supt. – See Fishersville
  ES, RURAL ROUTE 01 BOX 385 24482
    C. Landes, prin.

Victoria, Lunenburg Co., Pop. Code 4
  Lunenburg County SD
  Sch. Sys. Enr. Code 4
  Supt. – Michael Basham, P O BOX X 23974
  Lunenburg MS, RURAL ROUTE 01 23974
    Wayne Staples, prin.
  Lunenburg ES 23974 – Michael Tisdale, prin.
  MS 23974 – Nancy Chappell, prin.
  Other Schools – See Kenbridge

Vienna, Fairfax Co., Pop. Code 7
Fairfax County SD
Supt. – See Fairfax
Kilmer MS, 8100 WOLFTRAP ROAD 22180
  Donald Thurston, prin.
Thoreau MS, 2505 CEDAR LANE 22180
  R. Boosley, prin.
Archer ES, 324 NUTLEY ST NW 22180
  Judith Azzara, prin.
Cunningham Park ES, 1001 PARK ST SE 22180
  Ednamae Trevey, prin.
Flint Hill ES, 2444 FLINT HILL RD 22180
  Linda Clark, prin.
Freedom Hill ES, 1945 LORD FAIRFAX RD 22180
  Cabell Lloyd, prin.
Marshall Road ES, 730 MARSHALL RD SW 22180
  David Meadows, prin.
Stenwood ES, 2620 GALLOWS RD 22180
  Dr. Douglas Dalton, prin.
ES, 128 CENTER ST S 22180
  Robert Pantall, prin.
Westbriar ES, 1741 PINE VALLEY DR 22180
  Dr. Dolores Varnon, prin.
Wolftrap ES, 1903 BEULAH RD 22180
  Nancy Poole, prin.

Our Lady of Good Counsel School
P O BOX 217 22180

Vinton, Roanoke Co., Pop. Code 6
Roanoke County SD
Supt. – See Salem
Cook ES, 412 POPLAR ST S 24179
  Ronald Weaver, prin.
Hardy Road ES, 1200 HARDY RD 24179
  Martha Blount, prin.
Horn ES, 1002 RUDDELL RD 24179
  Ronald Hodges, prin.

Virgilina, Halifax Co., Pop. Code 2
Halifax County SD
Supt. – See Halifax
ES, P O BOX 147 24598 – John Courtney, prin.

Virginia Beach, (Indep. City), Pop. Code 10
Virginia Beach CSD
Sch. Sys. Enr. Code 8
Supt. – Dr. James Melvin, P O BOX 6038 23456
Alanton ES, 1441 STEPHENS RD 23454
  Linda Tanner, prin.
Arrowhead ES, 5549 SUSQUEHANNA DR 23462
  Ramona Hurd, prin.
Bayside ES, 5649 BAYSIDE RD 23455
  Barbara Toncray, prin.
Birdneck ES, 957 S BIRDNECK RD 23451
  Thomas Gregory, prin.
Brookwood ES, 601 S LYNNHAVEN RD 23452
  Arthur Mae Lawson, prin.
Centerville ES, 2201 CENTERVILLE TPKE 23464
  Albert Williams, prin.
College Park ES, 1110 BENNINGTON RD 23464
  Ronald Sykes, prin.
Cooke ES, 15TH & MEDITERRANEAN AVE 23451
  Thomas Coggin, prin.
Creeds ES, RURAL ROUTE 04 BOX 4017 23457
  Gene Glasco, prin.
Dey ES, 1900 N GREAT NECK RD 23454
  Rhonda Skaggs, prin.
Fairfield ES, 5428 PROVIDENCE RD 23464
  Raymond Alexander, prin.
Green Run ES, 1200 GREEN GARDEN CIR 23456
  Lou Royal, prin.
Hermitage ES, 1701 PLEASURE HOUSE RD 23455
  Anthony Mencini, prin.
Holland ES, 3340 HOLLAND RD 23452
  William Vroman, prin.
Indian Lakes ES, 1240 HOMESTEAD DR 23464
  H. Smith, prin.
Kemps Landing MS
  525 KEMPSVILLE ROAD 23464
  Don Clement, prin.
Kempsville ES, 570 KEMPSVILLE RD 23464
  Dr. Nancy Hyatt, prin.
Kempsville Meadows ES, 736 EDWIN DR 23462
  Barbara Tourgee, prin.
Kings Grant ES, 612 N LYNNHAVEN RD 23452
  Robert Edwards, prin.
Kingston ES, 3532 KINGS GRANT RD 23452
  Robert Pearsall, prin.
Linkhorn Park ES, 1413 LASKIN RD 23451
  Carroll Monger, prin.
Luxford ES, 4808 HAYGOOD RD 23455
  Verlin Adams, prin.
Lynnhaven ES, 210 DILLON DR 23452
  William Skaggs, prin.
Malibu ES, 3632 EDINBURGH DR 23452
  Margaret Nicolls, prin.
Newtown Road ES, 900 NEWTOWN RD 23462
  Troy Perry, prin.
North Landing ES, 2929 N LANDING RD 23456
  Mary Butler, prin.
Parkway ES, 4080 OHARE DR 23456
  James Oglesby, prin.
Pembroke ES, 4622 JERICHO RD 23462
  Nancy Rosenblatt, prin.
Pembroke Meadows ES
  820 CATHEDRAL DR 23455 – Charles Ball, prin.
Plaza ES, 641 CARRIAGE HILL RD 23452
  Preston Holt, prin.
Point of View ES, 5400 PARLIAMENT DR 23462
  Olivia Dabney, prin.
Princess Anne ES, 2444 SEABOARD RD 23456
  David Portis, prin.

Providence ES, 4968 PROVIDENCE RD 23464
  Ronald Cowan, prin.
Rosemont ES, 1257 ROSEMONT RD 23456
  Ramona Stenzhorn, prin.
Rosemont Forest ES
  1716 GREY FRIARS CHASE 23456
  John Kalocay, prin.
Salem ES, 3961 SALEM LAKES BLVD 23456
  Andrew Carrington, prin.
Seatack ES, 411 BIRDNECK CIR 23451
  Hazel Wright, prin.
Shelton Park ES, 1700 SHELTON RD 23455
  Steven Alligood, prin.
Thalia ES, 421 THALIA RD 23452
  Shirley Barco, prin.
Thoroughgood ES, 1444 DUNSTAN LN 23455
  Ralph Mizelle, prin.
Trantwood ES, 2344 INLYNNVIEW RD 23454
  William Jenkins, prin.
White Oaks ES, 960 WINDSOR OAKS BLVD 23462
  Edna Bates, prin.
Williams ES, 892 NEWTOWN RD 23462
  Betsy Thigpen, prin.
Windsor Oaks ES, 3800 VAN BUREN DR 23452
  Dr. Pearl Moyers, prin.
Windsor Woods ES
  233 PRESIDENTIAL BLVD 23452 – W. Cox, prin.
Woodstock ES, 6016 PROVIDENCE RD 23464
  Perry Williams, prin.

Cape Henry Collegiate School
  1320 MILL DAM ROAD 23454
Hebrew Academy of Tidewater
  1244 THOMPKINS LN 23464
St. Gregory School
  5345 VIRGINIA BEACH BLVD 23462
St. Matthew School, 3316 SANDRA LN 23464
Star of the Sea School, 311 ARTIC CIR 23451

Wakefield, Sussex Co., Pop. Code 4
Sussex County SD
Supt. – See Sussex
Chambliss ES 23888 – W. Goodwyn III, prin.

Warm Springs, Bath Co.
Bath County SD
Sch. Sys. Enr. Code 3
Supt. – P. Nowlin III, P O BOX 67 24484
Other Schools – See Hot Springs, Millboro

Warrenton, Fauquier Co., Pop. Code 5
Fauquier County SD
Sch. Sys. Enr. Code 6
Supt. – S. Lamm, 10 HOTEL ST 22186
Bradley MS, 674 HASTINGS LN 22186
  Douglas White, prin.
Central ES, 430 E SHIRLEY AVE 22186
  Doralee Magyar, prin.
Smith ES, RURAL ROUTE 605 22186
  Alfred Bell, prin.
Other Schools – See Bealeton, Catlett, Marshall,
  Midland, Remington

Highland School, 597 BROADVIEW AVE 22186
St. John School, 285 WINCHESTER ST 22186

Warsaw, Richmond Co., Pop. Code 3
Richmond County SD
Sch. Sys. Enr. Code 4
Supt. – Frederick Pitman, P O BOX 735 22572
Richmond County MS 22572
  William Brann, prin.
Richmond County ES 22572
  Virginia Brown, prin.

Waterford, Loudoun Co.
Loudoun County SD
Supt. – See Leesburg
ES 22190 – Mary Morris, prin.

Waverly, Sussex Co., Pop. Code 4
Sussex County SD
Supt. – See Sussex
Jackson MS 23890 – A. Marks, prin.

Waynesboro, (Indep. City), Pop. Code 7
Augusta County SD
Supt. – See Fishersville
Cassell ES, RURAL ROUTE 01 BOX 31 22980
  R. Davis, prin.
Ladd ES, 1930 ROSSER AVE 22980
  John Chase,Jr., prin.

Waynesboro CSD
Sch. Sys. Enr. Code 5
Supt. – Dr. Thomas L. Varner
  301 PINE AVE 22980
Berkeley Glenn ES, 1020 JEFFERSON AVE 22980
  Rodney Bradt, prin.
Collins ES, 1625 IVY ST 22980
  William Bateman, prin.
Shenandoah Heights ES
  1201 SHENANDOAH AVE 22980
  Irene Kaufman, prin.
Wenonah ES, 125 N BAYARD AVE 22980
  Joseph King, prin.
Westwood Hills ES, 548 ROSSER AVE 22980
  Stephen Braintwain, prin.

Weber City, Scott Co., Pop. Code 4
Scott County SD
Supt. – See Gate City
ES, 145 JENNINGS ST 24251 – Joe Rusek, prin.

West Point, King William Co., Pop. Code 5
West Point CSD
Supt. – See King William
ES 23181 – Duane Carlton, prin.

Weyers Cave, Augusta Co.
Augusta County SD
Supt. – See Fishersville
ES, P O BOX 63 24486 – Ronald Robinson, prin.

Whitetop, Grayson Co.
Grayson County SD
Supt. – See Independence
Mt. Rogers S, RURAL ROUTE 01 BOX 193 24292
  Wilma Testerman, prin.

Whitewood, Buchanan Co.
Buchanan County SD
Supt. – See Grundy
ES 24657 – Bob Ashby, prin.

Wicomico, Gloucester Co.
Gloucester County SD
Supt. – See Gloucester
Abingdon ES, P O BOX 88 23184
  Florence White, prin.

Williamsburg, (Indep. City), Pop. Code 6
Williamsburg- James City SD
Sch. Sys. Enr. Code 6
Supt. – Dr. John Allen, P O BOX 179 23187
Blair MS, IRONBOUND ROAD 23185
  Shade Palmer, prin.
Berkley MS, 1118 IRONBOUND RD 23185
  Eudice Meyers, prin.
Bruton Heights MS, 301 1ST ST 23185
  Lawrence Walk, prin.
Byrd ES, 112 LAUREL LN 23185
  Carol Beers, prin.
Norge ES, 7311 RICHMOND RD 23185
  Betti Shahmouradian, prin.
Whaley ES, SCOTLAND ST 23185
  Parker Land, prin.

York County SD
Supt. – See Grafton
Queens Lake MS, W QUEENS DRIVE 23185
  Ivey Hawkins, prin.
Magruder ES, 710 PENNIMAN RD 23185
  Nancy Dutro, prin.
Waller Mill ES, 314 WALLER MILL RD 23185
  Peggy McMaster, prin.

Walsingham Academy, P O BOX 159 23187

Willis, Floyd Co.
Floyd County SD
Supt. – See Floyd
ES 24380 – Janet Peak, prin.

Winchester, (Indep. City), Pop. Code 7
Frederick County SD
Sch. Sys. Enr. Code 6
Supt. – Dr. Kenneth Walker, P O BOX 3508 22601
Frederick MS, 441 LINDEN DRIVE 22601
  Fred Jefferson, prin.
Apple Pie Ridge ES
  RURAL ROUTE 08 BOX 1093 22601
  Thomas Hanisch, prin.
Indian Hollow ES
  RURAL ROUTE 02 BOX 360 22601
  David Welling, prin.
Robinson Memorial ES
  2400 ROOSEVELT BLVD 22601
  Wayne Davis, prin.
Senseny Road ES, 1400 SENSENY RD 22601
  James Plaugher, prin.
Other Schools – See Clear Brook, Stephens City

Winchester CSD
Sch. Sys. Enr. Code 5
Supt. – Dr. John Capehart, P O BOX 551 22601
Morgan MS, 48 S PURCELL AVE 22601
  Dick Blackwell, prin.
Douglass ES, NORTH KENT ST 22601
  Jack Booth, prin.
Kerr ES, 536 JEFFERSON ST 22601
  Ray Chapman, prin.
Quarles ES, KENT AND SOUTHWERK STS 22601
  Mary Joyner, prin.
Virginia Avenue ES
  VIRGINIA AVENUE AND KERR ST 22601
  William Askew III, prin.

Sacred Heart Academy, 1713 AMHERST ST 22601

Windsor, Isle of Wight Co., Pop. Code 3
Isle of Wight County SD
Supt. – See Isle of Wight
ES, P O BOX 287 23487 – William Joyner III, prin.

Wirtz, Franklin Co.
Franklin County SD
Supt. – See Rocky Mount
Burnt Chimney ES, RURAL ROUTE 01 24184
  Paul Strickler, prin.
Dudley ES, RURAL ROUTE 01 24184
  John Hollandsworth, prin.

Wise, Wise Co., Pop. Code 5
Wise County SD
Sch. Sys. Enr. Code 6
Supt. – Dr. J. Graham, P O BOX 1217 24293
Addington MS, P O BOX 977 24293
  Jack Turner, prin.
PS, P O BOX 947 24293 – Carter Collins, prin.

Other Schools – See Appalachia, Big Stone Gap, Coeburn, Pound, Saint Paul

Woodbridge, Prince William Co., Pop. Code 7
Prince William County SD
Supt. – See Manassas
Godwin MS, 14800 DARBYDALE AVE 22193
  William Perry, prin.
Lynn MS, 2451 LONGVIEW DRIVE 22191
  William Stephens, prin.
Rippon MS, 15101 BLACKBURN ROAD 22191
  Theresa Yeldell, prin.
MS, 2201 YORK DRIVE 22191 – Rob Stine, prin.
Bel Air ES, 14150 FERNDALE RD 22193
  Richard Clark II, prin.
Belmont ES, 751 NORWOOD LN 22191
  William Huber, prin.
Dale City ES, 14450 BROOK DR 22193
  James Bailey, prin.
Enterprise ES, 13900 LINDENDALE RD 22193
  John Phillips,Jr., prin.
Featherstone ES, 14805 BLACKBURN RD 22191
  Alison Miller, prin.
Kerrydale ES, 13199 KERRYDALE RD 22193
  David Critchfield, prin.
Kilby ES, 1800 HORNER RD 22191
  Betty Covington, prin.
King ES, 13224 NICKLESON DR 22193
  Dr. Natialy Walker, prin.
Lake Ridge ES, 11920 HEDGES RUN DR 22192
  John Scott, prin.

Marumsco Hills ES, 14100 PAGE ST 22191
  Harold Secord, prin.
Minnieville ES, 13639 GREENWOOD DR 22193
  Jeanette Brown, prin.
Neabsco ES, 3800 CORDELL AVE 22193
  Faye Patterson, prin.
Occoquan ES, 12915 OCCOQUAN RD 22192
  Bruce Leiby, prin.
Potomac View ES, 14601 LAMAR RD 22191
  Ralph Johnson, prin.
Rippon ES, 15101 BLACKBURN RD 22191
  Freddie Smith, prin.
Rockledge ES, 2300 MARINER LN 22192
  James Robbins, prin.
Springwoods ES, 3815 MARQUIS PL 22192
  Frank Gastley, prin.
Vaughan ES, 2200 YORK DR 22191
  Robin Sweeney, prin.

———————

Aquinas School, 13750 MARYS WAY 22191

Woodlawn, Carroll Co., Pop. Code 1
Carroll County SD
Supt. – See Hillsville
ES, RURAL ROUTE 01 BOX 6-B 24381
  Arthur Noblett, prin.

Woodstock, Shenandoah Co., Pop. Code 5
Shenandoah County SD
Sch. Sys. Enr. Code 5
Supt. – Dr. Jerry Webb, P O BOX 488 22664

MS, P O BOX 465 22664 – John Kagey, prin.
Robinson ES, 1231 SUSAN AVE 22664
  Harold Ebersole, prin.
Other Schools – See Edinburg, Mount Jackson, New
  Market, Seven Fountains, Strasburg, Toms Brook

Woolwine, Patrick Co.
Patrick County SD
Supt. – See Stuart
ES, RURAL ROUTE 01 BOX 2 24185
  Bill Dillon,Jr., prin.

Wytheville, Wythe Co., Pop. Code 6
Wythe County SD
Sch. Sys. Enr. Code 5
Supt. – Robert McCoy
  1570 RESERVOIR ST W 24382
Scott MS, 7 S 7TH ST 24382
  Charles Patterson, prin.
Sheffey ES, RURAL ROUTE 03 24382
  E. Cassell, prin.
Spiller ES, TAZEWELL ST 24382
  Richard Lawson, prin.
Other Schools – See Austinville, Max Meadows, Rural
  Retreat, Speedwell

Yorktown, York Co., Pop. Code 2
York County SD
Supt. – See Grafton
MS, RURAL ROUTE 17 23690
  Herbert Deppe, prin.
ES, 131 SIEGE LN 23692 – Marsha Brown, prin.

WASHINGTON

STATE DEPARTMENT OF EDUCATION
Old Capitol Building
Mail Stop FG-11, Olympia 98504
(206) 753-6738

Superintendent of Public Instruction	Dr. Frank Brouillet
Deputy Superintendent	Dr. Charles Marshall
Assistant Superintendent Financial Services	Perry Keithley
Assistant Superintendent Special Services & Support Programs	Dr. Judy Schrag
Assistant Superintendent Vocational-Technical Services	Jan Carlson
Assistant Superintendent Instructional Programs & Services	Cheryl Chow

STATE BOARD OF EDUCATION
Dr. Monica Schmidt, *Executive Director*   Old Capitol Building, Olympia   98504

HIGHER EDUCATION COORDINATING BOARD
A. Robert Thoeny, *Executive Director*   917 Lakeridge Way, Olympia   98504

EDUCATIONAL SERVICE DISTRICTS

ESD 101, Dr. Brian Talbott, Supt.
  1025 W INDIANA AVE, Spokane 99205
ESD 105, Michael Bernazzani, Supt.
  33 S 2ND AVE, Yakima 98902
ESD 112, Bill Fromhold, Supt.
  1313 NE 134TH ST, Vancouver 98685

ESD 113, Fred Tidwell, Supt.
  601 MCPHEE ROAD SW, Olympia 98502
ESD 114, Frank Deebach, Supt.
  105 NATIONAL AVE N, Bremerton 98312
ESD 121, Dr. Doyle Winter, Supt.
  12320 80TH AVE S, Seattle 98178

ESD 123, John Thrasher, Supt.
  705 W ROSE ST, Walla Walla 99362
ESD 171, Dennis Peterson, Supt.
  640 MISSION AVE S, Wenatchee 98801
ESD 189, Dennis Couch, Supt.
  330 PACIFIC PLACE, Mount Vernon 98273

PUBLIC, PRIVATE, AND PAROCHIAL ELEMENTARY SCHOOLS

Aberdeen, Grays Harbor Co., Pop. Code 3
Aberdeen SD 5
Sch. Sys. Enr. Code 5
Supt. – Dr. Richard B. Voege, 216 N G ST 98520
Miller JHS, 100 LINDSTROM ST 98520
  Fred Easter, prin.
Central Park ES, 601 SCHOOL ROAD 98520
  Robert Sevey, prin.
Gray ES, 900 CLEVELAND ST 98520
  Leif Tangvald, prin.
McDermoth ES, 409 N K ST 98520
  Peter Rattie, prin.
Stevens ES, 301 S FARRAGUT ST 98520
  Francis Connors, prin.
West ES, 1801 BAY AVE 98520
  Sue Torrens, prin.
Young ES, 1700 CHERRY ST 98520
  Mitch Rajcich, prin.

Wishkah Valley SD 117
Sch. Sys. Enr. Code 2
Supt. – Richard Throgmorton
  RURAL ROUTE 01 BOX 308 98520
Wishkah Valley ES
  RURAL ROUTE 01 BOX 308 98520
  Mike Jacobs, prin.

———————

St. Mary's ES, 518 N H ST 98520

Acme, Whatcom Co.
Mt. Baker SD 507
Supt. – See Deming
ES 98220 – Donna Mellander, prin.

Addy, Stevens Co.
Summit Valley SD 202
Sch. Sys. Enr. Code 1
Supt. – Suellen White
  HCR ROUTE BOX 10A 99101
Summit ES, HCR BOX 10A 99101 – (—), prin.

Adna, Lewis Co.
Adna SD 226
Sch. Sys. Enr. Code 2
Supt. – Bernard Rodgers, P O BOX 118 98522
ES, P O BOX 26 98522 – Lynn Roberts, prin.

Airway Heights, Spokane Co., Pop. Code 4
Cheney SD 360
Supt. – See Cheney
Sunset ES, P O BOX 396 99001
  John Fishback, prin.

Alderwood Manor, Snohomish Co., Pop. Code 5
Mukilteo SD 6
Supt. – See Everett
Lake Stickney ES, 1625 MADISON WAY 98036
Sue Lerner, prin.

Almira, Lincoln Co., Pop. Code 2
Almira SD 17
Sch. Sys. Enr. Code 2
Supt. – John Magers 99103
ES 99103 – Joan Secrest, prin.

Amanda Park, Grays Harbor Co.
Quinault Lake SD 97
Sch. Sys. Enr. Code 2
Supt. – Ray Lorton, P O BOX 38 98526
Lake Quinault ES, P O BOX 38 98526
Thomas Byrne, prin.

Amboy, Clark Co.
Battle Ground SD 119
Supt. – See Battle Ground
IS 98601 – Bob Legato, prin.

Anacortes, Skagit Co., Pop. Code 6
Anacortes SD 103
Sch. Sys. Enr. Code 4
Supt. – Dr. C. Duane Lowell, 2200 M AVE 98221
MS, 22ND & M STS 98221 – Charles Kiel, prin.
Fidalgo ES, 1360 GIBRALTER ROAD 98221
Chris Borgen, prin.
Island View ES, 26TH & J 98221
Dick Canfield, prin.
Mount Erie ES, 41ST & M 98221 – Bob Knorr, prin.
Whitney ES, 12TH & M 98221 – Bob Knorr, prin.

Ariel, Cowlitz Co.
Woodland SD 404
Supt. – See Woodland
Yale ES, 11842 LEWIS RIVER ROAD 98603
John Huffman, prin.

Arlington, Snohomish Co., Pop. Code 5
Arlington SD 16
Sch. Sys. Enr. Code 5
Supt. – Robert Schmitt, P O BOX 309 98223
MS, 1220 E 5TH ST 98223 – Herbert Hower, prin.
IS, 319 N FRENCH AVE 98223
Suzanne Baier, prin.
PS, 315 N FRENCH AVE 98223
Deannie Dunbar, prin.
Trafton ES, HWY 30 & JIM CREEK ROAD 98223
Chris Sharp, prin.

Ashford, Pierce Co.
Eatonville SD 404
Supt. – See Eatonville
Columbia Crest ES 98304 – Lucile Fountain, prin.

Asotin, Asotin Co., Pop. Code 3
Asotin-Anatone SD 420
Sch. Sys. Enr. Code 2
Supt. – Richard A. Riggs, P O BOX 489 99402
ES, P O BOX 489 99402 – Jack Pease, prin.

Auburn, King Co., Pop. Code 8
Auburn SD 408
Sch. Sys. Enr. Code 6
Supt. – Dr. James P. Fugate, 915 4TH ST NE 98002
Chinook ES, 3502 AUBURN WAY S 98002
Thomas Jacka, prin.
Evergreen Heights ES, 5602 S 316TH ST 98001
Joseph Binetti, prin.
Gildo Rey ES, 1005 37TH ST SE 98002
Mark Boynton, prin.
Lake View ES, 16401 SE 318TH ST 98002
Sterling Kuhlman, prin.
Lea Hill ES, 30908 124TH AVE SE 98002
Randal DeKoker, prin.
Pioneer ES, 2301 M ST SE 98002
L. Allen Price, prin.
Scobee ES, 1031 14TH ST NE 98002
Donald Lapinski, prin.
Teminal Park ES, 1101 D ST SE 98002
Sandra Turner, prin.
Washington ES, 20 E ST NE 98002
Molly Ringo, prin.
Other Schools – See Pacific

Federal Way SD 210
Supt. – See Federal Way
Camelot ES, 4041 S 298TH ST 98001
Phyllis Tellari, prin.
Lake Dolloff ES, 4200 S 308TH ST 98001
Robert Otterstad, prin.
Lakeland ES, 35675 43ND AVE S 98001
Ed Novak, prin.
Valhalla ES, 27847 42ND AVE S 98001
Maurice Huggins, prin.

Auburn Christian ES
3535 AUBURN WAY S 98002
Buena Vista SDA ES
3320 ACADEMY DR SE 98002
Green River Montessori, 922 12TH ST NE 98002
Holy Family ES, 505 17TH ST SE 98002
Valley Christian ES, 1312 2ND ST SE 98002

Bainbridge Island, Kitsap Co.
Bainbridge Island SD 303
Sch. Sys. Enr. Code 5
Supt. – Dr. Michael Boring
8489 MADISON AVE NE 98110
Commodore Bainbridge MS 98110
Jerrold McLaughlin, prin.
Blakely ES, 4704 BLAKELY AVE NE 98110
Brent Peterson, prin.

Ordway ES, 8555 MADISON AVE NE 98110
William Hoots, prin.
Wilkes ES, 12781 MADISON AVE NE 98110
Edward Thompson, prin.

Battle Ground, Clark Co., Pop. Code 5
Battle Ground SD 119
Sch. Sys. Enr. Code 6
Supt. – Dr. Merle I. Locke 98604
Lewisville IS 98604 – Chuck Anderson, prin.
Chief Umtuch ES 98604 – Paul Walden, prin.
Maple Grove ES, 12500 NE 199TH ST 98604
Tom Nadal, prin.
Other Schools – See Amboy, Vancouver, Yacolt

Meadow Glade SDA ES
18717 NE 109TH AVE 98604

Belfair, Mason Co., Pop. Code 5
North Mason SD 403
Sch. Sys. Enr. Code 4
Supt. – Dr. Marie Pickel, P O BOX 167 98528
Hawkins MS 98528 – Thomas Marrs, prin.
ES 98528 – Lea Harmon, prin.
Sand Hill ES 98528 – Rodger DeBritz, prin.

Bellevue, King Co., Pop. Code 8
Bellevue SD 405
Sch. Sys. Enr. Code 7
Supt. – Dr. Don O'Neil, P O BOX C-90010 98009
Chinook MS, 2001 98TH AVE NE 98004
Don Matheson, prin.
Highland MS
15027 BELLEVUE-REDMND ROAD 98007
Shuzo Takeuchi, prin.
Odle MS, 14401 NE 8TH ST 98007
Ian Armitage, prin.
Tillicum MS, 16020 SE 16TH ST 98008
Jim Hoff, prin.
Tyee MS, 13630 SE ALLEN ROAD 98006
Jan Toner, prin.
Ardmore ES, 16616 NE 32ND ST 98008
Angelo Righi, prin.
Bennett ES, 17900 NE 16TH ST 98008
George McDonald, prin.
Cherry Crest ES, 12400 NE 32ND ST 98005
Henry Gacek, prin.
Clyde Hill ES, 9601 NE 24TH ST 98004
Marilyn Volwiler, prin.
Eastgate ES, 4255 153RD AVE SE 98006
John Jester, prin.
Enatai ES, 10615 SE 23RD ST 98004
Bob Peterson, prin.
Lake Hills ES, 14310 SE 12TH ST 98007
Michael McBride, prin.
Medina ES, 8001 NE 8TH ST 98004
Joe Egan, prin.
Newport Heights ES, 12635 SE 56TH ST 98006
Dr. Jill Matthies, prin.
Phantom Lake ES, 1050 160TH AVE SE 98008
Arland Tangeman, prin.
Sherwood Forest ES, 16411 NE 24TH ST 98008
Jan Johnson, prin.
Somerset ES, 14100 SE SOMERSET BLVD 98006
Sylvia Hayden, prin.
Spiritridge ES, 16401 SE 24TH ST 98008
Gary St. George, prin.
Stevenson ES, 14220 NE 8TH ST 98007
Ron Jones, prin.
Sunset ES, 3810 132ND AVE SE 98006
Jan Zuber, prin.
Woodridge ES, 12619 SE 20TH PL 98005
William Pinnick, prin.

Bellevue Christian Lower ES
7800 NE 28TH ST 98004
Bellevue Montessori ES
2411 112TH AVE NE 98004
Cougar Mountain Academy, P O BOX 1441 98009
Eton ES
2701 BELLEVUE-REDMOND ROAD 98008
Jewish Day ES of Metro Seattle
15749 NE 4TH ST 98008
Neighborhood Christian ES
625 140TH AVE NE 98005
Sacred Heart ES, 9450 NE 14TH ST 98004
St. Louise ES, 133 156TH SE 98007
St. Thomas ES, 84TH NE AND NE 12TH 98039
The Little ES, 2812 116TH AVE NE 98004

Bellingham, Whatcom Co., Pop. Code 8
Bellingham SD 501
Sch. Sys. Enr. Code 6
Supt. – Dr. Lee Olsen, P O BOX 878 98227
Fairhaven MS, 110 PARK RIDGE ROAD 98225
Gregory Cowan, prin.
Shuksan MS, 2713 ALDERWOOD AVE 98225
Donald Young, prin.
Whatcom MS, 810 HALLECK ST 98225
William Fox, prin.
Alderwood ES, 3400 HOLLYWOOD AVE 98225
Sidney Hammond, prin.
Birchwood ES, 3200 PINEWOOD ST 98225
Dr. Norma Jean Williams, prin.
Columbia ES, 2508 UTTER ST 98225
Jack Wayerski, prin.
Cozier ES, 1330 LINCOLN ST 98226
Stephanie Sadler, prin.
Geneva ES, 1401 GENEVA ST 98226
Robert Austin, prin.
Happy Valley ES, 1041 24TH ST 98225
Terry Jorgenson, prin.
Larrabee ES, 1409 18TH ST 98225
Charlotte Owens, prin.

Lowell ES, 935 14TH ST 98225
Robert Brand, prin.
Parkview ES, 3033 COOLIDGE DR 98225
Gary Karlberg, prin.
Roosevelt ES, 2900 YEW ST 98226
Rodger Teig, prin.
Silver Beach ES, 4101 ACADEMY ST 98226
Roberta Bullock, prin.
Sunnyland ES, 2800 JAMES ST 98225
Gregory Freeman, prin.

Ferndale SD 502
Supt. – See Ferndale
North Bellingham ES
5275 NORTHWEST ROAD 98226
Tim Smith, prin.

Meridian SD 505
Sch. Sys. Enr. Code 4
Supt. – Dr. Donald Bauthues
194 LAUREL ROAD W 98226
Other Schools – See Everson, Lynden

Mt. Baker SD 507
Supt. – See Deming
Harmony ES, 5060 SAND ROAD 98226
Bruce Burpee, prin.

Assumption ES, 2116 CORNWALL AVE 98225

Benge, Adams Co.
Benge SD 122
Sch. Sys. Enr. Code 1
Supt. – (—) 99105
ES 99105 – Mary Ault, prin.

Benton City, Benton Co., Pop. Code 4
Kiona-Benton City SD 52
Sch. Sys. Enr. Code 4
Supt. – Gary Henderson, P O BOX 488 99320
Kiona-Benton City MS, P O BOX 488 99320
Steve Chestnut, prin.
Kiona-Benton City ES, P O BOX 488 99320
Leroy Fulfs, prin.

Bickleton, Klickitat Co.
Bickleton SD 203
Sch. Sys. Enr. Code 1
Supt. – Donald Newhall, P O BOX 10 99322
ES, P O BOX 10 99322 – Donald Newhall, prin.

Black Diamond, King Co., Pop. Code 4
Enumclaw SD 216
Supt. – See Enumclaw
ES, P O BOX 285 98010
David Wickersham, prin.

Blaine, Whatcom Co., Pop. Code 4
Blaine SD 503
Sch. Sys. Enr. Code 4
Supt. – Robert Gilden, P O BOX S 98230
MS, P O BOX S 98230 – William Kelly, prin.
ES, P O BOX S 98230 – E. Warren Aller, prin.

Bothell, King Co., Pop. Code 6
Everett SD 2
Supt. – See Everett
Mill Creek ES, 3400 148TH STREET SE 98012
Lynnette Lifirig, prin.
Woodside ES, 17000 23RD AVE SE 98012
Leslie Elsaesser, prin.

Northshore SD 417
Sch. Sys. Enr. Code 7
Supt. – Lee Maxwell
18315 BOTHELL WAY NE 98011
Arrowhead ES, 14925 67TH AVE NE 98011
Paulette Payseno, prin.
Canyon Creek ES, 21400 35TH AVE SE 98021
Ella Larrick, prin.
Crystal Springs ES, 21615 9TH AVE 98021
Blake Puckett, prin.
Kenmore ES, 19121 71ST AVE NE 98011
Ed Young, prin.
Lockwood ES, 24118 LOCKWOOD ROAD 98021
Jeane Lundgren, prin.
Maywood Hills ES, 19510 104TH AVE NE 98011
Gretchen Evans, prin.
Moorlands ES, 15115 104TH AVE NE 98011
Sylvia Lesser, prin.
Shelton View ES, 23400 5TH AVE W 98021
Charles Wheaton, prin.
Westhill ES, 19515 88TH AVE NE 98011
Ron Belcher, prin.
Woodin ES, 12950 NE 195TH ST 98011
Paul Bodnar, prin.
Other Schools – See Redmond, Woodinville

Heritage Christian ES
19527 104TH AVE NE 98011
Cedar Park Christian ES
16300 112TH AVE NE 98011
Montessori House ES
16017 118TH PLACE NE 98011
St. Brendan's ES, P O BOX 626 98011

Bow, Skagit Co., Pop. Code 5
Burlington-Edison SD 100
Supt. – See Burlington
Allen ES, 1517 COOK EXT ROAD 98232
Michael C. Miller, prin.

Bremerton, Kitsap Co., Pop. Code 8
Bremerton SD 100-C
Sch. Sys. Enr. Code 6
Supt. – Dr.DeWayne Boyd
300 N MONTGOMERY AVE 98312

MS, 2442 PERRY AVE 98310
  Flint Walpole, prin.
Crownhill ES, 1537 BERTHA AVE 98312
  Gerald Johnson, prin.
Jahr ES, 900 DIBB ST 98310
  Dwight Mickels, prin.
Naval Avenue ES, 900 OLYMPIC AVE 98312
  Richard Barich, prin.
Olympic View ES, 2442 PERRY AVE 98310
  Lloyd Sayer, prin.
View Bridge ES, 3220 WHEATON WAY 98310
  Donald Rogers, prin.
West Hills ES, 599 NATIONAL AVE S 98312
  Ernest Feser, prin.

Central Kitsap SD 401
Supt. – See Silverdale
Brownsville ES, 8795 ILLAHEE RD NE 98310
  David McVicker, prin.
Cottonwood ES, 330 FOSTER RD NE 98310
  Greg Cleven, prin.
Esquire Hills ES
  2650 NE JOHN CARLSON RD 98310
  Pamela Johnson, prin.
Jackson Park ES, 6200 DOWELL DR 98310
  Kimberly Marcum, prin.
Tracyton ES, 5550 TRACYTON BLVD NW 98310
  Ann Lawrie, prin.
Woodlands ES
  7420 CENTRAL VALLEY RD NE 98310
  Bruce Hobert, prin.

Bremerton Christian School
  4012 CHICO WAY NW 98312
Our Lady Star of the Sea ES, 1513 6TH ST 98310
Peace Lutheran ES
  1234 NE RIDDELL ROAD 98310

Brewster, Okanogan Co., Pop. Code 4
Brewster SD 111
Sch. Sys. Enr. Code 3
Supt. – Mark Jacobson, P O BOX 97 98812
ES 98812 – Donald Mueller, prin.

Bridgeport, Douglas Co., Pop. Code 4
Bridgeport SD 75
Sch. Sys. Enr. Code 2
Supt. – Robert Allen, P O BOX 1060 98813
ES, P O BOX 1060 98813 – Jean Homer, prin.

Brinnon, Jefferson Co.
Brinnon SD 46
Sch. Sys. Enr. Code 1
Supt. – Carolyn Enzler
  46 SCHOOLHOUSE ROAD 98320
ES, 46 SCHOOLHOUSE ROAD 98320
  (—), prin.

Brush Prairie, Clark Co.
Hockinson SD 98
Sch. Sys. Enr. Code 3
Supt. – Dr. Roger L. Bieber
  15916 NE 182ND AVE 98606
Hockinson MS, 15916 NE 182ND AVE 98606
  Vern Freeman, prin.
Hockinson Hts. ES, 20000 NE 164TH ST 98606
  Steve Wright, prin.

Buckley, Pierce Co., Pop. Code 5
White River SD 416
Sch. Sys. Enr. Code 5
Supt. – Richard Andrews, P O BOX G 98321
White River MS, P O BOX G 98321
  Patricia Cullen, prin.
Foothills ES, P O BOX G 98321 – Norm Ross, prin.
White River ES, P O BOX G 98321
  Patricia Brown, prin.
Other Schools – See Wilkeson

Burbank, Walla Walla Co., Pop. Code 5
Columbia SD 400
Sch. Sys. Enr. Code 3
Supt. – Larry Sappington, P O BOX 8 99323
Columbia Mid.S 99323 – Larry Sappington, prin.
Columbia ES 99323 – Robert Nolan, prin.

Burlington, Skagit Co., Pop. Code 5
Burlington-Edison SD 100
Sch. Sys. Enr. Code 4
Supt. – Dr. Paul Chaplik
  936 VICTORIA AVE E 98233
Umbarger ES, 820 SKAGIT ST S 98233
  Donald C. Zorn, prin.
West View ES, 515 VICTORIA AVE W 98233
  Louie J. Spane, prin.
Other Schools – See Bow, Edison

Camas, Clark Co., Pop. Code 6
Camas SD 117
Sch. Sys. Enr. Code 4
Supt. – Dr. Richard Mariotti
  2028 NE GARFIELD ST 98607
Zellerbach MS, 841 NE 22ND AVE 98607
  Patricia Boles, prin.
Fox ES, 2623 NW SIERRA ST 98607
  James Dunn, prin.
Lacamas Hts. ES, 1120 SE 262ND AVE 98607
  Patricia Edwards, prin.

Carbonado, Pierce Co., Pop. Code 2
Carbonado SD 406
Sch. Sys. Enr. Code 2
Supt. – Richard Carter 98323
ES 98323 – Richard Carter, prin.

Carnation, King Co., Pop. Code 3
Riverview SD 407
Sch. Sys. Enr. Code 4
Supt. – Dr. Karen Forys
  4900 TOLD RIVER ROAD NE 98014
Tolt MS, 3740 TOLT RIVER ROAD NE 98014
  Kathleen McMahon, prin.
ES, 4950 TOLT RIV RD NE 98014
  Jim Jordan, prin.
Other Schools – See Duvall

Carrolls, Cowlitz Co.
Kelso SD 453
Supt. – See Kelso
ES, P O BOX 3 98609 – Susan Baxter, prin.

Cashmere, Chelan Co., Pop. Code 4
Cashmere SD 222
Sch. Sys. Enr. Code 4
Supt. – Randall Hauff, 210 S DIVISION ST 98815
MS, 300 TIGNER ROAD 98815 – Ed Tuggle, prin.
Vale ES, 101 PIONEER AVE 98815
  Conrad Lautensleger, prin.

Castle Rock, Cowlitz Co., Pop. Code 4
Castle Rock SD 401
Sch. Sys. Enr. Code 4
Supt. – Dr. Richard Galt, P O BOX 218 98611
MS, P O BOX 100 98611 – Lyle Swanson, prin.
Castle Rock Upper MS, P O BOX 160 98611
  Tom Quigley, prin.
ES, P O BOX 160 98611 – Tom Quigley, prin.

Cathlamet, Wahkiakum Co., Pop. Code 3
Wahkiakum SD 200
Sch. Sys. Enr. Code 2
Supt. – John Thomas, P O BOX 398 98612
Wendt ES, P O BOX 398 98612 – Tom Colby, prin.

Centerville, Klickitat Co.
Centerville SD 215
Sch. Sys. Enr. Code 1
Supt. – Arthur Hoisington, P O BOX 357 98613
ES 98613 – (—), prin.

Centralia, Lewis Co., Pop. Code 7
Centralia SD 401
Sch. Sys. Enr. Code 5
Supt. – Dr. L. Dean Sorenson, P O BOX 610 98531
MS, 901 JOHNSON ROAD 98531
  Brian Glaspell, prin.
Edison ES, 607 H ST 98531 – Joe Gunther, prin.
Fords-Prairie ES, 1620 HARRISON AVE 98531
  Don Meek, prin.
Jefferson Lincoln ES, 400 W SUMMA ST 98531
  Anita Lloyd, prin.
Oakview MS, 201 OAKVIEW AVE 98531
  Robert Carter, prin.
Washington MS, FIELD & SPRUCE STS 98531
  Jerry Eacker, prin.

Centralia Christian ES, 1215 W MAIN ST 98531

Chattaroy, Spokane Co.
Riverside SD 416
Sch. Sys. Enr. Code 4
Supt. – Jerry M. Wilson
  RURAL ROUTE 01 BOX 287 99003
Riverside Mid.S
  RURAL ROUTE 01 BOX 278 99003
  Mark Gorman, prin.
ES, RURAL ROUTE 02 BOX 192 99003
  Cindy Benzel, prin.
Riverside ES, RURAL ROUTE 01 BOX 279 99003
  Michael Jordan, prin.

Chehalis, Lewis Co., Pop. Code 6
Chehalis SD 302
Sch. Sys. Enr. Code 4
Supt. – Gene Sharratt, 16TH AND WILSON 98532
Olympic Mid.S, 2057 SW SALSBURY AVE 98532
  Gerald Pierson, prin.
Bennett MS, 233 SW 3RD ST 98532
  Raymond Gundersen, prin.
Cascade ES, 89 SW 3RD ST 98532
  Glynn Gibson, prin.

St. Joseph ES, 123 SW 6TH ST 98532

Chelan, Chelan Co., Pop. Code 5
Lake Chelan SD 129
Sch. Sys. Enr. Code 3
Supt. – Carol Anderson 98816
MS 98816 – Larry Bowers, prin.
Morgen Owings ES 98816 – Thomas Baker, prin.

Cheney, Spokane Co., Pop. Code 6
Cheney SD 360
Sch. Sys. Enr. Code 5
Supt. – James Jungers, 520 4TH ST 99004
Betz ES, 317 N 7TH ST 99004 – Mary Shea, prin.
Reid Elementary School, 210 7TH ST 99004
  Delitha Spear, prin.
Salnave ES, 1015 SALNAVE ROAD 99004
  Joseph Mirich, prin.
Other Schools – See Airway Heights, Spokane

Chewelah, Stevens Co., Pop. Code 4
Chewelah SD 36
Sch. Sys. Enr. Code 4
Supt. – Steve Deal, P O BOX 47 99109
Jenkins MS, P O BOX 47 99109
  Sharon Horstman, prin.
Gess ES, P O BOX 47 99109
  Richard H. Brown, prin.

Chimacum, Jefferson Co., Pop. Code 2
Chimacum SD 49
Sch. Sys. Enr. Code 4
Supt. – L. D. Olson, P O BOX 278 98325
JHS, P O BOX 278 98325 – Mike O'Donnell, prin.
ES 98325 – Gary Breitstein, prin.

Clarkston, Asotin Co., Pop. Code 6
Clarkston SD J 250-185
Sch. Sys. Enr. Code 5
Supt. – Dr. H. O. Beggs, P O BOX 70 99403
Lincoln MS, 1945 4TH AVE 99403
  Jack Adams, prin.
Grantham ES, 1253 POPLAR ST 99403
  Norman Garrett, prin.
Highland ES, 1432 HIGHLAND AVE 99403
  David Brown, prin.
Parkway ES, 1103 4TH ST 99403
  Richard Schutte, prin.

Holy Family ES, 1002 CHESTNUT STREET 99403

Cle Elum, Kittitas Co., Pop. Code 4
Cle Elum-Roslyn SD 404
Sch. Sys. Enr. Code 3
Supt. – Dale Almlie, HRC 60 BOX 5010 98922
Cle Elum-Roslyn ES, 201 E 2ND ST 98922
  William Tracy, prin.
Other Schools – See Roslyn

Clearlake, Skagit Co.
Sedro Woolley SD 101
Supt. – See Sedro Woolley
ES, P O BOX 128 98235 – Richard Ruhl, prin.

Colbert, Spokane Co., Pop. Code 5
Mead SD 354
Supt. – See Mead
ES, RURAL ROUTE 03 BOX 94 99005
  Conn Wittwer, prin.
Midway ES, 821 E MIDWAY ROAD 99005
  Orval Janssen, prin.

Colfax, Whitman Co., Pop. Code 5
Colfax SD 300
Sch. Sys. Enr. Code 3
Supt. – Richard Langum
  1110 N MORTON ST 99111
Jennings ES, 1207 N MORTON ST 99111
  Jim Rosenbeck, prin.

College Place, Walla Walla Co., Pop. Code 6
College Place SD 250
Sch. Sys. Enr. Code 3
Supt. – C. E. Murphy
  1755 S COLLEGE AVE 99324
Sager MS, 1755 S COLLEGE AVE 99324
  Miles Kinzer, prin.
Davis ES, 31 SE ASH AVE 99324
  Jack Brennan, prin.

Clara E. Rogers ES, P O BOX 428 · 99324

Colton, Whitman Co., Pop. Code 2
Colton SD 306
Sch. Sys. Enr. Code 2
Supt. – Dr. Mike Johnson 99113
ES 99113 – Greg Reault, prin.

Colville, Stevens Co., Pop. Code 5
Colville SD 115
Sch. Sys. Enr. Code 4
Supt. – Dr. James Hitter
  430 E HAWTHORNE AVE 99114
Aster MS, 225 S HOFSTETTER ST 99114
  Dr. George Carnie, prin.
Fort Colville MS, 1212 E IVY 99114
  Elaine Porter Cole, prin.
Hofstetter ES, 640 N HOFSTETTER ST 99114
  Chuck Salina, prin.

Onion Creek SD 30
Sch. Sys. Enr. Code 1
Supt. – Suellen White
  RURAL ROUTE 02 BOX 301 99114
Onion Creek ES
  RURAL ROUTE 02 BOX 301 99114
  Joel Anderson, prin.

Concrete, Skagit Co., Pop. Code 3
Concrete SD 11
Sch. Sys. Enr. Code 3
Supt. – Dr. Gil Holt, P O BOX 386 98237
ES, P O BOX 387 98237
  Dr. Donald Jeanroy, prin.

Connell, Franklin Co., Pop. Code 4
North Franklin SD J 51-162
Sch. Sys. Enr. Code 4
Supt. – Dr. Dale Clark 99326
Olds JHS 99326 – Kenneth Behrends, prin.
ES 99326 – Terry Atwood, prin.
Other Schools – See Mesa

Cook, Klickitat Co.
Mill A SD 31
Sch. Sys. Enr. Code 1
Supt. – Jerry Harding, 11 R JESSUP ROAD 98605
Mill A ES, MPO 1.11 R JESSUP ROAD 98605
  (—), prin.

Copalis Beach, Grays Harbor Co., Pop. Code 2
North Beach SD 64
Sch. Sys. Enr. Code 3
Supt. – Richard Torrens, P O BOX 344 98535
Other Schools – See Ocean Shores, Pacific Beach

Cosmopolis, Grays Harbor Co.
Cosmopolis SD 99
Sch. Sys. Enr. Code 2
Supt. – Dr. Jake Henderson, P O BOX 479 98537
ES, P O BOX 479 98537
  K. Marcella Bramstedt, prin.

North River SD 200
Sch. Sys. Enr. Code 2
Supt. – Robert Tomisser, HCR 77 BOX 395 98537
North River ES, HCR 77 BOX 395 98537
  Robert Tomisser, prin.

Coulee City, Grant Co., Pop. Code 3
Coulee-Hartline SD 151
Sch. Sys. Enr. Code 2
Supt. – Dr. Raymond Phillips, P O BOX 428 99115
Coulee-Hartline ES 99115
  Raymond Phillips, prin.
Other Schools – See Hartline

Coulee Dam, Grant Co., Pop. Code 4
Grand Coulee Dam SD 301J
Sch. Sys. Enr. Code 4
Supt. – James Keene, W STEVENS 99116
Wright ES, 201 CREST DRIVE 99116
  Raymond Gilman, prin.
Other Schools – See Grand Coulee

Coupeville, Island Co., Pop. Code 4
Coupeville SD 204
Sch. Sys. Enr. Code 3
Supt. – Dr. Ernie Bartelson, P O BOX 726 98239
ES, 2 S MAIN ST 98239 – Virginia Moon, prin.

Cowiche, Yakima Co.
Highland SD 203
Sch. Sys. Enr. Code 3
Supt. – Robert Jundt, P O BOX 38 98923
Whitman-Cowiche ES
  1181 THOMPSON ROAD 98923
  Dean Mondor, prin.
Other Schools – See Tieton

Creston, Lincoln Co., Pop. Code 2
Creston SD 73
Sch. Sys. Enr. Code 2
Supt. – Michael Crowell, P O BOX 17 99117
ES, P O BOX 17 99117 – Wayne Kannberg, prin.

Curlew, Ferry Co., Pop. Code 4
Curlew SD 50
Sch. Sys. Enr. Code 2
Supt. – Jerry Davis, P O BOX 9 99118
S, P O BOX 9 99118 – S. Tedrow, prin.

Curtis, Lewis Co.
Boistfort SD 234
Sch. Sys. Enr. Code 2
Supt. – Thomas Wood
  983 BOISTFORT ROAD 98538
Boistfort ES, 983 BOISTFORT RD 98538
  Thomas Wood, prin.

Cusick, Pend Oreille Co., Pop. Code 2
Cusick SD 59
Sch. Sys. Enr. Code 2
Supt. – Charles Crickman 99119
ES 99119 – Charles Crickman, prin.

Custer, Whatcom Co.
Ferndale SD 502
Supt. – See Ferndale
ES, P O BOX 470 98240
  Margaret Thompson, prin.

Dallesport, Klickitat Co.
Lyle SD 406
Supt. – See Lyle
ES 98617 – Dean Oldenburg, prin.

Darrington, Snohomish Co., Pop. Code 4
Darrington SD 330
Sch. Sys. Enr. Code 3
Supt. – William Edwards, P O BOX 27 98241
ES, P O BOX 27 98241 – Beryl O. Mauldin, prin.

Davenport, Lincoln Co., Pop. Code 4
Davenport SD 207
Sch. Sys. Enr. Code 2
Supt. – Dave Iverson, P O BOX 8 99122
ES, P O BOX 8 99122 – Harold Patterson, prin.

Dayton, Columbia Co., Pop. Code 5
Dayton SD 2
Sch. Sys. Enr. Code 3
Supt. – Lynn Lupfer, 609 S 2ND ST 99328
ES, 302 PARK ST 99328 – Lynn Lupfer, prin.

Decatur Island, San Juan Co.
Lopez SD 144
Supt. – See Lopez
ES 98221 – Karen Lamb, prin.

Deer Park, Spokane Co., Pop. Code 4
Deer Park SD 414
Sch. Sys. Enr. Code 4
Supt. – Carl M. Maw 99006
JHS 99006 – Darell Cain, prin.
Arcadia MS 99006 – Jean Chandler, prin.
ES 99006 – Robert Rundell, prin.

Deming, Whatcom Co., Pop. Code 2
Mt. Baker SD 507
Sch. Sys. Enr. Code 4
Supt. – William A. Boulton 98244
ES 98244 – Donna Mellander, prin.
Other Schools – See Acme, Bellingham, Maple Falls

Des Moines, King Co., Pop. Code 6
Highline SD 401
Supt. – See Seattle
Chinook MS, 18367 8TH AVE S 98148
  Lamar Strain, prin.
Pacific MS, 22705 24TH AVE S 98188
  Larry Reynolds, prin.
ES, 22001 9TH AVE S 98198
  Helen Clement, prin.
Midway ES, 22447 24TH AVE S 98198
  Dr. Ron Lynch, prin.

St. Philomena's ES, 1815 S 220TH ST 98198

Dixie, Walla Walla Co.
Dixie SD 101
Sch. Sys. Enr. Code 1
Supt. – (—), P O BOX 77 99329
ES, P O BOX 77 99329 – Ray E. Yoder, prin.

Duvall, King Co., Pop. Code 3
Riverview SD 407
Supt. – See Carnation
Cherry Valley ES
  26701 NE CHERRY VALLEY ROAD 98019
  Karen Koester, prin.

East Olympia, Thurston Co., Pop. Code 7
Tumwater SD 33
Supt. – See Tumwater
ES 98540 – Charlene Allen, prin.

East Wenatchee, Douglas Co., Pop. Code 3
Eastmont SD 206
Sch. Sys. Enr. Code 5
Supt. – Walt Bigby, 460 9TH ST NE 98801
Sterling MS, 600 JAMES AVE N 98801
  Ed Barnhart, prin.
Cascade ES, 2330 BAKER AVE N 98801
  James Yancey, prin.
Grant ES, 1430 1ST ST SE 98801
  Beverly Jagla, prin.
Kenroy ES, 601 N JONOTHAN ST 98801
  Roy Henson, prin.
Lee ES, 1455 BAKER AVE N 98801
  James Malloy, prin.
Other Schools – See Wenatchee

Easton, Kittitas Co., Pop. Code 2
Easton SD 28
Sch. Sys. Enr. Code 1
Supt. – Jerry Kappenman, P O BOX 8 98925
S, P O BOX 8 98925 – Jerry Kappenman, prin.

Eastsound, San Juan Co., Pop. Code 2
Orcas Island SD 137
Sch. Sys. Enr. Code 2
Supt. – Thomas O'Brien, P O BOX 167 98245
Orcas Island MS, P O BOX 167 98245
  Kathleen Barner, prin.
Milton ES, P O BOX 167 98245
  Kathleen Barner, prin.
Other Schools – See Waldron

Eatonville, Pierce Co., Pop. Code 3
Eatonville SD 404
Sch. Sys. Enr. Code 4
Supt. – Dr. S. M. Martin, P O BOX 698 98328
MS, P O BOX 910 98328 – Deborah Brewer, prin.
ES, P O BOX 669 98328 – Robert Schaub, prin.
Weyerhaeuser ES, 6105 365TH ST E 98328
  Lewis Linington, prin.
Other Schools – See Ashford

Edison, Skagit Co.
Burlington-Edison SD 100
Supt. – See Burlington
ES, 577 MAIN AVE 98232
  David E. Johnson, prin.

Edmonds, Snohomish Co., Pop. Code 8
Edmonds SD 15
Supt. – See Lynnwood
Chase Lake ES, 21603 84TH AVE W 98020
  Laura Park, prin.
Seaview Heights ES, 8426 188TH ST SW 98020
  Marcia Nashem, prin.
Sherwood ES, 22901 106TH AVE W 98020
  Joe Rice, prin.
Westgate ES, 9601 220TH ST SW 98020
  Michael Hanrahan, prin.

Mukilteo SD 6
Supt. – See Everett
Picnic Point ES, 5819 140TH ST SW 98020
  Neil Cummings, prin.
Serene Lake ES, 4709 PICNIC POINT ROAD 98020
  Gerry Hussey, prin.

Holy Rosary ES, P O BOX 206 98020
The Stein ES, 7218 208TH ST SW 98020

Ellensburg, Kittitas Co., Pop. Code 7
Damman SD 7
Sch. Sys. Enr. Code 1
Supt. – Marsha Smith
  RURAL ROUTE 06 BOX 1266 98926
Damman ES, RURAL ROUTE 06 BOX 1740 98926
  Jacqueline Pratt, prin.

Ellensburg SD 401
Sch. Sys. Enr. Code 4
Supt. – Dr. Lew Moormann
  1300 E 3RD AVE 98926
Morgan MS, 400 E 1ST 98926
  Donald Price, prin.

Lincoln ES, 200 S SAMPSON 98926
  Rod Goosman, prin.
Mount Stuart ES, 705 W 15TH 98926
  Dick Robinson, prin.
Washington ES, 506 N SPRAGUE 98926
  Eugene Jump, prin.

Elma, Grays Harbor Co., Pop. Code 5
Elma SD 68
Sch. Sys. Enr. Code 4
Supt. – Gary Logan, P O BOX 698 98541
MS, P O BOX 698 98541 – Tami Hickle, prin.
ES, 30 ELMA MONTE ROAD 98541
  Lyle Burbidge, prin.

Endicott, Whitman Co., Pop. Code 2
Endicott SD 308
Sch. Sys. Enr. Code 2
Supt. – Dr Donald Simpson 98125
Endicott-St. John MS 99125
  Richard Scheuerman, prin.
ES 99125 – Richard Scheuerman, prin.

Entiat, Chelan Co., Pop. Code 2
Entiat SD 127
Sch. Sys. Enr. Code 2
Supt. – Virgil H. King, 2650 ENTIAT WAY 98822
ES, 2650 ENTIAT WAY 98822
  Monte Swenson, prin.

Enumclaw, King Co., Pop. Code 6
Enumclaw SD 216
Sch. Sys. Enr. Code 5
Supt. – Dr. James Barchek
  1118 MYRTLE AVE 98022
JHS, 550 SEMANSKI ST 98022
  Lea Anna Portmann, prin.
Kibler ES, 2057 KIBLER AVE 98022
  Mary O'Connor, prin.
Smith MS, 1640 FELL ST 98022
  Ronald May, prin.
Southwood ES, 3240 MCDOUGALL AVE 98022
  James Bolton, prin.
Westwood ES, 21200 SE 416TH ST 98022
  Wesley Hanson, prin.
Other Schools – See Black Diamond

Ephrata, Grant Co., Pop. Code 6
Ephrata SD 165
Sch. Sys. Enr. Code 4
Supt. – Dick Kinart, P O BOX 788 98823
MS, 384 A ST SE 98823 – Pat Flannery, prin.
Columbia Ridge ES, 60 H S E 98823
  Paul Oliver, prin.
Grant ES, 3RD & F NW 98823 – Dan Martell, prin.

St. Rose of Lima ES, P O BOX 1025 98823

Everett, Snohomish Co., Pop. Code 8
Everett SD 2
Sch. Sys. Enr. Code 7
Supt. – Dr. Paul Sjunnesen, P O BOX 2098 98203
Eisenhower MS, 2500 100TH ST SE 98204
  Judy Heidman, prin.
Evergreen MS, 7621 BEVERLY LANE 98203
  Les Hazen, prin.
Heatherwood MS 98203 – Bill Palmer, prin.
North MS, 2514 RAINIER AVE 98201
  Tom Romerdahl, prin.
Emerson ES, 8702 7TH AVE SE 98208
  Gaylor Schank, prin.
Garfield ES, 23RD & PINE 98201
  Betty Cobbs, prin.
Hawthorne ES, 1110 POPLAR ST 98201
  Wally Hall, prin.
Jackson ES, 3700 FEDERAL AVE 98201
  Robert Timm, prin.
Jefferson ES, 2500 CADET WAY 98208
  James McNally, prin.
Lowell ES, 5010 VIEW DRIVE 98203
  Joy Landsdowne, prin.
Madison ES, 616 PECKS DRIVE 98203
  Dana Gilroy, prin.
Monroe ES, 10901 27TH AVE SE 98208
  Kitty England, prin.
Silver Firs ES, 5909 146TH PLACE SE 98208
  Anne Martinis, prin.
Silver Lake ES, 12815 BOTHELL WAY 98204
  Sue Dedrick, prin.
View Ridge ES, 202 ALDER ST 98203
  Leann Torgerson, prin.
Whittier ES, 916 OAKES AVE 98201
  Bette Story, prin.
Other Schools – See Bothell

Lake Stevens SD 4
Supt. – See Lake Stevens
Lake Stevens MS, 1031 91ST AVE SE 98205
  David Minch, prin.
Hillcrest ES, 9315 4TH ST SE 98205
  Steven L. Smedley, prin.

Mukilteo SD 6
Sch. Sys. Enr. Code 6
Supt. – Dr. James Shoemake
  9401 SHARON DRIVE 98204
Challenger ES, 9600 SHARON DR 98204
  Ron Wick, prin.
Fairmount ES, 11401 HOLLY DR 98204
  Jean Boris, prin.
Olivia Park ES, 200 108TH ST SW 98204
  Dr. Dixie Young, prin.
Other Schools – See Alderwood Manor, Edmonds,
  Mukilteo

Snohomish SD 201
Supt. — See Snohomish
Seattle Hill ES, 12711 51ST AVE SE   98208
  Judy Edmonds, prin.

Immaculate Conception ES
  2508 HOYT AVE   98201
Silver Lake Christian ES
  2027 132ND ST SE   98208
St. Mary Magdalen ES, 8615 7TH AVE SE   98208

Everson, Whatcom Co., Pop. Code 3
Meridian SD 505
Supt. — See Bellingham
Reither PS, 954 E HEMMI ROAD   98247
  Richard Clark, prin.

Nooksack Valley SD 506
Supt. — See Nooksack
Nooksack Valley ES, P O BOX 278   98247
  Dale Steele, prin.

Fairchild AFB, Spokane Co.
Medical Lake SD 326
Supt. — See Medical Lake
Blair ES   99011 — Femme Munn, prin.

Fall City, King Co.
Snoqualmie Valley SD 410
Supt. — See Snoqualmie
ES, P O BOX 220   98024 — Lester Jones, prin.

Federal Way, King Co., Pop. Code 7
Federal Way SD 210
Sch. Sys. Enr. Code 7
Supt. — Dr. G. Richard Harris
  31405 18TH AVE S   98003
Adelaide ES, 1635 SW 304TH ST   98023
  Dr. Jill Hearne, prin.
Brigadoon ES, 3601 SW 336TH ST   98023
  Darwin Springer, prin.
Lake Grove ES, 303 SW 308TH ST   98023
  Carol Golden, prin.
Mirror Lake ES, 624 S 314TH ST   98003
  Patricia Smithson, prin.
Nautilus ES, 1000 S 289TH ST   98003
  Katrina Frank, prin.
Olympic View ES, 2626 SW 327TH ST   98023
  Richard Cornwell, prin.
Panther Lake ES, 34424 1ST AVE S   98003
  Sharon Stenersen, prin.
Twin Lakes ES, 4400 SW 320TH ST   98023
  Carolanne Watness, prin.
Wildwood ES, 2405 S 300TH ST   98003
  Carol Matsui, prin.
Other Schools — See Auburn, Kent

Colonial Christian ES
  1232 SW DASH POINT ROAD   98023
Spring Vall Montessori ES
  36605 PACIFIC HIGHWAY S   98003
St. Vincent De Paul ES, 30527 8TH AVE S   98003

Ferndale, Whatcom Co., Pop. Code 5
Ferndale SD 502
Sch. Sys. Enr. Code 5
Supt. — Dr. Jack Thompson, P O BOX 698   98248
Vista MS, P O BOX 1328   98248
  Christine Kuhnly, prin.
Central ES, P O BOX 187   98248
  Bruce Berry, prin.
Mountain View ES, P O BOX 935   98248
  Georgia Peterson, prin.
Skyline ES, P O BOX 905   98248
  Dave Boeringa, prin.
Other Schools — See Bellingham, Custer, Lummi
  Island

Forks, Clallam Co., Pop. Code 5
Queets Clearwater SD 20
Sch. Sys. Enr. Code 1
Supt. — Frances Hansen, HCR 01 BOX 1750   98331
Queets-Clearwater ES, HCR 80 BOX 1750   98331
  Ted Knivila, prin.

Quillayute Valley SD 402
Sch. Sys. Enr. Code 4
Supt. — Lew McGill, P O BOX 60   98331
IS, P O BOX 60   98331 — William Berglund, prin.
PS, P O BOX 60   98331 — Samuel McElravy, prin.

Fort Lewis, Pierce Co., Pop. Code 8
Clover Park SD 400
Supt. — See Tacoma
Beachwood ES, AMERICAN LAKE AVE A   98433
  Knute Adams, prin.
Clarkmoor ES, S DIVISION AND LIGGETT   98433
  Jerry Fritts, prin.
Greenwood ES, N DIVISION AND IDAHO   98433
  Gerald Stevenson, prin.
Hillside ES
  GARCIA BLVD AND MAGNOLIA BL   98433
  Rolene Peterkin, prin.
Parkway ES, 41ST DIVISION DRIVE   98433
  Maria deVilla, prin.

Friday Harbor, San Juan Co., Pop. Code 4
San Juan Island SD 149
Sch. Sys. Enr. Code 3
Supt. — Frank Kelly, P O BOX 458   98250
ES, P O BOX 458   98250 — Jan Thomas, prin.
Stuart Island ES, HCR   98250 — Jan Thomas, prin.

Garfield, Whitman Co., Pop. Code 3
Garfield SD 302
Sch. Sys. Enr. Code 2
Supt. — Larry Warner, P O BOX 398   99130

Garfield/Palouse MS   99130
  Robert Richards, prin.
ES   99130 — Robert Richards, prin.

George, Grant Co., Pop. Code 2
Quincy SD 144-101
Supt. — See Quincy
ES, P O BOX 5265   98824 — Dave Rossing, prin.

Gig Harbor, Pierce Co., Pop. Code 4
Peninsula SD 401
Sch. Sys. Enr. Code 6
Supt. — Tom Hulst, 14015 62ND AVE NW   98335
Goodman MS, 9010 PRENTICE AVE   98335
  Rod Mitchell, prin.
Kopachuck MS, 10414 56TH ST NW   98335
  Earl LaBerge, prin.
Artondale ES, 6219 40TH ST NW   98335
  Dave Watson, prin.
Discovery ES, 4905 ROSEDALE ST NW   98335
  Gary Williamson, prin.
Evergreen ES
  1820 KEY PENINSULA HWY KPS   98349
  David Trochim, prin.
Harbor Heights ES, 3510 GRANDVIEW ST   98335
  Steve Aspden, prin.
Minter ES, 12617 118TH AVE NW   98335
  Dave Southwick, prin.
Purdy ES, 13815 62ND AVE NW   98335
  Forbes Gildersleeve, prin.
Other Schools — See Lakebay, Vaughn

Glenoma, Lewis Co.
White Pass SD 303
Supt. — See Randle
ES   98336 — Robert Weller, prin.

Glenwood, Klickitat Co., Pop. Code 2
Glenwood SD 401
Sch. Sys. Enr. Code 2
Supt. — James Sikes, P O BOX 12   98619
S, P O BOX 12   98619 — (—), prin.

Goldendale, Klickitat Co., Pop. Code 5
Goldendale SD 404
Sch. Sys. Enr. Code 4
Supt. — Pat Martin, 603 S ROOSEVELT AVE   98620
Goldendale Middle School, 520 E COLLINS   98620
  Jerry Lynch, prin.
PS, 820 S SCHUSTER   98620 — Sue Thrasher, prin.

Graham, Pierce Co.
Bethel SD 403
Supt. — See Spanaway
Graham ES, 10026 E 204TH STREET   98338
  E. Platt, prin.
Kapowsin ES, 10412 264TH ST E   98338
  F. Keith Brown, prin.
Rocky Ridge ES, 6514 260TH ST E   98338
  Norman Standley, prin.

New Hope Christian ES, 25713 70TH AVE E   98338

Grand Coulee, Grant Co., Pop. Code 4
Grand Coulee Dam SD 301J
Supt. — See Coulee Dam
Center MS, P O BOX 700   99133
  Leon Johnson, prin.

Grandview, Yakima Co., Pop. Code 6
Grandview SD 116-200
Sch. Sys. Enr. Code 4
Supt. — Dr. M. S. Palanuk, 913 W 2ND ST   98930
MS, 1401 W 2ND ST   98930
  Richard T. Miller, prin.
McClure ES, 913 W 2ND ST   98930
  Steve Kaufman, prin.
Smith ES, 205 FIR ST   98930 — Monte Haag, prin.
Thompson ES, 114 EUCLID ST   98930
  Darrel McCallum, prin.

Granger, Yakima Co., Pop. Code 4
Granger SD 204
Sch. Sys. Enr. Code 3
Supt. — Dr. Lorence Simonsen, P O BOX 400   98932
Roosevelt ES, P O BOX 400   98932
  Ron Higgins, prin.

Granite Falls, Snohomish Co., Pop. Code 3
Granite Falls SD 332
Sch. Sys. Enr. Code 4
Supt. — Gale Hogan, P O BOX H   98252
MS   98252 — Brian Anderson, prin.
ES   98252 — Gail Thompson, prin.

Grapeview, Mason Co.
Grapeview SD 54
Sch. Sys. Enr. Code 2
Supt. — Evelyn Savage
  822 MASON BENSON ROAD   98546
ES   98546 — Evelyn Savage, prin.

Greenacres, Spokane Co., Pop. Code 4
Central Valley SD 356
Sch. Sys. Enr. Code 7
Supt. — Dr. Richard Sovde
  E 19307 CATALDO   99016
ES, 17915 E 4TH AVE   99016
  Fran Erickson, prin.
Other Schools — See Spokane, Veradale

Harrah, Yakima Co., Pop. Code 2
Mount Adams SD 209
Supt. — See White Swan
ES, P O BOX 159   98933 — Ted Filer, prin.

Harrington, Lincoln Co., Pop. Code 3
Harrington SD 204
Sch. Sys. Enr. Code 2
Supt. — Richard McBride, P O BOX 204   99134
ES, P O BOX 204   99134 — Jeffrey Miller, prin.

Hartline, Grant Co., Pop. Code 2
Coulee-Hartline SD 151
Supt. — See Coulee City
Coulee-Hartline JHS   99135 — (—), prin.

Hoquiam, Grays Harbor Co., Pop. Code 6
Hoquiam SD 28
Sch. Sys. Enr. Code 4
Supt. — Stanley Pinnick, 312 SIMPSON AVE   98550
MS, 203 W EKLUND AVE   98550
  Loran Northcutt, prin.
Central ES, 311 3RD ST   98550
  Mark Maxfield, prin.
Lincoln ES, 700 WOOD AVE   98550
  Edward Rosi, prin.
Washington ES, 3003 CHERRY ST   98550
  David Wayman, prin.

Hunters, Stevens Co., Pop. Code 2
Columbia SD 206
Sch. Sys. Enr. Code 2
Supt. — Roy W. Graffis   99137
Columbia S   99137 — Fred Pflugrath, prin.

Evergreen SD 205
Sch. Sys. Enr. Code 1
Supt. — Roy Graffis, P O BOX 7   99137
Evergreen ES, P O BOX 7   99137 — (—), prin.

Ilwaco, Pacific Co., Pop. Code 3
Ocean Beach SD 101
Sch. Sys. Enr. Code 4
Supt. — Gilbert Johnson, P O BOX F   98624
Hilltop MS, P O BOX 860   98624
  John Billups, prin.
Other Schools — See Long Beach, Ocean Park

Inchelium, Ferry Co.
Inchelium SD 70
Sch. Sys. Enr. Code 2
Supt. — Brian Lewis, P O BOX E   99138
S, P O BOX E   99138 — Neal Kirby, prin.
Hazelmere ES, HCR 01 BOX 324   99138
  Neal Kirby, prin.

Index, Snohomish Co., Pop. Code 2
Index SD 63
Sch. Sys. Enr. Code 1
Supt. — William Detmering, P O BOX 206   98256
ES, P O BOX 206   98256 — (—), prin.

Ione, Pend Oreille Co., Pop. Code 3
Selkirk SD 70
Supt. — See Metaline Falls
PS, P O BOX 77   99139 — Joseph Newbry, prin.

Issaquah, King Co., Pop. Code 6
Issaquah SD 411
Sch. Sys. Enr. Code 6
Supt. — Kateri Brow, 22211 SE 72ND ST   98027
MS, 22211 SE 72ND ST   98027 — Tina Butt, prin.
Maywood MS, 22211 SE 72ND ST   98027
  Larry Griffith, prin.
Pine Lake MS, 22211 SE 72ND ST   98027
  Bette De Salvo, prin.
Apollo ES, 565 NW HOLLY ST   98027
  Robert Koontz, prin.
Briarwood ES, 565 NW HOLLY ST   98027
  Dr. Abby Adams, prin.
Challenger ES, 565 NW HOLLY ST   98027
  Janet Kophs, prin.
Clark ES, 565 NW HOLLY ST   98027
  Thomas Bradley, prin.
Issaquah Valley ES, 565 NW HOLLY ST   98027
  Paty Festor, prin.
Maple Hills ES, 565 NW HOLLY ST   98027
  Shirley Roberts, prin.
Sunny Hills ES, 565 NW HOLLY ST   98027
  Lois White, prin.

Rainbow ES, 950 7TH AVE NW   98027

Joyce, Clallam Co., Pop. Code 2
Crescent SD 313
Sch. Sys. Enr. Code 2
Supt. — Richard Wilson, P O BOX 2   98343
Cresent ES, P O BOX 2   98343
  Doug Kugalek, prin.

Kahlotus, Franklin Co., Pop. Code 2
Kahlotus SD 56
Sch. Sys. Enr. Code 1
Supt. — J. Glenn Sorensen   99335
ES, P O BOX 69   99335 — J. Glenn Sorenson, prin.

Kalama, Cowlitz Co., Pop. Code 4
Kalama SD 402
Sch. Sys. Enr. Code 3
Supt. — Mal Swanson, P O BOX 1097   98625
MS, 548 CHINA GARDEN RD   98625
  Rich Frazer, prin.
ES, 548 CHINA GARDEN ROAD   98625
  Page Dettman, prin.

Keller, Ferry Co.
Keller SD 3
Sch. Sys. Enr. Code 1
Supt. — Joyce Nee, P O BOX 367   99140
Keller ES   99140 — Darlene Morava, prin.

Kelso, Cowlitz Co., Pop. Code 7
Kelso SD 453
Sch. Sys. Enr. Code 5
Supt. – Dr. Gay Selby, 601 CRAWFORD ST　98626
Barnes ES, 401 BARNES ST　98626
　Roger Peterson, prin.
Butler Acres ES, 1600 BURCHAM ST　98626
　Stanley Riedesel, prin.
Catlin ES, 404 LONG AVE　98626
　Jack O'Brien, prin.
Rose Valley ES, 1502 ROSE VALLEY ROAD　98626
　Bonita Decker, prin.
Wallace ES, 410 ELM ST　98626
　Gary Brumsickle, prin.
Other Schools – See Carrolls, Longview

Kennewick, Benton Co., Pop. Code 8
Finley SD 53
Sch. Sys. Enr. Code 3
Supt. – Rodney Hahn
　RURAL ROUTE 02 BOX 2670　99337
Finley ES, RURAL ROUTE 02 BOX 2670　99337
　Linda Eggers, prin.

Kennewick SD 17
Sch. Sys. Enr. Code 7
Supt. – Dr. Donald N. Anderson
　200 S DAYTON ST　99336
Desert Hills MS, 6011 W 10TH AVE　99336
　Marlis Lindbloom, prin.
Highlands MS, 425 S TWEEDT ST　99336
　Kenneth Pointer, prin.
Park MS, 1011 W 10TH AVE　99336
　James Ezell, prin.
Canyon View ES, 1229 W 22ND　99337
　Greg Fancher, prin.
Cascade ES, 505 HIGHLANDS DR　99337
　Terry Barber, prin.
Eastgate ES, 910 E 10TH AVE　99336
　Joseph Sullivan, prin.
Edison ES, 201 S DAWES ST　99336
　Charles Watson, prin.
Hawthorne ES, 3520 W JOHN DAY AVE　99336
　Gail Still, prin.
Lincoln ES, 4901 W 21ST　99337
　Linda Rash, prin.
Southgate ES, 3121 W 19TH AVE　99336
　Jack Shopbell, prin.
Sunset View ES, 711 CENTER PKWY　99337
　Harry Clemmons, prin.
Vista ES, 1701 N YOUNG ST　99336
　Barbara Ding, prin.
Washington ES, 105 W 21ST AVE　99337
　David Montague, prin.
Westgate ES, 2514 W 4TH AVE　99336
　Ted Mansfield, prin.

Bethlehem Lutheran ES, 1409 S GARFIELD　99337
St. Joseph's ES, 901 W 4TH ST　99336

Kent, King Co., Pop. Code 7
Federal Way SD 210
Supt. – See Federal Way
Star Lake ES, 4014 S 270TH ST　98032
　Don Swanson, prin.
Sunnycrest ES, 24629 42ND AVE S　98032
　Mary Pachek, prin.
Woodmont ES, 26454 16TH AVE S　98032
　George Kaess, prin.

Highline SD 401
Supt. – See Seattle
Parkside ES, 2104 S 247TH　98031
　Virginia Robinson, prin.

Kent SD 415
Sch. Sys. Enr. Code 7
Supt. – Dr. George T. Daniel
　12033 SE 256TH ST　98031
Cedar Valley ES
　26500 TIMBERLANE DRIVE SE　98042
　John Love, prin.
Covington ES, 17070 SE WAX ROAD　98042
　Dr. Charlene Behrns, prin.
Crestwood ES, 25225 180TH AVE SE　98042
　Claude Acree, prin.
East Hill ES, 9825 S 240TH ST　98031
　Janet Rowe, prin.
Grass Lake ES, 28700 191ST PL SE　98042
　Dennis McClellan, prin.
Jenkins Creek ES, 26915 186TH AVE SE　98042
　Tom Reilly, prin.
ES, 317 4TH AVE S　98032
　Dr. William Zimmerman, prin.
Lake Youngs ES, 19660 142ND AVE SE　98042
　Jerry Byers, prin.
Meridan ES, 25621 140TH AVE SE　98042
　Brian Meyer, prin.
O'Brien ES, 6804 S 212TH ST　98032
　Dr. Linda Barker, prin.
Panther Lake ES, 20831 108TH AVE SE　98031
　Jim Del Gianni, prin.
Park Orchard ES, 11010 SE 232ND ST　98031
　John Schmella, prin.
Pine Tree ES, 27825 118TH AVE SE　98031
　Dr. Dennis Johnson, prin.
Scenic Hill ES, 26025 SE 98TH　98031
　Robert Hayes, prin.
Soos Creek ES, 12651 SE 218TH PL　98031
　Dean Ficken, prin.
Sortun ES, 12711 SE 248TH　98031
　Gary Myers, prin.
Springbrook ES, 20035 100TH AVE SE　98031
　Wayne Watanabe, prin.
Other Schools – See Renton

Kent View Christian ES, 930 E JAMES ST　98031
St. James ES, 24447 94TH AVE S　98031

Kettle Falls, Stevens Co., Pop. Code 4
Kettle Falls SD 212
Sch. Sys. Enr. Code 3
Supt. – Gerald Hunter　99141
Mid.S　99141 – Dennis Gibson, prin.
ES　99141 – Jeff Peterson, prin.

Kingston, Kitsap Co., Pop. Code 5
North Kitsap SD 400
Supt. – See Poulsbo
David Wolfe ES
　27089 HIGHLAND ROAD NE　98346
　Don Todd, prin.

Kirkland, King Co., Pop. Code 7
Lake Washington SD 414
Sch. Sys. Enr. Code 7
Supt. – Dr. L. E. Scarr, P O BOX 2909　98033
Bell ES, 11212 NE 112TH ST　98033
　Ann Marie Hanel, prin.
Franklin ES, 12434 NE 60TH ST　98033
　Teresa Fewel, prin.
Frost ES, 11801 NE 140TH　98034
　Mike Baerwald, prin.
Juanita ES, 9635 NE 132ND ST　98034
　Tom Green, prin.
Keller ES, 13820 108TH AVE NE　98034
　Bryant Robinson, prin.
Kirk ES, 1312 6TH ST　98033
　Sherrill Adams, prin.
Lakeview ES, 10400 NE 68TH ST　98033
　Joyce McGlaston, prin.
Muir ES, 14012 132ND AVE NE　98034
　Larry Pollock, prin.
Rose Hill ES, 8044 128TH AVE NE　98033
　Dori Matsen, prin.
Sandberg ES, 12801 84TH AVE NE　98034
　Brad Stolz, prin.
Thoreau ES, 8224 NE 138TH ST　98034
　Don Hanson, prin.
Twain ES, 9525 130TH AVE NE　98033
　Greg Gelderman, prin.
Other Schools – See Redmond

Holy Family ES, 7300 120TH AVE NE　98033
Kirkland SDA ES, 5320 108TH AVE NE　98033

Kittitas, Kittitas Co., Pop. Code 3
Kittitas SD 403
Sch. Sys. Enr. Code 2
Supt. – Wallace Ramsey, P O BOX 599　98934
ES, P O BOX 599　98934 – Wallace Ramsey, prin.

Klickitat, Klickitat Co., Pop. Code 3
Klickitat SD 402
Sch. Sys. Enr. Code 2
Supt. – Roger Mortensen, P O BOX 37　98628
ES, P O BOX 37　98628 – Roger Mortensen, prin.

La Center, Clark Co., Pop. Code 1
La Center SD 101
Sch. Sys. Enr. Code 3
Supt. – Dr. John H. Thomas, P O BOX 168　98629
ES, P O BOX 168　98629 – Linda McGeachy, prin.

La Conner, Skagit Co., Pop. Code 3
La Conner SD 311
Sch. Sys. Enr. Code 2
Supt. – Norman Hoffman, P O BOX D　98257
La Conner Middle School, P O BOX D　98257
　Steff Steinhorst, prin.
ES, P O BOX D　98257 – Catherine Zaklan, prin.

Lacey, Thurston Co., Pop. Code 7
North Thurston SD 3
Sch. Sys. Enr. Code 6
Supt. – Dr. John W. Gott
　6202 PACIFIC AVE SE　98503
Chinook MS, 4301 8TH AVE NE　98506
　Kevin Evoy, prin.
Nisqually MS
　8100 STEILACOOM ROAD SE　98503
　Norman Bykerk, prin.
Evergreen Forest ES
　3025 MARVIN ROAD SE　98503
　John Oliver, prin.
ES, 1800 HOMANN DRIVE SE　98503
　John Feeney, prin.
Lakes ES, 6211 MULLEN ROAD SE　98503
　Craig Shanafelt, prin.
Mountain View ES, 1900 COLLEGE ST SE　98503
　Gloria Humter, prin.
Other Schools – See Olympia

Holy Family ES
　2606 CARPENTER ROAD SE　98503

Lacrosse, Whitman Co., Pop. Code 2
Lacrosse SD 126
Sch. Sys. Enr. Code 2
Supt. – Ronald Daron　99143
ES　99143 – Mark Hummel, prin.

Lake Stevens, Snohomish Co., Pop. Code 4
Lake Stevens SD 4
Sch. Sys. Enr. Code 5
Supt. – Donald M. Christensen
　12708 20TH ST NE　98258
Mount Pilchuck ES, 12806 20TH ST NE　98258
　Dr. Frank R. Howard, prin.

Sunnycrest ES, 3411 99TH AVE NE　98258
　Dr. Ardis M. Shirk, prin.
Other Schools – See Everett

Lakebay, Pierce Co.
Peninsula SD 401
Supt. – See Gig Harbor
Key Penninsula MS
　5510 KEY PENINSULA HWY N　98349
　John Robinson, prin.

Lakewood, Snohomish Co.
Lakewood SD 306
Sch. Sys. Enr. Code 4
Supt. – Wayne Robertson, P O BOX 220　98259
ES, P O BOX 40　98259 – David LaMont, prin.

Lamont, Whitman Co., Pop. Code 2
Lamont SD 264
Sch. Sys. Enr. Code 1
Supt. – Richard Hattrup, P O BOX 503　99017
MS, P O BOX 503　99017 – Joseph Whipple, prin.

Langley, Island Co., Pop. Code 3
South Whidbey SD 206
Sch. Sys. Enr. Code 4
Supt. – Arthur Jarvis, P O BOX 346　98260
MS, P O BOX 370　98260 – Greg Willis, prin.
South Whidbey IS, P O BOX 314　98260
　Sally Harrison, prin.
South Whidbey PS, P O BOX 350　98260
　Steve Stansberry, prin.

Leavenworth, Chelan Co., Pop. Code 4
Cascade SD 228
Sch. Sys. Enr. Code 4
Supt. – Norm Veach, SCHOOL ROAD　98826
Osborn ES, 225 CENTRAL AVE　98826
　Dan Miller, prin.
Winton ES, HCR　98826
　Connie Schwarzkopf, prin.
Other Schools – See Peshastin

Lind, Adams Co., Pop. Code 3
Lind SD 158
Sch. Sys. Enr. Code 2
Supt. – Dan Jeremiah, P O BOX 340　99341
ES, P O BOX 340　99341 – Dan Jeremiah, prin.

Littlerock, Thurston Co.
Tumwater SD 33
Supt. – See Tumwater
ES, P O BOX 7　98556 – Terry Borden, prin.

Long Beach, Pacific Co., Pop. Code 4
Ocean Beach SD 101
Supt. – See Ilwaco
ES, P O BOX 758　98631 – Tom Akerlund, prin.

Longview, Cowlitz Co., Pop. Code 8
Kelso SD 453
Supt. – See Kelso
Beacon Hill Elementary Sch
　257 ALPHA DR　98632 – Robert Rice, prin.

Longview SD 122
Sch. Sys. Enr. Code 6
Supt. – Dr. Grant Hendrickson
　28TH & LILAC STS　98632
Cascade MS, 2821 PARKVIEW DRIVE　98632
　Joan Landau, prin.
Monticello MS, 28TH & HEMLOCK　98632
　Mark Hottowe, prin.
Columbia Hts. ES, 2820 PARKVIEW DRIVE　98632
　Chuck Bergquist, prin.
Columbia Valley Gardens ES
　2650 30TH AVE　98632 – Jo Ann Robinson, prin.
Gray ES, 46TH & OHIO　98632
　Jerry Westendorf, prin.
Kessler ES, 1902 E KESSLER BLVD　98632
　Conrad Bankson, prin.
Mint Valley ES, 2745 38TH AVE　98632
　Mark Rosin, prin.
Olympic ES, 30TH & HUDSON　98632
　Glenn DeGallier, prin.
St. Helens ES, 27TH & BEECH　98632
　Mike Mendenhall, prin.

Columbia Heights Christian Academy
　3609 COLUMBIA HEIGHTS ROAD　98632
Longview Christian ES
　2610 OCIEAN BEACH HIGHWAY　98632
St. Rose ES, 25TH AND NICHOLS BLVD　98632

Loon Lake, Stevens Co.
Loon Lake SD 183
Sch. Sys. Enr. Code 1
Supt. – Vicki Simonsen, P O BOX 159　99148
ES, P O BOX 159　99148 – Vicki K. Simonsen, prin.

Lopez, San Juan Co., Pop. Code 4
Lopez SD 144
Sch. Sys. Enr. Code 2
Supt. – James Kiefert
　RURAL ROUTE 01 BOX 1190　98261
ES, RURAL ROUTE 01 BOX 1190　98261
　James Kiefert, prin.
Other Schools – See Decatur Island

Lummi Island, Whatcom Co.
Ferndale SD 502
Supt. – See Ferndale
Beach ES　98262 – Patty Helm, prin.

Lyle, Klickitat Co., Pop. Code 2
Lyle SD 406
Sch. Sys. Enr. Code 2
Supt. – W. Robert Garrett
7TH & KEASEY STS 98635
Lyle Primary School 98635 – (—), prin.
Other Schools – See Dallesport

Lyman, Skagit Co., Pop. Code 2
Sedro Woolley SD 101
Supt. – See Sedro Woolley
ES, P O BOX 1386 98263 – Jim Abrahamson, prin.

Lynden, Whatcom Co., Pop. Code 5
Lynden SD 504
Sch. Sys. Enr. Code 4
Supt. – Howard Heppner
1203 BRADLEY ROAD 98264
MS 98264 – Mark Helt, prin.
Fisher ES 98264 – Randy Flowers, prin.

Meridian SD 505
Supt. – See Bellingham
Meridian MS, 861 TEN MILE ROAD 98264
Bruce Taubenheim, prin.

Lynden Christian HS, 515 DRAYTON ST 98264

Lynnwood, Snohomish Co., Pop. Code 7
Edmonds SD 15
Sch. Sys. Enr. Code 7
Supt. – Brian Benzel, 3800 196TH ST SW 98036
Brier Terrace MS, 22200 BRIER ROAD 98036
Dorothy Wright, prin.
College Place MS, 7501 208TH ST SW 98036
Ann Foley, prin.
Meadowdale MS, 6500 168TH ST SW 98037
Don Denton, prin.
Beverly ES, 5221 168TH ST SW 98037
Janice Johnson, prin.
Brier ES, 3625 232ND SW 98036
Cliff Nelson, prin.
Cedar Valley ES, 20525 52ND AVE W 98036
Craig Madsen, prin.
College Place ES, 20401 76TH AVE W 98036
Steve Bodnar, prin.
Hazelwood ES, 3300 204TH ST SW 98036
Gloria Steberl, prin.
Hilltop ES, 20425 DAMSON ROAD 98036
Judy Ullock, prin.
Lynndale ES, 7200 191ST PL SW 98036
Dick Angus, prin.
ES, 18638 44TH AVE W 98037 – Frank Tylia, prin.
Martha Lake ES, 1000 172ND SW 98037
Phil Sorensen, prin.
Meadowdale ES, 6505 168TH ST SW 98037
Joe Miller, prin.
Oak Heights ES, 15500 18TH AVE W 98037
Karen Funkhouser, prin.
Spruce ES, 17405 42ND AVE W 98037
Lynda Tripp, prin.
Other Schools – See Edmonds, Mountlake Terrace

Snohomish County Christian HS
17913 64TH AVE W 98037
Bright and Early PS, 21316 66TH AVE W 98036
Christian Life ES, 1000 172ND ST SW 98037
Montessori Schools, P O BOX 206 98406
St. Thomas More ES, 6511 176TH ST SW 98037

Mabton, Yakima Co., Pop. Code 4
Mabton SD 120
Sch. Sys. Enr. Code 3
Supt. – S. Dale Knott, P O BOX 37 98935
Artz-Fox ES, P O BOX 40 98935
Charles Plesha, prin.

Malott, Okanogan Co.
Okanogan SD 105
Supt. – See Okanogan
MS 98829 – James Derting, prin.

Mansfield, Douglas Co., Pop. Code 2
Mansfield SD 207
Sch. Sys. Enr. Code 1
Supt. – Ronald Cummings, P O BOX 188 98830
ES, P O BOX 188 98830 – Ronald Cummings, prin.

Manson, Chelan Co., Pop. Code 2
Manson SD 19
Sch. Sys. Enr. Code 2
Supt. – Debbra House, P O BOX A 98831
ES 98831 – Sherman Young, prin.

Maple Falls, Whatcom Co.
Mt. Baker SD 507
Supt. – See Deming
ES 98266 – Bruce Burpee, prin.

Maple Valley, King Co., Pop. Code 2
Tahoma SD 409
Sch. Sys. Enr. Code 5
Supt. – Dr. Edward Heiser
23015 SE 216TH WAY 98038
Tahoma JHS, 24425 SE 216TH ST 98038
Donald Tirk, prin.
Cedar River MS
22615 SWEENEY ROAD SE 98038
Gary Morgan, prin.
Lake Wilderness ES, 24216 WITTE RD SE 98038
Wesley Bredin, prin.
Shadow Lake ES, 22620 SWEENEY RD SE 98038
Joan Watt, prin.

Marysville, Snohomish Co., Pop. Code 6
Marysville SD 25
Sch. Sys. Enr. Code 6
Supt. – Richard Huselton
4220 80TH ST NE 98270
Cascade ES, 5200 100TH ST NE 98270
Norman L. Colon, prin.
Liberty ES, 1000 LIBERTY AVE 98270
Betty Robertson, prin.
Marshall ES, 4400 116TH ST NE 98270
Melvin L. Beauchamp, prin.
Marysville MS, 4923 67TH ST NE 98270
Tim Culver, prin.
Pinewood ES, 5115 84TH ST NE 98270
Chriss Burgess, prin.
Shoultes ES, 13525 51ST AVE NE 98270
Donald Hazen, prin.
Sunnyside ES, 3619 63RD NE 98270
Charles H. Thacker, prin.
Tulalip ES, 7730 36TH AVE NW 98270
Gerard Buron, prin.

Grace Baptist Academy
8521 67TH AVE NE 98270

Mattawa, Grant Co., Pop. Code 1
Wahluke SD 73
Sch. Sys. Enr. Code 1
Supt. – Marvin Stevens, P O BOX 907 99344
Schott MS, P O BOX 907 99344
Gene Schmidt, prin.
ES, P O BOX 907 99344 – Robert Hahn, prin.

McCleary, Grays Harbor Co., Pop. Code 4
McCleary SD 65
Sch. Sys. Enr. Code 2
Supt. – Jim Ryder, P O BOX 8 98557
ES, P O BOX 08 98557 – Jim Ryder, prin.

Mead, Spokane Co., Pop. Code 4
Mead SD 354
Sch. Sys. Enr. Code 6
Supt. – Gary Ferney, 12508 N FREYA ST 99021
Other Schools – See Colbert, Spokane

Medical Lake, Spokane Co., Pop. Code 5
Medical Lake SD 326
Sch. Sys. Enr. Code 4
Supt. – Jim Van Matre, P O BOX 128 99022
MS, P O BOX 128 99022 – Richard Cerenzia, prin.
ES, P O BOX 128 99022 – Ben Merrill, prin.
Other Schools – See Fairchild AFB

Menlo, Pacific Co., Pop. Code 2
Willapa Valley SD 160
Sch. Sys. Enr. Code 2
Supt. – Lafe Bretthauer 98561
MS 98561 – Steve Rogers, prin.
Lebam ES 98561 – Charles Werley, prin.
Willpa ES 98561 – Charles Werley, prin.

Mercer Island, King Co., Pop. Code 7
Mercer Island SD 400
Sch. Sys. Enr. Code 5
Supt. – Dr. Wilma Smith
4160 86TH AVE SE 98040
Islander MS, 8225 SE 72ND ST 98040
Sue Galletti, prin.
Island Park ES, 5437 88TH AVE SE 98040
John Evans, prin.
Lakeridge ES, 8215 SE 78TH ST 98040
John Cameron, prin.
West Mercer ES, 4141 81ST AVE SE 98040
Nancy Emerson, prin.

St. Monica's ES, 4320 87TH AVE SE 98040

Mesa, Franklin Co., Pop. Code 2
North Franklin SD J 51-162
Supt. – See Connell
Basin City ES 99343 – JoAnn Henke, prin.
ES 99343 – Mick Ewart, prin.

Metaline Falls, Pend Oreille Co., Pop. Code 2
Selkirk SD 70
Sch. Sys. Enr. Code 2
Supt. – Richard Cole, P O BOX 566 99153
Bailey MS, P O BOX 566 99153
Joseph Newbry, prin.
Other Schools – See Ione

Milton, Pierce Co., Pop. Code 5
Fife SD 417
Supt. – See Tacoma
Surprise Lake MS, P O BOX 789 98354
John Ratko, prin.
ES, P O BOX 819 98354 – Beverly Cheney, prin.

Mineral, Lewis Co., Pop. Code 4
Morton SD 214
Supt. – See Morton
ES, P O BOX 176 98355 – Terresa Hodge, prin.

Monroe, Snohomish Co., Pop. Code 5
Monroe SD 103
Sch. Sys. Enr. Code 5
Supt. – William McCleary, P O BOX 687 98272
Salem Woods ES, 12802 219TH AVE SE 98272
Raymon Straub, prin.
Wagner IS, W MAIN ST 98272
Dr. James Lattyak, prin.
Wagner PS, DICKINSON ROAD 98272
Roy Harding, prin.
Other Schools – See Snohomish

Montesano, Grays Harbor Co., Pop. Code 5
Montesano SD 66
Sch. Sys. Enr. Code 4
Supt. – William Denholm, Jr.
106 MARCY AVE W 98563
Beacon Avenue ES, 1717 BEACON AVE E 98563
Marion Bogdanovich, prin.
Simpson Avenue ES, 519 SIMPSON AVE W 98563
Gary Mickelson, prin.

Morton, Lewis Co., Pop. Code 4
Morton SD 214
Sch. Sys. Enr. Code 3
Supt. – Richard Morton, P O BOX H 98356
ES, P O BOX L 98356 – C. Lowther, prin.
Other Schools – See Mineral

Moses Lake, Grant Co., Pop. Code 7
Moses Lake SD 161
Sch. Sys. Enr. Code 6
Supt. – Ben Edlund, 1318 W IVY ST 98837
Garden Hts. ES, 707 E NELSON ROAD 98837
Dan Martin, prin.
Knolls Vista MS, 454 W RIDGE RD 98837
Ken Yancey, prin.
Lakeview MS, 1048 E LARK AVE 98837
Robert Bonner, prin.
Larson Hts. ES
VANDENBURG AVE & LINDBERG 98837
Patricia Low, prin.
Longview ES, MAPLE DR 98837
George Rapozo, prin.
Midway ES, 502 S C ST 98837
Pete Doumit, prin.
North MS, LARSON BLVD & WEST DRIVE 98837
Lamonte Redal, prin.
Peninsula ES, 2406 W TEXAS ST 98837
Doug Luiten, prin.

Mossyrock, Lewis Co., Pop. Code 2
Mossyrock SD 206
Sch. Sys. Enr. Code 2
Supt. – Dr. Patrick Hoban, P O BOX 478 98564
MS, P O BOX 455 98564 – Gary Haslett, prin.
ES, P O BOX 455 98564 – Gary Haslett, prin.

Mount Vernon, Skagit Co., Pop. Code 7
Conway SD 317
Sch. Sys. Enr. Code 2
Supt. – Robert Warnecke
1798 CONWAY HILL LANE E 98273
Conway Consolidated ES
1798 CONWAY HILL LANE E 98273
(—), prin.

Mount Vernon SD 320
Sch. Sys. Enr. Code 5
Supt. – Thomas J. Pollino
124 E LAWRENCE ST 98273
LaVenture MS, 1200 LAVENTURE ROAD 98273
John Clark, prin.
Jefferson ES, 18TH & BLACKBURN 98273
Martin W. Kay, prin.
Lincoln ES, 1005 S 11TH ST 98273
Roger L. Trucker, prin.
Madison ES, 907 E FIR ST 98273
P. William Lupinacci, prin.
Washington ES, 1020 MCLEAN ROAD 98273
Linda M. Jenkins, prin.

Sedro Woolley SD 101
Supt. – See Sedro Woolley
Big Lake ES, 1676 STATE HWY 9 98273
Richard Ruhl, prin.

Immaculate Conception ES
1321 E DIVISION ST 98273
Mount Vernon Christian School
820 BLACKBURN ROAD 98273

Mountlake Terrace, Snohomish Co., Pop. Code 7
Edmonds SD 15
Supt. – See Lynnwood
Alderwood MS, 5409 228TH SW 98043
Wayne Sweeney, prin.
Cedar Way ES, 22222 39TH AVE W 98043
Jeanne Pedersen, prin.
Evergreen ES, 6004 237TH ST SW 98043
Janice Link, prin.
ES, 22001 52ND AVE W 98043
Spence Thunder, prin.

St. Pius X ES, 22105 58TH AVE W 98043

Moxee City, Yakima Co., Pop. Code 3
East Valley SD 90
Supt. – See Yakima
Moxee ES 98936 – Monica Masias, prin.

Mukilteo, Snohomish Co., Pop. Code 4
Mukilteo SD 6
Supt. – See Everett
ES, 2600 MUKILTEO DRIVE 98275
Dr. Jon Evavold, prin.

Naches, Yakima Co., Pop. Code 3
Naches Valley SD JT3
Sch. Sys. Enr. Code 4
Supt. – John Jones, P O BOX 66 98937
Naches Valley MS, P O BOX 39 98937
James Seamons, prin.
Naches Valley Inter. Sch., P O BOX 39 98937
James Seamons, prin.
Other Schools – See Yakima

Napavine, Lewis Co., Pop. Code 3
Napavine SD 14
Sch. Sys. Enr. Code 2
Supt. – Win Pearson   98565
ES   98565 – Richard Dickinson, prin.

Naselle, Pacific Co., Pop. Code 4
Naselle-Grays River Valley SD 155
Sch. Sys. Enr. Code 2
Supt. – Gerald Black, HCR 78 BOX 471-S   98638
ES, P O BOX 46   98638 – Daniel Edmondson, prin.
Other Schools – See Rosburg

Neah Bay, Clallam Co., Pop. Code 3
Cape Flattery SD 401
Supt. – See Sekiu
S, P O BOX 96   98357 – Dr. Dean Hunter, prin.

Nespelem, Okanogan Co., Pop. Code 2
Nespelem SD 14
Sch. Sys. Enr. Code 2
Supt. – Ed Hyde, P O BOX 291   99155
ES, P O BOX 291   99155 – Ed Hyde, prin.

Newman Lake, Spokane Co.
East Valley SD 361
Supt. – See Spokane
East Farms ES, 26203 E ROWAN AVE   99025
Lawana Embrey, prin.

Newport, Pend Oreille Co., Pop. Code 4
Newport SD 56-415
Sch. Sys. Enr. Code 4
Supt. – David Smith   99156
JHS, P O BOX 70   99156 – Dale Munson, prin.
Halstead ES, P O BOX 70   99156
Carol Bourassa, prin.

Nine Mile Falls, Spokane Co.
Nine Mile Falls SD 325
Sch. Sys. Enr. Code 4
Supt. – Robert LaLonde   99026
Lake Spokane ES, RURAL ROUTE 02   99026
David Nees, prin.
ES, 10102 W CHARLES ROAD   99026
Larry Guenther, prin.

Nooksack, Whatcom Co., Pop. Code 2
Nooksack Valley SD 506
Sch. Sys. Enr. Code 4
Supt. – Leo Groves   98276
Other Schools – See Everson, Sumas

North Bend, King Co., Pop. Code 4
Snoqualmie Valley SD 410
Supt. – See Snoqualmie
ES, 400 E 3RD ST   98045 – Frank Cernick, prin.
Opstad ES, 1345 STILSON AVE S E   98045
Marci Larsen, prin.

Northport, Stevens Co., Pop. Code 2
Northport SD 211
Sch. Sys. Enr. Code 2
Supt. – Neil Hutchens   99157
ES   99157 – (—), prin.

Oak Harbor, Island Co., Pop. Code 7
Oak Harbor SD 201
Sch. Sys. Enr. Code 6
Supt. – Roger Woehl, 8616 800TH AVE W   98277
MS, 1250 MIDWAY BLVD   98277
Mike Frankhauser, prin.
Broad View ES, 1250 MIDWAY BLVD   98277
James Matthews, prin.
Clover Valley ES, 600 CHEROKEE ST   98277
Mherling Luce, prin.
Crescent Harbor ES, 1250 MIDWAY BLVD   98277
Kathleen Vohland, prin.
ES, 1250 MIDWAY BLVD   98277
Bud Larson, prin.
Olympic View ES, 1250 MIDWAY BLVD   98277
Susan McCloskey, prin.

Oak Harbor Christian ES
7171 700TH AVE W   98277

Oakesdale, Whitman Co., Pop. Code 2
Oakesdale SD 324
Sch. Sys. Enr. Code 2
Supt. – Melvin J. Louk, P O BOX 228   99158
ES, P O BOX 228   99158 – Buddy Gibson, prin.

Oakville, Grays Harbor Co., Pop. Code 3
Oakville SD 400
Sch. Sys. Enr. Code 2
Supt. – Dennis Brandon, P O BOX H   98568
ES, P O BOX H   98568 – Eleanor Weisenbach, prin.

Ocean Park, Pacific Co.
Ocean Beach SD 101
Supt. – See Ilwaco
ES, P O BOX 631   98640 – Tom Akerlund, prin.

Ocean Shores, Grays Harbor Co., Pop. Code 4
North Beach SD 64
Supt. – See Copalis Beach
North Beach MS, P O BOX 1088   98569
Ronald Roberts, prin.
ES   98551 – Ronald Roberts, prin.

Odessa, Lincoln Co., Pop. Code 4
Odessa SD 105-157-166 J
Sch. Sys. Enr. Code 2
Supt. – Gordon Wallace, P O BOX 248   99159
Jantz ES   99159 – Leo Hutchins, prin.

Okanogan, Okanogan Co., Pop. Code 4
Okanogan SD 105
Sch. Sys. Enr. Code 3
Supt. – Richard Johnson, P O BOX 592   98840
MS, P O BOX 592   98840 – Dean Radke, prin.
Grainger ES, P O BOX 592   98840
James Derting, prin.
O'Keefe Primary   98840 – James Derting, prin.
Other Schools – See Malott

Olalla, Kitsap Co.
South Kitsap SD 402
Supt. – See Port Orchard
ES, 6100 OLALLA BURLEY ROAD SE   98359
Denny Bond, prin.

Olympia, Thurston Co., Pop. Code 8
Griffin SD 324
Sch. Sys. Enr. Code 2
Supt. – Nickolus Johnson
6530 33RD AVE NW   98502
Griffin ES, 6530 33RD AVE NW   98502
Barbara Murphy, prin.

North Thurston SD 3
Supt. – See Lacey
Hawk ES, 7600 5TH AVE SE   98503
Harry Hawkins, prin.
Meadows ES, 836 DEERBRUSH DR SE   98503
Hertica Martin, prin.
Olympic View ES, 1330 HORNE ST NE   98506
Carol O'Connell, prin.
Pleasant Glade ES
1920 ABERNETHY ROAD NE   98506
Mike Brennan, prin.
South Bay ES
3845 SLEATER KINNEY ROAD NE   98506
Alan Hoover, prin.
Woodland ES, 4630 CARPENTER ROAD SE   98503
Larry Stranz, prin.

Olympia SD 111
Sch. Sys. Enr. Code 6
Supt. – Richard Hunter
1113 LEGION WAY E   98501
Jefferson MS, 2200 CONGER ST NW   98502
Bob Duke, prin.
Reeves MS, 2200 N QUINCE   98506
Douglas Beach, prin.
Washington MS, 3100 CAIN ROAD SE   98501
Norman Josephson, prin.
Boston Harbor ES, 7300 ZANGLE ROAD NE   98506
Alward Tweit, prin.
Brown ES, 2000 26TH AVE NW   98502
Mickey Lahmann, prin.
Garfield ES, 325 PLYMOUTH ST NW   98502
Britt Nederhood, prin.
Lincoln ES, 213 E 21ST   98501 – Bob Markey, prin.
Madison ES, 812 CENTRAL ST SE   98501
Mark Haddock, prin.
McKinley ES, 1412 GRAND BLVD   98501
Darcie Bigelow, prin.
McLane ES, 200 DELPHI ROAD SW   98502
Barbara Eliason, prin.
Pioneer ES, 1655 CARLYON AVE SE   98501
Terresa Hodge, prin.
Rogers ES, 2001 SPRINGER ROAD   98506
Rick Bird, prin.
Roosevelt ES
1417 SAN FRANCISCO ST NE   98506
Larry Ash, prin.

Tumwater SD 33
Supt. – See Tumwater
Black Lake ES
6345 BELMORE-BLACK LAKE RD   98502
Bradley Smith, prin.

Evergreen Christian ES
1000 BLACK LAKE BLVD SW   98502
Faith Lutheran School
7075 PACIFIC AVE SE   98503
St. Michael's ES, 1203 10TH AVE SE   98501

Omak, Okanogan Co., Pop. Code 5
Omak SD 19
Sch. Sys. Enr. Code 4
Supt. – Myrl Power, P O BOX 833   98841
East Omak MS, P O BOX 833   98841
Rick Jones, prin.
MS, P O BOX 833   98841 – Judy Tassielli, prin.
North Omak ES, P O BOX 833   98841
Betty McKee, prin.

Paschal Sherman Indian ES   98841

Onalaska, Lewis Co., Pop. Code 2
Onalaska SD 300
Sch. Sys. Enr. Code 3
Supt. – Robert Kraig, 540 CARLISLE AVE   98570
ES, 540 CARLISLE AVE   98570
Mark Stedman, prin.

Orient, Ferry Co.
Orient SD 65
Sch. Sys. Enr. Code 1
Supt. – Barry McCombs   99160
ES   99160 – (—), prin.

Orondo, Douglas Co.
Orondo SD 13
Sch. Sys. Enr. Code 2
Supt. – Tom Reese, HC ROUTE BOX 18   98843
ES, HCR BOX 18   98843 – Tom Reese, prin.

Oroville, Okanogan Co., Pop. Code 4
Oroville SD 410
Sch. Sys. Enr. Code 3
Supt. – J. E. Gilman, 10TH & IRONWOOD   98844
ES   98844 – Phil Rohn, prin.

Orting, Pierce Co., Pop. Code 4
Orting SD 344
Sch. Sys. Enr. Code 3
Supt. – Lee Thoren, P O BOX 460   98360
MS, P O BOX 460   98360 – Al Burke, prin.
ES, P O BOX 460   98360 – Jan Donaldson, prin.

Othello, Adams Co., Pop. Code 5
Othello SD 147-163-55
Sch. Sys. Enr. Code 3
Supt. – Dennis Carter, P O BOX 588   99344
McFarland JHS, 790 S 10TH AVE   99344
H. Wayne Smith, prin.
Hiawatha ES, 506 E 7TH   99344
James Davis, prin.
Lutacaga ES, 795 S 7TH AVE   99344
Michael Kilpatrick, prin.
Scootney Springs MS, 601 14TH AND ASH   99344
Grace Tweten, prin.

Otis Orchards, Spokane Co.
East Valley SD 361
Supt. – See Spokane
ES, E 22000 WELLESLEY   99027
James Hammond, prin.

Outlook, Yakima Co.
Sunnyside SD 201
Supt. – See Sunnyside
ES, RURAL ROUTE 01   98938
Catherine Mears, prin.

Pacific, King Co., Pop. Code 4
Auburn SD 408
Supt. – See Auburn
Alpac ES, 310 MILWAUKEE BLVD N   98047
Bill Ray, prin.

Pacific Beach, Grays Harbor Co.
North Beach SD 64
Supt. – See Copalis Beach
ES   98571 – Del Talley, prin.

Packwood, Lewis Co.
White Pass SD 303
Supt. – See Randle
ES   98361 – Catherine Sadler, prin.

Palisades, Douglas Co.
Palisades SD 102
Sch. Sys. Enr. Code 1
Supt. – Charlotte Billingsley   98845
ES   98845 – (—), prin.

Palouse, Whitman Co., Pop. Code 4
Palouse SD 301
Sch. Sys. Enr. Code 2
Supt. – Larry Warner
RURAL ROUTE 1 BOX 100   99161
ES, RURAL ROUTE 01 BOX 100   99161
Alan Lee, prin.

Pasco, Franklin Co., Pop. Code 7
Pasco SD 1
Sch. Sys. Enr. Code 6
Supt. – Dr. Lawrence Nyland
1004 N 16TH AVE   99301
Emerson ES, 18TH & MARGARET   99301
Leonard Herrick, prin.
Frost ES, ROAD 22 & PEARL ST   99301
Suzanne Riley, prin.
Captain Gray ES, W COURT & 10TH   99301
C. Les Domingos, prin.
Livingston ES, 2515 ROAD 84   99301
Steve Droke, prin.
Longfellow ES, EIGHTH & W SHOSHONE   99301
Joe Mosebar, prin.
Markham ES, ELM & TAYLOR FLATS   99301
Katie Hales, prin.
McGee ES, 4601 N HORIZON DR   99301
Wes Hurst, prin.
Twain ES, 1801 ROAD 40   99301
Dianna Veleke, prin.

Star SD 54
Sch. Sys. Enr. Code 1
Supt. – (—)
24180 PASCO KAHLOTUS ROAD   99301
Star ES, 24180 PASCO KAHLOTUS RD   99301
Lucy Loeber, prin.

St. Patrick ES, 1016 N 14TH AVE   99301

Pateros, Okanogan Co., Pop. Code 3
Pateros SD 122
Sch. Sys. Enr. Code 2
Supt. – Gary Patterson, P O BOX 98   98846
ES   98846 – Gary Patterson, prin.

Paterson, Benton Co.
Paterson SD 50
Sch. Sys. Enr. Code 1
Supt. – Glenn Powell   99345
ES, P O BOX 189   99345 – Glenn Powell, prin.

Pe Ell, Lewis Co., Pop. Code 3
Pe Ell SD 301
Sch. Sys. Enr. Code 2
Supt. – James Haugen, P O BOX 368   98572
ES   98572 – L Feuchter, prin.

Peshastin, Chelan Co.
Cascade SD 228
Supt. – See Leavenworth
ES, SCHOOL ST 98847 – Rich Stewart, prin.

Plymouth, Benton Co.
Kennewick SD 17
Supt. – See Kennewick
Plymouth ES 99346 – Donald Campbell, prin.

Pomeroy, Garfield Co., Pop. Code 4
Pomeroy SD 110
Sch. Sys. Enr. Code 2
Supt. – Rick Anthony, P O BOX 950 99347
ES 99347 – Richard Goodwin, prin.

Port Angeles, Clallam Co., Pop. Code 7
Port Angeles SD 121
Sch. Sys. Enr. Code 5
Supt. – John Pope, 216 4TH 98362
Roosevelt MS, 400 S MONROE ROAD 98362
　Tom Anderson, prin.
Stevens MS, 1139 W 14TH ST 98362
　John Norton, prin.
Dry Creek ES, 1812 EDGEWOOD DRIVE 98362
　Ron Carr, prin.
Fairview ES, 2095 LAKE FARM ROAD 98362
　Mary Slehofer, prin.
Franklin ES, 2505 S WASHINGTON ST 98362
　Beverly Kinney, prin.
Hamilton ES, 1822 W 7TH ST 98362
　James Malvey, prin.
Jefferson ES, 218 E 12TH ST 98362
　Merton Thornton, prin.
Monroe ES, 300 S MONROE RD 98362
　Darold Powell, prin.

Queen of Angels ES, 1007 S OAK ST 98362

Port Orchard, Kitsap Co., Pop. Code 5
South Kitsap SD 402
Sch. Sys. Enr. Code 6
Supt. – Dr. DeWayne Gower
　1962 HOOVER AVE SE 98366
Burley-Glenwood ES
　100 SW LAKEWAY BLVD 98366
　Deane Robinson, prin.
East Port Orchard ES
　1964 HOOVER AVE SE 98366
　Lawrence Hill, prin.
Givens ES, 1026 SIDNEY AVE 98366
　Gerald Willson, prin.
Manchester ES, 1901 CALIFORNIA AVE SE 98366
　Patricia Rylander, prin.
Orchard Heights ES
　2288 FIRCREST DRIVE SE 98366
　Bill Wyant, prin.
South Colby ES, 3281 BANNER ROAD SE 98366
　John Lindley, prin.
Sunnyslope ES
　4183 SUNNYSLOPE ROAD SW 98366
　John Richardson, prin.
Other Schools – See Olalla

Port Townsend, Jefferson Co., Pop. Code 6
Port Townsend SD 50
Sch. Sys. Enr. Code 4
Supt. – Dr. Ron Johnson, 1610 BLAINE ST 98368
Inter. Sch 98368 – Lee Arey, prin.
Grant Street ES 98368 – Steven Lien, prin.

Poulsbo, Kitsap Co., Pop. Code 5
North Kitsap SD 400
Sch. Sys. Enr. Code 5
Supt. – Dr. Clifford Campbell
　18360 CALDART AVE NE 98370
North Kitsap MS, 2003 NE HOSTMARK ST 98370
　Gregg Epperson, prin.
Pearson ES
　15650 CENTRAL VALLEY RD NW 98370
　Steve Richards, prin.
ES, 18531 NOLL ROAD NE 98370
　John Sebastian, prin.
Other Schools – See Kingston, Suquamish

Christ the King Academy
　705 NE LINCOLN ROAD 98370

Prescott, Walla Walla Co., Pop. Code 2
Prescott SD 402-37
Sch. Sys. Enr. Code 2
Supt. – Mary Tompkins, P O BOX 65 99348
ES, P O BOX 65 99348 – Mary Tompkins, prin.

Prosser, Benton Co., Pop. Code 5
Prosser SD 116
Sch. Sys. Enr. Code 4
Supt. – Dr. Loyd Waite, P O BOX 430 99350
Housel MS, 2001 HIGHLAND DRIVE 99350
　Arden Smith, prin.
Keene-Riverview ES, 832 PARK AVE 99350
　William Bourn, prin.
Prosser Heights MS
　ALEXANDER COURT & MILLER AV 99350
　Richard Dorsett, prin.
Whitstran ES, RURAL ROUTE 02 BOX 2197 99350
　Dr. Lou Gates, prin.

Pullman, Whitman Co., Pop. Code 7
Pullman SD 267
Sch. Sys. Enr. Code 4
Supt. – Clayton Dunn, 115 NW STATE ST 99163
Lincoln MS, SE 315 CRESTVIEW 99163
　Phyllis Vettrus, prin.
Franklin ES, 240 SE DEXTER ST 99163
　Ardith Pierce, prin.

Jefferson ES, 1150 NW BRYANT ST 99163
　James Heidenreich, prin.
Sunnyside ES, 425 SW SHIRLEY ST 99163
　Fritz Hughes, prin.

Puyallup, Pierce Co., Pop. Code 7
Puyallup SD 3
Sch. Sys. Enr. Code 7
Supt. – Dr. Herbert Berg, P O BOX 370 98371
Ferrucci JHS
　3213 WILDWOOD PARK DRIVE 98373
　Larry Olson, prin.
Firgrove ES, 13918 MERIDIAN AVE S 98373
　Ken Benny, prin.
Fruitland ES, 1515 FRUITLAND AVE E 98371
　Nancy Wheeler, prin.
Hilltop ES, 2210 110TH AVE E 98372
　Harry Diseth, prin.
Karshner ES, 1328 8TH AVE NW 98371
　Bob Busk, prin.
Maplewood ES, 1110 PIONEER WAY W 98371
　Harold Esterbrook, prin.
Meeker ES, 409 5TH ST SW 98371
　Gwen Fletcher, prin.
Mountain View ES, 3411 119TH AVE E 98372
　Vince Pecchia, prin.
Northwood ES, 9805 24TH ST E 98371
　Dr. Geri Nyegaard, prin.
Pope ES, 15102 122ND AVE E 98374
　Ed Zeiger, prin.
Ridgecrest ES, 12616 NAHUNTA DRIVE 98374
　Brian Lewis, prin.
Riverside ES, 5515 44TH ST E 98371
　Lauren Orheim, prin.
Spinning ES, 1306 PIONEER WAY E 98372
　Michael Williams, prin.
Stewart ES, 309 4TH ST NE 98372
　Verna Smith, prin.
Sunrise ES, 2323 39TH AVE SE 98374
　Nancy Stephan, prin.
Wildwood Park ES
　2601 WILDWOOD PARK DRIVE 98374
　Jim King, prin.
Woodland ES, 11119 FRUITLAND AVE E 98373
　Julie Gearheard, prin.
Other Schools – See Tacoma

Sumner SD 320
Supt. – See Sumner
Mcalder ES, 15502 96TH ST E 98372
　Kathleen Bailey, prin.

All Saints ES, 504 2ND ST SW 98371
Puyallup Valley Christian ES
　601 9TH AVE SE 98372

Quilcene, Jefferson Co., Pop. Code 4
Quilcene SD 48
Sch. Sys. Enr. Code 2
Supt. – Dr. Marshall Jeffries, P O BOX 40 98376
S, P O BOX 40 98376 – Ted Knivila, prin.

Quincy, Grant Co., Pop. Code 5
Quincy SD 144-101
Sch. Sys. Enr. Code 4
Supt. – Tom Pickett, 119 J ST SW 98848
JHS, 417 C ST SE 98848 – Gary Carlton, prin.
Mountain View ES, 119 D ST NW 98848
　Dave Rossing, prin.
Pioneer MS, 224 J ST SE 98848 – James Culp, prin.
Other Schools – See George

Rainier, Thurston Co., Pop. Code 3
Rainier SD 307
Sch. Sys. Enr. Code 3
Supt. – Bob Golphenee 98576
JHS 98576 – John Dekker, prin.
Rainier SD 98576 – Joanne Goodwin, prin.

Randle, Lewis Co., Pop. Code 2
White Pass SD 303
Sch. Sys. Enr. Code 3
Supt. – Charles TenPas 98377
ES 98377 – Elmer Bailey, prin.
Other Schools – See Glenoma, Packwood

Raymond, Pacific Co., Pop. Code 5
Raymond SD 116
Sch. Sys. Enr. Code 3
Supt. – Chuck Hall, 1016 COMMERCIAL ST 98577
Ninth Street MS, 825 COMMERCIAL ST 98577
　Westbrook Snow, prin.
Riverview PS, 550 WASHINGTON ST 98577
　Westbrook Snow, prin.

Reardan, Lincoln Co., Pop. Code 2
Reardan-Edwall SD 9
Sch. Sys. Enr. Code 3
Supt. – Thomas Crowley, P O BOX 225 99029
ES 99029 – John Freeman, prin.

Redmond, King Co., Pop. Code 8
Lake Washington SD 414
Supt. – See Kirkland
Alcott ES, 4213 228TH AVE NE 98053
　Kris Griggs, prin.
Audubon ES, 3045 180TH AVE NE 98052
　Liz Wells, prin.
Dickinson ES, 7300 208TH AVE NE 98053
　Chuck Leicester, prin.
Mann ES, 17001 104TH ST 98052
　Al Blomquist, prin.
Mead ES, 1725 216TH AVE NE 98053
　Diane Hay, prin.
ES, 16600 NE 80TH ST 98052
　Dr. Marcia Morrison, prin.

Rockwell ES, 11125 162ND AVE NE 98052
　Virginia Searls, prin.
Rush ES, 6101 152ND AVE NE 98052
　Nancy Wilson, prin.
Smith ES, 23305 N E 14TH 98053
　Connie Perry, prin.

Northshore SD 417
Supt. – See Bothell
Sunrise ES, 14075 172ND AVE NE 98052
　Dudley Hallworth, prin.

Redmond Christian ES
　2315 173RD AVE NE 98052

Renton, King Co., Pop. Code 8
Kent SD 415
Supt. – See Kent
Fairwood ES, 16600 148TH AVE SE 98058
　Audrian Fowler, prin.
Ridgewood Elementary School
　18030 162ND PL SE 98058
　Marcia Woehlbrandt, prin.
Spring Glen ES, 2607 JONES AVE S 98055
　Del Morton, prin.

Renton SD 403
Sch. Sys. Enr. Code 7
Supt. – Dr. Gary Kohlwes, 435 MAIN AVE S 98055
McKnight MS, 2600 NE 12TH ST 98056
　Patricia Blix, prin.
Nelson MS, 2403 JONES AVE S 98055
　Sandra Chock-Eng, prin.
Benson Hill ES, 18665 116TH AVE SE 98058
　Joseph Brabant, prin.
Cascade ES, 16022 116TH AVE SE 98058
　Marsha Hallett, prin.
Hazelwood ES, 6928 116TH AVE SE 98056
　Vera Risdon, prin.
Highlands ES, 2727 NE 9TH ST 98056
　William Gladsjo, prin.
Kennydale ES, 1700 NE 28TH ST 98055
　Jim Ventris, prin.
Maplewood Hts ES, 13430 144TH AVE SE 98056
　Robert Hendrickson, prin.
Renton Park ES, 16828 128TH AVE SE 98058
　James Noddings, prin.
Sierra Hts., 9901 132ND AVE SE 98056
　Sherrill Herbel, prin.
Talbot Hill ES, 2300 TALBOT RD S 98055
　Fred Swatman, prin.
Tiffany Park ES
　1601 LAKE YOUNGS WAY SE 98058
　Edith Porter, prin.
Other Schools – See Seattle

Maple Valley Christian ES
　16700 174TH AVE SE 98058
Renton Christian ES, 221 HARDIE AVE NW 98055
St. Anthony ES, 336 SHATTUCK AVE S 98055

Republic, Ferry Co., Pop. Code 4
Republic SD 309
Sch. Sys. Enr. Code 3
Supt. – Terry Heindl, 915 HWY 20 EAST 99166
ES 99166 – Marjorie Sager, prin.

Richland, Benton Co., Pop. Code 8
Richland SD 400
Sch. Sys. Enr. Code 6
Supt. – Dr. Marge Chow, 615 SNOW AVE 99352
Carmichael JHS, 620 THAYER DRIVE 99352
　Nancy Kyle, prin.
Badger Mountain ES
　1515 MOUNTAIN VIEW LANE 99352
　Hershel Griggs, prin.
Jefferson ES, 1525 HUNT AVE 99352
　Gerald Lane, prin.
Lee ES, 1702 VAN GIESEN ST 99532
　Pricilla Cannon, prin.
Lewis & Clark ES, 800 DOWNING ST 99352
　Paul Dowdy, prin.
Sacajawea ES, 518 CATSKILL ST 99352
　Marriner Rigby, prin.
Whitman ES, 1704 GRAY ST 99352
　Gary Northrop, prin.
Other Schools – See West Richland

Christ the King ES, 1122 LONG AVE 99352
Liberty Christian ES
　1104 RICHMOND BLVD 99352
Tri-City Community Church Montessori
　RURAL ROUTE 03 BOX 8065 99352

Ridgefield, Clark Co., Pop. Code 4
Ridgefield SD 122
Sch. Sys. Enr. Code 4
Supt. – John Sullivan, P O BOX 468 98642
View Ridge MS, 510 PIONEER AVE 98642
　Geral Cox, prin.
South Ridge ES, 502 NW 199TH ST 98642
　Allan Heritage, prin.
Union Ridge ES, 330 N 5TH 98642
　Geral Cox, prin.

Mountain View Christian ES
　2810 NE 259TH ST 98642

Ritzville, Adams Co., Pop. Code 4
Ritzville SD 160-67
Sch. Sys. Enr. Code 2
Supt. – Dennis Hauff
　WELLSTANDT ROAD 99169
ES, 601 S CHELAN ST 99169
　Robert Babbitt, prin.

Rochester, Thurston Co., Pop. Code 2
Rochester SD 401
Sch. Sys. Enr. Code 4
Supt. – Larry Wise, P O BOX 457   98579
Grand Mound MS, 7710 JAMES ROAD SW   98579
  Clarence Surridge, prin.
Rochester ES, P O BOX 370   98579
  Sharon Mowry, prin.

Rockford, Spokane Co., Pop. Code 2
Freeman SD 358
Sch. Sys. Enr. Code 3
Supt. – Charles Stocker
  RURAL ROUTE 01 BOX 51   99030
Freeman ES   99030 – Mike Marshall, prin.

Roosevelt, Klickitat Co.
Roosevelt SD 403
Sch. Sys. Enr. Code 1
Supt. – Arthur Hoisington, P O BOX 247   99356
ES, P O BOX 247   99356 – (—), prin.

Rosalia, Whitman Co., Pop. Code 3
Rosalia SD 320
Sch. Sys. Enr. Code 2
Supt. – William Parks, P O BOX 128   99170
ES, P O BOX 128   99170 – Steve Warner, prin.

Rosburg, Pacific Co.
Naselle-Grays River Valley SD 155
Supt. – See Naselle
Grays River Valley MS, P O BOX 117   98643
  (—), prin.

Roslyn, Kittitas Co., Pop. Code 3
Cle Elum-Roslyn SD 404
Supt. – See Cle Elum
Strom JHS, 20 IDAHO AVE   98941
  Leon Maras, prin.

Roy, Pierce Co., Pop. Code 2
Bethel SD 403
Supt. – See Spanaway
ES, P O BOX 238   98580 – Leslie Tollefson, prin.

Royal City, Grant Co., Pop. Code 3
Royal SD 160
Sch. Sys. Enr. Code 3
Supt. – David James, P O BOX 486   99357
Royal MS, P O BOX 486   99357
  P. Andersen, prin.
Red Rock ES, P O BOX 486   99357
  Boyd Lindholm, prin.

Saint John, Whitman Co., Pop. Code 3
St. John SD 322
Sch. Sys. Enr. Code 2
Supt. – Dr. Donald Simpson, P O BOX 58   99171
ES, P O BOX 58   99171 – Terry Munther, prin.

Satsop, Grays Harbor Co.
Satsop SD 104
Sch. Sys. Enr. Code 1
Supt. – (—), P O BOX 96   98583
ES, P O BOX 96   98583
  Marsha Epperly-Hendrick, prin.

Seabeck, Kitsap Co.
Central Kitsap SD 401
Supt. – See Silverdale
ES, P O BOX 160   98380
  Dr. Ronald Bigelow, prin.

Seahurst, King Co.
_____
St. Francis of Assisi ES, P O BOX 870   98062

Seattle, King Co., Pop. Code 10
Highline SD 401
Sch. Sys. Enr. Code 7
Supt. – Dr. Kent Matheson, P O BOX 66100   98166
Cascade MS, 1201 S 104TH ST   98168
  Roy Adler, prin.
Sylvester MS
  16222 SYLVESTER ROAD SW   98166
  Tom Sawyer, prin.
Beverly Park ES, 11427 3RD AVE S   98168
  Michael Fuller, prin.
Bow Lake ES, 18237 42ND AVE S   98188
  Linda Wagner, prin.
Cedarhurst ES, 611 S 132ND ST   98168
  Tina Livingston, prin.
Gregory Heights ES, 16216 19TH AVE SW   98166
  Ken Pederson, prin.
Hazel Valley ES, 402 SW 132ND ST   98146
  Louis Barei, prin.
Madrona ES, 1121 33RD AVE   98122
  Charles Wetzel, prin.
Marvista ES, 19800 MARINE VIEW DR SW   98166
  Walter Lobdell, prin.
McMicken Heights ES, 3708 S 168TH ST   98188
  Dr. Don Savan, prin.
Mount View ES, 10811 12TH AVE SW   98146
  Albert Campbell, prin.
Olympic ES, 615 S 247TH   98198
  Charles Tuman, prin.
Riverton Heights ES, 3011 S 148TH ST   98168
  Keith Criss, prin.
Salmon Creek ES, 614 SW 120TH ST   98146
  Judy Beckon, prin.
Seahurst ES, 14603 14TH AVE SW   98166
  Ruth Amoe, prin.
Shorewood ES, 2725 SW 116TH ST   98146
  Darrell Finley, prin.

Southern Heights ES, 11249 14TH AVE S   98168
  Marsha Campbell, prin.
Valley View ES, 17622 46TH AVE S   98188
  Jay Hambly, prin.
White Center Heights ES
  712 SW 102ND ST   98146 – Richard Hanks, prin.
Other Schools – See Des Moines, Kent

Renton SD 403
Supt. – See Renton
Bryn Mawr ES, 8212 S 118TH ST   98178
  Fred Anderson, prin.
Campbell Hill ES, 6418 S 124TH ST   98178
  Shirley Patterson, prin.
Lakeridge ES, 7400 S 115TH ST   98178
  Gwen Dupree, prin.

Seattle SD 1
Sch. Sys. Enr. Code 8
Supt. – William Kendrick, 815 4TH AVE N   98109
Denny MS, 8402 30TH AVE SW   98126
  Joan Allen, prin.
Eckstein MS, 3003 NE 75TH ST   98115
  Lynn Caldwell, prin.
Hamilton MS, 1610 N 41ST ST   98103
  Dave Stevens, prin.
Madison MS, 3429 45TH AVE SW   98116
  John DuGay, prin.
Mcclure MS, 1915 1ST AVE W   98119
  Ben Nakagawa, prin.
Meany MS, 301 21ST AVE E   98112
  Bruce Hunter, prin.
Mercer MS, 1600 S COLUMBIAN WAY   98108
  Dean Sanders, prin.
South Shore MS, 8825 RAINIER AVE S   98118
  Robert Gary, prin.
Washington MS, 2101 S JACKSON ST   98144
  John Thorp, prin.
Whitman MS, 9201 15TH AVE NW   98117
  Bi Hoa Caldwell, prin.
Adams ES, 2418 28TH AVE W   98199
  Joanne Franey, prin.
Alki ES, 3010 59TH AVE SW   98116
  Patricia Sander, prin.
Arbor Heights ES, 3701 SW 104TH ST   98146
  Bruce Fowler, prin.
Bagley ES, 7821 STONE AVE N   98103
  Ora Franklin, prin.
Beacon Hill ES, 2025 14TH AVE S   98144
  Sonja Hampton, prin.
Blaine ES, 2550 34TH AVE W   98199
  Tim O'Brien, prin.
Brighton ES, 4425 S HOLLY ST   98118
  Bill Lagreid, prin.
Broadview Thompson ES
  13052 GREENWOOD AVE N   98133
  Norman Smith, prin.
Bryant ES, 3311 NE 60TH ST   98115
  Terry Acena, prin.
Coe ES, 2433 6TH AVE W   98119
  Carl Leatherman, prin.
Columbia ES, 3528 S FERDINAND ST   98118
  Larry Jacobs, prin.
Concord ES, 723 S CONCORD ST   98108
  Toby Gonzales, prin.
Cooper ES, 4408 DELRIDGE WAY SW   98106
  Doug Nuetzmann, prin.
Day/Orca ES, 3921 LINDEN AVE N   98103
  Carole Williams, prin.
Dearborn Park ES, 2820 S ORCAS ST   98108
  Carmen Tsubol Chan, prin.
Decatur ES, 7711 43RD AVE NE   98115
  Pat Tolliver, prin.
Dunlap ES, 8621 46TH AVE S   98118
  John Moffitt, prin.
Emerson ES, 9709 60TH AVE S   98118
  Ed James, prin.
Fairmount Park ES, 3800 SW FINDLAY ST   98126
  Victoria Yee, prin.
Gatewood ES, 4320 SW MYRTLE ST   98136
  Marie Floyd, prin.
Gatzert ES, 2101 S JACKSON ST   98144
  Robert Bass, prin.
Genesee Hill ES, 5012 SW GENESEE ST   98116
  Lillie Brown, prin.
Graham Hill ES, 5149 S GRAHAM ST   98118
  Margaret Reeder, prin.
Green Lake ES, 2400 N 65TH ST   98103
  Harvey Deutsch, prin.
Greenwood ES, 144 NW 80TH ST   98117
  Joanna Cairns, prin.
Hay ES, 411 BOSTON ST   98109
  Evette Mardesich, prin.
High Point ES, 6760 34TH AVE SW   98126
  Dave Ward, prin.
Highland Park ES, 1012 SW TRENTON ST   98106
  Venus Placer-Barber, prin.
Hughes ES, 7740 34TH AVE SW   98126
  Elizabeth Berg, prin.
Kimball ES, 3200 23RD AVE S   98144
  Victoria Foreman, prin.
Lafayette ES, 2645 CALIFORNIA AVE SW   98116
  James Abernethy, prin.
Latona ES, 401 NE 42ND ST   98105
  Wade Haggard, prin.
Laurelhurst ES, 4530 46TH AVE NE   98105
  Ken Seno, prin.
Lawton ES, 4017 26TH AVE W   98199
  William Johnson, prin.
Leschi ES, 135 32ND AVE   98122
  Wilbur Roberson, prin.
Lowell ES, 1058 E MERCER ST   98102
  Merlyn Simmons, prin.

Loyal Heights ES, 2511 NW 80TH ST   98117
  Thomas Slawson, prin.
Madrona ES, 3030 S 204TH ST   98198
  Margie Kates, prin.
Maple ES, 4925 CORSON AVE S   98108
  Lynn Fuller, prin.
Mcgilvra ES, 1617 38TH AVE E   98112
  James Oftebro, prin.
Minor ES, 18TH AND E UNION ST   98122
  Karen Hoo, prin.
Montlake ES, 2409 22ND AVE E   98112
  LaVaun Dennett, prin.
Muir ES, 3301 S HORTON ST   98144
  Harry Nelson, prin.
North Beach ES, 9018 24TH AVE NW   98117
  Kathleen Lindsey, prin.
Northgate ES, 11725 1ST AVE NE   98125
  Dorothy Woods, prin.
Olympic Hills ES, 13018 20TH AVE NE   98125
  Lawrence Matsuda, prin.
Olympic View ES, 500 NE 95TH ST   98115
  Robert Stone, prin.
Ranier View ES, 11650 BEACON AVE S   98178
  Ed Jefferson, prin.
Rogers ES, 4030 NE 109TH ST   98125
  Lyle Staley, prin.
Roxhill ES, 9430 30TH AVE SW   98126
  Roger Barron, prin.
Sacajawea ES, 9501 20TH AVE NE   98115
  Beverly Walker, prin.
Sand Point ES, 6208 60TH AVE NE   98115
  Jerry Takasaki, prin.
Sanislo ES, 1812 SW MYRTLE ST   98106
  Don Damon, prin.
Schmitz Park ES, 5000 SW SPOKANE ST   98116
  Joan Armitage, prin.
Seward ES, 2515 BOYLSTON AVE E   98102
  Nora Adams, prin.
Stevens ES, 1242 18TH AVE E   98112
  Karen Kodama, prin.
University Heights ES
  5031 UNIVERSITY WAY NE   98105
  Delores Pattee, prin.
Van Asselt ES, 7201 BEACON AVE S   98108
  William Cook, prin.
View Ridge ES, 7047 50TH AVE NE   98115
  Teo Cadiente, prin.
Viewlands ES, 10525 3RD AVE NW   98177
  Lois Freeborn, prin.
Wedgewood ES, 2720 NE 85TH ST   98115
  Cherryl Leeson, prin.
West Woodland ES, 5634 5TH AVE NW   98107
  Jim Alexander, prin.
Whittier ES, 7501 13TH AVE NW   98117
  Clarence Brown, prin.
Whitworth ES, 5215 46TH AVE S   98118
  Gary Tubbs, prin.
Wing Luke ES, 3701 S KENYON ST   98118
  Sybil Brown, prin.

Shoreline SD 412
Sch. Sys. Enr. Code 6
Supt. – Dr. Roy Duncan
  17077 MERIDIAN AVENUE N   98133
Einstein MS, 325 NW 195TH ST   98177
  Edward Merlino, prin.
Kellogg MS, 2545 NE 200TH ST   98155
  Michael Malan, prin.
Briarcrest IS, 2715 NE 158TH   98155
  Travis Wills, prin.
Brookside ES, 17447 37TH AVE NE   98155
  Nancy Kerwin, prin.
Echo Lake ES, 2800 NE 200TH   98155
  Judy Albrecht, prin.
Highland Terrace PS, 100 N 160TH ST   98133
  Delia Broderick, prin.
Lake Forest Park ES, 18500 37TH AVE NE   98155
  Nancy McMann, prin.
North City ES, 2800 NE 200TH ST   98155
  John Oordt, prin.
Parkwood ES, 17077 MERIDIAN AVE N   98133
  Dr. Leslie Winstead, prin.
Ridgecrest ES, 16516 10TH AVE NE   98155
  James Schaffner, prin.
Sunset IS, 17800 10TH AVE NW   98177
  Mary Petra, prin.
Syre ES, 19545 12TH AVE NW   98177
  Linda Stubbs, prin.

South Central SD 406
Sch. Sys. Enr. Code 4
Supt. – Dr. Michael Silver
  4640 S 144TH ST   98168
Showalter MS, 4628 S 144TH ST   98168
  Dr. Paul Highsmith, prin.
Thorndyke ES, 4415 S 150TH ST   98148
  Jim Miles, prin.
Tukwila ES, 5939 S 149TH ST   98168
  Dick Fain, prin.

_____
Bush School, 405 36TH AVE E   98112
Community Chapel Christian HS
  18635 8TH AVE S   98148
Lakeside MS, 13510 1ST AVE NE   98125
Seattle Christian School
  19639 28TH AVE S   98188
Watson Groen Christian HS
  2400 NE 147TH ST   98155
Amazing Grace Luthern ES
  10056 RENTON AVE S   98178
Assumption ES, 6220 32ND AVE NE   98115
Calvary Lutheran School
  3420 SW CLOVERDALE   98126
Christ Church ES, 12345 8TH AVE NE   98125

Christ the King ES, 415 N 117TH ST 98133
Christian Faith ES, P O BOX 28800 98198
Concordia Lutheran ES, 7040 36TH AVE NE 98115
Epiphany ES, 3710 E HOWELL ST 98122
Evergreen Gifted Children ES
　15201 MERIDIAN AVE N 98133
Holy Family ES, 9615 20TH AVE SW 98106
Holy Family ES, 9615 20TH AVE SW 98106
Holy Rosary ES, 4142 42ND AVE SW 98116
Hope Lutheran ES, 4446 42ND AVE SW 98116
Kings ES, 19531 DAYTON AVE N 98133
Northwest Montessori, 7400 25TH AVE NE 98115
Our Lady of Fatima ES
　3301 W DRAVUS ST 98199
Our Lady of Guadalupe ES
　3401 SW MYRTLE ST 98126
Our Lady of Lourdes ES
　10240 12TH AVE S 98168
Our Lady of Perpetual Help ES
　3520 NE 89TH ST 98115
Our Lady of the Lake ES, 3520 NE 89TH ST 98115
Pegasus ES, 15801 AMBAUM BLVD SW 98166
Perkins ES, 4649 SUNNYSIDE AVE N 98103
Seattle Country Day ES, 2619 4TH AVE N 98109
Seattle Hebrew Academy
　16167 INTERLAKEN DR E 98112
St. Alphonsus ES, 5816 15TH AVE NW 98107
St. Annes ES, 101 W LEE ST 98119
St. Benedict's ES
　4811 WALLINGFORD AVE N 98103
St. Bernadette ES, 1028 SW 128TH ST 98146
St. Catherine ES, 8524 8TH AVE NE 98115
St. Edward ES, 4212 S MEAD ST 98118
St. George ES, 5117 13TH AVE S 98108
St. John's ES, 120 N 79TH ST 98103
St. Joseph's ES, 700 18TH AVE E 98112
St. Luke ES, 17533 SAINT LUKE PLACE N 98133
St. Mark's ES, 18033 15TH PLACE NE 98155
St. Matthew's ES, 1230 NE 127TH ST 98125
St. Paul's ES, 10001 57TH AVE S 98178
St. Therese ES, 900 35TH AVE E 98122
Villa Academy, 5001 NE 50TH ST 98105
West Seattle Christian ES
　4401 42ND AVE SW 98116
West Seattle Montessori ES
　4536 38TH AVE SW 98126
Zion Christian ES, 620 20TH AVE S 98144

Sedro Woolley, Skagit Co., Pop. Code 6
Sedro Woolley SD 101
Sch. Sys. Enr. Code 5
Supt. – Dr. Pamela Carnahan
　2079 COOK ROAD 98284
Cascade MS, 201 N TOWNSHIP ST 98284
　Dr. Virginia Beck, prin.
Evergreen ES, 1111 MCGARGILE ROAD 98284
　Wendy Brown, prin.
Purcell ES, 7TH & BENNETT 98284
　Barbara Dow, prin.
Samish ES, 2195 PRAIRIE ROAD 98284
　Jim Abrahamson, prin.
Other Schools – See Clearlake, Lyman, Mount Vernon

Sekiu, Clallam Co., Pop. Code 2
Cape Flattery SD 401
Sch. Sys. Enr. Code 3
Supt. – David Woodruff, P O BOX 109 98381
Clallam Bay S, P O BOX 109 98381
　Roy E. Morris, prin.
Other Schools – See Neah Bay

Selah, Yakima Co., Pop. Code 5
Selah SD 119
Sch. Sys. Enr. Code 5
Supt. – Dr. J. Tuman, P O BOX 398 98942
MS, 411 N 1ST ST 98942 – Burlan Johnson, prin.
Campbell ES, N 1ST ST 98942 – Don Martin, prin.
Lince IS, 411 1ST ST 98942
　Frank Rowland, prin.

Sequim, Clallam Co., Pop. Code 5
Sequim SD 323
Sch. Sys. Enr. Code 4
Supt. – Kenneth Anderson
　503 N SEQUIM AVE 98382
MS, 503 N SEQUIM AVE 98382
　Norman Heggenes, prin.
Haller ES, 503 N SEQUIM AVE 98382
　Ronald Dalen, prin.

Shaw Island, San Juan Co.
Shaw Island SD 10
Sch. Sys. Enr. Code 1
Supt. – (—) 98286
ES 98286 – Nathan B. Smothers, prin.

Shelton, Mason Co., Pop. Code 6
Hood Canal SD 404
Sch. Sys. Enr. Code 2
Supt. – Robert Weir, N 111 HWY 106 98584
Hood Canal JHS, N 111 HIGHWAY 106 98584
　Daniel Bolender, prin.
Hood Canal ES, N 111 HIGHWAY 106 98584
　Daniel Bolender, prin.

Pioneer SD 402
Sch. Sys. Enr. Code 3
Supt. – Bert Miller, 611 E AGATE ROAD 98584
Pioneer MS, 611 E AGATE ROAD 98584
　Doug Lampi, prin.
Pioneer ES, 611 E AGATE ROAD 98584
　Doug Lampi, prin.

Shelton SD 309
Sch. Sys. Enr. Code 5
Supt. – H. Hansen, 811 W PINE ST 98584

MS, 9TH & FRANKLIN 98584
　Paul Johansson, prin.
Bordeaux ES, 250 W UNIVERSITY AVE 98584
　Dr. Fred Ebey, prin.
Evergreen ES, 8TH AND PINE 98584
　Tom River, prin.
Mountain View ES, CALLANAN & K ST 98584
　John Hill, prin.

Southside SD 42
Sch. Sys. Enr. Code 2
Supt. – Ronald Mills
　161 SE COLLIER ROAD 98584
Southside ES, 161 SE COLLIER ROAD 98584
　Ronald Mills, prin.

Silverdale, Kitsap Co., Pop. Code 3
Central Kitsap SD 401
Sch. Sys. Enr. Code 6
Supt. – Dr. Eugene R. Hertzke, P O BOX 8 98383
Clear Creek ES, 3999 NW SUNDE RD 98383
　Bonnie Hinton, prin.
Jenne-Wright ES, P O BOX 8 98383
　Elizabeth Wise, prin.
Public ES 12
　13200 OLYMPIC VIEW RD N W 98383
　Steven Anderson, prin.
ES, P O BOX 8 98383 – Thomas Gobeske, prin.
Other Schools – See Bremerton, Seabeck

Skykomish, King Co., Pop. Code 2
Skykomish SD 404
Sch. Sys. Enr. Code 1
Supt. – Gene Laes 98288
ES 98288 – (—), prin.

Snohomish, Snohomish Co., Pop. Code 6
Monroe SD 103
Supt. – See Monroe
Maltby ES, 9700 212TH ST SE 98290
　Alan Sall, prin.

Snohomish SD 201
Sch. Sys. Enr. Code 6
Supt. – Dr. Ronald Crawford, 1506 5TH ST 98290
Cathcart ES, 8201 188TH ST SE 98290
　Rowena Richardson, prin.
Central ES, 221 UNION ST 98290
　Don Shaw, prin.
Dutch Hill ES, 8231 131ST AVE SE 98290
　Karl Myhre, prin.
Emerson ES, 1103 PINE ST 98290
　Maureen Cornwell, prin.
Machias ES, 231 147TH AVE SE 98290
　Larry Aalbu, prin.
Riverview ES, 7322 64TH ST SE 98290
　Don Hultgren, prin.
Other Schools – See Everett

Liberty Christian ES, 7407 197TH ST SE 98290
Zion Lutheran ES, 331 UNION AVE 98290

Snoqualmie, King Co., Pop. Code 4
Snoqualmie Valley SD 410
Sch. Sys. Enr. Code 5
Supt. – Richard McCullough, P O BOX 400 98065
MS, RURAL ROUTE 01 BOX 500 98065
　Dennis Botten, prin.
ES, 755 PARK ST 98065 – Jack McCullough, prin.
Other Schools – See Fall City, North Bend

Soap Lake, Grant Co., Pop. Code 4
Soap Lake SD 156
Sch. Sys. Enr. Code 2
Supt. – Ashley Watson, P O BOX 158 98851
ES, P O BOX 158 98851 – William Woodford, prin.

South Bend, Pacific Co., Pop. Code 4
South Bend SD 118
Sch. Sys. Enr. Code 3
Supt. – David R. Spogen, P O BOX 437 98586
ES 98586 – Orson Giles, prin.

Spanaway, Pierce Co., Pop. Code 6
Bethel SD 403
Sch. Sys. Enr. Code 7
Supt. – Dr. Gerald Hosman
　516 E 176TH ST 98387
Camas Prairie ES, 320 E 176TH STREET 98387
　Carl Peterson, prin.
Elk Plain ES, 22015 22ND AVE E 98387
　Karl Bond, prin.
Evergreen ES, 1311 172ND ST E 98387
　Virginia Paul, prin.
Shining Mountain MS, 21615 38TH AVE E 98387
　Bradley Graham, prin.
ES, 215 166TH ST E 98387 – Cherie Brines, prin.
Other Schools – See Graham, Roy, Tacoma

Spangle, Spokane Co., Pop. Code 2
Liberty SD 362
Sch. Sys. Enr. Code 3
Supt. – Armin Vogt
　S 29818 N PINE CREEK ROAD 99031
Liberty ES, S 29818 N PINE CREEK ROAD 99031
　Ed Aylward, prin.

Spokane, Spokane Co., Pop. Code 9
Central Valley SD 356
Supt. – See Greenacres
Blake ES, 13313 E BROADWAY AVE 99216
　Dennis Olson, prin.
Broadway ES, 11016 E BROADWAY AVE 99206
　Geri Branch, prin.
Chester ES, 3525 S PINES ROAD 99206
　Julius Presta, prin.

Keystone ES, 612 S MCDONALD ROAD 99216
　Karen Toreson, prin.
Mcdonald ES, 1512 S MCDONALD ROAD 99216
　Harvey Hagen, prin.
Opportunity ES, 1109 S WILBUR ROAD 99206
　Glenn Bailey, prin.
Ponderosa ES, 10105 E CIMARRON ROAD 99206
　Carol Peterson, prin.
South Pines ES, 12021 E 24TH AVE 99206
　Robert J. Walter, prin.
University ES, 1613 S UNIVERSITY 99206
　Stanley Hughes, prin.

Cheney SD 360
Supt. – See Cheney
Garden Springs ES
　5116 W GARDEN SPRINGS ROAD 99204
　Marjean Scheele, prin.
Windsor ES, 5504 W HALLET ROAD 99204
　Richard D. Dierckins, prin.

East Valley SD 361
Sch. Sys. Enr. Code 5
Supt. – Ed Jenkins, 3415 N PINES ROAD 99206
Skyview ES, 16924 E WELLESLEY AVE 99216
　William D. Ferger, prin.
Trent ES, 3303 N PINES ROAD 99206
　William C. McCrorey Jr., prin.
Trentwood ES, E 14701 WELLESLEY 99216
　Jan Bernhart, prin.
Other Schools – See Newman Lake, Otis Orchards

Great Northern SD 312
Sch. Sys. Enr. Code 1
Supt. – Marcia Olson
　3115 N SPOTTED ROAD 99204
Great Northern ES
　N 3115 SPOTTED ROAD 99204 – (—), prin.

Mead SD 354
Supt. – See Mead
Brentwood ES, W 406 REGINA 99218
　Gerry Sperling, prin.
Evergreen ES, W 215 EDDY AVE 99216
　Richard Olsen, prin.
Farwell ES, N 13005 CRESTLINE 99208
　Paul Doneen, prin.
Shiloh ES, 505 E STONEWALL AVE 99208
　Dr. Nancy Isaacson, prin.

Orchard Prairie SD 123
Sch. Sys. Enr. Code 1
Supt. – Robert McMillan
　7626 N ORCHARD PRAIRIE ROAD 99207
Orchard Prairie ES
　7626 N ORCHARD PRAIRIE ROAD 99207
　Edward M. McCarthy, prin.

Spokane SD 81
Sch. Sys. Enr. Code 8
Supt. – Dr. Gerald L. Hester
　200 N BERNARD ST 99201
Garry JHS, 725 E JOSEPH AVE 99207
　Don Miller, prin.
Glover JHS, 2404 W LONGFELLOW AVE 99205
　Bill Leinweber, prin.
Libby JHS, 2900 E 1ST AVE 99202
　Nancy Stowell, prin.
Sacajawea JHS, 401 E 33RD AVE 99203
　George Renner, prin.
Salk JHS, 6411 N ALBERTA ST 99208
　Mary Haugen, prin.
Shaw JHS, 4106 N COOK ST 99207
　Clifford Truscott, prin.
Adams ES, 2909 E 37TH AVE 99223
　Marilyn Highberg, prin.
Arlington ES, 6363 N SMITH ST 99207
　Earl J. Buri, prin.
Audubon ES, 2020 W CARLISLE AVE 99205
　Gloria Morris, prin.
Balboa ES, 3010 W HOLYOKE AVE 99208
　Elva Mote, prin.
Bemiss ES, 2323 E BRIDGEPORT AVE 99207
　Dale McDonald, prin.
Browne ES, N 5134 DRISCOLL BLVD 99205
　Margaret McGilvray, prin.
Cooper ES, 3200 N FERRALL ST 99207
　Paul Ircink, prin.
Finch ES, 3717 N MILTON ST 99205
　Shari Y. Kirihara, prin.
Franklin ES, E 2627 17TH AVE 99223
　Linda Haladyna, prin.
Garfield ES, 222 W KNOX AVE 99205
　Phillip Snowdon, prin.
Grant ES, 1300 E 9TH AVE 99202
　William Reuter, prin.
Hamblen ES, 4005 S NAPA ST 99203
　Delbert V. Steele, prin.
Holmes ES, W 2600 SHARP 99201
　Thomas H. Jones, prin.
Hutton ES, 908 E 24TH AVE 99203
　Nelda Gaffney, prin.
Indian Trail ES, W 4102 WOODSIDE 99208
　Celeste Stoddard, prin.
Jefferson ES, 3612 S GRAND BLVD 99203
　Mary Wooley, prin.
Lidgerwood ES, 325 E ROWAN AVE 99207
　Deborah Johnson, prin.
Lincoln Heights ES, 3322 E 22ND AVE 99223
　Don A. Sesso, prin.
Linwood ES, 906 W WEILE AVE 99208
　Jim Rogers, prin.
Logan ES, 915 E MONTGOMERY AVE 99207
　Celia Dodd, prin.
Longfellow ES, 800 E PROVIDENCE AVE 99207
　Richard Stannard, prin.

Madison ES, W 319 NEBRASKA AVE 99205
  Marylou Mundy, prin.
Mullan Road ES, 2616 E 63RD AVE 99223
  Richard Clauss, prin.
Pratt ES, 6903 E 4TH AVE 99212
  Dana Lyman, prin.
Regal ES, 2707 E RICH AVE 99207
  Verner Hogberg, prin.
Ridgeview ES, 5608 N MAPLE ST 99205
  Michael J. Crabtree, prin.
Roosevelt ES, 333 W 14TH AVE 99204
  Gene Wooley, prin.
Sheridan ES, 3737 E 5TH AVE 99202
  Karin Short, prin.
Stevens ES, 1815 E SINTO AVE 99202
  Donna M. Burt, prin.
Westview ES, N 6104 MOORE ST 99205
  Jerry Senn, prin.
Whitman ES, 5400 N HELENA ST 99207
  James C Frye, prin.
Willard ES, 500 W LONGFELLOW AVE 99205
  Diana Moon, prin.
Wilson ES, 911 W 25TH AVE 99203
  Val Chadwick, prin.
Woodridge ES, 5100 W SHAWNEE AVE 99208
  Sonia Ault, prin.

West Valley SD 363
  Sch. Sys. Enr. Code 5
  Supt. – Dr. Leo Beck, P O BOX 11739 99211
Argonne JHS, 8823 E TRENT AVE 99212
  Joseph Dawson, prin.
Millwood PS, E 8818 GRACE 99212
  Franklin Koth, prin.
Ness PS, 9612 E CATALDO AVE 99206
  Fred Traher, prin.
Orchard Center ES, 7519 E BUCKEYE AVE 99212
  R.E. Richeson, prin.
Park MS, 915 N ELLA ROAD 99212
  James Howard, prin.
Pasadena Park PS, E 8508 UPRIVER DR 99212
  Amy Bragdon, prin.

All Saints MS, E 1428 33RD AVE 99203
Northwest Christian School Inc.
  W 1412 CENTRAL AVE 99205
Saint George's School
  2929 W WAIKIKI ROAD 99208
All Saints PS, E 3406 18TH AVE 99203
Assumption ES, 3400 W WEILE AVE #2 99208
Cataldo ES, W 455 18TH AVE 99203
Spokane Christian Academy
  E 8909 BIGELOW GULCH ROAD 99205
Spokane Junior Academy
  1505 W CLEVELAND AVE 99205
Spokane Lutheran/LCMS ES
  4001 W FREMONT AVE 99204
St. Aloysius ES, 611 E MISSION AVE 99202
St. Charles ES, 4515 N ALBERTA ST 99205
St. Francis Xavier of Assisi ES
  544 E PROVIDENCE AVE 99207
St. John Vianney ES
  N 501 WALNUT ROAD 99206
St. Mary's ES, E 14601 4TH AVE 99216
St. Paschal School, 2521 NORTH PARK RD 99212
St. Patrick ES, E 2706 QUEEN 99207
St. Thomas More ES
  515 W SAINT THOMAS MORE WAY 99208
Trinity ES, 1306 W MONTGOMERY AVE 99205

Sprague, Lincoln Co., Pop. Code 2
Sprague SD 8
  Sch. Sys. Enr. Code 2
  Supt. – Richard Hattrup, P O BOX 305 99032
ES, P O BOX 305 99032 – Richard Hattrup, prin.

Springdale, Stevens Co., Pop. Code 2
Mary Walker SD 207
  Sch. Sys. Enr. Code 2
  Supt. – Donald Fekete 99173
Springdale MS 99173 – Joyce Prairie, prin.
ES 99173 – Joyce W. Prairie, prin.

Stanwood, Snohomish Co., Pop. Code 5
Stanwood SD 401
  Sch. Sys. Enr. Code 4
  Supt. – Raymond Reid, P O BOX 430 98292
MS, P O BOX 879 98292 – Ron Hendricks, prin.
Church Creek MS, 7600 272ND ST NW 98292
  Richard Reim, prin.
PS, 10227 273RD PL NW 98292
  Eldon Allen, prin.

Starbuck, Columbia Co., Pop. Code 2
Starbuck SD 35
  Sch. Sys. Enr. Code 1
  Supt. – Frederick Yancey, P O BOX 188 99359
ES 99359 – (—), prin.

Stehekin, Chelan Co., Pop. Code 2
Stehekin SD 69
  Sch. Sys. Enr. Code 1
  Supt. – Riberta Pitts 98852
ES 98852 – Ron Scutt, prin.

Steilacoom, Pierce Co., Pop. Code 5
Steilacoom Historical SD 1
  Sch. Sys. Enr. Code 4
  Supt. – Dr. James Maw, 54 SENTINEL 98388
Pioneer MS, 54 SENTINEL 98388
  Varney Alvernaz, prin.
Anderson Island ES, 510 CHAMBERS ST 98388
  Donna Rivers, prin.
Cherrydale ES, 510 CHAMBERS ST 98338
  Donna Rivers, prin.

Salters Point MS, 510 CHAMBERS ST 98388
  Pamela Berger, prin.
Taylor ES, 510 CHAMBERS ST 98388
  Pamela Berger, prin.

Steptoe, Whitman Co.
Steptoe SD 304
  Sch. Sys. Enr. Code 1
  Supt. – Clifford Zinke, P O BOX 66 99174
ES, P O BOX 138 99174 – Clifford Zinke, prin.

Stevenson, Skamania Co., Pop. Code 4
Skamania SD 2
  Sch. Sys. Enr. Code 4
  Supt. – Clayton Anderson
    12 BUTLER LOOP 98648
Skamania ES, MPO 12R BUTLER LOOP 98648
  (—), prin.

Stevenson-Carson SD 303
  Sch. Sys. Enr. Code 4
  Supt. – Anthony Feldhausen, P O BOX 850 98648
Wind River MS, P O BOX 850 98648
  Donald Boyk, prin.
Carson ES, P O BOX 850 98648
  David Teitzel, prin.
ES, P O BOX 850 98648
  N. William Townsend, prin.

Sultan, Snohomish Co., Pop. Code 4
Sultan SD 311
  Sch. Sys. Enr. Code 4
  Supt. – Dr. Bill Tilley, P O BOX 399 98294
MS, P O BOX 399 98294 – Jann Siegert, prin.
ES, P O BOX 399 98294 – Thomas Dramer, prin.

Sumas, Whatcom Co., Pop. Code 3
Nooksack Valley SD 506
  Supt. – See Nooksack
Nooksack Valley ES, P O BOX 589 98295
  Gerald Bauthues, prin.

Sumner, Pierce Co., Pop. Code 5
Dieringer SD 343
  Sch. Sys. Enr. Code 3
  Supt. – Dr Curtis Horne, 1320 178TH AVE E 98390
Dieringer MS, 1808 VALLEY HIGHWAY 98390
  James Denton, prin.
Lake Tapps ES, 1320 176TH AVE E 98390
  James Milden, prin.

Sumner SD 320
  Sch. Sys. Enr. Code 5
  Supt. – Donald Eismann, 1202 WOOD AVE 98390
Bonney Lake ES, 18715 80TH ST E 98390
  Douglas Gall, prin.
Daffodil Valley ES, 1509 VALLEY AVE E 98390
  Julianne Hult, prin.
Emerald Hills Elem School
  19515 TAPPS DR 98390
  Jacqueline Carlstrom, prin.
Maple Lawn ES, 230 WOOD AVE 98390
  Sue Hall, prin.
Victor Falls ES
  18605 RHODES LAKE ROAD E 98390
  Michael Healy, prin.
Other Schools – See Puyallup

Sunnyside, Yakima Co., Pop. Code 6
Sunnyside SD 201
  Sch. Sys. Enr. Code 5
  Supt. – Jack Middleton, 1110 S 6TH ST 98944
IS, 1700 E LINCOLN AVE 98944
  Stanley Davis, prin.
Washington ES, 800 JACKSON 98944
  James Chambers, prin.
Other Schools – See Outlook

St. Joseph's ES, 907 S 6TH ST 98944
Sunnyside Christian ES, 811 NORTH AVE 98944

Suquamish, Kitsap Co.
North Kitsap SD 400
  Supt. – See Poulsbo
ES, 18950 PARK AVE NE 98392
  Marylou Murphy, prin.

Tacoma, Pierce Co., Pop. Code 9
Bethel SD 403
  Supt. – See Spanaway
Clover Creek ES, 16715 36TH AVE E 98446
  Patrick Plamondon, prin.
Naches Trail ES, 15305 WALLER ROAD E 98446
  Doyle Shaffer, prin.
Thompson ES, 15605 B ST E 98445
  Cherry Goudeau, prin.

Clover Park SD 400
  Sch. Sys. Enr. Code 7
  Supt. – Charles Alexander
    10020 GRAVELLY LAKE DR SW 98499
Carter Lake ES, 3415 LINCOLN BLVD SW 98439
  Erling Molver, prin.
Custer ES, 7700 STEILACOOM BLVD SW 98498
  Jeannie Haugh, prin.
Dower ES, 7817 JOHN DOWER RD W 98467
  Kevin Brooks, prin.
Heartwood ES, 4010 WOODBROOK RD SW 98439
  Gary Wilson, prin.
Idlewild ES, 10806 IDLEWILD RD SW 98498
  Georgene Mellom, prin.
Lake City ES, 8800 121ST ST SW 98498
  Frerel Gines, prin.
Lake Louise ES, 11014 HOLDEN RD SW 98498
  Lawrence Roberson, prin.
Lakeview ES, 10501 47TH AVE SW 98499
  Joe Fosnick, prin.

Oakbrook ES, 7802 83RD AVE SW 98498
  Lois Ping, prin.
Oakwood ES, 3220 KETELL ST S 98409
  Betty Lauritzen, prin.
Southgate ES, 10202 EARLEY AVE SW 98499
  J. Bruce Piland, prin.
Tillicum ES, 8514 MAPLE ST SW 98498
  Kenneth Haag, prin.
Tyee Park ES, 11920 SEMINOLE RD SW 98499
  Thomas Prentice, prin.
Other Schools – See Fort Lewis

Fife SD 417
  Sch. Sys. Enr. Code 4
  Supt. – Larry Crouch, 5602 20TH ST E 98424
Fife ES, 5802 20TH ST E 98424
  Gerald Lankford, prin.
Other Schools – See Milton

Franklin Pierce SD 402
  Sch. Sys. Enr. Code 6
  Supt. – Robert Whitehead, 315 129TH ST S 98444
Ford MS, 1602 104TH ST E 98445
  Alan Hokenstad, prin.
Keithley MS, 12324 L ST S 98444
  Lois Hosman, prin.
Brookdale ES, 611 132ND ST S 98444
  Larry Poulsen, prin.
Central Avenue ES, 4505 104TH ST E 98446
  Stephen Kvinsland, prin.
Christensen ES, 10232 BARNES LANE S 98444
  Iver Eliason, prin.
Collins ES, 4608 128TH ST E 98446
  Michael Gayda, prin.
Elmhurst ES, 420 133RD ST E 98445
  Linda Heade, prin.
Harvard ES, 1709 85TH ST E 98445
  Dennis Hammermaster, prin.
Sales ES, 11213 S SHERIDAN 98444
  Marie Korsmo, prin.

Puyallup SD 3
  Supt. – See Puyallup
Waller Road ES, 6312 WALLER ROAD E 98443
  Ken Keener, prin.

Tacoma SD 10
  Sch. Sys. Enr. Code 8
  Supt. – Lillian Barna, P O BOX 1357 98401
Arlington ES, 3002 S 72ND ST 98409
  Melvin O Gidley, prin.
Birney ES, 1202 S 76TH ST 98408
  Vernon T. Reis, prin.
Boze ES, 1140 E 65TH ST 98404
  Terry Burns, prin.
Browns Point MS, 1502 51ST ST NE 98422
  Theron Wheeler, prin.
Bryant ES, 717 S GRANT AVE 98405
  Kenneth Brownlee, prin.
Dash Point ES
  6546 DASH POINT BLVD NE 98422
  Theron Wheeler, prin.
Delong ES, 1229 S MOORLANDS DRIVE 98405
  Darlene Schoenwald, prin.
Downing ES, 2502 N ORCHARD ST 98406
  Daryl Ashpole, prin.
Edison ES, 3114 S 58TH ST 98409
  Robert Orlando, prin.
Fawcett ES, 126 E 60TH ST 98404
  Kenneth Klubberud, prin.
Fern Hill ES, 8442 S PARK AVE 98444
  Dr. Dale Scott, prin.
Franklin ES, 3202 S 12TH ST 98405
  Charles Harkins, prin.
Geiger ES, 621 S JACKSON AVE 98465
  Gail Miller, prin.
Grant ES, 1018 N PROSPECT ST 98406
  Erling Mellum, prin.
Hoyt ES, 2708 N UNION AVE 98407
  Sandra Roszman, prin.
Jefferson ES, 4302 N 13TH ST 98406
  Dr. Constance Lassiter, prin.
Larchmont ES, 8601 E B ST 98445
  Paul A. Wangsmo, prin.
Lister ES, 2106 E 44TH ST 98404
  Sharon D. Krause, prin.
Lowell ES, 810 N 13TH ST 98403
  John Armour, prin.
Lyon ES, 101 E 46TH ST 98404
  Paulette Williams, prin.
Manitou ES, 4806 S 66TH ST 98409
  Michael E. Crosby, prin.
Mann ES, 5211 S K ST 98408
  Donald R. Kvamme, prin.
McCarver ES, 2111 S J ST 98405
  Dorothy A. Dedrick, prin.
McKinley ES, 3702 MCKINLEY AVE 98404
  Frank Johnson, prin.
Northeast Tacoma ES, 5412 29TH ST NE 98422
  Dick Hopkins, prin.
Point Defiance ES, 6002 N 45TH ST 98407
  Coralee P. Kinney, prin.
Reed ES, 1802 S 36TH ST 98408
  Banasree Mallick, prin.
Rogers ES, 1301 E 34TH ST 98404
  Lei Lani Jackson, prin.
Roosevelt ES, 3550 E ROOSEVELT AVE 98404
  Richard S. Klumpar, prin.
Seward ES, 4902 S ALASKA ST 98408
  Kathleen Bergman, prin.
Sheridan ES, 5317 MCKINLEY AVE 98404
  Emma H. Sneed, prin.
Sherman ES, 4502 N 39TH ST 98407
  H. George Weeks, prin.

Skyline ES, 2301 N MILDRED ST 98406
  Donald B. Gillis, prin.
Stanley ES, 1712 S 17TH 98405 – Al Svinth, prin.
Wainwright ES, 130 ALAMEDA AVE 98466
  James W. Dewey, prin.
Washington ES, 3701 N 26TH ST 98407
  Sandra Roszman, prin.
Whitman ES, 1120 S 39TH ST 98408
  Dorothy Williams, prin.
Whittier ES, 777 ELM TREE LANE 98466
  William L. Rossman, prin.

University Place SD 83
  Sch. Sys. Enr. Code 5
  Supt. – Dr. Gregory Paus, 8805 40TH ST W 98466
Chambers ES, 9101 56TH ST W 98467
  Judie Bilderback, prin.
Narrows View ES, 7813 44TH ST W 98466
  Mario Marsillo, prin.
Sunset ES, 4523 97TH AVE W 98466
  Dallas Blair, prin.
University Place ES
  2708 GRANDVIEW DRIVE W 98466
  Jo Ellen McGrath, prin.

Annie Wright School, 827 TACOMA AVE N 98403
Charles Wright Academy
  7723 CHAMBERS CREEK ROAD W 98467
Tacoma Baptist HS, 2052 S 64TH ST 98409
Central Lutheran Christian ES
  409 TACOMA AVE N 98403
Concordia Lutheran ES, 202 E 56TH ST 98404
Heritage Christian ES, 5412 67TH AVE W 98467
Holy Rosary ES, 504 S 30TH ST 98402
Life Christian ES
  1717 S PUGET SOUND AVE 98405
New Horizon Christian ES
  17408 36TH AVE E 98446
Peoples Christian ES, 1819 E 72ND ST 98404
Puget Sound Christian ES, 1740 S 84TH ST 98444
St. Charles Borromeo ES, 7112 S 12TH ST 98465
St. Frances Cabrini ES, 5621 108TH ST SW 98499
St. Patrick ES, 1112 N G ST 98403
Visitation ES, 3306 S 58TH ST 98409

Taholah, Grays Harbor Co.
Taholah SD 77
  Sch. Sys. Enr. Code 2
  Supt. – Darrell Olson, P O BOX 249 98587
ES, P O BOX 249 98587 – Rich Culver, prin.

Tekoa, Whitman Co., Pop. Code 3
Tekoa SD 265
  Sch. Sys. Enr. Code 2
  Supt. – Jim Menzies, P O BOX 869 99033
ES 99033 – Wayne Roellich, prin.

Tenino, Thurston Co., Pop. Code 4
Tenino SD 402
  Sch. Sys. Enr. Code 4
  Supt. – Jack L. Jutte 98589
MS 98589 – Hal Williams, prin.
Tenino ES 98589 – Jeff Petra, prin.

Thorp, Kittitas Co., Pop. Code 2
Thorp SD 400
  Sch. Sys. Enr. Code 2
  Supt. – Richard Omans, P O BOX 155 98946
ES, P O BOX 155 98946 – Richard Omans, prin.

Tieton, Yakima Co., Pop. Code 3
Highland SD 203
  Supt. – See Cowiche
MS, P O BOX 6 98947 – F. David Jaeger, prin.

Toledo, Lewis Co., Pop. Code 3
Toledo SD 237
  Sch. Sys. Enr. Code 3
  Supt. – John Simpson 98591
MS 98591 – Dave Filla, prin.
ES 98591 – Tom Lahmann, prin.

Tonasket, Okanogan Co., Pop. Code 3
Tonasket SD 404
  Sch. Sys. Enr. Code 4
  Supt. – Jerry Mills, P O BOX 468 98855
MS, P O BOX 448 98855 – William Roberts, prin.
ES, P O BOX 448 98855 – William Roberts, prin.

Toppenish, Yakima Co., Pop. Code 6
Toppenish SD 202
  Sch. Sys. Enr. Code 5
  Supt. – Dr. Roy Williams
  106 FRANKLIN AVE 98948
MS, 106 FRANKLIN AVE 98948 – Fred Diaz, prin.
Garfield ES, 505 MADISON AVE 98948
  Roy DeBoer, prin.
Kirkwood-Mt. Adams IS, 403 JUNIPER ST 98948
  Gail Puryear, prin.
Lincoln ES, 309 N ALDER ST 98948
  Jan Esquivel, prin.

Touchet, Walla Walla Co., Pop. Code 4
Touchet SD 300
  Sch. Sys. Enr. Code 2
  Supt. – Terry Carlson, P O BOX 1135 99360
ES, P O BOX 1135 99360 – Terry Carlson, prin.

Toutle, Cowlitz Co., Pop. Code 2
Toutle Lake SD 130
  Sch. Sys. Enr. Code 3
  Supt. – Jack Adams
  5050 SPIRIT LAKE HIGHWAY 98649
Toutle Lake JHS
  5050 SPIRIT LAKE HIGHWAY 98649
  Roy Frizzel, prin.

Toutle Lake ES
  5050 SPIRIT LAKE MEM HWY 98649
  Roger Calhoun, prin.

Trout Lake, Klickitat Co., Pop. Code 2
Trout Lake SD R-400
  Sch. Sys. Enr. Code 2
  Supt. – Manuel Borge, P O BOX 10 98650
ES 98650 – Manuel Borge, prin.

Tumwater, Thurston Co., Pop. Code 6
Tumwater SD 33
  Sch. Sys. Enr. Code 5
  Supt. – Norman Wisner
  419 LINWOOD AVE SW 98502
MS, 6335 LITTLE ROCK ROAD SW 98502
  Richard Martin, prin.
Schmidt ES, 6600 CAPITOL BLVD S 98501
  Dennis Eygabroad, prin.
Simmons ES, 1205 2ND AVE S 98502
  Beth Kennedy, prin.
Other Schools – See East Olympia, Littlerock, Olympia

Twisp, Okanogan Co., Pop. Code 3
Methow Valley SD 350
  Sch. Sys. Enr. Code 3
  Supt. – Peter Ansingh 98856
Methow Valley JHS 98856 – Paul Arneson, prin.
Allen ES 98856 – Dr. Peter Ansingh, prin.

Union Gap, Yakima Co., Pop. Code 5
Union Gap SD 2
  Sch. Sys. Enr. Code 2
  Supt. – Noah Palmer, 3200 S 2ND ST 98903
ES, 3200 S 2ND ST 98903 – Tom Smith, prin.

Vader, Lewis Co., Pop. Code 2
Vader SD 18
  Sch. Sys. Enr. Code 2
  Supt. – Dennis Charlton, P O BOX 149 98593
ES 98593 – Dennis Charlton, prin.

Valley, Stevens Co.
Valley SD 70
  Sch. Sys. Enr. Code 2
  Supt. – Donald Munson, P O BOX 157 99181
JHS 99181 – Gerald Ely, prin.
ES 99181 – Gerald Ely, prin.

Vancouver, Clark Co., Pop. Code 8
Battle Ground SD 119
  Supt. – See Battle Ground
Laurin IS, 13601 NE 97TH AVE 98662
  Jim Kuhlman, prin.
Pleasant Valley IS, 14320 NE 50TH AVE 98686
  Teresa Baldwin, prin.
Glenwood Hts. ES, 9716 NE 134TH ST 98662
  Jeff Newport, prin.
Pleasant Valley ES, 14320 NE 50TH AVE 98686
  Teresia Hazen, prin.

Evergreen SD 114
  Sch. Sys. Enr. Code 7
  Supt. – Dr. K. C. Schmauder
  13905 NE 28TH ST 98682
Burton ES, 14015 NE 28TH ST 98682
  Robert Sanborn, prin.
Crestline ES, 13003 SE 7TH ST 98684
  Susan Porter, prin.
Ellsworth ES, 512 SE ELLSWORTH ROAD 98664
  Annie Arkebauer, prin.
Fircrest ES, 12001 NE 9TH ST 98684
  Dave Dyment, prin.
Hearthwood ES
  801 NE HEARTHWOOD BLVD 98684
  Kurt Smith, prin.
Image ES, 4400 NE 122ND AVE 98682
  Charles Whittey, prin.
Marrion ES, 10119 NE 14TH ST 98664
  Gloria Pappas, prin.
Mill Plain ES, 400 SE 164TH AVE 98684
  Max Schliewe, prin.
Orchards ES, 7000 NE 117TH AVE 98662
  Calvin Getty, prin.
Riverview ES, 12601 SE RIVERIDGE DRIVE 98684
  Joe Segram, prin.
Sifton ES, 7301 NE 137TH AVE 98682
  James Dixon, prin.
Silver Star ES, 10500 NE 86TH ST 98662
  Dianne Kennedy, prin.
Sunset ES, 9001 NE 95TH ST 98662
  Norman Brown, prin.

Vancouver SD 37
  Sch. Sys. Enr. Code 7
  Supt. – Dr. James F. Parsley, Jr.
  605 N DEVINE ROAD 98661
Lee MS, 8500 NW 9TH AVE 98665
  Dean Ramsey, prin.
Anderson ES, 2215 NE 104TH ST 98686
  Bertha Stuurmans, prin.
Eisenhower ES, 9201 NW 9TH AVE 98665
  Barbara Scott-Johnson, prin.
Felida ES, 2700 NW 119TH ST 98685
  Gary Ludke, prin.
Franklin ES, 5206 FRANKLIN ST 98663
  Annette Pokornowski, prin.
Fruit Valley ES, 3301 FRUIT VALLEY RD 98660
  Jeanne Mack, prin.
Harney ES, 3212 E EVERGREEN BLVD 98661
  Ron Porterfield, prin.
Hazel Dell ES, 511 E ANDERSON ROAD 98665
  Claude Gove, prin.
Hough ES, 1900 DANIELS ST 98660
  Gary Adams, prin.
King ES, 4801 IDAHO ST 98661 – Ed Little, prin.

Lake Shore ES, 9300 NW 21ST AVE 98665
  Henry Maas, prin.
Lieser ES, 301 S LIESER ROAD 98664
  Arlene Scarpelli, prin.
Lincoln ES, 4200 DANIELS ST 98660
  Genevieve Robinson, prin.
Marshall ES, 6400 MACARTHUR BLVD 98661
  Peter Loop, prin.
Minnehaha ES, 2800 NE 54TH ST 98663
  Elizabeth Gordon, prin.
Ogden ES, 8100 NE 54TH ST 98662
  David Lindblom, prin.
Rogers ES, 2000 NORRIS ROAD 98661
  Dr. Ronald Albough, prin.
Sacajawea ES, 700 NE 112TH 98665
  Scott Williams, prin.
Salmon Creek ES, 1601 NE 129TH ST 98685
  Darrell Brandenberg, prin.
Truman ES, 4505 NE 42ND AVE 98661
  Meddie Dale, prin.
Walnut Grove ES, 6103 NE 72ND AVE 98661
  Ellen Bucek, prin.
Washington ES, 2908 S ST 98663
  Bernice Burgess, prin.

Clark County Christian School
  7915 NE BURTON ROAD 98662
Cornerstone Christian School
  7708 NE 78TH ST 98662
Fir Grove SDA ES, 2920 FALK ROAD 98661
Kings Way Christian ES, 3300 NE 78TH ST 98665
Our Lady of Lourdes /St. James ES
  4701 FRANKLIN ST 98663
St. Joseph's ES, 6500 HIGHLAND DRIVE 98661

Vashon, King Co., Pop. Code 2
Vashon Island SD 402
  Sch. Sys. Enr. Code 4
  Supt. – Dr. Gary Hall, P O BOX 429 98070
McMurray ES, RURAL ROUTE 02 BOX 320 98070
  Michael Kirk, prin.
Burton ES, RURAL ROUTE 03 BOX 425 98070
  David Jarvis, prin.
MS, RURAL ROUTE 05 BOX 31 98070
  Ronald Meyer, prin.

Vaughn, Pierce Co.
Peninsula SD 401
  Supt. – See Gig Harbor
ES, 17521 HALL RD KPN 98394
  Larry Hawkins, prin.

Veradale, Spokane Co., Pop. Code 4
Central Valley SD 356
  Supt. – See Greenacres
Adams ES, E 14707 8TH AVE 99037
  Sid Crowe, prin.
Progress ES, 710 N PROGRESS ROAD 99037
  James Berry, prin.
Sunrise ES, 14603 E 24TH AVE 99037
  Ralph Larsen, prin.

Waitsburg, Walla Walla Co., Pop. Code 4
Waitsburg SD 401-100
  Sch. Sys. Enr. Code 2
  Supt. – Edward Larsen, P O BOX 217 99361
Waitsburg MS, P O 217 99361 – Jerald Scott, prin.
ES, P O 217 99361 – Glynn Davis, prin.

Waldron, San Juan Co.
Orcas Island SD 137
  Supt. – See Eastsound
Waldron Island ES 98297 – Kathleen Barner, prin.

Walla Walla, Walla Walla Co., Pop. Code 8
Walla Walla SD 140
  Sch. Sys. Enr. Code 6
  Supt. – Dennis A. Ray, 364 S PARK ST 99362
Berney ES, PLEASANT & SCHOOL 99362
  Dennis Maguire, prin.
Blue Ridge ES, 1150 W CHESTNUT ST 99362
  Buddy Heimbigner, prin.
Edison ES, 1315 E ALDER ST 99362
  Helen Polzin, prin.
Green Park ES, ISAACS & CLINTON 99362
  Charlene Bailey, prin.
Prospect Point ES
  HOWARD & RESER ROAD 99362
  Richard L. Moore, prin.
Sharpstein ES, 410 HOWARD ST 99362
  Bill Thompson, prin.

Assumption ES, 2066 E ALDER ST 99362
Liberty Christian ES
  1850 THE DALLES MILITARY RD 99362

Wapato, Yakima Co., Pop. Code 5
Wapato SD 207
  Sch. Sys. Enr. Code 5
  Supt. – Harold Ott, P O BOX 38 98951
JHS, P O BOX 38 98951 – Scott Dolquist, prin.
IS, P O BOX 38 98951 – Jim Devine, prin.
PS, P O BOX 38 98951 – Julene Miller, prin.

Warden, Grant Co., Pop. Code 4
Warden SD 146-161
  Sch. Sys. Enr. Code 3
  Supt. – John Eikum, P O BOX 308 98857
MS, P O BOX 308 98857 – Russ Davis, prin.
Evans ES, P O BOX 308 98857 – Ken Ibach, prin.

Washougal, Clark Co., Pop. Code 5
Mount Pleasant SD 29-93
  Sch. Sys. Enr. Code 1
  Supt. – L. Miller, 15 R MARBLE ROAD 98671

Mount Pleasant ES
  MPO 15 MARBLE ROAD 98671 – (—), prin.

Washougal SD 112-6
  Sch. Sys. Enr. Code 4
  Supt. – Brent C. Garrett, 2349 B ST 98671
  Jemtegaard MS
    35300 SE EVERGREEN BLVD 98671
    Claire Schozman, prin.
  Cape Horn-Skye ES
    MPO 9.80 STATE ROAD 140 98671
    Rodger Sitko, prin.
  Gause MS, 1100 34TH ST 98671
    Cheryl Silk, prin.
  Hathaway ES, 630 24TH ST 98671
    Dr. Donna Carman, prin.

Washtucna, Adams Co., Pop. Code 2
  Washtucna SD 109-43
  Sch. Sys. Enr. Code 1
  Supt. – David Randall, P O BOX 688 99371
  ES 99371 – Neils Peterson, prin.

Waterville, Douglas Co., Pop. Code 3
  Waterville SD 209
  Sch. Sys. Enr. Code 2
  Supt. – Larry Utzinger, P O BOX 490 98858
  ES, P O BOX 490 98858 – Kirsten Thomsen, prin.

Wellpinit, Stevens Co.
  Wellpinit SD 49
  Sch. Sys. Enr. Code 2
  Supt. – Jess Cruzen, P O BOX 390 99040
  ES, P O BOX 390 99040 – Ron Hunter, prin.

Wenatchee, Chelan Co., Pop. Code 7
  Eastmont SD 206
  Supt. – See East Wenatchee
  Rock Island ES, RURAL ROUTE 05 98801
    Scott McKay, prin.

  Wenatchee SD 246
  Sch. Sys. Enr. Code 5
  Supt. – Richard Johnson, 235 SUNSET AVE 98801
  Orchard MS, 1024 ORCHARD ST 98801
    Mike Franza, prin.
  Pioneer MS, 1620 RUSSELL ST 98801
    Gary Callison, prin.
  Columbia ES, 700 ORONDO ST 98801
    Dennis Friedrich, prin.
  Lewis & Clark ES, 1200 SPRINGWATER ST 98801
    Kevin Pearl, prin.
  Lincoln ES, 1224 METHOW ST 98801
    Jerry Yeager, prin.
  Mission View ES, 60 TERMINAL AVE 98801
    Joseph St. Jean, prin.
  Sunnyslope ES, 3109 SCHOOL ST 98801
    Catherine Reasor, prin.
  Washington ES, 1401 WASHINGTON ST 98801
    Charles Sears, prin.

  St. Joseph's ES, 600 SAINT JOSEPH PLACE 98801
  Wenatchee Adventist ES
    600 WESTERN AVE N 98801

West Richland, Benton Co., Pop. Code 5
  Richland SD 400
  Supt. – See Richland
  Tapteal ES, 705 N 62ND AVE 99352
    Larry Dale, prin.

Westport, Grays Harbor Co., Pop. Code 4
  Ocosta SD 172
  Sch. Sys. Enr. Code 3
  Supt. – William A. Gallacher 98595
  Ocosta ES 98595 – William Stuckrath, prin.

White Salmon, Klickitat Co., Pop. Code 4
  White Salmon Valley SD 405-17
  Sch. Sys. Enr. Code 4
  Supt. – Edward Fisk, P O BOX 157 98672
  MS, RURAL ROUTE 02 98672
    Robert Kochis, prin.
  ES, P O BOX 157 98672 – Cathie Mendonsa, prin.

White Swan, Yakima Co., Pop. Code 2
  Mount Adams SD 209
  Sch. Sys. Enr. Code 3
  Supt. – William Parker, P O BOX 361 98952
  MS, P O BOX 291 98952 – Furman Wheeler, prin.
  Other Schools – See Harrah

Wilbur, Lincoln Co., Pop. Code 4
  Wilbur SD 200
  Sch. Sys. Enr. Code 2
  Supt. – Nancy Lomas, P O BOX 1090 99185
  ES, P O BOX 1090 99185 – Nancy Lomas, prin.

Wilkeson, Pierce Co., Pop. Code 2
  White River SD 416
  Supt. – See Buckley
  ES, P O BOX A 98396 – Patricia Swift, prin.

Wilson Creek, Grant Co., Pop. Code 2
  Wilson Creek SD 167-202
  Sch. Sys. Enr. Code 2
  Supt. – Bob Periman, P O BOX 46 98860
  ES 98860 – Bob Periman, prin.

Winlock, Lewis Co., Pop. Code 4
  Evaline SD 36
  Sch. Sys. Enr. Code 1
  Supt. – Linda Godat
    111 SCHOOLHOUSE ROAD 98596
  Evaline ES, 111 SCHOOLHOUSE ROAD 98596
    (—), prin.

  Winlock SD 232
  Sch. Sys. Enr. Code 3
  Supt. – Dale Cummins, 311 NW FIR ST 98596
  Miller ES, 405 NW BENTON ST 98596
    Dale Cummins, prin.

Wishram, Klickitat Co., Pop. Code 3
  Wishram SD 94
  Sch. Sys. Enr. Code 1
  Supt. – Dennis Agar, P O BOX 268 98673
  S, P O BOX 268 98673 – Dennis Agar, prin.

Woodinville, King Co., Pop. Code 2
  Northshore SD 417
  Supt. – See Bothell
  Cottage Lake ES, 15940 192ND AVE NE 98072
    Brad Portin, prin.
  Hollywood Hill ES, 17110 148TH AVE NE 98072
    Becky Clausen, prin.
  Wellington ES, 16501 NE 195TH ST 98072
    Norman Moudry, prin.
  MS, 13209 NE 175TH ST 98072
    Dr. John Seremeta, prin.

Woodland, Cowlitz Co., Pop. Code 4
  Green Mountain SD 103
  Sch. Sys. Enr. Code 1
  Supt. – Rodney Hascall
    RURAL ROUTE 01 BOX 66 98674
  Green Mountain ES
    RURAL ROUTE 01 BOX 66 98674 – (—), prin.

  Woodland SD 404
  Sch. Sys. Enr. Code 4
  Supt. – D. W. Fluke, P O BOX 370 98674
  MS, P O BOX 370 98674 – Terry Gatz, prin.
  ES, P O BOX 370 98674 – Kerry Quorn, prin.
  Other Schools – See Ariel

Yacolt, Clark Co., Pop. Code 3
  Battle Ground SD 119
  Supt. – See Battle Ground
  Yacolt ES 98675 – Ron Spanjer, prin.

Yakima, Yakima Co., Pop. Code 8
  East Valley SD 90
  Sch. Sys. Enr. Code 4
  Supt. – Dr. Ronald Whittaker
    2020 BEAUDRY ROAD 98901
  East Valley Central MS
    2010 BEAUDRY ROAD 98901
    Stan Schmick, prin.

Terrace Heights ES
  4209 TERRACE HTS ROAD 98901
  Jean Steitzmiller, prin.
Other Schools – See Moxee City

Naches Valley SD JT3
  Supt. – See Naches
  Naches Valley PS
    2700 OLD NACHES HWY 98908
    R. Karen Craig, prin.

West Valley SD 208
  Sch. Sys. Enr. Code 5
  Supt. – Joseph J. Batali, 8902 ZIER ROAD 98908
  Ahtanum Valley ES, 3006 S WILEY ROAD 98903
    A. Streich, prin.
  Apple Valley ES, 7 N 88TH AVE 98902
    Norman Drake, prin.
  Mountainview ES, 830 STONE ROAD 98908
    David Levad, prin.
  Summitview ES, 6305 W CHESTNUT AVE 98908
    Bill Bennett, prin.
  Wide Hollow ES, 1000 S 72ND AVE 98908
    Stephen Hansen, prin.

Yakima SD 7
  Sch. Sys. Enr. Code 7
  Supt. – Dr. W. D. Starr, 104 N 4TH AVE 98902
  Adams MS, 723 S 8TH ST 98901
    Rod Bryant, prin.
  Barge-Lincoln ES, 219 E 1 ST 98901
    Bob Hibbs, prin.
  Garfield ES, 612 N 6TH AVE 98902
    Ed Trotter, prin.
  Gilbert ES, 410 N 44TH AVE 98908
    Jim Meyer, prin.
  Hoover ES, 400 W VIOLA AVE 98902
    Gary Hill, prin.
  King ES, 2000 S 18TH ST 98903
    Frank Naasz, prin.
  McClure ES, 1222 S 22ND AVE 98902
    Ron Edwards, prin.
  McKinley ES, 621 S 13TH AVE 98902
    Ray Foisy, prin.
  Nob Hill ES, 801 S 34TH AVE 98902
    Dr. Don Breitenfeldt, prin.
  Ridgeview ES, 609 W WASHINGTON AVE 98903
    Jim Williams, prin.
  Robertson ES, 2807 W LINCOLN AVE 98902
    Esperanza Lemos, prin.
  Roosevelt ES, 120 N 16TH AVE 98902
    John Gilmore, prin.
  Whitney ES, 4411 W NOB HILL BLVD 98908
    Don Ramsey, prin.

St. Joseph ES, 212 N 4TH ST 98901
St. Paul Cathedral ES
  1214 W CHESTNUT AVE 98902

Yelm, Thurston Co., Pop. Code 4
  Yelm SD 2
  Sch. Sys. Enr. Code 5
  Supt. – Dr. Glen L. Nutter
    404 YELM AVE W 98597
  MS, P O BOX 476 98597 – Jerry House, prin.
  McKenna ES, P O BOX 476 98597
    Jack Coates, prin.
  Southworth ES, P O BOX 476 98597
    Sharon Welsh, prin.
  Yelm Prairie ES, P O BOX 476 98597
    James Eisenhardt, prin.

Zillah, Yakima Co., Pop. Code 4
  Zillah SD 205
  Sch. Sys. Enr. Code 3
  Supt. – Gary Holmberg, P O BOX 225 98953
  MS, P O BOX 225 98953 – Jim Busey, prin.
  Hilton ES, P O BOX 685 98953
    Myrtle Dahlin, prin.

WEST VIRGINIA

STATE DEPARTMENT OF EDUCATION
1900 Washington St., Charleston 25305
(304) 348-2681

State Superintendent of Schools	Tom McNeel
Deputy Superintendent	James Smith
Assistant Superintendent Finance & Services	James Gladwell
Assistant Superintendent Special & Professional Education	John Pisapia
Assistant Superintendent Vocational, Technical & Adult Education	Clarence Burdette

STATE BOARD OF EDUCATION
Frances Seago, *President*   Executive Offices, Charleston   25305

WEST VIRGINIA BOARD OF REGENTS
William Simmons, *Chancellor*   950 Kanawha Blvd., E., Charleston   25333

PUBLIC, PRIVATE, AND PAROCHIAL ELEMENTARY SCHOOLS

Accoville, Logan Co.
Logan County SD
Supt. – See Logan
Buffalo ES, GENERAL DELIVERY 25606
  Brenda Williamson, prin.

Alderson, Greenbrier Co., Pop. Code 4
Greenbrier County SD
Supt. – See Lewisburg
ES, VIRGINIA ST 24910 – Mary Jones, prin.

Alkol, Lincoln Co.
Lincoln County SD
Supt. – See Hamlin
Martin ES, RURAL ROUTE 01 BOX 117 25501
  Yvonne Hill, prin.
Woodville ES, P O BOX 100 25501
  Bob France, prin.

Alum Bridge, Lewis Co.
Lewis County SD
Supt. – See Weston
ES 26321 – Opal Marsh, prin.

Alum Creek, Kanawha Co.
Lincoln County SD
Supt. – See Hamlin
Midway ES, RURAL ROUTE 01 BOX 130 25003
  Pauline Rymer, prin.

Amherstdale, Logan Co., Pop. Code 3
Logan County SD
Supt. – See Logan
ES, P O BOX 29 25607 – Charles Christian, prin.

Anawalt, McDowell Co., Pop. Code 3
McDowell County SD
Supt. – See Welch
ES, P O BOX 280 24808 – Donald Hoback, prin.

Ansted, Fayette Co., Pop. Code 4
Fayette County SD
Supt. – See Fayetteville
MS, P O BOX 776 25812 – Charles Garvin III, prin.
ES, P O BOX 609 25812 – Ralph Winter, prin.

Apple Grove, Mason Co.
Mason County SD
Supt. – See Point Pleasant
Sunnyside ES, RURAL ROUTE 01 BOX 121 25502
  Vickie Hall, prin.

Arnoldsburg, Calhoun Co.
Calhoun County SD
Supt. – See Grantsville
ES, GENERAL DELIVERY 25234
  Robert Berdine, prin.

Arthurdale, Preston Co., Pop. Code 3
Preston County SD
Supt. – See Kingwood
Valley JHS, P O BOX 690 26520
  Michael Teets, prin.
Valley ES, P O BOX 700 26520
  Denzil Devisson, prin.

Ashford, Boone Co.
Boone County SD
Supt. – See Madison
Ashford-Rumble ES, P O BOX 540 25009
  Dan Kirk, prin.

Ashton, Mason Co.
Mason County SD
Supt. – See Point Pleasant
Hannan ES, P O BOX 71 25503
  Bruce Faulkner, prin.

Athens, Mercer Co., Pop. Code 4
Mercer County SD
Supt. – See Princeton
ES, HCR BOX 172G 24712 – Betty Martin, prin.
Sun Valley ES, HCR BOX 185 24712
  Betty Snider, prin.

Augusta, Hampshire Co.
Hampshire County SD
Supt. – See Romney
ES, P O BOX 264 26704 – Jill Parker, prin.

Aurora, Preston Co.
Preston County SD
Supt. – See Kingwood
ES, RURAL ROUTE 01 BOX A 26705
  William Mathias, prin.

Baisden, Mingo Co.
Mingo County SD
Supt. – See Williamson
Cline ES, GENERAL DELIVERY 25608
  Jerry Thompson, prin.

Ballard, Monroe Co.
Monroe County SD
Supt. – See Union
ES 24918 – Danny Lively, prin.

Barboursville, Cabell Co., Pop. Code 5
Cabell County SD
Supt. – See Huntington
ES, 718 CENTRAL AVE 25504 – Ben Horton, prin.
Davis Creek ES
  RURAL ROUTE 02 BOX 498 25504
  Sonja Wagner, prin.
Martha ES, RURAL ROUTE 02 25504
  Paul Holton, prin.
Nichols ES, RURAL ROUTE 01 25504
  James Hanna, prin.

Barrackville, Marion Co., Pop. Code 4
Marion County SD
Supt. – See Fairmont
ES 26559 – Gary Price, prin.

Bartley, McDowell Co., Pop. Code 3
McDowell County SD
Supt. – See Welch
ES, P O BOX 113 24813 – Phyllis Murensky, prin.

Beards Fork, Fayette Co.
Fayette County SD
Supt. – See Fayetteville
ES, P O BOX 31 25014 – Joyce Floyd, prin.

Beaver, Raleigh Co., Pop. Code 4
Raleigh County SD
Supt. – See Beckley
ES, P O BOX 288 25813 – Wayne Keaton, prin.

Beckley, Raleigh Co., Pop. Code 7
Raleigh County SD
Sch. Sys. Enr. Code 7
Supt. – Ronald Cantley, 105 ADAIR ST 25801

Central ES, 320 S KANAWHA ST 25801
  Terry Farley, prin.
Cranberry-Prosprty ES
  100 CRANBERRY DR 25801 – Dan Petfry, prin.
Crescent ES, 205 CRESCENT RD 25801
  Don Shipe, prin.
Institute ES, 301 PARK AVE 25801
  Michael Sweeney, prin.
Lincoln ES, 1010 S KANAWHA ST 25801
  Sherman Meadows, prin.
Maxwell Hill ES, 1001 MAXWELL HILL RD 25801
  Charlotte Hutchens, prin.
Richmond ES, 105 ADAIR ST 25801
  Jerry Redden, prin.
Sylvia ES, 2001 S KANAWHA ST 25801
  Dewey Bone, prin.
Other Schools – See Beaver, Bradley, Clear Creek,
  Coal City, Crab Orchard, Daniels, Eccles, Fairdale,
  Ghent, Lester, Mabscott, Mac Arthur, Midway, Odd,
  Piney View, Princewick, Rock Creek, Shady Spring,
  Sophia, Stanaford, Sundial, Surveyor, Whitesville

St. Francis DeSales ES
  622 S OAKWOOD AVE 25801

Beech Bottom, Brooke Co., Pop. Code 3
Brooke County SD
Supt. – See Wellsburg
PS, HIGH ST 26030 – Edward Kalifut, prin.

Belington, Barbour Co., Pop. Code 4
Barbour County SD
Supt. – See Philippi
MS, P O BOX 98 26250 – Dana Stemple, prin.
ES, RURAL ROUTE 02 26250
  David Dodds.Jr,, prin.

Belle, Kanawha Co., Pop. Code 4
Kanawha County SD
Supt. – See Charleston
ES, 401 E 6TH ST 25015 – Yvonne Fawcett, prin.
Midland Trail ES, 200 FERRY ST 25015
  George Gray, prin.

Belleville, Wood Co.
Wood County SD
Supt. – See Parkersburg
Humphrey ES, RURAL ROUTE 01 BOX 107 26133
  Edward Stephens, prin.

Belmont, Pleasants Co., Pop. Code 3
Pleasants County SD
Supt. – See Saint Mary's
Pleasants County MS, P O BOX 179 26134
  Donna Barksdale, prin.
ES, P O BOX 468 26134 – Thomas Braun, prin.

Benwood, Marshall Co., Pop. Code 4
Marshall County SD
Supt. – See Moundsville
Boggs Run ES, P O BOX 577 26031
  Byron Freeland, prin.

Berkeley Springs, Morgan Co., Pop. Code 3
Morgan County SD
Sch. Sys. Enr. Code 4
Supt. – Dwight Dials
  903 S WASHINGTON ST 25411
Greenwood ES, RURAL ROUTE 03 25411
  John Rowland, prin.

North Berkeley ES, 213 HARRISON AVE 25411
Leonard Davis, prin.
Widmyer MS, ROUTE 522 S 25411
Rick Powell, prin.
Other Schools – See Great Cacapon, Hedgesville, Paw
Paw

Berwind, McDowell Co., Pop. Code 3
McDowell County SD
Supt. – See Welch
ES, P O BOX 128 24815 – Dorothy Cortellisi, prin.

Bethany, Brooke Co., Pop. Code 4
Brooke County SD
Supt. – See Wellsburg
ES, P O BOX H 26032 – Joyce Springborn, prin.

Beverly, Randolph Co., Pop. Code 2
Randolph County SD
Supt. – See Elkins
ES, P O BOX 209 26253 – Robert Frazer, prin.

Bigbend, Calhoun Co.
Calhoun County SD
Supt. – See Grantsville
Brooksville ES, GENERAL DELIVERY 26136
Robert Rentschler, prin.

Big Creek, Logan Co.
Logan County SD
Supt. – See Logan
ES, P O BOX 187 25505 – Richard Smith, prin.

Big Sandy, McDowell Co.
McDowell County SD
Supt. – See Welch
Fall River ES, P O BOX 70 24816
Virginia Hornick, prin.

Birch River, Nicholas Co.
Nicholas County SD
Supt. – See Summersville
ES, P O BOX 350 26610 – Glen Tyree, prin.

Blacksville, Monongalia Co., Pop. Code 2
Monongalia County SD
Supt. – See Morgantown
MS, P O BOX 46 26521 – June Kerr, prin.

Blandville, Doddridge Co.
Doddridge County SD
Supt. – See West Union
Middle Island ES 26328 – Janice Michels, prin.

Blue Creek, Kanawha Co.
Kanawha County SD
Supt. – See Charleston
Kenton ES 25026 – Sharon Stutler, prin.

Bluefield, Mercer Co., Pop. Code 7
Mercer County SD
Supt. – See Princeton
ES, RURAL ROUTE 04 BOX 480 24701
Rick Ball, prin.
ES, RURAL ROUTE 04 BOX 93 24701
William Sherwood, prin.
Ceres ES, RURAL ROUTE 02 BOX 189 24701
Gayle Pochick, prin.
Cumberland Heights ES
3318 E CUMBERLAND RD 24701
Chester Sword, prin.
Memorial ES, 319 MEMORIAL AVE 24701
Mona Poling, prin.
Preston ES, 321 PRESTON ST 24701
John Grittith, prin.
Ramsey ES, 300 RAMSEY ST 24701
John Fleming, prin.
Wade ES, 1400 HIGHLAND AVE 24701
Everette Gravely, prin.
Whitethorn ES, 1919 MARYLAND AVE 24701
Robert Rounion, prin.

Bomont, Clay Co.
Clay County SD
Supt. – See Clay
White ES, GENERAL DELIVERY 25030
David Derby, prin.

Bradley, Raleigh Co., Pop. Code 3
Raleigh County SD
Supt. – See Beckley
ES, P O BOX K 25818 – Mary Hartsog, prin.

Bradshaw, McDowell Co., Pop. Code 4
McDowell County SD
Supt. – See Welch
ES, P O BOX 70 24817 – Charles Vance, prin.

Bramwell, Mercer Co., Pop. Code 3
Mercer County SD
Supt. – See Princeton
ES, P O BOX 358 24715 – Terry Quesenberry, prin.

Branchland, Lincoln Co., Pop. Code 2
Lincoln County SD
Supt. – See Hamlin
ES, P O BOX 98 25506 – Chris Baker, prin.
Fez ES, RURAL ROUTE 03 BOX 410 25506
Haskell Holley, prin.
Pleasant View ES, 110 BEECH ST 25506
James Nelson, prin.

Brandywine, Pendleton Co.
Pendleton County SD
Supt. – See Franklin
ES 26802 – Lynn Vandevander, prin.

Brenton, Wyoming Co.
Wyoming County SD
Supt. – See Pineville
Baileysville ES, GENERAL DELIVERY 24818
Harry Cook, prin.

Bridgeport, Harrison Co., Pop. Code 6
Harrison County SD
Supt. – See Clarksburg
Johnson ES, 531 JOHNSON AVE 26330
Barry Buffington, prin.
Simpson ES, 250 WORTHINGTON DR 26330
James Harki, prin.

Taylor County SD
Supt. – See Grafton
Hepzibah ES, RURAL ROUTE 03 BOX 198 26330
Charles Kolb, prin.

Brownton, Barbour Co., Pop. Code 3
Barbour County SD
Supt. – See Philippi
Mt. Vernon ES 26334 – John Armentrout, prin.

Bruceton Mills, Preston Co., Pop. Code 2
Preston County SD
Supt. – See Kingwood
Bruceton-Brandonville ES, P O BOX 141 26525
Le Jay Graffious, prin.

Buckeye, Pocahontas Co.
Pocahontas County SD
Supt. – See Marlinton
Marlinton MS
RURAL ROUTE 02 BOX 52S 24924
Thomas Sanders, prin.

Buckhannon, Upshur Co., Pop. Code 6
Upshur County SD
Sch. Sys. Enr. Code 5
Supt. – Lynn Westfall, 102 SMITHFIELD ST 26201
Buckhannon-Upshur MS, P O BOX 250 26201
Alan Sturm, prin.
Academy PS, 2 COLLEGE AVE 26201
Dorothea Davis, prin.
Buckhannon-Upshr IS, 18 COLLEGE AVE 26201
John Haymond, prin.
Central ES, 5 BAXTER ST 26201
Scott Lampinen, prin.
East Main Street PS, EAST MAIN ST 26201
Roy Wager, prin.
Hodgesville ES
RURAL ROUTE 05 BOX 383 26201
Elizabeth Lee, prin.
Tennerton ES, RURAL ROUTE 06 BOX 513 26201
(—), prin.
Washington Distrct ES
RURAL ROUTE 07 BOX 234 26201
Darla Edgell, prin.
Other Schools – See French Creek, Rock Cave

Buffalo, Putnam Co., Pop. Code 4
Putnam County SD
Supt. – See Winfield
ES, RURAL ROUTE 01 BOX 93 25033
Robert Hull, prin.

Bunker Hill, Berkeley Co., Pop. Code 2
Berkeley County SD
Supt. – See Martinsburg
Musselman MS
RURAL ROUTE 02 BOX 119 25413
Earl Skidmore, prin.
ES, RURAL ROUTE 02 BOX 335 25413
Roger Williams, prin.

Burlington, Mineral Co.
Mineral County SD
Supt. – See Keyser
ES, RURAL ROUTE 01 BOX 126 26710
Eleanore Grubbs, prin.

Burnsville, Braxton Co., Pop. Code 3
Braxton County SD
Supt. – See Sutton
MS, P O BOX 35 26335 – Charles McCoy, prin.
ES, P O BOX 35 26335 – Charles McCoy, prin.

Cairo, Ritchie Co.
Ritchie County SD
Supt. – See Harrisville
MS 26337 – Edward Cumpston, prin.
PS 26337 – Edward Cumpston, prin.

Cameron, Marshall Co., Pop. Code 4
Marshall County SD
Supt. – See Moundsville
ES, 12 CHURCH ST 26033 – W. Simms, prin.

Canvas, Nicholas Co.
Nicholas County SD
Supt. – See Summersville
ES, P O BOX 233 26662 – Joseph Butler, prin.

Capon Bridge, Hampshire Co., Pop. Code 2
Hampshire County SD
Supt. – See Romney
ES, P O BOX 45 26711 – Stephen Keener, prin.

Carbon, Kanawha Co.
Kanawha County SD
Supt. – See Charleston
Decota ES 25037 – Karen Hessom, prin.

Cedar Grove, Kanawha Co., Pop. Code 4
Kanawha County SD
Supt. – See Charleston
Cedar Grove Community ES 25039
Kenneth Carvey, prin.

Center Point, Doddridge Co.
Doddridge County SD
Supt. – See West Union
MS 26339 – Tracy Stackpole, prin.

Ceredo, Wayne Co., Pop. Code 4
Wayne County SD
Supt. – See Wayne
Ceredo-Kenova MS, PO BOX 1000 25507
Emma Lou Akers, prin.
ES, P O BOX 635 25507 – Kenneth Cathell, prin.

Chapmanville, Logan Co., Pop. Code 4
Boone County SD
Supt. – See Madison
Manilla ES, 7 DOG FORK RD 25508
James Burgess, prin.

Logan County SD
Supt. – See Logan
Chapmanville East ES, P O BOX 340 25508
Lanna Adams, prin.
West Chapmanville ES, P O BOX 310 25508
Betty Hinkle, prin.

Charleston, Kanawha Co., Pop. Code 8
Kanawha County SD
Sch. Sys. Enr. Code 8
Supt. – Richard Trumble
200 ELIZABETH ST 25311
Big Chimney ES, 4710 CHIMNEY DR 25302
Steve Knighton, prin.
Bonham ES, RURAL ROUTE 01 BOX 425 25312
Julia Hedge, prin.
Boreman ES, 5113 ROCKY FORK RD 25313
Denzil Woods, prin.
Buena Vista ES, 1975 KELMONT LN 25320
Donna Sybert, prin.
Chamberlain ES, 4901 VENABLE AVE SE 25305
Nancy Evans, prin.
Chandler ES, 1900 SCHOOL ST 25312
Richard Evans, prin.
Cross Lanes ES, 5525 BIG TYLER RD 25313
James Brannon, prin.
Flinn ES, 2006 MCCLURE PKY 25312
Arthur Fisher, prin.
Ft. Hill ES, 810 WILKIE DR 25314
Bonnie Wood, prin.
Glenwood ES, 810 GRANT ST 25302
Mary Snow, prin.
Grandview ES, 959 WOODWARD DR 25312
Ronald Duerring, prin.
Holz ES, 1505 HAMPTON RD 25314
Diane Adkins, prin.
Kanawha City ES
3701 STAUNTON AVE SE 25304
Brenda Valentine, prin.
Kenna ES, 198 EUREKA RD 25314
Lorena Green, prin.
Loudendale ES
RURAL ROUTE 02 BOX 286 25314
Dorothea Fuqua, prin.
Malden ES, 4001 SALINES DR 25306
Nancy Pauley, prin.
Midway ES, 421 CAMPBELLS CREEK DR 25306
Charles Stevens, prin.
Oakwood ES, 909 OAKHURST DR 25314
Carolyn Meadows, prin.
Overbrook ES, 218 OAKWOOD RD 25314
Joyce Booher, prin.
Piedmont ES, 203 BRADFORD ST 25301
Carolyn Miller, prin.
Rand ES, 5701 CHURCH DR 25306
Boyd Mynes, prin.
Robins ES, 915 BEECH AVE 25302
Barbara Redman, prin.
Ruffner ES, 808 LITZ DR 25311
Darlena Reynolds, prin.
Shoals ES, 100 DUTCH RD 25302
David Zeitz, prin.
Sissonville ES, GENERAL DELIVERY 25301
Freda Burdette, prin.
Spring Hill ES, 517 CHESTNUT ST 25309
Tom Bunting, prin.
Staunton ES, 261 STAUNTON AVE SW 25303
Karen Wellman, prin.
Sugar Creek ES, 1898 SUGAR CREEK DR 25312
David Canterbury, prin.
Taft ES, 1719 BIGLEY AVE 25302
Clara Jett, prin.
Tiskelwah ES, 600 FLORIDA ST 25302
Barbara Hill, prin.
Tyler ES, 4277 WASHINGTON ST W 25313
Lois Moran, prin.
Valley Grove ES, 195-C RUTLEDGE RD 25311
Alice Robertson, prin.
Wallace Heights ES, 5801 SISSONVILLE DR 25312
Fred Keen, prin.
Watts ES, 230 COSTELLO ST 25302
Melanie Vickers, prin.
Woodlawn MS, 2425 HAMPSHIRE DR 25312
David Canterbury, prin.
Other Schools – See Belle, Blue Creek, Carbon, Cedar
Grove, Chelyan, Chesapeake, Clendenin, Cross
Lanes, Dunbar, Elkview, Falling Rock, Marmet,
Miami, Nitro, Pratt, Saint Albans, South Charleston,
Tad, Tornado

Sacred Heart ES
QUARRIER AND BROAD STS 25301
St. Agnes ES, 4801 STAUNTON AVE SE 25304
St. Anthony ES, 1027 SIXTH ST 25302

Charles Town, Jefferson Co., Pop. Code 5
Jefferson County SD
Sch. Sys. Enr. Code 6
Supt. – Raymond Frazier
   110 MORDINGTON PLACE   25414
Page Jackson Solar ES
   RURAL ROUTE 01 BOX 322M   25414
   John Ritchey, prin.
South Jefferson ES
   RURAL ROUTE 02 BOX 151-B   25414
   Gretchen Vancamp, prin.
Wright Denny IS, WEST CONGRESS ST   25414
   William Willingham, prin.
Other Schools – See Harpers Ferry, Kearneysville,
   Ranson, Shepherdstown

Charlton Heights, Fayette Co.
Fayette County SD
Supt. – See Fayetteville
Falls View ES, P O BOX 179   25040
   Edgar Friedrichs, prin.

Chattaroy, Mings Co., Pop. Code 4
Mingo County SD
Supt. – See Williamson
ES, GENERAL DELIVERY   25667
   Samuel Pauley, prin.

Chelyan, Kanawha Co.
Kanawha County SD
Supt. – See Charleston
ES, GENERAL DELIVERY   25041
   David Embrey, prin.

Chesapeake, Kanawha Co., Pop. Code 4
Kanawha County SD
Supt. – See Charleston
ES, 13620 MACCORKLE AVE   25315
   Jean Peters, prin.

Chester, Hancock Co., Pop. Code 5
Hancock County SD
Supt. – See New Cumberland
Allison ES, 600 RAILROAD ST   26034
   William Allison, prin.

Circleville, Pendleton Co., Pop. Code 4
Pendleton County SD
Supt. – See Franklin
S   26804 – Gary Wilson, prin.

Clarksburg, Harrison Co., Pop. Code 7
Harrison County SD
Sch. Sys. Enr. Code 7
Supt. – Robert Kittle, 408 WATER ST   26301
Adamston ES, 1636 W PIKE ST   26301
   James Eakle, prin.
Alta Vista ES, 261 HAYMOND HWY   26301
   Freda Perkins, prin.
Chestnut Hills ES, 106 FREDERICK ST   26301
   Richard Skinner, prin.
Hartman ES, 1201 N 15TH ST   26301
   Joseph Peet, prin.
Linden ES, 120 S LINDEN AVE   26301
   Richard Lantz, prin.
Morgan ES, 435 DUFF AVE   26301
   Allen Gorrell, prin.
North View ES, NORTH 19TH ST   26301
   Wather Pritchard, prin.
Pierpont ES, 100 SYCAMORE ST   26301
   Richard Skinner, prin.
Summit Park ES
   RURAL ROUTE 02 BOX 888   26301
   Doug Robbins, prin.
Towers ES, 120 S LINDEN AVE   26301
   Susan Collins, prin.
Wilsonburg ES, RURAL ROUTE 04 BOX 1   26301
   Rosalee Dolan, prin.
Other Schools – See Bridgeport, Enterprise, Lost
   Creek, Lumberport, Nutter Fort Stonewood, Salem,
   Shinnston, Wallace, West Milford, Wyatt

St. Mary Central ES, 107 E PIKE ST   26301

Clay, Clay Co., Pop. Code 3
Clay County SD
Sch. Sys. Enr. Code 5
Supt. – James Dawson, P O BOX 120   25043
JHS, P O BOX 489   25043 – L. Gillespie, prin.
ES, P O BOX 600   25043 – D. Jarvis, prin.
Other Schools – See Bomont, Dille, Indore, Ivydale,
   Lizemores, Nebo, Valley Fork

Clear Creek, Raleigh Co.
Raleigh County SD
Supt. – See Beckley
Clear Fork Distrct ES, GENERAL DELIVERY   25044
   E. Gallagher, prin.

Clendenin, Kanawha Co., Pop. Code 4
Kanawha County SD
Supt. – See Charleston
ES, P O BOX 462   25045 – Melissa Cisco, prin.

Coal City, Raleigh Co., Pop. Code 3
Raleigh County SD
Supt. – See Beckley
ES, P O BOX 278   25823 – James Hartsog, prin.

Coal Mountain, Wyoming Co.
Wyoming County SD
Supt. – See Pineville
ES, P O BOX 34   24823 – James Morgan, prin.

Coalton, Randolph Co.
Randolph County SD
Supt. – See Elkins
S, P O BOX 255   26257 – Thomas Wheeler, prin.

Colfax, Marion Co.
Marion County SD
Supt. – See Fairmont
ES   26566 – Joann Bradley, prin.

Colliers, Brooke Co., Pop. Code 3
Brooke County SD
Supt. – See Wellsburg
PS, PENN ST   26035 – James Missonak, prin.

Comfort, Boone Co.
Boone County SD
Supt. – See Madison
ES   25049 – Jackie Seacrist, prin.

Core, Monongalia Co.
Monongalia County SD
Supt. – See Morgantown
ES   26529 – Robert Glock, prin.

Cottageville, Jackson Co.
Jackson County SD
Supt. – See Ripley
ES   25239 – Kathleen Ranson, prin.

Cowen, Webster Co., Pop. Code 3
Webster County SD
Supt. – See Webster Springs
Glade ES, P O BOX 218   26206
   William Friend, prin.

Crab Orchard, Raleigh Co., Pop. Code 4
Raleigh County SD
Supt. – See Beckley
ES, P O BOX 727   25827 – Franklin Crawford, prin.

Craigsville, Nicholas Co., Pop. Code 2
Nicholas County SD
Supt. – See Summersville
Beaver ES, P O BOX 27   26205
   Thomas Neil, prin.
ES, RURAL ROUTE 01 BOX 313   26205
   Ann Blackshire, prin.

Cross Lanes, Kanawha Co.
Kanawha County SD
Supt. – See Charleston
Point Harmony ES, 5312 BIG TYLER RD   25313
   Phillip Jepson, prin.

Crum, Wayne Co., Pop. Code 2
Wayne County SD
Supt. – See Wayne
MS, RURAL ROUTE 02   25669 – (—), prin.
ES, P O BOX 69   25669 – Ralph Dawson, prin.

Culloden, Cabell Co., Pop. Code 4
Cabell County SD
Supt. – See Huntington
ES   25510 – Jack Nichols, prin.

Cyclone, Wyoming Co.
Wyoming County SD
Supt. – See Pineville
Road Branch ES, P O BOX 59   24827
   Robert Cook, prin.

Dailey, Randolph Co.
Randolph County SD
Supt. – See Elkins
Homestead ES, P O BOX 158   26259
   Franklin Collier, prin.

Dallas, Marshall Co.
Marshall County SD
Supt. – See Moundsville
Sand Hill ES, RURAL ROUTE 01 BOX 87   26036
   Lawrence Rine, prin.

Danese, Fayette Co.
Fayette County SD
Supt. – See Fayetteville
ES, P O BOX 69   25831 – Raymona Marlow, prin.

Daniels, Raleigh Co.
Raleigh County SD
Supt. – See Beckley
ES   25832 – Patra Janney, prin.

Danville, Boone Co., Pop. Code 3
Boone County SD
Supt. – See Madison
ES   25053 – Macel Miller, prin.
Ramage ES, RURAL ROUTE 01 BOX 293   25053
   Claudia Mabe, prin.

Davisville, Wood Co.
Wood County SD
Supt. – See Parkersburg
Kanawha ES, RURAL ROUTE 01 BOX 38A   26142
   Jeffrey Payne, prin.
Murphytown ES
   RURAL ROUTE 01 BOX 103   26142
   Wayne Meiser, prin.

Deep Water, Fayette Co.
Fayette County SD
Supt. – See Fayetteville
ES, P O BOX 98   25057 – James Dempsey, prin.

Dehue, Logan Co.
Logan County SD
Supt. – See Logan
Dehue Chambers ES, GENERAL DELIVERY   25618
   Ray Albright, prin.

Delbarton, Mingo Co., Pop. Code 3
Mingo County SD
Supt. – See Williamson

ES, GENERAL DELIVERY   25670
   Don Roberson, prin.
Myrtle ES, RURAL ROUTE 01 BOX 620   25670
   Eldean Wellman, prin.

Diana, Webster Co.
Webster County SD
Supt. – See Webster Springs
ES, P O BOX 90   26217 – Jerry Young, prin.

Dille, Clay Co.
Clay County SD
Supt. – See Clay
ES, GENERAL DELIVERY   26617 – T. Grittith, prin.

Dingess, Mingo Co.
Mingo County SD
Supt. – See Williamson
ES, P O BOX 34   25671 – Noble Harper, prin.

Dixie, Nicholas Co.
Nicholas County SD
Supt. – See Summersville
ES, GENERAL DELIVERY   25059
   Joseph Hoffman, prin.

Dorcas, Grant Co.
Grant County SD
Supt. – See Petersburg
ES   26835 – Joe Cunningham, prin.

Dunbar, Kanawha Co., Pop. Code 6
Kanawha County SD
Supt. – See Charleston
ES, 2401 MYERS AVE   25064 – Gary Ellis, prin.
Ford ES, 137 6TH ST   25064 – Betty Spencer, prin.
Mound ES, 501 19TH ST   25064
   Lewis Elliott, prin.
Roxalana ES, 1004 MIDWAY DR   25064
   Lauretha Kellum, prin.

Dunlow, Wayne Co.
Wayne County SD
Supt. – See Wayne
ES   25511 – Roy Matthews, prin.

Dunmore, Pocahontas Co.
Pocahontas County SD
Supt. – See Marlinton
Green Bank MS
   RURAL ROUTE 02 BOX 33A   24934
   Kenneth Vance, prin.

Earling, Logan Co.
Logan County SD
Supt. – See Logan
ES, GENERAL DELIVERY   25619
   Evelyn Whited, prin.

East Lynn, Wayne Co.
Wayne County SD
Supt. – See Wayne
MS, P O BOX 3   25512 – Samuel Thompson, prin.
Beech Fork ES, RURAL ROUTE 01 BOX 184   25512
   Dianna Buchman, prin.
ES, HCR 3   25512 – Samuel Thompson, prin.

Eccles, Raleigh Co.
Raleigh County SD
Supt. – See Beckley
ES   25836 – Robert Coburn, prin.

Eleanor, Putnam Co., Pop. Code 4
Putnam County SD
Supt. – See Winfield
Washington MS, P O BOX 547   25070
   Virgil Rice, prin.
Washington ES, P O BOX 564   25070
   James Studyvin, prin.

Elizabeth, Wirt Co., Pop. Code 3
Wirt County SD
Sch. Sys. Enr. Code 4
Supt. – Charles Murray, P O BOX 189   26143
ES, P O BOX 220   26143 – Sandra Hunton, prin.
Newark ES, RURAL ROUTE 03   26143
   Daniel Metz, prin.

Elk Garden, Mineral Co., Pop. Code 2
Mineral County SD
Supt. – See Keyser
S, P O BOX 10   26717 – Charles Keller, prin.

Elkhorn, McDowell Co.
McDowell County SD
Supt. – See Welch
Switchback ES, P O BOX 245   24831
   Jeff Nash, prin.

Elkins, Randolph Co., Pop. Code 6
Randolph County SD
Sch. Sys. Enr. Code 6
Supt. – Billy Ray Dunn, 40 11TH ST   26241
Elkins Third Ward ES, NATHAN ST   26241
   Barry Band, prin.
Jennings Randolph ES
   SCOTT FORD ROAD   26241
   Vincent Delconte, prin.
Midland ES, RURAL ROUTE 03 BOX 245   26241
   Roy Moss, prin.
North ES, RURAL ROUTE 02 BOX 320   26241
   Jeannie Galner, prin.
Other Schools – See Beverly, Coalton, Dailey,
   Harman, Mill Creek, Pickens, Valley Head

Elkview, Kanawha Co., Pop. Code 4
Kanawha County SD
Supt. – See Charleston
ES, 902 MAIN ST   25071 – John Eagle, prin.

Frame ES, 265 FRAME RD 25071
Patsy Smith, prin.
Pinch ES, 300 S PINCH RD 25071
Jean Jones, prin.

Ellenboro, Ritchie Co., Pop. Code 2
Ritchie County SD
Supt. – See Harrisville
PS 26346 – Samuel Jones, prin.

Enterprise, Harrison Co., Pop. Code 3
Harrison County SD
Supt. – See Clarksburg
ES, P O BOX 327 26568 – John Van Tromp, prin.

Evans, Jackson Co.
Jackson County SD
Supt. – See Ripley
ES, P O BOX 20 25241 – Vivian Poling, prin.

Fairdale, Raleigh Co.
Raleigh County SD
Supt. – See Beckley
ES, P O BOX 10 25839 – E. Moye, prin.

Fairmont, Marion Co., Pop. Code 7
Marion County SD
Sch. Sys. Enr. Code 7
Supt. – John Myers, P O BOX 712 26555
Miller JHS, 2 PENNSYLVANIA AVE 26554
James Feltz, prin.
State Street MS, 601 STATE ST 26554
Larry Hylton, prin.
Barnes ES, 100 NAOMI ST 26554
Ernestine Moore, prin.
Central ES, 316 COLUMBIA ST 26554
Janice Lake, prin.
Dunbar MS, 101 HIGH ST 26554
William Postlethwait, prin.
East Dale ES, RURAL ROUTE 03 26554
Janet Crescenzi, prin.
East Park ES, 1025 FAIRFAX ST 26554
(—), prin.
Jayenne ES, COUNTRY CLUB ROAD 26554
(—), prin.
Pleasant Valley ES, RURAL ROUTE 05 26554
Roger Pratt, prin.
Watson ES, 1579 MARY LOU RETTON DR 26554
George Risinger, prin.
White Hall ES, RURAL ROUTE 07 26554
Richard Petras, prin.
Other Schools – See Barrackville, Colfax, Fairview,
Farmington, Mannington, Monongah, Rachel,
Rivesville

Fairmont ES, 416 MADISON ST 26554

Fairview, Marion Co., Pop. Code 3
Marion County SD
Supt. – See Fairmont
MS 26570 – Judith Robinson, prin.
ES 26570 – Paul Vincent, prin.

Monongalia County SD
Supt. – See Morgantown
Daybrook ES, RURAL ROUTE 02 26570
Charlene Copeland, prin.
Jakes Run ES, RURAL ROUTE 02 26570
Charlene Copeland, prin.

Falling Rock, Kanawha Co.
Kanawha County SD
Supt. – See Charleston
Bridge ES, P O BOX 99 25079
Robert Paxton, prin.

Falling Waters, Berkeley Co.
Berkeley County SD
Supt. – See Martinsburg
Marlowe ES, P O BOX 880 25419
Jack Cornell, prin.

Farmington, Marion Co., Pop. Code 3
Marion County SD
Supt. – See Fairmont
ES 26571 – Masel Rogers, prin.

Fayetteville, Fayette Co., Pop. Code 4
Fayette County SD
Sch. Sys. Enr. Code 7
Supt. – Gerald Stover, 111 FAYETTE AVE 25840
MS, 135 HIGH ST 25840 – Peggy Freeman, prin.
Beckwith ES, P O BOX 506 25840
Rhodes Randall, prin.
Fayetteville Consolidated ES, P O BOX 510 25840
Wilhelmina Ashworth, prin.
ES, 200 WISEMAN AVE W 25840
Gary Milton, prin.
Gatewood ES
RURAL ROUTE 01 BOX 156-A 25840
David Radcliff, prin.
Other Schools – See Ansted, Beards Fork, Charlton
Heights, Danese, Deep Water, Gauley Bridge, Glen
Jean, Kimberly, Lookout, Meadow Bridge, Minden,
Montgomery, Mount Hope, Oak Hill, Page, Pax,
Powelltown, Scarbro, Smithers

Fenwick, Nicholas Co.
Nicholas County SD
Supt. – See Summersville
New Hope ES, HCR 2 BOX 447 26202
Charles Frazee, prin.

Flatwoods, Braxton Co., Pop. Code 2
Braxton County SD
Supt. – See Sutton
ES, P O BOX 130 26621 – Wesley Dobbins, prin.

Flemington, Taylor Co., Pop. Code 2
Taylor County SD
Supt. – See Grafton
ES 26347 – Richard Teagarden, prin.

Follansbee, Brook Co., Pop. Code 5
Brooke County SD
Supt. – See Wellsburg
MS, 1400 MAIN ST 26037 – Robert Guio, prin.
Hooverson Heights PS, 200 ROCKDALE RD 26037
Richard Baker, prin.
Jefferson PS, 1098 JEFFERSON ST 26037
C. Schupbach, prin.

St. Anthony ES, 1017 JEFFERSON ST 26037

Forest Hill, Summers Co.
Summers County SD
Supt. – See Hinton
ES 24935 – Sarah Brown, prin.

Fort Ashby, Mineral Co., Pop. Code 4
Mineral County SD
Supt. – See Keyser
MS, P O BOX 427 26719 – James Spataro, prin.
PS, P O BOX 1050 26719 – Robert Amtower, prin.

Fort Gay, Wayne Co., Pop. Code 3
Wayne County SD
Supt. – See Wayne
ES 25514 – Woodle Simpkins, prin.
Thompson ES, RURAL ROUTE 02 BOX 74 25514
Mavis Martin, prin.

Foster, Boone Co.
Boone County SD
Supt. – See Madison
ES, HCR BOX 8A 25081 – Fred Bell, prin.

Frametown, Braxton Co.
Braxton County SD
Supt. – See Sutton
ES, RURAL ROUTE 04 BOX 14 26623
Kathryn Lampe, prin.

Frankford, Greenbrier Co.
Greenbrier County SD
Supt. – See Lewisburg
ES, ROUTE 219 NORTH 24938
Bedford McClintic, prin.

Franklin, Pendleton Co., Pop. Code 3
Pendleton County SD
Sch. Sys. Enr. Code 4
Supt. – John Bowers, P O BOX 888 26807
ES 26807 – Craig Hutchinson, prin.
Other Schools – See Brandywine, Circleville, Seneca
Rocks, Upper Tract

French Creek, Upshur Co.
Upshur County SD
Supt. – See Buckhannon
ES, RURAL ROUTE 02 BOX 305 26218
Patricia McComas, prin.

Gallipolis Ferry, Mason Co.
Mason County SD
Supt. – See Point Pleasant
Beale ES, RURAL ROUTE 01 BOX 27 25515
Lewis Frum, prin.

Gap Mills, Monroe Co.
Monroe County SD
Supt. – See Union
ES 24941 – Larry Mustain, prin.

Gary, McDowell Co., Pop. Code 4
McDowell County SD
Supt. – See Welch
ES, P O BOX 250 24836 – Wallace Lavender, prin.

Gassaway, Braxton Co., Pop. Code 4
Braxton County SD
Supt. – See Sutton
MS, 106 BIRCH ST 26624
Virginia Chapman, prin.
Davis ES, 113 FIFTH ST 26624
James Lambert, prin.

Gauley Bridge, Fayette Co., Pop. Code 4
Fayette County SD
Supt. – See Fayetteville
MS, P O BOX 427 25085 – Mary Morris, prin.
ES, P O BOX 519 25085 – Mary Morris, prin.

Genoa, Wayne Co.
Wayne County SD
Supt. – See Wayne
ES, RURAL ROUTE 01 BOX 10 25517
Deborah Russell, prin.

Gerrardstown, Berkeley Co.
Berkeley County SD
Supt. – See Martinsburg
ES, GENERAL DELIVERY 25420
Manual Arvon, prin.

Ghent, Raleigh Co.
Raleigh County SD
Supt. – See Beckley
ES, P O BOX 350 25843 – Patsy Hill, prin.

Gilbert, Mingo Co., Pop. Code 3
Mingo County SD
Supt. – See Williamson
ES, P O BOX 365 25621 – Phyllis White, prin.

Glen Dale, Marshall Co., Pop. Code 4
Marshall County SD
Supt. – See Moundsville
ES, 407 7TH ST 26038 – David Gill, prin.

Glen Fork, Wyoming Co., Pop. Code 3
Wyoming County SD
Supt. – See Pineville
ES 25845 – Elmer Price, prin.

Glen Jean, Fayette Co.
Fayette County SD
Supt. – See Fayetteville
ES, P O BOX 245 25846 – Elena Green, prin.

Glen Rogers, Wyoming Co.
Wyoming County SD
Supt. – See Pineville
ES 25848 – Richard Garretson, prin.

Glenville, Gilmer Co., Pop. Code 4
Gilmer County SD
Sch. Sys. Enr. Code 4
Supt. – Clacy Williams, 201 N COURT ST 26351
ES, 44 VANHORN DR 26351 – James Phares, prin.
Other Schools – See Normantown, Sand Fork, Tanner,
Troy

Grafton, Taylor Co., Pop. Code 6
Taylor County SD
Sch. Sys. Enr. Code 5
Supt. – Ronald Dellinger, 306 BEECH ST 26354
MS, 225 W WASHINGTON ST 26354
Kermit Bias, prin.
Haymond ES, RURAL ROUTE 03 BOX 233 26354
Phyllis Leonard, prin.
Jarvis ES, 650 N PIKE ST 26354
Daniel Mankins, prin.
Pruntytown ES
RURAL ROUTE 02 BOX 157 26354
Suzann Murphy, prin.
Other Schools – See Bridgeport, Flemington, Thornton

Grantsville, Calhoun Co., Pop. Code 3
Calhoun County SD
Sch. Sys. Enr. Code 4
Supt. – Ronald Blankenship, HIGH ST 26147
Pleasant Hill ES, RURAL ROUTE 02 BOX 2 26147
Larry Stinn, prin.
Other Schools – See Arnoldsburg, Bigbend, Minnora

Great Cacapon, Morgan Co.
Morgan County SD
Supt. – See Berkeley Springs
ES, P O BOX 179 25422 – Lyle Colebank, prin.

Green Bank, Pocahontas Co.
Pocahontas County SD
Supt. – See Marlinton
ES, P O BOX 128 24944 – Charles Young, prin.

Greenville, Monroe Co.
Monroe County SD
Supt. – See Union
ES 24945 – Michael Allen, prin.

Greenwood, Tyler Co.
Doddridge County SD
Supt. – See West Union
ES 26360 – Rodney Jones, prin.

Griffithsville, Lincoln Co., Pop. Code 2
Lincoln County SD
Supt. – See Hamlin
ES, GENERAL DELIVERY 25521
Betty McComas, prin.

Hacker Valley, Webster Co.
Webster County SD
Supt. – See Webster Springs
ES, P O BOX 69 26222 – William Kavanagh, prin.

Hambleton, Tucker Co., Pop. Code 2
Tucker County SD
Supt. – See Parsons
Hamrick ES, P O BOX 8 26269
Larry McCune, prin.

Hamlin, Lincoln Co., Pop. Code 4
Lincoln County SD
Sch. Sys. Enr. Code 6
Supt. – Harold Smith, 238 MAIN ST 25523
ES, GENERAL DELIVERY 25523
Forrest Cummings, prin.
Other Schools – See Alkol, Alum Creek, Branchland,
Griffithsville, Harts, Leet, Midkiff, Ranger, Sod,
West Hamlin

Hanover, Wyoming Co.
Wyoming County SD
Supt. – See Pineville
Huff Consolidated ES, P O BOX E 24839
Tim Walls, prin.

Harman, Randolph Co., Pop. Code 2
Randolph County SD
Supt. – See Elkins
S, P O BOX 135 26270 – Wayne Kennedy, prin.

Harpers Ferry, Jefferson Co., Pop. Code 2
Jefferson County SD
Supt. – See Charles Town
Blue Ridge ES, RURAL ROUTE 02 BOX 362 25425
Nancy McManus, prin.
Shipley ES, RURAL ROUTE 03 BOX 270 25425
Cedric Sullivan, prin.

Harrisville, Ritchie Co., Pop. Code 4
Ritchie County SD
Sch. Sys. Enr. Code 4
Supt. – F. Dixon Law, P O BOX 216   26362
PS, 1201 E MAIN ST   26362 – Marion Roby, prin.
Other Schools – See Cairo, Ellenboro, Pennsboro,
   Smithville

Hartford, Mason Co., Pop. Code 3
Mason County SD
Supt. – See Point Pleasant
ES, P O BOX 278   25247 – Kim Neal, prin.

Harts, Lincoln Co.
Lincoln County SD
Supt. – See Hamlin
Atenville ES, RURAL ROUTE 02 BOX 12   25524
   Peggy Adkins, prin.
Ferrellsburg ES, GENERAL DELIVERY   25524
   Bill Bryant, prin.

Logan County SD
Supt. – See Logan
Dingess ES, GENERAL DELIVERY   25524
   Sam Dalton, prin.

Hedgesville, Berkeley Co., Pop. Code 2
Berkeley County SD
Supt. – See Martinsburg
MS, 101 POPLAR ST   25427
   Gary Greenfield, prin.
Back Creek Valley ES
   RURAL ROUTE 02 BOX 185   25427
   William Hull, prin.
ES, RURAL ROUTE 01 BOX 5   25427
   David McClung, prin.

Morgan County SD
Supt. – See Berkeley Springs
Pleasant View ES
   RURAL ROUTE 03 BOX 365 • 25427
   Jacqueline Davis, prin.

Hemphill, McDowell Co.
McDowell County SD
Supt. – See Welch
ES, P O BOX 151   24842 – Vincent Mullins, prin.

Henlawson, Logan Co., Pop. Code 3
Logan County SD
Supt. – See Logan
ES, GENERAL DELIVERY   25624
   Charles Slate, prin.

Herndon, Wyoming Co., Pop. Code 2
Wyoming County SD
Supt. – See Pineville
Herndon Consolidated ES, P O BOX 99   24726
   Walter Nixon, prin.

Hewett, Boone Co., Pop. Code 3
Boone County SD
Supt. – See Madison
Jeffrey-Spencer ES   25108 – Gary Bell, prin.

Hillsboro, Pocahontas Co., Pop. Code 2
Pocahontas County SD
Supt. – See Marlinton
ES, GENERAL DELIVERY   24946
   Kenneth Nottingham, prin.

Hinton, Summers Co., Pop. Code 5
Summers County SD
Sch. Sys. Enr. Code 5
Supt. – Demetrius Tassos, P O BOX 430   25951
Bellepoint ES, MILLER AVE   25951
   Harry Keaton, prin.
Hinton Area ES, 121 PARK AVE   25951
   Gary Irwin, prin.
Other Schools – See Forest Hill, Jumping Branch,
   Pipestem, Sandstone, Talcott

Holden, Logan Co., Pop. Code 4
Logan County SD
Supt. – See Logan
Holden Central ES, P O BOX M   25625
   Patsy Ferguson, prin.

Hometown, Putnam Co., Pop. Code 3
Putnam County SD
Supt. – See Winfield
ES, P O BOX 249   25109 – Ernest Page, prin.

Huntington, Cabell Co., Pop. Code 8
Cabell County SD
Sch. Sys. Enr. Code 7
Supt. – Robert Frum, P O BOX 446   25709
Altizer ES, THIRD ST   25705
   Walter Summers, prin.
Cammack ES, 200 10TH AVE   25701
   William Demmier, prin.
Emmons ES, 2746 4TH AVE   25702
   Deloris Baisden, prin.
Gallaher ES, 335 NORWAY AVE   25705
   Bill Adams, prin.
Geneva Kent ES, HOLLEY AVE   25705
   Lottie Simms, prin.
Guyandotte ES, FIFTH AVE & B&O RR   25702
   Ralph Rood, prin.
Highlawn ES, 2549 1ST AVE   25703
   Betty Smith, prin.
Hite-Saunders ES
   3708 GREEN VALLEY RD   25701
   Samuel Clay, prin.
Jefferson ES
   19TH ST W AND JEFFERSON AVE   25704
   Dortha Williamson, prin.

Johnston ES, 300 7TH AVE W   25701
   James Nester, prin.
Meadows ES
   16TH ST & WASHINGTON BLVD   25701
   John Hawkins, prin.
Miller ES, 12TH AVE & SEVENTH ST   25701
   Jon Walton, prin.
Monroe ES
   11TH ST WEST & MONROE AVE   25704
   Dennis Caldwell, prin.
Park Hills ES, 2001 MCCOY RD   25701
   Dorothy Scott, prin.
Pea Ridge ES, 5930 MAHOOD DR   25705
   Claudia Bryant, prin.
Peyton ES, PRIDDIE ST & ROTARY ROAD   25705
   Mary Johnson, prin.
Spring Hill ES, 1901 HALL AVE   25701
   Elmer Hayes, prin.
Washington ES, 2100 WASHINGTON AVE`   25704
   Bennie Thomas, prin.
Other Schools – See Barboursville, Culloden, Lesage,
   Milton, Ona, Salt Rock

Wayne County SD
Supt. – See Wayne
Westmoreland MS, 3609 HUGHES ST   25704
   Jesse Jones, prin.
Kellogg ES, 4415 PIEDMONT RD   25704
   Kenneth Adkins, prin.

Our Lady of Fatima ES, 535 NORWAY AVE   25705
St. Joseph ES, 520 13TH ST   25701

Hurricane, Putnam Co., Pop. Code 5
Putnam County SD
Supt. – See Winfield
MS, 518 MIDLAND TRAIL   25526
   Allen Messinger, prin.
Conner Street ES, 445 CONNER ST   25526
   Connie Linville, prin.
Hurricane Town ES
   RURAL ROUTE 02 BOX 28-1A   25526
   Nancy White, prin.
Lakeside ES, RURAL ROUTE 03 BOX 14B   25526
   Frances Courtright, prin.
West Teays ES, 3676 TEAYS VALLEY RD   25526
   Joanna Craigo, prin.

Iaeger, McDowell Co., Pop. Code 3
McDowell County SD
Supt. – See Welch
IS, P O BOX 308   24844 – Claude Roberts, prin.
ES, P O BOX 359   24844 – Gene Kennedy, prin.

Indore, Clay Co.
Clay County SD
Supt. – See Clay
Brown ES, GENERAL DELIVERY   25111
   Mark Jeffers, prin.

Inwood, Berkeley Co.
Berkeley County SD
Supt. – See Martinsburg
PS, P O BOX 509   25428 – Karen Waldo, prin.

Isaban, McDowell Co.
Mingo County SD
Supt. – See Williamson
Hardy Union ES, P O BOX B   24846
   Patricia Moore, prin.

Ivydale, Clay Co.
Clay County SD
Supt. – See Clay
ES, GENERAL DELIVERY   25113
   John Gency, prin.

Jane Lew, Lewis Co., Pop. Code 2
Lewis County SD
Supt. – See Weston
ES, P O BOX 431   26378 – Patsy Hite, prin.

Jolo, McDowell Co.
McDowell County SD
Supt. – See Welch
ES, P O BOX 299   24850 – Sam Breeding, prin.

Julian, Boone Co.
Boone County SD
Supt. – See Madison
Lory-Julian ES, 142 HWY 119   25529
   Carol Hager, prin.

Jumping Branch, Summers Co.
Summers County SD
Supt. – See Hinton
ES, P O BOX 9   25969 – David Quisenberry, prin.

Junior, Barbour Co., Pop. Code 3
Barbour County SD
Supt. – See Philippi
ES   26275 – Tommy Ramsey, prin.

Kearneysville, Jefferson Co.
Jefferson County SD
Supt. – See Charles Town
North Jefferson ES
   RURAL ROUTE 02 BOX 76   25430
   Carl Barr, prin.

Kenna, Jackson Co.
Jackson County SD
Supt. – See Ripley
ES   25248 – Betty Casto, prin.

Kenova, Wayne Co., Pop. Code 5
Wayne County SD
Supt. – See Wayne

Buffalo MS, RURAL ROUTE 01   25530
   Bernice Ray, prin.
Buffalo ES, RURAL ROUTE 01   25530
   Armilda Daniels, prin.
ES, 1400 POPLAR ST   25530 – Barbara Hicks, prin.

Kermit, Mingo Co., Pop. Code 3
Mingo County SD
Supt. – See Williamson
ES, P O BOX 295   25674 – Thomas Brewer, prin.
Marrowbone ES, RURAL ROUTE 01   25674
   Jewell Williamson, prin.

Keslers Cross Lanes, Nicholas Co.
Nicholas County SD
Supt. – See Summersville
ES, P O BOX 238   26675 – Terrance Beam, prin.

Keyser, Mineral Co., Pop. Code 6
Mineral County SD
Sch. Sys. Enr. Code 6
Supt. – Shirley Ball, 1 BAKER PLACE   26726
MS, 700 S WATER ST   26726
   George McCrum, prin.
Fountain PS, RURAL ROUTE 02 BOX 9   26726
   Gary Bowen, prin.
Other Schools – See Burlington, Elk Garden, Fort
   Ashby, New Creek, Ridgeley, Wiley Ford

St. Frances ES, 251 W PIEDMONT ST   26726

Keystone, McDowell Co., Pop. Code 3
McDowell County SD
Supt. – See Welch
ES, P O BOX W   24852 – Emma Holland, prin.

Kiahsville, Wayne Co.
Wayne County SD
Supt. – See Wayne
Cove Gap ES   25534 – Norman Adkins, prin.

Kimball, McDowell Co., Pop. Code 3
McDowell County SD
Supt. – See Welch
ES, P O BOX 308   24853 – Guy Sutphin, prin.

Kimberly, Fayette Co., Pop. Code 3
Fayette County SD
Supt. – See Fayetteville
ES, P O BOX 187   25118 – Sylvia Holliday, prin.

Kingwood, Preston Co., Pop. Code 5
Preston County SD
Sch. Sys. Enr. Code 6
Supt. – Elmer Pritt, P O BOX 566   26537
Albright ES, RURAL ROUTE 01 BOX 11F   26537
   Randal Zinn, prin.
ES, 207 S PRICE ST   26537 – Gary Henline, prin.
Other Schools – See Arthurdale, Aurora, Bruceton
   Mills, Newburg, Rowlesburg, Terra Alta, Tunnelton

Kirby, Hampshire Co.
Hampshire County SD
Supt. – See Romney
Grassy Lick ES, GENERAL DELIVERY   26729
   Karen Hott, prin.

Kopperston, Wyoming Co., Pop. Code 3
Wyoming County SD
Supt. – See Pineville
ES, P O BOX 12   24854 – Alvin Proffit, prin.

Lake, Logan Co.
Logan County SD
Supt. – See Logan
ES, GENERAL DELIVERY   25121
   Darrell Blas, prin.

Lashmeet, Mercer Co.
Mercer County SD
Supt. – See Princeton
ES, P O BOX 280   24733 – Margaret Walthall, prin.

Lavalette, Wayne Co., Pop. Code 3
Wayne County SD
Supt. – See Wayne
ES, P O BOX 380   25535 – Joan Chambers, prin.

Leet, Lincoln Co.
Lincoln County SD
Supt. – See Hamlin
Big Ugly ES, GENERAL DELIVERY   25536
   Larry Stratton, prin.

Left Hand, Roane Co.
Roane County SD
Supt. – See Spencer
Geary ES   25251 – Tim Holsclaw, prin.

Leivasy, Nicholas Co.
Nicholas County SD
Supt. – See Summersville
ES, GENERAL DELIVERY   26676
   James Amick, prin.

Lenore, Mingo Co.
Mingo County SD
Supt. – See Williamson
ES, GENERAL DELIVERY   25676
   John Preece, prin.

Leon, Mason Co., Pop. Code 2
Mason County SD
Supt. – See Point Pleasant
ES, RURAL ROUTE 03 BOX 2-A   25123
   Kennith Evans, prin.
Mt. Flower ES, RURAL ROUTE 02   25123
   Kennith Evans, prin.

Lesage, Cabell Co., Pop. Code 2
Cabell County SD
Supt. – See Huntington
Central ES, RURAL ROUTE 01 25537
John Hanna, prin.
Cox Landing ES, COX LN 25537
Larry Lambert, prin.

Lester, Raleigh Co., Pop. Code 3
Raleigh County SD
Supt. – See Beckley
ES 25865 – Ramona Jarrell, prin.

Levels, Hampshire Co.
Hampshire County SD
Supt. – See Romney
Cornwell ES, HCR BOX 73 25431
Phillip Painter, prin.

Lewisburg, Greenbrier Co., Pop. Code 5
Greenbrier County SD
Sch. Sys. Enr. Code 6
Supt. – Gordon Hanson, 202 CHESTNUT ST 24901
ES, 206 N LEE ST 24901 – William Fox, prin.
IS, 321 OAK ST 24901 – Andrea Phillips, prin.
Other Schools – See Alderson, Frankford, Quinwood,
Rainelle, Ronceverte, Rupert, Smoot, White
Sulphur Springs, Williamsburg

Liberty, Putnam Co.
Putnam County SD
Supt. – See Winfield
ES, P O BOX 89 25124 – Gary Hoffman, prin.

Little Birch, Braxton Co.
Braxton County SD
Supt. – See Sutton
ES, GENERAL DELIVERY 26629
Carolyn Long, prin.

Lizemores, Clay Co.
Clay County SD
Supt. – See Clay
ES, GENERAL DELIVERY 25125
Gordon Moore, prin.

Lockwood, Nicholas Co.
Nicholas County SD
Supt. – See Summersville
Otter Creek ES, GENERAL DELIVERY 26677
Allan Groves, prin.

Logan, Logan Co., Pop. Code 5
Logan County SD
Sch. Sys. Enr. Code 7
Supt. – Wesley Martin, P O BOX 477 25601
Justice ES, 407 CIRCLE DR 25601
Linda Heatherman, prin.
ES, 101 MIDDLEBURG IS 25601
Wilson Gore, prin.
West Logan ES, 506 HOLLY AVE 25601
Evelyn Adams, prin.
Other Schools – See Accoville, Amherstdale, Big
Creek, Chapmanville, Dehue, Earling, Harts,
Henlawson, Holden, Lake, Mallory, Man,
Monaville, Omar, Pecks Mill, Sharples, Stirrat,
Stollings, Verdunville, Whitman

Lookout, Fayette Co.
Fayette County SD
Supt. – See Fayetteville
Nuttall MS, P O BOX 68 25868
Donald Lockett, prin.
Divide ES, P O BOX 8 25868
Albert Pennington, prin.

Lost Creek, Harrison Co., Pop. Code 3
Harrison County SD
Supt. – See Clarksburg
ES, P O BOX 128 26385 – Frank Mariino, prin.

Lumberport, Harrison Co., Pop. Code 3
Harrison County SD
Supt. – See Clarksburg
MS, P O BOX 328 26386 – R. Nile Goff, prin.
ES, CHESTNUT & LYNDON STS 26386
Norman Van Meter, prin.

Mabscott, Raleigh Co., Pop. Code 4
Raleigh County SD
Supt. – See Beckley
ES, P O BOX 174 25871 – Jim Pennington, prin.

Mac Arthur, Raleigh Co.
Raleigh County SD
Supt. – See Beckley
Hollywood ES, P O BOX 7 25873
Carl Allen, prin.

Mc Graws, Wyoming Co.
Wyoming County SD
Supt. – See Pineville
ES, P O BOX 1190 25875 – James McGrady, prin.

McMechen, Marshall Co., Pop. Code 4
Marshall County SD
Supt. – See Moundsville
Center McMechen ES, 800 MARSHALL ST 26040
Phillip Devendra, prin.

Madison, Boone Co., Pop. Code 5
Boone County SD
Sch. Sys. Enr. Code 6
Supt. – Kenneth Mabe, 69 AVE B 25130
MS, 404 RIVERSIDE DR W 25130
Joe Tagliente, prin.
ES, 150 JOSEPHINE AVE 25130
Frederick Price, prin.

Other Schools – See Ashford, Chapmanville, Comfort,
Danville, Foster, Hewett, Julian, Nellis, Peytona,
Racine, Seth, Sylvester, Uneeda, Van, Wharton

Mallory, Logan Co., Pop. Code 3
Logan County SD
Supt. – See Logan
ES, P O BOX 68 25634 – Peggy Heatherman, prin.

Man, Logan Co., Pop. Code 4
Logan County SD
Supt. – See Logan
Christian ES, P O BOX 387 25635
Ray Miller, prin.
South Man ES, 301 MCDONALD AVE E 25635
Juanita Grimmett, prin.

Mannington, Marion Co., Pop. Code 5
Marion County SD
Supt. – See Fairmont
MS, 113 CLARKSBURG ST 26582
David Madigan, prin.
ES 26582 – Orval Price, prin.

Marlinton, Pocahontas Co., Pop. Code 4
Pocahontas County SD
Sch. Sys. Enr. Code 4
Supt. – Daniel Curry, P O BOX 88 24954
ES, 926 A FIFTH AVE 24954 – Wilma Dale, prin.
Other Schools – See Buckeye, Dunmore, Green Bank,
Hillsboro

Marmet, Kanawha Co., Pop. Code 4
Kanawha County SD
Supt. – See Charleston
ES, 408 94TH ST 25315 – Vollie Older, prin.

Martinsburg, Berkeley Co., Pop. Code 7
Berkeley County SD
Sch. Sys. Enr. Code 7
Supt. – Jackson Flanigan, 401 S QUEEN ST 25401
Martinsburg North MS, 105 EAST ROAD 25401
Wendell Christopher, prin.
Martinsburg South MS, 400 BUXTON ST 25401
George Michael, prin.
Bedington ES, RURAL ROUTE 02 BOX 276 25401
Janet Cookus, prin.
Berkeley Heights ES
RURAL ROUTE 05 BOX 490 25401
Martha Grove, prin.
Burke Street ES, 422 W BURKE ST 25401
James Moore, prin.
Opequon ES, 310 EAST RD 25401
Mark Grove, prin.
Rosemont ES, 301 S ALABAMA AVE 25401
John Morgan, prin.
Tuscarora ES, 200 TAVERN RD 25401
Samson Bland, prin.
Valley View MS
RURAL ROUTE 04 BOX 269 25401
Rodney Woods, prin.
Winchester Avenue ES
650 WINCHESTER AVE 25401
Stephen Crowell, prin.
Other Schools – See Bunker Hill, Falling Waters,
Gerrardstown, Hedgesville, Inwood

St. Joseph ES, 336 S QUEEN ST 25401

Mason, Mason Co., Pop. Code 4
Mason County SD
Supt. – See Point Pleasant
ES, ADAMS ST 25260 – Irene Shaw, prin.

Matewan, Mingo Co., Pop. Code 3
Mingo County SD
Supt. – See Williamson
ES, GENERAL DELIVERY 25678
Randy Keathley, prin.

Matheny, Wyoming Co.
Wyoming County SD
Supt. – See Pineville
ES, P O BOX 279 24860 – Freda Harless, prin.

Mathias, Hardy Co.
Hardy County SD
Supt. – See Moorefield
ES, P O BOX 10 26812 – Arland Schrock, prin.

Matoaka, Mercer Co., Pop. Code 3
Mercer County SD
Supt. – See Princeton
ES, P O BOX 378 24736 – Stephen Bailey, prin.

Maysville, Grant Co.
Grant County SD
Supt. – See Petersburg
ES 26833 – Caroll Michael, prin.

Meador, Mingo Co.
Mingo County SD
Supt. – See Williamson
Beech Creek ES, RURAL ROUTE 01 BOX 53 25682
Delmer Blankenship, prin.

Meadow Bridge, Fayette Co., Pop. Code 3
Fayette County SD
Supt. – See Fayetteville
ES, P O BOX 60 25976 – Grover Pack, prin.

Metz, Marion Co.
Wetzel County SD
Supt. – See New Martinsville
Long Drain ES
RURAL ROUTE 01 BOX 108-A 26585
William Jones, prin.

Miami, Kanawha Co.
Kanawha County SD
Supt. – See Charleston
Dawes ES, P O BOX 149 25134
Jana Tolliver, prin.

Middlebourne, Tyler Co., Pop. Code 3
Tyler County SD
Sch. Sys. Enr. Code 4
Supt. – Nick Zervos, P O BOX 25 26149
Ellsworth MS, PARK AVE 26149
Robert Wilt, prin.
Boreman ES, P O BOX 299 26149
Lynn Caseman, prin.
Other Schools – See Paden City, Sistersville

Midkiff, Lincoln Co.
Lincoln County SD
Supt. – See Hamlin
ES, GENERAL DELIVERY 25540
James Christian, prin.

Midway, Raleigh Co.
Raleigh County SD
Supt. – See Beckley
ES, P O BOX 277 25878 – Elizabeth Kennedy, prin.

Mill Creek, Randolph Co., Pop. Code 3
Randolph County SD
Supt. – See Elkins
Ward ES, P O BOX 278 26280 – David Roth, prin.

Milton, Cabell Co., Pop. Code 4
Cabell County SD
Supt. – See Huntington
ES, 1201 PIKE ST 25541 – Ivan Cooper, prin.

Minden, Fayette Co., Pop. Code 3
Fayette County SD
Supt. – See Fayetteville
ES, P O BOX 339 25879 – Gary Hough, prin.

Mineralwells, Wood Co., Pop. Code 3
Wood County SD
Supt. – See Parkersburg
ES, P O BOX 40 26150 – Bruce Goody, prin.

Minnora, Calhoun Co.
Calhoun County SD
Supt. – See Grantsville
S, RURAL ROUTE 02 BOX 24 25263
John Queen, prin.

Moatsville, Barbour Co.
Barbour County SD
Supt. – See Philippi
Kasson ES, RURAL RUOUTE 01 BOX 233A 26405
(—), prin.

Monaville, Logan Co.
Logan County SD
Supt. – See Logan
ES, GENERAL DELIVERY 25636
Marilyn Johnson, prin.

Monongah, Marion Co., Pop. Code 4
Marion County SD
Supt. – See Fairmont
MS 26554 – Ronald Wood, prin.
ES 26554 – Anna McCright, prin.

Sts. Peter & Paul ES, 695 CHURCH ST 26554

Montgomery, Fayette Co., Pop. Code 5
Fayette County SD
Supt. – See Fayetteville
MS, 514 5TH AVE 25136 – Jack Christ, prin.

Moorefield, Hardy Co., Pop. Code 4
Hardy County SD
Sch. Sys. Enr. Code 4
Supt. – John Miller, 510 ASHBY ST 26836
ES, 400 N MAIN ST 26836 – Peggy Hawse, prin.
Other Schools – See Mathias, Wardensville

Morgantown, Monongalia Co., Pop. Code 8
Monongalia County SD
Sch. Sys. Enr. Code 7
Supt. – Jack Dulaney, 263 PRAIRIE AVE 26505
Arnettsville ES
RURAL ROUTE 01 BOX 232 26505
Mariwynne Strong, prin.
Brookhaven ES, 1215 BAKER ST 26505
Leo Dandeo, prin.
Browns Chapel MS
RURAL ROUTE 09 BOX 142 26505
Loretta Florence, prin.
Central ES, 475 BAIRD ST 26505
Jean Williams, prin.
Cool Springs ES
RURAL ROUTE 10 BOX 85-B 26505
C. Collins, prin.
Dorsey ES 26505 – C. Collins, prin.
Easton ES, RURAL ROUTE 08 BOX 311 26505
Donna Talerico, prin.
First Ward ES, 301 MADIGAN AVE 26505
Kenneth Wolfe, prin.
Jerome Park ES, DENVER AT PUTNAM ST 26505
Leo Dandeo, prin.
Lazelle Union ES
RURAL ROUTE 13 BOX 441 26505
Robert Glock, prin.
Mt. Pleasant ES
RURAL ROUTE 07 BOX 191 26505
Mary Cocco, prin.
National ES, RURAL ROUTE 02 BOX 146 26505
Jerry Edens, prin.

North ES, 825 CHESTNUT RIDGE RD 26505
  Susanne Newbrough, prin.
Oak Grove ES, RURAL ROUTE 06 BOX 185 26505
  Mary Cocco, prin.
Phillips ES, RURAL ROUTE 01 BOX 50 26505
  Mariwynne Strong, prin.
Ridgedale ES, RURAL ROUTE 05 BOX 268 26505
  Loretta Florence, prin.
Riverside ES, 403 SCHLEY ST 26505
  Frank Mrazeck, prin.
Sabraton MS, 1737 LISTRAVIA AVE 26505
  Leo Dandeo, prin.
Second Ward ES
  WILSON AVE & KINGWOOD ST 26505
  Stephen King, prin.
Summers ES, RURAL ROUTE 03 BOX 117 26505
  C. Collins, prin.
Suncrest ES, 523 JUNIOR AVE 26505
  Susanne Newbrough, prin.
Wiles Hill ES, 287 EUREKA DR 26505
  Jean Williams, prin.
Woodburn ES
  CORNER PARSON & FORTNEY ST 26505
  Donna Talerico, prin.
Other Schools – See Blacksville, Core, Fairview,
  Pentress, Wadestown, Westover

St. Francis DeSales ES
  50 BEECHURST AVE 26505

Moundsville, Marshall Co., Pop. Code 7
Marshall County SD
Sch. Sys. Enr. Code 6
Supt. – Donald Haskins, P O BOX 578 26041
Central ES, 750 TOMLINSON AVE 26041
  David Wood, prin.
Limestone ES, RURAL ROUTE 01 BOX 245 26041
  William Hall, prin.
McNinch ES, 2600 4TH ST 26041
  Richard Redd, prin.
Park View ES, 21 PARK ST 26041
  C. McCreary, prin.
Sanford ES, 1600 3RD ST 26041
  Edward Sherman, prin.
Washington Lands ES
  RURAL ROUTE 04 BOX 255 26041
  James Loew, prin.
Other Schools – See Benwood, Cameron, Dallas, Glen
  Dale, McMechen, Wheeling

St. Francis Xavier ES, 600 JEFFERSON AVE 26041

Mount Hope, Fayette Co., Pop. Code 4
Fayette County SD
Supt. – See Fayetteville
MS, 510 MAIN ST 25880 – David Perry, prin.
ES, 408 LINCOLN ST 25880 – Robert Evans, prin.

Mount Lookout, Nicholas Co.
Nicholas County SD
Supt. – See Summersville
ES, RURAL ROUTE 04 BOX 319 26678
  Joyce Amick, prin.

Mount Nebo, Nicholas Co.
Nicholas County SD
Supt. – See Summersville
ES, P O BOX 160 26679 – Charlotte McClung, prin.

Mount Storm, Grant Co., Pop. Code 2
Grant County SD
Supt. – See Petersburg
Union ES 26739 – Jim Lent, prin.

Mullens, Wyoming Co., Pop. Code 5
Wyoming County SD
Supt. – See Pineville
MS, P O BOX 1025 25882 – Jan Caldwell, prin.
ES, 300 FRONT ST 25882 – Paul Ritchie, prin.

Nebo, Clay Co.
Clay County SD
Supt. – See Clay
ES, GENERAL DELIVERY 25141
  Brenda Krauklis, prin.

Nellis, Boone Co.
Boone County SD
Supt. – See Madison
ES 25142 – Bryan Elkins, prin.

Nettie, Nicholas Co., Pop. Code 3
Nicholas County SD
Supt. – See Summersville
ES, GENERAL DELIVERY 26681
  Jack Daugherty, prin.

Newburg, Preston Co.
Preston County SD
Supt. – See Kingwood
ES, P O BOX 247 26410 – Darrell Martin, prin.

New Creek, Mineral Co.
Mineral County SD
Supt. – See Keyser
ES 26743 – Joseph Hanna, prin.

New Cumberland, Hancock Co., Pop. Code 4
Hancock County SD
Sch. Sys. Enr. Code 6
Supt. – E. Russell Slack, 806 RIDGE AVE 26047
ES, COURT ST 26047
  Michael Swartzmiller, prin.
Other Schools – See Chester, Newell, New
  Manchester, Weirton

Newell, Hancock Co., Pop. Code 4
Hancock County SD
Supt. – See New Cumberland
Jefferson ES, JEFFERSON ST 26050
  Betty Buben, prin.

Newhall, McDowell Co., Pop. Code 4
McDowell County SD
Supt. – See Welch
ES, P O BOX 200 24866 – Juanita Hale, prin.

New Haven, Mason Co., Pop. Code 4
Mason County SD
Supt. – See Point Pleasant
ES, MILL ST 25265 – Joseph Scites, prin.

New Manchester, Hancock Co., Pop. Code 3
Hancock County SD
Supt. – See New Cumberland
ES, P O BOX 83 26056 – David Stevens, prin.

New Martinsville, Wetzel Co., Pop. Code 6
Wetzel County SD
Sch. Sys. Enr. Code 5
Supt. – Gerrita Postlewait
  333 FOUNDRY ST 26155
ES, 20 E BENJAMIN DR 26155
  Thomas Dvorak, prin.
Other Schools – See Metz, Paden City, Reader

Nitro, Kanawha Co., Pop. Code 6
Kanawha County SD
Supt. – See Charleston
Baker ES, 1201 PARK AVE 25143 – Kay Lee, prin.
ES, 1921 19TH ST 25143 – Ardith Rohmiller, prin.

Putnam County SD
Supt. – See Winfield
Nitro-Putnam ES, 3942 39TH ST E 25143
  Janice Sayre, prin.
Rock Branch ES, 4616 1ST AVE 25143
  Hattie Tincher, prin.

Nolan, Pike Co.
Mingo County SD
Supt. – See Williamson
ES, GEN DELIVERY 25687
  Mitchell Chapman, prin.

Normantown, Gilmer Co.
Gilmer County SD
Supt. – See Glenville
ES 25267 – Linda Whaley, prin.

Nutter Fort Stonewood, Harrison Co., Pop. Code 4
Harrison County SD
Supt. – See Clarksburg
Norwood ES, KIDD AVE 26301
  Phillip Brown, prin.
ES, 1302 BUCKHANNON PIKE 26301
  Terry McCloud, prin.

Oak Hill, Fayette Co., Pop. Code 6
Fayette County SD
Supt. – See Fayetteville
Collins MS, 601 JONES AVE 25901
  Bill Harless, prin.
Oak Hill East End ES, INGRAM ST 25901
  Jack Horrocks, prin.
ES, 140 SCHOOL ST 25901 – Peggy Tully, prin.
Rosedale ES, P O BOX 173 25901
  Arlos Arthur, prin.

Oakvale, Mercer Co., Pop. Code 2
Mercer County SD
Supt. – See Princeton
ES, OLD ROUTE 460 24739
  Joanna Fredeking, prin.

Oceana, Wyoming Co., Pop. Code 4
Wyoming County SD
Supt. – See Pineville
MS, P O BOX 520 24870 – Richard Cook, prin.
Berlin McKinney ES, P O BOX 628 24870
  Ruby Ford, prin.

Odd, Raleigh Co., Pop. Code 3
Raleigh County SD
Supt. – See Beckley
ES, P O BOX 127 25902 – Herb Lord, prin.

Omar, Logan Co., Pop. Code 3
Logan County SD
Supt. – See Logan
ES, GENERAL DELIVERY 25638
  Camilla Watson, prin.

Ona, Cabell Co.
Cabell County SD
Supt. – See Huntington
ES 25545 – Joe Noble, prin.

Paden City, Wetzel Co., Pop. Code 5
Tyler County SD
Supt. – See Middlebourne
MS, 425 S 4TH AVE 26159 – Duane Dober, prin.

Wetzel County SD
Supt. – See New Martinsville
ES, 510 N 2ND AVE 26159 – Kenneth Yoho, prin.

Page, Fayette Co.
Fayette County SD
Supt. – See Fayetteville
ES, P O BOX 338 25152 – Dale Arrington, prin.

Panther, McDowell Co.
McDowell County SD
Supt. – See Welch
ES, P O BOX 266 24872 – Brenda Owens, prin.

Parkersburg, Wood Co., Pop. Code 8
Wood County SD
Sch. Sys. Enr. Code 7
Supt. – William Staats, 1210 13TH ST 26101
Martin S, 1301 HILLCREST ST 26101
  Marie Held, prin.
Beechwood Center MS, 728 1/2 29TH ST 26101
  Manley Collins, prin.
Blennerhassett ES
  RURAL ROUTE 04 BOX 475A 26101
  Lawrence Hasbargen, prin.
Cedar Grove ES
  RURAL ROUTE 05 BOX 138 26101
  Jeffrey Payne, prin.
Criss ES, 2800 22ND ST 26101 – James Hall, prin.
Emerson ES, 1605 36TH ST 26104
  James Bredon, prin.
Fairplains ES, 615 BROADWAY AVE 26101
  Ralph Paugh, prin.
Gihon ES, RURAL ROUTE 07 26101
  Richard Wiblin, prin.
Jefferson ES, 1103 PLUM ST 26101
  Edward Alfred, prin.
Lincoln ES, 3010 MURDOCH AVE 26104
  Robert Harris, prin.
Lubeck ES, RURAL ROUTE 04 BOX 177 26101
  Edward Stephens, prin.
Madison ES, 1426 32ND ST 26104
  James Houck, prin.
McKinley ES, 1130 19TH ST 26101
  Earl Lucas, prin.
Nash ES, 1311 ANN ST 26101 – Max Powell, prin.
Park ES, 1500 PARK AVE 26101
  Manley Collins, prin.
Rayon ES, 1508 RAYON DR 26101
  Gregory Boso, prin.
Roosevelt ES, 800 CAMDEN AVE 26101
  B. Posey, prin.
Tavennerville ES, 2507 9TH AVE 26101
  David Stephens, prin.
Tygart ES, RURAL ROUTE 03 BOX 3 26101
  Denver Westfall, prin.
Worthington ES, 2500 36TH ST 26104
  Richard Kiser, prin.
Other Schools – See Belleville, Davisville,
  Mineralwells, Rockport, Vienna, Walker,
  Washington, Waverly, Williamstown

DeSales Heights Academy
  1600 MURDOCH AVE 26101
Parkersburg ES, 810 JULIANA ST 26101

Parsons, Tucker Co.
Tucker County SD
Sch. Sys. Enr. Code 4
Supt. – Mary Alice Klein, P O BOX 369 26287
ES, 501 CHESTNUT ST 26287
  Joel Goughnour, prin.
Other Schools – See Hambleton, Thomas

Paw Paw, Morgan Co., Pop. Code 3
Morgan County SD
Supt. – See Berkeley Springs
S 25434 – Dennis Beyer, prin.

Pax, Fayette Co., Pop. Code 2
Fayette County SD
Supt. – See Fayetteville
ES, P O BOX 38 25904 – Tom Spears, prin.

Pecks Mill, Logan Co.
Logan County SD
Supt. – See Logan
Mill Creek ES, P O BOX 399 25547
  Norma McCloud, prin.

Pennsboro, Ritchie Co., Pop. Code 4
Ritchie County SD
Supt. – See Harrisville
MS, 104 SCHOOL DR 26415
  Norma Hilvers, prin.
Creed Collins PS, 512 COLLINS AVE 26415
  David Meador, prin.

Pentress, Monongalia Co.
Monongalia County SD
Supt. – See Morgantown
ES, P O BOX 151 26544 – June Kerr, prin.

Petersburg, Grant Co., Pop. Code 4
Grant County SD
Sch. Sys. Enr. Code 4
Supt. – David Adkins, 204 JEFFERSON AVE 26847
ES, 333 RIG ST 26847 – Patricia Townshend, prin.
Other Schools – See Dorcas, Maysville, Mount Storm

Peterstown, Monroe Co., Pop. Code 3
Monroe County SD
Supt. – See Union
ES 24963 – Dan Lively, prin.

Peytona, Boone Co.
Boone County SD
Supt. – See Madison
MS 25154 – Brenda Hudson, prin.

Philippi, Barbour Co., Pop. Code 5
Barbour County SD
Sch. Sys. Enr. Code 5
Supt. – William Phillips, 50 S MAIN ST 26416
MS, RURAL ROUTE 03 26416
  Murlin Workman, prin.
ES, RURAL ROUTE 03 BOX 38 26416
  Charles Scheick, prin.
Other Schools – See Belington, Brownton, Junior,
  Moatsville, Volga

Pickens, Randolph Co., Pop. Code 2
Randolph County SD
Supt. – See Elkins
S, P O BOX 146   26230 – Leslie Edinger, prin.

Pineville, Wyoming Co., Pop. Code 4
Wyoming County SD
Sch. Sys. Enr. Code 6
Supt. – Gerald Short, P O BOX 69   24874
MS, P O BOX 470   24874 – Robert Adams, prin.
ES, P O BOX 700   24874 – E. Weaver, prin.
Pineville Riverside MS, P O BOX 1469   24874
   Joe Short, prin.
Other Schools – See Brenton, Coal Mountain,
   Cyclone, Glen Fork, Glen Rogers, Hanover,
   Herndon, Kopperston, Mc Graws, Matheny,
   Mullens, Oceana, Stephenson

Piney View, Raleigh Co., Pop. Code 3
Raleigh County SD
Supt. – See Beckley
ES, P O BOX A   25906 – Walter Peelish, prin.

Pipestem, Summers Co.
Summers County SD
Supt. – See Hinton
ES, P O BOX 17   25979 – Vicki Hinerman, prin.

Poca, Putnam Co., Pop. Code 4
Putnam County SD
Supt. – See Winfield
MS, P O BOX M   25159 – H. Scites, prin.
ES, P O BOX 430   25159 – Clinton Beaver, prin.

Point Pleasant, Mason Co., Pop. Code 6
Mason County SD
Sch. Sys. Enr. Code 6
Supt. – William Barker, 307 8TH ST   25550
Central ES, 1200 MAIN ST   25550
   Lois Shinn, prin.
North Point ES, 2200 LINCOLN AVE   25550
   Alan Alberchinski, prin.
Ordnance ES, 500 28TH ST   25550
   Grant Barnnette, prin.
Roosevelt ES, RURAL ROUTE 02 BOX 841   25550
   Betty Crouse, prin.
Other Schools – See Apple Grove, Ashton, Gallipolis
   Ferry, Hartford, Leon, Mason, New Haven,
   Southside, West Columbia

Powellton, Fayette Co., Pop. Code 4
Fayette County SD
Supt. – See Fayetteville
ES, P O BOX 9   25161 – Dennis O'Donnell, prin.

Pratt, Kanawha Co., Pop. Code 3
Kanawha County SD
Supt. – See Charleston
ES, P O BOX 36   25162 – Stephen Tolliver, prin.

Prichard, Wayne Co.
Wayne County SD
Supt. – See Wayne
ES   25555 – Grace Wiley, prin.

Princeton, Mercer Co., Pop. Code 6
Mercer County SD
Sch. Sys. Enr. Code 7
Supt. – William Baker
   1420 HONAKER AVE   24740
Glenwood ES, RURAL ROUTE 01 BOX 460   24740
   Loretta Raines, prin.
Knob ES, 706 KNOB ST   24740
   Billie Moorefield, prin.
Melrose ES, HCR BOX 357   24740
   Sharon Dove, prin.
Mercer ES, 1200 MERCER ST   24740
   Mary Kaufman, prin.
Silver Springs ES, 821 BROADWAY ST   24740
   Robert McGuire, prin.
Straley ES, 810 STRALEY AVE   24740
   Junie Dotyle, prin.
Thorn ES, 205 THORN ST   24740
   Michael McPherson, prin.
Other Schools – See Athens, Bluefield, Bramwell,
   Lashmeet, Matoaka, Oakvale, Rock, Spanishburg

Princewick, Raleigh Co.
Raleigh County SD
Supt. – See Beckley
Stoco ES, P O BOX 53   25908 – Larry Farley, prin.

Purgitsville, Hampshire Co.
Hampshire County SD
Supt. – See Romney
Mill Creek ES, P O BOX 45   26852
   Thomas Rowan, prin.

Quinwood, Greenbrier Co., Pop. Code 2
Greenbrier County SD
Supt. – See Lewisburg
Crichton ES, P O BOX 205   25981
   James Zopp, prin.

Rachel, Marion Co.
Marion County SD
Supt. – See Fairmont
Downs ES   26587 – Karen Richman, prin.

Racine, Boone Co., Pop. Code 3
Boone County SD
Supt. – See Madison
ES   25165 – Ina Hudson, prin.

Ragland, Mingo Co.
Mingo County SD
Supt. – See Williamson
Chafin ES, P O BOX 1   25690 – Robert Binion, prin.

Rainelle, Greenbrier Co., Pop. Code 4
Greenbrier County SD
Supt. – See Lewisburg
ES, 701 KANAWHA AVE   25962
   William Harris, prin.
East Rainelle MS, P O BOX 686   25962
   William Harris, prin.

Ranger, Lincoln Co.
Lincoln County SD
Supt. – See Hamlin
ES, GENERAL DELIVERY   25557
   Larry Prichard, prin.

Ranson, Jefferson Co., Pop. Code 4
Jefferson County SD
Supt. – See Charles Town
ES, 12TH AVE   25438 – (—), prin.

Ravenswood, Jackson Co., Pop. Code 5
Jackson County SD
Supt. – See Ripley
MS, 409 SYCAMORE ST   26164
   Dan Hunter, prin.
North ES, KAISER AVE   26164
   Gary Sampies, prin.
MS, RURAL ROUTE 01   26164
   Tilden Hackworth, prin.

Reader, Wetzel Co., Pop. Code 3
Wetzel County SD
Supt. – See New Martinsville
Short Line ES   26167 – T. Beckett, prin.

Red House, Putnam Co.
Putnam County SD
Supt. – See Winfield
Confidence ES, HCR BOX 163   25168
   Gary Hoffman, prin.

Red Jacket, Mingo Co., Pop. Code 3
Mingo County SD
Supt. – See Williamson
ES, P O BOX 91   25692 – Claude Chaflin, prin.

Reedy, Roane Co., Pop. Code 2
Roane County SD
Supt. – See Spencer
ES   25270 – Paulette Anderson, prin.

Richwood, Nicholas Co., Pop. Code 5
Nicholas County SD
Supt. – See Summersville
Cherry River ES
   RURAL ROUTE 09 BOX 142   26261
   J. Copley, prin.

Ridgeley, Mineral Co., Pop. Code 3
Mineral County SD
Supt. – See Keyser
ES, RURAL ROUTE 03   26753
   Clarence Golden, prin.
Short Gap PS, RURAL ROUTE 02 BOX 241   26753
   Doris Ours, prin.

Ripley, Jackson Co., Pop. Code 5
Jackson County SD
Sch. Sys. Enr. Code 6
Supt. – Carroll Staats, P O BOX 770   25271
MS, RURAL ROUTE 02 BOX 75A   25271
   Charles Cottrill, prin.
Fairplain ES, RURAL ROUTE 01   25271
   Gary Cross, prin.
ES, 404 SECOND AVE   25271
   Linn McClain, prin.
Other Schools – See Cottageville, Evans, Kenna,
   Ravenswood, Sandyville

Rivesville, Marion Co., Pop. Code 4
Marion County SD
Supt. – See Fairmont
ES   26588 – James Pulice, prin.

Roanoke, Lewis Co.
Lewis County SD
Supt. – See Weston
ES, RURAL ROUTE 02   26423
   Robert Barnett, prin.

Rock, Mercer Co.
Mercer County SD
Supt. – See Princeton
Montcalm ES, RURAL ROUTE 02 BOX 35   24747
   James Bailey, prin.

Rock Cave, Upshur Co.
Upshur County SD
Supt. – See Buckhannon
ES, RURAL ROUTE 02 BOX 2F   26234
   Jayne Carson, prin.

Rock Creek, Raleigh Co.
Raleigh County SD
Supt. – See Beckley
Mount View ES, P O BOX 127   25174
   Jerry Miller, prin.

Rockport, Wood Co.
Wood County SD
Supt. – See Parkersburg
ES, RURAL ROUTE 01 BOX 101-A   26169
   Bruce Goody, prin.

Romney, Hampshire Co., Pop. Code 4
Hampshire County SD
Sch. Sys. Enr. Code 5
Supt. – Grey Cassell, 46 S HIGH ST   26757
ES, SCHOOL ST   26757 – Allen Hott, prin.

Other Schools – See Augusta, Capon Bridge, Kirby,
   Levels, Purgitsville, Slanesville, Springfield

Ronceverte, Greenbrier Co., Pop. Code 4
Greenbrier County SD
Supt. – See Lewisburg
ES, 600 ACADEMY ST   24970
   Frank Adkins, prin.

Rowlesburg, Preston Co., Pop. Code 3
Preston County SD
Supt. – See Kingwood
ES, P O BOX 155   26425 – Robert McCrum, prin.

Rupert, Greenbrier Co., Pop. Code 4
Greenbrier County SD
Supt. – See Lewisburg
ES, P O BOX 518   25984 – Karen Cadle, prin.

Saint Albans, Kanawha Co., Pop. Code 7
Kanawha County SD
Supt. – See Charleston
Alban ES, 2030 HARRISON AVE   25177
   Ann Simmons, prin.
Bailey ES, 405 WINFIELD RD   25177
   Grace Angle, prin.
Belvil ES, 2009 WASHINGTON AVE   25177
   Rose Morris, prin.
Central ES, 900 HELENE ST   25177
   Norma Crede, prin.
Fairview ES, 101 HIGH ST   25177
   Ruth Perry, prin.
High Lawn ES, 2400 KANAWHA TER   25177
   Judith Reed, prin.
Lakewood ES, 2089 LAKEWOOD DR   25177
   Handley Burdette, prin.
Parkway ES, 205 PFAFF ST   25177
   Bille Santrock, prin.
Weimer ES, 3040 KANAWHA TER   25177
   John Handley, prin.

St. Francis of Assisi ES, 525 HOLLEY ST   25177

Saint Mary's, Pleasants Co., Pop. Code 4
Pleasants County SD
Sch. Sys. Enr. Code 4
Supt. – Harold Carl, 202 FAIRVIEW AVE   26170
ES, 315 WASHINGTON ST   26170
   Thomas Hardbarger, prin.
Other Schools – See Belmont

Salem, Harrison Co., Pop. Code 5
Doddridge County SD
Supt. – See West Union
Big Isaac ES, RURAL ROUTE 03   26426
   Betty Merritt, prin.
Greenbrier ES, RURAL ROUTE 01   26426
   John Trent, prin.
Sedalia ES, RURAL ROUTE 02 BOX 272   26426
   Lynn Bennett, prin.

Harrison County SD
Supt. – See Clarksburg
Harden ES, EAST MAIN ST   26426
   Geraldine Hawkinberry, prin.
Van Horn ES, 229 W MAIN ST   26426
   Carolyn Nutter, prin.

Salt Rock, Cabell Co.
Cabell County SD
Supt. – See Huntington
Merritts Creek ES, RURAL ROUTE 10   25559
   Mike O'Dell, prin.
ES   25559 – Curtis Ross, prin.

Sand Fork, Gilmer Co.
Gilmer County SD
Supt. – See Glenville
ES   26430 – Thomas Minney, prin.

Sandstone, Summers Co.
Summers County SD
Supt. – See Hinton
ES, P O BOX 129   25985 – James Withrow, prin.

Sandyville, Jackson Co.
Jackson County SD
Supt. – See Ripley
Gilmore ES   25275 – Jay Carnell, prin.

Scarbro, Fayette Co.
Fayette County SD
Supt. – See Fayetteville
ES, P O BOX 249   25917 – Lewis Williams, prin.

Scott Depot, Putnam Co.
Putnam County SD
Supt. – See Winfield
Scott Teays ES, 4308 TEAYS VALLEY RD   25560
   Dwight Childers, prin.

Seneca Rocks, Pendleton Co.
Pendleton County SD
Supt. – See Franklin
ES   26884 – Byron Bland, prin.

Seth, Boone Co., Pop. Code 2
Boone County SD
Supt. – See Madison
Sherman JHS   25181 – Carolyn Weaver, prin.

Shady Spring, Raleigh Co., Pop. Code 3
Raleigh County SD
Supt. – See Beckley
ES, P O BOX K   25918 – Gary Rumberg, prin.

Sharples, Logan Co.
Logan County SD
Supt. – See Logan

Spruce ES, GENERAL DELIVERY 25183
  Robert Adkins, prin.

Shepherdstown, Jefferson Co., Pop. Code 4
  Jefferson County SD
  Supt. – See Charles Town
  ES, P O BOX 216 25443 – Lawrence Hitt, prin.

Shinnston, Harrison Co., Pop. Code 5
  Harrison County SD
  Supt. – See Clarksburg
  MS, 811 PIKE ST 26431 – David Book, prin.
  ES, 93 MAHLON ST 26431
    Richard Nichols, prin.

Sistersville, Tyler Co., Pop. Code 4
  Tyler County SD
  Supt. – See Middlebourne
  MS, 501 MAIN ST 26175 – Kenneth Britton, prin.
  ES, RURAL ROUTE 02 BOX 31-7 26175
    Paul Ashby, prin.

Slanesville, Hampshire Co.
  Hampshire County SD
  Supt. – See Romney
  ES, P O BOX 515 25444 – Gary Kidwell, prin.

Smithburg, Doddridge Co.
  Doddridge County SD
  Supt. – See West Union
  ES 26436 – Partrick Curran, prin.

Smithers, Fayette Co., Pop. Code 4
  Fayette County SD
  Supt. – See Fayetteville
  Valley ES, P O BOX 215 25186
    Barbara Chaffins, prin.

Smithville, Ritchie Co.
  Ritchie County SD
  Supt. – See Harrisville
  PS 26178 – Donald Sheets, prin.

Smoot, Greenbrier Co.
  Greenbrier County SD
  Supt. – See Lewisburg
  ES, GENERAL DELIVERY 24977
    Robert Tharp, prin.

Sod, Lincoln Co.
  Lincoln County SD
  Supt. – See Hamlin
  Garretts Bend ES
    RURAL ROUTE 01 BOX 635A 25564
    Connie Runyon, prin.
  McCorkle ES, RURAL ROUTE 01 BOX 552 25564
    Connie Runyon, prin.

Sophia, Raleigh Co., Pop. Code 4
  Raleigh County SD
  Supt. – See Beckley
  Soak Creek ES, P O BOX 487 25921
    Michael Treadway, prin.
  MS, P O BOX 487 25921
    Michael Treadway, prin.

South Charleston, Kanawha Co., Pop. Code 7
  Kanawha County SD
  Supt. – See Charleston
  Alum Creek ES
    RURAL ROUTE 07 BOX 279A 25309
    Maryann Meadows, prin.
  Edison ES, 122 THIRD AVE SW 25303
    Sonja Smith, prin.
  Montrose ES, 631 MONTROSE DR 25303
    Lon Mitchell, prin.
  Richmond ES, 4620 SPRING HILL AVE 25309
    John Cummings, prin.
  Ruthlawn ES, RURAL ROUTE 08 BOX 248 25309
    James Burgess, prin.
  Village ES, 1213 VILLAGE DR 25309
    Jewell Copley, prin.
  Weberwood ES, 732 GORDON DR 25303
    Charlotte Richardson, prin.

Southside, Mason Co.
  Mason County SD
  Supt. – See Point Pleasant
  Beech Hill ES, 2745 US RT 35 25187
    Koneda Devrick, prin.

Spanishburg, Mercer Co.
  Mercer County SD
  Supt. – See Princeton
  ES, P O BOX 7 25922 – Gladys McComas, prin.

Spencer, Roane Co., Pop. Code 5
  Roane County SD
  Sch. Sys. Enr. Code 5
  Supt. – Charles Smith, P O BOX 669 25276
  MS, 811 MADISON ST 25276
    Woodrow Wilson, prin.
  Clover ES, CLAY ROUTE BOX 50A 25276
    Jack Sharp, prin.
  PS, 811 MADISON ST 25276
    Carolyn Patton, prin.
  Other Schools – See Left Hand, Reedy, Walton

Springfield, Hampshire Co.
  Hampshire County SD
  Supt. – See Romney
  Springfield-Green Spring ES, P O BOX 340 26763
    William Heavner, prin.

Stanaford, Raleigh Co.
  Raleigh County SD
  Supt. – See Beckley
  ES, P O BOX K 25927 – Eloise Jarrell, prin.

Stephenson, Wyoming Co.
  Wyoming County SD
  Supt. – See Pineville
  ES, GENERAL DELIVERY 25928
    Chester Ellison, prin.

Stirrat, Logan Co.
  Logan County SD
  Supt. – See Logan
  ES, P O BOX 302 25645 – Mary Cox, prin.

Stollings, Logan Co.
  Logan County SD
  Supt. – See Logan
  ES, P O BOX 487 25646
    Ernestine Sutherland, prin.

Summersville, Nicholas Co., Pop. Code 5
  Nicholas County SD
  Sch. Sys. Enr. Code 6
  Supt. – Robert Bailey, 715 BROAD ST 26651
  Glade Creek ES
    RURAL ROUTE 41 BOX 1646 26651
    Richard Legg, prin.
  Muddlety ES, RURAL ROUTE 01 BOX 90 26651
    Leonard Tyree, prin.
  ES, 307 MCKEES CREEK RD 26651
    Lowell Morriston, prin.
  Zela ES, P O BOX 1073 26651 – Terry Lewis, prin.
  Other Schools – See Birch River, Canvas, Craigsville,
    Dixie, Fenwick, Keslers Cross Lanes, Leivasy,
    Lockwood, Mount Lookout, Mount Nebo, Nettie,
    Richwood

Sundial, Raleigh Co.
  Raleigh County SD
  Supt. – See Beckley
  Marsh Fork MS 25189 – Donald Jarrell, prin.

Surveyor, Raleigh Co.
  Raleigh County SD
  Supt. – See Beckley
  Trap Hill MS 25932 – James Harmon, prin.

Sutton, Braxton Co., Pop. Code 4
  Braxton County SD
  Sch. Sys. Enr. Code 5
  Supt. – Kenna Seal, 400 4TH ST 26601
  MS, 411 N HILL ROAD 26601
    Robert Sigler, prin.
  ES, 228 NORTH HILL ROAD 26601
    Manoka McCue, prin.
  Other Schools – See Burnsville, Flatwoods,
    Frametown, Gassaway, Little Birch

Sylvester, Boone Co., Pop. Code 2
  Boone County SD
  Supt. – See Madison
  ES 25193 – Georgia Price, prin.

Tad, Kanawha Co.
  Kanawha County SD
  Supt. – See Charleston
  Ingles ES, P O BOX 120 25201
    William Reynolds, prin.

Talcott, Summers Co.
  Summers County SD
  Supt. – See Hinton
  ES, P O BOX 140 24981 – (—), prin.

Tanner, Gilmer Co.
  Gilmer County SD
  Supt. – See Glenville
  ES 26179 – Dorothy Rhoades, prin.

Terra Alta, Preston Co., Pop. Code 4
  Preston County SD
  Supt. – See Kingwood
  ES, 405 W STATE AVE 26764
    Russell McConnell, prin.

Thacker, Mingo Co.
  Mingo County SD
  Supt. – See Williamson
  ES, GENERAL DELIVERY 25694
    John Hatfield, prin.

Thomas, Tucker Co., Pop. Code 3
  Tucker County SD
  Supt. – See Parsons
  Davis-Thomas ES, P O BOX 250 26292
    Michael McClellan, prin.

Thornton, Taylor Co.
  Taylor County SD
  Supt. – See Grafton
  Knottsville ES, RURAL ROUTE 01 BOX 264 26440
    John Stallings, prin.

Tornado, Kanawha Co.
  Kanawha County SD
  Supt. – See Charleston
  Andrews Heights ES, P O BOX 158 25202
    Sue Shank, prin.

Triadelphia, Ohio Co., Pop. Code 4
  Ohio County SD
  Supt. – See Wheeling
  Middle Creek ES
    RURAL ROUTE 01 BOX 386 26059
    James Tecca, prin.

Troy, Gilmer Co.
  Gilmer County SD
  Supt. – See Glenville
  ES 26443 – Larry Barton, prin.

Tunnelton, Preston Co., Pop. Code 3
  Preston County SD
  Supt. – See Kingwood
  Central Preston JHS, P O BOX 188 26444
    Gerald Cline, prin.
  Fellowsville ES
    RURAL ROUTE 01 BOX 265 26444
    Donald Post, prin.
  Tunnelton-Denver ES, P O BOX 400 26444
    Francis Martin, prin.

Uneeda, Boone Co.
  Boone County SD
  Supt. – See Madison
  ES 25205 – Marion Workman, prin.

Union, Monroe Co., Pop. Code 3
  Monroe County SD
  Sch. Sys. Enr. Code 4
  Supt. – Bobby Via, P O BOX 330 24983
  ES 24983 – Linda Ballard, prin.
  Other Schools – See Ballard, Gap Mills, Greenville,
    Peterstown

Upper Tract, Pendleton Co.
  Pendleton County SD
  Supt. – See Franklin
  ES 26866 – Thomas Mooney, prin.

Valley Fork, Clay Co.
  Clay County SD
  Supt. – See Clay
  ES, GENERAL DELIVERY 25283
    Larry Legg, prin.

Valley Head, Randolph Co.
  Randolph County SD
  Supt. – See Elkins
  ES 26294 – Susan Hinzman, prin.

Van, Boone Co., Pop. Code 2
  Boone County SD
  Supt. – See Madison
  ES 25206 – Grady Hayner, prin.

Varney, Mingo Co.
  Mingo County SD
  Supt. – See Williamson
  ES, P O BOX 309 25696 – Dow Ooten, prin.

Verdunville, Logan Co.
  Logan County SD
  Supt. – See Logan
  ES, P O BOX J 25649 – Barbara Porter, prin.

Vienna, Wood Co., Pop. Code 7
  Wood County SD
  Supt. – See Parkersburg
  Greenmont ES, 209 58TH ST 26105
    Gary Bailey, prin.
  Maplewood ES, 1400 12TH ST 26105
    Sally Leech, prin.
  Neale ES, 2305 GRAND CENTRAL AVE 26105
    William Holbert, prin.
  ES, 700 41ST ST 26105 – Paul Armstrong, prin.

Volga, Barbour Co.
  Barbour County SD
  Supt. – See Philippi
  Volga-Century ES
    RURAL ROUTE 01 BOX 12S 26238
    Alice Tenney, prin.

Wadestown, Monongalia Co.
  Monongalia County SD
  Supt. – See Morgantown
  ES, P O BOX 189 26589 – June Kerr, prin.

Walker, Wood Co.
  Wood County SD
  Supt. – See Parkersburg
  Pleasant Valley ES
    RURAL ROUTE 02 BOX 221 26180
    Wayne Meiser, prin.
  ES, P O BOX 38 26180 – Jeffrey Payne, prin.

Walkersville, Lewis Co.
  Lewis County SD
  Supt. – See Weston
  ES 26447 – Danny Hinkle, prin.

Wallace, Harrison Co., Pop. Code 3
  Harrison County SD
  Supt. – See Clarksburg
  ES, RURAL ROUTE 01 BOX 4-A 26448
    Terryt McCloud, prin.

Walton, Roane Co., Pop. Code 2
  Roane County SD
  Supt. – See Spencer
  ES 25286 – Charles Poole, prin.

War, McDowell Co., Pop. Code 4
  McDowell County SD
  Supt. – See Welch
  ES, P O BOX 967 24892 – John Wargo, prin.

Wardensville, Hardy Co., Pop. Code 2
  Hardy County SD
  Supt. – See Moorefield
  ES, P O BOX 277 26851 – Douglas Hines, prin.

Washington, Wood Co.
  Wood County SD
  Supt. – See Parkersburg
  ES, RURAL ROUTE 01 26181
    Lawrence Hasbargen, prin.

Waverly, Wood Co., Pop. Code 2
Wood County SD
Supt. – See Parkersburg
ES 26814 – Robert Cutlip, prin.

Wayne, Wayne Co., Pop. Code 4
Wayne County SD
Sch. Sys. Enr. Code 6
Supt. – Michael Ferguson, P O BOX 68 25570
MS, P O BOX 458 25570 – Nancy Adkins, prin.
Crockett ES, RURAL ROUTE 02 BOX 2226 25570
Reba Thompson, prin.
ES 25570 – James Ross, prin.
Other Schools – See Ceredo, Crum, Dunlow, East
Lynn, Fort Gay, Genoa, Huntington, Kenova,
Kiahsville, Lavalette, Prichard

Webster Springs, Webster Co.
Webster County SD
Sch. Sys. Enr. Code 5
Supt. – Martha Dean, 327 RIVER DRIVE 26288
ES, 318 RIVER DR 26288 – Geoffrey Ezell, prin.
Other Schools – See Cowen, Diana, Hacker Valley

Weirton, Hancock Co., Pop. Code 7
Brooke County SD
Supt. – See Wellsburg
Edgewood ES, 4215 WELLS ST 26062
Michael Ferrell, prin.
Millsop PS
LEGION & SWEARINGEN ROAD 26062
Dolores Ginier, prin.

Hancock County SD
Supt. – See New Cumberland
Broadview ES, 189 CIRCLE DR 26062
Richard Barnabel, prin.
Cove ES, COVE ROAD 26062
Carole Bernardino, prin.
Liberty ES, 200 CULLER RD 26062
Betty Ann McGillen, prin.
Marland Heights ES, 3900 BRIGHTWAY ST 26062
Sue Oboryshko, prin.
Weirton Heights ES, 160 S 12TH ST 26062
James Piccirillo, prin.

Sacred Heart of Mary ES
200 PRESTON AVE 26062
St. Joseph the Worker ES
129 MICHAEL AVE 26062
St. Paul ES, 140 WALNUT ST 26062

Welch, McDowell Co., Pop. Code 5
McDowell County SD
Sch. Sys. Enr. Code 7
Supt. – J. Kenneth Roberts
30 CENTRAL AVE 24801
ES, P O BOX A 24801 – Tony Larkin, prin.
Other Schools – See Anawalt, Bartley, Berwind, Big
Sandy, Bradshaw, Elkhorn, Gary, Hemphill, Iaeger,
Jolo, Keystone, Kimball, Newhall, Panther, War

Wellsburg, Brooke Co., Pop. Code 5
Brooke County SD
Sch. Sys. Enr. Code 6
Supt. – Richard Whitehead
17TH AND CHARLES 26070
Hammond MS, RURAL ROUTE 02 BOX 99 26070
Charles Baker, prin.
MS, 1447 MAIN ST 26070 – Curtis Tarr, prin.
Franklin PS, 1305 WASHINGTON PIKE 26070
William Harvey, prin.
PS, EAST-12TH & PLEASANT AVENUE 26070
Paul Vandyke, prin.
Other Schools – See Beech Bottom, Bethany, Colliers,
Follansbee, Weirton

West Columbia, Mason Co.
Mason County SD
Supt. – See Point Pleasant
ES, GENERAL DELIVERY 25287 – (—), prin.

West Hamlin, Lincoln Co., Pop. Code 3
Lincoln County SD
Supt. – See Hamlin

ES, RURAL ROUTE 01 BOX 112 25571
Brenda Clay, prin.

West Liberty, Ohio Co., Pop. Code 5
Ohio County SD
Supt. – See Wheeling
ES, 204 CHATHAM ST 26074 – Larry Boron, prin.

West Milford, Harrison Co., Pop. Code 3
Harrison County SD
Supt. – See Clarksburg
ES, 226 SCHOOL ST 26451 – Frank Devono, prin.

Weston, Lewis Co., Pop. Code 6
Lewis County SD
Sch. Sys. Enr. Code 5
Supt. – Joseph Mace, P O BOX 888 26452
Kitsonville ES, 269 S MAIN AVE 26452
Robert Thompson, prin.
Peterson ES, RURAL ROUTE 03 BOX 101A 26452
Robert Clay, prin.
Polk Creek ES, 619 W 2ND ST 26452
Thomas Garrett, prin.
Shadybrook PS, 104 SCHOOL ST 26452
Mary Ann Hiteshew, prin.
Weston Central ES, 239 COURT AVE 26452
Marcella Linger, prin.
Other Schools – See Alum Bridge, Jane Lew, Roanoke,
Walkersville

Westover, Monongalia Co., Pop. Code 5
Monongalia County SD
Supt. – See Morgantown
ES, MORRISON AVE 26505
Jacqueline Sainato, prin.

West Union, Dodridge Co., Pop. Code 4
Doddridge County SD
Sch. Sys. Enr. Code 4
Supt. – Raymond Frazier
104 SISTERSVILLE PIKE 26456
Carr ES, RURAL ROUTE 02 26456
Elizabeth Yeager, prin.
Summers ES, RURAL ROUTE 01 26456
George Stansberry, prin.
ES 26456 – Delbert Murphy, prin.
Other Schools – See Blandville, Center Point,
Greenwood, Salem, Smithburg

Wharncliffe, Mingo Co.
Mingo County SD
Supt. – See Williamson
Ben Creek ES, GENERAL DELIVERY 25651
Bertie Cline, prin.

Wharton, Boone Co.
Boone County SD
Supt. – See Madison
MS 25208 – Gene Rizzo, prin.
ES 25208 – Gene Rizzo, prin.

Wheeling, Ohio Co., Pop. Code 8
Marshall County SD
Supt. – See Moundsville
Sherrard ES, RURAL ROUTE 03 BOX 505 26003
Roger Schrumpf, prin.

Ohio County SD
Sch. Sys. Enr. Code 6
Supt. – Henry Marockie
2203 NATIONAL ROAD 26003
Bethlehem PS, 22 CHAPEL RD 26003
Jonathan Duncan, prin.
Clay ES, 15TH & WOOD STS 26003
James Bock, prin.
Elm Grove ES, RURAL ROUTE 02 BOX 444 26003
Barbara Fassig, prin.
Kruger Street PS, 144 KRUGER ST 26003
Barbara Fassig, prin.
Madison ES, 91 ZANE ST 26003
Roge Warren, prin.
North Park ES, 94 FINCH AVE 26003
Jonathan Duncan, prin.
Park View ES, 111 PARK VIEW LN 26003
Jonathan Duncan, prin.

Ritchie ES, 3700 WOOD ST 26003
Robert Mosca, prin.
Steenrod PS, CHANTAL COURT 26003
Jonathan Duncan, prin.
Warwood ES, 1200 RICHLAND AVE 26003
John Rohal, prin.
Woodsdale ES, 19 BETHANY PIKE 26003
Ruth Ann Scherich, prin.
Other Schools – See Triadelphia, West Liberty

Mt. Dechantal Vistation Academy
410 WASHINGTON AVE 26003
Corpus Christi ES, 1512 WARWOOD AVE 26003
Our Lady of Peace ES
640 OLD FAIRMONT PIKE 26003
St. Michael ES, 1221 NATIONAL RD 26003
St. Vincent De Paul ES, 127 KEY AVE 26003

White Sulphur Springs, Greenbrier Co., Pop. Code 5
Greenbrier County SD
Supt. – See Lewisburg
ES, 150 REED ST 24986 – Pat Brackenrich, prin.

Whitesville, Boone Co., Pop. Code 3
Raleigh County SD
Supt. – See Beckley
Pettus ES, HCR 25209 – Brenda Jarrell, prin.

Whitman, Logan Co., Pop. Code 3
Logan County SD
Supt. – See Logan
ES, GENERAL DELIVERY 25652
Meri Saunders, prin.

Wiley Ford, Mineral Co.
Mineral County SD
Supt. – See Keyser
ES, P O BOX 20 26767 – Jane Kitzmiller, prin.

Williamsburg, Greenbrier Co.
Greenbrier County SD
Supt. – See Lewisburg
ES, P O BOX 39 24991 – Garry Moore, prin.

Williamson, Mingo Co., Pop. Code 6
Mingo County SD
Sch. Sys. Enr. Code 6
Supt. – Harry Cline, ALDERSON ST 25661
West Williamson ES, 1428 W 5TH AVE 25661
Fred Newsome, prin.
ES, RURAL ROUTE 01 BOX 310 25661
John Hatfield, prin.
Other Schools – See Baisden, Chattaroy, Delbarton,
Dingess, Gilbert, Isaban, Kermit, Lenore, Matewan,
Meador, Nolan, Ragland, Red Jacket, Thacker,
Varney, Wharncliffe

Williamstown, Wood Co., Pop. Code 5
Wood County SD
Supt. – See Parkersburg
ES, 418-430 WILLIAMS AVE 26187
Robert Cutlip, prin.

Winfield, Putnam Co., Pop. Code 2
Putnam County SD
Sch. Sys. Enr. Code 6
Supt. – Stephen Baldwin, P O BOX 47 25213
MS, P O BOX 118 25213 – E. Anderson, prin.
Eastbrook ES, 1600 BILLS CREEK RD 25213
Harold Hatfield, prin.
ES, P O BOX 8 25213 – Jack Gordon, prin.
Other Schools – See Buffalo, Eleanor, Hometown,
Hurricane, Liberty, Nitro, Poca, Red House, Scott
Depot

Wyatt, Harrison Co.
Harrison County SD
Supt. – See Clarksburg
ES, P O BOX 117 26463 – Ben Guido, prin.

WISCONSIN

STATE DEPARTMENT OF PUBLIC INSTRUCTION
P.O. Box 7841, Madison 53707
(608) 266-1771

Superintendent of Public Instruction	Herbert Grover
Deputy Superintendent	C. Richard Nelson
Assistant Superintendent Handicapped Children & Pupil Services	Victor Contrucci
Assistant Superintendent Instructional Services	John Benson
Assistant Superintendent Library Services	Leslyn Shires
Assistant Superintendent Management & Budget	Gary Johnson
Assistant Superintendent School Financial Resources & Management Services	Vacant

PUBLIC, PRIVATE, AND PAROCHIAL ELEMENTARY SCHOOLS

Abbotsford, Clark Co., Pop. Code 4
Abbotsford SD
Sch. Sys. Enr. Code 3
Supt. – James Hayes 54405
ES 54405 – Lawrence Stettler, prin.

Abrams, Oconto Co., Pop. Code 4
Oconto Falls SD
Supt. – See Oconto Falls
ES 54101 – Thomas Lutz, prin.

Adams, Adams Co., Pop. Code 4
Adams-Friendship Area SD
Sch. Sys. Enr. Code 4
Supt. – Robert Beaver, P O BOX 346 53910
ES, P O BOX 349 53910 – John Bratlund, prin.
Castle Rock ES
   RURAL ROUTE 01 BOX 255 53910
   Theodore Haschke, prin.
Other Schools – See Arkdale, Brooks, Friendship,
   Grand Marsh

Adell, Sheboygan Co., Pop. Code 3
Random Lake SD
Supt. – See Random Lake
Batavia ES, RURAL ROUTE 01 53001
   Roger Hoffman, prin.

Albany, Green Co., Pop. Code 4
Albany SD
Sch. Sys. Enr. Code 2
Supt. – Ervin Forgy, P O BOX 349 53502
ES 53502 – Ervin Forgy, prin.

Algoma, Kewaunee Co., Pop. Code 5
Algoma SD
Sch. Sys. Enr. Code 3
Supt. – Harold D. Gehrke
   1715 DIVISION ST 54201
ES 54201 – Dale Larson, prin.

St. Mary ES, 214 CHURCH ST 54201
St. Paul's Evangelist Lutheran ES
   1115 DIVISION ST 54201

Allenton, Washington Co.
Slinger SD
Supt. – See Slinger
ES 53002 – Michael Hohner, prin.

Alma, Buffalo Co., Pop. Code 3
Alma SD
Sch. Sys. Enr. Code 2
Supt. – V. Martzke
   RURAL ROUTE 02 BOX 11-A 54610
ES, RURAL ROUTE 02 BOX 11-A 54610
   Lois Balk, prin.

Alma Center, Jackson Co., Pop. Code 2
Alma Center SD
Sch. Sys. Enr. Code 3
Supt. – Larry Lienau 54611
Lincoln MS 54611 – Craig McIntosh, prin.
MS 54611 – Randy Stanley, prin.
Other Schools – See Merrillan

Almena, Barron Co., Pop. Code 3
Barron Area SD
Supt. – See Barron
ES, P O BOX 86 54805 – Richard Updike, prin.

Almond, Portage Co., Pop. Code 2
Almond-Bancroft SD
Sch. Sys. Enr. Code 2
Supt. – Ed Poock, P O BOX 130 54909
ES 54909 – (—), prin.
Other Schools – See Bancroft

Altoona, Eau Claire Co., Pop. Code 5
Altoona SD
Sch. Sys. Enr. Code 4
Supt. – Robert Bredesen
   1903 BARTLETT AVE 54720
MS, 1903 BARTLETT AVE 54720
   Arnold Johnson, prin.
Pederson ES, 1827 BARTLETT AVE 54720
   John Grafenauer, prin.

St. Mary's ES, 227 5TH ST W 54720

Amberg, Marinette Co., Pop. Code 3
Wausaukee SD
Supt. – See Wausaukee
ES 54102 – Carl Anderson, prin.

Amery, Polk Co., Pop. Code 4
Amery SD
Sch. Sys. Enr. Code 4
Supt. – Raymond Norsted
   115 DICKEYE ST N 54001
MS, 115 DICKEY ST N 54001
   Patricia Graves, prin.
Lien ES, 469 MINNEAPOLIS AVE S 54001
   James Grayden, prin.

Amherst, Portage Co., Pop. Code 3
Tomorrow River SD
Sch. Sys. Enr. Code 3
Supt. – Robert Barrett 54406
JHS 54406 – (—), prin.
ES 54406 – William Gilles, prin.

Aniwa, Shawand Co., Pop. Code 2
Antigo SD
Supt. – See Antigo
ES 54408 – (—), prin.

Antigo, Langlade Co., Pop. Code 6
Antigo SD
Sch. Sys. Enr. Code 5
Supt. – Craig Bangtson
   120 S DORR STREET 54409
Crestwood ES, W8464 CTH AA 54409
   Walt Pechman, prin.
East ES, 220 7TH AVE 54409
   Thomas Krueger, prin.
North ES, 506 GRAHAM AVE 54409
   (—), prin.
Pleasant View ES, W11141 HIGHWAY HH 54409
   Harry Arndt, Jr., prin.
Spring Valley ES, N4754 CTH BB 54409
   (—), prin.
West ES, 1232 7TH AVE 54409 – (—), prin.
Other Schools – See Aniwa, Deerbrook, Lily, Mattoon

Peace Lutheran ES, 300 LINCOLN ST 54409
St. John's ES, 419 FULTON ST 54409
St. Mary ES, 723 DELEGLISE ST 54409

Appleton, Outagamie Co., Pop. Code 8
Appleton Area SD
Sch. Sys. Enr. Code 7
Supt. – Jerome Boettcher, P O BOX 2019 54913
Badger ES 54911 – Ruth Finch, prin.
Columbus ES, 913 N ONEIDA ST 54911
   Gordon Foster, prin.
Edison ES, 412 N MEADE ST 54911
   William Premeau, prin.
Foster ES, 305 FOSTER ST 54915
   David Schmidt, prin.
Franklin ES, 2212 JARCHOW ST 54911
   Richard Goree, prin.
Highlands ES, 2137 ELINOR ST 54914
   Thomas O'hearn, prin.
Horizons ES, 2101 SCHAEFER CIR 54915
   Gerald McDermot, prin.

Huntley ES, 2224 ULLMAN ST 54911
   Richard Haas, prin.
Jefferson ES, 1000 S MASON ST 54914
   James Murphy, prin.
Johnston ES, 2525 FOREST ST 54915
   Joanne DeGroot, prin.
Lincoln ES, 1000 N MASON ST 54914
   Alan Schroeder, prin.
McKinley ES, 1125 E TAFT ST 54911
   Thomas Loveall, prin.
Planmann ES, RURAL ROUTE 03 54915
   Stephen Otto, prin.
Richmond ES, 1414 JOHN ST 54915
   Helga Eggener, prin.
Twin Willows ES, 3335 N LYNNDALE DR 54915
   Ruth Finch, prin.

St. Joseph MS, 323 W LAWRENCE ST 54911
Appleton Catholic Central ES
   313 S STATE ST 54911
Holy Angels ES, W3600 COUNTY KK 54915
Immanuel Evangelist Lutheran ES
   397 SCHOOL ROAD 54915
Mt. Oliver Evangelist Lutheran ES
   930 E FLORIDA AVE 54911
Riverview Lutheran ES, 136 SEYMOUR ST 54915
Sacred Heart ES, 1312 MONROE ST 54915
St. Bernadette ES, 2331 LOURDES DR 54915
St. Edward ES, RURAL ROUTE 03 54915
St. Matthew Lutheran ES
   1316 W LAWRENCE ST 54914
St. Paul Evangelist Lutheran ES
   225 E HARRIS ST 54911
St. Pius X ES, 500 W MARQUETTE ST 54911
St. Thomas More ES, 1810 MCDONALD ST 54911

Arcadia, Trempealeau Co., Pop. Code 4
Arcadia SD
Sch. Sys. Enr. Code 3
Supt. – Tom Westerhaus, 308 MAIN ST E 54612
ES, 358 W RIVER ST 54612 – Gary Paul, prin.

Arcadia Catholic ES
   341 WASHINGTON ST 54612

Arena, Iowa Co., Pop. Code 2
River Valley SD
Supt. – See Spring Green
ES 53503 – (—), prin.

Argonne, Forest Co., Pop. Code 2
Crandon SD
Supt. – See Crandon
ES 54511 – Dee Dailey, prin.

Argyle, Lafayette Co., Pop. Code 3
Argyle SD
Sch. Sys. Enr. Code 2
Supt. – Ronald Eastman 53504
ES 53504 – Robert Eastman, prin.

Arkansaw, Pepin Co., Pop. Code 2
Arkansaw SD
Sch. Sys. Enr. Code 2
Supt. – Gregory Van Dyke 54721
ES 54721 – (—), prin.

Arkdale, Adams Co.
Adams-Friendship Area SD
Supt. – See Adams
Roche A Cri ES, RURAL ROUTE 01 54613
   Glenn Rathermel, prin.

Arlington, Columbia Co., Pop. Code 2
De Forest SD
Supt. – See De Forest
Leeds ES, RURAL ROUTE 02 53911
   Deborah Fritsch, prin.

702

Poynette SD
Supt. – See Poynette
ES   53911 – Frank Zych, prin.

Ashland, Ashland Co., Pop. Code 6
Ashland SD
Sch. Sys. Enr. Code 4
Supt. – Hollister DeMotts, 203 11TH ST E   54806
MS, 203 11TH ST E   54806 – Mary Podlesny, prin.
Beaser ES, 618 BEASER AVE   54806
   Allan Lundquist, prin.
Ellis ES, 308 STUNTZ AVE   54806
   Alloy Chapinski, prin.
Ondossagon ES, RURAL ROUTE 03   54806
   Ronald Lahnala, prin.
Marengo Valley ES
   RURAL ROUTE 04 BOX 21   54806
   Sara Sarnstrom, prin.
Wilmarth ES, 901 3RD AVE W   54806
   Alloy Chapinski, prin.

Ashland SD
Sch. Sys. Enr. Code 4
Supt. – Hollister DeMotts, 203 11TH ST E   54806
MS, 203 11TH ST E   54806 – Mary Podlesny, prin.
Beaser ES, 618 BEASER AVE   54806
   Allan Lundquist, prin.
Ellis ES, 308 STUNTZ AVE   54806
   Alloy Chapinski, prin.
Ondossagon ES, RURAL ROUTE 03   54806
   Ronald Lahnala, prin.
Marengo Valley ES
   RURAL ROUTE 04 BOX 21   54806
   Sara Sarnstrom, prin.
Wilmarth ES, 901 3RD AVE W   54806
   Alloy Chapinski, prin.
Other Schools – See Benoit, Mason

St. Agnes Consolidated ES
   215 FRONT ST E   54806

Athens, Marathon Co., Pop. Code 3
Athens SD
Sch. Sys. Enr. Code 3
Supt. – William Anderson, P O BOX F   54411
MS   54411 – Guy Leavitt, prin.
Athens ES   54411 – Margaret Wolding, prin.

St. Anthony ES, 309 MUELLER BOX 1   54411

Auburndale, Wood Co., Pop. Code 3
Auburndale SD
Sch. Sys. Enr. Code 3
Supt. – Gary Rooney   54412
ES   54412 – Edward Dorff, prin.

St. Mary ES, 224 E MAIN ST   54412

Augusta, Eau Claire Co., Pop. Code 4
Augusta SD
Sch. Sys. Enr. Code 3
Supt. – Marvin Hopland   54722
JSHS, RURAL ROUTE 02 BOX 67   54722
   John Lacke, prin.
ES   54722 – Marvin Hopland, prin.

Avoca, Iowa Co., Pop. Code 3
Riverdale SD
Supt. – See Muscoda
ES   53806 – Mary Stanek, prin.

Baldwin, St. Croix Co., Pop. Code 4
Baldwin-Woodville Area SD
Sch. Sys. Enr. Code 4
Supt. – Duane Lones   54002
Greenfield ES   54002 – Patrick McCardle, prin.
Other Schools – See Woodville

Balsam Lake, Polk Co., Pop. Code 3
Unity SD
Sch. Sys. Enr. Code 4
Supt. – Milton Kier, P O BOX 307   54810
Unity MS, P O BOX 307   54810
   Richard O. Klatt, prin.
Unity ES   54810 – Gail Becker, prin.

Bancroft, Portage Co.
Almond-Bancroft SD
Supt. – See Almond
ES   54921 – (—), prin.

Bangor, La Crosse Co., Pop. Code 4
Bangor SD
Sch. Sys. Enr. Code 3
Supt. – Gene Wellman, P O BOX 7   54614
ES   54614 – Mike Richardson, prin.

St. Paul's Evangelist Lutheran ES
   1301 PEARL ST BOX 257   54614

Baraboo, Sauck Co., Pop. Code 6
Baraboo SD
Sch. Sys. Enr. Code 4
Supt. – Anthony Kujawa, 101 2ND AVE   53913
East ES, 815 6TH ST   53913 – Ann Sorg, prin.
Fairfield Center ES, RURAL ROUTE 01   53913
   David Holm, prin.
South ES, 400 MULBERRY ST   53913
   (—), prin.
West ES, 707 CENTER ST   53913
   Allegra Zick, prin.
Other Schools – See North Freedom, West Baraboo

St. John's Lutheran ES, 515 5TH ST   53913
St. Joseph ES, 310 2ND ST   53913

Barneveld, Iowa Co., Pop. Code 3
Barneveld SD
Sch. Sys. Enr. Code 2
Supt. – Janice Hardesty   53507
Barneveld ES   53507 – Janice Hardesty, prin.

Barron, Barron Co., Pop. Code 5
Barron Area SD
Sch. Sys. Enr. Code 4
Supt. – Ronald Novotny
   1190 MEMORIAL DRIVE   54812
Riverview MS, 135 W RIVER AVE   54812
   Kenneth Mosentine, prin.
Woodland ES, 808 E WOODLAND AVE   54812
   Harold Thorson, prin.
Other Schools – See Almena, Dallas, Ridgeland

Bassett, Kenosha Co.
Randall J1 SD
Sch. Sys. Enr. Code 2
Supt. – Y. Lemmerhirt, P O BOX 38   53101
Randall Consolidated ES, P O BOX 38   53101
   (—), prin.

Bayfield, Bayfield Co., Pop. Code 3
Bayfield SD
Sch. Sys. Enr. Code 2
Supt. – D. H. Anderson   54814
ES   54814 – John Anderson, prin.
Other Schools – See La Pointe

Bear Creek, Outagamie Co., Pop. Code 2
Clintonville SD
Supt. – See Clintonville
IS   54922 – (—), prin.
PS   54922 – (—), prin.

St. Mary's ES
   126 WELCOME AVE BOX 216   54922

Beaver Dam, Dodge Co., Pop. Code 7
Beaver Dam SD
Sch. Sys. Enr. Code 5
Supt. – Martin Richardson
   705 MCKINLEY ST   53916
Jefferson ES, BROOK & JEFFERSON ST   53916
   Jerald Lauritzen, prin.
Lincoln ES, 210 GOULD ST   53916
   Claryn Glewen, prin.
South Beaver Dam ES, RURAL ROUTE 03   53916
   John Da Valt, prin.
Trenton ES, RURAL ROUTE 04   53916
   Julie Bran, prin.
Washington ES, 600 GROVE ST   53916
   Robert Gartzke, prin.
Wilson ES, 310 WEST ST   53916
   John Da Valt, prin.
Other Schools – See Juneau

St. Stephen's Lutheran ES
   412 W MAPLE AVE   53916
Unified Catholic Parish ES
   503 S SPRING ST   53916

Belleville, Dane Co., Pop. Code 4
Belleville SD
Sch. Sys. Enr. Code 3
Supt. – Darrell Fitch, 101 N GRANT ST   53508
ES, 237 W PEARL ST   53508
   Gary Loertscher, prin.
MS, CHURCH ST   53508 – (—), prin.

Belmont, Lafayette Co., Pop. Code 3
Belmont Comm. SD
Sch. Sys. Enr. Code 2
Supt. – Harold Justman   53510
ES   53510 – Eugene Hawkinson, prin.

Beloit, Rock Co., Pop. Code 8
Beloit SD
Sch. Sys. Enr. Code 6
Supt. – Frank McKinzie, 1633 KEELER AVE   53511
Burge ES, 321 OLYMPIAN BLVD   53511
   Barbara Hickman, prin.
Converse ES, 1602 TOWNLINE AVE   53511
   Anthony Beardsly, prin.
Cunningham ES, 910 TOWNLINE AVE   53511
   Richard McGregory, prin.
Gaston ES, 610 MCKINLEY AVE   53511
   Ralph Napper, prin.
Hackett ES   53511 – (—), prin.
McLenegan ES, 2639 SUNSHINE LN   53511
   Booker Street, prin.
Merrill ES, 1333 COPELAND AVE   53511
   George Kolak, prin.
Morgan ES, LEE LANE   53511
   Merlin Nundahl, prin.
Robinson ES, 1801 CRANSTON RD   53511
   Thomas Teteak, prin.
Royce ES, 825 LIBERTY AVE   53511
   Robert Layman, prin.
Todd ES, 1621 OAKWOOD AVE   53511
   Deborah Carlson, prin.
Wright ES, 1033 WOODWARD AVE   53511
   Robert Harris, prin.

Beloit-Turner SD
Sch. Sys. Enr. Code 4
Supt. – Charles Melvin
   1231 INMAN PARKWAY   53511
Turner MS, 1237 INMAN PARKWAY   53511
   Andrew Toutloff, prin.
Powers ES, 620 HILLSIDE DR   53511
   Nancy Yoder, prin.
Town View MS, NEWARK RD   53511
   Michael Kuehne, prin.

Parkview SD
Supt. – See Orfordville
Newark ES, RURAL ROUTE 02   53511
   Dennis Socwell, prin.

Brother Dutton ES, 717 HACKETT ST   53511
Our Lady of Assumption ES
   2222 SHOPIERE RD   53511
St. John's Lutheran ES, 1000 BLUFF ST   53511

Benoit, Bayfield Co.
Ashland SD
Supt. – See Ashland
MS   54816 – Sam Dymesich, prin.

Benton, Lafayette Co., Pop. Code 3
Benton SD
Sch. Sys. Enr. Code 2
Supt. – Alfred Kluge, P O BOX 6   53803
ES   53803 – Loras Kruser, prin.

Berlin, Green Lake Co., Pop. Code 6
Berlin Area SD
Sch. Sys. Enr. Code 4
Supt. – Ray Kinziger, 265 E HURON ST   54923
Clay JHS, 259 E MARQUETTE ST   54923
   Larry Zarnot, prin.
Clay ES, 259 E MARQUETTE ST   54923
   Robert Sillanpaa, prin.
Washington ES, 344 BROADWAY ST   54923
   David Phelps, prin.
Other Schools – See Poy Sippi

Berlin Catholic ES, 315 SW CERESCO ST   54923
St. John Lutheran ES, 146 MOUND ST   54923

Big Bend, Waukesha Co., Pop. Code 4
Mukwonago SD
Supt. – See Mukwonago
ES, W230 S8695 BIG BEND DR   53103
   Robert Brueggeman, prin.

St. Joseph ES, ST JOSEPH DR   53103

Birchwood, Washburn Co., Pop. Code 2
Birchwood SD
Sch. Sys. Enr. Code 2
Supt. – James D. Landes   54817
ES   54817 – (—), prin.

Birnamwood, Shawano Co., Pop. Code 3
Wittenberg-Birnamwood SD
Supt. – See Wittenberg
ES   54414 – Mark Flynn, prin.

Black Creek, Outagamie Co., Pop. Code 4
Seymour Comm. SD
Supt. – See Seymour
ES   54106 – Timothy Moe, prin.

Black Earth, Dane Co., Pop. Code 4
Wisconsin Hts. SD
Supt. – See Mazomanie
ES, 1133 CENTER ST   53515
   Gene Brotzman, prin.

Black River Falls, Jackson Co., Pop. Code 5
Black River Falls SD
Sch. Sys. Enr. Code 4
Supt. – Dennis Richards, 301 N 4TH ST   54615
Black River Falls MS, 206 N 3RD ST   54615
   Warren Rosin, prin.
Forrest Street MS, 720 FORREST ST   54615
   David Yakes, prin.
Gebhardt ES, 411 GEBHARDT RD   54615
   Carlyle Button, prin.
Other Schools – See Hixton

Blair, Trempealeau Co., Pop. Code 4
Blair SD
Sch. Sys. Enr. Code 2
Supt. – William Urban   54616
ES   54616 – John Ibinger, prin.

Blanchardville, Lafayette Co., Pop. Code 3
Pecatonica SD
Sch. Sys. Enr. Code 3
Supt. – Terry Wiseman, P O BOX 117   53516
Other Schools – See Hollandale

Bloomer, Chippewa Co., Pop. Code 5
Bloomer SD
Sch. Sys. Enr. Code 4
Supt. – (—), 1310 17TH AVE   54724
MS, 1315 15TH AVE   54724
   Vernon Verkuilen, prin.
ES, 1726 OAK ST   54724 – Roger Berg, prin.

St. Paul ES, 1210 MAIN ST   54724

Bloomington, Grant Co., Pop. Code 3
Bloomington SD
Sch. Sys. Enr. Code 2
Supt. – John Cooper   53804
ES   53804 – Vandy Bloyer, prin.

St. Mary ES, 531 CONGRESS ST   53804

Blue River, Grant Co., Pop. Code 2
Richland SD
Supt. – See Richland Center
Akan ES, RURAL ROUTE 02   53518
   Pricilla Williams, prin.

Riverdale SD
Supt. – See Muscoda
Riverdale MS, P O BOX 97   53518
   John Melby, prin.

ES, P O BOX 97 53518 – Joyce Schwingel, prin.
Excelsior MS, P O BOX 97 53518
   Elizabeth Smith, prin.

Bonduel, Shawano Co., Pop. Code 4
Bonduel SD
Sch. Sys. Enr. Code 3
Supt. – Lyman Franzwa 54107
ES 54107 – John Reinke, prin.
Navarino ES, RURAL ROUTE 01 54107
   Karl Prien, prin.

St. Paul Lutheran ES, 240 E GREEN BAY ST 54107

Boscobel, Grant Co., Pop. Code 5
Boscobel SD
Sch. Sys. Enr. Code 4
Supt. – Albert Vanovermeer
   208 E BLUFF ST 53805
MS, 300 BRINDLEY ST 53805 – Gene Larsen, prin.
ES, 200 BUCHANAN ST 53805
   William Hughes, prin.

Bowler, Shawano Co., Pop. Code 2
Bowler SD
Sch. Sys. Enr. Code 3
Supt. – Otto Kolpack 54416
ES 54416 – (—), prin.

Boyceville, Dunn Co., Pop. Code 3
Boyceville Comm. SD
Sch. Sys. Enr. Code 3
Supt. – Stewart Waller, P O BOX 98 54725
ES 54725 – Ted Bissell, prin.
Connorsville MS, RURAL ROUTE 02 54725
   Ted Bissell, prin.
Other Schools – See Wheeler

Boyd, Chippewa Co., Pop. Code 3
Stanley-Boyd Area SD
Supt. – See Stanley
ES 54726 – Boyd McLellan, prin.

Brandon, Fond du Lac Co., Pop. Code 3
Rosendale-Brandon SD
Supt. – See Rosendale
ES 53919 – Joseph Cramer, prin.

Waupun SD
Supt. – See Waupun
Amity ES, RURAL ROUTE 02 53919
   John Omdahl, prin.

Brill, Barron Co.
Rice Lake Area SD
Supt. – See Rice Lake
MS 54818 – William Carlson, prin.

Brillion, Calumet Co., Pop. Code 5
Brillion SD
Sch. Sys. Enr. Code 3
Supt. – Richard E. Walker, 315 S MAIN ST 54110
ES, 315 S MAIN ST 54110 – Gerald Novak, prin.
Other Schools – See Forest Junction

St. Mary's ES, 209 N CUSTER ST 54110
Trinity Evangelist Lutheran ES
   234 W WATER ST 54110

Bristol, Kenosha Co., Pop. Code 5
Bristol #1 SD
Sch. Sys. Enr. Code 2
Supt. – Gale Ryczek, 20121 83RD ST 53104
Bristol Consolidated North ES 53104
   (—), prin.

Brodhead, Green Co., Pop. Code 5
Brodhead SD
Sch. Sys. Enr. Code 4
Supt. – Gene Hamele, HIGHWAY 11 S 53520
MS, P O BOX 258 53520 – Tom Simonson, prin.
ES, P O BOX 258 53520 – Ronald Albrecht, prin.

Brookfield, Waukesha Co., Pop. Code 8
Elmbrook SD
Sch. Sys. Enr. Code 6
Supt. – Ronald E. Goedken, 13780 HOPE ST 53005
ES, 2530 N BROOKFIELD RD 53005
   Gerald Ristow, prin.
Burleigh ES, 16185 BURLEIGH PL 53005
   Ruth Jahnke, prin.
Hillside ES, 2250 N LYNETTE LN 53005
   Scott Netzel, prin.
Wisconsin Hills ES
   18700 W WISCONSIN AVE 53005
   Landis Knutson, prin.
Other Schools – See Elm Grove

Brookfield Academy
   3600 N BROOKFIELD ROAD 53005
Immanuel Lutheran ES, 4780 N 135TH ST 53005
St. Dominic Catholic ES
   18105 W CAPITOL DR 53005
St. John Vianney ES, 17500 GEBHARDT RD 53005
St. Luke Catholic ES, 1305 DAVIDSON RD 53005

Brooklyn, Green Co., Pop. Code 3
Oregon SD
Supt. – See Oregon
ES, 204 DIVISION ST 53521 – Gerald Zibell, prin.

Brooks, Adams Co.
Adams-Friendship Area SD
Supt. – See Adams
ES 53921 – Edith Hoppe, prin.

Brown Deer, Milwaukee Co., Pop. Code 7
Brown Deer SD
Sch. Sys. Enr. Code 4
Supt. – Kenneth C. Moe, 8200 N 60TH ST 53223
MS, 5757 W DEAN ROAD 53223
   Charles Radtke, prin.
Dean ES, 8355 N 55TH ST 53223
   Robert Rossow, prin.

Bruce, Rusk Co., Pop. Code 3
Bruce SD
Sch. Sys. Enr. Code 3
Supt. – Lee Paul 54819
ES 54819 – David Lindau, prin.
Other Schools – See Exeland

Brussels, Door Co., Pop. Code 3
Southern Door SD
Sch. Sys. Enr. Code 4
Supt. – Mead Hansen
   8401 STATE HWY 57 54204
South Door MS, 8401 STATE HWY 57 54204
   Michael Reinert, prin.
South Door ES 54204 – Michael Reinert, prin.

Burlington, Racine Co., Pop. Code 6
Burlington Area SD
Sch. Sys. Enr. Code 5
Supt. – Gary Fields, 100 N KANE ST 53105
MS, 201 S KENDRIC AVE 53105 – J. L. Gulla, prin.
Cooper ES, 249 CONKEY ST 53105
   Gary Olson, prin.
Waller ES, 195 GARDNER AVE 53105
   Joseph Schiestle, prin.
Winkler ES, RURAL ROUTE 07 BOX 632 53105
   Joseph Schiestle, prin.

Wheatland J1 SD
Sch. Sys. Enr. Code 2
Supt. – C. Scott Huth, 6606 368TH AVE 53105
Wheatland Center ES, 6606 368TH AVE 53105
   C. Scott Huth, prin.

St. Charles ES, 441 CONKEY ST 53105
St. John's Lutheran ES
   198 WESTRIDGE AVE 53105
St. Mary ES, 225 W STATE ST 53105

Butler, Waukesha Co., Pop. Code 4

St. Agnes Catholic ES
   12801 W FAIRMOUNT AVE 53007

Butternut, Ashland Co., Pop. Code 2
Butternut SD
Sch. Sys. Enr. Code 2
Supt. – David Welter, P O BOX 247 54514
ES, P O BOX 247 54514 – (—), prin.

Cable, Bayfield Co., Pop. Code 2
Drummond SD
Supt. – See Drummond
ES 54821 – D. Craig Yakes, prin.

Cadott, Chippewa Co., Pop. Code 4
Cadott Comm. SD
Sch. Sys. Enr. Code 4
Supt. – Robert Butterfield 54727
Cadott JHS, P O BOX 115 54727 – (—), prin.
ES 54727 – A. Patrick Mrotek, prin.

St. Joseph ES, P O BOX 84 54727

Caledonia, Racine Co., Pop. Code 7
Racine SD
Supt. – See Racine
Caddy Vista ES, 10010 CADDY LN 53108
   Kathryn Bruhn, prin.

St. Louis ES, 13125 HWY G RTE 01 53108
Trinity Lutheran ES
   7852 NICHOLSON ROAD RTE 2 53108

Cambria, Columbia Co., Pop. Code 3
Cambria-Friesland SD
Sch. Sys. Enr. Code 2
Supt. – Richard Kloiber 53923
MS 53923 – (—), prin.
Other Schools – See Friesland

Cambridge, Dane Co., Pop. Code 3
Cambridge SD
Sch. Sys. Enr. Code 3
Supt. – George R. Nikolay, P O BOX 27 53523
ES, P O BOX 27 53523 – Michael Buehler, prin.

Cameron, Barron Co., Pop. Code 4
Cameron SD
Sch. Sys. Enr. Code 3
Supt. – William McDougall 54822
ES 54822 – Gerald Peterson, prin.

Campbellsport, Fond du Lac Co., Pop. Code 4
Campbellsport SD
Sch. Sys. Enr. Code 4
Supt. – Joseph Bertone 53010
ES 53010 – Ben Eder, prin.
Other Schools – See Eden

Kewaskum SD
Supt. – See Kewaskum
Wayne ES, RURAL ROUTE 03 53010
   Thomas Larsen, prin.

St. Matthew's ES, 423 MILL ST 53010
Waucousta Lutheran ES
   RURAL ROUTE 03 BOX 2010 53010

Camp Douglas, Juneau Co., Pop. Code 3
Tomah Area SD
Supt. – See Tomah
ES 54618 – Jerry Bauer, prin.

Cascade, Sheboygan Co., Pop. Code 3
Plymouth SD
Supt. – See Plymouth
ES 53011 – (—), prin.
Parnell ES, RURAL ROUTE 01 53011
   (—), prin.

Cashton, Monroe Co., Pop. Code 3
Cashton SD
Sch. Sys. Enr. Code 3
Supt. – M. P. Healy, 540 COE ST 54619
ES 54619 – Marie Brueggen, prin.

Clinton Amish ES, RURAL ROUTE 03 54619

Cassville, Grant Co., Pop. Code 4
Cassville SD
Sch. Sys. Enr. Code 2
Supt. – (—), P O BOX 588 53806
ES, P O BOX 588 53806 – James Adams, prin.

St. Charles ES, 521 E DEWEY ST 53806

Cataract, Monroe Co.
Sparta Area SD
Supt. – See Sparta
ES 54620 – James Liska, prin.

Catawba, Price Co., Pop. Code 2
Phillips SD
Supt. – See Phillips
MS 54515 – Robert Spence, prin.

Cato, Manitowoc Co., Pop. Code 4

St. Mary's Parochial ES, 19 SO CTY J 54206

Cazenovia, Richland Co., Pop. Code 2
Weston SD
Sch. Sys. Enr. Code 2
Supt. – Bruce Lemery, RURAL ROUTE 02 53924
Weston MS, RURAL ROUTE 02 53924
   James Miller, prin.
ES, P O BOX 186 53924 – Marge Brown, prin.
Other Schools – See Hillpoint

Cedarburg, Ozaukee Co., Pop. Code 6
Cedarburg SD
Sch. Sys. Enr. Code 4
Supt. – Frank M. Kennedy
   W68-N611 EVERGREEN BLVD 53012
Webster MS, W75-N624 WAUWATOSA 53012
   Thomas Pautsch, prin.
Parkview ES, W72 N 853 HARRISON AVE 53012
   Amy Echelard, prin.
Thorson ES, W51 N932 KEUP RD 53012
   Alan Schultz, prin.

First Immanuel Lutheran ES
   W67 N622 EVERGREEN 53012
St. Francis Borgia ES
   N43 W6005 HAMILTON ROAD 53012

Cedar Grove, Sheboygan Co., Pop. Code 4
Cedar Grove-Belgium SD
Sch. Sys. Enr. Code 3
Supt. – Mary Bowden, 50 W UNION AVE 53013
MS 53013 – (—), prin.
ES, 120 VAN ALTENA AVE 53013
   Karla Sloan, prin.

Chaseburg, Vernon Co., Pop. Code 2
Westby Area SD
Supt. – See Westby
ES 54621 – Raymond Beck, prin.

Chetek, Barron Co., Pop. Code 4
Chetek SD
Sch. Sys. Enr. Code 4
Supt. – Robert Rykal, 1001 KNAPP ST 54728
MS, 1001 KNAPP ST 54728 – Leo Eckerman, prin.
Roselawn ES, 1201 6TH ST 54728
   Colleen Hickey, prin.

Chili, Clark Co.
Marshfield SD
Supt. – See Marshfield
East Fremont ES 54420 – Curtis Hanson, prin.

Chilton, Calumet Co., Pop. Code 5
Chilton SD
Sch. Sys. Enr. Code 4
Supt. – W. I. Demaster
   509 SCHOOL COURT 53014
ES, 421 COURT ST 53014 – Robert Garfield, prin.

Chilton Catholic ES
   60 E WASHINGTON ST 53014

Chippewa Falls, Chippewa Co., Pop. Code 7
Chippewa Falls Area SD
Sch. Sys. Enr. Code 5
Supt. – James Ramsdell, 1130 MILES ST 54729
First Ward ES, 1000 E GRAND AVE 54729
   Wayne Sievert, prin.
Halmstad ES, 565 E SOUTH AVE 54729
   James Dimock, prin.
Hillcrest ES, 1200 MILES ST 54729
   George Pehler, prin.
Korger Chestnut ES, 140 W ELM ST 54729
   Darold Isaacson, prin.
South View ES, A STREET 54729
   Wayne Sievert, prin.

Stillson ES, RURAL ROUTE 04   54729
    Larry Bommersbach, prin.
Other Schools – See Jim Falls

Holy Ghost ES, 436 S MAIN ST   54729
Notre Dame ES, 3 HIGH ST   54729
St. Charles Borromeo ES
    429 W SPRUCE ST   54729

Clayton, Polk Co., Pop. Code 2
Clayton SD
Sch. Sys. Enr. Code 2
Supt. – Alan Beeler   54004
ES   54004 – (—), prin.

Clear Lake, Polk Co., Pop. Code 3
Clear Lake SD
Sch. Sys. Enr. Code 3
Supt. – Ray H. Smith   54005
MS   54005 – Scott Clifton, prin.
ES   54005 – Gary Twining, prin.

Cleveland, Manitowoc Co., Pop. Code 4
Sheboygan Area SD
Supt. – See Sheboygan
ES, 411 E WASHINGTON AVE   53015
    Eric Oleson, prin.

Clinton, Rock Co., Pop. Code 4
Clinton Comm. SD
Sch. Sys. Enr. Code 4
Supt. – Robert L. Jensen   53525
MS   53525 – Roger T. Noe, prin.
ES   53525 – Georgiann McKenna, prin.

Clintonville, Waupaca Co., Pop. Code 5
Clintonville SD
Sch. Sys. Enr. Code 4
Supt. – Jerald Schoenike, 28 9TH ST   54929
Dellwood ES, N HARRIET STREET   54929
    (—), prin.
Longfellow ES, S CLINTON AVE   54929
    (—), prin.
Other Schools – See Bear Creek

St. Martin Lutheran ES
    100 S CLINTON AVE   54929
St. Rose ES, 140 AUTO ST   54929

Clyman, Dodge Co., Pop. Code 2
Dodgeland SD
Supt. – See Juneau
ES, P O BOX 26   53016 – Arland Weber, prin.

Cobb, Iowa Co., Pop. Code 2
Iowa-Grant SD
Supt. – See Livingston
ES   53526 – Francis Fry, prin.

Colby, Clark Co., Pop. Code 4
Colby SD
Sch. Sys. Enr. Code 4
Supt. – Lloyd Rueb   54421
ES, 202 W DOLF ST   54421 – Ervin Lafave, prin.
Other Schools – See Dorchester, Unity

St. Mary's ES, 205 S 2ND ST   54421

Coleman, Marinette Co., Pop. Code 3
Coleman SD
Sch. Sys. Enr. Code 3
Supt. – Clifford Robbins   54112
ES, P O BOX 242   54112 – Paul Morstad, prin.

Faith Christian School, P O BOX 258   54112

Colfax, Dunn Co., Pop. Code 4
Colfax SD
Sch. Sys. Enr. Code 3
Supt. – Lee Bjurquist, P O BOX 528   54730
ES   54730 – Gary Hoffman, prin.

Colgate, Washington Co.
Germantown SD
Supt. – See Germantown
Bell ES, 3294 WILLOW CREEK RD   53017
    Robert Wisdom, prin.

Coloma, Waushara Co., Pop. Code 2
Westfield SD
Supt. – See Westfield
ES   54930 – John Blader, prin.

Columbus, Columbia Co., Pop. Code 5
Columbus SD
Sch. Sys. Enr. Code 4
Supt. – Timothy Gavigan
    200 W SCHOOL ST   53925
MS, 400 S DICKASON BLVD   53925
    Wayne Bobholz, prin.
Dickason MS, 400 S DICKASON BLVD   53925
    Wayne Bobholz, prin.
Fuller Street ES, 200 FULLER ST   53925
    Nikki Mason, prin.
Hampden ES, RURAL ROUTE 01   53925
    Nikki Mason, prin.

St. Jerome Parochial ES, HWY 89   53925
Zion Lutheran ES, 822 WESTERN AVE   53925

Combined Locks, Outagamie Co., Pop. Code 3
Kimberly Area SD
Supt. – See Kimberly
Janssen ES, 420 WALLACE ST   54113
    James Juetten, prin.

Conover, Vilas Co., Pop. Code 3
Northland Pines SD
Supt. – See Eagle River
MS   54519 – Eugene Olson, prin.

Conrath, Rusk Co., Pop. Code 1
Flambeau SD
Supt. – See Tony
ES   54731 – Patricia Rohrbach, prin.

Coon Valley, Vernon Co., Pop. Code 3
Westby Area SD
Supt. – See Westby
ES   54623 – Raymond Beck, prin.

Cornell, Chippewa Co., Pop. Code 4
Cornell SD
Sch. Sys. Enr. Code 3
Supt. – Bernard H. Bennett, P O BOX 517   54732
ES, P O BOX 517   54732 – Marvin Shufelt, prin.

Cottage Grove, Dane Co., Pop. Code 3
Monona Grove SD
Supt. – See Monona
ES, 470 N MAIN ST   53527 – Gary Kopitzke, prin.

Crandon, Forest Co., Pop. Code 4
Crandon SD
Sch. Sys. Enr. Code 3
Supt. – Robert Jaeger
    100 N PROSPECT AVE   54520
ES, 203 E GLEN ST   54520 – Deward Ison, prin.
Mole Lake ES, RURAL ROUTE 01   54520
    John Gruber, prin.
Other Schools – See Argonne

Crivitz, Marinette Co., Pop. Code 4
Crivitz SD
Sch. Sys. Enr. Code 3
Supt. – Gordon Rieden, P O BOX 130   54114
MS   54114 – Eugene Chapman, prin.
ES   54114 – Eugene Chapman, prin.

Cross Plains, Dane Co., Pop. Code 4
Middleton-Cross Plains SD
Supt. – See Middleton
Park ES, 1209 PARK ST   53528
    George Ferge, prin.

St. Francis Xavier ES, 2939 THINNES ST   53528

Cuba City, Grant Co., Pop. Code 4
Cuba City SD
Sch. Sys. Enr. Code 3
Supt. – Daniel Pulsfus, 101 N SCHOOL ST   53807
ES, 518 W ROOSEVELT ST   53807
    Jerome Goeman, prin.
Other Schools – See Dickeyville

St. Rose ES, 218 JACKSON   53807

Cudahy, Milwaukee Co., Pop. Code 7
Cudahy SD
Sch. Sys. Enr. Code 5
Supt. – John Watson, 3744 E RAMSEY AVE   53110
Jones ES, 5845 S SWIFT AVE   53110
    Gary Schlunz, prin.
Kosciuszko ES, 5252 S KIRKWOOD AVE   53110
    Gary Schlunz, prin.
Lincoln ES, 4416 S PACKARD AVE   53110
    Richard Jeffery, prin.
Mitchell ES, 5950 S ILLINOIS AVE   53110
    Neal White, prin.
Parkview ES, 5555 S NICHOLSON AVE   53110
    William Emanuelson, prin.

Holy Family ES, 3776 E HAMMOND AVE   53110
St. Paul's Evangelist Lutheran ES
    3766 E CUDAHY AVE   53110

Cumberland, Barron Co., Pop. Code 4
Cumberland SD
Sch. Sys. Enr. Code 3
Supt. – Merwin Moen, 1000 8TH AVE   54829
MS, P O BOX 67   54829 – John Banks, prin.
ES, P O BOX 458   54829 – John Modjeski, prin.

Cushing, Polk Co.
St. Croix Falls SD
Supt. – See Saint Croix Falls
ES   54024 – Jeanette Ramstrom, prin.

Dairyland, Douglas Co., Pop. Code 2
Webster SD
Supt. – See Webster
ES   54830 – William Plath, prin.

Dallas, Barron Co.
Barron Area SD
Supt. – See Barron
MS, P O BOX 152   54733 – Gayle Dague, prin.

Danbury, Douglas Co.
Webster SD
Supt. – See Webster
ES   54830 – William Plath, prin.

Dane, Dane Co., Pop. Code 3
Lodi SD
Supt. – See Lodi
ES   53529 – Carol Tierney, prin.

Darien, Walworth Co., Pop. Code 4
Delavan-Darien SD
Supt. – See Delavan
ES   53114 – James Easterday, prin.

Darlington, Lafayette Co., Pop. Code 4
Darlington Comm. SD
Sch. Sys. Enr. Code 3
Supt. – Howard J. Friske
    11838 CENTER HILL ROAD   53530
JHS, 627 MAIN ST   53530 – Joseph Galle, prin.
MS, 627 MAIN ST   53530 – (—), prin.
Fayette ES, RURAL ROUTE 04   53530
    (—), prin.
Willow Springs ES, RURAL ROUTE 02   53530
    (—), prin.
Other Schools – See Shullsburg

Holy Rosary ES, 744 WELLS ST   53530

Deerbrook, Langlade Co.
Antigo SD
Supt. – See Antigo
River Grove ES, N5620 HWY H   54424
    Luella Fleischman, prin.

Deerfield, Dane Co., Pop. Code 4
Deerfield Comm. SD
Sch. Sys. Enr. Code 3
Supt. – Linda Barrows
    300 SIMONSON BLVD   53531
MS, 300 SIMONSON BLVD   53531 – (—), prin.
ES, 10 LIBERTY ST   53531 – Chuck Wedig, prin.

De Forest, Dane Co., Pop. Code 5
De Forest SD
Sch. Sys. Enr. Code 4
Supt. – Augusto Munoz, 210 N MAIN ST   53532
MS, 520 E HOLUM ST   53532
    Frederick Aronson, prin.
ES, 201 N CLEVELAND AVE   53532
    Kenneth Stevens, prin.
Other Schools – See Arlington, Madison,
    Morrisonville, Windsor

Delafield, Waukesha Co., Pop. Code 5
Kettle Moraine SD
Supt. – See Wales
Cushing MS, 227 N GENESEE ST   53018
    Nancy Blair, prin.

Delavan, Walworth Co., Pop. Code 6
Delavan-Darien SD
Sch. Sys. Enr. Code 4
Supt. – James Ticknor, 324 BELOIT ST   53115
Phoenix MS, 414 BELOIT ST   53115
    Donald Carpenter, prin.
Park ES, 317 S MAIN ST   53115
    Eugene Schmig, prin.
Wileman ES, 1001 E GENEVA ST   53115
    Eugene Schmig, prin.
Other Schools – See Darien

Delavan Christian ES, 820 OAK ST   53115
St. Andrew's ES, 115 S 7TH ST   53115

Denmark, Brown Co., Pop. Code 4
Denmark SD
Sch. Sys. Enr. Code 4
Supt. – James Renier, WALL ST   54208
JHS, WALL ST   54208 – Karen Bauknecht, prin.
ES, WALL ST   54208 – David Ewald, prin.

All Saints ES, P O BOX 488   54208

De Pere, Brown Co., Pop. Code 7
De Pere SD
Sch. Sys. Enr. Code 4
Supt. – Richard Yenchesky
    1700 CHICAGO ST   54115
MS, 615 S BROADWAY   54115
    James N. Phelan, prin.
Dickinson ES, 435 S WASHINGTON ST   54115
    Hugh Allen, prin.

West De Pere SD
Sch. Sys. Enr. Code 4
Supt. – Neal O. Richtman
    1155 WESTWOOD ST   54115
Lincoln ES, 670 MAIN AVE   54115
    James Bach, prin.
Westwood MS, 1155 WESTWOOD ST   54115
    James Bach, prin.

Notre Dame Consolidated ES
    221 S WISCONSIN ST   54115
Notre Dame ES, 100 S HURON ST   54115
St. Boniface ES, 405 GRANT ST   54115
St. Joseph ES, 1307 LOURDES AVE   54115

De Soto, Crawford Co., Pop. Code 2
DeSoto Area SD
Sch. Sys. Enr. Code 3
Supt. – Robert Peterson   54624
JHS   54624 – (—), prin.
Prairie View ES, RFD   54624
    Robert Schnell, prin.
Other Schools – See Stoddard

Dickeyville, Grant Co., Pop. Code 4
Cuba City SD
Supt. – See Cuba City
ES   53808 – Jerome Goeman, prin.

Holy Ghost ES, P O BOX 40   53808

Dodgeville, Iowa Co., Pop. Code 5
Dodgeville SD
Sch. Sys. Enr. Code 4
Supt. – David Westhoff
    912 W CHAPPELL ST   53533

MS, 325 W CHAPPEL ST 53533
Bruce Rundle, prin.
ES, 404 N JOHNSON ST 53533
Paul Godfrey, prin.
Other Schools – See Ridgeway

St. Joseph ES, 305 E WALNUT ST 53533

Dorchester, Clark Co., Pop. Code 3
Colby SD
Supt. – See Colby
ES 54425 – Ervin Lafave, prin.

Dousman, Waukesha Co., Pop. Code 4
Kettle Moraine SD
Supt. – See Wales
Kettle Moraine MS, 301 E OTTAWA AVE 53118
R. B. DeBoer, prin.
ES, 341 E OTTAWA AVE 53118
Peter Christensen, prin.

St. Bruno ES, 246 W OTTAWA AVE 53118

Downsville, Dunn Co.
Menomonie Area SD
Supt. – See Menomonie
ES 54735 – Thomas Mangin, prin.

Dresser, Polk Co., Pop. Code 3
St. Croix Falls SD
Supt. – See Saint Croix Falls
ES 54009 – Donna Swenson, prin.

Drummond, Bayfield Co., Pop. Code 2
Drummond SD
Sch. Sys. Enr. Code 2
Supt. – James Adams, P O BOX 40 54832
Other Schools – See Cable

Durand, Pepin Co., Pop. Code 4
Durand SD
Sch. Sys. Enr. Code 4
Supt. – Vaughn Hoffman, 511 7TH AVE E 54736
HS, 604 7TH AVE E 54736 – Thomas Casey, prin.
MS, 604 7TH AVE E 54736 – (—), prin.
ES, CITY VIEW 54736 – Thomas Casey, prin.
Other Schools – See Mondovi

St. Mary's ES, 901 W PROSPECT ST 54736

Eagle, Waukesha Co., Pop. Code 4
Mukwonago SD
Supt. – See Mukwonago
Eagleville ES, RURAL ROUTE 02 53119
James Grimyser, prin.

Palmyra-Eagle Area SD
Supt. – See Palmyra
ES, P O BOX 8 53119 – Donna Kalnes, prin.

Eagle River, Vilas Co., Pop. Code 4
Northland Pines SD
Sch. Sys. Enr. Code 4
Supt. – Jann Peterson, EAGLE BLDG 54521
Northland Pines MS 54521
Thomas Thielke, prin.
ES 54521 – Eugene Olson, prin.
Other Schools – See Conover, Land O Lakes, Saint Germain

Eastman, Crawford Co., Pop. Code 2
Prairie Du Chien Area SD
Supt. – See Prairie Du Chien
ES 54626 – Merle Frommelt, prin.

Seneca SD
Supt. – See Seneca
South MS, RURAL ROUTE 01 54626
Joseph Zoeller, prin.

East Troy, Walworth Co., Pop. Code 4
East Troy Comm. SD
Sch. Sys. Enr. Code 4
Supt. – H. J. Brossard, P O BOX 137 53120
MS, P O BOX 587 53120
L. Patrick Showalter, prin.
ES, P O BOX 257 53120 – William Pokel, prin.
Stone ES, RURAL ROUTE 01 53120
(—), prin.
Troy Center ES, RURAL ROUTE 01 53120
(—), prin.

St. Peter ES, 3001 ELM ST 53120

Eau Claire, Eau Claire Co., Pop. Code 8
Eau Claire Area SD
Sch. Sys. Enr. Code 7
Supt. – Dr. Marvin Lansing, 500 MAIN ST 54701
Arlington Heights ES, 2025 KEITH ST 54701
Kimberly Hill, prin.
Black MS, 1519 PETERSON AVE 54703
Jane Robertson, prin.
Boyd ES, 1105 MAIN ST 54701
Mary Milbrandt, prin.
Davey ES, 3000 STARR AVE 54703
Robert Dawson, prin.
Lincoln ES, 1712 BABCOCK ST 54703
Richard Starnauld, prin.
Little Red ES, RURAL ROUTE 04 54701
Kim Hagen, prin.
Locust Lane ES, 3245 LOCUST LN 54703
Jacqueline Belka, prin.
Longfellow ES, 512 BALCOM ST 54703
Alvin Lechleitner, prin.
Lowes Creek ES, 1029 E LOWES CREED RD 54701
Mary Milbrandt, prin.

Manz ES, 1000 E FILLMORE AVE 54701
Terrance Sheridan, prin.
Mckinley ES, 1266 MCKINLEY RD 54703
Jane Robertson, prin.
Mount Washington ES
1710 MENOMONIE ST 54703 – Kim Hagen, prin.
Park ES, 1606 PARK AVE 54701
Kimberly Hill, prin.
Putnam Heights ES
633 W MACARTHUR AVE 54701
Richard Savolainen, prin.
Randall ES, 506 5TH AVE 54703
Donald Skamfer, prin.
Robbins ES, 3832 E HAMILTON AVE 54701
Patricia Popple, prin.
Roosevelt ES, 3010 8TH ST 54703
Roger Barstad, prin.
Sherman ES, 3110 VINE ST 54703
Susan Fitzsimons, prin.
Other Schools – See Eleva, Fall Creek

Eau Claire Lutheran School
1223 BELLINGER STREET 54703
Immaculate Conception ES
1703 SHERWIN AVE 54701
Sacred Heart ES, 418 N DEWEY ST 54703
St. James the Greater ES, 2502 11TH ST 54703
St. Olaf ES, 2407 NORTH LN 54703
St. Patrick's ES, 322 FULTON ST 54703

Eden, Fond du Lac Co., Pop. Code 3
Campbellsport SD
Supt. – See Campbellsport
ES 53019 – Thomas Koyen, prin.

St. Mary's ES, P O BOX 98 53019

Edgar, Marathon Co., Pop. Code 4
Edgar SD
Sch. Sys. Enr. Code 3
Supt. – Barkley Anderson 54426
ES, P O BOX 198 54426
Robert Christianson, prin.

St. John ES, P O BOX 66 54426

Edgerton, Rock Co., Pop. Code 5
Edgerton SD
Sch. Sys. Enr. Code 4
Supt. – K. F. Williams
200 ELM HIGH DRIVE 53534
MS, 116 SWIFT ST 53534 – Larry D. Miller, prin.
Edgerton Community ES
100 ELM HIGH DR 53534 – Donald Granger, prin.

Eland, Shawano Co., Pop. Code 2
Wittenberg-Birnamwood SD
Supt. – See Wittenberg
MS 54427 – Mark Flynn, prin.

Elcho, Langlade Co., Pop. Code 4
Elcho SD
Sch. Sys. Enr. Code 2
Supt. – Paul Roberts 54428
ES 54428 – (—), prin.

Elderon, Marathon Co., Pop. Code 2
Wittenberg-Birnamwood SD
Supt. – See Wittenberg
ES 54429 – Gordon Geurink, prin.

Eleva, Trempealeau Co., Pop. Code 3
Eau Claire Area SD
Supt. – See Eau Claire
Cleghorn ES, RURAL ROUTE 01 54738
Gayle Kleppe, prin.

Eleva-Strum SD
Supt. – See Strum
MS 54738 – (—), prin.

Elkhart Lake, Sheboygan Co., Pop. Code 4
Elkhart Lake-Glenbeul SD
Sch. Sys. Enr. Code 3
Supt. – David Magar, 201 N LINCOLN 53020
Other Schools – See Glenbeulah

Elkhorn, Walworth Co., Pop. Code 5
Elkhorn Area SD
Sch. Sys. Enr. Code 4
Supt. – Tony Serpe, 1887 BUILDING 53121
Elkhorn Area MS
JACKSON AT WALWORTH 53121
Robert Crist, prin.
Tibbets ES, RURAL ROUTE 02 53121
Clifford Schiefelbein, prin.
Westside ES, SUNSET DR 53121
Clifford Schiefelbein, prin.

St. Patrick ES, 529 SUNSET DR 53121

Elk Mound, Dunn Co., Pop. Code 3
Elk Mound Area SD
Sch. Sys. Enr. Code 3
Supt. – William J. Vincent 54739
MS 54739 – Delphine Rogalla, prin.
Springbrook ES, RURAL ROUTE 01 54739
Delphine Rogalla, prin.

Ellsworth, Pierce Co., Pop. Code 4
Ellsworth Comm. SD
Sch. Sys. Enr. Code 4
Supt. – Eugene Swanson, HILLCREST ST 54011
Hillcrest ES, 350 S GRANT 54011
Michael Perkins, prin.

Sunnyside ES, RURAL ROUTE 02 54011
Michael Perkins, prin.
Other Schools – See Hager City

St. Francis School, 244 WOODWORTH ST 54011

Elm Grove, Waukesha Co., Pop. Code 6
Elmbrook SD
Supt. – See Brookfield
MS, 1500 PILGRIM PARKWAY 53122
Donald Van Buskirk, prin.
Tonawanda ES, 13605 UNDERWOOD PKY 53122
Roger Bottoni, prin.

Elm Grove Lutheran ES, 945 TERRACE DR 53122
St. Mary ES, 13000 JUNEAU BLVD 53122

Elmwood, Pierce Co., Pop. Code 3
Elmwood SD
Sch. Sys. Enr. Code 2
Supt. – Frederic Schmit 54740
ES 54740 – (—), prin.

Elroy, Juneau Co., Pop. Code 4
Elroy-Kendall-Wilton SD
Sch. Sys. Enr. Code 4
Supt. – Allen Schraufnagel, ACADEMY ST 53929
ES, 2ND MAIN ST 53929 – Warren Brown, prin.
Other Schools – See Kendall, Wilton

Endeavor, Marquette Co., Pop. Code 2
Portage Comm. SD
Supt. – See Portage
ES 53930 – Russell Schultz, prin.

Ettrick, Trempealeau Co., Pop. Code 2
Galesville-Ettrick SD
Supt. – See Galesville
ES 54627 – Marvin Baures, prin.

Evansville, Rock Co., Pop. Code 5
Evansville Comm. SD
Sch. Sys. Enr. Code 4
Supt. – Thomas Benzinger, 321 S 1ST ST 53536
MS, 315 S 1ST ST 53636 – Vincent Maloney, prin.
ES, 401 S 3RD ST 53536 – Susan Masterson, prin.

Exeland, Sawyer Co., Pop. Code 2
Bruce SD
Supt. – See Bruce
ES 54835 – Norman Rademaker, prin.

Fairchild, Eau Claire Co., Pop. Code 3
Osseo-Fairchild SD
Supt. – See Osseo
ES 54741 – James Sutherland, prin.

Fall Creek, Eau Claire Co., Pop. Code 4
Eau Claire Area SD
Supt. – See Eau Claire
Brackett ES, 9480 USH 53 54742
Gayle Kleppe, prin.

Fall Creek SD
Sch. Sys. Enr. Code 3
Supt. – J. C. Kling, 336 E HOOVER AVE 54742
MS, 142 E WASHINGTON AVE 54742
Gregg Butler, prin.
ES, 242 E HOOVER AVE 54742
James Smith, prin.

Fall River, Columbia Co., Pop. Code 3
Fall River SD
Sch. Sys. Enr. Code 2
Supt. – Steven Rubert, P O BOX 116 53932
ES 53932 – (—), prin.

Fennimore, Grant Co., Pop. Code 4
Fennimore Comm. SD
Sch. Sys. Enr. Code 3
Supt. – Edgar Ryun, 1397 9TH ST 53809
ES, 830 MADISON ST 53809 – Lyle Lang, prin.

Florence, Florence Co., Pop. Code 4
Florence SD
Sch. Sys. Enr. Code 3
Supt. – Kenneth Brittingham 54121
ES, P O BOX 440 54121 – Gary Osterberg, prin.
Other Schools – See Niagara

Fond du Lac, Fond du Lac Co., Pop. Code 8
Fond Du Lac SD
Sch. Sys. Enr. Code 6
Supt. – Alan Osterndorf
72 S PORTLAND ST 54935
Chegwin ES, 109 E MERRILL AVE 54935
S. Ellen Ritchie, prin.
Evans ES, 140 PETERS AVE 54935
Alice Murphy, prin.
Franklin ES, 401 S MILITARY RD 54935
Eugene Harter, prin.
Lakeshore ES, 706 PRAIRIE RD 54935
John Theis, prin.
Parkside ES, 475 W ARNDT ST 54935
Delmar Coburn, prin.
Pier ES, 259 OLD PIONEER RD 54935
Harold Breit, prin.
Roberts ES, 270 CANDY LN 54935
Jerome Sullivan, prin.
Rosenow ES, 290 WEIS AVE 54935
Lydell Newby, prin.
Waters ES, 495 WABASH AVE 54935
Helen Stone, prin.

North Fond Du Lac SD
Supt. – See North Fond du Lac
Elmwood ES, 2213 W SCOTT ST 54935
Richard Carleton, prin.

Faith Lutheran ES
  55 N PRAIRIE ROAD ROUTE 6   54935
Redeemer Lutheran ES, 606 FOREST AVE   54935
SS Louis & Patrick ES, 37 E FOLLETT ST   54935
SS Mary & Joseph ES, 92 AMORY ST   54935
St. Peter's Lutheran ES, 35 E 2ND ST   54935

Fontana, Walworth Co., Pop. Code 4
Fontana J8 SD
  Sch. Sys. Enr. Code 2
  Supt. – Daniel Misner   53125
  ES   53125 – Daniel Misner, prin.

Footville, Rock Co., Pop. Code 3
Parkview SD
  Supt. – See Orfordville
  ES, P O BOX 327   53537 – Margarite Hamele, prin.

Forest Junction, Calumet Co.
Brillion SD
  Supt. – See Brillion
  MS   54123 – Harold Bertrand, prin.

Fort Atkinson, Jefferson Co., Pop. Code 6
Fort Atkinson SD
  Sch. Sys. Enr. Code 4
  Supt. – Gerald McGowen, 317 S HIGH ST   53538
  Luther JHS, 201 PARK ST   53538
    William Moran, prin.
  Barrie ES, 1000 HARRIETTE ST   53538
    Corliss Deets, prin.
  Purdy ES, 710 S AMIN ST   53538
    Russell Stevens, prin.
  Rockwell ES, 820 MONROE ST   53538
    Pauline Nikolay, prin.

St. Joseph ES, 310 N MAIN ST   53538
St. Paul's Evangelist Lutheran ES
  309 BLUFF ST   53538

Fountain City, Buffalo Co., Pop. Code 3
Cochrane-Fountain City SD
  Sch. Sys. Enr. Code 3
  Supt. – James Larson   54629
  Cochrane Fountain ES   54629
    Kenneth Wald, prin.

Fox Lake, Dodge Co., Pop. Code 4
Waupun SD
  Supt. – See Waupun
  ES, 200 DEPOT ST   53933 – Phillip Posard, prin.

Francis Creek, Manitowoc Co., Pop. Code 3

St. Anne School, 202 PACKER DR   54214

Franklin, Milwaukee Co., Pop. Code 7
Franklin SD
  Sch. Sys. Enr. Code 4
  Supt. – H. E. Guzniczak, P O BOX 307   53132
  Forest Park MS, 8225 W FOREST HILL AVE   53132
    Richard Pladies, prin.
  Country Dale ES, 7380 S N CAPE RD   53132
    Doug Rosenbecker, prin.
  ES, 8050 S 76TH ST   53132 – James Trotier, prin.
  Pleasant View ES
    4601 W MARQUETTE AVE   53132
    Karl Wegerbauer, prin.
  Robinwood ES, 10705 W ROBINWOOD LN   53132
    D. Anderson, prin.

Jubilee Christian School, 7509 S 27TH ST   53132
Sacred Hearts ES, 7933 S 116TH ST   53132
St. Paul's Lutheran ES, 6881 S 51ST ST   53132

Franksville, Racine Co.
Norway J7 SD
  Sch. Sys. Enr. Code 2
  Supt. – Loren Englund
    21016 7 MILE ROAD   53126
  Drought ES, 21016 7 MILE RD   53126
    Loren Englund, prin.

Raymond #14 SD
  Sch. Sys. Enr. Code 2
  Supt. – John Di Padova, 2659 76TH ST   53126
  Raymond ES, 2659 76TH ST   53126
    John Di Padova, prin.

Raymond J1 SD
  Sch. Sys. Enr. Code 2
  Supt. – Warren Beltz, 11926 HIGHWAY K   53126
  North Cape ES, 11926 HWY K   53126
    Donald Hafeman, prin.

Frederic, Polk Co., Pop. Code 4
Frederic SD
  Sch. Sys. Enr. Code 3
  Supt. – Wallace Koel   54837
  ES   54837 – Thomas Twining, prin.

Fredonia, Ozaukee Co., Pop. Code 4
Northern Ozaukee SD
  Sch. Sys. Enr. Code 3
  Supt. – Frank Parsons, 401 HIGHLAND DR   53021
  Ozaukee MS, 401 HIGHLAND DR   53021
    Thomas R. Maurer, prin.
  Maple Lawn ES, 242 FREDONIA AVE   53021
    Maryanna Meikrantz, prin.
  Other Schools – See Waubeka

Freedom, Outagamie Co., Pop. Code 5
Freedom Area SD
  Sch. Sys. Enr. Code 4
  Supt. – Gary Scheverell, P O BOX 101   54130
  JHS, P O BOX 1008   54131 – (—), prin.
  ES   54131 – Gerald Hedtke, prin.

St. Nicholas ES, P O BOX 1022   54131

Fremont, Waupaca Co., Pop. Code 3
Weyauwega-Fremont SD
  Supt. – See Weyauwega
  ES, P O BOX 308   54940 – Quintin Urban, prin.

Friendship, Adams Co., Pop. Code 3
Adams-Friendship Area SD
  Supt. – See Adams
  MS   53934 – Robert Showalter, prin.
  Pine Land ES, RURAL ROUTE 01   53934
    Lynn Hoernke, prin.

Friesland, Columbia Co., Pop. Code 2
Cambria-Friesland SD
  Supt. – See Cambria
  ES   53935 – Richard Lovett, prin.

Galesville, Trempealeau Co., Pop. Code 4
Galesville-Ettrick SD
  Sch. Sys. Enr. Code 4
  Supt. – R. J. Howard   54630
  ES   54630 – Marvin Baures, prin.
  Other Schools – See Ettrick, Trempealeau

Gays Mills, Crawford Co., Pop. Code 3
North Crawford SD
  Sch. Sys. Enr. Code 3
  Supt. – Michael Cox, P O BOX 68   54631
  Haney ES, RURAL ROUTE 02   54631
    John Lynch, prin.
  Other Schools – See Mount Sterling, Soldiers Grove

Genesee Depot, Waukesha Co., Pop. Code 6
Kettle Moraine SD
  Supt. – See Wales
  Magee ES, P O BOX 37   53127 – John Hanold, prin.

St. Paul ES   53127

Genoa City, Walworth Co., Pop. Code 4
Genoa City J2 SD
  Sch. Sys. Enr. Code 4
  Supt. – Paul Weber, KOSSUTH STREET   53128
  Brookwood ES, KOSSUTH ST   53128
    Jan Chambers, prin.

Germantown, Washington Co., Pop. Code 7
Germantown SD
  Sch. Sys. Enr. Code 5
  Supt. – William Josten
    N 104 W 13840 DONGES BAY RD   53022
  Kennedy MS
    W 160 N 11836 WASHINGTON ST   53022
    Jack Burant, prin.
  County Line ES
    W159N9939 SCHOOL ROAD   53022
    Richard Pautz, prin.
  MacArthur ES
    W154N11492 FOND DU LAC AVE   53022
    Anthony Clementi, prin.
  Other Schools – See Colgate, Richfield

St. Boniface ES
  W204 N11968 GOLDENLE ROAD   53022

Gillett, Oconto Co., Pop. Code 4
Gillett SD
  Sch. Sys. Enr. Code 3
  Supt. – Warren Eiseth   54124
  JHS   54124 – (—), prin.
  ES   54124 – Robert Hruska, prin.

Gilman, Tayor Co., Pop. Code 2
Gilman SD
  Sch. Sys. Enr. Code 3
  Supt. – Richard Stokes   54433
  ES   54433 – (—), prin.
  Jump River ES, W 14574 HWY 73   54433
    (—), prin.

Gilmanton, Buffalo Co., Pop. Code 2
Gilmanton SD
  Sch. Sys. Enr. Code 2
  Supt. – Glen Denk   54743
  Dover MS, P O BOX 28   54743
    Barbara Plank, prin.
  ES, P O BOX 28   54743 – Orla Sather, prin.

Gleason, Lincoln Co.
Merrill Area SD
  Supt. – See Merrill
  Midway ES, RURAL ROUTE 02   54435
    Thomas Genisot, prin.

Glenbeulah, Sheboygan Co., Pop. Code 2
Elkhart Lake-Glenbeul SD
  Supt. – See Elkhart Lake
  MS   53023 – Carlos Kreibich, prin.

Glen Flora, Rusk Co., Pop. Code 1
Flambeau SD
  Supt. – See Tony
  ES   54526 – Leon Warren, prin.

Glenwood City, St. Croix Co., Pop. Code 3
Glenwood City SD
  Sch. Sys. Enr. Code 3
  Supt. – Wallace L. Lindholm
    HIGHWAY 170   54013
  MS   54013 – Julian Bender, prin.
  MS, 3RD & OAK STS   54013
    Nancy Dimberio, prin.
  Saint Johns ES   54013 – Nancy Dimberio, prin.

Glidden, Ashland Co., Pop. Code 3
Glidden SD
  Sch. Sys. Enr. Code 2
  Supt. – Walter Mehr   54527
  ES   54527 – Walter Mehr, prin.

Goodman, Marinette Co., Pop. Code 3
Goodman-Armstrong SD
  Sch. Sys. Enr. Code 2
  Supt. – John Long, 7TH & MAIN   54125
  Goodman Armstrong ES
    CORNER 4TH & MAIN   54125 – (—), prin.

Grafton, Ozaukee Co., Pop. Code 6
Grafton SD
  Sch. Sys. Enr. Code 4
  Supt. – Edward Eckhardt
    1900 WASHINGTON ST   53024
  Long MS, 700 HICKORY ST   53024
    Donald Krueger, prin.
  ES, 1900 WASHINGTON ST   53024
    Michael Wifler, prin.
  Kennedy ES, 1629 11TH AVE   53024
    Alfred Lund, prin.
  Woodview ES, 600 5TH AVE   53024
    Irvin Luisier, prin.

St. Joseph ES, 1210 16TH AVE   53024
St. Paul Lutheran ES
  701 WASHINGTON ST   53024

Grand Marsh, Adams Co.
Adams-Friendship Area SD
  Supt. – See Adams
  MS   53936 – Jack Davies, prin.
  Lincoln ES, RURAL ROUTE 01   53936
    Harriet Dehlinger, prin.

Granton, Clark Co., Pop. Code 2
Granton Area SD
  Sch. Sys. Enr. Code 2
  Supt. – Roland M. Krueger   54436
  ES   54436 – Gordon Port, prin.

Grantsburg, Burnett Co., Pop. Code 4
Grantsburg SD
  Sch. Sys. Enr. Code 3
  Supt. – Merlin A. Johnson   54840
  MS   54840 – William A. Stapp, prin.
  ES   54840 – Byron Kopp, prin.
  Nelson MS, RURAL ROUTE 01   54840
    Clayton Jorgensen, prin.

Gratiot, Lafayette Co., Pop. Code 2
Black Hawk SD
  Supt. – See South Wayne
  Black Hawk MS   53541 – Jerry Mortimer, prin.
  ES   53541 – Harriett Rowe, prin.

Green Bay, Brown Co., Pop. Code 8
Ashwaubenon SD
  Sch. Sys. Enr. Code 5
  Supt. – Lawrence Heyerdahl
    1055 GRIFFITHS LANE   54304
  Parkview MS, 955 WILLARD DRIVE   54304
    Paul Kane, prin.
  Pioneer ES, 1360 PONDEROSA AVE   54313
    Wayne Bloch, prin.
  Valley View ES, 2200 TRUE LN   54304
    Corinne Gariepy, prin.

Green Bay SD
  Sch. Sys. Enr. Code 7
  Supt. – Lyle Martens, P O BOX 1387   54305
  Edison MS, 442 ALPINE DRIVE   54302
    Michael Hermans, prin.
  Franklin MS, 1234 W MASON ST   54303
    Vernon L. Schahczenski, prin.
  Lombardi MS, 1520 S POINT ROAD   54303
    Wayne D. Astin, prin.
  Washington MS, 314 S BAIRD ST   54301
    Jack T. Landes, prin.
  Allouez MS, 116 W ALLOUEZ AVE   54301
    Donald Dickinson, prin.
  Baird ES, 539 LAVERNE DR   54311
    Charles Decker, prin.
  Beaumont ES, 1505 GATEWOOD ST   54304
    James Wotruba, prin.
  Chappell ES, 205 N FISK ST   54303
    Kenneth Krueger, prin.
  Danz ES, 2130 BASTEN ST   54302
    Robert Blomiley, prin.
  Doty ES, 525 LONGVIEW AVE   54301
    Roger Winnie, prin.
  Eisenhower ES, 1770 AMY ST   54302
    James Anderson, prin.
  Elmore ES, 615 ETHEL AVE   54303
    Donald Bunker, prin.
  Fort Howard ES, 520 DOUSMAN ST   54303
    Gayle Frame, prin.
  Howe ES, 525 S MADISON ST   54301
    Margaret Hutchison, prin.
  Jackson ES, 1306 S RIDGE RD   54304
    Robert Deprey, prin.
  Keller ES, 1806 BOND ST   54303
    Rosemary Baloun, prin.
  Kennedy ES, 1754 NINTH ST   54304
    John Jirikovec, prin.
  Langlade ES, 400 BROADVIEW DR   54301
    Wayne Johnston, prin.
  Lincoln ES, 1105 SHAWANO AVE   54303
    Patrick Manning, prin.
  Mac Arthur ES, 1331 HOBART DR   54304
    Theodore Herzog, prin.
  Martin ES, 626 PINEHURST AVE   54302
    Merton Mueller, prin.

Nicolet ES, 600 N IRWIN AVE 54302
  Michael Reinert, prin.
Sullivan ES, 1567 DECKNER AVE 54302
  Graydon Axtell, prin.
Tank ES, 814 S OAKLAND AVE 54304
  Robert Kohl, prin.
Webster ES, 2101 S WEBSTER AVE 54301
  Donald Dickinson, prin.
Wequiock ES, RURAL ROUTE 01 54301
  Robert Blomiley, prin.

Howard-Suamico SD
Sch. Sys. Enr. Code 5
Supt. – Fredrick Stieg
  2700 LINEVILLE ROAD 54303
Bay View MS, 2700 LINEVILLE ROAD 54303
  Gordon Maki, prin.
Hillcrest Heights ES, 720 HILLCREST DR 54313
  Elmer Perala, prin.
Howard ES, 631 W IDLEWILD CT 54303
  Anthony Plansky, prin.
Suamico Central ES, RURAL ROUTE 04 54303
  Anthony Plansky, prin.

Pulaski Comm. SD
Supt. – See Pulaski
Lannoye ES, RURAL ROUTE 05 54301
  Bernard Olejniczak, prin.

Annunciation ES, 1087 KELLOGG ST 54303
Catholic Central ES, 640 S IRWIN AVE 54301
Green Bay Christian ES
  139 S MONROE AVE 54301
Holy Family ES, 1204 S FISK ST 54304
Holy Martyrs of Gorcum ES
  3542 FINGER RD 54311
Pilgrim Lutheran ES, 1731 ST AGNES DR 54304
Redeemer Lutheran ES, 205 HUDSON ST 54303
Resurrection ES, 333 HILLTOP DR 54301
SS Peter & Paul ES, 1420 HARVEY ST 54302
St. Bernard ES, 2020 HILLSIDE LN 54302
St. John the Baptist ES
  2561 GLENDALE AVE 54313
St. Joseph ES, 1224 TWELFTH AVE 54304
St. Jude ES, 1420 DIVISION ST 54303
St. Mark Evangelist Lutheran ES
  1167 KENWOOD ST 54304
St. Mary of Angles ES, 650 S IRWIN AVE 54301
St. Matthew ES, 2575 S WEBSTER AVE 54301
St. Philip's ES, 312 VICTORIA ST 54302

Greendale, Milwaukee Co., Pop. Code 7
Greendale SD
Sch. Sys. Enr. Code 5
Supt. – William D. Knapp, 5900 S 51ST ST 53129
MS, 6800 SCHOOLWAY 53129
  Charles Herman, prin.
Canterbury ES, 7000 ENFIELD AVE 53129
  Carolyn Krueger, prin.
College Park ES, 5701 W COLLEGE AVE 53129
  Jeanne Backes, prin.
Highland View ES, 5900 S 51ST ST 53129
  John Mortonson, prin.

St. Alphonsus ES, 6000 W LOOMIS RD 53129

Greenfield, Milwaukee Co., Pop. Code 8
Greenfield SD
Sch. Sys. Enr. Code 5
Supt. – Ronald C. Wojack
  3200 W BARNARD AVE 53221
MS, 3200 W BARNARD AVE 53221
  Clifford Sheldon, prin.
Edgewood ES, 4711 S 47TH ST 53220
  Donald Sickels, prin.
Glenwood ES, 3550 S 51ST ST 53220
  Dale Arsnow, prin.
Maple Grove ES, 6921 W COLD SPRING RD 53220
  James Ander, prin.
Other Schools – See Milwaukee

Whitnall SD
Sch. Sys. Enr. Code 4
Supt. – William Hittman, 5000 S 116TH ST 53228
Whitnall MS, 5025 S 116TH ST 53228
  Brian McCormack, prin.
Other Schools – See Hales Corners

St. Jacobi Lutheran ES
  8605 W FOREST HOME AVE 53228
St. John Evangelist ES
  8500 W COLD SPRING RD 53228

Green Lake, Green Lake Co., Pop. Code 4
Green Lake SD
Sch. Sys. Enr. Code 2
Supt. – Philip Baranowski, 612 MILL ST 54941
ES, P O BOX 369 54941 – (—), prin.

Greenleaf, Brown Co.

Zion Lutheran School-Wayside
  RURAL ROUTE 01 BOX 238 54126

Greenwood, Clark Co., Pop. Code 4
Greenwood SD
Sch. Sys. Enr. Code 3
Supt. – John Kammerud
  209 S HENDREN AVE 54437
ES 54437 – Wayne Ledin, prin.

Gresham, Shawano Co., Pop. Code 3
Shawano-Gresham SD
Supt. – See Shawano
ES 54128 – Robert Kurkiewicz, prin.

Hager City, Pierce Co.
Ellsworth Comm. SD
Supt. – See Ellsworth
Lindgren ES, RURAL ROUTE 01 54014
  Michael Perkins, prin.
Prairie View ES, RURAL ROUTE 01 54014
  Michael Perkins, prin.

Hales Corners, Milwaukee Co., Pop. Code 6
Muskego-Norway SD
Supt. – See Muskego
Tess Corners ES
  W147 S6800 DURHAM DR 53130
  Arnit Beske, prin.

Whitnall SD
Supt. – See Greenfield
ES, 11319 W GODSELL AVE 53130
  Joanne Kania, prin.

Hales Corners Lutheran ES
  5409 S 111TH ST 53130
St. Mary Parish ES
  9553 W EDGERTON AVE 53130

Hamburg, Marathon Co., Pop. Code 3
Merrill Area SD
Supt. – See Merrill
Maple Grove ES, RURAL ROUTE 01 54438
  Richard Monka, prin.

Wausau SD
Supt. – See Wausau
Berlin ES, RURAL ROUTE 01 54438
  George Klinker, prin.

Hammond, St. Croix Co., Pop. Code 3
St. Croix Central SD
Sch. Sys. Enr. Code 3
Supt. – Dan Woll 54015
Saint Croix JHS 54015 – (—), prin.
Other Schools – See Roberts

Harshaw, Oneida Co.
Rhinelander SD
Supt. – See Rhinelander
Cassian Woodboro ES 54529 – Erik Larsen, prin.

Hartford, Washington Co., Pop. Code 6
Erin #2 SD
Sch. Sys. Enr. Code 2
Supt. – Donald Hanrahan
  1697 HIGHWAY OO 53027
Erin ES, 1697 HYW O 53027 – (—), prin.

Hartford Jt. 1 SD
Sch. Sys. Enr. Code 4
Supt. – Glenn Broker, 600 HIGHLAND AVE 53027
Central MS, 60 MILL ST 53027
  Phillip May, prin.
Lincoln ES, 755 S RURAL ST 53027
  Mary Jensen, prin.
Rossman ES, 600 HIGHLAND AVE 53027
  Richard Harry, prin.

Richfield Jt. 11 SD
Supt. – See Hubertus
St. Augustine ES, 1810 HWY CC 53027
  (—), prin.

Peace Lutheran ES
  1025 PEACE LUTHERAN DR 53027
St. Kilian ES, 245 HIGH ST 53027

Hartland, Waukesha Co., Pop. Code 6
Hartland-Lakeside J3 SD
Sch. Sys. Enr. Code 4
Supt. – Patrick Kness
  651 E IMPERIAL DRIVE 53029
Hartland North MS, 232 CHURCH ST 53029
  John Lillethun, prin.
Hartland South MS, 651 E IMPERIAL DR 53029
  Timothy Kooi, prin.
Other Schools – See Pewaukee

Merton J8 SD
Sch. Sys. Enr. Code 2
Supt. – Heidi Schweizer
  W299 N5614 HIGHWAY E 53029
Swallow ES, W299 N5614 HWY E 53029
  (—), prin.

Nashotah-Delafield J1 SD
Supt. – See Nashotah
Bark River ES, 3325 HWY 83 53029
  Bernard Stankewicz, prin.

University Lake School, P O BOX 337 53029
Divine Redeemer Lutheran ES
  31385 W HILL ROAD 53029
St. Charles ES, 526 RENSON RD 53029

Hatley, Marathon Co., Pop. Code 2
D. C. Everest Area SD
Supt. – See Schofield
MS 54440 – Nancy Caskey, prin.

St. Florians ES, 500 CHURCH LN 54440

Haugen, Barron Co., Pop. Code 2
Rice Lake Area SD
Supt. – See Rice Lake
ES 54841 – Marjorie Johnson, prin.

Hawkins, Rusk Co., Pop. Code 2
Ladysmith-Hawkins SD
Supt. – See Ladysmith
ES 54530 – Mike Milutinovich, prin.

Hayward, Sawyer Co., Pop. Code 4
Hayward Comm. SD
Sch. Sys. Enr. Code 4
Supt. – Jack R. White, 316 W 5TH ST 54843
MS, 316 W 5TH ST 54843 – Douglas Beck, prin.
ES, 701 N IOWA AVE 54843
  Victor Wekkin, prin.
Other Schools – See Stone Lake

Ojibwa School, RURAL ROUTE 02 54843

Hazel Green, Grant Co., Pop. Code 4
Southwestern Wisconsin SD
Sch. Sys. Enr. Code 3
Supt. – Norbert Kalinosky, P O BOX 368 53811
Southwestern ES 53811 – Michael Hogan, prin.

Herbster, Bayfield Co.
South Shore SD
Supt. – See Port Wing
ES 54844 – Fred Schlichting, prin.

Highland, Iowa Co., Pop. Code 3
Highland SD
Sch. Sys. Enr. Code 2
Supt. – Ruthann Faber, P O BOX 285 53543
ES 53543 – Shirley Klar, prin.

Hilbert, Calumet Co., Pop. Code 4
Hilbert SD
Sch. Sys. Enr. Code 2
Supt. – F. W. Holewinski, 132 8TH ST 54129
ES, 132 EIGHTH ST 54129 – Martha Albers, prin.

Hillpoint, Sauk Co.
Weston SD
Supt. – See Cazenovia
Pine Crest MS, RFD 53937 – Edward Borton, prin.

Hillsboro, Vernon Co., Pop. Code 4
Hillsboro SD
Sch. Sys. Enr. Code 3
Supt. – Mark Heyerdahl 54634
City ES, 853 HILLSBOROUGH AVE 54634
  James Hoffman, prin.

Hingham, Sheboygan Co.
Oostburg SD
Supt. – See Oostburg
ES, RURAL ROUTE 01 53031 – Robert Shaul, prin.

Hixton, Jackson Co., Pop. Code 2
Black River Falls SD
Supt. – See Black River Falls
ES, 162 ELDER ST 54635 – Carlyle Button, prin.

Holcombe, Chippewa Co., Pop. Code 3
Lake Holcombe SD
Sch. Sys. Enr. Code 2
Supt. – Denis Kirkman, P O BOX 40 54745
ES, P O BOX 40 54745 – Don Lapp, prin.

Hollandale, Iowa Co., Pop. Code 2
Pecatonica SD
Supt. – See Blanchardville
Pecontonica ES 53544 – (—), prin.

Holmen, LaCrosse Co., Pop. Code 4
Holmen SD
Sch. Sys. Enr. Code 4
Supt. – Donald Jacobson
MS 54636 – Peter Tabor, prin.
Evergreen ES 54636 – Michael Smith, prin.
Oak Grove ES 54636 – Michael Smith, prin.
Viking ES 54636 – (—), prin.

Horicon, Dodge Co., Pop. Code 5
Horicon SD
Sch. Sys. Enr. Code 4
Supt. – Donald B. Mayo, 611 MILL ST 53032
MS, 611 MILL ST 53032 – Larry Ballwahn, prin.
ES, 611 MILL ST 53032 – Larry Ballwahn, prin.

St. Stephen's Lutheran ES
  505 N PALMATORY ST 53032

Hortonville, Outagamie Co., Pop. Code 4
Hortonville SD
Sch. Sys. Enr. Code 4
Supt. – Marvin Obry, 246 OLK ST 54944
ES, 246 OLK ST 54944 – Eugene Riedl, prin.

Bethlehem Evangelist Lutheran ES
  P O BOX 298 54944
SS Peter & Paul ES, 107 OLK ST 54944

Howards Grove, Sheboygan Co., Pop. Code 4
Howards Grove SD
Sch. Sys. Enr. Code 3
Supt. – Ronald E. Albert
  437 N WISCONSIN DRIVE 53081
Other Schools – See Sheboygan

Hubertus, Washington Co.
Richfield Jt. 11 SD
Sch. Sys. Enr. Code 2
Supt. – Richard Martzke, 1750 HIGHWAY J 53033
Friess Lake MS, 1750 HIGHWAY J 53033
  (—), prin.
Other Schools – See Hartford

St. Hubert ES, 3733 HUBERTUS RD 53033

Hudson, St. Croix Co., Pop. Code 6
Hudson SD
Sch. Sys. Enr. Code 5
Supt. – Ronald Rice, 416 SAINT CROIX ST 54016

Fourth Street ES, 4TH ST   54016
  Toby Garey, prin.
MS, 5TH & SAINT CROIX   54016
  William Hickox, prin.
North Hudson ES, 510 LEMON ST N   54016
  Toby Garey, prin.
Rock ES, SUMMER ST   54016 – Mary Kenne, prin.

St. Patrick's Catholic ES
  4TH AND SAINT CROIX   54016

Hurley, Iron Co., Pop. Code 4
Hurley SD
  Sch. Sys. Enr. Code 3
  Supt. – Roger Myren, P O BOX 157   54534
  South Side ES, 4TH AVE N   54534
    Lawrence Sobolewski, prin.
  Other Schools – See Montreal

St. Mary Seven Dolors ES, 205 5TH AVE S   54534

Hustisford, Dodge Co., Pop. Code 3
Hustisford SD
  Sch. Sys. Enr. Code 2
  Supt. – Roger Moore, P O BOX 326   53034
  ES, P O BOX 326   53034 – Roger Moore, prin.

Bethany Lutheran ES, P O BOX 374   53034

Independence, Trempealeau Co., Pop. Code 4
Independence SD
  Sch. Sys. Enr. Code 2
  Supt. – Dunae Sackett   54747
  ES   54747 – (—), prin.

SS Peter & Paul ES, 400 OSSEO RD   54747

Iola, Waupaca Co., Pop. Code 3
Iola-Scandinavia SD
  Sch. Sys. Enr. Code 3
  Supt. – Robert Crase   54945
  Iola Scandinavia ES   54945 – Robert Crase, prin.

Iron Ridge, Dodge Co., Pop. Code 3
Mayville SD
  Supt. – See Mayville
  Southview ES, RURAL ROUTE 01   53035
    Pat John, prin.

St. Matthew's Lutheran ES
  308 HERMAN ST   53035

Iron River, Bayfield Co., Pop. Code 3
Maple SD
  Supt. – See Maple
  ES   54847 – Thomas Peterson, prin.

South Shore SD
  Supt. – See Port Wing
  Oulu ES   54847 – Fred Schlichting, prin.

Ixonia, Jefferson Co., Pop. Code 5
Oconomowoc Area SD
  Supt. – See Oconomowoc
  ES   53036 – Robert Krause, prin.

Jackson, Washington Co., Pop. Code 4
West Bend SD
  Supt. – See West Bend
  ES   53037 – Janice King, prin.

Davids Star Evangelical Lutheran ES
  1401 WESTERN AVE   53037

Janesville, Rock Co., Pop. Code 8
Janesville SD
  Sch. Sys. Enr. Code 6
  Supt. – Donald Mrdjenovich
    527 S FRANKLIN ST   53545
  Adams ES, 1138 E MEMORIAL DR   53545
    Edward Connors, prin.
  Harrison ES, 760 PRINCETON RD   53546
    Wayne Flury, prin.
  Jackson ES, 441 BURBANK AVE   53546
    Helen Johns, prin.
  Jefferson ES, 1831 MOUNT ZION AVE   53545
    Jon Cousins, prin.
  Lincoln ES, 1835 S OAKHILL AVE   53545
    Dwane Kamla, prin.
  Madison ES, 331 N GRANT AVE   53545
    Niel Bender, prin.
  Monroe ES, 55 S PONTIAC DR   53545
    Patrick Meehan, prin.
  Roosevelt ES, 316 S RINGOLD ST   53545
    Edna Anderson, prin.
  Van Buren ES, 1515 LAPHAM ST   53545
    Jack Hackett, prin.
  Washington ES, 811 N PINE ST   53545
    James Bromley, prin.
  Wilson ES, 465 ROCKPORT RD   53545
    Norman Graper, prin.

Milton SD
  Supt. – See Milton
Janesville Consolidated ES
  RURAL ROUTE 06   53545 – Terry Risch, prin.

St. John Vianney ES, 1301 CLARK ST   53545
St. Mary ES, 307 E WALL ST   53545
St. Matthew's Lutheran ES
  709 MILTON AVE   53545
St. Patrick ES, 305 LINCOLN ST   53545
St. Pauls Lutheran School
  210 S RINGOLD ST   53545
St. Williams ES, 1822 RAVINE ST   53545

Jefferson, Jefferson Co., Pop. Code 6
Jefferson SD
  Sch. Sys. Enr. Code 4
  Supt. – Thomas Shepro, 206 S TAFT AVE   53549
  MS, 201 S COPELAND AVE   53549
    Allan D. Peters, prin.
  Jefferson East ES, 120 S SANBORN AVE   53549
    Wayne Sheil, prin.
  Jefferson West ES, 900 W MILWAUKEE ST   53549
    William Bluege, prin.
  Other Schools – See Sullivan

St. John the Baptist ES, 333 E CHURCH ST   53549
St. John's Evangelist Lutheran ES
  232 E CHURCH ST   53549

Jim Falls, Chippewa Co.
Chippewa Falls Area SD
  Supt. – See Chippewa Falls
  ES, RURAL ROUTE 01   54748 – Jon Hagen, prin.

Johnson Creek, Jefferson Co., Pop. Code 4
Johnson Creek SD
  Sch. Sys. Enr. Code 3
  Supt. – Allan Schaefer, 111 SOUTH ST   53038
  ES, 111 SOUTH ST   53038 – (—), prin.

Juda, Green Co.
Juda SD
  Sch. Sys. Enr. Code 2
  Supt. – Gordon Mortensen   53550
  ES   53550 – Scott Johnson, prin.

Junction City, Portage Co., Pop. Code 3
Stevens Point Area SD
  Supt. – See Stevens Point
  Kennedy ES   54443 – Steve Bogaczyk, prin.

Juneau, Dodge Co., Pop. Code 4
Beaver Dam SD
  Supt. – See Beaver Dam
  Hyland Praire MS, N6688 HIGHPOINT RD   53039
    Claryn Glewen, prin.

Dodgeland SD
  Sch. Sys. Enr. Code 3
  Supt. – Frederick Lampe, 302 S MAIN ST   53039
  ES, 302 S MAIN ST   53039 – Barbara Auten, prin.
  Other Schools – See Clyman, Lowell, Reeseville

St. John's Christian Day ES, 402 S MAIN ST   53039

Kansasville, Racine Co.
Brighton #1 SD
  Sch. Sys. Enr. Code 2
  Supt. – Gerald Mullins, RURAL ROUTE 01   53139
  Brighton ES, 1200 248TH AVE   53139
    Gerald Mullins, prin.

Dover #1 SD
  Sch. Sys. Enr. Code 1
  Supt. – Russ Clouse
    4101 S BEAUMONT AVE   53139
  ES, 4101 S BEAUMONT AVE   53139
    Russ Clouse, prin.

Kaukauna, Outagamie Co., Pop. Code 7
Kaukauna Area SD
  Sch. Sys. Enr. Code 5
  Supt. – Harold Goetz, 101 OAK ST   54130
  Nicolet ES, 109 E 8TH ST   54130
    John Moore, prin.
  Park ES, 509 LAWE ST   54130
    Sheldon Niquette, prin.
  Quinney ES, 2601 SULLIVAN AVE   54130
    Paul Haehlke, prin.
  Victor Haen ES, HAEN DR   54130
    Bernard Schmitt, prin.

Holy Cross ES, 220 DOTY ST   54130
St. Aloysius ES, 2401 MAIN AVE   54130
St. Mary ES, 112 W 8TH ST   54130
Trinity Lutheran ES, 800 AUGUSTINE ST   54130

Kendall, Monroe Co., Pop. Code 2
Elroy-Kendall-Wilton SD
  Supt. – See Elroy
  ES   54638 – George Vukich, prin.

Kennan, Price Co., Pop. Code 2
Phillips SD
  Supt. – See Phillips
  ES   54537 – Robert Spence, prin.

Kenosha, Kenosha Co., Pop. Code 8
Kenosha SD
  Sch. Sys. Enr. Code 7
  Supt. – John J. Hosmanek, 3600 52 ST   53142
  Bain ES, 2210 52ND ST   53140
    Blane McCann, prin.
  Bose ES, 1900 15TH ST   53140 – Gary Gayan, prin.
  Durkee ES, 839 62ND ST   53140
    James Marescalco, prin.
  Forest Park ES, 6810 45TH AVE   53142
    Richard Guttormsen, prin.
  Frank ES, 1816 57TH ST   53140
    Rosaria Jermanotta, prin.
  Grant ES, 1716 35TH ST   53140
    Stephen Blazevich, prin.
  Grewenow ES, 7714 20TH AVE   53140
    John Fountain, Jr., prin.
  Harvey ES, 2012 19TH AVE   53140
    Stephen Relich, prin.
  Jefferson ES, 1832 43RD ST   53140
    Linda Neilson, prin.
  Jeffery ES, 4011 87TH ST   53142
    Willis Zuberbuehler, prin.

Lincoln ES, 6811 18TH AVE   53140
  Leotis Swopes, prin.
Mckinley ES, 5520 32ND AVE   53142
  Patricia Hoffman, prin.
Pleasant Prairie ES, 9208 WILMOT RD   53142
  Charles Nelson, prin.
Prairie Lane ES, 10717 47TH AVE   53142
  Peter Pingitore, prin.
Roosevelt ES, 3322 ROOSEVELT RD   53142
  Richard Baas, prin.
Southport ES, 723 76TH ST   53140
  Michael Thome, prin.
Strange ES, 5414 49TH AVE   53142
  Lawrence Maurer, prin.
Vernon ES, 8518 22ND AVE   53140
  Robert Debelak, prin.
Vernon Wing ES, 8518 22ND AVE   53140
  Robert Debelak, prin.
Whittier ES, 8542 51ST AVE   53142
  Willis Zuberbuehler, prin.
Wilson ES, 4520 33RD AVE   53142
  Nora Ratliff, prin.
Other Schools – See Somers

Paris J1 SD
  Sch. Sys. Enr. Code 2
  Supt. – Conrad Chaffee, 1901 176TH AVE   53142
  Paris Consolidated ES, 1901 176TH AVE   53142
    (—), prin.

Christian Life School
  6009 PERSHING BLVD   53142
Bethany Lutheran Day ES, 2100 75TH ST   53140
Friedens Lutheran ES, 5043 20TH AVE   53140
Holy Rosary ES, 4400 22ND AVE   53140
Mt. Carmel ES, 5400 19TH AVE   53140
St. Casimir ES, 1011 WASHINGTON RD   53140
St. Mark ES, 7207 14TH AVE   53140
St. Mary's Catholic ES, 7400 39TH AVE   53142
St. Peter's ES, 2224 30TH AVE   53142
St. Therese ES, 2030 91ST ST   53140
St. Thomas ES, 6218 25TH AVE   53140

Keshena, Menominee Co., Pop. Code 2
Menominee Indian SD
  Sch. Sys. Enr. Code 3
  Supt. – Roger Klumb, P O BOX 399   54135
  Menominee JHS   54135 – (—), prin.
  ES   54135 – Jesse Stratton, prin.
  Other Schools – See Neopit

Kewaskum, Washington Co., Pop. Code 4
Kewaskum SD
  Sch. Sys. Enr. Code 4
  Supt. – Penelope Kleinhans, P O BOX 37   53040
  MS, P O BOX 432   53040 – Julie Backus, prin.
  Farmington ES
    RURAL ROUTE 01 BOX 8736   53040
    Thomas Larsen, prin.
  ES, 1550 REIGLE DR   53040
    Richard Zarling, prin.
  Other Schools – See Campbellsport

Holy Trinity ES, P O BOX 464   53040
St. Lucas ES, P O BOX 86   53040

Kewaunee, Kewaunee Co., Pop. Code 5
Kewaunee SD
  Sch. Sys. Enr. Code 4
  Supt. – R. F. Plantico, 911 3RD ST   54216
  Marquette MS, 317 DORELLE ST   54216
    Roy Stone, prin.
  Hillcrest ES, 915 2ND ST   54216 – Roy Stone, prin.

Holy Rosary ES, 519 KILBOURN ST   54216

Kiel, Calumet Co., Pop. Code 5
Kiel Area SD
  Sch. Sys. Enr. Code 4
  Supt. – Don Mattox, 210 RAIDER HEIGHTS   53042
  MS, 502 PAINE ST   53042 – Wayne Krueger, prin.
  Zielanis ES, ADAMS & NORTH ST   53042
    Marlys Gross, prin.
  Other Schools – See Newton

SS Peter & Paul ES, 423 FREMONT ST   53042

Kieler, Grant Co.

Immaculate Conception ES, P O BOX 109   53812

Kimberly, Outagamie Co., Pop. Code 6
Kimberly Area SD
  Sch. Sys. Enr. Code 4
  Supt. – Albert Brown
    217 E KIMBERLY AVE   54136
  JHS, 125 E KIMBERLY AVE   54136
    Edward Wulgaert, prin.
  Westside ES, 746 W 3RD ST   54136
    James Juetten, prin.
  Other Schools – See Combined Locks

Holy Name Of Jesus ES
  614 E KIMBERLY AVE   54136

Knapp, Dunn Co., Pop. Code 2
Menomonie Area SD
  Supt. – See Menomonie
  ES   54749 – Donald Heifner, prin.

Kohler, Sheboygan Co., Pop. Code 4
Kohler SD
  Sch. Sys. Enr. Code 3
  Supt. – John Egan, 230 SCHOOL ST   53044
  ES, 230 SCHOOL ST   53044 – John Egan, prin.

Krakow, Shawano Co.
Pulaski Comm. SD
Supt. – See Pulaski
Fairview ES, 2840 HWY 32   54137
James Brawner, prin.

Lac Du Flambeau, Vilas Co., Pop. Code 4
Lac Du Flambeau #1 SD
Sch. Sys. Enr. Code 2
Supt. – Alden Bauman, P O BOX 189   54538
Lac Du Flambeau ES, P O BOX 189   54538
Alden Bauman, prin.

La Crosse, La Crosse Co., Pop. Code 1
La Crosse SD
Sch. Sys. Enr. Code 6
Supt. – Richard A. Swantz
807 EAST AVE S   54601
Lincoln MS, 9TH & DIVISION   54601
A. K. Bassuener, prin.
Logan MS, LOGAN & AVON   54601
Roger Fish, prin.
Longfellow MS, 19TH & DENTON   54601
Melvin Jenkins, prin.
Emerson ES, 21ST & CAMPBELL RD   54601
Thomas Brobeck, prin.
Franklin ES, KANE & GILLETTE   54601
Terry Witzke, prin.
Hamilton ES, 1111 7TH ST S   54601
Hallie Marshall, prin.
Hintgen ES, 3505 28TH ST S   54601
Elmer Grassman, prin.
Jefferson ES, ST JAMES & CALEDONIA   54601
Jay Thurston, prin.
Roosevelt ES, WOOD & HAYES   54601
Tarry Hall, prin.
Spence ES, 22ND & BENNETT   54601
(—), prin.
State Road ES, 2350 HAGEN RD   54601
Jane Durham, prin.
Summit ES, 1800 LAKESHORE DR   54603
Mary McKnight, prin.

Blessed Sacrament ES, 2404 KING ST   54601
Cathedral ES, 13TH & FERRY ST   54601
First Evangelist Lutheran ES
520 WEST AVE S   54601
Holy Trinity Catholic ES, 1417 13TH ST S   54601
Mt. Calvary Lutheran ES, 1614 PARK AVE   54601
St. James ES, AVON & WINDSOR   54603
St. Pius X ES, 3710 EAST AVE S   54601
St. Thomas More ES, 20TH & WESTON STS   54601

Ladysmith, Rusk Co., Pop. Code 5
Ladysmith-Hawkins SD
Sch. Sys. Enr. Code 4
Supt. – William Bobbe   54848
MS, 115 E 6TH ST S   54848 – Robert Bricco, prin.
ES, LINDOO AND 6TH   54848
Marshall Frillici, prin.
Other Schools – See Hawkins

Our Lady of Sorrows ES
105 WASHINGTON AVE   54848

La Farge, Vernon Co., Pop. Code 3
La Farge SD
Sch. Sys. Enr. Code 2
Supt. – Paul Jacobson   54639
ES   54639 – Paul Jacobson, prin.

Lake Geneva, Walworth Co., Pop. Code 6
Geneva J4 SD
Sch. Sys. Enr. Code 1
Supt. – Robert Johnson
RURAL ROUTE 04 BOX 2000   53147
Woods ES, RURAL ROUTE 04 BOX 2000   53147
Robert Johnson, prin.

Lake Geneva Jt. 1 SD
Sch. Sys. Enr. Code 4
Supt. – Harry Van Dyke, 818 GENEVA ST   53147
Denison MS, 900 WISCONSIN ST   53147
(—), prin.
Central ES, 900 WISCONSIN ST   53147
Leo Baker, prin.
Eastview ES, SAGE ST   53147
Hollis Herbison, prin.
Star Center ES, RURAL ROUTE 03   53147
Tom Kwiatkowski, prin.

Linn J4 SD
Sch. Sys. Enr. Code 1
Supt. – Robert H. Schroeder
RURAL ROUTE 01   53147
Traver ES, RURAL ROUTE 01   53147
(—), prin.

Linn J6 SD
Sch. Sys. Enr. Code 2
Supt. – (—), RURAL ROUTE 01   53147
Reek ES, RURAL ROUTE 01   53147
Sharon Pankow, prin.

St. Francis DeSales ES, 130 W MAIN ST   53147

Lake Mills, Jefferson Co., Pop. Code 5
Lake Mills Area SD
Sch. Sys. Enr. Code 4
Supt. – Jon E. Litscher, 209 CHURCH ST   53551
MS, 318 COLLEGE ST   53551
Patrick Curtin, prin.
Prospect Street ES, 135 E PROSPECT ST   53551
Joseph Vanderzanden, prin.

St. Paul Evangelist Lutheran ES
229 FREMONT ST   53551

Lake Nebagamon, Douglas Co., Pop. Code 3
Maple SD
Supt. – See Maple
ES   54849 – Barbara Anderson, prin.

Lancaster, Grant Co., Pop. Code 5
Lancaster Comm. SD
Sch. Sys. Enr. Code 4
Supt. – Dan Dahlgren, 236 W MAPLE ST   53813
MS, 925 W MAPLE ST   53813
Marlin E. Phillips, prin.
Winskill ES, 861 W MAPLE ST   53813
Thomas Davies, prin.

St. Clement ES, 333 W CHERRY STREET   53813

Land O Lakes, Vilas Co., Pop. Code 3
Northland Pines SD
Supt. – See Eagle River
ES   54540 – Eugene Olson, prin.

Lannon, Waukesha Co., Pop. Code 3
Hamilton SD
Supt. – See Sussex
ES, P O BOX 376   53046
Sylvester Racinowski, prin.

St. John Lutheran ES
20813 W FOREST VIEW DR   53046

Laona, Forest Co., Pop. Code 4
Laona SD
Sch. Sys. Enr. Code 2
Supt. – Glenn Detro, FOREST AVE   54541
Robinson ES, FOREST AVE   54541 – (—), prin.

La Pointe, Ashland Co., Pop. Code 2
Bayfield SD
Supt. – See Bayfield
MS   54850 – John Anderson, prin.

Larsen, Winnebago Co.
Winneconne Comm. SD
Supt. – See Winneconne
Winchester ES, RURAL ROUTE 01   54947
Kenneth Schleinz, prin.

La Valle, Sauk Co., Pop. Code 2
Reedsburg SD
Supt. – See Reedsburg
Irontown La Valle ES   53941 – Paul Rosholt, prin.

Lena, Oconto Co., Pop. Code 3
Lena SD
Sch. Sys. Enr. Code 2
Supt. – Ray Artz   54139
MS   54139 – (—), prin.
ES   54139 – Ray Artz, prin.

Oconto Falls SD
Supt. – See Oconto Falls
Spruce ES, RURAL ROUTE 01   54139
Barbara Natelle, prin.

St. Charles Catholic ES, P O BOX 30   54139

Lily, Langlade Co.
Antigo SD
Supt. – See Antigo
ES   54445 – Sandra Gallagher, prin.

Little Chute, Outagamie Co., Pop. Code 6
Little Chute Area SD
Sch. Sys. Enr. Code 6
Supt. – Mark Stone, 1402 FREEDOM ROAD   54140
MS, 329 GRAND AVE   54140
Donald L. Bangert, prin.
ES, 625 GRAND AVE   54140
Barbara Neuhengen, prin.

St. John ES, 328 GRAND AVE   54140

Little Suamico, Oconto Co., Pop. Code 4
Oconto Falls SD
Supt. – See Oconto Falls
ES   54141 – Thomas Lutz, prin.

Livingston, Grant Co., Pop. Code 3
Iowa-Grant SD
Sch. Sys. Enr. Code 3
Supt. – J. Bruce Bradley, RURAL ROUTE 01   53554
ES   53554 – Paul Messling, prin.
Other Schools – See Cobb, Montfort, Rewey

Lodi, Columbia Co., Pop. Code 4
Lodi SD
Sch. Sys. Enr. Code 4
Supt. – John Sauerberg, 206 S MAIN ST   53555
MS, 101 SCHOOL ST   53555
John Casey Hurley, prin.
ES, 103 PLEASANT ST   53555
Carol Tierney, prin.
Other Schools – See Dane

Loganville, Sauk Co., Pop. Code 2
Reedsburg SD
Supt. – See Reedsburg
ES   53943 – Mary Liegel, prin.

Lomira, Dodge Co., Pop. Code 4
Lomira SD
Sch. Sys. Enr. Code 3
Supt. – John C. Mason   53048
JHS   53048 – (—), prin.
ES   53048 – Peter Runde, prin.

Other Schools – See Theresa

Consolidated Catholic ES
699 MILWAUKEE ST   53048

Lone Rock, Richland Co., Pop. Code 3
River Valley SD
Supt. – See Spring Green
ES   53556 – (—), prin.

Lowell, Dodge Co., Pop. Code 2
Dodgeland SD
Supt. – See Juneau
ES, P O BOX 429   53557 – Helen Petrich, prin.

Loyal, Clark Co., Pop. Code 4
Loyal SD
Sch. Sys. Enr. Code 3
Supt. – David Miskulin   54446
JHS   54446 – James Batchelor, prin.
ES   54446 – Lawrence Halida, prin.

St. Anthony ES, 212 W SPRING ST   54446

Luck, Polk Co., Pop. Code 3
Luck SD
Sch. Sys. Enr. Code 3
Supt. – Allen Ormson   54853
ES   54853 – John Nichols, prin.

Luxemburg, Kewaunee Co., Pop. Code 4
Luxemburg-Casco SD
Sch. Sys. Enr. Code 4
Supt. – Raymond A. Thillman, P O BOX 10   54217
Luxemburg-Casco ES, P O BOX 70   54217
Steven Pearson, prin.

St. Mary's ES, RURAL ROUTE 03 BOX 16   54217

Lyndon Station, Juneau Co., Pop. Code 2
Mauston SD
Supt. – See Mauston
ES   53944 – Frank Harrington, prin.

Lynxville, Crawford Co., Pop. Code 2
Seneca SD
Supt. – See Seneca
ES   53640 – Joseph Zoeller, prin.

Madison, Dane Co., Pop. Code 9
De Forest SD
Supt. – See De Forest
Pumpkin Hollow ES, 3956 HOEPKER RD   53704
Deborah Fritsch, prin.

Madison Metro SD
Sch. Sys. Enr. Code 7
Supt. – E. James Travis, 545 W DAYTON ST   53703
Cherokee Hts. MS, 4301 CHEROKEE DRIVE   53711
Donna Chandler, prin.
Gompers MS, 1402 WYOMING WAY   53704
Rollie Willan, prin.
Jefferson MS, 101 S GAMMON ROAD   53705
Roger Cerutti, prin.
Marquette MS, 510 S THORNTON AVE   53703
Michael Owens, prin.
Orchard Ridge MS, 5602 RUSSETT ROAD   53711
John Horton, prin.
Schenk MS, 230 SCHENK ST   53714
Robert Pellegrino, prin.
Sennett MS, 502 PFLAUM ROAD   53716
Samuel Barosko, prin.
Van Hise MS, 4801 WAUKESHA ST   53705
Marvin Meissen, prin.
Allis ES, 4201 BUCKEYE RD   53716
Allen Pease, prin.
Crestwood ES, 5930 OLD SAUK RD   53705
Joanne Yatvin, prin.
Elvehjem ES, 5106 ACADEMY DR   53716
Michael Mahaffey, prin.
Emerson ES, 2421 E JOHNSON ST   53704
Stephan Kailin, prin.
Falk ES, 6323 WOODINGTON WAY   53711
Jerry Dowden, prin.
Franklin ES, 305 W LAKESIDE ST   53715
Durward McVey, prin.
Glendale ES, 1201 TOMPKINS DR   53716
Joseph Cullen, prin.
Gompers ES, 1402 WYOMING WAY   53704
Harlan Siebrecht, prin.
Huegel ES, 2601 PRAIRIE RD   53711
Victor Mutter, prin.
Kennedy ES, 221 MEADOWLARK DR   53714
Jerry Johnson, prin.
Lake View ES, 1802 TENNYSON LN   53704
Eugene Sturdevant, prin.
Leopold ES, 2602 POST RD   53713
Donald Stern, prin.
Lincoln ES, 909 SEQUOIA TRL   53713
Merle Sweet, prin.
Lindbergh ES, 4500 KENNEDY RD   53704
Jack Moore, prin.
Lowell ES, 401 MAPLE AVE   53704
Jerrold Johnson, prin.
Marquette ES, 1501 JENIFER ST   53703
Nancy Haugen, prin.
Mendota ES, 4002 SCHOOL RD   53704
Donald Stoddard, prin.
Midvale ES, 502 CAROMAR DR   53711
Kathleen Marty, prin.
Muir ES, 6602 INNER DR   53705
Leonard Rush, prin.
Orchard Ridge ES, 5602 RUSSETT RD   53711
Margaret Planner, prin.
Randall MS, 1802 REGENT ST   53705
James Griffin, prin.

Sandberg ES, 4114 DONALD DR   53704
  Joanne Marshall, prin.
Schenk ES, 230 SCHENK ST   53714
  Richard Dickman, prin.
Shorewood Hills ES
  1105 SHOREWOOD BLVD   53705
  Eric Webb, prin.
Stephens ES, 120 S ROSA RD   53705
  Darlene Hancock, prin.
Thoreau ES, 3870 NAKOMA RD   53711
  Alice Benn, prin.
Van Hise ES, 4747 WAUKESHA ST   53705
  Booker Gardner, prin.

Verona Area SD
  Supt. – See Verona
Maple Grove ES, 3210 MAPLE GROVE DR   53719
  (—), prin.

Abundant Life Christian School
  4909 E BUCKEYE ROAD   53716
Blessed Sacrament ES
  2112 HOLLISTER AVE   53705
Eastside Evangelist Lutheran ES
  2310 INDEPENDENCE LN   53704
Edgewood Campus ES
  2324 EDGEWOOD DR   53711
Holy Cross Lutheran ES
  2670 MILWAUKEE ST   53704
Our Lady Queen of Peace ES
  418 HOLLY AVE   53711
St. Dennis ES, 409 DEMPSEY RD   53714
St. James ES, 1204 SAINT JAMES CT   53715
St. Maria Goretti ES, 5405 FLAD AVE   53711
Wingra ES Inc, 3200 MONROE ST   53711

Manawa, Waupaca Co., Pop. Code 4
Manawa SD
  Sch. Sys. Enr. Code 3
  Supt. – Douglas Smith, 585 E 4TH ST   54949
MS, 627 DEPOT ST   54949 – John Fossum, prin.
ES, P O BOX 400   54949 – John Fossum, prin.

St. Paul's Lutheran ES
  RURAL ROUTE 02 BOX 62   54949

Manchester, Green Lake Co., Pop. Code 3
Markesan SD
  Supt. – See Markesan
ES   53945 – Alice Kuehn, prin.

Manitowish Wtrs, Vilas Co., Pop. Code 3
Boulder Junction JI SD
  Sch. Sys. Enr. Code 2
  Supt. – William Sherer
  HWYS K & P BOX 120   54545
North Lakeland ES   54545 – Daniel Vernetti, prin.

Manitowoc, Manitowoc Co., Pop. Code 8
Manitowoc SD
  Sch. Sys. Enr. Code 5
  Supt. – Vernon Childs, P O BOX 1657   54220
Franklin ES, 800 S 35TH ST   54220
  Robert Kautzer, prin.
Jackson ES, 1201 N 18TH ST   54220
  Donald Desimowich, prin.
Jefferson ES, 1402 MANILA ST   54220
  Robert George, prin.
Madison ES, 701 N 4TH ST   54220
  Curtis Kittleson, prin.
Monroe ES, 2502 S 14TH ST   54220
  Steven Huebbe, prin.
Strangel ES, 1002 E CEDAR AVE   54220
  Diane Lawler, prin.

Bethany Evangelist Lutheran ES
  3209 MEADOW LN   54220
First German Evangelist Lutheran ES
  1025 S 8TH ST   54220
Holy Innocents ES, 1408 WALKO BLVD   54220
Immanuel Evangelist Lutheran ES
  916 PINE ST   54220
Sacred Heart ES, 702 STATE ST   54220
St. Andrew Catholic ES, 1418 GRAND AVE   54220
St. Mary ES, 2109 MARSHALL ST   54220
St. Paul Catholic ES, 2411 WOLLMER ST   54220

Maple, Douglas Co., Pop. Code 3
Maple SD
  Sch. Sys. Enr. Code 4
  Supt. – L. G. Kavajecz   54854
Maple Corner ES   54854 – Nancy Bartman, prin.
Other Schools – See Iron River, Lake Nebagamon,
  Poplar, Wentworth

Marathon, Marathon Co., Pop. Code 4
Marathon City SD
  Sch. Sys. Enr. Code 3
  Supt. – Robert Burmester, P O BOX 37   54448
ES, P O BOX 457   54448 – Larry Perrodin, prin.

St. Mary's ES, P O BOX 102   54448

Marinette, Marinette Co., Pop. Code 7
Marinette SD
  Sch. Sys. Enr. Code 5
  Supt. – Robert B. Froelich, 1010 MAIN ST   54143
MS, 1010 MAIN ST   54143
  Kathleen Sweningson, prin.
Garfield ES, 1615 CARNEY BLVD   54143
  Barbara Schaal, prin.
Menekaunee ES, 115 HANCOCK ST   54143
  Alfred Rasmussen, prin.
Merryman ES, 611 ELIZABETH AVE   54143
  George Hayes, prin.

Park ES, 1225 HOCKRIDGE ST   54143
  Kenneth Ducharme, prin.
Washington ES, 2502 TAYLOR ST   54143
  Thomas Polkinghorne, prin.
Other Schools – See Porterfield

Holy Family ES, 1228 ELIZABETH AVE   54143
Lourdes-Holy Family School
  1232 GARFIELD AVE   54143
Trinity Lutheran ES, 1216 COLFAX ST   54143

Marion, Waupaca Co., Pop. Code 4
Marion SD
  Sch. Sys. Enr. Code 3
  Supt. – Jerry Smith, 1001 N MAIN ST   54950
ES, 1001 N MAIN ST   54950 – Jerry Smith, prin.

Markesan, Green Lake Co., Pop. Code 4
Markesan SD
  Sch. Sys. Enr. Code 4
  Supt. – Lyle Plagenz   53946
Mackford ES, RURAL ROUTE 02   53946
  Roland Salter, prin.
MS   53946 – Lester Schruck, prin.
Other Schools – See Manchester

Marshall, Dane Co., Pop. Code 4
Marshall SD
  Sch. Sys. Enr. Code 3
  Supt. – Wayne Edwards, P O BOX 76   53559
MS, P O BOX 106   53559 – Robert C. Seyffer, prin.
ES, P O BOX 106   53559 – Robert Seyffer, prin.

Marshfield, Wood Co., Pop. Code 7
Marshfield SD
  Sch. Sys. Enr. Code 5
  Supt. – Alain G. Holt, 1010 E 4TH ST   54449
Grant ES, 605 KALSHED   54449
  Edward Whelihan, prin.
Jefferson ES, 1008 S CEDAR AVE   54449
  Curtis Hanson, prin.
Lincoln ES, 1201 E 17TH ST   54449
  Dennis Wiltgen, prin.
Madison ES, 501 N APPLE AVE   54449
  Edward Whelihan, prin.
Nasonville MS, 11044 HWY 10   54449
  Curtis Hanson, prin.
Washington ES, 600 W 5TH ST   54449
  James Cain, prin.
Other Schools – See Chili

Immanuel Lutheran ES
  610 S CHESTNUT AVE   54449
Our Lady of Peace ES, 1300 W 5TH ST   54449
Sacred Heart ES, 1017 S CENTRAL AVE   54449
St. John ES, 307 N WALNUT AVE   54449

Mason, Bayfield Co., Pop. Code 2
Ashland SD
  Supt. – See Ashland
ES   54856 – Richard Anderson, prin.

Mattoon, Shawano Co., Pop. Code 2
Antigo SD
  Supt. – See Antigo
ES   54450 – Theodore McAuly, prin.

Mauston, Juneau Co., Pop. Code 5
Mauston SD
  Sch. Sys. Enr. Code 4
  Supt. – Robert L. Hubert
  508 GRAYSIDE AVE   53948
Olson MS, 508 GRAYSIDE AVE   53948
  William Shaw, prin.
West Side ES, LOOMIS DR   53948
  Frank Harrington, prin.
Other Schools – See Lyndon Station

St. Patrick ES, 325 MANSION ST   53948

Mayville, Dodge Co., Pop. Code 5
Herman #22 SD
  Sch. Sys. Enr. Code 2
  Supt. – Dennis Mair, RURAL ROUTE 01   53050
Herman Consolidated ES, N6409 HWY P   53050
  (—), prin.

Mayville SD
  Sch. Sys. Enr. Code 4
  Supt. – Stephen Bushke, CLARK ST   53050
MS, MAIN & DAYTON ST   53050 – Pat John, prin.
Parkview ES, OAK STREET   53050
  Pat John, prin.
Other Schools – See Iron Ridge

St. John's Lutheran ES, 520 BRIDGE ST   53050
St. Mary's ES, 28 NABER ST   53050

Mazomanie, Dane Co., Pop. Code 4
Wisconsin Hts. SD
  Sch. Sys. Enr. Code 3
  Supt. – John Gehn, RURAL ROUTE 01   53560
ES, 314 ANNE ST   53560 – Mary Milbrandt, prin.
Other Schools – See Black Earth

McFarland, Dane Co., Pop. Code 5
McFarland SD
  Sch. Sys. Enr. Code 4
  Supt. – Patrick Kennedy
  5101 FARWELL ST   53558
Elvehjem MS, 6009 JOHNSON ST   53558
  Donald Barnes, prin.
ES, 6103 JOHNSON ST   53558
  Thomas Mooney, prin.

McAllister, Marinette Co.
Wausaukee SD
  Supt. – See Wausaukee
ES   54177 – John Moberg, prin.

Medford, Taylor Co., Pop. Code 5
Medford Area SD
  Sch. Sys. Enr. Code 4
  Supt. – Allen Christel, 215 PINE ST   54451
MS, 509 CLARK ST   54451 – John Patritto, prin.
ES, 1065 W BROADWAY AVE   54451
  Robert Kieslich, prin.
Other Schools – See Stetsonville

Holy Rosary Catholic ES
  215 S WASHINGTON AVE   54451
Immanuel Lutheran ES, 420 LINCOLN ST   54451

Mellen, Ashland Co., Pop. Code 4
Mellen SD
  Sch. Sys. Enr. Code 2
  Supt. – Eugene Johnson   54546
ES   54546 – Howard Leafblad, prin.

Melrose, Jackson Co., Pop. Code 3
Melrose-Mindoro SD
  Sch. Sys. Enr. Code 3
  Supt. – Edward Woods   54642
ES   54642 – (—), prin.
Other Schools – See Mindoro

Menasha, Winnebago Co., Pop. Code 7
Menasha SD
  Sch. Sys. Enr. Code 5
  Supt. – William Decker, P O BOX 360   54952
Butte des Morts JHS, 501 TAYCO ST   54952
  Harold Pelton, prin.
Banta, 6TH ST   54952 – Richard Geiger, prin.
Clovis Grove ES, 974 9TH ST   54952
  Terry Martin, prin.
Gegan ES, AIRPORT RD   54952
  Mark French, prin.
Jefferson ES, 2ND ST   54952 – Richard Geiger, prin.
Nicholet ES, 449 AHNAIP ST   54952
  Jean Stebbins-Mueller, prin.

St. John ES, 527 5TH ST   54952
St. Mary ES, 528 2ND ST   54952
Trinity Lutheran ES, 300 BROAD ST   54952

Menomonee Falls, Waukesha Co., Pop. Code 8
Hamilton SD
  Supt. – See Sussex
Marcy ES, W180 N4851 MARCY RD   53051
  Terry Tuttrup, prin.

Menomonee Falls SD
  Sch. Sys. Enr. Code 5
  Supt. – Jack T. Magnuson
  N 84 W-16579 MENOMONEE AVE   53051
North MS, N 88 W 16750 GARFIELD AVE   53051
  Donald Vogt, prin.
Franklin ES, N81 W14701 FRANKLIN DR   53051
  Beatrice Wurtz, prin.
Shady Lane ES
  W172 N 8959 SHADY LANE BLVD   53051
  Kenneth Semmann, prin.
Valley View ES
  W180 N 8130 TOWN HALL RD   53051
  Harry Goetz, prin.

Calvary Baptist School
  N84 W16971 MENOMONEE AVE   53051
Bethlehem Evangelist Lutheran ES
  N84 WI5252 MENOMONEE AVE   53051
Grace Evangelist Lutheran ES
  N87 W16173 KENWOOD BLVD   53051
St. Anthony ES
  N74 W13646 APPLETON AVE   53051
St. Mary ES, N89 W16215 CLEVELD AVE   53051
Zion Lutheran School
  W188 N4868 EMERALD HL DR   53051

Menomonie, Dunn Co., Pop. Code 7
Menomonie Area SD
  Sch. Sys. Enr. Code 5
  Supt. – David Ross, 718 BROADWAY ST N   54751
MS, 1715 5TH ST W   54751 – N. J. Fellrath, prin.
Cedar Falls ES, RURAL ROUTE 07 BOX 50   54751
  Stanley Huftel, prin.
East ES, MAIN ST   54751 – Stanley Huftel, prin.
Little Elk Creek ES, RURAL ROUTE 03   54751
  Stanley Huftel, prin.
Lucas ES, RURAL ROUTE 01   54751
  Donald Heifner, prin.
North ES, PINE RIVER   54751
  Donald Heifner, prin.
River Heights ES, 615 24TH AVE W   54751
  Thomas Mangin, prin.
Other Schools – See Downsville, Knapp

St. Joseph ES, 813 9TH AVE E   54751
St. Paul's Lutheran ES, 1116 9TH ST E   54751

Mequon, Ozaukee Co., Pop. Code 7
Mequon-Thiensville SD
  Sch. Sys. Enr. Code 5
  Supt. – Karl Hertz
  5000 W MEQUON ROAD 112 N   53092
Lake Shore MS
  11036 N RANGE LINE ROAD   53092
  Michael Dietz, prin.
Steffen MS, 6633 W STEFFEN DRIVE   53092
  Bernard Roeker, prin.
Donges Bay ES, 2400 W DONGES BAY RD   53092
  Carl Fahrenkrug, prin.

Oriole Lane ES, 12850 N ORIOLE LN   53092
  Shirley McCurdy, prin.
Range Line MS, 11040 N RANGE LINE RD   53092
  Shirley McCurdy, prin.
Wilson ES, 11001 N BUNTROCK AVE   53092
  Esther Silvers, prin.

SS Cecilia & James Catholic ES
  11300 N ST JAMES LN   53092
Trinity Lutheran ES
  10729 W FREISTADT RD 120 N   53092

Mercer, Iron Co., Pop. Code 4
Mercer SD
Sch. Sys. Enr. Code 2
Supt. – Randy Freese, P O BOX C   54547
ES   54547 – (—), prin.

Merrill, Lincoln Co., Pop. Code 6
Merrill Area SD
Sch. Sys. Enr. Code 5
Supt. – Thomas Strick, 1111 N SALES ST   54452
Franklin ES, 120 N GENESEE ST   54452
  David Donner, prin.
Jefferson ES, 1801 W MAIN ST   54452
  Gene Bebel, prin.
Lincoln ES, 101 N CENTER AVE   54452
  Ken Bashara, prin.
Pine River ES, RURAL ROUTE 06   54452
  Virginia Kohnke, prin.
Scott ES, RURAL ROUTE 04   54452
  Garth Swanson, prin.
Washington ES, 1900 E 6TH ST   54452
  Robert Gruling, prin.
Other Schools – See Gleason, Hamburg

St. John Lutheran ES, 1104 E 3RD ST   54452
St. Robert Bellarmine ES, P O OBX 586   54452
Trinity Lutheran ES, 611 W MAIN ST   54452

Merrillan, Jackson Co., Pop. Code 3
Alma Center SD
Supt. – See Alma Center
ES   54754 – Randy Stanley, prin.

Merrimac, Sauk Co., Pop. Code 2
Sauk-Prairie SD
Supt. – See Sauk City
ES, 260 SCHOOL ST   53561
  Christine Lefeber, prin.

Merton, Waukesha Co., Pop. Code 4
Merton J9 SD
Sch. Sys. Enr. Code 2
Supt. – Robert Gilpatrick   53056
ES, 6881 MAIN ST   53056 – (—), prin.

Middleton, Dane Co., Pop. Code 7
Middleton-Cross Plains SD
Sch. Sys. Enr. Code 5
Supt. – Gene Thieleke, 7106 SOUTH AVE   53562
Kromrey MS, 7009 DONNA DRIVE   53562
  Stanley S. Angell, prin.
Elm Lawn ES, 6701 WOODGATE ROAD   53562
  Harriet Forman, prin.
Northside ES, 3620 HIGH RD   53562
  Charles Welda, prin.
Sauk Trail ES, 2205 BRANCH ST   53562
  Gene Gray, prin.
Other Schools – See Cross Plains, Verona, Waunakee

Milton, Rock Co., Pop. Code 5
Milton SD
Sch. Sys. Enr. Code 4
Supt. – Jon C. Platts, 430 E HIGH ST #2   53563
MS, 20 E MADISON AVE   53563
  Allan Smejkal, prin.
Milton East ES, 725 GREENMAN ST   53563
  Joseph Ban, prin.
Milton West ES, 8L25 W MADISON AVE   53563
  Nathan Bruce, prin.
Other Schools – See Janesville

Milwaukee, Milwaukee Co., Pop. Code 3
Fox Point J8 SD
Sch. Sys. Enr. Code 3
Supt. – Robert Kattman
  8377 N PORT WASHINGTON ROAD   53217
Indian Hill ES, 1101 W BROWN DEER RD   53217
  Jean Morrow, prin.
Maple Dale MS
  8377 N PT WASHINGTON RD   53217
  James Zielinski, prin.

Fox Point Jt. 2 SD
Sch. Sys. Enr. Code 3
Supt. – Matthew Gibson
  7300 N LOMBARDY ROAD   53217
Bayside MS, 601 E ELLSWORTH LN   53217
  Salvatore DiStefano, prin.
Dunwood ES, 217 W DUNWOOD RD   53217
  Nancy Hoppe, prin.

Glendale Jt. 1 SD
Sch. Sys. Enr. Code 4
Supt. – Robert Kattman
  2600 W MILL ROAD   53209
Glen Hills MS, 2600 W MILL ROAD   53209
  Roger Tietz, prin.
Good Hope ES, 2315 W GOOD HOPE RD   53209
  Judith Le Sage, prin.
Parkway ES
  5910 N MILWAUKEE RIVER PKY   53209
  James Magestro, prin.

Greenfield SD
Supt. – See Greenfield

Elm Dale ES, 5300 S HONEY CREEK DR   53221
  James Edelstein, prin.

Milwaukee SD
Sch. Sys. Enr. Code 8
Supt. – (—), P O BOX 10-K   53201
Audubon MS, 3300 S 39TH ST   53215
  Avery Goodrich, prin.
Bell MS, 6506 W WARNIMONT AVE   53220
  Clarence Lawrence, prin.
Burroughs MS, 6700 N 80TH ST   53223
  Eugene Laatsh, prin.
Edison MS, 5372 N 37TH ST   53209
  E. G. Kane, prin.
Eighth Street MS, 609 N 8TH ST   53233
  Willie Kirk, prin.
Fritsche MS, 2969 S HOWELL AVE   53207
  Suzanne Lundin, prin.
Fulton MS, 2760 N 1ST ST   53212
  Saul Reeves, prin.
Kosciuszko MS, 971 W WINDLAKE AVE   53204
  Fermin Burgos, prin.
Morse MS, 4601 N 84TH ST   53225
  Avistine Davis, prin.
Muir MS, 5496 N 72ND ST   53218
  Frank Harper, prin.
Parkman MS, 3620 N 18TH ST   53206
  Dennis Schumacher, prin.
Robinson MS, 3245 N 37TH ST   53216
  Janice Sodos, prin.
Roosevelt MS, 800 W WALNUT ST   53205
  Josephine Koebert, prin.
Sholes MS, 4965 S 20TH ST   53221
  Wayne Brzezinski, prin.
Steuben MS, 2360 N 52ND ST   53210
  Donald C. Luebke, prin.
Walker MS, 1712 S 32ND ST   53215
  Marie Campos, prin.
Webster MS, 6850 N 53RD ST   53223
  Lafayette Golden, prin.
Wright MS, 8400 W BURLEIGH ST   53222
  Arthur McManus, prin.
Alcott ES, 3563 S 97TH ST   53228
  Ethel Cahill, prin.
Allen Field ES, 730 W LAPHAM BLVD   53204
  Anita Pietrykowski, prin.
Auer Avenue ES, 2319 W AUER AVE   53206
  Bobbye Vance, prin.
Barton ES, 5700 W GREEN TREE RD   53223
  Minnie Benson, prin.
Berger ES, 3275 N 3RD ST   53212
  James Thompson, prin.
Browning ES, 5575 N 76TH ST   53218
  Josie Gray, prin.
Bruce ES, 6453 N 89TH ST   53224
  Gordon Harrison, prin.
Bryant ES, 8718 W THURSTON AVE   53225
  Barbara Williams, prin.
Burbank ES, 6035 W ADLER ST   53214
  Margaret Mueller, prin.
Burdick ES, 4348 S GRIFFIN AVE   53207
  Theadoll Taylor, prin.
Carleton ES, 4116 W SILVER SPRING DR   53209
  Earl Johnson, prin.
Cass Street ES, 1647 N CASS ST   53202
  John Weatherall, prin.
Clarke Street ES, 2816 W CLARKE ST   53210
  Diane Neicheril, prin.
Clemens ES, 4229 N 36TH ST   53216
  Theresa O'Bee, prin.
Clement Avenue ES
  3666 S CLEMENT AVE   53207
  Janetta Trotman, prin.
Congress ES, 5225 W LINCOLN CREEK DR   53218
  Louis Fuhrman, prin.
Cooper ES, 5143 S 21ST ST   53221
  Patrick Driscoll, prin.
Curtin ES, 3450 S 32ND ST   53215
  Richard Kaiser, prin.
Doerfler ES, 3014 W SCOTT ST   53215
  Arthur Luse, prin.
Dover Street ES, 619 E DOVER ST   53207
  Emeric Dakich, prin.
Eighty Eighth Street ES, 3575 S 88TH ST   53228
  Shirley McCarty, prin.
Eighty First ES, 2964 N 81ST ST   53222
  Barbara Begale, prin.
Eighty Second Street ES, 3778 N 82ND ST   53222
  Dorie Sand, prin.
Elm ES, 2616 W GARFIELD AVE   53205
  Darrel Jacobs, prin.
Emerson ES, 9025 W LAWRENCE AVE   53225
  Roberta Wilkerson, prin.
Engelburg ES, 5100 N 91ST ST   53225
  Doreen Brittonlange, prin.
Fairview ES
  6500 W KINNICKINNIC RVR PWY   53219
  Carolyn Strutz, prin.
Fernwood ES
  3239 S PENNSYLVANIA AVE   53207
  Howard Hargis, prin.
Fifty Fifth Street ES, 2765 S 55TH ST   53219
  Jeanne Hochstatter, prin.
Fifty Third Street ES, 3618 N 53RD ST   53216
  William Laste, prin.
Forest Home Avenue ES
  1516 W FOREST HOME AVE   53204
  Margaret Werner, prin.
Franklin ES, 2308 W NASH ST   53206
  James Henry, prin.
Fratney ES, 3255 N FRATNEY ST   53212
  Richard Moring, prin.
Garden Homes ES, 4456 N TEUTONIA AVE   53209
  Rebecca Abraham, prin.

Garfield Avenue ES, 2215 N 4TH ST   53212
  Thomas McGinnity, prin.
Garland ES, 1420 W GOLDCREST AVE   53221
  Robert Helminiak, prin.
Goodrich ES, 8251 N CELINA ST   53224
  (—), prin.
Grandview ES, 12021 W FLORIST AVE   53225
  Barbara Birks, prin.
Grant ES, 2920 W GRANT ST   53215
  Mary Heitman, prin.
Grantosa Drive ES, 4850 N 82ND ST   53218
  Madeline Ferschl, prin.
Granville ES, 9520 W ALLYN ST   53224
  Lavera Laws, prin.
Green Bay Avenue ES, 3872 N 8TH ST   53206
  Gwen Leitgen, prin.
Greenfield ES, 1711 S 35TH ST   53215
  Steven Huffman, prin.
Hampton ES, 5000 N 53RD ST   53218
  David Pearson, prin.
Happy Hill ES, 7171 W BROWN DEER RD   53223
  Gregory Lott, prin.
Hartford Avenue ES
  2227 E HARTFORD AVE   53211
  Ronald Andryk, prin.
Hawley ES, 5610 W WISCONSIN AVE   53213
  James Friedel, prin.
Hawthorne ES, 6945 N 41ST ST   53209
  Douglas Roberts, prin.
Hi Mount Boulevard ES
  4921 W GARFIELD AVE   53208
  Spencer Korte, prin.
Holmes ES, 2463 N BUFFUM ST   53212
  Robert Kreilkamp, prin.
Hopkins Street ES, 1503 W HOPKINS ST   53206
  Harold Galitzer, prin.
Humboldt Park ES, 3230 S ADAMS AVE   53207
  Penelope Kroog, prin.
Irving ES, 7900 W ACACIA ST   53223
  Carl Nell, prin.
Kagel ES, 1210 W MINERAL ST   53204
  Rose Guajardo, prin.
Keefe Avenue ES, 1618 W KEEFE AVE   53206
  Gene Berman, prin.
Kilbourn ES, 5354 N 68TH ST   53218
  Juanita Sanders, prin.
Kluge ES, 5760 N 67TH ST   53218
  Joseph Plummer, prin.
Lafollette ES, 3239 N 9TH ST   53206
  Dorothy St. Charles, prin.
Lancaster ES, 4931 N 68TH ST   53218
  Willie Killins, prin.
Lee ES, 921 W MEINECKE AVE   53206
  George Hughes, prin.
Lincoln Avenue ES, 1817 W LINCOLN AVE   53215
  Gerald Gosenheimer, prin.
Lloyd Street ES, 1228 W LLOYD ST   53205
  Mary Wacholz-Hickey, prin.
Longfellow ES, 1021 S 21ST ST   53204
  Labelle Calaway, prin.
Lowell ES, 4360 S 20TH ST   53221
  Claudette St. Clair, prin.
Macdowell ES, 1706 W HIGHLAND AVE   53233
  John Schmuhl, prin.
Manitoba ES, 4040 W FOREST HOME AVE   53215
  Allan Nuhlicek, prin.
Maple Tree ES, 6644 N 107TH ST   53224
  Estelle Sprewer, prin.
Maryland Avenue ES
  2418 N MARYLAND AVE   53211 – (—), prin.
Meir ES, 1555 N MARTIN LUTHER KING   53212
  Albin Kaczmarek, prin.
Mitchell ES, 1728 S 23RD ST   53204
  Alton Townsel, prin.
Morgandale ES, 3635 S 17TH ST   53221
  Ramon Cruz, prin.
Neeskara ES, 1601 N HAWLEY RD   53208
  Mark Hughes, prin.
Ninety Fifth Street ES, 3707 N 94TH ST   53222
  Marshall Bullock, prin.
Palmer ES, 1900 N 1ST ST   53212 – (—), prin.
Parkview ES, 10825 W VILLARD AVE   53225
  Juliana Rhoten, prin.
Philipp ES, 4310 N 16TH ST   53209
  Marga Vann, prin.
Pierce ES, 2765 N FRATNEY ST   53212
  Frederick Carr, prin.
Pleasant View ES, 4920 W CAPITOL DR   53216
  John Sullivan, prin.
Riley ES, 2424 S 4TH ST   53207
  Marilyn Spicuzza, prin.
Seventy Eighth Street ES, 3727 S 78TH ST   53220
  John Thomas, prin.
Sherman ES, 5110 W LOCUST ST   53210
  Kay Mantilla, prin.
Siefert ES, 1547 N 14TH ST   53205
  Brenda Wood, prin.
Silver Spring ES, 5131 N GREEN BAY AVE   53209
  Elcendia Nord, prin.
Sixty Fifth Street ES, 6600 W MELVINA ST   53216
  Theresa Heimann, prin.
Sixty Seventh Street ES, 6701 W EDEN PL   53220
  Santa Consiglio, prin.
Story ES, 3815 W KILBOURN AVE   53208
  Paul Shebesta, prin.
Stuart ES, 7001 N 86TH ST   53224
  Walter Marshall, prin.
Thirty Eighth Street ES, 2623 N 38TH ST   53210
  Margaret Stalheim, prin.
Thirty Fifth Street ES
  3517 W COURTLAND AVE   53209
  Ann Cunningham, prin.
Thirty First Street ES, 1945 N 31ST ST   53208
  Patricia Unterholzner, prin.

Thirty Seventh Street ES, 1715 N 37TH ST 53208
LeRoy Freeman Jr., prin.
Thoreau ES, 7878 N 60TH ST 53223
Frederick Frommgen, prin.
Townsend Street ES
3360 N SHERMAN BLVD 53216
Robert Johnson, prin.
Trowbridge Street ES
1943 E TROWBRIDGE ST 53207
Quentin Borucki, prin.
Twentieth Street ES, 2442 N 20TH ST 53206
Albert Weiss, prin.
Twenty First Street ES
2121 W HADLEY ST 53206
Beatrice Beckley, prin.
Twenty Fourth Street ES, 4950 N 24TH ST 53209
Dorothy Thomas, prin.
Twenty Seventh Street ES, 1312 N 27TH ST 53208
Alice White, prin.
Victory ES, 2222 W HENRY AVE 53221
Ksenija Ignatjevs, prin.
Vieau ES, 823 S 4TH ST 53204
Robert Koeper, prin.
Whitman ES, 4200 S 54TH ST 53220
Bobbie Dawson, prin.
Whittier ES, 4382 S 3RD ST 53207
Patricia Holmes, prin.
Wisconsin Avenue ES
2708 W WISCONSIN AVE 53208
Glen Burk, prin.
Zablocki ES, 1016 W OKLAHOMA AVE 53215
Thelma Bradford, prin.

Wauwatosa SD
Sch. Sys. Enr. Code 6
Supt. – Maurice Sullivan
12121 W NORTH AVE 53226
Whitman JHS, 11100 W CENTER ST 53222
Carl Wossow, prin.
Eisenhower ES, 11600 W CENTER ST 53222
Daniel Hauser, prin.
Madison ES, 9925 W GLENDALE AVE 53225
John Shanahan, prin.
Other Schools – See Wauwatosa

West Allis SD
Supt. – See West Allis
Franklin ES, 2060 S 86TH ST 53227
Vern Messersmith, prin.
Irving ES, 10230 W GRANT ST 53227
Charlotte Blair, prin.
Jefferson ES, 7229 W BECHER ST 53219
Dean Mewhorter, prin.
Longfellow ES, 2211 S 60TH ST 53219
Terry Schubert, prin.
Mitchell ES, 10125 W MONTANA ST 53227
Richard Pilak, prin.

Whitefish Bay SD
Supt. – See Whitefish Bay
Cumberland ES
4780 N MARLBOROUGH DR 53211
Randall Hawley, prin.

University School
2100 W FAIRY CHASM ROAD 53217
Wisconsin VCY Central School
3434 W KILBOURN AVE 53208
Atonement Lutheran ES
4224 W RUBY AVE 53209
Beautiful Savior Lutheran ES
3012 N HOLTON ST 53212
Bethlehem Lutheran ES
2466 W MCKINLEY AVE 53205
Blessed Sacrament ES
4005 W OKLAHOMA AVE 53215
Bruce Guadalupe Community ES
825 N VAN BUREN ST 53202
Catholic East ES, 2461 N MURRAY AVE 53211
Centennial Lutheran ES, 3558 S 24TH ST 53221
Child of Christ Lutheran ES
3353 S WHITNALL AVE 53207
Christ Lutheran ES
2229 W GREENFIELD AVE 53204
Christ Memorial Lutheran ES
5719 N TEUTONIA AVE 53209
Corpus Christi Catholic ES
8545 W VILLARD AVE 53225
Ebenezer Lutheran ES, 1127 S 35TH ST 53215
Emmaus Lutheran ES, 2818 N 23RD ST 53206
Fairview Evangelist Lutheran ES
137 N 66TH ST 53213
Gardens Homes Lutheran ES
2475 W ROOSEVELT DR 53209
Gospel Lutheran Grade School
3965 N 15TH ST 53206
Harambee Community ES
110 W BURLEIGH ST 53212
Hillel Academy
6401 N SANTA MONICA BLVD 53217
Holy Angels ES, 3774 N 12TH ST 53206
Holy Cross ES, 5522 W BLUEMOUND RD 53208
Holy Spirit ES, 2251 S 31ST ST 53215
Immaculate Conception ES
1051 E RUSSELL AVE 53207
Jordan Lutheran ES, 8420 W BELOIT RD 53227
Mary Queen of Heaven ES
2360 S 106TH ST 53227
Milwaukee Jewish Day ES
6255 N SANTA MONICA BLVD 53217
Milwaukee Montessori ES
4610 W STATE ST 53208
Mother of Good Counsel ES
3021 N 68TH ST 53210

Mother of Perpetual Help ES
5140 N 55TH ST 53218
Mt. Calvary Lutheran ES, 2862 N 53RD ST 53210
Mt. Lebanon Lutheran ES
6100 W HAMPTON AVE 53218
Mt. Oliver Lutheran ES
5301 W WASHINGTON BLVD 53208
North Trinity Lutheran ES, 6090 N 35TH ST 53209
Northwest Lutheran ES, 4119 N 81ST ST 53222
Our Fathers Evangelist Lutheran ES
6023 S 27TH ST 53221
Our Lady Queen of Peace ES
2733 W EUCLID AVE 53215
Our Lady of Good Hope ES
7140 N 41ST ST 53209
Our Lady of Sorrows ES, 4059 N 64TH ST 53216
Pilgrim Evangelist Lutheran ES
6717 W CENTER ST 53210
SS Cyril & Methodius ES, 2433 S 15TH ST 53215
Sacred Heart ES, 917 N 49TH ST 53208
Salem Lutheran ES, 6844 N 107TH ST 53224
Siloah Lutheran ES, 3731 N 21ST ST 53206
St. Adalbert ES, 1913 W BECHER ST 53215
St. Albert ES, 5966 N 35TH ST 53209
St. Alexander ES, 3344 S 16TH ST 53215
St. Anthony ES, 1747 S 9TH ST 53204
St. Anthony of Padua ES
7632 W STEVENSON ST 53213
St. Augustine ES, 2507 S GRAHAM ST 53207
St. Augustine ES, 6753 W ROGERS ST 53219
St. Barbara ES, 2100 S 32ND ST 53215
St. Bernadette ES, 8202 W DENVER AVE 53223
St. Casimir ES, 924 E CLARKE ST 53212
St. Catherine ES, 2647 N 51ST ST 53210
St. Catherine ES, 8660 N 76TH PL 53223
St. Charles Borromeo ES
3100 W PARNELL AVE 53221
St. Eugene ES
7600 N PORT WASHINGTON RD 53217
St. Gregory Great ES, 3132 S 63RD ST 53219
St. Helen ES, 3329 S 10TH ST 53215
St. James Evangelist Lutheran ES
2028 N 60TH ST 53208
St. John Kanty ES, 2840 S 10TH ST 53215
St. John Lutheran ES
7877 N PORT WASHINGTON RD 53217
St. John's Evangelist Lutheran ES
4001 S 68TH ST 53220
St. Josaphat ES, 801 W LINCOLN AVE 53215
St. Joseph ES, 2750 N 122ND ST 53222
St. Lawrence ES, 1418 S LAYTON BLVD 53215
St. Leo ES, 2458 W LOCUST ST 53206
St. Lucas Lutheran ES, 648 E DOVER ST 53207
St. Margaret Mary ES, 3950 N 92ND ST 53222
St. Martin Lutheran ES
1557 W ORCHARD ST 53204
St. Mary Czestochowa ES
3027 N FRATNEY ST 53212
St. Matthew Evangelist Lutheran ES
8444 W MELVINA ST 53222
St. Matthew's ES, 1114 S 25TH ST 53204
St. Matthias ES, 9300 W BELOIT RD 53227
St. Nicholas ES, 5375 N GREEN BAY AVE 53209
St. Paul's Catholic ES
3945 S KANSAS AVE 53207
St. Paul's Lutheran ES
7821 W LINCOLN AVE 53219
St. Peter Immanuel Lutheran ES
7801 W ACACIA ST 53223
St. Philip Neri Catholic ES
5501 N 68TH ST 53218
St. Rita ES, 6021 W LINCOLN AVE 53219
St. Roman ES, 1810 W BOLIVAR AVE 53221
St. Rose ES, 514 N 31ST ST 53208
St. Sebastian ES, 1740 N 55TH ST 53208
St. Stephen ES, 4200 N 51ST ST 53216
St. Stephen's Catholic ES
5872 S HOWELL AVE 53207
St. Thomas Aquinas ES, 1940 N 36TH ST 53208
St. Veronica ES, 341 E NORWICH AVE 53207
St. Vincent De Paul ES, 1646 S 22ND ST 53204
Urban Day ES, 1441 N 24TH ST 53205
Walther Memorial Lutheran ES
3101 N 40TH ST 53216
Woodlawn Lutheran ES, 2217 S 99TH ST 53227

Mindoro, La Crosse Co.
Melrose-Mindoro SD
Supt. – See Melrose
ES 54644 – (—), prin.

Mineral Point, Iowa Co., Pop. Code 4
Mineral Point SD
Sch. Sys. Enr. Code 3
Supt. – Jeffrey Gruber, 607 COTHERN ST 53565
MS, 530 MAIDEN ST 53565
Marvin Hanson, prin.
ES, 607 COTHERN ST 53565
Jeffrey Gruber, prin.

Minocqua, Oneida Co., Pop. Code 5
Minocqua J1 SD
Sch. Sys. Enr. Code 2
Supt. – James Chillstrom 54548
ES 54548 – (—), prin.

Trinity Lutheran ES, 8781 BRUNSWICK RD 54548

Minong, Washburn Co., Pop. Code 3
Northwood SD
Sch. Sys. Enr. Code 2
Supt. – Robert Hecht, P O BOX 10 54859
Gordon MS, P O BOX 10 54859 – Tim Foley, prin.

Mishicot, Manitowoc Co., Pop. Code 4
Mishicot SD
Sch. Sys. Enr. Code 3
Supt. – John Risch 54228
Schultz ES 54228 – Kenneth Baroun, prin.

Holy Cross ES, 423 CHURCH ST 54228

Mondovi, Buffalo Co., Pop. Code 5
Durand SD
Supt. – See Durand
Grandview ES, RURAL ROUTE 04 54755
Thomas Casey, prin.

Mondovi SD
Sch. Sys. Enr. Code 4
Supt. – John P. Herpst, 337 JACKSON ST N 54755
Anthony ES, RURAL ROUTE 01 54755
James Harrison, prin.
ES, 426 MILL ST 54755 – James Harrison, prin.
Naples ES, RURAL ROUTE 01 54755
James Harrison, prin.

Monona, Dane Co., Pop. Code 6
Monona Grove SD
Sch. Sys. Enr. Code 4
Supt. – Jerome Coaty
5301 MONONA DRIVE 53716
Winnequah MS, 800 GREENWAY ROAD 53716
Charles Amera, prin.
Maywood ES, 902 NICHOLS RD 53716
William Breisch, prin.
Winnequah ES, 800 GREENWAY RD 53716
William Breisch, prin.
Other Schools – See Cottage Grove

Immaculate Heart Of Mary ES
4913 SCHOFIELD ST 53716

Monroe, Green Co., Pop. Code 7
Monroe SD
Sch. Sys. Enr. Code 5
Supt. – James Munro, 1510 13TH ST 53566
MS, 1510 13TH ST 53566 – Vincent Barnes, prin.
Abraham Lincoln ES, 2700 13TH AVE 53566
Virgil Leopold, prin.
Northside ES, 3005 8 1/2 ST 53566
Donald Sorn, prin.
Parkside ES, 920 4TH ST 53566
James Brunette, prin.

St. Victor ES, 1416 20TH AVE 53566

Montello, Marquette Co., Pop. Code 4
Montello SD
Sch. Sys. Enr. Code 3
Supt. – Roger Klug, 222 FOREST LANE 53949
Forest Lane ES, 222 FOREST LN 53949
William Knickerbocker, prin.

Montfort, Grant Co., Pop. Code 3
Iowa-Grant SD
Supt. – See Livingston
ES 53569 – Russell Messling, prin.

Monticello, Green Co., Pop. Code 4
Monticello SD
Sch. Sys. Enr. Code 2
Supt. – David Heather 53570
ES 53570 – David Heather, prin.

Montreal, Iron Co., Pop. Code 3
Hurley SD
Supt. – See Hurley
Roosevelt ES, MICHIGAN AVE 54540
Lawrence Sobolewski, prin.

Morrisonville
De Forest SD
Supt. – See De Forest
ES, 4649 WILLOW ST 53571
Deborah Fritsch, prin.

Mosinee, Marathon Co., Pop. Code 5
D. C. Everest Area SD
Supt. – See Schofield
Evergreen ES, 1610 PINE RD 54455
Phillip Mirasola, prin.

Mosinee SD
Sch. Sys. Enr. Code 4
Supt. – Louis Birchbauer
591 W HIGHWAY 153 54455
MS, 700 HIGH ST 54455 – James Ronca, prin.
ES, 600 12TH ST 54455 – Guy Habeck, prin.

St. Paul Parochial ES, 404 HIGH ST 54455

Mountain, Oconto Co.
Suring SD
Supt. – See Suring
ES 54149 – Marilyn Seis, prin.

Mount Calvary, Fond du Lac Co., Pop. Code 3

Consolidated Parochial ES
100 NOTRE DAME ST 53057

Mount Horeb, Dane Co., Pop. Code 5
Mt. Horeb Area SD
Sch. Sys. Enr. Code 4
Supt. – Ellen Meister, P O BOX 87 53572
MS, 207 ACADEMY ST 53572
Kendall Gladem, prin.
ES, 305 ACADEMY ST 53572
Kendall Gladem, prin.
PS, 300 SPELLMAN 53572
Steven Ashmore, prin.

Mount Sterling, Crawford Co., Pop. Code 2
North Crawford SD
Supt. – See Gays Mills
ES   54645 – William Kvigne, prin.

Mukwonago, Waukesha Co., Pop. Code 5
Mukwonago SD
Sch. Sys. Enr. Code 5
Supt. – Paul Strobel, 423 DIVISION ST   53149
Park View MS, 930 N ROCHESTER ST   53149
David Petersen, prin.
Clarendon Avenue ES
915 CLARENDON AVE   53149
Donald Skrepenski, prin.
Prairie View ES, RURAL ROUTE 01   53149
James Grimyser, prin.
Section ES   53149 – Roger Dickert, prin.
Other Schools – See Big Bend, Eagle

Waterford J1 (T) SD
Supt. – See Waterford
Caldwell ES, 8318 CALDWELL RD   53149
Norma Conners, prin.

St. James ES, 830 E HWY NN   53149
St. John's Lutheran ES, 509 GRAND AVE   53149

Muscoda, Grant Co., Pop. Code 4
Riverdale SD
Sch. Sys. Enr. Code 3
Supt. – Thane Uglow, P O BOX 66   53573
Eagle Orion IS, P O BOX 66   53573
Joseph Walsh, prin.
IS, P O BOX 66   53573 – Jeanette Arneson, prin.
PS, P O BOX 66   53573 – Sharon McDougal, prin.
Other Schools – See Avoca, Blue River

Muskego, Waukesha Co., Pop. Code 7
Muskego-Norway SD
Sch. Sys. Enr. Code 5
Supt. – Donald Matheson, P O BOX 48   53150
Bay Lane MS, P O BOX 22   53150
Charles Boerner, prin.
Mill Valley ES
W191 S 6445 HILLENDALE DR   53150
JoAnn Kehl, prin.
ES, S75 W17476 JANESVILLE RD   53150
Delores Papke, prin.
Other Schools – See Hales Corners, Wind Lake

St. Leonard's ES
W173 S7777 WESTWOOD DR   53150
St. Paul's Lutheran ES
S66 W14325 JANESVILLE ROAD   53150

Nashotah, Waukesha Co., Pop. Code 3
Nashotah-Delafield J1 SD
Sch. Sys. Enr. Code 2
Supt. – Jack Roller
W329 N4476 LAKELAND DRIVE   53058
ES, W329 N4476 LAKELAND DR   53058
(—), prin.
Other Schools – See Hartland

Necedah, Juneau Co., Pop. Code 3
Necedah Area SD
Sch. Sys. Enr. Code 3
Supt. – F. J. Worachek, P O BOX 3000   54646
ES, P O BOX 3000   54646 – R. Schelfhout, prin.
Rock View ES   54646 – R. Schelfhout, prin.

Neenah, Winnebago Co., Pop. Code 7
Neenah SD
Sch. Sys. Enr. Code 6
Supt. – G. R. Grigsby
410 S COMMERCIAL ST   54956
Clayton ES, 2916 W FAIRVIEW RD   54956
Stephen Rasmussen, prin.
Coolidge ES, 321 ALCOTT DR   54956
David Brotski, prin.
Hoover ES, 950 HUNT AVE   54956
Kurt Hollenbeck, prin.
Roosevelt ES, 215 E FOREST AVE   54956
Robert Lindner, prin.
Spring Road ES, 1191 WINCHESTER RD   54956
Loren Graunke, prin.
Taft ES, 133 WESTERN AVE   54956
Richard Nilson, prin.
Tullar ES, 925 TULLAR RD   54956
Lloyd Thede, prin.
Washington ES, 220 E FRANKLIN AVE   54956
Arthur Prosek, prin.
Wilson ES, 920 HIGGINS AVE   54956
Richard Olson, prin.

Fox Valley Christian Academy
293 S GREEN BAY RD   54956
Martin Luther Evangelist Lutheran ES
807 ADAMS ST   54956
St. Gabriel ES, 900 GEIGER ST   54956
St. Margaret Mary ES, 610 DIVISION ST   54956
Trinity Lutheran ES, 411 OAK ST   54956

Neillsville, Clark Co., Pop. Code 5
Neillsville SD
Sch. Sys. Enr. Code 4
Supt. – Richard Quast, 614 E 5TH ST   54456
City MS, 504 E FIFTH ST   54456
Kenneth Van Dam, prin.
City ES, 504 E 5TH ST   54456 – Mark Craig, prin.

Nekoosa, Wood Co., Pop. Code 5
Nekoosa SD
Sch. Sys. Enr. Code 4
Supt. – Robert Scamfer, 600 SECTION ST S   54457

Alexander MS, 310 1ST ST   54457
Peter Pavloski, prin.
Humke ES, 500 S SECTION ST   54457
Richard Millenbah, prin.

Sacred Heart ES, 710 VILAS AVE   54457

Neopit, Menominee Co.
Menominee Indian SD
Supt. – See Keshena
MS   54150 – Phillip Erickson, prin.

St. Anthony ES, P O BOX 241   54150

Neosho, Dodge Co., Pop. Code 3
Neosho J3 SD
Sch. Sys. Enr. Code 2
Supt. – Cyril Richter, P O BOX 17   53059
ES, P O BOX 17   53059 – (—), prin.

Neshkoro, Marquette Co., Pop. Code 2
Westfield SD
Supt. – See Westfield
ES   54960 – Ronald Chase, prin.

New Auburn, Chippewa Co., Pop. Code 2
New Auburn SD
Sch. Sys. Enr. Code 2
Supt. – Kenneth Rynish   54757
ES   54757 – Daniel Hickey, prin.

New Berlin, Waukesha Co., Pop. Code 8
New Berlin SD
Sch. Sys. Enr. Code 5
Supt. – Gerald Tuchalski
4333 S SUNNYSLOPE ROAD   53151
Eisenhower MS
4333 S SUNNYSLOPE ROAD   53151
Paul Holweck, prin.
MS, 18695 W CLEVELAND AVE   53151
J. F. Harder, prin.
Calhoun ES, 1500 S WEST LN   53146
Howard Mackin, prin.
Cleveland Heights ES
17401 W CLEVELAND AVE   53146
Douglas Dunlop, prin.
Glen Park ES, 3500 S GLEN PARK RD   53151
David Berglund, prin.
New Berlin Center ES
4385 S CALHOUN RD   53151 – David Smith, prin.
Orchard Lane ES, 2015 S SUNNYSLOPE RD   53151
James Brusky, prin.
Prospect Hill ES, 5330 S RACINE AVE   53146
Lester Graves, prin.

West Allis SD
Supt. – See West Allis
Hoover ES, 12705 W EUCLID AVE   53151
David Vogel, prin.

Holy Apostles ES, 3875 S 159TH ST   53151

New Glarus, Green Co., Pop. Code 4
New Glarus SD
Sch. Sys. Enr. Code 3
Supt. – Peter Etter, 413 6TH ST   53574
ES, 413 6TH ST   53574 – Rick Balko, prin.

New Holstein, Calumet Co., Pop. Code 5
New Holstein SD
Sch. Sys. Enr. Code 4
Supt. – Donald F. Fictum
1715 PLYMOUTH ST   53061
ES, 2226 PARK AVE   53061 – Joseph Wieser, prin.

Holy Rosary ES, 1814 MADISON ST   53061

New Lisbon, Juneau Co., Pop. Code 4
New Lisbon SD
Sch. Sys. Enr. Code 3
Supt. – Paul Keeney, 500 S FOREST ST   53950
ES, 500 S FOREST ST   53950 – Carl Paradise, prin.

New London, Waupaca Co., Pop. Code 6
New London SD
Sch. Sys. Enr. Code 4
Supt. – Kenneth G. Renning
901 W WASHINGTON ST   54961
Lincoln ES, 206 E HANCOCK ST   54961
Kenneth Laudolff, prin.
Parkview ES, WERNER ALLEN RD   54961
William Caskey, prin.
Sugar Bush ES, RURAL ROUTE 02   54961
Kenneth Laudolff, prin.
Other Schools – See Readfield

Emanuel Evangelist Lutheran ES
912 LAWRENCE ST   54961
Most Precious Blood ES
120 E WASHINGTON ST   54961

New Richmond, St. Croix Co., Pop. Code 5
New Richmond SD
Sch. Sys. Enr. Code 4
Supt. – Thomas Kleppe, 152 E 4TH ST   54017
MS, 450 S ARCH AVE   54017
Karen Warncke, prin.
ES, S STARR AVE   54017 – Donald Mayer, prin.

St. Mary's ES, 257 S WASHINGTON AVE   54017

Newton, Manitowoc Co., Pop. Code 4
Kiel Area SD
Supt. – See Kiel
Meeme ES, 12121 CTH XX   53063
Marlys Gross, prin.

Niagara, Marinette Co., Pop. Code 4
Florence SD
Supt. – See Florence
Hillcrest ES, RURAL ROUTE 01 BOX 112   54151
Gary Osterberg, prin.

Niagara SD
Sch. Sys. Enr. Code 3
Supt. – Samuel Welcher, 1200 RIVER ST   54151
ES, 700 JEFFERSON AVE   54151
Peter Behnke, prin.

Nichols, Outagamie Co., Pop. Code 2
Seymour Comm. SD
Supt. – See Seymour
ES   54152 – Timothy Moe, prin.

North Fond du Lac, Fond du Lac Co., Pop. Code 5
North Fond Du Lac SD
Sch. Sys. Enr. Code 4
Supt. – Donald Kellogg, 225 MCKINLEY ST   54935
Allen MS, 923 MINNESOTA AVE   54935
Donald Kellogg, prin.
Friendship ES, 1115 THURKE AVE   54935
Richard Carleton, prin.
Other Schools – See Fond du Lac

Presentation ES, 706 MINNESOTA AVE   54935

North Freedom, Sauk Co., Pop. Code 3
Baraboo SD
Supt. – See Baraboo
ES   53951 – Connie Sprecher, prin.

North Lake, Waukesha Co.
Merton J7 SD
Sch. Sys. Enr. Code 2
Supt. – William Woody, P O BOX 188   53064
ES, P O BOX 188   53064 – William Woody, prin.

Norwalk, Monroe Co., Pop. Code 3
Norwalk-Ontario SD
Supt. – See Ontario
ES   54648 – Lillian Rumppe, prin.

Oak Creek, Milwaukee Co., Pop. Code 7
Oak Creek-Franklin SD
Sch. Sys. Enr. Code 5
Supt. – Milton Bleeke
340 E PUERTZ ROAD   53154
MS, 9330 S SHEPARD AVE   53154
Gerald Murphy, prin.
Carollton ES, 8965 S CARROLLTON DR   53154
Carol Hansis, prin.
Cedar Hills ES, 2225 W SYCAMORE AVE   53154
Reginald Becker, prin.
Edgewood ES, 8545 S SHEPARD AVE   53154
James Butler, prin.
Meadowview ES, 10420 S MCGRAW DR   53154
Jon Good, prin.
Shepard Hills ES
9701 S SHEPARD HILLS DR   53154
Larry Tylke, prin.

Parkway Christian Academy
10940 S NICHOLSON ROAD   53154
Grace Lutheran School
3401 E PUETZ ROAD   53154
St. Matthew's ES, 9329 S CHICAGO RD   53154

Oakdale, Monroe Co., Pop. Code 3
Tomah Area SD
Supt. – See Tomah
MS, RURAL ROUTE 03   54649 – Jerry Bauer, prin.

Oakfield, Fond du Lac Co., Pop. Code 3
Oakfield SD
Sch. Sys. Enr. Code 3
Supt. – Anthony Evers, P O BOX 99   53065
MS, P O BOX 69   53065 – David Poeschl, prin.
Reynolds ES, P O BOX 99   53065
Milton Hurlbert, prin.

Oconomowoc, Waukesha Co., Pop. Code 6
Merton J4 SD
Sch. Sys. Enr. Code 2
Supt. – Michael Budisch
6786 HIGHWAY C   53066
Stone Bank ES, 6786 HWY C   53066
Michael Budisch, prin.

Oconomowoc Area SD
Sch. Sys. Enr. Code 5
Supt. – James Rickabaugh, 7077 BROWN ST   53066
Ashippun ES, 295A CTH O   53066
Robert Krause, prin.
Greenland ES, 440 COOLIDGE ST   53066
Rozanna Shadewald, prin.
Meadow View ES, 7077 BROWN ST   53066
Delwin Krueger, prin.
Park Lawn ES, PARK LAWN ST   53066
David Engen, prin.
Summit ES, 36316 VALLEY RD   53066
Michael Schutz, prin.
Other Schools – See Ixonia, Okauchee

Country Christian School, 6160 N HWY 67   53066
St. Jerome ES, 110 W 3RD ST   53066
St. Matthew Lutheran ES
818 W WISCONSIN AVE   53066
St. Paul's Evangelist Lutheran ES
210 E PLEASANT ST   53066

Oconto, Oconto Co., Pop. Code 5
Oconto SD
Sch. Sys. Enr. Code 4
Supt. – Jerome Sommer
  1717 SUPERIOR AVE 54153
Washington JHS, 400 MICHIGAN AVE 54153
  Carl Liebig, prin.
Jefferson ES, 223 MCDONALD ST 54153
  Carl Liebig, prin.
Washington ES, 400 MICHIGAN AVE 54153
  Carl Liebig, prin.

Holy Trinity ES, 310 ARBUTUS AVE 54153

Oconto Falls, Oconto Co., Pop. Code 4
Oconto Falls SD
Sch. Sys. Enr. Code 4
Supt. – Victor Rossetti, 200 FARM ROAD 54154
Washington MS, WASHINGTON ST 54154
  Daniel Strebig, prin.
Jefferson ES, GREENBAY AVE 54154
  Barbara Natelle, prin.
Washington MS, WASHINGTON ST 54154
  Daniel Strebig, prin.
Other Schools – See Abrams, Lena, Little Suamico

Ogema, Price Co., Pop. Code 3
Prentice SD
Supt. – See Prentice
ES 54459 – (—), prin.

Okauchee, Waukesha Co., Pop. Code 4
Oconomowoc Area SD
Supt. – See Oconomowoc
ES, P O BOX 176 53069 – Gary Schulze, prin.

Omro, Winnebago Co., Pop. Code 5
Omro SD
Sch. Sys. Enr. Code 4
Supt. – Oren Barker, P O BOX P 54963
MS, P O BOX 370 54963 – Art Zitt, prin.
Enterprise ES, 8389 LIBERTY SCHOOL RD 54963
  John Schiessl, prin.
Patch ES, 607 TYLER AVE 54963
  James Herman, prin.
Other Schools – See Oshkosh

Onalaska, La Crosse Co., Pop. Code 6
Onalaska SD
Sch. Sys. Enr. Code 4
Supt. – Claude Deck, 612 MAIN ST 54650
MS, 711 QUINCY ST 54650 – John Burnett, prin.
Northern Hills ES, 511 E SPRUCE ST 54650
  Catherine Berg, prin.
Pertzsch ES, 524 MAIN ST 54650
  James Urban, prin.

St. Patrick's ES, 127 11TH AVE N 54650
St. Paul's Evangelist Lutheran ES
  P O BOX 128 54650

Oneida, Outagamie Co., Pop. Code 5
Pulaski Comm. SD
Supt. – See Pulaski
Hillcrest ES, RURAL ROUTE 01 54155
  Bernard Olejniczak, prin.

Oneida Tribal ES, P O BOX 365 54155

Ontario, Vernon Co., Pop. Code 2
Norwalk-Ontario SD
Sch. Sys. Enr. Code 2
Supt. – Al Szepi, RURAL ROUTE 01 54651
ES 54651 – Robert Friske, prin.
Other Schools – See Norwalk

Oostburg, Sheboygan Co., Pop. Code 4
Oostburg SD
Sch. Sys. Enr. Code 3
Supt. – Edward Grosshuesch
  410 NEW YORK AVE 53070
MS, 110 N 10TH ST 53070 – Robert Shaul, prin.
ES, 630 NEW YORK AVE 53070
  Robert Shaul, prin.
Other Schools – See Hingham

Oostburg Christian ES
  610 SUPERIOR AVE 53070

Oregon, Dane Co., Pop. Code 5
Oregon SD
Sch. Sys. Enr. Code 4
Supt. – Phillip Helgesen, 200 N MAIN ST 53575
MS, 200 N MAIN ST 53575
  Edward F. Guziewski, prin.
MS, 300 SODEN DRIVE 53575 – Karl Ahrens, prin.
ES, 200 N MAIN ST 53575 – James Clark, prin.
Other Schools – See Brooklyn

Orfordville, Rock Co., Pop. Code 4
Parkview SD
Sch. Sys. Enr. Code 4
Supt. – David Romstad, P O BOX 464 53576
Parkview JHS 53576 – (—), prin.
ES 53576 – (—), prin.
Other Schools – See Beloit, Footville

Osceola, Polk Co., Pop. Code 4
Osceola SD
Sch. Sys. Enr. Code 4
Supt. – Robert Vesperman 54020
MS 54020 – Jean Neuman, prin.
ES 54020 – Floyd Woolson, prin.

Oshkosh, Winnebago Co., Pop. Code 8
Omro SD
Supt. – See Omro

Omro Junction MS, 1205 SAND PIT RD 54901
  Connie Koch, prin.
Plainview ES, 3077 UTICA RD 54904
  Kenlynn Akin, prin.

Oshkosh Area SD
Sch. Sys. Enr. Code 6
Supt. – James Henderson, P O BOX 3048 54903
Merrill MS, 108 W NEW YORK AVE 54901
  Donald Dutton, prin.
South Park MS, 1551 DELAWARE ST 54901
  William Holm, prin.
Stanley MS, 915 HAZEL ST 54901
  James McCartney, prin.
Tipler MS, 325 S EAGLE ST 54901
  Frank Bremberger, prin.
Cook ES, 1600 HAZEL ST 54901
  Sara Hawley, prin.
Franklin ES, 1401 W 5TH AVE 54901
  Jack Kolterjahn, prin.
Green Meadow ES, 3300 PICKETT RD 54904
  Edwin Schaefer, prin.
Jefferson ES, 244 W 11TH AVE 54901
  Ivan Werner, prin.
Lakeside ES, 4991 FOND DU LAC RD 54901
  Edwin Schaefer, prin.
Merrill ES, 108 W NEW YORK AVE 54901
  Henry Hauser, prin.
Oaklawn ES, 112 VIOLA OSCKOSH 54901
  Sara Hawley, prin.
Oakwood ES, 1225 N OAKWOOD RD 54904
  Raymond Wachholz, prin.
Read ES, 1120 ALGOMA BLVD 54901
  Gordon Russell, prin.
Roosevelt ES, 910 N SAWYER ST 54901
  Thomas Fischer, prin.
Shapiro ES, 1050 W 18TH AVE 54901
  Joyce Lloyd, prin.
Smith ES, 1745 OREGON ST 54901
  Ivan Werner, prin.
Stanley ES, 1109 E MELVIN AVE 54901
  James McCartney, prin.
Sunset ES, 3596 WINNECONNE RD 54904
  Thomas Fischer, prin.
Washington ES, 929 WINNEBAGO AVE 54901
  Henry Grasley, prin.

Grace Lutheran ES, 919 NEBRASKA ST 54901
Sacred Heart ES, 505 KNAPP ST 54901
St. Mary ES, 619 MERRITT AVE 54901
St. Peter ES, 449 HIGH AVE 54901
St. Vincent De Paul ES, 1207 OREGON ST 54901
Trinity Lutheran ES, 819 SCHOOL AVE 54901

Osseo, Trempealeau Co., Pop. Code 4
Osseo-Fairchild SD
Sch. Sys. Enr. Code 4
Supt. – Paul Pisani, 13TH & FRANCIS 54758
ES 54758 – Lee Eder, prin.
Other Schools – See Fairchild

Owen, Clark Co., Pop. Code 3
Owen-Withee SD
Sch. Sys. Enr. Code 3
Supt. – Gerald J. Nelson 54460
Owen Withee ES 54460 – Arthur Feldman, prin.

Oxford, Marquette Co., Pop. Code 2
Westfield SD
Supt. – See Westfield
ES 53952 – (—), prin.

Palmyra, Jefferson Co., Pop. Code 4
Palmyra-Eagle Area SD
Sch. Sys. Enr. Code 4
Supt. – Lance K. Fanshaw, 709 MAPLE ST 53156
ES, 701 MAPLE ST 53156 – Marlea Linse, prin.
Other Schools – See Eagle

Pardeeville, Columbia Co., Pop. Code 4
Pardeeville Area SD
Sch. Sys. Enr. Code 3
Supt. – Gerald Skaar, 120 S OAK ST 53954
MS, 403 W CHESTNUT ST 53954
  Terry D. Pease, prin.
Marcellon ES, RURAL ROUTE 01 53954
  Terry Pease, prin.
ES, 403 W CHESTNUT ST 53954
  Terry Pease, prin.

Portage Comm. SD
Supt. – See Portage
Pacific ES, RURAL ROUTE 02 53954
  Virginia Kramar, prin.

Park Falls, Price Co., Pop. Code 5
Park Falls SD
Sch. Sys. Enr. Code 4
Supt. – Michael Peterson, 477 1ST AVE N 54552
Lincoln MS, N 2ND AVE 54552
  Frank Campbell, prin.
ES 54552 – Charles Pouba, prin.

St. Anthony of Padua ES, 200 5TH AVE S 54552

Patch Grove, Grant Co., Pop. Code 2
West Grant SD
Sch. Sys. Enr. Code 2
Supt. – Richard Heidenreich 53817
West Grant MS 53817 – Richard Heidenreich, prin.
West Grant ES 53817 – Richard Heidenreich, prin.

Pembine, Mariette Co., Pop. Code 3
Beecher-Dunbar-Pembine SD
Sch. Sys. Enr. Code 2
Supt. – Cornelis Vander Zeyden
  P O BOX 247 54156

ES, P O BOX 247 54156
  Cornelis Vander Zeyden, prin.

Pepin, Pepin Co., Pop. Code 3
Pepin Area SD
Sch. Sys. Enr. Code 2
Supt. – Mark Collins 54759
ES 54759 – Rick Palmer, prin.

Peshtigo, Marinette Co., Pop. Code 5
Peshtigo SD
Sch. Sys. Enr. Code 3
Supt. – George A. Fox, BADGER ROAD 54157
ES, BADGER RD 54157 – H. David Lindbom, prin.

St. Mary's ES, 141 S WOOD AVE 54157

Pewaukee, Waukesha Co., Pop. Code 5
Hartland-Lakeside J3 SD
Supt. – See Hartland
Lakeside MS
  N 35 W29288 NORTH SHORE DR 53072
  Timothy Kooi, prin.

Kettle Moraine SD
Supt. – See Wales
Zion ES, N14 W29143 SILVERNAIL RD 53072
  Nancy Blair, prin.

Pewaukee SD
Sch. Sys. Enr. Code 4
Supt. – George Goens, 510 LAKE ST 53072
MS, 210 MAIN ST 53072 – (—), prin.
ES, 404 LAKE ST 53072 – Terrence Trotier, prin.

St. Anthony ES
  W280 N2101 HIGHWAY SS 53072
St. Mary ES, 449 W WISCONSIN AVE 53072

Phelps, Vilas Co., Pop. Code 4
Phelps SD
Sch. Sys. Enr. Code 2
Supt. – John Oxley 54554
ES 54554 – John Oxley, prin.

Phillips, Price Co., Pop. Code 4
Phillips SD
Sch. Sys. Enr. Code 4
Supt. – R. A. Weghorn, P O BOX 70 54555
MS, CHERRY ST 54555 – John Dill, prin.
ES 54555 – Rodger Nyberg, prin.
Other Schools – See Catawba, Kennan

Pigeon Falls, Trempealeau Co., Pop. Code 2
Whitehall SD
Supt. – See Whitehall
ES 54760 – Rodney Thompson, prin.

Pine River, Waushara Co.
Wild Rose SD
Supt. – See Wild Rose
Pleasant View ES
  RURAL ROUTE 01 BOX 120 54965
  Vernon Hess, prin.

Pittsville, Wood Co., Pop. Code 3
Pittsville SD
Sch. Sys. Enr. Code 3
Supt. – Milo Fossen 54466
ES 54466 – Dale Brux, prin.

Plain, Sauk Co., Pop. Code 3
River Valley SD
Supt. – See Spring Green
Sunnyside ES 53577 – (—), prin.

St. Luke ES, 1290 NACHREINER AVE 53577

Plainfield, Waushara Co., Pop. Code 3
Tri-County Area SD
Sch. Sys. Enr. Code 3
Supt. – Curtis Powell 54966
Tri County MS 54966 – James Mostek, prin.
Tri County ES 54966 – (—), prin.

Platteville, Grant Co., Pop. Code 6
Platteville SD
Sch. Sys. Enr. Code 4
Supt. – Donald Reinicke, 780 N 2ND ST 53818
MS, 40 E MADISON ST 53818
  Alan Eveland, prin.
Gray ES, 110 W ADAMS ST 53818
  Ronald Sime, prin.
Westview ES, 1205 CAMPT ST 53818
  Robert Bennett, prin.
Wilkins ES, 425 BROADWAY ST 53818
  Karen Schilling, prin.

St. Mary's Parish ES, 345 N COURT ST 53818

Plover, Portage Co., Pop. Code 6
Stevens Point Area SD
Supt. – See Stevens Point
Roosevelt ES, 600 WISCONSIN AVE 54467
  (—), prin.

Plum City, Pierce Co., Pop. Code 3
Plum City SD
Sch. Sys. Enr. Code 2
Supt. – Gerald Mikunda 54761
ES 54761 – William Fuller, prin.

Plymouth, Sheboygan Co., Pop. Code 6
Plymouth SD
Sch. Sys. Enr. Code 4
Supt. – Paul Brandl, 106 S HIGHLAND AVE 53073
Riverview MS, SMITH ST 53073
  Stephen Smith, prin.

Fairview ES 53073 – Amy Flood, prin.
Parkview ES, 500 PARKVIEW DR 53073
 Frederick Brietzke, prin.
Other Schools – See Cascade

St. John Lutheran ES, 222 N STAFFORD ST 53073
St. John the Baptist ES
 116 N PLEASANT ST 53073

Poplar, Douglas Co., Pop. Code 3
Maple SD
Supt. – See Maple
Northwestern MS 54864 – William Pelkey, prin.
ES 54864 – George Benlick, prin.

Portage, Columbia Co., Pop. Code 6
Portage Comm. SD
Sch. Sys. Enr. Code 4
Supt. – Marshall H. Boyd
 117 W FRANKLIN ST 53901
Caledonia ES, RURAL ROUTE 02 53901
 Mary Mittlesteadt, prin.
Fort Winnebago ES, RURAL ROUTE 01 53901
 Barbara Wade, prin.
Lewiston ES, RURAL ROUTE 03 53901
 Jane Engelland, prin.
Muir ES, 2600 WOODCREST DR 53901
 Gary O'hearn, prin.
Other Schools – See Endeavor, Pardeeville

St. John's Lutheran ES, 430 W EMMETT ST 53901
St. Mary's Parochial ES, 315 W COOK ST 53901

Port Edwards, Wood Co., Pop. Code 4
Port Edwards SD
Sch. Sys. Enr. Code 2
Supt. – Clifford Hudson, 801 2ND ST 54469
ES, 801 2ND ST 54469 – Edwin Heuer, prin.

Porterfield, Marinette Co., Pop. Code 4
Marinette SD
Supt. – See Marinette
ES, RURAL ROUTE 01 54159
 Joseph Beauclaire, prin.

Port Washington, Ozaukee Co., Pop. Code 6
Port Washington SD
Sch. Sys. Enr. Code 4
Supt. – Donald Tuler
 1234 W LINCOLN AVE 53074
Jefferson MS, 1403 N HOLDEN ST 53074
 Joseph Groh, prin.
Dunwiddie ES, 1243 N HOLDEN ST 53074
 Nancy Edelman, prin.
Lincoln ES, 1351 N THEIS LN 53074
 John Taylor, prin.
Other Schools – See Saukville

St. Mary ES, 446 JOHNSON ST 53074
St. Peter ES, 1800 N WISCONSIN ST 53074

Port Wing, Bayfield Co., Pop. Code 3
South Shore SD
Sch. Sys. Enr. Code 2
Supt. – Fred Schlichting, P O BOX 5 54865
Other Schools – See Herbster, Iron River

Potosi, Grant Co., Pop. Code 3
Potosi SD
Sch. Sys. Enr. Code 2
Supt. – Dennis Pratt 53820
ES, P O BOX 193 53820 – William Kline, prin.

SS Andrew & Thomas ES
 RURAL ROUTE 02 BOX 160 53820

Poynette, Columbia Co., Pop. Code 4
Poynette SD
Sch. Sys. Enr. Code 4
Supt. – (—), 108 N CLEVELAND 53955
MS, 108 N CLEVELAND 53955
 Paul Lareau, prin.
Dekorra ES 53955 – (—), prin.
ES 53955 – Paul Lareau, prin.
Other Schools – See Arlington

Poy Sippi, Waushara Co., Pop. Code 3
Berlin Area SD
Supt. – See Berlin
ES 54967 – Eugene Nickolai, prin.

Prairie Du Chien, Crawford Co., Pop. Code 6
Prairie Du Chien Area SD
Sch. Sys. Enr. Code 4
Supt. – John C. Mulrooney
 800 E CRAWFORD ST 53821
Kennedy ES, 420 S MINNESOTA ST 53821
 Gary Baxter, prin.
Other Schools – See Eastman

St. Gabriel ES, 515 N BEAUMONT RD 53821
St. John Nepomucene ES
 720 S WACOUTA AVE 53821

Prairie Du Sac, Sauk Co., Pop. Code 4
Sauk-Prairie SD
Supt. – See Sauk City
Grand Avenue MS, 225 GRAND AVE 53578
 Craig Bender, prin.
Tower Rock ES, RURAL ROUTE 01 53578
 John Lyon, prin.

Prairie Farm, Barron Co., Pop. Code 2
Prairie Farm SD
Sch. Sys. Enr. Code 2
Supt. – Howard Hanson 54762
ES 54762 – Howard Hanson, prin.

Prentice, Price Co., Pop. Code 3
Prentice SD
Sch. Sys. Enr. Code 3
Supt. – Gregory Krause 54556
ES 54556 – (—), prin.
Other Schools – See Ogema, Tripoli

Prescott, Pierce Co., Pop. Code 5
Prescott SD
Sch. Sys. Enr. Code 3
Supt. – B. L. Lepley, 1220 SAINT CROIX ST 54021
MS 54021 – R. W. Hoffmann, prin.
Malone ES 54021 – (—), prin.

St. Joseph Catholic ES, 281 DAKOTA ST S 54021

Princeton, Green Lake Co., Pop. Code 4
Princeton SD
Sch. Sys. Enr. Code 2
Supt. – Marvin Groskreutz 54968
ES 54968 – Marvin Groskreutz, prin.

St. John's Catholic ES, 125 CHBURCH ST 54968

Pulaski, Brown Co., Pop. Code 4
Pulaski Comm. SD
Sch. Sys. Enr. Code 5
Supt. – Thomas Joynt
 143 W GREEN BAY ST 54162
Glenbrook ES, 132 FRONT ST 54162
 James Brawner, prin.
Sunnyside ES, 720 COUNTY HWY C 54162
 Gerald Prosek, prin.
Other Schools – See Green Bay, Krakow, Oneida

Assumption of the BVM School
 P O BOX 57 54162

Racine, Racine Co., Pop. Code 8
Racine SD
Sch. Sys. Enr. Code 7
Supt. – Don Woods
 2220 NORTHWESTERN AVE 53404
Gilmore MS, 2201 HIGH ST 53404
 Ronald Olson, prin.
Jerst-Ager MS, 3601 LA SALLE ST 53402
 Richard Anderson, prin.
McKinley MS, 2326 MOHR AVE 53405
 Frank Osimitz, prin.
Mitchell MS, 2701 DREXEL AVE 53403
 Michael Frontier, prin.
Starbuck MS, 1516 OHIO ST 53405
 Jetha Pinkston, prin.
Washington MS, 914 SAINT PATRICK ST 53402
 Deborah Cora, prin.
Brown ES, 5915 ERIE ST 53402
 Charles Leonard, prin.
Fine Arts ES, 815 DE KOVEN AVE 53403
 Doug Julius, prin.
Fratt ES, 3501 KINZIE AVE 53405
 Donald Burant, prin.
Giese ES, 5120 BYRD AVE 53406
 George Knudtson, prin.
Gifford ES, 8332 NORTHWESTERN AVE 53406
 Rita Applebaum, prin.
Goodland ES, 4800 GRACELAND BLVD 53406
 Laverne Diem, prin.
Janes ES, 1425 N WISCONSIN ST 53402
 Lawrence Terry, prin.
Jefferson ES, 1722 W 6TH ST 53404
 Pat Rogers, prin.
Jerstad Ager ES, 3535 LA SALLE ST 53402
 Robert Hesse, prin.
Johnson ES, 2420 KENTUCKY ST 53405
 Chuck Groom, prin.
Jones ES, 3300 CHICKORY RD 53403
 Dawn Kloften, prin.
Knapp ES, 2701 17TH ST 53405
 Rick Fornal, prin.
Mitchell ES, 2713 DREXEL AVE 53403
 Michael Frontier, prin.
North Park ES, 4748 ELIZABETH ST 53402
 George Ginther, prin.
Red Apple ES, 914 ST PATRICK ST 53402
 Deborah Cora, prin.
Roosevelt ES, 915 ROMAYNE AVE 53402
 George Margosian, prin.
Wadewitz ES, 2700 YOUT ST 53404
 David Sweeney, prin.
West Ridge ES, 1347 S EMMERTSEN RD 53406
 (—), prin.
Wind Point ES, 4834 N MAIN ST 53402
 John Blickle, prin.
Winslow ES, 1325 PARK AVE 53403
 Doug Julius, prin.
Other Schools – See Caledonia, Sturtevant

Prairie School, 4050 LIGHTHOUSE DRIVE 53402
Concordia Lutheran ES
 3350 LATHROP AVE 53405
Holy Name ES, 1510 VILLA ST 53403
Sacred Heart ES
 2023 NORTHWESTERN AVE 53404
St. Edward ES, 1435 GROVE AVE 53405
St. John Nepomuk ES, 1923 GREEN ST 53402
St. John's Lutheran ES, 510 KEWAUNEE ST 53402
St. Joseph ES, 1525 ERIE ST 53402
St. Lucy's ES, 3035 DREXEL AVE 53403
St. Rita ES, 4433 DOUGLAS AVE 53402
Trinity Lutheran ES, 2035-65 GENEVA ST 53402
Wisconsin Lutheran ES, 734 VILLA ST 53403

Radisson, Sawyer Co., Pop. Code 2
Winter SD
Supt. – See Winter
ES 54867 – (—), prin.

Randolph, Columbia Co., Pop. Code 4
Randolph SD
Sch. Sys. Enr. Code 2
Supt. – Richard Kloiber
 110 MEADOW WOOD DRIVE 53956
ES, 265 N HIGH ST 53956 – Ronald Kolash, prin.

Randolph Christian ES, 457 2ND ST 53956

Random Lake, Sheboygan Co., Pop. Code 4
Random Lake SD
Sch. Sys. Enr. Code 4
Supt. – Russell Draeger 53075
ES, 605 RANDOM RD 53075
 Francis Murphy, prin.
Other Schools – See Adell

St. John Lutheran ES, 2281 HWY SS 53075
St. Mary ES, 306 BUTLER RD 53075

Readfield, Waupaca Co.
New London SD
Supt. – See New London
ES 54969 – William Caskey, prin.

Readstown, Vernon Co., Pop. Code 2
Kickapoo Area SD
Supt. – See Viola
ES 54664 – Hugh Parr, prin.

Redgranite, Waushara Co., Pop. Code 3
Wautoma Area SD
Supt. – See Wautoma
ES, P O BOX 49 54970 – Richard Getchius, prin.

Reedsburg, Sauk Co., Pop. Code 6
Reedsburg SD
Sch. Sys. Enr. Code 4
Supt. – Robert Allen, 710 N WEBB AVE 53959
MS, 1121 8TH ST 53959 – Charles Whitsell, prin.
South ES, 420 PLUM ST 53959
 Rachel Bauer, prin.
Westside ES, 401 ALEXANDER AVE 53959
 James Farrar, prin.
Other Schools – See La Valle, Loganville, Rock
 Springs

Sacred Heart ES, 545 N OAK ST 53959
St. Peter's Lutheran ES, 346 N LOCUST ST 53959

Reedsville, Manitowoc Co., Pop. Code 4
Reedsville SD
Sch. Sys. Enr. Code 3
Supt. – Jerome Runice, P O BOX 82 54230
JHS, P O BOX 82 54230 – (—), prin.
ES, 350 S PARK ST 54230
 Roger Ohlemacher, prin.

SS John & James Lutheran ES, P O BOX 211 54230
St. Mary's-Patricks ES, 628 MENASHA ST 54230

Reeseville, Dodge Co., Pop. Code 3
Dodgeland SD
Supt. – See Juneau
Dodgeland MS, P O BOX 8 53579
 Frederick Yarolimek, prin.

Rewey, Iowa Co., Pop. Code 2
Iowa-Grant SD
Supt. – See Livingston
ES 53580 – Doyle Hoke, prin.

Rhinelander, Oneida Co., Pop. Code 6
Rhinelander SD
Sch. Sys. Enr. Code 5
Supt. – Robert A. Hanson, ACACIA LANE 54501
Williams MS, ACACIA LANE 54501
 Robert Fabich, prin.
Central ES, 418 N PELHAM ST 54501
 Jean Nolte, prin.
Crescent ES, 3319 BOYCE DR 54501
 Jon Warmke, prin.
Newbold ES, RURAL ROUTE 01 54501
 (—), prin.
Pelican ES, RURAL ROUTE 04 54501
 Jean Nolte, prin.
Pine Lake ES, RURAL ROUTE 01 54501
 Gene Belmas, prin.
South Park ES, 511 S PELHAM ST 54501
 Jon Warmke, prin.
West ES, 309 MAPLE ST 54501 – (—), prin.
Other Schools – See Harshaw

Three Lakes SD
Supt. – See Three Lakes
Sugar Camp ES, 4066 CAMP FOUR RD 54501
 J. Lehman, prin.

Rhinelander Catholic Central ES
 103 E KING ST 54501
Zion Lutheran ES, 26 W FREDERICK ST 54501

Rib Lake, Taylor Co., Pop. Code 3
Rib Lake SD
Sch. Sys. Enr. Code 3
Supt. – Ramon Parks, P O BOX 278 54470
MS, P O BOX 278 54470 – (—), prin.
Clearview ES, P O BOX 278 54470 – (—), prin.
Other Schools – See Westboro

Rice Lake, Barron Co., Pop. Code 6
Rice Lake Area SD
Sch. Sys. Enr. Code 5
Supt. – Robert Foster, 700 AUGUSTA ST   54868
MS, 204 CAMERON ROAD   54868
  Richard Halverson, prin.
Franklin ES, 1011 S MAIN ST   54868
  Judith Klasell, prin.
Hill Top ES, 204 CAMERON RD   54868
  John Olesczuk, prin.
Jefferson ES, 30 PHIPPS AVE   54868
  Judith Klassell, prin.
Lincoln City ES, 426 N WILSON AVE   54868
  (—), prin.
Other Schools – See Brill, Haugen
_____

St. Joseph ES, 128 W HUMBIRD ST   54868

Richfield, Washington Co., Pop. Code 6
Germantown SD
Supt. – See Germantown
Highway View ES, RURAL ROUTE 01   53076
  Richard Pautz, prin.
Rockfield MS
  N132W18473 ROCKFIELD RD   53076
  Anthony Clementi, prin.

Richfield #2 SD
Sch. Sys. Enr. Code 2
Supt. – Scott Sarnow   53076
ES, HWY 167 & 175   53076 – James Anonich, prin.

Richland Center, Richland Co., Pop. Code 5
Ithaca SD
Sch. Sys. Enr. Code 2
Supt. – John Garner, RURAL ROUTE 02   53581
Ithaca JHS, RURAL ROUTE 02   53581
  Ernest Modjeski, prin.
Ithica ES, RURAL ROUTE 02   53581
  (—), prin.

Richland SD
Sch. Sys. Enr. Code 4
Supt. – Gerald Edwards
  125 S CENTRAL AVE   53581
Richland MS, RURAL ROUTE 02   53581
  David Siefkes, prin.
Doudna MS, BOHMANN DR   53581
  Robert Nugent, prin.
Jefferson ES, 586 N MAIN ST   53581
  Carol Troxel, prin.
Lincoln ES, 678 S PARK ST   53581
  Marjorie Sugden, prin.
Rockbridge ES, RURAL ROUTE 03   53581
  James Korb, prin.
Washington ES, RURAL ROUTE 01   53581
  Gary Garbe, prin.
Other Schools – See Blue River
_____

St. Mary ES, 155 W 5TH ST   53581

Ridgeland, Dunn Co., Pop. Code 2
Barron Area SD
Supt. – See Barron
ES, P O BOX 196   54763 – Mae Repp, prin.

Ridgeway, Iowa Co., Pop. Code 3
Dodgeville SD
Supt. – See Dodgeville
ES   53582 – Richard Grimoskas, prin.

Ringle, Marathon Co., Pop. Code 4
D. C. Everest Area SD
Supt. – See Schofield
Easton ES, RURAL ROUTE 01   54471
  Nancy Caskey, prin.
Riverside ES, RURAL ROUTE 01   54471
  Don Abel, prin.

Rio, Columbia Co., Pop. Code 3
Rio Comm. SD
Sch. Sys. Enr. Code 2
Supt. – David Carlson   53960
ES   53960 – David Carlson, prin.

Ripon, Fond du Lac Co., Pop. Code 6
Ripon SD
Sch. Sys. Enr. Code 4
Supt. – Michael Heckman, P O BOX 991   54971
MS, P O BOX 185   54971 – Leland Nelson, prin.
Adams ES, P O BOX 991   54971 – (—), prin.
Callan ES, P O BOX 991   54971
  James Thoma, prin.
Central MS, P O BOX 991   54971
  Mary Miritz, prin.
Ceresco ES, P O BOX 991   54971
  James Thoma, prin.
Roosevelt ES, P O BOX 991   54971
  James Thoma, prin.
Wayside ES, P O BOX 991   54971
  Mary Miritz, prin.

River Falls, Pierce Co., Pop. Code 6
River Falls SD
Sch. Sys. Enr. Code 4
Supt. – Charles Brenden, 104 LOCUST ST E   54022
Greenwood ES, 418 N 8TH ST   54022
  (—), prin.
Westside ES, 1007 W PINE ST   54022
  Jerene Mortenson, prin.
_____

St. Bridget Parochial ES, P O BOX 268   54022

Roberts, St. Croix Co., Pop. Code 3
St. Croix Central SD
Supt. – See Hammond
ES   54023 – Donald White, prin.

Rochester, Racine Co., Pop. Code 3
Waterford Jt. 1 V SD
Sch. Sys. Enr. Code 3
Supt. – R. M. Marta, P O BOX 98   53167
Other Schools – See Waterford

Rock Springs, Sauk Co., Pop. Code 2
Reedsburg SD
Supt. – See Reedsburg
ES   53961 – Robert Leopold, prin.

Rosendale, Fond du Lac Co., Pop. Code 3
Rosendale-Brandon SD
Sch. Sys. Enr. Code 4
Supt. – Terry Milfred   54974
MS   54974 – Ronald Milton, prin.
ES   54974 – Terry Milfred, prin.
Other Schools – See Brandon

Rosholt, Portage Co., Pop. Code 3
Rosholt SD
Sch. Sys. Enr. Code 3
Supt. – Orland McCollum   54473
ES   54473 – Kathleen Martinsen, prin.
_____

St. Adalbert ES, 252 ST ADALBERTS RD   54473

Rothschild, Marathon Co., Pop. Code 5
D. C. Everest Area SD
Supt. – See Schofield
ES, 810 1ST ST   54474 – James Harris, prin.
_____

St. Mark's ES, 602 MILITARY RD   54474

Rubicon, Dodge Co., Pop. Code 4
Rubicon J6 SD
Sch. Sys. Enr. Code 2
Supt. – Florence McDonald
  RURAL ROUTE 01   53078
Saylesville ES, RURAL ROUTE 01   53078
  Florence McDonald, prin.

Rudolph, Wood Co., Pop. Code 2
Wisconsin Rapids SD
Supt. – See Wisconsin Rapids
ES, 6950 KNOWLEDGE AVE   54475
  Edward Schmidt, Jr., prin.

Saint Croix Falls, Polk Co., Pop. Code 4
St. Croix Falls SD
Sch. Sys. Enr. Code 4
Supt. – Fred Johnson   54024
Sorensen MS   54024 – Jay Delano, prin.
ES   54024 – Larry Swanson, prin.
Other Schools – See Cushing, Dresser

Saint Francis, Milwaukee Co., Pop. Code 7
St. Francis SD
Sch. Sys. Enr. Code 4
Supt. – William F. Steinert
  4225 S LAKE DRIVE   53207
Faircrest ES, 3819 S IOWA AVE   53207
  Mary Kuxhause, prin.
Thompson ES, 3120 E NORWICH AVE   53207
  Frederick Kelroy, prin.
Willow Glen ES, 2600 E BOLIVAR AVE   53207
  Kenneth Knoll, prin.
_____

Sacred Heart of Jesus ES
  3641 S KINNICKINNIC AVE   53207

Saint Germain, Vilas Co., Pop. Code 4
Northland Pines SD
Supt. – See Eagle River
ES   54558 – Eugene Olson, prin.

Salem, Kenosha Co., Pop. Code 6
Salem J2 SD
Sch. Sys. Enr. Code 3
Supt. – Marvin Carby, P O BOX 160   53168
Salem Consolidated ES, P O BOX 160   53168
  Ronald Bousquet, prin.

Sauk City, Sauk Co., Pop. Code 5
Sauk-Prairie SD
Sch. Sys. Enr. Code 4
Supt. – Richard Magnuson, 213 MAPLE ST   53583
Sauk Prairie MS, 207 MAPLE ST   53583
  Ellen Paul, prin.
Blackhawk ES, RURAL ROUTE 01   53583
  William Henning, prin.
Spruce Street ES, 701 SPRUCE ST   53583
  Greg Hubanks, prin.
Other Schools – See Merrimac, Prairie Du Sac
_____

St. Aloysius ES, 608 OAK ST   53583

Saukville, Ozaukee Co., Pop. Code 5
Port Washington SD
Supt. – See Port Washington
ES, 333 N MILL ST   53080 – Lois Zahorik, prin.

Schofield, Marathon Co., Pop. Code 4
D. C. Everest Area SD
Sch. Sys. Enr. Code 5
Supt. – Gerald Makie, 6300 ALDERSON ST   54476
ES, 1310 GRAND AVE   54476
  Donald Wendorf, prin.
Weston ES, 5200 CAMP PHILLIPS RD   54476
  Gerald Ray, prin.
Other Schools – See Hatley, Mosinee, Ringle,
  Rothschild
_____

St. Therese ES, 113 KORT ST   54476
St. Peter Lutheran ES, 115 EAU CLAIRE ST   54476

Seneca, Crawford Co., Pop. Code 3
Seneca SD
Sch. Sys. Enr. Code 2
Supt. – Joseph Zoeller   54654
ES   54654 – Joseph Zoeller, prin.
Other Schools – See Eastman, Lynxville

Seymour, Outagamie Co., Pop. Code 5
Seymour Comm. SD
Sch. Sys. Enr. Code 4
Supt. – William Loasching
  10 CIRCLE DRIVE   54165
Rock Ledge ES, 330 W HICKORY ST   54165
  Douglas Watirovich, prin.
Other Schools – See Black Creek, Nichols
_____

St. John Baptist ES, 928 S MAIN ST   54165

Sharon, Walworth Co., Pop. Code 4
Sharon J11 SD
Sch. Sys. Enr. Code 2
Supt. – Dorothy Kaufmann
  104 E SCHOOL ST   53585
ES, 104 E SCHOOL ST   53585 – (—), prin.

Shawano, Shawano Co., Pop. Code 6
Shawano-Gresham SD
Sch. Sys. Enr. Code 4
Supt. – Frederick Davel
  204-210 S FRANKLIN ST   54166
Franklin MS, 204-210 S FRANKLIN ST   54166
  John Esse, prin.
Lincoln ES, 237 S SAWYER ST   54166
  William Prijic, prin.
Olga ES, 1300 S UNION ST   54166
  Harvey Steffan, prin.
Other Schools – See Gresham
_____

Sacred Heart ES, 124 E CENTER ST   54166
St. James Lutheran ES, 320 S ANDREWS ST   54166

Sheboygan, Sheboygan Co., Pop. Code 8
Howards Grove SD
Supt. – See Howards Grove
Northview MS, 902 TYLER RD   53083
  Paul Ten Pas, prin.
Mosel Lakeview ES, RURAL ROUTE 01   53083
  Paul Ten Pas, prin.
Riverview ES, 437 N WISCONSIN DR   53083
  Paul Ten Pas, prin.

Sheboygan Area SD
Sch. Sys. Enr. Code 6
Supt. – George Longo, 830 VIRGINIA AVE   53081
Farnsworth MS, 1017 UNION AVE   53081
  Roland Alger, prin.
Mann MS, 2820 UNION AVE   53081
  Warren Brewer, prin.
Urban MS, 1226 NORTH AVE   53081
  Bette Lang, prin.
Cooper ES, 2014 COOPER AVE   53083
  Carl Toepel, prin.
Grant ES, 1528 N 5TH ST   53081
  Allan Calabresa, prin.
Jackson ES, 4540 MOENNING RD   53081
  Carol Kalzow, prin.
Jefferson ES, 1538 N 15TH ST   53081
  John Pfaff, prin.
Lincoln ES, 4815 CO TRUCK J   53081
  Carol Kalzow, prin.
Longfellow ES, 1315 S 9TH ST   53081
  William Walter, prin.
Madison ES, 2302 DAVID AVE   53081
  Russell Groblewski, prin.
Pigeon River ES, 3508 N 21ST ST   53083
  Eric Oleson, prin.
Sheridan ES, 1412 MARYLAND AVE   53081
  James Orlenko, prin.
Washington ES, 1238 GEELE AVE   53083
  Wayne Blessing, prin.
Wilson ES, 1625 WILSON AVE   53081
  Thomas Binder, prin.
Other Schools – See Cleveland
_____

Bethlehem Lutheran ES
  1121 GEORGIA AVE   53081
Christ Child Academy, 2722 HENRY ST   53081
Holy Name ES, 814 SUPERIOR AVE   53081
Immanuel Lutheran ES
  1626 ILLINOIS AVE   53081
Sheboygan Christian ES, 418 GEELE AVE   53083
St. Dominic ES, 2100 N 21ST ST   53081
St. Paul's Lutheran ES, 1819 N 13TH ST   53081
Trinity Lutheran ES, 824 WISCONSIN AVE   53081

Sheboygan Falls, Sheboygan Co., Pop. Code 6
Sheboygan Falls SD
Sch. Sys. Enr. Code 4
Supt. – Norman Frakes
  220 AMHERST AVE   53085
MS   53085 – Michael Meissen, prin.
ES   53085 – (—), prin.
Other Schools – See Waldo
_____

St. Mary's ES, 313 GIDDINGS AVE   53085

Sheldon, Rusk Co., Pop. Code 2
Flambeau SD
Supt. – See Tony
ES   54766 – William Pfalzgraf, prin.

Shell Lake, Washburn Co., Pop. Code 4
Shell Lake SD
Sch. Sys. Enr. Code 3
Supt. – J. Lilyquist   54871

MS 54871 – Thomas Butler, prin.
ES 54871 – Thomas Butler, prin.

Sherwood, Calumet Co., Pop. Code 2

St. John Sacred Heart ES, P O BOX 78 54169

Shiocton, Outagamie Co., Pop. Code 3
Shiocton SD
Sch. Sys. Enr. Code 3
Supt. – Robert McCoy, P O BOX 68 54170
ES 54170 – Carl Gloede, prin.

Shorewood, Milwaukee Co., Pop. Code 7
Shorewood SD
Sch. Sys. Enr. Code 4
Supt. – Barbara Grohe
1701 E CAPITOL DRIVE 53211
JHS, 3830 N MORRIS BLVD 53211
John Hansen, prin.
Atwater ES, 2100 E CAPITOL DR 53211
Richard Cobb, prin.
Lake Bluff ES, 1600 E LAKE BLUFF BLVD 53211
Karen Petric, prin.

St. Robert ES, 2200 E CAPITOL DR 53211

Shullsburg, Lafayette Co., Pop. Code 4
Darlington Comm. SD
Supt. – See Darlington
Prairie View ES, RURAL ROUTE 01 53586
(—), prin.

Shullsburg SD
Sch. Sys. Enr. Code 2
Supt. – John Timmerman
444 JUDGEMENT ST 53586
Shullsburg ES, 444 JUDGEMENT ST 53586
Peter Wagner, prin.

Silver Lake, Kenosha Co., Pop. Code 4
Silver Lake J1 SD
Sch. Sys. Enr. Code 2
Supt. – Perry K. Hellum, 300 PROSSER ST 53170
Riverview ES, 300 PROSSER ST 53170
Douglas Field, prin.

Siren, Burnett Co., Pop. Code 3
Siren SD
Sch. Sys. Enr. Code 3
Supt. – Robert G. Lee, P O BOX 29 54872
ES, P O BOX 29 54872 – Emmett Byrne, prin.

Slinger, Washington Co., Pop. Code 4
Slinger SD
Sch. Sys. Enr. Code 4
Supt. – Ron J. Rueckl
207 E WASHINGTON ST 53086
ES, 207 E WASHINGTON ST 53086
Sarah Bernhard, prin.
Other Schools – See Allenton

St. Peter Roman Catholic ES
206 E WASHINGTON ST 53086

Soldiers Grove, Crawford Co., Pop. Code 3
North Crawford SD
Supt. – See Gays Mills
North Crawford ES, P O BOX 38 54655
Robert Knadle, prin.

Solon Springs, Douglas Co., Pop. Code 3
Solon Springs SD
Sch. Sys. Enr. Code 2
Supt. – Robert Houg
RURAL ROUTE 01 BOX 571 54873
Saint Croix ES
RURAL ROUTE 01 BOX 595A 54873
(—), prin.

Somers, Kenosha Co., Pop. Code 6
Kenosha SD
Supt. – See Kenosha
ES, 1245 72ND AVE 53171 – Gary Gillmore, prin.

Somerset, St. Croix Co., Pop. Code 3
Somerset SD
Sch. Sys. Enr. Code 3
Supt. – Dianne Beeler, 400 SPRING ST 54025
ES, P O BOX 100 54025 – Janet Muellner, prin.

St. Anne ES, RURAL ROUTE 01 BOX 12A 54025

South Milwaukee, Milwaukee Co., Pop. Code 7
South Milwaukee SD
Sch. Sys. Enr. Code 5
Supt. – Michael Wiziarde, 1001 15TH AVE 53172
Blakewood ES, 3501 BLAKEWOOD AVE 53172
Ervin Nowak, prin.
Lakeview ES, 711 MARION AVE 53172
Gerald Schumacher, prin.
Luther ES, 718 HAWTHORNE AVE 53172
Carolyn Keeler, prin.
Rawson ES, 1410 RAWSON AVE 53172
Gregory Maass, prin.

St. Adalbert ES, 1610 MINNESOTA AVE 53172
St. John's Parish ES, 805 MARQUETTE AVE 53172
St. Mary's ES, 1314 MANITOBA AVE 53172
St. Sylvester ES, 695 COLLEGE AVE 53172
Zion Evangelist Lutheran ES
2200 9TH AVE 53172

South Wayne, Lafayette Co., Pop. Code 2
Black Hawk SD
Sch. Sys. Enr. Code 3
Supt. – Robert Beaver 53587

ES 53587 – Joyce Mau, prin.
Other Schools – See Gratiot

Sparta, Monroe Co., Pop. Code 6
Sparta Area SD
Sch. Sys. Enr. Code 4
Supt. – Douglas Schroeder
506 N BLACK RIVER ST 54656
Angelo ES, RURAL ROUTE 04 54656
Richard Baudek, prin.
Lakeview ES, 711 PINE ST 54656
Richard Baudek, prin.
Lawson ES, BLACK RIVER ST 54656
James Liska, prin.
Leon ES, RURAL ROUTE 03 54656
James Liska, prin.
Southside ES, WALRATH ST 54656
Richard Baudek, prin.
Other Schools – See Cataract

St. Patrick's ES, 318 W OAK ST 54656

Spencer, Marathon Co., Pop. Code 4
Spencer SD
Sch. Sys. Enr. Code 3
Supt. – Donald Stevens, 300 SCHOOL ST 54479
ES, 300 SCHOOL ST 54479 – Mark McQuire, prin.

Spooner, Washburn Co., Pop. Code 4
Spooner SD
Sch. Sys. Enr. Code 4
Supt. – John W. McDermott
500 COLLEGE ST 54801
MS, 500 COLLEGE ST 54801
John Tourville, prin.
ES, SCRIBNER ST 54801 – James Dohm, prin.

St. Francis DeSales ES, 406 OAK ST 54801

Spring Green, Sauk Co., Pop. Code 4
River Valley SD
Sch. Sys. Enr. Code 4
Supt. – Miles Turner 53588
ES 53588 – (—), prin.
Other Schools – See Arena, Lone Rock, Plain

St. John Evangelist ES
209 N WASHINGTON ST 53588

Spring Valley, Pierce Co., Pop. Code 3
Spring Valley SD
Sch. Sys. Enr. Code 3
Supt. – Gene Roland 54767
Gilman ES 54767 – Helen Sandve, prin.
MS 54767 – Leroy Nelson, prin.
Wilson ES 54767 – Nancy Cleveland, prin.

Stanley, Chippewa Co., Pop. Code 4
Stanley-Boyd Area SD
Sch. Sys. Enr. Code 4
Supt. – Charles Poulter, E 4TH AVE 54768
Stanley-Boyd MS, E 4TH AVE 54768
Gene Luoma, prin.
Dodge ES 54768 – Marion Peterson, prin.
Other Schools – See Boyd

Stetsonville, Taylor Co., Pop. Code 2
Medford Area SD
Supt. – See Medford
ES 54480 – Barbara Larson, prin.

Stevens Point, Portage Co., Pop. Code 7
Stevens Point Area SD
Sch. Sys. Enr. Code 6
Supt. – Dwight Stevens, 1900 POLK ST 54481
Emerson MS, 1401 E AVE 54481
Loran Volland, prin.
Jackson ES, 1900 W ZINDA DR 54481
John Legro, prin.
Jefferson ES, 1800 E AVE 54481
Loren Volland, prin.
Madison ES, 600 AMRIA DR 54481
Bob Schroeder, prin.
McDill ES, 2516 SCHOOL ST 54481
Eugene LaRose, prin.
McKinley ES, 2926 BLAINE ST 54481
Jerome Corgiat, prin.
Plover Whiting ES, 3931 HOOVER AVE 54481
William King, prin.
Washington ES, 3500 PRAIS ST 54481
Patricia Lewis, prin.
Other Schools – See Junction City, Plover

SS Joseph & Stephen ES, 1335 CLARK ST 54481
St. Paul Lutheran ES, 1919 WYATT AVE 54481
St. Peter ES, 708 1ST ST 54481
St. Stanislaus ES, 2150 HIGH ST 54481

Stockbridge, Calumet Co., Pop. Code 3
Stockbridge SD
Sch. Sys. Enr. Code 2
Supt. – Harold Brennan, P O BOX 188 53088
ES, 110 SCHOOL ST 53088
Barkley Anderson, prin.

Stoddard, Vernon Co., Pop. Code 3
DeSoto Area SD
Supt. – See De Soto
ES 54658 – Gary Husmann, prin.

St. Matthew's Evangelist Lutheran ES
P O BOX 208 54658

Stone Lake, Sawyer Co.
Hayward Comm. SD
Supt. – See Hayward
ES 54876 – John Becker, prin.

St. Francis Solanus ES, RURAL ROUTE 02 54876

Stoughton, Dane Co., Pop. Code 6
Stoughton Area SD
Sch. Sys. Enr. Code 5
Supt. – James P. Fricke, P O BOX 189 53589
MS, P O BOX 189 53589 – Mark Mulholland, prin.
Kegonsa ES, P O BOX 189 53589
Robert Soderbloom, prin.
Yahara ES, P O BOX 189 53589
Barbara Wood, prin.

Saint Ann's ES, 324 N HARRISON ST 53589

Stratford, Marathon Co., Pop. Code 4
Stratford SD
Sch. Sys. Enr. Code 3
Supt. – Edwin E. Otto 54484
MS 54484 – (—), prin.
Raleigh ES 54484 – Barbara Gaulke, prin.

St. Joseph ES, RURAL ROUTE 02 BOX 347 54484

Strum, Trempealeau Co., Pop. Code 3
Eleva-Strum SD
Sch. Sys. Enr. Code 3
Supt. – Gary Marine, RURAL ROUTE 01 54770
ES 54770 – (—), prin.
Other Schools – See Eleva

Sturgeon Bay, Door Co., Pop. Code 6
Sevastopol SD
Sch. Sys. Enr. Code 3
Supt. – Carl Scholz, 4550 HIGHWAY 57 54235
Sevastopol ES, 4550 HWY 57 54235
Ann Jerdee, prin.

Sturgeon Bay SD
Sch. Sys. Enr. Code 4
Supt. – Jerome Kain, 1230 MICHIGAN ST 54235
Walker MS, 19 N 14TH AVE 54235
Robert White, prin.
Sunrise ES, 1414 RHODE ISLAND ST 54235
Joseph McMahon, prin.
Sunset ES, 757 DELAWARE ST 54235
Joseph McMahon, prin.
West ES, 17 W PINE ST 54235
Joseph McMahon, prin.

Corpus Christi ES, 731 W JUNIPER ST 54235
SS Peter & Paul ES, 4761 DUNN RD 54235
St. Joseph ES, 130 N 5TH AVE 54235
St. Peter's Evangelist Lutheran ES
116 W MAPLE ST 54235

Sturtevant, Racine Co., Pop. Code 5
Racine SD
Supt. – See Racine
Schulte ES, 8515 WESTMINSTER DR 53177
Steve Miley, prin.

St. Sebastian's ES, 3030 95TH ST 53177

Sullivan, Jefferson Co., Pop. Code 2
Jefferson SD
Supt. – See Jefferson
ES, RURAL ROUTE 02 53178
Daniel Wenkman, prin.

Watertown SD
Supt. – See Watertown
Concord ES, RURAL ROUTE 01 53178
Charles Bruce, prin.

Sun Prairie, Dane Co., Pop. Code 7
Sun Prairie SD
Sch. Sys. Enr. Code 5
Supt. – Robert Fritsch
509 COMMERCIAL AVE 53590
MS, 160 SOUTH ST 53590
Dennis J. Ferriter, prin.
Bird ES, 1170 N BIRD ST 53590
Judith Braught, prin.
Eastside ES, 661 ELIZABETH LN 53590
Phillip Wilms, prin.
Northside ES, 230 KLUBERTZANZ DR 53590
Kenneth Hammond, prin.
Royal Oaks ES, 2215 PENNSYLVANIA AVE 53590
Robert Demrow, prin.
Westside ES, 1320 BUENA VISTA DR 53590
Arzetta Witalison, prin.

Sacred Hearts ES, 221 COLUMBUS ST 53590

Superior, Douglas Co., Pop. Code 8
Superior SD
Sch. Sys. Enr. Code 6
Supt. – Benjamin Kanninen
823 BELKNAP ST 54880
Blaine ES, 823 BELKNAP ST 54880
Patrick Dorin, prin.
Bryant ES, 6010 JOHN AVE 54880
Beverly Sutherland, prin.
Cooper ES, 1812 WYOMING AVE 54880
Dennis Mertzig, prin.
Dewey ES, 611 24TH AVE E 54880
Yvonne Cloutier, prin.
Four Corners ES 54880 – Alan Nelson, prin.
Lake Superior ES, 6200 E 3RD ST 54880
Kenneth Leland, prin.
Lincoln ES, 309 6TH AVE E 54880
Beth Arnson, prin.
Pattison ES, 1016 N 21ST ST 54880
Roger Bare, prin.

Cathedral School, 1419 BAXTER AVE 54880

Suring, Oconto Co., Pop. Code 3
Suring SD
Sch. Sys. Enr. Code 3
Supt. – William Kean, P O BOX 158 54174
ES 54174 – Arthur Schelk, Jr., prin.
Other Schools – See Mountain

Sussex, Waukesha Co., Pop. Code 5
Hamilton SD
Sch. Sys. Enr. Code 5
Supt. – Ralph Lenz
W 220 N 6151 TOWN LINE ROAD 53089
Templeton MS
N 59 W 22490 SILVER SPRING 53089
Gordon Heier, prin.
Maple Avenue ES
W240N6059 MAPLE AVE 53089
Doyle Alexander, prin.
Other Schools – See Lannon, Menomonee Falls

Lisbon J2 SD
Sch. Sys. Enr. Code 2
Supt. – Dennis Kruse
N56 W26530 RICHMOND ROAD 53089
Richmond ES
N56 W26530 RICHMOND RD 53089
(—), prin.

Taylor, Jackson Co., Pop. Code 2
Taylor SD
Sch. Sys. Enr. Code 2
Supt. – William Urban 54659
ES 54659 – Nora Olson, prin.

Theresa, Dodge Co., Pop. Code 3
Lomira SD
Supt. – See Lomira
ES 53091 – Delores Justman, prin.

Thorp, Clark Co., Pop. Code 4
Thorp SD
Sch. Sys. Enr. Code 3
Supt. – Terry Olson, P O BOX 449 54771
ES, P O BOX 409 54771 – Jerome Fiene, prin.

Thorp Catholic ES, 411 E SCHOOL ST 54771

Three Lakes, Oneida Co., Pop. Code 4
Three Lakes SD
Sch. Sys. Enr. Code 3
Supt. – George St. Catherine 54562
JHS, P O BOX 280 54562 – (—), prin.
ES, P O BOX 280 54562 – Thomas Bredesen, prin.
Other Schools – See Rhinelander

Tigerton, Shawano Co., Pop. Code 3
Tigerton SD
Sch. Sys. Enr. Code 2
Supt. – Walter W. Barker 54486
ES 54486 – Walter Barker, prin.

Tomah, Monroe Co., Pop. Code 6
Tomah Area SD
Sch. Sys. Enr. Code 5
Supt. – Anthony Hinden
801 LINCOLN AVE 54660
Lemonweir ES, N GLENDALE AVE 54660
Jerry Bauer, prin.
Miller ES, 813 OAK AVE 54660
Dennis Raabe, prin.
Other Schools – See Camp Douglas, Oakdale,
Warrens, Wyeville

St. Mary ES, 315 W MONROE ST 54660
St. Paul Lutheran ES, 505 SUPERIOR AVE 54660

Tomahawk, Lincoln Co., Pop. Code 5
Tomahawk SD
Sch. Sys. Enr. Code 4
Supt. – Robert Stirn, E WASHINGTON AVE 54487
MS, E KINGS ROAD 54487 – John Penn, prin.
ES, E KINGS RD 54487 – Herbert Sosinsky, prin.

St. Mary's ES, 110 N 7TH ST 54487

Tony, Rusk Co., Pop. Code 2
Flambeau SD
Sch. Sys. Enr. Code 3
Supt. – John Schomisch, P O BOX 86 54563
Other Schools – See Conrath, Glen Flora, Sheldon

Trempealeau, Trempealeau Co., Pop. Code 3
Galesville-Ettrick SD
Supt. – See Galesville
Gale-Ettr-Tremp MS 54661 – Warren Selck, prin.
ES 54661 – Warren Selck, prin.

Trevor, Kenosha Co.
Salem #7 SD
Sch. Sys. Enr. Code 2
Supt. – (—), 26325 WILMOT ROAD 53179
ES, 26325 WILMOT RD 53179 – (—), prin.

Tripoli, Oneida Co.
Prentice SD
Supt. – See Prentice
ES 54564 – (—), prin.

Turtle Lake, Barron Co., Pop. Code 3
Turtle Lake SD
Sch. Sys. Enr. Code 3
Supt. – Douglas Hendrickson 54889
ES 54889 – William Burhop, prin.

Twin Lakes, Kenosha Co., Pop. Code 5
Twin Lakes #4 SD
Sch. Sys. Enr. Code 2
Supt. – Ronald Bullens 53181
Lakewood ES, 1218 WILMOT AVE 53181
Dan Armstrong, prin.

Two Rivers, Manitowoc Co., Pop. Code 7
Two Rivers SD
Sch. Sys. Enr. Code 4
Supt. – Keith Martin, 1500 27TH ST 54241
Clarke MS, 4606 BELLEVUE PLACE 54241
Richard Vogt, prin.
Case ES, 1322 33RD ST 54241
Frederic Willert, prin.
Koening ES, 1114 LOWELL ST 54241
Robert Dewane, prin.
Magee ES, 3502 GLENWOOD ST 54241
Garth Landon, prin.

Two Rivers Catholic Central MS
1800 JEFFERSON ST 54241
St. John's Lutheran ES, 17TH & E PARK ST 54241
Two Rivers Catholic Central School
2203 12TH ST 54241

Union Grove, Racine Co., Pop. Code 5
Union Grove Jt. 1 SD
Sch. Sys. Enr. Code 3
Supt. – Giles Williams
1745 MILLDRUM ST 53182
Union Grove MS, 1745 MILLDRUM ST 53182
Giles Williams, prin.
ES, 810 14TH AVE 53182 – (—), prin.

Yorkville J2 SD
Sch. Sys. Enr. Code 2
Supt. – Gilbert Nilsen
18621 WASHINGTON AVE 53182
Yorkville ES, 18621 WASHINGTON AVE 53182
Gilbert Nilsen, prin.

Union Grove Christian School
P O BOX 103 53182

Unity, Marathon Co., Pop. Code 2
Colby SD
Supt. – See Colby
ES 54488 – Ervin Lafave, prin.

Valders, Manitowoc Co., Pop. Code 3
Valders SD
Sch. Sys. Enr. Code 4
Supt. – Ronald Ertner, 138 JEFFERSON ST 54245
MS, JEFFERSON ST 54245 – Derrick Krey, prin.
ES, 300 W WILSON ST 54245
Mark Swanson, prin.

Verona, Dane Co., Pop. Code 5
Middleton-Cross Plains SD
Supt. – See Middleton
West Middleton ES
RURAL ROUTE 07 BOX 7627 53593
Patrick Kinney, prin.

Verona Area SD
Sch. Sys. Enr. Code 4
Supt. – Wayne Diekrager, 300 CHURCH ST 53593
MS, 400 N MAIN ST 53593 – Judy Peppard, prin.
ES, 420 CHURCH AVE 53593 – (—), prin.
Other Schools – See Madison

Vesper, Wood Co., Pop. Code 3
Wisconsin Rapids SD
Supt. – See Wisconsin Rapids
ES, 217 S VIRGINIA ST 54489
Edward Schmidt, Jr., prin.

Viola, Richland Co., Pop. Code 3
Kickapoo Area SD
Sch. Sys. Enr. Code 3
Supt. – Jeanetta Kirkpatrick 54664
ES 54664 – (—), prin.
Other Schools – See Readstown

Viroqua, Vernon Co., Pop. Code 5
Viroqua Area SD
Sch. Sys. Enr. Code 4
Supt. – Roland J. Hill 54665
MS, 100 BLACKHAWK DRIVE 54665
Jerry Sines, prin.
ES 54665 – Chester Lee, prin.

Wabeno, Forest Co., Pop. Code 4
Wabeno Area SD
Sch. Sys. Enr. Code 3
Supt. – Joseph Innis 54566
MS 54566 – (—), prin.
ES 54566 – Richard Huisman, prin.

Waldo, Sheboygan Co., Pop. Code 2
Sheboygan Falls SD
Supt. – See Sheboygan Falls
ES 53093 – (—), prin.

Wales, Waukesha Co., Pop. Code 4
Kettle Moraine SD
Sch. Sys. Enr. Code 5
Supt. – E. W. Brakken, P O BOX 901 53183
ES, P O BOX 130 53183 – Judith Wojta, prin.
Other Schools – See Delafield, Dousman, Genesee
Depot, Pewaukee

Walworth, Walworth Co., Pop. Code 4
Walworth J1 SD
Sch. Sys. Enr. Code 2
Supt. – Lee Siudzinski 53184
ES, 121 BELOIT ST 53184 – (—), prin.

Warrens, Monroe Co., Pop. Code 2
Tomah Area SD
Supt. – See Tomah
ES 54666 – Paul Wiese, prin.

Washburn, Bayfield Co., Pop. Code 4
Washburn SD
Sch. Sys. Enr. Code 2
Supt. – Donald Kolek, 309 W 4TH ST 54891
Dupont ES, 305 W 4TH ST 54891
Clyde Sukanen, prin.

Washington Island, Door Co.
Washington SD
Sch. Sys. Enr. Code 1
Supt. – James Kenyon 54246
ES 54246 – James Kenyon, prin.

Waterford, Racine Co., Pop. Code 4
Waterford J1 (T) SD
Sch. Sys. Enr. Code 2
Supt. – (—), 8937 BIG BEND ROAD 53185
Washington MS, 8937 BIG BEND RD 53185
Norma Conners, prin.
Other Schools – See Mukwonago

Waterford Jt. 1 V SD
Supt. – See Rochester
Fox River MS, 921 W MAIN ST 53185
Gary D. Tilleros, prin.
ES, 405 W MAIN ST 53185
Douglas Robbins, prin.

St. Thomas Aquinas ES, 302 S 2ND ST 53185

Waterloo, Jefferson Co., Pop. Code 4
Waterloo SD
Sch. Sys. Enr. Code 3
Supt. – Wayne Benson, 785 N MONROE ST 53594
ES, 785 N MONROE ST 53594
Mary Gavigan, prin.

St. John's ES, 413 E MADISON ST 53594

Watertown, Jefferson Co., Pop. Code 7
Watertown SD
Sch. Sys. Enr. Code 5
Supt. – Richard Stolsmark, 111 DODGE ST 53094
Douglas ES, 1120 CENTER ST 53094
Charles Bruce, prin.
Lebanon ES, RURAL ROUTE 02 53094
Wayne Simon, prin.
Lincoln ES, 210 N MONTGOMERY ST 53094
Martin Kerwin, prin.
Schurz ES, 1508 NEENAH ST 53094
Martin Kerwin, prin.
Webster ES, 634 12TH ST 53094
Wayne Simon, prin.
Other Schools – See Sullivan

Calvary Baptist Christian ES
792 MILFORD ST 53094
Lebanon Lutheran ES, N534 HWY 109 53094
St. Bernard ES, 111 S MONTGOMERY ST 53094
St. Henry ES, 300 E CADY ST 53094
St. John Lutheran ES, 317 N 6TH ST 53094
St. Mark's Lutheran ES, 310 N 8TH ST 53094
Trinity-St. Luke's Lutheran ES
801 S 5TH ST 53094

Waubeka, Ozaukee Co.
Northern Ozaukee SD
Supt. – See Fredonia
Grandview ES, N5470 SCHOOL RD 53021
Maryanna Meikrantz, prin.

Waukesha, Waukesha Co., Pop. Code 8
Waukesha SD
Sch. Sys. Enr. Code 7
Supt. – George Shiroda, 222 MAPLE AVE 53186
Banting ES, 2019 BUTLER DR 53186
Joseph Vitale, prin.
Bethesda ES, 730 S UNIVERSITY DR 53188
Nancy Marsho, prin.
Blair ES, 618 CHICAGO AVE 53188
William Hempel, prin.
Hadfield ES, 618 OAKLAND AVE 53186
Gary Weber, prin.
Hawthorne ES, 1111 MAITLAND DR 53188
(—), prin.
Heyer ES, 1209 HEYER DR 53186
Philip Ziegler, prin.
Hillcrest ES, 21950 W DAVIDSON RD 53186
Barbara Brzenk, prin.
Lowell ES, 140 N GRANDVIEW BLVD 53188
James Chermak, prin.
Meadowbrook ES
W269 N 1182 MEADOWBROOK RD 53188
Fred Jones, prin.
North View ES, 1721 N VIEW RD 53188
Dennis Bissett, prin.
Pleasant Hill ES, 175 S BARKER RD 53186
Thomas Kotlarek, prin.
Prairie ES, 1801 S CENTER RD 53186
Dale Heinen, prin.
Randall ES, 114 S CHARLES ST 53186
George Ruecktenwald, prin.
Rose Glen ES
W273 S 3845 BROOK HILL DR 53188
John Schliecker, prin.
Saratoga ES, 130 WALTON AVE 53186
Bonnie Schlais, prin.
White Rock ES, 1150 WHITEROCK AVE 53186
Carlos Gamino, prin.
Whittier ES, 1103 S EAST AVE 53186
Peter Johnson, prin.

Waukesha Christian Academy, P O BOX 31   53187
St. Joseph ES, 818 N EAST AVE   53186
St. Mary ES, 520 E NEWHALL AVE   53186
St. William ES, 444 N MORELAND BLVD   53188
Trinity Lutheran ES
    1060 WHITEROCK AVE   53186

Waunakee, Dane Co., Pop. Code 5
Middleton-Cross Plains SD
Supt. – See Middleton
Springfield ES
    RURAL ROUTE 01 BOX 6039   53597
    Patrick Kinney, prin.

Waunakee Comm. SD
Sch. Sys. Enr. Code 4
Supt. – Allen Rosenthal, SCHOOL DRIVE   53597
MS, 303 SOUTH ST   53597 – Richard Hagen, prin.
ES, 501 SOUTH ST   53597 – Beverly Grove, prin.

St. John's ES, 114 E 3RD ST   53597

Waupaca, Waupaca Co., Pop. Code 5
Waupaca SD
Sch. Sys. Enr. Code 4
Supt. – Robert Groshek, RURAL ROUTE 01   54981
MS, 407 SCHOOL ST   54981
    Joseph McClone, prin.
Central MS, 425 SCHOOL ST   54981
    Boyd Simonson, prin.
Chain O Lakes ES, RURAL ROUTE 01   54981
    (—), prin.
Riverside ES, PARK AVE   54981 – (—), prin.
Westwood ES, 615 W UNION ST   54981
    (—), prin.

First Baptist Christian School
    1500 ROMAN ROAD   54981

Waupun, Fond du Lac Co., Pop. Code 6
Waupun SD
Sch. Sys. Enr. Code 4
Supt. – G. E. Thompson, 950 WILCOX ST   53963
MS, 450 E FRANKLIN ST   53963
    Richard Steinbach, prin.
Alto ES, RURAL ROUTE 03   53963
    Vernon Wanish, prin.
Jefferson ES, 601 GRANDVIEW AVE   53963
    Vernon Wanish, prin.
Washington ES, 101 YOUNG ST   53963
    John Omdahl, prin.
Other Schools – See Brandon, Fox Lake

Waupun Christian ES, 520 MCKINLEY ST   53963

Wausau, Marathon Co., Pop. Code 8
Wausau SD
Sch. Sys. Enr. Code 6
Supt. – Theodore H. Nicholson
    P O BOX 359   54401
Muir MS, 1400 STEWART AVE   54401
    Charles Morrill, prin.
Franklin ES, 1509 N 5TH ST   54401
    Glenn Schwede, prin.
Grant ES, 500 N 4TH AVE   54401
    Donn Sharer, prin.
Hawthorn Hills ES, 1600 KICKBUSCH ST   54401
    Berland Meyer, prin.
Hewitt Texas ES, RURAL ROUTE 02   54401
    Faith Kettner, prin.
Jefferson ES, 500 RANDOLPH ST   54401
    Arden Hoffmann, prin.
Jones ES, 1018 S 12TH AVE   54401
    Don Christianson, prin.
Lincoln ES, 720 S 6TH AVE   54401
    Arlon Parkin, prin.
Maine ES, RURAL ROUTE 01   54401
    George Klinker, prin.
Marshall ES, 1918 LAMONT ST   54401
    Todd Orthmann, prin.
Rib Mountain ES, 2701 ROBIN LANE   54401
    Claudette Harring, prin.
Riverview ES, 4303 TROY ST   54401
    William Paul, prin.
Stettin ES, 3115 STEWART AVE   54401
    Donn Sharer, prin.
Other Schools – See Hamburg

Holy Name ES, 1122 S 9TGH AVE   54401
St. Anne ES, 604 N 6TH AVE   54401
St. Frances Cabrini ES, 602 2ND ST   54401
St. Matthew ES, 225 S 28TH AVE   54401
St. Michael ES, 614 STEUBEN ST   54401
Trinity Lutheran ES, 501 STEWART AVE   54401
Zion Lutheran ES, 616 GRANT ST   54401

Wausaukee, Marinette Co., Pop. Code 3
Wausaukee SD
Sch. Sys. Enr. Code 3
Supt. – (—)   54177
MS   54177 – Frank Rynish, prin.
ES   54177 – Carl Anderson, prin.
Other Schools – See Amberg, McAllister

Wautoma, Washara Co., Pop. Code 4
Wautoma Area SD
Sch. Sys. Enr. Code 4
Supt. – Thomas Yager, CAMBRIDGE ST   54982
Dafoe MS, P O BOX 870   54982
    Charles Riley, prin.
Riverview ES, P O BOX 870   54982
    Allen Hasselquist, prin.
Other Schools – See Redgranite

Wauwatosa, Milwaukee Co., Pop. Code 4
Wauwatosa SD
Supt. – See Milwaukee
Longfellow MS, 7600 W NORTH AVE   53213
    Richard Hess, prin.
Catc MS
    9501 W WATERTOWN PLANK RD   53226
    Richard Huenkink, prin.
Jefferson ES, 6927 MAPLE TER   53213
    Scott Kellogg, prin.
Lincoln ES, 1741 N WAUWATOSA AVE   53213
    Jean Carron, prin.
McKinley ES, 2435 N 89TH ST   53226
    Roland Groddy, prin.
Roosevelt ES, 2535 N 73RD ST   53213
    (—), prin.
Underwood ES, 11132 W POTTER RD   53226
    Robert Muske, prin.
Washington ES, 2166 N 68TH ST   53213
    Dennis Kayon, prin.
Wilson ES, 1060 GLENVIEW AVE   53213
    Thomas Engel, prin.

Christ King ES, 2646 N SWAN BLVD   53226
Our Redeemer Lutheran ES
    10025 W NORTH AVE   53226
St. Bernard ES, 7440 HARWOOD AVE   53213
St. John's Evangelist Lutheran ES
    1278 DEWEY AVE   53213
St. Jude the Apostle ES, 8042 ST JUDE CT   53213
St. Pius X ES, 2520 N WAUWATOSA AVE   53213

Wauzeka, Crawford Co., Pop. Code 3
Wauzeka-Steuben SD
Sch. Sys. Enr. Code 2
Supt. – David Polashek   53826
ES   53826 – (—), prin.

Webster, Burnett Co., Pop. Code 3
Webster SD
Sch. Sys. Enr. Code 3
Supt. – William V. Keigan   54893
ES   54893 – William Plath, prin.
Other Schools – See Dairyland, Danbury

Wentworth, Douglas Co.
Maple SD
Supt. – See Maple
Lakeside ES   54894 – Susan Vojacek, prin.

West Allis, Milwaukee Co., Pop. Code 8
West Allis SD
Sch. Sys. Enr. Code 6
Supt. – Sam J. Castagna
    9333 W LINCOLN AVE   53227
Mann MS, 6213 W LAPHAM ST   53214
    William Swasey, prin.
Wright MS, 9501 W CLEVELAND AVE   53227
    Duane Stowell, prin.
Lincoln ES, 7815 W LAPHAM ST   53214
    Richard Henske, prin.
Madison ES, 1117 S 104TH ST   53214
    Christopher Drobka, prin.
Roosevelt ES, 932 S 69TH ST   53214
    Beverly Fochs-Jeide, prin.
Walker ES, 1435 S 119TH ST   53214
    Howard Kumbier, prin.
Wilson ES, 8710 W ORCHARD ST   53214
    Norman Domach, prin.
Other Schools – See Milwaukee, New Berlin, West
Milwaukee

Heritage Christian School
    1300 S 109TH ST   53214
Good Shepherds Evangelist Lutheran ES
    1337 S 100TH ST   53214
Holy Assmmption ES, 1526 S 72ND ST   53214
Immaculate Heart Of Mary ES
    1227 S 116TH ST   53214
St. Aloysius ES, 1435 S 92ND ST   53214
St. Mary Help Christians ES
    1230 S 61ST ST   53214

West Baraboo, Sauk Co., Pop. Code 3
Baraboo SD
Supt. – See Baraboo
Willson MS, 146 BERKLEY BLVD   53913
    Mary Haugsby, prin.

West Bend, Washington Co., Pop. Code 7
West Bend SD
Sch. Sys. Enr. Code 6
Supt. – Dwain Ehrlich, 697 S 5TH AVE   53095
Badger MS, 710 S MAIN ST   53095
    Richard Osterhaus, prin.
Silverbrook MS
    120 N SILVERBROOK DRIVE   53095
    Paul Zavitkowsky, prin.
Barton ES, 614 SCHOOL PL   53095
    Dale Westby, prin.
Decorah ES, 1225 SYLVAN WAY   53095
    Dennis Kayon, prin.
Fair Park ES, 519 N INDIANA AVE   53095
    John Cain, prin.
Green Tree ES, 1330 GREEN TREE RD   53095
    Robert Walden, prin.
Mclane ES, 833 CHESTNUT ST   53095
    Toni Bauman, prin.
Other Schools – See Jackson

Calvary Life Academy, P O BOX 365   53095
Good Shepherd Lutheran ES
    777 S INDIANA AVE   53095
Holy Angels ES, 230 N 8TH AVE   53095

St. Frances Cabrini ES
    529 HAWTHORN DR   53095
St. John's Lutheran ES, 899 S 6TH AVE   53095
St. Mary Immaculate Conception ES
    415 ROOSEVELT DR   53095

Westboro, Taylor Co., Pop. Code 3
Rib Lake SD
Supt. – See Rib Lake
Silver Creek ES, P O BOX 187   54490
    (—), prin.

Westby, Vernon Co., Pop. Code 4
Westby Area SD
Sch. Sys. Enr. Code 4
Supt. – Paul Schoenberger
    206 WEST AVE S   54667
ES, 206 W AVE SOUTH   54667 – Janice Lee, prin.
Other Schools – See Chaseburg, Coon Valley

Westfield, Marquette Co., Pop. Code 4
Westfield SD
Sch. Sys. Enr. Code 4
Supt. – Kenneth Ripple   53964
ES   53964 – Dale Kongslie, prin.
Other Schools – See Coloma, Neshkoro, Oxford

West Milwaukee, Milwaukee Co., Pop. Code 5
West Allis SD
Supt. – See West Allis
Pershing ES, 1330 S 47TH ST   53214
    Neal Janssen, prin.

St. Florian ES, 1215 S 45TH ST   53214

West Salem, La Crosse Co., Pop. Code 5
West Salem SD
Sch. Sys. Enr. Code 4
Supt. – Eugene Ertz, 405 E HAMLIN ST   54669
MS, 450 N MARK ST   54669
    Randy Fredrickson, prin.
ES, 230 W GARLAND ST   54669 – (—), prin.

Christ Lutheran ES, 124 S YOULON ST   54669

Weyauwega, Waupaca Co., Pop. Code 4
Weyauwega-Fremont SD
Sch. Sys. Enr. Code 3
Supt. – James Stillman, P O BOX 580   54983
MS, P O BOX 580   54983 – David Elliott, prin.
ES, P O BOX 580   54983 – Quintin Urban, prin.
Other Schools – See Fremont

St. Peter Lutheran ES
    RURAL ROUTE 02 BOX 230-S   54983

Weyerhaeuser, Rusk Co., Pop. Code 2
Weyerhaeuser Area SD
Sch. Sys. Enr. Code 2
Supt. – Jim Schuchardt, 310 E MAIN ST   54895
ES   54895 – Barbara Lorkowski, prin.

Wheeler, Dunn Co., Pop. Code 2
Boyceville Comm. SD
Supt. – See Boyceville
ES   54772 – Ted Bissell, prin.

Whitefish Bay, Milwaukee Co., Pop. Code 7
Whitefish Bay SD
Sch. Sys. Enr. Code 4
Supt. – Leroy E. Rieck
    1200 E FAIRMOUNT AVE   53217
Richards ES
    5812 N SANTA MONICA BLVD   53217
    James Smith, prin.
Other Schools – See Milwaukee

Holy Family ES, 4849 N WILDWOOD AVE   53217
St. Monica ES
    5635 N SANTA MONICA BLVD   53217

Whitehall, Trempealeau Co., Pop. Code 4
Whitehall SD
Sch. Sys. Enr. Code 3
Supt. – Marlene Hanson, 2405 HOBSON ST   54773
MS, 1817 DEWEY ST   54773
    Gerald Freimark, prin.
Sunset ES, 2305 HOBSON ST   54773
    Rodney Thompson, prin.
Other Schools – See Pigeon Falls

White Lake, Langlade Co., Pop. Code 2
White Lake SD
Sch. Sys. Enr. Code 2
Supt. – Howard Seeman   54491
ES   54491 – Howard Seeman, prin.

Whitewater, Walworth Co., Pop. Code 7
Whitewater SD
Sch. Sys. Enr. Code 4
Supt. – John Negley, 401 S ELIZABETH ST   53190
Franklin MS, 118 S SUMMIT ST   53190
    James Jacobson, prin.
Lakeview ES, RURAL ROUTE 03   53190
    Jack Trojan, prin.
Lincoln ES, 242 S PRINCE ST   53190
    Darrell Millard, prin.
Washington ES, 506 E MAIN ST   53190
    Tom Christofferson, prin.

Wild Rose, Waushara Co., Pop. Code 3
Wild Rose SD
Sch. Sys. Enr. Code 3
Supt. – William Thompson, P O BOX 276   54984
ES   54984 – Gwen Ocull, prin.
Other Schools – See Pine River

Williams Bay, Walworth Co., Pop. Code 4
Williams Bay SD
Sch. Sys. Enr. Code 2
Supt. – (—), 139 CONGRESS ST   53191
ES, 139 CONGRESS ST   53191
    Peter Geissal, prin.

Wilmot, Kenosha Co., Pop. Code 2
Salem J9 SD
Sch. Sys. Enr. Code 2
Supt. – Richard Goetsch, P O BOX 68   53192
ES, P O BOX 68   53192 – Robert Goetsch, prin.

Wilton, Monroe Co., Pop. Code 2
Elroy-Kendall-Wilton SD
Supt. – See Elroy
ES   54670 – George Vukich, prin.

Wind Lake, Racine Co., Pop. Code 4
Muskego-Norway SD
Supt. – See Muskego
Lakeview ES, 26335 FRIES LN   53185
    Thomas Brown, prin.

Windsor, Dane Co., Pop. Code 5
De Forest SD
Supt. – See De Forest
ES, 4352 WINDSOR RD   53598
    Deborah Fritsch, prin.

Winneconne, Winnebago Co., Pop. Code 4
Winneconne Comm. SD
Sch. Sys. Enr. Code 4
Supt. – Alan Johnson, 233 S 3RD AVE   54986
MS, 233 S 3RD AVE   54986
    Frederick Gierke, prin.
ES, 233 S THIRD AVE   54986
    Kenneth Schleinz, prin.
Other Schools – See Larsen

Winter, Sawyer Co., Pop. Code 2
Winter SD
Sch. Sys. Enr. Code 3
Supt. – Barry Bay   54896

ES   54896 – (—), prin.
Other Schools – See Radisson

Wisconsin Dells, Columbia Co., Pop. Code 5
Wisconsin Dells SD
Sch. Sys. Enr. Code 4
Supt. – Gerald Peterson
    400 WASHINGTON AVE   53965
MS, 400 WASHINGTON AVE   53965
    Samuel Hagerman, prin.
ES, 400 WASHINGTON AVE   53965
    Kurt Hollenbeck, prin.

Wisconsin Rapids, Wood Co., Pop. Code 7
Wisconsin Rapids SD
Sch. Sys. Enr. Code 6
Supt. – Richard Wasson, 510 PEACH ST   54494
Childrens Choice ES, 2390 48TH ST S   54494
    John Orluske, prin.
Grant ES, 8511 COUNTY TRUNK WW   54494
    Bernard Fowler, prin.
Grove ES, 2750 LINCOLN ST   54494
    Robert Wells, prin.
Howe ES, 221 8TH ST N   54494
    Yvonne Ellie, prin.
Mead ES, 241 17TH AVE S   54494
    Richard Belke, prin.
Pitsch ES, 501 17TH ST S   54494
    Patricia Flanagan, prin.
Washington ES, 1010 28RTH ST N   54494
    John Orluske, prin.
Woodside ES, 611 TWO MILE AVE   54494
    Leo Mueller, prin.
Other Schools – See Rudolph, Vesper

Immanuel Lutheran ES, 111-161 11TH ST N   54494
Our Lady Queen of Heaven ES
    750 10TH AVE S   54494
St. Lawrence ES, 551 10TH AVE N   54494
St. Paul Evangelist Lutheran ES
    311 14TH AVE S   54494
St. Vincent De Paul ES, 831 12TH ST S   54494
SS Peter & Paul School, 1140 2ND ST N   54494

Wittenberg, Shawano Co., Pop. Code 3
Wittenberg-Birnamwood SD
Sch. Sys. Enr. Code 4
Supt. – Gerald Jackson   54499
ES   54499 – Gordon Geurink, prin.
Other Schools – See Birnamwood, Eland, Elderon

Wonewoc, Juneau Co., Pop. Code 3
Wonewoc-Union Center SD
Sch. Sys. Enr. Code 3
Supt. – Oscar Pynnonen   53968
MS   53968 – Richard Cathcart, prin.
ES   53968 – Donald Urban, prin.

St. Paul's Evangelist Lutheran ES
    P O BOX 325   53968

Woodruff, Oneida Co., Pop. Code 4
Woodruff J1 SD
Sch. Sys. Enr. Code 2
Supt. – Martin Holmquist, P O BOX 670   54568
Arbor Vitae Wood ES   54568 – (—), prin.

Woodville, St. Croix Co., Pop. Code 3
Baldwin-Woodville Area SD
Supt. – See Baldwin
Viking MS   54028 – Geroge Streeck, prin.

Wrightstown, Brown Co., Pop. Code 4
Wrightstown Comm. SD
Sch. Sys. Enr. Code 3
Supt. – Larry J. Lark   54180
ES   54180 – Richard Calaway, prin.

St. Paul ES, 425 MAIN ST   54180

Wyeville, Monroe Co., Pop. Code 2
Tomah Area SD
Supt. – See Tomah
ES   54671 – Paul Wiese, prin.

WYOMING

STATE DEPARTMENT OF EDUCATION
Hathaway Building
Cheyenne 82002
(307) 777-7675

Superintendent of Public Instruction   Lynn Simons
Deputy Superintendent   Audrey Cotherman
Assistant Superintendent Certification, Accreditation & Programs   Alan Wheeler
Assistant Superintendent Administrative Services   Tom Morris

STATE BOARD OF EDUCATION
Kathryn Kelly, *Chairperson*   3288 Monte Vista, Torrington   82240

PUBLIC, PRIVATE, AND PAROCHIAL ELEMENTARY SCHOOLS

Afton, Lincoln Co., Pop. Code 4
Lincoln County ESD 2
Sch. Sys. Enr. Code 4
Supt. – Dr. J. Allen Lowe   83110
Star Valley JHS   83110 – Alan Lindford, prin.
ES   83110 – Dee Hokanson, prin.
Osmond ES   83110 – Ron Tolman, prin.
Other Schools – See Cokeville, Etna, Thayne

Aladdin, Crook Co.
Crook County SD 1
Supt. – See Sundance
Four Oaks ES   82710 – (—), prin.

Albin, Laramie Co., Pop. Code 2
Laramie County SD 2
Supt. – See Pine Bluffs
S   82050 – Richard Goodschmidt, prin.

Alcova, Natrona Co.
Natrona County SD 1
Supt. – See Casper
ES   82620 – Gene Thompson, prin.

Arapahoe, Fremont Co.
Fremont County ESD 38
Sch. Sys. Enr. Code 2
Supt. – Thomas Rouse, P O BOX 211   82510
ES   82510 – Jack Blair, prin.

Arvada, Sheridan Co.
Sheridan County SD 3
Supt. – See Clearmont
ES   82831 – (—), prin.

Baggs, Carbon Co., Pop. Code 2
Carbon County SD 1
Supt. – See Rawlins
Little Snake River Valley ES, P O BOX 9   82321
    George Linthicum, prin.

Bairoil, Sweetwater Co., Pop. Code 2
Carbon County SD 1
Supt. – See Rawlins
ES, P O BOX 27   82322 – Karen Heeren, prin.

Banner, Sheridan Co.
Johnson County SD 1
Supt. – See Buffalo
Kearney ES   82832 – Elbert Beauneir, prin.

Basin, Big Horn Co., Pop. Code 4
Big Horn County SD 4
Sch. Sys. Enr. Code 2
Supt. – Donald Markley, P O BOX 151   82410
Irwin ES, 101 S 12   82410 – David Foreman, prin.
Other Schools – See Hyattville, Manderson

Big Horn, Sheridan Co., Pop. Code 2
Sheridan County SD 1
Supt. – See Ranchester
MS, P O BOX 490   82833 – John Baggett, prin.
ES, P O BOX 932   82833 – Colleen Model, prin.

Big Piney, Sublette Co., Pop. Code 3
Sublette County SD 9
Sch. Sys. Enr. Code 3
Supt. – Dwight Parrish
    FINE ARTS CENTER   83113
MS, 510 NICHOLS ST S   83113 – Bill Lehr, prin.
ES, 511 NICHOLS ST S   83113 – Jim Rugh, prin.
Other Schools – See Labarge

Bondurant, Sublette Co.
Sublette County SD 1
Supt. – See Pinedale
ES   82922 – David Lehtoma, prin.

Buffalo, Johnson Co., Pop. Code 5
Johnson County SD 1
Sch. Sys. Enr. Code 4
Supt. – Von Dahl, 601 W LOTT ST 82834
Clear Creek MS, 58 N ADAMS AVE 82834
　Donald Tavegle, prin.
Billy Creek ES, KAYCEE ROUTE BOX 29 82834
　Elbert Beaunier, prin.
Meadowlark ES, 550 S BURRITT AVE 82834
　Elbert Beaunier, prin.
Other Schools – See Banner, Kaycee, Linch

Burlington, Big Horn Co., Pop. Code 1
Big Horn County SD 1
Supt. – See Cowley
S 82411 – Laird Jenkins, prin.

Burns, Laramie Co., Pop. Code 2
Laramie County SD 2
Supt. – See Pine Bluffs
West ES 82053 – Stephen Hutchinson, prin.

Byron, Big Horn Co., Pop. Code 3
Big Horn County SD 1
Supt. – See Cowley
ES, P O BOX 176 82412 – Judy Devine, prin.

Carpenter, Laramie Co.
Laramie County SD 2
Supt. – See Pine Bluffs
ES 82054 – James Benoit, prin.

Casper, Natrona Co., Pop. Code 8
Natrona County SD 1
Sch. Sys. Enr. Code 7
Supt. – Dr. Jacob E. Dailey
　970 N GLENN ROAD 82601
Bar Nunn ES, 100 TRISHA DR 82601
　Dr. Gerald Ross, prin.
Crest Hill ES, 4445 S POPLAR ST 82601
　William Jones, prin.
Fairdale ES, 1400 S FAIRDALE AVE 82601
　James Kirby, prin.
Ft. Caspar ES, 2000 LARAMIE AVE 82604
　Janice Thomas, prin.
Garfield ES, 1927 S WALNUT ST 82601
　Charles Huber, prin.
Grant ES, 1536 OAKCREST AVE 82601
　Mary Hein, prin.
James ES, 701 CARRIAGE LN 82609
　Bill Hambrick, prin.
Jefferson ES, 522 S JEFFERSON ST 82601
　Mary Lou Reynolds, prin.
Manor Heights ES, 3201 E 15TH ST 82609
　Wayne Mohr, prin.
McKinley ES, 1217 W 14TH ST 82604
　Norman Carrell, prin.
Mountain View ES, 400 N 3RD AVE 82604
　Terrance Gerhardt, prin.
North Casper ES, 1014 GLENARM ST 82601
　Thomas Chapman, prin.
Oregon Trail ES, 6332 BUCKBOARD ROAD 82604
　Gene Thompson, prin.
Paradise Valley ES
　MAGNOLIA & RIVER BEND ROAD 82604
　Dr. Harold Andrew, prin.
Park ES, 823 S DAVID ST 82601
　Larry Regnier, prin.
Pineview ES, 639 PAYNE AVE 82609
　Robert Hogan, prin.
Poison Spider ES
　6150 RADERVILLE ROUTE 82604
　Don Reno, prin.
Red Creek ES, BATES CREEK ROUTE 82604
　Gene Thompson, prin.
Sagewood ES, 2451 SHATTUCK AVE 82601
　Charles Adelman, prin.
Southridge ES, 1600 W 29TH ST 82604
　Larry Jones, prin.
University Park ES, 600 N HUBER DR 82609
　Robert Hogan, prin.
Westwood ES, 2300 BELLAIRE DR 82604
　Milton Johnson, prin.
Willard ES, 129 N ELK ST 82601
　James Hoppe, prin.
Other Schools – See Alcova, Evansville, Kaycee,
　Midwest, Mills, Powder River

　St. Anthony's School, 218 E 7TH ST 82601

Centennial, Albany Co.
Albany County SD 1
Supt. – See Laramie
ES 82055 – Richard Greenlee, prin.

Cheyenne, Laramie Co., Pop. Code 8
Laramie County SD 1
Sch. Sys. Enr. Code 7
Supt. – Dr. Dennis Peterson
　2810 HOUSE AVE 82001
Afflerbach ES, 400 W WALLICK ROAD 82007
　Ray Willard, prin.
Alta Vista ES, 1620 LOGAN AVE 82001
　Tom Rooney, prin.
Anderson ES, 2204 PLAIN VIEW ROAD 82009
　Weldon Borgaard, prin.
Arp ES, 1216 E REINER CT 82007
　Dave Johnson, prin.
Baggs ES, 3705 CHEYENNE ST 82001
　Eugene Wanner, prin.
Bain ES, 903 ADAMS AVE 82001
　Roger Bengtson, prin.
Buffalo Ridge ES, 5331 PINERIDGE AVE 82009
　Lloyd McKean, prin.
Churchill MS, 510 W 29TH ST 82001
　Margaret Lucero, prin.

Cole ES, 820 O NEIL AVE 82007 – Dan Pratz, prin.
Corlett ES, 600 W 22ND ST 82001
　Margaret Lucero, prin.
Davis ES, 6309 YELLOWSTONE RD 82009
　Monica Beglau, prin.
Deming ES, 715 W 5TH AVE 82001
　Dennis Dix, prin.
Dildine ES, 4312 VAN BUREN AVE 82001
　Rick Melmer, prin.
Eastrdige ES, 3323 CONCORD ROAD 82001
　Marc Lahiff, prin.
Fairview MS, 2801 E 10TH ST 82001
　Len McVay, prin.
Gilchrist ES, 1108 HAPPY JACK ROAD 82007
　Mike Beeman, prin.
Goins ES, 201 CRIBBON AVE 82007
　Terry Bridwell, prin.
Hebard ES, 413 SEYMOUR AVE 82007
　Nancy Dredge, prin.
Henderson MS, 2820 HENDERSON DR 82001
　Marc Lahiff, prin.
Hobbs ES, 5710 SYRACUSE ROAD 82009
　Lynn Westbrook, prin.
Jessup ES, 6113 EVERS BLVD 82009
　Marian Bondurant, prin.
Lebhart ES, 807 COOLIDGE ST 82001
　Len McVay, prin.
Miller MS, 3501 EVANS AVE 82001
　Dennis Dix, prin.
Pioneer Park ES, 1407 COSGRIFF COURT 82001
　Bill Hardesty, prin.
Rossman ES, 916 W COLLEGE DR 82007
　Dr. Ken Davis, prin.
Other Schools – See Granite Canon, Horse Creek

Our Savior Lutheran School
　5101 DELL RANGE BLVD 82009
St. Mary's ES, 112 E 24TH ST 82001
Trinity Lutheran School, 1111 E 22ND ST 82001

Chugwater, Platte Co., Pop. Code 2
Platte County SD 1
Supt. – See Wheatland
S 82210 – Larry Bowman, prin.

Clearmont, Sheridan Co., Pop. Code 2
Sheridan County SD 3
Sch. Sys. Enr. Code 2
Supt. – W. S. Beaver 82835
ES 82835 – (—), prin.
Fence Creek ES 82835 – (—), prin.
Hanging Woman ES 82835 – (—), prin.
Other Schools – See Arvada

Cody, Park Co., Pop. Code 6
Park County SD 6
Sch. Sys. Enr. Code 4
Supt. – Charles L. Flake, 919 CODY AVE 82414
Eastside ES, 1601 BLEISTEIN AVE 82414
　Robert McLeod, prin.
Livingston ES, 2001 12TH ST 82414
　Melvin Faber, prin.
Sunset ES, 1520 21ST ST 82414
　Loren Rohloff, prin.
Valley ES, 3566 SF ROAD 82414
　Melvin Faber, prin.
Other Schools – See Wapiti

Cokeville, Lincoln Co., Pop. Code 3
Lincoln County SD 2
Supt. – See Afton
ES 83114 – Max Excell, prin.

Cowley, Big Horn Co., Pop. Code 2
Big Horn County SD 1
Sch. Sys. Enr. Code 3
Supt. – Grant Sanders, P O BOX 688 82420
ES, P O BOX 38 82420 – Judy Devine, prin.
Other Schools – See Burlington, Byron, Deaver,
　Frannie

Crowheart, Fremont Co.
Fremont County SD 6
Supt. – See Kinnear
ES 82512 – Anne LaPlante, prin.

Deaver, Big Horn Co., Pop. Code 2
Big Horn County SD 1
Supt. – See Cowley
Rocky Mountain MS 82421 – Billie Bymers, prin.

Diamondville, Lincoln Co., Pop. Code 3
Lincoln County SD 1
Sch. Sys. Enr. Code 4
Supt. – B. L. Mowry, P O BOX 335 83116
Burgoon ES, P O BOX 335 83116
　James Provance, prin.
Canyon MS, P O BOX 335 83116
　Mike Vassallo, prin.
Kemmerer ES, P O BOX 335 83116
　James Provance, prin.

Douglas, Converse Co., Pop. Code 6
Converse County SD 1
Sch. Sys. Enr. Code 4
Supt. – M. I. Meredith, P O BOX 1028 82633
MS, 615 HAMILTON STREET 82633
　Wayne Porter, prin.
Cheyenne River ES, P O BOX 1028 82633
　(—), prin.
Dry Creek ES, P O BOX 1028 82633
　(—), prin.
East Douglas ES, P O BOX 1028 82633
　(—), prin.
Moss Agate ES, P O BOX 1028 82633
　(—), prin.

Shawnee ES, P O BOX 1028 82633 – (—), prin.
Wagonhound ES, P O BOX 1028 82633
　(—), prin.
Walker Creek ES, P O BOX 1028 82633
　(—), prin.
West Douglas ES, P O BOX 1028 82633
　Elizabeth Groff, prin.
White ES, P O BOX 1028 82633 – (—), prin.

Converse County SD 2
Supt. – See Glenrock
Ogallala ES, RURAL ROUTE 03 82633
　Sid Applegate, prin.

Dubois, Fremont Co., Pop. Code 1
Fremont County SD 2
Sch. Sys. Enr. Code 2
Supt. – James Robinson, P O BOX 188 82513
ES, P O BOX 188 82513 – Denise Wheeler, prin.

Elk Mountain, Carbon Co., Pop. Code 2
Carbon County SD 2
Supt. – See Saratoga
ES, P O BOX 22 82324 – Dick Close, prin.

Encampment, Carbon Co., Pop. Code 3
Carbon County SD 2
Supt. – See Saratoga
S, P O BOX 277 82325 – John Sackman, prin.

Ethete, Fremont Co.
Fremont County SD 14
Sch. Sys. Enr. Code 3
Supt. – Raymond Streeter
　BOX 340 LANDER ROUTE 82520
Wyoming Indian MS
　BOX 340 LANDER ROUTE 82520
　Scott Wiblemo, prin.
Wyoming Indian ES, P O BOX 340 82520
　Scott Wiblemo, prin.

Etna, Lincoln Co.
Lincoln County SD 2
Supt. – See Afton
Metcalf ES 83118 – Alan Allred, prin.

Evanston, Uinta Co., Pop. Code 6
Uinta County SD 1
Sch. Sys. Enr. Code 5
Supt. – Norman Gaines, P O BOX 6002 82930
Davis MS, P O BOX 6002 82930
　Diane Galloway, prin.
Evanston MS, 341 SUMMIT ST 82930
　Vaughn Thacker, prin.
Aspen ES, 225 BROKEN CIRCLE DR 82930
　Ruth Anderson, prin.
Clark ES, 600 13TH ST 82930 – Bob Addy, prin.
North Evanston ES, P O BOX 6002 82931
　Douglas McCombie, prin.
Uinta Meadows ES, 90 CHEYENNE DR 82930
　Rob Robinson, prin.

Evansville, Natrona Co., Pop. Code 5
Natrona County SD 1
Supt. – See Casper
ES, 435 ALBANY 82636 – Robert Leathers, prin.

Farson, Sweetwater Co.
Sweetwater County SD 1
Supt. – See Rock Springs
Farson-Eden S, P O BOX A 82932
　James Roach, prin.

Fort Laramie, Goshen Co., Pop. Code 2
Goshen County SD 1
Supt. – See Torrington
MS 82212 – Roger Fuss, prin.

Fort Washakie, Fremont Co., Pop. Code 2
Fremont County ESD 21
Sch. Sys. Enr. Code 2
Supt. – V. Zerga, P O BOX 110 82514
ES, P O BOX 110 82514 – Danny Coe, prin.

Foxpark, Albany Co.
Albany County SD 1
Supt. – See Laramie
ES 82057 – Bill Ratliff, prin.

Frannie, Park Co., Pop. Code 2
Big Horn County SD 1
Supt. – See Cowley
Deaver-Frannie ES 82423 – Judy Devine, prin.

Gillette, Campbell Co., Pop. Code 7
Campbell County SD 1
Sch. Sys. Enr. Code 6
Supt. – Mark Higdon, 1000 W 8TH ST 82716
4J ES, 283 S HWY 50 82716 – (—), prin.
Alcott ES, TECKLA ROUTE 82716
　Kareen Skillestad, prin.
Conestoga ES
　4901 SLEEPY HOLLOW BLVD 82716
　Jo Campbell, prin.
Hillcrest ES, 800 BUTLER SPAETH ROAD 82716
　Regan Lefdahl, prin.
Lakeview ES, 410 LAKESIDE DRIVE 82716
　Al McClelland, prin.
Meadowlark MS, 816 E 7TH ST 82716
　Mike Porter, prin.
Paintbrush ES, 1001 W LAKEWAY ROAD 82716
　David Olsen, prin.
Rawhide ES
　PROSPECTOR/PKWY RAWHIDE RD 82716
　Sue Wurbs, prin.
Stocktrail ES, 800 STOCKTRAIL AVE 82716
　Steve Fenton, prin.

Sunflower ES, 2500 DOGWOOD AVE 82716
  George Mathes, prin.
Wagonwheel ES, 800 HEMLOCK AVE 82716
  Ron Butler, prin.
Other Schools – See Recluse, Rozet, Weston, Wright

Glendo, Platte Co., Pop. Code 2
Platte County SD 1
Supt. – See Wheatland
S 82213 – Duane Synoground, prin.

Glenrock, Converse Co., Pop. Code 5
Converse County SD 2
Sch. Sys. Enr. Code 3
Supt. – James Hoyt, P O BOX 1300 82637
MS, P O BOX 1270 82637 – John Binning, prin.
Boxelder ES, BOXELDER ROUTE 82637
  Sid Appelgate, prin.
Grant ES, P O BOX 1240 82637
  Sidney Applegate, prin.
Other Schools – See Douglas

Granger, Sweetwater Co., Pop. Code 2
Sweetwater County SD 2
Supt. – See Green River
ES, 200 1ST 82934 – Eileen Rountree, prin.

Granite Canon, Laramie Co.
Laramie County SD 1
Supt. – See Cheyenne
Willadsen ES, 645 HARRIMAN RD 82059
  Mike Beeman, prin.

Green River, Sweetwater Co., Pop. Code 7
Sweetwater County SD 2
Sch. Sys. Enr. Code 5
Supt. – Curtis Sokness, 400 N 1ST EAST ST 82935
Lincoln MS, 600 W 3RD NORTH ST 82935
  John Grenevitch, prin.
Monroe MS, 250 MONROE AVE 82935
  Monte Silk, prin.
Harrison ES, 1825 ALABAMA DR 82935
  Michael Caffrey, prin.
Jackson ES, 2500 W TETEN 82935
  Morris Anderson, prin.
Roosevelt ES, 550 UINTA DR 82935
  Douglas Wray, prin.
Truman ES, 1055 W TETON BLVD 82935
  Jerri Tomlin, prin.
Washington ES, 750 W 5TH N ST 82935
  Jeff Brewer, prin.
Wilson ES, 351 MONROE AVE 82935
  Burl Hoopes, prin.
Other Schools – See Granger, Mc Kinnon

Greybull, Big Horn Co., Pop. Code 4
Big Horn County SD 3
Sch. Sys. Enr. Code 3
Supt. – J. Franklin Houk, 636 14TH AVE N 82426
MS, 640 8TH AVE N 82426 – Gary Lehnhoff, prin.
ES, 413 3RD AVE N 82426 – Mark Mayer, prin.
Other Schools – See Shell

Guernsey, Platte Co., Pop. Code 4
Platte County SD 2
Sch. Sys. Enr. Code 2
Supt. – David Swantek
  555 S WYOMING ST 82214
Guernsey-Sunrise ES
  555 SOUTH WYOMING ST 82214
  Bruce Heimbuck, prin.

Hamilton Dome, Hot Springs Co.
Hot Springs County SD 1
Supt. – See Thermopolis
ES 82427 – John Lawrence, prin.

Hanna, Carbon Co., Pop. Code 4
Carbon County SD 2
Supt. – See Saratoga
Austin Creek ES, LEO ROUTE 82327
  Dick Close, prin.
ES, P O BOX 1000 82327 – Dick Close, prin.
Kortes Dam ES, LEO ROUTE 82327
  Dick Close, prin.

Horse Creek, Laramie Co.
Laramie County SD 1
Supt. – See Cheyenne
Ingleside ES, 376 RD 228A 82061
  Dr. Ken Davis, prin.

Hudson, Fremont Co., Pop. Code 3
Fremont County SD 1
Supt. – See Lander
ES 82515 – Pat Flynn, prin.

Hulett, Crook Co., Pop. Code 2
Crook County SD 1
Supt. – See Sundance
S 82720 – Jeff Carrier, prin.
Homestake ES 82720 – (—), prin.

Huntley, Goshen Co.
Goshen County SD 1
Supt. – See Torrington
ES 82218 – Mike Durfee, prin.

Hyattville, Big Horn Co.
Big Horn County SD 4
Supt. – See Basin
ES 82428 – Donald Markley, prin.

Jackson, Teton Co., Pop. Code 5
Teton County SD 1
Sch. Sys. Enr. Code 4
Supt. – Tom Cusack, P O BOX 568 83001

Jackson Hole JHS, 275 N JEAN 83001
  Terry Roice, prin.
ES, 155 N JEAN 83001 – Richard McDowell, prin.
Jackson Hole IS, 220 S GLENWOOD 83001
  Dale Jeske, prin.
Other Schools – See Kelly, Moran, Wilson

Jeffrey City, Fremont Co., Pop. Code 3
Fremont County SD 9
Sch. Sys. Enr. Code 1
Supt. – Gene Patch, P O BOX 130 82310
ES, P O BOX 130 82310 – (—), prin.

Kaycee, Johnson Co., Pop. Code 2
Johnson County SD 1
Supt. – See Buffalo
ES, P O BOX F 82639 – Rosemary Doyle, prin.

Natrona County SD 1
Supt. – See Casper
Willow Creek ES, WILLOW CREEK ROUTE 82639
  Larry Jones, prin.

Kelly, Teton Co.
Teton County SD 1
Supt. – See Jackson
ES 83011 – Dale Jeske, prin.

Kinnear, Fremont Co.
Fremont County SD 6
Sch. Sys. Enr. Code 2
Supt. – Carol Larson 82516
Other Schools – See Crowheart, Pavillion

Labarge, Lincoln Co., Pop. Code 2
Sublette County SD 9
Supt. – See Big Piney
ES 83123 – Thomas Megown, prin.

La Grange, Goshen Co., Pop. Code 1
Goshen County SD 1
Supt. – See Torrington
S 82221 – Mike Durfee, prin.

Lance Creek, Niobrara Co.
Niobrara County SD 1
Supt. – See Lusk
ES 82222 – Gail Crook, prin.

Lander, Fremont Co., Pop. Code 6
Fremont County SD 1
Sch. Sys. Enr. Code 4
Supt. – Gene Young
  100 BALDWIN CREEK ROAD 82520
Starrett JHS, 863 SWEETWATER ST 82520
  Gary Stover, prin.
Atlantic City ES 82520 – Wayne King, prin.
Northside ES, 6TH & WASHINGTON 82520
  Jack Slagle, prin.
Southside ES, 6TH & POPO AGIE 82520
  Wayne King, prin.
Westside ES, 350 SMITH ST 82520
  Pat Flynn, prin.
Other Schools – See Hudson

Laramie, Albany Co., Pop. Code 7
Albany County SD 1
Sch. Sys. Enr. Code 5
Supt. – William Conklin
  1948 E GRAND AVE 82070
Beitel ES, 17TH & SHERIDAN 82070
  David Williams, prin.
Harmony ES, COALMONT ROUTE 82070
  Ronald Langton, prin.
Linford ES, 120 S JOHNSON ST 82070
  Diane Smith, prin.
Nellie Iles ES, 518 E ORD ST 82070
  Bill Ratliff, prin.
Slade ES, 11TH & SULLY 82070
  Norman Bock, prin.
Thayer ES, 801 S 24TH ST 82070
  Richard Greenlee, prin.
Valley View ES
  RURAL ROUTE 01 BOX 288 82070
  David Williams, prin.
Washington MS, 309 S 9TH ST 82070
  Ronald Langton, prin.
Whiting ES, 9TH & CUSTER 82070
  Ronald Langton, prin.
Other Schools – See Centennial, Foxpark, Rock River, Wheatland

St. Laurence O'Toole School, 608 S 4TH ST 82070

Linch, Johnson Co.
Johnson County SD 1
Supt. – See Buffalo
ES 82640 – Rosemary Doyle, prin.

Lingle, Goshen Co., Pop. Code 2
Goshen County SD 1
Supt. – See Torrington
Lingle-Ft. Laramie ES 82223 – Roger Fuss, prin.

Lovell, Big Horn Co., Pop. Code 4
Big Horn County SD 2
Sch. Sys. Enr. Code 3
Supt. – Glenn Engelking
  502 HAMPSHIRE AVE 82431
MS, 520 SHOSHONE AVE 82431
  Norman L. Opp, prin.
ES, 600 SHOSHONE AVE 82431
  Don Burbank, prin.

Lusk, Niobrara Co., Pop. Code 4
Niobrara County SD 1
Sch. Sys. Enr. Code 3
Supt. – Richard Claycomb, P O BOX 629 82225

ES, HCR 01 BOX 151 82225 – Gail Crook, prin.
Zerbst ES, HCR, 01, BOX 151 82225
  Gail Crook, prin.
Other Schools – See Lance Creek

Lyman, Uinta Co., Pop. Code 4
Uinta County SD 6
Sch. Sys. Enr. Code 4
Supt. – Randy Hillstead, P O BOX 1090 82937
MS, P O BOX 1090 82937 – James McKim, prin.
MS, P O BOX 1090 82937 – Joseph Tanner, prin.
Urie ES, P O BOX 1090 82937
  James Bingham, prin.

Mc Fadden, Carbon Co.
Carbon County SD 2
Supt. – See Saratoga
ES, P O BOX 757 82080 – Larry Mowry, prin.

Mc Kinnon, Sweetwater Co.
Sweetwater County SD 2
Supt. – See Green River
ES 82938 – William Duncan, prin.

Manderson, Big Horn Co., Pop. Code 2
Big Horn County SD 4
Supt. – See Basin
Cloud Peak MS 82432 – Donald Markley, prin.
ES 82432 – Don Markley, prin.

Medicine Bow, Carbon Co., Pop. Code 3
Carbon County SD 2
Supt. – See Saratoga
S, P O BOX 185 82329 – Larry Mowry, prin.

Meeteetse, Park Co., Pop. Code 2
Park County SD 16
Sch. Sys. Enr. Code 2
Supt. – Glenn Schimke, P O BOX 218 82433
ES, 2107 IDAHO 82433 – Kent Cook, prin.

Midwest, Natrona Co., Pop. Code 3
Natrona County SD 1
Supt. – See Casper
S 82643 – John Iszler, prin.

Mills, Natrona Co., Pop. Code 4
Natrona County SD 1
Supt. – See Casper
ES, P O BOX 268 82644 – Andrew Johnson, prin.

Moorcroft, Crook Co., Pop. Code 3
Crook County SD 1
Supt. – See Sundance
ES, 101 SOUTH BELLE FOURCHE 82721
  James Henman, prin.

Moran, Teton Co.
Teton County SD 1
Supt. – See Jackson
ES 82013 – Dale Jeske, prin.

Mountain View, Uinta Co., Pop. Code 3
Uinta County SD 4
Sch. Sys. Enr. Code 3
Supt. – Allen Knapp, P O BOX 130 82939
MS, P O BOX 130 82939 – William Kolton, prin.
Ft. Bridger MS, P O BOX 130 82939
  John Metcalfe, prin.
ES, P O BOX 130 82939 – John Metcalfe, prin.

Newcastle, Weston Co., Pop. Code 5
Weston County SD 1
Sch. Sys. Enr. Code 4
Supt. – John Nuspl, 116 CASPER AVE 82701
MS, 15 STAMPEDE ST 82701 – Bob Miller, prin.
Burns ES, 627 PINE ST 82701
  Terry Sherven, prin.
Other Schools – See Osage

Osage, Weston Co.
Weston County SD 1
Supt. – See Newcastle
Moats ES 82723 – E. Dummer, prin.

Oshoto, Crook Co.
Crook County SD 1
Supt. – See Sundance
Nebraska ES 82724 – (—), prin.

Parkman, Sheridan Co.
Sheridan County SD 1
Supt. – See Ranchester
Slack ES, PASS CREEK ROUTE 82838
  Evalyn Bailey, prin.

Pavillion, Fremont Co., Pop. Code 2
Fremont County SD 6
Supt. – See Kinnear
Wind River ES 82523 – Anne Laplante, prin.

Pine Bluffs, Laramie Co., Pop. Code 4
Laramie County SD 2
Sch. Sys. Enr. Code 3
Supt. – Dr. Ronald White, P O BOX 368 82082
JHS, 5TH & ELM 82082 – Gary Datus, prin.
ES, 5TH & ELM 82082
  Michael Klopfenstein, prin.
Other Schools – See Albin, Burns, Carpenter

Pinedale, Sublette Co., Pop. Code 4
Sublette County SD 1
Sch. Sys. Enr. Code 3
Supt. – Don Bryngelson, P O BOX 549 82941
MS, P O BOX 549 82941 – Larry Newland, prin.
ES, P O BOX 549 82941 – David Lehtoma, prin.
Other Schools – See Bondurant

Powder River, Natrona Co.
Natrona County SD 1
Supt. – See Casper
ES 82648 – Dr. Gerald Ross, prin.

Powell, Park Co., Pop. Code 6
Park County SD 1
Sch. Sys. Enr. Code 4
Supt. – Dr. Ralph Reed, 160 N EVARTS ST 82435
MS, 368 E 3RD ST 82435 – Merton Rustad, prin.
Clark ES, 956 AVENUE K 82435
Brent Walker, prin.
Parkside ES, 1ST & DOUGLAS STS 82435
Steve Sexton, prin.
Southside ES, 532 E MADISON ST 82435
Steve Sexton, prin.
Westside ES, 956 AVENUE K 82435
Brent Walker, prin.

Ranchester, Sheridan Co., Pop. Code 3
Sheridan County SD 1
Sch. Sys. Enr. Code 3
Supt. – Doug Cobb, P O BOX 66 82839
Tongue River MS, P O BOX 879 82839
Suzanne Elliott, prin.
Burgess Junction ES, P O BOX 849 82839
Evalyn Bailey, prin.
Tongue River ES, P O BOX 849 82839
Evalyn Bailey, prin.
Other Schools – See Big Horn, Parkman

Rawlins, Carbon Co., Pop. Code 7
Carbon County SD 1
Sch. Sys. Enr. Code 5
Supt. – Mary Gibson, P O BOX 160 82301
MS, 801 E BROOKS ST 82301
Harvey Soulek, prin.
Highland Hills ES
DARNLEY & INVERNESS 82301
Marvin Austin, prin.
Mountain View ES, 11TH & BIRCH 82301
Joseph Omelia, prin.
Pershing ES, DAVIS & PERSHING 82301
Robert Johnson, prin.
Sinclair ES, 9TH & CLEVELAND 82301
Joseph Omelia, prin.
Sunnyside ES, 600 MAHONEY ST 82301
Karen Heeren, prin.
Other Schools – See Baggs, Bairoil

Recluse, Campbell Co.
Campbell County SD 1
Supt. – See Gillette
ES 82725 – Sue Wurbs, prin.

Riverton, Fremont Co., Pop. Code 6
Fremont County SD 25
Sch. Sys. Enr. Code 5
Supt. – Weldon Shelley, 121 N 5TH ST W 82501
MS, 413 N 4TH ST W 82501 – Terry Statton, prin.
Ashgrove ES, 510 N 1ST ST 82501
Mary Ann Atwood, prin.
Jackson ES, 720 W JACKSON AVE 82501
Jim Matson, prin.
Jefferson ES, 313 E JEFFERSON AVE 82501
Delene Berg, prin.
Lincoln ES, 1304 E LINCOLN AVE 82501
Owen Lampert, prin.

St. Margaret's School, 220 N 7TH ST E 82501

Rock River, Albany Co., Pop. Code 2
Albany County SD 1
Supt. – See Laramie
S 82083 – Gordon Kendall, prin.
River Bridge ES, GARRETT ROUTE 82083
Gordon Kendall, prin.

Rock Springs, Sweetwater Co., Pop. Code 7
Sweetwater County SD 1
Sch. Sys. Enr. Code 6
Supt. – Don Baumberger, P O BOX 1089 82902
Desert View ES, DESERT VIEW ADDITION 82901
William Schoonmaker, prin.
Lincoln ES, 915 EDGAR ST 82901
Arlen Ruff, prin.
Lowell ES, 1302 LOWELL AVE 82901
Dana Coletti, prin.
Northpark ES, SIGNAL DR 82901
Douglas O'Brien, prin.
Overland ES, FOOTHILL BLVD 82902
Paul Westberry, prin.
Reliance ES, P O BOX 1089 82902
William Schoonmaker, prin.

Roosevelt ES, 440 DEWAR DR 82901
Sandra Kuhn, prin.
Walnut ES, 1115 WALNUT ST 82901
James Peterson, prin.
Washington ES, 625 AHSAY ST 82901
Dana Coletti, prin.
Westridge ES, 3501 DEWAR DR 82901
Gerald Wolfe, prin.
Yellowstone ES, 725 C ST 82901
Sandra Kuhn, prin.
Other Schools – See Farson, Superior, Wamsutter

Rock Springs Catholic School
615 ELIAS AVE 82901

Rozet, Campbell Co.
Campbell County SD 1
Supt. – See Gillette
ES 82727 – Larry Klaassen, prin.

Saratoga, Carbon Co., Pop. Code 4
Carbon County SD 2
Sch. Sys. Enr. Code 4
Supt. – Ken Olson, P O BOX 1530 82331
MS 82331 – Karen Ammann, prin.
ES, P O BOX 1710 82331 – Jeriann James, prin.
Other Schools – See Elk Mountain, Encampment,
Hanna, Mc Fadden, Medicine Bow, Shirley Basin

Shell, Big Horn Co.
Big Horn County SD 3
Supt. – See Greybull
ES 82441 – (—), prin.

Sheridan, Sheridan Co.
Sheridan County SD 2
Sch. Sys. Enr. Code 5
Supt. – Russell Carlson, P O BOX 919 82801
Beckton ES, RURAL ROUTE 02 82801
William Schott, prin.
Central MS, 25 SOUTH CUSTER 82801
Maurice Fuller, prin.
Coffeen ES, 1053 S SHERIDAN AVE 82801
Lester Engelter, prin.
Highland Park ES, 1301 AVON ST 82801
William Schott, prin.
Meadowlark ES, 1410 DESMET AVE 82801
Walter Wragge, prin.
Sagebrush ES, 1685 HILLPOND DR 82801
Morris Zempel, prin.
Woodland Park ES, 5135 COFFEEN AVE 82801
George Mathis, prin.
Other Schools – See Story

Holy Name School, 121 S CONNOR ST 82801

Shirley Basin, Natrona Co.
Carbon County SD 2
Supt. – See Saratoga
ES, P O BOX 8087 82615 – Larry Mowry, prin.

Shoshoni, Fremont Co., Pop. Code 3
Fremont County SD 24
Sch. Sys. Enr. Code 2
Supt. – John Meeks, P O BOX 327 82649
ES, P O BOX 327 82649 – Edward Pickett, prin.

Story, Sheridan Co.
Sheridan County SD 2
Supt. – See Sheridan
ES, P O BOX 129 82842 – George Mathis, prin.

Sundance, Crook Co., Pop. Code 4
Crook County SD 1
Sch. Sys. Enr. Code 4
Supt. – Dr. Ottlin A. Wegner, P O BOX 830 82729
ES, P O BOX 870 82729 – Delbert Harbaugh, prin.
Other Schools – See Aladdin, Hulett, Moorcroft,
Oshoto

Superior, Sweetwater Co., Pop. Code 3
Sweetwater County SD 1
Supt. – See Rock Springs
ES, 61 SUMMIT 82945 – James Etherington, prin.

Ten Sleep, Washakie Co., Pop. Code 2
Washakie County SD 2
Sch. Sys. Enr. Code 2
Supt. – Leslie Stencel, P O BOX 115 82442
S 82442 – Dr. Marilyn White, prin.

Thayne, Lincoln Co., Pop. Code 2
Lincoln County SD 2
Supt. – See Afton
Holdaway ES 83127 – Reynold Johnson, prin.

Thermopolis, Hot Springs Co., Pop. Code 5
Hot Springs County SD 1
Sch. Sys. Enr. Code 4
Supt. – Neal Carroll, 101 S 10TH ST 82443
MS, 315 SPRINGVIEW ST 82443
Jerry Pauli, prin.
Lucerne ES, LUCERNE ROUTE 82443
Lilly Brewster, prin.
Witters ES, 215 SPRINGVIEW ST 82443
John Lawrence, prin.
Other Schools – See Hamilton Dome

Torrington, Goshen Co., Pop. Code 6
Goshen County SD 1
Sch. Sys. Enr. Code 4
Supt. – Paul Novak, 2602 W E ST 82240
MS, 25TH & WEST E ST 82240
Marvin Haimen, prin.
Lincoln ES, 436 E 22ND AVE 82240
Dina Ohman, prin.
Prairie Center ES, NORTH HCR 82240
Diana Ohman, prin.
Trail MS, 1601 EAST M ST 82240
Glenn Reynick, prin.
Other Schools – See Fort Laramie, Huntley, La
Grange, Lingle, Yoder

Upton, Weston Co., Pop. Code 4
Weston County SD 7
Sch. Sys. Enr. Code 2
Supt. – Randal Wendling, P O BOX 470 82730
Nelson ES 82730 – James Everingham, prin.
MS 82730 – James Everingham, prin.

Wamsutter, Sweetwater Co., Pop. Code 3
Sweetwater County SD 1
Supt. – See Rock Springs
Desert ES 82336 – Richard Horsley, prin.

Wapiti, Park Co.
Park County SD 6
Supt. – See Cody
ES 82450 – Loren Rohloff, prin.

Weston, Campbell Co.
Campbell County SD 1
Supt. – See Gillette
Little Powder ES 82731 – Mike Peterson, prin.

Wheatland, Platte Co., Pop. Code 4
Albany County SD 1
Supt. – See Laramie
Cottonwood ES, HARRIS PARK ROUTE 82201
Gordon Kendall, prin.

Platte County SD 1
Sch. Sys. Enr. Code 4
Supt. – Lucien Trouchon, 1350 OAK ST 82201
JHS, 1150 PINE ST 82201
Mark Knickerbocker, prin.
Libbey ES, 13TH AT OAK 82201
Mary Alice Stapleton, prin.
Sybille ES, 3284 HWY 34 82201
Mary Alice Stapleton, prin.
West MS, 201 20TH ST 82201
John Hazaleus, prin.
Other Schools – See Chugwater, Glendo

Wilson, Teton Co.
Teton County SD 1
Supt. – See Jackson
ES 83014 – Len Geiger, prin.

Worland, Washakie Co., Pop. Code 6
Washakie County SD 1
Sch. Sys. Enr. Code 4
Supt. – Jerry Maurer, 220 BIG HORN AVE 82401
MS, 1200 CULBERTSON AVE 82401
Ted Mills, prin.
East Side ES, 203 N 15TH ST 82401
Dean Carrell, prin.
South Side ES, 1229 HOWELL AVE 82401
Donald Neihart, prin.
West Side ES, 810 S 6TH ST 82401
Mike Hejtmanek, prin.

Wright, Campbell Co.
Campbell County SD 1
Supt. – See Gillette
Cottonwood ES, P O BOX 330 82732
Kareen Skillestad, prin.

Yoder, Goshen Co., Pop. Code 2
Goshen County SD 1
Supt. – See Torrington
Southeast ES 82244 – Brian Grasmick, prin.

DIOCESAN SUPERINTENDENTS OF ROMAN CATHOLIC SCHOOLS
(State, Archdiocese or Diocese, Supervising Officer, and Address)

ALABAMA
Birmingham
  Brice A. Hendrick, Supt.
  P.O. Box 186, Birmingham 35201
Mobile
  Gwen Byrd, Supt.
  P.O. Box 129, Mobile 36601

ALASKA
Anchorage
  Sr. Diane Bardol, GNSH, Supt.
  P.O. Box 2455, Kodiak 99615
Juneau
  Sr. Clara Dischler, Supt.
  433 Jackson St., Ketchikan 99901
Fairbanks
  Nancy Cook, Supt.
  615 Monroe St., Fairbanks 99701

ARIZONA
Phoenix
  Sr. E. Meegan, Supt.
  400 E. Monroe St., Phoenix 85004
Tucson
  John McCarthy, Supt.
  8800 E. 22nd St., Tucson 85710

ARKANSAS
Little Rock
  Sr. Henrietta Hockle, OSB, Supt.
  P.O. Box 7565, Little Rock 72217

CALIFORNIA
Fresno
  Richard Sexton, Supt.
  P.O. Box 4273, Fresno 93744
Los Angeles
  Rev. Msgr. A. Carroll, Supt.
  Rev. Msgr. John A. Mihan, (Elem.) Supt.
  1520 W. 9th St., Los Angeles 90015
Monterey
  A. Leonardich, Supt.
  P.O. Box 350, Monterey 93940
Oakland
  Sr. Hennessy, Supt.
  2910 Lakeshore Ave., Oakland 94610
Orange
  Sr. Leydon, SSL, Supt.
  2811 Villa Real Dr., Orange 92667
Sacramento
  James Adams, Supt.
  1121 "K" St., Sacramento 95814
San Bernardino
  Sr. Ann Muckerman, SSND, Supt.
  1739 North D St.
  San Bernardino 92405
San Diego
  Rev. Marc Antonio, Supt.
  P.O. Box 11277, San Diego 92111
San Francisco
  Sr. Glenn McPhee, Supt.
  443 Church St., San Francisco 94114
San Jose
  Sr. Mary Claude Power, PBVM, Supt.
  7600X St. Joseph Ave., Los Altos 94022
Santa Rosa
  Sr. O'Connor, Supt.
  P.O. Box 6654, Santa Rosa 95406
Stockton
  Sr. Gschwind, Supt.
  P.O. Box 4237, Stockton 95204

COLORADO
Colorado Springs
  Sr. J. Kasel, SSND, Supt.
  29 W. Kiowa, Colorado Springs 80903
Denver
  M. Franken, Supt.
  P.O. Box 1620, Denver 80201
Pueblo
  Sr. Vasquez, OSB, Supt.
  1001 N. Grand Ave., Pueblo 81003

CONNECTICUT
Bridgeport
  Bernard Helfrich, Supt.
  238 Jewett Ave., Bridgeport 06606

Hartford
  Rev. James G. Fanelli, Supt.
  125 Market St., Hartford 06103
Norwich
  Sr. Patricia Barry, RSM, Supt.
  43 Perkins Ave., Norwich 06360

DELAWARE
Wilmington
  Sr. Marie Kelly, SND, Supt.
  1626 N. Union St., Wilmington 19806

DISTRICT OF COLUMBIA
Washington
  J. Porath, Supt.
  P.O. Box 29260, Washington, DC 20017

FLORIDA
Miami
  Sr. Danielle, SSND, Supt.
  6180 N.E. 4th Court, Miami 33137
Orlando
  Dr. Fenchak, Supt.
  P.O. Box 2569, Orlando 32802
Palm Beach
  Sr. Daehn, Supt.
  9995 N. Military Trail, Palm Beach 33410
Pensacola-Tallahassee
  Sr. Cianciolo, CND, Supt.
  P.O. Box 17329, Pensacola 32522
St. Augustine
  Patricia Tierney, Coor. for Schs.
  P.O. Box 24000, Jacksonville 32217
St. Petersburg
  Sr. Dawson, OSF, Supt.
  P.O. Box 40200, St. Petersburg 33743
Venice
  Sr. Decosty, SNJM, Supt.
  1000 Pinebrook Rd., Venice 34292

GEORGIA
Atlanta
  Sr. Roberta Schmidt, CSJ, Supt.
  680 Peachtree St., N.W., Atlanta 30308
Savannah
  Sr. Virginia Rose, CSJ, Supt.
  St. John Center
  Grimball Point Rd., Savannah 31406

GUAM
Agana
  Sr. Maria Ana Lee, Supt.
  P.O. Box 125, Agana 96910

HAWAII
Honolulu
  Rev. J. Dever, Supt.
  P.O. Box 1247, Kaneohe 96744

IDAHO
Boise
  Sr. Kerstiens, Supt.
  7003 Franklin Rd., Boise 83709

ILLINOIS
Belleville
  Sr. Korte, Supt.
  2620 Lebanon Ave., Belleville 62221
Chicago
  Sr. Costello, RSM, Supt.
  155 E. Superior St., Box 1979, Chicago 60690
Joliet
  Sr. Zielinski, Supt.
  425 Summit St., Joliet 60435
Peoria
  Sr. Kormelink, Supt.
  412 N.E. Madison Ave., Peoria 61604
Rockford
  Sr. Joella Miller, Supt.
  1260 N. Church St., Rockford 61101
Springfield
  Rev. Michaletz, CSV, Supt.
  P.O. Box 819, 67401

INDIANA
Evansville
  Rev. Kuper, Supt.
  P.O. Box 4169, Evansville 47711
Fort Wayne-South Bend
  L. Bowman, Supt.
  P.O. Box 390, Fort Wayne 46801
Gary
  Rev. McGrogan, Supt.
  P.O. Box M-356, Gary 46401
Indianapolis
  Frank Savage, Supt.
  P.O. Box 1410, Indianapolis 46206
Lafayette
  Eugene Piccolo, Supt.
  P.O. Box 260, Lafayette 47902

IOWA
Davenport
  Rev. Msgr. W. Robert Schmidt, Supt.
  2706 Gaines St., Davenport 52804
Des Moines
  Sr. Fitzpatrick, Supt.
  P.O. Box 1816, Des Moines 50306
Dubuque
  Rev. Thomas Toale, Supt.
  P.O. Box 1180, Dubuque 52001
Sioux City
  Rev. Hoffmann, Supt.
  P.O. Box 3105, Sioux City 51102

KANSAS
Dodge City
  Sr. Rother, Supt.
  P.O. Box 999, Dodge City 67801
Kansas City
  Sr. Michalle Faltus, OSF, Supt.
  P.O. Box 2329, Kansas City 66110
Salina
  Fr. McCarthy, Supt.
  P.O. Box 837, Salina 67401
Wichita
  Daniel Elsener, Supt.
  424 N. Broadway St., Wichita 67202

KENTUCKY
Covington
  Rev. Leonard Callahan, Supt.
  P.O. Box 18548, Covington 41018
Lexington
  Sr. Bankemper, Supt.
  P.O. Box 12350, Lexington 40582
Louisville
  Rev. Thomas Duerr, Supt.
  1516 Hepburn Ave., Louisville 40204
Owensboro
  Sr. Amelia Stenger, Supt.
  4005 Frederica St., Owensboro 42301

LOUISIANA
Alexandria-Shreveport
  Sr. Hebert, MSC, Supt.
  P.O. Box 7417, Alexandria 71306
Baton Rouge
  Sr. Mary Michaeline, OP, Supt.
  P.O. Box 2028, Baton Rouge 70821
Houma-Thibodaux
  Sr. Paisant, Supt.
  P.O. Box 9077, Houma 70361
Lafayette
  Sr. Banquer, Supt.
  P.O. Box E, Lafayette 70502
Lake Charles
  Sr. Gloria Cain, Supt.
  4029 Ave. G., Lake Charles 70601
New Orleans
  Howard Jenkins, Supt.
  7887 Walmsley Ave., New Orleans 70125
Shreveport
  Sr. Faltus, Supt.
  2500 Line Ave., Shreveport 71104

MAINE
Portland
  Sr. Cobb, RSM, Supt.
  P.O. Box 6750, Portland 04103

MARYLAND

Baltimore
  Lawerence Callahan, Co-Supt.
  320 Cathedral St., Baltimore 21201

MASSACHUSETTS

Boston
  Sr. Roach, OP, Supt.
  468 Beacon St., Boston 02115
Fall River
  Rev. Beaulieu, Supt.
  423 Highland Ave., Fall River 02720
Springfield
  Sr. Bette Gould, Supt.
  625 Carew St., Springfield 01104
Worcester
  Charles McManus, Supt.
  49 Elm St., Worcester 01609

MICHIGAN

Detroit
  John Klipp, Supt.
  305 Michigan Ave., Detroit 48226
Gaylord
  Timothy Dwyer, Supt.
  1665 W. M-32, Gaylord 49735
Grand Rapids
  Daniel Pierson, Supt.
  600 Burton Ave., S.E., Grand Rapids 49507
Kalamazoo
  Frank C. Wippel, Supt.
  P.O. Box 949, Kalamazoo 49005
Lansing
  Sr. Wotiska, Supt.
  228 N. Walnut, Lansing 48933
Marquette
  Joseph Sullivan, Supt.
  P.O. Box 280, Marquette 49855
Saginaw
  Dr. John T. Norris, Director of Education
  5800 Weiss St., Saginaw 48603

MINNESOTA

Crookston
  Sr. Kallhoff, Supt.
  1200 Memorial Dr., Crookston 56716
Duluth
  Sr. Williams, Supt.
  215 W. 4th St., Duluth 55806
New Ulm
  Sr. Fallon, Supt.
  1400 Chancery Drive, New Ulm 56073
St. Cloud
  Rev. David J. Rieder, Supt.
  305 7th Ave., N., St. Cloud 56301
St. Paul-Minneapolis
  Rev. Finucan, Supt.
  328 W. 6th St., St. Paul 55102
Winona
  Rev. Nelson, Supt.
  P.O. Box 588, Winona 55987

MISSISSIPPI

Biloxi
  Sr. Joanne Cozzi, OC, Supt.
  P.O. Box 1189, Biloxi 39533
Jackson
  Rev. Cullen, Supt.
  P.O. Box 2248, Jackson 39205

MISSOURI

Jefferson City
  Sr. Reck, SSND, Supt.
  P.O. Box 417, Jefferson City 65101
Kansas City-St. Joseph
  Sr. Perkins, Supt.
  P.O. Box 419037, Kansas City 64141
St. Louis
  Sr. Mary Ann Eckhoff, SSND, Supt.
  4140 Lindell Blvd., St. Louis 63108
Springfield-Cape Girardeau
  Rev. Edward M. Eftink, Ph.D., Supt.
  P.O. Box 50960, Springfield 65805

MONTANA

Great Falls-Billings
  Sr. Mary Editha Brown, BVM, Supt.
  P.O. Box 1399, Great Falls 59403
Helena
  James Tucker, Supt.
  P.O. Box 1729, Helena 59624

NEBRASKA

Grand Island
  Rev. Thomas Ryan, Supt.
  P.O. Box 996, Grand Island 68802

Lincoln
  Rev. James D. Dawson, Supt.
  P.O. Box 80328, Lincoln 68501
Omaha
  Sr. Mulcahey, Supt.
  8536 K St., Omaha 68127

NEVADA

Reno
  Sr. Mary Leonard Welcer, PBVM, Supt.
  P.O. Box 1211, Reno 89504

NEW HAMPSHIRE

Manchester
  Bro. Roger L. Lemoyne, SC, Supt.
  P.O. Box 310, Manchester 03105

NEW JERSEY

Camden
  Rev. Thomas McIntyre, Supt.
  P.O. Box 709, Camden 08101
Metuchen
  Dr. Defiore, Supt.
  103 Center St., Perth Amboy 08861
Newark
  Superintendent
  100 Linden Ave., Irvington 07111
Paterson
  Frank Petrucelli, Supt.
  777 Valley Rd., Clifton 07013
Trenton
  Sr. Moran, Supt.
  1018 Whitehead Rd., Trenton 08648

NEW MEXICO

Gallup
  Rev. Thomas R. Maikowski, Supt.
  P.O. Box 214, Farmington 87401
Las Cruces
  R. Cordonnier, Supt.
  P.O. Box 16318, Las Cruces 88004
Santa Fe
  R. Cordonnier, Supt.
  4000 St. Josephs Pl., N.W., Albuquerque 87120

NEW YORK

Albany
  Fr. Ingemie, Supt.
  40 N. Main Ave., Albany 12203
Brooklyn
  Rev. Vincent Breen, Supt.
  6025 6th Ave., Brooklyn 11220
Buffalo
  R. J. Cook, Supt.
  100 S. Elmwood Ave., Buffalo 14202
New York
  Br. Kearney, FMS, Supt.
  1011 1st Ave., New York 10022
Ogdensburg
  Rev. Lawrence Deno, Supt.
  622 Washington St., Box 369, Ogdensburg 13669
Rochester
  Br. Walsh, Supt.
  1150 Buffalo Rd., Rochester 14624
Rockville Centre
  Dr. Hugh F. Carroll, Supt.
  50 N. Park Ave., Rockville Center 11570
Syracuse
  Br. McGovern, Supt.
  P.O. Box 511, Syracuse 13201

NORTH CAROLINA

Charlotte
  Sr. Sullivan, RSM, Supt.
  1524 E. Morehead St., Charlotte 28207
Raleigh
  Sr. Regina Haney, OSF, Supt.
  300 Cardinal Gibbons Dr., Raleigh 27606

NORTH DAKOTA

Bismarck
  Steve Brannan, Supt.
  P.O. Box 1137, Bismarck 58502
Fargo
  Sr. Gust, Supt.
  1310 Broadway, Fargo 58107

OHIO

Cincinnati
  Sr. Connelly, Supt.
  100 E. 8th St., Cincinnati 45202
Cleveland
  Sr. Vladimiroff, Supt.
  1031 Superior Ave., Cleveland 44114
Columbus
  Dr. Coury, Supt.
  197 E. Gay St., Columbus 43215

Steubenville
  Sr. Mary Corr, Supt.
  422 Washington St., Steubenville 43952
Toledo
  Rev. John A. Thomas, Ph.D., Supt.
  436 W. Delaware Ave., Toledo 43610
Youngstown
  Dr. Wolsonovich, Supt.
  144 W. Wood St., Youngstown 44503

OKLAHOMA

Oklahoma City
  Sr. Loretta Gegen, Supt.
  P.O. Box 32184, Oklahoma City 73132
Tulsa
  Arden Glenn, Supt.
  P.O. Box 2009, Tulsa 74101

OREGON

Baker
  Rev. Stone, Supt.
  P.O. Box 987, Bend 97701
Portland
  Sr. Molly Giller, Supt.
  P.O. Box 351, Portland 97207

PENNSYLVANIA

Allentown
  Dr. James J. Cusimano, Supt.
  824 N. Graham St., P.O. Box 2607
    Lehigh Valley 18001
Altoona-Johnstown
  Sr. Grilliot, Supt.
  P.O. Box 126, Hollidaysburg 16648
Erie
  Sr. Lois Lorei, RSM, Supt., act'g.
  517 E. 26th St., Erie 16504
Greensburg
  Dr. Scatena, Supt.
  723 E. Pittsburgh, St., Greensburg 15601
Harrisburg
  Rev. Lawrence, Supt.
  P.O. Box 3553, Harrisburg 17105
Philadelphia
  Dr. Palestini, Supt.
  222 N. 17th St., Philadelphia 19103
Pittsburgh
  Dr. Cibik, Supt.
  111 Blvd. of the Allies, Pittsburgh 15222
Scranton
  Rev. Jordan, Supt.
  300 Wyoming Ave., Scranton 18503

PUERTO RICO

Arecibo
  Sr. Ernestina Duran, HCCS, Supt.
  P.O. Box 1683, Arecibo 00613
Caguas
  Rev. Ortiz, Supt.
  P.O. Box 8699, Casguas 00625
Ponce
  Sr. Maria Una Garcia
  P.O. Box 557, Station 6, Ponce 00731
Mayaguez
  Sr. Mary Owen, CSJ, Supt.
  P.O. Box 2272, Mayaguez 00709
San Juan
  Sla. DeArmas, Supt.
  Condominio Vick Center, Oficina C-402
    Avenida Munoz Rivera 867, Rio Piedras 00925

RHODE ISLAND

Providence
  Br. Cassey, Supt.
  One Cathedral Square, Providence 02903

SOUTH CAROLINA

Charleston
  Rev. Robert J. Kelly, Supt.
  P.O. Box 818, Charleston 29402

SOUTH DAKOTA

Rapid City
  Norman Graham, Supt.
  P.O. Box 678, Rapid City 57709
Sioux Falls
  Rev. Carroll, Supt.
  3000 W. 41st St., Sioux Falls 57105

TENNESSEE

Knoxville
  Steve Hammond, Supt.
  2701 Vermont Ave., Chattanooga 37404
Memphis
  Sr. Trojano, CSJ, Supt.
  P.O. Box 41679, Memphis 38104

Nashville
Steve Hammond, Supt.
2400 21st Ave., S., Nashville 37212

TEXAS

Amarillo
Sr. Lindner, DC, Supt.
P.O. Box 5644, Amarillo 79107
Austin
Sr. Loretta Raphael, OP, Supt.
9049 Jollyville Rd., Austin 78759
Beaumont
Sr. Rose Mary Cousins, Supt.
P.O. Box 3948, Beaumont 77704
Brownsville
Sr. Doyle, CCVI, Supt.
P.O. Box 2279, Brownsville 78520
Corpus Christi
Dr. Kamke, Supt.
620 Lipan, Corpus Christi 78401
Dallas
Sr. Caroleen Hensgen, SSND, Supt.
P.O. Box 190507, Dallas 75219
El Paso
Rev. Sescon, Supt.
1101 Birch St., El Paso 79930
Fort Worth
Edward Doherty, Supt.
800 W. Loop 820 S., Fort Worth 76111
Galveston-Houston
Sr. Colleen Hennessey, SSND, Supt.
2401 E. Holcombe Blvd., Houston 77021
Lubbock
Roberta Meyer, Supt.
P.O. Box 98700, Lubbock 79499

San Angelo
Edward Doherty, Supt.
612 E. 18th St., Odessa 79762
San Antonio
Br. Pontolillo, Supt.
P.O. Box 28410, San Antonio 78228
Tyler
Sr. Cousins, Supt.
P.O. Box 3948, Beaumont 77704
Victoria
Br. Pontolillo, Supt.
P.O. Box 28410, San Antonio 78228

UTAH

Salt Lake City
Sr. Allem, CSC, Supt.
27 C St., Salt Lake City 84103

VERMONT

Burlington
Sr. Ruth Ravey, RSM, Supt.
351 North Ave., Burlington 05401

VIRGINIA

Arlington
Marie Powell, Supt.
200 N. Glebe Rd. #703, Arlington 22203
Richmond
Lois King Draina, Supt.
811A Cathedral Pl., Richmond 23220

WASHINGTON

Seattle
Sr. Thielman, Supt.
232 Warren Ave., N., Seattle 98109
Spokane
(—), Supt.
P.O. Box 1453, Spokane 99210
Yakima
Sr. Brennan, Supt.
P.O. Box 2834, Yakima 98907

WEST VIRGINIA

Wheeling-Charleston
Judith Minear, Supt.
1310 Byron St., P.O. Box 230, Wheeling 26003

WISCONSIN

Green Bay
Jack Calareso, Supt.
P.O. Box 1825, Green Bay 54305
La Crosse
Donald Novotrey, Supt.
P.O. Box 4004, La Crosse 54601
Madison
Sr. Montgomery, Supt.
142 W. Johnson St., Madison 53703
Milwaukee
(—), Supt.
P.O. Box 2018, Milwaukee 53201
Superior
Richard Lyons, Supt.
1201 Hughitt Ave., Box 310, Superior 54880

WYOMING

Cheyenne
Br. Klietz, Supt.
P.O. Box 774, Cheyenne 82003

SUPERINTENDENTS OF LUTHERAN SCHOOLS

(District, States, Supervising Officer and Address)

LUTHERAN CHURCH — MISSOURI SYNOD
Board of Parish Education
3558 S. Jefferson Avenue, St. Louis, MO 63118

District and Supervising Officer(s)

Atlantic
Rev. Dwayne Mau
171 White Plains Rd. Bronxville, NY 10708

California-Nevada-Hawaii
Rev. Mark Haas
465 Woolsey St., San Francisco, CA 94134

Central Illinois
Rev. Paul Droegmueller
P.O. Box 7003, Springfield, IL 62791

Eastern
Rev. Folwaczny
2500 Kensington, Buffalo, NY 14226

English
William Hodgson
23001 Grand River, Detroit, MI 48219

Florida-Georgia
Robert Reed
441 Park Lake Circle, Orlando, FL 32803

Indiana
Rev. Ron Mueller
1145 S. Barr St., Ft. Wayne, IN 46802

Iowa East
Wayne King
4403 First Ave., S.E., Cedar Rapids, IA 52402

Iowa West
Rev. Robert Riggert
P.O. Box 1155, Fort Dodge, IA 50501

Kansas
Rick Soeken
2318 W. Tenth, Topeka, KS 66604

Michigan
Wayne Wentzel
3773 Geddes Rd., Ann Arbor, MI 48105

Mid-South
Robert Hentscher
1580 W. Massey Rd., Memphis, TN 38119

Minnesota North
Marvin Kading
P.O. Box 604, Brainerd, MN 56401

Minnesota South
Arthur Plath
14301 Grand Ave., Burnsville, MN 55337

Missouri
David Wiesner
3558 S. Jefferson Ave., St. Louis, MO 63118

Montana
Judy Williams
30 Broadwater Ave., Billings, MT 59101

Nebraska
Reed Sander
152 S. Columbia, Box 407, Seward, NE 68434

New England
Thomas Beineke
400 Wilbraham Rd., Springfield, MA 01109

New Jersey
Nancy White
1168 Springfield Ave., Mountainside, NJ 07092

North Dakota
Rev. Rob Pfau
2601 23rd Ave., Fargo, ND 58103

North Wisconsin
Gary Beyer
3103 Seymour Ln., Wausau, WI 54401

Northern Illinois
Rev. John Sternberg
2301 S. Wolf Road, Hillside, IL 60162

Northwest
Gordon Tagge
1700 Knott St., Portland, OR 97212

Ohio
Clarence Moses
6451 Columbia Road, Olmstead Falls, OH 44138

Oklahoma
Steven Wiederker
308 N.W. 164th St., Edmond, OK 73013

Rocky Mountain
Rev. Neal MacLachlan
P.O. Box 725, Aurora, CO 80040

SELC
Mr. Robert Flesch
2025 W. State Rd., Oviedo, FL 32765

South Dakota
Rev. Clark Gies
P.O. Box 89110, Sioux Falls, SD 57105

South Wisconsin
Gene Ladendorf
8100 W. Capitol Dr., Milwaukee, WI 53222

Southeastern
Rev. Bryant Clancy
P.O. Box 10415, Alexandria, VA 22310

Southern
Thomas Rogers
P.O. Box 8396, New Orleans, LA 70122

Southern California
Steven Kuschel
1530 Concordia, Irvine, CA 92715

Southern Illinois
Daniel Roth
2408 Lebanon, Belleville, IL 62221

Texas
Norman Stuemke
8100 U.S. 290 East, Austin, TX 78724

Wyoming
David Strain
2400 S. Hickory, Casper, WY 82604

GENERAL CONFERENCE OF SEVENTH-DAY ADVENTISTS

Charles B. Hirsh, Director, Department of Education
6840 Eastern Avenue, N.W., Washington, DC 20012

ATLANTIC UNION
Paul Kilgore, Director
Box 458, South Lancaster, MA 01561

Bermuda Mission
Carlyle Simmons, Supt.
Box 1170, Hamilton, Bermuda

Greater New York Conference
Leslie L. Lee, Supt.
P.O. Box 1029, Manhasset, NY 11030

New York Conference
G. N. Kovalski, Supt.
Box 67, Onondaga Branch, Syracuse, NY 13215

Northeastern Conference
Sandra Herndon, Acting Supt.
115-50 Merrick Blvd., Jamaica, NY 11434

Northern New England Conference
Ron Goodall, Supt.
Box 1340, Portland, ME 04104

Southern New England Conference
Eugene F. Armour, Supt.
South Lancaster, MA 01561

MID-AMERICA UNION CONFERENCE
Randall Fox, Director
P.O. Box 6127, Lincoln, NE 68506

Central States Conference
S. H. Cox, Acting Supt.
Box 1527, Kansas City, MO 64141

Dakota Conference
Jack Babshaw, Supt.
P.O. Box 520, Pierre, SD 57501

Iowa-Missouri Conference
Otis Graves, Supt.
Box 65665, W. Des Moines, IA 50265

Kansas-Nebraska Conference
Dwight Mayberry, Supt.
3440 Urish Road, Topeka, KS 66604

Minnesota Conference
Larry Kromann, Supt.
P.O. Box 27360, Minneapolis, MN 55427

Rocky Mountain Conference
Robert W. Rice, Supt.
2520 S. Downing St., Denver, CO 80210

COLUMBIA UNION CONFERENCE
F. Wayne Foster, Director
7710 Carroll Ave., Takoma Pk., MD 20012

Allegheny Conference, East
R. L. Booker, Supt.
Box 266, Pine Forge, PA 19548

Allegheny Conference, West
Cordell Williamson, Supt.
1339 E. Broad St., Columbus, OH 43205

Chesapeake Conference
Robert Skeggs, Supt.
6600 Martin Rd. Columbia, MD 21044

Mountain View Conference
Mark Walker, Supt.
1400 Liberty St., Parkersburg, WV 26101

New Jersey Conference
Merle Greenway, Supt.
2160 Brunswick Ave., Trenton, NJ 08648

Ohio Conference
James Clizbe, Supt.
Box 831, Mount Vernon, OH 43050

Pennsylvania Conference
Paul Roesel, Supt.
720 Museum Rd., Reading, PA 19611

Potomac Conference
Harry Mayden, Supt.
Box 1208, Staunton, VA 24401

LAKE UNION CONFERENCE
Warren E. Minder, Director
Box C, Berrien Springs, MI 49103

Illinois Conference
George Lloyd, Supt.
Box 89, Brookfield, IL 60513

Indiana Conference
Herbert Wrate, Supt.
P.O. Box 1950
Carmel, IN 46032

Lake Region Conference
Reginald D. Barnes, Supt.
8517 S. State St., Chicago, IL 60619

Michigan Conference
Gary Randolph, Supt.
P.O. Box 19009, Lansing, MI 48901

Wisconsin Conference
Robert Knutson, Supt.
P.O. Box 7310, Madison, WI 53707

NORTH PACIFIC UNION CONFERENCE
G. L. Plubell, Director
P.O. Box 16677, Portland, OR 97216

Alaska Mission
Glenn Gingery, Supt.
718 Barrow St., Anchorage, AK 99501

Idaho Conference
L. H. Opp, Supt.
7777 Fairview, Boise, ID 83704

Montana Conference
T. P. Bonney, Supt.
Box 743, Bozeman, MT 59715

Oregon Conference
Charles Dart, Supt.
13400 S.E. 97th Ave., Clackamas, OR 97015

Upper Columbia Conference
C. W. Jorgensen, Supt.
Box 19039, Spokane, WA 99219

Washington Conference
N. M. Merkel, Supt.
P.O. Box 1008, Bothell, WA 98011

PACIFIC UNION CONFERENCE
E. J. Anderson, Director
P.O. Box 5005, Westlake Village, CA 91359

Arizona Conference
Don Keele, Supt.
P.O. Box 5317, Phoenix, AZ 85010

Central California Conference
Jay H. Lantry, Supt.
P.O. Box 580, San Jose, CA 95106

Hawaiian Mission
Robert Wong, Supt.
P.O. Box 4037, Honolulu, HI 96813

Nevada-Utah Conference
Ronald W. Christensen, Supt.
P.O. Box 10730, Reno, NV 89510

Northern California Conference
K. W. Hutchins, Supt.
Box 23165, Pleasant Hill, CA 94523

Southeastern California Conference
Wallace D. Minder, Supt.
P.O. Box 8050, Riverside, CA 92515

Southern California Conference
H. D. Lawson, Supt.
Box 969, Glendale, CA 91209

SOUTHERN UNION CONFERENCE
D. K. Griffith, Director
P.O. Box 849, Decatur, GA 30031

Alabama-Mississippi Conference
Shirley Goodridge, Supt.
P.O. Box 17100, Montgomery, AL 36193

Carolina Conference
Louis Canosa, Supt.
P.O. Box 25848, Charlotte, NC 28212

Florida Conference
Harold E. Haas, Supt.
Box 1313, Orlando, FL 32802

Georgia-Cumberland Conference
James Epperson, Supt.
P.O. Box 12000, Calhoun, GA 30701

Kentucky-Tennessee Conference
Lyle Anderson, Supt.
Box 459, Madison, TN 37115

South Atlantic Conference
S.E. Gooden, Supt.
Morris Brown Station, Box 92447
Atlanta, GA 30314

South Central Conference
Joseph F. Dent, Supt.
P.O. Box 24936, Nashville, TN 37202

Southeastern Conference
G. Timpson, Supt.
P.O. Box 5978, Orlando, FL 32805

SOUTHWESTERN UNION CONFERENCE
Frances Clark, Director
P.O. Box 4000, Burleson, TX 76028

Arkansas-Louisiana Conference
J. Wayne Hancock, Supt.
Box 3100, Shreveport, LA 71130

Oklahoma Conference
Darrell Beyer, Supt.
Box 32098, Oklahoma City, OK 73123

Southwest Region Conference
James Ford, Supt.
Box 226289, Dallas, TX 75266

Texas Conference
H. E. Walker, Supt.
Box 11620, Fort Worth, TX 76109

Texico Conference
Sergio Hernandez, Supt.
P.O. Box 7770, Amarillo, TX 79109